MSU DETROIT COLLEGE OF LAW

Who'sWho in American Law®

Who's Who in American Law®

2002~2003

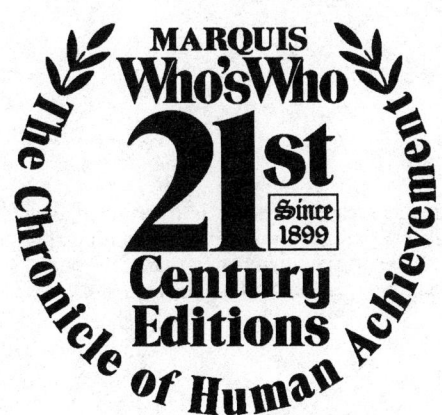

MARQUIS
Who'sWho
21st
Since 1899
Century Editions
The Chronicle of Human Achievement

12th Edition

MARQUIS
Who'sWho •121 Chanlon Road
New Providence, NJ 07974 U.S.A.
www.marquiswhoswho.com

Who's Who in American Law®

Marquis Who's Who®

Editorial Director   Fred Marks

Senior Managing Research Editor   Lisa Weissbard   **Managing Editor**   Eileen McGuinness

Editorial

Senior Editor	Francine Richardson
Associate Editor	Jessica Parkin
Assistant Editors	Laura Koserowski
	Jeffrey D. Ramesar
	Deanna Richmond
	Kate Spirito

Creative Services

Creative Services Director	Michael Noerr
Creative Services Coordinator	Rose Butkiewicz
Production Supervisor	Jeanne Danzig

Editorial Services

Senior Manager	Debby Nowicki
Production Manager	Paul Zema
Freelance Supervisor	Mary San Giovanni
Technical Coordinator	Sola Osofisan
Mail Processing Supervisor	Kara A. Seitz
Mail Processing Staff	Betty Gray
	Hattie Walker
Editorial Services Assistant	Ann Chavis

Research

Senior Research Editor	Musa Muromets
Associate Research Editor	Jennifer Podolsky
Assistant Research Editor	Willie Lee

Editorial Systems

Project Manager	Helene Davis
Programmers/Analysts	Tom Haggerty
	Sofia P. Pikulin

Published by Marquis Who's Who, a member of the Lexis-Nexis Group.

Chief Executive Officer   Andrew W. Meyer

Vice President and Publisher   Randy H. Mysel

Vice President, Database Production   Dean Hollister

Chief Information Officer   John Roney

For information, contact:

Marquis Who's Who
121 Chanlon Road
New Providence, New Jersey 07974
1-908-464-6800
www.marquiswhoswho.com

WHO'S WHO IN AMERICAN LAW is a registered trademark of Reed Publishing used under license.

Library of Congress Catalog Card Number 77-79896
International Standard Book Number   0-8379-3518-0 (Classic Edition)
                                     0-8379-3519-9 (Deluxe Edition)
International Standard Serial Number   0162-7880

Manufactured in the United States of America

Table of Contents

Preface

The twelfth edition of *Who's Who in American Law* provides biographical information on more than 15,000 lawyers and professionals in law-related areas including, among others, judges, legal educators, law librarians, legal historians, and social scientists.

The biographical sketches include such information as education, vital statistics, career history, awards, publications, memberships, address(es), and more. In addition, practicing lawyers were asked to include their fields of legal expertise or interest.

In this edition, there are separate indexes for individuals involved actively in the practice of law and for other legal professionals such as judges, law librarians, and legal educators. The "Fields of Practice Index" enables *Who's Who in American Law* users to access practicing lawyers geographically by city and state within fields such as federal or state civil litigation, corporate, taxation, criminal, and approximately 70 other fields of law. The "Professional Index" lists other professionals geographically by type of career such as education, government, or judicial administration.

The selection of the law field codes for the "Fields of Practice Index" was derived from three main sources, beginning with the specialty categories described by the American Bar Association Standing Committee on Specialization. Further information was supplied by state committees and boards on specialization, outlining the specialties recognized by or certified with the respective states. These lists reflect the varying degrees of specialty certification from state to state. Finally, an acknowledged expert on specialization in the legal profession provided valuable information and recommendations for a comprehensive list of recognized areas of law.

Practicing attorneys were asked to select up to three fields that reflected personal practice or interest. The Biographees' sketches reflect these fields. The "Fields of Practice Index" lists these lawyers under their selected fields. Individualized fields not encompassed in the list and newly emerging areas with relatively few practitioners are listed by Biographee name at the end of the index under the category "Other."

As in all Marquis Who's Who biographical volumes, the principle of current reference value determines selection of Biographees. Reference interest is based either on position of responsibility or noteworthy achievement. In the editorial evaluation that resulted in the ultimate selection of the names in this directory, an individual's desire to be listed was not sufficient reason for inclusion.

Each candidate is invited to submit biographical data about his or her life and professional career. Submitted information is reviewed by the Marquis editorial staff before being written in sketch form, and a prepublication proof of the composed sketch is sent to potential Biographees for verification. Every verified sketch returned by a candidate and accepted by the editorial staff is written in the final Marquis Who's Who format. This process ensures a high degree of accuracy.

In the event that individuals of significant reference interest fail to submit biographical data, the Marquis staff compiles the information through independent research. Sketches compiled in this manner are denoted by asterisks.

Marquis Who's Who editors diligently prepare each biographical sketch for publication. Occasionally, however, errors do appear. We regret all such errors and invite Biographees to notify the publisher so that corrections can be made in a subsequent edition.

Board of Advisors

Marquis Who's Who gratefully acknowledges the following distinguished individuals who have made themselves available for review, evaluation, and general comment with regard to the publication of the twelfth edition of *Who's Who in American Law.* The advisors have enhanced the reference value of this edition by the nomination of outstanding individuals for inclusion. However, the Board of Advisors, either collectively or individually, is in no way responsible for the final selection of names, or for the accuracy or comprehensiveness of the biographical information or other material contained herein.

Standards of Admission

Selection of Biographees for *Who's Who in American Law* is determined by reference interest. Such reference value is based on either of two factors: (1) incumbency in a defined position of responsibility or (2) attainment of a significant level of achievement.

Admission based on position includes the following examples:

Justices of the U.S. Supreme Court

Judges of the U.S. Circuit Courts

Judges of the U.S. District Courts

Attorney General of the United States and other high-ranking federal executive attorneys

Chief counsel of congressional committees

Justices of state and territorial courts of the highest appellate jurisdiction

State and territorial attorneys general

Chief judges of selected county courts, based on population

Deans and professors at leading law schools

General counsel of major corporations and labor unions

Officials of the American Bar Association and specialized bar groups

Officials of state and territorial bar associations

Officials of selected county and city bar associations, based on population

Highly rated lawyers in private practice

Editors of important legal journals

Admission by the factor of significant achievement is based on objective criteria for measuring accomplishments within the legal profession.

Key to Information

[1] **WATTS, BENJAMIN GREENE,** [2] lawyer; [3] b. May 21, 1935; [4] s. George and Sarah (Carson) W.; [5] m. Ellen Spencer, Sept. 12, 1960; [6] children: John Allen, Lucy Anne. [7] BS, Northwestern U., 1956; JD, U. Chgo., 1965. [8] Bar: Ill. 1965, U.S. Supreme Ct. 1980. [9] Mem. legal dept. Standard Publs. Corp., Chgo., 1965-73, asst. counsel, 1973-81, counsel, 1981-83; ptnr. Watts, Clayborn, Johnson & Miller, Oak Brook, Ill., 1983-85, sr. ptnr., 1985—; [10] lectr. Coll. of DuPage, 1980-94, U. Chgo., 1994—. [11] Author: Legal Aspects of Educational Publishing, 1985, Copyright Legalities, 1997. [12] Chmn. Downers Grove (Ill.) chpt. ARC, 1982-83; active DuPage council Boy Scouts Am.; trustee Elmhurst (Ill.) Hist. Mus., 1972—, pres. bd. trustees, 1995—. [13] Served to lt. USAF, 1959-61. [14] Recipient Outstanding Alumnus award Northwestern U., 1971. [15] Mem. ABA, Ill. Bar Assn., Chgo. Bar Assn., Am. Mgmt. Assn., Phi Delta Phi, Caxton Club, Tavern Club (Chgo.), Masons [16] Democrat. [17] Lutheran. [18] General practice, Trademark and copyright, General corporate. [19] Home: 543 Farwell Ave Elmhurst IL 60126 [20] Office: Watts Clayborn Johnson & Miller 1428 Industrial Ct Oak Brook IL 60521

KEY

[1]   Name
[2]   Occupation
[3]   Vital statistics
[4]   Parents
[5]   Marriage
[6]   Children
[7]   Education
[8]   Professional certifications
[9]   Career
[10]   Career-related activities
[11]   Writings and creative works
[12]   Civic and political activities
[13]   Military service
[14]   Awards and fellowships
[15]   Professional and association memberships, clubs and lodges
[16]   Political affiliation
[17]   Religion
[18]   Fields of legal practice
[19]   Home address
[20]   Office address

Table of Abbreviations

The following abbreviations and symbols are frequently used in this book.

*An asterisk following a sketch indicates that it was researched by the Marquis Who's Who editorial staff and has not been verified by the Biographee.
A Associate (used with academic degrees only)
AA, A.A. Associate in Arts, Associate of Arts
AAAL American Academy of Arts and Letters
AAAS American Association for the Advancement of Science
AACD American Association for Counseling and Development
AACN American Association of Critical Care Nurses
AAHA American Academy of Health Administrators
AAHP American Association of Hospital Planners
AAHPERD American Alliance for Health, Physical Education, Recreation, and Dance
AAS Associate of Applied Science
AASL American Association of School Librarians
AASPA American Association of School Personnel Administrators
AAU Amateur Athletic Union
AAUP American Association of University Professors
AAUW American Association of University Women
AB, A.B. Arts, Bachelor of
AB Alberta
ABA American Bar Association
ABC American Broadcasting Company
AC Air Corps
acad. academy, academic
acct. accountant
acctg. accounting
ACDA Arms Control and Disarmament Agency
ACHA American College of Hospital Administrators
ACLS Advanced Cardiac Life Support
ACLU American Civil Liberties Union
ACOG American College of Ob-Gyn
ACP American College of Physicians
ACS American College of Surgeons
ADA American Dental Association
a.d.c. aide-de-camp
adj. adjunct, adjutant
adj. gen. adjutant general
adm. admiral
adminstr. administrator
adminstrn. administration
adminstrv. administrative
ADN Associate's Degree in Nursing
ADP Automatic Data Processing
adv. advocate, advisory
advt. advertising
AE, A.E. Agricultural Engineer
A.E. and P. Ambassador Extraordinary and Plenipotentiary

AEC Atomic Energy Commission
aero. aeronautical, aeronautic
aerodyn. aerodynamic
AFB Air Force Base
AFL-CIO American Federation of Labor and Congress of Industrial Organizations
AFTRA American Federation of TV and Radio Artists
AFSCME American Federation of State, County and Municipal Employees
agr. agriculture
agrl. agricultural
agt. agent
AGVA American Guild of Variety Artists
agy. agency
A&I Agricultural and Industrial
AIA American Institute of Architects
AIAA American Institute of Aeronautics and Astronautics
AIChE American Institute of Chemical Engineers
AICPA American Institute of Certified Public Accountants
AID Agency for International Development
AIDS Acquired Immune Deficiency Syndrome
AIEE American Institute of Electrical Engineers
AIM American Institute of Management
AIME American Institute of Mining, Metallurgy, and Petroleum Engineers
AK Alaska
AL Alabama
ALA American Library Association
Ala. Alabama
alt. alternate
Alta. Alberta
A&M Agricultural and Mechanical
AM, A.M. Arts, Master of
Am. American, America
AMA American Medical Association
amb. ambassador
A.M.E. African Methodist Episcopal
Amtrak National Railroad Passenger Corporation
AMVETS American Veterans of World War II, Korea, Vietnam
ANA American Nurses Association
anat. anatomical
ANCC American Nurses Credentialing Center
ann. annual
ANTA American National Theatre and Academy
anthrop. anthropological
AP Associated Press
APA American Psychological Association
APGA American Personnel Guidance Association
APHA American Public Health Association
APO Army Post Office
apptd. appointed
Apr. April
apt. apartment

AR Arkansas
ARC American Red Cross
arch. architect
archeol. archeological
archtl. architectural
Ariz. Arizona
Ark. Arkansas
ArtsD, ArtsD. Arts, Doctor of
arty. artillery
AS American Samoa
AS Associate in Science
ASCAP American Society of Composers, Authors and Publishers
ASCD Association for Supervision and Curriculum Development
ASCE American Society of Civil Engineers
ASHRAE American Society of Heating, Refrigeration, and Air Conditioning Engineers
ASME American Society of Mechanical Engineers
ASNSA American Society for Nursing Service Administrators
ASPA American Society for Public Administration
ASPCA American Society for the Prevention of Cruelty to Animals
assn. association
assoc. associate
asst. assistant
ASTD American Society for Training and Development
ASTM American Society for Testing and Materials
astron. astronomical
astrophys. astrophysical
ATLA Association of Trial Lawyers of America
ATSC Air Technical Service Command
AT&T American Telephone & Telegraph Company
atty. attorney
Aug. August
AUS Army of the United States
aux. auxiliary
Ave. Avenue
AVMA American Veterinary Medical Association
AZ Arizona
AWHONN Association of Women's Health Obstetric and Neonatal Nurses

B. Bachelor
b. born
BA, B.A. Bachelor of Arts
BAgr, B.Agr. Bachelor of Agriculture
Balt. Baltimore
Bapt. Baptist
BArch, B.Arch. Bachelor of Architecture
BAS, B.A.S. Bachelor of Agricultural Science
BBA, B.B.A. Bachelor of Business Administration
BBB Better Business Bureau

BBC British Broadcasting Corporation
BC, B.C. British Columbia
BCE, B.C.E. Bachelor of Civil Engineering
BChir, B.Chir. Bachelor of Surgery
BCL, B.C.L. Bachelor of Civil Law
BCLS Basic Cardiac Life Support
BCS, B.C.S. Bachelor of Commercial Science
BD, B.D. Bachelor of Divinity
bd. board
BE, B.E. Bachelor of Education
BEE, B.E.E. Bachelor of Electrical Engineering
BFA, B.F.A. Bachelor of Fine Arts
bibl. biblical
bibliog. bibliographical
biog. biographical
biol. biological
BJ, B.J. Bachelor of Journalism
Bklyn. Brooklyn
BL, B.L. Bachelor of Letters
bldg. building
BLS, B.L.S. Bachelor of Library Science
BLS Basic Life Support
Blvd. Boulevard
BMI Broadcast Music, Inc.
BMW Bavarian Motor Works (Bayerische Motoren Werke)
bn. battalion
B.&O.R.R. Baltimore & Ohio Railroad
bot. botanical
BPE, B.P.E. Bachelor of Physical Education
BPhil, B.Phil. Bachelor of Philosophy
br. branch
BRE, B.R.E. Bachelor of Religious Education
brig. gen. brigadier general
Brit. British, Brittanica
Bros. Brothers
BS, B.S. Bachelor of Science
BSA, B.S.A. Bachelor of Agricultural Science
BSBA Bachelor of Science in Business Administration
BSChemE Bachelor of Science in Chemical Engineering
BSD, B.S.D. Bachelor of Didactic Science
BSEE Bachelor of Science in Electrical Engineering
BSN Bachelor of Science in Nursing
BST, B.S.T. Bachelor of Sacred Theology
BTh, B.Th. Bachelor of Theology
bull. bulletin
bur. bureau
bus. business
B.W.I. British West Indies

CA California
CAA Civil Aeronautics Administration
CAB Civil Aeronautics Board
CAD-CAM Computer Aided Design–Computer Aided Model
Calif. California
C.Am. Central America
Can. Canada, Canadian
CAP Civil Air Patrol
capt. captain
cardiol. cardiological
cardiovasc. cardiovascular
CARE Cooperative American Relief Everywhere
Cath. Catholic
cav. cavalry
CBC Canadian Broadcasting Company
CBI China, Burma, India Theatre of Operations
CBS Columbia Broadcasting Company
C.C. Community College
CCC Commodity Credit Corporation

CCNY City College of New York
CCRN Critical Care Registered Nurse
CCU Cardiac Care Unit
CD Civil Defense
CE, C.E. Corps of Engineers, Civil Engineer
CEN Certified Emergency Nurse
CENTO Central Treaty Organization
CEO chief executive officer
CERN European Organization of Nuclear Research
cert. certificate, certification, certified
CETA Comprehensive Employment Training Act
CFA Chartered Financial Analyst
CFL Canadian Football League
CFO chief financial officer
CFP Certified Financial Planner
ch. church
ChD, Ch.D. Doctor of Chemistry
chem. chemical
ChemE, Chem.E. Chemical Engineer
ChFC Chartered Financial Consultant
Chgo. Chicago
chirurg. chirurgical
chmn. chairman
chpt. chapter
CIA Central Intelligence Agency
Cin. Cincinnati
cir. circle, circuit
CLE Continuing Legal Education
Cleve. Cleveland
climatol. climatological
clin. clinical
clk. clerk
C.L.U. Chartered Life Underwriter
CM, C.M. Master in Surgery
CM Northern Mariana Islands
CMA Certified Medical Assistant
cmty. community
CNA Certified Nurse's Aide
CNOR Certified Nurse (Operating Room)
C.&N.W.Ry. Chicago & North Western Railway
CO Colorado
Co. Company
COF Catholic Order of Foresters
C. of C. Chamber of Commerce
col. colonel
coll. college
Colo. Colorado
com. committee
comd. commanded
comdg. commanding
comdr. commander
comdt. commandant
comm. communications
commd. commissioned
comml. commercial
commn. commission
commr. commissioner
compt. comptroller
condr. conductor
Conf. Conference
Congl. Congregational, Congressional
Conglist. Congregationalist
Conn. Connecticut
cons. consultant, consulting
consol. consolidated
constl. constitutional
constn. constitution
constrn. construction
contbd. contributed
contbg. contributing
contbn. contribution
contbr. contributor
contr. controller
Conv. Convention

COO chief operating officer
coop. cooperative
coord. coordinator
CORDS Civil Operations and Revolutionary Development Support
CORE Congress of Racial Equality
corp. corporation, corporate
corr. correspondent, corresponding, correspondence
C.&O.Ry. Chesapeake & Ohio Railway
coun. council
CPA Certified Public Accountant
CPCU Chartered Property and Casualty Underwriter
CPH, C.P.H. Certificate of Public Health
cpl. corporal
CPR Cardio-Pulmonary Resuscitation
C.P.Ry. Canadian Pacific Railway
CRT Cathode Ray Terminal
C.S. Christian Science
CSB, C.S.B. Bachelor of Christian Science
C.S.C. Civil Service Commission
CT Connecticut
ct. court
ctr. center
ctrl. central
CWS Chemical Warfare Service
C.Z. Canal Zone

D. Doctor
d. daughter
DAgr, D.Agr. Doctor of Agriculture
DAR Daughters of the American Revolution
dau. daughter
DAV Disabled American Veterans
DC, D.C. District of Columbia
DCL, D.C.L. Doctor of Civil Law
DCS, D.C.S. Doctor of Commercial Science
DD, D.D. Doctor of Divinity
DDS, D.D.S. Doctor of Dental Surgery
DE Delaware
Dec. December
dec. deceased
def. defense
Del. Delaware
del. delegate, delegation
Dem. Democrat, Democratic
DEng, D.Eng. Doctor of Engineering
denom. denomination, denominational
dep. deputy
dept. department
dermatol. dermatological
desc. descendant
devel. development, developmental
DFA, D.F.A. Doctor of Fine Arts
D.F.C. Distinguished Flying Cross
DHL, D.H.L. Doctor of Hebrew Literature
dir. director
dist. district
distbg. distributing
distbn. distribution
distbr. distributor
disting. distinguished
div. division, divinity, divorce
divsn. division
DLitt, D.Litt. Doctor of Literature
DMD, D.M.D. Doctor of Dental Medicine
DMS, D.M.S. Doctor of Medical Science
DO, D.O. Doctor of Osteopathy
docs. documents
DON Director of Nursing
DPH, D.P.H. Diploma in Public Health
DPhil, D.Phil. Doctor of Philosophy
D.R. Daughters of the Revolution
Dr. Drive, Doctor
DRE, D.R.E. Doctor of Religious Education
DrPH, Dr.P.H. Doctor of Public Health, Doctor of Public Hygiene

D.S.C. Distinguished Service Cross
DSc, D.Sc. Doctor of Science
DSChemE Doctor of Science in Chemical Engineering
D.S.M. Distinguished Service Medal
DST, D.S.T. Doctor of Sacred Theology
DTM, D.T.M. Doctor of Tropical Medicine
DVM, D.V.M. Doctor of Veterinary Medicine
DVS, D.V.S. Doctor of Veterinary Surgery

E, E. East
ea. eastern
E. and P. Extraordinary and Plenipotentiary
Eccles. Ecclesiastical
ecol. ecological
econ. economic
ECOSOC Economic and Social Council (of the UN)
ED, E.D. Doctor of Engineering
ed. educated
EdB, Ed.B. Bachelor of Education
EdD, Ed.D. Doctor of Education
edit. edition
editl. editorial
EdM, Ed.M. Master of Education
edn. education
ednl. educational
EDP Electronic Data Processing
EdS, Ed.S. Specialist in Education
EE, E.E. Electrical Engineer
E.E. and M.P. Envoy Extraordinary and Minister Plenipotentiary
EEC European Economic Community
EEG Electroencephalogram
EEO Equal Employment Opportunity
EEOC Equal Employment Opportunity Commission
E.Ger. German Democratic Republic
EKG Electrocardiogram
elec. electrical
electrochem. electrochemical
electrophys. electrophysical
elem. elementary
EM, E.M. Engineer of Mines
EMT Emergency Medical Technician
ency. encyclopedia
Eng. England
engr. engineer
engring. engineering
entomol. entomological
environ. environmental
EPA Environmental Protection Agency
epidemiol. epidemiological
Episc. Episcopalian
ERA Equal Rights Amendment
ERDA Energy Research and Development Administration
ESEA Elementary and Secondary Education Act
ESL English as Second Language
ESPN Entertainment and Sports Programming Network
ESSA Environmental Science Services Administration
ethnol. ethnological
ETO European Theatre of Operations
Evang. Evangelical
exam. examination, examining
Exch. Exchange
exec. executive
exhbn. exhibition
expdn. expedition
expn. exposition
expt. experiment
exptl. experimental
Expy. Expressway

Ext. Extension
F.A. Field Artillery
FAA Federal Aviation Administration
FAO Food and Agriculture Organization (of the UN)
FBA Federal Bar Association
FBI Federal Bureau of Investigation
FCA Farm Credit Administration
FCC Federal Communications Commission
FCDA Federal Civil Defense Administration
FDA Food and Drug Administration
FDIA Federal Deposit Insurance Administration
FDIC Federal Deposit Insurance Corporation
FE, F.E. Forest Engineer
FEA Federal Energy Administration
Feb. February
fed. federal
fedn. federation
FERC Federal Energy Regulatory Commission
fgn. foreign
FHA Federal Housing Administration
fin. financial, finance
FL Florida
Fl. Floor
Fla. Florida
FMC Federal Maritime Commission
FNP Family Nurse Practitioner
FOA Foreign Operations Administration
found. foundation
FPC Federal Power Commission
FPO Fleet Post Office
frat. fraternity
FRS Federal Reserve System
FSA Federal Security Agency
Ft. Fort
FTC Federal Trade Commission
Fwy. Freeway

G-1 (or other number) Division of General Staff
GA, Ga. Georgia
GAO General Accounting Office
gastroent. gastroenterological
GATE Gifted and Talented Educators
GATT General Agreement on Tariffs and Trade
GE General Electric Company
gen. general
geneal. genealogical
geod. geodetic
geog. geographic, geographical
geol. geological
geophys. geophysical
geriat. geriatrics
gerontol. gerontological
G.H.Q. General Headquarters
GM General Motors Corporation
GMAC General Motors Acceptance Corporation
G.N.Ry. Great Northern Railway
gov. governor
govt. government
govtl. governmental
GPO Government Printing Office
grad. graduate, graduated
GSA General Services Administration
Gt. Great
GTE General Telephone and ElectricCompany
GU Guam
gynecol. gynecological

HBO Home Box Office

hdqs. headquarters
HEW Department of Health, Education and Welfare
HHD, H.H.D. Doctor of Humanities
HHFA Housing and Home Finance Agency
HHS Department of Health and Human Services
HI Hawaii
hist. historical, historic
HM, H.M. Master of Humanities
HMO Health Maintenance Organization
homeo. homeopathic
hon. honorary, honorable
Ho. of Dels. House of Delegates
Ho. of Reps. House of Representatives
hort. horticultural
hosp. hospital
H.S. High School
HUD Department of Housing and Urban Development
Hwy. Highway
hydrog. hydrographic

IA Iowa
IAEA International Atomic Energy Agency
IATSE International Alliance of Theatrical and Stage Employees and Moving Picture Operators of the United States and Canada
IBM International Business Machines Corporation
IBRD International Bank for Reconstruction and Development
ICA International Cooperation Administration
ICC Interstate Commerce Commission
ICCE International Council for Computers in Education
ICU Intensive Care Unit
ID Idaho
IEEE Institute of Electrical and Electronics Engineers
IFC International Finance Corporation
IGY International Geophysical Year
IL Illinois
Ill. Illinois
illus. illustrated
ILO International Labor Organization
IMF International Monetary Fund
IN Indiana
Inc. Incorporated
Ind. Indiana
ind. independent
Indpls. Indianapolis
indsl. industrial
inf. infantry
info. information
ins. insurance
insp. inspector
insp. gen. inspector general
inst. institute
instl. institutional
instn. institution
instr. instructor
instrn. instruction
instrnl. instructional
internat. international
intro. introduction
IRE Institute of Radio Engineers
IRS Internal Revenue Service
ITT International Telephone & Telegraph Corporation

JAG Judge Advocate General
JAGC Judge Advocate General Corps
Jan. January
Jaycees Junior Chamber of Commerce
JB, J.B. Jurum Baccalaureus

JCB, J.C.B. Juris Canoni Baccalaureus
JCD, J.C.D. Juris Canonici Doctor, Juris Civilis Doctor
JCL, J.C.L. Juris Canonici Licentiatus
JD, J.D. Juris Doctor
jg. junior grade
jour. journal
jr. junior
JSD, J.S.D. Juris Scientiae Doctor
JUD, J.U.D. Juris Utriusque Doctor
jud. judicial

Kans. Kansas
K.C. Knights of Columbus
K.P. Knights of Pythias
KS Kansas
K.T. Knight Templar
KY, Ky. Kentucky

LA, La. Louisiana
L.A. Los Angeles
lab. laboratory
L.Am. Latin America
lang. language
laryngol. laryngological
LB Labrador
LDS Latter Day Saints
LDS Church Church of Jesus Christ of Latter Day Saints
lectr. lecturer
legis. legislation, legislative
LHD, L.H.D. Doctor of Humane Letters
L.I. Long Island
libr. librarian, library
lic. licensed, license
L.I.R.R. Long Island Railroad
lit. literature
litig. litigation
LittB, Litt.B. Bachelor of Letters
LittD, Litt.D. Doctor of Letters
LLB, LL.B. Bachelor of Laws
LLD, L.L.D. Doctor of Laws
LLM, L.L.M. Master of Laws
Ln. Lane
L.&N.R.R. Louisville & Nashville Railroad
LPGA Ladies Professional Golf Association
LPN Licensed Practical Nurse
LS, L.S. Library Science (in degree)
lt. lieutenant
Ltd. Limited
Luth. Lutheran
LWV League of Women Voters

M. Master
m. married
MA, M.A. Master of Arts
MA Massachusetts
MADD Mothers Against Drunk Driving
mag. magazine
MAgr, M.Agr. Master of Agriculture
maj. major
Man. Manitoba
Mar. March
MArch, M.Arch. Master in Architecture
Mass. Massachusetts
math. mathematics, mathematical
MATS Military Air Transport Service
MB, M.B. Bachelor of Medicine
MB Manitoba
MBA, M.B.A. Master of Business Administration
MBS Mutual Broadcasting System
M.C. Medical Corps
MCE, M.C.E. Master of Civil Engineering
mcht. merchant
mcpl. municipal

MCS, M.C.S. Master of Commercial Science
MD, M.D. Doctor of Medicine
MD, Md. Maryland
MDiv Master of Divinity
MDip, M.Dip. Master in Diplomacy
mdse. merchandise
MDV, M.D.V. Doctor of Veterinary Medicine
ME, M.E. Mechanical Engineer
ME Maine
M.E.Ch. Methodist Episcopal Church
mech. mechanical
MEd., M.Ed. Master of Education
med. medical
MEE, M.E.E. Master of Electrical Engineering
mem. member
meml. memorial
merc. mercantile
met. metropolitan
metall. metallurgical
MetE, Met.E. Metallurgical Engineer
meteorol. meteorological
Meth. Methodist
Mex. Mexico
MF, M.F. Master of Forestry
MFA, M.F.A. Master of Fine Arts
mfg. manufacturing
mfr. manufacturer
mgmt. management
mgr. manager
MHA, M.H.A. Master of Hospital Administration
M.I. Military Intelligence
MI Michigan
Mich. Michigan
micros. microscopic, microscopical
mid. middle
mil. military
Milw. Milwaukee
Min. Minister
mineral. mineralogical
Minn. Minnesota
MIS Management Information Systems
Miss. Mississippi
MIT Massachusetts Institute of Technology
mktg. marketing
ML, M.L. Master of Laws
MLA Modern Language Association
M.L.D. Magister Legnum Diplomatic
MLitt, M.Litt. Master of Literature, Master of Letters
MLS, M.L.S. Master of Library Science
MME, M.M.E. Master of Mechanical Engineering
MN Minnesota
mng. managing
MO, Mo. Missouri
moblzn. mobilization
Mont. Montana
MP Northern Mariana Islands
M.P. Member of Parliament
MPA Master of Public Administration
MPE, M.P.E. Master of Physical Education
MPH, M.P.H. Master of Public Health
MPhil, M.Phil. Master of Philosophy
MPL, M.P.L. Master of Patent Law
Mpls. Minneapolis
MRE, M.R.E. Master of Religious Education
MRI Magnetic Resonance Imaging
MS, M.S. Master of Science
MS, Ms. Mississippi
MSc, M.Sc. Master of Science
MSChemE Master of Science in Chemical Engineering

MSEE Master of Science in Electrical Engineering
MSF, M.S.F. Master of Science of Forestry
MSN Master of Science in Nursing
MST, M.S.T. Master of Sacred Theology
MSW, M.S.W. Master of Social Work
MT Montana
Mt. Mount
MTO Mediterranean Theatre of Operation
MTV Music Television
mus. museum, musical
MusB, Mus.B. Bachelor of Music
MusD, Mus.D. Doctor of Music
MusM, Mus.M. Master of Music
mut. mutual
MVP Most Valuable Player
mycol. mycological

N. North
NAACOG Nurses Association of the American College of Obstetricians and Gynecologists
NAACP National Association for the Advancement of Colored People
NACA National Advisory Committee for Aeronautics
NACDL National Association of Criminal Defense Lawyers
NACU National Association of Colleges and Universities
NAD National Academy of Design
NAE National Academy of Engineering, National Association of Educators
NAESP National Association of Elementary School Principals
NAFE National Association of Female Executives
N.Am. North America
NAM National Association of Manufacturers
NAMH National Association for Mental Health
NAPA National Association of Performing Artists
NARAS National Academy of Recording Arts and Sciences
NAREB National Association of Real Estate Boards
NARS National Archives and Record Service
NAS National Academy of Sciences
NASA National Aeronautics and Space Administration
NASP National Association of School Psychologists
NASW National Association of Social Workers
nat. national
NATAS National Academy of Television Arts and Sciences
NATO North Atlantic Treaty Organization
NATOUSA North African Theatre of Operations, United States Army
nav. navigation
NB, N.B. New Brunswick
NBA National Basketball Association
NBC National Broadcasting Company
NC, N.C. North Carolina
NCAA National College Athletic Association
NCCJ National Conference of Christians and Jews
ND, N.D. North Dakota
NDEA National Defense Education Act
NE Nebraska
NE, N.E. Northeast
NEA National Education Association
Nebr. Nebraska
NEH National Endowment for Humanities

neurol. neurological
Nev. Nevada
NF Newfoundland
NFL National Football League
Nfld. Newfoundland
NG National Guard
NH, N.H. New Hampshire
NHL National Hockey League
NIH National Institutes of Health
NIMH National Institute of Mental Health
NJ, N.J. New Jersey
NLRB National Labor Relations Board
NM New Mexico
N.Mex. New Mexico
No. Northern
NOAA National Oceanographic and Atmospheric Administration
NORAD North America Air Defense
Nov. November
NOW National Organization for Women
N.P.Ry. Northern Pacific Railway
nr. near
NRA National Rifle Association
NRC National Research Council
NS, N.S. Nova Scotia
NSC National Security Council
NSF National Science Foundation
NSTA National Science Teachers Association
NSW New South Wales
N.T. New Testament
NT Northwest Territories
nuc. nuclear
numis. numismatic
NV Nevada
NW, N.W. Northwest
N.W.T. Northwest Territories
NY, N.Y. New York
N.Y.C. New York City
NYU New York University
N.Z. New Zealand

OAS Organization of American States
ob-gyn obstetrics-gynecology
obs. observatory
obstet. obstetrical
occupl. occupational
oceanog. oceanographic
Oct. October
OD, O.D. Doctor of Optometry
OECD Organization for Economic Cooperation and Development
OEEC Organization of European Economic Cooperation
OEO Office of Economic Opportunity
ofcl. official
OH Ohio
OK Oklahoma
Okla. Oklahoma
ON Ontario
Ont. Ontario
oper. operating
ophthal. ophthalmological
ops. operations
OR Oregon
orch. orchestra
Oreg. Oregon
orgn. organization
orgnl. organizational
ornithol. ornithological
orthop. orthopedic
OSHA Occupational Safety and Health Administration
OSRD Office of Scientific Research and Development
OSS Office of Strategic Services
osteo. osteopathic
otol. otological

otolaryn. otolaryngological

PA, Pa. Pennsylvania
P.A. Professional Association
paleontol. paleontological
path. pathological
PBS Public Broadcasting System
P.C. Professional Corporation
PE Prince Edward Island
pediat. pediatrics
P.E.I. Prince Edward Island
PEN Poets, Playwrights, Editors, Essayists and Novelists (international association)
penol. penological
P.E.O. women's organization (full name not disclosed)
pers. personnel
pfc. private first class
PGA Professional Golfers' Association of America
PHA Public Housing Administration
pharm. pharmaceutical
PharmD, Pharm.D. Doctor of Pharmacy
PharmM, Pharm.M. Master of Pharmacy
PhB, Ph.B. Bachelor of Philosophy
PhD, Ph.D. Doctor of Philosophy
PhDChemE Doctor of Science in Chemical Engineering
PhM, Ph.M. Master of Philosophy
Phila. Philadelphia
philharm. philharmonic
philol. philological
philos. philosophical
photog. photographic
phys. physical
physiol. physiological
Pitts. Pittsburgh
Pk. Park
Pky. Parkway
Pl. Place
P.&L.E.R.R. Pittsburgh & Lake Erie Railroad
Plz. Plaza
PNP Pediatric Nurse Practitioner
P.O. Post Office
PO Box Post Office Box
polit. political
poly. polytechnic, polytechnical
PQ Province of Quebec
PR, P.R. Puerto Rico
prep. preparatory
pres. president
Presbyn. Presbyterian
presdl. presidential
prin. principal
procs. proceedings
prod. produced (play production)
prodn. production
prodr. producer
prof. professor
profl. professional
prog. progressive
propr. proprietor
pros. atty. prosecuting attorney
pro tem. pro tempore
PSRO Professional Services Review Organization
psychiat. psychiatric
psychol. psychological
PTA Parent-Teachers Association
ptnr. partner
PTO Pacific Theatre of Operations, Parent Teacher Organization
pub. publisher, publishing, published
pub. public
publ. publication
pvt. private

quar. quarterly
qm. quartermaster
Q.M.C. Quartermaster Corps
Que. Quebec

radiol. radiological
RAF Royal Air Force
RCA Radio Corporation of America
RCAF Royal Canadian Air Force
RD Rural Delivery
Rd. Road
R&D Research & Development
REA Rural Electrification Administration
rec. recording
ref. reformed
regt. regiment
regtl. regimental
rehab. rehabilitation
rels. relations
Rep. Republican
rep. representative
Res. Reserve
ret. retired
Rev. Reverend
rev. review, revised
RFC Reconstruction Finance Corporation
RFD Rural Free Delivery
rhinol. rhinological
RI, R.I. Rhode Island
RISD Rhode Island School of Design
Rlwy. Railway
Rm. Room
RN, R.N. Registered Nurse
roentgenol. roentgenological
ROTC Reserve Officers Training Corps
RR Rural Route
R.R. Railroad
rsch. research
rschr. researcher
Rt. Route

S. South
s. son
SAC Strategic Air Command
SAG Screen Actors Guild
SALT Strategic Arms Limitation Talks
S.Am. South America
san. sanitary
SAR Sons of the American Revolution
Sask. Saskatchewan
savs. savings
SB, S.B. Bachelor of Science
SBA Small Business Administration
SC, S.C. South Carolina
SCAP Supreme Command Allies Pacific
ScB, Sc.B. Bachelor of Science
SCD, S.C.D. Doctor of Commercial Science
ScD, Sc.D. Doctor of Science
sch. school
sci. science, scientific
SCLC Southern Christian Leadership Conference
SCV Sons of Confederate Veterans
SD, S.D. South Dakota
SE, S.E. Southeast
SEATO Southeast Asia Treaty Organization
SEC Securities and Exchange Commission
sec. secretary
sect. section
seismol. seismological
sem. seminary
Sept. September
s.g. senior grade
sgt. sergeant
SHAEF Supreme Headquarters Allied Expeditionary Forces
SHAPE Supreme Headquarters Allied Powers

in Europe
S.I. Staten Island
S.J. Society of Jesus (Jesuit)
SJD Scientiae Juridicae Doctor
SK Saskatchewan
SM, S.M. Master of Science
SNP Society of Nursing Professionals
So. Southern
soc. society
sociol. sociological
S.P.Co. Southern Pacific Company
spkr. speaker
spl. special
splty. specialty
Sq. Square
S.R. Sons of the Revolution
sr. senior
SS Steamship
SSS Selective Service System
St. Saint, Street
sta. station
stats. statistics
statis. statistical
STB, S.T.B. Bachelor of Sacred Theology
stblzn. stabilization
STD, S.T.D. Doctor of Sacred Theology
std. standard
Ste. Suite
subs. subsidiary
SUNY State University of New York
supr. supervisor
supt. superintendent
surg. surgical
svc. service
SW, S.W. Southwest
sys. system

TAPPI Technical Association of the Pulp and Paper Industry
tb. tuberculosis
tchg. teaching
tchr. teacher
tech. technical, technology
technol. technological
tel. telephone
Tel. & Tel. Telephone & Telegraph
telecom. telecommunications
temp. temporary
Tenn. Tennessee
Ter. Territory
Ter. Terrace
TESOL Teachers of English to Speakers of Other Languages
Tex. Texas
ThD, Th.D. Doctor of Theology

theol. theological
ThM, Th.M. Master of Theology
TN Tennessee
tng. training
topog. topographical
trans. transaction, transferred
transl. translation, translated
transp. transportation
treas. treasurer
TT Trust Territory
TV television
TVA Tennessee Valley Authority
TWA Trans World Airlines
twp. township
TX Texas
typog. typographical

U. University
UAW United Auto Workers
UCLA University of California at Los Angeles
UDC United Daughters of the Confederacy
U.K. United Kingdom
UN United Nations
UNESCO United Nations Educational, Scientific and Cultural Organization
UNICEF United Nations International Children's Emergency Fund
univ. university
UNRRA United Nations Relief and Rehabilitation Administration
UPI United Press International
U.P.R.R. United Pacific Railroad
urol. urological
U.S. United States
U.S.A. United States of America
USAAF United States Army Air Force
USAF United States Air Force
USAFR United States Air Force Reserve
USAR United States Army Reserve
USCG United States Coast Guard
USCGR United States Coast Guard Reserve
USES United States Employment Service
USIA United States Information Agency
USMC United States Marine Corps
USMCR United States Marine Corps Reserve
USN United States Navy
USNG United States National Guard
USNR United States Naval Reserve
USO United Service Organizations
USPHS United States Public Health Service
USS United States Ship
USSR Union of the Soviet Socialist Republics
USTA United States Tennis Association

USV United States Volunteers
UT Utah

VA Veterans Administration
VA, Va. Virginia
vet. veteran, veterinary
VFW Veterans of Foreign Wars
VI, V.I. Virgin Islands
vice pres. vice president
vis. visiting
VISTA Volunteers in Service to America
VITA Volunteers in Technical Assistance
vocat. vocational
vol. volunteer, volume
v.p. vice president
vs. versus
VT, Vt. Vermont

W, W. West
WA Washington (state)
WAC Women's Army Corps
Wash. Washington (state)
WATS Wide Area Telecommunications Service
WAVES Women's Reserve, US Naval Reserve
WCTU Women's Christian Temperance Union
we. western
W. Ger. Germany, Federal Republic of
WHO World Health Organization
WI Wisconsin
W.I. West Indies
Wis. Wisconsin
WSB Wage Stabilization Board
WV West Virginia
W.Va. West Virginia
WWI World War I
WWII World War II
WY Wyoming
Wyo. Wyoming

YK Yukon Territory
YMCA Young Men's Christian Association
YMHA Young Men's Hebrew Association
YM & YWHA Young Men's and Young Women's Hebrew Association
yr. year
YT, Y.T. Yukon Territory
YWCA Young Women's Christian Association

zool. zoological

Alphabetical Practices

Names are arranged alphabetically according to the surnames, and under identical surnames according to the first given name. If both surname and first given name are identical, names are arranged alphabetically according to the second given name.

Surnames beginning with De, Des, Du, however capitalized or spaced, are recorded with the prefix preceding the surname and arranged alphabetically under the letter D.

Surnames beginning with Mac and Mc are arranged alphabetically under M.

Surnames beginning with Saint or St. appear after names that begin Sains, and are arranged according to the second part of the name, e.g. St. Clair before Saint Dennis.

Surnames beginning with Van, Von, or von are arranged alphabetically under the letter V.

Compound surnames are arranged according to the first member of the compound.

Many hyphenated Arabic names begin Al-, El-, or al-. These names are alphabetized according to each Biographee's designation of last name. Thus Al-Bahar, Neta may be listed either under Al- or under Bahar, depending on the preference of the listee.

Also, Arabic names have a variety of possible spellings when transposed to English. Spelling of these names is always based on the practice of the Biographee. Some Biographees use a Western form of word order, while others prefer the Arabic word sequence.

Similarly, Asian names may have no comma between family and given names, but some Biographees have chosen to add the comma. In each case, punctuation follows the preference of the Biographee.

Parentheses used in connection with a name indicate which part of the full name is usually deleted in common usage. Hence Chambers, E(lizabeth) Anne indicates that the usual form of the given name is E. Anne. In such a case, the parentheses are ignored in alphabetizing and the name would be arranged as Chambers, Elizabeth Anne. However, if the name is recorded Chambers, (Elizabeth) Anne, signifying that the entire name Elizabeth is not commonly used, the alphabetizing would be arranged as though the name were Chambers, Anne. If an entire middle or last name is enclosed in parentheses, that portion of the name is used in the alphabetical arrangement. Hence Chambers, Elizabeth (Anne) would be arranged as Chambers, Elizabeth Anne.

Where more than one spelling, word order, or name of an individual is frequently encountered, the sketch has been entered under the form preferred by the Biographee, with cross-references under alternate forms.

Who'sWho in American Law®

Biographies

AARON, KENNETH ELLYOT, lawyer; b. Phila., Nov. 3, 1948; s. Neal L. and Dorothea G. Aaron; m. Phyllis A. Carroll, May 29, 1969; children: Seth Joel, Joshua Scott. BS in Econs., U. Pa., 1970, JD, 1973. Bar: Pa. 1973, U.S. Dist. Ct. (ea. dist.) Pa. 1973, U.S. Ct. Appeals (3d cir.) 1974, U.S. Supreme Ct. 1977, U.S. Dist. Ct. (we. dist.) Pa. 1993, Del. 2001, Fla. 2001, U.S. Dist. Ct. Del. 2001; cert. bus.bankruptcy law specialist Am. Bankruptcy Bd, Cert. Assoc. Astor & Weiss, Phila., 1973-76; ptnr. Casper & Davidson, P.C., 1976-80; pvt. practice, 1980-83; ptnr. Garfinkel & Volpicelli, 1983-86, Mesirov, Gelman, Jaffe, Cramer & Jamieson, Phila., 1986-91, Buchanan Ingersoll P.C., Phila., 1991-2001, Weir & Ptnrs., Phila., 2001—. Mem. Ea. Dist. Pa. Bankruptcy Conf., vice chmn. edn. com. 1991, co-chmn. 1992, co-chmn. legis com., 1993; trustee Phila. Bar Found., 1997-2000. Author: Foreclosure and Repossession, 1989, (chpt.) Bus. Lawyer's Bankruptcy Guide, 1992, BNA's Environmental Due Diligence Guide, 1992, Matthew Bender's Environmental Law Practice Guide, 1992. Commr. Haverford (Pa.) Twp. Planning Bd., 1978—80; chmn. Lower Merton Zoning Bd., 1993—; planning commr. Lower Marion Twp. Planning Bd., Ardmore, Pa., 1992. Recipient Tax Writing award Nat. Assn. Accts., 1970, Am. Jr. award in Creditors' Rights, 1973. Mem.: Phila. Bar Assn. (chmn. commn. on insolvency issues in real estate 1989—), Phila. Bar Found. (trustee 1997—), Rotary (pres. Haverford Twp. 1982—83), Hias & Coun. (v.p. 1999—). Avocations: sports, camping, golfing. Bankruptcy, Contracts commercial, Insurance. Office: Weir & Ptnrs 1339 Chestnut St Ste 500 Philadelphia PA 19107

AARONS, STEPHEN D. lawyer; b. St. Louis, Nov. 23, 1954; s. Donale E. and Teddye W. Costello; m. Doris A. Valdez, Apr. 12, 1993; 1 child, Ian. BA, George Washington U., 1976; MA, Oxford (Eng.) U., 1984; JD, St. Louis U., 1979. Bar: N.Mex., U.S. Supreme Ct. VISTA lawyer Mont. Legal Svcs., Gt. Falls, 1979-80; judge advocate U.S. Army Intelligence Command, Augsburg, Germany, 1980-83; chief capital trial def. counsel N.Mex. Pub. Defender Dept., Santa Fe, 1984-89; assoc. Jones, Snead, Wertheim, 1989-92; mng. atty. Aarons Law Firm, PC, 1992—. Mem. faculty Nat. Inst. Trial Advocacy. Nat. pres. Coll. Dems. of Am., Washington, 1975-77. Lt. col. USAR, 1980—. Office: Aarons Law Firm PC 300 Catron St Santa Fe NM 87501-1807

AARONSON, DAVID ERNEST, law educator, lawyer; b. Washington, Sept. 19, 1940; s. Edward Allan and May (Rosett) A.; m. Laura Dine, 1991; stepchildren: Dara Prushansky, Jared Prushansky. B.A. in Econs, George Washington U., 1961, M.A., 1964, Ph.D., 1970; LL.B., Harvard U., 1964; LL.M. (E. Barrett Prettyman fellow), Georgetown U., 1965. Bar: D.C. bar 1965, Md. bar 1975, U.S. Supreme Ct. bar 1969. Research asst. Office of Commr., Bur. Labor Stats., U.S. Dept. Labor, Washington, 1961; staff atty. legal intern program Georgetown Grad. Law Center, 1964-65; research assoc. patent research project dept. econs. George Washington U., 1966; assoc. firm Aaronson and Aaronson, 1965-67, ptnr., 1967-70; prof., B.J. Tennery Scholar Am. U. Law Sch., Washington, 1970—; prof. Sch. Justice, Coll. Public and Internat. Affairs, 1981-92; dep. dir. Law and Policy Inst., Jerusalem, Israel, summer, 1978. Interim dir. clin. programs Md. Criminal Justice Clinic, 1971-73, founder prosecutor criminal litigation clinic, 1972, co-dir. trial practice litigation program, 1982—; vis. prof. Law Sch. of Hebrew U., Jerusalem, summer, 1978; trustee Montgomery-Prince George's Continuing Legal Edn. Inst., 1983—. Author: Maryland Criminal Jury Instructions and Commentary, 1975, (with N.N. Kittrie and D. Saari) Alternatives to Conventional Criminal Adjudication: Guidebook for Planners and Practitioners, 1977, (with B. Hoff, P. Jaszi, N.N. Kittrie and D. Saari) The New Justice: Alternatives to Conventional Criminal Adjudication, 1977, (with C.T. Dienes and M.C. Musheno) Decriminalization of Public Drunkenness: Tracing the Implementation of a Public Policy, 1981, Public Policy and Police Discretion: Processes of Decriminalization, 1984, (with R. Simon) The Insanity Defense: A Critical Assessment of Law and Policy in the Post-Hinckley Era, 1988, Maryland Criminal Jury Instructions and Commentary, 2d rev. edit., 1988; contbr. articles to legal and public policy jours. Mem. council Friendship Heights Village Council, 1979. Recipient Outstanding Community Service award, 1980; Outstanding Tchr. award Am. U. Law Sch., 1978, 81, Scholar/Tchr. of the Year award Am. U., 1989; Pauline Ruyle Moore scholar in Pub. Law, 1983 Mem. ABA (mem. criminal justice sect. rules of cr. prof. and evid. com. 1991—), D.C. Bar Assn. (chmn. criminal code rev. com. 1971-73), Md. State Bar Assn. (criminal law sect. coun. 1984—, chairperson 1989-90, Robert C. Heeney award 1999), Assn. Am. Law Schs. (elected to sect. coun., criminal justice sect. 1999—), Montgomery County (Md.) Bar Assn., Soc. for Reform of Criminal Law, Am. Law Inst., Phi Beta Kappa. Office: Am U Law Sch 4801 Massachusetts Ave NW Washington DC 20016-8196 E-mail: daarons@wcl.american.edu

ABAUNZA, DONALD RICHARD, lawyer; b. New Orleans, Oct. 25, 1945; s. Alfred E. and Virginia (White) A.; m. Carolyn Thompson; 1 child, Richard. BA, Vanderbilt U., 1966; JD, Tulane U., 1969. Bar: La. 1969, U.S. Dist. Ct. (ea. dist.) La. 1969, U.S. Dist. Ct. (we. dist.) La. 1980, U.S. Supreme Ct. 1986. Assoc. Lemle, Kelleher, Kohlmeyer, Dennery, Hunley, Moss & Frilot, New Orleans, 1969-76; ptnr. Liskow & Lewis, 1977-96, mng. ptnr., 1996—. Adj. faculty Tulane Sch. Law, 1981-89. Fellow Am. Coll. Trial Lawyers; mem. La. Bar Assn. (Pres.'s award 1988). Admiralty, General civil litigation, Insurance. Office: Liskow & Lewis 1 Shell Sq 50th Fl 701 Poydras St New Orleans LA 70139-5099

ABBOTT, BARRY ALEXANDER, lawyer; b. New Haven, Aug. 20, 1950; s. Harold and Norma (Kaufman) A.; 1 child, Anne Stewart. AB, Dartmouth Coll., 1972; JD, U. Fla., 1975; MBA, Stanford U., 1977. Bar: Fla. 1975, Calif. 1976, U.S. Dist. Ct. (so. dist.) Fla. 1976, U.S. Dist. Ct. (no. dist.) Calif. 1976, U.S. Ct. Appeals (9th cir.) 1976, U.S. Supreme Ct. 1979, D.C. 1985, N.Y. 1986. Assoc. Morrison & Foerster, San Francisco, 1977-83, ptnr., 1983-94; dir. Howard Rice Nemerovski Canady Falk & Rabkin, 1994—. Adj. faculty mem. Boalt Hall Sch. Law, U. Calif., Berkeley, 1998; lectr. corp., comml. and fin. inst. law various orgns.; mem. Fed. Res. Bd. Consumer Adv. Coun., 1992-94, chmn. consumer credit com., 1993-94, mem. governing com. Conf. on Consumer Fin. Law; mem. Am. Coll. Consumer Fin. Svcs. Attys., 1995—, bd. regents, 1995-98. Co-author: Truth in Lending: A Comprehensive Guide; contbr. articles to profl. jours. Named One of Outstanding Young Men of Am., U.S. Jaycees, 1980. Fellow Royal Soc. Arts (Silver medal 1972); mem. ABA (chmn. young lawyers divsn. bus. law com. 1987-88, chmn. ins. products subcom. 1987-92, vice chmn. consumer fin. svcs. commn. 1995-96, active various coms.), Calif. Bar Assn. (vice chair fin. instns. com. 1991-92, chair 1992-93, mem. ins. law com. 1994-96, mem. bus. law sect. exec. com. 1996-99, treas. 1997-98, vice chair 1998-99), Fla. Bar Assn., D.C. Bar Assn., N.Y. State Bar Assn., San Francisco Bar Assn. (chmn. membership com. 1984-86, bd. dirs. 1982, 87-88, Award of Merit 1985), Barristers Club (bd. dirs. 1981-83, treas., pres. 1982), Order of Coif, Phi Beta Kappa, Phi Kappa Phi. Republican. Clubs: World Trade (San Francisco), Commonwealth (Calif.). Banking, Contracts commercial, Insurance. Office: Howard Rice 3 Embarcadero Ctr Ste 700 San Francisco CA 94111-4065 E-mail: babbott@hrice.com

ABBOTT, BOB, state supreme court justice; b. Kans., Nov. 1, 1932; BS, Emporia State U.; JD, Washburn U.; LLM, U. Va. Bar: Kans. 1960. Pvt. practice, Junction City, Kans., from 1960; former chief judge Kans. Ct. Appeals; justice Kans. Supreme Ct., 1990—. Office: Kansas Supreme Court 374 Kansas Judicial Ctr 301 SW 10th St Topeka KS 66612-1507*

ABBOTT, CHARLES FAVOUR, lawyer; b. Sedro-Wolley, Wash., Oct. 12, 1937; s. Charles Favour and Violette Doris Abbott; m. Oranee Harward, Sept. 19, 1958; children: Patricia, Stephen, Nelson, Cynthia, Lisa, Alyson. BA in Econs., U. Wash., 1959, JD, 1962. BAr: Calif. 1962, Utah 1981. Law clk. Judge M. Oliver Koelsch, U.S. Ct. Appeals (9th cir.), San Francisco, 1963; assoc. Jones, Hatfield & Abbott, Escondido, Calif., 1964; pvt. practice, 1964-77, Provo, Utah, 1983-93; of counsel Mueller & Abbott, Escondido, 1997—; ptnr. Abbott, Thorn & Hill, Provo, 1981-83, Abbott & Abbott, Provo, 1993—. Author: How to Do Your Own Legal Work, 1976, 2d edit., 1981, How to Win in Small Claims Court, 1981, How to Be Free of Debt in 24 Hours, 1981, How to Hire the Best Lawyer at the Lowest Fee, 1981, The Lawyers's Inside Method of Making Money, 1979, The Millionaire Mindset, 1987, How to Make Big Money in the Next 30 Days, 1989, Business Legal Manual and Forms, 1990, How to Make Millions in Marketing, 1990, Telemarketing Training Course, 1990, How to Form A Corporation in Any State, 1990, The Complete Asset Protection Plan, 1990, Personal Injury and the Law, 1997, Fen-Phen Fallout--The Medical and Legal Crisis, 1998; mem. editl. bd. Wash. Law Rev. and State Bar Assn. Jour., 1961-62; bd. editors Phen-fen Litigation Strategist, 1998-2000; contbr. articles to profl. jours. Mem. ATLA, Utah Bar Assn., Calif. Bar Assn., U.S. Supreme Ct. Bar Assn. Administrative and regulatory, General civil litigation, Personal injury. Home: 2830 N Marrcrest Circle Provo UT 84058 Office: Abbott & Abbott 3651 N 100 E Ste 300 Provo UT 84604-4521

ABBOTT, CHARLES HENRY, lawyer; b. Rumford, Maine, Oct. 26, 1935; s. Warren Salisbury and Lucille (Hicks) A.; m. Mary Myers; children: Woods, Edward, Ann. AB, Bowdoin Coll., 1957; LLB, Yale U., 1963. Bar: Maine 1963, U.S. Dist. Ct. Maine 1963, U.S. Ct. Appeals (1st cir.) 1965, U.S. Supreme Ct. 1980. Ptnr. Skelton, Taintor & Abbott, Auburn, Maine, 1964—; bd. dirs. Cen. Maine Power Co.; mem. First Circuit Judge Selection Panel, Boston, 1979-80. Contbr. articles to profl. jours. Mem. Gov.'s Exec. Council, State of Maine, 1975-76. Served to lt. CIC, U.S. Army, 1958-60. Fellow Am. Coll. Trial Lawyers; mem. Am. Judicature Soc. Democrat. Federal civil litigation, State civil litigation. Office: Skelton Taintor & Abbott PO Box 3200 Auburn ME 04212-3200

ABBOTT, CHARLES WARREN, lawyer; b. Miami, Jan. 16, 1930; s. Voyle E. and Katherine (Paschall) A.; m. Betty Jo Eckholdt, Jan. 9, 1959; children: Brenda Jean, Katherine Louise, Abigail Jill. BS in Bus. Adminstrn., U. Fla., 1951, JD, 1953. Bar: Fla. 1955, U.S. Dist. Ct. (so. dist.) Fla. 1955, U.S. Dist. Ct. (ctrl. dist.) Fla., U.S. Supreme Ct. 1960, U.S. Ct. Appeals (11th cir.) 1981, U.S. Dist. Ct. (no. dist.) Fla. 1981; cert. mediator Supreme Ct. Fla. Assoc. Maguire, Voorhis & Wells, P.A., Orlando, Fla., 1955-59, ptnr., 1959-68, dir., 1968-95; ptnr. Holland & Knight LLP, 1998—. Mem. judicial nominating commn. Fifth Appellate Dist., 1984-88, chmn. 1987-88. Chmn. Goldenrod Fire Control Dist., 1966-79; mem. Orange County Emergency Med. Svcs. Coun., 1984, 91-94; dir. Fla. Found. for Spl. Children. Served with JAGC, USAF, 1953-55; served to capt. USAFR, 1951-62. Fellow Am. Coll. Trial Lawyers; mem. ABA, Fla. Bar Assn., Orange County Bar Asns., Fla. Def. Lawyers Assn. (sec.-treas. 1983, v.p. 1984, pres. 1985), Def. Rsch. Inst. (state chmn. 1981-85, so. regional v.p. 1986-88, nat. dir. 1988-91), Fedn. Ins. Corp. Counsel, Internat. Assn. Def. Counsel, Am. Bd. Trial Advs. (charter, treas. 1991-92, sec. 1992-93), Am. Inns of Ct. (charter mem., treas. 1st ctrl. Fla., pres. 1992-93), Phi Delta Phi. Democrat. Presbyterian. General civil litigation, Personal injury. Home: 2035 Summerland Ave Winter Park FL 32789-1453 Office: Holland & Knight LLP PO Box 1526 200 S Orange Ave Ste 2600 Orlando FL 32801

ABBOTT, HIRSCHEL THERON, JR. lawyer; b. Clarksdale, Miss., Jan. 11, 1942; s. Hirschel Theron Sr. and Ona Belle (Williamson) A.; m. Mimi Eugenia DuPre, June 14, 1969; children: Barkley, Chip. BBA in Acct., U. Miss., Oxford, 1964; JD, U. Va., Charlottesville, 1971. Bar: La. 1971, Miss. 1971, U.S. Dist. Ct. (ea. dist.) La. 1971, U.S. Ct. Appeals (5th cir.) 1981, U.S. Tax Ct. 1988; bd. cert. tax law specialist. Lawyer Stone, Pigman, Walther, Wittmann & Hutchinson, New Orleans, 1971-75, ptnr., 1975—. Bd. dirs. Episcopal Housing for Srs., Inc., Lambeth House, Inc.; past trustee, sec. Preservation Resource Ctr., New Orleans; past bd. mem., chmn. Trinity Episcopal Sch. Bd. Trustees; past trustee, treas. La. Civil Svc. League; past bd. mem. Uptown Neighborhood Improvement Assn.; past mem., chmn. Jefferson Scholarship Selection Com. U. Va.; past regional chmn. U. Va. Law Sch. Annual Giving Fund; past mem. of vestry Trinity Episcopal Ch.; past mem. Adv. Bd. Jr. League New Orleans. Recipient Monte M. Lemann award, La. Civil Svc. League, 1989. Fellow Am. Coll. Trust and Estate Counsel (past mem. charitable planning and exempt orgns. com.), La. Bar Found.; mem. ABA (tax sect., bus. law sect., real property trusts probate sect.), La. Bar Assn. (past chmn. tax law specialization commn., tax sect., corp. sect., successions, donations and trusts sect.), Miss. State Bar Assn., New Orleans Estate Planning Coun., Assn. Employee Benefit Planners. Epicopalian. General corporate, Estate planning, Taxation, general. Office: Stone Pigman Walther et al 546 Carondelet St New Orleans LA 70130-3588 E-mail: habbott@stonepigman.com

ABBOTT, WILLIAM ANTHONY, lawyer; b. Austin, Minn., May 25, 1951; s. Robert Elmer and Marion Iris (Edel) A.; m. Deborah Lynn Hunt, Apr. 23, 1982; 1 child, Whitney Hunt. BBA with distinction, U. Wis., 1973, JD cum laude, 1975. Bar: Wis. 1976, U.S. Dist. Ct. (we. dist.) Wis. 1976, U.S. Tax Ct. 1981. Ptnr., Bell, Metzner, Gierhart & Moore, S.C., Madison, Wis., 1980— . V.p. Briarpatch, Inc. for runaway youth, Madison, 1979-87, pres. 1988; ambassador Picada; sec. Energy Assistance, Inc., Madison, 1983; committeeman United Way Pres.'s Council, Madison, 1984—. Mem. ABA, Wis. Bar Assn., Dane County Bar Assn., Middleton Jaycees (pres. 1978), Order of Coif, Airplane Owners and Pilots Assn., Phi Kappa Phi, Beta Gamma Sigma. Clubs: Bklyn. Flying (v.p. 1987—), Wis. Fun Flyers, Inc. (v.p. 1987—). Lodge: Optimists (bd. dirs. 1985-86). General corporate, Real property, Corporate taxation. Office: Bell Metzner Gierhart & Moore SC 2472 Thatcher Ln Mc Farland WI 53558-9737

ABBOTT, WILLIAM SAUNDERS, lawyer; b. Medford, Mass., June 2, 1938; s. Charles Theodoric and Evelyn (Saunders) A.; m. Susan Shaw, June 24, 1961; children: Cathryn, Stephen, David. AB, Harvard U., 1960, LLB, 1966. Bar: Mass. 1967, U.S. Dist. Ct. Mass., U.S. Ct. Appeals (D.C. cir.). White House fellow, 1966-67; regional coord. U.S. Agrl. Programs Asia USDA, 1967-68; gen. counsel Cabot, Cabot & Forbes Co., Boston, 1968-77; prin. Simonds, Winslow, Willis & Abbott, 1977—. With Harvard Law Review. Bd. dirs. Bay Tower Restaurant, Arlington Bd. Selectmen, 1970-73; pres. Plymouth County Wildlands Trust, 1984-90, 96-97; pres. Nat. Found. to Improve TV, 1970—. Lt. USN, 1963-66. Mem. Mass. Bar Assn., Boston Bar Assn., Phi Beta Kappa. General corporate, Real property. Home: 33 Herring Way Plymouth MA 02360-3225 Office: Simonds Winslow Willis & Abbott 50 Congress St Ste 925 Boston MA 02109-4075 E-mail: wabbott1@aol.com

ABELE, ROBERT CHRISTOPHER, lawyer; b. Boonville, Mo., Mar. 24, 1958; s. William Arved and Joyce (Gowan) A. AB, U. Mo., 1980; JD, U. Mo., Kansas City, 1983. Bar: Mo. 1983, U.S. Dist. Ct. (we. dist.) Mo. 1983, U.S. Dist. Ct. Kans. 1998, U.S. Ct. Appeals (8th cir.) 1983, U.S. Ct. Appeals (10th cir.) 1985, U.S. Supreme Ct. 1991, U.S. Ct. Appeals (11th cir.) 1993. Law clk. to judge U.S. Ct. Appeals (8th cir.), 1983-85; assoc. Morrison, Hecker, Curtis, Kuder & Parrish, Kansas City, Mo., 1985-90, ptnr., 1990-91, Morrison & Hecker, Kansas City, 1991-95, Badger & Levings, Kansas City, 1995-2000; atty. law dept. Sprint, 2001—. Adj. prof. U. Mo. Kansas City Sch. Law, 1988. Chmn. Mo. Coun. on Arts, 1989-94; trustee U. Mo.-Kansas City Law Found., 1986-99, pres., 1997-98; bd. dirs. Mid.-Am. Arts Alliance, 1989-98, treas. Nat. Assembly of State Art Agys, 1994-95, 95-96. Recipient Decade award U. Mo.-Kansas City Law Found., 1991. Mem. Kansas City Met. Bar Assn. (exec. com. 1999-2001). Republican. Avocation: classical vocal music. Federal civil litigation, Insurance, Product liability. Home: 4616 Wyoming St Kansas City MO 64112-1136 Office: Sprint Law Dept 8140 Ward Pkwy Kansas City MO 64114

ABELL, DAVID ROBERT, lawyer; b. Raleigh, N.C., Nov. 24, 1934; s. De Witt Sterling and Edna Renilde (Doughty) A.; children: David Charles, Elizabeth A. Harrington, Kimberly A. Creasman, Hilary Ayres, Glenn Bryan; m. Ellen Penrod Hackmann, July 27, 1985. BA, Denison U., 1956; JD (Internat. fellow), Columbia U., 1963. Bar: Pa. 1963, Ill. 1973. Assoc. Ballard, Spahr, Andrews & Ingersoll, Phila., 1963-68; sec., counsel Hurst Performance, Inc., Warminster, Pa., 1969-70; sec., gen. counsel STP Corp., Des Plaines, Ill., 1970-72; ptnr. David R. Abell Ltd., Winnetka, 1974-96, Rooks, Pitts & Poust, Chgo., 1996-2000, Schuyler, Roche & Zwirner, Chgo. and Evanston, Ill., 2000—. Author: Residential Real Estate System, 1977, 2d edit., 1990. Trustee Music Inst. Chgo., 1988-96; bd. govs. Winnetka Cmty. House, 1993-96. Aviator USMCR, 1956-60. Mem. ABA, Ill. Bar Assn., Chgo. Bar Assn., Rotary (pres. Winnetka 1977-78). Episcopalian. Estate planning, Probate, Estate taxation. Home: 740 Oak St Winnetka IL 60093-2521 Office: One Prudential Plz Ste 3800 130 E Randolph St Chicago IL 60601 E-mail: dabell@srzlaw.com

ABELL, RICHARD BENDER (RICHARD LON WELCH), lawyer, federal judicial official; b. Phila., Dec. 2, 1943; s. Lon Edward Welch, Jr. and Charlotte Amelia (Bender) A., stepfather Ernest George Abell; m. Lucia del Carmen Lombana-Cadavid, Dec. 2, 1968; chldren David, Christian, Rachel. BA in Internat. Affairs, George Washington U., 1966, JD, 1974. Bar: Pa. 1974. Vol. Peace Corps, Colombia, 1967-69; assoc. Reilly & Fogwell, West Chester, Pa., 1974-80; asst. dist. atty. Chester County, 1974-79; staff mem. U.S. Senator Richard Schweiker, Washington, 1979-80; dir. Office of Program Devel. Peace Corp., 1981-83; dep. asst. atty. gen. U.S. Dept. Justice, 1983-86, asst. atty. gen., 1986-90; special master U.S. Ct. Fed. Claims, 1991—. Mem. adj. faculty Del. Law Sch., Wilmington, 1975-77, West Chester State U., 1976; bd. dirs. Fed. Prison Industries, Inc., 1985-91; chmn. Nat. Crime Prevention Coalition, 1986-90; mem. adv. bd. Nat. Inst. Corrections, 1986-90; co-chmn. adv. com. Nat. Ctr. for State and Local Law Enforcement Tng., 1987-90; vice chmn. rsch. and devel. rev. bd. Dept. Justice, 1987-89; mem. nat. drug policy bd. Enforcement Coordinating Group and Coordinating Group for Drug Abuse Prevention and Health, The White House, Washington, 1988-89. Author: Peter Smith of Westmoreland County, Va. (Died 1741) and Some Descendents, 1996, Sojourns of a Patriot: Field and Prison Papers of An Unreconstructed Confederate, 1998. Chmn. Young Rep. Nat. Fedn., Washington, 1979-81; mem. exec. com. Rep. Nat. Com., 1979-81; mem. fed. coordinating coun. on Juvenile Justice and Delinquency Prevention, 1986-90; mem. Pres.'s Task Force on Adoption, 1987-88; mem. Pres.'s Commn. on Agrl. Workers, 1988-93. With U.S. Army, 1969-71. Decorated Purple Heart, Army Commendation medal for heroism, Air medal; recipient Jefferson Davis Hist. gold medal, 2000. Episcopalian. Home: 8209 Chancery Ct Alexandria VA 22308-1514

ABELLE, PATSY CAPLES, lawyer; b. Waukegan, Ill., Aug. 20, 1935; d. Roy Lee Caples and Lee Self (Rosamond) Henderson. BS in Fin., DePaul U., 1964, JD, 1967; LLM, NYU, 1968. Bar: Ill. 1967, NY 1968, U.S. Dist. Ct. (no. dist.) Ill. 1967, U.S. Ct. Mil. Appeals 1968, U.S. Supreme Ct. 1968. Chief securities Fed. Res. Bank, N.Y.C., 1968-73; assoc. Willkie Farr & Gallagher, N.Y.C., 1973-78; sr. atty. Fed. Res. Bd, Washington, 1978-81; sr. assoc. Cravath, Swaine & Moore, N.Y.C., 1981—. Contbr. articles to law jours. Chmn. Fed. Women's Program Adv. Com., Washington, 1980. Mem. Blue Sky Lawyers Assn. (chmn. 1984-85). Securities. Office: Cravath Swaine & Moore 825 8th Ave Fl 38 New York NY 10019-7475

ABELMAN, ARTHUR F. lawyer; b. N.Y.C., June 12, 1933; s. Bert and Myra (Dickoff) A. AB, Harvard U., 1954, JD, 1957. Bar: N.Y. 1958, U.S. Dist. Ct. (so. and ea. dist.) N.Y. 1958, U.S. Ct. Appeals (2d cir.) 1958. Assoc. Casey Lane & Mittendorf, N.Y.C., 1957-59; counsel Am. Petroleum Inst., 1959-61; corp. sec. Pocket Books, Inc., 1961-65; assoc. Weil Gotshal Manges, 1965-79; counsel Moses & Singer, 1979—; pres. Millan House, Inc., 1982—. Pres. Sculpture Ctr., Inc., N.Y.C., 1979-85, trustee, 1971-2000, exec. com., 1988-2000, treas., 1991-2000; trustee Norman Rockwell Art Collection Trust, E.E. Cummings Trust, James Beard Found. Inc., mem. exec. com., 1995—. Mem. ABA, N.Y. Bar Assn., Assn. of Bar of City of N.Y. Republican. Jewish. Club: Harvard. Libel, Real property, Trademark and copyright. Home: 116 E 68th St New York NY 10021-5955 Office: Moses & Singer LLP 1301 Avenue Of The Americas New York NY 10019-6022

ABELSON, ELIAS, lawyer; b. N.Y.C., Nov. 17, 1932; s. Harry and Lucille (Margulies) A.; m. Isobel Faith Schiffman, Sept. 8, 1957; children: Adam Samuel, Joshua Tobin, Matthew Noah. BA, U. Pa., 1954; JD, Columbia U., 1959. Bar: N.J. 1960, U.S. Dist. Ct. N.J. 1960, U.S. Ct. Appeals (3d cir.) 1969, U.S. Ct. Appeals (7th cir.) 1973, U.S. Claims Ct. 1969, U.S. Tax Ct. 1969, U.S. Supreme Ct. 1965. Dep. atty. gen. State of N.J., Trenton, 1960-63, 64-68, asst. atty. gen., 1968-88; assoc. Green, Robinson & Deitz, Trenton, 1963-64; gen. counsel Bucknell U., Lewisburg, Pa., 1988—; mem. N.J. Supreme Ct. Dist. Ethics Com., 1985-88; lectr. in field. Contbr. articles to legal publs. Sec. Princeton Folk Music Soc., 1976-78; vice chmn. Princeton U. Concerts Com., 1978-82; trustee Gr. Princeton Youth Orch., 1984-88, vice-chmn., 1985-86, chmn., 1986-88. Served to 1st lt. U.S. Army, 1954-56. Mem. Nat. Assn. Coll. & Univ. Attys., N.J. Bar Assn., Pa. Bar Assn., Union County Bar Assn., Columbia Law Sch. Alumni Assn. N.J. (sec. 1982-84, trustee 1984-88). Jewish. Home: 100 Eastwood Dr Portsmouth NH 03801-6070

ABERSON, LESLIE DONALD, lawyer; b. St. Louis, May 30, 1936; s. Hillard and Adele (Wenneker) A.; m. Regene Jo Lowenstein, Oct. 16, 1960; children: Karen, Angie, Leslie. BS, U. Ky., 1957, JD, 1960. Bar: Ky. 1960, U.S. Dist. Ct. (we. dist.) Ky. 1964, U.S. Tax Ct. 1968, U.S. Supreme Ct. 1975. Assoc. Rothschild, Aberson & Miller, Louisville, 1963-65, ptnr., 1965—. Dir. Bank of Louisville. Bd. dirs. Ky. Athletic Hall of Fame, 1965—, NCCJ; past bd. dirs. Jewish Hosp. Louisville, Louisville Med. Rsch. Found.; bd. dirs., past pres. B'rith Sholom Temple; bd. dirs., past v.p. Jewish Cmty. Fedn. Louisville; bd. dirs. Louisville Free Pub. Libr. Found. Recipient Louis Cole Young Leadership award Louisville C. of C. Mem. Ky. Bar Assn., Louisville Bar Assn., Ky. Trial Lawyers Assn., Am. Trial Lawyers Assn., Louisville C. of C. (instl. rev. com.), U. Ky. Law Sch. Alumni Assn. (bd. dirs.). General corporate, Estate planning, Real property. Home: 5431 Harbortown Cir Prospect KY 40059-9257 Office: Rothschild Aberson & Miller Suite 102 5940 Timber Ridge Dr Prospect KY 40059

ABNEY, JOE L. lawyer; b. Wetumka, Okla., June 5, 1941; s. Virgil Lawrence and Wanda (Bachus) A.; m. Paula Katherine Fowler, Sept. 21, 1963; 1 child, Lisa Jo. B.A., E. Central U., 1963; J.D., S. Tex. Coll. Law, 1974. Bar: Tex. 1974. Prin., Lake Mt. Sch. Dist., Covelo, Calif., 1963; tchr. Davis Sch. Dist., Okla., 1964; claims supr. Liberty Mut. Ins., New Orleans, 1965-71, Home Ins. Co., Houston, 1971-74; mem. firm Smith, Abney & Woolf, Houston, 1974— . Advisor, Grangerland 4H Club, Conroe, 1981-83; pres. River Plantation Horse Owners Assn., 1980-81, Hughes County Young Dems., 1962-64; sec. E. Central U. Young Dems., Ada, Okla., 1963. Mem. So. Assn. Workmen's Compensation Adminstrs., Tex. Trial Lawyers Assn., Harris County Criminal Lawyers Assn. Baptist. Club: Montgomery County Genealogy, Soc. War of 1812. Lodge: Elks. Labor, Personal injury, Workers' compensation. Home: 150 Stonewall Jackson Dr Conroe TX 77302-1158 Office: 150 Stonewall Jackson Dr Conroe TX 77302-1158

ABRAHAM, KENNETH SAMUEL, law educator; b. Kearny, N.J., June 19, 1946; s. Saul Jerome and Helen Beverly (Godin) A.; m. Susan R. Stein, Apr. 5, 1981. AB, Ind. U., 1967; JD, Yale U., 1971. Bar: Md. 1977, Va. 1988. Assoc. Mazer & Lesemann, Hackensack, N.J., 1971-73; asst. prof. law U. Md., Balt., 1974-77, assoc. prof., 1977-80, prof., 1980-84; prof. law U. Va., Charlottesville, 1984—. Assoc. reporter Am. Law Inst., Phila., 1986-91. Author: Distributing Risk: Insurance, Legal Theory, and Pub. Policy, 1986, Insurance Law and Regulaiton, 1999, 3d edit., 2001, Environmental Liability Insurance Law, 1991, The Forms and Functions of Tort Law, 1997; also articles. Mem. Am. Law Inst. (coun.), Phi Beta Kappa. Home: 770 Covey Hill Rd Charlottesville VA 22901-3268 Office: U Va Sch Law 580 Massie Rd Charlottesville VA 22903-1738

ABRAHAM, RICHARD PAUL, lawyer; b. Phila., Oct. 27, 1945; s. Hans Alfred and Lillian Elizabeth (Fredericks) A.; divorced; children: Jacob, Daniel. BA, Temple U., 1967, JD, 1970. Bar: Pa. 1970, U.S. Dist. Ct. (ea. dist.) Pa. 1970, U.S. Ct. Appeals (3d cir.) 1971, U.S. Dist. Ct. (mid. dist.) Pa. 1979, U.S. Supreme Ct. 1989. Law clk. to judge Montgomery County Ct. Common Pleas, Norristown, Pa., 1970-71; sole practice, Phila., 1971-73; ptnr. Abraham, Pressman and Bauer, Phila., 1973—. Contbr. article to Temple U. Law Quar., 1970 (J. Howard Reber award). Mem. Phila. Bar Assn., Assn. Trial Lawyers Am., Phila. Trial Lawyers Assn., Pa. Trial Lawyers Assn. Democrat. Jewish. Club: Germantown Cricket (Phila.). State civil litigation, Personal injury, Workers' compensation. Office: 1818 Market St 35th Fl Philadelphia PA 19103

ABRAHAM, WILLIAM JOHN, JR. lawyer; b. Jan. 17, 1948; s. William John and Constance (Dudley) A.; m. Linda Omeis, Aug. 31, 1968; children: Richard S., Heidi K. BA with honors, U. Ill., 1969; JD magna cum laude, U. Mich., Ann Arbor, 1972. Bar: Wis. 1973, U.S. Supreme Ct. 1975. Jud. clk. U.S. Ct. Appeals (D.C. cir.), Washington, 1972-73; ptnr. Foley & Lardner, Milw., 1973—. Former mem. mgmt. com., former chmn. bus. law dept; bd. dirs. The Vollrath Co., Windway Capital Corp., Phillips Plastics Corp., Sirco, Inc., Park Bank, TransPro, Inc.; lectr. MBA program U. Wis. Past bd. dirs. United Way of Greater Milw., Family Svc. of Milw., Milw. Zool. Soc.; bd. dirs., former chmn. Children's Hosp. Found., All-Am. Big 10 Fencing Champion, 1968-69, Greater Milw. Com., Children's Hosp. of Milw.; adv. bd. Wis. Policy Rsch. Inst. Mem. ABA, State Bar of Wis. (chmn. legis. com.), Milw. Bar Assn., Barristers, Tripoli Country Club (bd. dirs., pres.), Milw. Athletic Club, Univ. Club, Desert Mountain Country Club. General corporate, Real property, Securities. Office: Foley & Lardner 777 E Wisconsin Ave Ste 3800 Milwaukee WI 53202-5367

ABRAHAMSON, A. CRAIG, lawyer; b. Washington, May 24, 1954; s. Joseph Labe and Helen Dorothy (Selis) A.; m. Mary Ellen Bernard, Dec. 29, 1979; children: Nicholas Eric, Amy Nicole. BA, U. Minn., 1976; JD, U. Tulsa, 1979. Bar: Minn. 1979, U.S. Dist. Ct. Minn. 1979, Okla. 1982, U.S. Dist. Ct. (no. and ea. dists.) Okla. 1983, Mo. 1991. Assoc. Law Office of Joseph L. Abrahamson, Mpls., 1979-82, Freese & March, Tulsa, 1982-83, Barlow & Cox, Tulsa, 1983-86; pvt. practice, 1986-95, 2000—; ptnr. Levinson, Smith & Abrahamson, 1995-2000; gen. counsel Sandman Property Svcs., Inc. & The Sanditen Cos., 2001. V.p. program com. Youth Svcs., Tulsa, Inc., Leadership Tulsa Class XVII, 1989-92; sec. Great Expectations Educators, Inc., 1995-99; mem. bd. trustees Am. Theatre Co., 1999—. Recipient Am. Jurisprudence Evidence award Lawyers Co-operative Pub. Co. Bancroft-Whitney Co., 1978. Mem. ATLA, ABA (litigation sect.), Okla. Bar Assn. (family law sect., real property sect.), Okla. Trial Lawyers Assn., Tulsa County Bar Assn. (profl. responsibility com.). Democrat. Jewish. Lodge: Masons. Avocations: fishing, camping, travel, tennis. Bankruptcy, State civil litigation, Family and matrimonial. Home: 7518 S 107th East Ave Tulsa OK 74133-2530 Office: A Craig Abrahamson 3314 E 51st St Ste 200-A Tulsa OK 74135 E-mail: craiga@abrahamsonlaw.com, litgatr120@aol.com

ABRAHAMSON, SHIRLEY SCHLANGER, state supreme court chief justice; b. N.Y.C., Dec. 17, 1933; d. Leo and Ceil (Sauerteig) Schlanger; m. Seymour Abrahamson, Aug. 26, 1953; 1 son, Daniel Nathan. AB, NYU, 1953; JD, Ind. U., 1956; SJD, U. Wis., 1962. Bar: Ind. 1956, N.Y. 1961, Wis. 1962. Asst. dir. Legis. Drafting Research Fund, Columbia U. Law Sch., 1957-60; since practiced in Madison, Wis., 1962-76; mem. firm LaFollette, Sinykin, Anderson & Abrahamson, 1962-76; justice Supreme Ct. Wis., Madison, 1976-96, chief justice, 1996—; prof. U. Wis. Sch. Law, 1966-92. Bd. visitors Ind. U. Sch. Law, 1972—, U. Miami Sch. Law, 1982-97, U. Chgo. Law Sch., 1988-92, Brigham Young U., Sch. Law, 1986-88, Northwestern U. Law Sch., 1989-94; chmn. Wis. Rhodes Scholarship Com., 1992-95; chmn. nat. adv. com. on ct.-adjudicated and ct.-ordered health care George Washington U. Ctr. Health Policy, Washington, 1993-95; mem. DNA adv. bd. FBI, U.S. Dept. Justice, 1995—; bd. dirs. Inst. Jud. Adminstrn., Inc., NYU Sch. Law; chair Nat. Inst. Justice's Commn. Future DNA Evidence, 1997—. Editor: Constitutions of the United States (National and State) 2 vols, 1962. Mem. study group program of rsch., mental health and the law John D. and Catherine T. MacArthur Found., 1988-96; mem. coun. fund for rsch. on dispute resolution Ford Found., 1987-91; bd. dirs. Wis. Civil Liberties Union, 1968-72; mem. ct. reform adv. panel Internat. Human Rights Law Group Cambodia Project, 1995-97. Mem. ABA (coun., sect. legal edn. and admissions to bar 1976-86, mem. commn. on undergrad. edn. in law and the humanities 1978-79, standing com. on pub. edn. 1991-95, mem. commn. on access to justice/2000 1993—, mem. adv. bd. Ctrl. and East European law initiative 1994—, mem. consortium on legal svcs. and the public 1995—, vice-chair ABA Coalition for Justice 1997—), Wis. Bar Assn., Dane County Bar Assn., 7th Cir. Bar Assn., Nat. Assn. Women Judges, Am. Law Inst. (mem. coun. 1985—). Office: Wis Supreme Ct PO Box 1688 Madison WI 53702-1688*

ABRAMOVSKY, ABRAHAM, law educator, lawyer; b. Jerusalem, Aug. 12, 1946; came to U.S., 1956; s. Abba and Ahuva (Kruglikov) A.; m. Deborah Lee Wright, Sept. 21, 1970; children: Aviva, Abba, Ari, Dov. BA, Queens Coll., 1967; JD cum laude, SUNY, Buffalo, 1970; LLM, Columbia U., 1971, JSD, 1976. Bar: N.Y. 1971, U.S. Dist. Ct. (so. and ea. dists.) N.Y. 1982, U.S. Supreme Ct. 1982. Pvt. practice, N.Y.C., 1971-75; asst. prof. U. Toledo Coll Law, 1975-77; assoc. prof. Pace U. Sch. Law, White Plains, N.Y., 1977-79; prof. Fordham U. Sch. Law, N.Y.C., 1979—; dir. Internat. Criminal Law Ctr. Fordham U., 1990—. Editor: Federal Criminal Law and the Corporate Counsel, 1979; columnist N.Y. Law Jour., N.Y.C., 1982—; guest host Cable TV, N.Y.C.; interviewee CBS Nightwatch, ABC News, Daily News, Newsday, L.A. Time, N.Y. Times, San Francisco Chronicle; contbr. articles to profl. jours. Fordham U. grant, 1987; vis. fellow U. Warwick Sch. of Law, Coventry, Eng., 1976; Charles Evans Hughes fellow Columbia U., 1972-73. Mem. ABA (vice-chair internat. criminal law com.), Anti-Defamation League (bd. dirs. L.I. chpt.). Jewish. Office: Fordham U Sch Law 140 W 62nd St New York NY 10023-7407

ABRAMOWITZ, ELKAN, lawyer; b. N.Y.C., Mar. 10, 1940; S. Harry and Claire L. (Liebreich) A.; m. Susan Isaacs, Dec. 7, 1943; children: Andrew, Elizabeth. AB, Brown U., 1961; LLB, N.Y. U., 1964. Bar: N.Y. 1964. Law clk. U.S. Dist. Ct. (so. dist.) N.Y., 1964-66; asst. U.S. atty. So. Dist. N.Y., 1966-70, chief criminal divsn., 1976-77; pvt. practice N.Y.C., 1970-76, 77-79; with Morvillo Abramowitz Grand Iason & Silberberg, 1979—. Mem. faculty Nat. Inst. Trial Advocacy, 1977—. Mem. ABA, N.Y. State Bar Assn., Assn. Bar City of N.Y., Fed. Bar Coun. Federal civil litigation, State civil litigation, Criminal. Home: 96 Middle Rd Port Washington NY 11050-2634 Office: 565 5th Ave New York NY 10017 E-mail: eabramowitz@magislaw.com

ABRAMOWITZ, ROBERT LESLIE, lawyer; b. Phila., May 1950; s. Nathan P. and Lucille H. (Rader) A.; m. Susan Margaret Stewart, Dec. 1, 1974; children: David, Catherine. BA, Yale U., 1971; JD, Harvard U., 1974. Bar: Pa. 1974, N.J. 1975. Assoc. Ballard, Spahr, Andrews & Ingersoll, Phila., 1974-81, ptnr., 1981-90; ptrn. Morgan Lewis & Bockius, LLP, 1990—. Adj. prof. law Villanova U., 1986—. Trustee Moorestown (N.J.) Friends Sch., 1981-90, Rock Sch. of Pa. Ballet, 1990—; pres. Harvard Law Sch. Assn. Greater Phila., 1999-2001. Mem. ABA, Am. Coll. of Employee Benefits Counsel, Phila. Bar Assn. (exec. com. probate sect. 1982-85, pension com. 1985-94, chair 1987-89), Yale Club, Merion Cricket Club. Estate planning, Pension, profit-sharing, and employee benefits. Home: 623 Pembroke Rd Bryn Mawr PA 19010-3613 Office: Morgan Lewis & Bockius LLP 1701 Market St Philadelphia PA 19103-2903

ABRAMS, NORMAN, law educator, university administrator; b. Chgo., July 7, 1933; s. Harry A. and Gertrude (Dick) A.; m. Toshka Alster, 1977; children: Marshall David, Julie, Hanna, Naomi. AB, U. Chgo., 1952, JD, 1955. Bar: Ill. 1956, U.S. Supreme Ct. 1967. Assoc. in law Columbia U., 1955-57; rsch. assoc. Harvard U., 1957-59; sec. Harvard-Brandeis Coop. Rsch. for Israel's Legal Devel., 1957-58, dir., 1959; mem. faculty law sch. UCLA, 1959—, prof. law, 1964—, assoc. dean law, 1989-91, vice chancellor acad. pers., 1991-2001, interim exec. v. chancellor, spring 1998, co-dir. Ctr. for internat. and strategic studies, 1982-83, chmn. steering com., 1985-87, 88-89; vis. prof. Hebrew U., 1969-70, Forchheimer vis. prof., 1986; vis. prof. Bar Ilan U., 1970-71, 78, U. So. Calif., 1972, 73, Stanford U., 1977, U. Calif. at Berkeley, 1977, Loyola U., Los Angeles, summers 1974, 75, 76, 79; spl. asst. to U.S. atty. gen., also prof.-in-residence criminal div. Dept. Justice, 1966-67. Reporter for So. Calif. indigent accused persons study Am. Bar Found., 1963; cons. Gov. Calif. Commn. L.A. Riots, 1965, Pres.'s Commn. Law Enforcement and Adminstrn. Justice, 1966-67, Nat. Commn. on Reform of Fed. Criminal Laws, 1967-69, Rand Corp., 1968-74, Ctr. for Adminstrv. Justice, ABA, 1973-77, Nat. Adv. Commn. on Criminal Justice Stds., Organized Crime Task Force, 1976; spl. hearing officer conscientious objector cases Dept. Justice, 1967-68; vis. scholar Inst. for Advanced Studies, Hebrew U., summer, 1994. Author: (with others) Evidence, Cases and Materials, 7th edit., 1983, 8th edit., 1988, 9th edit., 1997, Federal Criminal Law and Its Enforcement, 1986, 2d and 3d edits. (with S. Beale), 1993, 2000; mem. editl. bd. Criminal Law Forum, 1990—. Chmn. Jewish Conciliation Bd., L.A., 1975-81; bd. dirs. Bet Tzedek, 1975-85, L.A. Hillel Coun., 1979-82, Shalhevet High Sch., 1998—; chmn. So. Calif. region Am. Profs. for Peace in Middle East, 1981-83; bd. dirs. met. region Jewish Fedn., 1982-88, v.p. 1982-83; pres. Westwood Kehillah Congregation, 1985. Mem. Soc. for Reform of Criminal Law (mem. exec. com. 1994—), Phi Beta Kappa. Office: UCLA Law School 405 Hilgard Ave Los Angeles CA 90095-9000 E-mail: abrams@Law.UCLA.EDU

ABRAMS, ROBERT, lawyer, former state attorney general; b. Bronx, N.Y., July 4, 1938; s. Benjamin and Dorothy (Kaplan) A.; m. Diane B. Schulder, Sept. 15, 1974; children: Rachel Schulder, Becky Schulder. B.A., Columbia U., 1960; J.D., NYU, 1963; LL.D. (hon.), Hofstra U., 1979; Lugum Doctoris (hon.), Yeshiva U., 1984; LLD (hon.), L.I. U., 1989, Pace U., 1991. Mem. N.Y. State Assembly, 1965-69; pres. Borough of Bronx, 1970-78; atty. gen. State of N.Y., 1979-93; ptnr. Stroock & Stroock & Lavan, N.Y.C., 1994—. Panel mem. of disting. neutrals CPR Inst.; dir. Sterling Nat. Bank, Sterling Bancorp. Contbr. articles to profl. publs.; writer column Nat. Law Jour., N.Y. Law Jour., N.Y. Times, N.Y. Newsday, N.Y. Post, N.Y. Daily News, Buffalo News, Albany Times Union, Ganette Suburban Newspapers, The Harvard Environ. Law Rev., NYU Law Rev., Columbia Jour. Environ. Law, Pace Environ. Law Rev., Washburn Law Rev., Albany Law Rev., Pace Law Rev., The Jour. of State Gov. Del. Dem. Nat. Conv., 1972, 76, 80, 84, mem. platform com., 1988; elector Electoral Coll., 1988. Recipient Adam Clayton Powell Pub. Svc. award, Interfaith award Coun. Chs., N.Y.C., Bronx Community Coll. medallion for Svc., Scroll of Honor plaque United Jewish Appeal, Benjamin Cardozo award for legal excellence Jewish Lawyers Guild, Brotherhood award B'nai B'rith, Man of Yr. award NAACP, Alumni Achievement award NYU Sch. Law, Environmentalist of Yr. award Environ. Planning Lobby N.Y., Disting. Pub. Svc. Citation Bus. Coun. N.Y. State, N.Y. State Sheriff's Assn. award, Nat. Crime Victims award, Torch of Liberty award Anti-Defamation League, Anatoly Scharansky Freedom award N.Y. Conf. Soviet Jewry, Environmentalist of Yr. award L.I. Pine Barrens Soc., Il Leone de San Marco Hon. Italian Am. award, Cavaliere medal Pres. Italy, Pres. award Marist Coll., Hubert Humphrey Humanitarian award United Fedn. Tchrs., Law Day award N.Y. State Trial Lawyers Assn., Contbns. to Urban Law award Fordham Law Jour., Deans medal Law Sch. NYU, Margaret Sanger award N.Y. State Family Planning Advocates, Lehman/LaGuardia Civic Achievement award Anti-Defamation League B'nai B'rith and Commn. on Social Justice of the Order of Sons of Italy, Father of the Yr. award Nat. Father's Day Com., B'nai Zion Bill of Rights award, Avodah award Jewish Tchr's. Assn., Man of the Yr. award N.Y. State Consumer Assembly, Rodef Tzedek Pursuer of Justice award Restructionist Rabbinical Coll., Humanitarian award Rochester Labor and Religious Coalition, Special Recognition award Profl. Women in Construction and Allied Industries, Humanitarian award Long Island Assn. for Children with Learning Disabilities, Man of the Yr. award Mental Ilness Found., N.Y. State Ct's. Man of the Yr. award Shamrai Tzedek Soc., Grand Marshall award Schenectady Labor Coun. Labor Day Parade, Louis Brandeis award Zionist Orgn. Am., Lubavich Tzivos Hashem award, Chassidius in Am. Exemplary Leadership award Bostoner Chassidum, Recognition for Pub. Svc. award Greater Buffalo AFL-CIO Coun., Effort on Behalf of the Elderly award Workmen's Circle Home & Infirmary For the Aged, Dedication Concerning Reproductive Rights award N.Y. Coun. of Jewish Women, Citation of Appreciation N.Y. State Assn. of Architects, Pesach-Tikvah Hope Developer award, Pub. Svc. award N.Y. Soc. Clin. Psychologists, Cmty. Achievement award Am. Orthodox Fedn., State Svc. award Nat. Columbus Day Com., Environmentalist of the Yr. award Sierra Club, Svc. award N.Y. State Jewish War Veterans, Cadet award N.Y.C. Mission Soc., Disting. Achievement award AMIT Women, Man of the Yr. award Nassau County Police Res. Assn., Ann. award Lubavitch Youth Orgn., Appreciation award Japanese C. of C. of N.Y., Friend of the Cmty. award Empire State Pride Agenda, Roland Smith award Capital Region chpt. N.Y. Civil Liberties Union, Scharansky Freedom award L.I. Com. on Soviet Jewry, Cert. of Honor award N.Y. League of Histadrut, Scouting For the Handicapped Outstanding Svc. award Greater N.Y. Coun. of Boy Scouts of Am., Citizen of the Yr. award We. N.Y. Labor Coalition, Svc. award Citizen's Coun. for the Cmty. of Mentally Retarded, Rockland Hosp. Guild, Man of the Yr. award The Shield Inst. for Retarded Children, Maccabean Svc. award N.Y. Bd. of Rabbis, Thurgood Marshall award Bridge Builders Albany, Pro Choice award Naral N.Y., Dist. Humanitarian award Insts. Applied Human Dynamics, Life-Long Dedication award Holocaust Meml. Com.; named Man of Yr. St. Patrick's Home Aged and Infirm, Man of Yr. State Israel Bonds. Mem. N.Y. State Bar Assn. (Environ. Acheivement award), Nat. Assn. of Attys. Gen. (pres. 1988-89, chmn. environ. protection com. 1982-85, chmn. antitrust com. 1985-88, chmn. civil rights com. 1990-92, chmn. ea. regional conf. of attys. gen. 1983-84, Wyman award for Outstanding Atty. Gen. in the Nation 1991, commn. campaign finance reform). Democrat. Administrative and regulatory. Office: Stroock & Stroock & Lavan 180 Maiden Ln Ste 3989 New York NY 10038-4937 Office Fax: 212-806-6006

ABRAMS, ROGER IAN, law educator, arbitrator; b. Newark, July 30, 1945; s. Avel S. and Myrna (Posner) A.; m. Frances Elise Kovitz, June 1, 1969; children: Jason, Seth. BA, Cornell U., 1967; JD, Harvard U., 1970. Bar: Mass. 1970, U.S. Dist. Ct. Mass. 1971, U.S. Ct. Appeals (1st cir.) 1971. Law clk. to Judge Frank M. Coffin U.S. Ct. Appeals (1st cir.), Boston, 1970-71; assoc. Foley, Hoag & Eliot, 1971-74; prof. law Law. Sch. Case Western Res. U., Cleve., 1974-86; dean Law Ctr. Nova U., Ft. Lauderdale, Fla., 1986-93; dean Law Sch. Rutgers U., Newark, 1993-1998; prof. law sch. Rutger U., 1993-99; Herbert J. Hannuch scholar Rutgers U., 1998-99; dean, Richardson prof. law Northeastern U., Boston, 1999—. Labor arbitrator Fed. Mediation Svc., 1975—; mem. gender bias report implementation com. Fla. Supreme Ct. Author: Legal Bases: Baseball and the Law, 1998, The Money Pitch: Baseball Free Agency and Salary Arbitration, 2000; contbr. articles to law jours. Bd. dirs. Inst. for Continuing Legal Edn., N.J., 1993-98. Recipient Gen. Counsel's Advocacy award NAACP, Boston, 1974; inductee Union N.J. Hall of Fame, 1995. Mem. Am. Law Inst., Am. Bar Found., Am. Arbitration Assn. (labor arbitrator). Democrat. Jewish. Avocations: swimming, distance walking, reading. Office: Northeastern Univ Sch Law 400 Huntington Ave Boston MA 02115-5005 E-mail: rabrams@neu.edu

ABRAMS, RUTH IDA, retired state supreme court justice; b. Boston, Dec. 26, 1930; d. Samuel and Matilda A. BA, Radcliffe Coll., 1953; LLB, Harvard U., 1956; hon. degree, Mt. Holyoke Coll., 1977, Suffolk U., 1977, New Eng. Sch. Law, 1978. Bar: Mass. 1957. Ptnr. Abrams Abrams & Abrams, Boston, 1957-60; asst. dist. atty. Middlesex County, Mass., 1961-69; asst. atty. gen. Mass., chief appellate sect. criminal div., 1969-71; spl. counsel Supreme Jud. Ct. Mass., 1971-72, assoc. justice, 1977-2000; retired Supreme Jud. Ct., 2000; assoc. justice Superior Ct. Commonwealth of Mass., 1972-77. Mem. Gov.'s Commn. on Child Abuse, 1970-71, Mass. Law Revision Commn. Proposed Criminal Code for Mass., 1969-71; trustee Radcliffe Coll., from 1981 Editor: Handbook for Law Enforcement Officers, 1969-71. Recipient Radcliffe Coll. Achievement award, 1976, Radcliffe Grad. Soc. medal, 1977 Mem. ABA (com. on proposed fed. code from 1977), Mass. Bar Assn., Am. Law Inst., Am. Judicature Soc. (dir. 1978), Am. Judges Assn., Mass. Assn. Women Lawyers. Home: Supreme Jud Ct Mass 100 Memorial Dr 8-11A Cambridge MA 02142-1330

ABRAMS, STAN, lawyer; b. Hollywood, Calif., June 14, 1969; m. Claire Zhang, Oct. 15, 2000. JD, Boston Coll., 1996. Bar: Mass. 1996. Atty. Lehman, Lee & Xu, Beijing, China, 1999—. Mem. Internat. Trademark Assn., Am. Intellectual Property Lawyers Assn., Intellectual Property Owners Assn. Office: Lehman Lee & Xu 188 Beijing Int Cl Jianguomenwai Beijin China 100020 Fax: 8610 6532 3877. E-mail: sabrams@chilalaw.cc

ABRAVANEL, ALLAN RAY, lawyer; b. N.Y.C., Mar. 11, 1947; s. Leon and Sydelle (Berenson) A.; m. Susan Ava Paikin, Dec. 28, 1971; children: Karen, David. BA magna cum laude, Yale U., 1968; JD cum laude, Harvard U., 1971. Bar: N.Y. 1972, Oreg. 1976. Assoc. Paul, Weiss, Rifkind, Wharton & Garrison, N.Y.C., 1971-72, 74-76; fellow Internat. Legal Ctr., Lima, Peru, 1972-74; from assoc. to ptnr. Stoel, Rives, Boley, Fraser & Wyse, Portland, Oreg., 1976-83; ptnr. Perkins Coie, 1983—. Editor, pub. Abravanel Family Newsletter. Chair Oreg. Internat. Trade Com., Oreg. Dist. Export Coun. Mem. ABA, Portland Met. C. of C. General corporate, Private international, Municipal (including bonds). Office: Perkins Coie 1211 SW 5th Ave Portland OR 97204-3713

ABT, RALPH EDWIN, lawyer; b. Chgo., Apr. 9, 1960; s. Wendel Peter and Hedi Lucie (Wieder) A. BA, Loyola U., Chgo., 1982; JD, John Marshall Law Sch., Chgo., 1987. Bar: Ill. 1987, U.S. Dist. Ct. (no. dist.) Ill. 1987, U.S. Ct. Appeals (7th cir.) Ill. 1988. Pvt. practice, Chgo., 1987-88; staff atty. Sec. of State's Office, 1988-95, Ill. Dept. Pub. Aid, Chgo., 1995—. Poll watcher, Chgo., 1981, 83, precinct capt., 1983, 93-2000. Mem. ABA, Ill. Bar Assn., Chgo. Bar Assn., Trade Law Assn. (charter mem., chmn. charter membership drive 1986), Phi Alpha Delta. Lutheran. Avocations: reading, tennis, bicycling, weight lifting. Home: 5067 W Balmoral Ave Chicago IL 60630-1547 Office: Ill Dept Pub Aid 32 W Randolph St Ste 927 Chicago IL 60601-3470

ABUT, CHARLES C. lawyer; b. Jan. 11, 1944; BA, Columbia U., 1969; JD, Cornell U., 1972. Bar: N.J. 1972, U.S. Supreme Ct. 1976, D.C. 1979, N.Y. 1980; cert. matrimonial atty. Assoc. Hannoch & Weisman, Newark, 1972-74; arbitrator Am. Arbitration Assn., 1978—. Lectr. Inst. CLE, 1989-2000. Author: Celebrity Goodwill, 1989. With Mil. Police, U.S. Army, 1964-67. Fellow Am. Acad. Matrimonial Attys.; mem. ABA, ATLA, N.J. Trial Lawyers Assn., Masons, Psi Upsilon. General civil litigation, Family and matrimonial, General practice. Office: 1 Executive Dr Fort Lee NJ 07024-3309 E-mail: ccaesq@att.net

ACHAMPONG, FRANCIS KOFI, law educator, consultant; b. Kumasi, Ghana, Feb. 18, 1955; came to U.S., 1981; s. John Wilberforce and Salome (Mensa) A.; m. Nicole Victoria Blache. LLB, U. Ghana, 1976; LLM, U. London, 1977, PhD, 1981; LLM, Georgetown U., 1985. Bar: N.Y. 1986, Va. 1988, U.S. Dist. Ct. (ea. dist.) Va. 1988, U.S. Ct. Appeals (4th cir.) 1988, U.S. Supreme Ct. 1990. Adj. lectr. George Washington U., Washington, 1981-82; asst. prof. Howard U., 1981-85; prof. Norfolk (Va.) State U., 1985—, chair dept. entrepreneurial studies, 1998—; of counsel Shelton & Malone, Norfolk, 1998—. Cons. Aetna Life & Casualty, Hartford, Conn., 1981-82, Profl. Ins. Assn. of Md., Pa., 1986, Shapiro, Meiselman & Greene, P.C., Rockville, Md., 1987, Crowell & Moring, Washington, 1988, Clark & Stant, Virginia Beach, Va., 1988. Author: Workplace Sexual Harassment, 1999; contbr. articles to profl. jours. Mem. Am. Risk and Ins. Assn., Acad. Legal Studies in Bus. Avocations: gospel music, exercise, reading, movies. Home: 1509 Colebrook Dr Virginia Beach VA 23464-7206 Office: Norfolk State U 700 Park Ave Norfolk VA 23504-8090 Fax: 757-823-2506. E-mail: fachampong@nsu.edu

ACHESON, AMY J. lawyer; b. Pitts., July 16, 1963; d. Willard Phillips and Patricia Louise (Marshall) A. BA, Haverford Coll., 1984; JD cum laude, U. S.C., 1987. Bar: Pa. 1987, U.S. Dist. Ct. (we. dist.) Pa. 1987, U.S. Ct. Appeals (10th cir.) 1989, U.S. Ct. Appeals (3d cir.) 1988, U.S. Ct. Appeals (4th cir.) 1993. Assoc. Reed, Smith, Shaw & McClay, Pitts., 1987-95; shareholder Berger Law Firm, 1995-99, Ogg, Jones, Cordes & Ignelzi, Pitts., 1999—. Mem. S.C. Law Rev., 1985-87. Fin. officer Ret. Sr. Vol. Program Allegheny County, Pitts., 1990-91; treas. Parents League for Emotional Adjustments, Pitts., 1990-91; mem. adv. bd. Pa. Dept. Correction, Community Svc. Ctr. No. 1, Pitts., 1990-97; bd. mgrs. The Woodwell, Pitts., 1992-97, v.p., 1998-2000. Mem. ABA (jud. adminstrn. div. com., chmn. subcom. on discipline of fed. judges, 1990-91), Pa. Bar Assn., Allegheny County Bar Assn. (young lawyers sect. coun. 1990-91), Order of the Coif, Order of the Wig and Robe. Federal civil litigation, State civil litigation. Office: Riverview Pl 245 Fort Pitt Blvd Pittsburgh PA 15222-1511 E-mail: amyacheson@aol.com

ACKER, ANN, lawyer; b. Chgo., July 21, 1948; BA, St. Mary's Coll.; JD, Loyola U. Bar: Ill. 1973. Mem. Chapman and Cutler, Chgo. Office: Chapman and Cutler 111 W Monroe St Ste 1700 Chicago IL 60603-4006

ACKER, FREDERICK GEORGE, lawyer; b. Defiance, Ohio, May 7, 1934; s. Julius William and Orah Louise (Dowler) A.; m. Cynthia Ann Wayne, Dec. 1, 1962; children: Frederick Wayne, Mary Katherine, Richard Hoghton, Jennifer Ruth. Student, Ind. U., 1952-54; BA, Valparaiso U., 1956; MA, Harvard U., 1957, JD, 1961; postgrad., U. Manchester (Eng.), 1957-58. Bar: Ill. 1961, Ind. 1961. Ptnr. Winston & Strawn, Chgo., 1961-88, McDermott, Will & Emery, Chgo., 1988—. Co-chmn. Joint Prin. and Income Act. com., Chgo., 1976-81. Co-author: (portfolio) Generation-Skipping Tax, 1991; contbr. articles to profl. jours. Bd. dirs. Max McGraw Wildlife Found., Dundee, Ill., 1984—, chmn., pres. 1997-2001; trustee L.S. Wood Ednl. Trust, Chgo., 1975—; trustee Ill. chpt. The Nature Conservancy, Chgo., 1981-90, chmn., 1986-90. Danforth Found. fellow, 1956; Fulbright scholar, 1957. Fellow Am. Coll. Trust and Estate Counsel; mem. ABA, Ill. Bar Assn., Trout Unlimited, Fulbright Assn. (bd. dirs. 1994-2000, pres. 2000), Met. Chgo. Club, Anglers Club, Chgo. Farmers Club. Lutheran. Avocations: hunting, fishing. Estate planning, Probate, Estate taxation. Home: 543 N Madison St Hinsdale IL 60521-3213 Office: McDermott Will & Emery 227 W Monroe St Ste 3100 Chicago IL 60606-5096

ACKER, RODNEY, lawyer; b. Jacksonville, Tex., Sept. 29, 1949; s. Mike and Dorothy (Kennedy) A.; m. Judy Bruyere, Sept. 2, 1972; children: Amy, Shelley, Rachel, Sam. BBA, U. Tex., Arlington, 1971; JD with honors, Tex. Tech, 1974. Bar: Tex. 1974, U.S. Dist. Ct. (no., so., ea., we. dists.) Tex., U.S. Ct. Appeals (5th and 11th cirs.), U.S. Supreme Ct.; cert. in civil trial law. Law clk. to Hon. Eldon Mahon, U.S. Dist. Ct., Ft. Worth, 1974-76; assoc. Kendrick, Kendrick & Bradley, Dallas, 1976, Jenkens & Gilcrist, Dallas, 1976-79, ptnr., then shareholder, 1979—. Fellow Am. Bar Found., Tex. Bar Found., Dallas Bar Found.; mem. ABA, Am. Coll. Trial Lawyers, State Bar Tex., Dallas Bar Assn., Patrick Higginbotham Am. Inns of Ct., Phi Delta Phi. Baptist. Federal civil litigation, General civil litigation, Securities. Home: 9639 Hilldale Dr Dallas TX 75231-2705 Office: Jenkens & Gilcrist 1445 Ross Ave Ste 3200 Dallas TX 75202-2785

ACKERMAN, BRUCE ARNOLD, law educator, lawyer; b. N.Y.C., Aug. 19, 1943; s. Nathan and Jean (Rosenberg) A.; m. Susan Gould Rose, May 29, 1967; children: Sybil Rose, John Mill. BA summa cum laude, Harvard U., 1964; LLB with honors, Yale U., 1967. Bar: Pa. 1970. Law clk. U.S. Ct. Appeals (2d cir.), New York, 1967-68; law clk. to assoc. justice John M. Harlan U.S. Supreme Ct., Washington, 1968-69; prof. law and public policy analysis U. Pa., Phila., 1969-74; prof. law Yale U., New Haven, 1974-82, Sterling prof. law and polit. sci., 1987—; Beekman prof. law and philosophy Columbia U., N.Y.C., 1982-87. Author: Private Property and the Constitution, 1977, Social Justice in the Liberal State, 1980 (Gavel award ABA), (with Hassler) Clean Coal/Dirty Air, 1981, Reconstructing American Law, 1984, We the People: Foundations, 1991, The Future of Liberal Revolution, 1992, (with Golove) Is NAFTA Constitutional?, 1995, We the People: Transformations, 1998, (with others) The Uncertain Search for Environmental Quality, 1974 (Henderson prize Harvard Law Sch.). Guggenheim fellow, 1985. Fellow Am. Acad. Arts and Scis.; mem. Am. Law Inst. Office: Yale U Law Sch PO Box 208215 New Haven CT 06520-8215

ACKERMAN, KENNETH EDWARD, lawyer, educator; b. Bronx, May 25, 1946; s. Kenneth L. and Anna (McCarthy) A.; m. Kathryn H. Hartnett, July 10, 1972; children: Andrew, Carl, Sheila, Edward, Daniel, Kenneth. Student, Talladega Coll., 1966; BA, Fordham Coll., 1968; JD, Cornell U., 1971. Bar: N.Y. 1972, Pa. 1994, U.S. Ct. Appeals (2d cir.) 1975, U.S. Supreme Ct. 1976. Clk. legal dept. Port Authority N.Y. and N.J., 1969, IBM, 1970; ptnr. Mackenzie Hughes LLP, Syracuse, N.Y., 1971 . Adj. prof. banking law and negotiable instruments Am. Inst. Banking program Onondaga Community Coll., 1984—, Syracuse U. Coll., lectr. Author: Alcoholism-Prognosis for Recovery in the Reconstituted Soviet Republics, 1991; contbr. articles to profl. jours. Chmn. Ctrl. N.Y. chpt. March of Dimes, 1972-82; mem. A.A.-USSR Travel Group, 1987; bd. dirs. Ctrl. N.Y. Health Systems Agy., Inc., 1982-83, Syracuse Sr. Citizens Housong Corp., 1992—. Mem. ABA, N.Y. State Bar Assn. (chmn. com. lawyer alcoholism and drug abuse 1993-95), Onondaga County Bar Assn. (bd. dirs. 1990-93, commr. Ballacosa spl. commn. alcohol and drug abuse in profession 1999-2001). Banking, Bankruptcy, Contracts commercial. Office: 600 Onondaga Savs Bank Bldg Syracuse NY 13202

ACKERSON, NELS J(OHN), lawyer; b. Indpls., Apr. 12, 1944; s. Ralph D. and Mariel F. (Maze) A.; m. Sharon Carroll Ackerson, June 11, 1983; children by previous marriage: Betsy Virginia, Peter Nels; stepchildren: Stacia Carroll Loveall, Joshua Michael Loveall. BS with distinction, Purdue U., 1967, M in Pub. Policy, 1971; JD cum laude, Harvard U., 1971. Bar: Ind. 1971, U.S. Dist. Ct. (so. dist.) Ind. 1971, U.S. Ct. Appeals (7th cir.) 1971, D.C. 1985, U.S. Ct. Appeals (D.C. cir.) 1985, U.S. Supreme Ct. 1989, U.S. Ct. Internat. Trade, 1991, U.S. Ct. Appeals (6th cir.), 1996, U.S. Ct. Appeals (4th cir.) 1999. Advisor Harvard Adv. Mission to Republic of Columbia, 1970; assoc. Barnes, Hickam, Pantzer & Boyd, Indpls., 1971-76; chief counsel U.S. Senate Subcom. Constl. Amendments, Washington, 1976-77; chief counsel, exec. dir. U.S. Senate Subcom. on Constn., 1977-79; ptnr. Campbell, Kyle & Proffitt, Noblesville, Ind., 1979-82, Sidley, Austin & Naguib, Cairo, 1982-84, Sidley & Austin, Cairo, Washington, 1982-91; chmn. Ackerson & Bishop Chartered, The Ackerson Group, Chartered, Washington, 1991—, Class Corridor LLC, 2001—. Class counsel AT&T Fiber Optic Litigation; bd. advisors Telecom Real Estate Advisor. Bd. editors Harvard Law Rev., 1968-71. Dem. nominee for U.S. Congress, 5th dist., Ind., 1980; mem. liberal arts adv. coun. Purdue U., 1997-2001. Mem. ABA (litigation sect., bus. and banking sect., internat. law sect., adminstrv. law sect.), Am. Agrl. Law Assn., Ctr. Nat. Policy, Nat. Policy Assn. (food and agr. com.), Am. C. of C. in Egypt (pres. 1984), Assn. Trial Lawyers Am. Presbyterian. Federal civil litigation, Private international, Legislative. Office: Ackerson Group Chartered 1666 K St NW Ste 1010 Washington DC 20006-1217 Fax: (202) 833-8831

ACKERT, T(ERRENCE) W(ILLIAM), lawyer; b. N.Y.C., June 8, 1946; s. T.W. and M. Ackert; m. MP. Ackert, July 4, 1970. BA in History, U. West Fla., 1969; JD, U. Fla., 1972. Bar: Fla. 1972, U.S. Dist. Ct. (mid. dist.) Fla. 1972, U.S. Supreme Ct. 1977, U.S. Ct. Appeals (fed. cir.) 1981. Pvt. practice, Orlando, Fla., 1972—; counsel Sharks Success, Inc., 1988-93, U.S. Ct. Internat. Trade, 2001—. Adj. prof. U. Cen. Fla., Orlando, 1988-93; gen. counsel (Fla.) Morgran Stiftung , Liechtenstein, 1991-95; law lectr. Profl. Skills Inst., Fla., 1981-85. Co-author: Florida Dissolution Manual, 1991; contbr. articles to profl. jours. Chmn. 9th Cir. Grievance Com., Orlando, 1989; mem. Human Svc. Planning Com., Orange County, Fla., 1984. Mem. Seminole County Bar (LAS pres. 1979, Pres. award 1980-83), Orange County Bar (LAS dir. 1980), Fla. Bar (trial lawyers sect., chmn. bar delivery of legal svc. com. 1986-88, chmn. mid-yr. conv. family law 1981, Pres.'s Svc. award 1985, 87). Avocations: pro bono service, travel. Federal civil litigation, State civil litigation, Contracts commercial. Office: PO Box 2548 Winter Park FL 32790-2548 also: 1133 Louisiana Ave Ste 209 Winter Park FL 32789-2350

ACKLEY, ROBERT O. lawyer; b. Chgo., July 24, 1952; s. William O. and Jeannette E. (Mitchell) A.; m. Patricia Ann Cerney, May 24, 1980; children: Matthew, Allison, Elizabeth, Anne, Kathryn, Kimberly. BA, No. Ill. U., 1974; MA., No. Mich. U., 1977; JD, John Marshall Law Sch., Chgo., 1988. Bar: Ill. 1988, U.S. Dist. Ct. (no. dist.) Ill. 1988. Adminstrv. intern, asst. to city mgr. City of Marquette, Mich., 1976-77; adminstrv. asst. to town mgr. Town of Glastonbury, Conn., 1978; supr. Continental Bank, Chgo., 1979; chief methods analyst dept. fin. City of Chgo., 1980-81, chief supr. ops. dept. revenue, 1981-84; pres. Ackley & Assocs., Chgo., 1984-88; law clk., adminstrv. asst. to chief justice Thomas J. Moran Supreme Ct. of Ill., Lake Forest, 1988-90; atty. Cassiday, Schade & Gloor, Chgo., 1990-91; pvt. practice, 1991—. Bd. dirs. Ill. Pro Bono Ctr.; adj. prof. Roosevelt U., Chgo., 1989-90; mem. panel arbitrators Cir. Ctr. of 19th Jud. Cir., 1991-97, Cir. Ct. Cook County, 1993-97; detention screening atty. pretrial svcs. Cir. Ct. of Cook County, 1991—; drugs panel atty. Office of State Appellate Defender, 1992—. Bd. dirs. Bryn Mawr-Broadway Ridge Mchts. Assn., Chgo., 1984-87; panel mem. Capital Resource Ctr., 1991, Community Econ. Devel. Law Project. Fellow Ill. Bar Found.; mem. ABA, Nat. Assn. Counsel Children, Ill. Bar Assn., Chgo. Bar Assn., Lake County Bar Assn. (pro bono svc. award 2000), Ill. Appellate Lawyers Assn., Acad. Polit. Sci. (life). General civil litigation, Family and matrimonial, Juvenile. Home: 606 Buckingham Pl Libertyville IL 60048-3326 Office: 500 N Lake St Ste 109 Mundelein IL 60060-1860 E-mail: ackley@wundeleinlaw.com

ACOBA, SIMEON RIVERA, JR. state supreme court justice, educator; b. Honolulu, Mar. 11, 1944; s. Simeon R. and Martina (Domingo) A.. BA, U. Hawaii, 1966; JD, Northwestern U., Chgo., 1969. Bar: Hawaii 1969, U.S. Dist. Ct. Hawaii, U.S. Ct. Appeals (9th cir.). Law clk. Hawaii Supreme Ct., Honolulu, 1969-70; housing officer U. Hawaii, 1970-71; dep. atty. gen. State of Hawaii, 1971-73; pvt. practice, 1973-80; judge 1st Circuit Ct. Hawaii, 1980-94, Intermediate Ct. Appeals Hawaii, Honolulu, 1994-2000; assoc. justice Hawaii Supreme Ct., 2000—. Instr. criminal law Hawaii Pacific U., 1992—; atty. on spl. contract divsn. OSHA, Dept. Labor, Honolulu, 1975—77, Pub. Utilities divsn., State of Hawaii, 1976—77; campaign spending com. State of Hawaii, 1976—; staff atty. Hawaii State Legislature, 1975. Bd. dirs. Hawaii Mental Health Assn., 1975—77, Nuuanu YMCA, 1975—78, Hawaii Youth at Risk, 1990—91; mem. Gov.'s Conf. on Yr. 2000, Honolulu, 1970, Citizens Com. on Adminstrn. of Justice, 1972, State Drug Abuse Commn., 1975—76, Com. to Consider the Adoption of ABA Model Rules of Profl. Conduct, 1989—91; mem. Judicial Edn. Com., 1992—93, Hawaii State Bar Assn. Jud. Adminstrn. Com., 1992—94, Permanent Com. Rules Penal Procedure and Cir. Ct. Rules, 1992—96; subcom. chmn. Supreme Ct. Com. Pattern Jury Instrns., 1990—91; mem. Hawaii Supreme Ct. Ad Hoc Com. Jury Master List, 1991—92. Recipient Liberty Bell award, 1964. Mem.: ABA, ATLA, Hawaii Bar Assn. (dir. young lawyers sect. 1973). Office: Hawaii Supreme Ct 417 S King St Honolulu HI 96813-2912

ACOSTA, RAYMOND LUIS, federal judge; b. N.Y.C., May 31, 1925; s. Ramon J. and Carmen J. (Acha-Jimenez) Acosta-Colon; m. Marie Hatcher, Nov. 2, 1957; children: Regina, Gregory, Ann Marie. Student, Princeton U., 1948; JD, Rutgers U., 1951. Bar: N.J. 1953, U.S. Supreme Ct. 1956, P.R. 1959. Sole practice, Hackensack, N.J., 1953-54; spl. agt. FBI, San Diego, Washington, Miami, Fla., 1954-58; asst. U.S. atty. San Juan, P.R., 1958-61; sole practice, 1961-67; trust officer Banco Credito y Ahorro Ponceno, 1967-80; U.S. atty. Dist. P.R., Hato Rey, 1980-82; judge U.S. Dist. Ct. P.R., San Juan, 1982—. Alt. del. U.S.-P.R. Commn. on Status, 1962-63; mem. Gov.'s Spl. Com. to Study Structure and Orgn. Police Dept., P.R., 1969 Contbr. articles to profl. jours. Pres. United Fund, P.R., 1979. Served with USN, 1943-46. Recipient Merit cert. Mayor of San Juan, 1973. Mem. Fed. Bar Assn. (pres., P.R. 1967), P.R. Bankers Assn. (chmn. trust div. 1971, 75, 77), P.R. Bar Assn., Soc. Former Spl. Agts. FBI. Office: US Courthouse & PO Bldg Ste 348 300 Recinto Sur St San Juan PR 00901

ACREE, ANGELA DENISE, lawyer; b. Portales, N.Mex., Oct. 29, 1959; d. Elick Henry and Velma Joan Acree; m. Robert Franklin Torp, May 23, 1998. BS, U. Houston, 1986; MBA, S.W. Mo. State U., 1991; JD, U. Mo., 1997. Bar: Mo. 1997, Ill. 1998. Sole practice, Murphysboro, Ill., 1998—. Contbr. articles to profl. jours. With USAF, 1979-83. Mem. ABA, ATLA, Ill. State Bar Assn., Jackson County Bar Assn. Avocations: golf, canoeing, paragliding. Criminal, Family and matrimonial, General practice. Home: 6685 Old Hwy 13 Apt C-1 Carbondale IL 62901 Office: 617 Walnut Ste 2 Murphysboro IL 62966

ADAIR, DONALD ROBERT, lawyer; b. Rochester, N.Y., July 24, 1943; s. Robert Voigt and Esca Lois (Naas) A.; m. Susanne Jonsson, Nov. 1969; 1 child, Emily Elsebeth; m. Judith Ann Jameson, Nov. 29, 1975 (div. Nov. 1995); children: Thomas, Abigail, Kathryn Carrie. BA, Harvard U., 1965; JD, Cornell U., 1968. Bar: N.Y. 1968, U.S. Dist. Ct. (we. dist.) N.Y. 1968. Assoc. Nixon, Hargrave, Devans & Doyle, Rochester, 1968-76, ptnr., 1977-87; prin. Adair Law Firm and predecessor firms, 1988—. Bd. dirs. NetLink Transaction Svcs., LLC, Victor, N.Y., Stone Constrn. Equip., Inc., Honeoye, N.Y., Victor Insulators, Inc., Victor, N.Y. Contbr. chpt. to book New York Limited Liability Companies and Partnerships, 1995. Active Greater Rochester chpt. ARC, 1973—, chair, 1991-93; mem. Consumer Credit Counseling Svc. of Rochester, Inc., 1972—, chair, 1994-96. Recipient Spl. Citation for Exceptional Vol. Svc., Greater Rochester chpt. ARC, 1991. Fellow Am. Bar Found. (life); mem. ABA, N.Y. State Bar Assn., Monroe County Bar Assn. General corporate, Finance, Mergers and acquisitions. Office: Adair Law Firm 30 Corporate Woods Rochester NY 14623-1469

ADAMEK, CHARLES ANDREW, lawyer; b. Chgo., Dec. 24, 1944; s. Stanley Charles and Virginia Marie (Budzban) A.; m. Lori Merriel Klein; children: Donald Steven, Elizabeth Jean. BA with honors, U. Mich., 1966, JD, 1969. Bar: Ill. 1969, Calif. 1978. Clk. U.S. Dist. Judge U.S. Fed. Cts., Chgo., 1969-71; assoc. atty. Lord Bissell & Brook, 1971-77, ptnr., 1977-78, L.A., 1978—. Mem. ABA, Ill. State Bar Assn., State Bar Calif., Nat. Assn. Railroad Trial Counsel (Western Region exec. com. 1985—). Roman Catholic. Avocations: Bluegrass banjo, sr. ice hockey. General civil litigation, Insurance, Product liability. Office: Lord Bissell & Brook 300 S Grand Ave Ste 800 Los Angeles CA 90071-3119 E-mail: cadamek@lordbissell.com

ADAMI, PAUL E. lawyer; b. Peoria, Ill., Oct. 7, 1950; s. Richard R. and Dorothy M. (Crawford) A.; m. Jane Flatley, Dec. 10, 1982; children: Mary Elizabeth, Megan Marie. BS, U. Ill., 1972, JD, 1975. Bar: Ill. 1975, U.S. Dist. Ct. (cen. dist.) Ill. 1976, U.S. Ct. Appeals (7th cir.) 1979. Law clk. to presiding justice U.S. Dist. Ct. (cen. dist.) Ill., Peoria, 1975-76; assoc. Mohan, Alewett & Prillaman & Adami, Springfield, Ill., 1976-81, ptnr., 1981—. Ill. Bankers' Assn. scholar, 1971. Mem. ABA, Ill. State Bar Assn. Contracts commercial, Family and matrimonial, Personal injury. Home: 7165 Hermes Ln New Berlin IL 62670-6627 Office: Mohan Alewelt Prillaman & Adami Ste 325 1 N Old Cap Plz Springfield IL 62701 E-mail: adami@mohanlaw.com

ADAMO, KENNETH R. lawyer; b. Staten Island, N.Y., Sept. 27, 1950; BS, ChE, Rensselaer Polytech. Inst., 1972; JD, Union U., Albany, 1975; LLM, John Marshall Law Sch., 1989. Bar: Ill. 1975, N.Y. 1976, Ohio 1984, Tex. 1988, U.S. Patent and Trademark Office. Ptnr. Jones, Day, Reavis & Pogue, Cleve. Mem. Internat. Bar Assn. Federal civil litigation, Intellectual property. Office: Jones Day Reavis & Pogue N Point 901 Lakeside Ave Cleveland OH 44114

ADAMS, ANNE CLAIRE, lawyer; b. Santa Barbara, Calif., Dec. 15, 1956; d. John Franklin and Carol Louise (Snyder) A.; m. William Paul Thurber, Mar. 24, 1990. BA, UCLA, 1979; MBA, Golden Gate U., 1986; JD, Southwestern U., 1993. Bar: Calif., 1994. Investment exec. Wedbush, Noble, Cooke, Inc., L.A., 1980-84; affil. coord. SelecTV, Marina del Rey, Calif., 1985-86, affil. mgr., 1986-87; sales rep. Continental Cablevision, Culver City, Calif., 1987-88, acct. mgr. L.A., 1988-95; bus. affairs exec. MediaOne, 1995-99; sole practice Canoga Park, Calif., 1999—. Bd. dirs. L.A. Women's Appt. Collaboration, 1995—, bd. dirs. L.A. coun. Camp Fire Boys and Girls, 1996—, pres., 1997-99; asst. pub. policy dir. Jr. League L.A., 1998-99. Recipient Disting. Svc. award Harriet Buhai Ctr. Family Law, 1995, Cert. Recognition Calif. State Assembly, 1997, Cert. Commendation City L.A., 1997, Outstanding Vol. award L.A. coun. Camp Fire Boys and Girls, 1996-97. Avocations: community service, travel. Bankruptcy, Consumer commercial, Contracts commercial. Address: Law Offices Anne C Adams 6928 Owensmouth Ave Ste 101 Canoga Park CA 91303-2095

ADAMS, DANIEL FENTON, law educator; b. Reading, Pa., July 29, 1922; s. Daniel Snyder and Carrie Betsy (Vought) A.; m. Eloise Williams, Sept. 6, 1968 A.B., Dickinson Coll., 1947; LL.B., Dickinson Sch. Law, 1949. Bar: Pa. 1951, Ark. 1984. Prof. law Dickinson Sch. Law, Carlisle, Pa., 1949-65, asst. to dean, 1952-54, 56-60, acting dean, 1954-56, asst. dean, 1960-65; prof. Sch. Law U. Ark., Little Rock, 1965-70, 77-93, prof. emeritus, 1993—; asst. dean U. Ark. Sch. Law, 1966-70, acting dean, 1981-82, interim dean, 1989-91; prof. U. Miss. Sch. Law, Oxford, 1970-77. Vis. prof. Stetson U. Sch. Law, St. Petersburg, Fla., 1976-77, 99-00, U. Tenn. Coll. Law, 1993. Contbr. articles to profl. jours. Served with U.S. Army, 1943-44 Mem. ABA, Pa. Bar Assn., Ark. Bar Assn. Home: 4717 Osprey Dr Orange Beach AL 36561-5755

ADAMS, DANIEL LEE, lawyer; b. Beaver, Ohio, Oct. 3, 1936; s. Paul D. and Margaret (Rhea) A.; m. Julianne Faller, Aug. 13, 1960; children: Cristin Ann, Meghan Kathleen. BA, Ohio State U., 1957, JD, 1960. Bar: Fla. 1962. Atty. Attys.' Title Services, Inc., Ft. Lauderdale, Fla., 1960-62, also bd. dirs.; atty. Attys. Title Ins. Fund, Inc., 1962-69; ptnr. English, McCaughan and O'Bryan, Ft. Lauderdale, 1969—. Trustee, dir. 17th Jud. Cir. of Attys.' Title Ins. Fund, Orlando, Fla.; mem. MRTA Commn., Tallahassee, 1985-86; dir. Atty.'s Title Guaranty Fund, Inc., Colo. Mem. ABA, Broward County Bar Assn., Fla. Bar Assn. (exec. coun. real property, probate and trust law sect., grievance com.), Broward County Club 100 (pres. 1992-93, bd. dirs. 1988-94). Democrat. Roman Catholic. Avocations: bicycling, reading, wood working. Real property. Home: 600 Petunia Dr Fort Lauderdale FL 33317-1926 Office: English McCaughan & O'Bryan 100 NE 3rd Ave Ste 1100 Fort Lauderdale FL 33301-1144 E-mail: dadams@emolaw.com

ADAMS, DAVID HUNTINGTON, judge; b. Cleve., May 30, 1942; s. Donald Croxton and Nancy (Downer) A.; m. Ann Arendell Rawls, Oct. 2, 1965 (div. 1982); children: Ann Arendell, David Huntington, Susanna Camp; m. Mary Watson, Dec. 4, 1982. AB, Washington and Lee U., 1965, JD, 1968. Bar: Va. 1968, U.S. Dist. Ct. (ea. dist.) Va. 1968, U.S. Ct. Appeals (4th cir.) 1968, U.S. Supreme Ct. 1973. Law clk. U.S. Dist. Ct., Norfolk, Va., 1968-69; assoc. law firm Willcox, Savage, 1969-72; ptnr. law firm Agelasto, Bernard & Adams, 1972-74, Taylor, Walker, Bernard & Adams, Norfolk, 1974-78, Taylor, Walker & Adams, Norfolk, 1974-87, Clark & Stant, P.C., 1987-93; judge U.S. Bankruptcy Ct. (ea. dist. Va.), 1993—. Master of the bench James Kent Am. Inn of Ct., 1994-99, pres., 1995; lectr. bankruptcy practice joint com. on cont. legal edn. Va. Bar Found., 1981, 89; adminstrv. hearing officer Commonwealth of Va., 1974-89. Author: Virginia Landlord/Tenant Law, 1980. Bd. dirs. Heritage Mus., Norfolk, 1991-94, Virginia Beach Neptune Fest., 1997—, King Neptune XXVI; pres. Bay Colony Civic League, Virginia Beach, 1978, Princess Anne Hills Civic League, Virginia Beach, 1988; mem. 4th Cir. Jud. Conf., 1974—; mem. 2d dist. ethics com. Va. State Bar, 1983-84. Mem. ABA, Am. Bankruptcy Inst., Nat. Conf. Bankruptcy Judges (bd. govs. 1996—, sec. 2000), Norfolk-Portsmouth Bar Assn., Virginia Beach Bar Assn., Va. Bar Assn. (bd. dirs. bankruptcy sect. 1990-93, mem. coun. jud. sect. 1995—, chmn. 1997), Hampton Roads Coun. Navy League of U.S. (life mem., pres. 2000—), Cavalier Golf and Yacht Club (commodore 1994, bd. dirs. 1993—), N.Y. Yacht Club. Episcopalian. Avocations: yachting, swimming, cycling. E-mail: David. Office: United States Bankruptcy Ct Walter E Hoffman US Courthouse 600 Granby St Norfolk VA 23510-1915 E-mail: Adams@vaeb.uscourts.gov

ADAMS, DEBORAH ROWLAND, lawyer; b. Princeton, N.J., July 28, 1952; d. Bernard S. and Natalie S. Adams; m. Charles L. Campbell, June 16, 1990. BA, Colo. Coll., Colorado Springs, 1974; JD, U. Colo., 1978. Bar: Ind. 1978, Colo. 1978, U.S. Dist. Ct. Colo. 1978. Atty. Legal Svcs. Orgn. Ind., Indpls., 1978-79, Pikes Peak Legal Svcs., Colorado Springs, 1979-80, Pub. Defender's Office, Colorado Springs, 1980-81; assoc. Ranson, Thomas, Cook and Livingston, 1982-84, Ranson, Thomas, Adams, Petinga and Yukawa, Colorado Springs, 1984; pvt. practice, 1985—. Mem. state Jud. Nominating Comm. for 4th Jud. Dist., 1994-99; Colo. State Grievance Com., 1997-98, Atty. Regulation Com., 1999. Bd. dirs. Domestic Violence Prevention Ctr., 1980-86, pres., 1982-84; bd. dirs. Pikes Peak Legal Svcs., 1983-88, pres., 1986-87, pro bono advocacy sch. faculty, 1990-92; co-chairperson Colo. Springs Devel. Com., Colo. Women's Found., 1987, mem. grant selection com., 1988, 90; bd. dirs. Vis. Nurses Assn., 1989-91, Colo. Coll. Bus. and Cmty. Alliance Bd., 1999—, Citizens Project Bd., 1999—; bd. dirs. CASA, 1999—, Colo. Bar Found., 2000—, Chins Up, 1991-97, pres., 1997-98; co-chairperson El Paso County sect. COLTAF Fundraising Com. for benefit of Colo. Legal Aid Found., 1991-99, chairperson, 1994-95; mem. state bd. dirs. Legal Aid Found., 1994-2000, v.p., 1997-99. Recipient Pro Bono award Pikes Peak Legal Svcs., 1988; named Atty of Yr. El Paso County Legal Secs. Assn., 1990; selected to attend First Colo. Springs Leadership Class, Colorado Springs Leadership Inst., 1997. Mem. Colo. Bar Assn. (family law sect. 1991-2001, conciliation panel subcom. of profls. com. 1992, bd. govs. 1994-97, exec. com. 1995-97, nominating com. 1996), Colo. Bar Found., Colo. Women's Bar Assn., El Paso County Bar Assn. (pres.-elect 1994-95, pres. 1995-96, Trial Advocacy Sch. faculty 1990, 94, Moot Ct. judge 1992, 95, fee arbitration dispute com. 1995), Women Lawyer's Assn. Fourth Jud. Dist.(chairperson jud. nominating com. 1991-93, Portia award 1992), Zonta Club Colorado Springs (pres. 1989-90, co-chairperson dist. 12 regional conf. 1991-92, Zontian of Yr. 1990-91). Democrat. Avocations: reading, skiing, tennis, running, mountain biking. Family and matrimonial. Office: 2 N Cascade Ave Ste 1010 Colorado Springs CO 80903-1629

ADAMS, EDMUND JOHN, lawyer; b. Lansing, Mich., June 6, 1938; s. John Edmund and Helen Kathryn (Pavlick) A.; m. Mary Louise Riegler, Aug. 11, 1962. BA, Xavier U., 1960; LLB, U. Notre Dame, 1963. Bar: Ohio 1963. Assoc. Paxton & Seasongood, Cin., 1965-70, Frost & Jacobs, 1970-71, ptnr., 1971-2000, mem. exec. com., 1985-88, 90-96, mng. ptnr., 1994-96, chmn., 1996-2000, of counsel, 2000—. Author: Catholic Trails West, The Founding Catholic Families of Pennsylvania, Vol. 1, 1988, Vol. 2, 1989. Mem. Ohio Bd. Regents, 1999—; trustee Jewish Hosp., 1995—, Cin. Internat. Visitors Ctr., 1989-91, Japan Am. Soc. Greater Cin., 1988-96,

Ursuline Acad., 1992-94; trustee S.W. Ohio Regional Transit Authority, 1980-91, pres., 1983, 88; trustee Sister Cities Assn. Greater Cin., 1984-91, chmn., 1984-90; trustee Greater Cin. Ctr. for Econ. Edn., 1996—, mem. exec. com., 1999—; chmn. USTA Nat. Father and Son Clay Ct. Tennis Championships, 1990-92; mem. Hamilton County Rep. Exec. Com., 1982—; mem. Hamilton County Rep. Fin. Com., 1990—, chmn., 1992-94; mem. Hamilton County Rep. Ctrl. Com., 2000—. 1st lt. U.S. Army, 1963-65. Fellow Am. Coll. Bankruptcy; mem. ABA, Ohio Bar Assn., Cin. Bar Assn., Cin. Tennis Club (trustee 1990-98, treas. 1992-93, sec. 1994-95, pres. 1996-98, historian 2001—), Queen City Club, Met. Club. (bd. dirs. 1996—). Roman Catholic. Bankruptcy, Contracts commercial, General corporate. Home: 3210 Columbia Pky Cincinnati OH 45226-1042 Office: Frost Brown Todd 2500 PNC Ctr 201 E 5th St Cincinnati OH 45202-4182 E-mail: adamschoice@fuse.net, eadams@fbtlaw.com

ADAMS, JAMES CHARLES, lawyer; b. Cleve., June 20, 1949; s. Charles Otterbein and Loraine Ida (Bagnoli) A.; m. Donna Elaine Roe, Aug. 7, 1971 (dec. 1983); 1 dau., Heather Anne; Kathleen Ann Dunham, Oct. 22, 1983. B.A., Mich. State U., 1971; J.D., U. Mich., 1974. Bar: Mich. 1974, U.S. Dist. Ct. (ea. dist.) Mich., 1974. Assoc. Honigman Miller Schwartz, Detroit, 1974-75, Dykema, Gossett, Spencer, Goodnow & Trigg, Detroit, 1975-82, ptnr., 1982-86; ptnr. Simpson & Moran, Birmingham, Mich., 1986-87; prin. James C. Adams, Traverse City, Mich., 1987-93, Adams & Assocs., Traverse City, 1993—. Mem. ABA, Detroit Bar Assn., Order of Coif, Phi Kappa Phi. Presbyterian. Real property. Home: 155 Lake Village Dr Apt 201 Ann Arbor MI 48103-6538 Office: Dykema Gossett Spencer Goodnow & Trigg 400 Renaissance Ctr Ste 35 Detroit MI 48243-1501

ADAMS, JAMES G., JR. judge, lawyer; b. Hopkinsville, Ky., Nov. 4, 1954; s. J. Granville Sr. and Levina (Simmons) A.; m. Betty Veatch; children: James G. III, William H. II, Robert Lynn. AA, Hopkinsville Community Coll., 1974; BA, U. Ky., 1976; paralegal degree, No. Ky. U., 1979. Bar: Ky. 1979, U.S. Dist. Ct. (we. dist.) Ky. 1980. Assoc. Trimble, Soyars, Breathitt & Foster, Hopkinsville, Ky., 1979-80; ptnr. Trimble & Foster & Adams, 1980-87, Trimble, Foster Adams & Powell, Hopkinsville, 1988-93. Asst. county atty. Christian County, 1980-93; dist. judge divsn. I 3rd Jud. Dist., 1994—. Bd. chmn. Pennyroyal Area Mus., Hopkinsville, 1984-88; pres. Buddies Inc., Hopkinsville, 1982-83. Named Boss of the Yr., Hopkinsville Legal Secs., 1983-84. Mem. Jaycees (pres. 1982-83, named Outstanding Local Pres. Ky. Jaycees, 1982-83), Rotary. Democrat. Methodist. Avocations: golf, hunting, fishing, boating, cooking. Office: Christian County Hall of Justice 216 W 7th St Hopkinsville KY 42240-2104 E-mail: jamesadams@mail.aoc.state.ky.us

ADAMS, JOSEPH KEITH, lawyer; b. Provo, Utah, Apr. 3, 1949; s. Joseph S. and Marian (Bellows) A.; m. Myrle June Overly, Sept. 2, 1971; children: Derek J., Bret K., Stephanie, Julie K., Scott J., Laura. BA summa cum laude, Brigham Young U., 1973; JD, Harvard U., 1976. Bar: Utah 1976, U.S. Dist. Ct. Utah 1976, U.S. Tax Ct. 1983. Assoc. Van Cott, Bagley, Cornwall & McCarthy, Salt Lake City, 1976-82, shareholder, 1982-98; also bd. dirs. Van Cott, Bagley, et al, 1993-97, chmn. tax and estate planning sect., 1995-98; ptnr. Stoel, Rives, LLP, 1998—. Adj. faculty Brigham Young U. Law Sch., Provo, 1993. Co-author: Practical Estate Planning Techniques, 1990. Planned giving com. Restoration Cathedral Madeleine, Salt Lake City, 1991-93; pres. Utah Planned Giving Roundtable, Salt Lake City, 1994, Salt Lake City Estate Planning Coun.; planned giving com. U. Utah Hosp. Found., 1994; bd. dirs. Salt Lake C.C. Found., 1982-98; stake pres. LDS Ch. David O. Mackay scholar Brigham Young U., 1967-73. Fellow Am. Coll. Trust and Estate Counsel; mem. ABA (real property, probate and trust sect., taxation sect.), Utah State Bar (exec. com., past chmn. estate planning probate sect.), Harvard Alumni Assn. Utah (chair bd. dirs. 1980-90), Harvard Law Sch. Assn. Utah (vice chair). Republican. Mem. LDS Ch. Avocations: skiing, reading, golfing. Estate planning, Probate, Estate taxation. Office: Stoel Rives LLP 201 S Main St Ste 1100 Salt Lake City UT 84111-4904 E-mail: jkadams@stoel.com

ADAMS, LEE STEPHEN, lawyer, banker; b. St. Louis, June 3, 1949; s. Albert L. and Margaret C. (Donoghue) A. A.B., Rutgers Coll., 1971; J.D., Georgetown U., 1974. Bar: D.C. 1975, Mo. 1975, Ohio 1982, Calif. 1995. Asst. dean Georgetown U. Law Ctr., Washington, 1974-76, adj. prof. law, 1973-76; sr. counsel to bd. govs. FRS, 1976-81; v.p., gen. counsel Fed. Res. Bank, Cleve., 1981-82, sr. v.p., gen. counsel, 1982-86; dep. gen. counsel Bank One Corp., Columbus, Ohio, 1986-95, v.p., gen. counsel, 1986-91; of counsel Morrison & Foerster, San Francisco, 1995-98, ptnr. Washington, 1999—, group chair fin. svcs. Lectr. law Cath. U. Law Sch., Washington, 1977-81 Mem. Columbus Country Club. Administrative and regulatory, Banking. Home: 4309 Torchlight Cir Bethesda MD 20816-1846 Office: Morrison & Foerster 2000 Pennsylvania Ave NW Washington DC 20006-1812

ADAMS, MORGAN GOODPASTURE, lawyer; b. Nashville, Feb. 2, 1964; s. David Porterfield Jr. and Elizabeth Devereux (Morgan) Spiegel. BA, Bowdoin Coll., 1985; JD, Ga. State U., 1989. Bar: Ga. 1989, Tenn. 1989, D.C. 1990, U.S. Ct. Mil. Appeals 1990, U.S. Dist. Ct. (ea. dist.) Tenn. 1994, U.S. Ct. Vets. Appeals 1994, U.S. Supreme Ct. 1997. Litigation assoc. Luther Anderson Cleary & Ruth, Chattanooga, 1993-95; litig. ptnr. Hatfield, Van Cleave, Akers & Adams, 1995-97; pvt. practice, 1997—. Contbg. editor ABA Family Law Lit. newsletter, 1998-99. Pres. Advantage Hunter, Hunter Mus., Chattanooga, 1994-95; vice-chmn. Hamilton County Rep. Com., Chattanooga, 1997-99; Leadership Chattanooga Class of 1999; senator Ga. State Coll. Law. With USMC, 1989-93; maj. USMCR. Bosch-Duisberg scholar Ga. State U. Coll. Law, Germany, 1989. Mem. Chattanooga Bar Assn. (chmn. family law sect. 1999-2000), Chattanooga Trial Lawyers Assn. (pres.-elect 2001), Army Navy Club. Pachyderm Club (pres. 1997-98). Avocations: rugby, tennis, running. General civil litigation, Family and matrimonial, Personal injury. Office: 410 Mccallie Ave Chattanooga TN 37402-2009 E-mail: adams@chattanoogainjurylaw.com

ADAMS, SAMUEL FRANKLIN, lawyer; b. Jacksonville, Fla., Jan. 9, 1958; s. Samuel Eugene and Lucille (Quinn) A.; m. Beverly June Walls, Sept. 27, 1986 (div. 1996); m. Ronda Jean Pence, Sept. 7, 1996; children: Samuel Matthew, Stephen Mikell. BA in Polit. Sci., Stetson U., 1980; JD, Samford U., 1983. Bar: Fla. 1983, S.C. 1987, U.S. Dist. Ct. S.C. 1988. Assoc. Phil Trovillo, P.A., Ocala, Fla., 1983-86; v.p.adminstrn. Good Shepherd Meml. Pk., Spartanburg, S.C., 1986-88, C & C Properties, Spartanburg, 1988—; pvt. practice law, 1988-95; assoc. Dallis Law Firm, PA, 1995-97; ptnr. Adams & Charles, Attys. at Law, P.A., 1997-98, Adams Law Firm, 1998—. Atty. for City of Chesnee, S.C., 1991-92; magistrate Spartanburg County, 1992—; city judge Pallot Mills, 1992-96. Pres. Boiling Springs Jaycees, 1996-97. Mem. ABA, Fla. Bar Assn., Am. Assn. Trial Lawyers, Jaycees (v.p. enrollment and growth Spartanburg 1988, legal counsel Boiling Springs 1991-92, 96, pres. 1996-97), Optimists (sec., treas. Ocala chpt. 1984-85). Democrat. Presbyterian. Avocations: hiking, jogging, basketball. General civil litigation, General corporate, Probate.

ADAMS, THOMAS LAWRENCE, lawyer; b. Jersey City, Apr. 14, 1948; s. Lawrence Ignatius and Dorothy Tekla (Halgas) A.; m. Elizabeth Anne Russell, June 14, 1969 (div. 1981); children: Thomas, Katherine; m. Deanna Louise Mollo, July 30, 1983; stepchildren: Kathy, Kerry. BS, N.J. Inst. Tech., 1969; JD, Seton Hall U., 1975. Bar: N.J. 1975, U.S. Dist. Ct. N.J. 1975, U.S. Patent Office 1975, N.Y. 1976. Sys. engr. Grumman Aerospace, Bethpage, N.Y., 1969-71; sr. engr. Weston Instruments, Newark, 1971-74; mem. patent staff RCA, Princeton, N.J., 1974-75; corp. atty. Otis Elevator, N.Y.C., 1975-77; ptnr. Goebel & Adams, Morristown, N.J., 1978-80, Behr & Adams, Morristown and Edison, 1981—. Mem. Seton Hall Law Rev. Mem. Livingston (N.J.) Twp. Coun., 1985-88, dep. mayor, 1987; mem. Livingston Environ. Commn., 1984-87; chmn. Livingston Rep. County Com., 1992-98. Mem. N.J. Patent Law Assn., Trial Attys. N.J., N.J. Bar Assn. (chmn. patent, trademark, copyright law and unfair competiton 1991), Morris County Bar Assn., KC (grand knight 1980), Tau Beta Pi, Eta Kappa Nu. State civil litigation, Patent, Trademark and copyright. E-mail: adams@newidea.com

ADAMSEN, JOHN HOLGER, lawyer; b. Aarhus, Jutland, Denmark, July 29, 1965; s. Hans Joachim and Lilian Maja A.; m. Helle Birgitte Breuning-Hansen, July 8, 2000. Degree in Law, Aarhus U., 1988. Jr. atty. Hjejle, Gersted & Mogensen, Copenhagen, 1988-91; lawyer Nielsen & Noerager, 1991-94; ptnr. Pedersen & Jantzen, 1994-97, Andreassen & Ptnrs., Copenhagen, 1997-98, Zenith Law Firm, Copenhagen, 1998. Avocations: history, tennis. Home: 8 Loevstraede 2100 Copenhagen Selandia Denmark Office: Zenith Law Firm 2 Oslo Plads 2100 Copenhagen Selandia Denmark Fax: 4533470010. E-mail: jha@zenith-law.dk

ADAMSON, LARRY ROBERTSON, lawyer; b. Tucson, Mar. 17, 1935; s. Harold David and Manie (Robertson) A.; m. Florence Anna Obad, May 31, 1969; children— Larry Robertson, Michael Marion. B.S. in Bus. Adminstrn., U. Ariz., 1957, postgrad., 1960-61; J.D., U. San Francisco, 1969; LL.M. in Taxation, NYU, 1970. Bar: Calif. 1970, Ariz., 1971, U.S. Dist. Ct. Ariz. 1971, U.S. Tax Ct. 1970. Staff acct. with various C.P.A. firms in Los Angeles and San Francisco, 1961-69; assoc., then mem. Duffield, Young, Adamson & Alfred, P.C. and predecessors, Tucson, 1970— ; guest lectr. U. Ariz. Law Sch., 1974-83, Ariz. Law Inst., 1978-79, So. Ariz. Estate Planning Council, 1976, 83, Tucson Legal Secs. Assn., 1984, State Bar Ariz., 1990, 97, also for various civic, charitable orgns. and tax study groups. Bd. dir. Tucson Airport Authority, 1993-98, pres. 1998; Bd. dirs. Tucson Symphony Soc., 1980-85, mem. exec. com. 1981-84, sec., 1982-84; mem. deferred giving com. Ariz. Sonora Desert Mus., Tucson, 1980-84, bd. dirs. U. Ariz. Found., 1983-88; mem. Tucson Com. on Fgn. Relations, 1984—; bd. dirs. Tucson Med. Ctr. Found., 1985-93, chmn. planned giving com., mem. exec. com., 1985-93, Ariz. Children's Found., 1993-97; exec. com. Planned Giving Roundtable So. Ariz., 1985—, pres., 1997. Served to comdr. USNR, 1953-76. Mem. ABA, Ariz. Bar Assn., Pima County Bar Assn., Am. Inst. C.P.A.s, Ariz. Soc. C.P.A.s, Calif. Soc. C.P.A.s., Am. Assn. Atty.-C.P.A.s, Ariz. Assn. Atty.-C.P.A.s (pres. 1981—), So. Ariz. Estate Planning Council (dir. 1976-84, pres. 1982-83). Clubs: Rotary (dir. club 1975-77, pres. 1985-86, treas. club 1975-76, sec. club 1976-77, dir. and pres. Rotary Club of Tucson Found. 1975—), Tucson Country, Mountain Oyster, U. Ariz. Found. Pres.'s (Tucson). Estate planning, Estate taxation, Personal income taxation. Office: Duffield Young Adamson & Alfred PC 3430 E Sunrise Dr Ste 200 Tucson AZ 85718-3236

ADANIYA, KEVIN SEISHO, lawyer; b. San Francisco, Sept. 24, 1968; s. Roy Seijin and Lavern Gay Adaniya. BA in Polit. Sci., U. Calif., Santa Barbara, 1990; JD, U. of the Pacific, Sacramento, 1995. Bar: Hawaii 1996, U.S. Dist. Ct. Hawaii 1997. Law clk. State of Hawaii, Hilo, 1995-96; sole practitioner Honolulu, 1996—. Mem. faculty Inst. for Paralegal Edn., 1999; facilitator Ohana Conferencing, 1999—. Co-author: Paralegals in Family Law Practice, 1999. Vol., Kids First Program, Honolulu, 1998—, Vol. guardian Ad Litem Program, Honolulu, 1998—; atty. mem. AmeriCorps/Students and Advs. for Victims of Domestic Violence, 1996-97, 98-99. Recipient cert. of spl. commendation Vol. Legal Svcs. Hawaii, 1997,Outstanding Local V.P. award U.S. Jr. C. of C., 1998. Mem. ABA, ATLA, Hawaii State Bar Assn. (dir. young lawyers divsn. 1999-2001, treas. child and parent adv. sect. 2000), Hawaii Bus. Jaycees (v.p. 1997-2000, Edward R. Nakano Meml. award 1998, Daniel K. Inouye award 1999). Bankruptcy, Family and matrimonial. Office: 33 S King St Ste 140 Honolulu HI 96813-4319 E-mail: kevinadaniya@msn.com

ADDIS, RICHARD BARTON, lawyer; b. Columbus, Ohio, April 9, 1929; s. Wilbur Jennings and Leila Olive (Grant) A.; m. Marguerite C. Christjohn, Feb. 9, 1957; children: Jacqueline Carol, Barton David. BA, Ohio State U., 1954, JD, 1955. Bar: Ohio 1956, U.S. Dist. Ct. (no. dist.) Ohio 1957, N.Mex. 1963, U.S. Dist. Ct. N.Mex. 1963, Laguna Pueblo (N.Mex.) Tribal Ct. 1986. Pvt. practice, Canton, Ohio, 1956-63, Albuquerque, 1963—, Laguna Pueblo, 1986—. Co-developer The Woodlands Subdivsn., Albuquerque; co-owner Cerro del Oro Mine, Valencia County, N.Mex., 1977—. With USMC, 1946-48, 50-52. Mem. Ohio Bar Assn., N.Mex. Bar Assn. Oil, gas, and mineral, General practice. Office: PO Box 25923 Albuquerque NM 87125-0923

ADDISON, DAVID DUNHAM, lawyer; b. Richmond, Va., Aug. 23, 1941; s. Grafton Dulany and Anne (Withers) A.; m. Marion Lee Wood, Aug. 21, 1965; children: David Dunham Jr., Marion Lee, Elizabeth Townshend. BA, Hampden-Sydney Coll., 1964; LLB, U. Va., 1967. Bar: Va. 1967. Assoc. Browder, Russell, Morris & Butcher, Richmond, 1967-72; ptnr., dir. Browder & Russell, P.C., 1972-90; mem. firm, shareholder Williams, Mullen, Clark & Dobbins, P.C., 1990—. Contbr. articles to profl. jours. Fellow Am. Coll. Trust and Estate Counsel (state chmn. 1986-92); mem. ABA (com. chmn. 1987-94), S.R., Va. Bar Assn., Richmond Bar Assn., Estate Planning Coun. Richmond (pres. 1987-88), Richmond Trust Adminstrs. Coun. (pres. 1986-87), Kiwanis Club of Richmond (pres. 1998-99), Country Club of Va., Commonwealth Club. Episcopalian. Avocations: travel, golf. Estate planning, Probate, Taxation, general. Office: Williams Mullen Clark & Dobbins 2 James Center 1021 E Cary St Richmond VA 23219-4000

ADDUCCI, JAMES DOMINICK, lawyer; b. Chgo., Dec. 2, 1951; s. John James and Frances Mary (Violante) A.; m. Elizabeth Anne Clark, Apr. 29, 1978; children: John James, Marian Elizabeth. BA, Loyola U., Chgo., 1973; JD, Harvard U., 1976. Bar: Ill. 1976, U.S. dist. Ct. (no. dist.) Ill. 1977, U.S. Ct. Appeals (7th cir.) 1977, U.S. Ct. Appeals (8th cir.) 1990, U.S. Ct. Appeals (3d cir.) 1991, U.S. Ct. Appeals (fed.cir.) 1991. Law clk. Judge Decker, U.S. Dist. Ct. (no. dist.) Ill., Chgo., 1976-77; assoc. Kirkland & Ellis, Chgo., 1977-82; assoc. Schuyler, Roche & Zwirner, Chgo., 1982-84, ptnr., 1984—. Mem. Chgo. Council Lawyers. Democrat. Roman Catholic. Federal civil litigation, State civil litigation, Trademark and copyright. Office: Schuyler Roche & Zwirner 130 E Randolph St Ste 3700 Chicago IL 60601-6342

ADELMAN, GRAHAM LEWIS, lawyer; b. Frankfurt, Germany, Sept. 23, 1949; s. Louis and Helen (Howell) A.; m. Sharon Louise Stabile, May 16, 1975; children: Victor, Neal, Owen. BA, U. Va., 1971; JD cum laude, U. Miami, 1974. Bar: Fla. 1974. Law clk. High Ct. of Am. Samoa, 1975-76; asst. counsel Am. Fina Inc., Dallas, 1976-78; assoc. gen. counsel The Western Co. of N.Am., Ft. Worth, 1978-80, gen. counsel, 1980-86, v.p., gen. counsel, sec., 1986-90, dir., 1989—. Sr. v.p., gen. counsel, sec., 1990-95; sr. v.p., gen. counsel, dir. Global Indsl. Techs., Inc., 1995-2000. Contbr. articles to law revs. Mem. ABA, Maritime Law Assn., Southwest Legal Found. (com. transnat. arbitration). Admiralty, General corporate, Private international. Home: 2433 Rogers Ave Fort Worth TX 76109-1014 Office: Global Industrial Technologies Inc 2121 San Jacinto St Ste 2500 Dallas TX 75201-6707

ADELMAN, ROGER MARK, lawyer, educator; b. Norristown, Pa., June 25, 1941; s. Lewis D. and Mary (Butz) A. B.A., Dartmouth Coll., 1963; LL.B., U. Pa., 1966. Bar: D.C. 1967, Pa. 1969. Asst. U.S. atty. D.C., 1969-87; ptnr. Kirkpatrick & Lockhart, Washington, 1988—; adj. prof. Georgetown U. Law Ctr., Washington, 1975— . Served with U.S. Army, 1967-68. Mem. D.C. Bar Assn., Assn. Bar D.C. Office: 1800 M St NW Washington DC 20036-5802

ADELMAN, STANLEY JOSEPH, lawyer; b. Devils Lake, N.D., May 20, 1942; s. Isadore Russell Adelman and Eva Claire (Robins) Stoller; m. Mary Beth Petchaft, Jan. 30, 1972; children: Laura E., Sarah A. BS, U. Wis., 1964, JD, 1967. Bar: Ill. 1967, U.S. Dist. Ct. (no. dist.) Ill. 1967, Wis. 1968, U.S. Ct. Appeals (7th cir.), U.S. Dist. Ct. (ea. dist.) Wis. 1979, U.S. Supreme Ct. 1982, U.S. Ct. Appeals (10th cir.) 1984, U.S. Ct. Appeals (fed. cir.) 1987. Assoc. Sonnenchein, Carlin, Nath & Rosenthal, Chgo., 1967-75, ptnr., 1975-85; co-chmn. litigation dept. Rudnick & Wolfe, 1985-91, 96-97, ptnr., 1985—, profl. responsibility ptnr., 1992-94, mem. mgmt. policy com., 1985-97, co-chmn. complex litigation practices group, 1997-98. Bd. dirs. Legal Assistance Found., Chgo., 1982-83. Fellow Nat. Inst. Trial Advocacy; mem. Chgo. Bar Assn., Chgo. Coun. Lawyers, Am. Inns of Ct. (pres. Markey/Wigmore chpt. 1998-99), Lawyers Club Chgo., Order of Coif. Jewish. Federal civil litigation, General civil litigation, State civil litigation. Home: 115 Crescent Dr Glencoe IL 60022-1303 Office: Piper Marbury Rudnick & Wolfe 203 N La Salle St Ste 1800 Chicago IL 60601-1210 E-mail: stanley.adelman@piperrudnick.com

ADELMAN, STEVEN HERBERT, lawyer; b. Dec. 21, 1945; s. Irving and Sylvia (Cohen) A.; m. Pamela Bernice Kozoll, June 30, 1968; children: David, Robert. BS, U. Wis., Madison, 1967; JD, DePaul U., 1970. Bar: Ill. 1970, U.S. Dist. Ct. (no. dist.) Ill. 1970, U.S. Ct. Appeals (7th cir.) 1975. Ptnr. Keck, Mahin & Cate, Chgo., 1970-93, Lord, Bissell & Brook, Chgo., 1993—. Bd. dirs. Bur. Jewish Employment Problems, Chgo., 1983—, pres. 1991, 92; employment relations com. Chgo. Assn. Commerce and Industry, 1982-90. Contbr. chpts. to books, articles to profl. jours. Mem. ABA (Silver key award 1969), Chgo. Bar Assn. (chmn. labor and employment law com. 1988-89), Ill. State Bar Assn., Chgo. Coun. Lawyers, Decalogue Soc. Labor. Office: Lord Bissell & Brook 115 S La Salle St Ste 3200 Chicago IL 60603-3902 E-mail: sadelman@lordbissell.com

ADELSON, BENEDICT JAMES, lawyer; b. Cleve., July 3, 1930; s. Joseph Stanley and Sara J. (Joffe) A.; m. Sybil Schar, Apr. 12, 1981. BS in Econs., U. Pa., 1952; JD, Harvard U., 1955. Bar: Ohio 1955, Calif. 1970. Assoc. Schleshinger, Galvin, Kohn & Landefeld, Cleve., 1963-68, Gendel, Raskoff, Shapiro & Quittner, L.A., 1970-77, Fierstein & Sturman, L.A., 1977-87. General corporate, Real property, Corporate taxation. Home: 830 Glorietta Blvd Coronado CA 92118-2306

ADERSON, SANFORD M. lawyer; b. Pitts., July 15, 1949; s. Sanford C. and Marjorie S. (Stern) A.; m. Leslie S. Sertner, Aug. 12, 1972; children: Benjamin, Jonathan. BSBA, Boston U., 1971, JD, 1974. Bar: Pa. 1974, U.S. Dist. Ct. (we. dist.) Pa. 1974, U.S. Tax Ct. 1978, U.S. Ct. Appeals (3d cir.) 1986. Law clk. to judge Ct. of Common Pleas, Pitts., 1974-83; with Aderson, Frank, Steiner & Blechman, 1976-2001; gen. counsel, exec. v.p. Luttner Fin. Group, 1999-2001, pres., 2001—. Bd. dirs. Jewish Cmty. Ctr. of Pitts., 1993-98, chmn. sports, fitness and recreation com.; bd. dirs. Make-A-Wish, 2000—; mem. bus. com. Pitts. Cultural Trust, 2001—. Mem. ABA, Pa. Bar Assn., Allegheny County Bar Assn. (bankruptcy sect. mem. of coun. 1993-98), Westmoreland Country Club (bd. dirs. 1987—, chmn. legal adv. com., chmn. greens com. 1992-96, v.p. 1997—). Bankruptcy, General corporate, Mergers and acquisitions. Office: Luttner Fin Group Ltd 244 Blvd of the Allies Pittsburgh PA 15222 E-mail: sanford_m_aderson@glic.com

ADIN, RICHARD H(ENRY), lawyer, editor, publisher; b. Kingston, N.Y., May 19, 1948; s. Aaron and Lenore (Glasner) A.; m. Mary Grace Francioli, Nov. 10, 1972 (div. 1995); children: Mariah Pompea, Justin Richard. Student Hebrew U., Jerusalem, 1968-69, BA, SUNY, Fredonia, 1970, JD, U. San Fernando Valley, 1977. Bar: Ind. 1977, U.S. Dist. Ct. (so. dist.) Ind. 1977, U.S. Ct. Appeals (7th cir.) 1979, U.S. Supreme Ct. 1980, U.S. Ct. Appeals (6th cir.) 1982. Assoc. Law Office of Jack Davis, Evansville, Ind., 1977-78; ptnr. Matthews, Shaw & Adin, Evansville, 1978-81, Fields & Adin, Evansville, 1981-82; assoc. Bates Law Office, Evansville, 1982-83; sole practice, Evansville, 1983-84; exec. editor, atty. Matthew Bender & Co., Inc., N.Y.C., 1984-89; mng. editor, atty. Prentice Hall Law & Bus., Englewood Cliffs, N.J., 1989-92; pres. Richard H. Adin Freelance Editorial Svcs., Gardiner, N.Y., 1992—; pres., publisher Rhache Publishers, Ltd., Gardiner, N.Y. 1994—; gen. counsel, sec. AmCor Land, Ltd. Plattekill, N.Y., 1986-88, also bd. dirs.; instr. in evidence, U. Evansville, 1979-80; instr. in pub. Rhinebeck (N.Y.) Ctrl. Sch. Dist., 1995—; Mem. U. San Fernando Valley Law Rev., 1976-77. Atty., bd. dirs. Deaf Social Services Agy., Evansville, 1978-80; bd. dirs. Evansville Legal Aid Soc., 1980-81, Plattekill Library Assn., Modena, N.Y., 1985, Plattekill Library Chess Club, Modena, 1986-87; litigation atty. Hoosiers for License Br. Reform, Evansville, 1981-83; social worker Hawthorne (N.Y.) Cedar Knolls Sch., 1970-72; welfare frauds investigator Ulster County Dept. Social Svcs., Kingston, N.Y., 1972-73; asst. cashier First Nat. Bank, Ellenville, N.Y., 1973-74. Scholar N.Y. State Regents, 1966-70, Friends of Hebrew U., 1968-69. Mem. Ind. State Bar Assn., Editorial Freelancers Assn., Mid-Hudson Pubs. Assn. (founder). Criminal, Health. Office: 52 Oakwood Blvd Poughkeepsie NY 12603-4112

ADKISON, RON, lawyer; b. Nacogdoches, Tex., Jan. 8, 1955; s. Robert Edward and Doris Ozelle (Pollard) A.; m. Tanya Regina Williamson, June 2, 1979 (div. Dec. 1984); 1 child, Veronica Alexis Adkison; m. Donna Elaine Dennis, Apr. 1, 1990 (divorced); 1 child, Alexander Aron. BA, Stephen F. Austin U., 1976; JD, Baylor U., 1978. Bar: Tex. 1979, U.S. Dist. Ct. (ea., we., so. and no. dists.) Tex., U.S. Ct. Appeals (5th cir.), U.S. Supreme Ct. Atty. Wellborn & Houston, Henderson, Tex., 1979; ptnr. Wellborn, Houston, Adkison et al., 1980—. Regent Stephen F. Austin State U., Nacogdoches, 1993—; chair bd. regents, 1995-96. Fellow Am. Bd. Trial Advs.; mem. Coll. State Bar Tex. (Disciplinary Rev. com., Adminstrn. Rules Civil Evidence com.), Tex. Trial Lawyers Assn. (dir., chair Toxic Torts com.), Henderson Country Club (pres. 1989-94). Avocations: golf, aviation. General civil litigation, Contracts commercial, Environmental. Office: Wellborn Houston Adkison et 300 W Main St Henderson TX 75652-3109

ADLER, DAVID NEIL, lawyer; b. Bklyn., Apr. 11, 1955; s. Leonard Howard and Elaine (Holder) A. Student, Colgate U., 1973-75; BA, NYU, 1977; JD, St. John's U., 1980. Bar: N.Y. 1981, U.S. Dist. Ct. (ea. and so. dists.) N.Y. 1986, U.S. Tax Ct. 1989. Pvt. practice, Kew Gardens, N.Y., 1982—. Contbr. articles to profl. jours. Mem. Queens County Bar Assn. (com. chmn. 1983—, co-editor Queens Bar Bull. 1987—, bd. mgrs. 1989—, officer 1993—, pres. 1998), N.Y. State Bar Assn. (exec. com. trusts and estates). Estate planning, Probate, Estate taxation. Office: 12510 Queens Blvd Kew Gardens NY 11415-1519

ADLER, ERWIN ELLERY, lawyer; b. Flint, Mich., July 22, 1941; s. Ben and Helen M. (Schwartz) A.; m. Stephanie Ruskin, June 8, 1967; children: Lauren, Michael, Jonathan B.A., U. Mich., 1963, LL.M., 1967; J.D., Harvard U., 1966. Bar: Mich. 1966, Calif. 1967. Assoc. Pillsbury, Madison & Sutro, San Francisco, 1967-73; assoc. Lawler, Felix & Hall, L.A., 1973-76, ptnr., 1977-80, Rogers & Wells, L.A., 1981-83, Richards, Watson & Gershon, L.A., 1983—. Bd. dirs. Hollywood Civic Opera Assn., 1975-76, Children's Scholarships Inc., 1979-80 Mem. ABA (vice chmn. appellate advocacy com. 1982-87), Calif. Bar Assn., Phi Beta Kappa, Phi Kappa Phi Jewish General civil litigation, State civil litigation, Insurance. Office: Richards Watson & Gershon 333 S Hope St Bldg 38 Los Angeles CA 90071-1406

ADLER, IRA JAY, lawyer; b. N.Y.C., Jan. 1, 1942; s. Ralph and Beatrice (Rosenblum) A.; m. Laraine Sheila Garfinkel, July 4, 1965; children: Jodi, Michael. BA, NYU, 1963, JD, 1966. Bar: N.Y. 1966. Ptnr. Certilman, Balin, Adler & Hyman, LLP, East Meadow, N.Y., 1973—. Bd. dirs. Queens County Builders and Contractors, Flushing, N.Y. Contbr. to profl. publs. Mem. ABA, N.Y. State Bar Assn., Nassau County Bar Assn., L.I. Builders Inst. (bd. dirs. 1985—), Real Estate Inst. C.W. Post (bd. dirs. 1986—), N.Y. State Builders Assn. (bd. dirs. 1988—). Real property. Office: Certilman Balin Adler & Hyman LLP 90 Merrick Ave East Meadow NY 11554-1571

ADLER, LEWIS GERARD, lawyer; b. N.Y.C., Sept. 13, 1960; s. Sherman and Esther (Weiss) A.; m. Kim Adler, Sept. 5, 1988; children: Craig, Stephanie, Katie, Samantha. AS, Vanderbilt U., 1981; JD, Rutgers U., 1985. Bar: N.J. 1986, Pa. 1985, U.S. Dist. Ct. N.J. 1986, U.S. Dist. Ct. Pa. 1990, U.S. Supreme Ct. 1990, U.S. Tax Ct. 2000, U.S. Ct. Appeals (3d cir.) 2000. Solicitor Gloucester County Constrn. Bd. Appeals, Woodbury, N.J., 1987-88; atty. Gloucester County Sr. Citizen Will Program, 1987-88; pvt. practice N.J., 1989—; spl. counsel Gloucester County, 1990—. Pub. defender Deptford Township, 1996, zoning bd. solicitor, 1997-2000. Designer computer software. V.p. Haddonfield Plays & Players, 2001—. Mem. ABA, N.J. Bar Assn., Gloucester County Bar Assn., Phila. Trial Lawyers, Pa. Bar Assn. Democrat. Avocations: water and snow skiing, spelunking, chess, bicycling, rappelling. State civil litigation, Computer, Environmental. Home: 215 Douglass Ave Haddonfield NJ 08033-1626 Office: 57 Euclid St Woodbury NJ 08096-4633

ADLER, NADIA C. lawyer; b. Salford, Lancashire, Eng., Feb. 26, 1945; came to U.S., 1948; d. David Colin and Rose (Bolton) Cohen; m. David J. Adler, Mar. 1977 (div. 1992); m. Robert Bernstein, May, 1997. BA, CCNY, 1966; JD, N.Y.U., 1973. Bar: N.Y. 1974, U.S. Dist. Ct. (so. and ea. dists.) N.Y. 1974, U.S. Ct. Appeals (2d cir.) 1975, U.S. Supreme Ct. 1983. Assoc. Rosenman Colin Freund Lewis & Cohen and predecessor firms, N.Y.C., 1973-82; ptnr. Rosenman & Colin, 1983-87; v.p., gen. counsel Montefiore Med. Ctr., 1987-89, sr. v.p., gen. counsel, 1989-98; v.p., gen. counsel, corp. sec. C.R. Bard, Inc., Murray Hill, N.J., 1999—. Mem. legal affairs com. Greater N.Y. Hosp. Assn., N.Y.C., 1987-99; mem. bioethics task force, subcoms. on patient decision making, reproductive techs. and physician-assisted suicide, commn. women's equality Am. Jewish Congress, N.Y.C., 1989—; mem. bd. ethics Village Briarcliff Manor, N.Y., 1997—. Bd. dirs. Berkeley-in-Scarsdale (N.Y.) Assn., 1989-91. Mem. ABA (mem. forum on health care), Assn. of Bar of City of N.Y., Am. Health Lawyers Assn. and predecessor assns., N.Y. State Bar Assn. (co-chair in-house counsel com. health law sect., mem. exec. com. health law sect. 1996-99). Democrat. Administrative and regulatory, General corporate, Health. Office: C R Bard Inc 730 Central Ave New Providence NJ 07974-1199

ADMAY, CATHERINE ADCOCK, law lecturer, researcher; b. Johannesburg, South Africa, Oct. 16, 1965; came to U.S., 1981; d. Roger Sydney Edmund Wyatt and Patricia Laura (Tennant) Adcock; m. Thomas Raden Admay, Aug. 1997. MA, U. Strasbourg, France, 1987; BA, Yale U., 1988, JD, 1992. Atty. vol. Legal Resources Ctr., Pretoria, South Africa, 1988-89; law clk. to Hon. Betty Fletcher 9th Cir. Ct. Appeals, Seattle, 1992-93; assoc. Heller, Elvman, White & McCauliff, 1993; law lectr. NYU Law Sch., N.Y.C., 1994-96, Duke U. Law Sch., Durham, N.C., 1996—. Rschr. Govt. of South Africa, 1996—. Co-author appendix Truth and Reconciliation Commission of South Africa Report, 1998. Numerous civic activities. Internat. Humanitarian fellow Hauser Found./ICRC, Geneva, 1998. Mem. numerous profl. orgns. Avocations: reading, hiking, kayaking, exploring. Office: Duke Law Sch PO Box 90360 Durham NC 27708-0360

AFFELDT, DAVID ALLAN, lawyer, legal consultant; b. Cedar Rapids, Iowa, Jan. 15, 1941; s. Chester Nicholas and Helen (May) A.; m. Judy Cook, Aug. 29, 1964 (dec.); 1 child, Christine A. BA, U. Iowa, 1963; JD, U. Tex., 1966. Bar: D.C., U.S. Dist. Ct. D.C. 1993, U.S. Ct. Appeals (D.C.) 1993. Asst. atty. gen. Iowa Dept. Justice, Des Moines, 1966; asst. counsel Iowa Senate, 1967; legis. aide to Congress Neal Smith, U.S. Ho. of Reps., Washington, 1968-69; chief counsel Senate Com. on Aging, 1969-79; spl. asst. to commr. Social Security Adminstrn., 1979-80; cons. to nat. aging orgns., 1980—. Cons. Assn. for Gerontology in Higher Edn.; author numerous laws impacting older Americans. Author numerous reports on the elderly. Cons. on older Ams. issues Pamela Harriman/Dems. for the 80s, Washington, 1982-86. With D.C. N.G., 1966-72. Recipient resolutions and certs. of commendation from nat. aging orgns. and U.S. Senate. Mem. D.C. Bar Assn. Avocations: reading, swimming, tennis, mini-triathlon, travel. Home and Office: 10404 Joiners Ln Potomac MD 20854-1941

AGATA, BURTON C. law educator, lawyer; b. N.Y.C., Feb. 7, 1928; s. Max and Augusta (Steger) A.; m. Dale S. Granirer, Dec. 24, 1955; children: Seth Hugh, Abby Fran. AB, U. Mich., 1947, JD, 1950; LLM in Trade Regulation, NYU, 1951. Bar: N.Y. 1951. Counsel div. N.Y. State Banking Dept., 1955-59; ptnr. firm Burstein & Agata, Mineola and N.Y.C., 1959-61; prof. Mont. U., 1961-62, N.Mex. U., 1962-63, Houston U., 1963-69; counsel Nat. Commn. on Reform Fed. Criminal Laws, 1968-70; prof. law Hofstra U., 1970-2001, Max Schmertz disting. prof. law, 1982-2001, disting. prof. emeritus, 2001—, interim dean, 1989; mem. faculty Nat. Inst. Trial Advocacy, 1977-81; dir. N.E. Regional Program, 1981-84. Spl. counsel N.Y. City Charter Revision Commn., 1987-89, N.Y. State Senate Minority, 1982-87; cons. Fed. Jud. Center, 1972, Inst. Jud. Adminstrn., 1973, HEW, 1971, White House Spl. Action Office Drug Abuse Prevention, 1973, N.Y. State Temp. Com. on Constnl. Revision, 1993-95; Chmn. N.Y. State Task Force, Standards and Go als for Prosecution and Def., 1977-79; cons. Adv. Com. on Qualifications of Counsel, 2d Ct., 1977; bd. dirs. Nassau Economic Opportunity Commn., 1972-73; reporter-cons. action unit on criminal justice system N.Y. State Bar Assn., 1986-90. Contbr. articles to law jours. With JAGC U.S. Army, 1951-54. Food Law fellow NYU, 1951, fellow U. Wis., 1963. Fellow Am. Bar Found. (life); mem. Am. Law Inst. (life), ABA (state antitrust law commn. 1980—, vice chair com. on professionalism sr. lawyers divsn. 1996-2000), N.Y. State Bar Assn. (exec. com. criminal justice sect., chmn. com. rev. of criminal law 1987—, spl. com. on pre-sentence reports 1989-2001, Donnelly Act com. 1990-2001), Assn. of Bar of City of N.Y. (criminal cts. com. 1970-73, penology com. 1973-76, criminal justice coun. 1983-85, antitrust com. 1986-89), Fed. Jud. Coun., Assn. Am. Law Schs. (chmn. criminal law sect. 1973) Home and Office: PO Box 727 Hudson NY 12534 E-mail: vze2vnja@verison.net

AGCAOILI, JOSE LUIS VILLAFRANCA, lawyer; b. Manila, Philippines, Apr. 10, 1960; s. Antonio Villasenor and Maria Luz Villafranca A.; m. Marybeth Webb, Mar. 17, 1990; 1 child, Juan Loranzo. BS, Dela Salle U., Manila, Philippines, 1981; B of Law, U. Santo Tomas, Manila, Philippines, 1987. Assoc. Agcaoili & Assocs., Philippines, 1987-95; chief staff Philippine Senate, 1992-98; sr. assoc. Agcaoili & Assocs., 1995—. Aviation, General corporate, General practice. Office: Agcaoili & Assocs 7th Fl citibank Ctr Makati 918-1868 The Philippines Fax: 819-1868. E-mail: avaslaw@info.com.ph

AGGER, JAMES H. retired lawyer; b. 1936; married. AB, St. Joseph's U., 1958; JD, U. Pa., 1961. Mem. Krusen, Evans & Byrne, 1965-69; gen. counsel Catalytic Inc., Air Products and Chems. Inc., 1969-77; asst. gen. counsel Air Products and Chems., Inc., Trexlertown, Pa., 1977-80, gen. counsel, 1980—, v.p., 1982-97, corp. sec., 1990, sr. v.p., 1997-99; ret., 1999. General corporate. Office: Air Products & Chems Inc 7201 Hamilton Blvd Allentown PA 18195-1526*

AGOSTI, DEBORAH ANN, state supreme court justice; Justice Nev. Supreme Court, Carson City, 1999—. Office: Supreme Ct Nev 201 S Carson St Carson City NV 89701-4702*

AGRANOFF, GERALD NEAL, lawyer; b. Detroit, Nov. 24, 1946; s. Carl and Frances (Solomon) A.; children: Lindsay Sara, Dana Jill. BS, Wayne State U., 1969, JD, 1972; LLM, NYU, 1973. Bar: Mich. 1973, N.Y. 1975, U.S. Tax Ct. 1974, U.S. Ct. Claims 1974. Atty.-advisor U.S. Tax Ct., Washington, 1973-75; assoc. law firm Baker & McKenzie, N.Y.C., 1975-79, Baer Marks & Upham, N.Y.C., 1979-80; counsel Pryor, Cashman et al, 1980-82; gen. counsel Arbitrage Securities Co., Plaza Securities Co., 1982—; gen. ptnr. Edelman Securities Co., 1984—. Trustee, Mgmt. Assistance Inc., Liquidating Trust; bd. dirs. Canal Capital Corp., N.Y.C., Bull Run Corp., Dynacore Holdings Corp., Atlantic Gulf Cmtys.; adj. instr. NYU Inst. on Fed. Taxation, 1980-81. Bd. dirs. Soho Repertory Theatre, N.Y.C., 1982; mem. N.Y. com. UNICEF. Corporate taxation, Personal income taxation, State and local taxation. Office: The Edelman Cos 717 5th Ave New York NY 10022-8101 E-mail: gagranoff@edelco.com

AGRAZ, FRANCISCO JAVIER, SR. lawyer, public affairs representative; b. Laredo, Tex., Aug. 21, 1947; s. Jose Jesus and Irene (Garcia-Gomez) A.; m. Rosalinda Varela, Aug. 23, 1969 (div. Feb. 1980); children: Francisco Javier Jr., Raquel Jeanne; m. Ruth Urquidi, Jan. 1, 1984. BA in Journalism, U. Tex. at El Paso, 1970; JD, U. Houston, 1987. Bar: Tex. 1988, U.S. Dist. Ct. (so. dist.) Tex. 1988. Anchor reporter KENS-TV, San Antonio, 1970; corr. ABC Capital Cities Comms., Chgo., Houston, N.Y., 1970-77; pub. affairs analyst Exxon Corp., Houston and Memphis, 1977-83; assoc. Wood, Burney, Cohn & Bradley, Corpus Christi, Tex., 1987-89, Redford, Wray & Woolsey, P.C., Corpus Christi, 1989-91; pres., atty. at law Francisco J. Agraz P.C., Houston, 1991—; gen. mgr. The MRAM Co., 1996-98; pub. affairs officer FBI, 1998—. Bd. govs. United Way of Coastal Bend, Corpus Christi, Tex., 1987-91. Mem. State Bar of Tex. (grievance com., pub. rels. com.). Roman Catholic. Avocations: Spanish translator. General corporate, Private international. E-mail: agrazfj@worldnet.att.net

AHARONI, EREZ, lawyer; b. Israel, Oct. 20, 1957; s. Aharon and Yael A.; m. Iris Aharoni; children: Ofir, Itamar, Almog. LLB, Tel Aviv U., 1985. Bar: Israel, 1985. Ptnr. Zysman, Aharoni, Gayer & Co., Tel Aviv, 1986—. Served with Israeli Air Force. Consumer commercial, Communications, Real property. Office: Zysman Aharoni Gayer & Co 52 A Hayrkon St Tel Aviv 63432 Israel Fax: 972-3-7955550. E-mail: mail@zag-law.co.il

AHLERS, GLEN-PETER, SR. law library director, educator, consultant; b. N.Y.C., Mar. 15, 1955; s. LeGrande Jacob and Joan (Stoltz) A.; m. Sondra Sue Wadley, May 17, 1987; children: Glen-Peter II, Sandia Marie, Gavin Patrick, Sierra Le Ann Rose, Stacia Camille. BS, U. N.Mex., Albuquerque, 1979; MA, U. of South Fla., 1983; JD, Washburn U., 1987. Bar: Kans. 1987, U.S. Dist. Ct. Kans. 1987, U.S. Ct. Mil. Appeals 1988, D.C. 1990. Reference asst. U. N.Mex. Sch. Law, Albuquerque, 1979-83; asst. dir. Washburn Sch. Law Libr., Topeka, 1983-87; assoc. libr. dir. Wake Forest U., Winston-Salem, N.C., 1987-90; libr. dir., assoc. prof. D.C. Sch. Law, Washington, 1990-92, U. Ark., Fayetteville, 1992-2000, prof., 2001—. Computer and libr. cons. Ctr. for R&D in Law-Related Edn., Winston-Salem, 1987-90; adj. prof. Sch. of Law Wake Forest U., Winston-Salem, N.C., 1987-90; bd. dirs. Mid-Am. Law Sch. Libr. Consortium, 1992—, Consortium of Southestern Law Librs., 1988-90. Author: Election Laws of the United States, 1995; co-author: Notary Law and Practice, 1997; editor The Maall Newsletter, 1984-87, The Scrivener, 1992—; tech. editor Washburn Law Jour., 1985-86; contbr. articles to profl. jours. Mediator N.C. Neighborhood Justice Ctr., Winston-Salem, 1989-90. Mem. ABA, ALA, Ark. Bar Assn., Am. Assn. Law Librs., Southwestern Assn. Law Librs. (pres. 1995-97), Mid Am. Assn. Law Librs. (pres. 1999-2000), Scribes (exec. dir. 1997—), Phi Kappa Phi, Kappa Delta Pi, Beta Phi Mu. Avocation: writing. Home: 2139 Revere Ln Fayetteville AR 72701-2711 Office: U Ark Leflar Law Ctr Fayetteville AR 72701-1201 E-mail: gahlers@uark.edu

AHLSCHWEDE, EARL DAVID, lawyer; b. Friend, Nebr., Nov. 12, 1940; s. Clarence Jefferson and Phyllis D. (Kleinholz) A.; m. Virginia S. Chudly, Apr. 15, 1972; children: Mathew, James and John (twins). BS, U. Nebr., 1962, JD, 1964. Bar: Nebr. 1964, U.S. Dist. Ct. Nebr. 1964. Adminstrv. asst. Nebr. Dept. Agr., Lincoln, 1964-66; county atty. York County, Nebr., 1967-68; city atty. Beatrice, 1969-74; city mgr., atty. City of Grand Island, 1974-77; ptnr. Ahlschwede, De Backer & Truell, Grand Island, 1977-87. Bd. dirs. St. Francis Med. Ctr., Grand Island, 1981-87; chmn. Hall County Housing Authority, Grand Island, 1983-93. Mem. ABA, 11th Jud. Dist. Bar Assn., Nebr. State Bar Assn. (ho. of dels. 1983-89), Am. Judicature Soc. State civil litigation, Criminal, General practice. Home: 1620 Coventry Ln Grand Island NE 68801-7026 Office: Mayer Burns & Ahlschwede Norwest Bank Bldg Third and Locust Sts Grand Island NE 68802

AHLSTROM, MICHAEL JOSEPH, lawyer; b. N.Y.C., June 1, 1953; s. Albert Warren and Bernadette Patricia (Flynn) A.; m. Mary Lou Donnelly, Apr. 19, 1980; 1 child, Courtney Leigh. BS, St. Francis Coll., 1975; JD, U. San Francisco, 1978. Bar: N.Y. 1980, U.S. Dist. Ct. (so. and ea. dists.) N.Y. 1980, Ga. 1982, U.S. Dist. Ct. (no. dist.) Ga. 1983, U.S. Ct. Appeals (11th cir.) 1984, U.S. Supreme Ct. 1987; registered neutral, Ga. Counsel Gear Design, Inc., N.Y.C., 1979-80; ptnr. Ahlstrom & Ahlstrom, 1981-83; gen. counsel Network Rental, Inc., Atlanta, 1984-87; assoc. John Marshall and Assocs., P.C., 1987; ptnr. Marshall & Ahlstrom, P.C., 1987-88; mng. atty. UAW-GM-Ford Chrysler Legal Plan Ga., 1993-96; pvt. practice, Marietta, Ga., 1988-92, 96—. Arbitrator Nat Assn. Securities Dealers, Superior Ct. Fulton County, Ga., 1987—, Ga. Lemon Law, 1991—; panel atty. Cobb County Circuit Defender; spl. master Cobb County Superior Ct., mediator, 1966—; mediator domestic cases Fulton County Superior Ct., 1998—, mediator juvenile cases; guardian ad litem Cobb County Superior Ct. Mem. N.Y. Bar Assn., Ga. Bar Assn. (pub. rels. com. 1989-91), Cobb County Bar Assn., Am. Corp.Counsel Assn. (program chmn. 1986-87), Am. Arbitration Assn. (comml. panel 1987—), KC, Phi Delta Phi, Alpha Kappa Psi. Republican. Roman Catholic. Avocations: fishing, hunting, tennis, golf, croquet. Contracts commercial, General corporate, General practice. Home: 613 Fairway Ct Marietta GA 30068-4159

AHOLA, JUHANI ILMARI, lawyer; b. Helsinki, Feb. 5, 1943; s. Vaino and Ines A.; m. Irmelin Panelius, July 23, 1967; children: Pauliina Kallio, Kasimir, Johanna. LLM, Helsinki U., 1968. Advisor Min. Transports, Helsinki, 1969-70; chief legal dept., asst. dir. Ctrl. C. of C. Finland, 1970-74. Treas. Jaycees Internat., Coral Gables, Fla., 1981. Lt. Finnish Mil., 1962-63. Mem. Finnish Fowarders Assn. (legal advisor, adv. com. 1990-2000). Avocations: classical music, sailing, golf. General corporate, Mergers and acquisitions, Transportation. Office: Ahola & Sokka Italahdenkatu 15-17 FI-00210 Helsinki Finland Fax: 358 9 58 445 445. E-mail: juhani.ahola@ahola-sokka.fi

AHRENSFELD, THOMAS FREDERICK, lawyer; b. Bklyn., June 30, 1923; s. Frederick Herman and Madeline Florence (Moffett) A.; m. Joan Ann McGowan, Mar. 17, 1944; 1 child, Thomas Frederick. A.B., Bklyn. Coll., 1948; LL.B., Columbia U., 1948. Bar: N.Y. 1948. Assoc., then ptnr. Conboy, Hewitt, O'Brien & Boardman, N.Y.C., 1948-58; sec., assoc. gen. counsel Philip Morris Inc., 1959-70, v.p., gen. counsel, 1970-76, sr. v.p., gen. counsel, 1976-85, Philip Morris Cos., Inc., N.Y.C., 1985-88; pvt. practice law Pleasantville, N.Y., 1988—. Trustee Trinity-Pawling Sch. Corp., 1976-98; elder Presbyn. Ch. 1st lt. USAAF, 1942-45. Decorated D.F.C., Air medal with oak leaf clusters. Mem. ABA, N.Y.C. Bar Assn., N.Y. Athletic Club, Mt. Kisco (N.Y.) Country Club, Johns Island (Fla.) Club. General corporate. Home and Office: 85 Nannahagan Rd Pleasantville NY 10570-2314

AH-TYE, KIRK THOMAS, lawyer; b. L.A., Mar. 31, 1951; s. Thomas and Ruth Elizabeth (Liu) Ah-T.; m. Deborah Ann Wells, Jan. 31, 1981; 1 child, Torrey Ann. BA, U. Calif., Santa Barbara, 1973; JD, Boston Coll., 1976. Bar: Calif. 1977, U.S. Dist. Ct. (cen. dist.) Calif. 1978, U.S. Dist. Ct. (ea. dist.) Calif. 1994, U.S. Ct. Appeals (9th cir.) 1978, U.S. Supreme Ct. 1981. Co-exec. dir., mng. atty. Channel Counties Legal Svcs. Assn., Santa Barbara, 1977—. Expert witness Assembly Com. on Edn., Calif. Legis., Sacramento; panelist Ctr. for the Study of Dem. Instns., Santa Barbara; panelist, instr. CLE approved classes; past legal cons. Santa Barbara chpt. calif. Assn. Bilingual Educators; inaugural prodr., moderator Santa Barbara Law, Sta. KTMS-AM, 1994—. Editor (bar newsletter) Santa Barbara Lawyer, 1992-93, (monthly legal series) Santa Barbara News-Press; contbr. articles to profl. jours. Trustee Montessori Ctr. Sch., Santa Barbara, 1991-93; bd. dirs., v.p. Santa Barbara Internat. Film Festival, 1991-93; chair adv. bd. Santa Barbara Regional Health Authority, 1985; mem. blue-ribbon com. County Bd. Suprs., Santa Barbara, 1988; chair Santa Barbara County Affirmative Action Commn., 1987-88; mem. grant-making com. Fund for Santa Barbara, 1988-92. Recipient Local Hero award Santa Barbara Ind., 1988. Master Santa Barbara Am. Inns of Ct.; mem. State Bar Calif. (state resolutions com. to state bar conf. of dels. 1994-96, exec. com. to conf. dels. 1997, ann. legal svcs. achievement award for so. Calif. 1997, Achievement award for legal svc. 1997), Santa Barbara County Bar Assn. (jud. svc. award com. 1992, chmn. pro bono com. 1993, bd. dirs., sec., CFO 1992—, pres. 1997-98), Lawyer Referral Svc. Santa Barbara (bd. dirs., pres. 1992). Avocations: sports, film, literature, weights, tennis. General civil litigation, Education and schools, Health. Office: Channel Counties Legal Svcs Assn 324 E Carrillo St Ste B Santa Barbara CA 93101-7438

AHUMADA, RICARDO, lawyer; b. Nuevo Laredo, Tamaulipas, Mex., Sept. 18, 1970; s. Rene Ahumada and Isabel Reyes; m. Pamela Garcia, Nov. 11, 1994. Degree in law, U. Autonoma Mex., 1993. Assoc. Martinez, Algaba, Estrella, De Haro y galvan-Duque, S.C., Mexico City, 1994-95; fgn. assoc. Shearman & Sterling, N.Y.C., 1997-98; assoc. Chevez, Ruiz, Zamarripa y Cia, S.C., Mexico City, 1995—2001; ptnr. Deloitte and Touchle, 2001—. Mem. Mex. Bar Assn. Avocations: golfing, bowling, traveling. Constitutional, Taxation, general. Office: Jaime Blarres 11 Edificio B 11510 Mexico City Mexico Fax: 525 283-4699. E-mail: rahumada@dttmx.com

AIBEL, HOWARD J. lawyer, arbitrator/mediator; b. N.Y.C., Mar. 24, 1929; m. Katherine Webster, June 6, 1952; children: David Webster, Daniel Walter, Jonathan Brown. AB magna cum laude, 1950; JD cum laude, Harvard U., 1951. Bar: N.Y. 1952. Assoc. White & Case, N.Y.C., 1952-57; trade regulation counsel GE, 1957-60, spl. litigation counsel elec. equipment antitrust cases, 1960-64; antitrust counsel ITT Corp., N.Y.C., 1964-66, v.p., assoc. gen. counsel, 1966-68, sr. v.p., gen. counsel, 1968-87, exec. v.p., gen. counsel, 1987-92, exec. v.p., chief legal officer, 1992-94; ptnr. LeBoeuf Lamb Greene & MacRae, 1994-99, of counsel, 1999-2001. Bd. dirs. Farrel Corp., Transparancy, Internat.-USA; vice chmn. Fund for Modern Cts., 1985-95; mem. AAA/ABA/AMA Com. Health Care Dispute Resolution, 1997-2000. Mem. vis. com. Northwestern U. Law Sch., 1984-90; mem. adv. com. Corp. Counsel Ctr., chmn., 1986-87; bd. dirs. Alliance of Resident Theatres, N.Y.. 1986—, chmn., 1989—; trustee Lawyers Com. for Civil Rights, 1991-95; trustee U. Bridgeport, 1989-91, chmn. adv. com. Sch. Law, 1987-92; cons. trustee Westport Nature Ctr. for Environ. Activities; bd. dirs., 1st v.p. Westport Arts Ctr., 1993-96. Fellow Am. Bar Found. (life); mem. ABA (bus. law sect. corp. governance 1994-98), Am. Law Inst. (elected mem.), Am. Arbitration Assn. (chmn. exec. com. 1992-95, chmn. bd. dirs. 1995-98), Assn. Gen. Counsel, pres. Harvard Law Sch. Assn. NY, 1992-94, v.p. Harvard Law Sch. Assn., 1994—, Am. Judicature Soc. (bd. dirs. 1994-2001, exec. com. 1996-2001). Home and Office: 183 Steep Hill Rd Weston CT 06883-1924 E-mail: hjaibel@optonline.net

AIDINOFF, M(ERTON) BERNARD, lawyer; b. Newport, R.I., Feb. 2, 1929; s. Simon and Esther (Miller) A.; m. Celia Spiro, May 30, 1956 (dec. June 28, 1984); children: Seth G., Gail M.; m. Elsie V. Newburg, Nov. 29, 1996. BA, U. Mich., 1950; LLB magna cum laude, Harvard U., 1953. Bar: D.C. 1953, N.Y. 1954. Law clk. to Judge Learned Hand, U.S. Ct. of Appeals, N.Y.C., 1955-56; with Sullivan & Cromwell, 1956-63, ptnr., 1963-96, sr. counsel, 1997—. Dir. Am. Internat. Group Inc., Gibbs & Cox, Inc.; adv. com. to IRS commr., 1979-80, 85-86. Editor in chief The Tax Lawyer, 1974-77. Trustee Spence Sch., 1971-79; mem. adv. com. Gibbs Bros. Fedn., 1965-94; mem. vis. com. Harvard U. Law Sch., 1976-82, 99—; adv. dir. Met. Opera Assn., 1989—; chmn. bd. dirs. St. Luke's Chamber Ensemble, 1988-2001, chmn. emeritus, 2001—. 1st lt. JAGC, AUS, 1953-55. Recipient Judge Learned Hand Human Rels. award Am. Jewish Com., 1997. Mem. ABA (vice-chmn. sect. taxation 1974-77, chmn.-elect 1981-82, chmn. 1982-83, chmn. commn. taxpayer compliance 1983-88, Ho. of Dels. 1988-91), N.Y. State Bar Assn., Assn. Bar of City of N.Y. (exec. com. 1974-78, chmn. exec. com. 1977-78, v.p. 1978-79, chmn. taxation com. 1979-81, chmn. govt. ethics com. 1988-90), East Hampton Hist. Soc. (trustee 1983-89, 90-95), Am. Law Inst. (cons. fed. income tax project 1974—, chmn. tax program com. 1988—, John Minor Wisdom award 1995), Found. for a Civil Soc. (bd. dirs. 1994—, vice chmn. 1997-98, chmn. 1999—), Coun. Fgn. Rels., Guild Hall (trustee1989-94, 95—, treas. 1993-94, 95—), Lawyers Com. for Human Rights (bd. dirs. 1986—, treas. 1997—), Confrerie des Chevaliers du Tavestin, Commanderie de Bordeaux, The Parks Coun. (bd. dirs. 1995-97), Century Assn., India House, Met. Club, Phi Beta Kappa. Corporate taxation, Taxation, general. Home: 980 5th Ave New York NY 10021-0126 Office: Sullivan & Cromwell 125 Broad St New York NY 10004-2498 E-mail: aidnoffmb@sullcrom.com

AIELLO, JAMES ANDREW, lawyer; b. Phoenix, Mar. 5, 1940; s. James Francis and Ethel Swea Aiello; m. Helene Sarah Aiello, June 21, 1964; children: James Anthony, Matthew Charles. BA, U. Ariz., 1962; JD, U. San Francisco, 1965. Bar: Calif. 1966, D.C. 1979, U.S. Supreme Ct. 1968. Dep. atty. gen. Office of Calif. Atty. Gen., San Francisco, 1965-70; asst. dist. atty. San Mateo County Calif. Dist. Atty., Redwood, City, 1970-79; chief of staff Hon. William Royer, U.S. Rep., Washington, 1979-81; dir. domestic govt. affairs Combustion Engring. Inc., 1981-92; v.p. govt. affairs Ogden Martin, Inc., 1992-95; acting CEO KBF Environtl., Inc., 1995-97; dir., chief of party PADCO, Inc., Midrand, South Africa, 1997—; acting CEO, MIIU, South Africa, 2000—. Prin. Oakton (Va.) Cons. Group, 1995-97; dir. KBF Environtl. Inc., 1995-97, DGL Internat., Inc., Washington, 1995-98; mem. environ. adv. com. Conn. State Legis., Hartford, 1994-97, legis. adv. com. 1994-95; mem. environ. adv. com. Hawaii Legis., 1992-95. Contbr. articles to profl. jours. Chair, legis. and regulations com. Integrated Waste Svcs. Assn., 1993-95. Mem. Masons (San Carlos Lodge #690), Aircraft and Pilots and Owners Assn., Bar Assn. D.C., Bar Assn. of State of Calif. (ho. adminstrv. asst. assoc.), Westwood Country Club. Republican. Episcopalian. Avocations: opera, classical music, private pilot, South African wild game conservation. Office: PO Box 95427 Waterkloof 0145 South Africa E-mail: ocgp@icon.co.za

AIELLO, ROBERT JOHN, lawyer; b. Bklyn., July 23, 1959; s. John Frank Aiello and Adele Cavaliere; m. Sylvia Stone, Sept. 29, 1996. BA, Trinity Coll., 1981; JD, Fordham U., 1984. Bar: N.Y. 1985, D.C. 1988, U.S. Dist. Ct. (ea. and so. dists.) 1986, U.S. Supreme Ct. 1993. Assoc. Reid & Priest, N.Y.C., 1983; asst. dist. atty. Queens County Dist. Attys. Office, Kew Gardens, N.Y., 1984-91; ptnr. Aiello & Cannick, N.Y.C., 1992—. Counsel Assemblyman Joseph R. Lentol, 1992-95. Bd. govs. Columbus Citizens Found., chmn. H.S. scholarship com. Mem. N.Y. State Bar Assn., Columbian Lawyers Assn., Queens Bar Assn. (spkr. 1993—), Don Mont Meml. Rsch. Found. (bd. dirs.), Phi Beta Kappa, Pi Gamma Mu. Roman Catholic. Avocations: running, tennis, boating, skiing, reading. Criminal, Education and schools, Personal injury. Home: 67 Rockcrest Rd Manhasset NY 11030-3416 Office: Aiello & Cannick 233 Broadway Rm 4000 New York NY 10279-4099

AIN, SANFORD KING, lawyer; b. Glen Cove, N.Y., July 24, 1947; s. Herbert and Victoria (Ben Susan) A.; m. Miriam Luskin, July 12, 1980; children: David Lloyd, Daniel Jason. BA cum laude, U. Wis., 1969; JD, Georgetown U., 1972. Bar: Va. 1972, D.C. 1973, Md. 1982. Ptnr. Sherman, Meehan, Curtin & Ain P.C., Washington, 1972—. Mem. faculty continuing legal edn. program State Bar Va., D.C. Bar, Md. Bar. Fellow Am. Acad. Matrimonial Lawyers (pres. D.C. chpt. 1991-94, counsel 1999-2000), Am. Coll. Family Trial Lawyers, Va. Trial Lawyers Assn., Md. Bar Assn. Family and matrimonial, Real property. Office: Sherman Meehan Curtin & Ain PC 1900 M St NW Ste 600 Washington DC 20036-3519

AISENBERG, BENNETT S. lawyer; b. Feb. 17, 1931; s. Joseph Samuel and Minna Ruth (Cohan) A. BA, Brown U., 1952; JD, Harvard U., 1955. Bar: Mass. 1955, Colo. 1958, U.S. Dist. Ct. Colo. 1958, U.S. Ct. Appeals (10th cir.) 1958. Ptnr. Gorsuch, Kirgis, Denver, 1958-80; pvt. practice, 1980—. Mem. Nat. Acad. Arbitrators, Colo. Trial Lawyers Assn. (pres. 1984-85), Denver Bar Assn. (trustee 1982-85, 86-89, pres. 1991-92), Colo. Bar Assn. (pres. 1998-99). Alternative dispute resolution, State civil litigation, Personal injury. Office: Colorado State Bank Bldg 1600 Broadway Ste 2350 Denver CO 80202-4921

AISENSTARK, AVERY, lawyer, educator; b. Tel Aviv, May 11, 1945; came to U.S., 1947; s. Isaac Mayer and Hadasa Hinda (Goldberg) A.; m. Edith Gluck, June 19, 1968; 1 child, M. Daniel. J.D., U. Md., 1969. Bar: Md. 1969, U.S. Dist. Ct. Md. 1969. Assoc. Frank, Bernstein, Conaway & Goldman, Balt., 1969-73; asst. legis. officer Office of Gov., State of Md., Annapolis, 74; revisor statutes, dir. Gov.'s Commn. to Revise Annotated Code, 1974-77, spl. cons., 1978-79; asst. atty. gen., chief counsel for opinions and advice Office of Atty. Gen., Balt., 1979-85; ptnr. Frank, Bernstein, Conaway & Goldman, Balt., 1985—; lectr. law U. Md., 1981—; mem. standing com. on rules of practice and procedure Md. Ct. of Appeals, 1984—; mem. Gov.'s Commn. to Revise Annotated Code, 1977—. Sec., founding mem. bd. dirs. Md. Found. for Performing Arts, 1973-82; founding chmn. Balt. chpt. Nat. Jewish Commn. on Law and Pub. Affairs, 1977-79, mem. exec. bd., 1977—; v.p., bd. dirs. Collel Bayit Vegan Found., Inc.; pres., bd. dirs. Found. for Beth Jacob Tchrs. Coll., Inc. Mem. Md. State Bar Assn. (council, sect. on state and local govts. 1982—), Order of Coif. Democrat. Jewish. Home: 6700 Cross Country Blvd Baltimore MD 21215-2505 Office: Frank Bernstein Conaway Goldman 3908 N Charles St Apt 303 Baltimore MD 21218-1740

AJALAT, SOL PETER, lawyer; b. Chgo., July 12, 1932; s. Peter S. and Tesbina (Shahadie) Ajalat; m. Lily Mary Roum, Aug. 21, 1960; children: Stephen, Gregory, Denise, Lawrence. BS, UCLA, 1958, JD, 1962. Bar: Calif. 1963, U.S. Dist. Ct. (no., cen., ea. and so. dists.) Calif. 1963, U.S. Claims Ct. 1990. Pvt. practice, L.A., 1965—. Referee Calif. State Bar Ct., 1984-90. Pres. bd. dirs. St. Nicholas Orthodox Cath. Ch., L.A., 1976-78; pres. Toluca Lake Elem. Adv. Coun., L.A., 1979, L.A. Unified Sch. Dist. Area I Adv. Coun., 1980, Providence High Sch. Adv. Coun., L.A., 1985; bd. dirs. Med. Ctr. North Hollywood, 1991-98, Angels of the Yr. Awards, 1996—, Life Svcs., Inc., 1997-2001; mem. improvement adv. com. Burbank City media dist., 1997-2000. Mem. Calif. Bar Assn., L.A. County Bar Assn. (mem. L.A. Superior Ct. bench and bar com. 1987-96, chmn. mcpl. ct. com. 1985-86, trustee 1987-88), Calif. Trial Lawyers Assn., Conf. Bar Dels. (del. 1985—), L.A. County Trial Lawyers Assn., Lawyers Club L.A. County (pres. 1985-86), Toluca Lake C. of C. (pres. 1997), Wm. A. Neima Rep. Club (pres. 1978-79), Masons, Shriners, Kiwanis. Eastern Orthodox. Avocation: physical fitness. State civil litigation, General practice. Office: 3800 W Alameda Ave Ste 1150 Burbank CA 91505-4304

AKAR, VIRGINIA MAYA, lawyer; b. Bklyn., Aug. 29, 1967; d. Aron and Luisa Maya; m. Joseph Akar, June 12, 1993; children: Kaili, Kane. BS in Journalism, U. Fla., 1990; JD, St. Thomas U., 1994. Bar: Fla. 1994. Writer Miami (Fla.) Today newspaper, 1990-91; prosecutor Office of Miami-Dade State Atty., 1994-98; products liability atty. Seipp Flick & Kissane, Miami, 1998; pvt. practice, 1998—. Legal cons. Accar Ltd. Inc., Miami, 1994. Editor St. Thomas Law Rev. jour., 1992-94. Mem. ABA, Dade County Bar Assn. Avocations: running, kickboxing. Office: 1 NE 1st St Ste 35 Miami FL 33132-2437

AKERS, SAMUEL LEE, lawyer; b. Chattanooga, Oct. 20, 1943; s. Shelby Russell and Helen Louise (Crumley) A.; m. Mercedes Lilia Vuksanovic, Mar. 13, 1967; children: Bradford Lee, Camby Leigh. BA, Berry Coll., 1966; JD, Memphis State U., 1974. Bar: Tenn. 1974, U.S. Dist. Ct. (ea. dist.) Tenn. 1976, U.S. Ct. Appeals (6th cir.) 1985, U.S. Supreme Ct. 1987, U.S. Dist. Ct. (mid. dist.) Tenn. 1989. Trust examiner Office of the Compt. of the Currency, Memphis, 1975-76; assoc. Luther, Anderson, Cleary & Ruth, Chattanooga, 1976-78, 81-84, ptnr., 1985-93, Hatfield Van Cleave & Akers, Chattanooga, 1994, Hatfield Van Cleave Akers & Adams, P.L.C., Chattanooga, 1995-96; spl. agt. FBI, Orlando, Fla., 1978-81; clk. and master Chancery Ct. Hamilton County, 11th Jud. Dist., Chattanooga, 1996—. Mem. comml. panel Am. Arbitration Assn., N.Y.C., 1986-96. Asst. instr. SCUBA cert. Lt. comdr. USNR, 1967-71. Named Outstanding Young Man of Am. Jaycees, 1977. Mem. Tenn. Bar Assn., Chattanooga Bar Assn. (bd. govs. 1995-96, sec.-treas. 1997, pres.-elect 1998, pres. 1999-2000), Soc. Former Spl. Agts. of the FBI (chmn. Chattanooga chpt. 1987-88, 95-96). Republican. Roman Catholic. Avocations: jogging, bicycling, hiking, tennis, scuba diving. General civil litigation, State civil litigation, Probate. Home: 106 Westwood Dr Signal Mountain TN 37377-2525 Office: Chancery Ct Tenn 300 Courthouse Hamilton Co Chattanooga TN 37402 E-mail: leeakers@exch.hamiltonth.gov

AKERS-PARRY, DEBORAH (DEBORAH ROWLEY AKERS), lawyer; b. Troy, N.Y., Apr. 27, 1949; d. Samuel Lansing and Audrey (Relyea) Rowley. AB, Washington U., St. Louis, 1971; JD, Cleve. State U., 1976. Bar: Ohio 1976. Assoc. Wm. F. Manlove Co., L.P.A.; ptnr. Manlove, Manlove, Rowley & Fuhry, Chagrin Falls, Ohio, 1976-79; pvt. practice Avon Lake, 1979-84; assoc. Schwarzwald, Robiner, Wolf & Rock, L.P.A., Cleve., 1984-88; prin. Wolf & Akers, L.P.A., 1988—. Mem. faculty Ohio CLE Inst., 1985-87, 89-93, Ohio Supreme Ct. Jud. Coll. Teleconf., 1991. Co-author: Disqualification, Family Advocate, vol. 9, #3, 1987; mem. editorial bd. The Domestic Rels. Jour. of Ohio. Trial referee Medina County Ct. of Common Pleas, 1983-84; mem. Profl. Edn. systems, 1990-91; appointee 8th Ohio Appellate Dist. Jud. Conf., 1991, 98, Bench Bar Conf., 1990, 94. Fellow Am. Acad. Matrimonial Lawyers; mem. ABA (family law sect., litigation sect., 1989—, participant Advanced Family Law Advocacy Inst. 1987, faculty 1992-94, 97, publs. bd. 2000—), Nat. Inst. Trial Advocacy (participant Teacher Training Program, Harvard Law Sch., 1993); Ohio State Bar Assn. (chmn. family law com. 1994-96, chmn. legis. drafting subcom. 1989-93, del. coun. of dels. 1990—, family law specialty cert. bd. 1999—, chmn. specialization com. 2001—), Cuyahoga County Bar Assn. (chmn. family law com. 1992-93, trustee 1986-87, mem. grievance com. 1986-96, faculty Trial Advocacy Inst. 1988-89, co-chmn. 1990-91, chmn. 1993), Cleve. Bar Assn. (chmn. family law sect. 1989-90, profl. ethics com. 1986-93), Medina County Bar Assn. (lectr. 1983, 84, 87), Ohio Family Law Inst., Akron Bar Assn., Wayne County Bar Assn., Geauga County Bar Assn., Cleveland-Marshall Coll. of Law Alumni Assn. (trustee 1991-96, chmn. CLE com. 1994-96). Episcopalian. Family and matrimonial. Office: Wolf & Akers LPA 1515 East Ohio Bldg 1717 E 9th St Cleveland OH 44114-2803

AKSEN, GERALD, lawyer, educator, arbitrator; b. N.Y.C., Feb. 16, 1930; s. David and Bess (Stein) A.; m. Phyllis Schwadron, June 3, 1957 (dec.); 1 child, Lisa Susan. AB, CCNY, 1951; MA, Columbia U., 1952; LLB, NYU, 1958. Bar: N.Y. 1959, U.S. Dist. Ct. (so. and ea. dist.) N.Y. 1961, U.S. Supreme Ct. 1964. Assoc. Flood & Purvin, N.Y.C., 1958-61; assoc. gen. counsel Am. Arbitration Assn., 1962-63, gen. counsel, 1964-80; ptnr. Reid & Priest L.L.P., 1981-98, Thelen Reid & Priest L.L.P., N.Y.C., 1998—. Adj. prof. NYU, N.Y.C., 1968—; mem. First Dept. Jud. Screening Com., 1983-93; bd. dirs. U.S. Coun. Internat. Bus., 1982—; ICC Inst. World Bus. Law, 1992—; vice chmn. ICC Internat. Ct. Arbitration, 2000—; pres.-elect Coll. Coml. Arbitrations, 2001—. Bd. dirs. Nat. Inst. Consumer Justice, 1971-72, World Arbitration Inst. 1984—; adv. bd. Internat. and Comparative Law Ctr. of Southwestern Legal Found., 1988—; pvt. adjudications com. Ctr. for Pub. Resources, 1988—. 1st lt. U.S. Army, 1952-55. Fellow Am. Bar Found; mem. ABA (ho. of dels. 1985-87, chmn. sect. internat. law and practice 1982-83), N.Y. State Bar Assn., Assn. Bar City of N.Y. (chmn. adv. com. on ADR 1992-93), London Ct. Internat. Arbitration, Am. Arbitration Assn. (bd. dirs. 1982-95), Citizens Union (bd. dirs. 1983-86), Am. Soc. Internat. Law. Federal civil litigation, Private international. Office: Thelen Reid & Priest LLP 40 W 57th St Fl 28 New York NY 10019-4097 E-mail: gaksen@thelenreid.com

ALAIMO, ANTHONY A. federal judge; b. Sicily, Italy, Mar. 29, 1920; AB, Ohio No. U.; JD, Emory U. Bar: Ga. 1948, Ohio 1948. Assoc. Reuben A. Garland, 1949-51, 53-56; pvt. practice, Atlanta, 1967-63; ptnr. Highsmith, Highsmith, Alaimo & Knox, Brunswick, Ga., 1963-67, Cowart, Sapp, Alaimo & Gale, Brunswick, 1963-67, Alaimo, Taylor & Bishop, Brunswick, 1967-71; judge U.S. Dist. Ct. (so. dist.) Ga., 1971—, now sr. judge. Office: US Dist Ct PO Box 944 Brunswick GA 31521-0944

ALARCON, ARTHUR LAWRENCE, federal judge; b. L.A., Aug. 14, 1925; s. Lorenzo Marques and Margaret (Sais) A.; m. Sandra D. Paterson, Sept. 1, 1979; children— Jan Marie, Gregory, Lance B.A. in Polit. Sci, U. So. Calif., 1949, J.D., 1951. Bar: Calif. 1952. Dep. dist. atty. L.A. County, 1952-61; exec. asst. to Gov. Pat Brown State of Calif., Sacramento, 1962-64, legal adv. to gov., 1961-62; judge L.A. Superior Ct., 1964-78; assoc. justice Calif. Ct. Appeals, L.A., 1978-79; judge U.S. Ct. Appeals for 9th Circuit, 1979-92, sr. judge, 1992—. Served with U.S. Army, 1943-46, ETO Office: US Ct Appeals 9th Cir 1607 US Courthouse 312 N Spring St Los Angeles CA 90012-4701*

ALBANO, MICHAEL SANTO JOHN, lawyer; b. Bklyn., Jan. 13, 1944; s. Alexander Joseph and Josephine (Giannetto) A.; m. Grace Alma Hoelzel, Mar. 14, 1944; children: Christine Grace, Sarah Michelle. BA, U. Mo., Kansas City, 1965, JD, 1968. Bar: Mo. 1968, U.S. Dist. Ct. (we. dist.) Mo. 1968. From assoc. to shareholder Welch, Martin & Albano LLC, Independence, Mo., 1968—. Contbr. articles to profl. jours. Tchrs. Assn. scholar, 1963-64, U. Mo. scholar, Kansas City, 1963-66. Mem. ABA (vice-chmn. family law sect., chmn. 1984-85), Am. Acad. Matrimonial Lawyers (bd. govs. 1982-88, v.p. 1988-93, pres. 1993-94), Mo. Bar Assn., Kansas City Bar Assn., Internat. Acad. Matrimonial Lawyers (bd. govs. Am. chpt. 1986—), Phi Delta Phi. Democrat. Lutheran. Family and matrimonial. Office: 311 W Kansas Ave Independence MO 64050-3715

ALBER, PHILLIP GEORGE, lawyer; b. Lansing, Mich., Dec. 10, 1948; s. Phillip Karl and Audrey Irene (Putnam) A.; m. Shari Thornton; children: Emily Nicole, Phillip George, Elisabeth Whitney, Christian Thornton. BA magna cum laude, U. Mich., 1971; JD cum laude, Wayne State U., 1974. Bar: Mich. 1975, U.S. Dist. Ct. (ea. dist.) Mich. 1975, U.S. Ct. Appeals (6th cir.) 1978, U.S. Dist. Ct. (we. dist.) Mich. 1982. Assoc. Harvey, Kruse, Westen & Milan, Detroit, 1975-79, ptnr., 1979-85, Mager, Mercer and Alber, Detroit, 1985-2000, Alber Crafton, PLLC, Troy, Mich., 2001—. Lectr. Ill. Inst. Continuing Edn., Chgo., 1980. Mem. ABA (torts ins. practice sect., vice chair fidelity and surety law com.), Detroit Bar Assn. (pub. adv. com. 1979—, cir. ct. com. 1978—), Mich. Bar Assn. (rep. assembly 1970-80), Internat. Assn. Def. Counsel (fidelity and surety com. 1984—), Surety Claims Inst., Nat. Bd. Claim Assn. (pres. 1992-94, program chair 1990—), Assn. Def. Trial Counsel, Detroit Athletic Club, Hundred Club, Goodfellows Old Newsboys Club (Detroit). Republican. Roman Catholic. Federal civil litigation, State civil litigation, Construction. Home: 655 Rivard Blvd Grosse Pointe MI 48230-1253 Office: Alber Crafton PLLC Ste 300 2301 W Big Beaver Rd Troy MI 48084-4906 E-mail: palber@albercrafton.com

ALBERT, ROSS ALAN, lawyer; b. Boston, Nov. 22, 1958; s. Richmond G. and Mary (Day) A.; m. Nancy Ada Christian, July 16, 1983. AB, Harvard U., 1982, postgrad., 1985-86; JD, U. Calif., Berkeley, 1986. Bar: Mass. 1986, D.C. 1988, U.S. Dist. Ct. Md. 1987, U.S. Ct. Appeals (4th cir.) 1987, U.S. Ct. Appeals (5th cir.) 1993, U.S. Ct. Appeals D.C. cir. 1994, U.S. Ct. Appeals (2d cir.) 1994, U.S. Ct. Appeals (6th cir.) 1994, U.S. Ct. Appeals (9th cir.) 1994, U.S. Ct. Appeals (11th cir.) 1994, U.S. Supreme Ct. 1994, U.S. Ct. Appeal (8th cir.) 1995. Jud. law clk. U.S. Dist. Ct. Md., Balt., 1986-88; assoc. Wilmer, Cutler & Pickering, Washington, 1988-93; spl. counsel Office of Gen. Counsel-appellate group U.S. SEC, 1993-97, counsel to commr. Norman S. Johnson, 1997-2000, sr. spl. counsel Office Internet Enforcement, 2000-01; of counsel Morris, Manning & Martin LLP, Atlanta, 2001—. Assoc. editor Calif. Law Rev., 1985-86. Mem. Harvard Club Washington. Democrat. Appellate, Federal civil litigation, Securities. Office: Morris Manning & Martin LLP 1600 Atlanta Fin Ctr 3343 Peachtree Rd Atlanta GA 30326 E-mail: ra81@post.harvard.edu

ALBERTS, HAROLD, lawyer, b. San Antonio, Apr. 3, 1920; s. Bernard H. and Rose Alberts; m. Rose M. Gaskin, Mar. 25, 1945; children: Linda Rae, Barry Lawrence. LLB, U. Tex., 1942. Bar: Tex. 1943, U.S. Supreme Ct. 1950, U.S. Ct. Mil. Appeals 1959. Tchr. U. Tex., 1942, instr., 1941-42; legal officer Chase Field, 1944; sole practice Corpus Christi, Tex. Pres. Jewish Welfare Fund, Corpus Christi, 1948; chmn. S.W. Regional Anti-Defamation League, Tex. and Okla., 1970-71, chmn., 1969-72, chmn. Brotherhood Week, 1957; chmn. Nueces County (Tex.) Red Cross, 1959-61; mem. campaign exec. com., chmn. meetings United Cmty. Svcs., 1961; v.p. Little Theatre, Corpus Christi, 1964; chmn. Corpus Christi NCCJ, 1967-69, nat. dir., 1974-76; bd. dirs. Tex. State Assn. Mental Health; pres. Combined Jewish Appeal, Corpus Christi, 1974-76; moderator Friday Morning Group, 1975, 96. Served to lt. (sr. grade) USNR, 1942-46. Mem. ABA, Tex. Bar Assn., Corpus Christi Bar Assn., Kiwanis (pres. 1962), B'nai B'rith (pres. 1955), Masons (32d degree). State civil litigation, General practice, Probate. Home and Office: PO Box 271477 Corpus Christi TX 78427-1477

ALBICOCCO, SANTA, lawyer, county official; b. Bklyn. d. Frank Vincent and Mary Lucy (LaCava) Caputo; m. Samuel J. Rozzi, Ma. r7, 1981 (dec. July 1992); m. Sam A. Albicocco, Mar. 11, 1997. BA, Marymount Manhattan Coll., N.Y.C., 1971; JD, St. John's U., Jamaica, N.Y., 1981. Bar: N.Y. 1982. Insp. Nassau County, N.Y., 1981-82, dep. county atty., 1982-84, dep. county treas., 1984-86, chief Bur. of Real Estate, Ins. and Workers Compensation, 1986-88, dep. county exec., 1988-93, treas., 1993—. Mem. N.Y. State Banking Bd., 1998—. Recipient Tenth Ann. Achievers award L.I. Ctr. for Bus. and Profl. Women, 1989, commendation Women Econ. Developers of L.I., 1988; Nassau County Women's History Month honoree Nassau County Office of Women's Svcs., 1996. Mem. Mcpl. Forum of N.Y., Govt. Fin. Officers Assn., Bar Assn. Nassau County, Columbia Lawyers Assn. Nassau County. Republican. Roman Catholic. Office: Nassau County Treas 240 Old Country Rd Mineola NY 11501-4245

ALBRECHT, PETER LEFFINGWELL, lawyer; b. N.Y.C., Mar. 4, 1930; s. Ralph Gerhart and Aillinn (Leffingwell) A.; m. Constance Trowbridge, Sept. 10, 1955 (div. 1975); children— Kate, Cynthia Margaret, Mary Eugenie, David, Thomas Peter Salem, Matthew William Trotter; m. Margaret Page, Jan. 29, 1977. A.B., Harvard, 1952, LL.B., 1955. Bar: Mass. 1956. Assoc., Ropes & Gray, Boston, 1955-68, ptnr., 1968—. Mem. Lawyers Alliance for Nuclear Arms Control, ABA (mem. various coms. and subcoms. sect. corp., banking and bus. law). Banking, Bankruptcy, Entertainment. Office: Ropes & Gray 1 International Pl Fl 4 Boston MA 02110-2624

ALBRIGHT, AUDRA A. lawyer; b. Syracuse, N.Y., July 20, 1971; d. Willis James and Anita Ann A. BA, SUNY, Plattsburgh, 1993; legal asst. cert., Syracuse U., 1994; JD, Temple U., 1997. Bar: Pa. 1998, N.J. 1997. Assoc. Turner & McDonald P.C., Phila., 1997—. Mem. ABA. Democrat. Avocations: fencing, antique restoration, raising birds. Contracts commercial, General corporate, Private international. Home: Atp A-306 150 N Bethlehem Pike Ambler PA 19002

ALBRIGHT, JOSEPH P. state supreme court justice; b. Parkersburg, W.Va., Nov. 8, 1938; s. M.P. and Catherine (Rathbone) A.; m. Patricia Ann Deem, 1958 (dec. 1993); children: Terri Albright Cavi, Lettie Albright Elder, Joseph P. Jr., John Patrick (dec.); m. Nancie Gensert Divvens; stepchildren: Susan Divvens Bowman, Debbie Divvens Holcomb, Sandy Divvens Fox. BBA cum laude, U. Notre Dame, JD, 1962. Bar: W.Va. 1962, U.S. Dist. Ct. W.Va. 1962. Pvt. practice, Parkersburg, 1964-95; asst. prosecuting atty. Wood County, 1965-68; city atty. City of Parkersburg, W.Va., 1968-70; justice W.Va. Supreme Ct. of Appeals, Charleston, 1995—96, 2001—; pvt. practice Parkersburg and Charleston, 1997—2000. Mem. W.Va. State Ethics Commn.; bd. dirs. Belpre (Ohio) Inc. Former clk. Charter Bd. of Parkerburg; mem. W.Va. Ho. of Dels., 1970-86, freshman mem. of jud. com., chmn. of ho. com. on edn., chmn. ho. com. on judiciary, 52nd spkr. of Ho. of Dels., 1984-86; mem., chmn. Blennerhassett Hist. Park Commn.; co-chmn. Blennerhassett Hist. Commn.; mem. St. Francis Xavier Ch., Parkersburg, past pres. parish adv. coun. Named Freshman Legislator of Yr., Charleston Gazette, 1970. Office: WVa Supreme Ct Appeals State Capitol Complex Bldg 1 Room E308 1900 Kanawha Boulevard E Charleston WV 25305*

ALBRIGHT, TERRILL D. lawyer; b. Lebanon, Ind., June 23, 1938; s. David Henry and Georgia Pauline (Doty) A.; m. Judith Ann Stoelting, June 2, 1962; children: Robert T., Elizabeth A. AB, Ind. U., 1960, JD, 1965. Bar: Ind. 1965, U.S. Dist. Ct. (so. dist.) Ind. 1965, U.S. Dist. Ct. (no. dist.) Ind. 1980, U.S. Ct. Appeals (7th cir.) 1981, U.S. Ct. Appeals (3d and D.C. cirs.) 1982, U.S. Supreme Ct. 1972; cert. arbitrator for large complex cse program constrn. and internat. commercial cases Am. Arbitration Assn., cert. mediator. Assoc. Baker and Daniels Law Firm, Indpls., 1965-72, ptnr., 1972—. Mem. panel of disting. neutrals, nat. panel for constrn. and regional comml. panel, CPR Inst. for Dispute Resolution, N.Y.C. Bd. dirs., pres. Christamore House, Indpls., 1979-86; bd. dirs. Greater Indpls. YMCA, 1980-82; chmn. Jordan YMCA, Indpls., 1982; pres. Community Ctrs. Indpls., 1987-90. 1st lt. U.S. Army, 1960-62. Fellow Am. Bar Found., Ind. Bar Found., Indpls. Bar Found., Am. Coll. Trial Lawyers; mem. Nat. Conf. Bar Presidents (exec. coun. 1995-98), Ind. State Bar Assn. (chmn. young lawyer sect. 1971-72, rep. 11th dist. 1983-85, bd. dirs., v.p. 1991-92, pres. elect 1992-93, pres. 1993-94), Ind. U. Law Alumni Assn. (bd. dirs. 1974-80, pres. 1979-80). Democrat. Federal civil litigation, General civil litigation, Construction. Office: Baker & Daniels 300 N Meridian St Ste 2700 Indianapolis IN 46204-1782 E-mail: tdalbright@bakerd.com

ALBRITTON, WILLIAM HAROLD, III, federal judge; b. Andalusia, Ala., Dec. 19, 1936; s. Robert Bynum and Carrie (Veal) A.; m. Jane Rollins Howard, June 2, 1958; children: William Harold IV, Benjamin Howard, Thomas Bynum. A.B., U. Ala., 1959, LL.B., 1960. Bar: Ala. 1960. Assoc. firm Albrittons & Rankin, Andalusia, 1962-66, ptnr., 1966-76; ptnr. firm Albrittons & Givhan, Andalusia, 1976-86; ptnr. Albrittons, Givhan & Clifton, 1986-91; judge U.S. Dist. Ct. (mid. dist.) Ala., Montgomery, 1991-97, chief judge, 1998—. Mem. 11th Circuit Jud. Coun., 1998—. Pres. Ala. Law Sch. Found., 1988-91, Ala. Law Inst. Fellow Am. Coll. Trial Lawyers, Am. Bar Found.; mem. ABA, Fed. Judges Assn. (bd. dirs. 1999—), Jud. Conf. U.S. (com. on ct. adminstrn. and case mgmt. 1999—), Ala. State Bar (commr. 1981-89, disciplinary commn. 1981-84, v.p. 1985-86, pres.-elect 1989-90, pres. 1990-91), Am. Judicature Soc., Am. Inns of Ct., Bluewater Bay Sailing Club, Bluewater Bay Country Club, Phi Beta Kappa, Phi Delta Phi, Omicron Delta Kappa, Alpha Tau Omega.

ALBRITTON, WILLIAM HAROLD, IV, lawyer; b. Tuscaloosa, Ala., Mar. 21, 1960; s. William Harold III and Jane Rollins (Howard) A.; m. Lucille Smith, July 23, 1983; 1 child, Elizabeth Rollins. BA, U. Ala., Tuscaloosa, 1982, JD, 1985. Ptnr. Albrittons, Clifton, Alverson, Bowden, Moody P.C., Andalusia, Ala., 1985-2001; counsel Bradley, Arant, Rose & White, Birmingham, 2001—. Bd. dirs. The Bank, Andalusia; judge Mcpl. Ct. Andalusia, 1989-2000. Bd. dirs. Covington County Arts Coun., Andalusia, 1986-90, Andalusia City Schs. Found., 1991—, Andalusia Area C. of C., 1986-89; elder 1st Presbyn. Ch., Andalusia, 1990—. Mem. ABA, Ala. Bar Assn. (sec. pres.'s adv. task force 1986-88, chmn. com. on local bar activities 1990, task force on minority opportunity 1990-96, character and fitness com. 1991-96, chmn. 1993-96, chmn. com. solo practitioners & small firms 1997-99), Ala. Def. Lawyers Assn. (bd. dirs. young lawyers sect. 1991-96, amicus curiae com. 1992—), Internat. Assn. Def. Counsel, Am. Inns of Ct., Kiwanis. Avocations: scuba diving, music, photography, travel, sailing. General civil litigation, Insurance, Workers' compensation. Home: 3612 Rockhill Rd Birmingham AL 35223 Office: Bradley Arant Rose & White 2100 Park Pl Ste 1400 Birmingham AL 35223 E-mail: halbritton@bradleyarant.com

ALBUM, JERALD LEWIS, lawyer; b. Monroe, La., Oct. 18, 1947; s. Natt B. and Rose Marie (Pickens) A.; m. Joan Abbey Lurie, July 30, 1983; children: Nicole, Jeffrey. BS, Tulane U., 1969, JD, 1973. Bar: La. 1973, Colo. 1990, Tex. 1992, U.S. Dist. Ct. (ea. dist.) La. 1975, U.S. Dist. Ct. (mid. dist.) La. 1980, U.S. Dist. Ct. (we. dist.) La. 1983, U.S. Ct. Appeals (5th cir.) 1976. Assoc. Mmahat, Gagliano, Duffy & Giordano, Metairie, La., 1973-79; assoc. to ptnr. Lemle, Kelleher, Hunley, Moss & Frilot, New Orleans, 1980-85; shareholder Abbott Simses, Album & Knister, 1985-96; ptnr. Album, Stovall, Radecker & Giordano. Mem. La. Assn. of Def. Counsel, New Orleans Bar Assn., La. State Bar Assn. Avocations: golf, volleyball, gardening. Admiralty, General civil litigation, Personal injury. Home: 4637 Southshore Dr Metairie LA 70002-1430 Office: Album Stovall Radecker & Giordano 3850 N Causeway Blvd Ste 1130 Metairie LA 70002-7247

ALCOTT, MARK HOWARD, lawyer; b. N.Y.C., Aug. 11, 1939; s. Harvey and Rose (Eigerman) A.; m. Susan M. Bell, Sept. 3, 1961; children: Jill, Laura, Daniel, Elizabeth. AB cum laude, Harvard U., 1961, LLB cum laude, 1964. Bar: N.Y. 1965, U.S. Dist. Ct. (so. and ea. dists.) N.Y. 1966, U.S. Ct. Appeals (2d cir.) 1966, U.S. Ct. Appeals (9th and 10th cirs.) 1980, U.S. Ct. Internat. Trade 1980, U.S. Supreme Ct. 1982, U.S. Ct. Appeals (D.C. cir.) 1983, D.C. 1984, U.S. Tax Ct. 1985. Assoc. Paul, Weiss, Rifkind, Wharton & Garrison, N.Y.C., 1964-73, ptnr., 1973—. Mediator Mandatory Mediation Program, U.S Dist. Ct. (so. dist.) N.Y.; spl. master, mediator commercial divsn. N.Y. Supreme Ct. Mem. Community Planning Bd., Riverdale, N.Y., 1970-72; comr. Larchmont (N.Y.) Planning Commn., 1982-94; bd. dirs. Mosholu-Montefiore Community Ctr., Bronx, 1966-77. Fellow: Am. Coll. Trial Lawyers (chmn. downstate N.Y. com., chmn. internat. com.), N.Y. Bar Found.; mem.: ABA (litigation sect. internat. litigation com.), N.Y. State Bar Assn. (chmn. internat. litigation com. comml. and fed. litigation sect. 1989—92, sec. exec. com., exec. vice chmn. 1992—93, sect. chmn.-elect 1993—94, sect. chmn. 1994—95, mem. ho. of dels., mem. exec. com., v.p.), Assn. Bar City of N.Y. (fed. legis. com. 1970—73), Internat. Bar Assn. (bus. law sect., internat. litigation com.), Fed. Bar Coun. Avocation: sailing. Federal civil litigation, General civil litigation. Office: Paul Weiss Rifkind Wharton & Garrison Ste 419 1285 Avenue Of The Americas Fl 21 New York NY 10019-6065

ALDAVE, BARBARA BADER, law educator, lawyer; b. Tacoma, Dec. 28, 1938; d. Fred A. and Patricia W. (Burns) Bader; m. Ralph Theodore Aldave, Apr. 2, 1966; children— Anna Marie, Anthony John BS, Stanford U., 1960; JD, U. Calif.-Berkeley, 1966. Bar: Oreg. 1966, Tex. 1982. Assoc. law firm, Eugene, Oreg., 1967-70; asst. prof. U. Oreg., 1970-73, prof., 2000—; vis. prof. U. Calif., Berkeley, 1973-74; from vis. prof. to prof. U. Tex., Austin, 1974-89, co-holder James R. Dougherty chair for faculty excellence, 1981-82, Piper prof., 1982, Joe A. Worsham centennial prof., 1984-89, Liddell, Sapp, Zivley, Hill and LaBoon prof. banking financial and comml. law, 1989; dean Sch. Law, prof. St. Mary's U., San Antonio, 1989-98, Ernest W. Clemens prof. corp. law, 1996-98. Vis. prof. Northeastern U., 1985-88, 98; vis. prof. Boston Coll. 1999-2000; ABA rep. to Coun. Inter-ABA, 1995-99; NAFTA chpt. 19 panelist, 1994-96. Pres. NETWORK, 1985-89; chair Gender Bias Task Force of Supreme Ct. Tex., 1991-94; bd. dirs. Tex. Alliance Children's Rights, Lawyer's Com. for Civil Rights Under Law of Tex., 1995-2000; nat. chair Gray Panthers, 1999—. Recipient tchg. excellence award U. Tex. Student Bar Assn., 1976, Appreciation awards Thurgood Marshall Legal Soc. of U. Tex., 1979, 81, 85, 87, Tchg. Excellence award Chicano Law Students Assn. of U. Tex., 1984, Hermine Tobolowsky award Women's Law Caucus of U. Tex., 1985, Ethics award Kugle, Stewart, Dent & Frederick, 1988, Leadership award Women's Law Assn. St. Mary's U., 1989, Ann. Inspirational award Women's Advocacy Project, 1989, Appreciation award San Antonio Black Lawyers Assn., 1990, Spl. Recognition award Nat. Conv. Nat. Lawyers Guild, 1990, Spirit of the Am. Woman award J. C. Penney Co., 1992, Sarah T. Hughes award Women and the Law sect. State Bar Tex., 1994, Ann. Tchg. award Soc. Am. Law Tchrs., 1996, Legal Svcs. award Mexican-Am. Legal Def. and Ednl. Fund, 1996, Woman of Justice award NETWORK, 1997, Ann. Peacemaker award Camino a la Paz, 1997, Outstanding Profl. in the Cmty. award Dept. Pub. Justice, St. Mary's U., 1997, Charles Hamilton Houston award Black Allied Law Students Assn. St. Mary's U., 1998, Woman of Yr. award Tex. Women's Polit. Caucus, 1998, award Clin. Legal Edn. Assn., 1998, lifetime achievement award Jour. Law and Religion, 1998. Mem. ABA (com. on corp. laws sect., banking and bus. law 1982-88), Bexar County Women's Bar Assn. (Belva Lockwood Outstanding Lawyer award 1991), Harlan Soc., Stanford U. Alumni Assn., Tex. Appleseed, Tex.-Mexico Bar Assn., Order of Coif, Phi Delta Phi, Iota Sigma Pi, Omicron Delta Kappa, Delta Theta Phi (Outstanding Law Prof. award St. Mary's U. chpt. 1990, 91). Roman Catholic. Home: 86399 N Modesto Dr Eugene OR 97402-9031 Office: U Oreg Sch Law Eugene OR 97403-1221 E-mail: baldave@law.uoregon.edu, balaw98@aol.com

ALDEN, STEVEN MICHAEL, lawyer; b. L.A., May 19, 1945; s. Herbert and Sylvia Zina (Hochman) A.; m. Evelyn Mae Subotky, Dec. 31, 1977; children: Carissa Louise, Bramley Marshall, Darym Alexander. AB, UCLA, 1967; JD, U. Calif., Berkeley, 1970. Bar: Calif. 1971, N.Y. 1971. Assoc. Debevoise & Plimpton, N.Y.C., 1971-78, ptnr., 1979—. Lectr., seminar panelist Practising Law Inst., N.Y.C., 1981—; panelist, lectr. N.Y. State Bar, Albany, 1984. Contbr. articles to profl. jours. Mem. ABA (real estate fin. com.), Assn. of Bar of City of N.Y. (com. real property law), Am. Land Title Assn. (assoc. lender's counsel group), Am. Coll. Real Estate Lawyers, Order of Coif, Phi Beta Kappa, Board Room Club (N.Y.C.). Republican. Real property. Office: Debevoise & Plimpton 919 3rd Ave Fl 42 New York NY 10022

ALDERMAN, RICHARD MARK, legal educator, lawyer, television and radio commentator; b. Passaic, N.J., Feb. 18, 1947; s. Wilbur and Lois H. (Taub) A.; m. Janie Alderman; 1 child, Willie. B.A., Tulane U., 1968; J.D. cum laude, Syracuse U., 1971; LL.M., U. Va., 1973. Bar: N.Y. 1972, Tex. 1981, U.S. Supreme Ct. 1983. Staff atty. Legal Services, Syracuse, 1972-73; Dwight Olds chair in law U. Houston, 1973—, assoc. dean Law Ctr., 1993—; vis. prof. Loyola Law Sch., Los Angeles, 1976-77, Boston Coll., 1980-81; People's Lawyer, Sta. KTRK-TV, Houston, 1980—; It's the Law, 14 Tex. cities; dir. council on Legal Edn. Opportunity Summer Inst., Houston, 1975. Author: A Transactional Guide to the Uniform Commercial Code, 1982; Creditors' Rights in Texas, 1978; Uniform Commercial Code Series, 1984; Know Your Rights! Answers to your most Common Legal Questions, 1985, 4th rev. edit., 1995, Doing Business in Texas, 1987, 2d edit., 1992, Texas Deceptive Trade Practices, 1988, The Lawyer's Guide to the DTPA, 1990, Alderman's Texas Consumer and Commercial Laws Annotated, 1996. Contbr. articles to profl. jours. Recipient M.D. Anderson Scholarship award Found. Prof. U. Houston Law Ctr., 1977. Mem. ABA (Golden Gavel award 1985, 89), Tex. Bar Assn. (consumer law council 1984—, editor-in-chief Caveat Vendor 1984—), Order of the Coif, Phi Delta Phi. Jewish. Home: 4135 University Blvd Houston TX 77005-2713 Office: U Houston Law Ctr University Park 4800 Calhoun Rd Houston TX 77004-2610

ALDISERT, RUGGERO JOHN, federal judge; b. Carnegie, Pa., Nov. 10, 1919; s. John S. and Elizabeth (Magnacca) A.; m. Agatha Maria DeLacio, Oct. 4, 1952; children: Lisa Maria, Robert, Gregory. B.A., U. Pitts., 1941, J.D., 1947. Bar: Pa. bar 1947. Gen. practice law, Pitts., 1947-61; judge Ct. Common Pleas, Allegheny County, 1961-68, U.S. Ct. Appeals (3d cir.), Pitts., 1968-84, chief judge, 1984-87, sr. judge Pitts., Sanat Barbara, Calif., 1987—. Adj. prof. law U. Pitts. Sch. Law, 1964-87 ; faculty Appellate Judges Seminar, NYU, 1971-85 , asso. dir., 1979-85 ; lectr. internat. seminar legal medicine U. Rome, 1965, Law Soc. London, 1967, Internat. seminar comparative law, Rome, 1971; chmn. Fed. Appellate Judges Seminar; bd. dirs. Fed. Jud. Center, Washington, 1974-79; mem. Pa. Civil Procedural Rules Com., 1965-84 Jud. Conf. Com. on Adminstrn. Criminal Law, 1971-77; chmn. adv. com. on bankruptcy rules Jud. Conf. U.S., 1979-84; lectr. univs. in U.S. and abroad. Author: Il Ritorno al Paese, 1966-67, The Judicial Process, Readings, Materials and Cases, 1976, Logic for Lawyers: A Guide to Clear Legal Thinking, 1989, Opinion Writing, 1990, Winning on Appeal, 1992. Allegheny dist. chmn. Multiple Sclerosis Soc., 1961-68; pres. ISDA, Cultural Heritage Found., 1965-68; trustee U. Pitts., 1968— ; chmn. bd. visitors Pitts. Sch. Law, 1978—. Served to maj. USMCR, 1942-46. Recipient Outstanding Merit award Allegheny County Acad. Trial Lawyers, 1964. Mem. Inst. Jud. Adminstrn., Am. Law Inst., Italian Sons and Daus. of Am. (nat. pres. 1954-68), Italian Sons and Daus. Am. Fraternal Assn. (nat. pres. 1960-68), Phi Beta Kappa, Phi Alpha Delta, Omicron Delta Kappa. Democrat. Roman Catholic. Office: US Ct Appeals 120 Cremona Dr Ste D Santa Barbara CA 93117-5511*

ALDRICH, LOVELL W(ELD), lawyer; b. Port Chester, N.Y., Dec. 21, 1942; s. Laurence Weld and Leota A.; m. Sharon King, Aug. 20, 1966; children: Molly Colleen, Abigail Elizabeth. BBA in Fin., Tex. A&M U., 1965; JD, St. Mary's U., San Antonio, 1968. Bar: Tex. 1968, U.S. Dist. Ct. (so. dist.) Tex. 1971, U.S. Dist. Ct. (ea. dist.) Tex. 1980, U.S. Ct. Appeals (5th cir.) 1981. Assoc. Law Office of Fred Parks, Houston, 1970-72, Lloyd & Hoppess, Houston, 1972-75; pvt. practice, 1975-78; ptnr. Aldrich & Buttrill, 1978-81, Aldrich, Buttrill & Kuhn, Houston, 1981-87, Lovell W. Aldrich & Assocs., A Profl. Legal Corp., Houston, 1987-98; pvt. practice Sugar Land, Tex., 1998—. Capt. U.S. Army, 1968-70, Vietnam. Mem. Tex. Bar Assn. (cert. personal injury trial law, bd. cert. legal specialization personal injury trial law), Am. Bd. Trial Advs. Episcopalian. Avocations: travel, golf, photography, reading. General civil litigation, State civil litigation, Personal injury. Home: 1007 Horseshoe Dr Sugar Land TX 77478-3460 Office: Lovell W Aldrich PC PO Box 377 Sugar Land TX 77487-0377

ALDRICH, RICHARD KINGSLEY, lawyer; b. Denver, Dec. 31, 1943; s. Harold Eugene and Mary Frances (Kingsley) A.; m. Katherine Ann Kirwan, Sept. 26, 1970; children: Amy Marie Aldrich McAffee, Lori Ann Aldrich Selwyn, Sara Kathleen. Student, Tex. Tech. U., 1962-64; BA in History, U. Mont., 1966, JD, 1969. Bar: Mont. 1969, U.S. Dist. Ct. Mont. 1969. Staff atty. Office of Field Solicitor, Dept. of Interior, Billings, Mont., 1969-85, field solicitor, supervising atty., 1985—. Bd. dirs. Billings Pub. Edn. Found., 1992-97, Mont. State U. Parent Assn., Bozeman, 1993-96, Billings Sr. Bronc Booster Club; bd. dirs., pres. Billings Sr. High Parent Adv., 1991-95. Recipient cert. of appreciation, U.S. Dept. Justice, Nat. Park Svc. and U.S. Fish and Wildlife Svc., 1994, 96, Dept. of Interior Meritorious award, 1998. Mem. ABA (spkr. panel presentation 1997), Mont. State Bar, Phi Delta Phi, Sigma Nu. Avocations: long distance running, skiing, fly fishing, hiking, reading. Office: Dept of Interior Office of Field Solicitor 316 N 26th St Ste 3005 Billings MT 59101-1373

ALDRICH, STEPHEN CHARLES, judge; b. Mpls., Oct. 28, 1941; s. George Francis and Marjorie Belle (Shimel) A.; m. Myrna Sumption, Sept. 6, 1964; children: Jeffrey Stephen, David George. BA, Grinnell Coll., 1963; JD, U. Minn., 1971. Bar: Minn 1972, U.S. Dist. Ct. Minn. 1975. Staff asst. to Hon. Donald M. Fraser U.S. Congress, Washington, 1965; budget examiner U.S. Office of Mgmt. and Budget, 1965-67; admissions counselor Grinnell (Iowa) Coll., 1967-68; law clk. to Hon. Philip Neville U.S. Dist. Ct. Minn., Mpls., 1971-72; asst. senate counsel State of Minn., St. Paul, 1972-73; asst. city atty. City of St. Paul, 1973-75; sole practice Mpls., 1975-97; dist. judge Hennepin County, 1997—. Mem. Supreme Ct. Bd. on Continuing Legal Edn., St. Paul, 1985-92. Contbr. articles to profl. jours. Mem. City Charter Commn., Mpls., 1972-80; sec., bd. dirs. Powderhorn Devel. Corp. Mpls., 1975-80. Fellow Am. Acad. Matrimonial Lawyers; mem. Hennepin County Bar Assn. (chmn. family law sect. 1985-86, mem. ethics com. 1980-85, 89-96). Mem. United Ch. Christ. Office: Hennepin County Dist Ct C1200 Govt Ctr Minneapolis MN 55497 Business E-Mail: stephen.aldrich@co.hennepin.mn.us

ALEKSANDER, NICHOLAS P. lawyer; b. London, May 5, 1959; m. Tobe Bendeth, Sept. 1, 1985; children: Isabelle, Abigail. MA, U. Cambridge, Eng., 1983; Law Soc. Finals, London Guildhall U., 1984. Bar: solicitor Supreme Ct. Eng. and Wales 1986. Articled clk. Bristows, Cooke & Carpmael, London, 1984-86; assoc., 1986, Travers Smith Braithwaite, London, 1986-93; ptnr., 1993-2000, Gibson, Dunn & Crutcher, London, 2001—. Contbr. articles to profl. jours., chpts. to books. Fellow Royal Soc. Arts; mem. Internat. Commn. Jurists (mem. exec. bd. Brit. sect.), Internat. Fiscal Assn., Law Soc. Eng. and Wales. Corporate taxation, Taxation, general. Office: Gibson Dunn & Crutcher 2-4 Temple Ave Telephone Ho London EC4Y OHB England Fax: 44 20 7071 4244

ALESIA, JAMES H(ENRY), judge; b. Chgo., July 16, 1934; m. Kathryn P. Gibbons, July 8, 1961; children: Brian J., Daniel J. BS, Loyola U., Chgo., 1956; JD, Ill. Inst. Tech., Chgo., 1960; grad. Nat. Jud. Coll., U. Nev., 1976. Bar: Ill. 1960, Minn. 1970. Police officer City of Chgo., 1957-61; assoc. Law Office Anthony Scariano, Chicago Heights, Ill., 1960-61, Pretzel & Stouffer, Chgo., 1961-63; asst. gen. counsel Chgo. & North Western Transp. Co., 1963-70; assoc. Rerat Law, Mpls., 1970-71; asst. U.S. atty. No. Dist. Ill., Chgo., 1971-73; trial counsel Chessie Sys., 1973; U.S. adminstrv. law judge, 1973-82; ptnr. Reuben & Proctor (merged with Isham, Lincoln & Beale), 1982-87; judge U.S. Dist. Ct. for No. Dist. Ill., 1987—. Mem. faculty Nat. Jud. Coll., U. Nev., Reno, 1979-80. Mem. FBA, Justinian Soc. Lawyers, Celtic Legal Soc. Republican. Roman Catholic. Office: US Dist Ct 219 S Dearborn St Ste 2050 Chicago IL 60604-1800

ALESSI, ROBERT JOSEPH, lawyer, pharmacist, real estate developer; b. Rome, Aug. 22, 1958; s. William John and Mary Jean A.; m. Ellen Mary Paczkowski, May 21, 1988; children: Laura C., Grace E. BS in Pharmacy, Union U., 1982; JD cum laude, Albany Law Sch., 1985. Bar: N.Y. 1986, U.S. Dist. Ct. (no. dist.) N.Y. 1986, U.S. Dist. Ct. (we. dist.) N.Y. 1986, U.S. Dist. Ct. (ea. dist.) N.Y. 1993, U.S. Dist. Ct. (so. dist.) N.Y. 1993, U.S. Ct. Appeals (2d cir.) 1995, U.S. Supreme Ct. 1996. Assoc. Nixon, Hargrave, Devans & Doyle, Albany, N.Y., 1985-90, LeBoeuf, Lamb, Greene & MacRae, Albany, 1990-93, ptnr., 1994—, mng. ptnr., 1999—; mng. dir. Hudson Heritage, L.L.C., 1999—. Adj. prof. law Albany Law Sch., 1989-94; town atty. Town of Bethlehem, 2001—. Co-author: Year 2000 Deskbook, 1998. Mem. master plan com. Town of Bethlehem, Delmar, N.Y., 1989-89, mem. planning bd. counsel, 1990-94. Mem. N.Y. State Bar Assn., Albany Law Sch. Environ. Alumni Group, Rockefeller Found. (advisor Pocantico roundtable consensus on brownfields). Avocations: tennis, fitness training, reading. General civil litigation, Environmental, Public utilities. Home: 8 Partridge Rd Delmar NY 12054-3919 Office: LeBoeuf Lamb Greene & MacRae LLP One Commerce Plz Ste 2020 99 Washington Ave Albany NY 12210 Fax: 518-626-9010. E-mail: ralessi@llgm.com

ALEXANDER, CHARLES JACKSON, II, lawyer; b. Winston-Salem, N.C., Nov. 20, 1946; s. Jack C. and Mary Ann (Smitherman) A.; m. Dawn L. Sattenfield; children— Kristen, Joseph. B.A., Wake Forest U., 1969, J.D., 1972. Bar: N.C. 1972, U.S. Dist. Ct. (mid. dist.) N.C. 1972. Sole practice, Winston-Salem, N.C., 1972-76; sr. ptnr. Alexander & Hinshaw, Winston-Salem, 1976-82, Alexander, Wright, Parrish, Hinshaw & Tash, Winston-Salem, 1982-87; ptnr. Morrow, Alexander, Tash, Long & Black, 1987—. Pres. Cystic Fibrosis Found., Winston-Salem, Am. Cancer Soc., Winston-Salem, 1984. Mem. ABA, Assn. Trial Lawyers Am., N.C. Acad. Trial Lawyers (sustaining patron), N.C. Bar Assn., Criminal Def. Lawyers (pres. 1982-83), N.C. Jaycees (legal counsel 1981-82; recipient Outstanding Pres. award 1977-78, Disting. Service award 1983), Greater Winston-Salem C. of C. (dir. 1978). Democrat. Presbyterian. Criminal, Family and matrimonial, Personal injury. Home: 7600 Beechtree Ct Clemmons NC 27012-9142 Office: Morrow Alexander Tash Long & Black 3890 Vest Mill Rd Winston Salem NC 27103-1302

ALEXANDER, CLIFFORD JOSEPH, lawyer; b. New Orleans, Oct. 2, 1943; s. Charles Ernest and Lois Primus (Boley) A.; m. Elizabeth McAnany, June 11, 1966; children: Brian, Heather, Rachel. AB, Rockhurst Coll., 1966; JD, Georgetown U., 1969. Bar: Mass. 1970, D.C. 1977. Mem. staff SEC, Washington, 1967-70; assoc. Gaston Snow & Ely Bartlett, Boston, 1970-75; mem. staff U.S. Senate Banking Com., Washington, 1975-77; mem. Kirkpatrick & Lockhart LLP (formerly Kirkpatrick, Lockhart, Hill, Christopher & Phillips, and predecessor), 1977—. Co-editor: Money Managers Compliance Manual. Mem. ABA (corp., banking and bus. law sect.), Boston Bar Assn., Fed. Bar Assn. (securities and banking law sects.), D.C. Bar Assn., Mass. Bar Assn., U.S. Supreme Ct. Bar. Banking, Securities. Home: 8721 Bluedale St Alexandria VA 22308-2307 Office: Kirkpatrick & Lockhart 1800 Massachusetts Ave NW Fl 2 Washington DC 20036-1806

ALEXANDER, CLIFFORD L., JR. management consultant, lawyer, former secretary of army; b. N.Y.C., Sept. 21, 1933; s. Clifford L. and Edith (McAllister) A.; m. Adele Logan, July 11, 1959; children— Elizabeth, Mark Clifford. A.B. cum laude, Harvard, 1955; LL.B., Yale U., 1958; LL.D. (hon.), Malcolm X Coll., 1972, Morgan State U., 1978, Wake Forest U., 1978, U. Md., 1980, Atlanta U., 1982. Bar: N.Y. 1960, U.S. Supreme Ct 1960, D.C. 1960. Asst. to dist. atty., N.Y. County, 1959-61; exec. dir. Manhattanville Hamilton Grange (neighborhood conservation project), 1961-62; exec. program dir. HARYOU, Inc., also pvt. practice law, 1962-63; mem. staff Nat. Security Council, 1963- 64; dep. spl. asst. to Pres. Johnson, 1964-65, assoc. spl. counsel, 1965-66, dep. spl. counsel, 1966-67; chmn. Equal Employment Opportunity Commn., 1967-69; partner firm Arnold & Porter, 1969-75, Verner, Liipfert, Bernhard, McPherson & Alexander, 1975-76; sec. army, 1977-80; pres. Alexander & Assocs., Inc. (cons.), Washington, 1981—. Dir. Pa. Power & Light Co., Dreyfus Third Century Fund., Dreyfus Gen. Money Market Fund, Dreyfus Common Stock Fund, Dreyfus Govt. Securities Fund, Dreyfus Tax Exempt Fund, MCI Corp.; adj. prof. Georgetown U.; prof. Howard U., Washington.; Mem. Pres.'s Commn. on Income Maintenance Programs, 1967-68; Pres.'s spl. ambassador to the Independence of Swaziland, 1968; mem. Pres.' Commn. for Observation Human Rights Yr., 1968; bd. dirs. Mex.-Am. Legal Def. and Ednl. Fund, NAACP Legal Def. and Ednl. Fund; bd. overseers Harvard U., 1969-75; trustee Atlanta U. Host, co-producer: TV program Cliff Alexander: Black on White, 1971-74. Served with AUS, 1958-59. Named hon. citizen Kansas City, Mo., 1965; recipient Ames award Harvard, 1955; Frederick Douglass award, 1970; Outstanding Civilian Service award Dept. Army, 1980; Disting. Public Service award Dept. Def., 1981; others. Mem. Am., D.C. bar assns. Club: Reveille (N.Y.C.) (Annual Outstanding Achievement award 1966). Home: 512 A St SE Washington DC 20003-1139 Office: Alexander & Assocs 400 C St NE Washington DC 20002-5818

ALEXANDER, DONALD G. state supreme court justice; Grad., Bowdoin Coll.; JD, U. Chgo. Bar: Maine. Mem. Sen. Edmund Muskie's staff; asst. Maine atty. gen., 1974-76; dep. atty. gen.; judge Dist. Ct., 1978, Maine Superior Ct., 1980-98; justice Maine Supreme Jud. Ct., 1998—. Office: Cumberland County Courthouse PO Box 368 142 Federal St Portland ME 04112-0368*

ALEXANDER, GEORGE JONATHON, law educator, former dean; b. Berlin, Germany, Mar. 8, 1931; s. Walter and Sylvia (Grill) A.; m. Katharine Violet Sziklai, Sept. 6, 1958; children: Susan Katina, George Jonathon II. AB with maj. honors, U. Pa., 1953, JD cum laude, 1969; LLM, Yale U., 1965, JSD, 1969. Bar: Ill. 1960, N.Y. 1961, Calif. 1974. Instr. law, Bigelow fellow U. Chgo., 1959-60; instr. internat. relations Naval Res. Officers Sch., Forrest Park, Ill., 1959-60; prof. law Syracuse U. Coll. Law, 1960-70, assoc. dean, 1968-69; prof. law U. Santa Clara (Calif.) Law Sch., 1970—, disting. univ. prof., 1994-95, Elizabeth H. and John A. Sutro prof. law, 1995—, pres. faculty senate, 1996-97, dean, 1970-85, dir. Inst. Internat. and Comparative Law, 1986—, dir. grad. programs, 1998-2001. Dir. summer programs at Oxford, Geneva, Strasbourg, Budapest, Tokyo, Hong Kong, Beijing, Ho Chi Minh City, Singapore, Bangkok, Kuala Lumpur, Seoul, Munich; vis. prof. law U. So. Calif., 1963; vis. scholar Stanford (Calif.) U. Law Sch., 1985-86, 92; cons. in field. Author: Civil Rights, U.S.A., Public Schools, 1963, Honesty and Competition, 1967, Jury Instructing on Medical Issues, 1966, Cases and Materials on Space Law, 1971, The Aged and the Need for Surrogate Management, 1972, Commercial Torts, 1973, 2d edit. 1988, U.S. Antitrust Laws, 1980, Writing A Living Will: Using a Durable Power of Attorney, 1988, (with Scheflin) Law and Mental Disabilities, 1998; author, editor: International Perspectives on Aging, 1992; also articles, chpts. in books, one film. Dir. Domestic and Internat. Bus. Problems Honors Clinic, Syracuse U., 1966-69, Regulations in Space Project, 1968-70; ednl. cons. Comptroller Gen. U.S., 1977—; mem. Nat. Sr. Citizens Law Ctr., 1983-89, pres., 1986-90; co-founder Am. Assn. Abolition Involuntary Mental Hospitalization, 1970, dir., 1970-83. With USN, 1953-56. U.S. Navy scholar U. Pa., 1949-52; Law Bds. scholar, 1956-59; Sterling fellow Yale, 1964-65; recipient Ralph E. Kharas Civil Liberties award, Syracuse U. Sch. Law, 1970, Owens award as Alumnus of Yr., 1984, Disting. prof. Santa Clara Univ. Faculty Senate, 1994-95, 2000 award for outstanding contbns. to cause of civil liberties Freedom of Thought Found.; named Disting. Vis. Prof. Krens Dznube U., Vienna, 2001. Mem. Internat. Acad. Law Mental Health (mem. sci. com. 1997-99), Calif. Bar Assn. (first chmn. com. legal problems of aging), Assn. Am. Law Schs., Soc. Am. Law Tchrs. (dir., pres. 1979), AAUP (chpt. pres. 1962), N.Y. Civil Liberties Union (chpt. pres. 1965, dir., v.p. 1966-70), Am. Acad. Polit. and Social Sci., Order of Coif, Justinian Honor Soc., Phi Alpha Delta (chpt. faculty adviser 1967-70) Home: 11600 Summit Wood Ct Los Altos Hills CA 94022 Office: U Santa Clara Sch Law Santa Clara CA 95053-0001 E-mail: gjalexander@aya.yale.edu

ALEXANDER, GERRY L. state supreme court chief justice; b. Aberdeen, Wash., Apr. 28, 1936; BA, U. Wash., 1958, JD, 1964. Bar: Wash. 1964. Pvt. practice, Olympia, Wash., 1964-73; judge Wash. Superior Ct., 1973-85, Wash. Ct. Appeals Divsn. II, Tacoma, 1985-95; state supreme ct. justice Wash. Supreme Ct., Olympia, 1995-2000, state supreme ct. chief justice, 2000—. Mem. Statute Law Com. Lt. U.S. Army, 1958-61. Mem. ABA, Am. Judges Assn., Wash. State Bar Assn., Thurston-Mason County Assn. (pres. 1973), Puget Sound Inn of Ct. (pres. 1996), Bench-Bar-Press (chair), Washington Cts. Hist. Soc. Office: Temple of Justice PO Box 40929 Olympia WA 98504-0929 E-mail: j_g.alexander@courts.wa.gov

ALEXANDER, GREGORY STEWART, law educator, educator; b. 1948; BA, Ill. U., 1970; JD, Northwestern U., 1973; postgrad., U. Chgo., 1974-75. Law clk. to chief judge U.S. Ct. Appeals, 1972-74; asst. prof. law U. Ga., 1975-78, assoc. prof., 1978-84; prof. Cornell U., Ithaca, N.Y., 1984—, A. Robert Noll prof. law, 2000—. Vis. prof. Harvard Law Sch., 1997—. Bigelow fellow U. Chgo., 1974-75; fellow Max-Planck Inst. (Germany), 1995-96. Mem. Am. Soc. Politics and Legal Philosophy, Am. Soc. Legal History. E-mail. Office: Cornell U Law Sch Myron Taylor Hall Ithaca NY 14853 E-mail: gsa9@cornell.edu

ALEXANDER, JAMES PATRICK, lawyer, educator; b. Glendale, Calif., Oct. 14, 1944; s. Victor Elwin and Thelma Elizabeth (O'Donnell) A.; m. Jeanne Elizabeth Bannerman, June 10, 1967; children: Rene Leigh, Amy Lynne. AB, Duke U., 1966, JD, 1969. Bar: Ala. 1969. Assoc. Bradley, Arant, Rose & White, Birmingham, Ala., 1969-75, ptnr., 1975—. Adj. lectr. employment discrimination law U. Ala. Sch. Law, 1981—; exec. adv. com. spl. studies program U. Ala., Birmingham, 1991-93. Trustee Ala. chpt. Nat. Multiple Sclerosis Soc. (vice-chmn. 1987-89, chmn. 1990-91); bd. dirs. Birmingham Civil Right Inst., Inc. Fellow Coll. Labor and Employment Lawyers; mem. Birmingham Bar Assn., Ala. State Bar, ABA, Am.

Arbitration Assn. (comml. arbitrator, employment disputes arbitrator), Indsl. Rels. Rsch. Assn. (Ala. chpt.), Sigma Nu, Duke Law Alumni Assn. (pres. Ala. chpt. 1989-90). Antitrust, Federal civil litigation, Labor. Home: 4309 Altamont Rd Birmingham AL 35213-2407 Office: Bradley Arant Rose & White LLP 1400 Park Pl Tower 2001 Park Pl Ste 1400 Birmingham AL 35203 E-mail: jalexander@barw.com

ALEXANDER, KATHARINE VIOLET, lawyer; b. N.Y.C., Nov. 19, 1934; d. George Clifford and Violet (Jambor) Sziklai; m. George Jonathon Alexander, Sept. 6, 1958; children: Susan Katina, George J. II. Student, Smith Coll., Geneva, 1954-55; BA, Goucher Coll., 1956; JD, U. Pa., 1959; student specialized courses, U. Santa Clara, 1974-76. Bar: Calif. 1974, U.S. Dist. Ct. (no. dist.) Calif. 1974, U.S. Ct. Appeals (9th cir.) 1974; cert. criminal lawyer Calif. State Bar Bd. Legal Specialization. Research dir., adminstr. Am. Bar Found., Chgo., 1959-60; lectr. law San Jose (Calif.) State U., 1972-74; sr. atty. Santa Clara County, San Jose, 1974-97, ret., 1997. Editor: Mentally Disabled and the Law, 1961; contbg. author: The Aged and the Need for Surrogate Management, 1969-70, Jury Instructions on Medical Issues, 1965-67. Community rep. Office Econ. Opportunity Com., Syracuse, N.Y., 1969-70. Mem. AAUW, Food and Wine Inst., Calif. Bar Assn., Santa Clara County Bar Assn. (trustee 1981-82), Calif. Attys. for Criminal Justice (bd. govs. 1988-92), Jr. League, Anthropology and Stanford Museum of Arts. Presbyterian. Avocations: stock market, gourmet, traveling. Home and Office: 11600 Summit Wood Ct Los Altos Hills CA 94022-4500 Fax: 650-948-7596. E-mail: g.j.alexander@aya.yale.com

ALEXANDER, KENT B. lawyer; b. Atlanta, Nov. 7, 1958; BA in Polit. Sci. magna cum laude, Tufts U., 1980; JD, U. Va., 1983. Bar: Ga. 1983. Assoc. Long & Alridge, Atlanta, 1983-85; asst. U.S. atty. for no. dist. Ga., U.S. Dept. Justice, 1985-92, U.S. atty., 1994-97; of counsel, ptnr. King & Spalding, 1992-94, ptnr., 1997-99; sr. v.p., gen. counsel Emory Univ., 2000—. Co-founder Hands On Atlanta. Office: Emory Univ 401 Administration Bldg Atlanta GA 30322-0001

ALEXANDER, ROBERT GARDNER, lawyer; b. Madison, Wis., May 19, 1949; s. Charles Kohl and Jean (Gardner) A.; m. Karen Lynn Kaminski, Sept. 30, 1989; children: Elizabeth Jean, Sarah Lynn, Rebecca Ann. BA, U. Wis., 1971, JD, 1976; ML in Taxation, DePaul U., 1984. Bar: Wis. 1976, U.S. Dist. Ct. (we. dist.) Wis. 1976, U.S. Dist. Ct. (ea. dist.) Wis. 1978, U.S. Tax Ct. 1982, U.S. Ct. Appeals (7th cir.) 1983. Rsch. atty. U. Wis., Madison, 1976-77; atty. McLario Law Offices, Menomonee Falls, Wis., 1978-87, Alexander Law Offices, S.C., Wauwatosa, 1987—. Trustee, sec. Falls Bapt. Ch., Inc., Menomonee Falls, 1987—; dir. David Barba Evantelistic Assn., Downers Grove, Ill., 1989—, Preach the Word, Inc., Downers Grove, 1992—; adv. bd. Joy Bapt. Camp, Whitewater, Wis., 1992—. Mem. ABA, Nat. Acad. Elder Law Attys., Wis. State Bar, Milw. Estate Planning Counsel, Nat. Assn. Estate Planning Counselors (accredited estate planner), Ea. Wis. Planning Giving Counsel, Phi Kappa Phi. Republican. Avocations: music, art, sports. Estate planning, Probate, Estate taxation. Office: Alexander & Klemmer SC Ste 304 2675 N Mayfair Rd Wauwatosa WI 53226-1305 E-mail: alexlaw@exeepc.com

ALEXIS, CARL ODMAN, lawyer, earth scientist; b. Valparaiso, Nebr., Aug. 8, 1918; s. Joseph Emmanual Alexander Alexis and Marjorie Edith Odman; m. May Britt Lennerup, 1954 (div. 1962); children: Carl Eric, Karin Frenze; m. Mildred Craig Bartos, 1966 (dec. 1996); m. Jeanette Strain, Apr. 24, 1999. BS, U. Nebr., 1937; MS, U. Ariz., 1940, PhD, 1949; postgrad., Calif. Inst. Tech., 1939-40, NYU, 1943-44; JD, U. Nebr., 1966. Bar: Nebr. 1966. Chemist Am. Potash and Chem. Corp., 1940-41; mucker Phelps Dodge Corp., Bisbee, Ariz., 1941; instrument man Stanolind Oil and Gas Co., Tulsa, 1941-42; sr. supr. Plum Brook Ordnance Works, Sandusky, Ohio, 1942-43; grad. asst. U. Ariz., Tucson, 1947-48; field engr. Anaconda Copper Corp., Salt Lake City, 1948-49; geologist U.S. Geol. Survey, Washington, 1949-50; phys. sci. adminstr. Office Naval Rsch., 1950-62; spl. asst. atty. gen. Atty. Gen.-Dept. Rds., 1967-71. Lt. comdr. USN, 1943-46, USNR, 1946-69, ret. Mem. Neb. Bar Assn., Lincoln Bar Assn., Audubon Soc., Am. Legion, Friends of Nebr. State Mus., Nebr. State Hist. Soc., Nebr. Art Assn., Gt. Plains Assn., Sigma Xi, Phi Kappa Phi. Home: 1811 S Pershing Rd Lincoln NE 68502-4840

ALEXIS, GERALDINE M. lawyer; b. N.Y.C., Nov. 3, 1948; d. William J. and Margaret Daly; m. Marcus Alexis, June 15, 1969; children: Marcus L., Hilary I., Sean C. BA, U. Rochester, 1971; MBA, JD, Northwestern U., 1976. Bar: Ill. 1976, U.S. Dist. Ct. (no. dist.) Ill. 1976, U.S. Trial Bar 1985, U.S. Ct. Appeals (7th cir.) 1986, U.S. Ct. Appeals (5th cir.) 1996. Law clk. to Hon. John F. Grady, justice U.S. Dist. Ct. (no. dist.) Ill., Chgo., 1976-77; assoc. Sidley & Austin, 1977-79, 81-83, ptnr., 1983-2000; advisor U.S. Dept. Justice Office Legal Counsel, Washington, 1979-81; atty. McCutchen, Doyle, Brown & Enersen, San Francisco, 2000—. Mem. ABA (vice chair civil practice and procedure com. antitrust sect.), Law Club (pres.), 7th Cir. Bar Assn. (1st v.p.), Chgo. Bar Assn. Democrat. Antitrust, Federal civil litigation, Finance. Office: McCutchen Doyle Brown & Enersen 3 Embarcadero Ctr San Francisco CA 94111

ALFINI, JAMES JOSEPH, dean, educator, lawyer; b. Yonkers, N.Y., Oct. 12, 1943; s. James Joseph and Olga (Genish) A.; m. Carol Miller, Dec. 23, 1966; children: David James, Michael Steven. AB, Columbia U., 1965; JD, Northwestern U., 1972. Bar: N.Y. 1973, Ill. 1976, U.S. Dist. Ct. (no. dist.) Ill. 1976, U.S. Ct. Appeals (7th cir.) 1982, U.S. Supreme Ct. 1977. Reginald Heber Smith cmty. lawyer Monroe County Legal Assistance Corp., Rochester, N.Y., 1972-73; asst. dir. research Am. Judicature Soc., Chgo., 1973-77, dir. rsch., 1977-80, asst. exec. dir. programs, 1980-85; adj. prof. law IIT Chgo.-Kent Sch. Law, 1978-85; assoc. prof. of law Fla. State U., Tallahassee, 1985-90, prof. law, 1990-91; dean, prof. No. Ill. U. Coll. Law, 1991-97, prof., 1997—. Co-author: (books) Making Jury Instructions Understandable, 1982, Judicial Conduct and Ethics, 1990, 95, 2000, Mediation Theory and Practice, 2000; mem. Christian Ch. Bd. Editors Ohio State Jour. Dispute Resolution, 1994-98. Mem. governing bd. Cook County Legal Assistance Found., 1981-83; arbitration and mediation rules com. Fla. Supreme Ct., 1988-91; mem. Ill. Jud. Ethics com., 1993-97; chmn. coord. coun. Nat. Ct. Orgns., 1982-83; bd. govs. Chgo. Coun. Lawyers. 1st lt. U.S. Army, 1965-69. Decorated Army Commendation medal. Mem. ABA (sect. dispute resolution, chair), ACLU, Am. Law Inst., Law and Soc. Assn. Democrat. E-mail: jalfini@niu.edu. Home: 525 Wing Ln Saint Charles IL 60174-2339

ALFORD, BARRY JAMES, lawyer; b. Dallas, Nov. 13, 1965; s. James Arnold and Edwinna Ruth Alford; m. Lora Lyn Smith, Nov. 1, 1992 (div. Aug. 1996); 1 child, Tiffany Marie. BS in Econs., Tex. Christian U., 1988; JD, Oklahoma City U., 1992. Atty. Law Office of Jack Beech, Ft. Worth, 1993-94; pvt. practice law, 1994—. Mem. Tarrant County Criminal Def. Lawyers Assn., Tarrant County Bar Assn., Tarrant County Young Lawyers Assn. Criminal. Office: Ste 908 One Summit Ave Fort Worth TX 76102

ALFORD, MARGIE SEARCY, lawyer, author; b. Tuscaloosa, Ala., Dec. 20, 1949; d. Joseph Alexander and Margaret Tyler (Zehmer) Searcy; m. Andrew Ray Alford, Sept. 4, 1992. BS, U. Ala., 1967-69, 70-71; student, U. Ams., Mexico City, 1969, Emory U., Atlanta, 1970; JD, U. Ala., 1974. Bar: Ala. 1974; U.S. Dist. Ct. (no. dist.) Ala. 1975. Assoc. univ. counsel U. Ala., Tuscaloosa, 1974-75; pvt. practice, 1975-92, Birmingham, Ala., 1992—. Editor-in-chief, prin. author: Matthew Bender's A Guide to Toxic Torts, 4 vols., 1986; contbg. author: Matthew Bender's Drug Product Liability, 4 vols.; contbr. numerous articles to legal jours., freelance writer for numerous publs. Group leader Ea. Area Diabetes Support Group, 1997—; mem. Trussville Area C. of C., bd. dirs., 2000—. Named Most Outstanding Young Career Woman in Ala. Ala. Bus. and Profl. Women, 1986. Mem. ATLA (twice nat. chair environ. and toxic tort law sect., twice nat. chair of women trial lawyers caucus), Nat. Assn. Women Bus. Owners, Bus. and Profl. Women, Women Lawyers Lunch Bunch, Ala. State Bar, Ala. Media Profls. Presbyterian. Avocations: collecting antique furniture and paintings, chow chow dog breeder, gardening, traveling. Criminal, Environmental, Personal injury. Office: PO Box 610781 Birmingham AL 35261-0781 Fax: (205) 520-5083. E-mail: margialfor@aol.com

ALITO, SAMUEL ANTHONY, JR. federal judge; b. Trenton, N.J., Apr. 1, 1950; s. Samuel A. and Rose (Fradusco) A.; m. Martha-Ann Bomgardner, 1985; children: Philip Samuel, Laura Claire. AB, Princeton U., 1972; JD, Yale U., 1975. Bar: N.J. 1975, N.Y. 1982, U.S. Dist. Ct. N.J. 1975, U.S. Ct. Appeals (3d cir.) 1977, U.S. Ct. Appeals (2d cir.) 1980, U.S. Ct. Appeals (D.C. cir.) 1987, U.S. Supreme Ct. 1979. Law clk. to judge U.S. Ct. Appeals (3d cir.), Newark, 1976-77; asst. U.S. atty. U.S. Atty.'s Office, 1977-81, U.S. atty., 1987-90; asst. to solicitor gen. Office of Solicitor Gen. Dept. Justice, Washington, 1981-85; dep. asst. atty. gen. Office of Legal Counsel Dept. Justice, 1985-87; judge U.S. Ct. Appeals for 3d Cir., Newark, 1990—. Office: US Courthouse PO Box 999 Newark NJ 07101-0999

ALLAN, LIONEL MANNING, lawyer; b. Detroit, Aug. 3, 1943; AB cum laude, U. Mich., 1965; JD, Stanford U., 1968; student, U. Paris. BAr: Calif. 1969, U.S. Supreme Ct. 1972. Law clk. U.S. Dist. Ct. (no. dist.) Calif., 1969-70; pres. Allan Advisors, Inc., legal cons. firm. Speaker and writer in field of corp. securities and pvt. internat. law; sec. adv. com. San Jose Fed. Ct., 1969-85; mem. bd. visitors Stanford Law Sch., 1985-88; mem. com. comml. code State Bar Calif., 1974-77, corps. com., 1983-86. Co-author: How to Structure the Classic Venture Capital Deal, 1983, Equity Incentives for Start-up Companies, 1985, Master Limited Partnerships, 1987. Bd. dirs. San Jose Mus. Art, 1983-87; trustee KTEH-TV Channel 54 Found., 1987—; dir. NCCJ, 1995—, Harker Sch., 1998—. Served to capt. JAGC, USAR, 1968-74. Mem. ABA (com. on small bus. 1980—, chmn. internat. bus. subcom. 1985-88, chmn. small bus. com. 1989-93), Santa Clara Bar Assn. (chmn. fed. ct. sect. 1971, 77), Internat. Bar Assn., San Jose C. of C. (dir.), Pi Sigma Alpha, Phi Sigma Iota, Phi Delta Phi. General corporate, Private international, Securities. Office: Allan Advisors Inc 18222 Seebree Ln Monte Sereno CA 95030-3135 E-mail: lonallan@launchnet.com

ALLAN, RICHMOND FREDERICK, lawyer; b. Billings, Mont., Apr. 22, 1930; s. Roy F. and Edith (Prater) A.; m. Dorothy Frost, Aug. 9, 1954; children: Richmond P., David F., Michael R. BA, U. Mont., 1954, JD, 1957; postgrad., London Sch. of Econs., 1957-58. Bar: Mont. 1957, U.S. Supreme Ct. 1961, D.C. 1965. Law clk. U.S. Ct. Appeals (9th cir.), San Francisco, 1958-59; ptnr. Kurth, Conner, Jones & Allan, Billings, 1959-61; chief asst. U.S. atty. U.S. Dept. of Justice, 1961-64; assoc. solicitor U.S. Dept. of Interior, Washington, 1965-67, dep. solicitor, 1968-69; ptnr. Weissbrodt & Weissbrodt, 1969-77, Casey, Lane & Mittendorf, Washington, 1977-78, Duncan, Weinberg, Miller & Pembroke, P.C., Washington, 1979—. Fulbright Commn. scholar, 1957. Mem. Fed. Bar Assn. (pres. Mont. chpt. 1963-65). Avocations: trap and skeet shooting. Administrative and regulatory, Oil, gas, and mineral, Real property. Office: Duncan Weinberg Genzer & Pembroke PC 1615 M St NW Ste 800 Washington DC 20036-3219 E-mail: rfa@dwgp.com

ALLAN, WALTER ROBERT, lawyer; b. Detroit, Aug. 1, 1937; s. Walter Francis and Henrietta (Fairchild) A. AB, U. Mich., 1959, JD, 1962. Bar: Calif. 1964, U.S. Ct. Appeals (9th Cir.) 1964, U.S. Supreme Ct. 1972, U.S. Ct. Appeals (D.C. cir.) 1973, U.S. Ct. Appeals (5th cir.) 1977, U.S. Ct. Appeals (3d cir.) 1988. From assoc. to ptnr. Pillsbury, Madison & Sutro, San Francisco, 1963-67; sole practitioner Tiburon, Calif., 1967—. Appellate, Federal civil litigation, General civil litigation. Office: PO Box 771 Belvedere Tiburon CA 94920-0771

ALLARD, JAVIER, lawyer; b. Vina del Mar, Chile, Nov. 13, 1971; Lic. jud. and social scis., U. Chile, Santiago, 1996; M of Law, Columbia U., 1999. Legal asst. Aylwin Abogados, Santiago, Chile, 1992; atty. Carey y Cia Ltd., Chile, 1996-98, 2000—; fgn. atty. Cleary Gottlieb Steen & Hamilson, N.Y.C., 1999-2000. Recipient Columbia U. Sch. Law Comparative Law Achievement award, 1999; Acad. Excellence scholar, U. Chile, 1990, Fulbright scholar, 1997-99. Mem. Chilean Bar Assn., Columbia Law Sch. Assn. General corporate. Office: Carey y Cia Ltd Miraflores 222 Piso 24 Santiago Chile Fax: 562-633-1980

ALLCOCK, JOHN PAUL MAJOR, lawyer; b. London, July 8, 1941; BSc, U. London, 1963; MSc, Faculté Polytechnique, Mons, Belgium, 1964. Chartered elec. engr. 1974. Trainee patent agt. Gill Jennings & Every, London, 1964-68; patent mgr. Honeywell Ltd., Bracknell, Eng., 1968-71; chartered patent agt. Langner Parry, London, 1971-72; patent mgr. Clifford Chance (formerly Coward Chance), 1972-78; ptnr. Bristows, 1978—. Avocations: travel, sailing, walking. Computer, Intellectual property, Patent. Office: Bristows 3 Lincolns Inn Fields London WC2A 3AA England E-mail: john.allcock@bristows.com

ALLEGRUCCI, DONALD LEE, state supreme court justice; b. Pittsburg, Kans., Sept. 19, 1936; s. Nello and Josephine Marie (Funaro) A.; m. Joyce Ann Thompson, Nov. 30, 1963; children: Scott David, Bowen Jay. AB, Pittsburg State U., 1959; JD, Washburn U., 1963. Bar: Kans. 1963. Asst. county atty. Butler County, El Dorado, Kans., 1963-67; state senator Kans. Legislature, Topeka, 1976-80; mem. Kans. Pub. Relations Bd., 1981-82; dist. judge Kans. 11th Jud. Dist., Pittsburg, 1982-87, adminstrv. judge, 1983-87; justice Kans. Supreme Ct., Topeka, 1987—. Instr. Pittsburg State U., 1969-72; exec. dir. Mid-Kans. Community Action Program, Inc. Mem. Dem. State Com., 1974-80; candidate 5th Congl. Dist., 1978; past pres. Heart Assn.; bd. dirs. YMCA. Served with USAF, 1959-60. Mem. Kans. Bar Assn. Democrat. Office: Kansas Supreme Court 374 Kansas Judicial Ctr 301 SW 10th Ave Fl 3 Topeka KS 66612-1507*

ALLEN, DAVID JAMES, lawyer; b. East Chicago, Ind. BS, Ind. U., 1957, MA, 1959, JD, 1965. Bar: Ind. 1965, U.S. Dist. Ct. (so. dist.) Ind. 1965, U.S. Ct. Appeals 1965, U.S. Ct. Appeals (fed. and 7th cirs.) 1983, U.S. Tax Ct. 1965, U.S. Supreme Ct. 1965. Of counsel Hagemier, Allen and Smith, Indpls., 1975—. Adminstrv. asst. Gov. of Ind. Mathew E. Welsh, 1961—65; counsel Ind. Gov. Roger D. Branigin, 1965—69; asst. to Gov. Edgar D. Whitcomb, 1969—70; legis. counsel Ind. Gov. Evan Bayh, 1989—90; spl. counsel Gov. Frank O'Bannon State of Ind., 1999—; mem. Spl. Commn. on Ind. Exec. Reorgn., 1967—69; commr. Ind. Utility Regulatory Commn., 1970—75; mem. Ind. Law Enforcement Acad. Bd. and Adv. Coun., 1968—85, Ind. State Police Bd., 1968—; commr. for revision Ind. Commn. to REcommend Changes in Ind. Legis. Process, 1990—; commr. Ind. Criminal Code Revision Study Commn., 1998—; nat. judge adv. Acacia Frat., 1980—86, 1992—; chief counsel Ind. Ho. Reps., 1976—76, spl. counsel, 1979—89, Ind. Senate, 1990—97; adj. prof. pub. law Sch. Pub. and Environ. Affairs, Ind. U., Bloomington, 1976—. Author: New Governor In Indiana: Transition of Executive Power, 1965. Mem. ABA, Ind. State Bar Assn. (mem. adminstrv. law com. 1968-77, chmn. adminstrv. law com. 1973-76, mem. law sch. liaison com. 1977-78, criminal justice law exec. com. 1966-72), Indpls. Bar Assn. Administrative and regulatory, Legislative, Public utilities. Office: Hagemier Allen & Smith 1170 Market Tower 10 W Market St Ste 1170 Indianapolis IN 46204-5924 Office Fax: 317-464-8146. E-mail: allendindy@worldnet.att.net

ALLEN, FRANK CLINTON, JR. lawyer, chemical engineer; b. New Orleans, Apr. 14, 1934; s. Frank Clinton and Lucy Charlotte (Walters) A.; m. Cynthia Ann Church, June 7, 1958; children: Frank C. III, Thomas Church, C. Ann. BSChemE, Tulane U., 1955, LLB, 1964. Registered profl. engr., La.; bar: La. 1964, Miss. 1977, Tex. 1991, U.S. Supreme Ct. 1972. Process engr. Am. Oil Co., New Orleans, 1955-60, Chevron Oil Co., New Orleans, 1960-64; atty. Jones, Walker, Waechter, 1964-78; v.p., gen. counsel, corp. sec. McDermott Internat., Inc., 1978-99; atty. Jones, Walker, Waechter, Poitevent, Carrere, Devere, 1999—. Mem. AIChE, ABA, La. Bar Assn., Miss. Bar Assn., Tex. Bar Assn. Avocation: sailing. Environmental, Personal injury, Product liability. Office: Jones Walker et al 201 Saint Charles Ave Fl 48 New Orleans LA 70170-1000 E-mail: fallen@jwlaw.com, fallen@ametro.net

ALLEN, HARRY ROGER, lawyer; b. Memphis, June 13, 1933; s. Sam J. and Louise (Frazier) A.; children: Julie Ferriss, Steven J., Leslie Loraine Allen Anchor; m. Emily Ann Mason, May 4, 1990; 1 stepchild, Jeremy Myrick. Student, Tulane U., 1951-53; BBA, U. Miss., 1955, LLB, 1959. Bar: Miss. 1959, U.S. Dist. Ct. (so. dist.) Miss. 1961, U.S. Ct. Appeals (5th cir.) 1981, U.S. Supreme Ct. 1981. From assoc. to ptnr. Brunini Everett, Grantam & Quinn, Vicksburg, Miss., 1959-68; ptnr. Bryan, Nelson, Allen, Schroeder, Cobb & Hood, Gulfport, 1968-91; pres. Allen, Vaughn, Cobb & Hood, P.A., 1992—. Spl. asst. atty. gen. State of Miss., Gulfport, 1989-91. Mem. Harrison County com. region XIII commn. Mental Health and Mental Retardation, Gulfport, 1976—; fin. chmn. Miss. Rep. Party, 1982-84; Miss. Elector Bush/Quayle Ticket, Jackson, Miss., 1984; del. Rep. Nat. Conv., Dallas, 1984. Capt. USAF, 1955-58. Named to Best Lawyer in Am. publ., 1988-97. Mem. Internat. Assn. Def. Counsel, Miss. Bar Found. (bd. trustees), Miss. Bar Assn. (pres. Harrison County young lawyers sect. 1969-70, jud. liaison com. 1990-91), Miss. Fed. Bar Assn. (so. dist. commr. 1980-81), Miss. Bar Leadership Conf. (chmn. 1991), Harrison County Bar Assn. (pres. 1990), Lamar Order, Am. Inns of Ct. (pres. Russell 1995-96, Blass-Walker chpt. Republican. Methodist. Avocations: golf, skiing. General civil litigation, Insurance, Personal injury. Office: Allen Vaughn Cobb & Hood P A PO Box 4108 Gulfport MS 39502-4108 E-mail: kallen@nuchlaw.com

ALLEN, HENRY SERMONES, JR. lawyer; b. Bronxville, N.Y., Aug. 26, 1947; s. Henry S. and Cecelia Marie (Chartrand) A.; m. Patricia Stromberger, Nov. 26, 1988; children: David Beckman, Amy Louise, Jeffrey Roy. AB magna cum laude, Washington U., St. Louis, 1969; MPA, Cornell U., 1973, JD, 1974. Adminstrv. resident Montefiore Hosp. and Med. Ctr., Bronx, N.Y., 1971; rsch. trainee Nat. Ctr. Health Svcs. Rsch., HEW, 1974-75; assoc. Vedder, Price, Kaufman & Kammholz, Chgo., 1975-79; pvt. practice Springfield, 1979-81; ptnr. Allen & Reed, Chgo., 1981-86, McBride, Baker & Coles, 1986—. Adj. asst. prof. hosp. law Ithaca (N.Y.) Coll., 1974-75; adj. prof. Cornell U., 1995—. HUD fellow, 1969-71. Mem. Am. Health Lawyers Assn., Ill. Soc. Hosp. Attys., Nat. Health Lawyers Assn., Phi Beta Kappa, Omicron Delta Epsilon, Corneel U. of Chgo. Club. Antitrust, Federal civil litigation, Health. Office: Northwestern Atrium Ctr 500 W Madison St 40th Fl Chicago IL 60661

ALLEN, JAMES HENRY, SR. magistrate judge; b. Memphis, May 10, 1935; s. Henry L. and Hazel V. Allen; m. Charlene Anne Jayroe, July 29, 1961; children: James Henry, Elizabeth Hazel, Luanne Mae. AB, Memphis State U., 1957; LLB, Tulane U., 1960. Bar: La. 1960, Tenn. 1961, U.S. Dist. Ct. (we. dist.) Tenn. 1961, U.S. Supreme Ct. 1969, U.S. Ct. Appeals (6th cir.) 1973. Assoc. Tual, Allan, Keltner and Lee, Memphis, 1960, Nelson, Norvell & Floyd, Memphis, 1961; claims adjuster State Farm Mut. Automobile Ins. Co., 1961-65; adminstrv. asst. law clk. Bankruptcy Ct., 1965-67; assoc. Charles G. Black, 1967-69; asst. atty. gen. Shelby County, 1969-79; U.S. magistrate U.S. Dist. Ct., 1979—. Lectr. on criminal law, recruit class Shelby County Sheriff's Dept., Memphis, 1976; lectr. on fed. rules civil procedure CLE, Memphis, 1981. With USMCR, 1957-65. Scholar Tulane U., 1957-60. Mem. La. Bar Assn., Memphis and Shelby County Bar Assn., Nat. Coun. U.S. Magistrates, Phi Alpha Delta. Baptist. E-mail: James. Office: US Dist Ct 338 Federal Bldg 167 N Main St Memphis TN 38103-1816 Fax: 701-495-1384. E-mail: Allen@ck6.uscourts.gov

ALLEN, JAMES LEE, lawyer; b. Lakewood, Ohio, Apr. 21, 1952; s. Frank M. and Dorothy S. (Stone) A.; m. Sue Eveline Goble, July 25, 1981. BA with high distinction, U. Mich., 1974, JD, 1977; LLM, Wayne State U., 1988. Bar: Mich. 1977, U.S. Dist. Ct. (ea. dist.) Mich. 1978, U.S. Ct. Appeals (6th cir.) 1982, U.S. Tax Ct. 1981, U.S. Supreme Ct. 1984. Assoc. Hardig, Goetz, Heath, Merritt & Reebel, Birmingham, Mich., 1977-83; ptnr. Plunkett & Cooney, P.C., Detroit, 1983— ; instr. Walsh Coll., Troy, Mich., 1980. Vestryman Nativity Episcopal Ch., Birmingham, 1978-81; bd. dirs., treas. Common Ground, Birmingham, 1980; bd dirs. Birmingham Community House, 1983-86. Mem. U. Mich. Alumni Assn., Oakland County Bar Assn. (chmn. program com. (1979-82), Mich. Bar Assn. (mem. representation assembly 1978-90), Phi Beta Kappa. Republican. Banking, General corporate. Home: 3755 Ledge Ct Troy MI 48084-1142

ALLEN, JEFFREY MICHAEL, lawyer; b. Chgo., Dec. 13, 1948; s. Albert A. and Miriam (Feldman) A.; m. Anne Marie Guaraglia, Aug. 9, 1975; children: Jason M., Sara M. BA in Polit. Sci. with great distinction, U. Calif., Berkeley, 1970, JD, 1973. Bar: Calif. 1973, U.S. Dist. Ct. (no. and so. dists.) Calif. 1973, U.S. Ct. Appeals (9th cir.) 1973, U.S. Dist. Ct. (ea. dist.) Calif. 1974, U.S. Dist. Ct. (cen. dist.) Calif. 1977, U.S. Dist. Ct. (so. dist.) Calif., U.S. Supreme Ct.; lic. real estate broker. Prin. Graves & Allen, Oakland, Calif., 1973—. Teaching asst. dept. polit. sci. U. Calif., Berkeley, 1970-73; lectr. St. Mary's Coll., Moraga, Calif., 1976-90; mem. faculty Oakland Coll. of Law, 1996-98; bd. dirs. Family Svcs. of the East Bay, 1987-92, 1st v.p., 1988, pres., 1988-91; mem. panel arbitrators Ala. County Superior Ct.; arbitrator comml. arbitration panel Am. Arbitration Assn. Mem. editorial bd. U. Calif. Law Rev., 1971-73, project editor, 1972-73; mem. Ecology Law Quar., 1971-72; contbr. articles to profl. jours. Mem. U.S. Youth Soccer Consul. Commn., 1997—98, U.S. Youth Soccer Bylaws Com., 1998—; mem. region 4 regional coun. U.S. Youth Soccer, 1996—99, chmn. mediation and dispute resolution com., 1999—2000; treas. Hillcrest Elem. Sch. PTA, 1984—86, pres., 1986—88; past mem. GATE adv. com., strategic planning com. on fin. and budget, dist. budget adv. com., instructional strategy counsel Oakland Unified Sch. Dist., 1986—91; mem. Oakland Met. Forum, 1987—91, Oakland Strategic Planning Com., 1988—90; mem. adv. com. St. Mary's Coll.. Paralegal Prog.; commr. Bay Oaks Youth Soccer, 1988—94; asst. dist. commr. dist. 4 Calif. Youth Soccer Assn., 1990—92, also bd. dirs., pres. dist. 4 competitive league, 1990—93, sec. bd. dirs., 1993—96, chmn. bd. dirs., 1996—99; chmn. U.S. Soccer dateabase mktg. com. Calif. Soccer Assn., 1997—99; bd. dirs. Montera Sports Complex, 1988—89, Jack London Youth Soccer League, 1988—94, Calif. Soccer Assn., 1996—99. Mem.: ABA (chmn. real property com. gen. practice sect. 1987—91, mem. programs com. 1991—93, chmn. subcom. on use of computers in real estate trans. 1985—86, adv. coord. 1993—96, sect. coun. 1994—98, mktg. bd. 1996—98, mem. 1998—99, editor Tech. and Practice Guide 1998—, editl. bd. GP Solo 1999—), Calif. Bar Assn. (mem. ADR com. 2001—), Alameda County Bar Assn. (past vice chmn. com. continuing edn., exec. com. alternative dispute resolution programs, panel mediator, arbitrator), U.S. Soccer Assn. (database mktg. com., constl. commn.), Calif. Scholarship Fedn., U.S. Soccer Fedn. (nat. C lic. coach and state referee, state referee instr. and state referee assessor), Calif. North Referee Assn. (referee adminstr. dist. 4 1992—96, state bd. dirs. 1996—), Soc. for Profls. in

Dispute Resolution, Oakland C. of C., Rotary (bd. dirs. Oakland 1992—94). Avocations: reading, computers, photography, skiing, baseball, coaching and refereeing youth soccer. Bankruptcy, General civil litigation, Real property. Office: Graves & Allen 436 14th St Ste 1400 Oakland CA 94612-2716 E-mail: jallenlaw@aol.com, jallenlaw@gravesandallen.com

ALLEN, JEFFREY RODGERS, lawyer; b. West Point, N.Y., Aug. 15, 1953; s. James R. and Kathryn (Lewis) A.; m. Cynthia Lynn Colyer, Aug. 10, 1975; children: Emily Rodgers, Elizabeth Colyer, Richard Byrd. BA in History, U. Va., 1975; JD, U. Richmond, 1978. Bar: Va. 1978, U.S. Ct. Mil. Appeals 1981, U.S. Ct. Appeals (4th cir.) 1982, U.S. Supreme Ct. 1982. Trial atty. Michie, Hamlett, Donato & Lowry, Charlottesville, Va., 1982-86; chief counsel Va. Dept. Mil. Affairs, Blackstone, 1986-2000; with U.S. Property and Fiscal Office, 2001—. Atty., advisor U.S. Army Mobile Air Surg. Transport Team, Savannah, Ga., 1980-82; steering com. X-Car Litigation Group, 1983-85; lectr., organizer Law Everyone Should Know series Piedmont (Va.) C.C., Charlottesville, 1984-86; trial atty., of counsel Thorsen, Marchant & Scher, L.L.P., Richmond, 1986-98; mem. legal adv. com. Va. Gov.'s Mil. Adv. Commn., 1987-2000, judge advocate adv. coun. N.G. Bur., 1993-96, TJAG Air N.G. judge advocate adv. coun., 1997-, coord. strategic planning com. Pres. Regency Woods Condominium Assn., Richmond, 1976-78, Ashcroft Neighborhood Assn., Charlottesville, 1983-86; treas. Va. N.G. Found., 1986—. Capt. U.S. Army, 1978-82, lt. col. JAGC, Va. Air N.G., 1982-2000, col. USAF, 2001—. Mem. Assn. Trial Lawyers Am., Va. Trial Lawyers Assn., Richmond Bar Assn. Republican. Methodist. Avocations: jogging, mountain climbing, photography, fishing, swimming. Home: 2700 Cottage Cove Dr Richmond VA 23233-3318 Office: USPFO Bldg 316 Ft Pickett Blackstone VA 23824-6316 E-mail: jeff.allen@va.ngb.army.mil

ALLEN, JOHN THOMAS, JR. lawyer; b. St. Petersburg, Fla., Aug. 23, 1935; s. John Thomas and Mary Lita (Shields) A.; m. Joyce Ann Lindsey, June 16, 1958 (div. 1985); children: John Thomas III, Linda Joyce, Catherine Lee (dec.).; m. Janice Dearmin Hudson, Mar. 16, 1987. BSBA with honors, U. Fla., 1958; JD, Stetson U., 1961. Bar: Fla. 1961, U.S. Dist. Ct. (mid. dist.) Fla. 1962, U.S. Ct. Appeals (5th cir.) 1963, U.S. Ct. Appeals (11th cir.) 1983, U.S. Supreme Ct. 1970. Assoc. Mann, Harrison, Mann & Rowe and successor Greene, Mann, Rowe, Davenport & Stanton, St. Petersburg, 1961-67, ptnr., 1967-74; sole practice, 1974-95; pvt. practice Allen & Maller, P.A., 1996-98, Gulfport, Fla., 1998—. Counsel Pinellas County Legis. Del., 1974-75; counsel for Pinellas County as spl. counsel on water matters, 1975-98. Mem. Com of 100, St. Petersburg, 1975-98. Mem. ABA, Fla. Bar Assn., St. Petersburg Bar Assn., St. Petersburg C. of C., Lions, Beta Gamma Sigma. Republican. Methodist. State civil litigation, General practice, Personal injury. Home: 5929 Bayview Cir S Gulfport FL 33707-3929 Office: 5929 Bayview Cir S Gulfport FL 33707-3929

ALLEN, LAYMAN EDWARD, law educator, research scientist; b. Turtle Creek, Pa., June 9, 1927; s. Layman Grant and Viola Iris (Williams) A.; m. Christine R. Patmore, Mar. 29, 1950 (dec.); children: Layman G., Patricia R.; m. Emily C. Hall, Oct. 3, 1981 (div. 1992); children: Phyllip A. Hall, Kelly C. Hall; m. Leslie A. Olsen, June 10, 1995. Student, Washington and Jefferson Coll., 1945-46; AB, Princeton U., 1951; MPub. Admnstrn., Harvard U., 1952; LLB, Yale U., 1956. Bar: Conn. 1956. Fellow Ctr. for Advanced Study in Behavioral Scis., 1961-62; sr. fellow Yale Law Sch., 1956-57, lectr., 1957-58, instr., 1958-59, asst. prof., 1959-63, assoc. prof., 1963-66; assoc. prof. law U. Mich. Law Sch., Ann Arbor, 1966-71, prof., 1971—. Chmn. bd. trustees Accelerated Learning Found., 1998—; sr. rsch. scientist Mental Health Rsch. Inst., U. Mich., 1966-99; cons. legal drafting Nat. Life Ins. Co., Mich. Blue Cross & Blue Shield (various law firms); mem. electronic data retrieval com. Am. Bar Assn.; ops. rsch. analyst McKinsey & Co.; orgn. and methods analyst Office of Sec. Air Force.; trustee Ctr. for Study of Responsive Law. Editor: Games and Simulations, Artificial Intelligence and Law Jour.; author: WFF 'N Proof: The Game of Modern Logic, 1961, latest rev. edit., 1990, (with Robin B.S. Brooks, Patricia A. James) Automatic Retrieval of Legal Literature: Why and How, 1962, WFF: The Beginner's Game of Modern Logic, 1962, latest rev. edit., 1973, Equations: The Game of Creative Mathematics, 1963, latest rev. edit., 1994, (with Mary E. Caldwell) Reflections of the Communications Sciences and Law: The Jurimetrics Conference, 1965, (with J. Ross and P. Kugel) Queries 'N Theories: The Game of Science and Language, 1970, latest rev. edit., 1973, (with F. Goodman, D. Humphrey and J. Ross), On-Words: The Game of Word Structures, 1971, rev. edit., 1973; contbr. articles to profl. jours.; co-author/designer: (with J. Ross and C. Stratton) DIG (Diagnostic Instrnl. Gaming) Math; (with C. Saxon) Normalizer Clear Legal Drafting Program, 1986, MINT System for Generating Dynamically Multiple-Interpretation Legal Decision-Assistance Systems, 1991, The Legal Argument Game of Legal Relations, 1997. With USNR, 1945-46. Mem. ABA (coun. sect. sci. and tech.), AAAS, ACLU, Assn. Symbolic Logic, Nat. Coun. Tchrs. Math. Democrat. Unitarian. Home: 2114 Vinewood Blvd Ann Arbor MI 48104-2762 Office: U Mich Sch Law 625 S State St Ann Arbor MI 48109-1215 E-mail: laymanal@umich.edu

ALLEN, LEON ARTHUR, JR. lawyer; b. Springfield, Mass., July 15, 1933; s. Leon Arthur Sr. and Elsie (Shoemaker) A.; m. Patricia Mellion, June 23, 1961; 1 child, Christopher L. BEE, Cornell U., 1955; LLB, NYU, 1964. Bar: N.Y. 1964, U.S. Dist. Ct. (so. and ea. dists.) N.Y. 1965. Tech. editor McGraw Hill Pub. Co., N.Y.C., 1958-62; constrn. engr. Gilbert Assocs., 1962-64; assoc. LeBoeuf, Lamb, Leiby & MacRae, 1964-70; ptnr. LeBoeuf, Lamb, Leiby & MacRae (name changed to LeBoeuf, Lamb, Greene & MacRae), 1971—. Served with U.S. Army, 1956-58. Mem. ABA, Assn. of Bar of City of N.Y. (chmn. adminstrv. law com. 1972-74). Clubs: Racquet & Tennis (N.Y.C.); Union (N.Y.C.), Tuxedo (Tuxedo Park, N.Y.). Administrative and regulatory, FERC practice, Private international. Home: 530 E 86th St New York NY 10028-7535 Office: LeBoeuf Lamb Greene MacRae 125 W 55th St New York NY 10019-5369 E-mail: laallen@llgm.com

ALLEN, MARGUERITE E. legal association administrator; b. Vicksburg, Miss., July 25, 1947; d. John Austin and Laura-Frances (Martin) Holliday; 1 child, Laura-Ashley Allen. BA, Miss. State U., 1969; MA, La. Tech. U., 1995. Adminstr. asst. VA, Jackson, Miss.; residential realtor Towery Real Estate, Shreveport, La.; exec. dir. Shreveport Bar Assn. Bd. dirs. Shreveport Mental Health Assn., 1988-93; pub. relations Jr. League of Shreveport, 1992. Mem. Nat. Assn. Bar. Execs. Avocations: walking, reading, travel, gardening. Home: 11175 Heritage Oaks Shreveport LA 71106-8383 Office: Shreveport Bar Assn 509 Marshall St Shreveport LA 71101-3591

ALLEN, NEWTON PERKINS, lawyer; b. Memphis, Jan. 3, 1922; s. James Seddon and Sarah (Perkins) Allen; m. Malinda Lobdell Nobles, Oct. 04, 1947 (dec. Nov. 1986); children: John Lobdell, Malinda Allan Lewis, Newton Perkins Lewis, Cannon Fairfax Lewis; m. Malinda Lobdell Crutchfield, June 23, 1990. AB, Princeton, 1943; JD, U. Va., 1948. Bar: Tenn 1947, NC 1990. Assoc. Armstrong, Allen, Prewitt, Gentry, Johnston & Holmes, Memphis, 1948, ptnr., 1950-95; assoc. Dann & Allen, 1996—2001; pvt. practice Memphis, 2001—. Contbr. articles to profl jours. Mem Chickasaw coun Boy Scouts Am, 1958—60, mem exec bd, 1961—69; trustee LeBonheur Children's Hosp, Memphis, 1964—72, vice chmn bd, 1965; mem alumni coun Princeton, 1954—64, 1990—93; chmn Greater Memphis Coun Crime and Delinquency, 1976—80; bd dirs Memphis Orchestra Soc, pres, 1979—81; pres bd trustees St Mary's Episcopal Sch, 1966—67, vpres, 1972—73; co-chmn Memphis Conf Faith at Work, 1975, bd dirs, 1976—79. Mem.: ABA (ed bd sr lawyers div 1990, pub comt chair 1993—95, coun mem 1994—95, chair travel and leisure comt 1995—96, vice chair 1996—97, chair-elect 1997—98, chair 1998—99), Am Col Trust and Estate Coun, Tenn Bar Asn, Memphis Bar Asn, Tenn Def Lawyers Asn, NC Bar Asn, Princeton Alumni Asn Memphis (pres 1992), Memphis Lions (pres 1956). Republican. General civil litigation, General practice, Probate. Office: Law Office 840 Valleybrook Dr Memphis TN 38120

ALLEN, PAUL ALFRED, lawyer, educator; b. New Canaan, Conn., Feb. 18, 1948; s. Alfred J. and Wilma T. (DeWaters) A. BA, Johns Hopkins U., 1970; JD, NYU, 1974; MBA, U. Colo., 1989. Bar: Md. 1974, D.C. 1978, Colo. 1984, Calif. 1992. Exec. dir. Md. Environ. Trust, Balt., 1974-75; assoc. Bergson, Borkland, Margolis & Adler, Washington, 1975-79, ptnr., 1980-82; gen. counsel Plus System, Inc., Denver, 1983-91; counsel Visa USA, Inc., San Francisco, 1991-92, exec. v.p., gen. counsel, 1992—. Lectr. Grad. Sch. of Banking, Boulder, Colo., 1984-86, U. Denver Law Sch., 1985-90. Editor: How to Keep Your Company Out of Court, 1984; contbr. articles to profl. jours. Recipient Svc. award Supreme Ct. Colo. Mem. ABA, Calif. Bar Assn., Colo. Bar Assn., Am. Corp. Counsel Assn. Democrat. Antitrust, General civil litigation, General corporate. Office: Visa USA Inc PO Box 194607 San Francisco CA 94119-4607

ALLEN, RICHARD BLOSE, legal editor, lawyer; b. Aledo, Ill., May 10, 1919; s. James Albert and Claire (Smith) A.; m. Marion Treloar, Aug. 27, 1949; children: Penelope, Jennifer, Leslie Jean. BS, U. Ill., 1941, JD, 1947; LLD, Seton Hall U., 1977. Bar: Ill. 1947. Staff editor ABA Jour., 1947-48, 63-66, exec. editor, 1966-70, editor, 1970-83, editor, pub., 1983-86; pvt. practice Aledo, 1949-57; gen. counsel Ill. Bar Assn., 1957-63; mng. editor Def. Counsel Jour., Chgo., 1987—. Editor Sr. Lawyer, 1986-90, 94-2000. Maj. Q.M.C., AUS, 1941-46. Mem. ABA (mem. ho. of dels. 1996-99, chair sr. lawyers divsn. 2000-01), Ill. Bar Assn. (mem. assembly 1972-74), Chgo. Bar Assn., Am. Law Inst., Selden Soc., Scribes, Mich. Shores Club, Sigma Delta Chi, Kappa Tau Alpha, Phi Delta Phi, Alpha Tau Omega. Office: Def Counsel Jour 1 N Franklin St Ste 2400 Chicago IL 60606-2401 E-mail: dickall2@aol.com, rallen@iadclaw.org

ALLEN, RICHARD LEE, JR. lawyer, consultant; b. Piqua, Ohio, Mar. 12, 1954; s. Richard Lee and Marcella Marie (Reaster) A.; m. Judith Ellen Simpkin, June 28, 1978; children— Richard Lee III, John Christopher. B.S. in Pharmacy, U. Cin., 1977; J.D., Capital Law Sch., 1980. Bar: Ohio 1980. Risk mgr. Med. Ctr. Hosp., Chillicothe, Ohio, 1978-79; Spl. counsel Ohio Hosp. Ins. Co., Columbus, 1980— ; pharmacist Med. Ctr. Hosp., Chillicothe, 1977; adj. prof. Ohio State U., Columbus, 1982— . Mem. Assn. Trial Lawyers Am., Am. Soc. Law and Medicine, Ohio Bar Assn., Ohio Pharm. Assn., Columbus Bar Assn. Health, Insurance, Personal injury. Home: 678 Blackoak Ct Reynoldsburg OH 43068-1509 Office: Ohio Hosp Ins Co 155 E Broad St Fl 13 Columbus OH 43215-3609

ALLEN, ROBERT DEE, lawyer; b. Tulsa, Oct. 13, 1928; s. Harve and Olive Jean (Brown) A.; m. Mary Latimer Conner, May 18, 1957; children: Scott, Randy, Blake. BA, U. Okla., 1951, LLB, 1955, JD, 1970. Bar: Okla. 1955, Ill. 1979, U.S. Dist. Ct. (we., no. and ea. dists.) Okla. 1955, U.S. Dist. Ct. (no. dist.) Ill. 1979, U.S. Ct. Appeals (10th cir.) 1956, U.S. Ct. Appeals (7th cir.) 1980, U.S. Supreme Ct. 1985. Assoc. Abernathy & Abernathy, Shawnee, Okla., 1955; law clk. to judge 10th U.S. Ct. Appeals, Denver, 1956; to judge Western Dist. Okla., 1956-57; asst. ins. commr., gen. counsel Okla. Ins. Dept., 1957-63; partner firm Quinlan, Allen & Batchelor, Oklahoma City, 1963-65, DeBois & Allen, 1965-66; counsel AT&T, Washington, 1966-67; gen. atty. Southwestern Bell Telephone Co., Okla., 1967-79; v.p., gen. counsel Ill. Bell Telephone Co., Chgo., 1979-83; sole practice law Chgo. and Oklahoma City, 1983—; mcpl. counselor Oklahoma City, 1984-89; of counsel Hartzog, Conger & Cason, 1983-90, Kimball, Wilson, Walker and Ferguson, 1990-93, Berry & Durland, 1993-94, Durland & Durland, 1994-96, White, Coffey, Galt & Fite, P.C., 1996-97, Phillips, McFall, McCaffrey, McVay & Murrah, P.C., 1997-2000; asst. general counsel Okla. Corp. Commn. Public Utilities Divsn., 2000—. Spl. counsel Okla. Mcpl. Power Authority, 1990-94, City of Altus, Okla., 1990-95; mem. Gov.'s Ad Valorem Tax Structure and Sch. Fin. Commn., 1972; bd. dirs. Taxpayers Fedn. Ill., 1980-83; adv. bd. dirs. Southwestern Legal Found., 1985—; rsch. fellow Southwestern Legal Found., 1994—; adj. prof. ins. law Oklahoma City U. Coll. Law, 1985—, agy. and partnership law, U. Okla. Coll. Law, 1989—; Okla. State chmn. Nat. Inst. Mcpl. Law Officers, 1984-89; apptd. mem. Legis Task Force on Okla. Adminstrv. Code, 1987; founding mem. U. Okla. Assocs., 1980. Bd. dirs. Oklahoma County Legal Aid Soc., 1973—; trustee Oklahoma City Riverfront Redevel. Authority, 1997—. With U.S. Army, 1946-48, 1st lt., 51-53; lt. col. USAR. Fellow Am. Bar Found.; mem. ABA, Fed. Bar Assn. (v.p. Okla. Chpt. 1977—), Okla. Bar Assn., Okla. County Bar Assn., Am. Judicature Soc., Okla. Assn. Mcpl. Attys. (bd. dirs. 1984-89), English Speaking Union (dir. 2001—), Order of Coif, Chgo. Club, The Econs. Club of Okla., Oklahoma City Golf and Country Club, Phi Delta Phi, Sigma Phi Epsilon (dir.) Presbyterian. Home: 8101 Glenwood Ave Oklahoma City OK 73114-1107 E-mail: rdeeallen@aol.com

ALLEN, ROBERT EUGENE BARTON, lawyer; b. Bloomington, Ind., Mar. 16, 1940; s. Robert Eugene Barton and Berth R. A.; m. Cecelia Ward Dooley, Sept. 23, 1960 (div. 1971); children: Victoria, Elizabeth, Robert, Charles, Suzanne, William; m. Judith Elaine Hecht, May 27, 1979 (div. 1984); m. Suzanne Nickolson, Nov. 18, 1995. BS, Columbia U., 1962; LLB, Harvard U., 1965. Bar: Ariz. 1965, U.S. Dist. Ct. Ariz. 1965, U.S. Tax Ct., 1965, U.S. Supreme Ct. 1970, U.S. Ct. Customs and Patent Appeals 1971, U.S. Dist. Ct. D.C. 1972, U.S. Ct. Appeals (9th cir.) 1974, U.S. Ct. Appeals (10th, and D.C. cirs.) 1984, U.S. Dist. Ct. N.Mex., U.S. Dist. Ct. (no. dist.) Calif., U.S. Dist. Ct. (no. dist.) Tex. 1991, U.S. Ct. Appeals (fed. cir.) 1992, U.S. Dist. Ct. (ea. dist.) Wis. 1995. Ptnr., dir. Allen, Price & Padden, Phoenix; spl. asst. atty. gen. Ariz. Ct. Appeals, 1978, judge pro-tem, 1984, 92, 99; Ptnr., dir. Allen, Price & Padden, Phoenix, 2000—. Nat. pres. Young Dems. Clubs Am., 1971-73; mem. exec. com. Dem. Nat. Com., 1972-73, Ariz. Gov.'s Kitchen Cabinet working on a wide range of state projects; bd. dirs. Phoenix Bapt. Hosp., 1981-83, Phoenix and Valley of the Sun Conv. and Visitors Bur., United Cerebral Palsy Ariz., 1984-89, Planned Parenthood of Ctrl. and No. Ariz., 1984-87, Internat. Coun. Ariz. Heart Inst. Found., 1998—, Cordell Hull Found. for Internat. Edn., 1996—; trustee Environ. Health Found., 1994-97, Friends of Walnut Canyon, 1991-94; bd. dirs. Ariz. Aviation Futures Task Force, chmn. Ariz. Airport Devel. Criteria Subcom.; mem. Apache Junction Airport Rev. Com.; Am. rep. exec. bd. Atlantic Alliance of Young Polit. Leaders, 1973-77, 77-80; trustee Am. Counsel of Young Polit. Leaders, 1971-76, 81-85; mem. Am. delegations to Germany, 1971, 72, 76, 79, USSR, 1971, 76, 88, France, 1974, 79, Belgium, 1974, 77, Can., 1974, Eng., 1975, 79, Norway, 1975, Denmark, 1976, Yugoslavia and Hungary, 1985; Am. observer European Parliamentary elections, Eng., France, Germany, Belgium, 1979, Moscow Congressional, Journalist delegation, 1989, NAFTA Trade Conf., Mexico City, 1993, Atlantic Assembly, Copenhagen, 1993. Contbr. articles on comml. litigation to profl. jours. Mem. ABA, Ariz. Bar Assn., Maricopa County Bar Assn., N.Mex. State Bar, D.C. Bar Assn., Am. Judicature Soc., Fed. Bar Assn., Am. Arbitration Assn., Phi Beta Kappa, Harvard Club. Democrat. Episcopalian (lay reader). Antitrust, General civil litigation, Intellectual property. Office: Allen Price & Padden 3131 E Camelback Rd Phoenix AZ 85016-4500

ALLEN, RUSSELL G. lawyer; b. Ottumwa, Iowa, Nov. 7, 1946; BA, Grinnell Coll., 1968; JD, Stanford U., 1971. Bar: Calif. 1971. Ptnr. O'Melveny & Myers LLP, Newport Beach, Calif., 1975-2001; wealth advisor J.P. Morgan Chase & Co., 2001—. Trustee Grinnell Coll. Capt. JAGC, USAF, 1971-75. Fellow Am. Coll. Trust and Estate Counsel; mem. ABA (real property, probate and trust law and taxation sects.), Orange County Bar Assn. (estate planning, probate and trust sects.) Estate planning, Probate, Estate taxation. Office: JP Morgan Chase and Co Ste 200 888 San Clemente Dr Newport Beach CA 92660 E-mail: rallen@omm.com

ALLEN, WILBUR COLEMAN, lawyer; b. Victoria, Va., Apr. 30, 1925; s. George Edward and Mary Lee (Bridgforth) A.; m. Frances Brockenbrough Gayle, Sept. 16, 1950; children: Frances Gayle Allen Fitzgerald, Wilbur Coleman Jr., Robert Clayton, Edward Lefebvre, Courtney Allen Van Winkle. BA, U. Va., 1947, JD, 1950. Bar: Va. 1949, D.C. 1954, U.S. Dist. Ct. (ea. and we. dists.) Va. 1951, U.S. Ct. Appeals 1950, U.S. Supreme Ct. 1954. Ptnr. Allen, Allen, Allen & Allen, Richmond, Va., 1950—, pres., 1969-90. Lt. (j.g.) USN, 1942-45, PTO. Sunday Sch. supt. All Saints Episc. Ch., Richmond, 1960-65, vestryman, 1964-68, 70-74, 80-83, sr. warden, 1967-68, chmn. stewardship com., 1980-81; bd. visitors Va. Commonwealth U., 1984-87, property com., 1984-85, audit com., 1984-85. Fellow Am. Coll. Trial Lawyers; mem. ABA, ATLA, Am. Judicature Soc., Va. State Bar, Va. Bar Assn. (chmn. spl. com. on professionalism 1990-93), Va. State Bar Council, Va. Trial Lawyers Assn. (chmn. publicity com. 1968, chmn. spl. com. on ins. 1981), N.Y. State Trial Lawyers Assn., Richmond Bar Assn. (pres. 1979, outstanding contbn. award 1981), Country Club of Va., Rotary (pres. 1974-75, Rotarian of Yr. 1980). State civil litigation, Insurance, Personal injury. Home: 4803 Lockgreen Cir Richmond VA 23226-1746 Office: Allen Allen Allen & Allen 1809 Staples Mill Rd Richmond VA 23230-3515

ALLEN, WILLIAM HAYES, lawyer, educator; b. Palo Alto, Calif., Oct. 19, 1926; s. Ben Shannon and Victoria Rose (French) A.; m. Joan Webster Emmett, July 16, 1950; children: Edwin Hayes, Neal French, William Kent. Student, Deep Springs Coll., 1942-44; BA with gt. distinction, Stanford U., 1948, LLB, 1956. Bar: D.C. 1958. Corr. AP, Fresno, Calif., 1948-49, newsman Sacramento, 1950-53; law clk. to Chief Justice Earl Warren U.S. Supreme Ct., Washington, 1956-57; assoc. Covington & Burling, 1957-64, ptnr., 1964-92; ret., 1993—. Acting. prof. Stanford U. Law Sch., 1979; adj. prof. Howard U. Law Sch., 1981-83; lectr. George Mason U. Law Sch., 1983-86; practitioner-in-residence Cornell U. Law Sch., 1992; vis. prof. Deep Springs Coll., 1996; chmn. jud. rev. com. Adminstrv. Conf. U.S., 1972-82, 1973, sr. conf. fellow, 1982-95; mem. steering com. Nat. Prison Project, 1975-93. Pres. Stanford Law Rev., vol. 8, 1955-56; contbr. articles to legal jours. Trustee Deep Springs Coll., 1984-92, chmn. bd. trustees, 1992; mem. Fair Housing Bd., Arlington County, Va., 1974-79. With U.S. Army, 1945-47. Mem. ABA (mem. coun. adminstrv. law sect. 1969-72, 79-81, chmn. 1982-83), D.C. Bar (chmn. legal ethics com. 1976-78), Am. Law Inst., Nat. Press Club, Am. Acad. of Appellate Lawyers, Order of Coif. Democrat. Mem. United Ch. of Christ. Administrative and regulatory, Federal civil litigation. Office: Covington & Burling 1201 Pennsylvania Ave NW Washington DC 20004-2401 E-mail: allenwh@erols.com, wallsn@cov.com

ALLENDER, JOHN ROLAND, lawyer; b. Boone, Iowa, Oct. 22, 1950; s. John S. and C. Corinne (Hayes) A.; m. Patti Allender; children: Susan A., Andrew J. BS, Iowa State U., 1972; JD, U. San Diego, 1975; LLM in Taxation, NYU, 1976. Bar: Calif. 1976, Tex. 1977, U.S. Ct. Claims 1977, U.S. Tax. Ct. 1977, U.S. Dist. Ct. (so. dist.) Tex. 1977. Assoc. Fulbright & Jaworski, Houston, 1976-83, ptnr., 1983—. Mem. adv. commn. Tex. Bd. Legal Specialization, 1986-2000. Bd. dirs. Ronald McDonald House, Houston, 1990—. Mem. State Bar of Tex. (chmn. sect. taxation 1990), Houston Bar Assn. (chmn. sect. taxation 1979). General corporate, Corporate taxation, Taxation, general. Office: Fulbright & Jaworski 1301 Mckinney St Houston TX 77010-3031

ALLEY, WAYNE EDWARD, federal judge, retired army officer; b. Portland, Oreg., May 16, 1932; s. Leonard David and Hilda Myrtle (Blum) A.; m. Marie Winkelmann Dommer, Jan. 28, 1978; children: Elizabeth, David, John; stepchildren: Mark Dommer, Eric Dommer. A.B., Stanford U., 1952, J.D., 1957. Bar: Calif. 1957, Oreg. 1957, Okla. 1985. Ptnr. Williams & Alley, Portland, 1957-59; commd. officer JAGC, U.S. Army, advanced through grades to brig. gen., ret., 1981; dean Coll. Law, dir. Law Ctr. U. Okla., Norman, 1981-85; judge U.S. Dist. Ct. Western Dist. Okla., Oklahoma City, 1985—. Decorated D.S.M., Legion of Merit, Bronze Star Mem. Fed. Bar Assn., Oreg. Bar Assn., Okla. Bar Assn., Order of Coif, Phi Beta Kappa. Office: US Dist Ct 3102 US Courthouse 200 NW 4th St Ste 3102 Oklahoma City OK 73102-3027

ALLINGHAM, LYNN MARIE, lawyer; b. Seattle, Dec. 7, 1955; d. William D. and Ruth E. (Busse) A.; m. Gregory Joseph Gulik, Mar. 2, 1986; children: Geoffrey Joseph Allingham Galik, Jonathan-Paul Allingham Galik. BA magna cum laude, U. Wash., 1978, J.D., 1981. Bar: Wash. 1981, Alaska 1982; U.S. Dist. Ct. (we. dist.) Wash., 1981, Alaska, 1982, Ct. Appeals (9th cir.) 1983. Assoc. Guess & Rudd, Anchorage, 1982-86; pvt. practice, Anchorage, 1986-88; asst. atty. U.S. Attys. Office, Anchorage, 1988-91; pvt. practice, Anchorage, 1991—. Mem. ABA (dist. rep. young lawyers div. 1984-86, forum com. on communications 1984-86, co-chmn. internat. law com. 1986—, asst. editor The Affiliate Newsletter), Wash. Bar Assn., Alaska Bar Assn. (v.p. 1986—, chmn. Young Lawyers Sect. 1984-85). Alaska Bar Assn. (chmn. statutes, by-laws and rules com. 1984-86), Anchorage Assn. Women Lawyers, Anchorage Bar Assn. (bd. dirs. 1984—, 2d v.p. 1986—, chmn. young lawyers sect. 1985), Alaska Workd Affairs Council, Anchorage Resource Devel. Council, Phi Beta Kappa. General civil litigation, General practice, Private international. Office: 3300 C St Ste 200 Anchorage AK 99503-3942

ALLISON, JOHN ROBERT, lawyer, educator, author; b. Waco, Tex., Apr. 6, 1948; s. Lloyd Burton and Mary LaBertha (Fulps) A.; m. Margo Lu Armstrong, Dec. 22, 1971; children: Sarah Marie, Jill Elaine, Eric Forrest. Student Tex. A&M U., 1966-69; JD, Baylor U., 1972. Bar: Tex. 1972. Asst. prof. U. Tex., Austin, 1972-77, assoc. prof., 1977-81, prof. 1981-83, Mary John and Ralph Spence Centennial prof. in bus. adminstrn., 1983—; dir. Ctr. for Legal and Regulatory Studies, 1987—. Staff editor Am. Bus. Law Jour., Austin, 1974-78, co-editor, 1978-79, articles editor, 1979-81, mng. editor, 1981-83, editor-in-chief 1983-85, adv. editor 1985—; author: Business Law: Text and Cases, 1978, 6th edit., 1994; Business Law: Alternate Edition, 1979, 5th edit., 1992; The Legal Environment of Business, 1984, 4th edit., 1993; Fundamentals of Business Law, 1984; editor-in-chief Baylor Law Rev., 1971-72; contbr. articles to profl. jours. Mem. and contbr. Assn. for Retarded Citizens, 1974—, Am. Diabetes Assn., 1981—; bd. dirs. Dispute Resolution Ctr. Austin/Travis County, 1989-90. Recipient Best Article award Am. Bus. Law Jour., 1977; named Outstanding Prof. Grad. Sch. Bus., U. Tex., 1984. Mem. Acad. Legal Studies in Bus. (exec. com. 1983-84, Holmes/Cardozo award 1985, Faculty Excellence award 1987). Democrat. Home: 8616 Cameron Loop Austin TX 78745-7916 Office: U Tex Grad Sch Bus Mgmt Sci Info Systems Dept Austin TX 78712

ALLISON, JOHN ROBERT, lawyer; b. San Antonio, Feb. 9, 1945; s. Lyle (stepfather) and Beatrice (Kaliner) Forehand; m. Rebecca M. Picard; 1 child, Katharine. BS, Stanford U., 1966; JD, U. Wash., 1969. Bar: Wash. 1969, D.C. 1973, Minn. 1994, U.S. Supreme Ct. 1973. Assoc. Garvey, Schubert & Barer, Seattle, 1969-73; ptnr., 1973-86; prin. Betts, Patterson & Mines, P.S., 1986-94; sr. counsel Minn. Mining & Mfg. Co., 1994-2000, asst. gen. counsel, 2000—. Lectr. bus. law Seattle U., 1970, U. Wash.,

1970-73; judge pro tem, King County Superior Ct., 1983-94. Mem. ABA (vice chmn. toxic and hazardous substances and environ. law com. 1986-91, chair elect 1991-92, chair 1992-93), Minn. Bar Assn., Seattle-King County Bar Assn. (chmn. jud. evaln. polling com. 1982-83), Wash. State Bar Assn. (bd. bar examiners 1984-94), D.C. Bar Assn., Nat. Inst. Pollution Liability (co-chmn. 1988), Order of the Coif. Federal civil litigation, State civil litigation, Product liability. Office: Minn Mining & Mfg Co 3 M Ctr Saint Paul MN 55144-1000 E-mail: jrallison@mmm.com

ALLISON, JONATHAN, retired lawyer; b. Washington, Apr. 17, 1916; s. Albert Johnson and Etta (Tucker) A. BS, Washington and Jefferson Coll., 1937; JD, U. Pa., 1940; postgrad., Harvard Grad. Bus. Adminstrn., 1940-41. Bar: Pa. 1942. Pvt. practice, Washington, 1946-95; ret., 1995. Maj. AUS, 1941-46. Mem. ABA, Pa. Bar Assn., Washington County Bar Assn., Duquesne Club (Pitts.), Southpointe Golf Club, St. Clair Country Club (Upper St. Clair). Republican. Presbyterian. Home: 20 Fairmont Ave Washington PA 15301-3509 Office: 438 Washington Trust Bldg Washington PA 15301

ALLISON, RICHARD CLARK, judge; b. N.Y.C., July 10, 1924; s. Albert Fay and Anice (Clark) A.; m. Anne Elizabeth Johnston, Oct. 28, 1950; children: Anne Sidney, William Scott, Richard Clark. BA, U. Va., 1944, LLB, 1948. Bar: N.Y. 1948. Practiced in, N.Y.C., 1948-52, 54-60; ptnr. Reid & Priest, 1961-87; mem. Iran-U.S. Claims Tribunal, The Hague, 1988—. With USNR, 1942-46. Fellow Southwestern Legal Found., Am. Bar Found. (life); mem. ABA (chmn. com. Latin Am. Law 1964-68, chmn. Internat. Law Sect. 1977, chmn. Nat. Inst. on Doing Bus. in Far East 1972, chmn. internat. legal exchange program 1981-85), Internat. Bar Assn. (chmn. 1986 Conf., ethics com. 1986-89), Société Internat. des Avocats, Inter-Am. Bar Assn., Am. Fgn. Law Assn., Am. Arbitration Assn. (nat. panel), Inst. for Transnational Arbitration, Am. Soc. Internat. Law, Coun. on Fgn. Rels., Assn. Bar City N.Y., Raven Soc., SAR, St. Andrew's Soc. N.Y., Manhasset Bay Yacht Club, Phi Beta Kappa, Omicron Delta Kappa, Pi Kappa Alpha, Phi Delta Phi. Republican. Episcopalian. Home: 224 Circle Dr Manhasset NY 11030-1123 Office: c/o Iran-US Claims Tribunal Parkweg 13 2585 JH The Hague The Netherlands

ALLISON, STEPHEN PHILIP, lawyer; b. L.A., Jan. 4, 1947; s. Philip L. and Catherine (Lawder) A.; m. Margaret Ann Yochem, June 7, 1969; children— Brian Clayton, Todd Lawder. BA, Tex. Christian U., 1969; JD, U. Houston, 1972. Bar: Tex. 1972, U.S. Ct. Appeals (5th cir.) 1977, U.S. Supreme Ct. 1977, U.S. Dist. Ct. (we. dist.) Tex. 1981, U.S. Dist. Ct. (no. dist.) Tex. 1988, U.S. Dist. Ct. (so. dist.) Tex. 1990. Asst. dist. atty. Bexar County, San Antonio, 1973-77; assoc. Dobbins, Harris & Gonzalez, San Antonio, 1977-78, Sawtelle, Goode, Davidson & Troilo, San Antonio, 1978-89; ptnr. Haynes and Boone, 1989—; mcpl. judge City of Terrell Hills, 1987-91; admissions com. Tex. Supreme Ct., 1978-82. Author: Products Liability, Texas Practice Guide, 1985, Accident Investigation and Product Education: Defendant's Perspective, 1985, Obtaining and Presenting Evidence on Geographic Markets, 1987, Nonprice Predation Under Section 2 of the Sherman Act, 1991, Representing Financial Institutions in a Usury Case, 1992, Drafting and Responding to Interrogatories and Requests for Production of Documents, 1995, Document Control and Management in Complex Cases, 1995. Pres., Tex. Christian U.-San Antonio Alumni Club, 1978-83. Mem. Edn. Task Force, Greater San Antonio C. of C., 1991—; bd. trustees Alamo Heights Ind. Sch. Dist., 1992—, pres., 1995-96; active Meth. Hosp. Found., 1987-94, Golden Circle, SW Found. Biomedical Rsch., 1993—; mem. vestry St. Mark's Episcopal Ch., 1988-91. Fellow Tex. Bar Found.; mem. ABA, Def. Research Inst., State Bar of Tex. (mem. com. PEER 1983-86, mem. com. ct. costs, efficiency and delay 1985-87, Citizens and Law Focused Edn. 1988-91), Tex. Assn. Def. Counsel (dir. def. counsel San Antonio 1993—), San Antonio Bar Assn. (chmn. legal ethics com. 1992-94), San Antonio Bar Found., Tex. Assn. Sch. Bds. (mem. spl. com. on revenue and funding 1994-95), Tex. Christian U. Alumni Assn. (dir. 1979-83), Tex. Christian U. Frog Club (dir. 1992—, Alumni Svc. award 1996), Order of Alamo, Los Compadres, Town Club. Republican. Lodge: Olmos Kiwanis (San Antonio). Federal civil litigation, State civil litigation. Home: 200 Morningside Dr San Antonio TX 78209-4734

ALLOTTA, JOSEPH JOHN, lawyer; b. Rochester, N.Y., May 1, 1947; m. Elizabeth Dingwall, July 17, 1971; children: John Joseph, Leslie Denise, Jeffrey James. BA, Am. U., 1969; JD, Case Western Res. U., 1972. Bar: Ohio 1972. Law clk. to presiding judge U.S. Dist. Ct. (no. dist.) Ohio, 1972-74; assoc. Gallon, Kalniz & Iorio, 1974-79; sr. ptnr. Allotta & Farley, Toledo, 1979—. Instr. U. Toledo, 1975-76. Pres., St. Matthew's Found.; Dem. precinct committeeman Sylvania Twp., 1983—. With U.S. Army, 1969-75. Fellow: Labor and Employment Law Lodge; mem.: ABA (employment law sect., chmn. subcom. publs. 1990), Ohio State Bar Assn. (labor law sect., bd. govs. 1979—85), Internat. Boilermakers (hon.)), Health Club. Avocations: logging, writing. Federal civil litigation, Labor, Pension, profit-sharing, and employee benefits. Home: 6127 Cross Trails Rd Sylvania OH 43560-1715 Office: Allotta & Farley 2222 Centennial Rd Toledo OH 43617-1870 E-mail: jallotta@allotta-farley.com

ALM, STEVE, former prosecutor; m. Haunani Ho; 1 child. MEd, U. Oreg., 1979; JD, U. Pacific, 1983. Editor West Pub. Co., 1983-85; dep. prosecuting atty. City and County of Honolulu, 1985-87, line-dep., then felony team supr., 1987-90, dir. dist. and family ct. divsn., 1990-94; U.S. atty. for Hawaii U.S. Dept. Justice, Honolulu, 1994—2001. Adj. prof. Richardson Sch. Law U. Hawaii. Mem. ABA (mem. gov. com. on crime), Hawaii State Bar Assn. (ex-officio mem. domestic violence coordinating coun., v.p. criminal justice and corrections sect.).*

ALMAN, EMILY ARNOW, lawyer, sociologist; b. N.Y.C., Jan. 20, 1922; d. Joseph Michael and Cecilia (Greenstone) Arnow; B.A., Hunter Coll., 1948; Ph.D., New Sch. for Social Research, 1963; J.D., Rutgers U., Newark, 1977; m. David Alman, Aug. 1, 1940; children: Michelle Alman Harrison, Jennifer Alman Michaels. Bar: N.J. 1978, U.S. Supreme Ct. 1987. Probation officer, N.Y.C., 1945-48; assoc. prof. sociology Douglass Coll. Rutgers U., Newark, 1960-86, prof. emeritus, 1986—; sr. ptnr. Alman & Michaels, Highland Park, N.J., 1978—. Candidate for mayor, City of East Brunswick, 1972; chmn. Concerned Citizens of East Brunswick, 1970-78; pres. bd. trustees Concerned Citizens Environ. Fund., East Brunswick, 1977-78. Mem. ABA (com. family law) N.J. Bar Assn. (bd. dirs. legal svcs), Middlesex County Bar Assn. (Ann. Aldona Appleton award women lawyers sect. 1990, Ann. Svc. to Families award 1993), Am. Sociol. Assn., Assn. Fed. Bar State of N.J., Assn. Trial Lawyers Am., Trial Lawyers Assn. Middlesex County, Law and Soc. Assn., Am. Judicature Soc., Nat. Assn. Women Lawyers, N.J. Assn. Women Lawyers, ACLU, AAUP, Women Helping Women. Author: Ride The Long Night, 1963; screenplay, The Ninety-First Day, 1963. General civil litigation, Family and matrimonial, Probate. Home: 611 S Park Ave Highland Park NJ 08904-2928

ALONSO, ANTONIO ENRIQUE, lawyer; b. Havana, Cuba, Aug. 31, 1924; came to U.S., 1959; s. Enrique and Inocencia (Avila) A.; m. Daisy Ojeda, July 20, 1949; children: Margarita, Antonio, Enrique, Jorge. JD, U. Habana, Cuba, 1946; PhD, U. Habana, 1952; student, U. Fla., 1974-76. Bar: Fla. 1976. Pub. defendant High Ct. Las Villas, Cuba, 1946-49; atty. Provincial Gov., Cuba, 1950-52; under sec. Treasury, Cuba, 1952-54; mem. House of Reps. Congress of Cuba, 1954-58; prof. U. Jose Marti, 1952-58, Inst. Soc. Action, 1964-65; prof. modern lang. Coll. St. Teresa, 1968; sole practice Miami, 1976—. Adj. prof. St. Mary's Coll., Minn., summers, 1968-73. Author: (with others) Violation of Human Rights in Cuba, 1962, History of the Communist Party of Cuba, 1970; weekly columnist on real estate and law Diario Las Ams. newspaper; contbr. articles to profl. jours. Recipient Field Svc. Program award Nat. Assn. Student Affairs, 1973. Mem. AAUP, Am. Assn. Tchrs. Spanish and Portuguese, Fla. Bar Assn. Republican. Roman Catholic. General corporate, Real property. Home: 1900 SW 12th Ave Miami FL 33129-2613 Office: 1699 Coral Way Ste 315 Miami FL 33145-2860

ALPER, JOANNE FOGEL, lawyer; b. N.Y.C., Sept. 16, 1950; d. Ben R. and Florence D. (Schneider) Fogel; m. Paul Edward Alper, Aug. 4, 1973; children: Michael Ian, Brooke Lauren. BA, Syracuse U., 1972; JD, George Washington U., 1975. Bar: Va. 1975, U.S. Dist. Ct. (ea. dist.) Va. 1975, D.C. 1976, U.S. Dist. Ct. D.C. 1976, U.S. Ct. Appeals (4th and D.C. cirs.) 1978, U.S. Supreme Ct. 1980. Assoc. Leonard, Cohen & Gettings, Arlington, Va., 1975-79; ptnr. Cohen, Gettings, Alper & Dunham, Arlington, 1979—; subs. judge Juvenile and Domestic Rels. Ct., 17th Jud. Dist. Mem. Arlington County Fair Housing Bd., 1984-88, mem. Commn. on Arlington's Future, 1986. Fellow Am. Acad. Matrimonial Lawyers; mem. Arlington Bar Assn. (pres. 1982-83), Va. State Bar (bar coun. 1989—, pres. conf. local bar assns. 1984-85 , chmn. family law sect. 1985-86), Va. Trial Lawyers Assn. (dist. gov. 1983-87, gov. at large 1987—), No. Va. Young Lawyers Assn. (pres. 1979, v.p. Arlington County 1978). Federal civil litigation, State civil litigation, Family and matrimonial. Home: 5601 Little Falls Rd Arlington VA 22207-1566 Office: Cohen Gettings Alper & Dunham 2200 Wilson Blvd Arlington VA 22201-3324

ALPERT, JONATHAN LOUIS, lawyer; b. Balt., Aug. 4, 1945; s. Leo M. and Louise (Altheimer) A.; m. Elizabeth LaPinta, June 12, 1979; children: Sara Louise, Rachel Leah. BA, Johns Hopkins U., 1966; JD, U. Md., 1969; LLM, Harvard U., 1970. Bar: Fla. 1969, Md. 1969, U.S. Supreme Ct. 1973, U.S. Ct. Appeals (5th cir.) 1970, U.S. Ct. Appeals (11th cir.) 1981, U.S. Dist. Ct. (so. dist.) Fla., 1970, U.S. dist. Ct. (mid. dist.) Fla., 1977. Ptnr. Alpert & Alpert, Miami, Fla., 1970-77; judge indsl. claims State of Fla., St. Petersburg, 1977-79; assoc. prof. Stetson Law Sch., 1979-82; ptnr. Fowler, White, Gillen, et al., Tampa, Fla., 1982-86; sr. ptnr. Alpert & Ferrentino P.A., 1986—. Reporter Gov.'s Advisors on the Workers' Compensation Bill, 1979; lectr. numerous seminars, 1979—; bd. dirs. Suncoast chpt. Am. Concrete Inst., Tampa; adj. prof. Stetson Law Sch., St. Petersburg, 1977-79. Author: Florida Worker's Compensation Law, 5th edit., 1991, also current supplements, Florida Law Damages, 1990, Automobile Reparations--The Law in Florida, 1991, Florida Real Estate, 1991, also current supplements, Florida Settlement and Release, 1991, and current supplements, Florida Motor Vehicle No Fault Law, 1992, also current supplements; contbr. numerous articles to profl. jours. Bd. dirs. Pinellas Safety Coun., Clearwater, Fla., 1977-80; chmn. coll. law admissions com. Stetson U., 1980-81; com. west Fla. Johns Hopkins U., Tampa, 1985-86. Recipient Torch award Nat. Safety Coun., Pinellas County, 1989. Master Ferguson-White Inns of Ct.; mem. ABA, Am. Arbitration Assn., Am. Trial Lawyers Assn. (DRI Scribes), Am. Soc. Legal History, Fla. Bar Assn. (asst. sec. 1986—, co-chmn. adminstrv. law sect. 1981-82, others), Am. Judicature Soc., Selden Soc., Scribes. Avocations: reading, writing, boating, swimming. General civil litigation, Consumer commercial, Securities. Office: Alpert & Ferrentino PA 100 S Ashley Dr Ste 2000 Tampa FL 33602-5313

ALPERT, MICHAEL EDWARD, lawyer; b. Annapolis, Md., Nov. 13, 1942; s. Myron M. and Mary A. (Byrnes) A.; m. Deirdre Lehn Whittleton, Jan. 1, 1964; children: Lehn Patricia, Kristin Anne, Alison Daley. AB, Pomona Coll., 1965; JD, UCLA, 1969. Bar: Calif. 1970. Assoc. Gibson, Dunn & Crutcher, L.A., 1969-72, L.A. and San Diego, 1974-77; chief dep. commr. corps. State of Calif., 1972-74; ptnr. Gibson, Dunn & Crutcher, L.A. and San Diego, 1977-92, of counsel, 1992—. Mem. editl. bd. UCLA Law Rev., 1967-69. Bd. dirs. Foodmaker, Inc., 1992—, San Diego Repertory Theatre, 1978-89, pres., 1988; mem. San Diego County Juvenile Justice Commn., 1993-97, vice-chmn., 1995, chmn., 1996, Calif. Little Hoover Commn., 1994—, vice chmn., 1995—; bd. dirs. San Diego chpt. Assn. Corp. Growth, 1987-89; mem. exec. bd. Calif. State Dem. Party. Mem. State Bar Calif., San Diego County Bar Assn., San Diego Corp. Fin. Coun. (chmn. 1982-83), Order of Coif, Lomas Santa Fe Country Club (San Diego), Phi Sigma Alpha. General corporate, Mergers and acquisitions, Securities. Office: Gibson Dunn & Crutcher 401 W A St San Diego CA 92101-7901

ALSCHULER, ALBERT W. law educator; b. Aurora, Ill., Sept. 24, 1940; s. Sam and Winifred (King) A.; m. Louise Evans, Mar. 21, 1970 (div. 1977); 1 child, Samuel Jonathan. AB, Harvard U., 1962, LLB, 1965. Bar: Ill. 1965. Prof. law U. Tex., Austin, 1969-76, U. Colo., Boulder, 1976-84, U. Pa., Phila., 1984, U. Chgo., 1985-88, Wilson-Dickinson, 1988—. E-mail: al-alscholer@law.uchicago.edu. Office: U Chgo Sch Law 1111 E 60th St Chicago IL 60637-2776

ALSDORF, ROBERT HERMANN, lawyer; b. Ashland, Ohio, Mar. 5, 1946; s. Howard Alton and Henrietta (Bulleit) A.; m. Sarah Jane Schlick, Nov. 27, 1970; children: Matthew William, Paul August. B.A. magna cum laude, Carleton Coll., 1967; M.A. in U.S. History, Yale U., 1973, J.D., 1973. Bar: D.C. 1973, Wash. 1975, U.S. Dist. Ct. (we. dist.) Wash. 1975, U.S. Ct. Appeals (9th cir.) 1975, U.S. Dist. Ct. (ea. dist.) Wash. 1981, U.S. Supreme Ct. 1984. Trial atty. Dept. Justice, Washington, 1973-75; assoc. Culp, Dwyer, Guterson & Grader, Seattle, 1975-79; ptnr. Armstrong, Alsdorf, Bradbury & Maier P.C. and predecessor Armstrong & Alsdorf, Seattle, 1979-84, pres., 1984— ; speaker continuing legal edn. seminars; pvt. arbitrator of disputes. Author continuing legal edn. materials. Bd. dirs. Stevens Neighborhood Housing Improvement Program, Seattle, 1979-82, pres., 1980-81. Mem. ABA (antitrust sect.), Wash. State Bar Assn. (franchise law revision subcom. corp. bus. and banking com. 1985—, exec. com., sec.-treas. consumer protection antitrust and unfair bus. practices sect. 1987—), Seattle-King County Bar Assn. (com. mem. young lawyers sect. 1978-80, continuing legal edn. 1984-87), Phi Beta Kappa. Antitrust, Federal civil litigation, Securities. Home: 952 12th Ave E Seattle WA 98102-4516 Office: Armstrong Alsdorf Bradbury & Maier 1300 Hoge Bldg Seattle WA 98104

ALSOP, DONALD DOUGLAS, federal judge; b. Duluth, Minn., Aug. 28, 1927; s. Robert Alvin and Mathilda (Aaseng) A.; m. Jean Lois Tweeten, Aug. 16, 1952; children: David, Marcia, Robert. BS, U. Minn., 1950, LLB, 1952. Bar: Minn. 1952. Pvt. practice, New Ulm, Minn.; ptnr. Gislason, Alsop, Dosland & Hunter, 1954-75; judge U.S. Dist. Ct. Minn., St. Paul, 1975—, chief dist. judge, 1985-92, sr. dist. judge, 1992—. Mem. 8th cir. jud. coun., 1987-92, Jud. Conf. Com. to Implement Criminal Justice Act, 1979-87; mem. exec. com. Nat. Conf. Fed. Trial Judges, 1990-94. Chmn. Brown County (Minn.) Republican Com., 1960-64, 2d Congl. Dist. Rep. Com., 1968-72, Brown County chpt. ARC, 1968-74. Served with AUS, 1945-46. Mem. 8th Cir. Dist. Judges Assn. (pres. 1982-84), New Ulm C. of C. (pres. 1974-75), Order of Coif. Office: US Dist Ct 754 Fed Bldg 316 Robert St N Saint Paul MN 55101-1495

ALSTADT, LYNN JEFFERY, lawyer; b. Erie, Pa., Dec. 27, 1951; s. Willis Harry and Norma Margaret (Linn) A.; m. Nancy Ann Weiz, Apr. 16, 1977. BS, BA, U. Pitts., 1973, JD, 1976. Bar: Pa. 1976, U.S. Dist. Ct. (we. dist.) Pa. 1976, U.S. Patent and Trademark Office 1979, U.S. Ct. Appeals (3d cir.) 1980, U.S. Ct. Appeals (6th and Fed. cirs.)1983, U.S. Supreme Ct. 1982, U.S. Ct. Internat. Trade 1983. Assoc. Blenko, Buell, Ziesenheim & Beck, Pitts., 1976-79; ptnr. Buell, Blenko, Ziesenheim & Beck, 1979-84, Buell, Ziesenheim, Beck & Alstadt, Pitts., 1984-88, Buchanan Ingersoll, Pitts., 1988—. Adj. prof. U. Pitts. Sch. Law, 1988—, Duquesne U. Sch. Law, 1995—; dir. Internat. Congress on Tech., Pitts., 1983-84. Contbr. articles to legal jours. Treas. Moon Twp. Planning Agy., 1984; mem. Moon Twp. Vol. Fire Dept., 1981—. Recipient Samuel G. Wagner prize U. Pitts. Law Sch., 1976. Mem. ABA, Pa. Bar Assn., Allegheny County Bar Assn., Pitts. Intellectual Property Law Assn. (chmn. pub. rels. 1982-83, treas. 1993, chmn. ethics grievences and membership coms. 1994-95, dir. 2000-01, v.p. 2001-02), Rivers Club, Phi Alpha Delta. Republican. Patent, Trademark and copyright, Trade regulation. Home: 102 Greenlea Dr Moon Township PA 15108-2610

ALTEMOSE, MARK KENNETH, lawyer; b. Easton, Pa., July 21, 1965; s. Richard and Constance Irene (Silfies) Altemose; m. Jennifer Lou Abram, Nov. 24, 1995; children: Rachel Rebecca, Meghan Grace. BA in Econ., Lafayette Coll., 1987; JD, Villanova, 1990. Bar: Pa. 1990, N.J. 1990, U.S. Dist. Ct. N.J. 1991, U.S. Dist. Ct. (ea. dist.) Pa. 1991, U.S. Ct. Appeals (3rd cir.) 1991. Assoc. Korn, Kline & Kutner, Phila., 1990-91, Brown, Brown, Scott & Ferretti, Allentown, Pa., 1991-94, Knafo Law Offices, Allentown, 1994—. Hearing com. mem. Disciplinary Bd. Supreme Ct. of Pa., Harrisburg, 1995—, chmn., 1999—. Mem.: ATLA, Lehigh County Bar Assn. (co-chmn. Law Day 1995—), Pa. Trial Lawyers Assn. (bd. govs. 1998—), Pa. Bar Assn., Northampton County Bar Assn. Democrat. Presbyterian. Avocations: weightlifting, running, golf. Personal injury, Product liability, Workers' compensation. Office: Knafo Law Offices 4201 W Tilghman St Allentown PA 18104-4448 E-mail: maltemuse@knafo.com

ALTER, ELEANOR BREITEL, lawyer; b. N.Y.C., Nov. 10, 1938; d. Charles David and Jeanne (Hollander) Breitel; children: Richard B. Zabel, David B. Zabel. BA with honors, U. Mich., 1960; postgrad., Harvard U., 1960-61; LLB, Columbia U., 1964. Bar: N.Y. 1965. Atty., office of gen. counsel, ins. dept. State of N.Y., 1964-66; assoc. Miller & Carlson, N.Y.C., 1966-68, Marshall, Bratter, Greene, Allison & Tucker, N.Y.C., 1968-74, mem. firm, 1974-82, Rosenman & Colin, 1982-97, Kasowitz, Benson, Torres & Friedman, N.Y.C., 1997—. Fellow U. Chgo. Law Sch., 1988; adj. prof. law NYU Sch. Law, 1983-87; vis. prof. law U. Chgo., 1990-91, 93; lectr. in field. Editorial bd.: N.Y. Law Jour. Contbr. articles to profl. jours. Trustee Lawyers' Fund for Client Protection of the State of N.Y., 1983—, chmn., 1985—; bd. visitors U. Chgo. Law Sch., 1984-87. Mem. Am. Law Inst., Am. Coll. Family Trial Lawyers, N.Y. State Bar Assn., Assn. of Bar of City of N.Y. (libr. com. 1978-80, com. on matrimonial law 1977-81, 87-88, judiciary com. 1981-84, 94, 95, 96, exec. com. 1988-92), Am. Acad. Matrimonial Lawyers. Family and matrimonial. Office: Kasowitz Benson Et Al 1301 Avenue Of The Americas New York NY 10019-6022

ALTIERI, PETER LOUIS, lawyer; b. Norwalk, Conn., Dec. 7, 1955; s. John L. and Eileen Mary (Rudden) A.; m. Sandra Shelton White, Sept. 3, 1983; children: Brianna Burr, John Shelton. AB, Georgetown U., 1977; JD, Fordham Sch. Law, 1980. Bar: N.Y. 1981, U.S. Dist. Ct. (so. dist., ea. dist.) N.Y. 1981, U.S. Dist. Ct. (no. dist. and we. dist.) N.Y. 1983, U.S. Dist. Ct. Conn. 1983, U.S. Supreme Ct. 1984, U.S. Ct. Appeals (2d. cir.) 1986, Conn. 1987. Law clk. to judge U.S. Dist. Ct., 1978; intern U.S. Attys. Office, N.Y.C., 1978; assoc. Law Firm Malcolm A. Hoffmann, 1980-87; ptnr. Epstein, Becker & Green, 1987—. Mem. ABA, Conn. Bar Assn. (exec. com. antitrust sect. 1988—), Assn. Bar City N.Y. (com. uniform state laws 1985-88, com. on inter-Am. affairs 1997-99), The Patterson Club Conn., Union League Club N.Y.C. Antitrust, General civil litigation, Labor. Home: 140 Burr St Fairfield CT 06430-7105 Office: Epstein Becker & Green 250 Park Ave Ste 1201 New York NY 10177-0001 E-mail: paltieri@ebglaw.com

ALTMAN, LEO SIDNEY, lawyer; b. Denver, May 6, 1911; s. Simon and Gisela (Marmorstein) A.; m. Helen Kimball, Aug. 30, 1949 (dec. Dec. 28, 1999). JD, U. Colo., 1935. Bar: Colo. 1935. Ptnr. Koperlik & Altman, Pueblo, Colo., 1935-56, Preston & Altman, Pueblo, 1956-64, Preston, Altman & Parlapiano, Pueblo, 1964-80, Preston, Altman, Parlapiano, Keilbach & Lytle, Pueblo, 1981-94, Altman, Keilbach, Lytle & Parliapiano, Pueblo, 1994-96, Altman, Keilbach, Lytle, Parlapiano & Ware, Pueblo, 1996—. Mcpl. ct. judge, Pueblo, 1942-50; U.S. commr., Pueblo, 1937-41. V.p. Pueblo Met. Mus. Bd., 1970-76; mem. Pueblo Civic Symphony bd., 1968-69; bd. dirs. Pueblo chpt. ARC, 1959-72, chmn., 1961, resolutions com. nat. ARC, 1963, mem. We. Area adv. counsel ARC, 1970-73; pres. Temple Emanuel Congregation, 1952; pres. Allied Jewish Coun. of Pueblo, 1946-47; pres. Family Svc. Soc., 1951-52; comdr. Pueblo Post 2 Am. Legion, 1946, Dist. 8. Colo., 1948; mem. Pueblo Cmty. welfare coun., 1948. Served to lt. col. U.S. Army, 1942-46, Res., 1946-66. Fellow Am. Coll. Trust and Estate Counsel; mem. ABA, Colo. Bar Assn. (bd. govs. 1953-56, v.p. 1956), Pueblo County Bar Assn. (pres. 1952, chmn. grievance com. 1956-61), Colo. State Bd. Law Examiners (law com. 1964-68), B'nai B'rith (pres. Pueblo lodge 524 1940), Pueblo Knife and Fork Club (pres. 1946-47), Pueblo Monday Evening (pres. 1966-67), Pi Lambda Phi. Republican. Jewish. Estate planning, Probate, Estate taxation. Home: 1111 Bonforte Blvd Apt 810 Pueblo CO 81001-1830 Office: Altman Keilbach Lytle Parlapiano & Ware 229 Colorado Ave Pueblo CO 81004-2003

ALTMAN, LOUIS, lawyer, author, educator; b. N.Y.C., Aug. 6, 1933; s. Benjamin and Jean (Zimmerman) A.; m. Sally J. Schlesinger, Dec. 26, 1955 (dec.); 1 child: Andrew; m. Eleanor Silver, Oct. 30, 1966; 1 child: Robert. AB, Cornell U., 1955; LLB, Harvard U., 1958. Bar: N.Y. 1959, Conn. 1970, Ill. 1973. Assoc. Amster & Levy, N.Y.C., 1958-60; patent atty. Sperry Rand, 1960-63; chief patent counsel Gen. Time Corp., 1963-67; ptnr. Altman & Reens, Stamford, Conn., 1967-72; chief patent counsel Baxter Labs, Deerfield, Ill., 1972-76; assoc. prof. John Marshall Law Sch., 1976-79, adj. prof., 1979-96, Loyola Law Sch., 1996-97; of counsel Gerlach, O'Brien & Kleinke, Chgo., 1981-83; ptnr. Michael Best & Friedrich, 1983-2001; of counsel, 2001—. Author: Callmann on Unfair Competition, Trademarks & Monopolies, 4th edit., 1981, Business Competition Law Adviser, 1983; contbr. Construction Law, 1986, Legal Compliance Checkups, 1985, articles to legal jours. Recipient Gerald Rose Meml. award John Marshall Law Sch., 1988. Intellectual property, Patent, Trademark and copyright. Home: 3005 Manor Dr Northbrook IL 60062-6947 Office: Michael Best & Friedrich 401 N Michigan Ave Chicago IL 60611-4255 E-mail: LALTMAN@ATTglobal.net

ALTMAN, ROBERT, lawyer; b. St. Paul, Feb. 21, 1949; s. Milton and Helen (Horwitz) A.; m. Margo Geller, Mar. 28, 1998; children: (by previous marriage: Jesse, David, Aaron. BA, U. Calif., Berkeley, 1970; JD, U. Minn., 1973. Bar: Minn. 1975, Ga. 1978, U.S. Ct. Appeals (5th cir.) 1978, U.S. Ct. Appeals (11th cir.) 1981, U.S. Supreme Ct. 1981. Atty. Team Def. Project, Atlanta, 1976-77; assoc. dir. So. Prisoners Def. Com., New Orleans, 1978-79; exec. dir. Fed. Defender Program, Inc., 1980-84; pvt. practice Atlanta, 1984—; judge Mcpl. Ct. City of Atlanta, 1988-96. Bd. dirs. Fed. Defender Program, Inc., 1985-91, pres., 1990=91; instr. Nat. Inst. Trial Advocacy, Emory U., Atlanta, 1983—; mem. com. to rev. the criminal justice act U.S. Jud. Conf., 1991-93. Mem. Ga. Bar Assn., Atlanta Bar Assn. (Blue Ribbon commn.), Assn. Trial Lawyers Am., Ga. Trial Lawyers Assn. (chair bad faith ins. litigation group, mem. exec. com. 1999), Nat. Assn. Criminal Def. Lawyers, Ga. Assn. Criminal Def. Laywers. General civil litigation, Criminal, Insurance. Office: 1355 Peachtree St NE Ste 1560 Atlanta GA 30309-3275 E-mail: altlaw@mindspring.com

ALTON, ANN LESLIE, judge, lawyer, educator; b. Pipestone, Minn., Sept. 10, 1945; d. Howard Robert, Jr. and Camilla Ann (DeMong) A.; m. Gerald Russell Freeman Sr.; children: Brady Michael Alton Freeman, Matthew Alton Freeman (dec.). BA, Smith Coll., 1967; JD, U. Minn., 1970; postgrad., Nat. Jud. Coll., U. Nev., 1989. Bar: Minn. 1970, U.S. Dist. Ct. Minn. 1972, U.S. Supreme Ct. 1981. Apptd. gen. jurisdiction state trial ct. judge civil and criminal jurisdiction Dist. Ct., 4th Jud. Dist., Hennepin County, Minn., 1989—, elected, 1990, 96—; mem. exec. com., 1995-98; chair psychol. svcs. com., 1996-2000; vice chair adminstrv. com. Dist. Ct.,

4th Jud. Dist., Hennepin County, 1989-94, asst. county atty. Mpls., 1970-89, felony prosecutor, criminal divsn., 1970-75, acting chief citizen protection divsn., 1975-76, chief citizen protection/econ. crime divsn., 1976-79, chief econ. crime unit, 1979-85, sr. atty. civil divsn. handling labor and employment law, 1989-89, mem. civil com., 1989—, presiding judge probate/mental health div., 1995-98, mem. exec. com., 1995-98, chair psychol. svcs. to ct. com., 1997-2000. Adj. prof. law Hamline U. Law Sch., St. Paul, 1973-76, instr., 1977—; adj. prof. law William Mitchell Coll. Law, St. Paul, 1977—; adj. prof. U. Minn. Law Sch., 1978-82; lectr. in field, 1970—; sr. faculty Minn. Advocacy Inst., Minn. CLE, 1988—; mem. faculty Nat. Inst. Trial Advocacy, U. Notre Dame Law Sch., 1989—, asst. team leader North Ctrl. Regional Jury Trial Advocacy Course, 1991—; sr. critiquing judge Jud. Trial Skills Tng. Program Minn. Supreme Ct. Continuing Edn. Program for State Cts., 1993—; mem. faculty intensive trial advocacy program Widener U. Sch. of Law, Wilmington, Del., 1993-96; bd. dirs. Pan-O-Gold Realty Co., 1986-89, Alton Realty Co., 1986-89, Alton Found., 1999—. Author articles, pamphlet, manual. Vice-chmn. bd. dirs. Minn. Program on Victims of Sexual Assault, 1974-76; bd. dirs. Physician's Health Plan (now Allina), Health Maintenance Orgn., 1976-80, exec. com., 1977-80; mem. legal drug abuse subcom. Gov. Minn. Adv. Com. Drug Abuse, 1972-74; bd. visitors U. Minn. Law Sch., 1979-85; mem. child abuse project coordinating com. Hennepin County Med. Soc., 1982-83, chmn. corp., labor, ins. subcom., 1982. Recipient Honorable Mention Roscoe award for Excellance in Tchg. Trial Advocacy, Roscoe Pound Inst., Washington, 2000. Mem. ABA (jud. adminstrn. divsn.), Minn. Bar Assn. (criminal law, labor and employment law, civil litigation sects.), Hennepin County Bar Assn. (ethics com. 1973-76, criminal law com. 1973—, vice chmn. 1979-80, 83-84, unauthorized practice law com. 1977-78, individual rights and responsibilities com. 1977-78, labor and employment law com. 1985—, civil litigation com. 1985—), Minn. Dist. Judges Assn. (benefits com. 1991—, mem. program and edn. com. 1993—, mem. worker compensation risk mgmt. com. 1995-97), U. Minn. Law Sch. Alumni Assn. (bd. dirs. 1979-85). Office: 1251-C Hennepin County Govt Ctr 300 S 6th St Minneapolis MN 55487 also: 1251-C Hennepin County Govt Ctr Minneapolis MN 55487 E-mail: ann.alton@co.hennepin.mn.us

ALTON, HOWARD ROBERT, JR. lawyer, real estate and food company executive; b. Pipestone, Minn., May 12, 1927; s. Howard Robert Sr. and Vera Edna (Boehmke) A.; m. Camilla Ann DeMong; children: Ann, Jeanine, Howard R. III, Patricia, Michelle. BBA, U. Minn., 1950; JD cum laude, Hamline U., 1975. Bar: Minn., 1975, U.S. Ct. Appeals (8th cir.) 1975, U.S. Dist. Ct. Minn. 1976. Founder Hamline Sch. Law, 1972-74, Alton, Severson & Sovis, Apple Valley, Minn., 1978-86, Freeman, Alton & Dodd, Mpls., 1987-88; sr. counsel, chief exec. officer Pan-O-Gold Baking Co., Wayzata and St. Cloud, Minn.; now ret. With U.S. Marines, 1945-46. Mem. Minn. Young Pres. Orgn. (past chmn.), Minn. Execs. Orgn. Forum (past chmn.), The Mpls. Club, Old Port Cove Yacht Club, North Palm Beach City Club, Gt. Lakes Cruising Club, Wayzata Country Club, Ocean Reef Club. Avocations: conservation, wildlife preservation, power boating. General corporate. Home and Office: PO Box 619 Wayzata MN 55391-0619

ALWORTH, CHARLES WESLEY, lawyer, engineer; b. Buenos Aires, Aug. 23, 1943; s. Cecil Dwight and Kathleen Mary (Whitaker) A.; m. Sally Ann Wells, Dec. 21, 1967 (div. Nov. 1981); m. Madeline E. Wilson, Feb. 14, 1983; children: Cecil Dwight II, Barbara Diane. BSEE, U. Okla., 1965, M in Elec. Engring., 1967, PhD, 1969; JD, U. Tulsa, 1992. Bar: U.S. Patent Bar Office 1989, Tex. 1993, U.S. Dist. Ct. (ea. dist.) Tex. 1993; registered profl. engr., La., Okla., Tex. Tchg. asst. elec. engring. U. Okla., Norman, 1965, grad. asst. elec. engring., 1965-67, spl. instr. elec. engring., 1967-68; asst. prof. elec. engring. Tex. A&M U., College Station, Tex., 1968-74; chief, prin. cons. Conoco, Inc., Ponca City, Okla., 1974-90; rsch. assoc. profl. engr. U. Tulsa, 1990—; chief engr. Alworth Cons., Tyler, Tex., 1990—; of counsel Sefrna & Assocs., 1993-95; prin. Charles W. Alworth Engr. & Atty. at Law; assoc. prof. and head elec. engring. U. Tex., Tyler, 1997-98. Patentee in field; contbr. articles to profl. jours. Mem. Phi Delta Phi, Tau Beta Pi, Eta Kappa Nu, Sigma Xi. Episcopalian. Avocations: aviation, woodworking, gardening. Intellectual property, Patent, Trademark and copyright. Home: 505 Cumberland Rd Tyler TX 75703-9325

AMADEO, NATIAL SALVATORE, lawyer; b. Jersey City, Oct. 2, 1955; s. Nataile Michael and Gussie (Calato) A.; m. Jane Marie Drafke, Aug. 16, 1980; children:— Nataile, Anthony, Amalia, Andrew. A.B., U. Notre Dame, 1977; J.D., Duke U., 1980. Bar: N.J. 1980, Ill. 1981. Assoc. Arthur F. Lobbe, Jersey City, 1981-82; ptnr. Amadeo & Miller, Jersey City, 1982—. Officer bd. dirs. Hudson unit Assn. Retarded Citizens, Jersey City, 1983—, pres., 1985; bd. dirs. N.J. Youth Correctional Facility, 1983—. Mem. Hudson C. of C., Moose. Republican. State civil litigation, Family and matrimonial, Personal injury. Office: Amadeo & Miller 1767 John F Kennedy Blvd Jersey City NJ 07305-2023

AMADO, HONEY KESSLER, lawyer; b. Bklyn., July 20, 1949; d. Bernard and Mildred Kessler; m. Ralph Albert Amado, Oct. 24, 1976; children: Jessica Reina, Micah Solomon, Gabrielle Beth. BA in Polit. Sci., Calif. State Coll., Long Beach, 1971; JD, Western State U., Fullerton, Calif., 1976. Bar: Calif. 1977, U.S. Dist. Ct. (ctrl. dist.) Calif. 1981, U.S. Ct. Appeals (9th cir.) 1981, U.S. Supreme Ct. 1994. Assoc. Law Offices of Jack M. Lasky, Beverly Hills, Calif., 1977-78; pvt. practice, 1978—. Lectr. in field. Contbr. articles to profl. jours.; mem. editl. bd. L.A. Lawyer mag., 1996—, articles coord., 1999-2000, chair, 2000-01. Mem. Com. Concerned Lawyers for Soviet Jewry, 1979-90; nat. v.p. Jewish Nat. Fund, 1995-97; bd. dirs. Jewish Nat. Fund L.A., 1990-98; sec. L.A. region, bd. dirs. , 1991-94, Am. Jewish Congress, Jewish Feminist Ctr., 1992-99, co-chair steering com., 1994-96; mem. Commn. on Soviet Jewry of Jewish Fedn. Coun. Greater L.A., 1977-83, chmn., 1979-81, commn. on edn., 1982-83, cmty. rels. com., 1979-83. Mem. Calif. Women Lawyers (bd. govs. 1988-90, 1st v.p. 1989-90, jud. evaluations co-chair 1988-90), San Fernando Valley Bar Assn. (family law mediators and arbitrators planel 1983-94, judge pro-tem panel 1987-94), Beverly Hills Bar Assn. (family law mediators panel 1985-94), L.A. County Bar Assn. (family law sect., appellate cts. com. 1987—, chmn. subcom. to examine reorgn. Calif. Supreme Ct. 1990-94, judge pro tem panel 1985-95, appellate jud. evaluations com. 1989—, editl. bd. L.A. Lawyer mag. 1996—, articles coord. 1999—, dist. 2 settlement program 1996—), Calif. State Bar, Calif. Ct. Appeal. Democrat. Jewish. Appellate, General civil litigation, Family and matrimonial. Office: 261 S Wetherly Dr Beverly Hills CA 90211-2515

AMAN, ALFRED CHARLES, JR. dean; b. Rochester, N.Y., July 7, 1945; s. Alfred Charles, Sr. and Jeannette Mary (Czebatul) A.; m. Carol Jane Greenhouse, Sept. 23, 1976 AB, U. Rochester, 1967; JD, U. Chgo., 1970. Bar: D.C. 1971, Ga. 1972, N.Y. 1980. Law clk. U.S. Ct. Appeals, Atlanta, 1970-72; assoc. Sutherland, Asbill & Brennan, 1972-75, Washington, 1975-77; assoc. prof. Sch. Law, Cornell U., Ithaca, N.Y., 1977-82, prof. law, 1983-91, exec. dir. Internat. Legal Studies Program, 1988-90; prof. law, dean Sch. Law, Ind. U., Bloomington, 1991-99, dean, Roscoe C. O'Byrne chair in law, 1999—, disting. Fulbright chair in comparative constitutional law, 1998; vis. prof. law U. Paris II, 1998. Cons. U.S. Adminstrv. Conf., Washington, 1978-80, 86—; trustee U. Rochester, 1980—; vis. fellow Wolfson Coll., Cambridge U., 1983-84, 90-91. Author: Energy and Natural Resources, 1983, Administrative Law in a Global Era, 1992, Administrative Law Treatise, 1992, 2d edit., 2001. Chmn. Ithaca Bd. Zoning Appeals, 1980-82 Mem. ABA, Am. Assn. Law Schs., D.C. Bar Assn., Ga. Bar Assn., N.Y. State Bar Assn., Phi Beta Kappa Avocations: music; jazz drumming; piano; composition and arranging. Office: Ind U Sch Law 211 S Indiana Ave Bloomington IN 47405-7001

AMAN, GEORGE MATTHIAS, III, lawyer; b. Wayne, Pa., Mar. 2, 1930; s. George Matthias and Emily (Kalbach) A.; m. Ellen McMillan, June 20, 1959; children: James E., Catherine E., Peter T. A.B., Princeton U., 1952; LL.B., Harvard U., 1957. Bar: Pa. 1958. Assoc. Townsend Elliot & Munson, Phila., 1960-65; ptnr. Morgan Lewis & Bockius, 1965-93; of counsel High, Swartz, Roberts & Seidel, Norristown, Pa., 1993—. Commr. Radnor Twp., Pa., 1976-80, 86-92, planning commr., 1981-86; pres. bd. trustees Wayne Presbyn. Ch., Pa., 1981-84. Served to 1st lt. U.S. Army, 1952-54. Mem. ABA, Pa. Mcpl. Authorities Assn., Phila. Regional Mcpl. Fin. Officers Assn. (dir. 1983-87). Republican. Clubs: Merion Cricket (Haverford, Pa.); Princeton (Phila.) (dir 1977-79, treas. 1985-86). General corporate, Municipal (including bonds). Home: 246 Upland Way Wayne PA 19087-4859 Office: High Swartz Roberts Seidel 40 E Airy St Norristown PA 19401-4803 E-mail: georgcaman@aol.com, gaman@hsrs-law.com

AMANN, LESLIE KIEFER, lawyer, educator; b. Pensacola, Fla., Dec. 21, 1955; d. Robert C. and Marilyn Joan (Franklin) K.; m. Colin B. Amann, Apr. 12, 1985; children: Augustus Kiefer, Nicholas Jacob. BMEd, S.W. Tex. State U., 1976; JD, U. Houston, 1987. Bar: Tex. 1987, U.S. Dist. Ct. (so. dist.) Tex. 1988, U.S. Ct. Appeals (5th cir.), 1991, U.S. Dist. Ct. (no. dist.) Tex. 1992. Legis. aide to Lindon Williams Tex. State Senate, Austin, 1977-81; tchr. The Lincoln Sch., Guadalajara, Mex., 1979-82; legal asst. Koons Rasor Fuller & McCurley, Dallas, 1983-84; clk., assoc., participating assoc. Reynolds, Allen, Cook, Reynolds & Cunningham, Houston, 1984-93; shareholder Cunningham & Amann, 1993-94; asst. gen. counsel Charter Bank, 1995-96; sr. v.p., fiduciary counsel Bank of America, 1996—. Adj. faculty Law Sch., U. Houston, 1988-2000; mem. faculty Tex. Bankers Assn. Trust Sch., 1998-2001. Contbr. articles to profl. jours. Mem. adv. bd. Probate and Trust Law Inst., South Tex. Coll. Law, Houston, 1998, 99, 2000; vol. Annunciation Orthodox Sch., Houston, 1996-2001; vol. Greater Houston Partnership Texas Scholars, 2000-01. Recipient Adj. Faculty award Univ. Houston Law Sch., 1999. Fellow Tex. Bar Found. (life); mem. Houston Bar Assn. (vol. lawyers in pub. schs. 1998), Tex. State Bar., Women Attys. in Tax and Probate. Republican. Methodist. Avocations: writing, reading, book collecting. General civil litigation, Estate planning, Probate. Office: Bank of America PO Box 2518 700 Louisiana 6th Fl Houston TX 77252-2518

AMBER, DOUGLAS GEORGE, lawyer; b. East Chicago, Ind., Apr. 15, 1956; s. George and Margaret (Watson) A. BA in Polit. Sci., Ind. U., 1978; JD, U. Miami, 1985. Bar: Fla. 1985, US. Ct. Claims 1986, U.S. Ct. Internat. Trade 1986, U.S. Tax Ct. 1986, U.S. Ct. Appeals (11th cir.) 1986, U.S. Dist. Ct. (mid. and so. dists.) Fla. 1987, U.S. Ct. Mil. Appeals 1987, U.S. Ct. Appeals (fed. cir.) 1987, Ind. 1988, U.S. Dist. Ct. (no. and so. dists.) Ind. 1988, U.S. Ct. Appeals (7th cir.) 1989, U.S. Supreme Ct. 1989; registered civil mediator. Dep. prosecutor 31st Jud. Cir. Ind., Crown Point, 1988-93; pvt. practice Munster, 1993—. Adj. prof. polit. sci. Purdue U., 1997—. Mem. exec. bd. dirs. Calumet coun. Boy Scouts Am., 1994-96. Mem. ABA, Acad. Legal Studies in Bus., Nat. Dist. Attys. Assn., South Lake County Bar Assn., Ind. State Bar Assn., Lake County Bar Assn. (bd. dirs. 1990-96), Ind. Trial Lawyers Assn., Audio Engring. Soc., Soc. Audio Cons. (cert. video and audio cons.), Mensa, Delta Theta Phi. Avocations: bicycling, weight training. Office: Amber Golding & Hofstetter 9250 Columbia Ave Ste E-2 Munster IN 46321-3530 E-mail: amber@axp.calumet.purdue.edu

AMBER, LAURIE KAUFMAN, lawyer; b. N.Y.C., Apr. 15, 1954; d. Martin and Barbara (Schiffman) Kaufman; m. Henry Michael Amber, June 18, 1977; children: Ian, Kyle. BS, Cornell U., 1974, MBA, 1975; JD, U. Miami, 1978. Bar: Fla. 1978, U.S. Dist. Ct. (so. dist.) Fla. 1978, U.S. Tax Ct. 1978, U.S. Ct. Appeals (5th cir.) 1979, U.S. Ct. Customs and Patent Appeals 1979, U.S. Customs Ct. 1979, U.S. Ct. Appeals (11th cir.) 1981, U.S. Ct. Internat. Trade 1981, U.S. Supreme Ct. 1982, U.S. Claims Ct. 1985; cert. civil circuit mediator Supreme Ct. Fla.; cert. family mediator Supreme Ct. Fla. Staff mgr. Proctor & Gamble Mfg. Co., Staten Island, N.Y., 1975; adj. asst. prof. Nova U., Fort Lauderdale, Fla., 1976-77; atty., labor arbitrator Amber & Amber, P.A., South Miami, 1978—. Arbitrator nat. labor panel Am. Arbitration Assn., Miami, 1982—, Grievance Arbitration Panel of Fla. PERC, Tallahassee, 1979—; hearing examiner pers. appeals County of Dade, Miami, 1985-91, 2000—; dir. Kids That Care Pediat. Cancer Fund, 1996—. Pres. Office Village Condominium Assn., South Miami, 1994, Children's Cancer Fund, 1996-2000; bd. dirs. Jackson Meml. Found., 1996-2000, Kids That Care Pediatric and Cancer Fund, 2000—. Named Woman of Yr. ABWA, 1983. Mem. ABA, Zonta (bd. dirs. Coral Gables, Fla. club 1988). General practice, Probate, Real property. Office: Amber & Amber PA 7731 SW 62nd Ave Ste 202 Miami FL 33143-4908

AMBRO, THOMAS L. federal judge; b. Cambridge, Ohio, Dec. 27, 1949; BA, Georgetown U., 1971, JD, 1975. Bar: Del. 1976. Clk. hon. Daniel L. Herrmann Del. Supreme Ct., 1975-76; assoc. Richards, Layton and Finger, 1976-82, ptnr., 1982-2000; judge U.S. Ct. Appeals (3d cir.), 2000—. Mem. State Del. Gov.'s Commn. on Major Comml. Litigation Reform, 1993; arbitration panelist Am. Arbitration Assn.; mem. N.Y. TriBar Opinion Com., 1988—. Author: Third Party Legal Opinions in Asset Based Financing: A Transactional Guide, 1990; contbr. articles to profl. jours. Mem. ABA (mem. com. on uniform comml. code, mem. com. on negotiated acquistions, mem. bus. bankruptcy com., vice-chair com. on programs 1987-90, chair com. on meetings 1988-90, chair subcom. on opinion letters 1989-95, mem. com. on comml. fin. svcs. 1989-95, mem. drafting subcom. third-party legal opinion report 1989-91, participant Silverado Conf. on Legal Opinions, 1989, chair com. on meetings 1990-94, chair com. on legal opinions 1994-98, chair or co-chair com. on publs. 1994-97, mem. coun. sect. bus. law 1994-98, editl. bd. The Bus. Lawyer, 1998-99, editor, 1999—, sec. sect. bus. law 1998-99, vice-chair sect. bus. law 1999—), Del. State Bar Assn. (chmn. 1979-82, vice-chmn. 1982-83 comml. law sect., chair subcom. on uniform comml. code 1983—), Am. Coll. Bankruptcy, Am. Bankruptcy Inst., Am. Coll. Investment Counsel, Am. Coll. Comml. Fin. Lawyers (charter, bd. regents), Phi Beta Kappa. Office: J Caleb Boggs Fed Bldg 844 N King StRoom 5122 Wilmington DE 19801-3519*

AMBROSE, MYLES JOSEPH, lawyer; b. N.Y.C., July 21, 1926; s Arthur P.. and Ann (Campbell) A.; m. Elaine Miller, June 26, 1948 (dec. Sept. 1975); children: Myles Joseph, Kathleen Anne, Kevin Arthur, Elise Mary, Nora Jeanne, Christopher Miller; m. Lorraine Genovese, June 3, 1994. Grad., New Hampton Sch., N.H., 1944; BBA, Manhattan Coll., 1948, LLD (hon.), 1972; JD, N.Y. Law Sch., 1952. Bar: N.Y. 1952, U.S. Supreme Ct. 1969, D.C. 1973, U.S. Ct. Appeals (fed. cir.) 1970, U.S. Ct. Internat. Trade 1970, D.C. Ct. Appeals 1973. Pers. mgr. Devenco, Inc., 1948-49, 51-54; adminstrv. asst. U.S. atty. So. dist., N.Y., 1954-57; instr. econs. and indsl. rels. Manhattan Coll., 1955-57; asst. to sec. U.S. Treasury, 1957-60; exec. dir. Waterfront Commn. of N.Y. Harbor, 1960-63; pvt. practice law N.Y.C., 1963-69; chief counsel N.Y. State Joint Legislative Com. for Study Alcoholic Beverage Control Law, 1963-65; U.S. commr. customs Washington, 1969-72; spl. cons. to Pres., spl. asst. atty. gen., 1972-73; ptnr. Spear & Hill, 1973-75, Ambrose & Casselman, P.C., 1975-88, O'Connor & Hannan, Washington, 1988-98, Ross and Hardies, Washington, 1998—; of counsel Arter & Hadden, 1998—. U.S. observer 13th session UN Commn. on Narcotics, Geneva, Switzerland, 1958; chmn. U.S. del. 27th Gen. Assembly, Internat. Criminal Police Orgn., London, 1958, 28th Extraordinary Gen. Assembly, Paris, 1959; U.S. observer 29th Gen. Assembly, Washington, 1960; mem. U.S. del., Mexico City, 1969, Brussels, 1970, Ottawa, 1971, Frankfurt, 1972; chmn. U.S.-Mexico Conf. on Narcotics, Washington, 1960, mem. confs., Washington and; Mexico City, 1969, 70, 71, 72; chmn. U.S.-Canadian-Mexican Conf. on Customs Procedures, San Clemente, Calif., 1970; chmn. U.S. del. Customs Cooperation Coun., Brussels, 1970; chmn., Vienna, 1971, U.S.-European Customs Conf. Narcotics, Paris and; Vienna, 1971; organized Drug Enforcement Adminstrn. (DEA), 1973; hon. consul Principality of Monaco, Washington, 1973-98; mem. adv. com. on customs comml. ops. U.S. Treasury Dept., 1988-91; past chmn. ABA standing com. on customs law. Author: Primer on Customs Law. Bd. dirs. U. Coll. of Dublin-Grad. Bus. Sch., 1996-2001, Daytop Village; vice-chmn. Reagan-Bush Inaugural Com., 1980; mem. adv. bd. Eisenhower Inst. of World Affairs. Decorated chevalier Order of Grimaldi (Monaco), knight comdr. Order of Merit Italian Republic; ; recipient Presdl. Mgmt. Improvement cert. Pres. Nixon, 1970, Sec. Treasury Exceptional Svc. award, 1970, Disting. Alumnus award N.Y. Law Sch., 1973, Alumni award for pub. svc. Manhattan Coll., 1972 Fellow Am. Bar Found.; mem. Friendly Sons of St. Patrick, Univ. Club (D.C.), Alpha Sigma Beta, Phi Alpha Delta (hon.) Republican. Roman Catholic. Federal civil litigation, Criminal, Immigration, naturalization, and customs. Home: #912 19375 Cypress Ridge Ter Lansdowne VA 20176-5182 Office: Arter & Hadden 1801 K St NW Washington DC 20006-1301 E-mail: mambrose@arterhadden.com, ballyeagna@aol.com

AMDAHL, DOUGLAS KENNETH, retired state supreme court justice; b. Mabel, Minn., Jan. 23, 1919; B.B.A., U. Minn., 1945; J.D. summa cum laude, William Mitchell Coll. Law, 1951, L.L.D. (hon.), 1987. Bar: Minn. 1951, Fed. Dist. Ct. 1952. Ptnr. Amdahl & Scott, Mpls., 1951-55; asst. county atty. Hennepin County, Minn., 1955-61; judge Mcpl. Ct., Mpls., 1961-62, Dist. Ct. 4th Dist., Minn., 1962-80, chief judge, 1973-75; assoc. justice Minn. Supreme Ct., 1980-81, chief justice, 1981-89; of counsel Rider, Bennett, Egan & Arundel, Mpls., 1989-99; ret. Asst. registrar, then registrar Mpls. Coll. Law, 1951-65; moot ct. instr. U. Minn.; faculty mem. and advisor Nat. Coll. State Judiciary; mem. Nat. Bd. Trial Advocacy; chmn. Nat. Ctr. for State Cts. Delay Reduction Adv. Com., 1986-88, Nat. Ctr. for State Cts. Coordinating Coun. on Life-Sustaining Decisionmaking by the Cts., 1989-93. Mem. ABA (chmn. com. on stds. of jud. adminstrn. 1987-96), Minn. Bar Assn., Hennepin County Bar Assn., Internat. Acad. Trial Judges, State Dist. Ct. Judges Assn. (pres. 1976-77), Conf. of Chief Judges (bd. dirs. 1987-88), Delta Theta Phi (assoc. justice supreme ct.). Home: 2322 W 53rd St Minneapolis MN 55410-2501 E-mail: damdahl@aol.com

AMDUR, ARTHUR R. lawyer; b. Houston, Jan. 19, 1946; s. Paul S. and Florence Amdur; m. Dora B.; children— Josh, Jonny, Shira. B.A., 1967; J.D., 1970; LL.M., 1974. Bar: Tex. 1970, D.C. 1974; cert. immigration law Tex. Bd. Legal Specialization, 1988 . pvt. practice, Houston and Washington, 1970-76; asst. U.S. atty, Houston, 1976-82; pvt. practice, Houston, 1982—, lectr. on immigration law ; adj. prof. law South Tex. Coll. Law, Houston. Bd. dirs. YMCA Internat. Refugee Ctr., 1985—; spl. asst. to gen. counsel Republican Nat. Com., Washington, 1974. Named Adj. Law Prof. of Yr., South Tex. Coll. Law, 1983. Mem. Fed. Bar Assn. (pres. 1981), Tex. State Bar Assn., Am. Immigration Lawyers Assn., Immigration Law Examiner, State Bar Tex. (bd. legal specialization 1997—). Jewish. Club: Georgetown U. Alumni (pres. 1984) (Houston). Federal civil litigation, Immigration, naturalization, and customs, Private international. Office: Amdur Law Office 6161 Savoy Dr Ste 450 Houston TX 77036-3379

AMDUR, MARTIN BENNETT, lawyer; b. N.Y.C., Aug. 19, 1942; s. Charles and Helen (Freedman) A.; m. Shirley Bell, May 25, 1975; children: Richard J., Stephen B. AB, Cornell U., 1964; LLB, Yale U., 1967; LLM in Taxation, NYU, 1968. Bar: N.Y. 1968, U.S. Tax Ct. 1970, U.S. Dist. Ct. (so. and ea. dists.) N.Y. 1971. Assoc. Weil, Gotshal & Manges LLP, N.Y.C., 1968-75, ptnr., 1975—. Mem. ABA, Am. Coll. Tax Counsel, N.Y. State Bar Assn., Assn. Bar City N.Y. Corporate taxation, Personal income taxation. Home: 983 Park Ave Apt 6B New York NY 10028-0808 Office: Weil Gotshal & Manges LLP 767 Fifth Ave New York NY 10153-0119 Fax: 212-310-8995. E-mail: Martin.Amdur@Weil.com

AMEND, JAMES MICHAEL, lawyer; b. Chgo., July 19, 1942; s. Nathan and Edith (Greenberg) A.; m. Sheila Rae Cohen, Apr. 4, 1971; children: Allison, Anthony. BSE, U. Mich., 1964, JD, 1967. Bar: Ill. 1968, U.S. Dist. Ct. (no. dist.) Ill. 1968, U.S. Ct. Appeals (7th cir.) 1969, U.S. Supreme Ct. 1970, U.S. Ct. Appeals (9th cir.) 1985. Ptnr. Kirkland & Ellis, Chgo., 1968—. Prof. Stanford U. Law Sch., 1996-97. Editor U. Mich. Law Rev., 1966, Patent Law: A Primer for Federal District Court Judges, 1998; author: Intellectual Property Law, 1982. Chmn. Chgo. Lawyers Com. for Civil Rights Under Law, 1985-86. Fulbright scholar, 1967. Mem. ABA, U.S. Trademark Assn. Jewish. Clubs: Saddle and Cycle, Mid-Am. (Chgo.). Avocations: running, skiing, golf. Federal civil litigation, Patent, Trademark and copyright. Office: Kirkland & Ellis 200 E Randolph St Fl 54 Chicago IL 60601-6636

AMENDOEIRA, RUI, lawyer; b. Faro, Algarve, Portugal, July 7, 1968; s. Firmino C. and Maria F. A. Law, Lisbon Law Sch., 1991. Bar: Portugal 1993. Assoc. Azevedo Neves, Benjamin Mendes e P. Miranda, 1991-96; ptnr. Pereira de Miranda, Correia & Amendoeira, Lisbon, 1997—. Avocations: tennis, jogging. Contracts commercial, General corporate, Oil, gas, and mineral. Office: Pereira Miranda Correia Amendoeira Av António Augusto Aguiar 27-2D 1069-126 Lisbon Portugal Fax: 21 314 65 54. E-mail: apdmlaw@mail.telepac.pt

AMES, JOHN LEWIS, lawyer; b. Norfolk, Va., July 15, 1912; s. Harry Lee and Catherine I. (Betty) A.; m. Margaret Kilbon, Apr. 8, 1939 (dec. Sept. 1996); children: Margaret Lee, John Lewis. AB, Randolph-Macon Coll., 1933; JD, U. Richmond, 1937; postgrad., NYU, 1939-40. Bar: Va. 1936, N.Y. 1940. Mem. tax divsn. Home Life Ins. Co., N.Y.C., 1937-38; trial atty. Tanner, Sillocks & Friend, 1938-41; house counsel Ruthrauff & Ryan, Inc., 1941-42, house counsel and asst. to pres., 1945-48, sec., counsel, 1948-50, v.p., sec., 1950-55, v.p., sec., treas., 1955-57, also dir.; v.p., sec. Erwin, Wassey, Ruthrauff & Ryan, Inc., 1957-59; asst. dir. bus. affairs CBS TV Netowrk, Inc., N.Y.C., 1959-62; v.p., sec., treas. Kudner Agy., Inc., 1962-65, also dir.; sr. v.p. adminstrn. and fin. West, Weir & Bartel, Inc., N.Y.C., 1966, exec. v.p., dir., until 1968; v.p., sec. Lennen & Newell, Inc., 1968-73; v.p. bus. and legal affairs Dancer-Fitzgerald-Samplem Inc., 1973-83; legal cons. Saatchi & Saatchi DFS Inc., 1983-96. Dir. Carroll Products, Inc.; spl. agt. FBI, Washington and N.Y.C., 1942-45; spl. dept. atty. gen. N.Y. State, 1946-48; mem. Nassau County N.Y. Crime Commn., 1973-83. Trustee Randolph-Macon Coll., 1955-85, trustee emeritus, 1985—; mem. Massapequa Bd. Edn., 1952-79, pres. 1957-78; past pres. Nassau-Soffolk Sch. Bds. Assn.; past chmn. trustees Am. Assn. Advt. Agencies Group Ins.; trustee, chmn. bd. of trustees, vice chmn., chmn. adminstrv. bd. White Stone Unite Meth. Ch. Mem. N.Y. County Lawyers Assn., Am. Arbitration Assn. (mem. nat panel), Soc. Former Spl. Agts. FBI (past nat. sec.), Alumni Soc. Randolph-Macon Coll. (past pres.), Lancaster County Crime Solvers, Inc. (pres. 1991-94, 2001—), Indian Creek Yacht and Country Club, Windmill Point Yacht Club, Phi Kappa Sigma, Omicron Delta Kappa, Tau Kappa Alpha. Methodist. Home: PO Box 727 White Stone VA 22578-0727 Office: 375 Hudson St New York NY 10014-3658

AMESTOY, JEFFREY LEE, state supreme court chief justice; b. Rutland, Vt., July 24, 1946; s. William Joseph and Diana (Wood) A.; m. Susan Claire Lonergan, May 24, 1980; children: Katherine Leigh, Christina Elizabeth, Nancy Claire. BA, Hobart Coll., 1968; JD, U. Calif., San Francisco, 1972; MPA, Harvard U., 1982; D of Pub. Adminstrn. (hon.), Norwich U., 1994. Bar: Vt. 1973, U.S. Dist. Ct. Vt. 1973. Assoc. Mahady & Klevana, Windsor, Vt., 1973-74; legal counsel Gov.'s Justice Commn., Montpelier, 1974-77; asst. atty. gen., chief of Medicaid fraud div. State of Vt., 1978-81, commr. labor and industry, 1982-84, atty. gen., 1985-97, chief justice Supreme Ct. Vt., 1997—. Pres. Nat. Assn. of Attys. Gen.,

1992-93. Trustee Thomas Waterman Wood Gallery, Montpelier, 1986-92. With USAR, 1968-74. Mem. Vt. Bar Assn., Kennedy Sch. Govt. Harvard U. Alumni Exec. Coun., Conf. Chief Justices. Republican. Congregationalist Home: 503 Loomis Hill Rd Waterbury Center VT 05677-8280

AMMOUNA, SAMI SAED, lawyer, legal consultant; b. Lattakia, Syria, Apr. 1, 1938; s. Saed Mohammed Ammouna and Wisal Murad Jarkas; m. Mariam Al Adra Soubhi Al Hallaj, July 10, 1972; children: May, Natalie, Zaina. BA in Law with honors, U. Damascus, 1968. Head pvt. edn. sect. Ministry of Edn., Lattakia, Syria, 1963-73, legal rschr. Kuwait, 1973-76, head of legal affairs, 1976-85, head of interrogation, 1985-93, min. of edn.'s personal legal cons., 1993-98; legal cons., ptnr. Khatib & Ptnrs. Attys., 1985-90, Monawer & Ptnrs. Attys., Kuwait, 1990-94, Al Mashoura Advocates and Legal Cons., Kuwait, 1994—. Arbitrator Lattakia, 1988—; mem. arbitration com. C. of C., Kuwait, 1995—; legal cons. Syrian Embassy, 1991—. Contbr. articles to profl. jours. Syrian Mil., Damascus, 1959-60. Mem. Syrian Law Assn., Syrian Educators Assn. Liberal. Islam. Civil rights, Contract and Others. Home: St #10 Block 7 Jabriya PO Box 24325 Safat Kuwait Office: Al Mashoura Advocates 2d Fl Fahed Al Salam St Sheraton Safat Kuwait Home Fax: 00965 2459000; Office Fax: 00965 5319403. E-mail: sami.ammouna@usa.net

AMON, CAROL BAGLEY, federal judge; b. 1946; BS, Coll. William and Mary, 1968; JD, U. Va., 1971. Bar: Va. 1971, D.C. 1972, N.Y. 1980. Staff atty. Communications Satellite Corp., Washington, 1971-73; trial atty. U.S. Dept. Justice, 1973-74; asst. U.S. atty. Ea. Dist. N.Y., 1974-86, U.S. magistrate, 1986-90, dist. ct. judge, 1990—. Recipient John Marshall award U.S. Dept. Justice, 1983. Mem. Assn. Bar of City of N.Y., Va. State Bar Assn. Office: US District Court 225 Cadman Plz E Brooklyn NY 11201-1818

AMSCHLER, JAMES RALPH, lawyer, relocation company executive; b. Mpls., June 29, 1943; s. Ralph Frank Amschler and June Ann (Naslund) Petrovich; m. Judith Claire Ketterbaugh, Aug. 19, 1967; 1 child, Christy Hamilton. BS, U. Wis., 1965; LLB, Stanford U., 1968. Bar: Wis. 1968, U.S. Dist. Ct. (we. dist.) Wis. 1968, Utah 1969, U.S. Dist. Ct. Utah 1969, N.Y. 1975, Conn. 1992, U.S. Supreme Ct. 1975. Instr. law U. Wis., Madison, 1968-69; assoc. VanCott, Bagley, Cornwall & McCarthy, Salt Lake City, 1969-73; asst. gen. counsel Carrier Corp., Syracuse, N.Y., 1973-83; assoc. gen. counsel Federated Dept. Stores, Cin., 1983-85; sr. v.p., gen. counsel PHH Homequity Corp., Wilton, Conn., 1985-96; prin. Diversified Adv. Svcs., Ltd., Westport, 1996—. Adj. prof. law Syracuse U., 1981-82; chmn. FTC/antitrust sub-com. Nat. Assn. Mfrs., 1982-83. Bd. dirs. Wilton (Conn.) United Way, 1985-91. Mem. N.Y. State Bar Assn., Utah Bar Assn., Wis. State Bar Assn., Conn. State Bar. Lutheran. Avocations: golf, tennis, sailing. Antitrust, Federal civil litigation, Real property. Home: 17 Cardinal Ln Westport CT 06880-1714 Office: Diversified Advisory Services Ltd 17 Cardinal Ln Westport CT 06880-1714

AMSTERDAM, MARK LEMLE, lawyer; b. N.Y.C., June 10, 1944; s. Leonard M. and Erica (Lemle) A.; children: Lauren, Matthew. AB, Columbia U., 1966, JD cum laude, 1969. Bar: N.Y. 1969, U.S. Dist. Ct. (so., ea. and no. dists.) N.Y. 1972, U.S. Dist. Ct. (no. dist.) Tex., U.S. Supreme Ct. 1973. Assoc. Fried, Frank, Harris, N.Y.C., 1969-70; staff atty. Ctr. Constl. Rights, 1970-75; atty. pvt. practice, 1975-76, 81—; ptnr. Rubin Hanley & Amsterdam, 1976-79, Katz Amsterdam & Lewinter, N.Y.C., 1980, Amsterdam & Lewinter, N.Y.C., 1990—. Instr. N.Y. Law Sch., 1982-83. Contbr. articles to profl. jours. Fellow N.Y. State Bar Assn.; mem. Gardeners Bay Country Club, Columbia Club. Federal civil litigation, State civil litigation, Criminal. Home: 1220 Park Ave New York NY 10128-1733 Office: 9 E 40th St New York NY 10016-0402

AMUNDSON, ROBERT A. state supreme court justice; m. Katherine Amundson; children: Robert, Beth, Amy. BBA, Augustana Coll., 1961; JD, U. S.D., 1964. Asst. atty. gen. Atty. Gen's. Office, 1965-69; mem. firm Belle Fourche and Lead, 1970-89; cir. judge 2d Jud. Cir., 1989-91; justice Supreme Ct. of S.D., Vermillion, 1991—. Office: Supreme Court of South Dakota State Capitol Bldg 500 E Capitol Ave Pierre SD 57501-5070*

ANANI, TARIG, lawyer; b. Riyadh, Saudi Arabia, Jan. 22, 1965; s. Faisal Anani and Diane Katherine Hill. BA cum laude, Univ. Houston, 1988, JD, 1991; MBA, Rice Univ., 1992; MS of Jurisprudence, Stanford U., 1994. Bar: Tex. 1991, Calif. 1993, U.S. Supreme Ct. 1995. Corp. assoc. Curtis, Mallet-Prevost, Colt & Mosle, Manhattan, N.Y., 1994-97; gen. counsel SAP Arabia, Jeddah, Makkah, Saudi Arabia, 1998—. Dir. Mail2World, Inc., Century City, 2000-01. Computer, General corporate, Private international.

ANCEL, JERALD IRWIN, lawyer; b. Indpls., Jan. 29, 1944; s. Harry and Margaret (Schnieder) A.; m. Gayle Elizabeth Vogel, Aug. 21, 1965; children— Jason, Jennifer, Marc. B.S. in Acctg., Ind. U.-Bloomington, 1965, J.D., 1968. Bar: Ind. 1968, U.S. Dist. Ct. (so. dist.) Ind. 1968, U.S. Dist. Ct. (no. dist.) Ind. 1980. Adjudicator, State of Ind., Indpls., 1965-68; assoc. Law Offices of Steven H. Ancel, Indpls., 1968-73, ptnr. Ancel & Ancel, Indpls., 1974-76; mng. ptnr. Ancel, Friedlander, Miroff & Ancel, Indpls., 1976-80; mng. ptnr. Ancel, Miroff & Frank, P.C., Indpls., 1981— ; lectr. Ind. Continuing Legal Edn. Forum. Author: Save Our Farms, Farm Foreclosure Prevention and Reorganization, 1983; Survey of Bankruptcy Law from Creditor's View, 1983, 84. Mem. Gov.'s Com. to Study Mental Health Laws, Indpls., 1974-76, com. chmn., 1978-80; bd. dirs., sec. Marion County Assn. Retarded Citizens, Indpls., 1978-80. Mem. ABA, Ind. Bar Assn., Indpls. Bar Assn., Comml. Law League Am., Assn. Trial Lawyers Am., Am. Bankruptcy Inst., Phi Delta Phi. Club: Broad Ripple Sertoma (pres. 1973-74). Bankruptcy, Federal civil litigation, Contracts commercial. Home: 11090 Queens Way Cir Carmel IN 46032-9636 Office: Ancel Miroff & Frank 1000 Two Market Sq Ctr PO Box 44219 Indianapolis IN 46244-0219

ANDERS, MILTON HOWARD, lawyer; b. Shreveport, La., Apr. 28, 1930; s. Howard P. and Nora Lee (Whitman) A.; m. Patsy Ruth Hollis, Sept. 4, 1954; 1 child, Mary Alison. B.S., La. Tech. U., 1951; J.D., La. State U., 1957. Bar: La. 1957, Tex. 1971. Atty. Placid Oil Co., Shreveport, 1957-60, Barnwell Industries, Shreveport, 1960-65, Mobil Corp., Shreveport, 1965-69; ptnr. Vinson & Elkins, Houston, 1969— . Mem. La. Bar Assn., Tex. Bar Assn., La. Bank Counsel Assn., Tex. Assn. Bank Counsel. Baptist. Banking, Contracts commercial, Oil, gas, and mineral. Office: Vinson & Elkins 3300 1st City Tower 1001 Fannin St Ste 3300 Houston TX 77002-6706

ANDERSEN, JAMES A. retired state supreme court justice; b. Auburn, Wash., Sept. 21, 1924; s. James A. and Margaret Cecelia (Norgaard) A.; m. Billiette B. Andersen; children: James Blair, Tia Louise. BA, U. Wash., 1949, JD, 1951. Bar: Wash. 1952, U.S. Dist. Ct. (we. dist.) Wash. 1957, U.S. Ct. Appeals 1957. Dep. pros. atty. King County, Seattle, 1953-57; assoc. Lycette, Diamond & Sylvester, 1957-61; ptnr. Clinton, Andersen, Fleck & Glein, 1961-75; judge Wash. State Ct. of Appeals, 1975-84; justice Wash. State Supreme Ct., Olympia, 1984-92, chief justice, 1992-95; ret., 1995. Chair Legis. Ethics Bd. Mem. Wash. State Ho. of Reps., 1958-67, Wash. State Senate, 1967-72. Served with U.S. Army, 1943-45, ETO. Decorated Purple Heart; recipient Disting. Alumnus award U. Wash. Sch. of Law, 1995. Mem. ABA, Wash. State Bar Assn., Am. Judicature Soc. Home: 3008 98th Ave NE Bellevue WA 98004-1817

ANDERSEN, RICHARD ESTEN, lawyer; b. N.Y.C., Oct. 26, 1957; s. Arnold and Marianne (Singer) A.; m. Patricia Anne Woods, May 9, 1987; children: Benjamin Singer, David Woods. BA, Columbia U., 1978, JD, 1981; LLM, NYU, 1987. Bar: N.Y. 1982, U.S. Tax Ct. 1982. Ptnr. Arnold & Porter, N.Y.C. Mem. bd. advisors Jour. Internat. Taxation, Tax Mgmt. Inc. Author: Foreign Tax Credits, 1996, U.S. Income Tax Withholding (Fgn. Persons), 1997. Mem. ABA, N.Y. State Bar Assn., Internat. Tax Inst., Internat. Fiscal Assn. (mem. USA br. coun., N.Y. exec. com.), Internat. Tax Assn. (pres.). Finance, Private international, Corporate taxation. Office: Arnold & Porter 399 Park Ave New York NY 10022 E-mail: richard_andersen@aporter.com

ANDERSEN, ROBERT MICHAEL, lawyer; b. Council Bluffs, Iowa, June 4, 1950; s. Howard M. and Muriel Marie (Robinson) A.; m. Natalia Anne Nankovitch, May 1, 1982; children: Erica Nicole, Amelia Marie. BS, U. Iowa, 1972, JD, 1976; MPA, Harvard U., 1986. Bar: Ohio 1976, Iowa 1976, U.S. Ct. Appeals (2d, 6th, and 7th and D.C. cirs.) 1979, U.S. Supreme Ct. 1979. Assoc. Squire, Sanders & Dempsey, Cleve., 1976-78; pvt. practice Milw.; asst. regional counsel U.S. EPA, Chgo., 1980-82, assoc. regional counsel, 1982-84, dep. regional counsel, regional jud. officer, 1984-86; dep. gen. counsel NSF, Washington, 1986-90; gen. counsel Def. Nuclear Facilities Safety Bd., 1990-98; chiel counsel U.S. Army Corps Engrs., 1998—. Adj. prof. lectr. waste mgmt., dept. engring. George Washington U., 1994—; lectr. internat. environ. controls for Antarctica, regulation of sci. fraud and misconduct, and waste mgmt.; mgmt. cons. in field. Articles editor Iowa U. Law Rev., 1975-76; contbr. articles to profl. jours. Recipient Bronze medal EPA, 1982, Meritorious Svc. medal NSF, 1990, Antarctic Svc. medal NSF, 1990, Antarctic medallion, NSF, 1990, Presdl. Meritorious Exec. Rank award Pres. George Bush, 1992, Predl. Disting. Exec. Rank award Pres. William Jefferson Clinton, 1995, Meritorious Svc. award Def. Nuclear Facilities Safety Bd., 1998. Roman Catholic. Avocations: mountaineering, tennis, chess, writing, mathematics. Home: 7003 Petunia St Springfield VA 22152-3428 Office: USA CE Office of Chief Counsel 441 G St NW Rm 3A29 Washington DC 20314-1000 E-mail: robert.m.andersen@usace.army.mil

ANDERSEN, RONALD MEREDITH, lawyer; b. Blair, Nebr., Nov. 26, 1943; s. Henry Leonard and Dorthea Marie (Sorensen) A. BS, U. Wis., Madison, 1966; JD, U. Denver, 1971. Bar: Colo. 1971, Ariz. 1981, U.S. Dist. Ct. Colo. 1971, U.S. Dist. Ct. Ariz. 1981, U.S. Ct. Appeals (10th cir.) 1976. Ins. adjuster State Farm Ins. Cos., Greeley, Colo., 1967-69; law clk. Colo. Judiciary, Denver, 1969-71; appellate dep. Adams County Dist. Attys. Office, Brighton, Colo., 1971-73; ptnr. Johnston & Andersen, Denver, 1973-79; trial atty. EEOC, Phoenix, 1979-88; asst. atty. gen. State of Ariz., 1991-93; staff atty. Indsl. Commn. Ariz., Phoenix, 1993—. Mem. Ariz. Bar Assn. Office: Indsl Commn Ariz 800 W Washington #303 Phoenix AZ 85007 E-mail: rona@ica.state.az.us

ANDERSON, ALAN MARSHALL, lawyer; b. Postville, Iowa, Oct. 23, 1955; s. Hilbert Emil and Wilma Althea (Zummack) A.; m. Ann Marie Luken, Aug. 9, 1980. BA magna cum laude, Coe Coll., 1974-78; MBA with distinction, Cornell U., 1981, JD magna cum laude, 1982; cert. internat. comml. and bus. law, U. Pacific, 1988. Bar: Minn. 1983, U.S. Dist. Ct. Minn. 1983, U.S. Ct. Appeals (4th and 8th cirs.) 1983, U.S. Ct. Appeals (10th cir.) 1985, U.S. Ct. Appeals (fed. cir.) 1987, U.S. Supreme Ct. 1990, U.S. Ct. Appeals (7th cir.) 1992. Law clk. to cir. judge U.S. Ct. Appeals (4th cir.), Richmond, Va., 1982-83; assoc., then ptnr. Faegre & Benson, Mpls., 1983-90; ptnr. Robins, Kaplan, Miller & Ciresi, 1990-92; shareholder Larkin, Hoffman, Daly & Lindgren, 1992—. Bd. dirs. Compumedics, Ltd., Melbourne, Australia, 2000—. Contbr. articles to law revs. Mem. alumni coun. Coe Coll., 1998—; mem. bd. dirs. Compumedics, Ltd., Melbourne, Australia, 2000—. Recipient Chatman Labor Law Prize Cornell Law Sch. Faculty, 1982. Mem. ABA, Minn. Bar Assn. (cert. civil trial specialist, named leading Am. Atty. 1999), Am. Intellectual Property Law Assn., Fed. Cir. Bar Assn., Coe Coll. Alumni Coun., Nat. Assn. Securities Dealers (nat. bd. arbitrators 1990—), Am. Arbitration Assn. (panel of arbitrators 1993—), U.S. Judo Assn. (life mem., nat. bd. legal advisors 1989-94, Silver award), Order of Coif, Phi Beta Kappa, Phi Kappa Phi. Republican. Lutheran. Avocation: judo. Appellate, General civil litigation, Intellectual property. Office: Larkin Hoffman Daly & Lindgren 7900 Xerxes Ave S Ste 1500 Minneapolis MN 55431-1128

ANDERSON, ALBERT SYDNEY, III, lawyer; b. Atlanta, July 7, 1940; s. Albert S. Jr. and Constance S. (Spalding) A.; children: Judith, William. BA in Math., Emory U., 1962; MS in Physics, Stanford (Calif.) U., 1964, PhD in Physics, 1968, JD, 1977. Bar: Ga. 1978, U.S. Patent and Trademark Office 1980, U.S. Supreme Ct. 1981. Assoc. Stokes & Shapiro, Atlanta, 1978-81, Kutak, Rock & Huie, Atlanta, 1981-84; ptnr. Jones & Askew, 1984-96; pvt. practice Norcross, Ga., 1996—. Asst. atty. gen. State of Ga., Atlanta, 1984-88. Elder Trinity Presbyn. Ch., Atlanta, 1978-81; chmn. bd. trustees Trinity Sch., Atlanta, 1971-74. Mem. Am. Phys. Soc. Avocations: golf, hiking, music. Federal civil litigation, Patent, Trademark and copyright. Office: Patent Law Offices 35 Technology Pkwy S Ste 170 Norcross GA 30092-2928 E-mail: aanderson@andersonpatent.com

ANDERSON, ANTHONY LECLAIRE, lawyer; b. Davenport, Iowa, Sept. 15, 1938; s. Frederic Nielsen and Marie Louise (LeClaire) A.; m. Beulah M. Bassham, July 3, 1963; children: Timothy LeClaire, Mark LeClaire, Jonathan Frederic LeClaire. BS with final honors, Washington U., St. Louis, 1967; JD, St. Louis U., 1971. Bar: Mo. 1972, U.S. Dist. Ct. (we. dist.) Mo. 1972, U.S. Dist. Ct. (ea. dist.) Mo. 1972, U.S. Ct. Appeals (8th cir.) 1974, U.S. Ct. Appeals (7th cir.) 1992, U.S. Tax Ct. 1976, U.S. Supreme Ct. 1976. Dir. pub. affairs Key Comm., Inc., St. Louis, 1973-74, Anderson, Wollrab & Wilson, St. Louis, 1974-76, Anderson, Preuss, Mooney & Eickhorst, St. Louis, 1976-82, Anderson, Preuss & Bachman, St. Louis, 1982-87, Anderson & Preuss, St. Louis, 1987—. Dir. Shield Fire Ins. Co., St. Louis, 1976-83. Panel atty. Lawyers Reference Svc., St. Louis, 1972-92; mem. Nat. Rep. Congrl. Com., 1998. Served with U.S. Army, 1962-64. Recipient Law Enforcement Assistance cert. Bd. Police Commrs., 1967, Bi-Centennial Commn., Davenport, Iowa, 1976. Mem. ABA, ATLA, Am. Judicature Soc., Ill. Trial Lawyers Assn., Bar Assn. Met. st. Louis, Press (editor 1968-69), Phi Alpha Delta. Episcopalian. Bankruptcy, General corporate, Franchising. Home: 2919 Moniteau Dr Saint Louis MO 63121-4518 Address: Anderson And Preuss 201 S Central Ave Ste 103 Saint Louis MO 63105-3517

ANDERSON, ARLENE D. lawyer; b. Dec. 2, 1960; AB, Vassar Coll., 1983; JD summa cum laude, William Mitchell Coll. Law, 1996. With Bowman & Brooke LLP , Mpls. Avocations: drama, brass music, rock climbing. Contracts commercial, Product liability. Office: Bowman & Brooke LLP 150 S Fifth St Ste 2600 Minneapolis MN 55402

ANDERSON, AUSTIN GOTHARD, lawyer, university administrator; b. Calumet, Minn., June 30, 1931; s. Hugo Gothard and Turna Marie (Johnson) A.; m. Catherine Antoinette Spellacy, Jan. 2. 1954; children: Todd, Susan, Timothy, Linda, Mark. BA, U. Minn., 1954, JD, 1958. Bar: Minn. 1958, Ill. 1962, Mich. 1974. Assoc. Spellacy, Spellacy, Lano & Anderson, Marble, Minn, 1958-62; dir. Ill. Inst. Continuing Legal Edn., Springfield, 1962-64; dir. dept. continuing legal edn. U. Minn., Mpls., 1964-70, assoc. dean gen. extension divsn., 1968-70; ptnr. Dorsey, Marquart, Windhorst, West & Halladay, 1970-73; assoc. dir. Nat. Ctr. State Cts., St. Paul, 1973-74; dir. Inst. Continuing Legal Edn. U. Mich., Ann Arbor, 1973-92; dir. Inst. on Law Firm Mgmt., 1992-95; prin. AndersonBoyer Group, Ann Arbor; pres. Network of Leading Law Firms, 1995—. Adj. faculty U. Minn., 1974, Wayne State U., 1974-75; mem. adv. bd. Ctr. for Law Firm Mgmt. Nottingham Trent U., Eng.; draftsman ABA Guidelines for Approval of Legal Asst. Programs, 1973, Model Guidelines for Minimum Continuing Legal Edn., 1988; chair law practice mgmt. sect. State Bar Mich., 2000-2001; mem. Task Force on Court Filing, State Bar of Mich., 2000; mem. com. on quality of life; cons. in field. Co-editor, contbg. author: Lawyer's Handbook, 1975, co-editor 3d edit., 1992; author: A Plan for Lawyer Development, 1986, Marketing Your Practice: A Practical Guide to Client Development, 1986; cons. editor, contbg. author: Webster's Legal Secretaries Handbook, 1981; cons. editor Merriam Webster's Legal Secretarial Handbook, 2d edit., 1996; co-author: The Effective Associate Training Program-Improving Firm Performance, Profits and Prospective Partners; contbr. chpt. to book and articles to profl. jours. Chmn. City of Bloomington Park and Recreation Adv. Commn., Minn., 1970-72; chmn. Ann Arbor Citizens Recreation Adv. Com., 1981-89, Ann Arbor Parks Adv. Com., 1983-92, chair, 1991-92; rep. Class of '58 U. Minn. Law Sch., 1996—. Recipient Excellence award CLE sect. Assn. of Am. Law Schs., 1992. Fellow Am. Bar Found., State Bar Mich. Found.; mem. ABA (vice chmn. continuing legal edn. com. sect. legal edn. and admission to bar 1988-93, standing com. continuing edn. of bar 1984-90, chmn. law practice mgmt. sect. 1981-82, AII-ABA com. on continuing profl. edn. 1993-96, ALI-ABA com. on continuing profl. edn. 1999—, spl. com. on rsch. on future of legal profession 1998—, sec. Coll. of Law Practice Mgmt. 1993-97, house of dels. 1993-99, commn. on lawyer advt. 1994-97, futures com.), Internat. Bar Assn., Mich. Bar Assn., State Bar of Mich. (chair law practice mgmt. sect.), Ill. Bar Assn., Minn. Bar Assn., Assn. Continuing Legal Edn. Adminstrs.(pres. 1969-70), Ann Arbor Golf and Outing Club. Administrative and regulatory. Home: 4660 Bayberry Cir Ann Arbor MI 48105-9762 Office: AndersonBoyer Group 3840 Packard St # 110 Ann Arbor MI 48108-2280 E-mail: aga@andersonboyer.com

ANDERSON, CARL WEST, retired judge; b. Monterey Park, Calif., Sept. 11, 1935; s. Carl Ejnar and Mary Madeline (West) A.; m. Margo Hart, Aug. 15, 1964; children: Thomas Hart, Marnie Marie. AB in Pol. Sci., U. Calif., Berkeley, 1957, LLB, 1962; LLM in Jud. Process, U. Va., 1992. Bar: Calif. 1963. Dep. dist. atty. Alameda County (Calif.) Dist. Atty., 1964-72, sr. dep. dist. atty., 1972-75; judge Alameda County Superior Ct., 1975-84; assoc. justice Calif. Ct. Appeals, 1st dist., divsn. 3, San Fransisco, 1984; presiding justice divsn. 4, San Francisco, 1987-97, adminstrv. presiding justice, 1987-97; ret., 1997. Pvt. judge, assoc. Am. Arbitration Assn. and alternative adjucication, 1997—; mem. appellate performance stds. com. Nat. Ctr. for State Cts. Commn., 1994-95. Pres. Piedmont (Calif.) Coun. Boy Scouts Am., 1987, 88, 93. Capt. USAR, 1957-74. Scholar U. Calif. Alumni Assn., 1953; fellow U. Calif. Sch. Law and Ctr. for Study Law and Soc., Germany, 1962-63. Fellow ABA (commn. stds. jud. adminstrn. 1992-93, appellate judges conf. exec. com. JAD 1992, 93, chair-elect 1995—, chair 1996-97), Coun. Chief Judges Cts. Appeal (pres. 1992-93). Avocations: tennis, gardening, golf. Office: Am Arbitration Assn 225 Bush St 18th Fl San Francisco CA 94104-4211 E-mail: justicecanderson@sprynet.com

ANDERSON, CHARLES ANTHONY, lawyer; b. Ashtabula, Ohio, Nov. 21, 1945; s. Charles Lindley and Teresa (Silva) A.; m. Martha M. Bodnar, June 18, 1974; children: Charles Joshua, Kristin, Megan, Caitlin, Justin. BA, Bowling Green State U., 1967; postgrad., U. So. Calif., 1971-72; JD, U. San Francisco, 1975. Bar: Calif. 1976, Va. 1977, U.S. Ct. Appeals (D.C. cir.) 1977, U.S. Dist. Ct. (ea. dist.) Va. 1978. Staff rschr. Commn. on Fed Paperwork, Washington, 1976; com. atty. U.S. Ho. of Reps., 1977; pvt. practice Reston, Va., 1977-83; ptnr. Ralston, Redick, Norwitch, O'Connor, Craig, Anderson, 1983-88; trial atty., pvt. practice Charles A. Anderson, P.C., 1988-2000; mng. ptnr. Grenadier, Anderson, Simpson and Duffett, P.C., 2000—. Lt. USN, 1968-72. Mem. Va. Trial Lawyers' Assn. (family law exec. bd. 1990-96), KC (trustee 1993-97, Grand Knight 1994). Avocations: poker, reading, World War II history. General civil litigation, Family and matrimonial, General practice. Home: 2657 Unicorn Ct Herndon VA 20171-2425 Office: Grenadier Anderson Simpson & Duffett Ste 130 11710 Plaza America Dr Reston VA 20190 E-mail: bxqx61a@aol.com

ANDERSON, CHARLES HILL, lawyer; b. Chattanooga, June 16, 1930; s. Ray N. and Lois M. Anderson; (div.); children: Eric S., Alicia L., Burton H. JD, U. Tenn., 1953. Bar: Tenn. 1953, U.S. Dist. Ct. Tenn. 1953, U.S. Ct. Appeals (6th cir.) 1956, U.S. Supreme Ct. 1956, U.S. Ct. Mil. 1964. Pvt. practice, Chattanooga, 1953-59, 2001—; assoc. gen. counsel Life & Casualty Ins. Co. Tenn., Nashville, 1960-69; dist. atty. U.S. Dept. Justice, 1969-77; pvt. practice, 1977-79, 87—; asst. adj. gen. State of Tenn., 1979-87. Mem. U.S. Atty. Gen. Adv. Com., Washington, 1973-77; del. Tenn. Constl. Conv., Nashville, 1965-66; dir. Nashville Pub. TV Coun., 1994-99; chmn. Met. Bd. of Equalization, 1998-2001. Brig. gen. AUS, ret., 1987. Mem. ABA, Tenn. Bar Assn., Nashville Bar Assn., Fed. Bar Assn. (pres. Nashville chpt. 1972), Am. Arbitration Assn. (arbitrator), Assn. Life Ins. Counsel (mediator, approved Tenn. Supreme Ct., U.S. Dist. Ct.), Cumberland Club (pres. 1981-82), The Federalist Soc. Presbyterian. General corporate, Insurance, Labor. Home: 1310 Aswan Dr Signal Mountain TN 37377-2618 Office: POB 561 Signal Mountain TN 37377

ANDERSON, DAMON ERNEST, lawyer; b. Minot, N.D., June 20, 1946; s. Melvin Ernest and Maxine I. (Spaulding) A.; m. Julie Kay Severson, Oct. 23, 1982; children: Joshua Daniel, Philip Kyle. BA, Dickinson State U., 1968; JD, U. N.D., 1974. Bar: N.D. 1974, Minn. 1981, U.S. Dist. Ct. N.D. 1974, U.S. Ct. Appeals (8th cir.) 1980, U.S. Supreme Ct. 1980. Pvt. practice Kessler and Anderson, Grand Forks, N.D., 1974-78, 1978-98; asst. state's atty. Grand Forks County, 1978—. Past mem. divsnl. comdr. adv. coun. Salvation Army, Mpls., past mem. Salvation Army local adv. bd., Grand Forks. Sgt. U.S. Army, 1968-70. Mem. Am. Legion, Masons. Lutheran. Juvenile. Office: 151 S 4th St Ste 601 Grand Forks ND 58201-4715

ANDERSON, DAVID BOYD, lawyer, steel company executive; b. Moorhead, Minn., Mar. 10, 1942; children: Kimberly, Erik, Jonathan, Caroline J. BA, U. Minn., 1964, JD, 1967; LLM, DePaul U., 1983. Bar: Minn. 1967, Ill. 1978. Labor relations supr. Continental Can Co., N.Y.C., 1970-72; asst. gen. counsel Am. Hosp. Supply Co., Evanston, Ill., 1972-83; v.p. planning and gen. counsel Inland Steel Industries, Inc., Chgo., 1983—. Active adv. com. LISC, planning com. Northwestern U. Corp. Counsel Inst. Served as capt. U.S. Army, 1967-70. Mem. ABA, Ill. Bar Assn., Minn. Bar Assn. Office: 16th Fl 30 W Monroe St Fl 16 Chicago IL 60603-2495

ANDERSON, DORIS EHLINGER, lawyer; b. Houston; d. Joseph Otto and Cornelia Louise (Pagel) Ehlinger; m. Wiley Anderson, Jr. (dec.); children: Wiley Newton III, Joe E. BA, Rice U., 1946; permanent high sch. tchr. cert., U. Houston, 1948; JD, U. Tex., 1950; MLS in Muscology, U. Okla., 1985. Bar: Tex. 1950, U.S. Supreme Ct. Assoc. Ehlinger & Anderson, Houston, 1950-52, ptnr., 1965—; assoc. Price, Guinn, Wheat & Veltmann, 1952-55, Wheat, Dyche & Thornton, Houston, 1955-65; life mem. Rice Assocs., 1984—. Hist. lectr., Harvard Negotiation Seminar, 1992 Edn. for Ministry, U of South, 1999. Editor: Houston City of Destiny, 1980; contbr. articles to hist. pubs. and to Bayou Bend. Parliamentarian Harris County Flood Control Task Force, Houston, 1975—; bd. dirs. Houston Bapt. Mus Am. Architecture and Decorative Arts, 1980-90, curator costume, 1980; apptd. ambassador Inst. Texan Culture U. Tex, San Antonio; past pres. gen. San Jacinto Descendants; docent Bayou Bend Mus. Fine Arts, Houston. Recipient best interpretive exhibit award Tex. Hist. Commn., 1983, Outstanding Woman of Yr. award YWCA, Houston, 1983; named adm. Tex. Navy, 1980. Mem. ABA, UDC (pres. Jefferson Davis chpt.), Assn. Women Attys. Houston, Houston Bar Assn., Daus.

Republic Tex. (Chaplain Robert E. Lee chpt., parliamentarian gen.), Am. Mus. Soc., Harris County Heritage Soc., Kappa Beta Pi (pres. Lamda alumni). Episcopalian. Oil, gas, and mineral, Real property. Home: 5556 Cranbrook Rd Houston TX 77056-1600 Office: Ehlinger & Anderson 5556 Sturbridge Dr Houston TX 77056-1623

ANDERSON, DORIS ELAINE, lawyer; b. Nov. 6, 1934; d. Frederick John and Hazel Elizabeth (Bergman). A.B. in Mus., U. Mich., 1956; JD, U. Calif.-Berkeley, 1964. Bar: Calif., 1968. Atty. Fibreboard Corp., San Francisco, 1965-79; gen. counsel Internat. Diamond Corp., San Rafael, Calif., 1980-82; legal counsel Kaiser-Crebs Mgmt. Corp., Oakland, 1983-85; asst. sec., atty. Fibreboard Corp., Concord, 1989-93; mgr. corp. affairs and asst. sec. Fair, Isaac and Co., Inc., San Rafael, 1993-98. Mem. Am. SOc. Corp. Secs., Inc. Avocations: tennis, golf, music. Administrative and regulatory, General corporate, Securities. Home: 5570 Taft Ave Oakland CA 94618-1519 E-mail: dorisanderson@att.net

ANDERSON, EDWARD RILEY, state supreme court chief justice; b. Chattanooga, Aug. 10, 1932; BS, U. Tenn., 1955, JD, 1957. Bar: Tenn. 1958, U.S. Dist. Ct. (ea. dist.) Tenn. 1965, U.S. Ct. Appeals (4th cir.) 1985, U.S. Ct. Appeals (6th cir.), U.S. Supreme Ct. 1988. Assoc. Joyce & Wilson, Oak Ridge, Tenn., 1957-61; ptnr. Joyce, Anderson & Meredith, 1961-87; judge Tenn. Ct. Appeals, Knoxville, 1987-90; justice Tenn. Supreme Ct., 1990—, now chief justice. Mem. Tenn. Jud. Conf., 1987—; mem. bd. dirs. Conf. of Chief Justices, 1999-2000; chmn. Tenn. Jud. Coun., 1990-95, Select Senate/House Com. on Ct. Automation, 1990-94. Past commr. Oak Ridge City Charter. Named Judge of Yr. Am. Bd. Trial Advocates, 1998. Fellow Am. Bar Found., Tenn. Bar Found.; mem. ABA, Am. Bd. Trial Advocates (pres. Tenn. chpt. 1987-88), Tenn. Bar Assn., Anderson County Bar Assn. (pres. 1961), Tenn. Def. Lawyers Assn. (pres. 1980-81), Am. Inns of Ct. (pres. Tenn. chpt. 1988-90). Avocations: reading, tennis. Office: Tenn Supreme Ct Supreme Court Bldg 719 Locust St Knoxville TN 37902-2512

ANDERSON, EDWARD VIRGIL, lawyer; b. San Francisco, Oct. 17, 1953; s. Virgil P and Edna Pauline (Pedersen) A.; m. Kathleen Helen Dunbar, Sept. 3, 1983; children: Elizabeth D., Hilary J. AB in Econs., Stanford U., 1975, JD, 1978. Bar: Calif. 1978. Assoc. Pillsbury Madison & Sutro, San Francisco, 1978—, ptnr., 1987-94; mng. ptnr., mem. firm mgmt. com. Skjerven Morrill MacPherson LLP, San Jose, 1994—. Editor IP Litigator, 1995—; mem. bd. editors Antitrust Law Devel., 1983-86. Trustee Lick-Wilmerding H.S., San Francisco, 1980—, pres.; trustee Santa Clara Law Found., 1995—; trustee, v.p. Hamlin Sch. for Girls, San Francisco, 1998—, v.p. Mem. ABA, Calif. Bar Assn., San Francisco Bar Assn., Santa Clara Bar Assn. (counsel), City Club San Francisco, Stanford Golf Club, Phi Beta Kappa. Republican. Episcopal. Antitrust, Intellectual property, Patent. Home: 330 Santa Clara Ave San Francisco CA 94127-2035 Office: Skjerven Morrill MacPherson Franklin and Friel 25 Metro Dr Ste 700 San Jose CA 95110-1349 E-mail: eanderson@skjerven.com

ANDERSON, ERIC SEVERIN, lawyer; b. N.Y.C., Dec. 16, 1943; s. Edward Severin and Dorothy Elvira (Ekbloom) A. BA in History summa cum laude, St. Mary's U., San Antonio, 1968; JD cum laude, Harvard U., 1971. Bar: Tex. 1971. From assoc. to ptnr. Fulbright & Jaworski, L.L.P., Houston, 1971—. Served with USAF, 1961-65. Mem. ABA, State Bar Tex., Houston Bar Assn. Democrat. Clubs: Houston Ctr., Houston City. Avocations: classical music, theater, sports. General corporate, Municipal (including bonds), Securities. Home: 14 E Greenway Plz Unit 21-o Houston TX 77046-1406 Office: Fulbright & Jaworski LLP 1301 Mckinney St Houston TX 77010-3031

ANDERSON, EUGENE ROBERT, lawyer; b. Portland, Oreg., Oct. 24, 1927; s. Andrew E. and Ruth Beatrice (White) A.; m. Jenny Morgenthau, Nov. 8, 1986: children: Matthew, Martin. BS, UCLA, 1949; student, Oreg. State Coll., 1945; JD, Harvard U., 1952; LLM, NYU, 1960. Bar: N.Y. bar 1953, Mass., So. and Eastern dists. N.Y., Second Circuit, D.C. Circuit, U.S. Ct. Claims, U.S. Supreme Ct. bars 1953. Assoc. firm Chadbourne & Parke, N.Y.C., 1953-61, partner, 1965-69; asst. U.S. atty. So. Dist. N.Y., Foley Square, 1961-65, chief civil div., 1963-65; ptnr. firm Anderson Kill & Olick, P.C., N.Y.C., 1969—; asst. dist. atty. N.Y. County, 1977. Spl. hearing officer U.S. Dept. Justice, 1965-68; arbitrator Am. Arbitration Assn., 1965— , Small Claims Ct., 1970-76; mem. com. on trial practice and technique Second Circuit, 1967-73 Mem. N.Y.C. Mayor's Bus. Adv. Com., Mayor's Task Force Auto. Ins. Served with AUS, 1945-46. Mem. ABA, Fed. Bar Assn., Assn. Bar City N.Y., Police Athletic League (dir., gen. counsel). General practice, Insurance. Office: Anderson Kill & Olick PC 1251 Avenue of the Americas New York NY 10020-1182 E-mail: eanderson@andersonkill.com

ANDERSON, GENE S. lawyer. U.S. atty. Western Wash., Seattle. Office: US Atty Office 3600 Seafirst 5th Ave Pla 800 5th Ave Ste 3600 Seattle WA 98104-3176

ANDERSON, GEOFFREY ALLEN, retired lawyer; b. Chgo., Aug. 3, 1947; s. Roger Allen and Ruth (Teninga) A. BA cum laude, Yale U., 1969; JD, Columbia U., 1972. Bar: Ill. 1972. Assoc. Isham, Lincoln & Beale, Chgo., 1972-79, ptnr., 1980-81, Reuben & Proctor, Chgo., 1981-85; dep. gen. counsel Tribune Co., 1985-92; gen. counsel Chgo. Cubs, 1986-90, corp. counsel, 1991-92; v.p. Timber Trails Country Club, Inc., 1992—. Elder Fourth Presbyn. Ch., Chgo., chmn. worship and music com., 1990-92, trustee, 1992-95, 99—, v.p., 1993-94; bd. dirs. The James Chorale, Chgo., 1993-96, chmn. program com., 1994-96. Recipient Citizenship award Am. Legion, 1965. Mem. Chgo. Bar Assn. (chmn. entertainment com. 1981-82, Best Performance award 1977), Yale Club (N.Y.C.), Phi Delta Phi. General corporate, Securities.

ANDERSON, HAROLD LLOYD, lawyer; b. Bismarck, N.D., Feb. 15, 1927; s. Victor L. and Anna M. (Vollan) A.; m. Corynne O. Olson, Oct. 18, 1952; children: Eric, Odin, Sonna Marie, Thor. JD, U. N.D., 1952. Bar: N.D. 1952. Sole practice, Bismarck, 1952-54; states atty. Burleigh County, N.D., 1955-64; ptnr. Pearce, Anderson & Durick and predecessor firms, Bismarck, 1965-85, Anderson & Anderson, Bismarck, 1986-93, of counsel, 1993—. Temp. dist. judge, 1979. Pres. Bismarck Sch. Bd., 1972, 76-77, 80. Served with AUS, 1944-46. Mem. N.D. States Attys. Assn. (pres. 1958), State Bar Assn. N.D. (pres. 1978-79), Burleigh County Bar (pres. 1968), Dist. Bar Assn. (pres. 1969), Masons, Shriners, Elks. Lutheran. Avocations: reading, golf, fishing. Administrative and regulatory, Contracts commercial, General corporate. Office: PO Box 2574 PO Box 2574 Bismarck ND 58502-2574 E-mail: Harold@btigate.com

ANDERSON, HERBERT HATFIELD, lawyer, farmer; b. Rainier, Oreg., Aug. 2, 1920; s. Odin A. and Mae (Hatfield) A.; m. Barbara Stuart Bastine, June 3, 1949; children— Linda, Catherine, Thomas, Amy, Elizabeth, Kenneth B.A. in Bus. Adminstrn., U. Oreg., 1940; J.D., Yale U., 1949. Exec. trainee U.S. Steel Co., San Francisco, 1940-41; assoc. Spears, Lubersky, Campbell, Bledsoe, Anderson & Young, Portland, Oreg., 1949-54; ptnr. Spears, Lubersky, Bledsoe, Anderson, Young & Hilliard, 1954-90, Lane, Powell, Spears & Lubersky, Portland, 1990—. Instr. law Lewis and Clark Coll., Portland, 1950-70. Mem. planning adv. com. Yamhill County, Oreg., 1974-82; bd. dirs. Emanuel Hosp., 1967—; bd. dirs. Flyfisher Found., 1972—, pres., 1972-84; bd. dirs. Multnomah Law Library, 1958—, sec. 1962-68, 77-95, pres., 1964-74. Served to maj., parachute inf. U.S. Army, 1942-46, ETO Fellow Am. Bar Found. (chmn. Oreg. chpt. 1988—); mem. ABA (chmn. governing com. forum on health law 1984-89, chmn. standing com. on jud. selection, tenure and compensation 1978-80, Lawyer's Conf., exec. com. 1980-94, chmn. 1989-90, judicial adminstrn. divsn. coun. 1988-94, sr. lawyer's divsn. coun. 1987-89), Am. Judicature Soc. (bd. dirs. 1981-85), Soc. Law and Medicine, Nat. Health Lawyers Assn., Am. Acad. Hosp. Attys., Oreg. Soc. Hosp. Attys. (pres. 1984-85), Multnomah Bar Found. (bd. dirs. 1955—, pres. 1959-64, 87—), Nat. Bankruptcy Conf. (conferee 1964—, exec. com. 1976-79, chmn. farmer insolvency com. 1985-88), Nat. Assn. R.R. Trial Counsel, Oreg. Bar Assn. (del. to ABA 1966-68), Multnomah Bar Assn. (pres. 1955), Western States Bar Conf. (pres. 1967), Oreg. Asian Pear Coun. (pres. 1989-91), Sigma Chi. Democrat. Lutheran. Clubs: Multnomah Athletic, Michelbook Country, Flyfishers Oreg. (pres. 1972), Willamette Amateur Field Trial (pres. 1968-72). Lodge: Masons Bankruptcy, Health, Real property. Home: River Meadow Farm 19289 SE Neck Rd Dayton OR 97114-7815 Office: Lane Powell Spears & Lubersky 601 SW 2d Ave Ste 2100 Portland OR 97204-3158 E-mail: herband@open.org

ANDERSON, J. TRENT, lawyer; b. Indpls., July 22, 1939; s. Robert C. and Charlotte M. (Pfeifer) A.; m. Judith J. Zimmerman, Sept. 8, 1962; children: Evan M., Molly K. BS, Purdue U., 1961; LLB, U. Va., 1964. Bar: Ill. 1965, Ind. 1965. Teaching asst. U. Cal. Law Sch., Berkeley, 1964-65; assoc. Mayer, Brown & Platt, Chgo., 1965-72, ptnr., 1972—. Instr. Loyola U. Law Sch., Chgo., 1985. Mem. Law Club, Union League Club, Mich. Shores Club. Contracts commercial, General corporate, Mergers and acquisitions. Home: 3037 Iroquois Rd Wilmette IL 60091-1106 Office: Mayer Brown & Platt 190 S La Salle St Ste 3100 Chicago IL 60603-3441 E-mail: janderson@mayerbrown.com

ANDERSON, JAMES FRANCIS, lawyer; b. Glen Ridge, N.J., June 13, 1965; BA, Seton Hall U., 1987, JD, 1990. Bar: N.J. 1991, U.S. Supreme Ct. 1995. Pvt. practice, Spring Lake, N.J., 1991—. Pro bono atty. Ocean-Monmouth Legal Svcs., Freehold, N.J., 1991—; mentor Manasquan (N.J.) H.S., 1994. Mem. ABA, Masons. Criminal, General practice. Office: PO Box 144 Spring Lake NJ 07762-0144

ANDERSON, JAMES MILTON, lawyer; b. Chgo., Dec. 29, 1941; s. Milton H. and Eunice (Carlson) A.; m. Marjorie Henry Caldwell, Jan. 22, 1966; children: James Milton, Joseph H., Hilding F., Marjorie II. BA, Yale U., 1963; JD, Vanderbilt U., 1966. Bar: Ohio 1967. Assoc. rifm Taft, Stettinius & Hollister, Cin., 1968-75, ptnr., 1975-77, 82-96, mem. exec. com., 1975-77, 91-96; pres. U.S. ops., dir. Xomox Corp., 1977-81; sec. Access Corp., 1984-96; asst. sec. Carlisle Cos., 1985-90; bd. dirs. Cin. Stock Exch., 1978—, chmn., 1980-89. Bd. dirs. Command Sys. Inc.; trustee, chmn. Monarch Found., 1988—. Mem. Indian Hill Coun., 1981-89, vice-mayor, 1985-87, mayor, 1987-89; mem. Hamilton County Airport Authority, 1980-85; trustee Children's Hosp. Med. Ctr., 1977—, chmn. bd. trustees, 1991-96, pres., CEO, 1996—; trustee The Children's Hosp. Found., 1990—, chmn. bd. trustees, 1990-93; trustee Cin. Ctr. for Devel. Disorders, 1969—, pres., 1974-80; trustee Dan Beard coun. Boy Scouts Am., 1982—, chmn., 1984-87, area pres. Ea. Ctrl. Region, 1989-91; trustee Cin. Mus. Natural History, 1984-87, Coll. Mt. St. Joseph, 1990-98; trustee Joy Outdoor Edn. Ctr., 1984-2000, pres., 1991-93, chmn., 1993-95. Capt. AUS, 1966-68. Decorated Bronze Star with two oak leaf clusters, Air medal. Mem. ABA, Ohio Bar Assn., Cin. Bar Assn., Valve Mfrs. Assn., Young Pres. Orgn., Camargo Club, Queen City Club, Commonwealth Club, Yale Club of N.Y., Cin. Yale Club, Order of Coif. Avocation: sailing. General corporate, Finance, Mergers and acquisitions. Office: 1800 Star Bank Ctr 3333 Burnet Ave Cincinnati OH 45229-3026

ANDERSON, JOHN BAYARD, lawyer, educator, former congressman; b. Rockford, Ill., Feb. 15, 1922; s. E. Albin and Mabel Edna (Ring) A.; m. Keke Machakos, Jan. 4, 1953; children: Eleanora, John Bayard, Diane, Karen, Susan Kimberly. A.B., U. Ill., 1942, JD, 1946; LLM, Harvard U., 1949; hon. doctorates, No. Ill. U., Wheaton Coll., Shimer Coll., Biola Coll., Geneva Coll., North Park Coll. and Theol. Sem., Houghton Coll., Trinity Coll., Rockford Coll. Bar: Ill. 1946. Practice law Rockford, 1946-52; with U.S. Fgn. Service, 1952-55; assigned West Berlin, 1952-55; mem. 87th-95th Congresses from 16th Dist. Ill., mem. rules com.; chmn. Ho. Republican Conf., 1969-79; ind. candidate for Pres. U.S., 1980. Vis. prof. Stanford U., spring, 1981; vis. prof. law Nova-Southeastern U. Ctr. for Study Law, 1987-2001; vis. prof. polit. sci. Brandeis U., 1985, Oreg. State U., spring 1986, U. Mass., 1985—; vis. prof. law Washington Coll. Law Am. U., 1997—; lectr. polit. sci. Bryn Mawr Coll., spring 1985. Author: Between Two Worlds: A Congressman's Choice, 1970, Vision and Betrayal in America, 1976, The American Economy We Need, 1984, A Proper Institution: Guaranteeing Televised Presidential Debates, 1988; editor: Congress and Conscience, 1970. Ind. candidate for Pres. U.S., 1980. Mem. World Federalist Assn. (pres. 1992—), Ctr. for Voting and Democracy (pres. 1996—, co-chair nat. adv. bd. pub. campaign for campaign fin. reform 1997—), Coun. on Fgn. Rels., Phi Beta Kappa. Mem. Evang. Free Ch. (past trustee). Office: Nova Southeastern U Sch Law 3305 College Ave Fort Lauderdale FL 33301 E-mail: janderson@wfa.org, jbafed@aol.com

ANDERSON, JON ERIC, lawyer; b. Jacksonville, N.C., Feb. 1, 1956; m. Lori Jean Schumacher, June 30, 1979; children: Andrew Jon, Elizabeth Ruth, Margaret Mary. BA, U. Wis., 1978; JD, Marquette U., 1981. Bar: Wis. 1981, U.S. Dist. Ct. (ea. and we. dists.) Wis. 1981, U.S. Ct. Appeals (7th cir.) 1996, U.S. Supreme Ct. 1988. Assoc. Mulcahy & Wherry, S.C., Milw., 1981-84, mng. atty. Sheboygan, Wis., 1984-87, Madison, 1987-90; shareholder Godfrey & Kahn, S.C., 1991-99, Lafollette, Godfrey & Kahn, S.C., 2000—. Author: (with others) Comparable Worth-A Negotiator's Guide, 1985; contbg. author Pub. Sector Labor Rels., Wis., 1988. Thomas More Soc. scholar, 1979. Mem.: ABA, Edn. Law Assn., Wis. Bar Assn. (bd. dirs. labor law sect. 1988—91), Wis. Sch. Attys. Assn. (bd. dirs. 2000—), Nat. Assn. Coll. and Univ. Attys. (com. bd. operators 2001—), Blackhawk Country Club, Madison Club, Phi Delta Phi, Alpha Sigma Nu. Lutheran. Avocations: woodworking, music. Administrative and regulatory, Education and schools, Labor.

ANDERSON, KARL STEPHEN, editor; b. Chgo., Nov. 10, 1933; s. Karl William and Eleanor (Grell) a.; m. Saralee Hegland, Nov. 5, 1977; children by previous marriage: Matthew, Douglas, Eric. BS in Editl. Journalism, U. Ill., 1955. Asst. to pub., plant mgr. Pioneer Press, Oak Park, St. Charles, Ill., 1955-71; successively advt. mgr., asst. to pub., then pub. Crescent Newspapers, Downers Grove, 1971-73; assoc. pub., editor Chronicle Pub. Co., St. Charles, 1973-80; assoc. pub. Chgo. Daily Law Bull., 1981-88; dir. comms., editor Ill. State Bar Assn., 1988—. Past pres. Chgo. Pub. Rels. Forum. Trustee emeritus Chi Psi Ednl. Trust; trustee Leo Sowerby Found.; bd. dirs. Ill. Press Found., Chgo. Legal Svcs. Found. Recipient C.V. Amenoff award No. Ill. U. Dept. Journalism, 1976, Bd. Govs. award Ill. State Bar, 1987, Print Media Humanitarian award Coalition Sub Bar Assns., 1987, Robert C. Preble, Jr. award Chi Psi, 1991, Asian-Am. Bar Media Sensitivity award, 1991, Liberty Bell award DuPage County Bar Assn., 1993, Glass Ceiling Busters award Assn. Women Lawyers, 1993, Disting. Svc. award Chgo. Vol. Legal Svcs. Found., 1993, Gratitude award Lawyers Assistance Program, 1993, Outstanding Achievement in Comm. award Justinian Soc., 1994, Communicator of Yr. award, 1999, 3rd prize Nat. Libr. Poetry, 1995, Svc. award Women's Bar Assn. Ill., 1998, Peoria County Bar Assn., 1998. Mem. Am. Judicature Soc. (sec. Ill. chpt.), Nat. Assn. Bar Execs., Baltic Bar Assn., Chgo. Legal Sec. Assn., Chgo. Press Vets. Assn. (bd. sec.), Ill. Press assn. (Will Loomis award 1977, 80), Kane County Bar Assn., DuPage Women Lawyers Assn., West Suburban Bar Assn., N. Suburban Bar Assn. (Pub. Svc. award 1997), Bohemian Lawyers Assn. (Liberty award 1999), No. Ill. Newspaper Assn. (past pres.), Pub. Rels. Soc. Ctrl. Ill. (Master Communicator award of achievement 1997), Soc. Profl. Journalists, Headline Club (past pres.), Nordic Law Club, Nellie Fox Soc., Chgo. Athletic Assn., Chi Psi. Home: 3180 N Lake Shore Dr Apt 14D Chicago IL 60657-4851 Office: Ill State Bar Assn 20 S Clark St Ste 900 Chicago IL 60603-1885

ANDERSON, KATHLEEN GAY, mediator, hearing officer, arbitrator, trainer; b. Cin., July 27, 1950; d. Harold B. and Trudi L. (Chambers) Briggs; m. J.R. Carr, July 4, 1988; 1 child, Jesse J. Anderson. Student, U. Cin., 1971-72, Antioch Coll., 1973-74; cert., Nat. Jud. Coll., U. Nev., Reno, 1987, Inst. Applied Law, 1987, Acad. Family Mediators, 1991. Cert. Lemmon Mediation Inst., Acad. Family Mediators, U.S. Postal Svc. Panel, U.S. Forest Svc. Panel, State of Alaska, U. Alaska, pvt. sector panels. Paralegal Lauer & Lauer, Santa Fe, 1976-79, Wilkinson, Cragun & Barker, Anchorage, 1981-82; employment law paralegal specialist Hughes, Thorsness, Gantz, Powell & Brundin, 1983-91; investigator, mediator Alaska State Commn. Human Rights, 1991; mediator, arbitrator, trainer The Arbitration and Mediation Group, Anchorage, 1987—; hearing officer Municipality of Anchorage, 1993-99; State of Alaska, 1994—. Mem. faculty nat. Jud. Coll., U. Nev., Reno, 1988-89; adj. prof. U. Alaska, Anchorage, 1985-99, Alaska Pacific U., 1990-96, Chapman U., 1990; mem. Alaska Supreme Ct. Mediation Task Force, 1991-96; adv. com. Am. Arbitration Assn. for Alaska, 1995-99, ADR subcom. Supreme Ct. Civil Justice Reform task force, 1998-99; trainer mediation svcs. pvt. profit and nonprofit groups, pub. groups, U.S. mil., state and fed. govt.; arbitrator Anchorage Bd. Realtors, 1997-98, pvt. sector. Author, editor: Professional Responsibility Handbook for Legal Assistants and Paralegals, 1986; contbr. articles to profl. jours. Lectr. Alaska Bar Assn., NLRB, Bus. and Profl. Women, Coun. on Edn. and Mgmt., Small Bus. Devel. Coun., various employers and bus. groups. Mem. Assn. for Conflict Resolution, Alaska Bar Assn. (assoc., alt. dispute resolution sect.), Alaska Dispute Settlement Assn. (v.p. 1992-93, chair com. on credentialing and stds. of practice, pres. 1997-98). Avocations: jewelry design, antiques, gourmet cooking. Home: PO Box 111517 Anchorage AK 99511-1517 Office: PO Box 240783 Anchorage AK 99524-0783 E-mail: rankath@alaska.net

ANDERSON, MICHAEL STEVEN, lawyer; b. Mpls., May 25, 1954; s. Wesley James and Lorraine Kathrine (Sword) A.; m. Gail Karin Miller, June 18, 1977; children: Mark, Steven. BA magna cum laude, Cornell U., 1976; JD, Washington U., St. Louis, 1980. Bar: Wis. 1980, U.S. Dist. Ct. (ea. and we. dists.) Wis. 1980, U.S. Ct. Appeals (7th cir.) 1986, U.S. Supreme Ct. 1991. Ptnr. Axley Brynelson, Madison, Wis., 1980—; gen. counsel DEC, Internat., Inc., 1992—. Editor, author Washington U. Law Quarterly, 1979-80. Apptd. mem. local Bd. Attys. Profl. Responsibility, 1993—. Mem. Am. Corp. Counsel Assn., Lic. Exec. Soc., Order of Coif. Mem. Evangelical Free Ch. Avocation: family. General civil litigation, General corporate, Product liability. Home: 5882 Timber Ridge Trail Madison WI 53711-5180 Office: Axley Brynelson 2 E Mifflin St Madison WI 53703-2889 E-mail: manderson@axley.com

ANDERSON, PAUL HOLDEN, state supreme court justice; b. May 14, 1943; m. Janice M.; 2 children. BA cum laude, Macalester Coll., 1965; JD, U. Minn., 1968. Atty. Vols. in Svc. to Am., 1968-69; spl. asst. atty. gen. criminal divsn. dept. pub. safety Office Minn. Atty. Gen., 1970-71; from assoc. to ptnr. LeVander, Gillen & Miller, South St. Paul, Minn., 1971-92; chief judge Minn. Ct. Appeals, 1992-94; assoc. justice Minn. Supreme Ct., 1994—. Deacon, ruling elder, clk. of session House of Hope Presbyn. Ch., St. Paul; mem. PER coms. Ind. Sch. Dist. 199, 1982-84, chmn. cmty. svcs. adv. com., bd. dirs., chmn. bd. Mem. Dakota County Bar Assn. (bd. dirs., pres.), South St. Paul/Inver Grove Heights C. of C. (bd. dirs., exec. com.). Avocations: tennis, gourmet cooking, bike riding. Office: Minn Supreme Court 425 Minnesota Judicial Ctr Saint Paul MN 55155-0001 Fax: 651-282-5115. E-mail: paul.anderson@courts.state.mn.us

ANDERSON, PAUL STEWART, lawyer; b. Aug. 19, 1952; s. Robert Garfield and Ruth Helen (Hjorth) A.; m. Linda Joy Quinn, Sept. 29, 1984. BA, Wake Forest U., 1974; JD, Ill. Inst. Tech.-Chgo. Kent Law Sch., 1978; cert. in European Programs (hon.), U. Pacific, Sacramento and Salzburg, Austria, 1978. Bar: Ill. 1979, U.S. Ct. Appeals (7th cir.) 1979, U.S. Ct. Appeals (D.C. cir.) 1979, U.S. Ct. Internat. Trade 1979. Intern Mannheimer & Zetterlof, Gothenburg, Sweden, 1978; assoc. Barnes, Richardson & Colburn, Chgo., 1979-81; ptnr. Sonnenberg & Anderson, 1981—. Supporting mem. Union League Boys' Club, Chgo., 1984. Mem. ABA, Ill. Bar Assn., Chgo. Bar Assn. (customs law com. 1981—, vice chmn. 1986-87, chmn. 1987-88), Mid.-Am. Swedish Trade Assn. (bd. dirs. 1982-86), Norwegian-Am. C. of C. (v.p. 1984, pres. 1986—), Can. of Chgo. Club (bd. dirs. 1984—, v.p. 1986—, hon. consul gen. for Norway to Chgo. and Ill. 2000—). Methodist. Immigration, naturalization, and customs. Address: Sonnenberg & Anderson Atty At Law 333 W Wacker Dr Ste 2070 Chicago IL 60606-1293 E-mail: psa@sonnander.com

ANDERSON, PHILIP SIDNEY, lawyer; b. Little Rock, May 9, 1935; s. Philip Sidney and Frances (Walt) A,; m. Rosemary Gill Wright, Sept. 26, 1959; children: Sidney Walt (Mrs. Geoffrey R.T. Kenyon), Philip Wright, Catherine Gill (Mrs. Jess L. Askew III). BA, LLB, U. Ark., 1959. Bar: Ark. 1960, U.S. Supreme Ct. 1966. Assoc. Wright, Lindsey & Jennings, Little Rock, 1960-65, ptnr., 1965-88, Williams & Anderson, Little Rock, 1988—. Lectr. Ark. Law Sch., 1963-66; mem. com. on jury instrns. Ark. Supreme Ct., 1962-97; mem. panel for the 8th cir. U.S. Cir. Judge Nominating Commn., 1978-79; mem. fed. adv. com. U.S. Ct. Appeals 8th cir., 1983-88, co-chmn., 1987-88; bd. dirs. Camden News Pub. Co., Ark. Dem.-Gazette, Inc. Co-author: Arkansas Model Jury Instructions, 1965, 74, 89. Pres. Friends of Little Rock Pub. Libr., 1968-69, Little Rock Unltd. Progress, Inc., 1973-74; trustee Cen. Ark. Libr. System, 1981-87, pres. 1984; trustee George W. Donaghey Found., 1976—, pres. 1979-80; trustee Ctr. for Am. and Internat. Law, 1996—. 2d lt. AUS, 1959-60. Fellow Am. Bar Found., Ark. Bar Found. (pres. 1973-74), ABA (chair ho. of dels. 1992-94, bd. govs. 1990-94, 97-2000, pres. 1998-99); mem. Ark. Bar Assn. (spl. award meritorious svc.), Am. Law Inst. (mem. coun. 1982—). Episcopalian. Antitrust, Federal civil litigation, General corporate. Home: 4716 Crestwood Dr Little Rock AR 72207-5436 Office: Williams & Anderson 111 Center St Ste 2200 Little Rock AR 72201-4429 E-mail: psa@wiiiamsanderson.com

ANDERSON, R(OBERT) BRUCE, lawyer; b. Effingham, Ill., Feb. 4, 1956; s. Robert Dee and Annalee (Schreiner) A.; m. Shannon Elizabeth Whitcomb, Mar. 19, 1983. BS in Polit. Sci., Ill. State U., 1977; JD, Stetson U., 1981. Bar: Ill. 1981, Fla. 1981. Assoc. Law Offices of James R. DePew, Bloomington, Ill., 1981-82; chief asst. county atty., utilities counsel Collier County, Naples, Fla., 1982-88; ptnr. Young, Van Assenderp, Varnadoe and Anderson, P.A., Tallahassee and Naples, 1988—. Mem. editl. adv. com. Local Govt. Law Symposium, Stetson Law Rev., 1986-94. State chmn. Ill. Teenage Rep. Fedn., Springfield, 1974; alt. del. Rep. Nat. Conv., Kansas City, Mo., 1976, 80; mem. exec. com. Collier County Reps., Naples, Fla., 1986-96, treas. exec. com., 1987-88; active Collier County Devel. Svc. Adv. Com., 1994—, City-County Beach Renourishment Adv. Com., 1994-97, vice-chmn. 1996-97, Leadership Collier Class of 1995. Washington Crossing Found. scholar, 1974. Mem. Fla. Bar Assn., Am. Coll. Trial Lawyers (Excellence in Advocacy medal 1981), Collier County Bar Assn., Nat. Inst. Mcpl. Law (chmn. com. on municipally-owned utilities 1984-86), Naples Area C. of C., Tiger Bay Club, Alpha Kappa Lamda (Holmes award 1978). Republican. Methodist. Land use and zoning (including planning), Municipal (including bonds), Real property. Office: Young Van Assenderp Varnadoe and Anderson PA 801 Laurel Oak Dr Ste 300 Naples FL 34108-2771

ANDERSON, ROBERT EDWARD, lawyer; b. Spokane, Wash., Sept. 25, 1928; s. Ewald Godried and Hazel L. A.; m. Audrey May, Nov. 29, 1947; children: Mark, Eric, Kent, Carl. B in Law, Gonzaga U., 1950, LLB, 1954, JD, 1967. Bar: Wash. 1954, U.S. Dist. Ct. (ea. dist.) Wash. 1954, U.S. Supreme Ct. 1966. Pvt. practice, Spokane, 1954—. Recipient Silver Beaver award Boy Scouts Am., 1976, Lamb award Nat. Luth. Ch. Am., 1980. Mem. Kiwanis Internat. (lt. gov. 1967). Lutheran. State civil litigation, Family and matrimonial, General practice. Office: 2032 W Northwest Blvd Spokane WA 99205-3715

ANDERSON, ROBERT LANIER, III, federal judge; b. Macon, Ga., Nov. 12, 1936; s. Robert Lanier II and Helen A.; m. Nancy Briska, Aug. 18, 1962; children: Robert, William Hilliar, Browne McIntosh. AB magna cum laude, Yale U., 1958; LLB, Harvard U., 1961. Assoc. Anderson, Walkert, Reichert, Macon, Ga., 1963-79; judge U.S. Ct. Appeals (11th cir.), 1979—, chief judge Ga., 1999—. With USAR, 1058-61, capt. U.S. Army, 1961-63. Mem. ABA, Ga. Bar Assn., Macon Bar Assns., State Bar of Ga., Am. Judicature Soc. Office: US Ct Appeals PO Box 977 Macon GA 31202-0977*

ANDERSON, ROBERT MONTE, lawyer; b. Logan, Utah, Feb. 19, 1938; s. E. LeRoy and Grace (Rasmussen) A.; m. Kathleen Hansen, Aug. 12, 1966; children: Jennifer, Katrina, Alexander. AB, Columbia Coll., 1960; LLB, U. Utah, 1963. Bar: Utah 1963, U.S. Cir. Ct. Appeals (10th cir.) 1967, U.S. Supreme Ct. 1976. Assoc., shareholder, v.p. Van Cott, Bagley, Cornwall & McCarthy, Salt Lake City, 1963-82; pres., shareholder Berman & Anderson, 1982-86; v.p., shareholder Hansen & Anderson, 1986-90; pres., shareholder Anderson & Watkins, 1990-95; pres. Anderson & Smith, 1995-97; lawyer, shareholder, pres. Van Cott, Bagley Cornwall & McCarthy, 1998—. Bd. dirs., mem. exec. com. Anderson Lumber Co., Ogden, Utah, 1982-2000. Trustee The Children's Ctr., Salt Lake City, 1973-77; pres. Utah Legal Svcs., Salt Lake City, 1979. Mem. ABA, Utah State Bar Assn. (cts. and judges com. 1991-99), Am. Inns Ct., Alta Club, Cottonwood Club, Rotary. Avocations: tennis, skiing. General civil litigation, Construction, Real property. Office: Van Cott Bagley Cornwall & McCarthy 50 S Main St Ste 1600 Salt Lake City UT 84144-2044 E-mail: randerson@vancott.com

ANDERSON, RUSSELL A. state supreme court justice; b. Bemidji, Minn., May 28, 1942; m. Kristin Anderson; children: Rebecca, John, Sarah. BA, St. Olaf Coll., 1964; JD, U. Minn., 1968; LLM, George Washington U., 1977. Pvt. practice, 1976-82; atty. Beltrami County, 1978-82; dist. ct. judge 9th Jud. Dist., 1982-98; assoc. justice Minn. Supreme Ct., 1998—. Mem. Jud. Edn. Adv. Com., Sentencing Guidelines Commn.; Supreme Ct. Adv. Com. on Rules of Criminal Procedure; chair Supreme Ct. Gender Fairness Implementation Com. Mem. Sch. Dist. 593 Edn. Found., Crookston; mem. Fertile-Beltrami Edn. Found.; past pres., mem. ch. coun., 9th grade Sunday sch. tchr.; mem. Connect U.S.-Russian Domestic Violence Delegation to Russia, 1995, 97. Lt. comdr. USN, 1968-76. Mem. Minn. State Bar Assn., 14th Dist. Bar Assn. Office: Minn Supreme Ct 25 Constitution Ave Saint Paul MN 55155-1500

ANDERSON, STEPHEN HALE, federal judge; b. Salt Lake City, Jan. 12, 1932; m. Shirlee Gehring; two children. Student, Eastern Oreg. Coll. Edn., LaGrande, 1951, Brigham Young U., Provo, 1956; LLB, U. Utah, 1960. Bar: Utah 1960, U.S. Claims Ct. 1963, U.S. Tax Ct. 1967, U.S. Ct. Appeals (10th cir.) 1970, U.S. Supreme Ct. 1971, U.S. Ct. Appeals (9th cir.) 1972, various U.S. Dist. Cts. Tchr. South H.S., Salt Lake City, 1956-57; trial atty. tax div. U.S. Dept. Justice, 1960-64; ptnr. Ray, Quinney & Nebeker, 1964-85; judge U.S. Ct. Appeals (10th cir.), Salt Lake City, 1985—. Spl. counsel Salt Lake County Grand Jury, 1975; chmn. fed.-state jurisdiction com. Jud. Conf. U.S., 1995-98; mem. Nat. Jud. Coun. State and Fed. Cts., 1992-96; mem. ad hoc. com. on bankruptcy appellate panels 10th Cir. Jud. Coun., 1995-97; mem. various coms. U.S. Ct. Appeals (10th cir.). Editor-in-chief Utah Law Rev. Cpl. U.S. Army, 1953-55. Mem. Utah State Bar (pres. 1983-84, various offices), Salt Lake County Bar Assn. (pres. 1977-78), Am. Bar Found., Salt Lake Area C. of C. (bd. govs. 1984), U. Utah Coll. Law Alumni Assn. (trustee 1979-83, pres. 1982-83), Order of Coif. Office: US Ct Appeals 4201 Fed Bldg 125 S State St Salt Lake City UT 84138-1102

ANDERSON, SUELLEN, lawyer; b. L.A., Apr. 11, 1950; d. Robert Walter and Marian D. (Guild) Greiner; m. Dane Roger Anderson; children: Robert Joseph, Nicholas Drew. BA, Calif. State U., Los Angeles, 1974; JD, U. So. Calif., 1978. Bar: Calif. 1978, U.S. Dist. Ct. (cen. and ea. dist.) Calif. 1978. Corp. counsel, asst. sec. Tenneco West, Inc., Bakersfield, Calif., 1978-84; programs coordinator Greater Bakersfield Legal Assistance, 1985-89; assoc. Darling, Maclin and Thomson, Bakersfield, 1990-92; dean Calif. Pacific Sch. Laws, 1993-97; exec. dir. Kern County Bar Assn., 1997—2001; partner klein,DeNatale, Goldner, Cooper, Rosenlieb & Kimball , 2001—. Dir. Greater Bakersfield Legal Assistance, 1980-85; mem. coun. 100 Californian State U. Bakersfield, 1994—, steering com., 2001—. Comty. mem. editl. bd. The Bakersfield Californian, 1998. Assoc. dir. Alliance Against Family Violence, Bakersfield, 1985-89; bd. dirs. Tenneco Employees Fed. Credit Union, Bakersfield, 1981-83. Mem. Calif. Bar Assn. (vice chair legal svcs. sect. standing com. pvt. bar involvement 1992), Kern County Bar Assn. (bd. dirs. 1985—, sec.-treas. 1988-89, 1st v.p. 1991, pres. 1992), Kern County Women Lawyers Assn. (pres. 1982-83), Kern County Women Lawyers Scholarship Found. (pres. 1988-90, treas. 1990-91), Bakersfield Rotary (bd. dirs. 1999-2000, sec. 2001-2002). Democrat. Business E-Mail: sanderso@kleinlaw.com

ANDERSON, TERENCE JAMES, law educator; b. Chgo., Feb. 26, 1940; s. James E. and Charlotte (Flatley) A.; m. Carolyn Bugh; children: Michael, Kathleen, Jamie, Andrew. BA, Wabash Coll., 1961; JD, U. Chgo., 1964. Bar: Ill. 1967, D.C. 1973, Fla. 1977. Local cts. commr. Zomba, Malawa, Africa, 1964-66; assoc. Goldberg, Weigle, Mallin & Gitles, Chgo., 1966-69, ptnr., 1970-73; att. prof. Antioch Sch. of Law, Washington, 1973-78, acad. dean, 1975-76; vis. prof. U. Miami Sch. of Law, Coral Gables, Fla., 1976-78, prof., 1978—. Spl. counsel to gen. counsel SEC, Washington, summers 1980-81; dir. Legal Svcs. of Greater Miami, Inc., 1977 83. Bd. dirs. ACLU of South Fla., 1981-85; mem. dist. admissions com. U.S. Dist. Ct. (so. dist.) Fla.; counsel to former U.S. Judge Alcee L. Hastings and now mem. Ho. of Reps., 1982—. Netherlands Inst. Advanced Studies fellow, 1994-95. Author: (with William Twining) Analysis of Evidence, 1991, The Battle of Hastings: Four Stories in Search of a Meaning, 1996. Mem. ABA, Am. Assn. Law Schs. Office: Univ Miami Sch Law PO Box 248087 Miami FL 33124-8087

ANDERSSON, GUNNAR EINAR, lawyer; b. El Paso, Tex., Mar. 10, 1926; s. Kingsley Sherman and Laurella Florence (Hollis) A.; m. Anne N. H. Williams, June 26, 1948; children— Laura Anne Andersson Kirkland, Norman Hill. B.S., U.S. Mil. Acad., 1946; J.D., U. Denver, 1978. Bar: Colo. 1978, U.S. Dist. Ct. Colo. 1978, U.S. Ct. Appeals (10th cir.) 1978, U.S. Supreme Ct. 1986. Commd. 2d lt. U.S. Army, 1946, advanced through grades to lt. col., 1965, ret., 1973; ptnr. firm Andersson & Conter, Colorado Springs, 1978-80, Barber, Gross & Andersson, Colorado Springs, 1980-81, Gross & Andersson, 1981-85, Andersson, Gerig, Gross & Lederer, P.C., 1985-86; sole practice Gunnar E. Andersson, P.C., 1986—. Dist. chmn. Colorado Springs Rep. Com., 1978-86. Decorated Legion of Merit, Meritorious Service medal, Bronze Star medal. Fellow Explorer's Club; mem. Assn. Trial Lawyers Am., VFW (advocate 1978—), Phi Alpha Delta. Episcopalian. Clubs: Torch Internat. (past pres.). Lodge: Elks (advocate 1982—). Home: 312 Blue Windsor Ln Colorado Springs CO 80906-4427 Office: 625 N Cascade Ave Ste 350 Colorado Springs CO 80903-3238

ANDOLINA, LAWRENCE J. lawyer; b. Rochester, N.Y., Apr. 27, 1948; s. Michael Carl and Nina (Formicola) A.; m. Sharon Jean Cemino, Sept. 22, 1973; children: Lindsay, Lauren. BA, Boston Coll., 1970; JD, Albany Law Sch., 1974. Bar: N.Y. 1975, U.S. Dist. Ct. (we. dist.) N.Y. 1976 (no. dist.) 1995, U.S. Ct. Appeals 1980 (2nd cir.). Asst. dist. atty. Monroe County (N.Y.) Dist. Atty. Office, Rochester, 1975-78; atty., assoc. Palmiere, Passero & Crimi, 1978-80; atty., ptnr. Affronti, Jesserer, Andolina & Lamb, 1980-85, Jesserer, Andolina & Lamb, 1985-87, Jesserer & Andolina, 1987, Harris, Beach & Wilcox, Rochester, 1988-98; ptnr. Trevett Lenweaver & Salzer, N.Y., 1998—. Mem. Nat. Assn. Crim. Def. Lawyers, New York State Assn. Crim. Def. Lawyers, Monroe County Bar Assn. (past pres. 1991-92). Civil rights, Federal civil litigation, Criminal. Office: Trevett Lenweaver & Salzer 16 E Main St Rochester NY 14614-1808

ANDREASEN, JAMES HALLIS, retired state supreme court judge; b. Mpls., May 16, 1931; s. John A. and Alice M. Andreasen; m. Janet Andreasen, June 25, 1961 (dec. July 1985); children: Jon A., Amy E., Steven J.; m. Marilyn McGuire, May 17, 1987. BS in Commerce, U. Iowa, 1953, JD, 1958. Bar: Iowa 1958. Pvt. practice law, Algona, Iowa, 1958-75; with Algona City Coun., 1961-68; judge 3d Jud. Dist. Ct., 1975-87, Supreme Ct. Iowa, Des Moines, 1987-98, ret., sr. judge, 1998—. Lt. col. USAFR, 1954-75. Mem. ABA, Iowa State Bar Assn., Kossuth County Bar Assn. Methodist. Office: Kossuth County Courthouse Algona IA 50511

ANDREOFF, CHRISTOPHER ANDON, lawyer; b. Detroit, July 15, 1947; s. Andon Anastas and Mildred Dimitry (Kolinoff) A.; m. Nancy Anne Krochmal, Jan. 12, 1980; children: Alison Brianne, Lauren Kathleen. BA, Wayne State U., 1969; postgrad. in law, Washington U., St. Louis, 1969-70; JD, U. Detroit, 1972. Bar: Mich. 1972, U.S. Dist. Ct. (ea. dist.) Mich. 1972, U.S. Ct. Appeals (6th cir.) 1974, Fla. 1978, U.S. Supreme Ct. 1980. Legal intern Wayne County Prosecutor's Office, Detroit, 1970-72; law clk. Wayne County Cir. Ct., 1972-73; asst. U.S. atty. U.S. Dept. Justice, 1973-80; asst. chief criminal divsn. U.S. Atty.'s Office, 1977-80; spl. atty. organized crime and racketeering sect. U.S. Dept. Justice, 1980-84, dep. chief Detroit Organized Crime Strike Force, 1982-85, mem. narcotics adv. com., 1979-80; ptnr. Evans & Luptak, Detroit, 1985-93, Jaffe, Raitt, Heuer & Weiss, Detroit, 1995—. Lectr. U.S. Atty. Gen. Advocacy Inst., 1984. Recipient numerous spl. commendations FBI, U.S. Drug Enforcement Adminstrn., U.S. Dept. Justice, U.S. ATty. Gen. Mem. ABA, FBA (spkr. trial adv. and criminal law sect. Detroit 1983—, bd. dirs. 1989-91, chmn. criminal law sect. 1990-91), Mich. Bar Assn., Fla. Bar Assn., Nat. Assn. Criminal Def. Lawyers, Detroit Bar Assn. Greek Orthodox. Federal civil litigation, State civil litigation, Criminal. Home: 4661 Rivers Edge Dr Troy MI 48098-4161 Office: Jaffe Raitt Heuer & Weiss One Woodward Ave Ste 2400 Detroit MI 48226

ANDRES, KENNETH G., JR. lawyer; b. Trenton, N.J., Nov. 9, 1953; s. Kenneth George and Joan Margaret (Fredericks) A. BA, Swarthmore Coll., 1975; JD, Capital U., 1978. Bar: N.J. 1978, Pa. 1978, U.S. Dist. Ct. N.J. 1978, U.S. Ct. Appeals (3rd cir.) 1981, U.S. Supreme Ct. 1994; cert. civil trial atty., N.J., cert. advocate Am. Bd. Trial Advocates. Ptnr. Andres & Berger PC, Haddonfield, N.J. Adj. prof. law Mercer County C.C., 1983-89; faculty mem. Am. Trial Lawyers Assn. - N.J., 1989—. Contbr. articles to profl. publs. Mem. N.J. Supreme Ct. Dist. III ethics com., 1994-98; mem. N.J. Supreme Ct. Civil Jury Charge Com., 1996—. Named Profl. Lawyer of Yr., N.J. Commn. Professionalism in Law, 1998. Mem. ATLA (nat. gov. 2001—), ABA, Assn. Trial Lawyers of Am.-N.J. (bd. govs. 1986-90, parliamentarian 1990-91, from asst. sec. to pres. 1990-1999, N.J. Gold Medal award 1999), Pa. State Bar Assn., N.J. State Bar Assn., Burlington County Bar Assn. (chmn. civil bench and bar com. 1992-94, trustee 1993), Mercer County Bar Assn. (trustee 1982-91). State civil litigation, Personal injury, Product liability. Office: Andres & Berger PC 264 Kings Hwy E Haddonfield NJ 08033-1907 E-mail: kandres@andresberger.com

ANDREU-GARCIA, JOSE ANTONIO, territory supreme court chief justice; Chief justice Supreme Ct. of P.R. Office: Supreme Ct PR PO Box 9022392 San Juan PR 00902-2392 E-mail: andreujp@tld.net, josea2@tribunales.gobierno.net

ANDREW, JOHN HENRY, lawyer, retail corporation executive, author; b. Duluth, Minn., May 23, 1936; s. Frederick William and Florence Elizabeth (Phillips) A.; m. Floretta Claudette Townsend; children: Sean Townsend, Brett Townsend. BA cum laude with distinction, U. Minn., Duluth, 1958; JD, Northwestern U., 1961. Bar: Ill. 1961, Calif. 1975, N.Y. 1980. Assoc. Pattishall, McAuliffe & Hofstetter, Chgo., 1961-71; sr. atty. J.C. Penney Co., Inc., N.Y.C., 1971-74, sr. counsel legis. and regional ops., Western regional coun. L.A., Buena Park, Calif., 1974-93, sr. govt. rels. counsel Sacramento, 1993-97, chief counsel govt. rels., 1997. Author: The Hanging of Arthur Hodge: A Caribbean Anti-Slavery Milestone. Chmn. pub. affairs com. Planned Parenthood Assn. Chgo., 1970-71; mem. Calif. State Dem. Cen. Com., 1976-82. Mem. ABA, Ill. State Bar Assn. (chmn. internat. law sect. 1969-70), Calif. State Bar (com. on consumer fin. svcs. 1982-84, 90-93), Sacramento County Bar Assn., Renaissance Soc., Sacramento Pubs. Assn. (Best Gen. Non-Fiction award 2000-01), Cornwall Family History Soc., Sullivan County (Pa.) Hist. Soc. (life), Calif. C. of C. (regulatory, consumer and legal affairs com. 1974-86, mem. air and waste mgmt. com. 1994-97). Administrative and regulatory, Consumer commercial, Legislative. Home: 11359 Mother Lode Cir Gold River CA 95670-3025 E-mail: jandrew523@aol.com

ANDREWS, DAVID RALPH, lawyer; b. Oakland, Calif., Jan. 4, 1942; m. Rozan McCurdy, July 1, 1962; children: David, Linda. BA, U. Calif., Berkeley, 1968; JD, U. Calif., 1971. Bar: Calif. 1971, D.C. 1986, U.S. Dist. Ct. (no. dist.) Calif. 1971, U.S. Dist. Ct. Hawaii 1991, U.S. Supreme Ct. 1980. Assoc. McCutchen, Doyle, Brown & Enersen, San Francisco, 1971-75; regional counsel Reg. IX U.S. EPA, 1975-77; legal counsel and spl. asst. for policy U.S. EPA, Washington, 1977-79; dep. gen. counsel Dept. Health and Human Svcs., 1980-81; ptnr. McCutchen, Doyle, Brown & Enersen, San Francisco, 1981-97, chmn., 1991-95; legal adviser U.S. Dept. State, Washington, 1997-2000; ptnr. McCutchen, Doyle, Brown & Enersen, San Francisco, 2000—. Amb., spl. negotiator U.S./Iran Claims, 2000—; bd. dirs. Union Bank Calif., Kaiser Permanente, NetCel360 Holdings Ltd., PG&E Corp. Trustee San Francisco Mus. of Modern Art, 1988-97; bd. trustees Golden Gate Nat. Park Assn., 1992-95, Marin Cmty. Found., 1996-97; mem. U.S. Agy. for Internat. Devel. Energy Tng. Program Adv. Com. of the Inst. Internat. Edn.; mem. bd. dirs. Union Bank Calif., Kaiser Permanente and NetCel360 Holdings Ltd., 2000—. Fellow Max Planck Inst. of Pub. Internat. Law, Heidelberg, Fed. Republic of Germany, 1974. Mem. ABA (natural resources sect.), Calif. Bar Assn.), San Francisco Bar Assn. Avocations: photography, tennis, running. Administrative and regulatory, Environmental. Office: McCutchen Doyle Brown & Enersen 3 Embarcadero Ctr San Francisco CA 94111-4003

ANDREWS, MARK, lawyer; b. Cleve., Aug. 4, 1949; s. Andrew and Florence Mae (Spettigue) Ondrejko; m. Cheryl Anne Keepers, Feb. 21, 1981; children: Wesley Keepers, Laurel Keepers. BA cum laude, Miami U., Oxford, Ohio, 1971; JD, Georgetown U., 1975. Bar: D.C. 1975, Alaska 1981. Ptnr. Kalijarvi & Andrews, Washington, 1977-79; staff atty. Alaska Legal Svcs., Bethel, 1980-81, supervising atty., 1981-86; asst. borough atty. Fairbanks North Star Borough, 1986-93; risk mgr. Fairbanks North Star Borough and Sch. Dist., 1993-95; assoc. counsel Tanana Chiefs Conf., Inc., Fairbanks, 1995—. Mem. Phi Beta Kappa. Labor, Legislative, Native American. Office: Tanana Chiefs Conference Inc 122 1st Ave Ste 600 Fairbanks AK 99701-4871 E-mail: mandrews@tananachiefs.org

ANDREWS, MINERVA WILSON, retired lawyer; b. Rock Hill, S.C., Feb. 1, 1925; d. York Lowry and Minnie de Foix (Long) Wilson; m. Robert Taylor Andrews, Apr. 15, 1950; children: Susan Allison (Mrs. Robert N. Wiles), Stuart Davidson. AB, U. S.C., 1945; LLB, U. Va., 1948. Bar: Va. 1948. Trial atty. AntiTrust Divsn. U.S. Dept. Justice, Washington, 1949-55; assoc. atty. Bauknight, Prichard, McCanlish & Williams, Fairfax, Va., 1963-72, Boothe, Prichard & Dudley, 1972-80; ptnr. Boothe, Pritchard & Dudley, McGuire, Woods, et al. (merged), McLean, Va., 1980-91; ret., 1991. Author: Carolina-Virginia Recollections, 1999. Nat. pres. Nat. Soc. Arts & Letters, 1994—96; bd. dir. Mclean Citizen Asn., 1968—2000, Fairfax/Falls Church United Way, Vienna, 1988—2001; life elder Lewinsville Presby. Church, McLean, 1980—. Named Citizen of the Yr. Fairfax County Fedn. Citizen Assn. and Washington Post, 1997. Mem. Va. State Bar (past chmn. real property sect.), Va. Bar Assn. (past chmn. real estate com. 1981-84, William B. Spong Jr. Professionalism award 2001), Fairfax Bar Assn. (chmn. real property com. 1980-82), Nat. Soc. Arts and Letters (past nat. pres. 1994-96). Republican. Office: McGuireWoods LLP 1750 Tysons Blvd Ste 1800 Mc Lean VA 22102-4215

ANDREWS, WILLIAM DOREY, law educator, lawyer; b. N.Y.C., Feb. 25, 1931; s. Sidney Warren and Margaret (Dorey) A.; A.B., Amherst Coll., 1952, LL.D., 1977; LL.B., Harvard U., 1955; m. Shirley May Herrman, Dec. 26, 1953; children: Helen Estelle Andrews Noble, Roy Herrman, John Frederick, Margaret Dorey Andrews Davenport, Susan Louise, Carol Mary Andrews Reid. Bar: Mass. 1959. Practice in Boston, 1959-63; assoc. Ropes & Gray, 1959-63; lectr. Harvard Law Sch., Cambridge, Mass., 1961-63, asst. prof., 1963-65, prof., 1965—, Eli Goldston prof. law, 1986— ; cons. Sullivan & Worcester, 1964—; assoc. reporter for accessions tax proposal Am. Law Inst. Fed. Estate and Gift Tax Project; gen. reporter for subchpt. C, Am. Law Inst. Fed. Income Tax Project, 1974-82, 86-93; cons. U.S. Treasury Dept., 1965-68. Mem. Zoning Bd. Appeals, Concord, 1966-73. Served to lt. USNR, 1955-58. Mem. Am. Law Inst., Am. Bar Assn. Office: Harvard U Law Sch 1545 Massachusetts Ave Cambridge MA 02138-2903

ANFUSO, VICTOR L'EPISCOPO, lawyer, business consultant; b. Bklyn., Sept. 17, 1932; s. Victor L'Episcopo and Frances (Stallone) A.; m. Kathy Ann Shea, Apr. 8, 1967; children— Dina, Michelle, Victor T., William P., Adrienne. A.B. magna cum laude, St. John's U., 1954, J.D., 1959. Bar: N.Y. 1959, Oreg. 1986. Ptnr., Warner Birdsall & Anfuso, N.Y.C., 1959-62, Anfuso & Kroll, N.Y.C., 1965-69, Anfuso & Posmantur, N.Y.C., 1971-73; sole practice, N.Y.C., 1974-80; ptnr. Wildes Weinberg & Anfuso, N.Y.C., 1980-84; ch. adminstr. Bible Temple, Portland, Oreg., 1984-86; sr. cons. Anfuso Cons., Yuba City, Calif., 1981-82; pres., co-founder Portland Consulting Group, 1988. Contbr. articles to law jours. Pres., N.Y. State Young Citizens for Johnson, 1964; bd. dirs. World Rehab. Fund, 1972-78. Served to lt. USNR, 1955-57. Mem. N.Y. State Bar Assn., Oreg. State Bar Assn., Assn. Immigration and Nationality Lawyers, Full Gospel Businessmen's Assn. Mem. Christian Ch. Home: 3101 NE 156th Ave Portland OR 97230-5167 Office: 1515 SW 5th Ave Portland OR 97201-5406

ANGEL, ARTHUR RONALD, lawyer, consultant; b. Long Beach, Calif., May 10, 1948; s. Morris and Betty Estelle (Unger) A.; 1 child, Jamie Kathryn. BA, U. Calif.-Berkeley, 1969; JD, Harvard U., 1972. Bar: Mass. 1972, D.C. 1975, Okla. 1979, Calif. 2001, U.S. Dist. Ct. (we. dist.) Okla. 1980, U.S. Dist. Ct. (no. dist.) Okla. 1981, U.S. Dist. Ct. (ctrl. dist.) Calif. 2001, U.S. Supreme Ct. 1983. Atty. FTC, Washington, 1972-78; pvt. practice Oklahoma City, 1978-87; ptnr. Angel & Ikard, 1987-93; of counsel Abel, Musser Sokolosky & Assoc., L.A., 1994-2000; ptnr. Carrick Law Group, 2001—. Mem. adv. panel on cardiovascular devices, Washington, 1979-82; cons. FTC, 1978-79; adminstrv. law judge Okla. Dept. Labor, 1999-2000; spl. mcpl. judge City of Oklahoma City, 1999-2001. Recipient Meritorious Service award FTC, Washington, 1978. Fellow Inst. Law and Social Scis.; mem. Am. Arbitration Assn., Assn. Trial Lawyers Am., Okla. Trial Lawyers Assn., Okla. Bar Assn., D.C. Bar Assn., Mass. Bar Assn. Democrat. Jewish. Federal civil litigation, General practice, Personal injury. Home: 1236 N Fairfax Ave Los Angeles CA 90046 Office: Carrick Law Group 350 S Grand Ave Ste 2930 Los Angeles CA 90071-3406 E-mail: art@carricklawgroup.com

ANGEL, JAMES JOSEPH, lawyer; b. Racine, Wis., Apr. 1, 1956; s. William J. and Dorothy P. (Potman) A.; m. Catherine Anne Cowan, Oct. 17, 1982; children: Carter Anne, Riley James, Spenser Catherine. BA, W.Va. Wesleyan Coll., 1977; JD, U. Richmond, 1979. Dep. commonwealth atty. City of Lynchburg (Va.) Commonwealth Atty. Office, 1979-84; ptnr. Smith, Angel & Falcone, P.C., Lynchburg, 1984-87; pvt. practice, 1987—. Chmn. Boonsboro-Peakland Neighborhood Assn., Lynchburg, 1990-99. Mem. ATLA, Va. Trial Lawyers Assn., Va. Bar Assn., Va. Coll. Criminal Def. Attys., Lynchburg Bar Assn. (past pres. criminal law sect. 1992). Avocations: golf, whitewater rafting. Criminal, General practice, Personal injury. Office: 725 Church St Lynchburg VA 24504-1417 also: Allied Arts Bldg PO Box 1042 Lynchburg VA 24505-1042

ANGELICO, DENNIS MICHAEL, lawyer; b. New Orleans, Dec. 19, 1950; s. John Blase and Gladys (Dehring) A.; B.A., Tulane U., 1974, J.D., 1974. Bar: La. 1974, U.S. Dist. Ct. (ea., mid. and we. dists.) La. 1974, U.S. Supreme Ct. 1983, U.S. Ct. Appeals (5th cir.) 1975. Assoc., then ptnr. Hess & Washofsky, New Orleans, 1974— . Bd. dirs. Dashiki Project Theatre, New Orleans, 1982-85. Mem. ABA, La. Bar Assn. (sec.-treas. labor law sect. 1983, vice chmn. labor law sect. 1984, chmn. labor law sect. 1985), De La Salle Alumni Assn. (rec. sec. 1982), Tulane Alumni Assn. (Fellows Club), Phi Alpha Delta. Democrat. Roman Catholic. Labor, Pension, profit-sharing, and employee benefits. Home: PO Box 13945 New Orleans LA 70185-3945

ANGELL, M(ARY) FAITH, federal magistrate judge; b. Buffalo, May 7, 1938; d. San S. and Marie B. (Caboni) A.; m. Kenneth F. Carobus, Oct. 27, 1973; children: Andrew M. Carobus, Alexander P. Carobus. AB, Mt. Holyoke Coll., 1959; MSS, Bryn Mawr Coll., 1965; JD, Temple U., 1971. Bar: Pa. 1971, U.S. Dist. Ct. (ea. dist) Pa. 1971, U.S. Ct. Appeals (3rd cir.) Pa. 1974, U.S. Supreme Ct. 1979, Acad. Cert. Social Workers. Dir. social work, vol. svcs. Wills Eye Hosp., Phila., 1961-64, 65-69; dir. soc. work dept. juvenile divsn. Defender Assoc., 1969-71; asst. dist. atty. City of Phila., 1971-72; asst. atty. gen. Commonwealth of Pa., Phila., 1972-74, deputy atty. gen., 1974-78; regional counsel ICC, 1978-80, regional dir., 1980-88; administrv. law judge Social Security Administrn., 1988-90; U.S. magistrate judge U.S. Dist. Ct. (ea. dist.) Pa., 1990—. Adj. prof. Temple U. Law Sch., Phila., 1976-94, clin. instr., 1973-76; co-chmn. Commn. on Gender, 3d Cir. Task Force on Equal Treatment in Cts., 1994—; mem. com. on racial and gender bias in the justice sys. Supreme Ct. of Pa., 2000. Federal trustee Defender Assn. Phila., 1985-90; bd. dirs. Child Welfare Adv. Bd., Phila., 1984-90, Federal Cts. 200 Adv. Bd., Phila., 1987-88, Phila. Woman's Network, 1986-88. Recipient Sr. Exec. Svc. award U.S. Govt., 1980. Mem. NASW, FBA (chair exec. com., pres. 1990-92, recognition 1992), Nat. Assn. Women Judges, Fed. Magistrate Judges Assn. (dist. dir. 1994-98), Phila. Bar Assn. (chmn. com. 1976-77), Temple Am. Inn of Cts. (master 1993-98), Third Circuit Task Force on Equal Treatment in the Courts (co-chair Commn. on Gender 1994-97), Temple Law Alumni Exec. Bd. (Women's Law Caucus Honoree 1996). Office: US District Court 601 Market St 3030 US Courthouse Philadelphia PA 19106

ANGELL, SUSAN L. lawyer; b. San Francisco, Feb. 8, 1955; d. Vincent H. and Margaret A. Angell; m. Larry Kastelic, June 18, 1983 (div. Jan. 1994); children: Danny, Katie, Timmy. BSN, U. San Francisco, 1977; MSN, Calif. State U. Long Beach, 1988; JD, Thomas Jefferson Sch. Law, 1996. cert. RN; Bar: Calif. RN Oakland Children's Hosp., 1977-80; RN,

nurse practitioner Children's Hosp. Orange Co., 1982-85; hosp. mgr. FHP Hosp., Fountain Valley, Calif., 1986-88; RN ProCare, Santa Ana, 1989-95; atty. O'Flaherty, Cross, Martinez, Ovando & Hatton, Anaheim, 1997-98, Ginsberg, Stephan, Oringher & Richman, Costa Mesa, 1998—. Mem. Nursing Alumni Assn. (v.p.), Orange Co. Bar Assn., So. Calif. Assn. Health Care Risk Mgrs. Office: 535 Anton Blvd Ste 800 Costa Mesa CA 92626-7110 E-mail: sangwll@gsor.com

ANGINO, RICHARD CARMEN, lawyer; b. McKeesport, Pa., May 2, 1940; s. Carmen and Filomena (Lombardi) A.; m. Alice K. Angino, May 2, 1976; children: Elizabeth, Richard, William. BA in English, Franklin and Marshall Coll., Lancaster, Pa., 1958-62; JD, Villanova U., Pa., 1965. Bar: Pa. 1965, U.S. Supreme Ct. 1968, U.S. Ct. Appeals (3rd cir.) 1975, U.S. Dist. Ct. (ea. and cen. dist.) 1966. Ptnr., civil litigation specialist Angino & Rovner PC, Harrisburg, Pa., 1965—. Pres. Pa. Trial Lawyers Assn., Pa., 1982-83. Co-author: The Pennsylvania No-Fault Motor Vehicle Insurance Act, 1979, Pennsylvania Personal Injury Evidence, 1990. Pres. Leukemia Soc. Am., Ctrl. Pa., 1989-92; v.p. Am. Horticulture Soc., Alexandria. Va., 1990-92, Friends of Wildwood, Harrisburg, Pa., 1989-96; assoc. trustee Franklin and Marshall, 1979—; bd. cons. Villanova Univ. Sch. Law, 1994—, govs. residence preservation com., 1997—. Mem. Internat. Soc. Barristers, Dauphin County Bar Assn., Pa. Bar Assn., Pa. Trial Lawyers Assn., Assn. Trial Lawyers Am. Republican. Roman Catholic. Avocation: ornamental horticulture. Personal injury, Product liability, Professional liability. Home: 2040 Fishing Creek Valley Rd Harrisburg PA 17112-9245 Office: Angino & Rovner PC 4503 N Front St Harrisburg PA 17110-1799 E-mail: rca@angino-rouner.com

ANGST, GERALD L. lawyer; b. Chgo., Dec. 29, 1950; s. Gerald L. Sr. and Audrey M. (Hides) A.; m. Candace Simning, Jan. 29, 1983. BA magna cum laude, Loyola U., Chgo., 1972, JD cum laude, 1975. Assoc. Sidley Austin Brown & Wood, Chgo., 1975-82, ptnr., 1982—. Mem. ABA (constrn. litigation com. litigation sect.), Chgo. Bar Assn. (civil practice com.). General civil litigation, Construction, Insurance. Office: Sidley Austin Brown & Wood 47th Fl Bank One Plz Chicago IL 60603-2000 E-mail: gangst@sidley.com

ANGULO, CHARLES BONIN, foreign service officer, lawyer; b. N.Y.C., Aug. 6, 1943; s. Manuel R. and Carolyn C. (Bonin) A.; m. Penelope Snare, June 28, 1986. BA, U. Va., 1966; cert., U. Madrid, 1966; JD, Tulane U., 1969. Bar: Va. 1969. Assoc. Michael & Dent, Charlottesville, Va., 1969-73; assoc. editor The Michie Pub. Co., 1973; fgn. svc. officer U.S. Dept. State, Washington, 1973-75, Am. Embassy U.S. Dept. State, Brussels, 1976-78, Santo Domingo, 1981-85, Office of the Legal Advisor, U.S. Dept. State, Washington, 1978-81; exec. dir. office of insp. gen. U.S. Dept. State, 1985-86; asst. chief protocol U.S. State Dept., 1986-88, Am. Consulate Gen. U.S. Dept. State, Jeddah, Saudi Arabia, 1988-93; fgn. svc. officer Am. Embassy U.S. Dept. State, Quito, Ecuador, 1993—. Home and Office: 4517 17th Ave W Bradenton FL 34209-4316 E-mail: cpangulo@aol.com

ANNANON, SONGPHOL, lawyer, consultant; b. Trang, Thailand; LLB, Thammasat U., Bangkok, 1992. Sr. lawyer Mongkolnavin Law Office, Bangkok, 1998—. Mem. Thai Bar Assn., Law Soc. of Thailand. Bankruptcy, General civil litigation, Intellectual property. Office: Mongkolnavin Law Office 12 Sukhumvit 5 Sukhumvit St 10110 Bangkok Thailand Home: 48/18 Ngamwongwan 8 Ngamwongwan St 11000 Bangkhen Thailand Fax: 662-2535530

ANNOTICO, RICHARD ANTHONY, legal administration, real estate investor; b. Cleve., Sept. 17, 1930; s. Anthony and Grace (Kovarik) A. AB in Bus. with hons., Ohio U., 1953; LLB, Southwestern Law Sch., 1963; JD, UCLA, 1965. Dir. internat. sales then v.p. Liberty Records, L.A., 1957-64; real estate investment counselor Calif. Land Sales, Beverly Hills, 1964-66, R.A. Annotico & Assocs., L.A., 1966-68, real estate investor, 1969—. Spkr. in field.; mem. Bd. of Governors State Calif.; expert witness State Legis. Calif. Contbr. numerous articles to profl. jours. Commr. L.A. Transp. Commn., 1984-88, v.p. 1985-87; commr. L.A. Human Rels. Comm n., 1977-84, pres. 1983-84; mem. Calif. State Senate Small Bus. Adv. Bd., 1978-82, L.A. City County Adv. Commn. on Consolidation, 1976-77; pres. Federated Italian-Americans So. Calif., 1975-76; mem. Mayors Exec. Com. Christopher Columbus Quincentenary 1992. Lt. USAF, 1954-55. Decorated Cavaliere Ufficiale Order of Merit (Italy), Comdr. St. Lazarus Internat. Chivalric, Hospitaller and Mil. Order. Mem. Calif. State Bar Assn. (bd. govs., 1983-86, 86-89, 89-92, v.p. 1986, 89, 92). Office: RA Annotico & Assocs 4267 Marina City Dr Unit 1008 Marina Del Rey CA 90292

ANSBACHER, SIDNEY FRANKLYN, lawyer; b. Jacksonville, Fla., May 28, 1961; 1 child, Benjamin Alexander. BA, U. Fla., 1981; JD, Hamline U., 1985; LLM in Agrl. Law, U. Ark., 1989. Bar: Fla., U.S. Dist. Ct. (mid. dist.) Fla., U.S. Ct. Appeals (D.C. cir.). Atty. Fla. Dept. Natural Resources, Tallahassee, 1986-87; assoc. Turner, Ford, Buckingham, Jacksonville, Fla., 1987-90; ptnr., assoc. Brant, Moore et al, 1990-95; ptnr. Mahoney Adams & Criser, 1995-97, Upchurch Bailey & Upchurch, St. Augustine, 1997—. Contbr. articles to profl. jours.; mng. editor Fla. Bar Environ. and Land Use CLE Manual, 1998—. Bd. dirs. Fla. Forestry Found., 1993-96. Recipient Outstanding Achievement award Fla. Wildlife Fedn., 1990. Mem. Fla. Bar (treas. environ. and land use law sect. 1998-99, sec. 1999-2000, chair-elect 2000—, bd. dirs. 1994-98, Judy Florence Outstanding Svc. award 1992, 2000, Coun. of Sects. 2000—), Jacksonville Bar Assn. (chair environ. and land use law sect. 1994-96). Avocations: bicycling, tennis, reading. Office: Upchurch Bailey & Upchurch PA 780 N Ponce De Leon Blvd Saint Augustine FL 32084-3519 E-mail: sfansbacher@ubulaw.com

ANSELL, EDWARD ORIN, lawyer; b. Superior, Wis., Mar. 29, 1926; s. H. S. and Mollie (Rudnitzky) A.; m. Hanne B. Baer, Dec. 23, 1956; children: Deborah, William. BSEE, U. Wis., 1948; JD, George Washington U., 1955. Bar: D.C. 1955, Calif. 1960. Electronic engr. FCC, Buffalo and Washington, 1948-55; patent atty. RCA, Princeton, N.J., 1955-57; gen. mgr. AeroChem. Rsch. Labs., 1957-58; patent atty. Aerojet-Gen. Corp., La Jolla, Calif., 1958-63, corp. patent counsel, 1963-82, asst. sec., 1970-79, sec., 1979-82, assoc. gen. counsel, 1981-82; dir. patents and licensing Calif. Inst. Tech., Pasadena, 1982-92; pvt. practice Claremont, Calif., 1992—; co-founder Gryphon Scis., South San Francisco, 1993, Ciphergen Biosystems, Fremont, 1993. Adj. prof. U. La Verne (Calif.) Coll. Law, 1972-78; spl. advisor, task force chmn. U.S. Commn. Govt. Procurement, 1971 Editor: Intellectual Property in Academe: A Legal Compendium, 1991; contbr. articles to profl. publs. Recipient Alumni Svc. award George Washington U., 1975. Mem. Am. Intellectual Property Law Assn., Assn. Corp. Patent Counsel, Ea. Bar Assn. Los Angeles County, L.A. Intellectual Property Law Assn., Assn. Univ. Tech. Mgrs., State Bar Calif. (exec. com. intellectual property sect. 1983-86), Athenaeum Club Pasadena, Univ. Club Claremont. Intellectual property, Patent, Trademark and copyright. Office: 427 N Yale Ave # 204 Claremont CA 91711 E-mail: anselaw@att.net

ANSLEY, SHEPARD BRYAN, lawyer; b. July 31, 1939; s. William Bonneau and Florence Jackson (Bryan) A.; m. Boyce Lineberger, May 9, 1970; children-Anna Rankin, Florence Bryan. BA, U. Ga., 1961; LLB, U. Va., 1964. Bar: Ba. 1967. Assoc. Carter & Ansley and predecessor firm Carter, Ansley, Smith & McLendon, Atlanta, 1967-73, ptnr., 1973-84, of counsel, 1984-91; with Attkisson Carter & Akers Inc., 1991-2000, Attkisson Carter & Co., Atlanta, 2001—. Bd. dirs. Prime Bancshares, Inc., Prime Bank, FSB; chmn. bd. dirs., pres. Sodamaster Co. Am.; exec. v.p. Woodridge Realty, Inc.; sr. v.p., ACA Consulting, Inc.; fin. cons. Attkisson, Carter & Akers, Inc.; bd. dirs., sec. CRM Co., LLC, L.A. County, Calif. Mem. Vestry St. Luke's Episcopal Ch., Atlanta, 1971-74; treas., mem. exec. com., bd. dirs. Alliance Theatre Co., Atlanta, 1974-85; trustee Atlanta Music Festival Assn., Inc., 1975—; v.p., bd. dirs. Atlanta Preservation Ctr. Inc., pres., 1988-90; bd. visitors Lineberger Cancer Rsch. Ctr. U. N.C. at Chapel Hill, 1987-92; pres., bd. dirs. The Study Hall at Emmaus House, Inc.; bd. dirs., The Margaret Mitchell House, Inc.; bd. govs. Ga. Pub. Policy Found., Inc., 1999—. Capt. U.S. Army, 1965-67. Mem. ABA, Ga. Bar Assn., Atlanta Bar Assn., Atlanta Lawyers Club, Am. Coll. Mortgage Attys., Atlanta Jr. C. of C. (bd. dirs. 1968-72), Piedmont Driving Club. E-mail: sbansley@mindspring.com

ANSTEAD, HARRY LEE, state supreme court justice; Former judge, chief judge Fla. Ct. Appeals. (4th dist.), Fla.; justice Fla. Supreme Ct., Tallahassee, 1994—. Office: Supreme Ct Bldg 500 S Duval St Tallahassee FL 32399-6556

ANTHONY, ANDREW JOHN, lawyer; b. Newark, Jan. 26, 1950; s. Andrew and Mary (Norton) A.; m. Raquel Perez Montoya, Sept. 29, 1990; children: Nicholas, Natalie. BA, Kean Coll., 1973; JD cum laude, U. Miami, 1976. Bar: Fla. 1977, U.S. Dist. Ct. (so. dist.) Fla. 1977. Assoc. Knight, Peters, Hoeveler, Pickle, Niemoeller & Flynn, Miami, Fla., 1977-79, Vernis & Bowling, Miami, 1979, Ligman, Martin, Shiley & McGee, Coral Gables, Fla., 1979-86; sole practice, 1986—. Mem. ABA, Fla. Bar Assn. Democrat. Roman Catholic. Avocations: numismatics, fishing, reading. State civil litigation, Insurance, Personal injury. Home: 3703 Anderson Rd Coral Gables FL 33134-7052 Office: 866 S Dixie Hwy Coral Gables FL 33146 E-mail: ajanthony@ajalaw.com

ANTHONY, ROBERT ARMSTRONG, law educator, lawyer; b. Washington, Dec. 28, 1931; s. Emile Peter and Martha Graham (Armstrong) A.; m. Ruth Grace Barrons, Feb. 7, 1959 (div.); 1 child, Graham Barrons; m. Joan Patricia Caton, Jan 3, 1980; 1 child, Peter Christopher Caton. BA, Yale U., 1953; BA in Jurisprudence, Oxford U., 1955; JD, Stanford U., 1957. Bar: Calif. 1957, N.Y. 1971, D.C. 1972. Assoc. Pillsbury, Madison & Sutro, San Francisco, 1957-62, Kelso, Cotton & Ernst, San Francisco, 1962-64; assoc. prof. law Cornell U. Law Sch., 1964-68, prof., 1968-75, dir. internat. legal studies, 1964-74; chief counsel, later dir. Office Fgn. Direct Investments, Dept. Commerce, 1972-73; cons. Adminstrv. Conf. U.S., Washington, 1968-71, chmn., 1974-79; ptnr. McKenna, Conner & Cuneo, Washington, 1979-82; sole practice, 1982-83; prof. law George Mason U., Arlington, Va., 1983—. Fulbright lectr., Slovenia, 1994; lectr. Acad. Am. and Internat. Law, Southwestern Legal Found., Dallas, summers 1967-72, instr. Golden Gate U., 1961. Mem. editorial adv. bd. Jour. Law and Tech., 1986-91; contbr. articles to profl. jours. Active Pres.'s Inflation Program Regulatory Coun., 1978-79, Fairfax County (Va.) Rep. Com., 1984-86; chmn. panel U.S. Dept. Edn. Appeal Bd., 1981-83; cons., chmn. pubs. adv. bd. Internat. Law Inst., 1984—; cons. Inst. Pub. Adminstrn., Slovenia, 1994—; bd. dirs. Marin Shakespeare Festival, San Rafael, Calif., 1961-64, Nat. Ctr. for Adminstrv. Justice, 1974-79, Va. Assn. Scholars, 1990-98; commr. Sausalito (Calif.) City Planning Commn., 1962-64. Mem. ABA (coun., sec. sect. adminstrv. law and regulatory practice 1988-94), Assn. Am. Rhodes Scholars, Am. Law Inst., Stanford U. Law Soc. Washington (pres. 1982), Cosmos Club. Home: 2011 Lorraine Ave Mc Lean VA 22101-5331 Office: George Mason U Law Sch 3401 N Fairfax Dr Arlington VA 22201-4411 E-mail: ranthony@gmu.edu

ANTHONY, STEPHEN PIERCE, lawyer; b. Concord, Mass., Aug. 30, 1961; s. Reed Pierce and Barbara (Beatley) A.; m. Lisa Ann Battalia, June 2, 1990. AB, Dartmouth Coll., 1983; JD, Columbia U., 1988. Bar: Md. 1989, D.C. 1991, U.S. Dist. Ct. D.C. 1991, U.S. Ct. Appeals (D.C. cir.) 1991. Law clk. to Hon. Patricia M. Wald, U.S. Ct. Appeals for D.C. Cir., Washington, 1988-89; assoc. Wilmer, Cutler & Pickering, 1989-91; asst. U.S. atty. U.S. Atty.'s Office for D.C., 1991-96; trial atty. pub. integrity sect. criminal divsn. U.S. Dept. Justice, 1996—2000; with Covington & Burling, 2000—. Barrister Edward Bennett Williams Am. Inn of Ct., Washington, 1997—. Notes and comments editor Columbia Law Rev., 1987-88. Harlan Fiske Stone scholar Columbia U., 1985-86, 87-88, James Kent scholar, 1986-87. Office: Covington & Burling 1201 Pennsylvania Ave NW Washington DC 20004 E-mail: santhony@cov.com

ANTON, RONALD DAVID, lawyer; b. Phila., Nov. 9, 1933; s. Emil T. Anton and Mary E. Bishara; m. Suzanne J. Winker, Aug. 19, 1976; 1 child, Ronald J. JD, U. Buffalo, 1958; LLM, U. Pa., 1959, Yale U., 1960. Bar: N.Y. 1959. Ptnr. Boniello, Anton, Conti & B., Niagara Falls, N.Y., 1960—; corp. counsel City of Niagara Falls, 2000—. Lectr. Univ. Buffalo (N.Y.) Law Sch., 1960-62; cons. N.Y. State Legis., Buffalo, Greater Buffalo (N.Y.) Devel. Found.; past pres. Niagara (N.Y.) County Legal Aid, 1966-68, Niagara Falls (N.Y.) Bar, 1968; past dist. gov. N.Y. State Trial Lawyers, 1984-88; moderator (tv show) The Law For You, N.Y., 1967. Author: Jesus, Saviour, 1992; contbr. articles to profl. jours. Rep. candidate N.Y. State Atty. Gen., 1990; trustee Stella Niagara Edn. Pk., Lewiston, N.Y., 1988—. General civil litigation. Home: 175 White Tail Run Grand Island NY 14072-3223 Office: Boniello Anton Conti & B 770 Main St Niagara Falls NY 14301-1704

ANTONE, NAHIL PETER, lawyer, civil engineer; b. Baghdad, Iraq, Jan. 17, 1952; came to U.S., 1978; s. Peter and Salima (Kammoo) A. BS in Civil Engring. with highest distinction, U. Baghdad, 1971; MS in Structural Engring., U. Surrey, 1974; JD summa cum laude, Detroit Coll. Law, 1985. Bar: Mich. 1985, U.S. Dist. Ct. (ea. dist.) Mich. 1985; registered profl. engr., Mich. Constrn. engr. Ministry Constrn., Baghdad, 1971-73; project mgr. Ministry Oil, 1974-78; design engr. Harley Ellington Pierce Yee, Southfield, Mich., 1978-79; v.p. Hennessey Engring. Co., Trenton, 1979-85; assoc. Bodman, Longley & Dahling, Detroit, 1985-88; owner N. Peter Antone Profl. Corp., Southfield, 1988—; ptnr. Antone & Kuhn Law Offices, Farmington Hills, Mich., 1989-93; pvt. practice Southfield, 1993—. Lectr. Detroit Coll. Law, 1986-87. Govt. of Iraq scholar, 1974; scholar Det. Coll. Law, 1982. Mem. ABA, Detroit Bar Assn., ASCE (chmn. legis. com. Southeast Mich. chpt. 1981). Avocations: tennis, swimming, exercise, travel, music. Construction, Immigration, naturalization, and customs, Public international. Home: 28935 Murray Crescent Dr Southfield MI 48076-5563 Office: 16445 W 12 Mile Rd Southfield MI 48076-2949

ANUTA, MICHAEL JOSEPH, lawyer; b. Pound, Wis., Feb. 4, 1901; s. Michael Anuta and Charlotte Zudnochowsky; m. Marianne M. Strelec; children: Mary Hope Milidonis, Nancy Ellen Beauchamp, Janet Grace Dalquist, Michael John, Karl Frederick. LLB, LaSalle Extension U., 1956; LLD (hon.), Alma Coll., 1960; BS (hon.), San Vicinte De Paul, Maracaibo, Venezuela, 1965. Bar: Mich. 1929, U.S. Supreme Ct. 1932, U.S. Dist. Ct. Mich., U.S. Dist. Ct. Wis., Bar of Interstate Commerce Commn. Traffic mgr. M&M Traffic Assn., Menominee, Mich., 1938-48; pros. atty. Menominee County, 1938-48; mcpl. judge City of Menominee, 1958-68; reserve judge Menominee, 1929—. Author: East Prussians from Russia, 1979, Ships of our Ancestors, 1983, History of Rotary Clubs in Wisconsin-Michigan, 1993, Anuta Heritage Register, 1993. Dir., v.p. Mich. Children's Aid Soc.; active Boy Scouts Am., 1945—; moderator Synod Presbyn. Ch. Mich., 1953; chmn. Menominee County Def. Council, WWII, 1953. Lt. col. CAP, Mich. Recipient Silver Beaver award Boy Scouts Am., 1945, Silver Antelope, 1967, Disting. Svc. award community svc. Radio Sta. WAGN, 1963, Disting. citation, Govt. Legislature of Mich., 1989; named Man Yr. Menominee Area C. of C., 1971. Mem. ABA, State Bar Mich., Menominee County Bar Assn., Mich. Prosecuting Attys. Assn. (pres. 1945), Menominee County Hist. Soc. (pres. 1967-74, pres. emeritus), Am. Hist. Socs. Germans from Russia (dir. 1978-81), Hist. Soc. Mich. (dir. 1972-78, award merit 1980, Charles Follow award 1983), Am. Arbitrators Assn., Panel Arbitrators Res. Mich. Judge, Rotary (gov. dist. 1963-64, pres. 1934-35), Shriners, Masons (33 degree). Republican. Avocations: pilot, amateur radio. Antitrust, Aviation, General corporate. Home and Office: # 105 1200 Northland Terrace Ln Marinette WI 54143-4193 E-mail: Michael@webcntrl.com

ANUTTA, LUCILE JAMISON, lawyer; b. Nashville, July 10, 1943; d. Frederick Thomas and Roberta Bogle (Jamison) A.; m. Gerald Patrick McCarthy, May 21, 1977. BA, Duke U., 1965; MA, Middlebury Coll., 1966; JD, U. Mich., 1975. Bar: Va. 1976. Assoc. Hunton & Williams, Richmond, Va., 1975-79; tax atty. Reynolds Metal Co., 1979-2000; of counsel McGuire Woods LLP, 2000—. Pension, profit-sharing, and employee benefits, Corporate taxation. Home: 305 Marston Ln Richmond VA 23221-3705 Office: McGuire Woods LLP One James Ctr 901 E Cary St Richmond VA 23219-4030 E-mail: lanutta@mcguirewoods.com

ANZAI, EARL I. state attorney general; b. Honolulu; Student, Emroy U., Oreg. State U.; BA, U. Hawaii, 1964, MA, 1966. Law clk. First Cir. Ct., Honolulu, 1983-95; dir. Dept. Budget and Fin., 1995-99; atty. gen. State Senate Hawaii, 1999—. Office: Dept Atty Gen 425 Queen St Honolulu HI 96813-2903*

APFELBAUM, MARC, lawyer; b. Phila., Apr. 30, 1955; s. Herbert and Beatrice Bernice (Bitman) A. BA cum laude, U. Pa., 1978; JD magna cum laude, Georgetown U., 1983. Bar: N.Y. 1984, U.S. Dist. Ct. (so. and ea. dists.) N.Y. 1984, Conn. 1991. Assoc. Cravath, Swaine & Moore, N.Y.C., 1983-89; v.p., assoc. gen. counsel, asst. sec. Time Warner Cable, Stamford, Conn., 1989-96, sr. v.p., gen. counsel, sec., 1996—. Editor Georgetown Law Jour., 1982-83. Mem. ABA. Communications, General corporate. Home: 440 W End Ave Apt 14C New York NY 10024-5358 Office: Time Warner Cable 290 Harbor Dr Stamford CT 06902-7475 E-mail: marc.apfelbaum@twcable.com

APODACA, PATRICK VINCENT, lawyer; b. El Paso, Tex., Mar. 11, 1951; s. Richard Felix and Isabel (Ortega) A. B.S. in Fgn. Service, Georgetown U., 1972; J.D., Harvard U., 1975. Bar: D.C. 1975, N.Mex. 1984. Assoc. Silverstein & Mullens, Washington, 1975-76; spl. asst. Carter-Mondale Transition Group, Washington, 1976-77; assoc. counsel to pres., The White House, Washington, 1977-81; assoc. Finley, Kumble, Wagner, Washington, 1981-84, Keleher & McLeod, Albuquerque, 1984-86, ptnr., 1986—. Asst. coordinator get-out-the vote com. Dem. Nat. Com., Washington, 1976; voter registration coordinator N.Mex. Dem. Com., Albuquerque, 1984; mem. N.Mex. State Dem. Party Cen. Com., 1987—; del. Dem. Nat. Conv., 1988; mem. Pres.'s Adv. Com. on Arts, Washington, 1981; bd. dirs. Tex. Tech U. and Health Scis. Ctr. Research Found., 1987—, Presbyn. Heart Inst., 1986—. Mem. D.C. Bar Assn. (chmn. internat. law com. young lawyers div. 1982-84), ABA, N.Mex. Bar Assn. (com. on minority involvement in bar 1987—, com. on Lawyer Referral Project for Elderly 1986—), Albuquerque Bar Assn. Roman Catholic. Administrative and regulatory, General corporate, Securities. Office: Keleher & McLeod PO Drawer AA Albuquerque NM 87103

APOLINSKY, STEPHEN DOUGLAS, lawyer; b. Birmingham, Ala., Dec. 5, 1961; s. Harold Irwin and Sandra Jean (Rubenstein) A. BA, U. Mich., 1983; JD, Emory U., 1987. Bar: Ga. 1987, U.S. Dist. Ct. (no. dist.) Ga. 1987, D.C. 1989, Ala. 1994. Litigation assoc. Bentley, Karesh Seacrest Labovitz & Campbell, Atlanta, 1987-94; mem. Eastman, Stapleton & Apolinsky, LLC, 1995-97, Eastman & Apolinsky, L.L.P., Atlanta, 1997—. Mem. ATLA, Ga. Trial Lawyers Assn., Atlanta Bar Assn., Atlanta Claims Assn., Am.-Israel C. of C. (past bd. dirs. S.E. region), Druid Hills Civic Assn. Avocations: travel and sports. General civil litigation, Insurance, Personal injury. Office: Eastman & Apolinsky 114 E Ponce De Leon Ave Decatur GA 30030-2526 E-mail: gatriallawyer@msn.com

APPEL, ALBERT M. lawyer; b. N.Y.C., May 26, 1945; s. Morris and Belle (Kaplan) A.; m. Irena Uhl, June 10, 1979; 1 child, Elliott. BS in Econs., U. Pa., 1966; JD, NYU, 1969. Bar: N.Y. 1969, U.S. Dist. Ct. (so. and ea. dists.) N.Y. 1971, U.S. Ct. Appeals (2d cir.) 1974, U.S. Ct. Appeals (4th cir.) 1979. Assoc. Spear and Hill, N.Y.C., 1969-75, Webster & Sheffield, N.Y.C., 1976-80, ptnr., 1981-91; spl. counsel Stroock & Stroock & Lavan LLP, 1991-97, ptnr., 1998—. Mem. ABA, Am. Health Lawyers Assn., N.Y. State Bar Assn., Assn. of Bar of City of N.Y., Beta Alpha Psi. General civil litigation, Health. Home: 670 W End Ave New York NY 10025-7313 Office: Stroock & Stroock & Lavan LLP 180 Maiden Ln New York NY 10038-4925 E-mail: aappel@stroock.com

APPEL, NINA SCHICK, law educator, dean; b. Feb. 17, 1936; d. Leo and Nora Schick; m. Alfred Appel Jr.; children: Karen Oshman, Richard. Student, Cornell U.; JD, Columbia U., 1959. Instr. Columbia Law Sch., 1959-60; adminstr. Stanford U., mem. faculty, prof. law, 1973—, assoc. dean, 1976-83; dean Sch. Law Loyola U., 1983—. Mem. Am. Bar Found., Ill. Bar Found., Chgo. Bar Found., Chgo. Legal Club, Chgo. Network. Jewish. Office: Loyola U Sch Law 1 E Pearson St Chicago IL 60611-2055

APPEL, ROBERT EUGENE, lawyer, educator; b. Cleve., Oct. 18, 1958; s. Robert Donald and Jean Ann (Crites) A.; m. Margaret Rose Curley, Aug. 24, 1985. BS, Cen. Conn. State U., 1980; JD, U. Bridgeport, Conn., 1982; MBA, U. Conn., 1984; LLM, Boston U., 1984. Bar: Conn. 1983. Asst. mgr. fin. services Lexington Ins. Co., Boston, 1984-85; tax. cons. Touche Ross and Co., Stamford, Conn., 1985-86; asst. dir. nat. design CIGNA Corp., Bloomfield, 1986-88, dir. nat. design, 1988-98; asst. v.p. Lincoln Nat. Life Ins. Co., Hartford, 1999—. Lectr. Real Estate Tng. and Ednl. Svcs., Bridgeport, 1985-88; lectr. real estate Dare Inst., Southbury, 1991—. Div. coord. United Way, 1988. Mem. ABA, Conn. Bar Assn. Republican. Roman Catholic. Avocations: investing, running, weightlifting, motorcycling. Estate planning, Estate taxation, Personal income taxation. Home: 80 Kingston Dr East Hartford CT 06118-2450 Office: Lincoln Fin Group 350 Church St Hartford CT 06103-1106

APPERSON, BERNARD JAMES, lawyer; b. Washington, June 28, 1956; s. Bernard James Jr. and Ann Wentworth (Anderson) A. BA in Polit. Sci., Am. U., 1978; JD, Cumberland Sch. Law, 1981; LLM in Internat. Law, Georgetown U., 1985. Bar: Fla. 1981, Ga. 1981, D.C. 1983, U.S. Supreme Ct. 1985. Atty., U.S. trustee for so. dist. N.Y. U.S. Dept. Justice, N.Y.C., 1981; atty. EPA, Washington, 1981-83; atty. civil rights div. U.S. Dept. Justice, 1983-84, atty. office legis. affairs, 1986-87; asst. U.S. atty. Ea. Dist. Va., Alexandria, 1987-97; counsel to dir. Legal Services Corp., Washington, 1985-86; commr. U.S. Dist. Ct., Ea. Dist. Va., Alexandria, 1996-97; sr. counsel com. on govt. reform and oversight, spl. counsel subcom. Nat. Econ. Growth, Natural Resources etc. U.S. Ho. of Reps., Washington, 1997-98; assoc. ind. counsel Office of the Ind. Counsel, 1998-99, dep. ind. counsel, 1999-2000; chief counsel oversight and investigations Com. on Jud., U.S. Ho. of Reps., 2000, chief counsel subcom. on crime, 2000—. Instr. FBI Tng. Acad., Quantico, Va., 1990; lectr. law U. London and U. Ga., 1990. Assoc. editor Am. Jour. Trial Advocacy Cumberland Sch. Law, 1979-81. County chmn. Paula Hawkins for U.S. Senate, Volusia County, Fla., 1974; nat. staff Citizens for Reagan, Fla., Kansas City, Mo., 1976; cons. Reagan for Pres., Detroit, 1980; dep. northeastern regional dir. Reagan-Bush 1984, Washington, 1984. Lewis F. Powell Medal for Excellence in Advocacy Am. Coll Trial Lawyers, 1980. Mem. Federalist Soc. for Law and Pub. Policy Studies, Order of Barristers, St. Andrew's Soc. Republican. Anglican. Home: 545 E Braddock Rd Apt 704 Alexandria VA 22314-2171 Office: US Ho of Reps Com on Jud/ Subcom on Crime 207 Cannon House Office Bld Washington DC 20515

APPLEBAUM, CHARLES, lawyer; b. Newark, May 19, 1947; s. Harry I. and Francis (Gastwirth) A.; m. Patricia Gyurko; children: Matthew, David, Michael, Amanda. BA, U. Pa., 1969; JD, Rutgers U., 1973; LLM, NYU, 1978. Bar: U.S. Dist. Ct. N.J. 1973. Law clk. to Hon. Samuel A. Larner, Jersey City, 1973-74; assoc., then ptnr. Greenbaum, Rowe, Smith, Ravin, Davis & Himmel LLP, Woodbridge, N.J., 1974-89; gen. counsel Alfieri Orgn., Edison, 1989—. Adj. prof. Rutgers Law Sch., Newark, 1985-88. Co-author: New Jersey Real Estate Forms, 1988; contbr. articles to profl. jours. Mem. ABA (real property probate and trust, chmn. significant lit. and publs. 1985-97, co-editor The Acrel Papers 1992-94), Am. Coll. Real Estate Lawyers (editor publs. 1991—). Contracts commercial, Land use and zoning (including planning), Real property. Office: M Alfieri Co Inc PO Box 2911 399 Thornall St Edison NJ 08837-2236 E-mail: capplebaum@malfieri.com

APPLEGATE, KARL EDWIN, lawyer; b. Cicero, Ind., July 21, 1923; s. Karl Raymond and Gladys Mae (Worley) A.; m. Elizabeth Ann Dilts, June 10, 1944; children: Eric Edwin, Raymond Alan, Robert Dale, Beth Ann. BS, Ind. U., 1946, JD, 1948. Bar: Ind. 1949, Fed. Ct. (7th cir.), U.S. Supreme Ct. 1968, U.S. Tax Ct. 1983. U.S. commr. So. Dist., Ind., 1953-58; cert. family and civil mediator Indiana, Fla., 1992; dep. prosecutor Monroe County, Ind., 1959; mcpl. judge Bloomington, 1960-63; mem. Ind. Ho. of Reps., 1965-66; U.S. atty. So. Dist. Ind., 1967-70; sr. ptrn. Applegate Law Offices, Bloomington, 1970-92, sr. mem., 1991-93, Applegate, McDonald, Koch & Arnold, Bloomington, 1993—; now Applegate, McDonald, Koch, P.C. Legal cons. Ind. Masonic Home, Franklin, 1981-82. Trustee 1st United Meth. Ch., 1962-65. Staff sgt. AUS, 1941-44, ETO. Decorated Purple Heart; named Outstanding Young Man of Bloomington, Jaycees, 1956; recipient Disting. Svc. award U.S. Jr. C. of C., 1956, Good Govt. award 1961. Mem. ABA, Fed. Bar Assn., Ind. Bar Assn. (co-chair com. assistance to lawyers program 1990-94), Monroe County Bar Assn., Tri-County Bar Assn., Kiwanis, Elks, Masons, Alpha Kappa Psi. Federal civil litigation, General practice, Personal injury. Home: 509 S Swain Ave Bloomington IN 47401-5129 Office: Applegate McDonald & Koch PO Box 1030 Bloomington IN 47402-1030

APPLEMAN, JOLENE W. patent lawyer; b. New Castle, PA, June 5, 1945; d. Lawrence B. and Bertha L. Weinstein; m. Bernard R. Appleman, Aug. 31, 1969; children: Laura I., Beth H. BA, Case Western Res. U., 1967; MS Chem., Ohio State U., 1970; JD, Duquesne U., 1990. Bar: Pa. 1990, U.S. Patent Office, 1991, N.J. 1992. Lectr. in chem. Montgomery Coll., 1977-84, Union C.C., Cranford, NJ, 1984-87, Carnegie Mellon U., 1987-90; assoc. Cohen & Grigsby, Pitts., 1990-91, Eckert Seamans, Pitts., 1992-95, Reed, Smith, Shaw & McClay, Pitts., 1995-97; patent counsel Pfizer Inc., N.Y.C., 1997—. Lect., Food and Drug in Law School, Duquesne U., 1997—. Mem. ABA, Chem. and the Law. Office: Pfizer Inc 235 E 42nd St New York NY 10017-5755 E-mail: jolene.w.appleman@pfizer.com

APPLETON, RICHARD NEWELL, lawyer; b. Bronx, N.Y., Sept. 1, 1941; s. Harry Newell Appleton and Catherine (Burke) Haddon; m. Kathleen Pauline Sheehan Morrell, Oct. 5, 1963 (div. Apr. 1974); children: Heather, Cheryl; m. Alene Marie Appleton, Aug. 31, 1990; children: Brennan, Adriana. BA, Rutgers Coll., 1964; JD, Western State U., 1983. Bar: Calif. 1984, U.S. Dist. Ct. So. Calif. 1984. Time study engr. E.R. Squibb & Sons, New Brunswick, N.J., 1963-65; plant indsl. engr. Anaconda Wire and Cable, Anderson, Ind., 1965-69; budget analyst Marcona Mining Co., San Juan, Peru, S.A., 1969-73, dir. adminstrv. svcs. S.A., 1973-76; internal cons. Iron Ore Can., Sept Iles, Que., 1976-78; mgr. adminstrn. Mullen Engring., Casper, Wyo., 1978-79; consulting engr. Woodward Assocs., San Diego, 1979-81; law clerk Stutz, McCormick, Mitchell & Verlasky, 1981-84; assoc. McCormick & Mitchell, 1984-91, ptnr., 1991-93, mng. ptnr., 1993-99, ptnr., 1999-2001; prin. Appleton Dispute Solutions, Chula Vista, Calif., 2001—. Arbitrator and mediator San Diego County Mcpl. and Superior Ct., 1989—; judge pro tem Small Claims Ct., 1995—. Contbr. articles to profl. jours. and book revs. Precinct committeeman Rep. Party, Anderson, 1966-68. Recipient Cert. Merit award NASA, 1962, Amjur in Evidence award The Lawyers Co-Op Bancroft Whitney, 1983, Most Valuable Reporter award Stats, Inc., 1994. Mem. ATLA, Assn. So. Calif. Def. Counsel, Soc. Profls. in Dispute Resolution. Roman Catholic. Avocations: golf, baseball, statistical analysis, fiction and non-fiction writing. State civil litigation, Construction, Personal injury. Office: Appleton Dispute Solutions PO Box 212132 Chula Vista CA 91914 Address: 1261 Crystal Springs Dr Chula Vista CA 91915-2154 E-mail: rna9141@aol.com

APRUZZESE, VINCENT JOHN, lawyer; b. Newark, Nov. 1, 1928; s. John and Mildred (Cerefice) A.; m. Marie A. Yeager, July 10, 1955; children: Barbara, John, Donald, Lynn, Kathy. BA, Rutgers U., 1950; LLB, U. Pa., 1953. Bar: N.J. 1954, U.S. Dist. Ct. N.J. 1954, U.S. Ct. Appeals (3d cir.) 1962, U.S. Supreme Ct. 1970, U.S. Ct. Appeals (D.C. cir. 1973), U.S. Ct. Appeals (4th cir.) 1973, D.C. 1976, N.Y. 1983. Assoc. Lum, Fairlie & Foster, Newark, 1953-54; sole practice, 1954-55, 58-65; sr. ptnr. Apruzzese & McDermott, 1965-70, pres. Springfield, N.J., 1970-90, Liberty Corner and Newark. Mem. legal adv. bd. Martindale-Hubbell, 1991-98. Bd. dirs. St. Barnabas Hosp., Papermill Playhouse. With JAGC, USAF, 1956-57. Mem. ABA (mem. coun. labor and employment law sect. 1984-94, chair labor & employment law sect. 1992-93, bd. govs. 1988-91), Coll. of Labor and Employment Lawyers, Fed. Bar Assn., Internat. Labor Law Soc. (treas.), Am. Coll. Trial Lawyers, Am. Bar Found., Fed. Bar State N.J., N.J. State Bar Assn. (pres. 1982-84), Essex County Bar Assn., Somerset County Bar Assn., Baltusrol Country Club (Springfield), Chatham (Mass.) Beach and Tennis Club, Eastward Ho Country Club (Chatham). General practice, Labor. Office: Apruzzese McDermott Mastro & Murphy PO Box 112 25 Independence Blvd Liberty Corner NJ 07938 E-mail: vapruzzese@excite.com

AQUILINO, THOMAS JOSEPH, JR. federal judge, law educator; b. Mt. Kisco, N.Y., Dec. 7, 1939; s. Thomas Joseph and Virginia Burr (Doughty) A.; m. Edith Luise Berndt, Oct. 27, 1965; children: Christopher T., Philip A., Alexander B. Student, Cornell U., 1957-59, U. Munich, 1960-61; BA, Drew U., 1962; postgrad., Free U., Berlin, 1965 66; JD, Rutgers U., 1969. Bar: N.Y. 1972, U.S. Dist. Ct. (so., ea. and no. dists.) N.Y. 1973, U.S. Ct. Appeals (2nd cir.) 1973, U.S. Supreme Ct. 1976, U.S. Ct. Appeals (3rd cir.) 1977, Interstate Commerce Commn. 1978, U.S. Ct. Claims 1979, U.S. Ct. Internat. Trade 1984. Law clk. to judge U.S. Dist. Ct. (so. dist.) N.Y., N.Y.C., 1969-71; atty. Davis Polk & Wardwell, 1971-85; judge U.S. Ct. Internat. Trade, 1985—. Adj. prof. law Benjamin N. Cardozo Sch. of Law, 1984-95; mem. bd. visitors Drew U., 1997—. With U.S. Army, 1962-65. Mem. N.Y. State Bar Assn., Fed. Bar Coun. Roman Catholic. Avocations: sports, travel, linguistics, cinema. Office: US Ct Internat Trade 1 Federal Plz New York NY 10278-0001

ARABIAN, ARMAND, arbitrator, mediator, lawyer; b. N.Y.C., Dec. 12, 1934; s. John and Aghavnie (Yalian) A.; m. Nancy Arabian, Aug. 26, 1962; children: Allison Ann, Robert Armand. BSBA, Boston U., 1956, JD, 1961; LLM, U. So. Calif., L.A., 1970; LLD (hon.), Southwestern Sch. Law, 1990, Pepperdine U., 1990, U. West L.A., 1994, We. State U., 1997, Thomas Jefferson Sch. of Law, 1997, Am. Coll. Law, 2001. Bar: Calif. 1962, U.S. Supreme Ct. 1966. Dep. dist. atty. L.A. County, 1962-63; pvt. practice law Van Nuys, Calif., 1963-72; judge Mcpl. Ct., L.A., 1972-73, Superior Ct., L.A., 1973-83; assoc. justice U.S. Ct. Appeal, 1983-90, U.S. Supreme Ct. Calif., San Francisco, 1990-96; ret., 1996. Adj. prof. sch. law Pepperdine U., 1996—. 1st lt. U.S. Army, 1956-58. Recipient Stanley Litz Meml. award San Fernando Valley Bar Assn., 1986, Lifetime Achievement award San Fernando Valley Bar Assn., 1993; Pappas Disting. scholar Boston U. Sch. Law, 1987; Justice Armand Arabian Resource and Comm. Ctrs. named in honor of Van Nuys and San Fernando Calif. Courthouses, 1999. Republican. Office: 6259 Van Nuys Blvd Van Nuys CA 91401-2711 Fax: 818-781-6002. E-mail: honarabian@AOL.com

ARAK, VIKTOR, lawyer; b. Talinn, Estonia, Feb. 14, 1975; arrived in Sweden, 1990; s. Taivo and Veera Arak. LLM, Stockholm U., 1998. Assoc. Setterwalls, Stockholm, 1998—. Bd. dirs. SE2C Ab, Stockholm. Chmn. Borgerliga Studenter, Stockholm, 1995-96. Admiralty, Contracts commercial. Office: Setterwalls Arsenalsgatan 6 SE-11147 Stockholm Sweden E-mail: viktor.arak@settenwalls.se

ARANT, EUGENE WESLEY, lawyer; b. North Powder, Oreg., Dec. 21, 1920; s. Ernest Elbert and Wanda (Haller) A.; m. Juanita Clark Flowers, Mar. 15, 1953; children: Thomas W., Kenneth E., Richard W. B.S. in Elec. Engring, Oreg. State U., 1943; J.D., U. So. Calif., 1949. Bar: Calif. 1950. Mem. engring. faculty U. So. Calif., 1947-51; practiced in Los Angeles, 1950-51; patent atty. Hughes Aircraft Co., Culver City, Calif., 1953-56; pvt. practice, L.A., 1957-97, Ventura, Calif., 1997-2001, Gleneden Beach, Oreg., 2001—. Author articles. Mem. La Mirada (Calif.) City Council, 1958-60; trustee Beverly Hills Presbyn. Ch., 1976-78. Served with AUS, 1943-46, 51-53. Mem. ABA, Am. Intellectual Property Law Assn., State Bar Calif., Ala. State Bar, Santa Barbara Rotary, Univ. Club Santa Barbara. Democrat. E-mial. Patent, Trademark and copyright. Home: 100 NE Indian Shores Lincoln City OR 97367 Office: PO Box 0250 Ste A7 Gleneden Beach OR 97388 E-mail: gwapat@wcn.net

ARANTES-PEDROSO, FILIPA DE VILHENA, lawyer; b. Lisbon, Nov. 22, 1954; d. José Antonio Guedes de Sousa Arantes-Pedroso and Teresa Burnay De Vilhena. Law, U. Lisbon, 1978; EU Law, U. Louvain (Belgium), 1980. Lawyer J. Morais Leitão & Assocs., Lisbon, 1980-87; ptnr., 1987-93, Morais Leitão, J. Galvão Teles & Assocs., 1993—. Bd. dirs. Cidadele Soc. Inv. Tor. S.A., Cascais. Author: Competition Law in Western Europe and U.S.A., 1992. Founder Young Christian Dems., Lisbon, 1975-79. Mem. Portuguese Bar Assn., Portuguese European Law Assn. Antitrust, Contracts commercial, Communications. Office: Morais Leitão Galvão Teles & Associados Rua Castilho 75 1o 1250-068 Lisbon Portugal Fax: (351) 213817499. E-mail: fapedroso@mlgt.pt

ARBIT, BERYL ELLEN, legal assistant; b. L.A., Aug. 16, 1949; d. Harry A. and Norma K. (Michelson) A. BA, UCLA, 1970. From legal asst. to sr. legal asst. O'Melveny & Myers, LLP, L.A., 1977—. Guest lectr. atty. asst. tng. program UCLA, 1991. Mem. UCLA Atty. Asst. Alumni Assn. (bd. dirs. 1980-82), Alpha Omicron Pi (treas. Greater L.A. alumnae chpt. 1993—), Nu Lambda (corp. bd. pres. 1978-80, chpt. adv. 1976-78). Avocations: travel, theater, needlework, bridge. Office: O'Melveny & Myers, LLP 400 S Hope St Los Angeles CA 90071-2899 E-mail: barbit@omm.com

ARBIT, TERRY STEVEN, lawyer; b. Chgo., May 11, 1958; s. Jack and Sandra (Dwork) A.; m. Rhona Sue Schwartz, July 21, 1985; children: Julie Lyn, Michael Colin. BA, MA, U. Pa., 1980; JD, U. Chgo., 1983. Bar: Ill. 1983, Mich. 1984, U.S. Dist. Ct. (no. dist.) Ill. 1985, U.S. Ct. Appeals (7th and 9th cirs.) 1988, U.S. Dist. Ct. Colo. 1999. Law clk. to justice Mich. Supreme Ct., Southfield, 1983-84; assoc. Karon, Savikas & Horn, Ltd., Chgo., 1984-88, Goldberg, Kohn, Bell, Black, Rosenbloom & Moritz Ltd., Chgo., 1989-90; counsel profl. liability sect. FDIC, Washington, 1991-95; chief counsel's office divsn. of enforcement Commodity Futures Trading Commn., 1996—. Mem. ABA, Phi Beta Kappa, Pi Gamma Mu, Pi Sigma Alpha. Avocations: polit. studies, swimming, cycling. Home: 8 Botany Ct North Potomac MD 20878-4208 Office: Commodity Futures Trading Commn 1155 21st St NW Washington DC 20036-3308 E-mail: tarbit@cftc.gov

ARBOLEYA, CARLOS JOAQUIN, lawyer, broker; b. Havana, Cuba, Aug. 16, 1958; came to U.S., 1960; s. Carlos Jose and Marta Aurora (Quintana) A. ABA, Miami Dade C.C., 1977; BBA in Fin., U. Miami, 1980, MBA in Fin., 1981, JD, 1987. Bar: Fla. 1989, U.S. Ct. Appeals (D.C. cir.) 1990. From teller to br. mgr. Barnett Bank South Fla. N.A., North Miami Beach, 1975-84; realtor, assoc. Cervera Real Estate, 1980—; pres. Owner's Box Promotions, 1993-95; owner Carlos J. Arboleya, Jr., P.A., Coconut Grove, 1988—. Adv. bd. Exec. Nat. Bank, 1994—, Linda Ray Infant Ctr., 1990—; mem 20th Anniversary Gold Prix of Miami com, 2002; adv. bd, Ronald McDonald House, Twelve Good Men, 2000—01; bd, dirs. Pvt. Industry Coun. Jobs for Miami; Hispanic adv. com. U. Miami Sports Mktg., 1992—95. Bd. dirs. Greater Miami Tennis Found., 1995, U. Miami Ear Inst., 1993; vice chma. planning adv. bd. City of Miami, 1993-95, 98-99, chmn. 1995-98, chmn. code enforcement bd., 1990-91, vice chmn. 1989-90; asst. scoutmaster Boy Scouts Am.; participant joint civilian orientation conf. U.S. Dept. Def., 1995; pres. Cocogrove Villas Condominium Assn., 1998—; trustee United Way, Miami-Dade, 2000—. Named One of 12 Good Men of Miami, Ronald McDonald House, 2000-01. Mem. ABA, Nat. Soc. Hispanic MBAs, Nat. Eagle Scout Assn., Cuban Am. Bar Assn., Builders Assn. South Fla., Am. Title Ins. Co., Attys. Title Ins. Fund, Inc., Fla. Bar Assn., Latin Bus. Assn., Latin Builders Assn., Hispanic Law Students Assn., Coral Gables C. of C., Greater Miami C. of C. (sports coun., chmn., homestead motorsports complex com., 1994-97, co-chmn. existing events com., 1992-94), Leadership Miami (exec. com. 1990-93, task force 1984-88, Coconut Grove Jaycees, Phi Delta Phi, Delta Sigma Pi (Outstanding Alumni award 1982). Republican. Roman Catholic. Banking, General corporate, Real property. Office: Carlos J Arboleya Jr PA 2550 S Dixie Hwy Coconut Grove FL 33133-3137

ARBUTHNOT, ROBERT MURRAY, lawyer; b. Montreal, Quebec, Can., Oct. 23, 1936; s. Leland Claude and Winnifred Laura (Hodges) A.; m. Janet Marie O'Keefe, Oct. 6, 1968; children: Douglas, Michael, Mary Kathleen, Allison Anne. BA, Calif. State U., San Francisco, 1959; JD, U. Calif., San Francisco, 1966. Bar: Calif. 1967, U.S. Dist. Ct. (no. and cen. dists.) Calif. 1967, U.S. Ct. Appeals (9th cir.) 1967, U.S. Supreme Ct. 1975. Assoc. trial lawyer Rankin & Craddick, Oakland, Calif., 1967-69; assoc. atty. Ericksen, Arbuthnot, Brown, Kilduff & Day, Inc., San Francisco, 1970 73, ptnr., 1973 80, chmn. bd., mng. dir., 1980 . Gen. counsel CFS Ins. Svcs., San Francisco, 1990—; pro tem judge, arbitrator San Francisco Superior Ct., 1990—; lectr. in field. Bd. regents St. Mary's Coll. High Sch., Berkeley, Calif., 1988-91. With U.S. Army, 1959-62. Recipient Honors plaque St. Mary's Coll. High Sch., 1989. Mem. Internat. Assn. of Ins. Counsel, No. Calif. Assn. of Def. Counsel, Def. Rsch. Inst., Assn. Trial Lawyers Am., San Francisco Lawyers Club. Avocations: boating, family activities. General civil litigation, Personal injury, Product liability. Office: Ericksen Arbuthnot Kilduff Day & Lindstrom Inc 260 California St Ste 1100 San Francisco CA 94111-4300 E-mail: eakdlsf@aol.com

ARCENEAUX, M(ARTIN) THOMAS, lawyer; b. Lake Charles, La., Oct. 8, 1951; s. Felix Felicien and Betty Gordon (Gunn) A.; m. Elizabeth Montgomery, June 1, 1993; children: Anna Marie, Martin Thomas Jr., Jordan M. Lewis. BS, La. State U., 1972, JD, 1976. Bar: La. 1976, U.S. Dist. Ct. (we. dist.) La. 1976, Tex. 1978, U.S. Ct. Appeals (5th cir.) 1980. Law clk. to presiding judge U.S. Dist. Ct., Shreveport, La., 1976-78; assoc. Vinson & Elkins, Houston, 1978-79; ptnr. Beard, Arceneaux & Sutherland, Shreveport, 1979-81; land mgr., gen. counsel Despot Exploration Inc., 1981-83; sole practice, 1983-87; ptnr. Davidson, Nix, Arceneaux, Jones & Askew, 1987-96; city atty. City of Shreveport, 1995—; pvt. practice Shreveport, 1995—; instr. LSUS Paralegal Inst., 1996—; town atty. Town of Blanchard, 1996—. Exec. coun. Ark.-La.-Tex. Regional Export and Tech. Ctr., 1995—. Articles editor Law Rev., 1975-76. Bd. dirs. Shreveport Symphony Orchestra, 1992-95, Holy Angels Residential Facility, 1991-95; mem. Shreveport City Coun., 1982-90, chmn. 1986-87; chmn. audit fin. com., 1985-86, vice chmn. audit fin. com., 1985-86; mem. Caddo Parish Rep. Exec. Com., 1987-91 bd. dirs. Coordinating & Devel. Corp., 1990—. Named Outstanding Young Man of Yr., Shreveport Jaycees, 1985. Mem. La. Lawyers for Life, Rotary Club Shreveport (dir. 2000-01). Republican. Avocations: weight-lifting, writing, reading, singing. Bankruptcy, Oil, gas, and mineral, Real property. Home: 828 E Kings Hwy Shreveport LA 71105-3017

ARCHER, GLENN LEROY, JR. federal judge; b. Densmore, Kans., Mar. 21, 1929; s. Glenn LeRoy and Ruth Agnes (Ford) A.; m. Carole J. Thomas, 1990; children: Susan, Sharon, Glenn, Thomas. B.A., Yale U., 1951; J.D. with honors, George Washington U., 1954. Bar: D.C. 1954. Asst. atty. gen. U.S. Dept. Justice, Washington, 1981-85; circuit judge U.S. Ct. Appeals (fed. cir.), 1985-94, chief judge, 1994-97, sr. cir. judge, 1997—. Republican. Methodist. Office: US Ct of Appeals Fed Circuit 717 Madison Pl NW Washington DC 20439-0002

ARCHIBALD, JAMES KENWAY, lawyer; b. Mass., Mar. 29, 1949; s. John Lawrence and Jean (Kenway) A.; m. Joanne Mary Ricciuti, Aug. 16, 1975; children: Kathryn, John. BA, Johns Hopkins U., 1971; JD, U. Md., 1975. Bar: Md. 1975, D.C. 1985, U.S. Dist. Ct. Md. 1976, U.S. Ct. Appeals (4th cir.) 1978, U.S. Supreme Ct. 1979, U.S. Ct. Appeals (9th cir.) 1984, Maine 1998. Assoc. Venable, Baetjer and Howard, Balt., 1975-83, ptnr., 1983—. Co-author: Pleading Causes of Action in Maryland, 1990, Model Witness Examinations, 1997. Chmn. bd. trustees Md. State Colls. and Us., 1984-86; trustee Johns Hopkins U., 1997-2000; bd. dirs. Roland Park Country Sch., Inc., Balt., 1989-94; pres. Homeland Assn., Inc., Balt., 1990. Recipient Disting. Svc. award Litigation Sect. Md. State Bar, Md., 1981. Mem. ABA (litigation sect., co-chair com. 1987—), Internat. Assn. Def. Counsel, Def. Rsch. Inst. (Exceptional Performance award 1989, Md. state chair 1989-93), Md. Assn. Def. Trial Counsel (pres. 1988-89), Johns Hopkins Alumni Coun. (v.p. 1996-98, pres. 1998-2000), Johns Hopkins Second Decade Soc. (nat. chair 1989-91), Am. Law Inst. General civil litigation, Personal injury, Product liability. Home: 13037 Jerome Jay Dr Cockeysville MD 21030-1523 Office: Venable Baetjer & Howard 1800 Mercantile Bank Bldg 2 Hopkins Plz Ste 2100 Baltimore MD 21201-2982 E-mail: jkarchibald@venable.com

AREEN, JUDITH CAROL, law educator, university dean; b. Chgo., Aug. 2, 1944; d. Gordon Eric and Pauline Jeanette (Payberg) A.; m. Richard M. Cooper, Feb. 17, 1979; children: Benjamin Eric (dec.), Jonathan Gordon AB, Cornell U., 1966; JD, Yale U., 1969. Bar: Mass. 1970, D.C. 1972. Program planner for higher edn. Mayor's Office City of N.Y., 1969-70; dir. edn. voucher study Ctr. for Study Pub. Policy, Cambridge, Mass., 1970-72; mem. faculty Georgetown U., Washington, 1971—, assoc. prof. law, 1972-76, prof., 1976—, prof. cmty. and family medicine, 1980-89, assoc. dean Law Ctr., 1984-87; dean, exec. v.p. for law affairs Georgetown U, 1989—. Gen. counsel, coord. domestic reorgn. pres.' reorgn. project Office of Mgmt. and Budget, Washington, 1977-80; spl. counsel White House Task Force on Regulatory Reform, Washington, 1978-80; cons. NIH, 1984; cons. NRC, 1985, mem. com. film badge dosimetry; bd. dirs. WorldCom. Author: Youth Service Agencies, 1977, Cases and Materials on Family Law, 4th edit., 1999, Law, Science and Medicine, 1984, 2d edit., 1996. Mem. Def. Adv. Com. Women In Svcs., Washington, 1979-82; trustee Cornell Univ., 1997-2001. Woodrow Wilson Internat. Ctr. for Scholars fellow, 1988-89, Kennedy Inst. Ethics Sr. Rsch. fellow, Washington, 1982—. Mem. ABA, D.C. Bar Assn., Am. Law Inst. E-mail: areen@law.georgetown.edu

ARENCIBIA, RAUL ANTONIO, lawyer; b. N.Y.C., Dec. 18, 1955; s. Raul and Elba (Petrovitch) A.; m. Patricia Lucia Moore, Mar. 22, 1987; children: Adam Loell, Aaron Francis, Andrea GeorgeAnn. BA cum laude, NYU, 1977; JD, Harvard U., 1980. Bar: Fla. 1980, U.S. Dist. Ct. (so. dist.) Fla. 1980, U.S. Ct. Appeals (5th and 11th cirs.) 1981, U.S. Dist. Ct. (mid. dist.) Fla. 1985. Assoc. Paul & Thomson, Miami, Fla., 1980-81, Mahoney, Hadlow, et al, Miami, 1981-82, Frates & Novey, Miami, 1983-84, Dady, Siegfried, et al, Coral Gables, Fla., 1984-85; pvt. practice Miami, 1985-89; of counsel Goytisolo & Saez, 1988-89; mng. ptnr. Goytisolo, Saez & Arencibia, 1989-90; with Bailey, Harper & Arencivia, 1991—99; counsel Kilpatrick Stockton LLP, 2000—01; pvt. practice, 2001—. Contbg. author: Bonds: The Protective Layer in the Construction Process, 1987. Recipient NYU Founders Day award, 1977, NYU scholar, 1973. Mem. ABA, Fla. Bar Assn., Dade County Bar Assn., Cuban Am. Bar Assn. Republican. Roman Catholic. Avocation: chess. Appellate, Federal civil litigation, General civil litigation.

ARENSON, GREGORY K. lawyer; b. Chgo., Feb. 11, 1949; s. Donald L. and Marcia (Terman) A.; m. Karen H. Wattel, Sept. 4, 1970; 1 child, Morgan Elizabeth. BS in Econs., MIT, 1971; JD, U. Chgo., 1975. Bar: Ill. 1975, U.S. Dist. Ct. (no. dist.) Ill. 1975, N.Y. 1978, U.S. Dist. Ct. (so. and ea. dists.) N.Y. 1978, U.S. Supreme Ct. 1985, U.S. Ct. Appeals (2nd cir.) 1987, U.S. Dist. Ct. (ctrl. dist.) Ill. 1995, U.S. Ct. Appeals (7th cir.) 1997. Assoc. Rudnick & Wolfe, Chgo., 1975-77, Schwartz, Klink & Schreiber P.C., N.Y.C., 1977-81, ptnr., 1982-87, Proskauer, Rose, Goetz & Mendelsohn, N.Y.C., 1987-93, Kaplan& Fox & Kilsheimer LLP, N.Y.C., 1993—. Mediator U.S. Dist. Ct. (so. dist.) N.Y., 1993—; mem. MIT Corp., 1997—; mem. corp. devel. com. MIT, 1994—; mem. alumni/ae fund bd. MIT, 1989—, chair, 1994-96; mem. adv. bd. Fed. Discovery News, 1999—. Co-editor: Federal Rules of Civil Procedure, 1993 Amendments, A Practical Guide, 1994; contbr. articles to profl. jours. Mem. ABA, N.Y. State Bar Assn. (comml. and fed. litigation sect., chair com. on discovery 1989-97, chair com. fed. procedure 1997—), Assn. Bar City N.Y Bankruptcy, Federal civil litigation, Securities. Home: 125 W 76th St Apt 2A New York NY 10023-8334 Office: Kaplan Fox & Kilsheimer LLP 805 3d Ave New York NY 10022-7513

ARESTY, JEFFREY M. lawyer; b. Framingham, Mass., Dec. 31, 1951; s. Victor Joseph and Pola (Granek) A.; m. ELlen Louise Gould, Aug. 15, 1976; children: Joshua, Abigail, Joanne. BA, Johns Hopkins U., 1973; JD, Boston U., 1976, LLM in Taxation, 1978, LLM in Internat. Banking, 1993. Bar: Mass. 1977, D.C. 1982. Tax specialist Coopers & Lybrand, Boston, 1976-78; assoc. Meyers, Goldstein & Crossland, Brookline, Mass., 1978-79; ptnr. Crossland, Aresty & Levin, Boston, 1979-87, Aresty & Levin, Boston, 1987-91, Aresty Internat. Law Offices, Boston, 1992—. Cons. editor Tax Shelter Investment Rev., 1981-85. Recipient Disting. Achievement award Boston Safe Deposit and Trust, 1976, Grad. Banking Alumni Achievement award Boston U. Law Sch., 1993. Mem. ABA (membership chmn. 1981-84, coun. 1985-91, vice chmn. computer divsn. 1985-90, reporter TECH 2000 Task Force 1999—, chmn. internat. interest group 1992-96, chmn. internat. negotiations task force 1992-96, chmn. Mass. membership com. 1985-91, internat. law sect., chair law practice com. 1995-98, co-editor ABA Guide Internat. Bus. Negotiations 1994-2000, prodr. ABA/AT&T CD-Rom on Cross-Cultural Comm. 1997), Am. Bar Found. (standing com. tech. and info. systems 1998-99, pub. bd. gen. practice 1998—), Mass. Bar Assn. (bd. dels., exec. com. 1981-83, chmn. law practice sect. 1983-85), Mass. Bar Found. Alternative dispute resolution, Computer, Private international. Home: 35 Three Ponds Rd Wayland MA 01778-1732 Office: Aresty Internat Law Offices Bay 107 Union Wharf Boston MA 02109 E-mail: jaresty@abanet.org

ARGIROPOULOS, KATHLEEN O'NEILL, lawyer; b. Washington, July 31, 1948; d. Thomas Grover O'Neill and Elizabeth Jean (Nesbit) O'Neill Berry; m. John George Argiropoulos, July 10, 1976. BA, Mary Wash. Coll of U. Va., 1970, JD, George Washington U., 1973. Bar: D.C.

1973, Temporary Emergency Ct. Appeals 1976, U.S. Ct. Appeals (D.C. cir.) 1978, U.S. Supreme Ct. 1979. Staff atty. Consumer Product Safety Commn., Bethesda, Md., 1973-74; asst. v.p. law, sec. Air Transport Assn. Am., Washington, 1974-84; v.p., gen. counsel, sec. Airlines Reporting Corp., Washington, 1985—; dir. Washington Met. Area Corp. Counsel Assn. (1984—, treas. 1986—). Contbr. chpts. to book. Mem. ABA (standing com. on aeronautical law 1982, taxation com. 1983-84, forum com. on air and space law 1983—, bus. law 1985—). General corporate. Home: 4741 Rock Spring Rd Arlington VA 22207-4241 Office: Airlines Reporting Corp 1709 New York Ave NW Washington DC 20006-5206

ARGUE, JOHN CLIFFORD, business executive; b. Glendale, Calif., Jan. 25, 1932; s. J. Clifford and Catherine Emily (Clements) A.; m. Leah Elizabeth Moore, June 29, 1963; children: Elizabeth Anne, John Michael. AB in Commerce and Fin., Occidental Coll., 1953, LLD (hon.), 1987; LLB, U. So. Calif., 1956. Bar: Calif. 1957. Practiced in, L.A.; mem. firm Argue & Argue, 1958-59, Flint & MacKay, 1960-72, Argue, Pearson, Harbison & Myers, 1972-89, of counsel, 1990-99. Bd. dirs. Avery Dennison, Apex Mortgage Capital, TCW Convertible Fund, Nationwide Health Properties; mem. adv. bd. LAACO, Ltd., Mellon Fin. West Coast bd., TCW Galileo Funds; chmn. The Rose Hills Found., Amateur Athletic Found., L.A. Sports Coun., Kids in Sport, L.A. 2012 Bid Com. Pres. So. Calif. Com. Olympic Games, 1972—; founding chmn. L.A. Olympic Organizing Com., 1978-79; trustee emeritus Pomona Coll., U. So. Calif., chmn.; with Occidental Coll., Mus. Sci. and Industry; mem. nat. adv. coun. Autry Mus. Western Heritage; chmn. bd. Greater L.A. affiliate Am. Heart Assn., 1982; chmn. Verdugo Hills Hosp., 1979; pres. Town Hall of Calif., 1985, U. So. Calif. Assocs., 1988-93; chair Criminal Justice Legal Fund, 1994-99; chmn. PGA Championship, 1983, chmn. adv. bd., 1995; vice chmn., sec. L.A. 2000 Com., 1991 Olympic Sports Festival, 1993 Superbowl, 1994 World Cup. Mem. L.A. Bar Assn., Calif. Bar Assn. (inactive mem.), Southern Calif. Golf Assn. (pres. 1979), Calif. Golf Assn. (v.p. 1979), Calif. State Srs. Golf Assn. (pres. 2000), L.A. Area C. of C. (chmn. 1989), Chancery Club (pres. 1985-86), Calif. Club (pres. 1983-84), L.A. Athletic Club, Riviera Country Club, Oakmont Country Club (pres. 1972), L.A. Country Club, Rotary, Phi Delta Phi, Alpha Tau Omega. General corporate, Real property, Taxation, general. Home: 1314 Descanso Dr La Canada Flintridge CA 91011-3149 Office: The Rose Hills Found 444 S Flower St Ste 1450 Los Angeles CA 90071-2959

ARIS, JORAM JEHUDAH, lawyer; b. Haderah, Israel, Feb. 6, 1953; came to U.S., 1957; s. Joseph Koenigstein and Shoshanah (Lemberger) Aris; m. Gloria Bakash, Sept. 22, 1984; children: Giselle Dina, Danielle Lisa, Noah Elliot, Jonathan Joseph. Student, York U., Eng., 1972; BA magna cum laude, CUNY, 1973; JD, N.Y. Law Sch., 1978. Bar: N.J. 1978, N.Y. 1979. Assoc. U.S. Attys. Office (so. dist.) N.Y., N.Y.C., 1977, N.Y. State Atty. Gens. Office, N.Y.C., 1978; atty. First & First, 1978-79, Empire Mut. Ins. Co., N.Y.C., 1979-80; law sec. N.Y. State Supreme Ct., 1980-81; sole practice, 1981—. Chmn. Collective, N.Y.C., 1971-72. Mem. Riverdale Dem. Club, Bronx, N.Y., 1975-86, N.Y.C. Community Bd. #8, Bronx, 1980-86, Pub. Safety Com., Bronx, 1980-84, Environ. Safety and Sanitation, Bronx, 1985-86, Housing Com., Bronx, 1980-82, law com. 1984-86, ethics com. 1984-86; pres. Windsor Tenants Assn., Bronx, 1985-86; vol. N.Y.C. Adopt-A-Hwy.; active Hebrew Inst. Riverdale, N.Y.C., Conservative Synagogue Adath Israel, N.Y.C., Riverdale Temple, N.Y.C., Bene Naharayim (Iraqi) Synagogue, N.Y.C. Mem. ABA (elder care section), N.Y. State Bar Assn. (elder care sect.), N.Y. County Lawyers Assn. (trial atty.), Bronx County Bar Assn., Am.-Sephardic Orgn., Phi Delta Phi. Democrat. Jewish. General civil litigation, Personal injury, Probate. Home and Office: 3671 Hudson Manor Ter Bronx NY 10463-1137 E-mail: LawyerAris@aol.com

ARISTEI, J. CLARK, lawyer, educator; b. Washington, Sept. 6, 1948; s. Jerome and Eleanor Ruth (Clark) A. AA, L.A. Harbor Coll., 1968; BA cum laude, Calif. State U., Long Beach, 1971; JD, U. San Diego, 1975. Bar: Calif. 1975, U.S. Dist. Ct. (so. dist.) Calif. 1975, U.S. Dist. Ct. (cen. dist.) Calif. 1979, U.S. Dist. Ct. (ea. dist.) Calif. 1993, U.S. Dist. Ct. (no. dist.) N.Y. 1996, U.S. Ct. Appeals (7th cir.) 1997. Pvt. practice, San Diego, 1975; assoc. Bennett Olan Law Office, Beverly Hills, Calif., 1976-77, Fogel, Feldman, Kingler, Ostrov & Klevens, L.A., 1977-92, Kananack, Murgatroyd, Baum & Hedlund, L.A., 1993-94; shareholder Baum, Hedlund, Aristei et al, 1994—. Adj. prof. law U. West L.A., 1986-97, faculty libr. com., 1995-97. Lectr. in field. Mem. faculty libr. com. U. West L.A., 1995-97. Mem. State Bar Calif., Consumer Attys. Calif., Consumer Atty. Assn. L.A. Avocations: architecture, bicycling. Aviation, Personal injury, Product liability. Office: Baum Hedlund Aristei Guilford & Downey 12100 Wilshire Blvd Ste 950 Los Angeles CA 90025-7107 E-mail: caristei@baumhedlundlaw.com

ARKIN, L. JULES, lawyer; b. N.Y.C. s. Joseph and Mildred (Neidenberg) A.; m. Sandra Raughbord (div. 1983); children: Richard, Gary; m. Shirley Feldman. Student, Emory U., 1946-48; LLB, U. Miami, 1952. Bar: Fla. 1952. Ptnr. Meyer, Weiss, Rose, Arkin, Shampanier, Ziegler & Barash, PA, Miami Beach, Fla., 1954-85, Therrel Baisden & Meyer Weiss, 1985-96; pres., dir. Fin. Fed. Savs and Loan Assn. Dade County, 1980-84. Former mem., chmn. adv. bd. City of Miami Beach Social Svcs.; past pres., past chmn. Found. Jewish Philanthropies; bd. dirs. Hebrew Immigration Aid Soc., Coun. Jewish Fedns.; life trustee, past v.p. bd. Mt. Sinai Hosp. Greater Miami, alsp past pres. sustaining bd. fellows. Served to lt. comdr. USNR, 1948-54. Recipient Pres.'s Leadership award Greater Miami Jewish Fedn., 1967, Silver Medallion award NCCH, 1979; named Outstanding Civic Leader of Miami Beach, Civic League Miami Beach, 1971. Mem. ABA, Fla. Bar Assn., Dade County and Miami Beach Bar Assn., Miami Beach C. of C. (trustee, past pres., past mem. bd. govs.), Greater Miami C. of C. (bd. govs.), Masons, Kiwanis, Westview Country Club (Miami; pres.). Real property. E-mail: jylesarkin@email.com

ARLEN, JENNIFER HALL, law educator; b. Berkeley, Calif., Jan. 7, 1959; d. Michael John and Ann (Warner) A.; m. Robert Lee Hotz, May 21, 1988; children: Michael Arlen Hotz, Robert Arlen Hotz. BA, Harvard U., 1982; JD, NYU, 1986; PhD in Econs., NYU, 1992, 1992. Bar: N.Y. 1987, U.S. Ct. Appeals (11th cir.) 1987. Summer clk. U.S. Dist. Ct. (ea. dist.) N.Y., Bklyn., 1984; summer assoc. Davis Polk & Wardwell, N.Y.C., 1985; law clk. U.S. Cir. Judge, 11th cir., Savannah, Ga., 1986-87; asst. prof. law Emory U., Atlanta, 1987-91, assoc. prof. law, 1991-93; prof. law U. So. Calif., L.A., 1994—, Ivadelle and Theodore Johnson prof. law and bus., 1997—. Vis. prof. law U. So. Calif., 1993, Calif. Inst. Tech., (winter) 2001, Yale Law Sch., 2001-2002; dir. U. So. Calif. Ctr. in Law, Econs. and Orgn., 2000—. Olin fellow U. Calif. Sch. Law, Berkeley, 1991. Mem. ABA, Am. Assn. Law Schs. (chair remedies sect. 1994, chair elect 1993, mem. exec. com. 1990-91, 95, chair torts sect. 1995, chair-elect 1994, treas. 1991, sec. 1992-93, exec. com. bus. assns. sect. 1995-96, 2000—, chair law and econ., sect. 1996, chair-elect law and econs. sect. 1995, chair 1996), Am. Law and Econ. Assn. (bd. dirs. 1991-93, program com. 1999), Am. Econ. Assn., Order of Coif, Am. Law Inst. Democrat. Office: U So Calif Law Sch Los Angeles CA 90089-0001

ARMBRECHT, WILLIAM HENRY, III, retired lawyer; b. Mobile, Ala., Jan. 13, 1929; s. William Henry and Katherine (Little) A.; m. Dorothy Jean Taylor, Sept. 1, 1951; children— Katherine Handley, William Taylor, Alexander Paterson. B.S., U. Ala., 1950, J.D., 1952. Bar: Ala. 1952, U.S. Supreme Ct. 1972. Assoc. Inge, Twitty, Armbrecht & Jackson, Mobile, 1952-56; ptnr. Armbrecht, Jackson, McConnell & DeMouy, 1956-65, Armbrecht, Jackson & DeMouy, Mobile, 1965-75, Armbrecht, Jackson, DeMouy, Crowe, Holmes & Reeves, Mobile, 1976-94, Armbrecht, Jackson, DeMouy, Crowe, Holmes & Reeves, LLC, 1994-96. Served to 1st lt. JAGC, AUS, 1952-54. Mem. ABA, Ala. Bar Assn. (chmn. grievance com. 1973-74, chmn. sect. corp. banking and bus. law 1976-78), Mobile Bar Assn., Mobile Area C. of C. Found. (bd. dirs. 1990-92), Southeastern Corp. Law Inst. (mem. planning com. 1967-96), Phi Delta Phi, Delta Kappa Epsilon Episcopalian. Oil, gas, and mineral, Estate planning, General practice. Home: 600 Fairfax Rd E Mobile AL 36608-2931

ARMOUR, JAMES LOTT, lawyer; b. Jackson, Tenn., May 19, 1938; s. Quintin and Frances (Breeden) A.; m. Nancy Stokes Johnson, Mar. 17, 1962; 1 son, John Lawson. BA, Vanderbilt U., 1961, LLB, 1964; LLM, So. Meth. U., 1967. Bar: Tenn. 1964, Tex. 1965, U.S. Supreme Ct. 1967, N.Y. 1969, Okla. 1972. Assoc. firm Turner Rodgers Winn Scurlock & Terry, Dallas, 1965-67; internat. atty. Mobil Corp., N.Y.C. and London, 1967-71, Phillips Petroleum Co., Bartlesville, Okla., 1971-74; asst. gen. counsel Conoco, Inc., Stamford, Conn., 1974-83; ptnr. firm Locke Liddell & Sapp LLP, Dallas, 1984-2001; pvt. practice James L. Armour Atty. at Law, 2001—. Mem. adv. bd. oil and gas SW Legal Found., chair, 1996-99; mem. Dallas Com. on Fgn. Rels.; former mem. alumni bd. Vanderbilt Law Sch. Mem. ABA, Assn. of Bar of City of N.Y., State Bar Tex., Dallas Bar Assn., Petroleum Club, Phi Delta Phi, Kappa Sigma. Episcopalian. FERC practice, Oil, gas, and mineral, Private international. Home: 4541 Belfort Pl Dallas TX 75205-3618 Office: Law Offices of James L Armour Ste 2460 325 N St Paul St Dallas TX 75201-3857 Fax: 214 999 0603. E-mail: jlarmour@jlarmourlaw.com

ARMSTRONG, EDWIN ALAN, lawyer; b. Atlanta, June 20, 1950; s. Carl Edwin and Betty (Hawkins) A.; m. Marlene Bryant, Aug. 12, 1978. BA, Berry Coll., 1972; JD, Emory U., 1976. Bar: Ga. 1976, U.S. Dist. Ct. (no. dist.) Ga. 1977, U.S. Ct. Appeals (5th cir.) 1981, U.S. Ct. Appeals (11th cir.) 1982, U.S. Supreme Ct. 1989, U.S. Dist. Ct. (so. dist.) Ga., U.S. Ct. Appeals (4th cir.), U.S. Ct. Appeals (D.C. cir.) 1992, U.S. Ct. Appeals (6th cir.) 1992, U.S. Dist. Ct. (mid. dist.) Ga 1992. Atty. Flynt Jud. Cir. Pub. Defenders Office, McDonough, Ga., 1976-77; assoc. Neely, Neely & Player, Atlanta, 1977; pvt. practice, 1977-79, 81—; assoc. Stolz, Shulman & Loveless, 1979-81. Contbr. articles to profl. jours. Mem. ABA (forum com. on air and space law, tort and ins. practice sect.), ATLA, Atlanta Bar Assn., Decatur-DeKalb Bar Assn., State Bar Ga. (chmn. aviation law sect. 1998—), Ga. Trial Lawyers Assn., Nat. Transp. Safety Bd. Bar Assn. (founding, com. legis. and regulatory activity 1989—, editor newsletter 1991-92), Lawyer-Pilots Bar Assn. Episcopalian. Avocation: flying. Aviation, State civil litigation, Personal injury. Home: 4098 Northlake Creek Cv Tucker GA 30084-3416 E-mail: alanarmstrong@mindspring.com

ARMSTRONG, GORDON GRAY, III, lawyer; b. Mobile, Ala., Jan. 13, 1964; s. Gordon Gray Jr. and Margaret Claire A.; m. Simone Delaine Manley, Mar. 19, 1994; 1 child, Gordon Gray IV. BA, U. Ala., 1986, JD, 1989. Bar: Ala. 1989, U.S. Dist. Ct. (so. dist.) Ala. 1991, U.S. Ct. Appeals (11th cir.) 1992, U.S. Supreme Ct. 1995. Assoc. Clark, Deen & Copeland, Mobile, Ala., 1989-92; atty pvt. practice, 1992—. Mem. ABA (del. young lawyers divsn. 1993—), Nat. Assn. Criminal Def. Lawyers, Assn. Trial Lawyers Am., Am. Collectors Assn. (atty. program 1997—), Ala. State Bar Assn. (exec. com. young lawyers sect. 1992—, treas. 1995-96, sec. 1996-97, v.p. 1997-98, pres. 1998-99), Ala. Criminal Def. Lawyers Assn., Mobile Bar Assn. Avocations: fishing, golf, hunting, recreational sports, gardening. Consumer commercial, Criminal, Personal injury. Office: 205 Congress St Mobile AL 36603-6407

ARMSTRONG, HENRY JERE, judge, lawyer; b. Dothan, Ala., Mar. 5, 1941; s. Henry Jordan and Lillian (Taylor) A.; m. Jeanne Bachmann, June 3, 1963; children: April Heather, Ashley Brooke. BA, U. Ala., Tuscaloosa, 1964, JD, 1966; postgrad., JAGs Sch., Charlottesville, Va., 1972-73; grad., Armed Forces Staff Coll., 1978. Bar: Ala. 1966, D.C. 1974, Va. 1984, U.S. Ct. Mil. Appeals 1967, U.S. Supreme Ct. 1972. Commd. 2d lt. U.S. Army, 1964, advanced through grades to col., 1983; def. counsel, prosecutor Ft. Ord., Calif., 1967-68; chief criminal law, chief civil law, mil. judge Ft. Shafter, Hawaii, 1968-72; chief legis. br. criminal law divsn. Dept. Army, Washington, 1973-75, exec. asst. to JAG, 1975-77; staff judge adv. 2d inf. divsn. Korea, 1978-79; exec. officer U.S. Army Trial Def. Svc., Falls Church, Va., 1979-82; exec. officer litigation divsn. Dept. Army, Washington, 1982-84, ret., 1984; counsel to chief Immigration Judge of U.S., 1984-86; judge, asst. chief immigration judge U.S. Dept. Justice, 1986-97, dep. chief immigration judge, 1997—. Profl. responsibility adv. com. dept. Army; guest lectr. on ethics and def. advocacy U.S. Army Europe Continuing Legal Edn. seminars; faculty Nat. Judicial Coll., Reno, Nev. Contbr. articles to profl. jours. Elder Grace Presbyn. Ch., Springfield, Va. Decorated 2 oak leaf clusters, Legion of Merit; Inst. for Ct. Mgmt. fellow Nat. Ctr. for State Cts., Williamsburg, Va.; named hon. Ky. Col., 1982. Mem. ABA, Ala. State Bar Assn., D.C. Bar Assn., Va. State Bar Assn., Assn. Trial Lawyers Am., Fed. Bar Assn., Judge Advs. Assn. (bd. dirs.), Kappa Sigma Alumni Assn., Phi Alpha Delta. Home: 8208 Little River Tpke Annandale VA 22003-2305

ARMSTRONG, JACK GILLILAND, lawyer; b. Pitts., Aug. 10, 1929; s. Hugh Collins and Mary Elizabeth (Gilliland) A.; m. Ellen Lee Gliem, June 10, 1951 (dec.); children: Thomas G., Elizabeth Armstrong Pride; m. Elizabeth Lacewll White, March 27, 1993. AB, U. Mich., 1951, JD, 1956. Bar: Pa. 1956, Mich. 1956, U.S. Supreme Ct. 1968, Fla. 1981. Assoc. Buchanan, Ingersoll, Rodewald, Kyle & Buerger, Pitts., 1956-65; ptnr. Buchanan, Ingersoll, P.C., 1965-90, counsel, 1990-94, of counsel, 1995, Rothman Gordon, P.C., 1996—. Dir. Standard Steel Splty. Co., Greer, S.C. Trustee Union Dale Cemetery, 1972—, pres., 1992-95. Dir. Sigma Nu Ednl. Found., 1998—. Lt. U.S. Army, 1951-53. Mem. Pa. Bar Assn. (real property, probate, and trust law sect., mem. coun. 1981-84, treas. 1985, vice chmn. probate divsn. 1986-88, chmn. 1988-89, tax law sect.), Fla. Bar (real property, probate and trust law sect., tax sect.), Allegheny County Bar Assn. (probate and trust law), Estate Planning Coun. Pitts., Am. Coll. Trust and Estate Counsel (Pa. state chmn. 1990-95), Am. Coll. Tax Counsel, U. Mich. Alumni Assn. (Disting. Alumni Svc. award 1981), Am. Arbitration Assn. (nat. panel 1965—), Order of Coif, Duquesne Club, Univ. Club (pres. 1988-89), St. Clair Country Club, Town Club Jamestown, Delray Beach Club, Chautauqua Golf Club, Pine Tree Golf Club, Masons, Shriners, Jesters, Phi Alpha Delta, Signa Nu. Home: 4376 Pine Tree Dr Boynton Beach FL 33436-4818 Office: E-mail: jgarmstrong@rothmangordon.com

ARMSTRONG, JOHN DOUGLAS, lawyer, educator; b. Dayton, Ohio, July 9, 1956; s. Stephen Daniel and Barbar J. (McCoy) A.; m. Patti Kay Berry, June 26, 1976; children: Stephen Daniel, Patrick Cole. BS in Edn., U. Tex., 1978; JD, Oklahoma City U., 1981. Bar: Tex. 1982. Intern U.S. Congress, Washington, 1974-75; ptnr. Askins & Armstrong PC, LaPorte, Tex., 1981—. Mem. ABA, Houston Bar Assn., Bay Area Bar Assn., Rotary (class civil law sec. 1996—). Republican. Lutheran. Banking, Contracts commercial, Land use and zoning (including planning). Office: Askins & Armstrong PC 702 W Fairmont PO Box 1218 La Porte TX 77572-1218 E-mail: john-a@swbell.net

ARMSTRONG, ORVILLE, judge; b. Austin, Tex., Jan. 21, 1929; s. Orville Alexander and Velma Lucille (Reed) A.; m. Mary Dean Macfarlane; children: Anna Louise Glenn, John M., Paul Jefferson. BBA, U. Tex., Austin, 1953; LLB, U. So. Calif., 1956. Bar: Calif. 1957, U.S. Ct. Appeals (9th cir.) 1958, U.S. Supreme Ct. 1980. Ptnr. Gray, Binkley & Pfaelzer, 1956-61, Pfaelzer, Robertson, Armstrong & Woodard, L.A., 1961-66, Armstrong & Lloyd, L.A., 1966-74, Macdonald, Halsted & Laybourne, L.A., 1975-88, Baker & McKenzie, 1988-90; judge Superior Ct. State of Calif., 1991-92; assoc. justice ct. appeal State of Calif., 1993—. Lectr. Calif. Continuing Edn. of Bar. Served with USAF, 1946-49. Fellow ABA, Am. Coll. Trial Lawyers; mem. State Bar Calif. (gov. 1983-87, pres. 1986-87), L.A. County Bar Assn. (trustee 1971-72), Chancery Club (pres. 1988), Calif. Club. Baptist. Office: 300 S Spring St Los Angeles CA 90013-1230

ARMSTRONG, PAUL WHITE, lawyer, educator; b. Manchester, N.H., Mar. 30, 1945; s. Paul William and Ruth Marie (White) A.; m. Maria Luken, Apr. 26, 1975. MA, U. Dayton, 1969; JD, U. Notre Dame, 1972; LLM, NYU, 1978. Bar: N.J. 1973, Mich. 1974, U.S. Dist. Ct. N.J. 1973, U.S. Supreme Ct. 1976. Assoc. Rhoades, Mckee & Boer, Grand Rapids, Mich., 1973-74, Legal Aid Soc., Morristown, N.J., 1975; sole practitioner Bedminster, 1976-85; of counsel Weiner & Weiner, Morristown, 1986-93, Timmins, Larsen, Beacham & Hughes, Livingston, N.J., 1994-96, Kern, Augustine, Conroy & Schoppmann, Bridgewater, 1996—. Adj. prof. Rutgers Law Sch., Newark, 1985—, Robert Wood Johnson Med. Sch., New Brunswick, N.J., 1985—; lectr. nat. and internat. law and bioethics, 1976—. Author publs. in field. Chmn. N.J. Bioethics Commn., Princeton, 1990—; chmn. Gov.'s Coun. on AIDS, Trenton, N.J., 1989-92; chmn. N.J. Health Decisions, Princeton, 1994—; pres. Samaritan Homeless Interim Program, 1990—; trustee, founder, Karen Ann Quinlan Hospice, 1976—. Recipient Disting. Citizen award Acad. of Medicine (N.J.), 1989, Am. Law and Health award Boy Scouts Am., 1996; Victoria fellow Rutgers U., 1990. Home: 1051 Tall Oaks Dr Bridgewater NJ 08807-1237 Office: Kern Augustine et al 120 Route 22 West Bridgewater NJ 08807

ARMSTRONG, PHILLIP DALE, lawyer; b. Waukegan, Ill., Mar. 27, 1943; s. James Leonard and Bernice Frances (Nader) A.; m. Leila Robson; children: Leonard Hart, Theodore Nader, Leila VIII. BS in Chem. Engring., U. Mo., 1966; JD, Gonzaga U., 1978; LLM, U. Mo., Kansas City, 1979. Bar: N.D. 1979, U.S. Dist. Ct. N.D. 1979, U.S. Dist. Ct. Ariz. 1991, U.S. Tax Ct. 1980, U.S. Ct. Appeals 1983, U.S. Supreme Ct. 1984. Mktg. trainee Dow Chem. Co., Midland, Mich., 1966-68; chem. engr. Clark Oil and Refining, Hartford, Ill., 1968-70; life guard, pool attendant, pool mgr. various hotels and condominiums, Miami Beach, Fla., 1970-75; assoc. McCutcheon Law Firm, Minot, N.D., 1979-81; sole practice, 1981—, Mandan, N.D., 1995—; founder, pres. Producers Oil & Gas Corp., 1992—. Trustee in bankruptcy for chpts. 7, 12, and 13, N.W. and S.W. divs. Dist. of N.D., 1980-95; founder Armstrong Oilwell Ops., 1996. Mem. ABA, N.D. Bar Assn., Nat. Assn. Bankruptcy Trustees, Am. Bankruptcy Inst., Exch. Club (Minot). Republican. Episcopalian. Home: 1006 Valley View Dr Minot ND 58703-1642 Office: Armstrong Law Firm 12 Main St S Minot ND 58701-3871

ARMSTRONG, WILLIAM TUCKER, III, lawyer; b. Houston, Nov. 13, 1947; s. William Tucker Jr. and Jess (Nettles) A.; m. Nancy Bayliss Armstrong, Feb. 18, 1978; children: Will, Anne, Daniel. BA, Am. U., 1969; JD with honors, U. Tex., 1972. Bar: Tex. 1972, U.S. Ct. Appeals (5th cir.) 1972, U.S. Dist. Ct. (so. & we. dists.) Tex. 1978, U.S. Ct. Appeals (11th cir.) 1982, U.S. Ct. Appeals (D.C. cir.) 1983. Staff counsel for inmates Tex. Dept. Corrections, Huntsville, 1972-73; assoc. Foster, Lewis, Langley, Gardner & Banack, San Antonio, 1973-76, shareholder, 1976-96, Langley & Banack, 1996—. Active South Tex. Leukemia Soc., bd. dirs., 1989-92. Mem. Tex. State Bar Assn. (mem. coun. sch. law sect. 1985-87), Tex. Coun. Sch. Attys. (dir. 1999-2001), San Antonio Longhorn Club (pres. 1993-94), San Antonio Tex. Exes (pres. 1995-96), Oak Hills Country Club (dir. 1998-2001). Methodist. Avocation: golf. Civil rights, General civil litigation. Office: Langley & Banack Inc 745 E Mulberry Ave Ste 900 San Antonio TX 78212-3141 E-mail: warmstrong@langleybanack.com

ARNET, WILLIAM FRANCIS, lawyer; b. St. Louis, Mo., Mar. 13, 1948; s. Aloysius Richard and Grace Marie (Luenebrink) A.; m. Judith Ann Wissmann, June 13, 1970; children— Christina, Matthew, Benjamin. B.A. in Polit. Sci., S.E. Mo. State U., 1970; J.D., U. Mo.-Columbia, 1970-73. Bar: Mo. 1973, U.S. Dist. Ct. (we. dist.) Mo. 1975, U.S. Ct. Appeals (8th cir.) 1975, U.S. Supreme Ct. 1977. Asst. atty. gen. State of Mo., Jefferson City, 1973-81, 81-84; legis. aide Sen. John Danforth, Washington, 1981; counsel U. Mo., Columbia, 1984— . Contbr. to law rev., 1971-73. Mem. Mo. Bar Assn., Order of Coif, Roman Catholic. Home: 2205 Topaz Dr Columbia MO 65203-1445 Office: U Mo 227 University Hall Columbia MO 65211-3020

ARNETT, DEBRA JEAN, lawyer; b. Horton, Kans., July 15, 1956; d. Ralph E. and Margaret J. (Parry) A.; 1 child, Taylor Margaret Arnett. BSW, U. Kans., 1979, JD, 1982. Bar: Kans. 1982, U.S. Dist. Ct. Kans. 1982, U.S. Ct. Appeals (10th cir.) 1985. Atty., dir. McDonald, Tinker, Skaer, Quinn & Herrington, P.A., Wichita, Kans., 1982-91; judge pro tem State of Kans. 6th Judicial Dist., Miami County, 1993—; dir. Hartley, Nicholson, Hartley & Arnett, P.A., Paola, Kans., 1991-99; Law Offices of Debra J. Arnett, 1999—. Adj. assoc. prof. law Wichita State U., 1984-90. Rsch. asst. (book) Jurisdiction in Civil Actions, 1983. Vol., bd. dirs. Christmas in Oct., Miami County, Kans., sec. 1992—; bd. dirs., sec. Paola Free Libr. Found., 1992—, Lakemary Ctr., 1999—. Recipient Justice Lloyd Kagey Leadership award U. Kans. Sch. Law, 1982, Robert C. Foulston & George Siefkin prize for excellence in appellate advocacy, 1981; mem. Nat. Moot Ct. Team, U. Kans. Sch. Law, 1981; invited Hague (The Netherlands) Treaty Roundtable on Internat. Adoptions, U.S. State Dept., 1993. Mem. ABA (litigation, family law, and ins. practice sects.), Nat. Assn. Women Bus. Owners (sec. Wichita chpt. 1988-89, v.p. 1989-90, pres. 1990-91), Def. Rsch. Inst., Kans. Bar Assn. (sec. litigation sect. 1991-92, pres.-elect 1992-93, pres. 1993-94), Kans. Assn. Def. Counsel (bd. govs. 1983—), Miami County Bar Assn. (treas. 1995—), Wichita Bar Assn., Jenny Mitchell Kellogg Circle (bd. dirs. 1995—), Rotary (Paola chpt.). General civil litigation, Family and matrimonial, General practice. Office: 1 W Shawnee PO Box 211 Paola KS 66071-0211

ARNETT, FOSTER DEAVER, lawyer; b. Knoxville, Tenn., Nov. 28, 1920; s. Foster Greenwood and Edna (Deaver) A.; m. Jean Medlin, Mar. 3, 1951; children: Melissa Lee Arnett Campbell, Foster Jr. BA, U. Tenn., 1946; LLB, U. Va., 1948. Bar: Va. 1948, Tenn. 1948, U.S. Dist. Ct. (ea. dist.) Tenn. 1949, U.S. Ct. Appeals (6th cir.) 1954, U.S. Supreme Ct. 1958, U.S. Dist. Ct. (ea. dist.) Ky. 1978, U.S. Dist. Ct. (mid. dist.) Tenn. 1983, U.S. Dist. Ct. (ea. and we. dists.) Va. 1990. In practice, Knoxville, 1948—; ptnr. Arnett, Draper & Hagood (and predecessors), 1954—. Mem. Nat. Conf. Commrs. on Uniform State Laws, 1980-83; life mem. U.S. Ct. Appeals (6th cir.) Jud. Conf. Contbr. articles to profl. jours. Pres. Knox Children's Found., 1959-61, 75-76, East Tenn. Hearing and Speech Ctr., 1963-65, Knoxville Teen Ctr., 1969-71, Knoxville News-Sentinel Charities Inc., 1985—; v.p. Ft. Loudon Assn., 1972-75; del. Rep. Nat. Conv., 1964; bd. dirs., exec. com. Tenn. Mil. Inst., 1973-75; formerly active ARC, Am. Cancer Soc., United Fund. With AUS, 1942-46, PTO; to lt. col. USAR, ret. Decorated Silver Star, Bronze Star, Purple Heart. Fellow Am. Coll. Trial Lawyers (former chair legal ethics com., mem. atty.-client relationship com., mem. other coms.), Internat. Acad. Trial Lawyers (trustee Acad. Found. 1984-91, dean 1988-89, pres. 1992-93, mem. Found. Bd. 1983-92), Internat. Soc. Barristers, Am. Bar Found. (life), Tenn. Bar Found. (charter); mem. ATLA, ABA (mem. standing coms. on unauthorized practice of law and assn. comm., aviation and space law, state cert. legal specialist), Am. Bd. Trial Advs. (adv., charter, 1st pres. Tenn. chpt. 1985-86), Am. Inns of Ct. (charter, master of the bench emeritus Hamilton S. Burnett chpt.), Southea. Legal Found. (legal adv. bd.), Tenn. Bar Assn. (pres. 1968-69), Knoxville Bar Assn. (pres. 1959-60, Govs. award 1989), Internat. Assn. Def. Counsel (sec.-treas. 1981-84), S.E. Def. Counsel Assn. (v.p. 1966), Am. Acad. Hosp. Attys. of Am. Hosp. Assn. (charter), Tenn. Hosp. Assn., Am. Soc. Law, Medicine and Ethics, Fedn. Ins. and Corp. Counsel, Def.

Rsch. Inst. (charter), U.S. Supreme Ct. Hist. Soc. (founder), Tenn. Supreme Ct. Hist. Soc. (founder), Federalist Soc., SAR, Scribes, U. Tenn. Nat. Alumni Assn. (pres. 1961-62, chmn. nat. ann. giving program 1961-63), Scabbard and Blade, Scarrabbean, Torchbearer, U. Va. Law Sch. Alumni Assn. (pres. 1991-93, nat. chmn. appeals Law Sch. Found. 1986-88), Raven Soc., 511th Parachute Infantry Regiment Assn., Civitan Club, Farmington Country Club, Charlottesville, Va.), Cherokee Country Club, LeConte Club, Univ. Club (hon.), Men's Cotillion (bd. dirs. 1960-61, 63-64, 66-68, trustee 1962—), Appalachian Club (pres. 1974-76), 511th Parachute Infantry Regiment Assn., Phi Gamma Delta, Phi Delta Phi (hon.), Omicron Delta Kappa (hon.). Presbyterian. Aviation, General civil litigation, Health. Home: 4636 Alta Vista Way Knoxville TN 37919-7605 Office: Arnett Draper & Hagood Ste 2300 First Tennessee Plaza Knoxville TN 37929-2300

ARNETT, RICHARD LYNN, lawyer; b. Dallas, Sept. 13, 1950; s. Richard Alden and Sarah Emma (Conner) A.; m. Leslie Lynn Walker; children; John Alden, Richard Alden III, Alexandra Lynn. BS in Geophysics, Stanford U., 1972; JD, U. Tex., 1975. Bar: Tex. 1975, U.S. Ct. Appeals (5th cir.) 1977, U.S. Supreme Ct. 1979, U.S. Dist. Ct. (ea., no., so. and we. dists) Tex. Research asst. dept. geophysics So. Methodist U., Dallas, 1969-72; law clk. to atty. gen. of Tex. Austin, 1974-75; asst. atty. gen. State of Tex., 1975-79; assoc. Roberts & Weldon, 1979-81; asst. atty. gen. State of Tex., 1981-82; dep. commr. for legal services Tex. Edn. Agy., 1982-84, Brimm & Arnett, Austin, 1986-97; pres. Brim, Arnett & Robinett, P.C., 1997—. Mem. Tex. Bar Assn. (sch. law com.). Democrat. Methodist. Civil rights, General civil litigation, Education and schools. Home: 6501 Canon Wren Dr Austin TX 78746-3807 Office: Brim Arnett & Robinett 2525 Wallingwood Dr Bldg 14 Austin TX 78746-6900 E-mail: rarnett@barpc.net

ARNETT, WILLIAM GROVER, lawyer; b. Paintsville, Ky., Jan. 28, 1962; s. William O. and Easter (Howard) A.; m. Sabrina Roark, July 15, 1995; 1 chld, Katelynn Aydreanna. BA, Alice Lloyd Coll., 1985; JD, Chase Coll. Law, 1988. Assoc. Weinberg & Campbell, Hindman, Ky., 1988-90; asst. commonwealth atty. Ky. Prosecutorial Coun., Frankfort, 1989-90, Magoffin county atty., 1994-99; assoc. Perry & Preston, Paintsville, 1990-91; sole practice Salyersville, Ky., 1991—. Mem. Magoffin County Dem. Party, 1993—, A.B. Chandler Found., 1996—. Named to Outstanding Young Men of Am., 1985. Mem. ABA, DAR, Assn. Trial Attys. Am., Ky. Bar Assn., Ky. Acad. Trial Attys., Kiwanis Club. Pension, profit-sharing, and employee benefits, Personal injury, Workers' compensation. Office: PO Box 489 Salyersville KY 41465-0489 E-mail: groverarnett@grobearnett.com

ARNKRA, JOE, legal administrator, writer; b. Newark, Jan. 3, 1960; s. Sam F. and Jill E. Arnkraut. BS in Fin., UCLA, 1990. Legal adminstr., Santa Monica, Calif., 1990—; writing cons., trainer, 1990—. Democrat. Roman Catholic. Avocations: freelance writing, skydiving, spelunking, cross-country and super marathon races. Office: 2272 Colorado Blvd # 1228 Los Angeles CA 90041-1143 Fax: 310-559-6617

ARNOLD, ELIZABETH APPLEBY, law clerk, billboard designer; b. Harrisburg, Pa., Feb. 9, 1966; d. John Appleby and Barbara Crawford (Montgomery) A. BA summa cum laude, Yale U., New Haven, 1988; postgrad., Harvard U.; student, Trier (W. Ger.) U., 1986. Pres. Arnold & Assocs., Harrisburg, 1976-85; law clk. Freehill, Hollingdale & Page, Sydney, Australia, 1989. Recipient Addy award for billboard design, 1978. Mem. Am. Youth Found. (bd. dirs. Nat. Leadership Conf. 1987), Phi Beta Kappa. Republican. Presbyterian. Avocations: scuba diving, jazz, tae kwon do, poetry, skiing, baking, German literature. Address: 1098 Twin Lakes Dr Harrisburg PA 17111-3705

ARNOLD, JAMES LEONARD, lawyer; b. Bronx, N.Y., Sept. 4, 1946; s. Leonard Anthony and Veronica Ann (Van Dien) A., (div.); children: David James, Katherine Marie. AB, Georgetown U., 1968; JD, U. Va., 1971. Vice pres., gen. counsel The Nat. Legal Research Group Inc., Charlottesville, Va., 1971-82, Hadron Inc., Fairfax, Va., 1982—, pres., chief exec. officer, 1990—. Mem. Am. Corp. Counsel Assn., Va. Bar, D.C. Bar, N.Y. Bar, Washington Met. Corp. Counsel Assn. Republican. Roman Catholic. General corporate. Home: Quailsar Farm 1890 Calusa Ct Marco Island FL 34145-4207

ARNOLD, JOHN FOX, lawyer; b. St. Louis, Sept. 17, 1937; s. John Anderson and Mildred Chapin (Fox) A.; m. Martha Ann Freeman, June 29, 1963 (div. Oct. 1993); children: Lisa A. Galena, Laura Wray, Lynne A. Binder, Lesli Johnston. AB, U. Mo., 1959, LLB, 1961. Bar: Mo. 1961, U.S. Dist. Ct. (ea. dist.) Mo. 1961, U.S. Ct. Appeals (8th cir.) 1961, U.S. Supreme Ct. 1971. Ptnr. Green, Hennings, Henry & Arnold, St. Louis, 1963-70; mem. Lashly & Baer, P.C., 1970—, chmn., 1987—. Mem. St. Louis County Charter Revision Com., Mo., 1968; chmn. bd. overseers Lindenwood U., 1992-93, bd. dirs., 1993-95; chmn. St. Louis County Bd. Election Commrs., 1981-86, Downtown St. Louis Inc., bd. dirs., 1992-98, chmn. bd. dirs., 1996-98; chmn. bd. dirs. Downtown St. Louis Partnership, Inc., 1997-99. Lt. USAR, 1961-63. Recipient citation of merit U. Mo. Law Sch., Columbia, 1984. Fellow Am. Bar Found.; mem. ABA (mem. house of dels. 1986-90), Bar Assn. Met. St. Louis (pres. 1975-76), Mo. Bar (pres. 1984-85), Nat. Conf. Commrs. on Uniform State Laws (drafting com. Securities Act, Partnership Act, article 2 sales, 2A leases and 8 investment securities of Uniform Comml. Code), Am. Law Inst. Republican. Government contracts and claims, Municipal (including bonds), Securities. Office: Lashly & Baer 714 Locust St Saint Louis MO 63101-1699 E-mail: jfarnold@lashlybaer.com

ARNOLD, MORRIS SHEPPARD, judge; b. Texarkana, Tex., Oct. 8, 1941; BSEE, U. Ark., 1965, LLB, 1968; LLM, Harvard U., 1969, SJD, 1971; MA (hon.), U. Pa., 1977, JD (hon.), 1986; LLD (hon.), U. Ark., Little Rock. Bar: Ark. 1968, Pa. 1985. Tchg. fellow law Harvard U., 1969-70; from asst. prof. to prof. Ind. U. Law Sch., 1971-76, prof., 1976-77, dean, 1985; prof. law, history U. Pa., 1977-81; Ben J. Altheimer disting. prof. law U. Ark., Little Rock, 1981-84; judge U.S. dist. Ct. (we. dist.) Ark., Ft. Smith, 1985-92, U.S. Cir. Ct. (8th cir.), 1992—. Vis. fellow commoner Trinity Coll., Cambridge U., 1978; v.p., dir. office of pres., U. Pa., 1980-81; vis. prof. Stanford (Calif.) U. Law Sch., 1985. Author: Old Tenures and Natura Brevium, 1974, Yearbook 2 Richard II, 1378-79, 1975, On the Laws and Customs of England, 1980, Unequal Laws Unto a Savage Race, 1985, Select Cases of Treespass from the King's Courts, 1307-1399, 2 vols., 1985, 87, Arkansas Colonials, 1986, Colonial Arkansas 1686-1804: A Social and Cultural History, 1991, The Rumble of a Distant Drum: Quapaws and Old World Newcomers, 1673-1804. Rep. gen. counsel, Ark., 1982, chmn., 1983; bd. dirs. Nature Conservancy of Ark., 1982-87, Ark. Arts Ctr., 1981-84. Decorated chevalier Ordre Palmes Acad. (France); Frank Knox fellow Harvard U., U. London, 1970-71; Mus. Sci. Natural History fellow, 1986. Fellow Am. Soc. Legal History (hon.), Athenaeum Club London, Union League Club Phila., Country Club Little Rock. Office: US Cir Judge PO Box 2060 Little Rock AR 72203-2060

ARNOLD, RICHARD SHEPPARD, federal judge; b. Texarkana, Tex., Mar. 26, 1936; s. Richard Lewis and Janet (Sheppard) A.; m. Gale Hussman, June 14, 1958 (div.); children: Janet Sheppard, Arnold Hart, Lydia Palmer, Arnold Turnipseed; m. Kay Kelley, Oct. 27, 1979. BA summa cum laude, Yale U., 1957; LLB magna cum laude, Harvard U., 1960; LLD, U. Ark., 1992, U. Richmond, 1998. Bar: D.C. 1961, Ark. 1960. Pvt. practice, Washington, 1961-64, Texarkana, Ark., 1964-74; law clk. to justice Brennan U.S. Supreme Ct., 1960-61; assoc. Covington & Burling, 1961-64; ptnr. Arnold & Arnold, 1964-74; legis. sec. Gov. of Ark., 1973-74, staff coord., 1974; legis. asst. Senator Bumpers of Ark., Washington, 1975-78; judge U.S. Dist. Ct. (ea. and we. dists.) Ark., 1978-80, U.S. Ct. Appeals (8th cir.), Little Rock, 1980—, chief judge, 1992-98. Part-time instr. U. Va. Law Sch., 1962—64; mem. Ark. Constl. Revision Study Commn., 1967—68; chair spl. redaction rev. panel Jud. Conf. of the U.S., 2000—; vice chair Com. on the Jud. Br., 2001—; disting. vis. prof. law So. Meth. U. Law Sch., 2001. Case editor: Harvard Law Rev., 1959-60; contbr. articles to profl. jours. Gen. chmn. Texarkana United Way Crusade, 1969-70; pres. Texarkana Community Chest, 1970-71; mem. vis. com. Harvard Law Sch., 1973-79, U. Chgo. Law Sch., 1983-86, 94-97; candidate for Congress 4th Dist. Ark., 1966, 72; del. Democratic Nat. Conv., 1968, Ark. Constl. Conv., 1969-70; chmn. rules com. Ark. Dem. Com., 1968-74, mem. exec. com., 1972-74; mem. Com. on Legis. Orgn., 1971-72; trustee U. Ark., 1973-74; chmn. budget com. Jud. Conf. of U.S., 1987-96. Recipient Award of the Women Lawyers' Assn. of Greater St. Louis, 1998, Edward J. Devitt Disting. Svc. to Justice award, 1999, Meador-Rosenberg award, Standing Com. on Fed. Jud. Improvements of the ABA, 1999. Fellow Am. Bar Found.; mem. Am. Law Inst. (coun.), Jud. Conf. U.S. (exec. com. 1992-98), Cum Laude Soc., Phi Beta Kappa. Episcopalian. Office: 600 W Capitol Ave Ste 208 Little Rock AR 72201-3321

ARNOLD, W. H. (DUB ARNOLD), state supreme court justice; b. Arkadelphia, Ark., May 19, 1935; m. Betty Earlene Aud; three children. BA, Henderson State U., 1957; LLB, Ark. Law Sch., 1962. Dep. prosecuting atty. Clark County, Ark., 1965-66; prosecuting atty. 8th Jud. Dist., State of Ark., 1969-72; chmn.hief justice Ark. Workers Compensation Commn., 1973-77; prosecuting atty. 9th Jud. Dist. East, State of Ark., 1981-90; mcpl. judge Clark County, 1979-80; cir./chancery judge 9th Jud. Dist. East, State of Ark., 1991-96; chief justice Ark. Supreme Ct., 1997—. Law educator Ouachita Bapt. U., Arkadelphia, Ark., 1975-76, Ark. Law Enforcement Acad., 1990, Garland County C.C., 1993; lectr. Ark. Prosecuting Atty.'s Assn., 1988. Office: Justice Bldg 625 Marshall St Ste 1230 Little Rock AR 72201-1052*

ARNOLD, WILLIAM MCCAULEY, lawyer; b. Waco, Tex., May 3, 1947; s. Watson Caulfield and Mary Rebecca (Maxwell) A.; m. Karen Axtell, May 17, 1980; children: Margaret McCauley, William Axtell. BA, Duke U., 1969; JD, U. Tex., 1972. Bar: Tex. 1973, Va. 1975, D.C. 1977, Md. 1983, U.S. Dist. Ct. (ea. dist.) Va. 1975, U.S. Ct. Appeals (4th cir.) 1977, U.S. Ct. Claims 1977, U.S. Supreme Ct. 1978. Spl. atty. U.S. Dept. Justice, Newark, 1973-75; asst. county atty. County of Fairfax, Va., 1975-78; ptnr. Cowles, Rinaldi & Arnold, Ltd., Fairfax, 1978-95, McCandlish & Lillard, Fairfax, 1995—. Instr. No. Va. C.C., Alexandria. Pres. Clifton Betterment Assn., Va., 1979-81; chmn. Clifton Planning Commn., 1980-85, mem. Clifton Town Coun., 1985—; bd. dirs. Clifton Gentlemen's Social Club, 1981-84. Mem. ABA, Va. State Bar Assn., Fairfax County Bar Assn., Va. Trial Lawyers Assn., Associated Builders and Contractors. State civil litigation, Construction. Office: McCandlish & Lillard PC 11350 Random Hills Rd Ste 500 Fairfax VA 22030-6044 E-mail: marnold@mccandlaw.com

ARON, MARK G. lawyer, transportation executive; b. Hartford, Conn., Jan. 27, 1943; s. Samuel H. and Florence A.; m. Cindy Sondik, June 1, 1966; 1 child, Samantha. B.A. summa cum laude, Trinity Coll., 1965; LL.B., Harvard U., 1968. Bar: Va., Mass., D.C. Asst. prof. law Osgood Hall Law Sch., York U., Toronto, 1968-70; assoc. Goulston & Storrs, Boston, 1970-71; atty., asst. gen. counsel then dep. gen. counsel U.S. Dept. Transp., Washington, 1971-81; asst. gen. counsel CSX, Richmond, Va., 1981-83, gen. counsel spl. projects, 1983-85; sr. v.p. corp. svcs. Chessie System R.R., Balt., 1985-86; sr. v.p. law and pub. affairs CSX Corp., Richmond, 1986-95, exec. v.p. law and pub. affairs, 1995—2001, vice chmn., 2001—. Trustee Va. Union U.; bd. dirs. Va. Literacy Found. Mem. Va. Bar Assn., Mass. Bar Assn., D.C. Bar Assn., Bethesda Country Club. E-mail: mark. Office: CSX Corp Ste 560 National Pl 1331 Pennsylvania Ave NW Washington DC 20004 E-mail: aron@csx.com

ARON, ROBERTO, lawyer, writer, educator; b. Mendoza, Argentina, Nov. 1, 1915; s. David and Catalina (Trostanetzky) A.; m. Catalina Berstein, May 1, 1940 (dec. Oct. 1965); children: Jaim, Sylvia, Daniel; m. Eva Coriat, Dec. 14, 1968; stepchildren: Sonia, Aileen (twins). BA in Law, U. Chile, 1943; LLM in Internat. Law, NYU, 1977, LLM in Corp. Law, 1979, M in Hebrew and Judaic Studies, 1995. Bar: Israel 1960. Sr. ptnr. Aron and Cia, Santiago, Chile, 1943-57, Arón, Tamir and Arón, Tel Aviv, 1960—. Adj. tchr. NYU, 1983; lectr. Tel Aviv U., 1985—, bd. govs., 1982; vis. prof. faculty of law U. Chile, 1991; bd. dirs. Otzar Itiashvut Hayeudim Bank, Tel Aviv; mem. Israeli del. to UN, 1975; participant Oxford Trial Advocacy Program. Co-author: How To Prepare Witnesses for Trial, 1985, Trial Communications Skills, 1986, Cross-Examination and Impeachment of Witnesses, 1989. Mem. Nat. Inst. Trial Advocacy (participant workshops on teaching trial advocacy Harvard Law Sch.), Advocates Assn., Assn. Trial Lawyers Am. Avocations: golf, pipe collecting. General civil litigation, Contracts commercial, Criminal. Home: 985 5th Ave Apt 12A New York NY 10021-0142 Office: Paradise and Alberts 630 3rd Ave Rm 1701 New York NY 10017-6762 also: Arón and Stern 7 ABA Hillel St Ramat Gan 52522 Israel E-mail: aronbob@aol.com

ARONSON, MARK BERNE, retired consumer activist; b. Pitts., Aug. 24, 1941; s. Richard J and Jean (DeRoy) Aronson; m. Ellen Jane Askin, July 20, 1970 (div. Oct. 1993); children: Robert M, Andrew A, Michael D. BS in Econs., U. Pa., 1962; JD, U. Pitts., 1965. Pvt. practice law, Pitts., 1965-90; sr. ptnr. Behrend & Aronson Law Firm, 1967-80, Behrend, Aronson & Morrow Law Firm, Pitts., 1980-83; pres. Current Concepts Corp., 1992-2000. Real estate broker, 1972—94; consult to attys, 1991—; pvt consumer adv, 1991—. Trustee Pittsburgh Child Guidance Found, 1987—90; mem Pittsburgh Coun Educ, 1986—89; pres Community Day Sch, Pittsburgh, Pa., 1982—84; trustee Rodef Shalom Congregation, 1979—87, Jr Congregation, 1967—71, 1970—71, Brotherhood, 1990—92, 2000—01. Master: Masons; mem.: Am Arbitration Asn (mem nat panel arbitrators), Tau Epsilon Rho (chancellor Eta chpt 1964—65). Republican. Jewish. Address: Ste 506-507 Churchill Mansions 2525 Greensburg Pike Pittsburgh PA 15221 3691 E mail: mba9999@aol.com

ARONSTEIN, MARTIN JOSEPH, law educator, lawyer; b. N.Y.C., Jan. 25, 1925; s. William and Mollie (Mintz) A.; m. Sally K. Rosenau, Sept. 18, 1948 (dec.); children: Katherine Aronstein Porter, David M., James K. BE, Yale U., 1944; MBA, Harvard U., 1948; LLB, U. Pa., 1965. Bar: Pa. 1965. Bus. exec., Phila., 1948-65; assoc. firm Obermayer, Rebmann, Maxwell & Hippel, 1965-67, partner, 1968-69; assoc. prof. law U. Pa., 1969-72, prof., 1972-78; counsel firm Ballard, Spahr, Andrews & Ingersoll, Phila., 1978-80, partner, 1980-81; prof. law U. Pa., 1981-86, prof. emeritus, 1986—; of counsel firm Morgan, Lewis & Bockius, Phila., 1986-95. Contbr. articles to law revs.; mem. Permanent Editorial Bd. Uniform Comml. Code, 1978-80, counsel, 1980-87, counsel emeritus, 1987—. Served with USN, 1943-46. Mem. Am. Law Inst., ABA (reporter com. on stock certs. 1973-77, chmn. subcom. on investment securities 1982-84), Phila. Bar Assn., Order of Coif, Sigma Xi, Tau Beta Pi. Home: The Fountains at Logan Sq E Two Franklin Town Blvd 2213 Philadelphia PA 19103

AROUH, JEFFREY ALAN, lawyer; b. N.Y.C., May 2, 1945; s. Isaac E. and Jean J. (Halfon) A.; m. Karen Ann Wieder, Feb. 1, 1969; children: Russell Andrew, Ilonne A. BA, U. Mich., 1966; JD cum laude, NYU, 1969. Bar: N.Y. 1970; sr. cert. relocation profl. Assoc. Gilbert, Segall and Young, N.Y.C., 1969-74, ptnr., 1975-2001, Holland & Knight LLP, N.Y.C., 2001—. Spkr. in field. Editor NYU Law Rev., 1969; contbr. articles to legal publs. Recipient Founders Day award NYU. Mem. ABA, N.Y. State Bar Assn., Assn. Bar City N.Y., Employee Relocation Coun. (pub. policy com.), Order of Coif, Hampshire Country Club, Ibis Golf and Country Club. General corporate, General practice, Real property. Home: 3 Ridgeway Rd Larchmont NY 10538-1123 Office: 195 Broadway Fl 23 New York NY 10007

ARQUIT, KEVIN JAMES, lawyer; b. Ithaca, N.Y., Sept. 11, 1954; s. Gordon James and Nora (Harris) A. BA cum laude, St. Lawrence U., 1975; JD cum laude, Cornell U., 1978. Bar: Ohio 1978, N.Y. 1980, U.S. Dist. Ct. (so. and ea. dists.) N.Y. 1980, U.S. Dist. Ct. (we. dist.) N.Y. 1983, U.S. Dist. Ct. (no. dist.) Calif. 1983, U.S. Ct. Appeals (3d cir.) 1983, U.S. Dist. Ct. (no. dist.) N.Y. 1985, U.S. Ct. Appeals(2d cir.) 1985, U.S. Supreme Ct. 1989. Assoc. Arter & Hadden, Cleve., 1978, Fish & Neave, N.Y.C., 1978-83, Harris, Beach & Wilcox, Rochester, N.Y., 1983-86; atty. advisor to chmn. FTC, Washington, 1986-87, chief staff, 1987-88, gen. counsel, 1988-89; dir. Bur. Competition, 1989-92; ptnr., head Clifford Chance Rogers & Wells Antitrust Practice Group, N.Y.C., 1992—. Republican. Roman Catholic. Antitrust. Office: Clifford Chance Rogers & Wells LLP 200 Park Ave Fl 8E New York NY 10166-0899 E-mail: Kevin.Arquit@CliffordChance.com

ARRILLAGA, JOSEFINA, lawyer, banker; b. Bilbao, Spain, Feb. 5, 1933; d. Pedro and Mercedes (Lansorena) Arrillaga. Baccalaureate, Colegio Immaculada Concepcion, Madrid, Spain, 1950; Law Degree, Madrid, U., 1955, doctoral studies, 1955-57; Doctorate, Munich U., 1971. Atty., Madrid Legal Office, 1959-66; atty. dept. fgn. commerce Dresdner Bank A.G., Munich, 1974-75, legal advisor credit dept. Madrid br., 1979-81, head legal dept., 1981— ; asst. mgr. dept. fgn. banking Banco Urquijo, Madrid, 1974-75, head internat. legal dept., 1975-77; co-rep. Banco Urquijo and Banco de Quilnes, Frankfurt/Main, 1978-79; asst. lectr. dept. procedural law Madrid U., 1955-57. Mem. Internat. Bar Assn., Madrid Bar Assn., Internat. Union Lawyer (mem. permanent commn.), Spanish Nat. Found. Lyrical Arts (founding mem.), Spanish Assn. Friends of the Opera. Clubs: Club XXI, Ateneo, Club Liberal (Madrid). Author: The Responsibility of the Manufacturer, 1981. Home: Marceliano Santamaria 9 Madrid 16 Spain Office: Banco Exterior de Espana Carrera de San Jeronimo Madrid 16 Spain

ARRINGTON, JOHN LESLIE, JR. lawyer; b. Pawhuska, Okla., Oct. 15, 1931; s. John Leslie and Grace Louise (Moore) A.; m. Elizabeth Anne Waddington, 1956 (div.); children: Elizabeth Anne, John Leslie III, Winifred L., Katherine M.; m. Linda Vance, 1972. Grad., Lawrenceville Sch., 1949; AB, Princeton U., 1953; JD, Harvard U., 1956, LLM, 1957. Bar: Okla. 1956, U.S. Supreme Ct. 1960. Assoc. Arrington, Kihle, Gaberino & Dunn and predecessor firms, Tulsa, 1957-61, ptnr., 1961-93, chmn., CEO, 1994-96; gen. counsel ONEOK, Inc., 1997-98; of counsel Gable & Gotwals, Tulsa, 1998—. Chmn. bd. dirs. Woodland Bank of Tulsa, 1979-94. Prin. draftsman Okla. Supreme Ct. rules governing disciplinary proceedings, 1980-81; bd. dirs. Tulsa County Legal Aid Soc., 1965-70, pres. 1967-70; bd. dirs. Tulsa Family Mental Health Ctr., 1982-89. Named Outstanding Young Man, Tulsa Jaycees, 1963 Mem. ABA, Tulsa County Bar Assn. (Young Lawyer award 1962, pres. 1970, Pres.'s award 1984, Professionalism award 1993), Okla. Bar Assn. (mem. profl. responsiblity commn. 1977-84, vice chmn. 1983-84, Disting. svc. award 1984, Golden Gavel award 1985, Pres.'s award 1991, Masonic award for ethics 1995), So. Hills Country Club (Tulsa), Princeton Club (N.Y.C.). Republican. Episcopalian. General civil litigation, General corporate, Public utilities. Home: 2300 Riverside Dr Unit 3E Tulsa OK 74114-2402 Office: 100 W 5th St Ste 1000 Tulsa OK 74103-4293

ARTERTON, JANET BOND, judge; b. Philadelphia, Feb. 8, 1944; m. F. Christopher Arterton; two children. BA, Mt. Holyoke Coll., 1966; JD, Northeastern U., 1977. Law clk. to Hon. Herbert J. Stern U.S. Dist. Ct. N.J., 1977-78; ptnr. Garrison & Arterton, 1978-95; judge U.S. Dist. Ct. Conn., New Haven, 1995—. Fellow Am. Bar Found., Conn. Bar Found.; mem. ATLA, Nat. Employment Lawyers Assn., Conn. Employment Lawyers Assn., Conn. State Trial Lawyers Assn. (bd. govs. 1990-95), Conn. Bar Assn. (mem. adv. com. state ct. rules 1992, mem. fed. jud. selection com. 1991-93, mem. exec. com. women and the law sect. 1990-93, chairperson fed. practice sect. 1993-95. Office: US Dist Ct Conn 141 Church St New Haven CT 06510-2030

ARTHER, RICHARD OBERLIN, polygraphist, educator; b. Pitts., May 20, 1928; s. William Churchill Sr. and Florence Lind (Oberlin) A.; m. Mary-Esther Wuensch, Sept. 12, 1951; children: Catherine, Linda, William III. BS, Mich. State U., 1951; MA, Columbia U., 1960. Chief assoc. John E. Reid and Assocs., Chgo., 1951-53, dir. N.Y.C., 1953-58; pres. Sci. Lie Detection, Inc., 1958—, Nat. Tng. Ctr. Polygraph Sci., N.Y.C., 1958—. Author: Interrogation for Investigators, 1958, The Scientific Investigator, 1964, 6th edit., Arther Polygraph Reference Guide, 1964—; editor Jour. Polygraph Sci., 1966—. Fellow Acad. Cert. Polygraphists (exec. dir. 1962—), Am. Polygraph Assn. (founding mem.), Am. Assn. Police Polygraphists (founding mem., Polygraphist of Yr. 1980), N.Y. State Polygraphists (founder), N.J. Polygraphists (founder). Office: Sci Lie Detection Inc 200 W 57th St Ste 1400 New York NY 10019-3211

ARTHUR, LINDSAY GRIER, retired judge, author, editor; b. Mpls., July 30, 1917; s. Hugh and Alice (Grier) A.; m. Jean Johansen, Sept. 19, 1940; children: Lindsay G., Mollie K., Julie A. AB, Princeton U., 1939; postgrad., Harvard U., 1939-40; LLB, JD, U. Minn., 1946. Bar: Minn. 1946, U.S. Dist. Ct. Minn. 1948, U.S. Supreme Ct. 1964. Lawyer Nieman, Bosard & Arthur, Mpls., 1946-54; alderman Mpls. City Coun., 1951-54; judge Mcpl. Ct., Mpls., 1954-61; chief judge juvenile divsn. Dist. Ct., 1961-79, 87-93, judge felony, civil divsn., 1979-83, chief judge mental health divsn., 1983-87; mediator, 1987—. Arbitrator civil and family cts., 1991—. Author: Twin Cities Uncovered, 1996, A Manual for Mediators, 1995; editor Digest of Juvenile and Family Law, 1983-93; contbr. articles to profl. jours. Bd. dirs. Nat. Ctr. State Cts., Williamsburg, 1974-77, Metro YMCA, Mpls. area, 1981 85; chmn. trustees Bethlehem Luth. Ch., 1979-80. Lt. USNR, 1942-45, PTO. Mem. Nat. Coun. Juvenile Ct. Judges (pres. 1972-73, Jud. scholar 1985—), ABA (disabilities com. 1984-89), Am. Law Inst. (advisor divorce law 1989-93). Avocations: writing, walking. Home: 1201 Yale Pl Apt 205 Minneapolis MN 55403-1955 E-mail: lgasr@hotmail.com

ARTZ, CHERIE B. lawyer; b. Cin., Jan. 3, 1949; d. Joseph Meyer and Esther Epstein Fish; m. William Edward Artz, May 15, 1976; children: Rachel, Lindsey. BS, U. Cin., 1969; MA, George Washington U., 1973, JD with honors, 1985. Bar: Va. 1985, U.S. Ct. Appeals (fed. cir.) 1986, D.C. 1987, U.S. Supreme Ct. 1989, U.S. Ct. Appeals (4th cir.) 1990, U.S. Ct. Appeals (5th cir.) 1991, U.S. Ct. Appeals (6th cir.) 1992, Md. 1995. Tchr. Cin. Pub. Schs., 1969-71, Piscataway (N.J.) Pub. Schs., 1971-72; social worker Arlington (Va.) Juvenile Ct., 1973-82; law clk. U.S. Ct. Appeals Fed. Cir., Washington, 1985-86; lawyer Schnader Harrison Segal & Lewis, LLP, 1986—, ptnr., 1994—. Staff George Washington U.-New Horizons for Women Program, Washington, 1974-76. Mem. George Washington U. Law Rev., 1984. Bd. dirs. Temple Rodef Shalom, Falls Church, Va., 1991—, pres., 1996-98; bd. dirs. Mid. Atlantic coun. Union Am. Hebrew Congregations, Washington, 1998—; bd. overseers N.Y. Sch. Hebrew Union Coll., N.Y.C., 1999—. Avocations: tennis, travel. Home: 964 Saigon Rd Mc Lean VA 22102-2119 Office: Schnader Harrison Segal & Lewis LLP 1300 I St NW Ste 11E Washington DC 20005-3314

ASAI-SATO, CAROL YUKI, lawyer; b. Osaka, Japan, Oct. 22, 1951; came to U.S., 1953; d. Michael and Sumiko (Kamei) Asai; 1 child, Ryan Makoto Sato. BA cum laude, U. Hawaii, 1972; JD, Willamette Coll. Law, 1975. Bar: Hawaii 1975. Assoc. firm Ashford & Wriston, Honolulu, 1975-79; counsel Bank of New Eng., Boston, 1979-81; assoc. counsel Alexander & Baldwin, Honolulu, 1981-83, sr. counsel, 1984-88; of counsel Rush, Moore, Craven, Sutton, Morry, Beh, 1988-89, ptnr., 1989-97, Alston Hunt Floyd & Ing, 1997—. Willamette Coll. Law Bd. Trustees scholar, 1972-73. Mem. ABA, Hawaii Bar Assn., Hawaii Women Lawyers, Phi Beta Kappa, Phi Kappa Phi. Democrat. Contracts commercial, General corporate, Real property. Office: Alston Hunt Floyd & Ing Pacific Tower 18th Fl 1001 Bishop St Ste 1800 Honolulu HI 96813-3689

ASANTE, SAMUEL KWADWO BOATEN, lawyer, international official; b. Asokore, Ghana, May 11, 1933; s. Daniel Y. and Mary (Baafi) A.; m. Philomena Margaret Aidoo; children: Adlai, Joyce, Dominic, Philomena, Angela. J.S.D., Yale U., 1965; LL.M., U. London, 1958. Bar: Ghana 1960, Solicitor Sup. Ct. Eng. (hon.) 1960. Asst. state atty. Ghana, 1960-61; lectr. law U. Ghana, 1961-65, acting head dept. law, 1962; lectr. law U. Leeds, 1965-66; atty. legal dept. World Bank, Washington, 1966-69; adj. prof. law Howard U., 1967-69; solicitor gen. Ghana, 1969-77; chief adviser on legal matters UN Centre on Transnational Corp., N.Y.C., 1977-83, dir., 1983— ; dir. dept. econ, and social devel. UN, 1992—; chmn. Ghana constitutional drafting com., 1991-92; vis. prof. law and bus. Temple U., 1976; vis. fellow Clare Hall, mem. law faculty Cambridge U., 1978-79; lectr. in field. Fulbright fellow, 1963-65, Sterling fellow 1963-65; adv. to govts. on internat. econ. law and internat. bus. transactions. Patron Internat. Ctr. Pub. Law, London U., hon. friend Inst. Advanced Legal Studies. Bd. dirs. Internat. Development Law Inst.; arbitrator Internat. Ctr. Settlement of Investment Disputes. Fellow World Acad. Art and Sci., Ghana Acad. Art and Sci.; mem. Internat Law Assn., Am. Soc. Internat. Law, Soc. Pub. Tchrs. Law. Contbr. in field; mem. adv. bd. Jour. Fgn. Investment Law. Address: 412 Pinebrook Blvd New Rochelle NY 10804

ASCHER, RICHARD ALAN, lawyer; b. June 3, 1945; s. Richard Oscar and Bernice (Spiegel) Ascher; m. Barbara Haberman, May 22, 1967; children: Jonathan Colin, Andrew David. BA, SUNY, Buffalo, 1967, JD, 1970. Bar: Calif. 1991. Staff atty. Legal Aid Soc., Queens, NY, 1970—73; ptnr. Ascher & Goldstein, 1973—83, Ascher & Novitt, Queens, 1983—90. Counsel Assemblyman L. Stavisky, Albany, NY, 1974—75, Assemblyman I. Lafayette, Albany, 1976—90. Counsel, bd. dir. Jackson Heights Cmty. Devel. Corp., Queens, NY, 1980—82; pres. Queens Ind. Democrats, 1976; mem. lawyers com. Hart Presdl. Campaign, 1984; chmn. Com. to Make Watergate Perfectly Clear, Queens, 1973—74. Mem.: Queens County Bar Assn., Criminal Cts. Bar Assn., JFK Dem. Club (Jackson Heights chpt.) (exec. bd. 1987). Jewish. Criminal, Personal injury, Real property.

ASCHKINASI, DAVID JAY, lawyer; b. N.Y.C. BA, Brandeis U., 1972; JD, U. Colo., 1976. Bar: Colo. 1976, U.S. Dist Ct. Colo. 1976, U.S. Ct. Appeals (10th cir.) 1982. Sole practice, Boulder, Colo., 1976-77; asst. atty. gen. State of Colo., Denver, 1977-83; pvt. practice, 1983-84; div. counsel U.S. West Info. Systems, 1984-87; atty. U.S. West Communications, 1988—; corp. counsel Quest Comms., 2000—. Mem. ABA, Colo. Bar Assn., Denver Bar Assn., Am. Corp. Counsel Assn. Contracts commercial, General corporate. Office: Qwest Communications 1801 California St Ste 3800 Denver CO 80202-2610

ASH, DAVID CHARLES, lawyer; b. Bklyn., Nov. 28, 1951; s. Jerome William and Bernice (Kibrick) A.; m. Karen Artz Ash, June 11, 1977; children: Kimberly Barbara, Danielle Alexandra. AB magna cum laude, Brandeis U., 1973; JD, Harvard U., 1976. Bar: N.Y. 1977, U.S. Dist. Ct. (so. dist.) N.Y. 1977. Assoc. Rosenman Colin Freund Lewis & Cohen, N.Y.C., 1976-79, Trubin Sillcocks Edelman & Knapp, N.Y.C., 1979-82, Corbin Silverman & Sanseverino, N.Y.C., 1982-85; v.p., gen. counsel Sam Ash Music Corp., Hempstead, N.Y., 1985—, Samson Techs. Corp., Sam Ash Properties Corp., Sam Ash Music Inst., Inc. Mem. ABA, N.Y. State Bar Assn., Assn. of Bar of City of N.Y. Democrat. Jewish. Contracts commercial, Computer, Real property.

ASHCROFT, JOHN DAVID, attorney general; b. Chgo., May 9, 1942; m. Janet Elise; children: Martha, Jay, Andrew. B cum laude, Yale U., 1964; JD, U. Chgo., 1967. Bar: Mo., U.S. Supreme Ct. Assoc. prof. S.W. Mo. State U., Springfield, 1967-72; pvt. practice, 1967-73; state auditor State of Mo., 1973-75, asst. atty. gen., 1975-77, atty. gen., 1977-84, gov., 1985-92; atty. Suelthaus and Kaplan P.C., 1993-94; U.S. senator from Mo., 1995-2001; U.S. atty. gen. U.S. Dept. Justice, 2001—. Mem. commerce, sci. and transp. coms., aviation subcom., comm. subcom., chmn. consumer affairs, fgn. commerce & tourism subcom., mfg. and competitiveness subcom., mem. fgn. rels. com., European affairs subcom., Near Ea. & South Asian affairs subcom., Western Hemisphere Peace Corps subcom., mem. jud. com., chmn. constitution, fedn. and property rights subcom.; mem. Presdl. Adv. Coun. Intergovtl. Affairs, The Pres.'s Export Coun.; nat. chmn. Edn. Commn. States, 1987-88, Jud. Com., Subcom., chmn. constn.; chmn. Nat. Govs. Assn. Task Force on Coll. Quality, 1985, Nat. Govs. Assn. Task Force on Adult Literacy; co-chair Renewal Alliance. Gospel singer: records include In the Spirit of Life and Liberty, The Gospel According to John; author: Lessons from a Father to a Son, 1998, (with wife) College Law for Business, 7th, 8th, 9th, 10, 11th edits., It's the Law, 1979-91; contbr. articles to profl. jours. Chmn. Task Force on Adult Literacy, Task Force on College Quality Nat. Gov.'s Assn., 1991; chmn. Rep. Gov.'s Assn., 1990; co-chmn. Rep. Platform Com., 1992. Recipient Nat. Sheriffs Assn. award, 1996; named Christian Statesman of Yr., 1996. Mem. ABA (ho. of dels.), Mo. Bar Assn., Cole County Bar Assn., Nat. Assn. Attys. Gen. (pres. 1980-81, chmn. budget com., exec. com., Wyman award 1983), Nat. Govs. Assn. (vice chmn. 1990, chmn. 1991-92, chmn. Pres.'s Commn. on Urban Families 1992). Republican. Mem. Assembly of God Ch. Office: US Dept Justice 950 Pennsylvania Ave NW Washington DC 20530*

ASHE, BERNARD FLEMMING, arbitrator, educator, lawyer; b. Balt., Mar. 8, 1936; s. Victor Joseph Ashe and Frances Cecelia (Johnson) Flemming; m. Grace Nannette Pegram, Mar. 23, 1963; children: Walter Joseph, David Bernard. BA, Howard U., 1956, JD, 1961. Bar: Va. 1961, D.C. 1963, Mich. 1964, N.Y. 1971. Tchr. Balt. Pub. Schs., 1956-58; atty. NLRB, Washington, 1961-63; asst. gen. counsel Internat. Union United Auto Workers, Detroit, 1963-71; gen. counsel N.Y. State United Tchrs., Albany, 1971-96, arbitrator, 1996—. Mem. adj. faculty Cornell Sch. Indsl. and Labor Rels., Albany div., 1981, 87, Fordham U. Law Sch., 1996-00, Roger Williams U. Law Sch., 1996-98. Contbr. articles on labor and constnl. law to profl. jours. Bd. dirs. Urban League Albany, 1979-85, 1st v.p., 1981-85; trustee N.Y. Lawyers Fund for Client Protection, 1981—, Adelphi Univ., Garden City, N.Y., 1997—. Fellow Am. Bar Found. (life), Coll. Labor and Employment Lawyers (emeritus); mem. NAACP (Thurgood Marshall Justice award 2000), ABA (chmn. sect. labor and employment law sect. 1982-83, consortium on legal svcs. and the pub. 1979-84, commn. on pub. understanding about the law 1987-91, mem. standing com. on group and prepaid legal svcs. 1996-97, ho. of dels. 1985-96, 97—, nominating com. 1988-91, chair drafting com., 1998-2000, bd. govs. 1991-94, exec. com. 1993-94, accreditation com. sect. legal edn. and admission to the bar 1994-98, chmn. standing com. on group and prepaid legal svcs. 1996-97, sr. lawyers divsn. coun. 1994-2000, standing com. on client protection 1998-2001), Am. Law Inst., Nat. Bar Assn., Am. Arbitration Assn. (bd. dirs. 1982-98, Whitney North Seymour Sr. medal 1989), N.Y. State Bar Assn., Albany County Bar Assn.

ASHER, DAVID, lawyer; b. Dec. 8, 1964; BA, Calif. State U., Northridge, 1989; JD, U. West L.A., 1993. Pvt. practice, Calif., 1994-98. Office: 1968 19th St Ste 5 Santa Monica CA 90404-4708

ASHLEMAN, IVAN RENO, II, health care executive, lawyer; b. Kansas City, Mo., June 9, 1940; s. Ivan Reno and Ellen Lorraine (Fisher) A.; m. Susan Haase, July 25, 1986; children: Brian Eugene, Michael Scott. B.S., U. Nebr., 1963, J.D., 1963. Bar: Nev. 1963, U.S. Dist. Ct. Nebr. 1963, U.S. Dist. Ct. Nev. 1964, U.S. Tax Ct. 1975, U.S. Ct. Appeals (9th cir.) 1968, U.S. Supreme Ct. 1975. Sole practice, Las Vegas and Reno, Nev., 1966-69; ptnr. Davis, Cowell & Bowe, San Francisco and Las Vegas, 1969-80, Ashleman & Clontz, Las Vegas, 1982-83, Raggio, Ashleman, Wooster, Clontz & Lindell, Las Vegas and Reno, 1981, Ashleman, Evans & Kelly, 1987-88; pvt. practice, Reno, 1988—; Clark County dep. dist. atty., Las Vegas, 1964-66; pres. Ins. Services, Inc., 1983—; bd. dirs., pres. Geriatric Health Resources, Inc.; pres., bd. dirs. Sierra Health Care Mgmt. Assocs., Inc. Contbr. articles to profl. jours. Chmn. Nev. Bd. Museums and History, Carson City; exec. bd. dirs., treas. Nathan Adelson Hospice, Las Vegas, 1981—; pres. Young Dems. of Las Vegas, 1970; bd. dirs. Sparks Family Hosp., 1980-83, Spring Valley Community Hosp., 1980—; mem. Nev. Homebuilders. Mem. ABA, Am. Judicature Soc., Nev. Bar Assn., Nebr. Bar Assn., Washoe County Bar Assn., Clark County Bar Assn., So. Nev. Arbitration Assn., Indsl. Relations Reps. Assn., Am. Acad. Med. Adminstrs., Reno C. of C. Episcopalian. Clubs: Las Vegas Country, Hualapai (Las Vegas). Administrative and regulatory, General corporate, Health. Home: 485 Gonawabie Crystal Bay NV 89402 Office: 1661 E Flamingo Rd Ste 5A Las Vegas NV 89119-5291

ASHLEY-FARRAND, MARGALO, lawyer, mediator, private judge; b. N.Y.C., July 26, 1944; d. Joel Thomas and Margalo (Wilson) Ashley; m. Marvin H. Bennett, Mar. 5, 1964 (div. June 1974),; children: Marc, Aliza; m. Thomas Ashley-Farrand, Dec. 11, 1981. Student, UCLA, 1962-63, U. Pitts., 1972-74; BA cum laude, NYU, 1978; JD, Southwestern U., 1980. Bar: D.C. 1981, Md. 1981, Calif. 1983, U.S. Dist. Ct. (ctrl. and no. dists.) Calif. 1984; cert. family law specialist Calif. State Bar. Pvt. practice law, Washington, 1981-82; ptnr. Ashley-Farrand & Smith, Glendale, Calif., 1983-87; pvt. practice law, 1987-95; pvt. practice Pasadena, Calif., 1995—; v.p. Legal Inst. Fair Elections, 1995—; settlement officer L.A. Mcpl. Ct., 1990—. Judge pro tem L.A. Mcpl. Ct., 1989—, L.A. Superior Ct., 1993—. Convenor, pres. East Hills chpt. NOW, 1972-74, mem. Pa. state bd., 1972-74, pres. Hollywood chpt. 1974-75, mem. bd. N.Y.C. chpt. 1975-78; convenor, coord. L.A. Women's Coalition for Better Broadcasting, 1974-75; Dem. nominee Calif. State Assembly, 1994; convenor Shades of Culture Women's Club, 2000-2001. Themis soc. scholar, 1980; named one of Outstanding Young Women of Am., 1980. Mem. ABA, ACLU, NOW, NWPC, League of Conservation Voters, Calif. Women Lawyers, Women Lawyers Assn. L.A., Pasadena Interracial Women's Club (pres. 1993-94). Appellate, Family and matrimonial, Probate. Office: 215 N Marengo Ave Fl 3 Pasadena CA 91101-1504

ASHMAN, KENNETH J. lawyer; b. Chgo., Feb. 21, 1961; BA cum laude, Ariz. State U., 1983; JD, NYU, 1990. Bar: N.Y. 1990, Ill. 1996, N.Y. 1996; U.S. Dist. Ct. N.J., 1991, U.S. Dist. Ct. (so. and ea. dists.) N.Y. 1996, U.S. Dist. Ct. Hawaii, 1997, U.S. Dist. Ct. (no. dist.) Ill. 1998, U.S. Ct. Appeals (2nd cir.) 2000, U.S. Ct. Appeals (7th cir.), U.S. Supreme Ct., 1998. Assoc. Weil, Gotshal & Manges, LLP, 1990-94, LeBoeuf, Lamb, Green & MacRae, LLP, 1995-97. Mem. NYU mock trial team; law clk. to hon. Frederic Block, U.S. Dist. Judge, Ea. Dist. N.Y., 1994-95. Topics devel. editor: Boston U. Internat. Law Jour.; author: The Sky is Falling: Recovery of Lost Profits Caused by Construction Disasters, 1999, Class Action Settlements After Amchem, 1997, others; co-author: The Foreign Corrupt Practices Act in White Collar Crime: Business and Regulatory offenses, 2000, others. Recipient Am. Jurisprudence awards for excellence in trial advocacy and internat. trade law.

ASHTON, MARK ALFRED, lawyer; b. July 18, 1944; s. Alfred Jackson and Margarette Carolyn (Green) A.; m. Linda Diane Stroud, May 15, 1971; children: Kathryn, Hillary, Courtney. BBA, U. Okla., 1966; JD, 1969. Bar: Okla. 1969, U.S. Dist. Ct. (we. Dist.) Okla. 1969, U.S. Ct. Appeals. (10th cir.) 1970, D.C. Ct. Appeals 1970, U.S. Supreme Ct. 1973. Assoc. Rhoads, Ashton, Johnson & Schacher & Lawton, Okla., 1969-72; ptnr. Ashton and Ashton, Lawton, 1972-73; ptnr., pres. Ashton, Ashton, Wisener and Munkacsy, Inc., 1975—. Mem. com. apptd. by Okla. Supreme Ct. to write civil instrn. manual for all trial judges, 1978—; lectr. continuing legal edn. of bar; mem. Okla. Supreme Ct. Com. on Media in the Courtroom, 1978; commr. Okla. Jud. Nominating Comm., 1983-89; chmn., 1987; bd. dirs. Okla. Attys. Mutual Ins. Co., 1995—, exec. com., 1995—. Co-editor: Okla. Bar Assn. Desk Manual, 1976; editor: The Advocate, 1997—; contbr. articles on law to profl. jours. Mem. Comanche County Democratic party; 4th congl. dist. Okla. del. Dem. Nat. Conv., 1984, 2000; mem. Centenary United MEth. Ch., Lawton; chmn. City of Lawton Personnel Bd., 1975-80; past. chmn. Okla. chpt. Common Cause. Served to capt. Judge adv. Gen. USAF, 1969-72. Mem. Okla. Bar Assn. (lawyers ins. com. 1979, del. to ho. of dels. 1974, chmn. pub. info. com. 1982, 83, assoc. editor jour. 1983-87, editor, 1988-89; named Outstanding performance 1976, Golden Gavel award 1982, disting. svc. award 1988), SW Okla. Legal Inst. (pres. 1976), Okla. Trial Lawyers Assn. (pres. 1978, 87, bd. dirs. 1975-82, edn. chmn. 1976, pres., 1978, 87), ABA, Am. Trial Lawyers Assn., Okla. Bar Prof. Liability Co. (liability ins. com. 1979—, bd. dirs. 1979—, c.p. 1979-85, chmn. bd. 1985-87), Phi Delta Phi. Avocations: backpacking, photography. Federal civil litigation, General practice, Personal injury. Home: 1618 NW 34th St Lawton OK 73505-3814 Office: Ashton Wisener & Munkacsy PC 711 SW C Ave Lawton OK 73501-4311

ASHTON, MARK RANDOLPH, lawyer; b. Abington, Pa., Sept. 10, 1955; s. Frank E. and Charlotte (Wagenbaur) A. BA in Internat. Affairs, George Washington U., 1977; JD, John Marshall U., 1980. Bar: Pa. 1980. Law clk. to Hon. Mason Avrigian Ct. of Common Pleas of Montgomery County, Norristown, Pa., 1980-81; assoc. Abrahams & Loewenstein, 1982-87; dept. chmn. Riley, Riper, Hollin & Colagreco, 1987-90; ptnr. Fox, Rothschild, O'Brien & Frankel, Exton, Pa., 1990—. Mem. Montgomery Bar Assn. (bd. dirs. 1985-87), Chester County Bar Assn. (chmn. family law sect. 1988-90), Wissahickon Valley Hist. Soc. (pres.), D.J. Freed Am. Inn of Ct. (pres.). Republican. Episcopalian. Family and matrimonial. Home: 413 Stratford Ave Collegeville PA 19426-2553 Office: Fox Rothschild O'Brien & Frankel 760 Constitution Dr Ste 104 Exton PA 19341-1149

ASHWORTH, BRENT FERRIN, lawyer; b. Albany, Calif., Jan. 8, 1949; s. Dell Shepherd and Bette Jean (Brailsford) A.; m. Charlene Mills, Dec. 16, 1970; children: Amy, John, Matthew, Samuel (dec.), Adam, David, Emily, Luke, Benjamin. BA, Brigham Young U., 1972; JD, U. Utah, 1975. Bar: Utah 1977. Asst. county atty. Carbon County, Price, Utah, 1975-76; assoc. atty. Frandsen & Keller, 1976-77; v.p. legal affairs, sec., gen. counsel Nature's Sunshine Products, Provo, 1977—. Bd. dirs., gen. counsel Carbon County Nursing Home, Price, Utah, 1976-77; mem. Provo Landmarks Commn., 1997—, co-chair sesquicentennial com., 1998-99; active Provo Libr. Bd., 2001—; chmn. Utah County Cancer Crusade Com., 1981-83; chmn. Provo LCOC Arts subcom., 1998-99; city councilman Payson City, Utah, 1980-82, planning commn., 1980-82, mayor pro tem, 1982; bd. dirs. ARC, Utah County chpt., 1988-94, Springville Mus. Art, 1998-2001, Celebration of Health Found., 1999—; pres. Deseret Village Spani Fork, Utah, 1988-90; gen. counsel Brigham Young Acad. Found., 1995—; founder, chmn. George E. Freestone Boy Scout Mus., Provo, 2000—; exec. bd. Utah Nat. Park coun. Boy Scouts Am.; bd. dirs. Provo Sch. Dist. Found., 2001— Mem. ABA, SAR (pres. Utah County chpt. 1989-90, state chpts. 1st v.p. 1990-91, state soc. pres. 1991-92, chancellor 1992-94), ATLA, Southeastern Utah Bar Assn. (sec. 1977), Utah State Bar, Am. Corp. Counsel Assn. (sec. Intermountain chpt. 1990-91), Emily Dickinson Soc. Utah (pres. 1995-97), Sons Utah Pioneers, Kiwanis Club (v.p. 1995-96, pres. 1997-98, lt. gov. Utah Idaho dist. 2001—), Phi Kappa Phi, Phi Eta Sigma. General corporate, Private international. Home: 1377 Cambridge Ct Provo UT 84604-4178 Office: Natures Sunshine Products 1655 N Main St Spanish Fork UT 84660-1010

ASKEY, WILLIAM HARTMAN, US magistrate, judge, lawyer; b. Williamsport, Pa., June 21, 1919; s. Charles Fisher and Marguerite Kirlin (Hartman) A.; m. Betty Arlene Moore, July 3, 1942; 1 dau., Elizabeth Powell. BA, Bucknell U., 1941; JD, U. Pitts., 1951. Bar: Lycoming County Cts., 1951, Pa. 1952, U.S. Dist. Ct. (mid. dist.) Pa. 1952, U.S. Supreme Ct. 1960. Sole practice, Williamsport, Pa., 1951—; U.S. commr. U.S. Dist. Ct. (mid. dist.) Pa., 1964-71; part-time U.S. magistrate, judge, 1971—. With AAA, North Penn. Bd. dirs. Appalachia Ednl. Lab., Charleston, W.Va., 1967-85. Served to maj. USAAF, 1941-46. Mem. Lycoming Law Assn. (pres. 1968-69), Pa. Bar Assn., ABA (Nat. Conf. Spl. Ct. Judges), Fed. Bar Assn. (hon.), Fed. Magistrate Judges Assn., Charles F Greevy Jr Inn of Ct., Masons, Ross Club (Williamsport). E-mail: whaskey@sunlink.net

ASKIN, FRANK, law educator; b. Balt., Jan. 8, 1932; s. Abraham and Rose (Mervis) A.; m. Marilyn Klein, Aug. 6, 1960; children: Andrea Marcy, Jonathan Michael, Daniel Simon; 1 son from previous marriage, Steven. BA, CCNY, 1966; JD, Rutgers U., 1966. Bar: N.J. 1966, N.Y. 1983, U.S. Dist. Ct. (ea. dist.) N.Y., U.S. Ct. Appeals (2d, 3d cirs.), U.S. Supreme Ct. 1971. Journalist N.Y. Post, Bergen Record, Newark Star-Ledger; disting. prof. law Rutgers Law Sch., Newark, 1975—. Vis. prof. U. Hawaii Law Sch., 1975; spl. counsel edn. and labor com. U.S. Ho. of Reps., 1976-77, cons. govt. ops. com., 1989-92; gen. counsel ACLU, 1976—. Author: Defending Rights: A Life in Law and Politics, 1997; co-editor: Enforcing Fair Housing Laws, 1970; contbr. articles to profl. jours. Nat. bd. dirs. ACLU, 1968—, sec., 1971-75, gen. counsel, 1976—; del. Dem. Nat. Conv., 1980, 88; Dem. candidate 11th dist. U.S. Ho. of Reps., N.J., 1986—. Mem. Soc. Am. Law Tchrs. (treas. 1974-75). Office: Rutgers Law Sch 123 Washington St Newark NJ 07102-3192

ASLAKSEN, ASLAK, lawyer; b. Oslo, Apr. 24, 1959; m. Hanne Merete Jendal; children: Mads Aslaksøn, Bård AskaksRn, Oda Aslaksdatter Jendal. Degree in Law, U. Oslo, 1985; LLM, Harvard U., 1987. With legal dept. Aker AS, Oslo, 1985; head legal dept., Borar sec. Kosmos AS, 1987-89; assoc. IM Skaugen, 1990-92, Law Firm Schjødt AS, Oslo, 1992-95; with Advokatfirma Lyng & Co. Bd. dirs. numerous cos. Candidate Conservative party, Oslo, 1999—. Mem. Norwegian Bar Assn. Office: Advokatfirma Lyng & Co DA Fr Nansens Plass 7 Box 1494 Oslo 0116 Norway E-mail: aslak.aslaksen@lyngco.no

ASMUTH, GRETCHEN, law librarian, records manager; b. Stamford, Conn., Dec. 17, 1954; d. Vernon Paul and Marjorie (Hutchens) Wystrach; m. Walter Asmuth III, Oct. 11, 1986; 2 children. BA, U Conn., 1977; MSLS, Cath. U. Am., 1983. Asst. libr. Sutherland, Asbill & Brennan, Washington, 1981-82; dir. libr. and records svcs. Preston Gates Ellis & Rouvelas Meeds LLP, 1982—. Mem. Am. Assn. Law Librs., Am. Records Mgmt. Assn. Presbyterian. Office: Preston Gates et al 1735 New York Ave NW Washington DC 20006-5209

ASPEN, MARVIN EDWARD, federal judge; b. Chgo., July 11, 1934; s. George Abraham and Helen (Adelson) A.; m. Susan Alona Tubbs, Dec. 18, 1966; children: Jennifer Marion, Jessica Maile, Andrew Joseph. BS in Sociology, Loyola Univ., 1956; JD, Northwestern U., 1958. Bar: Ill., 1958. Individual practice, Chgo., 1958-59; draftsman joint com. to draft new Ill. criminal code Chgo. Bar Assn.-Ill. Bar Assn., 1959-60; asst. state's atty. Cook County, Ill., 1960-63; asst. corp. counsel City of Chgo., 1963-71; pvt. practice law, 1971; judge Cir. Ct. Cook County, Ill., 1971-79; judge ea. divsn. U.S. Dist. Ct. (no. dist.) Ill., Chgo., 1979-95, chief judge, 1995—. Edward Avery Harriman adj. prof. law Northwestern U. Law Sch.; past chmn. new judges, recent devels. in criminal law, and evidence coms. Ill. Judicial Conf., past chmn., adv. bd. Inst. Criminal Justice, John Marshall Sch. Law; past mem. Ill. Law Enforcement Commn., Gov. Ill. Adv. Commn. Criminal Justice, Cook County Bd. Corrections; past chmn. assoc. rules com. Ill. Supreme Ct., com. on ordinance violation problems; past vice chmn. com. on pattern jury instrns. in criminal cases; lectr. at judicial confs. and trial advocacy programs nationally and internationally; planner, participant in legal seminars at numerous schools including Harvard U., Emory U., U. Fla., Oxford U. (Eng.), U. Bologna, Nuremberg (Germany) U., U. Cairo, Egypt, U. Zimbabwe, U. Malta, U. The Philippines, U. Madrid; past mem. Georgetown U. Law Ctr. Project on Plea Bargaining in U.S., spl. faculty NITA advanced Trial Advocacy Program introducing Brit. trial techniques to experienced Am. litigators, spl. faculty of ABA designed to acquaint Scottish lawyers with modern litigation and tech.; frequent faculty mem. Nat. Judiciary Coll., Fed. Judicial Ctr., U. Nev. (Reno), Nat. Inst. for Trial Advocacy, Colo.; bd. dir. Fed. Judicial Ctr., past chair dir. search com.; past mem. Judicial Conf. Com. on Adminstrn. of the Bankruptcy System, Trial Bar Implementation Com. on Civility of the 7th Fed. Cir.; mem. Northwestern U. Law Bd. Co-author Criminal Law for the Layman-A Citizen's Guide, 2d edit., 1977, Criminal Evidence for the Police, 1972, Protective Security Law, 1983; contbr. over two dozen articles to legal publs. Past mem. vis. com. Northwestern U. Sch. Law, chmn. adv. com. for short courses (post law sch. ednl. program), mem. law bd.; past mem. vis. com. U. Chgo. Law Sch.; mem. vis. com. No. Ill. U. Sch. Law; organizer, past pres. Northwestern Univ. Sch. of Law chpt. Amincourt Program U.S. Judicial Conf; past mem. Cook County Bd. Corrections, John Howard Assn.; active CEELI programs in Bulgaria and Yugoslavia Ford Found. Jud. Tng. Program in China. With USAF, 1958-59; trustee Am. Inns Ct. Recipient Nat. Ctr. Freedom of Info. Studies award, Ctr. for Pub. Resources award, Merit award Northwestern U. Alumni Assn., Herbert Harley award Am. Judicature Soc.; named Person of Yr. Chgo. Lawyer, 1995. Mem. Am. Bar Found. (bd. dirs.), Judicature Soc. Ill. (past chmn. coms.), Chgo. Bar Assn. (bd. mgrs. 1978-79, past chmn. criminal law com., past bd. editors Chgo. Bar Record, mem. commn. on criminal justice. coms. on cont. legal edn., devel. of law, civil disorder and others), Ill. State Bar Assn. (past chmn. pub. rels., corrections, fair trial/free press, criminal law coms., mem. others), Northwestern U. Law Alumni Assn. (past pres., Merit award), ABA (co-chair, sec. of litigation Inst. for Trial practical task force, mem. standing com. on fed. jud. improvements, pres. ABA mus., mem. bd. Am. Bar Fedn., past mem. ABA bd. govs., mem. house dels., past chmn. exec com., mem. bd. editors ABA Jour.), Nat. Conf. Fed. Trial Judges (past mem. coun. sect., past chmn. exec. com. litigation, past chmn., coun. sect. criminal justice, mem. edn. bd. sect. criminal justice mag., past co-chmn. liason jud. com. sect. litigation, mem. jury comprehension study com., ho. dels., standing com. fed. jud. improvements, co-chmn. sect. litigation Inst. Trial Practice Task Force), Am. Inns Ct. E-mial: marvin. Office: US Dist Ct 2548 US Courthouse 219 S Dearborn St Ste 2050 Chicago IL 60604-1800 E-mail: aspen@ilnd.uscourts.gov

ASPERO, BENEDICT VINCENT, lawyer; b. Newton, N.J., Sept. 3, 1940; s. Umberto S. and Rose (Cerreta) A.; m. Sally Hennen, June 26, 1971; children: Benedict Vincent, Alexander Morgan. AB, U. Notre Dame, 1962, JD, 1966. Bar: N.J. 1970, N.Y. 1982, D.C. 1983, U.S. Dist. Ct. N.J. 1970, U.S. Supreme Ct. 1981. Assoc., then ptnr. Meyers, Lesser & Aspero, Sparta, N.J., 1971-76; atty. Benedict V. Aspero, Sparta and Morristown, 1976-82; ptnr. Broderick, Newmark, Grather & Aspero, Morristown, 1982-89, Courter, Kobert, Laufer, Purcell & Cohen, 1989-91; prin. Benedict V. Aspero, Esq., P.C., 1992—. Mem. adv. bd. Summit Bank, First Morris Bank; mem. adv. bd. Summit Bank, First Morris Bank, 2001—, GTI.net. Trustee, pres. Harding Twp. Civic Assn., 1982—85; trustee Craig

Sch., 1985—, pres. bd., 1986—; active Loyola Retreat House, 1992—99; chmn. bd. dirs. Craig Sch., bd. trustees, 1985—, pres. bd., 1992—; mem. adv. bd. First Morris Bank. Mem. ABA, N.J. Bar Assn., Morris County Bar Assn., Sussex County Bar Assn., Sorin Soc., Morristown Club, Essex Hunt Club. Republican. Roman Catholic. Contracts commercial, General corporate, Probate. Office: 222 Ridgedale Ave PO Box 1573 Morristown NJ 07962-1573 E-mail: bvatty@git.net

ASPEY, FREDERICK MORRIS (FRITZ ASPEY), lawyer; b. Phoenix, Jan. 12, 1947; s. Frederick Morris and Madge (Gieszl) A.; children: Tyler Jordan, Matthew Logan. B.S., No. Ariz. U., 1969; J.D., Ariz. State U., 1972. Bar: Ariz. 1972., U.S. Dist. Ct. Ariz. 1973, U.S. Ct. Appeals (9th cir.) 1974, U.S. Supreme Ct. 1978. Assoc. Law Office J.R. Babbitt, Flagstaff, Ariz., 1972-75; ptnr. firm Aspey, Watkins, & Diesel, Flagstaff, 1975—. Mem. Big Bros., Flagstaff, 1974—; mem. bd. visitors Ariz. State U. Coll. Law, Tempe, 1980—; cert. holder Flagstaff Med. Ctr., 1984—. Mem. ABA, Ariz. Bar Assn. (adminstrn. com. 1978-82, bd. govs. 1982-92, pres. 1991-92), Coconino County Bar Assn. (pres. 1980), Ariz. Trial Lawyers Assn., Assn. Trial Lawyers Am. Democrat. Methodist. Office: Aspey Watkins & Diesel PLLC 123 N San Francisco St Flagstaff AZ 86001-5231

ASPINWALL, DAVID CHARLES, lawyer; b. Denver, Apr. 15, 1955; s. Darrell David and Gwendolyn Beth (Skeels) A.; m. Inez Bussey Merritt, Dec. 5, 1981; children: Courtney Merritt, Johnathan Westbrook. B.Arts and Sci., Denver U., 1977, JD, 1980. Bar: Colo. 1980. Mem. Dunn, Crane & Burg, Denver, 1980-81, Michael S. Burg, P.C., Denver, 1981-83, Burg & Aspinwall, P.C., Denver, 1983-88; v.p. counsel, chief compliance officer Great West Life & Annuity Ins. Co., 1988—; mem. class action working group ACLI, 1995-2000; mem faculty, life ins. litigation ALIABA; mem. health issues task force Health Ins. Assn. Am., mem. subcom. on pilot life Employment Retirement Income Security Act, 1994-98, mem. legal adv. com., 1998-2001; instr. in field; corp. sponsor Denver U. Pres., Sundance Pride, 1987-90; pre-marital facilitation for Christ Episc. Ch., 1988-94; com. mem. St. Anne's Episc. Sch. Auction Underwriting Com., 1988-89. Mem. Arapahoe County Bar Assn., Def. Rsch. Inst., Colo. Bar Assn., Internat. Assn. Def. Counsel, Internat. Claims Assn. (mem. law com. 1990-93, panel mem. law com. presentation ann. conv. 1992), Phi Beta Kappa. Republican. Episcopalian. Federal civil litigation, General corporate, Insurance. Office: Great West Life & Annuity Ins Co 8515 E Orchard Rd Ste 100 Englewood CO 80111-5097 E-mail: david.aspinwall@gwl.com

ASSAEL, MICHAEL, lawyer, accountant; b. N.Y.C., July 20, 1949; s. Albert and Helen (Hope) A.; m. Eiko Sato. BA, George Washington U., 1971; MBA., Columbia U. Grad. Sch. Bus., 1973; JD, St. John's Law Sch., 1977. Bar: N.Y. 1978, U.S. Dist. Ct. (so. and ea. dists.) N.Y. 1980, U.S. Supreme Ct. 1982; CPA, N.Y. Tax sr. Price Waterhouse & Co., N.Y.C. and Tokyo, 1977-78; pvt. practice law, N.Y.C., 1978— ; pvt. practice acctg., N.Y.C., 1978— . Author: Money Smarts, 1982. Pres. bd. dirs. 200 Block East 74th Street Assn., 1982; bd. dirs. 200 E 74 Owners Corp., 1981— , treas., 1983-84, pres., 1984-85; mem. Yorkville Civic Council, tenant adv. com. Lenox Hill Neighborhood Assn., 1981-82. Recipient N.Y. Habitat/Citibank mgmt. achievement award, 1985. Mem. ABA, N.Y. State Bar Assn., N.Y. County Lawyers Assn., Am. Inst. CPA's, Am. Assn. Atty. CPA's, Inc., Nat. Assn. Accts., N.Y. State Soc. CPA's, Aircraft Owners and Pilots Assn. Clubs: N.Y. Road Runners, Columbia Bus. Sch. (N.Y.). Landlord-tenant, Real property, Personal income taxation.

ASSELIN, JOHN THOMAS, lawyer; b. Manshester, Conn., May 13, 1951; s. Oliver Joseph and MaryRose Mildred (Dondero) A.; children: Jessica Lynn, Kristina Anne. BA, U. Conn., 1973, JD, 1976. Bar: Conn. 1976, U.S. Dist. Ct. Conn. 1976. Pvt. practice, Willimantic, Conn., 1976—. Lectr. Practicing Law Inst. N.Y., Profl. Edn. Systems Inc. Author: Connecticut Workers' Compensation Practice Manual, The Trial Handbook for Connecticut Lawyers; contbr. articles to profl. jours. Served Conn. gov. Thomas J. Meskill, U.S. Rep. Robert Steele. Grantee Deerfield Found. Mem. ABA (lectr.), Conn. Bar Assn. (exec. com. civil justice sect.), Assn. Trial Lawyers Am., Conn. Trial Lawyers Assn. (bd. govs. 1981—), Phi Beta Kappa, Phi Kappa Phi, Pi Sigma Alpha. Roman Catholic. Avocations: horses, team penning. Family and matrimonial, Personal injury, Workers' compensation. Office: 661 Windham Rd South Windham CT 06266-1100

ASSIM, GARY DEAN, lawyer; b. London, May 3, 1961; s. Donna-Maria Cullen, Apr. 25, 1992; children: Alexander, Sam. Degree in law, Durham U., Eng., 1997. Mgmt. Lombard Tricity Fin. Ltd., London, 1981-84; lawyer Travers Smith Braithwaite, 1988-97; ptnr. Shoosmiths, Milton Keynes, 1997—. Contbr. articles to profl. jours.; contbr. numerous radio interviews. Recipient Fin. Houses diploma Fin. Houses Assn., 1981. Mem. Law Soc. Eng. and Wales, Milton Keynes Econ. Partnership, Inst. Dirs. Intellectual property, Patent, Trademark and copyright. Office: Shoosmiths 482 Midsummer Blvd Milton Keynes Bucks MK9 2SH England E-mail: gary.assim@shoosmiths.co.uk

ASTLEFORD, PETER DAVID, lawyer; LLB, Southampton U., 1983. Solicitor of Supreme Ct., Eng. and Wales. Lawyer Linklaters, London and Brussels; group legal adviser Invesco, London; now ptnr., head fin. svcs. Dechert. Co-author: Starting a Hedge Fund--A European Perspective, 1999. Avocation: scuba diving. Mergers and acquisitions, Securities, Financial. Office: Dechert 2 Serjeants Inn London EC4Y 1LT England Fax: 020 7353 3683. E-mail: peter.astleford@dechertEU.com

ATCHISON, RODNEY RAYMOND, retired lawyer, arbitrator; b. Hanford, Calif., Nov. 14, 1926; s. Clyde Raymond and Velma May (Watts) A.; m. Evaleen Mary McFadden, June 27, 1948; children: Cathlin Atchison, Susan Barisone, Kerry Dexter, Brian. Student, San Jose State Coll., 1946-49; JD, U. Santa Clara, 1952. Bar: Calif. 1953, U.S. Dist. Ct. (all dists.) Calif. 1953, U.S. Ct. Appeals (9th cir.) 1953, U.S. Supreme Ct. 1971. Assoc. Mullen & Filippi, Attys., San Francisco, 1953-55; dep. county counsel Santa Clara Calif. County Counsel, San Jose, 1955-57; city atty. City of Mountain View, Calif., 1957-62, City of Santa Cruz, 1962-90; pres. Atchison, Anderson, Hurley & Barisone, Profl. Law Corp., Santa Cruz, 1980-96; of counsel Atchison Barisone & Condotti, Profl. Law Corp., 1996, Law Offices of Rodney R. Atchison, 1996-2001. Arbitrator Am. Arbitration Assn., San Francisco, 1970-2001 Pres. Rotary Club Mountain View, Calif., 1961-62, Santa Cruz (Calif.) County Bar Assn., 1973. With USNR, 1944-46. Mem. ABA, Santa Cruz Rotary Club, Elks Lodge (life). Roman Catholic. Avocations: skiing, travel, golf. Alternative dispute resolution, Contracts commercial, Real property. E mail: rod7@aol.com

ATHAS, GUS JAMES, lawyer, director; b. Chgo., Aug. 6, 1936; s. James G. and Pauline (Parhas) A.; m. Marilyn Carres, July 12, 1964; children: Paula C. Vlahakos, James G., Christopher G. BS, U. Ill., 1958; JD cum laude, Loyola U., Chgo., 1965. Bar: Ill. 1965, U.S. Dist. Ct. (no. dist.) Ill. 1965, U.S. Ct. Appeals (7th cir.) 1970. With Isham, Lincoln & Beale, Chgo., 1965-69; group gen. counsel, asst. sec. ITT, Skokie, Ill., 1969-87; assoc. gen. counsel Itel Corp., Chgo., 1987; sr. v.p., gen. counsel, sec. Eagle Industries, Inc., 1987-97; exec. v.p. adminstrn., gen. counsel, sec. Falcon Bldg. Products, Inc., 1994-99; sr. v.p., gen. counsel Great Am. Mgmt. and Investment, Inc., 1995-97; ptnr. Stamos & Trucco, 2000—. Dir. Digistar Networks, Inc. Contbr. articles to profl. jours. 1st lt. U.S. Army, 1958-62. Mem. ABA, Am. Corp. Counsel Assn., Ill. Bar Assn., Chgo. Bar Assn. Greek Orthodox. General corporate, Private international, Mergers and acquisitions. Home: 1240 Hawthorne Ln Downers Grove IL 60515-4503 Office: Stamos & Trucco Sears Tower Ten North Dearborn 5th Fl Chicago IL 60602

ATKINS, AARON ARDENE, lawyer; b. Du Quoin, Ill., July 17, 1960; s. Thornton A. and Venita Lee (Thornton) A. BA, So. Ill. U., 1982, JD, 1985. Bar: Ill. 1985, U.S. Dist. Ct. (so. dist.) Ill. 1986. Ptnr. Miller & Atkins, Du Quoin, 1985-87; pvt. practice, 1987—. City atty. City of Du Quoin, Ill.; village atty. Village Dowell, Ill.; atty. Consol. Pub. Water Dist., Perry County Housing Authority, 1995—. Bd. dirs. Boys Club, Du Quoin, 1986-87, United Way, Du Quoin, 1987-94; cons. Sacred Heart Endowment Fund, Du Quoin, 1987-94; active in Sacred Heart Parish Coun., 1987-94, organist, 1974—. Mem. Ill. State Bar Assn., Perry County Bar Assn. (sec.-treas. 1995—), Du Quoin Bus. Assn., K.C. (4th degree), Elks (organist Du Quoin club 1992-94). Roman Catholic. Avocation: antiques. Banking, Probate. Home: 2372 Magnolia Rd Du Quoin IL 62832-3609 Office: 18 N Oak St Du Quoin IL 62832-1615

ATKINS, BRUCE ALEXANDER, lawyer; b. Newport News, Va., July 3, 1948; s. Alexander and Clara Belle (Parker) A.; children: Alexandra Patrice, Brandon Jarod; m. Marilyn S. Richardson, Apr. 10, 1991. BA with high honors, Hampton Inst., 1969; JD, U. Va., 1976. Bar: Ga. 1976, Tex. 1979, U.S. Ct. Appeals (4th and 5th cirs.) 1977, U.S. Ct. Appeals (11th cir.) 1981, U.S. Dist. Ct. (no. dist.) Ga. 1977, U.S. Dist. Ct. (so. dist.) Tex. 1982, U.S. Dist. Ct. (no. dist.) N.Y. 1983. Atty. Gulf Oil Corp., Atlanta, Houston, 1976-85; assoc. gen. counsel TransAmerican Natural Gas Corp., 1985-86; sr. assoc. Wood, Lucksinger & Epstein, 1986-88; pvt. practice Houston, 1988—. Vis. prof. Nat. Urban League, Tex. and La., 1981-84; chmn. creditors commn. Continental Airlines, Inc., Houston, 1984, Hill Petroleum Co., Houston, 1984. Mem. editl. bd. Tex. Collections Manual; contbr. articles to profl. jours. Conf. faculty U. Houston Law Found. Capt. U.S. Army, 1969-73. Earl Warren Legal Tng. fellow Earl Warren Found., 1973-76. Mem. Houston Bar Assn., Houston Lawyers Assn., Raveneaux Club (Spring, Tex.). Episcopalian. Federal civil litigation, State civil litigation, Contracts commercial. Home: 5707 Lookout Mountain Dr Houston TX 77069-2618 Office: Bruce A Atkins Atty at Law Ste 249 13700 Veterans Meml Dr Houston TX 77014-1026 E-mail: attyatkins@aol.com

ATKINS, PETER ALLAN, lawyer; b. N.Y.C., June 29, 1943; m. Lorraine Marilyn Feuerstadt, Apr. 3, 1966; children: Aileen Debra, Karen Jennifer. BA magna cum laude, CUNY, 1965; LLB cum laude, Harvard U., 1968. Bar: N.Y. 1969. Assoc. Skadden, Arps, Slate, Meagher & Flom LLP, N.Y.C., 1968-74, ptnr., 1975—. Mem. dean's adv. bd. Harvard Law Sch.; bd. dirs. A Better Chance, Inc. Contbr. articles to profl. jours. Mem. ABA, N.Y. State Bar Assn., Assn. of Bar of City of N.Y. General corporate, Mergers and acquisitions, Securities. Office: Skadden Arps Slate Meagher & Flom LLP 4 Times Sq Fl 46 New York NY 10036-6595 E-mail: patkins@skadden.com

ATKINS, ROBERT ALAN, lawyer; b. N.Y.C., Apr. 30, 1944; s. David Atkins and Tabbie Crystal Sas; m. Carol Anne Pierson, Dec. 26, 1966 (div. Aug. 1975); children: Laura, Christopher; m. Mari Beth Loria, May 21, 1982; children: Sascha, Jordan. BS in Philosophy cum laude, CUNY, 1964; MA in Philosophy, U. Calif., Berkeley, 1967, PhD, 1973, JD, 1979. Bar: Calif. 1980, U.S. Dist. Ct. (no. dist.) Calif. 1980, U.S. Dist. Ct. (cen. dist.) Calif. 1985. From instr. to assoc. prof. philosophy Antioch Coll., Yellow Springs, Ohio, 1968-75; asst. Gordon Lapides, San Francisco, 1979-80; assoc. Erickson, Beasley & Hewitt, 1980-85; pvt. practice Berkeley, 1986—. Prof. Union Grad. Sch., San Francisco, 1975—; lectr. U. Calif., Berkeley, 1983-88, sch. law New Coll. Calif., 1983-86. Contbr. articles to profl. jours. Commr. Berkeley Citizens Budget Rev. Commn. 1985-87; mem. adv. bd. U.S.-China Edn. Inst. 1981-86, steering com. Bay Area Lawyer's Alliance for Nuclear Arms Control 1982-84, chmn. symposium com., internat. com.; trustee, sec. Ann Martin Ctr. 1982-84; commentator on pub. affairs for radio sta. WYSO, Yellow Springs, 1971-73, producer children's show 1974-75; mem. adminstrv. coun. Antioch Coll., 1973-75, chmn. humanities area, mem. Chancellor's Cabinet, 1974-75; mem. Union Grad. Sch. Coun., 1979-84. Recipient Am. Jurisprudence award U. Calif., Berkeley, 1979; Ford Found. grantee, 1969. Mem. Order of Golden Bear. Civil rights, Labor, Personal injury. E-mail: ratkins700@aol.com

ATKINS, RONALD RAYMOND, lawyer; b. Kingston, N.Y., Mar. 8, 1933; s. A. Raymond and Charlotte S. A.; m. Mary-Elizabeth Empringham, June 23, 1956; children: Peter Herrick, Timothy Barnard, Suzanne Elizabeth. BS in Econs., U. Pa., 1954; JD, Columbia U., 1959. Bar: N.Y. 1959. Assoc. Pell, Butler, Curtis & LeViness, N.Y.C., 1959-61, ptnr., 1962-67; ptnr. Bisset & Atkins, N.Y.C., 1967—, also Greenwich, Conn., 1982—; also of counsel Davidson, Dawson & Clark, LLP, N.Y.C.; trustee Mianus Gorge Preserve, Inc., chmn., 1984-94. 1st lt. U.S. Army, 1954-56. Fellow Frick Collection, Piermont Morgan Libr.; mem. ABA, N.Y. State Bar Assn., Assn. Bar City N.Y. Republican. Episcopalian. Club: University (N.Y.C.), Grolier Club (N.Y.C.), Field Club (Greenwich, Conn.), U. Pa. Club (N.Y.C.). General corporate, Probate, Estate taxation. Home: Hobby Hill Farm Mianus River Rd Bedford NY 10506 also: 777 North St Greenwich CT 06831-3105

ATKINS, THOMAS JAY, lawyer, missionary and pastor; b. Detroit, Apr. 21, 1943; s. Robert Alfred and Dorothy Irene Atkins. BS in Applied Math. and Physics, Rensselaer Poly. Inst., 1965, MS in Engring., 1967; JD, UCLA, 1979; postgrad., Harvard Law Sch., 1979; MBA, UCLA, 1983; MDiv, MB Bibl. Sem., 2000. Bar: Calif. 1979. Ctr. for Advanced Studies, Gen. Electric Co., Washingon, Santa Barbara, Calif., 1967-70; prin. Cen. Valley Distbrs., Visalia, 1970—, Thomas Jay Atkins, P.C., Sacramento, 1979—, Calif. Merc. Inc., Tulare, Calif., 1980—, United Motors, San Jose, Fresno and Sacramento, 1986—; sr. cons. ptnr. Atkins Group, LLP, L.A., N.Y.C., London, Paris, 1989—. Founder Atkins Devel. Corp. (formerly Atkins Real Estate Corp.), L.A., 1985; chmn. bd. dirs., World Parts Corp., San Francisco; chmn. bd. dirs. Students Internat., Antigua, Guatemala, 1996—. Recipient rsch. commendation NASA, 1969 Mem. ABA, Am. Mgmt. Assn., UCLA Alumni Assn. (bd. dirs. 1991—), Santa Barbara Yacht Club, Visalia Country Club, Regency Club of L.A., Visalia Racquet Club Republican. Immigration, naturalization, and customs, Private international, Non-profit and tax-exempt organizations. Home: Badger Hill Ranch 363 Valley View Dr Exeter CA 93221-9798 Office: PO Box 3744 Visalia CA 93278-3744 also: 969 Hilgard Ave Ste 1007 Los Angeles CA 90024-3079 E-mail: tjatkins@lightspeed.net

ATKINSON, JANET E. lawyer; b. Detroit, Apr. 30, 1945; d. A.K. and Billie Dorothy Atkinson; m. Robert Joseph Kestell, Aug. 18, 1966 (div. Dec. 1992); children: Jeanette, Elizabeth, Robert, Katherine, Richard. BA, U. Wis., 1967; MLS, U. Md., 1972, JD, 1996. Libr. asst. Madison (Wis.) Pub. Libr., 1967-68; libr. Prince Georges (Md.) County Schs., 1972-74; real estate investor Kent County, Md., 1976-93, Washington, 1979; propr. Creative Cookery, Chestertown, Md., 1979-83; law clk. Shapiro & Olander, Balt., 1996-97; sr. assoc. Ctr. for Support of Families, Chevy Chase, Md., 1996—. Author: (with others) Year 2000 Family Law Update, 1999; contbr. articles to profl. jours. Chair Internat. Orgn. Family Rights Group, Washnigton, 1998-99; bd. dirs. Montgomery County NOW, Md., 1999—; mem. adv. bd. Divorce Roundtable, Montgomery County, 1999—. Mem. ABA (internat. com. chair family law sect. 1999—), Md. Bar Assn., Montgomery County Bar Assn., Women's Bar Assn. Roman Catholic. Office: Ctr for Support of Families 4 Leland Ct Chevy Chase MD 20815-4906 E-mail: jatkinson@thecsf.com

ATKINSON, MICHAEL PEARCE, lawyer; b. Ft. Worth, Feb. 19, 1946; s. Charles Pearce and Nancy Lou (Thompson) A.; m. Melissa Jan Potter, July 17, 1976; children: Charles Travis, Kellen Elizabeth. BA, U. Okla., 1968, JD, 1972; MS, U. Tex., 1975. Bar: Okla. 1972, U.S. Dist. Ct. (we. and ea. dists.) Okla. 1972, U.S. Dist. Ct. (no. dist.) Okla. 1975, U.S. Ct. Appeals (10th cir.) 1981. Ptnr. Jones, Atkinson, Williams, Bane & Klingenberg, Enid, Okla., 1972, Best Sharp Thomas Glass & Atkinson, Tulsa, 1980-87, Thomas Glass Atkinson Haskins Nellis & Boudreaux, Tulsa, 1980-93, Atkinson Haskins Nellis Holeman Phipps Brittingham & Gladd, Tulsa, 1994—; asst. pub. defender Office of Oklahoma County Pub. Defender, Oklahoma City, 1973; asst. dist. atty. Office of Oklahoma County Dist. Atty., 1974. Asst. adj. prof. Coll. Law U. Tulsa, 1976-77. With USAR, 1970-72. Master Am. Inns of Ct. (emeritus); fellow Internat. Acad. Trial Lawyers, Am. Coll. Trial Lawyers; mem. Internat. Assn. Def. Counsel (faculty trial acad. 1986), Am. Bd. Trial Advocates (pres. Okla. chpt. 1995, diplomate). Presbyterian. Avocations: hunting, fishing, running. Insurance, Personal injury, Product liability. Home: 2440 E 28th St Tulsa OK 74114-5611 Office: Aktinson Haskins Nellis Holeman Phipps Brittingham & Gladd 525 S Main St Tulsa OK 74103-4509 E-mail: matkinson@ahn-law.com

ATLASS, THEODORE BRUCE, lawyer, educator; b. Chgo., June 2, 1951; s. Ralph Louis Atlass and Opal Jeanne Collins. BSBA, U. Denver, 1972; JD, DePaul U., 1975; LLM, U. Miami, Coral Gables, Fla., 1976. Bar: Colo. 1975, U.S. Tax Ct. 1976, U.S. Supreme Ct. 1982. Shareholder Theodore B. Atlass, P.C., Denver, 1976-83, Atlass Profl. Corp., Denver, 1986—; ptnr. Welborn, Dufford, Brown & Tooley, 1983-85. Lectr. Colo. Soc. CPAs, 1977—, Coll. Law U. Denver, 1976—. Chmn. Advanced Estate Planning Symposium U. Denver, 1982—; bd. dirs. St. Joseph Hosp. Found., Denver, 1982-97, Colo. Ballet, Denver, 1985-92. Fellow Am. Coll. Tax Counsel, Am. Coll. Trust & Estate Counsel (Colo. state chair 1996-2001; fiduciary income tax com. chair 1997-2000); mem. Denver Estate Planning Coun. (pres. 1991-92), Denver Tax Assn. (pres. 1985), Centennial Estate Planning Coun. (pres. 1993-94). Republican. Presbyterian. Estate planning, Probate, Estate taxation. Office: Atlass Profl Corp Ste 100 3665 Cherry Creek North Dr Denver CO 80209-3712

ATTANASIO, JOHN BAPTIST, dean, law educator; b. Jersey City, Oct. 19, 1954; s. Gaetano and Madeline (Germinario) A.; m. Kathleen Mary Spartana, Aug. 20, 1977; children: Thomas, Michael. BA, U. Va., 1976; JD, NYU, 1979; diploma in law, Oxford U., 1982; LLM, Yale U., 1985. Bar: Md. 1979, U.S. Dist. Ct. Md. 1980, U.S. Ct. Appeals (4th cir.) 1980, U.S. Supreme Ct. 1983. Pvt. practice, Balt., 1979-81; vis. asst. prof. law U. Pitts., 1982-84; assoc. prof. law U. Notre Dame, Ind., 1985-88, prof. law, 1988-92; Regan dir. Kroc Inst. for Internat. Peace Studies, 1991-92; dean Sch. of Law St. Louis U., 1992-98; dean, William Hawley Atwell chair constnl. law So. Meth. U. Sch. Law, Dallas, 1998—. Co-author: Constitutional Law 1989. Chair adv. bd. Ctr. for Civil and Human Rights, 1990-92; mem. Fulbright awards area com., 1994-96; bd. dirs. Legal Svcs. Ea. Mo., 1996-98; bd. dirs. Ctr. for Internat. Understanding, 1993—. Recipient Legal Teaching award Sch. of Law, NYU, 1994. Mem. Ctrl. States Law Sch. Assn. (v.p. 1992-94), Phi Beta Kappa, Alpha Sigma Nu. Democrat. Roman Catholic. Office: So Meth U Dedman Sch Law PO Box 750116 3315 Daniel Ave Dallas TX 75275-0116*

ATTERBURY, ROBERT RENNIE, III, lawyer; b. Englewood, N.J., July 11, 1937; s. Robert Rennie Jr. and Beatrice May (Tether) A.; m. Lynda Duer Smith, Sept. 14, 1963; children: Stockton Ward, Kendall C. B. BA, U. Pa., 1960, LLB, 1963. Bar: N.Y. 1963, Ill. 1966. Assoc. Donovan, Leisure, Newton & Irvine, N.Y.C., 1963-66; atty. Caterpillar Tractor Co., Peoria, Ill., 1966-73; sr. atty. Caterpillar Overseas S.A., Geneva, 1973-78; gen. atty. Caterpillar Tractor Co., Peoria, 1978-83; assoc. gen. counsel Caterpillar Inc., 1983-91, v.p., sec., gen. counsel, 1991—. Mem. planning com. Ray Garrett Jr. Corp. and Securities Law Inst., Chgo., 1991—; mem. steering com. Civil Justice Reform Group; mem. adv. bd. Southwestern Legal Found., Internat. and Comparative Law Ctr., 1991—; mem. adv. coun. Asia/Pacific Ctr. for Resolution of Internat. Bus. Disputes, San Francisco, 1991—, corp. exec. bd., gen. counsel roundtable, 1999—; mem. Mfrs. Alliance Law Coun. I., Arlington, Va., 1992-98, vice chair, 1998-99, chair, 1999—; mem. The Forum for U.S.-European Union Legal-Econ. Affairs, Boston, 1995—, large law dept. coun., 1996—; mem. corp. counsel com. Nat. Ctr. for State Cts., 1998—; mem. adv. bd. Georgetown U. Law Ctr. Corp. Cousel Inst., 1999—; dir. Ill Equal Justice Found., 1999—; trustee Eureka Coll., 1999—. Pres. AMC Found., 1991—; bd. dirs. Lakeview Mus. Arts and Scis., 1995—98, vice chmn., 1998—99, chmn., 1999—2001; bd. dirs., sec. Lakeview Mus. Found., 1998—; bd. dirs. Prairie State Legal Svcs., 1998—. Mem. SAR, Am. Judicature Soc. (dir. 1998—), Am. Corp. Counsel Assn., Am. Soc. Corp. Secs., Assn. Gen. Counsel, Country Club Peoria (dir.), Rotary. Contracts commercial, General corporate, Private international. Home: 315 W Crestwood Dr Peoria IL 61614-7328 Office: Caterpillar Inc 100 NE Adams St Peoria IL 61629-7310

ATTRIDGE, DANIEL F. lawyer; b. Washington, Oct. 4, 1954; s. Patrick J. and Teresa (Glynn) A.; m. Anne Asbill, Aug. 23, 1980; children: James Winchester, William McKendrie, Thomas Sutherland. BA magna cum laude, U. Pa., 1976; JD cum laude, Georgetown U., 1979. Bar: D.C. 1980, U.S. Dist. Ct. D.C. 1980, U.S. Ct. Appeals (D.C. cir.) 1980, U.S. Supreme Ct. 1983, U.S. Dist. Ct. Md. 1985, U.S. Ct. Appeals (fed. cir.) 1985, U.S. Ct. Appeals (2d.cir.) 1987, U.S. Ct. Claims 1988, U.S. Ct. Appeals (4th and 6th cirs.) 1990, U.S. Ct. Appeals (8th cir.) 1997, U.S. Ct. Appeals (1st cir.) 2000. Law clk. to judge Oliver Gasch U.S. Dist. Ct. D.C., Washington, 1979-80; assoc. Kirkland & Ellis, 1980-85, ptnr., 1985—. Faculty Nat. Inst. Trial Advocacy, 1991—. Exec. editor Georgetown U. Law Jour., 1978-79. Fellow Am. Bar Found.; mem. ABA (vice chmn. antitrust sect. Sherman Act sect. 2 com. 1999-), D.C. Bar Assn. (bd. govs. 1996-99, co-chair litigation sect. 1993-96). Roman Catholic. General civil litigation. Home: 1249 Cherry Tree Ln Annapolis MD 21403-5023 Office: Kirkland & Ellis 655 15th St NW Fl 12 Washington DC 20005-5793 E-mail: daniel_attridge@kirkland.com

ATWOOD, JAMES R. lawyer; b. White Plains, N.Y., Feb. 21, 1944; s. Bernard D. and Joyce Rose A.; m. Wendy Fisler, Aug. 22, 1981 (div. July 1993); children: Christopher Charles, Carl Fisler. BA, Yale U., 1966; JD, Stanford U., 1969. Bar: Calif. 1969, D.C. 1970. Law clk. to judge U.S. Ct. Appeals, L.A., 1969-70; law clk. to Chief Justice Warren Burger U.S. Supreme Ct., 1970-71; mem. Covington & Burling, Washington, 1971-78, ptnr., 1977-78, 81—. Dep. asst. sec. for transp. affairs U.S. Dept. State, Washington, 1978-79, dep. legal adviser, 1979-80; acting prof. Law Sch. Stanford U., 1980 Author: (with Kingman Brewster) Antitrust and American Business Abroad, 2nd edit, 1981. Mem. bd. visitors Law Sch. Stanford U., 1995-97. Mem. ABA, Am. Soc. Internat. Law, D.C. Bar Assn. Antitrust, Federal civil litigation, Private international. Home: 8020 Greentree Rd Bethesda MD 20817-1304 Office: Covington & Burling 1201 Pennsylvania Ave NW Washington DC 20004-2401

AUBERT, FREDRIK SCHEEL, lawyer; b. 0slo, Norway, Oct. 1, 1971; Grad., U. Oslo, 1997. Asst. atty. Law Firm Rime & Co., Norway, 1997-99; assoc. Law Firm Lindh, Stabell, Horten, Norway, 1999—. Mem. Norwegian Bar Assn. Bankruptcy, Contracts commercial. Office: Lindh Stabell Horten Haakon VII Gate 2/PO Bx1364 N-0114 Oslo Norway

AUCUTT, RONALD DAVID, lawyer; b. St. Paul, Dec. 28, 1945; s. Howard Lewis and Eleanor May (Malcolm) A.; m. Grace Diane Kok, Apr. 3, 1976; children: David Gerard, James Andrew. BA, U. Minn., 1967, JD, 1975. Bar: Minn. 1975, D.C. 1976, Va. 1978, Tex. 1999, U.S. Supreme Ct. 1978, U.S. Tax Ct. 1980, U.S. Dist. Ct. D.C. 1980, U.S. Ct. Appeals (D.C. cir.) 1980, U.S. Ct. of Claims 1980, U.S. Claims Ct. 1982, U.S. Ct. Appeals (fed. cir.) 1982, U.S. Dist. Ct. (ea. dist.) Va. 1986, U.S. Ct. Appeals (4th cir.) 1986. Assoc. Miller & Chevalier, Chartered, Washington, 1975-81, ptnr., 1982-98, McGuireWoods LLP, McLean, Va., 1998—. Mem. bd. advisors IRS Practice Alert, N.Y.C., 1987-93; adj. prof. Sch. Law U. Va.,

1998—; mem. adv. com. Philip E. Heckerling Inst. on Estate Planning U. Miami, 1999—. Mem. bd. advisors Jour. Taxation Exempt Orgns., 1989-2000, Bus. Entities, N.Y.C., 1999—; mem. editl. bd. Estate Planning, N.Y.C., 1993—, mem. adv. bd. Tax Mgmt. Estates, Gifts, and Trusts Jour., 1999—; editl. adv. bd. Judges and Lawyers Bus. Valuation Update, Portland, Oreg., 1999—; contbr. articles to profl. publs. Sec.-treas. Miller and Chevalier Charitable Found., Washington, 1980-82, pres., 1993-97; bd. dirs. Evang. Free Ch. Am., Mpls., 1986-92, vice moderator, chmn. bd. dirs., 1993-95, moderator, 1995-97; bd. dirs. Coun. for Ct. Excellence, Washington, 1993-99, Advocates Internat., Fairfax, Va., 1997-2000, vice chmn. 1999-2000; Orgn. Security and Coop. in Europe internat. observer Bulgarian Parliamentary election, 1997; mem. adv. bd. Trinity Law Sch., Santa Ana, Calif., 1998—; bd. visitors U. Minn. Law Sch., 1998—; bd. regents Trinity Internat. U., Deerfield, Ill., 2000—. Lt. USN, 1970-73. Fellow Am. Bar Found., Am. Coll. Tax Counsel, Am. Coll. Trust and Estate Counsel (bd. regents 1996—, chmn. bus. planning com. 1997-2000, sec. 1999-2000, treas. 2000-01, v.p. 2001—); mem. ABA (chair taxation sect., com. on estate and gift taxes 1986-88, vice chmn. com. on govt. submissions 1989-91, chmn. 1991-93, com. 1993-97, liaison to sect. real property, probate and trust law 1990—, vice chair com. ops. 1998-2000), Internat. Acad. Estate and Trust Law (exec. coun. 2000—, academician), Christian Legal Soc., Met. Club Washington, Univ. Minn. Law Alumni Assn. (bd. dirs. 1998—). Estate planning, Estate taxation, Taxation, general. Home: 3417 Silver Maple Pl Falls Church VA 22042-3545 Office: McGuireWoods LLP 1750 Tysons Blvd Ste 1800 Mc Lean VA 22102-4231 E-mail: raucutt@mcguirewoods.com

AUERBACH, ERNEST SIGMUND, lawyer, company executive, writer; b. Berlin, Dec. 22, 1936; s. Frank L. and Gertrude A.; m. Jeanette Taylor, 1990; 1 child, Hans Kevin. AB, George Washington U., 1958, JD, 1961; postgrad., U.S. Army Gen. Staff Coll., 1975. Bar: D.C. 1962, Pa. 1978. Atty. So. Ry. Co., Washington, 1961-62; commd 1st lt. U.S. Army, 1962, advanced through grades to col.; served in Germany, Vietnam, Pentagon; div. counsel Xerox Corp., Stamford, Conn., 1970-75; mng. atty. NL Industries, Inc., N.Y.C., 1975-77; from asst. to assoc. gen. counsel, staff v.p. INA Corp., Phila., 1977-79; sr. v.p. INA Svc. Co., 1979-82; sr. v.p., chief of staff INA Internat., 1982-83; pres. internat. life and group ops. CIGNA Worldwide Corp. div. CIGNA Corp., 1984-89; mng. dir. Crusader Life Ins. PLC, Reigate, Eng., 1984-86, chmn. Eng., 1986-89; pres., COO N.Y. Life Worldwide Holding, Inc., N.Y.C., 1989-90; pres., CEO Paperless Claims, Inc., 1991-92; dir. gen. Seguros Azteca Ins. Co., Mexico City, 1992-93; sr. cons. Anderson Consulting, 1993-95; sr. v.p. United Ins. Cos., Inc., Irving, Tex., 1995-97, also pres., CEO student ins. divsn., 1996-97, pres., CEO ins. group, 1997; pres., COO Software Testing Assurance Corp., N.Y.C., 1998; pres., CEO Tesia Corp., 1998—. Bd. dirs. REVBOX, Inc., 1999—. Author: Joining the Inner Circle: How To Make It As A Senior Executive, 1990; contbg. author: The Wall St. Jour. on Mng., 1990; contbr. articles to legal, fin., news, and def. jours. Mem. Am. Coun. on Germany, 1980-2000; computer sys. tech. adv. com. Dept. Commerce, 1974-76; mem. bd. adv. dirs. Salvation Army, Mexico City, 1993-94; commr. bd. adjustment City of Coppell, Tex., 1996-97. Ret. col. USAR, 1985. Decorated Legion of Merit with oak leaf cluster, Bronze Star. Mem. Westchester-Fairfield Corp. Counsel Assn. (founding officer 1973-78), Audubon Soc. (pres., bd. dirs. Greenwich chpt. 1999—), Univ. Club, Nat. Arts Club (N.Y.C.), Army and Navy Club (Washington chpt.). General corporate, Private international, Public international. Home: 147 Southwoods Terr Southbury CT 06488 E-mail: colauerbach@earthlink.net

AUERBACH, JOSEPH, lawyer, educator, retired; b. Franklin, N.H., Dec. 3, 1916; s. Jacob and Besse Mae (Reamer) A.; m. Judith Evans, Nov. 10, 1941; children: Jonathan L., Hope B. Pym. AB, Harvard U., 1938, LLB, 1941. Bar: N.H. 1941, Mass. 1952, U.S. Ct. Appeals (1st, 2d, 3d, 5th, 7th and D.C. cirs.), U.S. Supreme Ct. 1948. Atty. SEC, Washington and Phila., 1941-43, prin. atty., 1946-49; fgn. service staff officer U.S. Dept. State, Dusseldorf, W. Ger., 1950-52; ptnr. Sullivan & Worcester, Boston, 1952-82, counsel, 1982—; lectr. Boston U. Law Sch., 1975-76, Harvard Bus. Sch., Boston, 1980-82, prof., 1982-83, Class of 1957 prof., 1983-87, prof. emeritus, 1987—; prof. Harvard Extension Sch., 1988, 91-95. Bd. dirs. Nat. Benefit Life Ins. Co., N.Y.C. Author: (with S.L. Hayes, III), Investment Banking and Diligence, 1986, Underwriting Regulation and Shelf Registration Phenomenon in Wall Street and Regulation, 1987, also chpt. to book, papers and articles in field. Trustee Mass. Eye and Ear Infirmary, Boston, 1981—, chmn. devel. com., 1985-88, chmn. nominating com., 1993-94; mem. adv. bd., former chmn. devel. com. Am. Repertory Theatre, Cambridge, Mass., 1985—; bd. dirs., past pres. Friends of Boston U. Librs., 1972—; past v.p., bd. dirs. Shakespeare Globe Ctr., N.A., 1983-90; overseer New Eng. Conservatory of Music, 1992-98, mem. fin. com.; bd. dirs. English Speaking Union, Boston, 1995-98; chair 1938 Harvard Pres. Assn.; active Harvard Coll. Fund, Harvard Law Sch. Fund. Decorated Army Commendation medal; recipient Disting. Svc. award Harvard Bus. Sch., 1996, Disting. Teaching award 1993, Exemplary Svc. award Harvard Extension Sch., 1995. Mem. ABA, Mass. Bar Assn., Boston Bar Assn., Harvard Mus. Assn., St. Botolph Club, Harvard Club N.Y.C., Shop Club, Downtown Club. Home: 300 Boylston St Apt 512 Boston MA 02116-3923 Office: Sullivan & Worcester 1 Post Office Sq Ste 2300 Boston MA 02109-2129 also: Harvard Bus Sch Cumnock Hall Rm 300 Boston MA 02163

AUKLAND, DUNCAN DAYTON, lawyer; b. Delaware, Ohio, July 6, 1954; s. Merrill Forrest and Elva Sampson (Dayton) A.; m. Diane Sue Clevenger, Aug. 7, 1982. BA, Va. Polytech. Inst., 1978; JD, Capital U., 1982. Bar: Ohio 1982, U.S. Dist. Ct. (so. dist.) Ohio 1982. Legal intern Ohio EPA, Columbus, 1982, staff atty., 1982-83, legal cons., 1983; sole practice, 1983-90; judge adv. USNG, 1990—. Atty. Clean Up and Recycling Backers of Clintonville, Columbus, 1983-89; deacon Overbrook Presbyn. Ch., Columbus, 1986-89. With JAGC, USAR, 1984-90. Mem. Ohio Bar Assn., Va. Poly. Alumni Assn. Cen. Ohio (pres. 1984-85), Ohio Gamma Alumni Corp. (trustee 1983-88, 91-95). Republican. Avocations: golf, home repairs. Home: 5789 Crescent Ct Worthington OH 43085-3804 Office: Ohio Adj Gen's Dept Attn: AGOH-JA 2825 W Dublin Granville Rd Columbus OH 43235-2789 E-mail: duncan.aukland@tagoh.org

AUSNEHMER, JOHN EDWARD, lawyer; b. Youngstown, Ohio, June 26, 1954; s. John Louis and Patricia Jean (Liguore) A.; m. Carole Marie Ausnehmer; children: Jill Ellen, Amber Layne. BS, Ohio State U., 1976; JD, U. Dayton, 1980. Bar: Ohio 1980, U.S. Dist. Ct. (no. dist.) Ohio 1981, U.S. Ct. Appeals (6th cir.) 1984, U.S. Supreme Ct. 1984. Law clk. Ohio Atty. Gen., Columbus, 1978, Green Schiavoni, Murphy, Haines & Sgambati Co., L.P.A., 1978; assoc. Dickson Law Office, Petersburg, Ohio, 1979-85; sole practice Youngstown, 1984—. Asst. pros. atty. Mahoning County, Ohio, 1986-89, 92—. Mem. Ohio Acad. Trial Lawyers, Ohio State Bar Assn, Mahoning County Bar Assn., Columbiana County Bar Assn., Mahonic Valley Soccer Club (rep. 1982-84), Phi Alpha Delta. Democrat. Roman Catholic. General practice, Personal injury, Workers' compensation. Home: 51 S Shore Dr Boardman OH 44512-5926 Office: PO Box 3965 120 Marwood Cir Youngstown OH 44513-3965

AUSTIN, ANN SHEREE, lawyer; b. Tyler, Tex., Aug. 25, 1960; d. George Patrick and Mary Jean (Brookshire) A. BA cum laude, U. Houston, 1983; JD, South Tex. Coll., 1987. Bar: Tex. 1987, U.S. Dist. Ct. (no. dist.) Tex. 1988, U.S. Ct. Appeals (5th cir.) 1989, U.S. Dist. Ct. (we. dist.) Tex. 1990, U.S. Ct. Appeals (D.C. cir.) 1992, U.S. Supreme Ct. 1992, U.S. Dist Ct. (ea. dist.) Tex. 1993. With First City Ops. Ctr., Houston, 1980-85; law clk. Lipstet, Singer, Hirsch & Wagner, 1985-86, Pizzitola, Hinton & Sussman, Houston, 1986-87; briefing atty. Hon. Hal M. Lattimore Ct. Appeals, 2d Jud. Dist., Ft. Worth, 1987-88; assoc. Cantey & Hanger, Ft. Worth and Dallas, 1988-93, Smith, Ralston & Russell, Dallas, 1993-94, Russell, Austin & Henschel, Dallas, 1994-95; pvt. practice Arlington, 1995-96; prin. Landau, Omahana & Kopka, Ltd., Dallas, 1996-97; asst. city atty. City of Dallas, 1997—. Tchr. Project Outreach State Bar of Tex., 1992; author Personnel Rules Recreation Dept., City of Dallas. Author: Personnel Rules, Park & Recreation Department, City of Dallas; co-author Annual Meeting of Invited Attorneys, Construction Law; chpt. editor: Cases and Materials on Civil Procedure, 1987; author chpt.: Erie Doctrine. Mem. Ft. Worth Hist. Preservation Soc., com. mem., 1992; fundraiser Nat. Com. Prevention Child Abuse, 1988—, Women's Haven. Mem. Tex. Young Lawyers Assn. (women in the profession com. 1992-94, profl. ethics and grievance awareness com. 1992-94, jud. rev. com. 1990), Dallas Bar Assn. (jud. com. 1992-94, ethics com. 1999—, comty. involvement com. 1999—, employment law sect. CLE com. 1999—), Dallas Assn. Young Lawyers, Dallas Women's Bar Assn. (CLE com. 1999—), Ft. Worth Tarrant County Young Lawyers Assn. (treas. 1989-90, dir. 1989, judge Teen Ct., co-chair Adopt-A-Sch. program), Tarrant County Women's Bar Assn., Am. Inns. of Ct. Methodist. Avocations: walking, reading, sky diving. Appellate, Federal civil litigation, Labor. Office: City Hall City Atty's Office 1500 Marilla St # 7dn Dallas TX 75201-6300

AUSTIN, BRADFORD LYLE, retired lawyer; b. Mpls., Dec. 16, 1946; s. John Freid and Mildred Dolores (Reynolds) A.; m. Sally Sands, Nov. 23, 1973. BS in Bus., U. Minn., 1972; JD, Drake U., 1976. Bar: Iowa 1976, U.S. Ct. Appeals (8th cir.) 1976, U.S. Supreme Ct. 1980. Assoc. Thoma, Schonthal, Davis, Hockenberg & Wine, Des Moines, 1976-78; sole practice Charles City, Iowa, 1978-80; mem. Nyemaster, Goode, McLaughlin, Emery & O'Brien, P.C., Des Moines, 1980—; ret. Lectr. bus. law Upper Iowa U., Fayette, 1978-79; jud. magistrate Iowa Dist. Ct., Floyd County, 1979-80; mem. alumni com. Drake Law Rev. Contbr. articles to legal publs. Mem. ABA, Iowa Bar Assn., Order of Coif. Contracts commercial, General corporate, Securities. Home: Apt 1600 700 Walnut St Ste 1600 Des Moines IA 50309-3800 Office: Nyemaster Goode McLaughlin Emery & O'Brien PC Hubbell # 10th Des Moines IA 50309

AUSTIN, DANIEL WILLIAM, lawyer; b. Springfield, Ill., Feb. 24, 1949; s. Daniel D. and Ruth A. (Ahrenkiel) A.; m. Lois Ann Austin, June 12, 1971; 1 child, Elizabeth Ann. BA, Millikin U., 1971; JD, Washington U., 1974. Bar: Ill. 1974, U.S. Dist. Ct. (cen. dist.) Ill. 1979, U.S. Ct. Appeals (7th cir.) 1980, U.S. Supreme Ct. 1980, U.S. Tax Ct. 1986. Assoc. Miley & Meyer, Taylorville, Ill., 1974-78; ptnr. Miley, Meyer & Austin, 1978-81; prin. Meyer, Austin & Romano P.C., 1981—, Meyer, Austin, Romano & Paisley, P.C., Taylorville. Pres. United Fund, Taylorville, 1980, Christian County YMCA, Taylorville, 1983-85, St. Vincent Meml. Hosp. Found., 1998—. Named one of Outstanding Young Men Am., 1985, Outstanding Citizen of City of Taylorville, 1993. Mem. ABA, Ill. Bar Assn., Christian County Bar Assn., Order of Barristers. Democrat. Presbyterian. Club: Taylorville Country (pres. 1985). Lodge: Sertoma (Taylorville pres. 1976). Avocations: golf, photography. General corporate, Probate, Real property. Home: 14 Westhaven Ct Taylorville IL 62568-9064 Office: Meyer Austin Romano & Paisley PC 210 S Washington St Taylorville IL 62568-2245

AUSTIN, JOHN DELONG, judge; b. Cambridge, N.Y., May 31, 1935; s. John DeLong and Mabel Cowles (Bascom) A.; m. Marcia Kay Behan, Aug. 15, 1969 (dec.); children: John DeLong, Susan Behan. AB, Dartmouth Coll., 1957; postgrad., u. Minn., 1959; JD, Albany Law Sch., 1969. Bar: N.Y. 1970. Editl. dir. Glens Falls (N.Y.) Times, 1960-66; sole practice Glens Falls, 1970-79; law asst. Warren County Judge and Surrogate, 1975-79, N.Y. State Supreme Ct., 1980-84; judge Warren County Family Ct., N.Y., 1984-99, Warren County Ct. and Surrogate's Ct., 1999—. Instr. Adirondack Comm. Coll., Glens Falls. Editor New Eng. Hist. and Geneal. Register, 1970-73; contbr. hist. and geneal. articles to various periodicals. Councilman Town of Queensbury, N.Y., 1969-71, supr., 1972-74; budget officer Warren County, N.Y., 1974; mem. N.Y. State Local Govt. Records Adv. Coun. With U.S. Army, 1958-60. Recipient Adminstrv. Law prize Albany Law Sch., 1969. Fellow Am. Soc. Genealogists; mem. N.Y. State Bar Assn., Warren County Bar Assn., Mohican Grange, Elks. Republican. Office: Warren County Mcpl Ctr Lake George NY 12845

AUSTIN, ROBERT EUGENE, JR. lawyer; b. Jacksonville, Fla., Oct. 10, 1937; s. Robert Eugene and Leta Fitch A.; children: Robert Eugene, George Harry Talley; m. Carolyn Rhea Songer. BA, Davidson Coll., 1959; JD, U. Fla., 1964. Bar: Fla. 1965, D.C. 1983, U.S. Supreme Ct. 1970; cert. in civil trial law Nat. Bd. Trial Advocacy, Fla. Bar. Legal asst. Fla. Ho. Reps., 1965; assoc. Jones & Sims, Pensacola, Fla., 1965-66; ptnr. Warren, Warren & Austin, Leesburg, 1966-68, McLin, Burnsed, Austin & Cyrus, Leesburg, 1968-77, Austin & Burleigh, Leesburg, 1977-81; sole practice, 1981-83, Leesburg and Orlando, Fla., 1984-86; ptnr. Austin & Lockett P.A., 1983-84, Austin, Lawrence & Landis, Leesburg and Orlando, 1986-92, Austin & Pepperman, Leesburg, 1992—. Asst. state atty., 1972; mem. Jud. Nominating Commn. and Grievance Com. 5th Dist. Fla.; gov. Fla. Bar, 1983; trustee U. Fla. Law Ctr. Chmn. Lake Dist. Boy Scouts Am.; asst. dean Leesburg Deanery Diocese Cen. Fla.; trustee Fla. House, Washington, U. Fla. Law Ctr., 1983—, chmn., 1988-90. Mem. Acad. Fla. Trial Lawyers, Am. Arbitration Assn., Am. Law Inst., Nat. Inst. Trial Advocacy, Lake County Bar Assn., Roscoe Pound Am. Trial Found., Kappa Alpha, Phi Delta Phi. Democrat. Episcopalian. General civil litigation, Personal injury, Product liability. Home: PO Box 490200 Leesburg FL 34749-0200 Office: Austin & Pepperman 1321 Citizens Blvd Ste C Leesburg FL 34748-3946 E-mail: reajr@aust-pep.com

AUTEN, DAVID CHARLES, lawyer; b. Phila., Apr. 4, 1938; s. Charles Raymond and Emily Lillian (Dickel) A.; m. Suzanne Crozier Plowman, Feb. 1, 1969; children: Anne Crozier, Meredith Smedley. BA, U. Pa., 1960, JD, 1963. Bar: Pa. 1963. Ptnr. Reed Smith Shaw & McClay (and predecessor), Phila., 1963—. Author articles in field. V.p. N.E. Cmty. Mental Health Ctr., 1971-72; vice chmn. alumni ann. giving U. Pa., 1975-77, 81-82, chmn., 1982-84, trustee, 1977-80, 83-88; pres. Gen. Alumni Soc., 1977-80; chmn. Benjamin Franklin Assocs., 1975-77, 81-82, bd. overseers Sch. Arts and Scis., 1983-96; trustee U. Pa. Health Sys., 1995—, Springside Sch., 1985-88, v.p., 1987-88; pres. Soc. of Coll., 1975-77; v.p. Assn. Reps. for Educated Action, 1971-79; bd. mgrs. Presbyn.-U. Pa. Med. Ctr., 1980—, vice chmn., 1983-85, 88-95; trustee Presbyn. Found. for Phila., 1986—, vice chm., 1996-98, chmn., 1998—; bd. mgrs. Phila. City Inst., 1981—, treas., 1990-99; bd. dirs. Kearsley Home, 1974—, treas., 1990-96, chmn., 1996—; bd. mgrs. St. Peter's Sch., 1975-88, pres., 1978-79; bd. dirs. Greater Phila. Internat. Network, 1989-94, Com. of Seventy, 1990—, Courtland Found., Del Pres Health Care Inc., Courtland Health Care, chmn., 1998—; mem. econ. devel. com. Greater Phila. First Corp.; rector's warden Christ Ch., Phila., 1996—. Mem. ABA, Pa. Bar Assn. (vice chmn. real property sect. 1985-87, chmn. 1987-88), Am. Land Title Assn., Phila. Bar Assn. (vice chmn. young lawyers sect. 1971-72), Juristic Soc. (pres.), Am. Coll. Real Estate Lawyers, Interfrat. Alumni Coun. U. Pa. (pres. 1970-74), French Am. C. of C. (bd. dirs. 1989—), Phi Beta Kappa, Theta Xi (pres. 1974-76, chmn. found. 1977-86), Rittenhouse Club (pres. 1979-82), Union League (bd. dirs., v.p., pres. 1993-94, chmn. Lincoln Found. 1996—), Fourth St. Club (bd. dirs. 1998-2000), Phila. Club. Episcopalian (vestryman). Banking, Finance, Real property. Home: 120 Delancey St Philadelphia PA 19106-4303 Office: Reed Smith Shaw & McClay 2500 One Liberty Pl Philadelphia PA 19103

AUTIN, DIANA MARIE THERESE KATHERINE, lawyer, educator; b. Golden Meadow, La., Sept. 16, 1954; d. Alphonse Adam and Lorraine (Leydecker) A.; m. W. Keith Hefner, Sept. 15, 1979; children: Peter Richard, Elena Lorraine, Emilia Lee Autin-Hefner. BA, U. Mich., 1974, JD, 1977. Bar: Mich. 1977, U.S. Dist. Ct. (ea. dist.) Mich. 1978, N.Y. 1982. Atty. Transp. Employees Union, Ann Arbor, Mich., 1977-79; atty., asst. dir. Downtown Welfare Adv. Ctr., N.Y.C., 1979-81; exec. dir. Fund Open Info. Accountability, Inc., 1981-84; dep. gen. counsel N.Y.C. Bur. Labor Services, 1984-87; exec. dir. Statewide Parent Advocacy Network, Newark. Adj. prof. Indsl. Labor Relations Sch. Cornell U.; apptd. mem. Mich. Ad Hoc Com. Juvenile Justice, Ann Arbor, 1978. Author: Young People and Law, 1979, Segregated and Second-Rate: Special Education in New York, 1992; also articles. Named Woman to Watch in the 1980's, Mademoiselle Mag., 1982, Advocate of the Yr. N.Y. State Commn. on the Quality of Care for the Mentally Disabled, 1993; Leadership fellow Advocacy Inst., 1994, Wasserstein Pub. Interest fellow Harvard Law Sch., 1993-94. Mem. Assn. Trial Lawyers Am., N.Y. Trial Lawyers Assn., N.Y. Bar Assn. (chair edn. health and early childhood subcom., mem. edn. com.), Nat. Lawyers Guild (cons. 1984). Home: 9 Lexington Ave Montclair NJ 07042-4501 Office: SPAN 35 Halsey St 4th Fl Newark NJ 07102

AVANT, GRADY, JR. lawyer; b. New Orleans, Mar. 1, 1932; s. Grady and Sarah (Rutherford) A.; m. Katherine Willis Yancey, Feb. 23, 1963; children: Grady M., Mary Willis Yancey. B.A. magna cum laude, Princeton U., 1954; J.D., Harvard U., 1960. Bar: N.Y. 1961, Ala. 1962, Mich. 1972. Assoc. Bradley, Arant, Rose & White, Birmingham, Ala., 1961-63; assoc., ptnr. Long, Preston, Kinnaird & Avant, Detroit, 1972-87; ptnr. Dickinson, Wright, Moon, Van Dusen & Freeman, 1988-94; sr. v.p. investment banking North Am. Capital Advisors, Inc., Bloomfield Hills, Mich., 1995-96; pvt. practice Grosse Pointe, 1996—. Contbr. articles to legal jours. Served to lt. USMC, 1954-57. Mem. ABA (bus. law sect., fed. regulation of securities com.), State Bar of Mich. (coun. sect. antitrust law 1978-85, chmn. sect. 1983-84, bus. law sect.), Detroit Com. on Fgn. Rels. (exec. com. 1979—, chmn. 1986-88), Grosse Pointe Club, Mountain Brook Club, Knickerbocker Club, Princeton Club of Mich. (pres. 1976-77, 94-95). Episcopalian. Antitrust, General corporate, Securities. Home and Office: 406 Lincoln Rd Grosse Pointe MI 48230-1607 Fax: 313-886-6556

AVENI, ANTHONY JOSEPH, lawyer, educator; b. Cleve., Aug. 1, 1938; s. Vincent James and Antoinette Elizabeth (Finelli) A.; m. Marie-Terese Sweeney, Aug. 22, 1964; children: Karen Marie, James Vincent, Laura Ann. BSCE, U. Notre Dame, 1961; MSCE, Stanford U., 1962; JD, Cleve.-Marshall Law Sch., 1966. Bar: Ohio 1966, U.S. Dist. Ct. (no. dist.) Ohio 1969. Ptnr. Sweeney & Aveni, Painesville, Ohio, 1966-75; assoc. Milburn, Cannon, Stern & Aveni, 1975-80; ptnr. Cannon, Stern, Aveni & Loiacono, Co. LPA, 1980—. Instr. real estate law Lakeland C.C., Mentor, Ohio, 1970—; lectr. in field. Mcpl. law dir. City of Mentor-on-the-Lake, 1983-88; asst. law dir. City of Willowick, 2000—; bd. atty. Lake County Assn. Realtors, mentor, 1982—; bd. dirs. Western Res. Counseling Svc., Painesville, 1968—; chmn., prof. div. United Way Lake County, 1978; county chmn. March of Dimes, Cleve., 1973. Mem.: Lake County Bar Assn. (chmn. real property com., pres. 1995—96), Ohio State Bar Assn. (bd. govs. real property sect.), Gyro-We. Res. Club (pres. Painesville chpt. 1973—74), Madison Country Club, K.C. Roman Catholic. Avocations: golf, fishing. Land use and zoning (including planning), Probate, Real property. Office: Cannon Stern Aveni & Loiacono LPA 41 E Erie St Painesville OH 44077-3947 E-mail: ajaveni@nls.net

AVERY, BRUCE EDWARD, lawyer; b. Boonville, N.Y., Aug. 16, 1949; s. Edward Cecil and Marian Alma (Pierce) A.; m. Margaret Calvert, June 21, 1969; children: Sarah, Prudence. BA in Sociology, Polit. Sci., Hobart Coll., 1971; JD, U. Louisville, 1976. Bar: Ky. 1976, U.S. Ct. Mil. Appeals 1977, U.S. Army Ct. Mil. Rev. 1984, U.S. Supreme Ct. 1984, Md. 1992, D.C., 1993, U.S. Ct. Vet. Appeals 1992, U.S. Dist. Ct. Md. 1993. Commd. capt. U.S. Army, 1976, advanced through grades to maj., 1983; rschr. U.S. Army Rsch. Inst., Ft. Knox, Ky., 1972-76, atty., 1976-77, U.S. Army, Camp Zama, Japan, 1977-80, U.S. Army Recruiting, Ft. Meade, Md., 1980-83, U.S. Army Claims Svc., Ft. Meade, 1984-87, U.S. Armed Forces Claims Svc., Seoul, Korea, 1987-89; chief claims V Corps, Frankfort, Germany, 1989-91; pvt. practice Rockville, Md., 1991—. Mem. Ft. Knox Bd. Edn., Ky., 1975-76. Mem. ABA, ATLA, FBA, D.C. Bar, Md. State Bar., Ky. Bar Assn. Family and matrimonial, General practice, Military. Office: 51 Monroe St Ste 1509 Rockville MD 20850-2414 E-mail: bavery@compuserve.com

AVERY, JAMES THOMAS, III, lawyer, management consultant; b. Richmond, Va., July 21, 1945; s. James Thomas Jr. and Hester Vail (Kraemer) A.; m. Nancy Carolyn Hoag, June 22, 1968; children: James Thomas IV, Carolyn Sears, John Dolph II. AB magna cum laude, Princeton U., 1967; MBA, JD, Harvard U., 1975. Bar: Mass. 1975, U.S. Dist. Ct. Mass. 1975, U.S. Ct. Appeals (1st cir.) 1975. Assoc. Choate, Hall & Stewart, Boston, 1975-79; dir. Cambridge (Mass.) Research Inst., 1979-85; pres. The Avery Co., Boston, 1985—; prin. Symmetrix, Inc., Lexington, Mass., 1992-94; pres./CEO PHH Fantus Cons., Inc., Hunt Valley, Md., 1995-97. Bd. dirs. Boston Pub. Co. Treas. All Saints Ch., Brookline, Mass., 1976-78; vestryman Ch. of Redeemer, Chestnut Hill, Mass., 1985-89. Capt. U.S. Army, 1967-71, Vietnam. Decorated Bronze Star, Air medal. Mem. ABA, Phi Beta Kappa. Republican. Episcopalian. Clubs: Somerset, Harvard, The Second (trustee, sec. 1980-91) (Boston); Brookline Thursday. Avocations: tennis, golf, skiing.

AVERY, REIGH KESSEN, legal assistant; b. Cin., Sept. 16, 1949; d. Henry Charles and Margaret Elizabeth (Dam) Kessen; m. Gerald L. Poe, Oct. 5, 1968 (div. Nov. 1989); children: Amy Kathleen, Michael Lee; m. Melvin L. Avery, May 6, 1996. AAS, El Centro Coll., Dallas, 1988. Legal sec. Victor C. McCrea Jr. & Co., Dallas, 1983-84, legal asst., 1986-90; legal sec. Fanning, Harper & Martinson, 1984-86, Thompson & Knight, Dallas, 1986; legal asst. Nacol, Wortham & Assocs., 1990-91; sr. legal asst. Snelling and Snelling, Inc., 1992-93; free-lance legal asst. Tex., 1993-95; sr. legal asst. Nationwide Mutual Ins. Co., 1995—. Chair comm. Fox Meadow Farms Homeowners Assn., Loveland, Ohio, 1972-74; pro bono vol. Child Support Clinic, Dallas, 1988, North Ctrl. Tex. Legal Svcs. Found., Inc., Dallas, 1988—; vol. Ramses The Gt. Exhbn. Dallas Mus. Nat. History Assn., 1989. Mem. Nat. Assn. Legal Assts., State Bar Tex. (legal assts. div.), Dallas Assn. Legal Assts. (litigation sect., com. nat. affairs 1988-89), Phi Theta Kappa, Phi Beta Lambda. Avocations: computers, Greek mythology, logic problems, crossword puzzles. Home and Office: 725 Pinoak Dr Grand Prairie TX 75052-6522

AVERY, ROBERT DEAN, lawyer; b. Youngstown, Ohio, Apr. 23, 1944; s. Donald Carson and Alta Belle (Simon) A.; m. Ann Mitchell Lashen, May 16, 1993; 1 child from previous marriage: Benjamin Robert. BA, Northwestern U., 1966; JD, Columbia U., 1969. Bar: Ohio 1971, Calif. 1973. Law clk. to Hon. Robert P. Anderson U.S. Ct. Appeals 2d Cir., N.Y.C., 1969-70; assoc. lawyer Jones, Day, Reavis & Pogue, Cleve., 1970-74, L.A., 1974-76, ptnr., 1977-98, adminstrv. ptnr., 1990-92, ptnr. Chgo., 1999—. Editor: Columbia Law Rev., 1968-69. Dir. Wilshire YMCA, L.A., 1981-88. Harlan Fiske Stone Scholar. Home: 45 E Division St Chicago IL 60610-2316 Office: Jones Day Reavis & Pogue 77 W Wacker Dr Fl 35 Chicago IL 60601-1662 E-mail: rdavery@jonesday.com

AVILEZ, VICTORIA MARIE, lawyer; b. Flint, Mich., Apr. 9, 1962; d. John Richard and Brenda Jean (Mitrage) Stevens; m. R. Antonio Avilez, Aug. 24, 1996. BA in History, Alma (Mich.) Coll., 1984; JD, Ariz. State U., Tempe, 1991. Bar: Ariz., 1991, U.S. Dist. Ct. Ariz., U.S. Ct. Appeals (9th cir.). Reporter The Ariz. Republic, Phoenix, 1984-88; assoc. Snell &

Wilmer LLD, 1991-97, Ryley, Carlock & Applewhite, Phoenix, 1998-99; ptnr. Cross, Meda & Avilez, 1999—. Mem. Fed. Bar Assn. (bd. mem., sec. Phoenix 1999—, chair bankruptcy practice and procedures com. 1998-99), Maricopa County Bar Assn. (bd. mem. 1995-99, pres. young lawyers divsn. 1997). Office: Cross Meda & Avilez PLC 411 N Central Ave Ste 700 Phoenix AZ 85004-2140 E-mail: vmavilez@uswest.net

AXELRAD, JEFFREY, lawyer; b. Uniontown, Pa., July 29, 1942; s. Louis M. and Leila (Husin) A.; children: Michelle G., Douglas R. BS, Carnegie Inst. Tech., 1964; JD cum laude, Northwestern U., 1967. Bar: Ill. 1967, D.C. 1969, U.S. Ct. Appeals (2d, 3d, 5th, 6th, 8th, 10th, 11th and D.C. cirs.), U.S. Supreme Ct. Trial atty. Dept. Justice, Washington, 1967-75, chief info. and privacy sect., 1975-77, chief torts sect., 1977-78, dir. torts br., 1978—. Mem. Fed. Bar Assn. Home: 4601 N Park Ave Apt 217 Bethesda MD 20815-4530 Office: Dept Justice PO Box 888 Washington DC 20044-0888 E-mail: ja729@aol.com

AXELROD, CHARLES PAUL, lawyer; b. N.Y.C., Oct. 23, 1941; s. Abraham and Lillian Rose (Neidetch) A.; m. Gail Y. Buksbaum, June 24, 1965; children: Seth Jordan, Tracy Brooke. BS, NYU, 1963; JD, Bklyn. Law Sch., 1966. Bar: N.Y. 1966, U.S. Ct. Appeals (2d cir.) 1967, U.S. Dist. Ct. (so. dist.) N.Y. 1970, U.S. Supreme Ct. 1974, U.S. Dist. Ct. (ea. dist.) N.Y. 1975, U.S. Ct. Appeals D.C. 1979. Ptnr. Goldstein & Axelrod, N.Y.C., 1980-94, Camhy, Karlinsky & Stein LLP, N.Y.C., 1994-99, Greenberg Traurig LLP, 1999—. Chmn. legis. sub-com. study of securities laws N.Y. State Assembly, 1972; adj. prof. law Pace U., Pleasantville, N.Y., 1976-77. Vol. atty. City of N.Y. Com. on Human Rights, 1972. Mem. ABA, N.Y. State Trial Lawyers Assn., N.Y. County Lawyers Assn., N.Y. State Bar Assn., Nat. Assn. Securities Dealers (bd. arbitrators), Com. on Securities and Exchs. (N.Y.C.). Democrat. Jewish. Lodge: B'Nai Brith. Contracts commercial, General corporate, Securities. Office: Camhy Karlinsky & Stein LLP 1740 Broadway Fl 16 New York NY 10019-4373

AXELROD, JONATHAN GANS, lawyer; b. N.Y.C., Oct. 23, 1946; s. Arthur and Rosalind (Gans) A.; m. Carol Jean Zachar, Jan. 16, 1983; children: Zachary Arthur, Tristan Gans. AB, Dartmouth Coll., 1968; JD, Columbia U., 1971; LLM in Labor Law, George Washington U., 1975. Bar: N.Y. 1971, D.C. 1975. Trial atty. App. Ct. Br. NLRB, 1971-74; asst. gen. csl Ea. Conf. Teamsters, 1974-80; ptnr. Beins, Axelrod, Osborne, Mooney & Green, Washington, 1980-96, Beins, Axelros & Kraft, Washington, 1996—. Contbr. articles to profl. jours. Mem. ABA, D.C. Bar Assn. (co-chmn. sect. on labor law 1985-89, steering com. 1990-91). E-mail: jaxelrod@bakfirm.com; jonathan@axelrod@cs.com. Federal civil litigation, Labor. Office: Beins Axelrod & Kraft PC 1717 Massachusetts Ave NW Washington DC 20036-2001 E-mail: jaxelrod@bakfirm.com

AXINN, STEPHEN MARK, lawyer; b. N.Y.C., Oct. 21, 1938; s. Mack N. and Lili H. (Tannenbaum) A.; m. Stephanie Chertok, May 12, 1963; children: Audrey, David, Jill. BS, Syracuse U., 1959; LLB, Columbia U., 1962. Bar: N.Y. 1962, U.S. Supreme Ct. 1962. Assoc. Cahill & Gordon, N.Y.C., 1963-64, Malcolm A. Hoffman, N.Y.C., 1964-66, Skadden, Arps, Slate, Meagher & Flom, N.Y.C., 1966-69, ptnr., 1970-97, Axinn, Veltrop & Harkrider LLP, N.Y.C., 1997—. Lead counsel WorldCom-Spring major investigation and litigation antitrust divsn. U.S. Dept. Justice, 1999-2000; adj. prof. Law Sch. NYU, 1981-83, Law Sch. Columbia U., 1983-85. Author: Acquisitions Under H-S-R, 1980; contbr. articles to profl. jours. Chmn. lawyers div. United Jewish Appeal, N.Y.C., 1985-87; mem. exec. com., treas. Jewish Theol. Sem. Am., 1984-96; mem. bd. visitors Columbia Law Sch., 1993-98; mem. adv. panel on environ. crimes by orngs. U.S. Sentencing Commn., 1992-94. Capt. U.S. Army, 1965-68. Mem. ABA (council antitrust sect. 1983-85), N.Y. State Bar Assn. (chmn. antitrust sect. 1982-83). Antitrust, Federal civil litigation, Securities. Office: Axinn Veltrop & Harkrider LLP 1370 Ave of the Americas New York NY 10019-6708 E-mail: sma@auhlaw.com

AXLEY, FREDERICK WILLIAM, lawyer; b. Chgo., June 23, 1941; s. Frederick R. and Elena (Hoffman-Pinther) A.; m. Cinda Jane Russell, Mar. 29, 1969; children: Sarah Elizabeth, Elizabeth Jane. BA, Holy Cross Coll., 1963; MA, U. Wis., 1966; JD, U. Chgo., 1969. Bar: Ill. 1969, U.S. Dist. Ct. (no. dist.) Ill. 1969, U.S. Ct. Appeals (7th cir.) 1970. Assoc. McDermott, Will & Emery, Chgo., 1969-74, jr. ptnr., 1974-80, sr. ptnr., 1980—. Trustee Wilmette Elem. Sch. Dist. #39, Ill., 1976-81, Ill. chpt. Nature Conservancy, 1983-91; bd. dirs. Bus. and Profl. People for the Pub. Interest, Chgo., 1984—; bd. dirs. Friends of the Chgo. River, 1994—, pres., 1998—; bd. dirs. Shore Line Place, 1994—, pres. 2001—, Interfaith Housing Devel. Corp., 1997—, 1st. v.p., 2000—. Served to lt. USN, 1963-65. Mem. Mich. Shores Club (Wilmette). Democrat. Roman Catholic. General corporate, Finance, Securities. Office: McDermott Will & Emery 227 W Monroe St Ste 3100 Chicago IL 60606-5096 E-mail: faxley@msn.com

AYERS, JEFFREY DAVID, lawyer; b. Grant, Nebr., Nov. 30, 1960; s. William D. and Lela R. (Gilmore) A.; m. Shelly Jo Dodds, June 11, 1988; children: Sydney Elizabeth, Bailey Anne. BS, Graceland U., 1982; MBA, JD, U. Iowa, 1985. Bar: Mo. 1985. Assoc. Stinson, Mag & Fizzell, Kansas City, Mo., 1985-88, Bryan, Cave, McPheeters & McRoberts, Kansas City, 1989-92; ptnr. Blackwell Sanders Peper Martin LLP, Mo., 1992-95, mng. ptnr. London, 1996-99; gen. counsel and corp. sec. Aquila, Inc., Kansas City, 1999—. Mayor City of Lake Tapawingo, Mo., 1993-96. Trustee Little Blue Valley Sewer Dist., 1994-95. Democrat. Mem. Cmtys. of Christ. Banking, Finance, Securities. Office: Aquila Inc 1100 Walnut St Ste 3300 Kansas City MO 64106-2109 E-mail: jayers@utilicorp.com

AYLWARD, RONALD LEE, lawyer; b. St. Louis, May 30, 1930; s. John Thomas and Edna (Ketcherside) A.; m. Margaret Cecilia Hellweg, Aug. 10, 1963; children: Susan Marie, Stephen Ronald, Carolyn Ann. AB, Washington U., St. Louis, 1952, JD, 1954; student, U. Va., 1955. Bar: Mo. 1954, Ill. 1961, U.S. Supreme Ct. 1968. Assoc. Heneghan, Roberts & Cole, St. Louis, 1958-59; asst. counsel Olin Corp., East Alton, Ill., 1960-64; asst. gen. counsel INTERCO, Inc., St. Louis, 1964-66, asso. gen. counsel, mgr. law dept., 1966-69, asst. sec., 1966-74, gen. counsel, 1969-81, mem. operating bd., 1970-92, v.p., 1971-81, mem. exec. com., dir., 1975-92, exec. v.p., 1981-85, vice chmn. bd. dirs., 1985-92; chmn., pres. Aylward & Assocs., Inc., St. Louis, 1992—. Mem. dist. export coun. U.S. Dept. Commerce, 1974-77; dir., mem. exec. com. Boatmen's Nat. Bank St. Louis, 1982-91, trust estates com., 1982-85, chmn. audit com., 1986-91; bd. dirs. Boatmen's Bancshares, Inc., mem. audit com., 1984-91, mem. compensation com., 1986-91; trustee Maryville U., 1989-92, chmn. bd., 1991-92. Bd. dirs. St. Louis chpt. Nat. Found. March of Dimes, 1974-84, sec., 1976-78, chmn., 1979-82; bd. dirs. Cardinal Ritter Inst., 1975-90, chmn. pers. com., 1986-90; bd. dirs. St. Louis chpt. ARC, 1977-82, Linda Vista Montessori Sch., 1975-77, BBB Greater St. Louis, 1978-81, YMCA Greater St. Louis, 1981-2001, adv. dir., 2001—, NCCJ, 1992-93; bd. dirs. Cardinal Glennon Children's Hosp., 1991-96, mem. exec. com., 1992-96, bd. dirs. Found., 1996-2001, dir. emeritus, 2001—; bd. dirs. Cath. Charities of St. Louis, 1994-2001, vice chmn., 1995-97, chmn. 1997-99; mem. coun. Archdiocesan Devel. Appeal, 1994-97, chmn. 1996-97, vice chmn ., 1995-97, mem. exec. com., 1995-97, chmn. rev./planning com., 1995-96, chmn., 1996-97, hon. life mem.; mem. fin. coun. Archdiocese of St. Louis, 1995-98, mem. investment com., 1995-97; bd. dirs., fin. United Way Greater St. Louis, 1986—; mem. in vestment com. St. Louis Cmty. Found., 1993-95; trustee St. Louis Coun. World Affairs, sec., 1977-84; chmn. lay bd. DePaul Health Ctr., 1979-81; mem. exec. com. lay bd., 1981-89; mem. lay adv. bd. Chaminade Coll. Prep Sch., 1980-84, chmn. bd. trustees, 1981-84; mem. lay bd. Acad. of the Visitation, 1981-85. With AUS, 1955-58. Recipient of Order of St. Louis's King, Archdiocese of St. Louis. Mem. Mo. Bar Assn., St. Louis Bar Assn., Am. Footwear Industries Assn. (nat. affairs vice chmn. 1970, chmn. 1971-75), Am. Apparel Mfrs. Assn. (dir. 1983-85), NAM (taxation com. 1970-76, pub. affairs com. 1973-76, govt. ops./expenditures com. 1973-78), St. Louis C. of C. (legis. and tax com. 1966-74, vice chmn. 1970-71), Assoc. Industries Mo. (dir. 1973-80, exec. com. 1974-80, 2d v.p. 1974-76, pres. 1976-78), Am. Soc. Corp. Secs. (pres. St. Louis regional group 1972-73), Rotary (bd. dirs. St. Louis Club 1976-79), Knights of Malta, Knights of Holy Sepulcher, Order of St. Louis King, Legatus, Mo. Athletic Club, Bellerive Country Club (dir. 1981-84), Delta Theta Phi (dist. chancellor Mo. 1970-79, pres. St. Louis Alumni 1963). Clubs: Mo. Athletic, Bellerive Country (dir. 1981-84). General corporate. Home: 55 Muirfield Saint Louis MO 63141-7372 Office: Aylward and Assoc Inc One City Plaza Dr Saint Louis MO 63141 Fax: (314) 434-6528

AYNES, RICHARD L(EE), law educator; b. Dayton, Ohio, June 12, 1949; s. Carl D. and B. Louise (Burton) A.; m. Kathleen H. Szokan, Aug. 20, 1971; children: Jennifer Elizabeth, Jeffrey Alexander. BS, Miami U., Oxford, Ohio, 1971; JD, Cleve.-Marshall Coll. Law, 1974. Bar: Ohio 1975, U.S. Supreme Ct. 1979. Inter, atty. Cleve. Legal Aid, 1974-75; law clk. 8th Dist. Ohio Ct. Appeals, Cleve., 1975-76; faculty U. Akron (Ohio) Sch. Law, 1976—, assoc. dean, 1984-93, interim athletic dir., 1993-94, prof. John F. Seiberling Constl. Law Chair, 1995, dean, 1995—. Trustee Western Res. Legal Svcs., Medina, Summit and Portage Counties, Ohio, 1982-93; chmn. Mayors Task Force on Mcpl. Campaign Fin., 1998; racial fairness implementation task force Ohio Supreme Ct., 2000—. U. Akron fellow, 1980. Mem. ABA (amicus com. criminal justice sect. 1982-88, cons. victims com. 1982-83, reporter spl. com. on evaluation jud. performance 1982-84, questionnaire com. 1999—). Office: U Akron Sch Law Akron OH 44325-0001 E-mail: raynes@uakron.edu

AYRES, TED DEAN, lawyer, academic counsel; b. Hamilton, Mo., July 14, 1947; m. Marcia Sue Busselle; children: John Corbett, Jackson Frazer, Joseph Dean. BSBA, Ctrl. Mo. State Coll., 1969; JD, U. Mo., 1972. Bar: Mo. 1972, U.S. Dist. Ct. (we. dist.) Mo. 1972, U.S. Ct. Appeals (8th cir.) 1977, U.S. Supreme Ct. 1977, Colo. 1984, U.S. Dist. Ct. Colo. 1984, U.S. Ct. Appeals (10th cir.) 1984, Kans. 1987. Law clk. to presiding justice Mo. Supreme Ct., Jefferson City, 1972-73; ptnr. Stubbs & Ayres, Chillicothe, Mo., 1973-74; atty. Southwestern Bell Tel. Co., St. Louis, 1974-76; counsel U. Mo., Columbia, 1976-84, U. Colo., Boulder, 1984-86; gen. counsel Kans. Bd. Regents, Topeka, 1986-92, gen. counsel, dir. govtl. rels., 1992-96; acting pres. Pitts. State U., 1995; gen. counsel, assoc. to pres. Wichita (Kans.) State U., 1996—, interim dir. Edwin A. Ulrich Mus. Art, 1999-2000. Adj. asst. prof. coll. bus. adminstrn. U. Colo., Denver, 1984-85, adj. assoc. prof., 1985-86; spl. asst. atty. gen. State of Colo., 1984-86, State of Kans., 1987—; presenter region II conf. Assn. Coll. Unions Internat., U. Mo., Rolla, 1983; spkr. Soc. Colo. Archivists, U. Colo., Boulder, 1985; adj. prof. Washburn U., Topeka, 1989; adj. prof. kinesiology and sport studies Wichita State U., 1999—. Contbr. articles to profl. jours. Active adv. com. Boone County (Mo.) Cmty. Svcs.; mem. com. social concerns Mo. United Meth. Ch., 1979-81, supervisory com. Mothers' Morning Out program, 1980-84; adminstv. bd., com. on fin. and stewardship 1st United Meth. Ch., Topeka, 1989-91, family life coun., 1994-95; trustee Mid-Mo. chpt. Nat. Multiple Sclerosis Soc., 1981-84; mem. bd. mgrs. Topeka YMCA-Downtown Br., 1991-96, fedn. coun. Indian Guides program, 1988-91; treas. pack 175 Cub Scouts, 1990-95; bd. dirs. Innovative Tech. Enterprise Corp., 1991-94, S.W. Youth Athletic Assn., Inc., 1994-96, Friends of Topeka Zoo, 1995-2000, Wichita Tech. Corp., 1997—, Wichita State U. Hist. Preservation Commn., 1998—, parents coun. Truman State U., 1997-99. Curator scholar, 1969-70, Omar E. Robinson scholar, 1970-71, John M. Dalton Endl. Trust scholar 1971-72. Mem. Mo. Bar Assn., Nat. Assn. Coll. and Univ. Attys. (chairperson Southwestern region 1979-81, bd. dirs. 1985-88, com. mem. 1979—, del. and presenter numerous CLE workshops), Friends of Topeka Zoo, U. Mo. Alumni Assn. (life). Home: 2214 SW Brookfield St Topeka KS 66614-4236 Office: Wichita State Univ 201 Morrison Hall Wichita KS 67260-0001 E-mail: ted.ayres@wichita.edu

AYSCUE, EDWIN OSBORNE, JR. lawyer; b. May 21, 1933; s. Edwin Osborne and Grace Elizabeth (Fields) A.; m. Emily Mizell Urquhart, Aug. 17, 1957; children: Grace Thompson, E. Osborne, Emily Hassel, Margaret Certain. Grad. cum laude, Phillips Acad., Andover, Mass., 1951; AB in Polit. Sci., U. N.C., Chapel Hill, 1954; LLB with honors, U. N.C., 1960. Bar: N.C. 1960, U.S. Supreme Ct. 1979. Ptnr. Smith Helms Mulliss & Moore, LLP (and predecessor firms), Charlotte, 1960—. Mem. Civil Justice Reform Act Com., Western Dist. N.C., 1991-95. Editor-in-chief: N.C. Law Rev., 1959-60; contbr. articles to profl. jours. Alumni rep. Phillips Acad., 1964-90; bd. dirs. Legal Svcs. of So. Piedmont, 1983-85, Legal Svcs. of N.C., 1984-85, 88-94; sr. warden Christ Episcopal Ch., 1990-91; bd. dirs. Friends of U. N.C. Libr., 1989-92, U.S. Supreme Ct. Hist. Soc., 1999—; trustee St. Mary's Sch., Raleigh, N.C., 2000—; bd. vis. U. N.C. Chapel Hill, 2000— . Lt. USNR, 1955-57. Fellow Am. Coll. Trial Lawyers (regent 1991-99, sec. 1995-97, pres.-elect 1997-98, pres, 1998-99), Am. Bar Found. (life); mem. ABA (ho. of dels. 1991-95), N.C. Bar Assn. (pres. 1984-85, Gen. Practice Hall of Fame), N.C. State Bar (mandatory continuing edn. com. 1987-92, vice-chair 1990-93), Mecklenburg County Bar Assn. (pres. 1980-81), U. N.C. Chapel Hill Law Alumni Assn. (pres. 1999-00), Mecklenburg Bar Found. (trustee 1987-93), Am. Judicature Soc. (bd. dirs. 1985-89), Order Golden Fleece, Nat. Conf. Bar Pres., 4th Cir. Jud. Conf., Charlotte Country Club, Order of Coif, Phi Beta Kappa. Democrat. Episcopalian. Antitrust, General civil litigation, Libel. Office: Smith Helms Mulliss & Moore LLP PO Box 31247 Charlotte NC 28231-1247

BAADE, HANS WOLFGANG, legal educator, law expert; b. Berlin, Dec. 16, 1920; s. Fritz and Edith (Wolff) B.; m. Anne Adams Johnston; children— Friedrich James, Hans Alastair. A.B., Syracuse U., 1949; J.D., Kiel U. (Germany), 1951; LL.B., LL.M., Duke U., 1955, diploma Hague Acad. Internat. Law, 1956. Assoc. Inst. Internat. Law, Kiel, 1955-60; assoc. prof. law Duke U., 1960-64, prof. law, 1964-70; prof. law U. Toronto, 1970-71; Hugh Lamar Stone prof. civil law U. Tex., Austin, 1971— ; arbitrator internat. comml. matters; dir. Am. Soc. Comparative Law. Mem. Am. Arbitration Assn. (nat. panel arbitrators); assoc. mem. Internat. Acad. Comparative Law. Editor: Law and Comparative Problems, 1961-66; bd. editors Am. Jour. Comparative Law, 1960— ; editorial sec. German Yr. Book Internat. Law, 1956-60; contbr. numerous articles to profl. jours. Hon. fellow faculty of law U. Edinburgh (Scotland), 1997—. Home: 6002 Mountainclimb Dr Austin TX 78731-3822 Office: U Tex Sch Law Austin TX 78705

BABBIN, JED LLOYD, lawyer; b. N.Y.C., Mar. 16, 1950; s. Harold H. and Pearl (Bander) B.; m. Frances Kloker, June 22, 1975 (div. 1990); children: Jacob Harold, Norman Tyler; m. Sharon Cohen. BE, Stevens Inst. Tech., Hoboken, N.J., 1970; JD, Samford U., 1973; LLM, Georgetown U., 1978. Bar: Ala. 1973, D.C. 1978. Assoc. McKenna, Connor & Cuneo, Washington, 1977-81; v.p., gen. counsel Shipbuilders Coun., 1977-81; dir. contract policy Lockheed Corp., 1985-90; dep. under sec. of def. acquisition planning Office Sec. of Def., 1990-91; ptnr. McGuire, Woods, Battle & Boothe, 1991-94, Tighe, Patton, Tabackman & Babbin, Washington, 1994-2000, O'Connor & Hannan, LLP, Washington, 2000—. Capt. USAF, 1973-77. Fellow Nat. Contract Mgmt. Assn.; mem. Nat. Lawyers Assn. (bd. dirs. 2000—). Republican. Jewish. Avocations: fishing, bird hunting. Administrative and regulatory, Criminal, Government contracts and claims. Business E-Mail: jbabbin@oconnorhannan.com

BABBY, LON S. lawyer; b. Bklyn., Feb. 21, 1951; BA, Lehigh U., 1973; JD, Yale U., 1976. Bar: Conn. 1976, D.C. 1977, U.S. Supreme Ct. 1981, U.S. Claims Ct., 1986; cert. agt. Nat. Basketball Players Assn., Nat. Football League Players Assn. Law clk. to Hon. M. Joseph Blumenfeld Dist. Conn., 1976-77; mem. Williams & Connolly, Washington, 1977—. Adj. faculty George Washington U. Law Sch., 1991-92. Editor Yale Law Jour., 1974-76; contbr. articles to profl. jours. Mem. ABA, D.C. Bar, Conn. Bar Assn., Phi Beta Kappa, Omicron Delta Kappa. Contracts commercial, Sports. Office: Williams & Connolly 725 12th St NW Washington DC 20005-5901 E-mail: lbabby@wc.com

BABCOCK, BARBARA ALLEN, law educator, lawyer; b. Washington, July 6, 1938; d. Henry Allen and Doris Lenore (Moses) B.; m. Thomas C. Grey, Aug. 19, 1979. AB, U. Pa., 1960; LLB, Yale U., 1963. Bar: Md. 1963, D.C. 1964, JD (hon.), U. San Diego 1983, U. Puget Sound, 1988. Law clk. U.S. Ct. Appeals D.C., 1963; assoc. Edward Bennett Williams, 1964-66; staff atty. Legal Aid Agy., Washington, 1966-68; dir. Pub. Defender Svc. (formerly Legal Aid Agy.), 1968-72; assoc. prof. Stanford U., 1972-77, prof., 1977—; asst. atty. gen. U.S. Dept. Justice, 1977-79. Ernest W. McFarland Prof. Law, 1986-97; Judge John Crown Prof. of Law, 1997—. Democrat. Author: (with others) Sex Discrimination and The Law: History, Theory and Practice, 1996; (with Massaro) Civil Procedure: Problems and Cases, 2001; contbr. articles to profl. jours. E-mail: bbabcock@stanford.edu. Home: 835 Mayfield Ave Palo Alto CA 94305-1052 Office: Stanford U Sch Law Stanford CA 94305

BABCOCK, CHARLES LYNDE, IV, lawyer; b. Bklyn., June 23, 1949; s. Charles Lynde III and Dorothy (Yates) B.; m. Janet Judd Laughlin, June 12, 1976; children: Katherine Kester, Barbara Yates. AB, Brown U., 1971; JD, Boston U., 1976. Bar: Tex. 1977, U.S. Dist. Ct. (no. dist.) Tex. 1977, U.S. Dist. Ct. (so. dist.) Tex. 1979, U.S. Ct. Appeals (5th and 11th cirs.) 1979, U.S. Supreme Ct. 1980, U.S. Dist. Ct. (we. dist.) Tex. 1981, U.S. Ct. Appeals (9th and 10th cirs.) 1982, U.S. Dist. Ct. (ea. dist.) Tex. 1982. Sportswriter Phila. Inquirer, 1971-73; law clk. to presiding justice U.S. Dist. Ct. (no. dist.) Tex., Dallas, 1976-78; assoc. Jackson, Walker, Winstead, Cantwell & Miller, 1978-83, ptnr., 1983—, now Jackson Walker LLP, Dallas. Author: Business Law for Executives, 1977, Texas Media Law handbook, 1984; contbr. articles to legal jours. Bd. dirs. Freedom of Info. Found. Tex., 1995—. Recipient Disting. Pro Bono Svc. award North Tex. Legal Svcs. Found., 1986. Fellow Tex. Bar Found., Am. Coll. Trial Lawyers; mem. ABA, Tex. Bar Assn. Mem. Soc. of Friends. Avocation: sports. Federal civil litigation, State civil litigation, Libel. Office: Jackson & Walker LLP Ste 6000 901 Main St Dallas TX 75202-3797

BABCOCK, KEITH MOSS, lawyer; b. Camden, N.J., Aug. 5, 1951; s. William Strong Jr. and Dinah Leslie (Moss) B.; m. Jacquelyn Sue Dickman, Aug. 16, 1975; children: Michael Arthur, Max William. AB, Princeton U., 1973; JD, George Washington U., 1976. Bar: S.C. 1977, U.S. Dist. Ct. S.C. 1977, U.S. Ct. Appeals (4th cir.) 1977, U.S. Supreme Ct. 1980. Staff atty. S.C. Atty. Gen.'s Office, Columbia, 1977-78, state atty., 1978-79, asst. atty. gen., 1979-81; ptnr. Barnes & Austin, 1981-82, Austin & Lewis, Columbia, 1982-84, Lewis, Babcock & Hawkins, Columbia, 1984—. Mem. civil justice adv. com. for dist. S.C., 1991-94; mem. S.C. Bd. Bar Examiners, 2001—. Bd. dirs. Columbia Jewish Community Pre-Sch., 1984, chmn., 1985-86; bd. dirs. Columbia Jewish Community Ctr., 1986-88. Mem. ABA, S.C. Bar Assn. (chmn. prof. resp. com. 1985-86), Richland County Bar Assn., S.C. Bd. Bar Examiners, Princeton Alumni Assn. of S.C. (v.p. 1980-86, 88-89, pres. 1990-93, 96-98), George Washington U. Law Sch. Alumni Assn. (bd. dirs. 1983-87), Summit Club, Spring Valley Country Club (Columbia). Democrat. Episcopalian. Federal civil litigation, State civil litigation, Condemnation. Home: 233 W Springs Rd Columbia SC 29223-6912 Office: Lewis Babcock & Hawkins 1513 Hampton St Columbia SC 29201-2928 E-mail: kmb@lbhlaw.com

BABER, WILBUR H., JR. lawyer; b. Shelby, N.C., Dec. 18, 1926; s. Wilbur H. and Martha Corinne (Allen) B.; BA, Emory U., 1949; postgrad. U. N.C., 1949-50, U. Houston, 1951-52; JD, Loyola U., New Orleans, 1965. Bar: La. 1965, Tex. 1966. Sole practice, Hallettsville, Tex., 1966—. Trustee Raymond Dickson Found. Served with U.S. Army. Mem. ABA, ASCE, La. Bar Assn., Tex. Bar Assn., La. Engring. Soc., Tex. Surveyors Assn. Methodist. Lodge: Rotary. State civil litigation, Oil, gas, and mineral, Probate. Office: PO Box 294 Hallettsville TX 77964-0294

BABIAK, JOANN U. lawyer; b. San Francisco, Jan. 1, 1956; d. Herman N. and Joyce M. Uhley; children: Joshua, Eva. BSc, Boston U., 1977; MA in Commicative Disorders, U. Pacific, 1980; JD, MA in Psychology, U. Tulsa, 1996. Bar: Okla. 1997, U.S. Dist. Ct. (no. dist.) Okla. 1997. Ind. contractor Romine & Pickering, P.C., Okla., 1997; pvt. practice, 1998; assoc. Legal Svcs. Ea. Okla., Tulsa, 1998—. Mediator early settlement program Supreme Ct. of Okla., 1995—. Mem. Access OK/ADA Roundtable, Tulsa, 1997-98. Equal justice fellow Nat. Assn. Pub. Interest Law, Mem. ATLA, Okla. Acad. Mediators and Arbitrators, Am. Inns of Ct. (assoc. Hudson-Hall-Wheaton chpt.). Alternative dispute resolution. Office: Legal Svcs Ea Okla 115 W 3d Ste 700 Tulsa OK 74103

BABIARZ, FRANCIS STANLEY, lawyer; b. Wilmington, Del., Feb. 23, 1948; s. John Edward and Adele Frances (Barczuk) B.; m. Joyce Elaine Pierson, Aug. 19, 1972. BA with honors, U. Del., 1970; JD cum laude, U. Mich., 1973; LLM, Temple U., 1976. Bar: Del. 1973. Atty. Biondi & Babiarz, P.A., Wilmington, 1974-79, Morris, Nicholas, Arsht & Tunnell, Wilmington, 1979-84; ptnr. Biggs & Battaglia, 1984-98, Manta & Welge, Wilmington, 1998-99; dir. legal affairs family ct. State of Del., 1999-2000, dep. bank commr for supervisory affairs, 2000—. Lawyer; b. Wilmington, Del., Feb. 23, 1948, s. John Edward and Adele Frances (Barczuk) B., m. Joyce Elaine Pierson, Aug. 19, 1972. BA with honors, U. Del., 1970; JD cum laude, U. Mich., 1973; LLM, Temple U., 1976. Bar: Del. 1973. Ptnr. Biondi & Babiarz, P.A., Wilmington, 1974-79, Morris, Nichols, Arsht & Tunnell, Wilmington, 1979-84, Biggs & Battaglia, Wilmington, 1984-98, Manta & Welge, Wilmington, 1998—; sec. Del. State Bd. Accountancy, 1977-80. Served to capt. USAR. Mem. Del. State Bar Assn. (profl. guidance com.), Am. Hort. Soc., Pa. Hort. Soc., Phi Beta Kappa, Phi Kappa Phi. Democrat. Roman Catholic. Staff mem. U. Mich. Jour. Law Reform, 1971-73. E-mail: 2237187@mcimail.com. Fax: 302-655-7004. Staff mem. U. Mich. Jour. Law Reform, 1971-73. Sec. Del. State Bd. Accountancy, 1977-80. Served to Capt. USAR. Mem. Del. State Bar Assn., Am. Hort. Soc., Pa. Hort. Soc., Phi Beta Kappa, Phi Kappa Phi. Democrat. Roman Catholic. General civil litigation, General practice, Labor. Office: 555 E Loockerman St Dover DE 19901-3779 Fax: 302-739-3609. E-mail: fbabiarz@state.de.us

BABINEAU, ANNE SERZAN, lawyer; b. Jersey City, Dec. 16, 1951; d. Joseph Edward and Mary (Golding) Serzan; m. Paul A. Babineau, Apr. 7, 1973; children: John Regis, Matthew Paul. BA, Coll. New Rochelle, 1973; JD, Seton Hall U., 1977. Bar: N.J. 1977, N.Y. 1983, U.S. Ct. Appeals (3d cir.) 1984. Staff atty. rate counsel div. N.J. Dept. Pub. Adv., Newark, 1977-78; assoc. Wilentz, Goldman & Spitzer, P.C., Woodbridge, N.J., 1979-85, ptnr., 1985—. Bd. dirs. Downtown New Jersey. Mem. ABA, N.J. State Bar Assn. (pub. utility sect.), Urban Land Inst. Roman Catholic. Administrative and regulatory, Public utilities, Real property. Office: Wilentz Goldman & Spitzer PO Box 10 90 Woodbridge Ctr Dr Ste 900 Woodbridge NJ 07095-1142

BABLER, WAYNE E. lawyer, retired telephone company executive; b. Orangeville, Ill., Dec. 8, 1915; s. Oscar E. and Mary (Bender) B.; m. Mary Blome, Dec. 27, 1940; children: Wayne Elroy Jr., Marilyn Anne Monson, Sally Jane Sperry. BA, Ind. Cen. Coll., 1935; JD, U. Mich., 1938; LLD, Ind. Cen. U., 1966. Bar: Mich. 1938, N.Y. 1949, Mo. 1955, Wis. 1963, U.S. Supreme Ct. 1963. Assoc. Bishop & Bishop, Detroit, 1938-42, ptnr., 1945-48; atty. AT&T, 1948-55; gen. solicitor Southwestern Bell Tel. Co., St. Louis, 1955-63, v.p., gen. counsel, sec., 1965-80, ret., 1980; v.p., gen. counsel Wis. Tel. Co., Milw., 1963-65. Bd. dirs., chmn. St. Louis Soc. Crippled Children; bd. dirs. St. Louis Symphony Soc. Mem. ABA (chmn. pub. utility sect. 1978-79), Fed. Communications Bar Assn., Mo. Bar. Assn., Delray Dunes Country Club, Ocean Club. Home: 11943 Date Palm Dr Boynton Beach FL 33436-5534

BABLITCH, WILLIAM A. state supreme court justice; b. Stevens Point, Wis., Mar. 1, 1941; B.S., U. Wis., Madison, 1963, J.D., 1968. Bar: Wis. 1968. Pvt. practice law, Stevens Point, Wis.; mem. Wis. Senate, 1972-85, senate majority leader, 1976-82; justice Wis. Supreme Ct., Madison, 1985—; dist. atty. Portage County, Wis., 1969-72. Mem. Nat. Conf. State Legislators (exec. com. 1979) Office: Wis Supreme Ct PO Box 1688 Madison WI 53702-1688*

BACA, JOSEPH FRANCIS, state supreme court justice; b. Albuquerque, Oct. 1, 1936; s. Amado and Inez (Pino) B.; m. Dorothy Lee Burrow, June 28, 1969; children: Jolynn, Andrea, Anna Marie. BA in Edn., U. N.Mex., 1960; JD, George Washington U., 1964; LLM, U. Va., 1992. Asst. dist. atty. 1st Jud. Dist., Santa Fe, 1965-66; pvt. practice Albuquerque, 1966-72; dist. judge 2d Jud. Dist., 1972-88; state supreme ct. justice N.Mex. Supreme Ct., Santa Fe, 1989—, chief justice, 1995-97. Spl. asst. to atty. gen. Office of N.Mex. Atty. Gen., Albuquerque, 1966-71. Dem. precinct chmn., albuquerque, 1968; del. N.Mex. Constl. Conv., Santa Fe, 1969; bd. dirs. State Justice Inst., 1994—, V.Chmn. 1999—. Recipient Judge of Yr. award Peoples Commn. for Criminal Justice, 1989, Quincentennial Commemoration Achievement award La Hispanidad Com., 1992, Luchando por la Justicia award Mex. Am. Law Students Assn. U. N.Mex. Law Sch., 1993; J. William Fulbright Disting. Pub. Svc. award George Washington U. Alumni Assn., 1994, Recognition and Achievement award Commn. on Opportunities for Minorities in the Profession, 1992, others; named one of 100 most influential Hispanics Hispanic Bus. Mag., 1997, 98. Mem. ABA, Hispanic Nat. Bar Assn. (Lincoln-Juarez award 2000), N.Mex. Bar Assn. (outstanding jud. svc. award 1998), Am. Law Inst., Scribes (bd. dirs. 1998—), Am. Jud. Soc. (bd. dirs. 1999—), Albuquerque Bar Assn., Santa Fe Bar Assn., N.Mex. Hispanic Bar Assn. (Outstanding Hispanic Atty. award 2000), Alumni Assn. (pres. 1980-81), Kiwanis (pres. Albuquerque chpt. 1984-85), KC (dep. grand knight 1968). Roman Catholic. Avocation: reading history. Office: Supreme Ct NMex Supreme Court Bldg PO Box 848 Santa Fe NM 87504-0848

BACCINI, LAURANCE ELLIS, lawyer; b. Darby, Pa., Nov. 16, 1945; m. Tracey Judith Lane, Dec. 20, 1969; 1 child, Allyson Alexandra Lane. BS, Drexel U., 1968; JD, Villanova U., 1971. Bar: Pa. 1971, U.S. Dist. Ct. (ea. dist.) Pa. 1973, U.S. Ct. Appeals (3d cir.) 1979. Law clk. to chief judge U.S. Dist. Ct. (ea. dist.) Pa., 1971-73; assoc. Schnader, Harrison, Segal & Lewis, Phila., 1973-78, ptnr., 1979—, mem. exec. com., 1990-91; ptnr. Wolf, Block, Schorr and Solis-Cohen, 1991—; speaker, faculty mem. on labor law Practising Law Inst., N.Y.C.; trustee Phila. Bar Found., 1986—; bd. dirs. Interest on Lawyers Inst. Account Bd. Author: NLRA Supervisor's Handbook; assoc. editor Villanova Law Rev. Recipient Drexel One Hundred honor award, 1992. Mem. Phila. Bar Assn. (bd. govs. 1978— , chmn. 1982, vice chancellor 1986, chancellor-elect 1987, chancellor 1988, commn. on jud. selection, retention and evaluation 1978-79), chmn. exec. com. young lawyers sect., chmn. long range planning com.), Pa. Bar Assn. (ho. of dels. 1983—), ABA (former chair, and dir. young lawyers div. 1981-82, chair long-range planning com., young lawyers div.'s Fed. practice com., fed. jucicial standards com., judicial conf. for 3d cir., house of dels. 1988—, mem. editorial bd. The Labor Lawyer), Greater Phila. C. of C.(bd. dirs. 1988). Labor. Office: Wolf Block Schorr and Solis-Cohen Packard Bldg 12th Flr SE Corner 15 St & Chestnut St Philadelphia PA 19102

BACH, THOMAS HANDFORD, lawyer, investor; b. Vineland, N.J., Dec. 25, 1928; s. Albert Ludwig and Edith May (Handford) B. A.B., Rutgers U., 1950; LL.B., Harvard U., 1956. Bar: N.Y. State bar 1957. Asso. firm Hawkins, Delafield & Wood, N.Y.C., 1956-61, Reed, Hoyt, Washburn & McCarthy, N.Y.C., 1961-62; ptnr. Bach & Condren, 1963-71, Bach & McAuliffe, N.Y.C., 1971-79, Stroock & Stroock & Lavan, N.Y.C., 1979-88, Sullivan & Donovan, N.Y.C., 1989-2000, of counsel, 2000—; arbitrator Nat. Assn of Securities Dealers Reg., 2000—. Co-counsel N.Y. State Senate Housing and Urban Devel. Com., 1971; fiscal cons. N.Y.C. Fin. Adminstrn., 1967-70; asst. counsel State Fin. Com., N.Y. State Constl. Conv. of, 1967; del. U.S./Japan Bilateral Session, 1988, Moscow Conf. on Law and Bilateral Econ. Rels., 1990; spkr. Practicing Law Inst., Mcpl. Bond Workshop, N.Y., 1995-97. Contbr. articles to profl. jours.; co-author: A Guide to Certificates of Participation, 1991, the Handbook of Municipal Bonds, 1994. Mem. N.Y. State Commn. to Study Constl. Tax Limitations, 1974-75; chmn. subcom. Pub. Securities Assn.; dir. Citizens Union of N.Y. Served with U.S. Army, 1951-53, 1st lt. U.S. Army, 1952-53, Japan. Mem. Am. Bar Assn. (internat. law. sect.), N.Y. State Bar Assn., Assn. of Bar of City of N.Y., N.J. Bar Assn., N.Y. Mcpl. Analysts Group (chmn. 1973-74), Mcpl. Forum of N.Y., Market Technicians Assn., Internat. Fin. Svcs. Vol. Corps. Episcopalian. Municipal (including bonds), Securities. Home: 4 E 89th St New York NY 10128-0636 also: 615 W Oak Rd Vineland NJ 08360-2262 Office: Sullivan & Donovan 16th Fl 415 Madison Ave New York NY 10017-1111

BACHELDER, JOSEPH ELMER, III, lawyer; b. Fulton, Mo., Nov. 13, 1932; s. Joseph Elmer and Frances Evelyn (Gray) B.; m. Louise Este Mason, June 12, 1955; children: Louise Stewart Bachelder Alcock, Christina Cathryn Bachelder Dufresne, Hilary Houston. BA magna cum laude, Yale U., 1955; LLB, Harvard U., 1958. Bar: N.Y. 1959. Assoc. Mudge, Rose, Guthrie & Alexander, N.Y.C., 1958-67, McKinsey and Co., Inc., N.Y.C., 1967-69; ptnr. Satterlee and Stephens, 1969-72, Leboeuf, Lamb, Lieby & MacRae, N.Y.C., 1972-80; founder, sr. ptnr. Law Offices Joseph E. Bachelder, 1980—; chmn. The Bachelder Group, Inc., 1989—. Lectr. NYU Ann. Inst. on Fed. Taxation, 1972-74, Practicing Law Inst., 1977-80, 2000, Am. Law Inst., 1980, 97, 98, The Conf. Bd., 1986. Co-author, editor: Employee Stock Ownership Plans, 1979; columnist N.Y. Law Jour. 1977—; speaker Academia Symposia Stanford Law Sch., 1999, 2000, Northwestern U. , Kellogg Sch. Bus., 1999, U. Del., 2000. Mem. Princeton Twp. (N.J.) Zoning Bd., 1981-82; trustee Concord (Mass.) Acad., 1986-92. Fellow Am. Coll. Tax Counsel; mem. ABA, N.Y. State Bar Assn., Assn. of Bar of N.Y.C. Republican. Congregationalist. Clubs: The Down Town Assn. (N.Y.), Yale Club N.Y.; Bedens Brook (Princeton), Nassau (Princeton); Siasconset Casino (Nantucket, Mass.). Home: 226 Constitution Dr Princeton NJ 08540-6712 Office: 780 3rd Ave New York NY 10017-2024

BACHMAN, KENNETH LEROY, JR. lawyer; b. Washington, Aug. 24, 1943; s. Kenneth Leroy and Audrey Teresa (Torrence) B.; m. Sharon Abel, June 18, 1966; children— Laura Ann, Eric Kenneth. A.B. summa cum laude, Ohio U., 1965; J.D. cum laude, Harvard U., 1968. Bar: D.C. 1968, U.S. Ct. Appeals (D.C. cir.) 1971, U.S. Supreme Ct. 1981. Law clk. to judge U.S. Dist. Ct. So. Dist. N.Y., 1968-70; assoc. Cleary, Gottlieb, Steen & Hamilton, Washington, 1970-76, ptnr., 1976— . Mem. ABA. Contbg. editor Oil and Gas Price Regulation Analyst, 1978-83, Natural Gas Journal, 1983-85; contbr. articles to profl. jours. Banking, Federal civil litigation, Public international. Home: 5332 Falmouth Rd Bethesda MD 20816-2915 Office: 1752 N St NW Washington DC 20036-2904

BACHMAN, RALPH WALTER, lawyer; b. Mpls., Sept. 16, 1944; s. Ralph W. and Marguerite L. (Curfman) B.; m. Mary K. Zakariasen, July 29, 1967; children— Melissa, Rachel, Matthew. B.A. summa cum laude, U. Minn., 1966; M.A., Oxford U., 1968; J.D., Stanford U., 1970. Bar: Minn. 1970. Assoc., Gray, Plant, Mooty, Mooty & Bennett, Mpls., 1970-71; ptnr. Broeker & Bachman, Mpls., 1971-76; dir. profl. conduct Minn. Lawyers Profl. Responsibility Bd., 1976-79; chief dep. Hennepin County Atty.'s Office, Minn., 1979-83; atty. Lindquist & Vennum, Mpls., 1983— ; adj. prof. U. Minn. Law Sch., 1980. Mem. ABA (com. on ethics and profl. responsibility 1980-83), Minn. State Bar Assn., Hennepin County Bar Assn. (pres. 1984-85). Federal civil litigation, State civil litigation. Office: Bachman's Inc 6010 Lyndale Ave S Minneapolis MN 55419-2289

BACK, MICHAEL WAYNE, lawyer; b. Gary, Ind., Oct. 27, 1949; s. Virlan and Eunice Inez (Dooley) B.; m. Deborah Lynn Martinez, Oct. 1, 1988; children: Michael Christiaan, Amelia Michelle, Mark W., Hillary E. BS, Purdue U., 1976; postgrad., John Marshall Law Sch., 1979, 1979. Bar: Ind. 1979, U.S. Dist. Ct. (no. and so. dists.) Ind. 1979. Pvt. practice (atty.), Crown Point, Ind., 1979-87; hearing officer Lake County Circuit Ct., Crown Pl., 1980-87, pvt. practice, 1987--. Sargeant USAF, 1969-71. Ind. State Bar Assn., Lake County Bar Assn. (bd. dirs. 1996—), Fed. Bar (bd. govs.), Ind. Trial Lawyers Assn. (bd. govs. 1996—). Democrat. Roman Catholic. Club: Innsbrook Country, Merrillville (sec. 1986-87, bd. dirs. 1985-93, pres. 1991-93). Avocations: golf, tennis. Office: Lake County Circuit Ct 1 Professional Ctr Ste 204 Crown Point IN 46307-1882

BACKES, ORLIN WILLIAM, lawyer; b. Glenburn, N.D., May 11, 1935; s. Leonard P. and Irene G.(Keller) B.; m. Millie Jensen, Oct. 15, 1958; children— Brent, Jon, Mary, Paul. B.S., Minot State Coll., 1958; J.D., U. N.D., 1963. Bar: N.D. Faculty Max Pub. Sch., N.D., 1958-60; ptnr. McGee Law Firm, Minot N.D., 1963— ; dir. First Western Bank, Minot., dir. Integrity Mutual Fund Board; Mayor, City of Minot, 1994-98, fellow, Am. Coll. of Trial Lawyers; Advocate Am. Bd. of Trial Advocates. bd. regents Minot State Coll., 1981. Recipient Golden award Minot State Coll., 1984. Mem. Order of Coif, Minot C. of C. (pres. 1974). Roman Catholic. E-mail: obackes@mcgeelaw.com. General civil litigation, Estate planning, Real property. Home: 948 13th Ave SE # 2 Minot ND 58701-2708 Office: McGee Law Firm Wells Fargo Bank Ctr Minot ND 58701

BACKMAN, GERALD STEPHEN, lawyer; b. N.Y.C., Apr. 16, 1938; s. Morris and Marion (London) B.; m. Susan Pergament, Sept. 3, 1961 (dec. May 1978); children: Jonathan A., Kenneth S.; m. Barbara Fried Kaynes, Nov. 3, 1979; children: Jonathan J. Kaynes, Adam R. Kaynes. BA, U. Pa., 1959; LLBcum laude, Harvard U., 1962. Assoc. Weil, Gotshal & Manges LLP, N.Y.C., 1962-70, ptnr., 1970—. House counsel The Associated Merchandising Corp., N.Y.C., 1965-68; lectr. N.Y.U., 1973, Irving Trust Co., N.Y.C., 1981-88; mem. Blue Ribbon Commission on Audit Coms. of Nat. Assn. Corp. Dirs.; adj. prof. law Fordham U. Sch. Law, N.Y.C., 2000—; mem. Tri-Bar Opinion Com., 2000—. Bd. dirs. Hewlett-East Rockaway (N.Y.) Jewish Ctr., 1976-97, chmn. legal com., 1974-85, sec., 1980-82; bd. dirs. 25 E. 86th St. Corp., N.Y.C., 1996-99. Mem. ABA, Am. Arbitration Assn. (arbitrator), N.Y. State Bar Assn. (trustee bus. law sect. 2000, chmn. securities regulation com. 2000—), Assn. Bar N.Y.C., Masons. Republican. Jewish. Avocations: golf, skiing, tennis, fishing. General corporate, Mergers and acquisitions, Securities. Home: 25 E 86th St Apt 9G New York NY 10028-0553 Office: Weil Gotshal & Manges LLP 767 5th Ave New York NY 10153-0119 E-mail: Gerald.Backman@Weil.com

BACON, BRETT KERMIT, lawyer; b. Perry, Iowa, Aug. 8, 1947; s. Royden S. and Aldeen A. (Zuker) B.; m. Bonnie Jeanne Hall; children: Jeffrey Brett, Scott Michael. BA, U. Dubuque, 1969; JD, Northwestern U., 1972. Bar: Ohio 1972, U.S. Ct. Appeals (6th cir.) 1972, U.S. Supreme Ct. 1980. Assoc. Thompson, Hine & Flory, Cleve., 1972-80, ptnr., 1980-2000; founding ptnr. Frantz Ward, 2000—. Spkr. in field. Author: Computer Law, 1982, 84. V.p. profl. sect. United Way, Cleve., 1982-86; pres. Shaker Heights Youth Ctr., Inc., Ohio, 1984-86; elder Ch. of Western Res., 1996—. Mem. Fedn. Ins. and Corp. Counsel, Bar Assn. Greater Cleve., Cleve. Play House Club (officer 1986-94, pres. 1991-93, pres. men's com. 1993-96), Pepper Pike Civic League (trustee and treas. 1994-97). General civil litigation, Contracts commercial, Personal injury. Home: 33076 Woodleigh Rd Cleveland OH 44124-5257 Office: Frantz Ward LLP Ste 1900 55 Public Sq Bldg Cleveland OH 44114

BACON, ROBERT DALE, lawyer; b. Huntington, W.Va., July 31, 1952; s. Omar Albert and Margaret (Grow) B. BA, Stanford U., 1973; JD, U. Calif., Davis, 1976. Bar: Alaska 1977, Calif. 1977, D.C. 1978, U.S. Supreme Ct. 1981. Law clk. Alaska Supreme Ct., Anchorage, 1976-77; staff atty. U.S. Ct. Appeals, Washington, 1977-78; clk. appellate cts. Alaska Ct. Sys., Anchorage, 1978-84; asst. atty. gen. Office of Spl. Prosecutions and Appeals, 1984-90; sr. dep. Office of State Pub. Defender, Calif., 1990-97; pvt. practice Oakland, 1997—. Democrat. Unitarian. Office: Office of State Pub Defender 484 Lake Park Ave # 110 Oakland CA 94610-2730 E-mail: bacon2254@aol.com

BADEL, JULIE, lawyer; b. Chgo., Sept. 14, 1946; d. Charles and Saima (Hrykas) Badel. Student, Knox Coll., 1963-65; BA, Columbia Coll., Chgo., 1967; JD, DePaul U., 1977. Bar: Ill. 1977, U.S. Dist. Ct. (no. dist.) Ill. 1977, U.S. Ct. Appeals (7th and D.C. cirs.) 1981, U.S. Supreme Ct. 1985, U.S. Dist. Ct. (ea. dist.) Mich. 1989. Hearings referee State of Ill., Chgo., 1974-78; assoc. Cohn, Lambert, Ryan & Schneider, 1978-80, McDermott, Will & Emery, Chgo., 1980-84, ptnr., 1985-2001, Epstein, Becker & Green, PC, Chgo., 2001—. Legal counsel, mem. adv. bd. Health Evaluation Referral Svc. Chgo., 1980-89; bd. dirs. Alternatives, Inc., Chgo. chpt. Asthma and Allergy Found., 1993-94, Glenwood Sch. for Boys. Author: Hospital Restructuring: Employment Law Pitfalls, 1985; editor DePaul U. Law Rev., 1976-77. Mem. ABA, Chgo. Bar Assn., Labor & Employment Alliance for Women, Columbia Coll. Alumni Assn. (1st v.p., bd. dirs. 1981-86), Pi Gamma Mu. Civil rights, Federal civil litigation, Labor. Office: Epstein Becker & Green 150 N Michigan Ave Ste 420 Chicago IL 60601-7553

BADGER, DAVID HARRY, lawyer; b. Indpls., June 16, 1931; s. David Henry and Mayme Pearl (Wright) B.; m. Donna Lee Bailey, June 24, 1954; children: David Mark, Lee Ann, Steven Michael. BEE, Rose Poly. Inst., 1953; JD, Ind. U., 1964. Bar: Ind. 1964, U.S. Dist. Ct. (so and no. dists.) Ind. 1964, U.S. Patent Office 1964, U.S. Ct. Customs and Patent Appeals 1971, U.S. Ct. Appeals (fed. cir.) 1982. Engr. GE, 1953-56, Ransburg Corp., Indpls., 1956-62; chief elec. engr. Rex Metal Craft, Inc., 1963-64; patent counsel, corp. sec. Ransburg Corp., 1974-76; legal counsel Ball Corp., Muncie, Ind., 1976-77; ptnr. Jenkins, Coffey, Hyland, Badger & Conard, Indpls., 1977-82; mng. ptnr. Brinks, Hofer, Gilson & Lione, 1982-98. Contbr. articles to profl. jours.; patentee in U.S. and fgn. countries. With USN, 1953-55, lt. comdr. USNR. Named Hon. Alumnus Rose Hulman Inst. Tech., 1987. Mem. ABA (various coms.), IEEE, Ind. Bar Assn. (various coms.), Am. Intellectual Property Law Assn. (various coms.), Licensing Execs. Soc. (various coms.), Indpls. Bar Assn., Internat. Assn. Intellectual Property Law, Indpls. Jazz Club (bd. dirs. 1983-85, 95-97), Junto of Indpls. (bd. dirs. 1997-99). Home: 3524 Inverness Blvd Carmel IN 46032-9379 Office: Brinks Hofer Gilson & Lione 1 Indiana Sq Ste 2425 Indianapolis IN 46204-2045 E-mail: badger938@aol.com

BADGER, RONALD KAY, lawyer; b. Horton, Jabs, Aug. 24, 1933; s. Clarence E. and Josephine L. (Rick) B.; m. Janet L. Horner, Feb. 16, 1963; children: Hellen J. Badger Haag, Ronald K. Jr., Laura J. Badger Davis. BS in Bus., U. Kans., 1958, BS in Law, 1961, JD, 1968. Bar: Kans. 1961, U.S. Dist. Ct. Kans. 1961, U.S. Ct. Appeals (10th cir.) 1973, U.S. Supreme Ct. 1982, U.S. Ct. Claims 1990. Law clk. to Judge Arthur J. STanley, U.S. Dist. for Kans., Kansas City, 1961-62; spl. asst. to U.S. atty. for dist. of Kans., Dept. Justice, Topeka, 1962-64; assoc. Foulston & Siefkin, Wichita, Kans., 1964-66; atty. in contract adminstrn. Boeing Co., 1966-68; pvt. practice, 1968—. Bd. dirs. Kans. Bar Jour., 1966-82; contbr. articles to legal jours. Bd. dirs. Wichita Symphony Soc., 1970—. Mem. FBA (pres. Kans. chpt. 1978-80), Kans. Bar Assn., Wichita Bar Assn., Wichita Estate Planning Coun. (sec. 1996-97, pres. 1997-98), Lions (pres. Wichita 1984-85), Christian Legal Soc. (pres. Wichita chpt. 2001—). Republican. Methodist. Environmental, Personal injury, Probate. Office: 330 N Main St Wichita KS 67202

BADGEROW, JOHN NICHOLAS, lawyer; b. Macon, Mo., Apr. 7, 1951; s. Harry Leroy Badgerow and Barbara Raines (Buell) Novaria; m. Teresa Ann Zvolanek, Aug. 7, 1976; children: Anthony Thornton, Andrew Cameron, James Terrill. BA in Bus. and English with honors, Principia Coll., 1972; JD, U. Mo., Kansas City, 1975. Bar: Kans. 1976, U.S. Dist. Ct. Kans. 1976, U.S. Ct. Appeals (10th cir.) 1977, U.S. Ct. Appeals (4th cir.) 1979, U.S. Supreme Ct. 1982, U.S. Ct. Appeals (fed. cir.) 1985, U.S. Ct. Appeals (8th cir.) 1986, Mo. 1986, U.S. Dist. Ct. (we. dist.) Mo. 1986. Ptnr. McAnany, VanCleave & Phillips, P.A., Kansas City, Kans., 1975-85; ptnr.-in-charge Spencer, Fane, Britt & Browne, Kansas City, Mo. and Overland Park, Kans., 1986—. Co-author, co-editor: Kansas Lawyer Ethics, 1996; chmn. ethics grievance com. Johnson County, 1988—; mem. Kans. Jud. Coun., 1995—, Kans. Bd. Discipline for Attys., 2000—. Co-author: Kansas Employment Law, 1992, 2d edit., 2001. Co-chmn. Civil Justice Reform Act Commn., Dist. of Kans., 1995-96. Mem. ABA, Kans. Jud. Coun., Kans. Bar Assn. (employment seminars, bd. editors 1982-88, CLE com. 1989-95, Outstanding Svc. award 1995, mem. ethics adv. opinion com. 1997—), Kans. Met. Bar Assn. (chmn. civil rights com.), Lawyers' Assn. Kansas City, Kans. Assn. Def. Counsel (age discrimination seminar), Mission Valley Hunt Club (Stilwell, Kans.), Kans. Bd. of Discipline for Attys. Republican. Christian Scientist. Avocations: horseback riding, carpentry, reading. Civil rights, Federal civil litigation, General civil litigation. Office: Spencer Fane Britt & Browne 9401 Indian Creek Pkwy Ste 700 Shawnee Mission KS 66210-2038

BADR, GAMAL MOURSI, legal consultant; b. Helwan, Egypt, Feb. 8, 1924; came to U.S., 1970; s. Ahmad Moursi and Aisha Morshida (Al-Alaily) B.; m. Fatima al-Zahraa Barakat, June 18, 1950; children: Hefni, Hussein. LLB, U. Alexandria, Arab Republic of Egypt, 1944, LLD summa cum laude, 1954; diploma in econs., U. Cairo, 1945, diploma in pvt. law, 1946. Asst. dist. atty. Mixed Cts. Egypt, Alexandria, 1945-49; from assoc. to ptnr. Vatimbella, Catzeflis, Garrana & Badr, 1949-63; legal advisor UN Congo Operation, Kinshasa, Congo, 1963-64; justice Supreme Ct. Algeria, Algiers, 1965-69; from mem. to dep. dir. legal dept. UN Secretariat, N.Y.C., 1970-84; legal advisor Mission of Qatar to UN, 1984-94; advisor Mission of Saudi Arabia to UN, 1998—. Permanent bur. mem. Pan-Arab Lawyers' Fedn., Cairo, 1959-61; adj. prof. law NYU, 1982-98; lectr. The Hague Acad. Internat. Law, 1984. Author: Agency, 1980, State Immunity, 1984; gen. editor Commercial Law of the Middle East; contbr. articles to profl. jours. Mem. Internat. Law Assn. (London), Am. Soc. Internat. Law, Am. Arbitration Assn. (panel of arbitrators), Am. Fgn. Law Assn. (v.p. 1985-87, 89-92), Egyptian-Am. Assn. (pres. 1987-90), Rotary (pres. Alexandria Club 1962-63). Muslim. Home: 18 Peter Lynas Ct Tenafly NJ 07670-1115

BAE, FRANK S. H. law educator, law library administrator; b. Chung King, Szechuan, China, Dec. 19, 1941; came to U.S., 1967; s. Tse H. and Yu F. (Wang) B.; m. Anne Rita Donavan, March 15, 1975; children: Stephen, David, Marie, Elizabeth. LLB, Nat. Chung Shing U., Taipei, Taiwan, 1965; MCL, U. Miami, Fla., 1968; MS, U. Wis., 1970; JurD (hon.), New England Sch. Law, Boston, 1977. Dir. law libr. New England Sch. Law, 1970—, asst. prof. law, 1970-73, assoc. prof. law, 1973-74, prof. law, 1974—. Co-author: Searching the Law, 2nd edit., 1999. Mem. New England Law Libr. Consortium (bd. dirs.). Office: New Eng Sch Law Libr 154 Stuart St Boston MA 02116-5616

BAECHTOLD, ROBERT LOUIS, lawyer; b. Jersey City, Dec. 18, 1937; s. Fred Jacob and Catherine (Lenning) B.; m. Henrietta Thelma Hornbaker, Jan. 24, 1959; children: Kathi Ann, Christina Lee, Theresa Lynn. BS, Rutgers U., 1958; JD summa cum laude, Seton Hall U., 1966. Bar: N.Y. 1967, N.J. 1971, Pa. 1994, U.S. Dist. Ct. (so. and ea. dists.) N.Y. 1967, U.S. Ct. Appeals (fed. cir.) 1971, U.S. Ct. Appeals (2d cir.) 1967. Rsch. chemist Am. Cyanamid Co., Bound Brook, N.J., 1958-62; patent agt. M&T Chems., Inc., Rahway, 1962-65; assoc. Ward, Haselton, Orme, McElhannon, Brooks & Fitzpatrick, N.Y.C., 1965-68, ptnr., 1969-71, Fitzpatrick, Cella, Harper & Scinto, N.Y.C., 1971—. Lectr. Am. Patent Law Assn., 1979, Practising Law Inst., 1981, 88, others; mem. adv. com. to Fed. Cir. Ct. Appeals, 1991-94. Contbg. author course handbook Practising Law Inst., 1981, 88; patentee chemistry field. Mem. Cranford (N.J.) Bd. Edn., 1970-73. Nat Starch Products scholar; Leopole Schepp Found. grantee, 1954-58. Mem. ABA, Am. Intellectual Property Law Assn. (com. chmn. 1981, bd. dirs. 1987-90), Fed. Cir. Bar Assn. (bd. dirs. 1997—), N.J. Patent Law Assn. (pres. 1978-80), N.Y. Intellectual Property Law Assn., N.Y. State Bar Assn., N.J. Bar Assn. Federal civil litigation, Patent, Trademark and copyright. Office: Fitzpatrick Cella Harper & Scinto 30 Rockefeller Plz New York NY 10112 E-mail: rbaechtold@fchs.com

BAENA, SCOTT LOUIS, lawyer; b. N.Y.C., Sept. 15, 1949; s. I. Alexander and Rose (Snofsky) B.; children: Jeffrey Lance, Brad Alexander. BBA in Acctg., Geogre Washington U., 1970, JD with honors, 1974. Bar: Fla. 1974. Ptnr. Helliwell, Melrose & DeWolf, Miami, Fla., 1974-79; mng. ptnr. Stroock & Stroock & Lavan, 1979-2000; founding ptnr. Bilzin Sumberg Dunn Baena Price & Axelrod, 2000—. Adj. prof. U. Miami Sch. of Law, 1983-89. Mem. Pres. Com. on Econ. Devel., 1970; pres. Coral Gables-Riviera Homeowners Assn., 1986; mem. Coral Gables Zoning and Planning Bd., Code Enforcement Bd., Hist. Preservation Task Force. Fellow Am. Bar Found.; mem. ABA (com. on comml. fin. svcs., corp., banking and bus. law sect. 1983—), Fla. Bar Assn. (chair bus. law sect. 1986-87, bd. govs.), Dade County Bar Assn. (bd. dirs. young lawyers div. 1977-79), Am. Law Inst. Jewish. Avocations: golf, horseback riding, woodworking. Bankruptcy, Contracts commercial. Office: Bilzin Sumberg et al Ste 2400 200 S Biscayne Blvd Miami FL 33131-2385 E-mail: sbaena@bilzin.com

BAER, JOHN RICHARD FREDERICK, lawyer; b. Melrose Park, Ill., Jan. 9, 1941; s. John Richard and Zena Edith (Ostreyko) B.; m. Linda Gail Chapman, Aug. 31, 1963; children: Brett Scott, Deborah Jill. BA, U. Ill., Champaign, 1963, JD, 1966. Bar: Ill. 1966, U.S. Dist. Ct. (no. dist.) Ill. 1967, U.S. Ct. Appeals (7th cir.) 1969, U.S. Ct. Appeals (D.C. cir.) 1975, U.S. Ct. Appeals (9th cir.) 1979, U.S. Supreme Ct. 1975. Assoc. Keck, Mahin & Cate, Chgo., 1966-73, ptnr., 1974-97; of counsel Sonnenschein Nath & Rosenthal, 1997-99, ptnr., 2000—. Mem. Ill. Atty. Gen.'s Franchise adv. bd., 1992-94, 96—, chair 1996—. Editor Commerce Clearing House

Sales Representative Law Guide, 1998—; mem editl. bd. U. Ill. Law Forum, 1964-65, asst. editor, 1965-66; contbg. editor: Commercial Liability Risk Management and Insurance, 1978. Mem. Plan Commn., Village of Deerfield (Ill.), 1976-79, chmn., 1978-79, mem. Home Rule Study Commn., 1974-75, mem. home rule implementation com., 1975-76. Mem. ABA (topics and articles editor Franchise Law jour. 1995-96, assoc. editor 1996-99, editor-in-chief The Franchise Lawyer 1999—), Internat. Franchise Assn. (legal/legis. com. 1990—), Inter-Pacfic Bar Assn., Ill. Bar Assn. (competition dir. region 8 nat. moot ct. 1974, profl. ethics com. 1977-84, chmn. 1982-83, spl. com. on individual lawyers advt. 1981-83, profl. responsibility com. 1983-84, standing com. on liaison with atty. registration and disciplinary commn. 1989-93, spl. com. on ethics 2000 1999—), Internat. Bar Assn. Administrative and regulatory, Contracts commercial, Franchising. Office: Sonnenschein Nath & Rosenthal 8000 Sears Tower 233 S Wacker Dr Ste 8000 Chicago IL 60606-6491 E-mail: jbaer@sonnenschein.com

BAETZ, W. TIMOTHY, lawyer; b. Cin., Aug. 5, 1944; s. William G. and Virginia (Fauntleroy) Baetz. BA, Harvard U., 1966; JD, U. Mich., 1969. Bar: Ill. 1969, D.C. 1980. Assoc. McDermott, Will & Emery, Chgo., 1969-74, income ptnr., 1975-78, capital ptnr., 1979—. Mem. mgmt. com. McDermott, Will & Emery, 1987-92, 95-2001. With U.S. Army, 1969-75. Fellow Am. Coll. Trust and Estate Counsel; mem. ABA, Ill. Bar Assn., Chgo. Bar Assn., Chgo. Coun. Lawyers, D.C. Bar Assn. Republican. Episcopalian. Estate planning, Probate. Home: 940 Golfview Rd Glenview IL 60025-3116 Office: McDermott Will & Emery 227 W Monroe St Ste 3100 Chicago IL 60606-5096

BAEUMER, ULRICH J.P. lawyer; b. Luedinghausen, Germany, May 31, 1970; s. Josef and Hilde Baeumer; m. Ayuska M. Motha, Nov. 10, 1997; 1 child, Kirana. Diploma, U. Wales, 1993; Staatsexamen, U. Cologne, Germany, 1996; LLM, George Washington U., 1997; Staatsexamen, Ct. of Appeals, Darmstadt, Germany, 1999. Bar: N.Y. 1997, Frankfurt. Fgn. lawyer Berliner, Corcoran & Rowe, Washington, 1996-97; referendar Heuking, Kuhn, Dusseldorf, Germany, 1997-98, PwC Veltins, Frankfurt, Germany, 1998, GM/Opel, Frankfurt, 1999; assoc. Price Waterhouse Coopers Veltins, 1999—. Editor-in-chief German Am. Law Jour., 1996-97; contbr. articles to profl. jours. Mem. ABA, DAJV. Computer, General corporate, Intellectual property. Home: Freiherr-vom-Stein 4 68512 Bad Soden, Hessen Germany Office: Pricewaterhouse Coopers Im Trutz Frankfurt 55 60322 Frankfurt/Main Germany E-mail: ulrich.baeumer@de.pwcglobal.com

BAGARIA, GAIL FARRELL, lawyer; b. Detroit, Oct. 6, 1942; d. Vincent Benjamin and Inez Elizabeth (Coffey) Farrell; m. William James Bagaria, Nov. 28, 1964; children: Bridget Ann, William James, Benjamin George. BA, U. Detroit, 1964; JD, Cath. U. Am., 1980. Bar: Md. 1980, U.S. Dist. Ct. Md., 1982. Cons. Miller & Webster, Clinton, Md., 1980-82; pvt. practice Bowie, 1982—. Prince George's County adv. com. on Aging, 1998—. Mem. Prince George's Women's Lawyers Caucus (sec. 1984, pres. 1986, treas. 1997), Md. State Bar Assn., Women's Bar Assn. Md., Prince George's County Bar Assn., Soroptimist Internat. (Bowie-Crofton chpt., pres. 1988-89, 93-94), Greater Bowie C. of C. (bd. dirs. 1995-97, 99-2000, sec. 1997-98, 98-99, Outstanding Bus. Person 1997). Democrat. Roman Catholic. Estate planning, Probate, Elder. Office: PO Box 759 Bowie MD 20718-0759

BAGATELOS, PETER ANTHONY, lawyer; b. San Francisco, Oct. 8, 1947; s. Anthony Peter and Emily B.; m. Anne Marie Hawkins, July 27, 1974; children: Catherine, Anthony. AA, George Washington U., 1967; BA, Stanford U., 1969; MA, Rutgers U., 1971; JD, U. San Francisco, 1974. Bar: Calif. 1975, U.S. Dist. Ct. (no. dist.) Calif. 1975, U.S. Ct. Appeals (9th cir.) 1975. Adminstrv. asst. San Francisco Bd. Suprs., 1974-76; assoc. Dobbs & Nielsen, San Francisco, 1976-83, Nielsen, Hodgson et al, San Francisco, 1983; ptnr. Bagatelos & Fadem, 1984—. Bd. dirs. Guadalupe Homes, Redlands, Calif., 1979-91. Recipient Cert. Honor, San Francisco Bd. Suprs., 1977. Republican. Greek Orthodox. General corporate, Contracts commercial. Office: Bagatelos & Fadem Ste 14-10 601 Claifornia St San Francisco CA 94108-2823

BAGBY, THOMAS RICHARD, lawyer; b. Roanoke, Va., Jan. 30, 1950; s. James Taylor and Mildred C. (Burnette) B.; m. Kathleen Thomasson, June 14, 1975. B.A., U. Va., 1972, J.D., 1975. Bar: Va. 1975, D.C. 1976, U.S. Supreme Ct. 1980. Law clk. Judge June L. Green, Washington, 1975-77; trial atty. Civil Rights div. U.S. Dept. Justice, Washington, 1977-81; assoc. McGuiness & Williams, Washington, 1981-83, ptnr., 1984— . Mem. ABA, Phi Beta Kappa. Federal civil litigation, Labor. Office: Epstein Becker & Green 1227 25th St NW Ste 700 Washington DC 20037-1175

BAGBY, WILLIAM RARDIN, lawyer; b. Grayson, Ky., Feb. 19, 1910; s. John Albert and Nano A. (Rardin) B.; m. Mary Carpenter, Sept. 3, 1939; 1 child, John Robert; m. Elizabeth Hinkel, Nov. 22, 1975. AB, Cornell U., 1933; JD, U. Mich., 1936; postgrad., Northwestern U., 1946-47. Bar: Ky. 1937, Ohio 1952, U.S. Tax Ct. 1948, U.S. Supreme Ct. 1950, U.S. Ct. Appeals (6th cir.) 1952. Pvt. practice, Grayson, 1937-43; atty., judge City of Grayson, 1939-43; counsel Treasury Dept., Chgo., Cleve. and Cin., 1946-54; pvt. practice Lexington, Ky., 1954—. Prof. U. Ky., 1956-57; gen. counsel Headley-Whitney Mus., 1974-84; mem. Bd. of Adjustment, Lexington-Urban County City Govt., 1965-98, chmn., 1980-98. Trustee Bagby Found. Musical Arts, N.Y.C., 1963-74; trustee, gen. counsel McDowell Cancer Found., 1979-91, pres., 1988-91. Lt. USN, 1943-46. Mem. ABA (hon. life), Am. Judicature Soc., Ky. Bar Assn. (hon. life), Fayette County Bar Assn., Lexington Club, U. Ky. Faculty Club, Rotary. Democrat. Probate, Taxation, general. Home: 228 Market St Lexington KY 40507-1030 Office: 1107 1st National Bldg Lexington KY 40507

BAGGETT, STEVEN RAY, lawyer; b. Fayetteville, Ark., July 3, 1963, s. Harold Ray and Norma June (King) B.; m. Amy Lynn Griggs, Jan. 2, 1999. BA, U. Ark., 1985; JD, So. Meth. U., 1988. Bar: Tex. 1988, U.S. Dist. Ct. (no. dist.) Tex. 1988, U.S. Ct. Appeals (5th cir.) 1992. Assoc. Thompson & Knight, Dallas, 1988-95, shareholder, ptnr., 1996—. Recipient Am. Jurisprudence awards Bancroft-Whitney Co., 1985-86. Mem. Tex. Bar Assn., Dallas Bar Assn. (spkrs. com. 1997—, state fair trial by jury com. 1998—, jud. com. 1999—, cmty. involvement com. 1999—, law in schs. and cmtys. com. 1999), Ark. U. Alumni Assn., So. Meth. U. Alumni Assn., Phi Beta Kappa. Avocations: weight training, running, ice skating, music. Federal civil litigation, General civil litigation, State civil litigation. Office: Thompson & Knight 1700 Pacific Ave Ste 3300 Dallas TX 75201-4693 E-mail: baggetts@tklaw.com

BAGLEY, CHARLES FRANK, III, lawyer; b. Dec. 3, 1944; m. Kirsten L., Aug. 19, 1967; children: Charles F. IV, Gordon T. BA, Southwestern U., 1966; JD, Washington & Lee U., 1969. Judge advocates gen. ct. lt. U.S. Navy, 1969-74; ptnr. Campbell, Woods, Bagley, Emerson, McNeer & Herndon, 1974—. Pres. bd. dirs. tri state coun. Boy Scouts of Am., 1982-85; bd. dirs. Contact Huntington, Hospice Huntington, chmn. 1987-89; active Huntington Area C. of C., Enslow Park Presbyn. Ch. Fellow Internat. Soc. Barristers, West Va. Bar Found.; mem. ABA, Va. Bar Assn., W.Va. State Bar Assn. (bd. govs. 1986-93, pres. 1991-92), W.Va. Bar Assn. (exec. coun. 1986-95, pres. 1993-94), Def. Trial Coun. W.Va. (bd. govs. 1985-90), Cabell County Bar Assn. (pres. 1985-86), Internat. Assn. Ins. Coun., Def. Rsch. Inst., Inc. (state chmn. 1985-90). Alternative dispute resolution, Insurance, Toxic tort. Address: 1123 12th Ave Huntington WV 25701-3423 E-mail: cbagley@campbellwoods.com

BAGLEY, CONSTANCE ELIZABETH, law educator, lawyer; b. Tucson, Dec. 18, 1952; d. Robert Porter Smith and Joanne Snow-Willstadter. AB in Polit. Sci. with distinction, with honors, Stanford U., 1974; JD magna cum laude, Harvard U., 1977. Bar: Calif. 1978, N.Y. 1978. Tchg. fellow Harvard U., 1975-77; assoc. Webster & Sheffield, N.Y.C., 1977-78, Heller, Ehrman, White & McAuliffe, San Francisco, 1978-79, McCutchen, Doyle, Brown & Enersen, San Francisco, 1979-84, ptnr., 1984-90; lectr. bus. law Stanford (Calif.) U., 1988-90, lectr. mgmt., 1990-91, lectr. law and mgmt., 1991-95, sr. lectr. law and mgmt., 1995-2000, GSB Trust faculty fellow, 1997-98, lectr. Stanford Exec. Program; lectr. Stanford Mktg. Mgmt. Exec. Program; sr. lectr. bus. adminstrn. Harvard Bus. Sch., Boston, 1999-2000, assoc. prof., 2000—. Bd. dirs. Alegre Enterprises, Inc., Latina Publ. LLC, 1995-2000; corp. practice series adv. bd. Bur. Nat. Affairs, 1984—; faculty adv. bd. Stanford Jour. Law, Bus. and Fin., 1994—; lectr., planning com. Calif. Continuing Edn. Bar, L.A., San Francisco, 1983, 85-87; lectr. So. Area Conf., Silverado, 1988, Young Pres. Orgn. Internat. U. for Pres., Hong Kong, 1988. Author: Mergers, Acquisitions and Tender Offers, 1983, Managers and the Legal Environment: Strategies for the 21st Century, 1991, 4th edit., 2002; co-author: Negotiated Acquisitions, 1992, Cutting Edge Cases in the Legal Environment of Business, 1993, 2d edit. 1998, Proxy Contests and Corporate Control: Strategic Considerations, 1997, Proxy Contests and Corporate Control: Conducting the Proxy Campaign, 1997, The Entrepreneur's Guide to Business Law, 1998; contbg. editor: Calif. Bus. Law Reporter, 1984-95; mem. editl. bd. Jour. Internet Law, 1997-99, 2001—; staff editor Am. Bus. Law Jour., 2000-. Vestry mem. Trinity Episcopal Ch., San Francisco, 1984-85; vol. Moffit Hosp. U. Calif., San Francisco, 1983-84; bd. dirs. Youth and Family Assistance, Redwood City, Calif., 1996-99. Mem. ABA, Acad. Mgmt., Acad. Legal Studies in Bus., Harvard Faculty Club, Cap and Gown Soc., Phi Beta Kappa. Republican. Office: Harvard Bus Sch Soldiers Field Boston MA 02163-1317 E-mail: cbagley@hbs.edu

BAGLEY, WILLIAM THOMPSON, lawyer; b. San Francisco, June 29, 1928; s. Nino J. and Rita V. (Thompson) Baglietto; m. Diane Lenore Oldham, June 20, 1965; children: Lynn Lorene, William Thompson, Walter William, Shana Angela, Tracy Elizabeth. AB, U. Calif., Berkeley, 1949, JD, 1952. Bar: Calif. 1953, U.S. Supreme Ct. 1967. Atty. Pacific Gas & Electric Co., 1952-56; assoc. Gardiner, Riede & Elliott, San Rafael, Calif., 1956-60; ptnr. Bagley Bernt & Bianchi, 1961-74; mem. Calif. Legis., 1961-74; chmn. Commodity Futures Trading Commn., Washington, 1975-79; ptnr. Nossaman, Guthner, Knox and Elliott, San Francisco, 1980—. Mem. Calif. Pub. Utilities Commn., 1983-86; mem. Calif. Transp. Commn., 1983-89, chmn., 1987-88. Bd. editors Calif. Law Rev., 1951-52. Bd. regents U. Calif., 1989—; bd. dirs. Nat. Futures Assn., Calif. Coun. Environ. and Econ. Balance, Edmund G. Brown Inst. Govtl. Affairs, L.A.; chmn. bd. Calif. Rep. League, 1980-82. Recipient Freedom of Info. award Sigma Delta Chi, 1970, Golden Bear award Calif. Pk. Commn., 1973; named Most Effective Assemblyman, Capitol Press Corps, 1969, Legislator of Yr., Calif. Trial Lawyers Assn., 1970. Mem. ABA, Calif. State Bar Assn., World Trade Club, Elks Club (life), Phi Beta Kappa, Alpha Tau Omega. Presbyterian. Administrative and regulatory, Legislative, Public utilities. E-mail: wbagley@nossaman.com

BAGSHAW, BRADLEY HOLMES, lawyer; b. Salem, Mass., Mar. 26, 1953; s. James Holmes and Hope (Bradley) B.; m. Suzanne LuBien, Aug. 23, 1975. AB summa cum laude, Bowdoin Coll., 1975; JD cum laude, Harvard U., 1981. Bar: Wash. 1981, U.S. Dist. Ct. (we. dist.) Wash. 1981, U.S. Dist. Ct. (ea. dist.) Wash. 1989, U.S. Ct. Appeals (9th cir.) 1989. Assoc. Helsell Fetterman, Seattle, 1981-88, ptnr., 1988—, mng. ptnr., 1991-97, ptnr., 1997—. Admiralty, Federal civil litigation, State civil litigation. Office: Helsell Fetterman 1325 4th Ave Ste 1500 Seattle WA 98101-2569 E-mail: bbagshaw@helsell.com

BAGWELL, LOUIS LEE, lawyer; b. Roswell, N.Mex., Dec. 29, 1947; s. Louis and Mary Sue (McNeil) B.; m. Mary Therese Schewendeman, July 16, 1971; children: Jessica, Laura. B.S. with honors, U. Tex., 1970; J.D. summa cum laude, U. Houston, 1974. Bar: Tex. 1974, U.S. Ct. Appeals (5th cir.) 1974, U.S. Dist. Ct. (so. and ea. dists.) Tex. 1974, U.S. Ct. Appeals (11th cir.) 1982. Assoc. Baker & Botts, Houston, 1974-80, ptnr., 1981-93; lectr. continuing legal edn. U. Houston, 1983-84. Bd. dirs. U. Houston Law Found., 1990-93. NCAA scholar Nat. Collegiate Athletic Assn., 1970. Fellow Houston Bar Found., Houston Bar Assn.; mem. ABA, State Bar Tex. (com. 1991-93, cert. civil trial specialist; grievance com. 1978-79), Assn. Civil Trial Specialists.Baptist. Avocations: golf, sailing, tennis. Federal civil litigation, State civil litigation. Office: Baker & Botts 1200 Smith St Ste 1200 Houston TX 77002-4592

BAHLER, GARY M. lawyer; BA, Houghton Coll., 1973; JD, Cornell U., 1976. Bar: N.Y. 1977. Sec., dep. gen. counsel Venator Group, Inc. (formerly Woolworth Corp.), N.Y.C., 1991-93, v.p., gen. counsel, sec., 1993-98, sr. v.p., gen. counsel, sec., 1998—. Office: Venator Group Inc 112 W 34th St New York NY 10120

BAHLS, STEVEN CARL, law educator, dean; b. Des Moines, Sept. 4, 1954; s. Carl Robert and Dorothy Rose (Jensen) B.; m. Jane Emily Easter, June 18, 1977; children: Daniel David, Timothy Carl, Angela Emily. BBA, U. Iowa, 1976; JD, Northwestern U., Chgo., 1979. Bar: Wis. 1979, Mont. 1989, Ohio 1994; CPA, Iowa. Assoc. Frisch, Dudek & Slattery, Milw., 1979-84, dir., 1985; assoc. dean and prof. U. Mont. Sch. of Law, Missoula, 1985-94; dean., prof. law sch. Capital U. Law Sch., Columbus, Ohio, 1994—. Coordinating exec. editor Northwestern U. Law Rev., 1979. Vice chair Columbus Works. Mem. ABA, Am. Agrl. Law Assn. (pres.), Wis. Bar Assn., Mont. Bar Assn., Ohio Bar Assn., Ohio State Bar Found. (bd. govs.), Order of Coif. Republican. Methodist. Avocations: photography, travel, hiking. Home: 499 N Columbia Ave Bexley OH 43209-1003 Office: Capital U Law Sch 303 E Broad St Columbus OH 43215-3200

BAILEY, CRAIG BERNARD, lawyer; b. Camden, N.J., Aug. 20, 1952; s. Bernard Thomas and Nora Frances (DiDomenico) B. BA and BS, Bucknell U., 1975; JD, George Washington U., 1978. Bar: U.S. Patent Office 1977, D.C. 1978, Calif. 1984, U.S. Ct. Claims, U.S. Ct. Internat. Trade, U.S. Tax Ct., U.S. Ct. Mil. Appeals, U.S. Ct. Appeals (1st, 4th, 5th, 7th, 8th, 9th, 10th, D.C. and fed. cirs.), U.S. Supreme Ct. Law clk. to chief judge U.S. Ct. Appeals (fed. cir.), Washington, 1978-80; assoc. Brenner & Wray, Arlington, Va., 1980-83; patent atty. Hughes Aircraft Co., El Segundo, Calif., 1983-86; assoc. Fulwider, Patton, Lee & Utecht, L.A., 1986-89, ptnr., 1990—. Mem. ABA, L.A. Patent Law Assn., Tau Beta Pi. Government contracts and claims, Patent, Trademark and copyright. Office: Fulwider Patton et al Hughes Ctr 6060 Center Dr Tenth Fl Los Angeles CA 90045

BAILEY, FRANCIS LEE, lawyer; b. Waltham, Mass., June 10, 1933; m. Florence Gott (div. 1961); m. Froma Portney (div. 1972); m. Lynda Hart, Aug. 26, 1972 (div. 1980); m. Patricia Shiers, June 10, 1985. Student, Harvard U., 1950-52, 57; LL.B., Boston U., 1960. Bar: Mass. 1960, U.S. Dist. Ct. Mass., 1961, U.S. Ct. Appeals (1st cir.) 1963, U.S. Tax Ct. 1964, U.S. Ct. Appeals (6th cir.) 1964, U.S. Supreme Ct. 1964, U.S. Ct. Appeals (2d cir.) 1967, U.S. Ct. Appeals (10th cir.) 1968, U.S. Ct. Appeals (3d cir.) 1969, U.S. Ct. Appeals (9th cir.) 1970, U.S. Ct. Appeals (4th and 7th cirs.) 1971, U.S. Dist. Ct. (we. and no. dists.) Tex. 1980, U.S. Ct. Mil. Appeals 1981, U.S. Ct. Appeals (8th and 11th cirs.) 1984, U.S. Ct. Appeals (5th cir.) 1985, Fla. 1989, U.S. Dist. Ct. (ea. dist.) Wis. 1991. Prin. Law Offices of F. Lee Bailey, West Palm Beach, Fla. Author: (with Harvey Aronson) The Defense Never Rests, 1971, Cleared for the Approach, 1977, (with John Greenya) For the Defense, 1976; novel Secrets, 1979; How to Protect Yourself Against Cops In California and Other Strange Places, 1982, To Be a Trial Lawyer, 1983; numerous works in field of criminal law (with Henry Rothblatt). Lt. USMC, 1952-56. Mem. ABA; ATLA. Aviation, General civil litigation, Criminal.

BAILEY, HENRY FRANKLIN, JR. lawyer; b. Buffalo, Wyo., May 10, 1953; s. Henry Franklin and Alma Oneita (Cotton) B.; m. Sandra Adele Shanor, Aug. 3, 1973; children— Brian, Jeffrey, Marcus, Douglas, Katherine. B.S. in Econs. with honors, U. Wyo., 1975, J.D. with honors, 1978. Bar: Wyo. 1978, U.S. Dist. Ct. Wyo. 1978, U.S. Ct. Appeals (10th cir.) 1978. Assoc. Loomis, Lazear, Wilson & Pickett, Cheyenne, Wyo., 1978-80, jr. ptnr., 1980-82, ptnr., 1982— ; instr. Summitt Bar Rev., Laramie, Wyo., 1980-83. Sr. editor Land and Water Law Rev., 1977. Bishop Ch. of Jesus Christ of Latter-Day Saints, Cheyenne, 1982— ; bd. dirs. Laramie County Community Coll. Booster Club, Cheyenne, 1978-80. Named Outstanding Young Man Am., U.S. Jaycees, 1980; Thurmond Arnold Law scholar, U. Wyo., 1975. Mem. ABA (trial practice com.), Wyo. Trial Lawyers Assn., Nat. Assn. R.R. Trial Lawyers (instr. 1982), Def. Research Inst., Def. Lawyers Assn. Wyo., Wyo. Bar Assn., Phi Kappa Phi, Beta Gamma Sigma. Club: Exchange (Cheyenne). Federal civil litigation, State civil litigation, Personal injury. Home: 5708 Blue Blf Cheyenne WY 82009-4419 Office: Loomis Lazear Wilson & Pickett 202 E 18th St Cheyenne WY 82001

BAILEY, K. RONALD, lawyer; b. Sandusky, Ohio, July 30, 1947; s. Kenneth White and Virginia McClung (Sheddan) B.; m. Sara Ann Geary Bressler, Mar. 14, 1969 (div. June 1973); 1 child, Matthew Scott; m. Lynn Darlene Kammer, Aug. 31, 1973; children: Thomas Keith, Kenneth Richard. B in Liberal Studies summa cum laude, Bowling Green State U., 1979; JD, Cleveland-Marshall Law Sch., 1982; grad., Gerry Spence's Trial Lawyers Coll., 1994. Bar: Ohio 1983, U.S. Dist. Ct. (no. dist.) Ohio 1983, U.S. Dist. Ct. (D.C. cir.) 2000, U.S. Ct. Appeals (6th cir.) 1985, U.S. Supreme Ct. 1992. Tool, diemaker Gen. Motors, Sandusky, 1968-84; sole practice Huron, Ohio, 1983-87; sr. trial atty. K. Ronald Bailey & Assocs. Co., Legal Profl. Assn., Sandusky, 1987—. Chmn. Charter Rev. Com. of Huron, 1984. Mem. ATLA, ABA (criminal justice sect., white collar crimes com.), Nat. Assn. Criminal Def. Lawyers, Ohio Bar Assn. (coun. dels. 1998—, criminal justice sect., white collar crimes com., criminal law com.), Erie County Bar Assn., Ohio Assn. Criminal Def. Lawyers (bd. dirs. 1988—, v.p. publs. 1991-93, 97-98, treas. 1994, pres. 1995-96, chmn. capital litigation 1997—, Pres.'s award 1989-95, 97-98, v.p. CLE 1997-98). Democrat. Pentecostal. Avocations: reading, photography, painting, swimming, drag racing. General civil litigation, Criminal, Personal injury. Home: 121 Sycamore Dr Norwalk OH 44857-1914 Office: K Ronald Bailey & Assocs Co, Legal Profl Assn 220 W Market St Sandusky OH 44870-2515 E-mail: krbailey@baileyandassoc.com

BAILEY, MARYANN GEORGE, lawyer; b. Citronelle, Ala., Jan. 30, 1951; d. William Everett Deese and Mary Alma Webb; m. Ronald F. George, Dec. 26, 1975 (div. Jan. 1983); 1 child, Kristen Leigh. BS, U. S. Ala., 1975; JD, U. Houston, 1980. Bar: Tex. 1980, U.S. Dist. Ct. (so. dist.) Tex. 1981, U.S. Dist. Ct. (we. dist.) Tex. 1991. Pvt. practice, Houston, 1980-88; assoc. then ptnr. Thornton, Summers, Biechlin, Dunham & Brown, LC, San Antonio, 1988—. Bd. dirs. Alamo Children's Adv. Ctr., San Antonio. Fellow Tex. Bar Found.; mem. San Antonio Bar Assn. Roman Catholic. Contracts commercial, Construction, Personal injury. Office: Thornton Summers Biechlin Dunhan & Brown 10100 Reunion Pl Ste 300 San Antonio TX 78216-4128

BAILEY, MICHAEL KEITH, lawyer; b. Washington, Feb. 19, 1956; s. Alda Merrill and Joan (Moyers) B.; m. Linda Ann Braswell, Dec. 18, 1982; children: Julia Anne, David Allen. AB in Econs. and Polit. Sci., Coll. William and Mary, 1978; JD, Stetson U., 1981. Bar: Fla. 1981, U.S. Dist. Ct. (mid. dist.) Fla. 1982, U.S. Ct. Appeals (11th cir.) 1982, U.S. Supreme Ct. 1986. Assoc. Pitts, Eubanks, et al, Orlando, Fla., 1981-86; ptnr. Parrish, Bailey & Myers, P.A., 1986-98, Bailey & Myers, P.A., Maitland, Fla., 1998—. Mem. ABA, ATLA (charter; pres.'s club), So. Trial Lawyers Assn., Def. Rsch. Inst., Orange County Bar Assn., Acad. Fla. Trial Lawyers (eagle patron), Nat. Bd. Trial Adv. (cert. civil trial advocate), Fla. Bar Bd. Ctr. (civil trial atty.). Republican. Presbyterian. General civil litigation, Insurance, Personal injury. Home: 701 E Lake Sue Ave Winter Park FL 32789-5804 Office: Bailey & Myers PA 100 E Sybelia Ave Ste 120 Maitland FL 32751-4777 E-mail: mbailey@baileymyers.com

BAILEY, PATRICIA PRICE, lawyer, former government official; b. Ft. Smith, Ark., June 20, 1937; m. Douglas L. Bailey; 2 children. BA in History cum laude, Lindenwood Coll., 1959; MA in Internat. Affairs, Tufts U., 1960; JD summa cum laude, Am. U., 1976. Bar: D.C., U.S. Ct. Appeals (D.C. cir.), U.S. Ct. Appeals (8th cir.), U.S. Supreme Ct. Editor, rsch. analyst Bur. of Intelligence and Rsch., U.S. Dept. State, 1960-61; exec. asst. Bur. for Latin Am., then asst. to dep. coordinator Alliance for Progress, AID, 1961-66; advisor fgn. affairs Rep. F. Bradford Morse, 1967-68; legal asst. Office of Counsel to Pres. in White House, 1976; spl. asst. to asst. atty. gen. U.S. Dept. Justice, 1977-79; exec. asst. to gen. counsel U.S. Merit systems Protection Bd., 1979; commr. FTC, Washington, 1979-88; ptnr., Squire, Sanders & Dempsey, Washington, 1989—; bd. dirs. Arbella Mut. Ins. Co.; bd. dirs., trustee Avdel PLC; mem. adv. com. Impact of Women in Pub. Office Rutgers U. Eagleton Inst. Politics. Contbr. articles to profl. jours. Bd. dirs. The Washington Ctr., 1987-89, Women's Legal Def. Fund, 1982-83, Lindenwood Coll., Found. for Women's Resources; mem. Dean's Adv. Coun. Washington Coll. Law of Am. U.; mem. Spl. Commn. to Rev. Honor System and Honor Code at West Point, 1988. Recipient Spl. Recognition award Nat. Assn. Attys. Gen., 1987, Philip Hart Pub. Svc. award Consumer Fedn. Am., 1985. Mem. Women's Bar Assn. of D.C. (bd. dirs. 1981-83, bd. dirs. Women's Bar Assn. Found. 1981-83, named Woman Lawyer of Yr., 1988). Office: Squire Sanders & Dempsey PO Box 407 1201 Pennsylvania Ave NW Washington DC 20044

BAILEY, THOMAS ANTHONY, lawyer; b. Milw., Nov. 20, 1942; s. Lawrence C. and Phyllis E. (Croasdaile) B.; m. Barbara Mary Dobbin, June 10, 1967; children: Mary Elizabeth, Kathleen, Erin, Brian, Sean, Bridget, Kevin, Michael. BS in Fin., Marquette U., 1964, JD, 1967; postgrad., U. Va. Law Sch., 1968-70. Bar: Wis. 1967, U.S. Supreme Ct. 1977. Asst. dist. atty. Milw. County, Milw., 1967-68; ptnr. Fricker & Bailey, 1972-92, Bailey Law Offices, Whitefish Bay, Wis., 1992—. Supr. Milw. County Bd., 1979—. Capt., U.S. Army, 1968-72. Fellow Am. Acad. Matrimonial Lawyers; mem. Milw. Bar Assn. (pres. 1984-85, chmn. family law sect.), Wis. Bar Assn., Wis. Acad. Trial Lawyers, St. Thomas More Lawyers Soc. (pres. 1980-81). Home and Office: Bailey Law Offices 130 W Silver Spring Dr Milwaukee WI 53217-4707

BAILEY, THOMAS CHARLES, lawyer; b. Rochester, N.Y., Nov. 26, 1948; s. Charles George and Teckla Barbara (Driscoll) B.; m. Rosalie Stoll, Sept. 24, 1974; children: Leah Isabelle, Molly Driscoll, Elizabeth Rose. BA, Princeton U., 1970; JD, SUNY, Buffalo, 1974. Bar: N.Y. 1975, Fla. 1977. Assoc. Little & Burt, Buffalo, 1974-78, ptnr., 1978-80, Saperston & Day, PC, Buffalo, 1980-92; pvt. practice, 1992-97; mem. Albrecht Maguire Heffern and Gregg PC, 1997-2000, Phillips, Lytle, Hitchcock, Blaine & Huber, LLP, Buffalo, 2000—. Bd. dirs., sec. Buffalo Therapeutic Riding Ctr. Inc., 1999-2001. Pres. St. Thomas Moore Guild, 1981; trustee Shea's O'Connell Preservation Guild, 1986-96, chmn., 1994; bd. dirs. Opera Niagara, Ltd., 1999—, pres., 2001-. Mem. ABA, N.Y. State Bar Assn. (exec. com. of real property law sect. 1994-2000), Fla. Bar Assn., Am. Assn. Franchisees and Dealers (fair franchising standards com.), Saturn

Club (dean 2000), Princeton U. Alumni Assn. Western N.Y. (pres. 1990-91), Brookhaven Trout Club. Avocations: fly fishing, boating, horses. General corporate, Franchising, Real property. Office: Phillips Lytle et al 3400 HSBC Tower Buffalo NY 14203

BAILLIE, JAMES LEONARD, lawyer; b. Mpls., Aug. 27, 1942; s. Leonard Thompson and Sylvia Alfreda (Fundberg) B.; m. Constance Samson, June 19, 1965; children: Jennifer, Craig, John. AB in History, 1964; JD, U. Chgo., 1967. Bar: Minn. 1967, U.S. Dist. Ct. Minn. 1968, U.S. Ct. Appeals (8th cir.) 1969, U.S. Ct. Appeals (5th cir.) 1980. Law clk. to presiding justice U.S. Dist. Ct., Mpls., 1967-68; assoc. Fredrikson & Byron, P.A., 1968-73, shareholder, 1973—. Mem. ABA (litigation sect. co-editor Bankruptcy Litigation 1998, bus. law sect. editl. bd. Bus. Law Today 1993-98, bus. sect. chair pro bono com. 1999—, standing com. on lawyer pub. svc. responsibility 1991-96, chmn. 1993-96, nat. pro bono award 1984, John Minor Wisdom award 1999), Minn. State Bar Assn. (chmn. bankruptcy sect. 1985-88, sec. 2000-01, treas. 2001-02) Hennepin County Bar Assn. (sec. 1992-93, treas. 1993-95, pres.-elect 1995-96, pres. 1996-97). Bankruptcy, General civil litigation, Contracts commercial. Home: 2851 E Lake Of The Isles Pky Minneapolis MN 55408-1055 Office: Fredrikson & Byron PA 1100 Internat Ctr 900 2nd Ave S Minneapolis MN 55402-3314 E-mail: jbaillie@fredlaw.com

BAIN, JAMES WILLIAM, lawyer; b. Suffern, N.Y., Dec. 19, 1949; s. William James and Agnes (Hoey) B.; m. Colleen K., Mar. 23, 1974; children: Rebecca, Meghan. BA, U. Conn., 1972; JD, U. Fla., 1976. Bar: Fla. 1977, U.S. Dist. Ct. (ea. dist.) Tenn. 1980, Tenn. 1984, U.S. Ct. Appeals (11th cir.) 1984, U.S. Ct. Appeals (D.C. cir.) 1984, Colo. 1986, U.S. Dist. Ct. Colo 1986, U.S. Ct. Appeals (10th cir.) 1988, U.S. Supreme Ct. 1998. Atty. trial Tenn. Valley Authority, Knoxville, 1977-85; atty. dir. Roath & Brega, P.C., Denver, 1985-89, Brega & Winters, P.C., Denver, 1989—. Instr. U. Fla., Gainesville, 1976, U. Colo., Boulder, 1987-90; seminar chmn. Inst. for Advanced Legal Study, Denver, 1987. Contbr. articles to profl. jours.; editor constrn. law column Colo. Lawyer. Recipient Civil Litigation Writing award for 1986-87, Denver Colo. Bar Assn., 1987. Mem. ATLA, Colo. Bar Assn., Fla. Bar Assn., Am. Judicature Soc., Am. Arbitration Assn. (arbitrator 1986), Internat. Platform Assn. Avocations: soccer, skiing, biking, basketball. Federal civil litigation, State civil litigation, Construction. Office: Brega & Winters PC 1700 Lincoln St Ste 2222 Denver CO 80203-4522

BAINBRIDGE, JOHN SEAMAN, retired law school administrator, law educator, lawyer; b. N.Y.C., Nov. 1, 1915; s. William Seaman and June Ellen (Wheeler) B.; m. Katharine Barker Garrett, Feb. 3, 1943 (div. July 24, 1968); 1 son, John Seaman; m. 2d, Elizabeth Kung-Ji Liu, May 13, 1978. B.S., Harvard U., 1938; LL.B., J.D., Columbia U., 1941. Bar: N.Y. 1941, Md. 1946, U.S. Dist. Ct. Md. 1946, U.S. Supreme Ct. 1946, U.S. Dist. Ct. (so. dist.) N.Y. 1948. Gen. practice law, Md. and N.Y., 1945-56; asst. dean Columbia U. Law Sch., 1956-65, assoc. dir. Internat. Fellows Program, 1960-62, asst. to pres. Columbia U., 1965-66; dir. Project on Staffing of African Instns. of Legal Edn. and Research, 1962-72; assoc. dir. Ctr. for Adminstrn. of Justice, Wayne State U., Detroit, 1972-74; dir. planning Sch. Law, Pace U., Westchester County, N.Y., 1974-76; assoc. dean, dean, prof. law No. Ill. U. Coll. Law, Glen Ellyn, 1976-81; vis. prof., assoc. dean Del. Law Sch., Wilmington, 1981-82; dean, prof. law Touro Coll. Sch. Law, Huntington, N.Y., 1982-85; cons. Edward John Noble Found., 1959-61, Inst. Internat. Edn., 1962-67; mem. adv. com. Peace Corps Lawyers Project, 1963; founder, dir. African Law Assn. in Am., Inc., 1965-72. Served to lt. comdr. USNR, 1940-46. Mem. ABA, Sons of Revolution, S.R. Presbyterian. Club: Harvard (N.Y.C.). Author: The Study and Teaching of Law in Africa, 1972. Home: 17 Ringfield Rd Chadds Ford PA 19317-9130

BAIR, BRUCE B. lawyer; b. St. Paul, May 26, 1928; s. Bruce B. and Emma N. (Stone) B.; m. Jane Lawler, July 19, 1952; children: Mary Jane, Thomas, Susan, Barbara, Patricia, James, Joan, Bruce, Jeffrey. BS, U. N.D., 1950, JD, 1952. Bar: N.D. 1952, U.S. Dist. Ct. N.D. 1955, U.S. Ct. Appeals (8th cir.) 1971, U.S. Supreme Ct. 1974. Assoc. Lord and Ulmer, Mandan, N.D., 1955-57; ptnr. Bair, Bair, Garrity and Kelsch, 1957—. Spl. asst. atty. gen. N.D. Milk Mktg. Bd., 1967—; chmn. bd. Bank of Tioga, 1984—, also dir. Rep. precinct committeeman, 1956-70, chmn. Morton County Rep. Com., 1958-62, mem. N.D. Rep. State Cen. Com., 1962-67; pres. sch. bd. St. Joseph's Cath. Ch., 1967-68; bd. dirs. Mandan Pub. Sch. Dist. #1, 1971-77; exec. com. Internat. Assn. Milk Control Agys., 1970-2000; bd. regents U. Mary, Bismarck, N.D., 1984— 1st lt. JAG Corps USAF, 1952-55. Fellow Am. Coll. Trust and Estate Counsel; mem. ABA, N.D. Bar Assn., Big Muddy Bar Assn., Am. Legion, Rotary, Elks. Roman Catholic. General civil litigation, Estate planning, Probate. Home: 901 3rd St NW Mandan ND 58554-2537 Office: 210 1st St NW Mandan ND 58554-3115

BAIRD, CHARLES BRUCE, lawyer, consultant; b. DeLand, Fla., Apr. 18, 1935; s. James Turner and Ethelyn Isabelle (Williams) B.; m. Barbara Ann Fabian, June 6, 1959 (div. Dec. 1979); children: C. Bruce Jr., Robert Arthur, Bryan James; m. Byung-Ran Cho, May 23, 1982; children: Merah-Iris, Haerah Violet. BSME, U. Miami, 1958; postgrad., UCLA, 1962-64; MBA, Calif. State U., 1966; JD, Am. U., 1971. Bar: Va. 1971, U.S. Dist. Ct. (ea. dist.) Va. 1971, D.C. 1973, U.S. Dist. Ct. D.C. 1973, U.S. Ct. Appeals (4th cir.) 1974, U.S. Supreme Ct. 1975. Rsch. engr. Naval Ordnance Lab., Corona, Calif., 1961-67; aerospace engr. Naval Air Systems Command, Washington, 1967-69; cons. engr. Bird Engring. Rsch. Assts., Vienna, 1969-71; prof. Def. Systems Mgmt. Coll., Ft. Belvoir, 1982; spl. asst. for policy compliance USIA Voice of Am., Washington, 1983-84. Cons. Booz, Allen & Hamilton, Inc., Bethesda, 1975-82, IBM, Bethesda, Md., 1984, Logistics Mgmt. Inst., McLean, Va., 1986-98, TelcoExchange.com, 1998-2000, 2001; adj. prof. Fla. Inst. Tech., 1988. Contbr. articles to profl. jours.; inventor computer-based comm. systems for the gravely handicapped. Bd. govs. Sch. Engring. U. Miami, 1957; trustee Galilee United Meth. Ch., Arlington, Va., 1983-87. Mem. Va. Trial Lawyers Assn., Internet. Soc., Fed. Comm. Bar Assn., United We Stand Am. (founding mem.), Sigma Alpha Epsilon. Home and Office: 5396 Gainsborough Dr Fairfax VA 22032-2744

BAIRD, DOUGLAS GORDON, law educator, dean; b. Phila., July 10, 1953; s. Henry Welles and Eleanora (Gordon) B. BA, Yale U., 1975; JD, Stanford U., 1979; LLD, U. Rochester, 1994. Law clk. U.S. Ct. Appeals (9th cir.), 1979, 80; asst. prof. law U. Chgo., 1980-83, prof. law, 1984—, assoc. dean, 1984-87, Bigelow prof. law, 1988—, dean, 1994-99. Author: (with others) Security Interests in Personal Property, 1984, 2d edit., 1987, Bankruptcy, 1985, 3d edit., 2000, Elements of Bankruptcy, 1992, 3d edit., 2001; (D. Baird, R. Gertner, R. Picker) Game Theory and the Law, 1994. Mem. AAAS, Order of Coif. E-mail: douglas. Office: U Chgo Sch Law 1111 E 60th St Chicago IL 60637-2776 E-mail: baird@law.uchicago.edu

BAIRD, THOMAS BRYAN, JR. lawyer; b. Newport News, Va., June 21, 1931; s. Thomas Bryan and Mary Florence (Rieker) B.; m. Mildred Katherine Clark, June 23, 1956; children: Sarah, Thomas Bryan III, William, Laura. BA, U. Va., 1952; LLB, U. Tenn., 1960. Bar: Tenn. 1964, Va. 1969, U.S. Dist. Ct. (we. dist.) 1970. With Stat Farm Ins., Knoxville, Tenn., 1960-68; asst. commonwealth atty. Wytheville, Va., 1969-71; commonwealth atty. Wythe County, 1972-98; prin. Thomas B. Baird, Jr. Trustee Simmerman Home for the Aged, 1972-83. Served with U.S. Army, 1953-55. Democrat. Presbyterian. Criminal, Insurance, Real property. Home: 875 N 18th St Wytheville VA 24382-1022

BAIRSTOW, RICHARD RAYMOND, retired lawyer; b. Waukegan, Ill., Sept. 26, 1917; s. Fred Raymond and Mildred (Wright) B.; m. Mary Kelley, Aug. 8, 1942 (dec. June 19, 1979); children: Kathleen Bairstow Young, Suzanne Bairstow Hicks, Mary Bairstow Neely; m. Agnes Macaitis Caldwell, July 22, 1980 (dec. July 22, 1995). AB, U. Ill., 1939, JD, 1947; postgrad., George Washington U., 1939-41. Bar: Ill. 1947, U.S. Dist. Ct. (no. dist.) Ill. 1964, U.S. Ct. Mil. Appeals 1963, U.S. SUpreme Ct. 1963. Assoc. Hall, Meyer & Carey, Waukegan, 1947-49; asst. state's atty. Lake County, 1949-53; ptnr. McClory & Bairstow, 1953-60, McClory, Bairstow, Lonchar & Nordigan, Waukegan, 1960-66; prin. Richard R. Bairstow & Assocs., 1966-98; ret., 1998. Dist. atty. Fox Lake Fire Protection Dist., Ingleside, Ill., 1948-98; adminstrv. law judge Ill. Dept. Revenue, Chgo., 1953-87. Bd. dirs. ARC, Lake County, 1947-73; mem., pres. Salvation Army, Waukegan, 1954-66; bd. dirs. Lake County Family YMCA, 1990-91. Col. AUS, 1941-46, ETO, USAR, 1946-71, ret. U.S. Army Command and Gen. Staff Coll., 1965. Mem. ABA, Ill. Lake County Bar Assn., Assn. U.S. Army, The Ret. Officers Assn., Am. Legion, Glen Flora Country Club, Waukegan City Club, Elks, Delta Tau Delta, Phi Alpha Delta. Republican. Episcopalian. General practice, Probate, Real property. Home: 2122 Ash St Waukegan IL 60087-5033

BAKER, ANITA DIANE, lawyer; b. Atlanta, Sept. 4, 1955; d. Byron Garnett and Anita (Swanson) B.; m. Thomas Johnstone Robison III, Sept. 26, 1995. BA summa cum laude, Oglethorpe U., 1977; JD with distinction, Emory U., 1980. Bar: Ga. 1980. Assoc. Hansell & Post, Atlanta, 1980-88, Kitchens, Kelley, Gaynes, Huprich & Shmerling, 1989-90; asst. gen. counsel NationsBank Corp., 1991-97; v.p., gen. counsel Adaris Corp., 1997-99; pvt. practice Atlanta, 1999—. Mem. Ga. Bar Assn., Atlanta Bar Assn., Ga. Assn. Women Lawyers, Atlanta Hist. Soc., Concourse Athletic Club, Ga. Alliance of Private Clubs, Pace Acad. Alumni Assn., Oglethorpe U. Alumni Assn., Stormy Petrel Bar Assn., Order of Coif, Phi Alpha Delta, Phi Alpha Theta, Alpha Chi, Omicron Delta Kappa. Contracts commercial, General corporate, Probate. Office: 1144 Canton St Ste 100 Roswell GA 30075 E-mail: dianebaker@adblaw.com

BAKER, BRUCE JAY, lawyer; b. Chgo., June 18, 1954; s. Kenneth and Beverly (Gould) B. Student, U. Leeds, Eng., 1974-75; BS, U. Ill., 1976; JD, Washington U., 1979. Bar: Ill. 1979, U.S. Dist. Ct. (no. dist.) Ill. 1984. Asst. atty. gen. antitrust divsn. State of Ill., Chgo., 1979-83; assoc. Mass, Miller & Josephson Ltd., 1983-86; sr. counsel Discover Card Services Inc., Riverwoods, Ill., 1986-89; sr. legis. counsel Dean Witter Fin. Svcs. Group, 1989-91; gen. counsel Ill. Commr. Banks and Trust Cos., Chgo., 1991-94; ptnr. Schiff Hardin & Waite, 1994-99, of counsel, 1999-2001, Barak, Ferrazzano, Kirschbaum, Perlman & Nagelberg, Chgo., 2001—; sr. v.p., gen. counsel Ill. Bankers Assn., 1999—. Contbr. articles to profl. jours. Registered lobbyist Ill. Legislature, Springfield, 1985-91, 94—. Named Ill. State scholar, 1972. Mem. ABA (antitrust com., banking com., chmn. state banking law devels. task force 1998—), Ill. State Bar Assn. (comml. banking and bankruptcy sect.), Chgo. Bar Assn. (fin. insts. com.), Ill. Bankers Assn. (legis. counsel 1985-86, gen. counsel 1994—, Disting. Bank Counsel award 1991, 97). Office: Ill Bankers Assn 111 W Jackson Blvd Ste 910 Chicago IL 60604-3502 also: Barack Ferrazzano Et Al 333 W Wacker Dr Ste 2700 Chicago IL 60606 E-mail: bbaker@ilbanker.com

BAKER, CAMERON, lawyer; b. Chgo., Dec. 24, 1937; s. David Cameron and Marion (Fitzpatrick) B.; m. Katharine Julia Solari, Sept. 2, 1961; children: Cameron III, Ann, John. Student, U. Notre Dame, 1954-57; AB, Stanford U., 1958; LLB, U. Calif., Berkeley, 1961. Bar: Calif. 1962, U.S. Dist. Ct. (so. dist.) Calif. 1962, U.S. Dist. Ct. (no. dist.) Calif. 1963, U.S. Ct. Appeals (9th) 1963. With Adams, Duque & Hazeltine, Los Angeles, 1961-62, Pettit & Martin, San Francisco, 1962-95, mng. ptnr., 1972-81, 84-87, exec. com., 1971-82, 84-88; with Farella, Braun & Martel, 1995—. Mayor City of Belvedere, Calif., 1978-79; owner Larkmead Vineyards, Napa Valley, Calif. Dir. Lassen Nat. Park Found., 1992—. Mem. ABA (sects. on bus. law and internat. law and practice), Calif. Bar Assn. (sect. bus., real property and internat. law), Bar Assn. San Francisco (bd. dirs. 1966, 72-73), Boalt Hall Alumni Assn. (dir. 1982-84), Bohemian Club, Tiburon Peninsula Club. General corporate, Private international, Mergers and acquisitions. Home: 38 Alcatraz Ave Belvedere CA 94920-2504 Office: Farella Braun Martel LLP 235 Montgomery St Fl 30 San Francisco CA 94104-2902 E-mail: cbaker@fbm.com

BAKER, CHARLES GEORGE, solicitor; b. London, Mar. 24, 1949; s. Geoffrey Harding and Valerie Stirling B.; m. Ragnhild Wilmann Nybo, June 22, 1974; children: Thomas, George, Simon. MA, Cambridge U., Eng., 1971. Cert. solicitor Supreme Ct. Eng., Wales, 1974. Trainee Clifford-Turner & Co., London, 1972-74, asst. solicitor, 1974, Holman, Fenwick & Willan, London, Paris, 1974-77, ptnr., 1978-89, Herbert Smith, London, 1989-99, Lawrence Graham, London, 1999—. Contbr. articles to profl. jours.; spkr. Internat. Congress Maritime Arbitrators, ABA, Maritime Law Assn. Australia and New Zealand, Tulane U., Lloyd's of London Maritime Law seminars, London Shipping Law Ctr. Gunner Hon. Arty. Co., 1972-76, London. Mem. Internat. C. of C. (arbitrator). Avocations: skiing, rugby football, golf, wine. Admiralty, Contracts commercial, Oil, gas, and mineral. Office: Lawrence Graham 61 St Mary Axe London EC3A 8JN England Fax: 44 20 7480 5156. E-mail: cg.baker@btinternet.com, charles.baker@lawgram.com

BAKER, DAVID REMEMBER, lawyer; b. Durham, N.C., Jan. 17, 1932; s. Roger Denio and Eleanor Elizabeth (Ussher) B.; m. Myra Augusta Mullins, Nov. 2, 1955 PhB, U. Chgo., 1949; BA, Birmingham-So. Coll., 1951; JD, Harvard U., 1954. Bar: Ala. 1954, N.Y. 1963, U.S. Supreme Ct. 1972. Assoc. Cabaniss & Johnston, Birmingham, Ala., 1957-62, Chadbourne, Parke, Whiteside & Wolff, N.Y.C., 1962-66, ptnr., 1967-86, Jones, Day, Reavis & Pogue, N.Y.C., 1986-93, ret. ptnr., 1993—; ptnr. Afridi, Angell & Baker, 1993-96, Gersen, Baker & Wood LLP, N.Y.C., 1997-98, Baker, Johnston & Wilson LLP, Birmingham and N.Y.C., 1998—; gen. counsel Econ. Club of N.Y., N.Y.C., 1977—. Co-editor Due Diligence, Disclosures and Warranties in the Corporate Acquisition Practice, 1988, 2d edit., 1992; author articles and book chpts. Pres. N.Y. Legis. Svc., N.Y.C., 1975-98, chmn., 1998—; mem. adv. com. Ctr. for N.Y.C. Law, 2000—; sec., dir. Jr. Achievement of N.Y., 1973-99; dir. Jr. Achievement of Greater Birmingham, 1999—; trustee Birmingham-So. Coll., 1985—. With U.S. Army, 1954-57. Mem.: ABA (liaison com. fin. acctg. stds. bd.), Am. Arbitration Assn. (nat. panel), Am. Law Inst., Am. Fgn. Law Assn., Am. Judicature Soc., Assn. Bar City N.Y. (chmn. com. on state legis. 1968—70), Ala. Bar Assn., Birmingham Bar Assn., Internat. Bar Assn. (vice chmn. bd. orgn. com. 1986—90, chmn. com. on trusts for bus. 1990—94, rep. to U.S. mems. N.Y. area 1988—2000, prin. rep. to UN in N.Y. 1993—, N.Am. adv. bd.), Internat. Law Assn., Assn. Lloyd's Mems., N.Y. State Bar Assn. (exec. com. bus. law sect. 1987—89, exec. com. internat. law and practice sect. 1991—92, chmn. internat. investment and devel. com. 1991—92), Internat. Ins. Soc., Musica Viva N.Y. (pres. 1994—96), Birmingham Athletic Club, Harvard Club N.Y.C., Met. Club N.Y.C. Democrat. Unitarian. Avocation: bridge (life master Am. Contract Bridge League). Private international, Mergers and acquisitions, Securities. Home: 1200 Beacon Pkwy E Apt 500 Birmingham AL 35209-1041 also: 315 E 72d St Apt 2-J New York NY 10021-4626 Office: Baker Johnston & Wilson LLP 1 Independence Plz Ste 322 Birmingham AL 35209-2634 also: 26th Fl 641 Lexington Ave New York NY 10022-4503 E-mail: drb@bakerjohnston.com

BAKER, FREDERICK MILTON, JR. lawyer; b. Flint, Mich., Nov. 2, 1949; s. Frederick Milton Baker and Mary Jean (Hallitt) Rarig; m. Irene Taylor; children: Jessica, Jordan. BA, U. Mich., 1971; JD, Washington U., St. Louis, 1975. Bar: Mich. 1975, U.S. Dist. Ct. (we. dist.) Mich. 1980, U.S. Dist. Ct. (ea. dist.) Mich. 1981, U.S. Ct. Appeals (6th cir.) 1983, U.S. Supreme Ct. 1986. Instr. law Wayne State U., Detroit, 1975-76; research atty. Mich. Ct. Appeals, Lansing, 1976-77, law clk. to chief judge, 1977; asst. prof. T.M. Cooley Law Sch., Mich., 1978-80; ptnr. Willingham & Cote, 1980-86, Honigman, Miller, Schwartz & Cohn, Lansing, 1986—. Adj. prof. Detroit Coll. Law Mich. State U., East Lansing, 2001—. Author: Michigan Bar Appeal Manual, 1982; editor Mich. Bar Jour., 1984—; contbr. articles to profl. jours. Founder, pres. Sixty Plus Law Ctr., Lansing, 1978-87, bd. dirs., 1987—; mem. community adv. bd. Lansing Jr. League, 1983-90; co-founder, dir., sec.-treas. John D. Voelker Found., 1989—; bd. dirs. Lansing chpt. ACLU, 1997—, bd. dirs. Greater Lansing chpt., 1997-99; treas. Kehillat Israel, 1996-98; trustee Thoman Found., 2000—. Recipient Disting. Brief award T.M. Cooley Law Rev., 1988, 99. Fellow Mich. State Bar Found.; mem. ABA (Outstanding Single Project award 1980, Disting. brief award 1988, 99, T.M. Cooley L. Rev.), Mich. Bar Assn. (vice chmn. jour. adv. bd. 1984-87, chmn. jour. adv. bd. 1987—, young lawyers sect. coun. 1980-84, grievance com. 1982-84, John W. Cummiskey award 1984), Ingham County Bar Assn. (Disting. Vol. award 2000). Unitarian. Club: Big Oak (Baldwin, Mich.). Avocations: photography, fishing, running, frisbee, squash. Federal civil litigation, State civil litigation, Insurance. Home: 5127 Barton Rd Williamston MI 48895-9304 Office: Honigman Miller Schwartz & Cohn 222 N Washington Sq Ste 400 Lansing MI 48933-1800 E-mail: fmb@honigman.com

BAKER, GAIL DYER, lawyer; b. West Point, N.Y, Mar. 16, 1954; s. Hillier Locke Jr. and Miriam Jane (Dyer) B. BA magna cum laude, U. Minn., 1978; JD, Suffolk U., 1981. Bar: Minn. 1981, U.S. Dist. Ct. Minn. 1981. Assoc. R.C. Ploetz & Assocs., Mpls., 1981-82; exec. dir., staff atty. Legal Assistance of Olmsted County, Rochester, Minn., 1982-85; assoc. Steward, Perry, Mahler & Bird, P.A., 1985-87, Ryan & VanDerHeyden, Rochester, 1987-88, Ryan & Grinde Ltd., Rochester, 1988-89; ptnr. Baker Law Offices, 1989—. Mem. task force on adoption and foster care Minn. Supreme Ct., 1996-97; co-chair Children in Need of Protection and Svcs. Rules Commn., 1997-99. Mem.: ABA (dist. rep. young lawyers divsn. 1985—87, publs. chmn. 1987—90, vice chmn. child adv. 1985—90, mem. pub.devel. bd.family law sect. 1989—, mediation com. 1989—90, children and law task force 1989—, task force creating atty. standards for child neglect and abuse cases 1994—96, steering com on unmet legal needs of children 1998—), Minn. Bar Assn. (family law sect., coach h.s. mock trials 1990—98), Olmsted County Bar Assn (treas. 1984—86, chair law day 1983—84, chair Bicentennial of Constitution 1988, v.p. 1996—97, pres. 1997—98, sec. 1999—2001), U. Minn. Alumni Assn., Phi Beta Kappa, Phi Delta Phi. Republican. Presbyterian. Family and matrimonial, General practice, Juvenile. Home: 1412 Berkman Ct SE Rochester MN 55904-4934 Office: Baker Law Offices Ste 210 1530 Greenview Dr SW Rochester MN 55902 E-mail: gboffice@millcomm.com

BAKER, GARY HUGH, lawyer; b. Broken Arrow, Okla., Nov. 18, 1947; s. Theodore Roosevelt and Maxine Gladys (Smittle) B.; m. Karen Louise DeLong, Aug. 29, 1970; 1 child, Katherine Elizabeth. B.A. with highest honors, U. Okla., 1970; J.D., U. Chgo., 1973. Bar: Okla. 1973, U.S. Dist. Cts. (no., we. and ea. dists.) Okla. 1973, U.S. Ct. Appeals (10th cir.) 1975. With Conner, Winters, Ballaine, Barry & McGowen Assocs., Tulsa, 1973-79, ptnr., 1979-81; ptnr. Baker & Hoster, Tulsa, 1981-97, dir. Crowe & Dunlevy, 1997—; dir. Legal Svc. Eastern Okla., Tulsa, 1980-84. Mem. Citizen's Coalition for Community Devel., Tulsa, 1980. Mem. Tulsa County Bar Assn. (sec. 1981, Outstanding Young Lawyer award 1979), Tulsa County Young Lawyers Assn. (chmn. 1979), Okla. Bar Assn. (banking Com. 1981—). Banking, Contracts commercial, Private international. Home: 28050 Us Highway 19 N Ste 201 Clearwater FL 33761-2627 Office: Crowe & Dumlevy 500 Kennedy Bldg Tulsa OK 74103

BAKER, GORDON EDWARD, political science educator; b. Poughkeepsie, N.Y., Dec. 6, 1923; s. Gordon Denzil and Emma (Calhoun) B.; m. June Sharpe, Sept. 2, 1947; children: Jefferson, Leslie Marie. BA, Reed Coll., 1948; MA, U. Wash., 1949; postgrad., Brown U., 1950; PhD, Princeton U., 1952. Mem. faculty U. Calif., Santa Barbara, 1952—, prof. polit. sci., 1965-93, chmn. dept., 1965-71, prof. emeritus, 1993—. Dir. NEH seminars, 1979, 80; spl. cons., Calif., 1973, 91. Author: Rural Versus Urban Political Power, 1955, The Reapportionment Revolution, 1966; co-author: Free Government in the Making, 1985; contbr. chpts. in books and articles to profl. jours. Mem. 20th Century Fund Conf. Rsch. Scholars and Polit. Scientists in Legis. Apportionment, 1962. Served with AUS, 1943-46. Guggenheim fellow, 1969; Social Sci. Rsch. Coun. faculty rsch. fellow, 1962. Mem. Am. Polit. Sci. Assn. (coun. 1968-70, exec. com. 1968-69), Nat. Mcpl. League. Office: U Calif at Santa Barbara Dept Polit Sci Santa Barbara CA 93106

BAKER, HERMAN DUPREE, lawyer; b. Statham, Ga., Apr. 18, 1928; s. William Grady and Mary O. (Gauntt) B.; m. Esther May Deal, May 17, 1953; children: Cynthia Jane Buchanan, Gloria Ann Baker Fondren, Joyce Hazel. AB, Mercer U., 1949, JD, 1952. Bar: Ga. 1965. Investigator U.S. Civil Svc. Commn., Augusta, Ga., 1953-59; asst. v.p. claims Pub. Savs. Ins. Co., Charleston, S.C., 1960-63; criminal investigator IRS, Atlanta, 1963-69, estate tax atty., 1969-76, appeals officer, 1976-86; pvt. practice probate and tax atty., 1986—. Chmn. fin. com., 1st Bapt. Ch., Decatur, Ga., 1982—. Served to comdr. USNR, 1945-46, PTO. Mem. Fed. Bar, State Bar Ga. Home: 2285 Winding Woods Dr Tucker GA 30084-3934 Office: 545 N McDonough St Ste 201 Decatur GA 30030 Fax: 404-377-8304. E-mail: hdbaker700@aol.com

BAKER, JAMES A. state supreme court justice; b. Evansville, Ind., Mar. 30, 1931; BBA, So. Meth. U., 1953, LLB, 1958. Bar: Tex. 1958, U.S. Dist. Ct. (no. dist.) Tex. 1958, U.S. Ct. Appeals (5th cir.) 1961, U.S. Ct. Appeals (11th cir.) 1981, U.S. Supreme Ct. 1980. Atty. Goldberg, Alexander and Baker, 1958-72, Weber, Baker and Allums, 1972-79; prin. Law Office of James A. Baker, 1979-86; judge U.S. Ct. Appeals (5th cir.), Dallas, 1986-95; justice Supreme Ct. of Tex., Austin, 1995—. Lectr. State Bar of Tex. Profl. Devel. Program; guest lectr. So. Meth. U. Sch. Law, Dallas Bar Assn., El Centro Dalls C.C. Contbg. author Tex. Collection Manual, 1980. Fellow Tex. Bar Found., Dallas Bar Found.; mem. ABA (mem. task force on appellate delay reduction 1991-92), State Bar Tex., Dallas Bar Assn. (former chair bankruptcy and comml. law sect. 1974, bd. dirs. 1995), Coll. of State Bar Tex., Am. Judicature Soc., Inst. Judicial Adminstrn., William Mac Taylor Jr. Inn of Ct. Office: Supreme Ct Bldg 201 W 14th Rm 104 PO Box 12248 Austin TX 78711-2248*

BAKER, JAMES EDWARD SPROUL, retired lawyer; b. Evanston, Ill., May 23, 1912; s. John Clark and Hester (Sproul) B.; m. Eleanor Lee Dodgson, Oct. 2, 1937 (dec. Sept. 1972); children: John Lee, Edward Graham (dec. Aug. 1988). A.B., Northwestern U., 1933, J.D., 1936. Bar: Ill. 1936, U.S. Supreme Ct. 1957. Practice in, Chgo., 1936—; assoc. Sidley & Austin, and predecessors, 1936-48, ptnr., 1948-81; of counsel Sidley & Austin, 1981-93. Lectr. Northwestern U. Law Sch., 1951-52; nat. chmn. Stanford U. Parents Com., 1970-75; mem. vis. com. Stanford Law Sch., 1976-79, 82-84, Northwestern U. Law Sch., 1980-89, DePaul U. Law Sch., 1982-87. Served to comdr. USNR, 1941-46. Fellow Am. Coll. Trial Lawyers (regent 1974-81, sec. 1977-79, pres. 1979-80); mem. ABA, Bar Assn. 7th Fed. Circuit, Ill. State Bar Assn., Chgo. Bar Assn., Soc. Trial Lawyers Ill., Northwestern U. Law Alumni Assn. (past pres.), Order of Coif, Phi Lambda Upsilon, Sigma Nu. Epublican. Methodist. Clubs: John

Evans (Northwestern U.) (chmn. 1982-85); University (Chgo.); John Henry Wigmore (past pres.); Legal (Chgo.), Law (Chgo.) (pres. 1983-85); Westmoreland Country (Wilmette, Ill.), Pauma Valley Country (Calif.). Home: 1300 N Lake Shore Dr Chicago IL 60610-2169 Office: Sidley & Austin Bank One Plz 10 S Dearborn St Chicago IL 60603

BAKER, KEITH LEON, lawyer; b. Columbus, Ind., Jan. 22, 1950; s. Richard Leon and Sarah Elizabeth (Wisehart) B. A.B., Princeton U., 1972; J.D., Syracuse U., 1975; LL.M. with highest honors, George Washington U., 1978. Bar: N.Y. 1976, D.C. 1976, U.S. Ct. Appeals (D.C. cir.) 1983, U.S. Ct. Internat. Trade 1983. Asst. bank examiner U.S. Treasury Dept., N.Y.C., 1974; law clk. U.S. Dept. of Justice, Syracuse, N.Y., 1974-75; atty.-adviser GAO, Washington, 1975-78; atty.-adviser U.S. EPA, Washington, 1978-80; assoc. Brownstein, Zeidman & Schomer, Washington, 1980-82; ptnr. Trammell, Chase & Lambert, Washington, 1982-84, Barnett & Alagia, Washington, 1984-89, Eckert, Seamans, Cherin & Mellott, 1989—. Author: Small Business Financing, 1983; contbr. articles to profl. jours. Mem. ABA, Fed. Bar Assn., Nat. Contract Mgmt. Assn. Methodist. General corporate, Government contracts and claims, Private international. Home: 6645 Hawthorne St Mc Lean VA 22101-4423 Office: Eckert Seamans Cherin & Mellott 2100 Pennsylvania Ave NW Washington DC 20037-3202

BAKER, MARK BRUCE, lawyer, educator; b. Bridgeport, Conn., Dec. 27, 1946; s. Phillip and Lillian (Islovitz) Bader; m. Sandra Fay Wolf, June 9, 1968 (div. 1982); 1 dau. Rachel Barrett Bader; m. Nora Kay Mandell, Dec. 30, 1984; 1 dau. Lisa Anne Baker. BBA, U. Miami, Coral Gables, Fla., 1968; JD, So. Meth. U., 1974. Bar: Tex. 1974. Assoc. firm Herndon, Girand and Dooley, Dallas, 1974-76; ptnr. firm Pailet and Bader, 1976-80; prof. internat. law U. Tex., Austin, 1980—; of counsel firm Bard and Groves, Houston, 1981-83; gen. counsel Embree Constrn. Group, Inc., Austin, Tex., 1987—; of counsel Goodall, Davison and Goldsmith, 1991—. Chmn. bd. Embree Health Care Group, Inc. Contbr. articles to legal publs. Bd. dirs. Jewish Cmty. Coun. Austin, 1983-86. Recipient Outstanding Asst. Prof. award U. Tex., 1982, Outstanding Class Lectr. award, 1984, Tex. Excellence Tchg. award U. Tex. Alumni Assn., 1983. Mem. ABA, Union Internat. des Avocats, Am. Friends Wilton Park (sec.-treas. 1982-84), Tex. Bar Assn. (internat. law sect.), Austin Fgn. Trade Coun., Am. Bus. Law Assn. (internat. law sect., pres. 1990-91). Home: 406 Brookhaven Trl Austin TX 78746-5413 Office: Bldg 2 Ste 400 1250 Capital of Tx Hwy S Austin TX 78746 E-mail: m.baker@mail.utexas.edu

BAKER, PATRICIA (JEAN), lawyer, mediator; b. June 28, 1948; BS summa cum laude, Wright State U., Dayton, Ohio, 1973; MBA, Northeastern U., Boston, 1989; JD, Calif. Western U., San Diego, 1993. Bar: Calif. 1993; cert. mediator. With GenRad Inc., Boston, 1974-82; mktg./sales staff GE Co., 1982-84; major accounts mgr. Fluke Mfg. Co., 1984-89; pub. rels. mgr. Racal Dana, Irvine, Calif., 1989-90; legal intern Pub. Defenders Dependancy, San Diego, 1992; law clk. Civil divsn. U.S. Atty., 1992; personal injury atty. L.H. Parker, Long Beach, Calif., 1993; mediator/atty. Baker & Assocs., San Diego, 1993-94; dir. Orange County region Am. Arbitration Assn., Irvine, 1994-97, v.p. Washington, 1997—. Mediator San Diego Mediation Ctr., 1993-97; trainer mediation skills Am. Arbitration Assn., 1994-97; adj. prof. Western State U., Irvine, 1995-96; MCLE presenter San Diego County Bar, 1994, State Bar of Calif., 1996, ABA, 1997; mediator Superior Ct., San Diego, 1994-97, U.S. Bankruptcy Ct. (cen. dist.) Calif., 1995-97; adj. prof. Columbus Sch. of Law, Washington, 1997—. Bd. dirs. Legal Aid Soc., San Diego, 1994, T. Homann Law Assn., San Diego, 1994. Recipient Am. Jurisprudence awards, 1992/ Mem. ABA (ADR sect.), D.C. Bar Assn., State Bar of Calif., San Diego County Bar Assn. (ADR sect.), Energy Bar Assn. (chmn. ADR com.), So. Calif. Mediation Assn. Avocations: tennis, golf. E-mial. E-mail: BakerJ@adr.org

BAKER, RICHARD SOUTHWORTH, lawyer; b. Lansing, Mich., Dec. 18, 1929; s. Paul Julius and Florence (Schmid) B.; m. Kathleen E. Yull, 1956 (dec. 1964); m. Marina J. Vidoli, 1965 (div. 1989); children: Garrick Richard, Lydia Joy; m. Barbara J. Walker, 1997. Student, DePauw U., 1947-49; AB cum laude, Harvard, 1951; JD, U. Mich., 1954. Bar: Ohio 1957, U.S. Dist. Ct. (no. dist.) Ohio 1958, U.S. Tax Ct. 1960, U.S. Supreme Ct. 1971, U.S. Ct. Appeals (6th cir.) 1972. Mem. firm Fuller & Henry, and predecessors, 1956-91; pvt. practice Toledo, 1991—. Chmn. nat. com. region IV Mich. Law Sch. Fund, 1967-69, mem.-at-large, 1970-85. Bd. dirs. Asso. Harvard Alumni, 1970-73. Served with AUS, 1954-56. Fellow Am. Coll. Trial Lawyers; mem. ABA, Ohio Bar Assn., Toledo Bar Assn., Toledo Club, Harvard Club (pres. Toledo chpt. 1968-77), Capital Club, Phi Delta Theta, Phi Delta Phi. General civil litigation, Environmental, Workers' compensation. Office: 2819 Falmouth Rd Toledo OH 43615-2215

BAKER, STEVEN WRIGHT, lawyer; b. Pitts., Oct. 23, 1947; s. Donald E. and Janet (Zahniser) B.; m. Louise G. Burrell, Oct. 31, 1970; children: Sara, Beth, Chad. BA, Allegheny Coll., 1969; JD, U. Calif.-San Francisco, 1974. Bar: Calif. 1974, U.S. Dist. Ct. (no. dist.) Calif. 1974, U.S. Ct. Internat. Trade 1974. U.S. Ct. Appeals (fed. cir.) 1975. Assoc. Glad, Tuttle and White, San Francisco, 1974-78; part. Bellsey & Baker, San Francisco, 1978— . Contbr. articles to profl. jours. Served with U.S. Army, 1969-71. Mem. ABA (internat. law sect.), Am. Inst. Internat. Steel (customs counsel), Am. Soc. Internat. Law, San Francisco Bar Assn., Customs Brokers and Forwarders Assn. No. Calif. Immigration, naturalization, and customs, Private international, Public international. Home: 190 Ignacio Valley Cir Novato CA 94949-5517 Office: Bellsey & Baker 100 California St Ste 670 San Francisco CA 94111-4584

BAKER, THOMAS EDWARD, lawyer, accountant; b. Washington, July 24, 1923; s. John Thad and Angelina E. (Rappa) B.; m. Mildred M. Younglove, Dec. 26, 1944 (dec. May 1995); children: Jean Ann Baker Holland, Cindy Baker Goralewicz, Linda Hogan; m. Helen Draughon, Nov. 3, 1996. BS, JD, U. Okla., 1950. Bar: Okla. 1950; CPA, Okla. Pvt. practice, Oklahoma City, 1950; agt., spl. agt. IRS, 1951-53; ptnr. Shutler Baker Simpson & Logsdon, Kingfisher, Okla., 1953-79, Baker, Logsdon, Schulte & Gibson, Kingfisher, 1979—. Trustee U. Okla. Found., Inc., 1987-89. WithAUS, 1943-46. Mem. Am. Legion (past svc. officer), Elks, Rotary (pres. Kingfisher club 1957). Democrat. Mem. Christian Ch. (Disciples of Christ). Oil, gas, and mineral, General practice, Probate. Home: 1211 Regency Ct Kingfisher OK 73750-4251 Office: Baker Logsdon Schulte & Gibson 302 N Main St Kingfisher OK 73750-2799

BAKER, THOMAS EUGENE, law educator; b. Youngstown, Ohio, Feb. 25, 1953; s. John M. and Helen Marie (Kish) B.; m. Jane Marie Schussler, June 15, 1974; 1 child, Thomas Athanasius. BS cum laude, Fla. State U., 1974; JD with high honors, U. Fla., 1977. Bars: Fla. 1979, U.S. Dist. Ct. (no. dist.) Tex. 1979, U.S. Supreme Ct. 1982, U.S. Ct. Appeals (5th cir.) 1979, U.S. Ct. Appeals (11th cir.) 1981. Law clk. to presiding judge U.S. Ct. Appeals (5th cir.) Ga., Atlanta, 1977-79; prof. law Tex. Tech. U., Lubbock, 1979-98, Alvin R. Allison prof., 1992-98; jud. fellow U.S. Supreme Ct., Washington, 1985-86, acting adminstrv. asst. to chief justice, 1986-87; James Madison chair constnl. law, dir. constnl. law ctr. Drake U. Law Sch., Des Moines, 1998—. Mem. adv. bd. Am. Criminal Law Rev., Washington, 1981-85; standing com. rules and procedures U.S. Jud. Conf., 1990-95; vis. prof. U. Fla., 1994; Fulbright prof. U. Athens, Greece, 1993; bd. editors Preview U.S. Supreme Ct. Cases, 1991—. Author: Rationing Justice on Appeal: The Problems of the U.S. Court of Appeals, 1994, The Most Wonderful Work: Our Constitution Interpreted, 1996; author: (with T. Floyd) Can a Good Christian Be a Good Lawyer?, 1998; author: Federal Court Practice and Procedure: A Third Branch Bibliography, 2001; mem. editl. bd. Jour. Supreme Ct. History, 1991—93;contbr. articles to profl. jours. Recipient Faculty Rsch. award Tex. Tech. U., 1996, 94, 83, Outstanding Law Prof. award, 1988, 89, Spencer A. Wells U. teaching award; Justice Tom C. Clark fellow Jud. Fellows, 1986. Mem. ABA (various sects. and coms.), Am. Law Inst. (elected), Am. Judicature Soc. (bd. dirs. 2000—), Sachems Club (Lubbock). Byzantine Catholic. Avocations: photography, racquet sports. Office: Drake U Law Sch 2507 University Ave Des Moines IA 50311-4516 E-mail: thomas.baker@drake.edu

BAKER, THURBERT E. state attorney general; b. Rocky Mount, N.C., Dec. 16, 1952; m. Catherine Baker; children: Jocelyn, Chelsea. BA in Polit. Sci., U. N.C.; JD, Emory U., 1979. Mem. Ga. Ho. of Reps., 1988-90, asst. adminstrn. floor leader, 1990-93, adminstrn. floor leader, 1993-97; atty. gen. State of Ga., 1997—. Trustee Statewide Ga. Diabetes Bd.; trustee Ebenezer Bapt. Ch., Atlanta, DeKalb Coll. Found. Mem. DeKalb County C. of C. (bd. dirs.), Nat. Med. Soc.-Emory U. Office: Atty Gen Dept Law 40 Capitol Sq SW Atlanta GA 30334-9003*

BAKER, WADE FRANKLIN, retired state bar executive; b. Jackson County, Ill., Dec. 30, 1919; s. Robert David Jr. and Lillian May (Damron) B.; m. Mary Eleanor LaClair, June 29, 1947; 1 child, Denise Ann. BEd, So. Ill. U., 1941; LLB, Lincoln Coll. Law, Springfield, Ill., 1950. Bar: Ill. 1950, Mo. 1957. Asst. sec., counsel Ill. Bar Assn., 1946-57; exec. dir., sec. The Mo. Bar, Jefferson City, 1957-84; pres. B.P. & G. Adv. Svcs., Inc., 1985-91. Former sec. Mo. Bar Found.; former sec.-treas. Mo. Bar Research, Inc., Mo. Legal Aid Soc.; former treas., asst. sec. Mo. Press Bar Commn. Chmn. adminstrv. bd., 1st United Meth. Ch., 1981-82; dir. for life Meml. Hosp. Served with AUUS, 1942-46, ETO; also 1951-52. Decorated Bronze Star; recipient Bicentennial award Mo. Bar, 1976, Fred Bolton award Nat. Assn. Bar Execs., 1978, Non-Alumni award U. Mo., 1975. Mem. Mo. Bar Assn., Jefferson City Rotary, Jefferson City YMCA (co-founder, former bd. mem.). Home: 2505 Orchard Ln Jefferson City MO 65109-0607

BAKER, WALTER WRAY, JR. lawyer; b. Raleigh, N.C., July 27, 1942; s. Walter Wray and Maggie Lee (Holland) B.; m. Jane Marlyn Green, June 14, 1964; children: Susan, Valerie, Walter. AA, Campbell Coll., 1962; AB, U. N.C., 1964, JD, 1966. Bar: N.C. 1966, U.S. Dist. Ct. (ea. and mid. dists.) N.C., U.S. Supreme Ct. 1974. Rsch. asst. to chief justice N.C. State Supreme Ct., Raleigh, 1966-67; pvt. practice High Point, 1967-94; ptnr. Baker & Boyan, PLLC, 1994—. Writer, lectr. continuing legal edn. personal injury & ethics; adj. prof. trial advocacy Wake Forest Sch. Law. Mem. N.C. Acad. Trial Lawyers (pres. 1985-86), High Point Bar Assn. (pres. 1985), N.C. State Bar (councillor 18th jud. dist.), Am. Bd. Trial Advocates, Joseph Br. Inn of Ct., Million Dollar Advocates Forum. Democrat. Mem. Wesleyan Ch. General civil litigation, Personal injury. Office: Baker & Boyan PLLC 820 N Elm St High Point NC 27262-3920

BAKER, WILLIAM PARR, lawyer; b. Balt., Sept. 5, 1946; s. George William and Jane (Parr) B.; m. Christine Corbett, Oct. 23, 1982; children: William Corbett, Brendan Parr, Laura Elizabeth. BA, St. Francis Univ., Loretto, Pa., 1968; JD, U. Md., 1971. Bar: Md. 1971, U.S. Dist. Ct. Md. 1972, U.S. Tax Ct. 1978, U.S. Supreme Ct. 1980, U.S. Ct. Appeals (4th cir.) 1982. Law clk. Md. Ct. Appeals, 1971-72; ptnr. Baker and Baker, PA and predecessors, Balt., 1972—. Civil case mediator Cir. Ct. for Balt. County; adj. prof. U. Md. Sch. Law. Contbr. articles to profl. jours. V.p. bd. dirs. Santa Claus Anonymous, 1973-76; bd. dirs. Balt. Assn. Retarded Citizens, 1981—. Mem. ABA, Md. Bar Assn., Bar Assn. Balt. City, Golfers Charitable Assn. (bd. dirs. 1989—), Am. Mensa, Balt. Country Club. Roman Catholic. Federal civil litigation, Contracts commercial, General practice. Office: Baker and Baker PA and predecessors 1000 Mercantile Trust Bldg 409 Washington Ave Baltimore MD 21204-4920

BAKKEN, GORDON MORRIS, law educator; b. Madison, Wis., Jan. 10, 1943; s. Elwood S. and Evelyn A. H. (Anderson) B.; m. Erika Reinhardt, Mar. 24, 1943; children: Angela E., Jeffrey E. BS, U. Wis., 1966, MS, 1967, PhD, 1970, JD, 1973. From asst. to assoc. prof. history Calif. State U., Fullerton, 1969-74, prof. history, 1974—, dir. faculty affairs, 1974-86. Cons. Calif. Sch. Employees Assn., 1976-78, Calif. Bar Commn. Hist. Law., 1985—; mgmt. task force on acad. grievance procedures Calif. State Univ. and Colls. Systems, 1975; mem. Calif. Jud. Coun. Com. Trial Ct. Records Mgmt., 1992-97. Author 7 books on Am. legal history; contbr. articles to profl. jours. Placentia Jusa referee coord., 1983. Russell Sag resident fellow law, 1971-72, Am. Bar Found. fellow in legal history, 1979-80, 84-85; Am. Coun. Learned Socs. grantee-in-ai d, 1979-80. Mem. Orgn. Am. Historians, Am. Soc. Legal History, Law and Soc. Assn., Western History Assn., Calif. Supreme Ct. Hist. Soc. (v.p.), Phi Alpha Theta (v.p. 1994-95, pres. 1996-97). Democrat. Lutheran. Office: Calif State U 800 N State College Blvd Fullerton CA 92834-6846 E-mail: gbakken@fullerton.edu

BAKKENSEN, JOHN RESER, lawyer; b. Pendleton, Oreg., Oct. 4, 1943; s. Manley John and Helen (Reser) B.; m. Ann Marie Dahlen, Sept. 30, 1978; children: Michael, Dana, Laura. AB magna cum laude, Harvard U., 1965; JD, Stanford U., 1968. Bar: Oreg. 1969, Calif. 1969, U.S. Dist. Ct. Oreg. 1969. Ptnr. Miller, Nash, Wiener, Hager & Carlsen, Portland, Oreg., 1968-99. Lawyer del. 9th Cir. Jud. Conf., San Francisco, 1980-82. Author: (with others) Advising Oregon Businesses, 1979, Arbitration and Mediation, supplement, 2000. Past bd. dirs. Assn. for Retarded Citizens, Portland; advisor Portland Youth Shelter House; mem. and counsel to bd. dirs. Friends of Pine Mountain Observatory, Portland. Mem. ABA (forum on constrn. industry), Oreg. State Bar, Oreg. Assoc. Gen. Contractors (legal com. 1991, counsel to bd. dirs. 1992), Multnomah Athletic Club. Avocation: astronomy. Alternative dispute resolution, State civil litigation, Construction.

BALASSA, TAMÁS, lawyer, educator; b. Budapest, Hungary, Dec. 11, 1970; s. Janos Balassa and Anna Weber; m. Susanna Radvany; 1 child, Adam. JD, ELTE U., Budapest, 1996. Assoc. Eorsi & Ptnrs., Budapest, 1996-99; tchr. ELTE Law Sch., 1996—; ptnr. Sandor, Bihary, Szegedi, Szent & Ivany, 1999—. Contbr. articles to legal publs. Contracts commercial, General corporate, Labor. Office: Sandor Bihary Szegedi Pasareti ut 59 1026 Budapest Hungary Fax: 36.1.392.4949. E-mail: balassat@advocat-sbsz.hu

BALDAUF, KENT EDWARD, lawyer; b. Pitts., Feb. 6, 1943; s. Walter William and Esther Baldauf; m. Kathleen Dian Abels, June 10, 1967; children: Kent Edward Jr., Krista K., Kara K. BS in Metall. Engring., Carnegie Mellon U., 1964; JD, Cleve. State U., 1970. Bar: Pa. 1970, U.S. Patent and Trademark Office 1971, U.S. Ct. Appeals (Fed. cir.) 1990, U.S. Supreme Ct. 1977. Shareholder, v.p., dir. Webb Law Firm, Pitts., 1988—. Editor Cleve. State U. Law Rev., 1969-70. Mem. ABA, Pa. Bar Assn., Allegheny County Bar Assn., Am. Intellectual Property Law Assn. (pres. 1998-99), Pitts. Intellectual Property Law Ass n., Engrs. Soc. Western Pa., Valley Brook Country Club, Duquesne Club. Federal civil litigation, Patent, Trademark and copyright. Office: The Webb Law Firm 436 7th Ave Pittsburgh PA 15219-1826

BALDINI, LAURA FLYNN, lawyer; b. Hartford, Conn. d. Daniel Francis and Barbara Lois Flynn; m. Matthew Alfred Baldini, June 13, 1998. BA, Yale U., 1992; JD, Seton Hall U., 1996. Bar: Conn. 1997, N.Y. 1997, U.S. Dist. Ct. Conn. 1998. Trial prep asst. Dist. Attys. Office N.Y. County, N.Y.C., 1992-93; law clk. Morgan, Melhush, Monaghan, Arvidson, Abrutyn & Lisowski, 1995-96; assoc. Chrenstein & Brown, 1996-98, Updike, Kelly & Spellacy, Hartford, Conn., 1998—. Author: Insider's Guide to Teenage Tennis, 1996. Vol. Jr. Achievement, Hartford, 1998—. Recipient Gilbert Shepard award Yale Club Hartford, 1989. Mem. ABA, Conn. Bar Assn., N.Y. Bar Assn., Hartford Golf Club, Jr. League Hartford. Roman Catholic. Avocations: tennis, golf, gardening, community service. Office: Updike Kelly & Spellacy PC One State St Hartford CT 06123

BALDOCK, BOBBY RAY, federal judge; b. Rocky, Okla., Jan. 24, 1936; s. W. Jay and S. Golden (Farrell) B.; m. Mary Jane (Spunky) Holt, June 2, 1956; children: Robert Jennings, Christopher Guy. Grad., N.Mex. Mil. Inst., 1956; JD, U. Ariz., 1960. Bar: Ariz. 1960, N.Mex. 1961, U.S. Dist. Ct. N.Mex., 1965. Ptnr. Sanders, Bruin & Baldock, Roswell, N.Mex., 1960-83; adj. prof. Eastern N.Mex. U., 1962-81; judge U.S. Dist. Ct. N.Mex., Albuquerque, 1983-86, U.S. Ct. Appeals (10th cir.), 1986-2001, sr. judge, 2001—. Mem. N.Mex. Bar Assn., Chaves County Bar Assn., Ariz. Bar Assn., Phi Alpha Delta. Office: US Ct Appeals PO Box 2388 Roswell NM 88202-2388*

BALDWIN, ALLEN ADAIL, lawyer, writer; b. St. Augustine, Fla., July 15, 1939; s. Larrie Paul and Bertha Mae (Capallia) B. BA, Brigham Young U., 1969; JD, So. U., Baton Rouge, 1975. Bar: Fla. 1975. Tchr. Putnam County Sch. Bd., Palatka, Fla., 1969-71; pvt. practice, 1975—. Author: Tricks to Make the Angels Weep, 1986, Call It Not Heaven, 1991, Redeem Us From Virtue, 1992. Mem. Latter-day Saints Ch. Avocations: reading, swimming, hiking. Family and matrimonial, General practice, Probate. Office: 308 St Johns Ave Palatka FL 32177-4723

BALDWIN, BRENT WINFIELD, lawyer; b. Wichita, Kans., July 10, 1952; s. Howard Stewart and Marguerite (Winfield) B.; m. Karen M. Altshuler, Sept. 27, 1974 (div. Apr. 1987); 1 child, Geoffrey W.; m. Scarlett J. Whitener, Aug. 17, 1991. BBA magna cum laude, U. Tex., 1974, JD, 1977. Bar: Mo. 1977, U.S. Dist. Ct. (ea. and we. dists.) Mo. 1977, Ill. 1978, U.S. Ct. Appeals (8th cir.) 1980, U.S. Ct. Appeals (7th cir.) 1981, U.S. Dist. Ct. (cen. dist.) Ill. 1981, U.S. Supreme Ct. 1982. Pvt. practice, St. Louis, 1977—; mng. ptnr. Baldwin & Hess, 1984-95, Hinshaw & Culbertson, St. Louis, 1995—. Contbr. articles to profl. jours. Chmn. bd. Deaconess Med. Ctrs. North & West, Deaconess Found. Mem. ABA, Mo. Bar Assn., Bar Assn. Met. St. Louis, Lawyers Assn. St. Louis, Mo. Orgn. Def. Lawyers, Am. Ins. Attys., Def. Rsch. Inst., Rotary (pres., Paul Harris fellow), Solar Found (bd. dirs.). Personal injury, Product liability, Professional liability. Office: Hinshaw & Culbertson 1010 Market St Ste 1400 Saint Louis MO 63101-2046

BALDWIN, CAROLYN WHITMORE, lawyer; b. Newton, Mass., July 9, 1932; d. Henry Jr. and Grace M. (Chase) W.; m. Peter Arthur Baldwin, Sept. 3, 1955; children: Sarah M., Robert H., Judith H. Student, U. Coll. of Southwest, Exeter, Eng., 1952-53; BA cum laude, Middlebury Coll., 1954; MA in Library Sci., U. Chgo., 1971; JD, Franklin Pierce Coll., Concord, N.H., 1977. Bar: N.H., 1977, U.S. Dist. Ct. N.H. 1977. Exhibits dir. U. Chgo. Library, 1970-73; manuscripts librarian N.H. Hist. Soc., Concord, 1973-74; library cataloger Franklin Pierce Law Ctr., 1973-77, dir. environ. law clinic, 1978-82; assoc. Murphy and McLaughlin, Laconia, N.H., 1977-78; sole practice Concord, 1983-90; ptnr. Baldwin & de Seve, 1991-97; of counsel Baldwin, Hogan, Callen & Kidd, 1997—. Of counsel McGregor & Shea, P.C., Boston, 1982—97. Supervising editor: Historic Districts in New Hampshire, a Handbook for Establishing and Administering Historic Districts, 1980; contbr. articles to profl. and other jours. Mem. Lakes Region Planning Commn., Meredith, N.H., 1977-90, chmn., 1982-83, 86-87; chmn. N.H. Natural Resources forum, Concord, 1983-86, Water Resources Action Project, 1985, Gilmanton (N.H.) Conservation Commn., 1974-80; mem. N.H. Commn. for Humanities, Concord, 1977-80; mem. Gilmanton Planning Bd., 1982-94, chmn., 1986-92; selectman Town of Gilmanton, 1995-98; bd. dirs. Granite State Pub. Radio, 1980-83, N.H. Main St. Ctr., 1997—; exec. dir. Environ. Law Coun., N.H., 1978-82; vice chmn. N.H. Hist. Preservation Task Force, 1983-84. Recipient Pres.'s medal N.H. Planner's Assn., 1985, Environ. Leadership award N.E. Environ. Network, 1989. Mem. N.H. Bar Assn. (mcpl., govt. law sect., mem. environ. law sect.), N.H. Assn. Regional Planning Commns. (chmn. legis. com. 1984-86), Franklin Pierce Law Ctr. Alumni Assn. (pres. 1979-80). Democrat. Mem. Unitarian Universalist Ch. Avocations: skiing, family, gardening. Environmental, Land use and zoning (including planning), Real property.

BALDWIN, GORDON BREWSTER, law educator, lawyer; b. Binghamton, N.Y., Sept. 3, 1929; s. Schuyler Forbes and Doris Ambeline (Hawkins) B.; m. Helen Louise Hochgraf, Feb., 1958; children: Schuyler, Mary Page. LLB, Cornell U., 1953; BA, Haverford Coll., 1950. Bar: N.Y. 1953, Wis. 1965. Pvt. practice, Rochester and Rome, N.Y., 1953-57; prof. law U. Wis., Madison, 1957-99, Evjue-Bascom profl. law, 1991-99, emeritus prof., 1999—, assoc. dean law, 1968-70, dir. officer edn., 1972-99; of counsel Murphy & Desmond, S.C., Madison, Wis., 1986-95. Chmn. internat. law U.S. Naval War Coll., 1963-64; Fulbright prof., Cairo, 1966-67, Tehran, Iran, 1970-71; lectr. State Dept., Cyprus, 1967, 1969, 1971; counselor internat. law U.S. Dept. State, Washington, 1975-76, cons., 1976-77; vis. prof. Chuo U., Tokyo, 1984, Giessen U., Fed. Republic Germany, 1987, 92, Thommasat U., Thailand, 1997; cons. U.S. Naval War Coll., 1961-65; chmn. screening com. on law Fulbright Program, 1974; mem. constl. law com. Multi-State Bar Exam, 1972-82; chmn. State Pub. Def. Bd., 1980-83, Wis. Elections Bd., 1991-96; cons., rep. Marshall Island Constn. Conv., 1990. Mem. Wis. Bd. Elections, 1991-95, Wis. Land Coun., 1998—, Wis. State Ethics Bd., 2000—. Ford Found. fellow, 1962-63 Fellow Am. Bar Found.; mem. AAUP (nat. coun. 1975-78, pres. Wis. conf. 1986-87), Bar Assn. (vice chmn. sect. on individual rights 1973-75), Fulbright Alumni Assn. (dir. 1979-82), Am. Law Inst., Order of Coif, Madison Club, Madison Lit. Club (pres. 1985-86), Univ. Club, Rotary (pres. Madison 1980, dist. gov. 1999-00), Phi Beta Kappa. Home: 3958 Plymouth Cir Madison WI 53705-5212 Office: U Wis 975 Bascom Mall Sch Law Madison WI 53706-1399 E-mail: gbaldwin@facstaff.wisc.edu

BALDWIN, JAMES EDWARD, lawyer, city administrator; b. Grand Rapids, Mich., Sept. 9, 1956; s. Bradford James and Emily Gertrude Baldwin; m. Mary Margaret Roberts, Sept. 6, 1986; children: James Patrick, Catherine Elizabeth. BS, Western Mich. U., Kalamazoo, 1984; JD, U. Cin., 1992. Bar: Ohio. Mgr. human resources Gold Circle Stores, Columbus, Ohio, 1985-86; prodn. supr. Gen. Dynamics and Systems, Lima, 1986-89; atty., sole practitioner, Cin., 1992—; dir. telecomms. City of Lebanon, Ohio, 1997—. Republican. Roman Catholic. Avocations: sports, history, travel. Home: 9036 Country View Ln Loveland OH 45140-1417 Office: City of Lebanon 50 S Broadway St Lebanon OH 45036-1777

BALDWIN, JEFFREY KENTON, lawyer, educator; b. Palestine, Ill., Aug. 8, 1954; s. Howard Keith and Annabelle Lee (Kirts) B.; m. Patricia Ann Mathews, Aug. 23, 1975; children: Matthew, Katy, Timothy, Philip R. BS summa cum laude, Ball State U., 1976; JD cum laude, Ind. U., 1979. Bar: Ind. 1979, U.S. Dist. Ct. (so. dist.) Ind. 1979, U.S. Ct. Appeals (7th cir.) 1979, U.S. Dist. Ct. (no. dist.) Ind. 1984. Majority leader's staff Ind. Senate, Indpls., 1976; instr. Beer Sch. Real Estate, 1977-78, Am. Inst. Paralegal Studies, Indpls., 1987—; dep. Office Atty. Gen., 1979-81; mng. ptnr. Baldwin & Baldwin, Danville, Ind., 1979—. Agt. Nat. Attys. Title Assurance Fund, Vevay, Ind., 1983—; officer, bd. dirs. Baldwin Realty, Inc., Danville; conf. participant White House Conf. on Small Bus. (Ind. meeting 1994), congl. appointee, 1995; bd. dirs. Small Bus. Coun. Bd. dirs. Hendricks Civic Theatre, Inc.; organizer, Hendricks County Young Republicans, 1972; sec. Hendricks County Rep. Com., 1978-84; bd. dirs. Hendricks County Assn. for Retarded Citizens, Danville, 1982-86; cons. Hendricks County Right for Life, Brownsburg, Ind., 1984—; mem.

philanthropy adv. com. Ball State U., Muncie, Ind., 1987—; judge Hendricks County unit Am. Cancer Soc., 1987; coordinator region 2 Young Leaders for Mutz, Indpls., 1987-88; cubmaster WaPaPh dist. Boy Scouts Am., 1988, S.M.E. chmn., 1988-89; steering com. Ind. Lawyers Bush/Quayle; founder, chmn. Christians for Positive Reform; candidate for Congress 7th Congl. Dist. of Ind.; del. to Annual Conf. South Ind. Conf. of United Meth. Ch., 1993, 95-98, 2000; host com. Midwest Rep. Leadership Conf., 1997; dist. coord. Hoosier Famiies for John Price for U.S. Senate; advisor John Price for Gov., 1999-2000; v.p. Danville Little League Baseball, 1998—. Recipient Presdl. award of honor Danville Jaycees, 1980; named hon. sec. State Ind., 1980. Mem. ABA, Ind. Bar Assn., Hendricks County Bar Assn., Indpls. Bar Assn., Internat. Platform Assn., Nat. Assn. Realtors, Ind. Assn. Realtors, Met. Indpls. Bd. Realtors (Hendricks County div.), Federalist Soc., Ind. Farm Bur., Nat. Fedn. Ind. Bus., Ind. C. of C., Danville C. of C. (sec. 1986), Moot Ct. Soc., Blue Key, Phi Soc. Methodist. General civil litigation, General practice, Legislative. Home: PO Box 63 Danville IN 46122-0063 E-mail: jbbfc@aol.com

BALDWIN, JOHN, legal association administrator, lawyer; b. Salt Lake City, Feb. 9, 1954; BA, U. Utah., 1977, JD, 1980. Bar: Utah 1980, U.S. Dist. Ct. Utah 1980, U.S. Ct. Appeals (10th cir.) 1984. Assoc. Jardine, Linebaugh, Brown & Dunn, Salt Lake City, 1980-82; asst. atty. gen. Utah Atty. Gen.'s Office, 1982-85; dir. Utah Divsn. Securities, 1985-90; exec. dir. Utah State Bar, 1990—. Adj. assoc. prof. mgmt. Eccles Sch. Bus., U. Utah. Mem. N.Am. Securities Adminstrs. Assn. (bd. dirs. 1987-90, pres. 1988-89), U. Utah Young Alumni Assn. (bd. dirs. 1987-90), U. Utah Beehive Honor Soc. (bd. dirs. 1993-97), U. Utah Alumni Assn. (bd. dirs. 1995-97). Office: Utah State Bar 645 S 200 E # 310 Salt Lake City UT 84111-3837

BALICK, HELEN SHAFFER, retired judge; b. Bloomsburg, Pa. d. Walter W. and Clarissa K. (Bennett) Shaffer; m. Bernard Balick, June 29, 1967. JD, Dickinson Sch. Law, 1966, LLD, 1997. Bar: Pa. 1967, Del. 1969. Probate adminstr. Girard Trust Bank, Phila., 1966-68; pvt. practice law Wilmington, Del., 1969-74; staff atty. Legal Aid Soc. Del., 1969-71; master Family Ct. Del., New Castle County, 1971-74; bankruptcy judge, U.S. magistrate Dist. Del., Wilmington, 1974-80, bankruptcy judge, 1974-94, chief judge, 1994-98. Guest lectr. Dickinson Sch. Law, 1981-87; lectr. Dickinson Forum, 1982. Pres. bd. trustees Cmty. Legal Aid Soc., Inc., 1972—74; trustee Dickinson Sch. Law, 1985—2000; mem. Citizens Adv. Com., Wilmington, 1973—74, Wilmington Bd. Edn., 1974; bd. dirs. Kutz Home, 1999—2001, Jewish Hist. Soc., 1999—; active U. Del. Libr. Assocs., 1998—, sec., 2000—, v.p., 2001; bd. govs. The Dickinson Sch. Law, Pa. State U., 2000—. Recipient Women's Leadership award Del. State Bar Assn., 1997; named to Hall of Fame of Del. Women, 1994. Mem.: Fed. Bar Assn., Nat. Conf. Bankruptcy Judges (bd. govs. 1986), Nat. Assn. Women Lawyers, Nat. Assn. Women Judges, Am. Judges Assn., Am. Coll. Bankruptcy, Am. Bankruptcy Inst., Del. Bar Assn., Del. Alliance Profl. Women (Trailblazer award 1984), Wilmington Women in Bus. (bd. dirs. 1980—83), Turnaround Mgmt. Assn. (bd. dirs. 1995—97), Dickinson Sch. Law Gen. Alumni Assn. (exec. bd. 1977—80, exec. bd. 1987—2000, v.p. 1981—84, pres. 1984—87, Outstanding Alumni award 1991, Career Achievement award 1998). Home: 2319 W 17th St Wilmington DE 19806-1330

BALILES, GERALD L. lawyer, former governor; b. Stuart, Va., July 8, 1940; BA, Wesleyan U., 1963; JD, U. Va., 1967. Bar: Va. 1967, U.S. Ct. Appeals (4th cir.), U.S. Supreme Ct. 1971. Ptnr. Bell, Lacy & Baliles, 1975-81; atty. gen. Commonwealth of Va., 1982-85, gov., 1986-90; with Hunton & Williams, 1986-90, now with Va. Mem. Va. Ho. of Dels., 1976-82, mem. appropriations com., 1978-82, com. corp. ins. and banking, 1976-82, com. conservation and natural resources, 1979-82; formerly ptnr. Lacy and Baliles, Richmond; chmn. Joint House-Senate Ins. Study Com., 1977-79; Legal Drafting Sub-Com., State Water Study Commn., 1977-81; vice chmn. Joint House-Senate Com. on Nuclear Power Generation Facilities, 1977-79; chmn. Nat. Commn. Ensure Strong Competitive Airline Industry, 1993. Chmn. PBS; chmn. so. regional edn. bd. Commn. Ednl. Quality. Mem. Richmond Bar Assn., Va. Bar Assn. (exec. com. 1979), ABA (environ. quality com., natural resources law sect. 1973—, environ. control com., corp., banking and bus. law sect. 1974—), Va. State Bar (chmn. environ. quality com. 1975-77). Criminal. Office: Hunton & Williams Riverfront Plz E Tower PO Box 1535 Richmond VA 23218-1535 Fax: 804-788-8218. E-mail: gbaliles@hunton.com

BALKA, SIGMUND RONELL, lawyer; b. Phila., Aug. 1, 1935; s. I. Edwin and Jane (Chernicoff) B.; m. Elinor Bernstein, May 29, 1966. AB, Williams Coll., 1956; JD, Harvard U., 1959. Bar: Pa. and D.C. 1961, N.Y. 1969, U.S. Supreme Ct. 1966. Sr. atty. Lilco, Mineola, N.Y., 1969-70; v.p., gen. counsel Brown Boveri Corp., North Brunswick, N.J., 1970-75; asst. gen. counsel Power Authority State N.Y., N.Y.C., 1975-80; gen. counsel Krasdale Foods, Inc., 1980—. Pres. Graphic Arts Coun. N.Y., 1980—. Chmn. Hunts Point Environ. Protection Coun., N.Y.C., 1980—; chmn. law com. N.Y.C. Community Bd. 6, Queens, 1980-88, chmn. econ. devel. com., 1988-99; chmn. Soc. for a Better Bronx, 1985—; bd. dirs. Bronx Arts Coun., 1981—, Greater N.Y. Met. Food Coun., 1986—; bd. dirs. Jewish Repertory Theatre, 1987—, co-chmn., 2000—; chmn. Bronx Borough Pres.'s Adv. Com. on Resource Recovery, 1988-90; chair fellows, mem. vis. com. Williams Coll. Mus. of Art, 1996-99. Fellow Am. Bar Found.; mem. ABA (co-chmn. pro bono project corp. law dept. 1986-88, chmn. 1988-90, com. of corp. gen. counsel 1974—, planning chmn. 1994-96, membership chmn. 1996-98, pro bono chair 2000—), Am. Corp. Counsel Assn. (bd. dirs. Met. N.Y. chpt. 1987—, bd. dirs. Found. 1992-99), Assn. Bar City N.Y. General corporate. Office: Krasdale Foods Inc 400 Food Center Dr Bronx NY 10474-7098

BALKAN, KENNETH J. lawyer; b. N.Y.C., Oct. 18, 1948; s. Robert and Leona (Brenner) B.; m. Berta Hochman, Aug. 16, 1970; children: Richard, Lauren, Adam. BA, Fairleigh Dickinson U., 1969; JD, St. John's U., 1972. Bar: N.Y. 1973, U.S. Dist. Ct. (so. and ea. dists.) N.Y. 1974, U.S. Ct. Appeals (2d cir.) 1975, U.S. Supreme Ct. 1978. Law intern Dist. Atty.'s Office County of Queens, N.Y.C., 1971; assoc. Kroll, Edelman, Elser & Wilson, 1972-77; ptnr. Wilson, Elser, Edelman & Dicker, 1977-81, L'Abbate & Balkan, Garden City, N.Y., 1981-94, L'Abbate, Balkan, Colavita & Contini, L.L.P., Garden City, 1995-98, of counsel, 1999—. Mem. editorial bd. Profl. Liability Reporter; mem. St. John's Law Rev., 1971-72; mediator for U.S. Dist. Ct. (ea. and so. dists.) N.Y.; lectr. in field. Contbr. articles to profl. jours. Mem. Def. Rsch. Inst. Mem. ABA (tort and ins. practice law and litigation subcoms., nat. reporter ins. coverage, profl. officer and dirs. law com., constrn. industry com.), N.Y. State Bar Assn. (former mem. com. profl. discipline, mem. ins. negligence and compensation law com., trial lawyers com.), Nassau County Bar Assn. (coms., ins. law, fee conciliation, profl. ethics vice-chair). General civil litigation, Insurance, Professional liability. Office: L'Abbate Balkan Colavita & Contini LLP 1050 Franklin Ave Rm 400 Garden City NY 11530-2929 E-mail: kbalkan@labbatebalkan.com

BALKO, GEORGE ANTHONY, III, lawyer, educator; b. Bklyn., June 22, 1955; s. George Anthony Jr. and Settimia (Palumbo) B. AB, Yale U., 1977; JD, U. Calif., San Francisco, 1986. Bar: Mass. 1986, U.S. Dist. Ct. Mass. 1987, U.S. Dist. Ct. Conn. 1999, U.S. Ct. Appeals (1st cir.) 1987, D.C 1990. Assoc. Swartz & Swartz, Boston, 1986-87, Bowditch & Dewey, Worcester, Mass., 1987-95, ptnr., 1996—. Adj. prof. Anna Maria Coll., Paxton, Mass., 1988—, mem. paralegal studies adv. bd., 1988-95. Author: Risk Management for Nursing Homes: A Primer In Long-Term Care Adminstration Handbook, 1993, Ambulatory Care and the Law: Lien Claims Where None Exist As of Right, 1995; legal columnist Jour. of Workers Compensation, 1996-99. Mem. Rice Sch. PTA, Holden, Mass., 1989-93; bd. health Town of Holden, 1995-99, chmn. 1996-99; moderator, 1999—; pres., bd. dirs. Elm Park Ctr. for Early Childhood Edn., 1994-96, mem. 1993-97. Recipient Am. Jurisprudence award for Ins. Law Lawyers Coop. Pub. Co. and Bancroft Whitney Co., 1985. Roman Catholic. Avocations: history, travel, tennis. Insurance, Personal injury, Product liability. Home: 4 Chestnut Hill Rd Holden MA 01520-1603 Office: Bowditch & Dewey 311 Main St Worcester MA 01608-1552

BALL, JAMES HERINGTON, retired lawyer; b. Kansas City, Mo., Sept. 20, 1942; s. James T. Jr. and Betty Sue (Herington) B.; m. Wendy Anne Wolfe, Dec. 28, 1964; children: James H. Jr., Steven Scott. AB, U. Mo., 1964; JD cum laude, St. Louis U., 1973. Bar: Mo. 1973. Asst. gen. counsel Anheuser-Busch, Inc., St. Louis, 1973-76; v.p., gen. counsel, sec. Stouffer Corp., Solon, Ohio, 1976-83; sr. v.p., gen. counsel Nestle Enterprises, Inc., 1983-91; gen. counsel, sr. v.p. Nestle USA, Inc., Glendale, Calif., 1991-99. Editor-in-chief St. Louis U. Law Jour., 1972-73. Bd. dirs. Alliance for Children's Rights, L.A., 1992-99, Am. Swiss Found., N.Y.C., 1996-99. Lt. comdr. USN, 1964-70, Vietnam. Mem. Mo. Bar Assn. General corporate, Mergers and acquisitions, Real property.

BALL, OWEN KEITH, JR. lawyer; b. Louisville, Feb. 19, 1950; s. Owen Keith and Martha Katherine (Guntherberg) B.; m. Shirley Marie Galinski, Sept. 16, 1972. BSCE, U. Kans., 1972, JD, 1980. Bar: Mo. 1980, U.S. Dist. Ct. (we. dist.) Mo. 1980, Kans. 1988, U.S. Dist. Ct. Kans. 1988. Ptnr. Smith, Gill, Fisher & Butts P.C., Kansas City, Mo., 1980-87; pvt. practice loan broker Lawrence, 1987-88; pvt. practice, 1988-91; legal counsel Marian Merrell Dow Inc., Kansas City, Mo., 1991-92; corp. counsel Marion Merrell Dow Inc., 1992-95, Hoechst Marion Roussel, Inc., Kansas City, 1995-99; sr. corp. counsel Aventis Pharms., Bridgewater, N.J., 1999—. Staff to investigate safety of the Hyatt Regency Hotel, Kansas City C. of C., 1981. Lt. USN, 1972-77. Mem. Am. Corp. Counsel Assn., Am. Soc. Corp. Secs., Mo. Bar Assn. Avocation: classical music. General corporate, Mergers and acquisitions, Securities. Office: Aventis Pharms Inc 300 Somerset Corporate Blvd Bridgewater NJ 08807-2854

BALLANFANT, RICHARD BURTON, lawyer; b. Houston, Aug. 15, 1947; s. Richard Edward and Selma Autrey (Lewis) B.; children: Andrea Lavon, Benjamin Burton, Amy Lamer. BA, U. Tex., 1969, JD, 1972. Bar: Tex. 1972, U.S. Ct. Appeals (5th cir.) 1976, U.S. Ct. Appeals (11th cir.) 1981, U.S. Ct. Appeals (8th cir.) 1988, U.S. Dist. Ct. (so. dist.) Tex. 1974. Atty. FCC, Washington, 1973-74; asst. U.S. atty. Dept. Justice, Houston, 1974-78; sr. asst. city atty. City of Houston, 1978-80; atty. Shell Oil Co., Houston, 1980—. Mem. Citizens Adv. Bd. Met. Transit Auth., Houston, 1979-83; del. Rep. State Conv., 1978, 80, 82, 88, 90, 92, 96, del. to Rep. Nat. Conv., 1992; chmn. Personnel Bd., West University Pl., Tex., 1975-85; appt. to Battleship Tex. Adv. Bd., 1989. Capt. USAR, 1972-82. Named Outstanding Asst. U.S. Atty. Dept. Justice, 1976, 77. Mem. Houston Bar Assn., Fed. Bar Assn. (pres. 1979-80), ABA, Houston C. of C. (govt. relations com.). Episcopalian. Federal civil litigation, State civil litigation, Environmental. Home: 3123 Amherst St Houston TX 77005-3009 Office: Shell Oil Co PO Box 2463 Houston TX 77001

BALLANTINE, JOHN TILDEN, lawyer; b. Louisville, Feb. 26, 1931; s. Thomas Austin and Anna Marie (Pfeiffer) B.; m. Mary January Strode, May 15, 1954 (div. 1964); children: John T. Jr., William Clayton, Douglas C.; m. Beverley Jo Hackley, Dec. 8, 1967; 1 child, Susan Marie. BA with high distinction, U. Ky., 1952; JD, Harvard U., 1957. Bar: Ky. 1957, U.S. Ct. Appeals (6th cir.) 1958, U.S. Supreme Ct. 1982. Law clk. to presiding judge U.S. Dist Ct. (we. dist.) Ky., 1957-58; assoc. then ptnr. Ogden Newell & Welch PLLC, Louisville, 1958—. Mem. civil rules com. Ky. Supreme Ct., 1988-96. Bd. dirs. Family and Children Agy., Louisville, 1965-75, pres., 1971-74; bd. dirs. Our Lady of Peace Hosp., Louisville, 1968-73, 88—, chmn., 1968-69, 91-93; bd. dirs. Met. United Way, Louisville, 1975-81; mem. Hist. Landmarks and Preservation Dists. Commn., Louisville, 1976-88; bd. dirs. Ky. Derby Festival, Louisville, 1975-81, v.p., 1975. 1st lt. USAF, 1952-54. Recipient Outstanding Young Man in Field of Law award Louisville Jaycees, 1966. Fellow Am. Coll. Trial Lawyers; mem. ABA, Ky. Bar Assn. (bd. govs. 1996—, ho. of dels. 1985-86, chmn. 1989-90, clients' security fund 1993-96, Ky. evidence rules rev. commn. 1995—), Louisville Bar Assn. (bd. dirs. 1969-71, 88, 89, 92, 93, 96—, pres. 1970, profl. responsibility com. 1988-93, past chmn. physician-atty. com.), U.S. 6th Cir. Ct. Appeals Jud. Conf. (life), Am. Bd. Trial Advs., Fed. Ins. and Corp. Counsel, Ky. Def. Counsel (pres. 1981-82), Louis D. Brandeis Am. Inn of Ct. (pres. 1997-98), Ky. Character and Fitness Com., Pendennis Club, The Law Club, Lawyers Club, Jefferson Club, Phi Beta Kappa. General civil litigation, Personal injury, Alternative dispute resolution. Office: Ogden Newell & Welch PLLC 1700 Citizens Plaza 500 W Jefferson St Ste 1700 Louisville KY 40202-2874 Business E-Mail: jballantine@ogdenlaw.com

BALLARD, RONALD MICHAEL, lawyer, political consultant; b. Covina, Calif., Apr. 17, 1958; s. Gonzy Steven and Eleanor (Guarino) B.; m. Jamie S. Kemmerer, Aug. 17, 1980; children: Nathaniel, Kaitlyn, Nolan, Devin, Casadei, Cameron, Aliza, Damian. BA, Claremont McKenna Coll., 1980; JD, UCLA, 1983. Bar: Calif. 1983, U.S. Dist. Ct. (cen. dist.) Calif. 1984. Assoc. Reid and Hellyer, San Bernardino, Calif., 1984-85; pvt. practice law Irvine, 1985-95, Lake Forest, CA, 95—; owner Centrilink.net, 1999—, RapidWeb Presence.com, 1999—, Form Of Title.com., 1999—. Mem., v.p. Charter Oak Unified Sch. Dist. Bd. Edn., Covina, 1977-81; mem., sec. 62d A.D. Rep. Cen. Com., Covina, 1978-81; lector, commentator St. Elizabeth Ann Seton Ch., Irvine, 1987-92; nat. sec. Caths. Respect Life, Westminster, Calif., 1990. Mem. State Bar Calif. (bus. law, estate, probate and trusts sect.), South Orange County C. of C. Contracts commercial, General corporate, Estate planning. Office: 22996 El Toro Rd Lake Forest CA 92630-4961 E-mail: rballard@ballardlaw.com

BALLMAN, B. GEORGE, lawyer; b. N.Y.C., Feb. 7, 1931; s. Bernard and Claire (Kahn) B.; m. Frances Hurst; children: Deborah, Lynda, B. George, Kimberly. AA, BS, Am. U., 1955, JD, 1957; LLM in Taxation, Georgetown U., 1960. Bar: Md. 1957, D.C. 1958, U.S. Supreme Ct. 1963. Mng. prin. Conroy, Ballman & Dameron, Rockville, Md., 1981—. Bd. dirs., treas. Bethesda-Chevy Chase Rescue Squad, 1948-50; co-founder, chancellor The Counsellors, 1963-64. Contbr. article to profl. jours. Mem. ABA, ATLA, Montgomery County Bar Assn. (treas. exec. com. 1960, chmn. law day com., 1962, pub. relations com. 1963, continuing legal edn. com. 1964, 65, 68, mem. grievance com. real estate sect. 1969—), D.C. Bar, Montgomery County Bar Assn., Congl. Country Club. Republican. Episcopalian. Administrative and regulatory, Estate planning, Land use and zoning (including planning). Office: 6 Montgomery Village Ave Gaithersburg MD 20879-3546

BALLON, CHARLES, lawyer; b. N.Y.C., Sept. 10, 1910; s. Herman and Anna (Platt) B.; m. Harriet Milk, Aug. 19, 1954; children— Howard, Hilary, Carla. B.A., Columbia U., 1930, LL.B., 1932. Bar: N.Y. 1933, U.S. Dist. Ct. (so. dist.) N.Y. 1935, U.S. Ct. Appeals (2d cir.) 1935, D.C. 1976, U.S. Dist. Ct. D.C. 1976, U.S. Ct. Appeals D.C. Ptnr., Hartman, Sheridan, Tekulsky & Pecora, N.Y.C., 1937-41; ptnr. Phillips, Nizer, Benjamin, Krim & Ballon, N.Y.C., 1946— . Bd. visitors Columbia U. Law Sch., 1975— ; chmn. bd. dirs. Benjamin N. Cardozo Sch. Law, Yeshiva U., N.Y.C., 1981-86, hon. chair, 1986—, trustee Yeshiva U., 1980— ; assoc. chmn. Fedn. Philanthropies of N.Y., 1979-86; v.p. United Jewish Appeal of N.Y., 1980-86, hon. chmn. . Served to lt. col. U.S. Army, 1942-46. Decorated Legion of Merit; recipient Proskauer medal Fedn. Jewish Philanthropies, 1973; Learned Hand award Am. Jewish Com., 1976; Israel Peace medal, Israel State Bonds, 1983; Disting. Service award Cardozo Sch. Law, 1979. Mem. Assn. Bar City of N.Y., N.Y. State Bar Assn. General corporate, General practice, Labor. Home: 800 5th Ave New York NY 10021-7216 Office: Phillips Nizer Benjamin Krim & Ballon 40 W 57th St New York NY 10019-4001

BALLOT, ALISSA E. lawyer; b. N.Y.C., Nov. 25, 1955; d. I. Martin and Barbara E. (Bendet) B. BA, Williams Coll., 1977; JD, Harvard U., 1980. Bar: N.Y. 1981, U.S. Dist. Ct. (so. and ea. dists.) N.Y. 1981. Assoc. Kramer, Levin et al, N.Y.C., 1980-83; counsel Lincoln Savs. Bank, 1983-85; assoc. gen. counsel Am. Savs. Bank, White Plains, N.Y., 1985-86, dep. gen. counsel, 1987-92; gen. counsel North Side Savs. Bank, Floral Park, 1992-96; sr. v.p. legal affairs, sec. Republic Security Bank, West Palm Beach, Fla., 1997-2001; sr. v.p. & gen. counsel Bank Atlantic, Ft. Laudersale, 2001—. Vice chmn. Williams Coll. Alumni Fund. Mem. ABA, Assn. of Corp. Counsel Am., Am. Soc. Corp. Secs. Jewish. Banking, General corporate. Home: 80 Monterey Pointe Dr Palm Beach Gardens FL 33418-5809 Office: Republic Security Bank 450 S Australian Ave West Palm Beach FL 33401-5008 E-mail: alissa.ballot@wachovia.com

BALLSUN, KATHRYN ANN, lawyer; b. Calif., May 8, 1946; d. Zan and Doris (Pratt) B. BA, U. So. Calif., 1969, MA, 1971; JD, Loyola U., L.A., 1976. Bar: Calif. 1976, U.S. Dist. Ct. (cen. dist.) Calif. 1977. Ptnr. Sherer, Bradford, Lyster & Ballsun, L.A. Vis. prof. UCLA Law Sch., Loyola U. Law Sch., L.A.; adj. prof. U. So. Calif. Law Sch.; mem. planning com. U. So. Calif. Progate and Trust Conf., 1985-87; lectr. various schs. Author: (with others) Estate Planning for the General Practitioner; editor: How to Live and Die with California Probate; contbr. articles to profl. jours. Mem. graphic arts coun. L.A. County Mus. Art, Children's Coun., Westwood Meth. Ch.; co-chmn. for Class of 1976 Greater Loyola Law Sch. Devel. Program, 1983; advisor Am. Cancer Soc. Program; radio vol. sta. KUSC; bd. dirs. Planned Protective Svcs. Inc.; bd. dirs. L.A. Philharm. Orch., com. profl. women, treas. 1985-86. Fellow Am. Coll. Probate Counsel; mem. ABA (real property, probate and trust law, taxation sects., pre-death planning com.), State Bar Calif. (resolutions com., exec. com., co-vice chair estate planning techniques, post death, pre-death com., trust and probate, bus. law, taxation sects., law revision study team 1983-85), L.A. County Bar Assn. (trustee, exec. com., trust and probate, taxation sects.), Beverly Hills Bar Assn. (treas. 1985-86, bd. govs. 1982-84, 84-86, probate and trust com., taxation com., sr. vice chair resolutions com., del. State Bar Conv. 1981-85, v.p. 1987-89, pres.-elect, pres. 1989—, panelist), Nat. Acad. Elder Law Attys., Inc., Calif. Women Lawyers, L.A. Women Lawyers, Women in Business (sec., polit. action com.), Beverly Hills Estate Planning Com., Estate Counselor's Forum (past pres., v.p., bd. dirs.), Los Angeles County Mus. Art, L.A. C. of C., ACLU (L.A. chpt.), UCLA Ctr. for Study of Women, ACLU (L.A. chpt.), Kappa Alpha Theta. Pension, profit-sharing, and employee benefits, Probate, Estate taxation. Office: Sherer Bradford Lyster & Ballsun 11th Fl 1901 AVe of the Americas Los Angeles CA 90067

BALMER, THOMAS ANCIL, judge; b. Longview, Wash., Jan. 31, 1952; s. Donald Gordon and Elisabeth Clare (Hill) B.; m. Mary Louise McClintock, Aug. 25, 1984; children: Rebecca Louise, Paul McClintock. AB, Oberlin Coll., 1974; JD, U. Chgo., 1977. Bar: Mass. 1977, D.C. 1981, U.S. Dist. Ct. Mass. 1977, Oreg. 1982, U.S. Dist. Ct. Oreg. 1982, U.S. Ct. Appeals (9th cir.) 1982, U.S. Ct. Appeals (D.C. cir.) 1983, U.S. Supreme Ct. 1987. Assoc. Choate, Hall & Stewart, Boston, 1977-79, Wald, Harkrader & Ross, Washington, 1980-82; trial atty. antitrust div. U.S. Dept. Justice, 1979-80; assoc. Lindsay, Hart, Neil & Weigler, Portland, Oreg., 1982-84, ptnr., 1985-90, Ater Wynne LLP, Portland, 1997—2001; dep. atty. gen. State of Oregon, Salem, 1993-97; justice Oreg. Supreme Court, 2001—. Adj. prof. of law Northwestern Sch. Law Lewis and Clark Coll., 1983-84, 90-92. Contbr. articles to law jours. Active mission and outreach com. United Ch. of Christ, Portland, 1984-87, Met. Svc. Dist. Budget Com., Portland, 1988-90; bd. dirs. Multnomah County Legal Aid Svc., Inc., 1989-93, chair 1992-93; bd. dirs. Chamber Music Northwest, 1997—, Classroom Law Project, 2000—. Mem. ABA, Oreg. Bar Assn. (chmn. antitrust sect. 1986-87, mem. fed. practice and procedure com. 1999—). Democrat. Home: 2521 NE 24th Ave Portland OR 97212-4831 Office: Supreme Ct Bldg 1163 State St Salem OR 97310*

BAMBERGER, MICHAEL ALBERT, lawyer; b. Berlin, Feb. 29, 1936; s. Fritz and Kate (Schwabe) B.; m. Phylis Skloot, Dec. 19, 1965; children— Kenneth A., Richard A. AB magna cum laude, Harvard U., 1957, LLB magna cum laude, 1960. Bar: N.Y. 1960, D.C. 1982. Assoc. Proskauer Rose Goetz & Mendelsohn, N.Y.C., 1960-69, Finley, Kumble, Wagner, Heine, Underberg, Manley, Myerson & Casey, N.Y.C., 1970, ptnr., 1971-87, Sonnenschein Nath & Rosenthal, N.Y.C., 1987—. Adj. prof. Benjamin Cardozo Sch. Law, Yeshiva U., 2001—; mem. faculty various legal seminars and insts.; mem. joint editl. bd. on uninc. orgn. acts. ABA/Nat. Conf. Commrs. on Uniform State Laws, 1994—; chmn. bd. Transcontinental Music Publs., New Jewish Music Press. Author: Reckless Legislation: How Lawmakers Ignore the Constitution, 2000; co-editor: State Limited Partnership Laws, 7 vols. and supplements, 1987—, State Limited Liability Company and Partnership Laws, 5 vols. and supplements, 1993—; editor Harvard Law Rev., 1958-60; contbr. articles to profl. jours. Vice chair bd. overseers Hebrew Union Coll.-Jewish Inst. Religion, N.Y.C.,; v.p., bd. dirs. Leo Baeck Inst., Selfhelp Cmty. Svcs.; bd. dirs. Ctr. Jewish History. Mem. ABA (com. on ltd. partnerships 1980—, chair com. on tech. and intellectual property 1992-95, chair, ad hoc com. on security interests in intellectual property 1990-98), First Amendment Lawyers Assn., N.Y. State Bar Assn. (exec. com. comml. and fed. litigation sect. 1989-93), Assn. Bar City N.Y. (com. on fed. legislation 1979-82, com. on civil rights 1982-86, chmn. 1983-86), N.Y. County Lawyers Assn. (securities com. 1980-82). Jewish. Constitutional, General corporate, Libel. Home: 172 E 93d St New York NY 10128-3711 Office: Sonnenschein Nath & Rosenthal 1221 Ave of Americas New York NY 10020-1001

BAMBERGER, PHYLIS SKLOOT, judge; b. N.Y.C., May 2, 1939; d. George Joseph and Martha (Wechselblatt) S.; m. Michael A. Bamberger, Dec. 19, 1965; children: Kenneth, Richard. BA, Bklyn. Coll., 1960; LLB, NYU, 1963. Bar: N.Y. 1963, U.S. Supreme Ct. 1967, U.S. Ct. Appeals (2d cir.) 1965, U.S. Dist. Ct. (so. dist.) N.Y. 1966, U.S. Dist. Ct. (ea. dist.) N.Y. 1979. Assoc. Legal Aid Soc., N.Y.C., 1963-67; assoc.-in-charge criminal appeals Bur. Legal Aid Soc., 1967-72; atty.-in-charge, fed. def. svcs. unit/appeal Legal Aid Soc., N.Y.C., 1972-88; judge N.Y. State Ct. Claims designated to sit in the N.Y. State Supreme Ct., Bronx County, 1988—. Mem. N.Y. State Chief Judge's Jury Project, 1993-94; mem. com. on alts. to incarceration Office of Ct. Adminstrn., 1994-96, mem. criminal law and procedure adv. com., 1994-98, co-chair 1998—. Author: Criminal Appeals Handbook, 1984; editor, contbr. Practice Under the Federal Sentencing Guidelines, 1988, 90, 93, 2000 (also supplements); author, compiler Recent Developments in State Constitutional Law, 1985; contbr. numerous articles to pubis. Mem. ABA, N.Y. State Bar assn. (co-chair presdl. com. on problems in criminal justice sys. 1986-88, mem. com. on the future of the profession), Assn. of Bar of City of N.Y. (chair com. on provision of legal svcs. to persons of moderate means 1995-98, 21st century com. 1992-95, chair com on probation 1993-94), Phi Beta Kappa. Office: Bronx County Courthouse 851 Grand Concourse Bronx NY 10451-2937

BAMFORD, TIMOTHY JAMES, lawyer; b. Gt. Britain, Aug. 13, 1960; BSc, London U., 1982. Solicitor, Eng., Wales, 1986. Ptnr. Charles Russell, London, 1996—. Computer, Entertainment, Intellectual property. Office: Charles Russell 8-10 New Fetter Ln London EC4A 1RS England Fax: 011-44-20-7203-5002. E-mail: timb@cr-law.co.uk

BANDER, EDWARD JULIUS, law librarian emeritus, lawyer; b. Boston, Aug. 10, 1923; s. Abraham and Ida (Lendman) B. BA, Boston U., 1949, LLB, 1951; MLS, Simmons Coll., 1955. Bar: Mass. 1951. Asst. reference libr. Harvard U., Cambridge, Mass., 1954-55; libr. U.S. Ct. Appeals (1st cir.), Boston, 1955-60; asst. libr., asst. prof. NYU, N.Y.C., 1960-70, assoc. prof., curator, assoc. libr., 1970-78; prof., libr. Suffolk U. Law Sch., Boston, 1978-90, libr., prof. emeritus, 1991—. Author: Mr. Dooley and the Choice of Law, 1963, Mr. Dooley and Mr. Dunne, 1981, Justice Holmes Ex Cathedra, 1966, 91, Searching the Law, 1986, Shakespeare on Lawyers and the Law, 1998; co-editor bi-monthly rev. law books, 1990—. Served with USN, 1942-46. Recipient Dean Frederick A. McDermott award Suffolk U. Student Bar Assn., 1980. Mem. Assn. Am. Law Schs., New Eng. Law Libr. Democrat. Jewish. Office: 50 Church St Concord MA 01742-3050 E-mail: ebander@acad.suffolk.edu

BANDES, SUSAN ANNE, lawyer; b. N.Y.C., May 19, 1951; d. Seymour and Lucille Janet (Coleman) B.; m. Christopher McElroy, May 23, 1976 (div. 1979). B.A., SUNY-Buffalo, 1973; J.D., U. Mich., 1976. Bar: Ill. 1976, U.S. Dist. Ct. (no. dist.) Ill. 1976, U.S. Ct Appeals (7th cir.) 1978. Staff atty. Office Ill. Appellate Defender, Chgo., 1977-81; staff counsel ACLU, Chgo., 1981-84; asst. prof. DePaul Coll. Law, Chgo., 1984— ; mem exec. com. Chgo. Law Enforcement Study Group, Chgo, 1981— . Mem. Chgo. Bar Assn., Chgo. Council Lawyers, Phi Beta Kappa. Democrat. Jewish. Office: De Paul Coll Law 25 E Jackson Blvd Chicago IL 60604-2289

BANDON, WILLIAM EDWARD, III, lawyer; b. Bklyn., June 12, 1961; s. William Edward Jr. and Lila Marie (Arida) B.; m. Patricia Linden McKeogh, Sept. 18, 1993; 1 child, John Robert. AB in History, Princeton U., 1983; JD, NYU, 1987. Bar: N.Y. 1988, U.S. Dist. Ct. (so. and ea. dists.) N.Y. 1988. Summer assoc. Cullen and Dykman, Bklyn., 1986, assoc., 1987-96, Brown Raysman Millstein Felder & Steiner LLP, N.Y.C., 1996-99, ptnr., 1999—. Trustee Lotte Kaliski Found. for Gifted Children, Inc., N.Y.C., 1996—; active Katonah (N.Y.) Hist. Mus., 1996—. Mem. ABA, N.Y. County Lawyers Assn. (chmn. com. tech. and automation 1997—), Computer Law Assn., Somers Hist. Soc. Democrat. Avocation: local history. Computer, General corporate, Intellectual property. Home: 5 Quicks Ln Katonah NY 10536-1005 Office: 120 W 45th St New York NY 10036-4041

BANDURKA, ANDREW ALAN, lawyer; b. Chesterfield, Derbyshire, Eng., Dec. 31, 1956; s. Leopold and Anthea B.; m. Sarah Mary Curran, Oct. 30, 1993; children: Leo, Maximilian, Thomas. BS, Sussex U., Brighton, Eng., 1978; MS, 1979. Bar: barrister Lincoln's Inn 1985; solicitor 1989. Analyst Brit. Airways, London, 1979-83; barrister 24, The Ropewalk, Nottingham, 1986-88; adjuster Internat. Ins. Svcs., London, 1989-93; asst. D.J. Freeman, 1989-93; ptnr. Holman Fenwick and Willan, 1993—. Contbr. articles to profl. jours. Upjohn scholar Lincoln's Inn, 1984. Mem. Chartered Inst. Arbitrators (assoc.). Avocations: walking, soccer, motorcycles. Alternative dispute resolution, Contracts commercial, Insurance. Office: Holman Fenwick and Willan Lloyds Ave London EC3N 3AL England Fax: 0207-4810316

BANDY, JACK D. lawyer; b. Galesburg, Ill., June 19, 1932; s. Homer O. and Gladys L. (Van Winkle) B.; m. Betty McMillan, Feb. 18, 1956; children: Jean A. Bandy Abramson, D. Michael, Jeffery K. BA, Knox Coll., 1954; LLB, U. La Verne, 1967. Bar: Calif. 1972, U.S. Supreme Ct. 2000. Safety engr. Indsl. Indemnity Co., L.A., 1960-65, sr. safety engr., 1965-69, resident safety engr., 1969-72; trial atty. Employers Ins. of Wausau, 1972-79; mng. atty. Wausau Ins. Cos., 1979-92; arbitrator, mediator L.A. Superior Mcpl. Ct., 1992—. Contbr. articles to profl. jours. Youth leader YMCA, Mission Hills, Calif., 1965-72. Served with U.S. Army, 1954-56. Mem. Calif. State Bar, Am. Soc. Safety Engrs. (cert. safety profl.). Alternative dispute resolution, Insurance, Personal injury. E-mail: bandy_jack@msn.com

BANEZ, WINTHROP HAWTHORNE REDOBLE, lawyer; b. Manila, May 11, 1969; s. Hawthorne Nejal and Elisea Redoble B.; m. Elizabeth Lorenzo, Dec. 21, 1988; 1 child: Lauren Andrea. BL, U. Philippines, Quezon City, 1995. Bar: The Philippines 1995. Jr. assoc. Catindig & Tiongco, Pasig City, The Philippines, 1995-97, Ponce Enrile Reyes & Manalastas, Makati City, The Philippines, 1997—. Mem. Integrated Bar Philippines. General corporate, Mergers and acquisitions, Securities. Office: Ponce Enrile Reyes Manalastas LP Leviste St 3/F VernidaIV Makati City 1227 The Philippines Fax: 632 8187355. E-mail: wrbanez@edsamail.com.ph, wrbanez@pecabar.com

BANGEL, HERBERT K. lawyer; b. Norfolk, Va., May 29, 1928; m. Carolyn Kroskin; children: Nancy Jo, Brad J. BS in Commerce, U. Va., 1947, JD, 1950. Bar: Va. 1949, U.S. Dist. Ct. (ea. dist.) Va., U.S. Ct. Appeals (4th cir.), U.S. Tax Ct., U.S. Bd. Immigration Appeals, D.C., U.S. Supreme Ct. Ptnr. Bangel, Bangel & Bangel, Portsmouth, Va., 1950—. Bd. dirs. Portsmouth Enterprises, Inc., Dominion Bank Greater Hampton Roads, Tidewater Profl. Sports Inc.; substitute judge Portsmouth Gen. Dist. Ct., 1979-84; mem. U.S. Ct. Appeals (4th cir.) Jud. Conf. Commr. Eastern Va. Med. Authority (named changed to Med. coll of Hampton Rds.), 1983-91, vice chmn., 1987-88; pres., chmn. Portsmouth Area United Fund, 1971-73; bd. dirs. Portsmouth Indsl. Found., 1968-90, bd. dirs. Urban League Tidewater (Va.), 1978-79, Tidewater chpt. Am. Heart Assn., 1983-84, Portsmouth Community Trust Distbn. Com., 1977-87, chmn., 1985-86; bd. dirs. Maryview Hosp., 1969-87; trustee Portsmouth-Chesapeake Area Found., 1968-72, United Community Funds and Councils Va., 1970-71, others; chmn. Portsmouth Redevel. and Housing Authority, 1977-83. Named First Citizen, City of Portsmouth, 1974. Mem. ABA, Va. Bar Assn., Portsmouth Bar Assn. (pres. 1964), Norfolk Bar Assn., Tidewater Trial Lawyers Assn. (bd. dirs. 1968-73), Va. Trial Lawyers Assn. (bd. govs. 1970), Assn. Trial Lawyers Am., Suburban Country Club (pres. 1961-62), Oceans Club (bd. dirs. 1973-76), Town Point Club (bd. govs. 1983—), Portsmouth Sports Club, Moose, Elks, B'nai B'rith. Democrat. Jewish. Personal injury. Home: 1 Crawford Pkwy Apt 1702 Portsmouth VA 23704-2613 Office: Bangel Bangel & Bangel PO Box 760 Portsmouth VA 23705-0760

BANKS, FRED LEE, JR. state supreme court presiding justice; b. Jackson, Miss., Sept. 1, 1942; s. Fred L. and Violet (Mabry) B.; m. Taunya Lovell, June 5, 1967 (div. 1975); children: Rachel R., Jonathan L.; m. Pamela Gipson, Jan. 28, 1978; 1 child, Gabrielle G. BA, Howard U., 1965, JD cum laude, 1968. Bar: Miss. 1968, U.S. Dist. Ct. (no. and so. dists.) Miss. 1968, U.S. Ct. Appeals (5th cir.) 1968, D.C. 1969, U.S. Supreme Ct. 1971. Ptnr. Banks, Owens & Byrd and predecessor firms Anderson, Banks, Nichols & Stewart; Anderson, Banks, Nichols & Leventhal; Anderson & Banks, Jackson, 1968-85; rep. Miss. Ho. of Reps., 1975; judge Miss. 7th Cir. Ct., Hinds County and Yazoo County, 1985-91; assoc. justice Miss. Supreme Ct, Jackson, 1991—; presiding justice Miss. Supreme Ct., Miss. Mem. Miss. Bd. Bar Admissions, 1978-81; pres. State Mut. Fed. Savs. and Loan, Jackson, 1976-89; mem. minority adv. com. U. Miss. Sch. of Law. Bd. dirs. NAACP, 1981—; mem. Nat. Adv. Com. for the Edn. of Disadvantaged Children, 1978-80; del. Dem. Nat. Conv., 1976, 1980; co-mgr. Miss. Carter-Mondale presidl. campaign, 1976; legislator Miss. Ho. of Reps., Jackson, 1976-85; bd. visitors Miss. Coll. Sch. of Law. Mem. ABA, Magnolia Bar Assn., Nat. Bar Assn., Hinds County Bar Assn., Am. Inns of Ct., Charles Clark Inn, Miss. Bar Assn. (chair criminal justice task force), D.C. Bar Assn., Sigma Pi Phi, Am. Inns of Ct., Chalres Clark Inn. Roman Catholic. Home: 976 Metairie Rd Jackson MS 39209-6948 Office: Mississippi Supreme Court 450 High St Jackson MS 39201-1006

BANKS, JOHN ROBERT, JR. lawyer; b. Balt., Mar. 15, 1958; s. John Robert and Ida Carol (Cromer) B. BA, Coll. William and Mary, Williamsburg, Va., 1980; JD, U. Houston, 1983. Bar: Tex. 1983, U.S. Dist. Ct. (so. dist.) Tex. 1983; cert. bus. bankruptcy law Tex. Bd. Legal Specialization. Assoc. Levin & Kasner, PC fka Levin, Roth & Kasner, PC, Houston, 1983-96; pvt. practice, 1997; ptnr. Mason, Coplen & Banks, LLP, 1998-99; shareholder Mason, Coplen, Shuchart, Hutchins & Banks, PC, 2000—. Dir. Cmty. Assn. Inst. Greater Houston, 1995-97, chmn. amb.'s subcom., 1995-97, chmn. legal com., 1995, vice-chmn. legal com., 1994, chmn. mem. svc. com., 1998; adminstrv. bd. Chapelwood United Meth. Ch., 1997-01, trustee, 1998-01. Mem. Am. Bar Assn. Republican. Avocation: stamp collecting. Telecopier: (713) 785-8651. Bankruptcy, General civil litigation, Consumer commercial. Office: Mason Coplen Shuchart Hutchins & Banks PC Attys at Law 7500 San Felipe St Ste 700 Houston TX 77063-1709 E-mail: johnbanksjr@msn.com

BANKS, LINDA T. legal assistant, massage therapist; b. Montgomery, Ala., Apr. 23, 1948; d. Robert Tillman and Margaret (Jackson) Tanner; m. R.O. Banks, Dec. 21, 1971 (div. Apr. 1978); 1 child, Charles R. BA, Brenau Coll., Gainesville, Ga., 1970; cert., Acad. Somatic Healing Arts, Atlanta, 1998. Cert. massage therapist. Legal asst. Powell, Goldstein et al, Atlanta, 1978-81, Martin & Young, Atlanta, 1981-84; adminstrv. asst. Yokogawa Corp., Peachtree City, Ga., 1984-86; legal asst. Sanders, Mottola & Haugen, Newnan, 1986-89; flight attendant ValuJet, Atlanta, 1996-98; self-employed massage therapist, Atlanta and Newnan, 1998—; legal asst. Sutherland Asbill & Brennan, Atlanta, 1989—. Bd. dirs. Manget-Brannon Alliance for Arts, Newnan, 1984; mem., patron Newnan Cmty. Theatre Co., 1981—. Mem. Internat. Massage Assn., Mu Phi Epsilon. Democrat. Episcopal/Methodist. Avocations: playing keyboards in local band, acting in local theatre, tennis, volunteer work for senior citizens. Home: 27 Chestnut Dr Newnan GA 30263-2201 Office: Sutherland Asbill & Brennan 999 Peachtree St NE Ste 2300 Atlanta GA 30309-3996

BANKS, ROBERT SHERWOOD, lawyer; b. Newark, Mar. 28, 1934; s. Howard Douglas and Amelia Violet (Del Bagno) B.; m. Judith Lee Henry; children— Teri, William; children by previous marriage— Robert, Paul, Stephen, Roger, Gregory, Catherine. A.B., Cornell U., 1956, LL.B., 1958. Bar: N.J. 1959, N.Y. 1968. Practice law, Newark, 1958-61; atty. E.I. duPont, Wilmington, Del., 1961-67; with Xerox Corp., Stamford, Conn., 1967-88, v.p., gen. counsel, 1975-88; sr. counsel Latham & Watkins, N.Y.C., 1988-89; gen. counsel Keystone Holdings, 1989-92. Bd. dirs. Cornell U. Found.; mem. panel of mediators, neutral advisors Ctr. for Pub. Resources. Mem. adv. coun. Cornell Law Sch.; past trustee U.S. Supreme Ct. Hist. Soc.; past bd. dirs. Ctr. for Pub. Resources. Mem. ABA, N.Y. Bar Assn., Am. Arbitration Assn. (panel arbitrators), Am. Judicature Soc. (exec. com., bd. dirs., pres. 1989-91), Cornell Law Assn., Am. Corp. Counsel Assn. (bd. dirs., chmn. 1982-83), Atlantic Athletic Club, Jonathan's Landing Club. General corporate. E-mail: RSBSR@mindspring.com

BANKSTON, WILLIAM MARCUS, lawyer; b. San Angelo, Tex., Feb. 16, 1946; s. Wyatt Lester and Mary Alice (Powell) B.; m. Janna Coe Herridge, Aug. 15, 1965 (div.); children: Darla Kae, Kendra Lynne; m. Judith Ann Railsback, Nov. 20, 1981 (div.); m. Frances J. Talbott. BA, BS, Tex. Tech U., 1968; JD, U. Tex., 1971. Bar: Alaska 1971, Tex. 1971, U.S. Tax Ct. 1983, U.S. Ct. Claims 1984, U.S. Supreme Ct. 1986. Assoc. Croft & Bailey, Anchorage, 1971-73; ptnr. Croft, Bailey, Gueschow & Bankston, 1973-74; instr. Anchorage C.C., 1972-74; ptnr. Greene & Bankston, Anchorage, 1974-76, Bankston & McCollum, Anchorage, 1976—. Mem. ABA, Alaska Bar Assn., State Bar Tex. Methodist. State civil litigation, General corporate, Securities. Office: Bankston & McCollum PC 550 W 7th Ave Ste 1800 Anchorage AK 99501-3569

BANNISTER, JOE, lawyer; BA, Cambridge U., Eng., 1984; MA, 1988. Assoc. Lovells, London, 1987-97; ptnr., 1997-98, Hong Kong, 1998—. Co-editor: Guide to Hong Kong Insolvency Regine, 2000. Mem. Hong Kong Soc. Accts. (mgmt. com. insolvency interests group). Bankruptcy. Office: Lovells 23/F Cheung Kong Ct 2 Queen's Rd Central Hong Kong China Fax: (852) 22190222. E-mail: joe.bannister@lovells.com

BANOFF, SHELDON IRWIN, lawyer; b. Chgo., July 10, 1949; BSBA in Acctg., U. Ill., 1971; JD, U. Chgo., 1974. Bar: Ill. 1974, U.S. Tax Ct. 1974. Ptnr. Katten Muchin Zavis, Chgo., 1974—. Chmn. tax conf. planning com. U. Chgo. Law Sch., 1993-94. Co-editor Jour. of Taxation, 1984—; contbr. articles to profl. jours. Mem. ABA, Chgo. Bar Assn. (fed. taxation com., mem. exec. coun. 1980—, chmn. large law firm com., 1999-2000), Chgo. Fed. Tax Forum, Am. Coll. Tax Counsel. E-mial. Corporate taxation, Taxation, general, Personal income taxation. Office: Katten Muchin Zavis 525 W Monroe St Ste 1600 Chicago IL 60661-3693 E-mail: sheldon.banoff@kmz.com

BÁNYAIOVÁ, ALENA, lawyer; b. Most, Czech Republic, May 2, 1949; d. Frantisek and Viola Novák; m. Frantisek Banyai; 1 child, Lucie. LLM, Charles U., Prague, 1972; LLD, 1973, PhD, 1988. Arbitrator Regional Arbitration Prague, 1972-76; mem. legis. dept. Fed. State Arbitration, Prague, 1976-88; scholar Inst. State and Law Acad. Scis., 1988-91; lawyer Altheimer & Gray, 1991—. Lectr. Charles U., 1999. Contbr. articles to profl. jours. Mem. Czech Adv. Chamber, Slovak Adv. Chamber, Internat. Bar Assn., Fedn. Jewish Orgns. (bd. dirs. 1998—). Contracts commercial, General corporate, Mergers and acquisitions. Office: Altheimer & Gray Platnérská 4 110 00 Prague 1 Czech Republic Fax: 00420-2-24810125. E-mail: banyaiovaa@altheimer.cz

BANZHAF, JOHN F., III, legal association administrator, lawyer; b. N.Y.C., July 2, 1940; s. John F., Jr. and Olga Banzhaf; m. Ursula Maag, 1971. B.S. in Elec. Engring, M.I.T., 1962; J.D. magna cum laude, Columbia U., 1965. Civilian research asst. Signal Corps Engring. Labs., 1957; research engr., cons. Lear Siegler Corp., 1959-62, editor Columbia Law Rev., 1964-65; research fellow Nat. Municipal League, 1965; law clk. to U.S. Dist. Judge Spottswood W. Robinson III, 1965-66; asso. firm Watson, Leavonworth, Kelton & Taggart, N.Y.C., 1967; founder, exec. dir. Action on Smoking and Health, Washington, 1968—, Nat. Inst. Legal Activism, 1980—, prof. law and legal activism Nat. Law Center, George Washington U., 1968—; exec. dir. Action on Safety and Health, 1971-80, Open America, 1975-80; founder Nat. Center for Law and the Deaf, 1975—. Bd. dirs. Consumers Union, 1971 Recipient 17th ann. Sat. Rev. award distinguished TV programming in pub. interest, 1969; Advt. Age award, 1967, 68; those who made advt. news, 1967, 68; Benjamin Franklin Lit. and Med. Soc. award, 1981 Mem. Sigma Xi, Eta Kappa Nu, Tau Beta Pi. Home: 2810 N Quebec St Arlington VA 22207-5215 Office: Nat Center for Law and the Deaf 2013 H St NW Washington DC 20006-4207

BARACK, PETER JOSEPH, lawyer, educator; b. Cleve., Nov. 3, 1943; s. Louis Barry and Florence (Schenberg) B.; m. Elise Hoffman, June 6, 1971; children: Sarah, Jonathan, David. AB summa cum laude, Princeton U., 1965; BPhil, Oxford (Eng.) U., 1067; JD magna cum laude, Harvard U., 1970. Bar: Ill. 1970, U.S. Ct. Appeals (7th cir.) 1976, U.S. Supreme Ct. 1978. Asst. prof. bus. adminstrn. Harvard U. Grad. Sch. Bus. Adminstrn., Cambridge, Mass., 1970-72; asst. prof. law Northwestern U. Sch. Law, Chgo., 1972-74, dir. JD-MM joint degree program, 1972-80, assoc. prof., 1974-79, adj. prof. corp. law, Edward Avery Harriman lectr., 1979—, adj. prof. fin. J.L. Kellogg Grad. Sch. Mgmt., 1999—; ptnr. Levy and Erens, 1969-74, Barcak, Ferrazzano, Kirschbaum Perlman & Nagelberg, Chgo., 1984—. Of counsel Mayer, Brown & Platt, Chgo., 1977-79; adj. prof. acctg., Kellogg Grad. Sch. of Mgmt., Northwestern U., 1998—; lectr. in field; pres. Chgo. Mgmt. Group, Inc., 1972—; bd. dirs. Christian Dior Perfumes, Inc., Duty Free Stores, Inc. Contbr. articles to legal jours. Pres. Highland Park (Ill.) Libr., 1982-84. Recipient Lt. John A. Larkin, Jr. Meml. prize, 1965; Marshall scholar, 1965; Nuffield scholar, 1966. Mem. ABA, Ill. State Bar Assn., Chgo. Bar Assn., Chgo. Coun. Lawyers, Assn. Marshall Scholars. General corporate, Private international, Securities. Home: 1379 Sheridan Rd Highland Park IL 60035-3406 Office: 333 W Wacker Dr Ste 2700 Chicago IL 60606-1227

BARAN, JAN WITOLD, lawyer, educator; b. Ingolstadt, Germany, May 14, 1948; came to U.S., 1951; s. Jerzy Leopold and Leonce Sidonie (Vanden Bussche) B.; m. Kathryn Kavanagh, June 16, 1979; children: Brendan Jerzy, Maria Leonce, Elise Jett, Anna Margaret. BA, Ohio Wesleyan U., 1970; JD, Vanderbilt U., 1973. Bar: Tenn. 1973, D.C. 1976, U.S. Dist. Ct. D.C. 1980, U.S. Ct. Appeals D.C. 1980, U.S. Ct. Appeals (10th cir.) 1994, U.S. Supreme Ct. 1980. Legal counsel Nat. Rep. Congl. Com., Washington, 1975-77; exec. asst. Fed. Election Commn., 1977-79; assoc. Baker & Hostetler, 1979-81, ptnr., 1981-85, Wiley, Rein & Fielding, Washington, 1985—. Gen. counsel, George Bush for Pres., Inc., 1987-88; gen. counsel, Bush-Quayle, Inc., 1988; lectr., co-chair Practicing Law Inst., Corp. Polit. Activities, Washington, 1978—. Author: The Election Law Primer for Corporations, 1984, 88, 92, 2000. Chmn. nat. adv. bd. Jour. of Law and Politics, 1983—; gen. counsel Am. bicentennial Presdl. Inaugural Inc., 1989, Rep. Nat. Com., 1989-92; mem. Pres. Commn. Fed. Ethics Law Reform; amb., head U.S. del. World Adminstrv. Radio Conf. WARC, Malaga, Spain, 1992; trustee Citizens Rsch. Found., 1995—; gen. counsel, dir. Bus.-Industry Polit. Action Com., 1996—. Patrick Wilson scholar, 1970-73. Mem. ABA (chmn. com. election law 1981-2000), D.C. Bar Assn., FBA (chmn. polit. campaign and election law com. 1981-83). Roman Catholic. Administrative and regulatory, Federal civil litigation. Home: 1608 Walleston Ct Alexandria VA 22302-3928 Office: Wiley Rein & Fielding 1776 K St NW Ste 900 Washington DC 20006-2332

BARANDES, ROBERT, lawyer; b. Bklyn., May 15, 1947; s. Max and Helen (Berger) B.; m. Joan Noveck, May 28, 1970 (div. Jan. 1981); m. Kathleen Lindsey, Aug. 22, 1982 (div. Jan. 1986). Student, U. Coll., London, 1967-68; BA magna cum laude, Union Coll., Schenectady, N.Y., 1969; JD, Harvard U., 1972. Bar: N.Y. 1973, U.S. Dist. Ct. (so. and ea. dists.) N.Y. 1976. From assoc. to ptnr. Barandes, Rabbino & Arnold, N.Y.C., 1972-81; ptnr. Roper, Barandes & Fertel, LLP, 1981-99; of counsel Beckman, Millman & Sanders LLP, 2000; ptnr. Beckman, Hillman, Barandes & Douglas, LLP, 2001—. Prodr. (on Broadway) The News, 1986, Broadway revival of Damn Yankees, 1994-96, (on Broadway) Epic Proportions, 1999, Broadway revival of Bells Are Ringing, 2001. Assoc. producer: (Broadway Play) On The Waterfront, 1995, Lyricist Musical Etched in Stone, 1984; writer, lyricist, musical Star Crossed Lovers, 1984; bookwriter, lyricist musical Almost Eden, 1990. Mem. ABA, League Am. Theatres and Producers, Phi Beta Kappa. Jewish. Avocations: writing, skiing, golf, tennis. General corporate, Entertainment, Securities. Office: Beckman Millman Barandes & Douglas LLP 116 John St Rm 1313 New York NY 10038-3303

BARASCH, AMY PITCAIRN, lawyer; b. N.Y.C., May 10, 1965; d. Mal Livingston and Sarah Ann (Beckley) B. BA, Brown U., 1986; JD, Columbia U., 1996. Bar: N.Y. 1997, U.S. Dist. Ct. (so. dist.) N.Y. 1997. Writer, editor 7 Days mag., N.Y.C., 1988-90; freelance journalist, Paris, 1990-93; assoc. Hughes Hubbard & Reed LLP, N.Y.C., 1997—. Mem. Assn. Bar City N.Y. Democrat. General civil litigation, Family and matrimonial. Office: Hughes Hubbard & Reed LLP One Battery Park Plz New York NY 10004

BARASCH, DAVID M. prosecutor; U.S. atty. U.S. Dist. Ct. (mid. dist.) Pa. Office: US Attorney Mid District of PA Federal Bldg PO Box 11754 Harrisburg PA 17108-1754

BARASCH, MAL LIVINGSTON, lawyer; b. N.Y.C., May 14, 1929; s. Joseph and Ernestine (Livingston) B.; m. S. Ann Beckley, May 19, 1962; children: Amy Pitcairn Barasch, Jody Taylor Barasch B.S. in Econs. with distinction, U. Pa., 1951; LL.B., Yale U., 1954. Bar: N.Y. 1957, U.S. Dist. Ct. (so. dist.) N.Y. 1960, U.S. Tax Ct. 1960. Assoc. Mudge Rose Guthrie Alexander & Ferdon, N.Y.C., 1957-62; assoc. Rosenman & Colin, 1962-67; ptnr. Rosenman & Colin, LLC, 1968-2000; council Rosenman & Colin LLP, 2000—. Mem. exec. com., 2d v.p. library N.Y. Law Inst., 1979-2000. Dist. leader, mem. exec. com. N.Y. County Dem. Com., 1961-65; treas., bd. dirs. Lenox Hill Neighborhood House; bd. dirs. Visions, Svcs. for the Blind and Visually Impaired. With U.S. Army, 1954-56. Fellow N.Y. Bar Found., Am. Coll. Trust and Estate Counsel; mem. ABA, N.Y. State Bar Assn., Assn. of Bar of City of N.Y. (chmn. com. on trusts, estates and surrogates cts. 2000—), Internat. Acad. Estate and Trust Law (academician, exec. coun.), Beta Gamma Sigma Club: University (N.Y.C.) Estate planning, Probate, Estate taxation. Home: 1088 Park Ave New York NY 10128-1132 E-mail: mlbarasch@rosenman.com, baraschNY@aol.com

BARASH, ANTHONY HARLAN, lawyer; b. Galesburg, Ill., Mar. 18, 1943; s. Burrel B. and Rosalyne J. (Silver) B.; m. Jean Anderson, May 17, 1965; children: Elizabeth, Matthew, Katherine, Andrew. AB cum laude, Harvard U., 1965; JD, U. Chgo., 1968. Bar: Calif. 1969, S.C. Assoc. Irell & Manella, L.A., 1968-71, Cox, Castle & Nicholson, L.A., 1971-74, ptnr., 1975-80, Barash & Hill, L.A., 1980-84, Wildman, Harrold, Allen, Dixon, Barash & Hill, L.A., 1984-87, Barash & Hill, L.A., 1988-93, Seyfarth, Shaw, Fairweather & Geraldson, L.A., 1993-96; sr. v.p. corp. affairs, gen. counsel Bowater, Inc., Greenville, S.C., 1996—. Bd. dirs. Deauville Restaurants, Inc. Trustee Pitzer Coll., 1981-98, vice-chmn., 1984-96; pres., bd. dirs. Beverly Hills Bar Assn. Found., 1983-96; bd. dirs. Nat. Equal Justice Libr., Urban League of the Upstate, Peace Ctr. for the Performing Arts. Fellow Am. Bar Found. (life); mem. ABA, S.C. Bar, State Bar Assn. Calif., Greenville County Bar Assn., Beverly Hills Bar Assn. (bd. govs. 1979-81, 88-94, pres. 1992-93), Harvard Club N.Y. Administrative and regulatory, Banking, Real property. Home: 1212 Shadow Way Greenville SC 29615-3843 Office: Bowater Inc 55 E Camperdown Way Greenville SC 29601-3597

BARBA, JULIUS WILLIAM, lawyer; b. Arlington, N.J., May 22, 1923; s. John and Rose (Lettiere) B.; m. Susan Vartanian, Oct. 24, 1970; children: Susan Elizabeth, Christina Barba. BA, Princeton U., 1947; LLB, U. Pa., 1950. Bar: N.J. 1950, N.Y. 1981, U.S. Supreme Ct. 1959, U.S. Ct. Appeals (D.C. cir.) 1960, U.S. Dist. Ct. D.C. 1969, U.S. Ct. Appeals (2d cir.) 1973. Assoc. Young, Shanley, Foehl, Congleton & Fisher, Newark, 1950-54; asst. spl. counsel to Pres. Eisenhower, Washington, 1954-57; ptnr. Shanley & Fisher, P.C., Morristown, 1957—; bd. dirs. Selective Ins. Group, Inc., Branchville, N.J., 1983. Bd. trustees Peck Sch., Morristown, N.J., 1982, Kent Place Sch., Summit, N.J.; mem. membership corp. Morristown Meml. Hosp., 1979, trustee, 1984; chmn. N.J. State Fin. Com., 1974-76; bd. dirs. Atlantic Health Systems, Inc. Served to lt. (j.g.) USNR, 1943-46, PTO. Mem. ABA, N.J. State Bar Assn., D.C. Bar Assn., Morris County Bar Assn., Essex County Bar Assn. Republican. Roman Catholic. Clubs: Met. (Washington); Baltusrol Golf (Springfield, N.J.), Morris County Golf (Convent, N.J.); Shinnecock Hills Golf (Southampton, N.Y.). Administrative and regulatory, Contracts commercial, General corporate. Home: Long Hill Rd New Vernon NJ 07976 Office: Shanley & Fisher PC 131 Madison Ave Morristown NJ 07960-6086

BARBADORO, PAUL JAMES, federal judge; b. Providence, June 4, 1955; s. Donald James and Elizabeth B.; m. Inez E. McDermott, Aug. 16, 1986; children: Katherine E., John James. BA cum laude, Gettysburg Coll., 1977; JD magna cum laude, Boston Coll., 1980. Bar: N.H. 1980. Asst. atty. gen. N.H. Atty. Gen., Concord, 1980-84; legal counsel U.S. Sen. Warren B. Rudman, Washington, 1984-86, Orr & Reno, Concord, 1986-87; dep. chief counsel U.S. Senate Iran-Contra Com., Washington, 1987; dir. Rath, Young, Pignatelli and Oyer, Concord, 1987-92; judge U.S. Dist. Ct., 1992-97, chief judge, 1997—. Mem. adv. group for dist. of N.H., Civil Justice Reform Act, Concord, 1992-94; mem. long range planning com. N.H. Supreme Ct., 1989-90; mem. 1st Cir. Jud. Coun., 1994-96; adj. prof. Franklin Pierce Law Ctr., 1997-98. Mem. N.H. Bar Assn. (chmn. unauthorized practice of law com. 1982-84, jud. conf. com. on automation and tech. 1996—, com. on cooperation with the cts. 1997—), U.S. Dist. Ct. N.H. Bar, 1st Cir. Ct. Appeals Bar, Order of Coif. Office: WB Rudman Courthouse 55 Pleasant St Rm 409 Concord NH 03301-3938

BARBEOSCH, WILLIAM PETER, banker, lawyer; b. N.Y.C., Nov. 25, 1954; s. Peter Joseph and Marie Delores (Slesiona) B.; m. Marta B. Varela, Sept. 6, 1986. AB magna cum laude, Brown U., 1976; JD, Columbia U., 1979; MBA, Yale U., 1989. Bar: N.Y. 1980, U.S. Tax Ct. 1985. Atty. Casey, Lane and Mittendorf (and successor firms), N.Y.C., 1979-86, Milbank, Tweed, Hadley and McCloy, N.Y.C., 1986-87; mgmt. assoc. Swiss Bank Corp., 1989-90; v.p. The J.P. Morgan Chase & Co., 1990-99; mng. dir. J.P. Morgan Chase & Co. and predecessor firms, 1999—, Internat. Wealth Adv., 1999—; dir. Chase Manhattan Bank & Trust Co. (Bahamas) Ltd., 2000—. Bd. advisors The Chase Jour., 1997—. Mem. N.Y. State Bar Assn., Assn. of the Bar of City of N.Y., Brown U. Club N.Y., Stone House Club, Yale Club (N.Y.C.), Phi Kappa Psi (sec. R.I. Alpha chpt. 1974-75). Republican. Roman Catholic. Avocations: swimming, history, politics. Home: 545 W 111th St Apt 7E New York NY 10025-1965 Office: JP Morgan Private Bank 345 Park Ave New York NY 10154 E-mail: bill.barbeosch@jpmorgan.com

BARBER, JANICE ANN, lawyer; b. Buffalo, May 30, 1947; d. Warren Richard and Betty A. (Stabler) B. BA with high distinction, U. Ky., 1969; JD cum laude, SUNY, Buffalo, 1977. Bar: N.Y. 1978, U.S. Dist. Ct. (we. dist.) N.Y. 1978. Reporter The Times-Union, Rochester, N.Y., 1969-74; assoc. Smith, Murphy & Schoepperle, Buffalo, 1977-84, ptnr., 1985-95, Brown & Tarantino, LLP, 1995—. Warden Episcopal Ch. of the Good Shepherd, 2001—; bd. dirs. Parkside Cmty. Assn., 1996—, Pro-Zoo, Buffalo Zool., 2000-2001. Mem. N.Y. State Bar Assn., Erie County Bar Assn., AAUW (Buffalo chap.), Audubon Soc., Roycrofters (life), Buffalo Olmstead Conservancy. Democrat. Episcopalian. State civil litigation, Insurance, Personal injury. Home: 139 Woodward Ave Buffalo NY 14214-2311 E-mail: janbfflo@cs.com

BARBER, MARK EDWARD, lawyer; b. Enumclaw, Wash., Dec. 30, 1952; s. Earl Marion Barber and Delila Mae Willis Lontz; m. Pamela Johnson, Aug. 30, 1974; 1 child, Matthew Edward. BA, U. Wash., 1975; JD, Pepperdine U., 1978. Bar: Wash. 1978, U.S. Dist. Ct. Wash. 1978, U.S. Ct. Appeals (9th cir.) 1980, U.S. Supreme Ct. 1985. Atty. Heavey & Woody, Inc. P.S., Seattle, 1978-79; sole practitioner, 1979-81; atty., prin. shareholder Warren Barber & Fontes, P.S., Renton, 1981—. Bd. dirs. Justice Polit. Action Com., Tacoma, 1993-95, Sunset Valley Farms Homeowners Assn., Issaquah, Wash., 1991-92, 95-96. Mem. ATLA, Wash. State Bar Assn., King County Bar Assn., Wash. State Trial Lawyers Assn. (pres. 1995-96). Personal injury, Product liability, Professional liability. Office: Warren Barber et al 100 S 2nd St Renton WA 98055-2013 E-mail: mebarber@seanet.com

BARBER, ROBERT CUSHMAN, lawyer; b. Columbus, Ga., Aug. 30, 1950; s. Robert Kennard and Kathleen (Cushman) B.; m. Bonnie A. Neilan, Apr. 30, 1983; children: Nicholas, Benjamin, Alexander. AB, Harvard U., 1972, M in City Planning, 1977; JD, Boston U., 1977. Bar: Mass. 1978, N.Y. 1978, U.S. Dist. Ct. Mass. 1981, U.S. Dist. Ct. (ea. and so. dist.) N.Y. 1981. Asst. dist. atty. N.Y. County, N.Y.C., 1977-81; assoc. Looney & Grossman, Boston, 1981-84, ptnr., 1985—, mng. ptnr., 2000—. Trial advisor Harvard Law Sch., 1985—. Bd. dirs. Fayerweather Edn. Found., 1995—; trustee Social Law Libr., 1998—. Mem. ABA, Boston Bar Assn. Federal civil litigation, Computer, Real property. Office: Looney & Grossman LLP 101 Arch St Ste 900 Boston MA 02110-1117 E-mail: rbarber@lgllp.com

BARBERY, PAUL SAUNDERS, lawyer; b. Keystone, W.Va., Dec. 5, 1936; s. Edwin Carrico and Mildred Marshall Barbery; m. Margaret Harris, July 21, 1961 (dec. July 1975); m. Sarah Davis, May 22, 1976; 1 child, Kevin Saunders. BS in Mining Engring., Va. Poly. Inst. and State U., 1959; LLB, U. Richmond, 1964. Bar: Va. 1964, W.Va. 1993, N.C. 1994, U.S. Dist. Ct. (ea. dist.) Va. 1964, U.S. Ct. Appeals (4th cir.) 1968, U.S. Dist. Ct. (so. dist.) W.Va. 1983. Ptnr. Martin Hopkins & Lemon, Roanoke, Va., 1964-74; gen. counsel PittstonCoal Group, Lebanon, 1974-75; gen. counsel, corp. sec. Va. Iron and Coke, Roanoke, 1975-76; sr. v.p., gen. counsel A.T. Massey Coal Co., Richmond, 1976-94; pvt. practice, 1994-97, Charlotte, N.C., 1997—. V.p., gen. counsel Am. Metals and Coal Internat., 1994—; chmn. bd. Elk Run Coal Co., Sylvester, W.Va., 1976-94; cons. in field. Trustee Eastern Mineral Law Found., Morgantown, W.Va., 1985-94; advisor Marshall U. Higher Edn. Learning Program, 1992-95; bd. dirs. Stonehenge County Club, Richmond, 1989-92. Named Disting. Alumni, Dept. Mines and Minerals, Va. Poly. Inst. and State U., 1990. Mem. McNeil Law Soc., Tau Beta Pi. Avocations: golf, boating. Contracts commercial, General corporate, General practice. Home: 481 Bay Harbour Rd Mooresville NC 28117-9059 Office: BB&T Center 200 S College St Ste 620 Charlotte NC 28202-2065

BARCAN, STEPHEN EMANUEL, lawyer; b. Buffalo, N.Y., July 10, 1942; s. Abe and Goldie (Irom) B.; m. Bettye Ann Grossman, June 13, 1965; children: Sara Ellen, Daniel Jonathan, Adam Michael. AB, Columbia Coll., 1963; JD cum laude, Rutgers U., 1966. Bar: N.J. 1966, U.S. Dist. Ct. N.J. 1966, U.S. Ct. Appeals (3d cir.) 1971. Law sec. to presiding judge Appellate div. N.J. Superior Ct., 1966-67; assoc. Wilentz, Goldman & Spitzer, P.A., Woodbridge, N.J., 1967-74, ptnr., 1974—. Pres. Temple Emanu-El, Westfield, N.J., 1984-86. Mem. N.J. Bar Assn., Middlesex County Bar Assn. Democrat. Jewish. Club: Raritan Yacht (Perth Amboy, N.J.). Administrative and regulatory, Federal civil litigation, Environmental. Office: Wilentz Goldman & Spitzer PO Box 10 90 Woodbridge Ctr Dr Ste 900 Woodbridge NJ 07095-1142

BARCELLA, ERNEST LAWRENCE, JR. lawyer; b. Washington, May 23, 1945; s. Ernest Lawrence and Louise Marion (Berniere) B.; m. Mary Elizabeth Lashley, June 1, 1970; 1 child, Laura Louise. AB, Dartmouth U., 1967; JD, Vanderbilt U., 1970. Bar: D.C. 1971, U.S. Dist. Ct. D.C. 1971, U.S. Ct. Appeals (D.C. cir.) 1971, U.S. Supreme Ct. 1976. Asst. U.S. atty., Washington, 1970-86; ptnr. Katten, Muchin, Zavis & Dombroff, 1991-94, Paul, Hastings, Janofsky & Walker, Washington, 1994—. Recipient John Marshall award, U.S. Dept. Justice, 1983. Fellow Am. Coll. Trial Lawyers; mem. ABA (white collar crimes com. criminal justice sect., complex crimes com. litigation sect.), Assn. Trial Lawyers Am., Fed. Bar Assn. (younger lawyer award 1979). Roman Catholic. Criminal. Office: Paul Hastings Janofsky and Walker 10th Fl 1299 Pennsylvania Ave NW Washington DC 20004-2400

BARCELO, JOHN JAMES, III, law educator; b. New Orleans, Sept. 23, 1940; s. John James Jr. and Elfrida Margaret (Bisso) B.; m. Lucy L. Wood, July 14, 1974; children— Lisa, Amy, Steven. B.A., Tulane U., 1962, J.D., 1966; S.J.D., Harvard U., 1977. Bar: La. 1967, D.C. 1974, U.S. Supreme Ct. 1974, N.Y. 1975. Fulbright scholar U. Bonn, Fed. Republic Germany, 1966-67; research assoc. Harvard U. Law Sch., Cambridge, Mass., 1968-69; prof. law Cornell U. Law Sch., Ithaca, N.Y., 1969—, A. Robert Noll. prof. of law, 1984-96, dir internat. legal studies, 1972-88, 90—, William Nelson Cromwell prof. internat. and comprative law, 1996—. Cons. Import Trade Adminstrn., Dept. Commerce Author: (with others) Law: Its Nature, Functions and Limits, 3rd edit., 1986, International Commercial Arbitration, 1999; co-editor: Lawyers' Practice and Ideals: A Comparative View, 1999; contbr. articles to profl. jours. Mem. Am. Assn. for Comparative Study of Law (bd. dirs.), Am. Soc. Internat. Law, Soc. Comparative Law, Maritime Law Assn. U.S. Office: Cornell U Law Sch Myron Taylor Hall Ithaca NY 14853

BARCLAY, H(UGH) DOUGLAS, lawyer, former state senator; b. N.Y.C., July 5, 1932; s. Hugh and Dorothy Barclay; m. Sara Seiter, Aug. 15, 1959; children: Kathryn D., David H., Dorothy G., Susan M., William A. BA, Yale U., 1955; JD, Syracuse U., 1961; LLD (hon.), St. Lawrence U., 1980; ScD (hon.), Clarkson Univ., 1981; LLD (hon.), SUNY, 1990, Syracuse U., 1997. Bar: N.Y. 1962. Ptnr. Hiscock & Barclay and predecessors, Syracuse, N.Y., 1961—. Sec., gen. counsel KeyCorp and subs., Albany, N.Y., 1971-89; mem. N.Y. State Senate, 1965-84, chmn. Judiciary com., chmn. Select Task Force on Ct. Reorgn., chmn. senate codes com.; dir., chmn. bd. Syracuse Supply Co; chmn. bd. Eagle Media, Inc. Mem. N.Y. State Econ. Power Allocation Bd., N.Y. Racing Assn., bd. trustees; pres. Met. Devel. Assn.; trustee, former chmn. Syracuse U., chair chancellor search com.; vice chmn. N.Y. State George Bush for Pres., 1988; chmn. N.Y. State Bush-Quayle campaign, 1992; mem. policy coun. Gov. Pataki's Transition Team; bd. visitors Syracuse U. Coll. Law; mem. Onondaga C.C. Found. Lt. arty. U.S. Army, 1955-57, Korea. Mem. ABA, N.Y. State Bar Assn. Banking, General corporate. Office: Hiscock & Barclay PO Box 4878 221 S Warren St Syracuse NY 13202-1633

BARDACKE, PAUL GREGORY, lawyer, former attorney general; b. Oakland, Calif., Dec. 16, 1944; s. Theodore Joseph and Frances (Woodward) B.; children: Julie, Brynn, Francheska, Chloe. BA cum laude, U. Calif.-Santa Barbara, 1966; JD, U. Calif.-Berkeley, 1969. Bar: Calif. 1969, N.Mex. 1970. Lawyer Legal Aid Soc., Albuquerque, 1969; assoc. firm Sutin, Thayer & Browne, 1970-82; atty. gen. State of N.Mex., Santa Fe, 1982-86; ptnr. Sutin, Thayer & Browne, 1987-90, Eaves, Bardacke, Baugh, Kierst & Kiernan, P.A., 1991—. Adj. prof. N.Mex. Law Sch., Albuquerque, 1973—; mem. faculty Nat. Inst. Trial Lawyers Advocacy, 1978— Bd. dirs. All Faiths Receiving Home, Albuquerque; bd. dirs. Friends of Art, 1974, Artspace Mag., 1979-80, Legal Aid Soc., 1970-74; bd. trustees Albuquerque Cmty. Found., 2001-. Reginald Heber Smith fellow, 1969 Fellow Am. Coll. Trial Lawyers; mem. ABA, Calif. Bar Assn., N.Mex. Bar Assn., Am. Bd. Trial Advocates (pres. N.Mex. chpt. 1992-93). Democrat. Antitrust, Federal civil litigation, State civil litigation. Office: Eaves Bardacke Baugh Kierst & Kiernan PA PO Box 35670 Albuquerque NM 87176-5670

BARDENWERPER, WILLIAM BURR, lawyer; b. Jan. 12, 1952; s. H. William and Dorothy (Weix) Bardenwerper; m. Gail Smith, Apr. 11, 1959. BA, U. Va., 1974; JD, U. Louisville, 1977. Bar: Ky. 1978, Wis. 1985, U.S. Dist. Ct. (we. dist.) Ky. 1978. Counsel, dir. intergovtl. affairs Jefferson County, Louisville, 1978—84; ptnr. Bardenwerper & Lobb P.L.L.C., 1984—. Author (editor): (books) Kentucky Methods of Practice (4 vols.), 1989, Kentucky Methods of Practice (4 vols.), 2d edit., 1998; editor (in-chief): (mag.) Louisville Lawyer mag., 1977—81. Vice chmn. Louisville C. of C., 1993—96; mayor City of Hurstbourne, Ky., 1994—; bd. dir. Homebuilders Assn. of Louisville, 1993—96. Recipient Disting. Svc. award, U. Louisville Sch. Law, 1977, Assoc. of Yr. award, Home Builders Assn. of Louisville, 1995. Mem.: ABA, Wis. Bar Assn., Ky. Bar Assn., Louisville Bar Assn. (chmn. real estate and zoning sect. 1988), Rotary (pres. Hurstbourne 1994—95). Roman Catholic. General corporate, Land use and zoning (including planning), Real property. Home: 8620 Blackpool Dr Louisville KY 40222-5667 Office: Bardenwerper & Lobb PLLC 8311 Shelbyville Rd Louisville KY 40222-5544

BARILLA, FRANK (ROCKY BARILLA), lawyer, consultant, educator; b. Los Angeles, Jan. 26, 1948; s. Bruno Frank and Lucera (Campos) B. Student Glendale Coll., 1966-68; B.A., U. So. Calif., 1970, J.D., 1975; M.B.A., Stanford U., 1972. Bar: Calif. 1975, Oreg. 1976, U.S. Dist. Ct. (no. dist.) Calif. 1976, U.S. Dist. Ct. Oreg. 1976, U.S. Ct. Appeals (9th cir.) 1977. Adj. asst. prof. immigration law Sch. Law, U. Oreg., Eugene, 1976-88; adj. asst. prof. Willamette U., Salem, Oreg., 1979, 83, 86; instr. bus. law Linfield Coll., McMinnville, Oreg., 1983; adminstr. labor and edn. com. Oreg. Legislature, Salem, 1979, 81, 83, legal counsel joint judiciary com., 1984-86, legislator, state rep. Oreg. Legis. Assembly, 1986-89; cons. Interface Cons., Portland, Oreg., 1981-84; hearings officer Oreg. Employment Div., Salem, 1982-83; adj. instr. Lewis and Clark Law Sch., Portland, Oreg., 1977, 80; cons. in field; vice chmn. Housing and Urban Devel. Com., mem. various other coms. Oreg. State Legislature; bd. dirs. La Alianza Legal de Oregon, 1983-88. Author tng. manual Enabling Legislation for Multicultural Education, 1981. Mem. Salem Pub. Schs. Affirmative Action, 1976-78; chmn. Salem Chpt. Hispanic Polit. Action Com., 1983-84; bd. dirs. Oreg. Soccer Assn., Salem, 1978, United Way, Portland, 1980. Recipient Civil Liberties award Oreg. chpt. ACLU, 1984. Calif. State fellow/scholar, 1968-72; fellow Merrill Trust, 1970-72, Council Grad. Mgmt. Edn., 1970-72, Kellogg Found., 1981-82. Mem. Oreg. State Bar (com. on affirmative action 1978-80, com. on fgn. and internat. law 1980-83, com. legal aid 1983-86), Calif. State Bar, Marion County Bar Assn. Home: 2429 Hastings Dr Belmont CA 94002-3319 Office: 1118 10th St Ste 200 Sacramento CA 95814-3504

BARKEN, BERNARD ALLEN, lawyer; b. St. Louis, July 20, 1924; s. Gottlieb and Hattie E. (Rubin) B.; m. Jocelyn Moss Kopman, Sept. 1, 1948; children: Thomas L., Dale Susan. JD, Washington U., 1947. Bar: Mo. 1947, U.S. Dist. Ct. (ea. dist.) Mo. 1947, U.S. Ct. Appeals (8th cir.) 1954, U.S. Tax Ct. 1966, U.S. Ct. Appeals 2nd cir.) 1985, U.S. Supreme Ct. 1984. Sole practice, St. Louis, 1947-80; ptnr. Shifrin & Treiman, 1980-88; pres. Bernard A. Barken, 1988-91; ptnr. Barken & Bakewell L.L.P., 1991—. With USAAF, 1943-44. Mem. ABA, Bar Assn. Met. St. Louis (v.p. 1958, chmn. young lawyers 1953). Jewish. Avocations: piano, tennis, gardening. General civil litigation, General corporate, General practice. Home: 30 Vouga Ln Saint Louis MO 63131-2628 Office: Barken & Bakewell LLP 500 N Broadway Ste 2000 Saint Louis MO 63102-2130 Fax: 314-444-7892. E-mail: babarken@hotmail.com

BARKER, DOUGLAS ALAN, lawyer; b. Martinsville, Va., Oct. 25, 1957; s. Cecil Ray and Virginia Adeline (Bryant) B.; children: Daryn Ruth, Dylan Victoria. BS, Va. Tech., 1981; MBA, The Citadel, 1988; JD cum laude, Pepperdine U., 1993. Bar: Calif. 1993, U.S. Dist. Ct. (ctrl. dist.) Calif. 1993, S.C. 1996, U.S. Dist. Ct. S.C. 1996. Assoc. Haight, Brown & Bonesteel, Santa Monica, Calif., 1993-96, Young Clement Rivers & Tisdale, Charleston, S.C., 1996-97; pvt. practice, 1997—. Lt. comdr. USN, 1981-87. Decorated Expeditionary medal USN, Beirut, Lebanon, 1983. Mem. ABA, L.A. Bar Assn., Charleston County Bar Assn., Assn. Bus. Trial Lawyers, L.A. JD/MBA Assn., Phi Delta Phi (magister 1992-93). Avocation: military history. General civil litigation, Intellectual property, Trademark and copyright. Home: 1253 Sam Snead Dr Mount Pleasant SC 29466-6923 Office: 171 Church St Ste 160 Charleston SC 29401-3137 E-mail: mail@douglasbarker.com

BARKER, ROBERT OSBORNE (BOB BARKER), mediator, educator; b. Cleve., June 13, 1932; m. Sharon Ann (div.); children: Debra, Stephen Robert, Dawn, Michael, Colleen. Student, Henry Ford C.C., 1950; BA in Comm. Arts and Sci., Mich. Ste U., 1954; postgrad., LaSalle U., 1966-69, U. Wis., 1989, U. Fla., 1996, 2000-01. Lic. cmty. assn. mgr., real estate agent; registered lobbyist Nat. Assn. Mfrs. With pub. rels. dept. Ford Motor Co., Dearborn, Mich., 1953; mgr. Kaiser Aluminum Co., Chgo., 1956-58; advt. mgr. Bastian Blessing Co., 1958-59; mgr. Sun Co., Ohio and Detroit, 1959-71, Goodyear Tire & Rubber Co., Detroit, 1971-72; mgr., v.p. Nat. Assn. Mfrs., Washington, Boston and, 1972-87; pres., CEO Barker Cons. Inc., 1987-96; mgr., v.p. seminars and materials dept. Am. Supplier Inst., 1987-90; nat. mdse./mktg. mgr. Costa del Mar Sunglasses, Ormond Beach, Fla., 1990-91; resort mgr. Oceanside 99 Condo, 1992-93, Outrigger Beach Club, 1994-95. Adj. prof. mktg., pub. rels., advt., retailing, sales fundamentals, global and internat. mktg. Daytona Beach C.C., 1994—; owner Dolphin Beach Club Condo, 1981-2001, bd. dirs., 1991-99; cert. and pvt. mediator, 1995—. Twp. trustee, Findlay, Ohio, 1962; lay min. Episcopal ch., 1960-85, vestry, 1981; mem. exec. bd. dirs. Volusia County Rep., 1991-2000; bd. dirs. Am. Cancer Soc., 1991-2001; adv., 2001—; bd. dirs. Dearborn Civic Theatre, 1980-84, Volusia Presdl. forum, 1991-99, Dearborn City Beautiful commr. emeritus, 1970-90; commr. Ormond Beach Quality of Life, Beautification and Planning bds., 1990-99; mem. adv. coun. bd. Habitat Humanity, 1995-99; res. police officer, Dearborn, 1968-88; pres. Dearborn High and Lindbergh Elem. PTA; bd. dirs. Bldg. Assn. Mgrs., 1991-95, Cmty. assoc. Inst., 1993-97, Volusia County Pers. Bd., 1991-93; mem. adv. coun. bd. Coun. of Aging, 1991-2000; mem. Fla. Police Benevolent Assn., Fla. Sheriffs Assn., Am. Fedn. Police; bd. dirs. Daytona and Ormond Beach Rep. Club, 1991-99, heritage mem. Ormond Meml. Art Mus., 1991-2001; amb. Daytona Internat. Airport; team selection scout Fla. Citrus Sports for New Year's Bowl football game, Orlando, Fla., 1997—; mem. elder voice focus group Genesis Elder Care, 2001—. Served with USNR, 1949-58, AFROTC, 1951-54; asst. publicity dir. bd. dirs. Ormond Sr. Games, 1994-96 Recipient Vol. of Yr. award Am. Cancer Soc., 1998. Mem. Meeting Planners Internat., Advt. Fedn., Assn. Execs., Fla. Pub. Rels. Soc. (Volusia chpt., former v.p. bd. dirs. 1996-98), Am. Legion (life), Mich. State U. Alumni (life, past. pres. 4 alumni clubs), Mich. State Varsity Alumni Club (life), U. Fla. Alumni Assn. (v.p. edn. 1999—), Ormond Beach C. of C. (amb., former chmn. pub. rels., Beatification, JazzMatazz, social com. 1990-2001), Nat. Assn. Sr. Friends of Volusia/Flagler Counties (pres. 2000—), Ormond Shrine Club (pres. 1994-95), Elks, Exch. Club, Rotary (pres. 1987-88), Masons, Moose-Legion, Shriners (dir. pub. rels. 1984, provost unit, Fez on Wheels and Vets. unit), Delta Tau Delta. E-mail: bobbarker13. Home: Unit 613 229 S Ridgewood Ave Daytona Beach FL 32114-4330 E-mail: 99@yahoo.com

BARKER, SARAH EVANS, judge; b. Mishawaka, Ind., June 10, 1943; d. James McCall and Sarah (Yarbrough) Evans; m. Kenneth R. Barker, Nov. 25, 1972. BS, Ind. U., 1965, LLD (hon.), 1999; JD, Am. U., 1969; LLD (hon.), U. Indpls., 1984; D in Pub. Svc. (hon.), Butler U., 1987; LLD (hon.), Marian Coll., 1991; LHD, U. Evansville, 1993; LLD (hon.), Wabash Coll., 1999, Hanover Coll., 2001. Bar: Ind. 1969, U.S. Dist. Ct. (so. dist.) Ind., 1969, U.S. Ct. Appeals (7th cir.) 1973, U.S. Supreme Ct., 1978. Legal asst. to senator U.S. Senate, 1969-71; spl. counsel to minority, govt. ops. com. permanent investigations subcom., 1971-72; dir. rsch. scheduling and advance Senator Percy Re-election Campaign, 1972; asst. U.S. atty. So. Dist. Ind., 1972-76, 1st asst. U.S. atty., 1976-77, U.S. atty., 1981-84; judge U.S. Dist. Ct. (so. dist.) Ind., 1984-94, chief judge, 1994—2000. Assoc., then ptnr. Bose, McKinney & Evans, Indpls., 1977-81; mem. long range planning com. Jud. Conf. U.S., 1991-96, exec. com., 1989-91, standing com. fed. rules of practice and procedure, 1987-91, dist. judge rep., 1988-91; mem. jud. coun. 7th cir. Ct. Appeals, 1988-2000, jud. fellows commn. U.S. Supreme Ct., 1993-98; jud. adv. com., sentencing commn., 1995-97, bd. advisors, Ind. U., Purdue U., Indpls., 1989—; mem. pres.'s cabinet Ind. U., 1995—; bd. visitors Ind. U. Sch. of Law, Bloomington, 1984—; bd. dirs. Clarian Health Ptnrs., 1996—, Christian Theol. Sem., 1999—; bd. dirs. Einstein Inst. for Sci., Health and the Cts., 2001—; mem. spl. redaction rev. panel U.S. Jud. Conf., 2000—. Recipient Peck award Wabash Coll., 1989, Touchstone award Girls Club of Greater Indpls., 1989, Leach Centennial 1st Woman award Valparaiso Law Sch., 1993, Most Influential Women award Indpls. Bus. Jour., 1996, Paul Buchanan award of excellence Indpls. Bar Found., 1998, Thomas J. Hennessy award Ind. U., 1995, Disting. Citizen fellow Ind. U., 1999-2001; named Ind. Woman of Yr., Women in Comm., 1986, Ind. Univ. Disting. Alumni, 1996, Disting. Citizen fellow Ind. U., 1999-2001, Singing Hoosiers Disting. Alumni award Ind. U., 2000, Man for All Seasons award St. Thomas More Soc., 2000. Mem. ABA, Ind. Bar Assn., Indpls. Bar Assn. (Antoinette Dakin Leach award 1993), Fed. Judges Assn. (exec. com., bd. dirs. 2001—), Am. Judicature Soc., Com. on Budget (judicial conf. 2001-), Einstein Inst. Sci., Health and Cts. (bd. dirs. 2001-), U.S. Judicial Conf. (spl. redaction rev. panel 2000-), Christian Theol. Sem. (bd. trustees 1999-), Lawyers Club, Kiwanis. Republican. Methodist. Office: US Dist Ct 210 US Courthouse 46 E Ohio St Indianapolis IN 46204-1903

BARKER, WILLIAM M. state supreme court justice; b. Chattanooga, Sept. 13, 1941; married; 3 children. BS, U. Chatanooga, 1964; JD, U. Cin., 1967. Bar: Tenn. 1967. Pvt. practice, 1967-83; cir. ct. judge, 1983-95; justice Ct. of Appeals, 1995-98, Tenn. Supreme Ct., 1998—. Adj. prof. U. Tenn., Chatanooga, 1984—. Chmn. bd. deacons 1st Presbyn. Ch. Chattanooga, 1995-97. With USAMC, 1967-69. Fellow Tenn. Bar Found., Chattanooga Bar Found.; mem. Am. Legion, Alpha Soc., U. Tenn. Chattanooga Alumni Coun., Chattanooga Rotary Club. Office: Tenn Supreme Ct 540 Mccallie Ave Ste 410 Chattanooga TN 37402-2067*

BARKER, WILLIAM THOMAS, lawyer; b. Feb. 28, 1947; s. V. Wayne and Cordelia (Whitten) B.; m. June K. Robinson, Jan. 30, 1981. BS, MS, Mich. State U., 1969; JD, U. Calif., Berkeley, 1974. Bar: Calif. 1975, Ill. 1976. Assoc. programmer-analyst Control Data Corp., Sunnyvale, Calif., 1969-71; law clk. Pa. Supreme Ct., Erie, 1974-75; assoc. Sonnenschein Carlin Nath & Rosenthal, Chgo., 1975-82, ptnr., 1982—. Moderator Ill. Ins. Law Forum, Counsel Connect, 1994-98; co-moderator Nat. Ins. Law gen. forum, 1996-98; moderator Ins. Law Forum, Lexis One, 2001. Bd. editors: Def. Counsel Jour., 1987—; editor Bad Faith Law Report, 1999-2001, contbg. editor 1990-99; mem. editl. bd. Ins. Litigation Reporter, 1987—. editl. dir. and sr. contbg. editor, 2001—; editor Covered Events, 1995-96, editor emeritus, 1996—; ins. law publs. bd. Def. Rsch. Inst., 1992-97; contbr. articles to profl. jours. Fellow Am. Bar Found.; mem. ABA (chair-elect com. on appellate advocacy, tort and ins. practice sect. 1994-95, chair 1995-96, chair gen. comm. bd. 1996-97), Internat. Assn. Def. Counsel (Yancey Meml. award for best article 1995, chair spl. com. on Amicus Curie 1996-97, chair ad hoc com. on interstate practice 2000—), Chgo. Coun. Lawyers (sec. 1987-88, bd. govs. 1989-91, chair com. profl. responsibility 1990-95), Chgo. Bar Assn. (chmn. com. constl. law 1984-85), Def. Rsch. Inst., Am. Law Inst., Ill. Assn. Def. Trial Coun. General civil litigation, Constitutional, Insurance. Home: 132 E Delaware Pl Apt 5806 Chicago IL 60611-4951 Office: Sonnenschein Nath Et Al 8000 Sears Tower 233 S Wacker Dr Ste 8000 Chicago IL 60606-6491

BARKETT, ROSEMARY, federal judge; b. Ciudad Victoria, Tamaulipas, Mex., Aug. 29, 1939; came to U.S., 1946, naturalized, 1958; BS summa cum laude, Spring Hill Coll., 1967; JD, U. Fla., 1970; LLD (hon.), Stetson U., St. Petersburg, Fla., 1987; LHD (hon.), Fla. Internat. U., Miami, 1987; LLD (hon.), John Marshall Law Sch., Chgo., 1990; LHD (hon.), U. So. Fla., Tampa, 1990; DCL (hon.), Spring Hill Coll., Mobile, Ala., 1990; LLD (hon.), Rollins Coll., Orlando, Fla., 1992, Nova U., Ft. Lauderdale, Fla., 1992. Bar: Fla., U.S. Dist. Ct. (so. dist.) Fla., U.S. Ct. Appeals (5th cir.), U.S. Supreme Ct. Pvt. practice, West Palm Beach, Fla., 1971-79; cir. judge

15th Jud. Cir. Ct., Palm Beach County, 1979-82, administrative judge civil divsn., 1982-83, chief judge, 1983-84; appellate judge 4th Dist. Ct. Appeal, West Palm Beach, Fla., 1984-85; justice Supreme Ct. Fla., Tallahassee, 1985-92, chief justice, 1992-94; cir. judge U.S. Ct. of Appeals (11th cir.) Fla., Miami, 1994—. Bd. dirs. Lawyers for Children, U.S. Assn. Constl. Law; mem. faculty U. Nev., Reno, Nat. Jud. Coll., Fla. Jud. Coll., Appellate Judges Seminar, Inst. Jud. Adminstrn., N.Y.U.; lectr. in field. Mem. editorial bd. The Florida Judges Manual. Mem. vis. com. Miami U. Law Sch.; mem. bd. visitors St. Thomas U. Recipient Woman of Achievement award Palm Beach County Commn. on Status of Women, 1985, Judge Mattie Belle Davis award Fla. Assn. Women Lawyers, 1991, Hannah G. Solomon award Nat. Coun. Jewish Women, 1991, Lifetime Achievement award Latin Bus. Profl. Women, 1992, Breaking the Glass Ceiling award Fla. Fedn. Bus. Profl. Women's Clubs, Inc., 1993, Disting. Jurist award Miss. State U., 1995, Margaret Brent Women Lawyers of Achievement award ABA Commn. Women in Profession, 1996, Harriette Glasner Freedom award ACLU Fla. Palm Beach Chpt., 1999,; named to Fla. Women's Hall of Fame, 1986, ABA Minority Justice Honoree, 1992, Miami Centennial Hall of Fame, 1996, Crohn's & Colitis Found. Women of Distinction, 1997, Nat. Assn. Women Judges Honoree of Year, 1999; Rosemary Barkett award named in her honor Acad. Fla. Trial Lawyers, 1992, Rosemary Barkett Outstanding Achievement award named in her honor Fla. Assn. Women Lawyers, 1999. Mem. ABA, Fla. Bar Assn. (family law sect., chairperson ct. stats. and workload com. and study commn. on guardianship law, lectr. on matrimonial media and criminal law continuing legal edn.), Palm Beach County Bar Assn., Am. Acad. Matrimonial Lawyers (award 1984), Fla. Assn. Women Lawyers (Palm Beach chpt.), Nat. Assn. Women Judges, Dade Marine Inst. (former chairperson), Palm Beach Marine Inst. (former chairperson, bd. trustees), Acad. Fla. Trial lawyers (Achievement award 1988), Assn. Trial Lawyers Am. (Achievement award 1986), Am. Law Inst., Fed. Judges Assn. Office: US Ct of Appeals (11th cir) Fla 99 NE 4th St Rm 1223 Miami FL 33132-2140*

BARKLEY, THIERRY VINCENT, lawyer; b. Paris, Mar. 21, 1955; s. Jacques and Michéline Marié (Rossi) B.; came to U.S., 1967, naturalized, 1974; m. Mary Ellen Gamble, June 18, 1983; children: Richard A., Robert V., Marriah E., Christopher R. BA in Polit. Sci., UCLA, 1976; JD, Calif. Western Sch. Law, San Diego, 1979. Bar: Nev. 1980, U.S. Dist. Ct. Nev. 1982, U.S. Supreme Ct. 1986. Intern, Calif. Ct. Appeals 4th Circuit, San Diego, 1978-79; law clk. Nev. Dist. Ct., 7th Jud. Dist., Ely, 1979-81; assoc. firm C.E. Horton, Ely, 1982-83; asst. city atty. Ely, 1982-83; assoc. firm Barker, Gillock & Perry, Reno, 1983-87, Perry & Spann, 1987-89, ptnr., 1990—. Editor Internat. Law Jour., 1979. Mem. Internat. Moot Ct. Team, 1978; recipient Dean's award Calif. Western Sch. Law, 1979. Mem. Rep. Presdl. Task Force, 1990. Mem. Nev. Bar Assn., Washoe Bar Assn., U.S. Jaycees (past pres. White Pine, Nev.). Republican. Roman Catholic. Lodge: Elks (past treas. Ely club). Federal civil litigation, State civil litigation, Insurance. Office: Perry & Spann 6130 Plumas St Reno NV 89509-6041

BARKMAN, JON ALBERT, lawyer; b. Somerset, Pa., Oct. 8, 1947; s. Blair Albert and Billie (Dietz) B.; m. Annette E. Shaulis, Dec. 1, 1983. BA, Washington and Jefferson U., 1969; JD, Duquesne U., 1975. Bar: Pa. 1975, U.S. Dist. Ct. (we. dist.) Pa. 1975, U.S. Supreme Ct. 1984, U.S. Ct. Appeals (3rd cir.) 1989. Mem. claims dept. Liberty Mut. Ins. Co., Pitts., 1969-71; dist. justice Commonwealth of Pa., Somerset, 1973-93; pvt. practice, 1975—; pres. Barkman Realty, Inc., Somerset County Settlement and Abstract Co. Inc. Advisor Com. Against Sexual Assault, Somerset, Pa., 1984; Pa. del. Nat. Spl. Ct. Judges Conv., Honolulu, 1989, Atlanta, 1991. Paul Harris fellow, 1989. Mem. ABA, ATLA, Pa. Trial Lawyers Assn., Somerset County Bar Assn. (pres. 1990—), Allegheny County Bar Assn., Elks, Rotary. Republican. Methodist. Home: 388 High St Somerset PA 15501-1301 Office: 116 N Center Ave Somerset PA 15501-2027

BARKOFF, RUPERT MITCHELL, lawyer; b. New Orleans, May 7, 1948; s. Samuel and Martha (Lewis) B.; m. Susan Joyce Levitt, May 31, 1970; children: Stuart, Jeffrey, Lisa. BA in Econs. with high distinction, U. Mich., 1970, JD magna cum laude, 1973. Bar: Ga. 1973. Assoc. Kilpatrick Stockton LLP, Atlanta, 1973-80, ptnr., 1980—. Contbr. articles to profl. jours. Mem. ABA (bus. law sect., antitrust sect., forum on franchising, panelist ann. forums 1980-92, chmn. 1989-92, assoc. editor Franchise Law Jour. 1981-86), Ga. Bar Assn. (corp. and banking sect.), Atlanta Bar Assn., Phi Beta Kappa. Democrat. Jewish. General corporate, Franchising. Home: 5215 Vernon Springs Trl NW Atlanta GA 30327-4511 Office: Kilpatrick Stockton LLP 1100 Peachtree St NE Ste 2800 Atlanta GA 30309-4530 E-mail: rbarkoff@kilpatrickstockton.com

BARKSDALE, RHESA HAWKINS, federal judge; b. Jackson, Miss., Aug. 8, 1944; s. John Woodson Jr. and Mary Bryan (Saunders) B. BS, U.S. Mil. Acad., 1966; JD, U. Miss., 1972. Law clk. to Hon. Byron R. White U.S. Supreme Ct., 1972-73; assoc., then ptnr. Butler, Snow, O'Mara, Stevens & Cannada, Jackson, 1973-90; judge U.S. Ct. Appeals (5th cir.), 1990—. Instr. U. Miss. Sch. Law, Jackson, 1975-76, Miss. Coll. Sch. Law, Jackson, 1976. Chmn. Miss. Vietnam Vets. Leadership Program, Jackson, 1982-85; del. Rep. Nat. Conv., New Orleans, 1988; elector election of Pres. of U.S., Jackson, 1988. Capt. U.S. Army, 1966-70, Vietnam. Decorated Silver Star, Bronze Star for Valor, Purple Heart; Cross of Gallantry with silver star (Republic of Vietnam). Mem. Am. Inn of Ct. (Charles Clark chpt.), Phi Delta Phi (Nat. Grad. of Yr. 1972). Episcopalian. Office: US Ct Appeals 5th Cir James O Eastland Courthouse 245 E Capitol St Ste 200 Jackson MS 39201-2414

BARLEY, JOHN ALVIN, lawyer; b. Jacksonville, Fla., Oct. 16, 1940; s. Lewis Alvin Barley and Catherine Alberta (Curran) McKendree; m. Mary Freida Szarowicz, Nov. 30, 1974 (div. Dec. 1991); children: Jared Scott, Jessica Lauren; m. Debora Ann Barber Brown, July 11, 1998. BS, Fla. State U., 1963; JD, U. Fla., 1968. Bar: Fla. 1969, U.S. Dist. Ct. (mid. and no. dists.) Fla. 1973, U.S. Ct. Appeals (5th and 11th cirs.) 1973, U.S. Supreme Ct. 1973. Law clk. to judge U.S. Dist. Ct. (so. dist.), Miami, Fla., 1968-69; exec. asst. to Hon. Ray C. Osborne Lt. Gov. Fla., Tallahassee, 1969-70; asst. dir. div. of labor Fla. Dept. Commerce, 1971; assoc. Maquire, Voorhis & Wells, Orlando, Fla., 1972-73; asst. atty. gen. Dept. of Legal Affairs, Tallahassee, 1974-75; gen. counsel Dept. of Gen. Services, 1976-78; pvt. practice, 1978—. Mem. Tallahassee Leon County Architectural Rev. Bd., 1994, 96. Mem. ABA, Fla. Bar Assn. (pub. contract law com., bd. govs. young lawyers div. 1974, rules of civil procedure com. 1974-88, 91-92), Tallahassee Bar Assn., Am. Judicature Soc., Phi Delta Phi. Roman Catholic. Avocations: camping, hunting, fishing, swimming, running. General civil litigation, Contracts commercial, Construction. Home: 4927 Heathe Dr Tallahassee FL 32308-2134 Office: 400 N Meridian St Tallahassee FL 32301-1254 also: PO Box 10166 Tallahassee FL 32302-2166

BARLIANT, RONALD, federal judge; b. Chgo., Aug. 25, 1945; s. Lois I. Barliant; children: Claire, Anne. BA in History, Roosevelt U., Chgo., 1966; postgrad., Northwestern U., Chgo., 1966-67; JD, Stanford U., 1969. Bar: Ill. 1969, U.S. Dist. Ct. (no. dist.) Ill., U.S. Ct. Appeals (7th cir.). VISTA vol., staff atty. Cook County Legal Assistance Found., Chgo., 1969-72; assoc. Miller, Shakman, Hamilton and Kurtzon, 1972-76, ptnr., 1976-88; judge U.S. Bankruptcy Ct. (no. dist.) Ill., 1988—. Adj. prof. debtor-creditor rels. John Marshall Law Sch., 1991-92; bd. dirs. Cook County Legal Assistance Found., 1975-82; gen. counsel Chgo. Coun. Lawyers, 1983-86. Mem. Fed. Bar Assn. (bd. dirs. 1992-94), Nat. Conf. Bankruptcy Judges (bd. govs. 1997—). Avocations: opera, theatre, golf, Cubs baseball. Office: US Bankruptcy Ct 219 S Dearborn St Rm 738 Chicago IL 60604-1702

BARLINE, JOHN, lawyer; b. Tacoma, Dec. 29, 1946; s. John Dean Barline and Jane (Greiwe) Moosey; m. Sally Harris, Oct. 21, 1984. B.A., Netherland Sch. Internat. Bus., Breukelen, 1968; B.A., U. Puget Sound, 1969; J.D., Willamette U., 1972; LL.M. in Taxation, NYU, 1973. Bar: Wash. 1972, U.S. Dist. Ct. (we. dist.) Wash. 1974. Ptnr., Dolack, Hansler, et al, Tacoma, 1973-85, ptnr. Williams, Kastner & Gibbs, Tacoma, 1985—. Bd. dirs., treas. Bldg. a Scholastic Heritage, Tacoma, 1980-85; bd. dirs., chmn. Bellarmine Prep. Sch., 1981— ; chmn. bd. dirs. Tacoma Community Coll. Found.; trustee U. Puget Sound, 1988—. Named among Leaders of Tomorrow, Time Mag., 1983. Mem. Wash. State Bar Assn. (com. mem., spl. dist. counsel, mem. gift and estate tax com.), Pierce County Bar Assn., ABA, U. Puget Sound Alumni Assn. (chmn. 1984—, bd. dirs. 1984). Republican. Roman Catholic. Clubs: Tacoma, Tacoma Yacht (bd. dirs. 1978-80), Tacoma Country and Golf. Lodge: Elks. General practice, Probate, Corporate taxation. Office: Williams Kastner & Gibbs 1000 Financial Ctr 1145 Bro Tacoma WA 98402

BARLOW, JOHN ADEN, lawyer; b. Columbus, Ohio, June 8, 1942; s. William Willard and Eleanore (Johnson) B.; m. Patricia Ann Mowry, Oct. 17, 1970 (div. Aug. 1982); children: William P., Allison J., Jonathan A.; m. Patricia Marion Palmer, Sept. 3, 1982. BSc in Edn., Ohio State U., 1963, JD cum laude, 1968. Bar: Ohio 1969, Wash. 1969, U.S. Dist. Ct. (we. dist.) Wash. 1969, U.S. Dist. Ct. (ea. dist.) Wash. 1992. Assoc. Skeel McKelvey Henke Evenson & Betts, Seattle, 1968-70; ptnr. Walstead Mertsching Husemoen Donaldson & Barlow, Longview, Wash., 1970—. Mem. Wash. State Ins. Commr.'s Tort Reform Com., 1987. Contbg. author to 2 books. Named Boss of Yr., Cowlitz County Legal Secs. Assn., 1989. Fellow Am. Coll. Trial Lawyers; mem. Wash. State Trial Lawyers Assn. (bd. dirs. 1981-90, v.p. for west 1989-90), Cowlitz County Bar Assn. (pres. 1974-75), Longview C. of C. (bd. dirs. 1977-80), Kiwanis (pres. Longview 1973). Democrat. Avocations: golf, antiques. Insurance, Personal injury. Home: 1506 23d Ave Longview WA 98632-3616 Office: Walstead Mertsching Husemoen Donaldson & Barlow 1000 12th Ave Ste 2 Longview WA 98632-2500

BARLOW, PETER HUGH, lawyer; b. Minot, N.D., Dec. 5, 1966; s. Lynn Burnham and Joan Yancey Barlow; m. Wendy Patricia Valiente, Oct. 13, 1990; children: Jessica Christine, Christopher Ryan, Brittany Lauren. BA in English, Brigham Young U., 1993; JD, U. Nebr., 1997. Bar: Utah 1997, U.S. Dist. Ct. Utah 1997. Assoc. Strong & Hanni, Salt Lake City, 1997—. Mem. ATLA, Utah Trial Lawyers Assn., Def. Rsch. Inst. Republican. Mem. LDS Ch. Avocations: sports, fishing, outdoor activities. Consumer commercial, Insurance, Personal injury. Office: Strong & Hanni 600 Boston Bldg 9 Exchange Pl Salt Lake City UT 84111

BARMANN, BERNARD CHARLES, SR. lawyer; b. Maryville, Mo., Aug. 5, 1932; s. Charles Anselm and Veronica Rose (Fisher) B.; m. Beatrice Margaret Murphy, Sept. 27, 1965; children: Bernard Charles Jr., Brigit. PhD, Stanford U., 1966; JD, U. San Diego, 1974; MPA, Calif. State U., Bakersfield. Bar: Calif. 1974, U.S. Dist. Ct. (so. dist.) Calif. 1974, U.S. Dist. Ct. (ea. dist.) Calif. 1978, U.S. Ct. Appeals (9th cir.) 1984, U.S. Supreme Ct. Asst. prof. Ohio State U., Columbus, 1966-69, U. Toronto, Ont., Can., 1969-71; dep. county counsel Kern County, Bakersfield, Calif., 1974-85, county counsel, 1985—. Adj. prof. Calif. State U., Bakersfield, 1986—. Editor: The Bottom Line, 1991-93, contbr. articles to profl. jours. Mem. exec. bd. So. Sierra coun. Boy Scouts Am., Bakersfield, 1986—; bd. dirs. Kern County Acad. Decathlon, Bakersfield, 1988—. Danforth Found. fellow, 1963-65; grantee Fulbright Found., 1963-65. Mem. Calif. Bar Assn. (law practice mgmt. sect. exec. com., jud. nominees evaluation commn. 1997-2000), County Counsel Assn. Calif. (bd. dirs. 1990—, chair 1993-94), Kern County Bar Assn. (pres. 2001), Rotary. Avocations: golf, skiing, travel, photography. Office: Kern County Office of County Counsel 1115 Truxtun Ave Bakersfield CA 93301-4639 E-mail: bbarmann@co.kern.ca.us

BARMETTLER, JOSEPH JOHN, lawyer; b. Omaha, Sept. 10, 1933; s. William Thomas and Dorothy Lucy (Flynn) B.; m. Jeanne Waller, June 21, 1958; children: Joseph Jr., Gregory, Richard, Katie, Peggy Carbullido, Timothy, Michael. BSC, Creighton U., 1956, JD, 1959. Bar: Nebr. 1959, U.S. Dist. Ct. Nebr. 1959, U.S. Ct. Appeals (8th cir.) 1963, U.S. Ct. Claims 1963. Assoc. Fitzgerald, Hamer, Brown & Leahy, Omaha, 1959-64; prin. Fitzgerald, Schorr, Barmettler & Brennan, P.C., L.L.O., 1964—, CEO, 1988—. Gen. counsel Met. C.C., Omaha, 1974—, Village of Boys Town, Nebr., 1991—, City of La Vista, Nebr., 1963—. Mem. devel. coun. Omaha Legal Aid Soc., 1989—; pres.'s coun. Creighton U., Omaha, 1990—; trustee La Vista Cmty. Found. Fellow Nebr. Bar Found.; mem. Nebr. Bar Assn. (chmn. ways, means and planning com. 1993-94, ho. of dels. 1985—, chmn. budget and adminstrn. com. 1993-94), Omaha Bar Assn., Omaha Downtown Rotary (dir. 1986-89, Paul Harris fellow). Republican. Avocations: golf, photography. General corporate, Municipal (including bonds), Real property. Office: Fitzgerald Schorr Barmettler & Brennan PC Ste 400 13320 California St Omaha NE 68154

BARNARD, ALLEN DONALD, lawyer; b. Williston, N.D., Feb. 22, 1944; s. Donald J. and Ruth E. (Franklin) B.; m. Andra Lynn Lebsock, Nov. 24, 1962; children: Alana, Aaron. BA in Social Scis., U. N.D., 1965; JD, U. Notre Dame, 1968. Bar: Minn. 1968, U.S. Dist. Ct. Minn. 1968, U.S. Ct. Appeals (8th cir.) 1971, U.S. Supreme Ct. 1973. Assoc. Best & Flanagan, Mpls., 1968-72, ptnr., 1972—, mng. ptnr., 1991-93. City atty. City of Golden Valley, Minn., 1988—, housing and redevel. authority atty., 1978—. Mem. ABA, Hennepin County Bar Assn., Mpls. Athletic Club, Madeline Island Yacht Club (bd. dirs. 1991-97). Avocations: sailing, skiing. General civil litigation, Condemnation, Land use and zoning (including planning). Office: Best & Flanagan 4000 US Bank Pl 601 2nd Ave S Ste 4000 Minneapolis MN 55402-4331 E-mail: abarnard@bestlaw.com

BARNARD, GEORGE SMITH, lawyer, former federal agency official; b. Opelika, Ala. s. George Smith and Caroline Elizabeth (Dowdell) B.; m. Muriel Elaine Outlaw, July 26, 1945; children: Elizabeth Elaine Barnard Crutcher, Charles Dowling, Beverly Laura Barnard Parker, Andrew Carey. BA, U. Ala., 1948, LLB, 1950. Bar: Fla. 1978, Ala. 1950, U.S. Tax Ct. 1950, U.S. Dist. Ct. Ala. 1950, U.S. Dist. Ct. Fla. 1978, U.S. Dist. Ct. (so. dist. trial bar) Fla. 1995, U.S. Supreme Ct. 1965, U.S. Ct. Claims 1979, U.S. Ct. Appeals (Fed. cir.) 1984, U.S. Ct. Appeals (11th cir.) 1985. Pvt. practice, Opelika, 1950-51; with IRS, 1951-78; attache, revenue service rep. Sao Paulo Brazil, S.Am. and Lesser Antilles, 1965-71, Mexico City, Bermuda Is., Bahamas, Panama, Major Antilles, C.Am., 1971-77; ptnr. Barnard, P.A., Miami, Fla., 1978-87, of counsel, 1987-91. Lectr. taxation U. Ala., 1958-60. Pres. Rocky Ridge Vol. Fire Dept., 1956-58, Rocky Ridge Civic Club, 1959, Ala. chpt. Nat. Assn. Internal Revenue Employees, 1962; commr. Rocky Ridge Civic Water Works, 1960-62; bd. dirs. S.E.Pompano Homeowners Assn., 1996-99. With USAAF, 1942-46. Recipient Albert Gallatin award U.S. Treasury Dept., 1978; named Hon. Citizen of Tex., 1979, Hon. Admiral in Tex. Navy, 1979. Mem. Fgn. Svc. Retirees Assn. of Fla. (advisor/dir. for S.E. Fla. 1987-98, dir. emeritus 1998—, original incumbent historian 1998—), Kappa Sigma. Republican. Private international, Estate taxation, Personal income taxation. Home: 671 SW 6th St Apt 602 Pompano Beach FL 33060-7739 Office: Charles D Barnard PA 3940 N Andrews Ave Fort Lauderdale FL 33309-5240 E-mail: memebarn@mediaone.net

BARNARD, ROBERT C. lawyer; b. 1913; s. Robert C. and Elsie (Francis) B.; m. Helen Hurd, Dec. 25, 1939; children— Robert Christopher, Mary Anne. BA, Reed Coll., 1935; postgrad. Columbia U. Law Sch. 1935-36; BA, Oxford (Eng.) U., 1938, BCL (Rhodes scholar), 1939, MA, 1951. Bar: Wash., 1940, D.C., 1947, U.S. Sup. Ct., 1943. Chief app. sect. antitrust div., chief legal adv. Office of Asst. Solicitor Gen., Dept. Justice, Washington, 1939-47; assoc. Cleary, Gottlieb, Steen & Hamilton, Washington, 1947-49, in charge Paris office, 1949-52, Washington, after 1952, sr. ptnr., 1961-84, of counsel, 1984— . Recipient Internat. Achievement award Internat. Soc. for Regulatory Toxicology and Pharmacology, 1995. Mem. ABA, Am. Indsl. Health Coun. (sci. advisor), Fed. Bar Assn., D.C. Bar Assn., Washington Bar Assn. Contbr. articles to profl. jours. Home: 5409 Dorset Ave Chevy Chase MD 20815-6627 Office: 2000 Pennsylvania Ave NW Washington DC 20006-1812

BARNARD, ROBERT N. lawyer; b. Madison, Wis., Dec. 15, 1947; s. Robert Julian and Dorothy Jane (Nichol) B.; m. Katherine Elaine Chott, Mar. 1, 1980; children: Suzanna Katherine, Sarah Elizabeth. AB, Harvard U., 1969; JD, Stanford U., 1975. Bar: Ill. 1975, U.S. Dist. Ct. (no. dist.) Ill. 1975. Assoc. Mayer, Brown & Platt, Chgo., 1975-81, ptnr. London, Eng., 1982-88, Chgo., 1988—. Trustee U. Notre Dame, London, 1986-88. Lt. U.S. Army, 1969-72. Banking, General corporate, Private international. Office: Mayer Brown & Platt 1675 Broadway New York NY 10019-5820

BARNES, DENNIS NORMAN, lawyer; b. Kingston, Pa., Feb. 10, 1940; s. Leslie Orland and Mary Whitney (Brown) B.; m. Ingrid Daubitz, Oct. 5, 1961; children: Richard, Kendra. AB, Dartmouth Coll., 1962; JD, Georgetown U., 1965. Bar: D.C. 1966, U.S. Ct. Appeals (D.C. cir.) 1966, U.S. Supreme Ct. 1995. Assoc. Morgan, Lewis & Bockius LLP, Washington, 1970-75, ptnr., 1975-2000; v.p. regulatory affairs Sun Country Airlines, 2000—. Capt. JAGC, U.S. Army, 1966-70. Mem. D.C. Bar Assn., Maritime Adminstrv. Bar Assn. (pres. 1991), Assn. Transp. Practitioners. Administrative and regulatory. Office: Sun Country Airlines Inc 1875 Connecticut Ave NW Ste 1100 Washington DC 20009 E-mail: dbarnes@suncountry.com

BARNES, DONALD MICHAEL, lawyer; b. Hazleton, Pa., June 15, 1943; s. Donald A. and Margaret (Resuta) B.; m. Mary Catherine Gibbons, June 3, 1967; children: Donald M., Stephanie A., Susan E. BS in Indsl. Engring., Pa. State U., 1965; JD cum laude, George Washington U., 1970. Bar: D.C. 1970, U.S. Dist. Ct. D.C. 1970, U.S. Ct. Appeals (D.C. cir.) 1970, U.S. Ct. Appeals (5th cir.) 1980, U.S. Ct. Appeals (4th cir.) 1980, U.S. Ct. Appeals (8th cir.) 1981, U.S. Ct. Appeals (6th cir.) 1993, U.S. Supreme Ct. 1975. Assoc. Arent, Fox, Kintner, Plotkin & Kahn, Washington, 1970-78, ptnr., 1978-97; mng. shareholder Jenkens & Gilchrist, Washington, 1997-2000; ptnr. Seyfarth Shaw, 2000—. Notes editor George Washington Law Rev., 1969-70 Mem. ABA (criminial justice, antitrust, litigation and adminstrv. law sects.), Fed. Bar Assn., D.C. Bar Assn., Order of Coif, Phi Delta Phi Administrative and regulatory, Antitrust, Federal civil litigation. Office: Seyfarth Shaw 815 Connecticut Ave NW Washington DC 20006-4004 E-mail: dbarnes@dc.seyfarth.com

BARNES, HARRY FRANCIS, federal judge; b. Memphis, May 14, 1932; m. Mary Milburn Mann, four children. Student, Vanderbilt U., 1950-52; BS, U.S. Naval Academy, 1956; LLB, U. Ark., 1964. With Pryor & Barnes, Camden, Ark., 1964-66, Barnes & Roberts, Camden, 1966-68, Gaughan, Laney, Barnes & Roberts, Camden, 1968-78, Gaughan, Laney & Barnes, Camden, 1978-82; mcpl. judge Camden and Ouachita Counties, 1975-82; circuit judge 13th jud. dist. State of Ark., 1982-93; judge U.S. Dist. Ct. (we. dist.) Ark., 1993—. Mem. Ark. Jud. Discipline and Disability Commn. With USMC, 1956-86, col. res. ret. Named Outstanding Trial Judge in Ark., Ark. Trial Lawyers Assn., 1986, 2000. Mem. ABA, Ark. Bar Assn., Ark. Jud. Coun. (bd. dirs.). Office: US Dist Ct We Dist PO Box 1735 El Dorado AR 71731-1735

BARNES, JAMES GARLAND, JR. lawyer; b. Ga., Mar. 3, 1940; s. James Garland Sr. and Carolyn L. (Stewart) B.; m. Lucy Curtis Ferguson, Nov. 1976; children: Susan Whitney, David Lawrence, Matthew Martin. BA, Yale U., 1961; LLB, U. Mich., 1966. Bar: Ill. 1967. With firm Baker & McKenzie, Chgo., 1966—, ptnr., 1973—. Co-author: The ABCs of the UCC Article 5: Letters of Credit. Mem. adv. com. Ill. Sec. of State's Corp. Acts, 1981-95; U.S. del. to UN Commn. on Internat. Trade Law, Internat. C. of C., 1994-2000. Mem. ABA (chmn. letter of credit subcom. 1991-96), Ill. Bar Assn. (chmn. corp. and security law sect. 1977-78), Chgo. Bar Assn. (chmn. corp. law com. 1982-83, chmn. profl. responsibility com. 1983-84), Legal Club Chgo. Contracts commercial, General corporate, Private international. Office: Baker & McKenzie 1 Prudential Pla 130 E Randolph St Ste 3700 Chicago IL 60601-6342 E-mail: james.g.barnes@bakernet.com

BARNES, JAMES NEIL, lawyer; b. Tulsa, June 28, 1944; s. William Harvey and Mildred E. (Norsworthy) B.; children: Deborah, Sociana; m. Anne E. Fuhrman, Dec. 18, 1992. BA, Northwestern U., 1966; JD, U. Mich., 1970. Bar: U.S. Dist. Ct. D.C. 1971, U.S. Ct. Appeals (D.C. cir.) 1973, U.S. Supreme Ct. 1977. Law clk. to judge U.S. Dist. Ct D.C., Washington, 1970-71; staff atty. Ctr. for Law and Social Policy, 1971-72, 77-81, co-dir., 1980-81; staff atty. Pub. Def. Svc., 1972-74; assoc. Hudson & Co., Port Vila, New Hebrides Islands, 1974-75; cons. Coun. for Pub. Interest Law, Washington, 1975-76; assoc. Wilmer, Cutler and Pickering, 1976-77; founder, dir. Antarctica Project, 1981-93; gen. counsel Antarctic and So. Ocean Coalition, Sydney, Australia and Washington, 1981—; treas. East coast dir. Threshold Internat. Ctr. for Environ. Renewal, Washington, 1981-87; sr. atty. Environ. Policy Inst. and Friends of Earth, Washington, 1987-94, head internat. dept. Friends of the Earth, 1990-94; counselor Les Amis de La Terre-France and Friends of the Earth Internat., 1994—; CEE Bankwatch Network, Prague, Czech Republic, 1995—, councilor and mem. statutory rev. com., 1998—; mem. nat. coun. Les Amis de la Terre-France, 1997—. Author: Let's Save Antarctica, 1982, Bankrolling Successes: A Portfolio of Sustainable Projects, 1988, 2d edit., 1995, Russian Roulette: Nuclear Power Reactors in Eastern Europe and Former Soviet Union, 1992-93, Promises, Promises: A Review of G-7 Economic Summit Declarations on Environment and Development, 1994; contbr. articles to profl. jours.; prodr.: (video) Antarctica: Soul of the Blue Planet; editor ECO, 1978—. UN rep. Greenpeace Internat., 1983-85, bd. dirs. Greenpeace USA, 1984-85; mem. State Dept. Adv. Com. on Law of the Sea, 1977-82, pub. adv. com. on Antarctica, 1978-92; mem. commn. on law and policy Internat. Union for Conservation of Nature and Natural Resources, 1980—; pres. Meridian Hill Studios Coop., 1987-90, treas., 1991-94. Recipient Golden Ark award His Royal Highness Prince Bernhard, The Netherlands, 1998; named Internat. Environmentalist of Yr., Nat. Wildlife Fedn., 1991; Ea. European projects grantee Rockefeller Bros. Fund, 1994—. Mem. Internat. Coun. Environ. Lawyers. Avocations: photography, guitar and harmonica, cycling. Home: 11 Ave Edouard Dupuy 24140 Villamblard Dordogne France E-mail: james.barnes@wanadoo.fr

BARNES, KAREN KAY, lawyer; b. June 22, 1950; d. Walter William and Vashti (Greenlee) Sessler; m. James Alan Barnes, Feb. 12, 1972; children: Timothy Matthew, Christopher Michael. BA, Valparaiso U., 1971; JD, DePaul U., 1978, LLM in Taxation, 1980. Bar: Ill. 1978, U.S. Dist. Ct. (no. dist.) Ill. 1978. Ptnr. McDermott, Will & Emery, Chgo., 1978-88; prin. William M. Mercer, Inc. and predecessor firm, 1989-93; staff dir. legal dept. McDonald's Corp., Oak Brook, Ill., 1993-95, home office dir. legal dept., 1995-97, regulatory practice group leader and mng. counsel, 1998—. Instr. John Marshall Grad. Sch. Law, Chgo., 1986-87; mem. adv. bd. John Marshall Sch. Law, 1996—; bd. dirs. Flutes Unlimited; mem. adv. bd. dirs. Plan Sponsor Mag., 2000—. Contbr. case note to DePaul Law Rev., 1976, note and comment editor DePaul Law Rev., 1976-77, editor Taxation For Lawyers, 1986-88. Mem. Am. Coll. Employee Benefit Attys., Chgo. Bar Assn. (chair employee benefits com. 1991-92, co-chair symphony orchestra 1999—), Midwest Pension Conf. (name chged to Midwest Benefits Coun.), WEB (pres. Chgo. chpt. 1986-88, v.p. nat. bd. 1988, pres. 1989-90), Profit Sharing Coun. Am. (legal and legis. com. 1994—, bd. dirs. 1997—, 2d vice

chair 1997-98, 1st vice chair 1998-2000, chair 2000—). Lutheran. Pension, profit-sharing, and employee benefits. Home: 3 S 102 Black Cherry Ln Glen Ellyn IL 60137 Office: McDonald's Corp McDonald's Plz Oak Brook IL 60523-1900 E-mail: karen.barnes@mcd.com

BARNES, OLIVER WILLIAM ABBOTT, solicitor; b. Nov. 13, 1950; married; children: Theo, Olivia, Ottilie. BA, Trinity Hall, Cambridge U., 1972. Trainee solicitor Travers Smith Braithwaite, London, 1973-76, ptnr., 1980—. Mem. Law Soc. (co. law com. 1998-). General corporate, Mergers and acquisitions, Securities. Office: Travers Smith Braithwaite 10 Snow Hill London EC1A 2AL England

BARNES, PETER, lawyer; b. Cambridge, Mass., Apr. 13, 1940; s. C. Tracy Barnes and Janet (White) Lawrence; children: K. Tracy, John E.; m. Jan Adair. BA magna cum laude, Yale U., 1962; LLB cum laude, Harvard U., 1965. Bar: D.C. 1966, Md. 1984. Assoc. Leva, Hawes, Symington, Martin & Oppenheimer, Washington, 1965-71, ptnr., 1972-83, Venable, Baetjer & Howard, Balt., 1983-86; mem., shareholder Swidler & Berlin, Chtd., Washington, 1987-98; ptnr. Swidler Berlin Shereff Friedman, LLP, 1998-99, counsel, 1999—. Bd. dirs. Walker & Dunlop, Inc., Washington. Mem. The Met. Club, The Elkridge Club. General civil litigation, Construction, Real property. Home: 4 Deep Run Ct Cockeysville MD 21030-1600 Office: Swidler Berlin Shereff Friedman LLP 3000 K St NW Ste 300 Washington DC 20007-5116 E-mail: PBarnes@swidlaw.com

BARNES, ROBERT NORTON, lawyer; b. Jan. 14, 1949; s. Bill and Mary Lou B.; m. Susan Eileen Ensch, Oct. 16, 1976; children: Megan Desiree, Allison Nichole. BA in English, U. Okla., 1970; J.D., 1974. Bar: Okla. 1974, Tex. 1992, U.S. Dist. Ct. (no. eist.) Okla. 1976, U.S. Dist. Ct. (ea. dist.) Okla. 1992, U.S. Ct. Appeals (10th cir.) 1984, U.S. Supreme Ct. 1989. Sole practice Tulsa, 1974-75; ptnr. Gibbon, Gladd, Clark, Barnes & Taylor, Tulsa, 1976-78; sr. dist. counsel Tex. Oil & Gas Corp., Oklahoma City, Dallas, 1978-80; v.p. Tex. Internat. Petroleum Corp., Oklahoma City, 1981-82; co-founder, atty. Stack & Barnes PC, 1982-92. Mem. Okla. Bar Assn., ABA, Oklahoma County Bar Assn., Okla. Mineral Lawyers Soc. Democrat. Episcopalian. Federal civil litigation, Oil, gas, and mineral, Environmental. Office: Barnes Smith Lewis PC 701 NW 63rd St Ste 500 Oklahoma City OK 73116-7650 E-mail: rbarnes@barneslewis.com

BARNES, THOMAS G. law educator; b. 1930; AB, Harvard U., 1952; DPhil, Oxford U., 1955. From asst. prof. to assoc. prof. Lycoming Coll., Williamsport, Pa., 1956-60; from lectr. to prof. history U. Calif., Berkeley, 1960—, humanities rsch. prof., 1971-72, prof. history and law, 1974—, co-chmn. Canadian studies program, 1982—. Dir. legal history project Am. Bar Found., 1965-86; com. mem. on ct. records 9th Cir. Ct. Author: Somerset 1625-1640: A County's Government During the Personal Rule, 1961, List and Index to Star Chamber Procs., James I, 3 vols., 1975, Lawes and Libertyes of Massachusetts, 1975, Hastings College of Law: The First Century, 1978; mem. editl. bd. Gryphon Legal Classics Libr.; editor Pub. Record Office. Huntington Libr. fellow, 1960, Am. Coun. Learned Socs. fellow, 1962-63, John Simon Guggenheim Found. fellow, 1970-71. Fellow Royal Hist. Soc.; mem. Selden Soc. (councillor, state corr.), Assn. Canadian Studies (v.p. 1999—). Office: U Calif Sch Law 454 Boalt Hl Berkeley CA 94720-7200

BARNES, WILLIE R. lawyer; b. Dallas, Dec. 9, 1931; m. Barbara Bailey; children: Michael, Sandra, Traci, Wendi, Brandi. BA, UCLA, 1953, JD, 1959. Bar: Calif. 1960, U.S. Dist. Ct. (cen. dist.) Calif. 1960. Various atty. positions Calif. Dept. of Corps., L.A., 1960-70, asst. commr. of corps., 1970-75, commr. of corps., 1975-79; ptnr., chmn. corp. dept. Manatt, Phelps, Rothenberg & Phillips, 1979-88; ptnr. Wyman, Bautzer, Kuchel & Silbert, 1989-91, Katten Muchin Zavis & Weitzman, L.A., 1991-92, Musick, Peeler & Garrett, L.A., 1992—. Chmn. svc. plan com. Knox-Keene Health Care, 1976-79; mem. securities regulatory reform com. State of Calif., 1979-81; mem. shareholders rights and securities transactions Calif. Senate Commn. on Corp. Governances, 1986—; chmn. Leveraged Real Estate Task Force, Inst. Cert. Planners, 1985-86; gen. counsel UCLA Alumni Assn., 1982-86; mem. listing qualifications panel NASDAQ. Co-mng. editor: Calif. Bus. Law Reporter, 1982-83. With U.S. Army , 1954-56. Named Law Alumnus of Year UCLA, 1976; recipient Resolution of Commendation Calif. Senate, 1979, Calif. Assembly, 1979. Mem. ABA (fed. regulation of securities and state regulation of securities coms., franchise forum, futures regulation com.), State Bar Calif. (bus. law sect. 1979, exec. com. 1983-86, vice chmn. 1985-86, com. on corps. 1982-83, ad hoc com. on corp. governance and takeovers 1986-88), Beverly Bar Assn. (corp. and comml. law sect.), L.A. Bar Assn., M.W. Securities Commrs. Assn., N.Am. Securities Assn., Ind. Commn. on L.A. Police Dept. Democrat. Avocations: tennis, basketball, photography. General corporate, Franchising, Securities. Office: Musick Peeler & Garrett One Wilshire Blvd Ste 2000 Los Angeles CA 90017 E-mail: w.barnes@mpglaw.com

BARNES-BROWN, PETER NEWTON, lawyer; b. Rutland, Vt., Aug. 22, 1948; s. Rufus Enoch and Julia Pottwin (Morgan) Brown; m. Susan Linda Barnes, Aug. 11, 1974; children: Diana Morgan, David Alexander, Julia Elizabeth. AB, Brown U., 1970; JD, U. Pa., 1976. Bar: Ga. 1978, N.Y. 1979, Mass. 1985. Law clk. Assoc. Justice Alfred H. Joslin R.I. Supreme Ct., Providence, 1977-78; assoc. Olwine, Connelly, Chase, O'Donnell & Weyher, N.Y.C., 1978-84, Goodwin, Procter & Hoar, Boston, 1984-86; internat. counsel Cullinet Software, Inc., Westwood, Mass., 1986-89; prin. Van Wert & Zimmer, P.C., Lexington, 1989-93; co-founder, mem. Morse, Barnes-Brown & Pendleton, P.C., Waltham, 1993—. Co-founding dir., clk. New Eng.-Latin Am. Bus. Coun., Inc., Boston, 1992-2000. Contbr. articles to profl. jours. Mem. ABA, Mass. Bar Assn., N.Y. State Bar Assn., State Bar Ga., Boston Bar Assn. Computer, General corporate, Private international. Office: Morse Barnes-Brown & Pendleton PC Reservoir Place 1601 Trapelo Rd Waltham MA 02451-7333

BARNETT, CHARLES DAWSON, lawyer; b. Louisville, Jan. 27, 1951; s. Bernard Harry and Marian (Spiesberger) B.; m. Maureen Liel Stewart, Nov. 17, 1980; children: Rachel Langfeld, Jacob Bernard, Hannah Marian. BS in Commerce, U. Louisville, 1973; JD, U. Fla., 1976. Bar: Fla. 1977, Ky. 1977, D.C. 1977, U.S. Dist. Ct. (so. dist.) Fla. 1981. Assoc. Barnett & Alagia, Louisville, 1977-81, ptnr., Palm Beach, Fla., 1981-88, Nat. Fin. Realty Trust, Louisville, 1986-88; pvt. practice, West Palm Beach, Fla., 1988—. Bd. dirs. Ralph E. Mills Found., Frankfort, Ky., 1980— . Active Louisville-Jefferson County Republican Exec. Com., 1978-80. Served with USCG, 1969-74. Jewish. General corporate, Private international, Corporate taxation. Home: 8412 Native Dancer Rd E Palm Beach Gardens FL 33418-7728 Office: 400 S Australian Ave Ste 700 West Palm Beach FL 33401-5044

BARNETT, CHARLES E. lawyer; BA, U. Mich., 1961, JD, 1964. Bar: N.Y. 1965, Conn. 1987. Assoc. Cadwalader, Wickersham & Taft, 1964-68; asst. counsel Macmillan, Inc., 1968-70; asst. gen. counsel Asarco Inc., 1970-73; v.p., gen. counsel, sec. St. Joe Minerals Corp., 1974-84; v.p., gen. counsel Combustion Engring., Inc., 1984-90, Reader's Digest Assn., Inc., 1990-94. General corporate. Office: Reader's Digest Assn Inc Reader's Digest Rd Pleasantville NY 10570-7000

BARNETT, EDWARD WILLIAM, lawyer; b. New Orleans, Jan. 2, 1933; s. Phillip Nelson and Katherine (Wilkinson) B.; m. Margaret Mauk, Apr. 3, 1933; children: Margaret Ann Stern, Edward William. B.A., Rice U., 1955; LL.B., U. Tex.-Austin, 1958. Bar: Tex. 1958. Mem. Baker Botts LLP, Houston, 1958—, mng. ptnr., 1984-98, sr. counsel, 1998—. Bd. dirs. J.P. Morgan Chase Bank of Tex., Louis Dreyfus Natural Gas; bd. dirs., chmn. Cen. Houston, Inc., 1989-91. Trustee Rice U., Houston, 1991—, chmn. bd. trustees, 1996—; trustee Baylor Coll. Medicine, St. Luke's Episcopal Health System, Tex. Heart Inst.; life trustee U. Tex. Law Sch. Found.; chmn. Greater Houston Partnership, 1992. Fellow Am. Coll. Trial Lawyers; mem. ABA (chmn. sect. antitrust law 1981-82), State Bar Tex., Houston Bar Assn., Coronado Club (pres. 1989), Houston Country Club, Old Baldy Club. Antitrust, General civil litigation. Office: Baker Botts LLP 3000 One Shell Plaza Houston TX 77002

BARNETT, JAMES MONROE, lawyer; b. Hulah, Okla., Dec. 24, 1933; s. Irvin M. and Ida Ruth (Loy) B.; m. Vicki L. Smith, Dec. 30, 1985. BBA, Washburn U., 1955, JD, 1959. Bar: Kans. 1959. Mem. firm Ross & Wells, Kansas City, Kans., 1959-63, Ross, Wells & Barnett, Kansas City, 1963-73; pres. Barnett & Ross, Chartered, 1973—. Bd. govs. Washburn Law Sch., 1974—, pres. 1982-83. Served with U.S. Army, 1956-58. Mem. ABA, Am. Judicature Soc., Wyandotte County Bar Assn., Kans. Bar Assn., Kans. Trial Lawyers Assn., Assn. Trial Lawyers Am. Republican. Methodist. Personal injury. Home: 14236 Benson St Overland Park KS 66221-2176 also: 9800 Metcalf St Gen Sq Bldg Overland Park KS 66206

BARNETT, MARK WILLIAM, state attorney general; b. Sioux Falls, S.D., Sept. 6, 1954; s. Thomas C. and Dorothy Ann (Lievrance) B.; m. Deborah Ann Barnett, July 14, 1979. BS in Govt., U. S.D., 1976, JD, 1978. Bar: S.D. Pvt. practice law, Sioux Falls, 1978-80; asst. atty. gen. State of S.D., Pierre, 1980-83, spl. prosecutor, 1984-90, atty. gen., 1990—; ptnr. Schmidt, Schroyer, Colwill and Barnett, 1984-90. Mem. S.D. Law Enforcement Tng. Commn., 1987—; mem. S.D. Bar Commn., 1986-88, 89-92, S.D. Corrections Commn., 1987. Bd. dirs. D.A.R.E., S.D. drug prevention prog., 1987—. Mem. S.D. Bar Assn. (pres. young lawyers' sect. 1985), Am. Judicature Soc. (nat. bd. dirs. 1984-88), State's Atty. Assn. (bd. dirs. 1987-90). Republican. Avocations: golf, weight lifting, snowmobiling. Office: Office Atty Gen 500 E Capitol Ave Pierre SD 57501-5070*

BARNETT, MARTHA WALTERS, lawyer; b. Dade City, Fla., June 1, 1947; d. William Haywood and Helen (Hancock) Walters; m. Richard Rawls Barnett, Jan. 4, 1969; children: Richard Rawls, Sarah Walters BA cum laude, Tulane U., 1969; JD cum laude, U. Fla., 1973. Bar: Fla. 1973, U.S. Dist. Ct. (mid. and so. dists.) Fla. 1973, U.S. Ct. Appeals (3d, 4th and 11th cirs.) 1975, D.C. 1989. Assoc. Holland & Knight LLP, Tallahassee, 1973-78, ptnr., 1979—. Bd. dirs., v.p. Fla. Lawyers Prepaid Legal Svc. Corp., 1978-80, pres., 1980-82, legis. com., 1983-84, mem. commn. on access to justice, 1984-86, exec. coun. tax sect., 1987-88, exec. coun. pub. interest sect., 1989-91; active Fla. Commn. Ethics, 1984-87, chairperson, 1986-87, Fla. Taxation and Budget Reform Commn., 1989—; Legal adv. bd. Martindale-Hubbell, 1990—; chair Ho. of Dels., 1994-96. Mem. Fla. Coun. Econ. Edn., Fla. Edn. Found.; bd. dirs. Lawyers Com. Civil Rights Under Law. Fellow Am. Bar Found. (life); mem. ABA (exec. coun. sect. on individual rights and responsibility 1974-86, bd. govs. 1986-89, task force on minorities in profession 1984-86, commn. on women in profession 1987-90, long range planning com. 1988-91, chair bd. govs. fin. com. 1988-89, bd. editors ABA Jour. 1990-94, exec. coun. sect. legal edn. and admission to bar 1990-94, chair commn. on pub. understanding about the law 1990-93, pres.-elect 1999-2000, pres. 2000-2001, others), Nat. Inst. Dispute Resolution (sec.-treas. 1988-94, bd. dirs. 1988-94, Gov. appt. Fla. Constitution revision Commn., 1997-98), Am. Law Inst., Fla. Bar Assn. (exec. coun. pub. interest law sect. 1989-91), Tallahassee Bar Assn. Administrative and regulatory, Legislative, State and local taxation. Office: Holland & Knight LLP PO Drawer 810 Tallahassee FL 32302-0810*

BARNETT, RANDY EVAN, law educator; b. Chgo., Feb. 5, 1952; s. Ronald Evan and Florice Jane (Abrahams) B.; m. Beth E. Black, Dec. 2, 1979; 2 children. B.A., Northwestern U., 1974; J.D., Harvard U., 1977. Bar: Ill. 1977, U.S. Dist. Ct. (no. dist.) Ill. 1977. Asst. State's Atty. Cook County, Chgo., 1977-81; research fellow U. Chgo. Law Sch., 1981-82; asst. prof. law Ill. Inst. Tech. Chgo.-Kent Coll. of Law, 1982-86, assoc. prof. law, 1986—; adj. scholarCato Inst.; adv. com. Speaker Ill. Ho. of Reps.; dir. law and philosophy program and Leonard P. Cassidy fellowship program Inst. for Human Studies, George Mason U., Fairfax, Va., 1982— . Editor: Assessing the Criminal, 1977. Contbr. articles to profl. jours. Mem. Mid Am. Legal Found. (chmn., bd. legal advisors), Wash. Legal Found. (bd. advisors), Heartland Inst. (bd. advisors).

BARNETT, RICHARD EARL, lawyer, film distributing company executive; b. Lake Charles, La., Aug. 1, 1927; s. George and Freida (Goldsmith) B.; student Princeton, 1944-45; B.A., Amherst Coll., 1950; LL.B., Columbia U., 1953; m. Harriet Schottland, July 21, 1950; children— Pamela Jane, James Richardson, Thomas Schuyler. Admitted to N.Y. bar, 1953; practiced in N.Y.C., 1953-56; atty. with gen. counsel's office N.Y. Central R.R., 1956-58; v.p., dir. Modern Film Corp., N.Y.C., 1958-71, sec., 1961-71, pres., 1971— ; chmn. Movies En Route, Inc., N.Y.C.; dir. Walport (Overseas) Ltd., London. Served to warrant officer U.S. Mcht. Marine, 1945-47. Mem. Am., N.Y.C. bar assns., Theta Xi, Phi Delta Phi. Home: 225 Clinton Ave Dobbs Ferry NY 10522-3003

BARNETT, ROBERT BRUCE, lawyer, educator; b. Waukegan, Ill., Aug. 26, 1946; s. Bernard and Betty Jane (Simon) B.; m. Rita Lynn Braver, Apr. 10, 1972; 1 child, Meredith Jane. BA, U. Wis., 1968; JD, U. Chgo., 1971. Bar: D.C. 1971. Law clk. to Hon. John Minor Wisdom U.S. Ct. Appeals (5th cir.), 1971-72; law clk. to assoc. justice Byron R. White U.S. Supreme Ct., Washington, 1972-73; legis. asst. Sen. Walter F. Mondale, 1973-75; assoc. Williams & Connolly, 1975-78, ptnr., 1979—. Adj. prof. Georgetown Law Sch., 1973-80. Trustee John F. Kennedy Ctr. for Performing Arts, 1994—; mem. bd. visitors Sanford Inst. of Pub. Policy, Duke U., 1998—, U. Chgo. Law Sch., 2001—. Democrat. General civil litigation, General corporate, Entertainment. Office: Williams & Connolly LLP 725 12th St NW Washington DC 20005-5901

BARNETT, ROBERT GLENN, lawyer; b. Oxford, Miss., July 30, 1933; s. Arden and Vera (Turner) B.; m. Rae Ragsdale, Apr. 21, 1962; children: Laura Lee, Mary Melissa. BA, U. Miss., 1959, JD, 1961. Ptnr. Houston & Barnett, Southaven, Miss., 1961-63, Neal, Houston, Elliott & Barnett, Jackson, 1963-65, Barnett & Barnett, Jackson, 1965-70; legal counsel Deposit Guaranty Nat. Bank, 1970-79, gen. counsel, sec. to bd., 1979-95; counsel Butler, Snow, O'Mara, Stevens and Cannada, 1996—. Vis. prof. U. Miss. Law Sch., Oxford, Miss., 1978-79, 85; banking law course coord., lectr. Sch. Banking of the South, Baton Rouge, 1978-79. Pres. Family Services Assn., Jackson, 1970-71; bd. dirs. Community Services Assn., 1968-70; bd. govs. Jackson Symphony Orch. Assn., 1981-85. Lt. (j.g.) USNR, 1954-58; capt. USNR, 1979. Fellow Young Lawyers of Miss. Bar (pres. 1995-96); mem. ABA (banking law com. 1982—), Miss. Bar Assn. (2d v.p. 1968-69), Jackson Legal Aid Bd. Trustees (pres. 1965-67), Miss. Bankers Assn. (chmn. bank lawyers com.), Miss. Jr. Bar Assn. (pres. 1967-68), Miss. Corp. Counsel Assn. (pres. 1988), So. Conf. Bank House Counsel (chmn. 1989), Lions (pres. North Jackson chpt. 1967-68), River Hills Tennis Club (dir. 1979-82, Patrick Farm Golf Club, Whisper Lake Golf Club. Baptist. Banking. Office: PO Box 22567 Jackson MS 39225-2567 E-mail: bbarnett@netdoor.com

BARNETTE, CURTIS HANDLEY, steel company executive, lawyer; b. St. Albans, W.Va., Jan. 9, 1935; s. Curtis Franklin and Garnett Drucella (Robinson) B.; m. Loris Joan Harner, Dec. 28, 1957; children: Curtis Kevin, James David. AB with High Honors, W.Va. U., 1956; postgrad. (Fulbright scholar), U. Manchester, 1956-57; J.D., Yale U., 1962; grad. advanced mgmt. program, Harvard U., 1974-75; LLD (hon.), W.Va. U., 1995, DeSales U., 1996, U. Charleston, 1998, Lehigh U., 1999. Bar: Conn. 1962, Pa. 1968, D.C. 1988, W.Va. 1990. Atty. Wiggin & Dana, New Haven, 1962-67, Bethlehem (Pa.) Steel Corp., 1967-92, sec., 1976-92, gen. counsel, 1977-92, sr. v.p., 1985-92, chmn., CEO, 1992-2000, also bd. dirs., 1986-2000; of counsel Skadden, Arps, Slate, Meagher & Flom, LLP, 2000—. Lectr. U. Md., 1958-59; law tutor Yale U., 1962-67; chmn., bd. dirs. Am. Iron and Steel Inst., 1997, dir., 1992-2000; bd. dirs. Met. Life Ins. Co., Lehigh Valley Partnership, Nat. Mus. Indsl. History; chmn. Internat. Iron and Steel Inst., 1994-95, dir. 1992-2000; Comenius prof., exec.-in-residence Moravian Coll., 2000—. Trustee Lehigh U., 1993—, Pa. Soc., 1993—; mem. Adminstrv. Conf. U.S., 1988-89; bd. adv. W.V. U., 1999—; dir. W.Va. U. Found., 1982—, chair, 1987-88; mem. adv. com. on Trade Policy and Negotiations, 1989—, Coal Commn., 1990, Pa. 21st Century Environ. Com., 1997-98. With U.S. Army Counterintelligence Corps, 1957-59, maj. USAR, 1959-67. Mem. ABA, Fed. Bar Assn., Pa. Bar Assn., Conn. Bar Assn., Northampton County Bar Assn., D.C. Bar Assn., W.Va. Bar Assn., Assn. Gen. Counsel (pres. 1988-90), Am. Soc. Corp. Secs. (chmn. 1986), Am. Law Inst., Pa. Chamber Bus. and Industry (dir. 1985-93), Bus. Coun., Bus. Roundtable (policy com. 1992-2000), Pa. Bus. Roundtable (dir. 1986-2000, chmn. 1994-95, Loblolly, Links, Saucon Valley Country Club, Bethlehem Club, Blooming Grove Hunting and Fishing Club, Yale Club of N.Y.C., Univ. Club of Washington, Met. Club, Phi Beta Kappa, Beta Theta Pi, Phi Alpha Theta, Phi Delta Phi. Home: 1112 Prospect Ave Bethlehem PA 18018-4914 Office: 1170 8th Ave Bethlehem PA 18016-7699 also: 1440 New York Ave Washington DC 20001 E-mail: barnette@bethsteel.com, hbarnett@skadden.com

BARNEY, JOHN CHARLES, lawyer; b. Nov. 18, 1939; s. Harold Lamont and Sara Eleanor (Johnston) B.; m. Joyce Marie Ebbinge; children: John C., Karen E., William L. BA, Wesleyan U., 1961; LLB, Columbia U., 1964. Bar: N.Y. 1964, U.S. Dist. Ct. (so. and ea. dists.) N.Y. 1966, U.S. Dist. Ct. (no. and we. dists) N.Y. 1977, U.S. Ct. Appeals (2d cir.) 1973, U.S. Supreme Ct. 1979. Assoc. Donovan, Leisure, Newton and Irvine, N.Y.C., 1964-66; staff atty. N.Y. State Law Revision Commn., Ithaca, 1966-68; ptnr. Barney, Grossman, Dubow & Marcus, 1968—. Asst. dist. atty. Tompkins County, N.Y., 1968-70; mem. N.Y. State Com. on Profl. Standards, 3d Jud. Dept., 1984-90, chmn. 1989-90. Chmn. Bd. Zoning Appeals, Lansing, N.Y., 1975-92; mem. Bd. Edn., Lansing, 1981-96, v.p., 1983-89, pres., 1989-96; bd. edn. Tompkins-Seneca-Tioga Bd. Coop. Ednl. Svcs., 1997—; bd. dirs. Challenge Industries (sheltered workshop), Ithaca, 1970-80. Mem. Tompkins County Bar Assn. (pres. 1983-84), N.Y. State Bar Assn. Republican. Unitarian. Contracts commercial, General practice, Real property. Home: 12 Stormy View Rd Ithaca NY 14850-9774 Office: Barney Grossman Dubow & Marcus 119 E Seneca St Ithaca NY 14850-4352

BARNHARDT, ZEB ELONZO, JR. lawyer; b. Winston-Salem, N.C., Dec. 28, 1941; s. Zeb Elonzo and Katie Sue (Taylor) B.; m. Pam Hall; children: Daniel Black, Kathleen Martin. AB, Duke U., 1964; JD, Vanderbilt U., 1969. Bar: N.C. 1969. Assoc. Womble Carlyle Sandridge & Rice, PLLC, Winston-Salem, 1969-75, mem., 1975-97, of counsel, 1997-98; owner, mgr., cons. Barnhardt & Assocs., Inc., 1998—; pvt. practice law, 1998—. Alumni admissions adv. com. Duke U., 1970-72; bd. dirs. Industries for Blind, Winston-Salem, 1973-85, vice chmn., 1983-84, chmn., 1985; bd. dirs. Goodwill Industries, Winston-Salem, 1973-80; bd. dirs. The Little Theatre, Winston-Salem, 1979-85, asst. treas., 1980, treas., 1981-82, v.p., 1983-84, pres., 1984-85; adv. bd. Salvation Army, Winston-Salem, 1973-85, chmn., 1979-80; bd. dirs. Leadership Winston-Salem, 1984-92, v.p. adminstrn., 1988-89, pres. 1989-90; com. mem. Winston-Salem Found., 1975-84, vice chmn., 1978-80, chmn., 1983-84; trustee High Point U., 1984-96. With USN, 1964-66. Recipient Disting. Service award as Young Man of Yr. Winston-Salem Jaycees, 1974; Disting. Alumni award Duke U., 1979 Mem. ABA (fed. regulation securities laws com., law firms com., com. on law and accounting, bus. law sect.), N.C. Bar Assn. (chmn. securities regulation com. 1985-87, vice chmn. bus. law sect. 1987-89, chmn. bus. law sect. 1989-91, bd. govs. 1991-94, chmn. membership recruitment and retention com. 1997-2000, chair lawyer effectiveness and quality of life com. 2001—), Forsyth County Bar Assn., Winston-Salem Jaycees (life, pres. 1973-74), N.C. Jaycees (regional dir. 1974-75, legal counsel 1975-77), Greater Winston-Salem C. of C. (bd. dirs. 1973-74), Forsyth Country Club, Rotary. Democrat. Methodist. General corporate, Securities. Office: Barnhardt & Assocs Inc 4389 Winterberry Ridge Ct Winston Salem NC 27103-9738 E-mail: zbarnhardtjr@triad.rr.com

BARNHART, FORREST GREGORY, lawyer; b. Alpine, Tex., Sept. 11, 1951; s. F. Neil and Jody (Ogg) B. AB, Vassar Coll., 1973; JD, Cornell U., 1976. Bar: Fla. 1976, U.S. Dist. Ct. (so. dist.) Fla. 1977, U.S. Ct. Appeals (5th and 11th cirs.) 1977; cert. civil trial lawyer. Assoc. Levy, Plisco, Perry, Shapiro, Kneen & Kincade, West Palm Beach, Fla., 1976-78, Montgomery Searcy & Denney, P.A., West Palm Beach, 1978-81, ptnr., 1981-89, Searcy, Denney, Scarola, Barnhart & Shipley, P.A., West Palm Beach, 1989—. Lectr. in field; moderator TV show Call the Lawyer, 1983-85; dir. WXEL-TV and FM, Pub. Radio and TV, West Palm Beach. Contbr. chpt. to The Advocates Primer, 1991. Spkr., com. mem. Floridians Against Constnl. Tampering, 1984; mem. Jud. Nominating Commn., 1986-90; trustee Fla. Lawyers Action Group; bd. dirs. 1000 Friends of Fla., Legal Aid Soc. Palm Beach County. Recipient Al J. Cone award; mem. Eagle Hall of Fame, 1991. Fellow ATKA, ABA, FBA (treas. 1983-84, sec., v.p. 1984-85, pres. 1986-87), Fla. Bar, Palm Beach County Bar Assn. (vice chmn. fed. ct. practice com. 1981-82, media law com. 1981-82, bench bar com. 1980-81, chmn. pub. rels. com. 1983-84, TV com. 1984—), Palm Beach Trial Lawyers Assn. (founding dir.), Acad. Fla. Trial Lawyers (sec. 1990-91, treas. 1991-92, pres.-elect 1992-93, pres. 1993—, bd. dirs. 1986-90, chmn., key man legis. com. 1986—, mem. coll. of diplomates, steering counsel continuing edn. com., Eagle Benefactor, Disting. Lectr. in Jurisprudence 1988, sec. 1990-91), Fla. Lawyers Action Group (chair bd. trustees), Cornell Club. General civil litigation, Personal injury, Product liability. Home: 236 Miraflores Dr Palm Beach FL 33480-3618 Office: Searcy Denney Scarola Barnhart & Shipley 2139 Palm Beach Lakes Blvd West Palm Beach FL 33409-6601

BARNHART, GENE, lawyer; b. Pineville, W.Va., Dec. 22, 1928; s. Forrest H. and Margaret (Harshman) B.; m. Shirley L. Dunn, Jan. 28, 1952; children: Sheryl Lynne (Mrs. John Dickey), Deborah Lee (Mrs. Kim Orians), Taffie Elise (Mrs. Tony Knight), Pamela Carole (Mrs. Michael Dean), Margaret Melanie (Mrs. Thomas Atkinson). Student, W.Va. U., 1946-48, Coll. Steubenville, 1949-50; JD, U. Cin., 1953. Bar: Ohio 1953. Counsel, clothing br. Armed Svcs. Procurement Agy., Washington and Phila., 1953-55; assoc. Black, McCuskey, Souers & Arbaugh, L.P.A., Canton, Ohio, 1955-60, ptnr., 1961-84, pres., 1984-86, vice chmn., 1986-88, chmn., 1988-98, of counsel, 1999—. Lectr. Ohio Legal Center Inst., Ohio Bar Assn., Am. Inst. Banking. Mem. Jackson Local Bd. Edn., 1966-74, pres., 1970; mem. Jackson Twp. Bd. Zoning Appeals, 1963-94, chmn., 1978-94; vice chmn. Jackson Zoning Ordinance Revision Com.; past pres. Coun. of Chs. of Ctrl. Stark County, Family Counseling Svcs. of Ctrl. Stark County; mem. Stark County Bd. Health, 1985-93; com. chmn. Congressional Action Com., Greater Canton Chamber; past pres., trustee Canton Preservation Soc.; deacon Grace Bible Ch. With USNR, 1948-49. Recipient Disting. Svc. award Jackson Twp. Jaycees, 1981, Cmty. award Jackson-Belden C. of C., 1982. Mem. Ohio State Bar Assn. (comml. law com., com. legal specialization), Stark County (grievance, disputed fee, meml., voluntary pro bono coms.), Order of Coif, Phi Alpha Delta. Land use and zoning (including planning), Probate, Real property. Home and Office: 2805 Coventry Ln NW Canton OH 44708-1321

BARNHILL, CHARLES JOSEPH, JR. lawyer; b. Indpls., May 22, 1943; s. Charles J. and Phyllis (Landis) B.; m. Elizabeth Louise Hayek, Aug. 14, 1971; children: Eric Charles, Colin Landis. BS in Econs., U. Pa., 1965; JD, U. Mich., 1968. Bar: Ill. 1968, U.S. Dist. Ct. (no. dist.) Ill. 1968, U.S. Ct. Appeals (7th cir.) 1969, U.S. Supreme Ct. 1972. Assoc. Kirkland & Ellis, Chgo., 1968; Reginald Heber Smith fellow Chgo. Legal Aid, 1968-69; assoc. Katz & Friedman, Chgo., 1969-72; ptnr. Davis, Miner, Barnhill & Galland, P.C. (now Miner, Barnhill & Galland), Madison, Wis., 1972—. Spl. master Fed. Dist. Ct. (no. dist.) Ill. Asst. editor Mich. Law Rev., 1968. Bd. dirs. Combined Health Appeal, Legal Assistance Found., Chgo., 1972-74, Old Town Triangle Assn., Chgo., 1972-75; chmn. Wis. Ctr. for Tobacco Rsch. and Intervention, 1996. Fellow: Am. Coll. Trial Lawers (chmn. employment litigation of litigation sect. 1975—78); mem.: ABA, Chgo. Coun. Lawyers (bd. dirs. 1974—76), Barristers Soc., Order of Coif. Antitrust, Civil rights. Office: Miner Barnhill & Galland 44 E Mifflin St Ste 803 Madison WI 53703-2800

BARNHILL, DAVID STAN, lawyer; b. Washington, May 10, 1949; s. Arthur David and Ida Bea (Cox) B.; m. Katherine C. Felger, July 26, 1975; children: Hannah Katherine, Mary Rachel. BS, Va. Poly. Inst., 1971, MS, 1973; doctoral studies, U. Va., 1976-79; JD magna cum laude, Washington and Lee U., 1983. Bar: Va. 1983, U.S. Ct. Appeals (4th cir.) 1983, U.S. Supreme Ct. 1990, Federal Ct. Claims 1994. Asst. prof. social sci. Va. Intermont Coll., Bristol, Va., 1973-76; soc. sci. researcher U. Va., Charlottesville, 1979-80; assoc. Woods, Rogers & Hazlegrove, Roanoke, 1983-88, ptnr., 1989—. Contbr. articles to profl. jours.; lead articles editor Washington & Lee Law Rev., 1982-83. Bd. dirs. Total Action Against Poverty, Roanoke, 1987-90, DePaul Children's Svcs., Roanoke, 1985-95, Legal Aid Roanoke Valley, 1990-92. Sgt. USNG, 1972-78. Named to Legal Elite, Va. Bus. Mag. (litigation), 2000, Best Lawyers in Am. (First Amendment Law), 2000—01. Mem.: ABA (forum on constrn. industry, civil litigation sect.), Va. State Bar (chmn. 6th dist. ethics com. 1990—91, bd. govs. constrn. law sect. 1991—99, chair 1998, state bar coun. 1995—2001, state bar disciplinary bd. 1995—2001, vice chair bench-bar and media rels. com. 1996—2000), Va. Bar Assn. (constrn. law coun., civil litigation coun. 1994—99), Roanoke Bar Assn. (bd. dirs. 1992—94), Va. Assoc. Gen. Contractors (legal affairs and contract documents coms. 1992—), Va. Tech. Alumni Assn., Order of the Coif. Democrat. Baptist. Avocations: middle distance running, writing. General civil litigation, Communications, Construction. Home: 5145 Falcon Ridge Rd Roanoke VA 24014-5720 Office: Woods Rogers & Hazlegrove 10 S Jefferson St Ste 1201 Roanoke VA 24011-1319 E-mail: barnhill@woodsrogers.com

BARNHILL, HENRY GRADY, JR. lawyer; b. Buena Vista, Ga., Aug. 24, 1930; s. Henry Grady and Imogene (Hogg) B.; m. Sarah Carolyn Haire, Oct. 29, 1953; children: Grady Michael, Stephen Drew, Kevin Scott, Carol Kelly. JD, Wake Forest U., Winston-Salem, N.C., 1958. Bar: N.C. 1958, U.S. Dist. Ct. (ea., mid. and we. dists.) N.C. 1958, U.S. Ct. Appeals (4th cir.) 1961, U.S. Supreme Ct. 1983, U.S. Ct. Appeals (fed. cir.) 1985. Assoc. Womble Carlyle Sandridge & Rice, Winston-Salem, 1958-61, ptnr., 1961—. Bd. visitors Sch. of Law Wake Forest U. Lt. USAF, 1951-55. Fellow Am. Coll. Trial Lawyers (state chmn. 1986-88); mem. Am. Bd. Trial Advs., N.C. Assn. Def. Attys., N.C. Bar Assn. (litigation sect.), 4th Cir. Jud. Conf., Forsyth County Bar (pres. 1979-80), Inns of Ct. (Chief Justice Joseph Branch). Democrat. Presbyterian. Avocation: tennis. Federal civil litigation, State civil litigation, Product liability. Home: 3121 Robinhood Rd Winston Salem NC 27106-5610 Office: Womble Carlyle Sandridge & Rice PLLC PO Drawer 84 1600 BB&T Financial Ctr Winston Salem NC 27102 E-mail: gbarnhill@wcsr.com

BARNICK, HELEN, retired judicial clerk; b. Max, N.D., Mar. 24, 1925; d. John K. and Stacy (Kankovsky) B. BS in Music cum laude, Minot State Coll., 1954; postgrad., Am. Conservatory of Music, Chgo., 1975-76. With Epton, Bohling & Druth, Chgo., 1968-69; sec. Wildman, Harrold, Allen & Dixon, 1969-75; part-time assignments for temporary agy., 1975-77; sec. Friedman & Koven, 1977-78; with Lawrence, Lawrence, Kamin & Saunders, 1978-81; sec. Hinshaw, Culbertson et al., 1982; sec. to magistrate judge U.S. Dist. Ct. (we. dist.) Wis., Madison, 1985-91; dep. clk., case adminstr. U.S. Bankruptcy Ct. (we. dist.) Wis., 1992-94; ret., 1994. Mem. chancel choir 1st Bapt. Ch., Mpls.; mem. choir, dir. sr. high choir Moody Ch., Chgo.; mem. chancel choir Fourth Presbyn. Ch., Chgo., Covenant Presbyn. Ch., Madison; dir. chancel choir 1st Bapt. Ch., Minot, N.D.; bd. dirs., sec.-treas. Peppertree at Tamarack Owners Assn., Inc., Wisconsin Dells, Wis.; mem. Festival Choir, Madison. Mem. Christian Bus. and Profl. Women (chmn.), Bus. and Profl. Women Assn., Participatory Learning and Tchg. Orgn., Madison Civics Club, Sigma Sigma Sigma. Home: 7364 Old Sauk Rd Madison WI 53717-1213

BARON, FREDERICK DAVID, lawyer; b. New Haven, Dec. 2, 1947; s. Charles Bates and Betty (Leventhal) B.; m. Kathryn Green Lazarus, Apr. 4, 1982; children: Andrew K. Lazarus, Peter D. Lazarus, Charles B. BA, Amherst Coll., 1969; JD, Stanford U., 1974. Bar: Calif. 1974, D.C. 1975, U.S. Supreme Ct. 1978, U.S. Dist. Ct. D.C. 1979, U.S. Ct. Appeals (D.C. cir.) 1979, U.S. Dist. Ct. (no. dist.) Calif. 1982, U.S. Ct. Appeals (9th cir.) 1982. Counsel select com. on intelligence U.S. Senate, Washington, 1975-76; spl. asst. to U.S. atty. gen., 1977-79; asst. U.S. atty. for D.C., 1980-82; atty. Clark, Baron & Korda, San Jose, Calif., 1982-83; ptnr. Cooley, Godward, Palo Alto, 1983—; assoc. dep. atty. gen., dir. Exec. Office for Nat. Security U.S. Dept. of Justice, 1995-96. Lectr. U.S. Info. Svc., 1979-80; pres. bd. trustees Keys Sch., Palo Alto, 19983-87; bd. dirs. Retail Resources, Inc., 1987-88. Co-author, editor U.S. Senate Select Com. on Intelligence Reports, 1975-76; also articles. Issues dir. election com. U.S. Senator Alan Cranston, 1974, Gov. Edmund G. Brown Jr., 1976; mem. transition team Pres. Carter, 1976-77, Pres. Clinton, 1992; del. Calif. Dem. Conv., 1989-90. Mem. ABA, Calif. Bar Assn., D.C. Bar Assn., Santa Clara County Bar Assn., Univ. Club. Federal civil litigation, State civil litigation. Office: Cooley Godward LLP 5 Palo Alto Sq Palo Alto CA 94306-2122

BAR-ON, OFER, lawyer; b. Haifa, Israel, Jan. 12, 1958; m. Carmit Friedlander Bar-on. LLB, Hebrew U., Jerusalem, 1985. Atty. gen. Min. of Justice, Jerusalem, Israel, 1985; lawyer Boazson Argon & Co., Israel, 1986; assoc. lawyer Kantor, Elhanani & Co., Tel Aviv, Israel, 1986-92. Coord. Assn. for Civil Rights in Israel, Jerusalem, 1982-84. Retired Major. Named Dean's list Oglethorpe U., Atlanta, 1980. Mem. Assn. for Civil Rights in Israel. Avocations: tennis. Contracts commercial, General corporate. Office: Shavit Bar-on Inbar 2 Kremnitsky St Engel Bldg 67899 Tel-Aviv Israel E-mail: obar-on@sbilaw.com

BARONI, BARRY JOSEPH, law educator, mediator, arbitrator; b. New Orleans, Dec. 21, 1939; s. Frank and Frances (Coniglio) B.; m. Eve Mary Davis, June 8, 1971. B.B.A., Loyola U., New Orleans, 1961, M.B.A., 1965, J.D., 1967; LL.M. in Labor Law, Tulane U., 1974. Bar: La. 1967, D.C. 1972, U.S. Dist. Ct. (ea. dist.) La. 1967, U.S. Ct. Appeals (5th cir.) 1967, U.S. Supreme Ct. 1971, U.S. Dist. Ct. D.C. 1971, U.S. Ct. Claims, U.S. Tax Ct., U.S. Ct. Mil. Appeals, U.S. Ct. Customs and Patent Appeals. Mem. faculty Coll. Bus., U. New Orleans, 1967— , prof. labor law and arbitration, 1967— ; mgmt. cons. and tng. specialist in indsl. relations, 1970— ; trial atty. enforcement div. SEC, Washington, summers 1971-75; prof. law U. Innsbruck, Austria, summers, 1979, 80, 82, 85, 87, 95, U. N.C., Chapel Hill, summer 1983; vis. prof. Coll. Bus., dep. gen. counsel NLRB, Washington, summer 1984; mem. arbitrator list Fed. Mediation and Conciliation Service, 1979—, Am. Arbitration Assn., 1975, Nat. Acad. of Arbitrators, 1987—. Editor Loyola U. Law Rev., 1965-66. Contbr. numerous articles to bus. and legal jours. Served to lt. comdr. JAGC, USNR, 1975-95. Mem. D.C. Bar Assn., La. Bar Assn., Am. Bus. Law Assn., So. Bus. Law Assn., Am. Arbitration Assn., Soc. for Profls. in Dispute Resolution. Office: U New Orleans Lakefront Coll Of Business New Orleans LA 70148-0001

BARR, CARLOS HARVEY, lawyer; b. Greeley, Colo., Oct. 12, 1936; s. Charles Allen B. and Zelma Arvilla (Sechler) Turner; m. Martha Lucía Sánchez-Morales, May 10, 1985. BA in Polit. Sci., U. Wash., 1959, MA in Polit. Sci., 1967; JD, George Wash. U., 1971. Bar: Wash. 1971, U.S. Dist. Ct. (ea. dist.) Wash. 1972, U.S. Dist. Ct. (we. dist.) Wash. 1979, U.S. Ct. Appeals (9th cir.) 1973, U.S. Supreme Ct. 1981, U.S. Tax Ct. 1985; cert. Spanish-English interpreter, Wash. Mgmt. intern U.S. Dept of Army, Ft. Lewis, Wash., 1960; joined Fgn. Svc., Dept. State, 1960, officer, 1960-61; vice consul U.S. Consulate Gen., Monterrey, Mex., 1961-64; consular officer, third sec. Am. Embassy, Khartoum, Sudan, 1964-66; analyst Latin Am. Bur., Washington, 1967-68; personnel officer, 1968-70; consular affairs officer, 1970-71, resigned; dir. legal svcs. Community Action Com. OEO, Pasco, Wash., 1971-72; lawyer Spokane (Wash.) County Legal Svc., 1972-73; pvt. practice Kennewick, Wash., 1973-75, Richland, 1975—. Mem. ABA, ATLA, Wash. Bar Assn., Wash. Trial Lawyers Assn., Hispanic Bar Assn. Wash., Nat. Hispanic Bar Assn. Avocation: Spanish literature. Personal injury, Product liability, Workers' compensation. Office: 1207 George Washington Way Richland WA 99352-3411

BARR, CHARLES F. lawyer, reinsurance company executive; BA, Boston Coll., 1972; JD, Suffolk U., 1976. Bar: Mass. 1977, Conn. 1993; CPCU. Counsel Comml. Union Ins. Cos., 1977-81; asst. gen. counsel Reliance Ins. Cos., 1981-87; v.p., gen. counsel United Pacific Life Ins. Co., 1984-87; gen. counsel Gen. Accident Ins. Co., 1987-89, Gen. Reins. Corp., Stamford, Conn., 1989-94, sr. v.p., gen. counsel, sec., 1994-2000; gen. counsel Benfield Blanch, Inc., Westport, 2000—. Office: Benfield Blanch Inc 327 Riverside Ave Westport CT 06880 E-mail: charles.barr@benfieldgroup.com

BARR, CHARLES JOSEPH GORE, lawyer; b. Saginaw, Mich., Sept. 17, 1940; s. Joseph Gore and Maja T. (Strand) B.; m. Carolyn Conn, Aug. 26, 1961; children: Maja Irene, Shannon Conn, Meaghan Won. BA, U. Mich., 1962, LLB, 1965. Bar: Mich. 1965, U.S. Dist. Ct. (ea. dist.) Mich. 1965, U.S. Ct. Appeals (6th cir.) 1968. Assoc. Clark Klein Winter, Detroit, 1965-67, Goodman, Eden, Millender & Bedrosian, Detroit, 1967-73; ptnr. Moore, Barr & Kerwin, 1974-78, Barr & Walker, Detroit, 1978-83, Barr & Arsenault, Detroit, 1984-90, Barr & Assocs., Detroit, 1990—. Mem. ABA, State Bar of Mich. (chmn. negligence sect. 1985-86), Assn. Trial Lawyers Am. (gov. 1982-85), Mich. Trial Lawyers Assn. (sec. 1986-87, pres. 1988-89), Nat. Lawyers Guild (pres. Detroit chpt. 1983-84, exec. bd.). General civil litigation, Personal injury, Product liability. Home: 19430 Cumberland Way Detroit MI 48203-1458 Office: 3315 Cadillac Tower Detroit MI 48226 Fax: 313-965-2043. E-mail: cbarr240@aol.com

BARR, HARVEY STEPHEN, lawyer; b. N.Y.C., June 4, 1941; s. Lillian (Meslin) B.; m. Willyce Selman, Dec. 18, 1962: children: Shari Lynn, Amy Sue, Pamela Jan, Matthew Scott. LLB, N.Y. Law Sch., 1964. Bar: N.Y. 1964, U.S. Ct. Appeals 1966, U.S. Dist. Ct. 1968, U.S. Supreme Ct. 1969. Village atty. Village of Spring Valley, N.Y., 1965-67, Village of Sloatsburg, N.Y., 1969-82, Village of Suffern, N.Y., 1975-77; asst. county atty. Rockland County, N.Y., 1970-74; ptnr. Barr & Faerber, Spring Valley, N.Y., 1979-90, Barr & Rosenbaum, 1990—. Editorial bd. N.Y. Law Forum, 1961-64. Active Rockland County Republican Com., 1964-82; chmn. Town of Ramapo Rep. Com. Mem. Rockland County Bar Assn. (com. chmn. 1980—), Bar Assn. State of N.Y. (program chmn. 1984-91). Jewish. Bankruptcy, Federal civil litigation, General corporate. Office: Barr & Rosenbaum 664 N Main St Spring Valley NY 10977-1901

BARR, JAMES HOUSTON, III, lawyer; b. Louisville, Nov. 2, 1941; s. James Houston Jr. and Elizabeth Hamilton (Pope) Barr; m. Sarah Jane Todd, Apr. 16, 1970 (div.); 1 child Lynn Jamison ; m. Cindy Ann Jeffries, May 31, 1997; children: Worden Pope Washington, Augustine Washington Jeffries. Student, U. Va., 1960-63, U. Tenn., 1963-64; BSL, JD, U. Louisville, 1966. Bar: Ky. 1966, U.S. Ct. Appeals (6th cir.) 1969, U.S. Supreme Ct. 1971, U.S. Ct. Mil. Appeals 1978. Law clk. Ky. Ct. Appeals, Frankfort, 1966-67; asst. atty. gen. Ky., 1967-71, 79-82; asst. U.S. atty. U.S. Dept. Justice, Louisville, 1971-79, 83—; 1st asst. U.S. Atty., 1978-79; asst. dist. counsel U.S. Army C.E., Louisville, 1982-83. Lt. comdr. USNR, 1967-81, lt. col. USAR, 1981-91. Mem. FBA (pres. Louisville chpt. 1975-76, Younger Fed. Lawyer award 1975), Ky. Bar Assn., Louisville Bar Assn., Soc. Colonial Wars, SAR, Washington Family Soc., Pendennis Club, Louisville Boat Club, Filson Club, Delta Upsilon. Republican. Episcopalian. Home: 100 Westwind Rd Louisville KY 40207-1520 Office: US Atty 510 W Broadway Ste 1000 Louisville KY 40202-2281

BARR, JAMES NORMAN, federal judge; b. Kewanee, Ill, Oct. 21, 1940; s. James Cecil and Dorothy Evelyn (Dorsey) B.; m. Trilla Anne Reeves, Oct. 31, 1964 (div. 1979); 1 child, James N. Jr.; m. Phyllis L. DeMent, May 30, 1986; children: Renae, Michele. BS, Ill. Wesleyan U., 1962; JD, Ill. Inst. Tech., 1971. Bar: Ill. 1972, Calif. 1977. Assoc. Pretzel, Stouffer, Nolan & Rooney, Chgo., 1974-76; claims counsel Safeco Title Ins. Co., L.A., 1977-78; assoc. Kamph & Jackman, Santa Ana, Calif., 1978-80; lawyer pvt. practice Law Offices of James N. Barr, 1980-86; judge U.S Bankruptcy Ct. Ctrl. Dist. Calif., Santa Anna, 1987—. Adj. prof. Chapman U. Sch. Law, 1996—. Lt. USN, 1962-67, Vietnam. Mem. Fed. Bar Assn. (Orange County chpt. bd. dirs. 1996-2000), Orange County Bar Assn. (cmty. outreach com.), Nat. Conf. Bankruptcy Judges, Orange County Bankruptcy Forum (bd. dirs. 1989—), Peter M. Elliott Inn Ct. (founder, first pres. 1990-91), Warren J. Ferguson Am. Inn of Ct. (founder). Office: US Bankruptcy Ct 411 W 4th St Santa Ana CA 92701-4500

BARR, JON-HENRY, lawyer; b. Livingston, N.J., Sept. 1, 1970; s. Gary and Susan Barr. BA, Lehigh U., 1992; JD, Seton Hall U., 1995. Bar: N.J. 1996, D.C. 1998, U.S. Dist. Ct. N.J. 1996, U.S. Ct. Appeals (3d cir.) 1997. Jud. law clk. Superior Ct. N.J., Freehold, N.J., 1995-96; assoc. Law Offices of Robert Blackman, Edison, 1996-98; ptnr. Barr & Canada, LLC, Clark, 1998—. Sec. Union Middlesex REACT, Woodbridge, N.J., 1989—; councilman Twp. of Clark, N.J., 1993-94; mem. Clark Rep. Civic Assn., 1996—. Named one of Outstanding Young Men of Am., 1998. Mem. N.J. State Bar Assn., Union County Bar Assn. (young lawyer trustee 2000-2001), Union County Mcpl. Prosecutors' Assn. (pres. 2001-2002). Jewish. Avocations: politics, travel. General civil litigation, Criminal, General practice. Home: 69 Fairview Rd Clark NJ 07066-2904 Office: Barr and Canada LLC 21 Brant Ave Clark NJ 07066-1512

BARR, MICHAEL BLANTON, lawyer; b. Freeport, N.Y., July 24, 1948; s. Harry Kyle and Rosemary (Blanton) B.; m. Nancy Nickeson, Aug. 11, 1979; children: Nicholas Upton, Jessica Nickeson, Alice Primrose. BS, Georgetown U., 1970; JD, George Washington U., 1973. Bar: D.C. 1973, U.S. Dist. Ct. D.C. 1973, U.S. Ct. Appeals (3d cir.) 1979, U.S. Ct. Appeals (4th cir.) 1976, U.S. Ct. Appeals (6th cir.) 1981, U.S. Supreme Ct. 1980. Assoc. LeBoeuf, Lamb, Lieby & McRae, Washington, 1973-76, Hunton & Williams, Washington, 1976-80, ptnr., 1980—, mng. ptnr. Washington office, 1985-2000, exec. com., 1985-94, 2000—. Contbr. articles to profl. jours. Bd. trustees Georgetown Day Sch., 1999—; bd. dirs. Am. Sch. of Tangier, Morocco, 1989—. Mem. ABA, Internat. Bar Assn., D.C. Bar Assn., City Tavern Club (Washington), Union League (N.Y.). General corporate, Finance, Private international. Home: 8004 Glendale Rd Chevy Chase MD 20815-5903 Office: Hunton & Williams 1900 K St NW Washington DC 20006-1110

BARRATT, JEFFREY VERNON, lawyer; b. London, Oct. 31, 1950; s. Arnold Douglas and Edith Joyce (Terry) Courtney-Lewis; m. Sharon Mary Tregaskis. LLB, Sydney U., 1973; postgrad., 1973-75. Trainee Giovanelli & Burks, Sydney, 1971-73; asst. Mallesons, 1973-75, Norton Rose, London, 1976-79; ptnr., 1979—. Avocations: cricket, skiing, opera, rugby. Banking, Oil, gas, and mineral. Office: Norton Rose Kempson House Camomile St EL3A 7AN London England Fax: 00442072836500

BARRAZA, HORACIO, lawyer; b. El Paso, Tex., June 11, 1967; s. Jorge and Carmen T. Barraza. BS, U. Tex., El Paso, 1989; JD, Western State U., 1993. Bar: Calif. 1995, U.S. Dist. Ct. (so. dist.) Calif. 1995. Assoc. Singleton & Dean, Escondido, Calif., 1995-97, Singleton & Assocs., Escondido, 1997—. Mem. ABA, ATLA, San Diego County Bar Assn., North San Diego County Bar Assn., San Diego Trial Lawyers Assn., Consumer Attys. of Calif., Am. Inns. of Ct. (assoc.). General civil litigation, Personal injury, Product liability. Office: Singleton & Assocs 120 Woodward Ave Escondido CA 92025-2637

BARRECA, CHRISTOPHER ANTHONY, lawyer; b. Pittsfield, Mass., Sept. 15, 1928; s. Christopher Joseph and Jennie (Cannici) B.; m. Alice Hazlehurst, Sept. 5, 1953. AA, Boston U., 1950, JD, 1953; LLM, Northwestern U., 1968. Bar: Mass. 1954, Ky. 1969, U.S. Dist. Ct. Ky. 1970, U.S. Dist. Ct. Mass. 1995, U.S. Ct. Appeals (6th cir.) 1970, Conn. 1988. With Gen. Electric Co., Fairfield, Conn., 1953-93, labor arbitration and litigation counsel, 1971-80, sr. labor and employment law counsel, 1980-93; ptnr., office chair, sr. counsel Paul, Hastings, Janolsky & Walker LLP, Stamford, 1993-99, sr. counsel, 1999—. Mem. arbitration services adv. com. Fed Mediation and Conciliation Service, 1973—; adj. prof. U. Louisville, 1970-71, U. Bridgeport (Conn.) Sch. of Law, 1986-90; selectman Weston, 1997-00. Co-author, editor: Labor Arbitrator Development, 1983, A Practical Guide for Advocates, 1990; contbr. articles to profl. jours. Chmn. Weston (Conn.) Bd. Edn., 1977-82; trustee, vice chair exec. com., chmn. com. legal affairs, sec. bd., 2001, sec. bd. Boston U., 1977—. Served with AUS, 1946-47. Mem. ABA (chmn. labor and employment law sect. com. labor arbitration advocacy, elected to governing council of labor and employment law sect. 1986—, chair 1996-97, elected to governing coun. dispute resolution sect. 2001—), Boston U. Sch. Law Alumni Assn. (Silver Shingle award 1982), Aspetuck Valley Country Club (Weston, pres. 1995-96). Administrative and regulatory, General corporate, Labor. Home: 6 Aspetuck Hill Ln Weston CT 06883-2601 Office: Paul Hastings Janolsky & Walker LLP 1055 Washington Blvd Stamford CT 06901-2216 E-mail: christopherbarreca@paulhastings.com

BARREIRA, BRIAN ERNEST, lawyer; b. Fall River, Mass., Sept. 1, 1958; s. Ernest R. and Lillian (Rego) B. BS in Ops. Mgmt., Boston Coll., 1980; JD, Boston U., 1984, LLM in Taxation, 1990. Bar: Mass. 1985. Estate settlement specialist State Street Bank and Trust Co., Boston, 1985-87; assoc. Barron & Stadfeld, 1987-88, Winokur, Winokur, Serkey, Rosenberg, & Hingham, P.C., Plymouth, 1988-96; pvt. practice, Plymouth and Hinghham, Mass., 1996—. Contbr. articles to profl. jours. Mem. ABA (chmn. elder law com. 1990-95, chmn. long-term health care issues com. 1992-96), Nat. Acad. Elder Law Attys., Mass. Bar Assn. (coun. probate sect. 1993-94, 95-97). Estate planning, Probate, Estate taxation. Home: 6 Cobblestone Ln Hanover MA 02339-1940 Office: 225 Water St Ste B110 Plymouth MA 02360-4054 E-mail: bb@lawyers.com

BARRERA, ERIC ISAAC, lawyer; b. Corpus Christi, Tex., Dec. 22, 1971; s. Isaac Jr. and Elva Quintanilla Barrera. BBA in Fin., U. Tex., 1994; JD, So. Meth. U., 1997. Bar: Tex. 1997, U.S. Dist. Ct. (so. dist.) Tex. 1997. Assoc. Gary, Thomasson, Hall & Marks, P.C., Corpus Christi, 1997—. Bd. dirs. Vol. Ctr. Coastal Bend, Cropus Christi, 1998—, Coastal Bend Youth City, 1998—. Mem. ABA, Tex. Bar Assn., Corpus Christi Bar Assn., Corpus Christi Young Lawyers Assn. (bd. dirs. 1998—), U. Tex. Silver Spurs, Phi Delta Phi. Methodist. Avocations: running, golf, tennis. General civil litigation, Personal injury. Office: Gary Thomasson Hall & Marks Ste 2888 201 S Carancahua St Corpus Christi TX 78401-3040

BARRETT, DAVID EUGENE, judge; b. Hiawassee, Ga., June 25, 1955; s. Homer and Laura Arispah (Wilson) B.; m. Donna L. Barrett; children: Laura Elizabeth, Thomas Jeffrey. BA summa cum laude, U. Ga., 1977, JD cum laude, 1980. Assoc. Erwin, Epting, et al, Athens, Ga., 1980-84, Blasingame, Burch, et al, Athens, 1984; pvt. practice Hiawassee, 1984-92; judge Recorders Ct., 1986-92, Superior Ct., Enotah Cir., 1992—. Counsel Towns County Humane Soc., Hiawassee, 1985-92; counselor Alzheimer Support, Hiawassee, 1985. Mem. ABA, Ga. Bar Assn., Mountain Bar Assn. (sec. 1987-88, v.p. 1988-89, pres. 1989-90), Western Bar Assn. (sec. 1983-84), Trial Lawyers Assn. Am., Towns County C. of C. (bd. dirs. 1986-87, 90-92, pres. 1988), Demosthenian Lit. Soc. (bd. dirs., sec. bd. trustees 1978-89, chmn. bd. 1986-89), Athens Jaycees (v.p. 1983-84). Home: 924 Mining Gap Ln Young Harris GA 30582-2324 Office: Superior Ct Enotah Cir 59 S Main St Ste K Cleveland GA 30528-1376

BARRETT, JAMES EMMETT, federal judge; b. Lusk, Wyo., Apr. 8, 1922; s. Frank A. and Alice C. (Donoghue) B.; m. Carmel Ann Martinez, Oct. 8, 1949; children: Ann Catherine Barrett Sandahl, Richard James, John Donoghue. Student, U. Wyo., 1940-42, LLB, 1949, student, St. Catherine's Coll., Oxford, Eng., 1945, Cath. U. Am., 1946. Bar: Wyo. 1949. Mem. firm Barrett and Barrett, Lusk, 1949-67; atty. Niobrara Sch. Dist., 1950-64; county and pros. atty. Niobrara County, Wyo., 1951-62; atty. Town of Lusk, 1952-54; atty. gen. State of Wyo., 1967-71; judge U.S. Circuit Ct. Appeals (10th cir.), 1971—, now sr. judge. Active Boy Scouts Am.; sec.-treas. Niobrara County Republican Central Com.; trustee St. Joseph's Children's Home, Torrington, Wyo., 1971-85. Served as cpl. AUS, 1942-45, ETO. Recipient Distinguished Alumni award U. Wyo., 1973 Mem. VFW, Am. Legion, Order of Coif (hon. mem. Wyo. Coll. Law/U. Wyo. chpt.).

BARRETT, JANE, lawyer; AB magna cum laude, Vassar Coll., 1969; MA in Chinese Studies, U. Mich., 1973; JD, NYU, 1976. Bar: N.Y. 1977, Mass. 1985. Staff atty. Legal Svcs. Corp., Bklyn., 1977-79; law asst. N.Y. County Supreme Ct., N.Y.C., 1979-81; asst. atty. gen. N.Y. State, 1981-84; asst. corp. counsel N.Y.C., 1984-87; sole practitioner N.Y.C., 1988-95; ptnr.

Spodek & Barrett LLP, 1995—. Bd. dirs. Bklyn. Legal Svcs. Corp. A. Contbg. author: Everywoman's Legal Guide, 1983; editor newsletter N.Y. County Lawyers Assn., 1977. Mem. N.Y. State Bar Assn., Assn. Bar City N.Y., N.Y. State Trial Lawyers, Nat. Assn. Ins. Women, Princeton Club. Office: Spodek & Barrett LLP 61 Broadway Rm 1050 New York NY 10006-2701

BARRETT, JOHN J(AMES), JR. lawyer; b. Phila., May 19, 1948; s. John J. and Carmela (DiJohn) B.; m. Rosemary A. Campagna, Aug. 23, 1969; children: Jeffrey, Kristin, Jacqueline. BA, Temple U., 1970, JD, 1973. Bar: Pa. 1973, N.J. 1987, U.S. Dist. Ct. (ea. dist.) Pa. 1973, U.S. Ct. Appeals (3rd cir.) 1975, U.S. Dist. Ct. (mid. dist.) Pa. 1986, U.S. Supreme Ct. 1986, U.S. Dist. Ct. N.J. 1987. Assoc. Saul, Ewing, Remick & Saul, Phila., 1973-80; ptnr. Saul Ewing LLP, 1980—. Mem. Nat. Assn. R.R. Trial Counsel, Phila. Assn. Def. Counsel. Federal civil litigation, State civil litigation, Product liability. Office: Saul Ewing LLP 3800 Centre Sq W Philadelphia PA 19102

BARRETT, KAREN MOORE, lawyer; b. Pitts., Jan. 16, 1950; d. James Newton and Grace Naomi (Gigax) Moore; m. Jay Elliott Barrett, June 24, 1972; children: Catherine Grace, Elizabeth Alice. AB, Bryn Mawr Coll., 1972; JD, Harvard U., 1977. Bar: Pa. 1977, U.S. Dist. Ct. (we. dist.) Pa. 1977. Assoc. Buchanan Ingersoll Profl. Corp., Pitts., 1977-84, ptnr., 1984-89; counsel CBS Corp. (formerly Westinghouse Electric Corp.), 1989-90, sr. counsel, 1990-93, asst. gen. counsel, 1993-2000; sr. counsel The PNC Fin. Svcs. Group, Inc., 2000—. Bd. dirs. Planned Parenthood of Western Pa., Inc., 1983-95, v.p., 1988-92; trustee Southminster Presbyn. Ch., 1995-98. Mem. ABA, Pa. Bar Assn., Allegheny County Bar Assn., Bryn Mawr of Western Pa. (Pitts., v.p. 1984-87, pres. 1987-91). Democrat. Banking, Mergers and acquisitions, Securities. Office: PNC Fin Svcs Group Inc 249 5th Ave Pittsburgh PA 15222-2707

BARRETT, PHILLIP HESTON, Nawyer; b. Detroit, May 7, 1943; s. Richard Hamilton and Jeanne Marcille (Webb) B.; m. Nancy Rose Samson, June 17, 1966 (div. Aug. 1979); children— Jeffrey Adam, Douglas Austin; m. Karen Lee Hock, Jan. 10, 1981 (div. Sept. 1999); 1 child, Andrew Hamilton. BS, Ohio State U., 1965, JD, 1968. Bar: Ohio 1968, U.S. Dist. Ct. (so. dist.) Ohio 1971, U.S. Ct. Appeals, 1982. Assoc. Porter, Wright, Morris & Arthur, Columbus, Ohio, 1970-74; ptnr. 1975—; Trustee United Way of Franklin County, Inc., 1985-96, chmn. 1992-94; trustee, Columbus Speech & Hearing Ctr., 1972-82 (chmn. 1978-80), Met. Human Svcs. Commn., 1986-91, chmn., 1987-89; trustee Children's Rsch. Inst., 1998—, Children's Hosp. Found., 1993—. Capt. Signal Corps, U.S. Army, 1968-70, Vietnam, Capt. JAG Corps, Ohio Nat. Fuard, 1971-73. Mem. ABA, Ohio Bar Assn., Columbus Bar Assn., D.C. Bar Assn., Columbus Bar Assn., Ohio State U. Pres.'s Club, New Albany Country Club, Capital Club, (Columbus). Avocations: squash, skiing, golf, photography. E-mail: pbarrett@porterwright.com. General corporate, Finance, Real property. Office: Porter Wright Morris & Arthur 41 S High St Ste 2800 Columbus OH 43215-6194

BARRETT, ROBERT MATTHEW, law educator, lawyer; b. Bronx, N.Y., Mar. 18, 1948; s. Harry and Rosalind B. AB summa cum laude, Georgetown U., 1976, MS in Fgn. Service, JD, 1980. Bar: Calif. 1981. Assoc. Latham & Watkins, L.A., 1980-82, Morgan, Lewis & Bockius, L.A., 1982-84, Skadden, Arps, Slate, Meagher & Flom, L.A., 1984-86, Shea & Gould, L.A., 1986-87, Donovan, Leisure, Newton & Irvine, L.A., 1988-90; ptnr. Barrett & Zipser, Calif., 1991-93; prof. law San Fernando Valley Law Sch., Woodland Hills, 1993—. Civilian vol. L.A. Sheriff's Dept., 1997-99. Mem. State Bar Calif. (standing com. on profl. responsibility and conduct 1995-99, chair 1997-98, spl. advisor 1998-99), L.A. Bar Assn. (bd. advisors vols. in parole com. 1981—). Address: 21300 Oxnard St Woodland Hills CA 91367-5058 Fax: 818-883-8142. E-mail: rmbarre@attglobal.net

BARRIE, JOHN PAUL, lawyer, educator; b. Burbank, Calif., Oct. 7, 1947; s. John and Virginia (Feagans) B.; children: Sean, Tyler. AB in Pol. Sci., UCLA, 1969; JD, U. Calif., San Francisco, 1972; LLM in Tax, NYU, 1973. Bar: Calif. 1972, D.C. 1975, Mo. 1977. Atty. advisor to judge U.S. Tax Ct., Washington, 1973-75; atty. office of gen. counsel Renegotiation Bd., 1975-77; assoc. Lewis & Rice, St. Louis, 1977-82, ptnr., 1982-86, Gallop, Johnson & Neuman, St. Louis, 1986-93, Bryan Cave L.L.P., St. Louis, 1993-98, Washington, 1998—. Adj. prof. Washington U. Sch. Law, St. Louis, 1979-99, Georgetown Law Ctr., 1999—; mem. IRS Dist. Dirs.'s Liaison Group, Practitioners Coun., IRS Kansas City Svc. Ctr. Liaison Group, Mo. Dept. Rev. Adv. Group, past chmn. Editor Mo. Bar Ct. and CLE Bull.; editl. advisor Jour. Multistate Taxation; contbr. articles on tax to profl. jours. Commr., Commn. Bot. Garden Subdist., St. Louis, 1989-99. Recipient Dir.'s award IRS, 1993. Fellow Am. Coll. Tax Counsel, Exec. Inst. for Advanced Study Washington U., St. Louis Tax Lawyers Group (past chmn.), St. Louis Corp. Tax Group (chmn.), St. Louis Internat. Tax Group; mem. ABA (tax sect., vice chmn. com. on govtl. submissions), Am. Tax Policy Inst. (life, sponsor), Mo. Bar Assn. (tax. sect., past chmn. tax com., Pres.'s award 1983), Calif. Bar Assn. (tax sect.), D.C. Bar Assn. (tax sec., steering com. 2001-), Bar Assn. Met. St. Louis (tax sect.), Nat. Assn. State Bar Tax Sects. (chmn. 1983-84), Noonday Club, City Club (Washington). Episcopalian. Corporate taxation, Taxation, general, State and local taxation. Home: 420 7th St NW Apt 1010 Washington DC 20004-2215 Office: Bryan Cave LLP 700 13th NW Ste 700 Washington DC 20005

BARRITT, KEITH ASHLEY, lawyer; b. Cedar Rapids, Iowa, Apr. 7, 1961; s. Paul Franklin and Joyce Anita (Hill) B.; m. Margarita Cuadra, Aug. 15, 1987; children: Alexander Ashley. David Franklin. BA with distinction, U. Va., 1983, JD, 1989. Bar: Va. 1989, D.C. 1991. Legis. aide to Congress John P. Murtha, U.S. Ho. of Reps., Washington, 1983-86; atty. Mintz, Levin, Cohn, Ferris, Glovsky & Popeo, 1989-93, Fish & Richardson, Washington, 1993—. Contbr. articles to law jours., including Intellectual Property Today, Legal Times, Nat. Law Jour., Radio Comm. Report. Sec. Collingwood-on-Potomac Citizens Assn., Alexandria, Va., 1999, pres., 2000—. Mem. Internat. Trademark Assn. Office: Fish & Richardson 601 13th St NW Ste 901S Washington DC 20005-3824 E-mail: barritt@fr.com

BARRON, HAROLD SHELDON, lawyer; b. Detroit, July 4, 1936; s. George Leslie and Rose (Weinstein) B.; m. Roberta Yellin, Nov. 17, 1963; children: Lawrence Ira, Jean Louise. A.B., U. Mich., 1958, J.D., 1961. Bar: N.Y. 1963, Mich. 1961, Ill. 1983, Pa. 1992. Pvt. practice, N.Y.C., 1962-68; practice in Southfield, Mich., 1968-83, Chgo., 1983-93, Pa., 1991—; atty. Hughes Hubbard & Reed, 1962-68; corp. counsel Bendix Corp., 1968-69, sec., assoc. gen. counsel, 1969-72, sec., gen. counsel, 1972-83, v.p., 1974-83; ptnr. Arnstein, Gluck, Lehr, Barron & Milligan, Chgo., 1983-86, Seyfarth, Shaw, Fairweather & Geraldson, Chgo., 1986-91; v.p., gen. counsel Unisys Corp., Blue Bell, Pa., 1991-92, sr. v.p., gen. counsel, 1992-94, sr. v.p., gen. counsel, sec., 1994-99, sr. v.p., gen. counsel, 1999-2001, vice chmn., 2001—. Mem. nat. adv. coun. and faculty Practising Law Inst., N.Y.C.; bd. dirs. Royal Maccabees Life Ins. Co., Southfield, 1983-94; chmn. bd. F.A. Tucker Group, Inc., 1991-95. Editor The Business Lawyer. Com. visitors U. Mich. Law Sch.; trustee Children's Hosp. Mich., Detroit, 1976-84; mem. Census Adv. Com. on Privacy and Confidentiality, 1975-76; mem. governing bd., adv. coun. Purdue U. Info. Privacy Rsch. Ctr.; bd. dirs. Citizens Rsch. Coun. of Mich., 1982-83, Greater Phila. Econ. Devel. Coalition. Served with AUS, 1961-62. Mem. ABA (coun. bus. law sect., chair elect bus. law sect., editor The Bus. Lawyer, Latin Am. legal initiatives coun., chmn. com. of corp. gen. counsel, sect. bus. law coun., com. corp. law and taxation, internat. bus. law com., com. devels. in investment svcs., com. long-range issues affecting bus. law practice, com. on corp. laws), Am. Arbitration Assn., Am. Soc. Corp. Secs. (securities law com.), CPR Inst. for Dispute Resolution (exec. com.), Mich. Bar Assn., Assn. Bar City N.Y. (com. corp. law depts.), Carlton Club, Chgo. Club, Bryn Mawr Country Club (Chgo.), The Reserve (Indian Wells, Calif.). General corporate, Mergers and acquisitions, Securities. Office: Unisys Corp Unisys Way Blue Bell PA 19424-0001

BARRON, JEROME AURE, law educator; b. Tewksbury, Mass., Sept. 25, 1933; s. Henry and Sadie (Shafmaster) B.; m. Myra Hymovich, June 18, 1961; children— Jonathan Nathaniel, David Jeremiah, Jennifer Leah A.B. magna cum laude, Tufts Coll., 1955; JD, Yale U., 1958; LL.M., George Washington U., 1960. Bar: Mass. 1959, D.C. 1960. Law clk. to chief judge U.S. Ct. Claims, Washington, 1960-61; assoc. firm Cross, Murphy & Smith, 1961-62; asst. prof. law U. N.D., Grand Forks, 1962-64; vis. assoc. prof. U. N.Mex., Albuquerque, 1964-65; dean Syracuse U. Coll. Law, 1972-73; assoc. prof. George Washington U., from 1965, prof., 1973—, dean, 1979-88, Lyle T. Alverson prof. law, 1987-2000, Harold H. Greene prof. law, 2000—. Author: (with Donald Gillmor and Todd Simon) Mass Communication Law, Cases and Comment, 6th edit., 1998, First Amendment in a Nutshell, 2d edit. 2000, Constitutional Law: Principles and Policy, 5th edit., 1996, (with C. Thomas Dienes) Constitutional Law In A Nutshell, 4th edit., 1999; contbr. articles, chpts. to profl. publs. Served with U.S. Army, 1959-60 Mem. ABA, D.C. Bar, Cosmos Club, Phi Beta Kappa. Office: George Washington U 2000 H St NW Washington DC 20006-4234

BARROWS, RONALD THOMAS, lawyer; b. Detroit, Jan. 19, 1954; s. Harland Wayne and Jeanette Edith (Authier) B. BA in English and Polit. Sci. magna cum laude, Oakland U., 1976; JD, Wayne State U., 1979. Bar: Mich. 1979, U.S. Dist. Ct. (ea. dist.) Mich. 1979, U.S. Ct. Appeals (6th cir.) 1983, U.S. Tax Ct. 1986; lic. real estate broker, Mich. Assoc. Abbott, Nicholson, Quilter, Esshaki & Youngblood, P.C., Detroit, 1979-80; counsel Lindon Land Co., Inc., Harper Woods, Mich., 1980-82; pvt. practice St. Clair Shores, 1981-87; ptnr. Barrows & Alt, P.C., Troy, 1987-90; sole practice Grosse Pointe, 1990—. Cons./counselor to corp. and pvt. real estate investors and developers; adj. prof. investment banking and venture capital formation, asset protection planning Oakland U. Paralegal Program, 1989-90. Contbr. articles to profl. jours. Mem. Mich. Comml. Investment Coun.; chmn. adv. com. Mich. chpt. Nat. Multiple Sclerosis Soc., co-chair coun. adv. com., mem. client programs com. Mem. ABA, ATLA, Mich. Bar Assn. (title stds. com. 1985—, real property coun. 1987-97, treas. 1994-97, chmn. water law com. 1985-90), Nat. Assn. Realtors, Mich. Assn. Realtors (sr. instr. 1980-91), Macomb County Assn. Realtors (lawyer realtor com. 1984-88), Nat. Order Barristers. Republican. Presbyterian. Avocations: sailing, billiards, theater, photography. Finance, Real property. Office: PO Box 36958 Grosse Pointe MI 48236-0958 E-mail: baron7@home.com

BARRY, DESMOND THOMAS, JR. lawyer; b. N.Y.C., Mar. 26, 1945; s. Desmond Thomas and Kathryn (O'Connor) B.; m. Patricia Mellicker, Aug. 28, 1971; children: Kathryn, Desmond Todd. AB, Princeton U., 1967; JD, Fordham U., 1973. Bar: N.Y. 1974, U.S. Dist. Ct. (so. and ea. dist.) N.Y. 1974, U.S. Ct. Appeals (2d cir.) 1974, U.S. Ct. Appeals (9th cir.) 1980, U.S. Ct. Appeals (5th cir.) 1983, U.S. Ct. Appeals (3d cir.) 1984, U.S. Supreme Ct. 1985. Assoc. Condon & Forsyth, N.Y.C., 1973-79, ptnr., 1979—. Trustee Canterbury Sch., New Milford, Conn., 1970-80. Capt. USMC, 1967-70, Vietnam. Decorated Navy Commendation medal with combat V, Combat Action medal, 1969, Vietnamese Cross of Gallantry, 1969. Mem. ABA (chmn. aviation & space law com. 1996-97), N.Y. State Bar Assn., Assn. of Bar of City of N.Y., Internat. Assn. Def. Counsel (exec. com. mem.), Univ. Club N.Y.C., Winged Foot Golf Club (bd. govs. 1999-01), Hawk's Nest Golf Culb, Vero Beach, Fla. Republican. Roman Catholic. Aviation, Insurance. Home: 40 Charter Oak Ln New Canaan CT 06840-6705 Office: Condon & Forsyth LLP 685 3rd Ave Fl 14 New York NY 10017-4024 E-mail: dbarry@condonlaw.com

BARRY, MARYANNE TRUMP, federal judge; b. N.Y.C., Apr. 5, 1937; d. Fred C. and Mary Trump; m. John J. Barry, Dec. 26, 1982; 1 child, David W. Desmond. BA, Mt. Holyoke Coll., 1958; MA, Columbia U., 1962; JD, Hofstra U., 1974, LLD (hon.), Seton Hall U., Caldwell Coll. Bar: N.J. 1974, N.Y. 1975, U.S. Ct. Appeals (3d cir.), U.S. Supreme Ct. Asst. U.S. Atty., 1974-75; dep. chief appeals div., 1976-77; chief appeals div., 1977-82; exec. asst. U.S. Atty., 1981-82; 1st asst., 1981-83; judge U.S. Dist. Ct., N.J., 1983-99, U.S. Ct. Appeals (3d cir.), Newark, 1999—. Chmn. Com. on Criminal Law Jud. Conf. of U.S., 1994-96. Fellow Am. Bar Found.; mem. ABA, N.J. Bar Assn., Am. Judicature Soc. (bd. dirs.), Assn. Fed. Bar State of N.Y. (pres. 1982-83). Office: US Ct Appeals PO & Courthouse Bldg Rm 333 PO Box 999 Newark NJ 07101-0999*

BARSAMIAN, J(OHN) ALBERT, lawyer, judge, educator, criminologist, arbitrator; b. Troy, N.Y., May 1, 1934; s. John and Virginia Barsamian; m. Alice Missirilan, Apr. 21, 1963; children: Bonnie, Tamara. BS in Psychology with honors, Union Coll., 1956; JD, 1968; LLB, Albany Law Sch., 1959; postgrad., SUNY, Albany, 1964, Nat. Jud. Coll., 1997. Bar: N.Y. 1961, U.S. Dist. Ct. (no. dist.) N.Y. 1961, U.S. Supreme Ct. 1967; fire tng. cert. N.Y. State Exec. Dept. Pvt. practice, 1961—; dir. criminal sci., chmn. dept. Russell Sage Coll., 1970-88, assoc. prof. criminal sci., 1977-82, prof., 1982-87, prof. emeritus, 1987—. Lectr. office local govt. divsn. criminal justice svcs. State N.Y., 1964—72, N.Y. State Police Acad., 1970; judge adminstrv. law N.Y. State Pub. Employment Rels. Bd., 1996—2001, supervising judge, asst. dir. pub. employment practice and representation, 2001—; faculty pub. affairs and policy pub. svc. tng. program Nelson A. Rockefeller Coll., 1986—91, Sch. Labor Rels. Ext. divsn. Cornell U., 1986; gaming cons. Gov's Office Indian Rels., NY, 1991—92; spl. counsel Office of Police Chief, Cohoes, NY, 1986—92, to city mgr., Troy, NY, 1993; counsel Watervliet Police Assn., 1967—74, Cohoes Police Assn., 1967—74, Colonie Police Assn., 1977—80, Troy Police Command Officers Assn., 1981—85, North Greenbush Police Assn., 1985—90, Office of the Police Chief, Syracuse, NY, 1985—90, Fire Dept. Union, Albany, NY, 1986, Shenectady Fire Fighters Union, 1992—95; gen. counsel Internat. Narcotic Enforcement Officers Assn., 1982—84, Troy Uniformed Firefighters Assn., 1977—97; spl. investigator Rensselaer County Dist. Atty., 1959—61; mem. law guardian panel N.Y. State Family Ct., 1967—77; mem. mediation panel N.Y. State Pub. Employment Rels. Bd., 1968—73; supervising judge, asst. dir. Pub. Employment Practices and Representation, 2001—. Founder, chmn. dept. police sci. Hudson Valley C.C., 1961-69; mem. adv. bd. History Ctr. Skidmore Coll., 1993—; bd. dirs. Rensselaer County ARC, 1966-70; memm. alumni coun. Union Coll., 1981-86; mem. parish coun. St. Peter Armenian Ch., Watervliet, N.Y., 1979-83, chmn., 1981-83, vice chmn., 1984; evaluator office of non-collegiate programs N.Y. State Dept. Edn., 1985—; hon. dep. sheriff St. Mary Parish (La.). Decorated chevalier, knight comdr. Sovereign Order of Cyprus; recipient Police Sci. Students award, Hudson Valley C.C., 1968, meritorious svc. to law enforcement award, Law Enforcement Officers Soc., 1969, Archbishop's cert. merit, Armenian Ch. Am., 1973, Lawyers Coop. Pub. Co. prize in criminal law, 1957; scholar Tarzian, Union Coll., 1952—56, Porter, Albany Law Sch., 1954—56, Saxton, 1956—59. Mem.: ATLA, ABA (com. on police selection and tng. 1967—69, mem. Rensselaer county criminal justice coord. coun. 1976—78), N.Y. Bar Assn. (chmn. com. on police 1970—72, trial lawyers sect. com. contg. legal edn. 1977—97, subcom. on adminstrv. law judges 2000), Nat. Assn. Adminstrv. Law Judges, Am. Arbitration Assn. (svc. award 1983), Acad. Criminal Justice Scis., Am. Coll. Barristers, N.Y. Vet. Police Assn. (life; counsel), N.Y. State Assn. Adminstrv. Law Judges (bd. dirs. 1999, bd. dirs. 2001), N.Y. State Trial Lawyers Assn., Am. Assn. Criminology, Union Coll. Alumni Assn. (Silver medal 1956), Les Amis d'Escoffier Soc., Masonic Vet. Assn. Troy (life)), Royal Order of Jesters, Shriners, Rose Crois (most wise master Delta chpt. 1986), Phi Delta Theat, Alpha Phi Sigma, Lambda Epsilon Chi. Administrative and regulatory, Criminal, Labor. Home and Office: 5 Sage Hill Ln Albany NY 12204-1315

BARTA, JAMES JOSEPH, judge; b. St. Louis, Nov. 5, 1940; BA, St. Mary's U., 1963; JD, St. Louis U., 1966. Bar: Mo. 1966, U.S. Supreme Ct. 1969. Spl. agt. FBI, Washington, Cleve., and N.Y.C, 1966-70; chief trial atty. St. Louis Cir. Atty., 1970-76; assoc. Guilfoil, Symington & Petzall, St. Louis, 1976-77; asst. U.S. atty. U.S. Dist. Ct. (ea. dist.) Mo., 1977-78, judge bankruptcy ct., 1978—, chief judge bankruptcy ct., 1986-89, 95-99. Lectr. Greater St. Louis Police Acad., 1970-76; mem. U.S. Supreme Ct. Adv. Com. on Bankruptcy Rules, 1987-94, chmn. tech. subcom.. 1990-94, style subcom., 1992-94; mem. tech. adv. com. St. Louis Coun. on Criminal Justice, 1972-74; dir. Organized Crime Task Force, St. Louis, 1972-74; project dir. St. Louis Crime Commn., 1975-77. Fellow Am. Coll. Bankruptcy (cir. chmn. 1990-94, bd. dirs. 1994-97, sec. bd. dirs. 1995-97); mem. ABA, Am. Bankruptcy Inst. (bd. dirs. 1989-94), Am. Judicature Soc., Mo. Bar Assn., St. Louis Bar Assn., St. Louis Bar Assn. CLE Inst. (at-large 1989-93), Former Spl. Agts. FBI. Office: US Bankruptcy Ct US Courthouse 111 S 10th St 7th Fl S Saint Louis MO 63102

BARTELL, ANGELA GINA BALDI, judge; b. Milw., Jan. 25, 1946; d. John Batiste and Marie Alma (Rank) Baldi; m. Jeffrey Bruce Bartell, Aug. 31, 1968; children: Jessica Marie, Carey Laurel, Chad Gerald, Dana Joyce, Nicholas John. BA, U. Wis., 1969, JD, 1971. Bar: Wis. 1972, U.S. Dist. Ct. (we. dist.) Wis. 1972. Intern Wis. Dept. Justice, Madison, 1970; law clk. to Hon. James E. Doyle U.S. Dist. Ct. (we. dist.) Wis., 1971-72; assoc., then ptnr. LaFollette Sinykin Law Firm, 1973-78; county judge Dane County Ct., 1978-79; chief judge Wis. Fifth Jud. Dist., 1982-88; cir. judge Dane County Cir. Ct., Madison, 1979—. Mem. Professionalism Commn., Madison, 1990-93; mem. Legal Edn. Commn., 1994-95; mem. adv. bd. Scan Child Abuse Prevention Project, Madison, 1988-90; assoc. dean Wis. Jud. Coll., 2000—. Jud. editor Wisconsin Judician Benchbooks, 3 vols., 1980-92 (Supreme Ct. award 1992), Wisconsin Jury Handbook, 1983; contbr.: State Bar Civil Forms Manual, 1992-99, Wisconsin Jury Instructions-Criminal, 1992—. Pres. Young Lawyers divsn. Wis. State Bar, Madision, 1974; bd. dirs. Dane County United Way, 1995—, chair bd., 2000-01; chair United Way Allocation Com.; planner, presenter Leadership Madison Forum, 1994. Fellow Am. Bar Found.; mem. Am. Law Inst., Nat. Assn. Women Judges, Rotary Club of Madison (bd. dirs. 2001—), Phi Beta Kappa. Office: Dane County Cir Ct 210 Martin Luther King Jr Blvd Madison WI 53709-0002

BARTEMES, AMY STRAKER, lawyer; b. Steubenville, Ohio, July 17, 1968; d. Ralph John and Martha Rose Straker; m. Brian Michael Bartemes, Oct. 5, 1996; 1 child, Cole Philip. BA, Purdue U., 1990; JD, Vanderbilt U., 1993. Bar: Ohio, 1993, U.S. Dist. Ct. (so. dist.) Ohio, 1996, U.S. Ct. Appeals (6th cir.), 1996, U.S. Dist. Ct. (no. dist.) Ohio, 1997. Assoc. atty. Shayne & Greenwald Co., LPA, Columbus, Ohio, 1993-97, Bricker & Eckler, LLP, Columbus, 1997—. Mem. Ohio State Bar Assn., Columbus Bar Assn., Phi Beta Kappa, Phi Delta Phi. Federal civil litigation, State civil litigation, Labor. Office: Bricker & Eckler LLP 100 S 3d St Columbus OH 43215

BARTH, J. EDWARD, lawyer, shareholder; b. Oklahoma City, Oct. 24, 1937; s. Richard L. and Vera S. Barth; m. Gene Bloomston, Apr. 15, 1972; children: Lance Rothstein, Rodney Rothstein, Lee P. Barth. BA, Yale U., 1959; JD, U. Mich., 1962. Bar: Okla. 1963, U.S. Dist. Ct. (we. dist.) Okla., U.S. Ct. Appeals (10th cir.) 1964. Law clk., Chief Judge A.P. Murrah U.S. Ct. Appeals 10th Cir., Oklahoma City, 1963-64; ptnr. Bohanon & Barth, 1964-79; shareholder, dir. Andrews Davis Legg Bixler Milsten & Price, 1979—. Chmn. com. on admissions and grievances, U.S. Dist. Ct. (we. dist.) Okla., 1987—; judge Okla. Temporary Ct. Appeals, Oklahoma City, 1991-92. Chmn. Met. Area Projects Oversight Bd., Oklahoma City, 1994—; pres., trustee Oklahoma City Cmty. Found., 1989-98; chmn., dir. ARC, Oklahoma County, 1979—. Mem. ABA, Okla. Bar Assn. (Lawyer of Month 1994), Oklahoma County Bar Assn. (dir. 1975-77). Contracts commercial, General corporate, Real property. Home: 6020 Riviera Dr Oklahoma City OK 73112-7356 Office: Andrews Davis Legg Bixler Milsten & Price 500 W Main St Ste 500 Oklahoma City OK 73102-2275

BARTKUS, ROBERT EDWARD, lawyer; b. Kearny, N.J., Sept. 30, 1946; s. Edward Charles and Dorothy Agnes (Konschott) B.; m. Mary Bartkus. BA with honors, Swarthmore Coll, 1968; JD, Stanford U., 1976. Bar: Calif. 1976, N.J. 1977, N.Y. 1977, U.S. Supreme Ct (3d, 2d cirs.), U.S. Dist. Ct. N.J., U.S. Dist. Ct. (so. and ea. dist.) N.Y. Spl. counsel Schulte, Roth & Zabel, N.Y.C., 1985-88. Tchg. asst. Stanford U. Law Sch., 1976; mem. Dist. X Ethics Com., 1992-97; lectr. N.J. Inst. for Continuing Edn., 1988—; master John J. Gibbons Intellectual Property Inn of Ct. Articles co-editor Stanford Law Rev., 1974-76; author Innovation Competition 28 Stanford Law Rev. 1976; author, editor: New Jersey Federal Civil Practice, 1992, N.J. Federal Civil Procedure, 1999; mem. editl. bd. N.J. Law Jour. (Alfred C. Clapp award 1995). Atty. Community Law Offfice, 1976-79, Legal Aid Soc., 1979-87; mem. alumni coun. Swarthmore Coll., 1977-78. Lt. USNR, 1968-73. Mem. ABA (ethics com. Dist. X), Nat. Assn. Securities Dealers (arbitrator), N.J. Bar Assn. (chair fed. practice com.), Assn. Fed. Bar of State of N.J., Morris County Bar Assn., Am. Arbitration Assn. (arbitrator), Delta Upsilon. Federal civil litigation, State civil litigation. Home: 6 Terrill Dr Califon NJ 07830-3443 Office: Profl Corp 90 Maple Ave Morristown NJ 07960-5221 E-mail: rbartkus@bartkus.com

BARTLE, HARVEY, III, federal judge; b. Bryn Mawr, Pa., June 6, 1941; s. Harvey Jr. and Dorothy L. (Baker) B.; m. Nathalie Akin Vanderpool, June 12, 1993; 3 children, 2 stepchildren. AB in History, Princeton U., 1962; LLB, U. Pa., 1965. Bar: Pa. 1965, U.S. Dist. Ct. (ea. dist.) Pa. 1965, U.S. Ct. Appeals (3d cir.) 1969, U.S. Supreme Ct. 1978. Law clk. to Hon. John Morgan Davis U.S. Dist. Ct. (ea. dist.) Pa., 1965-67; assoc. Dechert, Price & Rhoads, 1967-73, ptnr., 1973-79, 81-91; Pa. Ins. Commr., 1979-80; Pa. Atty. Gen., 1980-81; judge U.S. Dist. Ct. (ea. dist.) Pa., 1991—. Editor Law Review U. Pa. Capt. U.S. Army Res. Mem. ABA, Phila. Bar Assn., Am. Law Inst. Episcopalian. Office: US Dist Ct 601 Market St Philadelphia PA 19106-1713

BARTLETT, ALEX, lawyer; b. Warrensburg, Mo., Aug. 7, 1937; s. George Vest and May (Woolery) B.; m. Sue Gloyd, June 5, 1961 (div. June 1978); children: Ashley R., Nathan G.; m. Eleanor M. Veltrop, Oct. 27, 1978. BA, Cen. Mo. State U., 1959; LLB, U. Mo., 1961. Bar: Mo. 1962, U.S. Ct. Mil. Appeals 1963, U.S. Supreme Ct. 1965, U.S. Dist. Ct. (we. dist.) Mo. 1966, U.S. Ct. Appeals (8th cir.) 1968. From assoc. to ptnr. Hendren & Andrae, Jefferson City, Mo., 1965-79; mem. Bartlett, Venters, Pletz & Toppins, P.C., 1980-87; pvt. practice, 1987-90; mem. Husch & Eppenberger, LLC, 1990—. With Transit Casualty Co. Receivership, 1986-90, commr. claims, 1986-87, spl. claims counsel, 1987-89, dir. legal affairs dept., 1989-90; lectr. law U. Mo., Columbia, 1965-66. Contbr. editor Mo. Law Rev., 1960-61. Served to capt. JAGC, U.S. Army, 1962-65. Mem. ABA, FBA, Mo. Bar Assn. (chmn. young lawyers sect. 1972-73, ct. modernization com. 1972-74, jud. reform com. 1974-76, chmn. cts. and jud. com. 1978-79, legis. com. 1981-84, President's award 1976, Smithson award 1976), Cole County Bar Assn., Am. Coll. Trial Lawyers (chmn. Mo. 1994-96), Order of Coif. Democrat. Administrative and regulatory, Federal civil litigation, State civil litigation. Office: Husch and Eppenberger PO Box 1251 235 E High St Jefferson City MO 65102-3236

BARTLETT, CODY BLAKE, lawyer, educator; b. Syracuse, N.Y, Apr. 21, 1939; s. Stanley Jay and Izora Elizabeth (Blake) B.; m. Claudine Germaine Bouthillette, Dec. 27, 1968; 1 child, Cody Blake. AAS, Auburn C.C., 1960; BA with high honors, Mich. State U., 1963; JD, Harvard U., 1966. Bar: Mich. 1967, N.Y. 1967, U.S. Dist. Ct. (ea. dist.) Mich. 1967, U.S. Dist. Ct. (no. dist.) N.Y. 1967, U.S. Supreme Ct. 1984, U.S. Dist. Ct. (we. dist.) N.Y. 1985, Colo. 1993, U.S. Tax Ct. 1999, U.S. Ct. Fed. Claims 1999; cert. strength and conditioning specialist. Law clk. Onondaga County Dist. Atty.'s Office, Syracuse, 1965; assoc. Touche, Ross, Bailey & Smart, Detroit, 1966; law clk. Onondaga County Family Ct., Syracuse, 1967; assoc. Melvin & Melvin, 1967; budget and accounts officer Appellate Divsn., 4th Dept., Rochester, N.Y., 1967-69, dep. dir. adminstrn., 1969-72, dir. adminstrn., 1972-80; chief atty. State Commn. on Jud. Conduct, 1980-84; ptnr. Newman, Kehoe, Wunder and Bartlett, Lyons, N.Y., 1984-91, Kehoe, Bartlett & Kehoe, Wolcott, 1992-94, Bartlett Law Offices, Wolcott, 1994—. Spl. adminstr. N.Y. State Dangerous Drug Program, Western N.Y., 1973-75; adj. prof. polit. sci. dept. SUNY, Brockport, 1983-85, Grad. Sch. Pub. Adminstrn., 1985-90; adj. prof. Syracuse U. Coll. Law, 1980-84, Coll. Criminal Justice, Rochester Inst. Tech., 1979-80; grad. asst. polit. sci. dept. Mich. State U., 1962-63; lectr. jud. ethics and discipline Office Ct. Adminstrn., 1990. Author: Staying Fit Past Fifty, 1992; contbr. articles on legal issues and sports and fitness to publs.; drafter numerous legis. bills that became law. Mem. adv. com. Regional Criminal Justice Edn. and Tng. Ctr., Monroe C.C., Rochester, 1974-80; divsn. leader YMCA, Midtown Rochester membership drive, 1976; mem. East Bloomfield Planning Bd., 1984-87, chmn., 1985-87; trustee Village of East Bloomfield, 1985-87; mem. Sodus Point (N.Y.) Zoning Bd. Appeals, 1986-87; mem. adv. bd. Sodus Bay Hist. Soc., 1992; trustee Sodus Point Village, 1994-95; mem. adv. bd. Wolcott C. of C., 1993; mem. Circuit of Reebok Profls. and Specialists, 1992-94. Recipient Disting. Alumni award Assn. Bds. Trustees SUNY, 1980, nat., regional and state powerlifting and bench press champion, 1982, 83, 96-2000; N.Y. State and Am. nat. and world bench press record holder, 1996-99. Mem. N.Y. State Bar Assn. (spl. com. on jud. conduct 1984-90, profl. sports com. 1988-90), Wayne County Bar Assn., Onondaga County Bar Assn. (chmn. Syracuse City Ct. com. 1968-72), Nat. Strength and Conditioning Assn. (cert. specialist, bd. dirs., lectr. 1989-96), Phi Kappa Phi, Pi Sigma Alpha. Administrative and regulatory, General civil litigation, General practice. Home: 7094 Overlook Dr Sodus Point NY 14555-9620 Office: 12032 E Main St Wolcott NY 14590-1022 E-mail: bartlaw@dreamscape.com

BARTLETT, JAMES PATRICK, lawyer; b. Detroit, Apr. 15, 1971; s. James Patrick and Dolores Agnes Bartlett; m. Amy Louise Liedel. BAA, Ctrl. Mich. U., 1993; JD, U. Toledo, 1997. Bar: Mich., U.S. Dist. Ct. (ea. dist.) Mich., Ohio. Assoc. Czeryba and Godfroy, P.C., Monroe, Mich., 1997—. Administrative and regulatory, Criminal, General practice. Office: Czerba and Godfroy PC 19 E Front St Monroe MI 48161

BARTLETT, JAMES WILSON, III, lawyer; b. Pasadena, Calif., Mar. 21, 1946; s. James Wilson Jr. and Helen (Archbold) B.; m. Jane Edmunds Graves; children: Matthew Archbold, Polly Graves. BA, Washington & Lee U., 1968; JD, Vanderbilt U., 1975. Bar: Md. 1975, U.S. Dist. Ct. Md. 1975, U.S. Dist. Ct. (no. dist.) Ohio, 1992, U.S. Ct. Claims 1984, U.S. Ct. Appeals (4th cir.) 1976, U.S. Ct. Appeals (6th cir.) 1992, U.S. Supreme Ct. 1995. Assoc. Semmes, Bowen & Semmes, Balt., 1975-85; pvt. practice, 1985-86; ptnr. Kroll & Tract, 1986-87, Wilson, Elser, Moskowitz, Edelman & Dicker, Balt., 1987-98, mng. ptnr., 1998-2001; ptnr. Semmes, Bowen & Semmes, 2001—. Permanent mem. jud. conf. 4th Cir. Assoc. editor: Am. Maritime Cases, 1997—; contbr. articles to profl. jours. Chmn. law firm campaign United Fund, Balt., 1979; bd. dirs. Roland Park Civic League, 1987-90. 1st lt. U.S. Army, 1969-71. Mem. ABA (chmn. admiralty and maritime litigation com. litigation sect. 1997-99, vice chmn. 1985-88, chmn. admiralty and maritime law com. tort and ins. practice sect. 1990-91, vice chmn. 1992-95), Md. Bar Assn., Balt. City Bar Assn., Maritime Law Assn. U.S. (proctor, bd. dirs. 1998-2001, chair practice and proc. com. 2000—), Def. Rsch. Inst., Md. Assn. Def. Trial Counsel, Assn. Average Adjusters (Eng.), Assn. Average Adjusters U.S., Am. Boat and Yacht Coun., St. Andrews Soc., Md. Club, Propeller Club U.S. (gov. Balt. chpt. 1984-87, 97—, v.p. 1987-88, exec. v.p. 1988-89, pres. 1989-90, nat. regional v.p. 1991-92, nat. 3d v.p. 1995-96). Republican. Presbyterian. Admiralty, Product liability, Professional liability. Home: 307 Edgevale Rd Baltimore MD 21210-1913 Office: Semmes Bowen & Semmes 250 W Pratt St Baltimore MD 21201

BARTLETT, JOHN LAURENCE, lawyer; b. L.A., June 9, 1942; s. Oswald and Sarah Elisabeth (Caldwell) B.; m. Jane Helen Dormann, June 22, 1963; children: Jennifer Lynn, George Andrew. AB, UCLA, 1963; LLB, Stanford Law Sch., 1967. Bar: D.C. 1967, U.S. Dist. Ct. D.C. 1968, U.S. Ct. Appeals (D.C. cir.) 1969, U.S. Ct. Appeals (4th cir.) 1976, U.S. Supreme Ct. 1976, U.S. Ct. Appeals (2d cir.) 1977. Assoc. Kirkland & Ellis, Washington, 1967-72, ptnr., 1972-83, Wiley, Rein & Fielding, Washington, 1983—. Bd. dirs. Arinc Inc., Aeronautical Radio, Inc., Cmty. Residences Found., chmn. 1995—. Bd. dirs. Found. for Ministry of the Laity, Inc. Mem. ABA, Fed. Comm. Bar Assn., Computer Law Assn. Communications, Administrative and regulatory, Computer. Home: 2757 N Nelson St Arlington VA 22207-5033 Office: Wiley Rein & Fielding 1776 K St NW Washington DC 20006-2304 E-mail: jbartlett@wrf.com

BARTLETT, JOSEPH WARREN, lawyer; b. Boston, June 14, 1933; s. Charles W. and Barbara (Hastings) B.; m. May Parish, Apr. 28, 1956 (div.); children: Charles, Susan, Henry; m. Barbara Bemis, Sept. 20, 1980. AB, Harvard U., 1955; LLB, Stanford U., 1960. Bar: Mass. 1962, D.C. 1969, N.Y. 1981. Law clk. Chief Justice Warren, U.S. Supreme Ct., 1960-61; pvt. practice Boston, 1961-66, ptnr. Gaston & Snow, 1966-80, Gaston & Snow (formerly Gaston Snow Beekman & Bogue), N.Y.C., 1980-90, of counsel, 1990-91; ptnr. Mayer, Brown & Platt, 1991-96, Morrison & Foerster, N.Y.C., 1996-. Counsel Mass. Commn. Adminstrn., 1964-65; gen. counsel, under sec. Dept. Commerce, Washington, 1967-69; prin. adviser on universal social security coverage Sec. of HEW, Washington, 1978-79; acting prof. Stanford U., 1978; trustee, mem. fin. com. Montefiore Med. Ctr.; mem. Council on Fgn. Relations; adj. prof. NYU Law Sch. Served to 1st lt. U.S. Army, 1956-57. Fellow Am. Bar Found.; mem. Am. Law Inst., Am. Bar Assn., Boston Bar Assn. (pres. 1977-78) Democrat. Episcopalian. General corporate, Securities. Home: 200 E 71st St Apt 16C New York NY 10021-5147 Office: Morrison & Foerster 41st Fl 1290 Avenue of the Americas New York NY 10104-0050

BARTLETT, LINDA GAIL, lawyer; b. Bklyn., Apr. 6, 1943; d. Manny Max and Lottie (Sandler) Katz; m. Randall David Bartlett, Feb. 10, 1979; children: Gregory, Jeremy. AB, Bklyn. Coll., 1964; JD cum laude, U. Miami, 1977. Bar: U.S. Dist. Ct. (so., ea. and no. dists.) N.Y. 1979, U.S. Dist. Ct. N.Mex. 1979, U.S. Ct. Appeals (2d, 5th and 10th cirs.) 1979, U.S. Supreme Ct. 1980. Vol. U.S. Peace Corps, 1964-66; clin. intern U.S. NLRB, Coral Gables, Fla., 1976; assoc. Klecan & Roach, P.A., Albuquerque, 1977-78, Benjamin Wyle, N.Y.C., 1978-81; arbitrator Civil Ct. State of N.Y., 1981-90; pvt. practice law, 1990-94; ptnr. Bartlett, Bartlett & Ziegler, P.C., 1994—; mediator N.Y. County comml. divsn. N.Y. State Supreme Ct., 1996—. Adminstrv. law judge N.Y C. Dept. Environ. Protection, 1983-85; dep. gen. cunsel Dirs. Guild Am., Inc., N.Y.C., 1981-90, asst. exec. sec., 1985-90; adj. prof. law CUNY, 1986-87, 93—, vis prof. law, 1987-88; adj. prof. law Cornell U., 1989, N.Y. State Sch. Indsl. and Labor Rels., Ithaca. Bd. dirs. Lake Peekskill Civic Assn., 1972-73; planning and zoning chmn. LWV, 1972-73. Mem. ABA, Assn. Bar City N.Y. (labor rels. com., com. on labor arbitration), N.Y. State Bar Assn. (dist. del. employment and labor law sect. 1984-89, chair St. John's Law Sch., Ann. Employment Law Litigation Inst. 1996—, exec. com.). Avocations: sailing, skiing. Office: 10 E 40th St Fl 46 New York NY 10016-0301

BARTLETT, PETER LLEWELLYN, lawyer; b. Melbourne, Victoria, Australia, Dec. 13, 1947; sm. Carolyn M. Smith; 5 children. B. Jurisprudence, Monash U., Melbourne, 1970; LLB, 1972. Bar: barrister, solicitor Supreme Ct. Victoria, New South Wales, Queensland, Australian Capital Ter. Ptnr. Gillotts, Melbourne, 1974-87, Minter Ellison, Melbourne, 1987—; also bd. dirs. Trust mem. Victorian Sports Ctr. Trust, Melbourne Sports and Aquatic Ctr.; mem. disciplinary com., grievance officer Swimming Australia. Mem. Law Inst. Victoria (chair defamation com., immediate past chair litigation sect.), Law Coun. Australia (immediate past chair, communications and media com.), Law Asia (dep. chair, chair comms. and media sect.), Internat. Bar Assn. (dep. chair media law com.), Melbourne Press Club (dep. chair). Avocations: golf, tennis. Alternative dispute resolution, Communications, Libel. Office: Minter Ellison Rialto Tower 525 Collins St Melbourne VIC 3000 Australia Fax: 03 9620 5185. E-mail: peter.bartlett@minterellison.com

BARTLETT, ROBERT WILLIAM, lawyer; b. Chgo., Nov. 11, 1941; s. Robert C. and Rita E. Bartlett; m. Mary Lou Holtzman, Mar. 8, 1988; 1 child, Brooke Ann. AB, Stanford U., 1963; LLB, U. Va., 1966. Bar: Ill. 1966. Assoc. counsel U.S. League Savs. Instns., Chgo., 1970-77, assoc. gen. counsel, editor legal bull., 1977-81, sr. v.p., 1981-91; exec. editor bus. and fin. group Commerce Clearing House, Riverwoods, Ill., 1991-2000. Mem. ABA (mem. com. on savs. instns. 1973--). Roman Catholic. Avocation: running. Banking. Home: 8 Anglican Ln Lincolnshire IL 60069-3316 E-mail: bob_bartlett@att.net

BARTO, CHARLES O., JR. lawyer; b. Altoona, Pa., Aug. 12, 1946; s. Charles O. and Ernestine I. (Styers) B.; m. Marsha D. Packer, July 31, 1971; 1 child, Megan Suzanne. BA, Pa. State U., 1968; JD, Dickinson Sch. of Law, 1971. Bar: Pa. 1971, U.S. Dist. Ct. (mid. dist.) Pa. 1971, U.S. Supreme Ct. 1975, U.S. Ct. Appeals (3d cir.) 1979, U.S. Tax Ct. 1985. Asst. pub. defender Dauphin County Pub. Defender's Office, Harrisburg, Pa., 1971-73; assoc. Killian, Gephart & Snyder, 1971-74; ptnr. Killian & Gephart, 1975-83; prin. Charles O. Barto, Jr. & Assocs., 1983—. Gen. counsel Pa. Health Care Assn., Harrisburg, 1971—; conflicts counsel Hosp. Assn. Pa., Harrisburg, 1990—. Contbr. articles to books in field. V.p. St. Thomas Civic Assn., Linglestown, Pa., 1976-87; pres. consistory St. Thomas United Ch. of Christ, Linglestown, 1989, 92; chair constn. com. Pa. Coun. Chs., Harrisburg, 1990—, parliamentarian, 1990—; mem. Pa. Forestry Assn. Recipient Better Life award Pa. Health Care Assn., 1988, award of merit Health Care Facilities Assn. Pa., 1977, Boss of Yr. award Dauphin County Legal Secs. Assn., 1985-86. Mem. ABA, Pa. Bar Assn., Dauphin County Bar Assn., Assn. Trial Lawyers Am., Pa. Trial Lawyers Assn., Nat. Health Lawyers Assn. (bd. dirs. 1994—, pres. 1997-98), Kiwanis (lt. gov. divsn. 13N Pa. dist. 2001—), Koons Pool and Swim Club (pres. 1994—). Democrat. Avocations: tennis, skiing, coaching softball, computer programming, collecting pens. business e-mail: bartolawfirm-.com. Administrative and regulatory, State civil litigation, Health. Office: Charles O Barto Jr & Assocs 608 N 3rd St Harrisburg PA 17101-1102 E-mail: cbarto13@aol.com

BARTOL, ERNEST THOMAS, lawyer; b. Mineola, N.Y., Feb. 2, 1946; s. Frank Henry and Mary Ann (Kretlein) B.; m. Christine Ann Pillis; children: Jacqueline Marie, Aimee Elizabeth, Suzanne Melissa. BS in Acctg., Fordham U., 1967; JD, Villanova U., 1970. Bar: N.Y. 1971, U.S. Dist. Ct. (ea. and so. dists.) N.Y. 1973, U.S. Ct. Appeals (2d cir.) 1975, U.S. Supreme Ct. 1974. Staff acct. Pustorino, Puglisi, Behan & Co., N.Y.C., 1965-70; tax specialist Arthur Young & Co., Phila., 1970; acct. Arthur Andersen & Co., N.Y.C., 1970-71; assoc. Gehrig, Ritter, Coffey et al, Hempstead, N.Y., 1971-78; founder, sr. ptnr. Murphy, Bartol & O'Brien, LLP, Mineola, 1978—. Bd. dirs. numerous cos.; counsel to senator N.Y. State Senate, Garden City, 1985-90. Exec. com. United Cerebral Palsy Assn. Nassau County, 1978—, chmn. forget-me-not ball, 1987—92; pres., founder cmty. adv. com. Syosset Cmty. Hosp., 1987—92; exec. leader Nassau County Rep. Com., Westbury, NY, 1978—, Oyster Bay Rep. Com., 1978—; sec., mem. parish coun. and spl. sch. com. St. Edward Roman Cath. Ch., Syosset, NY, 1978—80; bd. dirs. L.I. Children's Mus., 1996—99; bd. trustees NY Inst. Tech., 1997—99; bd. dirs. L.I. Coalition for Fair Broadcasting, Inc., 2001. Named Man of Yr., United Cerebral Palsy Assn. Nassau County, 1993, Heart Coun. L.I., Inc., 2001. Mem. ABA, N.Y. State Bar Assn. (trusts and estates law com. 1983—, lectr. on estate topics), Nassau County Bar Assn. (estates and trusts law com. 1975—), profl. ethics com. 1980-86, 89-93), Criminal Cts. Bar Assn., Nassau Lawyers Assn. L.I. (bd. dirs. 1977—, chmn. 1992-93, rec. sec. 1993-94, corr. sec. 1994-95, 1st v.p. 1995-97, pres. 1997-98), Fed. Bar Coun., N.Y. State Trial Lawyers Assn., Cath. Lawyers Guild Diocese Rockville Centre, Chaminade H.S. Alumni Assn. (class rep. 1971, class dir. 1971-72, 1st v.p. 1972-74, pres. 1974-76), Rotary (sec.-treas. Syosset club 1980-90), Alpha Kappa Psi. Roman Catholic. Avocations: racquetball, tennis, fishing, softball, stamp collecting. General civil litigation, Estate planning, Probate. Office: Murphy Bartol & O'Brien LLP 22 Jericho Tpke Ste 103 Mineola NY 11501-2976 E-mail: mbolegal@aol.com

BARTOLINI, JAMES DANIEL, lawyer; b. New Haven, Apr. 13, 1946; s. Dante J. and Mariella (Cestaro) B.; m. Roni Goldstein, Dec. 22, 1975; 1 child, Jessica Marie. B.A., Trinity Coll., Hartford, Conn., 1968; M.A., Hartford Sem., 1970, M.Div., 1972; J.D., U. Conn., 1975. Bar: Conn. 1975, U.S. Ct. Appeals (2d cir.) 1975. Ptnr. RisCassi and Davis, Hartford, Conn., 1975— . Editor-in-chief Conn. Bar Jour., 1997—. Recipient Book award Harvard U., 1964. Mem. Am. Coll. Trial Lawyers, Nat. Bd. Trial Advocates (cert. Civil trial Specialist), Conn. Bar Assn. (bd. dirs. civil law sect. 1984—), Conn. Trial Lawyers Assn. (dir. 1982—, pres. 1988-89), Hartford County Med. Soc. (co-chmn. legal com. 1982—). Roman Catholic. Personal injury. Home: 47 Wood Pond Rd Glastonbury CT 06033-3703 Office: PO Box 6550 Hartford CT 06106

BARTON, BABETTE B. lawyer, educator; b. Los Angeles, Apr. 30, 1930; d. Milton Vernon and Ruth (Schreiber) Barancik; children: Jeffrey B. Barton, David R. Barton, Baird R. Barton. BS, U. Calif., Berkeley, 1951, LLB, 1954. Bar: Calif., U.S. Dist. Ct., U.S. Ct. Appeals 1955. Law clk. to Hon. Phil S. Gibson Calif. Supreme Ct., San Francisco, 1954-55; lectr., acting prof. U. Calif. Sch. Law, Berkeley, 1961-72, prof., 1972-99, prof. emeritus, 1999—; Adrian A. Kragen chair U. Calif., Berkeley. Cons. Calif. Inter Agy. Task Force on Electronic Funds Transfers, 1978-79, Dept. Treasury, 1963; adv. com. Calif. Bd. Legal Specialization, 1980-83. Contbr. chpts. to books in field. Adv. com. Alameda County Dir. Welfare, 1970-73; bd. dirs. Family Service Berkeley, 1967-74, Univ. Students' Coop. Assn., 1966-74. Recipient Citation award Boalt Hall Alumni Assn., 1997. Fellow Am. Law Inst., Am. Bar Found.; mem. ABA (taxation sect. chmn. tchg. tax. com. 1994-96, real property probate and trust sect. coun. 1977-79), Calif. State Bar (chmn. taxation sect. 1976-77, Joanne M. Garvey award taxation sect. 1997), Western Regional Bar Assn. (chmn. 1978-79), Am. Coll. Tax Counsel, San Francisco Tax Club, San Francisco Estate Planning Coun., Berkeley Tennis Club (bd. dirs. 1988-90, pres. 1990-91). Home: 16 Saint James Dr Piedmont CA 94611-3533 Office: U Calif Berkeley Sch Law 691 Simon Boalt Hl Berkeley CA 94720-0001

BARTON, BERNARD ALAN, JR. lawyer; b. Glens Falls, N.Y., Aug. 13, 1948; s. Bernard A. Sr. and Geraldine (Bushey) B.; children: Lindsey, Kylie. BA, U. Fla., 1969, JD, 1975, LLM, 1976. Bd. cert. tax lawyer. Ptnr. Holland & Knight, Tampa, Fla., 1976—. Editor, contbg. author Florida Taxation, State Taxation Series, 1994. Mem. ABA, Nat. Assn. Bond Attys., Fla. Bar Assn. (exec. coun. tax sect., chmn. various coms. 1980-99). Republican. Episcopalian. Corporate taxation, Taxation, general, State and local taxation. Office: Holland & Knight 400 N Ashley Dr PO Box 1288 Tampa FL 33601-1288

BARTON, JAMES CARY, lawyer; b. Raymondville, Tex., Sept. 1, 1940; s. Dewey Albert and Dorothy Marie (Keene) B.; m. Isabel Pattee Critz, Sept. 12, 1964 (div. June 1975); children: Hamilton Keene, James Albert, John Franklin; m. Carolyn Ann Cox, Dec. 20, 1975; stepchildren: Holly Ann Adams, Laura Lee Adams, Jennifer Lynn Adams. BA, Baylor U., 1962; LLB, Harvard U., 1965. Bar: Tex. 1965, U.S. Dist. Ct. (so. dist.) Tex. 1972, U.S. Tax Ct. 1977. Trial atty. FPC, Washington, 1965-67; atty.-advisor U.S. Tax Ct., 1967-68; assoc. to ptnr. Kleberg, Mobley, Lockett & Weil, Corpus Christi, Tex., 1969-75, Brown, Maroney, Rose, Baker & Barber, Austin, 1975-82; ptnr. to of counsel Johnson & Swanson, 1982-88; dir. Smith, Barshop, Stoffer & Millsap, Inc., San Antonio, 1988-91; prin. J. Cary Barton, P.C., 1991-93; prin Barton & Schneider, L.L.P., 1993—. Speaker in field. Sgt. USAF, 1968-69. Mem. ABA, State Bar Tex. (mem. coun. of real estate probate and trust law sect. 1982-85, mem. real estate forms com. 1986—), Am. Coll. Real Estate Lawyers, Tex. Bd. legal Specialization (cert. in comml. real estate law), Tex. Coll. Real Estate Attys. Democrat. Episcopalian. Real property. Office: Barton & Schneider LLP 700 N Saint Marys St Ste 1825 San Antonio TX 78205-3596

BARTON, JOHN HAYS, law educator; b. Chgo., Oct. 27, 1936; s. Jay and Agnes (Heisler) B.; m. Julianne Marie Gunnis, June 13, 1959; children: John II, Robert, Anne, Thomas, David. BS, Marquette U., 1958; JD, Stanford U., 1968. Bar: D.C. 1969. Engr. Sylvania Electronic Def. Labs., Mountain View, Calif., 1961-68; assoc. Wilmer, Cutler and Pickering, Washington, 1968-69; George E. Osborne prof. Stanford (Calif.) U. Law Sch., 1969—. Vis. prof. U. Mich. Law Sch., fall 1981, Harvard Law Sch., 1988. Author: Politics of Peace, 1981; co-author: Law in Radically Different Cultures, 1983 (Am. Soc. Internat. Lawe award 1984), International Trade and Investment, 1986; co-editor Words over War, 2000. Former chair Nat. Genetic Resources Adv. Coun.; mem. NAFTA Dispute Settlement Panel; mem. NRC Com. Intellectual Property Rights in Knowledge Based Econ., 2000-01; chair commn. intellectual property rights UK Dept. Internat. Devel., 2001—. Lt. (j.g.) USN, 1958-61. Rockefeller Found. fellow, 1976-77. Fellow AAAS, Chartered Inst. Arbitrators; mem. Am. Soc. Internat. Law. Home: 1340 Harwalt Dr Los Altos CA 94024-5815 Office: Stanford U Sch Law Stanford CA 94305

BARTON, ROBERT L(EROY), JR. judge, educator; b. Ballston Spa, N.Y., June 19, 1943; s. Robert L. Sr. and Bertha (Di Pasquale) B.; m. Jean M. Adamchic, Aug. 14, 1965; children: Robert Joseph, Katherine Anne. BA, U. Pitts., 1965; JD, Boston Coll., 1969. Bar: Mass. 1969, R.I. 1970, D.C. 1972, U.S. Ct. Appeals (1st cir.) 1970, U.S. Ct. Appeals (D.C. cir.) 1973, U.S. Dist. Ct. R.I., 1971, U.S. Dist. Ct. D.C. 1973, U.S. Dist. Ct. Md. 1973. Law clk. U.S. Dist. Ct. R.I., Providence, 1969-70; staff atty. R.I. Legal Svcs., 1970-71; spl. asst. to solicitor U.S. Dept. Labor, Washington, 1971-72; assoc. Sherman, Dunn, Cohen & Leifer, 1972-75; trial atty. FTC, 1975-88; judge Pa. Office of Hearing & Appeals, Pitts., 1988-90, Office of Hearings, Washington, 1990-95, Office of Adminstr. Law Judges, Washington, 1995—. Trial instr. Nat. Inst. Trial Advocacy, Washington, 1982-86, U.S. Dept. Justice, Washington, 1986-96. Chair com. Cath. League for Religious Rights, Milw., 1983-84. Master Am. Inn of Ct.; mem. Fed. Bar Assn. (co-chair adminstrv. jud. com.), Fed. Adminstrn. Law Judges Assn. (mem. exec. com.), Nat. Lawyers Assn. Roman Catholic. Avocations: travel tennis, swimming. Office: Office Adminstrv Law Judges 5107 Leesburg Pike Ste 1905 Falls Church VA 22041-3249 E-mail: robert.barton@usdaj.gov

BARTON, THOMAS DONALD, lawyer, educator; b. July 1, 1949; s. Donald Walter and Dorothy Louise (Farlin) B.; m. Sharon Lee Foster, July 26, 1980. BA, Tulane U., 1971; JD, Cornell U., 1974; PhD, Cambridge (Eng.) U., 1982. Bar: N.Y. 1974, Calif. 1990. Assoc. Harris, Beach & Wilcox, Rochester, N.Y., 1974-76; asst. prof. W.Va. U. Coll. Law, Morgantown, 1978-80; assoc. prof., assoc. dean acad. affairs, 1982-84; prof., 1984-87; posten prof. law, 1987-89; prof. Calif. Western Sch. Law, 1990—; dir. Brown Program in Preventive Law, 2000—. Mem. panel arbitrators, Am. Arbitration Assn.; mem. Morgantown Bd. Zoning Appeals, 1983-86; bd. dirs. W.Va. Tax Inst., 1978-80; cons. W.Va. State Elections Commn., 1979. NEH fellow, 1979. Contbr. articles to profl. jours. Recipient Gustavus Hill Robinson award, 1974; W.D.P. Carey Exhbn. prize, 1972. Mem. Phi Beta Kappa, Phi Sigma Delta, Delta Alpha Pi. Office: Calif Western Sch Law 225 Cedar St San Diego CA 92101-3046

BARTOSIC, FLORIAN, law educator, lawyer, arbitrator; b. Danville, Pa., Sept. 15, 1926; s. Florian W. and Elsie (Woodring) B.; m. Eileen M. Payne, 1952 (div. 1969); children: Florian, Ellen, Thomas, Stephen; m. Alberta C. Chew, 1990. B.A., Pontifical Coll., 1948; B.C.L., Coll. William and Mary, 1956; LL.M., Yale U., 1957. Bar: Va. 1956, U.S. Supreme Ct. 1959. Asst. instr. Yale U., 1956-57; assoc. prof. law Coll. William and Mary, 1957, Villanova U., 1957-59; atty. NLRB, Washington, 1956, 57, 59; counsel Internat. Brotherhood of Teamsters, 1959-71; prof. law Wayne State U., 1971-80, U. Calif., Davis, 1980-92; recalled to tchg., 1994-99; prof. emeritus law U. Calif., Davis, 1993—, dean law, 1980-90. Adj. prof. George Washington U., 1966-71, Cath. U. Am., 1960-71; mem. panel arbitrators Fed. Mediation and Conciliation Service, 1972— ; hearing officer Mich. Employment Relations Commn., 1972-80, Mich. Civil Rights Commn., 1974-80; bd. dirs. Mich. Legal Services Corp., 1973-80, Inst. Labor and Indsl. Relations, U. Mich., Wayne State U., 1976-80; mem. steering com. Inst. on Global Conflict and Cooperation, 1982-83; mem. adv. bd. Assn. for Union Democracy Inc., 1980—, adv. coms. Calif. Jud. Council, 1984-85, 87; vis. scholar Harvard Law Sch., 1987, Stanford Law Sch., 1987; sr. rsch. scholar ILO, 1990-91; acad. visitor Oxford U., London Sch. Econs., 1991; mem. exec. bd. Pub. Interest Clearinghouse, 1988-90. Co-author: Labor Relations Law in the Private Sector, 1977, 2d edit., 1986; contbr. articles to law jours. Mem. ABA (sec. labor relations law sect. 1974-75), Fed. Bar Assn., Am. Law Inst. (acad. mem. labor law adv. com. on continuing profl. edn.), Soc. Profls. in Dispute Resolution (regional v.p. 1979-80), Indsl. Rels. Rsch. Assn., Internat. Soc. Labor Law and Social Legis., Internat. Indsl. Rels. Assn., Am. Arbitration Assn., Nat Lawyers Guild, ACLU (dir. Detroit chpt. 1976-77), Order of Coif (hon.), Scribes. Home: 235 Ipanema Pl Davis CA 95616-0253 Office: U Calif Sch Law Mrak Hall Dr Davis CA 95616 E-mail: fbartosic@ucdavis.edu

BARTUNEK, ROBERT R(ICHARD), JR. lawyer; b. Cleve., July 2, 1946; s. Robert Richard and Clare Elizabeth (Lonsway) B.; 1 child, Kathryn Elizabeth. BS, Bucknell U., 1968; MBA, Ohio State U., 1974, JD, 1975; LLM, U. Mo., Kansas City, 1986. Bar: Mo. 1975, Kans. 1997, U.S. Dist. Ct. (we. dist.) Mo. 1975, U.S. Tax Ct. 1981, U.S. Dist. Ct. Kans. 1997. Ptnr. Beckett, Lolli & Bartunek, Kansas City, 1975-96, Swanson Midgley, LLC, Kansas City, 1997—. Mem. Men's Sr. Baseball League. Decorated Bronze Star. Mem. ABA, Lawyers Assn. Greater Kansas City, Kansas City Met. Bar Assn. (former chmn. tax law com.). Roman Catholic. General corporate, Estate taxation, Taxation, general. Home: 10314 Howe Ln Kansas City KS 66206- Office: Swanson Midgley LLC Crown Center 2420 Pershing Rd Ste 400 Kansas City MO 64108-2505 E-mail: rbartunek@swansonmidgley.com

BARTZ, DAVID JOHN, lawyer; b. Appleton, Wis., Feb. 15, 1955; s. Frederick Carl and Dorothy Lucille (Weckwerth) B. BA, U. Wis., 1976; MA in Pub. Affairs, U. Minn., 1979; JD, Ariz. State U., 1985. Bar: Ariz. 1985, U.S. Dist. Ct. Ariz. 1985, U.S. Ct. Appeals (9th cir.) 1985, Wis. 1989, U.S. Dist. Ct. (we. dist.) Wis. 1996, U.S. Dist. Ct. (ea. dist.) Wis. 1997. Policy analyst Minn. Dept. Transp., St. Paul, 1978-79; office dir. Wis. Senate, Madison, 1979-82, 86; pvt. practice, Phoenix, 1985-86; adminstr. Wis. Dept. Justice, Madison, 1987-91; pvt. practice, 1991—. Mem. ASPA (sec. Wis. Capital chpt. 1981-82), Ariz. Bar Assn., Wis. Bar Assn., Dane County Bar Assn. General corporate, Criminal, Labor.

BARUSCH, LAWRENCE ROOS, lawyer; b. Oakland, Calif., Aug. 23, 1949; s. Maurice Radston and Phyllis (Rose) B.; m. Susan Amanda Smith, Aug. 7, 1983; children: Nathaniel M., Ariana G. BA summa cum laude, Harvard U., 1971, JD cum laude, 1975. Bar: Calif. 1975. Assoc. Cotton, Seligman & Ray, San Francisco, 1975-77; gen. counsel Jones & Guerrero Co., Inc., Agana, Guam, 1977-82; ptnr. Klemm, Blair & Barusch, PC, Guam, 1982-85; assoc. Davis, Graham & Stubbs, Salt Lake City, 1986-87; counsel Parsons, Behl & Latimer, 1987-89, shareholder, 1989—; counsel Guam Tax Code Commn., 1990-94. Adj. prof. U. Utah Coll. Law, 1998-99, 2000—, vis. assoc. prof., 1999-2000; mem. com. U.S. activities of foreigners and tax treaties, tax sect. ABA, 1994—. Contbr. articles to profl. jours. including Guam Bar Jour., Utah Bar Jour., Offshore Investment and Tax Notes. Chmn. Dem. Party, Davis County, Utah, 1997-99. Sheldon fellow Harvard U., 1971. Mem. Guam Bar Assn. (pres. 1982-84), No. Marianas Bar Assn., Utah Bar Assn. (chmn. tax sect. 1994-95), Calif. Bar Assn., Utah Tax Review Comm., Phi Beta Kappa. Natural resources, Real property, Corporate taxation. Office: Parsons Behle & Latimer 201 S Main St Ste 1800 Salt Lake City UT 84111-2218 E-mail: lbarusch@pblutah.com

BARZ, PATRICIA, lawyer; b. Mattoon, Ill., Oct. 18, 1953; d. William E. Barz and Rosemary A. (Easton) Scott; m. Herbert P. Wiedemann, Feb. 12, 1983; children: Sarah Barz Wiedemann, Andrew Barz Wiedemann. BA, Yale U., 1974; JD, U. Va., 1978. Bar: Va. 1979, Conn. 1982, Ohio 1985. Assoc. Hunton & Williams, Richmond, Va., 1978-81, Davis, Graham & Stubbs, Denver, 1981-82; counsel legal dept. Aetna Life and Casualty Co., Hartford, Conn., 1982-84; assoc. Jones, Day, Reavis & Pogue, Cleve., 1984-92; dir. law Cleve. Metroparks, 1992—. Trustee St. Anthony Trust Assn., New Haven, 1983-86; class agt. Yale Alumni Fund, New Haven, 1985-89. Mem. ABA, Ohio State Bar Assn., Cleve. Bar Assn., Conn. Bar Assn., Va. Bar Assn., Yale Alumni Assn. (v.p. Cleve. chpt. 1986-88, trustee 1988-95, 98—, pres. 1995-98). Methodist. Avocations: figure skating, raquetball, theater, reading, travel. Contracts commercial, Landlord-tenant, Real property. Home: 18040 S Woodland Rd Shaker Heights OH 44120-1773 E-mail: pabarz@aol.com, pb@clevelandmetroparks.com

BARZA, HAROLD A. lawyer; b. Montreal, Que., Can., July 28, 1952; came to U.S., 1969; s. Solomon A. and Evelyn (Elkin) B. BA, Boston U., 1973; JD, Columbia U., 1976. Bar: N.Y. 1977, Calif. 1978, U.S. Dist. Ct. (ctrl. dist.) Calif. 1978. Law clk. to Hon. Milton Pollack U.S. Dist. Ct. (so. dist.) N.Y., 1976-77; assoc. Munger, Tolles & Rickershauser, L.A., 1978-81; ptnr. Gelles, Singer & Johnson, 1982-83, Gelles, Lawrence & Barza, L.A., 1983-87, Loeb & Loeb, L.A., 1987-99, Quinn, Emanuel, Urquehart, Oliver and Hedges, L.A., 1999—. Adj. prof. mass comm. law Southwestern U. Sch. Law, L.A., 1979-82; judge pro tem., L.A. Mcpl. Ct., 1985—. Mem. bd. editors Columbia Law Rev., 1975-76. Mem. steering com. Jewish Nat. Fund, L.A., 1983. James Kent scholar, 1974-76, Harlan Fiske Stone scholar, 1973-74. Mem. ABA (mem. com. on antitrust litigation), Los Angeles County Bar Assn. (trial lawyers, litigation and intellectual property sects.). Antitrust, Federal civil litigation, State civil litigation. Office: Quinn Emanuel Urquhart Oliver and Hedges 865 S Figueroa St Los Angeles CA 90017-2543 E-mail: hab@qeuo.com

BASILE, PAUL LOUIS, JR. lawyer; b. Oakland, Calif., Dec. 27, 1945; s. Paul Louis and Roma Florence (Paris) B.; m. Linda Lou Paige, June 20, 1970; m. 2d Diane Chierichetti, Sept. 2, 1977. BA, Occidental Coll., 1968; postgrad., U. Wash., 1969; JD, UCLA, 1971. Bar: Calif. 1972, U.S. Dist. Ct. (cen. dist.) Calif. 1972, U.S. Dist. Ct. (no. dist.) Calif. 1985, U.S. Ct. Appeals (9th cir.) 1972, U.S. Tax Ct. 1977, U.S. Ct. Claims. 1978, U.S. Customs Ct. 1979, U.S. Ct. Customs and Patent Appeals 1979, U.S. Ct. Internat. Trade 1981, U.S. Supreme Ct. 1977; cert. specialist in taxation law Bd. of Legal Specialization, State Bar of Calif. Assoc. Parker, Milliken, Kohlmeier, Clark & O'Hara, L.A., 1971-72; corp. counsel TFI Cos., Inc., Irvine, Calif., 1972-73; pvt. practice L.A., 1973-80, 90-96, 98-99; mem. Basile & Siener, 1980-86, Clark & Trevithick, L.A., 1986-90; ptnr. Wolf, Rifkin & Shapiro, 1990, of counsel, 1990-92; ptnr. Basile & Lane, LLP, 1996-97; of counsel Shaffer, Gold & Rubaum, L.L.P., 1996—; sr. ptnr. Basile & Assocs., L.A. and Pasadena, Calif., 1999—. Gen. counsel J.W. Brown, Inc., L.A., 1980—, asst. sec., 1984-92; sec., gen. counsel Souriau, Inc., Valencia, Calif., 1981-90; v.p., sec., dir., gen. counsel Pvt. Fin. Assocs., L.A., 1983-94; gen. counsel Quest Relocation Group, Toluca Lake, Calif., 1994-97, v.p. real estate, 1996—. Trustee, sec. Nat. Repertory Theatre Found., 1975-94, mem. exec. com., 1976-94, chmn. bd. dirs., 1991-94; mem. fin. com., bd. dirs. Calif. Music Theatre, 1988-92; bd. dirs. March of Dimes Birth Defects Found., Los Angeles County, 1982-87, mem. exec. com., 1983-86, sec., 1985-86; dist. fin. chmn. L.A. Area coun. Boy Scouts Am., 1982-83; trustee Occidental Coll., L.A., 1989-94; active L.A. Olympic Organizing Com., Ketchum Downtown YMCA, Vols. Am. L.A., others. Mem. ABA (taxation sect., corp. tax com., vice chmn. closely held bus. com. 1992-94, chair, 1994-96, chmn. subcom. on continuing legal edn. 1990-94, chmn. subcom. on estate planning 1992, sec. 1996-97, small firm lawyers com., bus. law sect., real property sect., probate and trust law sect., spl. problems of bus. owners com., estate planning and drafting, pre-death planning issues com.), State Bar Calif. (bus. law sect., nonprofit and unicorporated orgns. com. 1989-92, taxation sect., estate planning, trust and probate sect., taxation law adv. commn. 1994-97, vice chmn. 1995-96, chair 1996-97, mem. bd. legal specialization 1996-97), L.A. County Bar Assn. (taxation sect., com. on closely-held and pass-through entities, bus. and corps. law sect., sole practitioner section exec. com. 1995-99), Beverly Hills Bar Assn. (probate, trust & estate planning section, taxation section, vice chmn. Estate and Gift Tax Com., 1998—, law practice mgmt. section), Can. Calif. C. of C. (dir. 1980-89, 2d v.p. 1983-84, 1st v.p. 1984-85, pres. 1985-87), L.A.-Vancouver Sister City Assn. (dir., exec. com. 1987-92, treas. 1987-89, pres. 1989-92), French-Am. C. of C. (councilor 1979-84, v.p. 1980, 82-84), L.A. Area C. of C. (dir. 1980-81), Occidental Coll. Alumni Assn. (pres. 1979-80, v.p. 1978-79, alumni bd. govs. 1977-81, chmn. annual fund campaign 1990-91), Grand People (bd. dirs. 1985-92, chmn. bd. 1986-92), Rotary Club of L.A. (dir. 1994-96, sergeant-at-arms 1986-87, chmn. gateway com. 1993-94, chmn. world cmty. svc. com. 1991-93, chmn. vols. Am. of L.A. com. 1988-90, chmn. golf com. 1986-87, vice-chmn. pres. com. 1985-86), Rotary Internat. (chmn. club extension com. 1995-96, cmty. svc. dir. 1993-95, chmn. gift of life com. 1992-93), Small Bus. Coun. of Am., Inc. (legal adv. bd. 1989—), The Group, Inc., Attorneys for Family Held Enterprises. Democrat. Baptist. General corporate, Estate planning, Taxation, general. Home: 3937 Beverly Glen Blvd Sherman Oaks CA 91423-4404 Office: Basile and Assocs 12011 San Vicente Blvd Ste 600 Los Angeles CA 90049-4948 also: 180 S Lake Ave Ste 540 Pasadena CA 91101-2666

BASINGER, RICHARD LEE, lawyer; b. Canton, Ohio, Nov. 24, 1941; s. Eldon R. and Alice M. (Bartholomew) B.; m. Rita Evelyn Gover, May 14, 1965; children: David A., Darron M. BA in Edn., Ariz. State U., 1963; postgrad. Macalester Coll., 1968-69; JD, U. Ariz., 1973. Bar: Ariz. 1973, U.S. Dist. Ct. Ariz. 1973, U.S. Tax Ct. 1977, U.S. Ct. Appeals (6th cir.) 1975, U.S. Ct. Appeals (9th cir.) 1976, U.S. Supreme Ct. 1977; cert. arbitrator. Assoc. law offices, Phoenix, 1973-74; pvt. practice, Scottsdale, Ariz. 1974-75; pres. Basinger & Assocs., P.C., Scottsdale, 1975—, also bd. dirs. Contbr. articles to profl. jours. Bd. dirs. Masters Trail Ventures, Scottsdale, 1984-85, Here's Life, Ariz., Scottsdale, 1976—; precinct committeeman Republican Party, Phoenix, 1983—; bd. dir. Ariz. Coll. of the Bible, 1992-93. NSF grantee, 1968-69. Mem. ABA, Ariz. Bar Assn., Maricopa County Bar Assn., Ariz. State Horseman's Assn. (bd. dirs. 1984-86, 1st v.p. 1986), Scottsdale Bar Assn., Western Saddle Club (bd. dirs. 1983-86, pres. 1985-86), Scottsdale Saddle Club, Saguaro Saddle Club. Baptist. General corporate, Probate, Real property. Office: Mohave County Atty Dep County Atty Civil Divsn PO Box 7000 Kingman AZ 86402-7000

BASISZTA, MARTIN WINSTON, lawyer; b. Antioch, Calif., Jan. 10, 1943; m. Catherine Dawn Czarnecki, Mar. 3, 1978; children— Kelly Jane, Meghan Aileen. B.A. summa cum laude, U. Calif.-Davis, 1968; J.D., U. Calif.-Berkeley, 1972. Bar: Calif. 1973. Assoc., McNamara, Lewis & Craddick, Walnut Creek, Calif., 1973-75, Maloney, Chase, Fisher & Hurst, San Francisco, 1975-76; ptnr. Van Voorhis & Skaggs, Walnut Creek, 1976-78; sole practice law, Walnut Creek, 1978-83; ptnr. Basiszta & Daniels, Hayward, Calif., 1983— . Assoc. editor Calif. Law Rev., 1971-72. Contbr. articles to legal jours. Served with submarine service U.S. Navy, 1960-63. Recipient deptl. citation German studies U. Calif.-Davis, 1968; regents scholar U. Calif., 1966-68; German Govt. grad. grantee, German Govt. Grad. Exchange Program, 1969; John Woodward Ayer fellow in law, 1971-72; Alexander Von Humboldt grad. fellow in law, 1982; hon. Woodrow Wilson fellow, 1968. Mem. Bar Assn. San Francisco, Contra Costa County Bar Assn., Mt. Diablo Bar Assn., Santa Clara Bar Assn., San Mateo Bar Assn., Calif. Trial Lawyers Assn., Contra Costa/Alameda Trial Lawyers Assn., Assn. Def. Counsel, Def. Research Inst., Lawyers Club San Francisco, Barristers Club San Francisco, Phi Beta Kappa, Alpha Gamma Sigma, Phi Kappa Phi.

BASKERVILL, CHARLES THORNTON, lawyer; b. South Boston, Va., May 26, 1953; s. William Nelson and Julia Alice (Moore) B.; m. Pamela Temple Shell, July 17, 1976; children: Ann Cabell, Susannah Thornton. BA, Hampden-Sydney Coll., 1975; JD, U. Richmond, 1978. Bar: a. 1978, U.S. Dist. Ct. (ea. dist.) Va. 1978. Assoc. White, Hamilton, Wyche & Shell, P.C., Petersburg, Va., 1978-96; asst. commonwealth's atty, 1985—; assoc. Shell, Johnson, Andrews, Baskervill & Baskervill, P.C., 1996-2001, Shell, Johnson, Andrews & Baskervill, P.C., Petersburg, 2001—. Commr. of accts. City of Petersburg, Va., 1996—. Former dir. Petersburg Crime Prevention Found. Named to Athletic Hall of Fame, Hampden-Sydney Coll., 1988. Mem. Prince George County Bar Assn. (sec.-treas. 1990-91, pres. 1991-92), Petersburg Bar Assn. (pres. 2001—). Methodist. Avocations: golf, tennis. Estate planning, Family and matrimonial, Probate. Office: Shell Johnson Andrews Baskervill PC 43 Rives Rd Petersburg VA 23805-9255

BASS, DAVID STEVEN, lawyer, educational administrator; b. Bklyn., Dec. 10, 1946; s. Joseph and Thelma (Feingold) B.; m. Carol W. Palevsky, Aug. 17, 1969; children: Adam Brett, Wayne Jonathan. BA, Bklyn. Coll., 1967; JD, NYU, 1971, LLM, 1975. Bar: N.Y. 1972, U.S. Dist. Ct. (ea. dist.) N.Y. 1975. Atty. Office Labor Rels. and Collective Bargaining N.Y.C. Bd. Edn., 1973-80, dep. dir., 1980-84, dep. exec. dir., 1984—. Adj. prof. edn. law and pers. adminstrn. City Coll. CUNY, 1992—. Mem. Am. Arbitration Assn., N.Y. State Bar Assn. Democrat. Jewish. Home: 31 Whitney Dr Marlboro NJ 07746-1249 Office: Office Labor Relations and Collective Bargaining NYC B d Edn 110 Livingston St Brooklyn NY 11201

BASSECHES, ROBERT TREINIS, lawyer; b. N.Y.C., Jan. 24, 1934; s. Jacob Thomas and Paula (Treinis) B.; m. Harriet Itkin, July 6, 1958; children: K.B., Joshua, Jessica. BA, Amherst Coll., 1955; LLB, Yale U., 1958. Bar: D.C. 1962, U.S. Ct. Appeals (D.C. cir.) 1962, U.S. Ct. Appeals (2d cir.) 1978, U.S. Ct. Appeals (4th cir.) 1998. Law clk. to judge David L. Bazelon U.S. Ct. Appeals (D.C. cir.), Washington, 1958-59; law clk. to justice Hugo L. Black U.S. Supreme Ct., 1959; assoc. Shea & Gardner, 1959-63, ptnr., 1963—, adminstrv. ptnr., 1980-86, chmn., exec. com., 1988-93. Trustee Green Acres Sch., Rockville, Md., 1971-76, pres., chmn. bd. trustees, 1973-75; pres. Chevy Chase (Md.) Village Citizens Assn., 1976. Mem. Maritime Adminstrv. Bar Assn. (pres. 1969-71, sec. 1967-69), Phi Beta Kappa. Administrative and regulatory, Transportation. Office: Shea & Gardner Ste 800 1800 Massachusetts Ave NW Washington DC 20036-1872

BASSEN, NED HENRY, lawyer; b. N.Y.C., June 8, 1948; s. Harold Russell and Annette (Frankfeldt) B.; m. Susan Millington Campbell, July 2, 1999; children: Amanda Lee, Susannah Spence. BS, Cornell U., 1970, JD, 1973. Bar: N.Y. 1974, U.S. Dist. Ct. (so. and ea. dists.) N.Y. 1974, U.S. Ct. Appeals (11th cir.) 1984, U.S. Dist. Ct. (ea. dist.) Mich 1990. Assoc. Baer Marks & Upham, N.Y.C., 1975 80, Kelley Drye & Warren, N.Y.C., 1973-75, 80-83, ptnr., 1983-92; ptnr., labor group head Mudge Rose Guthrie Alexander & Ferdon, 1993-95; ptnr., chair labor and employment group Hughes Hubbard & Reed LLP, 1995—. Note and comment editor Cornell Law Rev., 1972-73. V.p. local condominium assn., 1988-93. Mem. ABA (labor and employment law sect.), U.S. Coun. for Internat. Bus., Indsl. Rels. Com., Indsl. Rels. Rsch. Assn., N.Y. State Bar Assn. (labor law sect., com. on equal employment opportunity law), N.Y. State Mgmt. Attys. Conf. Labor. Office: Hughes Hubbard & Reed LLP 1 Battery Park Plz Fl 12 New York NY 10004-1482

BASSETT, DEBRA LYN, lawyer; b. Pleasanton, Calif., Oct. 28, 1956; d. James Arthur and Shirley Ann (Russell) Bassett. BA, U. Vt., 1977; MS, San Diego State U., 1982; JD, U. Calif., Davis, 1987. Bar: Calif. 1987, D.C. 1990, U.S. Dist Ct. (no. and ea. dists.) Calif. 1988, U.S. Ct. Appeals (9th cir.), 1988, U.S. Supreme Ct., 1991. Guidance counselor Addison Cen. Supr. Union, Middlebury, Vt., 1982-83, Milton (Vt.) Elem. Sch., 1983-84; assoc. Morrison & Foerster, San Francisco, 1986; jud. clk. U.S. Ct. Appeals (9th cir.), Phoenix, 1987-88; assoc. Morrison & Foerster, San Francisco and Walnut Creek, Calif., 1988-92; sr. atty. Calif. Ct. Appeal (3d appellate dist.), Sacramento, 1992-99. Tutor civil procedure, rsch. asst. U. Calif., Davis, 1985-87; instr. U. Calif. at Davis Ext., 1995—; lectr. law U. Calif., Davis, 1997—; adj. prof. law McGeorge Sch. Law, 1998-99, vis. prof. law, 2000—, dir. legal process McGeorge Sch. Law, 1999-2000. Sr. articles editor U. Calif. Law Rev., Davis, 1986-87; editor, 1985-86. Mem. Sacramento Opera Chorus, 1998—, Music Soc. St. Cecilia, 2001—. Mem. APA, AAUW, ABA (vice chmn. ethics com. young lawyers divsn. 1989-91, exec. com. labor and employment law com. 1989-90), APA (assoc. mem.), Sacramento County Bar Assn., Calif. Women Lawyers, Women Lawyers of Sacramento, Scribes. Democrat. Avocations: music, tennis, travel, hiking. Home: 1541 39th St Sacramento CA 95816-6720 Office: U Calif Sch Law 400 Mark Hall Dr Davis CA 95616 E-mail: dlbassett@ucdavis.edu

BASSETT, EDWARD CALDWELL, JR. lawyer; b. Newton, Mass., July 4, 1952; s. Edward C. and Marie A. (Querfurth) B.; m. Nancy A. Bassett, May 17, 1981; children: Andrew, Allison, Christopher. AB, Boston Coll., 1974, JD, 1977. Bar: Mass. Ptnr., mem. mgmt. com. Mirick, O'Connell DeMallie & Lougee, Worcester, Mass., 1977—. Editor: Benders UCC Reporter Digest, 1977; contbr. articles to profl. jours. Chmn. Southboro (Mass.) Bd. Appeals, 1985-94; exec. com., trustee Anna Maria Coll., Paxton, Mass., 1992-94. Avocation: tennis. Condemnation, Personal injury, Product liability. Office: Mirick O'Connell et al 1700 Bank of Boston Twr Worcester MA 01608

BASSETT, JOHN WALDEN, JR. lawyer; b. Roswell, N.Mex., Mar. 21, 1938; s. John Walden Sr. and Evelyn (Thompson) B.; m. Patricia Lubben, May 22, 1965 (dec. Apr. 1995); children: John Walden III, Loren Patricia; m. Nolana Knight, May 2, 1998. AB in Econs., Stanford U., 1960; LLB with honors, U. Tex., 1964. Bar: Tex. 1964, N.Mex. 1964. Assoc. Atwood & Malone, Roswell, 1964-66; White House fellow, spl. asst. to U.S. Atty. Gen., Washington, 1966-67; ptnr. Atwood, Malone, Mann & Turner and predecessors, Roswell, 1967-95, Bassett & Copple, LLP, Roswell, 1995—. Bd. dirs. A.H. Belo Corp., Dallas, AMMA Found., Washington. Assoc. editor U. Tex. Law Rev., 1962. Mem. N.Mex. State Bd. Edn., 1987-91; pres., chmn. bd. United Way of Chaves County, N.Mex., 1973; bd. dirs. Ednl. Achievement Found., Roswell, 1992—, N.Mex. Bus. Roundtable for Ednl. Excellence, Albuquerque. 1st lt. U.S. Army, 1961-68. Mem. ABA, Tex. Bar Assn., N.Mex. Bar Assn., Chaves County Bar Assn., Order of Coif, Rotary (pres. 1976), N.Mex. Amigos, Phi Delta Phi. Republican. Episcopalian. General practice, Probate, Real property. Home: 5060 Bright Sky Rd Roswell NM 88201-8800 Office: Bassett & Copple 400 N Pennsylvania Ave Ste 250 Roswell NM 88201-4788 E-mail: bassett@trailnet.com

BASTIAANSE, GERARD C. lawyer; b. Holyoke, Mass., Oct. 21, 1935; s. Gerard C. and Margaret (Lally) B.; m. Paula E. Paliska, June 1, 1963; children: Elizabeth, Gerard. BSBA, Boston U., 1960; JD, U. Va., 1964. Bar: Mass. 1964, Calif. 1970. Assoc. Nutter, McClennen & Fish, Boston, 1964-65; counsel Campbell Soup Co., Camden, N.J., 1965-67; gen. counsel A&W Internat. (United Fruit Co.), Santa Monica, Calif., 1968-70; ptnr. Kindel & Anderson, Los Angeles, 1970—. Mem. ABA, Calif. Bar Assn., Mass. Bar Assn., Japan Am. Soc., Asia Soc., World Trade Ctr. Assn. Clubs: California (Los Angeles); Big Canyon Country (Newport Beach, Calif.). General corporate, Private international. Home: 2 San Sebastian Newport Beach CA 92660-6828 Office: Kindel & Anderson 2030 Main St Ste 1300 Irvine CA 92614-7220

BASTIAN, GARY WARREN, judge; b. St. Paul, Nov. 7, 1948; s. Warren John and Virginia (Brower) Bastian; children from previous marriage: Alexander, Christopher. BS, Wis. State U., 1970; JD, William Mitchell Co., 1974. Bar: Minn. 1975. Rschr. Minn. Taxpayers Assn., 1970-73; dir. IR rsch. staff Minn. Senate, 1974-85; project dir. labor mgmt. com. Minn. Sch., 1985-87; pvt. practice, 1987-91; asst. commr. Dept. Labor and Industry, 1991, dep. commr., 1991-95, commr., 1995-97; judge 2d Jud. Dist. Ramsey County, 1997—. Mem. Maplewood City council, Minn., 1980-90. mayor 1990-97; bd. dirs. East Communities Family Ctr., 1986-90, Minn. League of Cities, 1988-92, Nat. Assn. Govt. Labor Officials, 1995-97, sec.-treas., 1996-97, Ramsey-Washington Counties Suburban Cable Commn., 1991-97, State Fund Mut. Ins. Co., 1995-97, Minn. Safety Coun., 1996-97; chmn. Minn. Workers' Compensation Adv. Coun., 1995-97. Mem. Criminal Def. Svcs. Bd., 1998—; bd. dirs. U. Wis.-River Falls Found., 1997—; mem. Ramsey County Violence Coord. Coun., 1999—. Recipient award of merit Local 320, Pub. and Law Enforcement Teamsters Mpls., 1979. Mem. Assn. Met. Municipalities (bd. dirs. 1981-89), Suburban C. of C. (bd. dirs. 1979-84), Polar Wrestling Club. Roman Catholic. Home: 2042 Holloway Saint Paul MN 55109 Office: Ramsey County Courthouse Saint Paul MN 55102

BATA, RUDOLPH ANDREW, JR. lawyer; b. Akron, Ohio, Jan. 9, 1947; s. Rudolph Andrew and Margaret Eleanor (Ellis) B.; m. Genevieve Ruth Brannan, Aug. 25, 1968 (div. May 1985); 1 child, Seth Andrew; m. Linda Lee Waldo, May 7, 1985; 1 child, Sarah Ariel. BS, So. Coll., Collegedale, Tenn., 1969; JD, Emory U., 1972. Bar: D.C. 1973, N.C. 1978, U.S. Dist. Ct. N.C. 1991, U.S. Ct. Appeals (4th cir.) 1991; cert. arbitrator, mediator AOC. Assoc. ICC, Washington, 1972-73; in house counsel B.F. Saul Real Estate Investment Trust, Chevy Chase, Md., 1973-74; staff atty. Martha, Cafferky, Powers & Jordan, Washington, 1974-75; asst. corp. counsel Hardee's Food Systems, Inc., Rocky Mount, N.C., 1975-78; ptnr. Bata & Blomeley, Murphy, 1978-87, 88-90, Bata & Sumpter, Murphy, 1987-88; sole practice, 1990—. Bd. dirs. Cherokee County United Fund, Murphy, 1981-83. Mem. ABA, N.C. Bar Assn., D.C. Bar Assn., 30th Jud. Dist. Bar Assn., So. Soc. of Adventist Attys. (pres. 1984-85), Cherokee County C. of C. (bd. dirs. 1980-82). Avocations: golf, tennis, hiking. Banking, Probate, Real property. Office: 225 Valley River Ave Ste A Murphy NC 28906-3000 E-mail: batalaw@dnet.net

BATCHELDER, ALICE M. federal judge; b. Aug. 15, 1944; m. William G. Batchelder III; children: William G. IV, Elisabeth. BA, Ohio Wesleyan U., 1964; JD, Akron U., 1971; LLM, U. Va., 1988. Tchr. Plain Local Sch. Dist., Franklin County, Ohio, 1965-66, Jones Jr. High Sch., 1966-67, Buckeye High Sch., Medina County, 1967-68; assoc. Williams & Batchelder, Medina, Ohio, 1971-83; judge U.S. Bankruptcy Ct., 1983-85, U.S. Dist. Ct. (no. dist.) Ohio, Cleve., 1985-91, U.S. Ct. of Appeals (6th cir.), Cleveland, 1991—. Mem. ABA, Fed. Judge's Assn., Fed. Bar Assn., Medina County Bar Assn. Office: US Ct of Appeals (6th cir) 143 W Liberty St Medina OH 44256-2215

BATCHELDER, DRAKE MILLER, lawyer; b. Indpls., Dec. 12, 1941; s. Keith Drake and Anna (Miller) B.; divorced; children: Brian, Michael, David. BS in Indsl. Engring., U. Fla., 1965, JD with honors, 1969. Bar: Fla. Assoc. Mershon, Sawyer, Johnston, Dunwody & Cole, Miami, 1969-71; ptnr. Rimes, Greaton, Murphy & Batchelder, Ft. Lauderdale, Fla., 1971-79, English, McCaughan & O'Bryan, Ft. Lauderdale, 1979-86, Finley, Kumble Wagner, Ft. Lauderdale, 1986-88, Heinrich, Gordon, Batchelder, Hargrove & Weihe, Ft. Lauderdale, 1988-95, Tripp, Scott, Conklin & Smith, Ft. Lauderdale, 1995-98, Akerman, Senterfitt & Eidson, Ft. Lauderdale, 1998—. Editor U. Fla. Law Rev., 1969. Trustee Fla. Oaks Sch. Bd., Ft. Lauderdale, 1981-87, chmn. sch. bd., 1985-86; trustee St. Thomas Aquinas Found., Ft. Lauderdale, 1982-87. Mem. Broward County Bar Assn. (pres. young lawyers sect. 1973-74), Fla. Bar Assn. (bd. of govs. 1974-78, 79-84, chmn. merit retention commn. 1981-82), Ft. Lauderdale C. of C. (chmn. task force 1981-82). Republican. Roman Catholic. Clubs: Touchdown (pres. Ft. Lauderdale 1980-81), Lauderdale Yacht, Lago Mar County. Contracts commercial, Finance, Real property. Home: 9301 S Orchard Rd N Davie FL 33328 Office: Akerman Senterfitt & Eidson Ste 1600 350 E Las Olas Blvd Fort Lauderdale FL 33301-2292 E-mail: dbatchelder@akerman.com

BATCHELOR, JAMES KENT, lawyer; b. Long Beach, Calif., Oct. 4, 1934; s. Jack Morrell and Edith Marie (Ottinger) B.; m. Jeanette Lou Dyer, Mar. 27, 1959; children: John, Suzanne; m. Susan Mary Leonard, Dec. 4, 1976. AA, Sacramento City Coll., 1954; BA, Calif. State U., Long Beach, 1956; JD, U. Calif., 1959. Bar: Calif. 1960, U.S. Dist. Ct. (cen. dist.) Calif. 1960, U.S. Supreme Ct. 1968; cert. family law specialist Calif. Bd. Legal Specialization, 1980. Dep. dist. atty., Orange County, Calif., 1960-62; assoc. Miller, Nisson, Kogler & Wenke, Santa Ana, 1962-64; ptnr. Batchelor, Cohen & Oster, 1964-67, Kurilich, Ballard, Batchelor, Fullerton, 1967-72; pres. James K. Batchelor, Inc. Tchr. paralegal sect. Santa Ana City Coll.; judge pro-tem Superior Ct., 1974—; lectr. family law Calif. Continuing Edn. of Bar, 1973—. Contbr. articles to profl. jours. Fellow Am. Acad. Matrimonial Lawyers (pres. So. Calif. chpt. 1989-90); mem. ABA, Calif. State Bar (plaque chmn. family law sect. 1975-76, advisor 1976-78), Orange County Barristers (founder, pres., plaque 1963), Calif. State Barristers (plaque 1964, v.p.), Orange County Bar Assn. (plaque sec. 1977, pres. family law sect. 1968-71). Republican. Methodist. Family and matrimonial. Office: 765 The City Dr S Ste 270 Orange CA 92868-6908

BATEMAN, DAVID ALFRED, lawyer; b. Pitts., Jan. 28, 1946; s. Alfred V. and Ruth G. (Howe) B.; m. Trudy A. Heath, Mar. 13, 1948; children: Devin C., Mark C. AB in Geology, U. Calif., Riverside, 1966; JD, U. San Diego, 1969; LLM, Georgetown U., 1978. Bar: Calif. 1970, U.S. Dist. Ct. (so. dist.) Calif. 1970, U.S. Ct. Mil. Appeals 1972, Wash. 1973, U.S. Dist. Ct. (we. dist.) Wash. 1973, U.S. Supreme Ct. 1974, D.C. 1976, U.S. Dist. Ct. Appeals (9th cir.) 1981. Assoc. Daubney, Banche, Patterson & Nares, Oceanside, Calif., 1969-72; asst. atty. gen. State of Wash., Olympia, 1977-81; ptnr. Bateman & Woodring, 1981-85, Woodring, Bateman & Westbrook, Olympia, 1985-89, Hanemann & Batemann, Olympia, 1989-92, Hanemann, Bateman & Jones, Olympia, 1992—. Instr. Am. Inst. Banking, San Diego, 1972, U. Puget Sound, Olympia campus, spring, 1979; assoc. broker Coldwell Banker Comml., Tacoma, Wash. Served to capt. JAGC, USAF, 1972-77; col. JAGC, USAFR, 1977-97. Mem. Calif. State Bar Assn., D.C. Bar Assn., Wash. State Bar Assn., Rotary (past chmn. internat. svcs. com.). Roman Catholic. Private international, Land use and zoning (including planning), Real property.

BATEMAN, THOMAS ROBERT, lawyer; b. Winchester, Mass., Dec. 9, 1944; s. Richard Holt and Phyllis (Brown) B.; m. Katherine Elizabeth Elliott, Sept. 9, 1972; children: Kyra Elizabeth, Richard Holt, Robert Elliott. BA, Harvard U., 1967; JD, NYU, 1971. Bar: N.Y. 1972, U.S. Dist. Ct. (so. dist.) N.Y. 1973, U.S. Ct. Appeals (2d cir.) 1974, Mass. 1978, U.S. Dist. Ct. Mass. 1978, U.S. Ct. Appeals (1st cir.) 1978. Assoc. Winthrop, Stimson, Putnam & Roberts, N.Y.C., 1971-77, Skadden, Arps, Slate, Meagher & Flom, Boston, 1977-79, ptnr., 1980—. Class agent Phillips Exeter Acad., N.H., 1969—; class steering com. Harvard U., Cambridge, Mass. 1985—. Mem. ABA, N.Y. State Bar Assn., Assn. of Bar of City of N.Y. Episcopalian. Club: Harvard (Boston). General corporate, Public international, Securities. Home: 33 Bullard Rd Weston MA 02493-2203

BATES, HAROLD MARTIN, lawyer; b. Wise County, Va., Mar. 11, 1928; s. William Jennings and Reba (Williams) B.; m. Audrey Rose Doll, Nov. 1, 1952 (div. Mar. 1978); children: Linda, Carl; m. Judith Lee Farmer, June 23, 1978. BA in Econs., Coll. William and Mary, 1952; LLB, Washington and Lee U., 1961. Bar: Va. 1961, Ky. 1961. Spl. agt. FBI, Newark and N.Y.C., 1952-56; tech. sales rep. Hercules Powder Co., Wilmington, Del., 1956-58; investigator U.S. Def. Dept., Lexington, Va., 1959-62, Louisville, 1959-62; practice law, 1961-62; sec.-treas., dir., house counsel Life Ins. Co. of Ky., 1962-66; practice law Roanoke, Va., 1966—; sec., dir. James River Limestone Co., Buchanan, 1970-96; sec. Eastern Ins. Co., Roanoke, 1984-87. Pres., Skil, Inc., orgn. for rehab. Vietnam vets., Salem, Va., 1972-75; freshman football coach Washington and Lee U., 1958-60. Capt. U.S. Army Airborne, 1946-67, PTO. Mem. Va. Bar Assn., Roanoke Bar Assn., William and Mary Alumni Assn. 9bd. dirs. 1972-76), Soc. Former Spl. Agts. of FBI (chmn. Blue Ridge chpt. 1971-72). Republican. General corporate, Estate planning, Corporate taxation. Home: 209 Summit Way Roanoke VA 24016 Office: 320 Elm Ave Roanoke VA 24016 E-mail: hbates6802@aol.com

BATES, JOHN WYTHE, III, lawyer; b. Richmond, Aug. 22, 1941; s. John Wythe, Jr. and Virginia (Wellington) B.; m. Beverly Jane Estes, June 20, 1964; children: Elizabeth Puller, Kathryn Wellington. BS, Va. Tech., 1963; LLB, U. Va., 1966. Assoc. McGuire Woods Battle & Boothe, L.L.P., Richmond, 1966-71, pntr., 1971—, mng. ptnr., 1989-96. Mem. Va. Racing Commn., 1997-2000; chmn. Richmond Renaissance, Inc., 1998—. Chmn. United Way Gtr. Richmond, 1975-76; pres. Family and Children's Svc. Richmond, 1978-80; trustee St. Paul's Coll., 1989-96, Va. Found. Ind. Colls., 1994—; sr. warden St. Stephen's Ch., 1985-86; mem. exec. com. Va. Tech. Found. Bd., 1994-2000. Va. Law Found. fellow, 1997. Mem. Am. Coll. Real Estate Lawyers, Richmond Real Estate Group, Forum Club, River Rd. Citizens Assn. (pres. 1983-84), Country Club Va. (pres. 1987-88), Bull and Bear Club (pres. 1980-81), Commonwealth Club. Episcopalian. Avocations: golf, waterfowl hunting. Land use and zoning (including planning), Landlord-tenant, Real property. Office: McGuire Woods LLP One James Ctr 901 E Cary St Richmond VA 23219-4057 E-mail: jbates@mcguirewoods.com

BATLA, RAYMOND JOHN, JR. lawyer; b. Cameron, Tex., Sept. 1, 1947; s. Raymond John and Della Alvina (Jezek) B.; m. Susan Marie Clark, Oct. 1, 1983; children: Sara, Charles, Michael, Traci. BS with highest honors, U. Tex., 1970, JD with honors, 1973. Bar: Tex. 1973, D.C. 1973, U.S. Dist. Ct. (so. dist.) Tex. 1982, U.S. Ct. Appeals (D.C. cir.) 1974, U.S. Ct. Appeals (5th cir.) 1982, U.S. Ct. Appeals (10th cir.) 1978, U.S. Supreme Ct. 1977. Structural engr. Tex. Hwy. Dept., Austin, 1970; assoc. Hogan & Hatson, Washington, 1973-82, gen. ptrn., 1983—. Mem. Am. Endowment for Democracy Internat. Observer Del. to Czechoslovakia, 1990; sec. Coun. on Alt. Fuels, 1987-97. Author: Petroleum Regulation Handbook, 1980, Natural Gas Yearbook, 1991; columnist, mem. editorial bd. Natural Gas mag., 1984-91, Energy Law Jour., 1991-93; contbr. articles to profl. jours. Mem. ABA (mem. spl. com. for energy fin., vice chmn. energy com. 1981), Fed. Energy Bar Assn. (chmn. internat. energy transactions com. 1993-94), Fed. Bar Assn., D.C. Bar Assn., State Bar Tex., City Club of Wash., London Capital Club, Order of Coif, Chi Epsilon, Tau Beta Pi. Private international, Public international, Public utilities. Home: 12406 Shari Hunt Grv Clifton VA 20124-2056 also: 5 Half Moon St London W1Y 7RA England Office: Hogan & Hartson 555 13th St NW Ste 800W Washington DC 20004-1109 also: Hogan & Hartson One Angel Ct London EC2R 7HJ England E-mail: rjbatla@hhlaw.com

BATSON, DAVID WARREN, lawyer; b. Wichita Falls, Tex., Jan. 4, 1956; s. Warren M. Batson and Jacqueline (Latham) B. BBA, Midwestern State U., 1976; JD, U. Tex., 1979. Bar: Tex. 1980, U.S. Dist. Ct. (no. dist.) Tex. 1981, U.S. Tax Ct. 1981, U.S. Ct. Appeals (5th cir.) 1983, U.S. Ct. Appeals (D.C. cir.) 1983, U.S. Ct. Claims 1984, U.S. Supreme Ct. 1984. Atty. Arthur Andersen & Co., Ft. Worth, 1980-81; tax atty. The Western Co. of N.Am., 1981-85; sr. tax atty. Alcon Labs., Inc., 1985; gen. counsel Data Tailor, Inc., 1985-87; sr. tax atty. Arco, 1988-90; atty. pvt. practice, Wichita Falls, Tex., 1990—99; pvt. practice Strohencille, 1999—. Lectr. U. of Tex., Arlington, 1984-85; of counsel Means & Means, Corsicana, Tex., 1985-86. Contbr. articles to profl. jours. Speaker A Wish With Wings, Arlington, Tex., 1984-85, Habitat for Humanity (bd. dirs. 1999-). Mem. Assn. Trial Lawyers Am., Tex. Bar Assn., Christian Legal Soc., Tex. Trial Lawyers Assn., State Bar at Tex. Coll., Phi Delta Phi. Avocations: negotiations, camping, self improvement. Contracts commercial, Private international, Mergers and acquisitions. Address: PO Box 585 Stephenville TX 76401-0585

BATSON, RICHARD NEAL, lawyer; b. Nashville, May 1, 1941; s. John H. and Mildred (Neal) B.; m. Jean Elizabeth Flanagan; children: John Hayes, Richard Davis. BA cum laude, Vanderbilt U., 1963, JD, 1966. Bar: Ga. 1967. Law clk. to Judge Griffin B. Bell U.S. Ct. Appeals (5th cir.), Atlanta, 1966-67; assoc. Alston & Bird (formerly Alston, Miller & Gaines), 1967-71, ptnr., 1971—. Spkr. Nat. Conf. Bankruptcy Judges, 1982, 86, 87, 88, 94, 96, Bank Lending Inst., 1986-87, also other instns. and assns.; adj. prof. Emory U. Sch. Law, 1994-95; co-lectr. Ga. State U., fall 1984; mem. bankruptcy rules com. Jud. Conf. U.S., 1993-99. Co-author: Problem Loan Strategies, 1985, rev. 1998; contbg. author Bankruptcy Litigation Manual, 1990—; contbg. editor Norton Bankruptcy Law and Practice, 1990—. Sgt. USAF, 1967-73. Fellow Am. Coll. Trial Lawyers, Am. Coll. Bankruptcy (bd. dirs., pres. 1997-2001, chmn. bd. dirs. 2001—); mem. Atlanta Bar Assn. (pres. 1979-80), Am. Law Inst., Southeastern Bankruptcy Law Inst. (bd. dirs., pres. 1986-87), Nat. Bankruptcy Conf. Avocations: hiking, outdoor activities. Office: Alston & Bird 1 Atlantic Ctr Atlanta GA 30309-3400

BATT, NICK, property and investment executive; b. Defiance, Ohio, May 6, 1952; s. Dan and Zenith (Dreher) B. BS, Purdue U., 1972; JD, U. Toledo, 1976. Asst. prosecutor Lucas County, Toledo, 1976-80, civil divsn. chief, 1980-83; village atty. Village of Holland, Ohio, 1980-91; law dir. City of Oregon, 1984-91; spl. counsel State of Ohio, 1983-93; pres. Property & Mgmt. Connection, Inc., Toledo, 1993—. Mem. Maumee Valley Girl Scout Coun., Toledo, 1977-80; bd. mem. Bd. Cmty. Rels., Toledo, 1975-76; mem. Lucas County Dem. Exec. Com., 1981-83. Named One of Toledo's Outstanding Young Men, Toledo Jaycees, 1979. Mem. KC, Elks. Democrat. Roman Catholic. Office: Property & Mgmt Connection Inc 1732 Arlington Ave Toledo OH 43609-3050 E-mail: battnick@aol.com

BATTAGLIA, BRIAN PETER, lawyer; b. St. Petersburg, Fla., Oct. 10, 1960; s. Anthony S. and Virginia A. (Knopick) B.; m. Nancy L. Pateras, Sept. 27, 1986; children: Jason Michael, Matthew Brian. BS in Criminology, Fla. State U., 1982; JD, Drake U., 1985; LLM in Health Law, Loyola U., Chgo. Bar: Fla. 1986, U.S. Dist. Ct. (mid. dist.) Fla. 1987, U.S. Ct. Appeals (11th cir.) 1992, U.S. Supreme Ct. 1993. Cert. mediator cir. and county ct., Fla., 1995—. Assoc. Battaglia, Ross, Dicus and Wein, P.A., Tampa, St. Petersburg, 1986-90, shareholder litigation dept., 1990—, chair health law practice group. Adj. prof. St. Petersburg Jr. Coll. People's Law Sch., 1988-92, Stetson U. Coll. of Law, 1997-2001; mem. 6th cir. unlicensed practice of law com. Fla. Supreme Ct., 1993-95, chmn., 1995. Contbr. articles to law jours. Bd. dirs. Pinellas Opportunity Coun., 1988-92, pres., 1990-92; bd. dirs. Head Start, 1989-91, Bay Area Legal Svcs., 1994-97; v.p. Comty. Law Program, 1990-92, pres., 1992-95. Recipient pro bono cert. of appreciation Cmty. Law Program, 1993. Mem. ABA (com. on condemnation, zoning and land use litigation 1991-95), Am. Health Lawyers Assn., Fla. Bar (vice chmn. eminent domain com. 1994-95, health law sect. 1996-2001, Pres.'s Pro Bono Svc. award 6th jud. cir. 1994), Hillsborough County Bar Assn., St. Petersburg Bar Assn. (exec. com. 1993-95, 1999-2000, sec. 2000-01, Pro Bono award 1990, chair law day com. 1999), Delta Theta Phi, Alpha Phi Sigma. General civil litigation, Condemnation, Health. Office: Battaglia Ross Dicus and Wein PA 980 Tyrone Blvd N Saint Petersburg FL 33710-6382 E-mail: BPBlaw@aol.com

BATTAGLIA, LYNNE ANN, judge; b. Buffalo, 1945; BA Intl Relations, Amer. Univ., 1967, MA, 1968; JD, Univ. of Maryland, 1974. U.S. atty., Md., 1993-2001; chief of staff Office of U.S. Sen. Barbara A. Mikulski; judge Md. Ct. Appeals, 2001—. Office: Md Ct Appeals Robert C Murphy Bldg 361 Rowe Blvd Annapolis MD 21401*

BATTAGLIA, PHILIP MAHER, lawyer; b. Pasadena, Calif., Jan. 18, 1935; s. Philip N. and Helen Margaret (Maher) B.; m. Lorraine Marie Moore, Dec. 29, 1962; children: Karen, Steven, Kristen, Scott. B.S.L., U. So. Calif., 1956, LL.B., 1958. Bar: Calif. 1959, U.S. Dist. Ct. (cen. dist.) Calif. 1959, U.S. Supreme Ct. 1967. Assoc., then sr. ptnr. Flint & MacKay, Los Angeles, 1960—; with Donovan Leisure Newton, L.A., 1986-94; with Sidley & Austin, L.A. 1994—. adminstrv. asst. to Gov. Ronald Reagan, 1966-67; dir. First Colony Life Ins. Co. (Va.), others. Past pres. Santa Barbara (Calif.) Theatrefest. Served to 1st lt. USAF. Mem. Los Angeles County Bar Assn., U. So. Calif. Law Alumni Assn. (pres.), Trojan Barristers (pres.), Calif. Jr. Chamber (named Outstanding Young Man of Yr. 1967-68), Los Angeles Jr. Chamber, Phi Alpha Delta. Republican. Roman Catholic. Clubs: Chancery, Lincoln (Los Angeles). General corporate, Libel, Real property. Office: Sidley & Austin 555 W 5th St Fl 40 Los Angeles CA 90013-1010

BATTEN, MELISSA C. lawyer; b. Dalton, Ga., Mar. 2, 1972; d. William Cooper and Patricia Glenn Brooks; m. Joseph Eugene Batten, Apr. 11, 1998. BA in Polit. Sci. summa cum laude, U. Ga., 1994; JD cum laude, Harvard U., 1997. Bar: N.C. 1997, U.S. Dist. Ct. (we. dist.) N.C. 1997. Assoc. Fennebresque, Clarke, Swindel & Hay, Charlotte, N.C., 1997—. Mem. ACLU, Meddenburg County Bar Assn. (law firm pro bono coord. 1998—). Contracts commercial, Criminal. Office: Fennebresque Clark Swindell & Hay 100 N Tryon ST Ste 2900 Charlotte NC 28202

BATTIS, DAVID GREGORY, lawyer; b. Rahway, N.J., July 25, 1945; s. Robert A. and Ruth (Augustine) B.; m. Florence B. Daly, Sept. 9, 1967; children— Seth, Melissa, Anna. B.A., Swarthmore Coll., 1967; M.A., Stanford U., 1968; J.D., U. Pa., 1975. Bar: Pa. 1975, U.S. Dist. Ct. (ea. dist.) Pa. 1976, U.S. Ct. Appeals (3d cir.) 1981. Law clk. U.S. Ct. Appeals 3d circuit Phila., 1975-76; assoc. Schnader, Harrison, Segal & Lewis, Phila., 1976-83, ptnr., 1984— . Rec. clk. sch. com. Germantown Friends Sch., Phila., 1980— ; bd. mgrs. Springfield Retirement Residence-All Saints Rehab. Hosp., Phila., 1983-87; trustee Alfred Cope Book Trust, 1986—. Mem. ABA, Pa. Bar Assn., Phila. Bar Assn., Order of Coif. Mem. Soc. of Friends. Federal civil litigation, State civil litigation, Environmental. Office: Schnader Harrison Segal 1600 Market St Ste 3600 Philadelphia PA 19103-7287

BATTLE, LEONARD CARROLL, lawyer; b. Toronto, Ont., Can., Oct. 25, 1929; s. Leonard Conlon and Beatrice Hester Battle; m. Marjory Estelle Holland, Dec. 28, 1953; children: David, Tracy, Thomas, Patricia, John, Mary. AB, U. Mich., 1950; JD, Ind. U., 1958. Bar: Mich. 1961, Ind. 1961, U.S. Ct. Mil. Appeals 1964, U.S. Supreme Ct. 1964. Claims adjuster State Farm Ins. Co., 1959-61; asst. pros. atty. Midland County, Mich., 1961-67; pvt. practice, Midland, 1967—. Lt. col. JAG, USAFR, 1950-84. Mem. ATLA, Mich. Bar Assn. (mil. law com.), Midland County Bar Assn. (pres.), Air Force Ret. Judge Advs. Assn. Bankruptcy, Federal civil litigation, State civil litigation. Home: 408 Harper Ln Midland MI 48640-7321 Office: 200 E Main St Midland MI 48640-6510 E-mail: afjag05ret@webtv.net

BATTLES, JOHN MARTIN, lawyer; b. Pitts., May 10, 1957; s. John and Rosemarie B.; m. Mary Ann Battles; children: John David, Katherine Rose. BA, U. Pitts., 1978; BA in Bus. Adminstrn., U. Cin., 1980, JD, 1990. Asst. corp. counsel Cincom Systems, Cin.; now corp. counsel Lexis-Nexis Group, divsn. Reed Elsevier Inc., Dayton, Ohio. Contracts commercial, Computer, Intellectual property. Home: 7 Crescent Ct Fort Thomas KY 41075-2113 Office: Lexis Nexis Group Div Reed Elsevier Inc 9443 Springboro Pike Miamisburg OH 45342-4425

BAUCH, THOMAS JAY, financial/investment advisor, lawyer, educator, former apparel company executive; b. Indpls., May 24, 1943; s. Thomas and Violet (Smith) B.; m. Ellen L. Burstein, Oct. 31, 1982; children: Chelsea Sara, Elizabeth Tree. BS with honors, U. Wis., 1964, JD with highest honors, 1966. Bar: Ill. 1966, Calif. 1978. Assoc. Lord, Bissell & Brook, Chgo., 1966-72; lawyer, asst. sec. Marcor-Montgomery Ward, 1973-75; spl. asst. to solicitor Dept. Labor, Washington, 1975-77; dep. gen. counsel Levi Strauss & Co., San Francisco, 1977-81, sr. v.p., gen. counsel, 1981-96, of counsel, 1996-2000; pvt. practice, Tiburon, Calif., 1996-2000; mng. dir. Laurel Mgmt. Co., L.L.C., San Francisco, 2000—. Cons. prof. Stanford (Calif.) U. Law Sch., 1997—; ptnr. Ika Enterprises. Mem. U. Wis. Law Rev., 1964-66. Bd. dirs. Urban Sch., San Francisco, 1986-91, Gateway H.S., San Francisco, Charles Armstrong Sch., Belmont, Calif., 1998-2001, San Francisco Opera Assn., Telluride Acad., Corinthian Acad.; bd. visitors U. Wis. Law Sch., 1991-95. Mem. Am. Assn. Corp. Counsel (bd. dirs. 1984-87), Bay Area Gen. Counsel Assn. (chmn. 1994), Univ. Club, Villa Taverna Club, Corinthian Yacht Club, Order of Coif, San Francisco Yacht Club. General corporate. Office: Laurel Mgmt Co LLC Ste 1450 One Maritime Plaza San Francisco CA 94111 E-mail: tbauch@laurelmanagement.com

BAUER, GEORGE A., III, lawyer; b. Queens, N.Y., Nov. 2, 1954; s. George A. Jr. and Mariella (Hoffman) B.; m. Marcy F. Greenberg, Aug. 6, 1978; children: Garrett J., Melissa I., Maren A.A. BBA magna cum laude, CUNY, 1976; JD, NYU, 1979. Bar: N.Y. 1980, U.S. Dist. Ct. (so. and ea. dists.) N.Y. 1980, U.S. Ct. Appeals (2d and 4th cirs.) 1988, U.S. Supreme Ct. 1988. Ptnr. Milberg Weiss Bershad Hynes & Lerach LLP, N.Y.C., 1979—. Mem. ATLA, ABA, N.Y. State Bar Assn., N.Y. County Lawyers Assn. Federal civil litigation, State civil litigation, Securities. Office: Milberg Weiss Bershad Hynes & Lerach LLP 1 Penn Plz New York NY 10119-0002

BAUER, HENRY LELAND, lawyer; b. Portland, Oreg., June 7, 1928; s. Henry and Emma L. (Peterson) B.; m. Doris Jane Philbrick, Sept. 11, 1952 (dec.); children: Henry Stephen, Thomas Leland. BS in Bus., Oreg. State U., 1950; JD, U. Oreg., 1953. Bar: Oreg. 1953, U.S. Dist. Ct. Oreg. 1956, U.S. Ct. Appeals (9th cir.) 1960. Mem. Bauer & Bauer, Portland, 1955-70, Bauer, Murphy, Bayless & Fundingsland, and successor firms, Portland, 1970-75; prin. Henry L. Bauer & Assocs., P.C., 1975—. Past mem. adv. coun. Oreg. State U. Coll. Bus. Past bd. dirs., vice chmn. St. Vincent Hosp. and Med. Ctr.; mem., past pres. coun. trustees St. Vincent Med. Found.; lifetime trustee Kappa Sigma Endowment Fund; bd. dirs., past pres. Nat. Interfrat. Conf.; trustee Nat. Interfrat. Found.; past pres. Columbia Pacific coun. Boy Scouts Am.; past pres. Portland Civic Theatre; bd. visitors U. Oreg. Sch. Law, 1979-83; trustee Oreg. State U. Found.; chmn. Oreg. State U. Pres.'s Club. 1st lt. USAF, 1953-55. Recipient Silver Antelope award Boy Scouts Am.; named Disting. Alumnus, Oreg. State U., 1994. Mem. ABA, Oreg. Bar Assn., Multnomah County Bar Assn., Am. Judicature Soc., Lang Syne Soc., German-Am. Soc., Oreg. State U. Alumni Assn. (bd. dirs.), Delta Theta Phi, Kappa Sigma (past nat. pres.), Multnomah Athletic Club, Arlington Club, Masons. Republican. Presbyterian. Estate planning, Probate, Real property. Office: Henry L Bauer & Assocs PC 5440 SW Westgate Dr Ste 250 Portland OR 97221-2422

BAUER, MARVIN AGATHER, lawyer; b. Milw., June 28, 1940; m. Gray Bauer; children: Laura, Andrew. BS, U. Wis., 1962; JD, U. Chgo., 1965. Bar: Calif. 1966. Dep. atty. gen. State of Calif., Los Angeles, 1965-69; ptnr. Archbald & Spray, Santa Barbara, Calif., 1969-82, Bauer, Harris Clinkenbeard & Ramsey, Santa Barbara, 1982—. Lectr. U. Calif., 1975-77. Bd. dirs. Carpinteria Valley Assn., Calif., 1980-83, Carpinteria Boys Club, 1983-84. Mem. Am. Coll. Trial Lawyers, Am. Bd. Trial Advocates, Santa Barbara Bar Assn. (pres. 1978-79, bd. dirs. 1974-80), Calif. Med.-Legal Com., Santa Barbara Med. Legal Com. State civil litigation, Insurance, Personal injury. Home: PO Box 1307 Summerland CA 93067-1307 Office: Bauer Harris Clinkenbeard & Ramsey 925 De La Vina St Santa Barbara CA 93101-3243

BAUER, MICHAEL, lawyer; b. Chgo., Nov. 8, 1952; s. Morris and Tema (Posalski) B.; B.A., Northwestern U., 1973, J.D., 1976. Bar: Ill. 1976, D.C. 1977. Assoc. firm Williams & Jensen, P.C., Washington, 1976-78; atty. Am. Hosp. Supply Corp., Evanston, Ill., 1978-81; asst. gen. counsel AM Internat., Inc., Chgo., 1981-83; group counsel Bell & Howell Co., Chgo., 1983— . Class gift chmn. Norhtwestern U. Ten-Yr. Reunion, Evanston, 1983. Mem. ABA, Ill. Bar Assn., D.C. Bar Assn., Chgo. Bar Assn., Northwestern U. Coll. Arts and Scis. Alumni Assn. (bd. dirs. 1984). Jewish. Club: John Evans (Evanston). Bankruptcy, General corporate, Labor. Home: 1636 N Wells St Apt 2805 Chicago IL 60614-6022 Office: Bell & Howell Co 5215 Old Orchard Rd Skokie IL 60077-1035

BAUER, WILLIAM JOSEPH, federal judge; b. Chgo., Sept. 15, 1926; s. William Francis and Lucille (Gleason) B.; m. Mary Nicol, Jan. 28, 1950; children— Patricia, Linda. A.B., Elmhurst Coll., 1949, LLD, 1969; JD, DePaul U., 1952, LLD (hon.), 1993, John Marshall Law Sch., 1987; LLD (hon.), Roosevelt U., 1994. Bar: Ill. 1951. Ptnr. Erlenborn, Bauer & Hotte, Elmhurst, Ill., 1953-64; asst. state's atty. Du Page County, 1952-56; 1st asst. state's atty., 1956-58; state's atty., 1959-64; judge 18th Jud. Cir. Ct., 1964-70; U.S. dist. atty. No. Ill. Chgo., 1970-71; judge U.S. Dist. Ct. (no. dist.), 1971-75, U.S. Ct. Appeals (7th cir.), 1975-86, chief judge, 1986-93, senior judge, 1994-. Instr. bus. law Elmhurst Coll., 1952-59; adj. prof. law DePaul U., 1978-91; former mem. Ill. Supreme Ct. Com. on Pattern Criminal Jury Instrns.; chmn. Fed. Criminal Jury Instrn. Com. 7th Cir. Trustee Elmhurst Coll., 1979—, De Paul U., 1984—, DuPage Meml. Hosp.; bd. advisors Mercy Hosp. Served with AUS, 1945-47. Mem. ABA, Ill. Bar Assn., Du Page County Bar Assn. (past pres.), Chgo. Bar Assn., Fed. Bar Assn. (former bd. dirs.). Roman Catholic. Clubs: Union League, Law, Legal (Chgo.). Office: US Ct Appeals 219 S Dearborn St Ste 2754 Chicago IL 60604-1803*

BAUGH, JERRY PHELPS, lawyer; b. Evansville, Ind., July 20, 1933; s. Emmanuel Henry and Elva Lorene (Winkler) B.; m. Mary Frances Jones, July 16, 1960; children: David E., Matthew K., Carolyn G. Student, Exeter (Eng.) U., 1953-54; AB, DePauw U., 1955; JD, U. Mich., 1958. Bar: Ind. 1958, U.S. Dist. Ct. (so. dist.) Ind. 1958, U.S. Supreme Ct. 1971. Fgn. service officer U.S. Dept. State, Washington, 1958-66; ptnr. Baugh & Baugh, Evansville, Ind., 1966-74; asst. city atty. City of Evansville, 1967-70, city atty., 1970-71; ptnr. Lacey, Terrell, Annakin, Heldt & Baugh, Evansville, 1974—, Terrell, Baugh, Salmon & Born LLP, Evansville, 1998—. Asst. sec., dir. Cen. Ind., Evansville, 1982-91, sec., 1991-98. Mem. ABA, Ind. State Bar Assn., Evansville Estate Planning Coun. (pres. 1982-83), Evansville Bar Assn. (pres. 1983-84), Order of Coif. Democrat. Episcopalian. General corporate, Estate planning, Probate. Home: 100 NW 1st St Unit 104 Evansville IN 47708-1223 Office: Terrell Baugh Salmon & Born 5011 Washington Ave Evansville IN 47715-4865 E-mail: jpmfb@aol.com

BAUGHMAN, R(OBERT) PATRICK, lawyer; b. Zanesville, Ohio, Nov. 10, 1930; s. Robert O. and Kathryn E. B.; m. Joyce Hall, June 17, 1959; 1 dau., Patricia. B.S., Ohio State U., 1960, J.D., 1963. Bar: Ohio 1963. Assoc. firm Sindell & Sindell, Cleve., 1964-71, Jones, Day, Reavis & Pogue, Cleve., 1972-73; asst. atty. gen. State of Ohio, Columbus, 1971-72; pres., prin. firm Baughman & Assocs., Cleve., 1973— . Mem. ABA, Ohio Bar Assn., Cuyahoga County Bar Assn., Nat. Council Self-Insurers, Internat. Assn. Indsl. Accident Bds. and Commns., Internat. Platform Assn. Episcopalian. Club: Columbia Hills Country. Admiralty, Product liability, Workers' compensation. Office: Baughman & Assocs 55 Public Sq Ste 2215 Cleveland OH 44113-1996

BAUM, ALISSA L. lawyer; b. Ft. Worth, Jan. 21, 1968; d. Kenneth Sidney and Sandra B. BA, U. Tex., 1990, JD, 1993. Bar: Tex. 1993, DC 1995. Legis. asst. Office of Congressman Martin Frost, Washington, 1993-96; assoc. McLeod, Watkinson & Miller, 1996—. Democrat. Jewish. Office: McLeod Watkinson & Miller One Massachusetts Ave NW Washington DC 20001

BAUM, E. HARRIS, lawyer; b. Phila., June 20, 1933; s. Albert I. and Rose Blanche (Nathanson) B.; m. Joyce L. Blumberg, June 24, 1957 (dec. Jan. 1981); children: Sharon, Susan, Lewis; m. Myrna Field, Mar. 25, 1983. BS, Temple U., 1954, LLB, 1957. Bar: Phila. 1958, Pa. 1958, U.S. Cir. Ct. (3rd cir.) 1958, U.S. Supreme Ct. Assoc. Harry Norman Ball, Esq., Phila., 1958-62; sr. ptnr. Zarwin, Prince & Baum, 1962-68, Zarwin & Baum, Phila., 1968-94; sr. ptnr., chief litigation dept. Zarwin, Baum, DeVito, Kaplan, O'Donnell & Schaer, 1995—. Lectr. in field. Pres. Keneseth Israel Synagogue, Elkins Park, Pa., 1996-98; exec. bd. Headhouse Conservancy, Phila., 1993—; adv. bd. Phila. Blind Assn.; active ASSIST Disabled Police Fire Fighters, Phila., 1994. With USAR, 1954-56. Mem. Pa. Trial Lawyers,

Phila. Trial Lawyers, Athenaeum of Phila., Lawyer's Club, Bala Country Club, Million Dollar Adv. Forum. Avocations: cycling, traveling, sailing, golfing. General civil litigation, Contracts commercial, General corporate. Office: Zarwin Baum DeVito Kaplan O'Donnell & Schaer 1515 Market St Ste 1200 Philadelphia PA 19102-1981

BAUM, JOSEPH THOMAS, lawyer; b. Amsterdam, N.Y., May 25, 1944; s. Joseph W. and Margaret M. (Wilt) B.; children: Jason, Daniel. BA, Siena Coll., 1966; JD, Albany Law Sch., 1972. Bar: N.Y. 1973, U.S. Dist. Ct. (no. dist.) N.Y. 1973. Instr. Alfred U., N.Y., 1973-74; assigned counsel Allegany County, Belmont, 1973-74, law sec. Family Ct., 1974; asst. atty. gen. N.Y. State, Albany, 1974-79; clin. dir. Albany Law Sch., 1981—. Town atty. Town of Sand Lake, N.Y., 1980-82, 84, 98-2000, town councilman, 1992-96; bd. dirs. YMCA, Albany, 1984-87. Recipient Disting. Pro Bono Svc. award Legal Aid Northeastern N.Y., 1987, 98. Mem. ABA, N.Y. State Bar Assn., Rensselaer County Bar Assn., Am. Assn. Law Schs. (clin. sect.), Adirondack Mountain Club. Office: Albany Law Sch 80 New Scotland Ave Albany NY 12208-3434

BAUM, MICHAEL LIN, lawyer; b. Clinton, Okla., Apr. 10, 1952; s. William Eldon and Patricia (Schumacher) B.; m. Colleen Margaret Condon, Apr. 6, 1991; children: Elizabeth, Alexandra, Kevin. BA summa cum laude, UCLA, 1982, JD, 1985. Bar: Calif. 1985, D.C. 1993, U.S. Dist. Ct. (ctrl. dist.) Calif. 1986, U.S. Dist. Ct. (ea. and no. dists.) Calif. 1989, U.S. Dist. Ct. (we. dist.) Mich. 1991, U.S. Dist. Ct. (no. dist.) Ohio 1993, U.S. Dist. Ct. (no. dist.) N.Y. 1996, U.S. Ct. Appeals (9th cir.) 1990, U.S. Ct. Appeals (4th cir.) 1996, U.S. Ct. Appeals (7th cir.) 1997, U.S. Supreme Ct. 1991. Assoc. Kananack, Murgatroyd, Baum & Hedlund,and predecessors, L.A., 1985-87; ptnr., shareholder Baum, Hedlund, Aristei, Guilford & Downey, 1987—. Mem. discovery and trial teams MDL 817 United Airlines 1989 aircrash at Sioux City, Iowa, Chgo.; mem. plaintiffs' steering com. MDL 891 Northwest Airlines 1990 aircrash at Detroit Met. Airport, Ill. State Ct. procs. for USAir 427 crash near Aliquippa, Pa., 1994, MDL 1041 USAir 1994 crash at Charlotte, N.C.; trial team for consolidated hemophilia-AIDS cases, New Orleans, 1999. Mem. State Bar Calif., D.C. Bar, Bar Assn. D.C., Consumer Attys. Calif., Consumer Attys. L.A. Aviation, Personal injury, Product liability. Office: Baum Hedlund Aristei Guilford & Downey 12100 Wilshire Blvd Ste 950 Los Angeles CA 90025-7107 E-mail: mbaum@baumhedlundlaw.com

BAUM, PETER ALAN, lawyer; b. Jamaica, N.Y., Sept. 22, 1947; s. Morris and Elsa (Sturtz) B.; m. Barbara Hartman, Nov. 29, 1969; children: Benjamin, Lisa, Alexander. BA, Colgate U., 1969; JD, Syracuse U., 1972. Bar: N.Y. 1973, U.S. Dist. Ct. (no. dist.) N.Y. 1974. House counsel William Porter Real Estate Co., Syracuse, N.Y., 1972-73; pvt. practice, 1973-82; ptnr. DiStefano and Baum, 1983-85, Baum and Woodard, Syracuse, 1985-90; prin. Peter A. Baum Law Offices, Chittenango, N.Y., 1990-96; ptnr. Iaconis, Iaconis and Baum, 1997—. Lectr. Onondaga C.C., Syracuse, 1976-79. Chmn. bd. dirs. Syracuse Area Landmark Theater, 1982-83; bd. dirs. Syracuse Opera Co., 1979-85. Mem. N.Y. State Bar Assn. (ho. of dels. 1992-93), Madison County Bar Assn. (pres. 1993), Onondaga County Bar Assn. (continuing edn. chmn. 1977-78), Onondaga Title Assn. Landlord-tenant, Real property. Office: Iaconis Iaconis & Baum 282 Genesee St Chittenango NY 13037-1705

BAUM, STANLEY DAVID, lawyer; b. Bklyn., Feb. 22, 1954; s. Irwin and Muriel A. (Margolis) B.; m. Ilyne Rhona Fried, June 9, 1979; children: Andrew, Miranda. BS, U. Pa., 1976, JD, 1980; LLM, NYU, 1984. Bar: N.Y. 1981, U.S. Tax Ct. 1993. Lawyer Carter, Ledyard & Milburn, N.Y.C., 1988-98; of counsel Swidler, Berlin, Shereff, Friedman, LLP, 1998—. Contbr. articles to profl. jours. Mem. N.Y. State Bar Assn. (com. on employee benefits tax sect.). E-mail: sdbaum@swidlaw.com

BAUM, STANLEY M. lawyer; b. Bronx, N.Y., Mar. 6, 1944; s. Abraham S. and Mae (Weiner) B.; m. Louise Rae Iteld, Aug. 30, 1970; children: Rachel Jennifer, Lauren Amy. BS in Commerce, Rider Coll., 1966; JD summa cum laude, John Marshall Law Sch., 1969. Bar: Ga. 1970, U.S. Dist. Ct. (no. dist.) Ga. 1970, U.S. Ct. Appeals (5th cir.) 1970, U.S. Supreme Ct. 1973, U.S. Ct. Appeals (11th cir.) 1981, U.S. Tax Ct. 1983. Law clk. to U.S. atty. No. Dist. Ga., 1969; legal aide Ga. Gen. Assembly, 1970-71; asst. U.S. atty. No. Dist. Ga., 1971-74; ptnr. Bates & Baum, 1974—. Pres. Congregation Shearith Israel, 1976-78; chmn. Rep. Party of DeKalb County, 1983-85, 4th Dist. FRep. Party, 1985-89; pre.s Resurgens, Atlanta, 1987-88, Electoral Coll., 1988; del. Rep. Nat. Conv., 1992; mem. DeKalb County Bd. Ethics, 1991—, chair, 1993-95, 2001—; mem. Met. Atlanta Rapid Transit Authority Bd. Ethics, 1993—. Mem. ABA (criminal justice sect. white collar com.), Ga. Bar Assn., Atlanta Bar Assn. (chmn. criminal law sect. 1985-86, bd. dirs. 1986-87), Fed. Bar Assn. (pres. Atlanta chpt. 1976-77, nat. council 1974-77), DeKalb Bar Assn. (pres. 1989-90), Am. Judicature Soc., Nat. Dist. Attys. Assn. Clubs: Atlanta Lawyers. Lodge: Masons. Office: 3151 Maple Dr NE Atlanta GA 30305-2503

BAUMAN, FREDERICK CARL, lawyer; b. Harrisburg, Pa., July 31, 1952; s. Carl Frederick Jr. and June Edna (Roeder) B. BA, U. Del., 1974; JD, Harvard U., 1977. Bar: N.Y. 1978, Pa. 1985, Tex. 1988, N.J. 1989, Ariz. 1996. Assoc. Davis Polk & Wardwell, N.Y.C., 1977-81, Hawkins Delafield & Wood, N.Y.C., 1981-83; atty. Bell Atlantic Corp., Phila., 1983-86; v.p., counsel Bell Atlantic Compushop, Dallas, 1986-88; v.p., spl. counsel Bell Atlantic Capital Corp., Paramus, N.J., 1988; v.p., counsel, sec. Bell Atlantic TriCon Leasing Corp., 1989, sr. v.p., gen. counsel, sec., 1990-94, TriCon Capital Corp., Paramus, 1993-94; v.p., assoc. gen. counsel FINOVA Capital Corp. (f/k/a Greyhound Fin. Corp.), Phoenix, 1994—. Vice chmn. U.S. Olympic Com., Ariz., 1998—. C. Rodney Sharp scholar, 1970, Harvard Club of Del. scholar, 1976. Mem. ABA, Am. Corp. Counsel Assn. (Ariz. chpt. bd. dirs.), Tex. Bar Assn., Ariz. Bar Assn., Phi Beta Kappa. Presbyterian. General corporate, Finance, Mergers and acquisitions. Office: FINOVA Capital Corp 1850 N Central Ave Phoenix AZ 85004-4527

BAUMAN, JOHN ANDREW, law educator; b. 1921. BSL, U. Minn., 1942, LLB, 1947; JSD, Columbia U., 1958. Bar: Wis. 1947, Minn. 1948. Spl. fellow Columbia U., 1950-51; assoc. prof. U. N. Mex., 1947-54; assoc. prof. Ind. U., 1954-59, prof., 1959-60; prof. UCLA, 1960-91, prof. emeritus, 1991; exec. dir. Assn. Am. Law Schs., Washington, 1980-83, Mem. Order of Coif (sec.-treas. 1983-92). Author: (with York) Cases and Materials on Remedies, 1967, 5th edit., 1991. Office: UCLA Sch Law 405 Hilgard Ave Los Angeles CA 90095-9000

BAUMANN, JULIAN HENRY, JR. lawyer; b. Ft. Leavenworth, Kans., Feb. 20, 1943; s. Julian Henry and Helene (Claiborne) B.; m. Karen Ann Hofman, July 14, 1973; children: Andrew H., Allison C. BS, Clemson U., 1965; postgrad., U. Tenn., 1966; JD, U. S.C., 1968; LLM in Taxation, NYU, 1975. Bar: S.C. 1968, Del. 1976. Assoc. Richards, Layton & Fingers, Wilmington, Del., 1975-80, dir., 1980—. Served to capt., JAGC, U.S. Army, 1969-74. Fellow Am. Coll. Tax Counsel; mem. ABA, S.C. Bar Assn., Del. State Bar (chmn., sec. taxation 1990-91), Wilmington Tax Group (chmn. 1988-89), The Com. of 100 (pres. 1994-96), Bd. of Mgrs., The Nemours Found., Wilmington Club, Greenville Country Club. Democrat. Roman Catholic. Corporate taxation, Taxation, general, Personal income taxation. Home: 8 Brendle Ln Wilmington DE 19807-1300 Office: Richards Layton & Finger One Rodney Sq 10th & King Sts Wilmington DE 19801

BAUMANN, LARRY R(OGER), lawyer; b. Chadron, Nebr., Feb. 19, 1946; s. Robert R. and Mary Nadine (Simpson) B.; children: Brenda Sue, Andrea Lynn; m. Marcia Lynn Bliefernich; children: Abigail Lynn, Jeffrey Scott. BA, Chadron State Coll., 1968; JD, U. Nebr., 1974. Bar: Nebr. 1974, U.S. Dist. Ct. Nebr. 1974, U.S. Ct. Appeals (8th cir.) 1989, U.S. Tax Ct. 1983. Ptnr. Fillman & Baumann, York, Nebr., 1974-80, Kelley, Scritsmier & Byrne PC, North Platte, 1981—. Pres. York Jaycees, 1976; bd. dirs. C. of C., Nebraskaland Days, Inc. With U.S. Army, 1968-71, Vietnam. Mem. Nebr. Bar Assn., Lincoln County Bar Assn., Western Nebr. Bar Assn., Nebr. Coun. Sch. Attys. (pres. 1988-89). Democrat. Methodist. Federal civil litigation, State civil litigation, Education and schools. Office: Kelley Scritsmier & Byrne PC 221 W 2nd St North Platte NE 69103-1669 E-mail: lbaum@nponline.net

BAUMBERGER, CHARLES HENRY, lawyer; b. Port Huron, Mich., Sept. 13, 1941; s. Peter Julius and Evelyn Margaret (Jackson) B.; m. Martha Carolyn Megathlin, Aug. 8, 1969; children: Peter Scott, Charles Henry Jr. BA, Vanderbilt U., 1963; JD, U. Fla., 1966. Bar: Fla. 1966, U.S. Dist. Ct. (so. dist.) Fla. 1967; cert. civil trial lawyer. Atty. Stephens, Demos & Magill, Miami, Fla., 1967-68; ptnr. Hastings, Goldman & Baumberger, 1969-74; founding ptnr. Rossman & Baumberger P.A., 1974—. Lectr. various continuing legal edn. programs; guest on numerous radio, TV talk shows, 1987—. Contbr. articles to profl. jours. Mem. Gov.'s Task Force on Emergency Room and Trauma Care, 1987; So. Fla. Health Action Coalition, Inc., 1984; task force on trauma and trauma systems Dept. Transp., 1987—. Served to 1st lt. U.S. Army Res., 1966-72. Mem. ABA, ATLA (past chair of Profl. Negligence Sect.), Internat. Soc. Barristers, Fed. Bar Assn., Dade County Bar Assn. (bd. dirs. 1977-88, pres. 1989-90), Fla. Bar (exec. coun. trial lawyers sect. 1983-89, chmn. 1990-91), Acad. Fla. Trial Lawyers (bd. dirs. 1980-89), Dade County Trial Lawyers Assn. (founding mem. bd. dirs. 1981-84), Am. Bd. Trial Advocates (Miami chpt. past pres.), Fla. Lawyers Action Group, So. Trial Lawyers Assn., Trial Lawyers for Pub. Justice (founding mem. 1982—), Am. Coll. Trial Lawyers, Internat. Soc. Barristers, Coral Reef Yacht Club, Univ. Club. Democrat. Methodist. Personal injury. Home: 5755 Suncrest Dr Miami FL 33156-5704 Office: Rossman Baumberger & Reboso 44 W Flagler St Fl 23 Miami FL 33130-1808

BAUMGARDNER, JOHN ELLWOOD, JR. lawyer; b. Balt., Jan. 6, 1951; s. John Ellwood and Nancy G. (Brandenburg) B.; m. Astrid Rehl, Sept. 7, 1974; children: Jeffrey Mark, Julia Alexis. Bar: N.Y. 1976. Assoc. Sullivan & Cromwell, N.Y.C., 1975-83, ptnr., 1983—. Supervisory dir. The Turkish Pvt. Equity Investment Co., 1991-93; trustee JPM Advisor Funds, 1996. Mem. ABA, N.Y. State Bar Assn., Assn. of Bar of City of N.Y., Nat. Dance Inst. (bd. dirs. 1988-89), Princeton Club. General corporate. Office: Sullivan & Cromwell 125 Broad St Fl 28 New York NY 10004-2498 E-mail: baumgardnerj@sullcrom.com

BAUMGARTEN, SIDNEY, lawyer, company executive; b. N.Y.C., July 30, 1933; s. Abraham and Doris (Kanarick) B.; children: Douglas, Frederick, Roger, Julia. AB, Brown U., 1954; JD, NYU, 1960. Bar: N.Y. 1961, U.S. Dist. Ct. (ea. and so. dists.) N.Y. 1961, U.S. Ct. Claims 1961, U.S. Ct. Appeals (2d cir.) 1961. Asst. mgmt., field underwriter Home Life Ins. Co., 1957-61; sole practice, 1961-67; asst. dist. atty. Queens County, N.Y., 1967-68; law sec. to presiding justice State of N.Y., Queens, 1968-73; asst. to Mayor City of N.Y., 1974-77; gen. counsel Phoenix House Found., 1978-80; sr. ptnr. Baumgarten, Swiedler & Waxman, N.Y.C., 1980-88; pvt. practice, 1989-94; pres., CEO Spectral Biosci. Corp., 1994—. Lectr. various seminars, assns. and ednl. instns; adj. prof. law N.Y. Inst. Tech.; vis. prof. Found. U. Cardiology, Brazil, 1996. Co-chmn. area interviews alumni schs. program Brown U.; committeeman county Boy Scouts Am.; pres. N.Y.'s Finest Found., 1993; bd. dirs., chmn. N.Y. Therapeutic Communities, Inc.; trustee Lawrence Country Day Sch. (pres. 1985-87). Served with U.S. Army, 1954-56, with Res. 1956-73; lt. col. 88th brigade N.Y. Guard. Mem. East Side C. of C. (pres. 1983-86, chmn. 1987—), VFW, NRA (life), Am. Legion. Club: Brown U. (N.Y.C.). Criminal, General practice. Office: 350 Fifth Ave Ste 7310 New York NY 10118

BAUMKEL, MARK S. lawyer; b. Flint, Mich., Feb. 17, 1951; s. Sherwood and Marilyn (Schiff) B.; m. Julie A. Kimbrell, Oct. 20, 1978; 1 child, Molly. BA cum laude, Oakland U., Rochester,Mich., 1973; JD cum laude, Wayne State U., 1977. Bar: Mich. 1977, U.S. Dist. Ct. Mich. 1977, U.S. Ct. Appeals (6th cir.) 1985. Assoc. dist. counsel U.S. SBA, Detroit, 1977-78; asst. pros. atty. Ingham County Prosecutor's Office, Lansing, Mich., 1978-79; assoc. atty. Shifman & Goodman, P.C., Southfield, 1979-81, Kaufman & Friedman, Southfield, 1981-84; sole practitioner Troy, Mich., 1984-94; ptnr. Provizer & Phillips, P.C., Southfield, 1994—. Mem. Assn. Trial Lawyers Am. (sustaining), Mich. Trial Lawyers Assn. (PAC contbr.), Oakland County Bar Assn., Wayne County Mediation Tribunal (mediator), Am. Arbitration Assn. (arbitrator), Oakland County Mediation (mediator). Avocations: long-distance running and biking, guitar. E-mial. General civil litigation, Personal injury, Product liability. Home: 3826 Lakecrest Dr Bloomfield Hills MI 48304-3040 Office: Provizer & Phillips PC 6785 Telegraph Rd Ste 400 Bloomfield Hills MI 48301-3149 E-mail: baumkelm@aol.com

BAVERO, RONALD JOSEPH, lawyer, legal educator; b. N.Y.C., Jan. 11, 1950; s. Joseph Carmine and Nancy (Martino) B.; m. Carolyn Angela Grippi, Aug. 20, 1972; children— Christen, Theresa, James, Joanna. B.A., Fordham U., 1971; J.D., St. John's U., N.Y.C., 1974. Bar: N.Y. 1975, U.S. Ct. Appeals (2d cir.) 1975, U.S. Dist. Ct. (ea. and so. dists.) N.Y. 1975, U.S. Supreme Ct., 1990. Law asst. appellate div. N.Y. State Supreme Ct., 1974-76; asst. dist. atty. Westchester County Dist. Atty.'s Office, White Plains, N.Y., 1976-82; prin. law sec. N.Y. State Family Ct., White Plains, 1982-85; ptnr. Fink & Weinberger, P.C., 1985-93, Hall Dickler Kent Friedman and Wood, 1993—; acting village justice Village of Elmsford, 1987-89; prof. law Pace U., Pleasantville, N.Y., 1982— . Editor Symposium on Law of Condominiums, 1974; assoc. editor St. John's Law Rev., 1974. Mem. N.Y. State Bar Assn., Westchester County Bar Assn., Columbian Lawyers Assn. Republican. Roman Catholic. Criminal, Family and matrimonial. Address: 11 Martine Ave White Plains NY 10606-1934

BAXTER, HOWARD H. lawyer; b. Cleve., July 31, 1931; s. Harold H. and Bessie (Bovee) B.; m. Ona Mae Miller, June 25, 1955; children: Kevin, Douglas, John, Susan. BS, Iowa State Coll., 1953; JD, Case Western Res. U., 1956. Bar: Ohio 1956, D.C. 1982; U.S. Dist. Ct. (no. dist.) Ohio 1962, U.S. Ct. Appeals (3rd cir.) 1978, U.S. Supreme Ct. 1978, U.S. Ct. Appeals (fed. cir.) 1982. Assoc. McNeal & Schick, Cleve., 1956-60; group counsel Harris Corp., 1960-76; sec., gen. counsel Molins USA Inc., Richmond, Va., 1976-79; v.p., gen. counsel The Langston Co., Inc., Cherry Hill, N.J., 1976-79, Cuyahoga County Hosp. System, Cleve., 1979-81; v.p., sec., gen. counsel Macey Machine Co., Inc., 1981-88, exec. v.p., 1988-91; ptnr. Kasdan & Baxter Co., 1992-2000; pvt. practice, 2000—. Chmn. zoning com. Lakewood (Ohio) Rep. Club, 1959-60; vestry, sr. warden St. Stephens Episcopal Ch., Beverly, N.J., 1977-79, Lakewood, 1981—, Ch. of the Ascension, Lakewood. Mem. NRA, Ohio State Bar Assn., Cleve. Bar Assn., Great Lakes Hist. Soc. (vice chmn. 1981-88, exec. v.p 1968-76, trustee 1968—, chmn. exec. com. 1982-94), Ohio Gun Collectors Assn., Inc., Edgewater Yacht Club. Avocations: Marine history, sailing, shooting sports, scale model railroading. Contracts commercial, General corporate, Private international. Home: 18107 Clifton Rd Lakewood OH 44107-1024 Office: Howard H Baxter Co Superior Bldg 815 Superior Ave E Ste 1920 Cleveland OH 44114-2701

BAXTER, MARVIN RAY, state supreme court justice; b. Fowler, Calif., Jan. 9, 1940; m. Jane Pippert, June 22, 1963; children: Laura, Brent. BA in Econs., Calif. State U., 1962; JD, U. Calif.-Hasting Coll. Law, 1966. Bar: Calif. 1966. Appointments sec. to Gov. George Deukmejian, 1983-88; dep. dist. atty. Fresno County, Calif., 1967-68; assoc. Andrews, Andrews, Thaxter & Jones, 1968-70, ptnr., 1971-82; apptd. sec. to Gov. George Deukmejian, 1983-88; assoc. justice Calif. Ct. Appeal (5th dist.), 1988-90; state supreme ct. assoc. justice Calif. Supreme Ct., 1991—. Mem. Jud. Coun. of Calif., chmn. policy coord. and liaison com., 1996—. Mem. Fresno County Bar Assn. (bd. dirs. 1977-82, pres. 1981), Calif. Young Lawyers Assn. (bd. gov. 1973-76, sec.-treas. 1974-75), Fresno County Young Lawyers Assn. (pres. 1973-74), Fresno County Legal Svcs., Inc. (bd. dirs. 1973-74), Fresno State U. Alumni Assn. (pres. 1970-71), Fresno State U. Alumni Trust Coun. (pres. 1970-75). Office: Calif Supreme Ct 350 Mcallister St San Francisco CA 94102-4712

BAXTER-SMITH, GREGORY JOHN, lawyer; b. Davenport, Iowa, Sept. 27, 1949; s. James Sanford Baxter and Doris Arlene (Olson) Smith; m. Carolyn Imes, June 10, 1975 (div. Oct. 1980); children: Bradley Imes, Brian McBride; m. Karen Ruth Thomas, Dec. 12, 1986. BA in English, Bucknell U., 1971; JD, U. Mo., 1974. Bar: Mo. 1974, U.S. Dist. Ct. (we. dist.) Mo. 1975, U.S. Tax Ct. 1975. Clk. Hon. Charles Shangler Mo. Ct. Appeals, Kansas City, 1974-75; assoc. Miller & Poole, Springfield, Mo., 1975-76; shareholder Poole & Smith, P.C., 1976-78, Gregory J. Smith, P.C., Springfield, 1978-86, Poole, Smith & Wieland, P.C., Springfield, 1986-90, Smith & Fels, P.C., Springfield, 1990—. Mem. Springfield Met. Bar Assn., Greene County Estate Planning Coun., Mo. Bar Assn., Elks. Republican. Lutheran. Avocation: golf. General civil litigation, General corporate, Estate taxation. Home: 5027 S Glenhaven Ave Springfield MO 65804-7800 Office: Smith & Fels PC 528 W Battlefield St Ste 103 Springfield MO 65807-4122

BAYBAYAN, RONALD ALAN, lawyer; b. Paia, Hawaii, July 4, 1946; s. Celedonio Ladresa and Carlina (Domingo) B.; m. Dianne Lea, June 14, 1969 (div. June 1985); children: Alycia Kay, Amber Lea; m. Sharyn Dee Huckins, Dec. 31, 1985 (div. Oct. 1996). BA, Coe Coll., 1968; JD, Drake U., 1974. Bar: Iowa 1977, U.S. Dist. Ct. (so. dist.) Iowa 1977, U.S. Tax Ct. 1978, U.S. Dist. Ct. (no. dist.) Iowa 1980, U.S. Ct. Appeals (8th cir.) 1985, U.S. Supreme Ct. 1985, U.S. Dist. Ct. Hawaii 1986. Asst. law librarian Drake U., Des Moines, 1974-77; assoc. Law Office Mike Wilson, 1977-78; sole practice, 1978—. Bd. dirs. Berkley & Co. Amb.; presenter in field. Co-author: Paralegals in Family Law Practice in Iowa, 1995, How to Draft Wills and Trusts in Iowa, 1996, 99, A Practical Guide to Estate Administration in Iowa, 1997. Bd. dirs. Wakonda Christian Ch., 1989-90; dir. communique Victory Christian Ctr., 1991—; mem. bd. counselors Drake U. Law Sch., 1997—. Served with USAF, 1969-73. Mem. ABA, Iowa Bar Assn., Polk County Bar Assn., Am-Filipino Assn. Iowa (bd. dirs. 1986), Bass Anglers Sportsman Soc. (Iowa chpt. pres. 1979-82), Iowans for Better Fisheries (bd. dirs. 1991), Mid-Iowa Bassmasters (past pres., past v.p., past sec.). Republican. State civil litigation, Family and matrimonial, General practice. Home: 6217 Urbandale Ave Des Moines IA 50322-3541 Office: 4921 Douglas Ave Ste 3 Des Moines IA 50310-2749

BAYER, RICHARD STEWART, lawyer; b. Laurel, Md., July 7, 1951; s. James Theodore and Patricia Ruth (Stewart) B.; m. Roberta Ann Cruise, July 9, 1977; children: Andrew Stewart, Henry Eliot, Hannah Caitlin AB, Middlebury Coll., 1973; JD, Colo. U., 1976. Bar: Colo. 1976, U.S. Dist. Ct. Colo. 1976, U.S. Ct. Appeals (10th cir.) 1976, U.S. Supreme Ct. 1987, Calif. 1989. Assoc. Brownstein Hyatt, Farber & Madden, Denver, 1976-81, ptnr., 1981-86, Kutak, Rock & Campbell, Denver, 1987-89; gen. counsel Hoskings Trust, San Diego, 1989—. Author: Colorado Appellate Advocacy, 1984; contbr. articles to legal jours. Mem. ABA (chmn. 10th cir. comml., banking, fin. transactions subcom., litigation sect. 1984-89), Denver Bar Assn., Denver Law Club (sec. 1982-83) Democrat. Federal civil litigation, State civil litigation. Home: 785 Bellevue Pl La Jolla CA 92037-8023 Office: Hoskings Trust 4817 Santa Monica Ave San Diego CA 92107-2850

BAYERN, ARTHUR HERBERT, lawyer; b. Jan. 28, 1934; s. Henry V. and Rose (Strumer) Bayern; m. Janice O'Banion, June 10, 1961; children: William T., Robert M.(dec.). AB, Colgate U., 1954; JD, U. Tex., 1965. Bar: Tex. 1965, U.S. Dist. Ct. (we. dist.) Tex. 1966, U.S. Tax Ct. 1968, U.S. Ct. Appeals (5th cir.) 1970, U.S. Supreme Ct. 1978. Salesman IBM, Houston, 1959—62; ptnr. Remy, Bayern & Paterson, San Antonio, 1965—84, Bayern, Paterson & Aycock, San Antonio, 1984—98, Bayern & Aycock, San Antonio, 1998—. Pres. San Antonio Estate Planners Coun., 1972—73. Co-editor: (non-fiction) How to Live and Die with Texas Probate, 1983; editor (contbg.): Texas Probate System, 1974, Texas Guardianship System, 1983. Capt. USAF, 1954—57. Fellow: Am. Coll. Probate Counsel; mem.: State Bar Tex. (bd. dir. 1982—85, chmn. real estate, probate and trust law sect. 1981—82), San Antonio Bar Assn. (pres. 1980—81), ABA (chmn. com. on post-mortem estate and tax planning). Estate planning, Probate, Estate taxation. Office: Bayern & Aycock 745 E Mulberry Ave Ste 300 San Antonio TX 78212-3167

BAYKO, EMIL THOMAS, lawyer; b. Pitts., Mar. 5, 1947; s. Emil and Ruth (Alberti) B.; m. Ruth Ann Loucks, Nov. 5, 1967; children: Anthony M., Keith C., Paul S. BA in Polit. Sci., Kent State U., 1970; JD cum laude, U. Ill., Urbana-Champaign, 1973. Bar: Ill. 1973, U.S. Dist. Ct. (no. dist.) Ill. 1973, U.S. Ct. Appeals (7th cir.) 1974, D.C. 1975, N.Y. 1975, U.S. Ct. Appeals (2d cir.) 1975, U.S. Ct. Claims 1976, U.S. Dist. Ct. (so. dist.) N.Y. 1976, U.S. Ct. Appeals (D.C. cir.) 1976, U.S. Supreme Ct. 1976, U.S. Dist. Ct. (ea dist.) Pa. 1978, U.S. Ct. Appeals (3d cir.) 1978, Tex. 1980, U.S. Dist. Ct. (so. dist., no. dist., ea. dist., we. dist.) Tex. 1981, U.S. Ct. Appeals (5th cir.) 1981. Assoc. Chapman & Cutler, Chgo., 1973-74, White & Case, N.Y.C., 1975-80; ptnr. Liddell, Sapp, Zivley, Hill & LaBoon, Houston, 1981, Holtzman Urquhart Bayko & Moore, Houston, 1982-95, Bayko Gibson Carnegie & Hagan, Houston, 1995-2000, Jones, Day, Reavis & Pogue, Internat., Houston, 2001—. Co-author: Essays on American Law, 1971, Home Rule, 1972. Harno fellow U. Ill., 1971-73. Mem. ABA, Assn. of Bar of City of N.Y., Houston Bar Assn., Chgo. Bar Assn., Tex. Bar Assn., D.C. Bar Assn., Order of Coif. Democrat. Presbyterian. Clubs: Tex., Houston. Federal civil litigation, State civil litigation, Environmental. Office: Jones Day Reavis & Pogue Internat Chase Tower 65th Fl 600 Travis St Houston TX 77002-3008 E-mail: tbayko@jonesday.com

BAYLY, JOHN HENRY, JR. judge; b. Washington, Jan. 26, 1944; s. John Henry and Salome Carole (Winters) B.; m. Barbara Jean Downey, Feb. 16, 1974 (dec. Jan. 1977); 1 child, Anne Louise; m. Katherine Bridget Kenny, Dec. 1, 1979; children: Johanna, Georgia. AB, Fordham U., 1966; JD, Harvard U., 1969. Bar: U.S. Dist. Ct. D.C. 1969, U.S. Ct. Appeals (D.C. cir.) 1969, D.C. 1971, U.S. Supreme Ct. 1974. Atty., advisor FCC, Washington, 1969-71; asst. atty. Office of U.S. Atty., 1971-75, 78-85; dep. minority counsel Senate Select Com. on Intelligence, 1975-76; acting asst. gen. counsel Corp. for Pub. Broadcasting, 1976-78; gen. counsel Legal Services Corp., 1985-87, pres., 1987-88; of counsel Stein, Mitchell & Mezines, 1988-90; judge D.C. Superior Ct., 1990—. Mem. D.C. Bar Assn., John Carroll Soc., Counsellors, Bryant Inn of Ct., Lawyers Club Washington, Phi Beta Kappa. Republican. Roman Catholic. Home: 3512 Runnymede Pl NW Washington DC 20015-2420 Office: DC Superior Ct 500 Indiana Ave NW Ste 1 Washington DC 20001-2131

BAZLER, FRANK ELLIS, retired lawyer; b. Columbus, Ohio, Jan. 17, 1930; s. Frank Hayes and Minnie Maybrum (Rucker) B.; m. Virginia Ann Hutchison, Oct. 17, 1954. BSBA, Ohio State U., 1951, JD, 1953. Bar: Ohio 1953, U.S. Dist. Ct. (we. dist.) Ohio 1956, U.S. Ct. Mil. Appeals 1957, U.S.

Supreme Ct. 1957, U.S. Ct. Appeals (6th cir.) 1964. Assoc. Robert S. Miller, Atty., Troy, Ohio, 1955-57; ptnr. Miller, Bazler & Schlemmer, 1957-71; asst. corp. counsel Hobart Mfg. Co., 1971-74; corp. atty., asst. sec. Hobart Corp., 1974-95; ret., 1995; of counsel Dungan & LeFevre, Troy, 1995—. V.p. Bazler Transfer & Storage, Inc., Columbus, Ohio, 1950-58; sec., bd. dirs. Golden Triangle Farms, Inc., Troy, 1972-2001. Pres. Troy United Fund, Inc., 1960, Troy Mus. Corp., 1990; chmn. Miami County chpt. ARC, 1955-59, Miami County (Ohio) Rep. Fin. Com., 1981-84; mem. Miami County Gen. Bd. Health, 1992—, pres. pro-tem, 1998—; commn. on cert. of Attys. as Specialists of Supreme Ct. of Ohio, 1994-99, chmn., 1994-96. Capt. JAG, USAFR, 1953-61. Named one of Outstanding Young Men in Troy and Ohio, Troy Jaycees, 1957, Ohio Jaycees, 1961; recipient Disting. Citizen award Troy C. of C., 1985, Citizenship award Ohio State U., 1993. Fellow: Am. Bar Found. (Ohio chair 1995—), Ohio State Bar Found. (pres. 1992); mem.: ABA (ho. of dels. 1984—2000, mem. gen. practice sect. 1967—, coun. 1976—80, mem. standing com. on specialization 1999—), Nat. Caucus State Bar Assns. (Ohio rep. 1993—, exec com. 1997—, pres. 2000—01), Ohio State Bar Assn. (prs. 1984—85, coun. of dels. 1979—88, Ohio Bar medal 1990), Miami County Bar Assn. (pres. 1966, Meritorious Svc. award 1985), Nat. Conf. Bar Pres. (exec. coun. 1988—91), Brukner Nature Ctr. (trustee 1998—, pres. 1999—), Indsl. Heritage Mus. of Miami County (trustee, sec. 1997—), Overfield Tavern Mus. (pres. 2001—), Masons, Scottish Rite, Kiwanis (pres. 1964). Republican. Presbyterian. Avocations: photography, travel, golf. Home: 1156 Premwood Dr Troy OH 45373-3877 Office: Dungan & LeFevre 210 W Main St Troy OH 45373-3287

BEACH, ARTHUR O'NEAL, lawyer; b. Albuquerque, Feb. 8, 1945; s. William Pearce and Vivian Lucille (Kronig) B.; m. Alex Clark Doyle, Sept. 12, 1970; 1 child, Eric Kronig. BBA, U. N.Mex., 1967, JD, 1970. Bar: N.Mex. 1970. Assoc. Smith & Ransom, Albuquerque, 1970-74, Keleher & McLeod, Albuquerque, 1974-75, ptnr., 1976-78; shareholder Keleher & McLeod, P.A., 1978—. Tchg. asst. U. N.Mex., 1970. Bd. editors Natural Resources Jour., 1968-70. Mem. ABA, State Bar N.Mex. (unauthorized practice of law com., adv. opinions com., med.-legal panel, legal-dental-osteo.-podiatry com., jud. selection com., specialization bd.), Albuquerque Bar Assn. (dir. 1978-82). Democrat. Mem. Christian Sci. Ch. General civil litigation, Insurance, Personal injury. Home: 2015 Dietz Pl NW Albuquerque NM 87107-3240 Office: Keleher & McLeod PA PO Drawer AA Albuquerque NM 87103

BEACH, BARBARA PURSE, lawyer; b. Washington, June 12, 1947; d. Clifford John and Lillian (Natarus) B. BA, U. Ky., 1968; MSW, U. Md., 1972; JD, Am. U., 1980. Bar: D.C. 1980, Va. 1980. Law clk. to presiding justice benefit rev. bd. U.S. Dept. Labor, Washington, 1980; asst. city atty. City of Alexandria, Va., 1981-85; atty. Ross, Marsh, Foster, Myers & Quiggle, Alexandria, 1985-90, Beach, Butt & Assocs., PC, Alexandria, 1990-92; prin. Beach & Assocs., 1992—; town atty. Town of Herndon, Va., 1992-94. 4th dist. com. disciplinary bd. dirs. Va. State Bd., chmn., 2000-01. Vice-chmn. Va. Health Svcs. Cost Rev. Coun., 1989-92; mem. Va. Commn. on Women and Minorities, 1990-92; bd. dirs. Am. Heart Assn., Alexandria, 1996-2000, divsn. pres., 1998-99. Mem. Va. Trial Lawyers Assn., Alexandria Bar Assn. (pres. 1987-88), Kiwanis. General corporate, General practice, Land use and zoning (including planning). Office: Beach & Assocs 416 Prince St Alexandria VA 22314-3114

BEACH, DOUGLAS RYDER, lawyer, educator; b. Kittery, Maine, Sept. 20, 1948; s. Raymond Homer and Carolyn (Ryder) B.; m. Deborah C.M. Henry; children: Lindsay Alison, Garrett Wesley, Katherine Henry. BS, Central Conn. State U., 1970; JD cum laude, New Eng. Sch. Law, 1973; grad. with honors, U.S. Army Judge Sch., U. Va., 1976. Bar: Mass. 1973, Mo. 1977, U.S. Dist. Ct. (ea. and we. dists.) Mo. 1977, U.S. Ct. Mil. Appeals, 1973. Gen. ptnr. Paule & Beach, Inc., Clayton, Mo., 1977-81, Kaveney, Beach, Russell, Bond & Mittleman, Clayton, 1981-88, Beach, Burcke & Helfers, P.C., 1988—. Instr. bus. law Washington U., St. Louis, 1980-89; city atty. Cit y Chesterfield, Mo. Contbr. chpt. to Medical Records, Property Distribution, Trial Tactics in Domestic Relations, 1984, Elder Bonhomme Presbyterian Ch., Chesterfield, Mo., 1984. Treas. Y's Men's Internat., St. Louis, 1977-80; mem. exec. bd. John Marshall Rep. Club, 1969-72. Lt. col. USMCR, 1973-91. Mem. ABA, Am. Acad. Matrimony Lawyers (pres. Mo. chpt., Best Atty. U.S. Am. 1990-91, 92-93, 94-95, 96-97, 98-99, 99-2000), St. Louis County Bar Assn. (named Outstanding Young Lawyer 1983, pres. 1984-85), Met. Bar St. Louis, Trial Lawyers Assn. St. Louis. State civil litigation, Family and matrimonial, General practice. Home: 14565 Ansonborough Ct Chesterfield MO 63017-4614 Office: Beach Stuart Higgie & Mettleman 222 S Central Ave Ste 900 Saint Louis MO 63105-3575

BEACH, STEPHEN HOLBROOK, lawyer; b. Highland Park, Mich., June 3, 1915; s. Stephen Holbrook and Katherine Jean (Campbell) B.; m. Mary Frances Mulvihill, July 6, 1951; children: Jennifer Katherine Beach Buda, Stephen Holbrook III. AB with honors in Polit. Sci, Kalamazoo Coll., 1936; LLB cum laude, U. Detroit, 1941; postgrad., Georgetown U., 1945, Columbia U., 1970. Bar: Mich. 1941, U.S. Dist. Ct. (ea. dist.) Mich., 1941, U.S. Supreme Ct. 1944, N.Y. 1947, U.S. Dist. Ct. (so. dist.) N.Y. 1947, U.S. Dist. Ct. (ea. dist.) N.Y. 1949, D.C. 1949, Conn. 1975. Assoc. Winthrop, Stimson, Putnam & Roberts, N.Y.C., 1946-48, Cann, Lamb & Kittelle, N.Y.C., 1948-56, Willkie, Farr, Gallagher, Walton and Fitzgibbon, N.Y.C., 1956-60; staff atty. IBM Corp., 1960-61, of counsel supplies div. N.Y.C. and Dayton, N.J., 1961-65; v.p., gen. counsel, sec. The Svc. Bur. Corp., N.Y.C., 1965-75; v.p., gen. counsel Data Svcs. Control Data Corp., Greenwich, Conn., 1976-78, gen. counsel Computer Co. Mpls., 1979-80, v.p., assoc., gen. counsel, 1980-82, sr. v.p. telecommunications policy, corp. sec., 1983-85; of counsel Rogers, Hoge & Hills, White Plains, N.Y., 1985-86; pvt. practice law Greenwich and Stamford, Conn., 1986—. Bd. dirs., corp. sec. Dataware Techs., Inc. Editor-in-chief U. Detroit Law Jour., 1937-41. Capt. U.S. Army, 1943-46. Mem. ABA (sci. and tech. sect., banking and bus. law sect.), Conn. Bar Assn (intellectual property and computer law sects.), N.Y. State Bar Assn. (banking and bus. law sect.), D.C. Bar Assn., Assn. of Data Processing Svcs. Orgns. (v.p. govt. rels., bd. dirs. 1978-84), The Wee Burn Country Club, Delray Dunes Golf and Country Club. Republican. Episcopalian. Avocation: golf. Communications, Computer, General corporate. Home: 52 Brushy Hill Rd Darien CT 06820-6007 Office: PO Box 1202 Darien CT 06820-1202

BEAHM, FRANKLIN D. lawyer; b. Independence, Kans., Jan. 18, 1953; s. Edgar Hiram and Dorothy S.; m. Tawny L. McIntyre, Jan. 7, 1994; children: F. David, Patrick Stuart, Kristin Sanders, Stephen McWilliams. BBA, So. Methodist U., 1975; JD, Tulane U., 1977. Bar: La. 1977, Colo. 1993, Tex. 2000, U.S. Dist. Ct. (ea. dist.) La. 1977, U.S. Dist. Ct. (mid. dist.) La. 1980, U.S. Dist. Ct. (we. dist.) La. 1985, U.S. Ct. Appeals (5th cir.), U.S. Tax Ct. 1989, U.S. Supreme Ct. 1993. Assoc. Manard & Scheonberger, New Orleans, 1977-80, Bourgeois, Bennett, Metairie, La., 1980, Hammett, Leake & Hammett, New Orleans, 1980-83, ptnr., 1983-85, Thomas, Hayes & Beahm, New Orleans, 1985-95, Chehardy, Sherman, Ellis, Breslin, Murray, Metairie, 1995-97, Beahm & Green, New Orleans, 1997—. Mem. Am. Health Lawyers Assn., Am. Soc. Law and Medicine, La. Assn. Def. Counsel, La. Bar Assn. (Interprofl. com. 1997-98, professionalism com. 1999—), La. Med. Soc. (Interprofl. com. 1997-98), La. Soc. Hosp. Attys. of the La. Hosp. Assn., Denver Bar Assn., Def. Rsch. Inst. (med. malpractice com., product liability com.), Beta Alpha Psi. General corporate, Health, Professional liability. Office: 145 Robert E Lee Blvd Ste 408 New Orleans LA 70124-2581 E-mail: frank@beahm.com

BEAIRD, JAMES RALPH, law educator, dean; b. 1925. BS, U. Ala., 1949, LLB, 1951; LLM, George Washington U., 1953. Bar: Ala. 1951, D.C. 1973. Atty. U.S. Dept. Labor, 1951-56, asst. solicitor, 1956-59; assoc. gen. counsel NLRB, 1959-60; assoc. solicitor U.S. Dept. Labor, 1960-65; vis. prof. U. Ga., 1965-66, prof. law, 1967-89, prof. emeritus, dean, 1976-87, dean emeritus; John Sparkman Vis. Disting. Prof., U. Ala., 1988—; mem. Sec. Labor's Adv. Council on Welfare and Pension Plans, 1968—. Mem. adv. com. for Ga. SBA, 1969—. Mem. Farrah Order Jurisprudence. Office: U Ga Sch Law Athens GA 30602

BEAL, CAROL ANN, lawyer; b. N.Y.C., Aug. 8, 1962; d. Harry Steven and Margot Sanders; m. Kenneth I. Beal, Dc. 4, 1988; children: Zachary, Eric. BA in Psychology, SUNY, Binghamton, 1983; JD, St. John's U., 1986. Bar: N.Y. 1987, U.S. Dist. Ct. (ea. dist.) Conn. Sr. assoc. A.F. Pennisi, Forest Hills, N.Y., 1986-88, jr. ptnr., 1988-90; ptnr. C.A. Beal, 1990-93, Beal & Beal, Jericho, N.Y., 1993—. Lectr. on landlord-tenant law, co-operatives and condominiums, wills, trusts and estates, 1986—. Mem. Queens Bar Assn., Landlord Tenant Assn., Nassau Bar Assn., Syosset Tennis Acad. Avocations: tennis, skiing. Bankruptcy, Landlord-tenant, Probate. Office: Beal & Beal 34 Birchwood Park Cres Jericho NY 11753-2343 E-mail: carolabeal@aol.com

BEALES, RANDOLPH A. state attorney general; m. Julie Leftwich; 1 child. BA in Govt. with high honors, Coll. William and Mary; JD, U. Va. Exec. dir. Gov. George Allen's Commn. on Champion Schs., Va. Business-Edn. Partnership; dep. atty. gen. Commonwealth of Va., 1998—2001, atty. gen., 2001—. Episcopalian. Office: Office Atty Gen 900 E Main St Richmond VA 23219*

BEAL-GWARTNEY, TORE, lawyer; b. St. Maries, Idaho, July 2, 1959; d. James Jergon and Ingrid Ann Beal; m. C. Ryan McCaene (div. May 1991); m. John Michael Gwartney, Dec. 31, 1992. BA, Boise State U., 1982; JD, U. Idaho, 1993. Bar: Idaho 1993. Pvt. practice investment cons., fin. planner, Boise, Idaho, 1982-90; assoc. Cosho Humphrey Greener & Welsh, 1993—, ptnr., shareholder, 1999—. Apptd. mem. Coun. on Domestic Violence, Boise, 1997; Idaho Family Law Sect. Coun. mem. Mem. ABA, Idaho State Bar. Lutheran. Avocations: golf, horse back riding. Estate planning, Family and matrimonial. Home: 955 S Tranquil Ln Eagle ID 83616-4366 Office: Cosho Humphrey Greener & Welsh 815 W Washington St Boise ID 83702-5558

BEALL, KENNETH SUTTER, JR. lawyer; b. Evanston, Ill., Aug. 9, 1938; s. Kenneth Sutter and Helen Cantlon (Koenig) B.; m. Blair Hamilton Bissett, May 25, 1975; children: Kevina Anne, Hunter Bissett, Baret Bissett. BA, Washington and Lee U., 1961, LLB, 1963. Bar: Fla. 1964. With Gunster, Yoakley & Stewart, P.A., West Palm Beach, Fla., 1964—, ptnr., 1970—, pres., 1994—. Bd. dirs. The Whitehall Found., The Wells Family Found.; chmn. Palm Beach County Environ. Control Hearing Bd., 1970-92; mem. law coun. Washington and Lee U., 1997—; trustee, sec. Caribbean/Latin Am. Action. Served with USMCR, 1963-68. Mem. ABA, Fla. Bar (Pres.'s Pro Bono Svc. award 1983), Palm Beach County Bar Assn., Fed. Bar Assn. (pres. Palm Beach County chpt. 1981). Democrat. Roman Catholic. Contracts commercial, General corporate, Agriculture. Office: 777 S Flagler Dr Ste 500E West Palm Beach FL 33401-6121

BEAM, CLARENCE ARLEN, federal judge; b. Stapleton, Nebr., Jan. 14, 1930; s. Clarence Wilson and Cecile Mary (Harvey) B.; m. Betty Lou Fletcher, July 22, 1951; children— Randal, James, Thomas, Bradley, Gregory BS, U. Nebr., 1951, JD, 1965. Feature writer Nebr. Farmer Mag., Lincoln, 1951; with sales dept. Steckley Seed Co., Mount Sterling, Ill., 1954-58, advt. mgr., 1958-63; from assoc. to ptnr. Chambers, Holland, Dudgeon & Knudsen, Berkheimer, Beam, et al, Lincoln, 1965-82; judge U.S. Dist. Ct. Nebr., Omaha, 1982-87, chief judge, 1986-87; cir. judge U.S. Ct. Appeals (8th cir.), 1987—. Mem. com. on lawyer discipline Nebr. Supreme Ct., 1974-82; mem. Conf. Commrs. on Uniform State Laws, 1979—, chmn. Nebr. sect., 1980-82; mem. jud. conf. com. on ct. and jud. security, 1989-93, chmn., 1992-93. Contbr. articles to profl. jours. Mem. Nebr. Rep. Cen. Com., 1970-78. Capt. U.S. Army, 1951-53, Korea. Regents scholar U. Nebr., Lincoln, 1947, Roscoe Pound scholar U. Nebr., Lincoln, 1964 Mem. Nebr. State Bar Assn. Office: US Ct Appeals 8th Cir 435 Federal Bldg 100 Centennial Mall N Lincoln NE 68508-3859

BEAM, ROBERT CHARLES, lawyer; b. Phila., Dec. 21, 1946; s. Thomas Joseph and Jeannette Hortense (Templin) B.; m. Maureen McCauley, Aug. 21, 1976.; children: Davis McCauley B., Morgan McCauley B. BS in Commerce and Engring. Scis., Drexel U., 1970; JD, Temple U., 1977. Bar: U.S. Patent Office 1976, Pa. 1977, U.S. Dist. Ct. (ea. dist.) Pa. 1977, N.Y. 1978, D.C. 1979, U.S. Ct. Customs and Patent Appeals 1980, U.S. Ct. Appeals (3d and fed. cirs.) 1982, N.J. 1983, U.S. Dist. Ct. N.J. 1983, Can. Patent Office 1985. Law clk. U.S. Dist. Ct., Phila., 1976-77; assoc. Firzpatrick, Cella, Harper & Scinto, N.Y.C., 1977-79; patent atty. Hercules Inc., Wilmington, Del., 1979-81, CPC Internat. Inc., Englewood Cliffs, N.J., 1981-83; patent counsel and asst. gen. counsel Congoleum Corp., Kearny, N.J., 1983-85; pvt. practice, 1985—. Mem. ABA, Phila. Bar Assn., D.C. Bar Assn., Phila. Patent Law Assn., Am. Intellectual Property Law Assn. Contracts commercial, Patent, Trademark and copyright. Office: U City Sci Ctr Office 3624 Market St Philadelphia PA 19104-2614

BEANE, FRANK LLEWELLYN, lawyer; b. Canton, Ohio, Feb. 17, 1943; s. Frank Clarence and Lillian Ruth (Powell) B.; m. Patricia Jean Johnson, Sept. 16, 1967; children— Frank Clarence II, Adam Tyler. B.A., Central State U., Wilberforce, Ohio, 1965; J.D., U. Toledo, 1972. Bar: Ohio 1973, U.S. Dist. Ct. (no. dist.) Ohio 1973, U.S. Ct. Appeals (6th cir.) 1973. Asst. prosecutor Canton Police, 1973-74; pub. defender U.S. Dist. Ct. (no. dist.) Ohio, Cleve., 1974-81; assoc. Matecheck, Ferrero, and Stefanko, Massillon, Ohio, 1981— . Bd. dirs. Urban League, Massillon, 1981— , Boy's Club, Massillon, 1984— . Republican. Criminal. Home: 1134 3rd St SE Massillon OH 44646-8029 Office: 46 Federal Ave NW Massillon OH 44647-5467

BEAR, DINAH, lawyer; b. Lynnwood, Calif., Oct. 22, 1951; d. Henry Louis and Betty Jean (Isenhart) B. BJ, U. Mo., 1974; JD, McGeorge Sch. Law, 1977. Bar: Calif. 1978, D.C. 1981, U.S. Supreme Ct. 1982. Dep. gen. counsel Council on Environ. Quality, Washington, 1981-83, gen. counsel, 1983—. Contbr. articles to profl. publs. Recipient Disting. Svc. award Sierra Club, 1993, Chmn.'s award Natural Resources Coun. of Am., 1993. Mem. ABA (chmn. standing com. on environ. law), D.C. Bar Assn. Jewish. Avocation: gardening. Office: Coun Environ Quality 722 Jackson Pl NW Washington DC 20503-0002

BEAR, HENRY LOUIS, lawyer; b. Kansas City, Kans. s. Max and Mary (Kagon) B.; m. Betty Jean Isenhart, Jan. 4, 1951; 1 child, Dinah. JD, U. Mo., 1939. Bar: Mo. 1939, Calif. 1949, U.S. Dist. Ct. (so. dist.) Calif. 1949, U.S. Supreme Ct. 1959. Assoc. O'Hern & O'Hern, Kansas City, Mo., 1939-42; ptnr. Bear, Kotob, Ruby & Gross, and predecessors, Downey, Calif., 1949—. Sec., dir. Pyrotronics Corp.; dir. Bank of Irvine. Author: California Law of Corporations, Partnerships and Associations, 1970. Chmn. Midland dist. coun. Boy Scouts Am., 1954; active Cmty. Chest, Lynwood, Calif. Served to lt. USAF, 1942-46. Named Lynwood Man of Yr., 1952. Fellow Am. Coll. Probate Counsel; mem. ABA, Mo. Bar Assn., Calif. Bar Assn., Calif. Trial Lawyers Assn., L.A. County Bar Assn., Exec. Dinner Club (pres.), Rotary, Elks. Banking, General corporate, Probate. Office: Bear Kotob Ruby & Gross 10841 Paramount Blvd PO Box 747 Downey CA 90241-0747

BEAR, LARRY ALAN, lawyer, educator; b. Melrose, Mass., Feb. 28, 1928; s. Joseph E. and Pearl Florence B.; m. Rita Maldonado, Mar. 29, 1975; children: Peter, Jonathan, Steven. BA, Duke U., 1949; JD, Harvard U., 1953; LLM, (James Kent fellow), Columbia U., 1966. Bar: Mass. 1953, P.R. 1963, N.Y. 1967. Trial lawyer Bear & Bear, Boston, 1953-60; cons. legal medicine P.R. Dept. Justice, 1960-65; prof. law sch. U. P.R., 1960-65; legal counsel, then commr. addiction svcs. City of N.Y., 1967-70; dir. Nat. Action Com. Drug Edn. U. Rochester, N.Y., 1970-77; pvt. practice N.Y.C., 1970-82; pub. affairs radio broadcaster Sta. WABC, 1970-82; U.S. legal counsel Master Enterprises of P.R., 1982-90. Pres. Found. for a Drug Free Pa., 1991-92; adj. prof. markets, ethics and law Stern Sch. Bus., NYU, 1986-99, vis. prof. bus. ethics, 2000—; lectr. in legislation and ethics Wharton Sch. Exec. Program, 1996-2000; vis. prof. legal medicine Rutgers U. Law Sch., 1969; vis. prof. legal, social and ethical context of bus. Athens Lab. for Bus. Adminstrn., Greece, 1996; mem. alcohol and drug com. Nat. Safety Coun., 1972-82; cons. in field of substance abuse prevention, edn. programming, 1980—; mem. Atty. Gen.'s Med./Legal Adv. Bd. on Drug Abuse, Pa., 1992. Author: Law, Medicine, Science and Justice, 1964, The Glass House Revolution: Inner City War for Interdependence, 1990, Free Markets, Finance, Ethics, and Law, 1994; contbr. articles to profl. jours. Adv. com. on pub. issues Advt. Coun., 1972-95; mem.-at-large Nat. coun. Boy Scouts Am., 1972-85; chmn. Bd. Ethics, Twp. of Mahwah (N.J.), 1990-91; alumni admissions adv. com. Duke U., 1987—. Mem. ABA, N.Y. State Bar Assn., Forensic Sci. Soc. Great Britain, Acad. Colombiana de Ciencias Medico-Forenses, Harvard Club (N.Y.C.). Education and schools, Finance, Legislative. Home: 95 Tam Oshanter Dr Mahwah NJ 07430-1526 Office: Markets Ethicso and Law Program NYU Stern Sch Bus 40 W 4th St Ste 3-305 New York NY 10012-1106 E-mail: lbear@stern.nyu.edu

BEARD, RONALD STRATTON, lawyer; b. Flushing, N.Y., Feb. 13, 1939; s. Charles Henry and Ethel Mary (Stratton) B.; m. Karin Paridee, Jan. 24, 1991; children: D. Karen, Jonathan D., Dana K. BA, Denison U., 1961; LLB, Yale U., 1964. Bar: Calif. 1964, U.S. Ct. Appeals (9th cir.) 1980, U.S. Dist. Ct. (cen. dist.) Calif. 1964. Ptnr. Gibson, Dunn & Crutcher, L.A., 1964—, mng. ptnr., 1991-97, chmn., 1991—. Trustee Denison U., Granville, Ohio, 1975—, chmn., 1998—; mem. steering com. Calif. Minority Coun. Program, 1991—; mem. Constl. Rights Found., 1994—, Orange County Art Mus., Chapman Exec. Fellows; CEO roundtable U. Calif., Irvine. Mem. ABA, Calif. Bar Assn., L.A. Bar Assn., Calif. Club, City Club, Chancery Club, Bear Creek Golf Club. Avocations: sports, travel, golf. General corporate, Private international. Home: 27442 Hidden Trail Rd Laguna Hills CA 92653-5876 Office: Gibson Dunn & Crutcher 4 Park Plz Ste 1700 Irvine CA 92614-8560

BEARMON, LEE, lawyer; BBA, JD, U. Minn. Bar: Minn. 1956. Sr. v.p., exec. cons. Carlson Cos., Inc, Mpls.; of counsel Briggs & Morgan, 2000—. Office: Carlson Cos Inc PO Box 59159 Minneapolis MN 55459-8200 also: Briggs and Morgan 2400 IDS Ctr 80 S 8th St Minneapolis MN 55402-2100

BEASLEY, JAMES EDWIN, lawyer; s. James Edwin and Margaret Ann (Patterson) B.; children: Pamela Jane, Kimberly Ann, James Edwin. BS, Temple U., 1953, JD, 1956. Bar: Pa. 1956. Law clk. U.S. Dist. Ct. (ea. dist.) Pa., Phila., 1954-56; prin., owner Beasley, Casey & Erbstein, 1966—. Instr. law Temple U., 1976-80, adj. prof., 1994; permanent del. 3d Cir. Jud. Conf.; chmn. standard civil jury inst. Pa. Supreme Ct.; bd. dirs. NATA; past trustee Pop Warner Little Scholars. Author: Products Liability and the Unreasonably Dangerous Requirement; contbr. articles to profl. jours. With USN, 1943-45, Comdr. USAR, 1951-57. Mem.: ABA, ATLA, Fed. Bar Assn., Am. Judicature Soc., Am. Law Inst., Am. Bd. Trial Advs., Nat. Transp. Safety Bd. Bar Assn., Pa. Bar Assn., Phila. Bar Assn., Phila. Trial Lawyers Assn. (pres. 1970—71, Justice Michael Musmanno award), Pa. Trial Lawyers Assn. (pres. 1969—70), Inner Cir. Advs., Am. Bd. Profl. Liability Attys., Temple U. Gen. Alumni Assn. (cert. of honor), Pa. Soc., Aircraft Owners and Pilots Assn. (cert. flight instr. single-multi engine airplane and instrument FAA), Six Diamonds Aerobatic Flight Team, Nat. Air Racing Group, Union League, QB Phl Hanger, QB Phl Hanger. Episcopalian. Libel, Personal injury. Office: 1125 Walnut St Philadelphia PA 19107-4918 Fax: 215-592-8360. E-mail: lawyers@tortlaw.com

BEASLEY, JAMES W., JR. lawyer; b. Atlanta, July 13, 1943; s. James W. and Sara Capal (Tucker) B.; m. Elizabeth Barno Marshall-Beasley, Nov. 28, 1986. AB cum laude, Davidson Coll., 1965; LLB cum laude, Harvard U., 1968. Bar: N.Y. 1969, D.C. 1971, Fla. 1972, U.S. Supreme Ct. 1973. Assoc. Sullivan & Cromwell, N.Y.C., 1968, Wilmer, Cutler & Pickering, Washington, 1970-72; assoc., then ptnr. Paul & Thomson, Miami, Fla., 1972-78; mng. ptnr. Beasley, Olle & Downs, 1978-88; ptnr. Tew , Jordan, Schulte & Beasley, 1988-89, Cadwalader, Wickersham & Taft, Palm Beach, Fla., 1989-94, Tew & Beasley LLP, Palm Beach, 1994-97, Beasley, Leacock & Hauser, P.A., Palm Beach, 1997—. Author: Florida Corporations, 1985; contbr. articles to profl. jours. Chmn. County Conv. Ctr. Adv. Bd., 1994-96. Capt. U.S. Army, 1968-70. Mem. ABA, ATLA, Fla. Bar Assn. (chmn. securities regulation com. bus. law sect. 1975-77), Acad. Fla. Trial Lawyers. Appellate, General civil litigation, Securities.

BEASLEY, OSCAR HOMER, lawyer, educator; b. Denver, Sept. 30, 1925; m. Shirlee Beasley; 4 children. BA, U. Omaha, 1949; JD, U. Iowa, 1950. Bar: Iowa 1949, N.Mex. 1952, Calif. 1964, Hawaii 1982. Assoc. Joseph L. Smith, Albuquerque, 1955-59; ptnr. Ertz & Beasley, 1959-62, Beasley & Colberg, Albuquerque, 1962-64; atty. 1st Am. Title Ins. Co., Santa Ana, Calif., 1964-70, sr. v.p., sr. title counsel, 1970—; mem. N.Mex. Ho. of Reps., 1958-62. Instr. Western State U. Coll. Law, Fullerton, Calif., 1970-96, also mem. adv. bd. Mem. N.Mex. Ho. of Reps., 1958-62. Mem. ABA, Calif. Bar Assn., Orange County Bar Assn., L.A. County Bar Assn., N.Mex. Bar Assn., Iowa Bar Assn., Am. Coll. Real Estate Lawyers, Am. Land Title Assn. (hon. mem., Indian Land Claims Com.). Real property. Home: 1100 Irvine Blvd # 511 Tustin CA 92780-3529 Office: First Am Title Ins Co 1 First American Way Santa Ana CA 92707-5913 E-mail: obeasley@firstam.com

BEATIE, RUSSEL HARRISON, JR. lawyer; b. Lawrence, Kans., Jan. 20, 1938; m. Julia Ferguson DuVall; children: Benjamin Wilson Parkhill, Amy Wilder. BA cum laude, Princeton U., 1959; LLB cum laude, Columbia U., 1964. Bar: N.Y. 1964, U.S. Dist. Ct. (so. and ea. dists.) N.Y., U.S. Ct. Appeals (2d, 3d, 5th, 6th, 7th, 9th and 10th cirs.), U.S. Supreme Ct. Assoc. Dewey, Ballantine, Bushby, Palmer & Wood, N.Y.C., 1964-66, 68-72, Rogers & Wells, 1966-68; ptnr. Dewey Ballatine, 1972-83; pvt. practice, 1983-88; ptnr. Brown & Wood, N.Y.C., 1989-93, Beatlie, King & Abate, N.Y.C., 1993-97, Beatie and Osborn, 1997—. Author: Road to Manassas, 1961, The Army of the Potomac: A Study in Command, vol. 1, Birth of Command, 2001. 1st lt. arty. U.S. Army, 1959-61. Mem. Assn. of Bar of City of N.Y., Union Club, Princeton Club. Republican. Federal civil litigation, State civil litigation.

BEATTIE, DONALD GILBERT, lawyer; b. Des Moines, Nov. 30, 1947; s. Max and Rowena Jean (Gilbert) B.; divorced; children: Brett Joseph, Ryan Troy, Adam Ross, Nicholas Gilbert. BA, Simpson Coll., 1970; JD, Drake U., 1977. Bar: Iowa 1977, U.S. Dist. Ct. (no. and so. dist.) Iowa 1977. Ptnr. Beattie Law Firm, Pleasant Hill, Iowa, 1975—. City atty. Runnells, Iowa, 1977—. Mem. ATLA, Assn. Trial Lawyers of Iowa, Iowa State Bar Assn., Polk County Bar Assn., Nat. Bd. Trial Advocacy, Drake Law Rev. Alumni Assn. (bd. dirs.), Am. Legion, Order of Coif. Democrat. Lodge: Masons (master 1980). E-mial. Federal civil litigation, State civil litigation, Personal injury. E-mail: beattielaw@aol.com

BEATTY, WILLIAM GLENN, lawyer; b. Moline, Ill., July 13, 1953; s. Glenn Willard and Mary Frances (Karlson) B.; m. Carla Ann Busse, Feb. 25, 1978; children— Andrew Glenn, Mark William. B.A. cum laude, Augustana Coll., Rock Island, Ill., 1975; postgrad. Creighton U., 1975-76; J.D. with honors, Chgo.-Kent Coll. Law, 1978. Bar: Ill. 1978, U.S. Dist. Ct. (no. dist.) Ill. 1979, U.S. Ct. Appeals (7th cir.) 1979, U.S. Ct. Claims 1979. Assoc. Johnson, Cusack & Bell, Ltd., Chgo., 1978-84, ptnr., 1985— ; asst. instr. Chgo.-Kent Coll. Law, 1978; lectr. in field. Mem ABA, Ill. Bar Assn., Chgo. Bar Assn., Ill. Def. Counsel, Trial Lawyers Club Chgo., Def. Research Inst. Republican. Roman Catholic. State civil litigation, Insurance, Personal injury. Office: Johnson Cusack & Bell Ltd 211 W Wacker Dr Chicago IL 60606-1217

BEATTY, WILLIAM LOUIS, federal judge; b. Mendota, Ill., Sept. 4, 1925; s. Raphael H. and Teresa A. (Collins) B.; m. Dorothy Jeanne Starnes, June 12, 1948; children: William S., Steven M., Thomas D., Mary C. Student, Washington U., St. Louis, 1945-47; LL.B., St. Louis U., 1950. Bar: Ill. 1950. Gen. practice law, Granite City, 1950-68; circuit judge 3d Jud. Circuit Ill., 1968-79; U.S. dist. judge So. Dist. Ill., 1979—. Served with AUS, 1943-45. Mem. Madison County Bar Assn., Tri-City Bar Assn. Roman Catholic. Office: So Dist Ct 750 Missouri Ave Rm 377 East Saint Louis IL 62201-2954 Died July 22, 2001.

BEAUGRAND, KENNETH LOUIS, lawyer, business executive; b. N.Y.C., Oct. 19, 1938; BA, Brown U., 1960; LLB, Columbia U., 1963; LLM, U. London, 1964; m. Augusta Newell Wood Barnard, Nov. 22, 1969; 3 children. Bar: N.Y. 1964, Ont. 1977. Assoc. Willkie, Farr & Gallagher, N.Y.C., 1964-68; solicitor I.O.S. Ltd. Fin. Services, Geneva, 1968-69, sec., 1969-71, v.p., dir., gen. counsel, 1972-73; v.p., dir., gen. counsel Value Capital Services, Amsterdam, 1971-72; assoc. Aird, Zimmerman & Berlis, 1973-77; v.p., sec., gen. counsel Eaton Bay Fin. Services Ltd., Toronto, 1977-79, sr. v.p., gen. counsel, 1979-82, sr. v.p. ins. and fund. divs., 1982-83, sr. v.p. ops., 1983-85; exec. v.p. 1985-86, sr. v.p. investments The Imperial Life Assurance Co. of Can., Toronto, 1986-87, exec. v.p., chief operating officer, 1987—. Bd. dirs. Laurentian Mut. Funds, Viking Mut. Funds, Eaton Funds Mgmt., Ltd., Laurier Life, chmn., chief exec. officer, bd. dirs. Imbrook Properties, Ltd. Avocations: tennis, skiing, sailing. Clubs: University, Toronto Lawn Tennis. Office: The Imperial Life Assurance Co of Can 95 St Clair Ave W Toronto ON Canada M4V 1N7

BEBCHICK, LEONARD NORMAN, lawyer; b. New Bedford, Mass., Dec. 11, 1932; s. Samuel and Frances (Hait) B.; m. Gabriela Meyerhoff, Aug. 31, 1968; children: Ilana, Brian AB, Cornell U., 1955; LLB, Yale U., 1958. Bar: Mass. 1958, D.C. 1960, Md. 1989. Atty. CAB, Washington, 1959-60; assoc. Ginsburg & Leventhal, 1960-64; ptnr. Bebchick, Sher & Kushnick, 1964-74, Martin, Whitfield, Smith & Bebchick, Washington, 1974-82; pres. Leonard N. Bebchick P.C., 1982-88; ptnr. Leva, Hawes, Mason, Martin & Bebchick, 1988-89; pvt. practice as lawyer, 1989—. Joint co. sec. Brit Caledonian Airways, Eng., 1963-88; bd. dirs. British Caledonian Group, Eng., 1978-88, London Transport Internat. Cons., U.S., 1990-92; spl. counsel D.C. Pub. Svc. Commn., Washington, 1965-66, V.I. Pub. Utilities Commn., 1967-70. Pres. Congregation Beth El of Montgomery County, 1993-95; bd. dirs. United Synagogue of Conservative Judaism, 1993—, Jewish Fedn. Greater, Washington, 1996—; bd. govs. coms. Jewish Agy. Israel, 1998—; v.p. Muss H.S., Israel, 1997—. Mem. ABA (chmn. adv. com. on aero. law 1982-83), FBA, Internat. Bar Assn., Inst. of Dirs. (London), U.S. Nat. Student Assn. (v.p. internat. affairs 1953-54). Democrat. Jewish. Administrative and regulatory, Federal civil litigation, General corporate. Home: 6321 Lenox Rd Bethesda MD 20817-6023 Office: 1101 Connecticut Ave NW Washington DC 20036 E-mail: beblaw@erols.com

BEBER, ROBERT H. lawyer, financial services executive; b. N.Y.C., Aug. 17, 1933; s. Morris and Martha (Pollock) B.; m. Joan Parsons, June 14, 1957; children: Andrea, Judith, Deborah. A.B. in Econs, Duke U., 1955, J.D., 1957. Bar: N.Y., N.C. With Everett, Everett & Everett, N.C., 1957-58; atty. SBA, Washington, 1961-63; with RCA, 1963-81; sr. v.p., gen. counsel, sec. GAF Corp., N.Y.C., 1981-83, exec. v.p., dir., 1983-84, dir. subs.; sr. v.p., gen. counsel, sec. Phlcorp, Inc. (formerly Baldwin United Corp.), Phila., 1984-88; asst. gen. counsel litigation W.R. Grace & Co., N.Y.C., 1988-89, v.p., dir. litigation, 1989-91, sr. v.p., gen. counsel, 1991-93, exec. v.p., 1993-98, ret., 1999, cons., 1999—. Bd. dirs. Advantage Bank. Bd. vis. Sch. Law, Duke U., 1996—; chmn. bd. Health Care Plan N.J., 1975-78; v.p. South Jersey C. of C., 1974-77; dir. Advantage Bank, Palm Beach, Fla., 1999—. Served with U.S. Army, 1958-61. Mem. ABA. Republican. Jewish. General civil litigation, General corporate. Home: 7228 Queenferry Cir Boca Raton FL 33496-5953 Office: WR Grace & Co 5400 Broken Sound Blvd NW Boca Raton FL 33487-3511

BECERRA, ROBERT JOHN, lawyer; b. Jersey City, Jan. 26, 1962; s. Joseph Hercules and Blanche (Rosado) B.; m. Christiana Marie Carroll, Oct. 30, 1993. BBA, U. Miami, 1986, JD, 1990. Bar: Fla. 1990, U.S. Dist. Ct. (so. and mid dists.) Fla. 1991, U.S. Ct. Appeals (11th cir.) 1991, U.S. Dist. Ct. (ea. dist.) Mich. 1994, U.S. Supreme Ct. 1994, U.S. Ct. Appeals (3d cir.) 1997. Assoc. Raskin & Raskin, Miami, Fla., 1990-96, ptnr., 1997—. Mem. Fed. Bar Assn., Dade County Bar Assn. (fed. cts. com., Certificate of Merit 1993), Phi Kappa Phi. Democrat. Roman Catholic. Avocations: sailplane pilot, scuba diving, boating, skiing. Aviation, Federal civil litigation, Criminal. Office: Raskin & Raskin 2937 SW 27th Ave Ste 206 Miami FL 33133-3772 E-mail: bbecerra@raskinlaw.com

BECH, DOUGLAS YORK, lawyer, resort executive; b. Seattle, Aug. 18, 1945; s. Albert Richard and Vera Evelyn (Peterson) B.; m. Sheryl Annette Tucker, Aug. 9, 1968; children: Kristen Elizabeth, Allison York. BA, Baylor U., 1967; JD, U. Tex., 1970. Bar: Tex. 1970, N.Y. 1993. Ptnr. Andrews & Kurth, Houston, 1970-93, Akin, Gump, Strauss, Hauer & Feld, 1994-97; mng. dir. Raintree Capital Co., Houston, 1994—. Chmn., CEO Raintree Resorts Internat., Inc., Club Regina Resorts, Inc.; bd. dirs. Frontier Oil, efax.com, Pride Cos., Drexler Found. Sgt. USAR, 1968-74. Republican. Baptist. Avocations: running, snowskiing, travel, big game hunting, golf. General corporate, Mergers and acquisitions, Securities. Office: Raintree Resorts Internat 10000 Memorial Dr Ste 480 Houston TX 77024-3409 E-mail: dybech@raintreeresotrs.com

BECK, ANDREW JAMES, lawyer; b. Washington, Feb. 19, 1948; s. Leonard Norman and Frances (Greif) B.; children: Carter, Lowell, Justin. BA, Carleton Coll., 1969; JD, Stanford U., 1972; MBA, Long Island U., 1975. Bar: Va. 1972, N.Y. 1973, Pa., 1992. Assoc. Casey, Lane & Mittendorf, N.Y.C., 1972-80, ptnr., 1980-82, Haythe & Curley, N.Y.C., 1982-99, Torys, N.Y.C., 1999—, exec. com., 2000—. Bd. dirs. Capita Rsch. Group, Inc. Bd. dirs. Allied Devices Corp., 1994-98, Capita Rsch. Group; trustee Bklyn. Heights Synagogue, 1980-81, Bklyn. Heights Montessori Sch., 1988-92, treas., 1990-92. Mem. ABA, Va. State Bar Assn., N.Y. Stat Bar Assn., Pa. Bar Assn., Assn. of Bar of City of N.Y., Nat. Stroke Assn. (gen. counsel 1992—, sec., bd. dirs. 2000—). Avocation: bridge. General corporate, Securities. Home: 71 Willow St Apt 1 Brooklyn NY 11201-1657 Office: Torys 237 Park Ave Fl 20 New York NY 10017-3142 E-mail: abeck@torys.com

BECK, JAN SCOTT, lawyer; b. Newark, May 5, 1955; s. Robert William and Dorothy (Warhaftig) B.; m. Marla Terri Klein, Sept. 27, 1981; children: Jamie Kyle, Bryan Michael, Sean Jason. BA in Acctg., Rider Coll., 1977; JD, Villanova U., 1980, LLM in Taxation, 1985. Bar: N.J. 1980, U.S. Dist. Ct. N.J. 1980, N.Y. 1981, U.S. Tax Ct. 1981, D.C. 1985, U.S. Supreme Ct. 1986. Pvt. practice, Westfield, N.J., 1980-86; atty. Inspiration Resources Corp., N.Y.C., 1986-88; dir. taxation ADT Inc., Boca Raton, Fla., 1988-89, v.p., gen. counsel, 1989-96; sr. v.p., dir. ADT Security Svcs., Inc., 1996-97; mng. dir., CEO The Turbary Group, Boca Raton, Fla., 1997—. Atty. Laventhol & Horwath, Phila., 1979-80, Touche Ross & Co., N.Y.C., 1980-86; dir. taxation Inspiration Resources Corp., N.Y.C., Monsoon Internat. LLC, 2000—. Author: The Strike: Student Involvement, 1975. Mem. ABA, N.Y. State Bar Assn., N.J. Bar Assn., AICPA, N.J. Soc. CPAs, Tax Exec. Inst., Omicron Delta Epsilon, Delta Epsilon Kappa. Avocations: camping, backpacking, mountain climbing, writing, skiing. General corporate, Mergers and acquisitions, Corporate taxation. Home: 20988 Solano Way Boca Raton FL 33433-1621 Office: The Turbary Group 7280 W Palmetto Park Rd Boca Raton FL 33433-3422 E-mail: jbeck@turbary.com

BECK, PAUL AUGUSTINE, lawyer; b. Pitts., Aug. 16, 1936; s. August W. and Agnes (Heyl) B.; m. Nancy Flaherty; children: Jennifer, Bradford, Michael. BS, Carnegie-Mellon U., 1957; LLB, Duquesne U., 1962. Bar: Pa. 1962, U.S. Ct. Appeals (4th cir.) 1963, U.S. Supreme Ct. 1966, U.S. Ct. Appeals (2d and 3d cirs.) 1971, U.S. Ct. Appeals (7th cir.) 1974, U.S. Ct. Appeals (Fed. cir.) 1982. Ptnr. Buell, Ziesenheim, Beck & Alstadt, Pitts., 1962-88, Buchanan Ingersoll, Pitts., 1988-95; propr. Paul A. Beck & Assocs., 1995—. Del. U.S. Ct. Appeals (3d cir.) Jud. Conf., 1983. Chmn. alumni forum com. Carnegie-Mellon U., Pitts., 1966-67. Capt. U.S. Army, 1957-59. Mem. ABA, Pa. Bar Assn. (ho. of dels. 1984—), Nat. Coun. Pat. Law Assn., Allegheny County Bar Assn. (gov. 1977-79, chmn. intellectual property law sect. 1979-84), Pitts. Intellectual Property Law Assn. (bd. dirs., pres. 1989-90), Duquesne U. Law Sch. Alumni Assn. (v.p. 1997-98, pres. 1999—). Intellectual property, Patent, Trademark and copyright. Office: Paul A Beck & Assocs Ste 100 1575 McFarland Rd Pittsburgh PA 15216-1808

BECK, PHILIP S. lawyer; b. Chgo., Apr. 30, 1951; BA, U. Wis., 1973; JD, Boston U., 1976. Bar: Ill. 1977. Clerk U.S. Ct. Appeals DC Cir., 1976-77; ptnr. Bartlit Beck Herman Palenchar & Scott, Chgo. Office: Bartlit Beck Herman et al 54 W Hubbard St Chicago IL 60610-4645 E-mail: philip.beck@bartlit-beck.com

BECK, STEPHANIE G. lawyer; b. Endicott, N.Y., Jan. 10, 1964; d. Ray A. and Donna E. (Geesey) B. BA with honors, SUNY, Binghamton, 1986; JD, Syracuse U., 1989. Bar: N.Y. 1990, U.S. Dist. Ct. (no. dist.) N.Y. 1990. Atty. Young & Paniccia, Binghamton, 1990—. Advisor/vol. Drama Club for Mentally and Physically Impaired, Binghamton, 1992-96; mem. ch. coun. Our Saviour Luth. Ch., Endwell, N.Y., 1990-94, 96; asst. coach Boys and Girls Club, Endwell, 1986-91. Mem. N.Y. State Bar Assn., Broome County Bar Assn. (bd. dirs.). Democrat. Lutheran. Avocations: softball, volleyball. Family and matrimonial, General practice, Probate. Office: Young and Paniccia 22 Riverside Dr Binghamton NY 13905-4612

BECK, STUART EDWIN, lawyer; b. Phila., Aug. 12, 1940; s. Louis M. and Anna (Cooper) B.; m. Elaine Kushner, June 20, 1964; children: Adam, Barry, Caroline. BSME, Drexel U., 1964; JD, George Washington U., 1968. Bar: Va. 1968, U.S. Dist. Ct. D.C. 1969, Pa. 1970, U.S. Dist. Ct. (ea. dist.) Pa. 1971, U.S. Ct. Appeals (3d cir.) 1971, U.S. Supreme Ct. 1980, U.S. Ct. Appeals (4th cir.) 1989, U.S. Patent and Trademark Office. Assoc. Seidel, Gonda & Goldhammer, Phila., 1969-73; atty. pvt. practice, 1974-79, 91—; ptnr. Trachman, Jacobs & Beck, 1979-88, Weinstein, Trachtman, Beck & Kimmelman, Phila., 1988-91. Adj. prof. patent law Rutgers U. Law Sch., Camden, N.J.; instr. patent, trademark and copyright law The Phila. Inst.; lectr. patent, trademark and copyright law Newmann Coll., 1999. Capt. Am. Cancer Soc., 1974, 75; bd. dirs. Jewish Family and Children Svc. Phila., 1973-89, legal, fin. and budget com., 1979—, spkrs. com., 1979—, bldg. and grounds com., 1980-82, trustee, 1989; bd. dirs., by-laws revision com., bldgs. and grounds com., edn. com. Temple Beth Hillel; bd. dirs. Phila. Vol. Lawyers for Arts, 1980-84, treas., 1980-82. Mem. ABA (patent trademark and copyright law sect., litigation sect., antitrust law sect.), Am. Intellectual Property Law Assn. (com. patent contracts other than govt. 1971-75), Pa. Bar Assn., Phila. Bar Assn. (com. profl. responsibility 1975-93, com. election procedures 1976-84, com. law and arts 1976-80), Phila. Patent Law Assn. (com. ethics 1977-83, com. pub. rels. 1974-77, com. profl. responsibility 1975-79). Avocations: sailing, travel. Intellectual property, Patent, Trademark and copyright.

BECK, WILLIAM G. lawyer; b. Kansas City, Mo., Mar. 4, 1954; s. Raymond W. Beck and Wanda Williams; 1 child, Collin M. BA in Econs., U. Mo., Kansas City, 1974, JD, 1978. Bar: Mo. 1978, U.S. Dist. Ct. (we. dist.) Mo. 1978, U.S. Ct. Appeals (5th cir.) 1988, U.S. Dist. Ct. (ea. dist.) Mich. 1991, U.S. Dist. Ct. (no. dist.) Ill. 1992, U.S. Ct. Appeals (6th cir.) 1992, U.S. Dist. Ct. (ea. dist.) Wis. 1997, U.S. Ct. Appeals (2d cir.) 1997, U.S. Ct. Appeals (10th cir.) 1997, U.S. Supreme Ct. 1997, U.S. Ct. Appeals (1st cir.) 1998, U.S. Ct. Appeals (7th cir.) 1999, U.S. Dist. Ct. Colo. 2000. Shareholder Field, Gentry, Benjamin & Robertson, P.C., Kansas City, 1978-89; ptnr. Lathrop & Norquist, 1989-95, Lathrop & Gage, L.C., Kansas City, 1996—. Commr. Human Rels. Commn., Jackson County, Mo., 1985-89; chmn. Citizens Assn., Kansas City, 1991-92, 95—; mem. Pub. Improvement Adv. Com., Kansas City, 1991—, vice chmn., 1995-98, chmn. 1998—, fin. chmn. cmty. infrastructure com., 1996—; mem. Waste Minimization Com., Kansas City, 1990-91. Federal civil litigation, Environmental, Toxic tort. Office: Lathrop & Gage LC 2345 Grand Blvd Ste 2800 Kansas City MO 64108-2684

BECK, WILLIAM HAROLD, JR. lawyer; b. Clarksdale, Miss., Aug. 18, 1928; s. William Harold and Mary (McGaha) B.; m. Nancy Cassity House, Jan. 30, 1954; children: Mary, Nancy, Katherine. BA, Vanderbilt U., 1950; JD, U. Miss., 1954. Bar: Miss. 1954, La. 1960. Atty., Clarksdale, 1954-57; asst. prof. Tulane U., 1957-59; ptnr. Foley & Judell, New Orleans, 1959-88, of counsel, 1988—. Capt. AUS, 1951-53. Mem. La. Bar Assn., Miss. Bar Assn., SAR, Soc. Colonial Wars, S.R., Mil and Hospitaller Order of St. Lazarus of Jerusalem, Huguenot Soc., Mil. Order Fgn. Wars. Municipal (including bonds). Office: Foley & Judell 1 Canal Pl 365 Canal St Ste 2600 New Orleans LA 70130-1138 E-mail: wandnbeck@aol.com

BECKER, ALISON LEA, lawyer; b. Covington, Ky., Apr. 5, 1963; d. Richard L. and Rosalind M. (Schuppert) Ante; m. Patrick J. Becker, Apr. 4, 1992; 1 child, Christopher P. BA, No. Ky. U., 1984, JD, 1987. Bar: Ohio 1988, Fla. 1998, U.S. Dist. Ct. (so. dist.) Ohio 1988, U.S. Ct. Appeals (6th cir.) 1988, U.S. Army Ct. Mil. Rev. 1990, U.S. Ct. Mil. Appeals 1992, U.S. Supreme Ct. 1992, Fla. 1998, U.S. Dist. Ct. (mid. dist.) Fla. 1998, U.S. Ct. Appeals (11th cir.) 1999. Sole practice, Cin., 1988-89; trial def. atty. U.S. Army JAG Corps, Goeppingen, Germany, 1990-91, trial counsel, legal assistance atty. Stuttgart, Germany, 1991-92, def. appellate counsel Falls Church, Va., 1992-94, chief claims and adminstrv. law Atlanta, 1994-97; sr. atty. Office Atty. Gen., Tampa, Fla., 1998—. Coord. for appellate def. before U.S. Supreme Ct., U.S. Army, Falls Church, 1992-94. Office: Office Atty Gen 501 E Kennedy Blvd Ste 775 Tampa FL 33602

BECKER, CARL FREDERICK, lawyer; b. Endicott, N.Y., Jan. 31, 1948; m. Christine Hill, July 06, 1974; children: Valeria, Jonathan. BS in Indsl. Mgmt., Clarkson Coll., 1970; JD, Albany Law Sch., 1973. Bar: N.Y. 1974. Ptnr. Govern, McDowell & Becker, Stamford, N.Y., 1973—. Social svcs. atty. Delaware County Dept. Social Svcs., Delhi, N.Y., 1974— ; village atty. Village of Hobart, N.Y., 1976—, Village of Stamford, N.Y., 1989—. Mem. N.Y. State Bar Assn., Delaware County Bar Assn. (pres. 2001—), N.Y. State Pub. Welfare Assn. (v.p. atty.'s sect. 1989-92, pres. 1993), Rotary (pres. Stamford 1978-79, chair dist. 7170 youth exch. com. 1999-2001). Republican. Presbyterian. Municipal (including bonds), Probate, Real property. Office: Govern McDowell & Becker 72 Main St Stamford NY 12167-1141

BECKER, EDWARD ROY, federal judge; b. Phila., May 4, 1933; s. Herman A. and Jeannette (Levit) B.; m. Flora Lyman, Aug. 11, 1957; children: James Daniel (dec. 1969), Jonathan Robert, Susan Rose, Charles Lyman. BA, U. Pa., 1954; LLB, Yale U., 1957. Bar: Pa. 1957. Ptnr. Becker, Becker & Fryman, Phila., 1957-70; U.S. Dist. Judge, 1970-82; judge U.S. Ct. Appeals (3d cir.), 1982—, chief judge, 1998—. Counsel Rep. City Com., Phila., 1965-70; mem. task force on implementation of new jud. article Joint State Govt. Commn., 1969; lectr. law U. Pa. Law Sch., 1978-83; mem. edn. adv. com. concerning Comprehensive Crime Control Act, Fed. Jud. Ctr., 1981-90, Fed. Jud. Ctr. Com. on Sentencing, Probation and Pretrial Svcs., 1985-90; bd. dirs. Fed. Jud. Ctr., 1991-95; mem. faculty sr. appellate judges seminar Inst. Jud. Adminstrn., N.Y.C., 1992-94. Bd. editors Manual for Complex Litigation, 1981-90; contbr. articles to profl. jours. Trustee Magna Carta Found., Phila.; vis. com. U. Chgo. Law Sch., 1988-91; chair Rhodes Scholarship Selection Com. Dist. II (Pa., N.Y., Vt., N.H.), 1996-98. Mem. ABA (jud. rep. antitrust sect. 1983-86), Phila. Bar Assn., Am. Judicature Soc., Am. Law Inst. (adv. com. restatement conflict of laws 2d, mem. ALI-ABA com. 1992—, chmn. program subcom. 1996-99), Jud. Conf. U.S. (com. on adminstrn. probation system 1979-87, chmn. com. on criminal law and probation adminstrn. 1987-90, com. on long range planning 1991-96, exec. com. 1998—), Phi Beta Kappa. Jewish. Home: 936 Herbert St Philadelphia PA 19124-2417 Office: US Ct Appeals 19613 US Courthouse 601 Market St Philadelphia PA 19106-1713

BECKER, NANCY ANNE, state supreme court justice; b. Las Vegas, May 23, 1955; d. Arthur William and Margaret Mary (McLoughlin) B. BA, U.S. Internat. U., 1976; JD, George Washington U., 1979. Bar: Nev. 1979, D.C. 1980, Md. 1982, U.S. Dist. Ct. Nev. 1987, U.S. Ct. Appeals (9th cir.) 1987. Legis. cons. D.C. Office on Aging, Washington, 1979-83; assoc. Goldstein & Ahalt, College Park, Md., 1980-82; pvt. practice Washington, 1982-83; dep. city atty., prosecutor criminal div. City of Las Vegas, 1983; judge Las Vegas Mcpl. Ct., 1987-89, Clark County Dist. Ct., Las Vegas, 1989-99; now assoc. state supreme ct. justice Nev. Supreme Ct. Cons. MADD, Las Vegas, 1983-87. Contbr. articles to profl. publs. Pres. Clark County Pro Bono Project, Las Vegas, 1984-95. Mem. So. Nev. Assn. Women Attys. (past officer), Am. Businesswomen's Assn. (treas. Las Vegas chpt. 1985-86), NCCJ, Las Vegas and Latin C. of C., Vietnam Vets Am., Soroptimist Internat. Office: Nevada Supreme Court Capital Complex 316 Bridger Ave Las Vegas NV 89101-5906

BECKER, SANDRA NEIMAN HAMMER, lawyer; b. N.Y.C., June 17, 1947; d. Melvin and Bernice (Lebowitz) N.; m. Otto R. Hammer, Aug. 25, 1969 (div.); m. Brandon Becker, May 20, 1978; children: Elliott M.N., Gabriel W. BA, CCNY, 1969; JD, U. San Diego, 1978; LLM, NYU, 1981. Bar: Calif. 1978, U.S. Dist. Ct. (so. dist.) Calif. 1979, U.S. Ct. Appeals (9th cir.) 1979. Adminstrv. analyst Consumer Affairs Unit, Syracuse, N.Y., 1973-75; atty. food and drug advt. FTC, Washington, 1978-79, atty. advt. practices div., 1984-88; with Office Gen. Counsel, Electric Rates Fed. Energy Regulatory Commn., Dept. Energy, 1988-92. Mng. editor Food Drug Cosmetic Law Jour., Washington, 1981-85. Food and Drug fellow Food and Drug Law Inst., 1978-80. Home: 713 Lamberton Dr Silver Spring MD 20902-3036 E-mail: srnb@aol.com

BECKETT, THEODORE CHARLES, lawyer; b. Boonville, Mo., May 6, 1929; s. Theodore Cooper and Gladys (Watson) B.; m. Daysie Margaret Cornwall, 1950; children: Elizabeth Gayle, Theodore Cornwall, Margaret Lynn, William Harrison, Anne Marie. BS, U. Mo., Columbia, 1950, JD, 1957. Bar: Mo. 1957. Of counsel Baker, Sterchi, Cowden & Rice, LLC; instr. polit. sci. U. Mo., Columbia, 1956-57; asst. atty. gen. State of Mo., 1961-64. Mem. City Plan Commn., Kansas City, 1976-80; bd. curators U. Mo., 1995-2001, pres. 1998. 1st lt. U.S. Army, 1950-53. Mem. Am., Mo., Kansas City bar assns., Lawyers Assn. Kansas City, Newcomen Soc. N.Am., SAR, Order of Coif, Sigma Nu, Phi Alpha Delta. Presbyterian. Clubs: Kansas City (Kansas City, Mo.), Blue Hills Country (Kansas City, Mo.). Federal civil litigation, State civil litigation. Office: 2400 Pershing Rd Ste 500 Kansas City MO 64108

BECKETT, THEODORE CORNWALL, lawyer; b. Heidelberg, Fed. Republic Germany, Nov. 21, 1952; (parents Am. Citizens); s. Theodore Charles and Daysie Margaret (Cornwall) B.; m. Patricia Anne McKelvy, June 18, 1983; children: Anna Kathleen, Kerry Christine, Cooper Charles. BA, U. Mo., 1975, JD, 1978. Bar: Mo. 1978, U.S. Dist. Ct. (we. dist.) Mo. 1978. Ptnr. Beckett & Hensley L.C., Kansas City, Mo., 1994—. Bd. dirs. Kans. Spl. Olympics, 1979-84, legal advisor, 1984—, Kans. City Metro Spl. Olympics, 1993—. Mem. ABA, Mo. Bar Assn., Kansas City Bar Assn., Mo. Assn. Trial Attys., Assn. Trial Lawyers Am., Kansas City Club, Carriage Club, Beta Theta Pi Democrat. Presbyterian. General civil litigation, Construction, Personal injury. Office: Beckett & Hensley LC PO Box 13185 610 Commerce Tower Kansas City MO 64199

BECKEY, SYLVIA LOUISE, lawyer; b. L.A., Feb. 8, 1946; d. Andrew Gabriel and Rita Jane (Mayer) B. BA with spl. honors, U. Tex., 1968, postgrad., 1968-69; JD, Duke U., 1971; MA, Johns Hopkins Sch. Advanced Internat. Studies, 1973-74; LLM, NYU, 1981. Bar: D.C. 1972, N.Y. 1975, U.S. Dist. Ct. (so. and ea. dists.) N.Y. 1975, U.S. Supreme Ct. 1975, U.S. Ct. Appeals (2d cir.) 1980, U.S. Dist. Ct. (so. and we. dists) Tex. 1995. Legis. atty. Am. law div. Congl. Rsch. Svc., Libr. of Congress, Washington, 1971-74; assoc. Cole & Deitz, N.Y.C., 1975-76, Milberg, Weiss, Bershad & Specthrie, N.Y.C., 1976-78; law. clk. to Judge Mary Johnson Lowe U.S. Dist. Ct. (so. dist.) N.Y., 1979-80; asst. chief div. comml. litigation Office of Corp. Counsel of City of N.Y., 1980-86; spl. master Supreme Ct. State of N.Y./N.Y. County, 1984-86; spl. counsel-enforcement U.S. Securities and Exch. Commn., N.Y.C., 1986-89; exec. dir., counselor at law Am. Inst. Law, Econs. and Comparative Studies, N.Y., 1990—; v.p. internat., house counsel Am. Sino Trade Devel. Coun., N.Y.C., 1997—. Guest speaker U. Witwatersrand Sch. Law, Johannesburg, Republic of South Africa, 1973; guest researcher Ct. Libr., Nairobi, Kenya, 1973; pro bono Internat. League Human Rights, N.Y.C., 1974-75, 8th ann. Conf. for World Peace Through Law, Abidjan, Ivory Coast, West Africa, 1973; law instr. Baruch Coll., N.Y.C. Co-author: Handbook for Drafting Jury Instructions, U.S. Dept. Justice Civil Rights Div., 1970; assoc. editor: The Constitution of the United States of America-Analysis and Interpretation, 1972; author legis. reports on Equal Credit Opportunity Act; referee Am. Bus. Law Jour., 1980-81. Bd. dirs. Chalon Coop. Bldg., Washington, 1972-73; chmn. fine arts com., mem. bd. dirs. St. Bartholomew's Community Club, St. Bartholomew's Episcopal Ch., N.Y.C., 1982-83; mem. organizing com. Annual Clio Awards China Road Show, 1999—. Hinds Webbs Fund grantee, 1967. Mem. Women's Bar Assn. City of N.Y., NYU Law Alumni Assn., Duke U. Law Alumni Assn., Fed. Bar Coun., Am. Fgn. Law Assn., Consular Law Soc., Dramatists Guild, English Speaking Union, Met. Mus. Art. Democrat. E-mail: SylviaBeckey@aol.com

BECKHAM, WALTER HULL, III, lawyer; b. Boston, Feb. 12, 1948; s. Walter Hull Jr. and Ethel Brooks (Koger) B. BA, Emory U., 1970, JD, 1977; MBA, U. Mich., 1972. Bar: Ga. 1977, U.S. Dist. Ct. (no. dist.) Ga. 1978, U.S. Dist. Ct. (so. dist.) Ga. 1980, U.S. Dist. Ct. (mid. dist.) Ga. 1988, U.S. Ct. Appeals (11th cir.) 1982. Investment analyst, portfolio mgr. Life of Ga., Atlanta, 1972-74; assoc. Jessee, Ritchie & Duncan, P.C., 1977-81, ptnr., 1981-82; pvt. practice, 1982—. Bd. dirs. Cmty. Outreach

YMCA, Atlanta, 1973—75; Brookhaven Boys Club, 1976; pres. Sr. Hon. Soc. Emory U., 1984—85, mem. Law Sch. Coun., 1993—, mem. bd. govs., 2001—. Mem.: ABA (tort and ins. practice sect., long range planning com. 1986—90, chmn. satellite seminars and videotapes com. 1990—92, chmn. pub. rels. com. 1993, com. coord. 1993, coun. 1990—93, sect. chmn. 1995—96), Ga. Bar Assn. (co-chmn. com. on professionalism 1997—2000, jud. procedure ande adminstrn. com. 2000—), Atlanta Bar Assn. (state ct. com. 1985), Internat. Acad. Trial Lawyers, Ga. Trial Lawyers Assn. (long range planning com. 1982—86), Kappa Alpha (Hardeman Province Ct. of Honor). Avocations: hunting, fishing, skiing. General civil litigation, Personal injury, Securities. Home: 1208 Village Run NE Atlanta GA 30319-5303 Office: Ste 2600 75 14th St Atlanta GA 30309

BECKMAN, MICHAEL, lawyer; b. N.Y.C., Oct. 8, 1945; s. Albert Beckman and Cecille Bronson; m. Susan Liebowitz, June 26, 1970 (separated Dec. 1987); children: Andrew D., Jason D. Bar: N.Y. 1969, U.S. Dist. Ct. (so. dist.) N.Y. 1972. Atty. Gordon Brady Keller & Ballen, N.Y.C., 1969-71; ptnr. Wolkowitz & Beckman, 1971-74; sr. ptnr. Bell Kalnick Beckman Klee & Green, 1974-88; sole practice, 1988-92; sr. ptnr. Beckman & Millman PC, 1992-96, Beckman Millman & Sanders LLP, N.Y.C., 1996—2000, Beckman, Millman, Barandes, & Douglass, LLP, N.Y.C., 2000—. Adj. prof. law NYU, 1981-93. Dir. N.Y. Jr. Tennis League, N.Y.C., 1986-95, Sports & Arts in Schs. Found. Mem. West Side Tennis Club. Avocations: tennis, skiing. General corporate, Real property, Securities. Home: 437 W 24th St New York NY 10011-1253 Office: Beckman Millman & Sanders LLP 116 John St Rm 1313 New York NY 10038-3303

BECKWITH, EDWARD JAY, lawyer; b. Paterson, N.J., July 18, 1949; s. David and Beverly Beckwith; m. Iris Kailo; children: Jessica, Jason, Jenna. BS, Pa. State U., 1971; JD, Georgetown U., 1974, ML in Taxation, 1983. Bar: D.C., U.S. Supreme Ct., U.S. Ct. Appeals (fed. cir.), U.S. Ct. Appeals (D.C. cir.), U.S. Dist. Ct. D.C., U.S. Tax Ct., U.S. Claims Ct. Staff asst. Coun. on Environ. Quality Exec. Office of Pres., Washington, 1973; assoc. Fried, Frank, Harris, Shriver & Kampelman, 1974-82, Baker & Hostetler, Washington, 1982-83, ptnr., 1984—. Adj. prof. law Georgetown U. Law Ctr., Washington, 1984—; bd. advisors Jour. Taxation Trusts and Estates, 1989-92; mem. Greater Washington Bd. Trade. Contbr. articles to profl. publs. Mem. steering com. sect. on trusts and probate law D.C. Bar, 1985-87; chmn. planned giving adv. coun. Pa. State U., 2000—. Alumni fellow honoree Pa. State U., 1998. Fellow Am. Coll. Trust and Estate Counsel (state chair, chmn. philanthropy study com. 2000—, chmn. charitable planning and exempt orgns. com. 2001—); mem. ABA, Am. Law Inst. (estate planning coun. Washington chpt.), Pa. State U. Alumni Assn., Omicron Delta Kappa. General corporate, Non-profit and tax-exempt organizations, Probate. Office: Baker & Hostetler 1050 Connecticut Ave NW Washington DC 20036-5304 E-mail: beckwith@bakerlaw.com

BECKWITH, SANDRA SHANK, judge; b. Norfolk, Va., Dec. 4, 1943; d. Charles Langdale and Loraine (Sterneberg) Shank; m. James Beckwith, Mar. 31, 1965 (div. June 1978); m. Thomas R. Ammann, Mar. 3, 1979. BA, U. Cin., 1965, JD, 1968. Bar: Ohio 1969, Ind. 1976, Fla. 1979, U.S. Dist. Ct. (so. dist.) Ohio 1971, U.S. Dist. Ct. Ind. 1976, U.S. Supreme Ct. 1977. Sole practice, Harrison, Ohio, 1969-77, 79-81; judge Hamilton County Mcpl. Ct., Cin., 1977-79, 81-86, commr., 1989-91; judge Ct. Common Pleas, Hamilton County Divsn. Domestic Rels., 1987-89; assoc. Graydon, Head and Ritchey, 1989-91; judge U.S. Dist. Ct. (so. dist.) Ohio, 1992—. Mem. Ohio Chief Justice's Code of Profl. Responsibility Commn., 1984, Ohio Gov.'s Com. on Prison Crowding, 1984-90, State Fed. Com. on Death Penalty Habeas Corpus, 1995—; pres. 6th Cir. Dist. Judges Assn., 1998-99; chair So. Dist. Ohio Automation Com., 1997—. Bd. dirs. Cin. chpt. ARC, 1996—, Tender Mercies. Mem. Fed. Judges Assn., Am. Judges Assn., Am. Judicature Soc., Fed. Bar Assn. (exec. com.), Fed. Cir. Bar Assn. Office: Potter Stewart US Courthouse Ste 810 Cincinnati OH 45202

BECRAFT, CHARLES D., JR. lawyer; b. Corning, N.Y., June 1, 1939; s. Charles D. and Mary A. (Szepansky) B. BS in Bus. Adminstrn., Syracuse U., 1961; LLB, JD, Union U., 1964. Bar: N.Y. 1967. Assoc. Flynn Law Offices, Bath, N.Y., 1967-68, Nasser Law Offices, Corning, 1968-70; prin., owner Becraft Law Offices, 1970-75, 80—; ptnr. Becraft, Knox & Kahl, 1975-80. Asst. dist. atty. County of Steuben, N.Y., 1970-73; city judge City of Corning, 1977-80. With U.S. Army, 1965-67. Mem. N.Y. Bar Assn., Steuben County Bar Assn. (pres. 1981-83), Corning City Bar Assn., Kiwanis, Lions. Republican. Methodist. Avocations: tennis, skiing, wine making. Estate planning, General practice, Real property. Office: 135 Cedar St Corning NY 14830-2634

BEDDOW, RICHARD HAROLD, judge; b. Springfield, Mass., Jan. 3, 1932; s. Richard Harold and Elizabeth Christine (Geehern) B.; m. Trudy C. Howells, Jan. 14, 1967; children: Catherine Elizabeth Almand, Elissa Christine. BS, U. Mass., 1953; LLB, Boston Coll, 1959. Bar: Mass. 1960. Atty. ICC, Washington, 1959-69, mem. rev. bd., 1969-73, adminstrv. law judge, 1973-81, NLRB, Washington, 1981—. With USN, 1953-55. Roman Catholic. Avocation: landscape gardening. Home: 2406 Rockwood Rd Accokeek MD 20607-9584 Office: NLRB 1099 14th St NW Washington DC 20570-0001

BEDNAR, RICHARD JOHN, lawyer, law educator; b. Omaha, Oct. 30, 1931; s. John Stanley and Frances Julia (Zikas) B.; m. Judith Ann Jaudon, Feb. 8, 1969; children— Linda, Elizabeth, John, Paul. LL.B., Creighton U., 1954; LL.M., George Washington U., 1969. Bar: Nebr. 1954, D.C. 1985. Commd. 2d lt. U.S. Army, 1954, advanced through grades to brig. gen., 1979; staff judge adv., Ft. Leavenworth, Kans., 1971-72; exec. to Judge Adv. Gen., Dept. Army, 1973-75, chief trial atty., 1975-76, chief litigation div., 1976-77, judge adv. U.S. Forces, Korea, 1977-79; asst. judge adv. gen. for civil law Dept. Army, 1979-81; judge adv. U.S. Army Europe, 1981-83; asst. judge adv. gen. for civil law Dept. Army, 1983-84, ret., 1984; dir. govt. contracts program George Washington U., Nat. Law Ctr., Washington, 1984— . Decorated Bronze Star, Legion of Merit with 2 oak leaf clusters, D.S.M. Mem. Assn. U.S. Army (past. pres. European dept.), ABA, Fed. Bar Assn., Nebr. Bar Assn., Nat. contract Mgmt. Assn. Republican. Episcopalian. Club: Army-Navy Country (Arlington, Va.). Home: 3805 Ft Worth Ave Alexandria VA 22304-1708 Office: Nat Law Ctr Washington DC 20052-0001

BEELER, PATRICIA, court administrator; b. Troy, N.Y., June 25, 1955; d. Andrew John and Virginia Ann (Catone) Beeler. AAS in Criminal Sci., Hudson Valley C.C., Troy; BA, Coll. St. Rose, Alabny, N.Y., MA in Comm. Arts. Lt. in charge of security Burns Security Svcs., Albany, 1973-75; chief clk. Rensselaer County Family Ct., Troy, 1975—. Bd. dirs. The Next Step, Inc., Albany, 1994—; mem. Dist. Atty.'s Task Force on Violence, Troy, 1995—; mem. City of Troy Mayor's Task Force. Mem. Family Ct. Clks. Assn. (bd. dirs., sec.), Women's Bar Assn. N.Y., Single Ski Club Albany. Avocations: running, alpine and cross-country skiing. Home: 15 Carroll Ter Albany NY 12209-1702 Office: Rensselaer County Family Ct 1504 5th Ave Troy NY 12180-4192

BEEMER, JOHN BARRY, lawyer; b. Scranton, Pa., Sept. 4, 1941; s. Ellis and Rose Mary (Costello) B.; m. Diane Montgomery Fletcher, July 18, 1964 (dec. July 1999); children: David, Bruce. BS, U. Scranton, 1963; LL.B., George Washington U., 1966. Bar: Pa. 1966, U.S. Supreme Ct. 1980; cert. civil trial adv. Nat. Bd. Trial Advocacy. Law clk. U.S. Ct. Claims, 1966-67; clk. to judge U.S. Dist. Ct. (mid. dist.) Pa., 1967-68; assoc. Warren, Hill, Henkelman & McMenamin, Scranton, 1968-72; ptnr. Beemer, Brier, Rinaldi & Fendrick, 1972-77; pres. Beemer, Rinaldi, Fendrick & Mellody, P.C., Scranton, 1977-83; ptnr. Beemer & Beemer, 1984—. Lectr. in law U. Scranton, 1969-70. Chmn. com. constn. and by-laws revision Lackawanna (county Pa.) United Fund., 1971; nat. chmn. U. Scranton Alumni Fund Drive, 1972. Mem. ABA, Pa. Bar Assn., Lackawanna Bar Assn. (bd. dirs. 1988—), Assn. Trial Lawyers Am., Pa. Trial Lawyers Assn., Phi Delta Phi. Federal civil litigation, State civil litigation, Criminal. Office: 114-116 N Abington Rd Clarks Summit PA 18411

BEER, PETER HILL, federal judge; b. New Orleans, Apr. 12, 1928; s. Mose Haas and Henret (Lowenburg) B.; children: Kimberly Beer Bailes, Kenneth, Dana Beer Long-Innes; m. Marjorie Barry, July 14, 1985. BBA, Tulane U., 1949, LLB, 1952; LLM, U. Va., 1986. Bar: La. 1952. Successively assoc., ptnr., sr. ptnr. Montgomery, Barnett, Brown & Read, New Orleans, 1955-74; judge La. Ct. Appeal, 1974-79, U.S. Dist. Ct. (ea. dist.) La., New Orleans, 1979—. Vice chmn. La. Appellate Judges Conf.; apptd. by chief justice of U.S. to state-fed. com. Jud. Conf. U.S., 1985-89; apptd. by chief justice of U.S. to Nat. Jud. Coun. State and Fed. Cts., 1993—. Mem. bd. mgrs. Touro Infirmary, New Orleans, 1969-74; mem. exec. com. Bur. Govtl. Rsch., 1965-69; chmn. profl. divsn. United Fund New Orleans, 1966-69; mem. New Orleans City Coun., 1969-74, v.p., 1972-74. Capt. USAF, 1952-55. Decorated Bronze Star. Mem. ABA (mem. ho. dels.), Am. Judicature Soc., Fed. Bar Assn., La. Bar Assn., Fed. Judges Assn. U.S. (bd. dirs. 1985, 5th cir. rep. bd. govs.), Nat. Lawyers Club, So. Yacht Club, St. John Golf Club. Jewish. Home: 133 Bellaire Dr New Orleans LA 70124-1008 also: 204 3rd Ave Pass Christian MS 39571-3214 Office: US Dist Ct US Courthouse 500 Camp St New Orleans LA 70130-3313

BEEZER, ROBERT RENAUT, federal judge; b. Seattle, July 21, 1928; s. Arnold Roswell and Josephine (May) B.; m. Hazlehurst Plant Smith, June 15, 1957; children: Robert Arnold, John Leighton, Mary Allison. Student, U. Wash., 1946-48, 51; BA, U. Va., 1951, LLB, 1956. Bar: Wash. 1956, U.S. Supreme Ct. 1968. Ptnr. Schweppe, Krug, Tausend & Beezer, P.S., Seattle, 1956-84; judge U.S. Ct. Appeals (9th cir.), 1984-96, sr. judge, 1996—. Alt. mem. Wash. Jud. Qualifications Commn., Olympia, 1981-84 1st lt. USMCR, 1951-53 Fellow Am. Coll. Trust and Estate Counsel, Am. Bar Found.; mem. ABA, Seattle-King County Bar Assn. (pres. 1975-76), Wash. Bar Assn. (bd. govs. 1980-83) Clubs: Rainier, Tennis (Seattle) E-mail: robert. Office: US Ct Appeals 802 US Courthouse 1010 5th Ave Seattle WA 98104-1195 E-mail: beezer@ca9.uscourts.gov

BEGAM, ROBERT GEORGE, lawyer; b. N.Y.C., Apr. 5, 1928; s. George and Hilda M. (Hirt) B.; m. Helen C. Clark, July 24, 1949; children— Richard, Lorinda, Michael. B.A., Yale U., 1949, LL.B., 1952. Bar: N.Y. bar 1952, Ariz. bar 1956, U.S. Dist. Ct. Ariz. 1957, U.S. Ct. Appeals (9th cir.) 1958, U.S Supreme Ct. 1973. Assoc. firm Cravath, Swaine & Moore, N.Y.C., 1952-54; spl. counsel State of Ariz., Colorado River Litigation in U.S. Supreme Ct., 1956-58; pres. Begam, Lewis Marks & Wolfe, P.A., Phoenix. Author: Fireball, 1987. Pres. Ariz. Repertory Theater, 1960—66; trustee Atla Roscoe Pound Found.; bd. dirs. Boys Clubs of Met. Phoenix; bd. govs. Welzmann Inst. Sci., Rehovot, Israel; pres. Am. Com. for Welzmann Inst. of Sci., 1996—98, chmn. fin. resource devel., 2000—; bd. dirs. Phoenix Theater Ctr., 1955—60, 1987—92, Ariz. Theatre Co., 2001—, Shakespeare-Sedona Theatre Co. Fellow: Internat. Soc. Barristers; mem.: ATLA (pres. 1976—77, chmn. polit. action com. 1979—86), Western Trial Lawyers Assn. (pres. 1970), State Bar Ariz. (cert. specialist in injury and wrongful death litication), Am. Bd. Trial Advocates (bd. dirs.), Yale Club (N.Y.C.), Desert Highlands Country (Scottsdale, Ariz.), Wig and Pen (London). Avocations: writing, theater, golf. Personal injury, Product liability. Office: Begam Lewis Marks & Wolfe 111 W Monroe St Ste 1400 Phoenix AZ 85003-1787 E-mail: begam@fastq.com

BEGG, DEREK JONATHON, lawyer; b. Melbourne, Australia, Nov. 3, 1966; s. Alan Keogh and Patricia (Rankin) B.; m. Ruzandra Lazarescu, Nov. 25, 1995. BA, U. Melbourne, 1987, LLB, 1990. Bar: Supreme Ct. of Victoria 1992, High Ct. of Australia 1992. Articled clk. Price Brent, Melbourne, 1991-92; solicitor Middletons Moore & Bevins, 1992-97, Sr. assoc., 1997—. Mem. state com. Australian Kidney Found., Victoria, 2000—. Mem. Nat. Product Liability Assn., Australian Ins. Law Assn., Australian Club, Melbourne Cricket Club. FaxL 613 9205 2055. Insurance, Product liability, Professional liability. Office: Middletons Moore & Bevins 200 Queen St Level 29 Melbourne VIC 3000 Australia E-mail: derek_begg@mmb.com.au

BEGGS, HARRY MARK, lawyer; b. Los Angeles, Nov. 15, 1941; s. John Edgar and Agnes (Kentro) B.; m. Sandra Lynne Mikal, May 25, 1963; children: Brendan, Sean, Corey, Michael. Student, Ariz. State U., 1959-61, Phoenix Coll., 1961; LLB, U. Ariz., 1964. Bar: Ariz. 1964, U.S. Dist. Ct. Ariz. 1964, U.S. Ct. Appeals (9th cir.) 1973, U.S. Ct. Appeals (fed. cir.) 1995, U.S. Supreme Ct. 1991. Assoc. Carson Messinger Elliott Laughlin & Ragan, Phoenix, 1964-69, ptnr., 1969-93; mem., mng. lawyer Carson Messinger Elliott Laughlin & Ragan, P.L.L.C., 1994—. Mem. editorial bd. Ariz. Law Rev. 1963-64; contbr. articles to profl. jours. Recipient award for highest grade on state bar exam. Atty. Gen. Ariz., 1964; Fegtly Moot Ct. award, 1963, 64; Abner S. Lipscomb scholar U. Ariz. Law Sch., 1963. Fellow Ariz. Bar Found. (founder); mem. State Bar Ariz., Ariz. Acad., Maricopa County Bar Assn. Federal civil litigation, General civil litigation, State civil litigation. Office: PO Box 33907 Phoenix AZ 85067-3907 E-mail: hbeggs@carsonlaw-az.com

BEGHE, RENATO, federal judge; b. Chgo., Mar. 12, 1933; s. Bruno and Emmavve (Frymire) B.; m. Bina House, July 10, 1954; children: Eliza Ashley, Francesca Forbes, Adam House, Jason Deneen. B.A., U. Chgo., 1951, J.D., 1954. Bar: N.Y. 1955. Practiced in, N.Y.C.; assoc. Carter, Ledyard & Milburn, 1954-65, ptnr., 1965-83, Morgan, Lewis & Bockius, 1983-89; judge U.S. Tax Ct., Washington, 1991—. Lectr. N.Y. U. Fed. Tax Inst., 1967, 78, U. Chgo. Fed. Tax Conf., 1974, 80, 86, also other profl. confs. Mng. editor U. Chgo. Law Rev., 1953-54; contbr. articles to profl. jours. Mem. ABA, Internat. Bar Assn., N.Y. State Bar Assn. (chmn. tax sect. 1977-78), Assn. of Bar of City of N.Y. (chmn. art law com. 1980-83), Am. Law Inst., Internat. Fiscal Assn., Am. Coll. Tax Counsel, America-Italy Soc. Inc. (bd. dirs. 1980-92), Phi Beta Kappa, Order of Coif, Phi Gamma Delta. Home: 633 E St SE Washington DC 20003-2716 Office: US Tax Ct 400 2nd St NW Washington DC 20217-0002

BEGLEITER, MARTIN DAVID, law educator, consultant; b. Middletown, Conn., Oct. 31, 1945; s. Walter and Anne Begleiter; m. Ronni Ann Frankel, Aug. 17, 1969; children: Wendy Cara, Hilary Ann. BA, U. Rochester, 1967; JD, Cornell U., 1970. Bar: N.Y. 1970, U.S. Dist. Ct. (ea. dist.) N.Y. 1971, U.S. Ct. Appeals (2d cir.) 1975. Assoc. Kelley Drye & Warren, N.Y.C., 1970-77; assoc. prof. Law Sch., Drake U., Des Moines, 1977-80, prof., 1980-87, 93—, Richard M. and Anita Calkins disting. prof. law, 1987-93. Contbr. articles to legal jours. Mem. ABA (com. on estate and gift taxes, taxation sect. 1980—, com. on tax legislation and regulations, lifetime transfers, real property, probate and trust law sect. 1980—, study com. law reform 1996—, chmn. task force on spl. use valuation 1988-93, advisor Nat. Conf. Commns. on Uniform State Laws 1988-93), Iowa Bar Assn. (adviser, resource person, probate, trust sect. 1983-89, 93—), Am. Law Inst. (adviser restatement 3d trusts 1994—). Jewish. Avocations: science fiction, golf. Office: Drake U Sch Law 27th & Carpenter Sts Des Moines IA 50311 E-mail: martin.begleiter@drake.edu

BEHLING, PAUL LAWRENCE, lawyer, educator; b. Washington, Feb. 15, 1948; s. John Lawrence Behling and Elizabeth (Freer) Nicholson; m. Christina Grande, Jan. 13, 1979; children: Cassandra, Catrina, Jonathan. B.S. cum laude, U. Hartford, 1970; J.D. with high honors, U. Conn., 1973; LL.M. in Taxation, NYU, 1974. Bar: Conn. 1973, U.S. Dist. Ct. Conn. 1974, U.S. Tax Ct. 1974, U.S. Ct. Appeals (2d cir.) 1974, D.C. 1980, U.S. Supreme Ct. 1980. Assoc. firm Solomon & Brown, Meriden, Conn., 1974-75; assoc. firm Copelon, Schiff & Zangri, New Haven, 1975-78, ptnr., 1978-86; ptnr. Siegel, O'Connor & Schiff, 1987-88; ptnr. Wiggin & Dana, New Haven, Conn.. 1988-95; prin. Bergman Horowitz & Reynolds PC, 1995—; adj. prof. law Quinnipiac Coll., 1982—, U. New Haven (Conn.) 1982—. Author: Taxation of Real Estate, 1984, Taxation of 401 (K) and Other Salary Reduction Plans, 1994; contbr. articles to profl. publs. Served to sgt. U.S. Army, 1965-67. Mem. ABA (chmn. sect. taxation closely held corp. 1982-85), Conn. Bar Assn. (chmn. tax sect. 1981-85). Democrat. Roman Catholic. Club: New Haven Lawn. Lodge: Kiwanis (v.p. New Haven 1978-81). General corporate, Corporate taxation, Estate taxation. Home: 1670 Hartford Tpke North Haven CT 06473-1247 Office: Bergman Horowitz & Reynolds 157 Church St Ste 19 New Haven CT 06510-2101

BEHRINGER, SAMUEL JOSEPH, JR. lawyer; b. Detroit, Oct. 6, 1948; s. Samuel Joseph and Evania Theresa (Cherry) B.; m. Linda Suzanne Gross, Sept. 7, 1979; 1 child, Kathryn Elizabeth. BS in Labor & Indsl. Rels., Mich. State U., 1970; JD, U. Detroit, 1973. Bar: Mich. 1974, U.S. Dist. Ct. (ea. dist.) Mich. 1974, U.S. Ct. Claims 1975, U.S. Tax Ct. 1975, U.S. Ct. Appeals (6th cir.) 1974, U.S. Supreme Ct. 1980. Asst. U.S. atty. Ea. Dist. Mich., Detroit, 1974-80; group v.p., gen. counsel Mich. Nat. Bank, 1980-83; atty. pvt. practice, Grosse Pointe Farms, Mich., 1983—. Chmn. young lawyers sect. 6th cir. admission ceremony State Bar Mich., 1975-83. Contbr. articles to profl. jours. Recipient Merit commendations U.S. Dept. Justice, 1977, 78, Spl. commendation Outstanding Svc. U.S. Atty. Gen., 1979. Mem. NRA, ABA, Fed. Bar Assn. (chmn. chpt. host. com. of nat. conv. Detroit 1985, mem. exec. bd. Detroit chpt. 1979-81), Detroit Bar Assn., Comml. Law League Am., Oakland County Bar Assn., Am. Corp. Counsel Assn., Assn. Trial Lawyers Am., Elks, Phi Kappa Tau, Gamma Eta Gamma. Banking, Bankruptcy, Contracts commercial. Home: 333 McKinley Ave Grosse Pointe MI 48236-3420

BEIDLER, MARSHA WOLF, lawyer; b. Bridgeton, N.J., Feb. 29, 1948; d. Benjamin and Esther (Lourie) Wolf; m. John Nathan Beidler, Aug. 18, 1974; children: Dora E., Evan A. BA, Dickinson Coll., Carlisle, Pa., 1969; JD, Rutgers U., Camden, N.J., 1972; LLM in Taxation, NYU, 1979. Bar: Pa. 1972, Fla. 1973, N.J. 1975; Fla. bar bd. cert. tax lawyer. Estate and gift tax atty. IRS, Phila., 1972-74, Trenton, N.J., 1974-76; atty. McCarthy & Hicks, Princeton, 1976-81; ptnr. Pinto & Beidler, 1981-83; prin. Smith, Lambert, Hicks & Miller, 1983-88; ptnr. Drinker, Biddle & Reath, 1988—. Sec. Mercer County Estate Planning Council, 1977-86; prof. paralegal studies Rider Coll., Trenton, 1982; lectr. estate planning various corps. and univs. Bd. dirs. Birth Alternatives, Princeton, 1980; bd. dirs. Mercer Council on Alcoholism, Trenton, 1985-86. Fellow Am. Coll. Trusts and Estate Counsel; mem. ABA (taxation sect., real property, probate and trust sect.), Fla. Bar Assn., N.J. Bar Assn. (taxation sect.). Estate planning, Probate, Personal income taxation. Office: Drinker Biddle & Reath 105 College Rd E PO Box 627 Princeton NJ 08542-0627 E-mail: beidlemw@dbr.com

BEIRNE, MARTIN DOUGLAS, lawyer; b. N.Y.C., Oct. 24, 1944; s. Martin Douglas and Catherine Anne Beirne; m. Kathleen Harrington; children: Martin, Shannon, Kelley. BS, Spring Hill Coll., 1966; JD with honors, St. Mary's U., 1969. Bar: Tex. 1969, U.S. Dist. Ct. (ea. dist.) Tex. 1972, U.S. Dist. Ct. (so. dist.) Tex. 1971, U.S. Dist. Ct. (no. dist.) Tex., U.S. Dist. Ct. (we. dist.) Tex., U.S. Ct. Appeals (5th and 11th cirs.) 1974, U.S. Dist. Ct. (ea. dist.) Calif., U.S. Supreme Ct. 1975. Ptnr. Fulbright & Jaworski, Houston, 1971-85; mng. ptnr. Beirne, Maynard & Parsons, 1985—. Editor-in-chief St. Mary's Law Rev. Bd. dirs. St. Thomas U., Houston Law Rev. Found., NCCJ. Capt. U.S. Army, 1969-71. Fellow Am. Bar Found., Tex. Bar Found.; mem. ABA, Tex. Bar Assn., Houston Bar Assn., Coronado Club, The Houstonian Club, Legatus-U. Houston Law Sch. Found. Roman Catholic. Federal civil litigation, State civil litigation, General corporate. Office: Beirne Maynard & Parsons LLP 1300 Post Oak Blvd Fl 24 Houston TX 77056-3028

BEISNER, JOHN HERBERT, lawyer; b. Salina, Kans., Feb. 24, 1953; s. Herbert J. and Matilda (Cordel) B.; m. Diane G. Klinke, Apr. 26, 1980; 1 child, Laura Ann. BA, U. Kans., 1975; JD, U. Mich, 1978. Bar: Calif. 1978, D.C. 1980. Assoc. O'Melveny & Myers, Washington, 1978-85, ptnr., 1985—, mng. ptnr. Washington office, 2000—. Mem. State Colls. Coord. Com. Kans. Bd. Regents, 1974-75. Mem. ABA, Am. Law Inst., Fed. Comm. Bar Assn. Administrative and regulatory, Federal civil litigation, Communications. Office: O'Melveny & Myers 555 13th St NW Ste 500W Washington DC 20004-1159 E-mail: jbeisner@omm.com

BEISWANGER, GARY LEE, lawyer; b. Billings, Mont., May 31, 1938; BA in Philosophy, History-Polit. Sci., U. Mont., 1960, LLB, 1963. Bar: Mont. 1963, U.S. Dist. Ct. Mont. 1963, U.S. Ct. Appeals (9th cir.) 1987. Pvt. practice, Billings, 1965—. Mem. ABA, ATLA, State Bar Mont., Mont. Trial Lawyers Assn., Yellowstone County Bar Assn. General civil litigation, General corporate, Real property. Office: Rocky Village Ctr I 1500 Poly Dr Billings MT 59102-1748 E-mail: gary1beiswanger@lawyer.com

BEIZER, LANCE KURT, lawyer; b. Hartford, Conn., Sept. 8, 1938; s. Lawrence Sidney and Victoria Merriam (Kaplan) B. BA in Sociology, Brandeis U., 1967; MA in English, San Jose State U., 1967; JD, U. San Diego, 1975. Bar: Calif. 1975. Selective svc. affairs coord. U. Calif., 1969-73, vet. affairs coord., 1973-75; vet. outreach coord. San Diego Community Coll. Dist., 1975-76; dep. dist. atty. Santa Clara County, Calif., 1976—. Bd. mgrs. Santa Clara Valley S.W. YMCA, Saratoga, Calif., 1988, chair, 1991-93; bd. dirs. The Lumen Found., San Francisco, 1985—. Bd. dirs. Fedn. Cmty. Ministries, Calif., 1992—, chair, 1996—; bd. dirs. Apistolic Cath. orthodox Ch., 1997—. Lt. USNR, 1961-65. Mem. Calif. Dist. Attys. Assn., Am. Profl. Soc. on Abuse of Children, Nat. Assn. Counsel for Children, Am. Weil Soc., Mensa, Commonwealth Club. Republican. Episcopalian. Home: 1197 Capri Dr Campbell CA 95008-6002 Office: Santa Clara County Dist Atty 70 W Hedding St San Jose CA 95110-1768 E-mail: LBeizer@yahoo.com

BEJNAR, THADDEUS PUTNAM, law librarian, lawyer; b. Carmel, Calif., Aug. 19, 1948; s. Waldemere and Katherine (Marble) B.; m. Susan Mavis Richards, Mar. 25, 1976 (div. Jan. 1986); m. Catherine Slade Baudoin, Apr. 10, 1988 (div. Apr. 1995). AB in Philosophy, U. So. Calif., 1971; JD, Georgetown U., 1978; MLIS, U. Tex., 1986. Bar: N.Mex. 1978, U.S. Dist. Ct. N.Mex. 1980, U.S. Ct. Appeals (10th cir.) 1981. Atty. Indian Pueblo Legal Svcs., Zuni, N.Mex., 1978-80; pvt. practice law Albuquerque, 1980-84; legal rsch. libr. U. N.Mex., 1984-87; law libr. Supreme Ct. Law Libr. State of N.Mex., Santa Fe, 1987—. Tchr. legal admisibility electronic records Advanced Legal Rsch. C.L.E., 1984-95; bd. dirs. Waldemere, Bejnar & Assocs., Spectra Rsch. Inst., 1995-2001. Author: Jurisdictional Guide to Jury Instructions, 1986; editor N.Mex. Jud. Conduct Handbook, 1989-93, Manual of Citation for the Ctrs. of the State of N.Mex., 1991-92, 2d edit., 1997; sr. editor N.Mex. Legal Forms, 1991-94. Chmn. N.Mex. del. White House Conf. Librs., 1991; chmn. N.Mex. Adv. Com. on Rules and Publs., 1992-96; ptnr. Legal Informatics, an internat. cons. firm, 1992—; bd. dirs. N.Mex. Libr. Found., 1997-2001. Lt. USAF, 1971-74. Mem. ALA (councilor 2000—), Am. Assn. Law Librs., N.Mex.

Libr. Assn., Spl. Libr. Assn., Adirondack Mt. Club, Order of Coif, Phi Kappa Phi, Phi Alpha Delta, Beta Phi Mu. Mem. Soc. of Friends. Avocations: philately, hiking, conservation. Home: Rt 2 Box 94 Socorro NM 87801 Office: Supreme Ct Law Libr PO Drawer L 237 Don Gaspar Ave Santa Fe NM 87501-2178 E-mail: thaddeus@trail.com

BELAY, STEPHEN JOSEPH, lawyer; b. Joliet, Ill., May 30, 1958; s. Donald L. and Miriam A. (Madden) B.; m. Trudy L. Patterson, Nov. 7, 1987; children: Jacob, Katherine. BA, U. Iowa, 1980, JD, 1983. Bar: Iowa 1983, U.S. Dist. Ct. (no. dist.) Iowa 1985. Pvt. practice, Cedar Rapids, Iowa, 1983-88; asst. county atty. State of Iowa, Burlington, 1988-89, Decorah, 1989-92, 95—; assoc. Anderson, Wilmarth & Van Der Maaten, 1993-96; ptnr. Anderson, Wilmarth, Van Der Maaten & Belay, 1997—. Chair Winneshiek County Rep. Party, Decorah, 1992-94. Mem. ABA (chair juvenile justice com. young lawyers divsn. 1992-93), Iowa State Bar Assn. (chair juvenile law com. young lawyers divsn. 1992-94), Lions (bd. dirs. 1991-93). Roman Catholic. Avocations: trout fishing, bicycling, camping. General civil litigation, Family and matrimonial. Home: 903 Pine Ridge Ct Decorah IA 52101-1135 Office: Anderson Wilmarth Van Der Maaten & Belay PO Box 450 Decorah IA 52101-0450

BELCHER, DENNIS IRL, lawyer; b. Wheeling, W.Va., Aug. 24, 1951; s. Finley Duncan Belcher and Ellen Jane (Huffman) Good; m. Vickie Marie Early, Aug. 2, 1975; children: Sarah Anne, Matthew Irl, Benjamin Scott. BA, Coll. William and Mary, 1973; JD, U. Richmond, 1976. Bar: Va. 1976, U.S. Tax Ct. 1978. Assoc. McGuire, Woods, Battle & Boothe, Richmond, Va., 1976-83, ptnr., 1983—, mem. exec. com., 1996—. Adj. prof. taxation Va. Commonwealth U., Richmond, 1985-88. Co-author: Business Tax Planning Forms for Businesses and Individuals, 1985. Chmn. Richmond chpt. Am. Heart Assn., 1984-85; trustee St. Christopher's Sch., 1993—. Fellow Am. Coll. Trust and Estate Counsel (bd. regents. 1999—); mem. ABA (real property and probate sect., sec. 1997-98, chmn. marital deduction com., vice chmn. lifetime transfers com., ho. of dels. 1998-99, vice chair probate divsn. 1999—), Va. Bar Assn. (ho. of dels. 1998-99, wills and trusts and taxations sects.), Bull and Bear Club, Country Club of Va. Presbyterian. Avocations: golf, farming. General corporate, Probate, Estate taxation. Office: McGuire Woods 1 James Ctr 901 East Cary St Richmond VA 23219 E-mail: dbelcher@mcguirewoods.com

BELDEN, H. REGINALD, JR. lawyer; b. Greensburg, Pa., Jan. 20, 1942; BA, Lafayette Coll., 1963; JD, U. Pitts., 1966. Bar: Pa. 1966. County solicitor, 1972—76; mng. ptnr. Belden, Belden, Persin & Johnston, Greensburg. Fellow: Am. Coll. Trial Lawyers, Am. Bar Found. (life)), Pa. Bar Found. (life)); mem.: ABA (ho. dels. 2000—), Am. Judicature Soc., Pa. Bar Assn. (bd. govs. 1985—88, bd. govs. 1995—97, pres. 2001—), Westmoreland County Bar Assn. (pres. 1986—87). Professional liability, General civil litigation, Business litigation. Office: Belden Belden Persin & Johnston Belden Bldg 117 N Main St Greensburg PA 15601*

BELDOCK, MYRON, lawyer; b. N.Y.C., Mar. 27, 1929; s. George J. and Irene (Goldstein) B.; m. Elizabeth G. Pease, June 28, 1953 (div. 1969); children: David, Jennifer, Hannah, Benjamin, Adam Schmalholz; m. Karen L. Dippold, June 19, 1986. BA, Hamilton Coll., 1950; LLB, Harvard U., 1958. Bar: N.Y. 1958, U.S. Dist. Ct. (ea. and so. dists.) N.Y. 1960, U.S. Ct. Appeals (2d cir.) 1960, U.S. Supreme Ct. 1973, U.S. Dist. Ct. (no. dist.) N.Y. 1983, U.S. Ct. Appeals (3d cir.) 1985, U.S. Ct. Appeals (5th cir.) 1992. Asst. U.S. Atty. U.S. Atty's Office, Eastern Dist., N.Y., 1958-60; assoc. Geist, Netter & Marx, N.Y.C., 1960-62; sole practice, 1962-64; ptnr. Beldock Levine & Hoffman LLP, 1964—. Bd. dirs., v.p. Brotherhood-In-Action, N.Y.C., 1972—; bd. dirs. Brookdale Revolving Fund., N.Y.C., 1973-76. Served with U.S. Army, 1951-54. Mem. Assn. of Bar of City of N.Y. (spl. com. penology 1974-80, com. on judiciary 2000-2003), N.Y. County Lawyers Assn., Bklyn. Bar Assn., Kings County Criminal Bar Assn., N.Y. County Criminal Bar Assn., N.Y. State Assn. Criminal Def. Lawyers, Nat. Assn. Criminal Def. Lawyers, Nat. Lawyers Guild. Civil rights, General civil litigation, Criminal.

BELKNAP, JERRY P. lawyer; b. Napoleon, Ohio, Aug. 22, 1917; s. Nathaniel J. and Mary E. (Ragan) B.; m. Maryellen Pilliod, Nov. 29, 1945; children: Nathaniel J., Raymond V., Caroline M. Belknap Russell, Mary Elizabeth Belknap Brann, Sarah A. Belknap Boonstra. AB, U. Mich., 1939, JD, 1941. Bar: Ohio 1941, Ind. 1942, U.S. Ct. Appeals (7th cir.) 1942, U.S. Supreme Ct. Ptnr. Barnes, Hickam, Pantzer & Boyd, and successor firm Barnes & Thornburg, Indpls., 1941—; chmn. Ind. Supreme Ct. com. on rules and practice, 1981-93. Mem. Indpls. Sch. Bd., 1968-72; treas. Episcopal Diocese of Indpls., 1964-71. Served with USAAF, 1942-45. Decorated Bronze Star, Air medal. Mem. Ind. State Bar Assn., ABA, Indpls. Bar Assn., Bar Assn. 7th Fed. Cir. Republican. Contbr. articles to legal jours. Federal civil litigation, State civil litigation, Public utilities. Home: 9539 Cedar Spring Dr Indianapolis IN 46260-1282 Office: 11 S Meridian St Merchants Bank Bldg Ste 1313 Indianapolis IN 46204-3506

BELL, ALBERT LEO, retired lawyer; b. Columbus, Ohio, May 22, 1930; s. Jerome E. and Elizabeth Mary Bell; m. Jean M. DiFino, Aug. 22, 1959; children: Albert, Kathleen, Paul. BA in Journalism, Ohio State U., 1956, JD, 1958. Bar: Ohio 1959. Cert. assn. exec. Ptnr. Walter & Bell, Columbus, Ohio, 1959-64; referee Franklin County Probate Ct., 1964-65; ptnr. Maguire and Bell, 1965-71; gen. counsel Ohio State Bar Assn., 1971-87, 89-97; ret. Judge Franklin County Common Pleas Ct., Columbus, 1988; adj. prof. law Capital U., Columbus, 1986-88. Contbr. articles on legal ethics to profl. jours. Chair Ohio Elections Com., 1990-92. Sgt. U.S. Army, 1948-52. Mem. ABA, Ohio State Bar Assn., Ohio Soc. Assn. Exec. (pres. 1995), Columbus Bar Assn., Nat. Orgn. Bar Counsel (pres. 1975-76), Am. Soc. Assn. Execs. (cert. assn. exec.), Am. Legion, U.S. Power Squadron, Ohio State U. Alumni Assn., Sigma Delta Chi, Phi Delta Phi. Home and Office: 1103 Bryan Dr Westerville OH 43081-1904 Fax: (614) 899-6174. E-mail: alleobell@aol.com

BELL, DERRICK ALBERT, law educator, author, lecturer; b. Pitts., Nov. 6, 1930; s. Derrick Albert and Ada Elizabeth (Childress) B.; m. Jewel Allison Hairston, June 26, 1960 (dec. Aug. 1990); m. Janet Dewart, June 28, 1992; children: Derrick Albert III, Douglass Dubois, Carter Robeson. AB, Duquesne U., 1952; LLB, U. Pitts., 1957; hon. degree in law, Toogaloo Coll., 1983, Northeastern U., 1985, Mercy Coll., 1988, Allegheny Coll., 1989, Howard U., 1995, Bates Coll., 1997, Medgar Evers Coll., 1998. Bar: D.C. 1957, Pa. 1959, N.Y. State 1966, Calif. 1969. Atty. civil rights div. Dept. Justice, Washington, 1957-59; 1st asst. counsel NAACP Legal Def. Edn. Fund, N.Y.C., 1960-66; dep. dir. Office Civil Rights, HEW, Washington, 1966-68; exec. dir. Western Ctr. on Law and Poverty, 1968-69; lectr. law Harvard U., Cambridge, Mass., 1969-71, prof. law, 1971-80, 86-92; dean U. Oreg. Law Sch., 1981-85;, 1991-93. Vis. prof. NYU Sch. Law, 1991—, scholar-in-residence, 1993-94. Author: Race, Racism and American Law, 1973, 4th edit., 2000, Constitutional Conflicts, 1992, Shades of Brown: New Perspectives on School Desegregation, 1980, And We Are Not Saved: The Elusive Quest for Racial Justice, 1987, Faces at the Bottom of the Well: The Permanence of American Racism, 1992, Confronting Authority: Reflections of an Ardent Protester, 1994. Mem. gospel choirs Psalms of Survival in an Alien Land Called Home, 1996, Constitutional Conflicts, 1997. 1st lt. USAF, 1952-54. Grantee Ford Found., 1972, 75, 91, 93, 94-96, NEH, 1980-81. Home: 444 Central Park W Apt 14B New York NY 10025-4358 Office: NYU Sch Law 40 Washington Sq S New York NY 10012-1005

BELL, JAMES L. lawyer; b. Tuscaloosa, Ala., July 8, 1947; s. Archie and Margaret B. BA in Internat. Studies, U. S.C., 1970, JD, 1973. Bar: S.C., U.S. Dist. Ct. S.C., Fla., U.S. Tax Ct., U.S. Ct. Appeals (4th, 5th and 11th cirs.), U.S. Dist. Ct. (no., so. and mid. dists.) Fla., U.S. Supreme Ct. 1980. Sr. ptnr. The Bell Law Firm, P.A., Charleston, S.C. Gen. counsel S.C. Homeowners Assn., Chopstick Theater, Inc., BIROM, Inc.; counsel S.C. Disabled Am. Vets., Tacht Cove, Lowco Concrete Pumping, Inc.; bd. dirs. Fla. Legal Svcs., Inc. Contbr. articles to profl. jours. Mem. S.C. Bar (mem. unauthorized practice of law com. 2000—, mem. access and justice com. 2000—), Phi Delta Phi (life mem.). Pension, profit-sharing, and employee benefits, Personal injury, Product liability. Office: The Bell Law Firm PA 184 E Bay St Ste 303 Charleston SC 29401-2142 Fax: 843-722-7028. E-mail: jbell@lawyer.com

BELL, JOHN ALTON, lawyer, judge; b. Greer, S.C., Dec. 1, 1958; s. Dallas Frank Sr. and Una Merle (Gay) B.; m. Vida Ivy, June 30, 1984; children: Luke, Meredith. BA, Carson-Newman Coll., 1980; JD, Memphis State U., 1982. Bar: Tenn. 1983, U.S. Dist. Ct. (we. dist.) Tenn. 1983, U.S. Army Ct. Mil. Rev. 1984, U.S. Ct. Mil. Appeals 1987, U.S. Dist. (ea. dist.) Tenn. 1988. Assoc. Litigation Support, Inc., Memphis, 1983; officer ops. and tng. U.S. Army, Ft. Knox, Ky., 1983-84, legal assistance atty., 1984-86, defense counsel, 1986-87; assoc. King & King, Greeneville, Tenn., 1987-89; ptnr. King, King & Bell, Greeneville and Newport, 1989-90, Bell & Bell P.C., Newport, 1990-98; judge Cooke County Sessions and Juvenile Ct., 1998—. Instr. bus. law Sullivan Jr. Coll., Ft. Knox, 1986-87; adj. prof. bus. law Walter State C.C., 1989-90, 97—. Columnist It's The Law, Newport Plain Talk, 1984-85, 89-98. Bd. dirs. Extended Sch. Program, Greeneville, 1988; co-vice chmn. Rep. Com. Cocke County, Tenn., 1989-95. Named Ky. Col., Gov. Ky., 1986. Mem. ABA, Fed. Bar Assn., Tenn. Bar Assn., Assn. Trial Lawyers Am., Judge Advocate Gen.'s Assn. Republican. Baptist. Avocations: sports, church activities. General practice, Military, Personal injury. Office: Cooke County Sessions Ct 111 Court Ave Newport TN 37821-3102

BELL, JOHN WILLIAM, lawyer; b. Chgo., May 3, 1946; s. John and Barbara Bell; m. Deborah Bell, Aug. 25, 1974; children: Jason, Alicia. Student, U. So. Calif., 1964-65; BA, Northwestern U., 1968; JD cum laude, Loyola U., Chgo., 1971. Bar: Ill. 1971. Assoc. Kirkland & Ellis, Chgo., 1972-75; ptnr. Johnson & Bell, Ltd. (formerly Johnson, Cusack & Bell, Ltd.), 1975—. Mem. ABA (vice chmn. products, gen. liability and consumer law com. sect. tort and ins. practice 1986-87, 88—, com. on torts and ins. practice sect.), Ill. Bar Assn., Chgo. Bar Assn. (tort liability sect., aviation com. 1982—, chmn. med.-legal rels. com. 1994-95), Internat. Assn. Ins. Def. Counsel, Ill. Def. Coun. (faculty mem. trial acad. 1994), Soc. Trial Lawyers Am., Ill. Trial Lawyers Assn., Am. Coll. Trial Lawyers, Fed. Trial Bar. General civil litigation, Insurance, Personal injury.

BELL, JONATHAN ROBERT, lawyer; b. Bklyn., Oct. 2, 1947; s. Saul A. and Hope R. (Rosenblat) B.; children: Gabriel J., Nicholas R.; m. Catherine Janow, May 5, 1989. BA, Yale U., 1969; JD, Harvard U., 1973. Bar: Mass. 1974, U.S. Tax Ct. 1977, N.Y. 1978, U.S. Dist. Ct. (so. dist.) N.Y. 1980. Assoc. Nutter, McClennen & Fish, Boston, 1973-77, Debevoise & Plimpton, N.Y.C., 1977-83, ptnr., 1984-93, Paul. Weiss, Rifkind, Wharton & Garrison, N.Y.C., 1993—. Bd. dirs. United Way, N.Y.C., 1984-95, N.Y.C. Ballet, 1995—; bd. dirs. Studio in A School, 1988, v.p., 1991-98. Fellow Am. Coll. Trust and Estate Counsel; mem. N.Y. State Bar Assn. (trusts and estates law sect.), Assn. Bar City N.Y. (chair trusts, estates and surrogate cts. com. 1995-98). Estate planning, Probate, Estate taxation. Home: 99 Jane St New York NY 10014-7221 Office: Paul Weiss Rifkind Wharton & Garrison Rm 202 1285 Avenue Of The Americas Fl 21 New York NY 10019-6028 E-mail: jbell@paulweiss.com

BELL, MILDRED BAILEY, law educator, lawyer; b. Sanford, Fla., June 28, 1928; d. William F. and Frances E. (Williford) Bailey; m. j. Thomas Bell, Jr., Sept. 18, 1948 (div.); children: Tom, Elizabeth, Ansley. AB, U. Ga., 1950, JD cum laude, 1969; LLM in Taxation, N.Y. U., 1977. Bar: Ga. 1969. Law clk. U.S. Dist. Ct. No. Dist. Ga., 1969-70; prof. law Mercer U., Macon, Ga., 1970-94, prof. emeritus, 1994—. Mem. Ga. Com. Constl. Revision, 1978-79. Bd. editors Ga. State Bar Jour., 1974-76; contbr. articles to profl. jours., chpts. in books. Mem. ABA, Ga. Bar Assn., Phi Beta Kappa, Phi Kappa Phi,. Republican. Episcopalian. Address: 6 Sea Eagle Ct Amelia Island FL 32034-4949

BELL, ROBERT BROOKS, lawyer; b. Norman, Okla., Aug. 31, 1953; m. Susan F. Krause, Apr. 15, 1989. BA, Dartmouth Coll., 1975; MA, Cambridge U., 1977; JD, Stanford U., 1980. Bar: U.S. Dist. Ct. D.C. 1981, U.S. Ct. Appeals (D.C. cir.) 1981, U.S. Dist. Ct. Md. 1985; N.Y. 1987. Law clk. to judge U.S. Dist. Ct. D.C., 1980-81; law clk. to Justice Byron White U.S. Supreme Ct., Washington, 1981-82; assoc. Sullivan & Cromwell, 1982-88; of counsel Gibson, Dunn & Crutcher, 1988-90; ptnr. Wiley, Rein & Fielding, 1990-99, Wilmer, Cutler & Pickering, Washington, 1999—. Contbr. articles to profl. jours. Deacon Georgetown Presbyn. Ch., 1983-85, trustee, 1987-88, pres. bd. trustees, 1989, elder, 1991—; trustee Nat. Capital Chpt. Trout Unltd., Washington, 1984-86. Mem. ABA (litigation, antitrust sects.), Order of the Coif, Phi Beta Kappa. Democrat. Antitrust, Federal civil litigation. Office: Wilmer Cutler & Pickering 2445 M St NW Washington DC 20037 E-mail: rbell@wilmer.com

BELL, ROBERT HOLMES, county judge; b. Lansing, Mich., Apr. 19, 1944; s. Preston C. and Eileen (Holmes) B.; m. Helen Mortensen, June 28, 1968; children: Robert Holmes Jr., Ruth Eileen, Jonathan Neil. BA, Wheaton Coll., 1966; JD, Wayne State U., 1969. Bar: Mich. 1970, U.S. Dist. Ct. (we. dist.) Mich. 1970. Asst. prosecutor Ingham County Prosecutor's Office, Lansing, Mich., 1969-72; state dist. judge Mich. State Cts., 1973-78, state cir. judge, 1979-87; judge U.S. Dist. Ct. Mich., Grand Rapids, Mich., 1987-2001, chief judge, 2001—. Office: US Dist Ct 402 Fed Bldg 110 Michigan St NW Grand Rapids MI 49503-2363 E-mail: kim@miwd.uscourts.gov

BELL, ROBERT M. state supreme court justice; b. Rocky Mount, N.C., July 6, 1943; AB with honors, Morgan State Coll., 1966; JD, Harvard U., 1969. Bar: Md. 1969. Judge Md. Dist. Ct. Dist. 1, Balt., 1975-79; former judge Cir. Ct. Md. 8th Jud. Cir.; assoc. judge Md. Ct. Spl. Appeals, 1980-91, Md. Ct. Appeals, Balt., 1991-96, chief judge, 1996—. Mem. ABA, Nat. Bar Assn., Md. State Bar Assn., Inc., Bar Assn. Balt. City, Monumental City Bar Assn. Office: Court of Appeals 634 Courthouse East 111 N Calvert St Baltimore MD 21202-1904 also: Court of Appeals 361 Rowe Blvd Annapolis MD 21401-1672*

BELL, ROBERT MORRALL, lawyer; b. Graniteville, S.C., Feb. 15, 1936; s. Jonathan F. and Ruby Lee (Carpenter) B.; m. Cecelia Richardson Coker, June 11, 1965 (dec.). AB, U. S.C., 1958, LLB, 1965. Bar: S.C. 1965, U.S. Dist. Ct. S.C. 1965, U.S. Ct. Appeals (4th cir.) 1970. With Watkins, Vandiver, Kirven & Long, Anderson, S.C., 1965-67; sr. law clk. to chief judge U.S. Dist. Ct. S.C., Greenville, 1967-69; mem. Abram, Bowen & Townes, 1969-71, Bell, Surasky and Brown, P.A., Langley, S.C., 1971-76, sr. ptnr., 1976—. County atty. Aiken County (S.C.), 1982—. Mem. S.C. Hwy Commn., 1982-86; state exec. committeeman S.C. Dem. Com., 1980-86; mem. S.C. Bd. Chiropractic Examiners, 1978-80; mem. Svc. Coun. of Aiken County, 1976-82, Aiken County Planning Commn., 1976-80; chmn. Aiken County Transp. Com., 1993-96; bd. dirs. Aiken County Crippled Children's Soc., 1976-82; bd. dirs. Gregg-Graniteville Found., 1984—, chmn., 1998—; del. gen. and jurisdictional confs. United Meth. Ch., 1988-92; mem. S.C. Midlands Citizens Com. on Jud. Qualifications, 1996—. Served with USAR, 1959-60. Named to Order Ky. Cols., 1989—. Mem. ABA, ATLA, Aiken County Bar Assn., S.C. Bar Assn., S.C. Trial Lawyers Assn., Masons, Shriners, Kappa Sigma Kappa, Tau Kappa Alpha, Phi Delta Phi, Chi Psi. Democrat. Personal injury, Workers' compensation. Office: Bell Surasky and Brown PA PO Box 2625 Jefferson Davis Hwy Langley SC 29834 E-mail: psichi7@cs.com, bellbsb1890@cs.com

BELL, SAMUEL H. federal judge, educator; b. Rochester, N.Y., Dec. 31, 1925; s. Samuel H. and Marie C. (Williams) B.; m. Joyce Elaine Shaw, 1948 (dec.): children: Henry W., Steven D.; m. Jennie Lee McCall, 1983 BA, Coll. Wooster, 1947; JD, U. Akron, 1952. Pvt. practice, Cuyahoga Falls, Ohio, 1956-68; asst. pros. atty. Summit County, 1956-58; judge Cuyahoga Falls Mcpl. Ct., 1968-73, Ct. of Common Pleas, Akron, 1973-77, Ohio Ct. Appeals, 9th Jud. Dist., Akron, 1977-82, U.S. Dist. Ct. (no. dist.) Ohio, Akron, 1982-2000, sr. status, 1996; sr. judge. Adj. prof. Coll. Wooster, 1987—; adj. prof., adv. bd. U. Akron Sch. Law, past trustee Dean's club; bd. dirs. Jos. R. Miller Found. Co-author: Federal Practice Guide 6th Cir., 1996. Recipient Disting. Alumni award U. Akron, 1988, St. Thomas More award, 1987. Fellow Akron Bar Found. (trustee 1989-94, pres. 1993-94); mem. Fed. Bar Assn., Akron Bar Assn., Akron U. Sch. Law Alumni Assn. (Disting. Alumni award 1983), Charles F. Scanlon Akron Inn Ct. (pres. 1990-92), Akron City Club, Masons, Phi Alpha Delta. Republican. Presbyterian. Office: US Dist Ct 526 Fed Bldg & US Courthouse 2 S Main St Akron OH 44308-1813

BELL, STEPHEN ROBERT, lawyer; b. Menominee, Mich., July 10, 1942; s. John Martin and Catherine Irene (Goodman) B.; m. Linden Tucker, May 22, 1976. AB, Georgetown U., 1964; JD, U. Wis., 1967. Bar: D.C. 1971, Minn. 1967, Wis. 1967, U.S. Ct. Appeals (4th and 5th cirs.), U.S. Supreme Ct. Assoc. Dorsey & Whitney, Mpls., 1967-68; ptnr. Wilkinson, Cragun & Barker, Washington, 1971-82, Squire, Sanders & Dempsey, Washington, 1982-96, Willkie, Farr & Gallagher, Washington, 1996—. Contbr. article to profl. jours. Lt. USNR, 1968-71. Mem. ABA, D.C. Bar Assn., Fed. Communications Bar Assn., Computer Law Assn. (bd. dirs. 1987-93), Order of Coif. Administrative and regulatory, Communications, Computer. Office: Wilkie Farr & Gallagher Three Lafayette Ctr 1155 21st St NW Ste 600 Washington DC 20036-3384 E-mail: sbell@willkie.com

BELL, STEVEN DENNIS, lawyer; b. Akron, Ohio, Feb. 11, 1953; s. Sam H. and Joyce E. (Shaw) B.; m. E. Jane White (div. Feb. 1995); children: Colleen, Patrick. BA, U. Notre Dame, 1975; JD, U. Akron, 1978. Bar: Ohio 1979, D.C. 1989, U.S. Dist. Ct. (no. dist.) Ohio 1980, U.S. Ct. Appeals (6th cir.) 1980, U.S. Ct. Appeals (D.C. cir.) 1987, U.S. Supreme Ct. 1989, U.S. Dist. Ct. (so. dist.) Ohio 1990, U.S. Dist. Ct. (ea. dist.) Mich. 1996. Pvt. practice, Akron, 1979-81; chief trial atty. City of Akron, 1981-84; asst. U.S. atty. no. dist. Ohio U.S. Atty.'s Office, Cleve., 1984-88, chief civil divsn., 1986-88, chief appellate litigation, 1987; ptnr. Janik & Bell, 1988-91, Ulmer & Berne LLP, Cleve., 1991—. Mem. ABA, Ohio State Bar Assn., Nat. Health Lawyers Assn. Federal civil litigation, Criminal, Environmental. Office: Bond Ct Bldg 1300 E 9th St Lbby 9 Cleveland OH 44114-1503

BELL, WAYNE S. lawyer, state agency official; b. L.A., June 24, 1954; s. Joseph and Jane Barbara (Barsook) B.; m. M. Susan Modzelewski, Apr. 1, 1989; 1 child, Seth Joseph Bell. BA magna cum laude, UCLA, 1976; JD, Loyola U., L.A., 1979; Advanced Mgmt. Program, Rutgers U., 1992. Bar: Calif. 1980, U.S. Dist. Ct. (cen. dist.) 1981, U.S. Tax Ct. 1981, U.S. Ct. Appeals (9th cir.) 1981, U.S. Dist. Ct. (so. and no. dists.) Calif. 1983, U.S. Supreme Ct. 1984, D.C. 1986, Tex. 1995; lic. real estate broker, Calif. Intern office of gov. State of Calif., Sacramento, summer 1976; assoc. Levinson, Rowen, Miller, Jacobs & Kabrins, L.A., 1980-82; sr. assoc. Montgomery, Gascou, Gemmill & Thornton, 1982-84; counsel, project developer Thomas Safran & Assocs., 1984-85; of counsel Greenspan, Glasser & Medina, Santa Monica, Calif., 1984-86; assoc. gen. counsel Am. Diversified Cos., Costa Mesa, 1985-88; legal cons. Project Atty., L.A., 1988-89; sr. counsel, asst. sec. Ralphs Grocery Co., 1989-99, v.p., sr. counsel, asst. sec., 1999; dep. sec., gen. counsel Calif. Bus., Transp. and Housing Agy., Sacramento, 1999—, spl. counsel to Gov.'s Legal Affairs Sec., 1999—. Judge pro tem Mcpl. Ct. South Bay Jud. Dist., 1987, L.A. Superior Ct., 1991, 94, 97; settlement officer L.A. Mcpl. Ct., Settlement Officer Program, 1990-92; spl. master State Bar Calif., 1991-92. Chief note and comment editor Loyola U. Law Rev., 1978-79; contbr. articles to profl. jours. and gen. pubs. Vol. atty. Westside Legal Svcs., Santa Monica, 1982-87; legal ombudsman Olympics Ombudsman Program L.A. County Bar Assn., 1984; gov. apptd. mem. Calif. adv. coun. Legal Svcs. Corp., 1982-88, Autism Soc. Am., Amnesty Internat.; contbg. mem. Dem. Nat. Com.; mem. leadership coun. So. Poverty Law Ctr.; charter mem. presdl. task force Ams. for Change; bd. dirs. Am. Theatre Arts, Hollywood, Calif., 1983-84; pres., exec. com., bd. dirs. Programs for the Developmentally Handicapped, Inc., L.A., 1987-92; chmn. bd. appeals handicapped accommodations City of Manhattan Beach, 1986-88; bd. dirs. The Foodbank of So. Calif., 1991-94, sec., 1993; legal oversight com. Legal Corps L.A., 1995-97; sec. bd. trustees The Ralphs/Food 4 Less Found., 1995-99; vol. L.A. County Bar Assn., Barristers Homeless Shelter Advocacy Project, 1996-99, exec. com. labor and employment law sect., 1997-99; mem. coordinating com. Lake Tahoe Interagy Coun., 2001—. Mem. Calif. Bar Assn. (legal svcs. sect. standing com. legal problems of aging 1983-86, chmn. legis. subcom. 1984-86, conf. dels. alternate 1987), D.C. Bar Assn. (real estate sect. com. on comml. real estate), Legal Assistance Assn. Calif. (bd. dirs., mem. exec. com., legis. strategy com. 1984-86), Loyola Law Sch. (advocate), Sacramento County Bar Assn. (pub. and adminstrv. law sects.). Democrat. Avocations: sailing, hiking, human behavior study, photography, travel. State civil litigation, Government contracts and claims, Labor. Office: Calif Bus Transp and Housing Agy 980 9th St Ste 2450 Sacramento CA 95814-2742

BELL, WILLIAM WOODWARD, lawyer; b. May 15, 1938; s. Charles Smith and Janie Mae (Woodward) B.; m. Mary Elizabeth Beniteau, May 31, 1969; children: Susan Elizabeth, Carol Ann. BBA, Baylor U., 1960, JD, 1965. Bar: U.S. Dist. Ct. (we. dist.) Tex. 1967, U.S. Supreme Ct. 1971. Ptnr. Sleeper, Boynton, Burleson, Williams & Johnson, Waco, Tex., 1965-68, Holloway, Slagle & Bell, Brownwood, 1968-71, Johnson, Slagle & Bell, Brownwood, 1971-74; pvt. practice, 1974—. Capt. USMC, 1960-63. Named Vol., 1991, Developer of Yr., Tex. Indsl. Devel. Coun. Fellow Tex. Bar Found.; mem. ATLA, ABA, Tex. Bar Assn., Brown County Bar Assn., Am. Judicature Soc., Phi Alpha Delta. Baptist. State civil litigation, General practice. Home: PO Box 1564 Brownwood TX 76804-1564 Office: PO Box 1726 115 S Broadway Brownwood TX 76804-1726

BELLER, HERBERT N. lawyer; b. Ill., 1943; BSBA, Northwestern U., 1964, JD cum laude, 1967. Bar: Ill. 1967, D.C. 1969; CPA, Ill. Law clk. to Hon. Theodore Tannenwald, Jr. U.S. Tax Ct., 1967-68; ptnr. Sutherland, Asbill & Brennan, Washington. Adj. prof. law Georgetown U., Washington, 1972-81. Editor-in-chief: The Tax Lawyer, 1993-96. Mem. ABA (mem. sect. taxation, vice chair 1993-96, mem. coun. 1989-92, liaison to AICPA tax div. 1998-2000, chmn. govt. submissions com. 1988-89, chmn. closely held corps. com. 1981-83), Am. Coll. Tax Counsel (regent), D.C. Bar Assn., Ill. State Bar Assn., Nat. Conf. Lawyers and CPAs. Office: Sutherland Asbill & Brennan LLP 1275 Pennysylvania Ave NW Washington DC 20004

BELLEVILLE, PHILIP FREDERICK, lawyer; b. Flint, Mich., Apr. 24, 1934; s. Frederick Charles and Sarah (Adelaine) B.; m. Geraldean Bickford, Sept. 2, 1953; children— Stacy L., Philip Frederick II, Jeffrey A. BA in Econs. with high distinction and honors, U. Mich., 1956, J.D., 1960, MS in Psychology CCU, 1997. Bar: Calif. 1961. Assoc. Latham &

Watkins, LA., 1960-68, ptnr. L.A. and Newport Beach, Calif., 1968-98, chmn. litigation dept., 1973-80, ptnr. L.A., Newport Beach, San Diego, Washington, 1980-98, Chgo., 1983-98, N.Y.C., 1985-98, London and San Francisco, 1990-98, Moscow, 1992-98, Hong Kong, 1995-98, Tokyo, 1995-98, Singapore, 1997-98, Silicon Valley, 1997-98. Asst. editor Mich. Law Rev., Ann Arbor, 1959-60 Past mem. So. Calif. steering com. NAACP Legal Def. Fund, Inc., L.A.; mem. cmty. adv. bd. San Pedro Peninsula Hosp., Calif., 1980-88; mem. Harbor Interfaith Bd. James B. Angell scholar U. Mich., 1955-56 Mem. ABA (antitrust and trade regulation and bus. law sects.), L.A. County Bar Assn. (bus. trial lawyers sect.), Assn. Bus. Trial Lawyers, Order of Coif, Portuguese Bend (Calif.) Club, Palos Verdes (Calif.) Golf Club, Caballeros, Phi Beta Kappa, Phi Kappa Phi, Alpha Kappa Psi. Republican. Avocations: antique and classic autos, public service, sports, art, antiques. Antitrust, Federal civil litigation, State civil litigation. Office: Latham & Watkins 633 W 5th St Ste 4000 Los Angeles CA 90071-2005

BELLINGER, EDGAR THOMSON, lawyer; b. N.Y.C., Sept. 23, 1929; s. John and Margaret (Thomson) B.; children from previous marriage: Edgar Jr., Robert, Margaret; m. Ann Clark, Feb. 25, 1989. BA, Haverford Coll., 1951; JD with honors, George Washington U., 1955. Bar: D.C. 1955, Md. 1955. Law clk. to chief judge U.S. Dist. Ct. D.C., 1955-57; asst. U.S. aty for Washington, 1957-59; ptnr. Pope, Ballard & Loos, Washington, 1959-81, Zuckert, Scoutt and Rasenberger, Washington, 1981-94, Bellinger & Assocs., Washington and Md., 1995—. Chmn. unauthorized practice com. D.C. Ct. Appeals, 1972-78; mem. D.C. jud. conf., 1972-90; bd. mgrs. Chevy Chase Village, 1983-86. Mem. ABA (mem. fidelity and surety com., mem. forum on constrn. industry, past chmn. bonds, liens and ins. divsn.), Am. Arbitration Assn. (panel of arbitrators), D.C. Bar Assn. (D.C. Ct. Appeals orgn. com. 1972), Md. Bar Assn., Talbot County Bar Assn., Nat. Assn. Securities Dealers (panel of arbitrators), Met. Club, Chevy Chase Club (bd. govs. 1972-77, pres. 1976-77). State civil litigation, Insurance, Probate. Home: 27497 West Point Rd Easton MD 21601-8439 Office: 888 17th St NW Washington DC 20006-3939 also: PO Box 739 Easton MD 21601-8914

BELLIS, DAWN MICHELE, lawyer, mediator; b. Lexington, Ky., June 23, 1968; d. Eddie Kay and Bernadette Grigsby B. BA in Architectural Design, Clemson (S.C.) U., 1990; JD, U. Ky., 1997. Bar: Ky. 1998, S.C. 1998; cert. mediator. Mediator Mediation Ctr. of Ky., Inc., Lexington, 1997—; atty. Peter Perlman Law Office, 1998—2001, Elam & Miller PSC, Lexington, 2001—. Small claims ct. mediator Small Claims Ct., Lexington, 1998—. Recipient C.A.L.I. award U. Ky. Capital Punishment Sem., 1996. Mem. ABA, Am. Trial Lawyers Assn., Ky. Acad. of Trial Attys., S.C. Trial Lawyers Assn., Trial Lawyers for Pub. Justice. Office: PO Box 21761 Lexington KY 40522

BELLISARIO, DOMENIC ANTHONY, lawyer; b. Pitts., May 14, 1953; s. Domenic and Mary (Murgia) B. BA, U. Pitts., 1975, JD, 1978. Bar: Pa. 1978, U.S. Dist. Ct. (we. dist.) Pa. 1978, U.S. Ct. Appeals (3d cir.) 1985, U.S. Dist. Ct. (no. dist.) Ohio 1999. Trial atty. Nat. Labor Rels. Bd., Pitts., 1978-83; human resource counsel Western Res. Care Sys., Youngstown, Ohio, 1986-89; ptnr. Bellisario & Pontier, Pitts., 1984-90; pvt. practice, 1991—. Author: Preventing and Defending Sexual Harassment Claims in Pennsylvania, 1996, Basic Wage and Hour Law in Pennsylvania, 1997. Mem. coun. Nat. Italian Am. Found., Washington, 1991. Mem. ABA, Nat. Italian Am. Found., Pa. Bar Assn., Allegheny County Bar Assn., Pa. Trial Lawyers Assn., Italian Cultural Heritage Soc. West Pa. Avocations: travel, skiing. Labor, Personal injury. Office: 1000 Law & Finance Bldg Pittsburgh PA 15219 E-mail: domenic@bellisario.com

BELLIZZI, JOHN J. law enforcement association administrator, educator, pharmacist; b. N.Y.C., July 26, 1919; s. Francis X. and Carmela (Bruno) B.; m. Celeste Morga, Sept. 1, 1942; children: John J. Jr., Robert F. PhG, St. John's U., N.Y.C., 1939; LLB, Albany Law Sch., 1960; JD, Union U., 1968; LLD, St. John's U., 1981. Pharmacist St. Luke's Hosp., N.Y.C., 1939-44; police officer N.Y.C. Police Dept., 1944-53; narcotics agt. N.Y. Bur. Narcotics Enforcement, N.Y.C., 1953-59, dir. Albany, 1959-81; exec. dir. N.Y. State Drug Abuse Commn., 1981-84, Internat. Narcotics Enforcement Assn., Albany, 1984—. Prof. pharmacy law St. John's U., N.Y.C., 1962-76; lectr. in field. Contbr. articles to profl. jours. Recipient Papal medal Vatican, 1965. Mem. Internat. Narcotics Enforcement Officers Assn. (pres. 1960-62, Anslinger medal 1979, chmn. law enforcement com. Paramount Pictures, 1972-75, Svc. award 1975), Ft. Orange Club, Albany Country Club, Univ. Club (Albany), Am. Friends of Law Enforcement Found. (bd. dirs., sec. Japanese), Phi Alpha Delta, Phi Sigma Chi (pres. 1939), Sigma Chi (fellow). Office: Internat Narcotics Enforcement Officers Assn 112 State St Albany NY 12207-2005

BELLOCCHI, LUKE PETER, lawyer; b. Oct. 4, 1969; s. Nat Hans and Lilan B. BA, U. Rochester, 1991; JD, SUNY, Buffalo, 1995; LLM, Georgetown U. Law Sch., 1996. Bar: Md., D.C., N.J. Staff Baker & McKenzie, Taipei, Taiwan, 1991-92; intern World Bank, Washington, 1993, cons., 1994; law clk. Preston Gates Ellis & Meeds, 1995-96; assoc. Wasserman Mancini & Chang, 1996; atty. advisor U.S. Dept. State, 1996—. Mem. Am. Soc. Internat. Law (exec. sec. 1998-99), Georgetown Club. Home: 5618 Lamar Rd Bethesda MD 20816-1350 Office: US State Dept 2201 C St NW Washington DC 20520-0001

BELLOWS, LAUREL GORDON, lawyer; b. Chgo., Apr. 9, 1948; d. Michael M. Gordon and Lois (Loren) Gross; m. Joel J. Bellows, June 9, 1978. BA, U. Pa., 1969; JD, Loyola U., Chgo., 1974. Bar: Ill. 1974, Fla. 1975, U.S. Dist. Ct. (no. dist.) Ill. 1975, U.S. Dist. Ct. (no. dist.) Ga. 1980, Calif. 1981, U.S. Dist. Ct. (cen. dist.) Calif. 1980. Ptnr. Bellows and Bellows, Chgo., 1975—. Editor Loyola U. Law Rev., 1973-74; co-author: Trial Techniques in Business and Commercial Cases, 1988-2000. Past pres. women's bd. Traveller's Aid Soc., Chgo.; past chmn. Chgo. Network, 1992—; mentor Woman of Destiny program, 1990-91. Mem. ABA (bd. govs. 2001—, sec.-treas. 1991-92, past chmn. commn. on women 1993-95, mem. fed. jud. com. 1999—), Ill. Bar Assn., Chgo. Bar Assn. (bd. mgrs. 1983-85, sec. 1987-89, pres. 1991-92), Women's Bar Assn. Ill., Women's Bar Assn. Ill. Found. (bd. dirs. 1988—), Am. Arbitration Assn. (arbitrator 1976—, award 1990). Club: The Arts. Federal civil litigation, State civil litigation, Securities. Office: Bellows and Bellows 79 W Monroe St Ste 800 Chicago IL 60603-4906 E-mail: lbellows@bellowspc.com

BELOFF, MICHAEL JACOB, barrister; b. Adlington, Eng., Apr. 18, 1942; s. Max and Helen (Dobrin) B.; m. Judith Mary Arkinstall, Dec. 6, 1969; children:Rupert, Natasha. BA in History 1st Class, U. Oxford, 1963, BA in Jurisprudence, 1965, MA, 1967. Bar: Eng. 1967, Queen's Counsel 1981. Recorder Crown Ct., Eng., 1984-96; dep. high ct. judge Queen's Bench Divsn., Eng., 1988-98; judge Ct. Appeals Jersey and Guernsey, Eng., 1996—; pres. Trinity Coll., Oxford, Eng., 1996—; named Master of Bench Gray's Inn, 1988. Mem. Ct. Arbitration for Sport, 1996—; dept. chmn. Data Protection Tribunal, Nat. Security, 2000—; vis. prof. Tulane Law Sch., 2001. Author: The Sex Discrimination Act, 1976, Halsbury's Law, 15th edit., 1999, Sports Law, 1999; editor: Judicial Review, 1992—; assoc. editor: Dictionary of National Biography; editor: Internat. Sports Law Review, 1999—; contbr. articles to profl. jours. Fellow Inst. Advanced Legal Studies (hon.), Royal Soc. Arts; mem. Reform Club (with polit. com. 1963—), Royal Automobile Club (steward 1999—). Avocations: watching athletics, French films, dining in interesting company.

BELSER, HOWARD MCGRIFF, JR. lawyer; b. Decatur, Ala., June 19, 1947; s. Howard McGriff and Geneva (Beard) B.; m. Suzanne F. Belser, Aug. 15, 1969; children: Howard M. III, Crawford Patterson. BA, Athens Coll., 1970; JD, Sanford U., 1973. Bar: Ala. 1983. Law clk. to Justice James W. Bloodworth Supreme Ct. Ala., Montgomery, 1973-74; atty. Hutson, Elrod, and Belser, Decatur, 1974-79, Hardwick, Knight & Belser, Decatur, 1979-81; pvt. practice, 1981—. Mem. Ala. State Bar Assn., Morgan County Bar Assn. Democrat. Methodist. Avocations: golf, duck hunting. Office: PO Box 2126 Decatur AL 35602-2126

BELSKY, MARTIN HENRY, law educator, lawyer; b. May 29, 1944; s. Abraham and Fannie (Turnoff) Belsky; m. Kathleen Waits, Mar. 09, 1985; children: Allen Frederick, Marcia Elizabeth. BA cum laude, Temple U., 1965; JD cum laude, Columbia U., 1968; cert. of study, Hague Acad. Internat. Law, The Netherlands, 1968; diploma in Criminology, Cambridge U., England, 1969. Bar: Pa. 1969, Fla. 1983, N.Y. 1987, U.S. Dist. Ct. (ea. dist.) Pa. 1969, U.S. Ct. Appeals (3d cir.) 1970, U.S. Supreme Ct. 1973. Chief asst. dist. atty. Phila. Dist. Atty.'s Office, Pa., 1969—74; assoc. Blank, Rome, Klaus & Comisky, Phila., 1975; chief counsel U.S. Ho. of Reps., Washington, 1975—78; asst. adminstr. NOAA, 1979—82; dir. ctr. for govtl. responsibility, assoc. prof. law U. Fla. Holand Law Ctr., 1982—86; dean Albany Law Sch., 1986—91, dean emeritus, prof. law, 1991—95; dean U. Tulsa Coll. of Law, Okla., 1995—. Chmn. Select Commn. on Disabilities, NY, Spl. Commn. on Fire Svcs.; bd. advs. Ctr. Oceans Law and Policy; mem. corrections task force Pa. Gov.'s Justice Commn., 1971—75; adv. task force on cts. Nat. Adv. Commn. on Criminal Justice Standards and Goals, 1972—74; mem. com. on proposed standard jury instrns. Pa. Supreme Ct., 1974—81; lectr. in law Temple U., 1971—75; mem. faculty Pa. Coll. Judiciary, 1975—77; adj. prof. law Georgetown U., 1977—81. Author (with Steven H. Goldblatt): (nonfiction) Analysis and Commentary to the Pennsylvania Crimes Codes, 1973; author: Handbook for Trial Judges, 1976, Oceans and Capital Law and Policy, 1994;contbr. articles to legal pubs.; editor (in chief): (jour.) Jour. Transnat. Law, Columbia Law Sch., 1968; mem. bd. adv.: jour. Territorial Sea Jour. Chmn. Phila. coun. Anti-Defamation League, 1975; chmn. N.Y. region, mem. D.C. bd. Anti-Defamation League, 1977—78, chmn. N.Y. region, mem. nat. leadership coun.; exec. v.p. Urban League Northeastern N.Y.; bd. dir. Coun. on Aging & Disability. Fellow Intenat., Columbia U. Law Sch.; scholar Stone. Mem.: ABA (del. young lawyers sect. exec. bd. 1973—75), N.Y. State Bar Assn., Albany County Bar Assn., Fla. Bar Assn., Am. Judicature Soc., Am. Soc. Internat. Law, Am. Arbitration Assn. (referee N.Y. State Commn. on Jud. Discipline), Fund for Modern Cts. (bd. dirs.), Am. Law Inst., Nat. Dist. Attys. Assn., Fed. Bar Assn., Phila. Bar Assn. (chmn. young lawyers sect. 1974—75), Pa. Bar Assn. (exec. com. young lawyers sect. 1973—75), Temple U. Liberal Arts Alumni Assn. (v.p. 1971—75), Hudson-Mohawk Assn. Coll. and Univs. (v.p.), Sword Soc., B'nai B'rith (v.p. lodge 1973—75), Cardoto Soc., United Jewish Fedn. Northeastern N.Y. (v.p., pres. elect). Office: U Tulsa Coll Law 3120 E 4th Pl Tulsa OK 74104-2418

BELSON, JAMES ANTHONY, judge; b. Milw., Sept. 23, 1931; s. Walter W. and Margaret (Taugher) B.; m. Rosemary P. Greenslade, Jan. 11, 1958; children: Anthony James, Marie Taylor, Elizabeth Ann, Stephen Griffin. AB cum laude, Georgetown U., 1953, JD, 1956, LLM, 1962. Bar: D.C. 1956, Md. 1962. Law clk. U.S. Ct. Appeals (D.C. cir.), 1956-57; assoc. Hogan & Hartson, Washington, 1960-67, ptnr., 1967-68; trial judge D.C. Superior Ct., 1968-81, presiding judge civil divsn., 1978-81; assoc. judge D.C. Ct. Appeals, Washington, 1981-91, sr. judge, 1991—. Faculty Nat. Jud. Coll., 1973-80; bd. dirs. Coun. for Ct. Excellence, 1981—; bencher Am. Inn of Ct. VI, 1983-90. Bd. editors Georgetown Law Jour., 1955-56. Bd. dirs. Project SHARE D.C., Inc., 1992—, chmn., 1997-99; bd. dirs. Cath. Legal Immigration Network, 1994-98. With JAGC, U.S. Army, 1957-60. Mem. ABA, Bar Assn. of D.C. (bd. dirs. 1966-67, chmn. jr. bar 1965-66), Am. Judicature Soc. (bd. dirs. 1980-85), Am. Bar Found., John Carroll Soc. (bd. govs. 1978-85, 1st v.p. 1989-91), Sovereign Mil. Order of Malta Fed. Assn. (pres. 1991-94, bd. dirs. 1988-95, 97—, chmn. task force on Cuba 1994-2000). Home: 12 W Severn Ridge Rd Annapolis MD 21401-5844 Office: DC Ct Appeals 500 Indiana Ave NW Washington DC 20001-2131 E-mail: jbelson@dcca.dc.us

BELT, DAVID LEVIN, lawyer; b. Wheeling, W.Va., Jan. 13, 1944; s. David Homer and Mae Jean (Duffy) B.; m. Carolyn Emery Copeland Belt, July 22, 1967; children: David Clifford, Amy Elizabeth. BA, Yale U., 1965, LLB, 1970. Bar: Conn. 1970. Assoc. Jacobs, Grudberg, Belt & Dow, P.C., New Haven, 1970-74, mem., 1974—. Co-author: The Connecticut Unfair Trade Practices Act, 1994; contbr. articles to profl. jours. 1 lt. USAR, 1965-67, Vietnam. Fellow Conn. Bar Found. (life); mem. Conn. Bar Assn. (exec. com. antitrust and trade regulation sect. 1978—), Conn. Trial Lawyers Assn., Yale Club N.Y.C. Antitrust, Federal civil litigation, General civil litigation. Office: Jacobs Grudberg Belt & Dow PC 350 Orange St New Haven CT 06511-6415

BELTHOFF, RICHARD CHARLES, JR. lawyer; b. Denville, N.J., Jan. 28, 1958; s. Richard Charles and Barbara Ann (Erdmann) B.; m. Vicki Shannon Alligood, June 13, 1981; children: Ashley Nicole, Jason Michael. BSP, East Caroline U., 1980; JD, U. N.C., 1984. Bar: N.C. 1984, U.S. Dist. Ct. (we. dist.) N.C. 1984, U.S. Ct. Appeals (4th cir.) 1987. Assoc. Grier & Grier, Charlotte, N.C., 1984-89; ptnr. Grier Belthoff & Furr PA, 1989-98; chief ops. counsel, dir. real estate, asst. sec. Compass Group USA, Inc., 1998—. Contbr. articles to legal jours. Mem. ABA, N.C. Bar Assn., Mecklenburg County Bar Assn. General corporate, Environmental, Labor. Home: 426 Shasta Ln Charlotte NC 28211-4054 Office: Compass Group Legal Dept 2400 Yorkmont Rd Charlotte NC 28217-4545 E-mail: richard.belthoff@exch.compass-usa.com

BELTON, JOHN THOMAS, lawyer; b. Yonkers, N.Y., Feb. 24, 1947; s. Harry James and Anne Marie (Kupko) B.; m. Linda Susanne Cheugh, jan. 6, 1973; 1 child, Joseph Timothy. BA, Ohio State U., 1972, postgrad. in bus. adminstrn., 1972-73; JD, Ohio No. U., 1976. Bar: Ohio 1977, U.S. Ct. of Claims. Sole practice, Columbus, Ohio, 1976-83; ptnr. Belton & Marlin, and predecessor firm Belton, Goldwin & Cheugh, Columbus, 1983—; arbitrator Franklin County Ct. Common Pleas, 1983—; dir. Weeks-Finneran Inc. Rep. precinct chmn., 1983. V.p. Far Northwest Coalition, 1984. Mem. ch. coun. St. Peter's Parish, 1984—, Pub. Bd. Zoning Appeals, 1991—; pres. Dublin Youth Athletics, 1985—. With USAF, 1968-71. Mem. ABA, ATLA, Columbus Bar Assn. (com. chmn. 1976—), U.S. Dist. Ct. Fed. Bar, U.S. Supreme Ct. Bar, Ohio Bar Assn. (bd. govs. 1993—), Dublin Jr. C. of C., The Pres., Ohio State Alumni, Republican Glee, Columbus Shamrock, K.C., Order of Barristers, Omicron Delta Kappa, Phi Alpha Delta (justice 1975). Roman Catholic. Avocations: reading, chess, golfing, racquetball, recreational activities. State civil litigation, Criminal, Personal injury. Home: 8649 Dunsinane Dr Dublin OH 43017-8757 Office: Belton & Marlin 2066 Henderson Rd Columbus OH 43220-2452 E-mail: lsbjib@cs.com

BELTON, ROBERT, law educator; b. 1935; BA, U. Conn., 1961; JD, Boston U., 1965. Bar: N.Y. 1966, N.C. 1970, Tenn. 1980. Asst. counsel legal def. fund NAACP, N.Y.C., 1966-70; ptnr. Chambers, Stein, Ferguson & Lanning, Charlotte, N.C., 1970-75; lectr., dir. fair employment clinic Vanderbilt U., Nashville, 1975-77, assoc. prof., 1977-82, prof., 1982—. Vis. prof. Harvard U. Law Sch., Cambridge, Mass., 1986-87, U. No. Car., 1990-91, Charles Hamilton Houston Disting. vis. prof. N.C. Ctrl. Law Sch., 1997. Author: Remedies in Employment Discrimination Law, 1992; co-author Casebook on Employment Discrimination Law, 1999; contbr. articles to profl. jours. Fellow Coll. Labor and Employment Lawyers, Inc.; mem. ABA, Nat. Bar Assn., Am. Assn. Law Schs. (exec. com. 1991-94), Am. Law Inst., Nat. Employment Lawyers' Assn. (exec. bd. 1996—). Office: Vanderbilt U Sch Law 21st Ave S Nashville TN 37203-1181

BENAK, JAMES DONALD, lawyer; b. Omaha, Jan. 22, 1954; s. James R. and Norma Lea (Roberts) B.; Patricia Ann Duffy, Mar. 1995; 1 child, James Duffy. BA, U. Nebr., 1977; JD, Creighton U., 1980. Bar: Nebr. 1980, U.S. Dist. Ct. Nebr. 1980, U.S. Ct. Appeals (7th cir.) 1988, U.S. Ct. Appeals (6th cir.) 1989, Ill. 1990, U.S. Dist. Ct. (no. and ctrl. dists.) Ill. 1991, U.S. Ct. Appeals (fed. cir.) 2001. Assoc. Kennedy, Holland, DeLacy & Svoboda, Omaha, 1980-84; asst. gen. atty. Union Pacific R.R. Co., 1984-87, gen. atty., 1987-90; ptnr. Jenner & Block, Chgo., 1990—. Bd. dirs. Combined Health Agys. Drive/Nebr., 1985-90, Automated Monitoring and Control Internat., Inc., 1987-90, Coll. World Series, 1989-90. Mem. ABA (litig. and intellectual property sects.), Nebr. Bar Assn., Chgo. Bar Assn. (pub. utility and ins. law com.). Roman Catholic. General civil litigation, Intellectual property, Transportation. Home: 335 N Garfield Ave Hinsdale IL 60521-3723 Office: Jenner & Block One IBM Plz Chicago IL 60611 E-mail: jbenak@jenner.com

BENAVIDES, FORTUNATO PEDRO (PETE BENAVIDES), federal judge; b. Mission, Tex., 1947; BBA, U. Houston, 1968, JD, 1972. Atty. Rankin, Kern & Martinez, McAllen, Tex., 1972-74, Cisneros, Beery & Benavides, McAllen, 1974, Cisneros, Brown & Benavides, McAllen, 1975, Cisneros & Benavides, McAllen, 1976; pvt. practice, 1977; judge Hidalgo County Ct.-at-Law # 2, Edinburg, Tex., 1977-79; prin. Law Offices of Fortunato P. Benavides, McAllen, 1980-81; judge 92nd Dist. Ct. of Hidalgo County, Tex., 1981-84, 13th Ct. Appeals, Corpus Christi, 1984-91, Tex. Ct. Criminal Appeals, Austin, 1991-92; atty. Atlas & Hall, McAllen, 1993-94; judge U.S. Ct. Appeals (5th cir.), Austin, 1994—. Commr. Tex. Juvenile Probation Commn., 1983-89; vis. judge to cts. in Tex., 1993. Active Mex.-Am. Dems. of Tex., 1990-92, Mustangs of Corpus Christi, 1990-91, hon. mem., 1992, St. Michael Episc. Ch., Austin, 1992—. Mem. ABA, State Bar Tex., Hidalgo County Bar Assn. Office: US Ct Appeals 5th cir Homer Thornberry Judicial Bldg 903 San Jacinto Blvd Ste 450 Austin TX 78701-2450*

BENDER, JACK SINCLAIR, III, retired lawyer; b. Kansas City, Mo., July 12, 1944; s. Jack Sinclair Jr. and Ruby June (Blake) B.; m. Donna Lou LaMar, Aug. 28, 1965; children: Kelley Ann, Heather Christine, Marcia Lynn. BA, Washburn U., 1966, JD, 1969; grad., Air Command and Staff Coll., 1979, Air War Coll., 1989. Bar: Kans. 1969, U.S. Dist. Ct. Kans. 1969, U.S. Supreme Ct. 1973. Asst. atty. gen. State of Kans., 1969; sr. atty. Boeing Co., Wichita, Kans., 1974-90, constrn. mgmt., 1990-99; ret., 1999. Cons. Boeing Employees' Assn., 1976-99, Boeing Mgmt. Bd. of Control, 1986-88; mobilization augmentee to gen. counsel Def. Logistics Agy., 1994-96. Author: The Law Can Help You, 1973. Ch. officer, 1st Presbyn. Ch., Wichita, 1981-87. Served to capt., JAG, USAF, 1966-74; served to col., JAG-USAFR, 1974-96 (ret.), USAF Acad. Liaison Officer, 1994—. Recipient Younger Fed. Lawyer award Fed. Bar Assn., 1973, Outstanding Air Force Res. Lawyer of Yr. award, 1983. Mem. ABA, Kans. Bar Assn., Wichita Bar Assn., Corp. Counsel Soc. Wichita (v.p. 1975-76, pres. 1976-77, 85-86), Res. Officers Assn., Jaycees (bd. dirs. 1978-80, Pres.'s award 1979), Air Force Assn. (life), Air War Coll. Alumni Assn., Am. Legion, Phi Alpha Delta. Construction, General corporate, Military. Home: 9431 Epping Ln Halstead KS 67056-9355 E-mail: galaxy2010@aol.com

BENDER, JOEL CHARLES, lawyer; b. Bklyn., Dec. 12, 1939; s. Harry and Edna (Bogolowitz) B.; m. Terry Bender; children: Lisa, Andrew, Gary. BA, Cornell U., 1961; JD, NYU, 1964. Bar: N.Y. 1964, U.S. Supreme Ct. 1970, Fla. 1980; diplomate Am. Coll. Family Trial Lawyers. Ptnr. Bender, Jenson & Silverstein, LLP, White Plains, N.Y., 1999—. Councilman Greenburgh, N.Y. 1977-89; dep. supv., police commr. Greenburgh, 1979-89. Fellow Am. Assn. Matrimonial Lawyers; mem. ABA, Am. Acad. Matrimonial Lawyers (pres. N.Y. chpt. 1999-2001, former officer, bd. mgrs.), N.Y. State Bar Assn., Fla. Bar, Westchester County Bar Assn. Democrat. State civil litigation, General corporate, Family and matrimonial. Office: Bender & Bodnar 140 Grand St Ste 701 White Plains NY 10601-4836 E-mail: jbender@jcbender.com

BENDER, JOHN CHARLES, lawyer; b. N.Y.C., May 17, 1940; s. John H. and Cecilia B.; m. Helen Hadjiyannakis; 1 child, Marianna Celene. BSME, Northea. U., 1964; JD, NYU, 1968, LLM, 1971. Bar: N.Y. 1968, U.S. Dist. Ct. (so. dist.) N.Y. 1972, U.S. Supreme Ct. 1997. Atty. Marshall, Bratter, Greene, Allison and Tucker, 1968-69; asst. dir, NYU Ctr. for Internat. Studies, N.Y.C., 1969-71; atty. Poletti Freidin Prashker Feldman & Gartner, 1971-75; spl. counsel Moreland Act Commn. on Nursing Homes and Residential Facilities, 1975-76; gen. counsel N.Y. State Fin. Control Bd., 1976-80; v.p., gen. counsel News Am. Pub. Inc., 1980-85; group v.p., gen. counsel Simon & Schuster Inc., 1985-90; sr. v.p., dir., gen. counsel Maxwell Macmillan Group, 1991-95; dir. Black Book Mktg. Group, Inc., 1994-96. Chmn., trustee Trust for Cultural Resources of City of N.Y., 1981-99; chmn., trustee Mary McDowell Ctr. for Learning, 1993—. Mem. ABA, Assn. of Bar of City of N.Y. (mem. com. on comm. law 1981-85, mem. spl. com. on edn. and the law 1982-85). Communications, General corporate, Intellectual property. Home: 27 W 67th St New York NY 10023-6258 Office: 708 3d Ave New York NY 10017-4201

BENDER, MICHAEL LEE, state supreme court justice; b. N.Y.C., Jan. 7, 1942; s. Louis and Jean (Waterman) B.; m. Judith Jones, Feb. 27, 1967 (div. Mar. 1977); children: Jeremy, Aviva; m. Helen H. Hand, Sept. 10, 1977; children: Maryjean Hand-Bender, Tess Hand-Bender, Benjamin Hand-Bender. BA in Philosophy, Dartmouth Coll., 1964; JD, U. Colo., 1967. Bar: Colo. 1967, D.C. 1967, U.S. Supreme Ct. 1980. Pub. defender City and County Denver, 1968-71; assoc. regional atty. EEOC, 1974-75; supr. atty. Jefferson County Pub. Defender, 1975-77; divsn. chief Denver Pub. Defender, Denver, 1977-78; atty. Gibson, Dunn & Crutcher, L.A., 1979-80; ptnr. Bender & Treece P.C., Denver, 1983-93; pres., shareholder Michael L. Bender PC, 1993-97; also pres. Bender & Treece P.C.; state supreme ct. justice Colo. Supreme Ct., 1997—. Adj. faculty U. Denver Coll. Law, 1981-86, chair. ABA Criminal Justice sect., Washington, 1990-91, NACD Lawyers Assistant Com., 1989-90; dir. Nat. Assn. Criminal Def. Lawyers, 1984-90; mem. practitioner's adv. com. U.S. Sentencing Com., 1990-91; mem. com. for Criminal Justice Act for Dist. Colo. U.S. Dist. Ct., 1991-93, domestic rels. reform com.; liason mem. Colo. Pub. Edn. com., Ct. Svcs., 1998—, atty. regulation adv. com., 1998-99; co-chair civil justice com. Supreme Ct., 1998—. Contbr. articles to profl. jours. Bd. govs. Colo. Bar, 1989-91. Recipient Fireman award Colo. State Pub., 1990; Robert C. Heeney Meml. award Nat. Assn. Criminal Def. Lawyers, 1990; named Vol. of Yr. Denver Bar Assn., 1988. Mem. Colo. Bar Assn. (ethics com. 1980—), ABA (chair criminal justice sect. 1990-91, criminal justice standards com. 1997—). Democrat. Jewish. Avocations: aerobics, skiing, bicycling, camping. Office: Colo Supreme Ct State Jud Bldg 2 E 14th Ave Fl 4 Denver CO 80203-2115

BENDER, PAUL, lawyer, educator; b. 1933; AB, Harvard U., 1954, LLB, 1957. Law clk. to Judge Learned Hand, 1958-59; law clk. to Justice Felix Frankfurter, U.S. Supreme Ct., 1959-60; asst. to Solicitor Gen., Dept. Justice, 1964-66; asst. prof. U. Pa. Law Sch., Phila., 1960-63, assoc. prof., 1963-66, prof., 1966-84; dean Coll. Law, Ariz. State U., Tempe, 1984-89, prof., 1989—. Prin. dep. solicitor gen. U.S., 1993-96; gen. counsel Nat.

Commn. on Obscenity and Pornography, 1968-70; reporter UN Assn. Panel on human rights, Am. fgn. policy, 1978; justice Supreme Ct. of the Ft. MacDowell Yavapai Nation, 2000—. Author: (with Dorsen and Neuborne) Political and Civil Rights in the United States, 1976, 78. Recipient Cert. of Merit, ABA, 1973. Office: Coll Law Ariz State U Tempe AZ 85287

BENDER, PAUL EDWARD, lawyer; b. Decatur, Ill., Dec. 5, 1951; s. Kenneth Donald and Martha Rosalis (Heinzelmann) B.; m. Anne Marie Scartabello, Dec. 31, 1976 (div. 1978). BA, Millikin U., 1973; JD cum laude, Hamline U., 1976; MBA, U. Phoenix, 1997. Bar: Minn. 1976, Ill 1977, U.S. Dist Ct. (cen. dist.) Ill. 1982. Assoc. Halloran & Alfuby, Mpls., 1976-77; sole practice Bender Law Office, Arthur, Ill., 1977-79; sr. title atty Chgo. Title Ins. Co., Peoria, 1979-82; ptnr. Cordis & Bender, Princeville, 1982-84; sr. title atty. Chgo. Title Co., Champaign, 1984-88, asst. v.p., mgr., 1990-92, resident v.p., (Champaign County mgr., 1992-96; mgr. McLean County Title Co., 1996—, Decatur Title, 1997—. Mem. AVA, Peoria Bar Assn. (chmn. real estate com. 1983-84, mem. continuing legal edn. 1981-83), Champaign County Bar Assn., Ill. Bar Assn., Bloomington YMCA Svc. Club, Optimist Club (Peoria chpt., prs. 1981-82, lt. gov. zone 6 Ill. 1982-83), Champaign C. of C. (zoning com. 1990-96), Lions, Mason, Shriners. Republican. Methodist. Bankruptcy, Real property. Home: 303 N Cottage Ave Normal IL 61761-4264 E-mail: benderpa@ctt.com

BENDER, RONALD ANDREW, lawyer; b. Butte, Mont., Sept. 29, 1946; s. John A. and Mary R. (Sullivan) B.; m. Jane K. Pozega, June 28, 1969; children: Andrew P., Kelly B. BA, Carroll Coll., Helena, Mont., 1968; JD, U. Mont., 1971. Bar: Mont. 1971, U.S. Dist. Ct. (fed. dist.) Mont. 1971, U.S. Ct. Appeals (9th cir.) 1974. Law clk. to Hon. Russell E. Smith U.S. Dist. Ct., Missoula, Mont., 1971-73; atty. Worden, Thane & Haines, P.C., 1973—. Contbr. articles to law rev. Bd. dirs. Five Valleys Land Trust, Missoula, 1990-96. Recipient Am. Jurisprudence Achievement award, 1969, 70, 71. Mem. ABA, Mont. Bar Assn., Am. Bd. Trial Advocates, Assn. Trial Lawyers Am., Mont. Def. Trial Lawyers, Def. Rsch. Inst., Missoula C. of C. (bd. dirs. 1990-93), Rotary (bd. dirs. 1990-93). Banking, General civil litigation, Labor. Office: Worden Thane & Haines PC 111 N Higgins Ave Ste 600 Missoula MT 59802-4494

BENEDICT, JAMES NELSON, lawyer; b. Norwich, N.Y., Oct. 6, 1949; s. Nelson H. and Helen (Wilson) B.; m. Janet E. Fagal, May 8, 1982. BA magna cum laude, St. Lawrence U., 1971; JD, Albany Law Sch. of Union U., 1974. Bar: N.Y. 1975, U.S. Dist. Ct. (no., ea. and so. dists.) N.Y. 1975, U.S. Ct. Appeals (2d cir.) 1975, U.S. Ct. Appeals (8th cir.) 1977, U.S. Ct. Appeals (10th cir.) 1978, U.S. Ct. Appeals (11th cir.) 1982, U.S. Supreme Ct. 1978. Assoc. Rogers & Wells, N.Y.C., 1974-82; ptnr. Clifford Chance Rogers & Wells, 1982—. Mem. bd. contbg. editors and advisors The Corp. Law Rev., 1976-86; contbr. articles to profl. jours. Bd. dirs. Reece Sch., N.Y.C., 1984-89, Stanley Isaacs Neighborhood Ctr., N.Y.C., 1984-89; trustee St. Lawrence U., Canton, N.Y., 1985-91. Mem. ABA (chmn. securities litigation subcom. on 1940 Act matters 1984-86, 96—), Fed. Bar Coun. N.Y. State Bar Assn., Assn. Bar City N.Y. (com. on securities regulaton, fed. legislation com., fed. cts. com.), Am. Soc. Writers on Legal Subjects, Sky Club (N.Y.C.), Scarsdale Golf Club, Phi Beta Kappa. Federal civil litigation, State civil litigation, Securities. Home: 26 Kensington Rd Scarsdale NY 10583-2217 Office: Rogers & Wells 200 Park Ave Fl 8E New York NY 10166-0800

BENEDICT, PETER BEHRENDS, lawyer; b. Pittsfield, Mass., Feb. 28, 1951; s. Bruce Merrill and Eleanor Jean (Hamel) B.; m. Jan Elizabeth Roina, May 20, 1972; children— Seth Behrends, Sarah Krapf. B.A. in English, Central Conn. State Coll., New Britain, 1973; J.D. cum laude, New Eng. Sch. Law, Boston, 1976. Bar: Conn. 1976, U.S. Dist. Ct. Conn. 1978, Mass. 1977, U.S. Supreme Ct. 1980. Atty., R. Richard Roina, Norwalk, Conn., 1976-78, Roina & Benedict, Norwalk, 1978, Roina, Benedict & Fiore, Norwalk, 1979, Rapaport & Manheim, Stamford, Conn., 1979-83, Rapaport, Manheim & Benedict, Stamford, 1983— . Bd. dirs. Norwalk YMCA, 1979-82, Literacy Vols. of Stamford, 1981— . Mem. ABA, Conn. Bar Assn., Stamford Bar Assn., Assn. Trial Lawyers Am., Conn. Trial Lawyers Assn. Independent. Congregational. Clubs: Bridgeport Rifle, Greenwich Boat and Yacht. State civil litigation, General practice, Personal injury. Home: 33 Sachem Ln Greenwich CT 06830-7229 Office: Rapaport & Benedict PC 750 Summer St Stamford CT 06901-1020

BENEDICT, RONALD LOUIS, lawyer; b. Cin., Feb. 22, 1942; s. Harold Lloyd and Thelma (Bryant) B.; m. Carol Joyce Worthington, Sept. 9, 1961 (div. Sept. 1980); children: Karen Elizabeth Benedict Sterwerf, Jennifer Lynn Benedict Suttle; m. Deborah Ann Taggart, Aug. 14, 1982. BA in Polit. Sci., U. Cin., 1964; JD, Salmon P. Chase Coll., 1968. BAr: Ohio 1968, U.S. Supreme Ct. 1985. Methods analyst Western-So. Life Ins. Co., Cin., 1964-69; atty. Ohio Nat. Life Ins. Co., 1969-71, sr. atty., 1971-73, asst. gen. counsel, 1973-80, assoc. counsel, 1980-94, corp. v.p., counsel, sec., 1994—. Sec., dir. Ohio Nat. Fund, Inc., Cin., 1973—; sec. Ohio Nat. Investment Mgmt. Co., Cin., 1971—, sec., bd. dirs. Ohio Nat. Equity Sales Co., Cin., 1971—. Author, lectr.: (treatise and course) Trial and Exection of Jesus, 1978, Pseudochristian Cults, 1977. Arbitrator, Ct. Common Pleas, Hamilton County, Ohio, 1973—; mem. and counsel Tri-State Billy Graham Cursade Com., Cin., 1977; trustee Southwestern Trails Assn., Greater Cin. Mut. Funds Assn. Recipient cert. Adult Christian Edn. Found., 1977; Life Office Mgmt. Inst. fellow, 1971. Mem. ABA, Ohio State Bar Assn. (corp. counsel com.), Cin. Bar Assn. (securities law com., spkrs. bur.), Aassn. Life Ins. Counsel (securities law com.), Investment Co. Inst. (SEC rules com.), League Am. Bicyclists, Alpha Tau Omega. Republican. Presbyterian. Avocations: theology, Bible teaching, church leadership, bicycle touring, outdoor activities. General corporate, Insurance, Securities. Home: 216 Norman Ln Lebanon OH 45036-1500 E-mail: Ronald_Benedict@Ohionational.com

BENHAM, ROBERT, state supreme court justice; m. Nell (Dodson) B.; children: Corey Brevard, Austin Tyler. BS in Polit. Sci. with honors, Tuskegee U.; JD, U. Ga.; LLM, U. Va. Judge Ga. Ct. Appeals, Ga., 1984-89; justice Supreme Ct., State of Ga., Atlanta, 1989—, presiding justice, chief justice. Mem. adv. bd. 1st So. Bank. Chmn. Gov.'s Commn. on Drug Awareness and Prevention, State of Ga.; mem. Ga. Hist. Soc.; trustee Fa. Legal Hist. Found.; bd. dirs. Cartersville (Ga.) Devel. Authority, Cartersville-Bartow C. of C.; deacon, former Sunday Sch. supt. The Greater Mt. Olive Bapt. Ch.; notably one of first black individuals elected to a statewide position in the history of Ga. Mem Atlanta Bar Assn. (bd. dirs. jud. sect.), Ga. Bar Found., Lawyers Club Atlanta, Masons, Shriners, Elks. Office: Ga Supreme Ct 244 Washington St SW Rm 572 Atlanta GA 30334-9007 Fax: (404) 657-4329

BENIGNO, THOMAS DANIEL, lawyer; b. Queens, N.Y., July 29, 1954; s. John Baptiste and Ernesta Mary (Yannaco) B.; m. Maria Angelica Vasquez, Jan. 26, 1980; children: Diana Maria, Laura Michelle, John Frederick. BA with honors, Hofstra U., 1976; JD, Benjamin Cardozo Law Sch., 1979. Bar: N.Y. 1981, U.S. Dist. Ct. (so. and ea. dists.) N.Y. 1985. Atty. Legal Aid Soc., Bronx, N.Y., 1979-84; ptnr. Benigno, Cassisi & Casissi, Floral Park, 1984-87; mng. ptnr., gen. counsel Benigno/Gurrieri Real Estate Mgmt. and Devel., Bklyn., 1984-95. Pres. Gurben Properties, Inc., Floral Park, 1987-88, Movies for Kids Inc., Valley Stream, N.Y., 1989-90; gen. counsel Our Gang Assocs. Inc. (doing bus. as Thin White Line), Cedarhurst, N.Y., 1988-90. Mem. N.Y. Bar Assn., Rotary Internat. Contracts commercial, Construction, Real property. Office: 269 Hempstead Ave Ste 2 Malverne NY 11565-1224

BENJAMIN, EDWARD BERNARD, JR. lawyer; b. New Orleans, Feb. 11, 1923; s. Edward Bernard and Blanche (Sternberger) B.; m. Adelaide Wisdom, May 11, 1957; children: Edward Wisdom, Mary Dabney, Ann Leith, Stuart Minor. BS, Yale U., 1944; JD, Tulane U., 1952. Bar: La. 1952. Practiced in, New Orleans, since 1952; ptnr. Jones, Walker, Waechter, Poitevent, Carrere & Denegre, 1967—. Pres. Am. Coll. Probate Counsel, 1986-87, Internat. Acad. Estate and Trust Law, 1976-78; vice chmn. bd. trustees Southwestern Legal Found., 1980-88, bd. dirs., 1988-90; chmn. bd. Starmount Co., Greensboro, N.C., 1968-88, chmn. emeritus, 1988—. Editor-in-chief Tulane U. Law Rev., 1951-52; mem. editorial bd. Community Property Jour., 1974-89. Trustee Hollins Coll., 1966-87; chancellor Episcopal Diocese of La., 1984—, Trinity Episcopal Ch., New Orleans, 1974-92; mem. adv. bd. CCH Estate & Fin. Planning Svc., 1982-88; chmn. Salavation Army City Commd. Adv. Bd., 1965-68; pres. New Orleans Jr. C. of C., 1953. 1st lt., F.A. pilot, U.S. Army, 1943-46. Mem. Am. Coll. Tax Counsel, Am. Law Inst., ABA (sec. taxation sect. 1967-68, coun. 1976-79, coun. real property, probate and trust law sect. 1978-81), La. Bar Assn. (chmn. taxation sect. 1959-60), La. Law Inst., La. Bar Found. (trustee 1998-99), New Orleans Country Club, Southern Yacht Club, New Orleans Lawn Tennis Clu Estate planning, Corporate taxation, Estate taxation. Home: 1837 Palmer Ave New Orleans LA 70118-6215 Office: Jones Walker Waechter Poitevent Carrere & Denegre 201 Saint Charles Ave Fl 51 New Orleans LA 70170-1000

BENJAMIN, JAMES SCOTT, lawyer; b. Miami Beach, Fla., Aug. 28, 1954; s. Julian R. Benjamin and June Lois Garvin; m. Laura Cipolla, Mar. 5, 1989; children: Kaitlyn, Courtney. BS in Advt., U. Fla., 1976; JD, Samford U., 1979. Bar: Fla. 1980, U.S. Dist. Ct. (so. dist.) Fla. 1981, U.S. Dist. Ct. (mid. dist.) Fla. 1989, U.S. Ct. Appeals (11th cir.) 1989, U.S. Dist. Ct. (we. dist.) Tex. 1993, U.S. Supreme Ct. 1994. Assoc. Krause Reinhard & Pozen, Miami, Fla., 1980-81; asst. state atty. 17th Jud. Cir. Broward County, Ft. Lauderdale, 1981-84; shareholder Benjamin & Aaronson P.A., 1984—. Presenter, lectr. in field. Author, columnist Xcitement Mag., 1990—, Screw Mag., 1998. Bd. dirs. Arthritis Found., Ft. Lauderdale, 1998, treas., 1999—. Mem. Fla. Assn. Criminal Def. Attys. (bd. dirs. 1998—), Broward County Assn. Criminal Def. Lawyers (v.p. 1997-98, pres. 1998-99), First Amendment Lawyers Assn. (nat. sec. 2000—), Free Speech Coalition, Inns of Ct. Avocation: fly fishing. Constitutional, Criminal, Entertainment. Office: Benjamin & Aaronson PA Ste 1615 One Financial Plaza Fort Lauderdale FL 33394

BENJAMIN, JEFF, lawyer, pharmaceutical executive; b. Bklyn., Dec. 28, 1945; s. Haskell and Lillian (Sikofski) B.; m. Betty Gae Meckler, Mar. 21, 1971; children: Lily Meckler, Ross Meckler. BA, Cornell U., 1967; JD cum laude, NYU, 1971. Bar: N.Y. 1971, U.S. Dist. Cts. (so. and ea. dists.) N.Y. 1972. Assoc. Kronish, Lieb, Shainswit, Weiner & Hellman, N.Y.C., 1971-74; atty. Ciba-Geigy Corp., Ardsley and Tarrytown, N.Y., 1974—, counsel for regulatory affairs, 1976—, divsn. counsel, 1978—, asst. gen. counsel, 1985—, dir. legal dept., assoc. gen. counsel, 1986-89, v.p., gen. counsel, 1996-97; assoc. gen. counsel, ethics and law compliance officer Novartis Corp., N.Y.C., 1997—. Lectr. in field. Contbr. articles to law jours. Mem. Citizens Adv. Com., Ramapo, N.Y. With USAR, 1969-74. Mem. ABA, Cornell U. Alumni Assn. (admissions amb.), Order of Coif. Antitrust, General corporate, Environmental. Home: 13 Park Ave New City NY 10956-1107 Office: Novartis Corp 608 Fifth Ave 10th Fl New York NY 10020-2305

BENN, SARA KITCHEN, lawyer, educator; b. Holden, Mass., Jan. 25, 1949; d. Charles Grant and Helen (Mansfield) Kitchen; m. Joel Dennis Benn, Feb. 14, 1976; children: Julia Ruth, Leon Matthew. AB, Trinity Coll., 1971; JD, Villanova U., 1975. Bar: Pa. 1975. Asst. pub. defender Pub. Defender's Office, Bucks County, Pa., 1975-77; mem. adj. faculty Gwynedd-Mercy Coll., Gwynedd Valley, Pa., 1977-85; asst. prof., chair sociology dept. Chestnut Hill Coll., Phila., 1985—; instr. Beaver Coll., Glenside, Pa., 1979; instr. in criminal law Temple U., Ambler, Pa., 1984-85; resource person Juvenile Justice Ctr. Pa., Phila., 1975-77; cons. Youth Services Agy., Doylestown, Pa., 1979; sec. bd. dirs. Alpha Pregnancy Services, Phila., 1983—; mem. edn. com. Phila. UNICEF. Editor: Bucks County on Youth Diversion, 1979. Mem. Nat. Right to Life Com., Washington, 1981—. Mary D. Walsh scholar Trinity Coll., 1967-71; Thomas J. Watson fellow, 1971-72. Mem. ABA (criminal justice div. and family law sect.), Phila. Bar Assn., Pennsylvanians for Human Life, Def. for Children itnernat.-U.S.A. Roman Catholic. Home: 9003 Ayrdale Cres # A Philadelphia PA 19128-1048

BENNETT, BIANCA CHERIE, lawyer; b. Washington, May 14, 1971; d. Carl Roosevelt and Barbara Jean (Pope) B. Grad., Princeton U., 1993; JD, U. Va., 1996. Bar: D.C., 1997. Assoc. Zuckert, Scoutt & Rosenberger, Washington, 1996—; mgr. Law Dept. General Dynamics Corp., Falls Church, Virginia, 1998-2000; dir. business affairs Paramount Pictures, Hollywood, Calif., 2000—. Mem. Washington Bar Assn., Black Entertainment and Sports Lawyers' Assn., Washington Area Lawyers for the Arts, Delta Sigma Theta Sorority, Inc. Avocations: photography, music, fgn. travel, long-distance running, fashion design. Entertainment. Home: 1460 N Mansfield Avenue ste 307 Hollywood CA 90028 E-mail: red_carpet2000@hotmail.com

BENNETT, CLARENCE J. lawyer; b. Springfield, Mass., Oct. 6, 1946; s. Nathaniel N. and Bess E. (Schneiderman) B.; m. Leslie G. Kimball, Aug. 31, 1969; children: Jonathan D., Alissa P. BA, McGill U., 1972, LLB, 1975. Bar: Mass. 1975, U.S. Dist. Ct. Mass. 1975. Assoc. Kimball & Bennett, Springfield, 1975—. Served with U.S. Army, 1967-79, Vietnam. Decorated Purple Heart, Bronze Star. Mem. DAV, VFW, Mil. Order Purple Heart, Jewish War Vets., Mass. Bar Assn., Hampden County Bar Assn. Criminal, Personal injury, Workers' compensation. Home: 96 White Oak Dr Longmeadow MA 01106-1739 Office: Kimball & Bennett 101 State St Ste 708 Springfield MA 01103-2072 E-mail: nitecourt@niteocourt.com

BENNETT, DAVID HINKLEY, lawyer; b. Portage, Wis., Sept. 18, 1928; s. Ross and Helen (Hinkley) B.; m. LaVonne Wilson, Feb. 3, 1955; children: Mark H., Todd W., John D. BBA, U. Wis., 1952, LLB, 1956. Bar: Wis. 1956, U.S. Ct. Appeals (7th cir.) 1962, U.S. Supreme Ct. 1966. Ptnr. Bennett & Bennett, Portage, 1956—. Dist. atty. Columbia County, Wis., 1959-67; regent Wis. State Univs., 1965-71. Served to 2d lt. AUS, 1953-56. Mem. Wis. Bar Assn. Republican. Presbyterian. Lodge: Masons. Estate planning, General practice, Personal injury. Home: 215 W Franklin St Portage WI 53901 Office: Bennett and Bennett 135 W Cook St # 30 Portage WI 53901-0030

BENNETT, EDWARD JAMES, lawyer; b. Newton, Iowa, Dec. 27, 1941; s. Erskine Francis and Malvina Esther (Goodhue) B.; m. Virginia Lee Cook, Jan. 30, 1965; children: Susan Elizabeth, Edward James. BA, U. Iowa, 1964, JD, 1966. Bar: Iowa 1966, U.S. Dist. Ct. (so. dist.) Iowa 1967. Atty. Diehl, Clayton & Cleverley, Newton, 1966-70, The Maytag Co., Newton, 1970-74, sr. atty., 1974-80, assoc. counsel, 1980-85, asst. sec., asst. gen. counsel, 1985-86, Maytag Corp. (formerly The Maytag Co.), Newton, 1986-90; sec., asst. gen. counsel Maytag Corp., 1990-99. Sec. The Hoover Co., 1990-99, Dixie-Narco Inc., 1990-99, Maytag Internat. Inc., 1990-99, Hoover Holdings Inc., 1990-99, Maytag Fin. Svcs. Corp., 1990-99, Maytag Corp. Found., 1990-99; dir. Progress Industries, 1993—, sec., 1994—. Mem. Civil Svc. Commn., Newton, 1980-86; mem. Newton Zoning Bd. Adjustment, 1978-96, chmn., 1978-85; sec., trustee Newton Cmty. Ctr., Inc., 1976-94; trustee Newton Cmty. Schs. Found., 1994—, v.p., 1996, pres., 1997; bd. dirs. Des Moines Metro Opera, 1998—, sec. 1998-99, pres. 2001—. Mem. ABA, Iowa State Bar Assn. (mem. trade regulation com. 1981-92, 93-97, 99—), Iowa Assn. Bus. and Industry (chmn. unemployment compensation com. 1976-94), Assn. Home Appliance Mfrs. (mem. product safety com. 1975-92). Republican. Presbyterian. Antitrust, General corporate, Securities. Home and Office: 203 Foster Dr Des Moines IA 50312-2539

BENNETT, FRED GILBERT, lawyer; b. May 28, 1946; HBA magna cum laude, U. Utah, 1970; JD, U. Calif., 1973. Bar: Calif. 1974. Ptnr. Gibson, Dunn & Crutcher, L.A., 1980-98; sr. ptnr. Quinn Emanuel Urquhart Oliver & Hedges, 1998—. Mem. nat. com. on arbitration U.S. Coun. for Internat. Bus., 1984—, chmn. western subcom., 1989—; comml. and constrn. arbitrator Internat. C. of C./Am. Arbitration Assn. Large Complex Case Panel; chmn. continuing edn. com. Am. Arbitration Assn. Large Complex Case Panel. Mng. editor UCLA Law Rev., 1972-73. Mem. ABA, Internat. Bar Assn., L.A. County Bar Assn., Phi Beta Kappa. Contracts commercial. Office: Quinn Emanuel Urquhart Oliver & Hedges 865 S Figueroa St Los Angeles CA 90017-2543

BENNETT, HERD LEON, lawyer; b. Portsmouth, Ohio, Oct. 17, 1934; BA, Duke U., 1956; JD, Cornell U., 1959. Bar: Ohio 1959. Ptnr. Bennett & Bennett, Eaton, Ohio, 1959—. Asst. atty. gen. of Ohio, 1962-63; spl. counsel to atty. gen. of Ohio, 1963-70; trustee Ohio State Bar Found., 1984-92, chair planning and rsch. com., 1986-92, awards com., 1988-90, pres. 1991-92; trustee Preble County Law Libr. Assn., 1970-72; trustee Ohio Continuing Legal Edn. Inst., 1990-91, 93-99, treas., 1993-94, vice chmn., 1994-95, chmn., 1995-96; trustee Eaton Found., 1978—, v.p., 1980—; trustee Nat. Hummel Found. and Mus., 1982—; bd. dirs. Ohio Bar Title Ins. Co., 1991-98, Northedge Shopping Ctr., Inc., Miller's Super Markets, Inc. Trustee Eaton Cmty. Improvement Corp., 1981-94 (v.p. 1987-94), trustee Preble County Area Cmty. Improvement Corp., 1994— (pres. 1994—); mem. Eaton Area C. of C., 1959—; mem., moderator, Sunday Sch. tchr. Concord United Ch. of Christ, Eaton H.S. Alumni Assn. (pres. 1983-84, permanent advisor); exec. officer Duke U. Office Devel., 1956-90, admissions interview chmn. for S.W. Ohio, 1994-97. Mem. ABA (real property, probate and trust law sect.), Nat. Assn. Criminal Def. Lawyers, Am. Judicature Soc., Ohio State Bar Assn. (mem. bd. govs. 1997—, mem. legal ethics and profl. conduct com. 1981—, coun. dels. 1981—), Preble County Bar Assn. (v.p. 1972-74, pres. 1974-76). Office: Bennett & Bennett 200 W Main St Eaton OH 45320-1748

BENNETT, JAMES DAVISON, lawyer; b. Mineola, N.Y., Dec. 2, 1938; BA, Cornell U., 1960, JD, 1963. Bar: N.Y. 1963. Ptnr. Bennett, Scholly, Pape, Rice & Schure, Rockvile Centre, N.Y., 1968—. Councilman Town of Hempstead, 1968-87, supr., 1978-87; active Nassau County Bd. Suprs., 1978-87, L.I. Power Authority, 1995-98; commr. N.Y.S. Pub. Svc. Commn., 1998—; apptd. to N.Y. State Conservation and Wildlife Fund, 1975-78; chmn. L.I. Area Devel. Agy., 1988-90, L.I. Regional Export Coun., 1988-90. Recipient citation Practising Law Inst., 1982-73, others. Mem. ABA, N.Y. State Bar Assn. (jud. conf. 1989, lectr. 1990), Nassau County Bar Assn. General corporate, Estate planning, Probate. Home: 34 Hilton Ave Garden City NY 11530-4414 Office: 255 Merrick Rd Rockville Centre NY 11570-5211

BENNETT, JOHN K. lawyer; b. Newark, Apr. 4, 1955; BA magna cum laude, Lafayette Coll., 1977; JD cum laude, Seton Hall U., 1980; LLM in Labor Law with honors, NYU, 1988. Bar: N.J. 1980, U.S. Dist. Ct. N.J., U.S. Dist. Ct. N.Y. (ea., so. and no. dists.), U.S. Ct. Appeals (2d and 3d cirs.), U.S. Supreme Ct. Law sec. to Hon. Robert L. Clifford Supreme Ct. N.J., 1980-81; assoc. to sr. ptnr. Carpenter, Bennett & Morrissey, Newark, 1981-98; ptnr., chair labor and employment law practice Connell, Foley & Geiser LLP, 1998—. Articles editor Seton Hall Law Rev., 1979-80; contbr. articles to profl. jours. Mem. ABA (litigation and labor and employment law sects., state labor law devel. com.), N.J. State Bar Assn. (exec. com. labor and employment law sect.), Essex County Bar Assn. General civil litigation, Labor. Office: Connell Foley LLP 85 Livingston Ave Roseland NJ 07068-3702 Fax: 973-535-9217. E-mail: jbennett@connellfoley.com

BENNETT, MAXINE TAYLOR, lawyer; b. Owensboro, Ky., Apr. 6, 1938; d. John Clevis and Alice Elizabeth (Siebe) Taylor; m. Wilford Thomas Bennett, Jan 19. 1957 (div. Dec. 1976); children: Cynthia Bennett Radseck, Jonathan Taylor Bennett; m. Edwin R. Druker, May 13, 1978. BA, Ky. Wesleyan Coll., 1959; MA, Western Ky. U., 1967; JD, Ind. U., Indpls., 1977. Bar: Ind. 1977, U.S. Dist. Ct. (so. and no. dists.) Ind. 1977, U.S. Ct. Appeals (7th cir.) 1984, U.S. Supreme Ct. 1986. Clk. Indpls. Corp. Counsel, 1975-77; atty. Commodities Dealers Licensing Bur. State of Ind., Indpls., 1977-78; sole practice, 1977—; assoc. Buck, Berry, Landau & Breunig, 1984—. Mem. People of Vision (Soc. to Prevent Blindness), Indpls., 1986—, Indpls. Symphony Guild, 1986—, Family Support Ctr. Aux., Indpls., 1985—, Block Lecture Soc.; mem. steering com. Indpls. Hebrew Congregation, 1982—, bd. dirs. Women's Haven, Indpls., 1981-82; trustee E.A. Block Charitable Trust, Indpls., 1982—; active Ind. Ballet Theatre Aux., 1988—. Recipient Nat. Career Woman of Yr. award Women's Expo, 1988-89. Mem. ABA, Ind. State Bar Assn., Ind. Trial Lawyers Assn. Indpls. Bar Assn. (Disting. fellow 1993), Columbia Club. Republican. Avocations: world travel, reading, creative needlework, gourmet cooking. Family and matrimonial, Personal injury, Probate. Office: Buck Berry Landau & Breunig 302 N Alabama St Indianapolis IN 46204-2166 E-mail: MAXBEN302@aol.com

BENNETT, SCOTT LAWRENCE, lawyer; b. N.Y.C., July 8, 1949; s. Allen J. and Rhoda (Maltz) B. AB with high distinction, U. Mich., 1971; JD, Cornell U., 1974. Bar: N.Y. 1975, U.S. Dist. Ct. (so. dist.) N.Y. 1976, U.S. Ct. Appeals (2d cir.) 1976, U.S. Supreme Ct. 1977. Assoc. Donovan, Leisure, Newton & Irvine, N.Y.C., 1974-79; sr. v.p., assoc. gen. counsel, sec. The McGraw-Hill Cos., Inc., 1979—. Mem. ABA, N.Y. State Bar Assn., Assn. Bar City N.Y., Assn. Am. Pubs. (lawyers com.), Phi Beta Kappa. E-mail: Scott. General corporate, Real property, Securities. Home: 101 W 12th St Apt 10J New York NY 10011-8120 Office: The McGraw Hill Co Inc Ste 383 1221 Avenue Of The Americas New York NY 10020-1095 E-mail: Bennett@Mcgraw-Hill.com

BENNETT, STEVEN ALAN, lawyer; b. Rock Island, Ill., Jan. 15, 1953; s. Ralph O. and Anne E. B.; m. Jeanne Aring; children: Preston, Spencer, Hunter, Whitney. BA in Art History, U. Notre Dame, 1975; JD, U. Kans., 1982. Bar: Tex. 1983, Ohio 1995, U.S. Dist. Ct. (no. dist.) Tex. 1983, U.S. Ct. Appeals (5th cir.) 1983, U.S. Supreme Ct. 1995. Atty. Freytag, Marshall et al, Dallas, 1982-84, Baker, Mills & Glast, Dallas, 1984-87; ptnr. Shank, Irwin, Conant et al, 1987-89; gen. counsel Bank One, Tex., N.A., 1989-94; sr. v.p., gen. counsel, sec. Banc One Corp., Columbus, Ohio, 1994-99; exec. v.p., chief legal officer, sec. Cardinal Health, Inc., Dublin, 1999-2001; pvt. practice Columbus, 2001—. City councilman, Mesquite, Tex., 1984-86, mayor pro tem, 1995; trustee Meadowview Sch., Mesquite, 1985-92; chair fin. com. St. Brendan Ch., Hilliard, Ohio, 1998—; pres., bd. dirs. Dallas Dem. Forum, 1993-94; bd. dirs. Ohio Hunger Task Force, Columbus; trustee Woodrow Wilson Internat. Ctr. for Scholars, Washington, 1996—, vice-chmn., 1999—; bd. dirs. Capital U. Law Sch., Columbus, Ctr. for Thomas More Studies, Dallas. Fellow, Ohio State Bar Found.; mem. ABA (banking law com.), Tex. Assn. Bank Counsel, Dallas Bar Assn., Ohio State Bar Assn., Columbus Bar Assn., St. Thomas More Soc. (Dallas bd. dirs. 1990-94), Am. Corp. Counsel Assn. (sec. 1999—, bd. dirs. 1996—, chair policy com. 1997-99), Phi Beta Kappa. Avocation: landscape photography. Administrative and regulatory, Banking, General corporate. E-mail: sbennett@columbus.rr.com

BENNINGFIELD, CAROL ANN, lawyer; b. San Antonio, Dec. 8, 1952; d. Gordon Lane Benningfield and Ann Benningfield McCraw. BA in Polit. Sci., S.W. Tex. State U., 1975; JD, U. Tex., 1979. Bar: Tex. 1979, U.S. Dist. Ct. (so. dist.) Tex. 1995. Staff atty. Tex. Dept. Labor and Stds., Austin, 1979; staff counsel Tex. Chem. Coun., 1979-80; assoc. Wiley, Garwood, San Antonio, 1981-83; account exec. Dean-Witter Reynolds, 1983-89; pvt. practice, Rockport, Tex., 1990—. Mem. gala com. San Antonio Stock Show and Rodeo, 1981-83; mem. Target 90 Goals for San Antonio, 1984-85; deacon First Presbyn. Ch., Rockport, 1992-95, mem. choir, 1990-96; mem. Rockport Art Assn., 1990—, Coll. State Bar of Tex.; trustee Aransas County Ind. Sch. Dist., Rockport, 1993-96, sec., 1993-96. Fellow Tex. Bar Found. Tex.; mem. San Antonio Young Lawyers (membership chmn. 1982), Rockport Fulton C. of C. (dir. 1992-94, awards com. chmn., v.p. 1993), Rotary. General civil litigation, Family and matrimonial, General practice. Office: 614 E Market Street Rockport TX 78382 E-mail: cabfield@dbstech.com

BENNION, DAVID JACOBSEN, lawyer; b. Glendale, Calif., Jan. 29, 1940; s. Donald Clark and Margaret (Jacobson) B.; m. Constance Wilson, Jan. 27, 1966; children: Marian, Margaret, Elizabeth, David, Sarah, Heidi. BA, Stanford U., 1964, JD, 1966. Bar: Calif. 1966. Ptnr. Boccardo Law Firm, San Jose, Calif., 1966-79; mission pres. LDS Ch., Geneva, 1979-82; ptnr. Packard, Packard and Bennion, Palo Alto, Calif., 1982-90, Bohn, Bennion & Niland, San Jose, 1993-98; pvt. practice, 1998—. Instr. continuing edn. of bar, personal injury trial. TMem. ABA, ATLA, Am. Bd. Trial Advs., Calif. State Bar, Am. Inns Ct. (pres. Santa Clara County chpt.). Republican. General civil litigation, Personal injury, Product liability. Home: 650 Center Dr Palo Alto CA 94301 Office: 95 S Market St Ste 360 San Jose CA 95113-2301 E-mail: djb@djbennion.com

BENSON, STUART WELLS, III, lawyer; b. Sewickley, Pa., Jan. 6, 1951; s. Stuart Wells and Rosalie (Sassin) B.; m. Ruthanne Ackerman, July 15, 1978; children: Kate Eileen, Laura Elizabeth, Sarah Wells. BA, Northwestern U., 1972; JD, U. Pitts., 1975. Bar: Pa. 1975, U.S. Dist. Ct. (we. dist.) Pa. 1975, U.S. Supreme Ct. 1982. Assoc. Brandt McManus Brandt & Malone, Pitts., 1975-80; ptnr. Dickie, McCamey & Chilcote, P.C., Pitts., 1980— . Contbr. articles to legal jours. Bd. dirs. North Hills YMCA, Pitts., 1981-84. Mem. Am. Arbitration Assn. (Appreciation award 1980, arbitrator), Pa. Def. Inst., Pa. Claims Assn., Pitts. Claims Assn., Allegheny County Bar Assn., Pa. Bar Assn., ABA, Internat. Assn. Indsl. Accident Bds. and Commns., Oakmont Country Club, Wildwood Golf Club, Rotary (pres. 1985, bd. dirs. 1979-87) Republican. Episcopalian. Workers' compensation. Home: 2116 Grandeur Dr Gibsonia PA 15044-7498

BENTLEY, FRED DOUGLAS, SR. lawyer; b. Marietta, Ga., Oct. 15, 1926; s. Oscar Andrew and Ima Irene (Prather) B.; children from previous marriage: Fred Douglas, Robert Randall; m. Jane Morrill McNeel, Nov. 7, 1997. BA, Presbyn. Coll., 1949; JD, Emory U., 1948; HHD (hon.), PhD (hon.), LHD (hon.), Kennesaw State U., 2000. Bar: Ga. 1948. Sr. mem. Bentley & Dew, Marietta, 1948-51; ptnr. Bentley, Awtrey & Bartlett, 1951-56, Edwards, Bentley, Awtrey & Parker, Marietta, 1956-75, Bentley & Schindelar, Marietta, 1975-80, Bentley, Bentley & Bentley, Marietta, 1975—. Pres. Beneficial Investment Co., Newmarket, Inc., Happy Valley, Inc., Bentley & Sons, Inc., Market Square, Inc., Market Square II L.L.C.; founder, chmn. bd. Charter Bank and Trust Co.; founder, trustee emeritus Kennesaw Coll. Mem. Ga. Ho. Reps., 1951-57, Ga. Senate, 1958; past pres. Cobb County (Ga.) C. of C.; founder, hon. curator Bentley Rare Book Galleries-Brenau U., Kennesaw State U.; mem., past chmn. Ga. Coun. Arts, 1976-89; mem. Gov.'s Fine Arts Com., 1990-92, Cummer Mus. of Art (hon. life); attache Ghana Olympic Com.; founder Cobb Emergency Svcs. Served with USN. Recipient Blue Key Cmty. Svc. award, Founder's award, 1992, Clarisse Baquell award for outstanding svc., Spl. Svc. award Kennesaw State U., Robert Cleveland award for lifetime achievement in law; named Citizen of Yr., C. of C., 1951, Leader of Tomorrow, Time mag., 1953, Vol. Citizen of Yr., Atlanta Jour./Constn., 1981, Kennesaw Hist. Soc. Man of Yr., 1996, Brenau U.. Man of Yr. award, 1996, President's award Kennesaw State U., 1999, Disting. Alumna Marietta H.S.; fellow J. Pierpont Morgan Libr.; Oct. 15 Fred Bentley Day City & Coun.; Bridge named in his honor, 2000. Mem. Ga. Bar Assn., Ga. Mus. Art (bd. advisors, hon. life mem.), Nat. PTA (hon. life), Cobb Landmarks Soc. (founder), Kennesaw Mountain Jaycees (founder), Rotary (hon. life), Georgian Club (bd. dirs.), The Grolier Club (hon.), Fellows of Marietta Cobb Mus. of Art (founder). Republican. Presbyterian. General practice. Home: 1441 Beaumont Dr Kennesaw GA 30152-3201 Office: 241 Washington Ave NE Marietta GA 30060-1958

BENTON, DONALD STEWART, publishing company executive, lawyer; b. Marlboro, N.Y., Jan. 2, 1924; s. Fred Stanton and Agnes (Townsend) B. Student, U. Leeds, Eng., 1945; BA, Columbia U., 1947, JD, 1949; LLM, NYU, 1953. Bar: N.Y. 1953. Practiced in N.Y.C., 1953-56; atty. N.Y. State Banking Dept., 1954-55; v.p. Found. Press, Inc., Bklyn., 1957-60; exec. asst. to exec. v.p. N.Y. Stock Exchange, 1960-61; dir. reference book dept. and spl. projects editor Appleton Century Crofts, N.Y.C., 1962-71; sr. editor Matthew Bender & Co., Inc., 1974-77; sr. legal editor Warren, Gorham & Lamont, Inc., 1977-89. Author: Thorndike Encyclopedia of Banking and Financial Tables, 3rd edit., 2000 yearbook, Federal Banking Laws, 3rd edit., 2000, Real Estate Tax Digest, 1984, Criminal Law Digest, 3rd edit., 1983, Modern Real Estate and Mortgage Checklists, 1979. Mem. Cresskill (N.J.) Zoning Bd. Adjustment, 1969-71, 82-83, 86—, Cresskill Planning Bd., 1971-74; councilman City of Cresskill, 1972-74. With AUS, 1943-46, 50-52. Decorated Bronze Star. Mem. Phi Delta Phi. Mem. Reformed Ch. in Am. Home: 117 Heatherhill Rd Cresskill NJ 07626-1020 Office: AS Pratt & Sons- Warren Gorham & Lamont 395 Hudson St New York NY 10014-3669

BENTON, W. DUANE, judge; b. Springfield, Mo., Sept. 8, 1950; s. William Max and Patricia F. (Nicholson) B.; m. Sandra Snyder, Nov. 15, 1980; children: Megan Blair, William Grant. BA in Polit. Sci. summa cum laude, Northwestern U., 1972; JD, Yale U., 1975; MBA in Accounting, Memphis State U., 1979; student Inst. Jud. Adminstrn., NYU, 1992; LLD (hon.), Ctrl. Mo. State U., 1994; LLM, U. Va., 1995; LLD (hon.), Westminster Coll., 1999. Bar: Mo. 1975; CPA, Mo. Ensign USN, 1972; advanced through grades to capt., 1993; judge advocate USN, Memphis, 1975-79; chief of staff for Congressman Wendell Bailey, Washington, 1980-82; pvt. practice Jefferson City, Mo., 1983-89; dir. revenue Mo. Dept. of Revenue, 1989-91; judge Mo. Supreme Ct., 1991—, chief justice, 1997-99. Adj. prof. Westminster Coll., U. Mo.-Columbia Sch. Law. Contbr. articles to profl. jours.; mng. editor Yale Law Jour., 1974-75 Chmn. Multistate Tax Commn. Washington, 1990-91; chmn. Mo. State Employees Retirement System, Jefferson City, 1989-93; regent Ctrl. Mo. State U., 1987-89; dir. Coun. for Drug Free Youth, Jefferson City, 1989-97; mem. Mo. Mil. Adv. Com., 1989-91; mem. Mo. Commn. Intergovernmental Coop., Jefferson City, 1989-91; trustee, deacon 1st Bapt. Ch., Jefferson City. Danforth fellow JFK Sch. Govt. Harvard U., 1990. Mem. AICPA (tax com. 1983—), Mo. Bar Assn. (tax com. 1975—), Mo. Soc. CPA's (tax com. 1983—), Navy League, Mil. Order of World Wars, Vietnam Vets of Am., VFW, Am. Legion, Phi Beta Kappa, Beta Gamma Sigma, Rotary. Baptist. Lt. USN, 1975-80. Capt. JAGC USNR. Office: Supreme Court PO Box 150 Jefferson City MO 65102-0150 E-mail: dbenton@osca.state.mo.us

BERALL, FRANK STEWART, lawyer; b. N.Y.C., Feb. 10, 1929; s. Louis J. and Jeannette F.; m. Christiana Johnson, July 5, 1958 (dec. July 1972); children: Erik Dustin, Elissa Alexandra; m. Jenefer M. Carey, Sept. 1, 1980. BS, Yale U., 1950, JD, 1955; LLM in Tax, NYU, 1959. Bar: N.Y. 1955, Conn. 1960; accredited estate planner. Assoc. firm Mudge, Stern, Baldwin & Todd, N.Y.C., 1955-57, Townley, Updike, Carter & Rodgers, N.Y.C., 1957-60; atty. Conn. Gen. Life Ins. Co., Bloomfield, Conn., 1960-65; atty. trust dept. Hartford Nat. Bank & Trust Co., 1965-67; assoc. Cooney & Scully, Hartford, 1968-70; ptnr. Copp & Berall and predecessors, 1970—. V.p., sec., gen. counsel John M. Blewer, Inc., Essex, Conn., 1969-86; asst. in instrn. Yale U. Law Sch., 1954-55; lectr. U. Conn. Sch. Ins., 1964-72, Law Sch., 1972-73; instr. estate planning Am. Coll. Life Ins., 1968-69; adj. asst. prof. grad. tax program U. Hartford, 1973-74; counsel Conn. Gov.'s Strike Force for Full Employment, 1971-72, Conn. Gov.'s Commn. on Tax Reform, 1972-73, State Tax Commr.'s Commn., 1972-75, Com. on Tax Law Clarification, 1984-88; lectr., spkr. in field. Co-author: A Practitioners Guide to the Tax Reform Act of 1969, 1970, Estate Planning and the Close Corporation, 1970, Planning Large Estates, 1970, Revocable Inter Vivos Trusts, 1985, The Migrant Client: Tax, Commnity Property, and Other Considerations, 1994; sr. editor Conn. Bar Jour., 1969—; mem. editl. bd. Estate Planning mag., 1973—, Practical Tax Lawyer, 1988—, Jour. Taxation of Trusts and Estates, 1988-92. Bd. dirs. Bloomfield Interfaith Homes, 1967-71; adv. council U. Hartford Tax Inst., 1970-82; trustee Cluber Ednl. Found., 1997-99; co-chmn. adv. council Hartford Tax Inst., 1986-94; co-chmn. Notre Dame Estate Planning Inst., 1977—. 1st lt., F.A. U.S. Army, 1951-52. Fellow Am. Coll. Trust and Estate Counsel (chmn. Conn. chpt. 1975-81, editl. bd. 1975-87, chmn. estate and gift tax com. 1976-81, chmn. accessions tax com. 1984-88, regent 1977-83), Am. Coll. Tax Counsel; mem. ABA (chmn. com. estate planning and ins. 1979-85, chmn. task force on retroactivity and constitutionality of tax law changes 1985-89, vice-chmn. comm. estate planning and drafting 1992-96, co-chmn. com. non-tax issues in drafting wills and recovable trusts and co-chmn. tax litig. and controversy of real property probate and trust sect. 1995—, chmn. mem. com. 1977-79, chmn. com. on income of estates and trusts 1983-85, chmn. com. econ. tax practice 1987-89, chmn. CLE com. tax sect., co-founder, convener estate planning seminar group 1972-78), Conn. Bar Assn. (exec. com., estates and probate sect. 1973—, chmn. 1984-86, chmn. tax sect. 1969-72, exec. com. 1969—, vice chmn. com. on specialization 1974-77), Hartford County Bar Assn. (chmn. com. liaison with IRS 1972-74, com. charter and by-laws 1975), Am. Law Inst. (tax adv. group 1980-89), Internat. Acad. Estate and Trust Law (exec. coun. 1978-82), Tax Club of Hartford (pres. 1975-76), Culver Summer Schs. Alumni Assn. (v.p. 1975-85, pres. 1997-99, bd. dirs. 1985-91, 93—), Culver Club Ctrl. New Eng. (pres. 1996—), Yale Club of Harford (dir. 1998—, pres. 1999—). E-mial. Probate, Estate taxation, State and local taxation. Home: 9 Penwood Rd Bloomfield CT 06002-1520 Office: Copp & Berall LLP 55 Farmington Ave Ste 703 Hartford CT 06105-3790 E-mail: cb@connix.com

BERDON, ROBERT IRWIN, judge trial referee, retired state supreme court justice; b. New Haven, Dec. 24, 1929; s. Louis J. and Jean (Cohen) B.; m. Nancy Tarr, Aug. 30, 1964 (dec. Mar. 1992); 1 child, Peter A. BS, U. Conn., 1951, JD, 1957; LLM in Jud. Process, U. Va., 1988. With Bank of Manhattan, 1953-54; pvt. practice New Haven, 1957-73; treas. State of Conn., 1971-73; judge Superior Ct., State of Conn., New Haven, 1973-91; justice Supreme Ct., State of Conn., 1991-99, ret., 1999—99, judge trial referee, 2000—. Adj. prof. law U. Bridgeport Sch. Law, 1986-91; lectr. in law U. Conn. Sch. of Law, 1993; assoc. fellow Saybrook Coll., Yale U., 1986—; lectr. Am. Bd. Trial Advs., 1986; mem. Conn. Bd. Pardons, 1991-92. Contbr. articles to profl. jours. Recipient Judiciary award Conn. Trial Lawyers Assn., 1976, Disting. Alumni award U. Conn., 1977, Outstanding State Trial Judge in U.S. award Assn. Trial Lawyers in Am., 1982, Pub. Svc. award U. Conn. Sch. Law Alumni Assn., 1989, Judiciary award Conn. Bar Assn., 1991, Hartford Neighborhood Housing Coalition award, 1992, RosCossi - Koskoff Justice award Conn. Trial Lawyers Assn., 1999, Jud. Recognition award Conn. Def. Lawyers Assn., 1999. Home: 245 Pleasant Point Rd Branford CT 06405-5609 Office: Superior Ct 235 Church St New Haven CT 06510

BERENDT, ROBERT TRYON, lawyer; b. Chgo., Mar. 8, 1939; s. Alex E. and Ethel L. (Tryon) B.; m. Sara Probert, June 15, 1963; children: David, Elizabeth, Katherine. BA, Monmouth Coll., 1961; JD with distinction, U. Iowa, 1965. Bar: Iowa 1965, Ill. 1968, U.S. Dist. Ct. (no. dist.) Ill. 1968, U.S. Ct. Appeals (7th cir.) 1968, Mo. 1979, U.S. Dist. Ct. (ea. dist.) Mo. 1979. Assoc. Schiff Hardin & Waite, Chgo., 1968-73, ptnr., 1973-78; litigation counsel Monsanto Co., St. Louis, 1978-83, asst. gen. counsel, 1983-85, assoc. gen. counsel, 1986-96; of counsel Thompson Coburn, 1996—. Disting. Neutral, Ctr. for Pub. Resources; editl. adv. bd. Alternatives, Inside Litigation, Product Safety and Liability Reporter-Bur. Nat. Affairs. Contbr. articles to profl. jours. Lt. USNR, 1965-68. Mem. ABA (litigation sect., coun. mem. 1993-96), Mo. Bar Assn., Ill. Bar Assn., Iowa Bar Assn., Bar Assn. Met. St. Louis, Product Liability Adv. Coun. (bd. dirs., exec. com., Inst. for the Judiciary, pres.-trustee Found. 1992-98). Avocations: golf, tennis, reading. Antitrust, General civil litigation, Environmental. Office: Thompson Coburn 1 Mercantile Ctr Ste 3400 Saint Louis MO 63101-1643

BERENZWEIG, JACK CHARLES, lawyer; b. Bklyn., Sept. 29, 1942; s. Sidney A. and Anne R. (Dubowe) B.; m. Susan J. Berenzweig, Aug. 8, 1968; children: Mindy, Andrew. B.E.E., Cornell U., 1964; J.D., Am. U., 1968. Bar: Va. 1968, Ill. 1969. Examiner U.S. Pat. Off., Washington, 1964-66; pat. adviser U.S. Naval Air Systems Command, 1966-68; ptnr. Brinks, Hofer, Gilson & Lione and predecessor firm, Chgo., 1968—. Editorial staff Am. U. Law Rev., 1966-68; contbr. articles to profl. jours. Mem. ABA, Chgo. Bar Assn., Ill. State Bar Assn., Bar Assn. 7th Fed. Cir., Va. State Bar, Internat. Trademark Assn. (bd. dirs. 1983-85), Brand Names Edn. Found. (bd. dirs. 1993-2000), Meadow Club (Rolling Meadows, Ill.), Miramar Club (Naples, Fla., Delta Theta Phi. Federal civil litigation, Patent, Trademark and copyright. Home: 127 W Oak St Apt A Chicago IL 60610-5422 Office: Brinks Hofer Gilson & Lione Ltd Ste 3600 455 N Cityfront Plaza Dr Chicago IL 60611-5599 E-mail: jcb@brinkshofer.com

BERESFORD, DOUGLAS LINCOLN, lawyer; b. Washington, June 1, 1956; s. Spencer Moxon and Ann (Lincoln) B.; m. Lori Anne Mainous, Sept. 22, 1990; children: Alexander Gould, Erik Mainous. AB cum laude, Harvard U., 1978; JD, Georgetown U., 1982. Bar: D.C. 1982, U.S. Ct. Appeals (D.C. cir.) 1984, U.S. Supreme Ct. 1986. Assoc. Morgan, Lewis & Bockius, Washington, 1982-83, Newman & Holtzinger, P.C., Washington, 1983-89, ptnr., 1989-94, Long, Aldridge & Norman, Washington, 1994-2000, Hogan & Hartson LLP, Washington, 2000—. Administrative and regulatory, FERC practice, Public utilities. Office: Hogan & Hartson LLP 555 13th St NW Ste 800W Washington DC 20004-1161 E-mail: dlberesford@hhlaw.com

BERESIN, MARTA ILENE, lawyer; b. Phila., July 27, 1965; d. Carl Morris and Constance (Goldman) Beresin; m. William Jacob Scher, July 9, 1995; 1 child, Razi Esther Beresin Scher. BA, Pa. State U., 1987; JD with honors, George Washington U., 1991. Bar: Md. 1991, D.C. 1998, U.S. Dist. Ct. Md. Law clk. Women's Legal Def. Fund, Washington, 1990, ACLU, Washington, 1990; assoc. Mitterhoff & Henrichsen, 1991-92; staff atty. Legal Aid Bur., Inc., Hughesville, Md., 1992-95, acting chief atty., 1995; staff atty. Homeless Persons Representation Project, Balt., 1995-97. Vol. HIV counselor Washington Free Clinic, 1992-97, bd. dirs., 1994, sec. bd. dirs., 1995; vol. shelter atty. Homeless Persons Representation Project, Bethesda, Md., 1999. Equal Justice Found. grantee, 1990. Mem. Law Assn. for Women (exec. bd. 1990-91). Democrat. Jewish. Avocations: yoga, running, photography. E-mail: berscher@erols.com

BERG, DAVID HOWARD, lawyer; b. Springfield, Ohio, Mar. 4, 1942; s. Nathan Stewart Berg and Mildred (Besser) Berg-Filion; children: Geoffrey Alan, Gabriel Adam, Caitlin Hannah; m. Kathryn Page, July 10, 1994. Student, Tulane U., 1963; BA in English, U. Houston, 1964, JD, 1967. Bar: Tex. 1967, U.S. Dist. Ct. Tex. 1967, N.Y. 1989, U.S. Dist. Ct. (so. dist.) N.Y. 1990, U.S. Ct. Appeals (2d, 4th, 5th, 8th and 11th cirs.) 1990, U.S. Supreme Ct. 1990. Law clk. NLRB, Washington, 1967-68; ptnr. David Berg & Assocs., Houston, 1968-77, Berg & Androphy, 1977—. Mem. fed. ct. lawyers adv. com. U.S. Dist. Ct. (so. dist.) Tex.; mem. U. Houston Law Found., 1996—; spl. counsel commn. on lawyer discipline, Tex. State Bar, 1996—. Contbr. articles and essays to mags. Issues staff Jimmy Carter Campaign, Atlanta, 1976; adviser Jimmy Carter Transition Govt., Washington, 1976; adviser Mayor Kathy Whitmire campaigns, 1980-91; patron Friends of Menil Collection, 1990-91; adviser campaign Mayor Bob Lanier, 1991; chmn. City of Houston's "Imagine Houston"; bd. dirs. "Camp for All"; bd. dirs. U. Houston Law Found., 1996. Recipient 1st pl. for best feature article in a scholarly jour. Nat. Assn. Publ., 1991. Fellow Internat. Acad. Trial Lawyers, Houston Bar Found.; mem. ATLA, Tex. Bar Assn. (chmn. grievance com. 1984-85), Tex. Bar Found., N.Y. State Bar Assn., Tex. Trial Lawyers Assn., Houston Trial Lawyers Assn., U. Houston Law Alumni Assn. (bd. dirs. 1992-95), Am. Bd. Trial Advocates (assoc.). Democrat. Jewish. Avocations: writing, running, fishing. Criminal, Personal injury. Home: 16 Sunset Blvd Houston TX 77005-1838 Office: Berg & Androphy 3704 Travis St Houston TX 77002-9550

BERG, GALE DIANE, lawyer; b. Bklyn., June 24, 1951; d. Sidney and Evelyn (Schulman) B.; m. Joel Hochdorf, Feb. 8, 1981; children: Jillian, Rachel. BA, Am. U., 1972; JD, Vt. Law Sch., 1976. Bar: N.Y. 1977, D.C. 1978, U.S. Dist. Ct. (so. and ea. dists.) N.Y. 1978, U.S. Ct. Appeals (2d cir.) 1978. Asst. atty. gen. N.Y. State Dept. Law, N.Y.C., 1977-80; assoc. Fischbein, Olivieri, Rozenholc & Badillo, N.Y.C., 1980; pvt. practice, N.Y.C., 1981-84; asst. counsel N.Y. State Racing and Wagering Bd., N.Y.C., 1984—; asst. adj. prof. bus. contract law Baruch Coll., 1982, asst. adj. prof. domestic relations, 1983; arbitrator N.Y.C. Civil Ct., 1983-84. Vol. Friends of Mario Cuomo, N.Y.C., 1984. Mem. ABA (chmn. subcom. on atty.'s fees of com. sole practitioners and small firms 1981-84, N.Y. State Bar Assn., N.Y. State Women's Bar Assn. (chmn. membership 1981-82). Office: NY State Racing and Wagering Bd 400 Broome St New York NY 10013-3238

BERG, STEPHANIE A. lawyer; b. Detroit, May 28, 1971; d. Lawrence J. and Beatrice S. Berg; m. Kevin A.S. Fanning, Sept. 4, 1998. BA, Wayne State U., 1993; JD, U. Detroit, 1997. Bar: Mich. Atty. Kepes, Wine & McNeilage, Southfield, Mich., 1997—. Mem. Mich. Trial Lawyers Assn. (exec. bd. dirs. 1998, women's caucus lobby days 1997). Avocations: mountain biking, running, tennis. Personal injury, Product liability. Office: Kepes Wine & McNeilage PC 27200 Lahser Southfield MI 48034

BERGAN, EDMUND PAUL, JR. lawyer; b. N.Y.C., May 6, 1950; s. Edmund Paul and Alice (Gordon) P. B.; m. Patricia Ann Gallagher, Jan. 31, 1987; children: Annabel (dec.), Caroline. BA, Holy Cross Coll., 1971; JD, Fordham U., 1975. Bar: N.Y. 1976. Staff atty. SEC, Washington, 1975-77; v.p., assoc. gen. counsel Securities Industry Assn., N.Y.C., 1977-81; v.p., asst. gen. counsel Alliance Capital Mgmt. LP, 1981-88; v.p. gen. counsel Alliance Fund Distbrs., 1988-94; v.p., gen. counsel Alliance Fund Svc. Subs., 1988-94; sr. v.p., gen. counsel Alliance Fund Distbrs. and Alliance Fund Svcs., 1994—. Mem. ABA (mem. fed. securities com. 1982—, investment advisers and cos. subcom. 1999—), Investment Co. Inst. (SEC rules com. 1986—, closed-end fund com. 1989—, chmn. 1992-97, various subcoms.), Bar Assn. City N.Y. (investment mgmt. com. 1999—). Republican. Roman Catholic. Avocations: historical studies, athletics. Securities. Office: Alliance Capital Mgmt LP 1345 Ave of Americas New York NY 10105-3198

BERGAN, PHILIP JAMES, lawyer; b. White Plains, N.Y., Apr. 13, 1938; s. Raymond Patrick and Marjorie (Ward) B. m. Susan Ellen Bancroft, Sept. 18, 1965; children: David Andrew, Jeffrey Matthew. AB, Holy Cross Coll., 1960; MA, Stanford U., 1963; LLB, Yale U., 1964. Bar: N.Y. 1966, U.S. Ct. Appeals (2d cir.) 1966, U.S. Supreme Ct. 1971, U.S. Dist. Ct. (so. dist.) N.Y 1973. Assoc. Shearman & Sterling, N.Y.C., Paris, London, 1964-77; gen. counsel merchant banking group Citicorp/Citibank, N.A., N.Y.C., 1978-82; v.p. gen. counsel's office Citicorp/Citibank N.A., 1982-84; assoc. gen. counsel Citicorp/Citibank, N.A., 1984-91; from counsel to ptnr. D'Amato & Lynch, 1992—. Bd. dirs. Household Bank, Prospect Heights, Ill., 1993—; 1st Ctrl. Nat. Life Ins. Co. of N.Y., N.Y.C., 1998—. Contbr. articles to prof. jours. Mem. ABA (banking law com. bus. law sect. 1992—), N.Y. State Bar Assn., Assn. Bar City N.Y. (banking law com. 1993-96, legal history com. 1995-98), Down Town Assn. Banking, Finance, Securities. Banking, Finance, Securities. Home: 935 Park Ave New York NY 10028-0212 Office: D'Amato & Lynch 70 Pine St Fl 47 New York NY 10270-0002

BERGER, CHARLES LEE, lawyer; b. Evansville, Ind., Oct. 14, 1947; s. Sydney L. and Sadelle (Kaplan) B.; m. Leslie Lilly, Apr. 20, 1973; children: Sarah, Rebecca, Leah. BA, U. Evansville, 1969; JD (cum laude), Ind. U., 1972. Bar: Ind. 1972, U.S. Dist. Ct. (so. dist.) Ind. 1972, U.S. Ct. Appeals (7th cir.) 1972, U.S. Ct. Appeals D.C. 1975, U.S. Supreme Ct. 1977, U.S. Dist. Ct. (we. dist.) Ky. 1981, U.S. Ct. Appeals (6th cir.) 1984. Ptnr. Berger & Berger, Evansville, 1972—. Mem. study com. Ind. Supreme Ct. Rules of Evidence, 1993—; mem. Ind. Jud. Qualifications Disciplinary Commn., 1998—. $Den— Sarah, Rebecca, Leah. B.A., U. Evansville, 1969; J.D. cum laude, Ind. U., 1972. Bar: Ind. 1972, U.S. Dist. Ct. (so. dist.) Ind. 1972, U.S. Ct. Appeals (7th cir.) 1972, U.S. Ct. Appeals D.C. 1975, U.S. Supreme Ct. 1977, U.S. Dist. Ct. (we. dist.) Ky. 1981, U.S. Ct. Appeals (6th cir.) 1984. Ptnr., Berger & Berger, Evansville, 1972—; mem. study com. Ind. Supreme Ct. Rules of Evidence, 1993—; mem. Ind. Jud. Qualifications Disciplinary Commn., 1998—. Bd. dirs. Leadership Evansville, 1977. Fellow Ind. Bar Found.; mem. Ind. Bar Assn. (chmn. trial lawyers sect. 1982-83), Am. Bd. Trial Advocates, Ind. Trial Lawyers Assn. (bd. dirs. 1973-77, 77-84, v.p. 1984—). Bd. dirs. Leadership Evansville, 1977. Fellow Ind. Bar Found.; mem. Ind. Bar Assn. (chmn. trial lawyers sect. 1982-83), Am. Bd. Trial Advocates, Ind. Trial Lawyers Assn. (bd. dirs. 1973-77, 77-84, v.p. 1984—). Jewish. Federal civil litigation, State civil litigation, Personal injury. Home: 7408 E Sycamore St Evansville IN 47715-3762 Office: Berger & Berger 313 Main St Evansville IN 47708-1485 E-mail: cberger@bergerlaw.com

BERGER, DAVID, lawyer; b. Archbald, Pa., Sept. 6, 1912; s. Jonas and Anna (Raker) B.; m. Barbara Simmons Wainscott, Nov. 5, 1997; children: Jonathan, Daniel. AB cum laude, U. Pa., 1932, LLB cum laude, 1936. Bar: Pa. 1938, D.C., N.Y. Asst. to prof. U. Pa. Law Sch., Phila., 1936-38, spl. asst. to dean; law clk. Pa. Supreme Ct., 1939-40; spl. asst. to dir. enemy alien identification program U.S. Dept. Justice, Washington, 1941-42; law clk. U.S. Ct. Appeals, 1946; pvt. practice Phila., Washington and N.Y.C.; city solicitor Phila., 1956-63; founder, chmn. Berger & Montague, P.C. Former counsel Sch. Dist. Phila.; former chmn. adv. com. Pa. Superior Ct.; mem. drafting com. fed. rules evidence U.S. Supreme Ct.; lectr. on legal subjects. Author numerous articles on law. Nat. commr. Anti-Defamation League; assoc. trustee U. Pa., mem. bd. overseers Law Sch.; Presdl. appointee U.S. Holocaust Meml. Coun.; dir. Internat. Tennis Hall of Fame; bd. dirs. ARC, Palm Beach, Fla.; founder, mem. Friends of Art and Preservation in Embassies. Decorated Silver Star and Presdl. Unit Citation; Fellow Duke of Edinburgh's Award World Fellowship; David Berger chair of law for the improvement of the adminstrn. of justice established at U. Pa. Law Sch.; enshrined in U. Pa. Tennis Hall of Fame, 1997. Fellow Am. Coll. Trial Lawyers, Internat. Acad. Trial Lawyers, Internat. Soc. Barristers;

mem. ABA (vice-chair tort and ins. practice sect. com. on comml. torts 1988-89), Phila. Bar Assn. (pres., bd. govs., chancellor), Phila. Bar Found. (past pres.), The Athenaeum Phila., Penn Club (N.Y.C., founder), Order of Coif, The Queens Club (London), Royal Ascot Racing Club (Ascot, Eng.). Antitrust, Bankruptcy, Federal civil litigation. Home: Elephant Walk 109 Jungle Rd Palm Beach FL 33480-4809 Office: Berger & Montague PC 1622 Locust St Philadelphia PA 19103-6305

BERGER, HAROLD, lawyer, engineer; b. Archbald, Pa., June 10, 1925; s. Jonas and Anna (Raker) B.; m. Renee Margareten, Aug. 26, 1951; children: Jill Ellen, Jonathan David. BS in Elec. Engring, U. Pa., 1948, JD, 1951. Bar: Pa. 1951. Practiced in, Phila.; judge Ct. of Common Pleas, Phila. County, 1971-72; chmn., moderator Internat. Aerospace Meetings Princeton U., 1965-66; chmn. Western Hemisphere Internat. Law Conf., San Jose, Costa Rica, 1967; chmn. internat. Confs. on Aerospace and Internat. Law, Coll. William and Mary; permanent mem. Jud. Conf. 3d Circuit Ct. of Appeals; mem. County Bd. Law Examiners, Phila. County, 1961-71; chmn. World Conf. Internat. Law and Aerospace, Caracas, Venezuela, Internat. Conf. on Environ. and Internat. Law, U. Pa., 1974, Internat. Confs. on Global Interdependence, Princeton U., 1975, 79; mem. Pa. State Conf. Trial Judges, 1972-80, Nat. Conf. State Trial Judges, 1972—; chmn. Pa. Com. for Independent Judiciary, 1973—. Adv. coun. Biddle Law Libr., U. Pa., 1991—; mem. bd. overseers Sch. Engring. & Applied Scis., U. Pa., 1998—. Mem. editorial advisory bd.: Jour. of Space Law, U. Miss. Sch. of Law, 1973— ; contbr. articles to profl. jours. Mem. We the People 200 Com. for Constn. Bicentennial, 1991. Served with Signal Corps, AUS, 1944-46. Recipient Alumnus of Year award Thomas McKean Law Club, U. Pa. Law Sch., 1965, Gen. Electric Co. Space award, 1966, Nat. Disting. Achievement award Tau Epsilon Rho, 1972, Spl. Pa. Jud. Conf. award, 1981. Mem. Inter-Am. Bar Assn. (past chmn. aerospace law com.), Fed. Bar Assn. (past nat. chmn. com. on aerospace law, pres. Phila. chpt. 1983-84, mem. nat. exec. coun., past nat. chmn. fed. jud. com., Presdl. award 1970, Nat. Disting. Svc. award 1978, nat. com. 1987 bi-centennial of U.S. Constn., chmn. class action and complex litigation com. 3d cir. 1990—, nat. chmn., alternate dispute resolution com. 1992-95, pres. eastern dist. Pa. chpt. 1996—), ABA (Spl. Presdl. Program medal 1975, past chmn. aerospace law com., mem. state and fed. ct. com., nat. conf. of state trial judges), Phila. Bar Assn. (past chmn. jud. liaison com. 1975, chmn. internat. law com. 1977), Assn. U.S. Mems. Internat. Inst. Space Law Internat. Astronautical Fedn. (former bd. dirs.), Internat. Acad. Astronautics Paris. Alternative dispute resolution, Federal civil litigation, Entertainment. Office: 1622 Locust St Philadelphia PA 19103-6305

BERGER, LAWRENCE HOWARD, lawyer; b. Phila., May 19, 1947; s. Howard Merrill Berger and Doris Eleanor Cummins; m. Julie Mitchell Collins, Aug. 8, 1970; children: Colby Shaw, Ryan Lawrence, Lindsey Wade. BS, Mich. State U., 1969; JD, U. Va., 1972. Bar: Pa. 1972, U.S. Dist. Ct. (ea. dist.) Pa. 1973, U.S. Ct. Appeals (3d cir.) 1986. Assoc. Morgan, Lewis & Bockius LLP, Phila., 1972-79, ptnr., 1979—. Bd. dirs. INROADS/Phila., Lacrosse Found. Trustee Agnes Irwin Sch., 1984-86, Naomi Wood Charitable Trust-Woodford Mansion Mus., 1986—, Fairmount Park Coun. for Hist. Sites, 1989-95, Fairmont Park Hist. Trust, 1993-95; dir. Phila. Lacrosse Assn., 1992—. Recipient Frank Carr Community Svc. award, 1991. Fellow Am. Bar Found.; mem. ABA (sec. com. on nonprofit corps. 1980-90), Pa. Bar Assn. (chmn. com. on uniform comml. code 1978-80), Phila. Bar Assn., Pa. Bar Inst., Banking Law Inst. (lectr. 1985), Pa. Bankers Assn. (lectr. 1980, 89), Martins Dam Club, Blue Key, Omicron Delta Kappa. Banking, General corporate, Non-profit and tax-exempt organizations. Home: 360 Pond View Rd Devon PA 19333-1732 Office: Morgan Lewis & Bockius LLP 1701 Market St Philadelphia PA 19103-2903

BERGER, MICHAEL GARY, lawyer; b. New Haven, Apr. 16, 1946; s. Jacob and Edith (Axelrod) B.; m. Miriam Janet Haines, July 24, 1977; children: Richard, Daniel. BS, Yale Coll., 1968; JD, Columbia U., 1973. Asst. dist. atty. New York County Office of Dist. Atty., N.Y.C., 1973-76; pvt. practice, 1981—. Arbitrator Am. Arbitration Assn., 1994—; mem. Criminal Justice Act Panel, N.Y.C., 1976-79; legal rep. clients in various fields icluding bus., medicine, profl. sports and entertainment; spkr. at cmty. client and bar groups. Commentator on legal manners for Ct. TV, CNBC, Fox News, nat. and local TV programs; contbr. book revs. to law publs. Criminal Justice Act atty. for indigent clients accused of fed. crimes. Mem. ABA, Fed. Bar Coun., Nat. Assn. Criminal Def. Lawyers, N.Y. State Bar Assn., Assn. of Bar of City of N.Y. Avocation: tennis. General civil litigation, Criminal, Entertainment. Office: 250 Park Ave 20th Fl New York NY 10177-0001 E-mail: mberger@mgberger.com

BERGER, ROBERT BERTRAM, lawyer; b. N.Y.C., Sept. 1, 1924; s. Edward William and Sophie (Berkowitz) B.; m. Phyllis Ann Korona, June 14, 1947; children: Barry Robert, Mark Alan, Karen Elizabeth Berger Adametz, James Michael; m. 2d, Arlene Kidder Wills, Dec. 27, 1980; 1 stepchild, Kimberly Kidder Wills Campbell. BS, Georgetown U., 1948; JD, U. Conn., 1952. Bar: Conn. 1952, U.S. Dist. Ct. Conn. 1953, U.S. Tax Ct. 1967, U.S. Ct. Appeals (2d cir.) 1968. Sole practice law, 1952-56; ptnr. Berger & Alaimo, Enfield, Conn., 1956-82, Berger, Alaimo, Santy & McGuire, Enfield, 1982-91, Berger, Santy & McGuire, Enfield, 1991-94, Berger & Santy, Enfield, 1994—2001, Berger, Santy & Barbieri, Enfield, 2001—. Judge Probate Dist. of Enfield, 1989-94; dir. Enfield Vis. Nuses Assn., 1993-96; bd. dirs., mem. exec. com. Conn. Attys. Title Ins. Co., Rocky Hill. Chmn. Enfield Dem. Town Com., 1979-87, Conn. Psychiat. Security Review Bd., 1985—. Contbr. monthly polit. column Enfield Press, 1980-84. Pres. United Way North Ctrl. Conn., 1981-84; trustee St. Bernard's Roman Cath. Ch., 1977-90, 99-2000; trustee, exec. bd. mem. Johnson Meml. Hosp., Johnson Meml. Corp., Stafford, Conn.; bd. dirs. United Way of Capitol Area, 1981-85, United Way North Ctrl. Conn., 1977—. With USMCR, 1942-45. Decorated Purple Heart; recipient disting. svc. award Enfield Jr. C. of C., 1955, Clayton Frost award U.S. Jr. C. of C., 1959-60. Mem. ABA, Conn. Bar Assn., Hartford County Bar Assn., Enfield Lawyers Assn. (pres. 1973-74), Am. Judicature Soc., Enfield Rotary (pres. 1970-71, Paul Harris fellow 1984). General corporate, Probate, Real property. Office: PO Box 1163 Enfield CT 06083-1163

BERGER, STEVEN R. lawyer, state official; b. Miami, Aug. 23, 1945; s. Jerome J. and Jeanne B. B.; m. Francine Blake, Aug. 20, 1966; children: Amy, Charlie. BS, U. Ala., 1967; JD, 1969. Bar: Fla. 1969, U.S. Dist. Ct. (no. dist.) Fla. 1969, U.S. Dist. Ct. (so. dist.) Fla. 1971, U.S. Ct. Appeals (5th cir.) 1971, U.S. Supreme Ct. 1972, U.S. Ct. Claims 1977, U.S. Ct. Appeals (11th cir.) 1981, U.S. Dist. Ct. (mid. dist.) Fla. 1989, N.Y. 1990, Nev. 1991, U.S. Dist. Ct. Nev. 1991, U.S. Ct. Appeals (2nd and 9th cirs.) 1991; cert. appellate specialist Fla. Bar Bd. Assoc. W. Dexter Douglass, Tallahassee, 1969-71, William R. Dawes, Miami, 1971; ptnr. Carey, Dwyer, Cole Selwood & Bernard, 1971-81; sole practice Steven R. Berger, P.A., 1981-89; ptnr. Wolpe, Leibowitz, Berger & Brotman, 1989-94, Berger & Chafetz, 1994-99; asst. atty. gen. State of Fla., 1999—. Mem. faculty Nat. Appellate Advocacy Inst., Washington, 1980; vice chmn. bench and bar adv. com. Ct. Appeals. 4th Dist., 1986-92. Chmn. City Miramar Planning Bd., 1975-76. Mem. ABA (vice chmn. app. practice com. litigation sect. 1981-83, chmn. 5th cir. subcom. appellate practice com. 1978-81), Am. Judicature Soc., Am. Arbitration Assn., Tallahassee Bar Assn. Appellate, General civil litigation, Criminal. Office: Office of Atty Gen 444 Brickell Ave Ste 950 Miami FL 33131-2407

BERGERE, C(LIFFORD) WENDELL, JR. lawyer; b. Winchester, Mass., Sept. 30, 1945; s. Clifford Wendell and Grace Elizabeth (Dunk) B.; m. Carol Eileen Clampett, Nov. 4, 1974; children— Jennifer Macy, Sarah Hampton. B.A. in Soviet History, St. Lawrence U., Canton, N.Y., 1967; J.D., George Washington U., 1972. Bar: D.C. 1972, U.S. Ct. Appeals (D.C. cir.) 1972. Atty. internat. matters Communications Satellite Corp., Washington, 1972-77; sr. corp. atty., asst. sec. Perkin-Elmer Corp., Norwalk, Conn., 1977-82, gen. counsel, asst. sec., 1982-86, v.p., gen. counsel, sec., 1986—. Bd. dirs. Danbury (Conn.) Hosp. Served with U.S. Army, 1969-70. Episcopalian. Antitrust, Federal civil litigation, Contracts commercial. Office: Perkin-Elmer Corp 761 Main Ave Norwalk CT 06859-0003

BERGERSON, DAVID RAYMOND, lawyer; b. Mpls., Nov. 23, 1939; s. Raymond Kenneth and Katherine Cecille (Langworthy) B.; m. Nancy Anne Heeter, Dec. 22, 1962; children: W. Thomas C., Kirsten Finch, David Raymond BA, Yale U., 1961; JD, U. Minn., 1964. Bar: Minn. 1964. Assoc. Fredrikson Law Firm, Mpls., 1964-67; atty. Honeywell Inc., 1967-74, asst. gen. counsel, 1974-82, v.p., asst. gen. counsel, 1983-84, v.p., gen. counsel, 1984-92; pvt. practice law, 1992-94; v.p., sec. Telcom Sys. Svcs., Inc., Plymouth, Minn., 1994-96, dir., cons., 1996-97; v.p. bd. dirs. Hogan Bergerson, Inc., Mpls., 1997—. Bd. dirs. Pillsbury Neighborhood Svcs., Inc., Mpls., 1983-92. Republican. Club: Minneapolis. Avocations: scuba, tennis, bird-hunting. General corporate, Mergers and acquisitions, Securities. Home: 2303 Huntington Point Rd E Wayzata MN 55391-9740 Office: Hogan Bergerson Inc 4040 IDS Ctr Minneapolis MN 55402 E-mail: dbergatmb@aol.com, dbergerson@qwest.net

BERGMAN, DANIEL CHARLES, county official, lawyer, environmental manager; b. Corpus Christi, Tex., Aug. 18, 1943; s. Benjamin and Pearl H. B.; m. Susan Lee Axall, Aug. 15, 1965 (div. 1987); children: Erica Catherine, Kelli Lorraine. B.S. in Biology, San Diego State U., 1965, M.S., 1971; J.D., U. San Diego, 1975. Bar: Calif. 1976, U.S. Dist. Ct. (so. dist.) Calif. 1976, U.S. Ct. Appeals (9th cir.) 1977; registered environ. health specialist Calif., Ill.; cert. community coll. tchr., vector ecologist, 1971-72, supervising environ. health specialist Dept. Health Services, 1972-79, chief div. environ. health mgr., 1979-81; environ. health cons. Contra Costa (Calif.) Dept. Health Services, 1981, asst. health services dir. Div. Environ. Health, 1981-89; pres., CFO Pyrite Canyon Group, Inc., 1991—; sole practice law, San Diego and Danville, Calif., 1976— ; lectr. in field. Recipient Am. Jurisprudence awards. Mem. Am. Pub. Health Assn., Nat. Environ. Health Assn. (Presdl. citation 1977), Calif. Environ. Health Assn. (Presdl. citation 1977, 78), ABA, Calif. State Bar Assn. Office: 3200C Pyrite St Riverside CA 92509-1109

BERGSCHNEIDER, DAVID PHILIP, legal administrator; b. Springfield, Ill., Nov. 19, 1951; s. Fred J. and Ruby A. (Martin) B.; m. Dawn E. Combes, Sept. 23, 1989; children: Alec, Bryant, Cale. Student, Bradley U., 1969-71; BA, Ill. Coll., 1973; JD, Marquette U., 1976. Bar: Ill. 1976, Wis. 1976, U.S. Ct. Appeals (7th cir.) 1990, U.S. Supreme Ct. 1980. Mem. legis. staff Ill. Gen. Assembly, Springfield, 1976-77; asst. defender Office State Appellate Defender, 1977-93, legal dir., 1993—. Co-author: Defending Illinois Criminal Cases, 1988, Illinois Criminal Practice, 1980, Brief Writing and Oral Argument Handbook, 1988, 94, 97; author: Illinois Handbook of Criminal Law Decisions, 1993, 2d edit., 1998; also articles. Recipient Award of Excellence Ill. Pub. Defender Assn., 1989. Mem. ABA, Ill. Bar Assn. (criminal justice sect. coun. 1987-91, 94-98, sec. 1995-96, chmn. 1996-97), Ill. Attys. for Criminal Justice, Aircraft Owners and Pilots Assn. Office: Office State Appellate Def PO Box 5780 Springfield IL 62705-5780

BERK, ALAN S. law firm executive; b. N.Y.C., May 11, 1934; s. Phil and Mae (Buchberg) B.; m. Barbara Binder, Dec. 18, 1960; children— Charles M., Peter M., Nancy M. BS in Econs., U. Pa., 1955; MS in Bus., Columbia U., 1956. CPA, 1960. Staff acct. Arthur Young & Co., N.Y.C., 1956-62, mgr., prin., 1962-67; sr. v.p. Avco Corp., Greenwich, Conn., 1967-75; dir. Arthur Young & Co., 1975—, ptnr., 1976—, chief fin. officer, 1979-89; nat. dir. fin., treas. Ernst & Young, 1989-92; exec. dir. Kelley, Drye & Warren, N.Y.C., 1993-94. Mem. nat. adv. group Nat. Tech. Inst. for the Deaf, Rochester, N.Y.; chmn. bd. dirs. Jewish Home for the Elderly of Fairfield County, Inc., 1997—; 1st v.p., treas. Bruce Mus., Greenwich, Conn.; mem. golf bd. Town of Greenwich, Conn.; commn. on aging Town of Greenwich. With U.S. Army, 1957. Mem. AICPA, N.Y. State Soc. CPAs, Fin. Execs. Inst., Landmark Club, Stockbridge (Mass.) Golf Club, Stockbridge Sportmen's Club, Lake Dr. Homeowner's Assn., 1st v.p. Stockbridge Bowl Assn. Home: 14 Cornelia Dr Greenwich CT 06830-3906

BERKENSTADT, JAMES ALLAN, lawyer; b. Chgo., June 26, 1956; s. Edward Jules and Lois Marion (Solomon) B.; m. Holly Lynn Cremer, Aug. 3, 1985; children: Rebecca, Bradley. BA, Northwestern U., 1978; JD, So. Ill. U., 1981. Bar: Ill., Wis. Litigation atty. Pollina & Phelan, Chgo., 1982-85; atty. for security dept. Chgo. Cubs Nat. League Ball Club, 1982-84; litigation atty. Axley & Brynelson, Madison, Wis., 1986-87; v.p., corporate counsel The Wisconsin Cheeseman, Inc., 1987—. Author: Black Market Beatles: The Story Behind The Lost Recordings, 1995, Nevermind: Nirvana, 1998; prodr. The Beatles Tapes CD, 1994—, Live At The Edgewater: vol. 1 and 2 CD; contbr. articles to Musician mag. Bd. dirs. Cremer Charitable Found., Madison, 1989—; historian/archivist for rock band Garbage. Mem. NARAS. Avocations: racquetball, golf, music archivist, writer. General corporate. Office: The Wisconsin Cheeseman Inc 301 Broadway Dr Sun Prairie WI 53590-1799

BERKETT, MARIAN MAYER, lawyer; b. Mar. 29, 1913; d. Maurice J. and Beulah (Lob) Mayer; m. George David B., Jan. 26, 1943. BA, La. State U., 1933, MA, 1935; LLB, Tulane U., 1937. Bar: La. 1937. Assoc. firm Deutsch, Kerrigan & Stiles, New Orleans, 1937—61, ptnr., 1961—. Bd. dir. New Orleans Lawyer Referral Svc. Author: (non-fiction) Workmen's Compensation Law in Louisiana, 1937;contbr. articles to Tulane Law Rev. Mem. charter commn., Jefferson Parish, La., 1953; vice chmn. La. Civil Svc. Commn., Baton Rouge, 1963—75; mem. adv. com. on charter reform Jefferson Parish; bd. dir., officer Family Svc. Soc. of New Orleans; mem. budget com. Cmty. Chest of New Orleans; contbr. to Bur. Govtl. Rsch. New Orleans Met. Area Com. ACLU; bd. dir., officer, hon. pres. La. Civil Svc. League; bd. dir. New Orleans chpt. NCCJ. Recipient Monte Lemann award, La. Civil Svc. League, 1973, award, Am. Coun. for Career Women, 1989, Disting. Grad. award, Tulane Law Sch., Industry Lifetime Achievement award, La. Civil Svc. League. Mem.: ABA (vice chmn. fidelity and surety com. ins. sect., governing com. forum on constrn. industry, Cornerstone award), Am. Law Inst., La. Bar Assn., New Orleans Bar Assn., Order of Coif. Construction, Estate planning, Probate. Home: 332 Iona St Metairie LA 70005-4140 Office: Deutsch Kerrigan & Stiles 755 Magazine St New Orleans LA 70130-3698

BERKLEY, BURTON, federal judge; b. Chgo., May 10, 1934; s. Ralph Albert and Frieda (Fleischman) Berkowitz; m. Carol Grace Goldberg, Dec. 22, 1955; children: David Saul (dec.), Florence Melissa Berkley-Yokie. AB, Harvard U., 1955, JD, 1958. Bar: Ill. 1958, U.S. Supreme Ct. 1962, N.Y. 1969, D.C. 1978. Asst. atty. gen. Ill. Atty. Gen.'s Office, Chgo., 1958-59; asst. U.S. atty. Dept. of Justice, 1959-61, appellate trial atty. Tax Div., Washington, 1961-67; dep. tax counsel GE, N.Y.C., 1967-70; legal advisor NIH, HEW, Washington, 1971-72, dep. gen. counsel, 1972-77; spl. counsel to assoc. commr. Office of Hearings and Appeal, Social Security Adminstrn., Arlington, Va., 1977-80, dep. chmn. appeals coun. Office of Hearings and Appeals, 1980-88, chief adminstrv. law judge Hearing Office, Washington, 1988-97, adminstrv. law judge, 1997—. Co-editor: Ethical Issues in Human Genetics, 1973. Avocations: reading, music, theatre, travel. Office: Social Security Adminstrn Office Hearings and Appeals 820 1st St NE 8th Fl Washington DC 20002-4243

BERKOFF, MARK ANDREW, lawyer; b. Boston, Aug. 8, 1961; s. Marshall Richard and Bebe R. B.; m. Susan Lynn Ochalek; children: Alexander, Rachel. BA with honors, U. Wis., 1983; JD, U. Chgo., 1986. Bar: Ill. 1987, U.S. Dist. Ct. (no. dist. Ill.) 1987, U.S. Ct. Appeals (7th cir.) 1990. Ptnr. Piper Marbury Rudnick & Wolfe, Chgo., 1986—. Vol. Am. Cancer Soc., Chgo., 1993-96, Make-A-Wish Found. No. Ill., 1998—. Mem. ABA, Chgo. Bar Assn., Turnaround Mgmt. Assn. Avocations: sports, collecting Currier & Ives prints, numismatics, family. Bankruptcy, Consumer commercial. Office: Piper Marbury Rudnick & Wolfe 203 N Lasalle St Ste 1800 Chicago IL 60601-1210

BERKSON, JACOB BENJAMIN, lawyer, author, conservationist; b. Washington County, Md., Dec. 6, 1925; s. Meyer and Ida Evelyn (Berman) B.; m. Ann Goldstein, June 25, 1955 (div.); children: Daniel Jeremy, Susan Kay, James Meyer. BA, U. Va., 1947, LLB, 1949, JD, 1970; grad., Fed. Exec. Inst., Charlottesville, Va., 1972. Bar: Md. 1949, Va. 1949, U.S. Supreme Ct. 1965, Calif. 1975. Sole practice, Hagerstown, Md., 1949-52, 54-64; ptnr. McCauley, Cooey, Berkson & Wright, 1964-70; dep. gen. counsel U.S. GSA, Washington, 1970-76; pvt. practice law Hagerstown, 1976—. Instr. Law Hagerstown Bus. Coll., 1986; trial magistrate, Hagerstown and Washington County, Md., 1951-52; mem. Legis. Coun. Md., 1955-58; del. Md. Legislature, 1955-58; trial magistrate, Hagerstown, 1958-59. Recipient commendation for svc. to U.S. Naval Acad. and pub. interest Chief of Naval Personnel, 1956. Lt. USNR, 1944-46, 52-54. Author: Shingahi Saburo and Short Stories, 1978, Comin' Home, 1993, A Canary's Tale, 1996; case editor, co-founder Va. Law Weekly, 1948; contbr. articles to profl. jours., address to Congrl. Record. Scoutmaster local coun. Boy Scouts Am.; organizer, dir. County Youth Conservation Corps; active Big Bros.; bd. dirs. Doub's Woods County Park, Devil's Backbone County Park; assisted in establishment of C&O Canal Nat. Histo. Park, 1954-70; camp sponsor YMCA; adv. Model Youth Legis.; pres. PTA; chmn. Washington County Park Commn., 1961-66; bd. dirs. Rachel Carson Coun., Inc., Chevy Chase, Md., 1996—. Mem. ABA, Calif. Bar Assn., Va. Bar Assn., Md. Assn. County Civil Attys. (pres., award for svc. as pres. 1966), Washington County Bar Assn. (pres.), Am. Legion, Hagerstown Club, Lions (pres.), Speakers Soc., Elks, Torch Club (Hagerstown), Thomas Jefferson Soc. Alumni. Republican. Jewish. Environmental, General practice, Personal injury. Home and Office: 1419 Potomac Ave Hagerstown MD 21742-3315

BERLAGE, JAN INGHAM, lawyer; b. Lewiston, N.Y., Nov. 17, 1969; s. Jan Coxe and Gai Elizabeth (Ingham) B. BA, Wesleyan U., Middletown, Conn., 1992; postgrad., Oxford U., 1992; JD, U. Va., 1995. Law clk. to Hon. E. Stephen Derby U.S. Bankruptcy Ct. Dist. Md., Balt., 1995-96; assoc. Day, Berry & Howard, Hartford, Conn., 1996-2001, Ballard Spahr Andrews & Ingersoll, Balt., 2001—. Exec. editor Jour. of Law and Politics, Charlottesville, 1994-95, editl. bd., 1993-94; author: (short story) Aguilar Expression, 1990. Deacon Avon Congl. Ch., 1997-2001; mem. Rep. Town Com., Avon, 1998-2001; mem. Avon Zoning Bd. Appeals, 1999-2001. Mem. ABA (v. chmn. young lawyers sect. indiv. rights and responsibilities com. 2001—), Federalist Soc. (pres. U. Va. chpt. 1994-95, co-chmn. Hartford chpt. 1997-2001), Conn. Young Lawyers Assn. (co-chmn. comml. law and bankruptcy sect. 1997-2000, co-chmn. civil rights sect. 2000-01), N.Y. Bar Assn. (mem. comml. law and fed. litigation sects., intellectual property subcom. 1998-2001), Jefferson Literary and Debating Soc., N.Am. Securities Adminstrn. Assn. (task force mem. 1994), Oxford U. Legal Soc., United Oxford/Cambridge U. Club, Phi Delta Phi, Psi Upsilon, Phi Beta Kappa. Bankruptcy, General civil litigation, Intellectual property. Office: Ballard Spahr Andrews & Ingersoll 300 East Lombard St Baltimore MD 21202-3268 E-mail: Berlageji@ballardspahr.com

BERLEY, DAVID RICHARD, lawyer; b. Bklyn., Apr. 9, 1942; s. Alexander and Ruth (Ginsburg) B.; m. Sharon Lee Freeman, Aug. 10, 1964 (div. 1975); children: Steven N., Barbara Robin; m. Katalin Fine, Feb. 14, 1992. BS, Boston U., 1963; JD, Boston Coll., 1966. Bar: Mass. 1966, U.S. Dist. Ct. Mass. 1966, U.S. Ct. Claims 1970, Fla. 1977, U.S. Dist. Ct. (so. dist.) Fla. 1977, U.S. Tax Ct., U.S. Ct. Appeals (11th cir.). Pvt. practice, 1966-77; gen. counsel Econocar Internat. Inc., Miami, Fla., 1976-77; v.p., gen. counsel Emergency Med. Services Assn., Inc., 1977-79, pvt. practice, 1979-85; ptnr. Berley & Littman, PA, 1985-94; pvt. practice, 1994—. Active Greater Miami Heart Assn., Jewish Fedn. Greater Miami, Bus. Vols. for Arts; past chmn. City of Miami Waterfront adv. bd., Coconut Grove Playhouse Soc. of Stars; mem. citizens' adv. bd. Sta.-WLRN Pub. Radio; mem. City of Miami Fin. Com. Mem. Mass. Bar Assn., Fla. Bar Assn. (grievance com.), Fla. Internat. Bankers Assn., Boston Coll. Law Sch. Alumni Assn., Greater Miami C. of C., Coconut Grove C. of C., Coconut Grove Playhouse Soc. Stars. Banking, General corporate, Private international. Office: 848 Brickell Ave Ste 200 Miami FL 33131-2981

BERLIN, ALAN DANIEL, lawyer, international energy and legal consultant; b. Bklyn., Oct. 20, 1939; s. Joseph Jacob and Rose (Smith) B.; m. Renee Wellinger, Dec. 22, 1962; children— Nicole Suzanne, Allison Leigh. BBA, CCNY, 1960; LLB, NYU, 1963, LLM, 1968. Bar: N.Y. 1963. Assoc. Aranow, Brodsky, Bohlinger, Einhorn & Dann, N.Y.C., 1965-68; asst. counsel Gen. Electric Co., 1968-70; tax counsel Norton Simon Inc., 1970-77; asst. prof. Pace U. Grad. Sch. Bus., 1977-85; pres. Belco Petroleum Corp., N.Y.C., 1977-88, The Crown Group, White Plains, N.Y., 1988-95; ptnr. Aitken Irvin Berlin & Vrooman L.L.P., 1995—. Spl. cons. to UN Dept. Tech. Cooperation for Devel., 1989—, UN Ctr. for Transnat. Corps., 1990—; hon. assoc. Ctr. for Petroleum and Mineral Law & Policy, U. Dundee, Scotland, 1993—; bd. dirs. Belco Oil & Gas Corp. Author monographs on fed. income tax. With U.S. Army, 1963-65. Mem. ABA, Internat. Bar Assn., N.Y. State Bar Assn., Assn. of Bar of City of N.Y., Inter-Am. Bar Assn., Assn. Internat. Petroleum Negotiators. Lodge: Masons. General corporate, Oil, gas, and mineral, Taxation, general. Office: Aitken Irvin Berlin & Vrooman LLP 2 Gannett Dr White Plains NY 10604-3403 E-mail: aberlin273@aol.com, aibvlaw@yahoo.com

BERLOW, ROBERT ALAN, lawyer; b. Detroit, Feb. 11, 1947; s. Henry and Shirley (Solovich) B.; m. Elizabeth Ann Goldin, Sept. 20, 1972; children: Stuart, Lisa. BA, U. Mich., 1968; JD, Wayne State U., 1971. Bar: Mich. 1971, U.S. Supreme Ct. 1978. Asst. to dean, instr. law sch. Wayne State U., Detroit, 1971-72; mem. Radner, Radner, Shefman, Bayer and Berlow, P.C., Southfield, Mich., 1972-78; gen. counsel Perry Drug Stores, Inc., Pontiac, 1978-80, gen. counsel, sec., 1980-82, v.p., gen. counsel, sec., 1982-88, sr. v.p., gen. counsel, sec., 1988-93, sr. v.p., chief adminstrn. officer, gen. counsel, sec., 1993-94, exec. v.p., gen. counsel, sec., 1994-95; sr. mem. Dykema Gossett, PLLC, Bloomfield Hills, 1995—, also chmn. retail practice group. Pres. Agy. for Jewish Edn., Metro Detroit, 1993-95, v.p., 1987-93; bd. dirs. Jewish Cmty. Ctr. Met. Detroit, 1989-2001, v.p., 1992-93, treas., 1996-97, sec., 1997-98. Mem. ABA, Mich. Bar Assn. (chair comml. leasing and mgmt. com. of real estate com. of real property law sect. 1993-98, chmn. real property law sect. 2001—, frequent spkr. continuing legal edn. programs), Internat. Coun. Shopping Ctrs. (roundtable leader nat. law conf.). Avocations: sports, photography. General corporate, Landlord-tenant, Real property. Office: Dykema Gossett PLLC 39577 N Woodward Ave Bloomfield Hills MI 48304-2837 E-mail: r.berlow@dykema.com

BERMAN, BRUCE JUDSON, lawyer; b. Roslyn, N.Y., Oct. 9, 1946; s. Howard M. Berman and Soosha T. (Draizen) Marks; children: Daniel H., Ann N., Andrew J., Josie A.; m. Susan Leigh Readinger, Dec. 29, 1991. BA, Williams Coll., 1968; MBA, Columbia U., 1970; JD, Boston U., 1972. Bar: Fla. 1973, U.S. Dist. Ct. (so. dist.) Fla. 1980, U.S. Dist. Ct. (mid. dist.) Fla. 1990, U.S. Ct. Appeals (5th cir.) 1980, U.S. Ct. Appeals (11th cir.) 1981, U.S. Supreme Ct. 1976. Assoc. Guggenheimer & Untermyer, N.Y.C., 1973-79; from assoc. to ptnr. Myers, Kenin, Levinson, Frank & Richards, Miami, Fla., 1979-85; ptnr. Weil, Gotshal & Manges LLP, 1985-2000, McDermott, Will & Emery, Miami, 2000—. Spl. ad hoc trial com. to Dade County (Fla.) Cir. Ct., 1988—; apptd. Supreme Ct. court reporter cert. planning com., 1995; apptd. Supreme Ct. Com. on Standard Jury Instrns. in Civil Cases, 2000, Supreme Ct. workgroup on access to pub. records, 2000. Author: Florida Civil Procedure, 1998, 99, 2000. Mem. New World Symphony Cmty. Bd., Miami Beach, Fla., 1991-2000. Mem. Fla. Bar (civil procedure rules com. 1984—, chmn. 1988-90, jud. adminstrn. rules com. 1988—, chmn. 1993-94), Dade County Bar. Federal civil litigation, State civil litigation, General practice. Office: McDermott Will & Emery 201 S Biscayne Blvd 22d Fl Miami FL 33131 E-mail: bberman@mwe.com

BERMAN, DAVID, lawyer, poet; b. N.Y.C., Sept. 11, 1934; s. Joseph and Sophie (Hersh) B. BA with honors, U. Fla., 1955; postgrad. Johns Hopkins U., 1955-56; JD, Harvard U., 1963. Bar: Mass. 1963. Teaching fellow Harvard Coll., 1962-63, 66-67; law clk. to justice Mass. Supreme Ct., 1963-64; asst. atty. gen. Commonwealth of Mass., 1964-67; assoc. Zamparelli & White, 1967, ptnr., 1968-74; pvt. practice, 1974-82, 1990—; ptnr. Berman & Moren, Medford, Mass., 1982-89. Author: Future Imperfect, 1982, Slippage, 1996, Early Mandamus in Massachusetts, Massachusetts Legal History, 1998. Trustee Cantata Singers, 1981—. Mem. ABA, Mass. Bar Assn., Mass. Bar Found., Middlesex Bar Assn. (Most Outstanding Trial Lawyer Appelate award, 1998), Harvard Club (Boston), Signet Soc., Confrerie de la Chaine des Rotisseurs, Ordre Mondial, Masons. Republican. Unitarian. Federal civil litigation, General civil litigation, State civil litigation. Home: 33 Birch Hill Rd Belmont MA 02478-1729 Office: 100 George P Hassett Dr Medford MA 02155-3264

BERMAN, ERIC M. lawyer, musician; b. Bklyn., Apr. 1, 1948; s. Bernard and Florence (Grier) B.; m. Christine Beck, Aug. 5, 1973 (div. Apr. 1986); m. Sheri Klein, July 31, 1988. BS in Music Edn., Hofstra U., 1970; MA in Music, NYU, 1971, PhD in Music, NYU, 1981; JD, St. John's U., 1981. Bar: N.Y. 1982, U.S. Dist. Ct. (so. and ea. dists.) N.Y. 1982. Instr. pub. schs., N.Y., 1970-71, 73-84; prin. tubaist San Antonio Symphony, 1971-73; musician, bus. mgr. Kapelye Klezmer Band, N.Y.C., 1981—; sole practice , N.Y.C., 1982-87; ptnr. Smith Carroad Levy and Victor, 1987-89; head litigation collection div. Finkelstein, Borah, Schwartz, Altschuler & Goldstein, 1990; pvt. practice Eric M. Berman, P.C., 1991—; dir., counsel Nassau Symphony Orch., Garden City, N.Y., 1982—, New Classical Consort, N.Y.C., 1983-86, Melville (N.Y.) Brass Ensemble, 1983-84; impartial hearing officer N.Y. State Dept. Edn., 1996—. Contbr. Music Sound Output, 1983-88, Modern Musician and Recording, 1983-88, Music and the Law, 1983-84; musician: (recs.) Levine and His Flying Machine, 1985, Kapelye's Chicken, 1987, Kapelye's On the Air, 1995. Mem. ABA, Nat. Assn. Retail Collection Attys. (comml. law league), N.Y. State Bar Assn. (exec. com., entertainment arts and sports law sect., editor of sect. pubs., comml. and fed. litigation sect., com. on comml. litigation), Am. Arbitration Assn. (panelist 1987—), Assn. of Bar of City of N.Y., N.Y. State Sch. Music Assn. Avocations: antiques, tennis, table tennis. Consumer commercial, Entertainment. Office: Eric M Berman PC 185 Willis Ave Mineola NY 11501-2622

BERMAN, HENRY STEPHEN, lawyer; b. N.Y.C., Aug. 5, 1942; s. Bernard Barry and Julia (Friedman) B.; children from previous marriage: Daniel, Elissa; m. Ronnie Parker Gouz, Dec. 6, 1992. BA, CUNY, 1964; JD, St. John's U., 1967; LLM, NYU, 1968. Bar: N.Y. 1967, U.S. Dist. Ct. (so. dist.) N.Y. 1969. Atty. U.S. Fed. Trade Commn., N.Y.C., 1967; law asst. Appellate divsn. 2d dept., Monroe Pl., Brooklyn, 1967-74; sec. Hon. Morrie Slifkin, Westchester City, 1974-77; ptnr. Fink, Weinberger, Fredman, Berman & Lowell, P.C., White Plains, N.Y., 1981-93, Hall, Dickier, Kent, Friemdna & Wood, 1993-96, Beiman, Bavero, Frucco & Govz, P.C., White Plains, 1996—. Contbr. articles to profl. jours. Fellow Am. Acad. Matrimonial Lawyers; mem. N.Y. State Bar Assn. (fin. officer family law sect. 1982-84, sec. family law sect. 1984-86, chmn. family law sect. 1988-90, co-chair CLE com. 1985—), Westchester County Bar Assn. (editor domestic law rev. family law sect. 1982-90, chair 1990-92). Family and matrimonial. Home: 81 Boulder Rdg Scarsdale NY 10583-3152 Office: 123 Main St White Plains NY 10601-3104

BERMAN, JOSHUA MORDECAI, lawyer, manufacturing company executive; b. Rochester, N.Y., Aug. 4, 1938; s. Jeremiah Joseph and Rose (Rappaport) B.; m. Ruth Freed, Mar. 17, 1996; children: Marc Ethan, Eve. BBA summa cum laude, CCNY, 1958; JD cum laude, Harvard U., 1961. Bar: Mass. 1961, N.Y. 1984. With Goodwin, Procter & Hoar, Boston, 1961-80, ptnr., 1969-80; pres. Berman Engel P.C., 1980-85; counsel Kramer, Levin, Naftalis & Frankel, 1985-2000. Adviser Fidelity Investments, 1971—, Rank Group Ltd., Auckland, New Zealand, 1996—; bd. dirs. Tyco Internat. Ltd., chmn. bd., CEO, 1970-73, v.p., 1997—. Founder, pres. Boston Children's Sch., 1965-66. General corporate, Mergers and acquisitions, Securities. Home: Alexandra La Frasse 1837 Chateau d'Oex Switzerland

BERMAN, LEONARD KEITH, lawyer; b. Dearborn, Mich., Mar. 30, 1963; s. Hyman Jack and Doris (Grushky) B.; m. Sharon Elizabeth Williams, Oct. 8, 1988; children: Sarah, Rebbeca. BA, Mich. State U., 1985; JD cum laude, Wayne State U., 1988. Bar: Mich. 1988, U.S. Dist. Ct. (ea. and we. dists.) Mich. 1988. Assoc. Bodman, Longley & Dahling P.C., Troy, Mich., 1987-91; staff atty. Elias Bros. Restaurants Inc., Warren, 1991-94; assoc. Hainer & Demorest P.C., Troy, 1994—. Of counsel Fin. Law Assocs., Troy, 1994—, Robert Riely P.C., Dearborn, 1996—. Pres. Cedar Springs Homeowners Assn., Novi, Mich., 1992—. Mem. ABA, State Bar Mich. Republican. Contracts commercial, General practice, Labor. Office: Hainer & Demorest PC 888 W Big Beaver Rd Ste 1400 Troy MI 48084-4738

BERMAN, MYLES LEE, lawyer; b. Chgo., July 11, 1954; s. Jordan and Eunice (Berg) B.; m. Mitra Moghimi, Dec. 19, 1981; children: Elizabeth, Calvin, Justin. BA, U. Ill., 1976; JD, Chgo.- Kent Coll. of Law, 1979. Bar: Ill. 1980, Calif. 1987, U.S. Dist. Ct. (no. dist.) Ill. 1980, U.S. Dist. Ct. (cen. dist.) Calif. 1988, U.S. Supreme Ct. 1992. Asst. state's atty. Cook County State's Atty.'s Office, Chgo., 1980-82; pvt. practice Offices of Myles L. Berman, 1982-91; pvt. practice, L.A., 1988—. Founder Nat. Drunk Driving Def. Task Force; traffic ct. judge pro tem Beverly Hills Mcpl. Ct., 1990—; traffic ct. judge pro tem adminstr. Culver Mcpl. Ct., 1991—; probation monitor State Bar Calif., 1992—. Editor: Century City Lawyer, 1992—. Mem. ABA, Santa Monica Bar Assn., Los Angeles County Bar Assn., Calif. Attys. for Criminal Justice, Nat. Assn. Criminal Def. Lawyers, Beverly Hills Bar Assn., Century City Bar Assn. (chmn. criminal law sect. 1989—, bd. govs. 1991—, Outstanding Svc. award 1990, 92, 93, 94, Spl. Recognition 1994, treas. 1994, sec. 1995, v.p. 1996, pres.-elect 1997, pres. 1998), Criminal Cts. Bar Assn. (evaluation profl. stds. and state bar com. 1996-97), Orange County Bar Assn., South Orange County Bar Assn., Cyberspace Bar Assn. Avocations: family, sports. Criminal. Office: 9255 Sunset Blvd Ste 720 Los Angeles CA 90069-3304 also: #9 3075 E Thousand Oaks Blvd Westlake Village CA 91362 also: 4665 MacArthur Ct Ste 240 Newport Beach CA 92660

BERMAN, PAUL JUSTIN, lawyer; b. Chgo., Jan. 7, 1951; s. Barry L. and Judith M. (Mendelsohn) B.; m. Susan Elizabeth Schonberger, June 25, 1972; children: David Benjamin, Michael Jonathan. BA, Harvard U., 1972, JD, 1975. Bar: D.C., U.S. Ct. Appeals (3rd , federal and D.C. cirs.), U.S. Patent Office, U.S. Supreme Ct. Assoc. Covington & Burling, Washington, 1975-83, ptnr., 1983—. Dir. Harvard Ctr. for Info. Polcy Rsch., Cambridge, Mass., 1976—. Co-author: High and Low Politics: Information Resources for the 1980's, 1977. V.p. Temple Emanuel, Kensington, Md., 1987—. Mem. Am. Intellectual Property Law Assn., Fed. Communications Bar Assn. (internat. practice com., ad hoc com. on alternate dispute resolution). Communications, Computer, Trademark and copyright. Office: Covington & Burling PO Box 7566 1201 Pennsylvania Ave NW Washington DC 20004-2401

BERMAN, RICHARD BRUCE, lawyer; b. Freeport, N.Y., Sept. 26, 1951; s. Nathan and Helen Dorothy (Raiden) B.; m. Laurie Michael, Nov. 2, 1985. BA in Speech Communication, Am. U., 1973; JD, U. Miami, 1976. Bar: Fla. 1976, U.S. Dist. Ct. (so. dist.) Fla. 1976, D.C. 1978. Atty. Travelers Ins. Co., Ft. Lauderdale, Fla., 1977-84; assoc. Frank & Flaster P.A., Sunrise, 1984-88, DeCasare & Salerno, Ft. Lauderdale, 1988-89; pvt. practice, 1989—. Bd. dirs. Frosch Health Care Cons., Inc., Landerhill; mem. worker's compensation rules com. Fla. Bar, 1991-94; mem. Fla. Workers Advs., 1991—, chmn. media rels. com., 2000—, bd. dirs. Mem. panel health care Dem. Legis. Task Force, Ft. Lauderdale, 1985-87; mem. adv. bd. Reflex Sympathetic Dystrophy Syndrome Assn. Fla., 1992—; mem. B'nai Brith; bd. dirs. Mommy & Me Enterprises, 1997—. Mem. ABA, ATLA, D.C. Bar, Fla. Bar Assn., Broward County Trial Lawyers Assn. Avocations: writing and performing music, theatre, writing children's music. Insurance, Personal injury, Workers' compensation. E-mail: rbberman@gate.net

BERMAN, RONALD CHARLES, lawyer, accountant; b. Chgo., July 7, 1949; s. Joseph and Helen Berman; m. Kristine K. Topp, May 1, 1993; children: Daniel J. Lohr, Joseph James. BBS with highest honors, U. Ill., 1971, JD with honors, 1974. Bar: Ill. 1974, Wis. 1976; CPA, Wis. Mem. tax staff Grant Thornton, Chgo., 1974-76, tax supr. Madison, Wis., 1976-78, tax mgr., 1978-81, ptnr. tax dept., 1991-94; assoc. Neider & Boucher, 1995, shareholder, 1996—. Lectr. cont. legal edn. U. Wis., 1999—. Mem. editl. adv. bd. Physician's Tax Advisor Newsletter, 1986-89, Physician's Tax and Investment Advisor, 1989-93. Scoutmaster Boy Scouts Am., Middleton, Wis., 1978—, fin. chmn. Mohawk Dist. Four Lakes coun., Madison, 1981-85, chmn. endowment fund, 1984-92, v.p. fin., 1992-94, exec. bd., 1982—, treas., 1994-96, nat. rep., 1996—; bd. dirs. Scouts on Stamps Soc. Internat., 1986-96, v.p., 1996—; bd. dirs. Madison Pension Coun., 1986-98, pres., 1988-89. Recipient Silver Beaver award Boy Scouts Am., 1981, Middleton Good Neighbor award Middleton Good Neighbor Festival, 2000. Mem. ABA (employee benefits com. taxation sect.), AICPA, Wis. Soc. CPAs (chmn. fed. tax com. 1990-92), State Bar Wis., Ill. Bar Assn., Madison Estate Coun. (bd. dirs. 1991-97, pres. 1995-96), Wis. Planned Giving Coun., Nat. Com. Planned Giving, Web Network Benefits Profls., Optimists, Order of Coif, Alpha Pi Omega, Phi Kappa Phi, Phi Alpha Delta. Avocations: photogrphy, philately, camping. Estate planning, Pension, profit-sharing, and employee benefits, Taxation, general. Home: 3906 Rolling Hill Dr Middleton WI 53562-1224 E-mail: rberman@neiderboucher.com

BERN, MARC JAY, lawyer; b. Milw., June 19, 1950; s. James Ellis and Harriet (Kramer) B.; children: Lindsay, Jesse, Noah, Erica; m. Bonnie Webster. BA with distinction, U. Wis., 1972; JD, Ill. Inst. Tech., 1975. Bar: Wis. 1975, U.S. Dist. Ct. (ea. and we. dists.) Wis., N.Y. 1983, U.S. Dist. Ct. (so. and ea. dists.) N.Y., U.S. Dist. Ct. (we. dist.) N.Y. 1990. Assoc. Habush, Gillick, Habush, Davis & Murphy, Milw., 1975-79; ptnr. Gillick, Murphy, Gillick, Bern & Wicht, 1979-82; assoc. Lipsig, Sullivan, Liapakis, N.Y.C., 1983-84; sr. trial assoc. Julien & Schlesinger, P.C., 1984-86, Trolman & Glaser, P.C., N.Y.C., 1986-88; pvt. practice law, 1988-91; counsel Weitz & Luxembourg PC, 1992-95; sr. ptnr. Napoli, Kaiser, Bern & Assocs. LLP, 1995—. Lectr. Milw. Area Tech. Coll., 1979-80, Continuing Edn. State Bar Wis., 1978—, Melvin Belli Seminar, Am. Trial Lawyers Assn., 1982—, Hahneman Med. Coll., 1980, Practicing Law Inst., 1984—, Wis. Acad. Trial Lawyers, Madison, 1981—, NYU Sch. Continuing Edn., 1985—, Inst. Continuing Profl. Edn., 1981-82, N.Y. State Trial Lawyers Assn., 1986-88, Mealeys Seminars, 1999—, Fen-Phen, Rezulin, Methyl Tertiary Butyl Ether. Mem. Am. Trial Lawyers Assn., State Bar Wis., State Bar N.Y., Am. Judicature Soc., Am. Soc. Law and Medicine, N.Y. State Trial Lawyers Assn., Assn. Trial Lawyers Am. (ann. conv. lectr. 1991), Delta Theta Phi. General civil litigation, Personal injury, Product liability. Home: 65 First Neck Ln Southampton NY 11968 Office: 115 Broadway 127th Fl New York NY 10006 E-mail: Lawbern@aol.com, mjbern@nkblaw.com

BERNABEI, LYNNE ANN, lawyer; b. Highland Park, Ill., Apr. 11, 1950; d. Guy and Anna (Tamarri) B. BA, Harvard U., 1972, JD, 1977. Bar: D.C. 1979, U.S. Supreme Ct. 1988, U.S. Dist. Ct. D.C. 1977, U.S. Ct. Appeals (D.C. cir.) 1979, U.S. Ct. Appeals (3d cir.) 1985, U.S. Ct. Appeals (fed. cir.) 1988, U.S. Ct. Appeals (4th cir.) 1992, U.S. Ct. Appeals (6th cir.) 1990. Clk. U.S. Dist. Ct. Judge William Bryant, Washington, 1977-78; assoc. Tigar & Buffone, 1978-80; clin. instr. Georgetown U., 1980-81; gen. counsel Govt. Accountability Project, 1981-85; ptnr. Newman, Sobol, Trister & OWens, 1985-87, Bernabei & Katz, Washington, 1987—. Co-author: The High Citadel: On the Influence of Harvard Law School, 1978; author articles. Recipient Achievement award Lambda Legal Defense and Edn. Fund, Washington, 1990. Mem. ABA, ATLA, Nat. Lawyers Guild (bd. dirs. D.C. chpt. 1992-95). Civil rights, General civil litigation, Labor. Office: Bernabei & Katz 1773 T St NW Ste 100 Washington DC 20009-7139 E-mail: lbernabei@aol.com

BERNARD, DONALD RAY, law educator, international business counselor; b. San Antonio, June 5, 1932; s. Horatio J. and Amber (McDonald) B.; children: Doren, Kevin, Koby; m. Elizabeth Priscilla Gilpin, 1986. Student, U. Mich., 1950-52; JD, U. Tex., 1958, BA, 1954, JD, 1958, LLM, 1964. Bar: Tex. 1958, U.S. Ct. Mil. Appeals, 1959, U.S. Supreme Ct. 1959; lic. comml. pilot. Commd. ensign U.S. Navy, 1954, advanced through grades to commdr., 1956-75, retired, 1975; briefing atty. Supreme Ct. Tex., Austin, 1958-59; asst. atty. gen. State of Tex., 1959-60; ptnr. Bernard & Bernard, Houston, 1960-80; pvt. practice law, 1980-94; prof. internat. law U. St. Thomas, 1991-94; guest lectr. Sch. Bus. Mont. State U., 1995-96. Mem. faculty S.W. Sch. Real Estate, 1968-77. Author: Origin of the Special Verdict As Now Practiced in Texas, 1964; co-author: (novel) Bullion, 1982. Bd. dirs. Nat. Kidney Found., Houston, 1960-63; chmn. Bd. Adjustment, Hedwig Village, Houston, 1972-76; bd. regents Angeles U. Found., The Philippines; chmn. of the bd. Metro Verde Devel. Corp., The Philippines;; bd. dirs. Gloria Dei Luth. Ch., Endowment Found. Comdr. USN, 1950-92; ret., air show pilot Confederate Air Force, 1970-80. Mem. Lawyers Soc. Houston (pres. 1973-74), Houston Bd. Realtors, ABA, Inter-Am. Bar Assn., Tex. Bar Assn. (com. liaison Mex. legal profession), Houston Bar Assn. (chairperson emeritus internat. law sect.), Internat. Bar Assn. (del. to 1st seminar with Assn. Soviet Lawyers, Moscow, 1988), Assn. Soviet Lawyers , Lawyer-Pilot Bar Assn., Sons of the Republic of Tex., Lic. Execs. Soc., St. James's Club, Masons, Shriners, Alpha Tau Omega, Phi Delta Phi. Lutheran. Home: 14 Scenic Dr Whitehall MT 59759-9789 E-mail: donbernard@msn.com

BERNARD, JOHN MARLEY, lawyer, educator; b. Phila., Feb. 6, 1941; s. Edward and Opal (Marley) B.; children: John Marley Jr., Kendall M., Katherine M., James M.; m. Esther L. von Laue, May 31, 1986. BA, Swarthmore Coll., 1963; LLB, Harvard U., 1967. Bar: Pa. 1967. Assoc. Montgomery McCracken Walker & Rhoads, Phila., 1967-73, ptnr., 1973-86, Ballard Spahr Andrews & Ingersoll, LLP, Phila., 1986—. Lectr. Temple U. Law Sch., Phila., 1975-95; instr. Phila. Acad. for Employee Benefits Tng., 1996-99; guest instr. U.S. Dept. Labor, Washington, 1984-96; instr. U. Pa. Wharton Sch., Phila., 1989-90; bd. dirs. PENJERDEL Employee Benefits Assn., Phila. Contbg. author: Handbook of Employee Benefits, 1989. Mem. ABA, Pa. Bar Assn. Labor, Pension, profit-sharing, and employee benefits, Corporate taxation. Office: Ballard Spahr Andrews & Ingersoll LLP 1735 Market St Fl 51 Philadelphia PA 19103-7599 E-mail: bernard@ballardspahr.com

BERNARD, MICHAEL MARK, lawyer, city planning consultant; b. N.Y.C., Sept. 5, 1926; s. H.L. and Henryetta (Siegel) B.; m. Laura Jane Pincus, Aug. 28, 1958; 1 dau., Daphne Michelle. AB, U. Chgo., 1949; JD, Northwestern U., 1953; MCity Planning, Harvard U., 1959. Bar: Ill. 1952, U.S. Dist. Ct. (no. dist.) Ill. 1953, N.Y. 1955, U.S. Ct. Appeals (1st cir.) 1956. Pvt. practice law, Chgo. and N.Y.C., 1953-55; rsch. asst. Law Sch. Harvard U., 1955-56; city planning cons., atty.-adviser Puerto Rico, 1956-58; rsch. atty. Model Laws Project Am. Bar Found., 1959-60; city planner, legal adviser Chgo. Dept. City Planning, 1960-64; cons. planning and land regulation, 1964—; cons. Chgo. Area Transp. Study, 1964-65; mem. exec. faculty Boston Archtl. Ctr., 1967—. Adv. to Gov.'s Exec. Office on reorgn. Commonwealth Mass., 1968-72; chmn. 1st Nat. Transp. Needs Study Mass.; cons. A.I.A. Rsch. Corp., 1974; cons. Mass. Atty. Gen., 1981—; mem. com. urban devel. and housing World Peace Through Law Ctr., 1965—; mem. com. transp. law transp. research bd. NRC-NAS, 1966—; cons. White House Policy Adv. Com. to D.C., 1966; del. World Congress Housing and Planning, Paris, France, 1962, Tokyo, Japan, 1966; fellow Ctr. Advanced Visual Studies, M.I.T.; prin. investigator Northwestern U. Transp. Ctr.; lectr. in field; vis. prof. urban and regional planning U. Iowa, 1969-70; vis. lectr. Harvard U., MIT, U. Mich.; mem. faculty Am. Law Inst., 1978—. Author: Constitutions, Taxation and Land Policy, 2 vols., 1979-80, Airspace in Urban Development, 1963; co-editor: Policy Studies Jour.; editor, pub.: Reflections on Space; revision project mgr.: Constitutional Uniformity & Equality in State Taxation, 2 vols., 1984, Transformation of Property Rights in the "Space Age", 1993, (U.S. Govt. manual) Transportation Planning for Small Cities, 1973; spl. editor: Urban Law Ann. Washington U. Sch. Law; columnist: Jour. Real Estate Devel.; bd. editors: Real Estate Fin.; contbr. articles to profl. jours. Patron Hull House Assn., Chgo., 1965; v.p., trustee Cambridge Community Art Ctr., 1971-73; mem. standing com. Unitarian Ch.; mem. founding site com. Mus. Contemporary Art, Chgo. With USN, 1944-46. Recipient cert. of commendation for teaching Boston Archtl. Ctr., 1984; grantee NRC-NAS, 1964-66. Fellow Lincoln Inst. Land Policy; mem. ABA (urban law, planning and zoning com., chmn. T.D.R. subcom. 1984-89, air and space com.), Internat. Fedn. Housing and Planning, Am. Arbitration Assn. (cert., bldg. and constrn. arbitrator),Am. Soc. Pub. Adminstrn., Policy Studies Orgn., Am. Planning Assn. (chmn. legis. com. Met. Chgo. sect. 1963-65, Mass. state reporter planning and law div. 1990—), Boston Soc. Architects (affiliate), Nat. Space Soc. (bd. dirs., space law com. Boston chpt.), Am. Underground Space Assn., Internat. Ctr. for Land Policy Studies, Urban Affairs Assn. (jour. rev. editor), Am. Crafts Coun., Mass. Assn. Craftsmen (v.p. 1975-78). Boston Visual Artists Union (hon., sec.-gen. 1971-72), New England Poetry Club (life), U. Chgo. Club Boston (bd. dirs.), Boston Athenaeum (life, dir. Poetry program). Home: 25 Stanton Ave Auburndale MA 02466-3005

BERNARD, RICHARD PHILLIP, lawyer; b. Chgo., May 29, 1950; s. Martin Joseph Jr. and Ruth (Hadka) B.; m. Svetlana Shoutova; children: Rachel, Benjamin, Alex. BA, Mich. State U., 1972; JD, NYU, 1976; M of Pub. Affairs, Princeton U., 1976; grad. Advanced Mgmt. Program, Harvard U., 1998. Bar: N.Y. 1977. Assoc. Milbank, Tweed, Hadley & McCloy, N.Y.C., 1976-84, ptnr., 1985-94; exec. v.p., gen. counsel New York Stock Exchange, 1996—; exec. dir., resource sec. Russian Securities Commn., Moscow, 1995. Participating atty. Legal Aid Soc. Community Law Offices, N.Y.C., 1977-80. Mem. ABA (banking and bus. sects., com. on fed. regulation of securities). Democrat. Avocations: Russia, carpentry. General corporate, Private international, Securities. Office: New York Stock Exchange 11 Wall St New York NY 10005-1905

BERNER, ARTHUR SAMUEL, lawyer; b. N.Y.C., Nov. 12, 1943; s. Hyman and Sylvia Berner; children: Jocelyn, Evan, Christina, Sara. BA, CCNY, 1964; JD, NYU, 1967. Bar: N.Y. 1967, Tex. 1980. Assoc. Cahill & Gordon, N.Y.C., 1967-70; with Inexco Oil Co., Houston, 1970-85; v.p. legal, sec. United Fin. Group Inc., 1985-91; shareholder Winstead, Sechrest & Minick, 1991—99, Haynes and Boone, LLP, 1999—. Bd. dirs. Ctr. Internat. Affairs. Bd. dirs. Soc. Performing Arts, Houston Grand Opera, Houston Symphony, Tex. Opera Theatre, Delia Stuart Dance Co., Jewish Fedn., Jewish Cmty. Ctr., Jewish Family Svc., Anti-Defamation League; pres. Am. Jewish Com. Mem. ABA, Houston Bar Assn., City Bar Assn., Tex. Bar Assn., N.Y. State Bar Assn. Jewish. General corporate, Finance, Securities. Office: Haynes and Boone LLP 1000 Louisiana St Ste 4300 Houston TX 77002

BERNER, FREDERIC GEORGE, JR. lawyer; b. Washington, May 7, 1943; s. Frederic George and Florence Grace (Carlton) B.; m. Lorraine Ann Ouellette, Sept. 28, 1968; children: Frederic George, III, Christina Lorraine, Jennifer Jane. BA, Middlebury Coll., 1965; MBA, Am. U., 1970; JD, George Washington U., 1973. Bar: D.C. 1973, U.S. Dist. Ct. (D.C. Dist.) 1973, U.S. Ct. Appeals (D.C. cir.) 1974, U.S. Ct. Appeals (4th cir.) 1977, U.S. Supreme Ct. 1980, U.S. Ct. Appeals (11th cir.) 1984, U.S. Ct. Appeals (10th cir.) 1994. Econ. intelligence officer CIA, Washington, 1965-67, 70; assoc. Sidley & Austin, 1973-80, ptnr., 1980—. Contbr. articles to legal publs.; bd. editl. advisors Pub. Utilites Fortnightly. Gen. counsel, bd. dirs. Washington chpt. Nat. Hemophilia Found., 1976-80. Served to 1st lt. U.S. Army, 1967-70. Mem. Fed. Energy Bar Assn. (com. chmn. 1983-89, bd. dirs.), D.C. Bar, ABA, Order of Coif. Republican. Presbyterian. Administrative and regulatory, Antitrust, FERC practice. Home: 7605 Glenbrook Rd Bethesda MD 20814-1319 Office: Sidley Austin Brown & Wood 1722 I St NW Fl 7 Washington DC 20006-3705 E-mail: fberner@sidley.com

BERNHARD, ALEXANDER ALFRED, lawyer; b. New Orleans, Sept. 20, 1936; s. John Helanus and Dora (Solosko) B.; m. Martha Ruggles, Nov. 21, 1959 (div.); children: John, Jason, Frederic; m. Joyce Harrington, Dec. 30, 1976 (div.); m. Myra Mayman, Nov. 2, 1986. BS, MIT, 1957; LLB, Harvard U., 1964. Bar: Calif. 1964, Oreg. 1965, Mass. 1966, N.H. 1991. Law clk. to judge U.S. Ct. Appeals (9th cir.), 1964-65; assoc. Johnson, Johnson & Harrang, Eugene, Oreg., 1965-66, Bingham, Dana & Gould, Boston, 1966-71, Hale and Dorr, Boston, 1971-73, jr. ptnr., 1973-75, sr. ptnr., 1975—. Trustee, bd. dirs. Mass. Eye and Ear Infirmary, chmn., 1992-96, chmn. emeritus, 1996—. Lt. submarines USNR, 1957-61. Mem. ABA, Boston Bar Assn., Union Boat Club, Longwood Cricket Club. Democrat. General corporate, Private international, Corporate taxation. Office: Hale and Dorr LLP 60 State St Ste 25 Boston MA 02109-1803 E-mail: alexander.bernhard@haledorr.com

BERNICK, ALAN E. lawyer, accountant; b. St. Paul, June 20, 1958; s. Herbert Jay and Marcia Bernick; m. Elisa Kim Neff, Aug. 24, 1986; children: Joshua Norton, Daniel Noah, Matthew David. BA, U. Minn., 1980, JD, 1983. Bar: Minn. 1983, U.S. Dist. Ct. Minn. 1983, U.S. Tax Ct. 1985; CPA, Minn. Ptnr. Oppenheimer Wolff & Donnelly LLP, St. Paul, 1983-2000; gen. counsel, asst. corp. sec. Andersen Corp., Bayport, Minn.,

2000—. Mem. exec. bd. Indianhead coun. Boy Scouts Am., 1993—. Mem. AICPA, Minn. State Bar Assn. (chair tax sect. 1995-97), Minn. Soc. CPAs (chair 1995-96). Avocations: family, outdoor activities, golf. General corporate, Corporate taxation, State and local taxation. Home: 621 Hampshire Dr Mendota Heights MN 55120-1935 Office: Andersen Corp 100 4th Ave N Bayport MN 55003-1096

BERNICK, DAVID M. lawyer; b. San Francisco, June 16, 1954; s. Herman Charles and Joan (Schutz) B.; m. Christine A. Clougherty, Aug. 13, 1983; 1 child, Evan Daniel. BA, U. Chgo., 1974, JD, 1978; MA, Yale U., 1975. Bar: Ill. 1978. Ptnr. Kirkland & Ellis, Chgo., 1984—. Mem. Univ. Club, Mid-Am. Club, Phi Beta Kappa. Litigation. Office: Kirkland & Ellis 200 E Randolph St Fl 54 Chicago IL 60601-6636

BERNING, LARRY D. lawyer; b. Kendallville, Ind., Oct. 21, 1940; s. Melvin and Dolores (Sorge) B.; m. Phyllis Low Cameron, Oct. 24, 1987; children: Emily Lyn, Scott Michael. AB, Ind. U., 1963, JD, 1968. Bar: Ill. 1968, Ind. 1968. Assoc. Sidley & Austin, Chgo., 1968-74, ptnr., 1974—. Trustee Old People's Home of Chgo.; pres. William H. Miner Found. Served with U.S. Army, 1963-65. Mem. ABA, Ill. Bar Assn., Chgo. Bar Assn., Ind. Bar Assn., Am. Coll. Truste and Estate Counsel, Chgo. Estate Planning Coun., Mid-Day Cub. Law Club, Legal Club, Skokie Country Club. Estate planning, Probate, Personal income taxation. Office: Sidley & Austin Bank One Plz 10 S Dearborn St Chicago IL 60603-2279 E-mail: lberning@sidley.com

BERNING, PAUL WILSON, lawyer; b. Marceline, Mo., Apr. 22, 1948; s. Harold John and Doris (Wilson) B. BJ, U. Mo., 1970; JD with honors, U. San Francisco, 1986. Bar: Calif. 1986, U.S. Dist. Ct. (no. dist., ea. dist., so. dist.) Calif. 1986, U. S. Dist. Ct. (cen. dist.) Calif. 1989, U.S. Ct. Appeals (9th cir.) 1986, U.S. Ct. Claims 1992, U.S. Supreme Ct. 1992. Copy editor Chgo. Sun-Times, 1970-74, nat., fgn. editor, 1974-78; asst. news editor San Francisco Examiner, 1978-83; law clerk San Francisco dist. atty. Consumer Fraud Divsn., 1984; extern Calif. Supreme Ct., San Francisco, 1985, San Francisco Superior Ct., 1986; assoc. Thelen, Marrin, Johnson & Bridges, San Francisco, 1986-94, ptnr., 1995-98, Thelen Reid & Priest, San Francisco, 1998—. Co-author: (book chpt.) Proving and Pricing Construction Claims, 1990; contbr. speeches and papers to profl. confs.; editor: Construction Web Links.Com, 2000—. Mem. ABA (forum on constrn. industry 1986—), State Bar Assn. Calif., Bar Assn. San Francisco (coord. legal assistance for mil. pers. 1991-92, assoc. liaison to San Francisco lawyers com. for urban affairs 1987-92). Avocations: horseback riding, sailing, reading. General civil litigation, Construction, Transportation. Office: Thelen Reid & Priest LLP 101 2nd St Ste 1800 San Francisco CA 94105-3659 Business E-Mail: pwberning@thelenreid.com

BERNS, PHILIP ALLAN, lawyer; b. N.Y.C., Mar. 18, 1933; s. Milton Benjamin and Rose (Aberman) Bernstein; m. Jane Klaw, June 7, 1959; children: David, Peter, Jay. BS in Marine Transp., N.Y. State Maritime Coll., 1955; LLB, Bklyn. Law Sch., 1960. Bar: N.Y. 1960, Calif. 1990, U.S. Ct. Appeals (2d cir.) 1962, U.S. Ct. Appeals (9th cir.) 1982. Admiralty atty. admiralty sect. U.S. Dept. Justice, N.Y.C., 1960-71, asst. atty. in charge admiralty sect., 1971-77, atty. in charge torts br. San Francisco, 1977—, rep. to Supreme Ct. subcom. on admiralty rules, 1996—. Adj. prof. McGeorge Law Sch., Sacramento, 1978-88; bd. dirs. Pacific Admiralty Seminar, San Francisco. Assoc. editor Am. Maritime Cases, 1978—. Chmn. exec. com. S.I. (N.Y.) Community Bds., 1969-70, 1st vice chmn. no. 3 bd., 1975-77, treas. no. 3 bd., 1973-74; chmn. 122d Precinct, Community Counsel, S.I., 1968-71; pres. Walnut Creek (Calif.) Little League, 1984-85, v.p. 1978-83; pres. Chestnut Hill Civic Assn., S.I., 1968-74, Congregation B'nai Jeshurun, S.I., 1973-76, v.p., 1971-73; cub pack leader Boy Scouts Am., S.I., 1969-70; bd. dirs. Mid-Island Little League, S.I., 1972-77, Jewish Community Ctr., S.I., 1976, Little League Dist. 4, Contra Costa (Calif.) County, 1984-90. Lt. USN, 1955-57 Named United Jewish Appeal Man of Yr., Congregation B'Nai Jeshurun, 1976. Mem. ABA (admiralty and maritime law com. 1991-94), Maritime Law Assn. U.S. (exec. com. 1991-94, vice chmn. practice and rules com. 1976-91, chmn. govt. liaison com. 1994—, no. dist. Calif. admiralty rules com. 1998—). Avocations: athletics, volunteer work. Home: 3506 Sugarberry Ln Walnut Creek CA 94598-1746 Office: US Dept Justice Torts Br PO Box 36028 450 Golden Gate Ave San Francisco CA 94102-3661

BERNSTEIN, BARRY JOEL, lawyer; b. Charleston, S.C., Feb. 11, 1961; s. Charles Stanley Bernstein and Sara Blum Baumwald; m. Charlene Wilkins, May 29, 1998; children: Brandi Nicole, Alexander Nicholas. BA, U. S.C., 1983, JD, 1995; postgrad., U.S. Army Command & Gen. Staff Coll., 2001. Bar: S.C., U.S. Dist. Ct. S.C. Security mgr. Boeing, Wichita, Kans., 1986-88; pres. Security Cons., Inc., Charleston, S.C., 1988-92; law clk. Bernstein and Bernstein, P.A., 1992-95; ptnr. Breland and Bernstein, Greenville, S.C., 1995-97; owner, pres. Bernstein Law Firm, 1998-2000; gen. counsel Adjutant Gen. of S.C., 2000—. Dir. Homeless Animal Res. and Placement, Greenville, 1995 2000. 1st lt. U.S. Army, 1983-86, ltc. JAG S.C. N.G., 1978—. S.C. Nat. Guard scholar U. S.C., 1980, Helen Gullickson scholar U. S.C. Sch. of Law, 1994; named Officer of Yr. ROA, Kans.. Mem. ABA, S.C. Trial Lawyers Assn., Comml. Law League Am., Masons (past master), Phi Delta Phi (magister 1994-95, province pres. 1996-98), Zeta Beta Tau. Jewish. Home: 304 Lost Creek Columbia SC 29212 Office: Adjutant General of SC 1 National Guard Rd Columbia SC 29201-4766 E-mail: bernsteinbj@sc-arng.ngb.army.mil

BERNSTEIN, DONALD SCOTT, lawyer; b. Bklyn., July 11, 1953; s. Emanuel and Shirley (Smithline) B.; m. Jo Ellen Finkel, May 31, 1987; children: Daniel Emanuel, Julia Clare. BA, Princeton U., 1975; JD, U. Chgo., 1978. Bar: N.Y. 1979, U.S. Dist. Ct. (ea. and so. dists.) N.Y. 1979. Assoc. Davis Polk & Wardwell, N.Y.C., 1978-86, ptnr., 1986—. Panelist Practicing Law Inst., N.Y.C., 1983—, Am. Law Inst., ABA, 1991—, Am. Bankruptcy Inst., 1991—; mem. vis. com. U. Chgo. Law Sch., 1995-98, chmn., 1997-98; mem. ofcl. U.S. del. Insolvency Working Group, UN Commn. on Internat. Trade Law. Contbg. author Collier on Bankruptcy, 1996—, bd. editors, 2000—. Bd. dirs. Altro Health and Rehab. Svcs., Bronx, N.Y., 1988-90, N.Y. chpt. Am. Diabetes Assn., 1992-96; mem. exec. com. bankruptcy lawyers div. United Jewish Appeal Fedn., 1985—. Mem. ABA (bus. bankruptcy com., com. on legal opinions), Am. Coll. Bankruptcy (bd. dirs., 2001—), New York County Lawyers Assn. (bd. dirs. 1992-94), Nat. Bankruptcy Conf. (exec. com. 1996-99), Am. Bankruptcy Inst., Assn. Bar City N.Y. (audit com. chmn., 2000—, com. on bankruptcy and corp. reorgn. 1979-83, 85-88, chmn. 1993-96, mem. tribar opinion com. 1988—, chmn. 1998—), Internat. Insolvency Inst. (bd. dirs.). Banking, Bankruptcy, Contracts commercial. Office: Davis Polk & Wardwell 450 Lexington Ave Fl 31 New York NY 10017-3982

BERNSTEIN, EDWIN S. judge; b. Long Beach, N.Y., Aug. 15, 1930; s. Harry and Lena (Strizver) B.; children: Andrea, David. BA, U. Pa., 1952; LLB, Columbia U., 1955. Bar: N.Y. 1955, U.S. Ct. Appeals (2d cir.) 1962, U.S. Dist. Ct. (ea. and so. dists.) N.Y. 1962, U.S. Tax Ct. 1962, U.S. Supreme Ct. 1964, Md. 1981, D.C. 1982. Mem. bd. contract appeals Dept. Army, Heidelberg, Fed. Republic Germany, 1968-72; regional counsel U.S. Navy, Quincy, Mass., 1972-73; adminstrv. law judge U.S. Dept. Labor, Washington, 1973-79, Fed. Mine Safety and Health Rev. Commn., Washington, 1979-81, U.S. Postal Svc., Washington, 1981-87, USDA, Washington, 1987-2000. Liaison rep. Administrv. Conf. of U.S., Washington, 1983-84; guest lectr. SUNY-Albany, 1978, U. Md., 1982, George Washington U., 1984. Author: U.S. Army Procurement Handbook, 1971; Establishing Federal Administrative Law Judges as an Independent Corps, 1984, also articles Bd. dirs. Washington Hebrew Congregation, 1985-88. Recipient Meritorious Civilian Svc. award Dept. Army, 1972. Mem. ABA, Fed. Bar Assn., D.C. Bar Assn., Fed. Adminstr. Law Judges Conf. (pres. 1983-84), Papermill Assn. (pres. 1980-81). Lodge: Masons Avocations: golf; bridge; sailing; wines; opera. Home and Office: 5702 Balsam Grove Ct Rockville MD 20852-5551

BERNSTEIN, ERIC MARTIN, lawyer; b. Passaic, N.J., May 5, 1957; s. Abbot Alan and Jean Hausman (Schwartz) B. BA, Drew U., 1979; JD, U. Okla., 1982; MS in Indsl. and Labor Rels., Cornell U., 1985. Bar: N.J. 1982, U.S. Dist. Ct. N.J. 1982, D.C. 1985, U.S. Ct. Appeals (3d cir.) 1985, U.S. Supreme Ct. 1986. Assoc. Mandelbaum Salsburg Gold & Lazaris, East Orange, N.J., 1982-83; pvt. practice Clifton, 1983-84; sr. assoc. Gerald L. Dorf, P.A., Rahway, 1984-87; of counsel Vaida & Vaida, P.C., Flemington, 1987-88; pvt. practice Bridgewater, Clifton and Three Bridges, N.J., 1988-92; ptnr. Weiner Lesniak, Parsippany, N.J., 1992-97, Mauro Savo Camerino & Grant, Somerville, 1998-00, Eric M. Bernstein & Assocs., LLC, Warren, 2000—. Lectr. Bur. Govt. Rsch., Rutgers U., New Brunswick, N.J., 1983—; mem. adj. faculty Raritan Valley C.C., Somerville, N.J., 1988-90; city atty. City of Passaic, N.J., 1990-92; mcpl. atty. Washington Twp.-Warren County, 1991—, Hardwick Twp.-Warren County, 1992-2001, West Windsor-Mercer County, 1993-97, North Plainfield-Somerset County, 1997—, Bethlehem Twp.-Hunterdon County, 1998-2000, Stillwater Twp.-Sussex County, 1998-2000, Paramus Borough-Bergen County, 1999-2001, Franklin Township-Hunterdon County, 1999—, Union City-Hudson County, 1999-2000, Lebanon Twp.-Hunterdon County, 2001—; bd. atty. Englewood Bd. Edn.-Bergen County, 1996-99, Lincoln Park Bd. Edn.-Morris County, 1997-2000; planning bd. atty. Bethlehem Twp.-Hunterdon County, 2000—, Hillsborough Twp.-Somerset County, 2001—. Asst. editor, co-author: Governing New Jersey Municipalities, 1984, co-editor, author, 6th edit., 1995; asst. editor N.J. Mcpl. Attys. Mag., 1984-92; editor N.J. State Bar Assn. Local Govt. Law Newsletter, 1995—. Vol. atty. Lawyers for the Arts, N.J., 1986—. Mem. ABA, Fed. Bar Assn., N.J. Bar Assn. (1st vice chair local govt. law sect. 1995—), D.C. Bar Assn., Passaic County Bar Assn., Somerset County Bar Assn. Republican. Jewish. Avocations: tennis, golf, stamp collecting, classical and jazz music. Education and schools, Labor, Municipal (including bonds). Home: 10 Timberline Dr Bridgewater NJ 08807-1204 Office: 2 North Rd PO Box 4922 Warren NJ 07059-0922 E-mail: embernstein@embalaw.com

BERNSTEIN, GEORGE L. lawyer, accountant; b. Phila., Feb. 22, 1932; s. Leon B. and Elizabeth (Seidman) B.; m. Phyllis Wagner, June 27, 1954; children: Harris, Lisa. BS in Econs., U. Pa., 1953, JD cum laude, 1956. Bar: Pa. 1957; CPA, Pa. Accountant Laventhol & Horwath, Phila., 1950-90, exec. ptnr., chief exec. officer, 1980-90; chief oper. officer Dilworth, Paxon, Attys., 1991-94; CFO, CAO HFA, Inc., Exec. Search Cons., 1994—. Nat. chmn. profl. divsn. State of Israel Bonds, 1988-90; co-chmn. bd. trustees Am. Jewish Congress, Phila., 1988-90; bd. dirs. Mann Ctr. for Performing Arts, Phila.; trustee Einstein Health Care Network, Phila. Recipient Humanitarian award State of Israel Bonds, 1989. Mem. AICPA (coun. 1976-79, 81-87, strategic planning com. 1986-90, v.p. 1986-87, bd. dirs. 1981-84, com. small and medium sized firms 1978-80, MAS exec. com. 1971-75), Pa. Inst. CPAs (pres. 1976-77, com.m on past pres., chmn. MAS com., long-range objectives com., budget and fin. com.), Locust Club (pres. 1990-92, exec. com., bd. dirs.). Democrat. Avocations: golf, walking, music, theatre.

BERNSTEIN, HOWARD MARK, lawyer; b. Washington, May 3, 1952; s. Howard and Mary Delia (Sliney) B.; m. Alice Ruth Huneycutt, Nov. 28, 1981; children: Ashley Laughton, Laura Whitney. Bar: Fla. 1976, U.S. Dist. Ct. (so. dist.) Fla. 1976, U.S. Ct. Appeals (5th cir.) 1981, U.S. Ct. Appeals (11th cir.) 1981, U.S. Dist. Ct. (mid. dist.) Fla. 1982, U.S. Ct. Claims 1982, U.S. Supreme Ct. 1982, U.S. Ct. Appeals (fed. cir.) 1982, U.S. Tax Ct. 1982. Assoc. Bradford, Williams, McKay, Kimbrell, Hamman & Jennings, P.A., Miami, Fla., 1976-78, Lane, Mitchell & Harris, P.A., Miami, 1978-81, Jacobs, Robbins, Gaynor, Hampp, Burns, Cole & Shasteen, P.A., St. Petersburg, Fla., 1981-83, Schultz & Walsh, P.A., Brandenton, Fla., 1983-85; asst. county atty. Pinellas County, Clearwater, Fla., 1985-97, Fisher & Sauls, P.A., 1997—. Mem. ABA, Clearwater Bar Assn., St. Petersburg Bar Assn., Barristers Soc. (lord high chancellor 1975-76). Democrat. Roman Catholic. Federal civil litigation, Communications, Land use and zoning (including planning). Home: 1916 Karly Ct Panama City FL 32405-1468 Office: Fisher & Sauls PA 100 2d Ave S Ste 701 Saint Petersburg FL 33701

BERNSTEIN, JAN LENORE, lawyer; b. N.Y.C., Apr. 24, 1957; d. James Hanley and Joan Mathilda (Wertheimer) B. BA magna cum laude, U. Pa., 1979; JD, Rutgers U., 1982. Bar: N.J. 1982, Pa.1983, N.Y. 1990. Law clk. to hon. Herbert S. Glickman, Newark, 1982-83; ptnr. Riker, Danzig, Scherer, Hyland and Perretti LLP, Morristown, N.J., 1983—. Mem. jud. performance com., jud. and prosecutorial appts. commn., econ. consequences of dissolution com., dis. X fee arbitration com. N.J. Supreme Ct.; mem. exec. com. family law sect.; past mem. family practice com.; presenter in field. Mem. editl. bd. N.J. Lawyer mag.; bd. dirs. N.J. Lawyer newspaper; contbr. articles to profl. jours. Dem. committeeperson; assoc. trustee U. Pa., chair woemn's atheltic bd., mem. trustee coun. Penn Women, bd. of athletic advisors. Mem. N.J. Bar Assn. (past chair women's rights sect.), Morris County (N.J.) Bar Assn. (family law com.). Family and matrimonial. Office: Riker Danzig Scherer Hyland & Perreti LLP Headquarters Plaza Speedwell Ave Morristown NJ 07962 also: 50 W State St Ste 1010 Trenton NJ 08608-1220 Fax: 973-538-1984. E-mail: jbernstein@riker.com

BERNSTEIN, JOSEPH, lawyer; b. New Orleans, Feb. 12, 1930; s. Eugene Julian and Lola (Schlemoff) B.; m. Phyllis Maxine Askanase, Sept. 4, 1955; children: Jill, Barbara, Elizabeth R, Jonathan Joseph. BS, U. Ala., 1952, LLB, Tulane U., 1957. Bar: La., 1957. Clk. to Justice E. Howard McCaleb of La. Supreme Ct., 1957; assoc. Jones, Walker, Waechter, Poitevent, Carrere & Denegre, 1957-60, ptnr., 1960-65; pvt. practice New Orleans, 1965—; former gen. counsel Alliance for Affordable Energy. Past pres. New Orleans Jewish Community Ctr., Met. New Orleans chpt. March of Dimes. Trustee New Orleans Symphony Soc.; past mem. adv. council New Orleans Mus. Art; past nat. exec. com. Am. Jewish Com. 2d lt. AUS, 1952-54. Mem. ABA, La. Bar Assn., New Orleans Bar Assn., Phi Delta Phi, Zeta Beta Tau. Republican. Jewish. General corporate, General practice, Public utilities. Home: 708 Explanade Ave Bay Saint Louis MS 39520

BERNSTEIN, KENNETH ALAN, lawyer; b. Bklyn., Oct. 11, 1956; s. Jay M. and Marjorie J. (Rosenthal) B.; m. Joy S. Smilon, Aug. 10, 1980; children; Lisa, Lauren. BA, SUNY, Binghamton, 1978; JD, Am. U., 1981. Bar: N.Y. 1982, U.S. Dist. Ct. (so. and ea. dists.) N.Y. 1982. Asst. dist. atty. N.Y. County Dist. Atty's. Office, N.Y.C., 1981-86; assoc. Law Office of Robert I. Elan/Kenneth A. Bernstein, Lake Success, N.Y., 1986-92, Torino & Singer, P.C., Mineola, from 1992; ptnr. Torino & Bernstein, P.C. Mem. ABA, N.Y. State Trial Lawyers Assn., N.Y. Bar Assn., Nassau County Bar Assn. State civil litigation, Criminal, Personal injury. Home: 309 Syosset Woodbury Rd Woodbury NY 11797-1214 Office: Torino & Bernstein PC 200 Old Country Rd Mineola NY 11501 E-mail: kenneth.bernstein@torinoandbernstein.com

BERNSTEIN, MARK R. retired lawyer; b. York, Pa., Apr. 7, 1930; s. Phillip G. Bernstein and Evelyn (Greenfield) Spielman; m. E. Louise Bernstein, May 10, 1955; children: Phillip, Cary, Adam, Andrew, Jonathan, Evan. BA, U. Pa., 1952; JD, Yale U., 1957. Bar: N.C., U.S. Dist. Ct. (we. dist.) N.C., U.S. Ct. Appeals, U.S. Custom Ct. Atty. Kennedy, Covington, Lobdell, & Hickman, Charlotte, N.C., 1957-60, Haynes, Graham, Bernstein & Baucom, Charlotte, 1960-67, Parker, Poe, Adams & Bernstein, Charlotte, 1968-98, chmn., 1992-97. Bd. dirs. Family Dollar Stores, Inc., Nat. Welders Supply Co., Inc. Bd. dirs., chmn. The Found. of the Carolinas, Inc., The Wildacres Found.; past pres. Charlotte Symphony Assn.; past chmn. mayor's com. for a Performing Arts Ctr., 1983-85, com. mem. Performing Arts Ctr. Task Force, 1987; chmn. N.C. Econ. Devel. Bd.; past pres. Temple Beth El, Charlotte Jewish Cmty. Ctr., Charlotte Civitan Club, Am. Symphony Orch. League, Golden Circle Theatre, Found. of Shalom Park; past mem. exec. com. Yale Law Sch.; past mem. bd. N.C. Blumenthal Performing Arts Ctr. Recipient Disting. Svc. award Jaycees, 1961, State of Israel Humanitarian award, 1981, Charlotte Fedn. of Jewish Charities A Man of the Ages award, 1985, Silver Medallion award NCCJ, 1995, Israel Humanitarian award, The Vanguard award for personal svcs. Arts and Sci. Coun., 1998. Mem. Mecklenburg County Bar Assn. (past pres.), Charlotte City Club, The Tower Club (bd. dirs.), Olde Providence Racquet Club (past pres.). Democrat. General corporate, Mergers and acquisitions. Home: 5300 Hardison Rd Charlotte NC 28226-6426

BERNSTEIN, MERTON CLAY, law educator, lawyer, arbitrator; b. N.Y.C., Mar. 26, 1923; s. Benjamin and Ruth (Frederica (Kleeblatt)) B.; m. Joan Barbara Brodshaug, Dec. 17, 1955; children: Johanna Karin, Inga Saterlie, Matthew Curtis, Rachel Libby. B.A., Oberlin Coll., 1943; LL.B., Columbia U., 1948. Bar: N.Y. 1948, U.S. Supreme Ct. 1952. Assoc. Schlesinger & Schlesinger, 1948; atty. NLRB, 1949-50, 50-51, Office of Solicitor, U.S. Dept. Labor, 1950; counsel Nat. Enforcement Commn., 1951, U.S. Senate Subcom. on Labor, 1952; legis. asst. to U.S. Sen. Wayne L. Morse, 1953-56; counsel U.S. Senate Com. on R.R. Retirement, 1957-58; spl. counsel U.S. Senate Subcom. on Labor, 1958; assoc. prof. law U. Nebr., 1958-59; lectr., sr. fellow Yale U. Law Sch., 1960-65; prof. law Ohio State U., 1965-75; Walter D. Coles prof. law Washington U., St. Louis, 1975-96, Walter D. Coles prof. emeritus, 1997—; mem. adv. com. to Sec. of Treas. on Coordination of Social Security and pvt. pension plans, 1967-68. Prin. cons. Nat. Commn. on Social Security Reform, 1982-83; vis. prof. Columbia U. Law Sch., 1967-68, Leiden U., 1975-76; mem. adv. com. rsch. U.S. Social Security Adminstrn., 1967-68, chmn., 1969-70; cons. Adminstrv. Conf. of the U.S., 1989, Dept. Labor, 1966-67, Russell Sage Found., 1967-68, NSF, 1970-71, Ctr. for the Study of Contemporary Problems, 1968-71. Author: The Future of Private Pensions, 1964, Private Dispute Settlement, 1969, (with Joan B. Bernstein) Social Security: The System That Works, 1988; contbr. articles to profl. jours. Mem. Bethany (Conn.) Planning and Zoning Commn., 1962-65, Ohio Retirement Study Commn., 1967-68; co-chmn. transition team for St. Louis Mayor Freeman Bosley Jr., 1993; mem. Bd. of Health, City of St. Louis, 1993-2000; bd. dirs. St. Louis Theatre Project, 1981-84; pres. bd. Met. Sch. Columbus, Ohio, 1974-75; del. White House Conf. Aging, 1995. With AUS, 1943-45. Fulbright fellow, 1975-76, Elizur Wright award, 1965. Mem. ABA (sec. sect. labor rels. law 1968-69), Internat. Assn. for Labor Law and Social Security (bd. dirs. U.S. chpt. 1973-83, 88-91), Fulbright Alumni Assn. (bd. dirs. 1976-78), Indsl. Rels. Rsch. Assn., Am. Arbitration Assn. (mem. adv. com. St. Louis region 1987—), Nat. Acad. Social Ins. (founding mem., bd. dirs. 1986-91). Democrat. Jewish. E-mail: bernstein@wulaw.wustl.edu

BERNSTEIN, MITCHELL HARRIS, lawyer; b. N.Y.C., Sept. 19, 1949; s. Melvin and Gladys (Weissman) B.; m. Barbara Veitch, Oct. 8, 1978; children: Jonathan, Matthew, Emily. AB, U. Pa., 1970; JD, Yale U., 1973. Bar: N.Y. 1974, U.S. Ct. Appeals (2d cir.) 1974, U.S. Dist. Ct. (so. and ea. dists.) N.Y. 1974, U.S. Ct. Appeals (5th and D.C. cirs.) 1980, U.S. Supreme Ct. 1980, D.C. 1981, U.S. Ct. Appeals (4th cir.) 1981, U.S. Dist. Ct. D.C. 1982, U.S. Ct. Appeals (3d cir.) 1985. Assoc. Breed, Abbott & Morgan, N.Y.C., 1974-77; sr. atty. U.S. EPA, Washington, 1977-81; assoc. Skadden, Arps, Slate, Meagher & Flom, 1981-83, ptnr., 1983-93; mem. Van Ness Feldman, 1994—. Bd. advisors Chem. Waste Litigation Reporter, Washington, 1985—. Mem. ABA, D.C. Bar. Assn. Administrative and regulatory, Environmental. Office: Van Ness Feldman Ste 7 1050 Thomas Jefferson St NW Washington DC 20007-3837 E-mail: mhb@vnf.com

BERNSTEIN, ROBERT JAY, lawyer; b. Bklyn., July 1, 1948; s. Martin Emanuel and Vera (Muter) B.; m. Janet Rodolico, Oct. 28, 1978. BA cum laude, cert. in pub. and internat. affairs, Princeton U., 1970; JD cum laude, U. Mich., 1975. Bar: Colo. 1976, N.Y. 1977. Law clk. to judge Richard P. Matsch U.S. Dist. Ct., Denver, 1975-76; assoc. Fried, Frank, Harris, Shriver & Jacobson, N.Y.C., 1976-80, Cowan, Liebowitz & Latman, P.C., N.Y.C., 1980-82, ptnr., 1982—. Mem. faculty, lectr. on copyright devels. Practicing Law Inst. Program, 1986, 88, 91, New Music Sem., 1987; guest lectr. on entertainment law U. Mich., 1987, 90; lectr. copyright law and litigation Copyright Soc. U.S.A., 1985, 87. Co-author column on copyright law N.Y. Law Jour., 1987—; contbr. articles on copyright law to Billboard mag., Entertainment and Sports Lawyer mag., others. Grantee Princeton U., 1969. Mem. ABA (sec. of patent, trademark and copyright lawyers, 1980—, forum com. on entertainment and sports law Music and Personal Appearances Div., 1980—, com. internat. copyright treaties and laws 1982-84, sub-com. on People's Republic of China., lectr. copyright law, forum com. on the entertainment and sports industries 1986), Am. Intellectual Property Law Assn. (sec., bd. dirs. 1990—, chmn. copyright law com. 1988-90, moderator panel on negotiation recording contracts, 1990, lectr. current devel. copyright law ann. meeting 1989, 93), Assn. Am. Pubs. (lawyers com. 1990—), Copyright Soc. of the USA (v.p. to pres.-elect, 1998-2000), Princeton Club, Fairview Country Club, Greenwich Reform Synagogue Men's Club. Avocations: tennis, jazz saxophone, piano, skiing, golf, Romance languages. General civil litigation, Entertainment, Trademark and copyright. Office: Cowan Liebowitz & Latman PC Fl 35 1133 Avenue Of The Americas New York NY 10036-6710 Fax: 212-575-0671. E-mail: RJB@CLL.com

BERNSTINE, DANIEL O'NEAL, law educator, university president; b. Berkeley, Calif., Sept. 7, 1947; s. Annias and Emma (Jones) B.; m. Nancy Jean Tyler, July 27, 1971 (div. Mar. 1986); children: Quincy Tyler, Justin Tyler. BA, U. Calif., Berkeley, 1969; JD, Northwestern U., Chgo., 1972; LLM, U. Wis., 1975; LLD (hon.), Hanyang U., Seoul, Korea, 1999. Bar: D.C. 1970, Wis. 1979. Prof. law Howard U. Law Sch., Washington, 1975-78, gen. counsel, interim dean, 1987-90; prof. law U. Wis. Law Sch., Madison, 1978-97, dean, 1990-97; pres. Portland (Ore.) State Univ., 1997—. Author: Wisconsin and Federal Civil Procedure, 1986. Bd. dirs. Madison Cmty. Found., 1990-94, Portland Urban League, Legacy Health Sys., Willamette United Way, 2001—; mem. Portland Multnomah Progress Bd., 1998—, Kellogg Commn. on the Future of State and Land-Grant Univs., 1997-2000. Mem. Am. Law Inst., Portland C. of C. (bd. dirs.). Office: Portland State Univ PO Box 751 Portland OR 97207-0751

BEROLZHEIMER, KARL, lawyer; b. Chgo., Mar. 31, 1932; s. Leon J. and Rae Gloss (Lowenthal) B.; m. Diane Glick, July 10, 1954; children: Alan, Eric, Paul, Lisa. BA, U. Ill., 1953; JD, Harvard U., 1958. Bar: Ill. 1958, U.S. Ct. Appeals (7th cir.) 1964, U.S. Ct. Appeals (9th cir.) 1969, U.S. Supreme Ct. 1976. Assoc. Ross & Hardies, Chgo., 1958-66, ptnr., 1966-76, of counsel, 1993—; v.p. legal Centel Corp., 1976-77, v.p., gen. counsel, 1977-82, sr. v.p., gen. counsel, 1982-88, sr. v.p., gen. counsel, sec., 1988-93. Nat. adv. bd. Ctr. for Informatics Law, John Marshall Law Sch., Chgo., 1988-93; mem. Corp. Counsel Ctr., Northwestern U. Law Sch., 1987-93, mem. emeritus, 1993—; mem. adv. bd. Litigation Risk Mgmt. Inst., 1989-95; bd. dirs. Milton Industries, Chgo., Devon Bank, Chgo.; cons. Mt. Pulaski Tel. and Elec. Co., Lincoln, Ill., 1981-86; sec., gen. counsel Consol. Water Co., Chgo., 1968-72; mem. human rels. task force Chgo. Cmty. Trust, 1988-90. Bd. dirs. The Nat. Conf. Commn. and Justice, Chgo., presiding co-chmn., 1987-90, mem. nat. exec. bd. dirs., 1988-98,

chair investment com., 1991-94, nat. co-chair, 1992-95, pres., 1993-94, chair, 1995-98; exec. bd. Internat. Coun. Christians and Jews, 1996-2000, v.p., 1998-2000; bd. dirs. Evanston (Ill.) Mental Health, 1975-82, chair, 1978-80; dir. Evanston Comty. Found., 1996—, vice chair, chair grants com., 1996-98, chair, 1999-2001; bd. dirs. Beth Emet Found., 1997; trustee Northlight Theatre, Evanston, 1992—, vice-chair, 1993-99; mem. coun. The Communitarian Network, 1993-96; trustee Beth Emet Synagogue, Evanston, 1985-87, 89, sec., 1985-89; chair Capital Campaign Plan com., 1994-97; discrimination priority com. United Way, 1990-97, vice-chair, 1993; mem. assembly Parliament of the World's Religions, 1993; mem. Ill. atty. gen.'s ad hoc com. for creation of justice commn., 1994; adv. com. Ill. Justice Commn., 1995-96; adv. bd. Nat. Underground R.R. Freedom Ctr., 1997—. 1st lt. U.S. Army, 1953-55. Fellow Am. Bar Found.; mem. ABA (chair telcom. com. bus. law sect. 1982-86, dispute resolution com. 1986-90, office com. 1991-95, mem. Coalition for Justice 1993-97, bd. editors Bus. Law Today 1995-97, co-chair conflicts of interest com. 1997-2001), Chgo. Bar Assn. (devel. of law com. 1963-77, chair 1971-73), Chgo. Coun. Lawyers. Democrat. Home: 414 Ashland Ave Evanston IL 60202-3208 Office: Ross & Hardies 150 N Michigan Ave Ste 2500 Chicago IL 60601-7567 E-mail: dkberolz@aol.com

BERRIDGE, GEORGE BRADFORD, retired lawyer; b. Detroit, June 9, 1928; s. William Lloyd and Marjorie (George) B.; m. Mary Lee Robinson, July 6, 1957; children: George Bradford, Elizabeth A., Mary L., Robert L. AB, U. Mich., 1950, MBA, 1953, JD, 1954. Bar: N.Y. 1954. Assoc. Chadbourne & Parke, N.Y.C., 1954-61; gen. atty., v.p. law Am. Airlines, Inc., 1961-71; sr. v.p., gen. counsel Americana Hotels, Inc., 1971-74, Nat. Westminster Bank U.S.A., N.Y.C., 1975-89, Nat. Westminster Bancorp, N.Y.C., 1989-93; ret., 1993. Contbr. articles to U. Mich. Law Rev. Served to lt. (j.g.) USN, 1951-53. Recipient Howard P. Coblentz prize U. Mich. Law Sch., 1954. Episcopalian. Administrative and regulatory, Banking, Private international. Home: 2 Circle Ave Larchmont NY 10538-4219 E-mail: gberr2@aol.com

BERRING, ROBERT CHARLES, JR. law educator, law librarian, former dean; b. Canton, Ohio, Nov. 20, 1949; s. Robert Charles and Rita Pauline (Franta) B.; m. Leslie Applegarth, May 20, 1998; children: Simon Robert, Daniel Fredrick. B.A. cum laude, Harvard U., 1971; J.D., M.L.S., U. Calif.-Berkeley, 1974. Asst. prof. and reference librarian U. Ill. Law Sch., Champaign, 1974-76; assoc. librarian U. Tex. Law Sch., Austin, 1976-78; dep. librarian Harvard Law Sch., Cambridge, Mass., 1978-81; prof. law, law librarian U. Wash. Law Sch., Seattle, 1981-82, U. Calif., Boalt Hall Law Sch., Berkeley, Calif., 1982—, dean sch. library and info. scis., 1986-89, Walter Perry Johnson chair, 1998—. Mem. Westlaw Adv. Bd., St. Paul, 1984-91; cons. various law firms; mem. on Legal Exch. with China, 1983—, chmn., 1991-93.; vis. prof. U. Cologne, 1993. Author: How to Find the Law, 8th edit., 1984, 9th edit., 1989, Great American Law Revs., 1985, Finding the Law, 1999; co-author: Authors Guide, 1981; editor Legal Reference Svc. Quar., 1981—; author videotape series Commando Legal Rsch., 1989. Chmn. Com. Legal Ednl. Exch. with China, 1991-93. Robinson Cox fellow U. Western Australia, 1988; named West Publishing Co. Acad. Libr. of Yr., 1994. Mem. Am. Assn. Law Libraries (pres. 1985-86), Calif. Bar Assn., ABA, ALA, Am. Law Inst. Office: U Calif Law Sch Boalt Hl Rm 345 Berkeley CA 94720-0001

BERRINGTON, CRAIG ANTHONY, lawyer; b. Chgo., Aug. 9, 1943; s. Leo and Geraldine (Dale) Berrington; m. Susan Dale Olsen, Sept. 3, 1967; children: Jennifer, Emily, Lacy. BA, Am. U., 1965; JD, Northwestern U., 1968. Bar: D.C. 1969, U.S. Supreme Ct. 1989. Atty. U.S. Dept. Labor, Washington, 1968-75, assoc. solicitor, 1975-77, exec. asst. to under sec., 1977-79, dep. asst. sec. Employment Standards Adminstrn., 1979-86; sr. v.p., gen. counsel Am. Ins. Assn., 1986—. Mem. ABA, U.S. Supreme Ct. Bar, D.C. Bar. Administrative and regulatory, Insurance, Corporate taxation. Home: 5920 Granby Rd Rockville MD 20855-1419 Office: Am Ins Assn 1130 Connecticut Ave NW Washington DC 20036-3904 E-mail: cberrington@aiadc.org

BERRITT, HAROLD EDWARD, lawyer; b. N.Y.C., Jan. 3, 1936; s. Philip H. and Anne L. (Rimer) B.; m. Charlotte Bayer, July 1957 (div. Nov. 1976); children: Gail J., Richard E.; m. Nancy A. Brown, Jan. 8, 1977; children: Matthew P., Alexis C. BBA, U. Mich., 1957, JD, 1960. Bar: N.Y. 1961. Assoc. Stroock & Stroock & Lavan, N.Y.C., 1961-69; ptnr. Pryor, Cashman, Sherman & Flynn, 1969-95, Rubin Baum Levin Constant & Friedman, N.Y.C., 1995-97; shareholder Greenberg Traurig, Miami, 1997—. Bd. dirs. Claire's Stores, Inc., Pembroke Pines, Fla. Trustee Nat. Found. for Advancement in the Arts, Miami. Mem. ABA, Fresh Meadow Country Club, Commanderie De Bordeaux. Avocations: classical music, wine, golf, tennis. General corporate, Securities. Office: Greenberg Traurig 1221 Brickell Ave Miami FL 33131-3224 E-mail: berritth@gtlaw.com

BERRY, BUFORD PRESTON, lawyer; b. Wichita Falls, Tex., Nov. 20, 1935; s. Buford P. and Fayette Jane (Herron) B.; children: Laura Lynn, Buford Preston III. B.B.A., U. Tex., 1958, LL.B., 1963. Bar: Tex. 1963, U.S. Tax Ct. 1963, U.S. Dist. Ct. (no. dist.) Tex. 1965, U.S. Dist. Ct. (we. dist.) Tex. 1968, U.S. Ct. Appeals (5th cir.) 1969, U.S. Ct. Claims 1974, U.S. Ct. Appeals (3d cir.) 1977, U.S. Ct. Appeals (10th cir.) 1981. Assoc. Thompson & Knight, Dallas, 1963-69, ptnr., 1969-74, sr. ptnr., 1974-80; shareholder, 1991; lectr. in taxation. Active Goodwill Industries of Dallas, 1979—. Lt. USNR, 1958-60. Fellow Am. Bar Found., Am. Coll. Tax Counsel, Tex. Bar Found.; mem. ABA (chmn. natural resource com. tax sect. 1983-85), Tex. Bar Assn., Southwestern Legal Found. (chmn. tax sect. 1984-85), Crescent Club, Brook Hollow Golf Club. Methodist. Corporate taxation, Personal income taxation. Office: Thompson & Knight 3300 1st City Ctr Dallas TX 75201

BERRY, JANIS MARIE, lawyer; b. Everett, Mass., Dec. 20, 1949; d. Joseph and Dorothy I. (Barbato) Sordillo; m. Richard G. Berry, Dec. 27, 1970; children: Alexis, Ashley, Lindsey. BA magna cum laude, Boston U., 1971, JD cum laude, 1974. Bar: Mass. 1974, U.S. Dist. Ct. Mass. 1975, U.S. Ct. Appeals (1st cir.), 1980, U.S. Supreme Ct. 1982. Law clk. Mass. Supreme Jud. Ct., Boston, 1974-75; assoc. Bingham, Dana & Gould, 1975-80; asst. U.S. atty., 1980-81; spl. atty. dept. justice N.E. Organized Crime Strike Force, 1981-84; chief atty. dept. justice N.E. Organized Crime Drug Task Force, 1984-86; ptnr. Ropes & Gray, 1986-94; pvt. practice, 1995; ptnr. Roche, Carens & DeGiacomo, 1996-97, Rubin & Rudman LLP, 1997-2001; justice Mass. Appeals Ct., 2001—. Instr. Harvard Law Sch., 1983-86, Inst. Trial Advocacy, Boston, 1984-87; lectr. Dept. Justice Advocacy Inst., 1986; mem. Mass. Bd. of Bar Overseers, 1989-93; bd. mem. Mass. Housing Fin. Agy., 1995-2001; chmn. merit selection panel U.S. Magistrate, 1989, Mass. Jud. Nominating Coun., 1991-92; trustee Social Law Libr., 1999-2001. Author: Defending Corporations Public Contracts Jour., (with others) Federal Criminal Practice, 1987. Candidate Mass. Atty. Gen., 1994; mem. Mass. Com. for Pub. Counsel Svcs., Boston, 1986-91; v.p. Boston Inn of Ct., 1990-91; trustee Atlanticare Hosp., 1990-94. Spl. Commendation award Dept. of Justice, Washington, 1983. Mem. Mass. Bar Assn., Boston Bar Assn., Am. Law Inst., Phi Beta Kappa. General civil litigation, Criminal, Personal injury. Office: Mass Appeals Ct 1500 New Courthouse Boston MA 02108

BERRY, L. CLYEL, lawyer; b. Twin Falls, Idaho, July 17, 1949; s. Clyel J. and Nellie B.; m. Jill Brunzell, July 17, 1970; children: Jacob Clyel, Matthew Robert. BABA, Wash. State U., 1973; JD, U. Idaho, 1975. Bar: Idaho 1976, U.S. Dist. Ct. (dis. Idaho) 1976, U.S. Ct. Appeals (ninth cir.) 1982. Assoc. Emil F. Pike, Twin Falls, 1976-78; ptnr. Pike and Berry, 1978-83; prin., 1983—. Sec., dir. Theisen Motors, Inc., Twin Falls. Mem. Idaho State Bar Assn., Idaho Trial Lawyer Assn. (regional dir. 1981-82), Assn. Trial Lawyers of Am., Fifth Jud. Dist. Bar Assn. (sec.-treas. 1977-78). Avocations: whitewater rafting, kayaking, lic. Alaska guide, skiing, fishing, travel. General practice, Personal injury, Workers' compensation. Office: PO Box 302 Twin Falls ID 83303-0302

BERRY, PHILLIP SAMUEL, lawyer; b. Berkeley, Calif., Jan. 30, 1937; s. Samuel Harper and Jean Mobley (Kramer) B.; m. Michele Ann Perrault, Jan. 16, 1982; children: David, Douglas, Dylan, Shane, Matthew. AB, Stanford U., 1958, LLB, 1961. Bar: Calif. 1962. Ptnr. Berry, Davis & McInerney, Oakland, Calif., 1968-76; owner Berry & Berry, 1976—, pres., 1977—. Adv. com. Coll. Natural Resources, U. Calif., Berkeley; mem. Calif. State Bd. Forestry, 1974-86, vice-chmn., 1976-86. Trustee So. Calif. Ctr. for Law in Pub. Interest, 1970-87, Sierra Club Legal Def. Fund, 1975-90, Pub. Advs., 1971-86, chmn. bd., 1980-82; dir. Pacific Environment Resources Ctr., 1997—. With AUS, 1961-67. Mem. ABA, Calif. State Bar Assn., Sierra Club (nat. pres. 1969-71, 91-92, v.p. conservation law 1971—, v.p. polit. affairs 1983-85, John Muir award), Am. Alpine Club. General civil litigation, Personal injury, Product liability. Office: Berry & Berry 2930 Lakeshore Blvd Oakland CA 94612-1425

BERRY, RICHARD MORGAN, lawyer; b. Newport, R.I., Jan. 29, 1945; s. George Morgan and Eleanor (Prior) B.; m. Jane D'Esti; 1 child, David Alric. BA, Pa. State U., 1967; MS in Mgmt. Scis., SUNY, Binghamton, 1973; JD, Bklyn. Law Sch., 1973. Bar: N.Y. 1974, Ill. 1982. Staff atty. med. soc. State of N.Y., Lake Success, 1973-77; mgr. profl. relations med. soc. County of N.Y., N.Y.C., 1977-78; sr. research atty. The Research Group, Inc., Charlottesville, Va., 1978-81; state legis. counsel ADA, Chgo., 1981-85, asst. gen. counsel, 1984-85, assoc. gen. counsel, 1985-93, dep. gen. counsel, 1993—. Lectr. various nat. health orgns., 1982—. Columnist legislation and litigation JADA, 1981-94. Mem. ABA. Roman Catholic. Avocations: golf, travel, writing, cartooning. General corporate, Health. Home: 1499 Shermer Rd Northbrook IL 60062-5367 Office: ADA 211 E Chicago Ave Chicago IL 60611-2637

BERRY, ROBERT WORTH, lawyer, educator, retired army officer; b. Ryderwood, Wash., Mar. 2, 1926; s. John Franklin and Anita Louise (Worth) B. B.A. in Polit. Sci., Wash. State U., 1950; J.D., Harvard U., 1955; M.A., John Jay Coll. Criminal Justice, 1981. Bar: D.C. 1956, U.S. Dist. Ct. (D.C.) 1956, U.S. Ct. of Appeals (D.C. cir.) 1957, U.S. Ct. Mil. Appeals 1957, Pa. 1961, U.S. Dist. Ct. (ea. dist.) Pa. 1961, U.S. Dist. Ct. (ctrl. dist.) Calif. 1967, U.S. Supreme Ct. 1961, Calif. 1967, U.S. Ct. Claims 1975, Colo. 1997, U.S. Dist. Ct. Colo. 1997, U.S. Ct. Appeals (10th cir.) 1997, U.S. Tax Ct. 1959. Research assoc. Harvard U., 1955-56; atty. Office Gen. Counsel U.S. Dept. Def., Washington, 1956-60; staff counsel Philco Ford Co., Phila., 1960-63; dir. Washington office Litton Industries, 1967-71; gen. counsel U.S. Dept. Army, Washington, 1971-74, civilian aide to sec. army, 1975-77; col. U.S. Army, 1978-87; prof., head dept. law U.S. Mil. Acad., West Point, N.Y., 1978-86; ret. as brig. gen. U.S. Army, 1987; mil. asst. to asst. sec. of army, Manpower and Res. Affairs Dept. of Army, 1986-87; asst. gen. counsel pub. affairs Litton Industries, Beverly Hills, Calif., 1963-67; chair Coun. of Def. Space Industries Assns., 1968; resident ptnr. Quarles and Brady, Washington, 1971-74; dir., corp. sec., treas., gen. counsel G.A. Wright, Inc., Denver, 1987-92, dir., 1987-2000; pvt. practice law Fort Bragg, Calif., 1993-96; spl. counsel Messner & Reeves LLC, Denver, 1997—. Bd. dirs. G.A. Wright Mktg., Inc., v.p./gen. counsel, 2001-; foreman Mendocino County Grand Jury, 1995-96. Served with U.S. Army, 1944-46, 51-53, Korea. Decorated Bronze Star, Legion of Merit, Disting. Service Medal; recipient Disting. Civilian Service medal U.S. Dept. Army, 1973, 74, Outstanding Civilian Service medal, 1977. Mem. FBA, Bar Assn. D.C., Calif. Bar Assn., Pa. Bar Assn., Colo. State Bar Assn., Denver Bar Assn., Army-Navy Club, Army-Navy Country Club, Phi Beta Kappa, Phi Kappa Phi, Sigma Delta Chi, Lambda Chi Alpha. Protestant. Contracts commercial, General corporate, Private international. E-mail: rberry@mprlaw.com

BERRY, WILLIAM WELLS, lawyer; b. Nashville, Sept. 10, 1917; s. Allen Douglas and Agnes Wilkie (Vance) B.; m. Mary John Atwell, May 31, 1941 (dec.); children: William W. (dec.), Edith Allen Berry Collier; m. Virginia N. Buntin, Jan. 4, 1986 B.A., Vanderbilt U., 1938, LL.B., 1940. Bar: Tenn. 1940. Pvt. practice law, Nashville, 1940-42, 46—; ptnr. Bass, Berry & Sims, 1965—. Mem. Tenn. Inheritance Tax Study Com., 1977, 82; mem. adv. com. dental divsn. Tenn. Dept. Pub. Health, 1953-57; pres. Bill Wilkerson Hearing and Speech Ctr., 1959-67; bd. dirs. Noel Meml. Found., 1954-68; trustee Tenn. Fed. Tax Inst., 1973-79, pres., 1976-77; trustee Monroe Harding Home, 1971-93, Washington Found., 1978—, Nashville Found., 1965-82, Nelson Found., 1997—. Capt. AUS, 1942-46. Decorated Air medal with oak leaf cluster Fellow Am. Coll. Estate and Trust Counsel (chmn. Tenn. chpt. 1975-81, bd. regents 1979-85), Internat. Acad. Trial Lawyers, Am. Bar Found., Tenn. Bar Found., Nashville Bar Found.; mem. ABA, Tenn. Bar Assn., Nashville Bar Assn. (bd. dirs. 1969-72, v.p. 1971-72), Am. Judicature Soc., Nashville Srs. Golf Assn. (pres. 1978-80), Nat. Soc. SAR, English Speaking Union (bd. dirs., past pres. Nashville chpt. 1991-93), 200 Club (bd. dirs., past comdr.), Belle Meade Country Club, Highlands Country Club. Republican. Presbyterian (deacon, elder). General corporate, Probate, Estate taxation. Home: 5110 Boxcroft Pl Nashville TN 37205-3702 also: 312 Pipers Ct Highlands NC 28741-6634 Office: Bass Berry & Sims 2700 AmSouth Center Nashville TN 37238 E-mail: wberry@bassberry.com

BERRYMAN, RICHARD BYRON, lawyer; b. Indpls., Aug. 16, 1932; s. Herbert Byron and Ruth Katherine (Mayerhoefer) B.; m. Virginia Marie Asti, June 9, 1957; children: Steven, Susan, Kenneth. BA, Carleton Coll., 1954; JD, U. Chgo., 1957. Bar: D.C. 1957. Atty. bur. of aeronautics U.S. Dept. Navy, Washington, 1957-59, atty. office gen. counsel, 1959-62; assoc. Cox, Langford & Brown, 1962-65, ptnr., 1965-68, Fried, Frank, Harris, Shriver & Jacobson, Washington, 1968-90; pvt. practice, 1990—. Mem. vis. com. Law Sch. U. Chgo., 1978-82; trustee Carleton Coll., Northfield, Minn., 1982-86; dir. Pericles Inst., Washington, 1996-2000. Mem. ABA. Administrative and regulatory, General corporate, Private international. Office: 1225 I St NW Ste 500 Washington DC 20005-3914

BERSI, ANN, lawyer; BA, MA, San Diego State U.; JD, Calif. Western Sch. of Law; PhD in Higher Edn. Adminstrn., U. Conn. Past mem. law firms Morris, Brignone & Pickering, Lionel, Sawyer & Collins, Las Vegas; dir. employee rels. State of Nev., 1981-83; exec. dir. State Bar Nev., 1983-89; dep. dist. atty. civil divsn. Clark County Dist. Atty.'s Office, Las Vegas. Past instr. pub. adminstrn. Pace U., N.Y.; legal counsel Clark County Sch. Dist. Bd. Trustees. Mem. State Bar Nev. (pres. bd. govs. 1999—). Office: District Attorneys Office PO Box 552215 Las Vegas NV 89155-2215*

BERSIN, ALAN DOUGLAS, lawyer, school system administrator; b. Bklyn., Oct. 15, 1946; s. Arthur and Mildred (Laikin) B.; m. Elisabeth Van Aggelen, Aug. 17, 1975 (div. Dec. 1983); 1 child, Alissa Ida; m. Lisa Foster, July 20, 1991; children, Madeleine Foster, Amalia Rose. AB magna cum laude, Harvard U., 1968; student, Oxford U., 1968-71; JD, Yale U., 1974; LLD (hon.), U. San Diego, 1994, Calif. Western Sch. Law, 1996, Thomas Jefferson Sch. Law, 2001. Bar: Calif. 1975, U.S. Dist. Ct. (ctrl. dist.) Calif. 1975, U.S. Ct. Appeals (9th cir.) 1977, Alaska 1983, U.S. Dist. Ct. Alaska 1983, U.S. Dist. Ct. Hawaii 1992, U.S. Dist. Ct. (so. dist.) Calif. 1992, U.S. Supreme Ct., 1996. Exec. asst. Bd. Police Commrs., L.A., 1974-75; assoc. Munger, Tolles & Olson, 1975-77, ptnr., 1978-92; spl. dep. dist. atty. Counties of Imperial and San Diego, Calif., 1993-98; supt. pub. edn. San Diego City Schs., 1998—. Adj. prof. of law U. So. Calif. Law Ctr.; vis. prof. Sch. Law U. San Diego, 1992-93; named spl. rep. for U.S. s.w. border by U.S. Atty. Gen., 1995-98; mem. Atty Gen.'s adv. com. of U.S. Attys., 1995-98; tech. adv. panel Nat. Inst. of Justice Law Enforcement, adv. com. FCC/NTIA Pub. Safety Wireless; founder U.S./Mex. Binat. Lab. Program; chmn. bd. dirs. U.S. Border Rsch. Tech. Ctr., S.W. Border Coun.; chmn. Calif. Commn. on Tchr. Credentialing, 2000—. Named Rhodes scholar 1968; recipient Resolution of Merit award Mayor and City Coun. L.A., 1991, Spl. Achievement award Hispanic Urban Ctr., 1992, Peacemaker's award San Diego Mediation Assn., 1997, Morgan award San Diego LEAD, 1998. Mem. Assn. Bus. Trial Lawyers (bd. govs. 1986-88), Inner City Law Ctr. (chmn. bd. dirs. 1987-90). Democrat. Jewish. Avocations: scuba diving, skiing, travel. Fax: 619-291-7182. E-mail: abersin@mail.sandi.net

BERTELSMAN, WILLIAM ODIS, federal judge; b. Cincinnati, Ohio, Jan. 31, 1936; s. Odis William and Dorothy (Gegan) B.; m. Margaret Ann Martin, June 13, 1959; children: Kathy, Terri, Nancy. B.A., Xavier U., 1958; J.D., U. Cin., 1961. Bar: Ky. 1961, Ohio 1962. Law clk. firm Taft, Stettinius & Hollister, Cin., 1960-61; mem. firm Bertelsman & Bertelsman, Newport, Ky., 1962-79; judge U.S. Dist. Ct. (ea. dist.) Ky., Covington, 1979—, chief judge, 1991-98; instr. Coll. Law U. Cin., 1965-72; city atty., prosecutor Highland Heights, Ky., 1962-69. Adj. prof. Chase Coll. of Law, 1989—. Contbr. articles to profl. jours. Served to capt. AUS, 1963-64. Mem.: ABA, Ky. Bar Assn. (bd. govs. 1978—79), U.S. Jud. Conf. (standing com. on practices and procedure 1989—95, liaison mem. adv. com. on civil rules 1989—95). Republican. Roman Catholic.

BERTHOLD, ROBERT VERNON, JR. lawyer; b. Charleston, W.Va., June 23, 1951; s. Robert V. and Betty Jeanne (Harkins) B.; m. Jacqueline G. Baisden, Aug. 9, 1976; children— Robert V., III, Matthew Chandler. B.S. cum laude, W.Va. U., 1973; J.D., 1976. Bar: W.Va. 1976, U.S. Dist. Cts. (no. and so. dists.) W.Va. 1976, U.S. Ct. Appeals (4th cir.) 1977. Assoc. Hoyer & Sergent, Charleston, W.Va., 1976-79; ptnr. Hoyer, Hoyer & Berthold, Charleston, 1979-87; pvt. practice , 1988— ; arbitrator Am. Arbitration Assn., 1978— . Mem. ABA, W.Va. Bar Assn., W.Va. Trial Lawyers Assn., (bd. dirs. 1984—), Assn. Trial Lawyers Am., Kanawha County Bar Assn. Democrat. Presbyterian. Avocation: sports. General civil litigation, General corporate, Personal injury. Home: 2 Monticello Pl Charleston WV 25314-2372 Office: 208 Capitol St Charleston WV 25301-2219

BERTRAM, MANYA M. retired lawyer; b. Denver; d. Samuel and Ruby (Feiner) Boran; m. Barry Bertram, June 19, 1938; children: H. Neal, Carel. JD magna cum laude, Southwestern U., 1962. Ptnr. Most and Bertram, L.A., 1963-83; of counsel Levin, Ballin, Plotkin, Zimring & Goffin, North Hollywood, Calif., 1983-92, Janice Fogg, 1993-97; ret. Former trustee Southwestern U. Sch. Law, former pres. Southwestern U. Sch. Law Alumni Assn.; former bd. advisors Whittier Coll. of Law, L.A., Beverly Coll. Law; commr. Calif. Commn. on Aging, Sacramento, 1977-82; bd. dirs. Jewish Family Svc., L.A., 1963-2001. Mem. ABA, Calif. State Bar Assn., L.A. County Bar Assn., Federacion Internac. de Abagados, Iota Tau Tau, B'nai B'rith (life mem.), Hadassah (life mem.). Avocation: geneology. E-mail: manyamin@aol.com

BERTSCHY, TIMOTHY L. lawyer; b. Pekin, Ill., Nov. 12, 1952; AB magna cum laude, U. Ill., 1974; JD, George Washington U., 1977. Bar: Ill. 1977, U.S. Dist. Ct. (cen. dist.) Ill., U.S. Ct. Appeals (7th cir.) 1982, U.S. Supreme Ct. Ptnr. Heyl, Royster, Voelker & Allen, Peoria, Ill., 1977—. Editor Bus. Torts Newsletter. Fellow Ill. State Bar Found., Am. Bar Found.; mem. ABA (ho. dels. 1995—), Ill. State Bar Assn. (pres. 1998-99), Peoria County Bar Assn. General civil litigation. Office: Heyl Royster Voelker & Allen PC 124 SW Adams St Ste 600 Peoria IL 61602-1352 E-mail: tbertschy@hrva.com

BERZON, MARSHA S. federal judge; BA, Radcliffe Coll., 1966; JD, Boalt Hall Sch. Law, 1973. Bar: Calif. 1973, D.C. 1975. Clerk Judge James Browning, 9th Cir., 1973-74, Justice William Brennan, 1974-75; atty. Woll & Meyer, Washington, 1975-77, Altshuler, Berzson, Nussbaum, Berzon & Rubin, San Francisco, 1978-2000; judge U.S. Ct. Appeals 9th Cir., 2000—. Office: US Ct Appeals 9th cir PO Box 193939 San Francisco CA 94119-3939

BERZOW, HAROLD STEVEN, lawyer; b. Bklyn., Oct. 22, 1946; s. Julius and Lillian (Hershkowitz) Brzozowsky; m. Lynore Kushner, Aug. 22, 1970; children: Alan, Jason, Rachel. BA, Bklyn. Coll., 1968; JD, Bklyn. Law Sch., 1971. Bar: N.Y. 1972, U.S. Dist. Ct. (so. and ea. dists.) N.Y. 1973, U.S. Ct. Appeals (2d cir.) 1975, U.S. Supreme Ct. 1978. Assoc. Finkel, Nadler & Goldstein, N.Y.C., 1971-77; ptnr. Finkel, Goldstein, Berzow, Rosenbloom & Nash, LLP, 1977—. Mem. ABA, N.Y. County Bar Assn., N.Y. State Bar Assn., Am. Bankruptcy Inst. Jewish. Bankruptcy, Contracts commercial, General corporate. Home: 15 Acorn Ln Plainview NY 11803-1901 Office: Finkel Goldstein Berzow Rosenbloom & Nash LLP 26 Broadway New York NY 10004-1703 E-mail: hsberzow@finkgold.com

BESHAR, ROBERT PETER, lawyer; b. N.Y.C., Mar. 3, 1928; m. Christine von Wedemeyer, Dec. 20, 1953; children: Cornelia, Jacqueline, Frederica, Peter. AB honors with exceptional distinction, Yale U., 1950, LLB, 1953. Bar: N.Y. 1954. Asst. gen. counsel Waterfront Commn. N.Y. Harbor, 1954-55; law sec. Hon. Charles D. Breitel, Appellate div. 1st dept. N.Y. Supreme Ct., N.Y.C., 1956-58; spl. hearing officer Justice Dept., 1967-68; dep. asst. sec. Commerce; dir. Bur. Internat. Commerce; nat. export expansion coordinator Commerce Dept., Washington, 1971-72; pvt. practice, N.Y.C., 1972-2000; pres. various family enterprises, 1993—. Bd. dirs. Nat. Semicondr. Corp. (audit and dir's. affairs coms., counsel to bd. dirs. 1972-98); mem. bus. adv. panel Nat. Commn. for Rev. of Antitrust Laws, 1978-79; mem. Mcpl. Securities Rulemaking Bd., 1982-85; bd. govs. Fgn. Policy Assn., 1991—. Author: Current Legal Aspects of Doing Business With Sino-Soviet Nations, 1973; editor: Manhattan Auto Study, 1973. Trustee Westchester Coll. Found., 1992—; mem. Planning Bd. of Somers, 1984-97. Scholar of the House, Yale U., 1950. Mem. ABA (chmn. corp. and antitrust law com. 1982-85), N.Y. State Bar Assn., Elizabethan and Gypsy Trail Clubs, Phi Beta Kappa. General corporate, General practice. Home: 120 E End Ave New York NY 10028-7552 Office: 1513 1st Ave at 79th St New York NY 10021-0901 also: PO Box 533 Somers NY 10589-0533 E-mail: beshar@met.connect.com

BESHEAR, STEVEN L. lawyer; b. Dawson Springs, Ky., Sept. 21, 1944; A.B., U. Ky., Lexington, 1966, J.D., 1968. Bar: N.Y. 1969, Ky. 1971. Assoc. White and Case, N.Y.C., 1968-70; later ptnr. Beshear, Meng and Green, Lexington; mem. Ky. Ho. of Reps., 1974-79; atty. gen. State of Ky., Frankfort, 1979-83, lt. gov., 1983-87; ptnr. Stites & Harbison, Lexington, 1987—. Bd. editors, Ky. Law Jour., (1967-68.). Mem. Fayette County Bar Assn., Ky. Bar Assn., ABA, Order of Coif, Phi Beta Kappa, Phi Delta Phi, Omicron Delta Kappa. Administrative and regulatory, General civil litigation, Government contracts and claims. Office: Stites & Harbison Lexington Fin Ctr 250 W Main St Ste 2300 Lexington KY 40507-1758 E-mail: sbeshear@stites.com

BESHEARS, ROBERT GENE, lawyer; b. Charleston, Ark., Aug. 24, 1931; s. Allen and Goldie (Stovall) B.; m. Doris M. Muchmore, Dec. 31, 1952 (div. Aug. 1978); children— John Robert, Michael Arthur, Charles Phillip; m. Ardys K. Frederick, Nov. 2, 1978; children— Jodi, Tami. B.S.B.A., U. Ariz., 1958, LL.B., 1959. Bar: Ariz. 1959, U.S. Dist. Ct. Ariz. 1959, U.S. Ct. Appeals (9th cir.) 1975. Assoc. Cavanagh & O'Connor, Phoenix, 1959-63; ptnr. O'Connor, Cavanagh, Anderson, Westover, Killingsworth & Beshears, Phoenix, 1963— . Bd. editors Ariz. Law Rev.,

1958-59. Contbr. articles to profl. jours. Active various civic fund-raising activities. Served with USAF, 1951-55. Pima County Bar Aux. scholar U. Ariz., 1958. Mem. Am. Bd. Trial Advs. (adv.), Internat. Assn. Def. Counsel (exec. com.), Fedn. Ins. Counsel, Phoenix Assn. Def. Counsel, Assn. Trial Lawyers Am., Personal Injury Trial lawyers Assn., Beta Gamma Sigma, Phi Kappa Phi. Republican. Episcopalian. Clubs: Paradise Valley Country, University, Plaza (Phoenix); Pinetop Country (Ariz.). Federal civil litigation, State civil litigation, Personal injury. Office: O'Connor Cavanagh Anderson 1 E Camelback Rd Ste 1100 Phoenix AZ 85012-1691

BESING, RAY GILBERT, lawyer, writer; b. Roswell, N.Mex., Sept. 14, 1934; s. Ray David and Maxine Mable (Jordan) B.; children: Christopher, Gilbert, Andrew, Paul. Student, Rice U., 1952-54; B.A., Ripon Coll., 1957; postgrad., Georgetown U., 1957; J.D., So. Methodist U., 1960. Bar: Tex. 1960. Ptnr. Geary, Brice, Barron, & Stahl, Dallas, 1960-74; sr. ptnr. Besing, Baker & Glast, 1974-77; prin. Law Offices of Ray G. Besing, P.C., 1977—. Lectr. trial procedures So. Meth. Sch. of Law, 1966-68; guest lectr. comm. law and policy, univs. and industry confs., 1984—; lectr. Bologna Ctr. of Johns Hopkins U., Nitze Sch. Advanced Internat. Studies, 1999. Author: Who Broke Up AT&T?: From Ma Bell to the Internet, 2000; mng. editor, So. Methodist U. Law Jour., 1959-60. Pres. Dallas Cerebral Palsy Found., 1970; bd. dirs. Dallas Symphony, 1972, Dallas Theatre Center, 1971; trustee Ripon Coll., 1969-76; mem. Tex. Gov.'s Transition Team on Telecom., 1982. Tex. Moot Ct. champion, 1958 Mem. Tex. Bar Assn., Dallas Bar Assn., Dallas Jr. C. of C. (v.p. 1964), Sigma Chi. Democrat. Episcopalian (mem. exec. council diocese Dallas, 1969-72). Home and Office: 400 Graham Ave Santa Fe NM 87501-1658 E-mail: rbesing@cybermesa.com

BESOZZI, PAUL CHARLES, lawyer; b. N.Y.C., Aug. 22, 1947; s, Alfio Joseph and Lucy Agnes (Ducibella) B.; m. Caroline Lisa Hesterberg, Oct. 7, 1978; 1 child, Christina Claire. BS cum laude in Int. Affairs, Georgetown U., 1969, JD, 1972; MBA in Bus./Govt. Rels., George Washington U., 1977. Bar: Va. 1972, D.C. 1973, U.S. Ct. Mil. Appeals 1972, U.S. Ct. Appeals (4th cir.) 1978, U.S. Ct Appeals (3d cir.) 1996, U.S. Supreme Ct. 1977. Assoc. Arnold & Porter, Washington, 1977-80; gen. counsel, minority counsel U.S. Senate Com. on Armed Svcs., 1980-84; ptnr. Hennesey, Stambler & Siebert, P.C., 1984-86, Besozzi & Gavin, Washington, 1987-93, Besozzi, Gavin & Craven, Washington, 1993-95, Besozzi, Gavin, Craven & Schmitz, Washington, 1995-96, Patton Boggs LLP, Washington, 1996—. Editor Georgetown Law Jour., 1971-72; contbr. articles and revs. to legal jours. Alumni interviewer Georgetown U. Alumni Assn., Washington, 1981—, dir. Procurement Roundtable, 1991—; mem. bd. visitors Georgetown U. Sch. Fgn. Svc. Capt. JAGC, U.S. Army, 1972-76. Mem. Fed. Comms. Bar Assn., Georgetown U. Alumni Assn. (bd. govs. 1993—), Phi Beta Kappa, Phi Alpha Theta, Pi Sigma Alpha. Communications, Legislative, Public utilities. Office: Patton Boggs LLP 2550 M St NW Ste 400 Washington DC 20037-1301 E-mail: pbesozzi@pattonboggs.com

BEST, FRANKLIN LUTHER, JR. lawyer; b. Lock Haven, Pa., Dec. 14, 1945; s. Franklin L. and Hazel M. (Yearick) B.; m. Kimberly R., May 1, 1982 BA, Yale U., 1967; JD, U. Pa., 1970; postgrad., Columbia U., 1994. Bar: Pa. 1970. Assoc. MacCoy, Evans & Lewis, Phila., 1970-74; asst. counsel Penn Mut. Life Ins. Co., 1974-77, asst. gen. counsel, 1978-84, assoc. gen. counsel, 1985-99, mng. corp. counsel, 1999—; counsel, asst. sec. Penn Ins. and Annuity Co., 1983-96, counsel, sec., 1996—. Lectr. Pa. Bar Inst., 1976-84. Author: Pennsylvania Insurance Law, 1991, 2d edit., 1998; contbr. articles to profl. jours. Bd. dirs. Ctr. City South Neighborhood Assn., 1979-80, pres., 1978-79; mem. Com. of Seventy, 1978-84; sec. Washington Sq. Assn., 1977-87; mem. 30th Ward Rep. Exec. Com., 1972-84, West Pikeland Twp. Open Spaces Com., 1987-99, chairperson, 1995-99, planning commn., 1994—, chairperson, 1996—. Mem. ABA, Internat. Claim Assn. (sec. 1995-2000, exec. com. 1979-81, 85-88, 95—, chairperson, 2000-01, pres. elect, 2001-), Phila. Bar Assn., Yale Club of Phila. Baptist. General civil litigation, Insurance, Probate. Office: Penn Mut Life Ins Co 600 Dresher Rd Horsham PA 19044-2204

BEST, JUDAH, lawyer; b. N.Y.C., Sept. 4, 1932; s. Sol and Ruth (Landau) B.; m. Sally Joan Dial, June 29, 1962; 1 child, Stephen Andrew AB, Cornell U., 1954; LLB, Columbia U., 1959. Bar: N.Y. 1959, D.C. 1961, U.S. Supreme Ct. 1963. Trial atty. Solicitor's Office, U.S. Dept. Labor, Washington, 1960-61; asst. U.S. atty. for D.C., 1961-64; assoc., then ptnr. Chapman, DiSalle & Friedman, Washington, 1964-70; ptnr. Dickstein, Shapiro & Morin, 1970-80, Steptoe & Johnson, Washington, 1980-87, Debevoise & Plimpton, Washington, 1987—. Participant trial advocacy program U. Va. Sch. Law, 1981—. Contbr. articles to profl. publs. Served with U.S. Army, 1954-56 Fellow Am. Coll. Trial Lawyers; mem. ABA (coun., litigation sect. 1977-81, chmn. subcom. on litigation 1982-84, mem. fed. regulation securities com., corp. bank and bus. law sect., pub. contracts sect., vice chmn. ABA Task Force Report on RICO 1983-85, chmn. litigation sect. 1988-89, sect. del. 1989—, mem. standing com. on fed. judiciary 1990-93, chmn. 1996-97, mem. spl. com. on governance 1993-93), Fed. Bar Assn., D.C. Bar Assn., Am. Bar Found., Am. Law Inst., Cosmos Club, Washington Golf and Country Club, City Club of Washington. Federal civil litigation, Criminal. Home: 2808 Woodland Dr NW Washington DC 20008-2742 Office: Debevoise & Plimpton 555 13th St NW Ste 1100E Washington DC 20004-1163 also: 875 3rd Ave New York NY 10022-6225 E-mail: jbest@debevoise.com

BETLEY, LEONARD JOHN, lawyer; b. Fort Wayne, Ind., June 30, 1933; s. Leonard Paul Betley and G. Margaret (Koch) Busse; m. Kathryn Gloin, Nov. 19, 1968; children: James R., Thomas L. BA, Yale U., 1955; JD, U. Mich., 1960. Bar: Ind. 1960, U.S. Dist. Ct. (so. dist.) Ind. 1960, U.S. Tax. Ct. 1962, U.S. Ct. Appeals (7th cir.) 1962. Assoc. Ice Miller Donadio & Ryan, Indpls., 1960-68, ptnr., 1969—; dir., sec. Fairbanks Communications, Palm Beach, Fla., 1975—, Design and Mfg., Connorsville, Ind., 1979-90. Bd. dirs. Hist. New Harmony, Inc., 1977-83, Park Tudor Sch., Indpls., 1982-91, Indpls. Mus. Art, 1990—; pres. bd. dirs. Regenstrief Found., 1987—; chmn. Ind. Nature Conservancy, 1991-93, Wishard Meml. Found., 1993. Served with U.S. Army, 1955-57. Mem. Ind. Bar Assn., Indpls. Bar Assn., Indpls. C. of C. (bd. dirs. 1982-93), Skyline Club (Indpls.). General corporate, Health, Corporate taxation. Home: 860 Williams Cove Dr Indianapolis IN 46260-5343 Office: Ice Miller Donadio & Ryan PO Box 82001 1 Am Sq Indianapolis IN 46282

BETTAC, ROBERT EDWARD, lawyer; b. Ashland, Ohio, Aug. 13, 1949; s. Donald Albert and Ruth Lavina (Foos) B.; m. Suzanne Lee Shepherd, June 30, 1979; children: Jacqueline Lee, Robert Mitchell. BA in Polit. Sci., Ashland U., 1972; JD, U. Cin., 1979. Bar: U.S. Dist. Ct. (we. and so. dists.) Tex. 1983, U.S. Dist. Ct. (no. dist.) Tex. 1989, U.S. Ct. Appeals (5th and 11th cirs.) 1981. Assoc. Foster & Assocs., Inc., San Antonio, 1979-84; ptnr. Foster, Bettac & Heller, P.C., 1984-89, Akin Gump Strauss Hauer & Feld, San Antonio, 1989—. Author: (with others) Texas Practice Guide, 2d ed., 1983. Mem. Witte Mus. Coun., San Antonio, 1984—. Labor. Home: 126 Rosemary Ave San Antonio TX 78209-3841 Office: Akin Gump Strauss Hauer & Feld 300 Convent St Ste 1500 San Antonio TX 78205-3732 E-mail: bbettac@akingump.com

BETTENHAUSEN, MATTHEW ROBERT, lawyer; b. Joliet, Ill., Aug. 6, 1960; s. Robert Theodore and E. Colleen Bettenhausen. BS summa cum laude in Acctg., U. Ill., 1982, JD cum laude, 1985. Bar: Ill. 1985. Assoc. Sonnenschein, Carlin, Nath & Rosenthal, Chgo., 1985; law clk. to judge, 1985-87; asst. U.S. atty. U.S. Dept. Justice, 1987—; dep. gov. Criminal Justice and Pub. Safety, 2000—. Dep. chief Criminal Receiving and Gen. Crimes Sects. U.S. Attys. Office, dep. chief Organized Crime and Drug Enforcement Task Force, acting chief appeals, assoc. chief entire criminal divsn.; adj. prof. adv. trial advocacy and evidence John Marshal Law Sch., Chgo.; lectr. in field. Bd. dirs. Bicentennial of Constl. Commn., Tinley Park, Ill., 1985—. Recipient Civic award, C. of C. Tinley Park, 1985, scholarship, Nat. Inst. Trial Advocacy, 1987.

BETTS, BARBARA LANG, lawyer, rancher, realtor; b. Anaheim, Calif., Apr. 28, 1926; d. W. Harold and Helen (Thompson) Lang; m. Roby F. Hayes, July 22, 1948 (dec.); children: John Chauncey IV, Frederick Prescott, Roby Francis II; m. Bert A. Betts, July 11, 1962; 1 child, Bruce Harold; stepchildren: Bert Alan, Randy W., Sally Betts Joynt, Terry Betts Marsteller, Linda Betts Hansen, LeAnn Betts Wilson. BA magna cum laude, Stanford U., 1948; LLB, Balboa U., 1951. Bar: Calif. 1952, U.S. Supreme Ct. 1978. Pvt. practice, Oceanside, Calif., 1952-68, San Diego, 1960—, Sacramento, 1962—. Ptnr. Roby F. Hayes & Barbara Lang Hayes, 1952-60; city atty. Carlsbad, Calif., 1969-68; v.p. Isle & Oceans Marinas, Inc., 1970-80, W.H. Lang Corp., 1964-69; sec. Internat. Prodn. Assocs., 1968—, Margaret M. McCabe, M.D., Inc., 1977-78. Co-author: (with Bert A. Betts) A Citizen Answers. Chmn. Traveler's Aid, 1952-53; pres. Oceanside-Carlsbad Jr. Chambrettes, 1955-56; vice chmn. Carlsbad Planning Commn., 1959; mem. San Diego Planning commn., 1959; v.p. Oceanside Diamond Jubilee Com., 1958; candidate Calif. State Legislature, 77th Dist., 1954; mem. Calif. Dem. State Ctrl. Com., 1958-66, co-chmn. 1960-62; co-chmn. 28th Congl. Dist.; alt. del. Dem. Nat. Conv., 1960; co-sponsor All Am. B-24 Liberator Collings Found. Named to Fullerton Union H.S. Wall of Fame, 1986; recipient Block S award Stanford U. Mem. ABA, AAUW (legis. com. 1958-59, local pres. 1959-60, asst. state legis. chmn. 1958-59), DAR (regent Oceanside chpt. 1960-61), DFC Soc. (assoc.), Am. Judicature Soc., Nat. Inst. Mcpl. Officers, Calif. Bar Assn., San Diego County Bar Assn., Oceanside C. of C. (sec. 1957, v.p. 1958, dir. 1953-54, 57-59), Heritage League (2d divsn. 8th Air Force), No. San Diego County Assn. Cs. of C. (sec.-treas.), Bus. and Profl. Women's Club (so. dist. legislation chmn. 1958-59), San Diego C. of C., San Diego Hist. Soc., Fullerton Jr. Assistance League, Calif. Scholarship Fedn. (life), Loyola Guild of Jesuit H.S., Soroptimist Internat. (pres. Oceanside-Carlsbad 1958-59, sec. pub. affairs San Diego and Imperial Counties 1954, pres. pres.'s coun. San Diego and Imperial Counties, Mex. 1958-59), Barristers (Stanford, Sacramento), Disting. Flying Cross Soc. (assoc.), Stanford Mothers, Phi Beta Kappa. Pension, profit-sharing, and employee benefits, Probate, Real property. Home: 441 Sandburg Dr Sacramento CA 95819-2559 Office: Betts Ranch 8701 E Levee Rd Elverta CA 95626-9559 also: 1830 Avenida Del Mundo #1608 Coronado CA 92118-3018 E-mail: blbbabbetts@earthlink.net

BETTS, REBECCA A. lawyer; b. Memphis, Nov. 25, 1951; BA, Dickinson Coll., 1972; JD, W.Va. U., 1976. BAr: W.V., U.S. Dist. Ct. (so. dist.) W.Va. 1976, U.S. Ct. Appeals (4th cir.) 1978, U.S. Supreme Ct. 1984. Assoc. Spilman, Thomas, Battle & Klostermeyer, Charleston, W.Va., 1976-77; asst. U.S. atty. U.S. Atty.'s Office, 1977-81, chief civil divsn., 1979-81; founding ptnr. King, Betts & Allen, Charleston, W.Va.; U.S. atty. U.S. Dist. Ct. (So. Dist.), 1994—. Mem. 4th Cir. adv. com. on rules & procedures, 1995—, com. for local rules and subcom. on criminal rules for So. Dist. W.Va., 1992, mem. civil justice reform act adv. com., 1991. Assoc. editor: W.Va. Law Rev. Mem. W.Va. State Bar (past mem. com. on legal ethics), The Legal Aid Soc. of Charleston (bd. dirs.), Order of the Coif. Office: US Attorney for South Dist WV US Courthouse Rm 4000 300 Virginia St E Charleston WV 25301-2503

BEUCHERT, EDWARD WILLIAM, lawyer; b. N.Y.C., Feb. 13, 1937; s. August Vincent and Anna (Jaufmann) B.; m. Elizabeth Sadowely, Aug. 5, 1961; children: Edward, Jon, Philip, Suzanne, Alexandra. BA cum laude, Fordham U., 1958; JD cum laude, Harvard U., 1961. Bar: N.Y. 1962. Assoc., then ptnr. and counsel Seward & Kissel, N.Y.C., 1963-99. Bd. dirs. Cotswold Assn., Inc., v.p., 1979-80, 98-99, pres., 1980-82. Contbr. articles to profl. jours. Bd. dirs. Edgemont Cmty. Coun., Inc., 1984-90, sec., 1984-86, v.p., 1987-90. 1st lt. U.S. Army, 1961-63. Recipient Silver Box award, Edgemont Cmty. Coun., 1998. Mem. ABA, N.Y. State Bar Assn., Assn. of Bar of City of N.Y., Internat. Bar Assn. Republican. Roman Catholic. General corporate, Private international, Real property. Home: 53 Inverness Rd Scarsdale NY 10583-3525

BEUKEMA, JOHN FREDERICK, lawyer; b. Alpena, Mich., Jan. 30, 1947; s. Christian F. and Margaret Elizabeth (Robertson) B.; m. Cynthia Ann Parke, May 25, 1974; children: Frederick Parke, David Christian. BA, Carleton Coll., 1968; JD, U. Minn., 1971. Bar: Minn. 1971, U.S. Ct. Mil. Appeals 1974, U.S. Dist. Ct. Minn. 1975, U.S. Ct. Appeals (8th cir.) 1981, U.S. Ct. Appeals (fed. cir.) 1984, U.S. Supreme Ct. 1988, U.S. Dist. Ct. (we. dist.) Wis. 1997, U.S. Ct. Appeals (9th cir.) 1999. Assoc. Faegre & Benson, Mpls., 1971, 75-79, ptnr., 1980—. Vestryman Cathedral Ch. St. Mark, Mpls., 1983-86; bd. dirs. Neighborhood Involvement Program, Mpls., 1986-90, pres., 1989-90; bd. dirs. Ronald McDonald House of Twin Cities, 1991-97, sec., 1995-97. Lt. JAGC, USNR, 1972-75. Mem. ABA, Minn. State Bar Assn., Hennepin County Bar Assn. Republican. Episcopalian. Antitrust, Appellate, General civil litigation. E-mail: jbeukema@faegre.com

BEUTTENMULLER, RUDOLF WILLIAM, lawyer; b. St. Louis, Dec. 20, 1953; s. Paul A. and Doris R. (Henle) B.; m. Ragina Lee Winters, July 14, 1984. AB cum laude, Princeton U., 1976; JD with distinction, Duke U., 1980. Bar: Tex. 1980, U.S. Dist. Ct. (no. dist.) Tex. 1980. Assoc. Jenkens & Gilchrist, Dallas, 1980-83; ptnr. Gregory, Self & Beuttenmuller, 1983-88, Bradley, Bradley & Beuttenmuller, Irving, Tex., 1988-93; dir. Thomas & Self, Dallas, 1994—. Articles editor Duke Law Jour., Durham, 1979-80. Mem. Rep. Nat. Com., Washington, 1984. Mem. ABA, Dallas Bar Assn., Duke Law Alumni Assn., Princeton Alumni Assn. Banking, General corporate, Real property. Home: 4428 Irvin Simmons Dr Dallas TX 75229-4247 Office: Thomas & Self 5339 Spring Valley Rd Dallas TX 75240-3009 E-mail: RudyBeutt@aol.com

BEVAN, ROBERT LEWIS, lawyer; b. Springfield, Mo., Mar. 23, 1928; s. Gene Walter and Blanche Omega (Woods) B.; m. Ronice Diane Gartin, Jan 25, 1977; children: Matthew Gene, Lisa Ann. AB, U. Mo., 1950; LLB, U. Kansas City, 1957. Bar: Mo. 1957, D.C. 1969. Adminstrv. asst. U.S. Senator T. Hennings Jr., Washington, 1957-60; legis. asst. U.S. Senator E.V. Long, 1960-69; sr. govt. relations counsel Am. Bankers Assn., 1970-84; ptnr. Hopkins & Sutter, 1984-95; of counsel Stinson, Mag and Fizzell, Kansas City, Mo., 1995-2001. Ghost author: The Intruders, 1967; contbg. editor U.S. Banker, 1985-88. Fieldman Dem. Nat. Com., 1968. Served with U.S. Army, 1946-47, 1951-53. Mem. ABA (bus. law sect., chmn. banking law com. 1988-92, commn. on IOLTA 1997-2000, co-chmn. joint banking com. 1999-2000), Echequer Club. Avocations: art and antiques. Office: 4545 Wornall Rd Ste 805 Kansas City MO 64111

BEVERIDGE, NORWOOD PIERSON, law educator; b. Boston, Nov. 5, 1936; s. Norwood Pierson and Dorothy Winifred (Woodrow) B.; m. Martha Baldwin, Jan. 2, 1993; childrn: Norwood Pierson III, Richard W., Susan C. AB, Harvard U., 1958, LLB, 1962; LLM, NYU, 1985. Bar: N.Y. 1963. Assoc. Kramer, Marx, Greenlee & Backus, N.Y.C., 1962-68, ptnr., 1968-71; asst. sec., asst. gen. counsel Amerace Corp., 1971-73, sec., corp. counsel, 1973-84; asst. prof. Lubin Sch. Bus./Pace U., Pleasantville, N.Y., 1985-86; assoc. prof. Western State U. Coll. Law, Fullerton, Calif., 1986-89, Oklahoma City U. Law Sch., 1989-92, prof., 1992—. Fellow Am. Bar Found. (life); mem. ABA (com. corp. law depts. 1974-86, com. partnerships and unicorp. bus. orgns. 1990—), Harvard Club. Home: 3040 Browne Stone Rd Oklahoma City OK 73120-1816 Office: Oklahoma City U Sch Law 2501 N Blackwelder Ave Oklahoma City OK 73106-1402 E-mail: paladin@okcu.edu

BEYER, GERRY WAYNE, law educator, lawyer; b. Sept. 12, 1956; s. O. Frank and Lorraine Hazel (Kopper) B.; m. Margaret Mary Brewer, June 17, 1983. BA summa cum laude, Ea. Mich. U., 1976; JD summa cum laude, Ohio State U., 1979; LLM, U. Ill., 1983, JSD, 1990. Bar: Ohio 1980, Ill. 1980, Tex. 1984, U.S. Ct. Mil. Appeals 1990, U.S. Supreme Ct. 1991. Assoc. Knisley, Carpenter, Wilhelm & Nein, Columbus, Ohio, 1980; instr. law U. Ill., Champaign, 1980-81; asst. prof., assoc. prof. law St. Mary's U., San Antonio, 1981-87, prof., 1987—. Vis. prof. Boston Coll. Law Sch., 1992-93, U. N.Mex., 1995, So. Meth. U. Sch. Law, 1997, Santa Clara U. Sch. Law, 1999-2000; lectr. Inst. Tex. Bar Rev., Austin, 1984-88, BAR/BRI Bar Rev., Houston, 1984-90, 99—, SMH Bar Rev., Boston, 1990-95, West Bar Rev., 1996-97; adv. bd. paralegal divsn. S.W. Sch. Ct. Reporting, 1990-92. Author quar. jour. articles in Estate Planning Devels. for Tex. Profls., 1981—, Texas Wills and Estates: Cases and Materials, 1987, 91, 2000, Teaching Materials in Estate Planning, 1995, 2000, Wills, Trusts, and Estates: Examples and Explanations, 1999; co-author: West's Legal Forms - Real Estate Transactions (vols. 19-23), 1986, West's Texas Forms - Probate and Administration of Estates (vols. 12, 12A, 12B), 1996, Texas Law of Wills, 2d edit., 1992, ann. supplement to Tex. Will Manual, 1986—, Modern Dictionary for the Legal Profession, 1993, 3d edit., 2001. Mem. ABA (vice chair significant current lit. com., probate and trust divsn. of real property, probate and trust law sect. 1990-95, vice-chair non-tax issues in drafting wills and revocable trusts 1996-99), ATLA, Tex. Bar Assn., Ill. State Bar Assn., Order Coif, Order Barristers, Southwest Found. for Biomed. Rsch. (animal rsch. com. 1986-91). Home: 1633 Babcock Rd PMB 186 San Antonio TX 78229-4725 Office: St Mary's U Sch Law 1 Camino Santa Maria San Antonio TX 78228-8603 E-mail: gwb@professorbeyer.com

BEYER, HENRY ANTHONY, lawyer; b. Pitts., June 26, 1932; s. Henry Anthony and Kathryn Grace (Niland) B.; m. Janet Marthe Condrey, July 11, 1959; children: David A., Stephen D., Joseph H., Daniel J., Robert M. BS, Duquesne U., 1954; JD, Harvard U., 1973. Bar: Mass. 1973, U.S. Dist. Ct. Mass. 1975, U.S. Ct. Appeals (1st cir.) 1975. Staff engr., sect. leader Vitro Labs., Silver Spring, Md., 1958-61; project engr., dir. Howard Rsch. Corp., Arlington, Va., 1961-166; staff engr. Codex Corp., Watertown, Mass., 1966-71. Lectr. on law Boston U. Sch. Law, 1973-97; vaculty bd. editors Am. Jour. Law and Medicine, 1981— ; editor Mental Retardation and the Law, 1979-84. Contbr. articles to profl. jours. Exec. dir. Boston U. Sch. Law, Pike Inst. on Law and Disability, 1984-97; trustee Walter E. Fernald Sch. Corp., Waltham, Mass., 1979-85, 89-2000; chmn. peace and justice commn. St. Bernard Parish, Concord, Mass., 1984-85. Served to 1st lt. AUS, 1954-58. Office: 52 Authors Rd Concord MA 01742-2607

BEYER, WAYNE CARTWRIGHT, lawyer; b. Bklyn., Feb. 21, 1946; s. Gerhard Robert and Barbara Janeway (Fein) B. AB, Dartmouth Coll., 1967; MAT, Harvard U., 1970; Jd, Georgetown U., 1977. Bar: N.H. 1978, U.S. Dist. Ct. N.H. 1978, U.S. Tax Ct. 1986, U.S. CT. Appeals (1st cir.) 1979, U.S. Supreme Ct. 1986, D.C. 1996. Mem. staff U.S. Ho. of Reps., Washington, 1973-75; atty. McLane, Graf, Raulerson, P.A., Manchester, N.H., 1978-83; chief of staff GSA, Washington, 1983-84, dep. gen. counsel, 1984-86; atty. Cleveland, Waters & Bass, P.A., Concord, N.H., 1986-94, Wayne C. Beyer & Assoc., Manchester, 1994-96; asst. corp. counsel Dist. of Columbia, 1996—. Lectr. civil rights. Contbr. articles to profl. jours. Mem. ABA, N.H. Bar Assn., Assn. Trial Lawyers Am., Def. Rsch. Inst., Internat. Assn. Chiefs of Police, Harvard Club, Bar Assn. of D.C. Civil rights, Federal civil litigation, Constitutional. Home: 2501 Porter St NW Apt 527 Washington DC 20008-1254 Office: Office Corp Counsel 441 4th St NW Fl 6 South Washington DC 20001-2714

BEZANSON, RANDALL PETER, law educator; b. Cedar Rapids, Iowa, Nov. 17, 1946; s. Peter Floyd and Larrayne (Bing) B.; m. Elaine Ruth Croyle, June 22, 1968; children: Peter, Melissa. BA, Northwestern U., 1968; JD summa cum laude, U. Iowa, 1971. Bar: Iowa 1971, Va. 1988. Law clk., presiding justice U.S. Ct. Appeals (D.C. cir.), 1971-72; law clk., Justice Harry Blackmun U.S. Supreme Ct., Washington, 1972-73; prof. law U. Iowa, Iowa City, 1973-88, 96-98, asst. to pres., 1976-77, v.p., 1979-84; dean of law Washington and Lee U., Lexington, Va., 1988-94, prof. law, 1994-96; Charles E. Floete Distinguished Prof. U. Iowa Coll. Law, Iowa City, 1998—. Commr. Nat. Conf. of Commrs. on Uniform State Laws, 1983-88; reporter Uniform Defamation Act, NCCUSL, 1988—; dir. City Nat. Bank, Cedar Rapids, 1977-88, 1st Nat. Bank, Iowa City, 1984-88. Author (with Cranberg and Soloski): Libel Law and the Press: Myth and Reality, 1987; author: (with Soliski) Reforming Libel Law, 1992; author: Taxes on Knowledge in America, 1994, Speech Stores: How Free Can Speech Be?, 1998; author: (with Cranberg and Soloski) Taking Stock: Journalism and the Publicly Traded Newspaper Company, 2001;contbr. articles to legal jours. Bd. dirs. Hawkeye Area Coun., Boy Scouts Am., Cedar Rapids, 1979-88; pres. Iowa City Pub. Libr. Bd. Trustees, 1978-80; mem. Iowa City Pub. Libr. Found. Bd. 1980. Murray scholar, U. Iowa, 1971. Mem. ABA, Iowa Bar Assn., Order of Coif, Beta Alpha Psi. Republican. Presbyterian. Avocations: nature, golf. Home: 12 Woodland Hts NE Iowa City IA 52240-9136 Office: U Iowa Coll Law Iowa City IA 52242 E-mail: Randy-Bezanson@uiowa.edu

BEZANSON, THOMAS EDWARD, lawyer; b. Hartford, Conn., Aug. 1, 1945; s. Philip Thomas and Lillian (Carlson) Bezanson; m. Janie R Bezanson, Aug. 10, 1969; children: Philip, Jeffrey. BA, Grinnell, 1967; MA, Rutgers U., 1971, JD, 1974. MSCE; bar: NY 1975, US Dist Ct (ea & no dists) 1975, US Ct Appeals (2d cir) 1975, US Ct Appeals (6th cir) 1980, US Supreme Ct 1991. Assoc. Chadbourne & Parke, N.Y.C., 1974-81, ptnr., 1981—. Author: 42 poems, 1993. Bd dirs Westchester Philharmonic, 1992—98, NY Lawyers Pub Interest Inc, 1997—, Legal Aid Soc, 1999—. With U.S. Army, 1967—69. Mem.: ABA, NY State Bar Asn, Asn Bar City New York. Federal civil litigation, State civil litigation, Product liability. Office: Chadbourne & Parke 30 Rockefeller Plz Fl 31 New York NY 10112-0129 Business E-Mail: tbezanson@chadbourne.com

BIALKIN, KENNETH JULES, lawyer, director; b. N.Y.C., Sept. 9, 1929; s. Samuel and Lillian (Kastner) B.; m. Ann Eskind, Aug. 19, 1956; children: Lisa Beth, Johanna. AB, U. Mich., 1950; cert. of attendance, London Sch. Econ., 1952; JD, Harvard U., 1953. Bar: N.Y. 1953, U.S. Dist. Ct. (ea. dist.) N.Y. 1955, U.S. Supreme Ct. 1964, U.S. Dist. Ct. (so. dist.) N.Y. 1972, U.S. Ct. Appeals (2d cir.) 1976. Assoc. Willkie Farr & Gallagher, N.Y.C., 1953-60, ptnr., 1960-88, Skadden, Arps, Slate, Meagher & Flom, N.Y.C., 1988—. Adj. prof. law NYU, 1967-87; lectr., commentator legal and fin. symposia; mem. N.Y. Stock Exch. Legal Adv. Commn., 1983-92, 98—, chmn. internat. securities subcom., 1989-98; bd. dirs. Citigroup Inc., Mcpl. Assistance Corp. City of N.Y., Sapiens Internat., Ltd., Tecnomatix Techs., Ltd.; mem. Adminstrv. Conf. of U.S., 1987-92; chmn. Com. on Fin. Svcs.; vis. com. grad. faculty New Sch. for Social Rsch., 1992—. Editor: The Business Lawyer, 1980; bd. editors Corp. Governance Jour., 1992—; contbr. articles on corp., fin. investment law to profl. jours. Chmn. Conf. Pres. Major Am. Jewish Orgns., 1984-86; chmn. Am.-Israel Friendship League, 1995—; nat. chmn. Anti-Defamation League B'nai Brith, 1982-86; pres. Jewish Cmty. Rels. Coun. N.Y., 1989-92; vice-chmn., dir. Jerusalem Found., Inc., 1975—. Mem. ABA (chmn. fed. regulation securities com. 1974-79, chmn. com. to study fgn. investment in U.S. 1978-80, chmn. ad hoc com. on insider trading regulation 1988—, chmn.

sect. corp. banking and bus. law 1981-82, 88), Am. Jewish Hist. Soc. (pres. 1997—), N.Y. County Lawyers Assn. (pres. 1986-88), Am. Bar Retirement Assn. (dir. 1981-84), Coun. Fgn. Rels., Harvard Club. General corporate, Mergers and acquisitions, Securities. Home: 211 Central Park W New York NY 10024-6020 Office: Skadden Arps Slate Meagher & Flom 4 Times Sq Fl 24 New York NY 10036-6595 E-mail: kbialkin@skadden.com

BIALO, KENNETH MARC, lawyer; b. N.Y.C., Nov. 21, 1946; s. Walter and Mildred (Miller) B.; m. Katherine Ann Burghard; children: Darren Andrew, Caralyn Alyssa, Jacquelyn Anne, Matthew Joseph Geronimo, Kelsey Elizabeth Ariel. BS, U. Rochester, 1968; JD cum laude (Univ. scholar), NYU, 1971; LLM, London Sch. Econs., 1973. Bar: N.Y. 1972, U.S. Ct. Appeals (2d cir.) 1974, U.S. Ct. Appeals (fed. cir.) 1988, U.S. Supreme Ct. 1975. Law clk. Hon. L.W. Pierce U.S. Dist. Ct. (so. dist.) N.Y., 1971-72; assoc. Sullivan & Cromwell, N.Y.C., 1973-80; counsel, sr. counsel Exxon Corp., 1980-90; sr. counsel, chief litigation atty. Exxon Chem. Co., Darien, Conn., 1990-91; ptnr. Baker Botts, LLP, N.Y.C., 1992—. Lectr. Practicing Law Inst., N.Y.C., 1982, 88, N.Y. State Bar Assn., 1997; vice chmn. bd. State of N.Y. Mcpl. Bond Bank Agy., N.Y.C., 2000—. Contbg. editor: Family Legal Guide, 1974; contbr. articles to profl. jours.; note and comment editor NYU Law Rev.; host The Larchmont Report, WVOX, Whitney Radio Group, New Rochelle, N.Y., 1995—; co-host Larchmont Today, LMC-TV, Mamaroneck, N.Y., 1995—; co-founder, prin. contbr. Plugged In, Rep. Party Newsletter, Larchmont, N.Y., 1996—. Trustee Village of Larchmont, N.Y., 1991—; mem. PLI Adv. Com. on Litig., 1994—; v.p., bd. dirs. Little League, Larchmont, 1985-94, mem. recreation com., 1987-89; treas., mem. exec. com. L.I. Sound Watershed Intermcpl. Coun., Westchester County, N.Y., 2000—. Mem. ABA (litig. sect. task force on client concerns 1994-95, subcom. class action, litig. sect.), N.Y. State Bar (antitrust com., fed. and comml. litig. sect., former chmn. corp. counsel com. 1989-91), Assn. of Bar of City of N.Y. (arbitration com. 1983-85), Fed. Bar Coun. (com. 2d cir. cts. 1985-87), Am. Arbitration Assn. (mem. arbitrators panel), Order of Coif, Univ. Club of Larchmont (bd. govs. 1995-99, pres. 1998-99). Avocations: tennis, baseball, opera, symphony. Antitrust, Federal civil litigation. Office: Baker Botts LLP 599 Lexington Ave New York NY 10022-6030

BIAS, DANA G. lawyer; b. Lexington, Ky., Mar. 12, 1959; d. Cyrus Dana and Betty Jo (Haddox) B. BA with highest honors, U. Louisville, 1981; JD magna cum laude, Boston U., 1984. Bar: Mass. 1985, N.Y. 1985, Ky. 1995, Tex. 2000, U.S. Dist. Ct. (so. and ea. dists.) N.Y. 1986, U.S. Dist. Ct. (ea. dist.) Tex. 2000. Counselor Mass. Half-Way Houses, Inc., Boston, 1982-83; sr. trial atty. Criminal Def. div. Legal Aid Soc., N.Y.C., 1984-89, mng. atty., 1989-94; sole practitioner Hauppauge, N.Y., 1995; sr. trial atty. Louisville-Jefferson County Pub. Defender Corp., 1995-97; asst. public advocate, capital trial atty. Dept. of Public Advocacy, 1997-2000; mng. atty. East Tex. Legal Svcs., Nacogdoches, 2000—. Lectr. N.Y.C. Pub. Schs., 1989, AAUW, 2001. Contbr. articles to profl. jours. Mem. ABA, ACLU, N.Y. State Bar Assn., Nat. Assn. Criminal Def. Lawyers, Mass. Bar Assn., Ky. Bar Assn., Tex. Bar Assn., NLADA, N.Y. Civil Liberties Union, Woodcock Soc., Mortar Bd., Phi Kappa Phi, Phi Eta Sigma. Democrat. Federal civil litigation, General civil litigation, State civil litigation. Office: East Tex Legal Svcs PO Box 631070 Nacogdoches TX 75963-1070 E-mail: dana.bias@etls.org

BIBLE, PAUL ALFRED, lawyer; b. Reno, Oct. 3, 1940; s. Alan and Loucile Pauline (Jacks) B.; m. Judith Lynn Schmidt, Mar. 21, 1970; children— Chad Alan, Patrick Marshall. Student U. Colo., 1958-59; B.A. in Econs., U. Nev., 1962; J.D., Georgetown U., 1965. Bar: D.C. 1965, Nev. 1965. Assoc. McDonald, Carano, Wilson, Bergin, Bible, Frankovich & Hicks, Reno, 1969-72, ptnr., 1972-83; sole practice, Reno, 1983-84; ptnr. Bible, Santini, Hoy & Miller, 1984-85; Bible, Santini, Hoy, Miller & Trachok, 1985-87; Bible, Hoy, Miller, Trachok & Wadhams, 1987-91; Bible, Hoy, Trachok & Wadhams, 1991-92; instr. Old Coll. Sch. Law, Reno, 1983; chmn. Nev. Gaming Commn., Reno, 1983-87. Contbr. articles to law revs. and profl. jours. Pres. DETRAP, Reno, 1971-73; mem. Nev. State Apprenticeship Council, Reno, 1971-83, chmn., 1971-83; mem. Truckee Meadows Community Coll. Found., 1982—; adv. bd. Truckee Meadows Community Coll., 1980-91. Served to capt. JAGC, U.S. Army, 1966-68. Recipient Henry Albert Pub. Service award U. Nev., 1962. Decorated Bronze Star medal. Mem. ABA, State Bar Nev., Assn. Trial Lawyers Am., Calif. Trial Lawyers Assn., Nev. Trial Lawyers Assn., Am. Arbitration Assn., Washoe County Bar Assn., Ducks Unltd. Democrat. Methodist. Club: Greenhead Hunting. Avocations: hunting, fishing, running, hiking. Administrative and regulatory, General civil litigation, Gaming. Office: Bible Hoy Trachok Wadhams & Zive 201 W Liberty St Ste 300 Reno NV 89501-2017

BICE, SCOTT HAAS, dean, lawyer, educator; b. Los Angeles, Mar. 19, 1943; s. Fred Haas and Virginia M. (Scott) B.; m. Barbara Franks, Dec. 21, 1968. B.S., U. So. Calif., 1965, J.D., 1968. Bar: Calif. bar 1971. Law clk. to Chief Justice Earl Warren, 1968-69; asst. prof., assoc. prof., prof. law U. So. Calif., Los Angeles, 1969-2000, assoc. dean, 1971-74, dean Law Sch., 1980-2000, Carl Mason Franklin prof., 1983-2000, Robert C. Packard prof. law, 2000—. Vis. prof. polit. sci. Calif. Inst. Tech., 1977; vis. prof. U. Va., 1978-79; bd.dirs. Western Mut. Ins. Co., Residence Mut. Ins. Co., Imagine Films Entertainment Co., Jenny Craig, Inc. Mem. editl. adv. bd. Calif. Lawyer, 1989-93; contbr. articles to law jours. Bd. dirs. L.A. Family Housing Corp., 1989-93, Stone Soup Child Care Programs, 1988—. Affiliated scholar Am. Bar Found., 1972-74 Fellow Am. Bar Found. (life); mem. Am. Law Inst., Calif. Bar, Los Angeles County Bar Assn., Am. Law Deans Assn. (pres. 1997-99), Am. Judicature Soc., Calif. Club, Chancery Club, Long Beach Yacht Club. Home: 787 S San Rafael Ave Pasadena CA 91105-2326 Office: U So Calif Sch Law Los Angeles CA 90089-0071 E-mail: sbice@law.usc.edu

BICKEL, JOHN W., II, lawyer; b. Champaign, Ill., Sept. 9, 1948; s. John William and Virginia Bickel; children: Hannah, Molly, Sarah. BS, U.S. Mil. Acad., 1970; JD, So. Meth. U., 1976. Bar: N.Y. 1988, Tex. 1976, U.S. Ct. Appeals (5th and 11th cirs.) 1980, U.S. Supreme Ct. 1983. Assoc. Thompson & Knight, Dallas, 1980-83; ptnr. Brown, Thomas, Karger & Bickel, 1983-84; co-mng., co-founder, ptnr. Bickel & Brewer, 1984—; co-founding ptnr. Bickel & Brewer Storefront, PLLC. Adv. mem. Tex. Supreme Ct. Jury Charge Task Force, 1992; mem. com. for qualified judiciary. Mem. exec. bd. So. Meth. U. Sch. Law.; mem. Hiram A. Boaz Soc. So. Meth. U.; mem. Tex. Com.: A Time to Lead--The Campaign for So. Meth. U.; mem. adv. com. Southwestern Ball, 1997—. Fellow Tex. Bar Found., Dallas Bar Found. (sustaining life); mem. ABA, State Bar Tex. (past chmn. litigation com. of environ. and natural resource law sect.), N.Y. Bar Assn., Dallas Bar Assn., Markey/Wigmore Inns of Ct. (Chgo. chpt.), West Point Assn. Grads. (trustee 1997-2000, strategic planning com. 1997—), West Point Soc. North Tex. (bd. dirs. 1992-). Federal civil litigation, General civil litigation, State civil litigation. Office: Bickel & Brewer 4800 Bank One Ctr 1717 Main St Ste 4800 Dallas TX 75201-4651 E-mail: jbickel@bickelbrewer.com

BICKSLER, DIANA GUIDO, lawyer; b. Berkeley, Calif., July 8, 1954; d. Salvador J. and Antonietta (D'Lessandro) G.; m. Gene Allen Bicksler, June 26, 1994. BA, U. Calif., Berkeley, 1976; MA, U. San Francisco, 1978; JD, U. Golden Gate, 1982. Bar: Calif. 1984, U.S. Dist. Ct. (no. dist.) Calif. 1984, U.S. Ct. Appeals (9th cir.) 1986. Assoc. Law Offices of James J. Duryea, San Francisco, 1982-85; assoc., mng. atty. Ericksen, Arbuthnot, Walsh, Paynter & Brown, San Jose, Calif., 1985-86; assoc. Tarkington, O'Connor & O'Neill, San Francisco, 1986-90; ptnr. Berding & Weil, Alamo, Calif., 1990-96; prin. Landmark Legal Profls., San Francisco, 1996-97, Cushing Bicksler Group, San Francisco, 1997—. Mem. ABA, San Francisco Bar Assn., Calif. Bus. Trial Lawyers Assn., Contra CostaBar Assn. State civil litigation, Insurance, Personal injury. Office: Cushing Bicksler Group 595 Market St Ste 2500 San Francisco CA 94105-2838 E-mail: dbicksler@cblawlink.com

BIDWELL, JAMES TRUMAN, JR. lawyer; b. N.Y.C., Jan. 2, 1934; s. James Truman and Mary (Kane) B.; m. Gail S. Bidwell, Mar. 6, 1965 (div.); children: Hillary Day Bidwell Mackay, Kimberley Wade, Cortney E.; m. Katherine T. O'Neil, July 15, 1988. BA, Yale U., 1956; LLB, Harvard U., 1959. Bar: N.Y. 1959. Atty. USAF, Austin, Tex., 1959-62; assoc. Donovan, Leisure, Newton & Irvine, N.Y.C., 1962-68, ptnr., 1968-84, White & Case, N.Y.C., 1984-98; sr. counsel Linklaters, 1998—. Pres. Youth Consultation Svc., 1973-78; trustee Berkeley Divinity Sch. Mem. ABA, Fed. Bar Assn., N.Y. State Bar Assn., N.Y. County Lawyers Assn. Episcopalian. Contracts commercial, General corporate, Private international. Office: Linklaters 1345 Avenue Of The Americas New York NY 10105-0302

BIEBEL, PAUL PHILIP, JR. lawyer; b. Chgo., Mar. 24, 1942; s. Paul Philip Sr. and Eleanor Mary (Sweeney) B.; divorced; children: Christine M., Brian E., Jennifer A., Susan E. AB, Marquette U., 1964; JD, Georgetown U., 1967. Bar: Ill. 1967, U.S. Dist. Ct. (no. dist.) Ill. 1967, U.S. Ct. Appeals (6th cir.) 1985, U.S. Supreme Ct. 1972. Asst. dean of men Loyola U., Chgo., 1967-69; asst. state's atty. Cook County State's Atty., 1969-75, dep. state's atty., 1975-81; 1st asst. atty. gen. Ill. Atty. Gen., 1981-85; pub. defender Cook County Pub. Defender, 1986-88; ptnr. Winston & Strawn, 1985-86, 88-94, Altheimer & Gray, Chgo., 1994-96; judge Cir. Ct. Cook County, Ill., 1996—. Contbr. articles to profl. pubis. Mem. Fed. Bar Assn. (bd. dirs., pres. 1994-95), Cath. Lawyers Guild (bd. dirs., Cath. Lawyer of Yr. 1988), Ill. Judges Assn., Ill. Appellate Lawyers, 7th Cir. Bar Assn., Chgo. Bar Assn. (chmn. com. 1991-93), Georgetown Law Alumni Assn. (bd. dirs. 1991-96). Roman Catholic. Avocations: reading, golf. State civil litigation. Home: 5415 N Forest Glen Ave Chicago IL 60630-1523 Office: Presiding Judge Criminal Divsn RM 101 2600 S California Ave Chicago IL 60608

BIECK, ROBERT BARTON, JR. lawyer; b. Wiesbaden, Germany, Apr. 13, 1952; s. Robert Barton and Mary-Jean (Boeck) B.; m. Julia A. Dietz, Apr. 20, 1991. BA in Polit. Sci., U. Nebr., 1974; JD with high honors, Tex. Tech. U., 1977. Bar: Tex. 1977, La. 1977, D.C. 1992, U.S. Dist. Ct. (ea. dist.) La. 1977, U.S. Dist. Ct. (mid. dist.) La. 1978, U.S. Dist. Ct. (we. dist.) La. 1979, U.S. Dist. Ct. (no. and so. dists.) Tex. 1991, U.S. Dist. Ct. D.C. (1994, U.S. Ct. Appeals (D.C. cir.) 1992, U.S. Ct. Appeals (5th and 11th cirs.) 1981, U.S. Supreme Ct. 1980. Assoc. firm Jones, Walker, Waechter, Poitevent, Carrere & Denegre, New Orleans, 1977-82, ptnr., 1982—. Chmn. profl. liability practice group, Jones, Walker, et al. Recipient West Horn Book award West Pub. Co., 1976; Fulbright and Jaworski scholar, 1976. Mem. ABA (litigation sect., bus. law sect., criminal laws com., federal regulation of securities com.), Securities Industry Assn., Nat. Soc. Compliance Profls., New Orleans Bar Assn., La. Bankers Assn., 5th Cir. Bar Assn., Order of Coif, Phi Kappa Phi, Phi Delta Phi. Banking, Federal civil litigation, Securities. Home: 1420 Marengo St New Orleans LA 70115-3815 Office: Jones Walker Waechter Poitevent Carrere & Denegre 201 Saint Charles Ave Ste 5200 New Orleans LA 70170-5100 E-mail: rbieck@joneswalker.com

BIEDERMAN, DONALD ELLIS, lawyer; b. N.Y.C., Aug. 23, 1934; s. William and Sophye (Groll) B.; m. Marna M. Leerburger, Dec. 22, 1962; children: Charles Jefferson, Melissa Anne. AB, Cornell U., 1955; JD, Harvard U., 1958; LLM in Taxation, NYU, 1970. Bar: N.Y. 1959, U.S. Dist. Ct. (so. dist.) N.Y. 1967, Calif. 1977. Assoc. Hale, Russell & Stentzel, N.Y.C., 1962-66; asst. corp. counsel City of N.Y., 1966-68; assoc. Delson & Gordon, N.Y.C., 1968-69; ptnr. Roe, Carman, Clerke, Berkman & Berkman, Jamaica, N.Y., 1969-72; gen. atty. CBS Records, N.Y.C., 1972-76; sr. v.p. legal affairs and adminstrn. ABC Records, L.A., 1977-79; ptnr. Mitchell, Silberberg & Knupp, 1979-83; exec. v.p., gen. counsel Warner/Chappell Music Inc., 1983-99, cons., 2000—. Adj. prof. Sch. Law Southwestern U., L.A., 1982-2000, prof. law, dir. entertainment and media law inst., 2000—, Pepperdine U., Malibu, Calif., 1985-87, Loyola Marymount U., L.A., 1992; lectr. Anderson Sch. Mgmt. UCLA, 1993, U. So. Calif. Law Ctr., 1995-97. Editor: Legal and Business Problems of the Music Industry, 1980; co-author: Law and Business of the Entertainment Industries, 1987, 2nd edit., 1991, 3d edit., 1995, 4th edit., 2001. Bd. dirs. Calif. Chamber Symphony Soc., L.A., 1981-92; dir. Entertainment Law Inst. U. So. Calif., 1993-2000. 1st lt. U.S. Army, 1959. Recipient Hon. Gold Record, Recording Industry Assn. Am., 1974, Trendsetter award Billboard mag., 1976, Gold Triangle award Am. Acad. Dermatology, 1999; named Entertainment Lawyer of Yr., Beverly Hills Bar Assn., 2000. Mem. N.Y. Bar Assn., Calif. Bar Assn., Riviera Country Club, Cornell Club. Democrat. Jewish. Avocations: golf, skiing, travel, reading. don. Entertainment, Intellectual property. Home: 2406 Pesquera Dr Los Angeles CA 90049-1225 Office: Warner/Chappell Music Inc 10585 Santa Monica Blvd Los Angeles CA 90025-4921 E-mail: dbiederman@swlaw.edu, biederman@warnerchappell.com

BIEHL, MICHAEL MELVIN, lawyer; b. Milw., Feb. 24, 1951; s. Michael Melvin Biehl and Frieda Margaret (Krieg) Davis. AB, Harvard U., 1973, JD, 1976. Bar: Wis. 1976, U.S. Dist. Ct. (ea. dist.) Wis. 1976. Assoc. Foley & Lardner, Milw., 1976-84, ptnr., 1984—. Author: Medical Staff Legal Issues, 1990; editor: Physician Organizations and Medical Staff, 1996. Mem. Mt. Sinai Med. Ctr. Clin. Investigations Com., Hastings Ctr.; election monitor first multi-party elections in Rep. Ga., 1990; dir. Colorlines Found. for Arts and Culture, Inc., chmn., bd. dirs. Milw. Psychiat. Hosp. and Aurora Behavioral Health Svcs. Mem. ABA, Am. Health Lawyers Assn., Am. Coll. of Med. Quality, Am. Soc. Law and Medicine. Mem. Unitarian Ch. Health, Real property. Home: 10315 N Versailles Ct Mequon WI 53092-5231 Office: Foley & Lardner 777 E Wisconsin Ave Ste 3800 Milwaukee WI 53202-5367

BIELE, HUGH IRVING, retired lawyer; b. Bridgeport, Conn., July 28, 1942; s. Ray James and Blanche (McClellan) B.; m. Pamela Althea Johnson, Aug. 21, 1965 (div.); children: Jonathan Christopher, Melissa Lynne. BA, St. Lawrence U., Canton, N.Y., 1965; JD, U. Utah, 1968. Bar: Utah 1968, U.S. Dist. Ct. Utah 1968, Calif. 1972, U.S. Dist. Ct. Calif. 1972, U.S. Ct. Appeals (9th and 10th cirs.). Instr. San Francisco Law Sch., 1971-73; atty. United Calif. Bank, San Francisco, 1971-74; v.p., sr. counsel First Interstate Bank, L.A., 1974-81; ptnr. Biele & Stuehrmann, 1981-83; sr. ptnr. Biele, Stuehrmann & Lapinski, 1983-84; founding ptnr. Biele & Lapinski, 1985-89; ptnr. Barton, Klugman & Detting, 1989-91; ptnr., dir. comml. law and litigation Grace, Skocypec, Cosgrove & Schirm, 1992-95; ret., 1995. Bd. govs. Fin. Lawyer Conf., L.A., 1976-2000, pres. 1984-85, original developer, ptnr. Engine Co. No. 28 rehabilitation, 1978-88, ptnr. Engine Co. No. 28 Restaurant, 1988—, owner Biele Enterprises. Author screenplay: Corporate Cancer, 1989, Hedge of Thorns, 1990. Chmn. Vols. in Parole, L.A., 1979—80, 1989—90, Lawyers for Human Rights, 1988—2000, co-pres. elect, 1998, co-pres., 1999; commr. Episc. Diocese AIDS Ministry, L.A., 1988—93; bd. dirs. Cmty. Counseling Svc. , 1989—99, pres., 1993—95, chmn. bd. dirs., 1995—99; bd. dirs. Casa de Rosa and the Sunshine Mission, 1997—, treas., 2001—; bd. dirs., v.p., sec. Project New Hope, Inc., L.A., 1990—92. Decorated Army Commendation medal, Bronze Star with oak leaf cluster. Mem.: ABA, FBA, Internat. Bar Assn., Fin. Lawyers Conf. (pres. 1986—87), L.A. County Bar Assn. (internat. sect. exec. com. 1978—97, chmn. 1981—82, exec. com. comml. law and bankruptcy sect. 1986—, chair 1992—93), Calif. State Bar (fin. inst. com.), Internat. Bankers Assn. Calif., St. Lawrence U. Alumni Assn. (pres. 1979—91). Republican. Episcopalian. Avocations: skiing, jogging, aerobics, travel. Banking, Bankruptcy, Contracts commercial. Office: PO Box 2068 Hollywood CA 90078-2068 Home: 3478 Wonder View Dr Los Angeles CA 90068-1536 E-mail: hughbiele@aol.com

BIELUCH, WILLIAM CHARLES, judge; b. Nov. 12, 1918; AB magna cum laude, Brown U., 1939; JD, Yale U., 1942. Bar: Conn. 1942. Assoc. Covington, Burling, Rublee, Acheson & Shorb, Washington, 1942-43; ptnr. Bieluch, Barry & Ramenda and predecessors, Hartford, 1946-68; judge Cir. Ct. Conn., 1968-73, Ct. Common Pleas Conn., 1973-76, Superior Ct. Conn., 1976-85, Appellate Session, 1979-83, Appellate Ct. Conn., 1985-88; ret., 1988; judge trial referee, 1988—. Trustee emeritus S. S. Cyril and Methodius Roman Cath. Ch., Hartford; corporator St. Francis Hosp. and Med. Ctr., Hartford. Lt. (j.g.) USCG, WWII. Decorated Knight St. Gregory, Pope Paul VI; recipient Merit award Polish Legion Am. Vets., 1952, Man of Yr. award United Polish Socs., 1968, Archdiocesan medal of appreciation Archbishop John F. Whealon, 1970, Disting. Grad. award Nat. Cath. Elem. Sch., 1995. Mem. Conn. Bar Assn. (chmn. Jr. Bar Sect. 1948-49), Hartford County Bar Assn., KC, Phi Beta Kappa. Republican. Office: 95 Washington St Hartford CT 06106-4431

BIENEN, LEIGH BUCHANAN, lawyer; b. Berkeley, Calif., Apr. 24, 1938; d. Norman Sharpe Buchanan and Janet Buchanan (Saniter) Arnold; m. Henry S Bienen, Apr. 28, 1961; children: Laura, Claire, Leslie. BA, Cornell U., 1960; MA, State U. Iowa, 1963; JD, Rutgers-Newark Sch. Law, 1975. Bar: NJ 1975, US Dist Ct NJ 1975, Pa 1977, NY 1982, US Supreme Ct 1982, DC 1983, Ill 1996. Rsch. atty. Ctr. for Rape Concern, Phila., 1975-76; law assoc. Boalt Hall, U. Calif., Berkeley, 1976-77; asst. dep. pub. defender Dept. Pub. Advocate, Trenton, N.J., 1977-91; adminstrv. dir. Princeton U. Woodrow Wilson Sch., 1991-94; sr. lectr. Northwestern U. Sch. Law, Evanston, Ill., 1995—. Lectr Univ Pa Sch Law, Philadelphia, Pa., 1981, Princeton Univ, Princeton, NJ, 1977, Princeton, 82, Princeton, 84, Princeton, 87, Princeton, 1991—94. Author: (book) Jurors and Rape, 1980, Learning from the Past, Living in the Present, 2000, (novels) The Left-Handed Marriage, 2001; author: ((with G Geis)) Crimes of the Century;contbr. articles to profl jours. Dir Chicago Hist Homicide Project, 2000; bd dirs NJ ACLU, 1982—92, Womens Rights Law Reporter, 1977—. Recipient Fiction Prize, O'Henry Prize Stories, 1983; fellow, MacDowell Colony, 1979, 1982, YADDO, 1984, Blue Mountain Ctr, 1986—87; grantee Wallace Eljabar Fund, 1974, Am Philos Soc, 1981—82, Fiction, NJ Coun Arts, 1986—87, Joyce Found, 1999; scholar Deans, Cornell Univ. Mem.: ABA (project on sex offender sentencing 1984—85). Office: Northwestern U Sch Law 357 E Chgo Ave Chicago IL 60611

BIENVENU, JOHN CHARLES, lawyer; b. Modesto, Calif., Sept. 11, 1957; s. Robert Charles and Martha Louise (Beard) B.; m. Sarah Luciene Brick, May 10, 1983; children: Reed Charles, Loren John. Student, U. Calif., Berkeley, 1975-78; BA summa cum laude, U. N.Mex., 1985; JD with distinction, Stanford U., 1988. Bar: Calif., 1988, N.Mex., 1990; U.S. Ct. Appeals (9th cir.) 1988, U.S. Ct. Appeals (10th cir.) 1990; U.S. Ct. Fed. Claims, 1991. Assoc. Brobeck, Phleger & Harrison, San Francisco, 1988-90, Rothstein, Walther, Donatelli, Hughes, Dahlstrom & Cron, Santa Fe, 1990-93; prin., 1993—. Mem. ACLU (cooperating atty. N.Mex.), N.Mex. State Bar. Democrat. Civil rights, General civil litigation. Home: 1580 Cerro Gordo Rd Santa Fe NM 87501-6143 Office: PO Box 2455 310 Mckenzie St Santa Fe NM 87501-1883

BIENVENU, ROBERT CHARLES, lawyer; b. Milw., Dec. 3, 1922; s. Harold John and Nellie (Davidson) B.; AB, U. Calif., Berkeley, 1947; JD, U. Pacific, 1953. Bar: Calif. 1954. m. Martha Beard, Mar. 28, 1945 (dec. 1969); children: Susan Krestan, Nancy Simas, John; m. Joyce Marlene Holley, Aug. 13, 1971. State parole officer Dept. Corrections, Sacramento, 1947-54; mem. Hoover, Lacy & Bienvenu, Modesto, Calif., 1954-66; pvt. practice, 1966—. Pres., Stanislaus County Sch. Bds. Assn., 1968-69; mem. Modesto City Schs. Bd. Edn., 1961-81; mem. Calif. Rep. Cen.Com. 1960-70; bd. dirs. Modesto Symphony Orch., 1966-72, Retarded Children's Soc. Stanislaus County, 1965-70, Am. Cancer Soc., 1955-60. With AUS, 1942-45. Mem. ABA, State Bar Calif., Stanislaus County Bar Assn., Am. Trial Lawyers Assn. Home: 218 Brook Way Modesto CA 95354-1314 Office: 726 10th St Modesto CA 95354-2302

BIERBOWER, JAMES J. lawyer; b. Giltner, Nebr., Mar. 17, 1923; married; 4 children. Student U. Nebr., 1940-42; B.S.S., Georgetown U., 1947, LL.B., 1950; LL.M., George Washington U., 1954. Bar: D.C. 1950, Nebr. 1951, Md. 1956, Va. 1960. Ptnr. Bierbower & Bierbower, Washington; adj. prof. law Georgetown Law Sch., 1962-92. Served with USMC, World War II. Decorated D.F.C., Air medal. Mem. ABA (state del. D.C. 1981-84, chmn. sect. gen. practice 1975-76, mem. ho. of dels. 1960-63, 70-84), D.C. Bar (pres. 1981-83), Bar Assn. D.C. (pres. 1978-79, mem. jud. selection com.), Fed. Bar Assn., Md. Bar Assn., Nebr. State Bar Assn., Va. State Bar Assn. General practice.

BIERCE, WILLIAM B. lawyer; b. Englewood, N.J., Dec. 15, 1949; s. Thurber and Joy Bierce; m. Martha Kenerson. BA, Yale U., 1971; Licence en Droit with honors, U. Grenoble, France, 1972; JD, NYU, 1975. Bar: N.J. 1975, N.Y. 1976, U.S. Ct. Internat. Trade 1980, U.S. Ct. Appeals (D.C. and 9th cirs.) 1984. Assoc. Coudert Bros., N.Y.C., 1975-78, Pisar and Huhs, N.Y.C., 1978-80, Windels, Marx, Davies and Ives, N.Y.C., 1980-85, ptnr., 1985-90, Bierce & Kenerson, P.C., N.Y.C., 1990—. Adj. asst. prof. Pace U. Grad. Sch. Bus., N.Y.C., 1981-86; bd. advisors Expertises des Systemes d'Information, Paris, 1985-98. Editor articles NYU jour. Internat. Law Politics, 1974-75; contbr. articles to profl. jours. Trustee Dwight-Englewood Sch., 1982-84. Grad. fellowship Rotary Found., 1971-72; nominee PriceWaterhouse Coopers/Corbett Assocs. Outstanding Achievement of Yr. award, 1999. Mem. Computer Law Assn., Union Internat. des Avocats (mem. U.S. bd. govs. 1997—), Am. Fgn. Law Assn. Computer, Mergers and acquisitions, Securities. E-mail: wbierce@biercekenerson.com

BIERIG, JACK R. lawyer, educator; b. Chgo., Apr. 10, 1947; s. Henry J. and Helga (Rothschild) B.; m. Barbara A. Winokur; children: Robert, Sarah. BA, Brandeis U., 1968; JD, Harvard U., 1972. Bar: Ill. 1972, U.S. Dist. Ct. (no. dist.) Ill. 1972, U.S. Ct. Appeals (1st-3d, 5th-11th and D.C. cirs.) 1974, U.S. Supreme Ct. 1980. Ptnr. Sidley & Austin (now Sidley Austin Brown & Wood), Chgo., 1972—; prof. Ill. Inst. Tech.-Chgo. Kent Coll. Law, 1974-95; lectr. law. U. Chgo. Law Sch. and Harris Sch. Pub. Policy , 2000—. Chmn. legal sect. Am. Soc. Assn. Execs., 1994-95. Contbr. articles to profl. jours. Pres. Neighborhood Justice Chgo., 1983-87; pres. Jewish Vocat. Svc., 1997-99. Mem. Ill. Assn. of Hosp. Attys. (pres. 1991), Chgo. Bar Assn. (bd. govs., 1982-84). Jewish. Club: Standard (Chgo.). Administrative and regulatory, Antitrust, Health. Office: Sidley Austin Brown & Wood 1 Bank One Plz Chicago IL 60603 E-mail: jbierig@sidley.com

BIERMAN, JAMES NORMAN, lawyer; b. St. Louis, Nov. 23, 1945; s. Norman and Margaret (Loeb) B.; m. Catherine Best, Apr. 10, 1983; 1 child, James Norman. AB magna cum laude, Washington U., 1967; JD, Harvard Law Sch., 1970. Assoc. Hogan & Hartson, Washington, 1970-72; asst. dean Harvard Law Sch., Cambridge, Mass., 1973-75; assoc. Foley & Lardner, Washington, 1975-79, ptnr., 1979—, ptnr. in charge, 1985-2001, mem. mgmt. com., 1989-98. Mem. nat. coun. Washington U. Coll. Arts and Scis., 1999—. Mng. editor Harvard Jour. Legis., 1969-70. Mem. Civil Rights Reviewing Authority HEW, Washington, 1979-80. Mem. ABA, Fed. Bar Assn., D.C. Bar Assn., Supreme Ct. Bar, Washington Lawyers Com. for

Civil Rights and Urban Affairs (bd. dirs.), Phi Beta Kappa, Omicron Delta Kappa, Pi Sigma Alpha, Phi Eta Sigma, City Club (Washington). Administrative and regulatory, Private international, Mergers and acquisitions. Home: 906 Peacock Station Rd Mc Lean VA 22102-1021 Office: Foley & Lardner 3000 K St NW Fl 5 Washington DC 20007-5109 E-mail: jbierman@foleylaw.com

BIERY, EVELYN HUDSON, lawyer; b. Lawton, Okla., Oct. 12, 1946; d. William Ray and Nellie Iris (Nunley) Hudson. BA in English and Latin summa cum laude, Abilene (Tex.) Christian U., 1968; JD, So. Meth. U., 1973. Bar: Tex. 1973, U.S. Dist. Ct. (we. dist.) Tex. 1975, U.S. Dist. Ct. (so. dist.) Tex. 1977, U.S. Dist. Ct. (no. dist.) Tex. 1979, U.S. Ct. Appeals (5th cir.) 1979, U.S. Ct. Appeals (11th cir.) 1981, U.S. Supreme Ct. 1981. Atty. Law Offices of Bruce Waitz, San Antonio, 1973-76; mem. LeLaurin & Adams, PC, 1976-81; ptnr. Fulbright & Jaworski, 1981—, head bankruptcy, reorganization and creditors' rights sect., 1990—. Policy com. Fulbright & Jaworski, San Antonio, 1996-98; speaker on creditors' rights, bankruptcy and reorganization law; lectr. Southwestern Grad. Sch. Banking, Dallas, 1980, La. State U. Sch. Banking, 1994; presiding officer, U. Tex. Sch. of Law Bankruptcy Conf., 1976, 94, State Bar Tex. Creditors' Rights Inst., 1985, State Bar Tex. Advanced Bus. Bankruptcy Law Inst., 1985, State Bar Tex. Inst. on Advising Officers, Dirs. and Ptnrs. in Troubled Bus., 1987, State Bar Tex. Advanced Creditors Rights Inst., 1988; pres. San Antonio Young Lawyers Assn., 1979-80; mem. bankruptcy adv. com. fifth cir. jud. coun., 1979-80; vice-chmn. bankruptcy com. Comml. Law League Am., 1981-83; mem. exec. bd. So. Meth. U. Sch. Law, 1983-91. Editor: Texas Collections Manual, 1978, Creditor's Rights in Texas, 2d edit., 1981; author: (with others) Collier Bankruptcy Practice Guide, 1993. Del. to U.S./Republic of China joint session on trade, investment and econ. law, Beijing, 1987; designated mem. Bankruptcy Judge Merit Screening Com. State of Tex. by Tex. State Bar Pres., 1979-82; patron McNay Mus., San Antonio; rsch. ptnr. Mind Sci. Found., San Antonio; diplomat World Affairs Coun., San Antonio. Recipient Outstanding Young Lawyer award San Antonio Young Lawyers Assn., 1979. Fellow Soc. Internat. Bus. Fellows (sec.), Am. Coll. Bankruptcy Attys., Tex. Bar Found. (life), San Antonio Bar Found. (life); mem. Tex. Bar Assn. (chair bankruptcy com. 1982-83, chair corp., banking and bus. law sect. 1989-90), Tex. Assn. Bank Counsel (bd. dirs. 1988-90), San Antonio Young Lawyers Assn. (pres. 1979-80), Plaza Club San Antonio (bd. dirs. 1982—), Zonta (Chair Z club com. 1989-90), Order of Coif. Bankruptcy, Federal civil litigation, General corporate. Office: Fulbright & Jaworski LLP 300 Convent St Ste 2200 San Antonio TX 78205-3720 also: 1301 Mckinney St Ste 5100 Houston TX 77010-3031

BIGELOW, ROBERT WILSON, trial lawyer; b. L.A., Oct. 22, 1964; s. William Phillips and Dona (Heath) B.; m. Madeline Garcia, Sept. 24, 1995; children: William, Emma. Student, UCLA, 1982-84; BA with distinction, U. N.Mex., 1990; JD, Georgetown U., 1993. Bar: N.Y. Intern FTC, Washington, 1992; mem. Georgetown Criminal Justice Clinic, 1992-93; sr. staff aty. Criminal Def. divsn. Legal Aid Soc., Bronx, N.Y., 1993-2001, supervising atty. N.Y.C., 2001—. Mentor John Jay Legal Svcs., Inc., White Plains, N.Y., 1997-2001. Mem. ABA (criminal justice sect. 1996—, def. function/svcs. com. 1996—), Assn. Legal Aid Attys. (rep. 1997-99, alt. v.p. 1999-2001). Democrat. Episcopalian. Avocation: baseball research. Home: 28 Cannon St West Orange NJ 07052 Office: Legal Aid Soc Criminal Def Divsn 49 Thomas St New York NY 10013

BIGLER, GLADE S. lawyer; b. Brigham City, Utah, Apr. 21, 1928; s. Horace J. and Marie (Schow) B.; m. Lois A Bigler, Sept. 4, 1951; children— Cathy, Nadine, Elaine, Thad, Pat. B.S. in Zoology, U. Utah 1950, J.D. 1956. Bar: Utah 1956, U.S. Dist. Ct. Utah 1956, U.S. Ct. Appeals (10th cir.) 1956, U.S. Supreme Ct. 1970. Ins. adjuster Travelers Ins. Co. 1956-58; gen. atty. VA, Salt Lake City 1958-60, loan guaranty atty. 1960-68, dist. counsel 1974-98, ret. 1998; adminstrv. law judge 1971-74; counsel 1974-95, ret. 1995; lectr. in field; pres. Nat. Fedn. Fed. Employees Local 990, 1961-62. Served with USN, 1950-53, USNR 1953-81. Fellow Am. Coll. Legal Medicine; mem. Fed. Bar Assn. (pres. 1964-65), Res. Officers Assn. (pres. Salt Lake chpt. 1978-79). Mormon. Home: 3003 Kenwood St Salt Lake City UT 84106-3704

BILANDIC, MICHAEL A. retired state supreme court justice, former mayor; b. Chgo., Feb. 13, 1923; s. Matthew and Domenica (Lebedina) B.; m. Heather Morgan, July 15, 1977; 1 son, Michael Morgan. JD, DePaul U., 1948. Bar: Ill. 1949. Master in chancery Cir. Ct. Cook County, Ill., 1964-67; spl. asst. to atty. gen., 1965-68; ptnr. Anixter, Bilandic & Pigott and predecessors, Chgo., 1963-77; acting mayor, 1976; mayor, 1977-79; ptnr. Bilandic, Neistein, Richman, Hauslinger and Young, 1979-84; justice Ill. Appellate Ct., 1984-90, Ill. Supreme Ct., 1990-2000. Mem. Chgo. City Coun., 1969-76, chmn. com. on environ. control, 1970-74, chmn. fin. com., 1974-76. 1st lt. USMC, 1942-46. Mem. Am., Ill., Chgo. bar assns., Cath. Lawyers Guild. Democrat. Roman Catholic. Office: 160 N La Salle St Fl 20 Chicago IL 60601-3119

BILDERSEE, ROBERT ALAN, lawyer; b. Albany, N.Y., Jan. 22, 1942; s. Max U. and Hannah (Marks) B.; m. Ellen Bernstein, June 9, 1963; 1 child, Jennifer M. BA, Columbia Coll., 1962, MA, 1964; LLB, Yale U., 1967. Assoc. Wolf Block Schorr & Solis Cohen, Phila., 1967-72; sole practice, 1972-73; assoc., then ptnr. Fox Rothschild, O'Brien & Frankel, 1973-80; ptnr. Morgan Lewis & Bockius LLP, 1980-97; founding ptnr. Bildersee & Silbert, LLP, 1997—. Lectr. Temple U. Sch. Law, Phila., 1978-91; asst. in instrn. Yale U. Law Sch., New Haven, 1966. Author: Pension Regulation Manual, Pension Administrator's Forms and Checklists, 1987; contbg. author: Employee Benefits Handbook, 1982-98; editor: Beyond the Fringes; contbr. articles to profl. jours. Woodrow Wilson fellow, 1962. Mem. ABA, Pa. Bar Assn., Phila. Bar Assn. Avocation: wildlife photography. Labor, Pension, profit-sharing, and employee benefits, Corporate taxation. Office: Bildersee and Silbert LLP 1617 Jfk Blvd Ste 1111 Philadelphia PA 19103-1826 E-mail: erisaplus@aol.com

BILGER, BRUCE R. lawyer; b. Balt., Feb. 27, 1952; BA, Dartmouth Coll., 1973; MBA, JD, U. Va., 1977. Bar: Tex. 1977. Mem. Vinson & Elkins, L.L.P., Houston. Mem. Phi Beta Kappa. E-mila. Finance, Private international, Mergers and acquisitions. Office: Vinson & Elkins LLP 2300 First City Tower 1001 Fannin St Houston TX 77002-6760 E-mail: bbilger@velaw.com

BILLAUER, BARBARA PFEFFER, lawyer, educator; b. Aug. 9, 1951; d. Harry George and Evelyn (Newman) Pfeffer. BS with honors, Cornell U., 1972; JD, Hofstra U., 1975; MA, NYU, 1982; cert. in risk scis. and pub. policy, Johns Hopkins U., 1999. Bar: N.Y. 1976, Fed. Dist. Ct. N.Y. 1977, U.S. Ct. Appeals (2d cir.) 1978, U.S. Supreme Ct. 1984. Assoc. Bower & Gardner, N.Y.C., 1974-78; sr. trial atty. Joseph W. Conklin, 1978-80; assoc. dept. head Curtis, Mallet-Prevost, Colt & Mosle, 1980-82; ptnr. Anderson, Russell, Kill & Olick, 1982-86, Stroock & Stroock & Lavan, N.Y.C., 1986-90; ptnr., chair environ. and toxic tort practice Keck, Mahin, Cate & Koether, 1990-93; prin. Barbara P. Billauer & Assocs., Lido Beach, N.Y., 1993—. Vis. scholar Johns Hopkins U. Sch. Pub. Health, 1998-99; faculty SUNY Stony Brook Med. Sch.; adj. assoc. prof. NYU Grad. Sch., 1982-88; lectr. Rutger's U. Med. Sch.; jud. screening com. Coordinated Bar Assn., 1983-86; mem. spl panel Citywide Ct. Adminstrn. 1982-85; bd. dirs. Weizmann Inst., Am. Com. Co-author: The Lender's Guide to Environmental Law: Risk and Liability, 1993. Fellow Am. Bar Found.; mem. ABA (indoor air polution 1990-93), Met. Womens Bar Assn. (v.p. 1981-83, pres. 1983-85, chmn. bd. 1985-87), Nat. Conf. Womens Bar Assn. (bd. dirs., v.p. 1989-95), Internat. Coun. Shopping Ctrs. (environ. com.), Brit. Occupl. Hygiene Soc., Environment Toxic Torts. Environmental, Health, Personal injury. E-mail: omniscience@starpower.net

BILLINGS, FRANKLIN SWIFT, JR. federal judge; b. Woodstock, Vt., June 5, 1922; s. Franklin S. and Gertrude (Curtis) B.; m. Pauline Gillingham, Oct. 13, 1951; children: Franklin, III, Jireh Swift, Elizabeth, Ann. S.B., Harvard U., 1943; postgrad., Yale U. law Sch., 1945; J.D., U. Va., 1947. Bar: Vt. 1948, U.S. Supreme Ct., 1958. With dept. electronics Gen. Electric Co., Schenectady, N.Y., 1943; bldg. dept. Vt. Marble Co., Proctor, 1945-46; pvt. practice law Woodstock, 1948-52; mem. firm Billings & Sherburne, 1952-66; asst. sec. Vt. Senate, 1949-55, sec., 1957-59; sec. civil and mil. affairs State of Vt., 1959-61; exec. clk. to gov., 1955-57; judge Hartford Mcpl. Ct., 1955-63; mem. Vt. Ho. of Reps., 1961-66, chmn. jud. com., 1961, speaker of ho., 1963-66; judge Vt. Superior Ct., 1966-75, assoc. justice, 1975-83, chief justice, 1983-84; judge U.S. Dist. Ct. Vt., 1984-94, chief judge, 1988-92, sr. ct. judge, 1994—. Active, Town of Woodstock, 1948-72. Served as warrant officer 1st class attached Brit. Army, 1944-45. Decorated Purple Heart; Brit. Empire medal. Mem. Vt. Bar Assn., Delta Theta Phi. Office: US Dist Ct PO Box 598 Woodstock VT 05091-0598

BILLINGSLEY, ROBERT THAINE, lawyer; b. Wichita, Kans., Jan. 9, 1954; s. Thaine Edward and Anita (Moore) B.; m. Anna Barron, Dec. 31, 1983; children: Carol Carothers, Leslie Hope. AB, Coll. of William and Mary, 1976; JD, U. Richmond, 1980. Bar: Va. 1980. Law clk. to presiding justice U.S. Dist. Ct., Roanoke, Va., 1980-81; assoc. McGuire, Woods & Battle, Richmond, 1981-87, Hirschler, Fleischer, Weinberg, Cox & Allen, Richmond, 1987-96; fin. advisr Kramnick & Assocs., Fredericksburg, 1996—. Bd. dirs. Make A Wish Found., Ctrl. and Western Va., 2000—. Bd. editors The Virginia Lawyer, 1984-86; mem. adv. bd. U. Richmond Law Rev., 1986-97; contbr. articles to profl. publs. Bd. dirs. Bethlehem Ctr., Richmond, 1985-89, United Meth. Found. of Va. Conf., Inc., 1993—, sec., 2000; bd. dirs. Hanover Indsl. Air Pk. Bus. Assn., 1994-96; mem. adminstrv. bd. Trinity United Meth. Ch., Richmond, 1986-89, trustee, 1988-96, chmn. bd. trustees, 1992-95, chmn. commitment campaign, 1995; team capt. United Way Greater Richmond, 1989, sect. chmn., 1991, divsn. chmn., 1993; team capt. Rappahannock Area United Way, 1998, divsn. chair, 1999; mem. Leadership Metro Richmond Class, 1992-93; bd. dirs. Arts Coun. of Richmond, Inc., 1994-96, exec. com., 1996; chmn. fin. com. Fredericksburg United Meth. Ch., 1999—; bd. dirs. College Heights Swimming Pool Assn. Mem. ABA (litigation sect., state memnership chmn. young lawyers divsn. 1985-89, state membership chmn. 1989-96), Va. Bar Assn. (com. on alternative dispute resolution), Va. State Bar Assn. (bd. govs. young lawyers conf. 1985-89, spl. com. on professionalism, legal edn., admission to bar), Richmond Bar Assn. (program com., vice chmn. 1990-91, chmn. 1991-92, adminstrn. of justice com. 1992-96), Fredericksburg Bar Assn., William and Mary Alumni Assn. (bd. dirs. Richmond chpt. 1993-95), Richmond Jaycees (bd. dirs. 1984-86), Rotary (Rappahannock chpt. bd. dirs. 2000—). Avocations: sports, travel, theatre. Federal civil litigation, General civil litigation, State civil litigation. Home: 1604 College Ave Fredericksburg VA 22401-4637 Office: Kramnick & Assocs 5444 Jefferson Davis Hwy Fredericksburg VA 22407-2627

BINDER, DAVID FRANKLIN, lawyer, author; b. Beaver Falls, Pa., Aug. 1, 1935; s. Walter Carl and Jessie Maivis (Bliss) B.; m. Deana Jacqueline Pines, Dec. 25, 1971; children: April, Bret. BA, Geneva Coll., 1956; JD, Harvard U., 1959. Bar: Pa. 1960, U.S. Ct. Appeals (3rd cir.) 1963, U.S. Supreme Ct. 1967. Law clk. to chief justice Pa. Supreme Ct., 1959-61; counsel Fidelity Mut. Life Ins. Co., Phila., 1964-66; ptnr. Bennett, Bricklin & Saltzburg, 1967-68; mem. Richter, Syken, Ross, and Binder, 1969-72, Raynes, McCarty, Binder, Ross and Mundy, Phila., 1972—. Mem. faculty Pa. Coll. Judiciary; judge pro tempore Phila. Common Pleas Ct., 1991-97; lectr., course planner Pa. Bar Inst.; mem. civil procedural rules com., ad hoc. com. on evidence Supreme Ct. Pa. Author: Hearsay Handbook, 1975, ann. supplements, 2nd edit., 1983, 3rd edit., 1991, Binder on Pennsylvania Evidence, 1999. Recipient Disting. Alumnus award Geneva Coll., 1981. Mem. ABA, Pa. Bar Assn., Phila. Bar Assn., Assn. Trial Lawyers Am. (lectr.), Pa. Trial Lawyers Assn., Harvard Law Sch. Assn., Am. Bd. Trial Advs., Am. Coll. Trial Lawyers, Union League. Federal civil litigation, State civil litigation, Personal injury. Home: 1412 Flat Rock Rd Narberth PA 19072-1216 Office: Raynes McCarty Binder Ross and Mundy 1845 Walnut St Ste 2000 Philadelphia PA 19103-4767 E-mail: dfbinder@raynesmccarty.com

BINES, HARVEY ERNEST, lawyer, educator, writer; b. Winthrop, Mass., Nov. 25, 1941; s. Carl and Lillian (Cooper) B.; m. Joan Carol Paller, Dec. 27, 1964; children: Jonathan W., Joel T., Susanne R., Benjamin E. BS, MIT, 1963; JD, U. Va., 1970. Bar: Mass 1971, Va. 1971, U.S. Dist. Ct. Mass., U.S. Dist. Ct. (ea. dist.) Va., U.S. Ct. Appeals (1st, 3d, 4th, 7th and D.C. cirs.), U.S. Supreme Ct. Law clk. to hon. John D. Butzner Jr. U.S. Ct. Appeals (4th cir.), Richmond, Va., 1970-71; asst. prof. Law Sch. U. Va., Charlottesville, 1971-74, assoc. prof. Law Sch., 1974-76; assoc. Sullivan & Worcester, Boston, 1976-79, ptnr., 1980—. Adj. prof. Boston Coll. Law Sch., Chestnut Hill, Mass., 1981-88, bd. dirs., treas. Schweitzer Fellowship, Boston. Author: Law of Investment Management, 1978, 1991. Lt. USNR, 1963-67. Mem. Am. Law Inst., Internat. Bar Assn., Boston Bar Assn. General corporate, Private international, Securities. Home: 36 Clarke St Lexington MA 02421-4916 Office: Sullivan & Worcester 1 Post Office Sq Ste 2300 Boston MA 02109-2129 E-mail: heb@sandw.com

BING, RICHARD MCPHAIL, lawyer; b. Lewes, Del., Aug. 23, 1950; s. Arden E. and Ellen Louise (Judd) B.; m. Valerie Lynn Wasson, Dec. 18, 1971; children: Jennifer Lynn, Kristin Tyler. BA, U. Richmond, 1972, JD, 1978. Bar: Va. 1978, U.S. Dist. Ct. (ea. and we. dists.) Va. 1979, U.S. Dist. Ct. (we. dist.) Pa. 1990, U.S. Dist. Ct. (no. dist.) N.Y. 1990, U.S. Dist. Ct. (ctrl. dist.) Ill. 1996, U.S. Ct. Appeals (4th cir.) 1979, U.S. Ct. appeals (2d cir.) 1990, U.S. Supreme Ct. 1994, U.S. Dist. Ct. (ctrl. dist.) Ill. 1996. Dir. ins. Bur. of Ins., Richmond, Va., 1978-79; resident gen counsel Va. Gasoline Retailers Assn., 1979-83; ptnr. Pearce & Bing, 1983-93, Bing & Assocs., P.C., Richmond, 1993—. Adj. prof. law J. Sargent Reynolds Community Coll., Richmond, 1984-85. Mem. Henrico County Rep. Com; bd. dirs. Three Chopt PTA, Richmond, 1984-85. Mem. ABA, Va. Bar Assn., Va. Bar, Richmond Bar Assn., Fed. bar Assn., Assn. Trial Lawyers Am., Va. Trial Lawyers Assn., Nat. Lawyers Club, Tcukahoe Jaycees (pres. 1981-82), Bull and Bear Club, Hermitage Country Club, Tobacco Co. Club, The Spider Club (bd. dirs.), Am. Assn. of Franchisees and Dealers, Svc. Sta. Dealers of Am., Inc., Affiliate Attys. Group. Avocations: golf, bicycling, photography. Federal civil litigation, General civil litigation, Contracts commercial. Home: 1701 Habwood Ln Richmond VA 23233-4451 Office: Bing & Assocs PC 300 Arboretum Pl Ste 140 Richmond VA 23236-3465

BINGHAM, A. WALKER, III, lawyer, business executive; b. N.Y.C., Nov. 5, 1928; s. Arthur Walker and Mary (Dunwody) B.; m. Nicolette Pathy, Oct. 28, 1967; children— Arthur Walker, IV, Alexander Dunwody, Nicole Pathy. B.A., Harvard U., 1951, LL.B., 1958. Bar: N.Y. 1959. Assoc. Milbank, Tweed Hadley & McCloy, N.Y.C., 1958-68; gen. atty. Abex Corp., N.Y.C., 1968-74, group counsel, Stamford, Conn., 1984— ; chmn. bd. Boorum & Pease Co., Elizabeth, N.J., 1974— . Served to lt. USN, 1951-54. Mem. Assn. Bar City N.Y. Clubs: Union, Harvard (N.Y.C.). Lodge: Holland. Contracts commercial, General corporate, Securities. Home: 19 E 72nd St New York NY 10021-4145 Office: Abex Corp 6 Landmark Sq Stamford CT 06904

BINNING, J. BOYD, lawyer; b. N.Y.C., July 7, 1944; s. James Edward and Lillian (Doughty) B.; m. Penelope Elizabeth Lancione, July 22, 1977; children: Alicia, Peter. AA, Wesley Coll., 1964; BS cum laude, Urbana Coll., Ohio, 1970; MA in Polit. Sci., Eastern Ky. U., 1971; JD, Ohio No. U., 1974. Bar: Ohio 1976, U.S. Dist. Ct. (so. dist.) Ohio 1977, U.S. Ct. Appeals (6th cir.) 1977, U.S. Dist. Ct. (no. dist.) Ohio 1979, U.S. Supreme Ct. 1979. Dep. sheriff Miami County, Troy, Ohio, 1971-74; investigator, legal intern Miami County prosecutor's office, Troy, 1973-75; spl. counsel for the Ohio Senate Jud. Com.; instr., advisor Iowa State Law Enforcement Acad., Des Moines, 1976; pvt. practice law, Columbus, 1976—; spl. counsel jud. com. Ohio Senate; judge moot ct. Capital Law Sch., Columbus. Author: Civil Rights and the Federal Courts, 1971. Grad. scholar Eastern Ky. U., 1970-71. Mem. Ohio State Bar Assn., Columbus Bar Assn., Columbus Bar Found., Ohio Acad. Trial Lawyers, Nat. Assn. Criminal Def. Lawyers. General civil litigation, Criminal, Personal injury. Office: 592 S 3rd St Columbus OH 43215-5754

BIOLATO, GIUSEPPE VITTORIO, lawyer; b. Savigliano, Piedmont, Italy, Apr. 29, 1943; s. Domenico Biolato and Ada Mioni. Degree in law, U. Perugia, Italy, 1965. Bar: Rome 1970, High Ct. 1986. Assoc. Studio Avv. Ercole Graziadei, Rome, 1966-71, ptnr., 1971-84; founding ptnr. Manca Amenta Biolato Corrao, 1984—. Lt. inf. Italian Mil., 1995-96. General corporate, Landlord-tenant, Real property. Office: Via del Babuino 51 00187 Rome Italy Fax: 06.3234238

BIOLCHINI, ROBERT FREDRICK, lawyer; b. Detroit, Sept. 22, 1939; s. Alfred and Erma (Barbetti) B.; m. Frances Lauinger, June 5, 1965; children: Robert F., Douglas C., Frances E., Tobin m., Thomas A., Christine M. BA, U. Notre Dame, 1962; LLB, George Washington U., 1965. Bar: Okla., Mich., 1965. Assoc. Doerner, Stuart, Saunders, Daniel, Anderson & Biolchini, Tulsa, 1968-71, ptnr., 1971-94, Stuart, Biolchini, Turner & Givray, Tulsa, 1994—. Pres., CEO Pennwell Corp.; chmn. bd. dirs., CEO, PennEnergy, Inc., Valley Nat. Bank, Ameritrust Holding Co., Old Faithful Underwriting Ltd.; mem. Lloyds of London, 1979—; bd. dirs. Lumen Energy Corp., Bank of The Lakes, Bank of Jackson Hole. Bd. dirs. Thomas Gilcrease Mus., past pres., chmn. bd., 1977-80, dir. emeritus, 1980—; bd. dirs., sec., legal clk. Tulsa Ballet Theatre, Inc., 1976-84; trustee Monte Cassino Endowment, 1978—; pres. Monte Cassino Sch. Bd., 1970-77; chmn. Christ the King Parish Coun., 1974-75; mem. adv. coun. U. Notre Dame Law Sch., 1982-2000, trustee U. Notre Dame, 2001—; chmn. Cath. Diocese Tulsa Fund for Future, 1998—; bd. dirs. legal counsel Tulsa Area United Way, 1986—; mem. pres.'s coun. Regis Coll., 1986—; Okla. chmn. Lawyers for Bush, 2000. Capt. U.S. Army, 1965-67. Mem. Okla. Bar Assn., Mich. Bar Assn., Met. Tulsa C. of C. (bd. dirs. 1992—), Summit Club, Southern Hills Country Club, Club Ltd., Knights of Malta, Knights of the Holy Sepulchre. Roman Catholic. Federal civil litigation, General corporate, Securities. Home: 1744 E 29th St Tulsa OK 74114-5402 Office: First Place Tower 15 E 5th St Ste 3300 Tulsa OK 74103-4340

BIRCH, ADOLPHO A., JR. state supreme court justice; b. Washington, Sept. 22, 1932; BA, JD, Howard U., 1956. Bar: Tenn. 1957. Pvt. practice, Nashville, 1958-66; asst. pub. defender, 1964-66; asst. dist. atty., 1966-69; judge Davidson County Gen. Sessions Ct., 1969-78, Tenn. Criminal Ct. (20th jud. dist.), 1978-87; former judge Tenn. Ct. Criminal Appeals; chief justice Tenn. Supreme Ct., Nashville, 1996-97, assoc. justice, 1997—. Assoc. prof. Nashville Sch. of Law. Served USNR, 1956-58. Mem. ABA, Nat. Bar Assn., Tenn. Bar Assn., Nashville Bar Assn., Napier Lobby Bar Assn. (past pres.). Office: 401 7th Ave N Nashville TN 37219-1407*

BIRCH, STANLEY FRANCIS, JR. federal judge; b. Langley Field, Va., Aug. 29, 1945; BA, U. Va., 1967; JD, Emory U., 1970, LLM in Taxation, 1976. Law clk. to Hon. Judge Sidney O. Smith Jr. U.S. Dist. Ct. (no. dist.) Ga.; mem. firm Greer, Sartain & Carey, Gainesville, Ga., 1974-76, Deal, Birch, Jarrard & Link, Gainesville, 1976-83, Birch, Hartness & Link, Gainesville, 1983-85, Vaughan, Davis, Birch & Murphy, Atlanta, 1985-90; judge U.S. Ct. Appeals (11th cir.), 1990—. Lt. U.S. Army 1970-72. Mem. State Bar Ga., Ga. Bar Found., Atlanta Bar Assn., Gainesville Northeastern Bar Assn., 11th Cir. Hist. Soc., Lawyers Club Atlanta, Ga. Legal History Found., U. Va. Alumni Assn., Emory U. Sch. Law Alumni Assn. (past pres.), Calvert Hall Alumni Assn., Old Warhorse Lawyers Club, Theta Delta Chi. Office: US Ct Appeals 11th Cir 56 Forsyth St NWRm 505 Atlanta GA 30303-2205*

BIRD, CHARLES ALBERT, lawyer; b. Stockton, Calif., July 1, 1947; s. Donald Gladstone and Elizabeth Clara (Jongeneel) B.; m. Charlotte Laura Soeters, June 28, 1969. BA, U. Calif., Davis, 1969, JD, 1973. Bar: Calif. 1973, U.S. Dist. Ct. (so. dist.) 1975, U.S. Dist. Ct. (cen. dist.) Calif. 1981, U.S. Ct. Appeals (9th cir.) 1975, U.S. Supreme Ct. 1980. Tchr. Woodland Unified Sch. Dist., Calif., 1969-70; law clk. justice Supreme Ct. Alaska, Juneau, 1973-74; assoc. Luce, Forward, Hamilton & Scripps, San Diego, 1975-79, ptnr., 1980—. Contbr. articles to profl. jours. Bd. dirs. Defenders Orgn., San Diego, 1982—, pres., 1990-92; founding dir. San Diego Vol. Lawyer Program, 1982-86. Fellow Am. Acad. Appellate Lawyers; mem. Calif. Acad. Appellate Lawyers, San Diego County Bar Assn. (legis. chmn. 1980-81, bd. dirs. 1982-85, sec. 1984, v.p. 1985), State Bar Assn. Calif. (exec. com. real property sect. 1982-86, chmn. exec. com. 1985-86). Democrat. Episcopalian. Appellate. Home: 4182 Ingalls St San Diego CA 92103-1354 Office: Luce Forward Hamilton 600 W Broadway Ste 2600 San Diego CA 92101-3372 E-mail: cbird@luce.com

BIRD, FRANCIS MARION, JR. lawyer; b. Atlanta, Jan. 14, 1938; s. Francis Marion Sr. and Mary Adair (Howell) B.; m. JoAnn Galvin, Aug. 1994; children from previous marriage: Barbara, Michael. AB, Princeton U., 1959; LLB, Emory U., 1964; LLM, Harvard U., 1966. Bar: Ga. 1964, U.S. Ct. Appeals (3d cir. and 11th cir.), U.S. Dist. Cts. (no. dist. and mid. dist.) Ga. Officer USN, 1959-62; assoc. Jones Bird & Howell, Atlanta, 1964-70, ptnr., 1971-82, Alston & Bird, Atlanta, 1982-88; pvt. practice, 1988—. Dir., sec. Summit Industries, Inc., 1980—. Adv. bd. mem. The Devereux Ga. Treatment Network, Kennesaw, Ga., 1989—. Mem. ABA, State Bar of Ga. (chmn. Standing Com. on Publs. 1977-78), Atlanta Bar Assn. (chmn. small firm/sole practitioner sect. 1995-96), Cobb County Bar Assn., Lawyers Club of Atlanta, Old War Horses Lawyers Club. Avocations: writing, walking. Alternative dispute resolution, Estate planning, Probate. Home: 110 Montgomery Ferry Dr NE Atlanta GA 30309-2713 Office: 400 Colony Sq NE Ste 1750 Atlanta GA 30361-6320

BIRD, WENDELL RALEIGH, lawyer; b. Atlanta, July 16, 1954; s. Raleigh Milton and R. Jean (Edwards) B. BA summa cum laude, Vanderbilt U., 1975; JD, Yale U., 1978. Bar: Ga. 1978, Ala. 1980, Calif. 1981, Fla. 1982, U.S. Ct. Appeals (2d, 3d, 4th, 5th, 6th, 7th, 8th, 9th, 10th and 11th cirs.) 1979-83, U.S. Supreme Ct. 1983. Law clk. to judge U.S. Ct. Appeals (4th cir.), Durham, N.C., 1978-79, U.S. Ct. Appeals (5th cir.), Birmingham, Ala., 1979-80; pvt. practice San Diego, 1980-82; atty. Parker, Johnson, Cook & Dunlevie, Atlanta, 1982-86; sr. ptnr. Bird & Assocs., P.C., 1986—. Adj. prof. Emory U. Law Sch., Atlanta, 1985-90; lectr. Washington Non-Profit Tax Conf., 1982—. Author: The Origin of Species Revisited, 2 vols., 1987; contbg. author: Federal and State Taxation of Exempt Organizations, 1994, CCH Federal Tax Service, 1988—; mem. bd. editors Yale U. Law Jour., 1977-78, others; contbr. articles to profl. jours. Bd. govs. Coun. for Nat. Policy, Washington, 1983—. Recipient Egger prize Yale U., 1978, Vanderbilt U. award, 1972. Mem. ABA (litigation sect., taxation sect., com. on exempt orgns., past chmn. subcom. on religious orgns., past chmn. subcom. on state and local taxes, chmn. subcom. on charitable contbns., sect. on real property probate and trust, com. charitable gifts), Am. Law Inst., Ga. Bar Assn., Fla. Bar Assn., Calif. Bar Assn., Ala. Bar Assn., Assn. Trial Lawyers Am., Phi Beta Kappa. Republican. Avocations:

science, skiing, photography, genealogy, piano, architecture. Constitutional, Non-profit and tax-exempt organizations. Home: 92 Blackland Rd NW Atlanta GA 30342-4420 Office: Bird & Assocs PC 1150 Monarch Plz 3414 Peachtree Rd NE Atlanta GA 30326-1153

BIRIBAUER, RICHARD FRANK, lawyer; b. Cranford, N.J., May 30, 1950; s. Frank Anton and Mary M. (Valle) B.; m. Linda Carey, Aug. 26, 1972; children: James Richard, David Tyler. A.B., Rutgers U., 1972; J.D., Washington and Lee U., 1975. Bar: Va. 1975, D.C. 1976. Assoc. Law Offices of Fulton Brylawski, Washington, 1975-77; trademark counsel Johnson & Johnson, New Brunswick, N.J., 1977-83, internat. trademark counsel, 1984-91, chief trademark counsel, 1991—. Contbr. articles to Washington and Lee U. Law Rev., Mng. Intellectual Property. Mem. ABA, D.C. Bar Assn., Va. State Bar Assn., Internat. Trademark Assn., Pharm. Trade Marks Group, Inter Am. Assn. Indsl. Property. Private international, Trademark and copyright, Intellectual property. Office: Johnson & Johnson One Johnson & Johnson Plz New Brunswick NJ 08933

BIRKELAND, BRYAN COLLIER, lawyer; b. Hibbing, Minn., May 29, 1951; s. Lionel Owen and Peggy Jean Birkeland; m. D.J. Loras, Jan. 5, 1974; children: Brett Holton, Blair Leigh, Blake Owen. Student, Washington and Jefferson Coll., 1969-70; BA with high honors, U. Tex., 1973, JD with honors, 1975. Bar: Tex. 1976. Ptnr. Jackson Walker, LLP, Dallas, 1982—. Moody Found. grantee, 1971. Mem. ABA, IBA, State Bar Tex., Dallas Bar Assn., Order of Coif, Phi Beta Kappa, Phi Kappa Phi, Delta Sigma Rho, Tau Kappa Alpha. Presbyterian. Banking, Private international, Real property. Home: 7639 Southwestern Blvd Dallas TX 75225-7927 Office: Jackson Walker LLP 901 Main St Ste 6000 Dallas TX 75202-3797 E-mail: bbirkeland@jw.com

BIRMINGHAM, PATRICK MICHAEL, lawyer; b. St. Paul, Apr. 2, 1947; s. George Thomas and Nona Birmingham; m. Karen Ann Moir, Oct. 17, 1992. BS, Portland State U., 1970; JD, Western State U., 1975. Bar: Calif. 1975, U.S. Dist. Ct. (ctrl. dist.) Calif. 1975, U.S. Supreme Ct. 1978, Oreg. 1978, U.S. Dist. Ct. Oreg. 1978. With Riverside County (Calif.) Office of Pub. Defender, 1975-78; pvt. practice Portland, Oreg., 1978—. With U.S. Army N.G., 1970-75. Named in Best Lawyers in Am. and Nar. Directory Criminal Def. Lawyers. Mem. Oreg. Criminal Def. Lawyers (life), Calif. Attys. for Criminal Justice, Nat. Assn. Criminal Def. Lawyers, Multnomah Defenders Inc. (bd. dirs. 1990-92), Multnomah County Bar Assn. (mentor program 1994-99). Criminal. Office: 1001 SW 5th Ave Ste 1625 Portland OR 97204-1132

BIRMINGHAM, RICHARD JOSEPH, lawyer; b. Seattle, Feb. 26, 1953; s. Joseph E. and Anita (Loomis) B. BA cum laude, Wash. State U., 1975; JD, Seattle U., 1978; LLM in Taxation, Boston U., 1980. Bar: Wash. 1978, Oreg. 1981, U.S. Dist. Ct. (we. dist.) Wash. 1978, U.S. Tax Ct. 1981. Ptnr. Davis Wright Tremaine, Seattle, 1982-93; shareholder Birmingham Thorson & Barnett, P.C., 1993—. Mem. King County Bar Employee Benefit Com., Seattle, 1986, U.S. Treasury ad hoc com. employee benefits, 1988—. Contbg. editor: Compensation and Benefits Mgmt., 1985—; contbr. articles to profl. jours. Mem. ABA (employee benefits and exec. compensation com. 1982—), Wash. State Bar Assn. (speaker 1984-86, tax sect. 1982—), Oreg. State Bar Assn. (tax sect. 1982—), Western Pension Conf. (speaker 1986), Seattle Pension Round table. Democrat. Avocations: jogging, bicycling, photography. Pension, profit-sharing, and employee benefits, Personal income taxation. Home: 3820 49th Ave NE Seattle WA 98105-5234 Office: Birmingham Thorson & Barnett PC 3315 Two Union Square 601 Union St Seattle WA 98101-2341 Business E-Mail: RBirmingham@BTBPC.com

BIRMINGHAM, WILLIAM JOSEPH, lawyer; b. Lynbrook, N.Y., Aug. 7, 1923; s. Daniel Joseph and Mary Elizabeth (Tighe) B.; m. Helen Elizabeth Roche, July 23, 1955; children: Deirdre, Patrick, Maureen, Kathleen, Brian. ME, Stevens Inst. Tech., 1944; MBA, Harvard U., 1948; JD, DePaul U., Chgo., 1953. Bar: Ill. 1953, U.S. Patent and Trademark Office, 1955, U.S. Dist. Ct. (no. dist.) Ill. 1960, U.S. Supreme Ct. 1961, U.S. Ct. Appeals (7th cir.) 1962, U.S. Ct. Appeals (3rd cir.) 1968, U.S. Ct. Mil. Appeals 1973, U.S. Ct. Appeals (Fed. cir.) 1982, U.S. Ct. Claims 1986; registered profl. engr., Ill., Ind. Chem. engr. Standard Oil Co. Ind., Chgo., 1948-53; patent atty., 1953-59; assoc. Neuman, Williams, Anderson & Olson, Chgo., 1959-60; ptnr., 1961-91, Leydig, Voit & Mayer, Ltd., Chgo., 1991-93; of counsel, 1994-96. Lawyer; b. Lynbrook, N.Y., Aug. 7, 1923; s. Daniel Joseph and Mary Elizabeth (Tighe) B.; m. Helen Elizabeth Roche, July 23, 1955; children: Deirdre, Patrick, Maureen, Kathleen, Brian. ME, Stevens Inst. Tech., 1944; MBA, Harvard U., 1948; JD, DePaul U., Chgo., 1953. Bar: Ill. 1953, U.S. Patent and Trademark Office, 1955, U.S. Dist. Ct. (no. dist.) Ill. 1960, U.S. Supreme Ct. 1961, U.S. Ct. Appeals (7th cir.) 1962, U.S. Ct. Appeals (3d cir.) 1968, U.S. Ct. Appeals (D.C. cir.) 1973, U.S. Ct. Mil. Appeals 1973, U.S. Ct. Appeals (fed. cir.) 1982, U.S. Ct. Claims 1986; registered profl. engr., Ill., Ind. Chem. engr. Standard Oil Co. Ind., Chgo., 1948-53, patent atty., 1953-59; assoc. Neuman, Williams, Anderson & Olson, Chgo., 1959-60, ptnr., 1961-91, Leydig, Voit & Mayer, Ltd., Chgo., 1991-93, of counsel, 1994-96. Served to capt. USNR, 1942-75. Mem. ABA, ASME, Fed. Cir. Bar Assn., Am. Intellectual Property Law Assn., Intellectual Property Law Assn. Chgo. Served to capt. USNR, 1942-75, ret. Mem. ABA, ASME, Fed. Cir. Bar Assn., Am. Intellectual Property Law Assn., Intellectual Property Law Assn. Chgo. Federal civil litigation, Patent, Trademark and copyright. Home: 233 Pine St Deerfield IL 60015-4853

BIRNBAUM, EDWARD LESTER, lawyer; b. Bklyn., Aug. 2, 1939; s. Isaac and Rita (Kuris) B.; m. Madeleine, Apr. 10, 1965; children—Amanda, Jordan. B.A., Queens Coll., CUNY, 1961; LL.B., N.Y.U., 1964. Bar: N.Y. 1964, U.S. Dist. Cts. (so. and ea. dists.) N.Y. 1967, U.S. Ct. Appeals (2d cir.) 1970, U.S. Supreme Ct. 1971, U.S. Dist. Ct. (we. dist.) 1983. Assoc. Korkus & Korkus, N.Y.C., 1964-66, I. Richman, Esq., N.Y.C., 1966-67; ptnr. Herzfeld & Rubin, P.C., N.Y.C., 1967— ; lectr. in field; faculty NYU Sch. Continuing Edn., Law and Taxation, 1987—; arbitrator small claims night ct. Contbr. articles on law to profl. jours. Coach Little League Baseball and Little League Basketball; candidate trustee Village of Saddle Rock, town counsel, N. Hempstead, N.Y.; pres., v.p. Village of Saddle Rock Civic Assn.; mem. Liberal Party County com., del. to jud. conv. Mem. ABA, N.Y. State Bar Assn. (chmn. com. on Supreme Ct., ho. of dels.), N.Y. County Bar Assn., Queens County Bar Assn., Nassau County Bar Assn., Am. Arbitration Assn. (arbitrator), Am. Trial Lawyers Assn., N.Y. State Trial Lawyers Assn., N.Y. Bar Found. Federal civil litigation, State civil litigation, Personal injury. Home: 70 Shelly Ln Great Neck NY 11023-1822 Office: Herzfeld & Rubin PC 40 Wall St Fl 56 New York NY 10005-2349

BIRNBAUM, IRWIN MORTON, lawyer; b. Bklyn., July 15, 1935; s. Sol N. and Rose (Cohen) B.; m. Arlene R. Burrows, June 8, 1957; children: Bruce J., Leslie R. Birnbaum Ventura, Amy G. Birnbaum Heath. BS in Acctg., Bklyn. Coll., 1956; JD, NYU, 1961. Bar: N.Y. 1962. Budget officer Montefiore Med. Ctr., Bronx, N.Y., 1962-70, v.p., chief fin. officer, 1970-86; counsel Proskauer & Rose LLP, N.Y.C., 1986-89, ptnr., 1989-97; COO Yale Univ. Sch. Medicine, New Haven, 1997—. Bd. dirs. N.Y. Regional Transplant Program, N.Y.C., treas., exec. com.; chmn. bd. dirs. FFH/N.E. Ins. Com.; mem. exec. com. and chair fin. com. MCIC Vt., Inc.; adj. prof. Robert Wagner Sch. Pub. Svc., NYU; lectr. pub. health, health policy, adminstrn. Sch. Medicine Yale U.; corporator South County Hosp., South Kingstown, R.I. Editor: Health Care Law Treatise, 1990. Bd. trustees, treas., exec. com. Malmonides Med. Ctr., Bklyn., 1988—; sec./treas., exec. com. Hosp. Trustees N.Y. State, 1990-97. Fellow N.Y. Acad. Medicine; mem. Assn. of Bar of City of N.Y. (sec. com. on medicine and law 1989-90, sec. health law com. 1995-96), Am. Acad. Hosp. Attys. (spl. com. in health care systems). Avocations: sailing, tennis, reading, travel. Health. Office: Yale Univ Sch Medicine 333 Cedar St I-209 SHM PO Box 208049 New Haven CT 06520-8049

BIRNBAUM, SHEILA L. lawyer, educator; b. 1940; B.A., Hunter Coll., 1960, M.A., 1962; LL.B., NYU, 1965. Bar: N.Y. 1965. Legal asst. Superior Ct., N.Y.C., 1965; assoc. Berman & Frost, 1965-70, ptnr., 1970-72; prof. Fordham U., 1972-78, NYU, N.Y.C., 1978-86, assoc. dean, 1982-84; ptnr. Skadden, Arps, Slate, Meagher & Flom, 1984—. Author: (with Rheingold) Products Liability, Law, Practice Science, 1974. Mem. N.Y.C. Bar Assn. (mem. exec. com. 1978—, jud. com. 1977), ABA (chmn. product gen. liability, consumer land coms.), Assn. of Bar of City of N.Y. (exec. com. 1978—, 2d century com. 1984-86), Phi Beta Kappa, Phi Alpha Theta, Alpha Chi Alpha. Insurance, Product liability, Toxic tort. Office: Skadden Arps Slate Meagher & Flom 4 Times Sq Fl 24 New York NY 10036-6595 E-mail: sburnbau@skadden.com

BIRNE, KENNETH ANDREW, lawyer; b. Englewood, N.J., Apr. 2, 1956; s. Alvin Aaron and Rita May (Gorsky) B.; m. Pamela Beth Ross; children: Jennafer Sara, Allison Francie, Jonathan Ross. BA in Polit. Sci., Ohio State U., 1978; JD, Case Western Res. U., 1981. Bar: Ohio 1981, U.S. Dist. Ct. (no. dist.) Ohio 1981. Sole practice, Cleve., 1981-85; ptnr. Peltz & Birne, 1985—. Instr. Am. Inst. Paralegal Studies, Cleve., 1982-93, pers. dir. Cleve. area, 1984-93; cons. in field. Mem. Ohio Bar Assn., Cleve. Bar Assn. (chmn. practice and procedure clinic 1984-86, vol. Call for Action 1986, meritorious service award 1986), Cuyahoga County Bar Assn., Phi Eta Sigma, Zeta Beta Tau, Phi Delta Phi. Lodge: Masons. State civil litigation, Personal injury, Workers' compensation. Office: Peltz & Birne Midland Bldg Ste 1880 Cleveland OH 44115-1093

BIRNEY, PHILIP RIPLEY, lawyer; b. Canton, Ohio, June 25, 1940; s. Forrest Earl and Jean Lois (Ripley) B.; m. Susanne Elaine St. John, July 11, 1964; children: Julie Michelle, Laurie Catherine, Nicole Susanne. BS in Bus. Adminstrn., Northwestern U., 1962; JD, U. Calif., L.A., 1965. Bar: Calif. 1966, U.S. Dist. Ct. (all dists.) Calif., U.S. Ct. Appeals (9th and 11th cirs.), U.S. Supreme Ct. 1975; diplomate, cert. specialist med. profl. liability Am. Bd. Profl. Liability Attys. Dep. atty. gen. State of Calif., Sacramento, 1966-68; dep. dist. atty. Sacramento County, 1968-70; sr. ptnr., chief trial lawyer Wilke, Fleury, Hoffelt, Gould & Birney, Sacramento, 1970—. Fellow Am. Coll. Trial Lawyers; mem. ABA, Calif. State Bar Assn., Sacramento County Bar Assn. (judiciary com. 1991-94, jud. rev. com. 1992—, chmn. 1995—), Am. Bd. Trial Advs. (bd. dirs. Sacramento Valley chpt. 1994—, pres. Sacramento Valley chpt. 1998-99, Civility award 1995), Calif. Med.-Legal Com., No. Calif. Assn. Def. Counsel (bd. dirs. 1986-88) Professional liability, Personal injury. Home: 832 Senior Way Sacramento CA 95831-2129 Office: Wilke Fleury Hoffelt Gould & Birney 400 Capitol Mall Fl 22 Sacramento CA 95814-4407 E-mail: sbi71164@aol.com, pbirney@wilkefleury.com

BIRNKRANT, SHERWIN MAURICE, lawyer; b. Pontiac, Mich., Dec. 20, 1927; BBA, U. Mich., 1949, MBA, 1951; JD with distinction, Wayne State U., 1954. Bar: Mich. 1955, U.S. Dist. Ct. (ea. dist.) 1960, U.S. Supreme Ct. 1960, U.S. Ct. Appeals (6th cir.) 1966. Mem. Oakland County Bd. Suprs., 1967-68; asst. atty. City of Pontiac, 1956-67, city atty., 1967-83; of counsel Schlussel, Lifton, Simon, Rands, Galvin & Jackier, Southfield, Mich., 1983-90, Sommers, Schwartz, Silver & Schwartz, Southfield, 1990-95; shareholder Birnkrant & Birnkrant P.C., Bloomfield Hills, 1995—. Mem. ABA (chmn. urban, state and local govt. law sect. 1987-88, Mich. chmn. pub. contract law sect. 1979-97, ho. of dels. 1990-93, alternate del. to ho. of dels., 1993-96, vice chmn. coordinating com. for model procurement code for state and local govt. 1974—), State Bar Mich. (chmn. pub. corp. law sect. 1973-74, coun. adminstrv. law sect. 1975-76), Oakland County Bar Assn. (chmn. ethics and unauthorized practices com. 1961-62), Am. Judicature Soc., Mich. Assn. Mcpl. Attys. (pres. 1975, coun. of pres. 1992—). Government contracts and claims, Land use and zoning (including planning), Municipal (excluding bonds). Office: Birnkrant & Birnkrant PC 7 W Square Lake Rd Bloomfield Hills MI 48302

BISBEE, DAVID GEORGE, lawyer; b. Council Bluffs, Iowa, June 7, 1947; s. George Kimball and Margaret Ruth (McMurry) B.; m. J. Gail Bower, May 19, 1999; children: Michael, Christopher, Tyler. Student, Iowa State U., 1965-67; BA, Augusta Coll., 1973; JD, U. Ga., 1975. Bar: Ga. 1975, U.S. Dist. Ct. (no. dist.) Ga. 1976, U.S. Ct. Appeals (5th cir.) 1978, U.S. Ct. Appeals (11th cir.) 1981. Assoc. Troutman, Sanders, et al, Atlanta, 1975-81; ptnr. Bisbee, Rickertsen & Zerog, 1981-95; pvt. practice, 1996-97; ptnr. McRae & Bisbee, LLP, 1997—. Lawyer, b. Council Bluffs, Iowa, June 7, 1947; s. George Kimball and Margaret Ruth (McMurry) B.; m. Rita Ann Bentley, May 21, 1981; children: Michael, Christopher, Tyler. Student Iowa State U., 1965-67; BA, Augusta Coll., 1973; JD, U. Ga., 1975. Bar: Ga. 1975, U.S. Dist. Ct. (no. dist.) Ga. 1976, U.S. Ct. Appeals (5th cir.) 1978, U.S. Ct. Appeals (11th cir.) 1981. Assoc. Troutman, Sanders, et al, Atlanta, 1975-81; ptnr. Bisbee, Rickertsen & Herzog, Atlanta, 1981-95; sole practice law, Atlanta, 1996—; ptnr. McRae & Bisbee, L.L.P., 1997—. Served to capt. U.S. Army, 1968-72. Mem. ABA (bus. bankruptcy com.), Am. Bankruptcy Inst. (subcom. on. internat. insolvencies), Atlanta Bankruptcy Bar Assn. (bd. dirs. 1980-86), Order of Coif. Republican. Methodist. Served to capt. U.S. Army, 1968-72. Mem. ABA (bus. bankruptcy com.), Am. Bankruptcy Inst. (subcom. on internat. involvencies), Atlanta Bankruptcy Bar Assn. (bd. dirs. 1980-86), Oil of Coil. Republican. Methodist. Bankruptcy, General corporate. Home: 2929 Tall Pines Way NE Atlanta GA 30345-1404 E-mail: dbisbee@mcraebisbee.com

BISGARD, EILEEN BERNICE REID, lawyer; b. Portland, Oreg., July 30, 1944; d. Elbert Hann and Bernice Elizabeth (Smythe) Reid; m. Stanley Howard Hargrove, Aug. 11, 1963 (div. 1973); children— Michael Dean, Kimberly Diane; m. William Harlow Bisgard, Nov. 27, 1974; children: Jeffery Beecher, Corrine Elizabeth, Alicia Naomi, Dawn Marie. B.S. with highest distinction, Colo. State U., 1966; J.D., U. Denver, 1977. Bar: Colo. 1977. Sole practice, Longmont, Colo., 1977-81; pres. Eileen B. Bisgard, P.C., Longmont, 1982-87 . Bd. dirs. Parents United, Boulder, Colo., 1983-85; founding pres., bd. dirs. Longmont Coalition Women in Crisis, 1979-82; bd. mgrs. St. Vrain Valley YMCA, Longmont, 1981-84; mem. youth ctr. adv. bd. City of Longmont, 1983-86; exec. dir. The Family Extension, Inc. (aka The Inn Between, Inc.), Longmont, 1986—. Mem. ABA, Colo. Bar Assn., Boulder County Bar Assn. (chmn. juvenile law com. 1984-85), Nat. Assn. Council Children, Child Welfare League Am. (steering com. western region, nat. standards com. for family foster care), Soroptimists. Family and matrimonial, Juvenile. Office: 525 3rd Ave Longmont CO 80501-5906

BISHOP, ALFRED CHILTON, JR. lawyer; b. Alexandria, Va., Oct. 3, 1942; s. Alfred Chilton and Margaret (Marshall) B.; divorced; 1 son, Alfred Chilton III; m. 2d Catherine Ann Keppel, May 17, 1980. B.A. with distinction, U. Va., 1965, LL.B., 1969; LL.M. in Taxation, Georgetown U., 1974. Bar: N.Y. 1970, U.S. Ct. Appeals (2d cir.), 1970, U.S. Tax Ct. 1971, U.S. Ct. Claims 1971, D.C. 1977. Assoc. Shearman and Sterling, N.Y.C., 1969-70; assoc. trial atty., Office of Chief Counsel IRS, Washington, 1970-74, sr. trial atty., 1974-80, sr. technician reviewer, 1980-81, br. chief, 1981— . Recipient Am. Jurisprudence award 1968, 1968. Mem. ABA (tax sec.), D.C. Bar Assn., Sr. Exec. Service Candidate Network (v.p. 1980-81, pres. 1981-82, dir. 1983), Sr. Exec. Assn., Phi Delta Phi. Episcopalian. Home: 7523 Thistledown Trl Fairfax Station VA 22039-2207

BISHOP, BRUCE TAYLOR, lawyer; b. Hartford, Conn., Sept. 13, 1951; s. Robert Wright Sr. and Barbara (Taylor) B.; m. Sarah M. Bishop, Aug. 31, 1974; children: Elizabeth, Margaret. BA in Polit. Sci., Old Dominion U., 1973; JD, U. Va., Charlottesville, 1976. Bar: Va. 1977, U.S. Supreme Ct., Va. 1976, U.S. Dist. Ct. (ea. dist.) Va., U.S. Dist. Ct. (we. dist.) Va., U.S. Ct. Appeals (4th cir.); diplomate Am. Bd. Trial Advocates. Law clk. to chief judge U.S. Dist. Ct. (ea. dist.) Va., 1976-77; assoc. Willcox & Savage, P.C., Norfolk, Va., 1977-82, ptnr., 1983—. Bd. dirs. Nautical Adventures, Inc., Norfolk FestEvents, Ltd., 1981—, pres., 1982-85; pres. Va. OpSail 2000 Found.; mem. bd. visitors Old Dominion U., 1972-83, sec., 1979-81, chmn., mem. various coms.; speaker in field. Treas. Norfolk Reps., 1978-82, also mem. numerous coms.; bd. dirs., chmn. regional Key Club campaign United Way South Hampton Roads; chmn., co-chmn. United Negro Coll. Fund, 1981, Four Cities United Way Campaign; trustee Va. Stage Co., 1982; pres. Community Promotion Corp.; commr. Norfolk Redevel. and Housing Authority, chmn., 2000—; active numerous other community orgns. Named Outstanding Young Man, Norfolk Jaycees; recipient Disting. Alumni award Old Dominion U., Dominion Vol. of Yr. award, 1993. Mem. ABA (mem. various sects.), Fed. Bar Assn. (pres. Tidewater chpt. 1980-81), Am. Bd. Trial Advocates, Va. Assn. Def. Lawyers, Va. Bar Assn., Va. Trial Lawyers Assn., Norfolk-Portsmouth Bar Assn., Def. Rsch. Inst., Internat. Assn. Def. Counsel (nat. trial acad. faculty 1997), Assn. Def. Attys., Def. Rsch. Inst., Old Dominion U. Alumni Assn. (bd. dirs. 1978-83), Old Dominion U. Ednl. Found. (bd. dirs. 1987—, sec. 2000—), Norfolk C. of C. (chmn. downtown devel. com. 1980-81), James Kent Am. Inn of Ct. (master). Avocations: basketball, tennis, gardening. Product liability, Toxic tort, Transportation. Office: Willcox & Savage PC One Commercial Place Norfolk VA 23510 E-mail: bbishop@wilsav.com

BISHOP, JAMES DODSON, lawyer, mediator; b. Washington, Sept. 28, 1957; s. James William and Jane Lillian (Dodson) B. BA magna cum laude in Polit. Sci., Lincoln (Pa.) U., 1979; JD, Howard U., Washington, 1982. Bar: Pa. 1985. Dir. Atty./Client Arbitration Bd. D.C. Bar, Washington, 1987-93; dir. Archdiocesan Legal Network of Cath. Charities, 1993—. Mediator, D.C. Superior Ct., Washington, 1987—; lay reader St. Georges Episcopal Ch., Washington, 1984—. Mem. ABA (vice chmn. State and Local Bar Dispute Resolution Com., 1993). Democrat. Episcopalian. Avocation: church activities. Home: 5157 33rd St NW Washington DC 20008-2011 Office: Catholic Charities 1221 Massachusetts Ave NW Washington DC 20005-5302

BISHOP, MAHLON LEE, lawyer, consultant, arbitrator; b. Pekin, Ill., Apr. 2, 1930; m. Joyce Ann Bresee, Apr. 27, 1952. BS, U. Ill., 1951, JD, 1956. Bar: Ill. 1956. Assoc. Winston & Strawn, Chgo., 1956-59; v.p., gen. counsel Wilson Foods Corp., Oklahoma City, 1958-77; sr. v.p. John Morrell & Co., Chgo., 1977-85; of counsel Isham, Lincoln & Beale, 1985-87; pvt. practice, Winnetka, Ill., 1987—. Founding chmn. Meat Industry Safety Com., Chgo., 1970-75; founding mem. Employee Retirement Ins. Com., Washington, 1975-77. Maj. USMC, 1951-54. Administrative and regulatory, Labor, Pension, profit-sharing, and employee benefits. Office: 722 Oak St Winnetka IL 60093-2521

BISSELL, JOHN W. federal judge; b. Exeter, N.H., June 7, 1940; s. H. Hamilton and Sarah W. B.; m. Caroline M.; July 15, 1967; children—Megan L., Katharine W. AB, Princeton U., 1962; LLB, U. Va., 1965. Law clk. U.S. Dist. Ct., N.J., 1965-66; assoc. Pitney, Hardin & Kipp, Newark and Morristown, 1966-69, ptnr., 1972-78; asst. U.S. atty., 1969-71; judge Essex County, 1978-81, N.J. Superior Ct., 1981-82, U.S. Dist. Ct. N.J., Trenton and Newark, 1983—. Office: US Dist Ct Federal Square PO Box 999 Newark NJ 07101-0999

BISSINGER, MARK CHRISTIAN, lawyer; b. Steubenville, Ohio, June 4, 1957; s. Emerson Melvin and Nancy (Osbun) B.; m. Julie Furber, Sept. 28, 1985; children: Lucas Christian, Nathan Kenneth. BS in Civil Engring., Purdue U., 1979; JD, U. Cin., 1983. Bar: Ohio 1983, U.S. Dist. Ct. (so. dist.) Ohio 1983, U.S. Ct. Appeals (6th cir.), Ky. 1993. Assoc. Dinsmore & Shohl, Cin., 1983-90, ptnr., 1990—. Spkr. Ohio Continuing Legal Edn., Cin., 1990—; lectr. Nat. Bus. Inst., 1990—; commn. cert. attys. as splsts. Supreme Ct. Ohio; mem. Supreme Ct. Ohio's Bd. Bar Examiners; lectr. Lorman Edn. Svcs. Pres. Ctr. for Comprehensive Alcoholism Treatment, Cin., 1989-92. Named Order of Coif, Cin., 1983; inducted class of 1999 Cin. Acad. of Leadership for Lawyers. Mem. ABA, Cin. Bar Assn., Ohio Bar Assn., No. Ky. Bar Assn., Ky. Bar Assn. Avocations: family, travel, sports. Bankruptcy, General civil litigation, Construction. Office: Dinsmore & Shohl 255 E 5th St Cincinnati OH 45202-4700

BISTLINE, F. WALTER, JR. lawyer; b. Lakeland, Fla., Sept. 30, 1950; s. Frederick Walter and Mary Carolyn (Stansell) B.; m. Rabun Huff, Mar. 18, 1972. BA, Emory U., 1972; JD, Boston U., 1975. Bar: N.Y. 1976, Tex. 1979. Assoc. firm White & Case, N.Y.C., 1975-79; assoc. Johnson & Gibbs, P.C., Dallas, 1979-81, ptnr./shareholder, 1981-95; ptnr. Porter & Hedges, L.L.P., Houston, 1995—. Lectr. So. Meth. U. Sch. of Law, 1991. Contbr. articles to profl. jours. Banking, Contracts commercial, Private international. Office: Porter & Hedges LLP 3500 Bank of America Ctr 700 Louisiana St Houston TX 77002-2700

BITENSKY, SUSAN HELEN, law educator; b. N.Y.C., Jan. 3, 1948; d. Reuben Bitensky; m. Elliott Lee Meyrowitz, Apr. 17, 1982; l child, William N. BA magna cum laude, Case Western Res. U., 1971; JD, U. Chgo., 1974. Bar: Pa. 1974, U.S. Dist. Ct. (we. dist.) Pa. 1974, U.S. Ct. Appeals (3d cir.) 1975, U.S. Ct. Appeals (2d cir.) 1977, N.Y. 1979, U.S. Dist. Ct. (so. and ea. dists.) N.Y. 1979, Mich. 1988. Asst. gen. counsel United Steelworkers Am., Pitts., 1974-77; assoc. Cohen, Weiss and Simon, N.Y.C., 1977-81; assoc. counsel N.Y.C. Bd. Edn., Bklyn., 1981-87; assoc. prof. law Mich. State U.-Detroit Coll. Law, 1988-93, prof. law, 1993—. Contbg. author: Children's Rights in America: UN Convention on the Rights of the Child Compared with U.S. Law; contbr. articles to profl. jours. Mem. ABA, Phi Beta Kappa. Office: Mich State Univ Detroit Coll Law 447 Law College Bldg East Lansing MI 48824-1300 E-mail: bitensky@msu.edu

BITZEGAIO, HAROLD JAMES, retired lawyer; b. Coalmont, Ind., Jan. 29, 1921; s. Nicholas Gilbert and Dora Belle (Burns) B.; m. Betty Jean Law, Apr. 15, 1950; children: Judith L. Bitzegaio Wallin, Gail Ann Bitzegaio Wright, Susan R. Bitzegaio Denyer, James R., Jane E. BS, Ind. State U., 1948; JD, Ind. U., 1953; grad., Ind. Jud. Coll., 1980. Bar: Ind. 1953, U.S. Dist. Ct. (so. dist.) Ind. 1953, U.S. Ct. Appeals (7th cir.) 1956. Sole practice, Terre Haute, Ind., 1953-58, 81-97; judge Vigo Superior Ct., 1959-80; of counsel Anderson & Nichols Law Office. Editor, contbr.: Indiana Pattern Jury Instructions, 1966. Mem. Ind. Adv. Com. Civil Rights, Indpls., 1961-70, Mayor's Com. Civil Rights, Terre Haute, 1967-68; bd. dirs. Wabash Valley Council Boy Scouts Am., Terre Haute, 1960-80. Served to lt. comdr. USN, 1941-46, PTO. Decorated D.F.C. with gold star, Air medal with two gold stars, Purple Heart; named Sagamore of the Wabash, Gov. of Ind., 1990. Mem. ABA, Ind. Bar Assn., Terre Haute Bar Assn., Ind. Judges Assn. (bd. mgrs. 1961-80, pres. 1977-78), Ind. U. Law Alumni Assn. (pres. 1973-74, recipient disting. service award 1974), VFW (life), Nat. Rifle Assn. (life), Ducks Unltd. (nat. trustee, emeritus). Democrat. Club: Terre Haute Country (bd. dirs. 1974-76). General practice. Home and Office: 2703 E Springhill Dr Terre Haute IN 47802-8406 E-mail: hbitz@gte.net

BIVENS, DONALD WAYNE, lawyer, judge; b. Ann Arbor, Mich., Feb. 5, 1952; s. Melvin Donley and Frances Lee (Speer) B.; children: Jody, Lisa. BA magna cum laude, Yale U., 1974; JD, U. Tex., 1977. Bar: Ariz. 1977, U.S. Dist. Ct. Ariz. 1977, U.S. Ct. Appeals (9th cir.) 1977, U.S. Ct. Appeals (fed. cir.) 1984, U.S. Supreme Ct. 1982. Ptnr. Meyer, Hendricks & Bivens, P.A., Phoenix, 1977—. Judge pro tem Maricopa County Superior Ct., Ariz., 1987—, Ariz. Ct. Appeals, Phoenix, 1999—; bd. dirs. Ctr. for Law in Pub. Interest, Phoenix, 1983-85. Note & Comment editor Tex. Law Rev., Austin, 1976-77. Pres. Ariz. Young Dems., 1980-82, Scottsdale Men's League, 1980-82; v.p., bd. dirs. Phoenix Symphony Assn., 1980-86; bd. dirs. Scottsdale Arts Ctr. Assn., 1981-84, Planned Parenthood Cen. and No. Ariz., 1989-92; adv. bd. Ariz. Theater Co., 1987-88. Recipient Consul award U. Tex. Sch. Law, 1977, Three Outstanding Young Men award Phoenix Jaycees, 1981. Mem. ABA (coun. litigation sect. 1995-98, chmn. computer litigation com. 1989-92, resource devel. com. litigation sect. 1992—, tech. task force 1998—, state del. to Ho. of Dels. 1999—), Am. Bar Found., Ariz. Bar Found., State Bar Ariz. (bd. govs. 1993-2000, pres. 1998-99—, peer rev. com. 1992—), Ariz. Trial Lawyers Assn., Maricopa County Bar Assn. (bd. dirs., chmn. Trial Adv. Inst. 1986-87, Mem. of Yr. 1998), Thurgood Marshall Inn of Ct. (pres. 1992-93). Democrat. Avocations: music, theater. Federal civil litigation, Computer, Securities. Home: 6311 E Naumann Dr Paradise Valley AZ 85253-1044 Office: Meyer Hendricks & Bivens PA 3003 N Central Ave Ste 1200 Phoenix AZ 85012-2921

BIVONA, JOHN VINCENT, lawyer; b. N.Y.C., July 14, 1941; s. Vincent James and Virginia Marie (Verno) B.; m. Anne Frances Carluccio, Jan. 13, 1968; children— Vincent John, Christopher John. B.A., Fordham U., 1963, J.D., 1966. Bar: N.Y. 1968, U.S. Dist. Ct. (so. and ea. dists.) N.Y. 1979. Law asst. N.Y. Supreme Ct., N.Y.C., 1969-71; assoc. firm Newman, Rich, Krinsly, Poses & Katz, N.Y.C., 1971-73; sr. ptng. Bivona & Cohen, N.Y.C., 1973— ; lectr. Def. Research Inst., Atlanta, 1982— . Contbr. articles to profl. jours. Bd. dirs. Neighborhood Council to Combat Poverty, N.Y.C., 1975— , Little Italy Restoration Soc., N.Y.C., 1977-80; pres. Heritage Theatre Nat. Arts Club, N.Y.C., 1974— ; co-pres. Tomorrow's Children's Fund, 1983— . Recipient Disting. Service award Heritage Theatre, N.Y.C., 1983. Mem. Def. Research Inst. (lectr. Atlanta 1982—) , N.Y. State Trial Lawyers (lectr. 1983—), N.Y. County Lawyers Assn., Columbian Lawyers. Republican. Roman Catholic. Federal civil litigation, Insurance, Personal injury. Home: 101 Chestnut Ridge Rd Saddle River NJ 07458-3124 Office: Bivona & Cohen Wall St Plz New York NY 10005 also: 4547 Cornhill London England

BIXENSTINE, KIM FENTON, lawyer; b. Providence, Feb. 26, 1958; d. Barry Jay Fenton and Gail Louise (Traverse) Weinstein; m. Barton Aaron Bixenstine, June 25, 1983; children: Paul Jay, Nathan Alexis. BA, Middlebury Coll., 1979; JD, U. Chgo., 1982. Bar: Ohio 1982, U.S. Dist. Ct. (no. and so. dists.) Ohio 1983, U.S. Ct. Appeals (6th cir.) 1983. Law clk. to presiding judge U.S. Dist. Ct. (so. dist.) Ohio, Cin., 1982-83; assoc. Jones, Day, Reavis & Pogue, Cleve., 1983-90, ptnr., 1991-99; sr. counsel TRW, Inc., 1999—. Fice chair comml. adv. coun. N.E. Ohio chpt. Am. Arbitration Assn. Bd. dirs. Planned Parenthood Greater Cleve., 1991-99, sec. 1992-93, v.p. 1994-96, pres. 1996-98; bd. dirs. Boys and Girls Clubs of Cleve., 2001—; chair corp. giving subcom. Cleve. Bar Found. Campaign, 2001—. Mem. Ohio Bar Assn. (bd. govs. litigation sect. 1994-98), Ohio Women's Bar Assn. (trustee 1995-97, chair legis. com., 1994-95), Cleve. Bar Assn. (bd. dirs. 1993-96, nominating com. 1997, 98, 99, chair nominating com. 1998-99, chair standing com. on lawyer professionalism 1994-96, bd. liaison to jud. selection com. 1996, minority outreach com. 1993-99, commn. on women in the law 1988-2001). Avocation: jogging. Federal civil litigation, State civil litigation, Product liability. Office: TRW Inc 1900 Richmond Rd Cleveland OH 44124-3760

BIZUB, JOHANNA CATHERINE, law librarian; b. Denville, N.J., Apr. 13, 1957; d. Stephen Bernard and Elizabeth Mary (Grizzle) B.; m. Scott Jeffrey Smith, 1992. BS in Criminal Justice, U. Dayton, 1979; MLS, Rutgers U., 1984. Law libr. Morris County Law Libr., 1981-83, Clapp & Eisenberg, Newark, 1984-86; dir. libr. Sills Cummis, 1986-94; libr. dir. Montville (N.J.) Twp. Pub. Libr., N.J., 1994-97; libr. dir. law dept. Prudential Ins. Co. Am., Newark, 1997—. Mem. ALA, N.J. Law Librs. Assn. (treas. 1987-89, v.p./pres.-elect 1989-90, 99-2000, pres. 1990-91, 2000-2001, past pres. 1991-92, 2001—), Am. Assn. Law Librs. (pvt. law librs. SIS, vice chair 1992-93, chair 1993-94, past chair 1994-95), N.J. Libr. Assn., Assoc. Libr. of Morris County (v.p. 1995, pres. 1996, treas. 1997-01), Spl. Libr. Assn. N.J. (treas. 1990-92), Am. Legion Aux. (treas. Rockden unit 175 1983-93). Democrat. Roman Catholic. Home: 11 Elm St Rockaway NJ 07866-3108 Office: Prudential Ins Co Am 22 Plz 751 Broad St Newark NJ 07102-3714

BJORK, ROBERT DAVID, JR. lawyer; b. Evanston, Ill., Sept. 29, 1946; s. Robert David and Lenore Evelyn (Loderhose) B.; m. Linda Louise Reese, Mar. 27, 1971; children: Heidi Lynne, Gretchen Anne. BBA, U. Wis., 1968; JD, Tulane U., 1974. Bar: La. 1974, U.S. Dist. Ct. (ea. dist.) La. 1974, U.S. Ct. Appeals (5th cir.) 1974, U.S. Dist. Ct. (mid. dist.) 1975, U.S. Supreme Ct. 1977, U.S. Dist. Ct. (we. dist.) 1978, U.S. Ct. Appeals (11th cir.) 1981, Calif. 1983, U.S. Dist. Ct. (no. dist.) Calif. 1983, U.S. Dist. Ct. (ea. dist.) Calif. 1984. Ptnr. Adams & Reese, New Orleans, 1974-83; assoc. Crosby, Heafey, Roach & May, Oakland, Calif., 1983-85; ptnr. Bjork Lawrence, 1985—. Instr. paralegal studies Tulane U., New Orleans, 1979-82. Mem. Tulane U. Law Rev., 1973-74; editor Med. Malpractice newsletter, 1983—. Bd. dirs. Piedmont (Calif.) Coun. Camp Fire, 1984-92, pres., 1987-89; treas. Couhig Congl. Com., New Orleans, 1980-82; bd. dirs. Camp Augusta Trust, 1990-2001. Lt. USNR, 1968-71. Mem. ABA, Internat. Assn. Def. Counsel, Calif. Bar Assn., La. Bar Assn. (chmn. young lawyers sect. 1982-83), Am. Soc. Law and Medicine. Federal civil litigation, State civil litigation, Personal injury. Home: 1909 Oakland Ave Piedmont CA 94611-3706 Office: Bjork Lawrence 1901 Harrison St Ste 1630 Oakland CA 94612-3501 E-mail: rbjork@bjorklaw.com

BLACHLY, JACK LEE, lawyer; b. Dallas, Mar. 8, 1942; s. Emery Lee and Thelma Jo (Budd) B.; m. Lucy Largent Rain, Jan. 15, 1972; 1 son, Michael Talbot. BBA, So. Meth. U., 1965, JD, 1968. Bar: Tex. 1968, U.S. Ct. Appeals (5th cir.) 1969, U.S. Supreme Ct. 1975, U.S. Tax Ct. 1977. Trust officer First Nat. Bank in Dallas, 1968-70; ptnr. firm Reese & Blachly, Dallas, 1970-71; assoc. firm Rain Harrell Emery Young & Doke, 1971-76; staff atty. Sabine Corp., 1976-77, mgr. legal dept., 1977-80, v.p., gen. counsel, 1980-89; asst. gen. counsel Pacific Enterprises Oil Co. USA (merger Sabine Corp. and Pacific Enterprise Oil Co. USA), 1989-90; pvt. practice, 1990—. Mem. Tex. Bar Assn., Dallas Bar Assn., Dallas Gun Club, Northwood Club. Baptist. General corporate, Oil, gas, and mineral, Securities. Office: 16012 Red Cedar Trl Dallas TX 75248-3901

BLACHMAN, MICHAEL JOEL, lawyer; b. Portsmouth, Va., Aug. 16, 1944; s. Zalmon I. and Rachel G. (Grossman) B.; m. Paula D. Levine, Nov. 23, 1969; children: Dara R., Erica Dale. BS, Am. U., 1966; JD, U. Tenn., 1969. Bar: Va. 1969, U.S. Dist. Ct. (ea. dist.) Va. 1971, U.S. Supreme Ct. 1974, U.S. Ct. Appeals (4th cir.) 1977. Asst. commonwealth's atty. Commonwealth of Va., Portsmouth, 1970-72; assoc. Bangel, Bangel & Bangel, 1972-77, ptnr., 1977—. Chmn. Portsmouth Juvenile Adv. Com., 1975-78. Mem. Va. Dem. Steering Com. 1980-85; vice chmn. Indsl. Devel. Authority and Port and Indsl. Commn., Portsmouth, 1987-89, chmn. 1989-93; bd. dirs. United Jewish Fedn. Tidewater, 1980—, v.p. 1989—. With USCGR, 1966-72. Recipient Young Leadership award United Jewish Fedn. Tidewater, 1983. Mem. ABA, Assn. Trial Lawyers Am., Va. Bar Assn., Va. Trial Lawyers Assn. (v.p. 1985-88, pres. 1989-90), So. Trial Lawyers Assn. (bd. dirs. 1991—), Portsmouth Bar Assn., Portsmouth C. of C., Kiwanis (bd. dirs. Portsmouth club 1973-75), B'nai B'rith. Jewish. Avocations: tennis, travel, reading. Personal injury. Office: Bangel Bangel & Bangel PO Box 760 Portsmouth VA 23705-0760

BLACK, BARBARA ARONSTEIN, legal history educator; b. Bklyn., May 6, 1933; d. Robert and Minnie (Polenberg) A.; m. Charles L. Black, Jr., Apr. 11, 1954; children— Gavin B., David A., Robin E. BA, Bklyn. Coll., 1953; LLB, Columbia U., 1955; MPhil, Yale U., 1970, PhD, 1975; LLD (hon.), N.Y. Law Sch., 1986, Marymount Manhattan Coll., 1986, Vt. Law Sch., 1987, Coll. of New Rochelle, 1987, Smith Coll., 1988, Bklyn. Coll., 1988, York U., Toronto, Can., 1990, Georgetown U., 1991. Assoc. in law Columbia U. Law Sch., N.Y.C., 1955-56; lectr. history Yale U., New Haven, 1974-76, asst. prof. history, 1976-79, assoc. prof. law, 1979-84; George Welwood Murray prof. legal history Columbia U. Law Sch., N.Y.C., 1984—, dean faculty of law, 1986-91. Editor Columbia Law Rev., 1953-55. Active N.Y. State Ethics Commn., 1992-95. Recipient Fed. Bar Assn. prize Columbia Law Sch., 1955 Mem. Am. Soc. Legal History (pres. 1986-90), Am. Acad. Arts and Scis., Am. Philos. Soc., Mass. Hist. Soc., Supreme Ct. Hist. Soc., Selden Soc., Century Assn. Office: Columbia U Sch Law 435 W 116th St New York NY 10027-7201

BLACK, BERT, state administrator, lawyer; b. N.Y.C., Mar. 6, 1956; s. Thomas and Evelyn Gretel (Florio) B.; m. Cynthia H. Daggett; children: Sarah, Amy. BA in Biology, SUNY, Buffalo, 1976; JD, U. Minn., 1979. Bar: Minn. 1979, U.S. Dist. Ct. Minn. 1979. Reporter Adv. Task Force on Minn. Corp. Law, Mpls., 1979-81; dir. corp. divsn. State of Minn., St. Paul, 1981-99; legal analyst Office of Sec. of State of Minn., 1999—. Lectr. various continuing legal edn. programs, 1981—; pres. Internat. Assn. Corp. Adminstrs., 1988-89; adj. prof. U. Minn. Law Sch., 1995; observer Revision of Revised Uniform Ltd. Partnership Act, Nat. Conf. Commrs. on Uniform State Laws. Editor: Minnesota Corporations Practice Manual, 1986. Chmn. Dem.-Farmer Labor Party, 59th Dist., 1982-84, chmn. Mpls. sect., 1983-85, assoc. chair, chair 5th congl. dist., 1986-94, mem. state exec. com., 1986-2000, mem. state ctrl. com. Minn., 1982—. Jewish. Home: 3932 Harriet Ave Minneapolis MN 55409-1439 Office: Sec of State of Minn Dept Legal Analyst 180 State Office Bldg Saint Paul MN 55155-1299 E-mail: Bert.Black@state.mn.us, Bert1956@aol.com

BLACK, D(EWITT) CARL(ISLE), JR. lawyer; b. Clarksdale, Miss., Aug. 17, 1930; s. DeWitt Carlisle Sr. and Alice Lucille (Hammond) B.; m. Ruth Buck Wallace, June 6, 1970; children: Elizabeth B. Smithson, D. Carl Black III. BA, Miss. Coll., 1951, LLB, 1963; MPA, Princeton U., 1953; LLM in Taxation, NYU, 1965. Bar: Miss. 1963, U.S. Dist. Ct. (so. dist.) Miss. 1963, U.S. Ct. Appeals (5th cir.) 1965. Rsch. asst. Pub. Affairs Rsch. Coun., Baton Rouge, 1956-57; asst. mgr., dir. rsch. Miss. Econ. Coun., Jackson, 1957-64; ptnr. Butler, Snow, O'Mara, Stevens & Cannada, 1965-98, of counsel, 1999—. Chair Miss. Tax Inst., Jackson, 1987. Treas. New Stage Theatre, Jackson, 1965-69; pres. Miss. Symphony Orch. Assn., Jackson, 1985-86, Miss. Symphony Found., Jackson, 1989-92. Cpl. U.S. Army, 1953-55. Fellow Am. Coll. Tax Counsel; mem. Miss. Bar Assn. (chair tax sect. 1989-90), Univ. Club, River Hills Club. Episcopalian. Avocations: fishing, reading. Estate planning, Pension, profit-sharing, and employee benefits, Taxation, general. Home: 1704 Poplar Blvd Jackson MS 39202-2119 Office: 1700 Am South Plz Jackson MS 39201 E-mail: carl.black@butlersnow.com

BLACK, FREDERICK A. b. July 2, 1949; s. John R. and Dorothy Black; m. Katie Black, Oct. 27, 1976; children: Shane, Shanthini, Sheena. BA, U. Calif., Berkeley, 1971; JD, Lewis and Clark Coll., 1975. Bar: Oreg. 1975, Guam 1976, U.S. Ct. Appeals (9th cir.) 1976. Dir. Office of Guam Pub. Defender, 1975-78; dep. dir. Office of Oreg. Fed. Defender, 1981-84; asst. U.S. atty. Dist. Guam and No. Mariana Islands , 1978-81, 84-89; 1st asst. U.S. atty. Dist. Guam and No. Mariana Islands, 1989-91; U.S. atty. Dept. Justice Dist. Agana, Guam and No. Mariana Islands, 1991—. Author: Oregon Search and Seizure Manual. Leader Boy Scouts Am. Recipient Spl. award Chief Postal Inspector, 1986, Drug Enforcement Adminstrn. award, 1986, 89. Mem. Guam Water Polo Team. Avocation: sailing. Office: US Atty's Office 108 Hernan Cortez Ave Ste 500 Agana GU 96910-5009*

BLACK, JAMES ISAAC, III, lawyer; b. Lakeland, Fla., Oct. 26, 1951; s. James Isaac Jr. and Juanita (Feemster) B.; m. Vikki Harrison, June 15, 1973; children: Jennifer Leigh, Katharine Ann, Stephanie Marie. BA, U. Fla., 1973; JD, Harvard U., 1976. Bar: Fla. 1976, N.Y. 1977, U.S. Tax Ct. 1984. Assoc. Sullivan & Cromwell, N.Y.C., 1976-84, ptnr., 1984—. Mem. ABA, N.Y. State Bar Assn. (persons under disability com. trusts and estates law sect. 1984-90), Assn. of Bar of City of N.Y. (sec. 1980-81, trusts estates and surrogates ct. com. 1980-83), Scarsdale Golf Club. Estate planning, Probate, Real property. Home: 23 Chesterfield Rd Scarsdale NY 10583-2205 Office: Sullivan & Cromwell 125 Broad St Fl 28 New York NY 10004-2489

BLACK, LOUIS ENGLEMAN, lawyer; b. Washington, Aug. 5, 1943; s. Fischer Sheffey and Elizabeth (Zemp) B.; m. Cecelia Whidden, Sept. 5, 1966; 1 child, Kerrison Todd. BA, NYU, 1968, JD, 1971, LLM in Taxation, 1978. Bar: N.Y. 1972. Assoc. Carter, Ledyard & Milburn, N.Y.C., 1972-79; ptnr. Van Ginkel & Benjamin, 1979-83; of counsel Zimet, Haines, Moss & Friedman, 1983-84, DeForest & Duer, N.Y.C., 1984-86, ptnr., 1986—. Vice-chmn. bd. dirs. MacMillan Ring-Free Oil Co., Inc., 1986-87; chmn. bd. Lee's Gourmet Farms, Inc., 1993-97. Editor: NYU Jour. Internat. Law and Politics, 1970-71; author: Partnership Buy/Sell Agreements, 1977. Mem. ABA, N.Y. State Bar Assn. Computer, General corporate, Taxation, general. Home: 220 E 65th St Apt 24M New York NY 10021-6629 Office: DeForest & Duer 90 Broad St Fl 18 New York NY 10004-2276 E-mail: lee@bigfoot.com

BLACK, ROBERT L., JR. retired judge; b. Dec. 11, 1917; s. Robert L. and Anna M. (Smith) B.; m. Helen Chatfield, July 27, 1946; children: William C., Stephen L., Luther F. AB, Yale U., 1939; LLB, Harvard U., 1942. Bar: Ohio 1946, U.S. Ct. Appeals (6th cir.) 1947, U.S. Supreme Ct. 1955. Pvt. practice, Cin., 1946-53; ptnr. Graydon, Head & Ritchey, 1953-72; judge Ct. Common Pleas, 1973-77, Ct. Appeals, Cin., 1977-89, vis. and assigned judge, 1989-92. Mem. jury instrns. com. Ohio Jud. Conf. 1973—, chmn. 1986-92. Contbr. articles on law to profl. jours. Councilman Village Indian Hill (Ohio), 1953-65, mayor, 1959-65; mem. standing com. Diocese of So. Ohio, Episcopal Ch., 1958-64, lay del. to gen. assembly, 1966, 69; vestryman, warden Indian Hill Episcopal Ch.; chmn. Cin. Human Rels. Commn., 1967-70. Served to Capt. U.S. Army, 1942-45. Decorated Bronze Star. Mem. Cin. Bar Assn., Ohio Bar Assn., ABA, Am. Judicature Soc., Nat. Legal Aid and Defender Assn., Phi Beta Kappa, Queen City Club, Camargo Club, Commonwealth (Cin.) Club. Republican. Episcopalian. Home: 5900 Drake Rd Cincinnati OH 45243-3306 E-mail: bopblack@aol.com

BLACK, SUSAN HARRELL, federal judge; b. Valdosta, Ga., Oct. 20, 1943; d. William H. and Ruth Elizabeth (Phillips) Harrell; m. Louis Eckert Black, Dec. 28, 1966. BA, Fla. State U., 1965; JD, U. Fla., 1967; LLM, U. Va., 1984. Bar: Fla. 1967. Atty. U.S. Army Corps of Engrs., Jacksonville, Fla., 1968-69; asst. state atty. Gen. Counsel's Office, 1969-72; judge County Ct. of Duval County, Fla., 1973-75; judge 4th Jud. Cir. Ct. of Fla., 1975-79; judge U.S. Dist. Ct. (mid. dist.) Fla., Jacksonville, 1979-90, chief judge, 1990-92; judge U.S. Ct. Appeals (11th cir.) Fla., 1992—. Faculty Fed. Jud. Ctr.; mem. U.S. Judicial Conf. Com. on Judicial Improvements; bd. trustees Am. Inns. Ct. Found. Trustee emeritus Law Sch. U. Fla.; past pres. Chester Bedell Inn of Ct. Mem. Am. Bar Assn., Fla. Bar Assn., Jacksonville Bar Assn. Episcopalian. Home: 4626 River Point Rd W Jacksonville FL 32207-1104*

BLACK, WALTER EVAN, JR. federal judge; b. Balt., July 7, 1926; s. Walter Evan and Margaret Luttrell (Rice) B.; m. Catharine Schall Foster, June 30, 1951; children: Walter Evan III, Charles Foster, James Rider. A.B. magna cum laude, Harvard U., 1947, LL.B., 1949. Bar: Md. 1949. Assoc. Hinkley & Singley, Balt., 1949-53, ptnr., 1957-67; asst. U.S. atty. Dist. Md., Balt., 1953-55, U.S. atty., 1956-57; ptnr. Clapp, Somerville, Black & Honemann, Balt., 1968-82; U.S. dist. judge Dist. Md., 1982—, chief judge, 1991-94; sr. status, 1994—. Sec.-treas. Parkwood Cemetery Co., Balt., 1967-82; also dir.; sec. So. Mech. Inc., Balt., 1971-82; also dir.; pres. Charles T. Brandt Inc., Balt., 1972-82; also dir. Chmn. Bd. Municipal and Zoning Appeals, Balt., 1963-67; mem. Jail Bd., Balt., 1971-73, Atty. Grievance Commn., 1978-82, Rev. Bd., 1975-78, chmn., 1975-76; mem. Gov.'s Commn. to Revise Annotated Code, 1975-82 Alt. Md. del. Republican Nat. Conv., 1960; chmn. Rep. City Com., Balt., 1962-66; Md. del. Rep. Nat. Conv., 1964; Bd. dirs. Balt. Urban League, 1963-69, 76-82; bd. dirs. Union Meml. Hosp.; dir. Hosp. for Consumptives of Md. Mem. Bar Assn. Balt. City, ABA, Md. Bar Assn., Rule Day Club, Lawyers' Round Table. Baptist. Office: US Dist Ct 101 W Lombard St Ste 710 Baltimore MD 21201-2605

BLACK, WILLIAM REA, lawyer; b. N.Y.C., Nov. 4, 1952; s. Thomas Howard and Dorothy Chambers (Dailey) B.; m. Kathleen Jane Owen, June 24, 1978; children: William Ryan, Jonathan Wesley. BSBA, U. Denver, 1978, MBA, 1981; JD, Western State U., Fullerton, Calif., 1987. Bar: Calif., U.S. Ct. Appeals (fed. cir.), U.S. Dist. Ct.; lic. real estate broker; lic. pvt. investigator. Bus. mgr. Deere & Co., Moline, Ill., 1979-85; dir. Mgmt. Resource Svcs. Co., Chgo., 1985-86; sr. v.p. Geneva Corp., Irvine, Calif., 1986-91; pvt. practice Newport Beach, 1991-92; gen. counsel Sunclipse, Inc., 1992-98; spl. counsel Amcor, Ltd., 1992-98; dir. gen. Amcor de Mex., S.A. de C.V., 1993-98; secretario KHL de Mex. S.A. de C.V., 1995-98; v.p., gen. counsel LL Knickerbocker Co., 1997-99; CEO Kuroi Kiku Corp., Kuroi Ryu Corp., First Reconnaissance Co., 1997—; v.p., gen. cousnel Thales Avionics, 1999—. Bd. dirs. Am. Employers Def., Inc., Kuroi Kiku Corp., Kuroi Ryu Corp. Mng. editor Western State U. Law Rev., Fullerton, 1984-87. Instr. Pai Lum Kung Fu Karate, Hartford, Conn., 1970-75, U.S. Judo Assn., Denver, 1975-80, United Studios Kenpo, L.A., 1995—. Recipient Am. Jurisprudence award Bancroft-Whitney Co., 1984, 85, 86; Pres.'s scholar full acad. merit scholarship, 1983. Mem. ABA, Am. Soc. Appraisers, Inst. Bus. Appraisers, Assn. Productivity Specialists, Am. Employment Law Coun., Profls. in Human Resources Assn., Am. Mgmt. Assn., Orange County Bar Assn., L.A. County Bar Assn., Mu Kappa Tau. Avocations: karate (2d degree black belt), judo, skiing, scuba, golf. General corporate, Labor, Mergers and acquisitions. Office: 17481 Red Hill Ave Irvine CA 92614-5630 E-mail: william.black@thales-ifs.com

BLACKBURN, JOHN D(AVID), legal educator, lawyer; b. Connersville, Ind., Dec. 19, 1949; s. James Edwin and Julia Jane (Hubbard) B.; m. Vitalia Berezina, Oct. 29, 1999; children— Jennifer Anne, Melissa Christine. B.S., Ind. State U., 1971; J.D., U. Cin., 1974. Bar: Ohio 1974. Instr. bus. adminstrn. U. Cin., 1974-75; asst. prof. bus. Ohio State U., Columbus, 1975-80, assoc. prof., 1981— ; vis. asst. prof. U. Pa., Phila., 1980-81, Ind. U., Bloomington, summer 1980. Author (with Elliot I. Klayman and Martin H. Malin): Legal Environment of Business, 5th edit. 1994; (with Julius Getman) Labor Relations: Law, Practice, and Policy, 1983; author (with others): Modern Business Law, 3d edit., 1990, Law and Business, 1987; (with Jack Steiber) Protecting Unorganized Employees Against Unjust Discharge, 1984; editor-in-chief: Jour. Legal Studies Edn., 1990-92, Am. Bus. Law Jour., 1986-89. Mem. Am. Bus. Law Assn. (best article award 1980). E-mail: blackburn.3@osu.edu.

BLACKBURN, JOHN GILMER, lawyer; b. Opelika, Ala., Oct. 21, 1927; s. John A. and Vera (Isley) B.; m. Phyllis Blackburn, May 12, 1951; children: Gay Blackburn Maloney, Allison Blackburn Akins, Lisa Blackburn Ayerst. BS in Acctg., Auburn U., 1950; JD, U. Ala., 1954; LLM in Taxation, NYU, 1956. Bar: Ala. 1954. Sole practice, Decatur, Ala., 1955-79; ptnr. Blackburn, Maloney & Schuppert, P.C., 1979—. Lectr. various tax seminars. Mayor, City of Decatur, 1962-68; mem. exec. com. Ala. Dems.; chmn. Auburn U. Found.; chmn. Ala. Rev. Com. on Higher Edn. With U.S. Army, 1946-47, to 1st lt., 1951-52, ETO. Mem. ABA (com. on life ins., cos. sect. taxation), Ala. Bar Assn. (chmn. tax sect.). Methodist. Lodge: Kiwanis. Estate planning, Corporate taxation, Estate taxation. Office: PO Box 1469 Decatur AL 35602-1469

BLACKBURN, ROBERT PARKER, lawyer; b. Tacoma, Sept. 24, 1956; s. John Griffin and Dorothy Joan (Parker) B. BS with honors, Case Western Res. U., 1978; JD, Am. U., 1981. Bar: D.C. 1982, Calif. 1987. Atty. Banner, Birch, McKie and Beckett, Washington, 1981-84; asst. patent counsel Agrigenetics Research Corp., Boulder, Colo., 1984-86; atty. Ciotti and Murashige, Menlo Park, Calif., 1986-87; ptnr. Irell & Manella, 1987-89; dir. intellectual property Chiron Corp., Emeryville, Cailf., 1989-91, v.p., chief patent counsel, 1991—. Disting. scholar Berkeley Ctr. for Law and Tech., U. Calif. Berkeley Sch. Law, 2001—. Mem. AAAS, ABA, Am. Chemical Soc., Am. Intellectual Property Law Assn. (biotech. task force mem., chem. practice com., biotechnology subcom. mem.). Federal civil litigation, Patent, Trademark and copyright. Office: Chiron Corp 4560 Horton St Emeryville CA 94608-2900

BLACKBURN, ROGER LLOYD, lawyer; b. Mobile, Ala., Mar. 18, 1946; s. Rogers Hammock and Louise (Megahee) B.; m. Linda McNulty, Mar. 29, 1969. BA, U. Fla., 1968, JD, 1971. Bar: Fla. 1971, U.S. Dist. Ct. (so. dist.) Fla. 1972, U.S. Tax Ct. 1979. Ptnr. Blackwell, Walker & Gray, Miami, Fla., 1971-76, Leesfield & Blackburn, P.A., Miami, 1976-92; pvt. practice North Ctrl. Fla., 1992—; of counsel Hicks Anderson and Kneale, P.A., Miami, 1995—. Mem. ATLA, Fla. Bar Assn., Dade County Bar Assn. (bd. dirs. 1974-86), Acad. Fla. Trial Lawyers (bd. dirs. 1985-91, exec. com. 1989-91), Dade County Trial Lawyers Assn. (pres. 1985-86), Am. Bd. Trial Advocates (pres. Miami chpt. 1991-92, nat. bd. dirs., chmn. seminar com., diplomate), Eighth Jud. Cir. Bar Assn., U. Fla. Law Ctr. Assn. (trustee 1986-95, trustee emeritus 1995—), U. Fla. Coll. Law Alumni Coun. (pres. 1984), Fla. Acad. Cert. Mediators, Fla. Blue Key. Democrat. E-mail. Federal civil litigation, General civil litigation, Personal injury. Office: 100 Biscayne Blvd Miami FL 33132-2304 E-mail: rblackburn1@mindspring.com

BLACKFORD, ROBERT NEWTON, lawyer, director; b. Cin., Feb. 5, 1937; s. Robert Criley and Virginia Pendleton (Yowell) B.; m. Margaret Ann Williams, July 22, 1961; children: William Pendleton, John Whitner. BSBA, U. Fla., 1960; JD, Emory U., 1968. Bar: Fla. 1968, Ga. 1968. Mem., dir. Maguire, Voorhis & Wells, P.A., Orlando, Fla., 1972-98, sec., treas., 1972-95; ptnr. Holland & Knight LLP, 1998—. Dir. Hughes Supply, Inc., Orlando, 1970—, sec., 1972-96, asst. sec., 1996-98; dir., sec. Princeton Fin. Corp., 1987-94. Mem. Orlando Mcpl. Planning Bd., 1969-75, Orlando Downtown Devel. Bd., 1972-77, chmn., 1975-77, bd. dirs. Crime Commn., Inc., 1985-88; mem. Orange County's Refuse Disposal Citizens Coordination Com., 1988-90, Orange County Solid Waste Adv. Bd., 1992-96; mem. neighborhood concerns com. Orlando Naval Tng. Ctr. Base Closing Commn., 1994-96; trustee Chelsey G. Magruder Found., Inc., 1981—, pres., 1982-85, 92-94, 2000—, sec./treas., 1998-2000; trustee Orlando Mus. Art, 1980-82, 85-91, pres. 1985-86,

chmn. bd., 1986-87, v.p. 1989-91; ruling elder First Presbyn. Ch., Orlando, 1989—, tchr., 1970-2000. Mem. ABA, Fla. Bar Assn., Ga. Bar Assn., Orange County Bar Assn., Orlando Area C. of C. (pres. 1980, chmn. bd. dirs. 1981), Orange County Hist. Soc. (bd. dirs. 1980-83), Univ. Club Orlando (bd. dirs. 1994-97, sec. 1994-96), Country Club Orlando, Rotary Club Orlando (pres. 1991-92). Democrat. General corporate, Mergers and acquisitions, Securities. Home: 2931 Nela Ave Orlando FL 32809-6178 Office: Holland & Knight LLP 200 S Orange Ave Ste 2600 Orlando FL 32801-3453 E-mail: bblackford@hklaw.com

BLACKMAN, KENNETH ROBERT, lawyer; b. Providence, May 19, 1941; s. Edward and Beatrice (Wolf) B.; m. Meryl June Rosenthal, June 7, 1964; children: Michael, Susan, Kevin. AB, Brown U., 1962; LLB, MBA, Columbia U., 1965. Bar: N.Y. 1966. Law clk. to U.S. Dist. Judge, 1965-66; ptnr. Fried, Frank, Harris, Shriver & Jacobson, N.Y.C., 1966—. Mem. ABA, N.Y. Bar Assn., Assn. Bar City of N.Y., Phi Beta Kappa, Beta Gamma Sigma Bankruptcy, General corporate, Securities. Office: Fried Frank Harris Shriver & Jacobson 1 New York Plz Fl 22 New York NY 10004-1980

BLACKMAR, CHARLES BLAKEY, state supreme court justice; b. Kansas City, Mo., Apr. 19, 1922; s. Charles Maxwell and Eleanor (Blakey) B.; m. Ellen Day Bonnifield, July 18, 1943 (dec. 1983); children: Charles A. (dec.), Thomas J., Lucy E. Blackmar Alpaugh, Elizabeth S., George B.; m. Jeanne Stephens Lee, Oct. 5, 1984. AB summa cum laude, Princeton U., 1942; JD, U. Mich., 1948; LLD (hon.), St. Louis U., 1991. Bar: Mo. 1948. Pvt. practice law, Kansas City; ptnr. Swanson, Midgley and predecessors, 1952-66; profl. lectr. U. Mo. at Kansas City, 1949-58; prof. law St. Louis U., 1966-82, prof. emeritus; judge Supreme Ct. Mo., 1982—89, chief justice, 1989-91, sr. status, 1992; spl. asst. atty. gen. Mo., 1969-77; labor arbitrator, active sr. judge, 1992—; judge Supreme Ct. Mo., 1991—92. Chmn. Fair Pub. Accommodations Commn. Kansas City, 1964-66; mem. Commn. Human Rels. Kansas City, 1965-66. Author: (with Volz and others) Missouri Practice, 1953, West's Federal Practice Manual, 1957, 71, (with Devitt) Federal Jury Practice and Instructions, 1970, 3d edit., 1977, (with Devitt, Wolff and O'Malley) 4th edit., 1988-92; contbr. numerous articles on probate and corp. law to profl. publs. Mem. Jackson County Rep. Com., 1952-58; mem. Mo. Rep. Com., 1956-58. 1st lt., inf. AUS, 1943-46. Decorated Silver Star, Purple Heart. Mem. Am. Law Inst., Nat. Acad. Arbitrators, Mo. Bar (spl. lectr. insts.), Disciples Peace Fellowship, Scribes (pres. 1986-87), Order of Coif, Phi Beta Kappa. Mem. Disciples of Christ Ch. Home: 612 Hobbs Rd Jefferson City MO 65109-1075 Home (Summer): 2 Sea Side Ln Belleair FL 33752-1989 E-mail: charlesblackmar@compuserve.com

BLACKMON, WILLIE EDWARD BONEY, lawyer; b. Houston, Apr. 16, 1951; s. A.L. and Florence (Joseph) B. BBA in Mktg., Tex. A&M U., 1973; JD, Tex. Southern U., 1982. Bar: Nebr. 1984, Mich. 1985, U.S. Dist. Ct. (ea. dist.) Mich., 1984, U.S. Ct. Mil. Appeals 1984, U.S. Supreme Ct. 1987, Tex. 1989, U.S. Dist. Ct. (no. dist.) Tex. 1990, U.S. Dist. Ct. (so. dist.) Tex. 1993. Terr. sales mgr. Gillette Co., 1977-79; sales and mktg. coord. Drilco divsn. Smith Internat., 1973-77; legal intern Gulf Coast Legal Found., Houston, 1982; intern, ind. counsel City of Detroit, 1982-84; judge advocate USAF, Ellsworth AFB, Offutt AFB, S.D., 1984-89, USAFR, Reese AFB, Randolph AFB, Tex., 1989-94; staff judge advocate lt. col. Tex. Air N.G., Ellington Field, 1994—. Asst. criminal dist. atty., Lubbock County, Tex., 1990-91; asst. criminal dist. atty., Harris County, Tex., 1991-92; pvt. practice, Houston, 1992-97; assoc. mcpl. judge City of Houston, 1995-97, mcpl. judge, 1997—; admissions liaison officer USAF Acad., 1990—; internat. election supr. Orgn. for Security and Coop. in Europe (OSCE), Bosnia, 1997; adj. instr. Judge Advocate Gen.'s Sch. Air Univ., Maxwell AFB, Ala., 1996—; exec. dir. Assn. Minority Mil. OFficers, 2000—; guest spkr., lectr. Tex. Tech. U., U. Nebr., Creighton U., Tex. A&M U., Tex. So. U. Recipient numerous mil. decorations and awards; named to Tex. A&M U. Athletic Hall of Fame, 1994. Mem. ABA, NAACP (Alex award 1999), State Bar Tex., Nebr. Bar Assn., State Bar Mich., Nat. Bar Assn. (Living Legend award 1990), Tex. Assn. African Am. Lawyers, Houston Lawyers Assn., Wolverine Bar Assn., Am. Judges Assn., Tex. Mcpl. Cts. Assn., , Mexican-Am. Bar Assn., Houston Bar Assn., Tex. Coalition Black Dems., Aggie Officers Assn., Coalition of Ivorian Intellectuals Am. (adv. com.), Masons. Baptist. Avocations: scuba diving, skiing, hiking, biking, dancing. Home: 8766 Pattibob St Houston TX 77029-3334 Office: 1400 Lubbock St Ste 214 Houston TX 77002-1526

BLACKSHEAR, A.T., JR. lawyer; b. Dallas, July 5, 1942; s. A.T. and Janie Louise (Florey) B.; m. Stuart Davis Blackshear. B.B.A. cum laude, Baylor U., 1964, J.D. cum laude, 1968. Bar: Tex. 1968, U.S. Ct. Appeals (5th cir.) 1970, U.S. Tax Ct. 1970; C.P.A., Tex. Acct. Arthur Andersen & Co., Dallas, 1964-66; assoc. Fulbright & Jaworski, Houston, 1969-75, ptnr., 1975—, chmn. exec. com., 1992—. Trustee Baylor Coll. Medicine, Meml./Hermann Healthcare Sys.; bd. dirs. Greater Houston Partnership. Mem. ABA, State Bar Tex., Houston Bar Assn., Houston Ctr. Club, Coronado Club, Houston Country Club. Baptist. Health, Corporate taxation, Personal income taxation. Office: Fulbright & Jaworski 1301 Mckinney St Fl 51 Houston TX 77010-3031

BLACKSTOCK, JAMES FIELDING, lawyer; b. L.A., Sept. 19, 1947; s. James Carne and Justine Fielding (Gibson) B.; m. Kathleen Ann Weigand, Dec. 12, 1969; children: Kristin Marie, James Fielding. AB, U. So. Calif., 1969, JD, 1976. Bar: Calif. 1976, Tenn. 1994, U.S. Dist. Ct. (ctrl. dist.) Calif. 1977, U.S. Supreme Ct. 1980. Assoc. Hill Farrer Burrill, L.A., 1976-80, Zobrist, Garner, Garrett, L.A., 1980-83; ptnr. Zobrist & Vienna, 1983; v.p., gen. counsel Tatum Petroleum, La Habra, Calif., 1983; atty. Thorpe, Sullivan, Workman & Thorpe, L.A. , 1984; ptnr. Sullivan, Workman & Dee, L.A., 1985-91; prin. James F. Blackstock, PLC, L.A. , 1992-93; v.p., gen. counsel Nat. Auto/Truckstops, Inc., Nashville, 1993-97, Cracker Barrel Old Country Store, Inc., Lebanon, 1997-98; sr. v.p., gen. counsel CBRL Group, Inc., 1998—. Pres. Commerce Assocs., U. So. Calif., 1990-93. Mem. Town Hall, L.A., 1980-90. Served to lt., USN, 1969-73; capt. USNR (ret.). Mem. ABA, Tenn. Bar Assn., Nashville Bar Assn., U. So. Calif. Alumni Assn. (bd. govs. 1990-92), Pasadena Tournament of Roses Assn., Saddle and Sirloin Club, Rancheros Visitadores. Republican. Roman Catholic. Please give city location for all career positions (in CAR section). General corporate, Real property, Securities. Home: 533 Turtle Creek Dr Brentwood TN 37027-5632 Office: 305 Hartman Dr Lebanon TN 37087-2519 E-mail: jblackst@cbrlgroup.com

BLACKWELL, BRUCE BEUFORD, lawyer; b. Gainesville, Fla., July 23, 1946; s. Benjamin B. and Doris Juanita (Heagy) B.; m. Julie McMillan, July 12, 1969; children: Blair Allison, Brooke McMillan. BA, Fla. State U., 1968, JD with honors, 1974. Bar: Fla. 1975, Ga. 1977, U.S. Supreme Ct. 1979, N.Y. 1980. Atty. So. Bell Tel. & Telegraph Co., Charlotte, N.C., 1975-76, Atlanta, 1976-78; antitrust atty. AT&T, Orlando and N.Y.C., 1978-80; atty. Sun Banks, Inc., Orlando, Fla., 1980; assoc. Peed & King, P.A., 1981-84; shareholder King & Blackwell, P.A., 1984-97, King, Blackwell & Downs, P.A., 1997—. Counselor, master to First Ctrl. Fla. Inns of Ct., 1999—. Bd. dirs. Legal Aid Soc., Orlando, 1986-88; chmn. Winter Park (Fla.) Civil Svc. Bd., 1992-94; trustee Fla. State U. Found., 1985-86. Capt. USAF, 1968-72. Recipient award of excellence Legal Aid Soc., 1993, Judge J.C. Stone Pro Bono Disting. Svc. award, 1996, Annual Friend of FAWL award Fla. Assn. Women Lawyers, 1998. Mem. Fla. Bar (chmn. 9th cir. grievance com. 1985-87, chmn. mid-yr. meeting 1986, chmn. 9th cir. fee arbitration com. 1992-94, bd. govs. 1994-98, vice chair statewide disciplinary rev. com. 1995-96, co-chair 1997-98, vice-chmn. access to cts. com. 1995-97, chmn. annual meeting com. 1997, mem. supreme ct. spl. com. on pro bono svcs. 1996-97, mem. com. to determine need for a new DCA 1998, Fla. Bar Presidents' Pro Bono Svc. award 1997, chair spl. com. on solo/small firm practice 1997-98, mem. rules com. 1997-98, mem. edn. work force 1996-97), Fla. Bar Found. (life mem., bd. dirs. exec. com., chmn., adminstrn. justice com. 1998-2004), Orange County Bar Assn. (exec. coun. 1983-86, pres. 1987-88, co-chair fair campaign practices com. 1998—), Fla. State U. Alumni Assn. (nat. pres. 1985-86), Orlando Touchdown Club (pres. 1996-97), Gold Key, Order of Omega, Omicron Delta Kappa. Democrat. Presbyterian. Avocation: study of China. General civil litigation, Family and matrimonial, Personal injury. Home: 1624 Roundelay Ln Winter Park FL 32789-4042 Office: PO Box 1631 Orlando FL 32802-1631

BLACKWELL, THOMAS FRANCIS, lawyer; b. Detroit, Nov. 25, 1942; m. Sandra L. Kroczek; children: Robert T., Katherine M. BA, U. Notre Dame, Ind., 1964; JD, U. Mich., 1967. Bar: Mich and U.S. Dist. Ct. (we. and ea. dists.) Mich. 1968, U.S. Ct. Appeals (6th cir.) 1969. Assoc. Smith, Haughey, Rice & Roegge, Grand Rapids, Mich., 1967-71, ptnr., 1971—, treas., 1979-85, 89—, exec. com., 1985-89. Spl. asst. atty. gen. State of Mich., 1972-82. Fellow Mich. State Bar Found.; mem. ABA, State Bar Mich., Grand Rapids Bar Assn., FBA, Products Liability Adv. Coun., Mich. Def. Trial Attys., Peninsular, Kent Country Club. General civil litigation, Personal injury, Product liability. Office: Smith Haughey Rice & Roegge 250 Monroe Ave NW Ste 200 Grand Rapids MI 49503-2251 E-mail: tblackwell@shrr.com

BLACKWOOD, GEORGE DEAN, JR. lawyer; b. Buffalo, Kans., Aug. 10, 1939; s. George Dean and Tillie (Johnson) B.; m. Toni Adams, Dec. 30, 1978; children: Kendrick George, Joanna Lynn. B.A., Baker U., 1961; A.M. in Polit. Sci., Boston U., 1962; J.D., Kans. U., 1965. Bar: Mo. 1965. Ptnr. Blackwood, Langworthy & Schmelzer, Washington. Mem. com. steering, administrn., and intergovernmental rels. Nat. League of Cities, 1992—; bd. dirs. Natl. Mutiple Sclerosis Soc., 1989—, trustee, 1992—, area vice chmn., 1990—; mayor pro tem, 6th dist. councilman at large, vice chair fin. City of Kansas, Mo., 1991—. Mem. ABA, Kansas City Bar Ass., Lawyers Assn. Kansas City. General corporate, Health, Probate. Office: Blackwood Langworthy & Schmelzer PC 1220 Washington St Ste 300 Kansas City MO 64105-1439

BLADEN, EDWIN MARK, lawyer, judge; b. Detroit, Feb. 2, 1939; s. Philip and Ruth Sara (Millstein) B.; m. Paula Dee Maskin, Sept. 2, 1962; children: Philip, Sara, Jeffrey. BA, Wayne State U., 1962, JD, 1965. Asst. atty. gen. State of Mich., Lansing, 1965-86; mng. atty. Moran & Bladen, 1987-93; pvt. practice, East Lansing, Mich., 1994-97; adminstrv. law judge USCG, 1999—. Author: Consumer Law of Michigan, 1978. Mem. Dem. Polit. Reform Comm., Mich., 1968. With U.S. Army Security, 1957-60, Korea. Recipient Alexander Freeman scholarship Wayne State U., Detroit, 1962-65. Mem. State Bar Mich. (chmn. anti-trust sect., treas./sec. 1990-94), Nat. Assn. Fraud Units (pres. 1985-86). Office: 3448 Jackson Fed Bldg 915 2nd Ave Seattle WA 98174-1009

BLAHER, NEAL JONATHAN, lawyer; b. Lowell, Mass., Nov. 6, 1960; BA in Psychology, U. Pa., 1981; JD, Villanova U., 1986. Bar: Pa. 1986, N.J. 1986, U.S. Dist. Ct. N.J. 1986, Fla. 1987, U.S. Dist. Ct. (ea. dist.) Pa. 1987, U.S. Ct. Appeals (3rd cir.) 1987, U.S. Ct. Appeals (11th cir.) 1988, U.S. Dist. Ct. (mid. dist.) Fla. 1988, U.S. Supreme Ct. 1997. Intern law clk. to presiding justice Cir. Ct., Phila., 1984-85; paralegal Fineman & Bach, 1982-83, assoc., 1986-88, Allen, Dyer, Doppelt, Milbrath & Gilchrist, P.A., Orlando, Fla., 1988-93; pvt. practice, 1993—. Mem. Fla. Bar, Orange County Bar Assn., Pub. Investors Arbitration Bar Assn. Avocation: music. Franchising, Securities, Trademark and copyright. Home and Office: PO Box 804 Orlando FL 32802-0804

BLAIN, PETER CHARLES, lawyer; b. Milw., Nov. 15, 1949; s. Emile Octave and Mary Catherine (Usalis) B.; m. Katherine Stauber, June 12, 1971; children: Thomas Peter, Timothy Charles, Katherine Elizabeth, Peter James. BS, Wis. State U., Stevens Point, 1971; JD, Georgetown U., 1978. Bar: Wis. 1978. Budget analyst VA, Washington, 1974-78; atty. Reinhart, Boerner, Van Deuren, Norris & Rieselbach S.C., Milw., 1978—. Chmn. Wis. State Bar Insolvency Sect., 1995-97; lectr. U. Wis., Milw., 1984—. Contbr. articles to profl. jours. 2d Lt. U.S. Army, 1972-74. Listed Best Lawyers in Am., Woodward/White, 1987—. Mem. Milw. Bar Bankruptcy Sect. (prog. chmn. 1984-85, sect. chmn. 1986-87, co-chair bankruptcy sect. bench/bar com. 1998—). Democrat. Roman Catholic. Avocation: reading. Bankruptcy. Office: Reinhart Boerner Van Deuren Norris & Rieselbach SC 1000 N Water St Ste 1800 Milwaukee WI 53202-6650 E-mail: pblain@reinhartlaw.com

BLAIR, ANDREW LANE, JR. lawyer, educator; b. Oct. 10, 1946; s. Andrew Lane and Catherine (Shaffer) B.; m. Catherine Lynn Kessler, June 21, 1969; children: Christopher Lane, Robert Brook. BA, Washington & Lee U., 1968; JD, U. Denver, 1972. Bar: Colo. 1972, U.S. Dist. Ct. Colo. 1972, U.S. Ct. Appeals (10th cir.) 1972. Assoc. Dawson, Nagel, Sherman & Howard, Denver, 1972-78; ptnr. Sherman & Howard, 1978—. Lectr. U. Denver Law Sch., 1980-83, U. Colo., Colorado Springs, 1984, U. Colo. Law Sch., Boulder, 1991. Author: Uniform Commercial Code sects. for Colorado Methods of Practice, 1982; contbr. articles to profl. jours. Mem. ABA, Colo. Bar Assn. Democrat. Methodist. Contracts commercial, General corporate, Securities. Home: 1111 Humboldt St Denver CO 80218-3123 Office: Sherman & Howard 633 17th St Ste 2900 Denver CO 80202-3665 E-mail: ablair@sah.com

BLAIR, M. WAYNE, lawyer; b. Spokane, Washington, Oct. 17, 1942; BS in Elec. Engr., U. Washington, 1965, JD, 1968. Bar: Wash. 1968. Mem. Wash. State Bd. for Jud. Adminstrn., 1995-2000. With USAF, 1968-72. Recipient Helen M. Geisness award, 1987, President's award, 1990. Mem. ABA (Ho. of Dels. 1988-91), Am. Judicature Soc., Washington State Bar Assn. (bd. govs. 1991-94, pres. 1998-99), Seattle-King County Bar Assn. (trustee 1981-83, pres. 1987-88). Alternative dispute resolution, General corporate, Real property. Office: 5800 Bank of America Twr 701 5th Ave Seattle WA 98104-7097

BLAIR, PAMELA S. lawyer; b. Canton, Ohio, July 15, 1968; d. Errol George and Bonnie Lee Huppert; m. Harry Gilson Blair, June 14, 1997. BA in Edn., U. Akron, 1991, JD, 1997. Bar: Ohio 1997, U.S. Dist. Ct. (no. dist.) Ohio 1998. Jud. clk. and bailiff to Hon. Harry E. Klide, Canton, 1993-96; assoc. Davis & Young, Akron and Cleve., 1996-98; dir. Trial Litigation Clinic, U. Akron Sch. Law, 1998—. Mem. Assn. for Practical and Profl. Ethics, Akron Bar Assn. (liasion to U. Akron Sch. Law 1997—, mem. ethics and professionalism com. 1998—), Akron Bar Assn.-Med. Liaison Soc. Methodist. Avocations: scuba diving, travel, sailing, skiing, reading. Office: U Akron Sch Law Akron OH 44325

BLAIR, RICHARD BRYSON, lawyer; b. Athens, Ohio, Oct. 1, 1945; s. Richard Holmes and Doris Ruth Blair; m. Ellen A. Riehl, Aug. 24, 1968; children: Heather Ann, Heidi Lynn, Richard Holmes II, Molly Jane. BA, Franklin and Marshall Coll., 1967; JD, Ohio Northern U., 1970. Bar: Ohio 1970, U.S. Dist. Ct. (no. dist.) Ohio 1972. Assoc. Roth and Stephens, Youngstown, Ohio, 1970-75, ptnr., 1976-77; ptnr., v.p. Roth, Stephens, Blair and Co. LPA, 1977—, Roth, Blair, Roberts, Strasfeld & Lodge, LPA, Youngstown. Bd. dirs. Greater Youngstown Coalition of Christians, 1994-98, co-chmn., 1996-98; trustee, mem. bd. edn. Eagle Hts. Acad. Mem. Ohio Bar Assn., Mahoning County Bar Assn., Internat. Assn. Ins. Counsel, Ohio Assn. Civil Trial Attys., Def. Rsch. Inst., Nat. Assn. R.R. Trial Counsel. Avocations: family, church activities, golf, jogging. General civil litigation, Insurance, Personal injury. Home: 253 Wildwood Dr Youngstown OH 44512-3340 Office: Roth Blair Roberts Strasfeld & Lodge LPA 1100 Bank 1 Bldg Youngstown OH 44503

BLAIR, SAMUEL RAY, lawyer; b. Aurora, Ill., June 19, 1941; s. Donald R. and Jeanette E. (Quirin) B.; m. Jean Jordan, Nov. 25, 1964 (div. 1977); children: Alissa Lynn Motzfeldt, Jason Jordan. BA, U. Denver, 1963; JD, Lewis & Clark Coll., 1969. Bar: Oreg. 1969, Hawaii 1990. Assoc. Hershizer, Mitchell et al, Portland, Oreg., 1970-73; pvt. practice law Salem, 1973—, Koloa, Hawaii, 1990—. Adj. prof. law Willamette U., Salem, 1985—. Mem. Marion County Bar Assn. (pres. 1985), Oreg. State Bar Assn., Kauai Bar Assn., Hawaii Bar Assn., Hawaii Def. Counsel Assn., Hawaii Trial Lawyers Assn., Assn. Trial Lawyers Am., Hospice, Million Dollar Advocates Forum. Avocations: travel, reading, trekking, martial arts (Aikido). General civil litigation, Personal injury, Product liability. Office: 2360 Kiahuna Plantation Dr Koloa HI 96756-9713

BLAIS, ROBERT HOWARD, lawyer; b. Muskegon, Mich., May 14, 1955; BA with high honors, Mich. State U., 1977; JD cum laude, U. Notre Dame, 1980. Ptnr. Bogle & Gates, Seattle, 1988-93; shareholder Gores & Blais, 1993—. Adj. prof. estate and tax planning Seattle U., 1982-83; chairperson Wash. State U. Planned Giving Adv. Bd., 1989-96. Mem. ABA, Wash. State Bar Assn. (real property, probate and trust coun. 1987-88), Seattle-King County Bar Assn., Estate Planning Coun. Seattle (pres. 1996-97), Am. Coll. Trust and Estate Counsel. Estate planning, Probate. Office: Gores & Blais 1420 5th Ave Ste 2600 Seattle WA 98101-1357

BLAKE, JOHN FREEMAN, financial lawyer; b. Santa Clara, Calif., June 29, 1950; s. Freeman Dawes and Teresa (Seneker) B.; divorced; children: William, Braden. AB cum laude, U. Calif., Berkeley, 1972; postgrad., Tufts U., 1972-73; JD, U. San Francisco, 1979. Bar: Calif., D.C., N.Y. Asst. v.p., fin. counselor Bank Am., San Francisco, 1974-79; assoc. McCutchen, Doyle, Brown & Enersen, 1979-80, McCabe, Schwartz, Evans , Levy & Dawe, Concord, Calif., 1980-83, Silverstein & Mullens, Washington, 1983-87; sole practice, 1987—. Mem. Joint Adv. Com. Calif. Continuing Edn. of Bar, 1981-83; adj. prof. estate planning Golden Gate U., San Francisco, 1982-83, George Washington U., Washington, 1984—; numerous seminars, lectures, forums. Author: Tax Management Financial Planning (4 vols.) 1985, also editor; author, editor: Financial Planning After the Tax Reform Act of 1986; author: The Role of Attorneys in Financial Planning, 1990; prepared numerous manuals, pamphlets on Calif. probate laws, estate planning; contbr. articles to profl. jours. Active Washington Estate Planning Council. Mem. ABA, State Bar of Calif., D.C. Bar Assn., N.Y. State Bar Assn., Internat. Assn. Fin. Planning (nat. bd. dirs. 1985-89), Registry Fin. Planning Practitioners, Cosmos Club, Phi Beta Kappa.

BLAKE, JONATHAN DEWEY, lawyer; b. Long Branch, N.J., June 14, 1938; s. Edgar Bond and Haven (Johnstone) B.; m. Prudence Anne Rowsell, Dec. 22, 1964 (div. June 1977); children: Juliet Haven, Deborah Anne, Susanna Rowsell; m. Elizabeth L. Shriver, Dec. 9, 1977; children: Jonathan Shriver-Blake, Molly Shriver-Blake. BA magna cum laude, Yale U., 1960, LLB cum laude, 1964; BA, MA, Oxford U., Eng., 1962. Bar: D.C. 1965, U.S. Supreme Ct. 1973, U.S. Dist. Ct. D.C. 1965, U.S. Dist. Ct. Md. 1985, U.S. Ct. Appeals (D.C. cir.) 1965, U.S. Ct. Appeals (2d cir.) 1973. Assoc. Covington & Burling, Washington, 1964-72, ptnr., 1972—, chmn. mgmt. com., 1996—. Tchr. Howard U., Washington, 1965-70, U. Va., Charlottesville, 1965-70. Contbr. articles to profl. jours. Pres. Great Falls Citizens Assn., Va., 1967-68; exec. com., bd. dirs. Deerfield Acad, Mass., 1980-85. Rhodes scholar, 1960; recipient Gordon Brown prize, 1959. Mem. ABA (chair internat. telecomm. com. 1993-2000), Fed. Comm. Bar Assn. (pres. 1980-85). Administrative and regulatory, Communications, Private international. Home: 4926 Hillbrook Ln NW Washington DC 20016-3208 Office: Covington & Burling PO Box 7566 1201 Pennsylvania Ave NW Washington DC 20044-7566 E-mail: jblake@cov.com

BLAKE, STANFORD, lawyer; b. Detroit, Sept. 13, 1948; s. Morris and Betty (Yaffe) B.; m. Ellen Perkins, Mar. 5, 1978; children— Cary, Brandon, Stephanie. B.S., U. Fla. 1970; J.D., U. Miami, 1973. Bar: Fla. 1973, U.S. Dist. Ct. (so. dist.) Fla. 1973, U.S. Supreme Ct. 1980, U.S. Ct. Appeals (5th and 11th cirs.) 1981. Asst. pub. defender Dade County, Miami, Fla., 1973-78; ptnr. Todd, Rosinek & Blake, Miami, 1978-84, Rosinek & Blake, Miami, 1984-86; pvt. practice law, Miami, 1986-90; ptnr. Blake & Lida P.A., 1990—. Chmn. Jr. Maccabiah Games S. Fla., Miami, 1984—. Co-chmn. Dade County Outstanding Citizen award, 1986; v.p. congregation Bet Breira, 1987—. Mem. ABA, Fla. State Bar Assn. (chmn. grievance com. 1987), Fed. Bar Assn., Nat. Assn. Criminal Def. Lawyers, Fla. Criminal Def. Attys. Assn. (pres. 1982-83, chmn. 1985-90), So. Miami Kendall Bar Assn. (pres. 1984-85), B'nai B'rith (pres. 1980-81). Democrat. Jewish. Criminal. Home: 7810 SW 164th St Miami FL 33157-3740

BLAKELY, JOHN T. lawyer; b. Beloit, Wis., May 26, 1944; s. Walter Edwin and Virginia (Treleaven) B.; m. Ellen Ford, Dec. 27, 1968 (div. Apr. 1988); children: Sara, Ford; m. Pamela Rose Westmoreland, Mar. 16, 1991. BA, Duke U., 1966; JD, U. Mich., 1969. Bar: Fla., U.S. Ct. Appeals (11th cir.), U.S. Dist. Ct. (mid. dist.) Fla., U.S. Supreme Ct.; bd. cert. personal injury lawyer; bd. cert. Nat. Bd. Trial Advocacy. Instr. law U. Wis., Madison, 1969-70; assoc. Carlton, Fields, Ward et al., Tampa, Fla., 1970-73; ptnr. Johnson, Blakely, Pope, Bokor, Ruppel & Burns, P.A., Clearwater, 1973—. Mem. ABA, ATLA, Fla. Bar (bd. cert. civil trial law), Acad. Fla. Trial Lawyers, Nat. Bd. Trial Advocacy. General civil litigation, Personal injury, Probate. Office: Johnson Blakely Pope Bokor Ruppel & Burns PA 915 Chestnut St Clearwater FL 33756

BLAKELY, ROBERT GEORGE, lawyer; b. Beloit, Wis., Aug. 21, 1947; s. George Knowlton and Catherine Lucille (Mitchell) B.; m. Susan Bradford Amsler; children: Robert, Alison; m. Louise A. Delahoyde. BA, Denison U., 1969; JD, Marquette U., 1972. Bar: Wis. 1972, U.S. Dist. Ct. (ea. and we. dists.) Wis. 1972. Assoc. Blakely & Long, Beloit, Wis., 1972-74, Hansen Law Firm, Beloit, 1974-80; ptnr. Hansen, Eggers & Blakely, 1980—. Instr. real estate law and continuing edn. Mem. Wis. State Bar (joint realtors com. 1997—), Beloit Jaycees (pres. 1972-84, Outstanding Young Man 1975). Republican. Congregationalist. Avocations: skiing, mountain biking. Contracts commercial, Family and matrimonial, Real property. Address: 416 College St Ste A Beloit WI 53511-6310

BLAKLEY, BENJAMIN SPENCER, III, lawyer; b. DuBois, Pa., Sept. 1, 1952; s. Benjamin Spencer Jr. and Mary Jane (Campney) B.; m. Kathleen M. Ellermeyer, Oct. 20, 1989; children: Benjamin Spencer IV, Kevin Charles, Kyra Jane. BA, Grove City Coll., 1974; JD, Duquesne U., 1977. Bar: Pa. 1977. Ptnr. Blakley, Jones & Mohney, DuBois, 1977—. Pub. defender Clearfield (Pa.) County, 1977-84; instr. Pa. State U., DuBois, 1979-85; solicitor City of DuBois, 2000. Mem. adv. bd. Salvation Army Pa. Corp., DuBois, 1978-98, chmn., 1988-91; mem. DuBois Area Youth Aid Panel, 1984-87; mem. Citizens for Effective Govt., DuBois, 1985-97; trustee DuBois Vol. Fire Dept., 1986-87, treas., 1987-90; mem. DuBois Ednl. Found., 1990—, Cath. Counseling and Adoption Svcs., 1996—; bd.

dirs. DuBois Sr. and Cmty. Ctr., 1992-97. Mem. Pa. Bar Assn., Clearfield County Bar Assn., DuBois Vol. Fire Dept. Relief Assn. (pres. 1998-2000). Democrat. Methodist. Criminal, Family and matrimonial, General practice. Office: Blakley Jones & Mohney PO Box 6 90 Beaver Dr Du Bois PA 15801-2440 E-mail: bjmlaw@penn.com

BLAN, KENNITH WILLIAM, JR. lawyer; b. Dec. 15, 1946; s. Kennith William and Sarah Shirley (Shane) B.; 1 child, Noah Winton; m. Lyndy r. Ervin, Sept. 1, 1995. BS, U. Ill., 1968, JD, 1971. Bar: Ill. 1972, U.S. Supreme Ct. 1978. With Office State's Atty., Vermilion County, Ill., 1971-72; atty. Chgo. Title & Trust Co., 1972; assoc. Graham, Meyer, Young, Welsch & Maton, Ill., Chgo., Springfield, Danville, 1972-74; pvt. practice Danville, 1975—. Spl. asst. atty. gen. Ill., 1974-76; atty. City of Georgetown, Ill., 1985-92, Village of Belgium, Ill., 1987-89, Village of Westville, Ill., 1988-91. Contbr. chpts. to books. Chmn. Vermilion County Young Rep. Club, 1975-77; founding sponsor Civil Justice Found.; mem. Christian Businessmen's Com., Christian Legal Soc. Capt. CAP. Mem. ABA, ATLA, Ill. Bar Assn., Vermilion County Bar Assn., Lawyer-Pilots Bar Assn., Ill. Trial Lawyers Assn. (bd. mgrs.), Ind. Trial Lawyers Assn., Am. Soc. Law and Medicine, Christian Legal Soc., Gideons Internat., Aircraft Owners and Pilots Assn., Elks. Federal civil litigation, State civil litigation, Personal injury. Office: PO Box 1995 Danville IL 61834-1995 E-mail: blanlaw@aol.com

BLANCHENAY, NICOLAS, lawyer; b. St. Maurice, France, Mar. 25, 1973; s. Pierre Andre and Anne-Marie Blanchenay. M in French Law, U. Paris, 1996; JD, U. Richmond, Va., 1998. Bar: N.Y. 1999, France 2001. Legal coord. Alstom Transp. Inc., Hawthorne, N.Y., 1998-2000; assoc. Hughes Hubbard & Reed, Paris, 2000—. Mem. Sanku no Yawaratori (dep. sec. 2000—). Avocations: judo, classical and electric guitar. Banking, , Mergers and acquisitions, Contracts commercial. Home: 24 rue Claude Terrasse Paris 75016 France Office: Hughes Hubbard & Reed 47 Ave Georges Mandel Paris France 75116 Fax: 33-1-45-53-15-04. E-mail: blanchen@hugheshubbard.com

BLANCHETTE, JAMES GRADY, JR. lawyer; b. Dallas, Apr. 29, 1922; s. James Grady and Thelma (Keys) B.; m. Bess Neblett, May 29, 1944; children: Linda Blanchette Ponti, Kay Blanchette Hill, Martha Blanchette Caschette. BBA, U. Tex., 1943, LLB, 1947; MBA, Harvard U., 1958. Bar: Tex. 2947. Chmn. exec. com. Chancellor's Coun. U. Tex. System, 1983; pres. Dads' Assn. U. Tex., 1972-73. Served to lt. USNR, 1943-45. Fellow Tex. Bar Found., Am. Coll. Trust and Estates Counsel; mem. ABA, Tex. Bar Assn., Dallas Bar Assn., Northwood Club (pres. 1971). Presbyterian. General corporate, Probate, Estate taxation. Address: 8600 Skyline Dr # 1212 Dallas TX 75243-4170

BLAND, JAMES THEODORE, JR. lawyer; b. Memphis, June 16, 1950; s. James Theodore and Martha Frances (Downen) B.; m. Pattie L. Martin, Apr. 12, 1974. BBA magna cum laude, Memphis State U., 1972, JD, 1974. Bar: Tenn. 1975, U.S. Dist. Ct. (we. dist.) Tenn. 1976, U.S. Tax Ct. 1976, U.S. Supreme Ct. 1983, U.S. Ct. Claims 1987; cert. Estate Planning specialist. Estate tax atty. IRS, Memphis, 1974-76; atty. Armstrong, Allen, Braden, Goodman, McBride & Prewitt, 1976-91; prin. James T. Bland, Jr. and Assocs., 1991—. Instr. in taxation, bus. law State Tchr.'s Inst., Memphis, 1975-83; bd. dirs. Thomas W. Briggs Found., Memphis. Fellow Am. Coll. Trust and Estate Counsel, Tenn. Bar Found., Memphis and Shelby County Bar Found. (pres. 1991-93); mem. ABA (legis. initiatives com., taxation sect., specialization in estate planning real property, probate and trust sect., Achievement award 1983, 85), Fed. Bar Assn. (pres. 1987-88, nat. coun. 1979—, bd. dirs. young lawyers divsn. 1979-84, pres. Memphis mid south chpt. 1979-80), Tenn. Bar Assn. (chmn. tax sect. 1984-85, bd. govs. 1984-85, 89-90, 90-91), Tenn. Young Lawyers Conf. (pres. 1985), Memphis Bar Assn. (bd. dirs. 1990-91), Tenn. Soc. CPA's. Republican. Methodist. General civil litigation, Probate, Taxation, general. Office: PO Box 770566 Memphis TN 38117-0566 E-mail: blandjr@worldnet.att.net

BLAND, J(OHN) RICHARD, lawyer; b. Denver, Oct. 30, 1946; s. Harry Edward and Julia Lenora (Bjelland) B.; m. Carole Jeanne Martin, Aug. 25, 1968. BS, Augustana Coll., 1968; JD, Drake U., 1971. Bar: Iowa 1971, Minn. 1971, U.S. Supreme Ct. 1976. Assoc. Meagher & Geer PLLP, Mpls., 1971-75, ptnr., 1975—. Lectr. Minn. Inst. of Legal Edn., Mpls., 1985—. Fellow Am. Coll. Trial Lawyers; mem. Minn. Bar Assn., Minn. Def. Lawyers Assn. (bd. dirs. 1986-88). General civil litigation, Personal injury, Professional liability. Home: 17225 5th Ave N Plymouth MN 55447-3593 Office: Meagher & Geer PLLP 33 S 6th St Ste 4200 Minneapolis MN 55402-3722 E-mail: DBland@Meagher.com

BLANK, A(NDREW) RUSSELL, lawyer; b. Bklyn., June 13, 1945; s. Lawrence and Joan B.; children: Adam, Marisa. Student, U. N.C., 1963-64; BA, U. Fla., 1966; postgrad., Law Sch., 1966-68; JD, U. Miami, 1970. Bar: Ga. 1971, Fla. 1970; cert. civil trial advocate Nat. Bd. Trial Advocacy. Law asst. Dist. Ct. Judge, Atlanta, 1970-72; ptnr. A. Russell Blank & Assocs., PC, 1985—. Contbr. articles to profl. jours. Pub. adv. com. Atlanta Regional Commn., 1972-74. Recipient Merit award Ga. Bar Assn., 1981. Mem. ABA, ATLA, Atlanta Bar Assn., Ga. Bar Assn. (Merit award 1981), Ga. Trial Lawyers Assn. (officer), Lawyers Club Atlanta, Fla. Bar Assn., Am. Bd. Trial Advocates (advocate, bd. dirs. 2000—, pres. Ga. chpt.), Xenix Soc. (bd. dirs.). Federal civil litigation, State civil litigation, Personal injury. Office: 230 Peachtree St NW Ste 2600 Atlanta GA 30303-1516

BLANK, PHILIP BERNARDINI, lawyer, educator; b. N.Y.C., May 22, 1934; s. Arthur J. and Consuelo Inez (de Pasquale) B.; m. Mary Grace Marcello, Sept. 8, 1962; children— Arthur, Philip, Jr., Tricia Ann, Gregory. B.S., Fordham U., 1956, LL.B., 1959. Assoc. atty. Law Offices-S.W. Rowe, White Plains, N.Y., 1962-66, staff atty. Allstate Ins. Co., White Plains, 1960-62, County Trust Co., White Plains, 1966-68; law asst./referee Surrogate's Ct., White Plains, 1968-79; prof. law Pace Law Sch., White Plains, 1979— , assoc. dean external affairs, 1985— ; faculty mem. N.Y. State Bar Assn., Albany, 1974— , Practising Law Inst., N.Y.C., 1977, NYU Sch. Continuing Edn., N.Y.C., 1975, Manhattanville Coll. Continuing Legal Edn., 1976-77. Author: textbook Wills, Intestate Succession and Trusts, 1983; contbr. articles to journs. Mem. Zoning Bd. Appeals, Mount Pleasant, N.Y. 1972— , chmn., 1978— . Served to staff sgt. USAR, 1960-66. Mem. White Plains Bar Assn., Westchester County Bar Assn. (chmn. trusts and estate sect. 1984—), N.Y. Bar Assn., ABA. Republican. Roman Catholic. Club: Westwood Swimming and Tennis Assn. (Thornwood, N.Y.). Office: Pace U Sch Law 78 N Broadway White Plains NY 10603-3710

BLANKE, RICHARD BRIAN, lawyer; b. St. Louis, Oct. 28, 1954; s. Robert H. and Phyllis I. (Kessler) Schaffler. BA, U. Pa., 1977; JD, U. Mo., 1980. Bar: Mo. 1980, U.S. Dist. Ct. (ea. and we. dists.) Mo. 1980. Ptnr. Blanke & Assocs., St. Louis County, Mo., 1980-90, Uthoff, Graeber, Bobinette & Blanke, St. Louis, 1991—. Mem. ABA, ATLA, Mo. Bar Assn., Mo. Assn. Trial Attys., St. Louis Met. Bar Assn. General civil litigation, Family and matrimonial, Personal injury. Office: Uthoff Graeber Bobinette & Blanke 906 Olive St Ste 300 Saint Louis MO 63101-1426 E-mail: rblanke@ugbblaw.com

BLANTON, HOOVER CLARENCE, lawyer; b. Green Sea, S.C., Oct. 13, 1925; s. Clarence Leo and Margaret (Hoover) B.; m. Cecilia Lopez, July 31, 1949; children: Lawson Hoover, Michael Lopez. JD, U. S.C., 1953. Bar: S.C. 1953. Ordained deacon, Bapt. Ch. Assoc. Whaley & McCutchen, Columbia, S.C., 1953-66; ptnr. McCutchen, Blanton, Rhodes and Johnson and predecessors, 1967—. Dir. Legal Aid Service Agy., Columbia, chmn. bd., 1972-73. Gen. counsel S.C. Rep. Conv., 1962; del. Rep. State Conv., 1962, 64, 66, 68, 70, 74; bd. dirs. Midlands Cmty. Action Agy., Columbia, vice chmn., 1972-73; bd. dirs. Wildewood Sch., 1976-78; mem. Gov.'s Legal Svcs. Adv. Coun., 1976-77, Commn. on Continuing Legal Edn. for Judiciary, 1977-84, Commn. on Continuing Lawyer Competence, 1988-92, Commn. on Continuing Legal Edn. and Specialization, 1992-2000, sec. 1995, chmn., 1996-99. Mem. ABA. S.C. Bar (ho. of dels. 1975-76, chmn. fee disputes bd. 1977-81), Richland County Bar Assn. (pres. 1980), S.C. Def. Trial Attys. Assn., Def. Trial Attys. (state chmn. 1971-77, 80-95, exec. coun. 1977-80), Am. Bd. Trial Advs. (pres. S.C. chpts. 1989), Toastmasters Club (pres. 1959), Palmetto Club, Phi Delta Phi. General civil litigation, Personal injury, Workers' compensation. Home: 3655 Deerfield Dr Columbia SC 29204-3730 Office: 1414 Lady St Columbia SC 29201-3304

BLANTON, MARY RUTHERFORD, lawyer, educator; b. Alexandria, Va., July 4, 1950; d. Arthur J. and Margaret (Cockrell) Rutherford; m. Theodore A. Blanton, May 27, 1972; children: William F., John A., Thomas Pennington, Mary Elizabeth. BA magna cum laude, Wake Forest U., 1972; postgrad., St. John's Grad. Inst., Santa Fe, 1973; JD cum laude, Georgetown U., 1981. Bar: Va. 1982, N.C. 1985. Tchr., chmn. English dept. Martin Spalding High Sch., Severn, Md., 1972-75; Legis. aide Ho. of Reps., Washington, 1976-77; sole practice Springfield, Va., 1982-83; assoc. Ketner & Rankin, Salisbury, N.C., 1984-86; ptnr. Crowell, Porter, Blanton & Blanton, 1986-90, Blanton & Blanton, 1990-94; prin. Mary Blanton & Assoc., Salisbury, 1994—. Instr. continuing edn. program Catawba Coll., Salisbury, 1985. Bd. mgrs. Salisbury-Rowan YMCA, Salisbury Planning Bd., Rowan County Libr. Bd.; mem., vice-chair Nat. Assessment Ednl. Progress, 1990-98. Carswell scholar, 1969-71. Mem. ABA, N.C. State Bar Assn., Va. State Bar Assn., Rowan County Bar Aux. (past pres.), Phi Beta Kappa. Episcopalian. Avocations: backpacking, skiing, reading. General practice. Home: 305 W Thomas St Salisbury NC 28144-5351 E-mail: mblanton@salisbury.net

BLANTON, W. C. lawyer; b. LaRue County, Ky., Apr. 13, 1946; s. Crawford and Lillian (Phelps) B. BS in Math., BA in Social Sci., Mich. State U., 1968; MEd, U. Vt., 1970; JD, U. Mich., 1975. Bar: Ind. 1975, U.S. Dist. Ct. (no. and so. dists.) Ind. 1975, U.S. Ct. Appeals (7th cir.) 1977, (8th cir.) 1996, Minn. 1996, U.S. Dist. Ct. Minn. 1996, U.S. Dist. Ct. Wisc. (we. dist.) 1996. Residence hall dir. U. Wis., Madison, 1970-72; assoc. Ice Miller Donadio & Ryan, Indpls., 1975-81, ptnr., 1982-94, Popham, Haik, Schnobrich & Kaufman, Ltd., 1995-97, Oppenheimer Wolff & Donnelly LLP, Mpls., 1997—. Mem. ABA. Democrat. Avocations: skiing, travel, bridge. General civil litigation, Environmental, Natural resources. Office: Oppenheimer Wolff & Donnelly LLP 3300 Plaza VII 45 S 7th St Ste 3400 Minneapolis MN 55402-1609 E-mail: wblanton@oppenheimer.com

BLATT, DAVID, lawyer, educator, dispute resolution consultant; b. Bklyn., Apr. 8, 1975; s. Abraham and Dawn B. BS in Bus. Mgmt., Yeshiva U., 1996; JD, Benjamin N. Cardoro Sch. Law, 1998; cert. in dispute resolution, Pepperdine U., 1998. Adminstrv. asst. Volcano Records, N.Y.C., 1997; cert. mediator N.Y. State, 1997—; law clk. Lester, Schwab Katz & Dwyer, LLP; prof. NYU; dispute resolution cons. ReSolution, Inc. Mem. ABA (sec. on alternative disputes 1998—), Assn. of the Bar of the City of N.Y. (com. for alternative dispute resolution 1998—), N.Y. State Bar Assn. (com. for alternative dispute resolution 1998—), Am. Arbitration Assn.

BLATT, RICHARD LEE, lawyer; b. Oak Park, Ill., May 24, 1940; s. B. Lee Gray and Madelyn Gertrude (Bentley) B.; m. Carol Milner Jenkinson, May 21, 1965 (div. Dec. 1984); children: Christopher Andrew Lee, Katherine Lee, Susannah Lee; m. Carolyn Elizabeth LeBlanc, Jan. 31, 1987; 1 child, Jennifer Lee DeNux Blatt. BA, U. Ill., 1962; JD, U. Mich., 1965. Bar: Ill. 1968, U.S. Dist. Ct. (no. dist.) Ill. 1968, U.S. Ct. Appeals (7th cir.) 1968, U.S. Supreme Ct. 1974, U.S. Dist. Ct. (so. dist.) Ill. 1977, U.S. Ct. Appeals (4th cir.) 1987, N.Y. 1989, U.S. Ct. Appeals (3rd cir.) 1990, U.S. Dist. Ct. (ea. and so. dists.) N.Y. 1998. Assoc. Peterson, Lowry, Rall, Barber & Ross, Chgo., 1968-75; ptnr. Peterson, Ross, Schloeb & Seidel, 1975-91, Peterson & Ross, Chgo., 1991-94; sr. ptnr. Blatt, Hammesfahr & Eaton, 1994-2000; sr. mem. Cozen & O'Connor, 2000—. Rep. Disting. Neutral Ctr. Pub. Resources Inst. for Dispute Resolution; regulation bd. arbitrators NASD; adv. bd. Exec. the Katie Ins. Sch./Ill. State U. Author: (with Robert G. Schloerb, Robert W. Hammesfahr, Lori S. Nugent) Punitive Damages: A Guide to the Insurability of Punitive Damages in the United States and Its Territories, 1988; (with Robert W. Hammesfahr and Lori S. Nugent) Punitive Damges: A State-by-State Guide to Law and Practice, 1991 (in Japanese 1995); (with Robert W. Hammesfahr and others) At Risk-Internet and E-Commerce Insurance and Reinsurance Legal Issues, 2000. Steering com. founders' coun. The Field Mus., Chgo. Capt. inf. USAR, 1965-67, Korea. Fellow Chartered Inst. Arbitrators; mem. ABA (mem. litigation sect., dispute resolution sect.), NSSAR (Ft. Dearborn chpt.), Ill. State Bar Assn., Chgo. Internat. Dispute Resolution Assn. (mem. planning com.), Soc. Mayflower Desc. State Ill., N.Y. State Bar Assn., Chgo. Bar Assn. (mem. alternative dispute resolution com.), Chgo. Club, Pi Kappa Alpha Ednl. Found. (trustee), Phi Beta Kappa, Phi Kappa Phi. Alternative dispute resolution, General civil litigation, Environmental. Home: 1415 N Dearborn Pkwy Chicago IL 60610-1559 Office: Cozen & O'Connor 222 S Riverside Plz Ste 1500 Chicago IL 60606-6000 Fax: 312-382-8910. E-mail: clblatt@earthlink.net, rblatt@cozen.com

BLATZ, KATHLEEN ANNE, state supreme court chief justice, state legislator; BA summa cum laude, U. Notre Dame, 1976; MSW, U. Minn., 1978, JD cum laude, 1984. Psychiat. social worker, 1979-81; mem. Minn. Ho. of Reps., St. Paul, 1979—93, chmn. crime and family law, fin. instns. and ins. coms., 1985-86; justice Minn. Supreme Ct., 1996-98, chief justice, 1998—. Office: Minn Judicial Ctr 25 Constitution Ave Rm 424 Saint Paul MN 55155-1500

BLAWIE, JAMES LOUIS, law educator; b. Newark, Mar. 26, 1928; s. Louis Paul and Cecelia Ruth (Grish) B.; m. Marilyn June Beyerle, May 30, 1952; children: Elias J., Cecelia R., Christiana L. BA, U. Conn., 1950; AM, Boston U., 1951, PhD, 1959; JD, U. Chgo., 1955. Bar: Conn. 1956, Calif. 1965, U.S. Dist. Ct. (no. dist.) Calif. 1965, U.S. Ct. Appeals (9th cir.) 1967, U.S. Supreme Ct. 1968. Instr. polit. sci. Mich. State U., East Lansing, 1955; assoc. prof. U. Akron, Ohio, 1956-57, Kent State U., 1956-57; asst. prof. bus. law U. Calif., Berkeley, 1958-60; assoc. prof. law Santa Clara U., Calif., 1960-63, prof. law, 1963—; vis. prof. polit. sci. Calif. State U., Hayward, 1966-67; adminstrv. law judge U.S. Equal Employment Opportunity Commn., Washington, 1982-85. Complaints examiner U.S. Equal Employment Opportunity Agy., Office Equal Employment Opportunity; cons. in field. Author: (handbook) The Michigan Township Board, 1957; contbr. articles to profl. jours. Mem. Citizen's Adv. Com. on Capital Improvements, 1962-65; bd. dirs. Washington Hosp., 1964-68. Maj. U.S. Army, 1963-74. Boston U. Faculty fellow, 1951-53; U. Chgo. Law Sch. scholar, 1953-55; grantee Mich. State U. grantee, 1955-56, Helsinki Govt. Ministry Edn. grantee, 1980-81. Mem. ABA, Fairfield County Bar Assn., Mensa. Republican. Avocations: computers, photography, travel, rare diseases databases. Home: 41752 Marigold Dr Fremont CA 94539-4779 also: PO Box 1102 Fremont CA 94538-0110 Office: Santa Clara U Sch Law Santa Clara CA 95053-0001 E-mail: jimblawie@aol.com, macfig@aol.com

BLAZEK-WHITE, DORIS, lawyer; b. Easton, Md., Nov. 17, 1943; d. George W. and Nola M. (Buterbaugh) Defibaugh; children: Christine T., Judson M.; m. Thacher W. White. BA, Goucher Coll., 1965; JD, Georgetown U., 1968. Bar: D.C. 1969, V.I. 1969, U.S. Ct. Appeals (3d cir. 1969), U.S. Ct. Appeals (D.C. cir.) 1971, Md. 1979. Gen. practice with Judge Warren H. Young, V.I., 1968-70; assoc. Covington & Burling, Washington, 1970-76, ptnr., 1976—. Mem. Am. Coll. Trust and Estate Counsel. Estate planning, Probate, Estate taxation. Office: Covington & Burling 1201 Pennsylvania Ave NW Washington DC 20004 E-mail: dbalzek-white@cov.com

BLAZZARD, NORSE NOVAR, lawyer; b. St. Johns, Ariz., July 8, 1937; s. Howard N. and Viola (Greer) B.; m. Mary Elizabeth Jecker, June 15, 1958; children: Howard Norse, Mary Catherine; m. Judith A. Hasenauer, July 2, 1977. AB, Stanford U., 1959; JD, U. Calif., Hastings, 1962. Bar: Calif. 1963, U.S. Dist. Ct. (no. dist.) Calif. 1966, Conn. 1974, U.S. Dist. Ct. Conn. 1975, U.S. Supreme Ct. 1975, U.S. Ct. Appeals (D.C. cir.) 1977, U.S. Ct. Appeals (2d cir.) 1978, Fla. 1993; CLU. Counsel Calif. Western Life Ins. Co., Sacramento, 1966-70; sr. v.p., gen. counsel NARE Life Svc. Co., Palo Alto, calif., 1970-74; pres. Blazzard, Grodd & Hasenauer, P.C., Westport, Conn., 1974—. Chmn. ins. products task force Fin. Products Stds. Bd., 1988-89; chmn. Nat. Assn. Variable Annuities, 1994. Bd. govs. Norwalk Symphony, 1979. Capt. JAGC, U.S. Army, 1962-66. Inductee Variable Annuity Hall of Fame, 1998. Mem. ABA, FBA, Calif. Bar Assn., Conn. Bar Assn., Fla. Bar Assn., D.C. Bar Assn., Am. Soc. CLU's (pres. Fairfield County chpt. 1977-79). Republican. Mormon. Insurance, Securities, Corporate taxation. E-mail: norse.blazzard@bghpc.com

BLEIER, MICHAEL E. lawyer; BA, U. Tulsa, 1962; JD, Georgetown U., 1965. Bar: Pa, D.C. Atty. Office of Gen. Counsel, Bd. Govs. Fed. Reserve System, 1971-78, sr. counsel, 1979-81, asst. gen. counsel, 1981-82; mng. counsel Mellon Bank Corp., Pitts., 1982-88; asst. gen. counsel Mellon Fin. Corp., 1989-91, dep. gen. counsel, 1991-92, gen. counsel, 1992—, sr. mgmt. com. Mem. Am. Bankers Assn. (vice chmn. bank counsel com. 1996—), Lawyers Coun. Fin. Svcs. Roundtable (chmn. 1993-98). Administrative and regulatory, Banking, Mergers and acquisitions. Office: Mellon Financial Corporation 1 Mellon Bank Ctr Fl 19 Pittsburgh PA 15258-0001 E-mail: bleier.me@mellon.com

BLEILER, CHARLES ARTHUR, lawyer; b. Boston, Mar. 16, 1945; s. Charles Edward and Grace Rita Bleiler; m. Joyce Ann Kohlmyer, Oct. 6, 1972; children: Charles Edward. BS, Tufts U., 1967; JD, U. San Diego, 1973. BAr: Calif. 1973, U.S. Dist. Ct. (so. dist.) Calif. 1973. Commd. ensign U.S. Navy, 1967, advanced through grades to lt. comdr., resigned, 1978; ptnr. Williams, Clodig & Bleiler, San Diego, 1974-85, Bleiler & Reiter, San Diego, 1985-91, Malowney, Chialtas & Bleiler, San Diego, 1991-93; pres. Charles A. Bleiler A.P.C., 1987—. Lectr. San Diego Trial Lawyers Assn., 1982. Bd. dirs. Rancho Santa Fe (Calif.) Cmty. Ctr., 1990-94, pres., 1993-94; mem. San Dieguito Soccer Bd., Encinitas, Calif., 1991-92; bd. dirs. Torrey Pines H.S. Found., Del Mar, Calif., 1996-98, pres., 1997-98; founding mem., lector Nativity Ch., Rancho Santa Fe; fundraiser for charitable orgns.; bd. dirs. Rancho Santa Fe Little League, 1989-92. Mem. ATLA, Calif. State Bar, San Diego County Bar Assn., Optimist Club (charter pres. Kearny Mesa club 1987-89). Republican. Roman Catholic. Avocations: sailing, horseback riding, skiing, coaching youth baseball and soccer. Construction, Labor, Personal injury. Home: PO Box 1653 Rancho Santa Fe CA 92067-1653 Office: 12770 High Bluff Dr Ste 380 San Diego CA 92130-2060 E-mail: bleiler@worldnet.att.net

BLENCOWE, PAUL SHERWOOD, lawyer, private investor; b. Amityville, N.Y., Feb. 10, 1953; s. Frederick Arthur and Dorothy Jeanne (Ballenger) B.; m. Mary Frances Faulk, Apr. 11, 1992; 1 child, Kristin Amanda. BA with honors, U. Wis., 1975; MBA, U. Pa., 1976; JD, Stanford U., 1979. Bar: Tex. 1979, Calif. 1989. Assoc. Fulbright & Jaworski, Houston, 1979-86, London, 1986-87, ptnr., 1988-89, Fulbright & Jaworski L.L.P., L.A., 1989-2000, of counsel, 2000—. Editor: China's Quest for Independence: Policy Evolution in the 1970s, 1980; editor-in-chief Stanford Jour. of Internat. Law, 1978-79; contbr. articles on U.S. securities and corp. law to profl. jours. Mem. ABA, The Calif. Club, Phi Beta Kappa, Phi Kappa Phi, Beta Theta Pi. General corporate, Mergers and acquisitions, Securities. Office: Fulbright & Jaworski LLP 865 S Figueroa St Fl 29 Los Angeles CA 90017-2543 E-mail: pblencowe@fulbright.com

BLENKO, WALTER JOHN, JR. lawyer; b. Pitts., June 15, 1926; s. Walter J. and Ardis Leah (Jones) B.; m. Joy Kinneman, Apr. 9, 1949; children: John W., Andrew W. BS, Carnegie-Mellon U., 1950; JD, U. Pitts., 1953. Bar: Pa. 1954. Pvt. practice law, Pitts., 1954—; ptnr. Eckert, Seamans, Cherin & Mellott, 1984-93, of counsel, 1993—. Mem. adv. bd. dept. mech. engring. Carnegie-Mellon U., 1992—. Active Churchill Vol. Fire Co., 1970-82; charter and hon. mem. Wilkinsburg Emergency Med. Svc.; sec. Hampton Twp. Zoning Hearing Bd., 1991-92, vice-chmn., 1993; mem. Hampton Twp. Sch. Bd., 1993-97, pres. 1996. With U.S. Army, 1944-46, ETO. Decorated Bronze Star, Combat Inf. badge; recipient Disting. Svc. award Carnegie-Mellon U. Alumni Assn., 1993. Fellow Am. Coll. Trial Lawyers, Allegheny County Bar Found.; mem. ASME, Pa. Bar Assn., Allegheny County Bar Assn., Assn. Bar of City of N.Y., Pitts. Intellectual Property Law Assn. (pres. 1977-78), Engrs. Soc. Western Pa., Internat. Patent and Trademark Assn., Carnegie-Mellon U. Alumni Assn. (exec. bd. 1996—, exec. com. 1997—), Duquesne Club, Univ. Club, Princeton Club (N.Y.), Rolls-Royce Owners Club (bd. dirs. 1982-84, v.p. publs. 1984-87, treas. 1987-89). Avocation: old cars. Federal civil litigation, Patent, Trademark and copyright. Home: 4073 Middle Rd Allison Park PA 15101-1207 Office: Eckert Seamans Cherin & Mellott 600 Grant St Pittsburgh PA 15219-2702

BLEVINS, JEFFREY ALEXANDER, lawyer; b. Forest Hills, N.Y., June 18, 1955; s. William E. and Mary J. Blevins; m. Pamela A. Manos, Nov. 26, 1983 (div. Mar. 1995); 1 child, Mary Alexandria; m. Diane L. Bannon, June 12, 1999; stepchildren: Meagan Elizabeth, Laura Leigh, Jeffrey Daniel. BA, Denison U., 1977; JD, DePaul U., 1981. Bar: Ill. 1981, U.S. Dist Ct. (no. dist.) Ill. 1981, U.S. Dist. Ct. (we. dist. Wis. 1984, U.S. Ct. Appeals (7th cir.) 1984, U.S. Supreme Ct. 1990. Personnel specialist Comerica Bank, Detroit, 1979-80; assoc. Bell, Boyd & Lloyd, Chgo., 1981-88, ptnr., mem., 1988—. Lectr., author Ill. Inst. Continuing Legal Edn., others; chair employment sect. Ctr. for Disability and Elder Law, 1999—. Editor in chief DePaul Law Rev., 1980. Mem. Ill. State Bar Assn. (labor and employment coun. 1992-95), Chgo. Bar Assn., Mid-day Club, Omicron Delta Epsilon. Republican. Lutheran. Federal civil litigation, State civil litigation, Labor.

BLINDER, ALBERT ALLAN, judge; b. N.Y.C., Nov. 27, 1925; s. William and Sarah (Gold) B.; m. Meredith Zaretzki, Nov. 16, 1961 (dec.); 1 child, Adam Z.; m. Joan Goodman, Jan. 20, 1985. AB, NYU, 1944, postgrad., 1944-45; JD, Harvard U., 1948. Bar: N.Y. 1949, U.S. Dist. Ct. (so. dist.) N.Y. 1953, U.S. Ct. Appeals (2d cir.) 1953, U.S. Supreme Ct. 1967. Asst. U.S. atty. for so. dist. N.Y., 1950-53; asst. counsel N.Y.C. Bd. High Edn., 1953-54; asst. dist. atty. County of Bronx, N.Y., 1954-60; ptnr. Saxe, Bacon & O'Shea, N.Y.C., 1960-64, Blinder, Steinhaus & Hochhauser, N.Y.C., 1965-73; judge N.Y. State Ct. Claims, 1973-96; jud.

hearing officer N.Y. State Supreme Ct., 1996—. Rsch. counsel N.Y. Commn. on Law of Estates, 1965; assoc. counsel N.Y. Commn. Revision of Penal Law, 1966-70; asst. counsel N.Y. Commn. on Eminent Domain, 1970-73; rsch. asst. N.Y. Commn. State Ct. System, 1971-73. Assoc. editor Am. Criminal Law Quar., 1968-70, mem. adv. bd., 1969-70. Mem.: ABA, Internat. Bar Assn., N.Y. State Bar Assn., Assn. Bar City N.Y., N.Y. County Lawyers Assn., Am. Arbitration Assn. (nat. panel arbitrators 1965—73), Am. Judges Assn. Office: 115 Broadway Fl 15 New York NY 10006-1604 E-mail: ABLINDER@aol.com

BLISS, DONALD TIFFANY, JR. lawyer; b. Norwalk, Conn., Nov. 24, 1941; s. Donald Tiffany and Marina (Popova) B.; m. Nancy Arnold, Sept. 14, 1974; children: Evan Hale, Bion Northam. JD, Harvard U., 1966. Bar: N.Y. 1969, D.C. 1971, U.S. Dist. Ct. D.C. 1975, U.S. Ct. Appeals (D.C. cir.) 1971, 84, U.S. Supreme Ct. 1975. Atty. Peace Corps, Micronesia, 1966-67; legis. counsel Congress of Micronesia, 1968; cons. judiciary, American Samoa, 1968; assoc. firm LeBoeuf, Lamb, Leiby & McCrae, N.Y.C., 1969; asst. to sec. HEW, 1969-72; spl. asst. to adminstr. EPA, 1972-73; exec. sec. AID, 1973-74; dep. gen. counsel U.S. Dept. Transp., 1975-77, acting. gen. counsel, 1976-77; ptnr. firm O'Melveny & Myers, Washington, 1979—. Mem. Maritime Adv. Com., 1984-85; pres. Harvard Law Sch. Assn. D.C., 1985-86; chmn. transp. sect. FBA, 1987-90; mem. interior task force Grace Commn.; nat. pres. The Ripon Soc. Author: Drug Testing and Federal Employees: Lessons from the Transportation Experience, 1988, Economic Deregulation and Safety: Are The Compatible, 1989, A Challenge to the U.S. Aviation Leadership: Launching the New Era of Global Aviation, 1991, Supreme Court Preemption Analysis: Differentiating the Hamiltonians and Jeffersonians, 1993. Trustee Studio Theatre; ex officio trustee Landon Sch.; trustee, 1st v.p. Arts for the Aging; pres. Dara's Canine Found., Inc. Recipient spl. citation HEW, 1972, 73, Pres.'s Cert. Exec. Mgmt., 1973, Superior Achievement award Dept. Transp., 1976. Mem. ABA (chmn. air and space forum 1997—), D.C. Bar Assn. (co-chmn. sect. adminstrv. law and agy. practice 1988-90), City Club D.C., Chevy Chase Club. Administrative and regulatory, Federal civil litigation. Home: 6732 Newbold Dr Bethesda MD 20817-2223 Office: O'Melveny & Myers 555 13th St NW Ste 500W Washington DC 20004-1159 E-mail: dbliss@omm.com

BLIWISE, LESTER MARTIN, lawyer; b. Phila., Dec. 22, 1945; s. Sanford and Mollie (Cohen) B.; m. Ilene Estelle Hisiger, June 23, 1968; children: Matthew Scott, Howard Michael. BA, Rutgers U., 1967; JD, Bklyn. Law Sch., 1970. Bar: N.Y. 1971, U.S. Dist. Ct. (no. dist.) N.Y. 1971, U.S. Dist. Ct. (so. dist.) N.Y. 1975. Law asst. appellate div. 3d dept. N.Y. State Supreme Ct., Albany, 1970-71, law sec. appellate div. 3d dept., 1971-72; assoc. Burstein and Marcus, White Plains, N.Y., 1972-73, Trubin Sillcocks Edelman & Knapp, N.Y.C., 1973-78, ptnr., 1978-84, Milgrim Thomajan Jacobs & Lee, N.Y.C., 1984-85, Curtis, Mallet-Prevost, Colt & Mosie, N.Y.C., 1985-87, Schulte Roth & Zabel, LLP, N.Y.C., 1987-97, LeBoeuf, Lamb, Greene & MacRae LLP, N.Y.C., 1997—. Mem. coun. advisors Ticor Title Ins. Co., N.Y.C., 1990—. Contbr. chpts. in books Real Estate Titles, 1984, rev., 1988, 2d edit., 1994, rev. edit., 1998, Foreign Investment in the U.S., 1989, rev. 1990, 92; notes editor Bklyn. Law Rev., 1969-70. Mem. planning bd. Town of Mamaroneck, N.Y., 1984-88. Mem. N.Y. Sate Bar Assn. (del. to Ho. of dels., 1992-94, chair real estate financing and liens com., real property law sect. 1980-88, 98—, chair real property law sect. 1991-92, sec. 1988-89, 2d vice chair 1989-90, 1st vice chair 1990-91), Am. Coll. Real Estate Lawyers. Finance, Real property. Home: 155 Franklin St New York NY 10013-2936 Office: LeBoeuf Lamb Greene & MacRae LLP 125 W 55th St New York NY 10019-5369

BLOCH, ALAN NEIL, federal judge; b. Pitts., Apr. 12, 1932; s. Gustave James and Molly Dorothy B.; m. Elaine Claire Amdur, Aug. 24, 1957; children: Rebecca Lee, Carolyn Jean, Evan Amdur. B.S. in Econs, U. Pa., 1953; J.D., U. Pitts., 1958. Bar: Pa. 1959. Indsl. engr. U.S. Steel Corp., 1953; practice law Pitts., 1959-79; judge U.S. Dist. Ct. (we. dist.) Pa., 1979-96, sr. judge, 1997—. Mem. Jud. Conf. U.S. Com. on Ct. Security, 1987-92; chmn. joint task force on death penalty representation Supreme Ct. Pa.-Ct. Appeals; past mem. Rule 11 task force Ct. Appeals (3d cir.). Contbr. articles to legal publs. Served with AUS, 1953-55. Mem. Am. Bar Assn., Acad. Trial Lawyers Allegheny County, Duquesne Club, Phi Delta Phi. Jewish. Club: River. Office: US Dist Ct We Dist US Post Office and Courthouse 700 Grant St Ste 837 Pittsburgh PA 15219-1934

BLOCH, FRANK SAMUEL, law educator; b. Jan. 16, 1945; s. Felix Jacob and Lore Clara (Misch) B.; m. Melissa Roth, Mar. 12, 1972; children: Julia Devi, Sara Shanti. BA, Brandeis U., 1966, MA, 1971, PhD, 1978; JD, Columbia U., 1969. Bar: Calif. 1970, Tenn. 1980, U.S. Dist. Ct. (no. dist.) Calif. 1971, U.S. Ct. Appeals (7th cir.) 1976, U.S. Dist. Ct. (mid. dist.) Tenn. 1980, U.S. Ct. Appeals (6th cir.) 1983. Assoc. atty. Calif. Rural Legal Assistance, Madera, Calif., 1971-72, directing atty., 1972-73; lectr. in law, clin. fellow U. Chgo., 1974-79; assoc. prof. law Vanderbilt U., Nashville, 1979-86, prof., 1986—, dir. clin. edn., 1979-2001. Pres. Legal Svcs. of Mid. Tenn., Inc., 1991-92, 95-96; cons. Internat. Social Security Assn., 1993-2000; cons. Adminstrv. Conf. of U.S., 1988-93. Author: Disability Determination, 1992, Bloch on Social Security Disability, 2000; editor: Who Returns to Work and Why?, 2001; contbr. articles to profl. jours. Rsch. fellow Internat. Social Security Assn., 1992-93; Fulbright grantee, 1986. Mem. ABA, Nat. Acad. Social Ins., Nashville Bar Assn., Nat. Legal Aid and Defender Assn. Democrat. Jewish. Home: 1119 Park Ridge Dr Nashville TN 37215-4515 Office: Vanderbilt U Sch Law 131 21st Ave S Nashville TN 37203-1120

BLOCH, MARC JOEL, lawyer; b. Cleve., Feb. 14, 1943; s. David R. and Sylvia C. (Levof) B.; m. Barbara Ann Bandler; children— Stephen, Robin. B.A., Miami U., 1965; J.D., Cleve. State Law Sch., 1969. Bar: Ohio 1969. Field atty NLRB, Cleve., 1969-72; assoc. Robert P. Duvin & Assocs., Cleve., 1973-79; prin. Duvin, Cahn & Hutton, Cleve., 1979— . Contbr. numerous articles to profl. jours. Pres. Pub. Sector Labor Relations Assn. Cleve. Mem. Greater Cleve. Bar Assn., ABA, Fed. Bar Assn., Beechmont Country Club (trustee), Phi Alpha Delta. Labor. Office: Erieview Tower 20th Fl 1301 E 9th St Cleveland OH 44114-1800

BLOCK, DAVID JEFFREY, lawyer, investment manager; b. Bklyn., Aug. 22, 1951; s. Herbert and Ruth Block. BA in Polit. Sci., SUNY, Buffalo, 1973; JD, Emory U., 1976. Bar: N.Y. 1977, D.C. 1978, Calif. 1979. Atty. advisor U.S. Comptroller of the Currency, Washington, 1977-79; assoc. Rosenblum, Parish and Bacigalupi, San Francisco, 1979-81; ptnr. Rosen Wachtell & Gilbert, 1983-86; pvt. practice law, 1981-83, 86-90; of counsel Adams, Sadler & Hovis, 1990-94, Leland Parachini Steinberg Matzger & Melnick, San Francisco, 1994—; investment mgr. Graver, Bokhof, Goodwin & Sullivan, investment counsel, 2000—. Lectr. in field. Contbr. articles to profl. jours. Mem. Olympic Club. Avocations: golf, cooking, wine collecting. Banking, Mergers and acquisitions, Securities. Office: 333 Market St San Francisco CA 94105-2102 also: 345 California St San Francisco CA 94104-2606

BLOCK, DENNIS JEFFREY, lawyer; b. Bronx, N.Y., Sept. 1, 1942; s. Martin and Betty (Berger) B.; m. Lauren Elizabeth Troupin, Nov. 27, 1967; children: Robert, Tracy, Meredith. BA, U. Buffalo, 1964; LLB, Bklyn. Law Sch., 1967. Bar: N.Y. 1968, U.S. Dist. Ct. (ea. dist.) N.Y., U.S. Dist. Ct. (so. dist.) N.Y., U.S. Ct. Appeals (2d, 3d, 5th, 6th, 7th, 8th, 9th, 10th and 11th cirs.), U.S. Supreme Ct. Br. chief SEC, N.Y.C., 1967-72; assoc. Weil, Gotshal & Manges, L.L.P., 1972-74, ptnr., 1974-98, Cadwalader, Wickersham & Taft, N.Y.C., 1998—. Co-author: The Business Judgment Rule: Fiduciary Duties of Corporate Directors and Officers, Law & Business, Inc., 1987, 5th edit., 1998; co-editor: The Corporate Counselor's Desk Book, 1982, 5th edit., 1999; contbr. articles to profl. jours. Chmn. major gifts lawyers div., United Jewish Appeal Fedn., 1987-89, chmn. lawyers div., 1989-91. Mem. ABA (coun. litigation sect., com. on corp. laws sect. bus. law), Assn. of Bar of City of N.Y., Am. Law Inst.

BLOCK, NEAL JAY, lawyer; b. Chgo., Oct. 4, 1942; s. William Emanual and Dorothy (Harrison) B.; m. Frances Keer Block, Apr. 19, 1970; children: Jessica, Andrew. BS, U. Ill., 1964; JD, U. Chgo., 1967. Bar: Ill. 1967, U.S. dist. Ct. (no. dist.) Ill. 1967, U.S. Ct. Appeals (3d and 6th cirs.) 1968, U.S. Claims Ct. 1990, U.S. Ct. Appeals (Fed. cir.) 1991. Atty., advisor U.S. Tax Ct., Washington, 1967-69; assoc. Baker & McKenzie, Chgo., 1969-74, ptnr., 1974—, client credit dir., 1989—. Adj. prof. law Kent Law Sch., Ill. Inst. Tech., Chgo., 1986-90. Mem. ABA, Chgo. Bar Assn. (chmn. fed. tax com. 1983-84), Ill. State Bar Assn., AICPA (honorable mention award 1964), Ill. Soc. CPA's. (silver medal 1964, Leading Ill. Atty. 1997). Public international, Corporate taxation, Personal income taxation. Office: Baker & McKenzie 1 Prudential Pla 130 E Randolph St Ste 3500 Chicago IL 60601-6342

BLOCK, RICHARD RAPHAEL, lawyer, arbitrator; b. Phila., Nov. 9, 1938; s. Harry and Ida (Brandes) B.; m. Joanne Kramer, July 1, 1943 (div. Jan. 1973); 1 child, Jeffrey. AB, Dickinson Coll., 1959; LLB cum laude, U. Pa., 1962. Bar: Pa. 1963, N.J. 1980, D.C. 1982. Assoc. Folz & Bard, Phila., 1963-64; ptnr. Melzer & Schiffrin, 1964-75, Beitch & Block, Phila., 1975-90; dir. community rels. Dist. Atty. of Phila., 1991-96; chief tech. officer Phila. Dept. of Commerce, 1996—. Chmn. hearing com Disciplinary Bd. Supreme Ct. Pa., 1982-90. Contbg. author: Handbook of Pennsylvania Courts, 1970, Divorce Mediation, 1985, Prenuptial Agreements, 1989, Encyclopedia on Matrimonial Practice, 1991; assoc. editor U. Pa. Law Rev.; contbr. articles to profl. jours. Vice pres. Am. Jewish Congress, Phila., 1975; campaign mgr. Elect Joan Specter to City Coun., Phila., 1978, 82, 86. Mem. Pa. Bar Assn. (arbitrator Inter-Atty. Dispute Resolution 1987—, speaker 1988) Am. Arbitration Assn., Phila. Coll. Judiciary (lectr. 1984). Republican. Avocations: horse racing, computers, music.

BLOCK, WILLIAM KENNETH, lawyer; b. N.Y.C., Oct. 23, 1950; s. Louis and Catherine Veronica (Kerr) B. BA, Colgate U., 1973; JD, Union U., Albany, N.Y., 1976. Bar: N.Y. 1977. Gen. counsel N.Y.C. Tax Commn., 1978-81; asst. commn. fin. N.Y.C. Dept. Fin., 1981-84, dep. commr. fin., 1984-89; assoc. Schwartz, Weiss, Steckler & Hoffman, P.C., N.Y.C., 1989-91; pvt. practice, William K. Block, P.C., 1992—. Adj. lectr. real estate NYU, 1992—. Contbr. articles on real property tax law and procedure to profl. jours. Mem. ABA, Internat. Assn. Assessing Officers (chmn. met. jurisdiction coun. 1987-88, presdl. citation 1986, McCareen award 1988), N.Y. State Assessors Assn., N.Y. State Bar Assn., New York County Bar Assn. (com. on City of N.Y., real property com., govt. counsel com.), Real Estate Rev. Bar Assn., dir. 1995—), Assn. Bar City of N.Y. (com. on tax certiorari), Real Estate Bd. N.Y. (com. on taxation). Democrat. Roman Catholic. Administrative and regulatory, Real property, State and local taxation. Home: 115 E 34th St Apt 20K New York NY 10016-4631 Office: 295 Madison Ave Fl 38 New York NY 10017-6304 E-mail: Williamkblock@aol.com

BLOEDE, VICTOR CARL, lawyer, academic executive; b. Woodwardville, Md., July 17, 1917; s. Carl Schon and Eleanor (Eck) B.; m. Ellen Louise Miller, May 9, 1947; children— Karl Abbott, Pamela Elena AB, Dartmouth Coll., 1940; JD cum laude, U. Md., Balt., 1950; LLM in Pub. Law, Georgetown U., 1967. Bar: Md. 1950, Fed. Hawaii 1958, U.S. Supreme Ct. 1971. Pvt. practice, Balt., 1950-64; mem. Goldman & Bloede, 1959-64; counsel Seven-Up Bottling Co., 1958-64; dep. atty. gen. Pacific Trust Ter., Honolulu, 1952-53; asst. solicitor for ters. Office of Solicitor, U.S. Dept. Interior, Washington, 1953-54; atty. U.S. Justice, Honolulu, 1955-58; assoc. gen. counsel Dept. Navy, Washington, 1960-61, 63-64; spl. legal cons. Md. Legislature, Legis. Council, 1963-64, 66-67; assoc. prof. U. Hawaii, 1961-63, dir. property mgmt., 1964-67; house counsel, dir. contracts and grants U. Hawaii System, 1967-82; house counsel U. Hawaii Research Corp., 1970-82; legal counsel Law of Sea Inst., 1978-82; legal cons. Rsch. Corp. and grad. rsch. divsn. U. Hawaii, 1982-92. Spl. counsel to Holifield Congl. Commn. on Govt. Procurement, 1970-73. Author: Hawaii Legislative Manual, 1962, Maori Affairs, New Zealand, 1964, Oceanographic Research Vessel Operations, and Liabilities, 1972, Hawaiian Archipelago, Legal Effects of a 200 Mile Territorial Sea, 1973, Copyright-Guidelines to the 1976 Act, 1977, Forms Manual, Inventions: Policy, Law and Procedure, 1982; writer, contbr. Coll. Law Digest and other publs. on legislation and pub. law. Mem. Gov.'s Task Force Hawaii and The Sea, 1969, Citizens Housing Com. Balt., 1952-64; bd. govs. Balt. Cmty. YMCA, 1954-64; bd. dirs. U. Hawaii Press, 1964-66, Coll. Housing Found., 1968-80; appointed to internat. rev. commn. Canada-France Hawaii Telescope Corp., 1973-82, chmn., 1973, 82; co-founder, incorporator First Unitarian Ch. Honolulu. Served to lt. comdr. USNR, 1942-45, PTO. Grantee ocean law studies NSF and NOAA, 1970-80. Mem. ABA, Balt. Bar Assn., Fed. Bar Assn., Am. Soc. Internat. Law, Nat. Assn. Univ. Attys. (founder & 1st chmn. patents & copyrights sect. 1974-76). Home: 635 Onaha St Honolulu HI 96816-4918

BLOM, DANIEL CHARLES, lawyer, investor; b. Portland, Oreg., Dec. 13, 1919; s. Charles D. and Anna (Reiner) B.; m. Ellen Lavon Stewart, June 28, 1952; children: Daniel Stewart (dec.), Nicole Jan Heath. BA magna cum laude, U. Wash., 1941, postgrad., 1941-42; JD, Harvard U., 1948; postgrad., U. Paris, 1954-55. Bar: Wash. 1949, U.S. Supreme Ct. 1970. Tchg. fellow speech U. Wash., 1941-42; law clk. to justice Supreme Ct. Wash., 1948-49; since practiced in Seattle; assoc. Graves, Kizer & Graves, 1949-51; gen. counsel Northwestern Life Ins. Co., 1952-54; ptnr. Case & Blom, 1952-54; assoc., ptnr., of counsel Ryan, Swanson & Cleveland, 1956—; exec. v.p., gen. counsel Family Life Ins. Co., 1977-85, spl. counsel, 1985-91. Vice chmn. Wash. Bd. Bar Examiners, 1970-72, chmn., 1972-75; mem. industry adv. com. Nat. Assn. Ins. Commrs., 1966-68; pres. Wash. Ins. Coun., 1971-73, gen. counsel, 1975-78; mediator Arbitration Forums, Inc. Editor Wash. State Bar Jour., 1951-52; assoc. editor The Brief, 1975-76; author: Life Insurance Law of the State of Washington, 1980, Banking and Insurance, Deregulatory Cross-Currents, 1985, Hostile Insurance Company Takeovers: New Frontier of the Law, 1990, Administrative Finality Under the Washington Insurance Code, 1991, Business and Professionalism, 1994, The Civility Problem, 1995, Technics and the Civilization of Law Practice, 1997, Varieties of Regulatory Experience, 1998. Chmn. jury selection Wash. Gov.'s Writer's Day Awards, 1976; bd. dirs. Crisis Clinic; trustee Bush Sch., 1971-79, v.p., 1976-77; trustee, v.p. Frye Mus., Seattle, 1976-82, World Affairs Coun. Seattle, 1972-94, Friends of Seattle Pub. Libr., 1982-87; bd. visitors U. Wash. Libr., 88-92, Friends of U. Wash. Librs., bd. dirs., 1991-95, pres., 1991-92. 2d lt. AUS, 1942-45, PTO. Decorated Bronze Star; Rhodes scholarship finalist, 1949. Fellow Am. Bar Found.; mem. ABA (vice chmn. com. on life ins. law, sect. tort and ins. practice 1971-76, chmn. 1976-78, sect. program chmn. 1978-79, mem. coun. 1979-83, chmn. pub. rels. com. 1981-83, chmn. com. on profl. independence of the lawyer 1984-85, chmn. com. on scope and correlation 1985-86, chmn. com. on handbook and bylaws 1987-88, chmn. hist. com. 1991-94, del. ABA to Union Internat. Des Avocats 1986-91, policy coord. tort and ins. practice sect. 1986-90), Wash. Bar Assn. (award of merit 1975, chmn. legal edn. liason com. 1977-78), Seattle Bar Assn., Union Internat. Des Avocats (v.p. 1987-92), N.Am. Found. for Internat. Legal Practice (dir. 1987-95, pres. 1987-89, chmn. 1990-95), Am. Judicature Soc., Assn. Life Ins. Counsel, Harvard Law Sch. Assn., Am. Coun. Life Ins. (legis. com. 1982-85), Am. Arbitration Assn., Found. UIA (coun. 1990-97), Fedn. Regulatory Counsel, (dir. 1995-97), Harvard Assn. Seattle and Western Wash. (trustee 1976-77), Rainier Club, Phi Beta Kappa, Tau Kappa Alpha. Administrative and regulatory, General corporate, Insurance. Home: 100 Ward St # 602-3 Seattle WA 98109-5613 Office: Ryan Swanson & Cleveland 1201 3rd Ave Ste 3400 Seattle WA 98101-3034 E-mail: blom@ryanlaw.com

BLOODWORTH, A(LBERT) W(ILLIAM) FRANKLIN, lawyer; b. Atlanta, Sept. 23, 1935; s. James Morgan Bartow and Elizabeth Westfield (Dimmock) B.; m. Elizabeth Howell, Nov. 24, 1967; 1 child, Elizabeth Howell AB in History and French, Davidson Coll., 1957; JD magna cum laude with 1st honors, U. Ga., 1963. Bar: Ga. 1962, U.S. Supreme Ct. 1971. Asst. dir. alumni and pub. relations Davidson Coll., N.C., 1959-60; assoc. Hansell & Post, Atlanta, 1963-68, ptnr., 1969-84, Bloodworth & Nix, Atlanta, 1984-95, Bloodworth & McSwain, Atlanta, 1996—. Counsel organized crime com. Met. Atlanta Commn. on Crime, 1965-67; asst. sec., counsel Met. Found. Atlanta, 1968-76 Bd. dirs. Atlanta Presbytery, 1974-78; trustee Synod of S.E., Presbyn. Ch. in U.S.A., Augusta, Ga., 1982-87; trustee Big Canoe Chapel, Ga., 1983-86, 88-91, chmn. bd. trustees, 1985-86, 90-91; mem. pres.'s adv. coun. Presbyn. Homes, 1989—; mem. president's adv. coun. Thornwell Home and Sch. for Children, 1998—. elder North Ave Presbyn. Ch., Atlanta. 1st lt. Intelligence Corps, USAR, 1957-59. Recipient Jessie Dan MacDougal Scholarship award U. Ga. Found., 1963, Outstanding Student Leadership award Student Bar Assn., U. Ga., 1963. Fellow Am. Coll. Trust and Estate Counsel; mem. ABA, State Bar Ga., Atlanta Bar Assn., Atlanta Estate Planning Coun., North Atlanta Estate Planning Coun., Capital City Club, Lawyers Club, Sphinx Club, Gridiron Club, Phi Beta Kappa, Phi Kappa Phi, Omicron Delta Kappa, Alpha Tau Omega (pres. chpt. 1957), Phi Delta Phi (grad. of yr. 1963, pres. chpt. 1963). Republican. Presbyterian. Estate planning, Probate, Estate taxation. Home: 3784 Club Dr NE Atlanta GA 30319-1108 Office: 706 Monarch Plz 3414 Peachtree Rd NE Atlanta GA 30326-1153 Fax: 404 231-9330. E-mail: bandm706@bellsouth.net

BLOOM, CHRISTOPHER ARTHUR, lawyer; b. Chgo., May 25, 1951; s. Charles G. and Lyra Anne (Eells) B.; m. Jo Anne Gazarek, Apr. 21, 1979; children: Anna Victoria, Mary Olivia. B.A. cum laude, Kenyon Coll., 1973; J.D., Ind. U., 1975. Bar: Ind. 1975, Pa. 1976, Ill. 1976, U.S. Dist. Ct. (so. dist.) Ind., 1975, U.S. Dist. Ct. (no. dist.) Ill. 1976, U.S. Dist. Ct. (no. dist.) Ind. 1980, U.S. Ct. Appeals (7th cir.) 1975, U.S. Ct. Appeals (2d cir.) 1976, U.S. Supreme Ct. 1979. Assoc. Green & Brandwein, Chgo., 1976-78; assoc. Fox & Grove, Chartered, Chgo., 1978-82, ptnr., 1982-84; ptnr. Alexander, Unikel, Bloom, Zalewa & Tenenbaum, Ltd., Chgo., 1984-86, ptnr. Keck, Mahin & Cate, 1986—; instr. Loyola U., Chgo., 1976-79; gen. counsel Orch. of Ill., Chgo., 1976— , Grant Park Concerts Soc., Chgo., 1977— . Mem. ABA, Ill. Bar Assn., Chgo. Bar Assn. (fed. tax commn.). Computer, General corporate, Private international. Home: 5490 S South Shore Dr Chicago IL 60615-5984

BLOOM, HOWARD MARTIN, lawyer; b. Brookline, Mass., Oct. 7, 1951; m. Cheryl Denise Goldstein, May 14, 1978. BA cum laude, U. Mass., 1973; JD cum laude, Suffolk U., 1977. Bar: Mass. 1977, U.S. Dist. Ct. Mass. 1978, U.S. Ct. Appeals (1st cir.) 1978, U.S. Dist. Ct. R.I. 1981, U.S. Dist. Ct. Conn. 1981, U.S. Supreme Ct. 1982. Sole practice, Boston, 1977-79; assoc. firm Siegel, O'Connor & Kainen, P.C., Boston, 1979-85, ptnr., 1985-86; of counsel, Jackson, Lewis, Schnitzler & Krupman, 1986-87, ptnr., 1988—. Co-author: Employer's Guide to Employment Law, 1984; contbr. articles to profl. jours. Mem. ABA, Mass. Bar Assn. (labor law sect. council 1983-86), Newton-Needham C. of C. (bd. dirs. 1983—). Labor. Office: Jackson Lewis Schnitzler & Krupman One Beacon St Ste 3300 Boston MA 02108

BLOOM, NORMAN DOUGLAS, JR. lawyer; b. Albuquerque, Apr. 6, 1928; s. Norman Douglas and Rose (Conway) B.; m. Janet Pierce, June 11, 1949 (div. June 1970); children— Ellen Clarie, Nancy Rose, Verna Madge; m. Betty Minter, Aug. 8, 1970; children— Dorothy Jane, Norma Jo, Deborah Kay, Brenda, Nathan Dean, Norman Douglas III. B.A., U. Colo., 1952; J.D., U. N.Mex., 1966; postgrad. Nat. Dist. Attys. Coll., 1972. Bar: N.Mex. 1966, U.S. Dist. Ct. N.Mex. 1966, U.S. Ct. Appeals (10th cir.) 1975, U.S. Supreme Ct. 1977, U.S. Ct. Claims 1979. Ptnr. Fettinger, Bloom & Overstreet, Alamogordo, N.Mex., 1966-71; dist. atty. 12th Jud. Dist., Otero and Lincoln Counties, N.Mex., 1971-75; ptnr. Fettinger & Bloom, Alamogordo, 1975-94, Fettinger, Bloom & Quinlan, P.C., 1994—. Organizer, founder La Placita Children's Home, Alamogordo, 1972, pres., 1975— . Served with AUS, 1946-47; PTO. Recipient Service to Mankind awards Sertoma Club, 1978, Sertoma Internat. of South N.Mex.-S.W. Tex., 1978, Greater Rocky Mountain Region, 1978. Mem. N.Mex. State Bar Assn. Otero County Bar Assn. (sec.-treas. 1967-68, pres. 1971-72, 84-85). Lodges: Kiwanis (bd. dirs. 1968-70, 76-78, Elks (trustee 1967-70) (Alamogordo), So. N.Mex. Am. Inns of Ct. (master bencher). State civil litigation, General practice, Juvenile. Home: 17 Indian Maid Ln Alamogordo NM 88310-9756 Office: Quinlan Bloom & Assoc PC PO Box 600 Alamogordo NM 88311

BLOOMER, HAROLD FRANKLIN, JR. retired lawyer; b. N.Y.C., Nov. 4, 1933; s. Harold Franklin and Allene (Cress) B.; m. Mary Jane Lloyd, July 16, 1955 (div. June 1976); children: Sarah Allene, Margaret Gail, Leslie Lloyd; m. Freya Donald, Nov. 30, 1985; children: Katharine Roma, Alice Donald. AB, Amherst Coll., 1956; LLB, Columbia U., 1967. Bar: Conn. 1967, N.Y. 1968, U.S. Dist. Ct. Conn. 1968, U.S. Dist. Ct. (so. and ea. dists.) N.Y. 1974, U.S. Ct. Appeals (2d cir.) 1974. Assoc. Debevoise, Plimpton, Lyons & Gates, N.Y.C., 1967-77; counsel Burlington, Underwood & Lord, Jeddah, Saudi Arabia, 1977-78; chief internat. counsel Saudi Rsch. & Devel. Corp., London, 1978-80; counsel Morgan, Lewis & Bockius LLP, London and N.Y.C., 1980-81, ptnr., 1981-2000; ret., 2000. Adj. prof. Pepperdine U. Sch. Law, London, 1985. Mem. Rep. Town Meeting, Greenwich, Conn., 1964-74, 92—, chmn. pub. works com., 1971-74, chmn. land use com., 1998—; mem. Rep. Town Com., Greenwich, 1973-74; trustee San. Products Trust, Riverside, Conn., 1965-74; trip leader Adventure Cycling Assn., Missoula, Mont., 2000—; mem. Conn. com. East Coast Greenway, 2001—. Lt. (j.g.) USNR, 1957-60. Kent scholar Columbia U., 1965-66, Stone scholar Columbia U., 1966-67. Mem. Am. Arbitration Assn. (panel of arbitrators 1990—), Riverside Yacht Club. Republican. Episcopalian. Avocations: sailing, canoeing, skiing, biking, running. Contracts commercial, Finance, Private international.

BLOOMFIELD, DAVID SOLOMON, lawyer, educator; b. Dec. 13, 1944; s. Jerome P. and Anne M. (Knoll) Bloomfield; m. Sally Ward, June 04, 1969; children: David S., Paul W. BS, Ohio State U., 1966, JD, 1969; postgrad. in Law, NYU, 1969—71. Bar: Ohio 1969, U.S. Dist. Ct. (so. dist.) Ohio 1970, U.S. Dist. Ct. (no. dist.) Ohioi 1972, U.S. Ct. Appeals (6th cir.) 1973, U.S. Tax Ct. 1970, U.S. Supreme Ct. 1973. Mem. staff Lybrand Ross Bros. & Montgomery, N.Y.C., NY, 1969—70; chief tax sect. Atty. Gen. Ohio, Columbus, 1970—71; assoc., then ptnr. Ward Kaps Bainbridge Maurer Bloomfield & Melvin, and predecessor, Ohio, 1971—92; ptnr. Bloomfield & Kempf, 1992—. Lectr. Capital U., 1972—78, Ohio Paralegal Inst., 1979; adj. prof. Capital U. Coll. Law, Columbus, 1980—, The Ohio State U., 1996—. Contbr. articles to profl. jours. Active Columbus United Way, 1979—; campaign chmn. Price for Judge, Columbus, 1980; bd. dir. N.W. Mental Health Assn., 1979—82. Recipient Merit award, Ohio Law Inst., 1975, Pub. Svc. award, U.S. Dept. Justice, 1996. Fellow: Ohio State Bar Assn.; mem.: ABA, Ohio Bar Assn. (coms.), Columbus Bar Assn. (chair coms., bd. commrs. on grievance and discipline of Supreme Ct.

Ohio, client security fund Supreme Ct. Ohio), Athletic Club, Ohio State U. Pres.'s Club (Columbus chpt.). Democrat. Jewish. Avocation: woodworking. Immigration, naturalization, and customs, Professional liability. Home: 3741 Romnay Rd Columbus OH 43220-4877 Office: Bloomfield & Kempf 199 S 5th St Columbus OH 43215-5234

BLOOMFIELD, NEIL JON, lawyer, law educator, real estate broker; b. N.Y.C., July 25, 1945; s. Elmer Joel and Charlotte (Orlov) B.; children— Jennifer, Violet. B.A. cum laude, Princeton U., 1966; J.D. cum laude, Harvard U., 1969. Bar: N.Y. 1969, Calif. 1972. Assoc., Willkie, Farr & Gallagher, N.Y.C., 1969-73, ptnr. Bloomfield & Greene, 1974-80; pres. Bloomfield White & Whitney, Inc., Sausalito, Calif., 1974-77, Law Offices of Neil Jon Bloomfield, 1980—; bd. dirs. Vol. Lawyers for the Arts, N.Y.C., 1970-72; adj. prof. law U. San Francisco, 1982-83; cert. expert in real estate law and trusts related to real estate Calif. Superior Ct. Mem. Marin County Bar Assn., San Francisco Bar Assn., Clolsrer Inn, Lincolns Inn Soc. (Cambridge). Editor: Community and Racial Crises, 1966. General civil litigation, Real property, Taxation, general. Office: 901 E St Ste 100 San Rafael CA 94901-2928

BLOUNT, CHARLES WILLIAM, III, lawyer; b. Independence, Mo., Nov. 14, 1946; s. Charles William and Mary Marguarette (Van Trump) B.; m. Susan Penny Smith Turner, Dec. 20, 1969 (div. Nov., 1987); children: Charles William IV, Chaille Elizabeth; m. Bonnie M. Harp., Jan. 1, 1991. BS in Journalism, U. Kans., 1968; JD cum laude, U. Toledo, 1981. Bar: Mo. 1981, U.S. Dist. Ct. (we. dist.) Mo. 1981, Tex. 1985, U.S. Dist. Ct. (no. dist.) Tex. 1988, U.S. Ct. Appeals (5th cir.) 1995, U.S. Supreme Ct. 1997; cert. in civil appellate law Tex. Bd. Legal Specialization. Litigation assoc. Shugart, Thomson & Kilroy, Kansas City, Mo., 1981-84, Hughes & Luce, Dallas, 1984-87, Simpson & Dowd L.L.P., Dallas, 1987-91, ptnr., 1991-94; mem. Dowd & Blount, 1994-99; ptnr. Perry-Miller & Blount, L.L.P., 1999—. Mem. West Group Tex. Editl. Bd., 1999. Bd. govs. U. Toledo Coll. Law, 1980-81; trustee Episcopal Diocese We. Mo., Kansas City, 1983-84; mem., chmn. com. Boy Scouts of Am., Kansas City, 1983-84, Richardson, Tex., 1984-92. 1st lt. U.S. Army, 1968-72. Mem. Phi Kappa Phi, Phi Kappa Tau (pledge pres., social chmn., activities chmn., 1965—). Avocations: music, reading. Appellate, State civil litigation, General corporate. Office: Perry-Miller & Blount LLP LB45 3300 Oak Lawn Ave Ste 675 Dallas TX 75219-4292 E-mail: cblount@pmblawfirm.com

BLOUNT, MICHAEL EUGENE, lawyer; b. Camden, N.J., July 9, 1949; s. Floyd Eugene and Dorothy Alice (Geyer) Durham; m. Janice Lynn Brown, Aug. 22, 1969; children: Kirsten Marie, Gretchen Elizabeth. BA, U. Tex., 1971; JD, U. Houston, 1974. Bar: Tex. 1974, Ill. 1980, D.C. 1981, U.S. Ct. Appeals (D.C. cir.) 1978, U.S. Ct. Mil. Appeals 1975, U.S. Supreme Ct. 1977. Atty. advisor Office of Gen. Counsel SEC, Washington, 1977-78, legal asst. to chmn., 1978-79; assoc. Gardner, Carton & Douglas, Chgo., 1980-84; ptnr. Arnstein, Gluck, Lehr, Barron & Milligan, 1984-86, Seyfarth Shaw, Chgo., 1987—. Trustee Assn. SEC Alumni. Lt. JAGC, USN, 1974-77. Mem. ABA (fed. regulation of securities com.), Chgo. Bar Assn., Order of Barons, Phi Alpha Delta (chpt. treas. 1973), Univ. Club (Chgo.). Private international, Mergers and acquisitions, Securities. Home: 1711 Galloway Dr Barrington IL 60010-5737 Office: Seyfarth Shaw 55 E Monroe St Ste 4200 Chicago IL 60603-5863

BLUCHER, PAUL ARTHUR, lawyer; b. Youngstown, Ohio, Aug. 1, 1958; s. Arthur E. and Lillian L. (McQuillan) B.; m. Brenda Lee Kilgore, Aug. 25, 1990. AS with honors, Youngstown State U., 1984, BS magna cum laude, 1986; JD, U. Pitts., 1990. Bar: Fla. 1990, U.S. Dist. Ct. (mid. dist.) Fla. 1997, U.S. Ct. Appeals (11th cir.) 1998. Police officer Mahoning County Sheriff, Youngstown, 1979-85, police detective, 1985-87; assoc. Brigham, Moore, et al., Sarasota, Fla., 1990-96, ptnr., 1996-97; pvt. practice Law Offices of Paul A. Blucher, P.A., Sarasota, Tampa, Fla. Mem. allocations & admissions com. United Way, Sarasota, 1996-2000 (Pathfinder Club Recognition award 1996); mem. Amyotrophic Lateral Sclerosis Assn. 1995—. Mem. ABA (state and local gov. com. 1990-99, real property sect. condemnation com. 1999—), Fla. Bar Assn. (stress mgmt. com. 1997-99, young lawyers 1990-95, eminent domain com. 1990—), Fla. Restaurant Assn., Assn. Eminent Domain Profls., Sarasota County Bar Assn. (chair 1990—, spkrs. bur. 2000-01). Democrat. Roman Catholic. Avocations: scuba diving, boating, flying. State civil litigation, Condemnation, Constitutional. Office: Law Offices of Paul A Blucher PA 2d Fl 434 S Washington Blvd Fl 2D Sarasota FL 34236-7100 E-mail: pblucher@fifthamendment.com

BLUE, JAMES MONROE, lawyer; b. St. Petersburg, Fla., Oct. 5, 1941; s. James Monroe and Mildred (Hobbs) B.; m. Barbara Ann Alderson, Jan. 3, 1981; children: Tammy Marlene, Kelli Christine, Shannon Kathlene. BA, Fla. State U., 1963; JD with honors, Stetson Coll., 1967. Bar: Fla. 1967, U.S. Dist. Ct. (mid. dist.) Fla. 1968, U.S. Ct. Appeals (11th cir.) 1968, U.S. Supreme Ct. 1978. Assoc. Carlton, Fields, Ward, Emmanuel, Smith & Cuttler, Tampa, Fla., 1967-69; ptnr. Alley, Alley & Blue, Miami, 1969-75, Smith, Young & Blue, Tallahassee, 1975-79, Allen, Norton & Blue, Tampa, 1979—. Mem. ABA, Fla. Bar Assn., Fla. Bar (chmn. labor law sect. 1978-79, Fla. C. of C. (human resources com. 1989—), Tampa C. of C. (com. of 100, 1987—). Republican. Presbyterian. Avocations: golf, boating, reading. Labor. Office: 324 S Hyde Park Ave Ste 350 Tampa FL 33606-4110 E-mail: jmb@anblaw.com

BLUESTONE, ANDREW LAVOOTT, lawyer; b. N.Y.C., Feb. 16, 1951; s. Henry Robert and Joan (Lavoott) B.; m. Janet Francesca Whelehan, May 1987; 1 child, Gabrielle. BA, Alfred U., 1973; MA, SUNY, Oswego, 1975; JD, Syracuse U., 1978. Bar: N.Y. 1979, U.S. Dist. Ct. (so. and ea. dists.) N.Y. 1979. Sr. trial asst. dist. atty. Kings County Dist. Atty., Bklyn., 1978-84; sr. assoc. Davis & Hoffman, N.Y.C., 1984-86, Donald Ayers, N.Y.C., 1986, Alexander, Ash, Schwartz & Cohen, N.Y.C., 1986-88, Trolman & Glaser, N.Y.C., 1988-89; pvt. practice, 1989—. Arbitrator Small Claims Civil Ct. City of N.Y.; lectr. NYCTL CLE. Bd. dirs. Scandia Symphony, N.Y.C., St. Luke's AME Ch., N.Y.C. Mem. ABA, N.Y.C.T.L.A., Def. Assn. N.Y., Assn. Trial Lawyers Am. (lectr.), N.Y. State Trial Lawyers Assn., Bklyn. Bar Assn. E-mail: Bluestoneatty.com. General civil litigation, Contracts commercial, Personal injury. Office: 233 Broadway Fl 51 New York NY 10279-5199

BLUM, IRVING RONALD, lawyer; b. Phila., Mar. 3, 1935; s. William and Dorothy (Gaskin) B.; m. Rochelle S. Klempner, June 17, 1956; children— Loren, Karen, Jill, Jason. BA, Wayne State U., 1956; JD, Detroit Coll. Law, 1959. Bar: Mich. 1959, U.S. Dist. Ct. (ea. dist.) Mich. 1959, Detroit. Ptnr., Akerman, Kaplan & Blum, Detroit, 1959-62, Blum, Brady & Rosenberg, Detroit, 1962-82, Blum, Kobheim, Elkin & Blum, Southfield, 1982—. Mem. Trial Lawyers Am., Mich. Trial Lawyers, 300 Club (bd. dirs.). Democrat. Jewish. Federal civil litigation, State civil litigation, Personal injury. Home: 132 Vintageisle Ln Palm Beach Gardens FL 33418-4603

BLUMBERG, EDWARD ROBERT, lawyer; b. Phila., Feb. 15, 1951; BA in Psychology, U. Ga., 1972; JD, Coll. William and Mary, 1975. Bar: Fla., 1975, U.S. Dist. Ct. Fla. 1975, U.S. Ct. Appeals, 1975, U.S. Supreme Ct. 1979. Assoc. Knight, Peters, Hoeveler & Pickle, Miami, Fla., 1976-77; ptnr. Deutsch & Blumberg, P.A., 1978—. Adj. prof. U. Miami Sch. Paralegal Studies. Author: Proof of Negligence, Mathew Bender Florida Torts, 1988. Mem. ABA (ho. of Dels. 1997—), ATLA, Dade County Bar Assn., Fla. State Bar (bd. govs., pres. elect 1996-97, pres. 1997-98), Acad. Fla. Trial Lawyers, Nat. Bd. Trial Advocacy (cert. civil trial adv.), Fla. Bar Found. (bd. dirs. 1996—, bd. govs. 1996-99). Federal civil litigation, State civil litigation, Personal injury. Office: Deutsch & Blumberg PA 100 Biscayne Blvd Fl 28 Miami FL 33132-2304

BLUMBERG, GRACE GANZ, law educator, lawyer; b. N.Y.C., Feb. 16, 1940; d. Samuel and Beatrice (Finkelstein) Ganz; m. Donald R. Blumberg, Sept. 9, 1959; 1 dau., Rachel. B.A. cum laude, U. Colo., 1960; J.D. summa cum laude, SUNY, 1971; LL.M., Harvard U., 1974. Bar: N.Y. 1971, Calif. 1989. Confidential law clk. Appellate Div., Supreme Ct., 4th Dept., Rochester, N.Y., 1971-72; teaching fellow Harvard Law Sch., Cambridge, Mass., 1972-74; prof. law SUNY, Buffalo, 1974-81, UCLA, 1981—. Reporter Am. Law Inst., Prins. of the Law of Family Dissolution. Author: Community Property in California, 1987, rev. edit., 1999, Blumberg's California Family Code Annotated (ann.); contbr. articles to profl. jours. Office: UCLA Sch Law Box 951476 Los Angeles CA 90095-1476

BLUMBERG, PHILLIP IRVIN, law educator; b. Balt., Sept. 6, 1919; s. Hyman and Bess (Simons) B.; m. Janet Helen Mitchell, Nov. 17, 1945 (dec. 1976); children: William A.M., Peter M., Elizabeth B., Bruce M.; m. Ellen Ash Peters, Sept. 16, 1979. AB, Harvard U., 1939, JD, 1942; LLD (hon.), U. Conn., 1994. Bar: N.Y. 1942, Mass. 1970. Assoc. Willkie, Owen, Otis, Farr & Gallagher, N.Y.C., 1942-43, Szold, Brandwen, Meyers and Blumberg, N.Y.C., 1946-66; pres., CEO United Ventures Inc., 1962-67; pres., CEO, trustee Federated Devel. Co., N.Y.C., 1966-68, chmn. fin. com., 1968-73; prof. law Boston U., 1966-74; dean U. Conn. Sch. Law, Hartford, 1974-84, prof. law, 1984-89, dean, prof. law emeritus, 1989—. Bd. dirs. Verde Exploration Ltd.; mem. legal adv. com. to bd. dirs. N.Y. Stock Exch., 1989-93; advisor corp. governance project, restatement of suretyship and restatement of agy. Am. Law Inst.; vis. lectr. U. Brabant, Tilburg, Netherlands, 1985, U. Internat. Bus. and Econs., Beijing, 1989, U. Sydney, 1992, Jagiellonian U., Cracow, Poland, 1992; adv. com. on transnat. corp. U.S. Dept. State. Author: Corporate Responsibility in a Changing Society, 1972, The Megacorporation in American Society, 1975, The Law of Corporate Groups: Procedure, 1983, The Law of Corporate Groups: Bankruptcy, 1985, The Law of Corporate Groups: Substantive Common Law, 1987, The Law of Corporate Groups: General Statutory Law, 1989, The Law of Corporate Groups: Specific Statutory Law, 1992, The Multinational Challenge to Corporation Law, 1993, The Law of Corporate Groups: State Statutory Law, 1995, The Law of Corporate Groups: Enterprise Liability, 1998; mem. editl. bd. Harvard Law Rev., 1940-42, treas., 1941-42; contbr. articles to profl. jours. Trustee Black Rock Forest Preserve, Inc.; trustee emeritus Conn. Bar Found. Capt. USAAF, 1943-46, ETO. Decorated Bronze Star Mem. ABA, Conn. Bar Assn., Am. Law Inst., Hartford Club, Harvard Club (Boston), Army & Navy Club (Washington), Phi Beta Kappa, Delta Upsilon. Home: 791 Prospect Ave Apt B-5 Hartford CT 06105-4224 Office: U Conn Sch Law 65 Elizabeth St Hartford CT 06105-2290 E-mail: pblumber@law.uconn.edu

BLUME, LAWRENCE DAYTON, lawyer; b. Kansas City, Mo., July 7, 1948; s. Dayton G. and Meredith L. B. BA, U. Ariz., 1970; JD, U. Mo., 1974. Bar: Mo. 1974, D.C. 1989, U.S. Dist. Ct. (we. dist.) Mo. 1974, U.S. Ct. Appeals (fed. cir.) 1984, U.S. Supreme Ct. 1978, U.S. Tax Ct. 1980, U.S. Ct. Internat. Trade 1981, N.Y. 1996. Ptnr. Swanson, Midgley, Gangwere, Clarke & Kitchin, Kansas City, 1974-80; prin. Miller & Blume, P.C., Washington, 1980-89; ptnr. Graham & James, 1989-2000, D.C. mng. ptnr., 1992-94; N.Y. mng. ptnr. Graham & James LLP, N.Y.C., 1994-98, firm chmn., 1998-2000; prin. Greenberg Traurig LLP, 2000—. Lectr. Nat. Assn. Fgn. Trade Zones, Washington, 1981—, Am. Assn. Exporters and Importers, N.Y.C., 1984—, various colls., univs. and trade groups, 1980—; prin. instr. Seminar on Internat. Bus. Transactions and Litigation Techniques. Mem.: ABA, Inter-Am. Bar Assn. (sr.)), Internat. Trade Bar Assn., Am.-Intellectual Property Law Assn., Customs and Internat. Bar Assn., Order of Barristers, Licensing Execs. Soc. Internat., Am. Assn. Exporters and Importers, Nat. Dem. Club. Democrat. Private international. Office: Greenberg Traurig 885 Third Ave Ste 2100 New York NY 10022 E-mail: blumel@gtlaw.com

BLUME, PAUL CHIAPPE, lawyer; b. Omaha, Oct. 11, 1929; s. Herman Alexander and Marie (Simoni) B.; m. Mary Lou Higgins, June 28, 1958; children: Nancy, Julie, Paul II, William. BS in Commerce, Loyola U., Chgo.; JD. Bar: Ill. 1957. Legal sect. mgr. Aldens Inc., 1957-58; assoc. Lord, Bissell & Brook, 1959-63, of counsel, 1983—; v.p., gen. counsel Nat. Assn. Ind. Insurers, Des Plaines, Ill., 1963-83, Ill. Ins. Info. Svc., 1987-96; pres. Ins. Briefs, Inc., 1984—. Capt. U.S. Army, 1951-53. Mem. Chgo. Bar Assn., Fedn. Ins. Counsel. Office: 115 S La Salle St Chicago IL 60603-3801

BLUMENFELD, JEFFREY, lawyer, educator; b. N.Y.C., May 13, 1948; s. Martin and Helen Kay (Smith) B.; m. Laura Madeline Ross, June 11, 1970; children: Jennifer Ross Blumenfeld, Joshua Ross Blumenfeld. AB in Religious Thought cum laude, Brown U., 1969; JD, U. Pa., 1973. Bar: D.C. 1973. Asst. U.S. atty. U.S. Atty. for D.C., Washington, 1975-79; trial atty. Antitrust div. U.S. Dept. of Justice, 1973-75, sr. trial atty. U.S. versus AT&T staff, 1979-82, asst. chief spl. regulated industries, 1982-84, chief U.S. versus AT&T staff, 1984, spl. counsel, 1995-97; ptnr. Blumenfeld & Cohen, 1984—; sr. trial counsel, antitrust divsn. U.S. Dept. Justice, 1996-97; gen. counsel, chief legal officer Rhythms Net Connections, 1997-2001. Adj. prof. Georgetown U. Law Ctr., Washington, 1983—; spl. counsel antitrust divsn. U.S. Dept. Justice, 1995-97. Bd. dirs. Charles E. Smith Jewish Day Sch., Washington, 1991-93. Democrat. Jewish. Antitrust, Federal civil litigation, Communications. Office: Blumenfeld & Cohen Ste 300 1625 Massachusetts Ave NW Washington DC 20036-2247

BLUMENTHAL, RICHARD, state attorney general; m. Cynthia Blumenthal; 4 children. BA, Harvard Coll.; JD, Yale U., 1973. Law clk. Justice Harry A. Blackmun, 1974-75; U.S. atty. State of Conn., 1977-81, former rep., 1984-87, senator, 1987-90, state atty. gen., 1990—. Sgt. USMCR. Office: Atty Gen Office 55 Elm St Hartford CT 06106-1746

BLUMENTHAL, WILLIAM, lawyer; b. White Plains, N.Y., Nov. 4, 1955; s. Louis and Mary (Meyer) B.; m. Marjory Susan Spodick, Dec. 30, 1979; 1 child, Deborah Louise. AB, MA, Brown U., 1977; JD, Harvard U., 1980. Bar: D.C. 1980, U.S. Dist. Ct. D.C. 1986. Cons. Policy & Mgmt. Assocs., Inc., Boston, 1977-80; teaching fellow Harvard U., Cambridge, Mass., 1978-80; assoc. Jones, Day, Reavis & Pogue, Washington, 1980-83, Sutherland, Asbill & Brennan, Washington, 1983-87, ptnr., 1988-93, Kelley Drye & Warren, Washington, 1993-95, King & Spalding, Washington, 1995—. Editor Horizontal Mergers: Law and Policy, 1986; contbr. to book: The Merger Review Process, 1995, Mergers & Acquisitions Handbook, 1986. Harvey A. Baker fellow Brown U., 1977. Mem. ABA (chmn. Clayton Act com. 1992-94, chmn. monograph com. 1989-92, vice chmn. antitrust sect. 1997-98). Antitrust, Federal civil litigation, Mergers and acquisitions. E-mail: wblumenthal@kslaw.com

BLUMKIN, LINDA RUTH, lawyer; b. N.Y.C., Aug. 25, 1944; d. Louis and Edith (Fortus) Blumkin. A.B. cum laude, Barnard Coll., 1964; LL.B. cum laude, Harvard U., 1967, LL.M., 1973. Bar: N.Y. 1968, U.S. dist. ct. (so. dist.) N.Y. 1969, U.S. Ct. Apls. (2nd cir.) 1969, U.S. Supreme Ct. 1982. Assoc. Fried, Frank, Harris, Shriver & Jacobson, N.Y.C., 1967-71, ptnr., 1979— ; lectr. Boston U., 1971, asst. prof. mgmt., 1972-73; assoc. Breed, Abbott & Morgan, N.Y.C., 1973-77; asst. dir. Bur. Competition FTC, 1977-79. Mem. ABA, N.Y.C. Bar Assn. Antitrust, Federal civil litigation. Office: Fried Frank Harris Shriver & Jacobson 1 New York Plz Fl 24 New York NY 10004-1901

BLUMROSEN, ALFRED WILLIAM, law educator; b. Detroit, Dec. 14, 1928; s. Sol and Frances (Netzorg) B.; m. Ruth L. Gerber, July 3, 1952; children: Steven Marshall, Alexander Bernet. BA, U. Mich., 1950, JD, 1953. Bar: Mich. 1953, N.J. 1961, N.Y. 1981. Solo practice, Detroit, 1953-55; mem. faculty Rutgers Law Sch., Newark, 1955—, prof., 1961—, acting dean, 1974-75, Herbert J. Hannoch scholar, 1984, Thomas A. Cowan prof., 1986—. Dir. fed.-state rels., chief conciliations U.S. EOOC, 1965-67, cons. to chmn., 1977-79; advisor U.S. Dept. Justice, HUD, 1968-72, U.S. Dept. Labor, 1995-96; of counsel Kaye, Scholer, Fierman, Hays & Handler, N.Y.C., 1979-82; dir. Ford Found. intentional discrimination project Rutgers U., Law Sch., 1998—. Author: Black Employment and the Law, 1971, Modern Law: The Law Transmission System and Equal Employment Opportunity, 1993; contbr. articles to profl. jours. Fulbright scholar, South Africa, 1993, Rockefeller Inst. Resident scholar Bellagio Conf. Ctr., 1995. Mem. ABA (Ross essay prize 1983), Internat. Soc. for Labor Law and Social Security, Indsl. Relations Rsch. Assn., Order of Coif. Office: Rutgers U Sch Law 123 Washington St Newark NJ 07102-3026 E-mail: theblumrosen@cs.com

BLUMROSEN, RUTH GERBER, lawyer, educator, arbitrator; b. N.Y.C., Mar. 7, 1927; d. Lipman Samuel and Dorothy (Finklebrand) Gerber; m. Alfred William Blumrosen, July 3, 1952; children: Steven Marshall, Alexander B. BA in Econs., U. Mich., 1947, JD, 1953. Bar: Mich. 1953, U.S. Supreme Ct. 1967, U.S. Ct. Appeals (3d cir.). Pvt. practice law, Detroit, 1953-55; cons. civil rights litigation, 1958-65; acting chief advice and analyses, acting dir. compliance EEOC, Washington, 1965; asst. dean Howard U., 1965-67; consul to chmn. EEOC, 1979-80; expert EEO HHS, Washington, 1980-81; assoc. prof. Grad. Sch. Mgmt. Rutgers U., Newark, 1972-87; adj. prof. Rutgers Law Sch., 1994—. Resident scholar rockefeller Found., Bellagio, Italy, 1995; adviser N.J. Commn. on Sex Discrimination in the Statutes, 1983-85; commr. N.J. Gov.'s Study Commn. on discrimination in Pub. Works Procurement and Constrn. Contracts, 1990-93; gen. advisor Rutgers Law Sch. Intentional Discrimination Proj., three year study of employment discrimination funded by The Ford Found., 1998—. Author: (with A. Blumrosen) Layoff or Worksharing: The Civil Rights Act of 1964 in the Recession if 1975; (with A. Blumrosen, et. al.) Downsizing and Employee Rights, 50 Rutgers Law Review 943, 1998; The Duty to Plan for Fair Employment Revisited: Worksharing in Hard times, 1975; Wage Discrimination, Job Segregation and Title VII of Civil Rights Act of 1964, 1979; Wage Discrimination and Job Segregation: The Survival of a Theory, 1980; An Analysis of Wage Discrimination in N.J. State Service, 1983; Remedies for Wage Discrimination, 1987, (with A. Blumrosen) The Flawed Foundation of Piscataway High, 1999. Fulbright scholar So. Africa, 1993. Mem. ABA, Fed. Bar Assn., Indsl. Rels. Rsch. Assn., Nat. Com. Pay Equity. Office: 123 Washington St # 915 Newark NJ 07102-3105 E-mail: theblumrosen@cs.com

BLUMSTEIN, EDWARD, lawyer; b. Phila., Aug. 24, 1933; s. Isaac and Mollye (Rodofsky) B.; m. Susan Perloff, Aug. 13, 1983; 1 child, Daniel Blumstein. BS in Econs., U. Pa., 1955; JD, Temple U., 1958. Bar: U.S. Dist. Ct. (ea. dist.) Pa. 1959, U.S. Ct. Appeals (3rd cir.) 1959. Pvt. practice, Phila., 1959-85; ptnr. Blumstein, Block & Pease, 1985—. Adj. prof. Sch. Law Temple U., 1994—. Gen. Counsel to North American Ski Journalists Assn. With U.S. Army, 1958-64. Mem. ABA, Pa. Bar Assn., Phila. Bar Assn. (bd. govs. 1984-85, past chmn. family law sect. 1984), Acad. Family Mediators and Family Mediation Assn. Del. Valley (pres. 1990-91), B'nai B'rith. Republican. Jewish. Avocations: skiing, sailing, reading, photography. Alternative dispute resolution, Family and matrimonial, Personal injury. Office: Blumstein Block & Pease 1518 Walnut St Fl 4 Philadelphia PA 19102-3403

BLY, ROBERT MAURICE, lawyer; b. Connersville, Ind., Oct. 31, 1944; s. Karl H. and Faye Virginia (DeHoff) B.; m. Ann Patrice Gleason, Aug. 24, 1968; 1 child, Thomas Robert. BS, Ball State U., 1966; JD, U. Tenn., 1973. Bar: Ill. 1973, Ind. 1974, U.S. Dist. Ct. (so. dist.) Ind. 1974, U.S. Dist. Ct. (no. dist.) Ind. 1978, U.S. Supreme Ct. 1981, Tenn. 1991, U.S. Dist. Ct. (ea. dist.) Tenn. 1992. Pub. sch. tchr. pub. schs., Ind., 1966-71; regional counsel's staff Chgo. (Ill.) Title & Trust Co., 1973-75; dep. prosecutor Porter County Ind., Valparaiso, 1975-76; pvt. practice law Valparaiso and Kokomo, Ind., 1976-91, Knoxville, 1992—. Adj. instr. Ind. U., Kokomo, 1987-91; del. Ho. of Dels., Ind. Bar Assn., Indpls., 1988; founder Southeast Estate Planning Inst.; guest lectr. in field. Columnist Fairfield Glade Sun, 1993-94; contb. author: Generations Planning Your Legacy, 1999. Pres. Vols. in Cmty. Svc., Kokomo, 1980-85; del. Ind. State Rep. Conv., Indpls., 1986; mem. Nat. Rep. Senatorial Com., Washington, 1993-96. Fellow: Offshore Inst., Mid South Estate Planning Forum (founding mem., pres. 1997—2001); mem.: Nat. Network Estate Planning Attys., Am.'s Assn. Asset Protection (gen. coun.), Tenn. Bar Assn. (tax, probate and trusts sect.). Episcopalian. Avocations: collecting and restoring classic automobiles, traveling. Estate planning, Private international, Estate taxation. Office: 9111 Cross Park Dr Ste D200 Knoxville TN 37923-4521

BLYTH, JOHN E. lawyer, educator; b. Rochester, N.Y., Oct. 19, 1931; s. Ray G. and Ruby Luella (Spaulding) B.; m. Joanna E. Jennings, Aug. 23, 1963; children: Geoffrey E., Jennifer E., Jane Blyth Warren, James E. AB, Colgate U., 1953; LLB, NYU, 1960; JD, Goethe U., 1962. Bar: N.Y. 1961. Ptnr. Harter, Secrest & Emery, Rochester, 1961-93, Hiscock & Barclay, Rochester, 1994-95, Blyth & Lamb, Rochester, 1995-2000, Fix Spindelman Brovitz & Goldman, Rochester, N.Y., 2000—. Speaker in field; adj. prof. Cornell U. Law Sch., Ithaca, N.Y., 1990—; former trustee Keuka Coll., Keuka Park, N.Y., 1986—. Contbr. articles to profl. jours. Pres. Palmyra (N.Y.) Macedon Sch. Bd., 1969-72, Citizen's Tax League, Rochester, 1984-86. Sgt. U.S. Army, 1954-57, ETO. Named Internat. Exec. of Yr., Rochester C. of C., 1994. Mem. N.Y. State Bar Assn. (chair real property law sect. 1990-91), Am. Coll. Real Estate Lawyers. Avocation: organist. E-mail jeb. Private international, Real property. Home: 1428 Hidden Pond Ln Walworth NY 14568-9538 Office: Fix Spindelman Brovitz & Goldman 14th Fl 2 State St Rochester NY 14614 E-mail: 2@frontiernet.net, jblyth@fixspin.com

BLYTHE, JAMES DAVID, II, lawyer; b. Indpls., Oct. 20, 1940; s. James David and Marjorie M. (Horne) B.; m. Sara S. Frantz, Nov. 21, 1974; 1 child; Amanda Renee. BS, Butler U., 1962; JD, Ind. U., 1966. Bar: Ind. 1966, U.S. Supreme Ct. (so. dist.) Ind., 1966, U.S. Supreme Ct. 1980, U.S. Ct. Appeals (7th cir.), 1993. Diplomate, U.S. congl. staff asst. Ct. Practice Inst., 1965-69; majority atty. Ind. Ho. of Reps., 1967, 69; dep. prosecutor Marion County Prosecutor's Office, 1966, 68; pvt. practice Indpls., 1966—; sr. ptnr. Blythe & Ost, 1994—. Mem. com. on character and fitness Ind. Supreme Ct., 1974-94; host TV show Ask a Lawyer, 1977-79. Bd. dirs. Marion County chpt. Am.Cncer Soc., 1971-76 (pres. 1975-76), Cen. Ind. coun. Boy Scouts Am., 1969-72, exec. com., 1969-71, Crossroads of Am. Coun., 1972-87, executive com. 1976-84, pres., 1979-81, life mem 1987, Salvation Army, 1975—, vice chmn., 1986, chmn., 1987, 88; Ind. chmn.

W.I. Amb. Exch., Jaycees, 1972-73; pres. North Ctrl. H.S. Alumni Assn., 1996-98; mem. lawyers fund raising com. Indpls. Mus. Art., 1973-74; co-membership chmn, Friends of Channel 20, 1975; hon. chmn. ann. dinner Muscular Dystrophy Family Found., 2001. Recipient cert. of Merit Am.Cancer Soc., 1971, 74-75, Outstanding Service award Indpls. br. Am. Cancer Soc., 1972-73, Richard E. Rowland award Jaycees, 1971-72, Stanley K. Lacy Meml. award Jaycees, 1974, Disting. Service award Ind. Jaycees, 1974, Silver Beaver award Boy Scouts Am., 1981, Live Mem. award Nat. Eagle Scout Assn., 1996; commendation Gov. State of Ind., 1973; named Man of Yr. Am. Cancer Soc., 1974; Jim Blythe Day named in his honor, Mayor of Indpls., 1976; named Sagamore of the Wabash, 1981, North Central H.S. Hall of Fame, 1999. Mem. Ind. Bar Assn. (legal ethics com. 1995—), Indpls. Bar Assn. (bd. mgrs. 1978-81, 89-90, chmn. grievance com. 1980-88), Kiwanis (v.p. Indpls 1986-87, pres. 1987-88, found pres. 1988-89, Indpls. Kiwanis found. 1989-99, pres. Ind. Dist. Found. 1995-98, pres. Indpls. found. 1989, civic award, 1991, Abe Lincoln Fellow, 1993, named Kiwanis Man of the Year, 1997), Gyro Club of Indpls. (bd. dirs. 2000—), Kappa Sigma, Phi Delta Phi. Republican. Presbyterian. General civil litigation, General corporate, Family and matrimonial. Home: 11028 E Lakeshore Dr Carmel IN 46033-4402 Office: 10585 N Meridian St Ste 200 Indianapolis IN 46290-1067 E-mail: jdb2@iquest.net

BOARDMAN, MARK SEYMOUR, lawyer; b. Birmingham, Ala., Mar. 16, 1958; s. Frank Seymour and Flora (Sarinopoulos) B.; m. Cathryn Dunkin, 1983; children:Wilson Paul, Joanna Christina. BA cum laude, U. Ala., 1979, JD, 1982. Bar: Ala. 1982, U.S. Dist. Ct. (no., so. and mid. dists.) Ala. 1982, U.S. Ct. Appeals (11th cir.) 1983, U.S. Supreme Ct. 1987. Assoc. Spain, Gillon, Riley, Tate & Etheredge, Birmingham, 1982-84; ptnr. Porterfield, Scholl, Bainbridge, Mims and Harper, P.A., 1984-93, Boardman Carr Weed & Hutcheson, P.C., Birmingham, 1993—. Pres. Holy Trinity Holy Cross Greek Orthodox Cathedral, 1991, 92, sec., 1987, asst. treas., 1986, treas., 1988, 89, v.p., 1990, 96-2001, bd. auditors, 1994; mem. coun. Greek Orthodox Diocese of Atlanta, 1992-95; mem. Shelby County (Ala.) Work Release Commn., sec., 1996; mem. ednl. adv. com. Homewood Bd. Edn., 1999-2001, strategic planning com., 2000-01. Mem. ABA, Ala. State Bar, Ala. Workers Compensation Claims Assn., Shelby County Bar Assn. (treas. 1992-93, sec. 1994, v.p. 1995, pres. 1996), Birmingham Bar Assn. (co-chmn. econs. of law com. 1997, local bar liaison com. 1997), Ala. Def. Lawyers Assn., Def. Rsch. Inst., Ala. Claims Assn., Order of Barristers, Phi Beta Kappa, Delta Sigma Rho-Tau Kappa Alpha, Pi Sigma Alpha. Greek Orthodox. General civil litigation, Insurance, Personal injury. Home: 1915 Wellington Rd Birmingham AL 35209-4026 Office: Boardman Carr Weed & Hutcheson PC PO Box 59465 Birmingham AL 35259-9465 also: 400 Boardman Dr Chelsea Birmingham AL 35043-8211

BOARDMAN, ROBERT A. lawyer; b. 1947; BA, Muskingum Coll., 1969; JD, Case Western Reserve U., 1972. Bar: Ohio 1972, Colo. 1976. Assoc. atty. Roetzel & Andress, 1972-75, atty., 1975-83; asst. gen. coun., sec. Manville Corp., Denver, 1983-87, v.p., sec., 1988-90; sr. v.p., gen. coun. Navistar Internat. Corp., Chgo., 1990—. General corporate, Finance, Securities. Office: Navistar Internat Corp 4201 Winfield Rd Warrenville IL 60555 E-mail: robert.boardman@nav-international.com*

BOAS, FRANK, retired lawyer; b. Amsterdam, North Holland, The Netherlands, July 22, 1930; came to U.S., 1940; s. Maurits Coenraad and Sophie (Brandel) B.; m. Edith Louise Bruce, June 30, 1981 (dec. July 1992); m. Jean Scripps, Aug. 6, 1993 (div. Dec. 2000). AB cum laude, Harvard U., 1951, JD, 1954. Bar: U.S. Dist. Ct. D.C. 1955, U.S. Ct. Appeals (D.C. cir.) 1955; U.S. Supreme Ct. 1958. Atty. Office of the Legal Adviser U.S. State Dept., Washington, 1957-59; pvt. practice, Brussels and London, 1959-79; of counsel Patton, Boggs & Blow, Washington, 1975-80; pres. Frank Boas Found., Inc., Cambridge, Mass., 1980—. Mem. U.S. delegation to UN confs. on law of sea, Geneva, 1958, 60; vice chmn. Commn. for Ednl. Exch., Brussels, 1980-87; mem. vis. com. Harvard Law Sch., 1987-91, Ctr. for Internat. Affairs, 1988—; dir. Found. European Orgn. for Research and Treatment of Cancer, Brussels, 1978-87, Paul-Henri Spaak Found., Brussels, 1981—, East-West Ctr. Found., Honolulu, 1990-01, Law of the Sea Inst., Honolulu, 1992-97, Pacific Forum CSIS, Honolulu, 1996—, Honolulu Acad. Arts, 1997—, U. Hawaii Found., 2000—; hon. sec. Am. C. of C. in Belgium, 1966-78. With U.S. Army, 1955-57. Decorated Officer of the Order of Leopold II, comdr. Order of the Crown (Belgium), comdr. Order of Merit (Luxembourg); recipient Tribute of Appreciation award U.S. State Dept., 1981, Harvard Alumni Assn. award, 1996. Mem. ABA, Fed. D.C. Bar Assn., Pacific and Asian Affairs Coun. (pres.), Honolulu Com. Fgn. Relations, Pacific, Outrigger Canoe (Honolulu), Travellers (London), Am. and Common Market (Brussels pres. 1981-85), Honolulu Social Sci. Assn. Education and schools, Private international, Public international. Home: 4463 Aukai Ave Honolulu HI 96816-4858

BOATNER, JERRA, legal assistant; b. Meridian, Miss., 11 June; d. Jerry Wayne and Marsha Jo (Shanks) B.; m. James Adrian Runnels, June 11, 1997. BA in Criminal Justice, U. So. Miss., 1995, MS in Criminal Justice, 1997. Dep. Metro Task Force, Hattiesburg, Miss., 1996; grad. asst. U. So. Miss., 1995-96, instr., 1996—; legal asst. Forrest Co. Dist. Atty., 1997—. Rschr.: (handbook) Mississippi Youth Court Handbook, 1995. Vol. Sexual Assault Crisis Ctr., Hattiesburg, Miss., 1995-96; campaign vol. Mayor John Robert Smith, Meridian, Miss., 1993. Recipient Alma B. Walters award Dept. Criminal Justice, U. So. Miss., 1995, Miss./Tenn. Lawman's Assn. scholarship, 1994. Mem. Phi Kappa Phi, Gamma Beta Phi. Democrat. Lutheran. Avocations: reading and rsch., walking, travel. Office: Forrest County Dist Atty PO Box 166 Hattiesburg MS 39403-0166

BOBIS, DANIEL HAROLD, lawyer; b. N.Y.C., May 1, 1918; s. Morris N. and Sarah C. Bobis; m. Selma Linder, May 15, 1960; children: Jodee E. Bobis Verbow, Stacee M. Bobis Miccio. LLB, St. Lawrence U., 1939; BS, Columbia U., 1947. Bar: N.Y. 1949, U.S. Patent and Trademark Office 1950, U.S. Supreme Ct. 1961, U.S. Ct. Appeals (3d cir.) 1963, N.J. 1964, U.S. Dist. Ct. N.J. 1964, U.S. Ct. Appeals (fed. cir.) 1982. Patent atty. Worthington Corp. (now Studebaker-Worthington Corp.), Harrison, N.J., 1946-1952, patent counsel, until 1969; mem. firm Popper, Bain, Bobis, Gilfillan & Rhoades, Newark, 1969-74, Popper & Bobis, Newark, 1974-79, Popper, Bobis & Jackson, Newark, 1979-88; of counsel Lerner, David, Littenberg, Krumholz & Mentlik, Westfield, 1988—. Founder Ann. Outstanding Patent Award, N.J. Coun. for R & D, 1966; former instr. on intellectual property matters and causes Horizon Sch. for Parlegal Tng., Linden, N.J. Capt. pilot AC, AUS, 1943-46; ETO. Decorated Air medal with one silver and 3 bronze oak leaf clusters, Purple Heart. Mem. ABA (chmn., mem. intellectual property coms.), N.J. Bar Assn. (chmn., mem. intellectual property coms.), N.J. Patent Law Assn. (pres. 1966, chmn., mem. intellectual property coms.), various N.J. county bar assns. (chmn., mem. intellectual property coms.). Home: 30 Burnham Ct Scotch Plains NJ 07076-3129 Office: Lerner David Littenberg Krumholz & Mentlik 600 South Ave W Ste 300 Westfield NJ 07090-1497 E-mail: dbobis@ldlkm.com

BOCCARDO, JAMES FREDERICK, lawyer; b. San Francisco, July 1, 1911; s. John Humbert and Erminia Gemma (Ferrando) B.; m. Lorraine Dimmett, Nov. 21, 1936; children: Leanne Boccardo Rees, John Humbert II. AB, San Jose State U., 1931; JD, Stanford U., 1934. Bar: Calif. 1934, D.C. Sole practice, San Jose, Calif., 1934—. Mem. ABA, Calif. Bar Assn., D.C. Bar Assn., Internat. Acad. Trial Lawyers, Assn. Trial Lawyers Am., Calif. Trial Lawyers Assn., Santa Clara County Trial Lawyers Assn., Inner Circle Advs. (past pres.). Republican. Avocations: golf, aviation. General civil litigation, Condemnation, Personal injury. Office: 985 University Ave Ste 12 Los Gatos CA 95032-7639 Fax: 408-354-1021

BOCCHINO, ANTHONY J. law educator, consultant; b. Meriden, Conn., July 31, 1947; s. Anthony and Kathryn (Wadilewski) B.; m. Linda L. Shafer, July 13, 1984. B.A., Bucknell U., 1969; J.D., U. Conn., 1972. Bar: Conn. 1972, N.C. 1973. Asst. prof. law Duke U. Law Sch., Durham, N.C., 1974-77, assoc. prof., 1977-79; sr. trial atty. Office of Insp.-Gen., GSA, Washington, 1979; assoc. prof. law Temple U. Law Sch., Phila., 1979-82, prof., 1982—; vis. George E. Allen prof. law U. Richmond Law Sch., Va., 1984; regional dir. Nat. Inst. Trial Advocacy, Phila., 1983, team leader, 1975; cons. on profl. tng. Steptoe & Johnson, Washington, 1982—. Author: North Carolina Trial Evidence Manual, 1976; Pennsylvania Evidence: Objections and Responses, 1983; Cases and Problems in Trial Advocacy, 1983, 84, 85. Bd. dirs. North Central Legal Services, Durham, 1977-79; guest lectr. Pa. Jud. Conf., Phila., John S. Bradway fellow Duke Law Sch., 1973-74; recipient award Mordecai Soc. Award, 1978, Williams Outstanding Teaching award Temple Law Sch., 1984. Mem. N.C. Bar Assn., ABA, Phila. Bar Assn., Conn. Bar Assn. Democrat. Roman Catholic. Home: 115 Edgewood Rd Ardmore PA 19003-2507 Office: Temple U Sch Law 1719 N Broad St Philadelphia PA 19122

BOCCIA, BARBARA, lawyer; b. Bklyn., Dec. 16, 1957; d. Daniel and Marie Boccia. BS with honors, U. Tenn., 1980; JD, U. of the Pacific, 1983. Bar: Calif. 1983, D.C, 1983. Litigation lawyer, ptnr. Mullen & Filippi, San Francisco, 1983-86; litigation lawyer Jones, Brown, Clifford & McDevitt, 1987-88; litigation lawyer, mng. lawyer Crymes, Hardie & Heer, 1988-89; pvt. practice Daly City, Calif., 1989-92; sr. trial atty., supervising atty. Akin & Carmody, San Francisco, 1992-94; prin. Law Office of Barbara Boccia, Inc., Daly City, Calif., 1994—. Arbitrator, corp. cons., writer, educator, speaker in field. Vol. Hotline and Spks. Bur., San Francisco AIDS Found., 1987-90; mem. founding bd. dirs. Northeast Ark. Regional AIDS Network; HIV instr. ARC, 1991. Named One of Outstanding Young Women in Am., 1980. Mem. San Francisco Bar Assn., Indsl. Claims Assn., Ins. Edn. Assn., Queen's Bench, Italian Welfare Agy. Avocations: jogging, basketball, aerobics, writing, being a mom. State civil litigation, Insurance, Workers' compensation. Office: PO Box 2210 Daly City CA 94017-2210 E-mail: bboc@mindspring.com

BOCHICCHIO, VITO SALVATORE, lawyer; b. Pitts. s. Richard John and Francesca (Romano) B.; m. Giovanna Febbraro, Nov. 21, 1992; children: Richard, Giosue, Francesco, Paolo. BA, MA, Duquesne U., 1984, JD, 1987. Bar: Pa. 1987, U.S. Dist. Ct. (we. dist.) Pa. 1987. Asst. dist. atty. Office Allegheny County Dist. Atty., Pitts., 1988-90; assoc. Rothman Gordon, 1990-94; ptnr. O'Brien, Rulis & Bochicchio, 1994—. Sec. Big Jim's Inc., Pitts., 1992—. Committeeman Allegheny County Dem. Com., Pitts., 1981—. Mem. Allegheny County Bar Assn., Small Mfrs. Coun., Calabria Club. Roman Catholic. Avocation: karate. Insurance, Personal injury, Workers' compensation. Office: O'Brien Rulis & Bochicchio 100 5th Ave Ste 500 Pittsburgh PA 15222-1821

BODANSKY, ROBERT LEE, lawyer; b. N.Y.C. BA cum laude, Syracuse U., 1974; JD with honors, George Washington U., 1977; cert. postgrad. studies, Ctr. Internat. Legal Studies, Salzburg, Austria, 1978. Bar: Md. 1978, D.C. 1978, Va. 2000, U.S. Dist. Ct. Md. 1978, U.S. Ct. Appeals (D.C. cir.) 1980, U.S. Dist. Ct. D.C. 1980, U.S. Ct. Appeals (4th cir.) 1981, U.S. Supreme Ct. 1982. First assoc., then ptnr. Feldman, Krieger, Goldman & Tish, Washington, 1978-83; ptnr. Feldman, Bodansky & Rubin, 1984-95; prin. Freer, McGarry, Bodansky & Rubin, P.C., 1995-97; ptnr. Nixon, Hargrave, Devans & Doyle, LLP (now Nixon Peabody LLP), 1997—. Advisor internat. bus. law and taxation programs McGeorge Sch. Law, Sacramento, Calif., 1985—. Author: Special Problems of Subcontractors and Suppliers, 1987. Legal advisor Parkwood Resident's Assn., Kensington, Md., 1984; bd. dirs. Ridgeleigh Residents' Assn., 1987—, Congregation Har Shalom, 1989-91; tchr. Adas Israel Congregation, Washington, 1975-91. Mem. ABA (chmn. subcom. internat. and foreign bus. law young lawyers div. 1978-80), Md. State Bar Assn., D.C. Bar Assn., Va. Bar Assn. Contracts commercial, General corporate, Real property. Office: Nixon Peabody LLP 401 9th St NW Ste 900 Washington DC 20004-2134 E-mail: rbodansky@nixonpeabody.com

BODDIE, REGINALD ALONZO, lawyer; b. New Haven, June 14, 1959; s. Gladys Geraldine (Harrell) B. BA, Brown U., 1981; JD, Northeastern U., 1984. Bar: N.Y., U.S. Dist. Ct. (ea. and so. dists.) N.Y. 1986, D.C. 1987, U.S. Ct. Appeals (2d cir.) 1989, U.S. Supreme Ct. 1990. Staff atty. Legal Aid Soc., N.Y.C., 1984-86, Harlem Legal Svcs., N.Y.C., 1986-88; asst. counsel Ctr. for Law and Social Justice Medgar Evers Coll. CUNY, 1988-95; pvt. practice Law Offices of Reginald A. Boddie, N.Y.C., 1995—. Arbitrator Lemon Law, N.Y. Atty. Gen. and Am. Arbitration Assn., N.Y.C., 1986-94. Founder, pres., exec. dir. United Youth Enterprises, Inc., New Haven, 1976—; founder, dir. Coll. Prep. program Ctrl. H.S., Providence, 1980-81; bd.dirs. Claremont Neighborhood Ctrs., Inc., Bronx, N.Y., 1994-96; vol. instr. ARC, New Haven, 1975-90; bd. dirs. Boys and Girls' Clubs of Union County, Union, N.J., 1996-97; vol. law edn. instr. N.Y.C. Pub. Schs., 1992—. Recipient Good Citizenship award Civitan Internat. Club, New Haven, 1977, 2 commendations Brown U., 1981, Outstanding Cmty. Svc. award New Haven Police Dept., 1984, Cmty. Svc. award Pub. Sch. 21, Bklyn., 1993, Trailblazer award for Cmty. Svc. Nat. Coun. of Negro Women, 2000, Cmty. Svc. award for Law Related Edn., Sch. Dist. 16, N.Y.C., 2000, others; named Vol. Lawyer of the Yr., N.Y.C. Civil Ct., 2000. Mem. Bklyn. Bar Assn., Optimist Internat. Club. Civil rights, General civil litigation, General practice. Office: Ste 2035 19 Fulton St Rm 408 New York NY 10038-2100

BODENSTEIN, IRA, lawyer; b. Atlantic City, Nov. 9, 1954; s. William and Beverly (Grossman) B.; m. Julia Elizabeth Smith, Mar. 9, 1991; children: Sarah Rose, George William, Jennie Kathryn. Student, Tel Aviv U., 1974-75; BA in Govt., Franklin & Marshall Coll., 1977; JD in Econs., U. Miami, 1980. Bar: Ill. 1980, U.S. Dist Ct. (no. dist.) Ill. 1980, U.S. Ct. Appeals (7th cir.) 1982, Fla. 1983. Assoc. James S. Gordon Ltd., Chgo., 1980-85, mem., 1985-89, Portes, Sharp, Herbst & Fox, Ltd., Chgo., 1990-91; shareholder Towbin & Zazove, Ltd., 1991-93; ptnr. D'Ancona & Pflaum, 1993-98; U.S. trustee Region 11, 1998—. Pres., bd. dirs., benefit chmn. Gus Giordano Jazz Dance, Chgo., 1990—; treas. Chgo. Pub. Art Group, 1995-99. Mem. ABA (bus. law sect., rep. young lawyers divsn. dist. 15, 1986-87, ann. meeting adv. com. 1990, spkr. spring meeting 1996, 97), Chgo. Bar Assn. (bd. dirs. young lawyers sect. 1985-87, chmn.-elect 1987-88, chmn. 1988-89, antitrust com., chmn. athletics com. 1984-85, bd. mgrs. 1990-92, chmn. pub. affairs and media rels. com., chmn. assn. meetings com., memberships com. 1996, cert. of appreciation 1984-93, 96-97). Democrat. Jewish. Home: 2848 W Wilson Ave Chicago IL 60625-3743 Office: Office US Trustee 227 W Monroe St Ste 3350 Chicago IL 60606-5099 E-mail: ira.bodenstein@usdoj.gov

BODKIN, HENRY GRATTAN, JR. lawyer; b. L.A., Dec. 8, 1921; s. Henry Grattan and Ruth May (Wallis) B.; m. Mary Louise Davis, June 28, 1943; children: Maureen L. Dixon, Sheila L. McCarthy, Timothy Grattan. B.S. cum laude, Loyola U., Los Angeles, 1943, J.D., 1948. Bar: Calif. 1948. Pvt. practice, Los Angeles, 1948-51, 53-95; ptnr. Bodkin, McCarthy, Sargent & Smith (predecessor firms), L.A.; of counsel Sullivan, Workman & Dee, 1995—. Mem. L.A. Bd. Water and Power Commrs., 1972-74, pres., 1973-74; regent Marymount Coll., 1962-67; trustee Loyola-Marymount U., 1967-91, vice chmn., 1985-86. With USNR, 1943-45, 51-53. Fellow Am. Coll. Trial Lawyers; mem. Calif. State Bar (mem. exec. com. conf. of dels. 1968-70, vice chmn. 1969-70), California Club, Riviera Tennis Club, Tuna Club, Chancery Club (pres. 1990-91), Phi Delta Phi. Republican. Roman Catholic. Federal civil litigation, State civil litigation, Insurance. Home: 956 Linda Flora Dr Los Angeles CA 90049-1631 Office: Sullivan Workman & Dee 800 S Figueroa St Fl 12 Los Angeles CA 90017-2521

BODNAR, PETER O. lawyer; b. Queens, N.Y., Mar. 19, 1945; s. John and Edith (Schultz) B. BA in Govt., NYU, 1966; JD, Fordham U., 1970. Bar: N.Y. 1971, U.S. Dist. Ct. (so. dist.) N.Y. 1973. Confidential law sec. to Hon. Evans V. Brewster Family Ct. and County Ct. Westchester County, N.Y., 1970-73; pvt. practice White Plains, 1973-77; ptnr. Bodnar & Greene, P.C., 1977-80, Bender & Bodnar, White Plains, 1980-98; prin. Law Offices of Peter O. Bodnar, 1998-99, Bodnar & Milone LLP, White Plains, 1999—. Pres., CEO P.A.J. Am. Ltd./The Olo Corp., 1990-97, CEO Organica, USA, Inc., 1998—. Trustee Village of Ossining, N.Y., 1975-77. Fellow Am. Acad. Matrimonial Lawyers; mem. ABA (family law sect.), N.Y. State Bar Assn. (family law sect., exec. com. 2000—), Westchester County Bar Assn. (family law sect., exec. com. 1992—, chair 2000—). Family and matrimonial. Office: 140 Grand St White Plains NY 10601-4831 E-mail: usorganica@aol.com

BODNER, MARC A. lawyer; b. Long Beach, N.Y., Mar. 16, 1970; s. Howard J. and Sandra A. B.; m. Amy J. Wilon, Oct. 31, 1996; 1 child, Isaac. BA in Polit. Sci., Queen's Coll., 1992; JD, Benjamin N. Cardozo Sch. Law, N.Y.C., 1997. Rsch. analyst Edward S. Gordon Co., N.Y.C., 1992-94; assoc. Goldberg, Corwin & Greenberg LLP, 1997—. Mack scholarship Benjamin N. Cardozo Sch. of Law, 1994. Mem. Assn. of the Bar of the City of N.Y., N.Y. State Bar Assn. Democrat. Jewish. Education and schools, General practice, Real property. Office: Goldberg Corwin & Greenberg LLP 331 Madison Ave 15th Fl New York NY 10017

BODNEY, DAVID JEREMY, lawyer; b. Kansas City, Mo., July 15, 1954; s. Daniel F. and Retha (Silby) B.; m. Sarah Hughes; children: Christian Steven, Anna Claire, Daniel Martin. BA cum laude, Yale U., 1976; MA in Fgn. Affairs, JD, U. Va., 1979. Bar: Ariz. 1979, U.S. Dist Ct. Ariz. 1980, U.S. Ct. Appeals (9th cir.) 1980, U.S. Supreme Ct. 1983. Legis. asst., speechwriter U.S. Senator John V. Tunney, Washington, 1975-76; sr. editor Va. Jour. of Internat. Law, 1978-79; assoc. Brown and Bain PA, Phoenix, 1979-85, ptnr., 1985-90; gen. counsel New Times, Inc., 1990-92; ptnr. Steptoe & Johnson, LLP, 1992—. Vis. prof. Ariz. State U., Tempe, 1985, 94—. Co-author: Libel Defense Resource Center: 50-State Survey, 1982—. Bd. dirs. Ariz. Ctr. for Law in the Pub. Interest, Phoenix, 1983—, pres., 1989-90; chmn. Yale Alumni Schs. Com., Phoenix, 1984-87; vice chmn. City of Phoenix Solicitation Bd., 1986-88, chmn., 1988-89; bd. dirs. Children's Action Alliance, 1995—, v.p., 1998—; mem. adv. panel on Civil Liberties to White House Commn. on Aviation Safety and Security, 1997. Mem. ABA (forum com. on communication law 1984—, concerned correspondents network com. 1979—), Ariz. Bar Assn. Democrat. Clubs: Yale (bd. dirs. Phoenix club 1979—), Ariz. Acad. General civil litigation, Communications, Libel. Office: Steptoe & Johnson 200 E Washington St 16th Fl0 Phoenix AZ 85004

BODOVITZ, JAMES PHILIP, lawyer; b. Evanston, Ill., Aug. 20, 1958; s. Philip Edward and Dosha (Laurman) B. BS, U. So. Calif., 1980, JD, 1984. Bar: N.Y. 1985, D.C. 1989, Calif. 1990. Assoc. Shearman & Sterling, N.Y.C., 1984-89, San Francisco, 1989-92; br. chief divsn. broker-dealer enforcement U.S. Securities Exch. Commn., N.Y.C., 1992-96; v.p., assoc. gen. counsel law dept. The Equitable Life Assurance Soc. of U.S., 1996—; sr. v.p., gen. counsel AXA Advisors, LLC, 1999—. Mem. ABA, Assn. Bar City N.Y. (Thurgood Marshall award 1998). Democrat. Federal civil litigation, General civil litigation, Securities. Office: AXA Financial Inc 12th Fl 1290 Ave of Americas New York NY 10104 E-mail: James.Bodovitz@axacs.com

BOE, MYRON TIMOTHY, lawyer; b. New Orleans, Oct. 30, 1948; s. Myron Roger and Elaine (Tracy) B. BA, U. Ark., 1970, JD, 1973; LLM in Labor, So. Methodist U., 1976. Bar: Ark. 1974, Tenn. 1977, U.S. Ct. Appeals (4th, 5th, 6th, 7th, 8th, 9th, l0th, 11th cirs.) 1978, U.S. Supreme Ct. 1978. City atty. City of Pine Bluff, Ark., 1974-75; sec.-treas. Ark. City Atty. Assn., 1975; sr. ptnr. Rose Law Firm, Little Rock, 1980—. Author: Handling the Title VII Case Practical Tips for the Employer, 1980. Served to 2d lt. USAR, 1972-73. Recipient Florentino-Ramirez Internat. Law award, 1975. Fellow Coll. Labor and Employment Lawyers, Inc., Ark. Bar Found. (bd. dirs.), Ark. Bd. Legal Specialization (sec. 1982-85, chmn. 1985-89, labor, employment discrimination, civil rights).; mem. ABA (labor sect. 1974—, employment law com. 1974—), ARC of Ark. (bd. dirs., v.p.), Ark. Bar Assn. (sec., chmn. labor sect. 1978-81, ho. of dels. 1979-82, Golden Gavel award 1983), Def. Rsch. Inst. (employment law com. 1982—), Am. Employment Law Coun. (charter), Ark. Assn. Def. Counsel. Civil rights, Labor. Office: Rose Law Firm 120 E 4th St Little Rock AR 72201-2893

BOEDIGHEIMER, ROBERT DAVID, lawyer; b. Mpls., Nov. 13, 1962; s. David Eugene and Phyllis Kay (Bylander) B.; m. Wendi Suzanne Lusk. BA in Philosophy, Polit. Sci. and Speech Comm. with distinction, U. Minn., 1985, JD, 1988. Bar: Minn. 1990, U.S. Dist. Ct. Minn. 1990. Law clk. to Hon. Lynn C. Olson, Anoka, Minn., 1989-90; assoc. Adams & Cesario, P.A., Bloomington, 1990-95; ptnr. McCloud & Boedigheimer, 1995—. Mem. ABA (litig. sect.), Minn. State Bar Assn., Minn. Trial Lawyers Assn., Nat. Employers Lawyers Assn., Wash. County Bar Assn., Dakota County Bar Assn., Nat. Bd. Trial Advocacy (cert. civil trial specialist). Republican. Roman Catholic. Avocations: racquetball, golf, weight training, skiing, watercolor painting. Family and matrimonial, Labor, Personal injury. Office: McCloud & Boedigheimer 5001 W 80th St Ste 201 Bloomington MN 55437-1110 E-mail: RDB@Boedigheimerlaw.com

BOEHM, THEODORE REED, judge; b. Evanston, Ill., Sept. 12, 1938; s. Hans George and Frances (Reed) B.; children from previous marriage: Elisabeth, Jennifer, Sarah, Macy; m. Margaret Stitt Harris, Jan. 27, 1985. AB summa cum laude, Brown U., 1960; JD magna cum laude, Harvard U., 1963. Bar: D.C. 1964, Ind. 1964, U.S. Supreme Ct. 1975. Law clk. to Chief Justices Warren, Reed and Burton, U.S. Supreme Ct., Washington, 1963-64; assoc. Baker & Daniels, Indpls., 1965-70, ptnr., 1970-88, 95-96, mng. ptnr., 1980-87; gen. counsel major appliances GE, Louisville, 1988-89; v.p., gen. counsel GE Aircraft Engines, Cin., 1989-91; dep. gen. counsel Eli Lilly & Co., 1991-95; justice Ind. Supreme Ct., Indpls., 1996—. Pres. Ind. Sports Corp., 1980-88; chmn. organizing com. 1987 Pan Am. Games, Indp.s. Mem. ABA, Am. Law Inst., Ind. Bar Assn. Office: Ind Supreme Ct State House Rm 324 Indianapolis IN 46204-2728 E-mail: thoehm@courts.state.in.us

BOEHNEN, DANIEL A. lawyer; b. Mitchell, S.D., Aug. 5, 1950; s. Lloyd and Mary Elizabeth (Buche) B.; m. Joan Bensing, May 22, 1976; children: Christopher, Lindsey. BS in Chem. Engring. cum laude, Notre Dame U., 1973; JD, Cornell U., 1976. Bar: Ill, U.S. Dist. Ct. (no. dist.) Ill., U.S. Ct. Appeals (7th and fed. cirs.), U.S. Supreme Ct. Atty. Allegretti, Newitt, Witcoff & McAndrews Ltd., Chgo., 1976—, assoc., 1982—; ptnr., exec. officer Allegretti & Witcoff, Ltd., 1986—, bd. dirs., 1993-96; founder, mng. ptnr. McDonnell Boehnen Hulbert & Berghoff, 1996—. Bd. dirs. Mitchell (S.D.) Prehist. Indian Village Soc., 1983—; commr. Northbrook Planning Commn., 1993—. Mem. ABA, AIPLA, Cornell Law Assn. Chg. (chmn.), Fed. Cir. Bar Assn. (bd. dirs.), Assn. Patent Law Firms (bd. dirs.). Avocations: skiing, photography, scuba diving. Federal civil litigation, Patent, Trademark and copyright. Office: McDonnell Boehnen Hulbert & Berghoff 300 S Wacker Dr Ste 3200 Chicago IL 60606-6709

BOEHNEN, DAVID LEO, grocery company executive, lawyer; b. Mitchell, S.D., Dec. 3, 1946; s. Lloyd L. Boehnen and Mary Elizabeth (Buche) Roby; m. Shari A. Bauhs, Aug. 9, 1969; children: Lesley, Michelle, Heather. AB, U. Notre Dame, 1968; JD with honors, Cornell U., 1971. Bar: Minn. 1971. Assoc. Dorsey & Whitney, Mpls., 1971-76, ptnr., 1977-89; sr. v.p. law and external rels. Supervalu Inc., Mpls., 1991-97, exec. v.p., 1997—; vis. prof. law Cornell U. Law Sch., Ithaca, N.Y., fall 1982; bd. dirs. ATM Med. Inc.. Mem. adv. coun. on arts and letters U. Notre Dame, 1993—; mem. adv. Coun. Cornell U. Law Sch., 1983-92, chmn. coun. 1986-90. Mem. Minn. Bar Assn. (chmn. bus. law sect., 1986), Greater Mpls. C. of C. (bd. dirs. 1988-90), Minikahda Club (Mpls.), Spring Hill Golf Club. Roman Catholic. Home: 71 Otis Ln Saint Paul MN 55104-5645

BOEHNER, LEONARD BRUCE, lawyer; b. Council Bluffs, Iowa, Apr. 19, 1930; s. Bruce and Flora (Kruse) B. AB, Harvard U., 1952, JD, 1955. Bar: N.Y. 1956, U.S. Dist. Ct. (so. dist.) N.Y. 1963, U.S. Ct. Appeals (2d cir.) 1963, U.S. Supreme Ct. 1964. Assoc. Dewey, Ballantine, Bushby, Palmer & Wood, N.Y.C., 1959-66; ptnr. Clare & Whitehead, N.Y.C., 1966-73, Morris & McVeigh LLP, N.Y.C. 1973—. Served to lt. USN, 1955-59. Mem. Assn. Bar City N.Y. Club: Union (N.Y.C.). General corporate, Estate planning, Securities. Office: Morris & McVeigh 767 3rd Ave New York NY 10017-2023

BOES, LAWRENCE WILLIAM, lawyer; b. Bklyn., Aug. 3, 1935; s. Lawrence and Elizabeth (Schaefer) B.; m. Joan Mary Elward, Oct. 2, 1965; children: Lawrence, Siobhan, Thomas. AB, Columbia Coll., 1961; JD, Columbia U., 1964. Bar: N.Y. 1965, U.S. Dist. Ct. (ea. dist.) N.Y. 1968, U.S. Dist. Ct. (so. dist.) N.Y. 1968, U.S. Ct. Appeals (2d cir.) 1971, U.S. Ct. Appeals (8th cir.) 1974, U.S. Supreme Ct. 1974, U.S. Ct. Appeals (9th cir.) 1982, U.S. Ct. Appeals (3d cir.) 1988. Law clk. to judge U.S. Ct. Appeals (2d cir.), 1964-65; assoc. Reavis & McGrath, N.Y.C., 1965-70, ptnr., 1970-88, Fulbright & Jaworski L.L.P., N.Y.C., 1989-00, ret. ptnr., 2001—; atty. Law Office of Lawrence W. Boes, 2001—. Revs. editor Columbia Law Rev., 1963-64. Mem. Village of Westbury Code Rev. Commn., N.Y., 1983—, chmn., 1991—. Cpl. U.S. Army, 1958-60. Pulitzer scholar N.Y.C. Bd. Edn., 1954; nat. scholar Columbia U., 1962. Mem. ABA, N.Y. State Bar Assn. (com. on stds. of atty. conduct 1999—), Bar Assn. Nassau County (chair 1998-00, profl. ethics com.), Univ. Glee Club N.Y.C. (sec. 1998—). Avocations: gardening, baseball, glee club singing. Alternative dispute resolution, Appellate, Municipal (including bonds). Office: Law Office Lawrence W Boes 256 Asbury Ave E Westbury NY 11590-2023 Fax: 516-997-2996. E-mail: larrywboes@aol.com

BOETTGER, ROY DENNIS, barrister, solicitor; b. Nelson, B.C., Can., Sept. 5, 1948; s. Robert Harold and Jean Velora (Lewis) B.; m. Lynn Irene Carroll, June 2, 1973; children: Kristin Jennie, Jill Rebecca. BA, U. Calgary, 1970; LLB, U. Alta., 1973. Bar: Alta. Student-at-law Atkinson McMahon, Calgary, Alta., 1973-74, assoc., 1974-77, ptnr., 1977—. Bioethics com. Rockyview Hosp., 1987-97. Dir., vice-chmn. The Calgary Found. Fellow Am. Coll. Trust and Estate Counsel; mem. Soc. Trust and Estate Practitioners, Calgary Bar Assn., Can. Bar Assn. (coun. mem. Alta. br. nat. exec. wills and trust sect. Ottawa br. 1979-85), Law Soc. Alta., Estate Planning Coun. Calgary (exec. mem. 1983-89), Rotary. Estate planning, Probate. Office: Field Atkinson Perraton 1900 350 7th Ave SW Calgary AB Canada T2P 3N9 E-mail: rboettger@fieldlaw.com

BOGAARD, WILLIAM JOSEPH, mayor, lawyer, educator; b. Sioux City, Iowa, Jan. 18, 1938; s. Joseph and Irene Marie (Hensing) B.; m. Claire Marie Whalen, Jan. 28, 1961; children: Michele, Jeannine, Joseph, Matthew. BS, Loyola Marymount U., L.A., 1959; JD with honors, U. Mich., 1965. Bar: Calif. 1966, U.S. Dist. Ct. (ctrl. dist.) Calif. 1966. Ptnr. Agnew, Miller & Carlson, L.A., 1970-82; exec. v.p., gen. counsel 1st Interstate Bancorp, 1982-96; vis. prof. securities regulation and banking Mich. Law Sch., Ann Arbor, 1996-97; lectr. securities regulation and corps. U. So. Calif. Law Sch., L.A., 1997—; mayor Pasadena, Calif., 1999—. Mem. Calif. Commn. on Jud. Nominees Evaluation, 1997-99. Mem. city coun., mayor City of Pasadena, Calif., 1978-86. Capt. USAF, 1959-62. Mem. Calif. State Bar, Los Angeles County Bar Assn. (Corp. Counsel of Yr. award 1988). Avocations: jogging, French and Spanish languages, hiking. Office: Pasadena City Hall 100 N Garfield Ave Pasadena CA 91109 E-mail: bbogaard@ci.pasadena.ca.us

BOGART, WILLIAM HARRY, lawyer; b. Sayre, Pa., Mar. 5, 1931; s. Harry M. and Luella C. Bogart; m. Karin Rudolph, Dec. 12, 1962 (div. Dec. 1987); children: Barbara, Silke. AB, Duke U., 1953; AAA, The Hague Acad. Internat. Law, 1962; JD, Syracuse U., 1963. Bar: N.Y. 1964. Mem. Ali, Gerber, Parr & Bogart, Syracuse, N.Y., 1966-67, Bogart & Andrews, Syracuse, 1967-77, Bogart & Assocs., P.C., Syracuse, 1977—. Cons. in field to various govts, fin. instns., ednl. instns.; lectr. in field; active with Acad. Scis. and Russian Govt. drawing comml., ins. and banking laws. Contbr. articles to profl. jours.; drafted civil rights laws for Czechoslovak constn. Mem. missionary com. Presbyn. Ch., 1974-77. With USMC, 1951-52. Mem. ABA, Am. Arbitration Assn., N.Y. State Bar Assn., N.Y. State Trial Lawyers Assn., Onandaga County Bar Assn., Assn. Attenders and Alumni, Lawyers Intergroups, World Ct., Assn. Atty. and Advocates, UN Assn., Witte Soc., Univ. Club, Army and Navy Club, The Hague Club, Masons (32d degree). Democrat. Contracts commercial, Private international, Personal injury. Home: 110 E Lake Rd Skaneateles NY 13152-9110 Office: 1600 State Tower Bldg 109 S Warren St Syracuse NY 13202-1798 E-mail: bogart@dreamscape.com

BOGDEN, DANIEL G. prosecutor; Grad., Ashland U.; JD, U. Toledo. Dep. dist. atty. Washoe County, 1987—90; asst. U.S. atty. Dist. Nev. U.S. Dept. Justice, 1990—2001, U.S. atty., 2001—. Office: 333 Las Vegas Blvd S Ste 5000 Las Vegas NV 89101*

BOGEN, ANDREW E. lawyer; b. L.A., Aug. 23, 1941; s. David and Edith B.; m. Deborah Bogen, Oct. 10, 1970; children: Elizabeth, Michael. BA, Pomona Coll., Claremont, Calif., 1963; LLB, Harvard U., 1966. Bar: Calif. 1966. Assoc. Gibson, Dunn & Crutcher, L.A., 1966-73, ptnr., 1973—. Trustee Exceptional Children's Found., L.A., 1976-89, Weingart Found., 1999—; bd. dirs. St. Anne's Maternity Home, 1990—. Securities. Office: Gibson Dunn & Crutcher 333 S Grand Ave Ste 4400 Los Angeles CA 90071-3197

BOGEN, DAVID SKILLEN, law educator; b. L.A., Aug. 24, 1941; s. Emil and Jane (Skillen) B.; m. Patricia Yolande Ciricillo, July6 8, 1940; children: Robert, Joshua, Jocelyn. BA, Harvard U., 1962, LLB, 1965; LLM, NYU, 1967. Bar: Mass. 1965, N.Y. 1967. Law clk. Mass. Supreme Jud. Ct., Boston, 1965-66; assoc. Debevoise, Plimpton, N.Y.C., 1967-69; asst. prof. Md. Law Sch., Balt., 1969-71, assoc. prof., 1971-74, prof. law, 1974—, assoc. dean, 1992-94, 97-99. Author: Bulwark of Liberty, 1984. Home: 4742 Rams Horn Row Ellicott City MD 21042-5979 Office: U Md Law Sch 500 W Baltimore St Baltimore MD 21201-1701

BOGENSCHUTZ, J. DAVID, lawyer; b. Covington, Ky., May 15, 1944; s. John Francis and Virginia Margaret (Dugan) B.; m. Mary H. McCleary, Oct. 24, 1981; children: Kathleen, Emily. BA, Miami U., Oxford, Ohio, 1966; JD, U. Cin., 1969. Bar: Ohio 1969, U.S. Dist. Ct. (so. dist.) Ohio 1970, U.S. Ct. Appeals (6th cir.) 1971, Fla. 1971, U.S. Dist. Ct. (so. dist.) Fla. 1972, U.S. Ct. Appeals (5th cir.) 1980, U.S. Dist. Ct. (mid. dist.) Fla. 1981, U.S. Ct. Appeals (4th and 11th cirs.) 1981, U.S. Dist. Ct. (ea. dist.) Wis. 1989, U.S. Ct. Appeals (3d cir.) 1999. Instr. Criminal Justice Inst. Nova U., 1977; instr. Broward County Criminal Justice Inst., 1972; asst. solicitor County of Broward, 1971, chief asst. state's atty., 1974-77; ptnr. Bogenschutz & Dutko, P.A., Ft. Lauderdale, Fla. Mem. Gov.'s Com. on Criminal Justice Standards and Goals, 1975-76; mem. bench bar liaison com. U.S. Dist. Ct. (so. dist.) Fla., 1985—. Mem. ATLA, NACDL, Broward County Bar Assn. (criminal law sect. chmn. 1980-81, exec. com. 1981-86, sec., treas. 1985-86), Ohio Bar Assn., Fla. Bar Assn. (criminal law sect., grievance com. 17th jud. cir. 1982-84), Fed. Bar Assn., Greene County Bar Assn., Fla. Pros. Atty.'s Assn., Nat. Dist. Atty.'s Assn. Democrat. Roman Catholic. Appellate, Criminal. Office: Bogenschutz & Dutko PA Colonial Bank Bldg 600 S Andrews Ave Ste 500 Fort Lauderdale FL 33301-2851

BOGGIO, MIRIAM ALTAGRACIA, lawyer; b. N.Y.C., July 28, 1952; d. Marco Antonio and Estella (Tejeda) B.; children: Andrew P. Boggio-Dandry, Edward M. Boggio-Dandry, Gregory A. Boggio-Dandry. BA in Polit. Sci. with honors, CUNY, 1973; JD, St. Johns U., 1976; AA in Fashion Design, Fashion Inst. Tech., 1984. Bar: N.Y. 1977, Fla. 1977, U.S. Dist. Ct. (ea. and so. dists.) N.Y. 1978, U.S. Tax Ct. 1982, U.S. Supreme Ct. 1982. Assoc. Schwartzman, Weinstock, Garelik & Mann PC, N.Y.C., 1977-84; counsel N.Y. Assembly Judiciary Com., Albany, 1977-84; dep. supt. N.Y. State Ins. Dept., N.Y.C., 1984-97; counsel govt. affairs, asst. corp. sec. Group Health Inc., 1997-99; prin. ct. atty. N.Y. State Supreme Ct., 2000—. SEEK scholar, 1973; recipient SEEK honors, 1973. Mem. Fla. Bar Assn., NY Co. Lawyers' Bar Assn., Phi Beta Kappa. Democrat. Roman Catholic. Office: NY State Supreme Ct 60 Centre St New York NY 10007

BOGGS, BETH CLEMENS, lawyer; b. Dubuque, Iowa, July 28, 1967; d. Theodore Alan and Mary Ann (Fleckenstein) Clemens; m. T. Darin Boggs, Mar. 9, 1991. BA, Govs. State U., 1987; JD, So. Ill. U., 1991. Bar: Ill. 1991, Mo. 1992, U.S. Dist. Ct. (so. dist.) Ill. 1991, U.S. Dist. Ct. (ea. dist.) Mo. 1992, U.S. Dist. Ct. (cen. dist.) Ill. 1997. Clk. R. Courtney Hughes & Assocs., Carbondale, Ill., 1990-91; lawyer Sandberg Phoenix & von Gontard, St. Louis, 1991-93; assoc. LaTourette, Schlueter & Byrne, 1993-95; mng. ptnr. Landau, Omahana & Kopka, P.C., 1995-99; mng. and founding ptnr. Boggs, Backer & Bates, LLC, 1999—. Adj. faculty Webster U., 1995—. Editor student articles So. Ill. U. Law Jour., 1991; contbr. articles to profl. jours. Mem. Young Lawyers divsn. of ABA (vice chair corp. counsel com. 1991-92, editor Corp. Counsel Newsletter 1991-92), Bus. Women St. Louis, Women Lawyers Assn., Lawyers Assn. St. Louis, Def. Rsch. inst., Mo. Orgn. Def. Lawyers. Avocations: tennis, softball, golf. General civil litigation, General corporate, Insurance. Office: BBB 7912 Bonhomme Ave Ste 400 Saint Louis MO 63105-3512 E-mail: bbblawyers@aol.com

BOGGS, DANNY JULIAN, federal judge; b. Havana, Cuba, Oct. 23, 1944; s. Robert Lilburn and Yolanda (Pereda) B.; m. Judith Susan Solow, Dec. 23, 1967; children: Rebecca, David, Jonathan. A.B., Harvard Coll., Cambridge, Mass., 1965; J.D., U. Chgo., 1968; LLD (hon.), U. Detroit Mercy, 1994. Dep. commr. Ky. Dept. Econ. Security, 1969-70; legal counsel, adminstrv. asst. Gov. Ky., 1970-71; legis. counsel to Rep. legislators Ky. Gen. Assembly, 1972; asst. to solicitor gen. U.S. Dept. Justice, Washington, 1973-75; asst. to chmn. FPC, 1975-77; dep. minority counsel Senate Energy Com., 1977-79; of counsel Bushnell, Gage, et al., 1979-80; spl. asst. to Pres. White House, 1981-83; dep. sec. U.S. Dept. Energy, 1983-86; judge U.S. Ct. Appeals (6th cir.), Cin., 1986—. Mem. adv. com. on appellate rules Jud. Conf. U.S., 1991-94, com. on automation and tech., 1994-2000. Mem. vis. com. U. Chgo. Law Sch., 1984-87, 99—; del. Republican Nat. Conv., 1972; staff dir. energy subcom. Rep. Platform Com., 1980; trustee Lexington Sch., 1999—. Mem. ABA (chair-elect, appellate judges conf. 2000-2001, sec. 1997-99), Ky. Bar Assn., Mont Pelerin Soc., Phila. Soc., Order of Coif, Phi Delta Phi Office: US Ct Appeals US Courthouse 601 W Broadway Ste 220 Louisville KY 40202-2227

BOGUS, CARL THOMAS, law educator; b. Fall River, Mass., May 14, 1948; s. Isidore E. and Carolyn (Dashoff) B.; m. Dale Shepard, Sept. 5, 1970 (div. 1987); children: Elizabeth Carol, Ian Troy; m. Cynthia J. Giles, Nov. 5, 1988; 1 child, Zoe Churchill. AB, Syracuse U., 1970, JD, 1972. Bar: Pa. 1973, U.S. Dist. Ct. (ea. dist.) Pa. 1973, U.S. Dist. Ct. Appeals (3d cir.) 1976, U.S. Supreme Ct. 1977. Assoc. Steinberg, Greenstein, Gorelick & Price, Phila., 1973-79, ptnr., 1979-83; assoc. Mesirov, Gelman, Jaffe, Cramer & Jamieson, 1983-84, ptnr., 1985-91; assoc. prof. Roger Williams U. Sch. Law, Camden, 1996—. Vis. prof. Rutgers U. Sch. Law, Camden, 1992-96; mem. bd. Visitors Coll. Law, Syracuse U., N.Y., 1976—; mem. nat. adv. panel Violence Policy Ctr., 1993—. Author: Why Lawyers Are Good for America: Disciplined Democracy, Big Business and the Common Law, 2001; editor: The Second Amendment in Law and History, 2001;contbr. articles to profl. jours. Bd. dirs. Handgun Control, Inc., 1987-89, bd. govs., 1992-93; bd. dirs. Ctr. to Prevent Handgun Violence, 1989-92, Lawyers Alliance for Nuclear Arms Control, 1987-89; mem. state governing bd. Common Cause R.I., 1999—. Mem. ABA (Ross Essay award 1991), Syracuse Law Coll. Assn. (exec. sec. 1979-83, 2d v.p. 1983-85). Democrat. Jewish. Office: Roger William U Sch Law 10 Metacom Ave Bristol RI 02809-5103 E-mail: ctb@rwulaw.rwu.edu

BOGUT, JOHN CARL, JR. lawyer; b. Billings, Mont., July 31, 1961; s. Jack Carl and Joan E. (Gibson) B. BA, Denison U., 1983; JD, Duquesne U., 1986. Bar: Pa. Supreme CT., U.S. Dist. Ct. (we. dist.) Pa., U.S. Ct. Appeals (3d cir.), U.S. Supreme Ct. Law clk. Meyer, Darragh, Buckler, Bebenek & Eck, Pitts., 1985; asst. dist. atty. County of Allegheny, 1986-89; litigation atty. Swensen, Perer & Johnson, 1989—; ptnr. Wayman, Irwin & McAuley, 1996—. Magistrate's Ct. prosecutor Pitts. Dist Atty.'s Office, 1988; cons. Bogut, Inc., Pitts., 1986—. Cons. Civic Light Opera Guild, Pitts., 1986—. Mem. ABA, Pa. Bar Assn., Allegheny County Bar Assn., Pa. Dist. Atty.'s Assn., Pitts. Ski Club, Young Republicans, Alpha Tau Omega. Lutheran. Avocations: skiing, sailing, ice hockey, lacrosse. General civil litigation, Criminal, General practice. Office: Wayman Irvin & McAuley 1624 Frick Bldg Pittsburgh PA 15219

BOGUTZ, JEROME EDWIN, lawyer, educator; b. Bridgeton, N.J., June 7, 1935; s. Charles and Gertrude (Lahn) B.; m. Helene Carole Ross, Nov. 20, 1960; children: Marc Lahn, Tami Lynne BS in Fin., Pa. State U., 1957; JD, Villanova U., 1962. Bar: Pa., U.S. Dist. Ct. (ea. dist.) Pa., U.S. Ct. Appeals (3d cir.), U.S. Supreme Ct. Assoc. Dash & Levy, Phila., 1962-63, Abrahams & Loewenstein, Phila., 1963-64; dep. dir., chief of litigation Community Legal Svcs., 1964-68, dir., 1968-78; emeritus, 1978—; pvt. practice law Phila., 1968-71; ptnr. Bogutz & Mazer, 1971-81, Fox Rothschild O'Brien & Frankel, Phila., 1981-98; judge Pro Tem Phila. Ct. Common Pleas, 1992—; ptnr. Christie, Pabarue, Mortensen & Young, P.C., Phila., 1998—. Adj. clin. prof. law Villanova (Pa.) U., 1969-72, lectr., 1987—, bd. consultors Law Sch., 1983—; pres. Internat. Mobile Machines, Phila., 1980-81, Interdigital Comm., 1980-81, also bd. dirs. ABA-JAD Lawyers Conf., 1987-92, mem. exec. coun., 1986-92, vice chmn., 1987-88, chmn., 1989-90, chmn. nominating com., 1989-90, mem. long range planning com., 1989-90; mem. adv. bd. Pa. Med. Profl. Liability Catastrophe Loss Fund, 2000—; bd. dirs. Jefferson Park Hosp., Phila. Bd. dirs. Am. Friends of Hebrew U., 1988-93, chmn. exec. com., 1991-93, pres., 1993-95, chmn. bd. 1995-98, chair steering com., pres. Pa. Futures Commn. on Justice in the 21st Century, 1993—, chmn. of bd., 1993-97. With USAR, 1956-60. Fellow Am. Bar Found. (life), Pa. Bar Found. (life, pres. 1986-88, bd. dirs. 1983—, lifetime dir. 1991—), Am. Judicature Soc. (life, bd. dirs. 1990—); mem. ABA (ho. of dels. 1980-84, 86-96, credentials and admissions com. 1987-88, nominating com. 1992, 93, chair ABA/JAD bench bar com., vice chmn. lawyer's conf. 1987-89, chair 1988-90, co-chair mid-yr. meeting com. 1987-88, planning com., conf. sect. officers, 1988-90, bd. mem. consortium on legal svcs. and pub. 1987-91, mem. disaster relief task force, bd. dirs., commr., chmn. ABA Commn. on Advt. 1988-91, adv. coun. ABA Commn. Responsibility 1999—), Pa. Bar Assn. (pres. 1985-86, bd. dirs. 1983-90, chair Governance Com., 1996-98), Phila. Bar Found. (pres. 1981), Phila. Bar Assn. (v.p. 1978, pres.-elect 1979, chancellor 1980, sec. 1975-78, trustee 1979—), Pa. Bar Trust (life mem., chmn. 1993-2001, chmn. emeritus 2001—), Pa. House of Dels. (life; chair governance com. 1996-98), Nat. Met. Bar Leaders (founder, pres. 1979-82, pres. emeritus 1983—), Nat. Conf. Bar Pres. (exec. coun. 1981-84), Phila. C. of C. (bd. dirs. 1980-83). Republican. Jewish Avocations: golf, sailing. General civil litigation, Communications, General corporate. Home: 110 S Somerset Ave Ventnor City NJ 08406-2848 Office: Christie Pabarue Mortensen & Young 1880 JFK Blvd Fl 10 Philadelphia PA 19103-7424

BOHANNON, CHARLES TAD, lawyer; b. Dallas, June 25, 1964; s. Charles Spencer and Donna Pauline (Smith) B.; m. Gayle Renee Alston, July 26, 1986. BA, Hendrix Coll., 1986; JD, U. Ark., Little Rock, 1992; LLM, Washington U., St. Louis, 1993. Bar: Ark. 1992, Tex. 1993, U.S. Dist. Ct. (ea. and we. dists.) Ark. 1992, U.S. Dist. Ct. (no. dist.) Tex. 1994, U.S. Ct. Appeals (5th and 8th cirs.) 1994, U.S. Tax Ct. 1994. Staff atty. U.S. Ct. Appeals (8th cir.), St. Louis, 1992-94; assoc. Gill Law Firm, Little Rock, 1994-98, Wright, Lindsey & Jennings, LLP, Little Rock, 1998—. Contbr. articles to profl. jours. Mem. ABA, Ark. Bar Assn., Pulaski County Bar Assn., Nat. Transp. Safety Bd., Bar Assn. State Bar of Tex., Nat. Assn. Bond Lawyers, Aircraft Owners and Pilots Assn. Avocations: soccer (player, referee, coach), flying, fly fishing, home renovation. Aviation, Municipal (including bonds), Taxation, general. Office: Wright Lindsey & Jennings 200 W Capitol Ave Ste 2200 Little Rock AR 72201-3699 E-mail: ctbohannon@wlj.com

BOHANON, LUTHER L. federal judge; b. Ft. Smith, Ark., Aug. 9, 1901; s. William Joseph and Artelia (Campbell) B.; m. Marie Swatek, July 17, 1933; 1 son, Richard L. LLB, U. Okla., 1927; LLD (hon.), Oklahoma City U., 1991. Bar: Okla. 1927, U.S. Supreme Ct. 1937. Gen. practice law, Seminole, Okla. and Oklahoma City, 1927-61; judge U.S. Dist. Ct. Okla. (no., ea., and we. dists.), 1961-74, sr. judge, 1974—. Mem. platform com. Democratic Nat. Conv., 1940. Served to maj. USAAF, 1942-45. Recipient citations and awards including citation from Okla. Senate and Ho. of Reps., 1979, Okla. County Bar Assn. and Jour. Record award, 1987, Humanitarian award NCCJ, 1991; Luther Bohanon Am. Inn of Ct. named in his honor Am. Inn of Ct. XXIII/U. Okla., 1991. Mem. U.S. Dist. Judges Assn. (10th cir.), Fed. Judges Assn., Okla. Bar Assn., Oklahoma County Bar Assn., Oklahoma City C. of C., Sigma Nu, Phi Alpha Delta. Methodist. Clubs: Mason (Shriner, 32 deg.), K.T, Jester, Kiwanis, Com.of 100, Men's Dinner Club. Home: 1617 Bedford Dr Oklahoma City OK 73116-5406 Office: US Dist Ct PO Box 1514 200 NW 4th St Ste 2001 Oklahoma City OK 73102-3028

BOHM, JOEL LAWRENCE, lawyer, securities industry executive; b. N.Y.C., Dec. 27, 1942; s. Ernest Jonas and Laura (Ullman) B.; m. Karen Rea Brandt, July 3, 1966; children: Michelle Elizabeth, Lori Allison. BA in Polit. Sci., Bklyn. Coll., 1965; JD, Bklyn. Law Sch., 1970. Bar: N.Y. 1971, U.S. Ct. Appeals (2d cir.) 1972, U.S. Dist. Ct. (so. and ea. dists.) N.Y. 1975, U.S. Supreme Ct. 1976. Staff atty. Mohawk Data Scis. Corp., N.Y.C., 1971-72; asst. gen. counsel Gen. Cable Corp., N.Y.C., 1972-73; v.p., gen. counsel Securities Industry Automation Corp., N.Y.C., 1973— ; referee, arbitrator small claims N.Y.C. Civil Ct., 1984—, arbitrator Better Bus. Bur. of Greater N.Y., Inc., 1986-89. Trustee Temple Shaari Emeth, Englishtown, N.J., 1981; mem. Manalapan Twp. Juvenile Conf. Com., 1987—. With USN, 1961. Mem. ABA, Assn. Arbitrators, N.Y. State Bar Assn., N.Y. County Lawyers Assn., Assn. of Bar of City of N.Y. Contracts commercial, Computer, General corporate. Office: Securities Industry Automation Corp 2 Metrotech Ctr Brooklyn NY 11201-3838

BOHN, CYNTHIA JANE, lawyer; b. Portsmouth, Ohio, June 3, 1963; d. Jerry Ray and Joy (Roberts) B. BS in Arts and Scis., Vanderbilt U., 1985; JD, Nashville Sch. Law, 1994. Bar: Tenn. 1994. Owner Laurells Raw Bar, Nashville, 1993; assoc. Law Office of Charlotte Fleming, 1994-97; pvt. practice, 1997—. Campaign mgr. Com. to Elect Andrei Lee, Nashville, 1997-98. Mem. TLAW, TTLA, Tenn. Bar Assn., Nashville Bar Assn., Lawyers Assn. for Women. Avocations: gardening, auctions, antiques. Office: 501 Union St Ste 502 Nashville TN 37219-1777

BOHN, ROBERT HERBERT, lawyer; b. Austin, Tex., Sept. 2, 1935; s. Herbert and Alice B.; m. Gay P. Maloy, June 4, 1957; children: Rebecca Shoemaker, Katherine Bernat, Robert H., Jr.. BBA, U. Tex., 1957, LLB, 1963. Bar: Tex. 1963, Calif. 1965. Ptnr. Boccardo Law Firm, San Jose, Calif., 1965-87, Alexander & Bohn, San Jose, 1987-91; Bohn, Bennion & Niland, 1992-97; Bohn & Bohn, 1998—. Spkr. Calif. Continuing Edn. of Bar; judge pro tem Superior Ct. of Calif., San Jose, 1975-96. Mem. ATLA, World Jurist Assn., Consumer Attys. Calif., Am. Bd. Trial Advocates, Santa Clara County Bar Assn., Calif. State Bar Assn., Santa Clara County Trial Lawyers Assn. (pres. 1999, Trial Lawyer of Yr. 2000), Trial Lawyers Pub. Justice, Roscoe Pound Found., Million Dollar Advocates Forum, Lawyers Arbitration Mediation Svc. (pres.), Commonwealth Club Calif., Silicon Valley Capital Club, Exec. Golfers (dir. gen.), Texas Cowboys Assn., Phi Gamma Delta. Alternative dispute resolution, General civil litigation, Personal injury. Home: 14124 Pike Rd Saratoga CA 95070-5380 Office: 152 N 3rd St Ste 200 San Jose CA 95112-5515 E-mail: bbohn@bohnlaw.com

BOHNEN, MICHAEL J. lawyer; b. Buffalo, Mar. 9, 1947; s. Joyce B. Oppenheim, June 19, 1969; children: Sharon, Deborah. BA, Harvard U., 1968, JD, 1972. Bar: Mass. 1972. Assoc. Nutter, McClennen & Fish, LLP, Boston, 1972-80, ptnr., 1980—. Lectr. Boston U. Law Sch., 1981-85. Co-author: Mass. Corporate Forms, 1990. Pres. Solomon Schechter Day Sch., Newton, 1980-82; pres. Jewish Cmty. Rels. Coun., Boston, 1991-93; chmn. Combined Jewish Philanthropies, 1993-95, New Jewish H.S., 1995—; vice chmn. Jewish Coun. for Pub. Affairs, 1995-99; trustee United Jewish Cmtys., 1999—. Mem. Boston Bar Assn. (chmn. corp. law com. 1997-99). General corporate, Mergers and acquisitions, Securities. Home: 60 Nathan Rd Newton MA 02459-1105 Office: Nutter McClennen & Fish LLP One International Pl Boston MA 02110

BOIES, WILBER H. lawyer; b. Bloomington, Ill., Mar. 15, 1944; s. W. H. and Martha Jane (Hutchison) B.; m. Victoria Joan Steinitz, Sept. 17, 1966; children: Andrew Charles, Carolyn Ursula. AB, Brown U., 1965; JD, U. Chgo., 1968. Bar: Ill. 1968, U.S. Dist. Ct. (no. dist.) Ill. 1968, U.S. Dist. Ct. (ea. dist.) Wis. 1973, U.S. Ct. Appeals (7th cir.) 1974, U.S. Ct. Appeals (5th cir.) 1975, U.S. Ct. Appeals (3d cir.) 1977, U.S. Supreme Ct. 1978, U.S. Ct. Appeals (8th cir.) 1994, U.S. Ct. Appeals (9th cir.) 1995. Assoc. Altheimer & Gray, Chgo., 1968-71; ptnr. McDermott, Will & Emery, 1971—. Contbr. articles to profl. jours. Active CPR Inst. for Dispute Resolution. Mem. ABA, Bar Assn. 7th Fed. Cir., Chgo. Bar Assn. (chmn. class litigation com. 1991-92), Chgo. Coun. Lawyers, Lawyers Club Chgo. (dir. 1996—), Met. Club, Chgo. Bar Found. Alternative dispute resolution, Federal civil litigation, State civil litigation. Office: McDermott Will & Emery 227 W Monroe St Ste 3100 Chicago IL 60606-5096 E-mail: bboies@mwe.com

BOK, DEREK, law educator, former university president; b. Bryn Mawr, Pa., Mar. 22, 1930; s. Curtis and Margaret (Plummer) B.; m. Sissela Ann Myrdal, May 7, 1955; children: Hilary Margaret, Victoria, Tomas Jeremy. B.A., Stanford U., 1951; J.D., Harvard U., 1954; M.A., George Washington U., 1958. Fulbright scholar, Paris, 1954-55; faculty Harvard U. Law Sch., Cambridge, Mass., 1958—, prof., 1961—, dean, 1968-71; pres. Harvard U., 1971-91, 300th anniversary univ. prof., 1991—. Editor: (with Archibald Cox) Cases and Materials on Labor Law, 1962; author: (with John T.

Dunlop) Labor and the American Community, 1970, Beyond the Ivory Tower: Social Responsibilities of the Modern University, 1982, Higher Learning, 1986, Universities and the Future of America, 1990, The Cost of Talent, 1993, (with William G. Bowen) The Shape of the River, 1998, The Trouble with Government, 2001; contbr.: In the Public Interest, 1980, The State of the Nation, 1997. Bd. dirs., nat. chmn. Common Cause, 1999—; chmn. bd. overseers Cts. Inst. Music, 1997—. Fellow Ctr. for Advanced Studies in the Behavioral Scis., 1991-92. Fellow Am. Acad. Arts and Scis., mem. Nat. Acad. Edn., Phi Beta Kappa. Office: Harvard U JFK Sch of Govt Cambridge MA 02138

BOLDEN, MELVIN WILBERFORCE, JR. lawyer; b. N.Y.C., Sept. 11, 1941; s. Melvin Wilberforce and Eloise (Thomas) B.; children: Danielle Lillian, Melvin Wilberforce, III. BA, Morgan State Coll., Balt., 1964; JD, Howard U., 1970. Bar: D.C. 1971, U.S. Dist. Ct. D.C. 1976, U.S. Ct. Appeals (D.C. cir.) 1976, U.S. Supreme Ct. 1987. Asst. gen. counsel NAACP, N.Y.C., 1970-72; atty. Commn. Human Rights City of N.Y., 1973-76; mng. atty. Neighborhood Legal Svcs., Washington, 1977-79; asst. chief Office of Corp. Counsel, Washington, 1980-82, chief, 1982—; mem. mental health rules com. D.C. Superior Ct., jud. conf. of D.C., 1982-91. Co-author The Search for Military Justice, Illinois Products Liability. Mem. ABA, Washington Bar Assn., D.C. Bar Assn., NAACP, Alpha Phi Alpha, Sigma Delta Tau. Democrat. Mem. African Methodist Episcopal Ch. Office: Office of Corp Counsel DC 451 Indiana Ave NW Rm 300 Washington DC 20001-2747

BOLDT, MICHAEL HERBERT, lawyer; b. Detroit, Oct. 11, 1950; s. Herbert M. and Mary Therese (Fitzgerald) B.; m. Margaret E. Clarke, May 25, 1974; children: Timothy (dec.), Matthew. Student, U. Detroit, 1968-70; BA, Wayne State U., 1972; JD, U. Mich., 1975. Bar: Ind. 1975, U.S. Dist. Ct. (so. dist.) Ind. 1975, U.S. Ct. Appeals (7th cir.) 1979, U.S. Supreme Ct. 1980, U.S. Ct. Appeals (D.C. cir.) 1983. Assoc. Ice Miller, Indpls., 1975-81, ptnr., 1982—. Bd. dirs. Star Alliance, Inc. Contbr. articles to profl. jours. Mem. Ind. State Bar Assn., Indpls. Bar Assn., Highland Golf and Country Club, Skyline Club. Labor, Pension, profit-sharing, and employee benefits. Office: Ice Miller Box 82001 1 American Sq Indianapolis IN 46282-0002 E-mail: boldt@icemiller.com

BOLES, DAVID LAVELLE, lawyer; b. Tulia, Tex., May 22, 1937; s. Jerry Hoytt and Irma Ruth (Walker) B.; m. Kerstin Gunilla Stenrudh, May 25, 1959 (div. 1984); children— David LaVelle Jr., Kerstin Regina Boles Davenport, William Gail-Holger. Student North Tex. U., 1955-57; B.S., Trinity U., 1959; J.D., U. Tex., 1963. Bar: Tex. 1963. Asst. atty. gen. Tex., Austin, 1963-67; sole practice, Denton, Tex., 1967-69; house counsel, corp. officer Sam P. Wallace Co., Inc., Dallas, 1969-73, adminstrv. mgr. contracts, labor, indsl. rels., ins., 1973-85, house counsel, corp. officer MMR/Wallace Group, Inc. and subs., 1985-90; pvt. practice, 1990—. Deacon Presbyn. Ch., Austin, Denton, 1963-74. Mem. Tex. Bar Assn., Denton County Bar Assn., Trinity Alumni Assn. (pres. 1965), Denton C. of C. Administrative and regulatory, Construction, Labor. Home and Office: HC 71 Box 100A Taos NM 87571-9501

BOLLAND, PIETER HEYME, lawyer; b. Leidschendam, Zuid-Holland, The Netherlands, Sept. 9, 1961; JD, Leyden (The Netherlands) U., 1984; LLM, Cornell U., 1988. Bar: civil law notary 1989. Assoc. Debrauw/Linklaters, Rotterdam, The Netherlands, 1984-97; mgmt. trainee Ing Bank NV, U.S. and The Netherlands, 1988-90; v.p. sales CNR Movies, Curaçao, 1990-91; acct. mgr. J&H, N.Y.C., 1991-93; sr. assoc. Loeff Clares Verbeke, Rotterdam, 1994; ptnr. Andersen Legal, 1995—. Lectr. Amsterdam U., 2001—. General corporate, Finance, Mergers and acquisitions. Office: Wouters Advocaten & Notaris Oostmaaslaan 71 3063 AN Rotterdam The Netherlands Fax: 010-880 1717. E-mail: pieterh.bolland@nl.andersenlegal.com

BOLLES, DONALD SCOTT, lawyer; b. Buffalo, Dec. 17, 1936; s. Theodore H. and Marie (Heth) B.; m. Jean Waytulonis Oct. 12, 1963 (dec. May 1983); children: Scott, Matthew; m. Geraldine Novinger, Feb. 14, 1988. BA, Alfred U., 1960; JD cum laude, U. San Diego, 1970. Bar: Calif. 1971, U.S. Dist. Ct. (so. and no. dists.) Calif. 1971. Ptnr. Hutton, Foley, Anderson & Bolles, Inc., King City, Calif., 1971-95, Anderson & Bolles, Inc., King City, 1995-99. Editor lead articles San Diego Law Rev., 1969-70. Trustee Mee Meml. Hosp., King City, 1974-78, chmn., 1978-80; chmn. King City Recreation Commn., 1974-77; candidate mcpl. ct. judge primary and gen. election, Monterey County, Calif., 1986; sec., founding mem. bd. dirs. Project Teen Ctr. Inc., 1986-90; bd. dirs. Sun St. Ctrs., 1991-99, Monterey Coll. Law, 1995—, pres., 2000-2001; pres. Corral de Tierra Homeowners Assn., 1996-98. Served to capt. U.S. Army, 1961-67, Vietnam. Decorated Combat Infantryman's badge, Army Commendation medal. Mem. Monterey County Bar Assn. (exec. com. 1985-86). Republican. Club: Toastmasters (King City) (pres. 1972-74). Lodge: Lions (pres. 1975-76, sec. 1984-86 King City club). Avocations: application of computer science to practice of law, tennis, golf, bridge, choir. State civil litigation, Family and matrimonial, General practice. Home: 23799-18 Monterey Salinas Hwy Salinas CA 93908-9328 E-mail: dsbolles@aol.com

BOLLINGER, LEE CARROLL, academic administrator, law educator; b. 1946; BS, U. Oreg., 1968; JD, Columbia U., 1971. Law clk. to Judge Wilfred Feinberg U.S. Ct. Appeals (2nd cir.), 1971-72; law clk. to Chief Justice Warren Burger U.S. Supreme Ct., 1972-73; asst. prof. law U. Mich., 1973-76, assoc. prof., 1976-78, prof., 1978-94, dean, 1987-94, pres., prof. law, 1997—; provost, prof. govt. Dartmouth Coll., 1994-96. Rsch. assoc. Clare Hall, Cambridge U., 1983. Author: (with Jackson) Contract Law in Modern Society, 1980; The Tolerant Soc., 1986, Images of a Free Press, 1991. Bd. dirs. Gerald R. Ford Found., Royal Shakespeare Co. Am. Rockefeller Humanities fellow. Fellow Am. Acad. Arts and Scis. Office: U Michigan 2074 Fleming Adminstrn Bldg Ann Arbor MI 48109-1340

BOLLMANN, HANS FELIX, lawyer; b. Zurich, Switzerland, Oct. 15, 1943; s. Hans and Berta (Walder) B.; m. L'Margrit Wenner, May 21, 1970; children: Jon, Fanny. Lic. iur., U. Zurich, 1972. Ct. clk. Lower Ct., Meilen, 1968; assoc. firm Winthrop, Stimson, Putnam & Roberts, N.Y.C., 1972-73, Pestalozzi & Gmuer, Zurich, 1974-75, ptnr., 1976—. Dir. Swiss subs of various U.S. firms. Author: On Joint Ventures, 1970; contbr. articles to profl. jours. Mem. City Appropriation com. Mem. Zurich Bar, Liberal Radical, Savoy (bd. dirs.), Constaffel (former dir.). Home: Schiedhaldenstr 50 CH-8700 Kusnacht Switzerland Office: Pestalozzi & Gmuer CH-8001 Zurich Switzerland E-mail: hans.bollmann@pgp.ch

BOLOCOFSKY, DAVID N. lawyer, psychology educator; b. Hartford, Conn., Sept. 29, 1947; s. Samuel and Olga Bolocofsky; m. Debra Stein, June 25, 1994; children: Vincent, Daniel, Charly. BA, Clark U., 1969; MS, Nova U., 1974, PhD, 1975; JD, U. Denver, 1988. Bar: Colo. 1988; cert. sch. psychologist, Colo. Tchr. high sch. Univ. Sch., Ft. Lauderdale, Fla., 1972-73; ednl. coord. Living and Learning Ctr., 1972-75; asst. prof. U. No. Colo., Greeley, 1975-79, assoc. prof., 1979-90, dir. sch. psychology program, 1979-82; assoc. Robert T. Hinds Jr. & Assocs., Littleton, Colo., 1988-93; hearing officer State of Colo., 1991—; pres. David N. Bolocofsky, P.C., Denver, 1993—. Psychol. cons. Clin. Assocs., Englewood, Colo., 1978—. Author: Enhancing Personal Adjustment, 1986, (chpts. in books) Children and Obesity, 1987, Obtaining and Utilizing a Custody Evaluation, 1989; contbr. numerous articles to profl. jours. Mem. Douglas-Elbert Bar Assn., Arapahoe Bar Assn., Colo. Soc. Sch. Psychologists (bd. dirs. 1978-96, treas. 1993-96), Interdisciplinary Commn. on Child Custody (pro bono com. 1988-93), Colo. Bar Assn. (family law sect., sec. juvenile law sect. 1990-92), Colo. Soc. Behavioral Analysis Therapy (treas. 1990-96), Arapmhc (bd. dirs. 1993-2001, bd. pres. 1995-97). Avocations: sailing, golf, skiing. Education and schools, Family and matrimonial, Juvenile. Home: 9848 E Maplewood Cir Englewood CO 80111-5401 Office: 7887 E Belleview Ave Ste 1275 Englewood CO 80111-6094 E-mail: familylawdoc@aol.com

BOLTON, JENNIFER SUZANNE, lawyer; b. Los Gatos, Calif., Aug. 15, 1969; d. Robert Winslow Bolton and Suzanne Perez. BA in Philosophy, U. So. Calif., 1992; JD, Whittier Law Sch, 1997. Day care dir. Saddleback Valley YMCA, Mission Viejo, Calif., 1985-92; law clk. Orange (Calif.) County Pub. Defenders, 1996-97; atty. Nersesian, Carter, Nelson, Bolton, Las Vegas, 1997—. Mem. ABA, Am. Trial Lawyers Assn. General civil litigation, Criminal, Family and matrimonial. Office: Mersesian Carter Nelson Bolton 333 S Third St Ste A Las Vegas NV 89101

BOLTON, JOHN ROBERT, lawyer, government official; b. Balt., Nov. 20, 1948; s. Edward Jackson and Virginia (Godfrey) B.; m. Gretchen Brainerd, Jan. 1986; 1 child, Jennifer Sarah. BA summa cum laude, Yale U., 1970, JD, 1974. Bar: D.C. 1975, U.S. Dist. Ct. D.C. 1975, U.S. Ct. Appeals (D.C. cir.) 1975, U.S. Ct. Appeals (4th cir.) 1977, U.S. Ct. Appeals (3d cir.) 1978, U.S. Supreme Ct. 1978, U.S. Ct. Appeals (5th and 11th cirs.) 1981, U.S. Ct. Appeals (10th cir.) 1983, U.S. Ct. Appeals (1st, 6th, 7th, 8th and 9th cirs.) 1988, U.S. Ct. Appeals (2d cir.) 1989. Assoc. Covington & Burling, Washington, 1974-81, ptnr., 1983-85; legal cons. The White House, 1981; gen. counsel Agy. for Internat. Devel., 1981-82, asst. adminstr., 1982-83; exec. dir. com. on resolutions Rep. Nat. Com., 1983-84; asst. atty. gen. legis. affairs U.S. Dept. Justice, 1985-88, asst. atty. gen. civil div., 1988-89; asst. sec. internat. orgn. affairs bur. U.S. Dept. State, 1989-93; ptnr. Lerner, Reed, Bolton & McManus (and predecessor firms), 1993-99; of counsel Kutak Rock, 1999-2001; under sec. state for arms control and internat. security U.S. Dept. State, Washington, 2001—. Adj. prof. George Mason U. Law Sch., 1994-2001; pres. Nat. Policy Forum, Washington, 1995-96; sr. v.p. Am. Enterprise Inst., Washington, 1997-2001. Contbr. articles to profl. jours. Mem. Phi Beta Kappa, Pi Sigma Alpha. Republican. Lutheran. Office: US Dept State 21st & C Sts NW Washington DC 20520 E-mail: j.bolton@state.gov

BOLTZ, GERALD EDMUND, lawyer; b. Dennison, Ohio, June 1, 1931; s. Harold E. and Margaret Eve (Hecky) B.; m. Janet Ruth Scott, Sept. 19, 1959; children: Gretchen Boltz Fields, Eric Scott, Jill Marie. BA, Ohio No. U., 1953, JD, 1955. Bar: Ohio 1955, U.S. Supreme Ct. 1964, Calif. 1978, U.S. Dist. Ct. (cen. dist.) Calif. 1978. Asst. atty. gen. State of Ohio, 1958; atty. spl. investigations unit SEC, 1959-60, legal asst. to commr., 1960-61, sr. trial and spl. counsel, 1961-66, regional adminstr. Ft. Worth, 1967-71, L.A., 1972-78; ptnr. Fine, Perzik& Friedman, 1979-83, Rogers & Wells, L.A., 1983-92, Bryan Cave, L.A., 1992—. Co-author: Securities Law Techniques. Served with U.S. Army, 1955-57. Mem. ABA, Fed. Bar Assn., L.A. Bar Assn., Ohio Bar Assn., Calif. Bar Assn., Bel Air Bay Club. Republican. Presbyn. (elder). Avocations: sailing, bridge, piano. General corporate. Home: 1105 Centinela Ave Santa Monica CA 90403-2316 Office: Bryan Cave 120 Broadway Ste 300 Santa Monica CA 90401-2386 E-mail: geboltz@bryancave.com

BOMAN, MARC ALLEN, lawyer; b. Cleve., Sept. 4, 1948; s. David S. and Shirley T. (Freier) B.; m. Leah Eilenberg, June 10, 1984; children: Autumn, Heidi, Jane, David. Student, Purdue U., 1966-68; BA, Case Western Res. U., 1971, JD, 1974. Bar: Ohio 1974, Wash. 1978, D.C. 1978, U.S. Dist. Ct. (we. dist.) Wash. 1980, U.S. Ct. Appeals (9th cir.), U.S. Dist. Ct. (ea. dist.) Wash. 1985, U.S. Ct. Appeals (fed. cir.) 1986. Atty.-advisor Office of Gen. Counsel U.S. Gen. Acctg. Office, Washington, 1974-78; dep. prosecuting atty. Office of Prosecuting Atty., King County, Wash., 1978-81; assoc. Perkins Coie, Seattle, 1981-86, ptnr., 1986—. Spl. ind. dep. prosecutor ethics investigation of county execs., 1994; mem. Seattle Ethics and Elections Commn., 1995-98; spkr. in field. Bd. dirs. Perkins Coie Cmty. Svcs. Fellowship, 1987-97, co-chmn., 1994-97; former bd. dirs. Totem coun. Girl Scouts U.S., Seattle Day Ctr. for Adults, Madrona Neighborhood Coun.; trustee Herzl-Ner Tamid Congregation, 1987-98, pres., 1994-96; mem. Leadership Tomorrow, United Way King County-Seattle C. of C., 1987-88; trustee King County Bar Found., 1995-2000, v.p., 1997-98, pres., 1998-99. Recipient Pres.'s award King County Bar Assn., 1999; Mayoral proclamation declaring Marc Boman Day named in honor of contbn. to citizens of Seattle, 1998. Mem. Seattle King Bar Assn. (trustee 1986-89, chmn. divsn. young lawyers 1984-85). General civil litigation, Construction, Government contracts and claims. Office: Perkins Coie 1201 3rd Ave Fl 40 Seattle WA 98101-3029

BONACORSI, MARY CATHERINE, lawyer; b. Henderson, Ky., Apr. 24, 1949; d. Harry E. and Johanna M. (Kelly) Mack; m. Louis F. Bonacorsi, Apr. 23, 1971; children: Anna, Kathryn, Louis. BA in Math., Washington U., St. Louis, 1971; JD, Washington U., 1977. Bar: Mo. 1977, Ill. 1981, U.S. Dist. Ct. (ea. dist.) Mo., U.S. Dist. Ct. (so. dist.) Ill., U.S. Ct. Appeals (8th cir.), U.S. Supreme Ct. 1995. Ptnr. Thompson Coburn, St. Louis, 1977—. Chairperson fed. practice com. eastern dist., St. Louis, 1987—, eight cir. jud. conf. com., St. Louis, 1987—. Mem. ABA, Assn. Trial Lawyers of Am., Mo. Bar Assn., Met. St. Louis Bar Assn., Order of Coif. Federal civil litigation, Labor. Office: Thompson Coburn Firstar Plz Ste 3100 Saint Louis MO 63101 E-mail: mbonacorsi@thompsoncoburn.com

BOND, MARC DOUGLAS, lawyer; b. Spokane, Wash., July 3, 1954; s. Richard Milton and Patricia (Hendrikson) B.; m. Cathy Sue Kasner, July 16, 1977; children: Travis Eliot, Carly Mariah, Katie McKenzie, Juli Sierra. BA in Polit. Sci., Willamette U., 1975, JD cum laude, 1978. Bar: Wash. 1978, Alaska 1979, U.S. Dist. Ct. Alaska 1979, U.S. Ct. Appeals (9th cir.) 1984, U.S. Supreme Ct. 1991. Law clk. to presiding judge Alaska Ct. System, Anchorage, 1978-79; assoc. Delaney, Wiles, Hayes, Reitman & Brubaker, Inc., 1979-83; shareholder Delaney, Wiles, Hayes, Gerety, Ellis & Young, Inc., 1983-97; gen. counsel Mount Roberts Tramway Ltd. Partnership, 1995-98; asst. counsel Union Oil Co. of Calif., 1997—; gen. counsel Alaska Nitrogen Products, LLC, 1998-2001. Co-founder, bd. dirs. Arctic Power!; spl. counsel Alaska Ski Areas Assn., 1992-97. Author: Alaska from Leasing to Production, 2000. Legal advisor Alaska div. Nat. Ski Patrol System Inc., Denver, 1982-89, dir. Alaska div., 1988-90, asst. nat. legal counsel, 1990-91, nat. legal counsel, 1991-97; dir. Sourdough Ski Patrol, Girdwood, Alaska, 1983-86; bd. dirs. ARC, Anchorage, 1983-86, Alaska Health Fair, Inc., 2001—; asst. scoutmaster Boy Scouts Am. Troop 209, 2001—. Mem. Wash. State Bar Assn., Alaska Bar Assn. (co-chair corp. counsel sect.), Federalist Soc., Asia Pacific Lawyers Assn. Republican. Avocations: skiing, hiking, camping, soccer. Contracts commercial, General corporate, Recreation. Office: Union Oil Co of Calif Unocal Alaska 909 W 9th Ave Anchorage AK 99501-3339 E-mail: mbond@unocal.com

BONDOC, ROMMEL, lawyer; b. June 23, 1938; s. Nicholas Rommel and Gladys Sue (Buckner) Bondoc; m. Ariel Guiberson, Aug. 20, 1960 (div. 1963); m. Alberta Linnea Young, Dec. 13, 1967; children: Daphne, Patience, Margaret, Nicholas. AB, Stanford U., 1959, JD, 1963. Bar: Calif. 1964, U.S. Ct. Appeals (9th cir.) 1965, U.S. Supreme Ct. 1969. Assoc. Melvin Belli, San Francisco, 1964—66, Vincent Hallinan, San Francisco, 1966—69; sole practice, 1969—. Mem.: San Francisco Bar Assn. (judiciary com. 1982—85), No. Calif. Criminal Trial Lawyers Assn. (bd. dir. 1972—, pres. 1978—79), Calif. Attys. for Criminal Justice (bd. dir. 1975—80). Democrat. Methodist. Criminal. Home: 509 Canyon Rd Novato CA 94947-4330 Office: 819 Eddy St San Francisco CA 94109-7701

BONEE, JOHN LEON, III, lawyer; b. Hartford, Conn., Dec. 16, 1947; s. John Leon, Jr. and M. Elaine (Sheridan) B. BA, Trinity Coll., Hartford, 1970; JD, Suffolk U., Boston, 1974; postgrad., Hague Acad. Internat. Law, The Netherlands, 1975. Bar: Conn. 1974, U.S. Dist. Ct. Conn. 1974; U.S. Ct. Appeals (2d cir.) 1975, U.S. Supreme Ct. 1979. Assoc. McCook, Kenyon and Bonee, Hartford, 1974-78; ptnr. The Bonee Law Offices, Conn., 1979—. Contbr. articles to profl. jours. Mem. bd. edn. Town West Hartford, 1981-83, corp. counsel, 1983, mem. community planning adv. com., 1984, mem. town coun., 1985-89; bd. dirs. World Affairs Coun., Hartford, 1980-91. Mem. ABA (gen. practice and internat. law sects., mem. ho. dels. 1996—), Conn. Bar Assn. (editor-at-large jour. 1978-84, probate and family law sects., mem. ho. of dels. 1995—, com. on professionalism 2000—), Hartford County Bar Assn. (bd. dirs. 1991-97, treas. 1992-93, sec. 1993-94, pres. elect 1994-95, pres. 1995-96, past pres. 1996-97, co-chair bench/bar leadership conf. com. 1992-93). General civil litigation, General practice, Probate. Office: 1 State St Hartford CT 06103-3100 E-mail: boneelaw@aol.com

BONESIO, WOODROW MICHAEL, lawyer; b. Hereford, Tex., Dec. 27, 1943; s. Harold Andre and Elizabeth (Ireland) B.; m. Michaele Ann Dougherty; children: Elizabeth Eaton, Jo Kristin, William Michael. B.A., Austin Coll., 1966; J.D., U. Houston, 1971. Bar: Tex. 1971, U.S. Dist. Ct. (we., no., so., and ea. dists.) Tex. 1973, U.S. Ct. Appeals (5th cir.) 1973, U.S. Ct. Appeals (11th cir.) 1981. Law clk. to U.S. dist. Judge Western Dist. Tex., San Antonio, 1971-73; ptnr. Akin, Gump, Strauss, Hauer & Feld, Dallas, 1973-92, Kuntz & Bonesio LLP, Dallas, 1992—. Speaker profl. confs. Precinct chmn. Dallas County Dems.; bd. dirs. Grace Presbytery Devel. Bd., 1986—89; ruling elder First Presbyterian Ch., Dallas, 1999—2001. Fellow: Tex. Bar Found.; mem.: ABA, FBA, Am. Arbitration Assn., Assn. Atty. Mediators, Am. Judicature Soc., Dallas Bar Assn., U. Houston Law Alumni Assn. (chpt. pres. 1982), Vocal Majority (bd. dirs., 1990—, pres. 2001), Nat. Assn. Rec. Artists, Austin Coll. Alumni Assn. (bd. dirs. 1983, Disting. Alumni award 2001), Tex. Bar Coll., Dallas Bar Found., Dallas Assn. Def. Counsel, Common Cause Tex., Soc. for Preservation and Encouragement Barber Shop Quartet Singing in Am. (internat. chorus champions 1975, 79, 82, 85, 88, 91, 94, 97, 2001.), Lake Highlands Exch. Club, Order of Barons, Phi Alpha Delta. General civil litigation, Consumer commercial, State and local taxation. Office: Kuntz & Bonesio LLP 1717 Main St Ste 4050 Dallas TX 75201-4639 E-mail: mbonesio@kuntz-bonesio.com

BONESTEEL, MICHAEL JOHN, lawyer; b. L.A., Dec. 22, 1939; s. Henry Theodore Samuel Becker and Kathleen Mansfield (Nolan) B.; children: Damon Becker, Kirsten Kathleen; m. Susan Elizabeth Schaff, June 1, 1980. AB in History, Stanford U., 1961; JD, U. So. Calif., 1966. Bar: Calif. 1967, U.S. Dist. Ct. (ctrl. and so. dists.) Calif, 1967, U.S. Ct. Appeals (9th cir.) 1967, U.S. Dist. Ct. (no. dist.) Calif. 1969, U.S. Dist. Ct. (ea. dist.) Calif. 1983, U.S. Supreme Ct. 1989. Assoc. Haight, Brown & Bonesteel, and predecessors, Santa Monica, Calif., 1967-71, ptnr., 1972—. Fellow Internat. Acad. Trial Lawyers, Am. Coll. Trial Lawyers; mem. ABA, State Bar Calif., Los Angeles County Bar Assn., Def. Rsch. Inst., Assn. So. Calif. Def. Counsel, Am. Soc. Most Venerable Order of Hospitaller St. John of Jerusalem, Hospitaller Order St. Lazarus of Jerusalem, Grand Priory of Am., Bel Air Bay Club, L.A. Country Club. Environmental, Personal injury, Product liability. Office: Haight Brown & BonesteelLLP 6080 Center Drive Suite 800 Los Angeles CA 90045-1574 Fax: 310-215-7300. E-mail: bonesteels@msn.com, bonesteelm@hbblaw.com

BONHAM-YEAMAN, DORIA, law educator; b. L.A., June 10, 1932; d. Carl Herschel and Edna Mae (Jones) Bonham; widowed; children: Carl Q., Doria Valerie-Constance. BA, U. Tenn., 1953, JD, 1957, MA, 1958; EdS in Computer Edn., Barry U., 1984. Instr. bus. law Palm Beach Jr. Coll., Lake Worth, Fla., 1960-69; instr. legal environment Fla. Atlantic U., Boca Raton, 1969-73; lectr. bus. law Fla. Internat. U., North Miami, 1973-83, assoc. prof. bus. law, 1983—. Editor: Anglo-Am. Law Conf., 1980; Developing Global Corporate Strategies, 1981; mem. editl. bd. Attys. Computer Report, 1984-85, Jour. Legal Studies Edn., 1985-97; contbr. articles to profl. jours. Bd. dirs. Palm Beach County Assn. for Deaf Children, 1960-63; mem. Fla. Commn. on Status of Women, Tallahassee, 1969-70; mem. Broward County Dem. Exec. Com., 1982-2000; pres. Dem. Women's Club Broward County, 1981; mem. Marine Coun. of Greater Miami, 1978-94, Svc. award, 1979. Recipient Faculty Devel. award Fla. Internat. U., Miami, 1980; grantee Notre Dame Law Sch., London, summer 1980. Mem. AAUW (pres. Palm Beach county chpt. 1965-66), U.S. Coun. for Internat. Bus., No. Dade C. of C., Acad. Legal Studies in Bus., Alpha Chi Omega (alumnae club pres. 1968-71), Tau Kappa Alpha. Episcopalian. Office: Fla Internat U Coll Bus Adminstrn North Miami FL 33181

BONNER, ROBERT CLEVE, lawyer; b. Wichita, Kans., Jan. 29, 1942; s. Benjamin Joseph and Caroline (Kirkwood) B.; m. Kimiko Tanaka, Oct. 11, 1969; 1 child, Justine M. BA magna cum laude, Md. U., 1963; JD, Georgetown U., 1966. Bar: D.C. 1966, Calif. 1967, Ct. Appeals (4th, 5th, 9th, 10th cirs.), U.S. Supreme Ct. Law clk. to judge U.S. Dist. Ct., L.A., 1966-67; asst. U.S. atty. U.S. Atty's Office (cen. dist.) Calif., 1971-75, U.S. atty., 1984-89; judge U.S. Dist. Ct. (cen. dist.) Calif., 1989-90; ptnr. Kadison, Pfaelzer, et al, Los Angeles, 1975-84; dir. Drug Enforcement Adminstrn., Washington, 1990-93; ptnr. Gibson, Dunn & Crutcher, L.A., 1993—. Chair Calif. Commn. on Jud. Performance, 1997-99. Served to lt. comdr. USN, 1967-70 Fellow Am. Coll. Trial Lawyers, Fed. Bar Assn. (pres. Los Angeles chpt. 1982-83); mem. L.A. C. of C. (bd. dirs. 1999—). Republican. Roman Catholic. Office: Gibson Dunn & Crutcher 333 S Grand Ave Ste 4400 Los Angeles CA 90071-3197

BONNER, WALTER JOSEPH, lawyer; b. N.Y.C., Nov. 18, 1925; s. Walter John and Marie Elizabeth (Guerin) B.; m. Maureen O'Malley; 1 child, Justin R.; children from previous marriage: Kevin P., Keith M., Barbara A., Susan E. A.B. cum laude, Cath. U. Am., 1951; J.D., Georgetown U., 1955. Bar: U.S. Supreme Ct., D.C., Va. Law clk. to judge U.S. Ct. Appeals D.C. Circuit, 1954-55; judge U.S. Dist. Ct., Washington, 1955-56; asst. U.S. dist. atty. for D.C., 1956-60; ptnr. firm Crowell & Moring, LLP, Washington. Adj. prof. Georgetown U. Law Ctr., 1957-58, 67-83. Trustee Lawrence E. Dean Meml. Scholarship Fund, Georgetown U. Med. Ctr. Served with USNR, 1943-85, capt. Res. ret. Fellow Am. Coll. Trial Lawyers; mem. ABA, Fed. Bar Assn., Bar Assn. of D.C., Va. State Bar, Va. Trial Lawyers Assn., Res. Officers Assn., Naval Res. Lawyers Assn., Naval Res. Assn., Phi Delta Phi. Clubs: Officers and Faculty (U.S. Naval Acad.) Federal civil litigation, State civil litigation, Criminal. Office: Crowell & Moring 1001 Pennsylvania Ave NW Washington DC 20004-2595 E-mail: wbonner@cromor.com

BONNEY, HAL JAMES, JR. federal judge; b. Norfolk, Va., Aug. 27, 1929; s. Hal J. and Mary (Shackelford) B.; m. Marie McBee, July 4, 1963 (div. 1979); children: David James, John Wesley. BA, U. Richmond, 1951, MA, 1953; JD, Coll. William and Mary, 1969. Bar: Va. 1969. Instr. Norfolk public schs., 1951-61; supt. Douglas MacArthur Acad., 1961-67; practiced law, 1969-71; law clk. U.S. Dist. Ct., 1969; prof. U. Va., 1964-71, Coll. William and Mary, 1969-71; U.S. bankruptcy judge Norfolk, 1971-95; ret., 1995. Adj. prof. law Regent U. Sch. Law, 1987-97; prodr. Hal Bonney Prodns. Tchr. Wesleymen Bible class Sta. WTAR-AM, 1962-98, tchr. emeritus, 1998; tchr. God News TV Network, 1989—; treas. Wesleymen Found., Inc., Billy Graham Crusades, 1974-76; pres. adv. coun. CBN U., 1986-95; vice-chmn. Va. Meth. Bd. Edn., Inc., 1991-99; bd. visitors Duke Div. Sch., 1991—; bd. dirs. Norfolk Union Mission, 1994—; mng. dir. The Tidewater Winds; mem. City of Norfolk Task Force on Pub. Housing, 1995-96; advisor Film Sch., Regent U., 1996-2000, assoc. prodr. 2000—;

vice chair rules com. Va. United Meth. conf., 1996—; bd. ordained ministry United Meth. Ch., Va. Recipient S.A.R. Good Citizenship medal, Woodmen of the World History medal, U. Richmond Gold medal, George Washington honor medal Freedoms Found., Alli award Cultural Alliance Greater Hampton Rds., 1998; Judge Hal Bonney Day named in honor by City of Norfolk, Jan. 27, 1998. Mem. Nat. Conf. Bankruptcy Judges (pres. 1983, chmn. editl. bd. The Am. Bankruptcy Law Jour.), Va. State Bar, Norfolk and Portsmouth Bar Assn., Nat. Film Soc., Am. Film Inst., Brit. Film Inst., Am. Cinematheque (mem. moving picture ball benefit com.), James Kent Inn of Ct. (pres. 1994-96, hon. mem.), Phi Alpha Theta, Pi Sigma Alpha, Phi Alpha Delta, Mason, Shriners, Elks. Methodist. Home: 1357 Windsor Point Rd Norfolk VA 23509-1311 Office: The Wesleymen 408 Boush St Norfolk VA 23510-1215 E-mail: halbonney@aol.com

BONNIE, RICHARD JEFFREY, law educator, lawyer; b. Richmond, Va., Aug. 22, 1945; s. Herbert Herman and Helene Selma (Berz) B.; m. Kathleen Ford, June 15, 1967; children: Joshua Ford, Zachary Andrew, Jessica Katherine. BA, Johns Hopkins U., 1966; LLB, U. Va., 1969. Var: Va. 1969, U.S. Dist. Ct. (ea. dist.) Va. 1969; U.S. Ct. Appeals (4th cir.) 1969, U.S. Supreme Ct. 1986. Asst. prof. law U. Va., Charlottesville, 1969-70, assoc. prof., 1973-77, prof., 1977-87, John S. Battle prof., 1987—; dir. Inst. Law, psychiatry, and Pub. Policy, 1979—. Vis. prof. Cornell Law Sch., 1993-94; assoc. dir. nat. Commn. Marijuana and Drug Abuse, 1971-73; reporter Nat. Conf. Commrs. on Uniform State Laws, 1972-74; cons. Spl. Action Office for Drug Abuse Prevention Exec. Office of the Pres., 1973-75; spl. asst. to U.S. Atty. Gen., 1975; mem. and sec. Nat. Adv. Coun. on Drug Abuse, 1975-80; mem. Com. on Problem of Drug Dependence, Inc., 1979-84; charter fellow Coll. Problems of Drug Dependence, 1992—; cons. Am. Psychiat. Assn., Coun. Psychiatry and Law, 1979—; mem. U.S. State Dept. Del. to investigate psychiat. practices in the Soviet Union, 1989; mem. World Psychiat. Assn. rev. team to investigate Soviet psychiatry, 1991; mem. adv. bd. permanent coordination office Reforms in psychiatry in Ctrl. and Ea. Europe, former Soviet Union, 1993—; bd. dirs. Geneva Initiative on Psychiatry, 1996—; pres. Am. Friends of Geneva Initiatives on Psychiatry, 1997—, mem. MacArthur Found. Network on Mental Health and the Law, 1988-96; bd. dirs. Va. Capital Representation Resource Ctr., 1994-97; mem. MacARthur Found. Network on Mandated Treatment, 2000—. Author: The Marijuana Conviction: The History of Marijuana Prohibition in the United States, 1974, 2d edit. 1999, Legal Aspects of Drug Dependence, 1975, Psychiatrists and the Legal Process: Diagnosis and Debate, 1977, Marijuana Use and Criminal Sanctions: Essays in the Theory and Practice of Decriminalization, 1980, Criminal Law: Cases and Materials, 1982, 2d edit., 1986, The Trial of John W. Hinckley, Jr.: A Case Study in the Insanity Defense, 1986, rev. edit. 2000, Criminal Law, 1997, Growing Up Tobacco Free, 1994, Mental Disorder, Work Disability and the Law, 1997, Reducing the Burden of Injury, 1999, The Evolution of Mental Health Law, 2001. Chmn. Va. Human Rights Com., Dept. mental Health and Mental Retardation, 1979-85; bd. dirs. Coll. on Problem of Drug Dependence, 1996-2000. Served to capt. USAF, 1970-73. Inst. Criminology fellow Cambridge U., 1977. Fellow Va. Law Found.; mem. Inst. Medicine of NAS (mem. bd. neurosci. and behavioral health, 1992—, mem. com. on preventing nicotine dependence in children and youths, 1993-94, mem. membership com. 1995-98, chair com. on opportunities in drug abuse rsch. 1995-96, chair com. injury prevention control 1997-98, mem. com. to assess sci. base for tobacco harm reduction 1999-2001, mem. com. to assess the sys. for the protection of human rsch. subjects 2000—), Nat. Rsch. Coun. (mem. comm. on data and rsch. for policy on illicit drugs 1998-2000, chair com. elder abuse and neglect 2001—), ABA (mem. criminal justice-mental health stds. project adv. bd. 1981-87), NAS, Am. Psychiat. Assn. (Isaac Ray award 1998), Va. Bar Assn. (chmn. com. mentally disabled 1981-90, mem. criminal law sect. coun. 1992-96), World Psychiat. Assn. (rev. team to investigate Soviet Psychiatry 1991), Am. Acad. Psychiat. Law (Amicus award 1994), Inst. Medicine, Va. Law Found. (fellow). Office: U Va Sch Law Charlottesville VA 22903

BONVILLIAN, WILLIAM BOONE, lawyer; b. Honolulu, Mar. 7, 1947; s. William Doughty and Florence Elizabeth (Boone) B.; m. Janis Ann Sposato, Apr. 12, 1980; children: Raphael William Boone, Marcus Doughty. AB, Columbia U., 1969; MA in Religion, Yale U., 1972; JD, Columbia U., 1974. Bar: Conn. 1975, D.C. 1976, U.S. Supreme Ct. 1983. Law clk. to Hon. Jack B. Weinstein U.S. Dist. Ct. (ea. dist.) N.Y., 1974-75; assoc. Steptoe & Johnson, Washington, 1975-77; dep. asst. sec., dir. congl. affairs, liaison officer U.S. Dept. Transp., 1977-81; ptnr. Brown, Roady, Bonvillian & Gold, 1981-85, Jenner & Block, Washington, 1985-89; chief counsel, legis. dir. to Sen. Joseph Lieberman U.S. Senate, 1989—. Editor Columbia Law Rev. 1973-74; contbr. articles to law and sci. jours. Recipient 2 outstanding Performance awards U.S. Sec. Transp., Washington, 1979, 80. Mem. Conn. Bar Assn., D.C. Bar Assn. Democrat. Episcopalian. Administrative and regulatory, Legislative, Real property. Home: 930 Hickory Run Ln Great Falls VA 22066-1903 Office: Office Sen Lieberman 706 Hart Senate Office Bldg Washington DC 20510-0001

BOOCHEVER, ROBERT, federal judge; b. N.Y.C., Oct. 2, 1917; s. Louis C and Miriam (Cohen) Boochever; m. Lois Colleen Maddox, Apr. 22, 1943 (dec.); children: Barbara K, Linda Lou, Ann Paula, Miriam Deon; m. Rose Marie Borden, Aug. 31, 2001. AB, Cornell U., 1939, JD, 1941; HD (hon.), U. Alaska, 1981. Bar: N.Y. 1944, Alaska 1947. Law clk. Nordlinger, Riegel & Cooper, 1941; asst. U.S. atty. Juneau, 1946-47; partner firm Faulkner, Banfield, Boochever & Doogan, 1947-72; asso. justice Alaska Supreme Ct., 1972-75, 78-80, chief justice, 1975-78; judge U.S. Ct. Appeals (9th cir.), Pasadena, Calif., 1980-86; sr. judge U.S. Ct. Appeals, 1986—. Mem. 9th cir. rules com. U.S. Ct. Appeals, 1983-85, chmn. 9th cir. libr. com., 1995-2001; chmn. Ala. Jud. Coun., 1975-78; mem. appellate judges seminar NYU Sch. Law, 1975; mem. Conf. Chief Justices, 1975-79, vice chmn., 1978-79; mem. adv. bd. Nat. Bank of Ala., 1968-72; guest spkr. Southwestern Law Sch. Disting. Lecture Series, 1992. Contbr. articles to profl. jours. Chmn. Juneau chpt. ARC, 1949-51, Juneau Planning Commn., 1956-61; mem. Alaska Devel. Bd., 1949-52, Alaska Jud. Qualification Commn., 1972-75; mem. adv. bd. Juneau-Douglas Community Coll. Served to Capt. U.S. Army, 1941-45. Named Juneau Man of Year, Rotary, 1974; recipient Disting. Alumnus award Cornell U., 1989; named in his honor The Boochever & Bird Chair for Study and Teaching of Freedom & Equality, U. Calif. Sch. Law, Davis, 2000. Fellow Am. Coll. Trial Attys.; mem. ABA, Alaska Bar Assn. (pres. 1961-62), Juneau Bar Assn. (pres. 1971-72), Am. Judicature Soc. (dir. 1970-74), Am. Law Inst., Juneau C. of C. (pres. 1952, 55), Alaskans United (chmn. 1972), Cornell Club L.A., Altadena Town and County Club. E-mail: robert. Office: US Ct Appeals PO Box 91510 125 S Grand Ave Pasadena CA 91105-1652 E-mail: boochever@ca9.uscourts.gov

BOOCOCK, STEPHEN WILLIAM, lawyer; b. Wilkinsburg, Pa., Sept. 25, 1948; s. William Samuel and Zelda Elizabeth (Heginbotham) B.; m. Carol Ann Bennett, July 11, 1970; children: Eric Alan, Allison Anne, Megan Leigh. BS in Acctg., Pa. State U., 1970; JD, U. Pitts., 1973. Bar: Pa. 1974, U.S. Dist. Ct. (we. dist.) Pa. 1973. Supervising tax specialist Coopers & Lybrand, Pitts., 1973-76; tax counsel Incom Internat., Inc., 1977-81; asst. treas., dir. tax Allegheny Ludlum Corp., 1981-93, asst. v.p. taxes, 1994-96, Allegheny Technologies, Inc., Pitts., 1996—. Treas. Meadow Wood Homeowner's Assn., 1990-2001. Served to capt. U.S. Army, 1970-79; with USAR. Mem. ABA, AICPA, Pa. Bar Assn., Allegheny County Bar Assn., Pa. Inst. CPAs, Pa. Chamber Bus. and Industry (tax subcom.), Pitts. C. of C. (tax subcom.), Com. on State Taxation, Tax Execs. Inst. (treas. Pitts. chpt. 1985-86, sec. 1986-87, sr. v.p. 1987-88, pres. 1988-89, nat. inst. dir. 1989-91, 99-2001, mem. nat. exec. com. 99-2001, nat. treas. 2001—, v.p. region VI 1992-93, mem. IRS adminstrv. affairs com. 1993—, vice chmn. 1995-97, chmn. 1997-99, membership com. 1993-97, mem. alternative tax sys. com. 1995-97, tax info. sys. com. 1995-97, nominating com. 1994-95, 97-98, 50th ann. task force 1993-95). Republican. Avocations: golf, hunting, fishing. Corporate taxation, Taxation, general, State and local taxation. Home: 2625 Woodmont Ln Wexford PA 15090-7978 Office: Allegheny Technologies Inc 1000 Six PPG Pl Pittsburgh PA 15222-5479

BOODELL, THOMAS JOSEPH, JR. lawyer; b. Chgo., Sept. 29, 1935; s. Thomas J. and Mary Elizabeth (Houze) B.; m. Beata Bergman Boodell, Aug. 4, 1962; children— Beata, Mary, Peter, David. A.B., Princeton U., 1957; J.D., Harvard U., 1964. Bar: Ill. 1964. Assoc. Boodell, Sears et al. Chgo., 1964-68; fellow Adlai Stevenson Inst. Internat. Affairs, Chgo., 1968-71; ptnr. Boodell, Sears, Giambalvo & Crowley, Chgo., 1971-84; ptnr. Keck, Mahin & Cate, Chgo., 1984— . Publisher, contbr. articles New City Mag., 1967-71. Pres. bd. dirs. Chgo. Children's Choir, 1979— ; bd. dirs. Wendy Will Case Cancer Fund, 1983— , Law in Am. Soc. Found., Chgo., 1972— ; trustee Chi Psi Ednl. Trust, Chgo., 1978-84. Lt. (j.g.) USN, 1957-60. Recipient Disting. Service award Chi Psi 1984, Disting. Service award Princeton Club Chgo., 1979. Fellow Am. Bar Found.; mem ABA, Chgo. Bar Assn., Ill. State Bar Assn., Law Club City Chgo., Legal Club Chgo., Univ. Club. Democrat. Federal civil litigation, General corporate, Private international. Home: 1229 E 56th St Chicago IL 60637-1616 Office: Keck Mahin & Cate 77 W Wacker Dr Ste 4900 Chicago IL 60601-1604

BOOHER, ALICE ANN, lawyer; b. Indpls., Oct. 6, 1941; d. Norman Rogers and Olga (Bonke) B. BA in Polit. Sci., Butler U., 1963; LLB, Ind. U., 1966, JD, 1967. Bar: Ind. 1966, U.S. Dist. Ct. (so. dist.) Ind. 1966, U.S. Tax Ct. 1970, U.S. Ct. Customs and Patent Appeals 1969, U.S. Ct. Mil. Appeals 1969, U.S. Ct. Appeals (D.C. cir.) 1969, U.S. Supreme Ct. 1969; cert. tchr., Ind. Rsch. asst., law clk. Supreme and Appellate Cts. Ind., Indpls., 1966; legal intern, atty., staff legal advisor Dept. State, Washington, 1966-69; staff legal adviser Bd. Vets. Appeals, 1969-78, sr. atty., 1978—, counsel, 1991—. Former counselor D.C. Penal Facilities and Shelters. Author: The Nuclear Test Ban Treaty and the Third Party Non-Nuclear States, also children's books; contbr. articles to various publs., chpts. to Whiteman Digest of International Law; exhibited crafts, needlepoint in juried artisan fairs; originator U.S. postage stamps Women in Mil. Svc., 1980-97, POWs/MIAs, 1986-96. Bd. dirs. numerous community groups, including D.C. Women's Commn. for Crime Prevention, 1980-81; pres., legal adviser VA employees Assn. Recipient various awards; named Ky. Col., 1988. Mem. DAV (life), VFW Aux. (life), LWV, Women's Bar Assn. D.C., D.C. Sexual Assault Coalition (chmn. legal com.), Judge Advocates Assn., Butler U. Alumni Assn., Nat. Mus. Women in Arts, Kennedy Ctr. Stars, Sackler Gallery (patron), Women in Mil. Svcs. to Am. Found. (charter), Bus. and Profl. Women (pres. D.C. 1980-81, nat. UN fellow 1974, nat. bd. dirs. 1980-82, 87—, Woman of Yr. award D.C. 1975, Marguerite Rawalt award D.C. 1986), USO, Women Officers Profl. Assns., Navy League U.S.A. (life), Am. Legion Aux. (life), Nat. Task Force on Women of the Mil. and Women Mil. POWS (chair Esther Peterson Tribute 1995, panel, paper moderator conf. 1997, book reviewer, contbr. to Stars & Stripes, Ex POWs Bull., others), U.S. Naval Inst., Army Women Officers Profl. Assn., Am. News Womens Club, Alliance Nat. Defense.

BOOKER, JAMES DOUGLAS, retired lawyer, government official; b. Columbus, Ohio, June 27, 1933; s. Homer Newton and Grace Bernice (Hermann) Booker; m. Onda Lee Minshall, Aug. 31, 1958; children: Christine E. Booker Garrett, Linda K. Booker Stanek, Molly A. Booker Lary, Andrew W. JD, Ohio State U., 1961. Bar: Ohio 1961, U.S. Dist. Ct. (so. dist.) Ohio 1962, U.S. Ct. Appeals (6th cir.) 1972, U.S. Supreme Ct. 1971. Asst. atty. gen. State of Ohio, Columbus, 1961-62; ptnr. Williams, Deeg, Ketcham, Booker & Obetz, 1962-75; adminstrv. law judge SSA, 1975-98. Former PTA officer, ch. deacon and Sunday Sch. tchr. Served with U.S. Army, 1953-55. Mem. Ohio State Bar Assn. Republican. Avocations: chess, music, history. Administrative and regulatory. Home: 1290 Smallwood Dr Columbus OH 43235-2503 E-mail: jamesdbooker@prodigy.net

BOOKER, RUSSELL STUART, lawyer; b. Maidstone, Kent, Eng., Aug. 21, 1957; s. Wilfred Bryan and Irene (Netherton) B.; m. Beverley Morel; children: Luke, Dominique. LLB with honors, Birmingham U., Eng., 1978. Assoc. Booth & Blackwell, London, 1981-86, Masons, London, 1986-88; ptnr., 1988—. Bd. dirs. Masons Ltd., London. Avocations: golf, sailing. General corporate, Mergers and acquisitions, Securities. Office: Masons 30 Aylesbury St EC1R 0ER London England Home Fax: 020 8295 4603; Office Fax: 020 7490 2545. E-mail: russell.booker@dataline.co.uk, russell.booker@masons.com

BOONE, CELIA TRIMBLE, lawyer; b. Clovis, N.Mex., Apr. 3, 1953; d. George Harold and Barbara Ruth (Foster) T.; m. Billy W. Boone, Apr. 21, 1990. BS, Ea. N.Mex. U., 1976, MA, 1977; JD, St. Mary's U., San Antonio, 1982. Bar: Tex. 1982, U.S. Dist. Ct. (no. dist.) Tex. 1983, U.S. Ct. Appeals (5th cir.) 1985, U.S. Supreme Ct. 1986. Instr. English Ea. N.Mex. U., Portales, 1977-78; editor Curry County Times, Clovis, 1978-79; assoc. Schultz & Robertson, Abilene, Tex., 1982-85, Scarborough, Black, Tarpley & Scarborough, Abilene, 1985-87; ptnr. Scarborough, Black, Tarpley & Trimble, 1988-90, Scarborough, Black, Tarpley & Boone, Abilene, 1990-94; of counsel Scarborough, Tarpley, Boone & Fouts, 1994-96; prin. Law Office of Celia Trimble Boone, 1996—. Instr. legal rsch. and writing St. Mary's Sch. Law, 1981-82. Legal adv. bd. to bd. dirs. Abilene Kennel Club, 1983-85; landmarks commn. City of Abilene, 1989-90. Recipient Outstanding Young Lawyer of Abilene, 1988. Mem. ABA, State Bar Tex. (disciplinary rev. com. 1989-93), Am. Trial Lawyers Assn., Tex. Trial Lawyers Assn., Tex. Criminal Def. Lawyers Assn., Tex. Acad. Family Law Specialists, Tex. Bd. Legal Specialization (cert.), Abilene Bar Assn. (bd. dirs. 1985-88, sec.-treas. 1985-86), Abilene Young Lawyers Assn. (bd. dirs. 1985-89, treas. 1985-86, pres.-elect 1987-88, pres. 1988-89), NOW, ACLU, Phi Alpha Delta. Democrat. Avocations: needlework, gardening. Bankruptcy, General civil litigation, Family and matrimonial. Office: 104 Pine St Ste 316 Abilene TX 79601-5930

BOONE, DAVID EASON, lawyer; b. Raleigh, N.C., July 5, 1948; s. Devan Duke and Virgil (Eason) B.; m. Beverly Ann Deem, Feb. 3, 1968; children: Rebecca Ann, Jacob Elisha, Courtney Keriann. BA, U. Va., 1970; JD, U. Richmond, 1975. Bar: Va. 1976, U.S. Dist. Ct. (ea. dist.) Va. 1976, U.S. Ct. Appeals (4th cir.) 1976, U.S. Supreme Ct. 1982. Law clk. Hon. Judge D. Dortch Warriner U.S. Dist. Ct., Richmond, Va., 1976-78; assoc. Francis, Hubard & Tice, 1978-80; ptnr. Boone, Beale, Cosby & Long, 1980—. Adj. instr. J. Sargeant Reynolds Community Coll., Richmond, 1977—. Served to lt. USN, 1970-73, Vietnam. Recipient NAACP Freedom Fund award, Richmond, 1982. Mem. ABA, Richmond Criminal Bar Assn., Nat. Assn. Criminal Def. Lawyers, Va. Coll. Criminal Def. Attys., Lawyers Pilots Bar Assn. Republican. Baptist. Avocations: flying, travel. Criminal. Office: Boone Beale Cosby & Long 27 N 17th St Richmond VA 23219-3607 E-mail: deboone27n17st@yahoo.com

BOONE, RICHARD WINSTON, SR. lawyer; b. Washington, July 19, 1941; s. Henry Shaffer and Anne Catherine (Huehne) B.; m. Jean Knox Logan, Dec. 17, 1966; children: Elizabeth Anne, Richard Winston, Jr., Katheryn Jeanne. BA with honors, U. Ala., 1963; JD, Georgetown U., 1970. Bar: Va. 1970, D.C. 1970, Md. 1984, U.S. Ct. Appeals (D.C. cir.) 1970, U.S. Ct. Appeals (2nd cir.) 1973, U.S. Ct. Appeals (4th cir.) 1972, U.S. Supreme Ct. 1974, U.S. Ct. Claims 1975. Ptnr. Carr, JOrdan, Coyne & Savits, Washington, 1977-81; shareholder, dir. Wilkes, Artis, Hedrick & Boone, P.C., McLean, Va., 1984-95; pres. Richard W. Boone, P.C., 1984-95, The Law Offices of Richard W. Boone, 1995-97, Boone & Assocs., P.C., 1998—. Capt. USAR, 1964-67. Mem. D.C. Def. Lawyers Assn., Va. Trial Lawyers Assn., Va. Assn. Def. Attys., Barristers Assn. Avocations: model railroading, personal computer. General civil litigation, Health, Personal injury. E-mail: rwboone@aol.com

BOONE, THEODORE SEBASTIAN, lawyer; b. Urbana, Ill., Jan. 7, 1961; s. William Werner and Eileen Georgeanna (Herweh) B. BA cum laude with highest deptl. distinction, U. Ill., 1983; JD, Columbia U., 1987. Bar: N.Y. 1988, D.C. 1989. Assoc. Arnold & Porter, Washington, 1991—. Translator, speaker in field. Contbr. book revs., articles to profl. jours. Grantee Internat. Rsch. and Exchs. Bd., Budapest, 1987-88, Fulbright and Bavarian State, Munich, 1983-84; Fgn. Lang. Area Studies/U.S. Dept. Edn., 1986-87. Mem. ABA (vice chmn. com. internat. investment, devel. and privatization), Am. Soc. Internat. Law, Am. C. of C. in Hungary (bd. govs. 1989-93, pres. 1991-93), N.Y. Bar Assn., D.C. Bar Assn., Phi Beta Kappa. Avocations: German and Hungarian language. General corporate, Private international, Legislative. Office: Arnold and Porter 555 12th St NW Washington DC 20004-1206

BOOTH, EDMUND A., JR. prosecutor; BA, U. Georgia; LLD, UGA Sch. Law. First asst. U.S. Atty., 1986—2001; U.S. Atty. Southern Dist., Savannah, Ga., 2001—. Office: PO Box 8999 Savannah GA 31412*

BOOTH, GORDON DEAN, JR. lawyer; b. Columbus, Ga., June 25, 1939; s. Gordon Dean and Lois Mildred (Bray) B.; m. Katherine Morris Campbell, June 17, 1961; children: Mary Katherine Williams, Abigail Kilgore Curvino, Sarah Elizabeth, Margaret Campbell, Celecia. BA, Emory U., 1961, JD, 1964, LLM, 1973. Bar: Ga. 1964, D.C. 1977, U.S. Supreme Ct. 1973. Pvt. practice, Atlanta, 1964-96; ptnr. Schreeder, Wheeler & Flint, 1995—. Bd. dirs., v.p. Stallion Music Inc., Nashville, BAA USA, Inc.; trustee, sec. Inst. for Polit. Econ., Washington. Contbr. articles to profl. jours. Trustee Met. Atlanta Crime Commn., 1977-80, chmn., 1979-80; mem. assembly for arts and scis. Emory Coll., 1971-86, chmn., 1983. Mem. Internat. Bar Assn. (coun. sect. bus. law 1974-88, chmn. aero. law com. 1971-86), State Bar Ga., Capital City Club, Piedmont Driving Club, Univ. Club (N.Y.C.), Advocates Club, Sigma Chi. Federal civil litigation, Private international, Transportation. Home: 3226 Paces Mill Rd SE Atlanta GA 30339-3787

BOOTH, HAROLD WAVERLY, lawyer, finance and investment company executive; b. Rochester, N.Y., Aug. 8, 1934; s. Herbert Nixon and Mildred B. (Anderson) B.; m. Flo Rae Spelts, July 4, 1957; children: Rebecca, William, Eva, Harold, Richard. B.S., Cornell U., 1955; J.D., Duke U., 1961. Bar: Nebr. 1961, Ill. 1967, Iowa 1974; CLU; chartered fin. counselor; cert. fin. planner. Staff atty. Bankers Life Nebr., Lincoln, 1961-67; pres. First Nat. Bank, Council Bluffs, Iowa, 1970-74; exec. v.p., treas. Blue Cross-Blue Shield Ill., Chgo., 1974-77; pres., chief exec. officer, chmn. Bankers Life Nebr., Lincoln, 1977-84; exec. v.p. Colonial Penn Group, Phila., 1985-87; chmn., chief exec. officer VGVR Cos., 1985—. Served to 1st lt. USAF, 1955-58. Fellow Life Mgmt. Inst. (pres. 1981-84); mem. Ins. Fedn. Nebr. (past pres.) Finance, Insurance. Home: 1000 Stony Ln Gladwyne PA 19035-1128

BOPP, JAMES, JR. lawyer; b. Terre Haute, Ind., Feb. 8, 1948; s. James and Helen Marguerite (Hope) B.; m. Cheryl Hahn, Aug. 8, 1970 (div.); m. Christine Marie Stanton, July 3, 1982; children: Kathleen Grace, Lydia Grace, Marguerite Grace. BA, Ind. U., 1970; JD, U. Fla., 1973. Bar: Ind. 1973, U.S. Supreme Ct. 1977. Dep. atty. gen. State of Ind., Indpls., 1973-75; ptnr. Bopp & Fife, 1975-79, Brames, Bopp, Abel & Oldham, Terre Haute, Ind., 1979-92, Bopp, Coleson & Bostrom, Terre Haute, 1992—; of counsel Webster, Chamberlain and Bean, Washington, 1997—. Dep. prosecutor Vigo County, Terre Haute, 1979-86; gen. counsel Nat. Right to Life Com., Washington, 1978—; pres. Nat. Legal Ctr. for Medically Dependent and Disabled, 1984—; gen. counsel James Madison Ctr. Free Speech, 1997—; instr. law Ind. U., 1977-78. Editor: Human Life and Health Care Ethics, 1985, Restoring the Right to Life: The Human Life Amendment, 1984; editor-in-chief Issues in Law and Medicine, 1985—. Mem. Pres.'s Com. on Mental Retardation, 1984-87, mem. congl. biomed. ethics adv. com., 1987-89; Vigo County Election Bd., 1991-93; vice chmn. Early for Gov., 1995-96; del. Rep. State Conv., Indpls., 1980, 82, 84, 86, 90, 92, 94, 96, 98, 2000; alt. del. Rep. Nat. Conv., 1992, 96, del., 2000; chmn. Vigo County Rep. Ctrl. Com., 1993-97, White House Conf. on Families, Washington, 1980, White House Conf. on Aging, Mpls., 1981; bd. dirs. Leadership Terre Haute, 1986-89, Nat. Rep. Pro-Life Com., Washington, 1983-91, Alliance for Growth and Progress, Terre Haute, 1993-97; chmn. bd. dirs. Hospice of Wabash Valley, Terre Haute, 1982-88; mem. The Federalist Soc., Free Speech & Election Law Practice Group, chmn. election law subcom., 1996—. Mem. Ind. State Bar Assn., Terre Haute Bar Assn., Terre Haute Rotary (bd. dirs. 1984-86). Roman Catholic. General civil litigation, Constitutional, Non-profit and tax-exempt organizations. Home: 1124 S Center St Terre Haute IN 47802-1116 Office: Bopp Coleson & Bostrom 1 S 6th St Terre Haute IN 47807-3510

BORCHARD, WILLIAM MARSHALL, lawyer; b. N.Y.C., Nov. 19, 1938; s. Bernard Philip and Helen (Marshall) B.; m. Myra Cohen, Dec. 13, 1969; children: Jillian, Thomas. BA, Princeton U., 1960; JD, Columbia U., 1964. Bar: N.Y. 1964, U.S. Dist. Ct. (so. and ea. dists.), U.S. Ct. Appeals (2d, 3d, fed. cirs.), U.S. Supreme Ct. Assoc. Kaye, Scholer, Fierman, Hays and Handler, N.Y.C., 1964-74, ptnr., 1974-83, Cowan, Liebowitz and Latman, N.Y.C., 1983—. Mem. editorial bds. Art and the Law, 1982—, The Trademark Reporter, 1983-99 Author: Trademarks and the Arts, 1999, A Trademark is Not a Copyright or a Patent, 2001. Staff sgt. USAFR, 1961-67. Stone scholar Columbia Law Sch. N.Y.C., 1962. Mem. ABA (coun. 1987-90), Am. Law Inst. (adv. com. 1986-92), Internat. Trademark Assn. (legal counsel 1988-91). Democrat. Jewish. Avocations: tennis, boating, biking. Trademark and copyright. Office: Cowan Liebowitz & Latman 1133 Ave of Americas New York NY 10036-6799 E-mail: wmb@cll.com

BORDELON, ALVIN JOSEPH, JR. lawyer; b. New Orleans, Nov. 1, 1945; s. Alvin Joseph and Mildred (Quarella) B.; m. Melanie Rose Bond; children by previous marriage: Peter Jude, Emily Aprill; m. Melanie Rose Bond. BA in English, U. New Orleans, 1968; JD, Loyola U., New Orleans, 1973. Bar: La. 1973, U.S. Ct. Appeals (5th cir.) 1975, U.S. Supreme Ct. 1983. Landman Chevron Oil Co., New Orleans, 1973-74; pvt. practice, 1974-75; ptnr. Douglas, Favre & Bordelon, 1975-76, Monroe & Lemann, New Orleans, 1976-81; sr. ptnr. Bordelon, Hamlin & Theriot, 1981—. Labor negotiator St. Tammany Parish Sch. Bd., Covington, La., 1991—, St. Bernard Parish Sch. Bd., Chalmette, La., 1986—; instr. criminal justice Loyola City Coll., 1975-76, Loyola U. Sch. Law, 1976-77. Mng. editor Loyola Law Rev., 1972-73. Chmn. Alcoholic Beverage Control Bd., New Orleans, 1983-84; mem. Mayor's Commn. on Crime, New Orleans, 1979; pres. Faubourg St. John Neighborhood Assn., New Orleans, 1977-80. With U.S. Army, 1968-70. Recipient Outstanding Civic Leadership award La. State Senate, Baton Rouge, 1982; named Short Story Competition 1st Place winner Writer's Digest, 1993. Mem. Profl. Assn. of Dive Instrs., La. Bar Assn. Republican. Roman Catholic. Avocations: poetry and short story writing, fishing, diving. Federal civil litigation, General civil litigation, State civil litigation. Office: Bordelon Hamlin & Theriot 701 S Peters St New Orleans LA 70130-1588 E-mail: alvinbordelon@msn.com

BORDEN, DAVID M. state supreme court justice; b. Hartford, Conn., Aug. 4, 1937; BA magna cum laude, Amherst Coll., 1959; LLB cum laude, Harvard U., 1962. Bar: Conn. 1962, U.S. Dist. Ct. Conn. 1962, U.S. Ct. Appeals (2d cir.) 1965, U.S. Supreme Ct. 1969. Pvt. practice, Hartford, Conn., 1962-77; judge Conn. Ct. Common Pleas, 1977-78, Conn. Superior Ct., 1978-83, Conn. Appellate Ct., 1983; assoc. justice Conn. Supreme Ct., 1990—. Chief counsel joint com. on judiciary Conn. Gen. Assembly, 1975-76; lectr. Law U. Conn. Sch. Law, 1970-73; exec. dir. Conn. Commn. to Revise Criminal Statutes, 1963-71. Mem. Conn. Bar Assn., Hartford County Bar Assn., Phi Beta Kappa. Democrat. Jewish. Avocations: hiking, reading. Office: Conn Supreme Ct Drawer N Sta A Hartford CT 06106-1548*

BORDES, JANE S. lawyer; b. New Orleans, Sept. 3, 1973; d. Bruce Gerald and Judith Mathews Bordes. BA in English summa cum laude, Loyola U. of New Orleans, 1994; JD, Tulane U., 1997. Bar: La. 1998. Assoc. Schafer and Schafer, New Orleans, 1997—. Office: Schafer and Schafer 328 Lafayette St New Orleans LA 70130-3244

BORDY, MICHAEL JEFFREY, lawyer; b. Kansas City, Mo., July 24, 1952; s. Marvin Dean and Alice Mae (Rostov) B.; m. Marjorie Enid Kanof, Dec. 27, 1973 (div. Dec. 1983); m. Melissa Anne Held, May 24, 1987; children: Shayna Robyn, Jenna Alexis, Samantha Falyn. Bar: Calif., 1986, U.S. Dist. Ct. (cen. dist.) Calif., 1986, (so. dist.) Calif., 1987, U.S. Ct. Appeals (9th cir.), 1986. Tchg. asst. biology U. Kans., Lawrence, 1975-76, rsch. asst. biology, 1976-80; post-doctoral fellow Johns Hopkins U., Balt., 1980-83; tchg. asst. U. So. Calif., L.A., 1984-86; assoc. Thelen, Marrin, Johnson & Bridges, 1986-87, Wood, Lucksinger & Epstein, L.A., 1987-89, Cooper, Epstein & Hurewitz, Beverly Hills, Calif., 1989-93; ptnr. Jacobson, Runes & Bordy, 1994-96, Jacobson, Sanders & Bordy, LLP, Beverly Hills, 1996-97, Jacobson White Diamond & Bordy, LLP, Beverly Hills, 1997—. Bd. govs. Beverly Hills (Calif.) Bar Barristers, 1988-90, chair real estate law sect. 1998-2000, exec. com. 2000—; bd. govs. Cedars-Sinai Med. Ctr., L.A., 1994—; bd. dirs. Sinai Temple, 1998—; cabinet United Jewish Fund/Real Estate, L.A., 1995—; mem. planning com. Am. Cancer Soc., 1996—; mem. Guardians of the Jewish Home for the Aging, 1995—, Fraternity of Friends, 1997-99; active Lawyers Against Hunger, 1995—. Pre-Doctoral fellow NIH, Lawrence, 1977-80; post-doctoral fellow Mellon Found., Balt., 1980-83. Mem. ABA, State Bar Calif., L.A. County Bar Assn., Beverly Hills Bar Assn. (gov., barrister 1988-92, chair real estate sect. 1998-00), Profl. Network Group. Democrat. Jewish. Avocations: running, reading. General corporate, Environmental, Real property. Office: Jacobson White Diamond & Bordy LLP 9777 Wilshire Blvd Ste 918 Beverly Hills CA 90212-1902 E-mail: mjbordy@jwdlo.com

BOREL, STEVEN JAMES, lawyer; b. Kansas City, Mo., Nov. 12, 1947; s. Mark and Margaret (Gibson) B.; m. Nancy Jean Dunaway, Aug. 31, 1967; children: Lindsay Kay, Emily Jean, Amy Lynn. BSBA, Pitts. State U., 1969; JD with distinction, U. Mo., Kansas City, 1972. Bar: Mo. 1972, Kans. 1989. Assoc. Stubbs, Epstein & Mann, Kansas City, 1972-79; pvt. practice, 1979—. Rsch. editor U. Mo.-Kansas City Law Rev., 1971-72. Capt. U.S. Army, 1969-74. Mem. ATLA, Mo. Assn. Trial Attys., Kans. Trial Lawyers Assn., Kansas City Met. Bar Assn. (chmn. workers' compensation com. 1991-93). Personal injury. Office: 1101 Walnut St Ste 1520 Kansas City MO 64106-2182 E-mail: sborel@borelfirm.com

BORENSTEIN, EUGENE REED, lawyer; b. Bklyn., July 19, 1944; s. Charles H. and Gloria (Seiden) B.; m. Maxine Herold, June 25, 1978. B.S., Mich. State U., 1966; J.D., New York Law Sbb., 1969. Bar: N.Y. 1969, U.S. Dist. Ct. (so. dist.) N.Y., 1969. Dep. chief housing and real estate divsn. Law Dept., City of N.Y., 1976-78, asst. chief comml. litigation, 1978-79, dep. chief affirmative litigation, 1979-81, chief worker compensation divsn., 1981-83, dep. chief tort divsn., 1981-92, chief tort divsn., 1992—. Home: 301 E 75th St New York NY 10021-3010 Office: City of NY Law Dept 100 Church St New York NY 10007-2601

BORENSTEIN, MILTON CONRAD, lawyer, manufacturing company executive; b. Boston, Oct. 21, 1914; s. Isadore Sidney and Eva Beatrice B.; m. Anne Shapiro, June 20, 1937; children: Roberta, Jeffrey. AB cum laude, Boston Coll., 1935; JD, Harvard U., 1938. Bar: Mass. 1938, U.S. Dist. Ct. 1939, U.S. Ct. Appeals 1944, U.S. Supreme Ct. 1944. Pvt. practice law, Boston, 1938—; officer, dir. Sweetheart Paper Products Co., Inc., Chelsea, Mass., 1944-61, pres., 1961-83, chmn. bd., 1984; with Sweetheart Plastics, Inc., Wilmington, Mass., 1958—, v.p., 1958-84, also dir.; v.p. Md. Cup Corp., Owings Mills, 1960-77, exec. v.p., treas., 1977-84, also dir.; ptnr. Concorde Assocs., Boston. Bd. dirs. Am. Assocs. Hebrew U., 1968—; trustee Combined Jewish Philanthropies, Boston, 1969—, N.E. Sinai Hosp., Stoughton, Mass., 1974—, Ben-Gurion U., 1975-85, 87—, Boston Coll., 1979-87, chmn. estate planning coun., 1981-83, mem. coun. exec. com. 1984—, assoc. trustee, 1987-96; mem. pres.'s coun. Sarah Lawrence Coll., 1970-79; bd. overseers Jewish Theol. Sem. Am., 1971—; mem. pres. Congregation Kehillath Israel, Brookline, Mass., 1977-79, hon. pres., 1979—; mem. pres's coun. Brandeis U., 1979-81, fellow, 1981—; v.p. Assoc. Synagogues of Mass., 1980-81; exec. com. New Eng. region Anti-Defamation League, 1980—; bd. dirs., nat. governing coun. Am. Jewish Congress, 1984—; assoc. chmn. scholarship com. Harvard Law Sch., 1964-66, mem. spl. gifts com., 1990, mem. Langdell com., 1991, 92, 93, 94, 95, 96, 97, 98, 99, Boston regional campaign com., 1992, chmn. class reunion gift, 1993, 98. Recipient Community Svc. award Jewish Theol. Sem. Am., 1970, Am. Jewish Congress, 1993, Bald Eagle Outstanding Alumnus award Boston Coll., 1991; named Rofeh Internat. Man of Yr., 1996. Fellow Mass. Bar Found.; mem. ABA, Mass. Bar Assn., Boston Bar Assn. (mem. bicentennial com. 1986-87), Harvard Club (Boston and N.Y.C.), Harvard Faculty Club. General corporate. Office: Concorde Assocs 1 Devonshire Pl Ste 2912 Boston MA 02109-3533

BORGER, JOHN PHILIP, lawyer; b. Wilmington, Del., Apr. 19, 1951; s. Philip E. and Jane (Smyth) B.; m. Judith Marie Yates, May 24, 1974; children: Jennifer, Christopher, Nicholas. BA in Journalism with high honors, Mich. State U., 1973; JD, Yale U., 1976. Bar: Minn. 1976, U.S. Dist. Ct. Minn. 1976, U.S. Ct. Appeals (8th cir.) 1979, U.S. Supreme Ct. 1982, N.D. 1988, U.S. Dist. Ct. N.D. 1988, Wis. 1993. Editor-in-chief Mich. State News, East Lansing, 1972-73; assoc. Faegre & Benson, LLP, Mpls., 1976-83, ptnr., 1984—. Bd. dirs. Milkweed Edits., 1995-01; adj. prof. U. Minn. Sch. Journalism and Mass Comm., 1999. Contbr. articles to profl. jours. Mem. ABA (chmn. media law and defamation torts com. torts and ins. practice sect. 1996-97), Minn. Bar Assn., State Bar Assn. N.D., Wis. Bar Assn., Hennepin County Bar Assn. Appellate, General civil litigation, Libel. Office: Faegre & Benson LLP 2200 Wells Fargo Ctr 90 S 7th St Ste 2200 Minneapolis MN 55402-3901 E-mail: jborger@faegre.com

BORGESON, EARL CHARLES, law librarian, educator; b. Boyd, Minn., Dec. 2, 1922; s. Hjalmer Nicarner and Doris (Danielson) B.; m. Barbara Ann Jones, Sept. 21, 1944; children— Barbara Gale, Geoffrey Charles, Steven Earl. BS in Law, U. Minn., 1947, LLB, 1949; BA in Law Librarianship, U. Wash., 1950. Libr. Harvard U. Law Sch. Libr., 1952-70; assoc. dir. Stanford U. Librs., 1970-75; assoc. law libr. Los Angeles County (Calif.) Law Libr., 1975-78; prof. and law libr. So. Meth. U., Dallas, 1978-88, prof. emeritus of law, 1988; lectr. UCLA Grad. Sch. Libr. Sci., 1975-78; adj. prof. Tex. Women's U., 1979-80; adj. prof. U. North Tex., Denton, 1988-90; librarian AccuFile, Inc., 1992—; cons. in field. With USNR, 1943-46. Mem. Am. Assn. Law Librs. Home: 1D Village Way Sherborn MA 01770-1536

BORISOFF, RICHARD STUART, lawyer; b. Rochester, N.Y., May 4, 1945; s. Samuel M. and Ida. B.; m. Risa W. Polgar, Aug. 17, 1967; children: Mindy, Dara. BA, U. Pa., 1967; JD, Columbia U., 1970. Bar: N.Y. 1971, D.C. 1981, U.S. Dist. Ct. (so. dist.) N.Y. 1973, U.S. Ct. Appeals (2nd cir.) 1973. Assoc. Paul, Weiss, Rifkind, Wharton & Garrison, N.Y.C., 1970-78, ptnr., 1978—. Office: Paul Weiss Rifkind Wharton & Garrison Ste 2330 1285 Avenue Of The Americas New York NY 10019-6028 E-mail: rborisoff@paulweiss.com

BORISON, SCOTT CRAIG, lawyer; b. N.Y.C., Feb. 8, 1961; s. E.B. and Joan B. Borison; m. Janet S. Legg, May 22, 1988; children: Ian, Madison. BA in Russian Studies, Fairleigh Dickinson U., 1982; JD, U. Okla., 1987. Bar: Okla. 1987, D.C. 1994, Md. 1995, U.S. Dist. Ct. Md., U.S. Dist. Ct. D.C., U.S. Ct. Appeals (4th and 10th cirs.), U.S. Tax Ct., U.S. Ct. Vets. Appeals. Law clk. Okla. Ct. Appeals, Oklahoma City, 1987-89; counsel Centurion Oil, Inc., 1989-93; atty., mem. Legg Law Firm, LLC, Frederick, Md., 1994—. Bd. dirs. Religious Coalition for Emergency Human Needs. Mem. Nat. Assn. Consumer Bankruptcy Attys., Frederick County Bar Assn., Bankruptcy Bar Dist. Md. Bankruptcy. Office: Legg Law Firm LLC 5500 Buckeystown Pike Frederick MD 21703-8331

BORK, ROBERT HERON, lawyer, author, educator, former federal judge; b. Pitts., Mar. 1, 1927; s. Harry Philip and Elizabeth (Kunkle) B.; m. Claire Davidson, June 15, 1952 (dec. 1980); children: Robert Heron, Charles E., Ellen E.; m. Mary Ellen Pohl, Oct. 30, 1982. BA, U. Chgo., 1948, JD, 1953; LLD (hon.), Creighton U., 1975, Notre Dame Law Sch., 1982; LHD, Wilkes-Barre Coll., 1976; JD (hon.), Bklyn. Law Sch., 1984; ThD, DeSales Sch. Theology, 1990; LLD honoris causa, Adelphi U., 1990. Bar: Ill. 1953, D.C. 1977. Assoc., then ptnr. Kirkland, Ellis, Hodson, Chaffetz & Masters, Chgo., 1955-62; assoc. prof. Yale Law Sch., 1962-65, prof. law, 1965-75, on leave, 1973-75; solicitor gen. U.S. Dept. Justice, Washington, 1973-77, acting atty. gen., 1973-74; Chancellor Kent prof. law Yale Law Sch., 1977-79, Alexander M. Bickel prof. pub. law, 1979-81; ptnr. Kirkland & Ellis, Washington, 1981-82; judge U.S. Ct. Appeals for D.C. Cir., 1982-88, resigned, 1988; resident scholar Am. Enterprise Inst. for Pub. Policy Rsch., Washington, 1977, adj. scholar, 1977-82, John M. Olin scholar in legal studies, 1988-99, sr. fellow, 2000—; prof. law Ave Maria Sch. Law, 2000—. Mem., trustee Woodrow Wilson Internat. Ctr. for Scholars, 1973-78; nominated for position assoc. justice U.S. Supreme Ct., 1987, confirmation denied by U.S. Senate. Author: The Antitrust Paradox: A Policy at War with Itself, 1978, 2d edit., 1993, The Tempting of America: The Political Seduction of the Law, 1990, Slouching Towards Gomorrah: Modern Liberalism and American Decline, 1996. With USMCR, 1945-46, 50-52. Recipient Francis Boyer award Am. Enterprise Inst., 1984, Henry Salvatori prize Intercollegiate Svcs. Inst., 1998. Fellow AAAS; mem. Federalist Soc. (co-chmn., bd. trustees). E-mail: rbork@aei.org

BORN, BROOKSLEY ELIZABETH, lawyer; b. San Francisco, Aug. 27, 1940; d. Ronald Henry and Mary Ellen (Bortner) B.; m. Alexander Elliot Bennett, Oct. 9, 1982; children: Nicholas Jacob Landau, Ariel Elizabeth Landau, Andrew E. Bennett, Laura F. Bennett, Peter J. Bennett. AB, Stanford U., 1961, JD, 1964. Bar: D.C. 1966. Law clk. U.S. Ct. Appeals, Washington, 1964-65; legal rschr. Harvard Law Sch., 1967-68; assoc. Arnold and Porter, Washington, 1965-67, 68-73, ptnr., 1974-96, 99—; chair U.S. Commodity Futures Trading Commn., 1996-99. Lectr. law Columbus Sch. Law, Cath. U. Am., 1972-74; adj. prof. Georgetown U. Law Center, Washington, 1972-73. Pres. Stanford Law Rev, 1963-64. Chair bd. visitors Stanford Law Sch., 1987; bd. dirs. Nat. Legal Aid and Defenders Assn., 1972-79, Washington Legal Clinic for Homeless, 1993-96, Lawyers Com. for Civil Rights Under Law, 1993-96, Am. Bar Found., 1989-99, Washington Lawyers Com. for Civil Rights and Urban Affairs, 1992-96, Nat. Women's Law Ctr., 1981—; trustee Ctr. for Law and Social Policy, Washington, 1977-96, Women's Bar Found., 1981-86. Mem. ABA (chair sect. ind. rights and responsibilities 1977-78, chair fed. judiciary com. 1980-83, chair consortium on legal svcs. and the pub. 1987-90, bd. govs. 1990-93, chair resource devel. coun. 1993-95, chair coun. Fund for Justice and Edn. 1995-96, state del. from D.C. 1994—), D.C. Bar (sec. 1975-76, mem. bd. govs. 1976-79), Am. Law Inst., Southwestern Legal Found. (trustee 1993-96), Order of Coif. Administrative and regulatory, Federal civil litigation, Finance. Office: Arnold & Porter 555 12th St NW Washington DC 20004-1206 E-mail: brooksley_born@aporter.com

BORN, DAWN SLATER, lawyer; BA in Pub. Justice summa cum laude, SUNY, Oswego, 1977; JD summa cum laude, U. Houston, 1981. Assoc. Wood, Campbell Moody & Gibbs, Houston, 1981-83, Bracewell & Patterson, LLP, Houston, 1983-88, ptnr., 1988-94; dir. corp. devel. Enron Capital & Trade Resources subs. Enron Corp., 1994-95, dir. restructuring, 1995-96; v.p., gen. counsel GNI Group, Inc., 1996-98; ptnr. LaBoeuf, Lamb, Greene & MacRae, LLP, 1998—. Bd. dirs., mem. fin. planning com. Queensland Alumina Ltd., bd. dirs. MedBusiness.net, Inc.; spkr. in field. Bd. dirs., exec., mem. nominating and endowment coms. Boys and Girls Country of Houston, Inc., 1996-99; mem. edn. com. River Oaks Bapt. Sch., 1994-97, gender com., 1994—, chair gender com. 1995-99, chair ad hoc com. to address mid. sch. disciplinary sys., 1996-97, mem. ad hoc com. to revise honor roll requirements, 1996-97, ad hoc com. for diversity and equity, 1998-99. Mem. ABA (bus. law and corp. counsel sects.), NAFE, State Bar Tex. (bus. law and corp. counsel sects., chair franchise and distbn. law com. 1993-94), D.C. Bar Assn., Houston Bar Assn., Coll. of State Bar Tex., Tex. Exec. Women (mentor and round table discussion group leader). General corporate, Mergers and acquisitions, Securities. Address: 3704 Plumb St Houston TX 77005-2810 Office: LeBoeuf Lamb Greene & MacRae LLP 1000 Louisiana St Houston TX 77002-5000

BORNHEIMER, ALLEN MILLARD, lawyer; b. Brewer, Maine, June 10, 1942; s. Millard Genthner and Gertrude Evelyn (Kinney) B.; m. Deborah Russell Hill, June 17, 1967; children: Anneliese, Charles, Elizabeth. Student, Phillips Exeter Acad., 1961; AB, Harvard U., 1965, LLB, 1968. Bar: Mich. 1968, Mass. 1971. Assoc. Dickinson, Wright, McKean & Cudlip, Detroit, 1968-70, Choate, Hall & Stewart, Boston, 1970-76, ptnr., 1976-99, mng. ptnr., 1988-95; principal, gen. counsel Cargex Properties, Inc., 2000—. Bd. dirs. Cargex Properties, Inc. and affiliated cos., Portland, Maine. Town moderator, Duxbury, Mass., 1982—, chmn. fin. com., 1974-76, mem. capital budget com., 1977; bd. dirs. Jordan Hosp., Plymouth, Mass., 1974-81; trustee North Yarmouth (Maine) Acad., 1976-79. Mem. ABA, Mass. Bar Assn., Boston Bar Assn., Am. Coll. Investment Counsel, Mass. Moderators Assn., Duxbury Yacht Club (bd. dirs. 1982-84), Harvard Club (Boston). Republican. Avocations: golf, piano, sailing. General corporate, Finance, Real property. Home: 15 Summerhouse Lane Duxbury MA 02332-3930 Office: 20th Fl 50 Milk St Boston MA 02109-5003 E-mail: allen.bornheimer@cargex.com

BOROD, DONALD LEE, lawyer; b. Cleve., June 22, 1947; s. Jules Arthur and Hortense Edith (Cowan) B.; m. Jane Duclos Hudson, Nov. 11, 1978; children: James Hudson, Catherine Duclos. B.A., U. Mich., 1969; J.D., Columbia U., 1972. Bar: N.Y. 1973, Conn. 1984. Assoc. firm Dewey, Ballantine, Bushby, Palmer & Wood, N.Y.C., 1972-81; assoc. gen. counsel Kollmorgen Corp., Hartford, Conn., 1981-83, gen. counsel, 1983-86, v.p., gen. counsel, 1986-91; counsel Pepe & Hazard, Hartford, 1992—. Harlan Fiske Stone scholar Columbia U., 1971. Mem. ABA, Conn. Bar Assn., Am. Corp. Counsel Assn., Assn. Bar City N.Y. Club: Hartford Golf. Federal civil litigation, General corporate, Private international. Office: Kollmorgen Corp 1601 Trapelo Rd Waltham MA 02451-7333

BORSTEIN, LEON BAER, lawyer; b. Camden, N.J., Mar. 21, 1939; s. Isadore and Mildred (Barr) B.; m. Virginia Henneberry; 1 child: Joseph Isaiah. BS, MIT, 1961; LLB, Columbia U., 1964. Bar: N.Y. 1968, U.S. Dist. Ct. (ea. and so. dists.) N.Y. 1974, U.S. Ct. Appeals (2d cir.) 1975, U.S. Supreme Ct. 1978. Prof. econs. Peace Corp, Santa Cruz, Bolivia, 1964-66; expert USAID, La Paz, Bolivia, 1966-68; atty. Jacobs Persinger & Parker, N.Y.C., 1968-69; asst. dist. atty., Bklyn., 1971-75; chief spl. asst. atty. gen. nursing home investigation, N.Y.C., 1975-76; ptnr. Borstein & Sheinbaum, N.Y.C., 1976—. Editor: Lawyers Guide to International Business Transaction, 1963; Transactional Guide to UCC, 1964. Author: Population and Housing Census of Santa Cruz Bolivia, 1967. Mem. edn. coun. MIT, 1975—. Federal civil litigation, State civil litigation, Criminal. Home: 120 E 34th St New York NY 10016-4609 Office: 420 Lexington Ave New York NY 10170-0002

BOSCA, PIA FEDERICA, lawyer, consultant; b. Asti, Italy, Feb. 2, 1969; JD, U. Turin, Italy, 1993; M of Comparative Jurisprudence, NYU, 1995; M in Corp. Law, U. Turin, Italy, 1998. Bar: New York 1996., Italy 1999. Assoc. Rubin, Baum, Levin, Constant & Friedman, N.Y.C., 1995—96, Frignani & Assocs., Turin, 1998-2000; cons. Bosca-Cora spa, Canelli, Italy, 2001—. Office: via Bosca 2 Canelli 14053 Italy E-mail: pia@bosca.it

BOSCIA, JAMES DOMINIC, lawyer; b. Elkhart, Ind., Aug. 26, 1948; s. James Matthew and Edith Theresa (Dente) B.; m. Susan Lee Brewer, Apr. 24, 1971; children— James E., Theresa L. B.S., Ind. U., 1970, J.D., 1975. Bar: Ind. 1975, U.S. Dist. Ct. (so. dist.) Ind. 1975, U.S. Dist. Ct. (no. dist.) Ind. 1977, Wis. 1986. Atty. student loan adminstrn. Ind. U., Bloomington, 1976-77; assoc. firm Borns, Quinn, Kopko & Lindquist, Merrillville, Ind., 1977-83; ptnr. firm Bowman & McPhee, P.C., Merrillville, 1983-85 , treas., 1983-87, pres. 1987—; ptnr. firm Borns & Quinn, P.C., 1985—; mem. State Bur. Wis.. Asst. soccer coach Southlake YMCA, Crown Point, Ind., 1983-84, head soccer coach, 1986—; treas. Cub Scout Pack, 1987—. Mem. ABA, Lake County Bar Assn., Comml. Law League Am. Justinian Soc. N.W. Ind., Am. Bankruptcy Inst. Roman Catholic. Bankruptcy, Consumer commercial. Home: 10699 Hanley St Crown Point IN 46307-2825 Office: Borns & Quinn Heintz Bowman & McPhee 1000 E 80th Pl Gary IN 46410-5608

BOSL, PHILLIP L. lawyer; b. Feb. 27, 1945; BA, U. Calif., Santa Barbara, 1968; JD, U. So. Calif., 1975. Bar: Calif. 1975. Ptnr. Gibson, Dunn & Crutcher LLP, L.A., 1983—. Mem. U. So. Calif. Law Rev., 1973-75. Officer USCG, 1969-72. Mem. ABA, Los Angeles County Bar Assn., Fed. Bar Assn., Assn. Bus. Trial Lawyers Am., Securities Industry Assn. (compliance and legal divsn.), Inst. Corp. Counsel (gov.), Nat. Assn. Securities Dealers (arbitrator), Order of Coif. General civil litigation, Securities. Home: 6226 Napoli Ct Long Beach CA 90803-4800 Office: Gibson Dunn & Crutcher LLP 333 S Grand Ave Ste 4400 Los Angeles CA 90071-3197 E-mail: pbosl@gibsondunn.com

BOSS, AMELIA HELEN, law educator, lawyer; b. Balt., Apr. 3, 1949; d. Myron Theodore and Loretta (Oakjones) B.; m. Roger S. Clark, Mar. 3, 1979; children: Melissa, Seymour, Edward, Ashley. Student, Oxford (Eng.) U., 1968; BA in Sociology, Bryn Mawr, 1970; JD, Rutgers U., 1975. Bar: N.J, Pa., U.S. Dist. Ct. (ea. dist.) N.J., U.S. Dist. Ct. (ea. dist.) Pa., U.S. Supreme Ct., U.S. Ct. Appeals (3d cir.). Law clk. Hon. Milton B. Cranford N.J. Supreme Ct., 1975-76; assoc. Pepper, Hamilton & Scheetz, Phila., 1976-78; assoc. prof. law Rutgers U. Sch. Law, Camden, N.J., 1983-87, Temple U., Phila., 1989-91; prof. law Temple U. Sch. Law, 1991—, Charles Klein prof. law, 1999—. Vis. prof. law U. Miami Sch. Law, Coral Gables, Fla., 1985-86; Leo Goodwin disting. vis. prof. law Nova U., Sch. Law, 1998; mem. coms. Nat. Conf. Commrs. on Uniform State Laws; U.S. rep. to UN Commn. on Internat. Trade Law. Author: (books) Electronic Data Interchange Agreements: A Guide and Sourcebook, 1993, ABCs of the UCC: Article 2A, ABCs of the UCC: Article 5; editor-in-chief The Data Law Report, 1993-97, The Business Lawyer, 1998-99, ABCs of the UCC; mem. permanent editl. bd. Uniform Comml. Code; contbr. articles to profl. jours. Named among top 50 women lawyers in U.S. Nat. Law Jour., 1998. Fellow Am. Bar Found.; mem. ABA (chmn. bus. law sect. 2000—), Internat. Bar Assn., Am. Law Inst. (coun. 2000—), Am. Bankruptcy Inst., Am. Coll. Comml. Fin. Lawyers, Nat. Assn. Women Lawyers. Home: 309 Westmont Ave Haddonfield NJ 08033-1714 Office: Temple U Sch Law 1719 N Broad St Philadelphia PA 19122-6002

BOSS, LENARD BARRETT, lawyer; b. Passaic, N.J., Mar. 6, 1960; s. Lawrence Steven and Laura (Ziegler) Boss. BA in Rhetoric, Bates Coll., 1982; JD with high honors, George Washington U., 1985. Bar: Pa 1985, DC 1986, US Ct Appeals (4th and 11th cirs) 1986, US Dist Ct DC 1987, US Ct Appeals (DC cir) 1987, US Ct Appeals (3d cir) 1988, US Supreme Ct 1989, Md 1995. Assoc. Asbill, Junkin, Myers & Buffone, Washington, 1986-91; ptnr. Asbill, Junkin & Myers, 1991-95; asst. fed. pub. defender Fed. Pub. Defender's Office, 1995-2000; ptnr. Asbill, Junkin, Moffitt & Boss, 2000—. Adj prof George Washington Univ Law Sch, 1999—. Avocations: films, music, sports. General civil litigation, Criminal. Office: Ste 200 1615 New Hampshire Ave NW Washington DC 20009-2520 E-mail: barry_boss@mindspring.com

BOSSES, STEVAN J. lawyer; b. Bronx, N.Y., July 29, 1937; s. Fred and Frieda (Picard) B.; m. Abbye Z. Bosses, May 24, 1964; children: Donna Lynne, David Keith, Gary Philip. BME, Cornell U., 1960; LLB, Columbia U., 1963. Bar: N.Y. 1963, U.S. Dist. Ct. (so. dist.) N.Y. 1964, U.S. Dist. Ct. (ea. dist.) N.Y. 1964, U.S. Patent Office 1964, U.S. Ct. Appeals (2d cir.) 1970, U.S. Ct. Appeals (3rd cir.) 1979, U.S. Ct. Appeals (fed. cir.) 1982, U.S. Supreme Ct. 1989. Assoc. Watson Leavenworth Kelton & Taggart, N.Y.C., 1963-71, ptnr., 1972-81, Fitzpatrick, Cella, Harper & Scinto, N.Y.C., 1981—. Mem. ABA, ASME, N.Y. State Bar Assn., Am. Intellectual Property Law Assn., Fed. Bar Coun. (trustee 1989-94), Fed. Cir. Bar Assn. N.Y. Intellectual Property Law Assn. Federal civil litigation, Patent, Trademark and copyright. Home: 19 Springdale Rd Scarsdale NY 10583-7330 Office: 30 Rockefeller Plz New York NY 10112-0002 E-mail: sbosses@fchs.com

BOSSIO, SALVATORE, lawyer; b. Spokane, Wash., Nov. 29, 1928; s. Salvatore N. and Rosa (Costanza) B.; m. Joan S. Smith, Feb. 16, 1957; children: Lora Jo, Deborah, Amy, Stephen, Bruce. B.A., Stanford U., 1951, J.D., 1953. Asso. firm Hassard, Bonnington, Rogers & Huber, San Francisco, 1955-64, partner, 1964—. Dir., sec. Swinerton & Walberg Co., San Francisco, 1988—. Served with U.S. Army, 1953-55. Recipient Pres.'s award for outstanding service Assn. Def. Counsel, 1979 Fellow Am. Coll. Trial Lawyers; mem. Am. Bar Assn., Bar Assn. San Francisco, State Bar Calif., Marin County Bar Assn., Am. Bd. Trial Advs., Internat. Assn. Ins. Counsel, Nat. Assn. R.R. Trial Counsel, Calif. Med.-Legal Assn. (chmn. 1978-79), Assn. Def. Counsel (dir. 1979-80), Am. Bd. Profl. Liability Attys. State civil litigation, Personal injury.

BOST, THOMAS GLEN, lawyer, educator; b. Oklahoma City, July 13, 1942; s. Burl John and Lorene Bell (Croka) B.; m. Sheila K. Pettigrew, Aug. 27, 1966; children: Amy Elizabeth, Stephen Luke, Emily Anne, Paul Alexander. BS in Acctg. summa cum laude, Abilene Christian U., 1964; JD, Vanderbilt U., 1967. Bar: Tenn. 1967, Calif. 1969. Instr. David Lipscomb Coll., Nashville, 1967; asst. prof. law Vanderbilt U., 1967-68; ptnr. Latham & Watkins, Los Angeles, 1968-99; prof. law Pepperdine U., 2000—. Lectr. on taxation subjects. Chmn. bd. regents, law sch. bd. visitors

Pepperdine U., Malibu, Calif., 1980-2000. Mem. ABA (chmn. standards of tax practice com., sec. taxation 1988-90), State Bar of Calif., Los Angeles County Bar Assn. (chmn. taxation sect. 1981-82), Calif. Club (L.A.), Beach Club (Santa Monica). Republican. Mem. Ch. of Christ. Corporate taxation, Personal income taxation, State and local taxation.

BOSTON, WILLIAM CLAYTON, lawyer; b. Hobart, Okla., Nov. 29, 1934; s. William Clayton and Dollie Jane (Gibbs) B.; m. Billie Gail Long, Jan. 20, 1962; children: Kathryn Gray, William Clayton III. BS, Okla. State U., 1958; LLB, U. Okla., 1962; LLM, NYU, 1967. Bar: Okla. 1961. Assoc. Mosteller, Fellers, Andrews, Snider & Baggett, Oklahoma City, 1962-64; ptnr. Fellers, Snider, Baggett, Blankenship & Boston, 1968-69, Andrews, Davis, Legg, Bixler, Milsten & Murrah, Oklahoma City, 1972-86; pvt. practice Boston & Boston PLLC, 1986—. Contbr. articles to profl. jours.; mem. adv. bd. The Jour. of Air Law and Commerce, 1995—. Past pres. and trustee Ballet Okla.; past v.p., bd. dirs. Oklahoma City Arts Coun.; past trustee Nichols Hills (Okla.) Methodist Ch.; past trustee, chmn. Okla. Found. for the Humanities; past trustee, vice-chmn., sec. Humanities in Okla., Inc., 1992-95. With U.S. Army, 1954-56. Mem. ABA (former chmn. subcom. on aircraft fin., former chmn. aircraft fin. and contract divsn. forum on air and space law), FBA, Internat. Bar Assn., Inter-Pacific Bar Assn., Okla. State Bar Assn., Oklahoma County Bar Assn. General practice. Home: 1701 Camden Way Oklahoma City OK 73116-5121 Office: 4005 NW Expressway St Oklahoma City OK 73116-1691

BOSTROM, ROBERT EVERETT, lawyer; b. Hartford, Conn., Nov. 20, 1952; m. Elizabeth Mitchell Leys, July 14, 1979; children: Leys, Ashley, Allison. BA, Franklin and Marshall Coll., 1974; M in Internat. Affairs, Columbia U., 1976; JD cum laude, Boston Coll., 1980. Bar: N.Y. 1981, U.S. Dist. Ct. (ea., so. dist.) N.Y. Atty. Fed. Res. Bank, N.Y.C., 1980-82; assoc. Windels, Marx, Davies & Ives, 1982-84, Brown & Wood, N.Y.C., 1984—; mng. ptnr., head fin. instns. practice. Exec. v.p. legal and regulatory affairs, gen. counsel Nat. Westminster Bancorp, 1992-96; mem. bd. advisors Mergers and Acquistions SNL Securities, 1994—; lectr., moderator, spkr., and chairperson in field; co-chmn. Strategic Rsch. Inst. Capital Markets Activities of Interant. Banks, 1994, 95. Contbr. articles to profl jours. and mags; editor-in-chief: Boston Coll. Internat. and Comparative Law Review, 1979-80; co-editor: Internat. Practioner's Notebook, 1988-93. Mem. Internat. Lawyers Assn. (exec. com. Am. br. 1992-94), ABA, N.Y. County Lawyers Assn. (banking com.). General corporate, Finance, Mergers and acquisitions. E-mail: rbostrom@winston.com

BOSTWICK, JAMES STEPHEN, lawyer; b. Pasadena, Calif., Jan. 15, 1943; s. Jack Raymond and Rhoda Loraine (Fox) B.; children from a previous marriage: Brenton Reid, Grant Evan, Blake Powell; m. Marti Philips; children: Taylor, Carter. MS, U. Wash., 1965; JD, Hastings Coll. Law, 1968. Bar: Calif. 1968, Hawaii 1981. Pvt. practice, San Francisco, 1968; assoc. Walkup, Downing, Sterns & Poore, 1968-73; ptnr. Walkup, Downing & Sterns, 1973-77, Sterns, Bostwick & Tehin, 1977-79; sr. ptnr. Bostwick & Tehin, 1979-96, Bostwick & Assocs., 1996—. Faculty Coll. Advocacy, 1976—, Hastings seminar on trial practice; lectr. in field. Recipient Trial Achievement award San Francisco Trial Lawyers Assn., 1979. Fellow Internat. Acad. Trial Lawyers (sec. internat. rels. 1997-99, bd. dirs. 1993—, dean 2000—); mem. ATLA, Calif. Trial Lawyers Assn. (chmn. profl. liability legis. com. 1975-77, bd. dirs. 1978-85), Am. Bd. Profl. Liability Attys., Hawaii Acad. Plaintiff's Attys., San Francisco Trial Lawyers Assn. (bd. dirs., chmn. patients litigation fund com., chmn. jud. liaison com., mem. nat. cert. com., Best Lawyer Am. personal injury litigation sect. 1987—). Democrat. General civil litigation, Personal injury, Professional liability. Office: 4 Embarcadero Ctr Ste 750 San Francisco CA 94111-4171 E-mail: james@bostwickfirm.com

BOSWELL, JOHN HOWARD, lawyer; b. Houston, Mar. 22, 1932; s. Henry Oliver and Opal Everest (Wineburg) B.; m. Sharon Lee Ueckert, Dec. 19, 1959; 1 child, Mark Richard. B.B.A., U. Houston, 1955; J.D., U. Houston, 1963. Bar: Tex. 1962, U.S. Supreme Ct. 1970, U.S. Ct. Appeals (5th cir.) 1970; cert. civil trial adv. Nat. Bd. Trial Advocacy, Tex. Bd. Legal Specialization. Sr. shareholder Boswell, Hallmark & Brothers, P.C., Houston; lectr. State Bar Tex. Continuing Legal Edn. Program, 1978-98, Pepperdine U. Coll. Law; faculty Tex. Coll. of Trial Advocacy, 1980-90. Served to lt. USNR, 1955-58. Mem. Am. Bd. Trial Advocates, Internat. Assn. Ins. Counsel, Tex. Assn. Def. Counsel, Def. Rsch. Inst. Federal civil litigation, State civil litigation, Personal injury. Home: 1247 Ripple Creek Dr Houston TX 77057-1764 Address: Boswell & Hallmark 1010 Lamar St Ste 900 Houston TX 77002-6314

BOSWELL, WILLIAM PARET, lawyer; b. Washington, Oct. 24, 1946; s. Yates Paret and Mary Frances (Hyland) B.; m. Barbara Stelle Schroeder, Sept. 6, 1969; children: Susan Anne, Sarah Mary, Christina Catherine. BA cum laude, Cath. U., 1968; JD, U. Va., 1971. Bar: Va. 1971, D.C. 1972, U.S. Ct. Mil. Appeals 1972, U.S. Supreme Ct. 1975, Pa. 1978. Atty. Peoples Natural Gas Co., Pitts., 1978-82, asst. sec., gen. atty., 1982-85, sec., gen. counsel, 1985-88, v.p., gen. counsel, sec., 1989-99; gen. counsel Hope Gas, Inc., 1998-2000; dep. gen. counsel Consol. Natural Gas Co., 1999-2000, Dominion Resources, Inc., Pitts., 2000; ptnr. McGuireWoods LLP, 2000—. Mem. exec. com. Gas Industry Stds. Bd., 1994-97, bd. dirs., 1998—, chmn., 2001—. Pres. Borough Coun., Osborne, Pa., 1984-97, mayor, 1998—; bd. dirs. Mendelssohn Choir Pitts., 1996—, pres. 1997-98; trustee Laughlin Found., 1995—. Capt. JAGC, USAF, 1971-78, col. USAFR, 1978-98, ret. Decorated Legion of Merit. Mem. ABA (chair gas com. 1995—), Pa. Bar Assn., D.C. Bar Assn., Va. Bar Assn., Am. Gas Assn. (chair regulatory com. 1996-98), Pa. Gas Assn. (chmn. 1989-90), Am. Corp. Counsel Assn. (pres. Pa. chpt. 1991-92, Excellence in Corporate Practice award 1998), Am. Soc. Corp. Secs., City Club Pitts., Army and Navy Club D.C. Republican. Roman Catholic. Avocations: reading, walking. General corporate, Oil, gas, and mineral, Public utilities. Home: 405 Hare Ln Sewickley PA 15143-2050 Office: Dominion Tower 23 Fl 625 Liberty Ave Pittsburgh PA 15222-3142

BOTELHO, BRUCE MANUEL, state attorney general, mayor; b. Juneau, Alaska, Oct. 6, 1948; s. Emmett Manuel and Harriet Iowa (Tieszen) B.; m. Guadalupe Alvarez Breton, Sept. 23, 1988; children: Alejandro Manuel, Adriana Regina. Student, U. Heidelberg, Federal Republic of Germany, 1970; BA, Willamette U., 1971, JD, 1976. Bar: Alaska 1976, U.S. Ct. Appeals (9th cir.), U.S. Supreme Ct. Asst. atty. gen. State of Alaska, Juneau, 1976-83, 87-90, dep. commr., acting commr. Dept. of Revenue, 1983-86; mayor City, Borough of Juneau, 1988-91, dep. atty. gen., 1991-94; atty. gen. State of AK, 1994—. Editor: Willamette Law Jour., 1975-76; contbr. articles profl. jours. Assembly mem. City, Borough of Juneau, 1983-86; pres. Juneau Human Rights Commn., 1978-80, Alaska Coun. Am. Youth Hostels, 1979-81, Juneau Arts and Humanities Coun., 1981-83, S.E.E Alaska Area coun. Boy Scouts Am., 1991-93, 2001—, coun. commr., 1993-2000; bd. dirs. Found. for Social Innovations, Alaska, 1990-93, Alaska Econ. Devel. Coun., 1985-87, Alaska Indsl. Devel. Corp., 1984-86; pres. Juneau World Affairs Coun., 2000—; chair adminstrv. law sect. Alaska Bar Assn., 1981-82; chair Alaska Resources Corp., 1984-86, Gov.'s Conf. on Youth and Justice, 1995-96; trustee Alaska Children's Trust, 1996-2000, Alaska Permanent Fund, 2000—; mem. exec. com. Conf. of Western Attys. Gen., 1997—, chair, 2000—; co-chair Alaska Justice Assessment Commn., 1997—, chair Gov. Task Force on Confidentiality of Chldns. Procs., 1998—; mem. Commn. for Justice Across the Atlantic, 1999—. Recipient Silver Beaver award Boy Scouts Am. Mem. Nat. Assn. Attys. Gen. (exec. com. 1998—). Democrat. Methodist. Avocation: international folk dance. Home: 401 F St Douglas AK 99824-5353 Office: State Alaska Dept Law PO Box 110300 Juneau AK 99811-0300

BOTTELLA, TAMMY ANN, lawyer; b. Cranston, R.I., Dec. 7, 1968; d. Ronald John and Louise Marie Bottella. AS, C.C. of R.I., 1989; BS, Bryant Coll., 1991; JD, Tulane U., 1994. Assoc. atty. Law Office of Charles Kirwan, Pawtucket, R.I., 1994-95, Law Office of Arlene Violet, East Providence, 1995-96; corp. counsel Great Am. Nursing Ctrs., Warwick, 1996-97; assoc. atty. Law Offices Winfred Eckenreiter, Fairhaven, Mass., 1997-99; pvt. practice Warwick, 1999—. Recipient Outstanding Bus. Student award Am. Mgmt. Soc., 1986. Mem. ABA, Million Dollar Advocates Forum, Assn. of Trial Lawyers of Am., R.I. Bar Assn., Conn. Bar Assn., Delta Mu Delta. Roman Catholic. Real property, General civil litigation, Personal injury. Home: 1108 Chopmist Hill Rd Scituate RI 02857-1046 Office: 255 Quaker Ln Ste 600 West Warwick RI 02893

BOTTITTA, JOSEPH ANTHONY, lawyer; b. Mar. 9, 1949; s. Anthony S. and Elizabeth (Bellisano) B.; m. Lynda Joan Kloss, Apr. 14, 1979;children: Michelle Emma, Gregory Joseph. BSBA, Seton Hall U., 1971, JD, 1974. Bar: U.S. Dist. Ct. N.J. 1974, U.S. Supreme Ct. 1981. Ptnr. Rusignola & Pugliese, Newark, 1974-78; sr. ptnr. Joseph A. Bottitta, West Orange, N.J., 1979-88, Gilbert, Gilbert, Schlossberg and Bottitta, 1988-89; pvt. practice, 1989-95; with Bottitta and Bascelli, 1995-99. Chmn. Supreme Ct. Fee Arbitration Com. Dist. V-B., 1984-85; mem. N.J. Uniform Law Commn., 1987-91; mem. N.J. Commn. on Professionalism in Law, 1997—; pres. N.J. Lawyers Svc., 2000—; pres., CEO E-Law.com, 2000—. Fellow Am. Bar Found.; mem. ABA, ATLA, N.J. State Bar Assn. (trustee 1988, sec. 1988-94, treas. 1994-95, v.p. 1995-97, pres.-elect 1997-98, pres. 1998-99), Essex County Bar Assn. (sec. 1983-84, treas. 1984-85, pres.-elect 1985-86, pres. 1986-87). Republican. Roman Catholic. Communications, Computer, General corporate. Office: c/o NJ Lawyers Svc 2333 Route 22 W Union NJ 07083-8517 E-mail: joeb@njls.com

BOUCHER, JOSEPH W(ILLIAM), lawyer, accountant, educator, writer; b. Menominee, Mich., Oct. 28, 1951; s. Joseph W. and Patricia (Coon) B.; m. Susan M. De Groot, June 4, 1977; children: Elizabeth, Bridget, Joseph William III. BA, St. Norbert Coll., 1973; JD, U. Wis., 1977, MBA in Fin., 1978. Bar: Wis. 1978, U.S. Dist. Ct. (we. dist.) Wis. 1978; CPA, Wis. Adminstrv. aide to Senator Wis. Senate, Madison, 1977; from assoc. to ptnr. Murphy, Stolper et al., 1977-84; ptnr. Stolper, Koritzinsky, Brewster & Neider, 1985-94; mng. ptnr. Stolper, Koritzinsky, Brewster, Neider, 1989-92, Neider & Boucher, S.C., 1995—. Lectr. bus. U. Wis., Madison, 1980—. Co-author: Organizing a Wisconsin Business Corporation, 1995, 99, Wisconsin LLCs and LLPs Handbook, 1996, 1999, 2000; contbr. articles to Wis. Bar Assn. Bd. dirs. Jackson Found., 1994—99, West Met. Bus. Assn., 1990—95, Dane County United Way., 1986—89, Wis. Chamber Orch., 1990—94, pres., 1993—94; bd. dirs. St. Coletta's, 1997—2001, Edgewood H.S., 1997—, chair, 2001—; mem. bd. advisors St. Mary's Med. Ctr., Madison, 1989—91. Named one of Outstanding Young Men of Am., 1979; named Wis. Lawyer Advocate of Yr., SBA, 1983. Mem. ABA, AICPA (mem. bd. examiners, mem. bus. law subcom. 1987-90), Wis. Bar Assn., Wis. State Bar Assn. (mem. corp. com. 1991—, co-chairperson interprofl. com. 1992-95, chair ltd. liability co. subcom.), Dane County Bar Assn., Wis. Inst. CPAs, U. Wis. Bus. Alumni Assn. (bd. dirs. 1980-87). Roman Catholic. Avocations: sports, reading. Contracts commercial, General corporate, Corporate taxation. Office: Neider & Boucher SC 440 Science Dr Madison WI 53711-1064

BOUDIN, MICHAEL, federal judge; b. N.Y.C., Nov. 29, 1939; s. Leonard B. and Jean (Roisman) B.; m. Martha A. Field, Sept. 14, 1984. B.A., Harvard Coll., 1961, LL.B., 1964. Bar: N.Y. 1964, D.C. 1967. Law clk. U.S. Ct. Appeals, 2d cir., 1964-65, U.S. Sup. Ct., 1965-66; assoc. firm Covington & Burling, Washington, 1966-72, ptnr., 1972-87; dep. asst. atty. gen. Anti-trust div. Dept. Justice, 1987-90; judge U.S. Dist. Ct. of D.C., 1990-92, U.S. Ct. Appeals, Boston, 1992-98. Vis. prof. Harvard Law Sch., 1982-83, lectr., 1983-98; lectr. U. Pa. Law Sch., 1984-85. Contbr. revs. to law jours. Mem. ABA, Am. Law Inst. Office: US Ct Appeals 1st Cir 1 Courthouse Way Ste 7710 Boston MA 02210-3009

BOUDREAU, DANIEL J. state supreme court justice; b. Natick, Mass., 1947; m. Faith Boudreau, 1972. BA, Boston Coll.; JD, U. Tulsa. Judge, then vice-chief judge Okla. Ct. of Civil Appeals, 1992-99; justice Okla. State Supreme Ct., Oklahoma City, 1999—.*

BOUGARTCHEV, KIRIL ALEXANDRE, lawyer; b. Paris, Aug. 28, 1961; s. Vladimir Bougartchev and Monique De Grave; m. Sylvie Praget, June 10, 1994; children: Nicolas, Juliette. M in Comml. Law, M ni Litigation, postgrad., Paris U. Paris Bar Exam. 1988. Trainee L'Oreal, Paris, 1982, Gide Loyrette Novel, Paris, 1983, Gen. Oils, Paris, 1985, Candert Bros./Klindel & Anderson, L.A., 1986, Kennedy Olmstead & Gardner, L.A., Jean Veil & Assocs., Paris, 1988, Arthur Andersen Internat., Paris, 1988; assoc. Gide Loyrette Novel, 1989, ptnr., 1999. Contbr.: (book) Bankruptcy Law, 1994; contbr. articles to legal jours. With Legal Office of Army, 1987-88. Mem. Paris Bar Assn. (sec. conf. du stage 1996). Avocations: tennis, hunting. Bankruptcy, Contracts commercial, Criminal. Office: Gide Loyrette Novel 26 Cours Albert 75008 Paris France

BOUKEMA, HENK JAN, lawyer; b. Eindhoven, Brabant, The Netherlands, Jan. 22, 1948; s. Johannes and Janny Maria (van den Heuvel) Boukema; m. Maria Monica Brigitta van Meel, May 18, 1984; children: Eleonora, Catherina, Tertius. ML, Vrije U., Amsterdam, 1973, MPhil, 1974, LLD, 1980. Mem. Bar of Amsterdam 1974, The Hague 2000. Member Amsterdam Bar Assn., 1974-99, The Hague Bar Assn., 2000—. Hon. judge, Regional Court of Arnhem, E. Netherlands, 2001. Author: Judging, 1980, Good Law, 1982, articles on Jurisprudence, 1974—. Legal adviser, Foundations on Arts, Culture, Sports. Officer in the Order of Oranje-Nassau by Her Majesty, 1999. Mem. Dutch Bar, Hague Bar, Intell. Prop. Orgn. First Lt., The Netherlands Artillery, 1968-69. Avocations: riding to hounds (Royal Dutch Hunt), opera. Office: Pels Rijcken & Droogleever Fortuijn Kon Julianaplein 30 2595 AA The Hague The Netherlands Fax: 0031 70 3830058. E-mail: hjm.boukema@prdf.nl

BOULGER, WILLIAM CHARLES, lawyer; b. Columbus, Ohio, Apr. 2, 1924; s. James Ignatius and Rebecca (Laughlin) B.; m. Ruth J. Schachtele, Dec. 29, 1954; children: Brigid Carolyn, Ruth Mary. AB, Harvard Coll., 1948; LLB, Law Sch. Cin., 1951. Bar: Ohio, 1951, U.S. Dist. Ct. (so. dist.) Ohio 1952, U.S. Supreme Ct. 1957. Ptnr. with Thomas A. Boulger, Chillicothe, Ohio, 1951-73; ptnr. Boulger and Boulger, Chillicothe, 1974—. Pres. Ross County Welfare Assn., Chillicothe, 1954-60; mem. Chillicothe. ARC, 1958-84, chmn., 1959-63, 1985—; mem. Democratic Exec. Com., Chillicothe, 1950s. Served as pfc. U.S. Army, 1943-45, ETO. Mem. Ross County Bar Assn. (pres. 1971), Ohio Bar Assn., ABA, Sunset Club, Symposiarchs Club (past pres.). Roman Catholic. Avocations: tennis, golf. General practice, Personal injury, Probate. Home: 31 Club Dr Chillicothe OH 45601-1129 Office: PO Box 204 Chillicothe OH 45601-0204

BOUMA, JOHN JACOB, lawyer; b. Ft. Dodge, Iowa, Jan. 13, 1937; s. Jacob and Gladys Glennie (Cooper) B.; m. Bonnie Jeanne Lane, Aug. 15, 1959; children: John Jeffrey, Wendy Sue, Laura Lynne, Jennifer Ann. BA, U. Iowa, 1958, JD, 1960. Bar: Iowa 1960, Wis. 1960, Ariz. 1962, U.S. Ct. Appeals (9th cir.) 1971, U.S. Ct. Appeals (D.C. cir.) 1971, U.S. Ct. Appeals (10th cir.) 1982, U.S. Tax Ct., 1983, U.S. Supreme Ct. 1975. Assoc. Foley, Sammond & Lardner, Milw., 1960, Snell & Wilmer, Phoenix, 1962-66, ptnr., 1967—, chmn., 1983—. Contbr. articles to profl. jours. Chmn. Phoenix Human Rels. Commn., 1972-75; mem. Phoenix Commn. on LEAP, 1971-72, Phoenix Cmty. Alliance, 1991—; bd. dirs. Phoenix Legal Aid Soc., 1970-76, Ariz. Econ. Coun., 1989-93, Mountain States Legal Found., 1977-95; trustee Ariz. Opera Co., 1984—, pres., 1989-91; trustee Phoenix Art Mus., 1994-2000, pres., 1996-98. Capt. JAGC, U.S. Army, 1960-62. Recipient Walter E. Craig Disting. Svc. award, 1998, Cmty. Legal Svcs. Decade of Dedication award, 1998, Disting. Achievement medal Ariz. State U. Coll. Law, 1998. Fellow Am. Coll. Trial Lawyers; mem. ABA (Ho. of Dels. 1989—, bd. govs. 1998-2001, editl. bd. 1996-98), Maricopa County Bar Assn. (pres. 1977-78), Nat. Conf. Bar Pres. (exec. coun. 1984-91, pres. 1989-90), Ariz. Bar Assn. (pres. 1983-84), Ariz. Bar Found. (pres. 1987-88), Iowa Bar Assn., Wis. Bar Assn., Phoenix Assn. Def. Counsel (pres. 1972), Attys. Liability Assurance Soc. Ltd. (bd. dirs. 1987—), Iowa Law Sch. Found. (bd. dirs. 1986—), Phoenix C. of C. (bd. dirs. 1988-94), Ariz. State Coll. Law Soc. (bd. dirs., pres. 1997-2000), Western States Bar Conf. (pres. 1988-89), Ariz. Suprme Ct. Spl. Com. on Lawyer Discipline and Profl. Conduct, Order of Coif, Phi Beta Kappa, Phi Eta Sigma, Omicron Delta Kappa. Avocations: fishing, hunting, skiing, travel, golf. Antitrust, General civil litigation, Professional liability. Home: 800 E Circle Rd Phoenix AZ 85020-4144 Office: Snell & Wilmer One Arizona Ctr Phoenix AZ 85004-2202

BOURCIER, JOHN PAUL, state supreme court justice; b. Providence, Mar. 27, 1927; s. Louis J. and Lydia E. (Garceau) B.; m. Norma M. DiLuglio, Aug. 20, 1951; children: Carol Bourcier Fargnoli, Norma J. Bourcier Bucci. BA, Brown U., 1950; LLB, Vanderbilt U., 1953. Bar: U.S. Dist. Ct. R.I. 1955, U.S. Ct. Appeals 1956, U.S. Immigration Svc. 1956, U.S. Ct. Mil. Appeals 1958, U.S. Tax Ct. 1960, U.S. Army Bd. Rev. 1965, U.S. Dist. Ct. Fla. 1965, N.H. 1965, Va. 1965. Trial atty. Bourcier & Bordieri, Providence, 1953-74; assoc. justice R.I. Superior Ct., 1974-95; justice R.I. Supreme Ct., 1995—. Chair Supreme Ct. Com. on Future of R.I. Cts.; invited judiciary panelist Rev. of Supreme Ct. Cases, 1987-92; lectr. in field; instr. Roger Williams Coll., 1982-95; guest lectr. Brown U., 1979-95, Bryant Coll., 1990-93, R.I. C.C., 1989-90; lectr. R.I. Fire Marshalls Arson Seminars, 1989—, New Eng. Fire Marshalls Arson Seminars, 1990-95; chmn. Superior Ct. Jury Trial Instrn. Rev. Com., mem. Civil Rules Rev. Com., others. Asst. editor Vanderbilt Law Rev., 1951-53. With USN, 1944-46. Named for life Assoc. Justice R.I. Supreme Ct. by Gov. Lincoln Almond, 1995—; inducted LaSalle Acad. Hall of Fame, 1998. Home and Office: RI Supreme Court 250 Benefit St Providence RI 02903-2719

BOUTIN, PETER RUCKER, lawyer; b. San Francisco, Oct. 6, 1950; s. Frank J. and Charlotte (Downey) B.; m. Suzanne Jones, Aug. 31, 1974; children: Jennifer, Lisa, Kevin. AB, Stanford U., 1972; JD magna cum laude, Santa Clara U., 1975. Bar: Calif. 1975, U.S. Dist. Ct. (no., ea., so. and ctrl. dists.) Calif. 1976, U.S. Ct. Appeals (9th cir.) 1977, U.S. Supreme Ct. 1982. Assoc. Keesal, Young & Logan, Long Beach, Calif., 1975-78, ptnr., 1978-84, mng. ptnr. San Francisco office San Francisco, 1984—. Arbitrator San Francisco Superior Ct., 1989—, Nat. Assn. Securities Dealers, San Francisco, 1980—; mediator San Francisco Superior Ct., 1989—; early neutral evaluation panel U.S. Dist. Ct., 1993—. Co-author Am. Arbitration Assn. Arbitrator Tng. Materials, 1992. Mem. Bar Assn. San Francisco, Assn. Bus. Trial Lawyers, Securities Industry Assn. Compliance and Legal Divsn., San Francisco Bond Club, Stanford Buck/Cardinal Club. General civil litigation, Labor, Securities. Office: Keesal Young & Logan 4 Embarcadero Ctr Ste 1500 San Francisco CA 94111-4122 E-mail: peter.boutin@kyl.com

BOVA, VINCENT ARTHUR, JR. lawyer, consultant, photographer; b. Pitts., Apr. 25, 1946; s. Vincent A. and Janie (Pope) B.; m. Breda Murphy, Mar. 20, 1971; 1 child, Kate Murphy Bova. BA in Bus. Adminstrn., Alma (Mich.) Coll., 1968; MPA, Ohio State U., 1972; JD, Oklahoma City U., 1975. Bar: Okla. 1975, N.Mex. 1976, U.S. Dist. Ct. 1976, U.S. Tax Ct., 1976, U.S. Ct. Appeals (10th cir.) 1976, U.S. Supreme Ct. 1979. Mktg. and systems rep., computer systems div. RCA, 1968-70; research analyst Research Atlanta, 1972-73; assoc. Threet, Threet, Glass, King & Maxwell, 1976-78; ptnr. Lill & Bova, P.A., 1978-81; sole practice Albuquerque, 1981—. Past pres. Bare Bulls Investment, 1982, Fumilan Investment, 1983, Toastmasters; rsch. analyst urban affairs Ohio Dept. Urban Affairs, Columbus, 1971; panel mem. N.Mex. Med. Rev. Commn., 1981—, N.Mex. Legal/Dental/Osteopathic Podiatry Com., 1981—; v.p. Albuquerque Com. on Fgn. Rels., 2001—. Contbr. articles on organizational behavior and mgmt. to profl. jours. Bd. dirs. Rio Grande Nature Ctr.; pres., v.p. spl. projects S.W. Arts and Crafts Festival, Albuquerque, 1986-89; pol. cons. Nov. Group; mem. N.Mex. Estate Planning Coun., 1978—; sec.-treas., vice-chmn. adv. bd. Salvation Army, 1987—; contbr. Ctr. for Home for Prevention of Domestic Violence, 1984-85, Ronald McDonald House, 1984; past chmn. N.Mex. Workers' Compensation Monthly; mem. advt. com. Supreme Ct. Panel; pres. Salvation Army Adv. Bd., Albuquerque; mem. Edn. Forum. With Air N.G., 1969-75. Recipient Pacesetters award Ohio State U., 1972; named one of Outstanding Young Men of Am., 1975, 76. Mem. ATLA (advanced grad. Nat. Coll. Advocacy), Ct. Practice Inst. (advanced diplomate), ABA, N.Mex. Bar Assn. (pres. small firm and solo sect.), State Bar N.Mex. (mem. med. legal panel, med.-dental podiatry legal panel, rep. probate, wills and trusts ann. report), Nat. Def. Lawyers, Assn. (staff chmn. 1986), N.Mex. Trial Lawyers Assn., Internat. Assn. Fin. Planners, Nat. Assn. Social Security Claimants Reps. (past state chmn.), Business Round Table, Albuquerque Bar Assn., N.Mex. Fin. Planning Assn., Sole Practitioners Assn., Internat. Credit Assn. (lectr.), Ohio State U. Alumni Assn. of N.Mex. (pres.), Image Profls. of the S.W. (bd. dirs., print chmn. 1996—), Image Profls. S.W. (photography award 1996, Best of Show 2000, 10 others, 14 awards 1999), Profl. Photography Assn., Photog. Soc. Am. (pres. chpt.), Toastmasters (past pres., v.p., edn. chmn., Able Toastmaster award), Millionaires Tip Club, Enchanted Lens Camera Club (pres.), Profl. Photographers Am. (8 awards 1999), Albuquerque Knife and Fork (pres., v.p., sec.-treas., bd. dirs.), Inn of the Ct., Zia Scuba Club, Phi Alpha Delta, Sigma Tau Gamma. Democrat. Presbyterian. Avocations: flower gardening, photography - video and still, computers, investing, reading. General civil litigation, Consumer commercial, Probate. Office: 5716 Osuna Rd NE Albuquerque NM 87109-2527

BOVAIRD, BRENDAN PETER, lawyer; b. N.Y.C., Mar. 9, 1948; s. John Francis and Margaret Mary (Endrizzi) B.; m. Carolyn Warren Boyle, Dec. 18, 1971; children: Anne Warren, Sarah Grant. BA, Fordham U., 1970; JD, U. Va., 1973. Bar: N.Y. 1974, D.C. 1980, Pa. 1983, U.S. Dist. Ct. (so. and ea. dists.) N.Y. 1974, U.S. Ct. Appeals (2d cir.) 1974. Atty., Dewey, Ballantine, Bushby, Palmer & Wood, N.Y.C., 1973-82; asst. gen. counsel Campbell Soup Co., Camden, N.J., 1982-90; sr. v.p., gen. counsel, sec. Orion Pictures Corp., N.Y.C., 1990-91; counsel, mem. exec. com. Wyeth-Ayerst Internat. Inc., St. Davids, Pa., 1992-95; pres. KDH Inc., 1994—; v.p., gen. counsel UGI Corp., Valley Forge, Pa., 1995—; v.p., gen. counsel AmeriGas Propane, Inc., Valley Forge, 1995—; bd. dirs. Motion Picture Export Assn. Am., Inc., 1990-91, United Valley Ins. Co. Mem. MPAA (legal com. 1990-91), ABA (corp., bus. law sect., internat. law sect.), Aircraft Owners and Pilots Assn., Phila. Country Club, Phi Delta Phi. General corporate, Private international, Mergers and acquisitions. Office: UGI Corp PO Box 858 Valley Forge PA 19482-0858

BOVASSO, LOUIS JOSEPH, lawyer; b. Jersey City, Aug. 16, 1935; s. Louis S. and Mildred (Blumetti) B.; m. Margaret Ann Wilt, Aug. 18, 1964 (div. Sept. 1977); children— Tracy, Marc, Shelley, Kari; m. Helen Schumow, July 14, 1984. B.S.M.E., Newark Coll. Engring., 1961; J.D., Catholic U. Am., 1966. Bar: Calif. 1973, U.S. Dist. Ct. (cen. dist.) Calif. 1973, U.S. Ct. Appeals (9th cir.) 1973, U.S. Ct. Appeals (5th cir.) 1975. Assoc. Poms, Smith, Lande & Rose, Los Angeles, 1973-79, ptnr., 1979—. Served to sgt. USAF, 1954-58. Mem. U.S. Trademark Assn., Century City Bar Assn., La. Patent Law Assn. Republican. Patent, Trademark and copyright. Home: 26081 Baldwin Pl Stevenson Ranch CA 91381-1135

BOWDEN, GEORGE NEWTON, judge; b. East Orange, N.J., Nov. 21, 1946; s. W. Paul and Catherine A. (Porter) B. BA, Bowdoin Coll., 1971; JD, U. Maine, 1974. Bar: Wash. 1974, Maine 1975, U.S. Dist. Ct. (we. dist.) Wash. 1978, U.S. Ct. Appeals (9th cir.) 1980, U.S. Supreme Ct. 1982. Asst. county atty. Lincoln County, Wiscasset, Maine, 1974; dep. pros. atty. Grays Harbor County, Montesano, Wash., 1974-76, King County, Seattle, 1976, Snohomish County, Everett, Wash., 1976-79; ptnr. Senter & Bowden, 1979-97; judge Snohomish County Superior Ct., 1997—. Bd. dirs. Everett Symphony Orch. 1993—, pres. 1996-98; v.p. Driftwood Players, Edmonds, Wash., 1978. Sgt. USMC, 1966-68. Mem. ATLA, NADCL, Wash. State Bar Assn. (CLE com., fee arbitration bd., legal aid and pro bono com.), Wash. Assn. Criminal Def. Lawyers (bd. govs., sec. 1993), Wash. State Trial Lawyers Assn., Snohomish County Bar Assn. (pres. 1995), Rotary. Avocations: scuba diving, skiing, bicycling. Office: Snohomish County Courthouse Superior Ct 3000 Rockefeller Ave M/S502 Everett WA 98201-4046

BOWDEN, HENRY LUMPKIN, JR. lawyer; b. Atlanta, Aug. 2, 1949; s. Henry Lumpkin and Ellen Marian (Fleming) B.; m. Roberta Jeanne Johnson, June 30, 1973; children: Caroline Bruton, Henry Lumpkin III. BA, U. Va., 1971; JD, Emory U., 1974. Bar: Ga. 1974. Law clk. for Hon. Griffin B. Bell U.S. Ct. Appeals (5th cir.), Atlanta, 1974-75; ptnr. King & Spalding, 1975-95; prin. Bowden Law Firm, P.C., 1995—. Trustee Atlanta Ballet, Inc., 1976-85, chmn., 1983-84; trustee Emory U., Atlanta, 1986—; trustee Hist. Oakland Found., Inc., Atlanta, 1987-95, chmn. 1992-95; trustee Westminster Schs., Atlanta, 1995-2000. Fellow Am. Coll. Trust and Estate Counsel (state chair 1991-96), Am. Bar Found.; mem. ABA, State Bar Ga. (chair fiduciary sect. 1990-91), Atlanta Bar Assn., Lawyers Club Atlanta, Piedmont Driving Club (dir. 1996-99), Capital City Club, Nine O'Clocks (pres. 1977-78), Farmington Country Club, Gridiron Secret Soc., Homosassa Fishing Club, The Ten, Phi Beta Kappa, Omicron Delta Kappa, Phi Delta Theta. Methodist. Home: 2542 Habersham Rd NW Atlanta GA 30305-3566 Office: 191 Peachtree St NE Ste 849 Atlanta GA 30303-1747 E-mail: henrybowdenjr@bowdenlaw.com

BOWE, RICHARD WELBOURN, lawyer; b. Balt., Nov. 4, 1949; s. Richard Eugene and Virginia Welbourn (Cooley) B.; m. Mary M. Vandeweghe (dec.); children: Richard Desmond Welbourn, Hollis Baldwin. AB in Politics, Princeton U., 1971; JD, Am. U., 1976. Bar: Md. 1976, D.C. 1977, U.S. Dist. Ct. D.C. 1977, U.S. Ct. Appeals (D.C. cir.) 1977. Assoc. Howrey & Simon, Washington, 1976-78, Cladouhos & Brashares, Washington, 1978-84; group counsel Md. Cup Corp., Balt., 1984-87; ptnr. Miles & Stockbridge, Washington and Balt., 1987-93; pvt. practice law Washington, 1993—. Advisor Dingman Ctr. Entrepreneurship, U. Md., College Park, 1992—; mem. small bus. devel. com. George Mason U., Fairfax, Va., 1992—. Contbr. articles to profl. jours. Active St. Albans Sch. Parent's Assn., 1992—. Mem. ABA, Md. State Bar Assn., D.C. Bar Assn. Episcopal. Avocations: sailing, golf, reading. Antitrust, General corporate, Mergers and acquisitions. Office: 5100 Wisconsin Ave NW Ste 401 Washington DC 20016-4119

BOWEN, DUDLEY HOLLINGSWORTH, JR. federal judge; b. Augusta, Ga., June 25, 1941; AB in Fgn. Lang., U. Ga., 1964, LLB, 1965; profesor invitado (hon.), Universidad Externada de Bogotá, 1987. Bar: Ga. 1965. Pvt. practice law, Augusta, 1968-72; bankruptcy judge U.S. Dist. Ct. (so. dist.) Ga., 1972-75, judge, 1979-97, chief judge, 1997—, Augusta; ptnr. firm Dye, Miller, Bowen & Tucker, 1975-79. Bd. dirs. Southeastern Bankruptcy Law Inst., 1976-87; mem. Ct. Security Com. Jud. Conf. U.S., 1987-92. Mem. bd. visitors U. Ga. Sch. Law, 1987-90. Served to 1st lt. inf., U.S. Army, 1966-68. Decorated Commendation medal. Mem. State Bar Ga. (chmn. bankruptcy law sect. 1977), Fed. Judges Assn. (bd. dirs. 1985-90), 11th Cir. Dist. Judges Assn. (sec.-treas. 1988-89, pres. 1991-92). Presbyterian. Office: US Dist Ct PO Box 2106 Augusta GA 30903-2106

BOWEN, PAUL HENRY, JR. lawyer; b. Troy, Ohio, Sept. 28, 1948; s. Paul Henry, Sr. and Dorathy Jane (Winters) B.; m. Linda Margaret Mary Eisenhart, Mar. 2, 1974. B.A., Pa. State U., 1970; J.D., U. Pitts., 1973. Bar: Pa. 1973, Fla. 1978, U.S. Dist. Ct. (mid. dist.) Fla. 1978, U.S. Ct. Appeals (5th cir.) 1984, U.S. Supreme Ct. 1983. Assoc., Vernon David, P.A., Winter Garden, Fla., 1980-81, Swann & Haddock, P.A., Orlando, Fla., 1981-85, Trenam, Simmons, Kemker, Scharf, Barkin, Frye & O'Neill, P.A., Tampa, Fla., 1985— . Precinct capt. to re-elect Mayor Frederick of Orlando, 1984. Served to capt. JAGC, USAF, 1975-80. Mem. ABA, Assn. Trial Lawyers Am., Acad. Fla. Trial Lawyers. Democrat. Methodist. Lodge: Kiwanis (citizenship com.). Civil rights, Federal civil litigation, Construction. Home: PO Box 814 Tampa FL 33601-0814

BOWEN, STEPHEN STEWART, lawyer; b. Peoria, Ill., Aug. 23, 1946; s. Gerald Raymond and Frances Arlene (Stewart) B.; m. Ellen Claire Newcomer, Sept. 23, 1972; children: David, Claire. BA cum laude, Wabash Coll., 1968; JD cum laude, U. Chgo., 1972. Bar: Ill. 1972, U.S. Dist. Ct. (no. dist.) Ill. 1972, U.S. Tax Ct. 1977. Assoc. Kirkland & Ellis, Chgo., 1972-78, ptnr., 1978-84, Latham & Watkins, Chgo., 1985—. Adj. prof. DePaul U. Masters in Taxation Program, Chgo., 1976 80; lectr. Practicing Law Inst., N.Y.C., Chgo., L.A., 1978-84, N.Y.C., 1986—. Mem. vis. com. U. Chgo. Div. Sch., 1984—, mem. vis. com. Sch. Law, 1991-93; mem. planning com. U. Chgo. Tax Conf., 1985—, chair, 1995-98; trustee Wabash Coll., 1996—. Fellow Am. Coll. Tax Counsel; mem. ABA, Ill. State Bar Assn., Order of Coif, Mich. Shores Club (Wilmette, Ill.), Met. Club (Chgo.), Econ. Club Chgo., Phi Beta Kappa. Corporate taxation. Office: Latham & Watkins Sears Tower Ste 5800 Chicago IL 60606-6306

BOWEN, STEVEN HOLMES, lawyer; b. Norwood, Mass., Mar. 14, 1946; s. Earl Kenneth and Dorothy Ethel (Holmes) B. B.A. magna cum laude, Harvard U., 1968; J.D., Boston U., 1974. Bar: Mass. 1974, U.S. Dist. Ct. Mass. 1975, U.S. Ct. Appeals, 1st cir. 1979, U.S. Supreme Ct. 1979. Law clk. Mass. Superior Ct., Boston, 1974-75; mem. firm Nicholas Macaronis, Lowell, Mass., 1975—. Served with U.S. Army, 1968-70. Mem. Mass. Bar Assn., Greater Lowell Bar Assn. State civil litigation, Criminal, Personal injury. Home: 356 Gray St Arlington MA 02476-6009 Office: Law Offices of Nicholas Macaronis 9 Central St Lowell MA 01852

BOWEN-MORRIS, NIGEL VAUGHAN, solicitor; b. Barmouth, Wales, Aug. 17, 1961; s. Bernard and Maureen (Towers) Bowen-M. BA with honors, St. Catherine's Coll., Oxford, 1980. Solicitor, Supreme Ct. of Eng. and Wales. Solicitor Watson, Farley & Williams, Greece, 1988-96; mng. ptnr., solicitor Stephenson Harwood, Greece, 1996—. Fellow Royal Geog. Soc. Admiralty, Banking, Finance. Office: Stephenson Harwood Cons Pal Trapezis & 7 Sachtouri 185 36 Piraeus Greece

BOWER, ALLAN MAXWELL, lawyer; b. Oak Park, Ill., May 21, 1936; s. David Robert and Frances Emily Bower; m. Deborah Ann Rottmayer, Dec. 28, 1959. BS, U. Iowa, 1962; JD, U. Miami, Fla., 1968. Bar: Calif. 1969, U.S. Supreme Ct. 1979. Internat. aviation law practice, L.A., 1969—; ptnr. Kern & Wooley, 1980-85, Bronson, Bronson & McKinnon, L.A., 1985-90, Lane Powell Spears Lubersky, L.A., 1990-99, Bailey & Marzano, Santa Monica, Calif., 1999—. Contbr. articles to profl. publs. Mem. Lawyer-Pilots Bar Assn. Republican. Presbyterian. Aviation, General civil litigation, Product liability. Office: Bailey & Marzano 2nd Fl 2828 Donald Douglas Loop N Santa Monica CA 90405-2959 Fax: 310-392-8091

BOWER, THOMAS MICHAEL, lawyer; b. N.Y.C., Apr. 6, 1952; s. John Joseph and Marianne Judith (Milch) B.; m. Sharon Misae Nakamoto, Dec. 1, 1979. BA magna cum laude, Cornell U., 1973; JD, Columbia U., 1976. Bar: N.Y. 1977, U.S. Ct. Mil. Appeals 1979, U.S. Dist. Ct. (so. dist. and ea. dists.) N.Y. 1980. Assoc. Bower & Gardner, N.Y.C., 1980-83, ptnr., 1984-91; prin. Newman & Bower, P.C., 1991-92; of counsel Bickford, Hahn & Haley, 1993-98; ptnr. Shaub Ahmuty Citrin & Spratt, LLP, N.Y.C., 1998—. Lt. JAGC, USNR, 1976-80. Mem. Fedn. Ins. and Corp. Counsel, Def. Rsch. Inst., Alpha Delta Phi. General civil litigation, Insurance. Office: Shaub Ahmuty Citrin & Spratt LLP 655 3rd Ave New York NY 10017-5617 E-mail: tbower@sacslaw.com

BOWIE, PETER WENTWORTH, judge, educator; b. Alexandria, Va., Sept. 27, 1942; s. Beverley Munford and Louise Wentworth (Boynton) B.; m. Sarah Virginia Haught, Mar. 25, 1967; children: Heather, Gavin. BA, Wake Forest Coll., 1964; JD magna cum laude, U. San Diego, 1971. Bar: Calif. 1972, D.C. 1972, U.S. Dist. Ct. D.C. 1972, U.S. Dist. Ct. Md. 1973, U.S. Dist. Ct. (so. dist.) Calif. 1974, U.S. Ct. Appeals (D.C. cir.) 1972, U.S. Ct. Appeals (9th cir.) 1974, U.S. Supreme Ct. 1980. Trial atty. honors program Dept. of Justice, Washington, 1971-74; asst. U.S. Atty. U.S. Atty.'s Office, San Diego, 1974, asst. chief civil div., 1974-82, chief asst. U.S. atty., 1982-88; lawyer rep. U.S. Ct. Appeals (9th cir.) Jud. Conf., 1977-78, 84-87; judge U.S. Bankruptcy Ct., San Diego, 1988—. Lectr. at law Calif. Western Sch. Law, 1979-83; exec. com. mem. 9th Cir. Judicial Conf., 1991-94; mem. com. on codes of conduct Jud. Conf. of U.S., 1995—. Bd. dirs. Presidio Little League, San Diego, 1984, coach, 1983-84; mem. alumni adv. bd. Sch. Law U. San Diego, 1998—. Lt. USN, 1964-68, Vietnam. Mem. State Bar Calif. (hearing referee ct. 1982-86, mem. rev. dept. 1986-90), Fed. Bar Assn. (pres. San diego chpt. 1981-83), San Diego County Bar Assn. (chmn. fed. ct. com. 1978-80, 83-85), Assn. Bus. Trial Lawyers (bd. govs.), San Diego Bankruptcy Forum (bd. dirs.), Phi Delta Phi. Republican. Mem. Unitarian Ch. Office: US Bankruptcy Court 325 W F St San Diego CA 92101-6017

BOWLER, MARIANNE BIANCA, judge; b. Boston, Feb. 15, 1947; d. Richard A. and Ann C. (Daly) B. BA, Regis Coll., 1967; JD cum laude, Suffolk U., 1976, LLD (hon.), 1994. Bar: Mass. 1978. Rsch. asst. Harvard Med. Sch., Boston, 1967-69; med. editor Mass. Dept. of Pub. Health, 1969-76; law clk. Mass. Superior Ct., 1976-77, dep. chief law clk., 1977-78; asst. dist. atty. Middlesex Dist. Atty.'s Office, Cambridge, Mass., 1978; asst. U.S. atty. U.S. Dept. of Justice, Boston, 1978-90, exec. asst. U.S. atty., 1988-89, sr. litigation counsel, 1989-90; magistrate judge U.S. Dist. Ct. Mass., 1990—. Chmn. bd. trustees New England Bapt. Hosp., Boston, 1990-95. Trustee Suffolk U., Boston, 1994—; bd. dirs. The Boston Found., 1995—; dir. South Cove Nursing Facilities Found., Inc., 1995—; co-pres. Boston Coll. Inn of Ct., 1998—. Mem. Jr. League Boston, Suffolk Law Sch. Alumni Assn. (pres. 1979-80), Vincent Club, Isabel O'Neil Found., Save Venice. Democrat. Roman Catholic. Avocations: faux finishing, trompe l'oeil painting. Office: US Dist Ct One Court House Way Ste 8420 Boston MA 02110

BOWMAN, CAROL ANN, lawyer; b. Marion, Ind., Jan. 20, 1952; d. James Russell and Carol Joan (Horner) B. BA with honors, Georgetown Coll., 1974; JD, Valparaiso U., 1977; postdoctoral, John Marshall Law Sch., 1980-81. Bar: Ind. 1977, U.S. Dist. Ct. (so. dist.) Ind. 1977, U.S. Dist. Ct. (no. dist.) Ind. 1978, U.S. Ct. Appeals (7th cir.) 1979; U.S. Supreme Ct., 1997. Dep. atty. gen. State of Ind., Indpls., 1977-79; gen. counsel, corp. sec. Whiteco Industries, Inc., Merrillville, Ind., 1979—, gen. counsel, 1995—, corp. sec., 1994—. Mem. adv. com. Atty. Gen. Ind., 1980-87; bd. dirs. The Caring Place, Inc. Trustee Unity in the Dunes, 2000—. Fellow Ind. Bar Found.; mem. ABA, Ind. Bar Assn., Women Lawyers Assn. Lake and Porter Counties (pres. 1982), Lake County Bar Assn., South Lake County Bar Assn., Valparaiso U. Law Sch. Alumni Assn. (bd. dirs. 1980-85, 94-97). Avocations: reading, golf, tennis, sailing, theater. Contracts commercial, General corporate, Real property. Home: 516 Glade Pl Valparaiso IN 46383-3162 Office: Whiteco Industries Inc 1000 E 80th Pl Ste 700 Merrillville IN 46410-5608 E-mail: abowman@whiteco.com

BOWMAN, CATHERINE MCKENZIE, lawyer; b. Tampa, Fla., Nov. 10, 1962; d. Herbert Alonza and Joan Bates (Baggs) McKenzie; m. Donald Campbell Bowman, Jr., May 21, 1988; children: Hunter Hall, Sarah McKenzie. BA in Psychology and Sociology, Vanderbilt U., 1984; JD, U. Ga., 1987. Bar: Ga. 1987, U.S. Dist. Ct. (so. dist.) Ga. 1987. Assoc. Ranitz, Mahoney, Forbes & Coolidge, P.C., Savannah, Ga., 1987-91; ptnr. Forbes and Bowman, 1991—. Bd. dirs. Greenbriar Children's Ctr., 1994-98, exec. com. 1995, pres. 1996-98; active Jr. League Savannah; mem. Leadership Savannah, 1994-96; mem. Savannah Found. Distbn. Com., 1994—. Mem. Am. Employment Law Coun., Ga. Def. Lawyers Assn., Savannah Young Lawyers Assn. (pres. 1996-97), 2000 Club (membership chair 1990-91, pres. 1992), South Atlantic Found. (bd. dirs. 1992). Email: cbowman@forbesand bowman.com. Insurance, Labor, Workers' compensation. Home: 21 Jameswood Ave Savannah GA 31406-5219 Office: Forbes and Bowman PO Box 13929 7505 Waters Ave Ste D-14 Savannah GA 31406-3824

BOWMAN, GEORGE ARTHUR, JR. retired judge; b. Milw., Dec. 1, 1917; s. George Arthur and Edna Oral (Hunter) B.; m. Rose Mary Thorpe, Aug. 8, 1947 (dec. 1980); children: George A. III, Daniel Andrew. Student, U. Wis., 1936-39; JD, Marquette U., 1943. Bar: Wis. 1943, U.S. Supreme Ct. 1943. Asst. dist. atty. Milw. County, 1947-48, children's ct. judge, 1967-72; asst. city atty. City of Milw., 1948-67; adminstrv. law judge Office of Hearing and Appeals Social Security Adminstrn. Dept. HHS, Chgo., 1973-97, adminstrv. law judge emeritus, 1997; pvt. practice, 1997—. Appointed Pres.'s Task Force, Law Enforcement Assistance Adminstrn., 1972; former counsel Milw. Police Dept.; advisor Nat. Council of Juvenile Ct. Judges, Nat. Conv., Atlanta; chmn. conv. com. Nat. Council of Juvenile Ct. Judges, Milw., 1972; chmn. State Task Force on Juvenile Delinquency, 1970-71; legis. com. Wis. Bd. Juvenile Ct. Judges, 1970-71; former mem. numerous legis. coms., Milw.; pioneered Legal Defender System in Children's Ct.; lecturer, Marquette U. Co-author: LEAA Uniform Standards for Police Departments, 1973 (Pres.'s citation). Bd. dirs. Am. Indian Info. and Action Group, Inc. "Project Phoenix", Juneau Acad.; chmn. Milw. County Rep. Party, 1961-62; active supporter numerous community juvenile programs, including Milw. Boys' Club, St. Joseph's Home for Children, Mt. Mary Coll. Proglram for Truant and Delinquent Girls, Operation Outreach, others; Social Security judge. With USN, 1943-46. Recipient Continious Svc. award Office of Hearings and Appeals Soc. Security Adminstr., 1991. Mem. Fed. Assn. Adminstrv. Law Judges, Assn. Office of Hearing and Appeals Adminstrv. Law Judges, Wis. State Bar Assn., Milw. Bar. Assn., Nat. Council Juvenile Ct. Judges, Am. Judicature Soc., Nat. Council of Sr. Citizens, Inc., Internat. Juvenile Officers Assn., Am. Legion (former post comdr.), Nat. Probate Judges Assn., New Trier Rep. Orgn., Committeeman's Club, Hawthorne Turf Club, Sigma Alpha Epsilon. Roman Catholic. Home: 2824 Orchard Ln Wilmette IL 60091-2144

BOWMAN, JEAN LOUISE, lawyer, civic worker; b. Albuquerque, Apr. 3, 1938; d. David Livingstone and Charlotte Louise (Smith) McArthur; children: Carolyn Louise, Joan Emily, Amy Elizabeth, Eric Daniel. Student, U. N.Mex., 1956-57, U. Pa., 1957-58, Rocky Mountain Coll., 1972-74; BA in Polit. Sci. with high honors, U. Mont., 1982, JD, 1985. Dir. Christian edn. St. Luke's Episcopal Ch., 1979-80; law clk. to assoc. justice Mont. Supreme Ct., 1985-87; exec. v.p. St. Peter's Cmty. Hosp. Found., 1987-91; exec. dir. Harrison Hosp. Found., Bremerton, Wash., 1991-93, St. Patrick Hosp. and Health Found., 1993—2001, Missoula Symphony Bd., 1993-99; pres. Missoula Symphony Assn., 1996-98. Bd. dirs. 1st Bank West. Trustee Rocky Mountain Coll., 1972-80; bd. dirs. Billings (Mont.) Area C. of C., 1977-80; mem. City-County Air Pollution Control Bd., 1969-74, chmn., 1970-71; del. Mont. State Constnl. Conv., 1971-72, sec., 1971-72; chmn. County Local Govt. Study Commn., 1973-76; mem. long range planning com. Billings Sch. Dist., 1978-79; bd. dirs. Billings LWV, 1970-72; pres. Helena LWV, 1988, 2d v.p. Mont. LWV, 1987-91; bd. dirs. Internat. Choral Festival, 1999—, Mont. Justice Found., 1999—. Named one of Billings' most influential citizens Billings Gazette, 1977; Bertha Morton scholar, 1982. Mem. Mont. State Bar, Missoula Rotary (pres. 1997-98). Republican. Home: 1911 E Broadway St Missoula MT 59802-4901 E-mail: jmbmslamt@msn.com

BOWMAN, PASCO MIDDLETON, II, federal judge; b. Timberville, Va., Dec. 20, 1933; s. Pasco Middleton and Katherine (Lohr) B.; m. Ruth Elaine Bowman, July 12, 1958; children: Ann Katherine, Helen Middleton, Benjamin Garber. BA, Bridgewater Coll., 1955; JD, NYU, 1958; LLM, U. Va., 1986; LLD (hon.), Bridgewater Coll., 1988. Bar: N.Y. 1958, Ga. 1965, Mo. 1980. Assoc. firm Cravath, Swaine & Moore, N.Y.C., 1958-61, 62-64; asst. prof. law U. Ga., 1964-65, assoc. prof., 1965-69, prof., 1969-70, Wake Forest U., 1970-78, dean, 1970-78; vis. prof. U. Va., 1978-79; prof., dean U. Mo., Kansas City, 1979-83; judge U.S. Ct. Appeals (8th cir.), Mo., 1983—8, chief judge, 1998-99. Mng. editor: NYU Law Rev, 1957-58; Reporter, chief draftsman: Georgia Corporation Code, 1965-68. Served to col. USAR, 1959-84. Fulbright scholar London Sch. Econs. and Polit. Sci., 1961-62, Root-Tilden scholar, 1955-58. Mem. N.Y. Bar, Mo. Bar Office: US Ct Appeals 8th Circuit 10-50 US Courthouse 400 E 9th St Kansas City MO 64106-2607

BOWMAN, PHILLIP BOYNTON, lawyer; b. Ames, Iowa, Feb. 28, 1936; s. Alfred Boynton and Susan Jean (Foxworthy) B.; m. Elizabeth Wales Porter, June 20, 1959; children: Susan Foxworthy, William Porter, Peter Wales. BS in Engring., Princeton U., 1958; JD, U. Mich., 1961. Bar: Ill. 1961, U.S. Dist. Ct. (no. dist.) Ill. 1962, U.S. Ct. Appeals (7th cir.) 1965. Assoc. then ptnr. Gorham, Adams, White & DeYoung, Chgo., 1961-75; ptnr. Gorham, Metge, Bowman & Hourigan, Chgo., 1976— . Pres., commr. Northbrook Park Dist., Ill., 1968-76; pres., bd. dirs., referee, coach, Northbrook Hockey League, 1962-86. Mem. ABA, Ill. Bar Assn., Chgo. Bar Assn., Chgo. Soc. Assn. Execs. (edn. com. 1984—), Ill. Bankers Assn. Republican. Episcopalian. Clubs: Skokie Country (Glencoe, Ill.) (golf com. 1984); Chgo. Curling (Northbrook) (bd. dirs., sec. 1980-87), Tavern (Chgo.), Law, Legal. Antitrust, General corporate, General practice. Home: 2060 Plymouth Ln Northbrook IL 60062-6064 Office: 300 W Washington St Chicago IL 60606-1707

BOWMAN, SCOTT MCMAHAN, lawyer; b. Shaker Heights, Ohio, Mar. 16, 1962; s. George Henry and Patricia (McMahan) B.; children: Chad Marshall, David Chandler, Elizabeth Brooks; stepchildren: Garrett Richard Sevek, Grant Allen Sevek. AA in Bus., Fullerton Coll., 1987; BBA, Calif. State U., Fullerton, 1989; JD, U. Cin., 1992. Pvt. practice, Salem, Ohio, 1992—. Asst. city solicitor Salem, 1992-94; advisor YWCA Salem, 1994—; advisor Butler Inst. Art, Salem, 1994—; intermediary, counsel Unorganized Militia, 1996—. Author: The Turning Point, 1997. Mem. Design Review Bd. City of Salem (Ohio), 1993-95, v.p., 1995; mem. Salem Planning and Zoning Commn., 1993-95, v.p., 1995; co-founder, trustee Salem Preservation Soc., 1993-95. Mem. Columbiana County Bar Assn. Episcopal. Avocations: camping, hunting, surfing, coaching football, politics. Estate planning, Probate, Real property. Office: PO Box 558 Salem OH 44460-0558 E-mail: SBowmanEsq@aol.com

BOWNES, HUGH HENRY, federal judge; b. N.Y.C., Mar. 10, 1920; s. Hugh Gray and Margaret (Henry) B.; m. Irja C. Martikainen, Dec. 30, 1944 (dec. Jan. 1991); children: Barbara Anne, David and Ernest (twins); m. Mary Davis, July 12, 1992. B.A., Columbia U., 1941, LL.B., 1948. Bar: N.H. bar 1948. Since practiced in, Laconia; ptnr. firm Nighswander, Lord & Bownes, 1951-66; assoc. justice N.H. Superior Ct., 1966-68; judge U.S. Dist. Ct. N.H., Concord, 1968-77, U.S. Ct. Appeals (1st cir.), 1977-90, sr. judge, 1990—. Mem. Laconia City Council, 1953-57; chmn. Laconia Democratic Com., 1954-57; mayor, Laconia, 1963-65; mem. Dem. Nat. Com. from N.H., 1963-66; Chmn. Laconia chpt. A.R.C., 1951-52; pres. bd. Laconia Hosp. Assn., 1963-64. Served to maj. USMCR, 1941-46. Decorated Silver Star, Purple Heart. Mem. ABA, Am. Law Inst., N.H. Bar Assn., Belknap County Bar Assn. (pres. 1965-67), Laconia C. of C. (past pres.), Lions Club (past pres. Laconia). Office: US Ct Appeals 1st Cir US Courthouse 1 Courthouse Way Ste 6730 Boston MA 02210-3008

BOYD, CRAIG STEPHEN, lawyer; b. Coatesville, Pa., Jan. 3, 1948; s. Clarence Clifford and Ellen (Hunsicker) B.; m. Pamela Kline, Aug. 30, 1969; children: David C., Jeffrey R., Steven D. B.S., Shippensburg U., Pa., 1970, M.S., Bowling Green State U., Ohio, 1971; J.D., U. Notre Dame, 1974; L.L.M. in Taxation, Villanova U., 1987. Bar: Pa. 1974, U.S. Dist. Ct. (ea. dist.) Pa. 1974. Assoc., E. Kenneth Nyce, Boyertown, Pa., 1974-77; sole practice law, Boyertown, Pa., 1977-83; mng. ptnr. Boyd & Karver, Boyertown, Pa., 1983—; lectr. law Ursinus Coll., Collegeville, Pa., 1974-76, Pa. State U., 1978-80; solicitor Hereford (Pa.) Twp. Zoning Bd., 1978—. Author: Domestic Relations Guide, 1984; research asst. book Lawyers, Law Students and People, 1974. Bd. dirs. Boyertown Area Community Trust, 1984— , Helping Hands, Inc., 1976-87; pres. Boyertown Area YMCA, 1978-83. Spencer Found. grantee, 1973-74; YMCA Service award, 1983, Red Triangle award, 1982, Exec. award, 1980. Mem. Pa. Bar Assn., Berks County Bar Assn., ABA. Democrat. Home: PO Box 114 Boyertown PA 19512-0114 Office: 7 E Philadelphia Ave Boyertown PA 19512-1154

BOYD, HARRY DALTON, lawyer, former insurance company executive; b. Huntington Park, Calif., June 13, 1923; s. Randall and Thelma L. (Lewis) B.; m. Margaret Jeanine Gamewell, June 13, 1948; children: Leslie Boyd Cotton, Wayne, Lynn Boyd Denby, Evan, Lance. LLB, U. So. Calif., 1949, LLM, 1960; A degree in Mgmt., Ins. Inst. Am., 1972. Bar: Calif. 1950. Pvt. practice, L.A.; assoc. Harvey & Viereck, 1952-55; assoc. gen. counsel, corp. sec. Farmers Ins. Group, 1955-77; group v.p., gen. counsel Swett & Crawford Group, 1977-83; gen. counsel, dir. Harbor Ins. Co., 1983-89; Calif. counsel Continental Ins. Co., 1987-89; of counsel Fidler & Bell, Burbank, Calif., 1990-93, Richard E. Garcia, Atty. at Law, L.A., 1994-96. Bd. dirs. FIG Fed. Credit Union, 1958-61, pres., 1960-61; mem. Sherman Oaks Property Owners Assn., 1967—, pres., 1969, 72; mem. Western Ins. Info. Svc., Spkrs. Bur., 1971-77; bd. dirs. Buffalo Reins. Co., 1983-87; expert witness in ins. litigation, 1990-2000; arbitrator reins., 1990-2000. Mem. adv. coun. Chandler Elementary Sch., 1970-73, Milliken Jr. H.S., 1973-74. With USAAF, 1943-46. Mem. Calif. Ins. Guarantee Assn. (bd. govs. 1972-77), Los Angeles County Bar Assn. (chmn. exec. com. corp. law depts. sect. 1971-72), Reins. Assn. Am. (legal com. 1979-81), Nat. Assn. Ind. Insurers (chmn. surplus lines com. 1980-82), Calif. Assn. Ins. Cos. (exec. com. 1979-83), Wilshire C. of C. (bd. dirs. 1971-79, pres. 1975), Nat. Assn. Ins. Commrs. (industry adv. com. on reins. regulation 1983-90), Am. Arbitration Assn. (arbitrator). Republican. Lutheran (pres. coun. 1964-65). Home: 13711 Weddington St Van Nuys CA 91401-5825

BOYD, JOSEPH ARTHUR, JR. lawyer; b. Hoschton, Ga., Nov. 16, 1916; s. Joseph Arthur and Esther Estelle (Puckett) B.; m. Ann Stripling, June 6, 1938; children: Joanne Louise Boyd Goldman, Betty Jean Boyd Jala, Joseph Robert, James Daniel, Jane N. Ohlin. Student, Piedmont Coll., Demorest, Ga., 1936-38, LLD, 1963; student, Mercer U., Macon, Ga., 1938-39; JD, U. Miami, Coral Gables, Fla., 1948; LLD, Western State U. Coll. Law, San Diego, 1981. Bar: Fla. 1948, U.S. Supreme Ct. 1959, D.C. 1973, N.Y. 1982. Practice law, Hialeah, 1948-68; city atty., 1951-58; mem.

Dade County Commn., Miami, Fla., 1958-68, chmn., 1963; vice mayor Dade County, 1967; justice Fla. Supreme Ct., Tallahassee, 1969-87, chief justice, 1984-86; assoc. Boyd Lindsey & Sliger P.A., 1987—. Mem. Hialeah Zoning Bd., 1946-48; juror Freedoms Found., Valley Forge, Pa., 1971, 73 Bd. dirs. Bapt. Hosp., Miami, 1962-66, Miami Coun. Chs., 1960-64; emeritus trustee Piedmont Coll. Recipient Nat. Top Hat award Bus. and Profl. Women in U.S. for advancing status of employed women, 1967 Mem. ABA, Fla. Bar Assn., Hialeah-Miami Springs Bar Assn. (pres. 1955), Tallahassee Bar Assn., Hialeah-Miami Springs C. of C. (pres. 1956), Am. Legion (comdr. Fla. 1953-54), VFW, Shriners, Masons (33 deg.), Lions, Elks, Wig and Robe, Iron Arrow, Phi Alpha Delta. Democrat. Baptist (deacon). Federal civil litigation, Probate. Office: Boyd Lindsey & Sliger PA 1407 Piedmont Dr E Tallahassee FL 32312-2943

BOYD, THOMAS MARSHALL, lawyer; b. Yorktown, Va., Sept. 10, 1946; s. Laurel Barnett and Mildred Warner Wellford (Marshall) B.; m. Torri Carol Tyler, Oct. 2, 1976; children: Brooke Warner, Tyler Randolph. BA in History, Va. Military Inst., 1968; JD, U. Va., 1971. Bar: Calif. 1973, D.C. 1974. Law clk. to fed. judge U.S. Dist. Ct. (cen. dist.) Calif., Los Angeles, 1973-74; trial atty., atty. advisor U.S. Dept. Justice, Washington, 1974-76; assoc. counsel com. on judiciary U.S. Ho. of Reps., 1976-86; dep. asst. atty. gen. Dept. Justice Office Legis. Affairs, 1986-88, asst. atty. gen., 1988-89, dir. office policy devel., 1989-91; dep. gen. counsel Kemper Corp., 1991-93, v.p. and legis. counsel, 1993-96; v.p. for legis. affairs Investment Co. Inst., 1996-98; ptnr. Ramsey, Cook, Looper & Kurlander LLP, 1998-99, Alston & Bird, LLP, Washington, 1999—. House counsel Presdl. Transition Com. on Criminal Justice, Washington, 1980-81; pub. mem. Adminstrv. Conf. U.S., 1992-95. Co-editor U.S. Atty.'s Criminal Trial Manual, 1971, Va. Bar Criminal Law Manual, 1971; contbr. articles to profl. jours. and pub. interest articles to newspapers. Served to capt. USAF, 1968-73. Recipient Nat. Media award Delta Soc., 1985, Edmund J. Randolph award, 1988. Mem. U.S. Supreme Ct. Bar Assn., Calif. Bar Assn., D.C. Bar Assn., Army-Navy Country Club, Leland Country Club. Republican. Episcopalian. Avocations: golf, jogging, writing. Constitutional, Legislative.

BOYD, WILLIAM ELKINS, lawyer; b. San Mateo, Calif., Oct. 13, 1947; s. William Sprott and Katherine (Elkins) Boyd. Stanford U., 1969; JD, Hastings Coll. of Law, 1974. Admitted to Calif. bar, 1975; ptnr. firm Boyd and McKay, San Francisco, 1980—; v.p. Boyd Bros., investments, San Francisco, 1980—. Spl. asst. to chmn. Calif. Republican Com., 1968; bd. dirs. San Mateo County Planned Parenthood, 1971-73, Hastings Child Care Center, 1974-76. Mem. Am. Bar Assn., State Bar Calif. Assn. (bus. law sect.), Stanford U. Alumni Assn., Hastings Alumni Assn. Episcopalian. Clubs: Burlingame Country, Hastings 1066 Club. Home: 590 Remillard Dr Burlingame CA 94010-6740 Office: 3 Embarcadero Ctr Ste 2360 San Francisco CA 94111-4026

BOYD, WILLIAM SPROTT, lawyer; b. San Francisco, Feb. 12, 1943; s. R. Mitchell S. and Mary (Mitchell) B.; children: Mitchell Sagar, Sterling McMicking. AB, Stanford U., 1964, JD, 1971. Bar: Calif. 1972, U.S. Dist. Ct. (no. dist.) 1972, U.S. Ct. Appeals (9th cir.) 1972, U.S. Dist. Ct. (cen. dist.) Calif. 1974, U.S. Dist. Ct. (ea. dist.) Calif. 1976. Assoc. Brobeck, Phleger & Harrison, San Francisco, 1971-77, ptnr., 1977—, of counsel. Mem. Lawyers Com for Urban Affairs, San Francisco, 1979—; bd. dirs. San Francisco Legal Aid Soc., 1980-85. Lt. USNR, 1965-68, Vietnam. Mem. ABA, Calif. Bar Assn., San Francisco Bar Assn. Antitrust, Federal civil litigation, State civil litigation. Office: Brobeck Phleger & Harrison 1 Market Pla Spear St Tower San Francisco CA 94105

BOYDSTUN, CHARLES BRYANT, JR. lawyer; b. Memphis, Sept. 10, 1949. B.A., U. Tenn., 1971, J.D., 1974. Bar: Fla. 1974, Tenn. 1981, U.S. Dist. Ct. (mid. dist.) Fla. 1974, U.S. Ct. Appeals (5th and 11th cirs.) 1981, U.S. Supreme Ct. 1978, U.S. Dist. Ct. (no. dist.) Fla. 1985; cert. civil trial lawyer Fla. Bar and Nat. Bd. Trial Advocacy. Assoc. Bradham, Lyle, Skipper & Cramer, St. Petersburg, Fla., 1974-76, Lyle, Skipper, Wood & Anderson, St. Petersburg, 1977-79; ptnr. Lyle & Skipper, P.A., St. Petersburg, 1979-93, Boydstun, Dabroski & Lyle, P.A., 1993-98; vice chmn. bd. trustees Pinellas County Law Library, St. Petersburg, 1978-98; chmn. 6th Jud. Circuit Unauthorized Practice of Law Com., St. Petersburg, 1983-85; mem. client security fund com. Fla. Bar, 1995-99. Author: How to Find a Good Lawyer, 1980. Pres. New Life Birthing Ctr., St. Petersburg, 1984-86; contbr. articles to profl. jours. V.p. Christian Legal Soc., St. Petersburg, 1982. Mem. Def. Research Inst., Fla. Acad. Trial Lawyers, ATLA, Am. Bd. Trial Advocates, Fla. Def. Lawyers, Fla. Bar Assn., Tenn. Bar Assn., St. Petersburg Bar Assn., St. Petersburg C. of C., Fla. C. of C., Barney Masterson Inn of Ct., Kiwanis (v.p. 1982-83, pres. 1984-85), Phi Alpha Delta. Democrat. Presbyterian. Federal civil litigation, State civil litigation, Insurance. Office: Boydstun Dabroski & Lyle PA 2600 9th St N Saint Petersburg FL 33704-2744

BOYER, DAVID DYER, lawyer, judge; b. Peoria, Ill., Oct. 6, 1960; s. John Harold and Sara Haskins Boyer; m. Rosene Marie Glenn, Nov. 22, 1995; stepchildren: Peter H. Monfore, Jennifer L. Monfore. BS, Bowling Green State U., 1982; JD, U. Ala., Tuscaloosa, 1985. Bar: Ala. 1985, U.S. Dist. Ct. (mid. dist.) Ala. 1986, U.S. Ct. Appeals (llth cir.) 1986, Calif. 1989, U.S. Dist. Ct. (ctrl. and so. dists.) Calif. 1990, U.S. Ct. Appeals (9th cir.) 1990. Jud. law clk. to Hon. H. Mark Kennedy, Montgomery, Ala., 1985-86; atty., mgr. Legal Svcs. Corp. Ala., Andalusia, 1986-88; atty., advisor HHS, San Bernardino, Calif., 1988-90; assoc. Kinkle, Rodiger & Spriggs, L.A., 1990-96; sr. assoc., leader litigation team McCormick, Kidman & Behrens, LLP, Costa Mesa, Calif., 1996-2000, ptnr., 2000—. Judge pro tem Orange County Superior Ct., Santa Ana, Calif., 1997—. Ex-officio 24th Stat Senate Dist., L.A. Rep. Com., 1994-98; Rep. nominee for Calif. Senate, 1994. With USMC, 1979-81. Frazier Reams fellow Bowling Green State U., 1981, Harold Anderson scholar, 1982. Mem. Bus. Trial Lawyers Assn., Orange County Bar Assn. Roman Catholic. Avocations: writing, tennis, golf, horse training and racing. General civil litigation, Insurance, Real property. Office: McCormick Kidman & Behrens 695 Town Center Dr Ste 1400 Costa Mesa CA 92626-7189

BOYER, TYRIE ALVIS, lawyer; b. Williston, Fla., Sept. 10, 1924; s. Alton Gordon and Mary Ethel (Strickland) B.; m. Elizabeth Everett Gale, June 9, 1945; children: Carol, Tyrie, Kennedy, Lee. BA, U. Fla., 1953, LLB, JD, 1954. Bar: Fla. Atty. Crawford, May & Boyer, Jacksonville, Fla., 1954-58, Boyer Law Offices, Jacksonville, 1958-60; judge Civil Ct. of Record, 1960-63; cir. judge 4th Jud. Cir. of Fla., 1963-67; atty. Dawson, Galant, Maddox, Boyer, Sulik & Nichols, 1967-73; appellate judge 1st Dist. Ct. Appeal, Tallahassee, 1973-79; chief judge 1st Dist. Ct. Appeals, 1975-76; atty. Boyer, Tanzler, Blackburn & Boyer, Jacksonville, 1979-84, Boyer, Tanzler & Sussman, Jacksonville, 1984—. Adj. prof. Fla. Coastal Sch. Law, Jacksonville, 1996—, U. North Fla., 1998—; chmn. Supreme Ct. Com. on Standard Conduct Governing Judges, Tallahassee, 1976-79. Contbr. articles to profl. jours. Chmn. Duval County Hosp. Authority, Jacksonville, 1970-73, Jacksonville Bldg. Fin. Authority, 1980-81; pres. Jacksonville Legal Aid Assn., 1954-61; bd. dirs. Jones Coll., Jacksonville, 1978-85; bd. advs. Fla. Coastal Sch. Law, 1996—; adj. prof. U. North Fla., 1998—. With USN, 1942-45, PTO. Mem. ABA, Am. Judicature Soc., Fla. Bar, Amer. Bar Assn., Jacksonville Bar Assn., Fla. Acad. Trial Lawyers, Am. Bd. Trial Advs., SCV (comdr.), Mil. Order Stars and Bars (comdr.), Masons, dir., Safari Club Internat., Fla. Blue Key, Order of Coif, Phi Beta Kappa, Phi Kappa Phi. Methodist. Avocation: big game hunting. Home: 3966 Cordova Ave Jacksonville FL 32207-6019 Office: Boyer Tanzler & Sussman 210 E Forsyth St Jacksonville FL 32202-3320

BOYKIN, HAMILTON HAIGHT, lawyer; b. N.Y.C., Feb. 3, 1939; s. Samuel Darrington and Alice (Haight) B.; m. Judith Panneton, Aug. 21, 1965; children: Lisa Ann, Samuel Scott, Allison Christine. B.A., Trinity Coll., Hartford, Conn., 1961; J.D., Georgetown U., 1964. Bar: D.C. 1964, Va. 1964. Ptnr. Colton and Boykin, Washington, 1965-93; ptnr. Boykin & Casano PC, Washington, 1994—. Mem. Va. State Bar Assn., DC Bar Ass. Democrat. Roman Catholic. Administrative and regulatory, General corporate, Real property. Home: 1100 Parrs Ridge Dr Spencerville MD 20868-9738 Office: Boykin & Casano PC 1620 L St NW Ste 900 Washington DC 20036-5628

BOYKO, CHRISTOPHER ALLAN, lawyer, judge; b. Cleve., Oct. 10, 1954; s. Andrew and Eva Dorothy (Zepko) B.; m. Roberta Ann Gentile, May 29, 1981; children: Philip, Ashley. B in Polit. Sci. cum laude, Mt. Union Coll., 1976; JD, Cleve. Marshall Coll. Law, 1979. Bar: Ohio 1979, U.S. Dist. Ct. (no. dist.) Ohio 1979, Fla. 1985, U.S. Tax Ct. 1986. Prin. Boyko & Boyko, Parma, Ohio, 1993, 94-95; asst. prosecutor City of Parma, 1981-87, dir. of law, 1987-93; exec. v.p., gen. counsel copy Am., Inc., 1993-94; judge Parma Mcpl. Court, 1993; ptnr. Boyko & Boyko, Attys., Parma, 1994—; judge Ct. Common Pleas, Cuyahoga County, Ohio, 1996—, Judicial Corrections Bd., 1999—. Guardian ad litem Juvenile Ct., 1979-93; legal advisor spl. weapons and tactics divsn. City of Parma Police Dept., 1984-93; chief counsel S.W. Enforcement Bur., 1991-93; mem. faculty Ohio Jud. Coll., Nat. Jud. Coll., lectr. FBI Nat. Acad.; jud. editor Law and Fact Com., 1999—. Active Citizens League of Greater Cleve., 1985—; trustee Cops & Kids, Inc., Cleve. Bar Assn., 2000—; mem. Parma Drug Task Force, 1987—; mem. adv. com. Parmadale Children's Svcs., 1991—; mem. St. Anthony's Sch. Commn. Mem. ABA, Fla. Bar Assn., Ohio Bar Assn., Cuyahoga County Bar Assn., Cleve. Bar Assn. (bd. trustee), Parma Bar Assn. (pres., trustee) Ukrainian Bar Assn., Cuyahoga County Police Chief Assn. (assoc.), Narcotics Law Officers Assn., Am. Inns of Ct. Found. (Harold Burton Inn of Ct., Master of Bench 2001—), Cleve. Am. Mid. Eastern Orgn., Mt. Union Coll. Alumni Assn., Cleve. Marshall Law Sch. Alumni Assn., Elks. Byzantine Catholic. Avocations: martial arts, running, weightlifting. General practice, Municipal (including bonds), Probate. Home: 5291 Huntington Reserve Dr Parma OH 44134-6172 Office: Justice Ctr 1200 Ontario St Cleveland OH 44113-1604

BOYLE, FRANCIS ANTHONY, law educator; b. Chgo., Mar. 25, 1950; AB in Polit. Sci., U. Chgo., 1971; JD magna cum laude, Harvard U., 1976, AM, 1978, PhD, 1983. Bar: Mass. 1977. Tcht. fellow, assoc. Ctr. Internat. Affairs Harvard U., 1976-78; tax atty. Bingman, Dana & Gould, Boston, 1977-78; prof. law U. Ill., Champaign, 1978—. Prof. USSR Summer U. Jurists, 1989; Parhad lectr. U. Calgary, 2001. Author: World Politics and International Law, 1985 (Outstanding Acad. Book, Choice mag. 1985-86), Defending Civil Resistance Under International Law, 1987, The Future of International Law and American Foreign Policy, 1989, The Bosnian People Charge Genocide, 1996, Foundations of World Order, 1999; contbr. legal article and book revs. to profl. jours. Mem. bur. polit.-mil. affairs (scholar-diplomat program) U.S. Dept. State, 1981; bd. dirs. coordinating council Lawyers Com. on Nuclear Policy, 1981—; cons. Amnesty Internat., 1983—; chmn., panel of jurists IPO Brussels Tribunal on Reagan Adminstrns. Fgn. Policy, 1984; advisor Coun. for Responsible Genetics, 1985—; cons. UN Com. on the Exercise of the Inalienable Rights of the Palestinian People, 1987—; bd. dirs. Amnesty Internat. USA, 1988-92. Mem. Am. Soc. Internat. Law (ad hoc guidelines com. 1978-80, Lieber group on laws of war 1979—), Phi Beta Kappa, Sigma Xi (award and prize in biology). Office: U Ill Coll Law 504 E Pennsylvania Ave Champaign IL 61820-6909 E-mail: fboyle@law.uluc.edu

BOYLE, GREGORY MICHAEL, lawyer; b. Chgo., June 9, 1971; s. James Wilson and Jaclyn Zeldine Boyle. BA, Carleton Coll., 1993; JD, Harvard U., 1997. Bar: Ill. 1997, U.S. Dist. Ct. (no. dist.) Ill. 1997. Assoc. Jenner & Block, Chgo., 1997—. Mem. ABA (sect. on litigation 1997—), Chgo. Coun. Lawyers. General civil litigation, Criminal. Office: Jenner & Block 1 IBM Plz Chicago IL 60611

BOYLE, MICHAEL FABIAN, lawyer; b. Lynwood, Calif., Apr. 11, 1949; s. Erwin Francis Boyle and Phanelphia (Gibson) Brunkow; 1 child, Conor Francis; m. Judy Pettigrew, May 14, 1986. B.A., San Diego State U., 1972; J.D., U. Calif., 1975. Bar: Calif. 1975, U.S. Dist. Ct. (no. dist.) Calif. 1975. Assoc. Connolley, Hothem & Flint, San Francisco, 1975-77; ptnr. Higgs, Flectcher & Mack, San Diego, 1978— . Contbr. articles to profl. jours. Bd. dirs. San Diego Hospice Corp. Bd., 1989-91, mem. The Mayor and City Coun. Citizens Fin. Com., 1990. Served as capt. USAR, 1971-82. Mem. ABA, Calif. Bar Assn., San Diego County Bar Assn. (chmn. ins. com.), San Diego State Univ. Alumni Assn. (officer, dir. 1984-89), Construction Fin. Mgnt. Assn. (officer, dir.) 1986-92. Democrat. Roman Catholic. State civil litigation, Construction, Personal injury. Home: 13482 Caminito Carmel Del Mar CA 92014-3847 Office: Higgs Fletcher & Mack 401 W A St Ste 2600 San Diego CA 92101-7913

BOYLE, PATRICIA JEAN, retired state supreme court justice; b. Detroit, Mar. 31, 1937; Student, U. Mich., 1955-57; B.A., J.D., Wayne State U., 1963. Bar: Mich. Practice law with Kenneth Davies, Detroit, 1963; law clk. to U.S. Dist. judge, 1963-64; asst. U.S. atty., Detroit, 1964-68; asst. pros. atty. Wayne County, dir. research, tng. and appeals, 1969-74; Recorders Ct. judge City of Detroit, 1976-78; U.S. dist. judge Eastern Dist. Mich., Detroit, 1978-83; assoc. justice Mich. Supreme Ct., 1983-98, ret., 1999. Active Women's Rape Crisis Task Force, Vols. of Am. Named Feminist of Year Detroit chpt. NOW, 1978; recipient Outstanding Achievement award Pros. Attys. Assn. Mich., 1978, 98, Mich. Women's Hall of Fame award, 1986, Law Day award ABA, 1998, Champion of Justice award State Bar Mich., 1998. Mem. Women Lawyers Assn. Mich., Fed. Bar Assn., Mich. Bar Assn., Detroit Bar Assn., Wayne State U. Law Alumni Assn. (Disting. Alumni award 1979) Avocation: reading. Address: 10765 Oxbow Lake Shore Dr White Lake MI 48386*

BOYLE, RICHARD EDWARD, lawyer; b. Westville, Ill., Mar. 27, 1937; s. Kelley George and Florence (Weisert) B.; m. Janet E. Peskar, Nov. 22, 1968; children: Kevin, Douglas, Leslie. BA, U. Ill., 1959, LLB, 1961. Bar: Ill. 1962, Mo. 1985, U.S. Dist. Ct. (so. dist.) Ill. 1962, U.S. Dist. Ct. (cen. dist.) Ill. 1962, U.S. Dist. Ct. (ea. dist.) Mo. 1991, U.S. Ct. Appeals (7th cir.) 1975, U.S. Supreme Ct. 1985. Assoc. Costello, Wiechert, Roberts & Gundlach, 1962-68; ptnr. Gundlach, Lee, Eggmann, Boyle & Roessler, Belleville, Ill., 1968—. With USAFR. Fellow Am. Coll. Trial Lawyers, Am. Bar Found. (mem. Adv. Group Civil Justice Reform Act 1990—); mem. Nat. Assn. R.R. Trial Counsel (pres. 1991-92), St. Clair County Bar Assn. (pres. 1979-80). General civil litigation, Personal injury, Product liability. Home: 13 Oak Knoll Pl Belleville IL 62223-1817 Office: Gundlach Lee Eggmann Boyle & Roessler Box 23560 5000 W Main St Belleville IL 62226-4727

BOYNTON, FREDERICK GEORGE, lawyer; b. Yokohama, Japan, May 9, 1948; s. Fred Wenderoth and Buelah Eleanor (Nygaard) B.; m. Nancy Jeanne McLendon, Aug. 3, 1985; children: Emily Margaret, Charlotte Clayton, Susan Jeanne. BA, The Citadel, 1970; JD, Tulane U., 1973. Bar: S.C. 1973, Ga. 1976, U.S. Dist. Ct. Ga. 1976, U.S. Ct. Appeals (5th and 11th cirs.). Assoc. Smith, Gambrell & Russell, and predecessors, Atlanta, 1976-82, ptnr., 1982-88; sole practice law, 1988—. Author: Criminal Defense Techniques, 1976; editor articles Tulane Sch. Law Rev. Exec. com. Southside Progress Assn., Atlanta, 1983-84, Leadership Sandy Springs, 1989-90; bd. dirs. Atlanta Union Mission, 1990-97, exec. com., 1991, sec., 1992, adv. bd., 1998—; mem. Local Advisory Coun., Ridgeview Middle Sch, 2001—. Served to capt. JAGC, U.S. Army, 1973-76. Fellow Lawyers Found. Ga.; mem. ABA, Fed. Bar Assn. (pres. Atlanta chpt. 1981-82, mem. exec. com. 1982—, dep. chmn. adminstrv. law sect. 1986-87, bd. dirs. younger lawyers divsn. 1981-84, v.p. 11th cir. 1985-87), State Bar Ga. (chmn. adminstrv. law sect. 1987-88), Lawyers Club Atlanta, Order of Coif. Real property, Federal civil litigation, State civil litigation. Home: 4860 Northway Dr NE Atlanta GA 30342-2424 Office: 6100 Lake Forrest Dr NW Ste 400 Atlanta GA 30328-3836 E-mail: fboynton@bellsouth.net

BOYTE, GEORGE GRIFFIN, lawyer; b. Humboldt, Tenn., Mar. 10, 1925; s. Hubert C. and Olga (Hogan) B.; m. Carol Dent, June 20, 1953; children: Katherine Dent Boyte McKee, Bonnie Carol Boyte Capsuto, George Griffin Jr. BA, Vanderbilt U., 1949, JD, 1952. Bar: Tenn. 1952. Mem. firm J. Frank Warmath, Humboldt, 1952-54; ptnr. Warmath & Boyte, Humboldt, 1954—; city atty. City of Humboldt, 1973-83. Mem. Tenn. Gen. Assembly, 1961-62; del. Tenn. Constl. Convs., 1959, 65. Served with USMCR, 1943-45. Recipient Pub. Trust award Humboldt Courier-Chronicle, 1976. Fellow Am. Bar Found., Tenn. Bar Found.; mem. ABA (mem. council gen. practice sect. 1974-79, ho. of dels. 1980-86), Am. Law Inst., Tenn. Def. Lawyers Assn. (v.p. 1980—), Tenn. Bar Assn. (pres. 1978-79, mem. ho. of dels. 1979-82), Gibson County Bar Assn. (pres. 1968-69), Humboldt C. of C. (pres. 1971-72), Rotary (pres. 1968-69), Golf and Country Club (pres. local club). Baptist. General practice. Home: 450 Forest St Humboldt TN 38343-3554 Office: Warmath and Boyte 314 N 22nd Ave Humboldt TN 38343-3010

BOZENTKA, LYNN M. lawyer; b. Wilmington, Del., Jan. 7, 1957; BS, Ohio U., 1976, U. Md., 1987; JD, Georgetown U., 1991. Bar: Md. 1991, Va. 1995, D.C. 1996. Assoc. Garson & Assocs., Bethesda, Md. Mem. ABA, Va. State Bar Assn., Md. State Bar Assn. Real property, Commercial leasing, Corporate litigation. Office: Garson & Assocs Ste 600 6905 Rockledge Dr Bethesda MD

BRACKEN, NANETTE BEATTIE, lawyer; b. Poughkeepsie, N.Y., Mar. 12, 1950; d. John Lindley and Margaret Jane (Brickner) Beattie; m. Paul Bracken, May 25, 1974; children: Kathleen John, James Beattie, Margaret Logue. BA, Vassar Coll., 1972; JD, U. Balt., 1975. Bar: N.Y. 1976, Conn. 1978, U.S. Dist. Ct. Conn. 1980. Chief clk. estate tax dept. Surrogate's Ct. Westchester County, N.Y. Dept. Taxation and Fin., White Plains, N.Y., 1976-78; assoc. Grehan & Fricke, Ridgefield, Conn., 1978-87; vol. Children's Ctr. Bedford Hills Correctional Facility, 1988—. Mem. Birthright, Danbury, Conn., 1978-80, Housatonic Mental Health Commn., Conn., 1980-83, Ridgefield Youth Commn., 1978-81; vice-chmn. Ridgefield Housing Commn., 1996—. Mem. ABA, N.Y. State Bar Assn., Conn. Bar Assn. Avocations: travel, gardening, dude ranching. Estate planning, Probate, Real property. Home and Office: 22 Green Ln Ridgefield CT 06877-3017 E-mail: bracken@ridgefieldlaw.com

BRACKETT, COLQUITT PRATER, JR. judge, lawyer; b. Norfolk, Va., Feb. 24, 1946; s. Colquitt Prater Sr. and Antoinette Gladys (Cacace) B.; m. Carol Ann Roberts, Dec. 29, 2000; 1 child, Susan Elizabeth Brackett Brooks. BS, U. Ga., 1966, MA, 1968, JD, 1973, LLM, 1976. Bar: Ga. 1973, U.S. Dist. Ct. (so. dist.) Ga. 1974, U.S. Dist. Ct. (mid. dist.) Ga. 1977, U.S. Supreme Ct. 1980, Tenn. 1987. Assoc. Surrett & CoCroft, Augusta, Ga., 1972-74; ptnr. Surrett & Brackett, 1974-76; faculty Sch. Law, U. Ga., Athens, 1977-82; mng. ptnr. Brackett, Prince & Neufeld, 1982-90; adminstrv. law judge Ga. Dept. Med. Assistance, 1990-98. Hearing officer Ga. State Bd. Edn., 1979-91; v.p. Mus. Dolls & Gifts, Inc., Pigeon Forge, Tenn., 1983—; pres. Bear Country Lodge and Conf. Ctr., Pigeon Forge, Tenn., 1996—, chmn. bd. Adventures in Toy Land. Author: Court Administration, 1972; (monograph) The Security Inventors Protection Corporation and the Operations of SIPC, 1976; (musical play) Americanization of Mary Poppins, 1995. Pres. Athens/Clarke Mental Health Assn., 1985; chmn. bd. dirs. N.E. Ga. Mental Health Assn., 1989-90; bd. dirs. Coalition for The Blue Ridge Pkwy., 1994-2000, Oconee Cultural Arts Found., 1995-97, Blue Ridge Pkwy. Assn., 1997-2001. Mem. ABA, Ga. State Bar Assn., Ga. Assn. Adminstrv. Law Judges (bd. dirs. 1990-91), Ga. Trial Lawyers Assn., Internat. Platform Assn., S.E. Tourism Soc., Rotary Internat., Ea. Nat. Parks Assn., Sevier County Bar Assn., Soc. Am. Poets, Soc. Magna Carta Barons. Episcopalian. Avocations: reading, music, golf, cross-country skiing. Mailing: 636 Middle Creek Rd Ste 4 Sevierville TN 37862-5013 Office: 2121 Chapman Hwy Sevierville TN 37826 E-mail: smokymts@ntown.net

BRACKETT, MARTIN LUTHER, JR. lawyer; b. Charlotte, N.C., Feb. 23, 1947; s. Martin Luther and Helen Virginia (Smith) B.; m. Lisa Nichol; children— Martin Hunter, Alexander Jones, Amelia Kathleen, Lauren Hart. B.A., Davidson Coll., 1969; J.D., U. N.C., 1972. Bar: N.C. 1972, U.S. Dist. Ct. (we. dist.) N.C. 1973, U.S. Ct. Appeals (4th cir.) 1975. Ptnr. Bailey, Brackett & Brackett, P.A., Charlotte, N.C., 1973-83, Brackett & Sitton, Charlotte, 1983-85, Robinson, Bradshaw & Hinson, P.A., 1985—. Mem. Auditorium-Coliseum-Conv. Ctr. Authority, Charlotte, 1981-87, chmn., 1985-87. Served to capt. U.S. Army, 1972-73. Recipient Van Hecke-Wettach award U. N.C., 1972. Fellow Am. Coll. Trial Lawyers; mem. N.C. Acad. Trial Lawyers (bd. govs. 1980-86, 88-95, v.p. 1984-86). Democrat. Presbyterian. Criminal, Family and matrimonial, Personal injury. Office: 1900 Independence Ctr 101 N Tryon St Charlotte NC 28246-0100

BRADDOCK, DONALD LAYTON, lawyer, accountant, real estate broker, investor; b. Jacksonville, Fla., Dec. 14, 1941; s. John Reddon and Harriet (Burgess) B.; children: Stella Helene Knowlton, Leslie Ann Meshad, Donald Layton Jr. BS in Bus. Adminstrn., U. Fla., 1963; JD, 1967. Bar: Fla. 1968, U.S. Dist. Ct. (mid. and no. dists.) Fla. 1968, U.S. Ct. Appeals (5th cir.) 1968, U.S. Ct. Appeals (4th and 11th cirs.) 1968, U.S. Supreme Ct. 1976, U.S. Tax Ct. 1970; CPA; registered real estate broker. Staff acct. Coopers and Lybrand, CPAs, 1964-65, Keith C. Austin, CPA, 1965-67; assoc. Kent, Durden & Kent, attys. at law, 1967-71; sole practice, 1971-73; ptnr. Howell, Kirby, Montgomery, D'Aiuto & Dean, attys. at law, 1974-76; pres., dir. Howell, Liles, Braddock & Milton, attys. at law, Jacksonville, Fla., 1976-88; ret., 1988. Bd. dirs., mem. exec. com. Fla. Lawyers Mutual Ins. Co., pres. 1996-97; bd. dirs. Doctors Lake Marina, Inc., 1993-99, pres., treas., 1993-99; pres., dir. SafeStop, Inc., 1990-99; pres., dir. Donald L. Braddock Chartered dba Mandarin Realty, 1970—; mgr. Wildcat Venture, LLC, 2000—; mgr. Bryant Hill, LLC, 2000—. Bd. dirs. Jacksonville Vocat. Edn. Authority, 1971-75; mem. Jacksonville Becentennial Commn., 1976; bd. govs. Fla. Bar Found., 1984-86, sec.-treas., 1986-88; sec., dir. Laurel Grove Plantation, Inc., 1988—. Served with Air N.G., 1963-69. Mem. Fla. Bar (bd. govs. young lawyers sec. 1972-77), Fla. Inst. CPAs, Jacksonville C. of C. (com. of 100), Jacksonville Bar Assn. (pres. 1983-84, bd. govs. 1978-84), U. Fla. Alumni Assn. (pres. 1975, bd. dirs. 1968-75), Fla. Blue Key, Friars Club, Phi Delta Phi, Alpha Tau Omega. Republican. General corporate, Real property, Estate taxation. Office: PO Box 57385 Jacksonville FL 32241-7385

BRADEN, BETTY JANE, legal association administrator; b. Sheboygan, Wis., Feb. 5, 1943; d. Otto Frank and Betty Donna (Beers) Huettner; children: Jennifer Tindall, Rebecca Leigh; m. Berwyn Bartow Braden, Nov. 5, 1983. BS, U. Wis., 1965. Cert. elem. tchr., Wis. Tchr. Madison (Wis.) Met. Sch. Dist., 1965-70, 71-72, sub. tchr., 1972-75; adminstrv. asst. ATS-CLE State Bar Wis., Madison, 1978, adminstrv. asst. Advanced Tng. Seminars-Continuing Legal Edn., 1979, coordinator, 1980, adminstr. coordinator, 1980-84, adminstrv. dir., 1984-87, dir. adminstrn., bar svcs., membership, 1987—; mem. rels. and pub. svcs. dir. Legal Edn., 1992—. Speaker Bar Leadership Inst. of ABA. Mem. Meeting Planners Internat. (sec. Wis. chpt. 1981-82, pres. 1982-83); Adminstrv. Mgmt. Soc., Am.

Mgmt. Assn., Am. Soc. for Personnel Adminstrn., Am. Soc. of Assn. Execs., Wis. Soc. of Assn. Execs., LWV, Nat. Assn. Bar Execs. (program chair 1995-96, sec. 1996-98, v.p. 1998-99, pres. elect 1999-2000, pres. 2000—). Avocations: tennis, scuba diving, reading, skiing. Home: 41 Golf Pkwy Madison WI 53704-7003 Office: State Bar of Wis 5302 Eastpark Blvd Madison WI 53718-2101

BRADFORD, CARL O. judge; b. Dallas, Nov. 16, 1932; s. Montie Leroy and Vivian Ila (Milan) B.; m. Claire Solange Chaloux, Jan. 15, 1955 (dec. 1972); children: Timothy, Kathleen, Elizabeth; m. Mary Ellen Sanborn, July 7, 1973; children: Bethany, Michael. Student, U. Detroit, 1956-59; JD, U. Maine, Portland, 1962. Bar: Maine 1963, U.S. Dist. Ct. Maine 1963, U.S. Ct. Appeals (1st cir.) 1963, U.S. supreme Ct. 1978. Asst. atty. gen. State of Maine, Augusta, 1963-64, justice Superior Ct., 1981-98, active-ret. justice Superior Ct., 1998—. Ptnr. Powers & Bradford, Freeport, Maine, 1964-81; commr. Uniform State Laws, 1972-76; mem. drafting com. Uniform Exemptions Act, 1974-76. With USN, 1951-55. Fellow Am. Bar Found., Maine Bar Found.; mem. Maine Bar Assn. (bd. govs. 1970-78, pres. 1977-78), Maine Trial Lawyers Assn. (bd. govs., sec. 1970-81), ABA (ho. of dels. 1978-81, 90-95, state bar del. 1978-81, bd. govs. 1st dist. 1990-93, bd. lisiaon to Nat. Conf. Spl. Ct. Judges 1990-91, liaison to Criminal Justice Sect. 1990-93, liaison to Nat. Conf. State Trial Judges 1991-93, chair subcom. nominations and awards com. 1991-93, bd. govs. program com. 1990-91, mem. oper. com. 1991-93, project 2000 subcom. 1991-93, bd. govs. chair compensation com. 1993, bd. govs. exec. com. 1993, bd. govs. exec. dir. search com. 1990, mem. comm. on multi-disciplinary practice 1998-2000), Nat. Conf. State Trial Judges (del. 1982-97, jud. immunity com. 1984-97, chair 1991-96, conf. vice chair 1993, chair-elect 1994-95, chair 1995-96), Am. Judicature Soc. Home: 225 Sea Meadows Ln Yarmouth ME 04096-5523 Office: Superior Ct PO Box 287 Portland ME 04112-0287

BRADFORD, DANA GIBSON, II, lawyer; b. Coral Gables, Fla., Sept. 29, 1948; s. Dana Gibson and Jeanette (Ellis) B.; m. Mary E. Bradford, June 20, 1970 (div. Jan. 1982); 1 child, Jeffrey Dana; m. Donna P. Bradford, Apr. 14, 1984; 1 child, Shannon Claire. BA, U. Fla., 1970; JD, Duke U., 1973. Bar: Fla. 1973, U.S. Dist. Ct. (mid. dist.) Fla. 1974, U.S. Dist. Ct. (so. and no. dists.) Fla. 1979, U.S. Ct. Appeals (5th cir.) 1974, U.S. Ct. Appeals (11th cir.) 1982, U.S. Supreme Ct. 1977. Lawyer, ptnr. Mahoney, Hadlow & Adams, Jacksonville, Fla., 1973-82, Baumer, Bradford & Walters, Jacksonville, 1982—, Smith, Gambrell & Russell, LLP, Jacksonville, 2000—. Mem. Fla. Bd. Bar Examiners, 1989-94, chmn. bd., 1992-93; mem. Fla. Supreme Ct. Commn. on Professionalism, 1996-98; seminar lectr. Contbr. chpt. to book, articles to profl. jours. Mem. Leadership Jacksonville, 1982; spl. counsel Jacksonville Sports Authority. Capt. U.S. Army Res., 1972-80. Mem. ABA, ATLA, Jacksonville Bar Assn. (bd. govs. young lawyers sect. 1976-78, chmn. trial sects. 1989-90), Jacksonville Assn. Def. Counsel (pres. 1978-79). Republican. Methodist. Federal civil litigation, General civil litigation, State civil litigation. Office: Baumer Bradford & Walters 50 N Laura St Ste 2200 Jacksonville FL 32202-3625 E-mail: dgbradford@sgrlaw.com

BRADIE, PETER RICHARD, lawyer, engineer; b. Bklyn., Feb. 19, 1937; s. Alexander Robert and Blanche Isabelle Bradie; m. Anna Barbara Corcoran, Jan. 22, 1960; children: Suzanne J., Barbara L., Michell S. BSME, Fairleigh Dickinson U., 1960; JD, South Tex. Coll. Law, 1978. Bar: Tex. 1978, U.S. Dist. Ct. (so. dist.) Tex. 1981; registered profl. engr., Ala. Performance engr. Pratt & Whitney Aircraft, West Palm Beach, Fla., 1961-63; sr. engr. Hayes Internat. Corp., Huntsville, Ala., 1963-64, Lockheed Missiles and Space, Huntsville, 1964-68; fluidics engr. Double A Products Co., Manchester, Mich., 1968-69; cons. Spectrum Controls, Montvale, N.J., 1969-72; sr. project mgr. Materials Research Corp., Orangebury, N.Y., 1972-74; sr. contracts adminstr. Brown & Root Inc., Houston, 1974-85; sole practice, 1985-91; ptnr. Bradie, Bradie & Bradie, 1991—. Counsel Inverness Forest C.A, Houston., 1978-80; sr. counsel Raymond-Brown & Root-Molem, J.V., Houston, 1982-84. Contbr. articles on fluidic controls to mags.; patentee. Dem. committeeman Bergen County, Haworth, N.J., 1959; del. Harris County Reps., Houston, 1984; officer, bd. dirs. Inverness Forest Civic Assn., Houston, 1975-78. Served to 2d lt. USMCR, 1958-61. Mem. ATLA, Tex. Bar Assn., Houston N.W. Bar Assn. (treas. 1986, bd. dirs. 1988, sec. 1988, pres.-elect 1988-89, pres. 1990-91), Comml. Law League Am., Rotary Club (Montvale bd. dirs. 1973-74), Am. Inn of Ct. Republican. Jewish. Avocations: classical music, history, computers. General civil litigation, Contracts commercial, General practice. Home: 22007 Kenchester Dr Houston TX 77073-1315 Office: 3845 Fm 1960 Rd W Ste 330 Houston TX 77068-3519 E-mail: bradiex3@bradie-law.com

BRADLEY, AMELIA JANE, lawyer; b. Columbia, S.C., Apr. 18, 1947; d. Hugh Wilson and Amelia Jane (Wylie) B.; m. Richard Bancroft Hovey, Apr. 1, 1977. BA, U. Va., 1968; MA, George Washington U., 1971. Bar: Va. 1976, D.C. 1985. Budget and mgmt. analyst NLRB, Washington, 1968-71, 72; clk. Cohen and Vitt, PC, Alexandria, Va., 1972-76; assoc. Cohen, Vitt & Annand, PC, 1976-80; White House fellow USDA, Washington, 1980-81, Office U.S. Trade Rep., Exec. Office of Pres., Washington, 1981, asst. gen. counsel, 1981-82, assoc. gen. counsel, 1982-84, legal advisor to U.S. GATT del. Geneva, 1984-87; prin. dep. gen. counsel Office U.S. Trade Rep., Exec Office of Pres., Washington, 1989-92; asst. U.S. trade rep. for dispute resolution Office U.S. Trade Rep., Exec. Office of Pres., 1994; assoc. dir. for global environment White House Office on Environ. Policy, 1994-95; assoc. dir. internat. trade and devel. Coun. on Environ. Quality, 1995; asst. U.S. trade rep. for monitoring, enforcement Exec. Office of Pres., 1996—. Chief negotiator U.S. GATT Uruguay Round Dispute Settlement Negotiating Group, 1986-87, 89-93; chmn. interagy. Sect. 301 Com., Washington, 1988-92; vis. rsch. assoc. Fletcher Sch. Law and Diplomacy, Tufts U., Medford, Mass., 1987-88; vis. rschr. Harvard U. Law Sch., Cambridge, Mass., 1988. Mem., chmn. Alexandria Human Rights Commn., 1975-80; pres., trustee Alexandria Law Libr., 1978-80; founding mem. Lawyer Referral Svc., Alexandria, 1978. NEH fellow, 1978. Mem. ABA, Va. State Bar (mem., chmn. com. on legal edn. and admission to bar 1977-84), D.C. Bar (chmn. internat. trade com. 1989-90). Episcopalian. Office: Office of US Trade Rep 600 17th St NW Washington DC 20508-0002

BRADLEY, ANN WALSH, state supreme court justice; Former judge Marathon County Circuit Ct., Wausau, Wis.; justice Wis. Supreme Ct., Madison. Office: PO Box 1688 Madison WI 53701-1688*

BRADLEY, CHARLES HARVEY, JR. lawyer; b. Indpls., July 17, 1923; s. Charles Harvey and Carolyn (Coffin) B.; m. Mary Jo Albright, Aug. 26, 1944; children: Sally A., Jane C. A.B., Yale U., 1945, LL.B., 1949. Bar: Ind. 1949. Ptnr., Thomson, O'Neal & Smith, Indpls., 1950-60; mgr. legal dept. Eli Lilly and Co., Indpls., 1960-63, asst. sec., dir. legal div., 1963, sec., gen. counsel, 1964-84, v.p., gen. counsel, 1984-86, v.p., gen. counsel, 1986-87. Mem. com. on character and fitness Ind. Supreme Ct., 1965-87, Supreme Ct. Com. on Continuing Legal Edn., 1984-87; trustee Hersey-Nofield Meml. Libr., Tinsville, Ind., 1990-96. Served to 2d lt. USMC, 1943-45, to capt., 1952-53. Decorated Air medal with 8 oak leaf clusters, D.F.C. with 3 oak leaf clusters. Fellow Ind. Bar Found.; mem. Ind. Bar Assn., Indpls. Bar Assn., Assn. Gen. Counsel, Indpls. Lawyers Club, Indpls. Legal Aid Soc., Indpls. C. of C. (dir. emeritus), Yale Law Sch. Assn. (pres. 1977-79, pres.'s commn. mgmt. AID programs 1991-92), Yale of Ind. Club (past pres.), Indpls. Athletic Club, Meridian Hills Country Club, Crooked Stick Golf Club. General corporate. Home: 1310 S Us Highway 421 Zionsville IN 46077-9762

BRADLEY, CRAIG MACDOWELL, law educator; b. Downers Grove, Ill., Dec. 5, 1945; s. Edward Russell and Ruth June Bradley; m. Cynthia Jane Decker, Apr. 29, 1978; children: Derek MacDowell, Kathleen Mae. AB, U. N.C., 1967; JD, U. Va., 1970. Bar: Va. 1970, D.C. 1972, U.S. Ct. Appeals (2nd and 7th cirs.) 1971, U.S. Ct. Appeals (D.C. cir.) 1972. Atty. criminal div. U.S. Dept. Justice, Washington, 1970; asst. U.S. atty., Washington, 1972-75, sr. trial atty. criminal div., 1976-78; law clk. to Justice Wm. Rehnquist, U.S. Supreme Ct., Washington, 1975-76; vis. assoc. prof. of law U. of N.C., Chapel Hill, N.C., 1978-79; assoc. prof. law Ind. U., Bloomington, 1979-85, prof., 1985-93, James Louis Calamaras prof., 1993—. Author: The Failure of the Criminal Procedure Revolution, 1993; editor: Criminal Procedure: A Worldwide Study; regular columnist: Trial Mag.; contbr. articles to law jours. Recipient Alexander von Humboldt award Alexander von Humboldt Found., 1982, 1992. Nat. Endowment for Humanities award Stanford U., 1987; Fulbright sr. scholar, Australia, 1988. E-mail: bradleyc@indiana.edu. Office: Sch Law Ind U Bloomington IN 47405

BRADLEY, E. MICHAEL, lawyer; b. N.Y.C., Apr. 13, 1939; s. Otis Treat Bradley and Marian Booth (Alling) Ward; m. Judith Allen Thompson, June 29, 1962; children: Jennifer Treat, Michael Thompson, Thomas Alcott, Samuel Allen. BA, Yale U., 1961; LLB, U. Va., 1964. Bar: N.Y., 1965. Assoc. Davis, Polk & Wardwell, N.Y.C., 1964-72, Brown & Wood, N.Y.C., 1972-73, ptnr., 1974-95, mem. policy com., 1981-94, mem. exec. com., 1989-94; ptnr. Jones, Day, Reavis & Poque, 1995—. Lectr. Practicing Law Inst., N.Y.C., 1970-79; 86, Am. Law Inst.-ABA, Phila., 1977-78; arbitrator Am. Arbitration Assn., N.Y.C., 1975—. Contbg. editor: The Use of Experts in Corporate Litigation, 1978, Securites Law Techniques, 1985. Bd. dirs. Bennett Coll. Found., N.Y.C., 1984—, Inst. Ams., La Jolla, Calif., 2001—; trustee Salisbury (Conn.) Sch., 1987—. Mem. ABA, N.Y. State Bar Assn., Fed. Bar Assn., Assn. of Bar of City of N.Y., Inst. of Americas (dir. 2001-), River Club, Union Club, Coral Beach Club, Quogue Field Club, Shinnecock Yacht Club, Nat. Golf Links of Am., L.I. Wyandanch Club. Republican. Presbyterian. Federal civil litigation, State civil litigation, Criminal. Home: 200 E 66th St New York NY 10021-9175 Office: Jones Day Reavis & Pogue 599 Lexington Ave Fl C1A New York NY 10022-6030 E-mail: embradley@jonesday.com

BRADLEY, PHILLIP ALDEN, lawyer; b. Madison, Wis., Dec. 2, 1954; s. Sterling Gaylen and Lois Evelyn (Lee) B. B.A. with honors, St. Andrews Coll., 1975; J.D., Antioch Sch. Law, 1978. Bar: Ga. 1978, U.S. Dist. Ct. (no. dist.) Ga. 1978, U.S. Dist. Ct. (mid. dist.) Ga. 1985, U.S. Dist. Ct. (so. dist.) Ga. 1987, U.S. Dist. Ct. (no. and so. dists.) Tex. 1991, U.S. Tax Ct. 1989, U.S. Ct. Appeals (5th cir.) 1978, U.S. Ct. Appeals (11th cir.) 1981, U.S. Ct. Appeals (4th cir.) 1992. Staff atty. Atlanta Legal Aid Soc., 1978-79; supervising atty. Ga. Legal Services, Conyers, 1980-81; assoc. Long, Aldridge & Norman, Atlanta, 1981-84, ptnr., 1985-94, mng. ptnr. sect. litigation, 1994—. Mem. ABA, Atlanta Bar Assn. Federal civil litigation, Labor, Securities. Office: Long Aldridge & Norman 303 Peachtree St NE Ste 5300 Atlanta GA 30308-3251

BRADLEY, WAYNE BERNARD, lawyer; b. Decatur, Ga., Oct. 11, 1944; s. Bernard Bell and Frances Eleanor (Copelan) B. A.B. in Econs. U. Ga.-Athens, 1966; J.D., John Marshall U., Atlanta, 1972; student Young Harris Jr. Coll., 1963-64. Bar: Ga. 1972, U.S. Supreme Ct. 1975. Asst. dist. atty. Ocmulgee Judicial Cir., Milledgeville, Ga., 1972-74; Peugh and Bradley, 1975-85; sole practice, Milledgeville, 1985—. Mem. Ga. Bar Assn., Ocmulgee Bar Assn., Baldwin County Bar Assn. (past pres.). Criminal, Personal injury, Workers' compensation. Home: 160 Tanya Rd NE Milledgeville GA 31061-7826 Office: 201 S Wilkinson St Milledgeville GA 31061-3351

BRADSHAW, CARL JOHN, investor, lawyer, consultant; b. Oelwein, Iowa, Nov. 1, 1930; s. Carl John and Lorraine Lillian (Thiele) B.; m. Katsuko Anno, Nov. 5, 1954; children: Carla K., Arthur Herbert, Vincent Marcus. BS, U. Minn., 1952, JD, 1957; LLM, U. Mich., 1958; MJur, Keio U., Tokyo, 1962. Bar: Minn. 1960, U.S. Supreme Ct., 1981, Calif. 1985. Assoc. Graham, James & Rolph, Tokyo, 1961-63; assoc. prof. law U. Wash., Seattle, 1963-64; sr. v.p. Oak Industries, Inc., Crystal Lake, Ill., 1964-84, dir. internat. ops., 1964-70, dir. corp. devel., 1970-72, pres. communications group, 1972-78, chief legal officer, 1979-84; counsel Seki & Jarvis, L.A., 1985-87, Bell, Boyd & Lloyd, L.A., 1987; prin. The Pacific Law Group, L.A., Tokyo and Palo Alto, Calif., 1987—, The Asian Mktg. Group, Torrance, 1992—. Participant Japanese-Am. program for cooperation in legal studies, 1957-61. Contbr. articles to legal and bus. jours Bd. dirs. Japan-Am. Soc., Chgo., 1966-72; bd. dirs., fin. dir. San Diego Symphony Orch. Assn., 1980-81. Served to lt. (j.g.) USN, 1952-55 Fulbright scholar, 1958-59, Ford Found. scholar, 1960-61. Fellow Radio Club Am.; mem. Minn. Bar Assn., Calif. Bar Assn., Am. Soc. Internat. Law, Internat. Fiscal Assn., Regency Club, Order of Coif. Avocation: reading, bible study. Home: 12958 Robleda Cv San Diego CA 92128-1126 Office: Pacific Law Group 12121 Wilshire Blvd Fl 2 Los Angeles CA 90025-1123

BRADSHAW, JEAN PAUL, II, lawyer; b. May 12, 1956; married; children: Andrew, Stephanie. BJ, JD, U. Mo., 1981. Bar: Mo. 1981, U.S. Dist. Ct. (we. dist.) Mo. 1982, U.S. Dist. Ct. (so. dist.) Ill. 1988, U.S. Ct. Appeals (8th cir.) 1986, U.S. Supreme Ct. 1987. Assoc. Neale, Newman, Bradshaw & Freeman, Springfield, Mo., 1981-87, ptnr., 1987-89; U.S. atty. we. dist. Mo. U.S. Dept. Justice, Kansas City, 1989-93; of counsel Lathrop & Gage, 1993-99, mem., 2000—. Named Spl. Asst. Atty. Gen. State of Mo., 1985-89; mem., chmn. elect U.S. Atty. Gen.'s adv. com., office mgmt. and budget subcom., sentencing guidelines subcom. Chmn. Greene County Rep. cen. com., 1988-89; pres. Mo. Assn. Reps., 1986-87; bd. dirs. Greene County TARGET, 1984-89; mem. com. on resolutions, family and community issues and del. 1988 Rep. Nat. Conv.; mem. platform com. Mo. Reps., 1988; chmn. Greene County campaign McNary for Gov., 1984, co-chmn. congl. dist. Dole for Pres., 1988, regional chmn. Danforth for Senate, 1988, co-chmn. 7th congl. dist. Webster for Atty. Gen., 1988; county chmn. U. Mo.-Columbia Alumni Assn., 1985-87; bd. dirs. Springfield Profl. Baseball Assn., Inc.; past mem. Mo. Adv. Coun. for Comprehensive Psychiat. Svcs., former bd. dirs. Ozarks Coun. Boy Scouts Am.; pres. bd. trustees St. Paul's Episcopal Day Sch., 1997—. Named Outstanding Recent Grad. U. Mo.-Columbia Sch. Law, 1991. Mem. ABA, Mo. Bar Assn., Kansas City Met. Bar Assn., U. Mo.-Columbia Law Sch. Alumni Assn. (v.p. 1988-89, pres. 1990-91), Law Soc. U. Mo.-Columbia Law Sch. Office: 2345 Grand Blvd Ste 2800 Kansas City MO 64108-2612 E-mail: jpbradshaw@rathropgage.com

BRADY, BRUCE MORGAN, lawyer; b. Oakland, Calif., Oct. 9, 1950; s. Alfred Foster and Anne Felton (Hazlewood) B.; m. Barbara Jean Gehrett, June 8, 1974; children: Morgan G., Evan L.G. BA in Anthropology, Columbia Coll., 1972; JD, Boston U., 1975. Asst. dist. atty. King's County Dist. Atty., Bklyn., 1975-81, dep. chief criminal ct., 1980-81; assoc. Gabrini & Scher, P.C., N.Y.C., 1981-84, ptnr., 1984-90; sr. ptnr. Callan, Koster, Brady, & Brennan, LLP, 1990—. Legal adv., vice-chmn. Children's Aid & Family Svcs., Paramus, N.J., 1990—; pres. Ridgewood (N.J.) Lacrosse Assn., 1993-99. Mem. N.Y. State Trial Lawyers Assn., N.Y.C. Med. Def. Bar Assn. (charter mem.). Avocations: golf, snow sports, theatre, personal computing. Insurance, Personal injury, Product liability. Office: Koster & Brady LLP 1 Whitehall St New York NY 10004-2109 E-mail: bbrady@crkbny.com

BRADY, EDMUND MATTHEW, JR. lawyer; b. Apr. 24, 1941; s. Edmund Matthew and Thelma (McDonald) B.; m. Marie Pierre Wayne, May 14, 1966; children: Edmund Matthew III, Meghan, Timothy BSS, John Carroll U., 1963; JD, U. Detroit, 1966; postgrad., Wayne State U., 1966-69; DHL (hon.), U. Detroit, 1998. Bar: Mich. 1966, U.S. Dist. Ct. (ea. dist.) Mich. 1966, U.S. Ct. Appeals (6th cir.) 1973, U.S. Supreme Ct. 1974. Sr. ptnr. Vandeveer & Garzia, 1973-90, Plunkett & Cooney, P.C., 1990—. Village clk. Grosse Pointe Shores, Mich., 1975-80; trustee St. John Hosp. and Med. Ctr., Detroit, 1992-2000, chmn., 1994-2000, Grosse Pointe Acad., Mich., 1977-83, adv. trustee, 1983-89; vice chmn. St. John Physicians Hosp. Orgn., 1994-95; supr. Grosse Pointe Twp., 1994-2000, trustee, 1989-2000; pres., dir. Grosse Pointe Hockey Assn., 1969-70; bd. dirs., chmn. maj. gifts divsn. 1st Fund, St. John Hosp. Guild; bd. dirs., pres. Friends of Bon Secours Hosp.; trustee, mem. exec. com., mem. fin. com. St. John Health Sys., 1998-2000. Recipient award of distinction U. Detroit Law Alumni, 1981, Michael Franck award State Bar of Mich. Rep. Assembly, 1998, Respected Advocate award Mich. Trial Lawyers Assn., 1998. Fellow Am. Bar Found, Mich. State Bar Found. (life); mem. ABA, Am. Coll. Trial Lawyers, Inter. Soc. Barristers, Am. Bd. Trial Advocates, Internat. Assn. Def. Counsel, Assn. Def. Trial Counsel (dir. 1975-80, pres. 1980-81), Mich. Def. Trial Counsel (dir. 1980-81), Def. Rsch. Inst. (Exceptional Performance citation 1981), Cath. Lawyers Soc., Soc. Irish-Am. Lawyers (founding dir. 1979-81), Mich. Soc. Health Law Attys., Mediation Tribunal Assn. (mem. panel Wayne County, Macomb County mediator 1989-98), Detroit Bar Assn. (dir. 1986-91, sec.-treas. 1988, pres.-elect 1989-90, pres. 1990-91), State Bar Mich. (commr. 1991-98, treas. 1994, v.p. 1995, pres.-elect 1996, pres. 1997-98), Country Club of Detroit, Detroit Athletic Club, Delta Theta Phi. Republican. Roman Catholic. Federal civil litigation, State civil litigation, Personal injury. Office: Plunkett & Cooney 243 W Congress St Ste 910 Detroit MI 48226-3253 E-mail: bradyed@plunkettlaw.com

BRADY, GEORGE CHARLES, III, lawyer; b. Darby, Pa., Mar. 13, 1947; s. George Charles Jr. and Lillian (Foster) B.; m. Joan Ann Kilkenny, Apr. 27, 1973; children— Jeffrey, Stephanie, Brent. A.B., Holy Cross Coll., 1969; J.D., Villanova U., 1972. Bar: Pa. 1972, U.S. Dist. Ct. (ea. dist.) Pa. 1972. Assoc. McDonnell & McDonnell, Drexel Hill, Pa., 1972-74; asst. dist. atty. Montgomery County, Pa., 1974-76; ptnr. Cox & Brady, Conshohocken, Pa., 1976-81; sole practice, Conshohocken, 1981-83; ptnr. Baughman & Brady, Conshohocken, 1983-85, Pizonka & Brady, Norristown, Pa., 1985—; dir. Personnel Data Systems, Conshohocken. Mem. Villanova Law Sch. Alumni Assn. (pres. 1980). Republican. Roman Catholic. Club: Whitemarsh Valley Country. State civil litigation, General corporate, General practice. Home: 1417 Uxbridge Way North Wales PA 19454-3683

BRADY, GEORGE EOGHAN, lawyer; b. Dublin, May 4, 1971; s. George and Margaret (Lysaght) B. Student, DePaul U., 1993; B of Civil Law, U. Coll. Dublin, 1994. Lawyer Matheson Ormsey Prentice, Dublin, 1994-98, assoc., 2000—, Baker & McKenzie, London, 1998-2000. Mem. Law Soc. Ireland, Law Soc. Eng. and Wales, Dublin Bar Assn. General corporate, Mergers and acquisitions. Office: Matheson Ormsby Prentice 30 Herbert St Dublin 2 Ireland E-mail: george.brady@mop.ie

BRADY, LAWRENCE PETER, lawyer; b. Jersey City, July 26, 1940; s. Lawrence Peter and Evelyn (Mauro) B.; div; children: Deegan, Tara, Kerry, Melissa, James; m. Mary Helen Reynolds, Mar. 28, 1984. BS in Acctg., St. Peters Coll., 1961; JD, Seton Hall U., 1964; LLM, Bklyn. Law Sch., 1966. Bar: N.J. 1964, U.S. Dist. Ct. N.J. 1964, U.S. Supreme Ct. 1969, U.S. Ct. Appeals (3rd cir.) 1972, N.Y. 1991; cert. civil trial atty. State of N.J. 1982; cert. Nat. Bd. Trial Advocacy 1989. Asst. prosecutor Hudson County, Jersey City, 1964-70; prosecutor Town of Kearny, N.J., 1971-74; sr. ptnr. Doyle & Brady, Kearny, 1974—. Dir. and founding incorporator Growth Bank, New Vernon, N.J. Mem. ATLA, Nat. Bd. Trial Advocacy, N.J. State Bar Assn., Hudson County Bar Assn., West Hudson Bar Assn. (sec. 1980, treas. 1981, v.p. 1982, pres. 1983), Am. Trial Lawyers N.J. (bd. govs.), Roxiticus Golf Club (Mendham, N.J.), Sandalfoot Country Club (Boca Raton, Fla.), Ocean Reef Club (Key Largo, Fla.), Ocean Reef Yacht Club. Roman Catholic. Avocations: golf, tennis, travel, fishing, boating. General civil litigation, State civil litigation, Personal injury. Office: Doyle & Brady 377 Kearny Ave Kearny NJ 07032-2600

BRADY, M. JANE, state attorney general; b. Wilmington, Del., Jan. 11, 1951; m. Michael Neal. BA, U. Del., 1973; JD, Villanova U., 1976. Dep. atty. gen. Wilmington and Kent County, 1977-87; chief prosecutor Sussex County, 1987-90; solo law practice, 1990-94; atty. gen. State of Del., Wilmington, 1995—. Office: Office of Atty Gen Carvel State Office Bldg 820 N French St Wilmington DE 19801-3509 E-mail: jbrady@state.de.us

BRADY, NORMAN CONRAD, lawyer, corporate executive; b. Dallas, June 29, 1934; s. Conrad and Louise Mabel (Norman) B.; m. Joyce Johnson, Sept., 1958 (div. 1967); 1 dau., Brigitte; m. Kornelia Jefferies Sichol, July 3, 1969; 1 son, Adam Conrad; step-children— Arthur, Tom, Timothy. B.A., Baylor U., 1956; J.D., U. Tex.-Austin, 1964. Bar: Tex. 1964, U.S. Dist. Ct. (no. dist.) Tex. 1967, U.S. Supreme Ct. 1984. Assoc. firm Rogers, Sayers & Brady, Austin, 1964-65; assoc. atty. Tex. Wholesale Beer Distbrs., Austin, 1965-67, Biesel, Zwieg, Diamond, Brady, Dallas, 1967-68; v.p. Service Corp. Internat., Houston, 1968— . Harris County campaign mgr. Gov. Preston Smith, 1968-70; mem. Harris County Fin. Com., Gov. Mark White, 1982. Served as 1st lt. USAF, 1956-58. Mem. SCV, SAR. Baptist. Clubs: Champions Golf, Houston, Inns of Court (Houston); Onion Creek Country, (Austin). Legislative. Home: 14118 Kiamesha Ct Houston TX 77069-1344 Office: Service Corp PO Box 13548 Houston TX 77219

BRADY, RUPERT JOSEPH, lawyer; b. Washington, Jan. 24, 1932; s. John Bernard and Mary Catherine (Rupert) B.; m. Maureen Mary MacIntosh, Apr. 20, 1954; children: Rupert Joseph Jr., Laureen Zegowitz, Kevin, Warren, Jeanine Hartnett, Jacqueline Rada, Brian, Barton. BEE, Cath. U. Am., 1953; JD, Georgetown U., 1959. Bar: Md. 1961, U.S. Ct. Appeals (D.C. cir.) 1964, U.S. Patent Trademark Office 1961, D.C. 1962, U.S. Supreme Ct. 1969, U.S. Ct. Appeals (fed. cir.) 1961. Elec. engr. Sperry Gyroscope Co., L.I., 1953-56; patent specifications writer John B. Brady, patent atty., 1956-59; patent agt. B.P. Fishburne, Jr., Washington, 1959-61; pvt. practice patent agt. Washington and Md., 1961; practice Washington, Md. and Va., 1961—; sr. ptnr. Brady, O'Boyle & Gates, Washington & Chevy Chase, Md., 1963-95; of counsel Birth, Stewart, Kolasch & Birch, LLP, Va., 1996—. V.p. Minstr-O-Media Inc. Patentee crane booms, moldboard support assembly. Mem. ABA, Am. Intellectual Property Law Assn., Md. Patent Law Assn., Senator's Club Alumni. Republican. Roman Catholic. Intellectual property, Patent, Trademark and copyright. Home: 7201 Pyle Rd Bethesda MD 20817-5623 Office: 8110 Gatehouse Rd Ste 500E Falls Church VA 22042-1210

BRADY, SCOTT EARL, lawyer; b. Baton Rouge, Dec. 6, 1969; s. Charles Bernard Sr. and Frances Elizabeth Tubre Brady; m. Jill Elizabeth LeBlanc, Jan. 3, 1997. BA in Polit. Sci., La. State U., 1994; JD magna cum laude, So. U., 1997. Bar: La. Atty. McKernan Law Firm, Baton Rouge, 1997—. Founder Brady-LeBlanc Acad. Achievement Award, So. U. Law Ctr. Mem. ABA, La. Trial Lawyers Assn., Baton Rouge Bar Assn., Phi Alpha Delta. Product liability, Toxic tort. Office: McKernan Law Firm 8710 Jefferson Hwy Baton Rouge LA 70809

BRADY, TERRENCE JOSEPH, judge; b. Chgo., Dec. 24, 1940; s. Harry J. and Othele R. Brady; m. Debra René, Dec. 6, 1969; children: Tara René, Dana Rose. BA cum laude, Coll. St. Thomas, 1963; JD, U. Ill., 1968. Bar: Ill. 1969, U.S. Dist. Ct. (no. dist.) Ill. 1970, U.S. Ct. Appeals (7th cir.) 1971. Pvt. practice, Crystal Lake, Ill., 1969-70, Waukegan, 1970-77; assoc. judge 19th Jud. Cir., Ill. Cir. Ct., 1977—. Lectr. Ann. Ill. Assoc. Judge Seminars, Statewide Ill. Traffic Conf., 1982, Lake County Bar Assn. Seminar, 1983, 88, others; invited participant Law and Econs. Seminar, U. Kans., 2000; mem. vis. jud. faculty Nat. Jud. Coll., U. Nev. Reno, 1997, condr. seminar civil mediation, 1999; presenter, lectr. in field; materials author, lectr. Pretrials and Negotiations Statewide Jud. Seminar, 1997; mem. long range planning com. 19th Jud. Circuit, Lake County, Ill., 1999. Contbr. articles to profl. jours. Served with U.S. Army, 1963-64, 68-69. Mem. Ill. Bar Assn. (com. on jud. adv. polls 1994—, vice-chair adv. polls 1998, task force on domestic violence 1998—, chair jud. adv. polls, 1999, sec. com. on jud. adv. polls 1997-99, bench and bar coms., judicial polls), Ill. Judges Assn. (bd. govs.), Ill. Bar Found., Lake County Bar Assn. (seminar materials author and lectr. 1997, 98, 99, 2000), Libertyville Racquet Club, Am. Inns of Ct. Avocations: tennis, golf, writing, reading. Office: Lake County Courthouse 18 N County St Waukegan IL 60085-4304 E-mail: tbrady@co.lake.il.us

BRADY, THOMAS CARL, lawyer; b. Malone, N.Y., Sept. 5, 1947; s. Francis Robert and Rosamond Ethel (South) B.; m. Joan Marie Murray, Dec. 4, 1971; children: Erin Marie, Ryan Thomas, Trevor Michael. BA, Niagara U., 1969; JD, SUNY, Buffalo, 1972. Bar: N.Y. 1973, U.S. Dist. Ct. (we. dist.) N.Y. 1973, Fla. 1981. City ct. judge City of Salamanca, N.Y., 1973; atty. County of Cattaraugus, Little Valley, N.Y., 1973-76; ptnr. Eldredge, Brady, Peters & Brooks, Salamanca and Ellicottville, 1976-82; sr. ptnr. Brady, Brooks & Smith, Salamanca, 1982-96, Brady, Brooks & O'Connell, L.L.P., Salamanca, 1996-2001, Brady & O'Connell, L.L.P., Salamanca, 2001—. Trustee St. Patrick's Roman Cath. Ch., Salamanca, 1991—; mem. N.Y. State Office Parks, Recreation and Hist. Preservation Allegany Region Commn., 1998—, vice chair, 1999—; mem. 8th Dist. Atty. Grievance Com., 1994-2000. Capt. USAR, 1969-76. Mem. ATLA, Nat. Lawyers Assn., Fla. Bar Assn., N.Y. State Trial Lawyers Assn., N.Y. State Bar Assn., Cattaraugus County Bar Assn. (pres. 1984), Kiwanis (pres. Salamanca club 1983-84). Republican. Roman Catholic. Avocations: skiing, golf, swimming, boating. General civil litigation, Municipal (including bonds), Personal injury. Home: 6894 Woodland Dr Great Valley NY 14741-9752 Office: Brady & O'Connell LLP 41 Main St Salamanca NY 14779-0227 Fax: 716-945-3566. E-mail: tbrady@bradyandoconnell.com

BRAFFORD, WILLIAM CHARLES, lawyer; b. Pike County, Ky., Aug. 7, 1932; s. William Charles and Minnie (Tacket) B.; m. Katherine Jane Prather, Nov. 13, 1954; children— William Charles III, David A. JD, U. Ky., 1957; LLM (fellow), U. Ill., 1958. Bar: Ky. 1957, Ga. 1965, Tax Ct. U.S 1965, Ct. Claims 1965, Ohio 1966, U.S. Ct. Appeals 1966, U.S. Supreme Ct. 1970, Pa. 1973. Trial atty. NLRB, Washington and Cin., 1958-60; atty. Louisville & Nashville R.R. Co., Louisville, 1960-63, So. Bell Telephone Co., Atlanta, 1963-65; asst. gen. counsel NCR Corp., Dayton, Ohio, 1965-72; v.p., sec., gen. counsel Betz Dearborn, inc., Trevose, Pa., 1972-97, ret., 1997. Former dir. Betz Process Chems., Inc., Betz, Ltd. U.K., Betz Paper Chem. Inc., Betz Energy Chems., Inc., Betz S.A. France, B.L. Chems., Inc., Betz GmbH, Germany, Betz Entec, Inc., Betz Ges. GmbH, Austria, Betz NV Belgium, Betz Sud S.p.A., Italy, Betz Internat. Inc., Betz Europe Inc., Primex Ltd., Barbados. Served as 1st lt. C.I.C. AUS, 1954-56. Mem. Am. Soc. Corp. Secs., Nat. Assn. Corp. Dirs., Atlantic Legal Found. Republican. Presbyterian.

BRAGG, ELLIS MEREDITH, JR. lawyer; b. Washington, Jan. 30, 1947; s. Ellis Meredith Sr. and Lucille (Tingstrum) B.; m. Judith Owens, Aug. 18, 1968; children: Michael Andrew, Jennifer Meredith. BA, King Coll., 1969; JD, Wake Forest U., 1973. Bar: N.C. 1973, U.S. Dist. Ct. (we. and mid. dists.) N.C. 1974, U.S. Ct. Appeals (4th cir.) 1980. Assoc. Bailey, Brackett & Brackett, P.A., Charlotte, N.C., 1973-76; ptnr. Howard & Bragg, 1976-77, McConnell, Howard, Johnson, Pruitt, Jenkins & Bragg, Charlotte, 1977-79; pvt. practice, 1979—. Dist. chmn. Mecklenburg County Dems., Charlotte, 1978; coach youth soccer program YMCA, Charlotte, 1982-83; mem. Headstart Policy Council, Charlotte, 1985. Mem. ABA, N.C. Bar Assn., N.C. Acad. Trial Lawyers. Presbyterian. Avocations: reading, jogging, gardening. State civil litigation, Family and matrimonial, General practice. Home: 6407 Honegger Dr Charlotte NC 28211-4718 Office: 500 E Morehead St Ste 210 Charlotte NC 28202-2694 E-mail: Bragglow@aol.com

BRAGG, MICHAEL ELLIS, lawyer, insurance company executive; b. Holdrege, Nebr., Oct. 6, 1947; s. Lionel C and Frances E (Klinginsmith) Bragg; m. Nancy Jo Aabel, Jan. 19, 1980; children: Brian Michael, Kyle Christopher, Jeffrey Douglas. BA, U. Nebr., 1971, JD, 1975. CLU; bar: Alaska 1976, Nebr 1976; cert. ChFC, CPCU. Assoc. White & Jones, Anchorage, 1976-77; field rep. State Farm Ins., 1977-79, atty. corp. law dept. Bloomington, Ill., 1979-81, sr. atty., 1981-84, asst. counsel, 1984-86, counsel, 1986-88; asst. v.p., counsel gen. claims dept. State Farm Fire and Casualty Co., 1988-94; v.p., counsel, gen. claims dept. State Farm Ins. Cos., Ill., 1994-97, assoc. gen. counsel corp. law dept., 1997—. Lectr, contbr legal seminars. Contbr, ed: articles to legal and ins jours. Pres McLean County Crime Detection Network, 1988—95. Recipient Disting Legal Serv Award, Corp Legal Times, 1998. Fellow: Am Bar Found; mem.: ABA (vice chmn property ins law comt 1986—91, chmn ins coverage litigation comt 1991—92, various offices tort and ins practices sect including coun 2000—, chair task force on ins staff counsel 2000—, mem standing comt on ethics and profl responsibility 2001—), Am Corp Counsel Asn, Def Research Inst, Fedn Def and Corp Counsel (chair industry coop sect 1995—97), Int Asn Def Counsel, Crestwick Country Club, Crestwicke Country Club. Republican. Avocations: golf, tennis. General civil litigation, Insurance, Personal injury. Office: State Farm Ins Cos Assoc Gen Counsel One State Farm Plz A-3 Bloomington IL 61710 E-mail: buck.bragg.achk@statefarm.com

BRAID, FREDERICK DONALD, lawyer; b. N.Y.C., Aug. 10, 1946; s. Donald Michael and Margaret Anna (Fluty) B.; m. Eleanor Mae Friedman, Oct. 23, 1980; children: Andrew Harris, Roy Leal, Josh Perry, David Barnett, Steven Gabriel. BS in Econs., St. John's U., Jamaica, N.Y., 1968; JD, St. John's U., Bklyn., 1971; LLM, NYU, 1979. Bar: N.Y. 1972, U.S. Dist. Ct. (so. and ea. dists.) N.Y. 1973, U.S. Ct. Appeals (2d cir.) 1973, (D.C. and 4th cirs.) 1997, U.S. Supreme Ct. 1975. Assoc. Rains & Pogrebin, Mineola and N.Y.C., N.Y., 1971-77, ptnr., 1978-99; bd. dirs. Rains & Pogrebin, P.C.; ptnr. Holland and Knight LLP, 2000—. Mem. adv. bd. NYU Sch. Law Ctr. for Labor and Employment Law, 1997—. Mng. editor St. John's Law Rev., 1970-71; contbr. articles to profl. jours. Served to capt. USAR, 1972-80. St. Thomas More scholar, St. John's U. Sch. Law, 1968-71. Mem. ABA, N.Y. Bar Assn., Assn. Trial Lawyers Am., Nassau County Bar Assn., Def. Rsch. Inst., Omicron Delta Epsilon, Delta Mu Delta. Federal civil litigation, State civil litigation, Labor. Home: 17 E 96th St New York NY 10128-0783 Office: Holland & Knight LLP 195 Broadway New York NY 10007-3100

BRAMBLE, RONALD LEE, business and legal consultant; b. Pauls Valley, Okla., Sept. 9, 1937; s. Homer Lee and Ethyle Juanita (Stephens) B.; m. Kathryn Louise Seiler, July 2, 1960; children: Julia Dawn, Kristin Lee. AA, San Antonio Coll., 1957; BS, Trinity U., 1959, MS, 1964; JD, St. Mary's U., 1975; DBA, Ind. No. U., 1973; cert. lay spkr. Meth. Ch. Mgr., buyer Fed-Mart, Inc., San Antonio, 1959-61; tchr. bus. San Antonio Ind. Sch. Dist., 1961-65, edn. coordinator, bus. tng. specialist, 1965-67; assoc. prof., chmn. dept. mgmt. San Antonio Coll., 1967-73; prin. Ron Bramble Assocs., San Antonio, 1967-77; pres. Adminstrv. Research Assocs., Inc., 1977-82; v.p. PIA, Inc., 1982-83; v.p. fin. Solar 21 Corp., 1983-84, sr. staff Ausburn, Astoria & Seale (formerly Ausburn, O'Neill & Assocs.), San Antonio, 1984-89; pvt. practice, 1990—; cons., comptr. TEL-STAR Systems, Inc., 1993-95; v.p. MegaTronics Internat. Corp., 1995—; lectr. bus., edn. and ch. groups, 1965—. Cons. editor: Prentice-Hall, Inc., Englewood Cliffs, N.J., 1969-71; contbr. articles to profl. jours. Mem. Am. Soc. Trial Cons., World Affairs Coun. of San Antonio, diplomat. Served with AUS, 1959. Recipient Wall Street Jour. award Trinity U., 1959, U.S. Law Week award St. Mary's Sch. of Law, 1975. Mem. ABA, Am. Soc. Trial Cons., San Antonio C. of C., Adminstrv. Mgmt. Soc. (pres. 1966-68, Merit award 1968), Bus. Edn. Tchrs. Assn. (pres. 1964), Sales and Mktg. Execs. San Antonio (bd. dirs. 1967-68, Disting. Salesman award 1967), Internat. Platform Assn., Internat. Assn. Cons. to Bus., Nat. Assn. Bus. Economists, Acad. Mgmt., Christian Legal Soc., Comml. Law League Am., Toastmasters, Phi Delta Phi, Lions. Republican. General corporate, Private international. Home: 127 Palo Duro St San Antonio TX 78232-3026

BRAME, JOSEPH ROBERT, III, lawyer; b. Hopkinsville, Ky., Apr. 18, 1942; s. Joseph Robert and Atwood Ruth (Davenport) B.; m. Mary Jane Blake, June 11, 1966; children: Rob, Blake, Virginia, John, Thomas. BA with high honors, Vanderbilt U., 1964; LLB, Yale U., 1967. Bar: Va. 1968, D.C. 2001. Assoc. McGuire, Woods, Battle & Boothe, Richmond, Va., 1967-72, ptnr., 1972-97; mem. NLRB, 1997-2000; shareholder Ogletree, Deakins, Nash, Smoak & Stewart, P.C., Washington, 2000—. Lectr. in field. Contbr. articles to profl. jours. Mem. adv. bd. Salvation Army, Richmond, 1980-97, chmn., 1989-91; troop com. chmn. Robert E. Lee coun. Boy Scouts Am., 1980-91; chair 10th Amendment Litig. com., Gov.'s Adv. Coun. on Federalism and Self Determination, 1994-97; gen. counsel Rep. Party Va., 1993-96. Mem. Am. Bar Found., Am. Coll. Labor and Employment Lawyers, Va. State Bar, Phi Beta Kappa. Presbyterian. Constitutional, Labor. Office: Deakins Nash Smoak & Stewart PC 2400 N St NW 5th Fl Washington DC 20037 E-mail: robert.brame@odnss.com

BRAMLETT, PAUL KENT, lawyer; b. Tupelo, Miss., May 31, 1944; s. Virgil Preston and McDuff (Goggans) B.; m. Shirley Marie Wilhelm, June 14, 1966; children: Paul Kent II (dec.), Robert Preston. AA with honors, Itawamba Jr. Coll., Fulton, Miss., 1962-64; BA, David Lipscomb Coll., 1966; postgrad., George Peabody Coll., 1966; JD, U. Miss., 1969. Bar: Miss. 1969, Tenn. 1980, U.S. Dist. Ct. (no. dist.) Miss. 1969, U.S. Dist. Ct. (we. dist.) Tenn. 1976, U.S. Dist. Ct. (mid. dist.) Tenn. 1980, U.S. Dist. Ct. (so. dist.) Miss. 1983, U.S. Dist. Ct. (we. dist.) Ky. 1988, U.S. Ct. Appeals (5th cir.) 1974, U.S. Ct. Appeals (6th cir.) 1980, U.S. Ct. Appeals (11th cir.) 1981, U.S. Supreme Ct. 1974. Pvt. practice, Tupelo, Miss., 1969-80, Nashville, 1980—. Mem. Million Dollar Advs. Forum, 1998. Mem. ABA, Miss. Trial Lawyers Assn. (bd. govs. 1976-79), Tenn. Bar Assn., Miss. Bar Assn. (pub. info. com. 1979-81), Nashville Bar Assn. (fed. ct. com. 1980-81), Million Dollar Advocates Forum, Am. Arbitration Assn. (comml. panel), Civitan Club (past gov. and legal counsel no. dist. Miss.). Mem. Ch. of Christ. Avocation: music. General civil litigation, Entertainment, Personal injury. Office: PO Box 150734 2828 Renaissance Tower Nashville TN 37215-0734

BRAMLETTE, DAVID C., III, federal judge; b. New Orleans, Nov. 27, 1939; BA, Princeton U., 1962; JD, U. Miss., 1965. Assoc., then ptnr. Adams, Forman, Truly, Ward & Bramlette, Natchez, Miss., 1975-91; spl. cir. judge Dist. Ct. (6th dist.) Miss., 1977, 79; fed. judge Dist. Ct. (so. dist.) Miss., 1991—. Trustee Miss. Nature Conservancy, 1990—; pres. BBCHA, 1989-90; active Arcole Hunting Camp, Ducks Unlimited, Nat. Wild Turkey Fedn.; mem. adv. bd. Natchez Lit. Celebration. Office: PO Box 928 Natchez MS 39121-0928 E-mail: connie_davis@mssd.uscourts.gov

BRANCH, JOHN WELLS (JACK TWIG), lawyer; b. Rochester, N.Y., May 1, 1912; s. John W. and Luna H. (Howell) B.; m. Caroline Wilbur, May 29, 1937 (dec. 1990); m. Margaret Zutterman, May 25, 1991. BA, Cornell U., 1934; J.S.D., 1937; MA in Econs., U. Rochester, 1937. Bar: N.Y. 1937, U.S. Ct. Appeals (2nd cir.) 1958. Assoc. Mann, Strang, Bodine & Wright, Rochester, N.Y., 1937-42; chief price atty. OPA, Rochester Dist., 1942-44; ptnr. and now of counsel Branch, Wise and Dewart, Rochester, 1945—; dir., legal advisor Hawthorne Villages, Inc., Asheville, N.C., 1998—. Pres. Nat. Planning Data Corp., Ithaca, N.Y., 1970-76; co-founder, pres. The Branch-Wilbur Fund, Inc., 1967—, Eldergard Svcs., Inc., 1988-94; co-founder Genesee-Volkhov Connection, Inc., 1994—. Recipient Civic award Rochester, N.Y 1995. Mem. N.Y. State Bar Assn., Monroe County Bar Assn., Estate Planning Coun. Monroe County, Rotary, Phi Beta Kappa. Democrat. Orthodox Christian. Avocations: composing, helping foreign students, reciting light verse. Estate planning, Probate. Home and Office: 34A Larkspur Ct Asheville NC 28805-1368

BRANCH, RONALD DREWITT, lawyer; b. Richmond, Va., Jan. 24, 1948; s. Cornell Drewitt and Virgie Ann (Pitts) B. B.A., Va. State U., 1970; J.D., Howard U., 1973. Bar: D.C. 1976, U.S. Dist. Ct. D.C. 1976. Atty., civil rights specialist U.S. Dept. Justice, Washington, 1976-78, GSA, 1978, U.S. Dept. Labor, 1978-79, HUD, Washington, 1979— ; arbitrator D.C. Superior Ct., 1984— . Div. leader Combined Fed. Campaign, Washington, 1982-83. CLEO scholar Howard U., 1970; Danforth intern U. Cin., 1970. Mem. ARC, D.C. Bar Assn. (pro bono), ABA, Wash. Bar Assn., Phi Alpha Delta. Baptist. Club: Nat. Lawyers. Home: 2450 Virginia Ave NW Washington DC 20037-2679 Office: US Dept of Housing & Urban Devel 451 7th St SW Washington DC 20410

BRANCH, THOMAS BROUGHTON, III, lawyer; b. Atlanta, June 5, 1936; s. Thomas Broughton Jr. and Alfred Iverson (Dews) B.; m. Trudi Schroetter, Dec. 27, 1963; children: Maria Barbara, Thomas B. IV. BA cum laude, Washington and Lee U., 1958, JD, 1960. Bar: Ga. 1960, U.S. Dist. Ct. (no. dist.) Ga. 1960, U.S. Ct. Appeals (5th cir.) 1960, U.S. Dist. Ct. (mid. dist.) Ga. 1980, U.S. Ct. Appeals (11th cir.) 1980, U.S. Dist. Ct. (so. dist.) N.Y. 1984, U.S. Ct. Appeals (2d cir.) 1984, U.S. Supreme Ct. 1991. Assoc. Kilpatrick & Cody, Atlanta, 1960-63; ptnr. Greene, Buckley et al, 1963-79, Wildman, Harrold, Allen, Dixon & Branch, Atlanta, 1979-89, Branch, Pike & Ganz, Atlanta, 1990-95, Holland & Knight, Atlanta, 1995—. Asst. prof. Woodrow Wilson Law Sch., Atlanta, 1964-68; trustee Washington and Lee U., Lexington, Va., 1979-90, trustee emeritus, 1991—; trustee, chmn. Atlanta Lawyers Found., Atlanta, 1980-81, Atlantis Aurora, Inc., 1970-74. Mem. Citizens Adv. Council on Urban Devel., Atlanta, 1977; trustee The Children's Sch., Inc., Atlanta, 1980-85; elder, clk. First Presbyn. Ch., Atlanta, 1967-79, 81-85, 97—. Fellow Am. Bar Found.; mem. ABA, Ga. Bar Assn., Atlanta Bar Assn. (mem. jud. selection and tenure com. 1988—), Am. Jud. Soc., Atlanta Lawyers Club (pres. 1976-77), Bleckley Inn of Ct. (master), Def. Rsch. Inst., Ansley Golf Club (pres., bd. dirs. 1976-87). Federal civil litigation, State civil litigation, Private international. Home: 160 The Prado NE Atlanta GA 30309-3388 E-mail: tbranch@hklaw.com

BRAND, MARK, lawyer; b. Sauk Centre, Minn., Feb. 1, 1952; s. Milton A. and Margaret (Kay) B.; m. Margrit B. Kuehn, Sept. 4, 1982; children: Peter, Erik, Natalie. BA cum laude, Concordia Coll., 1974; JD, U Notre Dame, 1979. Bar: Wash. 1979, U.S. Dist. Ct. (we. dist.) Wash. 1979, U.S. Ct. Appeals (9th cir.) 1979, Tex. 1981, U.S. Dist. Ct. (so. dist.) Tex. 1981, U.S. Ct. Appeals (5th and 11th cirs.) 1981, Ill. 1988, U.S. Dist. Ct. (no. dist) Ill. 1988, U.S. Ct. Appeals (7th cir.) 1988, U.S. Dist. Ct. (ea. dist.) Mich. 1992, U.S. Dist. Ct. (cent. dist.) Ill. 1996. Assoc. George, Hull & Porter, Seattle, 1979-80; atty. Gulf Oil Corp., Houston, 1980-85; assoc. Hutcheson & Grundy, LLP, 1985-87; ptnr. Phelan Pope & John Ltd., Chgo., 1987-93, Brand & Novak Ltd., Chgo., 1993-2000, Quarles & Brady LLC, Chgo., 2000—. Spkr., chair various seminars and trial practice, 1986—. Mem. ABA, Chgo. Bar. Assn. General civil litigation, Contracts commercial, Product liability. Office: Quarles & Brady LLC 500 W Madison St Ste 3700 Chicago IL 60611-2511

BRAND, STEVE AARON, lawyer; b. St. Paul, Sept. 5, 1948; s. Allen A. and Shirley Mae (Mintz) B.; m. Gail Idele Greenspoon, Oct. 9, 1977. BA, U. Minn., 1970; JD, U. Chgo., 1973. Bar: Minn. 1973, U.S. Dist. Ct. Minn. 1974, U.S. Supreme Ct. 1977. Assoc. Briggs & Morgan, St. Paul, 1973-78, ptnr., 1978-91, Robins, Kaplan, Miller & Ciresi, LLP, 1991—. Pres. Jewish Vocat. Svc., 1981—84, Sholom Found., 1996—99; bd. dirs. Friends of the St. Paul Libr., 1997—; pres. Mt. Zion Hebrew Congregation, 1985—87. Mem. ABA, Minn. Bar Assn. (chmn. probate and trust law sect. 1984-85), Hebrew Union Coll.-Jewish Inst. Religion (bd. overseers 1987—, vice-chmn. 1996—), Am. Coll. Trust and Estate Counsel (Minn. chair 1991-96, regent 1998—), Ramsey County Bar Found. (pres. 1995-2000), Phi Beta Kappa, B'nai Brith. Democrat. Estate planning, Probate, Estate taxation. Home: 1907 Hampshire Ave Saint Paul MN 55116-2401 Office: Robins Kaplan Miller & Ciresi LLP 2800 LaSalle Plz 800 Lasalle Ave Minneapolis MN 55402-2015 E-mail: sabrand@rkmc.com

BRANDEL, ROLAND ERIC, lawyer; b. Chgo., Nov. 30, 1938; s. Eric John and Louise Catherine (Covich) B.; m. Catherine Terry, July 3, 1963 (div. July 1970). BS in Econs., Ill. Inst. Tech., 1960; JD, U. Chgo., 1966; postgrad., Columbia U., 1970. Enlisted U.S. Navy, 1960, advanced through grades to lt. comdr., ret., 1970; clk. to presiding justice Calif. Supreme Ct., San Francisco, 1966-67; ptnr. Morrison & Foerster, 1967—. Vis. prof. law U. Calif., Berkeley, 1974-75; consumer adv. council Fed. Res. Bd., Washington, 1976-80; vis. com. U. Chgo. Law Sch., 1983-86, Golden Gate Law Sch., San Francisco, 1983—; study groups of EFT and Negotiable Instruments Sec. of State Adv. Commn., Washington, 1983—. Co-author: Law of EFT Systems, 1988, TIL: 4 Comp. Guide plus supplement, 1981-87, Community Reinvestment Act Manual, 1978, Financial Privacy Comp. Manual, 1979. Mem. Planning Commn. City of Berkeley, 1972-74; chmn. Waterfront Adv. Bd., Berkeley, 1973. Mem. ABA (council bus. law 1982-86, chmn. ad hoc com. payment systems 1983—), Inst. Marine Resources (adv.bd. 1983-86), Nat. Ctr. Fin. Services (chmn. legal adv. com. 1985—, mng. com. 1983—), U. Chgo. Law Sch. Alumni (pres. 1968—). Banking, Consumer commercial, General corporate. Home: 58 Roble Rd Berkeley CA 94705-2838 Office: Morrison & Foerster 345 California St San Francisco CA 94104-2606

BRANDRUP, DOUGLAS WARREN, lawyer; b. Mitchel, S.D., July 11, 1940; s. Clair L. and Ruth M. (Wolverton) B.; m. Patricia R. Tuck, Dec. 20, 1986; children: Kendra, Monika, Peter. AB in Econs., Middlebury Coll., 1963; JD, Boston U., 1966. Bar: N.Y. 1969, U.S. Dist. Ct. (so. dist.) N.Y. 1970, U.S. Ct. Appeals (2d cir.) 1970. Assoc. Donovan, Leisure, Newton & Irvine, N.Y.C., 1968-72; ptnr. Griggs, Baldwin & Baldwin, 1972-80, sr. ptnr., 1980—. Chmn. Equity Oil Co. Mem. Govs. Security Adv. Com., State of N.J., 1975-90. Capt. U.S. Army, 1966-68. Recipient Ellis Island medal of Honor, 1999. Mem. ABA, N.Y. County Bar Assn., N.Y. State Bar Assn., Met. Club (N.Y.C., pres.), Mashomack Preserve Club. Republican. Episcopalian. General corporate, Estate planning, General practice. Office: 57 Old Post Rd No 2 Greenwich CT 06830 Fax: 203-629-7983

BRANDT, WILLIAM ARTHUR, JR. consulting executive; b. Chgo., Sept. 5, 1949; s. William Arthur and Joan Virginia (Ashworth) B.; m. Patrice Bugelas, Jan. 19, 1980; children: Katherine Ashworth, William George, Joan Patrice, John Peter. BA with honors, St. Louis U., 1971; MA, U. Chgo., 1972, postgrad., 1972-74. Asst. to pres. Pyro Mining Co., Chgo., 1972-74; commentator Sta. WBBM-AM, 1977; with Melaniphy & Assocs., Inc., 1975-76; pres., cons. Devel. Specialists, Inc., 1976—. Mem. adv. bd. Sociol. Abstracts, Inc., San Diego, 1979-83. Contbr. articles to profl. jours. Trustee Fenwick H.S., 1991-2000, Comml. Law League of Am., Internat. Coun. Shopping Ctrs., Nat. Assn. Bankruptcy Trustees, Ill. Sociol. Assn., Midwest Sociol. Soc., Urban Land Inst.; mem. Fla. del. to Dem. Nat. Conv., 1996, also mem. Dem. Party Platform Com., 2000. LaVerne Noyes scholar, 1971-74. Mem. Am. Bankruptcy Inst., Am. Sociol. Assn., Amelia Island Plantation Club, Union League Club Chgo., City Club of Miami, gov. mem. Chicago Symphony, Clinton/Gore '96 Natl. Finance Bd., mnging. trustee Democratic Natl. Comm., maj. trust mem. Democratic Senatorial Campaign Comm., life mem. Zoological Soc. of the Miami Metro Zoo. Democrat. Roman Catholic. Home: 2000 S Bayshore Dr Apt 39 Coconut Grove FL 33133-3251 Office: 3 First Nat Plz Ste 2300 Chicago IL 60602 also: Wells Fargo Ctr 333 S Grand Ave Ste 2010 Los Angeles CA 90071-1524

BRANHAM, C. MICHAEL, lawyer; b. Columbia, S.C., Nov. 6, 1957; s. Mack C. and Jennie Louise (Jones) B.; m. Teresa Barrett; children: Anthony, Mark. BS, Auburn U., Montgomery, Ala., 1979; JD, U. S.C., 1983. Bar: S.C.; cert. tax law specialist; CPA. Acct. Wilson, Price, Barranco & Billingsley, CPAs, Montgomery, 1979-80; law clk. Atty. Gen.'s Office, State of S.C., Columbia, 1981-82; acct. Price, Waterhouse, 1983-86; tax lawyer Young, Clement, Rivers & Tisdale, LLP, Charleston, S.C., 1986—, chmn. tax, estate planning and probate group, 1999—, firm mgmt. com., 1999—, asst. mng. ptnr., 1999-2000. Chmn. taxation law specialization adv. bd. S.C. Supreme Ct., 1995-97; mem., pres. Charleston Tax. Coun., 1993-94; mem. dean's adv. bd. Med. U. S.C. Nursing Sch., Charleston, 1994-97; chmn. MUSC Planned Giving adv. coun., 1993-97; S.C. case reporter ABA sect. real property, probate and trust law, 1997—; mem. Bishop Gadsden Estate Planning Adv. Coun., Charleston, 1998—; bd. dirs., sec. S.C. Youth Soccer Assn. Soccer coach Hungryneck Internat. Soccer Assn., Mt. Pleasant, S.C., 1989-99, James Island/Trident United Soccer Assn., Charleston, 1999—; sec., bd. dirs. S.C. Youth Soccer Assn.; mem. Charleston Estate Planning Coun. Recipient Am. Jurisprudence award, 1983. Mem. ABA, AICPA, S.C. Assn. CPAs, S.C. Bar Assn., Charleston Breakfast Rotary, S.C. Youth Soccer Assn. (sec., mem. bd. dirs. 2000—). Avocations: soccer coaching, weight lifting. Estate planning, Probate, Estate taxation. Home: 829 Detyens Rd Mount Pleasant SC 29464-5181 Office: Young Clement Rivers & Tisdale LLP 28 Broad St Charleston SC 29401-3070

BRANHAM, MELANIE J. lawyer; b. Kansas City, Mo., Nov. 22, 1960; d. John Francis II and Annette (Bowers) B. BA, U. Kans., 1983, MUP, 1985; JD, We. New Eng. Coll., 1994. Bar: Kans. 1994, Mo. 1995, U.S. Ct. Appeals (10th cir.) 1994, U.S. Ct. Appeals (8th cir.) 1995, U.S. Supreme Ct. 1997. Grad. planner City of Lawrence, Kans., 1984; city planner City of Overland Park, 1984-85; asst. dir. planning and inspections City of Merriam, 1985-87; city adminstr. City of Westwood, 1987-89; town adminstr. Town of Sheffield, Mass., 1989-91; law clk. We. Mass. Legal Svcs., Springfield, 1992-93; atty./law clk. Kans. Legal Svcs., Olathe, 1993-94; assoc. Johnson County Dist. Atty.'s Office, 1994; pvt. practice, 1994-99; atty. Cohen, McNeile, Pappas & Shuttleworth, P.C., Leawood, Kans., 1999-2001, Branham Law Firm, Overland Park, 2001—. Active Nelson-Atkins Mus. of Art, Kansas City, Mo., 1986—; mem. ACLU of Kans. and We. Mo., Kansas City, Mo., 1992—. Lt. col. USAF, 1972-76. Named to Outstanding Young Women of Am., 1987, Vol. of Yr., United Way, 2001; recipient Am. Jurisprudence award, 1993. Mem. ABA, Kans. Trial Lawyers Assn., Johnson County Bar Assn., Kans. Bar Assn. (Pro Bono Atty. of Yr. 2001), Mo. Bar Assn. Episcopal. General civil litigation, Criminal, General practice. Office: Branham Law Firm PO Box 11567 Overland Park KS 66207 Fax: 913-652-6517

BRANNEN, JEFFREY RICHARD, lawyer; b. Tampa, Fla., Aug. 27, 1945; s. Jackson Edward and Tobiah M. (Lovitz) B.; m. Mary Elizabeth Strand, Nov. 24, 1972; 1 child, Samuel Jackson. BA in English, U. N.Mex., 1967, JD, 1970. Bar: N.Mex. 1970, U.S. Dist. Ct. N.Mex. 1970, U.S. Ct. Appeals (10th cir.) 1976, U.S. Supreme Ct. 1978. Law clk. N.Mex. State Supreme Ct., Santa Fe, 1970-71; from assoc. to pres., shareholder Montgomery & Andrews, pa, 1972-93; pres. Jeffrey R. Brannen, P.A., 1993—; of counsel Comeau, Maldegan, Templeman & Indall (formerly known as Carpenter, Maldegan, Templeman & Indall), 1995—. Faculty Nat. Inst. Trial Advocacy, Hastings Ctr. for Trial & Appellate Advocacy, 1980-93; co-chmn. Pers. Injury Inst., Hastings, 1992. Named one of Best Lawyers in Am. for personal injury and civil litig., 2001—. Mem. ABA, Am. Bd. Trial Advocates (N.Mex. pres. 1998), Assn. Def. Trial Attys. (state chmn. 1992—), Def. Rsch. Inst. (Exceptional Performance Citation 1989), N.Mex. Def. Lawyers Assn. (pres. 1989). Democrat. Avocations: skiing, soccer, fly fishing, travel. General civil litigation, Personal injury, Product liability. Office: Comeau Maldegan Templeman & Indall 141 E Palace Ave Santa Fe NM 87501-2041 Fax: (505) 982-4611. E-mail: jbrannen@cmtisantafe

BRANSON, ALBERT HAROLD (HARRY BRANSON), judge, educator; b. Chgo., May 20, 1935; s. Fred Brooks and Marie (Vowell) B.; m. Siri-Anne Gudrun Lindberg, Nov. 2, 1963; children: Gunnar John, Gulliver Dean, Hannah Marie, Siri Elizabeth. BA, Northwestern U., 1957; JD, U. Chgo., 1963. Bar: Pa. 1965, Alaska 1972. Atty. Richard McVeigh law offices, Anchorage, 1972-73; ptnr. Jacobs, Branson & Guetschow, 1973-76, Branson & Guetschow, Anchorage, 1976-82; pvt. practice Law Offices of Harry Branson, 1982-84, 85-89; atty. Branson, Bazeley & Chisolm, 1984-85; U.S. magistrate judge U.S. Dist. Ct., 1989—. Instr., adj. prof. U. Alaska Justice Ctr., 1980-93; U.S. magistrate, Anchorage, 1975-76. Mem. steering com. Access to Civil Justice Task Force, 1997-98. With U.S. Army, 1957-59. Mem. Alaska Bar Assn. (bd. dirs., v.p. bd. govs. 1977-80, 83-86, pres. bd. govs. 1986, Disting. Svc. award 1992, Spl. Svc. award 1988, editor-in-chief Alaska Bar Rag 1978-86), Anchorage Bar Assn. (bd. dirs., bd. govs. 1982-86), Anchorage Inn of Ct. (pres. 1995). Democrat. Avocations: book collecting, cooking, poetry. Office: US Dist Ct 222 W 7th Ave Unit 33 Anchorage AK 99513-7504

BRANSTETTER, CECIL DEWEY, SR. lawyer; b. Deer Lodge, Tenn., Dec. 15, 1920; s. Miller Henry and Lillie Mae (Adams) B.; m. Charlotte Virginia Coleman, Aug. 5, 1944; children: Kay Frances Johnson, Linda Charlotte Mauk, Kathy Jane Stranch , Cecil Dewey Jr. BA, George Washington U., 1947; JD, Vanderbilt U., 1949. Bar: U.S. Supreme Ct. 1957, U.S. Ct. Appeals (6th cir.) 1963. Ptnr. Branstetter, Kilgore, Stranch & Jennings, Nashville, 1990—. Chmn. Bd. Profl. Responsibility Supreme Ct. Tenn. Contbr. articles to profl. jours. Mem. Gen. Assembly Tenn., Nashville, 1950-53; chmn. Charter Commn. and Charter Revision Commn., Nashville, 1957-62, 78-90; mem. Met. Action Commn., Nashville, 1964-68; pres. Coun. Community Agys. and Tenn. Environ. Coun., Nashville, 1970, 71-73. Sgt. U.S. Army, 1943-46, lt. Res., 1946-52, ETO. Mem. ACLU (bd. dirs.), ABA, Met. Human Rels. Commn., Am. Judicature Soc., Tenn. Conservation League (Carter Patten award), Am. Trial Lawyers Assn., Tenn. Bar Assn., Tenn. Trial Lawyers Assn., Nashville Bar Assn., Davidson County Sportsman Club, Order of Coif. Democrat. Baptist. Avocations: farming, fishing, hunting, raising Angus cattle. Labor, Public utilities, Workers' compensation.

BRANTLEY, TERRY O. lawyer; b. Warner Robins, Ga., Aug. 8, 1972; s. William Wimmy and Rose Marie Brantley; m. Allison Mary Strazzella, Aug. 9, 1996. BS in Math., Jacksonville U., 1994; JD, Mercer U., 1997. Bar: Ga. 1997. Assoc. Dawson & Huddleston, Marietta, Ga., 1997—. Sec. Investor and Consumer Protection Sect., Atlanta, 1997-98; mem. Nat. Moot Ct. Competition Com. Mem. Mercer Law Rev., 1995-97. Mem. ATLA, Ga. Bar Assn. (mem. litigation com.), Order of Barristers. Avocations: golf, baseball. Office: Dawson & Huddleston 328 Alexander St Ste 10 Marietta GA 30060

BRANTON, JAMES LAVOY, lawyer; b. Albany, Tex., Apr. 19, 1938; s. George Lyndon Branton and Oletha Imogene (Westerman) Johnson; m. Molly Branton, May 18, 1968; children: Christina, Victoria, Claudia. BA, U. Tex., 1961, LLB, 1962. Bar: Tex., U.S. Dist. Ct. (we., so, ea. and no. dists.) Tex., U.S. Ct. Appeals (5th cir.). Ptnr. Hardberger, Branton & Herrera, Inc., San Antonio, 1974-78, Branton & Mendelsohn, Inc., San Antonio, 1978-83, Branton, Warncke, Hall & Gonzales, P.C., San Antonio, 1983-88, Branton & Hall, P.C., San Antonio, 1988—. Bd. dirs. Tex. Lawyers' Ins. Exch. Co-author: Trial Lawyer's Series, 1981-91. Capt. USAF, 1962-65. Fellow Am. Coll. Trial Lawyers (state com. 1993-95, chair 1996-98), Internat. Soc. Barristers, Internat. Acad. Trial Lawyers, Tex. Bar Found. (chair 1989-90); mem. Tex. Trial Lawyers Assn. (pres. 1975-76), State Bar Tex. (pres. 1994-95), Am. Bd. Trial Advocates (pres. San Antonio chpt. 1990-91, Tex. Trial Lawyer of Yr. 1994). Avocations: flying, scuba diving. Personal injury, Product liability, Professional liability. Home: 403 Evans Ave San Antonio TX 78209-3725 Office: Branton & Hall PC One Riverwalk Pl Ste 1700 700 N St Mary's St San Antonio TX 78205 E-mail: jimbraton@branton-hall.com

BRASWELL, BRUCE WAYNE, lawyer, educator; b. Amarillo, Tex., June 5, 1955; s. Harvey Leonard and Iva Pearl Braswell; m. Maureen Louise Conklin, June 18, 1988; children: Paul Leonard, Peter Wayne. BA in Math., BA in Psychology, Eastern Nazarene Coll., 1978; JD, Bklyn. Law Sch., 1983. Bar: N.Y. Sole practitioner, Peekskill, N.Y., 1985-88, Poughkeepsie, 1988—. Bd. dirs., sec. Ch. of Nazarene, 1988—. Mem. Rotary (newsletter editor 1988—). Conservative. Avocation: chess. Family and matrimonial, General practice, Real property. Home and Office: PO Box 50 South Plymouth NY 13844-0050

BRAUN, DAVID A(DLAI), lawyer; b. N.Y.C., Apr. 23, 1931; s. Morris and Betty Braunstein; m. Merna Feldman, Dec. 18, 1955; children: Lloyd Jeffrey, Kenneth Franklin, Evan Albert. AB, Columbia U., 1952, LLB, 1954. Bar: N.Y. 1955, Calif. 1974. Assoc. Ellis, Ellis and Ellis, N.Y.C., 1954-56, Davis and Gilbert, 1956-57; ptnr. Pryor, Cashman, Sherman and Flynn, 1957-73, Hardee, Barovick, Konecky & Braun, N.Y.C., 1973, L.A., 1974-81; pres., CEO Polygram Records, Inc., N.Y.C., 1980-81; counsel Wyman, Bautzer, Rothman, Kuchel & Silbert, L.A., 1982-85; ptnr. Braun, Margolis, Burrill & Besser, 1985-87; counsel Silverberg, Rosen, Leon & Behr, 1987-89, Silverberg, Katz, Thompson & Braun, 1989-91; spl. counsel Proskauer, Rose, Goetz & Mendelsohn, 1991-93; ptnr. Monasch Plotkin & Braun, 1993-94; pvt. practice, 1994-98; sr. counsel Akin, Gump, Strauss, Hauer & Feld, L.L.P., 1998—. Adj. prof. U. So. Calif. Sch. Cinema-TV; guest lectr. UCLA Ext.; mem. adv. com. Ctr. for Law, Media and the ARts, Columbia U. Sch. Law; internat. adv. bd. Nat. Inst. Entertainment and Media Law, Southwestern U. Sch. Law. Bd. visitors Columbia Coll., 1980-86, Columbia Law Sch., 1992-94; bd. dirs. Reprise! Broadway's Best in Concert, Musician's Assistance Program, 1994-98, Tu 'Um EST Cmty. Drug Rehab. Ctr., Rock and Roll Hall of Fame, 1985-93. Mem. Assn. of City of N.Y., L.A. County Bar Assn., Beverly Hills Bar Assn., Nat. Acad. Arts and Scis. (pres. N.Y. chpt. 1972-73), NATAS, Am. Arbitration Assn., Hollywood Radio and TV Soc. (bd. dirs. 1983-86), Sigma Chi, Phi Alpha Delta. Jewish. Entertainment, Intellectual property, Trademark and copyright. Home: 211 S Spalding Dr Apt 401S Beverly Hills CA 90212-3664 Office: Akin Gump Strauss Hauer & Feld LLP 24th Fl 2029 Century Park St Los Angeles CA 90067 E-mail: dbraun@akingump.com

BRAUN, FREDERICK B. lawyer, food company executive; b. Cin., Aug. 4, 1942; s. Roger K. and Ruth (Sheperd) B.; m. Susan Braun, Nov. 23, 1967 (div. 1983); 1 child, Roger Tracy. B.A., U. Cin., 1967; M.S., Case Western Res. U., 1969, J.D., 1973. Bar: Ohio, 1973, Ill., 1980, U.S. Dist. Ct. (so. and we. dists.) Ohio 1973, U.S. Ct. Appeals (6th cir.), U.S. Dist. Ct. (no. dist.) Ill. 1981, U.S. Ct. Appeals (7th cir.) 1981. Assoc. Beckman, Lavercombe Fox & Weil, Cin., 1973-78; ptnr. Buechner, Braun & Haffer, Cin., 1979-80; chief labor counsel Sara Lee Corp., Chgo., 1980-85, asst. counsel, 1985—. Assoc. editor Internat. Law Rev., 1972. Chmn. Title XX Social Security Adv. Bd., Columbus, Ohio, 1977-80. Mandell fellow Case Western Res. U., 1978. Mem. ABA, Ill. Bar Assn., Chgo. Bar Assn., Cin. Bar Assn., Ohio Bar Assn. Episcopalian. Club: University (Cin.). Federal civil litigation, General corporate, Labor. Home: 728 Cutter Ln Barrington IL 60010-1535 Office: Sara Lee Corp 3 1st Nat Plz Chicago IL 60602

BRAUN, JEROME IRWIN, lawyer; b. St. Joseph, Mo., Dec. 16, 1929; s. Martin H. and Bess (Donsker) B.; children: Aaron, Susan, Daniel; m. Dolores Ferriter, Aug. 16, 1987. AB with distinction, Stanford U., 1951, LLB, 1953. Bar: Mo. 1953, Calif. 1953, U.S. Dist. Ct. (no. dist.) Calif., U.S. Tax Ct., U.S. Ct. Mil. Appeals, U.S. Supreme Ct., U.S. Ct. Appeals (9th cir.). Assoc. Long & Levit, San Francisco, 1957-58, Law Offices of Jefferson Peyser, San Francisco, 1958-62; founding ptnr. Farella, Braun & Martel (formerly Elke, Farella & Braun), 1962—. Instr. San Francisco Law Sch., 1958-69; mem. U.S. Dist. Ct. Civil Justice Reform Act Adv. Com., 1991—; spkr. various state bar convs. in Calif., Ill., Nev., Mont.; request moderator/participant continuing edn. of bar programs; past chmn. 9th Cir. Sr. Adv. Bd., past chmn. lawyer reps. to 9th Cir. Jud. Conf.; mem. appellate lawyers liaison com. Calif. Ct. Appeals 1st dist.; jud.conf. U.S. Com. Long Range Planning; founder Jon Samuel Abramson Scholarship Endowment Stanford U. Law. Revising editor: Stanford U. Law Rev.; contbr. articles to profl. jours. Mem. Jewish Community Fedn. San Francisco, The Peninsula, Marin and Sonoma Counties, pres., 1979-80; past pres. United Jewish Community Ctrs. 1st lt. JAGC, U.S. Army, 1954-57, U.S. Army Res., 1957-64. Recipient Lloyd W. Dinkelspiel Outstanding Young Leader award Jewish Welfare Fedn., 1967, Professionalism award 9th cir. Am. Inns of Ct., 1999. Fellow Am. Acad. Appellate Lawyers, Am. Coll. Trial Lawyers (teaching trial and appellate advocacy com.), Am. Bar Found.; mem. ABA, Calif. Bar Assn. (chmn. adminstrn. justice com. 1977), Bar Assn. San Francisco (spl. com. on lawyers malpractice and malpractice ins.), San Francisco Bar Found. (past trustee), Calif. Acad. Appellate Lawyers (past pres., mem. U.S. Dist. Ct. Civil Justice Reform Act adv. com., Calif. Ct. of Appeals 1st Dist. Appellate Lawyers liaison com., jud. conf. of the U.S., com. on long-range planning, panelist 1994), Am. Judicature Soc. (past dir.), Stanford Law Sch. Bd. of Visitors, U.S. Dist. Ct. of No. Dist. Calif. Hist. Soc. (past pres., bd. dirs.), 9th Cir. Ct. of Appeals Hist. Soc. (past. pres.), Mex.-Am. Legal Def. Fund (honoree), Order of Coif. Antitrust, Federal civil litigation, General civil litigation. E-mail: jbraun@fbm.com

BRAUN, ROBERT ALAN, lawyer; b. Bronx, N.Y., Mar. 6, 1950; s. George and Sylvia (Feuerstein) B.; children: Alison, Scott, Brianna, Benjamin, Amanda; m. Laura Rosemarie Icolari. BA, Queens Coll., 1972; JD, St. Johns U., 1976. Bar: N.Y. 1977, U.S. Dist. Ct. (ea. and so. dists.) N.Y. 1977, U.S. Ct. Appeals (2d cir.) 1978, U.S. Supreme Ct. 1982. Asst. dist. atty. Kings County Dist. Atty., Bklyn., 1976-80; assoc. Robert Rivers PC, Hempstead, N.Y., 1980, Singer & Braun PC, Hempstead, 1980-82, Sarisohn, Sarisohn, Carner, LeBow, Braun & Shiebler, Commack, 1982-85, ptnr., 1985—. Committeeman Suffolk County Dem. Com., 1982—; trustee Temple Beth Sholom of Smithtown, 1999-2000, corres. sec., 2000—. Staff sgt. USANG, 1970-76. Mem. ABA, N.Y. State Bar Assn., Suffolk County Bar Assn. (com. mem. profl. ethics, grievences and fee disputes), Soc. Am. Magicians Assembly #1 (pres. 1981-82), Rotary. Democrat. Jewish. General corporate, Probate, Real property. Office: Sarisohn Sarisohn et al 350 Veterans Hwy Commack NY 11725-4330

BRAUNSDORF, PAUL RAYMOND, lawyer; b. South Bend, Ind., June 18, 1943; s. Robert Louis and Marjorie (Breitenstein) B.; m. Margaret Buckley, June 18, 1966; children: Christopher, Mark, Douglas, Amy. BA magna cum laude, U. Notre Dame, 1965; LLB, U. Va., 1968. Bar: N.Y. 1968; U.S. Dist. Ct. (we. dist.) N.Y. 1969, U.S. Dist. Ct. (no. dist.) N.Y. 1980; U.S. Ct. Appeals (2d cir.) 1975; U.S. Supreme Ct. 1980. Assoc. Harris, Beach & Wilcox, Rochester, N.Y., 1968-75; ptnr., 1976—. Instr. Nat. Inst. for Trial Advocacy, Rochester, 1988; lectr. in field. Contbg. author: Antitrust Health Care Handbook II, 1993, Antitrust Law in New York, 1995. Bd. dirs. Mercy Parents' Club, 1989-90, McQuaid Parents' Club, 1984-90, pres. 1986-87, Brighton Baseball, 1987-90. Republican. Roman Catholic. Avocations: tennis, photography, music. Antitrust, Federal civil litigation, State civil litigation. Office: Harris Beach LLP 99 Garnsey Rd Pittsford NY 14534

BRAVERMAN, ALAN N. lawyer; BA, Brandeis U., 1969; JD, Duquesne U., 1975. Bar: D.C. 1976. Assoc. Wilmer, Cutler & Pickering, 1976-82, ptnr., 1983-93; sr. v.p., gen. counsel ABC, Inc., N.Y.C., 1993-2000, exec. v.p., gen. counsel Burbank, Calif., 2000—. Office: ABC Inc 500 S Buena Vista St Burbank CA 91521-0922

BRAVERMAN, BURT ALAN, lawyer; b. N.Y.C., Apr. 20, 1946; BA, Miami U., Oxford, Ohio, 1966; JD with honors, George Washington U., 1969. Bar: Va. 1969, D.C. 1970, U.S. Supreme Ct. 1972. Ptnr. Cole, Raywid & Braverman, Washington, 1969—. Author treatise Information Law, 1985, Getting and Protecting Competitive Business Information, 1997; editor-in-chief Jour. Law and Econ. Devel., 1968-69; contbr. articles to profl. jours. Antitrust, Federal civil litigation, Communications. Office: Cole Raywid & Braverman 2d Fl 1919 Pennsylvania Ave NW Washington DC 20006-3404 E-mail: bbraverman@crblaw.com

BRAVERMAN, HERBERT LESLIE, lawyer; b. Buffalo, Apr. 24, 1947; s. David and Miriam P. (Cohen) B.; m. Janet Marx, June 11, 1972; children: Becca Danielle, Benjamin Howard. BS in Econs., U. Pa., 1969; JD, Harvard U., 1972. Bar: Ohio 1972, U.S. Dist. Ct. Ohio 1972, U.S. Supreme Ct. 1975, U.S. Ct. Appeals (6th cir.) 1980, U.S. Ct. Claims 1980. Assoc. Hahn, Loeser, Freedheim, Dean & Wellman, Cleve., 1972-75; sole practice, 1975-87; ptnr. Porter, Wright, Morris & Arthur, 1987-95, Walter & Haverfield LLP, Cleve., 1996—. Councilman Orange Village, Ohio, 1988—, pres., 1998-2001. Capt. USAR, 1970-82. Fellow Am. Coll. Trust and Estate Counsel; mem. ABA, Ohio Bar Assn., Bar Assn. Greater Cleve. (former chmn. estate planning trust and probate sect.), Suburban East Bar Assn. (pres. 1978-80), Rotary (Cleveland Heights pres. 1980), B'nai Brith (local pres. 1978-84), Wharton Club Cleve. (pres. 1991—), Am. Jewish Congress (Ohio pres. 1992—). Avocations: golf, symphony, reading. General corporate, Estate planning, Probate. Home: 3950 Orangewood Dr Cleveland OH 44122-7406 Office: Walter & Haverfield LLP 1300 Terminal Tower 50 Public Sq Ste 1300 Cleveland OH 44113-2253 also: 23240 Chagrin Blvd Ste 600 Beachwood OH 44122-5402 E-mail: hbraverman@walterhav.com, hlblaw@aol.com

BRAVERMAN, JANIS ANN BREGGIN, lawyer; b. Rochester, N.Y., Mar. 5, 1955; d. Arnold H. and Eleanor (Wingo) Breggin; m. Joseph T. Braverman; children: Rachel Tyler, Cadiz Safira, Theo Socrates, Arielle. BA, U. Denver, 1976, JD, 1980. Bar: Colo. 1980, U.S. Ct. Appeals (10th cir.) 1980. Assoc. Sherman & Howard, Denver, 1980-82, Jeffrey M. Nobel & Assocs., Denver, 1982-84; assoc. in house counsel Bill L. Walters Cos., Englewood, Colo., 1984-85; assoc. Deutsch & Sheldon, 1985-87; ptnr. Breggin & Assocs. P.C., Denver, 1987-95, The Breggin Law Firm, P.C., Denver, 1995—. Mem. Denver Women's Commn., 1990-93, chmn. 1991-92. Mem. Colo. Bar Assn., Denver Bar Assn., Colo. Women's Bar Assn. Real property. Office: The Breggin Law Firm PC 1546 Williams St # 101 Denver CO 80218-1635

BRAWER, MARC HARRIS, lawyer; b. N.Y.C., June 11, 1946; s. Leonard and Diana R. Brawer; m. Susan L. Brunswick, Nov. 23, 1975; 3 children. BA, Queens Coll., 1967; JD, Bklyn. Law Sch., 1969. Bar: N.Y. 1970, Fla. 1978, U.S. Dist. Ct. (ea. and so. dists.) N.Y. 1974, U.S. Ct. Appeals (2nd cir.) 1974, U.S. Supreme Ct. 1975, U.S. Dist. Ct. (so. dist.) Fla. 1981, U.S. Ct. Appeals (5th cir.) 1980; cert. marital and family lawyer, family mediator. Staff atty. Legal Aid Soc., N.Y.C., 1972-78; ptnr. Meyerson Resnicoff & Brawer, 1978-83, Meyerson & Brawer, Tamarac, Fla., 1983-84; head firm Marc H. Brawer, Sunrise, 1984—; of counsel Resnicoff, Samanowitz & Brawer, Great Neck, N.Y., 1985-91. Adj. prof. family law St. Thomas Law Sch., 1992; spkr. various orgns. and colls., 1980-96. Contbr. articles to profl. jours., 1970-84. Fellow Am. Acad. Matrimonial Lawyers; mem. Broward County Bar Assn., Queens County Bar Assn. (cert. of svc. 1982-83), Fla. Bar (sec. Family Law Commentator). Avocations: scuba diving, photography, ornamental horticulture. Family and matrimonial. Office: 7771 W Oakland Park Blvd Fort Lauderdale FL 33351-6749

BRAY, ABSALOM FRANCIS, JR. lawyer; b. San Francisco, Nov. 24, 1918; s. Absalom Francis and Leila Elizabeth (Veale) E.; m. Lorraine Cerena Paule, June 25, 1949; children: Oliver, Brian, Margot. BA, Stanford U., 1940; JD, U. So. Calif., 1949. Bar: Calif. 1949, U.S. Supreme Ct. 1960. Sr. ptnr. Bray & Baldin and successive firms to Bray & Bray, Martinez, Calif., 1949—, now pres. Founder, bd. dirs. John Muir Nat. Bank, Martinez. Chmn. Martinez Recreation Commn., 1949-54; chmn. nat. bd. dirs. Camp Fire Girls, 1959-61, 69-71; pres. Contra Costa County (Calif.) Devel. Assn., 1959-60, Contra Costa County Hist. Soc., 1995-97. Lt. USNR, 1942-46. Mem. State Bar Calif. (chmn. adoption com. 1955-56), Martinez His. Soc. (pres. 1984), Mohn Muir Meml. Assn. (pres. 1989-92), Navy League U.S. (pres. Contra Costsons, Rotary (pres. Martinez 1970-71). General practice, Probate. Home: 600 Flora St Martinez CA 94553-3268 Office: Bray & Bray Ward and Ferry Sts Martinez CA 94553-1697

BRAY, LAURACK DOYLE, lawyer; b. New Orleans, Nov. 13, 1949; s. Laudrack Doyle Bray and Helen Davis. AA, L.A. City Coll., 1969; BA, Long Beach State U., 1972, MS, 1977, MPA, 1981; JD, Howard U., 1984. Bar: Pa. 1986, D.C. 1986, U.S. Ct. Appeals (D.C. and fed. cirs.) 1987, U.S. Dist. Ct. D.C. 1987, U.S. Ct. Appeals (4th cir.) 1991, Md. 1991, U.S. Supreme Ct. 1992. Cmty. rsch. worker Crenshaw Consortium, L.A., 1977-79; adminstrv. intern City of Lawndale, Calif., 1981; legis. intern U.S. Congress, Washington, 1982; law clk. FDIC, 1983-84; pvt. practice, 1987—. Mem. moot ct. team Howard U., Washington. Contbr. articles to law jours. Recipient Am. Jurisprudence award, 1982, Best Brief award ABA, 1984. Mem. D.C. Bar Assn., Pi Alpha Alpha, Phi Kappa Phi. Democrat. Avocations: sports, dancing, travel. Appellate, Federal civil litigation, Criminal. Home and Office: 1019 E Santa Clara St Ventura CA 93001-3034

BREAKELL, DAVID JAMES, lawyer; b. Cuckfield, Sussex, Eng., Apr. 10, 1950; s. Frederick Lawrence and Hilda Lucy B. BA in Jurisprudence with honors, Oxford U., Eng., 1971; MA in Jurisprudence, 1975. Bar: solicitor Eng., Wales. Tng. solicitor Richards Butler, London, 1975-77; solicitor, 1977-84, Richards Butler & Assocs., Abu Dhabi, United Arab Emirates, 1980-82; ptnr. Saunders Sobell, London, 1984-93, DLA, London, 1993—. Co. sec. Focsa UK, 1989—. Mem. Law Soc. Banking, Contracts commercial, Finance. Office: DLA 3 Noble St London EC2V 7EE England Fax: (0) 20 7796 6367. E-mail: david.breakell@dla.com

BREAKSTONE, DONALD S. lawyer; b. Chgo., Feb. 13, 1945; s. Eugene A. and Julie K. (Kanstein) B.; m. Barbara R. Raife, Aug. 24, 1968; children: Elizabeth, Michael. BA in History, U. Mich., 1966; JD, Havard U., 1969. Bar: Ill. 1973, Ohio 1969. Editor Internat. Bur. of Fiscal Documentation, Amsterdam, The Netherlands, 1971-73; assoc. Mayer, Brown & Platt, Chgo., 1973-77, ptnr., 1977-94; v.p., gen. counsel Atty.'s Liability Assurance Soc., Inc., 1994-97, sr. v.p., gen. counsel, 1997—. Chmn. Glencoe Village Bd. of Appeals, 1987-88. Contbr. articles to profl. jours. Mem. ABA, Chgo. Council of Lawyers. Insurance, Private international. Office: Attys Liability Assurance Soc Inc 311 S Wacker Dr Ste 5700 Chicago IL 60606-6629

BREAULT, THEODORE EDWARD, lawyer; b. N.Y.C., Mar. 7, 1938; m. Gretchen S. Clements, Dec. 10, 1966; children: Victoria Ann, Theodore Edmund, Heidi Sherwin, Edmund Clements. BS, Manhattan Coll., 1960; JD, Cath. U. Am., 1963. Bar: D.C. 1964, Va. 1964, Pa. 1970, U.S. Ct. Appeals (D.C. cir.) 1964, (4th cir.) 1969, U.S. Supreme Ct. 1967. Assoc. Seltzer & Suskind, Washington, 1964-69, Egler & Reinstadtler, Pitts., 1969-77; pvt. practice Fairfax, Va., 1967-69, Pitts., 1977—. Lectr. Cath. U. Am. Sch. Nursing, Robert Morris Coll.; mem. Pa. Workmen's Compensation Sect.; spl. master Allegheny County Ct. of Common Pleas; arbitrator U.S. Dist. Ct. Pres. Sewickley (Pa.) Symphony Orch., 1974-75. Fellow: Pa. Bar Found. (life), mem.. Pa. Bar Assn. (civil litigation sect.), Va. State Bar Assn., D.C. Bar Assn., Allegheny County Bar Assn. (health law sect., chmn. workmen's compensation sect.), Am. Soc. Law and Medicine, Pa. Def. Inst., Am. Arbitration Assn. (arbitrator accident and comml. claims), Am. Coll. Legal Medicine (assoc. in law). General civil litigation, Personal injury, Workers' compensation. Home: 108 Claridge Dr Moon Township PA 15108-3204 Office: Breault & Assocs PC 428 Forbes Ave 1509 Lawyers Bldg Pittsburgh PA 15219

BREAUX, PAUL JOSEPH, lawyer, pharmacist; b. Franklin, La., Mar. 11, 1942; s. Sidney J. and Irene (Bodin) B.; m. Marilyn Anne Jones, Aug. 21, 1965; children: Jason E., James P. BS in Pharmacy, Northeast La. U., 1965; JD, La. State U., 1972. Bar: La. 1972, U.S. Supreme Ct. 1975. Pharmacist Belanger's Pharmacy, Morgan City, La., 1965-66, Clinic Pharmacy, Morgan City, 1966-69; pvt. practice of law Lafayette, 1972-73, 93—; assoc. Allen, Gooch, Bourgeois, Breaux, Robison, Theunissen Attys., 1973-75; ptnr. Allen, Gooch, Bourgeois, Breaux, Robison & Theunissen, 1975-93. Sec., bd. dirs. Bank of Lafayette. Bd. dirs. Lafayette Community Health Care Clinic, Inc., 1992—, vice chmn., 1996—; bd. dirs. Hospice of Acadiana, Inc., 1996—, v.p., 1999—; bd. dirs. The Hospice Found., pres. 1998—; mem. Gov.'s Universal Health Care Law Reform Commn., 1992—; active Boy Scouts Am., 1984-92. Named Vol. of Yr., Lafayette Cmty. Health Care Clinic, Inc., 2000. Mem. ABA, La. Bar Assn., Lafayette Parish Bar Assn., La. Bankers Assn. (mem. bank counsel com. 1983-85, 88-90, La. banking code legislation revision com. 1983), Am. Land Title Assn., Am. Pharm. Assn., La. Pharmacists Assn. (bd. dirs. 1991-99, Pharmacist of Yr. award 1992), Am. Compliance Inst., Nat. Assn. Retail Druggists, Am. Soc. Law and Medicine, Am. Soc. Pharmacy Law, Am. Health Lawyers Assn., Acad. Hosp. Attys. of Am. Hosp. Assn., Soc. Hosp. Attys. of La. Hosp. Assn., Lafayette C. of C., Kappa Psi, Phi Eta Sigma. Republican. Roman Catholic. General corporate, Health, Real property. Office: 600 Jefferson St Ste 503 Lafayette LA 70501-6998

BRECHBILL, SUSAN REYNOLDS, lawyer, educator; b. Washington, Aug. 22, 1943; d. Irving and Isabell Doyle (Reynolds) Levine; children: Jennifer Rae, Heather Lea. BA, Coll. William and Mary, 1965; JD, Marshall-Wythe Sch. Law, 1968. Bar: Va. 1969, Fed. Bar, 1970. Atty. AEC, Berkeley, Calif., 1968-73, indsl. rels. specialist Las Vegas, 1974-75; atty.

ERDA, Oakland, Calif., 1976-77, Dept. Energy, Oakland, 1977-78, dir. procurement divsn. San Francisco Ops. Office, 1978-85, asst. chief counsel for gen. law, 1985-93, acting asst. mgr. environ. mgmt. and support, 1992, acting asst. mgr. def. programs, 1993; chief counsel Dept. Energy Richland Ops. Office, 1994-99; mgr. Ohio field office Dept. of Energy, 1999—. Mem. faculty U. Calif. Extension; speaker Nat. Contract Mgmt. Assn. Ann. Symposiums, 1980, 81, 83, 84, 88, Weapons Complex Monitor Decision Makers forum, 1999, 2000, Fed. Agy. Environ. Clean-up forum, 2001. Contbr. articles to profl. jours. Spkr. on doing bus. with govt. leader Girl Scouts U.S.A., San Francisco area; bd. dirs. Am. Heart Assn. Eastern Wash., 1997-99, Sexual Assault Response Ctr., Tri Cities, Wash., 1997-99; vol. tchr. Jr. Achievement, 1999. Named Outstanding Young Woman Nev., 1974; recipient Meritorious Svc. award Dept. Energy, 1992, 2000. Mem. NAFE, Va. State Bar Assn., Fed. Bar Assn., Nat. Contract Mgmt. Assn. (pres. Golden Gate chpt. 1983-84, N.W. regional v.p. 1984-86). Republican. E-mail: susan.brechbill@ohio.doe.gov

BRECHER, ARMIN GEORGE, lawyer; b. Prague, Czechoslovakia, July 7, 1942; s. Gerhard and Eleanor Brecher; m. Elizabeth Pardue Rountree, July 2, 1966; children: Lindsay Brecher Cobb, Stefan Ryan, Alden Kelsey. BA summa cum laude, Emory U., Atlanta, 1966; LLB, U. Va., 1969. Ptnr., chair exec. com. and bd. ptnrs. Powell, Goldstein, Frazer & Murphy, Atlanta, 1969—. Mem. The ESOP Assn. Presbyterian. Administrative and regulatory, General corporate, Pension, profit-sharing, and employee benefits. Office: Powell Goldstein Frazer & Murphy LLP 191 Peachtree St NE Fl 16 Atlanta GA 30303-1740

BRECHER, HOWARD ARTHUR, lawyer; b. N.Y.C., Oct. 18, 1953; s. Milton and Dorothy (Zahler) B. AB magna cum laude, Harvard U., 1975, MBA, JD cum laude, Harvard U., 1979; LLM, NYU, 1984. Bar: N.Y. 1980, U.S. Dist. Ct. (so. dist.) N.Y. 1983, U.S. Tax Ct. 1981. Assoc. Roberts & Holland, N.Y.C., 1979-82, Chadbourne, Parke, Whiteside & Wolff, N.Y.C., 1982-84; atty. legal dept. N.Y. Telephone Co., 1984-91, legal counsel, 1991-96; v.p. Value Line, Inc., 1996—. Mem. tax com. N.Y.C. C. of C., 1985-88, 94—. Mem. ABA (tax sect.), N.Y. State Bar Assn. (tax sect., com. taxation of affiliated corps., trusts and estates sect.), Assn. of Bar of City of N.Y., Harvard Bus. Sch. Club of Greater N.Y. Democrat. Jewish. Clubs: Harvard (N.Y.C. and Boston). General corporate, Intellectual property, Taxation, general. Office: 220 E 42nd St Ste 6000 New York NY 10017-5891

BRECKER, JEFFREY ROSS, lawyer, educator; b. N.Y.C., June 9, 1953; s. Milton S. and Charlotte (Alpert) B.; m. Phyllis L. Gordon, Oct. 30, 1983. BA in Polit. Sci., NYU, 1975; JD, New Eng. Sch. Law, Boston, 1978. Bar: N.Y. 1979, U.S. Dist. Ct. (so. and ea. dists.) N.Y. 1979, U.S. Supreme Ct. 1982. Atty. Nassau (N.Y.) County Legal Svcs. Commn., 1978-80, Dist. Coun. 37 Legal Svcs., N.Y.C., 1980-82, Wingate & Shamis, N.Y.C., 1982-85; sr. trial atty., unit supr. Jacobowitz & Lysaght, 1985-89; mng. atty. Damashak Godosky & Gentile, 1989-95, Godosky & Gentile, N.Y.C., 1995—. Adj. prof. New Coll., Hofstra U., 1981; chairperson tort litigation com. Assn. Bar City of NY. State civil litigation, Personal injury, Product liability. Office: Godosky & Gentile 61 Broadway 20th Fl New York NY 10006-2701 Business E-Mail: JeffreyB@Godosky&Gentile.com

BREDEHOFT, ELAINE CHARLSON, lawyer; b. Fergus Falls, Minn., Nov. 22, 1958; d. Curtis Lyle and Marilyn Anne (Nesbitt) Charlson; children: Alexandra Charlson, Michelle Charlson. BA, U. Ariz., 1981; JD, Cath. U. Am., 1984. Bar: Va. 1984, U.S. Ct. Appeals (4th cir.) 1984, U.S. Bankruptcy Ct. (ea. dist.) Va. 1987, D.C. 1994, U.S. Ct. Appeals (D.C. cir.) 1994. Assoc. Walton and Adams, McLean, Va., 1984-88, ptnr., 1988-91, Charlson Bredehoft, P.C., Reston, 1991—. Spkr. Fairfax Bar Assn., CLE, 1992—, VB Assn., CLE, 1993—, 12th Ann. Multistate Labor and Employment Law Seminar, 1994, Va. CLE Ann. Employment Law Update, 1993—, Va. Women's Trial Lawyers Assn. Ann. Conf., 1998, Va. Bar Assn. Labor and Employment Conf., 1994-97, 99, Va. Trial Lawyers Assn., 1995, 97, Va. Law Found., 1995—, Va. Assn. Def. Attys., 1996; mem. faculty Va. State Bar Professionalism Courses, 1997-2000; invitee 4th Circuit Judicial Conf., 1997-99, permanent mem., 1999—; invitee Boyd Graves Conf., 1999—; substitute judge 19th Judicial Dist., 1998—; chair Fairfax Bar Assn. Diversity Taskforce, 1998-99 (Pres. Vol. award 1998). Bd. dirs. Va. Commn. on Women and Minorities in the Legal System, 1987-90, sec., 1988-90. Mem. Va. Bar Assn. (mem. exec. com. young lawyers sect., mem. litigation com., mem. nominating com., chmn. model jud. com.), Va. Trial Lawyers Assn. (vice chmn. ann. conv. 1996-98, mem. com. on long-range planning 1996-97, spkr. 1995, 97), Minn. State Soc., Fairfax Bar Assn. co-chair subcom. on minorities, Pres.'s Vol. award 1998, 99), George Mason Inns of Ct. (master 1996—). Civil rights, General civil litigation, Personal injury. Office: Charlson Bredehoft PC 11260 Roger Bacon Dr Ste 201 Reston VA 20190-5252

BREDEHOFT, JOHN MICHAEL, lawyer; b. N.Y.C., Feb. 22, 1958; s. John William and Viola (Struhar) B.; m. Ivana Terango; children: Alexandra Charlson Bredehoft, Michelle Charlson Bredehoft. AB magna cum laude, Harvard Coll., 1980, JD cum laude, 1983. Bar: D.C. 1983, U.S. Dist. Ct. D.C. 1985, U.S. Ct. Appeals (D.C. cir.) 1985, U.S. Ct. Appeals (1st cir.) 1986, U.S. Supreme Ct. 1987, U.S. Ct. Appeals (9th cir.) 1988, U.S. Ct. Appeals (3d and 5th cir.) 1989, U.S. Tax Ct. 1989, U.S. Ct. Appeals (4th Cir.) 1990, U.S. Dist. Ct. Mont. 1991, Va. 1992, U.S. Dist. Ct. (ea. dist.) Va. 1992. Assoc. Cleary, Gottlieb, Steen & Hamilton, Washington, 1983-91; prin. Charlson & Bredehoft, Fairfax, Va., 1991-98; ptnr. Venable, Baetjer & Howard L.L.P., McLean, 1998—. Contbg. editor Employment Law in Virginia, 1997. Bd. dirs. Falls Brook Assn., Herndon, Va., 1988-91; nat. class 1983 reunion gift chmn. Harvard Law Sch. Fund, Cambridge, 1988, class agt., 1994—; mem. Harvard Debate Centennial Com., 1992. Named Lawyer of Yr., Met. Washington Employment Lawyers Assn., 1996, Va. Legal Elite, Va. Bus., 2000. Mem. ABA (sect. on litigation), Va. Bar Assn. (sect. on labor and employment law, governing coun. mem.), Va. Trial Lawyers Assn. (founding officer, employment law sect.), Fairfax Bar Assn. (sect. on employment law, vice chmn. 1997-98, chmn. 1998-99), Def. Rsch. and Trial Inst. (appellate advocacy com.), Va. Law Found./Va. CLE (employment law com.), Va. Women Attys. Assn. Civil rights, Federal civil litigation, Labor. Office: 2010 Corp Ridge Ste 400 Mc Lean VA 22102-5203

BREEN, DAVID HART, lawyer; b. Ottawa, Ont., Can., Mar. 27, 1960; came to U.S., Aug. 19, 1978; naturalized, 1993; s. Harold John and Margaret Rae (Hart) B.; m. Pamela Annette Mitchell, Sept. 17, 1988; 1 child, Matthew Mitchell. BA cum laude, U. S.C., 1982, JD, 1986. Bar: S.C., U.S. Dist. Ct. S.C., U.S. Ct. Appeals (4th cir.), U.S. Bankruptcy Ct. S.C. 1987. Law clk. to Hon. Don S. Rushing Cir. Ct. (6th cir.), S.C., 1986-87; English instr. humanities U.S.C., Conway, 1987-88; criminal law instr. Horry-Georgetown Tech. Coll., 1987-88; sr. ptnr. David H. Breen, P.A., Myrtle Beach, 1988—. C.J.A. panel atty. U.S. Dist. Ct. S.C., 1991-97; mem. family ct. adv. com. 15th Jud. Ct., 1998—. Campaign asst. Joe Clark for Prime Minister, Ottawa, 1975-76. Mem. ABA, ATLA, S.C. Trial Lawyers Assn., S.C. Bar Assn., Horry County Bar Assn., Am. Bankruptcy Inst., Oshawa Gun Club, Phi Delta Phi. Methodist. Avocations: swimming, computers. Bankruptcy, Family and matrimonial, Personal injury. Home: Prestwick Country Club 2187 N Berwick Dr Myrtle Beach SC 29575-5835 Office: 4603 Oleander Dr Ste 6 Myrtle Beach SC 29577-5738

BREEN, NEIL THOMAS, publishing executive; b. N.Y.C., Oct. 14, 1944; s. Neil G. and Eileen M. Breen; m. Catherine M. Breen, Dec. 2, 1978. BA, Marquette U., 1966; JD, Creighton U., 1970. Bar: Nebr. 1970, U.S. Dist. Ct. Nebr. 1970. Editor-in-chief Shepard's/McGraw Hill, Colorado Springs, Colo., 1979-86, v.p. devel., 1987-89; Thomson Legal Pub., Stamford, Conn.; pres. Callaghan & Co., Deerfield, Ill., 1989-90; v.p., gen. mgr. litigation and fed. products group, 1991-92; v.p. legal divsn. McGraw Hill Ryerson, Whitby, Ont., Can., 1993-95; pres. Law Bull. Pub. Co., Chgo., 1996—. Author: Texas Law Locator, 1973, Illinois Law Locator, 1975. Mem. ABA, Assn. of trial Laywers of Am., Ill. State Bar Assn., Chgo. Bar Assn., Can. Bar Assn. Avocations: skiing, snowshoeing, hiking. Office: Law Bulletin Pub Co 415 N State St Ste 200 Chicago IL 60610-4631

BREESKIN, MICHAEL WAYNE, lawyer; b. Washington, Dec. 25, 1947; s. Nathan and Sylvia (Raine) B.; m. Frances Cox Lively, May 29, 1982; children: Molly Louise, Laura Rose. BA cum laude, U. Pitts., 1969; JD, Georgetown U., 1975. Bar: D.C. 1975, Colo. 1983, U.S. Dist. Ct. D.C. 1977, U.S. Dist. Ct. Colo. 1983, U.S. Ct. Appeals (D.C. cir.) 1978, U.S. Ct. Appeals (10th cir.) 1984, U.S. Supreme Ct. 1995. Mng. atty. Tobin & Covey, Washington, 1977-79; assoc. Donald M. Murtha & Assocs., 1979-80; counsel NLRB Office Rep. Appeals, 1980-83; trial atty. NLRB Denver Regional Office, 1983-88; assoc. Wherry & Wherry, Denver, 1989-91; sr. atty. The Legal Ctr. for People with Disabilities and Older People (formerly The Legal Ctr. Serving Persons with Disabilities), 1991-98; gen. counsel Assn. Cmty. Living Boulder County, Inc. (formerly the Assn. for Retarded Citizens in Boulder County, Inc.), 1998-2000; counsel Fox & Robertson, PC, Denver, 2000—. Presenter, lectr. in field. Adv. com. Domestic Violence Initiative for Women with Disabilities, 1997—. Recipient Outstanding Work for People with Disabilities acknowledgement Very Spl. Arts Colo., 1996; named Profl. of Yr., The Arc of Adams County, 1997; recipient Adv. of the Year award Assn. Cmty. Living in Boulder County Inc., 1996, Schenkein award Arc of Denver, Inc., 1997, award Disability Ctr. Ind. Living and Colo. Cross-Disability Coalition, 1999, Colo. Cross Disability Coalition Meml. award for Civil Rights Legal Advocacy, 2000. Mem. ABA, Colo. Bar Assn. (disability law forum com.), Arapahoe County Bar Assn., Disability Rights Roundtable. Avocations: bicycling, skiing, reading. Civil rights, Education and schools, Labor. Office: 910 16th St Ste 610 Denver CO 80202-2921

BREGMAN, ARTHUR RANDOLPH, lawyer, educator; b. Phila., Dec. 9, 1946; s. Nathan and Stella (Husock) B.; m. Patrice Rosalie Gancie, May 30, 1980. BA, Columbia U., 1968; MA, Yale U., 1969; JD, Georgetown U., 1985. Bar: D.C. 1985, U.S. Ct. Appeals (D.C. cir.) 1985, U.S. Dist. Ct. D.C. 1985, U.S. Claims Ct. 1985. Treas. Nat. Coun. for Soviet and E. European Rsch., Washington, 1981-83; law clk. Washington Lawyers' Com. for Civil Rights, 1983-84; assoc. Klores, Feldesman and Tucker, Washington, 1985-86; dir. Soviet and E. European Svcs. APCO, 1988-91; of counsel Steptoe & Johnson, Washington, Moscow, USSR, 1991-92, ptnr. Washington D.C. and Moscow, 1992-99; mng. ptnr. Squire, Sanders & Dempsey, Washington, 1999—. Adj. prof. Georgetown U. Law Ctr., Washington, 1986-89; program dir. Internat. Law Inst., Washington, 1986-91; chmn. bd. adv. U.S.-Russia Bus. Law Report, 1990—. Editor: U.S.-Soviet Contract Law, 1987. Recipient Civil Procedure prize Lawyers Coop. Pub. Co., Balt., 1982. Mem. ABA (internat. bar sect.), D.C. Bar. Private international, Public international. Home: 3059 Porter St NW Washington DC 20008-3272 Office: 1201 Pennsylvania Ave NW Washington DC 20004-2401 E-mail: rbregman@ssd.com

BREHL, JAMES WILLIAM, lawyer; BS engring., U. Notre Dame, 1956; JD, U. Mich., 1959. Bar: Wis. 1989; Minn. and various fed. cts. Lawyer Maun & Simon, St. Paul, 1963-2000; law practice and mediation/arbitration Nuetral Svcs., 2000—. Contbr. articles to law jours. Chmn. Minn. builder's adv. coun. Minn. Dept. Commerce, 1991-95; mem. planning commn. City of Afton, 1975-93; dir. Granville House Inc., 1985-95. Recipient Good Neighbor award WCCO, 1968. Mem. Minn. Bar Assn. (exec. com. 1996-97), Ramsey County Bar Assn. (exec. coun. 1977-80, 87-90, pres. 1993-94), Washington County Bar Assn. Labor, Real property. Fax: 651-436-5679

BREMER, HOWARD WALTER, consulting patenting and licensing lawyer; b. Milw., July 18, 1923; s. Walter Hugo and Lydia Martha (Schmidt) B.; m. Caryl Marie Faust, May 28, 1948; children: Katharine, William (dec.), Thomas, Timothy, Margaret. BSChemE, U. Wis., 1944, LLB, 1949. Bar: Wis. 1949, U.S. Patent and Trademark Office 1954, U.S. Supreme Ct. 1957, U.S. Ct. Appeals (fed. cir.) 1959, U.S. Dist. Ct. (so. dist.) Ohio 1960. Patent atty. Procter & Gamble Co., Cin., 1949-60; patent counsel Wis. Alumni Rsch. Found., Madison, 1960-88; cons., 1988—. Mem. adv. com. Coun. on Govtl. Rels., Washington, 1975-93; panel mem. Office Tech. Assessment, Washington, 1981-83; mem. Adv. Commn. on Patent Law Reform, Washington, 1991-92. Mem. internat. adv. bd. Industry and Higher Edn. Jour., 1996—; contbr. articles to profl. jours. Pres. Edgewood Campus Sch. PTA, Madison, 1967-69; mem. adv. bd. Edgewood H.S., 1971-80, chmn. adv. bd., 1973-74. With USN, 1944-46. Recipient alumni appreciation award Edgewood H.S., 1990, Hon. Recognition award, U. Wis. Coll. Agrl. and Life Scis., 2000. Mem. ABA (chmn. com. 1993—), Am. Intellectual Property Law Assn. (chmn. com. 1996-99), State Bar Wis. (chmn. intellectual property sect. 1967-68, 79-80), Wis. Intellectual Property Law Assn. (pres. 1989-90), Assn. Univ. Tech. Mgrs. (trustee 1977-78, 80-82, pres. 1978-80, com. chmn. 1985-93, mem. editl. bd. jour. 1990—, Birch award 1980). Avocations: building furniture, home maintenance, model railroading, travel, reading. Intellectual property, Legislative, Patent. Home: 1106 Brookwood Rd Madison WI 53711-3116 E-mail: hwbrewer@facstaff.wisc.edu

BREMER, JOHN M. lawyer; b. 1947; BA, Fordham U., 1969; JD, Duke U., 1974. Bar: Wis. 1974. Atty. law dept. Northwestern Mutual Life Ins., Milw., 1974-78, asst. gen. counsel, 1978-90, v.p., gen. counsel and sec., 1990-94, sr. v.p., gen. counsel, sec., 1995-98, exec. v.p., gen. counsel, sec., 1998-2000, sr. exec. v.p., sec., 2000-01, sr. exec. v.p., COO, 2001—. General corporate, Insurance, Real property. Office: Northwestern Mutual Life Ins Co 720 E Wisconsin Ave Milwaukee WI 53202-4703

BREMER, WILLIAM RICHARD, lawyer; b. San Francisco, Jan. 5, 1930; m. Margaret Herrington; children: Mark Richard (dec.), Karen Elizabeth, William Richard Jr. BS in Bus. Adminstrn., Menlo Coll., 1952; JD, U. San Francisco, 1958. Bar: Calif. 1959, U.S. Dist. Ct. (no. dist.) Calif. 1959, U.S. Ct. Appeals (9th cir.) 1959, U.S. Supreme Ct. 1965, U.S. Ct. Mil. Appeals 1973. Pvt. practice San Francisco Bay area, 1959—. Officer, dir. Marshall Hale Meml. Hosp., 1986-88, Childrens Hosp. San Francisco, 1988-91; bd. dirs. Bridgeway Plan for Health, 1988-92. Bd. dirs. Bay Area USO, 1980-89; arbitrator Marin County and San Francisco County Ct., 1977—, Animal control hearing officer, 1998—; coun; city councilman City of Tiburon (Calif.), 1966-70, mayor, 1968-69; v.p., bd. dirs. Tiburon Peninsula Found.; regional v.p. No. Calif. Naval War Coll. Found., 1997-2000. Lt. USMC, 1952-54, Korea; col. USMC Res. (ret.), 1954-82. Mem. Am. Arbitration Assn. (panel arbitrator 1965—), ATLA, San Francisco Trial Lawyers Assn., San Francisco Bar Assn., San Francisco Lawyers Club, Marin County Bar Assn., Calif. Trial Lawyers Assn., Navy League U.S. (life mem. San Francisco Coun., pres. 1978-80, nat. bd. dirs. 1978-88, no. Calif. state pres. 1981-82, nat. dep. JAG 1997-2001, nat. dir. emeritus 2000), Marine Corps Res. Officers Assn. (life), Res. Officers Assn. (life), Naval Order of U.S. (life, San Francisco commandery, comdr. 1982, 83, comdr. gen., nat. pres. 1993-95), Corinthian Yacht (commodore 1986-87), Montgomery St. Motorcycle (pres. 1974-75), Marines Meml. San Francisco (pres. 1985-86), Kiwanis (bd. dirs. San Francisco chpt. 1981-83), Tiburon-Belvedere Rotary (bd. dirs. 1997—, chair cmty. svc., pres. 2001—). General civil litigation, Criminal, Personal injury. Office: 120 Taylor Rd Belvedere Tiburon CA 94920-1061 E-mail: BillBrem@aol.com

BRENMAN, STEPHEN MORRIS, lawyer; b. San Francisco, Mar. 25, 1945; s. Irving I. and Vivian H. (Weiss) B.; m. Laura R. Yocum, Aug. 14, 1968; children: Jeremy S., Sara N. BS, Miami U., Oxford, Ohio, 1967; JD with distinction, Valparaiso (Ind.) U., 1970. Bar: Ind. 1970, U.S. Dist. Ct. (no. and so. dist.) Ind. 1970, U.S. Ct. Appeals (7th cir.) 1970, U.S. Supreme Ct. 1973, U.S. Tax Ct. 1973, U.S. Ct. Claims 1973. Assoc. Saul I. Ruman & Assocs., Hammond, Ind., 1970-73; ptnr. Katz & Brenman, Gary and Merrillville, 1973-78, mng. ptnr. Merrillville, 1978-99; pvt. practice, 2000—. Lectr. Valparaiso U. Sch. Law, 1970; chief pub. defender Gary City Ct., 1973-78, staff coord., 1973-78; dir. and officer Dunes Volkswagen, Inc., Gary, 1977-80, Len Pollak Buick, Inc., Gary, 1977-83, Merrillville Volkswagen, Porshe-Audi, Inc., Merrillville, 1980-83; lectr. alcoholic beverage laws in Ind., miscellaneous trade orgns., 1980—; temp. probate commr., pro-tem and temp. judge Superior Ct. Lake County, Civil Divsn., East Chicago, Ind., 1980—; lectr. estate planning and right to die Congregation Beth Israel, Inc., Hammond, 1989—, Jewish Fedn., Inc., Highland, Ind., 1989—. Note editor Valparaiso U. Law Rev., 1969-70; contbr. articles to profl. jours. Co-chmn. Ind. Alcoholic Beverage Commn. Study Com., Rules, Regulations and Forms Rev., 1990, 2000—; election judge and commr. Lake County Election Bd., Crown Point, Ind., 1973-78; dir. Munster (Ind.) Little League, 1980-84, umpire and coach, 1980-84; bd. dirs. Munster Youth Athletic Assn., 1980-84; bd. dirs. Jewish Fedn., Inc., Highland, 1980-85, Congregation Beth Israel, Inc., Hammond, 1980-85; dir. Hoosier Boys Town, Inc., Schererville, Ind., 1990-94, dir. and officer Hoosier Boys Town Found., 1990-94; mem. Munster H.S. Booster Club, 1987—; mem., dir., officer Alpha Epsilon Pi Parents Club, Inc., Bloomington, Ind., 1990-94./ Recipient Disting. Svc. award Jewish Fedn., 1980, 83, 84, Red and White Club, Munster H.S. Booster Club, 1989, Mustang Club, 1989; Valparaiso U. scholar, 1968-70. Mem. ABA (sect. bus. law, adminstrv. law and regulatory practice, real property, probate, trust law sects.), Nat. Assn. Estate Planners and Couns., Nat. Assn. Criminal Def. Attys., Ind. State Bar Assn., Fed. Bar Assn., Assn. Trial Lawyers Am., Ind. Trial Lawyers Assn., Lake County Bar Assn. (chmn. legal forms com.), Am. Judicature Soc. (corp. counsel inst. mem.), Phi Alpha Delta, B'nai B'rith, Miami U. Alumni Assn., Valparaiso U. Sch. Law Alumni Assn., Zeta Beta Tau. Democrat. Avocations: racquetball, tennis, boating, motor vehicle racing. Administrative and regulatory, Contracts commercial, Probate. Office: 107 West 79th Ave Merrillville IN 46410-5438

BRENNAN, DANIEL EDWARD, JR. state judge; b. Houston, Oct. 2, 1942; s. Daniel E. and Emily (Tabor) B.; m. Ruth Miriam Gonchar, Nov. 16, 1973; children: Danna Julie, Benjamin Tabor. AA, U. State N.Y., 1974, BS, 1976; JD, U. Bridgeport, 1981; IEM, Harvard U., 1974. Bar: Conn. 1981, U.S. Dist. Ct. Conn. 1981, U.S. Supreme Ct. Exec. asst. to pres. Hunter Coll., N.Y.C., 1970-77; pres. S&B Mgmt. Systems, 1977-80; ptnr. Brennan, McNamara & Baldwin, P.C., Bridgeport, Conn., 1981-96, The Brennan Law Firm, Trumbull, 1996-99; judge Superior Ct. Conn., 1999—. Trial referee Superior Ct., State of Conn.; chief legal advisor Bridgeport Police Dept., 1983-85; chief labor counsel City of Bridgeport, 1981-85, Town of Trumbull, 1982-87. Mem. Conn. Bar Assn. (former chair litigation sect.). State civil litigation, General practice, Labor. Home: 57 Gray Rock Rd Trumbull CT 06611-3307 Fax: 203-268-8498. E-mail: BDJudgeCT@aol.com, Daniel.Brennan@Jud.State.CT.us

BRENNAN, JAMES PATRICK, SR. lawyer; b. N.Y.C., June 20, 1947; s. Michael Joseph and Mary Patricia (Regan) B.; m. Ellen Margaret Hall, Nov. 6, 1970; children: James Patrick II, Liam Daniel. BS, Pratt Inst., 1969; JD, St. Mary's U., San Antonio, 1975. Bar: Tex. 1975. Atty. IRS, San Antonio, 1975-80, atty, life insurance securities and tax counsel USAA, San Antonio, 1980—, gen. counsel; instr. Am. Soc. CLU's., San Antonio, 1983-84. Assoc. editor law Jour. St. Mary's U., 1974. Mem. ABA, Tex. Bar Assn., Estate Planning Coun. San Antonio, Am. Soc. CLU's., Am. Soc. Charted Fin. Cons., Nat. Assn. Health Underwriters. Republican. Roman Catholic. Insurance, Securities, Taxation, general. Office: USAA VP Life Ins C-3-W 7800 Fredericksburg Rd San Antonio TX 78229-3418

BRENNAN, JOHN JOSEPH, lawyer, legal administrator; b. Troy, N.Y., Nov. 1, 1958; s. James Patrick and Grace Marie (Bartolomeo) B. AAS, Schenectady (N.Y) Community Coll., 1978; BA cum laude, Siena Coll., 1981; JD cum laude, Union U., 1985. Bar: N.Y. 1986, U.S. Dist. Ct. (no. dist.) N.Y. 1986, U.S. Supreme Ct. 1999. Law clk. to Appellate Divsn. Justice 4th Dept., Herkimer, N.Y., 1985-86; assoc. law ck. to justice State Supreme Ct., 1986-90; law clk. to U.S. Magistrate-Judge, Utica, N.Y., 1991-92; assoc. law clk. to justice N.Y. Supreme Ct., 1992—. Bd. dirs. Utica Symphony, Utica Zoo. Mem. ABA, N.Y. State Bar Assn., Oneida County Bar Assn., Herkimer County Bar Assn. (treas. 1990), KC, Pi Gamma Mu. Roman Catholic. Avocations: running, skiing. General practice. Home: 119 Court St Herkimer NY 13350-1923 Office: Oneida County Ct House Utica NY 13501

BRENNAN, WILLIAM COLLINS, JR. lawyer; b. Northampton, Mass., Nov. 23, 1951; s. William Collins and Doreen Angela (Murphy) B.; m. Ann Marie Simonetta, Aug. 18, 1973; 1 son, James P. B.A. magna cum laude, Boston Coll., 1973; J.D., Cath. U. Am., 1976. Bar: Md. 1976, D.C. 1977, U.S. Supreme Ct. 1980; cert. specialist in criminal trial advocacy Nat. Bd. Trial Advocacy. Assoc. DePaul, Willoner & Kenkel, P.A., College Park, Md., 1976-80; ptnr. Knight, Manzi, Brennan, Ostrom & Ham, P.A., Upper Marlboro, Md., 1980—; counselor Am. Inn of Ct. LXII, Prince George's County. Mem. Addictions Adv. Council Prince George's County, 1984. Mem. ABA, Assn. Trial Lawyers Am., Nat. Assn. Criminal Def. Lawyers, Md. State Bar Assn., Md. Trial Lawyers Assn., Md. Criminal Def. Attys. (bd. dirs. 1987—), Prince George's County Bar Assn., Phi Beta Kappa. Democrat. Roman Catholic. Lodge: KC. State civil litigation, Criminal, Personal injury. Home: 8221 Canning Ter Greenbelt MD 20770-2705 Office: Knight Manzi Brennan Ostrom & Ham PA 14440 Old Mill Rd Upper Marlboro MD 20772-3088

BRENNAN, WILLIAM JOSEPH, III, lawyer; b. Newark, Apr. 29, 1933; s. William J. Jr. and Marjory (Leonard) B.; m. Georgianna V. Franklin, Sept. 10, 1960; children: William J. IV, Alexandra V. BA, Colgate U., 1955; LLB, Yale U., 1962. Bar: N.Y. 1963, N.J. 1967, U.S. Dist. Ct. (so. and ea. dists.) N.Y. 1964, U.S. Dist. Ct. N.J. 1967, U.S. Ct. Appeals (1st cir.) 1987, U.S. Ct. Appeals (2nd cir.) 1968, U.S. Ct. Appeals (3rd cir.) 1968, U.S. Ct. Appeals (Fed. cir.) 1991, U.S. Supreme Ct. 1967. Assoc. Breed, Abbott & Morgan, N.Y.C., 1962-67; asst. atty. gen in charge of litigation Office of Atty. Gen. of N.J., Trenton, 1967-68; spl. counsel to gov. Office of the Gov. of the State of N.J., 1969; ptnr., mng. ptnr. Smith, Stratton, Wise, Heher & Brennan, Princeton, N.J., 1970—. Assoc. editor N.J. Law Jour., 1979—. Trustee St. Peter's Coll., Jersey City, 1988-94. Served to 1st lt. USMC, 1956-59. Recipient Award of Distinction, N.J. State Grand Jurors' Assn., 1969, Alumni Achievement award Newark Acad., 1986, Trial Bar award Trial Attys. N.J., 1994. Fellow Am. Coll. Trial Lawyers (chmn. com. on legal ethics 1987-93, chmn. com. on professionalism 1993-97), Internat. Acad. Trial Lawyers, Am. Acad. Appellate Lawyers, Am. Bar Found. (lie, state chmn. 1990); mem. ABA (mem. com. on legal ethics 1989, 3d cir. mem., com. on fed. judiciary 1989-93, ho. of dels. 1986-95), N.J. State Bar Assn. (pres. 1984-85), Assn. of Fed. Bar of State of N.J. (pres. 1992-94), Assn. of Bar of City of N.Y., Yale Law Sch. Assn. N.J., Am. Law Inst. Avocations: scuba diving, flying. Aviation, General civil litigation, Insurance. Office: Smith Stratton Wise Heher & Brennan 600 College Rd E Princeton NJ 08540-6636 E-mail: wjb@sswhb.com

BRENNECKE, ALLEN EUGENE, lawyer; b. Marshalltown, Iowa, Jan. 8, 1937; s. Arthur Lynn and Julia Alice (Allen) B; m. Billie Jean Johnstone, June 12, 1958; children: Scott, Stephen, Beth, Gregory, Kristen BBA, U. Iowa, 1959, JD, 1961. Bar: Iowa 1961. Law clk. U.S. Dist. Judge, Des Moines, 1961-62; assoc. Mote, Wilson & Welp, Marshalltown, Iowa, 1962-66; ptnr. Harrison, Brennecke, Moore, Smaha & McKibben, 1966—. Contr. articles to profl. jours. Bd. dirs. Marshalltown YMCA, 1966-71; mem. bd. trustees Iowa Law Sch. Found., 1973-86, United Meth. Ch., Marshalltown, 1978-81, 87-89; fin. chmn. Rep. party 4th Congl. Dist., Iowa, 1970-73, Marshall County Rep. Party, Iowa, 1967-70. Fellow ABA (chmn. ho. of dels. 1984-86, bd. govs. 1982-86), Nat. Jud. Coll. (bd. dirs. 1982-88), Am. Coll. Trusts and Estates Counsel, Am. Coll. Tax Counsel, Am. Bar Found., Iowa Bar Assn. (pres. 1990-91, award of merit 1987); mem. Masons, Shriners, Promise Keepers. Republican. Methodist. Avocations: golf; travel; sports. Home: 703 Circle Dr Marshalltown IA 50158-3809 Office: Harrison Brennecke Moore Smaha & McKibben 302 Masonic Temple Marshalltown IA 50158

BRENNEMAN, HUGH WARREN, JR. judge; b. Lansing, Mich., July 4, 1945; s. Hugh Warren and Irma June (Redman) Brenneman; m. Catherine Sheperd; 2 children. BA, Alma Coll., 1967; JD, U. Mich., 1970. Bar: Mich. 1970, D.C. 1975, U.S. Dist. Ct. (we. dist.) Mich. 1974, U.S. Dist. Ct. Md. 1973, U.S. Ct. Mil. Appeals 1971, U.S. Ct. Appeals (6th cir.) 1976, U.S. Ct. Appeals (D.C. cir.) 1981, U.S. Supreme Ct. 1980. Law clk. Mich. 30th Jud. Cir., Lansing, 1970-71; asst. U.S. atty. Dept. Justice, Grand Rapids, Mich., 1974-77; assoc. Bergstrom, Slykhouse & Shaw, P.C., 1977-80; U.S. magistrate judge U.S. Dist. Ct. (we. dist.) Mich., 1980—. Instr. Western Mich. U., Grand Valley State U., 1989-92. Mem. exec. bd. and adv. coun. Gerald R Ford coun. Boy Scouts Am., 1984—, v.p., 1988-92; mem. Grand Rapids Hist. Commn., 1991-97, pres., 1995-97; dir. Cmty. Reconciliation Ctr., 1991. Capt. JAGC, U.S. Army, 1971-74. Recipient Distng. Alumnus award Alma Coll., 1998. Fellow Mich. State Bar Found.; mem. FBA (pres. Western Mich. chpt. 1979-80, nat. del. 1980-84), State Bar Mich. (rep. assembly 1984-90), D.C. Bar Assn., Grand Rapids Bar Assn. (chmn. U.S. Constn. Bicentennial com., co-chmn. Law Day 1991), Fed. Magistrate Judges Assn., Am. Inns of Ct. (master of bench Grand Rapids chpt., pres.), Phi Delta Phi, Omicron Delta Kappa, Peninsular Club, Rotary (past pres., Charities Found. of Grand Rapids v.p., Paul Harris fellow), Econ. Club of Grand Rapids (past bd. dirs.). Congregationalist. Office: US Dist Ct West Mich 110 Michigan St NW Rm 580 Grand Rapids MI 49503-2313

BRENNER, EDGAR H. law administrator; b. N.Y.C., Jan. 4, 1930; s. Louis and Bertha B. (Guttman) B.; m. Janet Maybin, Aug. 4, 1979; children from previous marriage— Charles S., David M., Paul R. B.A., Carleton Coll., 1951; J.D., Yale U., 1954. Bar: D.C. 1954, U.S. Ct. Claims 1957, U.S. Supreme Ct. 1957. Mem. 2d Hoover Commn. Legal Task Force Staff, Washington, 1954; trial atty. U.S. Dept. Justice, 1954-57; assoc. Arnold & Porter, 1957-62, ptnr., 1962-89. Co-dir. Inter Univ. Ctr. for Legal Studies, 1999—. Contbr. articles to profl. jours. Commr. Fairfax County Econ. Devel. Corp., Va., 1963—78; v.p., bd. dirs. Stella and Charles Guttman Found., N.Y.C.; pres., bd. dirs. Ams. for Med. Progress, Arlington, Va. Fellow Coll. Problems of Drug Dependency. Mem.D.C. Bar Assn., Yale Club, Explorers Club (N.Y.C.). Democrat. Home: 340 Persimmon Ln Washington VA 22747-1845 Office: 4620 Lee Hwy Ste 216 Arlington VA 22207-3400 E-mail: edgarhbrenner@email.com

BRENNER, JANET MAYBIN WALKER, lawyer; b. Arkansas City, Kans. d. D. Arthur and Maybin (Gardner) Walker; children: Margaret Maybin Jonas, Theodore Kimball Jonas, Amanda Nash Freeman; m. Edgar H. Brenner, Aug. 4, 1979. AB, U. So. Calif.; JD, George Washington U., 1978. Bar: D.C. 1978, U.S. Dist. Ct. (D.C). Sponsor Brenner Women's Leadership com.; mem. women's com. Corcoran Gallery Art, Washington, 1969—, Pres.'s Cir., Planned Parenthood D.C., 1969—, Found. for Preservation of Hist. Georgetown. Mem. D.C. Bar Assn., Sulgrave Club (Washington). Real property. Home: 3325 R St NW Washington DC 20007-2310 also: Shadow Ridge Farm Washington VA 22747

BRESNAHAN, ARTHUR STEPHEN, lawyer; b. Chgo., Dec. 26, 1944; s. Arthur Patrick and Margaret Genevieve (Gleason) B.; m. Patricia Margaret Wetz, June 29, 1968; children: Arthur Patrick, Maureen Justina, Brian Michael, Brendan Robert, Sean Matthew. BA in Psychology, Loras Coll., 1967; JD, Ill. Inst. Tech., 1975. Bar: Ill. 1975, U.S. Dist. Ct. (no. dist.) Ill. 1975, U.S. Ct. Appeals (7th cir.) 1978, U.S. Supreme Ct. 1986, U.S Ct. Claims 1986. Assoc. Garbutt, Jacobson & Lee, Chgo., 1975-77; sr. assoc. atty. Purcell & Wardrope, 1977-83; ptnr. Bresnahan & Garvey, 1983-88, 1988-98; pvt. practice Arthur S. Bresnahan & Assocs., 1998—. Speaker in field. Asst. scoutmaster Boy Scouts Am., Chgo., 1980—, Webelos Den leader. Capt. USMC, 1967-72. Mem. ABA, VFW, Fed. Bar Assn., Ill. Bar Assn., Fed. Trial Bar, Chgo. Bar Assn., Trial Lawyers Club, Vietnam Vets. Am., Lawyer Pilots Bar Assn., Am. Legion. Democrat. Roman Catholic. Lodges: KC, Moose. Avocations: golf, Girl/Boy Scouts. Federal civil litigation, State civil litigation, Insurance. Home and Office: 4715 N Kenneth Ave Chicago IL 60630-4004

BRESSAN, PAUL LOUIS, lawyer; b. Rockville Centre, N.Y., June 15, 1947; s. Louis Charles Bressan and Nance Elizabeth Batteley. BA cum laude, Fordham Coll., 1969; JD, Columbia U., 1975. Bar: N.Y. 1976, Calif. 1987, U.S. Dist. Ct. (so., ea. and no. dists.) N.Y. 1976, U.S. Dist. Ct. (no. and ctrl. dists.) Calif. 1987, U.S. Ct. Appeals (2d cir.) 1980, U.S. Supreme Ct. 1980, U.S. Ct. Appeals (1st and 4th cirs.) 1981, U.S. Ct. Appeals (11th cir.) 1982, U.S. Ct. Appeals (9th cir.) 1987, U.S Ct. Appeals (7th cir.) 1991, U.S. Dist. Ct. (ea. dist.) Calif. 1995; U.S. Dist. Ct. (so. dist.) Calif. 1997. Assoc. Kelley, Drye & Warren, N.Y.C., 1975-84, ptnr. N.Y.C. and Los Angeles, 1984—. Served to lt. USNR, 1971-72. Named One of Outstanding Coll. Athletes of Am., 1969; Harlan Fiske Stone scholar Columbia Law Sch. Mem. ABA, Calif. Bar Assn., Phi Beta Kappa. Republican. Roman Catholic. Federal civil litigation, State civil litigation, Labor. Office: Kelley Drye & Warren LLP 777 S Figueroa St Ste 2700 Los Angeles CA 90017-5825 E-mail: pbressan@kelleydrye.com

BRESSLER, BARRY E. lawyer; b. Phila., Apr. 7, 1947; s. Joseph and Shirley M. (Eiseman) B.; m. Risé Sharon Cohen, June 14, 1970 (dec.); children: Allison Ivy, Michelle Amy. AB, Franklin and Marshall Coll., Lancaster, Pa., 1968; JD, U. Pa., 1971. Bar: Pa. 1971, U.S. Dist. Ct. (ea. dist.) Pa. 1973, U.S. Ct. Appeals (3d cir.) 1977, U.S. Supreme Ct. 1988, U.S. Dist. Ct. (mid. dist.) Pa. 1990. Law clk. to judge Superior Ct. Pa., Phila., 1971-73; assoc. Meltzer & Schiffrin, 1973-79, ptnr., 1979-86, Fox, Rothschild, O'Brien & Frankel, Phila., 1987-88; mem., sr. lawyer real estate litigation & creditors' rights Pelino & Lentz, P.C., 1988-2000; ptnr. Schnader, Harrison, Segal & Lewis, LLP, 2000—. Adj. instr. landlord-tenant law Delaware County C.C., Media, Pa., 1985—, Montgomery County C.C., Blue Bell, Pa., 1987—. V.p. English Ceramic Study Group, Phila.; v.p., sec. Temple Sinai, Dresher, Pa., 1991-97; grad. Leadership, Inc., Phila. Mem. ABA (litigation sect.), Pa. Bar Assn. (corp. banking and bus. sect.), Phila. Bar Assn. (real property sect.), Bankruptcy Conf. Ea. Dist. Pa. (treas. 1995-2000), Am. Arbitration Assn. Republican. Jewish. Avocations: tennis, ceramics, bridge. Bankruptcy, General civil litigation, Landlord-tenant. Office: Schnader Harrison Segal and Lewis LLP 1600 Market St Ste 3600 Philadelphia PA 19103-7286 E-mail: bbressler@schnader.com

BREST, PAUL A. law educator; b. Jacksonville, Fla., Aug. 9, 1940; s. Alexander and Mia (Deutsch) B.; m. Iris Lang, June 17, 1962; children: Hilary, Jeremy. AB, Swarthmore Coll., 1962; JD, Harvard U., 1965; LLD (hon.), Northeastern U., 1980, Swarthmore Coll., 1991. Bar: N.Y. 1966. Law clk. to Hon. Bailey Aldrich U.S. Ct. Appeals (1st cir.), Boston, 1965-66; atty. NAACP Legal Def. Fund, Jackson, Miss., 1966-68; law clk. Justice John Harlan, U.S. Supreme Ct., 1968-69; prof. law Stanford U., 1969—, Kenneth and Harle Montgomery Prof. pub. interest law, Richard E. Lang prof. and dean, 1987-99; pres. William and Flora Hewlett Found., Menlo Park, Calif., 1999—. Author: Processes of Constitutional Decision-making, 1992. Mem. Am. Acad. Arts and Scis. Home: 814 Tolman Dr Palo Alto CA 94305-1026 Office: William and Flora Hewlett Found 525 Middlefield Rd Menlo Park CA 94025-3460 E-mail: pbrest@hewlett.org

BRETT, ANTHONY HARVEY, lawyer; b. Ahoskie, N.C., Oct. 11, 1953; BA, Yale U., 1975; JD, Duke U., 1979. Bar: N.C. 1979, U.S. Supreme Ct. 1983. Ptnr. Womble, Carlyle, Sandridge & Rice, PLLC, Winston-Salem, N.C., 1979—. Mem. N.C. Bar Assn., N.C. Soc. Health Care Attys. Health. Office: Woble Carlyle Sandridge & Rice PLLC PO Box 84 Winston Salem NC 27102-0084 E-mail: abrett@wcsr.com

BRETT, JAY ELLIOT, lawyer; b. Somerville, N.J., June 4, 1931; s. Mac and Blanche (Kamerman) Brett; m. Marcia Barmon, July 17, 1955; children: Peter Barmon, Julie Picard, Amy Kamerman. BS, Cornell U., 1953; LLB, Harvard U., 1958. Bar: NY 1958, US Dist Ct (we dist) NY 1959, US Ct Int Trade 1965. Ptnr. Cohen & Roach LLP, Niagara Falls, NY, 1958—. Vice-chmn, mem exec comt Amherst Rep Comt, NY, 1970—83; del Rep Nat Conv, Kansas City, Mo., 1976. Maj U.S. Army, 1953—55, Korea, maj U.S. Army, 1961—62, Korea. Mem.: Assn Trial Lawyers Am, NY State Bar Asn, Erie County Bar Asn, Bar Asn City Niagara Falls (pres 1979), Niagara Club (bd dirs). Banking, Probate, Real property. Home: 212 Woodbury Dr Amherst NY 14226-2531 Office: Blair & Roach LLP PO Box 846 256 3rd St Niagara Falls NY 14303-0846 E-mail: jmbrett@msn.com, jebtalk@aol.com

BRETT, THOMAS RUTHERFORD, federal judge; b. Oklahoma City, Oct. 2, 1931; s. John A. and Norma (Dougherty) B.; m. Mary Jean James, Aug. 26, 1952; children: Laura Elizabeth Brett Tribble, James Ford, Susan Marie Brett Crump, Maricarolyn Swab. B.B.A., U. Okla., 1953, LL.B., 1957, J.D., 1971. Bar: Okla. 1957. Asst. county atty., Tulsa, 1957; mem. firm Hudson, Hudson, Wheaton, Kyle & Brett, 1958-69, Jones, Givens, Brett, Gotcher, Doyle & Bogan, 1969-79; judge U.S. Dist. Ct. (no. dist.) Okla., Tulsa, 1979—. Bd. regents U. Okla., 1971-78; mem. adv. bd. Salvation Army; trustee Okla. Bar Found. Col. JAG, USAR, 1953-83. Inductee Heritage Assn. Hall of Fame, 2000. Fellow Am. Coll. Trial Lawyers, Am. Bar Found.; mem. Okla. Bar Assn. (pres. 1970), Tulsa County Bar Assn. (pres. 1965), Am. Judicature Soc., U. Okla. Coll. Law Alumni Assn. (bd. dirs.), Order of Coif (hon.), Phi Alpha Delta. Democrat. Office: US Dist Ct US Courthouse 224 S Boulder Ave Rm 210 Tulsa OK 74103-3026

BRETTSCHNEIDER, RITA ROBERTA FISCHMAN, lawyer; b. Bklyn., Nov. 12, 1931; d. Isidore M. and Augusta T. (Singer) Fischman; m. Bertram D. Brettschneider, June 25, 1950 (dec. Nov. 17, 1986); children: Jane Brettschneider, Joseph Brettschneider; m. Bertram D. Cohn, June 30, 1991. BA, CUNY, 1953; JD, Bklyn. Law Sch., 1956; postgrad., NYU, 1968-69, Nat. Inst. Trial Advocacy, 1976. Bar: N.Y. 1961, U.S. Dist. Ct. N.Y. 1971. Pvt. practice, Huntington, N.Y., 1961—. Instr. women and the law C.W. Post Coll., Brookville, N.Y., 1969-70; arbitrator med. malpractice arbitration com. Suffolk County (N.Y.), 1974-76; spl. assoc. prof. philosophy and law New Coll. Hofstra U., Hempstead, N.Y., 1974-76; faculty N.Y. Law Jour. Conf. Changing Concepts in Matrimonial Law, 1976; legal advisor Am. Arbitration Assn., 1977-84; arbitrator night small claims ct. Nassau County, 1978-83; of counsel Nassau County Psychol. Assn., 1987—, Suffolk County Psychol. Assn., 1990-95. Contbr. numerous articles to profl. jours. Pres., bd. dirs. For Our Children and Us, 1992—. Mem. Nassau-Suffolk Women's Bar Assn. (chair judiciary com. 1974-80), Nassau County Bar Assn. (demonstrating atty. mock trial contested matrimonial action 1975), Suffolk County Bar Assn. (demonstrating atty. mock trial contested matrimonial action 1976), Am. Arbitration Assn. (legal advisor 1977-84), Nassau-Suffolk Women's Bar Assn. (pres. 1980-81). Family and matrimonial. Home: 2 Crosby Pl Cold Spring Harbor NY 11724-2403 Office: Brettschneider & Brettschneider 83 Prospect St Huntington NY 11743-3306 E-mail: vember@aol.com

BREWER, CHARLES BLAKE, SR. lawyer, corporation executive; b. Dallas, Dec. 24, 1948; s. Charles Albert and Maurine (Blake) B.; m. Patricia Carole Lee, Feb. 10, 1973; children: Christine Allyson, Kelley Amanda. B.A., So. Methodist U., 1971, J.D., 1974. Bar: Tex. 1974, U.S. Ct. Mil. Appeals 1975, U.S. Supreme Ct. 1980. Assoc. counsel Bonanza Internat., Inc., Dallas, 1979-81, v.p., gen. counsel, 1981-83; sr. v.p., gen. counsel, sec. USACafes, L.P., Dallas, 1983-88; exec. v.p., CEO, gen. counsel, sec. Southmark Corp, Dallas, 1989—. Served as capt. USMC, 1974-79. Mem. ABA, State Bar Tex., Dallas Bar Assn. General corporate, Securities. Office: Southmark Corp Ste 204 2711 Lyndon B Johnson Fwy ste 900 Dallas TX 75234-7325

BREWER, DANA, lawyer, educator; b. Concordia, Kans., Jan. 25, 1952; s. Dean Decker and Irma Elaine (Ames) B. BS cum laude, Kans. State U., 1974; JD, Washburn U., 1976. Bar: Kans. 1977, U.S. Dist. Ct. Kans. 1977. Assoc. Baldwin, Paulsen & Buechel, Chartered, Concordia, 1977-82; ptnr. Paulsen, Buechel, Swenson, Uri & Brewer, Chartered, Concordia, 1982—; educator Cloud County Community Coll., Concordia, 1979—. Chmn. United Lutheran Ministries, N. Central Kans., 1981-83; commr. Indsl. Devel. Adv. Commn., Concordia, 1982—; bd. dirs. Pan-Am. Hwy. Assn., 1984—, St. Joseph Hosp., Concordia, 1988—; bd. dirs. Brown Grand Theatre, Concordia, 1988—. Mem. Cloud County Bar Assn. (sec. 1977-79), Kans. Bar Assn. (com. on legal issues affecting elderly 1985—), ABA, Kans. Sch. Attys. Assn. (bd. dirs. 1984-88), Concordia C. of C. (bd. dirs. 1984—, chmn. 1986-88), Jaycees (community devel. v.p. 1983-84), Moose, Lions. Republican. Lutheran. Estate planning, Probate, Real property. Home: RR 2 Concordia KS 66901-9802 Office: Paulsen Buechel Swenson Uri & Brewer 613 Washington St # 327 Concordia KS 66901-2821

BREWER, DAVID MADISON, lawyer; b. Bordeaux, Gironde, France, July 8, 1953; s. Herbert L. and Paulyne B. (Ver Benec) B.; m. Andrea M. Bordiga, May 20, 1978; children: James David Madison, Caroline Elizabeth, Geoffrey Andrew. AB summa cum laude, Yale U., 1975, JD, 1978. Bar: N.Y. 1979. Assoc. atty. Cravath Swaine & Moore, N.Y.C., 1978-84; assoc. gen. tax counsel Union Pacific Corp., N.Y.C. and Bethlehem, Pa., 1984-89; pres. Madison Co., Inc., N.Y.C., 1990—; pres., CEO Madison Oil Co., 1993-2000, vice chmn., 2000—. Vice chmn. Madison Oil Co., 2000—; pres. Madison Oil Co., 1993-2000. Editor Yale Law Jour., 1977-78. Vice-chmn. Bush/Quayle '92 Fin. Com.; policy asst. Office of the Campaign Mgr., Bush-Quayle campaign, 1988; bd. dirs. Yale U. Law Sch. fund, 1989-93, Yale Alumni Fund, 1989-95; spl. gifts chmn. Yale U. Class of 1975 and Law Sch. Class of 1978, 1985—; mem. Yale Devel. Bd., 2000—; nat. vice-chmn. Smithsonian Friends of First Ladies, 1989-92; mem. world bd. USO, 1995—; trustee Pine Ridge Sch. (Vt.), 1998—. Fellow assoc. fellow, Saybrook Coll., Yale U., 2000—. Mem. N.Y. Bar Assn., Phi Beta Kappa. Republican. Episcopalian. Taxation, general. Office: 9400 N Central Expy Ste 1209 Dallas TX 75231-5045

BREWER, EDWARD CAGE, III, law educator; b. Clarksdale, Miss., Jan. 20, 1953; s. Edward Cage Brewer Jr. and Elizabeth Blair (Alford) Little; m. Nancy Corr Martin, Dec. 27, 1975 (div. Sept. 1985); children: Katherine Martin, Julia Blair; m. Laurie Carol Alley, June 27, 1993 (div. Dec. 1999); 1 child, Caroline Elizabeth McCarty; m. Karlyn A. Schnapp; 1 child, Matthew Karl Schnapp. BA, U. of the South, 1975; JD, Vanderbilt U., 1979. Bar: Ala. 1980, U.S. Ct. Appeals (5th and 11th cirs.) 1981, U.S. Dist. Ct. (so. dist.) Ala. 1981, Ga. 1982, U.S. Dist. Ct. (no. dist.) Ga. 1982, U.S. Dist. Ct. (so. dist.) Ga. 1988, U.S. Ct. Appeals (3d and 8th cirs.) 1983, U.S. Dist. Ct. (mid. dist.) Ga. 1992, U.S. Supreme Ct. 1996. Law clk. to Hon. Virgil Pittman U.S. Dist. Ct. (so. dist.) Ala., Mobile, 1979-81; law clk. to Hon. Albert J. Henderson U.S. Ct. Appeals (5th and 11th cirs.), Atlanta, 1981-82; pvt. practice, 1982-96; instr. Coll. of Law Ga. State U., 1992, 94; adj. prof. legal writing Emory U., 1994-96; asst. prof. law No. Ky. U., Highland Heights, 1996-2000, assoc. prof. law, 2000—. Co-author: Railway Labor Act of 1926: Legislative History, 1988, Georgia Appellate Practice, 1996, 2d edit., 2001; contbr. articles to profl. jours. Mem. Phi Beta Kappa, Omicron Delta Kappa. Episcopalian. Avocations: choral music, guitar, motorcycles, hiking, canoeing. Office: No Ky U Salmon P Chase Coll Law Nunn Dr Highland Heights KY 41099 E-mail: brewerec@nku.edu

BREWER, LEWIS GORDON, judge, lawyer, educator; b. New Martinsville, W.Va., Sept. 6, 1946; s. Harvey Lee and Ruth Carolyn (Zimmerman) B.; m. Kathryn Anne Yunker, May 25, 1985. BA, W.Va. U., 1968, JD, 1971; LLM, George Washington U., 1979. Bar: W.Va. 1971, Calif. 1978. Commd. 2d lt. USAF, 1968, advanced through grades to col., 1988, dep. staff judge adv. Calif., 1976-78, chief civil law San Antonio Air Logistics Ctr. Kelly AFB, Tex., 1979-83, staff judge adv. MacDill AFB, Fla., 1983-86, chief Air Force Cen. Labor Law Office Randolph AFB, Tex., 1987-88, dep. staff judge adv. Air Tng. Command, 1988-89, staff judge adv. 7th Air Force Osan AFB, Korea, 1989-91, 45 Space Wing Patrick AFB Fla., 1991-93; adminstrv. law judge W.Va. Edn. and State Employee Grievance Bd., Charleston, 1993-2000, mediator, 1994—; legal counsel W.Va. Ethics Commn., 2000—. Instr. bus. law No. Mich. U., Marquette, 1972, Solano Coll., Suisun City, Calif., 1978; instr. labor law Webster U., Ft. Sam Houston, 1983. Decorated Air Force Commendation medal, Meritorious Service medal, Legion of Merit. Mem. ABA, Assn. for Conflict Resolution, W.Va. Bar Assn., State Bar Calif., W.Va. U. Alumni Assn., George Washington U. Alumni Assn. Roman Catholic. office phone. Home: 528 Sheridan Cir Charleston WV 25314-1063 Office: 1207 Quarrier St Charleston WV 25301-1826 E-mail: Mede8wv@abanet.org, LBrewer@GWMail.state.wv.us

BREWER, STEPHANIE L. lawyer; b. Newport News, Dec. 8, 1969; d. M. Lynn and Constance Susan Taylor; m. Timothy F. Brewer, Apr. 25, 1998. BA, Ariz. State U., 1992; JD, Ind. U., Indpls., 1996. Bar: Ariz. 1996, U.S. Dist. Ct. Ariz. 1996. Assoc. account exec. Bronner Slosberg & Humphrey, Boston, 1992-93; assoc. Chester A. Yon, P.C., Fountain Hills, Ariz., 1997-98, Rhees Hopkins & Kreamer, Phoenix, 1998—. Editor Internat. and Comparative Law Rev., 1994-96. Mem. ABA, State Bar of Ariz. (constrn. law sect. 1998—), Maricopa County Bar Assn., Ariz. Women Lawyers Assn. Republican. Avocations: golf, hiking, sporting events. Office: Rhees Hopkins & Kreamer 4000 N Central Ave Ste 1750 Phoenix AZ 85012-3511

BREWSTER, CLARK OTTO, lawyer; b. Marlette, Mich., Nov. 5, 1956; s. Charles W. and June V. (Hoff) B.; m. Deborah K. Trowhill, Aug. 3, 1974; children: Cassie Mae, Corbin Clark, Cade Otto. BA cum laude, Cen. Mich. U., 1977; JD with honor, Tulsa U., 1980. Bar: Okla. 1981, U.S. Dist. Ct. (no. and ea. dists.) Okla. 1982, Tex. 1993. Assoc. Riddle and Assocs., Tulsa, 1981, Braly and McEachin, Tulsa, 1981-82; ptnr. Brewster & DeAngelis, 1982—. Bd. dirs. Redy Corp., Tulsa, Cottontail Oil Corp., Tulsa. Mem. ABA, ATLA, Okla. Bar Assn., Okla. Trial Lawyers Assn. (pres. 1998), Tulsa County Bar Assn., Order of Curule chair, Order of Barristers. Avocations: golf, hunting, horseback riding. Federal civil litigation, State civil litigation, Criminal. Home: 2109 E 30th Pl Tulsa OK 74114-5429 Office: Brewster & DeAngelis 2617 E 21st St Tulsa OK 74114

BREWSTER, RUDI MILTON, judge; b. Sioux Falls, S.D., May 18, 1932; s. Charles Edwin and Wilhemina Therese (Rud) B.; m. Gloria Jane Nanson, June 27, 1954; children: Scot Alan, Lauri Diane (Alan Lee), Julie Lynn Yahnke. AB in Pub. Affairs, Princeton U., 1954; JD, Stanford U., 1960. Bar: Calif. 1960. From assoc. to ptnr. Gray, Cary, Ames & Frye, San Diego, 1960-84; judge U.S. Dist. Ct. (so. dist.) Calif., 1994-98, sr. judge, 1998—. Served to capt. USNR, 1954-82 Ret. Fellow Am. Coll. Trial Lawyers; mem. Am. Bd. Trial Advs., Internat. Assn. Ins. Counsel, Am. Inns of Ct. Republican. Lutheran. Avocations: skiing, hunting, gardening. Office: US Dist Ct US Ct 4165 940 Front St San Diego CA 92101-8902 Fax: 619-702-9927. E-mail: Rudi_Brewster@casd.uscourts.gov

BREYER, STEPHEN GERALD, United States supreme court justice; b. San Francisco, Aug. 15, 1938; s. Irving G. and Anne R. B.; m. Joanna Hare, Sept. 4, 1967; children: Chloe, Nell, Michael. A.B., Stanford U., 1959; B.A. (Marshall scholar), Oxford U., 1961; LL.B., Harvard U., 1964; LL.D. (hon.), U. Rochester, 1983. Bar: Calif. 1966, D.C. 1966, Mass. 1971. Law clk. Justice Goldberg, U.S. Supreme Ct., 1964-65; spl. asst. to asst. atty. gen. U.S. Dept. Justice, 1965-67; asst. prof. law Harvard U., 1967-70, prof., 1970-81, lectr., 1981—, prof. govt. J.F. Kennedy Sch., 1978-81; asst. spl. prosecutor Watergate Spl. Prosecution Force, 1973; spl. counsel U.S. Senate Judiciary Com., 1974-75, chief counsel, 1979-81; judge U.S. Ct. Appeals (1st cir.), Boston, 1981-90, chief judge, 1990-94; Oliver Wendell Holmes lectr. Harvard Law Sch., 1992; assoc. justice U.S. Supreme Ct., Washington, 1994—. Mem. Judl. Conf. of U.S., 1990-94, U.S. Sentencing commn., 1985-89; vis. lectr. Coll. Law, Sydney, Australia, 1975, Salzburg (Austria) Seminar, 1978, 93; Jud. Conf. rep. to Adminstrv. Conf. U.S., 1981-94; vis. prof. U. Rome, 1993. Author: (with Paul MacAvoy) The Federal Power Commission and the Regulation of Energy, 1974, (with Richard Stewart) Adminstrative Law and Regulatory Policy, 1979, 3rd edit., 1992, Regulation and its Reform, 1982, Breaking the Vicious Circle, 1993; contbr. articles to profl. jours. Trustee U. Mass., 1974-81; bd. overseers Dana Farber Cancer Inst., Boston, 1977— . Mem. ABA, Am. Bar Found., Am. Law Inst., Am. Acad. Arts and Scis., Coun. Fgn. Rels. Office: US Supreme Ct Supreme Ct Bldg 1 1st St NE Washington DC 20543-0001

BRIACH, GEORGE GARY, lawyer, consultant; b. Youngstown, Ohio, Apr. 11, 1954; s. George William and Donna Jean (Phillips) B.; m. Loretta Ann Lepore, May 17, 1985; 1 child, Rachel Renee. BS magna cum laude, Youngstown State U., 1976; JD, U. Akron, Ohio, 1982. Bar: Ohio 1983, Mahoning County, 1983. Assoc. Flask & Policy, Youngstown, 1983-91; asst. atty. gen. State Atty. Gen.'s Office, 1984-90; solicitor Poland (Ohio) Village, 1988-89; cons., dir. Mahoning County (Ohio) Auditor, 1990—; ptnr. White & Briach, Youngstown, 1991—. Fundraiser United Way, Youngstown, 1989-92; bd. dirs., treas. D&E Counseling Ctr., Youngstown, 1992-98, 2000—; trustee, treas. Children' Challenge Found., Inc., 1998-2000; bd. dirs. Interfaith Home Maintenance, 1999—. Mem. Ohio Bar Assn., Mahoning County Bar Assn., Youngstown State U. Alumni Assn., Tippecanoe Country Club. Avocations: aerobic and weight training, golf, reading, travel. Family and matrimonial, General practice, Probate. Home: 45 Russo Dr Canfield OH 44406-9666 Office: White & Briach 755 Boardman Canfield Rd Youngstown OH 44512-4300

BRIAN, A(LEXIS) MORGAN, JR. lawyer; b. New Orleans, Oct. 4, 1928; s. Alexis Morgan and Evelyn (Thibaut) B.; m. Elizabeth Louise Graham, 1951; children: Robert Morgan, Ellen Graham. BA, La. State U., 1949; MS, Trinity U., 1954; JD, La. State U., 1956. Bar: La. 1956, U.S. Supreme Ct. 1971. Assoc. Deutsch, Kerrigan & Stiles, New Orleans, 1956-60, ptnr., 1961-79; sr. ptnr. Brian, Simon, Peragine, Smith & Redfearn, 1979-82, Fawer, Brian, Hardy & Zatzkis, New Orleans, 1982-86; sole practice, 1986—. Spl. asst. to La. Atty. Gen., 1982-87; spkr. profl. seminars; lectr. Inst. CLE, La. State U. Law Ctr., 1972—. Contbr. articles to profl. jours. Local merit badge counselor Boy Scouts Am., 1963—; bd.

dirs. Goodwill Industries New Orleans, 1969-84, v.p., mem. exec. com., 1975-77, mem. adv. bd., 1978, 86—; life deacon, past chmn., trustee, pres., lay preacher, Bible tchr., mem. coms. 1st Bapt. Ch., New Orleans; spkrs. convs., confs. So. Bapt. Conv., 1956—, La. Bapt. Conv., 1956—, Internat. Platform Assn.; past pres. bd. trustees New Orleans Bapt . Theol. Sem., 1961-74; bd. dirs. New Orleans Bapt. Theol. Sem. Found., 1972-81, Inter-Varsity Christian Fellowship, 1974—, La. State U. Found., 1976-81; mem. nat. legal adv. coun. Ams. United for Separation of Ch. and State, 1977-82. Staff sgt. USAF, 1951-55. Recipient Boss of Yr. award New Orleans Legal Secs. Assn., 1966. Fellow La. State Bar Assn. Found.; mem. ABA (TIPS fidelity and surety com., forum com. constrn. industry), La. State Bar Assn. (asst. examiner comm. on bar admissions 1968-89, fidelity, surety and constrn. sect. 1991—), New Orleans Bar Assn., Internat. Assn. Def. Counsel (vice chmn. fidelity and surety com. 1978-79, archs., engrs. and constrn. litig. com., advocacy com.), La. Assn. Def. Counsel, Def. Rsch. Inst., Am. Arbitration Assn. (arbitrator 1970—), La. Civil Svc. League, Internat. Ho., La. State U. Alumni Fedn. (life), Trinity U. Alumni Assn., La. State U. Law Ctr. Alumni Assn. (life) Upper Carrollton Neighborhood Assn. (v.p. 1976), Christian Legal Soc., Theta Xi, Phi Delta Phi. Democrat. Construction, Government contracts and claims, Insurance. Home: 5216 Pitt St New Orleans LA 70115-4107 Office: Box 534 5500 Prytania St New Orleans LA 70115-4237 Fax: (504) 895-4803. E-mail: ambrian@bellsouth.net

BRICE, ROGER THOMAS, lawyer; b. Chgo., May 7, 1948; s. William H. and Mary Loretta (Ryan) B.; m. Carol Coleman, Aug. 15, 1970; children: Caitlin, Coleman, Emily. AB, DePaul U., 1970; JD, U. Chgo., 1973. Bar: Ill. 1973, Iowa 1973, U.S. Ct. Appeals (10th, 4th, 6th and 7th cirs.) 1975, U.S. Dist. Ct. (no. and ctrl. dists.) Ill. 1977, 1995, U.S. Trial Bar (no. dist.) 1982, U.S. Supreme Ct. 1978. Staff atty. Office of Gen. Counsel NLRB, Washington, 1974-76; assoc. Kirkland & Ellis, Chgo., 1976-79, Reuben & Proctor, Chgo., 1979-80, ptnr., 1980-86, Isham, Lincoln & Beale, Chgo., 1986-88, Sonnenschein, Nath & Rosenthal, Chgo., 1988—, head of labor and employment group, 2000—. Legal counsel, bd. dirs. Boys and Girls Clubs Chgo., 1991—. Fellow Coll. Labor and Employment Lawyers. Roman Catholic. Civil rights, General civil litigation, Labor. Home: 3727 N Harding Ave Chicago IL 60618-4026 Office: Sonnenschein Nath & Rosenthal 233 S Wacker Dr Ste 8000 Chicago IL 60606-6491 E-mail: rbrice@sonnenschein.com

BRICK, ANN VETA, lawyer; b. Cheyenne, Wyo., Mar. 17, 1947; d. Gerald John and Margaret (Pasternack) Veta; m. Steven Alexander Brick, Dec. 29, 1968; children: Kate Elizabeth, Rachel Suzanne. B.A., Newcomb Coll., Tulane U., 1969; J.D., U. Calif.-Berkeley, 1975. Bar: Calif. 1975, U.S. Dist. Ct. (no. dist.) Calif. 1975, U.S. Ct. Appeals (5th cir.) 1978, U.S. Ct. Appeals (7th cir.) 1981, U.S. Ct. Appeals (9th cir.) 1988. Law clk. to judge U.S. Dist. Ct. (no. dist.) Calif., San Francisco, 1975-76; assoc. Howard, Rice, Nemerovski, Canady, Robertson & Falk, San Francisco, 1977-81, dir., 1981-84, of counsel, 1984—; dir. Legal Aid Soc. of San Francisco, 1982-87, Equal Rights Advocates, San Francisco, 1984—, ACLU of No. Calif., 1988—. Contbr. article to legal jour. Mem. Bar. Assn. Calif. (panelist Continuing Edn. of Bar 1983), State Bar of Calif. (com. on women in law 1986-88), Lawyers Com. for Urban Affairs, San Francisco Bar Assn. (judiciary com. 1982-84), ACLU (cooperating atty. 1978—), Order of Coif, Phi Beta Kappa. Democrat. Jewish. Office: 3 Embarcadero Ctr Ste 7 San Francisco CA 94111-4074

BRICKLER, JOHN WEISE, lawyer; b. Dayton, Ohio, Dec. 29, 1944; s. John Benjamin and Shirley Hilda (Weise) B.; m. Marilyn Louise Kuhlmann, July 2, 1966; children: John, James, Peter, Andrew, Matthew. AB, Washington U., St. Louis, 1966; JD, Washington U., 1968. Bar: Mo. 1968, U.S. Supreme Ct. 1972, U.S. Dist. Ct. (ea. dist.) Mo. 1974, U.S. Ct. Appeals (8th cir.) 1974. Assoc. Peper, Martin, Jensen, Maichel and Hetlage, St. Louis, 1973-77, ptnr., 1978-98, Blackwell Sanders Peper Martin LLP, St. Louis, 1998—. Bd. dirs. Concordia Pub. House, St. Louis, 1993-, chmn. 1998-2001. Bd. dirs. Luth. Family and Children's Svcs. Mo., St. Louis, 1988-93, vice chmn., 1988-89. Capt. JAGC, U.S. Army, 1969-73. Mem. ABA, Nat. Assn. Bond Lawyers, Bar Assn. Met. St. Louis. General corporate, Municipal (including bonds), Securities. Office: Blackwell Sanders Peper Martin LLP 720 Olive St Fl 24 Saint Louis MO 63101-2338 E-mail: jbrickler@bspmlaw.com

BRICKWEDDE, RICHARD JAMES, lawyer; b. Bklyn., Dec. 12, 1944; s. George L. and Rose M. (McCarthy) B.; m. June Minsch Gamber, Sept. 2, 1978; stepchildren: Stephanie, Karen, Frances. AB, Syracuse U., 1966; JD, Fordham U., 1969. Bar: N.Y. 1970, D.C. 1971, U.S. Tax Ct. 1972, U.S. Supreme Ct. 1991. Staff asst. Syracuse (N.Y.) office Senator Robert F. Kennedy, 1965-66; adminstrv. asst. U.S. P.O. and OEO/VISTA, Washington, 1966; mgmt. cons., 1969-71; gen. counsel The Student Vote, 1971; pvt. practice law Syracuse, 1971-80; regional counsel N.Y. State Dept. Environ. Conservation, 1980-91, acting regional dir., 1984; with Green & Seifter Attys. PC, 1992-2000; prin. Green, Seifter Attys. PLLC, 2000—. Head environ. law practice; assoc. counsel to majority leader N.Y. State Assembly, 1975, asst. counsel to spkr. N.Y. State Assembly, 1976-77. Author: The Student's Right to Vote, 1971, Duke's Tale, 1991, Interstate Garbage: The Carbone Case and the Commerce Clause, 1994, The Superfund Recycling Equity Act of 1999, 2000; contbg. editor Network, 1975-76; contbr. articles to profl. jours. and trade publs. Mem. Onondaga County (N.Y) Child Care Coun., Inc., 1978—83, treas., 1980—81, pres., 1981—82; mem. Internat. Ctr. of Syracuse, 1992—, pres., 1998—99; Internat. Goodwill amb., 2000; chmn. voting rights task force Dem. Nat. Com., 1970—71; bd. dirs. N.Y. Alpha Tau Omega Student Aid Fund, Inc., Syracuse, 1972—, Huntington Family Ctrs., Inc., Syracuse, 1971—89, v.p., 1980; bd. dirs. Onondanga County (N.Y) Child Care Coun., Inc., 1978—80, Appleseed Trust, 2000—, The Nature Conservancy of Ctrl. and Western N.Y., 2001—. Named Hon. Citizen State of Tex., 1976; recipient Pub. Citizenship award N.Y. Pub. Interest Rsch. Group 1980. Mem. ABA (vice chair spl. com. on solid waste 1998—), N.Y. Bar Assn., Onondaga County Bar Assn. (co-chair CLE com. 1999-2000), Nat. Solid Waste Mgmt. Assn. (mem. steering com. N.Y. chpt. 1992—). Democrat. Office: Green & Seifter Attys PLLC 1 Lincoln Ctr Ste 900 Syracuse NY 13202-1387 E-mail: rbrickwedde@greenseifter.com

BRICKWOOD, SUSAN CALLAGHAN, lawyer; b. Sydney, NSW, Australia, Dec. 6, 1946; d. Graham Callaghan Brickwood and Nan (Cahaley) Nichols). BA, Swarthmore Coll., 1969; postgrad., Harvard U., 1969-71; JD, U. So. Calif., 1980. Bar: Calif. 1980, U.S. Tax Ct. 1981. Controller Howard Smith, Ltd., Sydney, 1972-74; assoc. Rifkind & Sterling, Beverly Hills, Calif., 1980-81, Armstrong, Hendler & Hirsch, Century City, 1981-82; pvt. practice L.A., 1982—. Author: Start Over!, 1990. Bankruptcy. Office: 9107 Wilshire Blvd #500 Beverly Hills CA 90210-

BRIDENSTINE, LOUIS HENRY, JR. lawyer; b. Detroit, Nov. 13, 1940; s. Louis and Mary Ellen (O'Keefe) B.; m. Lucia Elizabeth Pucci, June 18, 1966; 1 child, Lucia McMullin. BS, John Carroll U., 1962; MA, U. Detroit, 1966, JD, 1965. Bar: Mich. 1966, U.S. Dist. Ct. (ea. dist.) Mich. 1966. Trial atty., atty.-advisor FTC, Washington, 1966-72; sr. legal counsel, v.p. dir. comms. Motor Vehicle Mfrs. Assn. U.S., Inc., Detroit, 1972-81; sr. v.p., gen. counsel, sec. Campbell-Ewald Co., Warren, Mich., 1981—. Exec. dir. Motorists Info., Inc., Detroit, 1977; legal affairs com. Am. Assn. Advt. Agys., N.Y.C., 1990—, chair, 2000—. Youth allocations panelist United Way Cmty Svcs., Detroit, 1991-98, chair, 1993-98, fund distbn. panelist, 1994-98; trustee, bd. dirs. Catholic Youth Orgn., Detroit, 1981-97, 99-2000, chair bd. dirs., 1990-92. Fellow Mich. State Bar Found. (life); mem. Mich. Bar Assn., Am. Corp. Counsel Assn., Alpha Sigma Nu, Blue Key, Detroit Athletic Club. Avocations: travel, reading. Administrative and regulatory, General corporate, Labor. Office: Campbell Ewald Co 30400 Van Dyke Ave Warren MI 48093-2368 E-mail: libridens@cecom.com

BRIDESTOWE, Lord See MOORE, THOMAS RONALD

BRIDGE, BOBBE J. state supreme court justice; m. Jonathan J. Bridge; children: Rebecca, Don. BA magna cum laude, U. Wash; MA, PhD in Polit. Sci., U. Mich.; JD, U. Wash., 1976. Superior Ct. judge King County, Wash., 1990-1999; chief judge King County Juvenile Ct., 1994-97, asst. presiding judge, 1997-98, presiding judge, 1998-99; judge Wash. State Supreme Ct., 1999—; mem. faculty Wash. State Jud. Coll. Chmn. King County Criminal Justice Coun., King County Truancy Steerin Com., Juvenile Justice Operational Master Plan Oversight Com., Pub. Trust and Confidence Com. Bd. Jud. Adminstrn.; co-chmn. Unified Family Ct. Bench-Bar Task Force. Bd. dirs. YWCA, Seattle Children's Home, Families for Kids Permanency Oversight Com., Tech. Adv. Com. Female Juvenile Offenders, Adv. Com. Adolescent Life Skills Program, Street Youth Law Program, Northwest Mediation Svc., Woodland Pk. Zoological Soc., Wash. Coun. Crime and Delinquency, Women's Funding Alliance, Alki Found., Privacy Fund, Seattle Arts Commn., U. Wash. Arts and Sci. Devel., Greater Seattle C. of C., Metrocenter YMCA, Juvenile Ct. Conf. Com.; mem. King County Task Force on Children and Families, Wash. State's Dept. Social and Health Svcs. Children., Youth, Family Svcs. Adv. Com., Child Protection Roundtable, Govs. Juvenile Justice Adv. Com.; chmn. State Task Force on Juvenile Issues, Coun. Youth Crisis Work Group, Families-at-Risk subcom., Bd. Dirs. Ctr. Career Alternatives, Candidate Evaluation Com. Seattle-King Mcpl. League, Law and justice Com. League Women Voters; co-chmn. Govs. Coun. on Families, Youth, and Justice; pres. Seattle Women's Commn., Seattle Chpt. Am. Jewish Com.,bd. dirs., asst. sec.-treas. Jewish Fedn. Greater Seattle, chmn., vice chmn. Cmty. Rels. Coun. Named Judge of Yr. Wash. Women Lawyers, 1996; recipient Hannah G. Solomon award Nat. Coun. Jewish Women, 1996, Cmty. Catalyst award Mother's Against Violence in Am., 1997, Women Making a Difference award Youthcare, 1998; honored "woman helping women" Soroptimist Internat. of Kent, 1999. Mem. Phi Beta Kappa. Office: Wash Supreme Ct PO Box 40929 Olympia WA 98504-0929

BRIDGELAND, JAMES RALPH, JR. lawyer; b. Cleve., Feb. 16, 1929; s. James Ralph and Alice Laura (Huth) B.; m. Margaret Louise Bates, March 24, 1950; children: Deborah, Cynthia, Rebekah, Alicia, John. BA magna cum laude, U. Akron, 1951; MA, Harvard U., 1955, JD, 1957. Bar: Ohio 1957. Mem. internat. staff Goodyear Tire & Rubber Co., Akron, Ohio, 1953-56; ptnr. Taft, Stettinius & Hollister, Cin., 1957—; dir., mem. exec. com. Firstar Corp. and Star Bank Cin.; dir. SHV N.Am., Inc., The David J. Joseph Co., Robert A. Cline Co., Art Stamping, Inc., Seinau-Fisher Studios, Inc.; instr., lectr. in lit. U. Cin.. Pres., trustee Cin. Symphony Orch.; sec., trustee Louise Taft Semple Found.; trustee Cin. Opera Co., Hillside Trust, Jobs for Cin. Grads., Cin. Inst. Fine Arts; past bd. dirs. Legal Aid Soc.; mayor, mem. coun. City of Indian Hill, Ohio, 1985-91; pres. Indian Hill Sch. Bd., 1971-77. 1st lt. USAF, 1951-53, Korea. Mem. ABA, Ohio Bar Assn., Cin. Bar Assn., Am. Arbitration Assn., Harvard Law Sch. Assn. (past pres. Cin. chpt.), Harvard Alumni Assn. (nat. v.p. 1978-85). Harvard Club (pres. 1983-84), Queen City Club, Commonwealth Club (treas. 1984-86), Queen City Optimist Club, Recess Club, Assn. Literary Scholars and Critics, Cin. Optimist Club, Cin. Literary Club. Republican. Episcopalian. Banking, General corporate, Private international. Home: 8175 Brill Rd Cincinnati OH 45243-3937

BRIDGES, ANNITA MARIE, lawyer; b. Columbia, S.C., Dec. 21, 1951; d. John R. and Anne M. (Wharton) B.; m. Robert H. Alexander, Jr. B.A., Howard U., 1973; J.D., Georgetown U., 1976. Bar: Okla. 1979, Colo. 1976, U.S. Dist. Ct. Colo. 1976, U.S. Dist. Ct. (we. dist.) Okla. 1980, U.S. Ct. Appeals (10th cir.) 1976. Legal intern SBA, Washington, 1974-75; asst. atty. gen. State of Colo., Denver, 1976-78; staff atty. Kerr-McGee Corp., Oklahoma City, 1978— ; lectr. U. Okla., Norman, 1982. Mem. Colo. Gov.'s Clemency Adv. Bd., 1977-78; mem. Gov.'s Adv. Commn. on Status Women; vol. in Oklahoma City Pub. Schs.; bd. dirs., past pres. Planned Parenthood Assn., Oklahoma City; bd. dirs. YWCA, Oklahoma City N.E. Devel. Corp., Black Liberated Arts Council. Recipient Outstanding Community Service award Community Council Central Okla., 1984. Mem. ABA, Okla. Bar Assn. (sec. labor law sect. 1979-80). Labor, Workers' compensation. Office: Kerr-McGee Corp PO Box 25861 Oklahoma City OK 73125-0861

BRIDGES, DAVID MANNING, lawyer; b. Berkeley, Calif., May 22, 1936; s. Robert Lysle and Alice Marion (Rodenberger) B.; m. Carmen Galante de Bridges, Aug. 16, 1973; children: David, Stuart. AB, U. Calif., Berkeley, 1957, JD, 1962. Assoc. Thelen, Marrin, Johnson & Bridges, San Francisco, 1962-70, ptnr., 1970-94, mng. ptnr. Houston, 1981-91. Served as lt. (j.g.) USN, 1957-59. Mem. ABA, State Bar of Tex., Tex. Bar Assn., Houston Bar Assn., Internat. Bar Assn., Houston Club, Coronado Club, Pacific-Union Club. Banking, Contracts commercial, Construction. Office: 700 Louisiana St Ste 4600 Houston TX 77002-2732 E-mail: dbridhou@aol.com

BRIDGMAN, SUSAN R. tax lawyer; b. Hamilton, Bermuda, Aug. 3, 1961; came to U.S., 1964; e. Matthew D. and Margaret A. Reddington; m. Charles J. Bridgman Jr., July 25, 1987; children: Rachael K., Emma C. BA in Italian, Ohio State U., 1984; JD cum laude, U. Dayton, Ohio, 1990. Bar: Ohio 1990. Corp. sales rep. Eastman Kodak Co., Dayton, 1984-87; jud. law clk. Montgomery County Ct. Common Pleas, 1989-90; staff atty. 2d Dist. Ct. Appeals of Ohio, 1990-93; tax atty. NCR Corp., 1993-97, Chernesky, Heyman & Kress, PLL, Dayton, 1997—. Mem. ABA, Ohio State Bar Assn., Dayton Bar Assn. Avocations: physical fitness, cooking travel, reading. Office: Chernesky Heyman & Kress PLL 10 Courthouse Plz SW Ste 1100 Dayton OH 45402-1868 E-mail: Srb@chklaw.com

BRIEANT, CHARLES LA MONTE, federal judge; b. Ossining, N.Y., Mar. 13, 1923; s. Charles La Monte and Marjorie (Hall) B.; m. Virginia Elizabeth Warfield, Sept. 10, 1948. B.A., Columbia U., 1947, LL.B., 1949. Bar: N.Y. 1949. Mem. firm Bleakley, Platt, Schmidt & Fritz, White Plains, 1949-71; water commr. Village of Ossining, 1948-51; town justice, 1952-58; town supr., 1960-63; village atty. Briarcliff Manor, N.Y.; also spl. asst. dist. atty. Westchester County, 1958-59; asst. counsel N.Y. State Joint Legis. Com. Fire Ins., 1968; judge U.S. Dist. Ct. (so. dist.) N.Y., N.Y.C., 1971-86, chief judge, 1986-93; judge U.S Dist Ct. So. Dist. N.Y., White Plains, 1993—. Adj. prof. Bklyn. Law Sch.; mem. Jud. Conf. U.S., 1989-95, mem. exec. com., 1991-95. Mem. Westchester County Republican Com., 1957-71; mem. Westchester County Legislature from 2d Dist., 1970-71. Served with AUS, World War II. Mem. ABA, N.Y. State Bar Assn., Westchester County Bar Assn., Ossining Bar Assn. Episcopalian (vestryman). Club: SAR. Office: US Dist Ct US Courthouse 300 Quarropas St White Plains NY 10601-4140

BRIEGER, GEORGE, lawyer; b. Hungary, Apr. 30, 1966; came to the U.S., 1977; s. Jenö and Miriam Brieger. BS in Computer Sci. cum laude, Bklyn. Coll., 1988; postgrad., Yeshiva U., 1988-90; JD, Cordozo Sch. Law, 1993; LLM in Intellectual Property, George Washington U., 2001. Bar: N.Y. 1994, U.S. Dist. Ct. (so. and ea. dists.) N.Y. 1995, U.S. Ct. Internat. Trade, 1999. Internat. counsel Bacher & Ptnrs. Atty. at Law, Budapest, Hungary, 1996-98; atty. Internat. Trade Litigation U.S. Customs Svc., N.Y.C., 1998-2000; atty. Sughrue Gion Zinn MacPeak & Seas, Washington, 2001—. Cons. Fin. Svcs. Vol. Corps, N.Y.C., 1996. Editor New Europe Law Rev. Cardozo Sch. Law, N.Y.C., 1992-93; contbr. chpt. to book. Adv. bd. Budapest-N.Y. Sister City Com., N.Y.C., 1996—. Scholar Revel Grad. Sch., N.Y.C., 1988-90. Mem. Am. Intellectual Property Law Assn. Avocations: linguistics, philosophy, computer technology, Tai Chi, swimming. E-mail: georgebrieger@yahoo.com

BRIER, BONNIE SUSAN, lawyer; b. Oct. 19, 1950; d. Jerome W. and Barbara (Srenco) B.; m. Bruce A. Rosenfield, Aug. 15, 1976; children: Rebecca, Elizabeth, Benjamin. AB in Econs. magna cum laude, Cornell U., 1972; JD, Stanford U., 1976. Bar: Pa. 1976, U.S. Dist. Ct. (ea. dist.) Pa., U.S. Tax Ct., U.S. Ct. Appeals (3d cir.), U.S. Supreme Ct. Law clk. to chief judge U.S. Dist. Ct. Pa. (ea. dist.), Phila., 1976-77, asst. U.S. atty. criminal prosecutor, 1977-79; from assoc. to ptnr. Ballard, Spahr, Andrews & Ingersoll, 1979-90; gen. counsel Children's Hosp. of Phila., 1990—. Legal counsel Womens Way, 1979—; lectr. U. Pa., 1988-95; lectr., speaker various orgns. and seminars. Editor Stanford Law Rev., 1974-76; contbr. articles to profl. jours. Bd. dirs. U.S. Com. for UNICEF, 1994—. Fellow Am. Coll. Tax Counsel; mem. ABA (exempt orgn. com. on tax sect., chair 1991-93, mem. health law sect.), Pa. Bar Assn. (tax sect.), Phila. Bar Assn. (tax sect.), Nat. Health Lawyers Assn., Am. Acad. Healthcare Attys. (bd. dirs. 1991-96), ABA (health law sec., bd. dirs. 1998—). Education and schools, Health, Taxation, general. Home: 132 Fairview Rd Narberth PA 19072-1331 Office: Children's Hosp of Pa 34th St and Civic Ctr Blvd Philadelphia PA 19104

BRIERTON, CHERYL LYNN, lawyer; b. Hartford, Conn., Nov. 11, 1947; d. Charles Greenwood and Elizabeth (Grechko) Wootton; m. David Martin Black, Oct. 12, 1968 (div. 1978); m. John Thomas Brierton, Sept. 6, 1982 (div. 1988); 1 child, John Greenwood. BA, Wellesley Coll., 1969; JD, U. San Diego, 1982. Bar: Calif. 1983. Tchr., libr. Anglican High Sch., Grenada, West Indies, 1972-74; dep. dir. Transalpino Student Travel, Paris, 1975-76; asst. dir. adminstn. Project OZ, YMCA, San Diego, 1976-78; asst. coord. policy and advocacy Community Congress San Diego, 1978-81; field dir. Calif. Child, Youth and Family Coalition, San Diego, 1981-83; asst. exec. dir. Community Congress San Diego, 1984-85; exec. dir. Calif. Child, Youth and Family Coalition, Sacramento, 1985-86; gen. atty. Def. Logistics Agy., Def. Depot Tracy, Calif., 1986-88; atty.-advisor Dept. of the Navy, Mare Island Naval Shipyard, Vallejo, 1988-89; staff atty. San Diego Superior Ct., 1989—. Mem. faculty Nat. Juvenile Judges Conf. Dispositional Alternatives Serious Offenders, 1982, 6th and 7th Nat. Confs. Juvenile Justice, 1979-80; cons. San Diego Youth Involvement Project, 1983-84, San Diego Youth and Community Svcs., 1983-84, South Bay Community Svcs., Chula Vista, 1983. Mem. Juvenile Justice Commn., Golden Hill Neighborhood Justice Cen. Planning Bd.; mem. com. jud. process Regional Criminal Justice Planning Bd. Scholar U. San Diego 1979. Mem. MENSA. Avocations: yachting, travel. General civil litigation, General practice. Home: 1329 Bancroft St San Diego CA 92102-2429 E-mail: cbriersp@co.san-diego.ca.us

BRIGGS, JOHN MANCEL, III, lawyer; b. Muskegon, Mich., May 24, 1942; s. John M. Jr. and Margaret Jane (Wren) B.; m. Janice R. Dykema, May 20, 1967; children: Jennifer Anne, Jill Margaret. BS, U. Mich., 1964, JD, 1967. Bar: Mich. 1968, U.S. Dist. Ct. (we. dist.) Mich. 1968, U.S. Ct. Appeals (6th cir.) 1974, U.S. Supreme Ct. 2000. Assoc. Parmenter, Forsythe, Rude, Van Epps, Briggs & Fauri and predecessors, Muskegon, 1967-70, ptnr., 1970-92; shareholder Parmenter O'Toole, Muskegon, Mich., 1992—. Active Muskegon United Appeal, 1968-73; bd. dirs. Big Bros., Muskegon, 1969-74; bd. dirs. Y Family Christian Assn., 1970-80, 81-83, 1st v.p., 1973-76, pres., 1977-78; bd. dirs. Muskegon-Oceana Legal Aid Soc., 1970-73, pres., 1972-73; bd. dirs. Berean Ch., 1985-86, 88-90, 93-94, 99-2001, sec., 1988-90, v.p., 1993, pres., 1994, 99, 2000. With USAR, 1967-73. Recipient Disting. Svc. award Muskegon Jaycees, 1977. Fellow Mich. State Bar Assn.; mem. ABA, Muskegon County Bar Assn. (sec. 1970-71, v.p. 1974-75, pres. 1975-76), Rotary (bd. dirs. 1981-85, pres.-elect 1982-83, pres. 1983-84, Presdl. Citation). Republican. Condemnation, Estate planning, Real property. Office: Parmenter O'Toole PO Box 786 175 W Apple Ave Muskegon MI 49443-0786

BRIGHAM, HENRY DAY, JR. retired lawyer; b. Pittsfield, Mass., Dec. 12, 1926; s. Henry Day and Gladys M. (Allen) B.; m. Catherine T. Van't Hul, Dec. 16, 1961; children: Henry Day, Johan Van't Hul, Alexander Frederick. BA, Yale U., 1947, JD, 1950. Bar: N.Y. 1951, Mass. 1966. Assoc. Milbank, Tweed, Hope & Hadley, N.Y.C., 1951-52, 54-56, Simpson, Thacher & Bartlett, N.Y.C., 1956-66; v.p., gen. counsel, dir. Eaton & Howard, Inc., Boston, 1966-73, 1973-79; v.p., chmn. exec. com. Eaton & Howard, Vance Sanders, Inc., 1979-81, Eaton Vance Corp., Boston, 1981—96; ret., 1996. Former trustee Eaton Vance Cash Mgmt. Fund, Boston; former v.p., trustee Eaton Vance Tax Free Reserves, Boston; former sec., clk., dir. Investors Bank & Trust Co., Boston; v.p., sec., trustee Wright Managed Income Trust, Boston, Wright Managed Equity Trust, Boston, Wright Blue Chip Master Portfolio Trust, Boston. Pres. Trustees of Donations of Episc. Diocese Mass., 1984-89; sr. warden Ch. of the Redeemer, Chestnut Hill, 1975-79; sec., bd. dirs. Chestnut Hill Assn. (Mass.), 1969—. Lt. USNR, 1952-54. Mem.: Investment Counsel Assn. Am. (bd. govs.), Assn. Yale Alumni (bd. govs.), Country Club (Brookline, Mass.), Tennis & Racquet Club, Downtown Club, Harvard Club, Longwood Cricket Club (Boston), Tarratine Yacht Club (Islesboro, Maine), Phi Beta Kappa, Phi Delta Phi. Republican. Episcopalian. General corporate.

BRIGHT, CRAIG BARTLEY, lawyer; b. Mineola, N.Y., May 23, 1931; s. Herbert Lester and Gertrude Lillian (Smith) B.; m. Judith Alice Pollard, July 31, 1955 (dec. Aug. 1956); m. Ann Sharpe, July 18, 1959. B.A. summa cum laude Colgate U., 1952; J.D. magna cum laude Harvard U., 1955. Bar; N.Y. 1956, U.S. Dist. Ct. (so. and ea. dists.) N.Y. 1961, U.S. Dist. Ct. Conn. 1961, U.S. Ct. Appeals (2d cir.) 1961. Staff judge advocate Judge Adv. Gen.'s Group, 1955-57; assoc. Patterson, Belknap, Webb & Tyler, N.Y.C., 1957-64, ptnr., 1965-92. Co-author: The Law and the Lore of Endowment Funds, 1969; The Developing Law of Endowment Funds, 1974; also law rev. articles. Served to capt. USAF, 1955-57. Mem. N.Y. State Bar Assn. (chmn. com. on profl. ethics 1981-84), Assn. of Bar of City of N.Y., ABA. Republican. Presbyterian. Club: Hermitage (Goochland, Va.). Contracts commercial, General corporate, Securities. Home and Office: 21 Hunting Ridge Rd Manakin Sabot VA 23103-2614

BRIGHT, JOSEPH CONVERSE, lawyer; b. Richmond, Va., July 28, 1940; s. Joseph Elliott and Marion (Converse) B.; m. Jill Giddens, May 5, 1989; children: Thomas Converse, Elizabeth Chase. BA, U. Va., 1962; LLB, U. Ga., 1965. Bar: Ga. 1964, U.S. Dist. Ct. (so. dist.) Ga. 1965, U.S. Dist. Ct. (mid. dist.) Ga. 1967, U.S. Dist. Ct. (no. dist.) Ga. 1983, U.S. Ct. Appeals (5th cir.) 1965, Fla. 1976, U.S. Dist. Ct. (mid. and no. dist.) Fla. 1982, U.S. Supreme Ct. 1976, U.S. Ct. Appeals (11th cir.) 1981, U.S. Dist. Ct. (no. dist.) Fla. 1998. Assoc. Joseph B. Bergen, Savannah, Ga., 1965-67; sole practice Valdosta, 1967-69; ptnr. Blackburn & Bright, 1969-91; pvt. practice, 1991—. Instr. part time Valdosta State U., 1967-81; mem. Ga. Bd. Bar Examiners. Fellow Am. Bd. Criminal Lawyers, Am. Coll. Trial Lawyers; mem. ATLA, Am. Bd. Trial Advocates (advocate), Nat. Assn. Criminal Def. Lawyers, Ga. Trial Lawyers Assn. (v.p.). Avocations: riding, English history, skeet shooting. Criminal, Personal injury, Product liability. Office: PO Box 5889 Valdosta GA 31603-5889 E-mail: jcblaw@bellsouth.net

BRIGHT, MYRON H. federal judge, educator; b. Eveleth, Minn., Mar. 5, 1919; s. Morris and Lena A. Bright; m. Frances Louise Reisler, Dec. 26, 1947; children: Dinah Ann, Joshua Robert. BSL, U. Minn., 1941, JD, 1947. Bar: N.D. 1947, Minn. 1947. Assoc. Wattam, Vogel, Vogel & Bright, Fargo,

N.D., 1947, ptnr., 1949-68; judge 8th U.S. Cir. Ct. Appeals, 1968-85, sr. judge, 1985—; disting. prof. law St. Louis U., 1985-88, emeritus prof. of law, 1989-95. Capt. AUS, 1942-46, CBI. Recipient Francis Rawle award ALI-ABA, 1996, Lifetime Achievement award U. N.D. Law Sch., 1998, Herbert Harley award, AJS, 2000. Mem.: ABA, N.D. Bar Assn., U.S. Jud. Conf. (com. on adminstrn. of probation sys. 1977—83, adv. com. on appellate rules 1987—90, com. on internat. jud. rels. 1996—). Office: US Ct Appeals 8th Cir 655 1st Ave N Ste 340 Fargo ND 58102-4952 E-mail: myron-bright@ca8.uscourts.gov

BRILL, STEVEN CHARLES, financial advisor, lawyer; b. Miami, Fla., Aug. 21, 1953; s. Arthur W. and Joan K. (Caveretta) B. AB, Boston U., 1975; JD, Western New Eng. Coll., 1978; LLM, NYU, 1986. Advanced underwriting cons. Equitable Life Assurance Soc., N.Y.C., 1978-79; sr. advanced underwriting cons. Met. Life Ins. Co., 1979-85; asst. v.p. personal fin. planning group Dean Witter Reynolds, 1985-87; v.p., dir. asset allocation group Chase Pvt. Bank, 1987-98; prin. Spielberger, Dampf, Brill & Levine, LLC, 1998—. Chmn. Cmty. Housing Innovations, Inc.; past pres., dir. Wychwood Owner's Corp., Great Neck, N.Y., Realty of Bay Terr. Inc., Bayside, N.Y. Contbr. articles to Mature Outlook Mag. Avocations: skiing, tennis, golf. Home: 16625 12th Ave Whitestone NY 11357-2261 E-mail: brilladvis@aol.com

BRIMMER, CLARENCE ADDISON, federal judge; b. Rawlins, Wyo., July 11, 1922; s. Clarence Addison and Geraldine (Zingsheim) B.; m. Emily O. Docken, Aug. 2, 1953; children: Geraldine Ann, Philip Andrew, Andrew Howard, Elizabeth Ann. BA, U. Mich., 1944, JD, 1947. Bar: Wyo. 1948. Pvt. practice law, Rawlins, 1948-71; mcpl. judge, 1948-54; U.S. commr., magistrate, 1963-71; atty. gen. Wyo. Cheyenne, 1971-74; U.S. atty., 1975; chief judge U.S. Dist. Ct. Wyo., Cheyenne, 1975-92, dist. judge, 1975—. Mem. panel multi-dist. litigation, 1992-2000; mem. Jud. Conf. U.S., 1994-97, exec., 1995-97. Sec. Rawlins Bd. Pub. Utilities, 1954-66; Rep. gubernatorial candidate, 1974; trustee Rocky Mountain Mineral Law Found., 1963-75. With USAAF, 1945-46. Mem. ABA, Wyo. Bar Assn., Laramie County Bar Assn., Carbon County Bar Assn., Am. Judicature Soc., Masons, Shriners, Rotary. Episcopalian. Office: US Dist Ct PO Box 985 Cheyenne WY 82003-0985

BRING, MURRAY H. retired lawyer; b. Denver, Jan. 19, 1935; s. Alfred Alexander and Ida (Molinsky) B.; m. Constance Brooks Evert, Dec. 30, 1963 (div. June 1989); children: Beth, Catherine, Peter; m. Kathleen Delaney, May 19, 1990. BA, U. So. Calif., 1956; LLB, NYU, 1959. Bar: N.Y. 1960, D.C. 1963, U.S. Supreme Ct. 1966. Law clk. to Chief Justice Earl Warren U.S. Supreme Ct., Washington, 1959-61; spl. asst. to asst. atty. gen. civil div. Dept. Justice, 1961-62; spl. asst to dep. undersec. state Dept. State, 1962-63; dir. policy planning anti-trust divsn., 1963-65; ptnr. Arnold & Porter, Washington, 1965-87; sr. v.p., gen. counsel Philip Morris Cos., Inc., N.Y.C., 1988-94, exec. v.p. external affairs and gen. counsel, 1994-97, vice chmn., gen. counsel, 1997-2000; ret., 2000. Editor-in-chief N.Y. Law Rev., 1958-59. Bd. dirs. Guild Hall East Hampton, NYU Law Sch. Found. Mem. ABA, Assn. Bar City N.Y., D.C. Bar Assn., Order of Coif, Phi Beta Kappa, Phi Kappa Phi. Avocations: photography; art. General corporate. Office: Philip Morris Cos Inc 120 Park Ave New York NY 10017-5592

BRINGARDNER, JOHN MICHAEL, lawyer, clergyman; b. Columbus, Ohio, Nov. 7, 1957; s. John Krepps and Elizabeth (Evans) B.; m. Emily Presley, June 19, 1982; children: John Taylor, Michael Steven, Malee Elizabeth. BA, U. Central Fla., Orlando, 1979; postgrad., Mercer U., 1979; JD, Fla. State U., 1981. Bar: Fla. 1982, Calif. 1994, U.S. Dist. Ct. (mid. dist.) Fla., U.S. Dist. Ct. (no. dist.) Fla., U.S. Ct. Appeals (11th cir.). Assoc. McFarlain, Bobo, Sternstein, Wiley & Cassidy, Tallahassee, 1982-87, Finley, Kumble Wagner, Tallahassee, 1987; minister Boston Ch. of Christ, 1987-90; evangelist Bankok Christian Ch., 1990-92, Metro Manila Christian Ch., 1992-93; gen. counsel Internat. Chs. of Christ, L.A., 1993—. Bd. dirs. Eye Care Corp., Orlando, Fla., Quality Coffee Corp., Tallahassee. Mem. ABA, Fla. Bar Assn. Avocations: football, baseball, triathlons, hiking, music. General civil litigation, Constitutional, Non-profit and tax-exempt organizations. Office: International Churches of Christ 3530 Wilshire Blvd Ste 1750 Los Angeles CA 90010-2238

BRINGMAN, JOSEPH EDWARD, lawyer; b. Elmhurst, N.Y., Jan. 31, 1958; s. Joseph Herman and Eileen Marie (Sheehy) B.; m. Laurie Lynn Cunningham, July 11, 1992; children: Joseph Edward Jr., Elizabeth Grace. BA, Yale U., 1980; JD, Stanford U., 1983. Bar: N.Y. 1984, Wash. 1985, U.S. Dist. Ct. (we. dist.) Wash. 1986, U.S. Ct. Appeals (9th cir.) 1986, U.S. Ct. Appeals (fed. cir.) 1988, U.S. Dist. Ct. (ea. dist.) Wash. 2000. Acting asst. prof. U. Wash. Law Sch., Seattle, 1983-85; assoc. Perkins Coie, 1985-91, of counsel, 1992—. Dir. Perkins Coie Cmty. Fellowship, Seattle, 1990-96, chair assoc. tng. com., 1997-2000. Editor: Stanford Jour. Internat. Law, 1980-83. Mem. Yale Alumni Schs. Com., Seattle, 1983—, Palo Alto, Calif., 1980-83. Nat. Merit scholar, 1976; recipient Pro Bono Publico award Trumbull Coll. (Yale U.), 1980. Mem. ABA, Wash. State Bar Assn., King County Bar Assn. (jud. screening com. 1993-96, chair fair campaign practices com. 1997-99, judiciary and cts. com. 1999—). Democrat. Roman Catholic. Federal civil litigation, State civil litigation, Professional liability. Office: Perkins Coie LLP 1201 3rd Ave Fl 48 Seattle WA 98101-3099 E-mail: brinj@perkinscoie.com

BRINKMAN, DALE THOMAS, lawyer; b. Columbus, Ohio, Dec. 10, 1952; s. Harry H. and Jean May (Sandel) B.; m. Martha Louise Johnson, Aug. 3, 1974; children: Marin Veronica, Lauren Elizabeth, Kelsey Renee. BA, U. Notre Dame, 1974; JD, Ohio State U., 1977. Bar: Ohio 1977, U.S. Dist. Ct. (so. dist.) Ohio 1979. Assoc. Schwartz, Shapiro, Kelm & Warren, Columbus, 1977-82; asst. tax counsel Am. Elect. Power, 1982; gen. counsel Worthington Industries, Inc., 1982-99, v.p. adminstrn., gen. counsel, sec., 1999—. Author: Ohio State U. Law Jour.,1975-76, editor, 1976-77. Trustee, officer Friends of Dahlberg Ctr., Columbus, 1980-86; dir., officer Assn. for Developmentally Disabled, Columbus, 1986-94. Mem. ABA, Ohio Bar Assn., Columbus Bar Assn. Republican. Roman Catholic. General corporate, Mergers and acquisitions, Securities. Office: Worthington Industries Inc 1205 Dearborn Dr Columbus OH 43085-4769 E-mail: dtbrinkm@worthingtonindustries.com

BRINKMANN, ROBERT JOSEPH, lawyer; b. Cin., Dec. 25, 1950; s. Robert Harry and Helen R. (Streuwing) B.; children: Christopher, Julia. BA, U. Notre Dame, 1972; postgrad., Alliance Française, 1974-75; AM, Brown U., 1977; JD, Loyola U., Los Angeles, 1980. Bar: Calif. 1980, D.C. 1981, U.S. Ct. Appeals (D.C. and 9th cirs.) 1981, U.S. Supreme Ct. 1984, U.S. Ct. Appeals (6th cir.) 1987. Tchr. secondary schs., Los Angeles and Paris, 1974-77; assoc. Hedrick & Lane, Washington, 1980-82; gen. counsel Nat. Newspaper Assn., 1982-92; exec. dir. Red Tag News Publs. Assn., 1990-92; v.p., counsel postal and regulatory affairs Newspaper Assn. Am., Reston, Va., 1992—. Mem. faculty Am. Press. Inst., Reston, Va., 1982-92; adj. faculty U. Md., 1996—. Mem. ABA, Fed. Communications Bar Assn. (former vice chmn. postal affairs com.). Roman Catholic. Administrative and regulatory, Communications, Legislative. Home: 204 Lynn Manor Dr Rockville MD 20850-4431 Office: Newspaper Assn Am National Press Bldg 529 14th St NW Ste 440 Washington DC 20045-1407 E-mail: brinb@naa.org

BRINSMADE, LYON LOUIS, retired lawyer; b. Mexico City, Feb. 24, 1924; s. Robert Bruce and Helen (Steenbock) B. (Am. citizens); m. Susannah Tucker, June 9, 1956 (div. 1978); children: Christine Fairchild, Louisa Calvert; m. Carolyn Hartman Lister, Sept. 22, 1979. Student, U. Wis., 1940-43; B.S., Mich. Technol. U., 1944; J.D., Harvard U., 1950. Bar: Tex. 1951. Assoc. Butler, Binion, Rice, Cook & Knapp, Houston, 1950-58, ptnr. in charge internat. dept., 1958-83, Porter & Clements, Houston, 1983-91; sr. counsel Porter & Hedges (formerly Porter & Clements), 1991-99. Bd. dirs. Houston br. English-Speaking Union of U.S., 1972-75. Served with AUS, 1946-47. Mem. ABA (chmn. com. internat. investment and devel. of sect. internat. law and practice 1970-76, council 1972-76, 81-82, vice chmn. 1976-79, chmn.-elect 1979-80, chmn. 1980-81, co-chmn. com. Mex. 1982-85), Internat. Bar Assn., Inter-Am. Bar Assn. (co-chmn. sect. oil and gas laws, com. natural resources 1973-76, council 1984-87), Houston Bar Assn., State Bar Tex. (chmn. internat. law com. 1970-74, mem. council sect. internat. law 1975-78), Am. Soc. Internat. Law (exec. council 1984-86), Houston World Trade Assn. (sec., dir. 1967-70), Houston World Trade Assn. (chmn. legis. com. 1967-72), Houston C. of C. (chmn. legis. subcom. internat. bus. com. 1970-72), SAR, Allegro of Houston, Houston Club, Petroleum Club, Harvard Club (Houston), Sigma Alpha Epsilon Episcopalian. Home: PO Box 1149 Wimberley TX 78676-1149

BRINSON, GAY CRESWELL, JR. retired lawyer; b. Kingsville, Tex., June 13, 1925; s. Gay Creswell and Lelia (Wendelkin) B.; m. Bette Lee Butter, June 17, 1979; children from former marriage: Thomas Wade, Mary Kaye. Student, U. Ill., Chgo., 1947-48; BS, U. Houston, 1953, JD, 1957. Bar: Tex. 1957, U.S. Dist. Ct. (so. dist.) Tex. 1959, U.S. ct. Appeals (5th cir.) 1962 U.S. Dist. Ct. (ea. dist.) Tex. 1965, U.S. Supreme Ct. 1974; U.S. Dist. Ct. (no. dist.) Tex. 1990; diplomate Am. Bd. Trial Advocates, Am. Bd. Profl. Liability Attys. Spl. agt. FBI, Washington and Salt Lake City, 1957-59; trial atty. Liberty Mut. Ins. Co., Houston, 1959-62; assoc. Horace Brown, 1962-64, Vinson & Elkins, Houston, 1964-67, ptnr., 1967-91; of counsel McFall, Sherwood & Sheehy, 1992-2000. Lectr. U. Houston Coll. Law, 1964-65; mem. staff Tex. Coll. Trial Advocacy, Houston, 1978-86; prosecutor Harris County Grievance Com.-State Bar Tex., Houston, 1965-70 Served with AUS, 1943-46, ETO. Fellow Tex. Bar Found. (life); mem. Tex. Acad. Family Law Specialists (cert.), Tex. Assn. Def. Counsel, Tex. Bd. Legal Specialization (cert.), Fedn. Ins. Counsel, Nat. Bd. Trial Advocacy (cert.), Houston Ctr. Club, Phi Delta Phi. Federal civil litigation, State civil litigation, Personal injury. Home: 3740 Del Monte Dr Houston TX 77019-3018 Office: McFall Sherwood & Sheehy 2500 2 Houston Ctr 909 Fannin St Houston TX 77010-1001 E-mail: gbrinson@houston.rr.com

BRIONES, DAVID, judge; b. El Paso, Tex., Feb. 26, 1943; m. Delia Garcia; four children. BA, U. Tex., El Paso, 1969; JD, U. Tex., Austin, 1971. Ptnr. Moreno & Briones, 1971-91; judge El Paso County Ct. No. 1, El Paso, 1991-94; dist. judge U.S. DIst. Ct. (we. dist.) Tex., 1994—. With U.S. Army, 1964-66. Fellow Tex. Bar Found.; mem. State Bar of Tex., El Paso Bar Assn., Mexican-Am. Bar Assn. Office: US Courthouse Courtroom 2 511 E San Antonio Ave El Paso TX 79901-2401 E-mail: David_Briones@txwd.uscourts.gov

BRISCOE, JOHN, lawyer; b. Stockton, Calif., July 1, 1948; s. John Lloyd and Doris (Olsen) B.; divorced; children: John Paul, Katherine. JD, U. San Francisco, 1972. Bar: Calif. 1972, U.S. Dist. Ct. (no., ea. and ctrl. dists.) Calif. 1972, U.S. Supreme Ct. 1978, U.S. Ct. Appeals (9th cir.) 1981. Dep. atty. gen. State of Calif., San Francisco, 1972-80; ptnr. Washburn and Kemp, 1980-88, Washburn, Briscoe & McCarthy, San Francisco, 1988—. Bd. dirs. San Francisco Bay Planning coalition, chmn., 1990-93; bd. dirs. U. Calif. Sea Grant Program, Friends of the Bancroft Libr., St. mary's Coll. MFA Program in Creative Writing, Historical Soc. US Dist. COunt, North Dist Calif.; vis. scholar U. Calif., Berkeley, 1990—; spl. adviser UN Compensation Commn., Geneva, Switzerland, 1998-99. Author: Surveying the Courtroom, 1984, rev. edit., 1999, Falsework, 1997; editor: Reports of Special Masters, 1991; contbr. articles to profl. and lit. jours. Mem. ABA, San Francisco Bar Assn., Law of the Sea Inst. Roman Catholic. General civil litigation, Land use and zoning (including planning), Real property. Office: Washburn Briscoe & McCarthy 55 Francisco St San Francisco CA 94133-2122

BRISCOE, MARY BECK, federal judge; b. Council Grove, Ks., Apr. 4, 1947; m. Charles Arthur Briscoe. BA, U. Kans., 1969, JD, 1973; LLM, U. Va., 1990. Rsch. asst. Harold L. Haun, Esq., 1973; atty.-examiner fin. divsn. ICC, 1973-74; asst. U.S. atty. for Wichita and Topeka, Kans. Dept. Justice, 1974-84; judge Kans. Ct. Appeals, 1984-95, chief judge, 1990-95; judge U.S. Ct. Appeals (10th cir.), Topeka, 1995—. Fellow Am. Bar Found., Kans. Bar Found.; mem. ABA, Am. Judicature Soc., Nat. Assn. Women Judges, Topeka Bar Assn., Kans. Bar Assn. (Outstanding Svc. award 1992), Women Attys. Assn. Topeka, Kans. Hist. Soc., Washburn Law Sch. Assn. (hon.), U. Kans. Law Soc. Office: US Ct Appeals 10th Cir 645 Massachusetts Ste 400 Lawrence KS 66044-2235*

BRISKMAN, LOUIS JACOB, lawyer; BA, U. Pitts., 1970; JD, Georgetown U., 1973. Bar: Pa. 1973. Chief counsel Westinghouse Electric Corp., 1978-81; v.p., sec., gen. counsel Group W Cable, Inc. divsn. Westinghouse, 1981-83; v.p., sec. Westinghouse Broadcasting Co., 1983-86; assoc. gen. counsel energy and advanced tech. & broadcasting divsn. Westinghouse, 1986-87; dep. gen. counsel Westinghouse Electric, 1987-92; sr. v.p., gen. counsel Westinghouse Electric Corp., 1993-98; exec. v.p., gen. counsel CBS Corp., N.Y.C., 1998-2000, CBS TV, N.Y.C., 2000—. Communications, General corporate. Office: CBS Corp 51 W 52nd St New York NY 10019-6119

BRISTER, BILL H. lawyer, former bankruptcy judge; b. Sieper, La., Mar. 5, 1930; s. Clayton Houston and Era (Price) B.; m. Carolyn Lee McDowell, June 11, 1955; children— Jeff, Julie. B.S. in Chemistry, Northwestern State U. Natchitoches, La., 1948; J.D., U. Tex., 1958. Bar: Tex. 1957, U.S. Dist. Ct. (no. dist.) Tex. 1959, U.S. Ct. Appeals (5th cir.) 1971, U.S. Supreme Ct. 1971. Pvt. practice, Lubbock, Tex., 1958-79; bankruptcy judge U.S. Dist. Ct. (no. dist.) Tex., 1979-85; of counsel Winstead, Sechrest & Minick and predecessor firm, 1986—. Served to col. USMCR, 1951-52. E-mail: billbrist@aol.com. Bankruptcy. Office: Winstead Sechrest & Minick 5400 Renaissance Tower 1201 Elm St Ste 5400 Dallas TX 75270-2199

BRISTOW, WALTER JAMES, JR. retired judge; b. Columbia, S.C., Oct. 14, 1924; s. Walter James and Caroline Belser (Melton) B.; m. Katherine Stewart Mullins, Sept. 12, 1952; children: Walter James III, Katherine Mullins (dec.). Student, Va. Mil. Inst., 1941-43; AB, U. N.C., 1947; LLB cum laude, U. S.C., 1947-50; LLM, Harvard U., 1950. Mem. Marchant, Bristow & Bates, 1953-76, S.C. Ho. of Reps., 1956-58, S.C. Senate, 1958-76; resident judge 5th Cir. Ct. S.C., 1976-88; ret., 1988. Nat. pres. Conf. Ins. Legislators, 1974-75. Trustee Elvira Wright Fund for Crippled Children, 1963-76; mem. bd. visitors ex officio The Citadel, Charleston, S.C., 1967-76. Served with AUS, 1943-45; ETO, brig. gen. S.C. Army N.G. Decorated Meritorious Svc. medal; recipient Order of Palmetto, 1999, Order of Cypress, 1999. Mem. ABA, Wig and Robe, S.C. Law Inst., S.C. Coun. on Holocaust, Capital City Club, Cotillion Club, Forest Lake Club, Palmetto Club, Columbia Ball Club, Sertoma, Alpha Tau Omega. Democrat. Office: PO Box 1147 Columbia SC 29202-1147

BRITT, W. EARL, federal judge; b. McDonald, N.C., Dec. 7, 1932; s. Dudley H. and Martha Mae (Hall) B.; m. Judith Moore, Apr. 17, 1976. Student, Campbell Jr. Coll., 1952; BS, Wake Forest U., 1956, JD, 1958. Bar: N.C. 1958. Pvt. practice law, Fairmont, N.C., 1959-72, Lumberton, 1972-80; judge U.S. Dist. Ct. (ea. dist.) N.C., from 1980, chief judge, 1983-90, sr. judge, 1997—. Mem. Jud. Conf. Com. on Automation and Tech., 1990-95; 4th cir. dist. judge rep. to Jud. Conf. U.S., 1991-97. Trustee Southeastern Community Coll., 1965-70, Southeastern Gen. Hosp., Lumberton, 1965-69, Pembroke State U., 1967-72; bd. govs. U. N.C. Served with U.S. Army, 1953-55. Mem. N.C. Bar Assn., Fed. Judges Assn. (bd. dirs., v.p., 1993-95, pres. 1995-97). Baptist. Office: US Dist Ct PO Box 27504 Raleigh NC 27611-7504

BRITTAIN, MAX GORDON, JR. lawyer; b. Glens Falls, N.Y., Dec. 22, 1947; s. Max Gordon and Eloise (Wilbur) B.; m. Teresa Ann Hochreiter, Sept. 28, 1984; children by previous marriage: Matthew Greer, Amanda Kelly. B.S., Bradley U., 1969; J.D. cum laude, Loyola U., Chgo., 1976. Bar: Ill. 1976, U.S. Dist. Ct. (no. dist.) Ill. 1976, U.S. Ct. Appeals (7th cir.) 1978, U.S. Supreme Ct. 1980, U.S. Ct. Appeals (fed. cir.) 1984. Assoc., Schiff Hardin & Waite, Chgo., 1976-79, Kovar & Smetana, Chgo., 1979-82; ptnr. Kovar, Nelson & Brittain, Chgo., 1982— ; instr. Loyola U., Chgo., 1981— ; lectr. on labor law. Mng. editor Loyola Law Rev., 1975-76; author: Wrongful Discharge Claims. Mem. ABA, Ill. Bar Assn. Republican. Methodist. Club: Union League (Chgo.). Federal civil litigation, Labor. Home: 515 S Beverly Ln Arlington Heights IL 60005-2103 Office: Kovar, Nelson, Brittain & Sledz 500 Marquette Bldg 400 S Dearborn St Chicago IL 60605-1107

BRITTIGAN, ROBERT LEE, lawyer; b. Columbus, Ohio, Aug. 24, 1942; s. Virgil Devan and Ruth (Clark) B.; m. Sharon Lynn Amore, Aug. 22, 1964; children: Eric Clark, Robert Lee II. BSBA cum laude, Ohio State U., 1964, JD summa cum laude, 1967. Bar: Ohio 1967, U.S. Ct. Mil. Appeals 1974, U.S. Ct. Claims 1977, U.S. Ct. Appeals (5th cir.) 1978, U.S. Ct. Appeals (6th cir.) 1992, U.S. Supreme Ct. 1974. Commd. 2d lt. U.S. Army, 1968, advanced through grades to maj., 1977, chief mil. justice Ga., 1972-73, dep. staff judge adv. 5th Inf. Divsn. (Mech.) Ft. Polk, La., 1974-76, action atty. litig. divsn. Office of JAG Washington, 1976-80, resigned, 1980; gen. counsel Def. Threat Reduction Agy., Washington, 1980—. Col. Res. ret. Decorated Bronze Star medal, Meritorious Svc. medal with oak leaf cluster; recipient Exceptional Civilian Svc. medal Def. Nuc. Agy., Meritorious Civilian Svc. medal, Sec. Defense, Presdl. Rank award, Meritorious Exec. Office: General Counsel Def Threat Reduction Agy 8725 John J Kingman Rd Fort Belvoir VA 22060-6201

BRITTON, CLAROLD LAWRENCE, lawyer, consultant; b. Soldier, Iowa, Nov. 1, 1932; s. Arnold Olaf and Florence Ruth (Gardner) B.; m. Joyce Helene Hamlett, Feb. 1, 1958; children: Laura, Eric, Val, Martha. BS in Engring., U. Mich., Ann Arbor, 1958, JD, 1961, postgrad. Bar: Ill. 1961, U.S. Dist. Ct. (no. dist.) Ill. 1962, U.S. Ct. Appeals (7th cir.) 1963, U.S. Supreme Ct. 1970, Mich. 1989. Assoc. Jenner & Block, Chgo., 1961-70, ptnr., 1970-88; pres. Britton Info. Systems, Inc., 1991—. Lectr. DePaul U., 1988. Author: Computerized Trial Ntoebook, 1991; asst. editor Mich. Law Rev., 1960. Comdr. USNR, 1952-57. Fellow Am. Coll. Trial Lawyers; mem. ABA (litigation sect., antitrust com., past regional chmn. discovery com. 1961), Ill. State Bar Assn. (chmn. Allerton House Conf. 1984, 86, 88, chmn. rule 23 com. 1985-87, chmn. civil practice and procedure coun. 1987-88, antitrust com.), Chgo. Bar Assn. (past chmn. fed. civil procedure com., mem. judiciary and computer law coms., civil practice com.), 7th Cir. Bar Assn., Def. Rsch. Inst. (com. on aerospace 1984), Mich. Bar Assn., Ill. Assn. Trial Lawyers, Order of Coif, Law Club (Chgo.), Racine Yacht Club (Wis.), Macatawa Yacht Club (Mich.), Masons, Alpha Phi Mu, Tau Beta Pi. Republican. Lutheran. Antitrust, Federal civil litigation, State civil litigation. Office: 411 E Washington St Ann Arbor MI 48104-2015 E-mail: britton@ic.net

BRITTON, LOUIS FRANKLIN, lawyer; b. Terre Haute, Ind., Mar. 5, 1953; s. Charles J. and Deneta (Reichert) B.; m. Debra Lynne Brown, May 15, 1977; children: Louis J., Laura Elizabeth. BA cum laude, Ind. U., 1974, JD magna cum laude, 1977. Bar: Ind. 1977, U.S. Dist. Ct. (so. dist.) Ind. 1977, U.S. Ct. Appeals (7th cir.) 1997. Assoc. Cox, Zwerner, Gambill & Sullivan, Terre Haute, 1977-81, ptnr., 1981—. Bd. dirs. Regional Mfrs. Coop. Parish coun. Sacred Heart Ch., 1978-81, St. Benedicts Ch., 1998—; treas. Vigo County Taxpayers Assn., 1995—; v.p. agy. rels., bd. rels., bd. dirs. United Way, 1981-84; v.p., bd. dirs. Terre Haute Humane Soc., 1982-84; pres., bd. dirs. Leadership Terre Haute Alumni Assn., 1984-85, Vigo Preservation Alliance, 1988-89; youth chmn., bd. dirs. local YMCA, 1987-88; bd. dirs. Terre Haute YMCA, 1985-88, Leadership Terre Haute, 1987-90, pres., 1989-90; active Friends of the Sisters of Providence, 1998—. Ira C. Batman fellow, 1976-77; named one of Outstanding Young Men Am., 1982; recipient Outstanding Svc. award Leadership Terre Haute, 1987. Mem. ABA, Ind. Bar Assn., Terre Haute Bar Assn., Terre Haute Area C. of C. (treas. 1999—), Order of Coif, Phi Beta Kappa. Contracts commercial, General practice, Real property. Home: 2206 N 7th St Terre Haute IN 47804-1802 Office: Cox Zwerner Gambill & Sullivan PO Box 1625 Terre Haute IN 47808-1625

BROADBENT, PETER EDWIN, JR. lawyer; b. Richmond, Va., May 16, 1951; s. Peter Edwin and Nancy Talbot (Norris) B.; m. Mary Anna Toms, June 5, 1976; children: Peter Edwin III, Christopher Toms, Elizabeth Talbot. BA, Duke U., 1973; JD, U. Va., 1976. Bar: Va. 1976, U.S. Dist. Ct. (ea. dist.) Va. 1976, U.S. Ct. Appeals (4th cir.) 1976. Assoc. Christian, Barton, Epps, Brent & Chappell, Richmond, Va., 1976-84; ptnr. Christian & Barton LLP, 1984—. Deacon First Presbyn. Ch. Mem. Richmond City Rep. Com., 1973—; nat. committeeman Young Rep. Nat. Com., Washington, 1974-75; mem. state ctrl. com. Rep. Party of Va., 2001—; former v.p., dir. Richmond Teams for Progress; former deacon First Presbyn. Ch.; bd. dirs. Libr. of Va.; bd. dirs. Friends of Va. State Archives. Mem. Va. State Bar Assn. (pub. info. com. 1977-82, 93—, chmn. 1982-85, bd. govs. Bus. Law Sect., 1997-2000, editor Va. Bus. Law, 1995-98), Va. Bar Assn., Richmond Bar Assn., Greater Richmond Intellectual Property Law Assn., Geneal. Rsch. Inst. Va. (past pres., dir. 1984—), Va. Geneal. Soc. (bd. dirs.), Soc. Colonial Wars in Va. (bd. dirs.). Republican. Presbyterian. Avocation: genealogy, politics. Communications, General corporate, Mergers and acquisitions. Home: 5307 Matoaka Rd Richmond VA 23226-2218 Office: Christian & Barton LLP 1200 Mutual Bldg 909 E Main St Richmond VA 23219-3002

BROCK, CHARLES MARQUIS, lawyer; b. Watseka, Ill., Oct. 8, 1941; s. Glen Westgate and Muriel Lucile (Bubeck) B.; m. Elizabeth Bonilla, Dec. 17, 1966; children: Henry Christopher, Anna Melissa. AB cum laude, Princeton U., 1963; JD, Georgetown U., 1968; MBA, U. Chgo., 1974. Bar: Ill. 1969, U.S. Dist. Ct. (no. dist.) Ill. 1969. Asst. trust counsel Continental Ill. Nat. Bank, Chgo., 1968-74; regional counsel Latin Am. Abbott Labs., Abbott Park, 1974-77, regional counsel Europe, Africa, Middle East, 1977-81, divsn. counsel domestic legal ops., 1981-88; assoc. gen. counsel internat. legal ops., asst. sec. Can. Abbott Labs., 1989-92, divsnl. v.p., assoc. gen. counsel, asst. sec., 1992-2000, divsnl. v.p., chief ethics and compliance officer, 2000—. Mem. Coun. Sr. Internat. Legal Officers, The Conf. Bd., N.Y.C., 1999-2000, global coun. bus. conduct, 2000—; bd. dirs. Inst. for Bus. and Profl. Ethics/DePaul U., Chgo. With U.S. Army, 1964-66. Mem. ABA, Ethics Officers Assn., Health Care Compliance Assn., Chgo. Bar Assn., Mich. Shores Club, Phi Beta Kappa. Republican. Contracts commercial, General corporate, Private international. Home: 1440 S Ridge Rd Lake Forest IL 60045-3880 Office: Abbott Labs 100 Abbott Park Rd Abbott Park IL 60064-3502 E-mail: charles.brock@abbott.com, ccmbrock@aol.com

BROCK, DAVID ALLEN, state supreme court chief justice; b. Stoneham, Mass., July 6, 1936; s. Herbert and Margaret B.; m. Sandra Ford, 1960; 6 children. AB, Dartmouth Coll., 1958; LLB, U. Mich., 1963; postgrad., Nat. Jud. Coll., 1977. Bar: N.H. 1963. Assoc. Devine, Millimet, McDonough, Stahl & Branch, Manchester, N.H., 1963-69; U.S. atty. State of N.H.,

1969-72; ptnr. Perkins, Douglas & Brock, Concord, N.H., 1972-74, Perkins & Brock, 1974-76; spl. counsel to gov. and exec. coun. N.H., 1974-76; legal counsel to gov. N.H., 1976; assoc. justice N.H. Superior Ct., 1976-78, N.H. Supreme Ct., 1978-86, chief justice, 1986—. Chmn. State of N.H. Legal Svcs. Adv. Commn., 1977-79; chmn. dist. ct. reform subcom. Gov.'s Commn. for Ct. System Improvement, 1974-75; chmn. N.H. Commn. Ct. Accreditation, 1986—; mem. Select Commn. on Unified Ct. System, 1980-84, chmn. N.H. Supreme Ct. Com. on Jud. Conduct, 1981-89, rules adv. com., 1985-97; mem. State N.H. Jud. Coun., 1979-87; mem. nat. adv. bd. Leadership Inst. for Jud. Edn., 1989-96, Nat. Jud. Coll. long range planning com., 1990-91; mem. Jud. Edn. and Tech. Assistance Consortium, 1989-97; chmn. Interbranch Coun. on Substance Abuse and the Criminal Justice System, 1991-95; bd. dirs. State Justice Inst., 1992-98, vice-chmn., 1994-95, co-chmn., 1995-98; bd. dirs. Conf. Chief Justices, 1993-94, v.p., 1996-97, pres-elect 1997-98, pres., 1998-99; bd. dirs. Nat. Ctr. for State Cts., 1996-2000, chmn.-elect, 1997-98, chmn., 1998-99; mem. Nat. Criminal Justice Info. Svcs. Adv. Policy Bd., 1999—. Bd. dirs. Manchester Cmty. Guidance Ctr., 1966-72, pres., 1969-72; chmn. Manchester Rep. Com., 1967-69; vice chmn. N.H. Rep. State Com., 1968-69; Rep. candidate U.S. Senate, 1972; del. N.H. Constl. Conv., 1974: mem. Gov.'s Commn. for Handicapped, 1978-79. Fellow ABA (mem. edn. com. of appellate judges conf. 1981-97, appellate advocacy com. 1982-84, faculty appellate judges' seminar program 1984-89, del. ho. of dels. 1994-96), N.H. Bar Assn. (chmn. constl. revision com. 1976-77), N.H. Bar Found. (hon.). Office: NH Supreme Ct Noble Dr Concord NH 03301

BROCK, DAVID GEORGE, lawyer; b. Buffalo, Oct. 13, 1945; s. Joseph Louis and Julia Strauss (Amram) B.; m. Marilyn Sandra Katz, May 25, 1969; children: Lauren, Joel. BA in English, Union Coll., 1967; JD, SUNY, Buffalo, 1972. Bar: N.Y. 1973, U.S. Dist. Ct. (we. dist.) N.Y. 1973; cert. civil trial specialist Nat. Bd. Trial Advocacy. Atty. Liberty Mut. Ins. Co., Buffalo, 1973-77; assoc. Jaeckle, Fleischmann & Mugel, 1977-79, ptnr., 1980—. Vice-chair N.Y. State Atty. Grievance Com. (8th judicial dist.), 1994-2000. Bd. dirs. Planned Parenthood Buffalo and Erie County, 1999—, treas., 2001; bd. dirs. Lower West Side Cmty. Enrichment Ctr.; bd. trustees Temple Beth Zion Buffalo, N.Y., 1988-98, pres., 1994-96. Mem. ABA, N.Y. State Bar Assn., Erie County Bar Assn. (chmn. profl. ethics com. 1991-95, bd. dirs. 1996-99), Western N.Y. Trial Lawyers Assn. (bd. dirs. 1993-95), Def. Rsch. Inst., Inc., Am. Arbitration Assn., Internat. Assn. Def. Counsel (bd. editors Def. Counsel Jour. 1992—), Nat. Inst. Trial Adv. Jewish. Avocations: reading, photography. General civil litigation, Insurance, Personal injury. Home: 49 Northington Dr East Amherst NY 14051-1721 Office: Jaeckle Fleischmann & Mugel LLP 12 Fountain Plz Buffalo NY 14202-2292 E-mail: dbrock@jaeckle.com

BROCK, MITCHELL, lawyer; b. Wyncote, Pa., Nov. 10, 1927; s. John W. and Mildred A. (Mitchell) B.; m. Gioia Connell, June 21, 1952; children: Felicity, Marina, Mitchell Hovey, Laura. AB, Princeton U., 1950; LLB, U. Pa., 1953. Bar: N.Y. 1954. Assoc. firm Sullivan & Cromwell, N.Y.C., 1953-59, ptnr., 1960-92, Paris, 1965-68, ptnr. in charge Tokyo, 1987-90. Bd. dirs. Frost Valley YMCA, Oliverea, N.Y., 1980-87, 1990-2000, Am. Found. Blind, 1967-87; pres., trustee Helen Keller Internat., N.Y.C., 1970-87, 90-94, chmn., trustee, 1994-96, sec., 1996—. Served with USN, 1945-46. Mem. Anglers Club, Princeton Club, Ivy Club, Boca Grande Pass Club. Republican. Episcopalian. General corporate, Private international. Home: PO Box 452 Boca Grande FL 33921-0452 E-mail: gimibrock@ewol.com

BROCKELMAN, KENT, lawyer; b. Danville, Ill., Mar. 25, 1959; s. Robert E. and Barbara (Perry) B. BA with high honors, U. Notre Dame, 1981; JD, UCLA, 1984. Bar: Ariz. 1984, U.S. Dist. Ct. 1984, U.S. Ct. Appeals (9th cir.) 1985. Assoc. Fennemore Craig, Phoenix, 1984-86; assoc. Daughton, Hawkins & Bacon, 1986-87, Bryan Cave, Phoenix, 1988-92; ptnr. Daughton, Hawkins, Brockelman & Guinan, 1992-96, Brockelman & Brodman, Phoenix, 1996—. Mem. Am. Inns of Ct., Phoenix, 1991—, pres. 1997-98; judge pro tempore Ariz. Ct. Appeals, Phoenix, 1994—. Editor-in-chief UCLA Law Rev., 1983-84. Mem., recorder Ariz. Town Hall, Phoenix, 1991—. Mem. ABA, State Bar Ariz., Maricopa County Bar Assn. General civil litigation, Labor. Office: Brockelman & Brodman 2 N Central Ave Ste 1750 Phoenix AZ 85004-2395 E-mail: kb@bblawfirm.com

BRODERICK, JOHN T., JR. state supreme court justice; BA magna cum laude, Coll. Holy Cross, 1969; JD, U. Va., 1972. Atty. Devine, Millimet, Stahl & Branch, Manchester, N.H., 1972-89; shareholder Broderick & Dean (formerly Merrill & Broderick), 1989-95; assoc. justice N.H. Supreme Ct., Concord, N.H., 1995—. Bd. dirs. Legal Svcs. Corp. Fellow Am. Coll. Trial Lawyers, N.H. Bar Found. (bd. dirs. 1985-91); mem. ABA, Mass. Bar Assn., N.H. Bar Assn. (bd. govs. 1985-91, pres. 1990-91), N.H. Trial Lawyers Assn. (bd. govs. 1977-82, pres. 1982-83). Office: NH Supreme Ct One Noble Dr Concord NH 03301*

BRODHEAD, DAVID CRAWMER, lawyer; b. Madison, Wis., Sept. 16, 1934; s. Richard Jacob and Irma (Crawmer) B.; m. Nancie Christensen, Aug. 17, 1963; children: Compton, Peter, Christoffer. B.S., U. Wis., 1956, LL.B., 1959. Bar: N.Y. 1960, Wis. 1959, D.C. 1979. Assoc. firm Paul, Weiss, Rifkind, Wharton & Garrison, N.Y.C., 1959-68, ptnr., 1969—. Dir. Centennial Industries, Inc., N.Y.C. Editor-in-chief: Wis. Law Rev, 1958-59. Trustee Collegiate Sch., N.Y.C., 1978-85; vestryman Christ and St. Stephen's Episcopal Ch., 1972-82. Mem. N.Y. State Bar, Assn. of Bar of City of N.Y., Wis. Bar. Assn., D.C. Bar Assn., ABA, Westside C. of C. of City of N.Y. (dir. 1970-83), Order of Coif, Delta Theta Phi Clubs: Washington (Conn.); Holland Soc. of N.Y. Contracts commercial, General corporate, Finance.

BRODSKY, DAVID MICHAEL, lawyer; b. Providence, Oct. 16, 1943; s. Irving and Naomi (Richman) B.; m. Stacey J. Moritz; children: Peter, Isabel, Nell. AB cum laude, Brown U., 1964; LLB, Harvard U., 1967. Bar: N.Y. 1968, U.S. Dist. Ct. (so. dist.) N.Y. 1969, U..S. Ct. Appeals (2d cir.) 1974, U.S. Dist. Ct. (ea. dist.) N.Y. 1977, U.S. Supreme Ct. 1977, U.S. Ct. Appeals (D.C. cir.) 1981, U.S. Ct. Appeals (3d cir.) 1984, U.S. Tax Ct. 1984, U.S. Dist. Ct. (no. dist.) Tex. 1986. Law clk. to U.S. Dist. judge U.S. Dist. Ct. (so. dist.) N.Y., 1967-69; asst. U.S. atty. So. Dist. N.Y., 1969-73; assoc. Guggenheimer & Untermyer, N.Y.C., 1973-75, ptnr., 1976-80; ptnr., chmn. litig. dept. Schulte Roth & Zabel, 1980-99; mng. dir., gen. counsel-Ams., Credit Suisse First Boston, 1999—. Lectr. in field. Co-author: Federal Securities Litigation: A Deskbook for the Practitioner, 1997. Chmn., bd. dirs. N.Y. Lawyers for Pub. Interest, Inc., 1991-94, vice-chmn., 1994-96. Recipient Pathways to Justice award. Fellow Am. Coll. Trial Lawyers (mem. access to justice com., mem. downstate N.Y. com.); mem. ABA, (litig. sect., co-chmn. ann. meeting 1998, co-chmn. trial practice com. 1990-94, task force on jury sys. 1995—), Assn. of Bar of City of N.Y., Anti-Defamation League (exec. com., legal com. 1994—), Am. Law Inst., N.Y. County Lawyers Assn., Fed. Bar Coun., Harvard Club, Scarsdale Golf Club. Jewish. General civil litigation, Criminal, Securities. E-mail: david.brodsky@csfb.com

BRODY, RICHARD ERIC, lawyer; b. N.Y.C., Sept. 9, 1947; s. Harold I. and Lillian C. (Albert) B.; m. V. Jane Cohen, May 25, 1974; children: Lauren, Erica. BA, Washington and Jefferson Coll., 1969; JD, Boston U., 1975. Bar: Mass. 1975, U.S. Dist. Ct. Mass. 1975, U.S. Ct. Appeals (1st cir.) 1975, U.S. Supreme Ct. 1987. Law clk. Mass. Superior Ct., Boston, 1975-76, chief law clk., 1976-77; assoc. Sisson, Lee & Bloomenthal, 1977-78; asst. dist. atty. Atty.'s Office Middlesex County Dist., Cambridge, Mass., 1978-82; assoc. Morrison, Mahoney & Miller, Boston, 1982-85, ptnr., 1985-95, Brody, Hardoon, Perkins & Kesten, Boston, 1995—. Lectr. Nat. Inst. Trial Advocacy, trial practice series Harvard U., Mass. Continuing Legal Edn., Def. Rsch. Inst.; evaluator Middlesex Multi-Door Courthouse, Cambridge, 1989—; mediator Arbitration Forums, Inc., Tarrytown, N.Y., 1989—, cons. Liability Cons., Inc., Sudbury, 1988—; mem. nat. adv. bd. Govtl. Liability Ins., Richmond, 1985—. Trustee Mass. Civil Liability Ins., Boston, 1983-89. Mem. Mass. Bar Assn. (civil litigation sect. coun.), Mass. Assn. Trial Lawyers, Boston Bar Assn., Def. Rsch. Inst., City Solicitors and Town Counsel Assn. Civil rights, General civil litigation, Personal injury. Office: Brody Hardoon Perkins & Kesten 1 Exeter Plz Fl 12 Boston MA 02116-2848

BROEKER, JOHN MILTON, lawyer; b. Berwyn, Ill., May 27, 1940; s. Milton Monroe and Marjorie Grace (Wilson) B.; m. Linda J. Broeker, Dec. 9, 1983; children: Sara Elizabeth, Ross Goddard; stepchildren: Terrance Mercil Jr., Johnny Mercil, Veronica Mercil. BA, Grinnell Coll., 1962; JD cum laude, U. Minn., 1965. Bar: Minn. 1965, Wis. 1982, U.S. Ct. Appeals (8th cir.) 1966, U.S. Dist. Ct. Minn. 1967,. U.S. Tax Ct. 1969, U.S. Ct. Appeals (5th cir.) 1971, U.S. Dist. Ct. (we. dist.) Wis. 1982, U.S. Supreme Ct. 1984. Law clk. to presiding judge U.S. Ct. Appeals (8th cir.), 1965-66; ptnr. Gray, Plant, Mooty, Mooty & Bennett, Mpls., 1966-71, Broeker, Geer, Fletcher & LaFond and predecessor firms, Mpls., 1971-91; v.p., gen. counsel NordicTrack, Inc., 1991-94; founder Broeker Enterprises, 1992—; pres. Legal Mgmt. Strategies, Inc., Mpls., 1994—; of counsel Popham, Haik, Schnobrich & Kaufman, Ltd., 1995-96, Halleland, Lewis, Nilan, Sipkins & Johnson, Mpls., 1996-97; pvt. practice, 1997—. Instr. U Minn. Law Sch., 1967-72; lectr. convs. and seminars, 1969—; lectr. U. Minn. Ctr. for Long Term Care Edn., 1972-77, Gt. Lakes Health Congress, 1972, Sister Kenney Inst., 1972. Contbr. articles to legal jours. Bd. dirs. Minn. Environ. Scis. Found., Inc., 1971-73; bd. dirs. Project Environ. Found., 1977-83, chmn., 1980-82; mem. alumni bd. Grinnell Coll., 1968-71; chmn. MInnetonka Environ. Quality and Natural Resources Commn., 1971-72; trustee The Writers Project, Inc., 1999—. Recipient Outstanding Alumni award Grinnell Coll., 1973. Mem. ABA (forum com. on health law 1978-91), Minn. Bar Assn. (chmn. environ. law com. 1970-72), State Bar Wis., Hennepin County Bar Assn. (chmn. environ. law com. 1976-77, legis. com. 1972-76, health law com. 1977-79), Am. Soc. Hosp. Attys., Minn. Soc. Hosp. Attys., Am. Health Care Assn. (legal coordinating com. 1970-75, labor com. 1973-74), Nat. Health Lawyers Assn., Minn. Thoroughbred Assn. (bd. dirs. 1991-92), Minn. Quarterhorse Racing Assn. (bd. dirs. 1994—, pres. 1997-99), Sierra Club (nat. dir. 1974-76, chmn. chpt. 1971-72, regional v.p. 1973-74). General corporate, Health, Labor. Home: 11402 Burr Ridge Ln Eden Prairie MN 55347-4717 Office: 8120 Penn Ave S Ste 151Q Bloomington MN 55431-1326 E-mail: jbroeker@msn.com

BROGDON, W.M. "ROWE", lawyer; b. Columbia, S.C., Oct. 14, 1953; s. Wallace M. and Helen (Deloach) B.; m. Cynthia S. Brogdon, Feb. 28, 1987; 1 child, Emily Elizabeth. BS in Biology magna cum laude, Ga. So. U., 1976; JD cum laude, Mercer U., 1982. Bar: Ga. 1982. Law clk. to Hon. B. Avant Edenfield U.S. Dist. Ct. (so. dist.) Ga.; ptnr. Smith & Brogdon Attys., Savannah, Ga., 1983-87, Brannan & Brogdon Attys., Claxton, 1987-93, Franklin, Taulbee, Rushing & Brogdon, P.C., Statesboro, 1994-2000; sole practitioner, 2000—. Contbr. articles to profl. jours. Vice chmn. bd. trustees Bulloch Acad. Sch., Statesboro, 1998—; bd. govs. Mercer U. Law Sch., 1979-81. State of Ga. law scholar, 1980. Mem. ATLA, Am. Bd. Trial Advocates, Ga. Trial Lawyers Assn. (chmn. Amicus com. 1996-98, v.p. mid. cir. 1996-97), Atlantic Cir. Bar Assn. (pres. 1991-92), Ogeechee Cir. Bar Assn. (pres. 1996-97), Nat. Bd. Trial Advocacy (cert.), Am. Bd. Trial Advocates, Rotary (treas. 1992-93), Phi Delta Phi. Methodist. Avocation: fishing. General civil litigation, Personal injury, Product liability. Home: 4599 Country Club Rd Statesboro GA 30458-9007 Office: PO Box 189 Statesboro GA 30459-1002 E-mail: rowebrog@frontiernet.net

BROMBERG, ALAN ROBERT, law educator; b. Dallas, Nov. 24, 1928; s. Alfred L. and Juanita (Kramer) B.; m. Anne Ruggles, July 26, 1959. A.B., Harvard U., 1949; J.D., Yale U., 1952. Bar: Tex. 1952. Assoc. firm Carrington, Gowan, Johnson, Bromberg and Leeds, Dallas, 1952-56; atty. and cons., 1956-76; of counsel firm Jenkens & Gilchrist, P.C., 1976—; asst. prof. law So. Meth. U., 1956-58, assoc. prof., 1958-62, prof., 1962-83, Univ. Disting. prof., 1983—, mem. presdl. search group, 1971-72. Faculty adviser Southwestern Law Jour., 1958-65; sr. fellow Yale U. Law Faculty, 1966-67; vis. prof. Stanford U., 1972-73; mem. adv. bd. U. Calif. Securities Regulation Inst., 1973-78, 79-87; counsel Internat. Data Systems, Inc., 1961-65, sec., dir., 1963-65; mem. Tex. Legis. Council Bus. and Commerce Code Adv. Com., 1966-67. Author: Supplementary Materials on Texas Corporations, 3d edit, 1971, Partnership Primer-Problems and Planning, 1961, Materials on Corporate Securities and Finance— A Growing Company's Search for Funds, 2d edit, 1965, Securities Fraud and Commodities Fraud, Vols. 1-7, 1967-93, 2nd edit., 2000, Crane and Bromberg on Partnership, 1968, Bromberg and Ribstein on Partnership, Vols. 1-2, 1988, Vols. 3-4, 1994-2000, Bromberg and Ribstein on Limited Liability Partnerships and the Revised Uniform Partnership Act, 1997-2000; mem. ednl. publs. adv. bd., Matthew Bender & Co., 1977-95, chmn., 1981-94; contbr. articles and revs. to law and bar jours.; adv. editor: Rev. Securities and Commodities Regulation, 1969—, Securities Regulation Law Jour, 1973—, Jour. Corp. Law, 1976—, Derivatives: Tax, Regulation, Finance, 1995-97. Sec., bd. dirs. Community Arts Fund, 1963-73; gen. atty. Dallas Mus. Contemporary Arts, 1956-63 ; bd. dirs. Dallas Theater Center, 1955-73, sec., 1957-66, fin. com., 1957-65, mem. exec. com., 1957-70, 79-85, life, 1973— , v.p., trustee endowment fund, 1974-85; trustee Found. for the Arts, 1996—; bd. dirs. Found. for the Arts, 1996—. Served as cpl. U.S. Army, 1952-54. Mem. ABA (comm. commodities, partnerships, fed. regulation securities), Dallas Bar Assn. (chmn. com. uniform partnership act 1959-61, libr. com. 1981-83), Tex. Bar Assn. (chmn. sect. corp. banking and bus. law 1967-68, vice chmn. 1965-67, com. corps. 1957—, mem. com. securities 1965—, chmn. 1965-69, mem. com. partnerships 1957—, chmn. 1979-81), Am. Law Inst. (life), Southwestern Legal Found. (co-chmn. securities com. 1982-85), Tex. Bus. Law Found. (bd. dirs. 1988—, co-chmn. legis. com. 1994—). Office: So Meth U Sch Law Dallas TX 75275-0001 also: 1445 Ross Ave Ste 3200 Dallas TX 75202-2785

BROMBERG, MYRON JAMES, lawyer; b. Paterson, N.J., Nov. 5, 1934; s. Abraham and Elsie (Baker) B.; m. Lisa Murtha, Nov. 28, 1987; children— Kenneth Karl, Eric Edward, Bruce Abraham. BA, Yale U., 1956; LLB, Columbia U., 1959. Bar: N.J. bar 1960, N.Y. bar 1981. Law asst. to dist. atty., N.Y. County, 1958; law asst. U.S. atty. So. Dist. N.Y., 1958-59; assoc. mem. firm Ralph Porzio, Morristown, N.J., 1960-61; ptnr. Porzio, Bromberg & Newman, 1962-77, mng. prin., 1980-96. Atty. Morris County Bd. Elections, 1963-64; town atty., Town of Morristown, 1965-67; lectr. trial practice Rutgers Inst. CLE, 1965-94; mem. faculty Kraft-Edison trial techniques seminar Emory U., 1997—. Chmn. fund and membership Morristown chpt. ARC, 1965; chmn. retail div. Community Chest Morris County, 1963; chmn. Keep Morristown Beautiful Com., 1963; mem. Morris Twp. Com., 1970-72; committeeman Morris County Democratic Com., 1962-63, 72-77; lay trustee Delbarton Sch., Morristown, 1972-75; trustee Morris Mus., 1973-79. Fellow Am. Coll. Trial Lawyers (chmn. com. on admission to fellowship 1986-91, com. on complex litigation 1992-98, com. on tchg. of trial and appellate advocacy 1998—), Am. Law Inst. (cons. group product libility), Am. Bar Found. (life); mem. ABA, Internat. Acad. Trial Lawyers (chair N.J. 1997-99, regional chair 3d jud. cir. 1997-2000), N.J. Bar Assn. (named outstanding young lawyer 1970, chmn. joint conf. com. with N.J. Med. Soc. 1970-72), Morris County Bar Assn., Am. Judicature Soc., Trial Attys. N.J. (pres. 1976-77, Trial Bar award 1989), Internat. Soc. Barristers (N.J. State chmn., bd. govs., sec.-treas. 1996-97, v.p. 1998-00, pres. 2000-2001), Internat. Assn. Def. Counsel (chair com. on toxic and hazardous substances 1994-96, dir. Def. Counsel Trial Acad. 1996), Andover Alumni Assn. N.Y.C., Columbia U. Law Sch. Assn. of N.J. (bd. dirs. 1986-95), Yale Club (N.Y.C. and ctrl. N.J.), Park Ave. (N.J.) Club, Chi Phi, Phi Delta Phi. Environmental, Product liability, Professional liability. Home: 9 Thompson Ct Morristown NJ 07960-6326 Office: PO Box 1997 100 Southgate Pkwy Morristown NJ 07962-1997 E-mail: mjbromberg@pbnlaw.com

BRONFIN, FRED, lawyer; b. New Orleans, Nov. 30, 1918; m. Carolyn Pick; children by previous marriage: Daniel R., Kenneth A. BA, Tulane U., 1938, JD, 1941. Bar: La. 1941, U.S. Dist. Ct. (ea. dist.) La. 1941, U.S. Ct. Appeals (5th cir.) 1951, U.S. Supreme Ct. 1973. Assoc. Rittenberg & Rittenberg, New Orleans, 1946-50; ptnr. Rittenberg, Weinstein & Bronfin, 1950-60, Weinstein & Bronfin, New Orleans, 1960-63, Bronfin, Heller, Steinberg & Berins and precessor firms, New Orleans, 1963-91; of counsel Bronfin & Heller, 1991-98, Heller, Draper, Hayden, Patrick & Horn, 1998—. With USN, 1942-46. Mem. ABA, La. Bar Assn., New Orleans Bar Assn., Order of Coif, Phi Beta Kappa. Office: Heller Draper Hayden Et Al 650 Poydras St Ste 2500 New Orleans LA 70130-6175 E-mail: fbronfin@hellerdraper.com

BRONIS, STEPHEN JAY, lawyer; b. Miami, Fla., Feb. 23, 1947; s. Larry and Thelma (Berger) B.; children: Jason Michael, Tyler Adam, Kenneth Lawrence. BSBA, U. Fla., 1969; JD, Duke U., 1972. Bar: Fla. 1972, D.C. 1973, U.S. Dist. Ct. (so. dist.) Fla. 1973, U.S. Ct. Appeals (5th cir.) 1977, U.S. Supreme Ct. 1978, U.S. Ct. Appeals (11th cir.) 1981, U.S. Dist. Ct. (mid. dist.) Fla. 1989, Colo. 1994, U.S. Dist. Ct. Colo. 1996, U.S. Ct. Appeals (10th cir.) 1996, U.S. Tax Ct. 1998. Asst. pub. defender 11th Jud. Cir. Fla., Miami, 1972-75; ptnr. Rosen & Bronis, P.A., 1975-77, Rosen, Portela, Bronis, et al, Miami, 1977-82, Bronis & Potela, P.A., Miami, 1982-90; pvt. practice, 1990-93; ptnr. Davis, Scott, Weber & Edwards, 1993-95, Zuckerman, Spaeder, Taylor & Evans, Miami, 1996—. Mem. faculty Nat. Inst. of Trial Adv., U. N.C., Yeshiva U, Nova Sch. Law; appointed to Fla. Supreme Ct. Commn. on Professionalism, 2000—; Fla. Bar rep. to 11th Cir. Jur. Conf., 2001—. Contbr. articles to profl. jours. Recipient Am. Jurisprudence award Bancroft-Whitney Co., 1972. Mem. ABA (ho. of dels. 1999—, Fla. rep. 2000—), ATLA, Nat. Criminal Def. Attys. Assn., Am. Bd. Criminal Lawyers (v.p. 1981-82), Fla. Criminal Def. Attys. Assn. (Outstanding Svc. award 1981), Calif. Attys. Criminal Justice, Acad. Fla. Trial Lawyers (criminal law sect. dir.). Democrat. General civil litigation, General corporate, Criminal. Home: 3 Grove Isle Dr Apt 1506 Miami FL 33133-4103 Office: 201 S Biscayne Blvd Ste 900 Miami FL 33131-4326 E-mail: sbronis@zuckerman.com

BRONNER, WILLIAM ROCHE, lawyer; b. N.Y.C., Mar. 13, 1946; s. Leonard and Gloria (Roche) Bronner; m. Nancy L. Bloomgarden, Oct. 14, 1973; children: Gregory R.B., Caitlin L.B. BA, Dartmouth Coll., 1967; JD, Columbia U., 1970. Bar: N.Y. 1970, U.S. Dist. Ct. (so. and ea. dists.) N.Y. 1972, U.S. Ct. Appeals (2d cir.) 1973, U.S. Ct. Claims 1977, U.S. Ct. Appeals (9th cir.) 1986, U.S. Dist. Ct. (we. dist.) N.Y. 1990, U.S. Ct. Appeals (fed. cir.) 1992, U.S. Internat. Trade, 1995. Law clk. to presiding judge U.S. Dist. Ct. (so. dist.) N.Y., N.Y.C., 1970-72; asst. U.S. atty. State of N.Y., 1972-76; assoc. Burns & Jacoby, 1977; counsel div. NL Industries, 1978-80, counsel govt. affairs, 1980-82, group counsel, 1982-84, assoc. gen. counsel, 1984-87; gen. counsel NL Chems., Inc., 1987-90; v.p., sec., gen. counsel Kronos, Inc., Hightstown, N.J., 1990—; v.p. Electro-Optical Scis., Inc., Irvington, N.Y., 2000—. Federal civil litigation, General corporate, Environmental. Office: Kronos Inc 5 Cedarbrook Dr Cranbury NJ 08512-3618 also: Electro Optical Scis Inc One Bridge St Irvington NY 10533 E-mail: william.bronner@nli-usa.com

BRONSON, BARBARA JUNE, lawyer; b. Malta, Ohio, June 12, 1949; d. Henry and Ilse (Rosenfeld) Bachman; m. Neal Barry Bronson, Aug. 14, 1971; children: Michael J., Alison A. BA, Lake Erie Coll., 1970; JD, U. Cin., 1973. Bar: Ohio 1973. Assoc. James D. Ruppert & Assoc., Franklin, Ohio, 1973-78; ptnr., officer Ruppert, Bronson, Chicarelli & Smith Co., L.P.A., 1978-99, Ruppert, Bronson & Ruppert Co., LPA, Franklin, 2000—. Law librarian Warren County Law Libr. Assn., Lebanon, Ohio, 1977-92. V.p. Warren County Women's Dem. Club, Lebanon, 1984; county coord. Anthony J. Celebrezze for State Atty. Gen., Warren County, 1986; county coord. Anthony J. Celebrezze for Gov., 1990; chmn. Civil Service Commn., Lebanon, 1987—; trustee Warren County Found., 1997—. Named one of Outstanding Young Women in Am., 1982-83, 85. Mem. Warren County Bar Assn. (v.p. 1985-86, pres. 1986-87). General practice, Probate, Real property. Home: 120 Wright Ave Lebanon OH 45036-2253 Office: Ruppert Bronson & Ruppert Co LPA 1063 E 2nd St # 369 Franklin OH 45005-1765 E-mail: bjbronson@ruppertlaw.com

BRONSON, MERIDITH J. lawyer; b. N.Y.C., Dec. 4, 1958; d. Ira D. and Carolyn Bronson; children: Logan Alexa, Jordan Alanna. BA, Drew U., 1980; JD, Seton Hall U., 1984. Cert. matrimonial atty. Jud. law clk., Newark, 1984-85; ptnr. Stern Steiger Croland, Paramus, 1985-95, Shapiro & Croland, Hackensack, N.J., 1995—. Master Family Law Inns of Ct., N.J., 1996—. Mem. Phi Beta Kappa. Family and matrimonial. Office: Shapiro & Croland 411 Hackensack Ave Fl 6 Hackensack NJ 07601-6365

BRONSTEIN, ALVIN J. lawyer; b. Bklyn., June 8, 1928; LLD, N.Y. Law Sch., 1951, LLD (hon.), 1990. Bar: N.Y. 1952, Miss. 1967, La. 1971, U.S. Ct. Appeals (D.C., 1st, 2d, 3d, 4th, 5th, 9th, 10th and 11th cirs.), U.S. Supreme Ct. 1961. Ptnr. Bronstein & Bronstein, Bklyn., 1952-63; pvt. practice Elizabethtown, N.Y., 1963-64; chief staff counsel Lawyers Constl. Def. Com., Jackson, Miss., 1964-68; fellow Inst. Politics, Kennedy Sch. Govt. Harvard U., Cambridge, Mass., 1968-69, assoc. dir. Inst. Politics, Kennedy Sch. Govt., 1969-71; ptnr. Elie, Bronstein, Strickler & Dennis, New Orleans, 1971-72; exec. dir. Nat. Prison Project, Nat. Jail Project ACLU Found., Washington, 1972-96, cons. nat. legal dept., 1996—. Cons., trial counsel CORE, NAACP, NAACP Legal Def. Fund, SCLC, SNCC, Miss. Freedom Dem. Party, Black Panther Party, Nat. Inst. for Edn. in Law and Poverty, and others; guest lectr. various law schs., 1964—; cons. various state corrections depts., 1972—; adj. prof. Am. U. Law Sch., 1973; expert witness in various prison litigations, 1978—; appointed mem. Fed. Jud. Ctr. Adv. Com. on Experimentation in the Law, 1978-81. Contbg. author: The Evolution of Criminal Justice, 1978, Prisoners' Rights Sourcebook, Vol. II, 1980, Confinement in Maximum Custody, 1980, Sage Criminal Justice Annual, Vol. 14, 1980, Readings in the Justice Model, 1980, Our Endangered Rights, 1984, Prisoners and the Courts: The American Experience, 1985; author: (with Rudovsky and Koren) The Rights of Prisoners, 1988; author, editor: Representing Prisoners, 1981; editor: Prisoners' Self-Help Litigation Manual, 1977; contbr. articles to profl. jours. MacArthur Found. fellow, 1989; named one of the 100 most influential lawyers in Am., Nat. Law Jour., 1985, 88, 91, 94; recipient Roscoe Pound award Nat. Coun. on Crime and Delinquency, 1981, Karl Menninger award Fortune Soc., 1982, Pa. Prison Soc. award, 1991. Office: Nat Prison Project ACLU Found 733 15th St NW Washington DC 20005

BROOKE, EDWARD WILLIAM, lawyer, former senator; b. Washington, Oct. 26, 1919; s. Edward W. and Helen (Seldon) B. B.S., Howard U., 1940, LL.D., 1967; LL.B. (editor Law Rev.), Boston U., 1948, LL.M., 1949, LL.D., 1968, George Washington U., 1967, Skidmore Coll., 1969, U. Mass., 1971, Amherst Coll., 1972; D.Sc., Lowell Tech. Inst., 1967; D.Sc. numerous other hon. degrees. Bar: Mass. 1948, D.C. Ct. Appeals 1979, D.C. Dist. Ct. 1982, U.S. Supreme Ct. 1962. Chmn. Boston Fin. Com., 1961-62; atty. gen. State of Mass., Boston, 1963-66; mem. U.S. Senate from Mass., 1967-79; chmn. Nat. Low-Income Housing Coalition; former ptnr. O'Connor & Hannan, Washington; formrly of counsel Csaplar & Bok, Boston. Former pub. mem. Adminstrv. Conf. U.S.; chmn. bd. dirs. Boston Bank Commerce; bd. dirs. Meditrust, Inc., Wellesley, Mass., Grumman

Corp., Bethpage, N.Y. Chmn. Boston Opera Co.; former commr. Pres.'s Commns. on Housing and of Wartime Relocation and Internment of Civilians; bd. dirs. Washington Performing Arts Soc. Served as capt. inf. AUS, World War II, ETO. Decorated Bronze Star; recipient Disting. Svc. award Amvets, 1952, Charles Evans Hughes award NCCJ, 1967, Springarn medal, NAACP, 1967 Fellow Am. Bar Assn., Am. Acad. Arts and Scis. Office: 6437 Blantyre Rd Warrenton VA 20187-7147

BROOKMAN, ANTHONY RAYMOND, lawyer; b. Chgo., Mar. 23, 1922; s. Raymond Charles and Marie Clara (Alberg) B.; m. Marilyn Joyce Brookman, June 5, 1982; children: Meribeth Brookman Farmer, Anthony Raymond, Lindsay Logan Christensen. Student, Ripon Coll., 1940-41; BS, Northwestern U., 1947; JD, U. Calif., San Francisco, 1953. Bar: Calif. 1954. Law clk. to presiding justice Calif. Supreme Ct., 1953-54; ptnr. Nichols, Williams, Morgan, Digardi & Brookman, 1954-68; sr. ptnr. Brookman & Talbot, Inc. (formerly Brookman & Hoffman, Inc.), Walnut Creek, Calif., 1969-92, Brookman & Talbot Inc., Sacramento, 1992—. Pres. Young Reps. Calif., San Mateo County, 1953-54. 1st lt. USAF. Mem. ABA, Alameda County Bar Assn., State Bar Calif., Lawyers Club Alameda County, Alameda-Contra Costa County Trial Lawyers Assn., Assn. Trial Lawyers Am., Calif. Trial Lawyers Assn., Athenian Nile Club, Masons, Shriners. Republican. General civil litigation, State civil litigation, Personal injury. Office: 901 H St Ste 200 Sacramento CA 95814-1808 also: Ste B-201 675 Ygnacio Valley Rd Walnut Creek CA 94596 also: 1746 Grand Canal Blvd Ste 11 Stockton CA 95207-8111

BROOKS, DANIEL TOWNLEY, lawyer; b. N.Y.C., Apr. 15, 1941; s. Robert Daniel and Mary (Lee) B.; m. Barbara Ann Badertscher, June 16, 1973; children: Daniel Townley, Jr., Andrei Matthew. BS in Engring. cum laude, Princeton U., 1963; LLB, Stanford U., 1967, MS in Engring., 1968. Bar: Calif. 1968, U.S. Dist. Ct. (no. dist.) Calif. 1968, U.S. Ct. Appeals (9th cir.) 1968, N.Y. 1970, U.S. Ct. Appeals (2d cir.) 1972, Va. 1982, D.C. 1998. Assoc. Cadwalader, Wickersham & Taft, N.Y.C., 1968-79; atty. U.S. SEC, Washington, 1979-81; with Computer Law Advisers, Springfield, Va., 1981-85; ptnr. Cadwalader, Wickersham & Taft, Washington, 1985-98, sr. counsel, 1998-2000; sr. v.p., gen. counsel Trading Edge, Inc., 2000—. Cons. and lectr. in computer law. Mem. ABA, IEEE, Calif. Bar Assn. (inactive), N.Y. State Bar Assn., Va. Bar Assn., D.C. Bar Assn., Computer Law Assn. Inc. (bd. advisors), Assn. Computing Machinery. Administrative and regulatory, Computer, General corporate. Home: 6106 Lorcom Ct Springfield VA 22152-1320 Office: Trading Edge Inc 1130 Connecticut Ave NW Washington DC 20036-3904 E-mail: dbrooks@tradingedge.com

BROOKS, DAVID VICTOR, lawyer; b. Sendai, Japan, May 22, 1948; came to U.S., 1951, naturalized, 1975; s. David Kenneth and Mary Victoria (Gooding) B.; m. Deborah Ann Gary, Nov. 14, 1970 (div. 1983); m. Mary Bonnie Kemp, July 7, 1984; children: Meredith Maxwell, Healther Branan, Matthew David, Sarah Rose. BA with high honors, N.C. State U., 1974; JD, U. N.C., 1977. Bar: N.C. 1977, U.S. Ct. Mil. Appeals 1978, U.S. Dist. Ct. (ea. dist.) N.C. 1980. Sr. trial atty. Naval Legal Svc. Office, Pearl Harbor, Hawaii, 1977-78; tort claims atty. Norfolk, Va., 1978-80; assoc. Maupin, Taylor & Ellis, P.A., Raleigh, N.C., 1980-84, ptnr., 1984-85; chmn. N.C. Indsl. Commn., 1985-87; mng. ptnr. Brooks, Stevens & Pope, P.A., Cary, N.C., 1987—. Author: The New Book of Rights, 1998. Bd. dirs. Mid-State Safety Coun., Henderson, N.C., 1983—; gen. counsel N.C. Rep. Party, Raleigh, 1983-85; dist. commr. Boy Scouts Am., Raleigh, 1981—. Capt. USMC, 1966-72, Vietnam; lt. comdr. USN, 1977-80. Decorated Silver Star medal, Navy and Marine Corps medal, Bronze Star, Purple Heart. Mem. ABA, N.C. Bar Assn., Am. Soc. Safety Engrs., Wake County Bar Assn., VFW, Lions. Lutheran. Republican. Labor, Workers' compensation. Home: 107 Redfern Dr Cary NC 27511-8610 Office: NC Indsl Commn Dobbs Bldg 2000 Regency Pkwy Ste 150 Cary NC 27511-8581

BROOKS, LARRY ROGER, judge; b. Oklahoma City, Mar. 8, 1949; s. Stanley James and Dorothy Marguerite (Miller) B.; m. Rebecca Jean Nix, June 5, 1971. BS in Agronomy, Okla. State U., 1971, MS in Agronomy, 1973; JD, U. Okla., 1976. Bar: Okla. 1976. Pvt. practice law, Idabel, Okla., 1977; asst. dist. atty. Craig County Dist. Attys. Office, Vinita, 1978, Logan County Dist. Attys. Office, Guthrie, 1979-94; assoc. judge Dist. Ct., Logan County, 1995—. Ch. bd. mem. Guthrie (Okla.) Ch. of the Nazarene. Mem. Okla. Bar Assn., Guthrie Lions Club (pres. 1991-92), Train Collectors Assn., Nat. Ry. Hist. Soc. Avocations: toy train and railroad memorabilia, railroad history, riding trains. Home: 324 N Capitol St Guthrie OK 73044-3640 Office: Assoc Dist Judge Logan County Courthouse Guthrie OK 73044

BROOKS, PATRICK WILLIAM, lawyer; b. May 11, 1943; s. Mark Dana and Madge Ellen (Walker) B.; m. Mary Jane Davey, Dec. 17, 1966; children: Carolyn Walker, Mark William. BA, State Coll. Iowa, 1966; JD, U. Iowa, 1971. Bar: Iowa 1971, U.S. dist. Ct. (so. dist.) Iowa 1972, U.S. Sup. Ct. 1974, U.S. Ct. apls. (8th cir.) 1979. Tchr. Waterloo (Iowa) Cmty. Schs., 1966-68; mem. staff Donahue & Brooks, West Union, Iowa, 1971-72; ptnr. Mowry, Irvine, Brooks & Ward, Marshalltown, 1972-84, 92—, Brooks, Ward & Trout, Marshalltown, 1984-92. Mem. Fayette County (Iowa) Republican Ctrl. com., chmn. platform resolutions com., 1971-72; pres. Marshall County Young Reps., 1974; trustee Iowa Law Sch. Found., 1970-71; bd. dirs. Iowa Hist. Found., 1991-96. Mem. Am. Judicature Soc., Iowa Bar Assn., Marshall County Bar Assn. (pres. 1985-86), Iowa Trial Lawyers Assn., Iowa Def. Counsel Assn., Buick Am. Club (bd. dir. 2001—). Lutheran. Avocations: international road rally driver and mechanic. Federal civil litigation, Insurance, Personal injury. Office: Box 908 6 W Main St Marshalltown IA 50158-4941

BROOKS, ROBERT FRANKLIN, SR. lawyer; b. Richmond, Va., July 13, 1939; s. Robert Noel Brooks and Annie Mae (Edwards) Miles; m. Patricia Wilson, May 6, 1972; children: Robert Franklin Jr., Thomas Noel, Courtenay M. Brooks Rainey. BA, U. Richmond, 1961, M of Humanities, 1993; JD, 1964. Bar: Va. 1964, N.Y. 1985, U.S. Dist. Ct. (ea. and we. dists.) Va. 1964, U.S. Ct. Appeals (4th cir.) 1965, U.S. Ct. Appeals (5th cir.) 1972, (2d cir.) 1979, (11th cir.) 1981, D.C. 1977, U.S. Supreme Ct. 1979. Assoc. Hunton & Williams, Richmond, 1964-71, ptnr., 1971—. Chmn. sect. II 3d Dist. Com., 1983; mem. rules evidence com. Supreme Ct. Va., 1984-85; mem. Fourth Cir. Judicial Conf. Trustee U. Richmond, chmn. exec. com., 1998-99, 99—. Fellow ABA, Am. Coll. Trial Lawyers (com. atty.-client relationships 1983-91, chmn. Va. state com. 1993-94), Am. Bar Found., Va. Law Found.; mem. N.Y. Bar Assn., D.C. Bar Assn., Va. State Bar (coun. 1986—, bd. govs. litigation sect. 1984-90, sec. 1985-86, chmn. 1986-87, com. lawyer fin. responsibility 1986-89, nominating com. 1990, spl. com. election methods 1989, chmn. bench-bar rels. com. 1987-88, faculty professionalism course 1988-90, governance com. 1990-91), Richmond Bar Assn. (chmn. judiciary com. 1985-87, chmm. com. on unprofl. conduct 1979-80, com. on improvement of adminstrn. of justice 1981-84), Va. Bar Assn. (profl. responsibility com. 1981-84). Federal civil litigation, State civil litigation. Home: 500 Kilmarnock Dr Richmond VA 23229-8102 Office: Hunton & Williams Riverfront Plz East Tower 951 E Byrd St Ste 200 Richmond VA 23219-4074

BROOKS, SONDRA, lawyer; b. Bklyn., Mar. 29, 1957; d. Frank Harry and Roslyn Louise Brooks; m. Lance Hillel Edwards, May 29, 1982; children: Devon Wesley, Alexandra Nell. BS, SUNY, Stony Brook, 1978; JD, Syracuse U., 1981. Bar: N.Y. 1982, U.S. Dist. Ct. (so. dist.) N.Y. 1982, U.S. Supreme Ct. 1985. Asst. dist. atty. Nassau County Dist. Attys. Office, Mineola, N.Y., 1981-87; asst. county atty. Suffolk County Attys. Office, Hauppauge, 1987-88; ptnr. Boland & Brooks, Smithtown, 1988—. Legal cons. Plaza Employment Agy., Lynbrook, N.Y., 1981—, Suffolk Ob-gyn. Assn., Pt. Jefferson, N.Y., 1981—. Editor Deviance and Delinquency, 1978, Syracuse Law Rev., 1980-81. Named Hon. Asst. Atty. Gen., State Ark., 1983, Outstanding Young Women of Am., 1986. Mem. NOW, Nassau County Bar Assn., Suffolk County Womens Bar Assn. (award 1995). Jewish. Avocations: weight training, tennis, reading, art history, travel. Criminal, Family and matrimonial, Personal injury. Home: 12 Crane Neck Rd East Setauket NY 11733-1628 Office: 222 E Main St Ste 212 Smithtown NY 11787-2814

BROOKS, SUSAN W. prosecutor; Grad., Miami U.; JD, Ind. U. Ptnr. McClure, McClure & Kammen, 1985—88, Kammen & Brooks, 1989—97; dep. mayor Indpls., 1998—99; of counsel Ice Miller Law Firm of Indpls.; U.S. atty. so. dist. Ind., 2001—. Office: 10 W Market St Ste 2100 Indianapolis IN 46204 Office Fax: 317-226-6125*

BROOKS, WILLIAM FERN, JR. lawyer; b. Kansas City, Mo., Sept. 2, 1926; s. William Fern and Gertrude Octavia (Kendig) B.; m. Jean A. Geggie, June 22, 1951; children— William Fern III, Elizabeth C. B.A., Union Coll., Schenectady, 1946; LL.B., U. Minn., 1961. Bar: Minn. 1961, U.S. Dist. Ct. Minn. 1961. Spl. asst. atty.-gen. State of Minn., 1961-64; ptnr. Chestnut, Jones, Brooks & Kennedy, Mpls., 1965-71; mem., officer Chestnut & Brooks, P.A., Mpls., 1971— . Pres. Newspaper Guild of Twin Cities, AFL-CIO, Mpls., 1958-60, The Lawyers Credit Union, 1986—, Minn. Tax Found., 1987—; chmn. Minn. Commn. on Alcohol Problems, St. Paul, 1971-75. With USNR, 1944-46, PTO. Mem. Minn. Bar Assn., ABA. Mem. Democratic Farm Labor Party. Episcopalian. Club: Minnesota (St. Paul). Administrative and regulatory, Legislative. Office: Chestnut & Brooks PA 3700 Piper Jaffray Towers Minneapolis MN 55402

BROOKS, WILLIAM JAMES, III, lawyer; b. West Palm Beach, Fla., Aug. 5, 1953; s. William James and Mary Helen (Olson) B; m. Anna Marie Frances Bourgeois, Sept. 29, 1979; children: William James IV, James Andrew. BA, Mt. Union Coll., 1974; JD, U. Notre Dame, 1977; LLM in Taxation, Emory U., 1985. Bar: Minn. 1977, U.S. Dist. Ct. Minn., 1977. Asst. revisor Revisor of Statutes, St. Paul, 1977-78; assoc. counsel Investors Diversified, Inc., Mpls., 1978-80; ptnr. Brooks & Moehn, P.A., 1981-84; asst. gen. counsel Farm Credit Services, St. Paul, 1985-86; ptnr. Brooks & Brooks, P.A., Bloomington, Minn., 1986-94. Bd. dirs. Common Line, Inc. Mem. Minn. Bar Assn. Republican. Roman Catholic. Estate planning, Estate taxation, Personal income taxation. Home and Office: 7712 Stonewood Ct Edina MN 55439-2641

BROOME, BARRY DEAN, lawyer, estate and financial planning consultant; b. Gaffney, S.C., Jan. 24, 1942; s. Walter Dean and Virginia Mae (Moss) B.; BA, U. Cen. Fla., 1973, J.D., Atlanta Law Sch., 1987; m. Janis M. Black, Feb. 14, 1969; children— Gina Michelle, Tina Marie, Jana Malia, Barry Dean II. Pres., Barry Broome Co., estate and fin. planning, Jacksonville, Fla., 1963-78; dir. tng. and sales devel. Gulf Life Ins. Co., Jacksonville, 1978-81; adj. instr. fin. planning Ga. State U.; cons. to ins. cos. in so. states, Dunwoody, Ga., 1981— ; advisor to securities industry in S.E. Mem. fin. com. North Fla. council Boy Scouts Am., 1978-81; fin. chmn. various Republican candidates on state and local level; mem. bishopric Ch. of Jesus Christ of Latter-day Saints, 1974-75, stake pres., 1976-80, mem. high council, 1975-76; bd. dirs. Housing Initiative of North Fulton Inc. Recipient spl. commendation Health Ins. Assn. Am., 1981; C.L.U.; chartered fin. cons. Mem. Am. Soc. C.L.U.s, Internat. Assn. Fin. Planning, Nat. Assn. Life Underwriters, Am. Arbitration Assn., Internat. Platform Assn. Contbr. articles on advanced underwriting to profl. publs. Home: 1125 Pinebloom Dr Roswell GA 30076-2633 Office: 9800 Old Dogwood Rd Roswell GA 30075-4612

BROOMFIELD, ROBERT CAMERON, federal judge; b. Detroit, June 18, 1933; s. David Campbell and Mabel Margaret (Van Deventer) B.; m. Cuma Lorena Cecil, Aug. 3, 1958; children: Robert Cameron Jr., Alyson Paige, Scott McKinley. BS, Pa. State U., 1955; LLB, U. Ariz., 1961. Bar: Ariz. 1961, U.S. Dist. Ct. Ariz. 1961. Assoc. Carson, Messinger, Elliot, Laughlin & Ragan, Phoenix, 1962-65, ptnr., 1966-71; judge Ariz. Superior Ct., 1971-85, presiding judge, 1974-85; judge U.S. Dist. Ct. Ariz., 1985—, chief judge, 1994-99. Faculty Nat. Jud. Coll., Reno, 1975-82. Contbr. articles to profl. jours. Adv. bd. Boy Scouts Am., Phoenix, 1968-75; tng. com. Ariz. Acad., Phoenix, 1980—; pres. Paradise Valley Sch. Bd., Phoenix, 1969-70; bd. dirs. Phoenix Together, 1982—, Crisis Nursery, Phoenix, 1976-81; chmn. 9th Cir. Task Force on Ct. Reporting, 1988—; space and facilities com. U.S. Jud. Conf., 1987-93, chmn., 1989-93, chmn. security, space and facilities com., 1993-95, budget com., 1997—. Recipient Faculty award Nat. Jud. Coll., 1979, Disting. Jurist award Miss. State U., 1986. Mem. ABA (chmn. Nat. Conf. State Trial Judges 1983-84, pres. Nat. Conf. Met. Cts. 1978-79, chmn. bd. dirs. 1980-82, Justice Tom Clark award 1980, bd. dirs. Nat. Ctr. for State Cts. 1980-85, Disting. Svc. award 1986), Ariz. Bar Assn., Maricopa County Bar Assn. (Disting. Pub. Svc. award 1980), Ariz. Judges Assn. (pres. 1981-82), Am. Judicature Soc. (spl. citation 1985), Maricopa County Med. Soc. (Disting. Svc. medal 1979). Lodge: Rotary. Office: US Dist Ct Sandra Day O'Connor Cthse 401 West Washington St #626 Phoenix AZ 85003-2158

BROOTEN, KENNETH EDWARD, JR. retired lawyer, writer, chief counsel United States Congress; b. Kirkland, Wash., Oct. 17, 1942; s. Kenneth Edward Sr. and Sadie Josephine (Assad) B.; m. Patricia Anne Folsom, Aug. 29, 1965 (div. Apr. 1986); children: Michelle Catherine, Justin Kenneth; m. Judy Diane Robinette, July 14, 2001. Diploma, Lewis Sch. Hotel, Restaurant and Club Mgmt., Washington, 1963; student, U. Md., 1964-66; AA with honors, Santa Fe C.C., Gainesville, Fla., 1969; BS in Journalism with highest honors, U. Fla., 1971, MA in Journalism and Communications with highest honors, 1972, JD with honors, 1975; law student, U. Idaho, 1972-73; diploma in internat. law, Polish Acad. Scis., Warsaw, 1974; postgrad. in Internat. Law, Cambridge (Eng.) U., Eng., 1974. Bar: Fla., D.C., U.S. Dist. Ct. (no., mid. and so. dists.) Fla., U.S. Dist. Ct. D.C., U.S. Tax Ct., U.S. Ct. Appeals (5th, 9th, 11th and D.C. circs.), U.S. Supreme Ct., Trial Counsel Her Majesty's Govt. of United Kingdom. Asst. to several congressmen U.S. Ho. of Reps., Washington, 1962-67; adminstrv. asst. VA Cen. Office, 1967, adminstrv. officer VA Hosp., Gainesville, Fla., 1967-72; ptnr. Carter & Brooten, P.A., 1975-78, Brooten & Fleisher, Chartered, Washington and Gainesville, 1978-80; pvt. practice, 1980-86, Washington, 1987-88, Washington and Orlando, Fla., 1988-91, Washington and Winter Park, 1991-98; ret., 1998. Permanent spl. counsel, acting chief counsel, dir. Select Com. Assassinations U.S. Ho. of Reps., 1976-77; counsel Her Majesty's Govt. of U.K. (in U.S.). Author: Malpractice Guide to Avoidance and Treatment, 1987; episode writer TV series Simon and Simon; nat. columnist Pvt. Practice, 1988-90, Physicians Mgmt., 1991-93; commentator Med. News Network, 1993-94; contbr. more than 250 articles to profl. jours.; composer. Served with USCGR, 1960-68. Named one of Outstanding Young Men Am., U.S. Jaycees, 1977. Mem. Fla. Bar Assn., D.C. Bar Assn., Sigma Delta Chi. Roman Catholic. Avocations: writing, marksmanship, dangerous game hunting. Federal civil litigation, Family and matrimonial, Public international. Address: 606 Overlook Dr Flat Rock NC 28731-9361

BRORBY, WADE, federal judge; b. 1934; BS, U. Wyo., 1956, JD with honor, 1958. Bar: Wyo. County and prosecuting atty. Campbell County, Wyo., 1963-70; ptnr. Morgan Brorby Price and Arp, Gillette, 1961-88; judge U.S. Ct. Appeals (10th cir.), Cheyenne, 1988-2001, sr. judge, 2001—. With USAF, 1958-61. Mem. ABA, Campbell County Bar Assn., Am. Judicature Soc., Def. Lawyers Wyo., Wyo Bar Assn. (commr. 1968-70). Office: US Ct Appeals 10th Cir O'Mahoney Fed Bldg Rm 2018 PO Box 1028 Cheyenne WY 82003-1028*

BROSS, JAMES LEE, law educator; b. Cin., June 17, 1944; s. Leo Joseph and Winifred Marie (Huber) B.; m. Nancy Marie Beale, Dec. 17, 1966; children: Jackson, Liesl. AB in English, Cath. U. Am., 1966, JD, 1969; LLM, U. Pa., 1971. Bar: D.C. 1969, Pa. 1969, U.S. Dist. Ct. (ea. dist.) Pa. 1970, U.S. Ct. Appeals (D.C. cir.) 1969. Staff atty. Cmty. Legal Svcs., Phila., 1969-71; prof. law Lewis and Clark Coll., Portland, Oreg., 1971-77; assoc. prof. IIT Chgo. Kent Law Sch., Chgo., 1977-81; prof. law Ga. State U., Atlanta, 1982—. Ptnr. Land Use Systems Assocs., Oak Park, Ill., 1981-82; cons. Oreg. Tenants Reform Coalition, Portland, 1972-74, Ga. Legislature, Atlanta, 1982—; dir. Neighborhood Law Inst., Portland, 1973-77. Author: Property Law, 1975; mem. editl. bd. Probate and Property, 1987-92; contbr. articles to profl. jours. Bd. dirs. Northwest Environ. Def. Ctr., Portland, 1974-75; active Cmty. Design Commn., Oak Park, 1978-82, Oak Park Com. on Sign Regulation, 1981-82; adviser DeKalb County Civic Assn., Ga., 1983—. Ford Found. fellow U. Pa., 1969-71. Mem. ABA, Am. Planning Assn., Soc. Am. Law Tchrs. Democrat. Mem. Soc. of Friends. Home: 1377 Mclendon Ave NE Atlanta GA 30307-2065 Office: Ga State U Sch Law PO Box 4037 140 Decatur St Atlanta GA 30302-4037

BROSS, STEWARD RICHARD, JR. lawyer; b. Lancaster, Pa., Oct. 25, 1922; s. Steward Richard and Katherine Mauk (Hoover) B.; m. Isabel Florence Kenney, May 10, 1943; 1 dau., Donna Isabel Bross Campagna. Student, McGill U., Montreal, Can., 1940-42; LLB, Columbia U., 1948. Bar: N.Y. 1948. Pvt. practice, N.Y.C.; ptnr. Cravath, Swaine & Moore, 1958-92, ret., 1992; adv. com. fgn. direct investment program Office of Sec. Dept. Commerce, 1969; adv. com. regulations Office Fgn. Direct Investment, 1968-70. Regent, trustee emeritus The Cathedral Ch. of St. John the Divine, N.Y.C.; warden emeritus Trinity Ch., N.Y.C. Served as officer Canadian Navy, 1942-45. Mem. ABA, N.Y. State Bar Assn., Assn. of Bar of City of N.Y., Pilgrims U.S., Econ. Club N.Y., Union Club, Rockefeller Center Club, Links Club, Univ. Club N.Y. General corporate. Home: 215 E 68th St New York NY 10021-5718 also: Ashgrove 130 Litchfield Rd Norfolk CT 06058-1252 also: 3200 Wailea Alanui Dr Apt 1101 Kihei HI 96753-7757 Office: Cravath Swaine & Moore 825 8th Ave New York NY 10019-7475

BROSSMAN, MARK EDWARD, lawyer; b. N.Y.C., Aug. 13, 1953; s. Isadore Jack and Blanche Brossman. BS, Cornell U., 1975; JD, NYU, 1978, LLM in Labor Law, 1981. Bar: N.Y. 1979, U.S. Dist. Ct. (so. and ea. dists.) N.Y. 1979, U.S. Dist. Ct. (no. and we. dists.) N.Y. 1981, U.S. Ct. Appeals (6th cir.) 1981, U.S. Ct. Appeals (2d cir.) 1983, U.S. Supreme Ct. 1983, U.S. Ct. Appeals (11th cir.) 1989. Assoc. Morgan, Lewis and Bockius, N.Y.C., 1978-83, Grutman, Miller et al, N.Y.C., 1984-85, ptnr., 1985-86; counsel Chadbourne and Parke, 1986-87, ptnr., 1987-98, Schulte, Roth & Zabel, N.Y.C., 1998—. Lectr. Cornell U., 1983—; adj. asst. prof. NYU, 1983—. Author: Social Investing for Pension Funds, 1982; contbr. articles to profl. jours. Mem. ABA, Assn. of Bar of City of N.Y. State Bar Assn., Indsl. Rels. Research Assn., Phi Kappa Phi. Office: Schulte Roth & Zabel LLP 919 Third Ave New York NY 10022

BROSTRON, JUDITH CURRAN, lawyer; b. Chgo., Feb. 2, 1950; d. Norman William and Marianne Cecelia (Baron) Curran; m. Kenneth C. Brostron, Nov. 22, 1989. Diploma Nursing, Evanston (Ill.) Hosp., 1971; BA, Nat. Coll. Edn., Evanston, 1981; JD, Chgo.-Kent Coll. Law, 1985; LLM, St. Louis U., 1999. Bar: Mo. 1985, U.S. Dist. Ct. (ea. dist.) Mo. 1985, Ill. 1986. Staff nurse Evanston Hosp., 1971-78, St. Francis Hosp., Evanston, Ill., 1979-81; assoc. Lashly & Baer, P.C., St. Louis, 1985-91, ptnr., 1991—. Mem. ABA, Am. Assn. Nurse Attys., Am. Soc. Law Medicine, Mo. Bar Assn., Ill. Bar Assn. Avocations: running, golf, gardening. Administrative and regulatory, Health, Personal injury. Office: Lashly & Baer P C 714 Locust St Saint Louis MO 63101-1699

BROUDE, RICHARD FREDERICK, lawyer, educator; b. L.A., June 6, 1936; s. Leo Martin and Frances (Goldman) B.; m. Paula Louise Galnick, June 8, 1958; children: Julie Sue, James Matthew, Mark Allen. BS, Washington U., St Louis, 1957; JD, U. Chgo., 1961. Bar: Ill. 1961, Calif. 1971, N.Y. 1989. Prof. law U. Nebr., Lincoln, 1966-69, Georgetown U., Washington, 1969-71; ptnr. Commons & Broude, L.A., 1974-77, Irell & Manella, L.A., 1977-80, Sidley & Austin, L.A., 1980-87, White & Case, L.A., 1987-90, Mayer, Brown & Platt, N.Y.C., 1990-99. Adj. prof. law U. So. Calif., L.A., 1978-90, St. Johns U., 2000—; adv. panel World Bank Insolvency Initiative. Author: Reorganizations Under Chapter 11, 1986-2001, Cases and Materials on Land Financing, 3d edit., 1985; editor: Insolvency and Finance in the Transportation Industry, 1993, Collier Internat. Bus. Guide; mem. editl. bd. Collier on Bankruptcy; contbg. editor Collier Bankruptcy Practice Guide. Fellow Am. Bar Found., Am. Coll. Bankruptcy; mem. ABA (com. on bus. bankruptcy), Am. Law Inst. (advisor Transnat. Insolvency Project), Internat. Bar Assn. (chair insolvency and credit rights com. 1996-2000), Bar Assn. of City of N.Y., Calif. Bar Assn., Nat. Bankruptcy Conf. (conferee, chair com. on internat. aspects, vice chair legis. com.). Bankruptcy, Contracts commercial. Office: Law Offices of Richard Broude 400 E 84th St # 22A New York NY 10028-5616 E-mail: rbroude@compuserve.com

BROUS, THOMAS RICHARD, lawyer; b. Fulton, Mo., Jan. 7, 1943; s. Richard Pendleton and Augusta (Gilpin) B.; m. Patricia Catlin, Sept. 12, 1964; (dec. Sept. 1999); children: Anna Catlin Brous, Joel Pendleton Brous; m. Mary Lou McClelland Kroh, Sept. 8, 2001. BSBA, Northwestern U., 1965; JD cum laude, U. Mich., 1968. Bar: Mo. 1968, U.S. Dist. Ct. (we. dist.) Mo. 1968, U.S. Ct. Mil. Appeals 1968, U.S. Supreme Ct. 1971. Assoc. Watson & Marshall L.C., Kansas City, Mo., 1968-78, ptnr., 1978-96, mng. ptrn., 1992-94; shareholder Stinson, Mag & Fizzell, P.C., 1996—. Mem. steering com. U. Mo. Kansas City Law Sch. Employee Benefits Inst., 1990—, chmn. 1992-93; mid-states key dist. EP/EO coun. IRS, 1997—. Author: Chapter 26, III Missouri Business Organizations, 1998; asst. editor Mich. Law Rev., 1966-68. Mem. vestry St. Andrews Episcopal Ch., Kansas City, 1974-77, Grace & Holy Trinity Cathedral, 1994—, chancellor, 1998—; trustee Mo. Repertory Theatre, Inc., Kansas City, 1990—, pres., 1995-98; v.p., treas. Barstow Sch., Kansas City, 1982-86; dir. Met. Orgn. to Counter Sexual Abuse, Kansas City, 1992-95. Capt. U.S. Army, 1968-72. Mem. ABA, Univ. Club (pres. 1988-89), Greater Kansas City Soc. Hosp. Attys., Kansas City Met. Bar Assn., Heart of Am. Employee Benefit Conf., The Mo. Bar Assn. (vice-chair employee benefits com. 1997-2000), Mo. Soc. Hosp. Attys., Delta Upsilon, Beta Gamma Sigma. Episcopalian. Avocations: reading, hiking, gardening. General corporate, Health, Pension, profit-sharing, and employee benefits. Office: Stinson Mag & Fizzell PC PO Box 419251 Kansas City MO 64141-6251 E-mail: tbrous@stinson.com

BROWDY, JOSEPH EUGENE, lawyer; b. Bklyn., July 23, 1937; s. Philip and Fannie (Asherowitz) B.; m. Anita Sue Rubenstein, June 18, 1958; childrenF: Jennifer, Daniel. BA, Oberlin Coll., 1958; LLB, NYU, 1961. Bar: N.Y. 1962, D.C. 1982. Assoc. Paul, Weiss, Rifkind, Wharton & Garrison, N.Y.C., 1962-71, ptnr., 1972-97, of counsel, 1998—. Adj. asst. prof. real estate NYU, 1976-86; lectr. in field. With U.S. Army Res., 1961-62. Mem. Assn. of Bar of City of N.Y. (com. real property law, chmn. subcom. on leasing 1989-92), Am. Coll. Real Estate Lawyers, Order of Coif, Phi Beta Kappa. Real property. Office: Paul Weiss Rifkind Wharton & Garrison 1285 Avenue of the Americas New York NY 10019-6065 E-mail: jbrowdy@paulweiss.com

BROWER, CHARLES NELSON, lawyer, judge; b. Plainfield, N.J., June 5, 1935; s. Charles Hendrickson and Mary Elizabeth (Nelson) B.; m. Carmen Elena Wiechmann-Yañez, May 23, 1987; children: Michael Claudio Joseph Hutchings, Carmen Désirée Ponti, Frederica Anne Amity,

Jasmin Maria Ponti, Charles Hendrickson II. BA cum laude, Harvard U., 1957, JD, 1961; cert. Parker Sch. Comp. & Internat. Law, Columbia U., 1962. Bar: N.Y. 1962, D.C. 1970, U.S. Supreme Ct. 1967, U.S. Ct. Appeals (D.C. cir., 2d, 5th, 6th, 7th, 8th, 9th, 11th and fed. cirs.), U.S. Ct. Inernat. Trade, U.S. Dist. Ct. (so. and ea. dists.) N.Y., U.S. Dist. Ct. D.C. Assoc., then ptnr. White & Case LLP, N.Y.C., 1961-69; asst. legal adviser European affairs Dept. State, Washington, 1969-71, dep. legal adviser, 1971-73, acting legal adviser, 1973; ptnr. White & Case LLP, 1973-84, 88-00, spl. counsel, 2001—; mem. 20 Essex St. Chambers, London, 2001—. Judge Iran-U.S. Claims Tribunal, The Hague, 1984-88, 2001—, substitute judge, 1983-84, 88-2000; dep. spl. counselor to the Pres., Washington, 1987; counsel and advocate for U.S., 1992, Costa Rica, 1998, Internat. Ct. Justice, The Hague, 1992; mem. Register of Experts, UN Compensation Commn., 1991—; mem. sec. of state adv. com. on internat. law, 1996—; mem. panel of arbitrators and conciliators Internat. Ctr. for Settlement of Investment Disputes, 1998—; judge ad hoc Inter-Am. Ct. of Human Rights, 1999—. Fulbright scholar Rheinische Friedrich-Wilhelms-Universitaet, Bonn, and Hochschule fuer Politik, Berlin, 1957-78. Mem. ABA (chmn. sect. internat. law 1981-82, mem. ho. of dels. 1982, 84-98, bd. govs. 1985-88, mem. nominating com. 1992-94), Internat. Law Assn. (hon. v.p. Am. br.), Internat. Bar Assn., Am. Soc. Internat. Law (v.p. 1994-96, pres. 1996-98, hon. v.p. 1998—), Am. Law Inst., Assn. of Bar of City of N.Y., Coun. Fgn. Rels., Inst. Transnat. Arbitration (chmn. adv. bd. 1994-2000), Southwestern Legal Found. (trustee 1996—), Met. Club, Chevy Chase Club. Episcopalian. Federal civil litigation, Private international, Public international. Home and Office: Parkweg 2585 JH The Hague The Netherlands E-mail: cbrower@20essexst.com, amarbs@compuserve.com, cbrower@whitecase.com

BROWER, DAVID JOHN, lawyer, urban planner, educator; b. Holland, Mich., Sept. 11, 1930; s. John J. and Helen (Olson) B.; m. Lou Ann Brown, Nov. 26, 1960; children: Timothy Seth, David John, II, Ann Lacey. B.A., U. Mich., 1956, J.D., 1960. Bar: Ill. 1960, Mich. 1961, Ind. 1961, U.S. Supreme Ct. 1971. Asst. dir. div. community planning Ind. U., Bloomington, 1960-70; rsch. prof. dept. city and regional planning U. N.C., Chapel Hill, 1970—, assoc. dir. Ctr. for Urban and Regional Studies, 1970-94; pres. Coastal Resources Collaborative, Ltd., Chapel Hill and Manteo, N.C., 1980—; counsel Robinson & Cole, Hartford, Conn., 1986—. Vis. prof., Vt. Law Sch., South Royalton, summers, 1994—. Author: (with others) Constitutional Issues of Growth Management, 1978; Growth Management, 1984, Managing Development in Small Towns, 1984, Special Area Management, 1985, Catastrophic Coastal Storms, 1989, Understanding Growth Management, 1989, Coastal Zone Management: An Evaluation, 1991, An Introduction to Coastal Zone Management, 1994, Natural Hazard Mitigation, 1999. Mem. Am. Planning Assn. (bd. dirs. 1982-85, chmn.-founder planning and law div. 1978, co-chmn. substainable devel. group 1995—), Am. Inst. Cert. Planners. Democrat. Episcopalian. Home: 612 Shady Lawn Rd Chapel Hill NC 27514-2009 Office: U NC Cb # 3140 Chapel Hill NC 27599-0001 E-mail: brower@email.unc.edu

BROWN, ALAN CRAWFORD, lawyer; b. Rockford, Ill., May 12, 1956; s. Gerald Crawford and Jane Ella (Herzberger) B.; m. Dawn Lestrud, Apr. 16, 1998; children: Parker Crawford, Sydney Danielle, Sarah Kate, Drew Kristen, Connor Austin. BA magna cum laude, Miami U., Oxford, Ohio, 1978; JD with honors, U. Chgo., 1981. Bar: Ill. 1981, U.S. Dist. Ct. (no. dist.) Ill. 1981, U.S. Tax Ct. 1986. Assoc. Kirkland & Ellis, Chgo., 1981-87; sr. assoc. Coffield Ungaretti Harris & Slavin, 1987-89; ptnr. McDermott, Will & Emery, 2001—, Neal, Gerber & Eisenberg, Chgo., 2001. Deacon Northminster Presbyn. Ch., Evanston, Ill., 1989-92; apiarist Chgo. Botanic Garden, Glencoe, Ill., 1988-97; active Kenilworth (Ill.) Union Ch. Mem. Order of Coif, Phi Beta Kappa. Estate planning, Probate, Estate taxation. Office: Neal Gerber & Eisenberg Ste 2200 LaSalle St Chicago IL 60602-3801 E-mail: acbrownesq@aol.com , abrown@ngelaw.com

BROWN, BONNIE MARYETTA, lawyer; b. North Plainfield, N.J., Oct. 31, 1953; d. Robert Jeffrey and Diana (Parket) B. AB, Washington U., St. Louis, 1975; JD, U. Louisville, 1978. Bar: Ky. 1978, U.S. Dist. Ct. (we. dist.) Ky. 1979, U.S. Dist. Ct. (ea. dist.) Ky. 1993. Pvt. practice, Louisville, 1978—; of counsel Morris, Garlove, Waterman and Johnson PLLC, 1998—. Lectr., seminar leader various profl., ednl., govtl. and civic groups; cons. marital rape; registered lobbyist 1994 Ky. Gen. Assembly for Ky. Assn. Marriage and Family Therapy. Editor Ky. Appellate Handbook, 1985; contbr. articles to profl. jours. Vol. legal panel Ky. Civil Liberties Union, Louisville, 1984—; author, chief lobbyist Marital Rape Bill, Ky. Coalition Against Rape and Sexual Assault, 1984-90, Sexual Harassment bill, 1996; vol. advocate Louisville RAPE Relief Ctr., 1975—; treas. Family Support Group/Family Readiness Program. of USAR, 1994-96, 3d Bat., 2nd. bge, 87th divsn., 1996-2000, acting coord. 10th bat., 6th bge, 100th divsn. Recipient Cert. Spl. Recognition RAPE Relief Ctr., 1980, Cert. Outstanding Contbn., Louisville YWCA, 1983, Cert. of Appreciation, James Graham Brown Cancer Ctr., 1984, Decade of Svc. award YWCA/Rape Relief Ctr., Outstanding Victim Adv. award Fayette County Govt., 1990, cert. of Recognition Jefferson County Family Ct., 1995. Mem. ABA (family law sect., apptd. to appellate handbook com., jud. adminstrn. divsn. lawyers conf.), Am. Acad. Matrimonial Lawyers (interdisciplinary com., legis. com., treas. Ky. chpt. 1999—), Ky. Bar Assn. (family law sect., chair 1996-97, seminar spkr., task force solo practtioners and small law firms 1992, chair subcom. on law office automation and networking, solo practitioner and small Law Firm sect., chmn. 1999-2000, CLE award 1981, 93, 97-2001, Louisville Bar Assn. (liaison to mental health sect., organizer marital rape seminar, chmn. family law sect., mediation com. property divsn., seminar spkr., organizer joint custody child abuse seminars, solo practitioner and small law firm sect., chair 1995, pro bono consortium), Ky. Acad. Trial Attys. (spkr. seminar, editor The Advocate family law sect. 1995-2001), Bus. and Profl. Women (pres. River City chpt. 1983-84), Ky. Fedn. (legis. chair 1986-87, 90-92, legal counsel 1992, 96, 97-2001, lobby corps chair 1993-95), Louisville Internat. Cultural Ctr. Republican. Avocations: basketball fan, classic cars. State civil litigation, Family and matrimonial. Office: Ste 1000 One Riverfront Plz Louisville KY 40202

BROWN, BRUCE ANDREW, lawyer; b. Cleve., Oct. 16, 1959; s. Andrew and Ruby Louise (Bishop) B. BA, Brown U., 1981; JD, Columbia U., 1984. Bar: N.Y. 1985, Ohio 1990. Assoc. Proskaver Rose Goetz and Mendelsohn, N.Y.C., 1983-86, Finley, Kumble Wagner Heine Vnderberg Manley Myerson & Casey, N.Y.C., 1986-87; pvt. practice B. Andrew Brown & Assocs., Cleve., 1987—. Mem. NAACP, Urban League (bd. dirs. 1988—), Omega Psi Phi. Democrat. Muslim. Avocation: golf. Office: B Andrew Brown & Assocs 1300 Bank One Ctr 600 Superior Ave E Cleveland OH 44114-2611

BROWN, CHARLES DODGSON, lawyer; b. N.Y.C., Dec. 31, 1928; s. James Dodgson and Leonora Rose (Nichols) B.; m. Martha Lockhart Spindler, Apr. 5, 1963; children: Gregory Spindler, William Howard. BA, NYU, 1949, JD, 1952. Bar: N.Y. 1952, U.S. Dist. Ct. (so. and ea. dists.) N.Y. 1955, U.S. Supreme Ct. 1958, U.S. Ct. Appeals (2d cir.) 1988. Counsel, former ptnr. Thacher Proffitt & Wood, N.Y.C., 1954—. Co-author: Equipment Leasing, 1995—. Chmn. zoning bd. Asharoken, N.Y., 1965, alt. chmn. environ. bd., 1967, trustee, 1967, village justice, 1980—; chmn. Boy Scout Am., Northport, N.Y., 1989—; elder 1st Presbyn. Ch., Northport; mem. admiralty law inst. faculty Tulane U. Sch. Law, 1999. With U.S. Army, 1952-54. Mem. ABA, N.Y. Bar Assn., Maritime Law Assn. U.S. (proctor in Admiralty 1956, former chair to marine fin. com. 1996-2000), N.Y. State Magistrate Assn., Suffolk County Magistrate Assn., Northport Tennis Club. Republican. Avocations: scuba diving, wind surfing, tennis. Admiralty. E-mail: cbrown@tpwlaw.com, cbrown2@tpwlaw.net

BROWN, DAVID JAMES, lawyer; b. Nyack, N.Y., Aug. 10, 1952; m. Liane Davis (dec. Oct. 1995); children: Elia Brown-Davis, Anthony Brown-Davis; m. Mary Klayder. BA in Journalism, U. Ky., 1976; JD, Union U., 1989. Bar: N.Y. 1990, Kans. 1990. Reporter, then asst. editor Rotterdam (N.Y.) Reporter, 1972; truck assembler Walter Motor Truck Co., Voorheesville, N.Y., 1973-75; news editor Corbin (Ky.) Times-Tribune, 1977-79; reporter, copy editor, then weekend regional editor Albany (N.Y.) Times Union, 1979-86; rsch. asst. Union U. Albany Law Sch., 1987-88; rsch. atty. ctrl. staff Kans. Ct. Appeals, Topeka, 1990-91, rsch. atty. for Chief Judge Mary Beck Briscoe, 1991-92; pvt. practice, Lawrence, Kans., 1992—. Legal asst. Prisoners' Legal Svcs., Albany, summer 1987; guest lectr. Rockefeller Coll. Pub. Affairs and Policy, SUNY, Albany, 1988; lectr. U. Kans., Sch. Journalism, 1989. Contbg. author: Practitioner's Guide to Kansas Family Law, 1997, update author 1999, 2001, Judicial Politics. Readings from Judicature, 2d edit., 1999. Bd. dirs. Douglas County AIDS Project, 1991-94, vice chmn., 1992-93, sec., 1993-94; vol. mediator Kans. Children's Svc. League, 1991-92; mem. Lawrence City Human Rels. Commn., 1994—, vice chmn., 1999-00, pres., 2000-2001. Named Ky. col., 1979. Mem. ABA, Kans. Bar Assn., Douglas County Def. Bar Assn. (joint organizer, pres. 1997-2000), Douglas County Bar Assn. (sec.-treas. 1997-98, v.p. 1999-00, pres. 2000-01), Judge Hugh Means Am. Inn Ct. (charter, recorder 1997-2001, membership chair 2001—, publicity chair 1999—), Douglas County Law Library (formation comm. 2000-2001, bd trustees 2001—). Family and matrimonial, General practice, Probate. Office: 1040 New Hampshire St Ste 14 Lawrence KS 66044-3044 E-mail: djbrown@IDIR.net

BROWN, DAVID NELSON, lawyer; b. Harrodsburg, Ky., May 29, 1940; s. Irmel Nelson and Pauline (Harmon) B.; m. Lois Aileen Everett, June 20, 1964; 1 child, Ian Richard. A.B., Cornell U., 1963; J.D., U. Chgo., 1966; Bar: D.C. 1967. Assoc., Covington & Burling, Washington, 1966-74, ptnr., 1974—. mgmt. com. Covington & Burling, 1989-93. Comment editor U. Chgo. Law Rev. Mem. ABA, Order of Coif, Cosmos Club. Episcopalian. General corporate, Private international, Securities. Office: Covington & Burling 1201 Pennsylvania Ave NW Washington DC 20004-2401 E-mail: dbrown@cov.com

BROWN, DAVID RONALD, lawyer; b. Turtle Creek, Pa., Jan. 25, 1939; s. James R. and Mary A. (Barnes) B.; children: Michelle, Adrienne, Aaron, Eden, Jeremy. Student, Brown U., 1956-57; BS, U. Pitts., 1960; JD, Duquesne U., 1967. Bar: Penn. 1967, U.S. Dist. Ct. (we. dist.) Penn. 1967, U.S. Ct. Appeals (3d cir. 1972, U.S. Tax Ct. 1986. Rschr. phys. chemistry Mellon Inst., Pitts., 1960-66; real estate lawyer Redevel. Authority of Allegheny County, 1966-69; ptnr. Litman, Litman, Harris & Brown, 1969-2000, Sherrard, German & Kelly, Pitts., 2000—. Lectr. Robert Morris Coll., 1978-84. Councilman Borough of Turtle Creek, Penn., 1963-67. Mem. ABA (real property and probate sect., com. title ins., bus. law sect.), Allegheny County Bar Assn. (com. legal svcs. 1973-74, real property com., probate and trust law com.). Contracts commercial, Probate, Real property. Home: 1411 Grandview Ave Apt 202 Pittsburgh PA 15211-1157 Office: Sherrard German & Kelly 35th Fl Free Markets Ctr Pittsburgh PA 15222

BROWN, DICK TERRELL, lawyer; b. Houston, Feb. 6, 1944; s. Archie Scales and Margaret Denman (Terrell) Brown; 1 child, Melissa Anne. BS in Mech. Engring., U. Tex.-Austin, 1965; JD, St. Mary's U., San Antonio, 1972. Bar: Tex. 1973, U.S. Dist. Ct. (we. dist.) Tex. 1977, U.S. Dist. Ct. D.C. 1984, U.S. Ct. Appeals (5th cir.) 1984. Assoc. Matthews, Nowlin, MacFarlane & Barrett, San Antonio, 1973-77; ptnr. McCamish, Martin, Brown and Loeffler, P.C., San Antonio, 1977-84, Austin, 1984-91, Brown & Lacallade, P.C., 1991—. Republican. Episcopalian. Administrative and regulatory, State civil litigation, Public utilities. Home: Ste Ii300 1250 S Capital Of Texas Hwy Austin TX 78746-6495 Office: Brown & Lacallade PC Ste Ii300 1250 S Capital Of Texas Hwy Austin TX 78746-6495

BROWN, DONALD JAMES, JR. lawyer; b. Chgo., Apr. 21, 1948; s. Donald James Sr. and Marian Constance (Scimeca) B.; m. Donna Bowen, Jan. 15, 1972; children: Megan, Maura. AB, John Carroll U., 1970; JD, Loyola U., Chgo., 1973. Bar: Ill. 1973, U.S. Dist. Ct. (no. dist.) Ill. 1973, U.S. Tax Ct. 1982. Asst. to state's atty. Cook County, Ill., 1973-75; assoc. Baker & McKenzie, Chgo., 1975-82, ptnr., 1982-95, Donohue, Brown, Mathewson & Smyth, Chgo., 1995—. State civil litigation, Personal injury. Office: Donohue Brown et al 140 S Dearborn St Chicago IL 60603-5202

BROWN, DOUGLAS COLTON, lawyer; b. N.Y.C., Sept. 2, 1948; s. Robin Colton and Catherine (Snyder) B. BA, Ohio Wesleyan U., 1970; JD., Calif. Western U., 1973. Bar: Wash. 1973, U.S. Ct. Mil. Appeals 1974, U.S. Supreme Ct. 1978, Calif. 1979, U.S. Dist. Ct. (so. dist.) Calif. 1979, U.S. Ct. Appeals (9th cir.) 1980, U.S. Dist. Ct. (ctrl. dist.) Calif. 1987. Judge adv. gen. Marine Corps, 1973-77; pvt. practice law, 1977—. Capt. USMC, 1973-77. Mem. Nat. Assn. Criminal Def. Attys., Calif. Attys. for Criminal Justice, San Diego Criminal Def. Lawyers Club. Avocation: travel. Criminal, Military. Office: Home Savings Tower 225 Broadway Ste 1400 San Diego CA 92101-5028

BROWN, EDWARD MAURICE, retired lawyer, business executive; b. Watertown, N.Y., Aug. 22, 1909; s. Ernest E. and Eunice (Lewis) B.; m. Anne Amos, Oct. 2, 1937; children— Edward Dustin, Ernest Amos. AB magna cum laude, Miami U., 1931, LLD, 1972; JD, Harvard U., 1934. Bar: Ohio 1934, N.Y. 1948, U.S. Supreme Ct. 1941. Assoc. Nichols, Wood, Marx & Ginter, 1934-47; asst. to pres. McCall Corp., N.Y.C., 1947-49, v.p., asst. sec., 1949-51, v.p., sec., dir., 1951-57; treas. Sperry Gyroscope Co. div. Sperry Rand Corp., 1958-59, v.p., treas., 1959-60, v.p., adminstr., 1960-65; v.p. Sperry Group, 1965-68; asst. treas. Sperry Rand Corp., 1958-68; group exec. of Teledyne, Inc., 1968-80; chmn. bd. Teledyne Can. Ltd., 1971-81. Trustee Village of Pelham Manor, N.Y., 1961-65, village mayor, 1965-67; mem. bd. govs. Nat. Ctr. for Disability Svcs., 1965-93. Lt. comdr. USNR, 1942-45. Decorated Bronze Star with Combat "V" award for svc. Mem. ABA, Phi Beta Kappa, Phi Eta Sigma, Phi Sigma, Beta Theta Pi. Republican. Episcopalian. Home and Office: 25 Ivywood Sq Oxford OH 45056-9494 E-mail: ebrown3@woh.rr.com

BROWN, FRANK EDWARD, lawyer; b. Roanoke, Va., Sept. 8, 1959; s. Robert Edward and Frances Geraldine B.; m. Elizabeth Barrett Wilson, Jan. 7, 1992. BA, U. N.C., 1983; JD, Fla. State U., 1987. Bar: Fla., U.S. Dist. Ct. (mid. dist.) Fla. 1988, U.S. Dist. Ct. (so. dist.) Fla. 1990, U.S. Dist. Ct. (no. dist.) Fla. 1991, U.S. Ct. Appeals (11th cir.) 1992. Assoc. Carlton, Fields, et al, Tampa, Fla., 1987-98; sr. asst. atty. gen. State of Fla., Tallahassee, 1989-94; assoc. Zinober & McCrea, P.A., Tampa, 1996, shareholder, 1997—. Author: (with others) 11th Circuit Civil Practice Guide, 1998. Mem. ABA, Fed. Bar Assn., Fla. Bar Assn. (co-chair employee benefits com. 1988—). Avocations: outdoor recreation, wine tasting. Civil rights, Labor. Office: Zinober & McCrea, P.A. Ste 800 201 E Kennedy Blvd Tampa FL 33602

BROWN, FRANK EUGENE, JR. lawyer; b. Okemah, Okla., May 30, 1941; s. Frank Eugene and Mary Lois (Knie) B.; m. Gail Hart, Sept. 30, 1967; children— Christopher Matthew, Meredith Claire. B.A. in Physics Engring., Washington and Lee U., 1963. J.D. summa cum laude, 1965. Bar: Va. 1965, U.S. Dist. Ct. (ea. and we. dists.) Va. 1965, U.S. Supreme Ct. 1971, U.S. Ct. Appeals (4th cir.) 1976, U.S. Ct. Appeals (D.C. cir.) 1978. Law clk. to chief judge U.S. Dist. Ct. (we. dist.) Va., Roanoke, 1965-66; teaching asst. Washington and Lee Sch. Law, Lexington, Va., 1965-66; ptnr. Adams, Porter, Radigan & Mays, Arlington, Va., 1970-74, Barham, Radigan, Suiters & Brown, P.C., Arlington, 1974-86, ptnr. Tolbert, Smith, Fitzgerald & Stackhouse, 1986-87, Mays & Valentine (merged with Tolbert, Smith & Fitzerald), Arlington, 1987—; adj. prof. Potomac Sch. Law, Washington, 1974-75. Mem. Christian social relations com. St. Paul's Episc. Ch., Alexandria, Va., 1981-82; trustee Randolph-Macon Acad., Front Royal, Va., Served to capt. USAF, 1966-70. Mem. Va. State Bar (10th dist. grievance com. 1976-79), Va. Bar Assn. (profl. responsibility com. 1981—), Phi Beta Kappa, Order of Coif, Omicron Delta Kappa, Sigma Phi Epsilon, Phi Alpha Delta. Republican. Federal civil litigation, State civil litigation, Contracts commercial. Home: 504 Woodland Ter Alexandria VA 22302-3317 Office: Mays & Valentine 1660 International Dr # 600 Mc Lean VA 22102-4848

BROWN, GARY WAYNE, lawyer; b. Picher, Okla., Apr. 7, 1942; s. Andrew Ellis and Rosabell (Duree) B.; m. Alice Jo Bell, Feb. 15, 1969; children— Marc Andrew, Joshua Lawrence. AA, Northeastern Okla. A&M Jr. Coll., 1962; BS, U. Okla., 1964, J.D., 1967. Bar: Okla. 1967, U.S. Ct. Appeals for the Armed Forces 1968, D.C. 1970, U.S. Dist. Ct. D.C. 1970, U.S. Supreme Ct. 1974, U.S. Ct. Fed. Claims 1976, Va. 1978, U.S. Dist. Ct. (ea. dist.) Va. 1978, U.S. Ct. Appeals D.C., U.S. Ct. Appeals (4th cir.). With Sachs, Greenebaum, Frohlich & Taylor, Washington, 1970-72; ptnr. Macleay, Lynch, Bernhard, Gregg & Attridge, Washington, 1972-85; ptnr. Bromley, Brown & Walsh, 1985-90; ptnr., managing ptnr. Miles & Stockbridge, Fairfax, 1970-75; prin., chmn. bd. McClandish & Lillard, P.C.; adj. prof. law Georgetown U., 1970-75, adj. asst. prof. med. sch., 1994-97. Contbg. author:Justice and the Military, 1972. Co-pres., bd. dirs. Juvenile Diabetes Found., No. Va. chpt., 1980-81; adv. bd. Salvation Army, Fairfax County, 1994—. Served to lt. JAG, USNR, 1967-70. Mem. Def. Rsch. Inst., D.C. Def. Lawyers (pres. 1984, Lawyer of Yr. 1996), Va. Def. Lawyers, Am. Health Lawyers Assn., The Counsellors. Democrat. Episcopalian. Federal civil litigation, Insurance, Personal injury. Home: 4909 Rock Spring Rd Arlington VA 22207-2705 Office: McLandlish & Lillard PC Fair Oaks Plaza 11350 Random Hills Rd Fairfax VA 22030-6044 E-mail: gwb@mclandlaw.com

BROWN, GEORGE E. judge, educator; b. Hammond, Ind., July 27, 1947; s. George E. and Violet M. (Matlon) B.; m. Patricia A. Schneider, June 6, 1970; children: Janet M., Elizabeth A. BS, Ball State U., 1969; JD, DePaul U., 1974; grad., Ind. Jud. Coll., 1996. Bar: Ind. 1974, Ill. 1974, U.S. Dist. Ct. (no. dist.) Ind. 1979, U.S. Supreme Ct. 1977, U.S. Tax Ct. 1977. Pvt. practice, LaGrange & Lake Counties, Ind., 1974-84; judge LaGrange County Ct., 1984-87, LaGrange Superior Ct., 1988—. Part-time chief dep. prosecutor LaGrange County, 1975—77; adj. faculty Tri-State U., Angola, Ind., 1991—. Vol. Jr. Achievement, 1997-2000, 01—. Mem.: ABA, Ind. State Bar Assn. (no. of dels., com. on written pub.), LaGrange County Bar Assn. (pres. 1978), Nat. Conf. State Trial Judges (criminal justice com.), Ind. Judges Assn. (com. protective orders), LaGrange Rotary (past dir., v.p. 1999—2000, pres. 2000—01). Office: Lagrange Superior Ct Courthouse Lagrange IN 46761

BROWN, G(LENN) WILLIAM, JR. bank executive; b. Waynesville, N.C., June 9, 1955; s. Glenn William and Evelyn Myralyn (Davis) B.; m. Amy Margaret Moss, Apr. 14, 1984; children: Elizabeth Quinn, Lauren Alexandra. BS in Biology, BS in Polit. Sci., MIT, 1977; JD, Duke U., 1980. Bar: N.Y., 1980. Assoc. Donovan Leisure Newton & Irvine, N.Y.C., 1980-84, Sidley & Austin, N.Y.C., 1984-87, ptnr., 1988-89; v.p. Goldman Sachs & Co., 1990-94; exec. dir. Goldman Sachs Internat. Fin., London, 1994-96; sr. v.p. AIG Internat. Inc., Greenwich, Conn., 1996-97; prin. Morgan Stanley & Co., Inc., N.Y.C., 1997, mng. dir., co-head at global FX sales, 1997—. Mem. ABA, Am. Fin. Assn. Presbyterian. Home: 31 Lindsay Dr Greenwich CT 06830-3402 Office: Morgan Stanley Co 1585 Broadway Frnt 4 New York NY 10036-8200 E-mail: bill.brown@morganstanley.com

BROWN, HAROLD MACVANE, lawyer; b. Colon, Panama, Oct. 2, 1940; s. Harold MacVane and Geraldine (Lynch) B.; m. Susan Murphy, June 20, 1970; children: Molly Curran, Katy Bradford. B.A., U. N.H., 1963; LL.M., Boston U., 1968. Bar: Mass. 1968, Alaska 1972, U.S. Dist. Ct. Mass. 1968, U.S. Dist. Ct. Alaska 1972. Assoc., Mahoney, McGrath, Atwood, Piper & Goldings, Boston, 1968-69; mem. atty.'s gen.'s office criminal div. Commonwealth of Mass., Boston, 1969-71; dist. atty. State of Alaska, 1971-73; ptnr. Ziegler, Cloudy, King, Brown & Peterson, Ketchikan, Alaska, 1974-85; atty. gen., State of Alaska, 1985-87; now ptnr. Heller, Ehrman, White & McAuliffe, Anchorage, Alaska. Mem. ABA, Alaska Bar Assn. (bd. govs. 1981—, pres., 1984). Mass. Bar Assn. Democrat. Episcopalian. Federal civil litigation, State civil litigation, Contracts commercial. Office: Heller Ehrman White & McAuliffe 1900 Enserch Ctr 550 W 7th Ave Ste 1900 Anchorage AK 99501-3578

BROWN, HERBERT RUSSELL, lawyer, writer; b. Columbus, Ohio, Sept. 27, 1931; s. Thomas Newton and Irene (Hankinson) B.; m. Beverly Ann Jenkins, Dec. 2, 1967; children: David Herbert, Andrew Jenkins. BA, Denison U., 1953; JD, U. Mich., 1956. Assoc. Vorys, Sater, Seymour and Pease, Columbus, Ohio, 1956, 60-64, ptnr., 1965-82; treas. Sunday Creek Coal Co., 1970-86; assoc. justice Ohio Supreme Ct., 1987-93. Examiner Ohio Bar, 1967-72, Multi-State Bar, 1971-76, Dist. Ct. Bar, 1968-71; commr. Fed. Lands, Columbus, 1967-68, Lake Lands, Columbus, 1981; bd. dirs. Thurber House, 1992-94, Sunday Creek Coal Co.; adj. prof. Ohio State U. Coll. Law, 1997-2000; panelist Am. Arbitration Assn., 1993—. Author: (novel) Presumption of Guilt, 1991, (novel) Shadows of Doubt, 1994, (play) You're My Boy, 1999, (play) Peace with Honor, 2000, (play) Mano A Mano, 2000; mem. editl. bd. U. Mich. Law Rev., 1955-56. Trustee Columbus Bar Found., 1993—, pres., 2001—; candidate Ohio State Legis.; deacon, mem. governing bd. 1st Cmty. Ch., 1966—80; bd. dirs. Ctrl. Cmty. House Columbus, 1967—75. Capt. JAGC U.S. Army, 1956—57. Fellow Am. Coll. Trial Lawyers; mem. Ohio Bar Assn., Columbus Bar Assn. Democrat. Office: 145 N High St Columbus OH 43215-3006

BROWN, IFIGENIA THEODORE, lawyer; b. Syracuse, N.Y., Mar. 14, 1930; d. Gus and Christine Theodore; m. Paul Frederick Brown, Sept. 16, 1956; 1 child, Paul Darrow. BA, Syracuse U., 1951, LLB, JD, 1954. Bar: N.Y. 1956. Acting police justice Village of Ballston Spa, N.Y., 1960-62; sr. ptnr. Brown & Brown, Ballston Spa, 1958-95; ptnr. Brown Brown & Peterson Esqs, 1995—; of counsel Brown, Peterson and Craig, 2000—. Chmn. N.Y. State Bd. Real Property Svcs., Albany, 1996—. Mem. Charlton Sch. Bd., 1989-93, Ballston Spa Libr. Bd., 1991-94; founder, pres. Saratoga County Women's Rep. Club; vice-chmn. Saratoga County Rep. Com., 1958-72. Mem. N.Y. State Bar Assn., Saratoga County Bar Assn. (treas. 1983-84, pres. 1984-85), Zonta (pres. Saratoga County 1962, 90), Order Ea. Star. Republican. Greek Orthodox. Avocations: church choir, piano. Family and matrimonial, Probate, Real property. Home: 42 Hyde Blvd Ballston Spa NY 12020-1608 Office: Brown Peterson and Craig One E High St Ballston Spa NY 12020

BROWN, JAMES BENTON, lawyer; b. Pitts., Jan. 18, 1945; s. Sidney J. and Marian R. (Bailiss) B.; m. Susan M. Brenner, Aug. 6, 1967; children: Jessica Lynn, Joshua David. BA, U. Louisville, 1967; JD, Duquesne U., 1971. Bar: Pa. 1971, U.S. Dist. Ct. (we. dist.) Pa. 1971, U.S. Ct. Appeals (3d cir.) 1974, U.S. Supreme Ct. 1982. Dir., prin., shareholders com. Cohen & Grigsby, P.C., head employment litigation group. Lectr. Pa. Bar Inst.; mediator Justus ADR; arbitrator Am. Arbitration Assn. Mem. ABA, Fed. Bar Assn., Am. Acad. Hosp. Attys., Pa. Bar Assn. (past vice chmn. labor and employment law sect.), Allegheny County Bar Assn., Internat. Assn. Def. Counsel. Democrat. Federal civil litigation, Labor. Home: 6739 Wilkins Ave Pittsburgh PA 15217-1318 Office: 15th fl 11 Stanwix St Ste 15 Pittsburgh PA 15222-1312 E-mail: jbrown@cohenlaw.com

BROWN, JAMES ELLIOTT, lawyer; b. Mt. Vernon, NY, Sept. 5, 1947; s. Gilbert E. and Doris (Elias) B.; m. Elizabeth Ferber, Nov. 16, 1970 (div. Jan. 1977); m. Virginia Linney Freeland, Nov. 26, 1977; children: Elias F., Benjamin J. BA, Cornell U., 1969; JD, U. Denver, 1974. Bar: Colo. 1974, U.S. Dist. Ct. Colo. 1974, U.S. Ct. Appeals (10th cir.) 1976. Assoc. Grant McHendrie Haines & Crouse, P.C., Denver, 1974-81, mng. ptnr. north office, 1984-89; pres. Brown & Harmon, 1993—. Bd. dirs. Turin Bicycles of Denver; guest lectr. U. Denver Coll. Law, 1980. Bd. govs. Adams County (Colo.) Econ. Devel., 1983-87; trustee Listen Found., Inc., 1988-91, v.p., 1991. Bd. govs. Adams County (Colo.) Econ. Devel., 1983-87. Mem. ABA, Colo. Bar Assn., Adams County Bar Assn., Denver Bar Assn., MetroNorth C. of C. (chmn. bd. dirs. 1986, bd. dirs. 1983-87, Econ. Developer of Yr. 1984), Rocky Mountain Rd. (pres. 1972-76), Rocky Mountain Radio League (Denver), Mile Hi DX Assn. (pres., v.p. 1990-93). Democrat. Jewish. Avocations: ham radio, running, bicycle riding, motor sports. Bankruptcy, Contracts commercial, Real property. Office: James E Brown & Assocs PC 1350 17th St Ste 306 Denver CO 80202-1525 E-mail: wy0j@aol.com

BROWN, JAMES KNIGHT, lawyer; b. Rainelle, W.Va., Sept. 25, 1929; s. Hugh Allen and Florence Catherine (Knight) B.; m. Sarah Elizabeth Droste, June 21, 1952; children: Carolyn, Patricia, Julia. BS, W.Va. U., 1951, LLB, 1956. Bar: W.Va. 1956, U.S. Ct. Appeals (4th and 6th cir.), U.S. Supreme Ct. Assoc. Jackson & Kelly, Charleston, W.Va., 1956-62, ptnr., 1962-98; mem. Jackson & Kelly PLLC, 1999—. W.Va. adv. bd. dirs. BB&T Corp. 1st lt. USAF, 1951-53. Fellow Am. Bar Found.; mem. ABA, W.Va. State Bar (pres. 1975-76), Order of Coif, Phi Beta Kappa. Democrat. Presbyterian. Avocations: woodworking, golf. General civil litigation, Contracts commercial, Oil, gas, and mineral. Office: Jackson & Kelly PLLC 1600 Laidley Tower Charleston WV 25301-2189

BROWN, JAMES MILTON, legal educator; b. Streator, Ill., July 16, 1921. BA, U. Ill., 1943; JD, U. Fla., 1963. Bar: Fla. 1963, D.C., 1968. Pres., gen. mgr. J.C. Ames Lumber Co., Streator, 1947-61, Brown-Vissering Constrn. Co., Streator, 1956-61; Sterling fellow Yale Law Sch., 1964-65; assoc. prof. law U. Miss., 1964-65; prof. law George Washington U., 1965-92, prof. emeritus, 1992—, dir. land use mgmt. and control program Nat. Law Ctr., 1965-92, sr. staff scientist Program of Policy Studies, 1965-82; commr. Md. Nat. Capital Park & Planning Commn., 1991—; mem. various panels Nat. Acad. Scis.; cons. in field. Contbr. articles to legal jours. Mem. ABA, D.C. Bar Assn., Fla. Bar Assn., Order of Coif, Phi Delta Phi, Lambda Alpha. Home: 7206 Westchester Dr Temple Hills MD 20748-4018 Office: Planning Bd Prince Georges County Adminstrn Bldg 14741 Governor Oden Bowie Dr Upper Marlboro MD 20772-3037

BROWN, JANICE ROGERS, state supreme court justice; Assoc. justice Calif. Supreme Ct., San Francisco, 1996—. Office: Calif Supreme Ct 350 Mcallister St Rm 1295 San Francisco CA 94102-4783*

BROWN, JEAN WILLIAMS, state supreme court justice; b. Birmingham, Ala. m. E. Terry Brown; 2 children. Grad. with honors, Samford U., 1974; JD, U. Ala., 1977. Bar: Ala. 1977, U.S. Ct. Appeals (11th cir.), U.S. Supreme Ct. Law clerk Tucker, Gray & Thigpen; asst. atty. gen. criminal appeals divsn. Ala. Atty. Gen.'s Office; judge Ala. Ct. Criminal Appeals, 1997-99; justice Supreme Ct. Ala., 1999—. Chief extradition officer Atty. Gen.'s Office; faculty Ala. Jud. Coll., 1982. Tchr. kindergarten Sunday sch. 1st Bapt. Ch. Mem. Montgomery Jr. League. Office: Ala Supreme Ct 300 Dexter Ave Montgomery AL 36104-3741

BROWN, JOE BLACKBURN, judge; b. Louisville, Dec. 9, 1940; s. Knox and Miriam (Blackburn) B.; m. Marilyn McGowen, Aug. 10, 1963; children: Jennifer Knox, Michael McGowen. BA cum laude, Vanderbilt U., 1962, JD, 1965. Bar: Ky. 1965, Tenn. 1972, U.S. Supreme Ct. 1979. Asst. U.S. atty. Dept. Justice, Nashville, 1971-73, 1st asst. U.S. atty., 1974-81, U.S. atty., 1981-91, spl. asst. U.S. trustee, 1991-98; U.S. magistrate judge, U.S. Dist. Ct. (mid. dist.) Tenn., 1998—. Lectr. law Atty. Gen.'s Advocacy Inst., 1982—; vice chmn. Atty. Gen.'s Adv. Com., 1986-87, chmn. subcom. on sentencing guidelines, mem. subcom. on budget and office mgmt., 1982-91; instr. math. and bus. law Augusta (Ga.) Coll., 1966-69; instr. law Nashville Sch. Law, 1999—. Contbr. articles to legal jours. Bd. dirs. Mid-Cumberland Drug Abuse Coun., Nashville, 1977-86; asst. scoutmastr Boy Scouts Am.; vestryman St. David's Episcopal Ch., sr. warden, 1982, 90; ch. atty. Episcopal Diocese of Tenn., 1995-98; lt. col. CAP, 1996—. Maj. U.S. Army, 1965-71; col. JAGC, USAR ret. Decorated Legion of Merit, Meritorious Svc. medal with 3 oak leaf clusters; recipient Disting. Svc. award Atty. Gen.'s Adv. Com., 1988. Fellow Tenn. Bar Assn., Nashville Bar Found.; mem. FBA (treas. 1978), Nashville Bar Assn. (bd. dirs. 1995-97, exec. com. 1996-97, v.p. 1997), Radio Amateur Transmitting Soc. (pres. 1997-98), Nat. Assn. Flight Instrs., Profl. Assn. Div Instrs., Ky. Bar Assn., NRA (life, Disting. Rifleman award), Harry Phillip Inn of Ct. (master of bench and bar 1994—), Order of Coif, Phi Beta Kappa. Republican. Home: 3427 Woodmont Blvd Nashville TN 37215-1421 Office: US Courthouse Rm 797 801 Broadway Nashville TN 37203-3816 E-mail: joe_b_brown@tnmd.uscourts.gov

BROWN, JOHN LEWIS, lawyer; b. Galesburg, Ill., July 2, 1955; s. Charles Lewis and Lois Maria (Nelson) B.; m. Cynthia Sue Bowen, Aug. 31, 1980; children: Whitney Rose, Vanessa Marie, Spencer Ross. BA, Northwestern U., 1977; JD, U. Iowa, 1980. Bar: Iowa 1980, Ill. 1980, Minn. 1984. Assoc. Lucas, Brown & McDonald, Galesburg, 1980-83; sr. atty., asst. v.p. ITT Consumer Fin. Corp., Mpls., 1983-93; asst. chief counsel John Deere Credit, Des Moines, 1993—. Mem. Iowa Bar Assn. Banking, Consumer commercial, General corporate. Home: 804 57th Pl West Des Moines IA 50266-7235

BROWN, JOHN ROBERT, lawyer, priest; b. Muskogee, Okla., Apr. 22, 1948; s. John Robert and Betty Jane (Singleterry) B. BA, MA, Cambridge U., 1972; STB, Gen. Theol. Sem., 1973; STM, Union Theol. Sem., 1978, Harvard U., 1981; MA, STL, U. Louvain, Belgium, 1983; JD, Howard U., 1991. Bar: Ga. 1991, D.C. 1991, U.S. Supreme Ct. 1997; ordained priest Episcopal Ch., 1972. Tchr., headmaster St. John's Sch., Oklahoma City, 1973-77; novice Soc. St. John the Evangelist, Cambridge, Mass., 1979-81; minor canon Pro-Cathedral of Holy Trinity, Brussels, Belgium, 1981-83; assoc. rector St. James Ch., L.A., 1983-87; hon. assisting priest Ch. of the Ascension and St. Agnes, Washington, 1987-91; legis. aide U.S. Ho. of Reps., 1987-91; hon. asst. priest Ch. of Our Savior, Atlanta, 1991—; staff atty. Ga. Legal Svcs., 1991-1995; asst. gen. counsel State Bar Ga., 1996—. Reader Ecumenical Inst. World Coun. Ch., Geneva, 1978, Huntington Libr., San Marino, Calif., 1985-86, Coll. of Preachers, Nat. Cathedral, Washington, 1987, fellow, Center for Ethics in Public Policy and the Professions, Emory U., 1996-98. Contbr. articles to profl. jours. Vol. NIH, 1987—88, Fed. Charitable Campaign, Washington, 1988—89, Atlanta Project, 1991—96; spiritual adv. com. AIDS Project, L.A., 1984—86; mem. Mayor's Task Force on Family Diversity, 1984—86, Mcpl. Elections Com. L.A., 1984—86; governing bd. Robert Wood Johnson Homeless Care Project, L.A., 1985—87; trustees com. Opera Am., 1994—; co-trustee Freeman Found., 1994—97; adv. bd. Caring Hands Programs, 1983—87; mem. United Way of Metro Atlanta, 1993—97; adv. bd. Metro Atlanta Cmty. Found., 1994—97; chmn. social justice grants com. Threshold Found., 1994—96; capt. The Old Guard of The Gate City Guard, Atlanta, 1998—; bd. dirs. S.W. Assn. Episcopal Schs., 1974—77, Anglican Roman Cath. Commn. of Beligum, 1981—83; chaplain Most Venerable Order of St. John of Jerusalem, 1996—; bd. dirs. Cmty. Counseling Svc., L.A., 1983—86, Acad. Performing Arts, L.A., 1984—85, Right to Life League So. Calif., 1984—86, Cape Coast Outreach Found., 1984—86, Coun. Battered Women, Atlanta, 1991—94, AID Atlanta, 1993—, Atlanta Opera, 1993—, ACLU of Ga., 1994—, Fund for So. Cmtys., 1995—98, OUT Fund, 1996—99, Funding Exch., 1997—99, Cathedral of St. Philip Bookstore, 1998—. Named one of Outstanding Young Men of Am., 1974; Yale U. rsch. fellow, 1983; recipient Mayor's Phoenix award, Atlanta, 1997. Fellow: Ga. Bar Found. (life); mem.: ABA (vice-chmn. fed. legis. com. gen. practice sect. 1989—91), Patrons of the Vatican Mus., United Oxford and Cambridge U. Club (London), Harvard Club (Washington), City Tavern, Lawyers Club (Atlanta), Commerce Club (Atlanta). Administrative and regulatory, General civil litigation, Health. Office: The Hurt Bldg # 800 50 Hurt Plz SE Atlanta GA 30303-2946

BROWN, JOHN THOMAS, lawyer; b. Ft. Dix, N.J., Dec. 16, 1948; s. Thomas Maurice and India Olean B.; m. Jerilyn Iris Post, June 24, 1972; children: India Claire, Solon Neville. BA with honors and distinction, Calif. State U., Chico, 1975; JD, U. Calif., San Francisco, 1978; grad. diploma in applied fin., Securities Inst. of Australia, 1999. Bar: Calif. 1978, Guam 1982, No. Mariana Islands 1983, NSW, 1999. Vol. VISTA, Gt. Lakes Region, 1968-69; assoc. Belzer & Jackl, Oakland, Calif., 1978-82; gen. counsel Jones & Guerrero Co., Inc., Agana, Guam, 1982—; v.p. Jones & Guerrero Co. Inc., Sydney, Australia, 1989—. Instr. Chabot Jr. Coll., Hayward, Calif., 1980-82; prin. broker Rimpac Realty, Agana, 1987—. Bd. dirs. Job Tng. Partnership Coun., Agana, 1987-89; hon. amb.-at-large for Guam. Fellow Australian Inst. Co. Dirs.; mem. ABA, Calif. Bar Assn., Guam Bar Assn. (ethics com.), Bar Assn. No. Mariana Islands, Lawasia Soc., Securities Inst. Australia (assoc.), Guam C. of C. (bd. dirs. 1986-89, chmn. ethics com. 1987-89, chmn. bd. dirs. 1988-89), Sydney Turf Club, Am. Nat. Club, Australia Jockey Club, Law Soc. of NSW. General corporate, Private international, Real property. Office: Jones & Guerrero GPO Box 3539 Sydney New South Wales 2001 Australia E-mail: netsuke@optushome.com.au, jngoz@ozemail.com.au

BROWN, LAMAR BEVAN, lawyer; b. Tooele, Utah, Apr. 26, 1951; s. John B. and Reva M. B.; children: Sean La Mar, Kyle Ross, Ian Lawrence. BA, Utah State U., 1974; JD, We. State U., 1980. Bar: Calif. 1980, U.S. Dist. Ct. (so. dist.) Calif. 1980, U.S. Ct. Appeals (9th cir.) 1986, U.S. Dist. Ct. (no. and ctrl. dist.) 1992. Assoc. Law Offices George Andrews, San Diego, 1980-82, Higgs, Fletcher & Mack, San Diego, 1982-90, Law Offices Craig McClellan, San Diego, 1990-95; mem. McClellan & Brown, 1995—. Mem. Consumer Attys. Calif., Consumer Attys. San Diego, Western Trial Lawyers Assn., San Diego County Bar Assn. Democrat. General civil litigation, Personal injury, Product liability. Office: McClellan & Brown 1144 State St San Diego CA 92101-3529 E-mail: lamarbrown@aol.com

BROWN, LEONARD ASHLEIGH, JR. lawyer; b. Newberry, S.C., July 24, 1969; s. Leonard Ashleigh and Sarah Gibson B.; m. Amy Durr, May 16, 1992; 1 child, Courtney. BA in History, Presbyn. Coll., 1991; JD, U. S.C. Sch. Law, 1997. Bar: S.C. Assoc. Welch Law Firm, Greenwood, SC, 1997—2001; owner, ptnr. Law Office of Smokey Brown, 2001—; assoc. mcpl. judge Town of Chapin, 2001—. Prosecutor City of Greenwood, 1998-2001, Lander U., Greenwood, 1999-2001; radio broadcaster Lander U. baseball, 1999-2000. Pres. Broken Ridge Homeowner's Assn., Greenwood, 1998-2000. Mem. ATLA, S.C. Assn. Criminal Def. Lawyers, S.C. Trial Lawyers Assn., Supreme Ct. Hist. Soc., Lake Murray-Irmo Rotary Club, Greater Irmo C. of C. Methodist. Avocations: baseball, historical traveling, hunting, reading, scuba diving. Home: 509 Sweet Thorne Rd Irmo SC 29063

BROWN, MARGARET DEBEERS, lawyer; b. Washington, Sept. 24, 1943; d. John Sterling and Marianna Hurd (Hill) deBeers; m. Timothy Nils, Aug. 28, 1965; children: Emeline Susan, Eric Franklin. BA magna cum laude, Radcliffe Coll., 1965; postgrad., Harvard U., 1965-67; JD, U. Calif., Berkeley, 1968. Bar: Calif. 1969, U.S. Ct. Appeals (ith cir.) 1971, U.S. Ct. Appeals (D.C. cir.) 1986, U.S. Ct. Appeals (2d cir.) 1987, U.S. Supreme Ct. 1972. Assoc. White, Hamilton, Wyche, Shell & Pollard, Petersburg, Va., 1968-70, Heller, Ehrman, White & McAuliffe, San Francisco, 1970-73; sole practice, 1973-77, 98—; atty. Pacific Telephone (name changed to Pacific Bell), 1977-83, sr. atty., 1983-85; sr. counsel Pacific Telesis Group, 1985-98, ret. 1998. Elder, deacon, sec.-treas. of deacons Calvary Presbyn. Ch., San Francisco; bd. dirs. No. Calif. Presbyn. Homes and Svcs. Mem. Calif. State Bar (mem. com. bar examiners 1994-98, chair subcom. on petitions and litigation 1996-98), San Francisco Bar Assn. (chmn. corp. law dept. sect. 1993, judiciary com. 1993-96, nominating com. 1993), Harvard Club of San Francisco (v.p. schs. 1998—, bd. dirs.), Radcliffe Club of San Francisco (bd. dirs.), Phi Beta Kappa. Administrative and regulatory, General civil litigation, Insurance.

BROWN, MATTHEW, lawyer; b. N.Y.C., Mar. 26, 1905; s. Jack Goddard and Pauline B. (Roth) B.; m. Edna Goodrich, Nov. 8, 1932; 1 child, Patricia Brown Specter. BS, NYU, 1925; LLB, Harvard U., 1928; LLD (hon.), Suffolk U., 1983. Bar: Mass. 1928, U.S. Supreme Ct. 1935. Sr. ptnr. Brown, Rudnick, Freed & Gesmer, Boston, 1940-88, counsel, 1988—; spl. justice Boston Mcpl. Ct., 1962-72. Chmn. Boston Broadcasters, 1972-81. Selectman Town of Brookline, Mass., 1953-64; trustee New Eng. Aquarium, Boston, 1981-88; mem. Nat. Jewish Coalition, Boston, 1984, Holocaust Meml. Coun., Washington. Fellow Brandeis U., Waltham, Mass., 1985 (hon.). Mem. ABA, Mass. Bar Assn., Boston Bar Assn., Am. Jewish Com. (hon. v.p.), Combined Jewish Philanthropies (hon. trustee, life), Belmont Country Club. Home (Summer): 180 Beacon St # 11G Boston MA 02116-1408 Office: Brown Rudnick Freed Gesmer One Fin Ctr Boston MA 02111 Home (Winter): 130 Sunrise Ave Palm Beach FL 33480-3961

BROWN, MEREDITH M. lawyer; b. N.Y.C., Oct. 18, 1940; s. John Mason Brown and Catherine (Screven) Meredith; m. Sylvia Lawrence Barnard, July 17, 1965; 1 child, Mason Barnard. AB, Harvard U., 1961, JD, 1965. Bar: N.Y. 1965, U.S. Ct. Appeals (2d cir.) 1966, U.S. Dist. Ct. (so. dist.) N.Y. 1976. Law clk. to Hon. Leonard P. Moore U.S. Ct. Appeals (2d cir.), N.Y.C., 1965-66; assoc. Debevoise & Plimpton, 1966-72, ptnr., 1973—, co-chair corp. dept., 1993—, chair or co-chair mergers and acquisitions group, 1985—. Author: (with others) Takeovers: A Strategic Guide to Mergers & Acquisitions, 2001, Global Offerings, 1994, Privatisations, 1994, Mechanics of Global Equity Offerings, 1995, International Mergers and Acquisitions: An Introduction, 1999; contbr. articles to profl. publs. Mem. ABA (fed. regulation of securities com., bus. law sect.), Assn. of Bar of City of N.Y. (chmn. profl. responsibility com. 1987-90), Internat. Bar Assn. (co-chmn. com. on issues and trading of securities, sect. on bus. law 1994-98, co-chmn. capital markets forum, sec. bus. law 1998—). General corporate, Mergers and acquisitions, Securities. Home: 1021 Park Ave New York NY 10028-0959 Office: Debevoise & Plimpton 875 3rd Ave Fl 23 New York NY 10022-6225 E-mail: mmbrown@debevoise.com

BROWN, MICHAEL DEWAYNE, lawyer; b. Guymon, Okla., Nov. 11, 1954; s. Wayne E. and R. Eloise (Ferguson) B.; m. Tamara Ann Oxley, July 19, 1973; children: Jared Michael, Amy Aryann. Student, Southeastern State Coll., 1973-75; BA in Polit. Sci. and English, Cen. State U., Edmond, Okla., 1978; JD, Oklahoma City U., 1981. Bar: Okla. 1982, Colo. 1992, U.S. Dist. Ct. (no. and we. dists.) Okla. 1982, U.S. Ct. Appeals (10th cir.) 1982, U.S. Ct. Appeals (D.C. cir.) 1987. Assoc. Long, Ford, Lester & Brown, Enid, Okla., 1982-87; pvt. practice, 1987—. Gen. counsel Fed. Emergency Mgmt. Agy., 2001—; adj. prof. state and local govt. law legis. Oklahoma City U.; cons. No. Okla. Devel. Assn., Enid, 1983-91; gen. counsel Alpha Oil Co., Duncan, Okla., 1985—, Physicians Mgmt. Svc. Corps., 1985-90, Physicians of Okla., Inc., Physicians Med. Plan Okla., Inc., City Nat. Bank & Trust Co., 1987-88, Stanfield Printing Co., 1987—, Hammell Newspapers, Inc., 1987-90, Dillingham Ins., 1989-91, Suits Rig Corp., Suits Drilling Co., 1989-91; chmn. bd. dirs. Okla. Mcpl. Power Authority, Edmond, 1982-88, judges & stewards commr. Internat. Arabian Horse Assn., 1991—. Councilman City of Edmond, 1981; cons. Okla. Reps., Oklahoma City, 1983; bd. dirs. Okla. Christian Home, Edmond, 1985; Rep. nominee 6th Dist. U.S. Congress, 1988; co-chmn. Nat. Challengers Polit. Coalition, 1989-91; trustee, co-chair fin. com. Theodore Roosevelt Assn., 1994—. Michael D. Brown Hydroelectric Power Plant and Dam named in his honor, Kaw Reservoir, Okla., 1987. Mem. Okla. Bar Assn. (assoc. bar examiner 1984—), MD Physicians Okla., Ariz. and La., MD Physicians of Tulsa. Mem. Christian Ch. (Disciples of Christ). Avocations: travel, photography, reading, wilderness adventures, swimming. General corporate, Legislative, Sports. Home: PO Box 1307 812 Tenacity Dr Longmont CO 80504-7332 Office: 500 C St SW Washington DC 20472 E-mail: michael.d.brown@fema.gov

BROWN, OMER FORREST, II, lawyer; b. Somerville, N.J., Mar. 4, 1947; s. George Alvin and Frances (Schnitzler) B.; m. Sandra J. Cannon, Apr. 3, 1982. AB, Rutgers U., 1969; JD, Cornell U., 1972. Bar: N.J. 1972, D.C. 1974, U.S. Supreme Ct. 1976. Dept. atty. gen. dept. law and pub. safety State of N.J., Trenton, 1972-75; sr. trial atty. U.S. Dept. Energy, Washington, 1979-83; ptnr. Davis Wright Tremaine, 1987-96, Harmon, Wilmot & Brown, LLP, Washington, 1997—. Bd. dirs., sec. VideoTakes, Inc., Arlington, Va., 1986—; mem. OECD Contact Group on Nuclear Safety Assistance for Eastern Europe, 1994—; mem. G-7 Joint Task Force on Ukrainian Nuclear Legislation, 1996—. Contbr. numerous articles on energy, enviro. and ins. law to legal jours. Capt. USAR, 1969-75. Recipient Class of 1931 award Rutgers U. Alumni Assn., 1979, Loyal Son of Rutgers award, 1980. Mem. ABA (various offices tort and ins. practice sect. 1981-96, coord. group on energy law 1995-99), Internat. Bar Assn., Fed. Bar Assn., Univ. Club (Washington). Democrat. Roman Catholic. Nuclear power, Environmental, Public international. Address: PO Box 419 Saint Michaels MD 21663-0419 E-mail: omerb@aol.com

BROWN, PATRICIA IRENE, retired law librarian, lawyer; b. Boston; d. Joseph Raymond and Harriet A. (Taylor) B. BA, Suffolk U., 1955, JD, 1965, MBA, 1970; MST, Gordon Conwell Theol. Sem., 1977. Bar: Mass. 1965. Libr. asst. Suffolk U., Boston, 1951-60, asst. libr., 1960-65, asst. law libr., 1965-85, assoc. law libr., 1985-92; ret.; human resources counselor Winthrop (Mass.) Sr. Ctr., 1993—. Dir. Referral/Resource Ctr., Union Congl. Ch., Winthrop, Mass.; vol. health benefits counselor Mass. Dept. Elder Affairs, 1994—. First Woman inducted into Nat. Baseball Hall of Fame, Cooperstown, N.Y., 1988, All- Am. Girls Profl. Baseball League, 1950-51. Mem. Assn. Am. Law Librs., Am. Congl. Assn. (bd. dirs. 1992—), Mass. Bar Assn. Avocations: television and movie history, walking, computers. Home: 1100 Governors Dr Apt 26 Winthrop MA 02152-3254 E-mail: pbrown@acad.suffolk.edu

BROWN, PAUL EDMONDSON, lawyer; b. Van Buren County, Iowa, Dec. 24, 1915; s. William Allen and Margaret (Edmondson) B.; m. Lorraine Hill, Jan. 9, 1944; 1 child, Scott. BA, U. Iowa, 1938, JD with distinction, 1941. Bar: Iowa 1941, U.S. Supreme Ct. 1966. Ptnr. Mahoney, Brown, Mahoney, Boone, Iowa, 1946-52; v.p., counsel Bankers Life Co. (now Prin. Fin. Group), Des Moines, 1952-80; of counsel Grefe & Sidney, 1980-84, Davis, Hockensberg, Wine, Brown, Koehn, Shors, Des Moines, 1984-91; pvt. practice, 1991—. Atty. County of Boone, Iowa, 1948-52; pres. Iowa Life Ins. Assn., Des Moines, 1980-85. With U.S. Army, 1942-46, col. USAR, 1946-70. Named Outstanding Young Man of Iowa, Iowa State Jr. C. of C., 1948; named to Iowa Ins. Hall of Fame, 2001. Mem. ABA, FBA, Iowa Bar Assn., Polk County Bar Assn., Assn. Life Ins. Counsel, U. Iowa Alumni Assn. (mem. Pres.' Club and various coms.), Civil War Roundtable, World War II State Monument Com., Downtown Des Moines Kiwanis Club (pres. 1961, Hixson fellow 1999). Republican. Congregationalist. General corporate, Insurance, Legislative. Home and Office: 5804 Harwood Dr Des Moines IA 50312-1206 Fax: 515-255-7900. E-mail: peb200@aol.com

BROWN, PAUL M. lawyer; b. Jan. 10, 1938; s. I. Harry and Rose L. (Kresge) B.; m. Helga J. Fischer, Aug. 4, 1962 (div. 1977); children: Stephanie J., William A.; m. Ruth Reiter, June 28, 1986. Student, Williams Coll., 1955-57; BS in Econs., U. Pa., 1959; LLB, Columbia U., 1962. Bar: N.Y. 1963, U.S. Ct. Appeals (2d cir.) 1963, U.S. Dist. Ct. (so. and ea. dists.) N.Y. 1964, U.S. Dist. Ct. Mass. 1981, U.S. Ct. Appeals (3d cir.), U.S. Ct. Appeals (1st cir.) 1982, U.S. Dist. Ct. (we. dist.) N.Y. 1983, U.S. Ct. Appeals (6th cir.) 1983, U.S. Dist. Ct. R.I. 1985, U.S. Dist. Ct. (ea. dist.) Mich. 1986. Assoc. Berman & Frost, N.Y.C., 1963-66; ptnr. Havens, Wandless, Slitt and Tighe, 1966-74, Whitman and Ransom, N.Y.C., 1975-94, Parson & Brown, N.Y.C., 1994-99, Satterlee Stephens Burke & Burke, N.Y.C., 1999—. Councilman Closter, N.J., 1970-74; police commr. Closter, 1970-73; trustee No. Valley Regional H.S., Demarest, N.J., 1972. With USAR, 1962-68. Mem. Assn. of Bar of City of N.Y., N.Y. State Bar Assn., Fed. Bar Coun., Am. Arbitration Assn. (panel of arbitrators), Univ. Club, Columbia Golf & Country Club, Las Campanas (N.Mex.) Club. Democrat. Federal civil litigation, State civil litigation, Construction. Office: Satterlee Stephens Burke & Burke 230 Park Ave New York NY 10169-0079 E-mail: pbrown@ssbb.com

BROWN, PAUL NEELEY, federal judge; b. Denison, Tex., Oct. 4, 1926; s. Arthur Chester and Nora Frances (Hunter) B.; m. Frances Morehead, May 8, 1955; children: Paul Gregory, David H. II. JD, U. Tex., 1950. Assoc. Keith & Brown, Sherman, Tex., 1951-53; ptnr. Brown & Brown, 1953; asst. U.S. atty. for Ea. Dist. Tex. Texarkana and Tyler, Tex., 1953-59; U.S. atty. Ea. Dist. Tex., Tyler, 1959-61; ptnr. Brown & Brown and Brown Brothers & Perkins, Sherman, 1961-65, Brown and Perkins, Sherman, 1965; sole practice, 1965-67; ptnr. Brown & Hill, 1967, Brown Kennedy Hill & Minshew, Sherman, 1967-71, Brown & Hill, Sherman, 1971-76, Brown Hill Ellis & Brown, Sherman, 1976-85; U.S. dist. judge U.S. Dist. Ct. (ea. dist.) Tex., 1985—. Served with USN, 1944-46, 50-51. Fellow Tex. Bar Found.; mem. Rotary. Presbyterian. Office: US Dist Ct Fed Bldg 101 E Pecan St Sherman TX 75090-5989

BROWN, PAUL SHERMAN, lawyer; b. St. Louis, June 26, 1921; s. Paul Michael and Norma (Sherman) B.; m. Ann Wilson, Feb. 7, 1959, 1 son, Paul S. BS in Commerce, St. Louis U., 1943, JD cum laude, 1951. Bar: Mo. 1951, U.S. Dist. Ct. (ea. dist.) Mo. 1951, U.S. Ct. Appeals (8th cir.) 1951, U.S. Supreme Ct. 1966. Shareholder, Brown & James , P.C., St. Louis, 1980— ; instr. St. Louis U. Night Law Sch., 1978— ; lectr. in field. Mem. St. Louis Amateur Athletic Assn. (dir. 1974-76, pres. 1976-78); mem. com. on civil pattern jury instructions, Mo. Supreme Ct. Fellow Am. Coll. Trial Lawyers, Internat. Acad. Trial Lawyers, Internat. Soc. Barristers; mem. ABA (vice-chmn. com. consumer products liability 1977-78), Mo. Bar Assn. (bd. govs. 1963-67), Am. Bd. Trial Advocates, Lawyers Assn. St. Louis, Bar Assn. Met. St. Louis (pres. 1970-71), Am. Judicature Soc., Order of Woolsack, Alpha Sigma Nu. Roman Catholic. Contbr. numerous articles to profl. jours. Federal civil litigation, State civil litigation, Insurance. Home: 7331 Kingsbury Blvd Saint Louis MO 63130-4143 Office: Brown & James 705 Olive St Ste 1100 Saint Louis MO 63101-2270

BROWN, PETER MEGARGEE, lawyer, writer, lecturer; b. Cleve., Mar. 15, 1922; s. George Estabrook and Miriam (Megargee) B.; m. Alexandra Johns Stoddard, May 18, 1974; children: Peter, Blair Tillyer, Andree de Rapalyee, Nathaniel Holmes; stepchildren: Alexandra, Brooke Stoddard, Wallace Davis. Student, U. Calif., Berkeley, 1943-44; BA, Yale U., 1945, JD, 1948. Bar: N.Y. 1949. Spl. asst. atty. gen. State N.Y. and asst. counsel N.Y. State Crime Commn., 1951-53; asst. U.S. atty. So. Dist. N.Y., 1953-55, spl. asst., 1956; ptnr. firm Cadwalader, Wickersham & Taft,

N.Y.C., 1959-82, head litigation and ethics coms.; ptnr. Brown & Seymour, 1983-96; counsellor-at-law Peter Megargee Brown, 1996—. Mem. Mayor's Com. on Judiciary, 1965-72, vice chmn., 1972-74 Author: The Art of Questioning: Thirty Maxims of Cross-Examination, 1987, Flights of Memory-Days Before Yesterday, 1989, Rascals: The Selling of the Legal Profession, 1989, One World at a Time: Tales of Murder, Joy and Love, 1991, Village: Where to Live and How to Live, 1997, Riot of the Century (Civil War Draft Riot 1863), 1999; author essays, articles on law profession, life and humor, pub. nationally. Mem. N.Y. County Rep. Com., 1958—; counsel on crime to Nelson Rockefeller, Campaign for Gov. N.Y.S., 1968; bd. dirs. Yale Alumni Fund, 1979-84; bd. dirs., pres. Episcopal Ch. Found., 1989-93; master of ceremonies Yale Class of 1944 50th Reunion, 1994, 55th reunion, 1999; chmn., co-founder Design and Art Soc., Ltd., N.Y.C.; pres. Trustees Riot Relief Fund; bd. regent Cath. St. John Divine; founding mem. Henry Morrison Flagler Mus., Palm Beach, Fla.; mediator, East Side N.Y. gang warfare, 1956-57; counsel Grand Jury Assn. N.Y. County, 1956-79; orientation specialist U.S. Army WWII, 1943-46; editor in ch. Camp Bowie Blade (commendation). Decorated knight Order St. John of Hosp. of Jerusalem, Soc. of Anchor Cross; recipient award for svc. to profession Fed. Bar Assn., N.Y., N.J. and Conn., 1962; recipient Trustees Gold medal for disting. svc., Fed. Bar Coun., 1971; Chmn.'s award Yale Alumni Fund, 1979, Disting. Svc. award Class of 1944, Yale U., 1983, Henry Knox Sherrill medal for outstanding svc. Episcopal Ch. Found., 1993, Speakers prize Browning Sch., Headmaster's medal for pub. svc. St. Andrew's Sch.; Named record scorer U.S. Army Phys. Efficiency Test 1943 (697 out of possible 700 a score still unbroken). Fellow Am. Bar Found., Am. Coll. Trial Lawyers, N.Y. State Bar Found.; mem. ABA, World Assn. Lawyers (founding), Soc. Colonial Wars, New England Soc., Sons of the Revolution, N.Y. State Bar Assn., Assn. of Bar of City of N.Y., Fed. Bar Coun. Found. (trustee, pres. 1961-62, chmn. bd. 1962-64, chmn. judiciary com. 1960-85), chmn. planning and program com. 2d cir. judicial conf. 1976-80), St. Nicholas Soc. (past pres.), Delta Kappa Epsilon (Phi chpt. Yale), Phi Delta Phi (magister Waite Inn 1947, pres. province I 1950-55). Episcopalian (vestryman, sr. warden 1961-77). Clubs: Union (N.Y.C.); Coral Beach (Bermuda). Federal civil litigation, General civil litigation, State civil litigation. Office: 1125 Park Ave Ste 6A New York NY 10128-1243

BROWN, RICHARD LAWRENCE, lawyer; b. Evansville, Ind., Dec. 8, 1932; s. William S. and Mildred (Tenbarge) B.; m. Alice Rae Costello, June 14, 1957; children: Richard, Catherine, Vanessa, Mary, James. AA, Vincennes U., 1953; BA, Ind. State U., 1957; JD, Ind. U., 1960. Bar: Ind., 1960, U.S. dist. ct. (so. dist.) Ind., 1961, U.S. Ct. Apls. (7th cir.), 1972, U.S. Sup. Ct., 1972. Mng. ptnr. Butler, Brown, Hahn and Little, and predecessor firms, Indpls., 1961-85, Butler, Brown and Blythe, Indpls., 1985-92; city atty. City of Beech Grove, Ind., 1967—; pvt. practice, Beech Grove, 1992-2001; of counsel Blythe & Ost, Indpls., 1994-96, Holwager, Byers & Caughy, Beech Grove, 1996-2001. Sec., treas. Internat. Bus. Inst., Dayton, Ohio, 1987—, Internat. Pub. Inst., Dayton, 1987-96; bd. dirs. Vincennes U. Found. Editor: Indiana Municipal Lawyers Assn. Newsletter, 1985—. Chmn. bd. zoning appeals small cities and towns Marion County, Ind., 1965-66; gen. counsel Habitat for Humanity Greater Indpls., 1985-95; parish chmn. St. Jude's Ch. With U.S. Army, 1953-55. Fellow Indpls. Bar Assn.; mem. ABA, Ind. Bar Assn., Ind. Mcpls. Lawyers Assn. (co-editor newsletter, bd. dirs., pres. 1987-88), Vincennes U. Alumni Assn. (pres., bd. dirs. 1990-92), KC, Delta Theta Phi. Roman Catholic. Avocation: golf. Federal civil litigation, State civil litigation. Office: 1818 Main St Beech Grove IN 46107-1418 E-mail: arqualfeather@aol.com

BROWN, ROBERT CARROLL, lawyer; b. Ridley Park, Pa., June 24, 1948; s. Robert Carroll Sr. and Marjorie Elizabeth (Nowell) B.; m. Charlene M. Lipp, Oct. 4, 1986; children: Robert Charles, Gregory Scott, Michael Joseph. AB in Polit. Sci., Pa. State U., 1970; JD, Temple U., 1973. Bar: Pa.; U.S. Dist. Ct. (ea. dist.) Pa. 1977, Pa. Supreme Ct. 1973, U.S. Ct. Appeals (3d cir.) 1980. Judicial law clk. Ct. Common Pleas/Northampton County, Easton, Pa., 1973-74; assoc. Fox & Oldt, 1974-82; ptnr. Fox, Oldt & Brown, 1982—. Sec. Greater Easton Corp., 1977-82, Two Rivers Area Commerce Coun., Easton, 1983-85; officer Lehigh Valley Flying Club, Allentown, Pa., 1979-99. Mem. Northampton County Bar Assn. (sec. 1983-84), Pa. Bar Assn., Pa. Trial Lawyers Assn., Pa. Def. Inst. Republican. Presbyterian. Avocations: private pilot, sports cars, golf, spectator sports. General civil litigation, Personal injury, Product liability. Home: 420 Wedgewood Dr Easton PA 18045-5753 Office: Fox Oldt & Brown 6 S 3rd St Ste 508 Easton PA 18042-4591 E-mail: rcbjr2001@csm.com

BROWN, ROBERT G. lawyer; b. Boston, Apr. 29, 1956; s. Roger Ellis and Ida Margaret (Roherty) B.; m. Margaret H. Brown Dec. 11, 1991. AA, Cape Cod C.C., 1976; BA, Northeastern U., 1979; JD, Suffolk U., 1982. Counsel Barnstable Conservation Found., Inc., 1983-1990, Hyannis (Mass.) Fire Dist., 1985-93, Cotuit (Mass.) Fire Dist., 1985-88, West Barnstable (Mass.) Fire Dist., 1987—, Old King's Hwy Region Hist. Dist. Com., 1984—, Mass. Dept. Correction, Boston, 1989-95. Dir. Barnstable Conservation Found. Inc., 1983-85. Mem. Barnstable Town Meeting, 1975-87, Barnstable Planning Com., Barnstable Charter Com., 1976-77, Barnstable Planning Bd., 1979-85. Mem. Mass. Bar Assn. (small firm mgmt. sect. coun. 1991-93), Mass. Acad. Trial Attys., Barnstable County Bar Assn., Phi Alpha Delta. Probate. Office: 86 Willow St Yarmouth Port MA 02675-1758

BROWN, ROBERT LAIDLAW, state supreme court justice; b. Houston, June 30, 1941; s. Robert Raymond and Warwick (Rust) B.; m. Charlotte Banks, June 18, 1966; 1 child, Stuart Laidlaw. BA, U. of the South, 1963; MA in English and Comparative Lit., Columbia U., 1965; JD, U. Va., 1968. Bar: Ark. 1968, U.S. Dist. Ct. (ea. and we. divs.) Ark. 1968. Assoc. Chowning, Mitchell, Hamilton & Burrow, Little Rock, 1968-71; dep. prosecuting atty. 6th Jud. Dist., Prosecuting Atty. Office, 1971-72; legal aide Office Gov. Dale Bumpers, 1972-74; legis. asst. U.S. Senator Dale Bumpers, Washington, 1975-76; adminstrv. asst. Congressman Jim Guy Tucker, 1977-78; ptnr. Harrison & Brown, P.A., Little Rock, 1978-85; pvt. practice law, 1985-90; assoc. justice Ark. Supreme Ct., Little Rock, 1991—. Contbr. articles to profl. jours. Trustee U. of the South, Sewanee, Tenn., 1983-89, bd. regents, 1989-95. Fellow ABA, Ark. Bar Found (cert. of recognition 1981); mem. Ark. Bar Assn. Episcopalian.

BROWN, ROBERT WAYNE, lawyer; b. Allentown, Pa., July 6, 1942; s. P.P. and Rose (Ferrara) B.; m. Rochelle Kaplan, Oct. 23, 1977; m. Shelley Sherman, Mar. 3, 1973; children: Courtney Sherman, Robin Thea, Ryan Palmer; m. Lupe Pearce, Nov. 22, 1996. AB, Franklin and Marshall Coll., 1964; JD, Cornell U., 1967. Bar: Ill. 1969, Pa. 1971. VISTA atty. Cmty. Legal Svcs., Detroit, 1967-68; asst. prof. law U. Ill., 1968-70; ct. adminstr., law clk. Lehigh County Ct. Common Pleas, 1971-72; ptnr. Gross & Brown, Allentown, 1972-76; pvt. practice law, 1976-77; sr. ptnr. Brown & Brown, 1977-82, Brown, Brown & Solt, Allentown, 1982-85, Brown, Brown, Solt & Krouse, Allentown, 1985-89, Brown, Brown, Solt & Ferretti, Allentown, 1989—. Instr. bus. law Muhlenburg Coll., 1973-76; pub. defender Lehigh County, 1973-74; mem. adv. bd. PNC Bank. Mem. Rape Crisis Coun. Lehigh Valley, 1978-84, Lehigh County Pre-trial Svcs., 1975-82; bd. dirs. Hispanic Am. Orgn., 1982-90, treas., 1983-86; bd. dirs. Lehigh County Sr. Citizens, 1980-88, pres., 1984-86; bd. dirs. Lehigh County Legal Svcs., 1973-77, Boys and Girls Club Allentown, 1994—, pres., 1998-2000; founding trustee Robert Clemente Charter Sch., 1998—. Recipient Cmty. Svc. award Hispanic Am. Orgn., 1985, Human Rels. Commn. award, Allentown, 1986; Lindback scholar Franklin and Marshall Coll., 1963-64. Mem. ABA, Pa. Bar Assn., Lehigh County Bar Assn., Order of Coif, Rotary (bd. dirs. Allentown 1998—). Democrat. State civil litigation, Contracts commercial, Real property. Home: 225 Parkview Ave Allentown PA 18104-5323 Office: 1425 W Hamilton St Allentown PA 18102-4224 E-mail: rwbrown@onemain.com

BROWN, RONALD WELLINGTON, lawyer, educator, consultant, business executive, entrepreneur; b. Oct. 17, 1945; s. Leroy Harry and Mollie (Fitch) Brown; m. Geraldine Reed, Aug. 20, 1972; children: Kimberly Diana, Michael David. BA, Rutgers U., 1967; JD, Harvard U., 1971, MBA, 1973; postgrad., Columbia U., 1975. Bar: N.Y. 1975, U.S. Dist. Ct. (so. and ea. dists.) N.Y. 1975, U.S. Ct. Appeals (2d cir.) 1975, U.S. Supreme Ct. 1978. From atty. legal dept. to staff counsel litigation ITT, N.Y.C., NY, 1973—84, staff counsel litigation, 1984—85; dir. N. Am. commonwealth antipiracy ops. Motion Picture Assn. Am., 1986—87; real estate devel. and property mgmt. N.J. Transit Corp., Newark, 1988; v.p. Reed, Brown Consulting Group, Montclair, 1991—; dir. bus. affairs Norjean Entertainment Mgmt., N.Y.C., 1997—. Vis. prof. Huston-tillotson Coll., Austin, Tex., 1978; of counsel Spooner & Burnett, N.Y.C., 1997—97; pres., CEO BRS & W Prodns., Inc., N.Y.C., 1992—94; adj. prof. law sch. Rutgers U., 1995; sec., dir., mem. exec. com. Studio Mus. in Harlem, N.Y.C., 1979—81. Author: (non-fiction) Economic and Trade Related Aspects of Transborder Flow: Elements of A Code for Transnational Commerce, 1986, Legal Aspects of Doing Business in the Middle East, 1975, Joint Ventures: A Tool for Small, Women, and Minority Owned Businesses, 2000;contbr. articles to profl. jours.; editor (mem. bd. editors): (law rev.) Harvard Civil Rights-Civil Liberties Law Rev., 1969—71; exec. prodr.(articles editor): (law rev.) Harvard Civil Rights-Civil Liberties Law Rev., 1970. Dir. Operation Crossroads Africa, Inc., N.Y.C., 1976—, v.p., 1981—86; pres., exec. dir., COO Sammy Davis Jr. Nat. Liver Inst., 1988—91; moderator White House Conf. Small Bus., 1995; mem. small bus. com. Prosperity N.J., 1996—; mem. N.J. Bd. Pub. Utilities Supplier Diversity Coun., 1997—; chmn. N.J. United Minority Bus. Brain Trust, 1997—2000, U.S. Small Bus. Adminstrn., 1999; CEO W.F. Golf Enterprises, Inc., 2000—; chmn. staff parish rels. com. St. Marks United Meth. Ch., 1998—2000, vice chmn. Ch. coun., 2001—; mem. Bd. Edn., Montclair, NJ, 1986—, v.p., 1987, pres., 1988—; bd. dirs. One Hundred Black Men, N.Y.C., 1982—88, 1st v.p., 1985—87; bd. dir. Friends of the Davis Ctr. for the Performing Arts, 1987—88, Leonard Davis Ctr. for the Performing Arts, N.Y.C., 1984—89; mem. Planning bd. Twp. of Montclair, 1997—. Named Black Achiever in Industry, Harlem YMCA, 1984. Mem.: ABA (mem. coun., chmn. Euripean law com., sect. internat. law and practice 1984—86, assoc. editor Internat. Law News 1983—86), Am. Arbitration Assn., Assn. Bar City N.Y. (chmn. subcom. on fed. legis. of com. on art law 1983—86), N.Y. State Bar Assn., Internat. Law Assn., Am. Soc. Internat. Law, Union Internat. des Avocats, Omega Psi Phi. Methodist. Entertainment, Private international, Real property. Home: 180 Union St Montclair NJ 07042-2125 Office: Reed-Brown Cons Group 180 Union St Montclair NJ 07042-2125

BROWN, SANFORD DONALD, lawyer; b. Neptune, N.J., May 16, 1952; s. Richard B. and Janet (Flint) B.; m. Joan Miller, Sept. 5, 1978; children: Jennifer, Sanford Flint, Edward. BA, Brown U., 1974; JD, Seton Hall U., Newark, 1978. Bar: N.J. 1978, U.S. Dist. Ct. N.J. 1978, U.S. Ct. Appeals (3d cir.) 1998, U.S. Supreme Ct. 1999. Law clk. to Hon. Patrick J. McGann, Freehold, N.J., 1978-79; assoc. Dawes & Youssouf, 1979-81; ptnr. Dawes & Brown, 1981-86, Cerrato, O'Connor, Dawes, Collins et al, Freehold, 1986-89, Cerrato, Dawes, Collins et al, Freehold, 1989—. Gen. counsel Manalapan-Englishtown Regional Bd. Edn., N.J., 1979-85, 87—, Monmouth Vocat. Bd. Edn., Colts Neck, N.J., 1979—, Allenhurst Bd. Edn., 1990-98, Interlaken (N.J.) Bd. Adjustment/Planning Bd., 1990—, Manasquan River Regional Sewer Authority, Howell, 1979-91, Pioneer Farm Credit, 1990—, United Meth. Homes N.J., 1992—, Ocean Twp. Bd. Adjustment Spl. Counsel, 1995—; fee arbitrator N.J. Supreme Ct., 1995-99, panel chair, 1998-99. Chancellor, So. N.J. Ann. Conf., United Meth. Ch., 1995-2000, co-chancellor Greater N.J. Ann. Conf., 2000—; coach Ocean Twp. (N.J.) Recreation League, 1986-97, Ocean Twp. Little League, 1992-95; chmn. bd. trustees United Meth. Ch., 1986-91; mem., chmn. county advancement com. Boy Scouts Am., 1989-92, atty., county exec. bd., 1992—, gen. counsel, 1995—, dist. chmn., 1996-9, at. rep., 1997-99, 2001—, v.p. 2000—. Recipient Monmouth Legal Sec. assn. Employer of the Year award, 1993, Monmouth Coun. Boy Scouts Disting. Adult Eagle Scout award, 1997, Silver Beaver award, 1998, Dist. Award of Merit, 1999. Mem. Monmouth Bar Assn., N.J. Bar Assn., N.J. Sch. Bd. Attys. Assn. (regional v.p. 1991), Brown U. Alumni Assn. (chpt. pres. 1986-89, 95—), Wemrock Profl. Condo Assn. (pres. 1988-96, v.p. 1996—), Nat. Eagle Scout Assn. (life), United Meth. Scouters Assn. (life), Rotary. Methodist. Avocation: swimming. General civil litigation, Education and schools, Land use and zoning (including planning). Office: Cerrato Dawes Collins 509 Stillwells Corner Rd Freehold NJ 07728-5302 E-mail: Sdbrown509@aol.com

BROWN, STANLEY MELVIN, lawyer; b. Derry, N.H., May 29, 1916; s. Norman Chandler and Ethel Violet (Hodgkins) B.; m. Thalia May Ryder, Nov. 10, 1942; 1 child, Kenneth Chad. AB, Dartmouth Coll., 1939; JD, Cornell U., 1942. Bar: N.Y. 1942, N.H. 1945, U.S. Ct. Appeals (1st cir.) 1947, U.S. Supreme Ct. 1948. Ptnr. McLane, Graf, Greene & Brown, Manchester, N.H., 1946-74, Brown & Nixon, P.A., Manchester, 1975-88; ptnr. Abramson, Reis, Brown & Dugan (formerly Abramson Reis & Brown), 1988—. Chmn., mem. planning bd. Bradford, N.H., 1948-58, town counsel, 1953-65, selectman, 1986-89; mem. N.H. Senate, 1951-53; del. Republican nat. conv., 1952, 72. Served to lt. (s.g.) USNR, 1942-46, PTO. Mem. Manchester Bar Assn., Merrimack County Bar Assn., N.H. Bar Assn. (pres. 1968-69), ABA (ho. of dels. 1968—, chmn. ho. of dels. 1976-78, bd. govs. 1969-72), ATLA, Internat. Soc. Barristers, N.H. Bar Found. (treas. 1973-83). Federal civil litigation, State civil litigation, General practice. Office: Abramson Reis Brown & Dugan 1819 Elm St Manchester NH 03104-2910

BROWN, STEPHEN PHILLIP, judge; b. Birmingham, Ala., June 29, 1941; s. William P. and Milledge (Anderson) B.; m. Dorothy Louise Ogden, Aug. 6, 1967; children: Katherine, Phillip, Steven. BSCE, Auburn U., 1963; LLB, Walter F. George Sch. Law, 1967. Bar: Ga. 1967, U.S. Dist. Ct. (mid. dist.) Ga. 1967, U.S. Ct. Appeals (11th cir.) Ga. 1967, U.S. Supreme Ct. 1967. Atty., regional counsel IRS, N.Y.C., 1967-69; ptnr. Brown, Katz, Flatau & Hasty, Macon, Ga., 1969-95. Rep. Ga. House of Reps., Atlanta, 1971-74. Democrat. Methodist. Avocations: organic gardening, woodworking. State civil litigation, General practice, Personal injury. Home: 2434 Wesleyan Dr N Macon GA 31210-6043 Office: Superior Ct Bibb City 310 Bibb County Courthouse Macon GA 31201

BROWN, STEPHEN THOMAS, judge; b. N.Y.C., Feb. 1, 1947; s. Albert and Ruth Hope (Kaff) B.; m. Yvonne Tobias Brown, Aug. 10, 1968. BS, Fla. State U., 1968; JD, U. Miami, Fla., 1972. Bar: Fla. 1972, U.S. Dist. Ct. (so. dist.) Fla. 1973, U.S. Dist. Ct. (mid. dist.) Fla. 1989, U.S. Ct. Appeals (11th cir.) 1973, U.S. Supreme Ct. 1976. Atty. Preddy, Kutner & Hardy, Miami, Fla., 1972-77, ptnr., 1977-86, Preddy, Kutner, Hardy, Rubinoff, Brown & Thompson, Miami, 1986-91; U.S. magistrate judge U.S. Dist. Ct. (so. dist.) Fla., 1991—. Adj. prof. U. Miami Sch. Law, 1983-84; vice chmn. auto ins. com. Fla. Bar, 1979-80, chmn. grievance com., 1981-84; mem. adv. com. on rules and procedures So. Dist. Fla., 1995-2001; mem. leadership coun. Fla. State U. Sch. of Arts & Scis. Mem. ABA, Acad. Fla. Trial Lawyers, Dade County Bar Assn., Fla. State U. Alumni Assn. (dist. v.p. 1993-99), Seminole Boosters Inc. (bd. dirs. 1988-93), Seminole Club Dade County (pres. 1984-87), U. Miami Law Sch. Alumni Assn. (bd. dirs. 1994—, v.p. 2000). Avocations: snow skiing, fishing, golf. Office: US Dist Ct 300 NE 1st Ave Miami FL 33132-2126

BROWN, STEVEN SPENCER, lawyer; b. Manhattan, Kans., Feb. 26, 1948; s. Gerald James and Buelah Marie (Spencer) B. BBA, U. Mo., 1970, JD, 1973. Bar: Mo. 1973, U.S. Tax Ct. 1974, Ill. 1977, U.S. Dist. (no. dist.) Ill. 1979, U.S. Ct. Appeals (7th cir.) 1980, U.S. Ct. Claims 1986, Calif. 1989, U.S. Ct. Appeals (11th cir.) 1989, U.S. Ct. Appeals (5th cir.) 2000. Trial atty. IRS Regional Counsel, Chgo., 1973-78; sr. trial atty. IRS Dist. Counsel, 1978-79; assoc. Silets & Martin Ltd., 1979-85, ptnr., 1985-92, Martin, Brown & Sullivan Ltd., Chgo., 1992—. Adj. prof. John Marshall, Chgo., 1985—. Republican. Presbyterian. Avocations: golf, tennis. Administrative and regulatory, Federal civil litigation, Personal income taxation. Home: 1340 N Astor St Apt 2903 Chicago IL 60610-8438 Office: Martin Brown & Sullivan Ltd 10th Fl 321 S Plymouth Ct Chicago IL 60604-3912 E-mail: brown@mbslaw.com

BROWN, T. ALAN, lawyer; b. Buffalo, Feb. 4, 1939; s. Edmund and Katherine (Welch) Brown; m. Marilyn Virginia DePan, July 02, 1969; children: Thomas, Edward. BS, John Carroll U., 1960; JD, Fordham U., 1963. Bar: NY 1963, US Dist Ct (we dist) NY 1964. With Roach, Brown, McCarthy & Gruber PC, Buffalo, 1964—, shareholder, 1970—, v.p., mng atty, 1990—. Mem.: ABA, NY Bar Asn, Erie County Bar Asn (dep treas 1999—2000), Western NY Trial Lawyers Asn (bd dirs 1989—91), Asn Def Trail Attys, Am Soc Law and Med, Am Arbit Asn (arbitrator), Int Asn Def Counsel, Mid-Day Club. General civil litigation, Personal injury, Professional liability. Home: 109 Depew Ave Buffalo NY 14214-1509 Office: Roach Brown McCarthy & Gruber PC & McCarthy P C 420 Main St Buffalo NY 14202-3502 E-mail: tabrown@roachbrown.com

BROWN, THOMAS CARTMEL, JR. lawyer; b. Marion, Va., June 20, 1945; m. Sally Lynch Guy; children: Sarah Preston, Taylor Caldwell. AB, Davidson Coll., 1967; JD, U. Va., 1970. Bar: Va 1971. Assoc. Boothe, Prichard & Dudley, Alexandria, Va., 1971-76, ptnr., 1976-86, McGuire-Woods LLP and predecessors, McLean, Va., 1986—. Mem lawyers comt Nat Ctr State Cts, 1993—; secy, gen counsel Potomac KnowledgeWay Project, Inc, 1995—99. Mem Va Child-Day Coun, Richmond, 1987—91, Northern Va Roundtable, 1995—; bd dirs Alexandria chpt Am Red Cross, 1982—88. Fellow: Am Bar Found, Va Law Found (bd dirs 1997—, vpres 2001); mem.: Va Bar Asn, Va State Bar (chmn bus law sect 1987—88, bd govs health law sect 1998—, vice-chair 2001), Omicron Delta Kappa. General corporate, Health. Office: McGuireWoods LLP 1750 Tysons Blvd Ste 1800 Mc Lean VA 22102-4231

BROWN, THOMAS PHILIP, III, lawyer; b. Washington, Dec. 18, 1931; s. Raymond T. and Beatrice (Cullen) B.; m. Alicia A. Sexton, July 28, 1955; children: Thomas, Mark, Alicia, Maria, Beatrice. B.S., Georgetown U., 1953, LL.B., 1956. Bar: D.C., Md. Pvt. practice law, 1958—. Author monograph and articles on legal malpractice. Pres. Cath. Youth Orgn. of Washington, 1972. Served to 1st lt. USMCR, 1955-58. Mem. Bar Assn. D.C. (pres. 1986, bd. dirs. 1987), Barristers Club, Columbia Country Club. Estate planning, General practice, Real property. Home: 5210 Norway Dr Chevy Chase MD 20815-6672 Office: 4948 Saint Elmo Ave Bethesda MD 20814-6013

BROWN, WADE EDWARD, retired lawyer; b. Blowing Rock, N.C., Nov. 5, 1907; s. Jefferson Davis and Etta Cornelia (Suddreth) B.; m. Gilma Baity (dec.); m. Euzelia Smart (dec.); children: Margaret Rose, Wade Edward, Sarah Baity Otey. Student, Mars Hill Coll., 1928; JD, Wake Forest U., 1931. Bar: N.C. 1930. Pvt. practice, Boone, N.C., 1931—; ret. Chmn. N.C. Bd. Paroles, Raleigh, 1967-72; cons. Atty. Gen., N.C. Dept. Justice, 1973; with student legal svcs., Appalachian State U. Author: Wade E. Brown: Recollections and Reflections, 1997. Mem. N.C. Senate, 1947-49, N.C. Ho. of Reps., 1951-53, Boone Merchants Assn.; mayor Town of Boone, 1961-67; chmn. Watauga County Hosp.; mem. gen. bd. Bapt. State Conv. N.C.; trustee Wake Forest U., now trustee emeritus; trustee Appalachian State U., Bapt. Found. N.C. Bapt. State Conv.; founder Watauga County Pub. Libr., 1996—. Probate, Real property. Office: PO Box 1776 Boone NC 28607-1776

BROWN, WESLEY ERNEST, federal judge; b. Hutchinson, Kans., June 22, 1907; s. Morrison H. H. and Julia (Wesley) B.; m. Mary A. Miller, Nov. 30, 1934 (dec.); children: Wesley Miller, Loy B. Wiley; m. Thadene N. Moore. Student, Kans. U., 1925-28; LLB, Kansas City Law Sch., 1933. Bar: Kans. 1933, Mo. 1933. Pvt. practice, Hutchinson, 1933-58; county atty. Reno County, Kans., 1935-39; referee in bankruptcy U.S. Dist. Ct. Kans., 1958-62, judge, 1962-79, sr. judge, 1979—. Apptd. Temporary Emergency Ct. of Appeals of U.S., 1980-93; dir. Nat. Assn. Referees in Bankruptcy, 1959-62; mem. bankruptcy divsn. Jud. Conf., 1963-70; mem. Jud. Conf., U.S., 1976-79. With USN, 1944-46. Mem. ABA, Kans. Bar Assn. (exec. council 1950-62, pres. 1964-65), Reno County Bar Assn. (pres. 1947), Wichita Bar Assn., S.W. Bar Kan., Delta Theta Phi. Office: US Dist Ct 414 US Courthouse 401 N Market St Wichita KS 67202-2089

BROWN, WILLIAM A. lawyer, mediator, arbitrator; b. Memphis, Nov. 6, 1957; s. Winn D. Sr. and Annie Ruth (Hurt) B.; m. Mary Lee Walker, Dec. 27, 1980. BBA, U. Miss., 1978, JD, 1981. Bar: Miss. 1981, U.S. Dist. Ct. (no. and so. dists.) Miss. 1981, U.S. Dist. Ct. (we. dist.) Tenn. 1987. Ptnr., pres. Walker, Brown & Brown, P.A., Hernando, Miss., 1981—. Pres. DeSoto Literacy Coun., Hernando, 1988, Am. Cancer Soc., Hernando, 1988, DeSoto County Econ. Devel. Coun., 1995-96; mem. Leadership 2000, 1990-91; vice-chmn. Hernando Preservation Commn., 1997-2000, chmn., 2001—; chmn. design com. Main Street Project, 1997-2000; allocations chmn. United Way of Mid-South Desoto County. James O. Eastland scholar, 1978-81; Paul Harris fellow Rotary Internat., 1997. Mem. Miss. Bar Assn. (bd. dirs. young lawyers sect. 1988-89), DeSoto County Bar Assn. (v.p. 1988-89, pres. 1996-98), Rotary (pres. Hernando chpt. 1989-90), Boy Scouts Am., N.W. Miss. (membership chmn. 1990, activities chmn. 1991). Methodist. Avocations: gardening, design and construction projects. Alternative dispute resolution, Personal injury, Real property. Home: PO Box 276 Hernando MS 38632-0276 Office: Walker Brown & Brown PA PO Box 276 Hernando MS 38632-0276

BROWN, WILLIAM ALLEY, lawyer; b. La Grange, Tex., Sept. 5, 1921; s. Leon Dancy and Mary (Alley) B.; m. Ann Dyke Shafer, June 27, 1953; children: Ann Lenora, William Alley. B.B.A., U. Tex., 1942; Indsl. Adminstr., Harvard Bus. Sch., 1943; J.D., U. Tex., 1948. Bar: Tex. 1948, U.S. Dist. Ct. (we. dist.) Tex. 1950, U.S. Dist. Ct. (so. dist.) Tex. 1959, U.S. Ct. Appeals (5th cir.) 1950, U.S. Ct. Appeals (11th cir.) 1983. Assoc., ptnr. Powell, Wirtz Rauhut, Austin, Tex., 1950-58; ptnr. Powell, Rauhut, McGinnis, Reavley & Brown, Houston, 1958-61; assoc. gen. counsel Brown & Root, Inc., Houston, 1961-76, v.p., gen. atty., 1976-83; prof. constrn. law Tex. A&M U., College Station, 1983-91; ptnr. Brown & Brown Attys., Houston, 1991—. Served to 1st lt. U.S. Army, 1942-46, ETO. Mem. Sons of Rep. of Tex., Alpha Tau Omega. Republican. Episcopalian. Clubs: Frisch Auf Country (La Grange, Tex.), Plaza (Wichita Falls, Tex.). Construction, Oil, gas, and mineral, Labor. Home: 777 N Post Oak Rd Apt 609 Houston TX 77024-3806 Office: 6343 Skyline Dr Houston TX 77057-6901

BROWN, WILLIAM HILL, III, lawyer; b. Phila., Jan. 19, 1928; s. William H. Jr. and Ethel L. (Washington) B.; m. Sonya Morgan Brown, Aug. 29, 1952 (div. 1975); 1 child, Michele D.; m. D. June Hairston, July 29, 1975; 1 child, Jeanne-Marie. BS, Temple U., 1952; JD, U. Pa., 1955. Bar: Pa. 1956, D.C. 1972, U.S. Ct. Appeals (3d cir.) 1959, U.S. Ct. Appeals (4th cir.) 1978, U.S. Dist. Ct. (ea. dist.) Pa. 1957, U.S. Ct. Appeals (10th cir.) 1986, U.S. Ct. Appeals (5th cir.) 1988, U.S. Dist. Ct. D.C. 1994, U.S. Ct. Appeals (D.C. cir.) 1994, U.S. Ct. Appeals (fed. cir.) 1997. Assoc. Norris, Schmidt, Phila., 1955-62; ptnr. Norris, Brown, Hall, 1962-68, Schnader, Harrison, Segal & Lewis, Phila., 1974—, mem. exec. com., 1983-87; chief of frauds Dist. Atty.'s Office, 1968, dep. dist. atty., 1968; commr. EEOC, Washington, 1968-69, chmn., 1969-73. Lectr. S.W. Legal Found., Practising Law Inst., Nat. Inst. Trial Advocacy; bd. dirs. United Parcel Svc., Inc., 1983—, Lawyers Com. Civil Rights Under Law; chmn. Phila. Spl. Investigation Commn. MOVE; pres. Nat. Black Child Devel., Inc., 1986-90; bd. dirs. Cmty. Legal Svcs., 1986—; mem. exec. com. Schnader, Harrison, Segal & Lewis, 1983-87; bd. dirs., mem. exec. com. Lawyers Com. Civil Rights Under law, 1977—, co-chair, 1991-93; mem. Commn. on Comml. Operation of U.S. Customs Svc., 1994-98. Contbr. articles to profl. jours. Bd. dirs. Mid. States Colls. and Secondary Schs., 1983-89, Main Line Acad., 1982—, Nat. Sr. Citizens Law Ctr., 1988-94; mem. nat. bd. govs. Am. Heart Assn., 1994-96, mem. audit com., mem. pub. affairs policy com., bd. dirs., 1986-94, mem. audit com., mem. pub. affairs policy com.; mem. adv. com. on appellate ct. rules Supreme Ct. Pa., 1989-95. With USAF, 1946-48. Recipient award of merit Fed. Bar Assn., Columbus, 1971, NAACP award, 1971, Dr. Edward S. Cooper award Am. Heart Assn., 1995, Whitney M. Young Jr. Leadership award Urban League, 1996, Whitney North Seymor award Lawyers Com. for Civil Rights Under Law, 1996, Champions for Social Justice and Equality award Black Law Students Assn. Rutgers-Camden, 1997, Earl G. Harrison Pro Bono award, 1998, law alumni award U. Pa., 2000. Fellow Internat. Acad. Trial Lawyers, Am. Law Inst.; mem. ABA, Phila. Bar Assn. (Fidelity award 1990), D.C. Bar Assn., Pa. Bar Assn., Fed. Bar Assn., Nat. Bar Assn., Inter-Am. Bar Assn., World Assn. Lawyers (founding mem.), Am. Arbitration Assn. (past bd. dirs.), Barrister's Assn. Phila., Inc. (J. Austin Norris award 1987), Citizens Commn. on Civil Rights, NAACP (bd. dirs. legal def. and ednl. fund), Alpha Phi Alpha (Recognition award 1969). Republican. Episcopalian Federal civil litigation, State civil litigation, Labor. Office: Schnader Harrison Segal & Lewis 1735 Market St Ste 3800 Philadelphia PA 19103-7598

BROWN, WILLIAM MICHAEL, scientist, consultant, writer, editor, lawyer; b. Poole, Dorset, England, Nov. 17, 1965; came to U.S., 1991, naturalized, 1999; s. Michael C. and Shirley L. (Rowney) B. BSc in Biochemistry summa cum laude, U. Southampton, England, 1988, PhD in Molecular Biology & Biochemistry, 1991; MBA, Fairleigh Dickinson U., 1997; JD magna cum laude, N.Y. Law Sch., 1998. Bar: N.J. 1998, U.S. Dist. Ct. N.J. 1998, N.Y. 1999, U.S. Dist. Ct. (so. dist.) N.Y. 1999, U.S. Ct. Appeals (fed. cir.) 1999, U.S. Patent and Trademark Office 1999; chartered European chemist, European Profl. biologist; cert. regulatory affairs. Awdrsch. fellow in neurology Ctr. Neurol. Diseases Harvard Med. Sch. and Brigham and Women's Hosp., Boston, 1991-92; fellow Johnson & Johnson's Skin Biology Rsch. Ctr., Raritan, N.J., 1992-93; rsch. fellow Meml.-Sloan Kettering Cancer Ctr., N.Y.C., 1993-94; sci. cons. Sills, Cummis, Zuckerman, Radin, Tischman, Epstein and Gross, Newark, 1994-96, Whitman, Breed, Abbott & Morgan, N.Y.C., 1996-97; sci. advisor/assoc. Kaye, Scholer, Fierman, Hays & Handler, 1997-99; patent counsel Taro Pharms., Hawthorne, N.Y., 1999-2000; v.p., chief intellectual property counsel Restoragon, Inc. (formerly BioNebraska, Inc.), Lincoln, Nebr., 2000—. Vis. fellow NIH, Balt., 1991-92; freelance sci. cons., writer, editor, 1993—; hon. rsch. fellow dept. physiology and anatomy U. Tasmania, Hobart, Tasmania, Australia, 1995—; reviewer/evaluator Current Drugs, 1997—, Fin. Times Pharms. Publ., 1998—. Author: Alzheimer's Disease: Current Treatments and Future Prospects, 1999; co-author: Fetuin, 1995, Transcription, 2001; articles editor N.Y. Law Sch. Law Rev., 1996-97; contbr. numerous articles to profl. jours. Recipient Brit. Assn. for Advancement of Sci. award, 1987, G. A. Kerkut prize, 1988, Maxwell Found. award, 1987, Woodrow Wilson Constl. Law award, 1998, Otto L. Walter Disting. Legal Writing award, 1998; Wellcome Trust rsch. scholar, 1987, Irving Mariash scholar N.Y. Law Sch., 1994-98; Vis. Rsch. fellow NIH, 1991-92. Fellow Royal Soc. Encouragement of Arts, Mfg. and Commerce; mem. AAAS, Am. Assn. Pharm. Scientists, Royal Soc. Chemistry, Inst. Biology, N.Y. Acad. Scis., Regulatory Affairs Profl. Soc., Federalist Soc., Sigma Xi, Epsilon Pi Tau, Delta Mu Delta. Achievements include cloning of the human tau gene with Dr. A. Andreadis; cloning of bovine, ovine and porcine fetuin cDNAs with Dr. K.M. Dziegielewska and Prof. N.R. Saunders; research in Alzheimer's disease. Office: Restoragon Inc 4130 NW 37th St Lincoln NE 68524 E-mail: wbrown@bionebraska.com

BROWNE, JEFFREY FRANCIS, lawyer; b. Clare, South Australia, Australia, Mar. 1, 1944; came to U.S., 1975; s. Patrick Joseph and Irene Kathleen (Cormack) B.; m. Deborah Mary Christine West, Aug. 28, 1971; children: Veronique Namur Irene, Jeffrey James, Nicholas Patrick, Sophie Christina, Amy Elizabeth. LLB, Adelaide U., South Australia, 1966; LLM, Sydney U., Australia, 1968, Harvard U., 1976. Bar: South Australia 1969, Australian Capital Territory 1973, N.Y. 1978, Victoria 1982, New South Wales 1983, Western Australia 1983. Assoc. High Ct. Australia, Canberra, Australian Capital Territory, 1967-68; diplomat Dept. Fgn. Affairs, 1969; 2d sec. Australian High Commn., London and Malaysia, 1970-71, acting high commr. Ghana, 1972; counsel nuclear tests case Internat. Ct. Justice, 1973-74; assoc. Sullivan & Cromwell, N.Y.C., 1976-81, ptnr., 1983—; gen. counsel Alcoa of Australia, Melbourne, 1981-82. Bd. dirs. Compinvest Pty. Ltd. Mem. Law Inst. Victoria, Australian Mining and Petroleum Law Assn., Law Coun. Australia (chmn. fin. and securities subcom., internat. trade and bus. law com.), Inst. Dirs. of Australia, Internat. Bar Assn. (sect. on energy and natural resources), Am. C. of C. in Australia (bd. dirs.), Am. Soc. Internat. Law, N.Y. Yacht Club, Melbourne Club. Contracts commercial, General corporate, Securities. Office: Sullivan & Cromwell 125 Broad St Fl 28 New York NY 10004-2489 also: 101 Collins St Melbourne Victoria 3000 Australia E-mail: brownej@sullcrom.com

BROWNE, RICHARD CULLEN, lawyer; b. Akron, Nov. 21, 1938; s. Francis Cedric and Elizabeth Ann (Cullen) B.; m. Patricia Anne Winkler, Apr. 23, 1962; children: Richard Cullen, Catherine Anne, Paulette Elizabeth, Maureen Frances, Colleen Marie. BS in Econs., Holy Cross Coll., 1960; JD, Cath. U. Am., 1963. Bar: Va. 1963, U.S. Ct. Claims 1963, U.S. Ct. Customs and Patent Appeals 1963, D.C. 1964, U.S. Ct. Mil. Appeals, 1963, U.S. Ct. Appeals (D.C. cir.) 1964, U.S. Supreme Ct. 1966, U.S. Ct. Appeals (fed. cir.) 1982, U.S. Ct. Appeals (9th cir.) 1983, U.S. Ct. Appeals (6th cir.) 1991, U.S. Ct. Appeals (7th cir.) 1998. Assoc. Browne, Beveridge, DeGrandi & Kline, Washington, 1963-68, ptnr., 1968-72, Schaffert, Miller & Browne, Washington, 1972-74; sr. counsel Office of Enforcement EPA, 1974-76; asst. chief hearing counsel U.S. Nuclear Regulatory Commn., 1976-78; sole practice, 1978-79; ptnr. Winston & Strawn, 1980-2001, of counsel, 2001—. Lectr. U. R.I., 1975 Washburn U., 1978, Legal Inst., CSC, 1975-78, Hofstra U., 1987—, Nat. Inst. for Trial Advocacy, 1986—. Del. Montgomery County Civic Fedn., 1970-74; chmn. Citizens Adv. Com. on Rockville Corridor, 1972-77; mem. Montgomery County Potomac River Basin Adv. Com., 1972-74; chmn. Cath. U. Am. Fund, 1996-2001. Served to capt. USAF JACG, 1963-66, USAFR, 1966-69. Named disting. mil. grad. Holy Cross Coll., 1960. Mem. Coll. Holy Cross Alulmni Assn. (bd. dirs. 1971-78, 98—, alumni senate 1978-97, nominations and elections com. 1995—, pres.-elect 2001—), Cath. U. Law Sch. Alumni Soc. (pres. 1992-93, dir. 1991—, bd. visitors 1998—), Cath. U. Gen. Alumni Assn. (bd. govs. 1992—, co-chair Gibbons medal com. 1995-2001, exec. com. 1995-2001). Republican. General corporate, Environmental, Trademark and copyright. Home: 7203 Old Stage Rd Rockville MD 20852-4438 Office: Winston & Strawn 1400 L St NW Ste 1000 Washington DC 20005-3508 E-mail: rbrowne@winston.com

BROWNING, DEBORAH LEA, lawyer; b. Helena, Ark., Aug. 16, 1955; d. William Herman Jr. and Mildred Kate (York) B. BS with honors, U. Ala., 1976; diploma, Oxford U., 1982; JD with honors, U. Tex., 1984. Bar: Tex. 1984, D.C. 1985. Drug abuse counselor Aletheia House, Birmingham, Ala., 1972-76; state parole officer Tex. Bd. Pardons and Parole, Houston, 1978-81; litigation clk. Harris County Dist. Attys. Office, 1983; appellate clk. Travis County Dist. Attys. Office, Austin, 1984; litigation assoc. Hogan & Hartson, Washington, 1984-92; pro bono atty. Internat. Human Rights Law Group, 1984—89, acting legal dir., 1988-89. Co-chair Working Group on Human Rights of Women, 1994—98; pres. W.E.A.R.E. for Human Rights, 1996—. Author: A Supplemental Report On The Chilean Plebiscite, 1988; co-author: Chile: The Plebiscite and Beyond, 1989, First Steps After Stroessner: An Analysis of the 1989 Paraguayan Elections, 1989; editor Am. Jour. Criminal Law, 1982-84. Vol. atty. Women's Legal Def. Fund., Washington, 1987-88; dir. Chile Election Observor Project and the Paraguay Working Group; crime prevention coord. East End. Civic Assn., Houston, 1979-81. Avocations: travel, crafts, alpacas. Federal civil litigation, Education and schools, Public international. Home: 7204 Central Ave Takoma Park MD 20912-6451

BROWNING, JAMES ROBERT, federal judge; b. Great Falls, Mont., Oct. 1, 1918; s. Nicholas Henry and Minnie Sally (Foley) B.; m. Marie Rose Chapell. BA, Mont. State U., Missoula, 1938; LLB with honors, U. Mont., 1941, LLD (hon.), 1961, Santa Clara U., 1989. Bar: Mont. 1941, D.C. 1950, U.S. Supreme Ct. 1952. Spl. atty. antitrust div. Dept. Justice, 1941-43, spl. atty. gen. litigation sect. antitrust div., 1946-48, chief antitrust dept. N.W. regional office, 1948-49; asst. chief gen. litigation sect. antitrust div. Dept. Justice (N.W. regional office), 1949-51, 1st asst. civil div., 1951-52; exec. asst. to atty. gen. U.S., 1952-53; chief U.S. (Exec. Office for U.S. Attys.), 1953; pvt. practice Washington, 1953-58; lectr. N.Y.U. Sch. Law, 1953, Georgetown U. Law Center, 1957-58; clk. Supreme Ct. U.S., 1958-61; judge U.S. Ct. Appeals 9th Circuit, 1961-76, chief judge, 1976-88, judge, 1988—. Mem. Jud. Conf. of U.S., 1976-88, exec. com. of conf., 1978-87, com. on internat. conf. of appellate judges, 1987-90, com. on ct. adminstrn., 1969-71, chmn. subcom. on jud. stats., 1969-71, com. on the budget, 1971-77, adminstrn. office, subom. on budget, 1974-76, com. to study U.S. jud. conf., 1986-88, com. to study the illustrative rules of jud. misconduct, 1985-87, com. on formulation of standard of conduct of fed. judges, 1969, Reed justice com. on cont. edn., tng. and adminstrn., 1967-68; David T. Lewis Disting. Judge-in-residence, U. Utah, 1987; Blankenbaker lectr. U. Mont., 1987, Sibley lectr. U. Ga., 1987, lectr. Human Rights Inst. Santa Clara U. Sch. Law, Strasbourg. Editor-in-chief, Mont. Law Rev. Dir. Western Justice Found.; chmn. 9th Cir. Hist. Soc. 1st lt. U.S. Army, 1943-46. Decorated Bronze Star; named to Order of the Grizzly, U. Mont., 1973; scholar in residence Santa Clara U., 1989, U. Mont., 1991; recipient Devitt Disting. Svc. to Justice award, 1990. Fellow ABA (judge adv. com. to standing com. on Ethics and Profl. Responsibility 1973-75); mem. D.C. Bar Assn., Mont. Bar Assn., Am. Law Inst., Fed. Bar Assn. (bd. dirs 1945-61, Nat. council 1958-62), Inst. Jud. Adminstrn., Am. Judicature Soc. (chmn. com. on fed. judiciary 1973-74, bd. dirs. 1972-75), Herbert Harley award 1984), Am. Soc. Legal History (adv. bd. jour.), Nat Lawyers Club (bd. govs. 1959-63). Office: US Ct Appeals 9th Cir PO Box 193939 San Francisco CA 94119-3939

BROWNING, WILLIAM DOCKER, federal judge; b. Tucson, May 19, 1931; s. Horace Benjamin and Mary Louise (Docker) B.; children: Christopher, Logan, Courtenay; m. Zerilda Sinclair, Dec. 17, 1974; 1 child, Benjamin. BBA, U. Ariz., 1954, LLB, 1960. Bar: Ariz. 1960, U.S. Dist. Ct. Ariz. 1960, U.S. Ct. Appeals (9th cir.) 1965, U.S. Supreme Ct. 1967. Pvt. practice, Tucson, 1960-84; judge U.S. Dist. Ct., 1984—. Mem. jud. nominating com. appellate ct. appointments, 1975-79; mem. Commn. on Structural Alternatives, Fed. Ct. Appeals, 1997-99. Del. 9th Cir. Jud. Conf., 1968-77, 79-82; trustee Inst. for Ct. Mgmt., 1978-84; mem. Ctr. for Pub. Resources Legal Program. 1st lt. USAF, 1954-57, capt. USNG, 1958-61. Recipient Disting. Citizen award U. Ariz., 1995. Fellow Am. Coll. Trial Lawyers, Am. Bar Found.; mem. ABA (spl. com. housing and urban devel. law 1973-76, com. urban problems and human affairs 1978-80), Ariz. Bar Assn. (chmn. merit selection of judges com. 1973-76, bd. gove. 1968-74, pres. 1972-73, Outstanding Mem. 1980), Pima County Bar Assn. (exec. com. 1964-68, med. legal screening panel 1965-75, pres. 1967-68), Am. Bd. Trial Advocates, Am. Judicature Soc. (bd. dirs. 1975-77), Fed. Judges Assn. (bd. dirs.). Office: US Courthouse 405 W Congress St Ste 6160 Tucson AZ 85701-5061

BROWNLEE, JOHN L. prosecutor; BA, Washington and Lee U.; MBA, Golden Gate U.; JD, Coll. William and Mary. Law clk. U.S. Dist. Ct. (we. dist.) Va., 1994—96; asst. U.S. atty. D.C., 1997—2001; assoc. Woods, Rogers and Hazelgrove, Richmond, Va., 2001; U.S. atty. We. Dist. Va. U.S. Dept. Justice, 2001—. With U.S. Army, 1987—91, Capt. JAG USAR. Office: PO Box 1709 Roanoke VA 24008*

BROWNRIGG, JOHN CLINTON, lawyer; b. Detroit, Aug. 7, 1948; s. John Arthur and Sheila Pauline (Taffe) B.; children: Brian M., Jennifer A., Katharine T. BA, Rockhurst Coll., 1970; JD cum laude, Creighton U., 1974. Bar: Nebr. 1974, U.S. Dist. Ct. Nebr. 1974, U.S. Tax Ct. 1977, U.S. Ct. Appeals (8th cir.) 1990. Ptnr. Eisenstatt, Higgins, Kinnamon, Okun & Brownrigg, P.C., Omaha, 1974-80, Erickson & Sederstrom, P.C., Omaha, 1980—. Lectr. law trial practice Creighton U. Sch. Law, Omaha, 1978-83; dir. Legal Aid Soc., Inc., Omaha, 1982-88, pres., 1987-88, devel. coun., 1989—; dir. Nebr. Continuing Legal Edn., Inc., 1991-93. Chmn. law sect. Archbishop's Capital Campaign, Omaha, 1991. Sgt. USAR, 1970-76. Fellow Nebr. State Bar Found. (dir. 1991-93); mem. Nebr. State Bar Assn. (pres. 1992-93), Nebr. Assn. Trial Attys., Omaha Bar Assn. (pres. 1990-91). Avocations: golf, bicycling, hiking. Alternative dispute resolution, Federal civil litigation, State civil litigation. Office: Erickson & Sederstrom PC Ste 100 10330 Regency Parkway Dr Omaha NE 68114-3761 E-mail: brownrigg@eslaw.com

BROWNSTEIN, RICHARD JOSEPH, lawyer; b. L.A., June 29, 1930; s. Alfred and Vera (Slifman) B.; m. Elisabeth B. Baer, July 15, 1955 (dec. Apr. 1973); children: J.B., Joyce A., Richard J., II; m. Shirley Jean Anderson, June 15, 1976 (div. Apr. 1983); m. Donna Oziel Sacks, Sept. 12, 1987. Student Reed Coll., 1948-50; LL.B., Willamette U., 1953. Bar: Oreg 1953, U.S Dist. Ct. Oreg. 1954. Assoc., then ptnr. White/Sutherland, Portland, Oreg., 1953-73; ptnr. Brownstein, Rask, Arenz, Sweeney, Kerr & Grim, Portland, 1973—; pres., bd dirs. Devel. Housing and Law Inst., Washington, 1984— . Mem., chmn. Met. Human Relations Commn., Portland, 1964-68, Oreg. adv. com. U.S. Civil Rights Commn., 1986-92, City of Portland Cable Regulatory Commn., 1986-93. Served to col. USAR, 1948-80. Mem. Oreg. Bar Assn. (corp. com. 1964-67, sec. civil rights com. 1967-70, group purchasing com. 1973-76, sec., chmn. legal secs. 1980-83, future of legal profession 1983-86, lawyers assistance com. 1986-89). Club: University (Portland). Lodge: B'nai B'rith (dist. pres. 1974-75). General corporate, Pension, profit-sharing, and employee benefits, Real property. Home: 763 NW Powhatan Ter Portland OR 97210-2734 Office: Brownstein Rask Arenz Sweeney Kerr & Grim 1200 SW Main St Portland OR 97205-2040

BROWNWOOD, DAVID OWEN, lawyer; b. L.A., May 24, 1935; s. Robert Scott Osgood and Ruth Elizabeth (Bellamy) B.; m. Sigrid Carlson, Mar. 3, 1956 (div. 1972); children: Jeffrey Owen, Kirsten, Scott David, Daniel Stuart; m. Susan Sloane Jannicky, July 4, 1975; 1 child, Mary Ruth Bellamy; stepchildren: Bradbury, Stephanie Ellington. AB with distinction, Stanford U., 1956; LLB magna cum laude, Harvard U., 1964. Bar: Calif. 1965, N.Y. 1969. Law clk. Ropes & Gray, Boston, 1963; assoc. McCutchen, Doyle, Brown & Enersen, San Francisco, 1964-66; lectr. law U. Khartoum, Sudan, 1966-67, Kenya Inst. Adminstrn., Lower Kabete, 1967-68; assoc. Cravath, Swaine & Moore, N.Y.C., 1968-72, ptnr., 1973—, recruiting ptnr., 1978-82, mng. ptnr. for legal staff, 1983-86; ptnr. in charge London office, 1995—2001. Treas. N.Y. Law Inst., 1978-83, chmn. exec. com., 1983-88, pres., 1988-93. Mem. editorial bd. Harvard U. Law Rev., 1963-64. Dir. Literacy Assistance Ctr., N.Y.C., 1983—94, co-chmn. bd. dirs., 1987—94; trustee Greenwich (Conn.) Country Day Sch., 1985—92, v.p., 1986—88, pres., chmn. bd. trustees, 1988—92; co-chmn. Harvard U. Law Sch. 25th Reunion Gift, 1988—89; N.Y. regional com. campaign Harvard Law Sch., 1991—95; com. on univ. resources Harvard U., 1991—, mem. Harvard law sch. vis. com., 1995—2001; keystone regional vice chair centennial campaign Stanford U., 1986—92; exec. com. Stanford U. N.Y. Coun., 1992—95; vice chmn. Stanford U. N.Y. Major Gifts Com., 1993—95; co-chair Stanford U. Ea. Coun., 1993; bd. govs. Stanford Assocs., 1993—95, pres., chmn. bd. govs., 1994—95; bd. advisors Stanford Trust (U.K.), 1995—; mem. nat. bd. Outward Bound USA, 1993—96. 1st lt. USAF, 1956—61. Recipient Centennial medallion Stanford U., Stanford Assocs. award. Fellow Am. Bar Found., N.Y. State Bar Found.; mem. ABA, Internat. Bar Assn., N.Y. State Bar Assn., Assn. Bar City N.Y., The Pilgrims, Round Hill Club (Greenwich), Field Club (Greenwich), Sankaty Head Club (Nantucket), Siasconset Casino Assn. (Nantucket), Harvard Club (N.Y.C.). Banking, General corporate, Securities. Home: 19 Pelham Crescent London SW7 2NR England also: 39 Baxter Rd Siasconset MA 02564 Office: Cravath Swaine & Moore City Point One Ropemaker St London EC2Y 9HR England also: Cravath Swaine & Moore 825 8th Ave Fl 46 New York NY 10019-7416 E-mail: dbrownwood@cravath.com

BRUCE, DANA GLENN, lawyer; b. Peoria, Ill., June 16, 1958; s. Glenn D. and Kathleen M. Bruce; m. Jeanne L. Foster, July 9, 1994; children: Joey Wallish, Jami Wallish, Josh Wallish, Jeremy Wallish. BA, Oral Roberts U., 1980; MDiv, So. Meth. U., 1984, JD, 1987. Intern min. Trinity United Meth. Ch., San Antonio, 1983; min. White Rock United Meth. Ch., Dallas, 1983-84; law clk. Gibson, Dunn & Crutcher, 1985-87, atty., 1987-93, Pryor & Bruce, Dallas, 1994—. Rancher, horse breeder Rising Star Ranch, Greenville, Tex., 1995—. Notes and comment editor Jour. Air Law and Commerce, 1986-87; patentee solar Powered Christmas Lights, 1999. Republican. Methodist. Avocations: horseback riding, fishing, tennis. Home: 4502 Scenic Ct Rowlett TX 75088-6877 Office: Pryor & Bruce 302 N San Jacinto St Rockwall TX 75087-2555

BRUCE, ERIKA LYNN, lawyer; b. Dallas, Sept. 17, 1969; BA in Polit. Sci., Washington U., St. Louis, 1992; JD, St. Mary's U., San Antonio, 1995. Bar: Tex. 1995. Atty. Law Office of Helene S. Cohen, Dallas, 1995-97, Donohoe, Jameson & Carroll, P.C., Dallas, 1997—. Editor St. Mary's Law Jour., 1994-95. Bd. dirs. Hebrew Free Loan Assn., Dallas, 1995—. Mem. ABA, Tex. State Bar Assn., Dallas Bar Assn. (cmty. outreach program). Avocations: marathon running, music, hiking, movies, books. Office: Donohoe Jameson & Carroll PC 3400 Renaissance Tower 1201 Elm St Dallas TX 75270-2102

BRUCE, JACKSON MARTIN, JR. lawyer; b. Milw., Apr. 10, 1931; s. Jackson Martin and Harriet (Edgell) B.; m. Lilias M. Morehouse, June 30, 1954; children: Lilias Stephanie, Andrew Edgell. AB magna cum laude, Harvard U., 1953, JD cum laude, 1957; MA with 1st class honors in Law, Cambridge U., 1955. Bar: Wis. 1957, Fla. 1973. Assoc. Quarles & Brady, Milw., 1957-64, ptnr., 1964-96; shareholder Dunwody, White & Landon, Naples, Fla., 1996—; counsel Michael Best & Friedrich, Milw., 1996—. Mem. joint editl. bd. Uniform Trusts and Estates Acts; contbr. articles to profl. jours. Bd. dirs. Living Ch. Found., Inc., 1965-98; trustee Univ. Sch. Milw., 1973-79. Fellow Am. Coll. Trust and Estate Counsel (bd. regents 1976-82, treas. 1990-91, sec. 1991-92, v.p. 1992-93, pres. 1994-95); mem. ABA (bd. govs. 1994-97, chmn. sect. real property, probate and trust law 1984-85, ho. dels., ethics com. 1998-2001), State Bar Wis. (chmn. bd. govs. 1979-80), Am. Bar Found., Am. Law Inst., Internat. Acad. Estate and Trust Law (mem. exec. coun. 1980-86), Nat. Conf. Bar Pres., Nat. Conf. Lawyers and Corp. Fiduciaries (chmn. 1984-90), Town Club, Milw. Club (bd. dirs.), The Club Pelican Bay. Estate planning, Probate, Estate taxation. Home: 6101 Pelican Bay Blvd Apt 1201 Naples FL 34108-8183 also: 9008 N Bayside Dr Milwaukee WI 53217-1913 Office: Dunwody White & Landon 4001 Tamiami Trl N Ste 200 Naples FL 34103-3591 also: Michael Best & Friedrich 100 E Wisconsin Ave Ste 3300 Milwaukee WI 53202-4107 Business E-Mail: jbruce@dwl-law.com, jmbruce@mbf-law.com

BRUCE, WILLIAM ROLAND, lawyer; b. Portsmouth, Va., July 13, 1935; s. William Roland Sr. and Elizabeth (Jack) B.; m. Katherine Martin, Sept. 1, 1956 (div. Apr. 1980); m. Rita Kay Glisson, Jan. 3, 1981; children: Kate, William, Elizabeth, Margaret, Andrew, Alexander. BA, U. Va., 1956, LLB, 1959. Bar: Va. 1959, Tenn. 1960, U.S. Supreme Ct. 1964. Assoc. Martin, Tate & Morrow, Memphis, 1959-62; sole practice, 1963-65; ptnr. Bruce & Southern, 1965-72; chmn. Bruce, Brandon & Regan, P.C., 1972-91; with Baker, Worthington, Crossley & Stansberry, Nashville, 1991-94, Stokes, Bartholomew, Evans & Petree, Nashville and Memphis, 1994—. Lectr. Vanderbilt U. Sch. Law, Nashville, 1977-79; mem. Tenn. Jud. Coun., 1997—; mem. Tenn. Housing devel. Agy., 1998—. Rep. Tenn. Ho. of Reps., Nashville, 1966-68; senator Tenn. Senate, Nashville, 1968-72; mem. Health Edn. and Housing Facility Bd. of Memphis, 1984—, chmn., 1984-87. Served to capt. U.S. Army, 1957-58. Named Tenn. Outstanding Young Man, Jaycees, 1969, Conservationist of Yr., Tenn. Conservation League, 1972. Fellow Am. Coll. Mortgage Attys., Tenn. Bar Found.; mem. ABA, Am. Bar Found., Tenn. Bar Assn., Nashville Bar Found. Democrat. Episcopalian. Avocation: sailing. Banking, Legislative, Real property. Home: 4996 Sparta Hwy Smithville TN 37166-5156 Office: Stokes Bartholomew Evans & Petree 424 Church St Ste 2800 Nashville TN 37219-2386 E-mail: bruces@dtccom.net

BRUCKEN, ROBERT MATTHEW, lawyer; b. Akron, Ohio, Sept. 15, 1934; s. Harold M. and Eunice B. (Boesel) B.; m. Lois R. Gilbert, June 30, 1960; children: Nancy, Elizabeth, Rowland, Gilbert. AB, Marietta Coll., 1956; JD, U. Mich., 1959. Bar: Ohio 1960. Assoc. Baker & Hostetler, Cleve., 1960-69; ptnr., 1970—. Trustee Lakeside Assn., 1979-97, Marietta Coll., 1983—; sec., treas. Leader Shape, Inc., 1990—. Served with AUS,

1959-60. Mem. ABA, Ohio State Bar Assn. (chmn. probate and trust law sect. 1981-83), Cleve. Bar Assn. (chmn. probate ct. com. 1973-75), Am. Coll. Trust and Estate Counsel, Phi Beta Kappa. Congregationalist. Estate planning, Probate, Estate taxation. Office: Baker & Hostetler 3200 Nat City Ctr 1900 E 9th St Ste 3200 Cleveland OH 44114-3475 E-mail: rbrucken@bakerlaw.com

BRUDER, GEORGE FREDERICK, lawyer; b. Ann Arbor, Mich., June 4, 1938; s. George G. and Mary Louise (Pfisterer) B.; m. Jean Riley, July 10, 1965; children: Roxanne, Stephanie. AB, Dartmouth Coll., 1960; JD, U. Chgo., 1963. Bar: D.C. 1964. Atty. FPC, Washington, 1964-67; atty. long lines dept. AT&T, Washington, 1967-68; assoc. Debevoise & Liberman, Washington, 1968-70, ptnr, 1971-75; ptnr. Bruder, Gentile & Marcoux, Washington, 1976-97. Mem. Fed. Energy Bar Assn. (pres. 1984-85). Democrat. Episcopalian. E-mail: gfbruder@erols.com Administrative and regulatory, FERC practice, Public utilities. Home: 8 E Lenox St Chevy Chase MD 20815-4211

BRUEMMER, RUSSELL JOHN, lawyer; b. Decorah, Iowa, Apr. 23, 1952; s. John William and Marion Jean (Wartinbee) B. BA, Luther Coll., 1974; JD, U. Mich., 1977. Bar: Minn. 1978, D.C. 1980, U.S. Dist. Ct. D.C. 1981, U.S. Supreme Ct. 1990, N.Y. 2001. Law clk. to judge U.S. Ct. Appeals (8th cir.), 1977-78; spl. asst. to the dir. FBI, Washington, 1978-80, chief counsel congl. affairs, 1980-81; assoc. Wilmer, Cutler & Pickering, 1981-84, ptnr., 1985-87, 90—, counsel to dir. of cen. intelligence, 1987-88; gen. counsel CIA, 1988-90. Speaker numerous profl. seminars. Editor-in-chief U. Mich. Jour. of Law Rev.; mem. editl. adv. bd. Electronic Banking Law and Commerce Report; contbr. articles to law and banking jours. Recipient Disting. Intelligence medal, 1990, Order of the Coif, 1977. Mem. ABA (banking law com. 1982—, subcom. on bank holding cos. and nonbanking activities, chmn. 1985-87, chmn. subcom. on securities activities 1994-96, 98-99, mem. standing com. on law and nat. security 1995-98), Am. Law Inst., Coun. on Fgn. Rels. Republican. Lutheran. Banking, Finance, Mergers and acquisitions. Home: 4024 40th St N Arlington VA 22207-4608 Office: Wilmer Cutler & Pickering 2445 M St NW Ste 500 Washington DC 20037-1487

BRUEN, JAMES A. lawyer; b. South Hampton, N.Y., Nov. 29, 1943; s. John Francis and Kathryn Jewell (Arthur) B.; m. Carol Lynn Heller, June 13, 1968; children: Jennifer Lynn, Garrett John. BA cum laude, Claremont Men's Coll., 1965; JD, Stanford U., 1968. Bar: Calif. 1968, U.S. Dist. Ct. (no., ea., so. and cen. dists.) Calif. 1970, U.S. Ct. Claims 1972, U.S. Tax Ct. 1972, U.S. Ct. Appeals (9th cir.) 1972, U.S. Supreme Ct. 1973, Ariz. 1993. Atty. FCC, Washington, 1968-70; asst. U.S. atty. criminal div. Office of US. Atty., San Francisco, 1970-73, asst. U.S. atty. civil div., 1973-75, chief of civil div., 1975-77; ptnr. Landels, Ripley & Diamond, 1977-2000, Farella Braun & Martel LLP, San Francisco, 2000—. Mem. faculty Nat. Jud. Coll. ABA; lectr. Am. Law Inst. Am. Bd. Trial Advocates, Practising Law Inst. Def. Rsch. Inst., others. Co-author: Pharmaceutical Products Liability, 1989; contbg. editor: Hazardous Waste and Toxic Torts Law and Strategy, 1987-92; contbr. numerous articles to profl. jours. Mem. ABA (vice chmn. environ. quality com. nat. resources sect. 1989-93, co-chmn. enforment litigation subcom. environ. litigation com. litigation sect. 1990-92), Am. Inn of Ct. (master-at-large), Internat. Soc. for Environ. Epidemiology. Avocations: scuba diving, travel. Criminal, Environmental, Product liability. Office: Farella Brown & Martel Russ Bldg 30th Fl 235 Montgomery St San Francisco CA 94104 Fax: (415) 954-4480. E-mail: jbruen@fbm.com

BRUESEKE, HAROLD EDWARD, magistrate; b. Sandusky, Ohio, Mar. 19, 1943; s. Edward W. and Jolanda (Sommer) B.; m. Bonnie A. Beaver, Aug. 12, 1967; children: Matthew E., Michael A. BA with honors, Elmhurst Coll., 1965; JD, Ind. U., 1968; grad., Ind. Judicial Coll., 2000. Bar: Ind., 1968, U.S. Dist. Ct. (no. and so. dists.) 1968, U.S. Supreme Ct. 1978; lic. real estate broker, Ind. Staff atty. Legal Svcs./Legal Edn., South Bend, Ind., 1968-70; pvt. practice, 1971-92; dep. pros. atty. St. Joseph County, 1971-73; juvenile referee St. Joseph Probate Ct., 1973-92, judge pro tem, 1993, magistrate, 1993—. Contbg. author: Juvenile Benchbook, 1980-92. Bd. dirs. Eden Theol. Sem., St. Louis, 1989-2001, various other civic orgns., South Bend, 1968—; bd. dirs., elder Zion United Ch. of Christ, South Bend, 1994-96. Mem. ABA, Ind. State Bar Assn., St. Joseph County Bar Assn., Nat. Coun. Juvenile and Family Ct. Judges, Ind. Coun. Juvenile and Family Ct. Judges (bd. dirs., sec., v.p. pres. 1980-2000), Jud. Conf. Ind. (dir. 1998-2000). Avocations: amateur radio, recreational vehicles, computers. Home: 52741 Arbor Dr South Bend IN 46635-1205 Office: Juvenile Justice Ctr 1000 S Michigan St South Bend IN 46601-3426 E-mail: bhbruese@home.com, hbrueseke@jjconline.org

BRUFF, HAROLD HASTINGS, dean; b. 1944; BA in Am. History and Lit., Williams Coll.; JD magna cum laude, Harvard U. Law faculty Ariz. State U., Tempe, 1971-79; sr. atty.-advisor Office of Legal Counsel, U.S. Dept. Justice, 1979-81; cons. to chmn. Pres.'s Commn. on the Accident at Three Mile Island, 1981; law faculty U. Tex., Austin, 1983-85, John S. Redditt prof. law, 1985-92; Donald Rothschild rsch. prof. George Washington U. Law Sch., Washington, 1992-96; dean U. Colo. Sch. Law, Boulder, 1996—. Contbr. articles to profl. jours. Mem. ABA, Phi Beta Kappa. Office: U Colo Boulder Sch Law Campus Box 401 Boulder CO 80309-0001*

BRUMM, JAMES EARL, lawyer, trading company executive; b. San Antonio, Dec. 19, 1942; s. John Edward and Marie Oletha (Gault) B.; m. Alicia Joan Pine, Aug. 17, 1968 (div. Mar. 1991); children: Christopher Kenji, Jennifer Kimiko, Laurie Kiyoko; m. Yuko Tsuchida, Apr. 17, 1991. AB, Calif. State U., Fresno, 1965; LLB, Columbia U., 1968. Bar: N.Y. 1969. Assoc. Reid & Priest, N.Y.C., 1968-72, Logan, Takashima & Nemoto, Tokyo, 1973-76; exec. v.p., gen. counsel, dir. Mitsubishi Internat. Corp., N.Y.C., 1977—; pres. Mitsubishi Internat. Corp. Found., 1992—; dir. Mitsubishi Corp., Japan, 1995—. Bd. dirs. Brunei LNG, Tembec, Inc. Trustee Spuyten Duyvil Nursery Sch., Bronx, N.Y., 1991-95; mem. lawyers com. for human rights, steering com. Internat. Rule of Law Coun., 1993—; bd. dirs. Jr. Achievement Internat., 1997-2000, Internat. Sch. Svcs., 1997-99; bd. dirs. Sanctuary for Families, 2000—; bd. visitors Columbia Law Sch., 1998—. Mem. ABA, Assn. Bar City N.Y. (chmn. com. on internat. trade 1990-93, chmn. task force on internat. legal svcs. 1998-2001), Univ. Club, Nippon Club. General corporate, Private international. Home: 255 W 84th St Apt 6C New York NY 10024-4327 Office: Mitsubishi Internat Corp 520 Madison Ave New York NY 10022-4213

BRUNE, KENNETH LEONARD, lawyer; b. Fort Madison, Iowa, Aug. 23, 1945; s. Bernard John and Colette Mary (Steffensmeier) B.; m. Judith Ann Sears, Oct. 17, 1970; children— James Bernard, Adrian Margaret, Sarah Anne. B.A., St. Ambrose Coll., 1967; M.A., U. Iowa, 1972; J.D., U. Tulsa, 1974. Bar: Iowa 1975, Okla. 1975, U.S. Dist. Ct. (we. and no. dist.) Okla. 1976, U.S. Ct. Appeals (10th cir.) 1976, U.S. Supreme Ct. 1980. Law clk. U.S. Dist. Ct. (no. dist.) Okla., Tulsa, 1975-77; asst. dist. atty., Tulsa County, Okla., 1977-78; judge dist. ct., Tulsa County, 1978-79; assoc. Holliman, Langholz, Runnels & Dorwart, Tulsa, 1980-81, ptnr., 1981— ; gen. counsel Make Today Count, Tulsa, 1979-83, Okla. Oncology Nursing Soc., Tulsa, 1980-83; chmn. bd. Legal Services Eastern Okla., Tulsa, 1981, bd. mem., 1980— ; judge temp. ct. appeals Okla. Supreme Ct., Tulsa, 1981; asst. prof. U. Tulsa Law Sch., 1984. Div. chmn. United Way, Tulsa, 1980-83. Served to 1st lt. U.S. Army, 1969-71, Vietnam. Decorated Bronze Star; St. Ambrose Coll. presdl. scholar, 1965-67. Mem. Okla. Bar Assn., Tulsa County Bar Assn. (speakers com. 1980-83), Delta Epsilon Sigma. Democrat. Roman Catholic. Federal civil litigation, General corporate, Oil, gas, and mineral. Home: 3519 S Florence Ave Tulsa OK 74105-2909 Office: Holliman Langholz Runnels & Dorwart 10 E 3d St 700 Holarud Bldg Tulsa OK 74103

BRUNENKANT, JON LODWICK, lawyer; b. Washington, June 17, 1950; s. Edward James and Jeanette (Lodwick) B. BA with honors, Northwestern U., 1972; JD with honors, George Washington U., 1975; MBA with honors, Iran Ctr. for Mgmt. Studies, 1977. Bar: D.C. 1978, Va. 1975, U.S. Supreme Ct. 1978, U.S. Ct. Appeals (3d, 5th, 6th, 7th, 8th, 10th, 11th and D.C. cirs.) 1978. Assoc. Grove, Jaskiewicz, Gilliam & Cobert, Washington, 1978-83, ptnr., 1983-89; ptnr. Travis & Gooch, Washington, 1990—. Mem. ABA, Fed. Energy Bar Assn. Administrative and regulatory, Federal civil litigation, FERC practice. Office: Travis & Gooch 1100 15th St NW Washington DC 20005-1707

BRUNER, PHILIP LANE, lawyer; b. Chgo., Sept. 26, 1939; s. Henry Pfeiffer and Mary Marjorie (Williamson) B.; m. Ellen Carole Germann, Mar. 21, 1964; children: Philip Richard, Stephen Reed, Carolyn Anne AB, Princeton U., 1961; JD, U. Mich., 1964; MBA, Syracuse U., 1967. Bar: Wis. 1964, Minn. 1968. Mem. Briggs and Morgan P.A., Mpls., St. Paul, 1967-83; founding shareholder Hart, Bruner and O'Brien P.A., Mpls., 1983-90; ptnr., head constrn. law group Faegre & Benson, 1991—. Adj. prof. William Mitchell Coll. Law, St. Paul, 1970-76; lectr. law seminars, univs., bar assns. and industry; chmn. Supreme Ct. Minn. Bd. Continuing Legal Edn., 1994-98. Contbr. articles to profl. jours. Mem. Bd. Edn., Mahtomedi Ind. Sch. Dist. 832, 1978-86; bd. dirs. Mahtomedi Area Ednl. Found., 1988-94, pres., 1988-91; bd. dirs. Minn. Ch. Found., 1975—, pres., 1989-97; chmn. constrn. industry adv. bd. West Group, 1991—. Capt. USAF, 1964-67. Decorated Air Force Commendation Medal; recipient Disting. Service award St. Paul Jaycees, 1974; named One of Ten Outstanding Young Minnesotans, Minn. Jaycees, 1975. Fellow Am. Coll. Constrn. Lawyers (founding mem., bd. govs.), Nat. Contract Mgmt. Assn., Am. Bar Found.; mem. ABA (chmn. internat. constrn. divsn. forum com. on constrn. industry 1989-91, chmn. fidelity and surety law com. 1994-95, regional chmn. pub. contract law sect. 1990-96), Internat. Bar Assn., Inter-Pacific Bar Assn. (vice chmn. internat. constrn. com. 1995-97), Fed. Bar Assn., Minn. Bar Assn. (vice chmn. litigation sect. 1979-81), Wis. Bar Assn., Hennepin Bar Assn., Internat. Assn. Def. Counsel, Am. Arbitration Assn. (nat. panel arbitrators), Mpls. Club. Presbyterian. General civil litigation, Construction, Government contracts and claims. Home: 8432 80th St N Stillwater MN 55082-9331 Office: Faegre & Benson 2200 Norwest Ctr 90 S 7th St Ste 2200 Minneapolis MN 55402-3901 E-mail: pbruner@faegre.com, Philipbruner@hotmail.com

BRUNER, STEPHEN C. lawyer; b. Chgo., Nov. 11, 1941; s. Henry Pfeiffer and Mary Marjorie (Williamson) B.; m. Elizabeth Erskine Osborn, Apr. 7, 1973; children: Elizabeth, David. B.A. summa cum laude, Yale U., 1963; J.D. cum laude, Harvard U., 1967. Bar: Ill. 1967, U.S. Dist. Ct. (no. dist.) Ill. 1971, U.S. Ct. Appeals (7th cir.) 1983, U.S. Supreme Ct. 1988. Assoc. Winston & Strawn, Chgo., 1971-76, ptnr., 1976-82, capital ptnr., 1982-01. Lectr. Northwestern U. Sch. of Law, 1983-84; cons. Commn. on Govt. Procurement, 1972; mem. Landmarks Commn., Oak Park, Ill., 1978-81; bd. govs. Oak Park-River Forest Community Chest, 1985-90; elected mem. Bd. Edn. Oak Park and River Forest High Sch., 1993-01. Served to lt. USN, 1968-71. Recipient Navy Achievement medal; Corning Found. travelling fellow, 1963-64. Mem. ABA (litigation and pub. contracts sects.), Chgo. Bar Assn., Am. Arbitration Assn. (panel of arbitrators), Chgo. Coun. on Fgn. Rels., Econ. Club, Univ. Club, Yale Club, Harvard Club (Chgo.). Federal civil litigation, Government contracts and claims. Office: Winston & Strawn 35 W Wacker Dr Chicago IL 60601-1695

BRUNETTI, MELVIN T. federal judge; b. 1933; m. Gail Dian Buchanan; children: Nancy, Bradley, Melvin Jr. BS, U. Nev., 1951-53, 1956-57, 1960; JD, U. Calif., San Francisco, 1964. Mem. firm Vargas, Bartlett & Dixon, 1964-69, Laxalt, Bell, Allison & Lebaron, 1970-78, Allison, Brunetti, MacKenzie, Hartman, Soumbeniotis & Russell, 1978-85; judge U.S. Ct. Appeals (9th cir.), Reno, 1985-99, sr. judge, 1999—. Mem. Council of Legal Advisors, Rep. Nat. Com., 1982-85. Served with U.S. Army N.G., 1954-56. Mem. ABA, State Bar of Nev. (pres. 1984-85, bd. govs. 1975-84). Office: US Ct Appeals US Courthouse 400 S Virginia St Ste 506 Reno NV 89501-2194*

BRUNING, ANTHONY STEVEN, lawyer; b. St. Louis, Oct. 24, 1955; s. Frederick Charles Jr. and Pauline (Shrum) B.; m. Cynthia Louise Leonard, Nov. 2, 1979; children: Anthony Steven Jr., Ryan Leonard, Michele Louise, Joseph Alexander. BA, U. Mo., 1977; JD, St. Louis U., 1980. Bar: Mo. 1980, U.S. Ct Appeals (8th cir.) 1980, U.S. Dist. Ct. (ea. dist.) Mo. 1980. Assoc. Leritz, Reinert & Duree PC, St. Louis, 1980-86, ptnr., 1986-90, Leritz, Plunkert and Bruning PC, St. Louis, 1990—. Speaker in field. Mem. Mo. Bar Assn. (rep. exec. com., young lawyers sect. coun. 1982-86), St. Louis Met. Bar Assn., ABA, Ill. Bar Assn., Mo. Assn. Trail Attys., Assn. Trail Lawyers Am., Mo. Athletic Club. Democrat. Avocations: fishing, hunting. Office: Leritz Plunkert & Bruning PC 1 City Ctr Ste 2001 Saint Louis MO 63101-2402 E-mail: abruning@leritzlaw.com

BRUNN, THOMAS LEO, SR. lawyer; b. Ionia, Mich., Mar. 14, 1937; s. Walter W. and Catherine M. (Fox) B.; m. Constance P. Perz, Sept. 28, 1963; children: Thomas Leo, Timothy J., Maribeth, Heather. BS, John Carroll U., 1959; JD, Cleve. Marshall Law Sch., 1967. Bar: ohio 1967. Pres. The Brunn Law Firm Co., L.P.A. Cleve. Served to 1st lt. U.S. Army, 1959-62. Mem. ABA, Ohio Bar Assn., Cleve. Assn. Civil Trial Attys. (pres. 1982-83), Fedn. Ins. Counsel (vice chmn. product liability com.), Chagrin Valley Country Club (Chagrin Falls, Ohio). State civil litigation, Family and matrimonial, Insurance. Office: 520 Standard Bldg Cleveland OH 44115 E-mail: brunn@core.com

BRUNO, ANTHONY D. lawyer; b. Newark, May 3, 1956; s. Frank and Delores (Fleming) B.; m. Gina Mabey, Aug. 1982; children: Chris, Dan, Will. BA in Polit. Sci., Syracuse U., 1978; JD, George Washington U., 1981. Bar: N.Y. 1981, N.J. 1981. Atty. Shearman & Sterling, N.Y.C., 1981-84; assoc. gen. counsel Warner-Lambert, Morris Plains, N.J., 1984-2000; sr. v.p., gen. counsel Galen Holdings Plc, Rockaway, 2001—. Office: 100 Enterprise Dr Ste 280 Rockaway NJ 07866 E-mail: tbruno@wclabs.com

BRUNSON, JOHN SOLES, lawyer; b. Houston, Jan. 8, 1934; s. Nathan Bryant and Jonnie E. (McMillian) B.; m. Joan Erwin, Dec. 26, 1953; children: W. Mark, Dana Ruth. BBA, Baylor U., 1956, LLB, 1958, JD, 1965. Bar: Tex., 1958, U.S. Supreme Ct., 1961. Assoc. Dillingham, Schleider & Lewis, Houston, 1958-64; ptnr. Brunson & Brill, 1964-70, Baker, Heard & Brunson, Houston, 1970-72, Brunson & Erwin, Houston, 1972-84. Pres. New Asia Products, Inc., 1984—; chmn. Clavis Investment Co., 1984—; bd. dirs. Ridgewood Devel. Mem. Harris County (Tex.) Dem. Exec. Com., 1959-65, Tex. Dem. Exec. Com., 1963-74; mem. exec. bd. Bapt. Gen. Conv. Tex., 1988-94; trustee First Bapt. Acad., 1996—, chmn., 2000—; trustee Houston Christian H.S., 1997—, Macedonian Call Found., 1991—, Ch. & Sch. Assn. Employee Group Benefit Plan, 2000—. Mem. ABA, State Bar Tex. Finance, Private international, Real property. Office: 7555 Katy Fwy Apt 70 Houston TX 77024-2119 E-mail: onejsb@swbell.net

BRUSTAD, ORIN DANIEL, lawyer; b. Chgo., Nov. 11, 1941; s. Marvin D. and Sylvia Evelyn (Peterson) B.; m. Ilona M. Fox, July 16, 1966; children: Caroline E., Katherine L., Mark D. BA in History, Yale U., 1963, MA, 1964; JD, Harvard U., 1968. Bar: Mich. 1968, U.S. Dist. Ct. (so. dist.) Mich. 1968. Assoc. Miller, Canfield, Paddock and Stone, Detroit, 1968-74, sr. ptnr., 1975—, chmn. employee benefits practice group, 1989-96, dep. chmn. tax dept., 1989-93. Bd. dirs. Electrocon Internat., Inc., Ann Arbor, Mich. Mem. editl. adv. bd. Benefits Law Jour.; contbr. articles to profl. jours. Fellow Am. Coun. Employee Benefits Counsel (charter); mem. ABA, Mich. Bar Assn., Detroit Bar Assn., Mich. Employee Benefits Conf. Avocations: sailing, skiing, reading, piano. General corporate, Pension, profit-sharing, and employee benefits. Home: 1422 Macgregor Ln Ann Arbor MI 48105-2836 Office: Miller Canfield Paddock & Stone 150 W Jefferson Ave Fl 25th Detroit MI 48226-4432 E-mail: odbrusta@aol.com, brustad@millercanfield.com

BRUSTEIN, MICHAEL LABE, lawyer; b. May 13, 1949; s. Louis and Flora Eva (Forman) B.; m. Joan Lorraine Goldfrank; 1 child, Tess. BA cum laude, NYU, 1971; MD, U. Conn., 1974. Bar: Conn. 1974. Chief adult and vocat. edn. br. Office Gen. Counsel HEW, Washington, 1974-79; legal cons. Dept. Edn. Transition Team, 1980; ptnr. Brustein & Manasevit, 1980—. Legal cons. Nat. Assn. Workforce Bds., Nat. Inst. Edn., State Edn. Agencies of N.Y., Calif., N.Mex., Tenn., Fla., R.I., Wyo., Ga., La., N.C., Mich., W.Va., Ark., P.R.; lawyers com. Civil Rights Under Law; gen. counsel Nat. Assn. Partnerships in Equity. Author: School-to-Work User's Guide: Understanding Federal Cost Principles and Avoiding Audit Liability, 1997, The AVA Guide to the School-to-Work Opportunities Act, 1994, The AVA Guide to Federal Funding for Tech-Prep, 1993, The AVA Audit Handbook: Avoiding Liability Under the 1990 Perkins Act, rev. edit., 1992; contbr. articles to profl. jours. Mem. Nat. Assn. Fed. Fin. Adminstrs. (gen. counsel), Nat. Assn. State Couns. Vocat. Edn. (gen. counsel), Nat. Coordinating Coun. Vocat. Student Orgns. (gen. counsel), D.C. Bar Assn., Conn. Bar Assn., N.Y. Bar Assn., Phi Beta Kappa, Phi Sigma Alpha. Home: 3726 Van Ness St NW Washington DC 20016-2226 Office: 3105 South St NW Washington DC 20007-4419 E-mail: mbrustein@bruman.com

BRUTON, CHARLES CLINTON, lawyer; b. Odessa, Tex., July 3, 1953; s. John Harley and Bonnie Jean (Woodson) B.; m. Janet Grubbs (div.). Student, Ea. N.Mex. U., 1971-73; BA in Polit. Sci. cum laude, Old Dominion U., 1979; JD magna cum laude, Oglethorpe U., 1982. Bar: Ga. 1983, U.S. Dist. Ct. (no. dist.) Ga. 1992, N.Mex. 1993, U.S. Dist. Ct. N.Mex. 1993, U.S. Ct. Appeals (11th cir.) 1993, U.S. Ct. Appeals (10th cir.) 1994. Legal sec. Macey & Zusmann, Atlanta, 1982-83; pvt. practice, Decatur, Ga., 1983-85; title ins. agt. Lincoln County Abstract, Ruidoso, N.Mex., 1985, Alamogordo (N.Mex.) Title Co., 1985-86; in house counsel, owner Otero Land & Title Co., Alamogordo, 1986-92; assoc. The Buck Firm, P.C., 1992-96; with N.Mex. Pub. Defender, Carlsbad, 1996—. Lawyer concerning Indian Child Welfare Act, Cherokee Nation, Tahlequah, Okla., 1992-94; alt. mem. N.Mex. Gov.s's Select Com. on Title Ins. Policy Changes, Santa Fe, 1991. Editor Woodrow Wilson Coll. Law Jour., 1981. Campaign sec. Judith Spear for Treas. Campaign, Alamogordo, 1988; elder Gateway Bapt. Ch., Alamogordo, 1993; mem. Lawyer's Co-op in Real Property and Bankruptcy, 1982. With USN, 1973-76. Mem. ABA, FBA, Lions (sec. Alamogordo 1992-93, tailtwister 1995), Otero County Bar Assn. (v.p. 1995-96, state bar com. on the unauthorized practice of law 1996—), Phi Mu Alpha Sinfonia. Republican. Avocations: computer programming, golf, fishing, role-playing games, music. Civil rights, General civil litigation, Native American. Office: NMex Pub Defenders 211 N Canal St Carlsbad NM 88220-5829

BRYAN, BARRY RICHARD, lawyer; b. Orange, N.J., Sept. 5, 1930; s. Lloyd Thomas and Amy Rufe (Swank) B.; m. Margaret Susannah Elliot, July 24, 1953; children— Elliot Christopher, Peter George (dec.), Susannah Margaret, Sallie Catharine. B.A., Yale U., 1952, J.D. cum laude, 1955; diploma in comparative legal studies, Cambridge U., Eng., 1956. Bar: N.Y. 1959. Legal advisor to gen. counsel Sec. of U.S. Air Force, Washington, 1956-58; assoc. Debevoise & Plimpton, N.Y.C., 1958-62, ptnr., 1963-93, presiding ptnr., 1993-98, of counsel, 1999—. Served to 1st lt. USAF, 1956-58. Fulbright scholar Trinity Coll., Cambridge U., 1956. Mem. ABA, Assn. of Bar of City of N.Y., Union Internationale des Avocats, Country Club of New Canaan, Polo de Paris, Fishers Island Club, Order of Coif, Phi Beta Kappa. Episcopalian. General corporate, Private international, Securities. Home: PO Box 197 Isabella Beach Rd Fishers Island NY 06390 Office: Debevoise & Plimpton 919 3rd Ave Fl 43 New York NY 10022

BRYAN, JAMES SPENCER, lawyer; b. Pitts., Oct. 26, 1944; s. Joseph and Zella Mae (Spencer) B.; m. Karen Smith, May 27, 1972. B.A., Harvard U., 1966; J.D., U. Pa., 1971; postgrad. Stanford U., 1967-68. Bar: Calif. 1972, U.S. Dist. Ct. (cen. dist.) Calif. 1973, U.S. Dist. Ct. (ea. and so. dists.) Calif. 1981. Jud. clk. U.S. Dist. Ct. (so. dist.) N.Y., N.Y.C., 1971-72; assoc. O'Melveny & Myers, Los Angeles, 1972-79, Seyfarth, Shaw, Fairweather & Geraldson, Los Angeles, 1979-82; ptnr. Dretzin & Kauff, Los Angeles, 1982-87, Lawler, Felix & Hall, L.A., 1987-90, Arter & Hadden, L.A., 1990—; judge pro tem Los Angeles Mcpl. Ct., 1983-84. Contbr. to Vanderbilt Law Rev., 1974, Loyola Law Rev., Los Angeles, 1981. NDEA fellow Stanford U., 1967. Mem. ABA, Calif. Bar Assn., Order of Coif. Democrat. Federal civil litigation, State civil litigation, Labor. Office: Arter & Hadden 700 S Flower St Los Angeles CA 90017-4101

BRYAN, ROBERT J. federal judge; b. Bremerton, Wash., Oct. 29, 1934; s. James W. and Vena Gladys (Jensen) B.; m. Cathy Ann Welander, June 14, 1958; children: Robert James, Ted Lorin, Ronald Terence. BA, U. Wash., 1956, JD, 1958. Bar: Wash. 1959, U.S. Dist. Ct. (we. dist.) Wash. 1959, U.S. Tax Ct. 1965, U.S. Ct. Appeals (9th cir.) 1985. Assoc., then ptnr. Bryan & Bryan, Bremerton, 1959-67; judge Superior Ct., Port Orchard, Wash., 1967-84; ptnr. Riddell, Williams, Bullitt & Walkinshaw, Seattle, 1984-86; judge U.S. Dist. Ct. (we. dist.) Wash., Tacoma, 1986—. Mem. State Jail Comm., Olympia, Wash., 1974-76, Criminal Justice Tng. Com., Olympia, 1978-81, State Bd. on Continuing Legal Edn., Seattle, 1984-86; mem., sec. Jud. Qualifications Commn., Olympia, 1982-83; chair Wash. Fed.-State Jud. Coun., 1997-98. Author: (with others) Washington Pattern Jury Instructions (civil and criminal vols. and supplements), 1970-85, Manual of Model Criminal Jury Instructions for the Ninth Circuit, 1992, Manual of Model Civil Jury Instruction for the Ninth Circuit, 1993. Chmn. 9th Ct. Jury Com., 1991-92; bd. dirs. Fed. Jud. Ctr., 2000—. Served to maj. USAR. Mem.: 9th Cir. Dist. Judges Assn. (sec.-treas. 1997—99, v.p. 1999—2001, pres. 2001—). Office: US Dist Ct 1717 Pacific Ave Rm 4427 Tacoma WA 98402-3234

BRYANS, RICHARD W. lawyer; b. Demver, May 29, 1931; s. William A. and Ruth W. (Waldron) B.; m. Carol Jean, Feb. 17, 1955; children: Richard W., Bridget Ann. BS, Denver U., 1954, JD, 1955. Bar: Colo., U.S. Supreme Ct. 1971. Sole practice, Boulder, Colo., 1958-63; ptnr. Kelly, Stansfield & O'Donnell, Denver, 1963-92, Bryans & Bryans, Denver, 1993—. Served to lt. (j.g.) USNR, 1955-58. State civil litigation, Condemnation, General corporate. Office: 1177 Grant St # 308 Denver CO 80203-2362

BRYANT, GEORGE MCEWAN, lawyer; b. N.Y.C., Nov. 24, 1941; s. Sydney James and Ruth Cutter (McEwan) B.; m. Barbara Ann Phyfe, Sept. 10, 1966; children: Meredith Lee, Scott McEwan. BA, Brown U., 1963; LLB, Columbia U., 1966. Bar: N.J. 1966, N.Y. 1969, U.S. Dist. Ct. N.J. 1966. Assoc. Cravath Swaine & Moore, N.Y.C., 1968-72, Marshall Brattner Greene Allison & Tucker, N.Y.C., 1972-74, Davies Hardy Ives & Lawther, N.Y.C., 1974-77; assoc. counsel N.Y. Life Ins. Co., 1977-96; asst. gen. counsel Met. Life Ins. Co., 1996—. Bd. dirs., v.p. United Way of Ridgewood, Glen Rock and Ho-Ho-Kus, 1978-80; vice chmn. Ridgewood

Republican Mcpl. Com., 1979-82; bd. dirs., treas. Ramapo Hunt and Polo Club Estates, 1983-90. Mem. ABA, Bergen County Bar Assn., The Moorings Country Club. Republican. Mem. Ref. Ch. in Am. General corporate, Probate, Real property. Home: 207 Phelps Rd Ridgewood NJ 07450-1420 Office: Met Life Ins Co One Madison Ave Area 6-H New York NY 10010-3690 E-mail: gbryant@metlife.com

BRYANT, J(AMES) BRUCE, lawyer; b. Dettlebach, Fed. Republic Germany, Jan. 23, 1961; came to U.S., 1964; s. John Thomas and Doris Jean (Hazenbuahler) B.; 1 child, James Bruce II. BA, Northwestern State U., Natchitoches, La., 1984; MJ, La. State, 1986; JD, Miss. Coll., 1989. Bar: Miss., Tex. 1995, U.S. Dist. Ct. (no. and so. dists.) Miss., U.S. Ct. Appeals (5th cir.) La. 1991, U.S. Dist. Ct. (we. dist.) La. 1994. With residential life La. State U., Baton Rouge, 1985-86; law libr. worker Miss. Coll. Sch. Law, Jackson, 1986-87; clk. Brunini Law Firm, 1987-88; ptnr. Cook & Bryant, Bay St. Louis, Miss., 1989-90; assoc. Cook, Yancey, King & Galloway, Shreveport, La., 1990-93; prof. bus. law La. State U., 1991-92, prof. paralegal sci., 1994-96; staff atty. State of La. Office of Support Enforcement, Shreveport, 1993-95; atty. Storm Operating Co. Inc. of La., 1994-98; sr. regional atty. State of La. Dept. Health and Hosps., Shreveport-Bossier City, La., 1995—; prof. comms. law, pub. rels and advt. Northwestern State U., 1996—; spl. asst. dist. atty. 1st Jud. Dist., Caddo Parish, La., 1998—. Bd. dirs. Extra Mile; cons. Wyman Fed. Credit Union, Geismar, La., 1989-90, Comml. Nat. Bank, Shreveport, 1990-93; owner, pres. SHOWBIZZ Entertainment Agys., Shreveport, 1992—; v.p. Godfather Prodns., Inc., Shreveport-Bossier City, La., 1994—; owner La. Ctr. for Law and Justice, 1995—; spl. asst. dist. atty. Caddo Parish, 1998—; owner, pres. Dreamworks Internat., 1999—. Editor, author (with others): Art & Bylaws for Moot Court, 1989; contbr. to The Silence Within, 2000. Del. Republican Dist. IV, 1994—; bd. dirs. Shreveport Little Theatre, 1995-2000, Extra Mile, 1996—; vol. N.W. La. Coalition for Mentally Ill, 1995—, Shreveport/Bossier Svc. Connection, 2001—. Mem. ABA, Miss. Pro Bono Project, Miss. Bar Assn., Assn. Trial Lawyers Am., La. Trial Lawyers Assn., Hancock County Bar Assn. (social chmn.), Shreveport Bar Assn. (comml. litigation sect., editor newsletter), L.A. Pro Bono Project, TKE Alumni Assn. (pres.), Univ. Club (mem. com. 1994—). Roman Catholic. Avocations: martial arts, weightlifting, skiing, shooting. Contracts commercial, Communications, Entertainment. Home: PO Box 444 Shreveport LA 71162-0444 Office: La Ctr for Law and Justice 711 Texas Advocates Bldg Shreveport LA 71120

BRYANT, RICHARD TODD, lawyer; b. Kansas City, Mo., Sept. 3, 1952; s. Francis Todd and Marion Audrey (Weum) B.; m. Carol H. Olsen, Mar. 24, 1979. A.A., A.A.S., Longview Community Coll., 1972; B.B.A., U. Mo.-Kansas City, 1974, M.P.A., 1975, J.D., 1978. Bar: Mo. 1978, D.C. 1995, U.S. Dist. Ct. (we. dist.) Mo. 1978, D.C. 1995, U.S. Dist. Ct. (ea. dist.) Mo. 1995, Kans. 1996, Territorial Ct. of the Virgin Islands 1999. Assoc. Harding & Copilevitz P.C., Kansas City, Mo., 1978-85; ptnr. Copilevitz, Bryant, Gray & Jennings, P.C., 1985-95; bailiff ct. Overland Park, Kans., 1974-84; ptnr. Richard T. Bryant & Assocs. PC, Kansas City, 1995-98, mng. shareholder, 1998—. Contbr. articles to legal jours. Cons. Westwood & Lenexa (Kans.) Police Dept., 1977-78; adminstrv. hearing officer Housing Authority of Kansas City, 1988—; chmn. ad hoc com. Kansas City (Mo.) City Coun., 1992. Mem. ABA (liaison standing com. assn. standards criminal justice 1978, com. adminstrn. criminal justice 1977-78), Am. Arbitration Assn. (bd. of arbitrators, bd. of mediators), Kansas City (Mo.) Bar Assn. (mcpl. ct. com., vice chmn. 1991-94, chmn. 1994-95), First Amendment Lawyers Assn., Phi Delta Phi, Omicron Delta Kappa, Phi Theta Kappa. Constitutional, Family and matrimonial, Insurance. Office: 804 Bryant Bldg 1102 Grand Blvd Kansas City MO 64106-2316

BRYCE, WILLIAM DELF, lawyer; b. Georgetown, Tex., Aug. 7, 1932; s. D.A. Bryce and Frances Maxine (Wilson) Bryce Bakke; m. Sarah Alice Riley, Dec. 20, 1954; children: Douglas Delf, David Dickson. BA, U. Tex., 1955; LLB, Yale U., 1960. Bar: Tex. 1960, U.S. Dist. Ct. (we. dist.) Tex. 1963, U.S. Ct. Claims 1964, U.S. Supreme Ct. 1971. Briefing atty. Tex. Supreme Ct., Austin, 1960-61; sole practice, 1961—. Lectr. U. Tex., 1965-66. Editor, Tex. Supreme Ct. Jour. Served to 1st lt. USAF

BRYDGES, THOMAS EUGENE, lawyer; b. Niagara Falls, N.Y., June 1, 1942; s. Earl W. and Eleanor M. (Mahoney) B.; m. Melissa May, May 26, 1990; children: Andrew MacLeod, Elizabeth Hendricks. BA in History, Syracuse U., 1971, JD, 1973. Bar: N.Y. 1974, U.S. Dist. (we. dist.) N.Y. 1974, U.S. Ct. Appeals (2d cir.) 1978. Assoc. Jaeckle, Fleischmann & Mugel, Buffalo, 1973-78, ptnr., 1979—. Bd. dirs., sec. Theodore Roosevelt Inagural site, 1999—. Author: (with others) Employment Discrimination Law, 1980—. Trustee Daemen Coll., Amherst, N.Y., 1988—; bd. dirs., v.p. Art Park & Co., Lewiston, N.Y., 1976—. Capt. U.S. Army, 1962-68, Vietnam. Decorated Bronze Star, Air medal, Army Commendation (2). Mem. ABA (labor sect.), Erie County Bar Assn., N.Y. Bar Assn. (labor law com.). Labor. Office: Jaeckle Fleischmann & Mugel 700 Fleet Bldg Buffalo NY 14202 E-mail: tbrydges@jaeckle.com

BRYNER, ALEXANDER O. state supreme court justice; b. Tientsin, China; m. Carol Crump; children: Paul, Mara. BA, Stanford U., 1966, JD, 1969. Law clk. to Chief Justice George Boney, Alaska Supreme Ct., 1969-71; legal editor Bancroft Whitney Co., San Francisco, 1971; with Pub. Defender Agy., Anchorage, 1972-74; ptnr. Bookman, Bryner & Shortell, 1974; Alaska dist. ct. judge Anchorage, 1975-77; U.S. atty. Alaska, 1977-80; chief judge Alaska Ct. Appeals, 1980-97; state supreme ct. justice Alaska Supreme Ct., Anchorage, 1997—. Office: Alaska Supreme Ct 303 K St Anchorage AK 99501-2013

BRYSON, WILLIAM CURTIS, federal judge; b. Houston, Aug. 19, 1945; m. Julia Penny Clark; two children. B.A. magna cum laude, Harvard Coll., 1969; J.D., U. of Tex. Sch. of Law, 1973. Law clerk to Justice Henry Friendly U.S. Ct. of Appeals, 2nd Circuit, 1973-74; law clerk to Justice Thurgood Marshall U.S. Supreme Ct., 1974-75; atty. Miller, Cassidy, Larroca & Lewin, 1975-78; asst. to the Solicitor General U.S. Dept. of Justice, 1978-79; chief Appellate Section, Criminal Div., 1979-82; special counsel Organized Crime & Racketeering Section, Criminal Div., 1982-86; dep. solicitor gen., 1986-94; dep. assoc. atty. & acting assoc. atty. gen., 1994; circuit judge Federal Circuit, Washington, 1994—. Office: 717 Madison Pl NW Washington DC 20439-0002*

BRYSON, WILLIAM HAMILTON, law educator; b. Richmond, Va., July 29, 1941; s. William Alexander and Lillian Sutton (Wilkinson) B. BA, Hampden_Sydney Coll., 1963; LLB, Harvard U., 1967; LLM, U. Va., 1968; PhD, Cambridge (Eng.) U., 1972. Bar: Va. 1967. Asst. prof. U. Richmond Sch. Law, 1973-76, assoc. prof., 1976-80, prof., 1980—. Adv. com. on rules of ct. Jud. Council Va. Author: Equity Side of the Exchequer, 1975, Legal Education in Virginia 1779-1979: A Biographical Approach, 1982, Virginia Civil Procedure, 1997, Virginia Circuit Court Opinions, 1985—, Virginia Law Books, 2000, Samuel Dodd's Reports, 2000; mem. editl. bd. Am. Jour. Legal History, 1976—. William Senior scholar, 1970-72; Max Planck Inst. fellow, Frankfurt, Germany, 1972-73; Fulbright grant, 1963, Am. Coun. Learned Socs. grant, 1980; recipient Yorke prize Cambridge U., 1973 Fellow Royal Hist. Soc.; mem. Selden Soc. (Va. corr.), Va. Hist. Soc., Va. Bar Assn., Am. Soc. Legal History (bd. dirs. 1981-84), Phi Beta Kappa. Episcopalian. Office: U Richmond Sch Law Richmond VA 23173

BRZOBOHATY, TOMAS, lawyer; b. Ceska Lipa, Czech Republic, Dec. 30, 1968; s. Josef and Libuse B.; m. Veronika Zelenkova, Sept. 7, 1990; children: Jan, Adela. LLM, Charles U., Prague, 1992, JD, PhD, Charles U., 1998. Laawyer Burns Schwartz, Czech Republic, 1991-95, ptnr. Czech Republic, 1996-00, Brzobohaty Broz & Honsa, Prague, Czech Republic, 2000—. Author: Securities Act and Related Legislation, 1993. Mem. Czech Bar Assn. Avocations: sports, music, poetry. Banking, Finance, Securities. Office: Brzobohaty Broz & Honsa Klimentska 10 11000 Prague 1 Czech Republic E-mail: tbrzobohaty@bbh.cz

BRZUSTOWICZ, JOHN CINQ-MARS, lawyer; b. Rochester, N.Y., Feb. 1, 1957; s. Richard J. and Alice (Cinq-Mars) B.; m. Diane Day, Aug. 22, 1981; children: Richard Reed, Megan Day, Emily Day-Hanson. BA, Coll. Wooster, 1979; JD, Case Western Res. U., 1985; cert., Cornell Inst. Labor Rels., 1982. Bar: Pa. 1985, U.S. Dist. Ct. (we. dist.) Pa. 1985, U.S. Ct. Appeals (3d cir.) 1986, U.S. Supreme Ct. 1990. Asst. to dir. Inst. Am. Music U. Rochester, Rochester, 1979-82; assoc. Peacock, Keller, Yohe, Day & Ecker, Washington, 1985-88, Sable, Makoroff & Libenson, Pitts., 1988-90; pvt. practice Brzustowicz Law Offices, McMurray, Washington, Pa., 1990-94; shareholder Day & Brzustowicz Law Offices, P.C., McMurray, 1995—. Chmn. bd. dirs. Inst. for Am. Music of Eastman Sch. Music, 1997—; chmn. law libr. Washington County (Pa.) Bar, 1992; mem. com. Jud. Inquiry Bd., Pa., 1991—; dir. Hanson Inst. of Am. Music of the Eastman Sch. of Music, U. Rochester, 1995. Co-author: Pennsylvania School Law, 1992, Pennsylvania Adminstrative Law, 1987; editor: So You Want to Be A Lawyer, 1990; advisor on PBC documentary: Life of Howard Hanson, An American Masterpiece, 1987. Pres. Newman Club, Coll. Wooster, 1976-79; v.p. Young Reps., Wooster, Ohio, 1977-79; co-founder, officer Wooster Polo and Hunt Club, 1976-79; bd. dirs. Hanson Inst. Am. Music of Eastman Sch. Music, 1996, Washington County Fund, 1998-2000, Pyramid Gallery, Rochester, N.Y., 1997—; mem. fin. com. JFK Sch., 1998—. Recipient Merit award Inst. Am. Music, 1981, Outstanding Scholar award Rotary, Albert H. Robbins award for Meritorious Svc. in Advancement of Am. Art, 2000. Mem. ABA, ATLA, Pa. Bar Assn. (del. 1992), Allegheny County Bar Assn., Washington County Bar Assn., Pa. Young Lawyers for Washington County (state rep. 1988), Peters Twp. C. of C., Wash. C. of C., K. of C. Roman Catholic. Avocations: reading, woodworking, biology. Bankruptcy, General civil litigation, General corporate. Home: 56 Mckennan Ave Washington PA 15301-3531 Office: 3821 Washington Rd Mc Murray PA 15317-2964 E-mail: dexterdawg@aol.com

BUC, NANCY LILLIAN, lawyer; b. Orange, N.J., July 27, 1944; d. George L. and Ethel Buc. AB, Brown U., 1965, LLD (hon.), 1994; LLB, U. Va., 1969. Bar: Va. 1969, N.Y. 1977, D.C. 1978. Atty. Fed. Trade Commn., Washington, 1969-72; assoc. Weil, Gotshal & Manges, N.Y., 1972-77, ptnr., 1977-78, Washington, 1978-80, 81-94, Buc & Beardsley, Washington, 1994—; chief counsel FDA, Rockville, Md., 1980-81. Mem. recombinant DNA adv. com. NIH, 1990-94; consensus panelist NIH Consensus Devel. Conf. on Effective Med. Treatment of Heroin Addiction, 1997; adj. prof. law Georgetown U. Law Ctr., 2000—. Mem. editl. bd. Food Drug and Cosmetic Law Jour., 1981-87, 94-97, Jour. of Products Liability, 1981-92, Health Span: The Jour. of Health, Bus. & Law, 1984-95. Mem. adv. com. on new devels. in biotech. 1986-89, mem. adv. com. on govt. policies and pharm. R & D, 1989-93, Office of Tech. Assessment, Washington, mem. com. to study drug abuse medications devel. and rsch., 1993-95; mem. com. on contraceptive R & D, Inst. Medicine, Washington, 1994-96; trustee Brown U., 1973-78, 1998—; fellow, 1980-92. Recipient Disting. Svc. award Fed. Trade Commn., Washington, 1972, Award of Merit FDA, Rockville, 1981, Sec.'s Spl. citation HHS, Washington, 1981, Ind. award Associated. Alumni of Brown U., 1991. Mem. ABA (mem. spl. com. to study FTC 1988-89), Com. of 200, Nat. Partnership for Women and Families (bd. dirs.). Administrative and regulatory. Office: Buc & Beardsley 919 18th St NW Ste 600 Washington DC 20006-5507

BUCCELLA, WILLIAM VICTOR, lawyer; b. Seattle, Oct. 23, 1943; s. Fred J. and Adeline J. (Carriero) B.; m. Mary A. O'Shea, Aug. 26, 1967; children: Mark Brendon, Jennifer Ball, Peter James. BS, Canisius Coll., 1965; JD, Cornell U., 1968. Bar: N.Y. 1968, U.S. Dist. Ct. (we. dist.) N.Y. 1972. Law clk. U.S. Dist. Ct. (we. dist.) N.Y., 1972-74; assoc. Diebold & Millonzi, Buffalo, 1974-77; assoc. gen. counsel Wheelabrator-Frye Inc., Hampton, N.H., 1977-81, gen. counsel, 1981-83; v.p., asst. gen. counsel The Signal Cos. Inc., La Jolla, Calif., 1983-86; mng. dir., gen. counsel The Henley Group Inc., La Jolla, 1986-90; ptnr. Hinckley, Allen, Snyder & Comen, Boston, 1990-92; ptnr. Goodwin, Proctor & Hoar, Boston, 1992—; dir. New Eng. Legal Found., Boston. chief counsel Rep. Nat. Conv., 1996. Lt. JAGC, USN, 1969-72. Mem. ABA, N.Y. State Bar Assn. General corporate. Office: Goodwin Procter & Hoar Exchange Pl Boston MA 02109-2803

BUCCINO, ERNEST JOHN, JR. lawyer; b. Oct. 29, 1945; s. Ernest J. and Rachel (Talarico) B.; m. Martha Mollinedo, Dec. 27, 1968; 1 child, Tasha. BS, Temple U., 1967, MEd, 1969, JD, 1973. Bar: Pa. 1973, N.J. 1974, U.S. Dist. Ct. (ea. dist.) Pa. 1973, U.S. Ct. Appeals (3d cir.) 1973, U.S. Supreme Ct. 1978. Officer, counsel Blue Cross Greater Phila., 1973-74; law clk. Supreme Ct. Pa., Phila., 1974; mem. Gross & Buccino, P.A., 1975-96; pvt. practice, 1996-97; prin. Buccino Law Office, 1997—. Lectr. Roscoe Pound, 1986, Trial Advocacy Found. Pa., Phila., 1984; mem. civil procedure rules com. Supreme Ct. Pa., 1994—. Author: The Barrister Vol. XVI, #3, 1985. Chmn. eastern dist. LAWPAC, Harrisburg, Pa., 1983—. Mem. ABA, ATLA, Pa. Bar Assn., Pa. Trial Lawyers Assn. (bd. dirs. 1982—), Phila. Trial Lawyers Assn. (bd. dirs. 1982—, lectr. luncheon series 1986), Justinian Soc. (bd. dirs. 1982—), Phila. Bar Assn. (chmn. econs. of law practice 1983, nominating com. 1982-83), Sons of Italy. Avocations. Personal injury. Office: 2112 Walnut St Philadelphia PA 19103-4808 E-mail: EJB@buccino.com

BUCHANAN, CALVIN D. (BUCK BUCHANAN), former prosecutor; b. Okolona, Miss., Feb. 12, 1958; m. Donna C. BA, U. Miss., 1980, JD, 1983. Bar: Miss. 1983, U.S. Mil. Ct. Rev. 1983, U.S. Dist. Ct. (no. dist.) 1983, U.S. Ct. Appeals (5th cir.) 1991. 1st Lt. MS Army NG, 1980-83; commd. U.S. Army, 1983; advanced through grades to capt., 1990; maj. Individual Ready Res., 1990—; asst. U.S. atty. No. Dist. Miss., 1990-97, U.S. atty., 1997—2001. Leonard B. Melvin scholar U. Miss. Sch. Law. Mem. Nat. Bar Assn., Miss. Bar Assn., Magnolia Bar Assn., Lafayette County Bar Assn., U. Miss. Alumni Assn. (mem. adv. coun. 1988-97), Inns of Court, Order of Omega, Phi Eta Sigma. Baptist.

BUCHANAN, DEENA LYNNA, lawyer; b. Washington, Dec. 29, 1973; d. Kenneth Mark and Joyce Marie B. BA summa cum laude, U. Pitts., 1995; JD cum laude, Georgetown U., 1998. Bar: N.Mex. 1998. Assoc. Modrall, Sperling, Roehl, Harris & Sisk, Albuquerque, 1998—. Adminstrv. editor Geo. Jour. Legal Ethics, 1997-98 (St. Thomas Aquinas award 1998). Bd. dirs. St. Mark's in the Valley Day Sch., Albuquerque, 1998. Mem. ABA, N.Mex. Bar Assn. (young lawyer's divsn. 1998—), Albuquerque Bar Assn. General civil litigation, Probate, State and local taxation. Office: Modrall Sperling Roehl Harris & Sisk PO Box 2168 Albuquerque NM 87103-2168

BUCHANAN, JAMES DOUGLAS, lawyer; b. Modesto, Calif., Aug. 7, 1941; s. James Monroe and Gladys Marian (Crowell) B.; m. Claudia Anne Dukes, May 26, 1963; children: Sarah, Jennifer, Amy, Andrew. BA in Journalism, U. Nev., 1963; JD, U. of the Pacific, 1975. Bar: Calif. 1975, U.S. Dist. Ct. (ea. dist.) Calif. 1976. Dep. dist. atty. Inyo County, Independence, Calif., 1976-77, pub. defender, 1977-78; ptnr. Smith & Buchanan, Bishop, Calif., 1978-86; legal counsel No. Inyo Hosp. Dist., 1980—; ptnr. Berger, Buchanan and Berger, 1989-91. Pipe major Loch Ness Scots Pipe Band, Bishop, 1982-99; mem. Selective Svc. Bd. 87, Bishop, 1982-97; deacon Episc. Ch., 1995; priest, 2000; vicar Trinity Meml. Episc. Ch., Lone Pine, Calif., 2000—. Mem. Inyo County Bar Assn. (pres. 1980). Office: 363 Academy Ave Bishop CA 93514

BUCHANAN, JOHN MACLENNAN, Canadian provincial official; b. Sydney, N.S., Can., Apr. 22, 1931; s. Murdoch William and Flora Isabel (Campbell) B.; m. Mavis Forsyth, Sept. 1, 1954; children: Murdoch, Travis, Nichola, Natalie, Natasha. BSc, Mt. Allison U., cert. engring., 1954; LLB, Dalhousie U., Halifax, N.S., 1958; DEng (hon.), N.S. Tech. Coll., 1979; LLD (hon.), St. Mary's U., 1982; DCL, Mt. Allison U., 1981; LLD (hon.), St. Francis Xavier U., 1986; D Polit. Sci. (hon.), U. de St. Anne, 1989. Bar: Called to bar, created queen's counsel 1972. Pvt. practice, Halifax, 1958-71; mem. N.S. Legislative Assembly, from 1967; min. public works, then fisheries; premier of N.S., 1978-90. Created Queen's Counsel, 1972; leader Progressive Conservative Party in N.S., from 1971; elected mem. legis. assembly for Halifax-Atlantic provinces gen. election, 1967, 70, 74, 78, 81, 84, 88, apptd. Privy Coun., 1972; apptd. to Senate of Can., 1990, bd. dirs. Legal Aid for N.S. Barristers Assn. Active Boy Scouts Am., pres. exec. oun., chmn. policy bd., 1978-90. Mem. Can. Bar Assn., N.S. Barristers Assn., Can.-U.S. Parliamentary Assn. (bd. dirs.), Royal Can. Legion, Buchanan Soc. of Glasgow, Scotland (bd. dirs.), Halifax Club, City Club, Lions, Masons, Shriners, Odd Fellows. Mem. United Ch. Can. Office: The Senate Ottawa ON K1A OA4 Canada

BUCHANAN, MARY BETH, prosecutor; BA, U. Pa.; JD, U. Pittsburgh Sch. Law. Assoc. Strassburger, McKenne, Gutnick and Potter, Pittsburgh, 1987—88; asst. US Atty. Western Dist. of Pa., 1988—2001, US Atty., 2001—. Office: US Attorney 633 US Post Office & Courthouse Pittsburgh PA 15219*

BUCHBINDER, DARRELL BRUCE, lawyer; b. N.Y.C., Oct. 17, 1946; s. Julian and Bernice (Levy) B.; m. Janet Grey McLean, Jan. 22, 1977; children: Julian Bradford, Andrew Grey, Ian Jeffress. BA in Politics with honors, NYU, 1968, JD, 1971. Bar: N.Y. 1972, U.S. Dist. Ct. (so. and ea. dists.) N.Y. 1973. Sole practice, N.Y.C., 1972-79; atty. Port Authority of N.Y. and N.J., 1979-83, prin. atty., 1983-86, dep. chief fin. divsn. Law Dept., 1986-92, chief pub. securities law divsn. aaw dept., 1992-2001, asst. gen. counsel, 2001—. Served with USNR, 1968-70. Mem. Nat. Assn. Bond Lawyers, Pi Sigma Alpha. Republican. E-mail: dbuchbin@panynj.gov

BUCHEN, PHILIP WILLIAM, lawyer; b. Sheboygan, Wis., Feb. 27, 1916; s. Gustav W. and Elenor (Jung) B.; m. Beatrice Loomis Gold, Feb. 27, 1947; children: Victoria Buchen Aler, Roderick L. A.B., U. Mich. at Ann Arbor, 1939, J.D., 1941. Bar: Mich. 1941. Pvt. practice law, Grand Rapids, Mich., 1941-74; partner law firm Ford & Buchen, 1941-42, Butterfield, Keeney & Amberg, Grand Rapids, 1943-47, Amberg, Law & Buchen, Grand Rapids, 1948-61; v.p. Grand Valley State Coll., Allendale, Mich., 1961-67; partner firm Law, Buchen, Weathers, Richardson & Dutcher, Grand Rapids, 1967-74; counsel to Pres. Ford, Washington, 1974-77; partner firm Dewey, Ballantine, Bushby, Palmer & Wood, 1977—. Dir. Communications Satellite Corp., Washington, 1969-74, Old Kent Fin. Corp., Grand Rapids, 1962-74, 77-86. Editor, Mich. Law Rev. Mem. U.S. Commn. on Fine Arts, Washington, 1977-81. Mem. D.C. Bar Assn., Order of Coif, Kent Country Club (Grand Rapids), Chevy Chase Club, Univ. Club (Washington), Phi Beta Kappa. Clubs: Kent Country (Grand Rapids); Chevy Chase (Washington), University (Washington). Home: 800 25th St NW Washington DC 20037-2207 Office: 1775 Pennsylvania Ave NW Washington DC 20006-4605

BUCHENROTH, STEPHEN RICHARD, lawyer; b. Bellefontaine, Ohio, Feb. 8, 1948; s. Richard G. and Patricia (Muller) B.; m. Vicki Anderson, June 6, 1974; children: Matthew Brian, Sarah Elizabeth. BA, Wittenburg U., Springfield, Ohio, 1970; JD, U. Chgo., 1974. Bar: Ohio 1974, U.S. Dist. Ct. (so. and no. dists.) Ohio 1974, U.S. Ct. Appeals (6th cir.) 1974. Ptnr. Vorys, Sater, Seymour & Pease, Columbus, Ohio, 1974—. Author: Ohio Mortgage Foreclosures, 1986, Ohio Franchising Law, 1990, also chpts. in books. Trustee, v.p. Godman Guild Assn., Columbus, 1977-83; trustee, sec. Neighborhood Homes, Inc., Columbus, 1977-85; mem. bd. rev. Worthington Pers., 1981—; pres. Worthington Alliance for Quality Edn., 1989-91; chmn. bd. advisors paralegal program Capitol U. Law Sch., 1991; pres. bd. trustees Worthington Edn. Found., 1997-98; mem. Ohio Supreme Ct. Commn. on CLE, 1994-2000, chmn., 1999; bd. advisors C.H.A.D.D. of Ctrl. Ohio, 1993-97; bd. trustees Wittenberg U., 2000—. Recipient Cmty. Svc. award Legal Assts. Ctrl. Ohio, 1987. Mem. ABA (forum com. franchising), Ohio State Bar Assn. (coun. dels., chmn. legal assts. com., bd. govs. real property sect.), Columbus Bar Assn. (bd. govs., pres. 1992-93), Am. Coll. Real Estate Lawyers. Republican. Lutheran. Contracts commercial, Franchising, Real property. Home: 2342 Collins Dr Columbus OH 43085-2810 Office: Vorys Sater Seymore & Pease 52 E Gay St PO Box 1008 Columbus OH 43215-3161 E-mail: SRBuchenroth@vssp.com

BUCHIGNANI, LEO JOSEPH, lawyer; b. Memphis, Nov. 4, 1922; s. Joseph Richard and Leonora B. (Shea) B.; m. Grace Elisabeth Crisler, Nov. 23, 1950; children: Leo, Crisler Quick, Joan Barnett. BA, Notre Dame U., 1944; LLB, Harvard U., 1948. BAr: Tenn. 1948, U.S. Dist. Ct. 1950, U.S. Supreme Ct. 1960. Assoc. Chandler, Shepherd, Heiskill & Williams, Memphis, 1948-50; ptnr. Buchignani & Greener, 1950-53, 58-80, Quick, Buchignani & Greener, Memphis, 1953-58, Buchignani & Neal, Memphis, 1981-83, Buchignani, Neal & Burnham, Memphis, 1983-88; co-founder, v.p., sec. Catherine's Stores, 1960-78. Mem. Tenn. Law Revision Commn., 1971-74. Mem. Tenn. Republican State Exec. Com., 1960-62. Served with USN, 1942-45. Mem. ABA, Tenn. Bar Assn., Memphis and Shelby County Bar Assn. (bd. dirs. 1959-61, sec.-treas. 1964-65, v.p. 1965-66, pres. 1966-67), Harvard Club, Notre Dame Club, Memphis Country Club, Colonial Country Club. Roman Catholic. Insurance, Personal injury, Probate. Home: 315 Kenilworth Pl Memphis TN 38112-5405

BUCHMAN, KENNETH WILLIAM, lawyer; b. Plant City, Fla., Nov. 20, 1956; s. Paul Sidney and Beryle (Solomon) B.; m. MarDee H. Buchman, May 9, 1985; 1 child, Katherine Elizabeth. AA, U. Fla., 1976, BBA, 1978, JD, 1981. Bar: Fla. 1981; U.S. Dist. Ct. (Mid. dist.) Fla. 1981; U.S. Ct. Appeals (11th cir.) 1986; U.S. Supreme Ct. 1988; bd. cert. city, county, local govt. law. Ptnr. Buchman and Buchman, Plant City, 1981-85, Buchman and Buchman, PA, Plant City, 1985-91; pvt. practice, 1991-2000; asst. city atty. City of Plant City, 1982-91, city atty., 1991—. City atty. San Antonio, Fla., 1995-2000; mem. exec. coun. city, county and local govt. law sect. Fla. Bar., 1997—. Mem. Fla. Mcpl. Attys. Assn. (steering com. 1999—), Attys. Title Ins. Fund, Plant City Bar Assn., Masons. Jewish. Municipal (including bonds), Real property. Office: 302 W Reynolds St Plant City FL 33566-3314

BUCHMAN, M. ABRAHAM, lawyer; b. Bklyn., Oct. 25, 1916; s. Judah Louis and Augusta Buchman; m. Ann P. Buchman, July 25, 1950; 1 child, Amy. BA cum laude, NYU, 1935; LLB cum laude, St. Lawrence U., 1938, JSD summa cum laude, 1939. Bar: N.Y. 1939, U.S. Dist. Ct. (so. dist.) N.Y. 1946, U.S. Ct. Appeals 1949, Supreme Ct. U.S. 1964. Plant mgr., contr. Atlas Import & Export Co., 1931-39; ptnr. Buchman & O'Brien, N.Y.C., Washington, 1940—, San Francisco. Cons. to sec. USAF, 1946-52; cons. to State Dept. at various meetings Coun. of Europe on prep. of conv. for wines and spirits; cons. Am. Wine Assn., 1993—, Vermouth Inst., Inc., 1943-64, Internat. Vermouth Inst., 1964—, Fedn. Italiana Industriali, Produttori ed Esportatori di Vini, Acquavit, Liquori, Sciroppi, Aceti ed Affini, 1962—; Am. Beverage Alcohol Assn., 1963—. Maj. USAF, 1942-46. Fellowship in

adminstrv. law named in his honor Columbia U. Law Sch., 1985—. Mem. ABA, FBA (pres. Empire State chpt. 1995-97), Assn. ICC Practitioners, Fed. Bar Coun., Internat. Bar Assn., Phi Beta Kappa. Administrative and regulatory. Home: 5301 Woodlands Blvd Tamarac FL 33319-3025 Office: Buchman & O'Brien LLP 10 E 40th St Rm 708 New York NY 10016-0200 also: 1331 Pennsylvania Ave NW Washington DC 20004-1710 also: 505 Sansome St San Francisco CA 94111-3106

BUCHMANN, ALAN PAUL, lawyer; b. Yonkers, N.Y., Sept. 5, 1934; s. Paul John and Jessie Gow (Perkins) B.; m. Lizabeth Ann Moody, Sept. 5, 1959. BA summa cum laude, Yale U., 1956; postgrad, U. Munich, 1956-57; LLB, Yale U., 1960. Bar: Ohio 1960, U.S. Dist. Ct. (no. dist.) Ohio 1963, U.S. Ct. Appeals (6th cir.) 1968, U.S. Supreme Ct. 1977, Fla. 1996. Assoc. Squire, Sanders & Dempsey, Cleve., 1960-70, ptnr., 1970-96; pvt. practice St. Petersburg, Fla. Contbr. articles to profl. jours. State chmn. Ohio Young reps., 1970-71, nat. committeeman, 1971-74; mem. exec. com. Cuyahoga County Reps., 1969-95, fin. com., 1987-94; mem. Selective svc. Bd., 1967-75; trustee Cleve. Internat. Program, 1979-82, 94-95; pres. English Speaking Union, 1981-83. Recipient Robert A. Taft award Young Reps., 1969, Outstanding State Chmn. award, 1971, James A. Rhodes award, 1974; Fulbright fellow U. Munich, 1956-57. Mem. ABA (chmn. pub. utility law sect. 1989-90, sect. del. 1996—, mem. coord. com. on legal edn. 1991-97), Fla. Bar Assn., Ohio State Bar Assn., St. Petersburg Bar Assn., Hillsborough County Bar Assn. General civil litigation, Public utilities. E-mail: buchmann1@netzero.net

BUCHWALD, DON DAVID, lawyer; b. Bklyn., May 10, 1944; m. Naomi Reice, Jan. 19, 1974; children: David, Jennifer. BA, Cornell U., 1965, JD, 1968. Assoc. Marshall, Bratter, Greene, Allison & Tucker, N.Y.C., 1970-73; asst. U.S. atty. So. Dist. of N.Y., 1973-80, dep. chief criminal, 1977-80; ptnr. Buchwald & Kaufman, N.Y.C., 1980-99; pvt. practice Don Buchwald, LLP, 1999—. Served to sgt. U.S. Army, 1968-70. Mem. ABA, Fed. Bar Council, Assn. of the Bar of the City of N.Y., N.Y. State Bar Assn. Federal civil litigation, State civil litigation, Criminal. Office: 100 Park Ave New York NY 10017-5516

BUCHWALD, NAOMI REICE, judge; b. Kingston, N.Y., Feb. 14, 1944; BA cum laude, Brandeis U., 1965; LLB cum laude, Columbia U., 1968. Bar: N.Y. 1968, U.S. Ct. Appeals (2d cir.) 1969, U.S. Dist. Ct. (so. and ea. dists.) N.Y. 1970, U.S. Supreme Ct. 1978. Litigation assoc. Marshall, Bratter, Greene, Allison & Tucker, N.Y.C., 1968-73; asst. U.S. atty. So. Dist. N.Y., 1973-80, dep. chief civil divsn., 1976-79, chief civil divsn., 1979-80; U.S. magistrate judge U.S. Dist. Ct. (so. dist.) N.Y., 1980-99, chief magistrate judge, 1994-96, U.S. dist. judge, 1999—. Editor Columbia Jour. Law and Social Problems, 1967-68. Recipient spl. citation FDA Commrs., 1978, Robert B. Fiske Jr. Assn. William B. Tendy award, Outstanding Pub. Svc. award Seymour Assn., Columbia Law Sch. Class of 1968 Excellence in Pub. Svc. award, 1998. Mem. Fed. Bar Coun. (trustee 1976-82, 97-2000, v.p. 1982-84), N.Y. State Bar Assn., Assn. of the Bar of the City of N.Y. (trademarks and unfair competition com. 1988-89, mem. long range planning com. 1993-95, litigation com. 1994-96, ad hoc com. on jud. conduct 1996-99), Phi Beta Kappa, Omicron Delta Epsilon. Office: US Ct House Foley Square New York NY 10007-1316

BUCK, DAVID PATRICK, lawyer; b. Rossville, Ga., Mar. 17, 1940; m. Maureen Nenno, May 11, 1968 (dec.); children— David, Jr., Teresa. B.S. in Acctg., U. Tenn., 1961, J.D., 1964; LL.M. in Internat. Law, U. Mich., 1972; student Air Command and Staff Coll., Air U., 1977. Bar: Tenn. 1965, U.S. Tax Ct. 1977, U.S. Ct. Claims 1977, U.S. Ct. Appeals (D.C. cir.) 1978, U.S. Supreme Ct. 1978, U.S. Ct. Appeals (fed. cir.) 1982, U.S. Ct. Appeals (4th cir.) 1982, U.S. Ct. Appeals (9th and 11th 1984. C.P.A., Md. 1994. Mem. staff law dept. USAF, 1965-85, U.S. Postal Service, 1985—; legal advisor Wilford Hall Med. Ctr., San Antonio, 1968-70; chief civil and internat. law, Torrejon Air Base, Madrid, 1972-76; trial atty. Gen. Litigation div. Office JAG, Washington, 1977-78; spl. atty. Office of Fgn. Litigation, Dept. Justice, Washington, 1978-80; chief civilian personnel and labor law br. Gen. Litigation div. Office JAG, Washington, 1980-85. Mem. Am. Soc. Internat. Law, Fed. Bar Assn., Beta Alpha Psi. Contbr. articles to internat. law jours., profl. jours. Home: PO Box 591 Riva MD 21140-0591 Office: HQ US Postal Service Office of Gen Counsel 475 Lenfant Plz SW Washington DC 20260-0004

BUCK, GURDON HALL, lawyer, urban planner; b. Hartford, Conn., Apr. 10, 1936; s. Richard Saltonstall and Aloha Frances (Hall) B.; children: Keith Saltonstall, Frances Josephine, Daniel Winthrop; m. Martha Finder, 1996. BA in English, Lehigh U., 1958; JD, U. Pa., 1965. Bar: Conn. 1965, U.S. Dist. Ct. 1966, U.S. Ct. Appeals (2d cir.) 1966. Assoc. Shipman & Goodwin, Hartford, 1965-67; v.p., counsel R. F. Broderick & Assocs., 1968-69; ptnr. Pelgrift, Byrne, Buck & Connolly, Hartford and Farmington, Conn., 1969-75, Byrne, Buck & Steiner and predecessor Byrne & Buck, Farmington, 1975-78; sr. ptnr. real estate and land use sects., chmn. common interest group Robinson & Cole, Farmington and Hartford, 1979—. Author: Condominium Development, Forms with Commentary, 1990, 2d edit., 1992; prin. co-author: The Connecticut Condominium Manual, 1972, Real Estate Brokers Community Associations Handbook, rev. edit., 1982, Connecticut Common Interest Ownership Manual, 1984, The Alaska Common Interest Ownership Manual, 1985, Attorney's and Lenders Guide to Common Interest Communities, 1989, 2nd edit., 1992; contbr. articles on zoning, condominiums, planned unit devels. to profl. jours.; columnist various newspapers. Lt. USCGR, 1958-62. Recipient Disting. Svc. award Glastonbury (Conn.) Jaycees, 1968. Mem. ABA (common interest com. law com., real property and probate, joint editl. bd. real property laws, adv. Uniform Planned Cmty. Act, Model Real Estate Coop. Act, Uniform Common Interest Ownership Act), Am. Law Inst. (advisor, restatement on property 3d servitudes), Am. Coll. Real Estate Lawyers (bd. dirs. 1986-92, common ownership com.), Anglo-Am. Real Property Inst. (bd. dirs. 1994-99), Cmty. Assns. Inst. (nat. trustee 1982-88, pres. Conn. chpt. 1980-83, sec. 1986-89, bd. dirs. 1992-98, pres. rsch. found. 1980-83, Century Club, Byron Hanke Disting. Svc. award, Acad. of Authors), Am. Planning Assn., Am. Inst. Cert. Planners, Internat. Bar Assn. (panelist common ownership consumer protection 1987), Conn. Bar Assn. (chmn. com. opinions, treas. real estate sect., pro bono com., chair comty. svc. com., ed. Conn. Bar Jour.), Statewide Legal Svcs. (bd. dirs., pres.), Hartford County Bar Assn., Conn. Assn. Homebuilders Orgn. (developer's coun.). Environmental, Land use and zoning (including planning), Real property. Office: 1 Commercial Plz Hartford CT 06103-3509

BUCK, THOMAS RANDOLPH, retired lawyer, financial services executive; b. Washington, Feb. 5, 1930; s. James Charles Francis and Mary Elizabeth (Marshall) B.; m. Alice Armistead James, June 20, 1953; children: Kathryn James, Thomas Randolph, Douglas Marshall, David Andrew; m. Sunny Clark, Sept. 15, 1971; 1 child, Carey Virginia; me. Yvonne Brackett, Nov. 27, 1981. B.A. summa cum laude, Am. U., 1951; JD, U. Va., 1954. Bar: Va. 1954, Ky. 1964, Fla. 1974. Asst. gen. atty. Seaboard Air Line R.R. Co., 1958-63; sec., gen. counsel Am. Comml. Lines. Inc., Houston, 1963-68; asst. gen. counsel Tex. Gas Transmission Corp., 1968-72; sec., gen. counsel Leadership Housing Inc., 1972-77; pres. law firm Buck and Golden, P.A., 1975-92; exec. v.p., gen. counsel Buck Fin. Svcs., Inc., Ft. Lauderdale, Fla., 1992-99. Past dir. Computer Resources Inc., Ft. Lauderdale, Fla., So. Aviation Inc., Opa Locka, Fla.; chmn. Hanover Bank of Fla. Bd. dirs. Sheridan House for Youth; trustee Fla. Bapt. Found. Served to capt. USMCR, 1954-58. Mem. Assn. ICC Practitioners (nat. v.p., mem. exec. com.), Maritime Law Assn. U.S., Am. Judicature Soc., Omicron Delta Kappa, Alpha Sigma Phi, Delta Theta Phi. Clubs: Kiwanian, Propeller of U.S. Banking, General corporate, Education and schools. Home: 2873 SW 13th Dr Deerfield Beach FL 33442

BUCKAWAY, WILLIAM ALLEN, JR. lawyer; b. Bowling Green, Ky., Dec. 3, 1934; s. William Allen and Kathryn Anne (Scoggin) B.; m. Bette Joan Cross, July 27, 1963; 1 child, William Allen III. AB, Centre Coll. of Ky., 1956; JD, U. Louisville, 1961. Bar: Ky. 1961, U.S. Dist Ct. (we. dist.) Ky. 1981, U.S. Dist. Ct. (ea. dist.) Ky. 1986, U.S. Supreme Ct. 1975. Assoc. Tilford, Dobbins, Caye & Alexander, Louisville, 1961-78; ptnr. Tilford, Dobbins, Alexander, Buckaway & Black, 1978—. Atty. Masonic Homes of Ky., Louisville, 1985—; gen. counsel Kosair Charitites. Elder 2d Presbyn. Ch., Louisville, 1975; emeritus mem. bd. govs. Lexington (Ky.) unit Shriners Hosp. for Cripled Children, 1986, sec., 1989-94; mem. children's oper. bd. Kosair Children's Hosp., 1986-99; mem. bd. govs. Norton Health Care, Louisville, 1999—. With USNR, 1956-58. Named Disting. Alumnus U. Louisville Sch. Law, 1986, Centre Coll., 1986. Mem. SAR (pres. Ky. soc. 1999-2000), Nat. Eagle Scout Assn., Soc. of the Cin. in State of Va., Sons Confederate Vets. (adj. John Hunt Morgan Camp 1993-96), Masons (33 deg., past master Crescent Hill lodge 1967, chmn. jurisprudence and law com. imperial coun. Shrine of N.Am. 1989-91), Kosair Shrine Temple (potentate 1986), Rotary, Soc. Colonial Wars (Ky. coun.), Soc. War of 1812 (pres. Ky. soc. 1998-2000), Sigma Chi, Phi Alpha Delta. General corporate, Non-profit and tax-exempt organizations, Probate. Home: 1761 Sulgrave Rd Louisville KY 40205-1643 E-mail: wbuckaway@tdabb.com, Bbuckaway@aol.com

BUCKLEY, CHARLES ROBINSON, III, lawyer; b. Richmond, Va., Oct. 9, 1942; s. Charles Robinson and Eleanor (Small) B.; m. Virginia Lee, Apr. 17, 1971; children: Richard, Rebecca. BS, U. N.C., 1965, JD, 1969. Bar: N.C. 1969, U.S. Supreme Ct. 1979. Asst. city atty. City of Charlotte, N.C., 1969-78; ptnr. Constagny, Goines, Buckley & Boyd, 1978-81, Taylor & Buckley, Charlotte, 1981-85, Buckley McMullen & Buie, P.A., Charlotte, 1994—. Town atty. Town of Matthew (N.C.), 1978—; faculty Ctrl. Piedmont C.C., 1970. Bd. dirs. Charlotte City Employees Credit Union, 1974-78; pre. PTA, 1980-82; bd. visitors Luth. Theol. So. Sem., 1989-93. Recipient Cert. of Merit, City of charlotte, 1982. Mem. N.C. Bar Assn., N.C. Assn. Mcpl. Lawyers (bd. dirs. 1979-81, v.p. 1995-96, 1st v.p. 1996-97, pres. 1997-98), Rotary, Optimist Club (pres. 1982-83), Phi Alpha Delta. Democrat. Lutheran. Consumer commercial, General practice, Municipal (including bonds). Home: 6813 Linda Lake Dr Charlotte NC 28215-4019 E-mail: CRB3@bellsouth.com

BUCKLEY, COLIN HUGH, lawyer; b. Chgo., June 27, 1960; s. Brian John and Joan (Langhorn) B. BA in English History with honors, Coll. William and Mary, 1982, JD, 1985; LLM in Legal History, U. Cambridge, Eng., 1986. Bar: Pa. 1986, Mass. 1993, U.S. Ct. Appeals (3d cir.) 1988. Assoc. Dechert Price & Rhoads, Phila., 1986-90, Day, Berry & Howard, Boston, 1990-96, counsel, 1997-98; mem. Brown Rudnick Freed & Gesmer, London, 1998—. Contbr. articles to profl. jours. Mem. ABA, Internat. Bar Assn., Pa. Bar Assn., Phila. Bar Assn., Selden Soc. Contracts commercial, General corporate, Mergers and acquisitions. Office: Brown Rudnick Freed & Gesmer Brown Rudnick Freed & Gesmr 8 Clifford St W1S 2IQ London England E-mail: cbuckley@brfg.co.uk

BUCKLEY, FREDERICK JEAN, lawyer; b. Wilmington, Ohio, Nov. 5, 1923; s. William Millard and Martha (Bright) B.; m. Josephine K. Buckley, Dec. 4, 1945; children: Daniel J., Fredrica Buckley Elder, Matthew J. Student, Wilmington Coll., 1941-42, Ohio State U., 1942-43; AB, U. Mich., 1948, LLB, 1949. Bar: Ohio 1950, U.S. Dist. Ct. (so. dist.) Ohio 1952, U.S. Supreme Ct. 1978, U.S. Ct. Appeals (6th cir.) 1981, Fla. 1982, U.S. Dist. Ct. (mid. dist.) Fla. 1991; cert. cir. ct. mediator, Fla.; cert. arbitrator Fla. state and fed. cts. Assoc. G.L. Schilling, Sr., Wilmington, 1951-52; ptnr. Schilling & Buckley, 1953-56; sole practice, 1956-62; sr. ptnr. Buckley, Miller & Wright, 1962—. Chmn., counsel The Wilmington Savs. Bank, 1971— , also dir.; solicitor City of Wilmington, 1954-63. Contbr. articles in field. With AUS, 1943-46, ETO. Joint program Mich. Inst. Pub. Adminstrn. fellow, 1948. Fellow Am. Coll. Trial Lawyers; mem. ABA, Am. Arbitration Assn. (comml. panel), Fed. Bar Assn., Ohio State Bar Assn., Clinton County Bar Assn., Fla. Bar, Fla. Acad. Profl. Mediators, Soc. Profls. in Dispute Resolution, Collier County Bar Assn., Ohio State Bar Found. Republican. Methodist. Alternative dispute resolution, General civil litigation, Probate. Office: 145 N South St Wilmington OH 45177-1646

BUCKLEY, JOHN JOSEPH, JR. lawyer; b. N.Y.C., May 18, 1947; m. Jane Emily Genster, Jan. 12, 1980; children: Emily, Darcy, Claire, Connor. AB, Georgetown U., 1969; JD, U. Chgo., 1972. Bar: N.Y. 1973, D.C. 1977. Law clk. to judge John Minor Wisdom U.S. Ct. Appeals, New Orleans, 1972-73; law clk. to justice Lewis F. Powell Jr. U.S. Supreme Ct., Washington, 1973-74; spl. asst. to atty. gen. Edward H. Levi U.S. Dept. Justice, 1975-77; assoc. Williams & Connolly, 1977-80, ptnr., 1981—. Mem. ABA, Order of Coif, Phi Beta Kappa. General civil litigation, Criminal. Home: 2955 Newark St NW Washington DC 20008-3339 Office: Williams & Connolly 725 12th St NW Washington DC 20005-5901 E-mail: JBuckley@wc.com

BUCKLEY, MICHAEL FRANCIS, lawyer; b. Saranac Lake, N.Y., Nov. 1, 1943; s. Francis Edward and Marjorie (Mooney) B.; m. Mary Thornton, June 26, 1965; children: Sean, Kathleen. BA, Dartmouth Coll., 1965; JD, Cornell U., 1968. Bar: N.Y. 1969, Fla. 1982, U.S. Dist. Ct. (we. dist.) N.Y. 1970. Assoc. Harter, Secrest & Emery, Rochester, N.Y., 1968-75, ptnr., 1976—. Contbg. author: Estate Planning and Probate in New York, 1985; co-editor: Administration of New York Estates, 1990. Bd. dirs. Highland Hosp. Found., Rochester, 1981-95, pres., 1984-87; bd. dirs. Highland Hosp., 1987—, pres., 1992-94; bd. dirs. Highland Health Sys., Inc., 1995-97, Strong Ptnrs. Health System, Inc., 1997—, YMCA of Greater Rochester, 1997—, Highland Cmty. Devel. Corp., 1998—, Highland Living Ctr., Inc., 1998—, Rochester Area Cmty. Found., 1999—, James B. Wilmot Found., Inc., 2000—, U. Rochester Med. Ctr., 2000—. Fellow Am. Coll. Trusts and Estates Counsel; mem. N.Y. State Bar Assn. (exec. com. trusts and estates law sect. 1988-92), Monroe County Bar Assn. (chmn. trusts and estates sect. 1984-85, banking liaison com. 1985-86), Fla. Bar Assn., Estate Planing Coun. Rochester, Internat. Assn. Fin. Planners, Dartmouth Club (Rochester). Roman Catholic. Avocations: basketball, platform tennis. Estate planning, Probate, Estate taxation. Home: 571 Thomas Ave Rochester NY 14617-1432 Office: Harter Secrest & Emery 1600 Bausch & Lomb Pl Rochester NY 14604-2711 E-mail: mbuckley@hselaw.com

BUCKLEY, MIKE CLIFFORD, lawyer; b. Atlanta, Sept. 1, 1944; s. Clifford Robert Buckley and Winifred Davis (Clayton) Coleman; m. Elizabeth Trimble, June 17, 1967. AB, U. Calif., Berkeley, 1966; JD, U. Calif., 1969. Bar: Calif. 1969. Assoc. Lawler, Felix & Hall, L.A., 1969-72; asst. West Coast counsel ITT, 1972-74; ptnr. Crosby, Heafey, Roach & May, Oakland, Calif., 1974—. Pres. TeleNetwork, Inc., Oakland, 1984-92; treas. Salem Luth. Home of the East Bay Inc., 1992-98; lectr. Calif. Continuing Edn. of Bar, Berkeley, 1978—; workshop leader Hastings Coll. Advocacy, San Francisco, 1981-85; adv. com. U.S. Bankruptcy Ct., San Francisco, 1984-89. Mem. ABA, Calif. Bar Assn., Alameda Bar Assn., San Francisco Bar Assn. Democrat. Bankruptcy, Contracts commercial. Home: 246 Pershing Dr Oakland CA 94611-3235 Office: Crosby Heafey Roach & May PO Box 2084 Oakland CA 94604-2084 E-mail: mbuckley@chrm.com

BUCKLIN, LEONARD HERBERT, lawyer; b. Mpls., Apr. 17, 1933; s. Leonard A. and Lilah B. (Nordland) B.; m. Charla Lee; children: Karen, Anne, David, Douglas, Lea, Gregory. BS in Law, U. Minn., 1955, JD, 1957. Bar: Minn. 1957, U.S. Dist. Ct. Minn. 1957, N.D. 1960, U.S. Dist. Ct. N.D. 1960, U.S. Ct. Appeals (8th cir.) 1971, U.S. Supreme Ct. 1973, Colo. 1989, U.S. Dist. Ct. Colo. 1989, Tex. 1992, U.S. Dist. Ct. Tex. 1993. Ptnr. Larson, Loevinger, Lindquist, Freeman & Fraser, Mpls., 1957-60, Zuger & Bucklin, Bismark, N.D., 1960-87; gen. counsel Provident Life Ins. Co., 1965-85; pres. Bucklin Trial Lawyers P.C., 1988-95; of counsel Bucklin and Klemine, Bismark, N.D., 1992—, Allison and Huerta, Corpus Christi, 1992-97; owner Bucklin of Counsel Attys., 1997—. Lectr. ethics & ins. coverage to various groups, cons. on ethics to attys. and bus., mem. trial procedures com. N.D. Supreme Ct., 1977-92. Author: Civil Practice of North Dakota, 1975, ann. supplements, 1976-92. Fellow Internat. Acad. Trial Lawyers (bd. dirs.); mem. ABA (ins. coverage and ethics coms., Ctr. Profl. Responsibility), United Network for Organ Sharing (patient affairs, ethics, profl. stds. com., bd. dirs.), ATLA, Tex. Trial Lawyers Assn., Winthrop Soc., Joseph Bucklin Soc. (exec. dir.), Chopin Soc. Tex., Tex. Ctr. for Legal Ethics, Million Dollar Advocates Forum, Rotary (Paul Harris fellow Corpus Christi), Order of Coif, Phi Delta Phi, Delta Sigma Rho. Methodist. Home and Office: 8063 S Michele Ln Tempe AZ 85284-1362 E-mail: director@bucklinsociety.net, ofcounsel@bigfoot.com

BUCKSTEIN, MARK AARON, lawyer, mediator, educator; b. N.Y.C., July 1, 1939; s. Henry Al and Minnie Sarah (Russ) B.; m. Rochelle Joan Buchman, Sept. 11, 1960; children: Robin Beth, Michael Alan. BS in Math., CCNY, 1960; JD, NYU, 1963. Bar: N.Y. 1963, U.S. Dist. Ct. (so. and ea. dists.) N.Y. 1965, U.S. Supreme Ct. 1981. Assoc. Russ & Weyl, Massapequa, N.Y., 1963-64; assoc. counsel Mut. Life Ins. Co. N.Y., N.Y.C., 1964-65; assoc. Moses & Singer, 1965-67, Leinwand, Maron & Hendler, N.Y.C., 1967-68; sr. ptnr. Baer Marks & Upham, 1968-86; sr. v.p. external affairs, gen. counsel TWA, Inc., 1986-92; exec. v.p. Am. Arbitration Assn., N.J., 1992-93; exec. v.p., gen. counsel GAF Corp. and Internat. Specialty Products, Wayne, 1993-96; counsel Greenberg Traurig, Ft. Lauderdale, Fla., 1996-99, Profl. Dispute Resolution, Inc., Boca Raton, 1999—. Spl. prof. law Hofstra U. Law Sch., Hempstead, N.Y., 1981-93; adj. prof. law Rutgers U. Law Sch., Newark, 1994-96; bd. dirs. Bayswater Realty & Capital Corp., N.Y.C., Travel Channel Inc., N.Y.C., TWA, GAF Corp., Internat. Specialty Products, Consultis; mem. exec. com. Herzfeld & Stern, N.Y.C., 1981-84; mem. nat. arbitration and mediation com. NASD, 1998-2001. Trustee Bronx H.S. Found., 1984-96. Mem. ABA, N.Y. Bar Assn., Assn. of Bar of City of N.Y., Soc. for Profls. in Dispute Resolution, KP (past dep. grand chancellor 1978). Democrat. Jewish. Avocations: tennis, music, theater, puzzles. Contracts commercial, General corporate, Securities. Office: Profl Dispute Resolution 1200 N Federal Hwy Boca Raton FL 33432-2803 E-mail: mabresolve@aol.com

BUCKWALTER, RONALD LAWRENCE, federal judge; b. Lancaster, Pa., Dec. 11, 1936; s. Noah Denlinger and Carolyn Marie (Lawrence) B.; m. Dollie May Fitting, May 9, 1963; children: Stephen Matthew, Wendy Susan. AB, Franklin and Marshall Coll., 1958; JD, Coll. William and Mary, 1962. Prin. Ronald L. Buckwalter, Esquire, Lancaster, 1963-71; ptnr. Shirk, Reist and Buckwalter, 1971-80; dist. atty. Lancaster County, 1978-80; judge 2nd Jud. Dist. Commonwealth Pa., 1980-90, U.S. Dist. Ct., Phila., 1990—. Sec. City Lancaster Authority, 1970; bd. dirs. Am. Cancer Soc., Lancaster, 1982, Boy Scouts Am., Lancaster, 1984, YMCA, Lancaster, 1990. 1st lt. U.S. Army NG, 1962-68. Recipient Pub. Life and Letter award Phi Sigma Alpha, 1990. Mem. Am. Judicature Soc., Fed. Bar Assn., Fed. Judges Assn., Pa. Bar Assn., Lancaster Bar Assn. (pres. 1988). Office: US Dist Ct 14614 US Courthouse 601 Market St Philadelphia PA 19106-1713

BUDANITSKY, SANDER, lawyer; b. Riga, Latvia, Feb. 9, 1972; came to the U.S., 1979; s. Grigory and Miriam Budanitsky; m. Kimberly Anne Rudolph, Nov. 16, 1997. BA, Dickinson Coll., 1993; JD, Widener U., 1996. Bar: N.J. 1996, Pa. 1996. Legal intern U.S. Dept. Justice, Office of the U.S. Trustee, Phila., 1995-96; assoc. Seigel & Mongiardo, P.C., Ridgewood, N.J., 1997-98, Robert C. Diorio, Elizabeth, 1998—. Avocation: rugby. General civil litigation, General corporate. Office: Law Offices Robert C Diorio 431 Morris Ave Elizabeth NJ 07208-3612

BUDD, DAVID GLENN, lawyer; b. Dayton, Ohio, May 19, 1934; s. Glenn E. and Anna Elizabeth (Purdy) B.; m. Barbarann Dumbaugh, Apr. 4, 1964; children: Anne Elizabeth, David Glenn II. AB with honors, Ohio U., 1959; JD with honors, U. Cin., 1962. Bar: Ohio 1962, U.S. Dist. Ct. (so. dist.) Ohio 1963, U.S. Dist. Ct. (no. dist.) Ohio 1967, U.S. Supreme Ct. 1967, Fla. 1980, U.S. Dist. Ct. (mid. dist.) Fla. 1981, U.S. Tax Ct. 1989. Assoc. Young, Pryor, Lynn, Strickland & Falke, Dayton, 1962-65; trial atty. U.S. Dept. Justice, Cleve., 1965-67; chief antitrust sect. Atty. Gen. Ohio, Columbus, Ohio, 1967-69; ptnr., sr. corp. atty. Cox & Brandabur Attys., Xenia, 1969-74; asst. v.p., asst. sec. law Jim Walter Corp., Tampa, Fla., 1974-76; sec., gen. counsel, asst. treas. Gardinier Big River, Inc., Gardinier, Inc., 1976-80; assoc. Young, Van Assenderp, Varnadoe & Benton, P.A., Naples, Fla., 1981-84; ptnr. Van Koughnet & Budd, 1984-85; sr. ptnr. Budd, Hines & Thompson, 1985-88, Budd & Thompson, Naples, 1989-92, Budd, Thompson & Zuccaro, Naples, 1993-95, Budd & Zuccaro, Naples, 1996-97, Budd and Bennett, Naples, 1998—. Legal counsel to bd. dirs. of numerous corps. Vol. Legal Aid Soc., Xenia, 1972; active Newcomen Soc. N.Am. With USN, 1952-54. Mem. ABA (bus. law sect.), Fla. Bar Assn., Collier County Bar Assn., Blue Key Club, Omicron Delta Kappa, Pi Gamma Mu, Phi Kappa Tau. Republican. Presbyterian. Avocations: health fitness club, tennis, golf, boating. General corporate, Probate, Real property. Home: 3757 Fountainhead Ln Naples FL 34103-2734 Office: Budd and Bennett 3033 Riviera Dr Ste 201 Naples FL 34103-2750 E-mail: buddbennett@aol.com

BUDD, THOMAS MATTHEW, solicitor; b. Murwillumbah, NSW, Australia, Sept. 12, 1958; arrived in U.K., 1984; s. Derek Knight and Gwenda Molly (Gregor) B.; m. Gillian Susan Grendale, June 27, 1992; children: Matthew Charles Hamilton, Rory Edward Andrew. B Comm., U. Queensland, Brisbane, Australia, 1980, LLB, 1982; LLM, U. Cambridge, Eng., 1985. Cert. solicitor, Queensland, New South Wales, Eng., Wales. Articled clk. Morris, Fletcher & Cross, Brisbane, 1982-84, solicitor, 1984, Slaughter and May, London, 1985-92; ptnr. Gouldens, 1992—. Mem. Internat. Bar Assn. Office: Gouldens 10 Old Bailey London EC4M 7NG England

BUDD, THOMAS WITBECK, lawyer; b. Phila., Nov. 1, 1939; s. Reginald Masten and Elizabeth (Charlton) B.; divorced; children: Kelly Budd Tinsley, Paige Budd Glickman; m. Bernadette Smith Budd, July 4, 1988; stepchildren: Amanda Rose Kronin, Karen Kronin Campisi. BA, Washington and Lee U., 1961, LLB, 1964. Bar: Va. 1964, N.Y. 1965, U.S. Supreme Ct. 1982. Assoc. Buell Clifton & Turner, N.Y.C., 1964-69, ptnr., 1969-70, Clifton Budd & Burke, N.Y.C., 1970-76, Clifton Budd Burke & Demaria, N.Y.C., 1976-88, Clifton, Budd & Demaria, N.Y.C., 1988—. Contbg. author, editor to Labor and Employment Law newsletter. Mem. law coun. Washington and Lee U., 1978-81, 84-85. Mem. ABA (labor law sect.), N.Y. Bar Assn. (labor law sect.), N.Y.C. Bar Assn. (labor law sect.), Washington Soc. Washington and Lee U., Princeton Club (N.Y.C.), St. George's Golf and Country Club (Stony Brook, N.Y.). Labor, Pension, profit-sharing, and employee benefits. Home: 3 Colgate Ct Shoreham NY 11786-1221 Office: Clifton Budd & Demaria 420 Lexington Ave New York NY 10170-0002 E-mail: twbudd@cbdm.com

BUECHEL, WILLIAM BENJAMIN, lawyer; b. Wichita, Kans., July 27, 1926; s. Donald William and Bonnie S. (Priddy) B.; m. Theresa Marie Girard, Nov. 3, 1955; children: Sarah Ann, Julia Elaine. Student, U. Wichita, 1947-49; BS, U. Kans., 1951; LLB, 1954. Sole practice, Concordia, Kans., 1954-56; stockholder Paulsen, Buechel, Swenson, Uri & Brewer Charterd, 1971-75; sec.-treas., 1975-77, 1975-77; pres., 1977-92; of counsel, 1993-95; ret. Bd. dirs. County Bank & Trust, Concordia,

1971-92, mem. trust and adminstrn. com. Citizens Nat. Bank, 1992—. Bd. dirs. Cloud County C.C. Found., 1983-89. Mem. ABA, Kans. Bar Assn. (mem. exec. coun. 1966-68, chmn. adv. sect. profl. ethics com. 1974-76), Cloud County Bar Assn. (pres. 1984-86), Elks, Moose, Rotary. Republican. Methodist. Estate planning, Probate, Estate taxation.

BUECHNER, JACK W(ILLIAM), lawyer, government affairs consultant; b. St. Louis, June 4, 1940; s. John Edward and Gertrude Emily (Richardson) B.; children from previous marriage: Patrick John, Terrence J.; m. Nancy Chanitz; 1 child, Charles Chanitz. BA, Benedictine Coll., 1962; JD, St. Louis U., 1965. Bar: Mo. 1965, U.S. Dist. Ct. (ea. dist.) Mo. 1965, U.S. Ct. Appeals (8th cir.) 1965, U.S. Ct. Appeals (D.C. cir.) 1998. Ptnr. Buechner, McCarthy, Leonard, Kaemmerer, Owen & Laderman, Chesterfield, Mo., 1965-93; mem. 100th-102d U.S. Congresses from 2d Mo. dist., 1987-91; dep. minority whip, 1989-90; vice-chmn. Rep. study group, pres. Internat. Rep. Inst., Washington, 1991-93; prin., dir. internat. svcs. The Hawthorn Group, Arlington, Va., 1993-95; ptnr. Manatt Phelps & Phillips, Washington, 1995—. State rep. 94th dist. Mo. Gen. Assembly, 1972-82, minority leader, 1974-78; mem. state adv. com. U.S. Commn. on Civil Rights, 1975-82; bd. dirs. Coun. Cmty. Democracies. Lay advisor St. Louis Med. Soc., 1989-92; Mo. Tourism Commn., 1976, 82-85; prin. Coun. for Excellence in Govt.; bd. dirs. Presdl. Classroom. Recipient Meritorious Svc. award St. Louis Globe-Democrat, 1973, Legis. Achievement award St. Louis Police Officers, 1982, Pub. Svc. award Women's Polit. Caucus, Mo., Disting. Svc. award Cardinal Glennon Hosp., Mo., 1982, Nat. Security Leadership award Am. Security Coun. Found., 1988, 89, Family and Freedom award, Golden Bulldog award, 1987, 88, Guardian of Small Bus. award Nat. Fedn. Ind. Bus., 1987, 88, 90, 91, Enterprise award U.S. C. of C., 1988, 89, 90, Sound Dollar award, 1988, Eagle of Freedom award Am. Security Coun. Foun., 1990. Mem. Mo. Bar Assn., D.C. Bar Assn., Met. Bar Assn., Mo. Soc. Washington (pres.), Nat. Conf. State Socs. (1st v.p.), Ctr. Nat. Policy (bd. dirs. 1997—, bd. dirs. Alliance for responsible Cuba policy), Assn. Former Mems. of Congress (bd. dirs., treas.), The Pericles Inst. (pres. 2001-), John Marshall Club (Outstanding Atty. award 1986), Lions, Phi Delta Phi. Republican. Episcopalian. Avocations: golf, reading, travel. Private international, Public international, Legislative. Home: 1303 Altamira Ct Mc Lean VA 22102-2201 Office: Manatt Phelps & Phillips 1501 M St NW Ste 700 Washington DC 20005-1737 E-mail: jbuechner@manatt.com

BUECHNER, ROBERT WILLIAM, lawyer, educator; b. Syracuse, N.Y., Oct. 29, 1947; s. Donald F. and Barbara (Northrup) B.; m. Angela Marian Hoetker, May 28, 1978; children: Julie Marie, Robert William Jr., Leslie Ann, James Bradley. BSE, Princeton U., 1969; JD, U. Mich., 1974. Bar: Ohio, 1974, Fla. 1974, U.S. Dist. Ct. (so. dist.) Ohio 1974, U.S. Tax Ct. 1974. Assoc. Frost & Jacobs, Cin., 1974-79; pres. Buechner, Haffer, O'Connell, Meyers & Healey Co., L.P.A., 1979—. Adj. prof. Salmon P. Chase Coll. Law, No. Ky., 1975-82; instr. Cin. chpt. Chartered Life Underwiters, 1976-96; lectr. Million Dollar Roundtable, Atlanta, 1981; prodr., host TV show Greater Cin. Bus. Rev., 1993—. Author: (with others) Why Universal Life, 1982, Prosper Through Tax Planning, 1982, Living Gangbusters, 1986, The 8 Pathways to Financial Success, 1987, 93, 98. Mem. planning divsn. Cin. Cmty. Chest, 1978-84; trustee Cin. Venture Assn., 1994-99, pres., 1997-98; trustee Cin. Country Day Sch., 1979-93, pres., 1990-93. Recipient Alumnus of Yr. award Cin. Country Day Sch., 1985, First winner of John Warrington Cmty. Svc. award, 1997. Mem. Cin. Bar Assn. (chmn. taxation sect. 1984-85), S.W. Ohio Tax Inst. (chmn. 1981-82), Cin. Assn. (trustee 1999—), Gyro Club (sec. 1982-83, v.p. 1999-2000), Princeton Club (pres. 1982-84). Republican. Methodist Avocations: golf, tennis, bridge. Estate planning, Probate, General corporate. Office: Buechner Haffer O'Connell Meyers Healey Co LPA 105 E 4th St Ste 300 Cincinnati OH 45202-4023 E-mail: rhuechner@bhomh.com

BUEHLER, JOHN WILSON, lawyer; b. Fresno, Calif., Aug. 16, 1950; s. John A. and Elizabeth (Wilson) B.; children: Nathaniel J., Christopher J. BA, U. Calif., Santa Cruz, 1973; JD magna cum laude, Willamette U., 1977. Bar: Oreg. 1977, U.S. Dist. Ct. Oreg. 1978, U.S. Ct. Appeals (9th. cir.) 1981. Law clk. to presiding justice U.S. Dist. Ct., Portland, Oreg., 1977-79; assoc. Bullivant, Wright et al, 1979-83; ptnr. Bullivant, Houser, Bailey, Pendergrass & Hoffman, 1984-95, Buehler & Buehler, Lake Oswego, 1995—. Bar examiner Bd. of Bar Examiners, Portland, Oreg., 1985-88 (chmn. 1987-88). Vol. atty. sr. law project City of Portland, 1980—. Mem. ABA, Oreg. Bar Assn., Multnomah Bar Assn, Def. Research Inst., Oreg. Assn. Def. Counsel., Democrat. Federal civil litigation, State civil litigation, Insurance.

BUELL, RODD RUSSELL, lawyer; b. Pitts., Mar. 31, 1946; s. Harold Ellsworth and Jeanne Charlotte (Russell) B. BS, Fla. State U., 1968; JD, U. Fla., 1970; LLM, U. Miami, 1978. Bar: Fla. 1971, U.S. Dist. Ct. (so., mid. and no. dists.) Fla. 1971, U.S. Ct. Appeals (5th and 11th cirs.) 1971. Gen. ptnr. Blackwell & Walker, P.A., Miami, 1970-95; shareholder Fleming, O'Bryan & Fleming, Ft. Lauderdale, Fla., 1995-97; pvt. practice, Coral Gables, 1997—. Mem. Dade County Def. Bar Assn. (pres. 1985-86), Def. Trial Attys. Assn. (exec. counsel 1986-88), Maritime Law Assn., Am. Bd. Trial Advs., Internat. Assn. Def. Counsel, Bath Club, Riviera Country Club, Miami Club, Univ. Club. Republican. Methodist. Admiralty, General civil litigation, Personal injury. Home: 11883 Maidstone Dr Wellington FL 33414 Office: 288 Aragon Ave Ste C Coral Gables FL 33134

BUESSER, ANTHONY CARPENTER, lawyer; b. Detroit, Oct. 15, 1929; s. Frederick Gustavis and Lela (Carpenter) B.; m. Carolyn Sue Pickle, Mar. 13, 1954; children: Kent Anderson, Anthony Carpenter, Andrew Clayton; m. Bettina Rieveschl, Dec. 14, 1973. B.A. in English with honors, U. Mich., 1952, M.A., 1953, J.D., 1960. Bar: Mich. 1961. Assoc. Chase, Goodenough & Buesser, Detroit, 1961-66; ptnr. Buesser, Buesser, Snyder & Blank, Detroit and Bloomfield Hills, Mich., 1966-81; sole practice Birmingham, 1981—. Trustee Detroit Country Day Sch., Beverly Hills, Mich., 1970-94, chmn. bd., 1977-82, 84-87, bd. chmn. emeritus, 1987—, chmn. nominating com., 1987-94. Served with AUS, 1953-55. Recipient Avery Hopwood award major fiction U. Mich., 1953, Outstanding Alumnus award Detroit Country Day Sch., 1988. Mem. ABA, State Bar Mich., Detroit Bar Assn. (pres. 1976-77), Oakland County Bar Assn., Am. Judicature Soc., Thomas M. Cooley Club (pres. 1974-76), Alpha Delta Phi, Phi Delta Phi. Office: 725 S Adams Rd Ste 260 Birmingham MI 48009-6913 Home: 756 Honey Creek Dr Ann Arbor MI 48103-1638

BUFFON, CHARLES EDWARD, lawyer; b. Topeka, Sept. 8, 1939; s. Merritt Woodbridge and Clare Marie (Waterfall) B.; m. Kathleen Craig Vreeland, June 6, 1964; children: Alexandra, Nathaniel Edward. AB in Internat. Rels. magna cum laude, Dartmouth Coll., 1961; LLB cum laude, Harvard U., 1964. Bar: D.C. 1965, U.S. Ct. Appeals (D.C. cir.) 1965, U.S. Ct. Appeals (6th cir.) 1966, U.S. Supreme Ct. 1971, U.S. Ct. Appeals (9th cir.) 1975, U.S. Ct. Appeals (2d cir.) 1980, U.S. Ct. Appeals (4th cir.) 1980, U.S. Ct. Appeals (3d cir.) 1981, U.S. Ct. Appeals (fed. cir.) 1982, U.S. Dist. Ct. Md. 1992, U.S. Ct. Appeals (11th cir.) 2000. Assoc. Covington & Burling, Washington, 1964-73, ptnr., 1973—. Adj. faculty U. Va. Law Sch., 1968-86, Am. U. 1988-92; lectr. in field. Contbr. articles to profl. jours. Fellow Am. Bar Found.; mem. ABA (litigation, intellectual property and antitrust sects.), D.C. Bar Assn. (past chmn. legal ethics com., spl. com. legal specialization, past mem. steering com. sect. cts., lawyers and adminstrn. justice, D.C. rules profl. conduct edn. com., spl. com. model rules profl. conduct, long range planning com., chmn. com. on multidisciplinary practice, Cert. Appreciation 1987), Phi Beta Kappa. Antitrust, Federal civil litigation, Intellectual property. Office: Covington & Burling 1201 Pennsylvania Ave NW PO Box 7566 Washington DC 20044-7566

BUFFORD, SAMUEL LAWRENCE, federal judge; b. Phoenix, Nov. 19, 1943; s. John Samuel and Evelyn Amelia (Rude) B.; m. Julia Marie Metzger, May 13, 1978. BA in Philosophy, Wheaton Coll., 1964; PhD, U. Tex., 1969; JD magna cum laude, U. Mich., 1973. Bar: Calif., N.Y., Ohio. Instr. philosophy La. State U., Baton Rouge, 1967-68; asst. prof. Ea. Mich. U., Ypsilanti, 1968-74; asst. prof. law Ohio State U., Columbus, 1975-77; assoc. Gendel, Raskoff, Shapiro & Quittner, L.A., 1982-85; atty. Paul, Weiss, Rifkind, Wharton & Garrison, N.Y.C., 1974-75, Sullivan Jones & Archer, San Francisco, 1977-79, Musick, Peeler & Garrett, L.A., 1979-81, Rifkind & Sterling, Beverly Hills, Calif., 1981-82, Gendel, Raskoff, Shapiro & Quittner, L.A., 1982-85; U.S. bankruptcy judge Ctrl. Dist. Calif., 1985—. Bd. dirs. Fin. Lawyers Conf., L.A., 1987-90, Bankruptcy Forum, L.A., 1986-88; lectr. U.S.-Romanian Jud. Delegation, 1991, Internat. Tng. Ctr. for Bankers, Budapest, 1993, Bankruptcy Technical Legal Assistance Workshop, Romania, 1994, Comml. Law Project for Ukraine, 1995-96, 99, Ea. Europe Enterprise Restructuring and Privitization Project, U.S. AID, 1995-96; cons. Calif. State Bar Bd. Examiners, 1989-90; bd. trustees Endowment for Edn.; bd. dirs. Nat. Conf. Bankruptcy Judges, 1994-2000; bd. dirs. San Pedro Enterprise Community, 1997—. Editor-in-chief Am. Bankruptcy Law Jour., 1990-94; contbr. articles to profl. jours. Younger Humanist fellowship NEH. Mem. ABA, L.A. County Bar Assn. (mem. profl. responsibility and ethics com. 1979—, chair profl. responsibility and ethics com. 1985-86, chair ethics 2000 liaison com. 1997—), Order of Coif. Office: US Bankruptcy Ct 255 E Temple St Ste 1582 Los Angeles CA 90012-3332

BUFORD, ROBERT PEGRAM, lawyer; b. Roanoke Rapids, N.C., Sept. 7, 1925; s. Robert Pegram and Edith (Rawlings) B.; m. Anne Bliss Whitehead, June 26, 1948; children: Robert, Bliss, Peyton. LLB, U. Va., 1950. Bar: Va. 1949. sr. counsel Hunton & Williams, Richmond, Va. Bd. visitors U. Va., Charlottesville, 1972-80; chmn. Met. Richmond C. of C., 1973; vice chmn., bd. trustees St. Paul's Coll., Lawrenceville, Va., 1977-85. Lt. (j.g.) USNR, 1943-46. Recipient Disting. Service award Jr. C. of C., 1961, Va. Profl. Assn., 1965, Good Govt. award Richmond First Club, 1967. Fellow Am. Bar Found., Va. Law Found.; mem. ABA, Va. Bar (assoc.), Country Club of Va., Commonwealth Club. Banking, General corporate, Securities. Home: 506 Kilmarnock Dr Richmond VA 23229-8102 Office: Hunton & Williams Riverfront Pla E Tower PO Box 1535 Richmond VA 23218-1535

BUGGE, LAWRENCE JOHN, lawyer, educator; b. Milw., June 1, 1936; s. Lawrence Anthony and Anita (Westenberg) B.; m. Mary Daly, Nov. 28, 1959 (div.); m. Elaine Andersen, Jan. 29, 1977; children: Kristin, Laura, Jill, David, Carol. AB, Marquette U., 1958; JD, Harvard U., 1963. Bar: Wis. 1963. Assoc. Foley and Lardner, Milw., Madison, Wis., 1963-70, ptnr., 1970-96, of counsel, 1996—. Pres. Nat. Conf. Commrs. on Uniform State Laws, 1989-91; adj. prof. law U. Wis. Law Sch., Madison, 1997—. Mem. Wis. Bar Assn. (pres. 1980-81), Mil. Bar Assn. (pres. 1974-75), Milw. Young Lawyers Assn. (pres. 1969-70). Home: 313 Walnut Grove Dr Madison WI 53717-1228 Office: Foley & Lardner PO Box 1497 150 E Gilman St Madison WI 53701-1497 E-mail: ljbugge@itis.com

BUHLER, GREGORY WALLACE, lawyer; b. Englewood, N.J., Oct. 17, 1949; s. Wallace and Mary Jane (Burton) B.; m. Jan Clark, Sept. 7, 1968; children— Jennifer, Casey. B.A., C.W. Post Coll., 1971, J.D., Hofstra Law Sch., 1974. Bar: N.Y. 1975, U.S. Dist. Ct. (so. and ea. dists.) N.Y. 1975, U.S. Ct. Claims 1979, U.S. Ct. Appeals (2d cir.) 1984, U.S. Supreme Ct. 1985, U.S. Ct. Appeals (5th cir.) 1989. Assoc. Whitman & Ransom, N.Y.C., 1974-76; from atty. to v.p. legal Pan Am. World Airways, Inc., N.Y.C., 1976—p; v.p., gen. coun. and sec. Kiwi Internat. Airlines, Inc., Newark, N.J., 1996—. Aviation, General civil litigation, Private international. Home: 633 Cardinal Rd Cortlandt Manor NY 10567-5201

BUILDER, J. LINDSAY, JR. lawyer; b. Miami, Fla., Feb. 6, 1943; s. John Lindsay and Majorie (Merrell) L.; m. Jean Fern, Aug. 3, 1968; children Margaret Merrell, John Lindsay III. BE, Vanderbilt U., 1965, JD, 1970. Bar: Fla. 1970, U.S. Dist Ct. (mid. dist.) Fla. 1971, U.S. Supreme Ct. 1976. Assoc., ptnr. Maguire, Voorhis & Wells P.A, Orlando, Fla., 1970-84; ptnr. Godbold, Allen, Brown & Builder P.A., Winter Park, 1984-88, Allen, Brown & Builder P.A., Winter Park, 1988-90, Honigman Miller Schwartz and Cohn., Detroit, Orlando, 1991-96, Graham, Clark, Jones, Builder, Pratt and Marks, Winter Park, Fla., 1996—. Mem. bd. trust Vanderbilt U., Nashville, 1990-92, Winter Park Mem. Hosp., chmn. 1994-96. Lt. (j.g) USN, 1965-67. Mem. Orange County Bar Assn. (pres. 1983-84), Vanderbilt U. Law Sch. Alumni (bd. dirs. 1985, pres.), Vanderbilt U. Alumni (pres. bd. dirs. 1989-90). Republican. Episcopalian. Avocations: golf, snow skiing, tennis. Office: Graham Builder Jones Pratt & Marks 369 N New York Ave Winter Park FL 32789-3124 E-mail: lbuilder@grahambuilder.com

BULL, HOWARD LIVINGSTON, lawyer; b. Binghamton, N.Y., Oct. 7, 1942; s. Glen Chapel Bull and Martha Gertrade (Mott) Skinner; m. Sheila Kay Settle, Apr. 22, 1977; children: John Keese, Jason Howard, Justin Thomas. AB, DePauw U., 1964; JD, U. Va., 1967. Bar: Calif. 1973, U.S. Dist. Ct. (no. dist.) Calif. 1973, U.S. Ct. Appeals (9th cir.) 1973. Assoc. Owen, Melbye & Rohlff, Redwood City, Calif., 1973-74; corp. atty. Varian Assocs., Inc., Palo Alto, 1974-99; pvt. practice Mountain View, 1999—. Pres. Midpeninsula chpt. UN Assn.-USA, 1985, Northern Calif. div., Palo Alto, 1987; trustee Ben Lomond (Calif.) Quaker Ctr., 1975-80. Served to capt. USAF, 1968-72. Mem. ABA, Am. Corp. Counsel Assn., Santa Clara County Bar Assn. (steering com. corp. counsel sect. 1984-86), Palo Alto Area Bar Assn., DePauw Alumni Club (pres. 1975). Republican. Mem. Soc. of Friends. Avocations: sports, camping, bicycling, woodworking. Contracts commercial, Computer. Home: 1457 Isabelle Ave Mountain View CA 94040-3039 Office: Counsel to Bus in Comml Lawt 1457 Isabelle Ave Mountain View CA 94040 E-mail: howardball@earthlink.net

BULLARD, ROCKWOOD WILDE, III, lawyer; b. Chgo., May 20, 1944; s. Rockwood Wilde, Jr. and Maryetta Moylen (Fitts) B.; m. Donna Rae Boles, Oct. 29, 1983; children: Elizabeth Ryan, Cathleen Stickney, Braley Boles, Rockwood Boles. BA, Wayne State U., 1971; JD with honors, New Eng. Sch. Law, 1974. Bar: D.C. 1974, Mich. 1976, U.S. Dist. Ct. (ea. dist.) Mich. 1976, U.S. Dist. Ct. (we. dist.) Mich. 1977, U.S. Ct. Appeals (6th cir.) 1978, U.S. Supreme Ct. 1979; panel chmn. Atty. Discipline Bd. State Bar Mich., 1984—; prin. Tower Internat. Co., Birmingham, Mich. Mem. instl. rev. com. Pontiac Gen. Hosp., 1976-83; chmn. attys.' div. United Way Oakland, Pontiac, 1983. Served as spl. agt. M.I., U.S. Army, 1967-69. Recipient Amos L. Taylor award New Eng. Law Sch., 1974. Mem. Oakland County C. of C. (bd. dirs. 1984-87), ABA, Mich. Bar. Assn., Oakland County Bar Assn., D.C. Bar Assn., Dickinson County Bar Assn. Federal civil litigation, General corporate, Trademark and copyright.

BULLOCK, BRUCE STANLEY, lawyer; b. Kissimmee, Fla., Oct. 29, 1933; s. Arthur Stanley and Athalia (Griffin) B.; m. Lydia Austill, July 8, 1960; children: Bruce Stanley Jr., Margaret Bullock Martin. BA, U. Fla., 1955, LLB, 1962. Bar: Fla. 1962, U.S. Dist. Ct. (mid. and no. dists.), U.S. Supreme Ct., U.S. Ct. Appeals (11th crct.); diplomate Am. Bd. Trial Advocates; cert. crct. ct. mediator. Atty. assoc. Marks Gray Conroy & Gibbs, Jacksonville, Fla., 1962-66, atty., ptnr., 1966-73; atty., pres. Bullock & Alexander, 1973-74, Bullock, Childs, Pendley & Reed, Jacksonville, 1974-95; ptnr. Bullock, Childs, Pendley & Reed, PA, 1995—. Pres. N.E. Fla. Med. Malpractice Claims Coun. Dir., committeeman, gen. counsel Duval County (Fla.) Rep. Party. Lt. USAF, 1955-59. Mem. Jacksonville Bar Assn., Jacksonville Assn. Def. Counsel (pres.), Fla. Def. Lawyers Assn., Def. Trial Lawyers Assn., Def. Rsch. Inst., U. Fla. Alumni Club (pres.), Rotary Club (v.p. S. Jacksonville chpt.), Am. Bd. Trial Advocates (pres. local chpt. 1999). Republican. Episcopalian. Avocations: fishing, boating, nature. General civil litigation, Personal injury, Product liability. Home: 2510 Hickory Bluff Ln Jacksonville FL 32223-6503 Office: Bullock Childs Pendley Reed 233 E Bay St Ste 711 Jacksonville FL 32202-3448 E-mail: bbullock@newsouth.net

BULLOCK, FRANK WILLIAM, JR. federal judge; b. Oxford, N.C., Nov. 3, 1938; s. Frank William and Wilma Jackson (Long) B.; m. Frances Dockery Haywood, May 5, 1984; 1 child, Frank William III BSBA, U. N.C., 1961, LLB, 1963. Bar: N.C. 1963. Assoc. Maupin, Taylor & Ellis, Raleigh, N.C., 1964-68; asst. dir. Adminstrv. Office of Cts. of N.C., 1968-73; ptnr. Douglas, Ravenel, Hardy, Crihfield & Bullock, Greensboro, N.C., 1973-82; judge U.S. Dist. Ct. N.C., 1982-92, chief judge, 1992-99. Mem. bd. editors N.C. Law Rev., 1962-63; contbr. articles to profl. jours. Mem. N.C. Bar Assn., Greensboro Bar Assn., N.C. Soc. of Cin., Fla. Soc. Colonial Wars, Greensboro Country Club. Republican. Presbyterian. Avocations: golf, tennis, running, history. Office: US Dist Ct PO Box 3223 Greensboro NC 27402-3223

BULLOCK, STEPHEN C. lawyer; b. Miami, Fla., May 9, 1949; BS, NYU, 1973; JD cum laude, Harvard U., 1989. Bar: Conn. 1989, Pa. 1989. Asst. counsel Pratt & Whitney; staff atty. United Tech. Corp.; asst. gen. counsel Carrier Corp., Syracuse, N.Y.; v.p., counsel Carrier Enterprises, LLC. Mem. ABA (mem. business law and antitrust sects.). Antitrust, General corporate, Mergers and acquisitions. Office: Carrier Corp Carrier Pkwy PO Box 4800 Syracuse NY 13221-4800

BULLOCK, STEVEN CARL, lawyer; b. Anderson, Ind., Jan. 19, 1949; s. Carl Pearson and Dorothy Mae (Colle) B.; m. Debra Bullock; children: Bradford, Christine, Justin, Evan. BA, Purdue U., 1971; JD, Detroit Coll., 1985. Bar: Mich. 1985, U.S. Dist. Ct. (ea. dist.) 1985, Ct. of Appeals (6th cir.) 1993, U.S. Supreme Ct. 1993. Pvt. pracitce, Inkster, Mich., 1985—. With USAF, 1971-75. Mem. Mich. Bar Assn. (criminal law sect.), Detroit Bar Assn., Detroit Funder's Soc., Recorder's Ct. Bar Assn., Suburban Bar Assn., Criminal Def. Lawyers of Mich. Avocations: golf, travel. Criminal, Family and matrimonial. Office: 2228 Inkster Rd Inkster MI 48141-1811 E-mail: lawone123@aol.com

BUMGARNER, JAMES MCNABB, judge; b. Peru, Ill., Sept. 13, 1919; s. Joshua Mills and Ethel (McNabb) Bumgarner; m. Helen D Welker, Feb. 07, 1942 (dec. May 1981); children: Barbara Malany, Sally Guth; m. Elizabeth L Miller, Feb. 12, 1983; 1 stepchild Tad Miller. BS in Psychology with honors, U. Ill., 1941, JD, 1946. Commd. 2nd lt. USAAF, 1942; advanced through grades to col. USAF, 1967, ret., 1974; pvt. practice Rantoul, Ill., 1947, Hannah, Mattoon; cir. judge 10th Jud. Cir. of Ill., 1979—. Mem.: VFW, Am Legion, Vietnam Vets Ill, Ret Judge Advs Asn, Ill Bar Asn, Putnam County Bar Asn, Timber Growers Asn, Air War Col Alumni Asn, Judge Advs Asn, Putnam County Hist Soc, Univ Ill Alumni Asn, Vietnam Vets Bar Asn, Ret Officers Asn, Ill Col Law Deans Club, Rotary, Phi Alpha Delta. Home: 1010 Market St PO Box 225 Hennepin IL 61327-0225 E-mail: jimbum@bumgarner.org

BUNT SMITH, HELEN MARGUERITE, lawyer; b. L.A., Oct. 8, 1942; d. Alan Verbanks and Nettie Virginia (Crandall) Bunt; m. Charles Robert Smith, Jan. 12, 1974; children: John, Sharon. BS, U. Calif., L.A., 1964; JD, Southwestern U., 1972. Bar: Calif. 1972; cert. secondary tchr., Calif. Tchr. L.A. City Schs., 1965-72; pvt. practice Pasadena, Calif., 1973—. Law Day chmn. Pasadena Bar Assn., 1980, sec., 1981. Editor (newsletter) Lawyer's Club, 1984-85. Sunday sch. tchr. Lake Ave. Congrl. Ch., Pasadena, church choir; sec. Pasadena Sister Cities Com., 1994-96. Mem. San Gabriel Bar Assn. (bd. dirs., sec. 1999—). Avocations: jogging, singing, stained glass. Office: 465 E Union St Ste 102 Pasadena CA 91101-1783

BURACK, MICHAEL LEONARD, lawyer; b. Willimantic, Conn., Oct. 10, 1942; s. Meyer and Rose Ann (Kravitz) B.; m. Maria Gallego, Oct. 20, 1978; children: Victoria Luisa, Cristina Maria. BA summa cum laude, Wesleyan U., Middletown, Conn., 1964; postgrad. in physics, Calif. Inst. Tech., 1965; MS in Applied Physics, Stanford U., 1967, JD, 1970. Bar: Calif. 1971, D.C. 1972. Law clk. to judge U.S. Ct. Appeals for 9th Cir., San Francisco, 1970-71; assoc. Wilmer, Cutler & Pickering, Washington, 1971-77, ptnr., 1978-2000, of counsel, 2001—. Mem. staff D.C. Jud. conf. Com. on Adminstrn. of Justice under Emergency Condition, 1972-73; mem. adv. com. govt. applications of ADR of Ctr. for Pub. Resources, 1988; mem. jud. evaluation com. D.C. Bar, 1991-94. Assoc. editor Jour. Pub. Contract Law, 1988-94. Mem. ABA, Order of the Coif, Phi Beta Kappa, Sigma Xi. Office: Wilmer Cutler & Pickering 2445 M St NW Washington DC 20037-1487 E-mail: mburack@wilmer.com

BURAK, H(OWARD) PAUL, lawyer; b. N.Y.C., July 9, 1934; s. Harry and Bette (Hauer) B.; m. Edna K. Goodman, Oct. 18, 1970; children: Hally Ann., Jason Lewis. BS, Cornell U., 1954; LLB, Columbia U., 1957. Bar: N.Y. 1958, D.C. 1967, U.S. Dist. Ct. (so. and ea. dists.) N.Y. 1967, U.S. Ct. Appeals (2d cir.) 1960, U.S. Supreme Ct. 1964. Assoc. Cadwalader, Wickersham & Taft, N.Y.C., 1957-63; dep. asst., asst. gen. counsel Agy. for Internat. Devel. U.S. State Dept., Washington, 1963-67; assoc. Rosenman Colin Kay Petschek & Freund, N.Y.C., 1967-69; ptnr. Rosenman & Colin, 1969—. Bd. dirs. Sony Corp. Am., N.Y.C., Sony Music Entertainment, Inc., N.Y.C., Sony Pictures Entertainment, Inc., Culver City, Calif., Sony USA Found., N.Y.C. Rev. editor Columbia Law Rev., 1956-57; author pamphlets. Mem. adv. bd. N.Y.C. Ballet. Mem. ABA, Assn. of Bar of City of N.Y., Fed. Bar Coun., N.Y. Bar Assn., Internat. Bar Assn., Univ. Club. General corporate, Private international, Mergers and acquisitions. Office: Rosenman & Colin 575 Madison Ave New York NY 10022-2585 E-mail: hpburak@rosenman.com

BURBANK, STEPHEN BRADNER, law educator; b. N.Y.C., Jan. 8, 1947; s. John Howard and Jean (Gedney) B.; m. Ellen Randolph Coolidge, June 13, 1970; 1 child, Peter Jefferson. AB, Harvard U., 1968, JD, 1973. Bar: Mass. 1973, Pa. 1976, U.S. Supreme Ct. 1977. Law clk. Supreme Jud. Ct. of Mass., Boston, 1973-74, Chief Justice Warren Burger, Washington, 1974-75; gen. counsel U. Pa., Phila., 1975-80, asst. prof. law, 1979-83, assoc. prof. law, 1983-86, prof. law, 1986—, Fuller prof. law, 1991-95; Berger prof. law, 1995—. Reporter 3rd Cir. Jud. Discipline Rules, Phila., 1981-82, 84, 3rd Cir. Task Force on Rule 11, Phila., 1987-89; mem. Nat. Commn. on Jud. Discipline and Removal, 1991-93; mediator, arbitrator Ctr. for Pub. Resources, New York, 1986—; cons. Dechert, Price & Rhoads, Phila., 1986—; mem. CPR Arbitration Commn., 1997-2000. Mem. Com. to Visit Harvard and Radcliffe Coll., Cambridge, Mass., 1979-85; mem. adv. bd. Inst. Contemporary Art, Phila., 1982-99; charter trustee Phillips Acad., Andover, Mass., 1980-97. Mem. Am. Law Inst. (adviser transnational rules of civil procedure 1997—, advisor internat. jurisdiction and judgments 1999—), Am. Arbitration Assn. (mem. panel of arbitrators 1985—), Century Assn., Am. Jud. Soc. (mem. exec. com., v.p. 1997-99), Phi Beta Kappa. Avocations: swimming, travel, tennis. Office: U Pa Sch Law 3400 Chestnut St Philadelphia PA 19104-6204 E-mail: sburbank@law.upenn.edu

BURCAT, JOEL ROBIN, lawyer; b. Phila., Oct. 28, 1954; s. David Sidney and Jessie (Goldberg) B.; m. Gail Rene Hartman, May 30, 1982; children: Dina Michelle, Shira Elizabeth. Student, Temple U., 1972-73; BS, Pa. State U., 1976; JD, Vt. Law Sch., 1980. Bar: Pa. 1980, U.S. Dist. Ct. (mid. dist.) Pa. 1980, U.S. Dist. Ct. (we. dist.) Pa. 1988, U.S. Dist. Ct. (ea. dist.) Pa. 1993, U.S. Ct. Appeals (3d cir.) 1981, U.S. Ct. Appeals (fed. cir.) 2001, U.S. Supreme Ct. 1984, U.S. Ct. Fed. Claims 2001. Asst. atty. gen. Pa. Dept. Environ. Resources, Harrisburg, 1980-83; assoc. Rhoads &

Sinon, 1983-88, Kirkpatrick & Lockhart, Harrisburg, 1988-91, ptnr., 1992—. Spl. counsel Pa. Senate Com. on Environ. Resources and Energy, Harrisburg, 1986-87; gen. counsel Nat. Wilderness Inst., Washington, 1991-93; mem. rules com. Pa. Environ. Hearing Bd., 1984-88. ; author, editor: Pennsylvania Environmental Law and Practice, 1994, Pennsylvania Environmental Law and Practice, 3d edit., 2001. Trustee United Jewish Cmty., Harrisburg, 1991-94, v.p., 1996-97; v.p. Yeshiva Acad. Harrisburg, 1986-96, pres., 1996-97; dir. Friends of State of Pa. Mus., 1999—. Recipient Best Publ. award Assn. Continuing Legal Edn., 1999. Mem. ABA (standing com. environ. law 1979-80, law student liaison), Pa. Bar Assn. (sec. environ. mineral and natural resource law sect. 1990-91, vice-chmn. 1991-92, chmn. 1992-93, ethics com. 1984-97, chmn. pro bono com. 1999—, Spl. Achievement award 1993, cert. of recognition 1994). Republican. Jewish. Avocations: guitar playing, classical music, jogging, hiking, gardening. Administrative and regulatory, General civil litigation, Environmental, Natural Resources. Office: Kirkpatrick & Lockhart 240 N 3d St Harrisburg PA 17101-1503 E-mail: jburcat@kl.com

BURCH, FRANCIS BOUCHER, JR. lawyer; b. Balt., Feb. 27, 1948; s. Francis Boucher and Mary Patricia (Howe) B.; m. Mary Ann Podesta, June 24, 1972; children: Sara E., Francis B. III, Michael F. Student, U. Fribourg, Switzerland, 1968-69; BA, Georgetown U., 1970; JD with honors, U. Md., 1974. Bar: Md. 1974, U.S. Ct. Appeals (4th cir.) 1975, U.S. Supreme Ct. 1994. Assoc. litigation dept. Piper & Marbury LLP, Balt., 1974-81, ptnr. litigation dept., 1981—, chmn. litigation dept., 1991-94, chmn., 1994-99; co-chmn. Piper, Marbury Rudnick & Wolfe LLP, 1999—. Contbr. articles to profl. jours. Bd. dirs. Greater Balt. Com., 1996—, vice-chmn., 1998—, mem. Leadership Program, 1990—, bd. dirs., 1993-98, vice-chmn., 1994-96, chmn., 1996-98, chmn. selection com., 1994-95; trustee Calvert Sch., 1989-2000, exec. com., 1991-2000, chmn., 1991-95, sec., 1991-95; trustee Western Md. Coll., 1996-2001, Johns Hopkins Health Sys. Corp., 1994-96, Johns Hopkins Hosp., 1994-96, Johns Hopkins Medicine, 1996—, Balt. Mus. Art., 1990-96, 98-2000, mem. exec. com., 1991-96, chmn. ann. giving com., 1991-93, treas., 1992-94, v.p., 1994-96, co-chmn. devel., 1994-96; bd. visitors U. Md. Sch. Law, Balt., 1993—, U. Md., 1995—; campaign cabinet, chmn. emerging markets United Way Ctrl. Md., 1994; chmn. Leadership Giving, 1999. With U.S. Army N.G., 1970-76. Fellow Am. Bar Found., Am. Coll. Trial Lawyers, Md. Bar Found.; mem. ABA, Am. Law Inst., Md. Bar Assn. (Disting. Svc. award litigation sect. 1981), Balt. City Bar Assn. (chmn. jud. appts. com. 1990-91, exec. coun. 1990-91), 4th Cir. Jud. Conf., Rule Day Club, Lawyers' Round Table Balt., Center Club, Md. Club, Balt. Country Club. Democrat. Roman Catholic. Avocations: skiing, surfing. General civil litigation, Product liability, Securities. Office: Piper Marbury Rudnick & Wolfe LLP 6225 Smith Ave Baltimore MD 21209-3600

BURCH, JOHN THOMAS, JR. lawyer; b. Balt., Feb. 22, 1942; s. John T. and Katheryn Estella (Peregoy) B.; m. Linda Anne Shearer, Nov. 1, 1969; children: John Thomas, Richard James. BA, U. Richmond, 1964, JD, 1966; LLM, George Washington U., 1971. Bar: Va. 1966, U.S. Supreme Ct. 1969, D.C. 1974, Mich. 1983, Md. 1993. Pvt. practice, Richmond, 1966, Washington, 1974-77; pres. Burch, Kerns and Klimek, 1977-82, Burch & Assocs., Washington, 1982-95, Burch & Bennett, P.C., Washington, 1983-85; ptnr. Alagia, Day, Marshall, Mintmire & Chauvin, 1985-90, Maloney & Burch, Washington, 1990-96; pres. Burch & Cronauer, P.C., 1995—, Burch & Assocs., Washington, 1982-95. Rep. committeeman, City of Alexandria, Va., 1975-92; aide-de-camp Brigadier Gen. to gov., State of Va., 1976—; alt. del. Rep. Nat. Conv., 1988, 94. Decorated Bronze Star, Meritorious Svc. medal, others; named Ky. Col. Mem. ABA (sec. pub. contract law sect. 1976-77), Fed. Bar Assn. (nat. coun., dep. sec. 1982-83), Am. Legion, VFW (dep. comdr. 1986-87), Spl. Forces Assn., Nat. Vietnam and Gulf War Vets. Coalition (nat. chmn. 1983—), Va. War Meml. Found. (trustee), Va. Soc. SAR (pres. 1975-76, Patriots medal 1978, Good Citizenship award 1970), Sons of Confederate Vets., Soc. of the War of 1812; Cheveliar, Order of St. Constantine Magna, Scabbard and Blade, Phi Alpha Delta, Phi Sigma Alpha. Republican. Episcopalian. State civil litigation, General practice, Government contracts and claims. Home: 1015 N Pelham St Alexandria VA 22304-1905 Office: Burch & Cronauer PC 910 17th St NW Ste 800 Washington DC 20006

BURCH, MARY SEELYE QUINN, law librarian, consultant; b. Worcester, Mass., Oct. 16, 1925; d. James Henry and Mary Seelye (O'Donnell) Quinn; m. Walter Douglas Burch, Aug. 18, 1972; children: Cathi, Andrew, David, John, Joan. BS, Suny, 1976; MLS, Pratt Inst., 1979. Law libr. N.Y. Supreme Ct., Troy, 1969-82; chief law libr. Office Ct. Adminstrn., Albany, N.Y., 1982-86; libr. N.Y. State Libr., 1986-89, ret., 1989; owner Mary S. Burch Law Libr. Svc., 1983—. Instr. legal rsch. SUNY, 1981; selected to meet with deans of law schs. in China for improvement of legal reference materials in China. Mem. N.Y. State Bar Assn. (lectr. 1980), Ulster County Bar Assn. (cons. 1980), Am. Assn. Law Librs., Assn. Law Librs. Upstate N.Y. (pres. 1971, v.p. 1981). Roman Catholic. Avocations: pilot, swimming, sewing. Home: 946 Hoosick Rd Troy NY 12180-6635 E-mail: msblaw2001@yahoo.com

BURCHFIELD, BOBBY ROY, lawyer; b. Middlesboro, Ky., Oct. 23, 1954; s. Roy and Anna Lee (McCreary) B.; m. Teresa J. Miller, Apr. 6, 1996; 1 child, Taylor Nicole. BA, Wake Forest U., 1976; JD, George Washington U., 1979. Bar: D.C. 1980, U.S. Ct. Appeals (3rd cir.) 1981, U.S. Dist. Ct. D.C. 1982, U.S. Dist. Ct. Md. 1982, U.S. Ct. Appeals (D.C. cir.) 1982, U.S. Ct. Appeals (9th cir.) 1985, U.S. Supreme Ct. 1986, U.S. Ct. Appeals (5th cir.) 1989, U.S. Ct. Appeals (6th cir.) 1993. Law clk. to Judge Ruggero J. Aldisert U.S. Ct. Appeals (3rd cir.), Pitts., 1979-81; assoc. Covington & Burling, Washington, 1981-87, ptnr., 1987—. Gen. counsel Bush-Quayle '92, 1992. Editor-in-chief George Washington U. Law Rev., 1978-79. Gen. counsel Rep. Nat. Lawyers Assn., 1991—92; nat. chmn. George Washington U. Nat. Law Ctr. Ann. Fund, 1990—91, Wake Forest U. Coll. Fund, 1999—2000; mem. Wake Forest U. Alumni Coun., 1990—91, 1997—2001; vol. George Bush for Pres., Washington, 1986—88. Named one of Best Lawyers in Am., 2001. Mem. ABA. Republican. Antitrust, Constitutional, Federal civil litigation. Office: Covington & Burling 1201 Pennsylvania Ave NW PO Box 7566 Washington DC 20044-7566 E-mail: BBurchfield@cov.com

BURD, MICHAEL, lawyer; b. N.Y.C., Feb. 7, 1958; arrived in Eng., 1978; s. Donald and Shane (Gale) B.; m. Jacqueline Margaret Thomas; children: Hannah Rebecca, Molly Rose, Sarah May. BA, Columbia U., 1980; MPhil, Cambridge (Eng.) U., 1982; law finals, Coll. Law, London, 1984. Solicitor Lewis Silkin, London, 1984-88, ptnr., 1988—. Editor: Employment Law Section-Practical Tax Planning and Precedents; adv. editor Managing Termination of Employment, 1996; contbr.: Employment Law Cases: Practical Implications for HR Managers. Kellett fellow Columbia U., Clare Coll., Cambridge, 1980-82. Mem. London Solicitors Litigation Assn. (com. mem. 1994—), City Westminster Law Soc. (pres. 1995-96). Labor. Office: Lewis Silkin 12 Gough Sq London EC4A 3DW England Office Fax: 44 0 20 7832 1722. E-mail: michael.burd@lewissilkin.com

BURDELIK, THOMAS L. lawyer; b. Chgo., June 4, 1959; s. Thomas L. and Roberta P. (Raber) B.; m. Mary Kathleen Igyarto; children: Clayton Thomas, Dylan Patrick. BA, North Cen. Coll., 1981; JD, John Marshall Sch. Law, 1984. Bar: Ill. 1984. Assoc. Parillo, Weiss & Moss, Chgo., 1984-87; sr. assoc. McSherry & Gray, 1987, Parillo, Weiss & Moss, Chgo., 1987-89; prin. Thomas L. Burdelik & Assocs., 1989—. Past guest lectr. on legal argument U. Ill. at Chgo. and St. Xavier Coll., Chgo.; co-mgr. Sheffield Garden Walk, 1997; instr. in fed. trial bar tng. Chgo. Bar Assn.; mock trial judge Northwestern U. Law Sch., 2001. Featured spkr. Chgo. Bar Assn. Seminars on Trial Practice, Cross Exam., Uninsured/Underinsured Motorist Claims, Role of Accident Reconstructionists and Jury Consultants in Trials in Cook County, spkr. sem. spon. by IL Trial Lawyers Assoc on Damages. Mem. Nat. Handgun Control, 1990-95, Nat. Abortion Rights Action League, 1990-95, Internat. CARE, 1991-95; vol. Northwestern Hosp., Chgo., 1991-95; mem. Ranch Triangle Comm. Orgn.; vol. fundraiser Off the Street Club of Chgo., 1991—. Mem. Chgo. Bar Assn. (instr. Fed. Trial Bar Tng. Course), Amnesty Internat., Randolph Athletic Club. Democrat. Roman Catholic. State civil litigation, Insurance, Personal injury. Office: 123 W Madison St Ste 19 Chicago IL 60602-4511

BURDEN, JAMES EWERS, lawyer; b. Sacramento, Oct. 24, 1939; s. Herbert Spencer and Ida Elizabeth (Brosemer) B.; m. Kathryn Lee Gardner, Aug. 21, 1965; children: Kara Elizabeth, Justin Gardner. BS, U. Calif., Berkeley, 1961; JD, U. Calif., Hastings, 1964; postgrad., U. So. Calif., 1964-65. Bar: Calif. 1965, Tax Ct. U.S. 1969, U.S. Supreme Ct. 1970. Assoc. Elliott and Aune, Santa Ana, Calif., 1965, White, Harbor, Fort & Schei, Sacramento, 1965-67, Miller, Starr & Regalia, Oakland, Calif., 1967-69, ptnr., 1969-73, Burden, Aiken, Mansuy & Stein, San Francisco, 1973-82, James E. Burden, Inc., San Francisco, 1982—. Of counsel, Aiken, Kramer & Cummings, Oakland and San Francisco; bd. dirs. IP Floor Products, Inc., San Leandro, Calif., Denver; founder, dir. Gloucestershire Innovation Centre, Gloucester, Eng., KineMed, Inc., San Francisco, Euro-Gen Pharmas. Ltd., Gloucester; underwriting mem. Lloyds of London, 1986-93; instr. U. Calif., Berkeley, Merritt Coll. 1968-74; prin. Dorset Capital LLC; founder, dir. Info4cars.com., Inc., Asheville, N.C., Landmk-t.com., Inc., San Francisco, Auto Ins. Advisor Agy., Inc. Contbr. articles to profl. jours. Mem. ABA, Claremont Country Club, Commonwealth of Calif., Inst. Dirs. (London), The Univ. Club. General corporate, Finance, Real property. Office: One Maritime Plz 4th Fl San Francisco CA 94111-3407 E-mail: jeburden@compuserve.com

BURG, BRENT LAWRENCE, lawyer; b. Houston, Mar. 2, 1940; s. Abner Danford and Bess (Levin) B.; m. Patricia S. Petitt, 1980; 1 child, Brook Lawrence. BA, U. Tex., 1962; JD, 1966. Bar: Tex. 1966, U.S. Dist. Ct. (so. dist.) Tex. 1966, U.S. Ct. Appeals (5th cir.) 1966, U.S. Supreme Ct. 1970, U.S. Ct. Appeals (4th cir.) 1976, U.S. Dist. Ct. Md. 1976, U.S. Ct. Appeals (11th cir.) 1981. Dist. judge 309th Dist. Ct., Harris County, Tex., 1981-82; assoc. mcpl. judge City of Piney Point Village, 1990-98, City of Bunker Hill Village, 1991-98; ptnr. Rentz, Burg and Assocs., Houston, 1983-95; pvt. practice Brent Burg, 1995-98; assoc. judge 312th Dist. Ct., 1999—; of counsel Fouts & Moore, L.L.P., 1996-98. Chairperson Houston Vol. Lawyers Program, Inc., 1988-89, 89-90. Fellow Tex. Bar Found.; mem. Houston Bar Found., State Bar Tex. (grievance com.), Houston Bar Assn. (family law sect. treas. 1978-79, chairperson elect 1980-81, dir. 1982-83, chairperson 1984-85; mem. Supreme Ct. of Tex. child support and visitation guidelines adv. com. 1986-87, 96-97), Phi Alpha Delta. Family and matrimonial. Office: 312th District Ct 1115 Congress St Houston TX 77002-1927

BURGDOERFER, JERRY, lawyer; b. Jeffersonville, Ind., May 3, 1958; s. Jerry Jack and Barbara Jean (Hofherr) B. BS, Ind. U., 1980, MBA, JD cum laude, Ind. U., 1983. Bar: Ill. 1984, U.S. Dist. Ct. (no. dist.) Ill. 1984, U.S. Tax Ct. 1984. Assoc. Adams, Fox, Adelstein, Rosen & Bell, Chgo., 1983-88, ptnr., 1988-89; assoc. Jenner & Block, 1989-90, ptnr., 1991—, co-chair corp., tax and bus. transactions, 1999—, co-chair securities practice group, 2000—; with Mori Sogo Law Offices, Tokyo, 1991-93. Author: Director and Officers Liability: Prevention, Insurance and Indemnification, 2000; contbr. articles to profl. jours. Vol. United Cerebral Palsy Assn., 1995—, dir., 1999—; mem. planning com. Northwestern U. Sch. Law Annual Garrett Corp. and Securities Law Inst. Named 2d Benton Nat. Moot Ct. Competition, 1982. Mem. ABA (fed. regulation of securities subcoms. on proxy statements and bus. combinations and disclosure and continuous reporting 2000—), Internat. Bar Assn., Inter Pacific Bar Assn., Ill. Bar Assn., Chgo. Bar Assn. (chairperson '34 Act Com. 1996-98, reporter, Securities Com. 1997-98, vice chair 1998-99, chair 1999-2000), Japan Am. Soc. Chgo., Ind. U. Alumni Club Chgo. (vol. 1988-89) , Econ. Club Chgo., Execs. Club Chgo., Chgo. Coun. on Fgn. Rels., Japan-Am. Soc. of Chgo., Phi Eta Sigma, Phi Delta Phi, Phi Delta Theta (sec. chpt. 1977-78, co-founder, steering com. Chgo. alumni club 1988-89). Avocations: bicycling, water skiing, Japanese language. General corporate, Private international, Securities. Office: Jenner & Block 1 E Ibm Plz Fl 4000 Chicago IL 60611-7603

BURGE, DAVID ALAN, patent lawyer, writer; b. Anderson, Ind., July 22, 1943; s. James Swisher and Esther M. (Sheppard) B.; m. Carolyn J. Alter, Nov. 24, 1966; children: Benjamin, Thomas. Bs in Gen. Engring. with highest honors, U. Ill., 1966; JD, U. Louisville, 1970. Registered patent atty. Pres. David A. Burge Co LPA, Cleve., 1975—. Author: Patent & Trademark Tactics and Practice, 1980, 3rd edition, 1999; contbr. chpts. in books. Pres. Gen. Engring. Constituent Alumni Assn., 1984, 85. Mem. ABA, Am. Intellectual Property Law Assn., Cleve. Bar Assn., Cleve. Patent Law Assn., Associated Locksmiths of Am., Burgess of Colonial Williamsburg, Phi Kappa Phi, Sigma Tau, Phi Eta Sigma, Gamma Epsilon, Sigma Delta Kappa. Avocations: antique tools, woodworking. Intellectual property, Patent, Trademark and copyright. Office: David A Burge Co LPA 2901 S Park Blvd Cleveland OH 44120-1842

BURGER, JOAN M. judge; b. Chgo., Mar. 15, 1944; d. Willaim James Herrmann and Cecile Dolores Malooly; m. Gary K. Burger, Mar. 19,1 966; children: Gary K. Jr., Christine M. Mattson, Eric W. BS, Loyola U., 1966; JD cum laude, St. Louis U., 1976. Legal officer Juvenile Ct., St. Louis, 1976-78; asst. circuit atty. 22nd Jud. Cir., 1978-80; cir. judge, 1995—; assoc. Law Offices Terry Flanagan, St. Louis, 1980-87; sole practice, 1987-95. Bd. dirs. Monsanto YMCA, St. Louis, 1983-94; mem. Leadership St. Louis, 1990-91; mem. venture grant United Way, St. Louis, 1991-95; mem. Aid to Victims of Crimes, St. Louis, 1992-94. Mem. Women Lawyers Assn. (pres. 1982-83, Pres.'s award 1988, chairperson women in profession com. 1983-85, sec. solo and small firm sect. 1993). Home: 3512 Crittenden St Saint Louis MO 63118-1108 Office: 22nd Jud Cir 10 N Tucker Blvd Saint Louis MO 63101-2044

BURGER, ROBERT THEODORE, lawyer, partner; b. Coral Gables, Fla., Oct. 20, 1949; s. Eugene Clifford Burger and Dorothy Irene Harrison; m. Janice Marie Colbert, Dec. 14, 1974; children: Melissa Anne, Amy Michelle, Kristin Reneé. BA, U. Fla., 1971, JD, 1974. Bar: Fla. 1974, U.S. Ct. Appeals (11th cir.) 1981, U.S. Dist. Ct. (mid. dist.) Fla. 1977; cert. civil trial lawyer, Fla. Assoc. Collins & Clark, Indian Harbour Beach, Fla., 1974-76; ptnr. Clark & Burger, 1976-86, Burger & Ville, Indian Harbour Beach, 1986-96, Burger & Paulk, Indian Harbour Beach, 1996—. Founding mem. Am. Inns of Ct., Brevard County Chpt., 1993-96. Pres., dir. Hacienda Girls Ranch, Melbourne, Fla., 1980-95, founder and pres. Community Christian Sch., Melbourne, 1984-88; mem. Brevard County Rep. Party Exec. Com., Melbourne, 1990-91; chmn., dir. Brevard County Jail Chaplain Ministry, Sharpes, Fla., 1994—. Mem. Assn. Trial Lawyers Am., Fla. Acad. Trial Lawyers, Christian Bus. Men's Com. (chmn. 1988-89). Presbyterian. Avocations: boating, horseback riding, fishing, tennis. Personal injury. Office: Burger & Paulk 1901 Hwy A1A Ste 6 Satellite Beach FL 32937-3526

BURGESS, DAVID, lawyer; b. Detroit, Nov. 30, 1948; s. Roger Edward and Claire Theresa (Sullivan) B.; m. Rebecca Culbertson Stuart, 1985 (dec. Dec. 1988); m. Catherine Mounteer, 1993; children: Jalil Riahi, Leila Riahi, Bryan Valentine, Grace Catherine. BS in Fgn. Svc., Georgetown U., 1970, MS in Fgn. Svc., JD, Georgetown U., 1978. Bar: D.C. 1978, U.S. Dist. Ct. D.C. 1979, U.S. Ct. Appeals (D.C. cir.) 1979, U.S. Ct. Appeals (fed. cir.) 1988, U.S. Ct. Internat. Trade 1988. Rsch. asst. Georgetown U. Sch. Bus. Adminstrn., Washington, 1975, asst. to dean, 1975-76; rsch. assoc., prof. Acad. in the Pub. Svc., 1976-79; asst. editor Securities Regulation Law Report; legal editor Internat. Trade Reporter Bur. Nat. Affairs, 1978-79; atty. Cadwalader, Wickersham & Taft, 1979-81; mng. editor Bur. Nat. Affairs, 1981-82; dir. U.S. Peace Corps, Niamey, Niger, 1982-84, Rabat, Morocco, 1984-85; dir. policy planning, mgmt. Peace Corps, Washington, 1985-87; dir. Bur. Human Rights and Humanitarian Affairs U.S. Dept. State, 1987-92; regional dir. Lawyers for Bush-Quayle Re-Election Campaign, 1992; chief party Rwanda Dem. and Governance Project, 1994, Russia NGO Sector Project, Moscow, 1994. Dir. democracy and civil soc. program, sr. advisor World Learning, Washington, 1995 (dir. U.S. Democracy Fellows program, Washington, 1995—); spkr. workshops Minority Legis. Edn. Program, Ind. Assn. Cities and Towns, Georgetown U. Continuing Edn. Program, Comms. Workers Am., Colo. State U., U. Wis. Alumni rep. Internat. Sch. Bangkok, 1972-74. Author: Financing Local Government, 1977, 2d edit., 1978, Preparation of the Local Budget, 2 vols., 1976, 2d edit., 1978, Local Government Accounting Fundamentals, 2d edit., 1977, Understanding Federal Assistance Programs, 2d edit., 1978, The POW/MIA Issue: Perspectives on the National League of Families, 1978; contbr. articles to publs. Adv. com. Arlington County Fiscal Affairs, 1993-94; mem. pres. coun. Mary Washington Coll.; mem. Rep. Nat. Com.; vol. G.W. Bush Campaign, 1999-2000. Mem. D.C. Bar Assn., Washington Fgn. Law Soc., Hoyas Unltd. (pres. 1992-94), Federalist Soc., Georgetown U. Alumni Assn. (bd. govs. 1975-00, class rep. 1971-91, mem. alumni senate 2000—), Rep. Nat. Lawyers Assn., Pachyderm Club No. Va. (pres. 1992-93), Pres.'s Club, RNC Eagle Club. Republican. Roman Catholic. Home: 3115 1st Pl N Arlington VA 22201-1037 Office: 1015 15th St NW Ste 750 Washington DC 20005-2605

BURGESS, HAYDEN FERN (POKA LAENUI), lawyer; b. Honolulu, May 5, 1946; s. Ned E. and Nora (Lee) B.; m. Puanani Sonoda, Aug. 28, 1968. B in Polit. Sci., U. Hawaii, JD, 1976. Bar: Hawaii 1976, U.S. Tax Ct., U.S. Ct. Appeals (9th cir.). Pvt. practice, Waianae, Hawaii, 1976—; pres. Hawaii Coun. for 1993 and Beyond, Honolulu, 1991—; exec. dir. Waianae Coast Cmty. Mental Health Ctr., 1997—. V.p. World Coun. Indigenous Peoples before UN, 1984-90; human rights adv., writer, speaker in field; pres. Pacific and Asia Coun. Indigenous Peoples; cons. on indigenous affairs, 1984; indigenous expert to ILO Conv.; expert UN seminar on effects of racism and racial discriminations on social and econ. rels. between indigenous peoples and states, 1989—; del. Native Hawaiian Convention. Trustee Office Hawaiian Affairs, Honolulu, 1982-86; mem. Swedish Nat. Commn. on Mus., 1986; leader Hawaiian Independence Movement; mem. Hawaiian Sovereignty Elections Coun. Mem. Law Assn. Asia and Western Pacific (steering com. on human rights 1988), Union of 3d World Journalists. General practice, Health, Public international. E-mail: plaenvi@pixi.com

BURGESS, ROBERT KYLE, lawyer; b. Fairfield, Iowa, Sept. 5, 1948; s. Charles and Eleanor Pearl (Morris) B.; children: Alyssa, Kristen, Ryan; m. Michelle Wenz. BS, Northwestern U., 1970, JD, 1973. Bar: Calif. 1973, U.S. Dist. Ct. (cen. dist.) Calif. 1974, U.S. Tax Ct. 1975, U.S. Ct. Appeals (9th cir.) 1976, U.S. Ct. Appeals (5th cir.) 1977, U.S. Supreme Ct. 1977, D.C. 1980, U.S. Dist. Ct. Md. 1980, U.S. Ct. Appeals (D.C. cir.) 1981, Ill. 1982. Assoc. Latham & Watkins, Los Angeles, 1973-78, Washington, 1978-81, ptnr., 1981-82, Chgo., 1982-95; sr. v.p., gen. counsel, sec. Am. Re Corp., Princeton, N.J., 1995-97, exec. v.p., gen. counsel, sec., 1997—. Mem. Calif. Bar Assn., Ill. Bar Assn., D.C. Bar Assn. General corporate, Mergers and acquisitions, Securities. Office: Am Re Corp 555 College Rd E Princeton NJ 08540-6616

BURGESS, TIMOTHY M. prosecutor; BA, MBA, U. of Alaska; JD, Northeastern U. Assoc. Gilmore and Franklin, Anchorage, 1987—89; Asst. U.S. Atty. Dist. of Alaska, 1989—2001, U.S. Atty., 2001—. Office: Fed Bldg & US Courthouse 222 W 7th Ave #9 Rm 253 Anchorage AK 99513-7567 Office Fax: 907-271-3224*

BURGIN, CHARLES EDWARD, lawyer; b. Marion, N.C., Dec. 16, 1938; m. Ellen Salsbury Burgin; children: Ellen, Lucy. BA, U. N.C., 1961; LLB, Duke U., 1964. Bar: N.C.; U.S. Supreme Ct. Law clk. to Hon. J. Braxton Craven Jr. U.S. Dist. Ct., U.S. Ct. Appeals, 1964-66; prosecuting atty. McDowell County Criminal Ct., 1966-68; sr. ptnr. Dameron, Burgin & Parker, P.A., Marion, N.C., 1968—. Bd. dirs. Shadowline, Inc.; lectr. in field. Contbr. articles to profl. jours. Bd. dirs. McDowell County Recreation Commn. 1977-87, First Union Nat. Bank 1975—; McDowell County Mountain Rescue Team 1980—; McDowell Arts and Crafts Assn. 1980—. Fellow Am. Coll. Trial Lawyers (state chmn. 1996-98, named Best Lawyers in Am. 1993—), Internat. Soc. Barristers, Am. Bar Found.; mem. ABA, N.C. Bar Assn. (pres. 1993-94), Defense Rsch. Inst., Am. Soc. Hosp. Attys., N.C. Assn. Defense Lawyers, U.S. Supreme Ct. Bar Assn. Insurance, Libel, Personal injury. Office: Dameron Burgin & Parker PA PO Drawer 1049 26 W Court St Marion NC 28752-3906 E-mail: cburgin@dameronburginlaw.com

BURGMAN, DIERDRE ANN, lawyer; b. Logansport, Ind., Mar. 25, 1948; d. Ferdinand William Jr. and Doreen Yvonne (Walsh) B. BA, Valparaiso U., 1970, JD, 1979; LLM, Yale U., 1985. Bar: Ind. 1979, U.S. Dist. Ct. (so. dist.) Ind. 1979, N.Y. 1982, U.S. Dist. Ct. (so. dist.) N.Y. 1982, U.S. Ct. Appeals (7th cir.) 1982, U.S. Ct. Appeals (D.C. and 2d cirs.) 1984, U.S. Supreme Ct. 1985, D.C. 1988, U.S. Dist. Ct. (ea. dist.) N.Y. 1992. Law clk. to chief judge Ind. Ct. Appeals, Indpls., 1979-80; prof. law Valparaiso (Ind.) U., 1980-81; assoc. Dewey, Ballantine, Bushby, Palmer & Wood, N.Y.C., 1981-84, Cahill Gordon & Reindel, N.Y.C., 1985-92; v.p., gen. counsel N.Y. State Urban Devel. Corp., 1992-95; dep. insp. gen. State N.Y., 1992-95; of counsel Vandenberg & Felin, N.Y.C., 1995-99; counsel Salans, Hertzfeld, Heilbronn, Christy & Viener, 1999—. Note editor Valparaiso U. law rev., 1978-79; contbr. articles to law jours. Mem. bd. visitors Valparaiso U. Sch. Law, 1986—, chmn., 1989-92. Ind. Bar Found. scholar, 1978. Mem. ABA (trial evidence com. 1983-86, profl. liability com. 1986-89, ins. coverage litigation com. 1990-92), Assn. Bar City N.Y. (com. profl. responsibility 1988-91, com. profl. and jud. ethics 1991-95, mem. coun. jud. adminstrn. 1997-99), New York County Lawyers Assn. (com. Supreme Ct. 1987-94, chmn. 1990-93, bd. dirs. 1991-97, exec. com. bd. dirs. 1992-95, fin. and pers. com. 1994-95), N.Y. State Bar Assn. (mem. Ho. Dels. 1994-98). Home: 345 E 56th St Apt 5C New York NY 10022-3744

BURGOON, BRIAN DAVID, lawyer; b. Lima, Ohio, Feb. 29, 1972; s. Richard Joseph Burgoon and Janet Constance Barrett. BA with honors, U. Fla., 1994, JD with high honors, 1997. Bar: Fla. 1997, Ga. 1998. Assoc. Sutherland Asbill & Brennan, Atlanta, 1997—. Mem. alumni coun. U. Fla. Coll. Law, Gainesville, 1997—; mem. Fla. Bar Bd. Govs., 2000—. Mem. ABA, Atlanta Bar Assn., Order of Coif, Atlanta Gator Club, Phi Beta Kappa. General civil litigation, Mergers and acquisitions, Securities. Home: 4282 Roswell Rd # A-4 Atlanta GA 30342 Office: Sutherland Asbill & Brennan LLP 999 Peachtree St NE Atlanta GA 30309

BURGWEGER, FRANCIS JOSEPH DEWES, JR. lawyer; b. Evanston, Ill., July 5, 1942; s. Francis Dewes and Helen Theodosia (Chancellor) B.; m. Kathleen Marie Wessel, Sept. 3, 1978; children: Lauren Elizabeth, Francis Joseph Dewes III, Sherman Ward Chancellor. BA, Yale U., 1964; JD, U. Pa., 1970. Bar: Calif. 1971, N.Y. 1988, U.S. Ct. Appeals (9th cir.) 1971, U.S. Dist. Ct. (cen. dist.) Calif. 1971. Law clk. to Hon. Shirley M. Hufstedler U.S. Ct. Appeals 9th Cir., L.A., 1970-71; assoc. O'Melveny & Myers, 1971-78, ptnr., 1978-85, O'Melveny & Myers LLP, N.Y.C.,

1985-97, sr. counsel, 1997—. Contbr. articles on environ. law. Capt. U.S. Army, 1964-67, Vietnam. Mem. Assn. of Bar of City of N.Y., N.Y. State Bar Assn., L.A. County Bar Assn. (exec. com. R.P. sect.). Avocations: books, wine, agriculture. Environmental, Finance, Real property. Office: O'Melveny & Myers LLP 153 E 53rd St Fl 54 New York NY 10022-4611

BURK, ROBERT S. lawyer; b. Mpls., Jan. 13, 1937; s. Harvey and Mayme (Cottle) B.; m. Eunice L. Silverman, Mar. 22, 1959; children: Bryan, Pam, Matt. BBA in Indsl. Rels., U. Minn., 1959; LLB, William Mitchell Coll. Law, 1965. Bar: Minn. 1966; qualified neutral under Rule 114 of the Minn. Gen. Rules of Practice, 1995—. Labor rels. cons. St. Paul Employers Assn., 1959-66; labor rels. mgr. Koch Refining Co., St. Paul, 1966-72, mgr. indsl. rels., 1972-75, mgr. indsl. rels., environ. affairs, 1975-77; sr. atty. Popham, Haik, Schnobrich & Kaufman, Ltd., Mpls., 1977-95, pres., CEO, 1986-90; ptnr. Burk & Seaton, P.A., Edina, Minn., 1995-2001, Burk & Landrum, P.A., Edina, 2001—. Chair bd. trustees William Mitchell Coll. Law, St. Paul, 1994-96, sec. 1991. Recipient Hon. Ronald E. Hachey Outstanding Alumnus award William Mitchell Coll. Law Alumni Assn., 1993. Mem. ABA (labor sect.), Minn. Bar Assn. (labor sect.). Administrative and regulatory, Labor. Office: Burk & Landrum PA 7400 Metro Blvd Ste 100 Edina MN 55439 Fax: 952-835-1867. E-mail: rburk@burklandrum.com

BURKE, DANIEL MARTIN, lawyer; b. Casper, Wyo., Sept. 9, 1946; s. Michael Joseph and Mary Josephine (Sirridge) B.; BA, U. Wyo., 1968, JD, 1970; m. Ellen Arden, July 3, 1970; children: Daniel Martin III, Kathleen Ellen, Brendan Arden, Anne Mary, Susan Theresa. Bar: Wyo. 1970. Law clk. to judge U.S. 10th Cir. Ct. Appeals (10th cir.), Cheyenne, Wyo., 1970; spl. asst. atty. gen. State of Wyo., Cheyenne, 1970-71; instr. Casper Coll., 1971-75; county and pros. atty. Natrona County, Casper, 1975-79; mem. Burke, Horn & Lewis, Casper, 1975-79; pres. Burke & Horn, P.C., Casper, 1979-82, Burke & Brown, P.C., Casper, 1983-86; pres. Daniel M. Burke, 1986— ; chmn. bd., pres. Rocky Mountain Communications Network, Inc., 1982-87; v.p., dir. Evco, Inc., 1982-86; dir. Guaranty Fed. Bank, First Nat. Bank Evanston (Wyo.), 1981-86, Wyo. Fin. Svcs., Inc., 1981-86; gen. ptnr. Bantry Bay Co., 1974-88; pres. The Chrysostom Corp.; sec. Shamrock Ranch Co., Casper, 1969—; asst. city atty. City of Casper, 1971-74. Mem. council St. Anthony Parish; mem. St. Anthony Parochial Sch. Bd.; bd. arbitrators Am. Arbitration Assn., Mem. ABA, Natrona County Bar Assn., Am. Judicature Soc., Nat. Assn. Dist. Attys. (dir. 1977-78), Wyo. Assn. County Attys. (pres. 1977-78), Casper C. of C., Casper Country Club, KC. Republican. Roman Catholic. Home: 1048 S Lincoln St Casper WY 82601-3331 Office: 231 E 10th St Casper WY 82601-3744

BURKE, HENRY PATRICK, lawyer; b. Scranton, Pa., May 12, 1942; s. Thomas and Dorothy Maria (McCloskey) B.; m. Alyce Louise McCrone, July 5, 1975; children: Henry Patrick, Daniel. BS, U. Scranton, 1964; JD, Villanova U., 1967. Bar: Pa. 1968; lic. real estate broker, Pa. Law clk. Ct. Common Pleas, Lackawanna County, Pa., 1968-69; lectr. bus. law U. Scranton, 1968-69; assoc. Haggerty & McDonnell, Scranton, 1969-75; assoc. counsel Scranton Redevel. Authority, 1969-70; spl. atty. gen. and legal opinion writer Pa. State Workers' Compensation Bd., 1972-97, legal opinion writer, 1972-97; sec., gen. counsel Opportunity Products Today, Inc., 1998; assoc. Burke and Douglass, Scranton, 1975-80; co-owner Directel Inc. Wireless, 1999-2000, Airport Taxi, Limousine and Courier Svc. Lehigh Valley, Inc., 1999-2000; pvt. practice law Scranton, 1969—. Author: The Burke-Duggan Family, From Opporession to Freedom, 1981. Mem. exec. com. Pa. unit Am. Heart Assn., 1973-74, asst. treas. Keystone chpt., 1972; del. Dem. Nat. Conv., 1972, chmn. econ. com. Dem. Nat. Platform Com., 1972; trustee Lackawanna Jr. Coll., 1977-79, solicitor, 1979-83; mem. alumni bd. govs. U. Scranton, 1969-75, pres. Nat. Alumni Soc., 1983-85; solicitor Cath. Social Svcs., 1978-95, bd. dirs., 1978-97; pres., owner Scranton-Wilkes Barre Twins, Inc., 1993-94; pres. Atlantic Collegiate Baseball League, 1995-97. Mem. ABA, Pa. Bar Assn., Lackawanna Bar Assn., Greater Scranton Bd. Realtors, Pa. Assn. Realtors, Nat. Assn. Realtors, Intertel, Internat. Soc. Philos. Enquiry, Mensa. Democrat. Roman Catholic. General civil litigation, Probate, Real property. Home: 319 Church St Dunmore PA 18512-1911 Office: Connell Bldg Ste 800 Scranton PA 18503

BURKE, JOHN MICHAEL, lawyer; b. Chgo., Oct. 9, 1941; s. John and Catherine Mary (Barrett) B.; m. Maureen Kay Fox, Oct. 5, 1968; children: Brian, Timothy, Michael. BBA, Loyola U., 1964, JD, 1965. Bar: Ill. 1965, U.S. Dist. Ct. (no. dist.) Ill. 1965, U.S. Ct. Appeals (7th cir.) 1968, U.S. Dist. Ct. (no.dist.) Ind. 1986. Assoc. Pretzel & Stouffer, Chgo., 1965-69, Shaheen, Lundberg & Callahan, Chgo., 1969-70; ptnr. Burke & Burke, Ltd., 1970—. Sgt. U.S. Army, 1965-68. Mem. ABA, Ill. Bar Assn. (chmn. tort council, service award 1984, mem. civil practice com. 1997—), Assn. Trial Lawyers Am., Ill. Trial Lawyers (bd. mgrs. 1988—), Appellate Lawyers Ill. Club: Westmoreland Country (Wilmette, Ill.). Federal civil litigation, State civil litigation, Personal injury. Home: 2241 Kenilworth Ave Wilmette IL 60091-1523 Office: Burke & Burke Ltd 20 S Clark St Ste 2200 Chicago IL 60603-1805 E-mail: jburke@burke-burke.com

BURKE, KATHLEEN MARY, lawyer; b. N.Y.C., Dec. 8, 1950; d. Hubert J. and Catherine (Painting) B. BA magna cum laude, Marymount Manhattan Coll., 1972; JD, U. Va., 1975. Bar: N.Y. 1976, Calif. 1979, U.S. Dist. Ct. (so. and ea. dists.) N.Y. 1977, U.S. Ct. Appeals (2d cir.) 1977, U.S. Ct. Appeals (9th cir.) 1980. Assoc. Donovan Leisure Newton & Irvine, N.Y.C., L.A., 1975-81, Kelley Drye & Warren, N.Y.C., 1981-84; assoc. counsel Soc. N.Y. Hosp., 1984-87, sec. and counsel, 1987—. Sec., coun. The N.Y. and Presbyn. Hosp. Healthcare Sys., 1991—; joint bd. N.Y. Hosp.-Cornell Med. Ctr.; sec. N.Y. Hosp-Cornell Med. Ctr. Fund, Inc., Soc. N.Y. Hosp. Fund, Inc., Royal Charter Properties, Inc., Royal Charter Properties-East, Inc., Royal Charter Properties-Westchester, Inc., Exec. Registry, Inc., N.Y. Hosp., Queens Med. Ctr., Presbyn. Hosp., N.Y.C., 1996—, N.Y. andPresbyn. Hosp. Health Care Sys., 1996—; faculty Concern for Dying, N.Y.C., 1985-90, NYU Sch. Continuing Edn., 1994-96; lectr. Cornell U. Med. Coll., 1994—. Contbr. articles to profl. jours. Trustee Marymount Manhattan Coll., N.Y.C., 1990—, N.Y. Meth. Hosp., 1995—, Wyckoff Heights Hosp., 1996—. Recipient McKay award, 1997. Mem. ABA, N.Y. State Bar Assn. (health law com. 1989-93), Am. Soc. Corp. Secs., Assn. of Bar of City of N.Y. (children and law com. 1986-89, law and medicine com. 1991-94), Am. Acad. Hosp. Attys. (speaker annual confs. 1987-92), Health Care Exec. Forum, Nat. Health Lawyers, Greater N.Y. Hosp. Assn. Legal Adv. Com. Roman Catholic. General civil litigation, Health. Office: Soc NY Hosp 525 E 68th St # 109 New York NY 10021-4870

BURKE, MICHAEL HENRY, lawyer; b. Washington, Oct. 28, 1952; s. John Joseph and Mary Catherine (Gaul) B.; m. Ann McFarland, Jan. 31, 1981; children: Allison M., Andrew M. BA magna cum laude, Tufts U., 1974; JD, Georgetown U., 1977. Bar: Mass. 1977, U.S. Dist. Ct. Mass. 1979. Assoc. Bulkley, Richardson and Gelinas L.L.P., Springfield, Mass., 1977-83, ptnr., 1983—. Pub. adminstr. Commonwealth of Mass., 1980-90. Mem. ABA, Mass. Bar Assn., Hampden County Bar Assn. Roman Catholic. Administrative and regulatory, Personal injury. Home: 50 Meadowbrook Rd Longmeadow MA 01106-1341 Office: Bulkley Richardson and Gelinas LLP 1500 Main St Springfield MA 01115-0001 E-mail: mburke@bulkley.com

BURKE, ROBERT BERTRAM, lawyer, political consultant, lobbyist; b. Cleve., July 9, 1942; s. Max and Eve (Miller) B.; m. Helen Choate Hall, May 5, 1979 (div. Oct. 1983). BA, UCLA, 1963, JD, 1966; LLM, London Sch. Econs., 1967. Bar: D.C. 1972, U.S. Supreme Ct. 1977, Calif. 1978. Exec. dir. Lawyer's Com. Civil Rights Under Law, Washington, 1968-69; ptnr. Fisk, Wolfe & Burke, Paris, 1969-71; assoc. O'Connor & Hannan, Washington, 1972-74; pvt. practice, 1974-79, L.A., 1978-93; lawyer, lobbyist, 1993—. Cons. Commonwealth Pa., Harrisburg, 1973. Chmn. So. Calif. Hollings for Pres., 1984; pres. Bldg. and Appeals Bd. City of L.A.; bd. dirs. Vols. of Am.; mem. exec. com. State Bar of Calif. pub. law sect. Mem. ABA UCLA Law Alumni Assn. (pres.). Jewish. Administrative and regulatory, Private international. Home: 277 S Irving Blvd Los Angeles CA 90004-3809 E-mail: bburke@rosekindel.com

BURKE, ROBERT THOMAS, lawyer; b. Phila., May 8, 1943. B.A., U. Santa Clara, 1965; M.A., UCLA, 1966, J.D., 1972. Bar: Calif. 1972. Ptnr. Pettit & Martin, San Francisco, 1972— . Chief article editor UCLA Law Rev., 1971-72. Lt. U.S. Army, 1967-69. Mem. ABA (mem. com. proprietary rights in software computer law divsn. 1982—), State Bar Calif., Bar Assn. San Francisco. General corporate, Trademark and copyright. Address: Pettit And Martin Ste 208 60 E Sir Francis Drake Blvd Larkspur CA 94939-1713

BURKE, THOMAS JOSEPH, JR. lawyer; b. Oct. 23, 1941; s. Thomas Joseph and Violet (Green) B.; m. Sharon Lynne Forke, Aug. 29, 1964; children: Lisa Lynne, Heather Ann. BA, Elmhurst Coll., 1963; JD, Chgo.-Kent Coll. Law, 1966. Bar: Ill. 1966, U.S. Dist. Ct. (no. dist.) Ill. 1967, U.S. Ct. Appeals (7th cir.) 1972, U.S. Supreme Ct. 1972, U.S. Ct. Appeals (11th cir.) 1994, U.S. Ct. Appeals (6th cir.) 1995. Assoc. Lord, Bissell & Brook, Chgo., 1966-74, ptnr., 1974—. Dir., pres. Buffalo Prairie Gang Camp. Fellow: Am. Coll. Trial Lawyers; mem.: ABA, Chgo. Bar Assn., Soc. Trial Lawyers, Trial Lawyers Club Chgo., Def. Rsch. Inst., Ill. Assn. Def. Trial Counsel, Product Liability Adv. Coun., Soc. Automotive Engrs., Assn. Advancement Automotive Medicine, Mid-Day Club, Pi Kappa Delta, Phi Delta Phi. Republican. Roman Catholic. Federal civil litigation, State civil litigation, Product liability. Office: Lord Bissell & Brook 115 S La Salle St Ste 3300 Chicago IL 60603-3801 E-mail: tburke@lordbissell.com

BURKE, THOMAS MICHAEL, lawyer; b. Summit, N.J., Feb. 10, 1956; s. Robert William and Eleanor Mary (Kelley) B.; m. Nancy Robin Mogab, Sept. 24, 1983; children: Colleen Margaret, Michael Thomas, Brendan Robert. BA, Notre Dame U., 1978; JD, St. Louis U., 1981. Bar: Mo. 1981, Ill. 1982, U.S. Dist. Ct. (ea. dist.) 1981. Assoc. Moser, Marsalek, Carpenter, Cleary & Jaeckel, St. Louis, 1981-86; ptnr. Noonan & Burke, 1986-92; prin. Thomas M. Burke, PC, 1992—. Bd. dirs. Legal Svcs. Ea. Mo., 1995-97. Active Vol. Lawyers program, St. Louis, St. Louis Hills Homeowner's Assn., 1984-94. Mem. Mo. Bar Assn. (bd. govs., 1998—, ethics and disciplinary commn.), Ill. Bar Assn., Interest On Lawyers' Trust Accounts (bd. dirs. 1997—, pres. 2000-2001), Bar Assn. Met. St. Louis (trial sect. asst. chmn. 1987-89, chmn. bylaws and election com. 1989—, treas. 1992-93. sec. 1993-94, v.p. 1994-95, pres.-elect 1995-96, pres. 1996-97), St. Louis Bar Found. (sec. 1993-94, treas. 1995-96), Lawyers Assn. St. Louis (exec. com. 1987-92, sec. 1992-93). General civil litigation, Personal injury, Workers' compensation. Office: 701 Market St Ste 1075 Saint Louis MO 63101-1886 E-mail: tburke@burkelawfirm.com

BURKE, TIMOTHY JOHN, lawyer; b. Syracuse, N.Y., June 5, 1946; s. Francis Joseph and Alice Marie Burke; m. Denise Kay Blied, Mar. 18, 1978; 1 child, Aimee Noel; 1 child from a previous marriage, Ryan Alexander. BA with distinction, Ariz. State U., 1967, JD cum laude, 1970. Bar: Ariz. 1970, U.S. Dist. Ct. Ariz. 1970, U.S. Ct. Appeals (9th cir.) 1974. Trial atty. Antitrust divsn. U.S. Dept. Justice, Washington, 1970-72, asst. to dir. ops., 1972-74; assoc. Fennemore Craig, Phoenix, 1974—, dir., 1978—. Part-time instr. legal writing Ariz. State U., 1974-75, adj. faculty assoc. profl. responsibility Coll. of Law, 2001. Mem. panel rev. bd. Phoenix United Way, 1975-76; bd. dirs. Florence Crittenton Svcs., Phoenix, 1980-88, pres., 1985-87; bd. dirs. Law Soc. Ariz. State U. Coll. Law, 1991-97, 99—, pres., 2000—; bd. dirs. Valley of Sn Cmtys. in Schs., 1995—. Recipient spl. commendation U.s. Dept. Justice, 1973. Fellow Am. Bar Found., Ariz. Bar Found.; mem. ABA (antitrust and litigation sects., vice chmn. bus. torts and unfair competition com. 1996-98, chair 1998-2001, vice chmn. state enforcement com., 2001-, editor Bus. Torts and Unfair Competition Newsletter 1996-98), FBA, Assn. Profl. Responsibility Lawyers (bd. dirs. 1993-98, pres. 1996-97), State Bar Ariz. (coun. antitrust sect., chmn. 1985-88, chmn. advt. com. 1992-94, ethics com. 1994-2001, chmn. 1995-2001, mem. task force on future of profession 2000—), Maricopa County Bar Assn. Antitrust. Office: Fennemore Craig 3003 N Central Ave Ste 2600 Phoenix AZ 85012-2913

BURKE, WILLIAM TEMPLE, JR. lawyer; b. San Antonio, Oct. 30, 1935; s. William Temple and Adelaide H. (Raba) B.; m. Mary Sue Johnson, June 8, 1957; children: William Patrick, Michael Edmond, Karen Elizabeth. BBA, St. Mary's U., San Antonio, JD, 1961. Bar: Tex. 1961. Practice law, Dallas; founder, pres. Burke Wright & Keiffer, PC, 1985-98; of counsel Hance/Scarborough/Wright, Dallas, 1998-2000, Hance, Scarborough, Wright Ginsberg and Brusilow, Dallas, 2000—. Co-founder, v.p., dir. Tex. Cath. Cmty. Credit Union, 1966-69, vice chmn. bd. dirs., 1990-91; pres., dir. Dallas County Small Bus. Devel. Ctr., 1966-67; v.p. Dallas County Hist. Survey Com., 1966; pres. Dallas Mil. Govt. Assn., 1962-63; pres. men's club St. Patrick's Parish Roman Cath. Ch., 1963, prin. jr. H.S. Christian devel. program, 1970, chmn. scout troop com., 1976-78, chmn. fin. com., 1984-87, mem. bldg. com., 1978-87, chmn. bd. consultors, 1978-81; bd. dirs. Dallas County War on Poverty, 1965-66; trustee Montserrat Jesuit Retreat House, 1995-2000, treas., 1996-97; bd. dirs. The Montserrat Found., 1999-2000; vice-chmn. Cath. Commn. Appeal Diocese of Dallas, 1993-97. 1st lt. U.S. Army, 1958-60; capt. USAR ret. Fellow Tex. Bar Found. (life), Coll. of State Bar Tex., Dallas Bar Found. (sr. life); mem. ABA, Tex. Bar Assn., Dallas Bar Assn. (chmn. bankruptcy and comml. law sect. 1976-77, 86-87, courthouse liaison com. 1985—, lectr. 1985—, chmn. spkrs. com. 2001—), Am. Bankruptcy Inst., John C. Ford Am. Inn Ct. (co-founder, pres. 2000—), Dallas C. of C., Dallas Safari Club, Serra Internat. Met. Club (pres. Met. Dallas 1997-98, Outstanding Mem. award 1995), Internat. Order Alhambra (exemplar 1978-95), KC (co-founder Greater Dallas, grand knight, trustee Dallas Coun. 1964-69, dist. examplar 4th degree 1968-69, Man of Yr. award 1970), Optimists (v.p., bd. dirs. Dallas 1965-66, Man of Yr. award 1966, Pres.'s award 1968), Phi Delta Phi, Tau Delta Sigma. Home: 9751 Larchcrest Dr Dallas TX 75238-2112 Office: 1401 Elm St Ste 4750 Dallas TX 75202 E-mail: wburke@hswgb.com

BURKE, WILLIAM THOMAS, law educator, lawyer; b. Brazil, Ind., Aug. 17, 1926; JD, U. Ind., 1953; JSD, Yale U., 1959. Bar: Ind. 1953. Rsch. assoc. and lectr. Yale U., 1956-62; assoc. prof. Ohio State U., 1962-64, prof., 1964-68, U. Wash. Sch. Law, Seattle, 1968-99, emeritus, 1999. Mem. adv. com. Law of Sea Task Force, Dept. State; mem. A217 Ocean Policy Com., Nat. Acad. Scis. Author: (with M. S. McDougal) The Public Order of the Oceans, 1962, Contemporary Legal Problems in Ocean Development, 1969, (with Legatski and Woodhead) National and International Law Enforcement in the Ocean, 1975, The New International Law of Fisheries, 1994, International Law of the Sea-Documents and Notes, 1997, 99. Office: U Wash Sch Law Condon Hall Seattle WA 98105 E-mail: sealaw1@home.com, burke@u.washington.edu

BURKETT, GERALD ARTHUR, lawyer, musician; b. Oklahoma City, Apr. 23, 1939; s. Francis Gerald and Leta Carey (Weaver) B.; m. Carolyn Ruth Hicks, Aug. 7, 1960; 1 child, Debora Lynne Burkett Nutt. BA, David Lipscomb U., 1962; MA, Peabody Coll., 1967; JD, Nashville Sch. of Law, 1974. Bar: Tenn. 1975, U.S. Dist. Ct. (mid. dist.) Tenn., 1976, U.S. Ct. Appeals (6th cir.), 1977, U.S. Tax Ct., 1981, U.S. Supreme Ct. 1993. Leader Fritz's German Band, Nashville, 1972-97; pvt. practice law office, 1975—; jud. commr. Met. Nashville/Davidson County, Tenn., 1999—. Adj. prof. Vol. State C.C., Gallatin, Tenn., 1979-93, 2001—, Nashville State Tech. Inst., 1984-89; band leader Strohaus, 1982 World's Fair, Knoxville, 1982; appears on Metro Night Ct., Channel 50, Nashville. Conductor of German band for commls. and concerts including Monday Night Football, 1994-2000, Super Bowl, 1995, Oktoberfest Concert, Soldier Field, Chgo., 1995; appears on weekly TV show Metro Night Ct., Channel 50, Nashville. Accordionist Charlie Rich's Bi-Centennial Album, 1976, film soundtrack Sweet Dreams, 1983. Mem. Nashville Assn. Musicians, Alliance Francaise (treas. 1985-86), Nashville Bar Assn., Tenn. Assn. of Spanish Spkg. Attys., Phi Delta Kappa (treas. 1967-68). Mem. Ch. of Christ. Avocations: travel, foreign languages. Criminal, Juvenile. Office: PO Box 8566 Hermitage TN 37076-8566 E-mail: geraldburkett@hotmail.com

BURKEY, LEE MELVILLE, lawyer; b. Beach, N.D., Mar. 21, 1914; s. Levi Melville and Mina Lou (Horner) B.; m. Lorraine Lillian Burghardt, June 11, 1938; 1 child, Lee Melville, III B.A., U. Ill., 1936, M.A., 1938; J.D. with honor, John Marshall Law Sch., 1943. Bar: Ill., 1944, U.S. Dist. Ct., 1947, U.S. Ct. Appeals, 1954, U.S. Supreme Ct.; 1983; cert. secondary tchr., Ill. Tchr. Princeton Twp. High Sch., Princeton, Ill., 1937-38, Thornton Twp. High Sch., Harvey, 1938-43; atty. Office of Solicitor, U.S. Dept. Labor, Chgo., 1944-51; ptnr. Asher, Gubbins & Segall and successor firms, 1951-94; of counsel, 1995—. Lectr. bus. law Roosevelt Coll., 1949-52; bd. dirs., pres. West Suburban Fin. Corp., 1975-94. Contbr. numerous articles on lie detector evidence. Trustee, Village of La Grange, Ill., 1962-68, mayor, 1968-73, village atty., 1973-87; commr., pres. Northeastern Ill. Planning Commn., Chgo., 1969-73; mem. bd. dirs. United Ch. Christ, Bd. of Homeland Ministries, 1981-87; mem. exec. com. Cook County Coun. Govts., 1968-70; life mem. La Grange Area Hist. Soc.; bd. dirs. Better Bus. Bur. Met. Chgo., Inc., 1975-82, Plymouth Place, Inc., 1973-82; mem. exec. bd., v.p. S.W. Suburban Ctr. on Aging, 1993—. Brevet 2nd Lt. Ill. Nat. Guard, 1932. Recipient Disting. Alumnus award John Marshall Law Sch., 1973, Good Citizenship medal S.A.R., 1973, Patriot medal S.A.R., 1977, Meritorious Svc. award Am. Legion Post 1941, 1974, Honor award LaGrange Area Hist. Soc., 1987, Cmty. Svc. award S.W. Suburban Ctr. on Aging, 2000; named to Order of Ky. Cols. Fellow Coll. Labor and Employment Lawyers (charter); mem. ABA (coun., sect. labor and employment law 1982-86, governance officer 1986-96), Ill. Bar Assn., Chgo. Bar Assn., SAR (state pres. 1977), S.R., La Grange Country Club, Masons, Order of John Marshall, Theta Delta Chi. Mem. United Ch. of Christ. Labor. Office: 125 S Wacker Dr Chicago IL 60606-4402

BURNETT, ARTHUR LOUIS, SR. judge; b. Spotsylvania County, Va., Mar. 15, 1935; s. Robert Louis and Lena Victoria (Bumbry) B.; m. Ann Lloyd, May 14, 1960; children: Darnellena, Arthur Louis II, Darryl, Darlisa, Dionne. BA summa cum laude, Howard U., 1957; LLB, NYU, 1958; grad., Fed. Exec. Inst., 1978. Bar: D.C. 1958, U.S. Dist. Ct. Md. 1963, U.S. Supreme Ct. 1964. Atty. Gen.'s Honor Program atty. fraud sect. criminal divsn. U.S. Dept. Justice, Washington, 1958, atty. to acting dep. chief gen. crimes sect., 1960-65; spl. asst. U.S. atty., Balt. and East St. Louis, Ill., 1961-63; asst. U.S. atty. D.C., 1965-68; legal adviser, gen. counsel D.C. Dept. Met. Police, 1968-69; U.S. magistrate U.S. Dist. Ct., Washington, 1969-75; asst. gen. counsel legal adv. divsn. U.S. CSC, 1975-78; assoc. gen. counsel Office of Personnel Mgmt., 1979-80; U.S. magistrate U.S. Dist. Ct. D.C., 1980-87; judge Superior Ct. D.C., 1987-98, sr. judge, 1998—; faculty Fed. Jud. Center, 1970—, Nat. Jud. Coll., 1974—. Judge-in-residence Children's Def. Fund, 1998—; program chmn. ann. meeting Nat. Conf. Spl. Ct. Judges, Washington, 1973, chmn. elect, acting chmn., 1974-75, chmn., 1975; program chmn. ann. meeting Nat. Council U.S. Magistrates, Williamsburg, Va., 1974, pres., 1983-84; program participant D.C. Circuit Jud. Conf., 1974, U.S. Ct. Claims Jud. Conf., 1979; adj. prof. Columbus Sch. Law, Cath. U. Am., 1997—, Cath. U., 1997—, Sch. Law Howard U., 1998—. Mem. NYU Law Rev., 1957-58 Recipient Founders Day award NYU, 1958, Sustained Superior Performance award U.S. Atty. Gen., 1963, Disting. Service award CSC, 1978, Meritorious Service award U.S. Office of Personnel Mgmt., 1980, Jud. award of excellence Washington Met. Trial Lawyers Assn., 1999, award of excellence Nat. Conf. State Trial Judges, 1999, Outstanding Disting. Service award Fed. Bar Assn., 1983. Mem. ABA (Franklin N. Flashner jud. award as outstanding judge on ct. of spl. jurisdiction 1985, coun. adminstrv. law and regulatory practice sect. 1987-90, liaison rep. of adminstrv. law and regulatory practice sect. to adminstrv. conf. of U.S. 1990-94, mem. JAD task force on improving opportunities for minorities 1988-97, 98—, judge Edward R. Finch Law Day USA speech award 1991, asst. sec. 1991-93, chair civil right and employment discrimination com. 1992-95, sec. adminstrv. law and regulatory practice 1993-95, chmn. CJS com. on criminal rules and evidence 1993-97, standing com. on substance abuse 1995-99, co-chmn. editl. bd. Criminal Justice Mag. 1997-2000), FBA (sect. coord. 1987-88, chmn. fed. litigation sect. 1984-85, chmn. standing com. on U.S. magistrates, dep. chmn. sect. adminstrn. of justice 1983-84, chmn. standing com. on U.S. magistrate, chmn. sect. adminstrn. of justice 1983-84, 95-97, pres. D.C. chpt. 1984-85, chmn. profl. ethics com. 1991-93, chmn. audit com. 1999—, Disting. Svc. award 1978, The Pres.'s award 1994), Washington Bar Assn. (chmn. jud. coun. 2000-01, Ollie Mae Cooper award 1997), Nat. Bar Assn. (chmn. cmty. and youth action com. jud. coun. 1995—, chmn. profl. ethics com., jud. coun. asst. sec., The Pres.'s award 1996), Bar Assn. D.C., D.C. Unified Bar, Am. Judicature Soc., Am. Judges Assn. (sec-treas. Prettyman-Leventhal Inn of Ct. Washington 1991-94, pres. 1994-95), Phi Beta Kappa, Omega Psi Phi. Office: Superior Ct DC Chambers JM-680 500 Indiana Ave NW Washington DC 20001-2131 E-mail: albsr2alb@aol.com, burnetta@dcsc.gov

BURNETT, E. C., III, state supreme court justice; b. Spartanburg, S.C., Jan. 26, 1942; s. E.C. Jr. and Lucy (Byars) B.; m. Jami Grant, 1963; children: Curry, Sharon, Jeffrey. AB, Wofford Coll., 1964; JD, U. S.C., 1969. Bar: S.C. 1969. Mem. S.C. Ho. of Reps., 1973-74; probate judge Spartanburg County, 1976-80; judge family ct., 1980-81, Seventh Jud. Cir., 1981-95; assoc. justice S.C. Supreme Ct., 1995—. Elder Mt. Calvary Presbyn. Ch. Mem. ABA, S.C. Bar Assn. Home: 200 Burnett Rd Pauline SC 29374-2610 Office: PO Box 804 Roebuck SC 29376*

BURNETTE, JAMES THOMAS, lawyer; b. Stuart, Va., Apr. 7, 1959; s. Edwin Lee and Marye Joanne (Minter) B.; m. Sarah Katherine Kelly, Dec. 2, 1989; children: Sarah Elizabeth, Thomas Pullen. BS, Campbell U., 1981; JD, Wake Forest U., 1984. Bar: N.C. 1985. Atty. Womble Carlyle Sandridge & Rice, Winston-Salem, N.C., 1985-86; ptnr. Edmundson & Burnette LLP, Oxford, 1986—; atty. City of Oxford, 1995—. Pres. 9th Jud. Dist. Bar Assn., 1998-2000. Mem. ATLA, Ninth Jud. Dist. Bar Assn. (pres. 2000), N.C. Acad. Trial Lawyers, N.C. State Bar, N.C. Bar Assn., Henderson Country Club. Episcopalian. Avocations: golf, traveling, reading. General civil litigation, Criminal, Personal injury. Home: 4129 Salem Farm Rd Oxford NC 27565-9199 Office: Edmundson & Burnette LLP 106 Main St Oxford NC 27565-3319 E-mail: edmundson@inet4u.com

BURNETTE, RALPH EDWIN, JR. judge; b. Lynchburg, Va., Sept. 25, 1953; s. Ralph Edwin and Carlease (Samuels) B. BA, Coll. William & Mary, 1975, JD, 1978. Bar: Va. 1978. Assoc. Edmunds & Williams, Lynchburg, 1978-83, ptnr., 1983-2001; gen. dist. ct. judge 24th Jud. Dist. Ct. Va., 2001—. Adj. prof. law Coll. William and Mary, 1996—. Deacon Peakland Bapt. Ch., Lynchburg, 1983-86; pres. Kaleidoscope Festival, Lynchburg, 1985, Lynchburg Symphony Orch., 1989-91; bd. dirs. Centra Health, Inc., 1987-97, United Way Cen. Va., 1989-90, Amazement Sq. Children's Mus. Mem. Va. Bar Assn., Va. State Bar (pres. 1993-94, pres.

young lawyers conf. 1985, chmn. com. on alternative dispute resolution 1985-89, mem. bar coun., 1986-95, vice chmn. standing com. on legal ethics 1986-88, chmn. com. on long range planning 1988-91, mem. exec. com. 1990-95), Lynchburg Bar Assn. (pres. 1991-92), Avocations: golf, music, boating. Office: Lynchburg Gen Dist Ct 905 Court St Lynchburg VA 24504

BURNETTE, SUSAN LYNN, lawyer; b. Sylva, N.C., Nov. 20, 1955; d. William M. and Mary (McGrady) B.; m. Mark Howard Morey, June 2, 1984; children: Barbara Elizabeth Morey, Marianne McGrady Morey. Student, Institut d'Etudes Politiques, Paris, 1974-75; BA, U. S.C., 1975, BS, 1976; JD, U. Va., 1979. Bar: Va. 1979, S.C. 1979, Tex. 1980, U.S. Dist. Ct. (no. dist.) Tex. 1980, U.S. Ct. Appeals (5th cir.) 1984, U.S. Tax Ct. 1985; bd. cert. estate planning and probate law Tex. Bd. of Legal Specialization. Ptnr. Whittenburg, Whittenburg & Schachter, Amarillo, Tex., 1983-90; shareholder Conant Whittenburg Whittenburg & Schachter, P.C., 1991-95, Conant Whittenburg French & Schachter, P.S.C., Amarillo, 1995-99, Whittenburg, Whittenburg & Schachter, P.C., Amarillo, 1999—. Lectr. in field. Fellow: Tex. Bar Found. (life); mem.: ABA, ATLA, Tex. Bar Assn. (dist. 13A grievance com. pres. 1994—95, coun. tax sect. 1999—, course dir. Advanced Tax Law Course 1999), S.C. Bar Assn., Va. Bar Assn., Tex. Acad. Probate and Trust Counsel, Amarillo Bar Assn. (v.p. 2001), Amarillo Area Estate Planning Coun. General civil litigation, Estate planning, Probate. Home: 2709 Sunlite St Amarillo TX 79106-6113 Office: Whittenburg Whittenburg & Schachter PC 1010 S Harrison St Amarillo TX 79101-3426 E-mail: sburnette@whittenburglaw.com

BURNISON, BOYD EDWARD, lawyer; b. Arnolds Park, Iowa, Dec. 12, 1934; s. Boyd WIlliam and Lucile (Harnden) B.; m. Mari Amaral; children: Erica Lafore, Alison Katherine. BS, Iowa State U., 1957; JD, U. Calif., Berkeley, 1961. Bar: Calif. 1962, U.S. Supreme Ct. 1971, U.S. Dist. Ct. (no. dist.) Calif. 1962, U.S. Ct. Appeals (9th cir.) 1962, U.S. Dist. Ct. (ea. dist.) Calif. 1970, U.S. Dist. Ct. (ctrl. dist.) Calif. 1992. Dep. counsel Yolo County, Calif., 1962-65; assoc. Steel & Arostegui, Marysville, 1965-66, St. Sure, Moore & Hoyt, Oakland, 1966-70; ptnr. St. Sure, Moore, Hoyt & Sizoo, Oakland and San Francisco, 1970-75; v.p. Crosby, Heafey, Roach & May, P.C., Oakland, 1975-2000, also bd. dirs.; pres. Boyd E Burnison A Profl. Law Corp., Walnut Creek, Calif., 2001—. Advisor Berkeley YMCA, 1971—, Yolo County YMCA, 1962—65, bd. dirs., 1965; trustee, sec., legal counsel Easter Seal Found., Alameda County, 1974—79, hon. trustee, 1979—; trustee Alameda County Law Libr., 2001—; bd. dirs. Easter Seal Soc. Crippled Children and Adults of Alameda County Calif., 1972—75, Moot Ct. Bd., U. Calif., 1960—61, East Bay Conservation Corps, 1997—2000, treas., 2000. Named Vol. of Yr., Berkeley YMCA, 1999. Fellow: ABA Found. (life); mem.: ABA (labor rels. and employment law sect., equal employment law com. 1972—), Nat. Conf. Bar Pres.'s, State Bar Calif. (spl. labor counsel 1981—84, labor and employment law sect. 1982—), Alameda County Bar Assn. (chmn. memberships and directory com. 1973—74, chmn. memberships and directory com. 1980, chmn. law office econs. com. 1975—77, assn. dir. 1981—85, pres. 1984, vice chmn. bench bar liaison com. 1983, chmn. 1984, Disting. Svc. award 1987), Alameda County Bar Found. (bd. dirs. 1993—95), Yolo County Bar Assn. (sec. 1965), Yuba Sutter Bar Assn., Bar Assn. San Francisco (labor law sect.), Contra Costa County Bar Assn. (labor law sect.), Indsl. Rels. Rsch. Assn., Sproul Assoc. Boalt Hall Law Sch. U. Calif. Berkeley, Iowa State Alumni Assn., Order Knoll, Round Hill Country Club, Rotary (Paul Harris fellow), Pi Kappa Alpha, Phi Delta Phi. Democrat. Labor. Home: PO Box 743 2500 Caballo Ranchero Dr Diablo CA 94528 Office: Boyd E Burnison A Profl Law Corp 1600 South Main Plz Ste 130 Walnut Creek CA 94596 Fax: (925) 817-2411

BURNS, BERNARD JOHN, III, public defender; b. Alexandria, Va., Apr. 28, 1956; s. Bernard John and Mary Theresa (O'Malley) B.; m. Pamela Sue Endres, June 9, 1990; 1 child, Kristie Keener. BA in Journalism, U. Iowa, 1982, JD with distinction, 1984. Bar: Iowa 1985, U.S. Dist. Ct. (so. dist.) Iowa 1987, U.S. Supreme Ct. 1989, U.S. Ct. Appeals (8th cir.) 1992. Asst. appellate defender Iowa Appellate Defender, Des Moines, 1985-94; asst. pub. defender Des Moines Adult Pub. Defender, 1994-99; asst. fed. defender Office of Fed. Defender, Des Moines, 1999—. Author: (with R. Rigg) Iowa Practice, Criminal Law and Procedure, 4 supplements, 2000—. Bd. dirs. Met. Arts Alliance Greater Des Moines, 1996—, pres., 2000; mem. Iowa Criminal and Juvenile Justice Planning Commn., 1993-99; chmn. Jazz in July Planning Com., Des Moines, 1997—; keyboard player Goodnight Dallas. Named Outstanding Sr., Iowa Sch. Journalism, 1982. Mem. Iowa Pub. Defenders Assn. (pres. 1991-99), Chopin Soc. (v.p. 1982), Phi Beta Kappa. Avocations: composer, actor, writer, Tae Kwon Do instructor, musician. Office: Fed Defender 300 Walnut St Ste 295 Des Moines IA 50309-2258

BURNS, CASSANDRA STROUD, prosecutor; b. Lynchburg, Va., May 22, 1960; d. James Wesley and Jeanette Lou (Garner) Stroud; m. Stephen Burns; children: Leila Jeanette, India Veronica. BA, U. Va., 1982; JD, N.C. Cen. U., 1985. Bar: Va. 1986, N.J. 1986, U.S. Dist. Ct. (ea. dist.) Va. 1987, U.S. Ct. Appeals (4th cir.) 1987, U.S. Bankruptcy Ct. (ea. dist.) Va. 1987; cert. in criminal law. Law clk. Office Atty. Gen. State of Va., Richmond, summer 1984; law intern Office Dist. Atty. State of N.C., Durham, 1985; staff atty. Tidewater Legal Aid Soc., Chesapeake, Va., 1987-89; asst. atty. Commonwealth of Va., Petersburg, 1989-90; assoc. atty. Bland and Stroud, 1990; asst. pub. defender City of Petersburg, 1990-91, Commonwealth's atty. Va., 1991—. Founder BED Task Force on Babies Exposed to Drugs, 1991, Buddies of Petersburg Program, 1997—. Sec. Chesapeake Task Force Coun. on Youth Svcs., 1987-89; ch. directress and organist; mem. NAACP; chair Petersburg-Dinwiddie Cmty. Criminal Justice Bd. Mem. Va. Bar Assn. (mem. coun. 1993—), Old Dominion Bar Assn., Va. Assn. Commonwealth Attys. (bd. dirs., mem. coun. 1993—), Legal Svcs. Corp. Va. (bd. dirs.), Nat. Bd. Trial Advocacy (cert.), Soutside Va. Legal Aid Soc. (bd. dirs.), Petersburg Bar Assn., Nat. Black Prosecutors Assn. (regional dir.), Petersburg Jaycees, Order Eastern Star, Peterburg C. of C., Kiwanis, Internat., Buddies Club, Phi Alpha Delta, Alpha Kappa Alpha. Democrat. Baptist. Avocations: piano, organ, volleyball, needlework, pets. E-mial. Home: 326 N Park Dr Petersburg VA 23805-2442 Office: Commonwealth's Atty 39 Bollingbrook St Petersburg VA 23803-4568 E-mail: bossyda@aol.com

BURNS, ELLEN BREE, federal judge; b. New Haven, Dec. 13, 1923; d. Vincent Thomas and Mildred Bridget (Bannon) Bree; m. Joseph Patrick Burns, Oct. 8, 1955 (dec.); children: Mary Ellen, Joseph Bree, Kevin James. BA, Albertus Magnus Coll., 1944, LLD (hon.), 1974; LLB, Yale U., 1947; LLD (hon.), U. New Haven, 1981, Sacred Heart U., 1986, Fairfield U., 1991. Bar: Conn. 1947. Dir. legis. legal svcs. State of Conn., 1949-73; judge Conn. Cir. Ct., 1973-74, Conn. Ct. of Common Pleas, 1974-76, Conn. Superior Ct., 1976-78, U.S. Dist. Ct. Conn., New Haven, 1978—, chief judge, 1988-92, sr. judge, 1992—. Trustee Fairfield U., 1978-85, Albertus Magnus Coll., 1985—. Recipient John Carroll of Carrollton award John Barry Council K.C., 1973, Judiciary award Conn. Trial Lawyers Assn., 1978, Cross Pro Ecclesia et Pontifice, 1981, Law Rev. award U. Conn. Law Rev., 1987, Judiciary award Conn. Bar Assn., 1987, Raymond E. Baldwin Pub. Svc. award Bridgeport Law Sch., 1992. Mem. ABA, Am. Bar Found., New Haven County Bar Assn., Conn. Bar Found. Roman Catholic. Office: US Dist Ct 141 Church St New Haven CT 06510-2030

BURNS, MARSHALL SHELBY, arbitrator, lawyer, retired judge; b. Cleve., Jan. 29, 1931; s. Marshall Shelby and Fairybelle (Moses) B.; m. Blanche Marie Coleman, Jan. 28, 1953; children: William M., Brian M. AA, Flint (Mich.) Jr. Coll., 1957; BA, U. Mich., Flint, 1972; JD, Thomas M. Cooley Law Sch., 1979; LLM, Wayne State U., 1984; grad., Nat. Jud. Coll., 1985. Bar; Mich. 1980, U.S. Dist. Ct. (ea. and we. dists.) Mich. 1980, U.S. Tax Ct. 1980, U.S. Supreme Ct. 1980. Tax supr. City of Flint, 1965-69; indsl. recreation adminstr. IMA, Flint, 1969-75; dir. personnel and labor relations Flint Gen. Hosp., 1975-76; asst. dir. personnel dept. pub. health State of Mich., Lansing, 1976-78, judge adminstrv. law, 1978-96. Gen. counsel Greater Lansing Urban League, 1983—; arbitrator Fed. Mediation and Conciliation Svc., Washington, 1983—, Better Bus. Bur., 1983—, Am. Arbitration Assn., 1983—; faculty advisor Nat. Jud. Coll., 1986. Mem. exec. bd. Tall Pine Counsel Boy Scouts Am., Flint, 1970-75; bd. dirs. Greater Lansing Urban League, 1982-84, Vol. Action Ctr. of Greater Lansing, 1982-84. Served to pvt. 1st class U.S. Army, 1953-55. Mem. NAACP, Am. Arbitration Assn. (arbitrator), Nat. Bar Assn., Indsl. Rels. Rsch. Assn., Rotary (v.p. East Lansing club 1990-91), Masons, Phi Alpha Delta (justice, treas. 1978-80), Alpha Phi Alpha (chpt. pres. 1989). Office: 417 N Pine St Lansing MI 48933-1025

BURNS, MARVIN GERALD, lawyer; b. Los Angeles, July 3, 1930; s. Milton and Belle (Cytron) B.; m. Barbara Irene Fisher, Aug. 23, 1953; children: Scott Douglas, Jody Lynn, Bradley Frederick. BA, U. Ariz., 1951; JD, Harvard U., 1954. Bar: Calif. 1955. Bd. dirs. Inner City Arts for Inner City Children. With AUS, 1955-56. Clubs: Beverly Hills Tennis, Sycamore Park Tennis. General civil litigation, Land use and zoning (including planning), Real property. Home: 10350 Wilshire Blvd Ph 4 Los Angeles CA 90024-4734 Office: 9107 Wilshire Blvd Ste 800 Beverly Hills CA 90210-5533 E-mail: mburns@lurie-zepeda.com

BURNS, RICHARD OWEN, lawyer; b. Bklyn., Nov. 16, 1942; s. James I. and Ida (Shore) B.; m. Lynda Gail Birnbaum, Dec. 24, 1967; children: Marc Adam, Lisa Ann, Susan Danielle. BS, Wilkes Coll., 1964; JD, Bklyn. Law Sch., 1967. Bar: N.Y. 1967, U.S. Dist. Ct. (so. dist.) N.Y. 1969, U.S. Dist. Ct. (ea. dist.) N.Y. 1979. Assoc. Clune & O'Brien, Mineola, N.Y., 1967-73, Clune, Burns, White & Nelson, Harrison, 1973-78; ptnr. Schurr & Burns, P.C., Spring Valley, 1978-98; pvt. practice, Chestnut Ridge, 1998—. Bd. dirs. Rockland County unit Am. Cancer Soc., West Nyack, N.Y., 1979-85, 86-92, pres., 1981-83; bd. dirs. Hudson Valley Health System Agy., Sterling Park, N.Y., 1979, Vets. Meml. Assn., Congers, N.Y., 1980-86; mem. Wilkes U. Coun., Wilkes-Barre, Pa., 1995—. Recipient Reese D. Jones award Wilkes Coll. Jr. C. of C., 1964. Mem. Rockland County Bar Assn., N.Y. State Bar Assn., N.Y. State Trial Lawyers Assn. Democrat. Jewish. State civil litigation, Labor, Personal injury. Home: 140 Waters Edge Congers NY 10920-2622 Office: 500 Chestnut Ridge Rd Chestnut Ridge NY 10977-5646

BURNS, RICHARD RAMSEY, lawyer; b. Duluth, Minn., May 3, 1946; s. Herbert Morgan and Janet (Strobel) B.; Jennifer, Brian; m. Elizabeth Murphy, June 15, 1984. BA with distinction, U. Mich., 1968, JD magna cum laude, 1971. Bar: Calif. 1972, U.S. Dist. Ct. (no. dist.) Calif. 1972, U.S. Ct. Appeals (9th cir.) 1972, Minn. 1976, U.S. Dist. Ct. Minn. 1976, Wis. 1983, U.S. Tax. Ct. 1983. Assoc. Orrick, Herrington, Rowley & Sutcliffe, San Francisco, 1971-76; ptnr. Hanft, Fride, P.A., Duluth, 1976—. Gen. counsel Evening Telegram Co., Superior, Wis., 1982—, Murphy TV Stas., Madison, Wis., 1982—. Chmn. Duluth-Superior Area Comty. Found., 1988-90; chair United Way of Greater Duluth, Inc., 1998-99; bd. dirs. Miller Dwan Found., Northland Coll., Ashland, Wis. Fellow Am. Coll. Trust and Estate Counsel; mem. Calif. Bar Assn., Wis. Bar Assn., Minn. Bar Assn. (exec. com. bd. govs., past chmn. probate and trust coun.), 11th Dist. Bar Assn. (past pres., past chmn. ethics com.), Arrowhead Estate Planning Coun. (pres. 1980), Northland Country Club (pres. 1982), Boulders Club, Kitchi Gammi Club (bd. dirs.), Mpls. Athletic Club, Kitchi Gammi Club. Republican. Avocations: travel, golf, tennis, fishing. Communications, Estate planning, Pension, profit-sharing, and employee benefits. Home: 180 Paine Farm Rd Duluth MN 55804-2609 Office: Hanft Fride PA 1000 First Bank Pl 130 W Superior St Ste 1000 Duluth MN 55802-2056

BURNS, ROBERT EDWARD, lawyer; b. Bedford, Ohio, June 18, 1953; s. Robert Joseph and Barbara (Charvat) B.; m. Patricia Bosler, Oct. 15, 1983. BA in Polit. Sci. magna cum laude, Marietta Coll., 1975; JD, Ohio State U., 1978. Bar: Ohio 1978. Research asst. Program for Energy Research, Edn. and Pub. Service Ohio State U., Columbus, 1978-80, research assoc. Nat. Regulatory Research Inst., 1980-81, sr. research assoc., 1981-90, sr. rsch. specialist, 1990—. Author, co-author numerous monographs, articles, speeches, presentations, papers and reports to profl. orgns. and journals. Mem. ABA (vice chmn. energy com. 1984—, adminstrv., antitrust and pub. utility law sects.), Nat. Assn. Regulatory Utility Commrs. (subcom. adminstrv. law judges 1985—, subcom. law 1980—, coord. info. conf. 1986-87), Sertoma (pres. University club 1984-85, dist. gov. 1992-94, Internat. Community Svc. award 1984-85, outstanding dist. gov. 1994). Democrat. Methodist. Avocation: reading. Home: 3180 Bowdoin Ct Columbus OH 43204-2167 Office: Ohio State U Nat Regulatory Rsch Inst 1080 Carmack Rd Columbus OH 43210-1002

BURNS, ROBERT WILLIAM, lawyer; b. Lewiston, Idaho, Aug. 26, 1943; s. William Harry and Mary Jane (Stephenson) B.; m. Sherry Lyn Ogle, Nov. 1963 (dec. Nov. 1964); m. Suzanne Loretta Cherry, Oct. 2, 1965; children— Rebecca Lyn, William Hardin. B.A. in Bus., U. Wash., 1966; J.D. Magna cum laude, Gonzaga U., 1973. Bar: Wash. 1973, U.S. Dist. Ct. (ea. and we. dists.) Wash. 1973, U.S. Ct. Appeals (9th cir.) 1981, U.S. Supreme Ct. 1982. Law clk., bailiff U.S. Dist. Ct. (ea. dist.) Wash., Spokane, 1971-74; assoc. Paine Lowe Coffin Herman & Okelly, Spokane, 1974-77; adj. prof. Gonzaga Law Sch., 1977; prin. Foulds Felker Burns & Johnson, P.S., Seattle, 1977-82; founder, pres. Burns & Ricketts, P.S., Seattle, 1982— . Served to capt. U.S. Army, 1966-68; Vietnam. Mem. Wash. State Bar Assn. (chmn. young lawyers sect. 1976-77), ABA, Def. Research Inst., Wash. Trial Lawyers Assn., Assn. Trial Lawyers Am. Republican. Presbyterian. Insurance, Personal injury. Office: Burns & Ricketts PS PO Box 21926 Seattle WA 98111-3926

BURNS, SANDRA, lawyer, educator; b. Bryan, Tex., Aug. 9, 1949; d. Clyde W. and Bert (Rychlik) B.; 1 son, Scott. BS, U. Houston, 1970; MA, U. Tex., 1972, PhD, 1975; JD, St. Mary's U., 1978. Bar: Tex. 1978; cert. tchr., adminstr., supr. instrn., Tex. Tchr. Austin (Tex.) Ind. Sch. Dist., 1970-71; prof. child devel./family life and home econs. edn. Coll. Nutrition, Textiles and Human Devel. Tex. Women's U., Denton, 1974-75; instrnl. devel. asst. Office of Ednl. Resources divsn. instr U. Tex. Health Sci., San Antonio, 1976-77; legis. aide William T. Moore Tex. Senate, Austin, fall 1978, com. clk.-counsel, spring 1979; legal cons. Colombotti & Assocs., Aberdeen, Scotland, 1980; corp. counsel 1st Internat. Oil and Gas, Inc., 1983; contracted atty. Humble Exploration Co., Inc., Dallas, 1984; assoc. Smith, Underwood, 1986-88; pvt. practice, 1988—. Atty. contracted to Republic Energy Inc., Bryan, Tex., 1981-82, ARCO, Dallas, 1985; vis. lectr. Tex. A&M U., fall 1981, summer, 1981; lectr. home econ. Our Lady of the Lake Coll., San Antonio, fall, 1975. Contbr. articles on law and edn. to profl. jours. Mem. ABA, State Bar of Tex., Phi Delta Kappa. Personal injury, Probate. Office: 8300 Douglas Ave Ste 800 Dallas TX 75225-5826 E-mail: burns@attorney-mediator.com

BURNS, SCOTT DAVID, lawyer; b. Camden, N.J., July 9, 1971; s. Paul Charles and Ida Julia Burns. BA in History, BA in Polit. Sci., Villanova U., 1993; JD, Widener U., 1996. Bar: N.J. 1996, Pa. 1996, U.S. Dist. Ct. N.J. 1996. Assoc. Sklar, Kwasnik & Sklar, Cherry Hill, N.J., 1997-98; ptnr. Kuasnik, Paston & Burns, Mt. Laurel, 1998—. Mem. ABA, Phila. Bar Assn., Camden County Bar Assn. Lutheran. Avocation: travel. Consumer commercial, Criminal. Office: Kwasnik Paston & Burns 139-H Gaither Dr Mount Laurel NJ 08054

BURNS, STEPHEN GILBERT, lawyer; b. N.Y.C., Apr. 29, 1953; s. Gilbert Leo and Ellen (Scully) B.; m. Joan Louise Wallace, Aug. 6, 1977; children: Christopher, Allison. Student, U. Vienna, Austria, 1974; BA, Colgate U., 1975; JD, George Washington U., 1978. Bar: D.C. 1978, U.S. Dist. Ct. D.C. 1979, U.S. Ct. Appeals (D.C. cir.) 1980. Atty. Nuclear Regulatory Commn., Washington, 1978-83, dep. chief counsel regional ops. and enforcement, 1983-86, legal asst. to commr., 1986-89, exec. asst. to chmn., 1989-91, dir. Office of Commn. Appellate Adjudication, 1991-94, assoc. gen. counsel, 1994-98, dep. gen. counsel, 1998—. Recipient Disting. Svc. medal, NRC, 2001. Mem. ABA. Presbyterian. Office: US Nuclear Regulatory Commn Office Of Gen Counsel Ms 15B Washington DC 20555-0001

BURNS, TERRENCE MICHAEL, lawyer; b. Evergreen Park, Ill., Mar. 2, 1954; s. Jerome Joseph Burns and Eileen Beatrice (Collins) Neary; m. Therese Porucznik, Mar. 24, 1979; children: David, Steven, Theresa, Daniel. BA, Loyola U., Chgo., 1975; JD, DePaul U., 1978. Bar: Ill. 1978, U.S. Dist. Ct. (no. dist.) Ill. 1978, U.S. Ct. Appeals (7th cir.) 1979, U.S. Supreme Ct. 1985, U.S. Dist. Ct. (no. dist.) Ind. 1989. Asst. state's atty. Cook County, Chgo., 1979-85; ptnr. Rooks, Pitts & Poust, 1985—. Mem. inquiry bd. Ill. Supreme Ct. Atty. Registration and Disciplinary Commn., Chgo., 1986-90, chair hearing bd., 1990—. Mem. ABA (ann. meeting adv. com.), Chgo. Bar Assn. (treas. 1997-99, 2d v.p. 1999-2000, 1st v.p. 2000-01, pres. 2001—, bd. mgrs. 1995-97, chair fin. com. 1997-99, criminal law com. 1979-83, jud. candidate evaluation com. 1981-86, 87-95, chmn. investigation divsn. evaluation com. 1991-92, chmn. hearing divsn. evaluation com. 1992-93, gen. chmn. 1993-95, ct. liaison com. 1993-95, tort reform subcom. 1997), Chgo. Bar Found. (bd. dirs. 1999-2000). Roman Catholic. General civil litigation, Personal injury. Office: Rooks Pitts & Poust 10 S Wacker Dr Ste 2300 Chicago IL 60606-7407

BURNS, THOMAS DAVID, lawyer; b. Andover, Mass., Apr. 4, 1921; s. Joseph Lawrence and Catherine (Horne) B.; m. Sylvia Lansing, Sept. 14, 1946 (div. 1982); children— Wendy Tilghman, Lansing, Diane Longley, Lisa; m. Marjorie Andrew Brown, Mar. 12, 1983 Student, Phillips Andover Acad., 1938, Brown U., 1938-41; LLB, Boston U., 1943. Bar: Mass. 1944, U.S. Dist. Ct. 1948, U.S. Ct. Appeals 1951, U.S. Supreme Ct. 1957. Assoc. Friedman, Atherton, King & Turner, Boston, 1946-50, ptnr., 1950-60; sr. and founding ptnr. Burns & Levinson, 1960—. Mem. Jud. Coun. Com. of Mass., 1973-77, mem. Mass. Jud. Nominating Commn., 1979-83; mem. Mass. Spl. Legis. Commn. on Malpractice, 1975—; chmn. Joint Com. Boston and Mass. Bar Com. on Jud. Selection, 1970-75; spl. counsel to Boston City Coun., 1981. Co-editor: Recollections of World War II Andover, 1938; contbr. articles to profl. jours Chmn. Planning Bd. Appeals, Andover, 1956-57; trustee Stratton Mountain Vt. Civic Assn., Mus. Am. Textile History, 1992—; v.p., bd. dirs. Birch Hill Corp., Stratton, Vt.; chmn. Andover Rep. Fin. Com., 1953-57; trustee, clk. Pike Sch., Andover; mem. alumni coun. and devel. com. Phillips Andover Acad., Boston U. Law Sch.; mem. Mass. Hist. Soc., Western Front Assn.; mem. adv. bd. PBS channel II WGBH, Boston. Lt. USNR, 1943-46, PTO, ETO. Fellow Am. Coll. Trial Lawyers, (state chmn. 1968, bd. regents 1970-76, treas. 1974-77), Am. Coll. Trial Lawyers Found. (dir.), Mass. Bar Found (trustee), Mass. Bar Assn. (mem. exec. com.), Am. Bar Found., ABA, Boston Bar Assn. (exec. coun.), Boston Vis. Nurse Assn., Boston Bar Found., Fed. Ins. and Corp. Counsel, Internat. Assn. Def. Counsel, Nat. Assn. R.R. Trial Counsel, Mass. Def. Lawyers Assn. (dir.), Delta Kappa Epsilon, North Andover Country Club, The Country Club (Brookline), Coral Beach Club (Bermuda), Duxbury Yacht Club, Boston City Club, Boston U. Law Sch. (alumni award, Disting. profl. svc. award 1996). Republican. General civil litigation, Insurance, Personal injury. Home: 5 Union Wharf Boston MA 02109-1202 Office: Burns & Levinson 125 Summer St Ste 602 Boston MA 02110-1616 E-mail: tburns@b-l.com

BURNSTEIN, DANIEL, lawyer; b. Hartford, Conn., Oct. 12, 1946; s. Lawrence J. and Margaret (Le Vien) B. AB, U. Calif., Berkeley, 1968; JD cum laude, New Eng. Sch. Law, 1975. Bar: Mass. 1975, U.S. Dist. Ct. Mass. 1976, U.S. Ct. Appeals (1st cir.) 1976. Pres. Beacon Expert Systems, Inc., 1989-99. Dir. Interactive Video Project Harvard Law Sch., Cambridge, 1985-89, clin. instr.; pres. Ctr. for Atomic Radiation Studies, Acton, Mass., 1982—; advisor Am. Mgmt. Assn. for Negotiation Curriculum to Mgrs., 1993; pres.-COO BuzzIT.com, 1999—. Editor: The Digital MBA, 1995. Mem. ABA, Mass. Adv. Coun. on Radiation Protection. Communications, Computer, Private international. Office: 35 Gardner Rd Brookline MA 02445-4512

BURROUGHS, CHARLES EDWARD, lawyer; b. Milw., June 9, 1939; s. Edward Albert and Ann Monica (Bussman) B.; m. Kathleen Walton, Jan. 30, 1965; children— James, Michael, Lauri, Stephanie. B.S., U. Wis.-Madison, 1962, LL.B., 1965; LL.M., George Washington U., 1968. Bar: Wis. 1965, U.S. Dist. Ct. (ea. and we. dists.) Wis. 1965, U.S. Ct. Clms. 1967, U.S. Ct. Mil. Apls. 1967, U.S. Ct. Apls. (7th cir.) 1969, U.S. Supreme Ct. 1968. Assoc., Porter & Porter, Milw., 1969-71, Purtell, Purcell, Wilmot & Burroughs, 1971-86; ptnr. VonBriesen & Purtell, 1986-91, Hinshaw & Culbertson, Milw. Served to capt. U.S. Army, 1965-69. Mem. ABA, AHLA, HFMA, State Bar Wis. (pres. health law sect.). Roman Catholic. Club: Milw. Athletic. Antitrust, Construction, Health. Home: 10937 N Hedgewood Ln Mequon WI 53092-4907

BURROW, ALISTAIR STEWART, solicitor; b. Glasgow, Scotland, Oct. 14, 1951; s. James Edward and Helen (Dickson) B.; m. Mary Anne Lockhart Crombie, Sept. 15, 1978; children: Sheona, Kirsty, Mairi. MA with hons., U. Glasgow, 1973, LLB, 1976. Notary nublic, 1978. Apprentice Boyds, Glasgow, 1976—78, asst. solicitor, 1978-81, Neill Clerk & Murray, Greenock, Scotland, 1981-82, ptnr. Glasgow, 1982-90, McClure Naismith, Glasgow, 1990—2001, Tods Murray WS, Glasgow, 2001—. Tutor law faculty U. Strathclyde, Scotland, 1980-83, U. Glasgow, 1988-91. Co-author: International Banking Law and Regulation, Offshore Financing: Security and Insolvency. Clerk Inc. Hammermen of Glasgow, 1988—; hon. treasurer World Conf., Eng., 1994—. Mem. Law Soc. Scotland, Internat. Bar Assn., Assn. Bus. Recovery Profls. Presbyterian. Avocations: youth leadership, hill walking, reading. Bankruptcy, General corporate, Mergers and acquisitions. Office: Tods Murray WS 33 Bothwell St Glasgow G2 6NL Scotland Fax: 0141 275 4781. E-mail: alistair.burrow@todsmurray.com

BURROWS, JON HANES, lawyer; b. Frederick, Okla., July 12, 1946; s. John Henry and Eula Elizabeth (Trull) B.; m. Katie Lea Royal, July 13, 1969; children: Justin Hanes, Kelly Elizabeth. BME, U. Okla., 1968, MME, 1969; JD, U. Tex., 1978. Bar: Tex. 1976, U.S. Dist. Ct. (we. dist.) Tex. 1978, U.S. Dist. Ct. (no. dist.) Tex. 1989; cert. residential and comml. real estate law Tex. Bd. Legal Specialization. Ptnr. Burrows & Cure, Temple, Tex., 1976-78; pvt. practice, 1978-81; ptnr. Burrows & Baird, 1982-85; pres. Burrows, Baird, Miller & Crews, PC, 1985-98; judge Bell County, Belton, Tex., 1999—. Mem. faculty in real estate law Temple Jr. Coll., 1980-89. Treas., bd. govs. Temple Civic Theatre, 1980; pres. Western Hills Elem. PTO, 1982; mem. human studies subcom. VA Hosp., 1983-86; bd. dirs. Temple United Way, 1983-86, 93—, campaign chmn., 1992;

trustee Temple Coll., 1989—. Capt. USAF, 1969-73, col. USAFR, ret. 2000. Mem. ABA, State Bar Tex., Bell-Lampasas-Mills Counties Bar Assn., USAF Res. Officers Assn., Temple C. of C. (bd. dirs. 1993-98, chmn. 1996-97), Lions (bd. dirs. 1980-86, pres. 1986-87), Phi Alpha Delta. Baptist. General practice, Probate, Real property. Home: 709 Clover Ln Temple TX 76502-4817 Office: Bell County Courthouse Compass Bank PO Box 768 Belton TX 76513-3162

BURROWS, KENNETH DAVID, lawyer; b. Bklyn., Mar. 26, 1941; s. Selig S. and Gladys (Spatt) B.; m. Erica Johng, Aug. 5, 1989. BA, Brown U., 1967; JD, Fordham U., 1970. Bar: N.Y. 1971, Conn. 1973, U.S. Dist. Ct. (so. dist.) N.Y. 1972, U.S. Dist. Ct. Conn. 1994, U.S. Sureme Ct. 1973. Assoc. Phillips, Nizer, Benjamin, Krim & Ballon, N.Y.C., 1970-77; ptnr. Kleinberg, Kaplan, Wolff, Cohen & Burrows, 1977-79, Burrows & Poster, N.Y.C., 1980-89, Burrows & Franzblau, N.Y.C., 1990-91; arbitrator small claims ct. City of N.Y., 1975-95; lectr. Practising Law Inst., 1996—; spl. master Supreme Ct. State of N.Y., N.Y. County, 1980-89; arbitrator U.S. Dist. Ct. (ea. dist.) N.Y., 1994—; mediator U.S. Dist. Ct. (so. dist.) N.Y., 1994—. Mem. Appellate Divsn. 1st Dept. Com. on Law Guardians. Served with USCGR, 1960-68. Mem. ABA, N.Y. State Bar Assn., Assn. Bar City N.Y., Am. Acad. Matrimonial Lawyers, N.Y. County Lawyers Assn., Am. Arbitration Assn. (mem. nat. arbitrators panel 1973-97). Federal civil litigation, State civil litigation, Family and matrimonial. Office: 425 Park Ave Ste 2600 New York NY 10022-3506

BURROWS, MICHAEL DONALD, lawyer; b. Oak Park, Ill., May 23, 1944; s. Milford Denton and Helen Jean (Spitali) B.; m. Sandi Miller, Feb. 6, 1982; 1 child, Matthew Denton. BA, Williams Coll., 1967; JD, N.Y. Law Sch., 1973. Bar: N.Y. 1974, U.S. Dist. Ct. (ea. and so. dists.) N.Y. 1974, U.S. Ct. Appeals (2d cir.) 1978, U.S. Supreme Ct. 1981. Assoc. Baker & McKenzie, N.Y.C., 1973-80, ptnr., 1980-95, of counsel, 1995-99, mem. internat. exec. com., 1986-88; ptnr. Winston & Strawn, 1999—, exec. com., 2000—. Co-author: The Practice of International Litigation, 1992. With USMC, 1968-70. Mem. ABA, Assn.of Bar of City of N.Y. Federal civil litigation, General civil litigation, State civil litigation. Office: Winston & Strawn 200 Park Ave New York NY 10166-0005

BURSLEY, KATHLEEN A. lawyer; b. Washington, Mar. 20, 1954; d. G.H. Patrick and Claire (Mulvany) B. BA, Pomona Coll., 1976; JD, Cornell U., 1979. Bar: N.Y. 1980, U.S. Dist. Ct. (ea. and so. dists.) N.Y. 1980, U.S. Ct. Appeals (5th and 11th cirs.) 1981, Fla. 1984, U.S. Dist. Ct. (mid. dist.) Fla. 1984, Tex. 1985, Mass. 1995. Assoc. Haight, Gardner, Poor & Havens, N.Y.C., 1979-81; counsel Harcourt Brace Jovanovich, Inc., N.Y.C. and Orlando, Fla., 1981-85, v.p. and counsel San Antonio and Orlando, 1985-92; assoc. gen. counsel pub. Harcourt Gen., Inc., Chestnut Hill, Mass., 1992—; gen. counsel Harcourt, Inc., 1992—; v.p. Harcourt Gen., Inc., 1998—. Mem. Maritime Law Assn. (proctor). Contracts commercial, Intellectual property, Trademark and copyright. Address: 41 Dwight St # 3 Brookline MA 02446 E-mail: kbursley@harcourtgeneral.com

BURSTEIN, HARVEY, lawyer, educator; b. St. Louis, Jan. 3, 1923; m. Morris and Rachel (Johannes) B.; m. Ina Bebchick, Sept. 25, 1947. LLB, Creighton U., 1948. Bar: Nebr. 1948, U.S. Supreme Ct. 1953, Mass. 1954, N.Y. 1963. Spl. agt. FBI, 1948-53; chief fgn. and domestic investigations, surveys and phys. U.S. Dept. State, 1953-54; pvt. practice, 1954—61, 1978—79; security officer M.I.T., Cambridge, 1956-61; v.p. and gen. counsel Norman Co., Inc., Valley Stream, N.Y., 1961-73; pres. Harvey Cons. Corp., 1961-73; corp. security dir. Sheraton Corp., Boston, 1973-74; dir. security and safety New Eng. Mut. Life Ins. Co., 1975-78; corp. dir. safety and security, staff atty. Data Gen. Corp., Westboro, 1979-90. Guest lectr. Ind. U., Mich. State U., Wellesley Coll., Babson Coll.; adj. asst. prof. Coll. Liberal Arts Fordham U.; adj. prof. Grad. Sch. Bus. Adminstr. Fordham U.; vis. prof. Sch. Hotel Adminstrn. Cornell U.; adj. assoc. prof. Coll. Criminal Justice Northeastern U., vis. prof., 1990-95, David B. Schulman prof. security, 1995—; arbitrator Civil Ct. of N.Y.C., 1971-73. Author: 10 books on security mgmt.;contbr. articles on security mgmt. and investigations to profl. jours. Liaison with aux. police for Chief of Police, Brookline, Mass., 1955—61; mem. Citizens Com. for Better Law Enforcement, Town of Mamaroneck, NY, 1971—73. Recipient Big Pi award Pi Lambda Phi, 1981. Mem.: Am. Judicature Soc., Soc. of Ex-FBI Agts., Am. Soc. for Indsl. Security, Boston Bar Assn., Masons, Pi Lambda Phi. Democrat. Jewish. Constitutional, Criminal. Home: 19 Linden Sq Wellesley MA 02482-4717 Office: Coll Criminal Justice Northeastern U Boston MA 02115

BURSTEIN, MERWYN JEROME, lawyer; b. Springfield, Mass., Apr. 6, 1938; s. Rubin Meyer and Sylvia (Burke) B.; m. Ruth B. Burstein, July 31, 1966; children: David, Judith, Jeffrey. BA in Psychology, Am. Internat. Coll., 1959; LLB, Boston Coll., 1960; JD, New Eng. Sch. Law, 1962. Bar: Mass. 1963, U.S. Dist. Ct. Mass. 1963, U.S. Dist. Ct. Conn. 1979, U.S. Tax Ct. 1981. Ptnr. Michelman & Burstein, Springfield, 1963-70; pvt. practice law, 1970-73; sr. ptnr. Burstein & Dupont, 1973-88, Burstein Law Offices, 1988—. Pres., treas. Springfield Investment Assocs., 1963—. Author: (pamphlet) You and the Law, 1963. Class chmn. alumni fund raising drive Am. Internat. Coll., 1969-76m life mem. Alumni Varsity Club; vice chmn. Longmeadow (Mass.) Dem. Com.; active Beth El Temple and Jewish Cmty. Ctr., Springfield. Mem. ATLA, Mass. Bar Assn., Hampden County Bar Assn., Masons, Shriners. Criminal, Family and matrimonial, Personal injury. Home: 29 Willett Dr Longmeadow MA 01106-2037 Office: 1331 E Columbus Ave Springfield MA 01105-2539

BURSTEIN, NEIL ALAN, lawyer; b. N.Y.C., June 24, 1951; s. Edward Stuart and Pauline (Linksman) B. B.S., Union Coll., Schenectady, 1973; J.D., Albany Law Sch., 1976; LL.M., NYU, 1983. Bar: N.Y. 1977, U.S. Dist. Ct. (so. dist.) N.Y. 1981. Assoc. Clayman, Mead & Gallo, Schenectady, 1976-78; gen. atty. Waldes Kohinour, Inc., Long Island City, N.Y., 1978-81; assoc. counsel Saks Fifth Ave., N.Y.C., 1981-86; mng. atty. Trans World Airlines Inc., 1986—; legis. counsel to N.Y. state senator A. Frederick Meyerson, Albany, 1973-76. Contbr. chpt. to Entertainment Law (Selz & Simensky), 1983, articles to profl. jours. William C. Saxton scholar Albany Law Sch., 1973. Mem. Assn. Bar City N.Y., ABA, N.Y. State Bar Assn. General corporate, Labor, Trademark and copyright. Home: 305 E 86th St New York NY 10028-4702 Office: Trans World Airlines 605 3rd Ave New York NY 10158-0180

BURSTEIN, RICHARD JOEL, lawyer; b. Detroit, Feb. 9, 1945; s. Harry Seymour and Florence (Rosen) B.; m. Gayle Lee Handmaker, Dec. 21, 1969; children: Stephanie Faith, Melissa Amy. Grad., U. Mich., 1966; JD, Wayne State U., 1969. Bar: Mich. 1969, U.S. Ct. Appeals (ea. dist.) Mich. 1969. Ptnr. Smith Miro Hirsch & Brody, Detroit, 1969-81, Honigman Miller Schwartz & Cohn, Detroit, 1981-96. Bd. dirs. Sandy Corp., Troy, Mich.; bd. dirs. Met. Affairs Corp., Detroit; co-chmn. Artrain. Mem. Am. Coll. Real Estate Lawyers. Real property. Office: Honigman Miller Schwartz & Cohn 32270 Telegraph RdSuite 225 Bingham Farms MI 48025*

BURT, JACQUELYN JEAN-MARIE, law school administrator; b. Pompton Plains, N.J., Feb. 17, 1963; d. John Joseph and Phyllis (Boob) B.; m. Frank John Tanzola, July 21, 1991; children: Alexandra, Harrison. AB, Harvard U., 1984; JD, Loyola U. Sch. Law, 1988. Bar: Ohio 1988, U.S. Ct. Appeals (6th cir.) 1988, N.J. 1989. Comml. litigation atty., Columbus, Ohio, 1988-89, Newark, 1989-92; dir. career svcs. Seton Hall U. Law Sch., 1993—. Adj. prof. law Seton Hall U. Law Sch., 1991—; mem. N.J. Supreme Ct. Com. on Women and the Law, 1994—. Co-author: Beyond LA Law, 1997. Class mother Hilltop Country Day Sch. Mem. Nat. Assn. Law Placement, ABA, N.J. Bar Assn., Sussex County Bar Assn. Avocations: movies, dance, swimming, collecting Dept. 56 Dickens houses. Home: 39 Heighwood Trl Sparta NJ 07871-1401 Office: Seton Hall U Sch Law One Newark Pl Newark NJ 07102

BURT, JEFFREY AMSTERDAM, lawyer; b. Phila., Apr. 27, 1944; s. Samuel Matthew and Esther (Amsterdam) B.; m. Sandra Cas, Dec. 17, 1967; children: Stephen, Daniel, Jonathan, Andrew. BA, Princeton, 1966; LLB, Yale U., 1970; MA in Econs., 1970. Bar: Md. 1971, DC 1971. Law clk. to judge U.S. Ct. Appeals (4th cir.), Balt., 1970-71; assoc. Arnold & Porter, Washington, 1971-77; ptnr., 1978—. Adj. prof. law Georgetown U., 1987-95; frequent lectr. Pres., Green Acres, Inc. Ind. Sch., Rockville, Md., 1984-86. Author: (with others) International Joint Ventures, 1986, 2nd edit., 1992; co-editor: Joint Ventures with Internat. Ptnrs., 1997. Mem. ABA (co-chairperson NIS Law Com. Sect. Internat. Law and Practice 1992-98), Russian Am. C. of C. (dir., sec.). Administrative and regulatory, Federal civil litigation, Private international. Office: Arnold & Porter 555 12th St NW Washington DC 20004-1206

BURT, ROBERT GENE, lawyer, educator; b. Tucson, Sept. 7, 1944; s. Jack A. and Eva Grace (Colton) B.; m. Stasia Payne, June 7, 1968; children: Jason R., Ashley A. AA, N.Mex. Mil. Inst., Roswell, 1964; BA, U. Ariz, 1965, JD, 1972; LLM in Taxation, Georgetown U., 1973. Bar: Ariz. 1972, D.C. 1973, Oreg. 1977. Appeals atty., spl. asst. to asst. atty. gen. tax div. U.S. Dept. Justice, 1973-75, trial atty., 1975-77; sole practice, Portland, Oreg., 1978; ptnr. Robert G. Burt, P.C., Portland, 1978-80, Burt & Hagen, P.C., Portland, 1980-85, Burt & Day, P.C., Portland, 1985-86; shareholder Burt & Assocs. P.C., Portland, 1986—; adj. prof. Lewis and Clark Coll.; editor: Professional Insight column, 1990-94. Capt. U.S. Army, 1967-71. Decorated Silver Star, Bronze Star with two oak leaf clusters, Purple Heart with one oak leaf cluster, Army Commendation medal with 4 oak leaf clusters, Air Medal with oak leaf cluster. Recipient Spl. Meritous award U.S. Dept. Justice, Washington, 1975. Mem. ABA, Oreg. Bar Assn. (chmn. taxation sect. 1988-89, chmn. CPA's joint com. 1989-90), Multnomah County Bar Assn., Oreg. Trial Lawyers Assn., Nat. Health Lawyers Assn., Oreg. Soc. Hosp. Attys., Ariz. State Bar, D.C. Bar. Episcopalian. Clubs: Multnomah Athletic (Portland). General corporate, Corporate taxation, Taxation, general. Office: 1515 SW 5th Ave Ste 600 Portland OR 97201-5449

BURTCH, JACK WILLARD, JR. lawyer; b. Youngstown, Ohio, Dec. 11, 1946; s. Jack Willard and Elizabeth Bentley (Robinson) B.; m. Susan Lee Thielemann, June 21, 1969; children: Anson James, Douglas Robinson. BA, Wesleyan U., 1969; JD, Vanderbilt U., 1972. Bar: Ohio 1972, Va. 1973. Assoc. Hunton and Williams, Richmond, Va., 1973-80; ptnr. McSweeney, Burtch & Crump PC, 1980-2001, Va. Law & Govt. Affairs PC, Richmond, 2001—. Active Episc. Diocese Va.; bd. dirs. Christchurch (Va.) Sch., 1995—. Capt. USAR, 1972-80. Republican. Labor. Home: 3205 Hawthorne Ave Richmond VA 23222-2518 Office: Va Law & Govt Affairs PC PO Box 8088 1015 E Main St 4th Fl Richmond VA 23223-0088 E-mail: jburtch@vlga.com

BURTON, JOHN PAUL (JACK BURTON), lawyer; b. New Orleans, Feb. 26, 1943; s. John Paul and Nancy (Key) B.; m. Anne Ward; children: Jennifer, Susanna, Derek, Catherine. BBA magna cum laude, La. Tech. U., 1965; LLB, Harvard U., 1968. Bar: N.Mex. 1968, U.S. Dist. Ct. N.Mex. 1968, U.S. Ct. Appeals (10th cir.) 1973, U.S. Supreme Ct. 1979. Assoc. Rodey, Dickason, Sloan, Akin & Robb, Albuquerque, 1968-74, dir., 1974—, chmn. comml. dept., 1980-81, mng. dir. Santa Fe, 1986-90. Co-author: Boundary Disputes in New Mexico, 1992, Unofficial Update on the Uniform Ltd. Liability Co. Act, 1994. Mem. Nat. Coun. Commrs. on Uniform State Laws, 1989—, drafting com. UCC Article 5, 1990-95, UCC Article 9, 1993-95, UCC Articles 2 and 2A, 1999—, Power-of Sale Foreclosure Act, 1999—, Uniform Ltd. Liability Co. Act, 1993-95, Legis. Coun., 1991-99, divsn. chair, 1993-95, 99—, chair legis. com., 1995-99, exec. com., 1995-99; joint editl. bd. Uninc. Bus. Orgns., 1994-95, Trust and Estates Acts, 1999—; pres. Brunn Sch., 1987-89. Fellow Am. Coll. Real Estate Lawyers, Lex Mundi Coll. Mediators; mem. ABA, Am. Law Inst. (rep. to UCC Article 5 drafting com. 1992-95), Am. Coll. Mortgage Attys., Am. Arbitration Assn. (mem. panel arbitrators), N.Mex. State Bar Assn. (chmn. comml. litig. and antitrust sect. 1985-86). Federal civil litigation, Contracts commercial, Real property. Office: Rodey Dickason Sloan Akin & Robb PA PO Box 1357 Santa Fe NM 87504-1357 E-mail: jpburton@rodey.com

BURTON, RANDALL JAMES, lawyer; b. Sacramento, Feb. 4, 1950; s. Edward Jay and Bernice Mae (Overton) B.; children: Kelly Jacquelyn, Andrew Jameson; m. Kimberly D. Rogers, Apr. 29, 1989. BA, Rutgers U., 1972; JD, Southwestern U., 1975. Bar: Calif. 1976, U.S. Dist. Ct. (ea. dist.) Calif. 1976, U.S. Dist. Ct. (no. dist.) Calif., 1990, U.S. Supreme Ct, 1991. Assoc. Brekke & Mathews, Citrus Heights, Calif., 1976; pvt. practice, Sacramento, 1976-93; ptnr. Burton & White, Sacramento, 1993—; judge pro tem Sacramento Small Claims Ct., 1982—. Bd. dirs. North Highlands Recreation and Park Dist., 1978-86, Family Svc. Agy. of Sacramento, 1991-96; active Local Bd. 22, Selective Svc., 1982—, Active 20-30 Club of Sacramento, 1979-90, pres., 1987. Recipient Disting. Citizen award, Golden Empire Council, Boy Scouts Am. Mem. Sacramento Bar Assn., Sacramento Young Lawyers Assn. Presbyterian. Lodge: Rotary (pres. Foothill-Highlands club 1980-81). Family and matrimonial, Personal injury, Probate. Office: 1540 River Park Dr Ste 224 Sacramento CA 95815-4609

BUSALD, E. ANDRÉ, lawyer; b. New Albany, Ind., Mar. 24, 1946; s. Edward Albert and Bernadine (Marsh) B.; m. Janis Kathman, July 16, 1966; children: Jacqueline, Andre, Ethan Ashley. BA, Holy Cross Coll., 1968; JD, U. Ky., 1970. Bar: Ky. 1971, Ohio 1989, U.S. Dist. Ct. (ea. and we. dist.) Ky., U.S. Dist. Ct. (so. dist.) Ohio, U.S. Supreme Ct. Trial lawyer Busald, Funk, Zevely, P.S.C., Florence, Ky., 1971—. Adj. prof. law Salmon P. Chase Law Sch., Highland Heights, Ky., 1976-86, bd. overseers, 1986—; lectr. in field; spl. justice Ky. Supreme Ct.; spl. judge U.S. Dist. Ct. (ea. dist.) Ky. Mem. Am. Trial Lawyers Assn. (bd.dirs. 1988-94), Ky. Acad. Trial Attys. (bd. dirs. 1972—, pres. 1985), No. Ky. Bar Assn. (pres. 1986, bd. dirs. 1985-97), Salmon P. Chase Inn of Ct. (pres. 1994). Federal civil litigation, General civil litigation, State civil litigation. Office: Busald Funk Zevely 226 Main St PO Box 6910 Florence KY 41022-6910

BUSBEE, KLINE DANIEL, JR. retired law educator, lawyer; b. Macon, Ga., Mar. 14, 1933; s. Kline Daniel and Bernice (Anderson) B.; children: Rodgers Christopher, Jon Edward. BBA, So. Meth. U., 1961, JD, 1962. Ptnr. Worsham, Forsythe, Sampels & Busbee, Dallas, 1962-70, Locke, Purnell, Rain & Harrell, P.C., Dallas, 1970-98, Gibson, Dunn & Crutcher, Dallas, 1998-99. Adj. prof. law So. Meth. U. Sch. Law, 1974-83, 92; adj. prof. pub. internat. law U. Tex. Grad. Sch. Mgmt., Dallas; bd. dirs. Atmos Energy Corp. Mem. ABA, Tex. Bar Assn., Dallas Country Club, Dallas Com. on Fgn. Rels., Snowmass Club, Petroleum Club. Home: 4360 San Carlos St Dallas TX 75205-2052 E-mail: kdbusbeelaw@aol.com

BUSEY, PHIL GORDON, lawyer; b. Oklahoma City, Jan. 22, 1952; s. C.L. and Hazel (Brown) B.; m. Catherine Jean Callaway, Sept. 17, 1977; children: Phil G. Jr., Brian Marshall, Emily C. BA in Polit. Sci. and History, Oklahoma City U., 1974; JD, Okla. U., 1977. Bar: Okla. 1978, U.S. Dist. Ct. (we. dist.) Okla., U.S. Ct. Appeals (10th cir.) 1987. Aircraft and ins. examiner Insured Aircraft Title Service, Inc., Oklahoma City, 1975-77; asst. v.p., trust officer Am.-First Title and Trust Co., 1977-79; asst. gen. counsel First Nat. Bank and Trust Co. and First Oklahoma Bancorp., Inc., 1979-81; atty. Linn, Helms, Kirk & Burkett, 1981-82; v.p., atty. Penn Sq. Bank, 1982; atty. Kornfeld Franklin & Phillips, 1982-84, Robinson, Boese & Davidson, Tulsa, 1984-85; of counsel Kirk & Chaney, 1985-91; shareholder Pats & Payne, P.C., 1987-91, Hall, Estill, Attys. at Law, 1991-95; of counsel Phillips McFadden, 1995-97; sr. v.p., global counsel Advanica Corp., 1997-99; pres., CEO ProForma Group Inc., 1999-2000, Busey Resource Group Inc., 2000—; atty. in pvt. practice, 2000—. Adj. prof. South Oklahoma City Jr. Coll. and Inst. of Banking, 1979-82, Oklahoma City U., 1983-95; mem. Okla. Regents Coun. for Career and Tech., 1999—. Contbr. articles to profl. jours. Baseball coach YMCA Youth Baseball team, Oklahoma City, 1977-93; bd. dirs. Ch. of the Servant, Oklahoma City, 1983; pres. Classen Awards Alumni Assn., Oklahoma City, 1983-95; mem. adminstrv. bd. St. Lukes United Meth. Ch., 1998—; mem. alumni bd. Oklahoma City U., 1997-99. Mem. ABA, Okla. Bar Assn., Oklahoma County Bar Assn., Nat. Assn. Bond Lawyers, Okla. State C. of C., So. Oklahoma City C. of C. (bd. dirs. 2000—), Phi Alpha Delta, Oklahoma City Young Men's Dinner Club. Democrat. Home: 6401 Winchester Dr Oklahoma City OK 73162-1722 Office: Kirk & Chaney 1300 Midland Center 134 Robert S Kerr Ave Oklahoma City OK 73102-6601 E-mail: buseypg@aol.com

BUSH, MICHAEL KEVIN, lawyer; b. Davenport, Iowa, May 23, 1952; s. Roy Alvin and A. Carmelita (Gilroy) B.; m. Kathleen M. Grace, Nov. 26, 1977; children: Kelly Anne, Daniel Stephen, Brendan Michael. BA, U. Notre Dame, South Bend, Ind., 1974; JD, Valparaiso (Ind.) U., 1977. Bar: Iowa 1977, U.S. Dist. Ct. (no. dist.) Iowa 1980, U.S. Ct. Appeals (7th cir.) 1980, U.S. Dist. Ct. (ctrl. dist.) Ill. 1983, U.S. Ct. Appeals (8th cir.) 1996, U.S. Supreme Ct. 1990, Ill. 1999. Mem. Wells, McNally & Bowman, Davenport, 1977-80; prosecutor Scott County Atty.'s Office, 1980-82; mem. Henninger & Henninger, 1979-82; founding ptnr. Walton, Creen & Bush, 1982-86; ptnr. Carlin, Hellstrom & Bittner, 1987—; sr. ptnr. Bush, Motto, Creen and Hoffman, 2000—. Recipient Iowa Trial Lawyer's Public Justice award, 2001. Mem. ATLA (sustaining mem.), Am. Bd. Trial Advocates (assoc.), Iowa Assn. Trial Lawyers (Down Pub. Justice award 2000), Million Dollar Advocates Forum, Iowa Bar Assn., Scott County Bar Assn., Am. Coll. Barristers (sr. counsel). Roman Catholic. Avocation: tennis. Personal injury. Home: 2806 E 42nd Ct Davenport IA 52807-1576 Office: Carlin Hellstrom & Bittner 5505 Victoria Ave Ste 100 Davenport IA 52807

BUSH, RAYMOND GEORGE, lawyer; b. Phila., Mar. 27, 1952; s. Raymond George and Florence Dorothy (Glassman) B.; children: Katherine Elizabeth, James Crisfield, Margaret Lindsley, Abigail Josephine. BA, Widener U., 1975; MPA, Temple U., 1980, postgrad., 1981-83, JD, 1988. Bar: Pa. 1988, N.J. 1989, U.S. Ct. Appeals (3d cir.) 1988, U.S. Ct. Appeals (fed. cir.) 1989, U.S. Ct. Mil. Appeals 1989, U.S. Dist. Ct. (ea. dist.) Pa. 1989, U.S. Dist. Ct. (mid. dist.) Pa. 1991, U.S. Supreme Ct. 1993, U.S. Dist. Ct. N.J. 1995; cert. estate practitioner. Employee rels. specialist regional office U.S. Dept. Health and Human Svcs., Phila., 1980-83; labor rels. officer U.S. VA, Coatsville, Pa., 1983; paralegal Office Gen. Counsel U.S. Dept. Health and Human Svcs., Phila., 1984; labor rels. specialist Fed. Labor Rels. Authority, 1984-88; mgmt. rep. U.S. Dept. Navy, 1988-89; assoc. Duane, Morris and Heckscher, 1989-90, Tallman, Hudders & Sorentino, Allentown, Pa., 1990-91; pvt. practice Bethlehem, 1991—. Lectr. at profl. meetings and confs.; adj. asst. prof. Widener U., Chester, Pa., 1988-89, instr. paralegal program; adj. faculty Nat. Bus. Inst.; adj. instr. Cedar Crest, Allentown, Pa., 1996-99, Muhlenberg Coll., Allentown, Pa., 1999—. Contbr. numerous articles to profl. publs. Bd. dirs. Community Dispute Settlement of Delaware County, Media, Pa., 1988-89; community mediator, bd. dirs. Common Ground, Bethlehem, Pa., 1989-90; personnel com. Cathedral Ch. of Nativity, Bethlehem, 1990, also vestry and solicitor; fundraising capt. Minsi Trail coun. Boy Scouts Am., 1990; active Leadership Lehigh Valley, 1991. Mem. ABA (labor and employment law sect., com. on fed. svc. labor and employment law), Pa. Bar Assn. (labor and employment law sect.), Phila. Bar Assn. (labor com.), Indsl. Rels. Rsch. Assn. (planning com. Phila. chpt. 1986-88, v.p. programming 1991—, mem. adv. bd., past pres. NE chpt.), Soc. Fed. Labor Rels. Profls. (pres. Mid-Atlantic chpt. 1981-88, exec. dir. 1988-89, nat. exec. bd. 1986-87), Northampton County Bar Assn. (chair labor rels. com. 1990-94, mem. pers. com. 1994—), Pi Gamma Mu, Phi Delta Phi. Republican. Episcopalian. Avocations: sailing, cross-country skiing, golf, photography, classical music. General civil litigation, Estate planning, Labor. Home: 226 E Wall St Bethlehem PA 18018-6118 Office: 65 E Elizabeth Ave Ste 901 Bethlehem PA 18018-6506 E-mail: RGBush@nni.com

BUSH, REX CURTIS, lawyer; b. Longview, Wash., Oct. 21, 1953; s. Rex Cole Bush and Arline (Quanstrom) Fitzgerald; m. Joy Ann Pallas, July 22, 1977 (div.); children: Alicia, Angela, Carrie; m. Janet Rae Hicks July 2, 1988; children: Jeni, Mykal. BA cum laude, Brigham Young U., 1980; JD, U. Utah, 1983. Bar: Utah 1983, U.S. Dist. Ct. (no. dist.) Utah 1983, U.S. Tax Ct. 1985. Tax atty. Arthur Andersen & Co., Houston, 1983-84; assoc. Mortensen & Neider, Midvale, Utah, 1984-85; in-house counsel Fin. Futures, Salt Lake City, 1985-87; registrar Hollander Cons., Portland, Oreg., 1987-88; in-house counsel Bennett Leasing, Salt Lake City, 1987-88; pres. Bush Law Firm, Sandy, Utah, 1988—. Judge pro tempore 3d Cir. Ct., Salt Lake City, 1985-87. Author: (booklet) What To Do in Case of an Automobile Accident, 1994. Mayor University Village, U. Utah, 1981-82; Rep. candidate Utah state senate, 1992; Rep. voting dist. sec., treas., 1992. Recipient Meritorious Leadership award, Nat. Com. for Employer Support of Guard and Reserve, 1990. Mem. ATLA, Utah Trial Lawyers Assn., Utah State Bar (chmn. small firm and solo practitioners com. 1994-96, honored for outstanding svc. to legal profession 1996). Personal injury. Office: Bush Law Firm 9615 S 700 E Sandy UT 84070-3557

BUSH, THOMAS NORMAN, lawyer; b. Lancaster County, Va., Nov. 13, 1947; s. T. Edwin and Willie Ann (Landman) B.; m. Carolyn Sue Brown; children: Jason, Jennifer. BS in Acctg., Va. Tech, 1970; JD, U. Richmond, 1977. Bar: Va.; CPA, Va. Staff acct. KPMG Peat Marwick, Richmond, Va., 1970-71; sr. auditor U.S. Army, Frankfurt, Germany, 1972-74; pvt. practice acctg. Richmond, 1974-77; tax mgr. PricewaterhouseCoopers, 1977-81; v.p., tax counsel Fort James Corp., 1981-98, Deerfield, Ill., 1999- . V.p. Fort James Found., 1993—; chmn. corp. matching gift U. Richmond Annual Fund steering com., 1996-97; mem. dept. acctg. adv. bd. Va. Tech., 1991—; mem. steering com. Ctr. for Leadership, Govt. and Global Econs., 1995-99. Mem. ABA, AICPA, Va. State Bar, Internat. Fiscal Assn., Am. Forest and Paper Assn. (tax com. 1986-94), Tax Execs. Inst. (pres. Va. chpt. 1989-90, regional v.p. 1995-96, bd. dirs. 1993-96, nominating com. 1996-97, vice chair IRS adminstrv. affairs com. 1997-99, mem. IRS customer satisfaction task force 1998-99), Tax Found. (program com. 1996—), Va. Soc. CPAs, Va. Mfrs. Assn. (tax com. 1988-99), Civitan (pres. West End Richmond 1982). Methodist. Avocations: coaching, baseball, travel. Finance, Mergers and acquisitions, Corporate taxation. Home: 4407 4 Winds Ln Northbrook IL 60062-1064 Office: Fort James Corp 1650 Lake Cook Rd Deerfield IL 60015-4753 E-mail: norm.bush@gapac.com

BUSH, WILLIAM MERRITT, lawyer; b. Long Beach, Calif., June 23, 1941; s. Lloyyd Merritt and Barbara Ann (Bufkin) B.; m. Dorothy Irene Vasvary, June 25, 1966; children: Steven Merritt, Amy Elizabeth. BA, Stanford U., 1963; JD, U. Calif., Hastings, 1966. Bar: Calif. 1967, U.S. Dist. Ct. (ctrl. dist.) Calif. 1967, U.S. Dist. Ct. (so. dist.) Calif. 1976. Assoc. Dannemeyer & Tuohey, Fullerton, Calif., 1967, Miller, Bush & Minnott, Fullerton, 1967-69, ptnr., 1970-88; pvt. practice, 1989—. Lectr. on fundamentals of family law Calif. Continuing Edn. of Bar, 1981—. Human rels. commr., City of Fullerton, 1971-77; mem. site coun., Fullerton H.S., 1986-88. Fellow Am. Acad. Matrimonial Lawyers; mem. ABA, Orange

County Bar Assn. (dir. 1982-85), Calif. State Bar (mem. family law cons. group, family law sect. 1979, mem. family law adv. commn. 1979-85, chmn. commn. 1982-85, bd. legal specialization 1982-89, chmn. 1987-88), Kiwanis. Republican. Methodist. Avocations: computers, jogging, body surfing. Family and matrimonial. Office: 110 E Wilshire Ave Ste 210 Fullerton CA 92832-1959 E-mail: wmbushesq@lawbush.com

BUSHNELL, GEORGE EDWARD, III, lawyer; b. Detroit, Feb. 18, 1952; s. George Edward Jr. and Elizabeth (Whelden) B.; m. Eileen Mary Maguire, Sept. 16, 1989; children: Ann-Elizabeth, Emily Spears, George Edward. BA, Bucknell U., 1974; JD, Emory U., 1981. Bar: Ga. 1981, D.C. 1983, N.Y. 1986. Vol. U.S. Peace Corps, Burkina Faso, 1974-76, tng. dir., 1976-77; staff asst. to hon. Lucien Nedzi U.S. Ho. of Reps., Washington, 1977-78; assoc. Duncan, Allen and Mitchell, Ivory Coast, Congo, 1981-85, Shearman & Sterling, N.Y.C., 1985-91; corp. counsel Joseph E. Seagram & Sons, Inc., 1991-2001; v.p., corp. counsel Vivendi Universal S.A., 2001—. Mem. ABA, N.Y. State Bar Assn. General corporate, Finance, Mergers and acquisitions. Home: 1075 Park Ave Apt 2A New York NY 10128-1003 Office: Joseph E Seagram & Sons Inc 800 3rd Ave New York NY 10022-7604

BUSHNELL, GEORGE EDWARD, JR. lawyer; b. Detroit, Nov. 15, 1924; s. George E. and Ida Mary (Bland) B.; children: George Edward III, Christopher Gilbert Whelden, Robina McLeod Bushnell Hogan. Mil. student, U. Kans., 1943; BA, Amherst Coll., 1948; LLB, U. Mich., 1951; LLD, Detroit Coll. Law, 1995. Bar: Mich. 1951, D.C. 1980, U.S. Dist. Ct. (ea. dist.) Mich. 1951, U.S. Dist. Ct. (we. dist.) Mich. 1971, U.S. Ct. Appeals (6th cir.) 1955, U.S. Ct. Appeals (fed. cir.) 1995, U.S. Ct. Appeals for the Armed Forces 1995, U.S. Supreme Ct. 1971, U.S. Ct. Internat. Trade 1995. From assoc. to sr. ptnr. Miller, Canfield, Paddock and Stone, Detroit, 1953-77, of counsel, 1989-2001; sr. ptnr. Bushnell, Gage, Doctoroff & Reizen, Southfield, Mich., 1977-89. Commr. Mich. Jud. Tenure Commn., 1969-83, chmn., 1978-80; pres. State Bar Mich., 1975-76; bd. dirs. Nat. Jud. Coll., 1985-89; mem. Mich. Atty. Discipline Bd., 1990-96; lectr. in field. Elder Grosse Pointe Meml. Ch.; moderator Detroit Presbytery, United Presbyn. Ch. U.S.A., 1972, pres. program agy. bd., 1972-76; bd. dirs. Econ. Devel. Corp. of Detroit, 1976—, Econ. Growth Corp. of Detroit, 1978-96, Tax Increment Fin. Authority, Detroit, 1984—, Econ. Devel. Authority, Detroit, 1988-98, Mich. Partnership to Prevent Gun Violence, 1995—, pres.-elect, 1999-2000; bd. trustees New Detroit, Inc., 1972—, chmn., 1974-75. Served with USAR, 1942-56. Decorated Bronze Star, Army Commendation medal. Mem. NAACP (life, co-chmn. fight for freedom fund dinner 1968), ABA (ho. of dels. 1976—, chmn. ho. of dels. 1988-90, pres.-elect 1993-94, pres. 1994-95, past pres. 1995-96, others, Trial Attys. of Am. (pres. 1971-89), State Bar Mich. . bd. of bar commrs. 1970-76, pres. 1975-76, John Hensel award for svcs. to the arts 1990, Roberts P. Hudson award for spl. svcs. to the bar and the people of Mich., 1979, 85, Cooley Law Sch. Louis A. Smith (disting. jurist award 1995), Detroit Bar Assn. (bd. dirs. 1958-65, pres. 1964-65, past pres. com. 1980—, bench & bar award for svc. to the judicial sys., the legal profession and the cmty. 1989), Nat. Conf. of Bar Pres. (pres. 1984-85), 6th Jud. Cir. Conf. (life), Am. Law Inst., Am. Arbitration Assn. (bd. dirs. 1970-82), Am. Coll. Trial Lawyers, Am. Bar Found. (life), Am. Judicature Soc. (bd. dirs. 1977-82), Can. Bar Assn. (hon.), Internat. Soc. Barristers, Fed. Bar Assn., Masons (33 deg.), Met. Club (N.Y.C.) Phi Delta Phi, Psi Upsilon. Democrat. Federal civil litigation, State civil litigation, General corporate. Office: Miller Canfield Paddock & Stone 150 W Jefferson Ave Ste 2500 Detroit MI 48226-4416 E-mail: bushness@millermanfield.com

BUSNER, PHILIP H. retired lawyer; b. Bklyn., Mar. 26, 1927; s. Joseph and Ray (Grajewer) B.; m. Naomi Marcia Greenfield, June 24, 1951; children: Joan Alexandra, Carey Elizabeth. BA cum laude, NYU, 1949; LLB, Harvard U., 1952. Bar: N.Y. 1953, U.S. Dist. Ct. (so. dist.) N.Y. 1956, U.S. Dist. Ct. (ea. dist.) N.Y. 1958, U.S. Ct. Appeals (2d cir.) 1956, U.S. Supreme Ct. 1974. Assoc. Rein, Mound & Cotton, N.Y.C., 1953, Hess, Mela, Segall, Popkin & Guterman, N.Y.C., 1954-55, Carroad & Carroad, N.Y.C., 1955-72; ptnr. Young, Sonnenfeld & Busner, 1972-75, Sonnenfeld & Busner, N.Y.C., 1976-78, Sonnenfeld, Busner & Weinstein, N.Y.C., 1978-85, Sonnenfeld, Busner & Richman, N.Y.C., 1986-88; pvt. practice Great Neck, N.Y., 1989-97; ret., 1998. Trustee Asthmatic Children's Found. N.Y., 1978-87; adminstrv. judge N.Y.C. Dept. Transp., 1989-93; arbitrator N.Y.C. Civil Ct., 1990-92, Nassau County Dist. Ct., 1990-95, Suffolk County Dist. Ct., 1990-93. With USAAF, 1945-47. Mem. Am. Arbitration Assn. (arbitrator 1990-92), Phi Beta Kappa. Home: One Todd Dr Sands Point NY 11050

BUSSEWITZ, ROY JON, lawyer; b. Hartford, Wis., Mar. 19, 1944; s. Reginald Max and Bernice (Kadolph) B.; m. Joyce Ann O'Donnell, Aug. 24, 1980; children: Kathleen Ann, Christine Marie. BS in Pharmacy, U. Wis., 1967; JD, Valparaiso U., 1973. Bar: Wis. 1973. Prof. health law U. Wis., Milw., 1973-78; legal cons. State of Wis., Madison, 1979; legis. asst., health U.S. Senator Gaylord Nelson, Washington, 1979-81; legis. counsel Am. Health Care Assn., 1981; exec. dir. Nat. Assn. Med. Equipment Suppliers, Alexandria, Va., 1982-84; dir. govt. rels. Nat. Assn. Pvt. Psychiat. Hosps., Washington, 1984-85; dir. fed. govt. affairs Glaxo Inc., Alexandria, 1984-88; cons., 1988-91; v.p. managed care/telecomms. Nat. Assn. Chain Drug Stores, Alexandria, 1991—. Bd. dirs., mem. working group Electronic Data Exch., Nat. Coun. Prescription Programs. Mem. Wis. Bar Assn. Avocations: tennis, golf, gardening, photography. Home: 1103 Potomac Ln Alexandria VA 22308-2534 Office: Nat Assn Chain Drug Stores 413 N Lee St Alexandria VA 22313 E-mail: rbussewitz@nacds.org

BUSTAMANTE, NESTOR, lawyer; b. Havana, Cuba, Apr. 20, 1960; came to the U.S., 1961; s. Nestor and Clara Rosa (Sanchez) B.; m. Marilyn Gonzalez, Sept. 20, 1986; children: Tiffany Alexandra, Nestor C. AA, U. Fla., 1980, BS in Journalism, 1982, JD, 1985. Bar: Fla. 1986, U.S. Dist. Ct. (so. dist.) Fla. 1989, U.S. Supreme Ct. 1991. Asst. state atty. State Atty.'s Office 11th Cir., Miami, 1986-88; juvenile serious offender prosecutor State Atty.'s Office, 1987-88, spl. prosecutor, gang prosecutor, 1987-88; asst. divsn. chief State Atty.'s Office-11th Jud. Cir., 1987-88; of counsel Fernandez-Caubi, Fernandez & Aguilar et al., 1988-89; atty. Ferencik, Libanoff, Brandt and Bustamante PA, Ft. Lauderdale, Fla., 1989—, ptnr., 1996—. Mem. code and rules of evidence com. The Fla. Bar, 1989-90, judicial evaluation com., 2000; adj. faculty dept constrn. mgmt. Fla. Internat. U. Contbr. articles to newsletters. Mem. Miami-Dade Constrn. Trades Qualifying Bd. Named Hon. mem. Quien es Quien Publs., Inc., N.Y.C., 1990. Mem. ATLA (scoring judge nat. finals student trial advocacy competition 1994, 95), Fed. Bar Assn., Dade County Bar Assn. (mem. juvenile divsn. com. 1988-92, mem. media and pub. rels. com. 1989-91, mem. constrn. law com. 1990-91), Phi Delta Phi, U. Fla. Alumni Assn. Contracts commercial, Construction, State civil litigation. Office: Ferencik Libanoff Brandt & Bustamante PA 150 S Pine Island Rd Ste 400 Fort Lauderdale FL 33324-2667 E-mail: flbbnb@mindspring.com

BUTCHER, BRUCE CAMERON, lawyer; b. N.Y.C., Feb. 17, 1947; s. John Richard and Dorothy Helen (Wehner) B.; m. Kathryn Ann Fiddler, Oct. 12, 1979; 1 child, Kristen Ann. BS, Belknap Coll., 1969; JD, St. John's U., N.Y.C., 1972. Bar: N.Y. 1973, U.S. Dist. Ct. (so. dist.) N.Y. 1974, La. 1980, U.S. Dist. Ct. (ea. dist.) La. 1980, U.S. Ct. Appeals (5th and 11th cirs.) 1981, Tex. 1993. Assoc. Laporte and Meyers, N.Y.C., 1972-73; asst. chief contract div. Corp. Counsel's Office City of N.Y., 1973-79; ptnr. Chaffe, McCall, Phillips, Toler & Sarpy, New Orleans, 1980-84; prin. Bruce C. Butcher, P.C., Metairie, La., 1985-93; of counsel Smith Martin & Schneider, New Orleans, 1993-94; gen. coun. The Vulcan Group, Birmingham, Ala., 1994-95, Favalora Constructors, Inc., 1995—; pres., gen. counsel Tailgators Restaurant, LLC, New Orleans, 1994-99. Mem. ABA (regional chmn. pub. report 1975, state chmn. pub. contracts sect. 1984-95, cert. of performance 1975), La. Bar Assn., Am. Arbitration Assn. (mem. arbitration panel U.S. Coun. on Internat. Bus. Arbitration 2001), New Orleans Country Club, New Orleans Athletic Club, Crescent Club. Home: 402 Julia St Apt 307 New Orleans LA 70130-3689 Office: 402 Julia St Ste 307 New Orleans LA 70130-3689 E-mail: bbutch@bellsouth.net

BUTLER, CHARLES RANDOLPH, JR. federal judge; b. N.Y.C., Mar. 28, 1940; BA, Washington and Lee U., 1962; LLB, U. Ala., 1966. Assoc. Hamilton Butler Riddick and LaTour, Mobile, Alal., 1966-69; asst. pub. defender Mobile County, 1969-70, dist. atty., 1971-75; ptnr. Butler and Sullivan, Mobile, 1975-84, Hamilton Butler Riddick Tarlton and Sullivan P.C., Mobile, 1984-88; dist. judge U.S. Dist. Ct. (so. dist.) Ala., 1988-94, chief dist. judge, 1994—. Adj. prof. criminal justice program U. So. Ala., 1972-76; mem. jud. coun. 11th cir., jud. conf. com. on criminal law, 1993-99, jud. conf. com., 1999—; past liaison mem. to long-range planning com. of the AO; past mem. program and adminstrn. subcom., planning for the future and automation subcom., probaton and pretrial umbrella group; mem. exec. com. Jud. Conf. of U.S., 2000—. Lst lt. USAR, 1962-64. Named One of Outstanding Young Men of Am., Mobile County Jaycees, 1971. Office: US Dist Ct 113 Saint Joseph St Mobile AL 36602-3683

BUTLER, JOHN EDWARD, lawyer; b. Teaneck N.J., Dec. 8, 1946; s. John Edward and Alice Mary (Knorr) B.;children: Jennifer, Kathryn, John Michael; m. Elizabeth M. Fair, Mar. 12, 1994. General practice, Personal injury, Probate. Home: 120 E Washington St Ste 825 Syracuse NY 13202-4014

BUTLER, PAUL BASCOMB, JR. lawyer; b. Charleston, S.C., Nov. 27, 1947; s. Paul B. and Mary Anna (Tisdale) B.; m. Virginia Eldridge, June 14, 1969; children: Jeffrey Bryan, Robert Paul. BA, Emory U., 1969, MDiv cum laude, 1972 JD with distinction, 1976. Bar: Ga. 1976, Fla. 1977; ordained to ministry United Meth. Ch., 1970. United Meth. Ch., 1970—; assoc. min. First United Meth. Ch., Phoenix, 1972-73; assoc. Swift, Currie, McGhee and Hiers, Atlanta, 1976-79; ptnr. Butler, Burnette & Pappas, Tampa, Fla., 1979-97, of counsel, 1998—. Chancellor Fla. Ann. Conf. United Meth. Ch., 1997—. Contbr. articles to profl. jours. Chair com. on new church devel. Fla. annual conf. United Meth. Ch., 1996-2000, chair bd. missions and ch. ext. Tampa dist. United Meth. Ch., Inc., 1992-96; pastor Temple Terrace United Meth., Tampa, 1998-2000, sr. pastor, 2000—; bd. dirs. United Meth. Ch. Found., 1999-2000. Mem. ABA (chmn. Nat. Inst. sect. of tort and ins. practice 1987-89, ho. of dels. 1993-95, coun. mem. sect. of tort and ins. practice 1990-93, chmn. task force on civil justice reform, chmn. property ins. law com. 1985-86, editor So. Region Annotated Homeowner's Policy), Fedn. of Ins. and Corp. Counsel (dean Litigation Mgmt. Coll. 1996-98, chair litigation mgmt. coll. adv. coun. 1998-2000, bd. deans 2000—), Def. Rsch. Inst. (chmn. ins. law com. 1989-92, chmn. Amcus com. 1994-97, bd. dirs. 1995-98, vice chair law inst. 1998-99, chair law inst. 1999—), Fla. Def. Lawyers Assn., Hillsborough County Bar Assn., Internat. Assn. Def. Counsel (vice chair property ins. com. 1993-96), Assn. Def. Trial Attys. Democrat. Clubs: Temple Terr. (Fla.) Golf and Country. Avocations: golf, tennis. Federal civil litigation, State civil litigation, Insurance. Office: Butler Burnette & Pappas Ste 1100 6200 W Courtney Campbell Cswy 1100 Tampa FL 33607-5946 E-mail: pbutler@bbplaw.com

BUTLER, REX LAMONT, lawyer; b. New Brunswick, N.J., Mar. 24, 1951; s. Ekker and Beatrice (Curry) B.; m. Stephanie Butler; children: Nijel Jaibrun, Vikteria Lamontra, Octavia Reneè Lamontra, Synclaire Lamontra. AA with honors, Fla. Jr. Coll.., 1975; BA, U. North Fla., 1977; JD, Howard U., 1983. Bar: Alaska 1983, U.S. Dist. Ct. Alaska 1983, U.S. Ct. Appeals (9th cir.) 1984, U.S. Ct. Appeals (D.C. cir.) 1984, U.S. Supreme Ct. 1996. Assoc. M. Ashley Dickerson, Inc., Anchorage, 1983-84; profl. legis. asst. State of Alaska, Juneau, 1984, asst. atty. gen. Anchorage, 1984-85; pvt. practice, 1985—. Adj. prof. law Anchorage C.C., 1985; adj. prof. U. Alaska, Anchorage, 1990—; mem. State Ct. Criminal Pattern Jury Instructions Com., 1997; chmn. lawyer rep. com. Alaska 9th Cir. Judicial Conf., 1997-98. Pres. Alaska Black Caucus, Anchorage, 1986, bd. dirs., 1987-88; gen. counsel NAACP, Anchorage, 1985-87, life mem.; commr. Anchorage Telephone Utility, 1985-87; trustee Anchorage Sr. Ctr., Inc., 1985-87, Shiloh Missionary Bapt. Ch., Anchorage, 1985—; bd. dirs. Ctr. Drug Problems, Anchorage, 1985-86, Alaska Civil Liberties Union, 1987-88; active fin. com. Dem. Cen. Com. Alaska. With USN, 1969-73. Named one of Outstanding Young Men Am., 1984; recipient Cert. Appreciation, African Relief Campaign, 1985. Mem. ABA, Nat. Bar Assn., Nat. Assn. Criminal Defense Lawyers, Alaska Bar Assn., Assn. Trial Lawyers Am., Anchorage Bar Assn., Alaska Trial Lawyers Assn., Lions Internat., Omega Psi Phi (dist. counselor 1995-96, 98—). Democrat. Criminal, Juvenile, Personal injury. Home: PO Box 200025 Anchorage AK 99520-0025 Office: 745 W 4th Ave Ste 300 Anchorage AK 99501-2157 Fax: 907-276-3306. E-mail: rexattys@alaska.net

BUTLER, ROBERT ANTHONY, lawyer; b. Akron, Ohio, Feb. 24, 1932; m. Elda Celli Butler, June 19, 1954 (div. 1976); children: Debra Zahara, Michael C., Dorothy Brundige; m. Carole Cronin Berry, 1976 (div. 1992); 1 child, Beth Ann Butler. JD, Ohio State U., 1955. Bar: Ohio 1956, U.S. Dist. Ct. Ohio 1956, U.S. Ct. Mil. Appeals, 1959; cert. specialist in worker's compensation. Ptnr. William J. Ahern, Columbus, 1960-63; founder, sr. ptnr. Butler, Cincione, DiCuccio & Barnhart, 1963—. Dir. spl. and continuing legal edn. Capitol U. Law Sch.; preceptor Ohio State U. Coll. of Medicine; presenter in field. Contbr. articles to profl. jours. 1st lt. USAF, 1957-60. Mem. Columbus Bar Assn. (former pres., Award of Merit), Franklin County Trial Lawyers Assn. (former pres.). Democrat. Avocations: fiction writing, water colors, calligraphy. Workers' compensation. Office: Butler Cincione DiCuccio & Barnhart 50 W Broad St Ste 700 Columbus OH 43215-3337

BUTLER, SAMUEL COLES, lawyer, director; b. Logansport, Ind., Mar. 10, 1930; s. Melvin Linwood and Jane Lavina (Flynn) B.; m. Sally Eugenia Thackston, June 28, 1952; children: Samuel Coles, Leigh F., Elizabeth J. AB magna cum laude, Harvard U., 1951, LLB magna cum laude, 1954. Bar: D.C. 1954, Ind. 1954, N.Y. 1957. Law clk. to Justice Minton U.S. Supreme Ct., 1954; assoc. Cravath, Swaine & Moore, N.Y.C., 1956-60, ptnr., 1961—. Dir. Ashland Inc., U.S. Trust Corp. Trustee Vassar Coll., 1969-77, N.Y. Pub. Libr., 1979—, chmn. bd., 1999—; trustee Am. Mus. Natural History, 1989-93; chmn. Harvard Coll. Fund, 1977-85; bd. overseers Harvard U., 1982-88, pres. bd., 1986-88; bd. dirs. Culver Ednl. Found., 1981-2001. With U.S. Army, 1954-56. Mem. Coun. Fgn. Rels. General corporate, Mergers and acquisitions, Securities. Home: 1220 Park Ave New York NY 10128-1733 Office: Cravath Swaine & Moore 825 8th Ave New York NY 10019-7475

BUTT, EDWARD THOMAS, JR. lawyer; b. Chgo., Oct. 27, 1947; s. Edward T. and Helen Kathryn (Guy) B.; m. Leslie Laidlaw Hilton, Oct. 20, 1972; children: Julie Guy, Andrew McNaughton. BA, Lawrence U., 1968; JD, U. Mich., 1971. Bar: Ill. 1971, U.S. Dist. Ct. (no. dist.) Ill. 1971, Wis. 1975, U.S. Dist. Ct. (ea. dist.) Wis. 1978, U.S. Ct. Appeals (7th cir.) 1978, U.S. Ct. Claims 1982, U.S. Ct. Appeals (6th cir.) 1986, U.S. Ct. Appeals (6th cir.) 1987, Mich. 1997. Assoc. Wildman, Harrold, Allen & Dixon, Chgo., 1971-75, 76-78, ptnr., 1979-94, Lund & Butt, S.C., Minocqua, Wis., 1975-76; of counsel Swanson, Martin & Bell, Chgo. and Wheaton, Ill., 1994—. Bd. dirs. Constl. Rights Found., Chgo. Mem. ABA, State Bar Wis., State Bar Mich., 7th Cir. Bar Assn., Def. Rsch. Inst., Crystal Lake Yacht Club, Crystal Downs Country Club. Avocations: distance running, sailing, golf. General civil litigation, Insurance, Product liability. Home: Michabou Shores 1006 Tiba Rd Frankfort MI 49635-9216 also: 3903 Forest Ave Western Springs IL 60558-1049 Office: Swanson Martin & Bell 2100 Manchester Rd Ste 1420 Wheaton IL 60187-4534

BUTTERFIELD, G. K., JR. judge; b. Wilson, N.C., Apr. 27, 1947; s. G. K. and Addie (Davis) Butterfield; children: Valeisha Monique, Jenetta Lenai. BS, NC Central U., 1971, JD, 1974. Sr. ptnr. law firm, 1974—88; resident judge NC Superior Ct Dist 7B, 1988—2001; assoc. justice Supreme Ct. N.C., 2001. Office: PO Box 1841 Raleigh NC 27602*

BUTTERKLEE, NEIL HOWARD, lawyer; b. Bklyn., Mar. 17, 1958; s. Samuel and Edith (Uday) B.; m. Arlene Marie Eberle, July 5, 1982. BA, SUNY, Stony Brook, 1980, MS, 1982; MBA, Adelphi U., Garden City, N.Y., 1987; JD, N.Y. Law Sch., 1992. Bar: Conn. 1992, N.Y. 1993, D.C. 1994, U.S. Dist. Ct. (ea. and so. dists.) N.Y. 1993, U.S. Ct. Appeals (D.C. cir.) 1997, U.S. Supreme Ct., 1997. Tech. writer Consolidated Edison Co. N.Y. Inc., N.Y.C., 1982-83, analyst, 1983-89, sr. analyst, 1989-93, atty., 1993-95, staff atty., 1995-99, sr. staff atty., 1999—. Editor: Law Review. Recipient Scholarship N.Y. Law Sch., N.Y.C., 1988-92; nationally ranked fencer U.S. Fencing Assn., 1984-88. Mem. ABA, N.Y. State Bar Assn., Conn. Bar Assn., Assn. Bar City N.Y., Energy Bar Assn. Avocations: golf, writing. Administrative and regulatory, Contracts commercial, FERC practice. Office: Consolidated Edison Co NY 4 Irving Pl Rm 1815 New York NY 10003-3598 E-mail: butterklee@coned.com

BUTTERWORTH, ROBERT A. state attorney general; b. Passaic, N.J., Aug. 20, 1942; m. Marta Prado. BA, BS, U. Fla.; JD, U. Miami. Prosecutor, Fla., 1970-74; circuit and county judge, 1974-78; sheriff Broward County Sheriff's Office, 1978-82; head Fla. Dept. Hwy. Safety and Motor Vehicles, Tallahassee, 1982-84; mayor City of Sunrise, 1984-87; atty. gen. State of Fla., Tallahassee, 1987—. Office: Capitol The Atty Gen Tallahassee FL 32399-1050*

BUTZBAUGH, ELDEN W., JR. lawyer; b. Benton Harbor, Mich., Dec. 2, 1937; s. Elden W. and Lucy Currie (Moore) B.; m. Judith Ann Wise, July 20, 1963; children: Daniel, T.D., Bud, Josh. BA, Western Mich. U., 1961, MBA, 1963; JD, U. Mich., 1968. Bar: Mich. 1968. Pres. Butzbaugh and Ehrenberg, St. Joseph, Mich., 1968—. Author: No-Fault Divorce: Practice and Procedure, 1978. Mem. ABA, State Bar Mich., Berrien County Bar Assn., Assn. Trial Lawyers Am., Mich. Trial Lawyers Assn., Berrien County Trial Lawyers Assn., Benton Harbor-St. Joseph Rotary Club, U. Mich. Alumni Assn., U. Mich. Pres. Club, U. Mich. Victors Club, Western Mich. 300 Club, St. Joseph River Yacht Club, St. Joseph Elks Club. General civil litigation, Personal injury, Product liability. Home: 101 N Pier St Saint Joseph MI 49085-1042 Office: Butzbaugh and Ehrenberg 316 Main St Saint Joseph MI 49085-1298

BUTZNER, JOHN DECKER, JR. federal judge; b. Scranton, Pa., Oct. 2, 1917; B.A., U. Scranton, 1939; LL.B., U. Va., 1941. Bar: Va. bar 1941. Pvt. practice law, Fredericksburg, 1941-58; judge 15th and 39th Jud. Cir. of Va., 1958-62; U.S. judge Ea. Dist. Va., 1962-67; cir. judge U.S. Ct. Appeals (4th cir.), Richmond, Va., 1967—; judge for appointment of ind. counsel U.S. Ct. Appeals for D.C. Cir., 1988-98. Served with USAAF, 1942-45.

BUXBAUM, RICHARD M. law educator, lawyer; b. 1930; AB, Cornell U., 1950, LLB, 1952; LLM, U. Calif., Berkeley, 1953; Dr. (hon.), U. Osnabrück, 1992, Eötvös Lorand U., Budapest, Hungary, 1993. Bar: Calif. 1953, N.Y. 1953. Practice law pvt. firm, Rochester, N.Y., 1957-61; prof. U. Calif., Berkeley, 1961—, dean internat. and area studies, 1993-99. Hon. prof. U. Peking, 1998. Editor-in-chief Am. Jour. Comparative Law. Property commn. mem. Found. for Responsibility, Remembrance, and the Future, Germany, 2001—. Recipient Humboldt prize, 1991, German Order of Merit, 1992, Officier Arts et Lettres, France, 1997, Order of Rio Branco, Brazil, 1998. Mem. German Soc. Comparative Law (corr.), Coun. on Fgn. Rels. Office: U Calif Sch Law 888 Simon Hall Berkeley CA 94720-0001 E-mail: bux@uclink.berkeley.edu

BUZAK, EDWARD JOSEPH, lawyer; b. Jersey City, Apr. 20, 1948; s. Edward and Nellie (Scalone) B.; m. Gail Marie Capizzi, July 24, 1971; children: Craig E., Lindsay T. BA, Union Coll., 1970; JD, Georgetown U., 1973. Bar: N.J. 1973, D.C. 1974. Assoc. Villoresi & Flanagan, Boonton, N.J., 1973-75; ptnr. Villoresi & Buzak, 1976-82; pvt. practice, Montville, N.J., 1983—. Trustee Housing Partnership of Morris County, Morristown, N.J., 1992—. Contbr. articles to profl. jours. Chmn. affordable housing com., asst. counsel N.J. State League of Municipalities, Trenton, N.J., 1986—; asst. counsel N.J. Planning Ofcls., 1998—. Mem. Assn. Environ. Authorities (chmn. legis. com. 1986-2000), N.J. Inst. Mcpl. Attys. (1st v.p.), N.J. Bar Assn. (chmn. local gov. com. 1985-87). Roman Catholic. Avocations: running, skiing, music, reading. Environmental, Land use and zoning (including planning), Municipal (including bonds). Office: 150 River Rd Ste N4 Montville NJ 07045-8920

BUZARD, DAVID ANDREW, lawyer; b. Evanston, Ill., Dec. 8, 1961; s. Clifford Howard and Mary Louise (Dole) B.; m. Véronique Elisabeth Marie Ravisé-Noël, Nov. 25, 1985; children: Clémentine, Victor. Student, Carleton Coll., 1980-82; BA in Linguistics, Northwestern U., 1984; JD, Tulane U., 1990. Bar: Ill. 1991, Va. 1997, U.S. Ct. Mil. Appeals 1991, U.S. Ct. Appeals (4th cir.) 1991, U.S. Dist. Ct. (ea. dist.) Va. 1997, U.S. Dist. Ct. (no. dist.) Ill. 1998, U.S. Supreme Ct. 1998. Law clk. U.S. Atty.'s Office, New Orleans, 1988-90; judge advocate U.S. Navy, 1990-97; assoc. Glasser & Glasser, PLC, Norfolk, Va., 1997-98, Bennett & Zydron, P.C., Virginia Beach, 1998—. V.p., counsel Alliance Française Chapitre de Grasse, Norfolk, Va., 1996—; judge Jessup Internat. Law Moot Ct. Competition, 1998. Contbr. articles to profl. jours. Lt. USN, 1990-97; lt. comdr. USNR, 1998—. Nat. Merit scholar. Mem. ATLA (vice chair fed. tort liability and mil advocacy sect., nursing homes litigation group), Va. State Bar (bd. govs. mil. law sect.), Va. Trial Lawyers Assn., Norfolk and Portsmouth Bar Assn. (founder, chair mil. law and lawyers com. 1997—, Walter E. Hoffman award 2001), Judge Advocates Assn., Disabled Am. Vets., Naval Res. Assn., Pan European Orgn. Personal Injury Lawyers Avocations: civic activities, travel. General civil litigation, Military, Personal injury. Office: Bennett & Zydron PC 120 S Lynnhaven Rd Virginia Beach VA 23452-7419 E-mail: dbuzard@exis.net

BUZUNIS, CONSTANTINE DINO, lawyer; b. Winnipeg, Man., Can., Feb. 3, 1958; came to U.S., 1982; s. Peter and Anastasia (Ginakes) B. BA, U. Man., 1980; JD, Thomas M. Cooley Law Sch., 1985. Bar: Mich. 1986, U.S. Dist. Ct. (ea. and we. dists.) Mich. 1986, Calif. 1986, U.S. Dist. Ct. (so. dist.) Calif. 1987, U.S. Supreme Ct. 1993. Assoc. Church, Kritselis, Wyble & Robinson, Lansing, Mich., 1986, Neil, Dymott, Perkins, Brown & Frank, San Diego, 1987-94, ptnr., 1994—. Arbitrator San Diego County Mcpl. and Superior Cts.; judge pro tem San Diego Mcpl. Ct. Sec., treas. Sixty Plus Law Ctr., Lansing, 1985; active Vols. in Parole, San Diego, 1988—; bd. dirs. Hellenic Cultural Soc., 1993-98. Mem. Mich. Bar Assn., Calif. Bar Assn., San Diego County Bar Assn., Desert Bar Assn., So. Calif. Def. Coun., State Bar Calif. (gov. 9th dist. young lawyers divsn. 1991-94, 1st v.p. 1993-94, pres. 1994-95, bd. govs. 1995-96) San Diego Barristers Soc. (bd. dirs. 1991-92), San Diego Def. Lawyers Assn., Risk Ins. Mgmt. Soc. (assoc.), San Diego Ins. Adjusters Assn. (assoc.), Pan Arcadian Fedn.,

Order of Ahepa (chpt. bd. dirs., v.p. 1995-98, chpt. pres. 2001—), Hellenic Cultural Soc., Phi Alpha Delta. Federal civil litigation, State civil litigation, Personal injury. Home: 3419 Overpark Rd San Diego CA 92130-1865 Office: Neil Dymott Perkins Brown & Frank 1010 2nd Ave Ste 2500 San Diego CA 92101-4959 Fax: 619-238-1562. E-mail: cbuzunis@neil-dymott.com

BUZZARD, STEVEN RAY, lawyer; b. Centralia, Wash., May 22, 1946; s. Richard James and Phylis Margaret (Bevington) B.; m. Joan Elizabeth Merrow, Nov. 11, 1967; children: Elizabeth Jane, Richard Wolcott, James Merrow. BA, Cen. Wash. State Coll., 1972; postgrad., U. Wash., 1973; JD, U. Puget Sound, 1975. Bar: Wash. 1975, U.S. Dist. Ct. (we. dist.) Wash. 1976, U.S. Supreme Ct. 1979, U.S. Tax Ct. 1983. Assoc. Shires, Kruse, Wallace, Roper & Kamps, Port Orchard, Wash., 1975-77; ptnr. Buzzard & O'Connell, Centralia, 1978-80, Buzzard & Tripp, Centralia, 1980-94, Buzzard & Assoc., Centralia, 1994—. City atty. Mossyrock, Wash., 1979-94, Vader, Wash., 1989-96, Bucoda, Wash., 1989-99; judge Centralia, 1980-84, Winlock, Wash., 1983—; sec. Consol. Enterprizes Inc., Centralia, 1986-88; judge Chehalis (Wash.) Mcpl. Ct., 1998—, Winlock Mcpl. Ct., 1983—, Napavine Mcpl. Ct., 2001—, Vader Mcpl. Ct., 2001—; past pres. Reliable Enterprises, Inc. Chmn. bd. dirs. Lewis County Cmty. Svcs., Chehalis, Wash., 1981-84; bd. dirs. Lewis County United Way, 1993-95; mem. adv. bd. Centralia Sch. Dist., 1995—; trustee, treas. Dollars for Scholars, Scholarship Found., 1997—. Mem. ABA (rural judges com. 1986), Wash. State Bar Assn. (ct. rules com. 1992-), Lewis County Bar Assn. (past pres.), Assn. Trial Lawyers Am., Wash. State Trial Lawyers Assn., Wash. State Govt. Lawyers Bar Assn. (trustee), Wash. State Dist. and Mcpl. Ct. Judges Assn. (dist. and mcpl. rural judges com.), Wash. Bd. Jud. Adminstrn. (best practices com. 2001—, ct. improvement com., 2001-), Dist. and Mcpl. Judges Assn. (ct. improvement com., long range planning com.), Kiwanis (pres.-elect 1991, pres. 1992-93, Disting. Past Pres. award 1994), Elks (trustee Centralia 1981—). Avocations: running, boating, hiking, biking, fishing. State civil litigation, General practice, Personal injury. Office: Buzzard & Assoc 314 Harrison Ave Centralia WA 98531-1326 Fax: (360) 330-2078

BYCZYNSKI, EDWARD FRANK, lawyer, financial executive; b. Chgo., Mar. 17, 1946; s. Edward James and Ann (Ruskey) B.; children: Stefan, Suzanne. BA, U. Wis., 1968; JD, U. Ill., 1972; Cert. de Droit, U. Caen (France), 1971. Bar: Ill. 1972, U.S.Dist. Ct. (no. dist.) Ill. 1972, U.S. Supreme Ct. 1976. Title officer Chgo. Title Inst. Co., 1972-73; ptnr. Haley, Pirok, Byczynski, Chgo., 1973-76; pres. Alderstreet Investments, Portland, Oreg., 1976-82, Nat. Tenant Network, Portland, 1981—. Asst. regional counsel SBA, Chgo., 1973-76; pres. Bay Venture Corp., Portland, 1984—. Contbr. articles to profl. jours. Mem. ABA, Ill. Bar Assn. Democrat. Banking, Franchising, Real property. Home: PO Box 2377 Lake Oswego OR 97035-0614 Office: 525 1st St Ste 105 Lake Oswego OR 97034-3100 E-mail: efb@ntnnet.com

BYE, KERMIT EDWARD, lawyer; b. Hatton, N.D., Jan. 13, 1937; s. Kermit Berthrand and Margaret B. (Brekke) B.; m. Carol Beth Soliah, Aug. 23, 1958; children— Laura Lee, William Edward, Bethany Ann. B.S., U. N.D., 1959, J.D., 1962. Bar: N.D. 1962, U.S. Dist. Ct. N.D. 1962, U.S. Ct. Appeals (8th cir.) 1969, U.S. Supreme Ct. 1974, Minn. 1981. Dep. securities commr. State of N.D., 1962-66, spl. asst. atty. gen., 1962-66; asst. U.S. Atty. Dist. N.D., 1966-68; ptnr. Vogel, Brantner, Kelly, Knutson, Weir & Bye, Fargo, N.D., 1968-2000; judge U.S. Ct. Appeals (8th cir.), Fargo, N.D., 2000—. Contbr. article to law rev. Chmn., Red River Human Services Found., 1980-83; bd. dirs. S.E. Mental Health and Retardation Ctr. Inc. Mem ABA, State Bar Assn. N.D. (pres. 1983-84), Cass County Bar Assn. Democrat. Lutheran. Office: Quentin Burdick US Courthouse 655 1st Ave N Rm 300 Fargo ND 58102*

BYERS, GARLAND FRANKLIN, JR. lawyer; b. Rutherfordton, N.C., Jan. 11, 1968; s. Garland Franklin Sr. and Helen Kathryn (Cannon) B.; m. Heather Kristina Emory, June 5, 1987; children: Amber Dianna, Jonathan Wesley. AAS in Criminal Justice, Isothermal C.C., Spindale, N.C., 1991; BS in Criminal Justice, U. S.C., Spartanburg, 1993; JD, N.C. Ctrl. Sch. Law, 1999. Bar: N.C. 2000, U.S. Dist. Ct. (we. dist.) N.C. 2000, U.S. Ct. Appeals (4th cir.) 2001. Chief of police Alexander Mills Police Dept., Forest City, N.C., 1988; police officer Rutherfordton Police Dept., 1988-90; cpl., dep. sheriff Rutherfordton County Sheriff's Dept., 1990-91; roving technician The New Cherokee Corp., Spindale, 1992-93; pvt. practice ins./loan agt. Primerica Fin. Svcs., 1994-95; criminal justice instr. Isothermal C.C., 1994-95; chief investigator N.C. State Dist. Attys. Office 29th Prosecutorial Dist., Rutherfordton, 1995-96; owner, pvt. investigator, counterintelligence specialist Byers Investigations, Hillsborough, N.C., 1997-99; atty. Byers & King, PLLC, Rutherfordton, 2000—. Mem. N.C. Bar Assn., Rutherford County Bar Assn., N.C. Acad. Trial Lawyers. Avocations: reading, martial arts, swimming. Appellate, Criminal, General practice. Office: 175 N Main St Rutherfordton NC 28139 E-mail: garlandbyersjr@aol.com

BYERS, MATTHEW T(ODD), lawyer, educator; b. Ridley Park, Pa., May 30, 1963; s. Richard Lynn and Joyce Ann (Ralston) B.; m. Lori Byers; children: Amanda Michelle, Amber, Helen, David, Saren, Loren. BA, U. N. Mex., 1985, JD, 1990. Bar: N.Mex. 1990, U.S. Dist. Ct. N.Mex. 1991, U.S. Ct. Appeals (10th cir.) 1991, U.S. Tax Ct. 1991, Pa. 1997. Staff Los Alamos (N.Mex.) Nat. Lab., 1989-90; assoc. Marek, Francis & Byers, P.A., Carlsbad, N.Mex., 1990—, ptnr., 1998—; assoc. Forry, Ullman, Ullman & Forry, Reading, Pa., 1997. Assoc. editor N. Mex. U. Law Review, 1990. Bd. dirs. United Way of Carlsbad, 1990-93. Recipient Cert. of Achievement Renaissance Program, Carlsbad, 1991. Mem. ABA, State Bar Assn. N.Mex., Eddy Cty. Bar Assn. (pres. 1993), George L. Reese Jr. Inn of Court, Pa. Bar Assn. Democrat. Baptist. Avocations: softball, music, reading. Bankruptcy, General practice, Probate. Office: Marek Francis & Byers PA 110 W Shaw St Carlsbad NM 88220-5878

BYRD, CHRISTINE WATERMAN SWENT, lawyer; b. Oakland, Calif., Apr. 11, 1951; d. Langan Waterman and Eleanor (Herz) Swent; m. Gary Lee Byrd, June 20, 1981; children: Amy, George. BA, Stanford U., 1972; JD, U. Va., 1975. Bar: Calif. 1976, U.S. Dist. Ct. (ctrl., so. no., ea. dists.) Calif., U.S. Ct. Appeals (9th cir.). Law clk. to Hon. William P. Gray, U.S. Dist. Ct., L.A., 1975-76; assoc. Jones, Day, Reavis & Pogue, 1976-82, ptnr., 1987-96; asst. U.S. atty. criminal divsn. U.S. Atty.'s Office-Cen. Dist. Calif., 1982-87; ptnr. Irell & Manella, 1996—. Mem. Calif. Law Revision Commn., 1992-97. Author: The Future of the U.S. Multinational Corporation, 1975; contbr. articles to profl. jours. Mem. Calif. State Bar (com. fed. cts. 1985-88), Los Angeles County Bar Assn., Women Lawyers Assn. Los Angeles County, Am. Arbitration Assn. (large and complex case panel 1992—, nat. energy panel 1998—, bd. dirs. 1999—), Stanford Prof. Women Los Angeles County, Stanford U. Alumni Assn., 9th Jud. Cir. Hist. Soc. (bd. dirs. 1986—, pres. 1997—), Assn. Bus. Trial Lawyers (bd. govs. 1996-99). Republican. General civil litigation, Criminal, General practice. Office: Irell & Manella LLP 1800 Ave Of Stars Ste 900 Los Angeles CA 90067-4276

BYRNE, GRANVILLE BLAND, III, lawyer; b. San Antonio, Jan. 26, 1952; s. Granville Bland and Mary (Dowling) B.; divorced; children: Peyton Smith, Fulton Buckner; m. Monique Renée Wise, 1999. AB, U. N.C., Chapel Hill, 1974; JD, Harvard U., 1978. Bar: Ga. 1978, U.S. Dist. Ct. (no. dist.) Ga. 1978, U.S. Ct. Appeals (5th cir.) 1978, U.S. Ct. Appeals (11th cir.) 1981. Assoc. Swift, Currie, McGhee & Hiers, Atlanta, 1978-84, ptnr., 1984-94; prin. Byrne, Eldridge, Moore & Davis, P.C., 1994-99, Byrne, Moore & Davis, P.C., Atlanta, 1999—. Bd. dirs. Compeer Atlanta, Inc., chmn., 1996—; bd. dirs. Cagle's, Inc. Elder, mem. session 1st Presbyn. Ch. Atlanta, 1993-96, 99—. Mem. ABA, Ga. Bar Assn., Atlanta Bar Assn. Democrat. Presbyterian. Contracts commercial, General corporate, Securities. Home: 3555 Castlegate Dr NW Atlanta GA 30327-2601 Office: Byrne Moore & Davis PC 3340 Peachtree Rd NE Atlanta GA 30326-1000 E-mail: gbb@bmdlaw.net

BYRNE, ROBERT WILLIAM, lawyer; b. Frankfurt, Germany, Dec. 12, 1958; s. Robert Patrick and Anne Lise (Brondelsbo) B. BA, Rutgers U., 1981; JD, Seton Hall U., 1984; postgrad., Colo. State U., 1998—. Bar: N.J. 1984, U.S. Dist. Ct. N.J. 1984, D.C. 1986, U.S. Ct. Appeals (3d cir.) 1987, U.S. Ct. Appeals (D.C. and fed. cirs.) 1988, (11th cir.), 1993, U.S. Dist. Ct. D.C. 1989, U.S. Supreme Ct. 1989, N.Y. 1991, U.S. Dist. Ct. (so. and ea. dists.) N.Y. 1991, Fla. 1992, U.S. Dist. Ct. (no. and mid. dists.) Fla. 1992, Calif. 2001., U.S. Dist. Ct. (no. dist.) Calif. 2001, U.S. Ct. Appeals (9th cir.) 2001. Law clk. to presiding judge Superior Ct. Passaic County N.J., 1984-85; asst. prosecutor Bergen County, N.J., 1985-88; assoc. Harwood Lloyd Esqs., Hackensack, 1988-90, Mudge Rose Guthrie Alexander & Ferdon, N.Y.C., 1990-91; sr. assoc. O'Connor, Reddy & Jensen, 1991-92; pvt. practice Panama City, Fla., 1992-94; v.p./gen. counsel Bay Bank & Trust Co., 1994-2000. Contbr. Seton Hall Legislative Jour., 1983-84. Henry Rutgers scholar, 1981. Mem. D.C. Bar, Fla. Bar, Bay County (Fla.) Bar Assn., Assn. Bar City N.Y., State Bar Calif., Bar Assn. San Francisco, Bay Area Lawyers Individual Freedom, Phi Alpha Delta, Pi Sigma Alpha. Democrat. Lutheran. Banking, Consumer commercial, Probate. Home: 767 Buena Vista Ave W # 304 San Francisco CA 94117-4135 E-mail: mobysfo@pacbell.net

BYRNE, THOMAS J. lawyer; b. Rochester, N.Y., June 17, 1944; m. Brenda C. Byrne, June 4, 1994; children: Thomas, David, Heather. AB, U. Rochester, 1967; JD, U. Denver, 1976. Bar: Colo. 1977, Calif. 1977, U.S. Ct. Appeals (10th cir.) 1977, U.S. Dist. Ct. Colo. 1977, U.S. Dist. Ct. (so. dist.) Tex. 1990, N.Y. 1990, U.S. Ct. Appeals (3d cir.) 1992, U.S. Dist. Ct. (ea. dist.) Pa. 1992, U.S. Dist. Ct. (ea. dist.) Va. 1992, U.S. Ct. Appeals (4th cir.) 1993, U.S. Dist. Ct. (no. dist.) Ill. 1993, U.S. Dist. Ct. Ariz. 1993, U.S. Dist. Ct. Utah 1996, U.S. Dist. Ct. (so. dist.) N.Y. 1997. Law clk. Dist. Ct. Colo., Denver, 1976-77; assoc. Ullstrom Law Offices, 1978-83; ptnr., Denver mgr. Conklin & Adler, Ltd., Denver and Chgo., 1983-86; mng. ptnr. Byrne, Kiely & White LLP, Denver, 1986—. Mem. fin. com. Citizens for Romer, Denver, 1990—. Capt. USAF, 1967-73. Mem. ABA (tort and ins. practice sect., vice chair aviation and space law com., litigation sect., forum on air and space law), Internat. Bar Assn., Colo. Bar Assn., Denver Bar Assn., State Bar Calif., N.Y. State Bar Assn., Def. Rsch. Inst., Colo. Def. Lawyers Assn., Nat. Bus. Aircraft Assn., Lawyer-Pilot Bar Assn., Aviation Ins. Assn. Avocations: flying, travel, sports. Aviation, Insurance, Product liability. Office: Byrne Kiely & White LLP 1120 Lincoln St Ste 1300 Denver CO 80203-2140

BYRNES, RICHARD JAMES, lawyer; b. Newark, Jan. 14, 1947; s. L. George and A. Marie (Ellis) B. A.B., Rutgers U., 1968; J.D., NYU, 1976. Bar: N.Y. 1976. Assoc. Weil, Gotshal & Manges, N.Y.C., 1976-77, Shearman & Sterling, N.Y.C., 1977-81; assoc. Hawkins, Delafield & Wood, N.Y.C., 1981-83, ptnr. 1984-85; sr. v.p. and co-mgr. William E. Pollack & Co., Inc., N.Y.C., 1985— ; ptnr. Kutak, Rock & Campbell, Washington, 1985—; dir. Pub. Space Collaborative, N.Y.C. Counsel N.Y. Sch. for Circus Arts, N.Y.C., 1978— . Served to capt. U.S. Army, 1968-71. Mem. ABA (internat. law com. 1983— , internat. fin. transactions com. 1984— , internat. trade com. 1984—), N.Y. Bar Assn., Am. Mgmt. Assn., Internat. Law Inst. (assoc.), Internat. Bar Assn., Inter-Am. Bar Assn. Banking, Private international, Securities. Office: William E Pollock & Co Inc 160 Water St New York NY 10038-4922

BYRNES, WILLIAM JOSEPH, lawyer; b. Bklyn., Apr. 11, 1940; s. William James and Margaret Mary (English) B.; m. Catherine Belle Rollings, Aug. 15, 1970; children: Jennifer, Suzanne. BS, Fordham U., 1961; JD, Yale U., 1964. Bar: N.Y. 1965, D.C. 1970, Va. 1992. Atty. AEC, Washington, 1964-68; internat. mgr. Comm. Satellite Corp., 1968-70; ptnr. Haley, Bader & Potts, Arlington, Va., 1970-95; of counsel Irwin Campbell & Tannenwald, Washington, 1995-96; pvt. practice, McLean, Va., 1997—. Author: Telecommunications Regulation: Something Old and Something New in the Communications Act: A Legislative History of the Major Amendments, 1934-1996, 1999; co-author: The Common Carrier Provisions--A Product of Evolutionary Development in A Legislative History of the Communications Act, 1989, Decency Redux: The Curious History of the New FCC Broadcast Indecency Policy, 1989, A New Telecommunications Paradigm, 1993; mem. Great Falls Players, Elden Street Players, Rockville Little Theatre, Am. Music Stage, Sterling Playmakers. Candidate Fairfax County Bd. Suprs., 1995; pres. McLean Citizens Found., McLean Orch. Recipient cert. U.S. Atomic Energy Commn., 1967. Mem. Fed. Comms. Bar Assn., Va. State Bar, D.C. Bar Assn., McLean Citizens Assn. (ex-pres.), Fairfax Com. 100. Avocations: acting, videography. Administrative and regulatory, Appellate, Communications. Office: 7921 Old Falls Rd Mc Lean VA 22102-2414

BYROM, JOE ALAN, lawyer; b. Duncan, Okla., Nov. 6, 1949; s. Joe Lane and Dorothy Adelle (Norton) B.; m. Carla Peters, June 25, 1977; children: Celeste Elizabeth, Russell Patrick. BA, U. Tex., 1972; JD, So. Meth. U., 1975. Bar: Tex. 1975, U.S. Dist. Ct. (no. and ea. dists.) Tex. 1976, U.S. Ct. Appeals (5th and 11th cirs.) 1981, U.S. Supreme Ct. 1985. Assoc. Blassingame & Osburn, Dallas, 1975-81, ptnr., 1981-88; ptnr. Brill, Siney and Hohmann, Dallas, 1989—. Mem. Assn. Trial Lawyers Assn. Am., Tex. Bar Assn., Dallas Bar Assn., Phi Delta Phi. Methodist. General civil litigation, Contracts commercial, General corporate. Home: 3505 Mockingbird Ln Dallas TX 75205-2225 Office: Brill Siney & Hohmann 2980 Lincoln Pla 500 N Akard St Dallas TX 75201-3320

CABEZAS-GIL, ROSA M. lawyer; b. Santa Cruz Canary Islands, Spain, Oct. 26, 1959; came to U.S., 1973; d. Alejandro and Maria Rosa (Darias) Cabezas; m. Jose D. Gil, July 10, 1982 (div. May 1997); children: Debby F. Gil, Lani Angelina Gil. AA in Humanities with honors, Gavilan Coll., Gilroy, Calif., 1978; BA in Internat. Rels., San Francisco State U., 1980; JD, St. Mary's U., 1987. Bar: Tex. 1987, U.S. Dist. Ct. (we. dist.) Tex. 1989, U.S. Ct. Appeals (5th cir.) 1989, U.S. Supreme Ct. 1991. News anchor, reporter Sta. KDTV-Channel 14, San Francisco, 1980-81; reporter, weather anchor Sta. KWEX-TV Channel 41, San Antonio, 1981-82; atty. Bexar County Legal Aid, 1988-91; pvt. practice, 1991—. Rep./liaison Canary Islands Govt., San Antonio, 1989-91; spkr. on probate and family law to various orgns., San Antonio. Treas. La Casa de España, San Antonio, 1984—. Nnamed Vol. Beyond Excellence McAulife Mid. Sch., 1994; recipient Cert. of Recognition Leadership, Club Mentor Tafoya Mid. Sch., 1992-93. Fellow San Antonio Bar Found. (bd. dirs. 1996—), State Bar of Tex. Found. 1998—, the College of the State Bar of Tex. 1989—; mem. State Bar Tex. (bd. dirs. women in the law sect. 1995-99, bd. dirs. local bar com. 1994—, bd. dirs. Dist. 10C gr ieveance com. 1996-99), Tex. Women Lawyers (charter bd. dirs., founding mem. 1994—, v.p. 1998), Bexar County Women's Bar Assn. (pres. 1994), San Antonio Mex. Am. Bar A ssn. (pres. 1993), Bexar County Legal Aid Assn. (bd. dirs. 1995—), St. Mary's Univ. Law Sch. Alumni Assn. (bd. dirs. 1992-97); mem. San Antonio Art leag. Mus. (bd. dirs. 1997—). Roman Catholic. Avocations: travel, reading. Family and matrimonial, Personal injury, Probate. Office: 111 Soledad St Ste 1230 San Antonio TX 78205-2296 E-mail: cabezasgil@aol.com

CABLE, PAUL ANDREW, lawyer; b. N.Y.C., Apr. 13, 1939; s. Sydney W. and Karen A. (Petersen) C.; m. Diana Kathleen Sybil Lee, June 17, 1972. B.A., Wesleyan U., 1961; M.A. in Econ., U. Manchester, 1963; LL.B., Harvard U., 1966. Bar: D.C. 1967, N.Y. 1970, Calif. 1976. Assoc., Anderson, Mori & Rabinowitz, Tokyo, Japan, 1966-69, Anderson & Martin, N.Y.C., 1969-70; ptnr. Anderson, Martin & Cable, 1970-72, Whitman & Ransom, N.Y.C. and Los Angeles, 1972-93; ptnr. Whitman, Breed, Abbott & Morgan, N.Y.C., 1993—. Contbg. author: International Business Operations, 1974, East-West Trade Transactions, 1976, International Trade, 1983, 3rd. edit., 1991. Marshall scholar, Brit. Govt., 1961-63. Mem. N.Y. City Bar Assn. (coms.), D.C. Bar Assn., Calif. Bar Assn., Phi Beta Kappa (hon.). Clubs: Stanwich; Harvard. Contracts commercial, General corporate, Private international. Home: 38 Birch Ln Greenwich CT 06830-3913 Office: Whitman Breed Abbott & Morgan 200 Park Ave New York NY 10166-0005

CABRANES, JOSÉ ALBERTO, federal judge; b. Mayaguez, P.R., Dec. 22, 1940; s. Manuel and Carmen (López) C.; children: Jennifer Ann, Amy Alexandra; m. Kate Stith, Sept. 15, 1984; children: Alejo, Benjamin José. AB, Columbia U., 1961; JD, Yale U., 1965; MLitt in Internat. Law, Cambridge (Eng.) U., 1967; LLD (hon.), Colgate U., 1988, nine other instns., 1989-2000. Bar: N.Y. 1968, D.C. 1975, U.S. Dist. Ct. Conn. 1976. Assoc. Casey, Lane & Mittendorf, N.Y.C., 1967-71; assoc. prof. law sch. Rutgers U., Newark, 1971-73; spl. counsel to gov. P.R., head Office Commonwealth P.R., Washington, 1973-75; gen. counsel Yale U., New Haven, 1975-79; judge U.S. Dist. Ct. Conn., 1979-94, chief judge, 1992-94; judge U.S. Ct. Appeals (2nd cir.), 1994—. Mem. Pres.'s Commn. White House Fellowships, 1993-96, Pres.'s Commn. Mental Health, 1977-78, U.S. del. Conf. Security and Coop. in Europe, Belgrade, 1977-78; mem. James Madison Meml. Fellowship Found., 1995—; founding mem. P.R. Legal Def. and Edn. Fund, 1972, chmn. bd., 1977-80; counsel Internat. League for Human Rights, 1971-77, v.p., 1977-80; cons. to sec. Dept. State, 1978; mem. Fed. Cts. Study Com., 1988-90; instr. history P.R. Colegio San Ignacio de Loyola, Rio Piedras, P.R., 1962; supr. in internat. law Queens Coll., Cambridge U., 1966-67. Author: Citizenship and the American Empire, 1979; co-author: (with Kate Stith) Fear of the Judging: Sentencing Guidelines in the Federal Courts, 1998; also articles on law and internat. affairs. Trustee Yale U., 1987-99, Yale-New Haven Hosp., 1978-80, 84-87, Colgate U., 1981-90, Century Found., N.Y.C., 1983-2000, Columbia U., 2000—, Fed. Jud. Ctr., 1986-90; bd. dirs. Aspira of N.Y. (Puerto Rican edn. agy.), 1970-74, chmn., 1971-73; mem. Coun. on Fgn. Rels. Recipient life achievement award Nat. P.R. Coalition, 1987, John Jay award Columbia Coll., 1991, life achievement award student divsn. Nat. Hispanic Bar Assn., 1991, Learned Hand medal for excellence in fed. jurisprudence Fed. Bar Coun., 2000; Kellett rsch. fellow Columbia Coll. at Cambridge U., 1965-67. Fellow Am. Bar Found., Mex.-Am. Lawyers Assn. (Spl. Recognition award 1994); mem. ABA, Conn. Bar Assn. (Naruk Jud. award 1993), Assn. of Bar of City of N.Y., Am. Law Inst., Nat. Hispanic Bar Assn. Roman Catholic. Office: US Ct of Appeals US Courthouse 141 Church St New Haven CT 06510-2030

CABRASER, ELIZABETH JOAN, lawyer; b. Oakland, Calif., June 23, 1952; AB, U. Calif., Berkeley, 1975; JD, U. Calif., 1978. Bar: Calif. 1978, U.S. Dist. Ct. (no., ea., cen. and so. dists.) Calif. 1979, U.S. Ct. Appeals (2d, 3rd, 5th, 6th, 9th, 10th, and 11th cirs.) 1979, U.S. Tax Ct. 1979, U.S. Dist. Ct. Hawaii 1986, U.S. Dist. Ct. Ariz. 1990, U.S. Supreme Ct. 1996. Ptnr. Lieff, Cabraser, Heimann & Bernstein LLP, San Francisco, 1978—. Contbr. articles to profl. jours. Named one of Top 50 Women Lawyers Nat. Law Jour., 1998, one of Top 100 U.S. Lawyers, 1997, 2000. Mem. ABA (tort and ins. practice sect., sect. litig. com. on class action and derivative skills, chair subcom. on mass torts), ATLA, Coun. Am. Law Inst., Calif. Constn. Rev. Commn., Nat. Ctr. for State Cts. (mass tort conf. planning com.), Women Trial Lawyer Caucus, Consumer Attys. Calif., Calif. Women Lawyers, Assn. Bus. Trial Lawyers, Nat. Assn. Securities and Comml. Attys., Bay Area Lawyers for Individual Freedom, Bar Assn. San Francisco (v.p. securities litig., bd. dirs.). Office: Lieff Cabraser Heimann & Bernstein LLP Embarcadero Ctr W 30th Fl 275 Battery St San Francisco CA 94111-3305 E-mail: ecabraser@lchb.com

CACACE, MICHAEL JOSEPH, lawyer; b. Mt. Vernon, N.Y., Apr. 20, 1952; s. Jerry F. and Margaret F. (Pesditsch) C.; m. Maureen R. Brown, May 24, 1975; children: Joseph M., Christine M. BA, Fordham U., 1974; JD, N.Y. Law Sch., 1978. Bar: Conn. 1978, N.Y. 1979, U.S. Dist. Ct. Conn. 1979, U.S. Ct. Appeals (2nd cir.) 1981, U.S. Dist. Ct. (so. dist.) N.Y. 1982. Law clk. Saxe, Bacon & Bolan, N.Y.C., 1976-78, atty., 1978-79; atty. Abate, Fox & Farrell, Stamford, Conn., 1979-82; pvt. practice law, Stamford, 1982-87; ptnr., D'Andrea & Cacace, 1988-94, Cacace Tusch & Santagata, Stamford, 1994—; bd. dirs. The Vol. Ctr., Stamford, 1980-86, pres. 1984-86; co.-chmn. 13th Charter Revision Com., Stamford, 1982-83; v.p. Gateway Cmtys., Inc., Stamford, 1981-89; bd. dirs. Stamford Commn. on Aging, 1975-80, chmn. 1978-80; instr. adminstrv. law Norwalk C.C., Conn., 1980-82. Author book chpt. Age Discrimination Law, 1981. Bd. dirs. Vis. Nurses Assn., Stamford, 1982-87, Shippan Point Assn., Stamford, 1980-83, Stamford Ctr. for the Arts, 1986—, v.p., 1989—, Stamford United Way, 1988-95, v.p., 1989-91, pres. 1991-94; mem. Conn. Com. Regional Plan, 1987—, United Way of Conn., 1988-94, pres. 1990-92. Named one of Outstanding Young Men of Am., 1977, Cmty. Leader of Yr., The Stamford Adv., 1986; recipient Dr. Max Reich award N.Y. Law Sch., Humanitarian award Southwestern Conn. Assn. Life Underwriters, 1987-88. Lawyers Co-op Book award Lawyers Co-op Book Co., 1977, Thomas F. Richardson Pres.'s award United Way Stamford, 1995, Citizen of Yr. The Fred Robbins Post # 142 Jewish Vets. of U.S., 1995. Mem. Am. Planning Assn. (Conn. chpt.), Urban Inst., Stamford/Darien Bar Assn. (mem. exec. com. 1980-92, treas. 1986-87, sec. 1987-87, 2d v.p. 1988-89, 1st v.p. 1989-90, pres. 1990-91), Conn. Bar Assn. (chair planning and zoning sect. 1994-97), N.Y. Bar Assn., Conn. Trial Lawyers Assn., Assn. Trial Lawyers Am., State St. Debating Soc. Democrat. Roman Catholic. Club: Roasters (Stamford), Landmark Club (bd. govs. 1995—). State civil litigation, General practice, Real property. Home: 316 Scofieldtown Rd Stamford CT 06903-4012 Office: Cacace Tusch & Santagata PO Box 15859 777 Summer St Stamford CT 06901-1022

CACCIATORE, RONALD KEITH, lawyer; b. Donaldsville, Ga., Feb. 5, 1937; s. Angelo D. and Myrtice E. (Williams) C.; children: Rhonda, Donna, Rex. Student, Spring Hill Coll., 1955-56; BA, U. Fla., 1960; JD, 1963. Bar: Fla. 1963, U.S. Supreme Ct. 1969. Asst. state atty. 13th Jud. Cir., 1963-65; pvt. practice Tampa, Fla., 1967. Lectr. criminal law, mem. 13th Jud. Cir. Jud. Nominating Commn., 1976-80, chmn., 1980; mem. Fed. Judiciary Adv. Commn. Fla., 1987—. Trustee Hillsborough C.C., 1979-83, chmn., 1982-83. Fellow Am. Coll. Trial Lawyers; mem. Hillsborough County Bar Assn. (pres. 1975-76, chmn. trial lawyers sect. 1983-85, Herbert G. Goldburg Meml. award 1991), Fla. Bar Assn. (chmn. criminal law sect. 1977-78), Fla. Coun. Bar Pres.'s (chmn. 1979-80), Fed. Bar Assn. (pres. Tampa Bay chpt. 1985-86, fed. jud. nominationcom. Fla. 1999—, George C. Carr Meml. award Tampa Bay chpt. 1996), Master of the Bar, White-Ferguson Inn, Herbert G. Goldburg Criminal Law Am. Inn of Ct. (pres. 2000—), Am. Inns of Ct., Palma Ceia Golf and Country Club, University Club. Criminal.

CADDY, MICHAEL DOUGLAS, lawyer; b. Long Beach, Calif., Mar. 23, 1938; s. Frank Edward and Tabitha (Miles) C. BS in Fgn. Svc., Georgetown U., 1960; JD, NYU, 1966. Bar: D.C. 1970, Tex. 1979. Practiced in, Washington and, Tex.; exec. dir. com. on pub. affairs McGraw-Edison Co., N.Y.C., 1960-61; asst. to lt. gov. State of N.Y., 1962-65; asst. to exec. v.p. NAM, N.Y.C., 1966-67; Washington liaison Gen. Foods Corp., 1968-70; assoc. Gail, Lane, Powell & Kilcullen, 1970-74; legis. counsel Nat. Assn. Realtors, Washington, 1975-76; atty. Office Tex. Sec. of State, Austin, 1980-81. Author: The Hundred Million Dollar Payoff, 1974, How They Rig Our Elections, 1975, Understanding Insurance, 1984, Legislative Trends in Insurance Regulation, 1985, Exploring America's Future, 1987. Mem. Rep. County Com., N.Y.C.,

1965-66; nat. dir. Young Ams. for Freedom, 1960-62; pres. Conservatives Hall of Fame. Scholar Intercollegiate Studies Inst., 1957-59. Mem. ABA, ATLA, ACLU, FBA, D.C. Bar, Tex. Bar, Houston Bar Assn., Houston Bar Assn. for Human Rights, Federalist Soc., Am. Conservative Union, Am. Judicature Soc., Assn. Former Intelligence Officers, Am. Econ. Assn., Am. Acad. Polit. and Social Sci., Internat. Platform Assn., Nat. Coun. Crime and Delinquency, Supreme Ct. Hist. Soc., People for Am. Way, Nat. Trust for Hist. Preservation, Human Rights Campaign. Home: 745 W Creekside Dr Houston TX 77024-3234 E-mail: douglascaddy@justice.com

CADLE, JERRY NEAL, lawyer; b. Swainsboro, Ga., June 3, 1951; s. F.H. and Eugenia (Baker) C.; m. Paula Kay Ferre, Dec. 27, 1971; children— Ivy Neal, Donald Jacob, Jean Marie. Student Middle Ga. Coll., 1969-70, Ga. So. Coll., 1970-71; BBA, U. Ga., 1972, JD, 1975. Bar: Ga. 1975, U.S. Dist. Ct. (so. dist.) Ga. 1975, U.S. Tax Ct. 1976, U.S. Ct. Appeals (11th cir.) 1981. Assoc. Rountree & Rountree, Swainsboro, Ga., 1975-76; ptnr. Rountree & Cadle, 1977-87, Roundtree Cadle & McNeely, 1987-91, Emanuel County Commisioner 1997-2000(chmn. 2000—), East Georgia Col. Found. chmn., 1990-2000. Bd. dirs. Emanuel County 4-H Found., 1975— , v.p., 1979— ; pres. Swainsboro Devel. Corp., 1977— ; deacon First Bapt. Ch., 1983-85, 87—, chmn. deacons, 1988-89, chmn. bd. trustees, 1984-85. Mem. Ga. Sch. Bd. Attys. Assn., Middle Judicial Cir. Bar Assn. (sec.-treas. 1978, 83, pres. 1988), Swainsboro Country Club (dir. 1981-85, pres. 1984). Contracts commercial, Probate, Real property. Home: 957 W Main St Swainsboro GA 30401 Office: Rountree & Cadle 130 S Main St Swainsboro GA 30401-3618

CADY, MARK S. state supreme court justice; b. Rapid City, S.D. married; 2 children. Undergrad. degree, Drake U., JD, 1978. Law clk. 2d Jud. Dist. Ct., 1978-79; asst. Webster County atty.; with law firm Ft. Dodge; dist. assoc. judge, 1983; dist. ct. judge, 1986; judge Iowa Ct. Appeals, 1994, chief judge, 1994; justice Iowa Supreme Ct., 1998—. Chmn. Supreme Ct. Task Force on Ct.'s and Cmty.'s Response to Domestic Abuse. Mem. ABA, Iowa State Bar Assn., Webster County Bar Assn. Office: Iowa Supreme Ct State House Des Moines IA 50319-0001 E-mail: MarkS.Cady@jb.state.ia.us*

CAFFEE, LORREN DALE, lawyer; b. Decatur, Ind., Oct. 22, 1947; s. Howard Dale and Maxine Faye (Smith) C.; m. Mary Katherine Hostetler, May 25, 1968 (div. Apr. 1982); children: Liesl Katherine, Evan Dale, Colin Dale (dec.); m. Mary Jannice Dyer, June 14, 1986. BA, Bluffton Coll., 1969; JD, Georgetown U., 1972. Bar: Ind. 1972, U.S. V.I. 1994, U.S. Dist. Ct. (no. dist.) Ind. 1974. Pvt. practice, Decatur, 1972-73, 74-76; assoc. DeVoss & DeVoss Law Offices, 1973-74; judge Adams County Ct., 1976-84, Adams Superior Ct., Decatur, 1985-90, Adams Cir. Ct., Decatur, 1991-99; assoc. A.J. Weiss & Assoc. Law Office, 1999—. Mem. county ct. com. Ind. Jud. Ctr., 1978-88, chmn., 1983-86; mem. juvenile benchbook com. Jud. Conf. of Ind., 1991-99, bd. dirs., 1995-99. Bd. dirs. Ind. Right to Life, 1974-76; mem. constn. and by-laws com. Ind. Young Reps. Fedn., 1974, of counsel, 1975-76; chmn. Adams County Young Reps., 1973-76. Mem. Ind. State Bar Assn., Adams County Bar Assn. (pres. 1975-76), Ind. Judges' Assn., Am. Judges Assn., Nat. Coun. Juvenile and Family Ct. Judges, Federalist Soc. Lutheran. Avocations: jazz music, aviation, sports cars, art, reading. Criminal. Home: PO Box 11479 Saint Thomas VI 00801-4479 Office: AJ Weiss and Assoc PO Box 1612 Saint Thomas VI 00804-1612

CAHILL, RICHARD FREDERICK, lawyer; b. Columbus, Nebr., June 18, 1953; s. Donald Francis and Hazel Fredeline (Garbers) C.; m. Helen Marie Girard, Dec. 4, 1982; children: Jacqueline Michelle, Catherine Elizabeth, Marc Alexander. Student, Worcester Coll., Oxford, 1973; BA with highest honors, UCLA, 1975; JD, U. Notre Dame, 1978. Bar: Calif. 1978, U.S. Dist. Ct. (ea. dist.) Calif. 1978, U.S. Dist. Ct. (cen. dist.) Calif. 1983, U.S. Dist. Ct. (so. dist.) Calif. 1992, U.S. Ct. Appeals (9th cir.) 1992. Dep. dist. atty. Tulare County Dist. Atty., Visalia, Calif., 1978-81; staff atty. Supreme Ct. of Nev., Carson City, 1981-83; assoc. Acret & Perochet, Brentwood, Calif., 1983-84, Thelen, Marrin, Johnson & Bridges, L.A., 1984-89; ptnr. Hammond Zuetel & Cahill, Pasadena, Calif., 1989-98, Pivo, Halbreich, Cahill & Yim, Irvine, 1999—. Mem. Pasadena Bar Assn., Los Angeles County Bar Assn., Assn. So. Calif. Defense Counsel, Notre Dame Legal Aid and Defender Assn. (assoc. dir.), Phi Beta Kappa, Phi Alpha Delta (charter, v.p. 1977-78), Pi Gamma Mu, Phi Alpha Theta (charter pres. 1973-74), Phi Eta Sigma, Sigma Chi. Republican. Roman Catholic. Avocation: tennis. State civil litigation. Home: 201 Windwood Ln Sierra Madre CA 91024-2677 Office: Pivo Halbreich Cahill & Yim 1920 Main St Ste 800 Irvine CA 92614-7227

CAHN, JAMES, lawyer, martial arts educator; b. Cleve., Apr. 16, 1946; s. Sherman D. and Barbara Cahn; m. Jean A. Johnson, May 20, 1978; children: Rachel, Lucy. BA, U. Pa., 1968; JD, Ohio State U., 1973; 7th Degree Black Belt, Oriental Martial Arts Coll., 2001. Bar: Ohio 1973. Assoc. Calfee, Halter & Griswold, Cleve., 1973-75; pvt. practice, 1975-77; ptnr. Hermann, Cahn & Schneider, 1977—. Instr., master Oriental Martial Arts Coll., Cleve. and Columbus, Ohio, 1975—; legal counsel U.S. Taekwondo Union, Colorado Springs, Colo., 1977-81, 85-86; lectr. Ohio Jud. Coll. Founding mem. Ctr. for Principled Family Advocacy. Fellow Am. Acad. Matrimonial Lawyers (pres. Ohio chpt. 1997-98); mem. ABA, Ohio State Bar Assn., Cuyahoga County Bar Assn. (chair family law sect. 1990-91), Cleve. Bar Assn. (family law sect.), Oakwood Club. Family and matrimonial. Office: Hermann Cahn & Schneider 1301 E 9th St Ste 500 Cleveland OH 44114-1876

CAHN, JEFFREY BARTON, lawyer; b. N.Y.C., Jan. 1, 1943; s. Harold Leon and Vivian (Loewy) C.; m. Miriam Epstein, Jan. 22, 1965; children: Lauren Samantha, Vanessa Shari. BA, Ind. U., 1964; JD, Rutgers U., 1967. Bar: N.J. 1967, U.S. Dist. Ct. N.J. 1967, U.S. Ct. Appeals (3d cir.) 1971, U.S. Supreme Ct. 1971, U.S. Tax Ct. 1973, U.S. Ct. Appeals (D.C. cir.), 1979, N.Y. 1980, U.S. Ct. Appeals (9th cir.) 1981, U.S. Claims Ct. 1981, U.S. Dist. Ct. (so. dist.) N.Y. 1992, U.S. Dist. Ct. (ea. dist.) N.Y. 1994, U.S. Ct. Appeals (2nd cir.) 1998. Law clk. to sr. presiding judge Appellate Div. N.J. Superior Ct., Trenton, N.J., 1967-68; assoc. Schapira, Steiner & Walder, Newark, 1968-72; ptnr. Sills, Cummis, Radin, Tischman, Epstein & Gross, 1972—. Author: (with others) New Jersey Transaction Guide, Vol. 12, 1993, The Use of Another's Trademark: A Review of the Law in The United States, Canada, and Western Europe, 1997; co-author, editor: Trademark Law Basics Coursebook, 2001; rsch. editor: Rutgers Law Rev., 1966-67; cons. editor Trademark Administration, 1999; contbr. articles to profl. jours. Mem. ATLA, ABA, N.J. State Bar Assn., Essex County Bar Assn., Internat. Trademark Assn. (publs. bd., 2002, projects editl. bd. 2001-), N.Y. State Bar Assn. (sect. intellectual property, chair copyright law com.), Am. Intellectual Property Law Assn., N.J. Intellectual Property Law Assn., Phi Delta Phi (Outstanding Grad. 1967). Jewish. Federal civil litigation, General civil litigation, Trademark and copyright. Home: 72 Winged Foot Dr Livingston NJ 07039-8229 Office: Sills Cummis Radin Tischman Epstein & Gross Legal Ctr 1 Riverfront Plz Fl 13 Newark NJ 07102-5401

CAHN, RICHARD CALEB, lawyer; b. Bklyn., June 11, 1932; s. Irving and Pearl (Abel) C.; m. Vivian Isabel Meksin, Dec. 24, 1961; children: Michael, Lisa, Daniel, Sara. AB, Dartmouth Coll., 1953; LLB, Yale U., 1956; U. London, 1959. Bar: N.Y. 1956, Fla. 1966, U.S. Supreme Ct. 1960. Student asst. U.S. atty. So. Dist. N.Y., N.Y.C., 1955; atty. U.S. Dept. Justice, Washington 1956-57; ptnr. Cahn Wishod & Lamb, Melville, N.Y.; prin. asst. dist. atty. Suffolk County (N.Y.), 1965-66; dep. atty. Town of Huntington (N.Y.), 1966-68; spl. counsel towns of Smithtown, Islip, Brookhaven, Babylon, Southhampton (N.Y.), 1967-68, Islip, N.Y., 1976-83, Huntington, N.Y., 1981-92; counsel Brentwood Sch. Dist., 1977-82, 86-90; spl. counsel Amityville Sch. Dist., 1978-79, Village of North Hills, 1978-79, Merrick Pub. Library; adj. prof. Touro Coll., 1987-90, 93—; hearing officer N.Y. State Edn. Dept., Nassau and Suffolk Counties, 1971-77; spl. dist. atty. Suffolk County, 1972; participant World Peace Through Law Conf., 1967, Malpractice Mediation Panel, 2d dept., 1974-84, Gov.'s Jud. Nominating Com. 2d dept., 1975-81; mem. screening com. bankruptcy judges U.S. Dist. Ct. Dist. N.Y., 1976-81, mem. screening com. U.S. magistrates, 1977-81; regional counsel SUNY-Stony Brook, 1972-90. Bd. dirs. Stony Brook Found., 1974-86, Ea. Dist. Civil Litigation Fund, 1982-86; del. Moscow Conf. on Law & Jurisprudence, 1990; trustee, sec. bd. trustees Adelphi U., 1997—. Fellow Soc. Values in Higher Edn., 1984-96; mem. ABA, N.Y. Bar Assn. (ho. of dels. 1981-83, chmn. condemnation, zoning and property use com. 1989—), Suffolk County Bar Assn. (pres. 1981-82), Fed. Bar Assn., Am. Judicature Soc., Fed. Bar Council (v.p. 1982-84, trustee 1984-89), Huntington Lawyers Club. Contbr. articles to profl. jours.; bd. editors Yale Law Jour., 1954. Federal civil litigation, State civil litigation. Office: 425 Broadhollow Rd Ste 315 Melville NY 11747-4701

CAIN, GEORGE HARVEY, lawyer, business executive; b. Washington, Aug. 3, 1920; s. J. Harvey and Madeleine (McGettigan) C.; m. Patricia J. Campbell, Apr. 23, 1946 (div.); children: George Harvey, James C., John P., Paul J.; m. Constance S. Collins, Aug. 10, 1985 BS, Georgetown U., 1942; JD, Harvard U., 1948. Bar: N.Y. 1949, Ohio 1972, Conn. 1977, U.S. Supreme Ct. 1995. Practiced law, N.Y. State, 1949-71, 73-76; pvt. practice Ohio, 1972-73; sec., gen. counsel Nat. Carloading Corp., 1949-54; mem. firm Spence & Hotchkiss, 1954-55; gen. atty., asst. sec. Cerro Corp., 1955-68, sec., gen. atty., 1968-72; v.p., gen. counsel Pickands Mather Co., Cleve., 1971-73; v.p., sec., gen. counsel Flintkote Co., White Plains, N.Y., 1973-76, Stamford, Conn., 1976-80; spl. counsel Day, Berry & Howard, Hartford and Stamford, 1980-82, ptnr. Stamford, 1983-90, of counsel, 1991—. Sec. Cerro Sales Corp., 1955-71; bd. dirs., sec. Leadership Housing Sys., Inc., 1970-71; bd. dirs., gen. counsel Atlantic Cement Co., Inc., 1962-71; bd. dirs. Hajoca Corp., 1975-79, Polymer Bldg. Sys., Inc.; adj. prof. U. Bridgeport Law Sch., 1983-86. Author: Turning Points: New Paths and Second Careers for Lawyers, 1994, Law Firm Partnership: Its Rights and Responsibilities, 1995, 2nd edit., 1999. Served to 1st lt. USAAF, 1942-46; to capt. USAF, 1951-52. Fellow Am. Bar Found.; mem. ABA (chair-elect sr. lawyers divsn. 2001—), N.Y. State Bar Assn., N.Y.C. Bar Assn., Ohio Bar Assn., Conn. Bar Assn., Am. Law Inst., Am. Soc. Corp. Secs., Georgetown U. Alumni Assn. (mem. Alumni senate), Harvard Club N.Y., Dutch Treat Club. Home: 14 Burnt Hill Rd Farmington CT 06032-2039 Office: Day Berry & Howard City Place I Hartford CT 06103-3499 E-mail: cainghsr@worldnet.att.net

CALABRESE, ARNOLD JOSEPH, lawyer; b. Summit, N.J., Nov. 18, 1960; s. Jack and Valentine (Pannullo) C.; m. Kathryn DeRosa, Aug. 16, 1986. BS in Econs. and Fin., Fairleigh Dickinson U., 1983; JD, U. Bridgeport, 1986. Bar: N.J. 1986, U.S. Dist. Ct. N.J. 1986. Law clk. intern to judge U.S. Dist. Ct. Conn., Hartford, 1985; assoc. Robert J. Hueston (merged with E. Richard Kennedy 1987), Florham Park, Montville, N.J., 1986-88, Rosenberg & Rosenberg, Florham Park, 1988-89; ptnr. Rosenberg, Rosenberg & Calabrese, 1990-96; atty. Law Offices Arnold J. Calabrese PC, 1996—. Lectr. N.J. chpt. Community Assn. Inst., Pennington, 1987—. Mem. ABA, N.J. Bar Assn., Morris County Bar Assn., Phi Delta Phi. State civil litigation, General corporate, Real property. Home: 4 Jolen Ct Florham Park NJ 07932-2519 Office: 171 Ridgedale Ave Ste A Florham Park NJ 07932-1764 E-mail: loajcpc@aol.com

CALABRESI, GUIDO, federal judge, law educator; b. Milan, Oct. 19, 1932; s. Massimo and Bianca Maria (Finzi Contini) C.; m. Anne Gordon Audubon Tyler, May 20, 1961; children: Bianca Finzi Contini, Anne Gordon Audubon, Massimo Franklin Tyler BS in Analytical Econs., Yale U., 1953, LLB, 1958, MA (hon.), 1962; BA in Politics, Philosophy and Econs., Oxford U., 1955, MA in Politics, Philosophy and Econs., 1959; LLD (hon.), Notre Dame U., 1979, Villanova U., 1984, U. Toronto, 1985, Boston Coll., 1986, Cath. U. Am., 1986, U. Chgo., 1988, Conn. Coll., 1988, Chgo.-Kent-I.T.T., 1989, William Mitchell Coll. Law, 1992, Princeton U., 1992, Detroit Mercy Sch. Law, 1994, Seton Hall U., 1995, Albertus Magnus Coll., 1995, Lewis and Clark Coll., 1996, St. John's U., 1997, Pace U., 1998, Iona Coll., 1998, Roger Williams U., 1999, Hofstra U., 1999, N.Y. Law Sch., 1999, Skidmore Coll., 2000, Colby Coll., 2001, U. San Diego, 2001; Dott. Ius SD (hon.), U. Turin, Italy, 1982; JD (hon.), U. Pavia, Italy, 1987, U. Stockholm, 1993; PhD (hon.), U. Haifa, Israel, 1988; DPhil, U. Tel Aviv, 1998; LHD (hon.), U. New Haven, 1989, Williams Coll., 1991, Quinnipiac Coll., 1993; DSc in Politics (hon.), U. Padua, Italy, 1990; Dott. Jur. (hon.), U. Bologna, Italy, 1991, U. Milan, 1998. Bar: Conn. 1958. Asst. instr. dept. econs. Yale U., New Haven, 1955-56; law clk. to Hon. Hugo Black U.S. Supreme Ct., Washington, 1958-59; asst. prof. Yale U. Law Sch., 1959-61, assoc. prof., 1961-62, prof., 1962-70, John Thomas Smith prof. law, 1970-78, Sterling prof. law, 1978-95; prof. emeritus, lectr. Yale U., 1995—; dean Yale U. Law Sch., 1985-94, Sterling prof. law emeritus, lectr., 1995—; judge U.S. Ct. Appeals 2d cir., 1994—. Fellow Timothy Dwight Coll., 1960—; vis. prof. Harvard U. Law Sch., 1969-70, Japan Am. Studies Seminar, Kyoto-Doshisha Univs., summer 1972, European U. Inst., Florence, Italy, 1979; Arthur L. Goodhart prof. legal sci. Cambridge U., also fellow St. John's Coll., 1980-81. Author: The Costs of Accidents: A Legal and Economic Analysis, 1970; (with P. Bobbitt) Tragic Choices, 1978; A Common Law for the Age of Statutes, 1983 (ABA citation of merit, Order of Coif Triennial Book award); Ideals, Beliefs, Attitudes and the Law: Private Law Perspectives on a Public Law Problem (Silver Gavel award ABA), 1985; contbr. articles to profl. jours. Hon. trustee Hopkins Grammar Sch., pres. 1976-80; trustee St. Thomas More Chapel, Yale U.; vice-chmn. bd. trustees Carolyn Found., Minn. Rhodes scholar, 1953; named one of Ten Outstanding Young Men Am., U.S. Jaycees, 1962; recipient Laetare Medal, U. Notre Dame, 1985, Marshall-Wythe medal Coll. William and Mary, 1985, award for outstanding rsch. in law and govt. Fellows of Am. Bar Found., 1998, Thomas Jefferson medal in law Jefferson Found./U. Va. Law Sch., 2000. Fellow Am. Acad. Arts & Scis., Associazione Italiana di Diritto Comparato, Brit. Acad. (corr.), Royal Swedish Acad. Scis. (fgn.), Nat. Acad. dei Lincei (fgn.), Acad. delle Sci. di Torino (fgn.); mem. Conn. Bar Assn., Assn. Am. Law Schs. (exec. com. 1986-89), Am. Philos. Soc. Home: 639 Amity Rd Woodbridge CT 06525-1206 Office: US Ct Appeals 2d Cir 157 Church St New Haven CT 06510-2100

CALDERWOOD, JAMES ALBERT, lawyer; b. Washington, Dec. 4, 1941; s. Charles Howard and Hilda Pauline (Dull) C.; m. Joyce M. Johnson, 1987 BS, U. Md., 1964; J.D. cum laude, George Washington U., 1970; postgrad., Oxford Ctr. Mgmt. Studies, Oxford, Eng., 1977. Bar: Md. 1970, D.C. 1973, U.S. Supreme Ct. 1974. Trial atty. antitrust div. U.S. Dept. Justice, Washington, 1970-73; spl. asst. U.S. Atty., $, 1973, trial atty. antitrust div., 1973-79; ptnr. Grove, Jaskiewicz, Gilliam & Cobert, Washington, 1979-90, Zuckert, Scoutt, Rasenberger, Washington, 1990—. Mem. faculty Transp. Law Inst. U. Denver; adj. prof. Washington Coll. Law, Am. U., 1983, 86; faculty Internat. Law Inst., 1995—; gen. counsel Soc. Fovt. Economists. Contbr. articles to profl. jours. Served to capt. USAF, 1964-68. George Washington U. Law Ctr. scholar, 1969. Mem. ABA (Achievement award 1973), Fed. Bar Assn. (nat. co chmn. council young lawyers 1972-73, chmn. regulated industries com. 1976-79), Fed. Energy Bar Assn. (chmn. antitrust com. 1985-86, 93-95), Transp. Lawyers Assn. (chmn. antitrust com. 1998—); Assn. for Transp. Law, Logistics & Policy (pres. D.C. chpt. 1998-99), Md. Bar Assn., D.C. Bar Assn., U. Md. Alumni Assn. (pres. elect 1984-85, pres. 1985-86) Coll. Bus. Alumni Club (pres. 1980-81), Nat. Press Club, Pi Sigma Alpha, Delta Sigma Pi, Delta Theta Phi, English Speaking Union. Episcopalian. Antitrust, Federal civil litigation, Transportation. Home: 5518 Western Ave Chevy Chase MD 20815-7122 Office: Zuckert Scoutt & Rasenberger 888 17th St NW Ste 600 Washington DC 20006-3309 E-mail: jacalderwood@zsrlaw.com

CALDWELL, COURTNEY LYNN, lawyer, real estate consultant; b. Washington, Mar. 5, 1948; d. Joseph Morton and Moselle (Smith) C. Student, Duke U., 1966-68, U. Calif., Berkeley, 1967, 1968-69; BA, U. Calif., Santa Barbara, 1970, MA, 1975; JD with highest honors, George Washington U., 1982. Bar: D.C. 1984, Wash. 1986, Calif. 1989. Jud. clk. U.S. Ct. Appeals for 9th Cir., Seattle, 1982-83; assoc. Arnold & Porter, Washington, 1983-85, Perkins Coie, Seattle, 1985-88; dir. western ops. Edn. Real Estate Svcs., Inc., Irvine, Calif., 1988-91, sr. v.p., 1991-98; ind. cons., Orange County, 1998—. Bd. dirs. Univ. Town Ctr. Assn., 1994; bd. dirs. Habitat for Humanity, Orange County, 1993-94, chair legal com., 1994. Named Nat. Law Ctr. Law Rev. Scholar, 1981-82. Mem. Calif. Bar Assn. Avocation: foreign languages. Home: 7204 West Esast Highway #46 Newport Beach CA 92663 Office: 537 Newport Center Dr # 163 Newport Beach CA 92660-6937 E-mail: clcaldwell@earthlink.net

CALDWELL, GILBERT RAYMOND, III, lawyer; b. Newton, Iowa, June 14, 1952; s. Gilbert Raymond and Frances Elizabeth (Ellingsworth) C.; m. Jeanne Sharon Myerscough, Dec. 23, 1974; 1 son: Kyle Myerscough. BA, U. Tulsa, 1974, JD, 1977. Bar: Iowa 1978, U.S. Dist. Ct. (no. and so. dists.) Iowa, U.S. Supreme Ct. 1988. Asst. city prosecutor, legal intern City of Tulsa, 1976-77; asst. county atty. Jasper County, Iowa, 1978; ptnr. Caldwell, Caldwell & Caldwell, Newton, 1979—. Presenter in field. Contbr. Iowa Juvenile Law Manual, 1990. Rep. precinct chmn. Fairview Twp., Iowa, 1982-83; mem. legis. study com. on family cts. in Iowa, Iowa Supreme Ct., 1990, mem. select com. to review ct. practices in child welfare matters, 1997; mem. Coun. on Chemically Exposed Children, 1990; mediator, bd. dirs. Prairie City-Monroe Sch. Edn. Found.; facilitator Improving Representation in Child in Need of Assistance Cases conf., 1998; mem. faculty panel Practical Solutions to Family Law Ethical Problems seminar, 1993; mem. faculty substance abuse conf., 1993. Mem. ABA (young lawyers divsn., exec. coun. family law, child advocacy and protection com., juvenile justice exec. com., family law sect., juvenile law and needs of children com., mental health com., gen. practice sect., vice chairperson family law com. 1990—, regional coord. juvenile law update 1988-89, 90, pres. 5A judicial dist. 1991-92), Am. Judicature Soc., Iowa State Bar Assn. (mem. young lawyers divsn. 1982-89, exec. coun. 1987-89, chairperson, v.p. juvenile law com., co-chairperson membership and minority affairs, chairperson family law sect. 1991-92, 98-99, exec. coun. family law sect, 1990-92, litigation sect. practice aides com., vice-chair mental health com., gen. practice sect., family law com. 1990-92, chair family and juvenile law sect., 1991-92, 98-99, exec. coun. family and juvenile law sect., 1997—, family law resource panel vol. lawyers project 1997—), Jasper County Bar Assn. (pres. 1989-90), Iowa Trial Lawyers Assn., Assn. Trial Lawyers Am., Nat. Assn. Counsel for Children, Newton Jaycees (sec. 1978-79, pres. 1979-80), Newton C. of C., Iowa Jaycees (state legal coun. 1979-80), Monroe Community Club, Jasper County Farm Bur., Kiwanis Noon Club (faculty panel mem. family law seminar 1993, chair com. family & juvenile law sect. 1993-94). General practice. Home: RR 2 Monroe IA 50170-9802 Office: Caldwell Caldwell & Caldwell 102 1st St N Newton IA 50208-3226

CALDWELL, RODNEY KENT, lawyer; b. Washington, Feb. 19, 1937; s. Rodney Huntington and Marion Elisabeth (Sasher) C.; m. Marjorie Lee Zink, Apr. 15, 1965 (div. 1975); children: Dana Kent, Susan Ashley; m. Yolanda Silva, June 22, 1979; 1 child, David Huntington. BChemE, U. Va., 1959; JD, U. Houston, 1969. Bar: Tex. 1969, U.S. Supreme Ct. 1975. With Howrey Simon Arnold & White, LLP (formerly Arnold, White & Durkee), Houston, 1970—. Author: Patent Litigation: Procedure & Tactics, 1978-84. Lt. USAF, 1959-62. Fellow Tex. Bar Found., Houston Bar Found.; mem. ABA, Am. Intellectual Property Law Assn., Internat. Bar Assn., Internat. Intellectual Property Assn., Univ. Club., Army and Navy Club. Methodist. Federal civil litigation, Patent, Trademark and copyright. Home: 4021 Ella Lee Ln Houston TX 77027-3910 Office: Howrey Simon Arnold & White LLP 750 Bering Dr Houston TX 77057-2149 E-mail: caldwellr@howrey.com

CALE, CHARLES GRIFFIN, lawyer, private investor; b. St. Louis, Aug. 19, 1940; s. Julian Dutro and Judith Hadley (Griffin) C.; m. Jessie Leete Rawn, Dec. 30, 1978; children: Whitney Rawn, Walter Griffin, Elizabeth Judith. BA, Principia Coll., Elsah, Ill., 1961; LLB, Stanford U., 1964; LLM, U. So. Calif., 1966. Bar: Calif. 1965. Pvt. practice, L.A., 1965-90; ptnr. Adams, Duque & Hazeltine, 1970-81, Morgan, Lewis & Bockius, L.A., 1981-91. Bd. dirs., co-chmn., CEO World Cup USA 1994, Inc., L.A., 1991. Group v.p. sports L.A. Olympic Organizing Com., 1982-84; assoc. counselor U.S. Olympic Com., 1985, spl. asst. to pres., 1985-89, asst. to pres, dir. olympic del., 1989-92; bd. dirs. Century 21 Real Estate-Can. Ltd., 1995-97, Rapattoui Corp., 2001-, Foresters Equity Services Corp., 2001-. Trustee St. Jhn's Hosp. and Med. Ctr., Santa Monica, Marymount H.S.; asst. chief de mission U.S. Olylmpic Team, 1988; bd. dirs. Hallum Prevention of Child Abuse Fund, 1976-96. Recipient Gold medal of Youth and Sports, France, 1984. Mem. State Bar Calif., Calif. Club, L.A. Country Club, The Beach Club, Ind. Order Foresters (bd. dirs. 1993-2001), Eagle Springs Golf Club, Country Club of the Rockies. Office: PO Box 688 Pacific Palisades CA 90272-0688

CALESELLA, GIORGIO, lawyer; b. Milan, Italy, June 4, 1955; s. Franco and Tina Calesella; m. Adriana Santurro, Nov. 3, 1956; children: Ilaria, Uberto, Fabrizio. LLB, U. Statale, Milan. Owner Studio Legale Calesella, Milan, 1987—. Contbr. articles to profl. jours. Mem. Rotary Internat. (chmn. commn. 1999-2000). Office: Studio Legale Calesella 14 Via M Camperio Milan 20121 Italy Fax: 39028051067. E-mail: gcalesel@tin.it

CALHOUN, DONALD EUGENE, JR. federal judge; b. Columbus, Ohio, May 15, 1926; s. Donald Eugene and Esther C.; m. Shirley Claggett, Aug. 28, 1948; children: Catherine C., Donald Eugene III, Elizabeth C. BA in Polit. Sci., Ohio State U., 1949, JD, 1951. Bar: Ohio 1951. Pvt. practice, 1951-68; ptnr. Folkerth, Calhoun, Webster, Maurer & O'Brien, 1968-82, Guren, Merritt, Feibel, Sogg & Cohen, 1982-84; of counsel Lane, Alton, Horst, 1984-85; judge U. S. Bankruptcy Ct., Columbus, 1985-99, ret., 1999, recalled, 2000—. Gen. counsel Ohio Conf. United Ch. of Christ, 1964-85 Chmn. City-wide Citizens Com. for Neighborhood Seminars on Sch. Program and Fin., 1963; mem. Columbus Bd. Edn., 1963-71, pres., 1966, 70. With USNR, 1944-46. Mem. Columbus Bar Assn. (pres. 1967-68, Community Svc. award 1972), Nat. Conf. Bar Pres., Am. Arbitration Assn., Columbus Jaycees (life), Athletic Club, Masons. Congregationalist. Office: US Bankruptcy Ct 170 N High St Columbus OH 43215-2403

CALHOUN, MONICA DODD, lawyer; b. Astoria, N.Y., June 3, 1953; d. Enda Aloysius and Christina (McGrath) Dodd; m. Charles H. Calhoun, Feb. 4, 1983. BA, SUNY, Albany, 1975; JD, SUNY, Buffalo, 1978; LLM, NYU, 1983. Bar: N.Y. 1979, U.S. Dist. Ct. (so. dist.) N.Y., 1982. Atty. Windsor Life Ins. Co., N.Y.C., 1978-79; assoc. gen. counsel Manhatten Life Ins. Co., 1979-84; from assoc. counsel to v.p. and chief counsel Tchrs. Ins. Annuity Assn.-Coll. Retirement Equities Fund, 1984—. Mem. ABA, Am. Life Ins. Counsel, N.Y. State Bar Assn. Insurance, Pension, profit-sharing, and employee benefits, Corporate taxation. Office: Tchrs Ins & Ann Assn Am 730 3rd Ave New York NY 10017-3206

CALHOUN, SCOTT DOUGLAS, lawyer; b. Aurora, Ill., May 1, 1959; s. Ellsworth L. Calhoun and Mary Louise (Mummert) Wire; m. Gloria Jean Fulvi, Aug. 1, 1987; 1 child, John Daniel. BA cum laude, Knox Coll., 1981; JD, Coll. of William and Mary, 1984. Bar: Ga. 1984, U.S. Dist. Ct. (no. dist.) Ga. 1984, U.S. Ct. Appeals (11th cir.) 1984. Assoc. Swift, Currie, McGhee & Hiers, Atlanta, 1984-90, ptnr., 1990-92; pvt. practice, 1992-94; prin. Byrne, Eldridge, Moore & Davis, PC, 1994-95; ptnr. Mozley, Finlayson & Loggins, 1996—. Spkr. in field. Bd. dirs. Atlanta Symphony Assocs., 1991-97, Wildwood Civic Assn., Atlanta, 1991-98; elder Trinity Presbyn. Ch., Atlanta, 1994-97, 2001—. Mem. Mortar Bd. Avocations: golf, music. Contracts commercial, General corporate, Estate planning. Office: Mozley Finlayson & Loggins 5605 Glenridge Dr NE Ste 900 Atlanta GA 30342-1380 E-mail: scalhoun@mfllaw.com

CALHOUN-SENGHOR, KEITH, lawyer; b. Richmond, Va., June 14, 1955; s. Clarence Calhoun Jr. and Senegal Senghor; m. Sharon White. AB with honors, Stanford U., 1977; JD, Harvard U., 1981. Bar: D.C. 1981, U.S. Ct. Appeals (4th cir.) 1982. Law clk. to judge U.S. Ct. Appeals for 4th Cir., Richmond, 1981-82; assoc. Gibson, Dunn & Crutcher, L.A. and Washington, 1983-85; fgn. legal fellow Kreuz, Niebler & Mittl, Munich, 1986; v.p., gen. counsel Tech. Applications, Inc., Alexandria, Va., 1986-90; pres. Noma Internat. Enterprises, Inc., Washington, 1990-93; of counsel Wood, Williams, Rafalsky & Harris, 1991-93; dir. Office of Space Commercialization U.S. Dept. Commerce, 1993-99; v.p. internat. and legal affairs, gen. counsel Edenspace Systems Corp., Reston, Va., 1999—. Fulbright scholar U. Bonn., 1977-78; German Acad. Exch. Svc. Fgn. fellow, 1985-86. Mem. ABA, D.C. Bar Assn. Office: Edenspace Systems Corp 11720 Sunrise Valley Dr Ste 500 Reston VA 20191-1413

CALICO, PAUL B. lawyer; b. Berea, Ky., Aug. 24, 1954; s. Thruman E. and Norma Jean (Brandenberg) C.; m. Ann Carol Rutherford, June 2, 1979; children: Austin Clay, Molly Elizabeth. Magna cum laude, Western Ky. U., 1976; JD with distinction, U. Ky., 1980. Bar: Ohio 1980, Ky. 1981, U.S. Dist. Ct. (so. dist.) Ohio 1980, U.S. Dist. Ct. ea. dist.) Ky. 1981. Ptnr. Strauss & Troy, LPA, Cin., 1980—. Mediator The Ctr. for Resolution Disputes, Inc.; spkr. in field. Contbr. articles to profl. jours. Trustee Collaborative Law Ctr., Women Helping Women, Inc., Vol. Lawyers Found., past pres.; adminstrv. bd. dirs., fin. com. sec. Anderson Hills United Meth. Ch. Decorated Order of Coif U. Ky. Mem. ABA, ATLA, Ohio Bar Assn., Ohio Acad. Civil Trial Attys., Ky. Bar Assn., Ky. Acad. Trial Attys., Cin. Bar Assn. (arbitrator 1982—, participant vol. lawyers for the poor project 1983—, common peas ct. com. 1985—, Alt. Dispute resolution com., employment law com. 1990—, ct. appeals com. 1987—), No. Ky. Bar Assn., Ohio Valley Scottish Soc. (trustee). Alternative dispute resolution, Federal civil litigation, State civil litigation. Home: 900 Birney Ln Cincinnati OH 45230-3718 Office: Strauss & Troy Fed Res Bldg 150 E 4th St Cincinnati OH 45202-4018 E-mail: pbcalico@strauss-troy.com

CALISE, NICHOLAS JAMES, lawyer; b. N.Y.C., Sept. 15, 1941; s. William J. and Adeline (Rota) C.; m. Mary G. Flannery, Nov. 10, 1965; children: James R., Lori K. AB, Middlebury Coll., 1962; MBA, LLB, Columbia U., 1965. Bar: N.Y. 1965, Conn., 1974, Ohio, 1986, Colo. 2000. Assoc., ptnr. Olvany, Eisner & Donnelly, N.Y.C., 1969-76; corp. staff atty. Richardson-Vicks Inc., Wilton, Conn., 1976-82, div. counsel, dir. planning and bus. devel. home care products div. Memphis, 1982-84; staff v.p., sec., asst. gen. counsel The B.F. Goodrich Co., Akron, Ohio, 1984-89, v.p., sec., assoc. gen. counsel, 1989-99. Mem. Flood and Erosion Control Bd., Darien, Conn., 1976, Rep. Town Meeting, Darien, 1977-78; chmn. Zoning Bd. Appeals, Darien, 1978-82; Justice of the Peace, Darien, 1982. Served to lt. USN, 1965-68, capt. JAGC, USNR, 1984-96, ret. Mem. ABA, Am. Soc. Corp. Secs. (bd. dirs. 1990-93, exec. steering com. 1992-93, chpt. treas. 1988-89, sec. 1989-90, v.p. 1990-91, pres. 1991-92, chmn. nat. conf. com. 1997, chmn. fin. com. 1998-2000, chmn. by-laws revision com. 1998-99, Bracebridge H. Young Distinguished Service award, 2001), Am. Corp. Counsel Assn., N.Y. State Bar Assn., Colo. Bar Assn., Ohio Bar Assn., U.S. Naval Inst., Navy League (life), Judge Advs. Assn. (life), Naval Res. Assn. (life), Res. Officers Assn. (life), Am. Legion, Club Cordillera. Roman Catholic. General corporate, Mergers and acquisitions, Securities. Home: PO Box 1916 2035-4 Cordillera Way Edwards CO 81632 Office: PO Box 1964 Edwards CO 81632-1964 E-mail: caliselaw@yahoo.com

CALISE, WILLIAM JOSEPH, JR. lawyer; b. N.Y.C., May 22, 1938; s. William Joseph and Adeline (Rota) C.; m. Elizabeth Mae Gagne, Apr. 16, 1966; children: Kimberly Elizabeth, Andrea Elizabeth. BA, Bucknell U., 1960; MBA, JD, Columbia U., 1963. Bar: N.Y. 1963, D.C. 1981. Assoc. then ptnr. Chadbourne & Parke, N.Y.C., 1967-94; sr. v.p., gen. counsel, sec. Rockwell Internat. Corp., Milw., 1994—. Dir. Henry St. Settlement, N.Y.C., 1977-94; mem. Allendale (N.J.) Sch. Bd., 1977-80. Capt. U.S. Army, 1964-66. Mem. Assn. Bar N.Y.C., Milw. Club. Roman Catholic. Office: Rockwell Internat Corp 777 E Wisconsin Ave Milwaukee WI 53202-5300 E-mail: wjcalise@corp.rockwell.com

CALKINS, STEPHEN, law educator, lawyer; b. Balt., Mar. 20, 1950; s. Evan and Virginia (Brady) C.; m. Joan Wadsworth, Oct. 18, 1981; children: Timothy, Geoffrey, Virginia. BA, Yale U., 1972; JD, Harvard U., 1975. Bar: N.Y. 1976, D.C. 1977, U.S. Dist. Ct. D.C. 1979. Law clk. to FTC commr. S. Nye, Washington, 1975-76; assoc. Covington & Burling, 1976-83; assoc. law prof. Wayne State U., Detroit, 1983-88, prof., 1988—; gen. counsel FTC, Washington, 1995-97; spl. counsel Covington & Burling, 1997—, program dir. conf. and annual antitrust conf., 2001—. Vis. assoc. prof. law U. Mich., Ann Arbor, 1985, U. Pa., Phila., 1987; vis. prof. law U. Utrecht, Netherlands, 1989; chair career devel. Wayne State U., 1990-91. Editor: Antitrust Law Developments, 1984, 86, 88, (legal book revs.) The Antitrust Bulletin, 1986—, (articles) Antitrust, 1991-95. Counsel Ind. Commn. on Admissions Practices in Cranbrook Sch., Detroit, 1984-85; mem. Northville Zoning Bd. Appeals, 1987-95; rep.-at-large Assn. Yale Alumni Assembly, 1989-92; elder First Presbyn. Ch. of Northville, 1989-92. Research fellow Wayne State U., 1984; USAID grantee, 1999-2000. Mem. ABA (coun. antitrust sect. 1988-91, 97-2000, counsel to com. on FTC 1988-89, co-chair 50th Anniversary com. adminstrv. law sect. 1997-2000, council 1999—), Am. Law Inst., Am. Assn. Law Schs. (sec. antitrust sect. 1987-91, chair-elect, 1991-93, chair, 1993-95), Harvard Club, Yale Club (Detroit), Northville Swim Club. Avocations: reading, skiing. E-mial. Administrative and regulatory, Antitrust, General corporate. Home: 317 W Dunlap St Northville MI 48167-1404 Office: Wayne State U Law Sch 471 W Palmer Detroit MI 48202 E-mail: calkins@wayne.edu

CALKINS, SUSAN W. state supreme court justice; Grad., U. Colo.; JD, U. Maine. Staff atty., exec. dir. Pine Tree Legal Assistance; judge Maine Dist. Ct., 1980-90, chief judge, 1990; judge Maine Superior Ct., 1995; justice Maine Supreme Jud. Ct., 1998—. Office: Cumberland County Courthouse PO Box 368 142 Federal St Portland ME 04112-0368*

CALLAHAN, GARY BRENT, lawyer; b. Ashland, Oreg., Apr. 24, 1942; s. Donald Burr and Joyce Valeri (Powers) C.; m. Nancy Kay King, Feb. 1967 (div. 1978); children: Shawn, Christopher; m. Sally Kornblight, Jan. 18, 1983; 1 child, Zachary. Student, Sacramento State U.; JD, U. of Pacific, 1970. Bar: Calif. 1971, U.S. Dist. Ct. (ea. dist.) Calif. 1971. Assoc. Rust & Mills, Sacramento, 1971-73, Barrett, Matheny & Newlon, Sacramento, 1973-77; ptnr. Westley & Callahan, 1977-80, Wilcoxen, Callahan, Montgomery & Harbison, Sacramento, 1980-94, Callahan & Deacon, Sacramento, 1994—. Instr., lectr. Continuing Edn. Bar, Berkeley, Calif., 1978—; faculty mem. advocacy skills workshop Sch. Law Stanford U., 1994—, Sch. Law U. San Francisco, 1994—. Served with USN, 1960-63. Recipient Outstanding Alumnus award U. The Pacific McGeorge Sch. of Law, 1989, Outstanding Advocate of Yr. award Sacramento Consumer Attys., 1999. Mem. Calif. Bar Assn., Assn. Trial Lawyers Am. (sustaining), Consumer Attys. Calif., Am. Bd. Profl. Liability Attys., Am. Bd. Trial Advs., Nat. Bd. Trial Advs., Sacramento Consumer Attys. (pres. 1984-85, Adv. of Yr. 1999). Democrat. Avocations: lecturing, instructing on trial advocacy, sailing, boating. State civil litigation, Insurance, Personal injury. Office: Callahan & Deacon 77 Cadillac Dr Ste 240 Sacramento CA 95825-8328 E-mail: gbc8esd@calweb.com

CALLAHAN, JOHN JOSEPH, lawyer; b. Toledo, Feb. 5, 1922; s. Hugh and Anna (Mackin) C.; m. Joyce Teague, Apr. 18, 1953. BA, John Carroll U., 1949; LLB, U. Mich., 1952. Bar: Ohio 1952, U.S. Supreme Ct. 1966, U.S. Mil. Ct. Appeals 1966, U.S. Ct. Appeals (6th cir.) 1973. Assoc. Burgess & Callahan, Toledo, 1952-72, Openlander, Callahan & Connelly, Toledo, 1972-77; ptnr. Secor, Ide & Callahan, 1977-92; prin. John J. Callahan Law Office, 1992—99; of counsel McHugh, Denune and McCarthy, Sylvania, 1999—. Served to Maj. USAF, 1942-46. Fellow ABA, Ohio State Bar Assn., Toledo Bar Assn. (pres. 1969-70). Democrat. Roman Catholic. Criminal. Home: 4203 Eaglehurst Rd Sylvania OH 43560-3410 Office: 5580 Monroe St Sylvania OH 43560-2561

CALLAHAN, J(OHN) WILLIAM (BILL CALLAHAN), judge; b. Rockville Centre, N.Y., Feb. 8, 1947; s. Peter Felix and Catherine Lucille (Walbroehl) C. BA, Mich. State U., 1971, JD cum laude, 1974. Atty. Bank of Commonwealth, Detroit, 1974-76; assoc. Hoops & Hudson, P.C., 1976-79, Tyler & Canham, P.C., Detroit, 1979-80, Stark & Reagan, P.C., Troy, Mich., 1980-81; pvt. practice Farmington Hills, 1981-86; mem. Plunkett & Cooney, P.C., Detroit, 1986-96; judge Wayne County Cir. Ct., 1996—. Bd. dirs. Vietnam Vets. Am. Chpt. 9, Detroit, 1981-85. With USMC, 1967-69, Vietnam. Mem. ABA, Detroit Bar Assn. Office: 1813 City-County Bldg Detroit MI 48226

CALLAHAN, MICHAEL THOMAS, lawyer, construction consultant; b. Kansas City, Mo., Oct. 7, 1948; s. Harry Leslie and Venita June (Yohn) C.; m. Stella Sue Paffenbach, Mar. 21, 1970; children: Molly Leigh, Michael Kroh. BA, U. Kans., 1970; JD, U. Mo., 1973, LLM, 1979; postgrad., Temple U., 1976-77. Bar: Kans. 1973, N.J. 1975, Mo. 1977. V.p. T.J. Constrn., Inc., Lenexa, Kans., 1973-74; sr. cons. Wagner-Hohns-Inglis, Inc., Mt. Holly, N.J., 1974-77, v.p. Kansas City, Mo., 1977-86; exec. v.p. CCL Constrn. Cons., Overland Park, Kans., 1986-88, pres., 1988—. Adj. prof. U. Kans., Iowa State U.; arbitrator, lectr. in field, author; chmn. CCL Pacific Corp.; pres. Handcrafted Wines Kans., Inc. Home: 9011 Delmar St Shawnee Mission KS 66207-2343 Office: CCL Constrn Cons 4600 College Blvd Ste 104 Overland Park KS 66211-1606

CALLAHAN, ROBERT JEREMIAH, retired state supreme court justice, trial referee; b. Norwalk, Conn., June 3, 1930; s. Jeremiah J. and Elizabeth A. (Connolly) C.; m. Dorothy B. Trudel, Jan. 24, 1959; children: Sheila, Kerry, Denise, Janine, Patrick, Megan, Jane, Robert Jr. BS in History and Govt., Boston Coll., 1952; JD, Fordham U., 1955. Judge Cir. Ct. Conn., 1970-75, Ct. Common Pleas, Conn., 1975-76, Conn. Superior Ct., 1976-85; assoc. justice Conn. Supreme Ct., 1985-96, chief justice, 1996-99; ret., 1999. Judge trial referee Superior Ct., Stamford, Conn.; mem. Bd. Pardons, Conn., 1985-87. Served with U.S. Army, 1956-58. Recipient Fordham U. Sch. Law Dean's medal of recognition, 1986, Fordham Law Alumni Assn. medal of excellence, 1997, Fordham Disting. Alumnus award, 1998, U. Conn. Alumni Assn. Disting. Svc. award, 1998. Roman Catholic. Office: Superior Ct 123 Hoyt St Stamford CT 06905

CALLAHAN, TENA TOYE, lawyer; b. Dallas, Dec. 5, 1954; d. Norman Lewis Callahan and Toye Mae Dennis; m. Dennis Bakos, May 27, 1977 (div. Dec., 1982); children: Randall A., Jesse D. BFA, U. Tex., 1977; JD, St. Mary's U., 1991. Bar: Tex. 1992, U.S. Dist. Ct. (no. dist.) Tex. 1992. Lawyer pvt. practice, Dallas, 1992-97; shareholder Callahan & Byrd P.C., 1997-98; pvt. practice Tena T. Callahan, P.C., 1998—. Named Parent of Yr. Big Brothers and Sisters of Am., Dallas, 1984. Mem. ATLA, Coll. of State Bar of Tex. Avocations: acting, singing, reading. State civil litigation, Family and matrimonial, Juvenile. Office: 4655 N Central Expy Dallas TX 75205-4022

CALLAHAN, THOMAS JAMES, lawyer; b. Cleve., Jan. 21, 1957; s. Thomas Joseph and Lucille Dorothy (DeVries) C.; m. Laura Jean Schwartz, Oct. 13, 1979; children: Thomas, Michael. BS cum laude in Acctg., Duke U., 1979; JD cum laude, Case Western Reserve U., 1985. Bar: Ohio 1985, U.S. Ct. Appeals (6th cir.) 1987, U.S. Tax Ct. 1987, U.S. Dist. Ct. (no. dist.) Ohio 1987, U.S. Ct. Fed. Claims 1987, U.S. Ct. Appeals (fed. cir.) 2000, U.S. Supreme Ct. 2000; CPA, Ohio 1981. Staff sr. acct. Price Waterhouse, Cleve., 1979-82, mgr., 1985-86; assoc. Thompson Hine LLP, 1986-96, ptnr., 1997—. Dir. The Ultrasonic Solution, Inc., Solon, Ohio, 1989—; asst. sec. The Phoenix Packaging Corp., 1997—. Vice chair allocations com. United Way Svcs., Cleve., 1992-96; mem. arbitration com. Cuyahoga Ct. Common Pleas, Cleve., 1989—. Mem. ABA (tax sect., adminstrv. practice com.), AICPA, Cleve. Bar Assn. (chmn. gen. tax com. 1999), Cleve. Tax Inst. (spkr. 1994-98, program chair 1999, vice chair 2000, chair 2001), Tax Club Cleve. (dir. 2000, treas. 2001). Corporate taxation, Taxation, general, Personal income taxation. Office: Thompson Hine LLP 3900 Key Ctr 127 Pub Sq Cleveland OH 44114-1216 E-mail: tom.callahan@thompsonhine.com

CALLAN, TERRENCE A. lawyer; b. San Francisco, Sept. 20, 1939; s. Harold A. and Viola A. (Briese) C.; m. Gail R. Raine, Apr. 20, 1968; 1 child, Ryan T. BA, U. San Francisco, 1961; JD, U. Calif., San Francisco, 1964. Bar: Calif. 1965, U.S. Dist. Ct. (no. dist.) Calif. 1965, U.S. Ct. Appeals (9th cir.) 1965, U.S. Dist. Ct. (cen. dist.) Calif. 1970, U.S. Supreme Ct. 1975, U.S. Dist. Ct. (so. dist.) Calif. 1981, U.S. Dist. Ct. (ea. dist.) Calif. 1996. Rsch. asst. Pillsbury, Madison & Sutro, San Francisco, 1964-65, assoc., 1965-72, ptnr., 1973—. Dir. sec., gen. counsel Presidio Soc., 1981-94; dir. sec., legal counsel Ft. Point and Presidio Hist. Assn., 1984—; bd. trustees 1066 Found., Mildred E. Stearns Found. Mem. ABA, Calif. State Bar Assn. (past chmn., exec. com. antitrust and trade regulation sect.), San Francisco Bar Assn. (past mem. judiciary com., antitrust, 9th cir. no. dist. merit screening com. for bankruptcy judgeships), Lawyers Club San Francisco (bd. govs.), U. Calif. Alumni Assn., Hastings Coll. of the Law Annual Campaign (nat. chair), U. San Francisco Alumni Assn. (bd. govs.), Order of Coif, Green and Gold Club (chmn. bd. dirs.), U. San Francisco Club, Phi Alpha Delta. Roman Catholic. Antitrust, Federal civil litigation, State civil litigation. Office: Pillsbury Madison Sutro LLP PO Box 7880 San Francisco CA 94120-7880

CALLENDER, JOHN FRANCIS, lawyer; b. Jacksonville, Fla., May 3, 1944; s. Francis Louis and Ethel (McLean) C.; m. Susan Carithers, June 13, 1969; children: John Francis Jr., Susanna McLean. AB cum laude, Davidson Coll., 1966; MA, U. N.C., 1969; JD with distinction, Duke U., 1976. Bar: Fla. 1976, U.S. Supreme Ct. 1982; Fla. bd. cert. civil trial lawyer, cert. cir. ct. mediator. Asst. states atty. State of Fla., Jacksonville, 1980-81; ptnr. Turner, Ford & Callender, P.A., 1981-84; pvt. practice, 1984—. Pres. Mental Health Clinic Jacksonville, Inc., 1985; bd. dirs. Vol. Jacksonville, Inc., 1981-84. Served with U.S. Army, 1970-73. Fellow Am. Soc. Papyrologists, 1969. Mem. ABA, ATLA, Acad. Fla. Trial Lawyers, Fla. Bar Assn., Jacksonville Bar Assn., Fla. Yacht Club, River Club, Rotary Club (pres. 1997, asst. dist. gov. 1999—), Am. Mensa Ltd., Phi Beta Kappa Alumni Assn. of N.E. Fla. (treas. 1996-99, pres. 1999-2000). Democrat. Episcopalian. Avocations: sailing, windsurfing, fishing, tennis, swimming. Federal civil litigation, State civil litigation, Personal injury. Home: 1745 Woodmere Dr Jacksonville FL 32210-2233 Office: 1301 Riverplace Blvd Ste 2105 Jacksonville FL 32207-9027 E-mail: jcallend@Fdn.com

CALLIES, DAVID LEE, lawyer, educator; b. Chgo., Apr. 21, 1943; s. Gustav E. and Ann D. Callies; m. Laurie Breeden, Dec. 28, 1996; 1 child, Sarah Anne. AB, DePauw U., 1965; JD, U. Mich., 1968; LLM, U. Nottingham, England, 1969. Bar: Ill. 1969, Hawaii 1978, U.S. Supreme Ct. 1974. Spl. asst. states atty., McHenry County, Ill., 1969; assoc. firm Ross, Hardies, O'Keefe, Babcock & Parsons, Chgo., 1969-75, ptnr., 1975-78; prof. law Richardson Sch. Law, U. Hawaii, Honolulu, 1978—; Benjamin A. Kudo prof. law U. Hawaii, 1995—. Mem. adv. com. on planning and growth mgmt. City and County of Honolulu Coun., 1978-88, mem. citizens adv. com. on State Functional Plan for Conservation Lands, 1979-93. Author: (with Fred P. Bosselman) the Quiet Revolution in Land Use Control, 1971 (with Fred P. Bosselman and John S. Banta) The Taking Issue, 1973, Regulating Paradise: Land Use Controls in Hawaii, 1984, (with Robert Freilich and Tom Roberts) Cases and Materials on Land Use, 1986, 3d edit., 1999, Preserving Paradise: Why Regulation Won't Work, 1994 (in Japanese 1994, in Chinese 1999), Land Use Law in the United States, 1994; editor: After Lucas: Land Use Regulation and the Taking of Property Without Compensation, 1993, Takings! Land Development Conditions and Regulatory Takings: After Dolan and Lucas, 1995, (with Hylton, Mandelker and Franzese) Property Law and the Public Interest, 1998; co-editor Environ. and Land Use Law Rev., 2000—. Life Fell., Clare Hall, Cambridge Univ. Named Best Prof., U. Hawaii Law Sch., 1990-91, 91-92; Mich. Ford Found. fellow U. Nottingham (Eng.), 1969, life mem. Clare Hall, Cambridge U., 1999. Mem. ABA (chmn. com. on land use, planning and zoning 1980-82, coun. sect. on state and local govt. 1981-85, 95—, exec. com. 1986-90, sec. 1986-87, chmn. 1989-90), Am. Law Inst., Am. Inst. Cert. Planners, Am. Planning Assn., Hawaii State Bar Assn. (chair, real property and fin. svc. sect., 1997), Am. Bar Found., Ill. Bar Assn., Internat. Bar Assn. (coun. Asia Pacific Forum 1993-96, co-chair Acads. Forum 1994-96, chair 1996-98), Nat. Trust for Hist. Preservation, Royal Oak Soc., Lambda Alpha Internat. (pres. Aloha chpt. 1989-90, internat. v.p. Asia-Pacific region 2001—, Internat. Mem. of Yr. 1994). Home: 1532 Kamole St Honolulu HI 96821-1424 Office: U Hawaii Richardson Sch Law 2515 Dole St Honolulu HI 96822-2328 E-mail: dcallies@hawaii.edu

CALLINAN, PATRICIA ANN, legal secretary; b. Harrisburg, Pa., Dec. 29, 1943; d. Albert Frances and Gilda Mary (Cifani) Pugliese; 1 child, Tricia Ann Corder. Comml. diploma, Bishop McDevitt, 1961. Chief enforcement sec. Commonwealth of Pa., Harrisburg, 1961-66; supt. sec. Cape May (N.J.) County Vocat. Tech. Ctr., 1966-67; asst. br. mgr. Continental Title Ins., Wildwood, N.J., 1967-91; legal sec. Corino & Dwyer, Esqs., 1991—. Past. pres., treas. Cape May County Legal Sec., 1968-70, St. Ann's PTA, Wildwood, 1980-84; past pres. Wildwood Cath. Parent Guild, 1986-88; bd. sec. Wildwood Crest Tourism Commn., 1990-93. Mem. Cape May County Women's Rep. Club; apptd. commr. Cape May County Mcpl. Utilities Authority, 1999; sunshine chmn. Cape May County Rep. Orgn. Named Legal Sec. of Yr., Cape May County Legal Sec., 1970, 73. Mem. Victoria Village Homeowners (sec. 1994-96), Lower Township Rep. Club, Lower Township Rep. Orgn. (committeewoman 1994-96, 96—, mem. exec. com. rec. sec. 1994—), Cape May County Legal Secs. Assn. Roman Catholic. Avocations: walking, dancing, reading, plays. Home: 36 Canterbury Way Cape May NJ 08204-4268 Office: Corino & Dwyer Esqs 9700 Pacific Ave Wildwood NJ 08260-3334

CALLISON, JAMES W. former lawyer, consultant, airline executive; b. Jamestown, N.Y., Sept. 8, 1928; s. J. Waldo and Gladys A. C.; m. Gladys I. Robinson, Oct. 3, 1959; children: Sharon Elizabeth, Maria Judith, Christopher James. AB with honors, U. Mich., 1950, JD with honors (Overbeck award 1952, Jerome S. Freud Meml. award 1953), 1953. Bar: D.C. 1954, Ga. 1960. Atty. Pogue & Neal, Washington, 1953-57; with Delta Air Lines, Inc., Atlanta, 1957-93, v.p. law and regulatory affairs, 1974-78, sr. v.p., gen. counsel, 1978-81, sr. v.p., gen. counsel, corp. sec., 1981-88; sr. v.p. legal and corp. affairs, sec. Delta Air Lines Inc., 1988-90; sr. v.p. corp. and external affairs Delta Air Lines, Inc., 1990-91, sr. v.p. corp. affairs, 1991-93; ret., 1993; cons. Inman Deming Internat., Washington. Contbr. articles to legal jours.; asst. editor: Mich. Law Rev, 1952-53. Bd. dirs. St. Joseph's Mercy Found.; mem. adv. bd. Village St. Joseph, Atlanta Union Mission; pres. Woodlands Assn., Inc., Dunwoody, Ga. Recipient Papal Pro Ecclesia Et Pontifice award, 1966 Mem. State Bar Ga. (chmn. corp. counsel sect. 1989-90, mem. emeritus), Atlanta Bar Assn. (life), Atlanta Athletic Club, Order of Coif. General corporate, Legislative, Transportation. Home: 2034 Dunwoody Club Way Dunwoody GA 30338-3024

CALLISON, RUSSELL JAMES, lawyer; b. Redding, Calif., Sept. 4, 1954; s. Walter M. and Norma A. (Bruce) C. BA in Polit. Sci., U. of Pacific, 1977, JD cum laude, 1980. Bar: Calif. 1980, U.S. Dist. Ct. (ea. dist.) Calif. 1981, U.S. Dist. Ct. (no. dist.) Calif. 1986, U.S. Ct. Appeals (9th cir.) 1989. Assoc. Memering & DeMers, Sacramento, 1980-85; pres. DeMers, Callison & Donovan, P.C., 1985-95; ptnr. Lewis, D'Amato, Brisbois & Bisgaard, San Francisco, 1995—. Spl. master Calif. State Bar, 1991—; arbitrator, judge pro tem Calif. Superior Cts., 1986—. Co-author: Premises Liability in California, 1996. Mem. ABA (litigation sect.), SAR (chpt. pres. 1992-93), Am. Arbitration Assn. (panel of arbitrators), Assn. Def. Counsel No. Calif., Commonwealth Club, Natomas Racquet Club, Order of Coif, Phi Alpha Delta. Republican. Episcopalian. Avocations: golf, hunting, fishing, antique restoration. General civil litigation, Insurance, Professional liability. Home: 3889 20th St San Francisco CA 94114-3018 Office: Lewis D'Amato Brisbois & Bisgaard One Sansome St Ste 1400 San Francisco CA 94104-4431 E-mail: callison@ldbb.com

CALLISTER, LOUIS HENRY, JR. lawyer, director; b. Aug. 11, 1935; s. Louis Henry and Isabel (Barton) C.; m. Ellen Gunnell, Nov. 27, 1957; children: Mark, Isabel, Jane, Edward, David, John Andrew, Ann. BS, U. Utah, 1958, JD, 1961. Bar: Utah 1961. Asst. atty. gen., Utah, 1961; sr. ptnr. Callister Nebeker & McCullough, Salt Lake City, 1961—. Bd. dirs. Am. Stores Co., 1985-97, Quailbluff Devel. Co., 1971-2000; Vice-chmn. Salt Lake City Zoning Bd. Adjustment, 1979-84; bd. govs. Salt Lake Valley Hosps., 1983-91; treas. exec. com. Utah Rep. Com., 1965-69; chmn. Utah chpt. Rockefeller for Pres. Com., 1964-68; sec., trustee Salt Lake Police/Sheriff Hon. Cols., 1982-97; trustee, mem. exec. com. Utah Econ. Devel. Corp., 1992—, chmn., 1998-2000; trustee U. Utah, 1987-99, vice-chmn., 1989-99, bd. dirs. U. Utah Hosp., 1993-99; trustee Grand Canyon Trust, 2001—. Mormon. Banking, General corporate, Mergers and acquisitions. Home: 3860 Highland Ct Bountiful UT 84010-3365 Office: Callister Nebeker & McCullough Gateway Tower E Ste 900 Salt Lake City UT 84133-1102 E-mail: 1hcallister@cnmlaw.com

CALLOW, KEITH MCLEAN, judge; b. Seattle, Jan. 11, 1925; s. Russell Stanley and Dollie (McLean) C.; m. Evelyn Case, July 9, 1949; children: Andrea, Douglas, Kerry. Student, Alfred U., 1943, CCNY, 1944, Biarritz Am. U., 1945; BA, U. Wash., 1949, JD, 1952. Bar: Wash. 1952, D.C. 1974. Asst. atty. gen., Wash., 1952; law clk. to justice Supreme Ct. Wash., 1953; dep. pros. atty. King County, 1954-56; ptnr. Little, LeSourd, Palmer, Scott & Slemmons, Seattle, 1957-62, Barker, Day, Callow & Taylor, 1964-68; judge King County Superior Ct., 1969-71, Ct. of Appeals Wash., Seattle, 1972-84, presiding chief judge, 1985-90; justice State Supreme Ct. Wash., Olympia, 1985-90, chief justice, 1989-90; cons. Prior-Martech, 1998—. 2d v.p. Conf. of Chief Justices; Booneville Power Admin. Rate Hearings Officer, 1995-96; lectr. bus. law U. Wash., 1956-62, Shefelman Disting. lectr., 1991; faculty Nat. Jud. Coll., 1980, Seattle U. Environ. Law, 1992, 94-95; co-organizer, sec. Coun. of Chief Justices of Cts. of Appeals; Rep. of Estonia, 1993-96, advisor Nat. Ct. and Ministry of Justice; advisor Kyrgyzstan, Kazakhstan, Georgia, Armenia, 1997; presenter in field. Editor-in-chief Commercial Law Desk Book, 1992-95; editor works in

field. Chief Seattle coun. Boy Scouts Am.; adviser Gov. Health Care Commn. State of Washington, 1991-92; pres. Young Men's Rep. Club, 1957. With AUS, 1943-46. Decorated Purple Heart; recipient Brandeis award Wash. State Trial Lawyers Assn., 1981, Douglas award, 1990. Fellow Am. Bar Found.; mem. ABA (chmn. com. on judiciary 1984-90), Wash. State Bar Assn. (mem. exec. com., appellate Judges Conf.), D.C. Bar Assn., Seattle-King County Bar Assn., Estate Planning Coun., Navy League, Rainier Club (sec. 1978, trustee 1989-92), Forty Nine Club (pres. 1972), Masons, Rotary, Psi Upsilon, Phi Delta Phi.

CALLOW, WILLIAM GRANT, retired state supreme court justice; b. Waukesha, Wis., Apr. 9, 1921; s. Curtis Grant and Mildred G. C.; m. Jean A. Zilavy, Apr. 15, 1950; children: William G., Christine S., Katherine H. PhB in Econs, U. Wis., 1943, JD, 1948. Bar: Wis.; cert. for Fla. mediation. Asst. city atty., Waukesha, 1948-52; city atty., 1952-60; county judge Waukesha, 1961-77; justice Supreme Ct. Wis., Madison, 1978-92. Asst. prof. U. Minn., 1951-52; mem. faculty Wis. Jud. Coll., 1968-75; Wis. commr. Nat. Conf. Commrs. on Uniform State Laws, 1967—; arbitrator Wis. Employment Rel. Commn.; arbitrator-mediator bus. disputes; arbitration and mediation nat. and internat. res. judge, 1992—. With USMC, 1943-45; with USAF, 1951-52, Korea. Recipient Outstanding Alumnus award U. Wis., 1973 Fellow Am. Bar Found.; mem. ABA, Dane County Bar Assn., Waukesha County Bar Assn. Episcopalian. Fax: 608-241-9923, 715-588-3452, 941-642-8889. E-mail: wgc@mymailstation.com, justice4@newnorth.net

CALMEIROS, JOSE MARIA ALBUQUERQUE, lawyer; b. Porto, Portugal, Nov. 26, 1965; s. Jorge and Maria Norton C.; m. Sofia Pidwell, July 18, 1998; children: Jose Maria, Maira da Piedade. Univ. law, Cath. U., 1988; M in Law, Lisbon U., 1992. Ptnr. Jose Maria Calmeiros and Assocs., Lisbon, 1992. Author: O Secton Bancanu e a Cre, 1993; Financas Europeias, 1998. Banking, Corporate taxation, Taxation, general. Office: Av Antonio Augusto de Aguiar 38-6 Lisbon 1050-016 Portugal

CALOGERO, PASCAL FRANK, JR. state supreme court chief justice; b. New Orleans, Nov. 9, 1931; s. Pascal Frank and Louise (Moore) C.; children— Deborah Ann Calogero Applebaum, David, Pascal III, Elizabeth, Thomas, Michael, Stephen, Gerald, Katie, Chrissy. Student, Loyola U., New Orleans, 1949-51, J.D., 1954; ML in the Jud. Process, U. Va., 1992; DLL (hon.), Loyola U., New Orleans, 1991. Bar: La. Ptnr. Landrieu, Calogero & Kronlage, 1958-69, Calogero & Kronlage, 1969-73; gen. counsel La. Stadium and Expn. Dist., 1970-73; assoc. justice Supreme Ct. La., New Orleans, 1973-90, chief justice, 1990—. Mem. La. Democratic State Central Com., 1963-71; mem. subcom. on del. selection La. Dem. Party, 1971; del. Dem. Nat. Conv., 1968. Served to capt. JAGC U.S. Army, 1954-57. Recipient Disting. Jurist award La. Bar Founds., 1991; Judge Bob Jones Meml. award, Am. Judges Assn., 1995. Mem. ABA, La. Bar Assn., New Orleans Bar Assn., Greater New Orleans Trial Lawyers Assn. (v.p. 1967-69), Order of the Coif. Office: Supreme Ct La 301 Loyola Ave New Orleans LA 70112-1814 E-mail: icaloger@lasc.org

CALVANI, TERRY, lawyer, former government official; b. Carlsbad, N.Mex., Jan. 29, 1947; s. torello Howard and Mary Virginia (Hawkins) C.; m. Mary Virginia Anderson, May 3, 1969; m. 2d, Judith Thompson, Aug. 28, 1980; children: Dominic Mario, Torello Howard. BA, U. N.Mex., 1969; JD with distinction, Cornell U., 1972. Bar: N.Mex. 1972, Calif. 1972, Tenn. 1978, D.C. 1992, U.S. Dist. Ct. N.Mex. 1972, U.S. Dist. Ct. (no. dist.) Calif. 1972, U.S. Dist. Ct. (mid. dist.) Tenn. 1978, U.S. Dist. Ct. D.C. 1994, U.S. Ct. Appeals (9th cir.) 1972, U.S. Ct. Appeals (6th cir.) 1977, U.S. Ct. Appeals (5th cir.) 1981, U.S. Ct. Appeals (11th cir.) 1981, U.S. Ct. Appeals (D.C. cir.) 1994, U.S. Supreme Ct. 1985. Tchg. fellow Stanford U. Law Sch., 1972-73; assoc. Pillsbury, Madison & Sutro (now Pillsbury Winthrop LLP), San Francisco, 1973-74, ptnr., 1990—. Asst. prof. law Vanderbilt U. Sch. Law, Nashville, 1974-77, assoc. prof., 1977-80, prof., 1980-83; vis. prof. law U. Va., Charlottesville, 1981-82; of counsel Haksell Slaughter & Young, Birmingham, Ala., 1980-83; commr. U.S. FTC, 1983-90, acting chmn., 1985-86; lectr. Harvard U. Sch. Law, 1998—; sr. lectrg. fellow Duke U. Sch. Law, 2000. Author: (with John Siegfried) Economic Analysis and Antitrust Law, 1979, 2d edit., 1988; bd. editors Antitrust Bull., 1982—, Bur. Nat. Affairs RICO Report, 1986-96. Mem. Am. Law Inst., ABA (chmn. spl. com. to study antitrust penalties and damages Antitrust Sect. 1979-82, chmn. Robinson-Patman com. antitrust sect. 1981-83, council mem. 1985-86, 90-93), 6th Cir. Jud. Conf. (life), Adminstrv. Conf. U.S. 1985-90, Order of Coif, The Club (Birmingham), The G.C. Club of Tenn. (Nashville), Olympic Club (San Francisco), Pacific Union Club (San Francisco), Riverside Country Club (Carlsbad), The Harvard Faculty Club (Cambridge, Mass.), Colonnade Club (Charlottesville). Roman Catholic. Antitrust. Office: Pillsbury Winthrop LLP 12th Flr 1133 Connecticut Ave NW Washington DC 20036 Office Fax: 202-833-8491. E-mail: tcalvani@pillsburywinthrop.com

CALVERT, JAY H., JR. lawyer; b. Charleston, S.C., Mar. 19, 1945; m. Ann E., June 14, 1969; children: Amanda, Emily, Sarah. BA, Amherst (Mass.) Coll., 1967; JD, U. Va., 1970. Bar: Pa. 1970, U.S. Dist. Ct. (ea. dist.) Pa. 1970, U.S. Ct. Appeals (3d cir.) 1971, U.S. Dist. Ct. (mid. dist.) Pa. 1973, U.S. Ct. Appeals (2d cir.) 1980, U.S. Ct. Appeals (8th cir.) 1987, U.S. Supreme Ct. 1989, U.S. Dist. Ct. Ariz. 1994, U.S. Dist. Ct. (we. dist.) Pa. 2000. Assoc. Morgan, Lewis & Bockius LLP, Phila., 1970-78, ptnr., 1978—, exec. ptnr., 1987-90, mng. ptnr., 1990-94; mgr. litigation sect., firm governing bd. Morgan Lewis & Bockius LLP, 1990-98, mem. exec. com., 1997-98, sr. ptnr. litigation sect., 1998—. Trustee Agnes Irwin Sch., Rosemont, Pa., 1988-94, Leukemia Soc. Am., Phila., 1982—; bd. dirs. St. David's Nursery Sch., Wayne, Pa., 1980-94; chmn. devel. com. Phila. Zool. Soc., 1993-96, chmn. facilities, exhibits and safety com., 1997—, bd. dirs., 1992—, vice-chmn. bd. dirs., 1994-96.; mem. ann. fund campaign com. Inglis House, 1998—. Mem. ABA, Pa. Bar Assn., Phila. Bar Assn., Lawyers Club of Phila. Avocations: biking, gardening, hiking, horseback riding, animal husbandry. Antitrust, General civil litigation, Health. Office: Morgan Lewis & Bockius LLP 1701 Market St Philadelphia PA 19103-2903 Fax: 215-963-5299. E-mail: jcalvert@morganlewis.com

CAMBRICE, ROBERT LOUIS, lawyer; b. Nov. 23, 1947; s. Eugene and Edna Bertha (Jackson) C.; m. Christine Jackson, Jan. 7, 1972; children: Bryan, Graham. BA cum laude, Tex. So. U., 1969; JD, U. Tex., 1972. Bar: Tex. 1973, U.S. Dist. Ct. (so. dist.) Tex. 1975, U.S. Ct. Appeals (5th cir.) 1975, U.S. Ct. Appeals (11th cir.) 1981, U.S. Supreme Ct. 1981. Asst. atty. City of Houston, 1974-76; pvt. practice, Houston, 1976-81; asst. atty. Harris County, Tex., 1981-85, City of Houston, 1986—, sr. trial atty. legal dept., 1990-92, chief def. litigation dept., 1992—. Earl Warren fellow, 1969-72. Mem. ABA, NAACP, Nat. Bar Assn., Alpha Kappa Mu. Roman Catholic. E-mail: Robert.Cambrice@cityofhouston.net

CAMERON, JOHN CLIFFORD, lawyer, health science facility administrator; b. Phila., Sept. 17, 1946; m. Eileen Duffy, July 12, 1975; children: Christopher, Meghan. BA, U. Pitts., 1969; MBA, Temple U., 1972; JD, Widener U., 1976; LLM, NYU, 1980. Bar: Pa. 1977, N.J. 1977, Md. 1995. Asst. adminstr. Phila. Psychiatric Ctr., 1972-76; jud. clk. to presiding justice N.J. Superior Ct., Newark, 1976-77; asst. adminstr. St. Elizabeth Hosp., Elizabeth, N.J., 1977; v.p. corp. legal affairs Methodist Hosp., Phila., 1978-94; solicitor, 1988-94; legal cons. North Penn Hosp, Lansdale, Pa., 1994-95; counsel, legal adminstr. Hodes, Ulman, Pessin & Katz, P.A., Towson, Md., 1995-96; asst. to pres. Temple U. Health Sys., Phila., 1996—; asst. sec. Neumann Med. Ctr., 1997—, Temple U. Children's Med. Ctr., Phila., 1997—, Jeanes Hosp., Phila., 1997—, Northwood Nursing Home, Phila., 1997—, Temple Physicians, Inc., Phila., 1997—, Temple Univ. Hosp., Phila., 1997—, Lower Bucks Hosp., Bristol, Pa., 1997—, Episcopal Hosp., Phila., 1997—, Temple U. Children's Med. Ctr., Phila., 1997—, Northeastern Hosp., Phila., 1997—, Temple Continuing Care Ctr., Phila., 1997—. Sec. Suthbrelt Properties, Ltd., Phila., 1981-94, Asbury Corp., Wilmington, Del., 1982-94, Healthmark, Inc., Moorestown, N.J., 1982-94, Meth. Hosp. Nursing Ctr., Phila., 1983-94; asst. sec. various hosps. and nursing homes, 1997—, instr. Grad. Sch. Mgmt., Pa. State U., 1991—; instr. mgmt. dept. Neumann Coll., 1991-96; instr. bus. divsn. Rosemont Coll., 1995-96. Contbr. articles to profl. jours. Mem. campaign United Way, Phila., 1979-94; mem. health and welfare com. United Meth. Eastern Pa. Conf., 1978-94; advisor Explorer Post, Boy Scouts Asm., 1988-94; mem. steering com. Golden Cross, Phila., 1984-94; sec. Tredyffrin Twp. Park and Recreation Bd., 1987-95; alumni rep. Widener U.; mem. environ. adv. com. and open space task force Tredyffrin Twp., 1991-95. Fellow Am. Coll. Healthcare Execs. (chmn. bylaws com. 1995-96); mem. ABA, N.J. Bar Assn., Pa. Bar Assn., Phila. Bar Assn., Am. Hosp. Assn., Hosp. Assn. Pa., Swedish Colonial Soc. (bd dirs. 1992—, gov. 1993-95), Sons of Union Vets. of Civil War, SAR. Avocations: swimming, music. General corporate, Health. Home: 1410 Church Rd Malvern PA 19355-9714

CAMERON, JOHN GRAY, JR. lawyer; b. Detroit, July 28, 1949; s. John Gray and Helen Jane (Schueler) C.; m. Ann Elizabeth Dargus, June 19, 1976; children— Clara Katherine. A.B., Albion Coll., 1971; J.D. cum laude, Wayne State U., 1974. Bar: Ill. 1974, Mich. 1978, Colo. 1998, N.C. 1999, U.S. Ct. Appeals (8th cir.) 1975, U.S. Dist. Ct. (ea. dist.) Mo. 1975, U.S. Dist. Ct. (no. dist.) Ill. 1975, U.S. Dist. Ct. (we. dist.) Mich. 1978, U.S. Ct. Appeals (6th cir.) 1980. Law clk. U.S. Ct. Appeals, St. Louis, 1974-75; assoc. Isham, Lincoln & Beale, Chgo., 1975-78; ptnr. Warner, Norcross & Judd, Grand Rapids, Mich., 1978— ; instr. Seidman Sch. Bus., Grand Valley State Coll., Allendale, Mich., 1979-85, Mich. Inst. Continuing Legal Edn., 1980-82; lectr. Mich. Bar, 1983. Author: Michigan Real Property Law: Principles and Commentary, 1984, 2nd edit. 1993, Michigan Real Estate Forms and Practice, 1988, A Practioner's Guide to Construction Law, 2000; contbg. author: Michigan Real Estate Form Book, 1982-83. Bd. dirs. Urban Inst. Contemporary Art, Grand Rapids, 1980-82; trustee East Congl. Ch., Grand Rapids, 1985-88, Mary Free Bed Hosp. and Rehab. Ctr., 1997—. Mem. ABA, Mich. Bar Assn., Grand Rapids Bar Assn., Grand Rapids Bar Found., Am. Land Title Assn., Omicron Delta Epsilon. Republican. Club: U. Real property. Home: 56 Campau Cir NW Grand Rapids MI 49503-2658 Office: Warner Norcross & Judd 900 Old Kent Bldg Grand Rapids MI 49503-2487

CAMIC, DAVID EDWARD, lawyer; b. Indpls., June 11, 1954; s. Edward Franklin Camic and Carolyn (Hooker) Camic-Longland. BA, Aurora U., 1982; postgrad., DePaul U., 1982-83; JD cum laude, John Marshall Law Sch., 1987. Bar: Ill. 1987, U.S. Dist. Ct. (no. dist.) Ill. 1990, N.Y. 1996. Ptnr. Camic, Johnson, Wilson & McCulloch P.C., Aurora, Ill., 1987—. Mem. faculty, lectr. Aurora U.; lectr. in criminal law Regional Police Tng., Aurora, 1987—. Contbr. articles to profl. jours. Chmn. Rape Def. Seminar, Aurora, 1986. Named Man of Yr. Todays Orgn. Youth, 1987. Mem. ATLA, ABA, Ill. Bar Assn. (past-chair criminal justice sect.), Kane County Bar Assn. (past chair criminal law com., bd. dirs. 2000-01), Nat. Assn. Criminal Lawyers, Phi Delta Phi. Criminal. Office: Camic Johnson Wilson & McCulloch PC 546 W Galena Blvd Aurora IL 60506-3855

CAMING, H. W. WILLIAM, lawyer, consultant; b. N.Y.C., Sept. 22, 1919; s. Arthur and Anne Winifred (Hayman) C.; m. Kathleen Marie White, Feb. 16, 1951; 1 child, Patricia Reynolds. BS summa cum laude, NYU, 1938; JD, Harvard U., 1941; LLM, NYU, 1956. Bar: N.Y. 1943, U.S. Dist. Ct. (so. dist.) N.Y. 1950, ICC 1954, FCC 1957. With office corp. counsel Brit. Ministry of Supply Mission, N.Y.C., Washington and Ottawa, Ont., Can., 1941-43; chief prosecutor and dep. dir. polit. ministries div. Office of U.S. Chief of Counsel for War Crimes, Nuremburg, Ger., 1946-49; spl. asst. atty. gen. State of N.Y., 1950-52; atty. Bell Telephone Labs., N.Y.C., 1953-57; labor counsel long lines dept. AT&T, 1957-65; chief co. spokesman; sr. counsel in charge privacy and corp. security AT&T, N.Y.C., 1965-76; Basking Ridge, N.J., 1977-84; cons. privacy matters, info. tech. and corp. security, 1984—. Mem. nat. adv. bd. Ctr. Info. Tech. and Privacy Law of John Marshall Law Sch., Chgo., 1983-88; lectr., panelist symposia internat. war crimes trials, and privacy matters, 1975—. Columnist Dubois (Pa.) Courier-Express, 1949-50; contbr. articles to profl. publs. Mem. Summit (N.J.) Bd. Edn., 1969-73, 85-88, pres., 1972; mem. adv. panels Congl. Office Tech. Assessment, 19987-88; mem. U.S. Privacy Coun. Served to capt. USAAF, 1943-46; capt. JAGC, USAR, 1946-53; PTO, CBI. Mem. ABA (chair com. privacy of criminal justice sect. 1981-83, vice chmn. 1980, 84-85, advisor on privacy matters to chair criminal justice sect. 1985-97), U.S. C. of C. (panel on privacy 1978-82, com. working group transborder data flow C. of C.'s U.S. and Can. 1984-85), U.S. Council Internat. Bus. (com. mem.), Nat. Dist. Attys. Assn., Computer Profls. for Social Responsibility, JAG Assn., Harvard Law Sch. Assn., Brotherhood of St. Andrew, Mil. Order World Wars, Organized Res. Corps Assn., Belmont Golf Club (Bermuda), Phi Beta Kappa. Republican. Episcopalian. Office: 17 Knob Hill Dr Summit NJ 07901-3024

CAMP, JACK TARPLEY, JR. federal judge; b. Newnan, Ga., Oct. 30, 1943; s. Jack Tarpley and Sophia (Stephens) C.; m. Elizabeth Thomas, Apr. 24, 1976; children: Thomas Henry, Sophia Rose. BA, The Citadel, Charleston, S.C., 1965; MA, U. Va., 1967, JD, 1973. Bar: Ala. 1973, Ga. 1975. Atty. Cabaniss, Johnston, Dumas & O'Neal, Birmingham, Ala., 1973-75, Glover & Davis, P.A., Newnan, 1975-88; U.S. dist. judge Atlanta, 1988—. Mgr. family timber land holdings. Mem. Newnan Hist. Soc., 1975—, Ga. Trust for Hist. Preservation, Atlanta, 1975—. Capt. U.S. Army, 1967-70, Vietnam. Decorated Bronze Star; Ford Found. fellow U. Va., 1965-66. Mem. Ga. State Bar (bd. govs. 1987-89), Newnan-Coweta Bar Assn. (pres. 1978), Fed. Judges Assn., Kiwanis. Presbyterian. Office: US Dist Ct 2142 US Courthouse 75 Spring St SW Atlanta GA 30303-3309

CAMPBELL, AMY TANNERY, lawyer; b. San Diego, June 15, 1971; d. Terrance J. and Sally A. Campbell. BA, U. Notre Dame, 1993; JD, Yale U., 1997. Bar: Pa. 1997. Assoc. Drinker Biddle & Reath LLP, Phila., 1997—. Mem. Young Am. Polit. Action Com. Mem. ABA, Am. Health Lawyers Assn., Pa. Bar Assn., Phila. Bar Assn. Democrat. Roman Catholic. Health. Office: Drinker Biddle & Reath LLP PNB Bldg 1345 Chestnut St Philadelphia PA 19107-3496

CAMPBELL, BRUCE IRVING, lawyer; b. Mason City, Iowa, July 7, 1947; s. E. Riley Jr. and Donna Mae (Andresen) C.; children: Anne, John; m. Beverly J. Evans. BA, Upper Iowa U., 1969; JD, Harvard U., 1973. Bar: Iowa 1973, U.S. Dist. Ct. (so. dist.) Iowa 1973, U.S. Dist. Ct. (no. dist.) Iowa 1974, U.S. Tax Ct. 1976, U.S. Ct. Appeals (8th cir.) 1977, U.S. Ct. Claims 1982. Shareholder Davis, Brown, Koehn, Shors & Roberts, P.C., Des Moines, 1973—. Adj. prof. law Drake U., Des Moines, 1974-90. Trustee Upper Iowa U., Fayette, 1978—, chair bd. trustees, 1992—; sec., dir Iowa Natural Heritage Found., 2001—. Mem. ABA, Iowa State Bar Assn., Polk County Bar Assn. Republican. Estate planning, Estate taxation, Taxation, general. Home: 62 Meadowbrook Cir Cumming IA 50061-1014 Office: Davis Brown Koehn Shors & Roberts PC 666 Walnut St Ste 2500 Des Moines IA 50309-3904 E-mail: bruce.campbell@lawiowa.com

CAMPBELL, DIANA BUTT, lawyer; b. Ayer, Mass., Nov. 14, 1943; d. Lester A. and Genevieve P. (Ash) Butt; m. James W. Campbell, Feb. 3, 1961; children: James R., Lisa J., Alan D. BS magna cum laude, Suffolk U., 1980; JD, New Eng. Sch. Law, 1984. Bar: Mass. 1984, U.S. Dist. Ct. Mass. 1986, U.S. Supreme Ct. 1988. Editor Danvers (Mass.) State Hosp. Newsletter, 1977, Mass. Press Assn. Bull., 1978-79; mediator, case coord. Salem (Mass.) Mediation Program, 1979-83; legal adv. Help for Abused Women and Their Children, Salem, 1980-82; pvt. practice, Hamilton, Mass., 1984—. Chair Hamilton Housing Authority, 1975-80; vol. Danvers State Hosp., 1978-92; mem. Cape Ann Area bd. Dept. Social Svc., Beverly, Mass., 1982-84; merit badge counselor Boy Scouts Am., Hamilton, 1984-93; assoc. mem. Hamilton Cable Adv. Bd., 1987-91; bd. dirs. United Way of North Shore, Beverly, 1988-94; adv. bd. of money mgmt. program North Shore Elder Svcs., 1993—. Mem. Nat. Acad. Elder Law Attys., Assn. Trial Lawyers Am., Mass. Acad. Trial Lawyers, Mass. Bar Assn., Soc. Profl. Journalists, Essex County Bar Assn., Salem Bar Assn., North Shore Women Lawyers' Assn., Kiwanis (pres. 1990-91). Avocations: Volkssporting, photography, travel. Family and matrimonial, Juvenile, Probate. Home: 30 East St Topsfield MA 01983 Office: 65 Railroad Ave South Hamilton MA 01982-2218

CAMPBELL, EDWARD ADOLPH, judge, electrical engineer; b. Boonville, Ind., Jan. 16, 1936; s.Revis Allen and Sarah Gertrude (Hunsaker) C.; m. Nancy Colleen Keys, July 26, 1957; children: Susan Elizabeth Campbell Frisse, Stephen Edward, Sara Lynne. BEE, U. Evansville, 1959; JD, Ind. U., 1965; grad. Nat. Coll. Dist. Attys., U. Houston, 1972; grad. Nat. Jud. Coll., U. Nev., 1978; grad. Am. Acad. Jud. Edn., U. Va., 1979; grad., Ind. Jud. Coll., 1981; grad. Ind. Grad. Program for Judges, Ind. Jud. Ctr., 1999. Bar: Ind. 1965, U.S. Dist. Ct. (so. dist.) Ind. 1965, U.S. Ct. of Customs and Patent Appeals 1967, U.S. Supreme Ct. 1973, U.S. Ct. Appeals (fed. cir.) 1982. Patent examiner U.S. Patent Office Digital Computer Divsn., Washington, 1959-60; patent adv. U.S. Naval Avionics, Indpls., 1960-65; patent atty. Gen. Elec. Co., Ft. Wayne, Ind., 1965-66; ptnr. Weyerbacher & Campbell, attys., Boonville, 1966-71; pros. atty. 2nd Jud. Cir., Warrick County, 1971-77; judge Warrick Superior Ct. No. 1, 1977-2001; sr. judge Ind. State Trial Cts., 2001—. Fellow Ind. Bar Found.; mem. IEEE, Ind.State Bar Assn., Evansville Bar Assn., Warrick County Bar Assn., Ind. Judges Assn., Nat. Coun. Juvenile and Family Ct. Judges, Ind. Coun. Juvenile and Family Ct. Judges, Warrick County C. of C. (bd. dirs. 1978-84, 97—), Lions Club, Kiwanis Club, Sigma Pi Sigma, Phi Delta Phi. Democrat. Methodist. Home: 911 Julian Dr Boonville IN 47601-9556

CAMPBELL, GEORGE EMERSON, lawyer; b. Piggott, Ark., Sept. 23, 1932; s. Sid and Mae (Harris) C.; m. Anna Claire Janes, June 22, 1960 (dec. Mar. 1971); children: Dianne, Carole; m. Joan Stafford Rule, Apr. 7, 1973. J.D., U. Ark., Fayetteville, 1955. Bar: Ark. 1955, U.S. Supreme Ct. 1971. Law clk. to judge Ark. Supreme Ct., 1959-60; mem. Rose Law Firm, P.A., Little Rock, 1960—; Del. 7th Ark. Constl. Conv., 1969-70; regional v.p. Nat. Mcpl. League, 1974-86. Mem. Ark. Ednl. TV Commn., 1976-92, chmn., 1980-82, 88-91; bd. dirs. Ark. Ednl. TV Found., 1984-92, chmn., 1988-91. Chmn. bd. Pulaski County Law Libr., 1980—; bd. dirs. Ark. Arts Ctr., 1991-95, sec. 1992-93), Ark. Symphony Orch. Soc., 1982-87, Ark. Capital Corp., Ark. Cert. Devel. Corp., Downtown Partnership; bd. dirs. Youth Home Inc., 1986-92, pres., 1991-92. With USNR, 1955-77, ret.. Fellow Am. Bar Found.; mem. ABA, Ark. Bar Assn., Pulaski County Bar Assn., Am. Law Inst., Am. Judicature Soc., Nat. Assn. Bond Lawyers. General corporate, Municipal (including bonds), Real property. Office: Rose Law Firm PA 120 E 4th St Little Rock AR 72201-2893 Office Fax: 501-375-1309. E-mail: gcambell@roselawfirm.com

CAMPBELL, HUGH BROWN, JR. judge; b. Charlotte, N.C., Feb. 19, 1937; s. Hugh Brown and Thelma Louise (Welles) C.; m. Mary Irving Carlyle, Nov. 3, 1962; children: Hugh B. III, Irving Carlyle, Thomas Lenoir. AB, Davidson Coll., 1959; JD, Harvard U., 1962. Atty. Craighill, Rendleman, Charlotte, 1964-77, Weinstein & Sturges, Charlotte, 1977-94, Cansler Lockhart Charlotte, 1995-2000; judge N.C. Ct. Appeals, Raleigh, 2001—. Chmn. Jury Commn., Mecklenburg County, N.C., 1985-97; exec. com. County Bar Assn., Mecklenburg County, 1989-92, civil cts. com. chair, 1990-92. Rep. N.C. House Reps., Raleigh, 1969-71; legis. liaison Charlotte/Mecklenburg County, Raleigh, 1971-72; state chmn. N.C. Zoo Bond Campaign, 1972; chmn. Carolinas Med. Ctr. Bond Campaign, 1976. Col. JAG U.S. Army, 1962-64, Res., 1964-92. Decorated Legion of Merit, Meritorious Svc. medal (2); Honored Order of Hornet, Mecklenburg County, 1976. Mem. N.C. Bar Coun. (exec. com., chair ethics 1981-90), Planned Parenthood Charlotte (bd. dirs., chmn. 1980-81), YMCA Charlotte (adv. bd. 1992—), Rotary Club E. Charlotte (pres. 1976-77). Democrat. Episcopalian. Avocations: tennis, swimming, hiking, reading, politics. Home: 1428 Scotland Ave Charlotte NC 28207-2561 Office: NC Ct Appeals PO Box 888 Raleigh NC 27602

CAMPBELL, LEVIN HICKS, federal judge; b. Summit, N.J., Jan. 2, 1927; s. Worthington and Louise (Hooper) C.; m. Eleanor Saltonstall Lewis, June 1, 1957; children: Eleanor S., Levin H., Sarah H. AB cum laude, Harvard U., 1948, LLB, 1951; postgrad., Nat. Coll. State Judiciary, 1970; LLD (hon.), Suffolk U., 1975. Bar: D.C. 1951, Mass. 1954. Assoc. firm Ropes & Gray, Boston, 1954-64; mem. Mass. Ho. of Reps., 1963-64; asst. atty. gen. State of Mass., 1965-66, spl. asst. atty. gen., 1966-67, 1st asst. atty. gen., 1967-68; assoc. justice Superior Ct. of Mass., 1969-72; judge U.S. Dist. Ct. Mass., Boston, 1972, U.S. Ct. Appeals (1st cir.), Boston, 1972—, chief judge, 1983-90, sr. judge, 1992—. Fellow Inst. of Politics J.F. Kennedy Sch. Govt. Harvard U., 1968-69, study group leader 1980; faculty chmn. law session Salzburg Seminar in Am. Studies, 1981 Pres. Cambridge 9 Neighborhood Assn., 1960-62; treas. Cambridge Ctr. for Adult Edn., 1961-64; campaign chmn. Cambridge United Fund, 1965; mem. bd. overseers Boston Symphony Orch., 1969-75, 77-80; pres. bd. overseers Shady Hill Sch., 1969-70; mem. vis. com. Harvard U. Press, 1958-64; v.p. Cambridge Community Svcs.; corp. mem. SEA Ednl. Assn., 1982—; trustee Colby Coll., Waterville, Maine 1981-90, 91-99, Asheville (N.C.) Sch.; overseer U.S. Constitution Mus. 1st lt. (j.g.) U.S. Army, 1951-54, Korea. Mem. ABA, Am. Law Inst., Am. Bar Found., Mass. Bar Found., Boston Bar Assn., U.S. Jud. Conf. (ct. adminstrn. com. 1975-83, chmn. subcom. on supporting pers. 1980-83, exec. com. 1985-90, chmn. com. to rev. cir. coun. conduct and disability orders 1989-94, ad hoc com. study jud. conf. 1987, fed. ct. study com. 1988-90, nat. commn. on jud. discipline and removal 1991-93), Mass. Hist. Soc. (coun. 1993-96, long range planning com. 1999-2000, v.p. 1996-99, pres. 2001—). Office: US Ct of Appeals US Courthouse 1 Courthouse Way Ste 6720 Boston MA 02210-3008

CAMPBELL, PAUL, III, lawyer; b. Chattanooga, Feb. 1, 1946; children: Paul IV, Kolter M. BA, Vanderbilt U., 1968; MA, Middlebury Coll., 1972; postgrad., So. Meth. U., 1971-72, Emory U., 1972-73; JD, U. Tenn., 1975. Bar: Tenn. 1976, Ga. 1977. Tchr. English St. Mark's Sch., Dallas, 1968-72; ptnr. Campbell & Campbell, Chattanooga, 1976-98; mem. Witt, Gaither & Whitaker, 1998—. Adj. prof. English, U. Tenn., Chattanooga, 1976, adj. prof. law, 1979-81, adj. prof. pre-trial litigation, Knoxville, 1996; mem. Tenn. Ct. of Judiciary, 1995—; mem. Tenn. Jud. Evaluation Guidelines Commn., 1994-95. Author: Tennessee Admissibility of Evidence in Civil Cases, 1987; co-author: Tennessee Automobile Liability Insurance, 1986, 95, 96, 99; editor-in-chief Tenn. Law Rev., 1975; contbr. articles to profl. jours. Bd. mgrs. YMCA Youth Residential Ctr., 1977-80; mem. McCallie Sch. Alumni Coun., 1987-93, U. Tenn. Dean's Alumni adv. coun. law coll., 1979—; trustee, Harbison Found., 1994-96. Recipient Am. Jurisprudence award U. Tenn., 1974, U. Tenn. Coll. Law Pub. Svc. award, 1995; Alumni Achievement award McCallie Sch., 1994. Mem. ABA, Am. Bar Found., Tenn. Bar Assn. (bd. govs. 1985-94, pres. 1992-93), Tenn. Bar Found., Chattanooga Bar Found., Chattanooga Bar Assn. (bd. govs. 1983-85), State Bar Ga., Fed. Bar Assn. (dir. chpt. 1983-88), Fed. Ins. and Corp. Counsel, Def. Rsch. Inst., Internat. Assn. Def. Counsel, Order of Coif, Phi Kappa Phi. Federal civil litigation, State civil litigation, Insurance. Office: Witt Gaither & Whitaker 736 Market St Ste 1100 Chattanooga TN 37402-4856

CAMPBELL, RICHARD BRUCE, lawyer; b. Phila., Jan. 5, 1947; s. George B. and Edith (Neithammer) C.; m. Patricia Ann James, Mar. 7, 1981; children: Ron Martin, Rebecca Joi. BA, U. S.C., 1968, JD, 1974. Bar: U.S. Dist. Ct. S.C. 1975, U.S. Ct. Appeals (4th cir.) 1976, U.S. Ct. Appeals (5th cir.) 1983, Colo. 1985, U.S. Dist. Ct. Colo. 1986, U.S. Ct. Appeals (fed. cir.) 1989, Fla. 1989, U.S. Dist. Ct. (mid. dist.) Fla., U.S. Ct. Appeals (11th cir.) 1992. Law clk. to presiding justice U.S. Dist. Ct., Columbia, S.C., 1975; ptnr. Henderson & Salley, Aiken, 1975-80; atty. TVA, Knoxville, 1980-85; ptnr. Wells, Love & Scoby, Boulder, Colo., 1986-89; shareholder Carlton, Fields, Ward, Emmanuel, Smith & Cutler, P.A., Tampa, Fla., 1989—. Lectr. in field. Contbr. articles to profl. jours. Served to capt. USAF, 1968-72. Mem. ABA, Am. Arbitration Assn. (panelist), Fla. Bar Assn., Colo. Bar Assn., Hillsborough County Bar Assn. Avocations: travel, skiing, photography. General civil litigation, Construction, Government contracts and claims. Office: Carlton Fields Ward Emmanuel Smith & Cutler PC PO Box 3239 Tampa FL 33601-3239 E-mail: rcamp@carltonfields.com

CAMPBELL, ROBERT HEDGCOCK, investment banker, lawyer; b. Ann Arbor, Mich., Jan. 16, 1948; s. Robert Miller and Ruth Adele (Hedgcock) C.; m. Katherine Kettering, June 17, 1972; children: Mollie DuPlan, Katherine Elizabeth, Anne Kettering. BA, U. Wash., 1970, JD, 1973. Bar. Wash. 1973, Wash. State Supreme Ct. 1973, Fed. 1973, U.S. Dist. Ct. (we. dist.) Wash. 1973, Ct. Appeals (9th cir.) 1981. Assoc. Roberts & Shefelman, Seattle, 1973-78, ptnr., 1978-85; sr. v.p. Lehman Bros., Inc., 1985-87, mng. dir., 1987—. Bd. dirs. Pogo Producing Co., 1999—; dir., treas. Nat. Assn. Bd. Lawyers, Hinsdale, Ill., 1982-85; pres., trustee Wash. State Soc. Hosp. Attys., Seattle, 1982-85; mem. econs. dept. vis. com. U. Wash., 1995-97; mem. Law Sch. dean's adv. bd. U. Wash., 1999—. Contbr. articles to profl. jours. Trustee Bellevue (Wash.) Schs. Found., 1988-91, pres., 1989-90; nation chief Bellevue Eastside YMCA Indian Princess Program, 1983-88; trustee Wash. Phikeia Found., 1983-91, Sandy Hook Yacht Club Estates, Inc., 1993-98; mem. Wash. Gov.'s Food Processing Coun., 1990-91. Mem. U. Wash. Varsity Swimming Alumni Bd. Republican. Avocations: skiing, wind surfing, bike riding, physical fitness, golf. Home: 8604 NE 10th St Medina WA 98039-3915 Office: Lehman Bros Columbia Seafirst Ctr 701 5th Ave Ste 7101 Seattle WA 98104-7016 E-mail: ibe2ski@aol.com, rhcampbe@lehman.com

CAMPBELL, ROY TIMOTHY, JR. lawyer; b. Newport, Tenn., Aug. 8, 1927; s. Roy Timothy and Polly Vance (Brittain) C. LLB, U. Tenn., 1950. Bar: Tenn. 1951, U.S. Dist. Ct. Tenn. 1953, U.S. Ct. Appeals (6th cir.) 1962. Pvt. practice, Newport, 1951-64; with Campbell & Hooper, 1964—; atty. Town of Newport, 1963—. Bd. dirs. Mchts. and Planters Bank; mem. Tenn. Senate, 1983. Bd. dirs. Indsl. Devel. Bd., Newport, 1964—; pres. Union Cemetery, Newport; chmn. adminstrn. bd. First United Meth. Ch., Newport, 1980-82; sec.-treas. Cocke County Rep. Exec. Com., Tenn., 1964—. With U.S. Army, 1946-47. Mem. Cocke County Bar Assn. (pres. 1973-74), Civic Club, Lions (Lion of Yr. 1980-81). General practice, Personal injury, Probate. Office: 335 E Main St Newport TN 37821-3131

CAMPBELL, SCOTT ROBERT, lawyer, former food company executive; b. Burbank, Calif., June 7, 1946; s. Robert Clyde and Jenevieve Anne (Olsen) C.; m. Teresa Melanie Mack, Oct. 23, 1965; 1 son, Donald Steven. BA, Claremont Men's Coll., 1970; JD, Cornell U., 1973. Bar: Ohio 1973, U.S. Dist. Ct. (so. dist.) Ohio 1974, Minn. 1976, Calif. 1989, U.S. Dist. Ct. (no. dist.) Calif. 1989, U.S. Ct. Appeals (9th cir.) 1989, U.S. Dist. Ct. (cen. and so. dists.) Calif. 1990, U.S. Ct. Appeals (5th cir.) 1991, U.S. Tax Ct. 1991. Assoc. Taft, Stettinius & Hollister, Cin., 1973-76; atty. Mpls. Star & Tribune, 1976-77; sr. v.p., gen. counsel, sec. Kellogg Co., Battle Creek, Mich., 1977-89; ptnr. Furth Fahrner Mason, San Francisco, 1989-2000, Zelle, Hofmann, Voelbel, Mason & Gette, LLP, San Francisco, 2000—. U.S. del. ILO Food and Beverage Conf., Geneva, 1984; participant, presenter first U.S.-USSR Legal Seminar, Moscow, 1988; speaker other legal seminars. Mem. ABA, Ohio Bar Assn., Minn. Bar Assn., Calif. Bar. Assn. Antitrust, General corporate, Securities. Office: Zelle Hofmann Voelbel Mason& Gette LLP 500 Sansome St Ste 400 San Francisco CA 94111-3219 E-mail: srclaw@ix.netcom.com, scampbel@zelle.com

CAMPBELL, SELAURA JOY, lawyer; b. Oklahoma City, Mar. 25, 1944; d. John Moore III and Gyda (Hallum) C. AA, Stephens Coll., 1963; BA, U. Okla., 1965; MEd, Chapel Hill U., 1974; JD, N.C. Cen. U., 1978; postgrad. atty. mediation courses, South Tex. Sch. of Law, Houston, 1991, Atty. Mediators Inst./Dallas, Dallas, 1992. Bar: Ariz 1983; lic. real estate broker, N.C.; cert. tchr. N.C. With flight svc. dept. Pan Am. World Airways, N.Y.C., 1966-91; lawyer Am. Women's Legal Clinic, Phoenix, 1987. Charter mem. Sony Corp. Indsl. Mgmt. Seminar, 1981; guest del. Rep. Nat. Conv., Houston, 1992; judge all-law sch. mediation competition for Tex., South Tex. Sch. Law, Houston, 1994. Mem. N.C. Cen. U. Law Rev., 1977-78. People-to-People del. People's Republic of China, 1987; guest del. Rep. Nat. Conv., Houston, 1992. Mem. Ariz. Bar Assn., Humane Soc. U.S., Nat. Wildlife Fedn., People for the Ethical Treatment of Animals, Amnesty Internat., Phi Alpha Delta. Republican. Episcopalian. Avocations: climbed Mt. Kilimanjaro, 1983, also Machu Pichu, Peru, Mt Kenya, Africa, horseback riding, photography. General civil litigation, Family and matrimonial, General practice. Home: 206 Taft Ave Cleveland TX 77327-4539

CAMPBELL, THOMAS DOUGLAS, lawyer, consultant; b. N.Y.C., Jan. 5, 1951; s. Edward Thomas and Dorothy Alice (Moore) C.; m. Mary Anne Makin, Dec. 22, 1978; 1 child, Kristen Anne. BA, U. Del., 1972; JD, U. Pa., 1976. Bar: Del. 1977. Law clk. Law Offices Bayard Brill & Handleman, Wilmington, Del., 1974-77; govt. affairs rep. Northeastern U.S. Std. Oil Co. Ind., 1977-78; Washington rep. Std. Oil Co., Ind., 1978-85; pres. Thomas D. Campbell and Assocs., Inc., Alexandria, Va., 1985—; chmn. bd. dirs. Compressus, inc., 2001—. Govt. affairs rep. Northeastern U.S., Std. Oil Co. Ind., 1977-78. With U.S. Army, 1968-69, Del. Air N.G., 1969-77. Elected to Wall of Fame, U. Del., 2000. Mem. ABA, Del. Bar Assn., Congl. Awards Found. (chmn. bd. dirs.), Duke of Edinburgh's Internat. Award Assn. (internat. trustee), Phi Beta Kappa, Phi Kappa Phi, Omicron Delta Epsilon, Omicron Delta Kappa. Republican. Episcopalian. Legislative. Home: 517 Queen St Alexandria VA 22314-2512 also: PO Box 37 Cruz Bay Saint John VI 00831

CAMPBELL, VINCENT BERNARD, judge, lawyer; b. Rochester, N.Y., Nov. 1, 1943; s. Paul and Lucy (Tarricone) C.; m. Geraldine Miceli, July 4, 1970; children: Dina, Tracy. BS, Syracuse U., 1965, LLD, 1968. Bar: N.Y. 1969. Lawyer Goldman and Shinder, Rochester, N.Y., 1970-74, Vincent B. Campbell Law Firm, Rochester, 1974—; businessman Flower City Builders Supply Corp., 1974—; real estate developer V.R.J.D. Devel. Inc., 40 West Ave. Properties, 1970—; judge Town of Greece, 1994—. V.p. Monroe County Legislature, Rochester, 1976-88; N.Y. state committeeman Rep. Party, Rochester, 1988-93; town councilman Town of Greece, 1990-94; bd. trustees N.Y. Chiropractic Coll., Seneca Falls, N.Y., 1992; econ. devel. com. Nazareth Coll., Rochester, 1991-93. Recipient Robert Roantree award Syracuse Credit Mfrs. Assn., 1965, Am. Jurisprudence award Lawyers Coop., 1969; named Legislator of the Yr., Monroe County Conservative Party, 1983-84. Mem. ABA, N.Y. State BarAssn., Monroe County Bar Assn., N.Y. State Magistrate's Assn., Rochester Yacht Club. Avocations: sailing, golfing, hunting, winemaking. Office: 1577 Ridge Rd W Ste 203 Rochester NY 14615-2511

CAMPOS, ELIZABETH BALLI, lawyer; b. McAllen, Tex., Oct. 9, 1970; d. S. Balli; m. Julio A. Campos; 1 child, Jacob Alex. BBA in Mgmt., Tex. A&M U., 1995; JD, Tex. So. U., Houston, 1998. Bar: Tex. 1998. Law clk. Howard Singleton & Assocs., Houston, 1996-97, Harris County Atty.'s Office, Houston, 1997-98, 61st Dist. Ct., Houston, 1998; atty. Law Office of Manuel Solis, 1999—. Mem. State Bar Tex., Tex. Young Lawyers Assn., Mex.-Am. Bar Assn. Roman Catholic. Avocation: water sports. Office: Law Office of Manuel E Solis 6657 Navigation Blvd Houston TX 77011-1341

CANARY, LEURA, prosecutor; Graduate, Huntington Coll.; JD, U. Ala. Asst. Atty. Gen. Ala. Atty. Gen. Office, 1981—90; trial atty. Dept. of Justice Civil Dist., Ala., 1990—94; asst. U.S. Atty. Middle Dist. , 1991—2001, U.S. Atty., 2001—. Office: US Attnoney's Office One Ct Sq Suite 201 Montgomery AL 36104 Fax: 334-223-7560*

CANBY, WILLIAM CAMERON, JR. federal judge; b. St. Paul, May 22, 1931; s. William Cameron and Margaret Leah (Lewis) C.; m. Jane Adams, June 18, 1954; children— William Nathan, John Adams, Margaret Lewis. A.B., Yale U., 1953; LL.B., U. Minn., 1956. Bar: Minn. 1956, Ariz. 1972. Law clk. U.S. Supreme Ct. Justice Charles E. Whittaker, 1958-59; asso. firm Oppenheimer, Hodgson, Brown, Baer & Wolff, St. Paul, 1959-62; asso., then dep. dir. Peace Corps, Ethiopia, 1962-64, dir. Uganda, 1964-66; asst. to U.S. Senator Walter Mondale, 1966; asst. to pres. SUNY, 1967; prof. law Ariz. State U., 1967-80; judge U.S. Ct. Appeals (9th cir.), Phoenix, 1980-96, sr. judge, 1996—; chief justice High Ct. of the Trust Ter. of the Pacific Islands, 1993-94. Bd. dirs. Ariz. Center Law in Public Interest, 1974-80, Maricopa County Legal Aid Soc., 1972-78, D.N.A.-People's Legal Services, 1978-80; Fulbright prof. Makerere U. Faculty Law, Kampala, Uganda, 1970-71 Author: American Indian Law, 1998; also articles; note editor: Minn. Law Rev, 1955-56. Precinct and state committeeman Democratic Party Ariz., 1972-80; bd. dirs. Central Ariz. Coalition for Right to Choose, 1976-80. Served with USAF, 1956-58. Mem. State Bar Ariz., Minn. Bar Assn., Maricopa County Bar Assn., Phi Beta Kappa, Order of Coif. Office: Sandra Day O'Connor US Courthouse 401 W Washington St SPC 55 Phoenix AZ 85003-2156

CANDLER, JAMES NALL, JR. lawyer; b. Detroit, Jan. 25, 1943; s. James Nall and Lorna Augusta (Blood) C.; m. Jean Ward McKinnon, Mar. 8, 1974; children: Christine, Elizabeth, Anne. AB, Princeton U., 1965; JD, U. Mich., 1970. Bar: Mich. 1970. Assoc. Dickinson Wright PLLC, Detroit, 1970-77, ptnr., 1977—. Adj. prof. real estate planning U. Detroit Sch. of Law, 1975-80. Bd. dirs. Detroit Inst. Ophthalmology Grosse Pointe Park, Mich., 1983—, chmn., 1994—. Lt. USNR, 1965-67. Mem. Internat. Assn. Attys. and Execs. in Corp. Real Estate, State Bar Mich. (chmn. real property law sect. 1998-99), Am. Coll. of Real Estate Lawyers, Grosse Pointe Club (chmn. 1987-89), Country Club of Detroit. Republican. Avocations: sailing, golf, platform tennis. Construction, Landlord-tenant, Real property. Home: 211 Country Club Dr Grosse Pointe MI 48236-2901 Office: 500 Woodward Ave Ste 4000 Detroit MI 48226-3416 E-mail: jcandler@dickinson-wright.com

CANDRIS, LAURA A. lawyer; b. Frankfort, Ky., Apr. 5, 1955; d. Charles M. and Dorothy (King) Sutton; m. Aris S. Candris, Dec. 22, 1974. AB with distinction in polit. sci., Transylvania Coll., 1975; postgrad., U. Pitts., 1975-77, U. Fla., 1977-78; JD, U. Pitts., 1978. Bar: Fla. 1978, U.S. Dist. Ct. (mid. dist.) Fla. 1978, U.S. Ct. Appeals (4th cir.) 1980, Pa. 1981, U.S. Dist. Ct. (we. dist.) Pa. 1982, U.S. Ct. Appeals (3d cir.) 1983. Assoc. Coffman, Coleman, Andrews & Grogan, Jacksonville, Fla., 1978-80, Manion, Alder & Cohen, Pitts., 1981-85, Eckert, Seamans, Cherin & Mellott, Pitts., 1985-86, ptnr., 1987-96, vice chmn. labor and employment law dept, mem. practice mgmt. com., mem. strategic planning com.; ptnr. Meyer Unkovic & Scott, LLP, 1996—, chair labor, employment law and employee benefits sect., mem. litigation and transactions depts. Counsel Nat. Assn. Women in Constrn. (chpt. 161), Pitts., 1985-86. Contbr. over 30 articles to profl. jours. including Forum Reporter, Pers. Law Update, Employment Law Inst. manuals, and Reference Manual for the 34th Annual Mid-West Labor Law Conf. Coun. mem. O'Hara Twp., 1986-90; mem. O'Hara Twp. Planning Commn., 1990; bd. dirs. Tri-State Employers Assn., 1991-93, Parent and Child Guidance Ctr., 1991-2001, v.p., 1998-99, mem. exec. com., 1998-2001, pres. 1999-2000, sec., 2000-01; treas., mem. exec. com. SMC Bus. Couns., 1993-94, bd. dirs., 1993-96; bd. dirs. Big Bros. & Big Sisters Greater Pitts., 1998—, v.p. planning, mem. exec. com., 2001—; bd. dirs. The Whale's Tale, 2000-01; bd. dirs., mem. exec. com. FamilyLinks, 2000-01. Nat. Merit Found. scholar 1972-75; named Ky. Col., 1974. Mem. ABA (EEO com. labor sect., labor and employment law com. litigation sect.), Fla. Bar Assn., Pa. Bar Assn. (employment sect.), Allegheny County Bar Assn. (coun. on professionalism, employment and fed. cts. sect., hdqrs. com. and pers. subcom.), Pitts. Human Resources Assn., Women's Bar Assn. Western Pa. Republican. Avocations: skiing, traveling, bicycling, reading. Federal civil litigation, Labor, Pension, profit-sharing, and employee benefits. Office: Meyer Unkovic & Scott LLP 1300 Oliver Bldg Pittsburgh PA 15222

CANE, BARBARA HAAK, lawyer; b. Mineola, N.Y., Mar. 5, 1945; d. Robert A. and Julia C. Haak; m. Mark A. Cane; children: Laura J., Jacob H.D. AB magna cum laude, Harvard U., 1966; MA, Columbia U., 1969; JD cum laude, Suffolk U., Boston, 1980. Bar: N.Y. 1985, Mass. 1980, U.S. Ct. Appeals (1st cir.), U.S. Dist. Ct. Mass. 1981, U.S. Supreme Ct. 1986. Law clk. Mass. Appeals Ct., 1980-81; assoc. Brown, Rudnick, Freed & Gesmer, Boston, 1981-84; corp. counsel Grand Met, USA, Montvale, N.J., 1984-86; v.p. legal and environ. affairs Polychrome Corp., Yonkers, N.Y., 1986-90; pvt. practice Nyack, 1991—. Lectr. Coll. City N.Y., pro-bono lectr. WNET-13, Leave a Legacy Rockland. Hospice, others. Writer monthly column The Rockland Jewish Reporter, 1994-99. Treas., bd. dirs. RSVP Internat., 1998-2000; mem. profl. adv. bd. Thirteen WNET; co-chair N.Y. Friends of Harvard-Radcliffe Hillel; past chair endowment com. UJA-Fedn. Rockland County. Mem. N.Y. State Bar Assn., Rockland County Bar Assn., Women's Bar Assn., N.Y.C. Bar Assn., Rockland County Women's Network, Planned Giving Group Greater N.Y., Nat. Coun. Planned Giving. Office: 8 Hart Pl Nyack NY 10960-2010 E-mail: bhcane@aol.com

CANE, MARILYN BLUMBERG, lawyer, educator; b. Rockville Center, N.Y., Feb. 26, 1949; d. Howard and Lilly Ruth (Goldberg); m. Edward M. Cane, Dec. 24, 1970 (div.); children: Daniel Eric, Jonathan Marc Howard; life ptnr. Karen E. Michaels, June 18, 2001. BA magna cum laude, Cornell U., 1971; JD cum laude, Boston Coll., 1974. Bar: N.Y. 1975, U.S. Dist. Ct. (so. dist.) N.Y. 1975, U.S. Ct. Appeals (2d cir.) 1976, Conn. 1977, Fla. 1981. With Reavis & McGrath, N.Y.C., 1974-76, Badger, Fisher & Assocs., Greenwich, Conn., 1977-80; counsel Corp Components divsn. GE, Fairfield, 1980-81; with Gunster, Yoakley & Assocs., Palm Beach, Fla., 1981-83; asst. prof. law Nova Southeastern U., Fort Lauderdale, 1983-85, assoc. prof. law, 1985-88, prof. law, 1988—. Author: Securities Arbitration: Law and Procedure, 1991; contbr. articles to profl. jours. Dir. Jewish Cmty. Day Sch. Palm Beach County, West Palm Beach, Fla., 1983-88; mem. adv. com. Conn. Banking Commn., Hartford, 1979-81; trustee Temple Beth Torah, Wellington, Fla., 1985-87, Sta. WXEL, 1992—. Fellow Am. Bar Found.; mem. ABA (bus. law sect., bank holding cos. subcom.), Fla. Bar Assn., (advisor exec. coun. bus. law sect. 1988—, chair corp./securities com. bus. law sect. 1992-93, vice chair 1999-2000), Am. Law Inst., Order of Coif, Human Rights Campaign. Home: 1580 NW 100th Terr Plantation FL 33322 Office: Nova Southeastern U Law Ctr 3305 College Ave Fort Lauderdale FL 33314-7721

CANFIELD, ANDREW TROTTER, lawyer, writer; b. N.Y.C., Apr. 30, 1953; s. Edward Francis and Janet Powell (Trotter) C.; m. Marguerite Southworth Dove, May 30, 1987; children: Augusta Phillips, Lilian Sinclair. BA in History, U. Va., 1976; JD, Am. U., 1991. Bar: Pa. 1991, D.C. 1993. Rsch. assoc. Planning Rsch. Corp., McLean, Va., 1977-79; legal asst. Casey, Scott and Canfield P.C., Washington, 1979-88, law clk., 1988-91, assoc., 1991-93, Canfield and Smith, Washington, 1993-94, of counsel, 1994—. Technical and legal writer on solar energy, environ. law, manufactured housing, computer products liability and govt. timber contracts, 1976—. Republican. Episcopalian. Avocations: history, audio, photography, poetry, skiing. Home: 204 Littlefield Dr Shelburne VT 05482-6357 Office: 1815 H St NW Ste 1001 Washington DC 20006-3604

CANFIELD, EDWARD FRANCIS, lawyer, business executive; b. Phila., Apr. 7, 1922; s. Frank James and Eunice C. (Sullivan) C.; m. Janet Powell Trotter, 1952 (div. 1991); children: Andrew Trotter, Janet Powell; m. Margaret Harvey O'Brien, 1993. B.A., St. Joseph's U., 1943; J.D., U. Pa., 1949. Bar: Pa. 1949, D.C. 1972. Practice in, Phila., 1949-51; with RCA, 1953-60, Philco-Ford Corp., 1960-69, corp. dir. govt. planning and mktg., 1961-69; pres. Leisure Time Industries, Inc., 1969; mng. ptnr. Casey, Scott & Canfield, 1971-93; ptnr. Canfield & Smith, Washington, 1993—. Lt. comdr. USNR, ret. Mem. Fed. Bar Assn., D.C. Bar Assn., Phila. Bar Assn., Congl. Country Club (Bethesda, Md.), Overbrook Golf Club (Bryn Mawr, Pa., Atlantic City (N.J.) Country Club. General civil litigation, Contracts commercial, General corporate. Home: 1 Andover Rd Haverford PA 19041-1002 Office: Canfield & Smith Fed Bar Bldg 1815 H St NW Ste 1001 Washington DC 20006-3604 also: 117 S 17th St Philadelphia PA 19103-5025

CANGANELLI, MICHAEL ANTONIO, lawyer, public service administrator; b. Indpls., Dec. 1, 1951; s. Vincent G. and Beverly Janice (Neal) C.; m. Toni Milana Oxley, Aug. 29, 1971 (div. Feb. 1982); m. Debra Ellen Krulik, Feb. 9, 1982 (div. Feb. 1990); m. Gail Denise Dent Sturgeon, Nov. 28, 1992; children: Joseph, David, Anastasia, Peter, Eli, Jeffrey, Alexandra. BA, Ind. U., 1974; JD, Ill. Inst. Tech., 1978. Bar: Ill. 1982, U.S. Ct. Appeals (7th cir.) 1982, U.S. Dist. Ct. (no. dist.) Ill. 1982, U.S. Dist. Ct. (ea. dist.) Wis. 1986, U.S. Dist. Ct. (no. dist.) Ind. 1986, U.S. Dist. Ct. (no. dist.) Ill. (Trial Bar) 1990, U.S. Dist. Ct. (so. dist.) Ind. 1994, U.S. Dist. Ct. (ctrl. dist.) Ill. 1995. With Wyo. State Office Bur. Land Mgmt. U.S. Dept. Interior, 1979-81; with Fed. Emergency Mgmt. Agy., Chgo., 1981-87; staff atty. Hyatt Legal Svcs., 1987-88, mng. atty., 1988-89; assoc. Klimek & Richiardi, Ltd., 1984-87; pvt. practice law, 1982—; pub. svc. adminstr. Ill. Dept. Employment Security, 1998—. Hearings referee adminstrv. law judge Ill. Dept. Employment Security, Chgo., 1990-98. Chief union contract spokesperson AFGE Local #1626; mem. atty. bargaining unit local #1006 AFSCME, 1991-92, 96-97, del. coun., 1997. Recipient Founders' Day Acad. Achievement award Ind. U., 1974, Outstanding Performance award, 1983, Quality Step Increase award, 1987, Fed. Emergency Mgmt. Agy.; named one of nominees for Congrl. Excalibur award, 1984; Gladys Isaacs Meml. scholar West Lafayette Ind. Sr. High Sch., 1970. Mem. ABA, Ill. Adminstrv. Law Judges (sec. 1992—), Kent Coll. Law Alumni Assn., Ind. U. Coll. Arts and Scis Alumni Assn., Knights (4th degree). Democrat. Roman Catholic. Administrative and regulatory, Bankruptcy, Family and matrimonial. Home: 1404 Boca Lago Dr Valparaiso IN 46383-4420 also: 401 S State St Fl 4 Chicago IL 60605 also: PO Box 2121 Chicago IL 60690-2121 E-mail: michaelantoniocanganelli@hotmail.com

CANNADY, TERESA LYNN, lawyer; b. Albertville, Ala., Aug. 16, 1963; d. Verlon Gene and Martha Ellen Cannady. AS, Snead State C.C., Boaz, Ala., 1982, 84; BS in Acctg., Jacksonville State U., 1988; JD, U. Ala., Tuscaloosa, 1991. Bar: Ala. 1991. Law clk. to Judge Inge Johnson, Tuscumbia, Ala., 1991-92; sole practitioner Albertville, 1992-97; atty. Engel, Walsh & Assocs., Mobile, Ala., 1997-98; gender issues legal specialist ABA.CEELI, Almaty, Kazakhstan, 1998—. Contbr. poetry to mags. Mem. Alice Meadows Coun., Mobile, 1998; bd. dirs. Salvation Army Women's Shelter, Mobile, 1998; chmn. bd. Big Bros./Big Sisters Marshall County, 1995. Mem. ABA, Ala. Bar Assn., Marshall County Bar Assn. Avocations: playing piano, writing poems and short stories. Home: 534 Seifullin Apt 172 Almaty Kazakhstan Office: ABA/CEELI 740 15th St NW Washington DC 20005-1019

CANNELL, JOHN REDFERNE, lawyer; b. Cambridge, Mass., Apr. 3, 1937; s. John and Thyra (Larson) C.; m. Elizabeth Ann May, May 28, 1960; children: John R. Jr. (dec.), James C., William H. AB, Princeton U., 1958; LLB, Columbia U., 1961. Bar: N.Y. 1961. Assoc. Simpson Thacher & Bartlett, N.Y.C., 1961-70, ptnr., 1970-95, of counsel, 1996—. Gov. Am. Bus. Council, Singapore, 1982-85, vice chmn., 1984-85. Trustee Kessler Inst. for Rehab., West Orange, N.J., 1986-97, vice chmn., 1989-92, chmn., 1992-95; trustee Henry H. Kessler Found., 1992—, chmn., 1996-99; trustee Marcus Ward Home, Maplewood, N.J., 1996—; dir. Kessler Rehab. Corp., 1992—, Kessler Med. Rehab. Rsch. and Edn. Corp., 1997—; bd. dirs. New Alternatives for Children, Inc., 1996—. Mem. ABA, Assn. of Bar of City of N.Y., Montclair Golf Club (trustee 2001—), Montclair Racquet Club, Univ. Club, Singapore Cricket Club, Tanglin Club. Episcopalian. Avocations: squash, golf. Bankruptcy, General corporate, Finance. Office: Simpson Thacher & Bartlett 425 Lexington Ave Fl 14 New York NY 10017-3903

CANNON, BENJAMIN WINTON, lawyer, business executive; b. Muncie, Ind., Sept. 17, 1944; s. Zane William and Gloria Gene (Phillips) C.; m. Diane Joan Koenig, June 24, 1967; children: Matthew Zane, Christine Elizabeth, Leslie Joan, Todd Graham. BA, Western Mich. U., 1965; postgrad., Notre Dame Law Sch., 1966-67; JD, Wayne State U., 1969; MBA, Mich. State U., 1979. Bar: Mich. 1970, Ill. 1981, Ohio 1994. Law clk. labor rels. staff Gen. Motors Corp., Detroit, 1966-69; tax atty. Plante & Moran CPAs, Southfield, 1969-71, atty. Burroughs Corp. (Unisys), Detroit, 1971-72; assoc. Nine and Maister, Attys., Bloomfield Hills, 1972-73; atty. Chrysler Fin. Corp., Troy, 1973-78, sr. atty., 1978-80; dep. gen. coun. DF Industries Inc., Long Grove, Ill., 1980-81; asst. gen. counsel, asst. sec. COMDISCO, Inc., Rosemont, 1981-82, pres. internat. group, 1982-86, v.p. capital equipment, 1986-90, v.p. gen. mgr. venture capital group, 1990-92; v.p. gen. counsel, sec., v.p. human resources LDI Corp., Cleve., 1992-94; v.p. Realtors Info. Network, 1995-96; pvt. practice Barrington, Ill., 1996—98, Bus. Lawyers Internat., Palatine, 1998—. Instr. law Oakland U., Rochester, Mich., 1980; legal counsel and cons. in field. Mem. Ill. Bar Assn., Assn. Corp. Counsel Am., Am. Soc. Corp. Secs., Gray's Inn Legal Soc., Omicron Delta Kappa, Kappa Delta Pi. Republican. Presbyterian. Computer, General corporate, Private international. Home: Apt 5 751 Pennsylvania Dr Palatine IL 60074-1978 E-mail: cannon007@att.net

CANNON, HUGH, lawyer; b. Albemarle, N.C., Oct. 11, 1931; s. Hubert Napoleon and Nettie (Harris) C.; m. Jo Anne Weisner, Mar. 21, 1988. AB, Davidson Coll., 1953; BA, Oxford U., 1955, MA, 1960; LLB, Harvard U., 1958. Bar: N.C. 1958, D.C. 1978, S.C. 1979. Mem. staff U. N.C. Inst. Govt., Chapel Hill, 1959; mem. firm Sanford, Phillips, McCoy & Weaver, Fayetteville, N.C., 1960; asst to Gov. of N.C., Raleigh, 1961; dir. adminstrn. State of N.C., 1962-65, state budget officer, 1963; mem., mng. ptnr. Sanford, Cannon, Adams & McCullough, Raleigh, 1965-79; pvt. practice Charleston, S.C., 1979—; mem. Everett, Gaskins, Hancock and Stevens attys., Raleigh, 1990—; v.p. gen. counsel Palmetto Ford, Inc., Charleston, 1979—. Author: Cannon's Concise Guide to Rules of Order, 1992. Parliamentarian NEA, 1965—; mem. nat. adv. coun. Am. Inst. Parliamentarians; pres. Friends of Coll., Raleigh, 1963; alt. de. Dem. Nat. Conv., 1964, chief parliamentarian, 1976, 80, 84, 88, 92, 96; bd. govs. U.

N.C., 1972-81; trustee Davidson Coll., 1966-74, N.C. Sch. Arts, 1963-72; mem. sch. bd. Charleston County, 2000—. Rhodes scholar, 1955. Mem. Phi Beta Kappa, Omicron Delta Kappa, Phi Gamma Delta. Episcopalian. Administrative and regulatory, General corporate. Home: PO Box 31820 Charleston SC 29417-1820 Office: 1625 Savannah Hwy Charleston SC 29407-2236

CANNON, JOHN, III, lawyer; b. Phila., Mar. 19, 1954; s. John and Edythe (Grebe) C. BA, Denison U., 1976; JD, Dickinson Sch. Law, 1983. Bar: Pa. 1983, Hawaii 1986, U.S. Dist. Ct. (ea. dist.) Pa. 1983, U.S. Ct. Appeals (3d cir.) 1985. Account exec. PRO Services, Inc., Flourtown, Pa., 1976-79, br. officer mgr. Pitts., 1979-80; law clk. Montgomery County Ct. of Common Pleas, Norristown, Pa., 1983-84; assoc. Rawle & Henderson, Phila., 1984-88; comml. litigation counsel CIGNA Corp., 1988-90; counsel CIGNA Internat. Fin. Svcs. Divsn., 1990-93; sr. counsel CIGNA Internat., 1993-95, v.p., sr. counsel, 1995-97, sr. v.p., chief counsel, 1997-2000, CIGNA Healthcare, Bloomfield, Conn., 1999—, Conn. Gen. Life Ins. Co., Bloomfield, 1999—. Bd. dirs. CIGNA Stu Zychie, Warsaw, Poland, INA Himawari Life Ins. Co. Ltd., Tokyo; v.p. Life Ins. Co. N.Am.; trustee U.S.-China Legal Coop. Fund, Washington, 1998—. Comments editor Dickinson Internat. Law Ann., 1983. Mem. ABA, Pa. Bar Assn., Hawaii State Bar Assn., Kappa Sigma (pres. 1975-76), Gamma Xi (v.p., trustee 1982-86). Republican. Episcopalian. General civil litigation, Private international, Pension, profit-sharing, and employee benefits. Office: Cigna Cos PO Box 7716 2 Liberty Pl Philadelphia PA 19192

CANNON, KATHLEEN, lawyer, educator; b. Monterey, Calif., Nov. 11, 1951; d. Jack Dempsey and Virginia Ann Cannon; m. Richard Eiden, May 26, 1979; children: Joncannon, Katrina. BS, Mich. State U., 1973; JD, Southwestern Law Sch., L.A., 1977. Bar: Calif. 1977. Paralegal VISTA/Peace Corps, Pacoima, Calif., 1973-74; prosecutor L.A. City Atty.'s Office, 1977-78; lawyer Los Angeles County Pub. Defender's Office, L.A., 1978-89, San Diego County Pub. Defender's Office, San Diego, 1989—. Instr. Nat. Inst. Trial Advocacy, 1992—; prof. Calif. Western Sch. Law, San Diego, 1993—, U. San Diego, 1995; spkr. Continuing Edn. Bar, San Diego, 1995-97. Bd. dirs., treas. North County Forum, Vista, Calif., 1997—. Mem. Calif. Pub. Defenders Assn. (bd. dirs. 1999—, spkr.). Avocations: hiking, travel. Office: San Diego County Pub Defender's Office 400 S Melrose Dr Ste 200 Vista CA 92083-6632

CANNON, KIM DECKER, lawyer; b. Salt Lake City, Oct. 15, 1948; s. Morris Nibley Cannon and Bette Jeanne (Decker) Sage; m. Jane B. Howard, June 10, 1972 (div. Sept. 1985); children: Sage, Meredith; m. Susan Margaret Clinch, Sept. 6, 1986; 1 child, Grace. AB, Dartmouth Coll., 1970; JD, U. Colo., 1974. Bar: Wyo. 1974, U.S. Dist. Ct. Wyo. 1974, U.S. Ct. Appeals (10th cir.) 1974. Ptnr. Burgess & Davis, Sheridan, Wyo., 1974-90, Burgess, Davis, Carmichael & Cannon, Sheridan and Cheyenne, 1990-94, Davis & Cannon, Sheridan and Cheyenne, 1994—. Pres. Sheridan County Fulmer Pub. Librs., 1980-85, Wyo. Theater, Inc., Sheridan, 1986-91, Wyo. Outdoor Coun., Lander, 1987-91; chmn. Wyo. Environ. Quality Coun., 1992-96; active Commn. on Jud. Conduct and Ethics, 1997-2001, chair, 2001—; chmn. Rhodes Scholarship Selection Com., Wyo., 1998—. Mem. Sheridan Bar Assn. (pres. 1982). Avocations: polo, training horses, fly fishing, skiing. General civil litigation, Environmental, Product liability. Home: PO Box 401 Big Horn WY 82833-0401 Office: Davis & Cannon 40 S Main St Sheridan WY 82801-4222 E-mail: cannon@davisandcannon.com

CANNON, THOMAS ROBERTS, lawyer; b. Durham, N.C., May 22, 1940; s. Edward Lee and Elizabeth Hendren (Roberts) C.; m. Martha Craig White, Feb. 19, 1966; children: Caroline Craig, Thomas Roberts Jr. AB, U. N.C., 1962, JD, 1965; postgrad., U. Va., 1962-63. Bar: N.C. 1965, U.S. Dist. Ct. (we. dist.) N.C. 1969, U.S. Ct. Appeals (4th cir.) 2000; cert. specialist in family law. Ptnr. Helms, Cannon, Hamel, & Henderson, P.A., Charlotte, N.C., 1981-2001, Horack, Talley, Pharr & Lowndes, Charlotte, 2001—. Served with USNR, 1968-89. Recipient John Motley Morehead scholarship, 1958-62. Fellow Am. Acad. Matrimonal Lawyers; mem. ABA, N.C. Bar Assn. (chmn. family law sect. 1982-83), N.C. State Bar (bd. legal specialization, family law certification com. 1988-94), Charlotte Country Club, Charlotte City Club. Presbyterian. State civil litigation, Family and matrimonial. Home: 2611 Beretania Cir Charlotte NC 28211-3635 Office: Horack Talley Pharr & Lowndes 301 S College St Ste 2600 Charlotte NC 28282 E-mail: cannont@htpl.com

CANNY, ANTHONY, lawyer; b. Witbank, South Africa, Apr. 25, 1950; s. Gordon Robert and Suzette Canny; m. Deborah Elaine Adams, Dec. 1, 1979; children: Tracy Loren, Brendan Ryan. B of Commerce, U. Witwaterstrand, South Africa, 1972, LLB, 1974. Bar: South Africa. Candidate assoc. Routledges Inc., Johannesburg, South Africa, 1975-77, assoc. South Africa, 1977-79, dir. South Africa, 1979—. Lt. South African Army, 1968—. Mem. Arbitration Found. So. Africa (bd. dirs. 1997—). Office: Routledges Inc PO Box 78333 Sandton City 2146 South Africa Office Fax: 0027113310711. E-mail: tonyc@routledges.co.za

CANO, MARIO STEPHEN, lawyer; b. Miami, Fla., Sept. 2, 1953; s. Mario Arturo Cano and Irene H. Moreno; m. Johanna Marie Van Rossum, Oct. 13, 1979. AA, Miami Dade Jr. Coll., 1973; BA, Fla. Internat. U., 1975; JD, U. Santa Clara, 1978. Bar: Fla. 1979, U.S. Dist. Ct. (so. dist.) Fla. 1979, U.S. Ct. Claims 1979, U.S. Tax Ct. 1979, U.S. Ct. Mil. Appeals 1979, U.S. Ct. Appeals (9th cir.) 1979, U.S. Dist. Ct. (no. and mid. dists.) Fla. 1980, U.S. Dist. Ct. (no. dist.) Calif. 1980, U.S. Ct. Appeals (3d cir.) 1980, U.S. Ct. Internat. Trade 1981, U.S. Ct. Appeals (11th cir.) 1981, U.S. Ct. Appeals (6th and 10th cirs.) 1983, U.S. Supreme Ct. 1983, Nebr. 1984, U.S. Dist. Ct. Nebr. 1984, U.S. Dist. Ct. (no. dist.) Okla. 1984, U.S. Dist. Ct. Hawaii 1984, U.S. Ct. Appeals (2d, 4th, 5th, 7th 8th and D.C. cirs.) 1984, N.Y. 1985, U.S. Dist. Ct. (no., we., ea. and so. dists.) N.Y. 1985, U.S. Ct. Appeals (1st cir.) 1987, U.S. Dist. Ct. (no. and so. dist.) Tex. 1988, U.S. Dist. Ct. (ea. dist.) Wis. 1988, U.S. Dist. Ct. (we. dist.) Pa. 1988, U.S. Dist. Ct. (no. dist.) Ill. 1991, Mass., 1998, U.S. Dist. Ct. Mass. 1999. Assoc. Orta and Assocs., Miami, 1979-80, Law Office of J. Ramirez, Coral Gables, Fla., 1980, Law Office of I.G. Lichter, Miami, 1980-82, Gelb & Spatz, Miami, 1982; pvt. practice Coral Gables, 1982—. Mem. Am. Immigration Lawyers Assn., Cuban Am. Bar Assn., Nat. Assn. Criminal Def. Lawyers. Democrat. Criminal, Family and matrimonial, Immigration, naturalization, and customs. Office: Ste 600 2121 Ponce De Leon Blvd Coral Gables FL 33134-5222 Fax: 305-448-2121

CANOFF, KAREN HUSTON, lawyer; b. Medford, Oreg., May 15, 1954; d. Loyd Stanley and Donna Lou (Wall) Huston; m. Lawrence Scott Canoff, May 30, 1981; children: Vincent Jared, Alyssa Rae. BS, U. Oreg., 1977; JD cum laude, Lewis & Clark Coll., 1981. Bar: Oreg. 1981, U.S. Dist. Ct. Oreg. 1982, U.S. Ct. Appeals (9th cir.) 1985, Calif. 1985, U.S. Dist. Ct. (so. dist.) Calif. 1985, U.S. Dist. Ct. (cen. dist.) Calif. 1986, U.S. Ct. Appeals (fed. cir.) 1991. Fin. cons. Stretch & Sew, Inc., Eugene, Oreg., 1975-78; assoc. Margaretta Eakin P.C., Portland, 1981-82, 83, Gary M. Bullock, Portland, 1982-83, Markowitz & Herbold, Portland, 1983-86; ptnr. Dorazio, Barnhorst & Bonar, San Diego, 1986-89, shareholder, 1989; ptnr. Hyde & Canoff, 1990-96; divsn. counsel, dir. human resources Nielsen Dillingham Builders, Inc., 1996—. Instr. People's Law Sch., Eugene, Oreg., 1978. Author: (with others) Legal Resource Guide, 1983; contbr. articles to profl. jours. Mem. Multnomah County Vol. Lawyers, Portland, Oreg., 1982-83, San Diego Vol. Lawyers Program, 1985-96, Vols. in Parole, San Diego, 1986-87, Charlotte Baker Soc., 1992-93; judge pro tem San Diego County mcpl. Ct., 1988—, San Diego Superior Ct, 1991—, 4th Dist. Ct. Appeals, 1995—; mem. nat. panel comml. arbitrators Am. Arbitration Assn., 1991-96; active Girl Scouts Am. Finalist San Diego Women Who Mean Bus. awards, 1995, 96, 97; recipient Am. Jurisprudence award, 1979. Mem. Calif. State Bar Assn. (bus. law, labor and employment, pub. law and real property sects.), San Diego County Bar Assn., (appellate ct. com. 1987—, editor It's the Law 1987, alternative dispute resolution sec. 1990-95, arbitration com. 1990-96, client rels. com. 1990-96, bus law, comml. law, constrn. law, corp. counsel and labor and employment law sects., editor Bar Briefs 1992, mem. ethics com. 1996), Lawyers Club San Diego (bd. dirs. 1988-91, editor Lawyers Club News 1986-88), Assn. Bus Trial Lawyers, Am. Corp. Counsel Assn., Associated Gen. Contractors (legal issues com.), Constrn. Defect Def. Action Coalition, Nat. Assn. Women Bus. Owners (bd. dirs. 1993-96, sec. 1993-94, chair govt. affairs 1995-96), Mortgage Bankers Assn. Am. (legal issues com. 1987-89), Phi Beta Kappa. Contracts commercial, Construction, General corporate.

CANTOR, BERNARD JACK, patent lawyer; b. N.Y.C., Aug. 18, 1927; s. Alexander J. and Tillie (Henzeloff) C.; m. Judith L. Levin, Mar. 25, 1951; children— Glenn H., Cliff A., James E., Ellen B., Mark E. B. Mech. Engring., Cornell, 1949; J.D., George Washington U., Washington, 1952. Bar: D.C. 1952, U.S. Patent Office 1952, Mich. 1953; registered patent atty. U.S., Can. Examiner U.S. Patent Office, Washington, 1949-52; pvt. practice Detroit, 1952-88; ptnr. firm Harness, Dickey & Pierce, Troy, Mich., 1988—. Lectr. in field. Contbr. articles on patent law to profl. jours. Mem. exec. council, legal officer Detroit Area Boy Scouts Am., 1972—. Served with U.S. Army, 1944-46. Recipient Ellsworth award patent law George Washington U., 1952, Shofar award Boy Scouts Am., 1975, Silver Beaver award, 1975, Disting. Eagle award, 1985. Fellow Mich. State Bar Found.; mem. ABA, Mich. Bar Assn. (dir. econs. sect., arbitrator State of Mich. grievance com.), Detroit Bar Assn., Oakland Bar Assn., Mich. Patent Law Assn., Am. Arbitration Assn. (arbitrator), Cornell Engring. Soc., Am. Technion Soc. (bd. dirs. Detroit 1970—), Pi Tau Sigma, Phi Delta Phi, Beta Sigma Rho. Intellectual property, Patent, Trademark and copyright. Home: 5685 Forman Dr Bloomfield Hills MI 48301-1154 Office: Harness Dickey & Pierce 5445 Corporate Dr Troy MI 48098-2617

CANTOR, HERBERT I. lawyer; b. N.Y.C., Dec. 10, 1935; s. David and Ethel C.; m. Lynn Hardie, July 8, 1972; children: David, Susan. BA in Chemistry, NYU, 1965; JD, Cath. U. Am., 1970. Bar: Md. 1970, U.S. Dist. Ct. Md. 1970, D.C. 1971, U.S. Dist. Ct. D.C. 1971, U.S. Ct. Appeals (5th, D.C. and fed. cirs.) 1971, U.S. Supreme Ct. 1974, U.S. Ct. Appeals (4th cir.) 1981, U.S. Ct. Claims 1987. Patent examiner U.S. Patent Office, Washington, 1965-67; agt. Jacobi, Davidson & Jacobi, 1967-68; pvt. practice, 1968-70; with Kraft, Cantor & Singer, Cantor & Lessler, 1971-85; ptnr. Cantor & Lessler, 1982-85, Wegner, Cantor, Mueller & Player, Washington, 1985-94; Evenson, McKeown, Edwards & Lenahan, 1994-2001; Crowell & Moring, 2001—. Adj. prof. Law Ctr. Georgetown Univ., Washington, 1988-89. Assoc. editor Cath. U. Law Rev., 1969-70. Mem. Am. Chem. Soc., Fedn. Internat. des Conseils Propriete Industrielle, Am. Intellectual Property Assn. Intellectual property, Patent, Trademark and copyright. Office: Crowell & Moring 1200 G St NW Ste 700 Washington DC 20005-6703 E-mail: hcantor@emel.com

CANTOR, JAMES ELLIOT, lawyer; b. Detroit, Mar. 14, 1958; s. Bernard J. and Judith (Levin) C.; m. Susan Elaine Finger, Dec. 26, 1983; children: Tilly Samantha, Brian Alexander. BS in Natural Resources, U. Mich., 1980; JD, Cornell U., 1986. Bar: Alaska 1986. Assoc. Perkins Coie, Anchorage, 1986-91; asst. atty. gen. environ. sect. Alaska, Atty. Gen.'s Office, 1991-98, supervising atty. transp. sect., 1998—. Mem. Eagle River (Alaska) Pk. and Recreation Bd. of Suprs., 1989-95, chmn., 1991-92; dir. Anchorage (Alaska) Trails and Greenways Coalition, 1994-97; commissioner Mcpl. of Anchorage, The Municipality of Anchorage Heritage Land Bank Adv. Commn., 1999—. Mem. Anchorage Inn of Ct. Avocations: dog sled racing. Office: Atty Gen Office 1031 W 4th Ave Ste 200 Anchorage AK 99501-5903

CANTOR, LOUIS, lawyer; b. Atlantic City, N.J., Sept. 17, 1921; s. Joseph B. and Miryl (Ginsberg) C.; m. Olga Yovu, Sept. 12, 1947; children— Diana Louise Dorman, David Joseph. B.S. in Social Scis., CCNY, 1942; J.D., Columbia U., 1949. Bar: N.Y. 1949, D.C. 1967, U.S. Dist. Ct. (so. and ea. dists.) N.Y. 1951. Assoc. Sol A. Herzog, N.Y.C., 1949-53, Max E. Greenberg, N.Y.C., 1953-67; sr. ptnr. Greenberg, Cantor, Trager & Toplitz, N.Y.C., 1968—; bd. dirs., sec. CCNY Alumni Fund, N.Y.C., 1980—; nat. chmn. Am. Red Mogen David for Israel, N.Y.C., 1980— . Served to cpl. U.S. Army, 1943-46, CBI. Mem. N.Y. County Lawyers Assn., N.Y. State Bar Assn., ABA. Jewish. Club: Robert F. Wagner, Sr. Democratic (pres. 1959-62). Contracts commercial, Construction, Government contracts and claims. Office: Greenberg Cantor & Reiss 100 Church St New York NY 10007-2601

CANTOR, RICHARD ALAN, lawyer; b. Terre Haute, Ind., Dec. 25, 1949; s. Oscar Edwin and Irene (Miller) C. B.A., Tulane U., 1972; J.D., Northeastern U., 1979. Bar: Fla. 1981, D.C. Press aide to Congressman Philip Ruppe, Washington, 1973-74; spl. asst. to Congressman James Mann, Washington, 1974-75; legis. cons., Washington, 1975-76; assoc. gen. counsel Oil Investment Inst., Washington, 1979-82, exec. dir., gen. counsel, 1982-86, Triad Artists, Los Angeles, 1987; atty., advisor office chief counsel Urban Mass Transp. Adminstrn., 1988—. Editorial bd. Petroleum Investment News, 1983-85. Fin. coordinator Buchanan for Senate Campaign, Washington, 1980; treas. Energy Edn. Com., Washington, 1982-85. Served with Air NG., 1972. Mem. ABA, State Bar Fla., U.S. Supreme Ct. Bar. Jewish. Office: 400 7th St SW Washington DC 20590-0001

CANTOR, SAMUEL C. lawyer, company executive; b. Phila., Mar. 11, 1919; s. Joseph and Miryl (Ginzberg) C.; m. Dorothy Van Brink, Apr. 9, 1943; children: Judith Ann Stone, Barbara Ann Palm. BSS, CCNY, 1940; JD, Columbia, 1943. Bar: N.Y. 1943, U.S. Dist. Ct. (so. and ea. dists.) N.Y. 1951, U.S. Supreme Ct 1969, D.C. 1971. Asst. dist. atty., N.Y.C., 1943-48; legislative counsel N.Y. State Senate; counsel N.Y.C. Affairs Com. N.Y. State Senate, 1949-59; mem. firm Newcomb, Woolsey & Cantor, Newcomb & Cantor, N.Y.C., 1951-59; 1st dep. supt. ins. State of N.Y., 1959-64, acting supt. ins., 1963-64; 2d v.p., gen. solicitor Mut. Life Ins. Co. N.Y., 1964-66, v.p., gen. counsel, 1967-72, sr. v.p., gen. counsel, 1973-74, sr. v.p. law and external affairs, 1974-75, sr. v.p. law and corp. affairs, 1975-78, exec. v.p. law and corp. affairs, 1978-84; counsel Rogers & Wells, 1984-89. Bd. dir. Mut. Life Ins. Co N.Y., Mony Reins. Corp., Monyco, Inc., Key Resources, Inc., Mony Advisors, Inc.; chmn. exec. com. N.Y. Life Ins. Guaranty Corp., 1974-84; mem. spl. com. on ins. holding holding cos. N.Y. Supt. Ins., 1967, N.Y. State select com. pub. employee pensions, 1973 Contbr. articles to Golf and other mags., legal and ins. jours. Fellow Am. Bar Found.; mem. Ins. Fedn. N.Y. (pres. 1967-68), Am. Bar Assn., N.Y. State Bar Assn., Am. Life Conv. (v.p. N.Y. State 1965-70), Am. Coun. Life Ins. (chmn. legal sect. 1977, chmn. legis. com. 1977-78, N.Y. State v.p. 1977-84), Health Ins. Assn. Am. (chmn. govt. rels. com. 1975, chmn. health care com. N.Y. State 1974-80), Assn. Life Ins. Counsel (dir.), Am. Judicature Soc., Bar Assn. City N.Y., N.Y. Law Inst., Nat. Attys. Assn., N.Y. State Dist. Attys. Assn., Union Internationale des Avocats, Columbia U. Law Sch. Alumni Assn. (dir.) Clubs: Mason. (N.Y.C.), University (N.Y.C.); Met., Univ. (Washington); Fort Orange (Albany, N.Y.); Sawgrass Country, Marsh Landing, Ponte Vedra (Fla.); La Costa Country (Carlsbad, Calif.); Confrérie des Chevaliers du Tastevin; Fairview Country (Greenwich, Conn.); Royal Dornoch Golf (Scotland), Am. Seniors Golf Assn., U.S. Golf Assn. (committeeman). Home: 10 Audubon Ln Greenwich CT 06831-2501 also: 22 Little Bay Harbor Dr Ponte Vedra Beach FL 32082-3707

CANTRELL, LUTHER E., JR. lawyer; b. Nashville, Aug. 6, 1933; s. Luther E. and Hattie Mai (Cassetty) C.; m. Barbara Ann Richardson, Oct. 4, 1960; children: Luther III, Timothy Richard, Christopher Thomas. BS in fin. and econs., U. Tenn., 1960; LLD, Nashville Sch. Law, 1965. Bar: Tenn., U.S. Dist. Ct. (mid. dist.) Tenn., U.S. Ct. Appeals (6th cir.), U.S. Supreme Ct. Assoc. Smith, Ortale & Smith, Nashville, 1965-70, Taylor, Schlater & Smith, Nashville, 1970-72; ptnr. Smith, Smith & Cantrell, 1972-73, Smith, Davies, Smith & Cantrell, Nashville, 1973-84, Davies, Cantrell, Humphreys & McCoy, Nashville, 1984-96; pvt. practice, 1997—. Mem. staff Nashville Sch. of Law, 1966—. Cpl. U.S. Army, 1954-55. Named Disting. Alumni Nashville Sch. Law, 1996. Mem. Tenn. Def. Lawyers Assn., Def. Rsch. Inst., Atlanta Claims Assn., Nashville Bar Assn., Tenn. Bar Assn., U.S. Supreme Ct Historical Soc., U. Tenn. Alumni Assn., Nashville Sch. Law Alumni Assn. (pres. 1971), Shriners, Am. Legion, Masons, Scottish Rite Masons, Optimist Club (pres. 1969, lt. gov. 1970-71, Honor Club 1969), Crime Stoppers Inc. (bd. dirs.), Royal Order Jesters (order of Quetzalcoatl). Avocations: music, photography, bowling, reading. General civil litigation, General practice, Personal injury. Home: 2813 Glenoaks Dr Nashville TN 37214-1605 Office: Law Offices Luther E Cantrell Jr 3d Fl Court Square Bldg 300 James Robertson Pkwy Nashville TN 37201-1107

CANTRILL, PATRICK, lawyer, trade association executive; b. Cheadle, Gt. Britain, Apr. 20, 1958; s. Frank Cantrill and Maureen Joan Lee; m. Carin Burchell, Aug. 8, 1987; children: Joshua, Elinor, Agatha. LLD, Univ. Coll. London, 1980. Solicitor Eng., Wales, 1984, Hong Kong, 1986. Solicitor Deacons, Hong Kong, 1986-89; ptnr. Crossman Block, London, 1989-92, Walker Morris, Leeds, U.K., 1992—; chmn. parallel imports subcom. Internat. Trademark Assn., N.Y.C., 1999—. Office: Walker Morris 12 King St Leeds LS1 2HL England Fax: 44-1132-459412. E-mail: pxc@walkermorris.co.uk

CAPECELATRO, MARK JOHN, lawyer; b. New Haven, June 2, 1948; s. Ralph Ettore and Elaine (Scialla) C.; m. Jane Beals, June 19, 1971; children: Christopher Beals, Kate Rowley, Jonathan Mark. BA, Colgate U., 1970; JD, U. Conn., 1973. Bar: Conn. 1973. Assoc. Ells, Quinlan, Eddy & Robinson, Canaan, Conn., 1973-77; ptnr. Ells, Quinlan & Robinson, 1977-90, Capecelatro & Nelligan LLP, Canaan, 1991—. Bd. advisors Canaan Nat. Bank, 1982—; mortgage counsel People's Bank, Canaan and Hartford, Conn., 1983—; trustee Sharon (Conn.) Hosp., 1984-91, vice chmn., 1990-91, chmn. exec. com., 1990-91; trustee Salisbury Congl. Ch., 1990-98, 2000—, vice chmn., 1990-93, chmn., 1993-98, fin. com., 1998—. Bd. dirs. Housatonic Homemaker Health Aide, West Cornwall, Conn., 1977-80, Housatonic Day Care Ctr., Inc., Lakeville, Conn., 1981-90, Salisbury Pub. Health Nursing, Lakeville, 1983-85, Salisbury Vol. Ambulance Svcs., Inc., 1997—, Salisbury Winter Sports Assn., 1983-87, Salisbury (Conn.) Congl. Ch.; mem. adv. com. Parkside Med. Svcs. Corp., 1988-93. Mem. ABA, Conn. Bar Assn., Litchfield County Bar Assn., Assn. Trial Lawyers Am., Conn. Assn. Trial Lawyers, Nat. Assn. Criminal Def. Lawyers. Republican. Avocations: guitar, fishing, skiing, canoeing, kayaking. General practice, Probate, Real property. Home: 196 Belgo Rd Lakeville CT 06039-1003 Office: Capecelatro & Nelligan LLP 117 Main St Canaan CT 06018-1045 Address: PO Box 1045 Canaan CT 06018 E-mail: mjc@mohawk.net

CAPEZZA, MICHELLE, lawyer; b. Edison, N.J., Dec. 21, 1971; d. Michael J. Capezza and Lenora Capezza-Byrne. BA with high honors, Rutgers Coll., 1993; JD, Seton Hall U., 1996. Bar: N.J. 1996, N.Y. 1997. Jud. clerk N.J. Superior Ct., New Brunswick, 1996-97; staff atty. The Ayco Co. LLP, Albany, N.Y., 1997-98; assoc. Salomon Smith Barney, N.Y.C., 1998-99, Proskauer Rose, LLP, N.Y.C., 1999-2000, Pitney Hardin Kipp & Szuch, LLP, Morristown, N.J., 2000—. Mem. ABA, N.Y. State Bar Assn., N.J. Bar Assn., Phi Beta Kappa. Avocations: music, art, foreign languages, gourmet cooking. Pension, profit-sharing, and employee benefits. Office: Pitney Hardin Kipp & Szuch LLP PO Box 1945 Morristown NJ 07962-1945 E-mail: mcapezza@phks.com

CAPIZZI, MICHAEL ROBERT, prosecutor; b. Detroit, Oct. 19, 1939; s. I.A. and Adelaide E. (Jennelle) C.; m. Sandra Jo Jones, June 22, 1963; children: Cori Anne, Pamela Jo. BS in Bus. Adminstrn., Ea. Mich. U., 1961; JD, U. Mich., 1964. Bar: Calif. 1965, U.S. Dist. Ct. (so. dist.) Calif. 1965, U.S. Ct. Appeals (9th cir.) 1970, U.S. Supreme Ct. 1971. Dep. dist. atty., Orange County, Calif., 1965-68; head writs, appeals and spl. assignments sect., 1968-71; asst. dist. atty., dir. spl. ops., 1971-86; legal counsel, mem. exec. bd. Interstate Organized Crime Index, 1971-79, Law Enforcement Intelligence Unit, 1971-95, chief asst. dist. atty., 1986-90, dist. atty., 1990-99. Instr. criminal justice Santa Ana Coll., 1967-76, Calif. State U., 196-87. Commr. City Planning Commn., Fountain Valley, Calif., 1971-80, vice chmn. 1972-73, chmn. 1973-75, 79-80; candidate for Rep. nomination Calif. Atty. Gen., 1998. Fellow Am. Coll. Trial Lawyers; mem. Nat. Dist. Attys. Assn. (bd. dirs. 1995-96, v.p. 1996-99), Calif. Dist. Attys. Assn. (outstanding prosecutor award 1980, v.p. 1995, pres. 1996), Calif. Bar Assn., Orange County Bar Assn. (chmn. cts. com. 1977, chmn. coll. of trial advocacy com. 1978-81, bd. dirs. 1977-81, sec.-treas. 1982, pres. 1984). Office: PO Box 1938 Santa Ana CA 92702-1938 E-mail: mrclaw@socal.rr.com

CAPORALE, D. NICK, lawyer; b. Omaha, Sept. 13, 1928; s. Michele and Lucia Caporale; m. Margaret Nilson, Aug. 5, 1950; children: Laura Diane Stevenson, Leland Alan. B.A., U. Nebr.-Omaha, 1949, M.Sc., 1954; J.D. with distinction, U. Nebr.-Lincoln, 1957. Bar: Nebr. 1957, U.S. Dist. Ct. Nebr. 1957, U.S. Ct. Appeals 8th cir. 1958, U.S. Supreme Ct. 1970. Judge Nebr. Dist. Ct., Omaha, 1979-81, Nebr. Supreme Ct., Lincoln, 1982-98; of counsel Baird Holm Law Firm, 1998—. Lectr. U. Nebr., Lincoln, 1982-84, 2000—. Pres. Omaha Community Playhouse, 1976. Served to 1st lt. U.S. Army, 1952-54, Korea. Decorated Bronze Star; recipient Alumni Achievement U. Nebr.-Omaha, 1972 Fellow Am. Coll. Trial Lawyers, Internat. Soc. Barristers; mem. Order of Coif. Office: Baird Holm Law Firm 1500 Woodmen Tower Omaha NE 68102 E-mail: ncaporale@bairdholm.com

CAPOUANO, ALBERT D. lawyer; b. Montgomery, Ala., 1945; BS, U. Ala., 1967, JD, 1970; LLM in Taxation, NYU, 1971. Bar: Ala. 1970, Fla. 1973. Mem. Dean, Mead, Egerton, Bloodworth, Capouano & Bozarth P.A., Orlando, Fla. Mem. Fla. Bar (computer law sect. 1984-87), Ala. State Bar. General corporate, Mergers and acquisitions, Taxation, general. Office: Dean Mead Egerton Bloodworth Capouano & Bozarth 800 N Magnolia Ave # 1500 PO Box 2346 Orlando FL 32802-2346 E-mail: acapouano@deanmead.com

CAPP, DAVID A. former prosecutor; Criminal divsn. chief U.S. Atty.'s Office, Dyer, 1988-91, 1st asst. atty., U.S. Atty, no. dist Ind, 1999—2001.*

CAPPY, RALPH JOSEPH, state supreme court justice; b. Pitts., Aug. 25, 1943; s. Joseph R. and Catherine (Miljus) C.; m. Janet Fry, Apr. 19, 1985; 1 child, Erik. BS in Psychology, U. Pitts., 1965, JD, 1968. Bar: Pa. 1968, U.S. Dist. Ct. (we. dist.) Pa. 1968, U.S. Supreme Ct. 1975. Law clk. to pres. judge Ct. Common Pleas of Allegeheny County, Pitts., 1968-70, apptd. judge, 1978-79, assigned family div., 1978-79, elected judge, 1979-85; judge criminal div. Ct. Common Pleas of Allegheny County, 1980-85; judge civil div. Allegheny County Ct. Common Pleas of Allegeheny County, 1985-86, former presiding adminstrv. judge, from 1986; pvt. practice, 1968-78; now justice Supreme Ct. Pa. Lectr. constl. law U. Pitts., 1970-72; instr. criminal law and trial tactics City of Pitts. Police Acad., Allegheny County Police Acad., 1970-74; trial defender, 1st asst. homicide atty. Office Pub. Defender Allegheny County, Pa., 1970-75; pub. defender

Allegheny County, Pa., 1975-78. Mem. Pitts. Health and Welfare Planning Agy., 1984—; mem. jud. ethics com. Pa. Law Jour., 1980-82; trustee U. Pitts., 1992—, bd. visitors, 1992—. Fellow Am. Bar Found.; mem. ABA, Pa. Bar Assn., Allegheny Bar Assn., Pa. Conf. State Trial Judges (legis. and planning com. 1978-83, legis. com., zone rep. 1984—, chmn. edn. com. 1985-88), Pa. Coll. Judiciary (lectr. 1983—, treas. 1987—, sec. 1988—), NACCP (life), Pitts. Athletic Assn. Office: Pa Supreme Ct 1 Oxford Ct Ste 3130 Pittsburgh PA 15219-1407

CAPSHAW, TOMMIE DEAN, judge; b. Oklahoma City, Sept. 20, 1936; m. Dian Shipp; 1 child, Charles W. BS in Bus., Oklahoma City U., 1958; postrad., U. Ark., 1958-59; JD, U. Okla., 1961. Bar: Okla. 1961, Wyo. 1971, Ind. 1975. Assoc. Looney, Watts, Looney, Nichols and Johnson, Oklahoma City, 1961-63, Pierce, Duncan, Couch and Hendrickson, Oklahoma City, 1963-70; trial atty., v.p. Capshaw Well Service Co., Liberty Pipe and Supply Co., Casper, Wyo.; adminstrv. law judge Evansville, Ind., 1973-75, 96-99; hearing office chief adminstrv. law judge Chgo., 1975-96; acting regional chief adminstrv. law judge, 1977-78; sr. adminstrv. law judge, 1999—. Acting appeals coun. mem., Arlington, Va., 1980, acting chief adminstrv. law judge, 1984; mem. faculty U. Evansville, 1977, Sch. Law Ill. U., 1988—, So. Ind. U., 1990; lectr. in field. Author: A Manual for Continuing Judicial Education, 1981, Practical Aspects of Handling Social Security Disability Claims, 1982, Judicial Practice Handbook, 1990, A Quest for Quality, Speedy Justice, 1991; contbr. numerous articles to profl. jours., chpt. to textbook. Mem. adv. coun. Boy Scouts Am., scoutmaster, den leader, 1969—, Nat. Jud. Coll. U. Nev.; bd. dirs. Casper Symphony, 1972-73, Casper United Fund, 1972-73, Midget Football Assn., Casper, 1972-73, German Twp. Water Dist., 1984-85; pres. Evansville Unitarian Universalist Ch., 1984-86; performer Evansville Philharmonic Orch., 1986-98; bd. dirs. German Twp. Vol. Fire Dept., 1998—. Recipient Kappa Alpha Order Ct. of Honor award, 1962, Silver Beaver award Boy Scouts Am., 1980, presentation for vol. svc. contbg. betterment of cmty. Office Hearings and Appeals, 1992, presentation outstanding jud. mentor tng. Supreme Ct. Iowa, 1992, presentation dising. mentor tng. Fla. Jud. Coll., 1992. Mem. Okla. Bar Assn., Okla. County Bar Assn. (v.p. 1967), Wyo. Bar Assn., Evansville Bar Assn. (jud. rep. 1986-87, James Bethel Gresham Freedom award 1988), Young Lawyers Assn., Assn. Adminstrv. Law Judges HHS (bd. dirs. 1979-82, Tic Vickery award 1998), Oklahoma City U. Alumni Assn. (bd. dirs. 1965). Home: 6105 School Rd # 6 Evansville IN 47720

CAPUTO, KATHRYN MARY, paralegal; b. Bklyn., June 29, 1948; d. Fortunato and Agnes (Iovino) Villacci; m. Joseph John Caputo, Apr. 4, 1976. AS in Bus. Adminstrn., Nassau C.C., Garden City, N.Y., 1989. Legal asst. Jacob Jacobson, Oceanside, N.Y., 1973-77; legal asst., office mgr. Joseph Kaldor, P.C., Franklin Square, 1978-82, William H. George, Valley Stream, 1983-89; exec. legal asst., office adminstr. Katz & Bernstein, Westbury, 1990-93; sr. paralegal and office adminstr. Blaustein & Weinick, Garden City, 1993—. Instr. adult continuing edn. legal sec. procedures Lawrence (N.Y.) H.S., 1992—. Spl. events coord. Bklyn.-Queens Marriage Encounter, 1981, 82, 83, 85, 86; mem. Lynbrook Civic Assn., St. Raymond's R.C. Ch. Pastoral Coun., 1999—, sec. 2000—, Renew 2001, mem. rev. bd.; mem. St. Vincent DePaul Soc., sec., 2001—. Mem. L.I. Paralegal Assn. Avocations: traveling, reading, theatre, gardening. Office: Blaustein & Weinick 1205 Franklin Ave Garden City NY 11530-1629 E-mail: kacapbwparalgl@hotmail.com

CARBAUGH, JOHN EDWARD, JR. lawyer; b. Greenville, S.C., Sept. 4, 1945; s. John Edward and Mary Lou (McCarley) C.; m. Mary Middleton Calhoun: children: John, Martha, Leacy, Miller. BA, U. of South, 1967; JD, U. S.C., 1973, postgrad., 1967-69, Georgetown U., 1977-79. Bar: S.C. 1973, U.S. Ct. Appeals (4th cir.) 1982, U.S. Supreme Ct. 1982. With White House Staff, Washington, 1969-70; campaign dir. re-elect Thurmond campaign, 1970-73; legis. asst. U.S. Senate, 1974-82; pvt. practice, 1982—. Bd. dirs. Westech. Internat., Inc., Washington Watch, Inc., Splty. Materials and Mfg., Inc., Tech. Holdings, Inc., The Stealth Corp., Inc.; mem. Pres. Commn. on Econ. Justice, Washington, 1985-87 Author: The Revisionists, 1991, We Need Each Other: U.S.-Japan Relations Approach the 21st Century, 1992; co-author: A Program for Military Independence, 1980; contbr. articles to profl. jours. Rep. Nat. Platform Staff, 1976, 80, 84, 88, 92, 96; Presdl. Transition Team, 1980-81. Sgt. USAR, 1969-77. Mem. Met. Club. Republican. Presbyterian. Avocations: tennis, travel, horticulture. Administrative and regulatory, Private international, Legislative. Address: 1300 N 17th St Ste 1100 Rosslyn VA 22209

CARBINE, JAMES EDMOND, lawyer; b. Scotts Bluff, Nebr., June 3, 1945; s. Edmond Horace Carbine and Mabel (Porterfield) Hukle; m. Marianne Lemly, Aug. 5, 1972; 1 child, Matthew. BA, Mich. State U., 1967; JD, U. Md., 1972. Bar: Md. 1972. Assoc. Weinberg and Green, Balt., 1972-79, ptnr., 1980-96, chmn. litigation dept., 1985-95; pvt. practice, 1996—. Panel mem. Nat. Press Club Symposium, 1974. Reporter Govs. Landlord Tenant Commn., Md., 1973-76; mem. Mayor's Bus. Roundtable, Balt., 1983-85; bd. dirs. Greater Homewood Community Corp., Balt., 1980-82; trustee Roland Park Found., 1986-87; bd. dirs. Md. Vol. Lawyers Svc., 1991—. With U.S. Army, 1968-70. Named one of Outstanding Young Men Am., Jaycees, 1977. Mem. ABA (computer litigation com., corp. coun. com., co-chair trial practice com. 1994-97), Md. Bar Assn., Balt. City Bar Assn., Nat. Press Club (panelist 1974). Avocation: outdoor sports. Federal civil litigation, State civil litigation. Office: 111 S Calvert St Ste 2700 Baltimore MD 21202-6143

CARDALENA, PETER PAUL, JR. lawyer, educator; b. Bklyn., Dec. 19, 1943; s. Peter Paul and Rose Rita (Femenella) C.; m. Rosalie Brunetti, Sept. 22, 1962; children: Peter Paul III (dec.), Lisa, Kim, Gina, Damian. AAS, St. John's U., Jamaica, N.Y., 1978, BS, 1980; JD, Touro Law Sch., 1984. Bar: N.Y. 1985. Supr. N.Y.C. Transit Authority, 1965—; sole practice law Floral Park, N.Y., 1984—; assoc. prof. law St. John's U., Jamaica, 1985—. Lectr. Katharine Gibbs Sch., N.Y.C., 1986—; legal advisor Nassau Co. Shields, 1985—, Sch. Adminstrs. Assn., Albany, N.Y., 1986—. Editor periodical Call Box, 1985; contbr. articles to profl. jours. Named Mem. of the Yr. Nassau Co. Shields, 1986. Mem. ABA, Nassau County Bar Assn., Bklyn. Bar Assn., Columbian Lawyers Assn. (Serafin Calabrese award 1984), N.Y.C. Transit Police Dept., Lt.'s Benevolent Assn. (counsel 1987—, exec. sec. 1987—), Nassau County Shields (counsel 1985—, Mem. of Yr. 1986). Roman Catholic. General practice, Labor. Home and Office: 37 Fern St Floral Park NY 11001-3207

CARDAMONE, RICHARD J. federal judge; b. Utica, N.Y., Oct. 10, 1925; s. Joseph J. and Josephine (Scala) C.; m. Catherine Baker Clarke, Aug. 28, 1946; 10 children. BA, Harvard U., 1948; LLB, Syracuse U., 1952. Bar: N.Y. 1952. Pvt. practice law, Utica, 1952-62; judge N.Y. State Supreme Ct., 1963-71, Appelate div. 4th Dept. N.Y. State Supreme Ct., 1971-81, U.S. Ct. Appeals (2d cir.), Utica, 1981—. Lt. (j.g.) USNR, 1943-46. Mem. Am. Law Inst., N.Y. State Bar Assn., Oneida County Bar Assn. Roman Catholic. Office: US Ct Appeals 10 Broad St Utica NY 13501-1233

CARDEN, CONSTANCE, lawyer, law professor; b. D.C., July 15, 1944; d. George Alexander and Constance (Sullivan) C.; m. John Dinsmore Adams, Jun. 7, 1975 (div. Jun. 1988); 1 child, Elizabeth; m. Bernard Lawrence Goldstein, Aug. 7, 1998. BA, Radcliffe Coll., 1966; MA in Teaching, Harvard Grad. Sch. Edn., 1967; JD, N.Y. Univ., 1972. Bar: N.Y. 1973. Assoc. Webster & Sheffield, N.Y.C., 1972-73; law clerk U.S. Dist. Judge Kevin Thomas Duffy, 1973-74; staff atty. Legal Aid Soc., 1974-81; sr. staff atty. Legal Svcs. for the Elderly, 1981-90; dir. litig. Bklyn. Neighborhood Office Legal Aid Soc., 1990-96; supervising atty. gen. legal svcs. N.Y. Legal Assistance Group, 1997-98, dir. spl. litig., 1998—. Revson fellow, City Coll. N.Y. Law Sch., N.Y.C., 1981-82; adj. asst. prof., Bkln. Law Sch., N.Y.C., 1985-86; adj. prof., Pace Law Sch., White Plains, NY, 1993—. Author, editor: Medical Assistance in New York State, 1988, revised annually. Pres., Project Greenhope Svcs. for Women, N.Y.C., 1986-97; bd. dirs. Medicare Rights Ctr., 1988-95, Correctional Assn., Osborne Assn., N.Y.C., Project Greenhope Svcs., 1986—. Recipient Legal Svcs. award, Bar Assn. City of N.Y., 1990. Mem. Century Assn., Canterbury Choral Soc., Essex Hunt Club. Avocations: running, singing, foxhunting, playing piano, reading. Home: 115 E 90th St New York NY 10128-1509 Office: New York Legal Asst Group 130 E 59th St New York NY 10022-1302 E-mail: ccarden@nylag.org

CARDILLO, JOHN POLLARA, lawyer; b. Ft. Lee, N.J., July 1, 1942; s. John E. and Margaret (Pollara) C.; m. Linda Bentey, Sept. 25, 1976; children: John Thomas, Joseph Pollara, Margaret Celia, Mark Luigi. BA, Furman U., 1964; postgrad., W.Va. U., 1965; JD, U. S.C., 1968. Bar: S.C. 1968, N.Y. 1970, Fla. 1972, U.S. Ct. Appeals (2d cir., 4th cir. 5th cir. 11th cir.) 1972, U.S. Dist. Ct. (ea. and so. dists.) N.Y. 1972, U.S. Dist. Ct. S.C. 1968, U.S. Dist. Ct. (so. and mid. dists.) Fla. 1974, U.S. Tax Ct. 1972, U.S. Supreme Ct. 1984. Assoc. Cardillo & Corbett, N.Y.C., 1968-71, Mays & McLellan, Columbia, S.C., 1971-72, Sorokoty, Monaco & Cervelli, Naples, Fla., 1972-75; ptnr. Monaco, Cardillo & Keith, P.A., 1975-96, Cardillo, Keith & Bonaquist, P.A., 1997—. Mem. Furman U. Alumni Bd. Dirs., 1984-89; active Environ. Adv. Coun., Collier County, Fla., 1983-87, past chmn.; past pres. Pine Ridge Civic Assn.; bd. dirs. YMCA Collier County, past pres., 1978-80, United Arts Coun. of Collier County, pres., 1991-92, bd. dirs. Big Bros., 1974-76; past pres. Naples Leadership Sch., 1987-88; mem. Leadership Collier, 1992; mem. Gov.'s Task Force on Drug Abuse, 1985; bd. advisors Gene and Mary Sarazen FDN, 1997—; bd. trustees Edison C.C., 1998-99; past chair 14th Congl. Dist., Fla. State Dem. Party, State Jud. Coun., Fla. Dem. Party; founding bd. dirs. Neighborhood Health Clinic, 1998—. Recipient Pioneer award YMCA, 1984, Fla. Bar Humanitarian award, 2001. Mem. ATLA, ABA, Am. Arbitration Assn., Acad. Fla. Trial Lawyers, Fla. Bar (20th jud. cir., bd. govs. 1992—), Fla. Criminal Def. Attys., Collier County Bar Assn. (past pres.), S.C. Bar Assn., Assn. Bar City N.Y., Maritime Law Assn., Naples Area C. of C. (bd. dirs. 1990-95, pres. 1994-95), Inns Of Ct. (founding bd. dirs. Thomas Biggs chpt.). General civil litigation, General practice, Personal injury. Home: 395 Ridge Dr Naples FL 34108-2933 Office: Cardillo Keith & Bonaquist PA 3550 Tamiami Trl E Naples FL 34112-4999 E-mail: jcardillo@ckblaw.com, ckblaw@ckblaw.com

CARETTI, RICHARD LOUIS, lawyer; b. Grosse Pointe, Mich., Dec. 17, 1953; s. Richard John and Doris Eleanor (Evans) C.; m. Lori Beth Resnick, Oct. 14, 1983; children: Katherine Lynn, Kristin Doris, Carly Makenna, Kendall Ricki. BA, Wayne State U., 1975; JD magna cum laude, Detroit Coll. Law, 1980. Bar: Mich. 1980, U.S. Dist. Ct. (ea dist.) Mich. 1980, U.S. Ct. Appeals (6th cir.) 1982, U.S. Supreme Ct. 1989. Assoc. and ptnr. Dickinson, Wright, Moon, Van Dusen & Freeman, Detroit, 1979-95; ptnr. Strobl, Cunningham, Caretty & Sharp, Bloomfield Hills, Mich., 1996—. Mem. ABA, Detroit Bar Assn., Def. Rsch. Inst., Mich. Def. Trial Counsel, Assn. Def. Trial Counsel, Macomb County Bar Assn., Delta Theta Phi. Roman Catholic. Club: Detroit Athletic (club open raquetball champion). Avocations: raquetball, softball, golf. State civil litigation, Insurance, Personal injury. Home: 22615 Lange St Saint Clair Shores MI 48080-2873 E-mail: rcaretti@stroblpc.com

CAREY, HUGH L. lawyer, former governor of New York; b. Bklyn.; s. Dennis and Margaret C.; m. Helen Owen, Feb. 27, 1947 (dec. Mar. 1974); children— Alexandria, Christopher, Susan, Peter (dec.), Hugh (dec.), Michael, Donald, Marianne, Nancy, Helen, Bryan, Paul, Kevin, Thomas; J.D., St. John's U. Mem. N.Y. Ho. of Reps., 1960-74, dep. whip; gov. N.Y., 1974-82; exec. v.p. W.R. Grace & Co., from 1987; of counsel, Whitman & Ransom. Served to col. in infantry N.Y.N.G., WWII, Decorated Bronze Star Medal, Croix de Guerre. Inf. Combat badge. Office: WR Grace & Co 919 18th St NW Ste 400 Washington DC 20006-5503 also: Whitman & Ransom 200 Park Ave Rm 2700 New York NY 10166-0005

CAREY, JOHN LEO, lawyer; b. Morris, Ill., Oct. 1, 1920; s. John Leo and Loretta (Conley) C.; m. Rhea M. White, July 15, 1950; children: John Leo III, Daniel Hobart, Deborah M. BS, St. Ambrose Coll., Davenport, Ia., 1941; JD, Georgetown U., 1947, LLM, 1949. Bar: Ind. 1954. Legislative asst. Sen. Scott W. Lucas, 1945-47; spl. atty. IRS, Washington, 1947-54; since practiced in South Bend; ptnr. Barnes & Thornburg, 1954—, now of counsel; law prof. taxation Notre Dame Law Sch., 1968-90. Trustee LaLumire Prep. Sch., Laporte, Ind. Served with USAAF, World War II; to lt. col. USAF, Korean War. Decorated D.F.C., Air medal. Mem. ABA (bd. govs. 1986-89, treas. 1990-93), Ind. Bar Assn. (pres. 1976-77), St. Joseph County Bar Assn., Signal Point Country Club. General corporate, Corporate taxation. Home: # 114 1250 W Southwinds Blvd Vero Beach FL 32963 Office: 600 1st Source Bank Ctr 100 N Michigan St South Bend IN 46601-1630

CAREY, ROBERT GEORGE, lawyer; b. Oil City, Pa., Sept. 22, 1934; s. James Herbert and Mary Catherine (Lonergan) C.; children— Leslie Erin, Jason Andrew. B.A., Gannon U., 1961; J.D., Temple U., 1967. Bar: Del. 1967, U.S. Dist. Ct. Del. 1968, U.S. Ct. Appeals (3d cir.) 1970, Pa. 1980, U.S. Supreme Ct. 1982. Assoc., Prickett Jones Elliott Kristol & Schnee and predecessors, Wilmington, Del., 1967-70, ptnr., 1970-85; pvt. practice, Wilmington, 1985—; counsel to Gov. Del., Dover, 1973-74; vice chmn. Del. Agy. to Reduce Crime, Office Gov. Del., Dover, 1974-77; chmn. Del. Gov.'s Crime Reduction Task Force, Dover, 1974-77; chmn. Del. Gov.'s Juvenile Justice Task Force, Dover, 1974-77; chmn. Council on Police Standards and Goals, 1979-82. Served with USAF, 1954-57. Mem. Del. Bar Assn. (ins. com. 1970-84, jud. selections com. 1975—, nominating com. 1980-84, vice chmn. fee dispute counciliation and mediation com. 1984—, gen. legislation com. 1985—), Pa. Bar Assn., ABA, Assn. Trial Lawyers Am., Del. Trial Lawyers Assn., Nat. Assn. R.R. Trial Counsel, Def. Research Inst., Am. Judicature Soc., VFW. Democrat. Roman Catholic. Clubs: University and Whist, Rodney Sq., Concord Country (Wilmington). Lodge; K.C. Federal civil litigation, State civil litigation, Personal injury. Home: 2302 Riddle Ave #407 Wilmington DE 19806-2199 Office: 1401 Pennsylvania Ave Ste 101 Wilmington DE 19806-4125

CARGILL, ROBERT MASON, lawyer; b. Atlanta, Nov. 15, 1948; s. George Slade Jr., and Emma Elizabeth (Matthews) C.; m. Sharon McEver, June 12, 1971; children: Ansley Lauren, Kristin Lucille. BS summa cum laude, Ga. Inst. Tech., 1970; JD magna cum laude, Harvard U., 1973. Bar: Ga. 1973, D.C. 1975. Assoc. atty. Hansell & Post, Atlanta, 1976-81, ptnr., 1981-89, Jones, Day, Reavis & Pogue, Atlanta, 1989—. Lt. USNR 1973-76. Mem. Swedish Am. C. of C. Atlanta (bd. dirs.), Swiss Am. C. of C. (bd. dirs. Atlanta chpt.), World Trade Ctr. Atlanta (bd. dirs.), Cherokee Town Country Club. Methodist. Avocations: tennis, travel. Contracts commercial, General corporate, Private international. Home: 230 Colewood Way NW Atlanta GA 30328-2923 Office: Jones Day Reavis & Pogue 303 Peachtree St NE Ste 3500 Atlanta GA 30308-3263 E-mail: rcargill@jonesday.com

CARIUS, JEFFREY RAPP, lawyer; b. Fukura, Japan, Aug. 29, 1949; s. Marvin Wilbur and Geraldine (Rapp) C.; m. Vicki Angia Williamson, June 2, 1973; children— Stephanie Lauren, Brian Timothy Marvin. B.A., U. Ill., 1971; J.D., Loyola U., New Orleans, 1975. Bar: Ill. 1975, Mo. 1995, U.S. Dist. Ct. (no. dist.) Ill. 1976, U.S. Ct. Appeals (7th cir.) 1976. Field atty. NLRB, Chgo., 1975-77; labor relations atty. Emerson Electric Co., St. Louis, 1977-83, sr. labor atty., 1983-90, asst. v.p. employee rels. & chief employment counsel. Served to capt. AUS, 1971-82. Mem. Ill. Bar Assn., Sigma Chi. Republican. Civil rights, Labor, Workers' compensation. Home: 14338 Willow Bend Park Apt 3 Town And Country MO 63017-8251 Office: Emerson Electric Co 8100 W Florissant Ave Saint Louis MO 63136-1494

CARLEY, GEORGE H. state supreme court justice; b. Jackson, Miss., Sept. 24, 1938; s. George L. Jr. and Dorothy (Holmes) C.; m. Sandra M. Lineberger, 1960; 1 child, George H. Jr. AB, U. Ga., 1960, LLB, 1962. Bar: Ga. 1961. Pvt. practice, Atlanta and Decatur, Ga., 1961-71; ptnr. McCurdy & Candler, Decatur, 1971-79; also spl. asst. atty. gen. Office. Atty. Gen.; judge Ct. Appeals Ga., 1979-89, chief judge, 1989-91, presiding judge, 1991-93; justice Supreme Ct. Ga., Atlanta, 1993—. Chmn. bd. visitors U. Ga. Law Sch., 1995-96. Bd. Visitors U. Ga. Law Sch.; past pres. U. Ga. Law Sch. Assn. Coun., 1989-90, active, 1986-91; trustee Ga. Legal History Found., Inc.; active Holy Trinity Episc. Ch., Decatur. Mem. ABA, State Bar Ga., Ga. Bar Found., Lawyers Club Atlanta, Old Warhorse Lawyers Club (pres. 1997-98), Joseph Henry Lumpkin Am. Inn of Ct. (pres. 1994-95), Pythagoras Lodge, Scottish Rite. Office: Supreme Court 504 State Judicial Bldg Atlanta GA 30334-9007

CARLIN, CLAIR MYRON, lawyer; b. Sharon, Pa., Apr. 20, 1947; s. Charles William and Carolyn L. (Vukasich) C.; children: Eric Richard, Elizabeth Marie, Alexander Myron. BS in Econs., Ohio State U., 1969, JD, 1972. Bar: Ohio 1973, Pa. 1973, U.S. Dist. Ct. (so. dist.) Ohio 1973, U.S. Dist. Ct. (no. dist.) Ohio 1975, U.S. Supreme Ct. 1976, U.S. Ct. Claims, 1983, U.S. Tax Ct. 1985. Staff atty. Ohio Dept. Taxation, Columbus, 1972-73; asst. atty. City of Warren, Ohio, 1973-75; assoc. McLaughlin, DiBlasio & Harshman, Youngstown, 1975-80; ptnr. McLaughlin, McNally & Carlin, 1980-98, Carlin & Vasvari, LLC, Poland, Ohio, 1998-2000, Clair M. Carlin, LLC, 2000—. Mem. editl. bd. Ohio Trial mag. Mem. Trumbull County Bicentennial Commn., Ohio, 1976; v.p. Svcs. for the Aging, Trumbull County, 1976-77; mem. Pres.' Club Ohio State U. Maj. Ohio NG, 1972-82. Fellow Ohio State Bar Found.; mem. ATLA (bd. govs. 1996—, trustee PAC 1996-98), ABA, Ohio State Bar Assn. (negligence law com. 1991—), Ohio State Bar Coll., Mahoning County Bar Assn. (chmn. legal edn. com. 1985-86, counsel 1986-87), Ohio Acad. Trial Lawyers (trustee 1988-92, polit. action com. chmn. 1991, exec. com. 1991-97, treas. 1992-93, sec. 1993-94, pres.-elect 1994-95, pres. 1995-96), Mahoning-Trumbull Acad. Trial Lawyers (pres. 1991), Ohio State U. Alumni Assn. (pres. Trumbull County chpt. 1985—), Cath. War Vets. (Ohio state commdr., Vet. of Yr. 1988), Rotary. Democrat. Roman Catholic. Personal injury, Product liability, Professional liability. Home: 3524 Hunters Hl Poland OH 44514-5303 Office: Clair M Carlin LLC PO Box 5369 Youngstown OH 44514-0369 E-mail: info@carlin-law.com

CARLIN, PAUL VICTOR, legal association executive; b. McKeesport, Pa., Nov. 11, 1945; BA, Grove City Coll., 1967; JD, Dickinson Law Sch., 1970. Bar: Pa. 1971, D.C. 1978, U.S. Dist. Ct. (we. dist.) Pa. 1971, U.S. Dist. Ct. D.C. 1978, U.S. Supreme Ct. 1979. Exec. dir. Balt. City Bar Assn., 1981-84, Conn. Bar Assn., Rocky Hill, 1984-85, Md. State Bar Assn., Balt., 1985—. Exec. v.p. Pro Bono Resource Ctr., 1990—; asst. sec. treas. Md. Bar Found. Mem. Am. Soc. Assn. Execs. (mem. devel. com. 1995-97, legal sect. coun. 1997—), Legal Mut. Liability Soc. Md. (charter, bd. dirs. 1986—), Phila. Bar Assn. (dir. legal svcs. 1975-77), ABA (standing com. lawyer referral 1977-80, standing com. delivery of legal svcs. com. 1987-89, standing com. assn. com. 1992-96, standing com. on legal assts. 1996-99), Nat. Assn. Bar Execs. (state del. 1987-89, treas. 1989-91, v.p. 1991, pres. elect 1992, pres. 1993, Bolton award for profl. excellence), Internat. Inst. Law Assn. Chief Execs. Office: Md State Bar Assn Inc 520 W Fayette St Baltimore MD 21201-1781

CARLING, FRANCIS, lawyer; b. N.Y.C., Nov. 2, 1945; s. James Andrew and Mary Amelia (Lorenzo) C.; m. Elisabeth Morse Kelley, Aug. 30, 1969 (div. Apr. 1979); 1 child, Duncan Campbell; m. Christina Ellen Black, Sept. 28, 1991 (div. Sept. 2000); children: Graham Black, Gillian Kirova. AB, Fordham U., 1967; JD, Yale U., 1970. Bar: Conn. 1970, U.S. Dist. Ct. Conn. 1971, N.Y. 1972, U.S. Dist. Ct. (so. and ea. dists.) N.Y. 1972, U.S. Ct. Appeals (2nd cir.) 1972, U.S. Supreme Ct. 1973, U.S. Dist. Ct. (no. dist.) Ohio 1978, U.S. Ct. Appeals (3d cir.) 1980, U.S. Dist. Ct. (we. dist.) N.Y. 1981, U.S. Ct. Appeals (6th cir.) 1986, U.S. Ct. Appeals (4th cir.) 1990. Staff atty. New Haven Legal Assistance Assn., 1970-72; assoc. Sullivan & Cromwell, N.Y.C., 1972-80, Winthrop, Stimson, Putnam & Roberts, N.Y.C., 1980-82, ptnr., 1982-97, Collazo Carling & Mish LLP, N.Y.C., 1997—. Author: Move Over: Students, Politics, Religion, 1969. Bd. dirs. Big Bros., Inc. N.Y., N.Y.C., 1974—, pres., 1993-95; v.p. Friends of Afghanistan, Inc., N.Y.C., 1985-90; bd. dirs. Vol. Cons. Group, Inc., N.Y.C., 1988-97. Mem. ABA, N.Y. State Bar Assn., Assn. Bar City N.Y., Union Club. Episcopalian. Avocation: music. General civil litigation, Labor, Pension, profit-sharing, and employee benefits. Home: 205 E 69th St New York NY 10021-5431 Office: Collazo Carling & Mish LLP 747 3rd Ave New York NY 10017-2803 E-mail: fcarling@ccmlaw.com

CARLISLE, DALE L. lawyer; With Gordon, Thomas, Honeywell, Malanca, Peterson & Daheim PLLC, Tacoma, 1966—, mng. ptnr., 1988—98. Mem.: Wash. State Bar Assn. (pres.-elect 2000—01, pres. 2001—). Securities. Address: 1201 Pacific Ave Ste 2200 Tacoma WA 98401-1157*

CARLOTTI, STEPHEN JON, lawyer; b. Providence, Apr. 28, 1942; s. Albert Edward and Rose C.; m. Nancy Ann Arnold, Sept. 16, 1961; children: Stephen J., Cristina C. AB, Dartmouth Coll., 1963; LLB, Yale U., 1966. Bar: R.I. 1966, U.S. Ct. Mil. Appeals 1967, U.S. Ct. Appeals (9th cir.) 1969, U.S. Dist. Ct. R.I. 1970, U.S. Supreme Ct. 1972. Assoc. Hinckley, Allen, Salisbury & Parsons, Providence, 1966, 70-72; ptnr. Hinckley, Allen, & Snyder, 1972-89, 91, mng. ptnr., 1986-89, 92-96; with The Mut. Benefit Life Ins. Co., Newark, 1989-91. Bd. dirs. Accessories Assoc., Inc. Chmn. Town Com., 1975-76; trustee Roger Williams U., 1978-93; chmn. Health Provider Svcs., R.I. Pub. Expenditures Coun. Capt. JAGC, U.S. Army, 1967-70. Mem. ABA, R.I. Bar Assn., R.I. Country Club, Univ. Club. Republican. Roman Catholic. Avocations: golf, tennis, sailing. General corporate, Real property, Securities. Office: Hinckley Allen & Snyder 1500 Fleet Ctr Providence RI 02903-2319 E-mail: scarlotti@haslaw.com

CARLSON, DAVID RUSCO, lawyer; b. San Antonio, Apr. 17, 1961; s. Robert Dalner C. and Penelope Rusco; m. Kay Marie Lethlean, Apr. 28, 1983; children: Josiah, Erica, Lauren, Noah, Japheth. BA in English, Portland State U., 1986; JD, Ariz. State U., 1989. Bar: Idaho 1990, Oreg. 1990, U.S. Dist. Ct. Oreg. 1990, U.S. Dist. Ct. Idaho 1990, Ariz. 1994. Prosecutor Malheur County Dist. Atty., Vale, Oreg., 1990-93; county atty. Malheur County, 1993-96; atty. pvt. practice, 1993—. Instr. Treasure Valley C.C., Ontario, Oreg., 1990-94, mem. budget bd., 1991-97, vice chair, 1997-2000, chair, 2000—, bd. dirs.; mem. Malheur County Commn. Juvenile Drug Ct. Policies and Implementation; lectr. theory and practice of "domestic violence" cases. Scout leader Boy Scouts Am., 1983—. Mem. Nat. Assn. Criminal Defense Lawyers, Oreg. Criminal Defense Lawyers Assn. (bd. dirs. 1995—). Republican. Mem. LDS Ch. Avocations: travel, current events, family, reading. Criminal. Office: 449 Washington St E Vale OR 97918-1254

CARLSON, JEFFERY JOHN, lawyer; b. Mpls., May 23, 1947; s. John Joseph and Sylvia Lorraine (Sandberg) C.; children: Erik John, Bryan Jeffery, Kimberly Anne. Student Augsburg Coll., 1965-66; BA summa cum laude, U. Minn., 1969, postgrad., 1970-71; JD, UCLA, 1974. Bar: Calif. 1974, U.S. Dist. Ct. (cen. dist.) Calif. 1974, U.S. Ct. Appeals (9th cir.) 1976. Teaching asst., rsch. asst. U. Minn., Mpls., 1970-71; assoc. Harwood & Adkinson, Newport Beach, Calif., 1974-77; assoc. Haight, Dickson, Brown & Bonesteel, Santa Monica, Calif., 1977-81, ptnr., 1981-88; sr. ptnr. Dickson, Carlson & Campillo, Santa Monica, 1988—; judge pro tem West Los Angeles Mcpl. Ct., 1981-83; arbitrator Panel of Arbitrators, Los Angeles, Orange and Ventura counties, 1980—; moderator, panel mem. program on recent devels. in tort practice; lectr. bus. law Calif. State U., Northridge, 1978. Author: Califorinia Tort Guide, 2d edit., (supplement to tort guide) California Continuing Education of the Bar, 2d. edit., 1990; cons. Punitive Damages and Restrictions on Recovery, of California Tort Damages Guide; contbr. articles to profl. jours. Mem. nominating com. Am. Soc. Pharmacy Law, pres. adv. com.; mem. ABA (vice-chmn. Com. on Toxic and Hazardous Substances and Environ. Law). Mem. So. Clif. Def. Counsel, Def. Research and Trial Lawyers Assn., Fedn. Ins. Corp. Counsel (chair pharm. litigation sect. 1995-96, mem. product liability adv. coun. 1995—), Phi Beta Kappa (James Harley Beal award 1987). Lutheran. Insurance, Personal injury, Product liability. Office: Dickson Carlson & Campillo 120 Broadway St Ste 300 Santa Monica CA 90401-2386

CARLSON, JON GORDON, lawyer; b. Wakefield, Mich., June 25, 1943; s. John Edwin and Irene Anne (Erickson) C.; m. Jane McCann, June 17, 1965; children: Christine, Eric, Susan. BA, U. Ill., 1965, JD, 1967. Bar: Ill. 1967, Mo. 1990. Assoc. Edward F. O'Malley, East St. Louis, Ill., 1967-68, Kassly, Weihl & Bone, Belleville, 1968-70; ptnr. Kassly, Weihl, Bone, Becker & Carlson, 1970-78, Chapman & Carlson, Ill., 1978-84, Talbert, Carlson & Mallon, 1985-86, Carlson & Alfeld, Edwardsville, 1986-87; prin. Jon G. Carlson & Assocs., P.C., 1987-94, Carlson, Wendler & Assocs., P.C., Edwardsville, 1994-99, St. Louis, 1996-99, Carlson & Carlson, P.C., 1999—. Mem. Ill. Trial Lawyers Assn. (pres. 1987-88). Democrat. Avocations: flying (multi-engine instrument rated pilot), walking, hiking. Labor, Personal injury, Product liability. Office: 90 Edwardsville Profl Park PO Box 527 Edwardsville IL 62025-0527

CARLSON, KATHLEEN BUSSART, law librarian; b. Charlotte, N.C., June 25, 1956; d. Dean Allyn and Joan (Parlette) Bussart; m. Gerald Mark Carlson, Aug. 15, 1987. BA in Polit. Sci., Ohio State U., 1977; JD, Capital U., 1980; MA in Libr. and Info. Sci., U. Iowa, 1986. Bar: Ohio 1980 (inactive). Editor Lawyers Coop. Pub. Co., Rochester, N.Y., 1980-83; asst. state law libr. State of Wyo., Cheyenne, 1987-88, state law libr., 1988—. 2d v.p., bd. dirs. Wyo. coun. Girl Scouts U.S., Casper, 1990-92, 1st v.p., bd. dirs., 1993-96. Mem. Am. Assn. Law Librs. (sec.-treas., State Ct. and County Law Librs. spl. interest sect. 1992-95, edn. com. 1991-92, chair grants com. 1997-98, nominating com. 1998-99, indexing legal periodical lit. adv. com. 1993-96, chair 1994-96, scholarship com. 1996-98, citation format com. 1998-2000, co-chair State, Court and Co. Librs. membership com. 2000-01, chair edn. com. 2000-01, mem. fair bus. practices com. 2000—), Western Pacific Assn. Law Librs. (pres. 1996-97), Wyo. Libr. Assn. (sec. acad. and spl. librs. sect. 1990-92, pres. 1994-95), Bibliog. Ctr. for Rsch. (trustee 1991-95), Zonta, Kappa Delta, Beta Phi Mu. Avocations: arts and crafts, baking, travel. Home: 911 E 18th St Cheyenne WY 82001-4722 Office: State Law Libr 2301 Capitol Ave Cheyenne WY 82002-0001 E-mail: kcarls@state.wy.us

CARLSON, MARY SUSAN, lawyer; b. Lincoln, Nebr., Nov. 2, 1949; d. Arnold Emil and Mary (Lloyd) C.; m. Gerald Phillip Greiman, May 2, 1982; children: David, Nora. AA, Cottey Coll., 1970; BFA in Edn., U. Nebr., 1972; postgrad., Notre Dame Law Sch., Tokyo, 1974; JD, U. Nebr., 1976. Bar: Nebr. 1977, D.C. 1979, U.S. Supreme Ct. 1986, Mo., 1987. Staff law clk. to presiding justice U.S. Ct. Appeals (8th cir.), St. Louis, 1976-78; assoc. Kilcullen, Smith & Heenan, Washington, 1978-79; trial atty. Guam land claims litigation U.S. Dept. Justice, Agana, 1981, trial atty. civil div. Washington, 1980-86; vis. asst. prof. law Washington U., St. Louis, 1987-90, vis. assoc. prof., 1990-94; ptnr. VanAmburg, Chackes, Carlson & Spritzer, LLP, 1995—. Lectr. Sichuan U. Sch. Law, Chengdu, P.R. China, 1991. Del.-at-large nat. steering com. Nat. Women's Polit. Caucus, 1991-98. Mem. ABA, Mo. Bar Assn., D.C. Bar Assn., Am. Arbitration Assn. (large complex case panel of arbitrators). Office: VanAmburg Chackes Carlson & Spritzer LLP 8420 Delmar Blvd Ste 406 Saint Louis MO 63124-2179 E-mail: scarlson@vccs-law.com

CARLTON, ALFRED PERSHING, JR. lawyer; b. Raleigh, N.C., Aug. 27, 1947; s. Alfred P. and Katherine (Singleton) C.; m. Blair Creech Carlton, Apr. 21, 2001; children: Mary Elizabeth, Troy Eugene. BSBA, U. N.C., 1969, JD, 1975; MPA, U. Dayton, 1973. Bar: N.C. 1975, U.S. Dist. Ct. (ea. dist.) N.C. 1975, U.S. Ct. Appeals (4th cir.) 1976, U.S. Supreme Ct. 1993. Pvt. practice, Raleigh, 1975-77; counsel N.C. Bankers Assn., 1977-79; sec., gen. counsel Bancshares N.C., Inc., 1979-82; adj. prof. law Campbell U., Buies Creek, N.C., 1979-82; ptnr. Sanford, Adams, Mc-Cullough & Beard, Raleigh, 1983-89; shareholder McNair & Sanford, 1990-95; ptnr. The Sanford Holshouser Law Firm, 1995—. Chmn. State Law Resources Inc., 1999—. Active City of Raleigh Hist. Properties and Hist. Dists. Commn., 1978-82; exec. bd. Occoneechee coun. Boy Scouts Am., 1983-94; trustee U. N.C. at Wilmington, 1997—; mem. Chief Justice's Commn. on Professionalism, 1998-2001. 1st lt. Med. Svc. Corps, USAF, 1970-73. Fellow Am. Bar Found.; mem. ABA (ho. of dels. 1987—, chmn. of the house 1996-98, bd. govs. 1996-98, chmn. standing com. on jud. independence 1998-2001, pres.-elect 2001—), N.C. Bar Assn. (bd. govs. 1981-82, 92-95), Am. Law Inst., N.C. Legis. Rsch. Commn. (study com. on pub. financing 1985-88). Democrat. Episcopalian. Avocations: tennis, gardening. Banking, Municipal (including bonds), Securities. Office: The Sanford Holshouser Law Firm PO Box 2447 Raleigh NC 27602-2447 E-mail: acarlton@shlf.com

CARLUCCI, JOSEPH P. lawyer; b. Port Chester, N.Y., Aug. 21, 1942; m. Elizabeth Smith; children: Susan Elizabeth, Kathleen Ann. BA in Econs., Georgetown U., 1964; JD, Fordham U., 1967. Bar: N.Y. 1969. Ptnr. Pierro & Carlucci, Port Chester, N.Y., 1969-76; pvt. practice, Rye, 1977-78; mng. ptnr. Cuddy & Feder & Worby LLP, White Plains, 1979-99. Chief legis. counsel to N.Y. senator from Westchester County, 1971-73; chief counsel N.Y. State Select Com. on State's Economy, 1973-74; part. Nat. Conf. Christians and Jews, 1999—. Co-founder, v.p. Rye Town-Port Chester Rep. Club, 1972; trustee Village of Port Chester, 1974-77; chmn. Port Chester Indsl. Devel. Agy., 1974-76; mem. Westchester County Econ. Devel. Coun., 1976-80, Narcotics Guidance Coun. Port Chester, 1970-74; chmn. Met. N.Y. YMCA Key Leaders Conf., 1984; mem. Parent's Coun., Wheaton Coll., 1986-87; bd. dirs. Port Chester YMCA, 1970-79, sec., 1972-77, v.p., 1978; mem. Port Chester Govt. Study Commn., 1971-73; commr. appraisal White Plains and Greenburgh Urban Renewal; counsel to South Shore Hotline, 1973-74; mem. Port Chester Pub. Employees Rels. Bd., 1973-77; mem. adv. bd. bd. dirs. Salvation Army, 1973-77; mem. adv. bd. Security Title and Guaranty Co., 1986-90; bd. dirs. Rye YMCA, 1979-87, pres., 1982-85, trustee, 1989—; trustee Rye Hist. Soc., 1979-83, 90-96, sec., 1980-81, v.p., 1982-83, 92-94, pres., 1994-96; interviewer alumni admissions program Georgetown U., 1988-96; bd. visitors Pace U. Sch. Law, 1990—; bd. dirs. Vol. Ctr. United Way Westchester County, 1991-97; mem. Westchester divsn. Cardinal's Com. for Laity, 1991—, vice chmn., 1992, chmn., 1993-95; mem. paralegal curriculum adv. com. SUNY-Westchester C.C., 1994; bd. dirs. March of Dimes Birth Defects Found., 1994-96, Westchester Bus. Partnership, 1995-98, Westchester Partnership for Econ. Devel., 1996—, Jacob Burns Film Ctr., Ind., 2000—; trustee Weschester Arts Coun., 2000—. Recipient Golden R award Renaissance Project, Inc., Gold Man award YMCA, 1985, Cmty. Svc. award Rotary Internat. Club, 1995. Mem. ABA (vice chmn. econs. of law practice com. on lawyering skills 1984-85), NCCJ, N.Y. State Bar Assn., Westchester County Bar Assn. (real property com. 1978-82), Port Chester-Rye Bar Assn. (sec. 1970-75, pres. 1976-77, bd. dirs. student assistance svcs. alcohol and drug abuse prevention program 1989-95, adv. bd. 1995—), Westchester C.C. Found. (bd. dirs. 1997—), NCCJ (bd. dirs. Westchester divsn. 1999—), Real Estate Fin. Assn. (bd. dirs. 2000—), Coveleigh Club (bd. govs. 1978-86, sec. 1979, v.p. 1980, pres. 1981-84), Georgetown U. Met. Club (bd. dirs. 1980-82), Hundred Club Westchester (bd. dirs.). General corporate, Probate, Real property.

CARMODY, JAMES ALBERT, lawyer; b. St. Louis, Nov. 21, 1945; m. Helen Tippy Valin, mar. 22, 1969; children: Paul Valin, Leigh Christin. BA, Vanderbilt U., 1967; JD, U. Ark., 1973. Bar: Tex. 1974, U.S. Dist. Ct. (so. dist.) Tex. 1974, U.S. Ct. Appeals (5th, 9th and 10th cirs.) 1975, U.S. Supreme Ct., 1996. Assoc. Mabry & Gunn, Texas City, Tex., 1974-75; mcpl. ct. judge, 1975; assoc. Chamberlain & Hrdlicka, Houston, 1975-78, ptnr., 1978-89, Keck Mahin & Cate, Houston, 1989-94, Carmody & Yokubaitis, L.L.P., Houston, 1995-2000. Assoc. editor U. Ark. Law Rev., 1973. Incorporator, Gulf Coast Big Bros. and Sisters, Inc., Galveston County, Tex., 1975; mem. St. Maximillian Cath. Community Bldg. Com., Houston, 1985-88. Served to lt. USN, 1967-71. Mem. Nat. Arbitration Forum, Galveston County Jr. Bar Assn. (pres. 1975, Outstanding Young Lawyer award 1975), Harris County Bar Assn. (arbitrator fee dispute com. 1997-99), Entrepreneurship Inst. Houston (chmn. 1991-94), Greater Houston Partnership (Mex. and Ams. com.), Delta Theta Phi (master insp. 1983-85, dean Houston alumni senate 1988, bd. dirs. Found.). Republican. Roman Catholic. Avocations: ham radio, international travel, satellite communications. General civil litigation, Contracts commercial, Private international. Office: 6363 Woodway Ste 910 Houston TX 77057 E-mail: carmody@lawyer.com

CARMODY, RICHARD PATRICK, lawyer; b. Chgo., June 2, 1942; s. Thomas Francis and Margaret (Tully) C.; m. Alison Pierce Cutter, Dec. 27, 1968; children: Elizabeth Hall Carmody, Emily Pierce Carmody. BA, U. Ill., 1964; JD, Vanderbilt U., 1975. Bar: Ala. 1975, U.S. Dist. Ct. (no., mid. and so. dists.) Ala. 1975, U.S. Ct. Appeals (11th cir.) 1985, U.S. Supreme Ct. 1988. Assoc. Lange, Simpson, Robinson & Somerville, Birmingham, Ala., 1975-81, ptnr., 1981—; chmn. exec. com. Lange, Simpson Robinson & Somerville, 1987-93. Mem. Am. Bankruptcy Inst., Washington, 1985—, co-chair ethics com. 1999—; bd. dirs. Am. Bd. Cert., 2000—, examining commn. 2001—; bd. cert. Bus. Bankruptcy Am. Bd. of Cert. Bd. dirs. Birmingham coun. Campfire Boys and Girls Inc., 1978-90, pres., 1983-85; bd. dirs. Ala. region NCCJ, 1995—, state chair, 2000—; mem. Leadership Birmingham, 1998—. Fellow Am. Coll. Bankruptcy, 1999—. Mem. Ala. Bar Assn. (chmn. bankruptcy and comml. law sect. 1985, exec. com. 1986-93), Greystone Golf & Country Club, Kiwanis. Roman Catholic. Avocations: golf, sports. Banking, Bankruptcy, Contracts commercial. E-mail: rcarmody@langesimpson.com

CARNAHAN, ROBERT NARVELL, lawyer; b. Littlefield, Tex., Nov. 22, 1928; s. C.D. and Wilma L. (Hartness) C.; children from previous marriage: Cynthia, Michael, Christopher; m. Natalie Kay Kowalik, May 8, 1993. BBA, Tex. Tech. Coll., 1950; JD with honors, U. Tex.-Austin, 1957. Bar: Tex. 1956. Asst. county atty. Potter County, Tex., Amarillo; ptnr. Stokes, Carnahan & Fields; sole practice Corpus Christi, Tex. Contbr. articles to profl. jours. 1st lt. USAF, 1954. Named one of top ten young lawyers in Am., Nat. Jaycees, 1967. Mem. State Bar Tex., Nueces County Bar Assn., Tex. Trial Lawyers Assn., Tex. Assn. Criminal Def. Lawyers, Am. Judicature Assn. Labor, Personal injury, Insurance. Office: 730 Wilson Plz Corpus Christi TX 78476 E-mail: carnahanlaw@sendero.net

CARNALL, GEORGE HURSEY, II, lawyer, business executive; b. Ft. Smith, Ark., Feb. 19, 1947; s. George and Kathleen (Browne) C.; m. Janet Spaulding, Aug. 28, 1971; children: Clayton Wilson, Abigail Browne, Kevin Joseph. BS in Econs. and Bus. Adminstrn., Millikin U., Decatur, Ill., 1969; JD, Vanderbilt U., 1974. Bar: Tenn. 1974, U.S. Dist. Ct. (we. dist.) Tenn. 1974. Assoc. Arnoult & May, Memphis, 1974-76, Watson Cox & Arnoult, Memphis, 1976-79; gen. counsel S.M.R. Enterprises, 1980-82, pres., 1982-87; pres. internat. divsn. Fantastic Sam's Internat., Inc., 1987-91; pres. LP Svcs., Inc., 1992-97, Mid South FS, Inc., Olive Branch, Miss., 1997—, Carnall Franchise Group, Memphis, 1991—. Contbr. articles to legal jours., mags., newspapers. Bd. dirs. Teen Challenge, Memphis, 1982-87. Served with U.S. Army, 1969-71. Mem. ABA, Tenn. Bar Assn., Memphis Bar Assn., Shelby Bar Assn. Mem. Assembly of God Ch. Franchising. Home: 6155 Timber Oaks Dr Olive Branch MS 38654-6935 Office: Carnall Franchise Group PO Box 725 Olive Branch MS 38654-0725

CARNES, EDWARD E. federal judge; b. 1950; BS, U. Ala., Tuscaloosa, 1972; JD, Harvard U., 1975. Asst. Ala. atty. gen. Office Atty. Gen., 1975-92; cir. judge U.S. Ct. Appeals (11th cir.), Montgomery, Ala., 1992—. Office: US Courthouse Frank M Johnson Jr Fed Bldg 15 Lee St Ste 408 Montgomery AL 36104-4096*

CARNES, JULIE ELIZABETH, federal judge; b. Atlanta, Oct. 31, 1950; m. Stephen S. Cowen. AB summa cum laude, U. Ga., 1972, JD magna cum laude, 1975. Bar: Ga. 1975. Law clk. to Hon. Lewis R. Morgan U.S. Ct. Appeals (5th cir.), 1975-77; spl. counsel U.S. Sentencing Commn., 1989, commr., 1990-96; asst. U.S. Atty. U.S. Dist. Ct. (no. dist.) Ga., Atlanta, 1978-90, judge, 1992—. Office: US Courthouse 75 Spring St SW Ste 2167 Atlanta GA 30303-3309

CARNEY, BRADFORD GEORGE YOST, lawyer, educator; b. Oct. 25, 1950; s. Blanchard Donald and Anne Carolyn (Yost) C.; m. Gail Elaine Hasson, Jan. 6, 1973: children: Jason Bradford, Brandon Burroughs. BA, Washington Coll., 1972; JD, U. Balt., 1976. Bar: Md. 1977, U.S. Dist. Ct. Md. 1978, U.S. Supreme Ct. 1982. Ptnr. Callahan, Calwell, Laudeman, Balt., 1982-87, Weinberg and Green, Balt., 1987-96; of counsel Royston, Mueller, McLean & Reid LLP, 1996—. Asst. prof. law Villa Julie Coll., Stevenson, Md., 1983-97, assoc. prof., 1997—. Bd. trustees Boys' Latin Sch., Md., 1988-93. Mem. ABA, Nat. Assn. Criminal Def. Lawyers, Md. State Bar Assn., Md. Criminal Def. Attys. Assn., Balt. County Bar Assn., Balt. City Bar Assn., U. Balt. Alumni Assn. (bd. govs. 1984-87), Boys' Latin Sch. Alumni Assn. (bd. dirs. 1983-86, pres. 1986-88). Federal civil litigation, State civil litigation, Criminal. Home: 474 Five Farms Ln Lutherville Timonium MD 21093-2954 Office: Royston Mueller McLean & Reid LLP 102 W Pennsylvania Ave Towson MD 21204-4526 E-mail: bcarney@rmmr.com

CARNEY, DEBORAH LEAH TURNER, lawyer; b. Great Bend, Kans., Aug. 19, 1952; d. Harold Lee and Elizabeth Lura Turner; m. Thomas J.T. Carney, Mar. 20, 1976; children: Amber Blythe, Sonia Briana, Ross Dillon. BA in Human Biology, Stanford U., 1974; JD, U. Denver, 1976. Bar: Kans. 1977, U.S. Dist. Ct. Kans. 1977, U.S. Ct. Appeals (10th cir.) 1982, Colo. 1984, U.S. Dist. Ct. Colo. 1984, U.S. Supreme Ct. 1989, U.S. Claims Ct. 1990. With Turner & Boisseau, Great Bend, 1976-84, of counsel, 1984-93; assoc. Lutz & Oliver, Arvada, Colo., 1984-85; prin. Deborah Turner Carney, P.C., Golden and Lakewood, 1985-92; shareholder Carney Law Office, Golden, 1992-95, owner, 1995—. Author (newsletter) Profl. Solutions, 1984, (chpt.) Courtroom Handbook, 1998; editor Apple Law newsletter, 1984-86; contbr. articles to profl. jours. Pres. Canyon Area Residents for the Environment (C.A.R.E.), 1998. Mem. Colo. Trial Lawyers Assn., 1st Jud. Dist. Bar Assn. (Colo.), Genesee Daytime Bookclub (co-chair 1997-98), Kiwanis (bd. dirs. Denver club 1988-90, trustee 1990-92, sec. 1992-93). Republican. Avocations: horses, dancing, computers. Federal civil litigation, State civil litigation, Personal injury. Office: 21789 Cabrini Blvd Golden CO 80401-9488 E-mail: deb@carneylaw.net

CARNEY, THOMAS DALY, lawyer; b. Detroit, Mar. 28, 1947; s. William C. and Mary L. (Daly) C.; m. Anne C. Filson; children: Thomas, David, Kristen. B.A., U. Mich., 1969, J.D., 1972. Bar: Mich. 1972. Assoc., Cross, Wrock, Miller & Vieson, Detroit, 1973-77, mem. firm, 1977-79; corp. counsel Hoover Universal, Inc., Ann Arbor, Mich., 1979-81, sec., gen. counsel, 1981-83, v.p., sec., gen. counsel, 1983-86; counsel Dickinson, Wright, Moon, Van Dusen & Freeman, Detroit, 1986-87, ptnr., 1988—. Mem. ABA, Mich. Bar Assn. Club: Barton Hills Country (Ann Arbor). General corporate. Office: Dickinson Wright Moon et al 500 Woodward Ave Ste 4000 Detroit MI 48226-3416

CAROME, PATRICK JOSEPH, lawyer; b. Cleve., Nov. 20, 1957; s. Edward Francis and Jeanne Marie (Carrabine) C.; m. Elsie Elizabeth Orr, Oct. 7, 1989. BA, Boston Coll., Chestnut Hill, Mass., 1980; JD, Harvard U., 1983. Bar: Mass. 1984, D.C. 1985, U.S. Dist. Ct. D.C. 1985, U.S. Ct. Appeals (D.C. cir.) 1987, U.S. Supreme Ct. 1988, U.S. Ct. Appeals (4th cir.) 1989, U.S. Ct. Appeals (9th cir.) 1993, U.S. Ct. Appeals (10th cir.) 1999. Law clk. to Judge Milton Pollack, U.S. Dist. Ct. for So. Dist. N.Y., N.Y.C., 1983-84; staff atty. Washington Post, 1984-86; staff counsel select com. to investigate covert arms trans. U.S. Ho. of Reps., Washington, 1987; assoc. Wilmer, Cutler & Pickering, 1986-87, 88-90, ptnr., 1991—. Mem. ABA (vice chmn. com. on govt. info. and right to privacy com. adminstrv. law sect. 1988-90, chmn. 1990-94). General civil litigation, Communications, Libel. Office: Wilmer Cutler & Pickering 2445 M St NW Ste 500 Washington DC 20037-1487

CARON, WILFRED RENE, retired lawyer; b. N.Y.C., July 23, 1931; s. Joseph Wilfred and Eva Caron; m. Anne Theresa Flanagan, AUg. 2, 1958. JD, St. John's U., 1956. Bar: N.Y. 1956, D.C. 1977, U.S. Dist. Ct. D.C. 1977, U.S. Dist. Ct. (no. dist.) N.Y. 1957, U.S. Dist. Ct. (so. and ea. dists.) N.Y. 1961, U.S. Ct. Appeals (2d cir.) 1965, U.S. Ct. Appeals (3d cir.) 1973, U.S. Ct. Appeals (5th cir.) 1977, U.S. Ct. Appeals (6th cir.) 1973, U.S. Ct. Appeals (8th cir.) 1975, U.S. Ct. Appeals (9th cir.) 1976, U.S. Ct. Appeals (D.C. cir.) 1975, U.S. Supreme Ct. 1961. Law clk. to chief judge N.Y. State Ct. Appeals, 1956-59; spl. asst. atty. gen. N.Y., 1959-60; assoc. Goldman & Drazen, 1960-64, Corner, Finn, Cuomo & Charles, N.Y.C., 1964-69; asst. gen. counsel Ronson Corp., Woodbridge, N.J., 1969-71; assoc. gen. counsel Securities Investor Protection Corp., Washington, 1972-80; gen. counsel U.S. Cath. Conf., Inc., 1980-87, Nat. Conf. Cath. Bishops, 1980-87, Cath. Telecom. Network Am., Inc., N.Y.C., 1981-88; ptnr. O'Connor & Hannan, Washington, 1987-88; sr. advisor Office of Policy Devel., U.S. Dept. of Justice, 1988-90; appellate counsel Travelers Ins. Co., 1990-92; ret., 1992. Contbr. articles to profl. jours. ADv. bd. St. Thomas More Inst. Legal Rsch., St. John's U. Sch. Law, N.Y.C., 1981-92; exec. bd. Ctr. for Ch.-State Studies, DePaul U. Law Coll., Chgo., 1982—. Served to 1st lt. U.S. Army, 1952-54, Korea. Mem. ABA, D.C. Bar Assn., N.Y. Bar Assn., VFW, Am. Legion. Roman Catholic. Home: 44 Old Main Rd Little Compton RI 02837-1321

CAROSELLI, WILLIAM R. lawyer; b. Braddock, Pa., Dec. 14, 1941; s. Rudolph G. and Josephine (Rodrequez) C.; m. Glenn H. De Zaldondo, July 8, 1968 (dec. 1984); children: Clay R., Alyssa; m. Carol Bodnar McCaw, Apr. 13, 1985. BA, Brown U., 1963; JD, Dickinson Sch. Law, 1966. Bar: U.S. Dist. Ct. (we. and mid. dists.) Pa. 1967, U.S. Ct. Appeals (3d cir.) 1968, U.S. Ct. Appeals (D.C. cir.) 1970. Assoc., McArdle, Harrington, Feeney & McLaughlin, Pitts., 1966-72; asst. solicitor Allegheny County Law Dept., Pitts., 1972-74; ptnr. Caroselli, Spagnolli & Beachler, Pitts., 1972—; mem. disciplinary bd. Pa. Supreme Ct., 1996—. Co-author: Pennsylvania Workers' Compensation Practices and Procedure, 1982, 85. Trustee Pa. Trial Lawyers Polit. Action Trust, Harrisburg, C.C. Mellor Library, Pitts., 1971-75; bd. dirs. Ea. Area Adult Svcs., Inc., Pitts.; Hearing Officer Disciplinary Bd. Supreme Ct. Pa., 1991-93; trustee St. Edmunds Acad., Pitts., 1982-88, Winchester Thurston Sch, 1989-94; bd. dirs. Greater Pitts. Coun. Boy Scouts of Am., 1989, 93; mem. Pa. Supreme Ct. Civil Rules Commn., 1989-95, Govs. Trial Ct. Nominating Commn.; permanent trustee Dickinson Sch. Law Pa. State U. Fellow Internat. Acad. Trial Lawyers; mem. ABA, Am. Bd. Trial Advocates, Pa. Bar Assn. (chmn. workers compensation sect. 1984), Pa. Trial Lawyers Assn. (pres. 1985-86), Western Pa. Trial Lawyers Assn. (pres. 1984), Assn. Trial Lawyers Am. (bd. govs. 1986-88, state del. 1980-82), The Rivers Club, Edgewood Club (pres. 1971-75), Pitts. Athletic Assn. Democrat. Federal civil litigation, Personal injury, Workers' compensation. Home: 433 Maple Ave Pittsburgh PA 15218-1501 Office: Caroselli Spagnolli & Beachler 322 Blvd Of The Allies Pittsburgh PA 15222-1925

CAROTENUTO, GIOVANNI, lawyer; b. Naples, Italy, Oct. 1, 1970; Degree in Law, U. Naples, 1995; LLM (hon.), U. London, 1997. Bar: Rome 1999. Assoc. Studio Legale Carnelutti, Rome, 1997-98; sr. assoc. Studio Legale Ughi e Nunziante, 1998—. Contbr. articles to legal jours. Mem. Alumni Assn. QMW London. Antitrust, Banking, Finance. Office: Studio Legal Ughi/Nunziante Via XX settembre 1 Rome Italy 00186 Fax: 06 4815912. E-mail: g.carotenuto@unlaw.it

CARPENTER, CHARLES ELFORD, JR. lawyer; b. Greenville, S.C., Nov. 3, 1944; s. Charles Elford and Mary Charlotte (Campbell) C.; m. Nancy Townsend, June 8, 1968; children: Charlotte Elizabeth, John Morrison. BA, Furman U., 1966; JD, U. Va., 1969; MPA, U. S.C., 1976. Bar: Va. 1969, S.C. 1972, U.S. Dist. Ct. S.C. 1974, U.S. Ct. Appeals (4th cir.) 1978, U.S. Ct. Appeals (11th cir.) 1984, U.S. Supreme Ct. 1983. Assoc. Leatherwood, Walker, Todd & Mann, Greenville, 1969, Richardson, Plowden, Grier & Howser, Columbia, S.C., 1974-78; ptnr. Richardson, Plowden, Carpenter & Robinson, P.A., 1978—. Mem. com. on grievances and discipline S.C. Supreme Ct., 1986-89, 1996; spkr. Law Seminars, Inc., Columbia, 1987, Outline for Post-Trial Practice, 1988, 89, 90; mem. S.C. Supreme Ct. Bd. Law Examiners, 1995-2001. Editor Appeal and Error, S.C. Jurisprudence; contbr. articles to legal jours. Mem. bd. visitors Presbyn. Coll., Clinton, S.C., 1983-87; trustee James H. Hammond Sch., Columbia, 1986-89, Trinity Presbytery; pres. A.C. Flora PTO; elder Eastminster Presbyn. Ch. Capt. U.S. Army, 1969-72. 'ellow Am. Acad. Appellate Lawyers (bd. dirs.); mem. ABA (speaker appellate process program 1990, editor Appellate Practice Jour. 1989-2000, co-chair oral arguement subcom. litigation sect., mem. task force on unreported opinions 1996—), S.C. Bar Assn. (mem. Richland County fee dispute com. 1984-88, speaker 1987, appellate practice, panel mem. proposed rules of appellate practicefor S.C. Bar ann. meeting 1989, mem. practice and procedure com., health and hosp. law subcom., appellate rules subcom., chmn. merit selection of judges subcom., alternative dispute resolution com. 1993—), Richland County Bar Assn., S.C. Def. Trial Attys. (chmn. amicus curiae com. 1981-85), Forest Lake Club, St. Andrews Soc., Tarantella Club, Columbia Ball Club, Torch Club. Avocations: reading, hunting, tennis, fishing. Administrative and regulatory, General civil litigation, Insurance. Office: Richardson Plowden Carpenter & Robinson PA 1600 Marion St # 7788 Columbia SC 29201-2913

CARPENTER, CHARLES FRANCIS, lawyer; b. Raleigh, N.C., Apr. 3, 1957; s. William Lester and Mattie Frances (Wallace) C.; m. Heidi Ann Athanas, June 14, 1980. BA with honors, U. N.C., 1979, JD, 1982. Bar: N.C. 1982, U.S. Dist. Ct. (mid. dist.) N.C. 1982, U.S. Dist. Ct. (ea. dist.) N.C. 1986, U.S. Ct. Appeals (4th cir.) 1986, U.S. Dist. Ct. (we. dist.) N.C. 1988. Assoc. Newsom, Graham, Hedrick, Murray, Bryson & Kennon,

Durham, N.C., 1982-87; ptnr. Newsom, Graham, Hedrick, Bryson & Kennon, 1988-93; pvt. practice Charles F. Carpenter, P.A., 1993-98; ptnr. Pulley, Watson, King & Lischer, PA, 1998—. Trustee N.C. Conf. United Meth. Ch., 1993—; mem. exec. bd. Occoneechee Coun. Boy Scouts Am., 1988—. Mem. ABA, N.C. State Bar, N.C. Bar Assn., Durham County Bar Assn. (medico-legal com. 1994—, bd. dirs. 1998—), Order of the Old Well, Honorable Order of Ky. Colonels, Phi Beta Kappa. Democrat. Avocations: karate, golf, softball, jogging, skiing. Bankruptcy, General civil litigation, Consumer commercial. Home: 1325 Arnette Ave Durham NC 27707-1601 Office: 905 W Main St Ste 21 F Durham NC 27701-2076 E-mail: cfc@pwkl.com

CARPENTER, DAVID ALLAN, lawyer; b. Cambridge, Mass., May 16, 1951; s. David Lawrence and Jane (Boucher) C.; m. Nancy Joan Surdyka, Apr. 29, 1973. BS in Bus. Adminstrn., Bucknell U., Lewisburg, Pa., 1972; MBA in Fin., Temple U., Phila., 1975; JD, Rutgers U., 1981. Banking officer Girard Bank, Phila., 1972-77, mng. ptnr., 1983-85, mng. ptnr. Mid Atlantic region, 1985-89, mng. ptnr. Atlantic region, 1989-92; nat. dir. litigation and claims svcs. Coopers & Lybrand, 1987-92, nat. dir. fin. adv. svcs. Boston, 1992-94; founding ptnr. Ptnrs. for Mkt. Leadership, Inc., Atlanta, 1995—; ptnr. Ptnrs. for Corp. Renewal, Phila., 1997—. Co-editor: Proving and Pricing Construction Claims, 1990, Environmental Dispute Handbook, 1991; contbr. articles to profl. jours., chpts. to books. Mem. Inst. Mgmt. Consultants, Turnaround Mgmt. Assn., Beta Gamma Sigma. Banking, Bankruptcy, General civil litigation. Address: PO Box 903 Great Barrington MA 01230-0903 Office: Ptnrs for Mkt Leadership Inc 100 Galleria Pkwy SE Ste 400 Atlanta GA 30339-3122

CARPENTER, GORDON RUSSELL, retired lawyer, banker; b. Denton, Tex., Feb. 6, 1920; s. Solomon Lafayette and Grace L. (Fowler) C.; m. Muriel E. James, Sept. 18, 1943 (dec.); m. Mary Alice Borah, Aug. 4, 1962. BS, North Tex. State U., 1940; postgrad., Georgetown U., 1941-42; LL.B., So. Meth. U., 1948. Bar: Tex. 1947, U.S. Supreme Ct. 1960. Announcer KDNT, Denton, Tex., 1940-41; spl. agent FBI, 1941-46; exec. sec. Southwestern Legal Found., Dallas, 1947-56; exec. dir., 1956-58; adminstrv. asst. to dean Law Sch. So. Meth. U., 1951-58, asst. prof. law, 1956-68, pres. Law Alumni, 1959-60; trust officer 1st Nat. Bank, Dallas, 1958-60, v.p., 1960-79; v.p., sr. fin. planning officer InterfFirst Bank, 1979-84. Pres. Law Alumni Assn., 1959. Bd. regents Tex. Sch. Trust Banking, 1981-82; bd. trustees Hatton W. Sumners Found., 1959—, exec. dir., 1985-95; chmn. North Tex. State U. Ednl. Found.; chmn. Luth. Med. Sys. Tex. Found., 1980-83; vice chmn. Farmers Br. Hosp. Authority, 1976-77. Recipient Pres.'s award State Bar Tex., 1963, Bd. Dirs. award, 1971, Gene Cavin award for excellence in con. legal edn., 1998, Disting. Law Alumni award So. Meth. U., 2001. Fellow Tex. Bar Found.; mem. ABA (chmn. publs. com. mineral and natural resources law sect. 1958-64), State Bar Tex. (chmn. cont. legal edn. com. 1952-54, 58-66, chmn. real estate, probate and trust law sect. 1964-65), Dallas Bar Assn. (dir. 1960-61, 65-66, chmn. centennial com. 1972-73), Dallas Bar Found. (trustee, sec.-treas.), Tex. Bankers Assn. (chmn. trust divsn. 1980-81), Soc. Former Spl. Agts. FBI (pres. 1963), Brookhaven Country Club, Masons, Delta Theta Phi. Republican. Presbyterian. Estate planning, Probate. Office: 325 N Saint Paul St Ste 3920 Dallas TX 75201-3821

CARPENTER, RANDLE BURT, lawyer; b. Raleigh, N.C., Oct. 19, 1939; s. Randle Burt and Adonis (Watson) C.; m. Suzanne Gronemeyer, Aug. 21, 1965; children: Randle III, Christine. BA in Internat. Rels., Duke U., 1962, LLB, 1965; LLM in Fgn. Law, NYU, 1969. Bar: N.Y. 1967, N.C. 1965, U.S. Supreme Ct., U.S. Ct. Appeals (2d cir.), U.S. Dist. Ct., U.S. Ct. Internat. Trade. Official asst. First Nat. City Bank, N.Y.C., 1965-67; with Exxon Internat. Inc., 1967-68; gen. counsel Occidental Crude Sales Inc., 1968-75; v.p. law Wesco Internat. Inc., 1975-76; gen. counsel A. Johnson & Co., Inc., 1976-81; ptnr. Davidson Dawson & Clark, 1981-84, Schoeman, Marsh & Updike, N.Y.C., 1984-97, Jackson & Nash, N.Y.C., 1997—. Adj. prof. law Pace U., White Plains, N.Y., 1984—. Contbr. articles to profl. jours. Angier B. Duke scholar Duke U., 1958. Mem. Am. Arbitration Assn., Assn. of Bar of City of N.Y. (inter-Am. affairs com.), Maritime Law Assn., Church Club N.Y., Colonial Order of the Acorn (companion). Bankruptcy, Environmental, Private international. Home: 29 Hazel Ln Larchmont NY 10538-4007 Office: Jackson & Nash 330 Madison Ave Rm 1800 New York NY 10017-5001

CARPENTER, RICHARD NORRIS, lawyer; b. Cortland, N.Y., Feb. 14, 1937; s. Robert P. and Sylvia (Norris) C.; m. Elizabeth Bigbee, Aug. 1961 (div. June 1975); 1 child, Andrew Norris; m. Leslie Nordby, July, 1991. BA magna cum laude, Syracuse U., 1958; LLB, Yale U., 1962. Bar: N.Y. 1962, N.Mex. 1963, U.S. Dist. Ct. (no. dist.) N.Y., U.S. Dist. Ct. N.Mex., U.S. Ct. Appeals (D.C. and 10th cirs.), U.S. Supreme Ct. Assoc. Breed, Abbott & Morgan, N.Y.C., 1962-63, Bigbee Law Firm, Santa Fe, 1963-78; ptnr. Carpenter Law Firm, 1978-2000, owner, 2000—. Spl. asst. atty. gen., State of N.Mex., 1963-74, 90-96; sec. Bokum Corp., Miami, Fla., 1969-70. Mem. adv. bd. Interstate Mining Compact, N.Mex., 1981-88; elder 1st Presbyn. Ch., Santa Fe, 1978-80, 86-89, trustee, 1975-77, pres., 1977; bd. dirs. Santa Fe Community Coun., 1965-67, St. Vincent Hosp. Found., Santa Fe, 1980-84; trustee Santa Fe Prep. Sch., 1981-84, pres., 1982-84; trustee St. Vincent Hosp., 1980-86, 87-2001, chmn. 1985-86, 90-93, 98-2000; bd. dirs. Santa Fe YMCA, 1964-69, pres., 1969; tr ustee Santa Fe Prep. Permanent Endowment Fund., 1987-90. Rotary Found. fellow, Panjab U., Pakistan, 1959-60. Mem. ABA, N.Mex. Bar Assn., 1st Jud. Bar Assn., N.Y. State Bar Assn., The Best Lawyers of Am., Phi Beta Kappa, Pi Sigma Alpha, Phi Beta Phi. Legislative, Natural resources, Public utilities. Home: 1048 Bishops Lodge Rd Santa Fe NM 87501-1009 Office: PO Box 1837 Santa Fe NM 87504-1837 E-mail: rncoffice@aol.com

CARPENTER, RUSSELL H., JR. lawyer; b. Providence, May 17, 1941; AB, Princeton U., 1963; BPhil in Politics, Oxford U., Eng., 1965; LLB, Yale U., 1968. Bar: D.C. 1968. Law clk. to Hon. David Bazelon U.S. Ct. Appeals (D.C. cir.), 1968-69; mem. Covington & Burling, Washington. Contbr. articles to profl. jours. Mem. Order Coif. Office: Covington & Burling PO Box 7566 1201 Pennsylvania Ave NW Washington DC 20004-2401 E-mail: rcarpenter@cov.com

CARPENTER, SUSAN KAREN, public defender; b. New Orleans, May 6, 1951; d. Donald Jack and Elise Ann (Diehl) C. BA magna cum laude with honors in English, Smith Coll., 1973; JD, Ind. U., 1976. Bar: Ind. 1976. Dep. pub. defender of Ind. State of Ind., Indpls., 1976-81, pub. defender of Ind., 1981—; chief pub. defender Wayne County, Richmond, Ind., 1981. Bd. dirs. Ind. Pub. Defender Coun., Indpls., 1981—; Ind. Lawyers Comm., Indpls., 1984-89; trustee Ind. Criminal Justice Inst., INdpls., 1983—. Mem. Criminal Code Study Commn., Indpls., 1981—, Supreme Ct. Records Mgmt. Com., Indpls., 1983—, Ind. Pub. Defender Commn., 1989—, Ind. Supreme Ct. Commn. on Race and Gender Fairness, 2000—. Mem. Ind. State Bar Assn. (criminal justice sect.), Nat. Legal Aid and Defender Assn., Nat. Assn. Defense Lawyers, Phi Beta Kappa. E-mail: scarpenter@iquest.net

CARPENTER, THOMAS MILTON, lawyer; b. Lubbock, Tex., Feb. 15, 1952; s. Charles Loren and Mildred Elaine (McDonald) C.; m. Betty Kathryn Wilkins, Mar. 26, 1983; children: Matthew T., Mark L. BA, Hendrix Coll., 1974; JD, U. Ark.-Fayetteville, 1977. Bar: Ark. 1977, U.S. Dist. Ct. (ea. dist.) Ark. 1978, U.S. Ct. Appeals (8th cir.) 1980, U.S. Supreme Ct. 1981, U.S. Ct. Mil. Appeals 1985, USAF Ct. Mil. Rev. 1985; cert. criminal trial specialist. Law clk. Ark. Supreme Ct., Little Rock, 1977-78; ptnr. Lessenberry & Carpenter, 1978-84; asst. city atty., 1984-90; chief comml. litigation divsn., city atty., 1991—. Coordinator Ark. Coalition Against the Death Penalty, 1978-83. Contbr. articles to profl. jours. Dist. commr. Boy Scouts Am., 1979; adminstrv. coun. Pulaski Heights Meth. Ch., Little Rock, 1982-85. Named Outstanding Asst. City Atty., Nat. Inst. Mcpl. Law Officers, 1991, Outstanding City Atty., Nat. Inst. Mcpl. Law Officers, 1994. Fellow Ark. Bar Assn. (exec. coun. 1991-94); mem. ABA, Nat. Bd. Trial Advocacy (bd. dirs. 1991—, v.p. 1995, pres.-elect 1996, pres. 1997-99), Ark. Bar Assn. (del. 1979-81, 83-85, tenured del., Golden Gavel award 1982, 1995), Assn. Trial Lawyers Am., Ark. City Atty.'s Assn. (pres. 1992-93), Pulaski County Bar Assn. Democrat. Office: Little Rock City Atty City Hall 500 W Markham St Ste 310 Little Rock AR 72201-1430 E-mail: tcarpenter@littlerock.state.ar.us

CARR, CYNTHIA, lawyer; b. San Antonio, Nov. 4, 1953; d. Robert Claude Carr and Alta Mae (Bletsch) Holmes; m. Marc Allan Wallman; children: Lydia Michael, Aidan Holmes. BA, Austin Coll., 1975; JD, Harvard U., 1984; LLM, NYU, 1990. Bar: N.Y. 1985, Conn. 1988. Coord. Cambodian sect. Internat. Rescue Com., Bangkok, Thailand, 1980-81; legal intern Mental Health Legal Advisers Com., Boston, 1982-83; assoc. White & Case, N.Y.C., 1984-87; assoc. gen. counsel, exec. dir. planned giving Yale U., New Haven, 1988-2000; gen. counsel Save the Children, Westport, Conn., 2000—. Vis. lectr. Yale U. Law Sch., New Haven, 1988-90. Vol. Peace Corps, West Africa, 1975-77, 79-80; bd. dirs. Yale Law Sch. Early Learning Ctr., 1990-95; trustee Yale U. Hong Kong Charitable Trust, 1997-2000, Oak Leaf Endowment Trust for Yale, 1997-2000. Mem. ABA (vice chair lifetime and charitable gift planning com. 2000—, probate and trust divsn. 2000-01), Conn. Bar Assn. (mem. charitable giving exempt orgns. subcom.), Trusts and Estates Mag. (charitable giving mini bd. mem. 1996-99), Jewish Found. New Haven (tax and legal com. 1999—), Conn. Planned Giving Group (bd. dirs. 2000-01). Estate planning, Taxation, general. Home: 30 Hawley Rd Hamden CT 06517-2128 Office: Save the Children 54 Wilton Rd Westport CT 06880-3131 E-mail: ccarr@savechildren.org

CARR, DAVIS HADEN, lawyer; b. Richmond, Va., July 21, 1940; s. Frederick Clifton Jr. and Bernice (Haden) C.; m. Judith A. Guerry, Aug. 1959 (div. Apr. 1979); children: Wendy Carr Conners, Julia Carr Stewart; m. Martha Cash, Feb. 12, 1983. BEE, U. Va., 1961; JD, Vanderbilt U., 1970. Bar: Tenn. 1970, Ky. 1989. Assoc. Boult, Cummings, Conners & Berry PLC, Nashville, 1970-74, ptnr., 1974—; mng. ptnr. Boult, Cummings, Conners & Berry, 1984-94, chmn., 1995-99. Active Leadership Nashville, 1977-78, chmn. alumni assn., 1978-79, bd. trustees 1997—, finance chair 2000-01; pres. Cumberland Museums, Nashville, 1978-80; bd. dirs. Greater Nashville Arts Found., 1991-97; bd. dirs. Jr. Achievement Mid. Tenn., 1991-99, chmn., 1995-97; trustee Vol. State Horesemen's Found., 1988-, Houghland Found., 1988—, The Bright Hour Trust, 2000—; mem. bd. trustees, exec. com. Fisk U., 1996—, vice-chmn., 2000—; bd. dirs. Nashville Downtown Partnership, 1994-99, chmn., 1994-95, exec. com., 1997-99. Mem. ABA, Tenn. Bar Found., Tenn. Bar Assn., Nashville Bar Found., Nashville Bar Assn., Vanderbilt U. Law Alumni Assn. (bd. dirs.), Cumberland Club (pres. 1986-87), Belle Meade Country Club, Nashville Area C. of C. (gen. counsel, mem. exec. com. 1992-96, bd. govs.). General corporate, Finance, Mergers and acquisitions. Home: Martlesham Heath 1344 Carnton Ln Franklin TN 37064-3258 Office: Boult Cummings Conners & Berry PO Box 198062 Nashville TN 37219-8062 E-mail: dcarr@bccb.com

CARR, EDWARD A. lawyer; b. Borger, Tex., July 31, 1962; AB with honors and distinction, Stanford U., 1984; JD, UCLA, 1987. Bar: Tex. 1988, D.C. 1989, U.S. Dist. Ct. (so. dist.) Tex. 1989, U.S. Ct. Appeals (5th cir.) 1989, U.S. Ct. Appeals (fed. cir.) 1989. Assoc. Vinson & Elkins, Houston, 1988-97, ptnr., 1997—. Lectr. in field. Contbr. articles to profl. jours., contbg. author: (6-vol. book set) Business and Commercial Litigation in Federal Courts, 1998, Texas Legal Ethics in the American Legal Ethics Library, Cornell Law School, 1998, Successful Partnering Between Inside and Outside Counsel, 2000; mem. UCLA Law Rev., 1985-87, mem. editl. bd., 1986-87. Fellow Tex. Bar Found. (life), Coll. State Bar Tex.; mem. ABA (sects. antitrust law, litigation), Am. Judicature Soc. (life), D.C. Bar, Fed. Bar Assn., State Bar Tex., Houston Bar Assn. Federal civil litigation, State civil litigation. Address: Vinson & Elkins LLP First City Tower 1001 Fannin St Ste 2300 Houston TX 77002-6760

CARR, GARY THOMAS, lawyer; b. El Reno, Okla., July 25, 1946; s. Thomas Clay and Bobbye Jean (Page) C.; m. Ann Elizabeth Smith, Jan. 5, 1985. AB, Washington U., St. Louis, 1968, BSCE, 1972, JD, 1975. Bar: Mo. 1975, U.S. Dist. Ct. (ea. and we. dists.) Mo. 1975, U.S. Ct. Appeals (8th cir.) 1977, U.S. Ct. Appeals (fed. cir.) 1980, U.S. Ct. Appeals (5th cir.) 1991. Jr. ptnr. Bryan, Cave, McPheeters & McRoberts, St. Louis, 1975-83, ptnr., 1984-99. Lectr. law Washington U., 1978-82, adj. prof., 1982-85; sec., dir. Bruton-Stroube Studios, Inc., 1978—, bd. dirs. Trustee Parkview Subdiv. Assn., St. Louis, 1982-90. 1st lt. U.S. Army, 1968-71, Vietnam. Mem. ABA, Mo. Bar Assn., St. Louis Bar Assn., Order of Coif. Avocations: woodworking, hunting, fishing, automobiles. General civil litigation, Contracts commercial, Government contracts and claims. Office: PO Box 3030 Saint Louis MO 63130-0430 E-mail: gtc10485@aol.com

CARR, JAMES FRANCIS, lawyer; b. Buffalo, May 7, 1946; s. Maurice Kilner and Cecelia Francis (Harmon) C.; children: James Robert, Marguerite Louise. BS, USAF Acad., 1968; JD, George Washington U., 1971. Bar: D.C. 1972, Mich. 1972, Pa. 1972, U.S. Dist. Ct. D.C. 1972, U.S. Ct. Appeals (D.C. cir.) 1972, U.S. Supreme Ct. 1975, Colo. 1979, U.S. Dist. Ct. Colo. 1979, U.S. Ct. Appeals (10th cir.) 1979. Atty. Unity Ctr., Meadville, Pa., 1971-73; asst. pros. atty. Genesee County, Flint, Mich., 1973-79; sr. asst. atty. gen. State of Colo., Denver, 1979-82, 85—; assoc. Sumners, Miller & Clark, 1982-83, Miles & McManus, Denver, 1983-85. Mem. Colo. Bd. Law Examiners, 1992—. Contbr. articles to profl. jours. Mem. Mich. Pub. Consultation Panel of Internat. Joint Commn., 1976-78; treas. Denver South High Sch. PTSA, 1988-91, pres., 1991-93; athletic dir. Most Precious Blood Sch., 1988-90; bd. dirs. Pioneer Jr. Hockey Assn., 1988-90. Mem. ABA (house of dels. 1997—, chair commn. on mental & physical disability law, 1998-2001, commn. on mental and phys. disability law 1995-2001, chmn. 1998-2001, standing com. pub. edn., 2001-, tort and ins. practice sect., chmn. environ. law com. 1978-81, liaison jud. adminstrn. divsn. 1987-90, chmn. govt. liability com. 1988-89, 92-93, chmn. emerging issues com. 1996-97, sect. sec. 1997-99, mem. TIPS coun. 1999—, mem. coun. govt. and pub. sector lawyers divsn. 1991-97, editor-in-chief The Brief 1981-87, spkr. ann. meeting 1991-94), ATLA, Denver Bar Assn. (chmn. pub. legal ednl. com. 1989-91, 99—, del. 1997—), Colo. Bar Assn. (spkr. ann. meetings 1991-95, chmn. health law sect. 1993-94, chmn. law edn. com. 1993-96, coun. licensure, enforcement and regulation, spkr. ann. meetings 1992-2001, chmn. profl. discipline com. 1992-93, 98-99, program chmn. ann. meeting 1993-94, chair publs. com. 1995-97). Democrat. Roman Catholic. Home: 10406 W Glasgow Ave Littleton CO 80127-3468 Office: Atty Gen Office 1525 Sherman St Fl 5 Denver CO 80203-1760 E-mail: jim.carr@state.co.us

CARR, JAMES GRAY, judge; b. Boston, Nov. 14, 1940; s. Edmund Albert and Anna Frances C.; m. Eileen Margaret Glynn, Dec. 17, 1966; children: Maureen M., Megan A., Darrah E., Caitlin E. AB, Kenyon Coll., 1962; LLB, Harvard U., 1966. Bar: Ill. 1966, Ohio 1972, U.S. Dist. Ct. (no. dist.) Ill. 1966, U.S. Dist. Ct. (no. dist.) Ohio 1970, U.S. Supreme Ct. 1980. Assoc. Gardner & Carton, et al., Chgo., 1966-68; staff atty. Cook County Legal Asst. Found., Evanston, Ill., 1968-70; prof. U. Toledo Law Sch., 1970-79; U.S. magistrate judge U.S. Dist. Ct., Toledo, 1979-94, U.S. dist. judge, 1994—. Adj. prof. law Chgo. Kent Law Sch., 1969, Loyola U., Chgo., 1970; reporter, juvenile rules com. Ohio Supreme Ct., Columbus, 1971-72; reporter, mem. nat. wiretap com. U.S. Congress, Washington, 1976-77. Contbr. articles to profl. law jours. Founder, bd. dirs. Child Abuse Ctr., Toledo, 1970-84; active Lucas County Mental Health Bd., Toledo, 1984-89, Lucas County Children Svcs. Bd., Toledo, 1989-94. Fulbright fellow, 1977-78. Mem. ABA (reporter, elec. survey stds. 1979-80, mem. task force on tech. and law enforcement 1995-99, mem. task force on jury initiatives 1995-98), Toledo Bar Assn. (bd. dirs.), Phi Beta Kappa. Roman Catholic. Office: US Dist Ct 203 US Courthouse 1716 Spielbusch Ave Toledo OH 43624-1363 E-mail: jcarr@ohnd.uscourts.gov

CARR, LAWRENCE EDWARD, JR. lawyer; b. Colorado Springs, Colo., Aug. 10, 1923; s. Lawrence Edward and Lelah R. (Rubert) C.; m. Agnes Isabel Dyer, Dec. 26, 1946; children— Mary Lee, James Patrick, Lawrence Edward III, Eileen Louise, Thomas Vincent. B.S., U. Notre Dame, 1948, LL.B., 1949; LL.M., George Washington U., 1954. Bar: Colo. 1949, D.C. 1952, Md. 1961. With Travelers Ins. Co., 1949-51; practiced in Washington, 1952—; sr. ptnr. Carr Goodson, P.C., 1984—. Mem. adv. coun. U. Notre Dame Coll. Law, 1985—. With USMCR, 1943-46, 51-52; col. Res.; ret. Fellow Am. Bar Found.; mem. ABA (ho. of dels. 1973-75), Bar Assn. D.C. (dir. 1969-71, pres. 1974-75), D.C. Def. Lawyers Assn. (pres. 1978-79), Bar Assn. D.C. Rsch. Found. (pres. 1985-86). Federal civil litigation, Environmental, Insurance. Home: 111 Storm Haven Ct Stevensville MD 21666-3707 Office: Carr Goodson PC 1667 K St NW 11th Fl Washington DC 20006-1605 E-mail: lec@cargoodso.com

CARR, OSCAR CLARK, III, lawyer; b. Apr. 9, 1951; s. Oscar Clark Carr Jr. and Billie (Fisher) Carr Houghton; m. Mary Leatherman, Aug. 4, 1973; children: Camilla Fisher, Oscar Clark V. BA in English with distinction, U. Va., 1973; JD with distinction, Emory U., 1976. Bar: Tenn. 1976, U.S. Dist. Ct. (we. dist.) Tenn. 1977, (no. dist.) Miss. 1977, U.S. Ct. Appeals (6th cir.) 1985, (5th cir.) 1995, U.S. Dist. Ct. (so. dist.) Miss. 2000; cert. mediator Tenn. Assoc. Glankler Brown, PLLC (formerly Glankler, Brown, et al, Memphis, 1976-82, ptnr., 1982—, chief mgr., 1998-00. Bd. dirs. Memphis Ballet Soc., 1980, Memphis-Shelby County Unit Am. Cancer Soc., Memphis Oral Sch. for Deaf, 1988-91; treas., vestryman St. John's Espiscopal Ch., Memphis, 1988-91, sr. warden, 1991; mem. Commn. on Ministry Diocese of West Tenn., 1987-90, King of Carnival memphis, 1994; pres., dir. Juvenile Diabetes Found. Memphis chpt., 1998; bd. dirs. Carnival Memphis. Mem. ABA, Tenn. Bar Assn. (we. dist. coun. environ. law 1992—), Memphis-Shelby County Bar Assn. (bd. dirs. 1985-87), Memphis Country Club (atty. 1997—), U. Va. Alumni Assn. Federal civil litigation, State civil litigation, Environmental. Office: Glankler Brown PLLC 1700 One Commerce Sq Memphis TN 38103 E-mail: ocarr@glankler.com

CARR, THOMAS ELDRIDGE, lawyer; b. Aug. 16, 1953; s. Peter Gordon and Margaret (Johnson) C.; children: Christopher Allen, Austin Thomas. BA, Tex. Tech. U., 1975, JD, 1977. Bar: Tex. 1978, U.S. Dist. Ct. (no. and we. dists.) Tex. 1978, U.S. Ct. Appeals (5th cir.) 1981, U.S. Supreme Ct. 1982. Assoc. Morgan, Gambill & Owen, Ft. Worth, 1978-81; ptnr. Morgan, Owen, & Carr, 1981-85, Quillin, Owen, Wilson & Carr, Ft. Worth, 1987-91, Owen & Carr, Ft. Worth, 1991-94, Taylor, Olson, Adkins, Sralla & Elam LLP, Ft. Worth, 1999—. Co-author: Of Counsel to Classrooms: A Resource Guide to Assist Attorneys and Teachers in Law Focused Education. Active Benbrook City Coun., Tex., 1984-86, Benbrook Park and Recreation Bd., 1981-84; mem. exec. bd. Longhorn coun. Boy Scouts Am., 1983-86; mem. Home Rule Charter Commn., Benbrook, 1983. Selected Outstanding Young Lawyer of Tarrant County, 1990. Mem. ABA (chmn. com.), Ft. Worth Tarrant County Young Lawyers Assn. (pres. 1983), State Bar Tex. (chmn. Sch. Law sect. 1991, bd. dirs. 1998-2001, Presdl. citation 2001), Tarrant county Bar Assn. (treas., sec. 1988), Tex. Young Lawyers Assn. (bd. dirs. 1984-86). General corporate, Education and schools, Probate. Office: East Tower Ste 200 6000 Western Pl Fort Worth TX 76107

CARR, WALTER STANLEY, lawyer; b. Chgo., May 5, 1945; s. Robert Adams and Margaret (Wiley) C.; m. Mary Baine, Sept. 20, 1969. BS, U. Pa., 1967; JD, U. Chgo., 1970. Bar: Ill. 1970. From assoc. to ptnr. McDermott, Will & Emery, Chgo., 1970-86; v.p. Miami Corp., 1987—. Pres. Hull House Assn., Chgo., 1989; bd. dirs. Planned Parenthood Assn. Chgo. Area, 1980—. Mem. ABA, Ill. Bar Assn., Chgo. Bar Assn., Chgo. Estate Planning Council. Club: Univ. (Chgo.). Estate planning, Probate, Estate taxation. Home: 507 W Briar Pl Chicago IL 60657-4633 Office: Miami Corp 410 N Michigan Ave Ste 590 Chicago IL 60611-4252

CARR, WILLARD ZELLER, JR. lawyer; b. Richmond, Ind., Dec. 18, 1927; s. Willard Zeller and Susan (Brownell) C.; m. Margaret Paterson, Feb. 15, 1952; children: Clayton Paterson, Jeffrey Westcott. BS, Purdue U., 1948; JD, Ind. U., 1951. Bar: Calif. 1951, U.S. Supreme Ct. 1963. Ptnr. Gibson, Dunn & Crutcher, Los Angeles, 1952—. Mem. nat. panel arbitrators Am. Arbitration Assn.; former labor relations cons. State of Alaska; lectr. bd. visitors Southwestern U. Law Sch.; mem. adv. council Southwestern Legal Found., Internat. and Comparative Law Ctr. Trustee Calif. Adminstrv. Law Coll.; bd. dirs. Employers' Group, Calif. State Pks. Found., Los Angeles coun. Boy Scouts Am.; mem. Mayor's Econ. Devel. Policies Com.; past chmn. Pacific Legal Found.; past chmn. men's adv. com. Los Angeles County-USC Med. Ctr. Aux. for Recruitment, Edn. and Service; past chmn. bd. Wilshire Republican Club; past mem. Rep. State Central Com.; past mem. pres.'s coun. Calif. Mus. Sci. and Industry; mem. Nat. Def. Exec. Res., Los Angeles World Affairs Coun.; bd. dirs., sec. Los Angeles Police Meml. Found.; past chmn. Los Angeles sect. United Way; mem. adv. com. Los Angeles County Human Rels. Commn., past commr., Calif. State World Trade Commn.; Los Angeles chpt. ARC. Fellow Am. Bar Found.; mem. Internat. Bar. Assn. (past chmn. labor law com. of bus. law sect.), chmn. Labor Employment Com., The Federalist Soc., Calif. Bar Assn., L.A. County Bar Assn., L.A. C. of C. (past chmn. 1991), Calif. C. of C. Administrative and regulatory, Labor. Home: 2185 Century Hl Los Angeles CA 90067-3516 Office: Gibson Dunn & Crutcher 333 S Grand Ave Ste 4400 Los Angeles CA 90071-3197 E-mail: wcarr@gdclaw.com

CARRELL, DANIEL ALLAN, lawyer; b. Louisville, Jan. 2, 1941; s. Elmer N. and Mary F. (Pfingst) C.; m. Janis M. Wilhelm, July 3, 1976; children: Mary Monroe, Courtney Adele. AB, Davidson Coll., 1963; BA, Oxford U., 1965, MA, 1969; JD, Stanford U., 1968. Bar: Va. 1972, U.S. Dist. Ct. (ea. dist.) Va. 1972, U.S. Ct. Appeals (4th cir.) 1975, U.S. Dist. Ct. (we. dist.) Va. 1985. Asst. prof. U.S. Mil. Acad., West Point, N.Y., 1968-71; assoc. Hunton & Williams, Richmond, Va., 1971-79, ptnr., 1979-95; prin. Carrell & Rice, 1996—. Hearing officer Commonwealth of Va., 2000—. Active Richmond Rep. Com., 1974—; co-counsel Dalton for Gov. campaign, Richmond, 1977; counsel Obenshain for Senate campaign, Richmond, 1978; treas. Va. Victory '92; state fin. chmn., fin. com., state ctrl. com. and budget com. Rep. Party Va., 1993-96; bd. dirs. Southampton Citizens Assn., 1985—; pres. Davidson Coll. Alumni Assn., 1987-88; trustee Davidson Coll., 1987-88; bd. dirs. Needles Eye Ministries, 1986-90, adv. bd., 1990—, bd. dirs. U-Turn, Inc., 2001-; elder, trustee Stony Point Reformed Presbyn. Ch., 1993—; moderator James River Presbytery Presbyn. Ch. Am., 1998, 2001. Rhodes scholar, 1962; recipient Merit award Sports Illustrated Mag., 1963. Mem. ABA (chmn. exemption and Noerr Doctrine com. 1986-87, antitrust sect.), Va. Bar Assn. (chmn. young lawyers joint law-related edn. com. 1978-79, young lawyers fellow award 1980), Va. State Bar (chmn. com. on legal edn. and admission to bar 1984-91, bd. govs. sect. edn. lawyers 1992-99. dist. com. discipline 2001-), Richmond Bar Assn., Christian Legal Soc., Westwood Club. Avocations: tennis, basketball, theatre, concerts. Antitrust, General civil litigation, General corporate. Home: 3724 Custis Rd Richmond VA 23225-1102 Office: Carrell & Rice 7275 Glen Forest Dr Richmond VA 23226-3772 E-mail: lexrex3dac@aol.com

CARRERA, VICTOR MANUEL, lawyer; b. Rio Grande City, Tex., Nov. 20, 1954; s. Eladio and Ines Olivia (Guerra) C. BS, U. Tex., 1975, BA with honors, 1976, JD, 1979. Bar: Tex. 1979, U.S. Dist. Ct. (so. dist.) Tex. 1980, U.S. Dist. Ct. (we. dist.) Tex. 1996, U.S. Dist. Ct. (no. dist.) Tex. 2001, U.S. Ct. Appeals (5th cir.) 1986; cert. civil trial law, personal injury trial law, civil appellate law, Tex. Assoc. Cardenas & Whitis, McAllen, Tex., 1979-80; briefing atty. U.S. Dist. Ct. (so. dist.) Tex., Brownsville, 1980-81; assoc. Keys, Russell & Seaman, Corpus Christi, Tex., 1981-84, Wood, Boykin, Wolter & Keys, Corpus Christi, 1984-86, ptnr., 1987-88; participating mem. Law Offices of Ramon Garcia, P.C., Edinburg, Tex., 1988-90; ptnr. Munoz, Hockema & Reed, McAllen, 1990-96, Reed & Carrera, Edinburg, 1997, Reed, Carrera & McLain, Edinburg, TX, 1997—. Lectr. South Tex. Coll. Law, Houston, 1987, U. Houston, 1989-90, 96-99, State Bar Tex., 1992. Mng. editor Tex. Internat. Law Jour., 1978-79. Recipient Outstanding Individual Contbn. Award Vol. Lawyers of Coastal Bend, 1985. Mem. Tex. Bar Assn., Tex. Trial Lawyers Assn. (dir. 1991-96, lectr. 1993-94), Hidalgo County Bar Assn. Democrat. Avocations: history, archaeology. General civil litigation, Private international, Personal injury. Home: 5400 N 1st St Mcallen TX 78504-2211 Office: Reed Carrera & McLain PO Box 9702 Mcallen TX 78502-9702 also: Reed Carrera & McLain Bldg 101 1 Paseo del Prado Edinburg TX 78539 E-mail: vmcarrera@rcmlaw.com

CARRERE, CHARLES SCOTT, law educator, judge; b. Dublin, Sept. 26, 1937; 1 son, Daniel Austin. BA, U. Ga., 1959; LLB, Stetson U., 1961. Bar: Ga. 1960, Fla. 1961. Law clk. U.S. Dist. Judge, Orlando, Fla., 1962-63; asst. U.S. Atty. Middle Dist. Fla., 1963-66, 68-69, chief trial atty., 1965-66, 68-69; ptnr. Harrison, Greene, Mann, Rowe & Stanton, 1970-80; judge Pinellas County, Fla., 1980-96; vis. prof. law Stetson Coll. Law, 1997-98, Cumberland Law Sch., 1998-99. Recipient Jud. Appreciation award St. Petersburg Bar Assn., 1996, Alumnus of Yr. award Stetson Student Bar Assn., 1998. Mem. State Bar Ga., Fla. Bar, Phi Beta Kappa. Presbyterian. Address: PO Box 22034 Gateway Mall Sta Saint Petersburg FL 33742

CARRES, LOUIS GEORGE, lawyer; b. Miami Beach, Fla., Aug. 14, 1943; s. Louis John and Helen (Davis) C.; m. Margaret Craig Good, July 10, 1983; children: Michele, Elliot. BA, Fla. Atlantic U., Boca Raton, 1965; JD, Stetson U., 1969. Bar: Fla. 1969, U.S. Dist. Ct. (so. dist.) Fla. 1971, U.S. Dist. Ct. (mid. dist.) Fla. 1974, U.S. Dist. Ct. (no. dist.) Fla. 1975, U.S. Ct. Appeals (5th cir.) 1973, U.S. Ct. Appeals (11th cir.) 1982, U.S. Supreme Ct. 1976. Staff atty. South Fla. Migrant Legal Svc.s, Delray Beach, 1969-71; mng. atty. Fla. Rural Legal Svcs. Delray Beach, 1971-73; chief appellate asst. Office of Pub. Defender, Tallahassee, Fla., 1977-80, asst., West Palm Beach, Fla., 1980— ; instr. bus. law Hillsborough Community Coll., Tampa, 1974. Mem. The Fla. Bar Assn. (appellate procedure rules com. 1987-91, criminal law sect. trial practice com. 1987-88), ABA, Palm Beach County Bar Assn. (mem. law reform com. 1971-72), Palm Beach Criminal Def. Assn., Am. Judicature Soc., Robert Bullington Law Soc. Democrat. Greek Orthodox. Home: 830 Palmetto St West Palm Beach FL 33405-3930 Office: Office of Pub Defender 6th Fl 421 3rd St Fl 6 West Palm Beach FL 33401-4203

CARREY, NEIL, lawyer, educator; b. Bronx, N.Y., Nov. 19, 1942; s. David L. and Betty (Kurtzburg) C.; m. Karen Krysher, Apr. 9, 1980; children: Jana, Christopher; children by previous marriage: Scott, Douglas, Dana. BS in Econs., U. Pa., 1964; JD, Stanford U., 1967. Bar: Calif. 1968. Mem. firm, v.p. corp. DeCastro, West, Chodorow, Inc., L.A., 1967-97; of counsel Jenkens & Gilchrist, 1998—. Instr. program legal paraprofls., U. So. Calif., 1977-89; lectr. U. So. Calif. Dental Sch., 1987—, Employee Benefits Inst., Kansas City, Mo., 1996; legal cons. 33rd Dist. Calif. PTA, 1997—. Author: Nonqualified Defered Compensation Plans-The Wave of the Future, 1985. Officer Vista Del Mar Child Care Ctr., L.A., 1968-84; treas. Nat. Little League Santa Monica, Calif., 1984-85, pres., 1985-86, coach, 1990-95; coach Bobby Sox Softball Team, Santa Monica, 1986-88, bd. dirs., 1988, umpire in chief, 1988; referee, coach Am. Soccer Youth Orgn., 1989-95; curriculum com. Santa Monica-Malibu Sch. Dist., 1983-84 comm. health adv. com., 1988-95, chmn., 1989-95, sports and phys. edn adv. com., 1991-2000, chmn., 1991-99, dist. com. for sch. based health ctr., 1991-94, title IX/gender equity com., chmn. 1992—, athletic study com., chmn., 1989-91, fin. adv. com., 1994, ad hoc com. dist. facilities chmn., 1998, fin. task force, 1999-2000, parcel renewal tax com., 2000; dir. The Santa Monica Youth Athletic Found., 1995—, exec. comm. 1997-98, v.p. 1998—, mem. parcel tax com., 1999; dir. The Small Bus. Coun. of Am. 1995—, dir. Santa Monica H.S. Booster Club, 1995-97, dir. Santa Monica Bay Rep. Club, 1995-96, Santa Monica Police Activities League, 1995-97, v.p. fin., 1997-98, pres.-elect, 1998-99, pres., 1999—; pres. Gail Dorin Music Found., 1994—; v.p. Sneaker Sisters, 1996—; pres. Santa Monical Bay Jr. Rowing, 1997—; legal cons. 33d Dist. Calif. PTA, 1997-99; recreation and parks commr. City of Santa Monica, 1999—; sec. Santa Monica Leaders Club, 1999-2000; mem. U. Pa. Women's Sports Adv. Bd., 1998—; mem. resource bd. Santa Monica-Malibu Edn. Found., 2000—; pres. Chris Carrey Charitable Found., 2000—; bd. dirs. Padres Contra el Cancer, 2001—. Mem. LWV (dir. 1997—), U. Pa. Alumni Soc. (pres. 1971-79, dir. 1979-87), Mountaingate Tennis Club, Alpha Kappa Psi (life), League of Women Voters (dir. 1999-), Children's Ctr. for Cancer and Blood Diseases, Childrens Hosp. Los Angeles. Jewish. General corporate, Health, Pension, profit-sharing, and employee benefits. Home: 616 23d St Santa Monica CA 90402-3130 Office: 12100 Wilshire Blvd Fl 15 Los Angeles CA 90025-7120 E-mail: ncarrey@aol.com, ncarrey@jenkens.com

CARRICO, HARRY LEE, state supreme court chief justice; b. Washington, Sept. 4, 1916; s. William Temple and Nellie Nadalia (Willett) C.; m. Betty Lou Peck, May 18, 1940 (dec. 1987); 1 child, Lucretia Ann; m. Lynn Brackenridge, July 1, 1994. Jr. cert., George Washington U., 1938, JD, 1942, LLD, 1987, U. Richmond, 1973, Coll. William & Mary, 1993. Bar: Va. 1941. With Rust & Rust, Fairfax, Va., 1941-43; trial justice, 1943-51; pvt. practice, 1951-56; judge 16th Jud. Cir., 1956-61; justice Va. Supreme Ct., Richmond, 1961-81, chief justice, 1981—. Chmn. bd dirs. Nat. Ctr. for State Cts., 1989-90. With USNR, 1945-46. Recipient Alumni Profl. Achievement award George Washington U., 1981. Mem. McNeill Law Soc., Conf. Chief Justices (bd. dirs. 1985-91, 1st v.p. 1987, pres.-elect. 1988, pres. 1989-90, co-chmn. nat. jud. coun. 1991-97), Order of Coif, Phi Delta Phi, Omicron Delta Kappa. Episcopalian.

CARRIGAN, JIM R. arbitrator, mediator, retired federal judge; b. Mobridge, S.D., Aug. 24, 1929; s. Leo Michael and Mildred Ione (Jaycox) C.; m. Beverly Jean Halpin, June 2, 1956. Ph.B., J.D., U. N.D., 1953; LL.M. in Taxation, NYU, 1956; LLD (hon.), U. Colo., 1989, Suffolk U., 1991, U. N.D., 1997. Bar: N.D. 1953, Colo. 1956. Asst. prof. law U. Denver, 1956-59; vis. assoc. prof. NYU Law Sch., 1958, U. Wash. Law Sch., 1959-60; Colo. jud. adminstr., 1960-61; prof. law U. Colo., 1961-67; partner firm Carrigan & Bragg (and predecessors), 1967-76; bd. regents U. Colo., 1975-76; justice Colo. Supreme Ct., 1976-79; judge U.S. Dist. Ct. Colo., 1979-95. Mem. Colo. Bd. Bar Examiners, 1969-71; lectr. Nat. Coll. State Judiciary, 1964-77, 95; bd. dirs. Nat. Inst. Trial Advocacy, 1971-73, 78—, chmn. bd. 1986-88, also mem. faculty, 1972—; adj. prof. law U. Colo, 1984, 1991—; bd. dirs. Denver Broncos Stadium Dist., 1996—. Editor-in-chief: N.D. Law Rev., 1952-53, Internat. Soc. Barristers Quar., 1972-79; editor: DICTA, 1957-59; contbr. articles to profl. jours. Bd. visitors U. N.D. Coll. Law, 1983-85. Recipient Disting. Svc. award Nat. Coll. State Judiciary, 1969, Outstanding Alumnus award U. N.D., 1973, Regent Emeritus award U. Colo., 1977, B'nai Brith Civil Rights award, 1986, Thomas More Outstanding Lawyer award Cath. Lawyers Guild, 1988, Oliphant Disting. Svc. award Nat. Inst. Trial Advocacy, 1993, Constl. Rights award Nat. Assn. Blacks in Criminal Justice (Colo. chpt.), 1992, Disting. Svc. award Colo. Bar Assn., 1994, Amicus Curiae award ATLA, 1995, Colo. Trial Lawyers Assn. Lifetime Achievement award, 2000. Fellow Colo. Bar Found., Boulder County Bar Found.; mem. ABA (action com. on tort system improvement 1985-87, TIPS sect. long range planning com., 1986-97; coun. 1987-91, task force on initiatives and referenda 1990-92, size of civil juries task force 1988-90, class actions task force 1995-97), Colo. Bar Assn., Boulder County Bar Assn., Denver Bar Assn., Cath. Lawyers Guild, Inns of Ct., Internat. Soc. Barristers, Internat. Acad. Trial Lawyers (bd. dirs. 1995—), Fed. Judges Assn. (bd. dirs. 1985-89), Am. Judicature Soc. (bd. dirs. 1985-89), Tenth Circuit Dist. Judges Assn. (sec. 1991-92, v.p. 1992-93, pres. 1994-95), Order of Coif, Phi Beta Kappa. Roman Catholic. Office: Judicial Arbiter Group 1601 Blake St Ste 400 Denver CO 80202-1328 E-mail: carrigan2350@earthlink.net

CARROL, ROBERT KELTON, lawyer; b. Washington, Ind., Sept. 28, 1952; s. Louis Leon and Beatrice (Colbert) C. BA with distinction, So. Meth. U., 1974, JD, 1977. Bar: Tex. 1977, Calif. 1978, U.S. Dist. Ct. (no. and ea. dists.) Calif. 1978, U.S. Dist. Ct. (cen. and so. dists.) Calif. 1984, U.S. Ct. Appeals (9th cir.) 1978, U.S. Ct. Appeals (D.C. cir.) 1983, U.S. Supreme Ct. 1983. Assoc. Littler, Mendelson, Fastiff & Tichy, San Francisco, 1977-82, ptnr., 1982—. Contbr. articles to profl. pubs. Vestry mem. St. Mary the Virgin Episc. Ch., San Francisco, 1982-85. Mem. ABA (labor law sect. 1977—, entertainment com. on devel. and sports law 1977—), State Bar Calif., State Bar Tex., Bar Assn. San Francisco, Phi Beta Kappa, Phi Delta Phi. Clubs: Lawyers' of San Francisco, Barristers of San Francisco. State civil litigation, Entertainment, Labor.

CARROLL, EARL HAMBLIN, federal judge; b. Tucson, Mar. 26, 1925; s. John Vernon and Ruby (Wood) C.; m. Louise Rowlands, Nov. 1, 1952; children— Katherine Carroll Pearson, Margaret Anne BSBA, U. Ariz., 1948, LLB, 1951. Bar: Ariz., U.S. Ct. Appeals (9th and 10th cirs.), U.S. Ct. of Claims, U.S. Supreme Ct. Law clk. Ariz. Supreme Ct., Phoenix, 1951-52; assoc. Evans, Kitchel & Jenckes, 1952-56, ptnr., 1956-80; judge U.S. Dist. Ct. Ariz., 1980—, sr. judge, 1994—. Spl. counsel City of Tombstone, Ariz., 1962-65, Maricopa County, Phoenix, 1968-75, City of Tucson, 1974, City of Phoenix, 1979; designated mem. U.S. Fgn. Intelligence Surveillance Court by Chief Justice U.S. Supreme Ct., 1993-99; chief judge Alien Terrorist Removal Ct., 1996-01, 2001—. Mem. City of Phoenix Bd. of Adjustment, 1955-58; trustee Phoenix Elem. Sch. Bd., 1961-72; mem. Gov.'s Council on Intergovtl. Relations, Phoenix, 1970-73; mem. Ariz. Bd. Regents, 1978-80. Served with USNR, 1943-46; PTO Recipient Nat. Service awards Campfire, 1973, 75, Alumni Service award U. Ariz., 1980, Disting. Citizen award No. Ariz. U., Flagstaff, 1983, Bicentenial award Georgetown U., 1988, Disting. Citizen award U. Ariz., 1990, Sidney S. Woods Alumni Svc. award, 2000. Fellow Am. Coll. Trial Lawyers, Am. Bar Found.; mem. ABA, Ariz. Bar Assn., U. Ariz. Law Coll. Assn. (pres. 1975), Sigma Chi (Significant Sig award 1991), Phi Delta Phi. Democrat. Office: US Dist Ct US Courthouse Ste 521 401 W Washington SPC 48 Phoenix AZ 85003-2151

CARROLL, FRANK JAMES, lawyer, educator; b. Albuquerque, Feb. 10, 1947; s. Francis J. and Dorothy (Bloom) C.; m. Marilyn Blume, Aug. 9, 1969; children: Christine, Kathleen, Emily. BS in Acctg., St. Louis U., 1969; JD, U. Ill., 1973. Bar: Iowa 1973, U.S. Dist. Ct. Iowa, U.S. Tax Ct., U.S. Ct. Appeals (8th cir.); CPA, Mo., Iowa. Acct. Arthur Young & Co., St. Louis, 1969-70; shareholder Davis, Brown, Koehn, Shors & Roberts, P.C., Des Moines, 1973—. Lectr. law Drake U. Law Sch., Des Moines, 1976-86, lectr. Sch. of Bus., 1988-92; bd. dirs. Newton Mfg. Co., Pella Plastics, Inc., Iowa Agr. Devel. Authority. Mem. commr.'s adv. group IRS, Washington, 1989; mem. grad. tax adv. bd. U. Mo. Kansas City Sch. Law, 1995. Mem. ABA, Iowa Bar Assn. (chair bus. law sect. 1995-98, chair corp. counsel sect. 2001—), Polk County Bar Assn., Des Moines C. of C., Wakonda Club, Des Moines Variety Club (bd. dirs. 1998), Beta Gamma Sigma. General corporate, Corporate taxation. Home: 5725 Harwood Dr Des Moines IA 50312-1203 Office: Davis Brown Koehn Shors Roberts PC 666 Walnut St Ste 2500 Des Moines IA 50309-3904

CARROLL, JAMES EDWARD, lawyer; b. Milford, Mass., July 9, 1952; s. James William and Anna (Bertoni) C.; m. Nancy Louise Baker, Oct. 12, 1974; children: Jonathan Patrick, Benjamin James, Jeremy David. BS, Fairfield U., 1974; MA, U. R.I., 1977; JD cum laude, Suffolk U., 1983. Bar: Mass. 1983, U.S. Dist. Ct. Mass. 1984, U.S. Ct. Appeals (1st cir.) 1984, U.S. Tax Ct. 1989, U.S. Supreme Ct. 1995. Tchr. Prout Meml. High Sch., Wakefield, R.I., 1974-76, Walpole (Mass.) High Sch., 1976-83; assoc. Gaston Snow & Ely Bartlett, Boston, 1983-86; trial atty. U.S. Dept. Justice, Washington, 1986-88; assoc. Hale & Dorr, Boston, 1988; ptnr. Peabody & Arnold, 1988-95; founding ptnr. Cetrulo & Capone, LLP, 1995—. Mem. criminal justice panel, U.S. Dist. Ct. Mass., 1993—. Contbr. articles to law rev. Bd. dirs. Am. Cancer Soc. Mem. ABA, Mass. Bar Assn. (speaker 1991-92), Boston Bar Assn., Nat. Assn. Criminal Def. Attys., Supreme Jud. Ct. Hist. Soc., Phi Delta Phi. Roman Catholic. Avocations: running, baseball, football, children's soccer. Federal civil litigation, General civil litigation, Criminal. Home: 139 Lawndale Rd Mansfield MA 02048-1621 Office: Cetrulo & Capone LLP 2 Seaport Ln Boston MA 02205

CARROLL, JAMES J. lawyer; b. Chgo., Jan. 10, 1948; BS magna cum laude, DePaul U., 1969, JD summa cum laude, 1972. Bar: Ill. 1972, U.S. Tax Ct. 1980, U.S. Supreme Ct. 1981. Of counsel Sidley & Austin, Chgo., 1995-99, ptnr., 1978-95; dir., pres. Wrigley Mgmt. Inc., 1995-99; trust counsel Northern Trust Co., 1999—. Lectr. Ill. Inst. for Continuing Legal Edn. Editor-in-chief DePaul Law Rev., 1971-72. Sec. Lakewood Estates Homeowners Assn.; bd. dirs. David and Ruth Barnow Found., 1979, Wrigley Family Found., 1993-99; active Ill. Atty. Gen.'s Charitable Adv. Coun. With USAR, 1970-76. Mem. Ill. State Bar Assn. (chmn. children's rights subcom. 1972-73), Chgo. Bar Assn. (probate practice com. 1977-88, lectr.), Law Club Chgo., Legal Club Chgo., Phi Eta Sigma, Beta Alpha Psi. Office: Northern Trust Co 181 W Madison St M 9 Chicago IL 60675-0001 E-mail: jjc@notes.ntrs.com

CARROLL, JAMES JOSEPH, lawyer; b. Cin., Aug. 1, 1946; s. John Daniel and Virgeal Catherine (Grever) C.; m. Marie Gemelli, May 7, 1977; children: Katharine, Emily. BBA, U. Cin., 1969; JD, No. Ky. U., 1978. Bar: Ohio 1978, U.S. Dist. Ct. (so. dist.) Ohio 1978, U.S. Tax Ct. 1979, U.S. Supreme Ct. 1979. Tax mgr. Main LaFrantz, Cin., 1974-77; sec., treas. R.E.S.C.O., Inc., 1977-80; owner, sec., treas. Sterling-Mead, Inc., 1980-87; pvt. practice, 1987-88; of counsel Cors & Bassett, 1989—. Candidate Hamilton County auditor, 1974; treas. for various polit. candidates, Hamilton County, 1980, 82, 84; bd. dirs., past pres. Hyde Park Neighborhood Council, Cin., 1980-88; pres., trustee Neighborhood Improvement Corp., 1986-96; treas. Hamilton County Dem. Party, 1990—. Served with USAR, 1969-75. Mem. Cin. Bar Assn., Ohio Soc. CPAs, Cin. C. of C. (trustee Leadership Cin. alumni 1986-92, v.p. membership 1989-91), Bankers Club. Democrat. Roman Catholic. General corporate, Real property, Personal income taxation. Office: Cors & Bassett 537 E Pete Rose Way Ste 400 Cincinnati OH 45202-3578 E-mail: jjc@corsbassatt.com

CARROLL, JAMES VINCENT, III, lawyer; b. Houston, Sept. 21, 1940; s. James Vincent and Adoline (Easley) C.; children: Mary Latham, James Vincent IV, David Carter. BBA, U. Tex., 1962, JD, 1964. Bar: Tex. 1965, D.C. 1983. Mem. Andrews & Kurth L.L.P. and predecessors, 1965-95; mng. ptnr. Washington, 1981-83; mng. shareholder Houston office of Littler, Mendelson, Fastiff, Tichy & Mathiason P.C., 1995-99; mem., mng. shareholder Houston Office of Littler Mendelson P.C., 1999—. Mem. U.S. del. 2d UN Conf. on Exploration and Peaceful Uses of Outer Space, 1982. Contbr. articles in field to profl. jours. Served with USCG, 1964-65, lt. comdr. USNR, 1965-69. Fellow Houston Bar Assn., ABA Found.; mem. NAM (labor law adv. com.), ABA (vice-chmn. oil com. natural resources sect. 1980-85, chmn. energy and natural resources litigation com. 1985-86, coun. mem. 1986-89), Tex. Bar Assn. (dir. labor law sect. 1974-76, chmn. fed. and state agy. subcom. com. on coordination with other state and fed. groups 1975-77), Houston Bar Assn. (founder and first chmn. labor and employment law sect. 1995-96, coun. mem. 1996-99), Tex. Assn. of Bus. (bd. dirs. 1986-89), U.S. C. of C. (labor law adv. com. 1984-87), East Tex. C. of C. (bd. dirs. 1984-87), U. Tex. Law Sch. Assn. (dir. 1980-83), Greater Houston Partnership (mem. govt. affairs coun. 1994-99), Houston Country Club, Bentwater Country Club, Tex. General civil litigation, Oil, gas, and mineral, Labor. Home: 5130 Holly Terrace Dr Houston TX 77056-2100 Office: Littler Mendelson PC 1301 Mckinney St Ste 1900 Houston TX 77010-3029 E-mail: jcarroll@littler.com

CARROLL, JOSEPH J(OHN), lawyer; b. N.Y.C., Sept. 18, 1936; s. James J. and M. Catherine (Molloy) C.; m. Barbara Ann Lediger, May 16, 1959; 1 child, Barbara Ann (dec.). BS, Manhattan Coll., 1958; LLB, St. John's U., 1963; LLM, NYU, 1968. Bar: N.Y. 1964, U.S. Supreme Ct. 1967. Ins. underwriter Atlantic Mut. Ins. Co., N.Y.C., 1959-63; pub. adminstrn. intern N.Y. State Housing Fin. Agy., 1963-64, adminstrv. asst., 1964-67; assoc. Mudge, Rose, Guthrie, Alexander & Ferdon, 1967-77, ptnr., 1977-95; of counsel Sullivan & Donovan, LLP, 1995—. Mem. nat. coun. trustees Nat. Jewish Med. and Rsch. Ctr., Denver; trustee Manhattan Coll., N.Y.C., Queen of the Most Holy Rosary Parish, Roosevelt, N.Y. Mem. ABA (health law and urban, state and local govt. sects.), N.Y. State Bar Assn. (mcpl. health law sects.), Am. Health Lawyers Assn., Am. Soc. Law, Medicine and Ethics, Nat. Assn. Coll. and Univ. Attys. E-mail: jjbacarroll@juno.com

CARROLL, MARK THOMAS, lawyer; b. Queens, N.Y., May 12, 1956; s. Bernard James and Thalia (Antypas) C.; m. Joanne Mary Grinnell, Aug. 4, 1979; children: Stephen, Thomas. BA, Columbia U., 1977; JD, Harvard U., 1980. Bar: Pa. 1980, U.S. Ct. Appeals (3d cir.) 1980, U.S. Dist. Ct. (ea. dist.) Pa. 1980. Assoc. Duane, Morris & Heckscher, Phila., 1980-82; asst. dir. ALI-ABA, 1982-85, dir. office of publs., 1985—. Bd. dirs. Bradford Glen Homeowners Assn., 1988-90; founding mem. Joseph's People Com. Mem. ABA, Assn. for Continuing Legal Edn. (treas.). Republican. Roman Catholic. Home: 1402 Ashcom Dr Downingtown PA 19335-3566 Office: ALI-ABA 4025 Chestnut St Ste 500 Philadelphia PA 19104-3099 E-mail: mcarroll@ali-aba.org

CARROW, MILTON MICHAEL, lawyer, educator; b. N.Y.C., Sept. 13, 1912; s. Samuel and Ethel (Berlin) Carrow; m. Betsey Wood Hall, Nov. 02, 1940 (div. 1968); children: David M, Thomas E, Deborah, James H, Emily W; m. Eve Wagner Cooper, Feb. 28, 1969 (div. 1986); m. Barbara M Barski, Nov. 02, 1996. AB, Syracuse U., 1933, postgrad., 1933-34; JD, Harvard U., 1937. Bar: NY 1938. Assoc. Legal Aid Soc., Rochester, N.Y., 1937-38, Lincoln Epworth & Nathan Sweedler, 1938-42, Emil Schlesinger, 1946-48; pvt. practice, 1948-53; ptnr. Lavine & Carrow, N.Y.C., 1953-59, Landis, Carrow, Benson & Tucker, N.Y.C., 1959-70, Carrow, Bernson, Hoeniger, Freitag & Abbey, 1970-73; dir. Ctr. for Adminstrv. Justice, ABA, 1973-77, Nat. Center for Adminstrv. Justice, Consortium of Univs. of Washington Met. Area, 1977-79; pres. Nat. Center for Adminstrv. Justice, 1979-82. Adj asst prof Law Sch NYU, 1964—68; consult Nat Adv Comt Civil Disorders, 1967; mem faculty appellate judges seminar Inst Jud Admin, 1969—70; vis prof Nat Law Ctr George Washington Univ, 1973—80, adj prof Nat Law Ctr, 1980—81, research prof pub policy, 1983—; vice chmn Weston Charter Communication, Conn., 1965—66; counsel UN We Believe, 1962—72; vis intervenor XVIII Int Congress Admin Scis, Madrid, 1980; US rep to standing comt law and sic pub admin Int INst Admin Scis, 1982; consult Block Island Charter Communications, 1988—89. Author: (book) Background of Administrative Law, 1948, The Licensing Power in New York City, 1968; author: ((with J D Nyhart)) Law and Science in Collaboration, 1983; editor ((with Robert Paul Churchill and Joseph J Cordes)): Democracy, Social Values and Public Policy, 1998;contbr. articles to profl jours; editor: Working Paper series, Grad Program in Pub Policy, 1985—. Dir Washington Cir George Washington Univ, 1988—. Mem.: ABA (chmn sect admin law 1971—72), Asn Bar City NY (chmn cont admin law 1964—67). Home: 914 25th St NW Washington DC 20037-2101 Office: George Washington Univ 805 21st St NW Rm 602 Washington DC 20052-0001 E-mail: mcarrow@earthlink.net

CARRUTHERS, ANDREW JAMES, lawyer, mediator, arbitrator; b. Croxley Green, Eng., Nov. 29, 1949; s. William Bevil and Joan (Bartlett) C.; m. Patricia Ann Burch; children: William Edward, James Alexander. JD, Oxford U., 1972. Solicitor, Supreme Ct. of Eng., 1975. Ptnr. Rowe & Maw, London, 1985—, mng. ptnr., 1998-99; head of litigation Aon Claims Solutions, 2000. Contbr. chpts. to legas text book Tolley's Pensions Law, 1999. Sec. pensions litigtion com., London, 1997—. Mem. Oxford Club, Cambridge Club, Avocations: music, reading, gardening. General civil litigation, Professional liability. Office: Rowe & Maw 20 Black Friars Ln London EC4V6HD England E-mail: acarruthers@roweandmaw.co.uk

CARSON, TIMOTHY JOSEPH, lawyer; b. Darby, Pa., Feb. 17, 1949; s. Joseph Timothy and Marian (Maloney) C.; m. Janet Louise Duffy, May 30, 1975; children: Lindsey, Anne, Timothy J. BS in Econs., U. Pa., 1970; JD, Villanova Sch. Law, 1975. Bar: Pa. 1975, U.S. Ct. Claims 1976, U.S. Tax Ct. 1976. Assoc. Lentz, Riley, Cantor, Kilgore & Massey, Paoli, Pa., 1975-77, Townsend, Elliott & Munson, Phila., 1977; assoc. Saul, Ewing, Remick & Saul, Phila., 1977-81, ptnr. 1981—, chmn. dept. pub. fin., mem. policy com., 1994—; Mng. editor Villanova Law Rev., 1974-75; contbr. articles to profl. jours. and newsletters. Chmn. Tri-State Rep. Alliance, 1984—; mem. SBA Adv. Coun., Phila., 1982-85, Del. Valley Regional Planning Commn., 1996—; spl. advisor Pa. Ho. Local Govt. Com., 1985-88, Pa. Senate Intergovt. Affairs Com., 1989-93; chmn. fin. com. Rep. State Com. Pa., 1986-90, mem. leadership com. 1986-93; del. 1988, alt. del. 1992, Rep. Nat. Conv. Recipient Spl. awards and commendations U. Pa. Bd. Trustees, U.S. Navy and NASA, 1971, Rep. State Com. Pa., 1989, March of Dimes Birth Defects Found., 1990. Fellow Am. Bar Found. (life), Pa. Bar Found., Phila. Bar Found. (trustee 1989-93, pres. 1992, Spl. award 1993), Am. Coll. Bond Lawyers; mem. ABA, Phila. Bar Assn. (exec. com. young lawyers sect. 1981-84), Pa. Bar Assn. (bd. govs. 1979-82, 96—, chmn. young lawyers sect. 1980-81, ho. of dels. 1979—, del. 3d cir. jud. conf. 1979, chmn. commn. mcpl. fin. mcpl. law sect. 1984-87, chmn.'s award young lawyers sect. 1981, exec. officer, mem. bd. govs. 1997—), Nat. Assn. Bond Lawyers, Pa. Assn. of Bond Lawyers (bd. dirs. 1988-90), Mcpl. Bond Club Phila. Republican. Roman Catholic. Clubs: Racquet (Phila.), U. Pa. Faculty, Merion Golf (Ardmore, Pa.). Municipal (including bonds). Office: Saul Ewing Remick & Saul 3800 Centre Sq W Philadelphia PA 19102-2174

CARSON, WALLACE PRESTON, JR. state supreme court chief justice; b. Salem, Oreg., June 10, 1934; s. Wallace Preston and Edith (Bragg) C.; m. Gloria Stolk, June 24, 1956; children: Scott, Carol, Steven (dec. 1981). BA in Politics, Stanford U., 1956; JD, Willamette U., 1962. Bar: Oreg. 1962, U.S. Dist. Ct. Oreg. 1963, U.S. Ct. Appeals (9th cir.) 1968, U.S. Supreme Ct. 1971, U.S. Ct. Mil. Appeals 1977; lic. comml. pilot FAA. Pvt. practice law, Salem, Oreg., 1962-77; judge Marion County Cir. Ct., 1977-82; assoc. justice Oreg. Supreme Ct., 1982-92, state supreme ct. chief justice, 1992—. Mem. Oreg. Ho. of Reps., 1967-71, maj. leader, 1969-71; mem. Oreg. State Senate, 1971-77, minority floor leader, 1971-77; dir. Salem Area Community Council, 1967-70, pres., 1969-70; mem. Salem Planning Commn., 1966-72, pres., 1970-71; co-chmn. Marion County Mental Health Planning Com., 1965-69; mem. Salem Community Goals Com., 1965; Republican precinct committeeman, 1963-66; mem. Marion County Rep. Central Exec. Com., 1963-66; com. predinct edn. Oreg. Rep.

Central Com., 1965; vestryman, acolyte, Sunday Sch. tchr., youth coach St. Paul's Episcopal Ch., 1935— ; task force on cts. Oreg. Council Crime and Delinquency, 1968-69; trustee Willamette U., 1970— ; adv. bd. Cath. Ctr. Community Services, 1976-77; mem. comporehensive planning com. Mid-Willamette Valley Council of Govts., 1970-71; adv. com. Oreg. Coll. Edn. Tchr. Edn., 1971-75; pres. Willamette regional Oreg. Lung Assn., 1974-75, state dir., exec. com., 1975-77; pub. relations com. Williamette council Campfire Girls, 1976-77; criminal justice adv. bd. Chemeketa Community Coll., 1977-79; mem. Oreg. Mental Health Com., 1979-80; mem. subcom. Gov's Task Force Mental Health, 1980; you and govt. adv. com. Oreg. YMCA, 1981— . Served to col. USAFR, 1956-59. Recipient Salem Disting. Svc. award, 1968; recipient Good Fellow award Marion County Fire Svc., 1974, Minuteman award Oreg. N.G. Assn., 1980; fellow Eagleton Inst. Politics, Rutgers U., 1971 Mem. Marion County Bar Assn. (sec.-treas. 1965-67, dir. 1968-70), Oreg. Bar Assn., ABA, Willamette U. Coll. Law Alumni Assn. (v.p. 1968-70), Salem Art Assn., Oreg. Hist. Soc., Marion County Hist. Soc., Stanford U. Club (pres. Salem chpt. 1963-64), Delta Theta Phi. Office: Oregon Supreme Ct Supreme Ct Bldg 1163 State St Salem OR 97310-1331*

CARSON, WILLIAM SCOTT, lawyer; b. Buffalo, Mar. 13, 1946; s. William Dana and Barbara Brenneman (Powell) C.; m. Elizabeth Karin Ellis, June 28, 1977; children— Bradley Robert, Karen Elizabeth. B.S., Brown U., 1969, A.B., 1969; J.D. with honors, George Washington U., 1973. Bar: Va. 1974, D.C. 1974, U.S. Patent and Trademark Office 1974, Colo. 1977, U.S. Ct. Appeals (D.C. cir.) 1982. Examiner, U.S. Patent Office, Arlington, Va., 1969-74; ptnr. Burton, Dorr and Carson, Denver, 1980-86, Dorr, Carson, Sloan & Peterson, 1987—. Mem. ABA, Colo. Bar Assn., Denver Bar Assn., Licensing Execs. Soc. Franchising, Patent, Trademark and copyright. Home: 101 Hudson St Denver CO 80220-5831 Office: Dorr Carson Sloan & Peterson 720 S Colorado Blvd Ste 1240 Denver CO 80246-1904

CARTEN, FRANCIS NOEL, lawyer; b. Bryn Mawr, Pa., Dec. 25, 1935; s. Francis Patrick and Louise Cathleen (Leach) C. BA, U. Notre Dame, 1960; JD, Villanova U., 1964. Bar: Pa. 1967, N.Y. 1967, Conn. 1976. Assoc. Eyre, Mann & Lucas, N.Y.C., 1966-74; pvt. practice Danbury and Stamford, Conn., 1975-78, Stamford, 1985-88; patent counsel TIE/Comm., Inc., Shelton, Conn., 1978-79, Automation Industries, Inc., Greenwich, 1979-85; ptnr. Wyatt, Gerber & O'Rourke), LLP, Stamford, 1988—. With U.S. Army, 1954-56. Mem. N.Y. State Bar Assn., N.Y. Intellectual Property Law Assn., Conn. Patent Law Assn., Seawanhaka Corinthian Yacht Club (Oyster Bay, N.Y.). Republican. Intellectual property, Patent, Trademark and copyright. E-mail: fncarten@att.net

CARTER, BARRY EDWARD, lawyer, educator, administrator; b. L.A., Oct. 14, 1942; s. Byron Edward and Ethel Catherine (Turner) C.; m. Kathleen Anne Ambrose, May 17, 1987; children: Gregory Ambrose, Meghan Elisabeth. A.B. with great distinction, Stanford U., 1964; M.P.A., Princeton U., 1966; J.D., Yale U., 1969. Bar: Calif. 1970, D.C. 1972. Program analyst Office of Sec. Def., Washington, 1969-70; mem. staff NSC, 1970-72; rsch. fellow Kennedy Sch., Harvard U., Cambridge, Mass., 1972; internat. affairs fellow Coun. on Fgn. Rels., 1972; assoc. Wilmer, Cutler & Pickering, Washington, 1973-75; sr. counsel Select Com. on Intelligence Activities, U.S. Senate, 1975; assoc. Morrison & Foerster, San Francisco, 1976-79; assoc. prof. law Georgetown U. Law Ctr., Washington, 1979-89, prof., 1989-93, 96—; exec. dir. Am. Soc. Internat. Law, 1992-93; acting undersec. for export adminstrn. U.S. Dept. Commerce, 1993-94, deputy undersec., 1994-96. Vis. prof. law Stanford U. Law Sch., 1990; bd. dirs. Nukem, Inc., 1998—; chmn. adv. bd. Def. Budget Project, 1990-93; mem. UN Assn. Soviet-Am. Parallel Studies Project, 1976-87. Author: International Economic Sanctions: Improving the Haphazard U.S. Legal Regime, 1988 (Am. Soc. Internat. Law Cert. of Merit 1989); co-author: International Law, 3d edit., 1999; co-editor: Internat. Law: Selected Documents, 2001-02; contbr. articles to profl. jours. With U.S. Army, 1969-71. Mem. ABA, Am. Bar Found., Calif. Bar Assn., D.C. Bar Assn., Coun. on Fgn. Rels., Am. Soc. Internat. Law (hon. v.p. 1993-99, counselor, 1999-2000), Phi Beta Kappa. Democrat. Roman Catholic. Home: 2922 45th St NW Washington DC 20016-3559 Office: Georgetown U Law Ctr 600 New Jersey Ave NW Washington DC 20001-2075 E-mail: carter@law.georgetown.edu

CARTER, GENE, federal judge; b. Milbridge, Maine, Nov. 1, 1935; s. K.W. and S. Loreta (Beal) C.; m. Judith Ann Kittredge, June 24, 1961; children: Matthew G., Mark G. BA, U. Maine, 1958, LLD (hon.), 1985; LLB, NYU, 1961. Bar: Maine 1962. Ptnr. Rudman, Winchell, Carter & Buckley (and predecessors), Bangor, Maine, 1965-80; assoc. justice Maine Supreme Jud. Ct., 1980-83; judge U.S. Dist. Ct. Maine, 1983-89, chief judge, 1989-96. Chmn. adv. com. on rules of civil procedure Maine Supreme Jud. Ct., 1976-80. Chmn. Bangor Housing Authority, 1970-77. Mem. Am. Trial Lawyers Assn., Internat. Soc. Barristers, Am. Coll. Trial Lawyers. Office: US Dist Ct 156 Federal St Portland ME 04101-4152

CARTER, GORDON THOMAS, lawyer; b. Birmingham, Ala., Sept. 20, 1956; s. George Gordon and Mildred Orene (Davis) C. BA, U. Ala.; JD, Cumberland Sch. of Law. Law clk. Ala. Civil Appeals Ct., Montgomery, 1981-82; asst. gen. counsel Alfa Mut. Ins. Co., Alfa Corp., 1982—. Legal advisor Montgomery Advt. Fedn. Mem. ABA, Ala. State Bar, Montgomery County Bar Assn., Sons Confederate Vets., Toastmasters (treas. Montgomery chpt. 1986, pres. 1987), Sunrise Exch. Club (pres. 1991), Phi Alpha Theta, Phi Alpha Delta, Phi Kappa Psi. Republican. Presbyterian. Avocations: reading, biking, swimming, geneaology. Insurance, Securities. Home: 8537 Plantation Ridge Rd Montgomery AL 36116-6652 Office: Alfa Mut Ins Co 2108 E South Blvd Montgomery AL 36116-2015

CARTER, J. DENISE, lawyer; b. Kansas City, Mo., Mar. 21, 1963; d. Ronald Ira and Sharon Kay (Williams) C. AA, Longview C.C., 1986; BA, U. Mo., Kansas City, 1989, JD, 1992. Bar: Mo. 1992. Pvt. practice, Kansas City, 1993—. Republican. Avocations: golf, tennis, scuba diving. Bankruptcy, Criminal, General practice. Office: 4218 Roanoke Rd Ste 300 Kansas City MO 64111-4735

CARTER, JAMES ALFRED, lawyer; b. Shelbyville, Tenn., June 29, 1941; s. Granville Thomas and Elaine (Thrasher) C.; m. Kathleen Shaughness, Oct. 6, 1967; children: James Byrne, Stephen Thomas. BBA, U. Tex., Arlington, 1962; JD, U. Tex., 1967. Bar: U.S. Dist. Ct. (no. dist.) Tex. 1969, U.S. Tax Ct. 1970, U.S. Ct. Claims 1977, U.S. Supreme Ct. 1980, U.S. Ct. Appeals (5th cir.) 1985; CPA, Tex. Acct. Price Waterhouse, Ft. Worth, 1967; assoc. Smith, Carter, Rose & Finley, San Angelo, Tex., 1969-71; ptnr. Smith, Carter, Rose, Finley & Griffis, 1971-97; pvt. practice James A. Carter & Assocs., 1997—. Chmn. estate planning, probate and tax law Tex. Bd. Legal Specialization, Austin, Tex., 1980-84. Chmn. March of Dimes, San Angelo, 1971; pres. West Tex. Boys Ranch, San Angelo, 1980-84; mem. St. John's Hosp. Yr. 2000, San Angelo, 1980-84, Century Club YMCA, San Angelo; bd. dirs. Rio Concho Manor, San Angelo, 1980-90; trustee San Angelo Ind. Sch. Dist., 1992-98, pres., 1997-98. Capt. U.S. Army, 1968-69. Fellow Tex. Bar Found.; mem. ABA, AICPA (chmn. regional trial bd.), Tex. Bar Assn. (cert. in tax law, estate planning, probate bd. legal specialization, chmn. tax specialization, estate planning and probate specialization coms., revision bd. Tex. guardianship statute, com. inheritance and state tax), Tex. State Soc. CPA's (chmn. by-laws com.), Kiwanis (pres. 1978-79). Republican. Mem. Ch. Christ. Avocations: handball, farming. Estate planning, Probate, State and local taxation. Home: 915 Montecito Dr San Angelo TX 76901-4555 Office: 515 W Harris Ave Ste 100 San Angelo TX 76903-6362 E-mail: jcartlaw@wcc.net

CARTER, JAMES H. state supreme court justice; b. Waverly, Iowa, Jan. 18, 1935; s. Harvey J. and Althea (Dominick) C.; m. Jeanne E. Carter, Aug. 1965; children: Carol, James. B.A., U. Iowa, 1956, J.D., 1960. Law clk. to judge U.S. Dist. Ct, 1960-62; assoc. Shuttleworth & Ingersoll, Cedar Rapids, Iowa, 1962-73; judge 6th Jud. Dist., 1973-76, Iowa Ct. Appeals, 1976-82; justice Iowa Supreme Ct., Des Moines, 1982—. Office: Iowa Supreme Ct State House Des Moines IA 50319-0001 E-mail: James.carter@jb.state.us

CARTER, JAMES HAL, JR. lawyer; b. Ames, Iowa, Sept. 25, 1943; s. James H. Sr. and Louise (Benge) C.; children: Janet, Faith, Katherine BA, Yale U., 1965, LLB, 1969. Bar: N.Y. 1971, U.S. Dist. Ct. (so. dist.) N.Y. 1972, U.S. Dist. Ct. (ea. dist.) N.Y. 1975, U.S. Dist. Ct. (no. dist.) N.Y. 1992, U.S. Dist. Ct. (west. dist.) Mich. 1992, U.S. Dist. Ct. Conn. 1981, U.S. Ct. Internat. Trade 1980, U.S. Ct. Appeals (2nd cir.) 1971, U.S. Supreme Ct. 1976, U.S. Ct. Appeals (1st and 5th cirs.) 1984, U.S. Ct. Appeals (fed. cir.) 1988, U.S. Ct. Appeals (3rd cir.) 1990. Fulbright scholar Cambridge U., Eng., 1965-66; law clk. U.S. Ct. Appeals (2d cir.), 1969-70; with Sullivan & Cromwell, N.Y.C., 1970, ptnr., 1977. Lectr. internat. comml. arbitration Practicing Law Inst.; bd. dirs., chmn. exec. com. Am. Arbitration Assn.; bd. dirs. Am. Assn. for Internat. Com. of Jurists, Am. Bar Found. Corr. editor: Internat. Legal Materials; contbr. articles to profl. jours. Mem. adv. bd. Southwestern Legal Found. Internat. and Comparative Law Ctr., Inst. for Transnational Arbitration. Mem. ABA (past chair internat. law and practice sect., former co-chmn. internat. comml. arbitration com.), U.S. Coun. Internat. Bus. (com. on arbitration), Am. Soc. Internat. Law (v.p.), Am. Law Inst., N.Y. State Bar Assn. (former chmn. internat. dispute resolution com.), Assn. of Bar of City of N.Y. (former chmn. internat. affairs coun.), Coun. on Fgn. Rels. Federal civil litigation, Private international. Office: Sullivan & Cromwell 125 Broad St 28th Fl New York NY 10004-2489 E-mail: carterj@sullcrom.com

CARTER, JAMES WOODFORD, JR. lawyer; b. Berwyn, Ill., Aug. 20, 1943; s. James Woodford and Doris Lavern (Olson) C.; m. Janet Gail Krill, Oct. 29, 1966; children: James W. III, Elizabeth, Sarah, David. BS, Western Mich. U., 1965; JD, U. Ill., 1972. Bar: Ill. 1972. Assoc., Hinshaw, Culbertson, Moelmann, Hoban & Fuller, Chgo., 1972-74; asst. counsel A.C. Nielsen Co., Northbrook, Ill., 1974-84, v.p., gen. counsel, 1984-88, sr. v.p., gen. counsel, 1988—, also bd. dirs., mem. exec. com.; bd. dirs. Petroleum Info. Corp. and Dataquest, Inc. div. Capt. USMC, 1966-69, Vietnam. Mem. ABA, Chgo. Bar Assn., Ill. State Bar Assn. Federal civil litigation, General corporate, Private international. Office: A C Nielsen Co Nielsen Pla Northbrook IL 60062

CARTER, JEANNE WILMOT, lawyer, publisher; b. Iowa City, Oct. 25, 1950; d. John Robert and Adelaide Wilmot (Briggs) Carter; m. Daniel Halpern, Dec. 31, 1982; 1 child, Lily Wilmot. BA cum laude, Barnard Coll., N.Y.C., 1973; MFA, Columbia U., 1977; JD, Yeshiva U., N.Y.C., 1986. Bar: N.Y. 1987. Assoc. Raoul Lionel Felder, P.C., N.Y.C., 1986—; pres., co-owner, dir. Ecco Press, Hopewell, N.J., 1992—. Author: Dirt Angel, 1997, Tales from the Rain Forest, 1997; editor: On Music, 1994; contbr. articles to profl. jours. and books including Reading the Fights, N.Am. Rev., O'Henry Prize Stories 1986, Antaeus, Antioch Rev., Arts and Entertainment Law Jour., Ont. Rev., Denver Quar., Jour. Blacks in Higher Edn., others. Bd. dirs. Nat. Poetry Series, 1981—, AIDS Helping Hand, N.Y.C., 1987-95, Planned Parenthood of Mercer County, 1998—; vol. litigator Womanspace, Princeton, N.J., 1994; mem. Jr. League of N.Y.C., 1980-91. N.Y. Found. of the Arts fellow, 1989. Mem. ABA, N.Y. State Bar Assn. Family and matrimonial. Home: 60 Pheasant Hill Rd Princeton NJ 08540-7502

CARTER, JOHN LOYD, lawyer; b. Clayton, N.Mex., Oct. 2, 1948; s. John Allen and Ruth (Laughlin) C.; m. Dorel Susan Payne, Sept. 20, 1975; children: Matthew, Caroline, Susan. BA, So. Meth. U., 1970, JD cum laude, 1973. Bar: Tex. 1973, U.S. Ct. Appeals (5th and 11th cirs.) 1975, U.S. Supreme Ct. 1976, U.S. Dist. Ct. (so. dist.) Tex. 1974, U.S. Dist. Ct. (no. dist.) Tex. 1978, U.S. Dist. Ct. (ea. dist.) Tex. 1985. Assoc. Vinson & Elkins, Houston, 1973-80, ptnr., 1980—. Fellow Am. Coll. Trial Lawyers, Am. Bar Found., Tex. Bar Found., Houston Bar Found. Antitrust, General civil litigation, Securities. Office: Vinson & Elkins 2300 First City Tower Houston TX 77002-6760 E-mail: jcarter@velaw.com

CARTER, RICHARD DENNIS, lawyer, educator; b. Newburgh, N.Y., Feb. 17, 1949; s. Edward Francis and Catherine Florence (Harding) C. BA, Pace U., 1977; JD, George Washington U., 1980. Bar: D.C. 1980, Va. 1991, Md. 1991, U.S. Dist. Ct. D.C. 1981, U.S. Dist. Ct. Md. 1990, U.S. Dist. Ct. (ea. dist.) Wis. 1994, U.S. Dist. Ct. Ariz. 1994, U.S. Ct. Appeals (4th cir.) 1991, U.S. Supreme Ct. 1987. Supervising atty., adj. prof. law D.C. Law Students in Ct., Washington, 1980-90, dep. dir., 1981-85, exec. dir., 1985-90; adj. prof. trial advocacy Georgetown U., 1982-2000; ptnr. Cunningham and Hudgins, Alexandria, Va., 1990, Hudgins, Carter & Coleman, Alexandria, 1990-98, Carter & Coleman, Alexandria, 1998—. Contbr. articles to profl. jours. Mem. ABA, D.C. Bar Assn., Washington Bar Assn., Alexandria Bar Assn., Am. Inns of Ct. Episcopalian. Avocation: motor sports. Federal civil litigation, State civil litigation, Health. Home: 3416 Sharon Chapel Rd Alexandria VA 22310-2311 Office: Carter & Coleman 602 Cameron St Alexandria VA 22314-2506

CARTER, STEVE, state attorney general; b. Lafayette, Ind. BA in Econs., Harvard U., 1976; JD, MBA, Ind. U. Chief city-county atty. Indpls.-Marion County; atty. gen. State of Ind., 2001—. Office: Ind Govt Ctr S 5th Fl 402 W Washington St Indianapolis IN 46204*

CARTER, THERESA, lawyer; b. Seoul, South Korea, Nov. 3, 1971; d. Dewey Allen and Soon Ye C. BBA, Loyola Marymount U., 1994; JD, Whittier Law Sch., 1997. Bar: N.Y., Calif. Ptnr. Carter, Nelson & Assoc., Las Vegas, 1997-98, Nersesian, Carter, Nelson, Bolton, Las Vegas, 1998—. Recipient Wiley M. Manual award for pro bono Calif. State Bar, 1996. Fellow Phi Delta Phi. Lutheran. Avocations: golf, arts and crafts, reading, nature hikes/walks. Office: Nersesian Carter Nelson Bolton 333 S 3rd St Ste A Las Vegas NV 89101

CARTER, T(HOMAS) BARTON, law educator; b. Dallas, Aug. 6, 1949; s. Sydney Hobart and Josephine (Wren) C.; m. Eleonore Dorothy Alexander, June 3, 1978 (div. 1988); 1 child, Richard Alexander. BA in Psychology, Yale U., 1971; JD, U. Pa., 1974; MS in Mass Communication, Boston U., 1978. Bar: Mass. 1974, U.S. Dist. Ct. Mass. 1975, U.S. Ct. Appeals (1st cir.) 1975. Asst. prof. law Boston U., 1979-85, assoc. prof., 1985-96, prof., 1996—; pvt. practice Boston, 1974—. Pres. Tanist Broadcasting Corp., Boston, 1981—. Co-author: The First Amendment and the Fourth Estate, 1985, 8th edit., 2000, The First Amendment and the Fifth Estate, 1986, 5th edit., 1999, Mass Communications Law in a Nutshell, 1988, 5th edit., 2000. Mem. ABA, Assn. for Edn. in Journalism and Mass Comm. (clk. 1981-82, asst. head 1982-83, head 1983-84), Broadcast Edn. Assn. (chair law and policy divsn. 1989-90, Fed. Comm. Bar Assn., Univ. Club. Avocation: bridge. Home: 109 Commonwealth Ave Apt 6 Boston MA 02116-2345 Office: Boston U 640 Commonwealth Ave Boston MA 02215-2422 E-mail: comlaw@bu.edu

CARTER, WILLIAM JOSEPH, lawyer; b. Balt., Sept. 1, 1949; s. Henry Merle and Florence (Rogan) C.; m. Monica Anne Urlock, July 17, 1976. BS in Psychology, Va. Poly. Inst., 1971; JD, Coll. William and Mary, 1974. Bar: Va. 1974, Pa. 1974, Md. 1980, U.S. Dist. Ct. D.C. 1981, U.S. Dist. Ct. Md. 1983, U.S. Dist. Ct. (ea. dist.) Va. 1985, U.S. Ct. Claims 1977, U.S. Tax Ct. 1977, U.S. Ct. Mil. Appeals 1975, U.S. Ct. Appeals (D.C. and 4th cirs.) 1979, U.S. Ct. Appeals (fed. cir.) 1982, D.C. 1980, U.S. Supreme Ct. 1977, U.S. Ct. Appeals (6th cir.) 1988, U.S. Ct. Appeals (3d and 5th cirs.) 1992. Commd. 2d lt. U.S. Army, 1971, advanced through grades to capt., 1974, served with JAGC, 1971-79, resigned, 1979; assoc. Carr, Jordan, Coyne & Savits, Washington, 1979-84; shareholder Carr, Goodson & Lee, P.C., 1984-95, Carr Goodson Lee & Warner Profl. Corp., Washington, 1996-98, Carr Goodson Warner Profl. Corp., Washington, 1999-2000, Carr Goodson, P.C., Washington, 2000—. Mem. Deans adv. roundtable Coll. Arts and Scis., Va. Poly. Inst. Author: Appellate Practice Handbook for Maryland, Virginia and District of Columbia, 1996; editor: Appellate Practice Manual for the District of Columbia Court of Appeals, 1992. Mem.: ABA, Bar Assn. D.C., Counselors, D.C. Bar Assn. (cts. and adminstrn. of justice sect., ct. rules com., chair 1998—2001), Rotary (pres. Olney, Md. chpt. 1999—2000). Episcopalian. Avocations: ice hockey, tennis, music, scuba diving, skiing. Appellate, General civil litigation, Insurance. Office: Carr Goodson PC Ste 1100 1667 K St NW Washington DC 20006

CARTER, ZACHARY W. lawyer; BA, Cornell U., 1972; JD, NYU, 1975. Bar: N.Y., U.S. Dist Ct. (ea. dist.) N.Y., U.S. Dist. Ct. (so. dist.) N.Y., U.S. Ct. Appeals (2d cir.), U.S. Supreme Ct. Asst. U.S. atty. U.S. Dist. Ct. (ea. dist.) N.Y., 1975-80; mem. Patterson, Belknap, Webb & Tyler, 1980-81; exec. asst. dist. atty. King County Dist. Atty's. Office, Bklyn., 1982-87; exec. asst. to dep. chief adminstrv. judge N.Y. City Cts., 1987; judge criminal ct. City of N.Y., 1987-91; U.S. magistrate judge E.D.N.Y., 1991-93; U.S. atty. ea. dist. N.Y. U.S. Dept. Justice, Bklyn., 1993-99; ptnr. Dorsey & Whitney, N.Y.C., 1999—. Mem. N.Y. Bar Assn. (mem. exec. com. criminal law sect.), Assn. Bar of the City of N.Y. (mem. com. to encourage judicial svc.). Office: Dorsey & Whitney LLP 250 Park Ave New York NY 10177-0001

CARTIER, RUDOLPH HENRI, JR. lawyer, legal educator; b. Yonkers, N.Y., Oct. 8, 1947; s. Rudolph Henri and Edith Edna (Hartling) C.; m. Linda Clair Truzzolino, Jan. 24, 1970 (div. July 1980); m. Mary Anne Lavorata, Aug. 16, 1980; children: Laura Anne, Stephen Robert. BA, LaSalle Coll., 1969; JD, St. John's U., Jamaica, N.Y., 1975. Bar: N.Y. 1976, U.S. Dist. Ct. (ea. and so. dists.) N.Y. 1976, U.S. Supreme Ct. 1982. Asst. dist. atty. Suffolk County Dist. Atty.'s Office, Riverhead, N.Y., 1975-77; sole practice, Selden, N.Y., 1977-82; ptnr. Rogers & Cartier, P.C., Patchogue, N.Y., 1982— ; gen. counsel Suffolk County Assn. Mcpl. Employees; asst. prof. Suffolk County Community Coll., Selden, N.Y., 1978-84, paralegal adv. bd.; spl. asst. dist. atty., Village of Head of the Harbor, 1985—. Atty., mem. steering com. Smithtown Citizens for Edn., N.Y., 1983—. Mem. N.Y. State Bar Assn. (criminal discovery and correctional services coms.), Suffolk County Bar Assn. (fee dispute resolution and criminal law coms.), Suffolk County Criminal Assn., L.I. Indsl. Relations Research Assn. Republican. Roman Catholic. State civil litigation, Criminal, Family and matrimonial. Home: 11 Peace Ln East Setauket NY 11733-1957 Office: Rogers and Cartier PC 180 E Main St Patchogue NY 11772-3171 also: 900 Ellison Ave Westbury NY 11590-5142

CARTY, PAUL VERNON, lawyer; b. Uchitomari, Okinawa, Aug. 2, 1954; s. Leo Sylvester and Dolores Iola (Inniss) C.; m. Kimberly Ann Fickett, Jan. 23, 1982; children: Rachel Lee, Paul Jr., Trevor Dudley. BA, Wesleyan U., Middletown, Conn., 1977; JD, U. Conn., 1985. Bar: Conn. 1985, U.S. Dist. Ct. (Conn.) 1992, Mashantucket Pequot Tribal Ct. 1995. Claims adjustor Liberty Mut. Ins. Co., Bklyn., 1977-80; sr. claims rep. Cigna Corp., Farmington, Conn., 1980-85; assoc. Farren & King, New Haven, 1985-97; solo practitioner, 1997—. Chmn. West Haven (Conn.) Bd. Ethics, 1987-90. Mem. ABA, Conn. Bar Assn., Conn. Trial Lawyers Assn., Conn. Criminal Def. Lawyers Assn., New Haven County Bar Assn., West Haven Bar Assn., George Crawford Law Assn. Episcopalian. Avocations: karate, photography. General civil litigation, Criminal, Personal injury. Home: 20 Swampscott St West Haven CT 06516-1424 Office: 506 Whalley Ave PO Box 3192 New Haven CT 06515-0292 E-mail: PVCartyEsq@aol.com

CARUSO, MARK JOHN, lawyer; b. L.A., Apr. 27, 1957; s. John Mondella and Joyce Dorothy C.; m. Judy F. Velarde, Aug. 15, 1987. BS cum laude, Pepperdine U., 1979, JD cum laude, 1982. Bar: Calif. 1982, N.Mex. 1987, U.S. Dist. Ct. (ctrl. dist.) Calif. 1982, U.S. Dist. Ct. N.Mex. 1987, U.S. Dist. Ct. (no. and so. dists.) Calif. 1995, U.S. Ct. Appeals (9th cir.) 1983, U.S. Ct. Appeals (10th cir.) 1987. Law clk. Fed. Trade Commn., L.A., 1981-82; pvt. practice, Burbank, Calif., 1982—, Albuquerque, 1987—. Mem. N.Mex. Ho. of Reps., 1990-94, mem. labor com., consumer and pub. affairs com., workers compensation oversight interim com., ct. correction and justice interim com., jud. com., labor com., workers compensation oversight com.; lobbyist Nat. Right to Work Com., 1984-86. Col., aide de camp to gov. State of N. Mex., 1987; chmn. N. Mex. Mcpl. Boundary Commn., 1988—; del. Rep. Nat. Conv., 1988, 92; lectr. breast implant litigation, Fen Phen diet drug litigation; Sandoval county chmn. George Bush for Pres., 1988; campaign mgr. Boulter for U.S. Congress, Tex., 1983-84. Recipient platinum award N.Mex. Free Enterprise Adv., 1986. Mem. ATLA, Breast Implant Litigation Group, Consumer Attys. of Calif., Albuquerque Hispano C. of C., Greater Albuquerque C. of C. General civil litigation, Personal injury, Product liability. Office: 4302 Carlisle Blvd NE Albuquerque NM 87107-4811 Fax: 505-883-5012. E-mail: mark@carusolaw.com

CARVER, GEORGE ALLEN, JR. retired lawyer; b. Washington, Nov. 8, 1940; s. George Allen and Barbara Ellen (Bristol) C.; m. Joan Page, Dec. 13, 1964; children: George Allen III, Robert William. BS, U.S. Mil. Acad., 1964; JD, U. Va., 1972. Bar: Va. 1972, D.C. 1978, U.S. Ct. Appeals (D.C. cir.) 1979, U.S. Ct. Appeals (9th cir.) 1986, U.S. Ct. Appeals (4th cir.) 1988. Trial atty. gen. crimes sect. Criminal divsn. U.S. Dept. Justice, Washington, 1972-76, trial atty. pub. integrity sect., 1976-81, dir. conflicts of interest crimes br., pub. integrity sect., 1981-88, dep. chief fraud sect., 1988-92, prin. dep. chief fraud sect., 1992-95, sr. counsel to chief asset forfeiture/money laundering sect., 1995-96, dep. chief, sr. counsel to the chief, 1996-2000; ret., 2000. Capt. inf. U.S. Army, 1964-69. Decorated Silver Star, Bronze Star, Purple Heart. Avocations: photography, fishing, boating, walking, reading. Home: 6049 Makely Dr Fairfax Station VA 22039-1324

CASE, BASIL TIMOTHY, lawyer; b. Florence, Ala., May 26, 1966; s. Basil Harvey and Virginia Nell Case. BA, U. No. Ala., 1987; JD, Samford U., 1992. Bar: U.S. Dist. Ct. (no. dist.) Ala. 1993. Pvt. practice, Florence, Ala. General civil litigation, Criminal. Office: 412 S Court St Ste 303 Florence AL 35630-5648

CASE, DAVID LEON, lawyer; b. Lansing, Mich., Sept. 22, 1948; s. Harlow Hoyt and Barbara Jean (Denman) C.; m. Cynthia Lou Rhinehart, Jan. 28, 1968; children: Beau, Ryan, Kimberly, Darren, Stephanie. BS with distinction, Ariz. State U., 1970, JD cum laude, 1973. Bar: Calif. 1973, U.S. Dist. Ct. (cen. dist.) Calif. 1973, U.S. Tax Ct. 1974, Ariz. 1976, U.S. Supreme Ct. 1997. Assoc. Willis, Butler & Scheifly, Los Angeles, 1973-75; from assoc. to mem. Ryley, Carlock & Applewhite, Phoenix, 1975—. Fellow Ariz. Bar Found., Am. Coll. Trust and Estate Counsel; mem. ABA (tax sect., corp. sect., probate and trust sect.), Ariz. Bar Assn., Ctrl. Ariz. Estate Planning Coun. (bd. dirs., pres. 1988-89), Beta Gamma Sigma. Republican. Presbyterian. Avocations: guitar, sports. General corporate, Estate planning, Taxation, general. Office: Ryley Carlock & Applewhite PO Box 634 Phoenix AZ 85001-0634 E-mail: dcase@rcalaw.com

CASE, DOUGLAS MANNING, lawyer; b. Cleve., Jan. 3, 1947; s. Manning Eugene and Ernestine (Bryan) C.; m. Marilyn Cooper, Aug. 23, 1969. BA, U. Pa., 1969; JD, MBA, Columbia U., 1973. Bar: N.Y. 1974, N.J. 1975, Calif. 1980, Ohio 1991, Fla. 2000. Assoc. Brown & Wood, N.Y.C., 1973-77; corp. counsel PepsiCo Inc., Purchase, N.Y. and Irvine, Calif., 1977-83, Nabisco Brands Inc., N.Y.C., East Hanover, N.J. and London, 1983-89; asst. gen. counsel Chiquita Brands Internat., Inc., Cin., 1989-92; prin. Douglas M. Case Law Offices, 1993-2001, Vero Beach, Fla., 2001—. Lectr. numerous seminars. Contbr. articles to profl. jours. Chmn. Olde Colonial Dist.; active Morris-Susssex Area coun. Boy Scouts Am., 1986-88; sec., trustee Marble Scholarship Com., N.Y.C., 1983-88; trustee Cin. Opera Guild, 1994-99, hon. trustee, 1999—, pres., 1997-98, chmn., 1998-99, Cin. Opera Assn., bd. dirs., exec. com. 1997-98. Mem. ABA, Internat. Bar Assn., Fla. Bar, Cin. Bar Assn. (chair solo and small firm practitioners com. 1995-97, continuing legal edn. chair internat. law com. 1994-96, sec. 1996-97, vice chair 1997-98, chair 1998-2000), Quality in Law (chmn. 1996-98), Munich Sister City Assn. of Greater Cin. (chmn. econ. devel. com. 1995-96), The Lawyers Club of Cin. (exec. com. 1995-2000, treas. 1996, sec. 1997, 2d v.p. 1998, 1st v.p. 1999, pres. 2000), Metropolitan Club (N.Y.C.), Morris County Golf Club, Columbia Bus. Sch. Club (N.Y.C., pres., bd. dirs. 1974-79), Kenwood Country Club. Avocation: golf. Contracts commercial, General corporate, Private international. Home: 501 Bay Dr Vero Beach FL 32963-2163 E-mail: dcaselaw@bellsouth.net

CASE, FORREST N., JR. lawyer; b. Albany, N.Y., July 14, 1932; s. Forrest N. and Helen (Reed) C.; m. Frances Watkins, June 4, 1988; children: Marjorie, Joanne, Kenneth. AB, Union Coll., 1954; LLB, Albany Law Sch., 1957. Bar: N.Y. 1957, U.S. Dist. Ct. (no. dist.) N.Y. 1957. Ptnr. Carter, Conboy & Case, Albany, 1961—. Treas. Northeastern N.Y. Def. Rsch. Inst., Albany, 1972-74. Fellow Am. Coll. Trial Lawyers; mem. ABA, N.Y. State Bar Assn., Albany County Bar Assn., Am. Bd. Trial Advocates (adv.), N.Y. State Trial Lawyers Assn., Def. Rsch. Inst. General civil litigation, Personal injury, Product liability. Office: Carter Conboy & Case 20 Corporate Woods Dr Albany NY 12211-2500

CASE, KAREN ANN, lawyer; b. Milw., Apr. 7, 1944; d. Alfred F. and Hilda M. (Tomich) Case. BS, Marquette U., 1963, JD, 1966; LLM, NYU, 1973. Bar: Wis. 1966, U.S. Ct. Claims 1973, U.S. Tax Ct. 1973. Ptnr. Meldman, Case & Weine, Milw., 1973-85, Meldman, Case & Weine divsn. Mulcahy & Wherry, S.C., 1985-87; Sec. of Revenue State of Wis., 1987-88; ptnr. Case & Drinka, S.C., Milw., 1989-91, Case, Drinka & Diel, S.C., Milw., 1991-97, CoVac, 1997—. Lectr. U. Wis., Milw., 1974-78; guest lectr. Marquette U. Law Sch., 1975-78; dir. WBBC, 1998—. Contbr. articles to legal jours. Mem. gov.'s Commn. on Taliesin, 1988, gov.'s Econ. Adv. Commn., 1989-91, pres.'s coun. Alverno Coll., 1988-94, nat. coun., 1998-2000; bd. dirs. WBCC, 1998—. Fellow Wis. Bar Found. (dir. 1977-90, treas. 1980-90); mem. ABA, Milw. Assn. Women Lawyers (founding mem., bd. dirs. 1975-78, 81-82), Milw. Bar Assn. (bd. dirs. 1985-87, law office mgmt. chair 1992-93), State Bar Wis. (bd. govs. 1981-85, 87-90, dir. taxation sect. 1981-87, vice chmn. 1986-87, 90-91, chmn. 1991-92), Am. Acad. Matrimonial Lawyers (bd. dirs. 1988-90), Nat. Assn. Women Lawyers (Wis. del. 1982-83), Milw. Rose Soc. (pres. 1981, dir. 1981-83), Friends of Boerner Bot. Gardens (founding mem., pres. 1984-90), Profl. Dimensions Club (dir. 1985-87), Tempo Club (sec. 1984-85). Probate, Corporate taxation, Personal income taxation. Home: 2212 Harbour Ct Longboat Key FL 34228-4174 Office: CoVac 9803 W Meadow Park Dr Hales Corners WI 53130-2261

CASE, STEPHEN SHEVLIN, lawyer; b. Mpls., Nov. 16, 1943; s. George Price and Helen (Beckwith) C.; m. Judy Elizabeth Everett, Apr. 5, 1969 (div. Feb. 1979); children: Mackenzie Beckwith, Julia Lee; m. Pamela Ellen Earl, Apr. 29, 1981 (div. 1992). BA, Washington and Lee U., 1966, LLB with honors, 1969. Bar: Ariz. 1969, U.S. Tax Ct. 1970, U.S. Ct. Appeals (9th cir.) 1984. Assoc., Fennemore, Craig, von Ammon & Udall, Phoenix, 1969-73; majority atty. (Rep.) Ariz. State Senate, 1973; trust counsel First Interstate Bank of Ariz., Phoenix, 1973-76; ptnr. Norris & Case, P.C., Sun City, Ariz., 1976-85, Case & Bennett, Sun City and Scottsdale, Ariz., 1985-95, Case and Siler, Sun City and Scottsdale, Ariz., 1995—; instr. Golden Gate U., Phoenix, 1983-87; lectr. in field. Bd. dirs. Cen. Ariz. Estate Planning Coun., 1978-81; mem. bd. adjustment Town of Paradise Valley, Ariz. 1987-91, Lukes Men of St. Lukes Hosp., 1976—, pres. 1981-82; bd. dirs. ARC (ctrl. Ariz. chpt.) 1992—, vice chmn., 1995-96, chmn., 1996—. Fellow Am. Coll. Trust and Estate Counsel; mem. ABA, State Bar Ariz. (chmn. sect. real property, probate and trust law 1981-82, chmn. sect. taxation 1983-84, disciplinary hearing com. 1989-96, chmn. 1994-96), Delta Theta Phi, Rotary (dir. Sun City Found. 1977-81, 95—, chmn. 1996—). Contbr. articles to profl. jours. Avocations: trout fishing, skiing, backpacking. Estate planning, Probate, Taxation, general. Office: 5725 N Scottsdale Rd Ste 195C Scottsdale AZ 85250-5908

CASE, THOMAS LOUIS, lawyer; b. Dallas, June 14, 1947; s. Donald L. and Ellen (Hanson) C.; m. Bonnie Nally, July 8, 1972. BA, Vanderbilt U., 1969, JD, 1972; cert. civil trial law, Tex. Bd. Legal Specialization. Bar: Tex. 1972, U.S. Dist. Ct. (no. dist.) Tex. 1973, U.S. Dist. Ct. (we. and ea. dists.) Tex. 1978, U.S. Dist. Ct. (so. dist.) Tex. 1979, U.S. Dist. Ct. (ea. dist.) Ark. 1981, U.S. Ct. Appeals (5th cir.) 1977, U.S. Supreme Ct. 1978, U.S. Ct. Appeals (8th cir.) 1984, U.S. Ct. Appeals (11th cir.) 1981. Assoc. Johnson, Bromberg, Leeds & Riggs, Dallas, 1972-77; ptnr. Bickel & Case, 1977-84, St. Claire & Case, Dallas, 1984-93, Thomas L. Case & Assocs., P.C., Dallas, 1993-2000; shareholder Case Carter Salyers & Henry, 2000—. Mem. ABA, Tex. Bar Assn., Tex. Assn. Def. Coun., Dallas Assn. of Def. Counsel, Dallas Bar Assn. Federal civil litigation, General civil litigation, Labor. Office: Case Carter Salyers & Henry PC 5910 N Central Expy Ste 1450 Dallas TX 75206-5146 E-mail: tcase@casecarter.com

CASEBOLT, JAMES STANTON, lawyer; b. Denver, Apr. 27, 1950; s. Stanton Taylor and Josephine Almira (Cole) C.; m. Joanne Ruth Tuthill, June 10, 1972; children— Matthew, Zachary. B.A. magna cum laude, Colo. Coll., 1972; J.D., U. Colo., 1975. Bar: Colo. 1975, U.S. Dist. Ct. Colo. 1975, U.S. Ct. Appeals (10th cir.) 1983. Assoc. Younge & Hockensmith, P.C., Grand Junction, Colo., 1975-78, dir., sec., 1978— , sr. litigation ptnr., 1984— . Author: Civil Jury Selection Procedure and Pattern Voir Dire. Mem. adv. bd. Salvation Army Grand Junction; trustee Presbytery Western Colo., 1982-85, chmn., 1984-85; cubmaster Boy Scouts Am., Grand Junction, 1984-87. Mem. ABA, Colo. Bar Assn. (litigation council 1982-85), Mesa County Bar Assn. (sec.-treas. 1980-83, bd. dirs.), Colo. Def. Lawyers, Phi Beta Kappa. State civil litigation, Insurance, Personal injury. Home: 836 E 17th Ave # 3-d Denver CO 80218-1449 Address: Younge & Hockensmith 743 Horizon Ct Ste 200 Grand Junction CO 81506-8716

CASELLA, PETER F(IORE), patent and licensing executive; b. June 5, 1922; s. Fiore Peter and Lucy (Grimaldi) C.; m. Marjorie Eloise Enos, March 9, 1946 (dec. Aug. 1989); children: William Peter, Susan Elaine, Richard Mark. BChE, Poly. U., Bklyn., 1943; student in chemistry, St. John's U., N.Y.C., 1940. Registered to practice by the U.S. Patent and Trademark Office, Can. Patent and Trademark Offices. Head patent sect. Hooker Electrochem. Co., Niagara Falls, N.Y., 1943-54; mgr. patent dept. Occidental Chem. Corp. (formerly Hooker Chem. Corp.), 1954-64, dir. patents and licensing, 1964-81, asst. sec., 1966-81, ret., 1981. Pres. TFA Products, Inc., Houston, Intra Gene Internat., Inc., Lewiston, N.Y., 1981-92; chmn. bd. In Vitro Internat., Inc., Linthicum, Md., 1983-86; cons. patents and licensing, Lewiston, N.Y., 1981—; Dept. Commerce del. on patents and licensing exchange, USSR, 1973, 90, Poland and German Dem. Rep., 1976. Editor: Drafting the Patent Application, 1957. Mem. Lewiston Bd. Edn., 1968-70. With AUS, 1944-46, Mediterranean Theater of Operation. Recipient Centennial citation Poly. U., Bklyn., 1955, Golden Jubilee Soc., 1993. Mem. ACS, AIChE, Assn. Corp. Patent Counsel (emeritus, exec. com. 1974-77, charter mem.), N.Y. Intellectual Property Law Assn. (Niagara Frontier chpt. pres. 1973-74, founder award 1974), Licensing Execs. Soc. (v.p. 1976-77, Trustees award 1977), Chartered Inst. Patent Agts. Gt. Britain (emeritus), Patent and Trademark Inst. Can., Internat. Patent and Trademark Assn. (emeritus), U.S. Trademark Assn., Nat. Assn. Mfrs. (patent com.), Mfg. Chemists Assn., Pacific Indsl. Property Assn., U.S. Patent Office Soc. (assoc.), U.S. Trademark Office Soc. (assoc.), Chemists Club (emeritus N.Y.C. chpt.), Niagara Club (Niagara Falls pres. 1973-74).

CASELLAS, SALVADOR E. judge; b. 1935; BS in Fgn. Svc. cum laude, Georgetown U., 1957; LLB magna cum laude, U. P.R., 1960; LLM, Harvard U., 1961. Ptnr. Fiddler, Gonzalez & Rodriguez, 1962-72, 77-94; judge U.S. Dist. Ct. P.R., San Juan, 1994—. Mem. P.R. Acad. Jurisprudence, P.R. Commn. on Bicentennial of U.S. Constn., 1987-89; aide to Sec. of U.S. Army, 1985-89, emeritus, 1990—. Dir. Alliance for Drug Free P.R., 1993-94. 1st lt. U.S. Army, 1961-62, Res., JAGC, 1963-67. Recipient Comdrs. medal Second U.S. Army, 1990, P.R. Nat. Guard medal, 1990. Mem. ABA, Am. Bar Found., P.R. Bar Assn., P.R. Bar Assn. Found., Caparra Country Club, Banker's Club. Office: US Dist Ct PR US Courthouse 150 Ave Carlos Chardon # 111 San Juan PR 00918-1703

CASEY, JOHN FREDERICK, lawyer; b. Martinsville, Ohio, May 19, 1939; s. Raymond J. and Esther E. (Read) C.; m. Karen S. Bollenbacher, Sept. 2, 1978. BS, Ohio State U., 1961, JD, 1965. Bar: Ohio, 1965, U.S. Dist. Ct. (so. dist.) Ohio 1967, D.C. 1981, U.S. Tax Ct. 1967. Ptnr. Means, Bichimer & Burkholder, Columbus, Ohio, 1965-70, Chamblin, Snyder & Casey, Columbus, 1971-75; pvt. practice, 1976-83, 91-93; ptnr., shareholder Wiles, Doucher, Van Buren, Boyle & Casey, 1984-85; ptnr. Thompson, Hine & Flory, 1986-88, Casey & Christensen, Columbus, 1989, Casey, McFadden & Winner, Columbus, 1990, Harris, McClellan, Binau & Cox, Columbus, 1994; prin. John F. Casey, A Legal Profl. Assn., 1994—. Adv. coun. mem. U.S. Small Bus. Adminstrn., Columbus, 1985-93. Mem. gov.'s Ohio Farmland Preservation Task Force, 1996-97. Mem. Ohio State Bar Assn. (bd. govs. 1990-99, emeritus 2000, estate planning, trust, and probate law sect.), Fin. Planning Assn. Ctrl. Ohio (founding trustee 2000), Columbus Bar Found., Ohio State U. Coll. Law (nat. coun.), Greater Columbus C. of C. Avocations: gardening, golf. General corporate, Estate planning, General practice. Home: 207 E Whittier St Columbus OH 43206-2638 Office: Lucas Predergast Albright Gibson & Newman 600 S High St Columbus OH 43215-5656

CASEY, KATHLEEN HEIRICH, lawyer, educator; b. Chgo., Mar. 10, 1937; d. Bruneau Ernest and Kathleen Brennan (Grogan) Heirich; m. John M. Casey, Nov. 18, 1959 (div. 1974); children: Sean M., Kyle L., Siobhan C. AB, Radcliffe Coll., 1959; JD, St. John's U., 1974. Bar: N.Y. 1975, U.S. Dist. Ct. (so. and ea. dists.) N.Y. 1975, U.S. Ct. Appeals (2d cir.) 1975, U.S. Supreme Ct. 1976, Calif. 1989, U.S. Dist. Ct. (no. dist.) Calif. 1989, U.S. Ct. Appeals (9th cir.) 1989. Asst. corp. counsel N.Y.C. Law Dept., 1974-76; appellate counsel Div. Criminal Justice, N.Y.C., 1976-77; asst. atty. gen. N.Y. Law Dept., 1977-78; prin. law clk. N.Y. State Supreme Ct., N.Y.C., 1978-81; assoc. Colton, Weissberg, Hartnick, Yamin & Sheresky, N.Y.C., 1981-83, Milbank, Tweed, Hadley & McCloy, N.Y.C., 1983-86; pvt. practice, N.Y.C., 1986—, Orinda, Calif., 1989—; adj. faculty N.Y. Law Sch., N.Y.C., 1983-85; mem. family dispute resolution and comml. panels Am. Arbitration Assn., N.Y.C., 1984—, Nat. Assn. Securities Dealers, 1989—. Contbr. articles to profl. jours. Nassau County committeewoman, 1972-79, 81-87; mem. law com. Nassau County Democratic Party, 1977-81, Navy League of U.S., N.Y. Council, 1980. Fellow Am. Acad. Matrimonial Law; mem. ABA, Calif. Bar Assn., Queen's Bench, N.Y. Women's Bar Assn. (officer 1985—), N.Y. State Bar Assn., Assn. of Bar of City of N.Y., N.Y.C. Lawyers Assn. Family and matrimonial. Office: 120 Village Sq Ste 64 Orinda CA 94563-2502

CASEY, PATRICK ANTHONY, lawyer; b. Apr. 20, 1944; s. Ivanhoe and Eutimia (Casados) C.; m. Gail Marie Johns, Aug. 1, 1970; children: Christopher Gaelen, Matthew Colin. BA, N.Mex. State U., 1970; JD, U. Ariz., 1973. Bar: N.Mex. 1973, Ariz. 1973, U.S. Dist. Ct. N.Mex. 1973, U.S. Ct. Appeals (10th cir.) 1979, U.S. Supreme Ct. 1980, U.S. Dist. Ct. Ariz. 1999. Assoc. Bachicha & Casey, Santa Fe, 1973-76; pvt. practice, 1976—. Bd. dirs. Santa Fe Sch. Arts and Crafts, 1974, Santa Fe Animal Shelter, 1975-81, Cath. Charities of Santa Fe, 1979-82, Old Santa Fe Assn., 1979-88, Santa Fe Fiesta Coun., 1982—; bd. dirs. United Way, 1986-89, N.Mex. State U. Found., 1985-93. With USN, 1961-67. Mem.: ATLA (state del. 1988—89, bd. govs. 1990—91, bd. govs. 1993—95), ABA, Western Trial Lawyers Assn. (bd. dirs. 1988—91, parliamentarian 1990—91, gov. 1987—90, treas. 1991—95, treas. 2000—01, sec. 1991—92, pres. 1996—97), N.Mex. Trial Lawyers Assn. (dir. 1977—79, dir. 1985—, treas. 1979—83, treas. 2000—01, pres. 1983—84), Bar Assn. 1st Jud. Dist. (pres. 1980), Hisbanic Bar Assn., Am. Legion, Vietnam Vets. of Am., VFW, Elks. General civil litigation, Personal injury, Product liability. Office: 1421 Luisa St Ste P Santa Fe NM 87505-4073

CASEY, PAULA JEAN, former prosecutor; b. Charleston, Ark., Feb. 16, 1951; d. Arthur Clinton and Mildred Aleene (Underwood) C.; m. Gilbert Louis Glover II, Mar. 13, 1981. BA, Ea. Cen. (Okla.) U., 1973; JD, U. Ark., 1977. Staff atty. Ctrl. Ark. Legal Services, Hot Springs, Ark., 1977-79; dep. pub. defender 6th Jud. Dist. Pub. Defender, Little Rock, 1979; clinic supr. U. Ark. at Little Rock Law Sch., 1979-81, asst. prof., 1981-84, assoc. prof., 1984-92, prof., 1992-93, assoc. dean, 1986-90; legis. dir., chief counsel U.S. Senator Dale Bumpers, 1990-92; lobbyist Ark. Bar Assn., 1993; U.S. atty. Ea. Dist. Ark., 1993—2001; prof. law U. Ark. at Little Rock Law Sch., 2001—. Cons. for juvenile affairs 6th Jud. Dist. Judges, Ark., 1987. Author, editor: Poverty Law Practice Manual, 1985. Sec. Pulaski County Dem. Com., Little Rock, 1984-89; mem. Ark. Dem. Com., 1984-89; mem. Juvenile Adv. Group, Little Rock, 1985-89; mem. Gov.'s Task Force on Juvenile Cts., Ark., 1987; chmn. Ark. Dem. Jud. Com., 1987; bd. dirs. Ctrl. Ark. Legal Svcs., Little Rock, 1986-89. Named One of Top 100 Women in Ark., Ark. Bus. Pubs., 1996, 98, 99; recipient Gale Pettus Pontz award U. Ark.-Fayetteville Law Sch. Women Students Assn., 1994, award of merit Organized Crime Drug Enforcement Task Force, 1997. Fellow Ark. Bar Found. (bd. dirs.); mem. Ark. Bar Assn. (del. 1986-90), Am. Inns Ct., Overton Am. Inns of Ct., 8th Cir. Ct. Appeals (fed. adv. comm. 2001-05). Democrat. Office: U Ark at Little Rock Sch Law 1201 McMath Blvd Little Rock AR 72202

CASEY, ROBERT FITZGERALD, lawyer, educator; b. Chgo., Sept. 28, 1943; s. John Francis and Gertrude Bernice (Fitzgerald) C. BA, Notre Dame U., 1964, MBA, 1987; MS in Edn., No. Ill. U., 1968; JD, DePaul U., 1974, LLM, 1980. Bar: Ill. 1975, Ind. 1976, Fla. 1977, U.S. Tax Ct. 1981, U.S. Ct. Claims 1982, U.S. Ct. Mil. Appeals 1982, U.S. Supreme Ct. 1982. Educator Carl Sandburg H.S., Orland Park, Ill., 1969-. Blue/gold liaison officer U.S. Naval Acad. Lt. comdr. JAGC USNR. Mem. Ill. Bar Assn., Ind. Bar Assn., Notre Dame Club (Chgo.), Phi Alpha Delta. Roman Catholic. General practice, Military, Real property. Home: 403 Country Club Dr Mchenry IL 60050-5677 Office: PO Box 11354 1210 White Oak Dr South Bend IN 46634-0354 Fax: 219-287-9872. E-mail: rcasey@dist230.org

CASH, RODERICK WILLIAM, JR. lawyer; b. N.Y.C., June 13, 1949; s. Roderick William and Fannie (Pisciotta) C.; m. Paulis Neila Waber, June 24, 1978; 1 child, Mason Roderick. B.A., Wesleyan U., 1971; J.D., Am. U., Washington, 1974. Bar: D.C. 1975, U.S. Dist. Ct. D.C. 1976, U.S. Ct. Appeals (Fed. cir.) 1976, U.S. Ct. Customs and Patent Appeals 1977, U.S. Customs Ct. 1978, U.S. Supreme Ct. 1978, U.S. Ct. Claims 1980, U.S. Tax Ct. 1980, N.Y. 1981. Atty., U.S. Customs Service, Dept. Treasury, Washington, 1975-77; ptnr. Cash & Cash, Washington, 1977-85; assoc. O'Connell & Kittrell, Washington, 1985-86; pres. Roderick Cash, Inc., 1986—; panelist Sta. WYCB Med. Malpractice Today, 1982, Sec., Dupont Circle Neighborhood Ecology Corp., Washington, 1976. Mem. Assn. Trial Lawyers Am., D.C. Bar Assn., Assn. Trial Attys. D.C., Assn. of Plaintiffs Trial Attys. (bd. govs. 1983—). Club: Univ. (Washington). Federal civil litigation, State civil litigation, Family and matrimonial. Home: 3915 Huntington St NW Washington DC 20015-1913 Office: O'Connell & Kittrell 1710 Rhode Island Ave NW Washington DC 20036-3007

CASILLAS, MARK, lawyer; b. Santa Monica, Calif., July 8, 1953; s. Rudolph and Elvia C.; m. Natalia Settembrini, June 2, 1984. BA in History, Loyola U., L.A., 1976; JD, Harvard U., 1979. Bar: N.Y. 1982, Calif. 1983. Clk. to chief judge U.S. Ct. Appeals (10th cir.), Santa Fe, 1979-80; assoc. Breed, Abbott & Morgan, N.Y.C., 1980-82; counsel Bank of Am. Nat. Trust and Savs. Assn., San Francisco, 1982-84; assoc. Lillick & Charles, 1984-87, ptnr., 1988-95, Russin & Vecchi LLP, San Francisco, 1995-96; of counsel LeBoeuf, Lamb, Greene & MacRae, LLP, 1997-2000; atty. Wilson Sonsini Goodrich & Rosati, Palo Alto, Calif., 2000—. Counsel Internat. Bankers Assn. in Calif., L.A., 1984-89, 94-97. Co-author: California Limited Liability Company: Forms and Practice Manual, 1994; mng. editor Harvard Civil Rights-Civil Liberties Law Rev., 1978-79. Mem. ABA (apptd. mem. airfin. subcom. 1991—), N.Y. Bar Assn., Calif. Bar Assn. (vice-chmn. fin. instn. com. 1987-88), Internat. Bar Assn., The Japan Soc., Bankers Club (bd. dirs. 1996—). Avocations: skiing, travel. Office: Wilson Sonsini Goodrich & Rosati 650 Page Mill Rd Palo Alto CA 94304 E-mail: mcasillas@wsgr.com

CASPER, ERIC MICHAEL, lawyer; b. Long Branch, N.J., Feb. 27, 1959; s. Walter Jr. and Lois Ann (Countryman) C. BS in Polit. Sci. with high honors, U. Iowa, 1980, MBA, JD with high honors, 1984. Bar: Ariz. 1985, U.S. Dist. Ct. Ariz. 1985, U.S. Tax Ct. 1986, U.S. Ct. Appeals (9th cir.) 1997. Assoc. Snell & Wilmer, Phoenix, 1984-91; trial atty. civil tax litigation Dept. Justice, Washington, 1991-95; pvt. practice Phoenix, 1995—; ptnr. Walker Silver, PLC. Contbr. articles to profl. publs. Tchr. Jr. Achievement, various Phoenix area jr. high and high schs., 1986-91; tutor Dept. Labor TEAM Project; vol. Phoenix chpt. Am. Cancer Soc., 1987-91. Mem. Ariz. Bar Assn. (tax and bankruptcy sects.), Mensa, Kiwanis (dir. Camelback), Am. Bankruptcy Inst. Methodist. Avocations: basketball, volleyball, science fiction. Home: 5778 W Corrine Dr Glendale AZ 85304-1890 Office: Walker Silver PLC 3200 N Central Ave Ste 1100 Phoenix AZ 85012-2431

CASPERSEN, R(ALPH) FREDERICK, lawyer; b. Mpls., Dec. 8, 1942; s. Ralph Bernhard and Mary Jane (Schmitt) C.; m. Patricia Niemi. A.B., Harvard U., 1964; J.D., Stanford U., 1971. Bar: Calif. 1972, U.S. Dist. Ct. (no. dist.) Calif. 1972, U.S. Tax Ct. 1974. Assoc. Farella, Braun & Martel, San Francisco, 1971-77, ptnr., 1977— . Served to lt. USNR, 1964-68; Vietnam. Mem. ABA, Calif. State Bar, Bar Assn. San Francisco. Republican. Club: Commercial. Lodge: Elks. Corporate taxation, Estate taxation, Personal income taxation. Office: Farella Braun & Martel 235 Montgomery St Ste 3000 San Francisco CA 94104-2902

CASS, ROBERT MICHAEL, lawyer, consultant; b. Carlisle, Pa., July 5, 1945; s. Robert Lau and Norma Jean (McCaleb) C.; m. Patricia Ann Garber, Aug. 12, 1967 (dec. Jan. 1999); children: Charles McCaleb, David Lau. BA, Pa. State U., 1967; JD, Temple U., 1971. Bar: N.Y. 1974; cert. arbitrator AIDA Reins. and Ins. Arbitration Soc. Benefit examiner Social Security Adminstrn., Phila., 1967-68; mktg. rep. Employers Comml. Union Ins. Co., 1968-70; asst. sec. Nat. Reins. Corp., N.Y.C., 1970-77; asst. v.p. Skandia Am. Reins. Corp., 1977-80; mgr. Allstate Reins. divsn., South Barrington, Ill., 1980-86, R.K. Carvill, Inc., Chgo., 1986-87; pres. R. M. Cass Assocs., 1987—. V.p. Assurance Alliance, Inc., Crystal Lake, Ill., 1989; lectr. Ins. Sch. Chgo., Coll. of Ins. N.Y., U. Wis., Am. Inst. for Chartered Property Casualty Underwriters. Author: (with others) Reinsurance Contract Wording, Reinsurance Practices, 2d edit.; editor, reviewer: (with others) The Legal Environment of Insurance, 4th edit. Mem. ABA (tort and ins. practice sect., past chair com. on excess, surplus lines and reins. law, standing com. on professionalism, standing com. on emerging issues, com. on long range planning, past chmn. internat. com., liaison to ABA Ctrl. & East European Law Initiative, chair 3rd Chinese-Am. law seminar, Guangzhou, China, 1999, chair 4th Chinese-Am. law seminar Beijing and Shanghai 2001, dispute resolution sect., past chair com. large complex case arbitration), Soc. CPCUs (past chair risk mgmt. sect. com., mem. excess, surplus and splty. lines sect. com., reinsurance sect. com., past officer Chgo. N.W. suburban chpt.), Am. Arbitration Assn. (panel neutrals), Assn. Ind. Reins. Cons. (pres.), Internat. Assn. Ins. Receivers (publs. com., past chair membership com.), Fellows of Am. Bar Found., N.Y. State Bar Assn., Assn. Internat. de Droit des Assurances, Ill. Captive and Alternative Risk Funding Ins. Assn. (pres. bd. dirs.), Coalition Alternative Risk Funding Mechanisms (bd. dirs.). Alternative dispute resolution, Insurance, Private international. Home: 330 N Jefferson Ct #1705 Chicago IL 60661-1212 Office: PO Box 543460 Chicago IL 60654-3460 E-mail: mikecassre@aol.com

CASS, RONALD ANDREW, dean; b. Washington, Aug. 12, 1949; s. Millard and Ruth Claire (Marx) C.; m. Valerie Christina Swanson, Aug. 24, 1969; children: Laura Rebecca, Alexander Stephan. BA with high distinction, U. Va., 1970; JD with honors, U. Chgo., 1973. Bar: Md. 1973, D.C. 1974, U.S. Dist. Ct. D.C. 1974, U.S. Ct. Appeals (D.C. cir.) 1974, U.S. Supreme Ct. 1977, Va. 1979. Law clk. to chief judge U.S. Ct. Appeals (3d cir.), Wilmington, Del., 1973-74; assoc. Arent, Fox, Kintner, Plotkin & Kahn, Washington, 1974-76; asst. prof. law U. Va. Sch. Law, Charlottesville, 1976-81; assoc. prof. law Boston U., 1981-83, prof., 1983-95; dean Boston U. Law Sch., 1990—; Melville Madison Bigelow prof. Boston U., 1995—; legal advisor Office Plans and Policy, FCC, Washington, 1987-88; mem. U.S. Internat. Trade Commn., 1988-90, vice chmn., 1989-90. Cons. comm. program Aspen (Colo.) Inst., 1977-78, Adminstrv. Conf. U.S. Washington, 1980-87, Helsell, Fetterman, Martin, Todd & Hokanson, Seattle, 1984-85, Assn. Trial Lawyers Am., Phila., 1985-87, UN Conf. Trade and Devel., Geneva, 1991, U.S. Dept. Justice, 1998, Microsoft Corp., 1998-; spl. cons. Nat. Econ. Rsch. Assn., Cambridge, Mass., 1990-94; arbitrator Biogen v. Schering-Plough, 1999-2000, Telesia Sistemas v. Lucent Tech., 2000-2001, UPS v. Canada, 2001-; adj. scholar Am. Enterprise Inst., Washington, 1993-; sr. fellow Internat. Ctr. Econ. Rsch., Turin, 1996-97, 99-; sesquicentennial assoc. Ctr. Advanced Studies U. Va. Law Sch., 1980-81; mem. nat. adv. bd. Case Western Res. U. Sch. Law, 1996-97; disting. lectr. U. Francisco Marroquin, Guatemala City, 1996; lectr. IMADEC Internat. Bus. Sch., Vienna, 2000. Author: Revolution in the Wasteland: Value and Diversity in Television, 1981, (with Colin S. Diver) Administrative Law: Cases and Materials, 1987, (with Colin S. Diver and Jack M. Beermann) Administrative Law: Cases and Materials, 2nd edit., 1994, 3rd edit., 1998, (with John R. Haring) International Trade in Telecommunications, 1998, The Rule of Law in America, 2001; contbr. articles and essays to profl. jours., also chpts. to books. Bd. dirs. Northwestern Va. Health Systems Agy., Culpeper, 1980, New Eng. Coun., 1995-; bd. govs. Sightsavers Internat., Washington, 1989-91; bd. dirs. Telecomm. Policy Rsch. Conf., Washington, 1989-91, sec.-treas. 1989-90, vice chmn., 1991-92; bd. dirs. New Eng. Legal Found., 1994-, New England Coun., 1995-; bd. overseers Boston Bar Found., 1992-94, Supreme Jud. Ct. Hist. Soc., 1997-2000; sr. Europe Discussion Group, Ctr. for Strategic and Internat. Studies, 1989-96; bd. advisors George Mason U. Law Sch. Law & Econs. Ctr., 1996-99, Inst. Dem. Comm., Boston, 1991-92, Fundación de la Commn. Social, MAdrid, 1995-, IMADEC Internat. Bus. Sch., Vienna, 1999-2001, Legal Issues in Econ. Integration,

Amsterdam, 2000-. Sr. fellow Internat. Ctr. Econ. Rsch., Turin, 1996-97, 99—. Fellow Am. Bar Found.; mem. ABA (adminstrv. law and regulatory practice sect., coun. 1993-95, chair 1998-99, legal edn. and admission bar sect., review commn. 1994-95, ho. of dels. 2000—), Am. Law Inst., Am. Law Deans Assn. (bd. dirs. 1995—, pres. 1995-97), Mont Pelerin Soc., Boston Bar Assn. (coun. 1992-95), Adminstrv. Conf. U.S. (pub. mem. 1990-95, govt. mem. 1988-90), Transatlantic Policy Network (U.S. Working Group), Spring Valley C. C., Order of Coif, Phi Beta Kappa, Bay Club. Republican. Jewish. Home: 36 Forest St Wellesley Hills MA 02481-6818 Office: Boston U Sch Law 765 Commonwealth Ave Boston MA 02215-1401

CASSERLY, JAMES LUND, lawyer; b. Norfolk, Va., Dec. 26, 1951; s. James Robert and Patricia (Lund) C.; m. Kathleen Ann Flynn, Apr. 25, 1981; 1 child Laura Flynn. AB magna cum laude, Tufts Coll., 1973; JD, Columbia U., 1976. Bar: D.C. 1976, U.S. Dist. Ct. D.C. 1980, U.S. Ct. Appeals (D.C. cir.) 1981. Law clk. to trial judges U.S. Ct. Fed. Claims, Washington, 1976-77; law clk. to judge Marion Bennett U.S. Ct. Appeals Fed. Cir., 1977-78; assoc. Wilkinson, Cragun & Barker, 1978-82, Squire Sanders & Dempsey, Washington, 1982-85, ptnr., 1985-94; sr. legal advisor to Commr. Susan Ness FCC, 1994-99; ptnr. Mintz Levin Cohn Ferris Glovsky & Popeo PC, 1999—. Communications, Legislative. Home: 2839 Allendale Pl NW Washington DC 20008 Office: Mintz Levin Cohn Ferris Glovsky & Popeo PC 701 Pennsylvania Ave NW Washington DC 20004-2608 E-mail: jlcasserly@mintz.com

CASSIDAY, BENJAMIN BUCKLES, III, lawyer; b. Honolulu, Sept. 6, 1950; s. Benjamin B. Jr. and Barbara (Dennison) C.; m. Maile Burgundy, May 8, 1996. BS, Stanford U., 1973; JD, Boston Coll., 1977. Bar: Colo. 1977, Hawaii 1980, U.S. Ct. Appeals (9th cir.) 1982. State pub. defender Pub. Defender's Office, Littleton, Colo., 1977-80; pvt. practice Honolulu, 1981-82, 88—; 1st dep. Fed. Pub. Defender's Office, 1982-87. Lawyer rep. 9th Cir., 1993-95. Mem. Am. Bd. Criminal Lawyers, Hawaii Assns. Criminal Def. Lawyers (bd. dirs.). Avocations: poker, pool. Federal civil litigation, Criminal, Private international. Home: 5699 Kalanianaole Hwy Honolulu HI 96821-2303 Office: Law Office of Ben Cassiday 841 Bishop St Ste 2201 Honolulu HI 96813-3921 E-mail: bencassiday@hotmail.com

CASSIDY, ROBERT CHARLES, JR. lawyer; b. Beaumont, Tex., May 16, 1946; s. Robert Charles and Peggy (Timken) C.; m. Leslie Fleming Iben, Sept. 2, 1949; children: Robert Charles III, Thomas Reinhard, Leslie Anne Valladingham. BA, Johns Hopkins U., 1968; JD, U. Pa., 1973; LLM, Georgetown U., 1977. Bar: Pa. 1973, U.S. Dist. Ct. D.C. 1975, U.S. Ct. Appeals (D.C. cir.) 1975, U.S. Ct. Internat. Trade 1982, U.S. Ct. Appeals (fed. cir.) 1982. Asst. counsel Office of Legis. Counsel U.S. Senate, 1973-75, internat. trade counsel Com. on Fin., 1975-79; gen. counsel Office of U.S. Trade Rep., Exec. Office of Pres., Washington, 1979-81; ptnr. Kaye, Scholer, Fierman, Hays & Handler, 1982-83, Wilmer, Cutler & Pickering, Washington, 1983—, internat. practice group leader, 1995-2000, trade group leader, 1985—. Bd. dirs. Cordell Hull Inst., 1999—. With U.S. Army, 1968—70. Mem.: ABA (chmn. internat. trade law com. 1986—89), D.C. Bar Assn., Am. Soc. Internat. Law. Administrative and regulatory, Private international, Legislative. Office: Wilmer Cutler & Pickering 2445 M St NW Washington DC 20037-1487 E-mail: rcassidy@wilmer.com

CASSON, RICHARD FREDERICK, lawyer, travel bureau executive; b. Boston, Apr. 11, 1939; s. Louis H. and Beatrix S. C. AB, Colby Coll., 1960; JD, U. Chgo., 1963. Bar: Ill. 1963, Mass. 1964. Ptnr. Casson & Casson, Boston, 1967-68; assoc. counsel, corp. sec. Bankers Leasing Corp., 1968-75; asst. gen. counsel, corp. sec. Commonwealth Planning Corp., 1975-76; assoc. gen. counsel, asst. sec. Prudential Capital Corp., 1976-92; pres. Autumn Crest Corp., 1991-98; v.p. Casseden Corp. Asst. innkeeper Jackson House Inn, Woodstock, Vt. Capt. JAGC U.S. Army, 1964-67. Decorated Bronze Star. Jewish. Home and Office: PO Box 233 Randolph Center VT 05061-0233 E-mail: rfc0439@together.net

CASTAGNA, WILLIAM JOHN, federal judge; Student, U. Pa., 1941-43; LLB, JD, U. Fla., 1949. Bar: Fla. 1949. Ptnr. MacKenzie, Castagna, Bennison & Gardner, 1970-79; judge U.S. Dist. Judge (mid. dist.) Fla., 1979—, now sr. judge. Democrat.

CASTAGNOLA, GEORGE JOSEPH, JR. lawyer, mediator, secondary education educator; b. Scotia, Calif., July 6, 1950; s. George Joseph and Olga Esther Castagnola; m. Sandra Annette Castagnola, June 7, 1975; children: George Joseph III, Laura, Joseph. Grad., U. San Francisco, 1974; JD, N.W. Calif. U., Sacramento, 1990, D Juridical Sci., 1992. BAr: Calif. 1990. Tchr. El Molino H.S., Forestville, Calif., 1977—; charter boat capt. Castagnola Fishing, Petaluma, 1971—; prof. law N.W. Calif. U., 1990—; atty., mediator Law and Mediation Office of George Castagnola, Petaluma, Calif., 1990—. Cpl. USMCR, 1968-74. Mem. Calif. Bar Assn., Sonoma County Bar Assn., Calif. Tchrs. Assn., Golden Gate Sport Fishing Assn. Roman Catholic. Avocations: weightlifting, fishing. Home and Office: 802 Wine Ct Petaluma CA 94954-7420

CASTANO, GREGORY JOSEPH, lawyer; b. Kearny, N.J., Feb. 17, 1929; s. Nicholas and Marianna (Prestinaci) C.; m. June Dwyer, Oct. 15, 1966; children: Gregory, Christopher, John, Timothy. BS, Seton Hall U., 1950; JD, Fordham U., 1953; LLM, NYU, 1956. Bar: N.J. 1956, U.S. Ct. Appeals (3d cir.) 1957, U.S. Supreme Ct. 1959, U.S. Tax Ct. 1974, N.Y. 1985. Sports writer Newark Star-Ledger, 1946-53; pvt. practice Harrison, N.J., 1959-78; atty. Bd. Adjustment, 1978; judge Superior Ct. N.J., Jersey City, 1978-85; ptnr. Tompkins, McGuire & Wachenfeld, Newark, 1985-88, Waters, McPherson & McNeill, Secaucus, N.J., 1988—. Asst. atty. Town of Harrison, 1959-64; asst. prosecutor County of Hudson, N.J., 1963-71; atty. Town of West New York, N.J., 1977-78, Town of Kearny, N.J., 1999—, Harrison Redevel. Agy., 1997—; adj. prof. Seton Hall U. Sch. Law, Newark, 1988—; master com. to computerize criminal cts. Essex County; mediator U.S. Dist. Ct., Superior Ct. Mem. editorial bd., The Cath. Adv., 1976-78. Tax assessor Town of Harrison, 1964-78; del. N.J. Constl. Conv., 1964; mem. juvenile conf. com. Twp. West Caldwell, N.J., 1977-78; trustee Caldwell (N.J.) Coll., 1985-91, chmn. acad. affairs com. bd. trustees, 1987-91; chmn. County Govt. Transition Com., Hudson County, 1987-88; mem. Hudson County Community Coll. Blue Ribbon Task Force, 1992-93. With U.S. Army, 1953-55. Named Man of Yr., Kearny Jaycees, 1963, Alumnus of Yr., Dorf Feature Service, 1987. Fellow Am. Bar Found.; mem. ABA, N.J. Bar Assn., Hudson County Bar Assn. (Justice medallion 1985), Essex County Bar Assn., West Hudson Bar Assn. (pres. 1977-78), Assn. Fed. Bar N.J., Essex Fells Country Club. General civil litigation, Municipal (including bonds), Real property. Home: 19 Sunset Rd West Caldwell NJ 07006-6540 Office: Waters McPherson & McNeill 300 Lighting Way PO Box 1560 Secaucus NJ 07096-1560

CASTILLE, RONALD D. state supreme court justice; b. Miami, Mar. 16, 1944; s. Henry and Marie Nash Castille. BS in Econs., Auburn U., 1966; JD, U. Va., 1971. Asst. dist. atty., 1971-81; chief asst. dist. atty. Career Criminal Unit, 1982-84; dep. dist. atty. Pre-Trial Unit, 1984-85; dist. atty. Phila., 1986-91; with litigation dept. Reed Smith Shaw & McClay, 1991-93; justice Supreme Ct. Pa., 1993—. Exec. bd. dirs. Criminal Justice Coordinating Commn., 1986-91; bd. dirs. Urban Coalition, 1988-91; co-chmn. Pa. Anti-Crime Coalition for George Bush for Pres., 1988, 92; commr. Pres.'s Commn. on Model State Drug Laws, 1992. Lt. USMC, 1966-68. Decorated Bronze Star with Combat V, Purple Heart (2); recipient Disting. Pub. Svc. award Pa. County and State Detectives Assn., 1987, Layman award Pa. Chiefs of Police Assn., 1987, Spirit of Am. award Inst. for Study of Am. Wars, 1988, Pres.'s award for Outstanding Svc., Nat. Dist. Attys. Assn., 1991; named Man of Yr., Fraternal Order of Police Lodge #5, 1988, Outstanding Disabled Vet. of Yr., Nat. Disabled Am. Vets., 1988. Mem. Nat. Dist. Attys. Assn. (v.p. 1986-91), Pa. Dist. Attys. Assn. (legis. chmn. 1986-91). Office: 1818 Market St Ste 3730 Philadelphia PA 19103-3639

CASTLEBERRY, JAMES NEWTON, JR. retired law educator, dean; b. Chatom, Ala., Dec. 28, 1921; s. James Newton and Nellie (Robbins) C.; m. Mary Ann Blocker, Feb. 12, 1944 (dec.); children: Jean, Nancy, James III (dec.), Elizabeth, Cynthia, Robert, Mary Ann. JD magna cum laude, St. Mary's U., 1952; diploma in comparative law, Nat. U. Mex., 1960; diploma in tchg. of comparative law, Strasburg, 1963. Bar: Tex. 1952. Asst. atty. gen. State of Tex., 1953-55; prof. law St. Mary's U., San Antonio, 1955-92, dean, 1978-89, dean emeritus, 1989—, ret., 1992. Dir. St. Mary's U. Summer Program in Internat. and Comparative Law, Innsbruck, Austria, 1986-89; exec. dir. Tex. Ctr. for Legal Ethics and Professionalism, 1990-92; lectr. comparative law fgn. legal study tours Corp. for Profl. Confs., 1990—. Co-author: Water & Water Rights, 1970; contbr. articles to law jours. Bd. dirs. Preservation Tex.; trustee Tex. Supreme Ct. Hist. Soc. Mem. ABA, Am. Bar Found., San Antonio Bar Assn., Tex. Bar Found., San Antonio Bar Found., Tex. State Bar, Phi Delta Phi (internat. pres. 1977-79). Home: 7727 Woodridge Dr San Antonio TX 78209-2223

CASTRATARO, BARBARA ANN, lawyer; b. Bethpage, N.Y., Apr. 25, 1958; d. Vincent James and Theresa (Chiarini) C. BA in Music, L.I. U., 1984; JD, N.Y. Law Sch., 1989. Bar: N.Y. 1990, U.S. Dist. Ct. (so. dist.) N.Y. 1990. Music dir. CBS Network, N.Y.C., 1979-81, exec. ops., 1985-88; music dir. NBC Network/Score Prodns., N.Y.C. and L.A., 1983-84, Score Prodns./ABC Network, N.Y.C. and L.A., 1980-84; assoc. Donald Frank Esq., N.Y.C., 1989-93, Law Offices of Joel C. Bender, White Plains, N.Y., 1993-99, Bender, Jenson, Silverstein & Castrataro, LLP, White Plains, 1999-2000; pvt. practice Law Offices of Barbara A. Castrataro, Chappaqua, N.Y., 2000—. Lectr. on divorce and separation; founder Castrataro Artist Mgmt., 1997-99; adj. faculty mem. Berkeley Coll., White Plains, N.Y. Recipient 3 Emmy nominations N.Y. Acad. TV Arts and Sci., 1979, 82-83. Mem. N.Y. State Bar Assn., Womens Bar Assn. Avocations: sailing, gourmet cooking, gardening. Entertainment, Family and matrimonial. Office: PO Box 132 Chappaqua NY 10514 E-mail: cambac233@aol.com

CASTRO, LEONARD EDWARD, lawyer; b. L.A., Mar. 18, 1934; s. Emil Galvez and Lily (Meyerholtz) C.; 1 son, Stephen Paul. A.B., UCLA, 1959, J.D., 1962. Bar: Calif. 1963, U.S. Supreme Ct. 1970. Assoc. Musick, Peeler & Garrett, Los Angeles, 1962-68, ptnr., 1968— . Mem. ABA, Los Angeles County Bar Assn.Bd. editors, note and comment editor: UCLA Law Review, 1961-62. Contbd. chpts. to books. Panelist, spkr., various legal edn. programs. General corporate, Private international, Securities. Office: Musick Peeler & Garrett 1 Wilshire Blvd Ste 2000 Los Angeles CA 90017-3876

CASTRO, LUIS D. lawyer; b. San Jose, Costa Rica, Mar. 1, 1966; s. Rodolfo Castro and Leda Chauarria; m. Mora Maria Catalina. Atty., UCR, Costa Rica, 1990. Ptnr. Castro & Pal, San Jose, 1993—. Editor Inventiva, 1998-2001. Coord. Free Legal Assistance, Betamia, 1997—. Mem. ABA, INTA, Colegio de Adogados CR. General corporate, Environmental, Trademark and copyright. Home: PO Box 10488-1000 San Jose Costa Rica Office: Castro y Pal Asociadoes Itan 225E 50 N 50E San Jose Costa Rica Fax: (506) 234-8337. E-mail: ldcastro@castropal.com

CATHCART, DAVID ARTHUR, lawyer; b. Pasadena, Calif., June 1, 1940; s. Arthur James and Martelle (Leeper) C.; m. Janet Eileen Farley, June 19, 1973; children: Sarah Emily, Rebecca Eileen. BA with gt. distinction, Stanford U., 1961; MA, Harvard U., 1966, LLB cum laude, 1967. Bar: Calif. 1968, U.S. Dist. Ct. (cen. dist.) Calif. 1969, U.S. Dist. Ct. (so., no. dists.) 1975, U.S. Dist. Ct. (ea. dist.) 1979, U.S. Ct. Appeals (9th cir.) 1975, U.S. Supreme Ct. 1979. Assoc. Gibson, Dunn & Crutcher LLP, L.A., 1968-70, 72-75, ptnr., 1975—. Legis. asst. U.S. Senate, Washington, 1971-72; mem. NLRB Adv. Com., 1994-98. Editor-in-chief: Employment Discrimination Law Five-Year Cumulative Supplement, 1989, Employment-At-Will: A 1989 State-By-State Survey, 1990; contbr. chpts. to legal texts, articles to profl. jours. Bd. dirs. Western Ctr. on Law and Poverty, L.A., 1985-88, U.S.-S. Africa Leadership Devel. Program, 1992—, The Employers Group, 2000—. Woodrow Wilson fellow, 1961-62, Danforth fellow, 1961-64. Fellow Coll. of Labor and Employment Lawyers; mem. ABA (mem. coun. 1997—, mgmt. co-chair equal employment opportunity law com., 1994-96, sect. of labor and employment law, co-chair employment and labor rels. law com., 1985-88, litigation sect.), L.A. County Bar Assn. (chair labor & employment law sect. 1991-92), Am. Employment Law Coun. (chair 1993—), Internat. Bar Assn. (vice-chmn. labor com., bus. law sect. 1987-90, U.S. country rep. 1989-93), Chancery Club, City Club on Bunker Hill, Harvard Club N.Y.C., Phi Beta Kappa. General civil litigation, Labor, Pension, profit-sharing, and employee benefits. Office: Gibson Dunn & Crutcher LLP 333 S Grand Ave Los Angeles CA 90071-3197

CATHELL, DALE ROBERTS, state supreme court justice; b. Berlin, July 30, 1937; s. Dale Parsons Cathell and Charlotte Robert (Hocker) Terrell; m. Charlotte M. Kerbin; children: Kelly Ann, Dale Kerbin, William Howard. Student, U. Md., 1962-64; LLB, U. Balt., 1967; cert., Nat. Jud. Coll., 1983. Bar: Md. 1967. Atty. City of Ocean City, Md., 1970-76; assoc. judge Md. Dist. Ct., Worcester County, 1980-81; judge Md. Cir. Ct., 1981-89, Ct. Spl. Appeals, 1st Appellate Cir., 1989-97, Ct. Appeals, 1997—. Adj. prof. law U. Balt., 1997—; mem. family and domestic rels. law com. Md. Jud. Conf., 1995-97, past mem. exec. com.; instr. WOR-WIC C.C., 1973, Salisbury State U., 1978. Mem. Pub. Service Commn. Adv. Panel, Md., 1970, charity revision com. Mayor City Council, Ocean City, 1970; mem. Worcester County Shoreline Com., Md., 1971; mem. charter revision com. City of Ocean City, 1973, mem. utility consumer adv. panel, 1978; creator Alt. Com. Service Program, Md., 1980—; organizer Legal Intern Program Pub. Schs., Worcester County, 1981—. Served with USAF, 1955-59. Mem. Md. Bar Assn. (jud. appointment com. 1970), Worcester County Bar Assn. (pres. 1970), Balt. City Bar Assn. Democrat. Episcopalian. Office: Ct Appeals Md Robert C Murphy Cts Apl Bld 361 Rowe Blvd Annapolis MD 21401-1672 also: PO Box 4306 Salisbury MD 21803-4306

CATLETT, S. GRAHAM, lawyer; b. Little Rock, Ark., Aug. 12, 1952; s. S. G. and Betty H. (Hubach) C.; m. Meredith Polk, June 29, 1974. B.B.A., U. Ark., 1974, J.D., 1977. Bar: Ark. 1977, U.S. Dist. Ct. Ark. 1977, U.S. Ct. Appeals (8th cir.) 1977, U.S. Tax Ct. 1977. Ptnr. Catlett & Stubblefield, Little Rock, 1977—; dir. Anderson's Cajun Wharf, Inc., Little Rock, 1986—; managing ptnr. Catlett Tower Partnership, Little Rock, 1986—; chmn. Mix Joint Venture, Moscow, 1989—; pres. Catlett, Inc., Little Rock, 1989—; lectr. continuing Legal Edn., 1982— . Chmn. fund drive Ballet Ark., 1984; treas. U.S. Senator David Pryor Com., 1978—. Mem. ABA, AICPA, Ark. Bar Assn., Ark. Soc. C.P.A.s, Greater Little Rock C. of C., U. Ark. Alumni Assn. (bd. dirs. 1984). Democrat. Presbyterian. General corporate, Real property, Taxation, general. Home: 323 Center St Ste 1800 Little Rock AR 72201-2607 Office: Catlett Stubblefield Bonds & Fleming 1800 Tower Bldg Little Rock AR 72201

CATRON, STEPHEN BARNARD, lawyer; b. Bowling Green, Ky., Feb. 4, 1949; s. Eugene and Gladys (Bell) C.; m. Deborah Faye Grigsby, Nov. 28, 1981. BA, Western Ky. U., Bowling Green, 1971; JD, U. Miss., 1974. Bar: Ky. 1974, Miss. 1974, Tenn. 1988, U.S. Dist. Ct. (we. dist.) Ky, 1974, U.S. Dist. Ct. (no. dist.) Miss. 1974, U.S. Supreme Ct. 1982, U.S. Ct. Appeals (6th cir.) 1983. Atty. Ky. Dept. Human Resources, Bowling Green, Ky., 1974-75; atty., ptnr. Reynolds, Catron, Johnson & Hinton, 1975-95, Lewis, King, Krieg, Waldrop and Catron, P.C., Bowling Green, 1995-2001; ptnr. Wyatt, Tarrant & Combs, LLP, 2001—. Pres. Bowling Green-Warren County Bar, 1989-90; chair., bd. trustees Ky. IOLTA Fund, Frankfort, Ky., 1990-94; bd. trustees Ky. Bar Found., Frankfort, Ky., 1990-94; bd. dirs. Nat. Assn. IOLTA Programs, Chgo., 1991-92. Author: Kentucky Corporations Law, 1989. Bd. dirs. Bowling Green (Ky.) Human Rights Commn., 1976-78; vice chair Ky. Ednl. TV Auth., Lexington, Ky., 1988-92; bd. regents Western Ky. U., Bowling Green., 1991-92; chairperson Bowling Green-Warren County Indsl. Authority; trustee Western Ky. U. Found. Fellow Am. Bar Found.; mem. Ky. Bar Assn. (bd. govs. 1992-2000, v.p. 2000-01, pres.-elect 2001—), Bowling Green C. of C. Democrat. Episcopalian. Avocations: reading, jogging, golf, computers. Banking, Contracts commercial, General corporate. Home: 231 Greenview Way Bowling Green KY 42103 Office: Wyatt Tarrant & Combs LLP PO Box 1220 918 Main St Bowling Green KY 42102-1220 E-mail: scatron@wyattfirm.com

CAULEY, MICHAEL A. prosecutor; U.S. atty. mid. dist., Fla. Office: 400 N Tampa St Ste 3200 Tampa FL 33602 Office Fax: 813-274-6246*

CAULFIELD, JEROME JOSEPH, lawyer; b. Phila., Aug. 9, 1949; s. Charles Patrick and Pauline Gertrude (Riley) C.; m. Rosita Noyes Murray, Aug. 4, 1973; children: Andrew, Alexandra. BS in Fgn. Svc., Georgetown U., 1971; JD, Am. U., 1974; LLM, NYU, 1977. Bar: N.Y. 1976, U.S. Tax Ct. 1980, U.S. Dist. Ct. (so. dist.) N.Y. 1986. Assoc. Carter, Ledyard & Milburn, N.Y.C., 1978-83, ptnr., 1984-99, mng. ptnr., 1999—. Contbr. articles to profl. jours. Bd. dirs. Impact on Hunger Inc., 1984-86. Mem. ABA, N.Y. State Bar Assn., Assn. of Bar of City of N.Y. Roman Catholic. Corporate taxation, Taxation, general, Personal income taxation. Home: 35 Stanwich Rd Greenwich CT 06830-4842 Office: Carter Ledyard & Milburn 2 Wall St Fl 13 New York NY 10005-2072 E-mail: caulfield@clm.com

CAULKINS, CHARLES S. lawyer; b. Great Bend, Kans., Sept. 22, 1949; s. Daniel P. Caulkins and Martha Taylor; m. Kelley D. Harris, Nov. 27, 1973; children: Kipp, Sloane, Sydney. BA, Monmouth Coll., 1971; JD, Creighton U., 1976; LLM in Labor Law, NYU, 1977. Bar: Kans. 1977, S.C. 1978, U.S. Dist. Ct. S.C. 1978, U.S. Ct. Appeals (4th and 10th cirs.) 1979, Fla. 1985, U.S. Dist. Ct. (so. dist.) Fla. 1985, U.S. Ct. Appeals (11th cir.) 1985, U.S. Supreme Ct. 1985. Ptnr. Thompson, Mann & Hutson, Greenville, S.C., 1977-84; mng. ptnr. Fisher & Phillips, Ft. Lauderdale, Fla., 1984—. Author: Florida Bar Journal, 1991. Immigration, naturalization, and customs, Labor, Pension, profit-sharing, and employee benefits. Office: Fisher & Phillips 1 Financial Plz Ste 2300 Fort Lauderdale FL 33394-0001

CAUTHRON, ROBIN J. federal judge; b. Edmond, Okla., July 14, 1950; d. Austin W. and Mary Louise (Adamson) Johnson. BA, U. Okla., 1970, JD, 1977; MEd, Cen. State U., Edmond, Okla., 1974. Bar: Okla. 1977. Law clk to Hon. Ralph G. Thompson U.S. Dist. Ct. (we. dist.) Okla., 1977-81; staff atty. Legal Svcs. Ea. Okla., 1981-82; pvt. practice law, 1982-83; spl. judge 17th Jud. Dist. State Okla., 1983-86; magistrate U.S. Dist. Ct. (we. dist.) Okla., Oklahoma City, 1986-91, judge, 1991—. Editor Okla. Law Rev. Bd. dirs. Juvenile Diabetes Found. Internat., 1989-92; mem. nominating com. Frontier Coun. Boy Scouts Am., 1987, Edmond Ednl. Endowment; trustee, sec. First United Meth. Ch., 1988-90. Mem. ABA, Okla. Bar Assn., Okla. County Bar Assn. (bd. dirs. 1990— bench and bar com.), McCurtain County Bar Assn. (pres. 1986), Am. Judicature Soc., Nat. Assn. Women Judges, Fed. Bar Assn., Nat. Coun. Women Magistrates (bd. dirs. 1990-91), Okla. Jud. Conf. (v.p. 1985), Am. Inns of Ct. (pres. 1991-92), Order of Coif, Phi Delta Phi. Office: US Courthouse 200 NW 4th St Ste 3108 Oklahoma City OK 73102-3029

CAVALIERE, FRANK JOSEPH, lawyer, educator; b. N.Y.C., Dec. 29, 1949; s. Alfred and Margaret Joan Cavaliere. BA in Econs., Bklyn. Coll., 1970; BBA in Acctg., Lamar U., 1976; JD, U. Tex., 1979. Bar: Tex. 1979. Atty. Coke & Coke, Dallas, 1979-81, Weller, Wheelus & Green, Beaumont, Tex., 1981-84; pvt. practice law, 1985—; from asst. to full prof. bus. law Lamar U., 1985—. Mem. editl. adv. bd. CPA Tech. and Internet Advisor, 2000—; tech. advisor Am. Law Inst.-ABA, 1998—, also continuing legal edn. spkr. Author (column) Web-Wise Lawyer, The Practical Lawyer, 19965; contbr. articles to profl. jours. Advisor Pi Kappa Alpha Fraternity, Beaumont, 1987-90, Delta Sigma Pi Fraternity, Beaumont, 1994-97. Lt. USNR, 1970-75. Mem. ABA, Tex. Bar Assn., Coll. of the State Bar Tex., Jefferson County Bar Assn., Phi Beta Kappa. Computer, General corporate, Estate planning. Office: 148 S Dowlen Rd PMB 683 Beaumont TX 77707-1755 E-mail: cavfj@prodigy.net, cavalierfj@hal.lamar.edu

CAVANAGH, MICHAEL FRANCIS, state supreme court justice; b. Detroit, Oct. 21, 1940; s. Sylvester J. and Mary Irene (Timmins) C.; m. Patricia E. Ferriss, Apr. 30, 1966; children: Jane Elizabeth, Michael F., Megan Kathleen BA, U. Detroit, 1962, JD, 1966. Bar: Mich. 1966. Law clk. to judge Ct. Appeals, Detroit, 1966-67; atty. City of Lansing, Mich., 1967-69; ptnr. Farhat, Story, et al., Lansing, 1969-73; judge 54-A Dist. Ct., 1973-75, Mich. Ct. Appeals, Lansing, 1975-82; justice Supreme Ct., 1983—, chief justice, 1991-94; Supreme Ct. liaison Mich. Indian Tribal Cts./Mich. State Cts. Supervising justice Sentencing Guidelines Com., Lansing, 1983-94, Mich. Jud. Inst., Lansing, 1986-94; bd. dirs. Thomas M. Cooley Law Sch., 1979-88; chair Mich. Justice Project, 1994-95, Nat. Interbranch Conf., Mpls., 1994-95. Bd. dirs. Am. Heart Assn. Mich., 1982—, chmn. bd. Am. Heart Assn. Mich., Lathrup Village, 1984-85; bd. dirs. YMCA, Lansing, 1978. Mem. ABA, Fed. Bar Assn., Ingham County Bar Assn., Inst. Jud. Adminstrn. (hon.), Inc. Soc. of Irish/Am. Lawyers (pres. 1987-88). Democrat. Roman Catholic Avocations: jogging, racquetball, fishing. Office: Mich Supreme Ct PO Box 30052 525 W Ottawa St Lansing MI 48933-1067

CAVANAUGH, MICHAEL EVERETT, lawyer, arbitrator, mediator; b. Seattle, Dec. 23, 1946; s. Wilbur R. Cavanaugh and Gladys E. (Herring) Barber; m. Susan P. Heckman, Sept. 7, 1968. AB, U. Calif., Berkeley, 1973; JD, U. Wash., 1976. Bar: Wash. 1976, U.S. Dist. Ct. (we. dist.) Wash. 1977, U.S. Ct. Appeals (9th cir.) 1977, U.S. Dist. Ct. (ea. dist.) Wash. 1978. Staff atty. U.S. Ct. of Appeals (9th crct.) Calif., San Francisco, 1976-77; from assoc. to ptnr. Preston & Thorgrimson, Seattle, 1981-85; ptnr. Bogle & Gates, 1985-97, assoc., 1977-81, ptnr., 1985-97; propr. Michael E. Cavanaugh, J.D., Arbitration and Mediation, 1997—. Contbg. author: Employment Discrimination Law, 3d edit., 1995. Avocations: sailing, creative writing, music. Alternative dispute resolution, Labor. Office: 1420 5th Ave # 2200 Seattle WA 98101-1346 E-mail: mec@cavanaugh-adr.com

CAYEA, DONALD JOSEPH, lawyer; b. Bklyn., Mar. 3, 1948; s. Glendon Vernon and Marie Nicola (Gesualdo) C. BA, L.I. U., 1969; JD, Western New Eng. Coll., 1975. Bar: N.Y. 1976, U.S. Dist. Ct. (so. and ea. dists.) N.Y. 1978, D.C. 1979, U.S. Supreme Ct. 1979. Prin. Donald J. Cayea & Assoc., N.Y.C., 1976—; ptnr. Kroll & Tract, 1988-90, Levitan, Frieland & Cayea, N.Y.C., 1990-94, Klepner & Cayea, N.Y.C., 1994-98, Brand, Cayea & Brand, LLC, N.Y.C., 1998—; gen. counsel Entertainment USA, 1990—. Lectr. Paralegal Inst., NYU, 1984—, adult edn. program Nassau County Bar Assn., Mineola, N.Y., 1978-79; panelist trial advocacy program Cardozo Law Sch., Yeshiva U., N.Y.C., 1984—; spkr. Ft. Lauderdale (Fla.) Film Festival, 1989, 90, Coun. on Mgmt. Worker's Compensation Update, N.Y.C., 1995, 96; guest panelist Property Loss Rsch. Bur., Washington, 1989, Chgo., 1991. Prodr.: (video) Dahmer, the Secret Life, 1993, (off Broadway) West Side Stories, Theatre Airelle, N.Y.C., 1993, Conversations with My Daughter; exec. prodr. (film) The

Hunt for CM24, 1997; prodr. (theatre) The Remarkable Thing About Star Dust, Mother Lode, 1999, (off-Broadway) Panache, 2000. Pres. Seascape Condominium, Westhampton Beach, N.Y., 1986-92; sponsor Richmond Roller Hocker Assn., Staten Island, N.Y., 1984-89; mem. Pres.'s Coun., L.I. Univ. Served in U.S. Army, 1970-71. Mem. ABA (editor TIPS publ. editorial bd. 1990-93), Assn. Trial Lawyers Am., N.Y. State Bar Assn., Internat. Bar Assn., Assn. of Bar of City of N.Y., New York County Lawyers Assn., Phi Epsilon Pi. Federal civil litigation, Insurance, Libel. Office: 720 5th Ave Fl 14 New York NY 10019-4107

CAYTAS, IVO GEORGE, lawyer; b. Plovdiv, Bulgaria, Feb. 3, 1958; s. George I. and Hilda (Plankl) Kaitasow. MA in Diplomacy, U. St Gallen, Switzerland, 1982, PhD in Law, 1984, PhD in Fin., 1986; LLM, Yale U., 1986. Bar: D.C. 1997, U.S. Ct. Internat. Trade, U.S. Claims Ct., U.S. Tax Ct., U.S. Dist. Ct. (so. and ea. dists.) N.Y. 1992, (no. and ctrl. dists.) Calif. 1992, U.S. Ct. Appeals (1st-11th cirs., fed. and D.C. cir.), U.S. Supreme Ct. 1996. Asst. to chmn. IMAG Corp., Vienna, Austria, 1979-80; ptnr. Caytas & Cie, St. Gallen, 1984-89, CCCC, St. Gallen, 1989-91; mng. dir. Swissconsult Corp., N.Y.C., 1990-91; pres., gen. counsel Swiss Am. Group Inc., 1991-95; ptnr. Caytas & Assocs., 1996—. Bd. dirs. The London Ct. of Internat. Abritration. Author: Investment Banking, 1988, Global Political Risk, Modern Financial Instruments, 1992, Transnational Legal Practice, 1992; contbr. articles to profl. publs. Fellow Swiss Nat. Sci. Found., 1985, 88, Max Planck Inst., 1987; recipient Walther-Hug Found. award, 1984. Mem. ABA (sect. of internat. law and practice, internat. investment com., internat. taxation com.), Assn. of Bar of City of N.Y. (com. on govt. ethics), Calif. Bar Assn. (internat. law com., task force on internat. legal svcs.), Yale Club. Roman Catholic. Banking, Finance, Securities. Office: 146 W 57th St New York NY 10019-3301

CECI, LOUIS J. former state supreme court justice; b. N.Y.C., Sept. 10, 1927; s. Louis and Filomena C.; m. Shirley; children— Joseph, Geraldine, David; children by previous marriage: Kristin, Remy, Louis Ph.B., Marquette U., 1951, J.D., 1954. Bar: Wis. 1954, U.S. Dist. Ct. (ea. dist.) Wis. 1954, U.S. Dist. Ct. (we. dist.) Wis. 1987; cert. mediator-arbitrator. Sole practice, Milw., 1954-58, 63-68; asst. city atty. City of Milw., 1958-63; mem. Wis. Assembly, Madison, 1965-66; judge Milw. County Ct., 1968-73, Milw. Circuit Ct., 1973-82; justice Wis. Supreme Ct., Madison, 1982-93, retired, 1993; res. judge State of Wis., 1993—. Lectr. Wis. Jud. Confs., 1970-79 Lectr. Badger Boys State, Ripon, Wis., 1961, 1982-84; asst. dist. commr. Boy Scouts Am., 1962. Recipient Wis. Civic Recognition PLAV, Milw., 1970; recipient Community Improvement Pompeii Men's Club, Milw., 1971, Good Govt. Milw Jaycees, 1973, Community-Judiciary Pompeii Men's Club, 1982 Mem. ABA, Wis. Bar Assn., Dane County Bar Assn., Milw. County Bar Assn., Waukesha County Bar Assn., Am. Legion (comdr. 1962-63). E-mail: appeal301@aol.com

CEDARBAUM, MIRIAM GOLDMAN, federal judge; b. N.Y.C., Sept. 16, 1929; d. Louis Albert and Sarah (Shapiro) Goldman; m. Bernard Cedarbaum, Aug. 25, 1957; children: Daniel Goldman C., Jonathan Goldman C. BA, Barnard Coll., 1950; LLB, Columbia U., 1953. Bar: N.Y. 1954, U.S. Dist. Ct. (so. dist.) N.Y. 1956, U.S. Ct. Appeals (2d cir.) 1956, U.S. Ct. Claims 1958, U.S. Supreme Ct. 1958, U.S. Dist. Ct. (ea. dist.) N.Y. 1980, U.S. Ct. Appeals (5th and 11th cirs.) 1981. Law clk. to judge Edward Jordan Dimock U.S. Dist. Ct. (so. dist.) N.Y., 1953-54, asst. U.S. atty., 1954-57; atty. Dept. Justice, Washington, 1958-59; part-time cons. to law firms in litig. matters, 1959-62; 1st asst. counsel N.Y. State Moreland Act Commn., 1963-64; assoc. counsel Mus. Modern Art, N.Y.C., 1965-79; assoc. litig. dept. Davis, Polk & Wardwell, 1979-83, sr. atty., 1983-86; acting justice Village of Scarsdale, N.Y., 1978-82, justice, 1982-86; judge U.S. Dist. Ct. (so. dist.) N.Y., 1986-98, sr. judge, 1998—. Mem. com. defender svcs. Jud. Conf. U.S., 1993-99; bd. vis. Columbia Law Sch.; trustee Barnard Coll.; co-counsel Scarsdale Open Soc. Assn., 1968-86. Contbr. articles to profl. jours. Mem. adv. com. on labor rels. Scarsdale Bd. Edn., 1976-77; mem. Scarsdale Bd. Archtl. Rev., 1977-78. Recipient Medal of Distinction Barnard Coll., 1991; James Kent scholar. Mem. ABA (chmn. com. on pictorial graphic sculptural and choreographic works 1979-81, copyright com. fed. practice and procedure 1983-84), Am. Law Inst., N.Y. State Bar Assn. (chmn. com. on fed. legis. 1978-80, com. on dist., city, village, and town cts. 1983-84), Assn. of Bar of City of N.Y. (com. on copyright and lit. property 1982-84, com. on the Bicentennial 1988-92), Fed. Bar Coun., Copyright Soc. U.S.A. (trustee, exec. com. 1979-82), Supreme Ct. Hist. Soc. Jewish. Office: US Dist Ct US Courthouse 500 Pearl St Rm 1330 New York NY 10007-1312

CEKALA, CHESTER, lawyer; b. Attleboro, Mass., May 18, 1959; s. Chester and Eileen (Polefka) C.; m. Suzanne Collette Cloutier, June 21, 1981 (div. May 1989); 1 child, Allison Rene; m. Carol Lee Raleigh, Oct. 7, 1990; children: Samuel Chester, Andrew Robin. BS, Worcester Poly. Inst., 1982; JD, Suffolk U., 1987, MBA, 2001. Bar: Ohio 1987, Mass. 1996, U.S. Ct. Appeals (fed. cir.) 1989, U.S. Patent and Trademark Office 1988, U.S. Supreme Ct. 1996. Chem. engr. Moleculon Biotech, Cambridge, Mass., 1981-87; patent atty. Procter & Gamble, Cin., 1987-90, W.R. Grace & Co., Lexington, Mass., 1990-91, The Gillette Co., Boston, 1991-2000, sr group patent counsel, 2000—. Mem. ABA, Am. Intellectual Property Assn., Boston Patent Law Assn., Cin. Intellectual Property Assn. (sec. 1987-88). Avocations: sailing, bicycling, skiing. General corporate, Intellectual property, Patent. Office: The Gillette Co Prudential Tower Bldg Boston MA 02199 E-mail: chet_cekala@gillette.com

CELEDONIA, BAILA HANDELMAN, lawyer; b. Bklyn., Jan. 8, 1945; s. Herman and Ida (Rubin) Handelman; m. Arthur Celedonia, Sept. 5, 1966; children: Miriam D., Loren E. BA, Carnegie Inst. Tech., 1965; JD summa cum laude, Bklyn. Law Sch., 1975. Bar: N.Y. 1976, U.S. Dist. Ct. (so. dist.) N.Y. 1976, U.S. Dist. Ct. (ea. dist.) N.Y. 1980, U.S. Ct. Appeals (9th, 10th and 11th cirs.) 1989, U.S. Supreme Ct. 1988. Law clk. U.S. Dist. Ct. (so. dist.) N.Y., N.Y.C., 1975-77; assoc. Cowan, Liebowitz & Latman, P.C., 1977-82, ptnr., 1983—. Adj. prof. Bklyn. Law Sch., 1987-88. Mng. editor Bklyn. Law Rev., 1974-75. Trustee Bklyn. Law Sch., 1984-86. Mem. ABA, Am. Intellectual Property Law Assn. (sec. 1997-2000, 1st v.p. Found. 2001—), Assn. Bar City N.Y., N.Y. State Bar Assn., Internat. Trademark Assn. (bd. dirs. 1990-92), Practicing Law Inst. (intellectual property adv. com. 1997—). Jewish. E-mial. Computer, Intellectual property, Trademark and copyright. Home: 35 Prospect Park W Brooklyn NY 11215-2370 Office: Cowan Liebowitz & Latman PC 1133 Avenue Of The Americas New York NY 10036-6710 E-mail: bhc@cll.com

CENATIEMPO, MICHAEL J. lawyer; b. Houston, June 16, 1946; s. Benedict S. and Mary E. C.; m. Mary Lou Rickel, May 31, 1970; children: Diana F., R. Matthew, Carla A. AB, St. Louis U., 1968; JD with honors, U. Houston, 1971. Bar: Tex. 1971; cert. estate planning and probate specialist. Briefing atty. to Hon. Ruel C. Walker Supreme Ct. Tex., 1971-72; with Butler, Binion, Rice, Cook & Knapp, Houston, 1972-78, Wyckoff, Russell, Frazier & Cenatiempo, Houston, 1978-85; ptnr. Cenatiempo & Ditta LLP, 1985—. Mem. Supreme Ct. Tex. Task Force on Jud. Appointments, 1991-93; presenter in field. Contbr. articles to profl. jours. Dir. St. Thomas H.S. Found., Houston, 1980-92, sec.-treas., 1989-92. Fellow Am. Coll. Trust and Estate Counsel (mem. state membership com. 1991-95, mem. estate and gift tax com. 1993, 97, mem. fiduciary litig. com. 1993-2000), Houston Bar Found. (dir. 1989, 90), State Bar Tex. Found.; mem. Houston Bar Assn. (chmn. probate, estates and trust law sect. 1983-84, media rep. on guardianship and mental health issues 1992—), State Bar Tex. (mem. real property, probate and trusts sect., mem. probate code subcom. 1995, mem. Tex. trust code com., statutory probate cts. liaison com.), Disability and Elder Law Attys. Assn., Houston Estate and Fin. Forum, Houston Bus. and Estate Planning Coun. Roman Catholic. Avocations: cycling, gardening, fly fishing, hunting, literature. Estate planning, Probate, Estate taxation. Office: Cenatiempo & Ditta 1550 Two Houston Ctr 909 Fannin St Houston TX 77010-1001 Fax: 713-655-9635. E-mail: mikecen@cenatiempo.com

CENTNER, CHARLES WILLIAM, lawyer, educator; b. Battle Creek, Mich., July 4, 1915; s. Charles William and Lucy Irene (Patterson) C.; m. Evi Rohr, Dec. 22, 1956; children: Charles Patterson, David William, Geoffrey Christopher. AB, U. Chgo., 1936, AM, 1938, 39, PhD, 1941; JD, Detroit Coll. Law, 1970; LLB, LaSalle Extension U., 1965. Bar: Mich. 1970. Asst. prof. U. N.D., 1940-41, Tulane U., New Orleans, 1941-42; liaison officer for Latin Am., Lend-Lease Adminstrn., 1942; assoc. dir. Western Hemisphere divsn. Nat. Fgn. Trade Coun., N.Y., 1946-52; exec. Ford Motor Co., Detroit, 1952-57, Chrysler Corp. and Chrysler Internat. S.A., Detroit and Geneva, Switzerland, 1957-70. Adj. prof. Wayne State U., U. Detroit, Wayne County C.C., 1970—. Author: Great Britian and Chile, 1810-1914, 1941. Lt. comdr. USNR, 1942-45. Mem. ABA, State Bar Mich., Oakland County Bar Assn., Masons. Republican. Episcopalian. Home: 936 Harcourt Rd Grosse Pointe MI 48230-1874

CERVONE, ANTHONY LOUIS, lawyer; b. Providence, Nov. 19, 1962; s. Anthony and Mary Gloria (Borrelli) C.; m. Joy D'Amico, Dec. 31, 1995. BA, R.I. Coll., 1984; JD, U. Bridgeport, 1988; Cert. Program Instrn. Lawyers, Harvard U., 1996. Bar: R.I. 1989, U.S. Dist. Ct. R. I. 1990, U.S. Ct. Appeals (1st cir.) 1991, U.S. Supreme Ct. 1996. Founder, prin. Cervone Law Firm, Cranston, R.I., 1989—; spl. coun. to The City of Providence, 1991-92. Mem. bench-bar com. R.I. Superior Ct., R.I. Family Ct., R.I. Dist. Ct.; affiliate atty. Am. Ctr. for Law and Justice, The Rutherford Inst. Mem. ABA, ATLA, R.I. Bar Assn., R.I. Trial Lawyers Assn., Supreme Ct. Hist. Soc., Smithsonian Instn., Library of Congress. Avocations: snowboarding, rollerhockey, golf, surfing, cycling, triathlons. Entertainment, Personal injury, Sports. Office: Renaissance Park 37 Sockanosset Crossroad Cranston RI 02920 E-mail: cervonelaw@aol.com

CHABANEIX, JEAN PAUL, lawyer; b. Cuscu, Peru, July 1964; s. Ferdinand and Luz Marina Chabaneix; m. Giselle Chabaneix; children: Benoit, François. Degree in law, Cath. U., Lima, Peru, 1990; LLM, NYU, 1995. Assoc. Rodrigo, Elias & Medrano, Lima, 1987-93, ptnr., 1994—. Fellow Org. Am. States, 1994. Contracts commercial, General corporate, Finance. Office: Rodrigo Elias & Medrano Ave San Felipe 758 Lima 11 Peru Office Fax: 511 4637300. E-mail: jpchabaneix@estudiorodrigo.com

CHABOT, ELLIOT CHARLES, lawyer; b. Anniston, Ala., Mar. 29, 1955; s. Herbert L. and Aleen (Kerwin) C.; m. Christine H. Swan, July 3, 1998. BA with honors, U. Md., 1977; JD, George Washington U., 1980. Bar: D.C. 1980, U.S. Dist. Ct. D.C. 1981, U.S. Ct. Fed. Claims 1981, U.S. Ct. Internat. Trade 1981, U.S. Tax Ct. 1981, U.S. Ct. Appeals Armed Forces 1981, U.S. Temporary Emergency Ct. Appeals 1981, U.S. Ct. Appeals (D.C. cir.) 1981, U.S. Ct. Appeals (4th, 5th, 8th, 9th, 10th, 11th, fed. cirs.) 1982, U.S. Ct. Appeals (7th cir.) 1983. Applications analyst, atty., House Info. Systems U.S. Ho. of Reps., Washington, 1980-81, project leader integrated law revision and retrieval project, 1981-89, legal support project leader House Info. Sys., 1989-95, webmaster internet law libr., 1994-99, legal sys. team leader House Info. Resources, 1995—. Bd. dirs. Am. Revenue Assn., Rockford, Iowa, 1983-87, Threshold Services, Inc., Silver Spring, Md., 1984-89; v.p. Banor Housing Inc., Kensington, Md., 1987-88, 90—, dir., 1987—. Columnist Aspen Hill Gazette, 1987-96. Pres. Aspen Hill (Md.) Civic Assn., 1985-95, dir. 1995-2000; pres. Parkland Community Sch. Coun., Aspen Hill, 1983-87, 94-96, v.p., 1971-73, mem. coun. 1970-74, 82-96; chmn. community svcs. com. Greater Wheaton (Md.) Citizens Adv. Bd., 1986-92; chmn. Ga. Ave. Men's Shelter Adv. Bd., Aspen Hill, 1989-96, Community Edn. Devel. subcom. of Citizens Adv. com. to the Interagency Coordinating Bd. for Community Use of Ednl. Facilities and Svcs., 1985-88; dist. 3 v.p. Montgomery County Civic Fedn., 1990-91; exec. com. Robert E. Peary High Sch. PTA, Aspen Hill, 1972-73; Montgomery County Coun. com. on re-use of Peary High Sch., 1986, task force to examine the regional dist. act, 1991; corr. sec. Area 2 adv. coun. Montgomery County Pub. Schs, 1972-74, adv. com. spl. edn. programs, 1974; commr. Gov.'s Commn. on Student Affairs, Md., 1976-77; adv. com. Aspen Hill Libr., 1972, 1986—; sec. Friends Aspen Hill Libr., 1994-96, dir., 1996—; rec. sec. Dist. 19 Dem. Club, Montgomery County, 1983-86, 2d v.p., 1986-89, 1st v.p., 1989-92; legal and acctg. div. steering com. Washington Israel Bonds, 1984-86; mem. exec. com. Allied Civic Group, Silver Spring, 1987-89, corr. sec., 1992-94; chmn. Kensington/Wheaton Human Svcs. Area Plan Adv. Group, 1988; mem. Sta. 21 com. Kensington Vol. Fire Dept., 1989; mem. Greater Layhill Community Night Com., 1989, Aspen Hill Master Plan Citizens Adv. com., 1990-94; sec. Montgomery County Dem. Party, 1994—, chmn. rules com., 1994—, chmn. Internet Svcs. com., 1995—, mem. ballot questions adv. com., 1988, 90, 98, 2000, vice chmn. precint orgn. com. of the party opers. task force, 1991-92; area coord. Dist. 19, 1992-94, chmn. Precinct 13-43, 1987-92, treas. Precinct 13-45, 1978-85; mem. Wheaton Action Group, 1990-95; campaign chmn. Dist. 19 Democratic Team, 1989-90; chmn. Wheaton Woods Recreation Ctr. Adv. Com., 1990; dir. dist 3 Montgomery Citizens Polit. Action Com., 1991-92; mem. Bauer Drive Community Ctr. Adv. Com., 1992—; vice chmn. homeless com. Temple Shalom, Chevy Chase, Md., 1992-93; sec. Montgomery County United Democrats, 1997-2000; mem. Md. State Dem. Ctrl. Com., 1994—; sec. Robert E. Peary H.S. Alumni Assn., Aspen Hill, MD, 2001—. Recipient George Washington award, George Washington U., 1980, Donald R. Spivak award Montgomery County Interagency Coordinating Bd. Community Use of Edn. Facilities and Services, 1987, Total Quality Team award Chief Adminstrv. Office of U.S. Ho. of Reps., 1996; named One of Outstanding Young Men, U.S. C. of C., 1982, Ky. Col. Hon. Order Ky. Cols., 1967, Citizen of Yr. Greater Wheaton Citizen's Adv. Bd., 1990, One of the Federal 100 Federal Computer Week, 1994. Mem. ABA, FBA, Internat. Law Inst. (mem. faculty legis. drafting 2000—), George Washington U. Law Alumni Assn. (pres. Capitol Hill chpt. 1987-89, sec. 1985-87), Phi Alpha Delta (clk. Jay chpt. 1979-80), Omicron Delta Kappa. Home: 12929 Magellan Ave Rockville MD 20853-3037 Office: US Congress House Info Resources H2-641 Ford Ho Office Bldg Washington DC 20515-6165 E-mail: elliotchabot@abanet.org

CHABOT, HERBERT L. judge; b. N.Y.C., July 17, 1931; s. Meyer and Esther (Mogilansky) C.; m. Aleen Carol Kerwin, June 16, 1951; children: Elliot C., Donald J., Lewis A., Nancy Jo. BA, CCNY, 1952; LLB, Columbia U., 1957; LLM, Georgetown U., 1964. Bar: N.Y. 1958. Staff counsel Am. Jewish Congress, 1957-60; law clk. U.S. Tax Ct., Washington, 1961-65, judge, 1978—, judge sr. status, 2001. Atty. Joint Congl. Com. Taxation, 1965-78, recalled to active svc., 2001. Del. Md. Constl. Conv., 1967-68. With U.S. Army, 1953-55. Mem. ABA, Fed. Bar Assn. Office: US Tax Ct 400 2nd St NW Washington DC 20217-0002

CHABROW, PENN BENJAMIN, lawyer; b. Phila., Feb. 16, 1939; s. Benjamin Penn and Annette (Shapiro) C.; m. Sheila Sue Steinberg, June 18, 1961; children: Michael Penn, Carolyn Debra, Frederick Penn. BS, Muhlenberg Coll., Allentown, Pa., 1959; JD, George Washington U., 1962, LLM in Taxation, 1968; postgrad. in econs. Harvard U. Bar: Va. 1963, D.C. 1964, U.S. Ct. Appeals (D.C. cir.) 1964, U.S. Tax Ct. 1964, U.S. Supreme Ct. 1966, Fla. 1972, U.S. Ct. Claims 1974, U.S. Ct. Appeals (5th and 11th cirs.) 1981; bd. cert. tax atty., Fla. Tax law specialist IRS, Washington, 1961-67; tax counsel C. of C. U.S., Washington, 1967-74; pvt. practice, Miami, Fla., 1974—; shareholder Wampler, Buchanan, Walker & Banciella, PA, Miami, 1993—; pres. Forum Realty Co., Phila., Pure Poultry Enterprises, Inc., Miami, Heartland Farms of Fla., Inc.; lectr. fed. taxation Barry U. Grad. Sch. of Bus., 1977-81. Founding dir. The Dan Marino Found., Inc., The Melissa Inst. for Violence Prevention and Treatment, Inc. Fellow Am. Coll. Tax Counsel; mem. ABA, Fla. Bar Assn., Fed. Bar Assn., Va. Bar Assn., D.C. Bar Assn., Greater Miami Estate Planning Coun., Muhlenberg Coll. Internat. Vis. Com., Phi Alpha Delta, Phi Sigma Tau. Contbr. articles profl. jours. General corporate, Estate planning, Taxation, general. Office: 777 Brickell Ave Ste 900 Miami FL 33131-2814

CHACKES, KENNETH MICHAEL, lawyer, legal educator; b. St. Louis, Sept. 12, 1949; s. Alex and Shirlee (Radloff) C.; m. Carole Gail Breen, June 14, 1970; children: Laura Michelle, Andrew Scott, Brian Carl. BA in Psychology, Tulane U., 1971; JD cum laude, St. Louis U., 1976. Bar: Mo. 1976, U.S. Dist. Ct. (ea. and we. dists.) Mo. 1976, U.S. Ct. Appeals (8th cir.) 1976, U.S. Ct. Appeals (D.C. cir.) 1979, U.S. Ct. Appeals (7th cir.) 1981. Ptnr. Chackes & Hoare, St. Louis, 1976-84; vis. asst. prof. law Washington U., 1984-87; atty. Mo. Protection & Advocacy Svcs., St. Louis and Jefferson City, 1988-90, mng. atty., 1990-92; pvt. practice, of counsel Vines, Frankel, Rubin, Bond & Dubin, P.C., St. Louis, 1992-96; ptnr. Van Amburg, Chackes, Carlson & Spritzer, LLP, 1996—. Adminstrv. hearing officer Mo. Dept. Elem. & Secondary Edn. Divsn. Spl. Edn., 1999—; adj. prof. law Washington U., 1982-83, 88, supr. clin. students, 1981-84, 88-89, 91—; appearances on TV shows Law Talk, 1985-86, Special People, Special Needs, 1989-90; judge Fed. Practice Tng. Inst., St. Louis, 1983, judge trial tng. program, 1986, 89, instr., 1984-85, 92; mem. fed. practice com. U.S. Dist. Ct. for Ea. Dist. Mo., chmn. subcom. on appointment of counsel in civil rights cases; mem. discovery abuse and civil jury instrns. subcom.; lectr. in field. Mem. editl. bd. St. Louis U. Law Jour. Exec. com. Access Resources of Mo., 1991—; mem. adv. com. on disabilities issues, HUD, 1990-91; mem. Coalition of Citizens with Disabilities of Greater St. Louis, 1989—, Mo. Coalition for Homeless, 1989—; steering com. St. Louis Lawyers' Project on Homelessness and Inadequate Housing, 1987-92. Recipient Legal Advocate award Mo. Assn. for Social Welfare, 1992, Equal Justice award Legal Svcs. of Ea. Mo., 1993. Mem. ABA (individual rights and responsibilities, labor and employment law and litigation sects.), Mo. Bar Assn., Nat. Employment Lawyers Assn. (pres. St. Louis chpt. 1995-98). Home: 8100 Gannon Ave Saint Louis MO 63130-3731 Office: 8420 Delmar Blvd Ste 406 Saint Louis MO 63124-2179 E-mail: kchackes@vccs-law.com

CHACON LOPEZ VELARDE, RICARDO, lawyer, educator; b. Mexico City, Mex., Apr. 25, 1971; Law degree, U. Panamericana, Mexico City, 1996, postgrad., 1996-97; LLM, U. Tex., 1998; postgrad., Escuela Libre de Derecho, Mexico City, 2000-2001, Inst. Tech. Autonomo Mex., 1999. Paralegal Rios Ferrer Y Guillen LLarena, S.C., Mexico City, 1992-97, jr. assoc., 1997-98, jr. ptnr., 1998—; law prof. negotiation and mediation U. Panamericana Sch. of Law, 1998—. Co-author: Global Telecommunications Law and Practice, 2000. Mem. Mexican Bar Assn. (com. telecomms.), Mexican Telecomms. Acad. Communications, General corporate, Mergers and acquisitions. Office: Rios Ferrer Guillen Llarena Insurgentes Sur 12th Fl 03900 Mexico City Mexico Fax: 52-56-62-63-50. E-mail: rchacon@riosferrer.com.mx

CHADWICK, ROBERT, lawyer, judge; b. Jackson, Miss., Apr. 5, 1924; s. Hudson and Annie (Eley) C.; m. Helen Faye Josey, Apr. 5, 1953; children: Robert Hudson, Celia, Dan, Lea Ann, Robin. BA, Auburn U., 1950; JD, Miss. Coll., 1957; postgrad., U. So. Calif., 1973, 75-76. Bar: Miss. 1963, U.S. Supreme Ct. 1970, U.S. Ct. Mil. Appeals 1975, Ky. 1980, U.S. Dist Ct. (ea. dist.) Ky. 1987. Chief regulation staff div. pesticide regulation USDA, Washington, 1965-70; atty., ecologist div. enforcement EPA, 1970-75, chmn. com. pesticide misuse rev., 1975-79; asst. gen. counsel Presdl. Clemency Bd. White House Dept. Justice, 1975; pvt. practice law Frankfort, Ky., 1980-82, 83—; law judge parole bd. Corrections Cabinet, 1982-83; asst. dir. div. hazardous materials Ky. Dept. Natural Resources and Environ. Protection, 1983—. Chmn. bd. Exis, Inc.; staff atty., gen. counsel Ky. Cabinet for Human Resources, 1989-90. Pres. PTA Oxon Hill (Md.) Jr. High Sch., 1974, Frankfort Audubon Soc., 1981-83. Cpl. U.S. Army, 1943-45. Mem. ABA, Nat. Assn. Adminstrv. Law Judges, Miss. State Bar Assn., Ky. State Bar Assn., Franklin County Bar Assn., VFW, Masons. Criminal, Environmental, General practice. Home and Office: 16 Ryswick Ln Frankfort KY 40601-3848

CHADWICK, VERNON HENRY, lawyer; b. Woodville, Miss., May 4, 1941; s. Carl A. and Elvena P. Chadwick; m. Julia B. Chadwick, Aug. 31, 1963; children: Price Conerly, Swayze Amelia. BS, Miss. Coll., 1978, LLB, 1966. Bar: Miss. 1966, U.S. Dist. Ct. (so. dist.) Miss. 1969. Ptnr. Chadwick & Chadwick, Natchez, Miss., 1966-71, Chadwick & McAllister, Jackson, 1973-85; pvt. practice, 1985—. Adj. prof. Miss. Coll., Clinton, 1980-90. Chmn. March of Dimes, Natchez, 1967; charter mem. Friends of the Jackson Zoo, 1977; active St. Andrew's Cathedral, Jackson, 1971—. With U.S. Army, 1959-62. Mem. ABA, Miss. Bar Assn., Hinds County Bar Assn. (chmn. libr. com. 1994-96), Adams County Bar Assn. (sec.-treas. 1968), Sigma Delta Kappa. Avocations: reading, writing, hiking, fishing. General practice, Probate, Real property. Home: 920 Meadowbrook Rd Jackson MS 39206-5944 Office: 1640 Lelia Dr Ste 210 Jackson MS 39216-4832

CHADWICK, WILLIAM JORDAN, lawyer; b. N.Y.C., Apr. 21, 1948; s. William Leroy and Mildred (Jordan) C.; B.A., St. Lawrence U., 1970; J.D., Vanderbilt U., 1973. Bar: Calif. 1973. Assoc. Paul, Hastings, Janofsky & Walker, Los Angeles, 1973-74, ptnr., 1977— ; atty advisor for tax policy U.S. Treasury Dept., Washington, 1974-75; spl. asst. to adminstr. Pension and Welfare Benefit Programs, U.S. Dept. Labor, Washington, 1975-76, adminstr., 1976-77; dir. Westam. Packaging, Los Angeles, Fin. Select Seminars, Inc., Santa Barbara, Calif., Prudential-Bache Broadcasting. Author: The Annotated Fiduciary, 1978; Regulation of Employee Benefits, 1978. Contbr. articles to profl. jours. Trustee St. Lawrence U., Canton, N.Y., 1977-83; bd. dirs. Internat. Found. Employee Benefits Plans, Brookfield, Wis., 1980-83. Served to 1st lt. U.S. Army, 1966-73. Recipient Spl. Achievement award U.S. Dept. Treasury, 1975, U.S. Dept. Labor, 1976, Sec's Spl. Commendation award U.S. Dept. Labor, 1977. Mem. ABA, Calif. Bar Assn., D.C. Bar Assn. Pension, profit-sharing, and employee benefits, Securities, Corporate taxation. Home: 901 Enchanted Way Pacific Palisades CA 90272-2824 Office: Paul Hastings Jonofsky & Walker 555 S Flower St Los Angeles CA 90071-2300

CHAFETZ, MARC EDWARD, lawyer; b. Boston, Apr. 21, 1953; s. Morris Edward and Marion (Donovan) C.; m. Andrea Laurie Barkan, Aug. 20, 1977; children: Drew Edward, Maria Caitlin. BA, Oberlin Coll., 1975; JD, U. Va., 1979. Bar: D.C. Ct. Appeals 1980, U.S. Dist. Ct. D.C. 1980, U.S. Ct. Appeals (D.C. cir.) 1982. Law clk. to presiding justice U.S. Dist. Ct., Bryan, Va., 1979-80; assoc. Fulbright & Jaworski, Washington, 1980-82; sr. counsel SEC, 1982-84; gen. counsel Health Comms., 1984—, also bd. dirs.; assoc. Ballard, Spahr, Andrews & Ingersoll, 1984-87; pres. Health Comms., Inc., 1987-94; COO The Tech. Group, Balt., 1996-97; of counsel Tighe, Patton, Tabackman & Babbin, Washington, 1996; CEO Train, Inc., 1995—; mng. dir. Bozman Ptnrs., LLC, 1997—; sr. v.p., gen. counsel In Touch Techs. Ltd., 1998-2000; chief strategy officer Net Compliance, Inc., 2001—. Contbr. articles to profl. jours. Trustee Health Edn. Found., 1979—, Nat. Child Rsch. Ctr., 1989-91; bd. dirs. Foodfit-.com., Washington. Mem. ABA, Fed. Bar Assn., D.C. Bar Assn. Federal civil litigation, Criminal, Securities. Home and Office: 900 19th St NW Ste 275 Washington DC 20006 E-mail: marc@bozmanpartners.com

CHAITMAN, HELEN DAVIS, lawyer; b. N.Y.C., July 5, 1941; d. Philip and Miriam (Pfeffer) D.; m. Edmund Chaitman, Feb. 29, 1964 (div. 1978); children: Jennifer, Alison; m. George B. Gelman, Oct. 21, 1979. AB cum laude, Bryn Mawr Coll., 1963; JD, Rutgers U., 1976. Bar: N.Y. 1976, N.J., U.S. Dist. Ct. N.Y., U.S. Dist. Ct. N.J., U.S. Ct. Appeals (3d cir.), U.S. Supreme Ct. Assoc. Paul, Weiss, Rifkind, Wharton & Garrison, N.Y.C., 1977-82; ptnr. Wilentz, Goldman & Spitzer, Woodbridge, N.J., 1983-87, Ross & Hardies, Somerset, 1987-99, Wolf Haldenstein Adler Freeman & Herz LLP, N.Y.C., 1999—. Author: The Law of Lender Liability, 1990; contbg. author: Commercial Damages, 1985; editor Emerging Theories of Lender Liability, 1985-87. Mem. ABA (chmn. comml. fin. svcs. com. 1994-97, sect. bus. law), Am. Law Inst. (sustaining mem. 1992-2001), Pub. Law Inst. Bankruptcy, Contracts commercial. Home: The Farm 115 Fairview Rd Frenchtown NJ 08825-3013 Office: Wolf Haldenstein Adler Freeman & Herz LLP 270 Madison Ave New York NY 10016-0601 also: Wolf Haldenstein Adler Freeman & Herz LLP 580 Howard Ave Somerset NJ 08873-1136 E-mail: chaitman@whafh.com

CHAMBERLAIN, JAMES ROBERT, lawyer; b. Cedar Rapids, Iowa, Nov. 13, 1949; s. Robert Glenn and Jane Helen (Newlin) C.; m. Marsha Lois Gurland, June 23, 1971; children: Jonathan J., Zachary T., Seth A., Jeremy D. BA, U. Wis., 1971, MS, 1973; JD, So. Meth. U., 1976. Bar: Tex. 1976, U.S. Dist. Ct. (no. dist.) Tex. 1978, Wis. 1980. Atty. trade regulation div. FTC, Dallas, 1976-80; sr. counsel antitrust div. Westinghouse Electric Corp., Pitts., 1980-92, asst. gen. counsel antitrust and Thermo King, 1992-95; v.p. and gen. counsel Thermo King Corp., Mpls., 1995—; asst. gen. counsel Ingersoll-Rand Co., 2000—. Adj. prof. antitrust law Duquesne U., 1986-92, William Mitchell Coll. of Law, 2000. Editor Human Rights Jour., 1975-76. Antitrust, General corporate. Home: 6604 Limerick Dr Minneapolis MN 55439-1260 Office: Thermo King Corp 314 W 90th St Minneapolis MN 55420-3693 E-mail: Jim_Chamberlain@ThermoKing.com

CHAMBERS, DAVID LAURANCE, III, legal educator; b. Indpls., Sept. 24, 1940; s. David L. and Estelle (Burpee) C.; ptnr. John G. Crane; children: Lucy, Abbot, Liza. AB, Princeton U., 1962; LLB, Harvard U., 1965. Bar: D.C. 1966, Mich. 1971. Assoc. Wilmer, Cutter & Pickering, Washington, 1965-67; spl. asst. to exec. dir. Nat. Adv. Com. on Civil Disorders, Washington, 1967-68; mem. faculty Sch. Law, U. Mich., Ann Arbor, now prof. law. Author: Making Fathers Pay: The Enforcement of Child Support, 1979. Mem. Soc. Am. Law Tchrs. (pres. 1977-79). Democrat. Home: 344 Quechee West Htfd Rd White River Junction VT 05001-2121 Office: U Mich Law School 625 S State St Ann Arbor MI 48109-1215

CHAMBERS, GUY WAYNE, lawyer; b. Harvey, Ill., Feb. 18, 1956; s. Robert Rood and Martha (Wayne) C. BS in Chem. Engring. with highest honors, U. Calif., Santa Barbara, 1978; JD, Columbia U., 1981. Bar: Calif. 1981, U.S. Ct. Appeals (fed. cir.) 1982, U.S. Patent and Trademark Office 1982, U.S. Ct. Appeals (9th cir.) 1992, U.S. Supreme Ct. 1995. Trial atty. civil div. U.S. Dept. Justice, Washington, 1981-84; assoc. Townsend and Townsend and Crew, San Francisco, 1984-91, ptnr., 1991—. Project mgr. NIH Patent Svcs. Contract. Contbr. articles to profl. publs. Mem. ABA, San Francisco Intellectual Property Law Assn. Federal civil litigation, Computer, Patent. Office: Townsend & Townsend & Crew 8th flr 2 Embarcadero Ctr San Francisco CA 94111 Office Fax: (415) 576-0300. E-mail: gwchambers@townsend.com

CHAMBERS, JULIUS LEVONNE, academic administrator, lawyer; b. Montgomery County, N.C., Oct. 6, 1936; BA, N.C. Cen. U., 1958; MA, U. Mich., 1959; LLB, U. N.C., 1962; LLM, Columbia U., 1963. Bar: N.C. 1962, N.Y. 1986. Ptnr. Chambers, Fertuson, Watt, Wallas, Adkins & Fuller, Charlotte, N.C., 1964-84; dir., counsel NAACP Legal Def. and Ednl. Fund, N.Y.C., 1984-92; chancellor N.C. Ctrl. U., Durham, 1993-2000; with Ferguson, Stein, Wallas, Adkins, Gresham & Sumter, Charlotte, 2000—. Bd. dirs. RJR Nabisco Holdings. Trustee N.J. State Bd. Higher Edn.; bd. visitors Harvard U., Columbia U. Law Sch.; trustee U. Pa., mem. bd. overseers Law Sch.; bd. dirs. Children's Def. Fund, Legal Aid Soc. N.Y. Mem. ABA (bd. editors ABA jour.), N.C. Bar Assn., Mecklenburg County Bar Assn., N.Y. State Bar Assn., Assn. of Bar of City of N.Y., Nat. Bar Assn., Assn. Black Lawyers N.C., Order of Coif, Order of Golden Fleece, Phi Alpha Theta. Office: Fergson Stein Wallas Adkins Gresham & Sumter 741 Kenilworth Ave Ste 300 Charlotte NC 28204

CHAMBERS, THOMAS JEFFERSON, lawyer; b. Yakima, Wash., Oct. 11, 1943; s. Thomas J. and Doris May (Ellyson) C.; m. Judy Larene Cable, June 11, 1967; children: Jolie, Jana, Tommy. BA in Polit. Sci., Wash. State U., 1966; JD, U. Wash., 1969. Bar: Wash., U.S. Dist. Ct. (we. and ea. dists.) Wash. 1969. Assoc. Lycette, Diamond & Sylvester, Seattle, 1969-71, Barokas & Martin, Seattle, 1972; sole practice, 1972—2001; justice Wash. State Supreme Ct., 2001—. Mem. congestion com. Wash. State Cts., 1984, King County Mandatory Arbitration Council, 1981-86, Damages Atty. Roundtable, 1983-86. Editorial adv. bd. Everday Law mag.; contbr. articles to profl. jours. Mem. jud. evaluation com. Mcpl. League, 1982. Mem. Wash. State Trial Lawyers Assn. (pres. 1985-86, pres.-elect 1984-85, bd. govs. 1976—, various coms.), Am. Bd. Trial Advs. (past. pres. Wash. chpt.), Am. Trial Lawyers Assn. (past mem. bd. govs.), Wash. State Bar Assn. (pres. 1996-97). Avocation: flying airplanes. Personal injury. Home: 4514 193rd Pl SE Issaquah WA 98027-9308 Office: PO Box 40929 Olympia WA 98504-0929*

CHAMBLEE, DANA ALICIA, lawyer; b. Tupelo, Miss. d. Don Allen and Diana Roberts Chamblee. BA, Rhodes Coll., 1994; JD, U. Mo., 1997. Bar: Mo. 1997, U.S. Dist. Ct. (we. dist.) 1998. Law clk. for judge John C. Crow Mo. So. Dist. Ct. Appeals, Springfield, 1997-98; assoc. William H. McDonald & Assocs., P.C., 1998—. Editor-in-chief Jour. Dispute Resolution, U. Mo. Sch. Law. Project chair Jr. League, Springfield, 1998—; mem. cmty. rels. bd. Habitat for Humanity, Springfield, 1998—. Mem. ABA, ATLA, Springfield Met. Bar Assn. (mem. young lawyers com. 1998—). Republican. Baptist. Antitrust, General civil litigation, Product liability. Home: 3660 S Cox # 101 Springfield MO 65807 Office: William H McDonald & Assocs PC 300 S Jefferson Ste 600 Springfield MO 65806

CHAMBLISS, PRINCE CAESAR, JR. lawyer; b. Birmingham, Ala., Oct. 3, 1948; s. Prince Caesar and Marguerite (Pearson) C.; m. Patricia Toney, Dec. 26, 1971; children: Patience Brandyn. Student Wesleyan U., Middletown, Conn., 1966-68; BA, U. Ala., Birmingham, 1969-71; JD, Harvard U., 1974. Bar: Ala. 1974, Tenn. 1976. Spl. asst. to pres. U. Ala., Birmingham, 1974-75; law clk. to judge U.S. Dist. Ct. (no. dist.) Ala., Birmingham, 1975-76; assoc. firm Armstrong, Allen, Braden, Goodman, McBride & Prewitt, Memphis, 1976-81, ptnr., 1981—; sec., treas. Tenn. Bd. Law Examiners, 1988-92, v.p., 1992—. Bd. dirs. ARC Memphis chpt., 1st vice chmn., 1988-89; trustee Miles Coll. Sch. Law, Birmingham, 1982-88. Recipient Community Service award Jud. Council Nat. Bar Assn., 1982; named Boss of Yr., Memphis Legal Secs. Assn., 1984. Mem. ABA, Memphis Bar Assn. (dir. 1983-85, pres. 1997-98), Fed. Bar Assn. (pres. Mid-South chpt. 1984-85), Nat. Bar Assn., Tenn. Bar Assn. (sec. 1995-97), Ala. Bar Assn, Memphis Council for Internat. Visitors (bd. dirs. 1983—). Federal civil litigation, State civil litigation, General corporate. Home: 1917 Miller Farms Rd Memphis TN 38138-2752 Office: Armstrong Allen Braden Goodman McBride & Prewitt 80 Monroe Ave Memphis TN 38103-2481

CHAMPION, SARA STEWART, lawyer; b. Boston, Apr. 1, 1942; d. William Julius Champion and Mary Stewart Cunningham; m. Wayne L. Kinsey, Dec. 12, 1964 (div. Feb. 1971); m. John Q. Adams, Apr. 25, 1998 (div. Oct. 2000). BA, Duke U., 1963; MA, U. Calif., Davis, 1974; JD cum laude, N.Y. Law Sch., 1992. Bar: N.Y. 1992, Conn. 1992. Rsch. analyst Nat. Security Agy., Ft. Meade, Md., 1963-65; instr. Russian Def. Lang. Inst., Monterey, Calif., 1970-72; claims rep. Social Security Adminstrn., San Francisco, 1974-78, claims rep., ops. supr. N.Y.C., 1978-87; office adminstr. Bachelder Law Offices, 1987-97, assoc., 1992-97, ptnr., 1997—. Mem. DAR, Soc. Mayflower Descendants Avocation: genealogy. Office: Bachelder Law Offices 780 3d Ave New York NY 10017 E-mail: ssc@jebachelder.com

CHAN, DANIEL CHUNG-YIN, lawyer; b. Kowloon, Hong Kong, June 5, 1948; came to U.S., 1969; s. David Chi-Kwong and Betty Wai-Lan (Kwok) C.; m. Mary Ching-Fay Wong, June 11, 1977; children: Pamila Wai-Sum (dec.), Derrick Ming-Deh. BA cum laude, Azusa Pacific U., 1972; postgrad., Calif. State U., L.A., 1973-75; JD, U. West L.A., 1983. Bar: Calif. 1984, U.S. Dist. Ct. (cen. dist.) Calif. 1984, U.S. Ct. Appeals (9th cir.) 1984, U.S. Dist. Ct. (so. dist.) Calif. 1985, U.S. Dist. Ct. (no. dist.) Calif. 1986. Mgr. Elegant Sewing Co., L.A., 1977; legal asst. Otto Frank Swanson Law Office, Marina Del Ray, Calif., 1978-84, assoc., 1984-87; pvt. practice, Pasadena, 1987—. Legal counsel Chinese Grace Missions Internat., Inc., Duarte, Calif., 1984—, Diao Jiou Chinese Christian Ch. L.A., Highland Park, Calif., 1988—, Ruth Hitchcock Found. Mem. ABA, Assn. Trial Lawyers Am., So. Calif. Chinese Lawyers Assn., Am. Immigration Lawyers Assn., Delta Epsilon Chi, Alpha Chi. Family and matrimonial, Immigration, naturalization, and customs, Private international. Office: 283 S Lake Ave Ste 219 Pasadena CA 91101-4818

CHAN, DAVID RONALD, tax specialist, lawyer; b. L.A., Aug. 3, 1948; s. David Yew and Anna May (Wong) C.; m. Mary Anne Chan, July 21, 1980; children: Eric, Christina. AB in Econs., UCLA, 1969, MS in Bus. Adminstrn., 1970, JD, 1973. Bar: Calif. 1973, U.S. Tax Ct. 1974, U.S. Ct. Appeals (9th cir.) 1974, U.S. Dist. Ct. (ctrl. dist.) Calif. 1980. Acct. Oxnard Celery Distbrs., L.A., 1968-73, Touche Ross & Co., L.A., 1970; tax prin. Kenneth Leventhal & Co. (name now E&Y Kenneth Leventhal Real Estate Group), 1973—. Contbr. chpts. to books and articles to profl. jours. Founder, dir. Chinese Hist. Soc. So. Calif., L.A., 1975—; mem. spkrs. bur. L.A. 200 Bicentennial, L.A., 1981; spkr. Project Follow Through, L.A., 1981, EY Tax Forum, UCLA Real Estate Forecast, Merril Lynch Symposium, Calif. CPA Soc. Recipient Forbes Gold medal Calif. Soc. CPAs, L.A., 1970, Elijah Watt Sells cert. AICPA, L.A., 1970, cert. recognition Chinese Hist. Soc. So. Calif., L.A., 1985. Mem. So. Calif. Chinese Lawyers Assn., L.A. County Bar Assn., Chinese Am. CPAs So. Calif., Asian Bus. League, Chinese For Affirmative Action. Republican. Avocations: Chinese cuisine, sports memorabilia, philately. Office: E&Y Kenneth Leventhal Real Estate Group Ste 1800 2049 Century Park E Los Angeles CA 90067-3119 E-mail: david.chan02@ey.com

CHANDLER, ALBERT BENJAMIN, III, attorney general; m. Jennifer Chandler; children: Lucie Brasher, Albert Benjamin IV, Russell Branham. BA in History with distinction, U. Ky., JD, 1986. Bar: Ky. 1986. Assoc. Brown, Todd & Heyburn, Lexington, Ky., Reeves & Graddy, Versailles; state auditor, atty. gen. Office of Atty. Gen. Recipient Achievement of the Yr. award Assn. Govt. Accts., 1993-94. Mem. ABA, Ky. Bar Assn. (named Outstanding Young Lawyer 1993), Woodford County Bar Assn. Office: Office of Atty Gen Ste 118 Capitol Bldg Frankfort KY 40601-2831

CHANDLER, EVERETT ALFRED, lawyer; b. Columbus, Ohio, Sept. 21, 1926; s. Everett P. and Mary C. (Turner) C.; children: Wayne B., Brian E., V. Rhette; m. Mittie Rene Olion, Mar. 20, 1987 (div. Sept. 1991); 1 child, Mae Evette. BEd, Ohio State U., 1955; JD, Howard U., 1958. Bar: Ohio 1958, U.S. Dist. Ct. (no. dist.) Ohio 1962, U.S. Ct. Appeals (6th cir.) 1991, U.S. Tax Ct. 1967. Asst. county pros., Cuyahoga County, 1968-71; chief pros. City of Cleve., 1971-75; prin. Everett A. Chandler, Atty., Cleve. Author book rev. Cleve. State Law Jour., 1974. Chair bd. dirs. Cmty. Action Against Addiction, Cleve., 1975—, Crisis Intervention Team, Cleve., 1976-91; trustee Legal Aid Soc., Cleve., 1982-84, Boys Club Cleve., 1969-72; Dem. candidate for judge, Cuyahoga County, 1994. With USN, 1945-53. Mem. Norman S. Minor Bar Assn., Kappa Alpha Psi (past pres. 1980-83, 76-80, chmn. bd.). Democrat. Baptist. Avocations: golfing, traveling. General civil litigation, Criminal, General practice. Home: 16010 Talford Ave Cleveland OH 44128-1237 Office: PO Box 28459 Cleveland OH 44128-0459

CHANDLER, GEORGE FRANCIS, III, lawyer, naval architect; b. Winthrop, Mass., Dec. 15, 1940; s. George Francis Jr. and Phyllis (McKay) C.; children: Heather Suzanne, George Francis IV. BSME, Va. Poly. Inst., 1963; JD, Suffolk U., 1972. Bar: Mass. 1972, N.Y. 1973, N.J. 1978, U.S. Dist. Ct. Mass. 1972, U.S. Dist. Ct. (so. dist.) N.Y. 1973, U.S. Dist. Ct. (ea. dist.) N.Y. 1977, U.S. Dist. Ct. (so. dist.) Tex. 1990), U.S. Dist. Ct. N.J. 1977, U.S. Ct. Appeals (2d cir.) 1973, U.S. Supreme Ct. 1977, U.S. Ct. Appeals (4th cir.) 1978, U.S. Ct. Appeals (11th cir.) 1983, U.S. Ct. Appeals (1st cir.) 1984, U.S. Ct. Appeals (5th cir.) 1992 ; profl. engr., Mass. Naval architect Dept. BuShips USN, Boston, 1958-63, 67-72; assoc. Bigham, Englar, Jones & Houston, N.Y.C., 1972-78; ptnr. Hill, Rivkins & Hayden LLP (and predecessor firm), 1978—. U.S. rep. to UNCITRAL for Electronic Commerce, 1991-96; mem. joint work group UNCITRAL/CMI, 1995-96; del. Comitè Maritime Internat., 1990, 98, 2001, CMI subcom. on H/V Rules, 1995-99, CMI steering commn. on transport law, 1997—; titulary mem. CMI Subcom. on Electronic B/L. Contbr. articles to profl. jours. Pres., founder Spl. Edn. PTA, Maplewood, N.J., 1984-87. Lt. USNR, 1963-67. Mem. ABA, Soc. Naval Archs. (chmn. N.Y. sect. 1986-87), Maritime Law Assn. (proctor, bd. dirs. 1993-96, chmn. com. on carriage of goods 1991-95, chmn. subcom. on electronic contracts of carriage 1990-91, chmn. electronic comm. com. 1995-99), Houston Maritime Arbitrators Assn. (founder, pres., bd. dirs. 1998—). Admiralty, Contracts commercial, Private international. Office: Hill Rivkins & Hayden LLP Ste 1515 712 Main St Houston TX 77002-3209

CHANDLER, KENT, JR. lawyer; b. Chgo., Jan. 10, 1920; s. Kent and Grace Emeret (Tuttle) C.; m. Frances Robertson, June 19, 1948; children: Gail, Robertson Kent. BA, Yale U., 1942; JD, U. Mich., 1949. Bar: Ill. 1949, U.S. Dist. Ct. (no. dist.) Ill. 1949, U.S. Ct. Appeals (7th cir.) 1955, U.S. Ct. Claims 1958. Assoc. Wilson & McIlvaine, Chgo., 1949-56, ptnr., 1957-94, spl. counsel to firm, 1994-98; of counsel Bell Jones & Quinlisk, 1998—. Bd. dirs. No. Trust Bank, Lake Forest, Ill., 1969-90, A.B. Dick Co., 1971-79, Internat. Crane Found., 1988—. Mem. zoning bd. appeals City of Lake Forest, Ill., 1953-63, chmn., 1963-67, mem. plan commn., 1955-69, chmn., 1969-70, pres. bd. local improvements, 1970-73, mayor, 1970-73, mem. bd. fire and police commn., 1975-82, chmn., 1982-84. Served to maj. USMCR, 1941-46. Mem. ABA, Ill. State Bar Assn., Chgo. Bar Assn., Lake County Bar Assn., Legal Club Chgo., Law Club (pres. 1985-86), Univ. Club, Onwentsia Club (Lake Forest), Old Elm Club (Highland Park, Ill.). Republican. Presbyterian. Estate planning, Pension, profit-sharing, and employee benefits, Personal income taxation. Office: 200 W Adams St Ste 2600 Chicago IL 60606-5233

CHANDLER, LAWRENCE BRADFORD, JR. lawyer; b. New Bedford, Mass., June 20, 1942; s. Lawrence Bradford and Anne (Crane) C.; m. Madeleine Bibeau, Sept. 7, 1963 (div. June 1984); children: Dawn, Colleen, Brad. BS in Bus. Adminstrn., Boston Coll., 1963; LLB, U. Va., 1966, JD, 1970. Bar: Mass. 1966, U.S. Supreme Ct. 1967, Va. 1970, W.Va. 1993; diplomate Nat. Bd. Trial Advocacy; advocate Am. Bd. Trial Advocates. Ptnr. Chandler, Franklin & O'Bryan, Charlottesville, Va., 1971—. Pres. Western Va. Chpt., 1992-93. Capt. U.S. Army, 1967-71. Mem. ABA, ATLA (chair state dels. 1993-94, exec. com. 1993-94, bd. govs. 1995—), Va. Trial Lawyers Assn. (pres. 1985-86), Am. Bd. Trial Advs. (pres. Va. chpt.), Nat. Bd. of Trial Advocacy (bd. examiners), Charlottesville Bar Assn., Assn. U.S. Army (pres. 1971-73), Am. Coll. Legal Medicine, Am. Soc. on Law, Medicine and Ethics, Am. Assn. Profl. Liability Attys. Roman Catholic. Personal injury. Home: 1445 Old Ballard Rd Charlottesville VA 22901-9469 Office: Chandler Franklin & O'Bryan PO Box 6747 Charlottesville VA 22906-6747 E-mail: goofyc@mindspring.com

CHANDLER, RICHARD GATES, lawyer; b. Stockton, Calif., July 6, 1952; s. Kensal Roberts and Barbara (Gates) C; m. Heidi Pankoke, Oct. 22, 1994. BA, Lawrence U., 1974; JD, U. Chgo., 1977. Bar: Wis. 1977. Assoc. Minahan & Peterson S.C., Milw., 1979-84; legis. counsel to State Rep. Tommy G. Thompson, Rep. leader, Wis. Assembly, Madison, 1985-86; legis. asst. Congressman Robert W. Kasten, Jr., Washington, 1977-78; budget dir. State of Wis., 1987-2001; sec. Dept. Revenue, Madison, 2001-. Mem. Phi Beta Kappa. Republican. Methodist. Home: 1618 Rutledge St Madison WI 53704-5539 Office: Dept Revenue PO Box 8933 Madison WI 53708-8933 E-mail: richards.chandler@dor.state.wi.us

CHANDLER, WILLIAM HENRY, lawyer; b. Heminway, S.C., May 5, 1948; s. William Jackson and Margaret Eloise (Nelson) C.; m. Ann Rodgers Timlison, July 31, 1982; children: Jared Witherspoon Nelson, Martha Elizabeth HArtman, Ann Paisley Snoden. AB, U. S.C., 1970, JD, 1973. Bar: S.C. 1973, U.S. Dist. Ct. (we. dist.) La. 1975, U.S. Dist. Ct. S.C. 1973, U.S. Ct. Mil. Appeals 1974. Ptnr. Chandler & Ruffin, Hemingway, S.C., 1978-84, Askins, Chandler, Ruffin & Askins, Hemingway, 1984—. Instr. bus. law Williamsburg Tech. Coll., Kingstree, S.C., 1978-79. Vice chmn. Williamsburg County Bd. Trustees, 1979—84, Williamsburg County Devel. Bd.; chmn. The Continuum of Care for Emotionally Disturbed Children; mem. State Hist. Records Adv. Bd., Williamsburg Co. Planning Commn.; supt. ch. sch. First Presbyn. Ch., Bossier City, La., 1975—77; law spkr. Presbytery of the Pines Presbyn. Ch. U.S., 1976—77; ruling elder Indiantown Presbyn. Ch., Hemingway, 1980—; bd. dirs. Francis Marion Coll. Found., Williamsburg County Farm Bur.; vice chmn. Pee Dee Heritage Found.; atty. Town of Stuckey, SC, 1979—. Mem. ABA, SAR, Am. Legion, S.C. Geneal. Soc., S.C. Libr. Soc., French Higuenot Soc., S.C. Hist. Soc., Williamsburg County Bar Assn., Williamsburg County Hist. Soc. (pres.), Three Rivers Hist. Soc. (pres.), St. Andrews Soc., Charleston Preservation Soc., Lions, Masons (Hemingway), Hog Crawl Hunting Club, Wilson Lake Fishing Club, Phi Eta Sigma, Omicron Delta Kappa, Phi Delta Phi. Home: Route 1 1949 Henry Rd Hemingway SC 29554-9725 Office: PO Box PO Box 218 Hemingway SC 29554-0218

CHANEY, JOHN LESTER, JR. lawyer; b. Sept. 20, 1926; s. John Lester and Gertrude Frances (Dunn) C.; m. Joan Theresa Muren, Sept. 10, 1955; children: John Robert, Catherine Ann, Donald Jeffrey, Ann Margaret. BA, George Washington U., 1953; LLB, 1957. Bar: Md. 1961. Tax law specialist IRS, Washington, 1957-61; atty. ICC, 1961-74; asst. chief atty., 1969-74; chief atty., interpretations, 1975-92; sr. spl. asst. office of compliance and consumer assistance, 1992-94. Pres. Seabrook Park Citizens Assn., Lanham, Md., 1961-63, St. Matthias PTA, Lanham, 1971-72. Served to lt. USN, 1953-55. Recipient Disting. Svc. award George Washington U. Gen. Alumni Assn., 1984. Mem. Md. Bar Assn., Nat. Law Assn. of George Washington U. Nat. Law Ctr., Gen. Alumni Assn. George Washington U. (sec. governing bd. 1982-84, pres. Columbian Coll. Assn., 1986-88, v.p. 1990-92, pres. 1992-96, immediate past pres. 1996—), George Washington U. Club (dir. 1983-84) (Washington). Roman Catholic. Home: 6954 Inverness Ct New Market MD 21774 Office: ICC 12th And Constitution Ave NW Washington DC 20423-0001

CHANG, JANICE MAY, lawyer, administrator, notary public; b. Loma Linda, Calif., May 24, 1970; d. Belden Shiu-Wah (dec.) and Sylvia (Tan) C. BA, cert. paralegal studies, Calif. State U., 1990, cert. creative writing, 1991; JD, LaSalle U., 1993; D in Naturopathy, Clayton Sch. Natural Healing, 1993; MS in Psychology, Calif. Coast U., 1997; PhD in Bus. Adminstrn., Columbia State U., 1997; DFA in Creative Writing: Poetry, Am. Internat. U., 1999. Notary pub., Calif. Victim/witness contact clk.-paralegal Dist. Atty.'s Office Victim/Witness Assistance Program, San Bernardino, Calif., 1990; gen. counsel JMC Enterprises, Inc., Riverside, 1993—; law prof. LaSalle U., Mandeville, La., 1994-97; corp. counsel, CFO, JDS Assocs., Inc., Loma Linda, 1998-99; corp. counsel, CFO DJS, L.P., 1998-99; with trust mgmt.-legal dept./trust svcs. Southeastern Calif. Conf. Seventh-Day Adventists, Riverside, 1998—. Spkr. Internat. U. Graduation Ceremony/Conv., Las Vegas, 1998; sponsor La Sierra U. Student Employment Recognition Banquet, Riverside, Calif., 1999, 2000, La Sierra U. Path of the Just Tree Project, 1998, vol. La Sierra U., Riverside, Ca. Health Fair Expo, 1988, 89, Am. Red Cross First Aid & CPR classes, 1994—. Contbr. poetry to anthologies, including Am. Poetry Anthology, 1987-90, The Pacific Rev., 1991, The Piquant, 1991, River of Dreams, 1994, Reflections of Light, 1994, Musings, 1994 (Honorable Mention award 1994), Best Poems of 1995 (Celebrating Excellence award 1995, Inspirations award 1995), Am. Poetry Annual, 1996, 99, Best New Poems of 1996, Interludes, 1996, Meditations, 1996, Perspectives, 1996 (Honorable Mention award 1996), Keepsakes, 1997 (Honorable Mention award 1997), Best Poems of 1997, Poetic Voices of America, 1997, The Isle of View, 1997, The Other Side of Midnight, 1997, Treasures, 1998, Best Poems of 1998, Writingscapes: Insights & Approaches to Creative Writing, 1998, Am. Poetry Ann., 1999, Mirrors, 1999 (Pres.'s Lit. Excellence award), America at the Millennium, 2000, Nature's Echoes, 2001; contbr. to photog. anthologies Tapestry of Dreams to Internat. Libr. Photography, 1999, Mystical Seasons to Internat. Libr. Photography, 1999, Candid Captures to Internat. Libr. Photography, 2001. Donor Loma Linda Indonesian SDA Ch. Belden S. Chang Meml. Fund-Bldg. Annex, 1998—. Recipient Poet of Merit award Am. Poetry Assn., San Francisco, 1989, Golden Poet award World of Poetry, Washington, 1989, Publisher's Choice award Watermark Press, 1990, Editor's Choice award The Nat. Libr. of Poetry, 1990-97, Pres.'s award for lit. excellence Iliad Press, 1995-97. Mem. APA, ATLA, Nat. Bar Assn., Nat. Notary Assn. Republican. Seventh-Day Adventist. Avocations: poetry writing, photography, music, drama, literature, numismatics. General corporate, Estate planning, Landlord-tenant. Home: 1025 Crestbrook Dr Riverside CA 92506-5662 Office: Southeastern Calif Conf 7th-Day Adventists PO Box 8050 11330 Pierce St Riverside CA 92515-8050 E-mail: ChangJM@secc-sda.org

CHANG, LEE-LEE, lawyer; b. Taipei, Taiwan, May 26, 1954; came to U.S., 1986; parents: T.S. and B.H. (Ong) C. LLB, Nat. Chung Hsing U., Taipei, 1976; JD, CUNY, 1990. Bar: N.Y. 1990. Chinese law specialist Stephen S. Lee & Assocs., Taipei, 1981-86; tchg. asst. CUNY Law Sch., Flushing, 1989-90; assoc. Wise, Lerman & Katz, P.C., N.Y.C., 1990-93; pvt. practice Flushing, 1994—. Cons. Dorcas & Kalam Co., Hicksville, N.Y., 1994—; adv. bd. mem. Chgo. Title Ins. Co., Garden City, N.Y., 1996—. Co-author: A Practical Usage Guide to Commercial Papers in R.O.C., 1983, Chinese Businessman's Guide to American Law-Business Practice-Taxation, 1993. Mem. Christian Legal Soc. Avocations: tennis, golf, traveling, swimming, reading. Contracts commercial, Probate, Real property. Office: 13621 Roosevelt Ave 3d Fl Flushing NY 11354-5507 E-mail: leeleechangesq@hotmail.com

CHANG, TA-KUANG, lawyer; b. Taipei, Taiwan, May 1, 1955; came to U.S., 1969; s. Tien-ding and Chih-chih (Lee) C.; m. Michele Cone, May 29, 1983; children: Ariane, Morgane. AB, Harvard U., 1977, MBA, JD, Harvard U., 1983; MA, Yale U., 1979. Bar: N.Y. 1984. Assoc. Milbank, Tweed, Hadley, McCloy, N.Y.C., 1983-84, Paul, Weiss, Rifkind, Wharton,

Beijing, N.Y.C., 1984-89, Latham & Watkins, N.Y.C., 1989-91; ptnr. Marks & Murase, 1991-96; Asia counsel Kaye, Scholer, Fierman, Hays & Handler, 1996-97; sr. fgn. legal cons. Allen & Overy, N.Y.C., 1997-98; ptnr. Coudert Bros., N.Y.C. and Hong Kong, 1998—. Co-author: Taxation in PRC, 1985, 87, 89; contbr. articles to profl. jours. Mem. ABA. General corporate, Finance, Private international. Office: Coudert Bros Swiss Bank Tower 1114 Ave of the Americas New York NY 10036-7710

CHANIN, JEFFREY, lawyer; b. Bklyn., Oct. 10, 1940; s. Louis and Julia (Levine) C.; m. Elizabeth Ann, June 15, 1963 (div. 1983); children: Joseph Robert, Jane Louise; m. Kristin Blaire, Dec. 17, 1983. AB, Bklyn. Coll., 1962; JD, Harvard U., 1965. Bar: Calif. 1966, U.S. Supreme Ct. 1967. Assoc. and ptnr. Statman, Treister & Glatt, L.A., 1965-77, of counsel, 1979-82; sr. v.p. and dir. Daylin Inc., L.A., 1977-79; pres. Handy Dan/Angels, L.A., 1978-79; exec. v.p. Wickes Cos., Inc., Santa Monica, Calif., 1982-84, also bd. dirs.; pres. Chamin & Co., 1984-87; mng. dir. Drexel Burnham Lambert Mdse., 1987—. Office: 131 S Rodeo Dr Beverly Hills CA 90212-2402

CHANIN, MICHAEL HENRY, lawyer; b. Atlanta, Nov. 11, 1943; s. Henry and Herma Irene (Blumenthal) C.; m. Margaret L. Jennings, June 15, 1968; children: Herma Louise, Richard Henry, Patrick Jennings. A.B., U. N.C., 1965; J.D., Emory U., 1968. Bar: Ga. 1968, D.C. 1981. Dir. So. Ctr. for Studies in Pub. Policy, Atlanta, 1968-69; asst. and acting legal officer 1st Coast Guard Dist., Boston, 1969-72; atty. Powell, Goldstein Frazer & Murphy, Atlanta, 1972-77; spl. asst. to sec. U.S. Dept. Commerce, Washington, 1977-78; dep. asst. to pres. The White House, 1978-81; ptnr. Powell, Goldstein, Frazer & Murphy, 1981—. Served to lt. USCGR, 1969-72. Mem. ABA, D.C. Bar Assn., State Bar Ga. Democrat. General corporate, Finance, Private international. Office: Powell Goldstein Frazer & Murphy 1001 Pennsylvania Ave NW Fl 6 Washington DC 20004-2505

CHANNICK, HERBERT S. lawyer, arbitrator, mediator; b. Phila., Aug. 27, 1929; s. Maurice and Rose (Rosenberg) C.; m. Nancy Abarbanel Wolfe, Dec. 1, 1950; children: Joan D., Robert L. AB, U. Ill., 1951; JD, Yale Law Sch., 1954. Assoc. Antonow & Weissbourd, Chgo., 1957 59; ptnr. Mct. Investment Co., 1960—. Mem. adv. bd. Ill. State Hist. Soc.; mem. Highland Park (Ill.) Planning Commn., 1972—74, Ill. Racing Bd., Chgo., 1974—76; bd. dirs. Ctr. for Transcultural Studies, 1977—96, Monmouth (Ill.) Coll., 1973—75. Capt. USAF, 1955—57. Mem. ABA, Am. Arbitration Assn., Ill. State Bar Assn., Abraham Lincoln Assn. Alternative dispute resolution. Home: 6526 Spring Brook Rd #210 Rockford IL 61114-8129 E-mail: hchannick@xta.com

CHAO, CEDRIC C. lawyer; b. Cambridge, Mass., Apr. 9, 1950; BA, Stanford U., 1972; JD, Harvard U., 1977. Bar: Calif. 1977, U.S. Dist. Ct. (no. dist.) Calif. 1977, U.S. Ct. Appeals (9th cir.) 1979, U.S. Supreme Ct. 1988. Law clk.to Hon. William H. Orrick U.S. Dist. Ct. (no. dist.) Calif., San Francisco, 1977-78; asst. U.S. atty. U.S. Atty.'s Office, 1978-81; assoc. Morrison & Foerster, 1981-83, ptnr., 1983—. Lawyer del. 9th cir. judicial conf., 1990-92; chair magistrate judge selection com. No. Dist. Calif., 1996. Author: Creating Your Discovery Plan, 1999. Named One of Calif.'s Top 25 Lawyers Under Age 45, Calif. Law Bus., 1994. Fellow Am. Bar Found.; mem. ABA (standing com. fed. judiciary, 1991-94), State Bar Calif. (com. profl. responsibility and conduct 1980-84, exec. com. litigation sect. 1986-91, vice chair 1989-90, chair 1990-91), San Francisco Bar Assn. (bd. dirs. 1988-90), Am. Law Inst., Asian Am. Bar Assn. Greater Bay Area (bd. dirs. 1977-82, pres. 1982), 9th Judicial Cir. Hist. Soc. (trustee 2000—), San Francisco C. of C. (bd. dirs. 1996-99), Singapore Am. Bus. Assn. (bd. dirs. 1999—, pres. 2001), World Affairs Coun. No. Calif. (trustee 1994-99), Commonwealth Club Calif. (quar. chair 1989). General civil litigation, Criminal, Private international. Office: Morrison & Foerster 425 Market St San Francisco CA 94105-2482 E-mail: cchao@mofo.com

CHAPLIN, ANSEL BURT, lawyer; b. Deerfield, Ill., June 12, 1931; s. Robert Tappan and Ruth (Burt) C.; m. Maud Denise Hazeltine, 1959 (div. 1993); children: Rawson, Margaret, Jane; m. Anne Carol Kenney, 1995. BA magna cum laude, Princeton U., 1953; postgrad., Inst. Polit. Sci., Paris, U. Algiers; JD, Harvard U., 1959. Bar: Mass. 1959. Law clk. to chief justice Mass. Supreme Ct., 1959-60; ptnr. Chaplin & Chaplin, Boston; practice, 1960-99, Cape Cod, Mass., 1981—. Owner Cape Cod Fishnet Industries, North Truro, Mass., 1980-96; chmn. com. legal edn. Mass. Supreme Ct., 1979-90, mem. com. lawyer advt., 1979-82; vice chmn. commn. on legal profession and the economy of New Eng., New Eng. Bd. Higher Edn., 1991; mem. U.S. Dist. Ct. Ad. Practice Com., 1981-85; chmn. vis. com. So. New England Sch. Law, 1992-93. Author papers in field. Pres. Truro Neighborhood Assn., 1979-83; mem. corp. Perkins Sch. for Blind, Watertown, Mass., 1973—, Winsor Sch., Boston, 1980-83; sec., adminstrv. trustee Truro Conservation Trust, 1981—, trustee Payomet Performing Arts Charitable Trust, 1998-2000, Dexter Keezer Cmty. Fund, 1998—; pres. Compact of Cape Cod Conservation Trusts, 1986-2001; pres. Friends of the Pamet, Inc., 1994-96; mem. bd. dirs. Mass. Appleseed Ctr. for Law and Justice, 1994-96; mem. Truro Planning Bd., 2001—. Recipient Thoreau award Cape Cod Mus. Natural History, 1987, Environmental Merit award EPA, 2000; Fulbright fellow, 1953-54 Fellow Am. Bar Found., Mass. Bar Found.; Mem. ABA, Am. Law Inst., Mass. Bar Assn. (chmn. law practice sect. 1978-80), Boston Bar Assn. (co-chair peer support com. 1997—), Harvard Law Sch. Assn. Mass. (pub. interest coord. 1994—), Harvard Law Sch. Assn. (mem. coun. 1997-2000), Wellesley Boat Club, Harvard Club (Boston). Democrat. Unitarian. General civil litigation, Environmental, General practice. Office: 203 S Orleans Rd Orleans MA 02653-4009 E-mail: abchaplin@cs.com

CHAPLIN, DOLCEY ELIZABETH, lawyer; b. Mt. Vernon, N.Y., Apr. 20, 1949; d. John Michael and Angelina Claire (Campanile) De Giacomo; m. James E. Chaplin III, June 24, 1972 (div. Apr. 1987); children: Tara Marie, James E. IV. BA, Ladycliff Coll., Highland Falls, 1971; MA, Wright State U., 1976; JD, Seton Hall U., 1984. Bar: N.J. 1985; cert. tchr., Ohio, N.J., N.Y. Tchr. Dayton (Ohio) Pub. Schs., 1972-75; contracts atty. ITT Avionics, Nutley, N.J., 1985-87; gen. counsel GEC Aerospace Inc., Whippany, 1988-92; contracts cons. ISSC(IBM), White Plains, N.Y., 1993; atty. Amex TRS, N.Y.C., 1994; pvt. practice Ridgewood, N.J., 1994—. Adj. prof. William Paterson U., Wayne, N.J., 1996—; dir. N.J. Inst. Tech., Newark, 1994—; dir. Def. Procurement Ctr., State of N.J., Newark, 1994—. Pro bono work Blessed Sacrament Re-Employment Ctr., Franklin Lakes, N.J., 1993—. N.Y. State Regents scholar, 1967. Mem. Nat. Contract Mgmt. Assn. (cert., nat. dir., chpt. v.p. 1994—), N.J. Assn. Women Bus. Owners (state chair 1996—). Avocation: biking. Administrative and regulatory, Government contracts and claims. Home: 448 Fairfield Ave Ridgewood NJ 07450-1838 Office: New Jersey Inst Tech DPTAC 240 Martin Luther King Blvd Newark NJ 07102

CHAPLIN, PEGGY LOUIE, lawyer; b. Guantanamo Bay Naval Base, Cuba, Nov. 22, 1940; d. Raymond Gerard Fannon and Joan Marie (Carguil) Boyce. BS, Johns Hopkins U., 1971; JD, U. Md., 1973; LLM in Internat. Comml. Law, Georgetown U., 1983. Bar: Md. 1973, U.S. Dist. Ct. Md. 1973, U.S. Ct. Internat. Trade 1975, U.S. Ct. Appeals (fed. cir.) 1986, (D.C. cir.) 1988. V.p. Vanguard Shipping & Import, Balt., 1972-77, F.W. Myers & Co., Inc., Balt., 1977-84; assoc. Ober, Kaler, Grimes & Shriver, 1984-91, ptnr., 1992-97, Sandler, Travis & Rosenberg, P.A., Balt., 1997—. Chair Johns Hopkins U. Inst. of Policy Studies com. Logistics and the Economy, 1996-99. Contbr. articles to bar jours. Mem. Gov.'s Commn. World Trade Efforts, 1984, Balt. City Wage Commn., 1986-90, Md. Trade Policy Com., 1986; chair 2d Ann. Md. Internat. Trade Conf.; chair air cargo devel. com. BWI Econ. Devel. Coun., 1993-96. Mem. NAFTA (chpt. 19 roster), Md. State Bar Assn. (chair internat. comml. law sect. 1991-92), Women's Bar Assn. Md. (pres. 1977-78), Md. Internat. Trade Assn. (pres. 1984-86), Md. C. of C. (chmn. internat. trade com. 1984-97), Am. Arbitration Assn. (panelist), Am. Assn. Exporters and Importers (chmn. logistics com.). Immigration, naturalization, and customs, Private international, Transportation. Office: Sandler Travis & Rosenberg PA 111 S Calvert St Ste 2700 Baltimore MD 21202-6143 E-mail: pchaplin@strtrade.com

CHAPMAN, CONRAD DANIEL, lawyer; b. Detroit, July 31, 1933; s. Conrad F. and Alexandrine C. (Baranski) C.; m. Carol Lynn DeBash, Sept. 1, 1956; children: Stephen Daniel, Richard Thomas, Suzanne Marie. BA, U. Detroit, 1954, JD summa cum laude, 1957; LLM in Taxation, Wayne State U., 1964. Bar: Mich. 1957, U.S. Dist. Ct. (so. dist.) Mich. 1957. Pres., chmn. bd. dirs. Powers, Chapman, DeAgostino, Meyers & Milia and predecessor firms, Troy, Mich., 1964—. Mem. ABA, Detroit Bar Assn., Oakland Bar Assn., Am. Arbitration Assn., Met. Detroit Estate Planning Coun., Nat. Assn. Estate Planning Coun., Detroit Athletic Club, Detroit Golf Club, Elks. General corporate, Estate planning, Corporate taxation. Office: Powers Chapman DeAgostino Meyers & Milia 3001 W Big Beaver Rd Ste 704 Troy MI 48084-3108

CHAPMAN, ROBERT FOSTER, federal judge; b. Inman, S.C., Apr. 24, 1926; s. James Alfred and Martha (Marshall) C.; m. Mary Winston Gwathmey, Dec. 21, 1951 (dec. Sept. 1998); children: Edward, Foster, Winston; m. Mary Vail St. Georges, Sept. 30, 2000. BS, U. S.C., 1945, LLB, 1949, LLD (hon.), 1986, Coll. Charleston, 1999. Bar: S.C. 1949. Asso. firm Butler & Moore, Spartanburg, 1949-51; partner firm Butler, Chapman & Morgan, 1953-71; U.S. dist. judge for S.C., 1971-81; U.S. cir. judge, 1981—. Chmn. S.C. Republican Party, 1961-63. Served to lt. USNR, 1943-46, 51-53. Recipient Nat. Patriot's award Congl. Medal of Honor Soc., 1985 Fellow Am. Coll. Trial Lawyers. Presbyn. (ruling elder). Home: PO Box 1043 Camden SC 29020-1043

CHAPOTON, JOHN EDGAR, lawyer, government official; b. Galveston, Tex., May 18, 1936; s. Otis Byron and Grace Donaldson (Wayman) C.; m. Sarah Eastham, Jan. 5, 1963; children: John Edgar, Clare Eastham. Student, Washington and Lee U., 1954-55; BBA with honors, U. Tex., 1958, LLB with honors, 1960. Bar: Tex. 1960, D.C. 1985. Assoc. Andrews, Kurth, Campbell & Jones, Houston, 1961-69; with Dept. Treasury, Washington, 1969-72, 81-84, tax legis. counsel, 1970-72, asst. sec. for tax policy, 1981-84; ptnr. Vinson & Elkins, Houston, 1972-81, mng. ptnr. Washington, 1984-01; ptnr. Brown Investment Adv. & Trust Co., 2001—. Chmn. law firms div. United Way Capital Area, Washington, 1988-90; bd. dirs. Boys and Girls Clubs Greater Washington, 1990—. Recipient Achievement award Tax Soc. NYU, 1984. Fellow Am. Coll. Tax Counsel; mem. ABA (sect. taxation, vice chair govt. rels.), Tex. State Bar Assn., D.C. Bar Assn., Am. Law Inst. Republican. Episcopalian. Avocations: golf. Corporate taxation, Taxation, general, Personal income taxation. Office: Vinson & Elkins LLP 1455 Pennsylvania Ave NW Washington DC 20004-1008

CHAPPARS, TIMOTHY STEPHEN, lawyer; b. Cin., July 23, 1952; s. Gregory S. and Helen (Maragos) C.; m. Laurie A. Kress, Dec. 24, 1986 (div. Sept. 1987); m. Laurie A. Kress, Apr. 18, 1990; children: Alexander T., Jake A. BS, Duke U., 1974; JD, U. Cin., 1978. Assoc. Cox & Chappars, Xenia, Ohio, 1978-94, Bryant Law Office, Wilmington, 1981—. Trial atty. Pub. Defender's Office, Clinton County, Wilmington, 1978-88; lectr. So. State Jr. Coll., Wilmington, 1982. Mem. Ohio Bar Assn., Am. Trial Lawyers Acad., Ohio Acad. Trial Lawyers. Methodist. Avocations: tennis, piano, hiking, cycling, skiing. Criminal, Personal injury. Home: 2025 Winding Brook Way Xenia OH 45385-9382 Office: PO Box 280 Xenia OH 45385-0280

CHAPPELL, MILTON LEROY, lawyer; b. Accra, Ghana, Mar. 25, 1951; (parents Am. citizens); s. Derwood Lee and Helen Jean (Freeman) C.; m. Margot Cecelia Shields, Dec. 18, 1972; children: Marton Gerald, Monet Louise. BA summa cum laude, Columbia Union Coll., 1973; JD, Cath. U., 1976; diploma, Nat. Inst. Trial Advocacy, Boulder, Colo., 1978; cert., U. Miami, 1982. Bar: Md. 1976, D.C. 1977, U.S. Ct. Appeals (4th, 5th, 9th and D.C. cirs.) 1977, U.S. Dist. Ct. D.C. 1978, U.S. Ct. Appeals (6th cir.) 1979, U.S. Supreme Ct. 1980, U.S. Ct. Appeals (11th cir.) 1981, U.S. Dist. Ct. Md. 1982, U.S. Ct. Appeals (7th cir.) 1988, U.S. Dist. Ct. (no. dist.) Calif., 1990, U.S. Ct. Appeals (3rd cir.) 2000. Sole practice, Silver Spring, Md., 1976—; staff atty. Nat. Right to Work Legal Def. Found., Springfield, Va., 1976—. Lectr. Columbia Union Coll., Takoma Park, Md., 1976-77; legal cons. JNA Elem. Sch., Takoma Park, 1980-83; gen. counsel Playgrounds Unltd., Inc., 1988-2000, Internat. Play Equipment Mfrs. Assn., Inc., 1995—, Park Dreams Internat., Ltd., 2000—; participant play settings subcom. recreation access adv. com. U.S. Archtl. and Transp. Barriers Compliance Bd., 1993-94. Contbr. to Ohio No. U. Law Rev., Govt. Union Rev., Calif. Pub. Employee Rels. Mem. Hillandale Civic Assn., Silver Spring, 1980—; legal cons., bd. dirs. Silver Spring Seventh-day Adventist Ch., 1976-84, Takoma Park.; participant U.S. Arch. and Trans. Barriers Compliance Bd., Recreation Access Adv. Com., Play Settings subcom., 1993-94. Mem. ABA, Md. Bar Assn. D.C. Bar Assn. Federal civil litigation, General practice, Labor. Home: 10321 Royal Rd Silver Spring MD 20903-1616 Office: Nat Right to Work Legal Def Found 8001 Braddock Rd # 600 Springfield VA 22151-2110 E-mail: mlc@nrtw.org

CHAR, VERNON FOOK LEONG, lawyer; b. Honolulu, Dec. 15, 1934; s. Charles A. and Annie (Ching) C.; m. Evelyn Lau, June 14, 1958; children: Richard, Daniel, Douglas, Charles, Elizabeth. BA, U. Hawaii, 1956; LLB, Harvard U., 1959. Bar: Hawaii 1959. Dep. atty. gen. Office of Atty. Gen., Honolulu, 1959-60, 62-65; ptnr. Damon Key Char & Bocken, 1965-89, Char, Sakamoto, Ishii, Lum & Ching, Honolulu, 1989—. Chmn. Hawaii Ethics Commn., Honolulu, 1968-75, Hawaii Bicentennial Com., 1986-91, 1st Hawaii Jud. Conf., 1985. Mem. ABA (bd. govs. 1991-94), Hawaii Bar Assn. (pres. 1985), U. Hawaii Alumni Assn. (pres. 1989-90). Antitrust, Aviation, General corporate. Home: 351 Anonia St Honolulu HI 96821-2052 Office: Char Sakamoto Ishii Lum & Ching Davies Pacific Ctr 841 Bishop St Ste 850 Honolulu HI 96813-3957 E-mail: vflchar@lawcsilc.com

CHARLES, ROBERT BRUCE, lawyer; b. Portsmouth, Va., Aug. 23, 1960; s. Roland Wilbur Charles Jr. and Doris Anne (Hassell) Barbineau; m. Marina Timasheff, Oct. 16, 1988; 1 child, Nicholas Westcote. AB, Dartmouth Coll., 1982; MA, Oxford U., 1984; JD, Columbia U., 1987. Bar: N.Y. 1989, Conn. 1989, Maine 1990. Law clk. to judge U.S. Ct. Appeals (9th cir.), Seattle, 1987-88; assoc. Kramer, Levin et al, N.Y.C., 1988-91, Weil, Gotshal & Manges, N.Y.C., 1991-92, Washington, 1993-95; dep. assoc. dir. office of policy devel The White House, 1992-93; chief staff, chief counsel nat. security, internat. affairs and criminal justice subcommittee U.S. Ho. of Reps., 1995-99; chief staffer Speaker's Task Force on Drug Free Am., 1997-99; prof. govt. and cyberlaw Harvard U. Extension Sch., 1998—; pres. Direct Impact, L.L.C., 1999—. Summer assoc. The White House, Washington, 1982-84, Supreme Ct. India, 1985. Contbr. articles to profl. jours., chpts. to books. Active Coun. on Fgn. Rels. Theodore Roosevelt Assn. Officer USNR, 1998—. Keasbey scholar, Phila. 1982, Tony Patino fellow Columbia U., 1984; recipient Petra T. Shattuck Disting. Tchg. award Harvard U., 2000. Republican. Avocations: distance running, cycling, hiking, writing. E-mail: RCharlesZZ@aol.com

CHARNEY, JONATHAN ISA, legal educator, lawyer; b. N.Y.C., Oct. 29, 1943; s. Wolfe R. and Rita Dorothy (Greenfield) C.; m. Sharon Renee Lehman, June 12, 1966; children— Tamar, Adam, Noah. B.A., NYU, 1965; J.D., U. Wis., 1968. Bar: Wis. 1968-93, Tenn. 1974, N.Y. 1980, U.S. Supreme Ct. 1971. Atty. Land and Natural Resources div. Dept. Justice, Washington, 1968-71, chief marine resources sect., 1972; asst. prof. law Vanderbilt U., Nashville, 1972-75, assoc. prof., 1975-78, prof., 1978— ; cons. in field; vis. prof. U. Pa., 1989. Bd. editors Wis. Law Rev., 1966-68. Mem. ABA (chair internat. law sect. internat. cts. com. 1988-89, dep. vice chair sect. on internat. law, pub. internat. law div. 1988-90), Am. Br. Internat. Law Assn. (chair com. on formation of internat. law 1986-90), Coun. Fgn. Rels., Woods Hole Oceanographic Inst., Marine Policy Ctr. (sr. advisors com. 1987-96, chair 1991-96), Am. Law Inst., Am. Soc. Internat. Law (exec. council 1982-85, v.p. 1994-96), Ocean Devel. and Internat. Law (bd. editors 1985—, editor-in-chief 1998—), Am. Jour. Internat. Law. (bd. editors 1986—, editor-in-chief 1998—), Assn. Am. Law Schs. (chmn. internat. law sect. 1985), Internat. Boundary Rsch. Unit (mem. bd. adv. 1993—), Order of Coif. Contbr. numerous articles to profl. jours. Office: Vanderbilt U 131 21st Ave S Ste 207 Nashville TN 37215-6706

CHASANOW, DEBORAH K. federal judge; b. 1948; BA, Rutgers U., 1970; JD, Stanford U., 1973. Pvt. practice atty. COle & Groner, Washington, 1975; asst. atty. gen. State of Md., 1975-79; chief criminal appeals divsn. Md. Atty. Gen.'s Office, 1979-87; U.S. magistrate judge U.S. Dist. Ct. Md., 1987-93, dist. judge, 1993—. Instr. law schs. U. Balt., U. Md., 1978-84. Mem. Fed. Magistrate Judges Assn., Md. Bar Assn., Prince George's County Bar Assn., Women's Bar Assn., Marlborough Am. Inn. Ct. (pres. 1988-90), Phi Beta Kappa. Office: US Courthouse 6500 Cherrywood Ln Rm 465A Greenbelt MD 20770-1249

CHASANOW, HOWARD STUART, retired judge, lecturer; b. Washington, Apr. 3, 1937; 1 child from previous marriage, Andrea; m. Deborah Hovis Koss, May 15, 11983. BA, U. Md., 1959, JD, 1961; LLM, Harvard U., 1962. Bar: Md. 1961, U.S. Supreme Ct. 1965. Asst. states atty. Prince George County, Upper Marlboro, Md., 1963-64, dep. states atty., 1964-67; judge Dist. Ct., 1971-77, 7th Jud. Cir., 1977-90, Ct. Appeals of Md., 1990-99, ret., 1999. Lectr. Sch. Law U. Md., Balt., 1973—, Nat. Jud. Coll., Reno, 1980—, Am. Acad. Jud. Edn., 1984—; founder Prince George's County Drinking Driving Sch.; chmn. adv. bd. Sentencing Guidelines, Md., 1982-90, chmn. jud. adminstrn. sect., 1982-84; mem. Md. Commn. on Criminal Sentencing Policy, 1996—; mem. standing com. on rules of practice and procedure Ct. Appeals, 1985-90; mem. govs. task force to Revise Criminal Code, 1992—. Contbr. law rev. articles. Served with USAF, 1968-69. Office: Ct Appeals Md Prince George County Courthouse PO Box 399 Upper Marlboro MD 20773-0399

CHASE, ERIC LEWIS, lawyer; b. Princeton, N.J., Sept. 21, 1946; s. Harold William and Bernice Mae (Fadden) C.; m. Jamie Campbell, Dec. 29, 1979; children: Eric Campbell, Kathryn Dianne, John Harold. BA, Princeton U., 1968; JD cum laude, U. Minn., 1974. Bar: N.J. 1974, D.C. 1975, U.S. Ct. Appeals (3d cir.) 1979, U.S. Supreme Ct. 1981, U.S. Claims Ct. 1982, U.S. Tax Ct. 1982, N.Y. 1983. Trial atty. FCC, 1974-78; asst. U.S. atty. Dist. N.J., Newark, 1978-80; ptnr. Margolis Chase, Verona, N.J., 1980-90, Hannoch Weisman, Roseland, 1990-93, Bressler, Amery & Ross, Florham Park, 1993—. Prof. law of war Marine Corps Command and Staff Coll., Quantico, Va., 1990-99. Author: Automobile Dealers and the Law, 1994, 7th edit., 2000; contbr. articles on law and mil. to profl. publs., including N.Y. Times, Washington Post, Newsweek mag. With USMC, 1968-71; col. Res., ret. Mem. ABA (mem. task force on internat. criminal ct.), N.J. State Bar Assn. (franchise com 1997—, co-chair franchise com. 1999-2001). General civil litigation, Communications, Franchising. Office: Bressler Amery & Ross 325 Columbia Tpke Ste 8 Florham Park NJ 07932-1212 E-mail: echase@bressler.com

CHASE, JONATHON B. law school dean, educator; b. Orange, N.J., June 6, 1939; s. David Boyd and Lillian (Reuben) C.; m. Nancy Markey, June 25, 1961; children— Tamara, Adam, Rebecca, Eli. B.A., Williams Coll., Williamstown, Mass., 1961; LL.B. cum laude, Columbia U., 1964. Bar: N.Y. 1964, Colo. 1969, U.S. Dist. Ct. (D.C. dist.), U.S. Dist. Ct. Colo., U.S. Ct. Appeals (10th cir.), U.S. Supreme Ct. Asst. prof. law Boston U., 1965-66; prof. law U. Colo., Boulder, 1966-82; exec. dir. Colo. Rural Legal Services, 1969-72; dean, prof. Sch. of Law, Vt. Law Sch., South Royalton, 1982—. Contbr. articles to profl. jours. Bd. dirs. Colo. br. ACLU, 1975-82, ACLU, Vt., 1982—, Vt. Planned Parenthood, 1982-84, Vt. Legal Aid, 1984—. Mem. ABA, Vt. Bar Assn. Democrat. Jewish. Home: PO Box 684 Norwich VT 05055-0684 Office: Vt Law Sch South Royalton VT 05068

CHASE, OSCAR G(OTTFRIED), law educator, consultant, author; s. Sidney and Helen G. Chase; m. Jane Monell, June 12, 1969; children: Arlo M., Oliver G. BA (hon.), NYU, 1960; JD, Yale U., 1963. Bar: N.Y. 1963, U.S. Dist. Ct. (so. and ea. dists.) N.Y. 1968, U.S. Ct. Appeals (2nd cir.) 1970, U.S. Supreme Ct. 1972, U.S. Ct. Appeals (D.C. cir.) 1975. Staff mem voter edn. project SNCC, Jackson, Miss., 1963-64; counsel Lower West Side Cmty. Corp., N.Y.C., 1966-67; lawyer M.F.Y. Legal Svcs., Inc., 1967-68; asst. gen. counsel, dir. law reform, 1968-72; prof. law Bklyn. Law Sch., 1972-78; vis. prof. law NYU, 1978-79; prof. law, 1979—. Assoc. dean law sch., 1990-94, vice dean law sch., 1994-99. Author: CPLR Manmual, rev. edit., 1980, Civil Litigation in New York, 1983, end. edit., 1990, 3d edit., 1996, New York Practice Guide: Negligence, 4 vols., 1989; co-author: Cases and Materials on Civil Procedure, 1987; contbr. New York Practice, bi-monthly column for N.Y. Law Jour., 1982-84; contbr. articles to profl. jours. Bd. dirs. Untapped Resources, Inc., 1970—81; mem. adv. com. ACLU Reproductive Freedom Project, 1977—82; mem. civil litigation com. Ea. Dist. N.Y.; mem. joint AALS, ABA, Law Sch. Admission Coun. on Fin. Aid, 1991—94; bd. dirs. Inst. Judicial Adminstrn., 1992, co-exec. dir., 2000—. Office: NYU Sch Law 40 Washington Sq S New York NY 10012-1099

CHASTAIN, MERRITT BANNING, JR. lawyer; b. Jan. 28, 1940; s. Merritt Banning and Lydia (Spock) Chastain; m. Virginia Anne Ferguson, July 21, 1962; children: Merritt Banning III, Grayson Anne Clark. BS, U. Okla., 1962; JD, La. State U., 1967. Bar: La. 1967, U.S. Dist. Ct. (we. dist.) La. 1968, U.S. Dist. Ct. (ea. dist.) La. 1972, U.S. Ct. Appeals (5th cir.) 1972, U.S. Supreme Ct. 1979. Law clk. La. Ct. Appeals (2d cir.), Shreveport, La., 1967—68; assoc. Smitherman, Lunn, Chastain & Hill, 1968—72, ptnr., 1972—. Mng. dir. Nat. Assn. of Pipe Coating Applicators, 1979—; spl. counsel La. Pub. Facilities Authority, 1985—87. Chmn. United Way of Shreveport/Bossier City, 1975, Ark.-La.-Tex. Ambs., Inc., 1989; pres. Vols. Am., 1976, Norwela Coun. Boy Scouts Am., 1977—78, Demoiselle Club, 1992, Cotillion Gov. Bd., 1989, Shreveport Opera, 1981—95, sec., 1981; trustee Loyola Coll. Prep. Sch., 1984—89, exec. com., 1985—89, pres. bd. trustees, 1986—87; chmn. bd. Loyola Found., Shreveport, La., 1987—88; corp. sponsor chmn. Arthritis Found. Telethon, 1990. Named Outstanding Young Man of La., La. Jaycees, 1975, Outstanding Young Man of Shreveport, Shreveport Jaycees, 1975. Mem.: ABA (La. mem. chmn. 1976—82), La. State Bar Assn. (spl. com. 1974—75), Shreveport Bar Assn. (exec. coun. 1971—75, sec.-treas. 1972, bd. govs. young lawyer's sect. 1967—74, pres. young lawyer's sect. 1974), La. Law Inst., Shreveport Club, Rotary, So. Trace Country Club (Shreveport). Democrat. Episcopalian. Contracts commercial, Estate planning, Real property. Home: 330 Corinne Cir Shreveport LA 71106-6004 Office: Smitherman Lunn Chastain & Hill 333 Texas St Ste 717 Shreveport LA 71101-3673

CHATIGNY, ROBERT NEIL, judge; b. 1951; AB, Brown U., 1973; JD, Georgetown U., 1978. Atty. Williams & Connolly, Washington, 1981-83; ptnr. Chatigny and Palmer, Hartford, Conn., 1984-86, Chatigny & Cowdery, Hartford, 1991-94; pvt. practice, 1986-90; dist. judge U.S. Dist. Ct., Conn., 1994—. Office: 450 Main St Hartford CT 06103-3022

CHATOFF, MICHAEL ALAN, lawyer; b. N.Y.C., Aug. 18, 1946; s. Alexander Zelig and Leona Rhoda (Weiss) C. BA, CUNY, 1967; JD, Bklyn. Law Sch., 1971; LLM, NYU, 1978. Bar: N.Y. 1971, U.S. Dist. Ct. (so. and ea. dists.) N.Y. 1978, U.S. Ct. Appeals (2d cir.) 1980, U.S. Supreme Ct. 1980. Reader Chgo. Title Ins. Co., N.Y.C., 1972; chief U.S. Code Congl. and Adminstrv. News West Pub. Co., Westbury, N.Y., 1972-97. Cons. N.Y. Sch. for Deaf, N.Y.C. Mayor's Office for Disabled, Westchester County Legis.; lectr. N.Y. State Dept. of Edn. Vocat. Ednl. Svcs. for Individuals with Disabilities, N.Y. Sch. Deaf, Lexington Sch. for Deaf, Parents for Deaf Awareness, Am. Profl. Soc. for Deaf, N.Y. Ctr. for Law and the Deaf, Coun. on Jewish Deaf Edn. and Rehab., Nat. Coun. on Deaf People and Deafness, NYU. Assoc. law editor Ency. on Deaf People and Deafness; contbr. articles to Nat. Law Jour., N.Y. Law Jour., Able Adv., Communication Outlook, Deaf Spectrum. Bd. dirs. Westchester Cmty. Svcs. for Hearing Impaired; counsel Conn. African-Am. Deaf Advocate; mem. Supreme Ct. Hist. Soc.; del. nominee Dem. Nat. Conv., 1992. Mem. ABA, Queens County Bar Assn., Assn. of Bar of City of N.Y., Nat. Assn. Deaf, Am. Contract Bridge League, Nassau Bar Assn. Avocations: bridge, jogging, weight-lifting. Civil rights, Education and schools, Legislative. Home: 26909T Grand Central Pkwy Floral Park NY 11005-1010

CHATROO, ARTHUR JAY, lawyer; b. N.Y.C., July 1, 1946; s. George and Lillian (Leibowitz) C.; m. Christina Daly, Aug. 6, 1994; 1 child, Alexander. BChemE, CCNY, 1968; JD cum laude, New York Law Sch., 1979; MBA with distinction, NYU, 1982. Bar: N.Y. 1980, Ohio 1992, Calif. 1993, U.S. Patent Office 1998. Process engr. Std. Oil Co. of Ohio, various locations, 1968-73; process specialist BP Oil, Inc., Marcus Hook, Pa., 1974-75; sr. process engr. Sci. Design Co., Inc., N.Y.C., 1975-78; mgr. spl. projects The Halcon SD Group, 1978-82; corp. counsel, tax and fin. The Lubrizol Corp., Wickliffe, Ohio, 1982-85, sr. counsel spl. investment projects, 1989-90; gen. counsel Lubrizol Enterprises, Inc., 1985-89; chmn. Correlation Genetics Corp., San Jose, Calif., 1990-91; gen. counsel Agrigenetics Co., Eastlake, Ohio, 1990-92; gen. counsel, dir. comml. contracting Agrigenetics, L.P., San Diego, 1992-93; counsel Agrigenetics, Inc. dba Mycogen Seeds, Mycogen Corp., 1994-97; dir. legal affairs Mycogen Corp., 1997-98; exec. v.p. bus. devel., legal and regulatory affairs Global Agro, Inc., Encinitas, Calif., 1998-99; exec. v.p., gen. counsel Akkadix Corp., San Diego, 1999—. Mem. Met. Parks Adv. com., Allen County, Ohio, 1973. Mem. ABA, AIChE, Am. Chem. Soc., N.Y. State Bar Assn., San Deigo County Bar Assn., Am. Corp. Counsel Assn., Jaycees (personnel dir. Lima, Ohio chpt. 1972-73), Licensing Execs. Soc., Toastmasters, Omega Chi Epsilon, Beta Gamma Sigma. Club: Toastmasters. Avocations: sailing, photography, skiing. General corporate, Intellectual property, Private international. Home: 3525 Del Mar Hts Rd # 285 San Diego CA 92130-2122 Office: Akkadix Corp Ste A 4204 Sorrento Valley Blvd San Diego CA 92121 E-mail: chatroo@akkadix.com, achatroo@earthlink.net

CHAUVIN, LEONARD STANLEY, JR. lawyer; b. Franklin, Ky., Feb. 13, 1935; s. Leonard Stanley Sr. C.; m. Cecilia McKay; children: Leonard Stanley III, Jacqueline, McKay. Grad., Castle Heights Mil. Acad., 1953; AB in Polit. Sci., U. Ky., 1957; JD, U. Louisville, 1961, LLD (hon.), 1990, Ohio No. U., 1990. Bar: Ky. 1961, U.S. Dist. Ct. (we. dist.) Ky. 1962, U.S. Ct. Appeals (6th cir.) 1964, U.S. Ct. Mil. Appeals 1966, U.S. Ct. Claims 1966, U.S. Supreme Ct. 1966, N.Y. 1983, Ind. 1983, Tenn. 1983, D.C. 1983, U.S. Dist. Ct. (so. and na. dists.) Ind. 1983, U.S. Dist. Ct. D.C. 1983, U.S. Ct. Appeals (7th, D.C. and Fed. cirs.) 1983, U.S. Tax Ct. 1983, U.S. Ct. Internat. Trade 1983, Wis. 1984, U.S. Dist. Ct. (so.and ea. dist.) 1984, U.S. Ct. Appeals (2d cir.) 1984, Fla. 1985, Nebr. 1985, Minn. 1985, Mass. 1986, W.Va. 1986. Assoc. Daniel B. Boone, Louisville, 1962-63, Laurence E. Higgins, Louisville, 1963-68; ptnr. Brown & Chauvin, 1968-78, Carroll, Chauvin, Miller & Conliffe, Louisville, 1978-82; sole practice, 1982-83; ptnr. Barnett & Alagia, 1983-92, Chauvin & White, Louisville, 1992-93, Chauvin & Chauvin, 1993—. Asst. Commonwealth atty. Jefferson County Commonwealth Attys. Office, Louisville, 1962-63; asst. gen. counsel dept. hwys. Commonwealth of Ky., Louisville; judge pro tem Louisville Police Ct.; master commr. Jefferson Cir. Ct., Louisville, 1992—; asst. county atty. of Jefferson County, 1978-87. Chmn. Registry of Election Fin.; mem. Ky. jud. retirement form system, Frankfort, Ky. Fellow Am. Bar Found. (chmn.); mem. ABA (chmn. ho. of dels. 1982-84, pres. 1989-90), Am. Coll. Tax Counsel, Ky. Bar Assn. (Lawyer of Yr. award), Nat. Jud. Coll., Am. Judicature Soc. (pres. 1986-88, Harley award), Am. Coll. Trust and Estate Counsel. Federal civil litigation, State civil litigation, Probate. Home: 1648 Cherokee Rd Louisville KY 40205-1369 Office: 1228 Starks Bldg Louisville KY 40202

CHAVEZ, JOHN ANTHONY, lawyer; b. Auburn, Calif., Oct. 5, 1955; s. Marco Antonio and Barbara Ann (Lawrence) Chavez-Rivas. BA, U. Calif., Santa Barbara, 1977; JD, Stanford U., 1981. Bar: Calif. 1981, Tex. 1982, U.S. Dist. Ct. (so. and no. dists.) Calif. 1982, (cen. dist.) Calif. 1983, U.S. Dist. Ct. (so. dist.) Tex. 1982, (we. dist.) Tex. 1983, (no. dist.) Tex. 1991, N.Y. 1986, U.S. Dist. Ct. (ea. and so. dists.) N.Y. 1986, U.S. Supreme Ct. 1986. With legal dept. Exxon Co. U.S.A., Houston, 1981-85, N.Y.C., 1985-86; assoc. gen. counsel Sybron Corp., Saddlebrook, N.J., 1986-88, Crown Equipment Corp., New Bremen, Ohio, 1989-90; trial atty. Exxon Co. U.S.A., Houston, 1990-92; counsel complex litigation Exxon Chem. Co., 1992-95; counsel internat. oil and gas exploration Exxon Exploration Co., 1995-96; counsel antitrust, mergers and acquisitions Exxon Chem. Co., 1996-2000; counsel intellectual property licensing ExxonMobil Chem. Co., Baytown, Tex., 2000—. Presenter numerous legal edn. seminars and programs. Contbr. articles to profl. jours. Mentor Ft. Bend Ind. Sch. Dist., 1998, Houston Bar Assn., 1998. Chancellor's scholar U. Calif., 1976; Univ. Svc. award for dist. svc. to campus cmty. U. Calif., Santa Barbara, 1977. Fellow Houston Bar Found.; mem. ABA (antitrust, bus. law, and litigation sects., joint venture agreements task force of the negotiated acquisitions com. 1998—, vice chair corp. counseling com. 1998-2000, vice chair intellectual property com. 2000—), Houston Bar Assn. (chair antitrust and trade regulation sect., 1997-98, vice-chair 1996-97, sec.-treas. 1995-96, coun. 1993-95), Wong Sun Soc. Republican. Avocations: hiking, theatre, travel. Antitrust, Federal civil litigation, Trade. Home: 7767 Cambridge St Houston TX 77054-2011 Office: Exxon Chem Co 5200 Bayway Dr Baytown TX 77520-2100 Fax: 281-834-2495. E-mail: anthony.chavez@exxon.com

CHAZEN, HARTLEY JAMES, lawyer; b. N.Y.C., Feb. 14, 1932; s. Joseph and Helen (Jacobson) C.; m. Lois Audrey, Dec. 12, 1967; 1 child, Nicole Joanna. AB, CCNY, 1953; LLB, Harvard U., 1958; LLM, NYU, 1959. Bar: N.Y. 1959. Assoc. Hays, St. John, Abramson & Heilbron, N.Y.C., 1959-65, Shea & Gould, N.Y.C., 1965-68, Rosenman & Colin, N.Y.C., 1968-70; ptnr. Monasch Chazen & Stream, 1970-82; pvt. practice, 1982-88; ptnr. Chazen & Fox, 1988—; of counsel McLaughlin & Stern, 1992-2000, Chazen & Fox, N.Y.C., 2000—. Lectr. in field. Capt. USAR, 1958-68. Mem. Assn. Bar City N.Y. (com. on trademark and unfair competition 1977-80), ABA (subcom. corp. taxation 1987—), Harvard Club. E-mal. Contracts commercial, General practice, Corporate taxation. Home: 75 Perkins Rd Greenwich CT 06830-3510 Office: Chazen & Fox 767 Madison Ave New York NY 10021-6509 E-mail: hchazen@chazenfox.com

CHEATHAM, ROBERT WILLIAM, lawyer; b. St. Paul, June 4, 1938; s. Robert William and Hildegard Frances Cheatam; m. Kay C. Sarnecki, Mar. 20, 1964; children: Ann Marie, Lynn Marie, Paul William BCE, U. Minn., 1961, JD, 1966. Bar: Calif. 1967, U.S. Dist. Ct. (no. dist.) Calif. 1967. Assoc. Brobeck, Phleger & Harrison, San Francisco, 1967-74, ptnr., 1974-88, Cheatham & Skovronski, San Francisco, 1988-96, Cheatham & Tomlinson, San Francisco, 1996-97, Cassidy, Cheatham, Shimko & Dawson, San Francisco, 1997-2000, Foley & Lardner, 2000—. Speaker on continuing legal edn., San Francisco. Co-author: Calif. Attorneys Guide to Real Estate Syndicates, 1970, Cheatham and Merritt California Real Estate Forms and Commentaries, 1984-90. Mem. ABA, Calif. Bar Assn. Real property, Securities. Office: Foley & Lardner 1 Maritime Plz Fl 6 San Francisco CA 94111-3416 E-mail: rcheatham@foleylaw.com

CHEATWOOD, ROY CLIFTON, lawyer; b. Rome, Aug. 27, 1946; s. Herman Arthur and Dorothy Mary (Griffin) C.; m. Cynthia Morrison, June 27, 1969; children: Clifton, Scott, Dancy. BA, U. South Fla., 1968; JD, Tulane U., 1974. Bar: La. 1974, U.S. Dist. Ct. (ea. dist.) La. 1974, U.S. Dist. Ct. (mid. dist.) La. 1975, U.S. Ct. Appeals (5th cir.) 1975, U.S. Dist. Ct. (we. dist.) La. 1977, U.S. Supreme Ct. 1977, U.S. Ct. Appeals (11th cir.) 1981, U.S. Dist. Ct. (no. dist.) Tex. 1990. Assoc. Jones, Walker, Waechter, Poitevent, Carrere & Denegre, New Orleans, 1974-78, ptnr., 1978-91, Phelps Dunbar, New Orleans, 1991—, practice coord., comml. litigation practice group, 1992—, mem. mgmt. com., 1995—. Adj. prof. La. State U., Baton Rouge, 1980, Loyola U., New Orleans, 1981, 84-86; faculty mem. Nat. Inst. Trial Advocacy, 1986—; master barrister Tulane Inn of Ct. Co-author: Louisiana Courtroom Evidence, 1993. Firm campaign rep. United Way, New Orleans, 1982, 98, recruiter, 1983-86, 88, acct. exec. area lawyers, 1989; bd. dirs. Children's Bur., New Orleans, 1988, 1st v.p., 1991, pres., 1993-95; mem. session St. Charles Presbyn. Ch., 1988-91, session New Covenant Presbyterian Church, 2000—, clk. of session, chair pastor-nominating com., 2000—. 1st lt. U.S. Army, 1968-71, Vietnam. Mem. ABA (vice chmn. 5th cir. trial practice com. 1975-76, co-chmn. 1976-78, judge regional nat. appellate adv. com. 1978, co-chmn. ann. litigation meeting 1981, judge nat. appellate adv. competition 1978, membership chmn. litigation sect. 1983-86), La. State Bar Assn. (bd. legal specialization 1998—). Federal civil litigation, State civil litigation, Construction. Office: Phelps Dunbar 365 Canal St Ste 2000 New Orleans LA 70130-6534 E-mail: cheatwood@phelps.com

CHEEK, MICHAEL CARROLL, lawyer; b. Fostoria, Ohio, Aug. 28, 1948; s. Carroll Wright and Mabel A. (Smith) C. BA, Hanover Coll., 1970; JD, U. Cin., 1974. Bar: Ohio 1974, Fla. 1974, U.S. Dist. Ct. (mid. dist.) Fla. 1975. Pub. defender, Clearwater, Fla., 1974-77; lawyer sole practice, 1977—. Vice chmn. bar grievance Clearwater, 1990-94; trustee Pinellas County Law Libr., Clearwater, 1977-92; chmn. Ct. Law Libr., 1982-89. Pres. 1st Step Corp., Clearwater, 1986-93; vice chmn. Long Ctr. Found., Clearwater, 1994-95; founder Head Start Learn-to-Swim Program, 1994. Mem. Nat. Assn. Criminal Def. Lawyers, Pinellas Criminal Def. Assn. (v.p. 1987), Am. Inn of Ct. Criminal. Office: 480 Poinsettia Rd Belleair FL 33756-1081

CHEELY, DANIEL JOSEPH, lawyer; b. Melrose Park, Ill., Oct. 24, 1949; s. Walter Hubbard and Edith Arlene (Orlandino) C.; m. Patricia Elizabeth Dorsey, May 14, 1977; children: Mary Elizabeth, Daniel, Katherine, Laura, Anne-Marie, Thomas, Susan, Michael, William. AB, Princeton U., 1971; JD, Harvard U., 1974. Bar: Ill. 1974, U.S. Dist. Ct (no. dist.) Ill. 1975, U.S. Ct. Appeals (7th cir.) 1975. With Baker & McKenzie, Chgo., 1974-81, ptnr. litigation, 1981-85, capital ptnr. litigation, 1985-94; ptnr. Mauck, Bellande & Cheely, 1994-2000, Bellande, Cheely & O'Flaherty, Chgo., 2000—. Liaison counsel Asbestos Claims Facility, Chgo., 1985-88, bus. devel. com., 1987-90, Chgo. assoc. train com., 1988-91, chmn. Chgo. assoc. evaluation; liaison coun. Com. for Claims Resolution, 1988-89. Advisor Midtown Sports and Cultural Ctr., Chgo., 1974—; mem. River Forest Regular Reps., Ill., 1980-88, Ill. Rep. Assembly, Chgo., 1984—; pres. Cath. Evidence Forum, 1984—; pres. Ch. History Forum, 1994—; dir. Cath. Citizens of Ill., 1997—; bd. dirs. Cath. Lawyers Guild, 2000—. Mem. ABA (vice chmn. environ. law sect. 1989-97), Ill. Bar Assn., Appellate Lawyers Soc. Ill., Chgo. Bar Assn., Trial Lawyers Club. Chgo., Serra Club (v.p. Chgo. chpt. 1988-89, 92-94, 96—, treas. 1989-92), United Rep. Fund, Phi Beta Kappa. Roman Catholic. Avocations: history, parent effectiveness training, education, Christian apologetics, travel consulting. Appellate, Personal injury, Product liability. Office: Bellande Cheely & O'Flaherty 19 S La Salle St Ste 1203 Chicago IL 60603-1406

CHEFITZ, JOEL GERALD, lawyer; b. Boston, Aug. 27, 1951; s. Melvin L and Bernice L (Kahn) Chefitz; m. Sharon P Garfinkel, June 18, 1972; children: Sandra Beth, Meira Sarah, Michael Hanan. AB cum laude, Boston U., 1972, JD magna cum laude, 1976. Bar: Ill 1976, US Dist Ct (no Dist) Ill 1977, US Ct Appeals (3d cir) 1981, US Supreme Ct 1983, US Ct Appeals (7th cir) 1984, US Ct Appeals (9th cir) 1993, US Ct Appeals (2d cir) 1994, US Ct Appeals (5th cir) 1996, US Ct Appeals (4th cir) 1998, US Ct Appeals (fed cir) 2000, US Ct Appeals (DC cir) 2001. Law clk. to presiding justice U.S. Dist. Ct. Mass., Boston, 1976-77; assoc. Kirkland & Ellis, Chgo., 1977-82, ptnr., 1982-86, Katten Muchin & Zavis, Chgo., 1986—. Editor: (jour) Boston Univ Law Rev, 1975—76;contbr. articles to profl jours. Bd dirs Legal Assistance Found Met Chicago. Scholar Am Jurisprudence, Boston Univ, 1973—76, CJS, 1975, Bigelow, 1976. Mem.: ABA, Chicago Bar Asn, 7th Cir Asn, East Bank Club. Antitrust, Federal civil litigation, Constitutional. Office: Katten Muchin & Zavis 525 W Monroe St Ste 1600 Chicago IL 60661-3693 E-mail: joel.chefitz@kmz.com

CHEMERS, ROBERT MARC, lawyer; b. Chgo., July 24, 1951; s. Donald and Florence (Weinberg) C.; m. Lenore Ziemann, Aug. 16, 1975; children: Brandon J., Derek M. BA, U. So. Calif., 1973; JD, Ind. U.-Indpls., 1976. Bar: Ind. 1976, Ill. 1976, U.S. Dist. Ct. (so. dist.) Ind. 1976, U.S. Dist. Ct. (no. and so. dists.) Ill. 1977, U.S. Ct. Appeals 7th cir.) 1977, U.S. Ct. Appeals (5th cir.) 1985. Assoc. Pretzel & Stouffer, Chgo., 1976-79, officer, 1979-81, dir., 1981—. Author: IICLE - Civil Practice, 1978, rev. edit. 1982, 87; IICLE Settlements, 1984. Mem. ABA, Ill. State Bar Assn., Chgo. Bar Assn., Def. Rsch. Inst., Ill. Def. Counsel, Appellate Lawyers Assn. Federal civil litigation, State civil litigation, Insurance. Office: Pretzel & Stouffer One S Wacker Dr Chicago IL 60606

CHEN, WEI DAVID, lawyer; b. Beijing, Jan. 14, 1972; came to U.S., 1992; s. Shun-Le Chen and Ming Ying Yang. BA, CUNY, 1995; JD, SUNY, Buffalo, 1998. Bar: N.Y., N.J. Asst. fundraiser Friends of Pataki, N.Y.C., 1995. Mem. ABA, N.Y. State Bar Assn., ASsn. Bar City N.Y., Golden Key, Phi Alpha Delta. Avocations: golf, gym, fishing, classical music. Home: 32 Canterbury Ave Staten Island NY 10314

CHEN, WESLEY, lawyer; b. N.Y.C., Nov. 29, 1954; s. Tom Y.M. and Mary (Don) C.; m. Vivien Wong, Dec. 10, 1983; 2 children: Marissa, Jocelyn. BA, N.Y. U., 1976, JD, 1980. Bar: N.Y. 1981, U.S. Dist. Ct. (so. and ea. dists.) N.Y. 1981. Lawyer Meissner, Tisch & Kleinberg, N.Y.C., 1980-81; pvt. practice, 1982-85, 89, 91—; of counsel Serchuk, Wolfe & Zelermyer, White Plains, N.Y., 1985-88; ptnr. Cantwell & Chen, N.Y.C., 1988, Kimmelman, Sexter, Warmflash & Leitner, N.Y.C., 1990-91, Krasner & Chen, N.Y.C., 1992-94, Serchuk & Zelermyer, N.Y.C., 1995—. Bd. dirs. United Orient Bank, N.Y.C., 1982-92, MFY Legal Svcs., Inc., 1993-96; mem. N.Y. State Banking Bd., 1992—. Vice pres., trustee Union Ch. of Pocantico Hills, 2000—. Mem. ABA, N.Y. State Bar Assn. (mem. banking law com.), N.Y.County Lawyers Assn. (mem. banking law com.), Asian-Am. Bar Assn. of N.Y., Chinese C. of C. (legal adviser 1982—). Banking, Contracts commercial, Real property. Office: 641 Lexington Ave Fl 20 New York NY 10022-4503

CHEN, ZHENSHENG, lawyer; b. Quanzhou, China, Mar. 17, 1957; married. BB of Navigation, Dalian Maritime U., China, 1982; LLM, Fudan U., Shanghai. Ct. clk. Shanghai Intermediate Ct., China, 1982-84; cheif judge Shanghai Maritime Ct., China, 1984-99; sr. PRC legal cons. Sinclair Roche & Temperley, Shanghai, China, 1999—. Vis. prof. law Shanghai Internat. Studies U., 1996, Jimei Maritime Coll, Xiamen, China, 1997; arbitrator China Arbitration Com., 2000—. Author: Journal of Dalian Maritime University, 1987, Navigation of China No. 2, 1994, Shanghai Judicial Practice No. 3 & No. 1, 1998. Vis. scholar, U. Calif., 1995-96. Mem. China Maritime Law Assn., Law Assn. China. Home: Bldg 7 Rm 3803 333 Linping North Rd Xinshi Rd Shanghai China Office: Sinclair Roche & Temperley HSBC Tower 101 Yin Cheng East Rd Shanghai 200120 China Fax: 86 21 6841 0525. E-mail: zhensheng.chen@srtlaw.com.cn

CHENAULT, JAMES STOUFFER, judge; b. Richmond, Ky., May 1, 1923; s. Joe Prewitt and Russell (Stouffer) C.; m. Dorothy Neff, Apr. 21, 1960; children: Jean Russell. AB, Ea. Ky. U., 1949, LLD (hon.), 1975; LLB, U. Ky., 1949. Bar: Ky. 1949, U.S. Ct. Mil. Appeals 1956, U.S. Supreme Ct. 1960. Prosecuting atty. City of Richmond, Ky., 1950-57; commonwealth's atty. 25th Jud. Ct. of Ky., Clark, Jessamine and Madison Counties, 1964-66, cir. judge, 1966-80, chief cir. judge Clark and Madison Counties, 1980-93; chief regional judge Bluegrass Region of Ky., 1978-93; spl. judge Ky. Ct. of Appeals, 1973, Ky. Supreme Ct., 1984. Ky. rep. Nat. Ctr. State Cts., 1972-78; mem. Ky. Commn. on Corrections and Community Svc., 1973-77, Ky. Crime Commn. Cts. Sect., 1972-80, chmn., 1976-80, Task Force on Office for Pub. Advocacy, 1981-82, Gov.'s Jud. Adv. Coun., 1972-75, Ky. Jud. Coun., 1977-81, State and Fed. Jud. Coun., 1979-84; vol. faculty intensive trial seminar U. Ky., 1983, 85, 87, 90; lectr. So. Police Inst., 1970-80, Nat. Conf. Appellate Ctr. Clks., 1985, Nat. Conf. U.S. Dist. Ct. Clks., 1988, Nat. Conf. on Tech. and the Cts., Chgo., 1984, Denver, 1988, 3rd Fed. Jud. Conc, 1987, Ala. Appellate Judges Conf., 1990; adj. faculty Sch. Law Enforcement Ea. Ky. U., 1967-73; lectr. numerous state jud. confs.; presenter 1st Nat. Jud. State of the Art Conf., Phoenix, 1987. Councilman City of Richmond, 1949-50. Lt. (j.g.) USN, 1943-46, PTO. Recipient Outstanding Contbn. award Ky. Coun. Crime and Delinquency, 1974, Outstanding Contbn. award City of Richmond, 1977, Disting. Svc. award Dept. Mass Comm. Ea. Ky. U., 1993, Outstanding Trial Judge award Ky. Acad. Trial Attys., 1993, Ky. Chief Justice Spl. award, 1994; named Outstanding Alumnus Ea. Ky. U., Richmond, 1982; inducted into U. Ky. Law Sch. Hall of Fame, 2000. Mem. ABA (lectr., presenter ann. meeting San Francisco chpt. 1987), Am. Judicature Soc., Internat. Acad. Trial Judges, Ky. Bar Assn. (pres. younger lawyers conf. 1956-57), Ky. Assn. Cir. Judges (pres. 1970-75, editor newsletter 1976-93, Outstanding Contbn. award 1978), Ky. Commonwealth's Attys. Assn. (pres. 1965-66), Richmond C. of C. (Outstanding Svc. award 1983, Outstanding Achievement award 1989), Exch. Club (pres. Richmond chpt. 1955), Elks. Avocations: Ky. history, home gardening. Home and Office: 302 High St Richmond KY 40475-1344

CHENAULT MINOT, MARILYN, legal executive; b. Mt. Vernon, Ill., Oct. 21, 1949; d. Nathan Bullock and Marguerite (Woodberry) Chenault; m. Tom Dee McFall, Aug. 29, 1969; children: Shannon, Nathan; m. Troy David Phillips, Aug. 14, 1981; stepchildren: Todd, Brittany; m. Winthrop Gardner Minot, June 6, 1998; stepchildren: Hilary, Amory, Constance. BS with honors, Okla. State U., 1970. Retail analyst Opticks, Inc. divsn. G. D. Searle, Dallas, 1977-78; dir. of adminstrn. Glast, Phillips and Murray, 1978-81; exec. dir. Haynes and Boone L.L.P., 1981-94; prin. Chenault and Co., 1994-95; exec. dir. Wolf, Greenfield & Sacks, P.C., 1995-96; COO Legalink Corp., 1997-98, Wolf, Greenfield & Sacks, P.C., Boston, 1999—. Adj. prof. So. Meth. U. Sch. Law, Dallas, 1981-94; instr. paralegal program So. Meth. U., 1981-85; legal adv. coun. Wang Labs., 1985-91, Pitney Bowes, 1991-96; mem. Tech. Task Force, 1989-93; chair Practicing Law Profitability Conf., 1984, Large Law Firm Tech. Conf., 1990; co-chair Law Net Inc. Conf., 1988. Contbr. articles to Nat. Law Jour., PC Week. Lou Wentz scholar Coll. Bus., Okla. State U., Stillwater, 1969-70, also C.V. Richardson scholar, 1969-70; named Outstanding Coll. Bus. Grad., 1970. Mem. NAFE, State Bar Tex. (law office mgmt. com. 1991-94), Dallas Bar Assn. (strategic planning com. 1990-94, chair mktg. subcom.), Tex. Lawyer Law Tech. Planning Com. 1992, Nat. Assn. Legal Adminstrs. (dir. of adminstrn. sect. 1979-85, large firm adminstrn. sect. 1985-91, com. mem. 1986-88, vice-chmn. 1989-90, chmn., 1990-91, chair in-house tng. task force, 1990-91, communication/governance/structure issues task force 1988-89, instr. law office adminstrn. course 1984, 87, pres. Dallas chpt. 1985-86, prin. adminstrs. team 1992-96, nat. nominating com. 1992-93, nat. certification task force 1996-97, vice-chair intellectual property affinity group 2000—). Home: 42 Nichols Rd Cohasset MA 02025-1166 Office: Wolf Greenfield & Sacks PC 600 Atlantic Ave Boston MA 02210-2211 E-mail: mminot@wgslaw.com

CHERAMIE, CARLTON JOSEPH, lawyer, business consultant; b. Raceland, La., Sept. 29, 1952; s. Antoine Joseph and Gladys Marie (Plaisance) C.; m. Myra Joan Diaz, July 15, 1973; 1 child, Andrea Ragan. B.A., Nicholls State U., Thibodaux, La., 1973; J.D., La. State U., 1976. Bar: La. 1976, U.S. Dist. Ct. (ea. dist.) La. 1977, U.S. Dist. Ct. (we. dist.) La. 1977, U.S. Ct. Appeals (5th cir.) 1982, U.S. Ct. Appeals (10th cir.) 1984, U.S. Supreme Ct. 1984. Law clk. Dist. Ct. 19th Jud. dist., Baton Rouge, 1975-76; assoc. Diaz & Herrin, Golden Meadow, La., 1976-77; assoc. Law Office of Ed Diaz, Golden Meadow, 1977-79; ptnr. Diaz & Cheramie, Golden Meadow, 1979-83, Cheramie & Smith, Cut Off, La., 1983—; pres., dir. Tradewinds Marine, Cut Off, 1982—; corp. cons. First Am. Investments, Dallas; atty. Town of Golden Meadow, 1980-83; dir. Westwind Capital, Cut Off. State advisor U.S. Congl. Adv. Bd., Cut Off, 1980. Mem. Fed. Bar Assn., Assn. Trial Lawyers Am., La. Trial Lawyers Assn., ABA, Phi Alpha Theta, Phi Delta Phi. Republican. Roman Catholic. Federal civil litigation, State civil litigation, General corporate. Home: 134 W 47th St Cut Off LA 70345-3129 Office: Cheramie & Smith 2024 W Main St Cut Off LA 70345-9408

CHERCHIGLIA, DEAN KENNETH, lawyer; b. Cold Springs, N.Y., Apr. 11, 1956; s. Patrick Joseph and Bella (Feld) C.; m. Susan Elaine Sonkin, July 5, 1980; children: Brian Alden, Evan James. BBA cum laude, Ohio U., 1977; JD, Case Western Res. U., 1984. Bar: Ohio 1984. Contract specialist NASA Lewis Rsch. Ctr., Cleve., 1980; atty. Hermann, Cahn & Schneider, 1984-85; assoc. Schwarzwald, Robiner, Wolf & Rock, 1985; asst. counsel HealthAm. Corp., 1986-87; atty. TransOhio Savs. Bank, 1987-91; asst. v.p., counsel Chase Fin. Corp., 1991-97; of counsel Benesch, Friedlander, Coplan & Aronoff, 1997-99; counsel CompliSource, LLC, 1999-2000; assoc. counsel, asst. sec. Ohio Savs. Bank, 2000—. Mem. Case Western Res. U. Law. Rev., 1982-84. Mem. Ohio State Bar Assn., Cleve. Bar Assn., Amnesty Internat. Avocations: photography, scuba diving, weightlifting. Consumer commercial, Contracts commercial, General corporate. Home: 3620 Stoer Rd Shaker Heights OH 44122-5116 E-mail: dcherchiglia@ohiosavings.com

CHEREWKA, MICHAEL, lawyer; b. Taylor, Pa., July 3, 1955; s. Michael Jr. and Anne (Regan) C.; m. Michele Mary Robinson, Aug. 2, 1980; children: Michael Colin, Matthew Bryan, Meaghan Kelly. Student, U. Bristol, Eng., 1976-77; BSBA cum laude, Bucknell U., 1978; JD cum laude, Dickinson Sch. Law, 1981. Bar: Pa. 1981, U.S. Dist. Ct. (mid. dist.) Pa. 1983, U.S. Tax Ct. 1983, U.S. Ct. Appeals (3d cir.) 1983, U.S. Supreme Ct. 1985. Sr. mem. tax staff Ernst & Whinney, Harrisburg, Pa., 1981-83; assoc. Ball, Skelly, Murren & Connell (formerly Ball & Skelly), 1983-89; pvt. practice, 1989-96; mng. ptnr. Cherewka & Radcliff, LLP, 1996—. Mem. Keystone Family Bus. Ctr., LLC, 2000—. Co-author: Pennsylvania Tax Service, 1987; contbg. editor (legal column) Cen. Penn Bus. Jour.,

1985-88; advisor Dauphin County Law Explorers Post, 1982-88. Mem. Country Club Park Civic Assn., 1983-98, pres., 1987-88; mem. Hist. Harrisburg Assn., 1982-84; active Tri-County United Way, 1985-90, cons. planning giving, mem. adv. com., 1988-90; bd. dirs. Capital divsn. Am. Heart Assn., chmn. 1989-91, bd. dirs. Pa. affiliate, 1989-98 , exec. com., 1989-90, 93, treas., 1994-95, incoming chmn. bd., 1995-96, chmn. 1996-97; chmn., bd. dirs. Concertante Chamber Ensemble, 1996-97; mem. planned giving com. Keystone Svc. Sys. Found., 1995—; mem. adv. bd. Found. Caths. United in Svc., Cath. Diocese of Harrisburg, 1991-97. Named Outstanding Young Man Am., U.S. Jaycees, 1983. Mem. Nat. Network Estate Planning Attys., Pa. Bar Assn. (tax sect. 1981—, real estate, probate and trust law sect. 1981—, com. state taxation 1984—, chmn. subcom. on compromise tax 1986-97), Dauphin County Bar Assn. (interprofl. rels. com. 1984-89, estate planning sect. 1992—), Estate Planning Coun. Cen. Pa. (chmn. CPA subcom. 1982-83, bd. dirs. 1988-96, treas. 1989-90, v.p. 1990-91, pres. 1991-92), Polit. Info. Com. CPAs Pa. (treas. 1982-83), Greater Harrisburg C. of C. (bus. liaison com. 1984-87, econ. devel. com. 1988-89, 92-93, reaccreditation task force 1996), Nat. Assn. Estate Planners (charter 1988—), Pa. Chamber Bus. and Industry (bus. subcom. 1989), Greater West Shore Area C. of C. (comml.-indsl. devel. com. 1987-89), Alzheimer's Assn. of So. Ctrl. Pa. (bd. dirs. 1998—), Pa. Assn. Nonprofit Orgns. (bd. dirs. 2000—), Delta Mu Delta, Omicron Delta Kappa. Republican. Orthodox Greek Catholic. Avocations: coin collecting, golf, basketball. General corporate, Estate planning, Taxation, general. Home: 125 Pelham Rd Camp Hill PA 17011-1353 Office: 624 N Front St Wormleysburg PA 17043-1022

CHERNEY, JAMES ALAN, lawyer; b. Boston, Mar. 19, 1948; s. Alvin George and Janice (Elaine) Cherney; m. Linda Bienenfeld. BA, Tufts U., 1969; JD, Columbia U., 1973. Bar: Ill. 1973, U.S. Supreme Ct. 1977, U.S. Ct. Appeals (7th cir.) 1979, U.S. Ct. Appeals (3d cir.) 1982, U.S. Ct. Appeals (10th cir.) 1984, U.S. Ct. Appeals (8th and 9th cirs.) 1987. Assoc. Kirkland & Ellis, Chgo., 1973-76, Hedlund, Hunter & Lynch, Chgo., 1976-79, ptnr., 1979-82, Latham & Watkins, Chgo., 1982—. Mem. ABA, Chgo. Bar Assn., Saddle and Cycle Club (sec. 1989, v.p. 1991-92, pres. 1992-94). Federal civil litigation, State civil litigation, Health. Office: Latham & Watkins Sears Tower Ste 5800 Chicago IL 60606-6306

CHERNOW, JEFFREY SCOTT, lawyer, educator, author; b. Phila., Mar. 8, 1951; s. William and Sylvia Ann (Rosenberg) C.; m. Debra Sharon Shapiro, Dec. 29, 1974; children: William Ross, Stephanie Lynne. BS, Pa. State U., 1972; JD, U. Balt., 1976. Bar: Md. 1976, U.S. Dist. Ct. Md. 1977, U.S. Supreme Ct. 1980, U.S. Ct. Claims 1991. Assoc. Goodman, Meagher & Enoch, Balt., 1977-79; asst. atty. gen. State of Md., 1980-85; assoc. Cardin & Cardin, P.A., 1985-86; pvt. practice law, 1986-89; ptnr. Kandel, Klitenic, Kotz, Betten & Chernow LLP, Owings Mills, Md., 1990—. Asst. prof. Towson (Md.) State U., 1978-83, assoc. prof., 1983-86; panel chmn. Md. Health Claims Arbitration Office, 1983-84; lectr. Md. Inst. for Continuing Profl. Edn. of Lawyers, Inc., 1986; dir. Altex Industries, Inc., 1989. Contbr. chpt. to book. Sec., trustee Basic Cancer Rsch. Found., Inc., 1986—; chmn. bldg. com. Congregation Adat Chaim, 1985-86, trustee, 1986-90. Mem. ABA, Md. Bar Assn., Bar Assn. Balt. City, N.Am. Securities Adminstrs. Assn. (mem. various coms. 1980-85, chmn. franchise and bus. opportunities com. 1984-85), Md. State Bar Assn. (sec. bus. law, franchise law com. 1991). General corporate, Franchising, Securities. Home: 214 Berry Vine Dr Owings Mills MD 21117-4500 Office: Kandel Klitenic Kotz Betten & Chernow LLP 1838 Greene Tree Rd Ste 370 Baltimore MD 21208-7102

CHEROVSKY, ERWIN LOUIS, lawyer, writer; b. Dover, N.J., Dec. 31, 1933; s. Sam and Ida (Bluestein) C.; m. Edith Mayer, June 26, 1966; children: Kim, Karen; children by previous marriage: Debra, Jill. AB, U. Rochester, 1955; LLB, Harvard U., 1958. Bar: N.Y. 1958, U.S. Dist. Ct. (so. dist.) N.Y. 1964, U.S. Ct. Appeals (2d cir.) 1964. Assoc. Stamer & Haft, N.Y.C., 1958-63, Summit Rovins & Feldesman, N.Y.C., 1963-68, ptnr., 1968-88, Proskauer Rose Goetz & Mendelsohn, 1988-89; chmn., legal cost containment cons. WIK Cons. Inc., N.Y.C., 1992-97; pres. Old Quarry Devel., Englewood, N.J., 1996—. Sec. Space & Leisure Time, Ltd., N.Y.C., 1972-80, Ghiordian Knot, Ltd., N.Y.C., 1978-88, ORS Automation, Inc., Princeton, N.J., 1983-86, Cook United, Inc., Cleve., 1986; lit. agt. for Random House Russian-English Dictionary of Idioms, 1995, From Central Park to Sinai, Roy S. Neuberger, 2000. Author: The Guide to New York Law Firms, 1991, Competent Counsel: The Business Guide to Hiring Lawyers and Monitoring Their Work, 1992; contbr. articles to profl. jours. Fellow Phi Beta Kappa Soc.; mem. N.Y.State Bar Assn., Assn. Bar City of N.Y., Fed. Bar Coun. (chmn. winter meeting 1980, mem. alternative dispute resolution com. 1984), Can. Club (N.Y.C.) (bd. govs. 1988-89, editor Maple Leaf 1984-89), Met. Club (N.Y.C.). General corporate, Securities, Corporate finance.

CHERPAS, CHRISTOPHER THEODORE, lawyer; b. Toledo, Mar. 23, 1924; s. Theodore C. and Mary (Veronie) C.; m. Ortha N. Mollis, June 23, 1946; children— Maria, Patricia, Christopher T. B.S. in Polit. Sci., Akron U., 1949; postgrad. Akron Law Sch., 1949-50, Western Res. U., 1951; J.D., Cleveland Marshall U., 1951. Bar: Ohio 1952, U.S. Dist. Ct. (7th dist.) Ohio 1954, U.S. Ct. Appeals (6th cir.) 1966. Counsel United Rubber Workers, Akron, Ohio, 1954-57; ptnr. Cherpas, Manos & Syracopoulos, Akron, 1957-74, Cherpas and Manos, Akron, 1974-79, Teodosio, Cherpas and Manos, Akron, 1979— . Served to capt. U.S. Army, ETO, PTO, Korea, 1942-46, 51-53. Mem. ABA, Ohio Bar Assn., Akron County Bar Assn., VFW, Am. Legion, Disabled Am. Vets, 37th Div. Assn. Democrat. Greek Orthodox. Clubs: Pan Arcadian Fedn. (Chgo.) (supreme pres. 1957-58); Fairlawn Country, Am. Hellenic Edn. Progressive Assn. (chpt. pres. 1979-80). Lodges: Masons, Shriners, K.T. Federal civil litigation, State civil litigation, Personal injury. Home: 1594 Alton Dr Akron OH 44313-6458 Office: Teodosio Cherpas Manos and Ward 907 Landmark Bldg 7 W Bowery St Akron OH 44308-1138

CHERRY, DAVID EARL, lawyer; b. Ft. Worth, Sept. 10, 1944; s. Leonard Earl and Dorothy Hazel (Brown) C.; m. Katherine Ann Yarborough, Dec. 23, 1967; children: Lisa, Craig. BBA, Tex. Christian U., 1967; JD, Baylor U., 1968. Bar: Tex. 1968, U.S. Dist. Ct. (we. dist.) Tex. 1970, U.S. Dist. Ct. (so. dist.) Tex. 1977, U.S. Ct. Appeals (5th cir.) 1977, U.S. Supreme Ct. 1978, U.S. Ct. Appeals (11th cir.) 1981, U.S. Ct. Claims 1985, U.S. Dist. Ct. (no. dist.) Tex. 1988, U.S. Dist. Ct. (ea. dist.) Tex. 1988. Ptnr. Pakis, Cherry, Beard & Giotes, Inc., Waco, Tex., 1968-91, Cherry, Davis, Harrison, Montez, Williams & Baird P.C., Waco, 1992-99, Campbell, Cherry, Harrison, Davis & Dove, P.C., Waco, 1999—. Mem. Charter Commn., Woodway, Tex., 1973; chmn. Planning and Zoning Commn., Woodway, 1976-79; bd. dirs. Heart of Tex. coun. Boy Scouts Am., Waco, 1985; mem. Nat. Exploring Com. Boy Scouts Am., Waco, 1977-82. Fellow Tex. Bar Found. (life); mem. ABA, Assn. Trial Lawyers Am., Tex. Bar Assn., Am. Bd. Trial Advocates, Tex. Trial Lawyers Assn., Tex. Bd. Legal Specialization (cert. civil trial law), Coll. of State Bar of Tex., Waco-McLennan County Bar Assn., Waco-McLennan County Legal Aid Soc. (dir. 1971-73), Waco-McLennan County Young Lawyers Assn. (pres. 1974-75, Outstanding Young Lawyer 1977). Avocations: running, camping, fishing, photography, hunting. Federal civil litigation, State civil litigation, Toxic tort. Office: Campbell Cherry Harrison Davis & Dove PC 5 Ritchie Rd Waco TX 76712

CHERRY, SANDRA WILSON, lawyer; b. Little Rock, Dec. 31, 1941; d. Berlin Alexander and Renna Glen (Barnes) Wilson; m. John Sandefur Cherry, Jr., Sept. 24, 1976; 1 dau., Jane Wilson. BA, U. Ark., 1962; JD, U. Ark. Sch. Law, 1975. Bar: Ark., 1975, U.S. Dist. Ct. (ea. dist.) Ark., 1979, U.S. Supreme Ct. 1979, U.S. Ct. Appeals (8th cir.) 1979. Tchr. social studies Little Rock Sch. Dist., 1966-70; chmn. social studies dept. Horace Mann Jr. High Sch., Little Rock, 1970-72; asst. U.S. atty. Dept. Justice, Little Rock, 1975-81, 83—; commr. Ark. Pub. Service Commn., Little Rock, 1981-83; adj. instr. U. Ark. at Little Rock Sch. Law, Little Rock, 1980. Contbr. case note to Ark. Law Rev., 1975. Pres. bd. dirs. Gaines House, Inc.; pres. U. Ark. at Little Rock Law Sch. Assn., 1980-81, bd. dirs., 1982; bd. dirs. Jr. League Little Rock, 1974, Ark. Cmty. Found., 1997—, Gov.'s Mansion Assn., 1998—. Recipient Gayle Pettus Pontz award U. Ark. Law Sch. Women Lawyers Assn., 1990. Mem. ABA, Ark. Bar Assn. (Ho. of Del. 1984-86, 89—, tenured del. 1994, sec., treas. 1986-89, exec. coun. chair 1995—, 8th cir. gender fairness task force, pres. 2001-), Pulaski County Bar Assn. (bd. dirs. 1989-90, 91-92, pres.-elect 1993-94, pres. 1994—), Ark. Women Lawyers Assn., Ark. Bar Assn. (Golden Gavel award 1992, com. on the status women and minorities), Little Rock C. of C. (met. coun.), Pi Beta Phi. Republican. Presbyterian. Home: 4100 S Lookout St Little Rock AR 72205-2030 Office: US Atty's Office PO Box 1229 Little Rock AR 72203-1229*

CHERWIN, JOEL IRA, lawyer; b. Winthrop, Mass., Apr. 29, 1942; s. Melvin Arthur and Martha C.; m. Sherry Lenore Cherwin, July 5, 1970; children: Alison, Matthew, Joshua. BS in Econs., U. Pa., 1963; JD, Boston U., 1966. Bar: Mass. 1966, U.S.. Dist. Ct. Mass. 1968, U.S. Tax Ct. 1969. Ptnr. Cherwin & Glickman, Boston, 1977-96, Cherwin, Glickman & Theise, Boston, 1996—2001, Cherwin, Theise, Adelson & Loria LLP, Boston, 2001—. Mem. ABA, Mass. Bar Assn. Democrat. Jewish. Banking, General corporate. Office: Cherwin Theise Adelson & Loria One International Pl Boston MA 02110

CHESBRO, ROBERT BRUCE, lawyer; b. Washington, May 14, 1945; s. Robert Cyril and Jeanne Marie (Gray) C.; m. Bettyann Casady, June 11, 1966; children: Robert Mark, Lawrence David. BS, St. Lawrence U., 1967; JD, SUNY-Buffalo, 1973. Bar: N.Y. 1974, U.S. Dist. Ct. (we. dist.) N.Y. 1974. Mgmt. trainee First Trust & Deposit Co., Syracuse, N.Y., 1967-68; assoc. Damon & Morey, Buffalo, 1973-79, ptnr., 1979—; bd. dirs. Hamburg N.Y. Devel. Corp., Hamburg Indsl. Devel. Agy., also sec.; instr. Hilbert Coll., Hamburg, 1987. Cub master, com. chmn. Cub Scout Pack 502, Hamburg, N.Y., 1976; com. chmn. Troop 502, Boy Scouts Am., Hamburg, 1978; bd. dirs., sec. Compass House, Buffalo, 1975. Served to 1st lt. U.S. Army, 1968-70; also to capt. USAR, 1970-73. Decorated Army Commendation medal; St. Lawrence U. Trustee scholar, 1963; N.Y. State Regents scholar, 1963; N.Y. State Regents War Svc. scholar, 1970. Mem. ABA, N.Y. State Bar Assn., Erie County Bar Assn., Willow Bend Club (pres. 1983-84). Republican. Presbyterian. Banking, Contracts commercial, Real property. Home: 6571 Taylor Rd Hamburg NY 14075-6509

CHESLER, EVAN ROBERT, lawyer; b. N.Y.C., July 17, 1949; s. Philip and Doris (Sims) C.; m. Diane Lynn Ackerman, May 30, 1970 (div. 1983); children: David Andrew, Matthew Lawrence, Rebecca Faye; m. Barbara Jean Gloven, Sept. 10, 1983. BA, NYU, 1970, JD, 1975; MA, Hunter Coll., 1973. Bar: N.Y. 1976, U.S. Dist. Ct. (so. dist.) N.Y. 1976, U.S. Supreme Ct. 1982, U.S. Ct. Appeals (2d cir.) 1982, U.S. Dist. Ct. (no. dist.) Calif. 1982. Tchr. N.Y.C. Bd. Edn., 1970-72; law clk. U.S. Dist. Ct. (so. dist.) N.Y., N.Y.C., 1975-76; assoc. Cravath, Swaine & Moore, N.Y.C., 1976-82, ptnr., 1982— . Author: The Russian Jewry Reader, 1973. Topics editor NYU Law Rev., 1974-75. Contbr. articles to legal jours. and chpts. to books. N.Y. Regents scholar, 1966-70, 72-75; Ctr. for Internat. Studies jr. fellow, 1974-75. Mem. Assn. of Bar of City of N.Y., N.Y. State Bar Assn., ABA, Order of Coif. Democrat. Jewish. Federal civil litigation, State civil litigation. Office: Cravath Swaine & Moore 825 8th Ave Fl 38 New York NY 10019-7475

CHESLER, STANLEY RICHARD, federal judge; b. Bklyn., June 15, 1947; s. Rubin and Beatrice (Horowitz) C.; m. Francine Richer, June 29, 1969; 1 child, Elizabeth. BA, SUNY, Binghamton, 1968; JD magna cum laude, St. John's U., 1974. Bar: N.Y. 1975, N.J. 1985, U.S. Dist. Ct. (ea. dist., so. dist.) N.Y. 1975, U.S. Dist. Ct. N.J. 1985, U.S. Ct. Appeals (2d cir.) 1975. Asst. dist. atty. Bronx County, N.Y., 1974-80, dep. chief investigations bur., 1976-78, chief investigations bur., 1978-79, chief rackets, narcotics bur., 1979-80; trial atty. U.S. Dept. Justice Organized Crime Strike Force, Newark, 1980-84, deputy chief, 1984-86; asst. U.S. atty. Dist. of N.J., 1987; U.S. magistrate judge U.S. Dist. Ct. N.J., 1987—. Fellow Am. Bar Found.; mem. Assn. Fed. Bar State of N.J. (bd. advisors), John J. Gibbons Am. Inn of Ct. (master). Avocations: cross country skiing, biking. Office: US Dist Ct NJ US PO Office & Courthouse Bldg Newark NJ 07101

CHESLEY, STANLEY MORRIS, lawyer; b. Cin., Mar. 26, 1936; s. Frankl and Rachel (Kinsburg) C.; children: Richard A., Lauren B. BA, U. Cin., 1958, LLB, 1960. Bar: Ohio 1960, Ky. 1978, W.Va. 1981, Tex. 1981, Nev. 1981. Ptnr. Waite, Schneider, Bayless & Chesley Co., Cin., 1960—. Contbr. articles to profl. jours. Past chmn. bd. commrs. on grievances and discipline Supreme Ct. Ohio; past pres. Jewish Fedn. Cin.; nat. vice chair, bd. govs., trustee, joint distbn. com. United Jewish Coms.; exec. bd., nat. bd. govs. Am. Jewish Com.; nat. bd. govs. Hebrew Union Coll.; exec. com. U.S. Holocaust Meml. Mus. Mem. ABA, ATLA, FBA, Am. Judicature Soc., Melvin M. Belli Soc., Ohio Bar Assn., Ky. Bar Assn., W.Va. Bar Assn., Tex. Bar Assn., Nev. Bar Assn., Cin. Bar Assn. General civil litigation, Personal injury, Product liability. Office: Waite Schneider Bayless & Chesley 1513 Central Trust Towers Cincinnati OH 45202 E-mail: wsbclaw@aol.com

CHESNUT, CAROL FITTING, lawyer; b. Pecos, Tex., June 17, 1937; d. Ralph Ulf and Carol (Lowe) Fitting; m. Dwayne A. Chesnut, Dec. 27, 1955; children: Carol Marie, Stephanie Michelle, Mark Steven. BA magna cum laude, U. Colo., 1971; JD, U. Calif., San Francisco, 1994. Rsch. asst. U. Colo., 1972; head quality controller Mathematics, Inc., Denver, 1973-74; cons. Mincome Man., Winnipeg, Can., 1974; cons. economist Energy Cons. Assocs. Inc., Denver, 1974-79; exec. v.p. tng. ECA Intercomp, 1980-81; gen. ptnr. Chestnut Consortium, S.F., 1981—. Sec. Critical Resources, Inc., 1981-83. Rep. Lakehurst Civic Assn., 1968; staff aide Senator Gary Hart, 1978; Dem. precinct capt., 1982-88. Mem. ABA, ACLU, AAUW (1st v.p. 1989-90), LWV, Soc. Petroleum Engrs., Am. Nuc. Soc. (chair conv. space activities 1989, chair of spouse activities 1989), Am. Geophys. Union, Assn. Women Geoscientists (treas. Denver 1983-85), Associated Students of Hastings (rep. 1994), Calif. State Bar, Nev. State Bar, Nat. Acad. Elder Law Attys., Clark County Bar Assn. (coun. com. 1999), Canyon Ranch Homeowners Assn. (sec. bd. dirs. 1994-97), Phi Beta Kappa, Phi Chi Theta, Phi Delta Phi. Uniterian. Estate planning, Probate, Elder. Office: Ste 319 2921 N Tenaya Way Las Vegas NV 89128-0454 E-mail: ladylawcfc@aol.com

CHESSER, DAVID MICHAEL, lawyer; b. Pensacola, Fla., Aug. 12, 1947; s. Julian Edward and Arabelle (Martin) C.; m. Carolyn Anne Miller, Aug. 31, 1968; children: Patrick, Lanie, Anna, Matthew. BA in Psychology, U. Fla., 1969, JD, 1971. Bar: Fla. 1972, U.S. Dist. Ct. (no. dist.) Fla. 1972, U.S. Ct. Appeals (5th and 11th cirs.) 1972, U.S. Tax Ct. 1974, U.S. Supreme Ct. 1976. Ptnr. Chesser, Wingard, Barr, Whitney, Flowers and Fleet, Ft. Walton Beach, Fla., 1971—, Chesser, Wingard, Barr and Fleet, Shalimar. City atty. Shalimar, Fla., 1972—, Ft. Walton Beach, 1982-84; founder, chmn. Baups Book Co., Inc.; pres. Old South Land Title; bd. dirs. Vanguard Bank and Trust Co. Chmn. Zoning Revision Panel, Okaloosa County, Fla., 1982, chmn. 911 devel. com.; pres. Okaloosa Guidance Clinic, Ft. Walton Beach, 1978, Okaloosa Guidance Found., Ft. Walton Beach, 1978—. Served to capt. U.S. Army, 1971-78. Mem. Fla. Bar Assn. (continuing edn. com.), Okaloosa-Walton Bar Assn. (pres. 1978), Niceville C. of C. (bd. dirs. 1980-82). Democrat. Methodist. Lodge: Kiwanis. Avocations: tennis, books, music, sports. Contracts commercial, General corporate, Real property. Office: Chesser Wingard Barr Fleet et al 1201 Eglin Pky Shalimar FL 32579-1206

CHESSER, STACEY C. lawyer; b. Elkhart, Ind. s. Floyd and Sandra Kay Chesser. BA, Ind. U., 1994; JD, Syracuse U., 1997. Atty. Cors & Bassett, Cin., 1997—. Exec. editor: Syracuse Jour. Internat. Law & Commerce, 1995-96 (Disting. Svc. award 1996). Mem. Ohio State Bar Assn., Cin. Bar Assn. Republican. Roman Catholic. Avocations: golf, music, snow skiing. Federal civil litigation, General civil litigation, Intellectual property. Home: 2507 Observatory Ave Cincinnati OH 45208 Office: Cors & Bassett 537 E Pete Rose Way Cincinnati OH 45202

CHESTER, MARK VINCENT, lawyer; b. Chgo., Apr. 22, 1952; s. Alvin L. and Barbara (Segal) C.; m. Shelly L. Beeber, May 20, 1979; children: Jonathan Harry, Michael Steven, Susan Gayle. BA, MA, Emory U., 1974; JD, Northwestern U., 1977. Bar: Ill. 1977, U.S. Dist. Ct. (no. dist.) Ill 1977, Ga. 1979, U.S. Ct. Appeals (7th, 11th and 5th cirs.) 1981, U.S. Supreme Ct. 1981. Asst. states atty. Cook County, Ill., 1977-81, spl. asst. states atty., 1981-96, spl. asst. atty. gen., 1981-83; assoc. Butler, Rubin, Newcomer & Saltarelli, Chgo., 1981-83; ptnr. Johnson and Colmar, 1983—. Bd. dirs. Project LEAP, 1976-94. Mem. Ill. Bar Assn., Ga. Bar Assn., Chgo. Bar Assn. State civil litigation, General corporate, Municipal (including bonds). Home: 1017 Prairie Ln Deerfield IL 60015-2814 Office: Johnson and Colmar 300 S Wacker Dr Ste 1000 Chicago IL 60606-6665 E-mail: mvchester@jocolaw.com

CHESTER, ROBERT SIMON GEORGE, lawyer; b. Chelmsford, Essex, England, Feb. 11, 1949; arrived in Can., 1971. s. Robert John and Elizabeth Poyitt (Forteath) C.; m. Anna Tharyan, Sept. 18, 1975; 1 child, Rahael Elizabeth Anna. BA, Oxford U., England, 1971, MA, 1979; postgrad., Osgoode Hall Law Sch., Toronto, 1971-72. Bar: Ontario 1982, England and Wales 1988. Vis. lectr. Osgoode Hall Law Sch., Toronto, 1972-74; rsch. staff Ontario Law Reform Commn., 1974-77; exec. counsel Dep. Atty. Gen. Ontario, 1977-82; counsel policy devel. Ministry Atty. Gen., Ontario, 1982-85; dir. rsch. McMillan Binch, Toronto, 1985—, ptnr., 1988—. Counsel Study on Access to Legal Svcs. by Disabled, Ontario, 1982-83; cons. Royal Commn. on Employment Equity, 1983-84, Royal Commn. on Electoral Reform, 1990-91, Royal Commn. on Aboriginal Peoples, 1992. Author: (with others) Environmental Rights in Canada, 1981, Barristers and Solicitors in Practice, 1998; co-editor: Winning with Computers, 1991, 2d vol., 1993; contbr. articles to profl. jours. Can. Rhodes Found. scholar, 1972; trustee and fellow Coll. Law Practice Mgmt. Mem. ABA (chmn. New Media and Internet bd., chmn. edn. bd. law practi mgmt. sect. 1994-96, chmn. Techshow 1992-93), Can. Bar Assn. (com. legal opinions 1992—). Anglican. Intellectual property, Private international, Libel. Home: 41 Walmsley Blvd Toronto ON Canada M4V 1X7 Office: McMillan Binch Royal Bank Plz PO Box 38 Toronto ON Canada M5J 2J7 E-mail: schester@mcbinch.com

CHESTER, STEPHANIE ANN, lawyer, banker; b. Oct. 8, 1951; d. Alden Runge and Nina Lavina (Hanson) C.; divorced. BA magna cum laude, Augustana Coll., 1973; JD, U. S.d., 1977; postgrad. C.F.S.C., ABA Nat. Grad. Trust Sch., Evanston, Ill., 1984. Bar: S.D. 1977, Minn. 1979. Asst. counselor Minnehaha County Juvenile Ct. Ctr., Sioux Falls, S.D., 1972-73; child care worker Project Threshold, 1973-74; legal intern Davenport, Evans, Hurwitz & Smith, 1976; law clk. S.D. Supreme Ct., Pierre, 1977-78; originations dept. buyer Dain Bosworth, Inc., Mpls., 1978-79; v.p., trust officer 1st Bank of S.D., N.A., Sioux Falls, 1979-86; v.p. First Trust Co., Inc., St. Paul, 1986-93; lawyer Westby, Chester & Lees, P.A., 1994-96; salesperson Coldwell Banker, Burnet Realty, 2000—. Pres. Sioux Falls Estate Planning Coun., 1983-85. Projects and rsch. editor S.d. Law Rev., 1977; author law rev. comment. Mem. fund raising coms. S.D. Symphony, Sioux Falls Cmty. Playhouse, Augustana Coll., 1982-83; mem. S.D. divsn. Nat. Women's Polit. Caucus; mem. events com. Augustana Coll. Fellows, Sioux Falls, 1984; bd. dirs. YWCA, Sioux Falls, 1984, Sioux Falls Arena/Coliseum, 1985; mem. Sioux Falls Jr. Svc. League, 1984. Augustana Coll. scholar, 1969-73; Augustana Coll. Bd. Regents scholar, 1973. Mem. ABA, S.D. Bar Assn., Minn. Bar Assn., 2d S.D. Jud. Cir. Bar Assn., Nat. Assn. Bank Women (state conv. com. 1983-85), Mensa, Network Club, Portia Club, Phi Delta Phi, Chi Epsilon. General corporate, Family and matrimonial, Probate. Home: 200 E 6th St Apt 412 Saint Paul MN 55101

CHESTNUTT, ELLEN JOANNE, state official; b. Milw., May 15, 1928; d. Arthur Herman and Lydia Boaz (Groff) Ziemann; m. William John Chestnutt, Sept. 3, 1954; children: David William C., Douglas John C., Gregory Mark C., Timothy Eric C. BS, U. Wis., 1950, JD, 1952. Bar: Wis. 1952, U.S. dist. Ct. Wis. 1952, Colo. 1964, U.S. Dist. Ct. Colo. 1964. Editor Shepards Citations, Colorado Springs, Colo., 1952-54; pvt. practice, 1964-68; chief dep. dist. atty., 1966-85; appeal referee Colo. Dept. Labor, 1985-86; instr. law Pikes Peak C.C., Colorado Springs, 1978-96; ret., 1996. Instr. law Chapman Coll. Contbr. articles to profl. jours. Task force on child support HEW, 1974; adv. com. Fed. Child Support Law Regulations, 1975, citizens adv. com. Dept. Social Svcs., 1988-93; spkr. Secs. Nat. Conf. on Fraud, Abuse, and Error, 1978; judge regional sci. fair, 1978-88; v.p. Longfellow Sch. PTA, Colorado Springs; vol. swimming instr. YMCA; bd. dirs. Salvation Army; citizens adv. com., block capt. Colorado Springs Police Dept. Recipient Disting. Faculty award Nat. Dist. Attys. Coll. Law, 1976, Dorothy Forney award United Coun. Welfare Fraud, 1988, Ted Cole Achievement award for lifetime excellence Colo. Welfare Fraud Coun., 1990, Portia award for outstanding female atty., 1999. Mem. Nat. Assn. Parliamentarians (pres. Henry Martyn Robert parliamentarian unit 1996—, registered parliamentarian), Wis. Bar Assn., Colo. Bar Assn., El Paso County Bar Assn. (past sec., trustee), Colo. Womens Bar Assn. (Silver honoree), Nat. Child Support Enforcement Assn. (hon. life), Nat. Dist. Attys. Assn., Colo. Family Support Coun. (past pres.), United Coun. on Welfare Fraud (past pres.), Colo. Welfare Fraud Coun. (past pres.), Nat. Reciprocal Family Support Enforcement Assn. (past pres.), Pikes Peak Geneal. Soc., Alpha Gamma Delta (past v.p. alumni assn.). Republican. Methodist. Home: 718 Pioneer Ln Colorado Springs CO 80904-1745

CHESTON, SHEILA CAROL, lawyer; b. Washington, Nov. 5, 1958; d. Theodore C. and Gabrielle Joan (Hellings) C. BA, Dartmouth Coll., 1980; JD, Columbia U., 1984. Bar: N.Y. 1986, D.C. 1986, U.S. Dist. Ct. D.C. 1987, U.S. Ct. Appeals (D.C. cir.) 1987, U.S. Dist. Ct. (so. and ea. dists.) N.Y. 1989, U.S. Ct. Appeals (2d cir.), U.S. Supreme Ct. 1989. Law clk. to judge U.S. Ct. Appeals for 9th Cir., L.A., 1984-85; assoc. Wilmer, Cutler & Pickering, Washington, 1985-92, ptnr., 1992-93; gen. counsel Def. Base Closure and Realignment Commn., 1993; spl. assoc. counsel to Pres. of U.S., 1994; dep. gen. counsel Dept. Air Force, 1993-95, gen. counsel, 1995-98; ptnr. Wilmer, Cutler & Pickering, Washington, 1998—. Adj. prof. in internat. litigation Georgetown Law Sch., 1991—. Mem. ABA, D.C. Bar Assn., Women's Bar Assn., Am. Soc. Internat. Law. Democrat. Episcopalian. Administrative and regulatory, Antitrust, Aviation. Office: Wilmer Cutler & Pickering 2445 M St NW Ste 500 Washington DC 20037-1487 E-mail: scheston@wilmer.com

CHIACCHIERE, MARK DOMINIC, lawyer; b. Phila., Dec. 10, 1966; s. Dominic Joseph and Diana (Alosi) C. BSBA, Georgetown U., 1989; JD, Villanova U., 1992. Bar: Pa. 1992, N.J. 1992,U.S. Dist. Ct. N.J. 1992, U.S. Dist. Ct. (ea. dist.) Pa. 1993, U.S. Ct. Appeals (3d cir.) 1993, U.S. Ct. Appeals (2d cir.) 2001. Assoc. O'Brien & Ryan, Plymouth Meeting, Pa.,

1992-94, White & Williams, Phila., 1994-97, Wyeth Ayerst Pharms., Phila., 1998-2000, Rifkin & Assocs., Phila., 2000—. Bd. dirs. The Savoy Co. Phila., treas., 1999—. Facilitator Parish Coun., Phila., 1996-97. Mem. ABA, Phila. Bar Assn., Savoy Co. (bd. dirs., treas.), Alpha Phi Omega (Mu Alpha alumni sec. 1991-97, bd. dirs. 1995—). General civil litigation, General corporate, Personal injury. Office: 222 W Lancaster Ave PO Box 1785 Paoli PA 19301 E-mail: mdc@rifleinlaw.com

CHIANG, YUNG FRANK, law educator; b. Taichung, Taiwan, Jan. 2, 1936; came to U.S., 1961; s. Ruey-ting and Yueh-yin (Ho) C.; m. Quay-yin Lin, Nov. 1, 1969; children: Amy P., David H. LLB, Nat. Taiwan U., 1958; LLM, Northwestern U., 1962; JD, U. Chgo., 1965. Bar: Taiwan 1960, N.Y. 1974. Assoc. Yen & Lai Law Office, Taipei, Taiwan, 1960-61; editor The Lawyers Co-op Pub. Co., Rochester, N.Y., 1965; rsch. assoc. Harvard Law Sch., Cambridge, Mass., 1965-67; asst. prof. U. Ga. Sch. Law, Athens, 1967-72; assoc. prof. Fordham U. Sch. Law, N.Y.C., 1972-76, prof., 1976—. Bd. dirs. Taiwan Ctr., N.Y.C.; legal cons., vice-chmn. Asia Bank, N.A., Flushing, N.Y., 1983-88, also bd. dirs.; leader N.Y. judge and lawyers del. to China and Hong Kong, People to People Internat., 1994; organizer, moderator 5 Russian delegations to U.S., People to People Amb. Program, 1994-95; pres. Fordham U. Law Faculty Union, 2000—. Contbr. articles to profl. jours. Organizer, bd. dirs. The Taiwan Mcht. Assn. N.Y., Flushing, 1976-96, pres., 1980-84; pres. N.Y. chpt. Formosan Assn. for Pub. Affairs, Washington, 1991-92. Mem. N.Y. State Bar Assn., N.Am. Taiwanese Profs. Assn. (bd. dirs. 1994-2000, v.p. 1997-98, pres. 1998-99), Nat. Assn. of Securities Dealers (arbitrator 1976-98), Order of Coif. Avocations: reading, skiing, archery, swimming. Office: Fordham U Sch Law 140 W 62nd St New York NY 10023-7407 E-mail: fchiang@mail.lawnet.fordham.edu

CHIARA, MARGARET, prosecutor; BA, Fordham U.; MA PAce U.; JD, Rutgers U. Assoc. French and Lawrence, Cassopolis, Mich., 1979—82; prosecuting atty. Cass County Dist. Atty.'s Office, 1982—86; asminstr. Trial Ct. Assessment Commn., 1987—98; policy and planning dir. Office of Chief Justice of Mich. Supreme Ct., 1999—2001; U.S. atty. We. Dist. Mich. U.S. Dept. Justice, 2001—. Office: PO Box 208 Grand Rapids MI 49501*

CHIARCHIARO, FRANK JOHN, lawyer; b. Sept. 11, 1945; s. Joseph Russell and Mary Catherine (Salmieri) C.; m. Judith Ann Penna, July 5, 1970; 1 child, Peter. BEE, Manhattan Coll., 1967; MSEE, NYU, 1970; JD, Bklyn. Law Sch., 1976. Bar: N.Y. 1977, U.S. Dist. Ct. (ea. and so. dists.) N.Y. 1977, U.S. Ct. Appeals (11th cir.) 1985, U.S. Ct. Appeals (4th cir.) 1989, U.S. Ct. Appeals (5th cir.) 1991, U.S. Supreme Ct. 1987. Engr. USN, Bklyn., 1968-72, USCG, N.Y.C., 1972-77; ptnr. Mendes & Mount, LLP., 1977—. Contbr. articles to profl. jours. Decorated knight commdr. of Holy Sepulchre. Mem. ABA, ATLA, N.Y. State Bar Assn., Def. Rsch. Inst. Roman Catholic. Aviation, Insurance, Product liability. Office: Mendes & Mount 750 7th Ave New York NY 10019-6834 E-mail: frank.chiarchiaro@mendes.com

CHIATE, KENNETH REED, lawyer; b. Phoenix, June 24, 1941; s. Mac Arthur and Lillian (Lavin) C.; m. Jeannette Jensen, Aug. 21, 1965; children: Gregory Jensen, Carley MkKay. BA with honors, Claremont Men's Coll., 1963; JD, Columbia U., 1966; postgrad., U. So. Calif. Law Sch., 1967. Bar: Calif. 1967, U.S. Dist. Ct. (cen. dist.) Calif. 1967, Ariz. 1971, U.S. Dist. Ct. Ariz. 1971, U.S. Dist. Ct. (no. Dist.) Calif. 1982. Law clk. presiding justice U.S. Dist. Ariz., 1971; ptnr. Lillick McHose & Charles, L.A., 1971-91, Pillsbury Winthrop, LLP (formerly Pillsbury Madison), L.A., 1991—. Arbitrator Los Angeles Superior Ct. Arbitration Panel, 1979-82; mcpl. ct. judge protem Los Angeles, 1979-81; vice chmn. Los Angeles Open Com., 1969-71. Named among Calif. Lawyers of Yr. 2000, Calif. Mag. Mem. ABA, L.A. County Bar Assn., Calif. State Bar Assn., Ariz. State Bar Assn., Maricopa County Bar Assn., Am. Trial Lawyers Assn., L.A. Bus. Trial Lawyers Assn. Federal civil litigation, State civil litigation, Personal injury. Office: Pillsbury Winthrop LLP 725 S Figueroa St Ste 2800 Los Angeles CA 90017-5443 E-mail: kchiate@pillsburywinthrop.com

CHIECHI, CAROLYN PHYLLIS, federal judge; b. Newark, Dec. 6, 1943; BS magna cum laude, Georgetown U., 1965, JD, 1969, LLM in Taxation, 1971; LLD honoris causa, 2000. Bar: D.C. 1969, U.S. Dist. Ct. D.C., U.S. Ct. Fed. Claims, U.S. Tax Ct., U.S. Ct. Appeals (5th, 6th, 9th, D.C. and fed. cirs.), U.S. Supreme Ct. Atty., advisor to Judge Leo H. Irwin U.S. Tax Ct., Washington, 1969-71; assoc. Sutherland, Asbill & Brennan, 1971-76, ptnr., 1976-92; judge U.S. Tax Ct., 1992—. Mem. bd. regents Georgetown U., Washington, 1988-94, 95-2001, mem. nat. law alumni bd., 1986-93; bd. dirs. Stuart Stiller Meml. Found., Washington, 1986—; prin. Coun. for Excellence in Govt., Washington, 1990-92. Dept. editor Jour. of Taxation, 1986-92; contbr. articles to profl. jours. Fellow Am. Bar Found., Am. Coll. Tax Counsel; mem. ABA, FBA, D.C. Bar Assn., Women's Bar Assn., Am. Judicature Soc., Georgetown U. Alumni Assn. (bd. govs. 1994-2000, Alumni award 1994, Alumnae awards 1998). Office: US Tax Ct 400 2nd St NW Washington DC 20217-0002

CHILDRESS, STEVEN ALAN, law educator; b. Mobile, Ala., Feb. 9, 1959; s. Roy and Mary Helen (Gillion) C.; children: Ani, Steven. BA, U. Ala., 1979; JD, Harvard U., 1982; PhD in Jurisprudence and Social Policy, U. Calif., Berkeley, 1995. Bar: Calif. 1983, U.S. Ct. Appeals (5th cir.) 1984, D.C. 1986, U.S. Ct. Appeals (9th cir.) 1986, U.S. Supreme Ct. 1987. Law clk. to judge U.S. Ct. Appeals (5th cir.), Shreveport, La., 1982-83; assoc. Morrison & Foerster, San Francisco, 1983-84; adj. lectr. law Golden Gate U. Sch. Law, 1984-86; grad. instr. U. Calif., Berkeley, 1985-86; assoc. Brobeck, Phleger & Harrison, San Francisco, 1987-88; assoc. prof. law Tulane U. Law Sch., New Orleans, 1988-96, prof. law, 1996—. Co-author: Federal Standards of Review, 1986, 3d edit., 1999; contbr. articles to profl. jours. Regents fellow U. Calif. at Berkeley, 1985. Mem. Law and Soc. Assn., Phi Beta Kappa. Office: Tulane U Sch Law School of Law New Orleans LA 70118 E-mail: achildress@law.tulane.edu

CHILES, STEPHEN MICHAEL, lawyer; b. July 15, 1942; s. Daniel Duncan and Helen Virginia (Hayes) C.; m. Deborah E. Nash, June 13, 1964; children: Stephen, Abigail. BA, Davidson Coll., 1964; JD, Duke U., 1967. Bar: N.Y. 1970, Pa. 1978, Wis. 1981, Ill. 1986, U.S. Dist. Ct. (ea. dist.) Pa. 1978, U.S. Tax Ct. 1978, U.S. Supreme Ct. 1978. Officer trust dept. Irving Trust Co., N.Y.C., 1970-75, v.p., 1975-77; assoc. atty. Stassen Kostos & Mason, Phila., 1978-79, mem., shareholder, 1979-85; ptnr. McDermott, Will & Emery, Chgo., 1986—. Contbr. articles to profl. jours. Served to capt. U.S. Army, 1967-69. Decorated Bronze Star, Army Commendation medal. Mem. ABA, State Bar Wis., Exmoor Country Club (Highland Park, Ill.). Republican. Episcopalian. Estate planning, Estate taxation. Office: McDermott Will & Emery 227 W Monroe St Ste 3100 Chicago IL 60606-5096

CHILIVIS, NICKOLAS PETER, lawyer; b. Athens, Ga., Jan. 12, 1931; s. Peter Nickolas and Wessie Mae (Tanner) C.; m. Patricia Kay Tumlin, June 3, 1967; children— Taryn Tumlin, Nicole Tumlin, Nickolas Peter Tumlin. LL.B., U. Ga., Athens, 1953; LL.M., Atlanta Law Sch., Ga., 1955. Bar: Ga. 1952, U.S. Supreme Ct. 1965. Ptnr. Lester & Chilivis, Athens, Ga., 1953-58; ptnr. Erwin, Epting, Gibson & Chilivis, 1958-75; commr. of revenue State of Ga., Atlanta, 1975-77; ptnr. Powell, Goldstein, Frazer & Murphy, 1977-84, Chilivis & Grindler, Atlanta, 1984-95, Chilivis, Cochran, Larkins & Bever, Atlanta, 1995—. Adj. prof. U. Ga. Sch. Law, Athens, 1965-75. Author: Termination Settlement, 1955. Contbr. chpts. to books, articles to profl. jours. Bd. visitors U. Ga., Athens, 1983-85; trustee Skandalakis Found., Atlanta, 1984, Found. of the Holy Apostles; former trustee U. Ga. Found.; former mem. U. Ga. Rsch. Found. Bd.; pres. and sr. warden Ch. of Apostles. With USAFR, 1953-55. Recipient Archdiocesan medal Archbishop of North and South Am., 1980. Fellow Internat. Soc. Barristers, Am. Coll. Trial Lawyers, Am. Acad. Appellate Lawyers; mem. Am. Inns. of Ct. (emeritus, master), Old War Horse Lawyers Club, Lawyers Club Atlanta, Commerce Club, Heritage Club, (Atlanta), Pres.'s Club (U. Ga.), Elks. Avocations: Handball; tennis; writing; lecturing. General civil litigation, Criminal. Home: 855 W Paces Ferry Rd NW Atlanta GA 30327-2655 Office: Chilivis Cochran Larkins & Bever Chilivis Bldg 3127 Maple Dr NE Atlanta GA 30305-2503

CHILSTROM, ROBERT MEADE, lawyer; b. San Diego, July 1, 1945; s. Arne Oswald and Margaret Myra (Kippax) C.; m. Buena Lelia Hamlin, Aug. 24, 1968; children: Per Benjamin, Mikaela Lynn. BA, Princeton U., 1967; MA, Columbia U., 1969; JD, Yale U., 1973. Bar: N.Y. State 1975, U.S. Dist. Ct. (so. dist., ea. dist.) N.Y. 1975, U.S. Ct. Appeals (2d cir.) 1975. Assoc. Cravath, Swaine & Moore, N.Y.C., Paris, London, 1973-85, Skadden, Arps, Slate, Meagher & Flom LLP, N.Y.C., 1985-87, ptnr., 1987—. General corporate, Finance, Private international. Office: Skadden Arps Slate Meagher & Flom LLP Rm 31-100 4 Times Sq New York NY 10036-6595 E-mail: rchilstr@skadden.com

CHILVERS, ROBERT MERRITT, lawyer; b. Long Beach, Calif., Oct. 23, 1942; s. James Merritt and Elizabeth Louise (Blackburn) C.; m. Sandra Lee Rigg, Sept. 5, 1969; children: Jeremy Merritt, Jessica Rigg. AB, U. Calif., Berkeley, 1972; JD, Harvard U., 1975. Bar: Calif. 1975, U.S. Dist. Ct. (no. dist.) Calif. 1975, U.S. Ct. Appeals (9th cir.) 1980, U.S. Supreme Ct. 1980, U.S. Dist. Ct. (ctrl. dist.) Calif. 1981, U.S. Ct. Fed. Claims, 1984, U.S. Dist. Ct. (ea. dist.) Calif. 1987, U.S. Ct. Appeals (fed. cir.) 1987. Assoc. Brobeck, Phleger & Harrison, San Francisco, 1975-82, ptnr., 1982-93; spl. master U.S. Dist. Ct. (no. dist.) Calif., 1994-99; shareholder Chilvers & Taylor, PC, San Rafael, Calif., 1996—. Faculty U. Calif., Hastings Sch. Law, San Francisco, 1983-89, Emory U., Atlanta, 1984-90, fed. practice program U.S. Dist. Ct. (no. dist.) Calif., 1984-86, Nat. Inst. for Trial Advocacy, 1986—, Cardozo Law Sch., Yeshiva U., N.Y.C., 1993—, Stanford U. Law Sch., 1994—, Widener U. Sch. Law, Wilmington, 1994-96, U. San Francisco Sch. Law, 1994—. Mem. Calif. Sch. Bds. Assn, 1985-89; trustee Mill Valley Sch. Dist., Calif., 1985-89, chmn., 1987-89; bd. dirs. Marin County Sch. Bds. Assn., Calif., 1985-86, Artisans, Mill Valley, Calif., 1999—. With USMC, 1964-71. Mem. Calif. Bar Assn. (commendation for Outstanding Contbns. to the delivery of vol. legal svcs. 1984), Marin County Bar Assn., Tau Beta Pi, Sigma Tau. Alternative dispute resolution, General civil litigation, State civil litigation. Office: Chilvers & Taylor PC 83 Vista Marin Dr San Rafael CA 94903-5228 E-mail: chilvers-taylor@home.com

CHIMPLES, GEORGE, lawyer; b. Canton, Ohio, Oct. 8, 1924; s. Mark and Katherine (Hines) C.; m. Margaret Joanna Cavalaris, July 31, 1949; children: Alicia Candace, Mark II, John Hines, Katherine Hines. AB, Princeton U., 1951; LLB, Harvard Coll., 1954. Bar: Pa. 1955, U.S. Dist. Ct. (ea. dist.) Pa. 1955, U.S. Ct. Appeals (3d cir.) 1955, U.S. Ct. Claims, 1965, U.S. Tax Ct., 1965. Assoc. Stradley, Ronon, Stevens & Young, Phila., 1954-61, gen. ptnr., 1961-92; pvt. practice Wayne, Pa., 1993—. Adj. prof. law U. Pa., Drexel U. Grad. Sch. Bus.; co-authored establishment of overseas infrastructure for securities mktg. in Europe and the Antilles. Trustee Christ Ch. Preservation Trust; permament assoc. Phila. Mus. Art. Capt. USAAF, 1942-46, ETO. Decorated D.F.C., Air medal with four oak leaf clusters, Air Force Commendation medal, Victory medal, four Battle Stars; recipient Royal Air Force plaque, 1994. Mem. ABA (chmn. subcom. regulated investment cos.), Phila. Bar Assn. (tax sect.), Internat. Bar Assn., Internat. Fiscal Assn. (tax treaty sect.), Mid-Atlantic Coun., Commanderie de Bordeaux aux Etats-Unis d'Amerique (archivist), Newcomen Soc. U.S. (com. chmn., nat. trustee, life mem.) Army and Navy Club (Washington chpt.), Penn Club (life, bd. dirs., historian) Athenaeum of Phila. (life), Libr. Co. of Phila. (life), Phila. Mus. Art (permanent assoc.), Phila. Club, Princeton Club N.Y., Cannon Club (Princeton chpt.), Merion Cricket Club. General corporate, Estate planning, Taxation, general. Home: 1179 Lafayette Rd Wayne PA 19087-2110 Office: 1522 Overington St Philadelphia PA 19124-5808

CHIN, DAVIS, lawyer; b. Evansville, Ind., Dec. 13, 1947; s. Frank S. M. and Mamie (Shu) C.; m. Pauline C., Aug. 3, 1974; 1 child, Davis M. BS, Rose-Hulman Inst. Tech., Terre Haute, Ind., 1969; JD, U. Balt., 1974; LLM in Taxation, John Marshall Law Sch., 1981. Bar: Ill. 1974, U.S. Dist. Ct. (no. dist.) 1974, U.S. Ct. Appeals (7th cir.) 1974, U.S. Patent and Trademark Office 1974, U.S. Claims Ct. 1977, U. S. Tax Ct. 1977, U.S. Supreme Ct. 1977, U.S. Ct. Appeals (fed. cir.) 1982. Staff atty. CTS Corp., Elkhart, Ind., 1974; assoc. Petherbridge, Lindgren & Gilhooly, Chtd., Chgo., 1974-78; staff atty. Borg-Warner Corp., 1978-80, Container Corp. Am., Chgo., 1980-84; pvt. practice, 1984—. Instr. Prairie State Coll., Chgo. Heights, 1987-90, 94, South Suburban Coll., South Holland, Ill., 1989-91, Roosevelt U., Olympia Fields, Ill., 1990-93. Elder United Presbyn. Ch., South Holland, 1986—; panel program atty. Chgo. Vol. Legal Svcs., 1988—. Mem. Am. Intellectual Property Law Assn., Chgo. Bar Assn., Intellectual Property Law Assn. Chgo., Patent Law Assn. Chgo. (bd. mgrs. 1985-87, 94-96). Avocations: tennis, golf, travel. General practice, Intellectual property, Taxation, general. Home: 11428 Plattner Dr Mokena IL 60448-9228 Office: 111 W Washington St Ste 1025 Chicago IL 60602-2745 E-mail: davischin@juno.com

CHIN, KELVIN HENRY, business consultant; b. Boston, Jan. 7, 1951; s. Henry W.F. and King (Lee) C.; m. Peggy Abbott, July 26, 1987; children: Jesse, Samantha. Student, U. Strasbourg, France, 1971; AB cum laude, high distinction in French, Dartmouth Coll., 1973; MA, Yale U., 1974; JD, Boston Coll., 1983. Dir. in East Asia, Found. for Creative Intelligence, Hong Kong, 1974-78; co-founder Microtex Corp., Cambridge, Mass., 1978-83; life ins. agent Sun Life of Canada, Wellesley, 1979-81; law clerk Bingham, Dana & Gould, Boston, 1980-83; summer assoc. to assoc. Choate, Hall & Stewart, 1982-84; employee benefits cons. Hicks Pension Svcs., Lexington, Mass., 1984-86; pres. Bus. Consulting Assocs., Boston, San Diego, 1986-92; dir. mediation Ctr. for Mediation, Am. Arbitration Assn., San Diego, 1992-93, regional v.p. Las Vegas, Nev., 1993-96, L.A., 1996-2000; co-founder The Health Accord LLC, N.Y.C., 2000; pres. AgreeOnline, Inc., L.A., 2000; bus. cons., 2000—. Mem. nat. adv. bd. Ctr. for Med. Ethics and Mediation, San Diego, 1992—; cons. Continuing Edn. of the Bar, Calif. 1992—. Editor: International Law Dictionary, 1983. Ombudsman Calif. Dept. on Aging, San Diego, 1991-93; com. mem. Waldorf Sch. of San Diego PTA, 1992-93; vol. mediator Ctr. for Mcpl. Dispute Resolution City Atty.'s Office, San Diego, 1990-93; bd. advs. U. W.L.A., 1996-97, TheLivingLibrary.com. Rufus Choate scholar Dartmouth Coll., 1971-73; Nat. Def. Fgn. Language fellow U.S. Dept. Edn., 1973-74. Mem. ABA (dispute resolution sect.), Am. Arbitration Assn. (blue ribbon mediator panel 1992—), San Diego County Bar Assn. (treas. alternative dispute resolution sect. 1991-93), Soc. Profls. in Dispute Resolution, So. Calif. Mediation Assn., The Ombudsman Assn., Nat. Panel of Mediators, New Media Advo Coun., Asian Bus. League, Asia Soc., Turnaround Mgmt. Assn., Internet CEO Roundtable. Avocations: basketball, philosophy. E-mail: Kelvin.Chin@verizon.net

CHIN, MING, state supreme court justice; b. Klamath Falls, Oreg., Aug. 31, 1942; m. Carol Lynn Joe, Dec. 19, 1971; children: Jennifer, Jason. BA in Polit. Sci., U. San Francisco, 1964, JD, 1967. Bar: Calif., 1970, U.S. Fed. Ct., U.S. Tax Ct. Assoc., head trial dept. Aiken, Kramer & Cummings, Oakland, Calif., 1973-76, prin., 1976-88; dep. dist. atty. Alameda County, 1970-72; judge Alameda County Superior Ct., 1988-90; assoc. justice divsn. 3 Ct. Appeal 1st Dist., 1990-94; presiding justice 1st Dist. Ct. Appeal Divsn. 3, San Francisco, 1994-96; state supreme ct. assoc. justice Calif. Supreme Ct., 1996—. Capt. U.S. Army, 1967-69, Vietnam, USAR, 1969-71. Mem. ABA, Calif. Judges Assn., State Bar Calif., Alameda County Bar Assn., San Francisco Dist. Atty.'s Commn. Hate Crimes, Commonwealth Club of Calif. (pres. 1998), Asian Am. Bar Assn., Alpha Sigma Nu. Office: Supreme Court Calif 350 Mcallister St Fl 1 San Francisco CA 94102-4783

CHIN, STEPHANIE ANNE, lawyer; b. San Francisco, Oct. 21, 1965; BSBA, U. Calif., Berkeley, 1987; JD, U. Calif., San Francisco, 1991; student, Hastings Coll. of Law. Bar: Hawaii 1991, U.S. Dist. Ct. Hawaii 1991. Dir., shareholder Torkildson, Katz, Fonseca, Jaffe, Moore, Hetherington, Honolulu, 1991—. Editor, mem. Hastings Law Jour., 1989-91. Recipient Am. Jurisprudence award Lawyer's Cool. Pub. Co., 1989. Mem. ABA, Nat. Assn. Pacific Am. Bar Assn., Hawaii Women Lawyers, Hawaii State Bar Assn., Arbitrator-Ct. Annexed Arbitration Program. General civil litigation, Contracts commercial. Office: Torkildson Katz Fonseca 700 Bishop St Fl 15 Honolulu HI 96813-4187

CHING, ANTHONY BARTHOLOMEW, lawyer, educator, consultant; b. Shanghai, China, Nov. 18, 1935; came to U.S., 1956; s. William L.K. and Christina Ching; m. Nancy Ann Prigge, Apr. 10, 1961; children: Anthony, Alice, Alexander, Andrew, Ann, Audrey, Anastasia, Albert. Student, Cath. U. West, France, 1953-54, Cambridgeshire Tech. Coll., 1954-55; matriculated, Cambridge (Eng.) U., 1955, St. John's Coll., 1956; BS in Geology, U. Ariz., 1959, postgrad., 1959-60, LLB, 1965; LLM, Harvard U., 1971. Bar: Ariz. 1965, U.S. Dist. Ct. Ariz. 1965, U.S. Ct. Appeals (9th cir.) 1969, U.S. Supreme Ct. 1969, U.S. Ct. Appeals (5th cir.) 1972. Geologist Duval Sulphur and Potash, Kingman and Tucson, Ariz., 1959-60; part-time geologist Am. Smelting and Refining Co., Tucson, 1960-61; engr. Marum and Marum Cons. Engrs., 1961-65; atty., sole practice, 1965-66; atty., chief trial counsel Pima County Legal Aid Soc., 1966-70; fellow clin. legal edn. Harvard Law Sch., Cambridge, Mass., 1970-71; acting prof. law Loyola U. Law Sch., L.A., 1971-73, 74-75, adj. prof., 1982; dir. litigation, acting project dir. Hawaii Legal Aid Soc., Honolulu, 1973-74; chief counsel Econ. Protection divsn. Atty. Gen.'s Office, State of Ariz., Phoenix, 1975-79; solicitor gen. Ariz. Dept. Law, 1979-91, asst. atty. gen., 1991-97; pvt. practice Tempe, Ariz., 1997—. Chmn. We. Attys. Gen. Litigation Action Com., 1983-86; pres. Nat. Consumer Law Ctr., Boston, 1979—; judge pro tem Maricopa County Superior Ct., 1983-93, 94—, Ct. Appeals, 1994. Mem. Pima County Dem. Com., 1966-70, Tucson Cmty. Coun., 1968-70, Pio Decimo Ctr., 1968-70; bd. dirs., Ariz. Consumer Coun., 1968-70; pres. Young Dems. Greater Tucson, 1969-70. Mem.: ABA, State Bar Ariz. (100 Women and Minority Lawyers in Ariz. award 2000), Nat. Legal Aid and Defender Assn. (treas. 1973—74, Reginald Heber Smith award 1969), Harvard Law Sch. Assn. Ariz. (pres. 1980—83). Home: 2632 S Fairfield Dr Tempe AZ 85282-2924 Office: 2043 E Southern Ave Tempe AZ 85282 E-mail: abching@azbar.org

CHING, LOUIS MICHAEL, lawyer; b. New Orleans, June 26, 1956; BS, Tulane U., 1979; JD, Willamette U., 1985. Bar: Oreg. 1986, Hawaii, 1986, U.S. Dist. Ct. Hawaii 1986, U.S. Ct. Appeals (9th cir.) 1989, U.S. Supreme Ct. 1990. Pvt. practice law, Honolulu, 1986-87, 90—; arbitrator, 1999. Mem. Hawaii Assn. Criminal Def. Lawyers, Phi Beta Kappa. Avocations: tennis, online Internet short-term stock trading. Criminal. E-mail: Alohajustice@hotmail.com

CHIPMAN, MARION WALTER, retired judge; b. Penokee, Kans., May 5, 1920; s. James Edwin and May Maude (Hatcher) C.; m. Thelma Nadine Clark, Nov. 1, 1941 (div. 1965); m. Nancy Jo Payne, May 28, 1983; children: Clark D., Jill Ellen. AB in Social Sci., Ft. Hays (Kans.) State U., 1942; JD, Washburn U., 1948. Bar: Kans. 1948, U.S. Dist. Ct. Kans. 1948, U.S. Ct. Appeals 1970, U.S. Supreme Ct. 1970. Supt. Prairieview (Kans.) Sch., 1942; atty. County of Graham, Hill City, Kans., 1949-53; counselor County of Johnson, Olathe, 1967-68; judge 10th Jud. Dist. Kans. Dist. Ct., 1980-91, sr. judge, 1996-2001. Sgt. USAAF, 1942-46. Mem. ABA (life), Johnson County Bar Assn. (life), Kans. Bar Assn. (life), Am. Judicature, Am. Judge's Assn., Am. Arbitration Assn., Am. Legion (life), Masons, Shriners, Elks. Methodist. Home: 100 Buckingham 6060 Shore Blvd S Gulfport FL 33707-5804

CHISHOLM, TOMMY, lawyer, utility company executive; b. Baldwyn, Miss., Apr. 14, 1941; s. Thomas Vaniver and Rubel (Duncan) C.; m. Janice McClanahan, June 20, 1964; children: Mark Alan (dec.), Andrea, Stephen Thomas, Patrick Ervin. BSCE, Tenn. Tech. U., 1963; JD, Samford U., 1969; MBA, Ga. State U., 1984. Registered profl. engr., Ala., Del., Ga., Fla., Ky., La., N.H., Miss., N., Pa., Tenn., S.C., Va., W.Va. Civil engr. TVA, Knoxville, Tenn., 1963-64; design engr. So. Co. Svcs., Birmingham, Ala., 1964-69, coord. spl. projects Atlanta, 1969-73, sec., house counsel, 1977-82, v.p., sec., house counsel, 1982-98; v.p., assoc. gen. counsel, sec. So. Co., 1998—, asst. to pres., 1973-75, sec., asst. treas., 1977—; mgr. adminstrv. svcs. Gulf Power Co., Pensacola, Fla., 1975-77; sec. So. Energy, Inc., Atlanta, 1981-82; v.p., sec. So. Energy Resources Inc., 1982-2000. Mem. ABA, State Bar Ala., Am. Soc. Corp. Secs., Am. Corp. Counsel Assn., Nat. Assn. Corp. Dirs., Phi Alpha Delta, Beta Gamma Sigma. General corporate. Office: The Southern Co 270 Peachtree St NW Ste 2200 Atlanta GA 30303-1247

CHMURA, MICHAEL J. news officer; b. Springfield, Mass., Aug. 17, 1957; s. Mitchell John and Angela C.; m. Susan Gene Sutherland; 1 child, Evan. BA, Northeastern U., 1981. News officer Harvard Law Sch., Cambridge, 1984—. Office: Harvard Law Sch 1563 Massachusetts Ave Cambridge MA 02138

CHO, CHI-HYOUNG, lawyer; b. Seoul, Mar. 9, 1959; m. In-Sook Kang, May 25, 1985; children: Sung-Ju, Tim Sunghoon. LLB, Sung Kyun Kwan U., Seoul, 1982; LLM, Seoul Nat. U., 1988, Tulane U., 1991; JD, Golden Gate U., 1995. Mil. prosecutor, judge, lectr. Army, Rep. of Korea, 1985-88; legal counsel, atty. at law Samsung Group, Seoul, 1989-90, 95-98; ptnr. Hwang Mok Park & Jim, 1998—. Lectr. Sung Kyun Kwan U., Seoul, 1998, Jud. Rsch. and Tng. Inst., Seoul, 2000. Co-editor: Law Dictionary (in Korean), 1991. Capt. Judge Adv. Army, 1985-88. Mem. Korean Bar Assn., Seoul Bar Assn., N.Y. Bar Assn. General corporate, Private international, Mergers and acquisitions. Office: Hwang Mok Park & Jim 9th Fl Dakyung Bldg 120 2-ka Taepyung-ro Chung-ku Seoul 100-724 Republic of Korea Fax: 82-2-772-2800. E-mail: chcho@hmpj.com

CHO, TAI YONG, lawyer; b. Seoul, Republic of Korea, May 27, 1943; came to U.S., 1966; s. Nam Suck and Sun Yeo (Yoon) C; m. Hea Sun Cho, July 14, 1973; children: Robert, Richard, Susan. BS, Seoul U., 1965; MS, Cooper Union, 1971; CE, Columbia U., 1971; JD, Fordham U., 1981. Bar: N.Y., 1982; registered profl. engr., N.Y., 1973. Engr. Ministry of Constrn., Seoul, 1965-66, Andrews & Clark, N.Y.C., 1967-68, Parsons, Brinckerhoff, Quade & Douglas, N.Y.C., 1969-71; v.p. John R. McCarthy Corp., 1972-80. Mem. ASCE, ABA, N.Y. State Bar Assn., Am. Arbitration Assn. (panel of arbitrators), Am.-Korean Lawyers Assn. of N.Y. (pres. 1988), Korean TV Broadcasters Assn., Am. (pres. 1990), Internat. Korean Lawyers Assn. (v.p. 1991). Contracts commercial, General corporate, Private international. Home: 56 Tuttle Rd Briarcliff Manor NY 10510-2233 Office: 309 5th Ave New York NY 10016-6509 E-mail: taicho@netzero.net

CHOBOT, JOHN CHARLES, lawyer; b. N.Y.C., Feb. 14, 1948; s. Arthur E. and Eleanore L. (Lotito) C.; m. Catherine Anne Moran, Aug. 24, 1974; children: Christine, Keith. BA, Cornell U., 1969; MS in Edn., CCNY, 1971; JD, Fordham U., 1975. Bar: N.Y. 1976, U.S. Dist. Ct. (we. dist.) N.Y. 1976, N.J. 1985, U.S. Dist. Ct. N.J. 1985. Assoc. Phillips, Lytle, Hitchcock, Blaine & Huber, Buffalo, 1975-85; with The CIT Group/Sales Financing, Inc., Livingston, N.J., 1985-90; sr. v.p., chief counsel bus. fin. divsn. AT&T Capital Corp., 1990-98; v.p. law, asst. gen. counsel Newcourt Credit Group Inc., Parsippany, N.J., 1998-99, The CIT Group, Inc., 1999-2000; counsel Am. Express Co., 2000-01; pvt. practice, 2001—. Adj. prof. law Seton Hall Law Sch., 2000—. Contbr. articles on equipment leasing, bankruptcy and secured transactions to legal jours. Mem. ABA, N.Y. State Bar Assn., Am. Bankruptcy Inst., Comml. Law League, Kappa Alpha Soc. Bankruptcy, Contracts commercial, General corporate. Home: 23 Laurel Hill Dr Randolph NJ 07869-4632 Office: Newcourt Credit Group Inc 2 Gatehall Dr Parsippany NJ 07054-4521 Fax: 973-355-7057. E-mail: johnchobot@newcourt.com

CHOI, UNGHWAN RAPHAEL, lawyer, economist; b. Pusan, Korea, Feb. 7, 1962; m. Grace Choi. BA in Econ., Seoul Nat. U., 1984; JD, PhD in Econ., UCLA, 1992. Bar: Calif. 1992, U.S. Dist. Ct. (ctrl. dist.) 1992. Internat. tax mgr., economist Coopers & Lybrand, L.A., 1992-96; sr. dir. KPMG, 1996-97; sr. atty. Kim & Chang, Seoul, 1997—. Author: Tax Management Foreign Income Portfolios: Transfer Pricing: Foreign Rules and Practice Outside of Europe, Part 2, 2000; contbr. articles to profl. jours. Earhart Found. fellow in econ., 1984-86; John Olin Found. fellow in law and econ., 1985; Inst. Superior Edn. fellow, 1981-84. Mem. Seoul Nat. U. Coll. Econ. and Bus. (bd. dirs. 1999). Mergers and acquisitions, Securities, Corporate taxation. Office: Kim & Chang 223 Naeja-Dong Chongro-Ku Seoul 110-720 Republic of Korea Fax: 822-737-9091. E-mail: uhchoi@kimchang.com

CHONG, STEPHEN CHU LING, lawyer; b. Lakewood, Ohio, Aug. 1, 1957; s. Richard Seng Hoon C. and Betty J. (Chong) Wamego; m. Sheryl Kay Horton, Nov. 23, 1984; children: Evan M. G., Erin M.L., Elena M.L., Eric M.K., Ethan M.L. BA, Calvin Coll., 1979; JD, Ohio State U., 1982. Bar: Fla. 1982, U.S. Dist. Ct. (mid. dist.) Fla. 1983, U.S. Ct. Appeals (11th cir.) 1982, U.S. Tax Ct. 1985; bd. cert. real estate lawyer Fla. Bar Bd. Legal Specialization and Edn. Assoc. Caudill, Drage, de Beaubien, Orlando, Fla., 1982-83; shareholder Caudill, Chong & Migliaccio, Winter Garden, 1983-84; assoc. Thomas R. Rogers & Assocs., Longwood, 1984-90; of counsel Litchford, Christopher, Orlando, 1990-92; pres., shareholder Marks & Chong, 1992-2001; ptnr. Arnold Matheny & Eagan PA, 2001—. Mem. nominating bd. City of Orlando, 1993-98, chmn. 1996-97; mem. area bus. com. Naval Tng. Ctr. Reuse Com., Orlando, 1994-95; bd. trustees Minority/Women Bus. Enterprise Alliance, Orlando, 1994-99; chair Realtor Rels. Com., Orlando, 1992-93; presenter in field. Contbr. articles to profl. jours. Mem. cultural diversity com. Orlando Sci. Ctr., 1993-2000; mem. cmty. adv. bd. WMFE-TV/FM, Orlando, 1994-95; mem. adv. bd. Ctrl. Fla. Family, Orlando, 1994-2000; pres. Asian Am. C. of C., Orlando, 1993-94; trustee Calvin Coll., Grand Rapids, Mich., 1999—. Recipient Vision award-Small Bus. Downtown Orlando Partnership, 1994. Mem. ABA, Fla. Bar Assn., Orange County Bar Assn., Christian Legal Soc. Ctr. Fla. (pres. 1999-2000). Presbyterian. General corporate, Franchising, Real property. Office: Arnold Matheny & Eagan PA 801 N Magnolia Ave Ste 201 Orlando FL 32803

CHOPIN, L. FRANK, lawyer; b. New Orleans, Apr. 29, 1942; s. Alton Francis and Floretta (Thensted) C.; children: Philip, Alexandra, Christopher. BBA, Loyola U., New Orleans, 1964, JD, 1966; diploma in mil. law, Judge Adv. Gen.'s Sch., U. Va. Sch. Law, 1966; postgrad., Nat. Law Ctr., George Wash. U., 1967-68; LLM in Taxation, U. Miami, Fla., 1976; PhD in Law, Cambridge U., Eng., 1986. Bar: La. 1966, Fla. 1968, Iowa 1980, U.S. Dist. Ct. (so. dist.) Fla. 1968, U.S. Ct. Appeals (5th cir.) 1968. Ptnr. Chopin & Chopin, Miami, 1969-77; assoc. prof. law Drake U., Des Moines, 1979-80; ptnr. Cadwalader, Wickersham & Taft, Palm Beach, Fla., 1980-94, Chopin, Miller & Yudenfreund, Palm Beach, 1994-98, Chopin & Miller, Palm Beach, 1999—. Adj. prof. law U. Miami, 1982-96, U. Sherbrooke, Can., 1982-94. Author: The New Residency Rules for Canadian Tax Considerations, 1985; also numerous articles in legal jours. Mem. Housing Fin. Authority; trustee Preservation Found., Palm Beach Community Chest, Inc. Served to capt. U.S. Army, 1966-68. Mem. ABA, Internat. Bar Assn., Fed. Bar Assn., Fla. Bar (tax sect.), Loyola U. Alumni Assn., U. Miami Alumni Assn., St. Thomas More Law Soc., Phi Alpha Delta (charter). Republican. Roman Catholic. Estate taxation, Taxation, general, Personal income taxation. Office: Chopin & Miller 505 S Flagler Dr Ste 300 West Palm Beach FL 33401-5942

CHOPIN, SUSAN GARDINER, lawyer; b. Miami, Fla., Feb. 23, 1947; d. Maurice and Judith (Warden) Gardiner; m. M.S. Rukeyser, Jr. Mar. 10, 1997; children: Philip, Alexandra, Christopher. BBA, Loyola U., New Orleans, 1966; JD cum laude, U. Miami, 1972; MLitt (Law), Oxford U., Eng., 1983. Bar: Fla. 1972, Iowa 1979. Sr. law clk. to judge U.S. Dist. Ct. (so. dist.) Fla., Miami, 1972-73; ptnr. Chopin & Chopin, 1973-77; assoc. prof. law sch. Drake U., Des Moines, 1979-80; pvt. practice law Palm Beach, Fla., 1981—; ptnr. Chopin & Chopin, 1999—. Lectr. in family law. Editor (mem. editl. bd.): (jour.) Fla. Bar Jour., 1975; editor: (co-chair editl. bd.) Fla. Bar Family Law Commentator, 2000—01. Trustee Preservation Found. of Palm Beach, 1986-89. Mem.: ABA, Fla. Bar Assn., Iowa Bar Assn., Fed. Bar Assn., Fla. Assn. Women Lawyers, Soc. Wig and Robe, Palm Beach County Bar Assn., Phi Kappa Phi, Phi Alpha Delta. State civil litigation, Family and matrimonial, General practice. Office: Esperante Bldg 222 Lakeview Ave Ste 1150 West Palm Beach FL 33401-6149

CHOU, YUNG-MING, lawyer; b. Tainan, Taiwan, Jan. 29, 1959; came to U.S., 1985; s. Ming-Chien and Hong-Hsi Chou; m. Chueh Wang; 1 child, Hsueh-Ting. LLB, Fu Jen Cath. U., Taipei, Taiwan, 1981; M of Criminal Justice Adminstrn., Oklahoma City U., 1986, JD, 1993. Bar: Calif. 1994, N.Y. 1994, U.S. Dist. (no. dist.) Calif. 1995, U.S. Dist. Ct. (ctrl. dist.) Calif. 1996, U.S. Tax Ct. 1998. In-house legal counsel, claim adjuster The First Ins. Co., Ltd., Taipei, 1983-85; lectr. Taiwan Police Coll., 1988-89; claims mgr. Ins. Co. N.Am., 1987-91; copr. counsel Aces Rsch., Inc., Fremont, Calif., 1994-96; pvt. practice Yung-Ming Chou, Atty. at Law, 1995—. Recipient Dr. Sun Yat Sen scholarship Kuomintang, Taipei, 1991-93; named Amb. at Large, Oklahoma City Mayor, 1986, Hon. Citizen, Oklahoma City Mayor, 1986. Mem. Alameda County Bar Assn. General civil litigation, Contracts commercial, General corporate. Office: 39111 Paseo Padre Pkwy Ste 207 Fremont CA 94538-1695

CHOUKAS-BRADLEY, JAMES RICHARD, lawyer; b. Hartford, Conn., Sept. 11, 1950; s. William Lee and Paula Ann (Elliott) Bradley; m. Melanie Rose Choukas, June 21, 1975; children: Sophia Crane, Jesse Elliott. BA cum laude, U. Vt., 1974; JD cum laude, Georgetown U., 1980. Bar: D.C. 1980, U.S. Ct. Appeals (D.C. cir.) 1981, U.S. Ct. Appeals (11th cir.) 1984, U.S. Ct. Appeals (10th cir.) 1985, U.S. Ct. Appeals (4th cir.) 1990, U.S. Ct. Appeals (6th cir.) 1993. Reporter, editor The Berlin (N.H.) Reporter, 1974; editor, pub., creative dir. Ad Lib, Gorham, N.H., 1974-75; asst. to city mgr. City of Berlin, 1975-77; legal intern Congl. Budget Office, Washington, 1978; rsch. assoc. Schlossberg-Cassidy & Assocs., 1978-80; assoc. Miller, Balis & O'Neil, P.C., 1980-84, mem., v.p., 1985—, exec. com., 1993-97. Legal advisor, first v.p. Sugarloaf Citizens Assn., Barnesville, Md., 1987-2000; counsel Mcpl. Gas Authority of Ga., Natural Gas Acquisition Corp. of City of Clarksville, Tenn., S.E. Ala. Gas Dist., Mcpl. Gas Authority of Miss.; gen. counsel Tenn. Energy Acquisition Corp., Lower Ala. Gas Dist.; spkr. in field; pioneer in joint action and pub. financing in deregulated natural gas industry. Author: The Early Days, 1975. Pres. D.C. Dukes Athletic Club, Washington, 1978-81, Montgomery Dukes, 1987-92; com. chmn. Berlin Bicentennial Commn., Berlin, 1975-76; youth soccer and flag football coach Seneca Sports Assn. Regents scholar State of N.Y., 1968. Mem.: Energy Bar Assn., Sugarloaf Citizens Assn., Nat. Youth Sports Coaches Assn., Dickerson Cmty. Assn., Historic Medley Dist., Energy Bar Assn., Sugarloaf Citizens Assn., Dickerson Cmty. Assn., Hist. Medley Dist., Nat. Youth Sports Coaches Assn., For A Rural Montgomery, Randolph Mountin Club, For a Rural Montgomery, Randolph Mountain Club, Phi Beta Kappa, Phi Beta Kappa. Avocations: softball, guitar, songwriting, hiking, travel. Administrative and regulatory, FERC practice, Municipal (including bonds). E-mail: jchoukasbradley@mbolaw.com

CHOVANES, EUGENE, lawyer; b. Hazleton, Penn., Jan. 1, 1926; s. Michael and Anna (Watro) C.; m. Claire Amelia Puhak, Mar. 27, 1952; children: Michael, George, Nicholas, Joseph, John. BS in Engring., Lehigh U., 1950; JD, Villanova U., 1960. Bar: Pa. 1961. Assoc. William Steell Jackson & Sons, Phila., 1957-63; ptnr. Jackson & Chovanes, Phila. and Bala-Cynwyd, Pa., 1963—. Lectr. patent law Villanova U., 1957-80. Sgt. U.S. Army, 1943-46, to 1st lt. Ordnance Corps, 1951-52. Mem. ABA, Phila. Intellectual Property Law Assn., Phila. Bar Assn., Soc. Registered Profl. Engrs., Am. Intellectual Property Law Assn. Patent, Trademark and copyright. Office: 1 Bala Plz Ste 319 Bala Cynwyd PA 19004-1405

CHOY, HERBERT YOUNG CHO, federal judge; b. Makaweli, Hawaii, Jan. 6, 1916; s. Doo Wook and Helen (Nahm) C.; m. Dorothy Helen Shular, June 16, 1945. BA, U. Hawaii, 1938; JD, Harvard U., 1941. Bar: Hawaii 1941. Law clk. City and County of Honolulu, 1941; assoc. Fong & Miho, 1947-48; ptnr. Fong, Miho and Choy, 1948-57; atty. gen. Territory of Hawaii, 1957-58; ptnr. Fong, Miho, Choy & Robinson, Honolulu, 1958-71; sr. judge U.S. Ct. Appeals (9th cir.), 1971—. Adv. com. on constrn. judiciary bldgs. Chief Justice Hawaii, 1970-71; compilation commn. to compile Revised Laws of Hawaii, 1955, 1953-57; com. to draft Hawaii rules of criminal procedure Supreme Ct., 1958-59; com. on pacific ocean territories Jud. Conf. the U.S., 1976-79. Dir. Legal Aid Soc. Hawaii, 1959-61; trustee Hawaii Loa Coll., 1963-79. Capt. U.S. Army, 1941-46, lt. col. Res. Recipient Order of Civil Merit award Republic of Korea, 1973. Fellow Am. Bar Found.; mem. ABA, Hawaii Bar Assn. (exec. com. 1953, 57, 61, legal ethics and unauthorized practices com. 1953, com. on legis. 1959). Office: US Ct Appeals 300 Ala Moana Blvd Rm C305 Honolulu HI 96850-0305

CHRISANT, ROSEMARIE KATHRYN, law library administrator; b. Chgo., Oct. 9, 1946; d. Theodore and Angeline Frances (Pawlik) Layne; 1 child, Paula Ellen Marie. BS in Edn., No. Ill. U., 1967; MLS, Rosary Coll., 1971. High sch. English tchr. Chgo. Sch. System, 1967-70; asst. libr. Akron (Ohio) Law Libr. Assn., 1971-76, libr. dir., 1976—. Cons. law firms, Akron. Contbr. articles to profl. jours. Mem. ABA, Am. Assn. Law Librs., Ohio Regional Assn. Law Librs. (Outstanding Svc. award 1986), Spl. Libr. Assn., Ohio Libr. Assn. Office: Akron Law Libr Assn Summit County Courthouse 209 S High St Rm 4 Akron OH 44308-1625 E-mail: allarkc@akronlawlib.org

CHRISS, TIMOTHY D. A. lawyer; b. Balt., Oct. 26, 1950; s. Evan Alevizatos and Ceres (Rogokos) C.; m. Karin Elizabeth Jones, Feb. 25, 1978; children: Alexander Wilhelm Alevizatos, Caroline Elizabeth. BA, Washington and Lee U., 1972; JD, Cath. U. Am., 1976. Bar: Md. 1976, U.S. Dist. Ct. Md. 1976. Assoc. Gordon, Feinblatt, Rothman, Hoffberger & Hollander, Balt., 1976-83, ptnr., 1983—. Com. on character Ct. Appeals Md., 1991—. Bd. dirs. Citizens Planning and Housing Assn., Balt.,1978-80, Devel. Credit Fund, Inc., 1996—, Union Meml. Hosp. Found., 1996—, Greater Homewood Cmty. Corp., 1997-99; trustee Gilman Sch., 1988-92, Maryvale Prep. Sch., 1997—. Fellow Md. Bar Found.; mem. ABA, Am. Coll. Real Estate Lawyers, Md. Bar Assn. (coun. real property sect. 1988-2000, sec. 1992-94, chmn.-elect 1994-96, chmn. 1996-98, chmn. real property code revision com. 1988-92), Bar Assn. Balt. City (exec. coun. 1988-90), Balt. City C. of C. (bd. dirs. 1993—), Balt. Country Club, Ctr. Club, Md. Club. Republican. Greek Orthodox. General corporate, Finance, Real property. Office: Gordon Feinblatt Rothman Hoffberger & Hollander 233 E Redwood St Baltimore MD 21202-3332 E-mail: tchriss@gfrlaw.com

CHRISTENBURY, EDWARD SAMUEL, lawyer; b. Boone, N.C., May 22, 1941; s. Edward S. Sr. and Frances (Timme) C.; m. Suzanne Bernfeld, Dec. 27, 1971. BS, U. Tenn., 1963, JD, 1965. Bar: Tenn. 1965, U.S. Supreme Ct. 1970, U.S. Ct. Appeals (D.C. cir.) 1972, U.S. Ct. Appeals (6th cir.) 1987, U.S. Ct. Appeals (5th cir.) 1999. Trial atty., dep. chief edn. sect. civil rights div. Dept. of Justice, Washington, 1968-71, dep. chief appellate and civil litigation sect. internal security div., 1971-73, chief spl. civil litigation unit criminal div., 1973-77, trial atty. civil div., 1977-79; asst. gen. counsel Nuclear Regulatory Commn., 1979-87; sr. v.p., gen. counsel TVA, Knoxville, 1987—. Lt. U.S. Army, 1966-67. Mem. Tenn. Bar Assn., Knoxville Bar Assn. Presbyterian. Avocation: reading. Office: TVA ET 11A 400 W Summit Hill Dr Knoxville TN 37902-1419 Fax: 865-632-3307. E-mail: eschristenbury@tva.gov

CHRISTENSEN, HAROLD GRAHAM, lawyer; b. Springville, Utah, June 25, 1926; s. Harold and Ruby (Graham) C.; m. Gayle Sutton, June 17, 1950; children: Steven H., David S., Susan; m. Jacquita W. Corry, Dec. 13, 1988. A.B., U. Utah, 1949; J.D., U. Mich., 1951. Bar: Utah 1952. Ptnr. firm Skeen, Worsley, Snow & Christensen (and successor firms), Salt Lake City; dep. atty. gen. of the U.S., 1988-89; of counsel Snow Christensen & Martineau, P.C., Salt Lake City, 1992—. Practitioner-in-residence, U. Utah, 1989; vis. prof. Coll. Law, U. Calif., San Francisco, 1990; disting. vis. prof. Bond U., Queensland, Australia, 1991. Served with USNR, 1944-46. Fellow Am. Coll. Trial Lawyers, Am. Bar Found.; mem. Utah State Bar (pres. 1975-76), Utah Bar Found. (trustee 1978), Salt Lake County Bar (pres. 1972-73), Am. Inns of Ct. Found. (trustee 1983-89). E-mial. Antitrust, Federal civil litigation, State civil litigation. Home: 2269 Pheasant Way Salt Lake City UT 84121-1312 Office: 10 Exchange Pl 11th Floor Salt Lake City UT 84111 E-mail: hchristensen@scmlaw.com

CHRISTENSEN, HENRY, III, lawyer; b. Jersey City, Nov. 8, 1944; s. Henry Jr. and M. Louise (Brooke) C.; m. Constance L. Cumpton, July 1, 1967; children: Alexander, Gustavus, Elizabeth, Katherine. BA, Yale U., 1966; JD, Harvard U., 1969. Bar: N.Y. 1970, U.S. Tax Ct. 1973, U.S. Ct. Appeals (2d. cir.) 1973, U.S. Supreme Ct. 1975. Assoc. Sullivan & Cromwell, N.Y.C., 1969-77, ptnr., 1977—. Adj. assoc. prof. NYU, N.Y.C., 1985-88, U. of Miami Law Sch., 1997—. Author: International Estate Planning, 1999; contbr. articles to profl. jours. Chmn. Prospect Park Alliance, Bklyn., 1985—; trustee, 1st vice chmn. Peddie Sch., Hightstown, N.J., 1986—; trustee Am. Fund for the Tate Gallery, 1987—, Bklyn. Acad. Music, 1992—, Vincent Astor Found., 1993—, Alex Hillman Family Found., 2000—, Friends of the Prince's Trust, 2001—; dir., sec. Freedom Inst., N.Y.C., 1980—, The Friends of Jiangnan U., 1987—; dir., v.p. Am. Friends of Whitechapel Art Gallery Found., 1991—; trustee, mem. exec. com. Am. Ctr. Oriental Rsch. in Amman, 1993—. Fellow Am. Coll. Trust and Estate Counsel; mem. N.Y. State Bar Assn. (chmn. estate and gift tax com. 1983-84, chmn. exempt orgn. com. 1986, chmn. income taxation of trusts com. 1984-85, 87-89, exec. com. tax sect. 1983-89), Internat. Acad. Estate and Trust Law (academician). Probate, Estate taxation, Personal income taxation. Home: 35 Prospect Park W Apt 8/9B Brooklyn NY 11215-2370 Office: Sullivan & Cromwell 125 Broad St Fl 29 New York NY 10004-2498

CHRISTENSEN, KAREN KAY, lawyer; b. Ann Arbor, Mich., Mar. 9, 1947; d. Jack Edward and Evangeline (Pitsch) C.; m. Kenneth Robert Kay, Sept. 2, 1977; children: Jeffrey Smithson, Braden, Bergen. BS, U. Mich., 1969; JD, U. Denver, 1975. Bar: Colo. 1975, D.C. 1976, U.S. Supreme Ct. 1979. Atty., advisor office of dep. atty. gen. U.S. Dept. of Justice, Washington, 1975-76, trial atty. civil rights div., 1976-79; legis. counsel ACLU, 1979-80; staff atty. D.C. Pub. Defender Service, 1980-85; asst. gen. counsel Nat. Pub. Radio, 1985-93; gen. counsel Nat. Endowment Arts, 1993-98, acting dep. chmn. for grants and partnership, 1997-98, dep. chmn. grants and awards, 1998—. Mem. D.C. Bd. Profl. Responsibility, 1990-98, chair, 1996-98. Mem. D.C. Bar Assn., NCA/ACLU (exec. bd. 1986-93, chair 1993), Phi Beta Kappa. Civil rights, Communications, Criminal. Office: 1100 Pennsylvania Ave NW Washington DC 20004-2501

CHRISTENSON, GORDON A. law educator; b. Salt Lake City, June 22, 1932; s. Gordon B. and Ruth Arzella (Anderson) C.; m. Katherine Joy deMik, Nov. 2, 1951 (div. 1977); children: Gordon Scott, Marjorie Lynne, Ruth Ann, Nanette; m. Fabienne Fadeley, Sept. 16, 1979. BS in Law, U. Utah, 1955, JD, 1956; SJD, George Washington U., 1961. Bar: Utah 1956, U.S. Supreme Ct. 1971, D.C. 1978. Law clk. to chief justice Utah Supreme Ct., 1956-57; assoc. firm Christenson & Callister, Salt Lake City, 1956-58; atty. Dept. of Army, Nat. Guard Bur., Washington, 1957-58; atty., acting asst. legal adviser Office of Legal Adviser, U.S. Dept. State, 1958-62; asst. gen. counsel for sci. and tech. U.S. Dept. Commerce, 1962-67, spl. asst. to undersec. of commerce, 1967, counsel to commerce tech. adv. bd., 1962-67, chmn. task force on telecommunications missions and orgn., 1967, counsel to panel on engring. and commodity standards, tech. adv. bd., 1963-65; assoc. prof. law U. Okla., Norman, 1967-70, exec. asst. to pres., 1967-70; univ. dean for ednl. devel., central adminstrn. State U. N.Y., Albany, 1970-71; prof. law Am. U. Law Sch., Washington, 1971-79, dean, 1971-77; on leave, 1977-79; Charles H. Stockton prof. internat. law U.S. Naval War Coll., Newport, R.I., 1977-79; dean, Nippert prof. law U. Cin. Coll. Law, 1979-85, univ. prof. law, 1985-99, prof. emeritus, dean emeritus, 1999—. Assoc. professorial lectr. in internat. affairs George Washington U., 1961-67; vis. scholar Harvard U. Law Sch., 1977-78, Yale Law Sch., 1985-86, Law Sch. U. Maine, Portland, 1997; Wallace S. Fujiyama vis. disting. prof. law Univ. Hawaii Law Sch., 1997; participant summer confs. on internat. law Cornell Law Sch., Ithaca, N.Y., 1962, 64; cons. in internat. law U.S. Naval War Coll., Newport, R.I., 1969; faculty mem., reporter seminars for experienced fed. dist. judges Fed. Jud. Center, Washington, 1972-77. Author: (with Richard B. Lillich) International Claims: Their Preparation and Presentation, 1962, The Future of the University, 1969; Contbr. articles to legal jours. Cons. to Center for Policy Alternatives Mass. Inst. Tech., Cambridge, 1970-81; mem. intergovtl. com. on Internat. Policy on Weather Modification, 1967; Vice pres. Procedural Aspects of Internat. Law Inst., N.Y.C., 1962— . Served with intelligence sect. USAF, 1951-52, Japan. Recipient Silver Medal award Dept. Commerce, 1967; fellow Grad. Sch. U. Cin. Mem. Am. Soc. Internat. Law (mem. panel on state responsibility), Utah Bar Assn., Cin. Bar Assn., Order of Coif, Phi Delta Phi, Kappa Sigma. Clubs: Literary (Cin.); Cosmos (Washington). Home and Office: 3465 Principio Ave Cincinnati OH 45208-4242 E-mail: christga@msn.com

CHRISTIAN, GARY IRVIN, lawyer; b. Albany, Ga., July 7, 1951; s. Rupert Irvin and Alice Amelia (Smith) C.; 1 child, Amy Margaret. BA in History, Polit. Sci., David Lipscomb Coll., 1973; MPA, U. Tenn., 1974; JD, Vanderbilt U., 1979. Bar: Fla. 1979, U.S. Dist. Ct. (no. and mid. dists.) Fla 1979. Rsch. dir. Ala. League of Mcpls., Montgomery, 1974-76; instr. in pub. adminstrn. David Lipscomb Coll., Nashville, 1977-79; assoc. Rogers, Towers, Bailey, Jones & Gay, Jacksonville, Fla., 1979-83, Foley & Lardner, Jacksonville, 1983-86; ptnr. Christian, Prom, Korn & Zehmer, 1986-92, Rumph, Stoddard & Christian, Jacksonville, 1992—. Editor-in-chief Vanderbilt Jour. of Transnational Law, 1978-79. Bd. dirs. PACE Ctr. for Girls, Inc., Jacksonville, 1984—, pres., 1984-86; mem. leadership Jacksonville, 1986-87; chmn. site selection com. St. Johns County Sch. Bd., 1993-95; mem. site selection com., St. Johns County Sch. Bd., 1989-91. Mem. ABA (condominiums and planned devels. com.), Jacksonville Bar Assn. (coord. continuing edn. 1984-85, vice chmn. real property sect. 1986-87, chmn. 1987-88, chmn. corps., banking & bus. sect. 1991-92), Wavemasters Soc. (pres. 1986-87), Jacksonville C. of C. (com. 100 1986-94), Southpoint Bus. Assn. (bd. dirs. 1990-2001, pres. 1991-93), Oak Bridge Country Club, Seminole Club, Salt Creek Homeowners Assn. (bd. dirs. 1993-97, pres. 1994-96), Univ. Club, Deer Creek Country Club. Republican. Mem. Ch. of Christ. Avocations: golf, fishing, racquetball, hunting, stamp collecting. Banking, Contracts commercial, Real property. Home: 1719 Girvin Rd Jacksonville FL 32225-2620 Office: Rumph Stoddard & Christian 3100 University Blvd S Ste 101 Jacksonville FL 32216-2777

CHRISTIAN, JOHN CATLETT, JR. lawyer; b. Springfield, Mo., Sept. 12, 1929; s. John Catlett and Alice Odelle (Milling) C.; m. Peggy Jeanne Cain, Apr. 12, 1953; children: Cathleen Marie, John Catlett, Alice Cain. AB, Drury Coll., 1951; LLB, Tulane U., 1956. Bar: La. 1956, Mo. 1956, U.S. Supreme Ct. 1975. Assoc. Porter & Stewart, Lake Charles, La., 1956-58, Wilkinson, Lewis, Wilkinson & Madison, Shreveport, 1958-62, ptnr., 1962-64, Milling, Benson, Woodward, Hillyer, Pierson & Miller, New Orleans, 1964-92, of counsel, 1993-94. Pres. Sherburne Land Co., 1974-83, Pointe-Martin Mgmt., Inc., 1990-2000; dir. Emerald Land Corp. Pres. Kathleen Elizabeth O'Brien Found., 1963—. Served with USMCR, 1951-53. Fellow Am. Coll. Trial Lawyers; mem. ABA, Fed. Bar Assn., Mo. Bar Assn., La. Bar Assn., La. Landowners Assn. (bd. dirs. 1983-2001), Boston Club, Beau Chene Country Club, Kappa Alpha Order, Omicron Delta Kappa, Phi Delta Phi. Home: 807 Tete Lours Dr Mandeville LA 70471-1774 Office: PO Box 1317 Mandeville LA 70470-1317 E-mail: jcchristiansr@aol.com

CHRISTIAN, TERRY CLIFTON, lawyer; b. Welch, W.Va., Aug. 4, 1952; s. Samuel Clifton and Mary Jane Christian; m. Wendy Lee McCoy, Feb. 14, 1991. BA, U. Del., 1984; JD, Ind. U., Indpls., 1987. Bar: Fla. 1988, U.S. Dist. Ct. (mid. dist.) Fla. 1989, U.S. Ct. Appeals (11th cir.) 1990, U.S. Dist. Ct. (no. and so. dists.) Fla. 1996, U.S. Supreme Ct. 1996; cert. Bd. Legal Edn. and Specialization, Fla.; cert. Nat. Bd. Trial Advocacy. Asst. state atty. Office of State Atty., Ft. Myers, Fla., 1988-89; mng. ptnr. Christian & Assocs., P.A., Tampa, 1989—. Mem. criminal justice act panel U.S. Dist. Ct. for Mid. Dist. Fla., 1989—, for No. Dist., 1996—, for So. Dist., 1998—; spl. asst. pub defender Capitol and RICO cases only, Tampa, 1989—. Author criminal law seminars. Capt. U.S. Army Res., 1986-90. Mem. FBA (exec. com. Tampa Bay chpt. 1996-2001, svc. award 1997-2001 Am. Immigration Lawyers Assn. (sec. Ctrl. Fla. chpt. 1992-94, treas. 1994-95, v.p. 1995-97, svc. award 1995-97), Fla. Bar, Hillsborough County Assn. Criminal Def. Lawyers (bd. dirs., sec. 1996-97, pres. 1997-98, svc. award 1998), Am. Inns. of Ct. (master Tampa Bay Inn 1995—, exec. com. 2000—, parliamentarian 2001—). Democrat. Roman Catholic. Avocations: reading, sports, physical exercise and weight training. E-mail: tcclawpa@aol.com.

CHRISTIAN, THOMAS WILLIAM, lawyer; b. Tuscaloosa, Ala., Aug. 23, 1938; s. George William and Grace (Mandeville) C.; m. Dorothy Rosamond, Jan. 23, 1965; children: George, Ed, Delia. AB, U. Ala., 1960, LLB, 1965. Bar: Ala. 1965, U.S. Dist. Ct. (no. dist.) Ala. 1965, U.S. Ct. Appeals (5th and 11th cirs.) 1971, U.S. Supreme Ct. 1973. Ptnr. Balch & Bingham, Birmingham, Ala., 1965-81; firm Rives & Peterson, 1981-2000, Christian & Small, Birmingham, 2000—. Lt. U.S. Army, 1961-63. Fellow Internat. Acad. Trial Lawyers, Am. Bar Found., Am. Coll. Trial Lawyers; mem. ABA, Ala. State Bar Assn., Birmingham Bar Assn. (pres. 1984), Ala.

Def. Lawyers Assn. (pres. 1979), Internat. Assn. Ins. Counsel, Birmingham Country Club, Redstone Club. Presbyterian. Avocations: fishing, jogging, nautilis. General civil litigation, Personal injury, Product liability. Home: 4012 Old Leeds Ln Birmingham AL 35213-3235 Office: Christian & Small 1800 Financial Ctr Birmingham AL 35203-2696 E-mail: twchristian@csattorneys.com

CHRISTIANSEN, MARK D. lawyer; b. Olney, Tex., June 10, 1955; s. Leon H. and Doris J. (Jennings) C. BA, U. Okla., 1977, JD, 1980. Bar: U.S. Dist. Ct. (we. dist.) Okla. 1984, U.S. Dist. Ct. (ea. dist.) Okla. 1993, U.S. Ct. Appeals (10th cir.) 1987. Assoc. Crowe & Dunlevy, Oklahoma City, 1980-85, mem., 1986—. Editor: The Oil and Gas Reporter. Mem.: ABA (chmn. energy and natural resources litigation 2001—, chmn. oil and natural gas exploration and prodn. com. 1999—2001), Oklahoma City Mineral Lawyers Soc. (pres. 1989—90), Okla. Bar Assn. General civil litigation, Oil, gas, and mineral. Home: 20 N Broadway Ave Ste 1800 Oklahoma City OK 73102-8296 Office: Crowe & Dunlevy Mid America Tower 20 N Broadway Ave Ste 1800 Oklahoma City OK 73102-8273

CHRISTIANSEN, PATRICK T. lawyer; b. Mpls., 1947; BSEE summa cum laude, U. Notre Dame, 1969; JD, Harvard U., 1972. Bar: Fla. 1972, Minn. 1974, U.S. Tax Ct. 1977, U.S. Supreme Ct. 1980. Mem. Akerman, Senterfitt & Eidson P.A., Orlando, Fla. Chmn. bd. Orlando Mus. Art; mem., bd. dirs. The Greater Orlando C. of C., Jobs and Edn. Partnership; chmn. Orange County Transp. Roundtable; mem. Orange County Blue Ribbon Commn., steering com., chmn. transp. com.; bd. dirs. United Arts Cen. Fla., Orlando Downtown Devel. Bd. Mem. ABA (sects. on bus. law, taxation, real property), Fla. Bar (trial lawyers sect., co-chmn. land trust com. real property, probate and trust law sect. 1978-82, dir. real property divsn. 1982-84, vice chmn. 1984-85, chmn. 1985-86, vice-chmn. UCC subcom. corp., banking and bus. law sect. 1979-84, bd. govs. young lawyers sect. 1981-83), Am. Coll. Real Estate Lawyers, Minn. State Bar Assn., Orange County Bar Assn. Banking, Consumer commercial, Real property. Office: Akerman Senterfitt & Eidson PA Citrus Ctr 17th Fl PO Box 231 255 S Orange Ave Orlando FL 32801-3445

CHRISTMAN, BRUCE LEE, lawyer; b. Bethlehem, Pa., Apr. 1, 1955; s. Raymond J. Jr. and Irene May (Bowman) C.; m. Lynn Eloise Brodt, Oct. 11, 1980; children: Jennifer Lynn, Amy Nicole. BA, Coll. William and Mary, 1977; JD, U. Pa., 1980. Bar: Va. 1980, U.S. Ct. Appeals (4th cir.) 1980, U.S. Dist. Ct. (ea. dist.) Va. 1980. Assoc. Hunton & Williams, Richmond, Va., 1980-84; prin., ptnr. Reed Smith LLP, Fairfax, 1984—. Adj. prof. George Mason Sch. Law; vice-chmn. bd. dirs. Luth. Social Svcs. Officer ch. coun., mem. exec. com., trustee St. Andrew Luth. Ch., Centreville, Va., 1988; mem. Leadership Fairfax Class of 1993, bd. dirs. 1997, 2000. Mem. Va. State Bar Assn., Phi Beta Kappa, Omicron Delta Kappa, Kappa Sigma. Democrat. Avocations: tennis, basketball, swimming, bicycling, camping. Banking, Finance, Real property. Home: 13610 Flintwood Pl Herndon VA 20171-3331 Office: Reed Smith LLP 3110 Fairview Park Dr Falls Church VA 22042-4503

CHRISTOPHER, WARREN, lawyer, former government official; b. Scranton, N.D., Oct. 27, 1925; s. Ernest W. and Catharine Anna (Lemen) C.; m. Marie Josephine Wyllis, Dec. 21, 1956; children— Lynn, Scott, Thomas, Kristen. Student, U. Redlands, 1942-43; B.S. magna cum laude, U. So. Calif., 1945; LL.B., Stanford, 1949; LL.D. (hon.), Occidental U., 1977, Bates Coll., 1981, Brown U., 1981, Claremont Coll., 1981. Bar: Calif. 1949, N.Y., U.S. Supreme Ct. 1949. Law clk. U.S. Supreme Ct. Justice William O. Douglas, Washington, 1949-50; practice in Los Angeles, 1950-67, 69-76, 81-93, 97—; mem. firm O'Melveny & Myers, LLP, 1950-67, 69, ptnr., 1958-67, 69-76, 81-93, sr. ptnr., 1997—; dep. atty. gen. U.S., Washington, 1967-69; dep. sec. of state Dept. State, 1977-81; sec. U.S. Dept. of State, 1993-97. Spl. counsel to Gov. Calif., 1959; cons. Office Under Sec. State, 1961-65; mem. bd. bar examiners State Bar Calif., 1966-67; dir. So. Calif. Edison Co., First Interstate Bancorp, Lockheed Corp.; chmn., trustee Carnegie Corp. N.Y.; mem. Calif. Coordinating Coun. for Higher Edn., 1960-67, pres., 1963-65; vice chmn. Gov.'s Commn. on L.A. Riots, 1965-66; chmn. U.S. delegations to U.S.-Japan Cotton Textile Negotiations, 1961, Geneva Conf. on Cotton Textiles, 1961; spl. rep. sec. state for Wool Textile Meetings, London, Rome, Tokyo, 1964-65; mem. Trilateral Commn., 1975-77, 81-88; mem. internat. adv. coun. Inst. Internat. Studies; chmn. Ind. Commn. on L.A. Police Dept., 1991. Author: In the Stream of History, 1998, Chances of a Lifetime, 2000; co-author: American Hostages in Iran: The Conduct of a Crisis, 1985. Trustee Stanford U., 1971-77, 81-93, pres. bd. trustees, 1985-88; bd. dirs., vice chmn. Coun. on Fgn. Rels., 1982-91; bd. dirs. L.A. World Affairs Coun.; mem. exec. com. Am. Agenda, 1988; mem. U.S.-Korea Wisemen Coun., 1991-93. Lt. (j.g.) USNR, 1943-46. Decorated Medal of Freedom 1981; recipient Harold Weill award NYU, 1981, Louis Stein award Fordham U., 1981, Jefferson award Am. Inst. for Pub. Svc., UCLA medal, Thomas Jefferson award in law U. Va. Fellow Am. Bar Found., Am. Coll. Trial Lawyers, AAAS; mem. ABA (ho. dels. 1975-77, chmn. standing com. fed. judiciary 1975-77), Calif. Bar Assn. (gov. 1975-77), L.A. County Bar Assn. (pres. 1974-75), Am. Law Inst., Order of Coif, Calif. Club, Chancery Club, Phi Kappa Phi. General civil litigation, General corporate, Public international. Office: O'Melveny & Meyers LLP 1999 Ave Of Stars Fl 7 Los Angeles CA 90067-6022

CHRISTOPHER, WILLIAM GARTH, lawyer; b. Beaumont, Tex., Oct. 14, 1940; s. Garth Daugherty and Ollye Mittie (Harkness) C.; m. Kathleen S. Christopher; children: John William, David Noah, Michael O'Hara. BS in Engring., U.S. Mil. Acad., 1962; JD, U. Va., 1970. Bar: Va. 1970, D.C. 1970, U.S. Supreme Ct. 1975, Mich. 1977, Fla. 1988, Tex. 1989. Assoc. Steptoe & Johnson, Washington, 1970-77; ptnr. Honigman Miller Schwartz & Cohn, Detroit, 1977-94, Holland & Knight, Tampa, Fla., 1994-95, Brown Clark, P.A., Sarasota, 1995—. Contbr. articles to legal publ. Pres. Birmingham (Mich.) Hockey Assn., 1982-84; mem. Epsc. Diocese of Mich. Commn. on Ministry, 1983-88, co-chmn., 1987-88, standing com., 1988. Capt. C.E. U.S. Army, 1962-67. Mem. ABA, VA. Bar, D.C. Bar, Fla. Bar (cert. bus. litigation law), Tex. Bar, Sarasota County Bar Assn., Raven Soc., Nat. Bd. Trial Advocacy (cert. civil trial advocacy), Order of Coif, Phi Delta Phi. Episcopalian. General civil litigation, Contracts commercial, Construction. Office: Brown Clark PA 1819 Main St Ste 500 Sarasota FL 34236-5975 E-mail: wchristopher@sarasotafirm.com

CHRISTY, GARY CHRISTOPHER, lawyer; b. L.A., July 23, 1948; s. Harry Voorhees and Theresa (Wolff) C.; m. Debra Deiter, June 29, 1984; 1 child, Casey. B.A., U. Tampa, 1971; J.D., Woodrow Wilson Coll. Law, Atlanta, 1976. Bar: Ga., U.S. Supreme Ct., U.S. Ct. Appeals (11th cir.), U.S. Dist. Ct. (no. and mid. dists.) Ga. Asst. dist. atty. Cordele Jud. Cir., Ga., 1976-79, dist. atty., 1979-85; ptnr. Davis, Pridgen, Jones & Christy, Vienna, Ga., 1985-86, Rainwater & Christy, Cordele, Ga., 1986-89, Davis, Gregory & Christy, 1990—; mem. faculty Ga. Inst. Trial Advocaty, Nat. Criminal Def. Coll. Mem. Organized Crime Prevention Coun. Ga., 1981-85; bd. dirs. Nat. Spinal Cord Injury Assn., Cordele, 1984. Recipient Disting. Svc. award Ga. Bur. Investigation, 1983. Fellow Ga. Bar Found.; mem. Nat. Dist. Attys. Assn., Assn. Trial Lawyers Am., Ga. Trial Lawyers Assn. (lectr. cross examination and closing argument 1986), Ga. Criminal Def Lawyers Assn. (lectr. 1990), State Bar Ga. (lectr.), Dist. Attys. Assn. Ga. (pres. 1984-85). Democrat. Roman Catholic. Home: Hwy 41 N PO Box 444 Vienna GA 31092-0444 Office: Davis Gregory Christy & Foxehand 708 16th Ave E PO Box 5230 Cordele GA 31010-5230

CHROMOW, SHERI P. lawyer; b. N.Y.C., Aug. 27, 1946; d. Abe and Sara L. Pinsky. BA, Barnard Coll., N.Y.C., 1968; JD, NYU, 1971. Ptnr. Shearman & Sterling, N.Y.C., 1979—. Lectr. Omega Enterprises, Practising Law Inst.; mem. steering com. N.Y. coun. U. L.I.; mem. adv. bd. N.Y.U. Law Sch. Real Estate Inst.; mem. adv. bd. Ticor Title Ins. Co. Mem. Urban Land Inst. Contracts commercial, Finance, Real property. Office: Shearman & Sterling 599 Lexington Ave C2 Fl New York NY 10022-6069 E-mail: schromow@shearman.com

CHUCK, WALTER G(OONSUN), lawyer, director; b. Wailuku, Maui, Hawaii, Sept. 10, 1920; s. Hong Yee and Aoe (Ting) C.; m. Marian Chun, Sept. 11, 1943; children: Jamie Allison, Walter Gregory, Meredith Jayne. Ed.B., U. Hawaii, 1941; J.D., Harvard U., 1948. Bar: Hawaii 1948. Navy auditor, Pearl Harbor, 1941; field agt. Social Security Bd., 1942; labor law insp. Terr. Dept. Labor, 1943; law clk. firm Ropes, Gray, Best, Coolidge & Rugg, 1948; asst. pub. prosecutor City and County of Honolulu, 1949; with Fong, Miho & Choy, 1950-53; ptnr. Fong, Miho, Choy & Chuck, 1953-58; pvt. practice law Honolulu, 1958-65, 78-80; ptnr. Chuck & Fujiyama, 1965-74; ptnr. firm Chuck, Wong & Tonaki, 1974-76, Chuck & Pai, Honolulu, 1976-78; pres. Walter G. Chuck Law Corp., 1980-94; pvt. practice, 1994—. Dist. magistrate Dist. Ct. Honolulu, 1956-63; gen. ptnr. M & W Assocs., Kapalama Investment Co.; bd. dirs. Aloha Airlines, Inc., Honolulu Painting Co., Ltd. Chmn. Hawaii Employment Rels. Bd., 1955-59; bd. dirs. Nat. Assn. State Labor Rels. Bds., 1957-58, Honolulu Theatre for Youth, 1977-80; chief clk. Hawaii Ho. of Reps., 1951, 53, Hawaii Senate, 1959-61; govt. appeal agt. SSS, 1953-72; former mem. jud. coun. State of Hawaii; former mem. exec. com. Hawaiian Open; former dir. Friends of Judiciary History Ctr. Inc., 1983-94; former mem. bd. dirs. YMCA. Capt. inf. Hawaii Terr. Guard. Recipient Ha'Aheo award for cmty. svc. Hawaii chpt. Am. Bd. Trial Advocates, 1995. Fellow Internat. Acad. Trial Lawyers (founder, dean, bd. dirs., state rep.), Am. Coll. Trial Lawyers; mem. ABA (former chmn. Hawaii sr. lawyers divsn., former mem. ho. of dels.), Hawaii Bar Assn. (pres. 1963), ATLA (former editor), U. Hawaii Alumni Assn. (Disting. Svc. award 1967, former dir., bd. govs.), Law Sci. Inst., Assoc. Students U. Hawaii (pres.), Am. Judicature Soc., Internat. Soc. Barristers, Am. Inst. Banking, Chinese C. of C., U. Hawaii Founders Alumni Assn. (v.p., bd. dirs., Lifetime Achievement award 1994), Harvard Club of Hawaii, Waialae Country Club (pres. 1975), Oahu Country Club. Republican. Federal civil litigation, State civil litigation, General practice. Home: 2691 Aaliamanu Pl Honolulu HI 96813-1216 Office: Pacific Tower 1001 Bishop St Ste 2450 Honolulu HI 96813-3430

CHUDACOFF, BRUCE MICHAEL, lawyer; b. Appleton, Wis., Oct. 1, 1944; s. Lester H. and Mollie (Goldin) C.; m. Nancy Lynn Wilets, June 9, 1968; children: Tanya Elizabeth, Tamara Ann, Joshua Aaron. AB, U. Mich., 1966; JD, Harvard U., 1969. Bar: Wis. 1969, U.S. Dist. Ct. (ea. dist.) Wis. 1971, U.S. Supreme Ct. 1972. Ptnr. Chudacoff & Liebzeit, Appleton, 1969—. Dir. 1st Interstate Bank Wis.-Appleton, 1976-91. V.p. ops. Bay Lakes Coun. Boy Scouts Am., 1983—; mem. Nat. Jewish Com. on Scouting, 1986—; state chmn. Israel Bond Orgn., Milw., 1984—85; comdr. Northeastern Wis. post Jewish War Vets, 1986—; chmn. NCCJ, Appleton, 1974—79, Outgamie County Rep. Party, 1998—2001. Served to capt. USAR, 1970—71, Vietnam. Recipient Disting. Merit citations, NCCJ, 1979, Gates of Jerusalem medal, Israel Bond Orgn., 1986. Mem. Outgamie County Bar Assn., State Bar Wis., Wis. Acad. Trial Lawyers, NE Wis. U. Mich. Alumni (pres. 1980), B'nai B'rith, Fox River Club. State civil litigation, Family and matrimonial, Personal injury. Home: 43 N Crestway Ct Appleton WI 54913-9510 Office: Chudacoff & Liebzeit 512 W College Ave Appleton WI 54911-5802

CHUDZINSKI, MARK ADAM, lawyer; b. Chgo., Oct. 13, 1956; s. Brunon and Maria (Chmielinski) C.; m. Barbara Podkul, July 31, 1993; 1 child, Anna. BA, Northwestern U., 1977, MBA, JD, Northwestern U., 1981; diplome d'etudes approfondies, U. Paris, 1982. Bar: N.Y. 1982, Ill. 1990, U.S. Supreme Ct. 1994. Assoc. Coudert Bros., N.Y.C., 1982-85, London, 1985-88, Sydney, Australia, 1988-89; sr. assoc. Winston & Strawn, Chgo., 1990-95, ptnr., 1995-96; gen. counsel Ameritech Internat., 1996-99; sr. v.p., gen. counsel and sec. Eziaz Inc., Chgo., 2000—. Bd. dirs. Tele Danmark A/S. Articles editor Northwestern Jour. Internat. Law and Bus., 1981. Trustee Window To The World Comm., Inc. (Stas. WTTW-TV and WFMT-FM), Chgo., Kosciuszko Found., N.Y.C.; adv. bd. Sta. WBEZ-FM, Chgo.; mem. Chgo. com. Chgo. Coun. Fgn. Rels.; bd. dirs. Chgo. Legal Clinic, Inc., Polish Mus. Am., 1991-98, Polish Am. Congress, 1992-96. Austin scholar 1978; fellow Leadership Greater Chgo., 1990; U.S. Champ Jessup Moot Ct., 1979. Mem. ABA, N.Y. State Bar Assn., Am. Soc. Internat. Law, French-Am. C. of C., German-Am. C. of C., U.S.-Poland C. of C. (founder, chmn. 1991-95), Chgo. Coun. Fgn. Rels. Roman Catholic. Communications, General corporate, Private international. Office: Eziaz Inc 550 W Van Buren St Chicago IL 60607-7600 E-mail: mark.chudzinski@eziaz.com

CHUNG, AMY TERESA, lawyer, property manager; b. San Francisco, Sept. 1, 1953; d. Burk Him and Mary Angeline (Lin) C.; m. Andrew Nathan Chang, May 5, 1979; children: Adrian Thomas, Alison Nicole. AB in Psychology, U. Calif., Berkeley, 1975; JD, U. Calif., San Francisco, 1978. Bar: Calif. Legal counsel M & B Assocs., San Francisco, 1978—; v.p. Anza Parking Corp., Burlingame, Calif., 1993—. Mem. adv. com. U. Calif., San Francisco, 1992—; v.p. Castle Peak Homeowners Assn., West Hills, Calif., 1987-89; v.p. Chinatown Stockton St. Mchts. Assn., San Francisco, 1981—; chair Chinese Cmty. Housing Corp., San Francisco, 1991—; project area com. Mid-Market, San Francisco, 1996—. Mem. Calif. Bar Assn. Avocations: piano, singing, ballet, swimming. Office: M & B Assocs 835 Washington St San Francisco CA 94108-1211

CHUNG, STEVEN KAMSEIN, lawyer; b. Honolulu, Oct. 13, 1947; s. Edward K.O. and Amy B.J. (Chun) C.; m. Evelyn Reiko, July 5, 1980; children: Chanelle Mari, Tiffany Rei. BA in Acctg., U. Hawaii, 1972; JD, U. Calif., San Francisco, 1976. Bar: Hawaii 1976, U.S. Dist. Ct. Hawaii 1976, U.S. Ct. Appeals (9th cir.) 1978, U.S. Supreme Ct. 1983. Assoc. Frank D. Padgett, Atty. at Law, Honolulu, 1976-80, ptnr. Chung, Lau, MacLaren & Lau, Honolulu, 1980-81, Walter G. Chuck & Assocs., Honolulu, 1981-86; pvt. practice, Honolulu, 1987-88; ptnr. Oshima, Chun, Fong & Chung, Honolulu, 1988—. Served to 1st lt. U.S. Army, 1966-69, Vietnam. Mem. Assn. Trial Lawyers Am., ABA, Hawaii Bar Assn. Roman Catholic. Bankruptcy, Federal civil litigation, State civil litigation. Home: 1826 Laukahi Pl Honolulu HI 96821-1337 Office: 841 Bishop St Ste 400 Honolulu HI 96813-3921

CHUNHAKASIKARN, SASIRUSM BULPAKDI, lawyer; b. Bangkok, Thailand, Aug. 26, 1971; B of Law, Chulalongkorn U., Bangkok, Thailand, 1993; M of Law, Howard U., 1998. Legal asst. Luang Thepnarin Law Office, Bangkok, Thailand, 1993-94; legal cons. A.B. Group Ltd., Thailand, 1993-95; atty. Luang Thepnarin Law Office, Thailand, 1994-95; legal rsch. asst., law clk. Bart Durham & Assocs., Tenn., 1999; atty. dispute resolution dept. Tilleke & Gibbins, Bangkok, 1999—. Mem. Law Soc. Thailand, Thai Bar Assn., Women Lawyers Assn. Thailand. General civil litigation, Contracts commercial, Private international. Office: Tilleke & Gibbins Internat 64/1 Soi Tonson Ploenchit Bangkok 10330 Thailand Fax: 66 2 6210172-3. E-mail: sasirusm@tillekeandgibbins.com

CHURCH, RANDOLPH WARNER, JR. lawyer; b. Richmond, Va., Nov. 6, 1934; s. Randolph Warner and Elizabeth Lewis (Gochnauer) C.; m. Lucy Ann Canary, July 4, 1970; children: Leslie R. Pennell, L. Weeks Kerr. BA with honors, U. Va., 1957, LLB, 1960. Bar: Va. 1960, U.S. Dist. Ct. (ea. dist.) Va. 1962, U.S. Ct. Appeals (4th cir.) 1981, U.S. Supreme Ct. 1999. Assoc. McCandlish, Lillard & Marsh, Fairfax, Va., 1960-63; ptnr. McCandlish, Lillard, Rust & Church, 1963-84; city atty., 1968-72; mng. ptnr. McCandlish, Lillard, Rust & Church, 1975-83, Hunton & Williams, Fairfax, 1984-99, mem. exec. com., 1988-94, sr. counsel, 2000—. Bd. dirs. George Mason Bank, George Mason Bankshares, Inc., George Mason Mortgage Co., 1991-98, Va. Found. for Rsch. and Econ. Edn., Inc., 1994-2000. Author: Appellate Civil Litigation, 1984; panelist: Lawyer Professionalism: Is Change in Order? 1988, Marketing Legal Services: What's Hot and What's Not, 1990, (with others) Equity Practice and Tips on Brief Writing. Active Fairfax Com. of 100, 1988—, bd. dirs., 1989-92; bd. visitors George Mason U., Fairfax, 1982-90, rector, 1983-86, chmn. adv. bd. Coll. Arts and Scis., 1999—; bd. dirs. Fairfax Symphony, 1991—, gen. counsel, exec. com., 1996—; bd. dirs. Va. Found. for Humanities and Pub. Policy, 1993-99, vice chmn., 1997-99; active Va. Mus. of Fine Arts Found., 2000—; pres. Fall for the Book, Inc., 2001—. Fellow Va. Law Found., Am. Bar Found.; mem. ABA, Am. Judicature Soc., Va. Bar Assn. (v.p. 1975), Tower Club, Country Club Fairfax County, U. Va. Club, Phi Beta Kappa. Episcopalian. State civil litigation, General corporate. Home: 5114 Forsgate Pl Fairfax VA 22030-4507 Office: Hunton & Williams 1751 Pinnacle Dr Ste 1700 Mc Lean VA 22102-3836

CHUTE, ALAN DALE, lawyer; b. International Falls, Minn. s. Lester Robert and Florence Adele (Jensen) C.; m. Sharon Marie McHenry, June 9, 1979; children: Andrew Alan, Anthony Lee, Alan Joseph. BS, U.S. Mil. Acad., 1977; JD, U. Minn., 1982; LLM, Judge Advocate Gen.'s Sch., Charlottesville, Va., 1987. Bar: Pa., Minn., U.S. Ct. Mil. Appeals, Army Ct. Mil. Rev., U.S. Ct. Appeals (3d, 9th cir.), U.S. Dist. Ct. (we. dist.) Pa. Commd. 2d lt. U.S. Army, 1977, advanced through grades to major, 1989, signal officer, 1977-79; claims judge adv. Office of Staff Judge Adv., Ft. Lewis, Wash., 1982-83, prosecutor, 1983-85; atty. U.S. Army Trial Def. Service, 1985-86, sr. def. counsel 2d inf. div. Korea, 1987-88; staff and faculty Judge Advocate Gen.'s Sch., Charlottesville, 1988-90; with Jones, Day, Reavis & Pogue, Pitts., 1990—. Editor-in-chief U. Minn. Law Rev., 1981-82. Mem. ABA, Pa. Bar Assn., Allegheny County Bar Assn. Roman Catholic. Lodge: KC. Home: 2595 Rossmoor Dr Pittsburgh PA 15241-2581 Address: Jones Day Reavis & Pogue 500 Grant St Pittsburgh PA 15219-2502 E-mail: adchute@jonesday.com

CHYTEN, EDWIN RICHARD, lawyer; b. Boston, May 15, 1925; s. William and Elizabeth (Carpenter) C.; m. Helen Siegal, Apr. 26, 1949 (div. Feb. 1981); children— Leslie. Kenneth, Neil; m. Rosalyn Levine, May 11, 1983. A.B., Harvard Coll., 1947; J.D., Boston Coll., 1971. Bar: Mass. 1971, U.S. Dist. Ct. Mass. 1971. Atty., legal counsel, v.p. Purity Supreme, Inc., North Billerica, Mass., 1974-79; ptnr. Meyers, Goldstein & Chyten, Chestnut Hill, Mass., 1979— . Served to lt. (j.g.) USN, 1943-46; PTO. Fellow Mass. Bar Assn., Mass. Acad. Trial Attys. Club: Newton Tennis (pres., 1978-80) (Mass.). State civil litigation, General corporate, General practice. Home: 250 Hammond Pond Pkwy Chestnut Hill MA 02467-1533 Office: Meyers Goldstein & Chyten 850 Boylston St Chestnut Hill MA 02467-2477

CIANI, JUDITH ELAINE, retired lawyer; b. Medford, Mass., July 24, 1943; d. A. Walter and Ruth Alice (Bowman) C.; m. Marion M. Smith, Sept. 29, 1982. Grad., Thayer Acad., Braintree, Mass., 1961; MA, Mt. Holyoke Coll., 1965; JD, Boston Coll., 1970. Bar: Calif. 1971, U.S. Dist. Ct. (no. dist.) Calif. 1971, U.S. Ct. Appeals (9th cir.) 1971. Aide/press sec. Rep. James A. Burke, Washington, 1965-67; atty. Pillsbury, Madison & Sutro, San Francisco, 1970-78, ptnr., 1978-90; ret., 1990. Del. Calif. Bar Conv., San Francisco, 1973-78, 83-85. Mem. San Francisco Police Commn., 1976-80, Juvenile Justice Task Force, San Francisco, 1981-83; bd. dirs. Bernard Osher Found., San Francisco, 1977—; pres. Common Fund for Legal Svcs., San Francisco, 1985—, Sinfonia San Francisco, 1985-86. Fellow Am. Bar Found.; mem. Bar Assn. San Francisco (bd. dirs., pres. Found. 1978—, bd. dirs. 1981-83, treas. 1987). Home: PO Box 960 Inverness CA 94937-0960 E-mail: jeciani@svn.net

CICCONI, CHRISTOPHER M. lawyer; b. Anaheim, Calif., Aug. 19, 1949; s. Samuel A. and Ercilia (Silva) C.; m. Cynthia Anne June 20, 1981; children: Christina Michelle, Kelly Melissa. BA in Comm. Arts, U. Notre Dame, 1971; JD, Villanova U., 1974; LLM in Taxation, Temple U., 1978. Bar: Pa., U.S. Dist. Ct. (ea. and mid. dists.) Pa., U.S. Ct. Appeals (3d dist.), U.S. Tax Ct., U.S. Supreme Ct. Assoc. Rocap, Rocap & Guinta, Media, Pa., 1974-77; 1st asst. pub. defender Pub. Defender's Office of Delaware County, 1977-78; ptnr. Hepford Zimmerman & Swartz, Harrisburg, Pa., 1978-90, mng. ptnr., 1985-90; atty., mem. Eckert Seamans Cherin & Mellott, 1990—, chairperson corp. dept., 1999—. Bd. dirs. York Saw & Knife Co., Inc., dBi Labs., Inc., Harrisburg, Ollie's Bargain Outlets, Inc., Harrisburg, sellstufflocal.com., Inc.; instr. Coll. Med., Pa. State U., 1992-98. Author, editor: Buying and Selling a Business, 1998. Mem., chair Zoning Hearing Bd., Derry Twp., Pa., 1984-89; mem. Preservation of Hershey Com., Derry Twp., 1987-88. Recipient Cmty. Achievement award Derry Twp., 1989, award of yr. Notre Dame Alumni Assn., 1995. Mem. Pa. Bar Assn. (chair legal affairs of older persons com. 1986-88, arbitrator dispute resolution com. 1988—), Dauphin County Bar Assn., Estate Planning Coun. Ctrl. Pa., Sorin Soc. of U. Notre Dame. Avocations: playing piano, wine collecting, travel, golf. Estate planning, Finance, Mergers and acquisitions. Home: 1045 Fairdell Dr Hummelstown PA 17036-8710 Office: Eckert Seamans et al 213 Market St Harrisburg PA 17101-2132 E-mail: cmc@escm.com

CICCONI, JAMES WILLIAM, lawyer; b. Elmira, N.Y., June 8, 1952; s. Raymond Joseph and Doris Arlene (Strong) C.; m. Patricia Olivia Burgess, Aug. 10, 1974; children: Jill, Sara, Rachel. BA, U. Tex., 1974, JD, 1977. Bar: Tex. 1977, D.C. 1985. Issues dir. Jim Baker for Atty. Gen. campaign, Austin, Tex., 1977-78; adminstrv. asst. to the gov. State of Tex., 1979-80, gen. counsel to the sec. of state, 1980-81; spl. asst. to the pres., to the chief of staff The White House, Washington, 1981-85; sr. issues advisor Bush-Quayle '88 campaign, 1987-88; asst. to the pres., dep. to the chief of staff The White House, 1989-90; atty. Akin Gump Strauss Hauer & Feld, 1985-88, 91-98, ptnr., 1991—; gen. counsel, exec. v.p. law and govt. affairs AT&T, N.Y.C., 1998—. Bd. dirs. Found. for Nat. Archives, Washington; issues dir. Bush-Quayle '92 Campaign; dep. dir. strategy Dole-Kemp '96 Campaign; dir. El Paso Electric Co., Am. Coun. Germany; cons. U.S. State Dept.; adv. Bush-Cheney transition. V.p. George Bush Presdl. Libr. Found., College Station, Tex., 1991—; del. Conf. Security Cooperation Europe (CSCE); mem. Adminstrv. Conf. U.S., U.S. Reform Observation Panel for UNESCO. Mem. D.C. Bar Assn., State Bar Tex. Republican. Roman Catholic. Avocations: baseball, tennis. Administrative and regulatory. Office: AT&T 1120 20th St NW Ste 1000 Washington DC 20036

CICERO, FRANK, JR. lawyer; b. Nov. 30, 1935; s. Frnk and Mary (Balma) Cicero; m. Janice Pickett, July 11, 1959; children: Erica, Caroline. AB with hons., Wheaton Coll., 1957; M in Pub. Affairs, Woodrow Wilson Sch. of Pub. & Internat. Affairs, 1962; JD, U. Chgo., 1965. Bar: Ill., U.S. Supreme Ct. 1965, various U.S. Ct. of Appeals and Dist. Cts. Polit. sci. instr. Wheaton Coll., Ill., 1957—58; spl. asst. Gov. Richard J. Hughes , NJ, 1962; assoc. Kirkland & Ellis, Chgo., 1965—70, ptnr., 1970—. Mem. vis. com. U. Chgo. Law Sch., 1971—74, 1996—99, lectr., 1989—90, 1991—92; del. 6th Ill. Constl. Conv., 1969—70. Bd. editors: law rev. U. Chgo. Law Rev.;contbr. articles to profl. jours. Recipient Joseph Henry Beale prize, U. Chgo., 1963, Outstanding Young Man award, Evanston Jaycees, 1970. Fellow: Am. Coll. Trial Lawyers, Internat. Acad. Trial Lawyers; mem.: ABA, Internat. Bar Assn., Ill. State Bar Assn., Bar Assn.

7th Fed. Cir., Am. Polit. Sci. Assn., Am. Acad. Polit. and Social Sci., Chgo. Club, Glen View Club, Cherry Hill Country Club, Ventana Canyon Golf Club, Mid-Am. Club (gov. 1981—84), Saddle and Cycle Club (gov. 1984). Federal civil litigation, State civil litigation, Private international. Office: Kirkland & Ellis 200 E Randolph Dr Ste 6000 Chicago IL 60601-6636

CICET, DONALD JAMES, lawyer; b. New Orleans, May 24, 1940; s. Arthur Alphonse and Myrtle (Ress) C.; m. Iona Perry. BA, Nicholls State U., 1963; JD, Loyola U., New Orleans, 1969. Bar: La. 1969, U.S. Dist. Ct. (ea. dist.) La. 1972, U.S. Dist. Ct. (mid. dist.) La. 1978, U.S. Dist. Ct. (we. dist.) La. 1979, U.S. Ct. Appeals (5th cir.) 1972, U.S. Supreme Ct. 1972. Pvt. practice, Reserve, La., 1969-88, LaPlace, 1988—; staff atty. La. Legis. Coun., 1972-73; legal counsel Nicholls State U. Alumni Fedn., 1974-76, 78-80; spl. counsel Pontchartrain Levee Dist., 1976—2001. Administrv. law judge La. Dept. Civil Svc., 1981—. Pres. Boys' State of La. Inc., 1990-92, bd. dirs., 1988—. With AUS, 1964, USNG, 1964-70. Recipient Am. Jurisprudence award Loyola U., 1968. Fellow La. Bar Found.; mem. ABA, La. Bar Assn. (ho. dels. 1973-77, 79-85), 40th Jud. Dist. Bar Assn. (pres. 1985-87). ATLA, La. Trial Lawyers Assn., Nicholls State U. Alumni Fedn. (exec. coun. 1972-76, 77-85, pres. 1982, James Lynn Powell award 1980), Am. Legion (post cmdr. 1976-77, dist. judge adv. 1975-95, judge adv. La. dept. 1990-92, 93-96, mem. La. dept. commn. on nat. security and govtl. affairs 1974-89, chmn. 1977-78, 79-81, 85-89, M.C. Gehr blue cap award 1983). Roman Catholic. Administrative and regulatory, Juvenile. Home: 263 Central Ave Reserve LA 70084-6003 Office: 197 Belle Terre Blvd PO Box 461 La Place LA 70069-0461

CICONTE, EDWARD THOMAS, lawyer; b. Wilmington, Del., Dec. 14, 1948; s. Joseph John and Josephine E. (Roda) C.; m. Diane Marie Penza, Mar. 3, 1973; children— Andrea, Michele, Jacklyn. B.S., St. Joseph's U., Phila., 1970; J.D., Villanova (Pa.) U., 1973. Bar: Del. 1973, U.S. Dist. Ct. Del. 1973. Ptnr. Ciconte and Roseman (formerly D'Angelo, Ciconte & Roseman), Wilmington, 1973—. Co-author: Delaware Collection Law, 1982. Served as capt. USAF, 1974. Mem. Del. Bar Assn., ABA, Am. Trial Lawyers Assn., Del. Trial Lawyers Assn., Comml. Law League Am. Democrat. Roman Catholic. Consumer commercial, Personal injury, Workers' compensation. Home: 4009 Springfield Ln Wilmington DE 19807-2251 Office: Ciconte and Roseman 1300 N King St Wilmington DE 19801-3220

CID, TIAGO, lawyer, tax consultant; b. Lisbon, Portugal, Aug. 4, 1971; s. Luis and Clarisse Cid; m. Vera Rosario, Sept. 14, 1974. Degree in Law, U. Lisbon, 1995; Postgrad., Univ. Inst. European Studies, Turin, Italy, 1996. Bar: 1997. Atty., ptnr. J.A. Pinto Ribiero & Assocs., Lisbon, 1996-2000; sr. cons. tax dept. Deloitte & Touche, 2000—. Mem. Ordem dos Advogados. Banking, General corporate, Taxation, general. Office: Deloittte & Touche Av E D Pacehco, Amoreiras Lisbon 1070-10P Portugal Fax: 351213859322. E-mail: tiago.cid@mail.deloitte.pt

CIFARELLI, THOMAS ABITABILE, lawyer; b. Queens, N.Y., Feb. 7, 1967; s. Philip S. and Gina A. Cifarelli; m. Lilian G. Cifarelli, Sept. 20, 1997; children: Vincent Thomas, Michael Greco. BA magna cum laude, UCLA, 1989; JD, Loyola U., 1992. Bar: Calif. 1992, U.S. Dist. Ct. (cen. dist.) Calif. 1994, U.S. Supreme Ct. 2001. Assoc. atty. Mazursky Schwartz & Angelo, L.A., 1992-94; trial atty. Law Offices of Philip Michels, 1994-97; trial atty., ptnr. The Cifarelli Law Firm, Santa Ana, Calif., 1997—. Lead trial & appellate atty. M.G. vs. Time Warner, Inc., etal. privacy rights case; lectr. Consumer Attys. Assn. Calif. Contbr. articles to law pubs. Mem. Million Dollar Advocates Forum (life), L.A. World Affairs Coun., 1998. Mem. ATLA, Consumer Attys. Assn. Calif. (seminar spkr., bd. govs. 2000—, diplomat's club), Orange County Trial Lawyers Assn. Avocations: fitness, writing, family, travel, reading. General civil litigation, Personal injury, Product liability. Office: The Cifarelli Law Firm Santa Ana CA 92701 E-mail: tomc@cifarellilaw.com

CILZ, DOUGLAS ARTHUR, lawyer; b. Rugby, N.D., Feb. 22, 1949; s. Fred W. and Arliene (Nelson) C.; m. Kathy Ann Walker, June 10, 1972; children: Jennifer, Nicholas. BS, Dickinson State U., 1976; JD, U. N.D., Grand Forks, 1980. Bar: N.D. 1980, U.S. Dist. Ct. N.D. 1980, Minn. 1981, U.S. Tax Ct. 1981, U.S. Claims Ct. 1981. Atty. Qualley Larson & Jones, Fargo, N.D., 1980-81, Pearson & Christensen, Grand Forks, 1981-87; ptnr. Juntunen, Cilz & Hagen, 1987-98; atty. N.D. Dept. Transp., 1998—. Instr. East Grand Forks (Minn.) Tech. Coll., 1989-92; apptd. spl. asst. atty. gen. Bank N.D., 1993—; apptd. temporary adminstrv. law judge N.D. Office Adminstrv. Hearings, 1995—. Sgt. USAF, 1968-71. Mem. ABA, Minn. Bar Assn., N.D. Bar Assn., Am. Trial Lawyers Assn., Grand Forks C. of C. Lutheran. Avocations: golf, sailing, fishing. General civil litigation, Estate planning, Taxation, general. Office: ND Dept Transportation 1951 N Washington St Grand Forks ND 58203-1420

CIMINI, JOSEPH FEDELE, law educator, lawyer, former magistrate; b. Scranton, Pa., Sept. 8, 1948; s. Frank Anthony and Dorothy Theresa (Musso) C. AB in German and Polit. Sci., U. Scranton, 1970; JD Columbus Sch. Law, Cath. U. Am., 1973. Bar: Pa. 1973, U.S. Dist. Ct. (mid. dist.) Pa. 1973, D.C. 1976, U.S. Ct. Appeals (3d cir.) 1978, U.S. Supreme Ct. 1978. Law clk. to judge Ct. Common Pleas Lackawanna County (Pa.), 1973-75; asst. U.S. atty. Middle Dist. Pa., Pa. Dept. Justice, 1975-80; spl. asst. to U.S. Atty. Middle Dist. Pa., 1980-81; asst. prof. sociology/criminal justice U. Scranton, 1980-94, assoc. prof., 1994—, chmn. dept., 2001—. U.S. magistrate judge U.S. Dist. Ct. (mid. dist.) Pa., 1981-92; spl. trial master Lackawanna County Ct. Common Pleas, 1995—. Past pres. Lackawanna Hist. Soc.; v.p. adv. bd. Holy Family Residence, Scranton, Pa., 1997—; v.p. pastoral coun. St. Francis Ch., 1994-96. Recipient Meritorious award Dept. Justice; German Acad. Exchange Service fgn. study travel grantee, W.Ger., 1981. Mem. ABA, Fed. Bar Assn. (past v.p. mid. dist. Pa. chpt.), Am. Judges Assn., Fed. Magistrate Judges Assn., Am. Justinian Soc. of Jurists, Acad. Criminal Justice Scis., Pa. Bar Assn., Northeastern Assn. Criminal Scis. (pres. 1987-88), Lackawanna Bar Assn., Pa. Sociol. Soc. (treas.), U. Scranton Alumni (nat. sec. 1997-99), Cath. U. Law Alumni, Purple Club, Victor Alfieri Lit. Soc., UNICO Nat. Republican. Roman Catholic. Address: Univ Scranton Dept Sociology/Criminal Justice Scranton PA 18510-4605 E-mail: ciminij1@scranton.edu

CINABRO, ROBERT HENRY, lawyer; b. Kalamazoo, June 10, 1948; s. Louis and Maria (Breviglieri) C.; m. Pamela Mae Eschenburg, Aug. 19, 1972; children: Jennifer Elise, Michael Thomas. BA cum laude, Kalamazoo Coll., 1970; JD, Cornell U., 1973. Bar: Mich. 1973, U.S. Dist. Ct. (we. dist.) Mich., 1975, U.S. Supreme Ct. 1979, U.S. Ct. Appeals (6th cir.) 1983, Fla. 1987. Law clk. to presiding judge 9th Judicial Ct., Kalamazoo, 1973-74; asst. city atty. City of Kalamazoo, 1974-77, dep. city atty., 1977-88, city atty., 1988—. Civil mediator 9th Jud. Cir. Ct., Kalamazoo, 1985—; civil arbitrator U.S. Dist. Ct. for We. Dist. Mich., Grand Rapids, 1986—; legal counsel Kalamazoo Met. Transit Authority, 1985-88. Mem. Kalamazoo Criminal Justice Commn., 1982-83, Kalamazoo Safety Coun., Drunk Driving Task Force, 1983—85 commr. Kalamazoo Hosp. Fin. Authority, 1988—; bd. dirs. Kalamazoo County Humane Soc., 1983-85. Mem. ABA, Kalamazoo County Bar Assn., Fed. Bar Assn., Fla. Bar Assn., Phi Beta Kappa. Roman Catholic. Avocations: civil war history, travel, animal welfare. Home: 2525 Frederick Ave Kalamazoo MI 49008-2149 Office: Office of City Atty 234 W Cedar St Kalamazoo MI 49007-5151 E-mail: kokatty@vvoyager.net

CINCIOTTA, LINDA ANN, lawyer, administrator; b. Washington, May 18, 1943; d. Nicholas Joseph and Laverne C.; m. John P. Olguin, Aug. 4, 1979. BS, Georgetown U., 1965; JD, George Washington U., 1970. Bar: D.C. 1970. Assoc. Arent, Fox, Plotkin & Kahn, Washington, 1970-77, ptnr., 1978-83; dir. Office Atty. Recruitment Mgmt. Dept. Justice, 1983—. Recipient U.S. Law Week award, George Washington U. Nat. Law Ctr., 1970. Mem. ABA (Nat. Assn. Law Placement liaison to commn. women in profession 1992-95), Fedn. Comm. Bar Assn. (pres. 1980-81, ABA del. 1977-79), D.C. Bar Assn., Order of Coif. Office: US Dept Justice Dir Office Atty Recruitment Mgmt 950 Pennsylvania Ave NW Washington DC 20530-0001

CINQUEGRANA, AMERICO RALPH, lawyer; b. July 8, 1942; s. Americo and Caroline (Pettine) C.; m. Hope Frances Meader, Aug. 24, 1968; children: Faith, Amelia. Cert., U. Md. Overseas, 1964; BA, U. N.H., 1968; JD, U. Va., 1973. Bar: Conn. 1973, U.S. Dist. Ct. Conn. 1973, U.S. Dist. Ct. (ea. and so. dists.) N.Y. 1973, U.S. Ct. Appeals (2d cir.) 1973. Intelligence officer CIA, Washington, 1968-70; asst. gen. counsel, 1976-79; dep. insp. gen. investigations, 1991-98; chief investigative counsel House Select Com. on Tech. Transfer to China, 1998; spl. counsel to CIA inspector gen., 1999; chief counsel Nat. Commn. for Review of Nat. Reconnaissance Office, 2000; spl. counsel Policy and Security Intelligence Cmty. Mgmt. Staff, 2001. Assoc. Day, Berry, & Howard, Hartford, Conn., 1973-76; dep. counsel to Atty. Gen. for Intelligece Policy, U.S. Dept. Justice, Washington, 1979-91; lectr. UVa. Law Sch., Charlottesville, 1983-85, Cath. U. Law Sch., Washington, 1986—; guest lectr. Brookings Inst., Washington, 1983, 84, Ctr. Law and Nat. Security U. Va. Law Sch., 1990—. Co-author course manual internation Simulation, 1968; author law rev. articles. Served with USAF, 1961-65. Ctr. for Law and Nat. Security grantee, 1983; named to Italian-Am. hall of Fame. Mem. U. N.H. ALumni Assn. (pres. Washington chpt. 1982). Office: Central & Intelligence Agy CIA 7722 Lewinsville Rd Mc Lean VA 22102

CIOFFI, MICHAEL LAWRENCE, lawyer; b. Cin., Feb. 2, 1953; s. Patrick Anthony and Patricia (Schroeder) C.; children: Michael A., David P., Gina M. BA magna cum laude, U. Notre Dame, 1975; JD, U. Cin., 1979. Bar: Ohio 1979, U.S. Dist. Ct. (so. dist.) Ohio 1980, U.S. Dist. Ct. (no. dist.) Ohio 1983, U.S. Ct. Appeals (6th cir.) 1985. Asst. atty. gen. Ohio Atty. Gen., Columbus, 1979-81; from assoc. to ptnr. Frost & Jacobs, Cin., 1981-87; staff v.p., asst. gen. counsel Penn Cen. Corp., 1988-93; v.p., asst. gen. counsel Am. Fin. Group, 1993-2000; ptnr. Blank Rome Comisky & McCauley, 2001—. Adj. prof. law U. Cin. Coll. Law, 1983—. Author: Ohio Pretrial Litigation, 1991; co-author: Sixth Circuit Federal Practice Manual, 1993. Bd. dirs. Charter Com. of Greater Cin., 1985-88. Recipient Goldman Prize for Tchg. Excellence U. Cin. Coll. Law, 1995, Nicholas Longworth Disting. Alumni award, 1996. Mem. ABA, Fed. Bar Assn. (mem. exec. com., pres.1994), Ohio Bar Assn., Cin. Bar Assn. Avocations: tennis, travel. Federal civil litigation, General civil litigation, Environmental. Office: Blank Rome Comisky & McCauley LLP 201 E 5th St Cincinnati OH 45202

CIOVACCO, ROBERT JOHN, lawyer; b. Bklyn., June 23, 1941; s. Frank and Frances (Grieci) C.; m. Phyllis Marie Russo, Aug. 14, 1966; children— Jennifer Jude, Lauren Marie. B.A., Adelphi U., 1963; LL.B., St. John's U., Bklyn., 1967 Bar: N.Y. 1967, U.S. Dist. Ct. (so. and ea. dists.) N.Y. 1975. Assoc., Roth Carlson Kwit Spengler & Mallin, N.Y.C., 1966-68; asst. counsel Celanese Corp., N.Y.C., 1968-71; ptnr., officer Whiteman, Ciovacco & Gorray, P.C., Westbury, N.Y., 1971— ; bd. dirs., sec., mem. exec. com. L.I. Forum for Tech., Farmingdale, N.Y., 1980-84. Bd. dirs. Community Program Ctrs. of L.I., Inc., Deer Park, N.Y., 1983—. Mem. Nassau Club (Glen Cove, N.Y.). Republican. Roman Catholic. Consumer commercial, General corporate, Real property. Office: Whiteman Ciovacco & Gorray PC 1600 Stewart Ave Westbury NY 11590-6696

CIPARICK, CARMEN BEAUCHAMP, state supreme court judge; b. N.Y.C., 1942; Grad., Hunter Coll., 1963; JD, St. John's U., 1967; LLD (hon.), CUNY, Queens Coll., 1994. Staff atty. Legal Aid Soc., N.Y.C.; asst. counsel Office of the Judicial Conf., 1969-72; chief law asst. N.Y.C. Criminal Ct., 1972-74; counsel Office of N.Y.C. Adminstrv. Judge, 1974-78; judge N.Y.C. Criminal Ct., 1978-82, N.Y. Supreme Ct, 1982-94; assoc. judge N.Y. State Ct. Appeals, N.Y.C., 1994—. Former mem. N.Y. State Commn. Judicial Conduct. Trustee Boricua Coll.; bd. dirs. St. John's U. Sch. of Law Alumni Assn. Named to Hunter Coll. Hall of Fame, 1991. Office: NY State Ct Appeals 122 E 42nd St New York NY 10168-0002

CIPOLLONE, ANTHONY DOMINIC, judge, educator; b. N.Y.C., Mar. 15, 1939; s. Domenico and Caterina (Brancazio) C.; m. Eileen Mary Patricia Kelly, Sept. 14, 1963; children: Catherine Mary, Kelly Ann, Mary Rose. BA, CCNY, 1961, MA, 1968; JD, Seton Hall U., 1978. Bar: N.J. 1978, Pa. 1978, U.S. Patent Office 1978, Fla. 1980, N.Y. 1984, D.C. 1985, Mass. 1988; cert. civil trial atty. N.J., 1987. Chemist Am. Chicle Co., Long Island City, N.Y., 1961-65; research chemist Denver Chem. Mfg. Co., Stamford, Conn., 1965-66; chem. sales engr. GAF Corp., N.Y.C., 1966-68; nat. acct. rep. Stauffer Chem., 1968-72; sales mgr. Rhone-Poulenc Inc., South Brunswick, N.J., 1972-78; prosecutor Town of Elmwood Park, 1981-85, Town of Paramus, 1982-85; mcpl. ct. judge Town of Paramus (N.J.), 1985-90, Town of Little Ferry (N.J.), 1986-89; atty. planning bd. Twp. Saddle Brook, 1986-87; mcpl. ct. judge Town of Elmwood Park (N.J.), 1991, Town of Saddle Brook (N.J.), 1991-94; atty. Twp. Saddle Brook, 1987-90. Adj. faculty MBA program for chmn. and pharm. mgrs. Fairleigh Dickinson U.; atty. Zoning Bd., City of Hackensack, N.J., 1989-90, atty. Planning Bd., 1991—. Served to sgt. USMC, 1961-66. Mem. ABA, Bergen Bar Assn., N.J. Bar Assn., Pa. Bar Assn., N.Y. Bar Assn., D.C. Bar Assn., Fla. Bar Assn., Mass. Bar Assn., Am. Chem. Soc., Am. Mensa. Roman Catholic. Home: 535 E Ridgewood Ave Apt 4 Ridgewood NJ 07450-3347 Office: 1 Essex St Hackensack NJ 07601-5414 E-mail: cipollone@verizon.net

CIRANDO, JOHN ANTHONY, lawyer; b. Syracuse, N.Y., June 25, 1942; s. Daniel John and Anne Marie (Farone) C.; m. Carolyn Joyce Lace, Sept. 17, 1966; children: Lisa Marie, Julie Lynn, Jennifer Mary. BA in History, St. Bonaventure (N.Y.) U., 1963; JD, SUNY, Buffalo, 1966. Bar: N.Y. 1966, U.S. Dist. Ct. (no. dist.) N.Y. 1966, U.S. Dist. Ct. (we. dist.) N.Y. 1994, U.S. Claims Ct. 1991, U.S. Ct. Mil. Appeals 1967, U.S. Ct. Appeals (2d cir.) 1985, U.S. Supreme Ct. 1974. Chief asst. dist. atty. Onondaga County Dist. Atty.'s Office, Syracuse, N.Y., 1971-87; atty. D.J. & J.A. Cirando, 1966—. Treas. N.Y. State Dist. Atty.'s Assn., 1977-87; chair Govs. Jud. Screening Com. 4th Jud. Dept., 1997—. Pres. bd. dirs. Vera House, Shelter for Women and Children in Crisis, Syracuse, 1988-90, gen. counsel, 1991—; bd. trustees Leukemia Soc. Am., 1995—, asst. sec., 1995-96, sec., 1996-2000, adv. bd., 2000—. Capt. JAG, U.S. Army, 1967-71. Mem. N.Y. State Bar Assn. (chair com. on county cts. 1975-78, chair com. on pub. rels. 1979-83), Onondaga County Bar Assn. (bd. dirs. 1974-77, sec. 1979). Appellate, Probate, Real property. Office: DJ & JA Cirando 101 S Salina St Ste 1010 Syracuse NY 13202-4303

CIRESI, MICHAEL VINCENT, lawyer; b. St. Paul, Apr. 18, 1946; s. Samuel Vincent and Selena Marie (Bloom) C.; m. Ann Ciresi; children: Dominic, Adam. BBA, U. St. Thomas; JD, U. Minn.; LLD, Southwestern U., 2001. Bar: Minn. 1971, U.S. Dist. Ct. Minn. 1974, U.S. Ct. Appeals (8th cir.) 1971, U.S. Supreme Ct. 1981, U.S. Ct. Appeals (2d cir.) 1986, U.S. Ct. Appeals (9th cir.) 1987, U.S. Ct. Appeals (10th cir.) 1990, N.Y. 1995, fed. cir., 1998, U.S. Ct. Appeals (5th cir.) 1999. Assoc. Robins, Kaplan, Miller & Ciresi, Mpls., 1971-78, ptnr., 1978—, exec. bd., 1983—, chmn. exec. bd., 1995—. Adv. bd. Ctr. Advanced Litigation, Nottingham (Eng.) Law Sch. Trustee U. St. Thomas. Named Product Liability Lawyer of Yr., Australian Nat. Consumer Law Assn., 1989, Trial Lawyer of Yr. Trial Lawyers for Public Justice Found., 1998. Mem. ABA, Minn. State Bar Assn., Hennepin County Bar Assn., Ramsey County Bar Assn., Assn. Trial Lawyers Am., Am. Bd. Trial Advocates, Internat. Bar. Assn., Inner Circle of Advocates, Trial Lawyers for Pub. Justice (bd. dirs.). Roman Catholic. Avocation: sports, U.S. history. Federal civil litigation, State civil litigation. Home: 1247 Culligan Ln Saint Paul MN 55118-4151 Office: Robins Kaplan Miller & Ciresi 2800 Lasalle Plz Minneapolis MN 55402

CISSELL, JAMES CHARLES, lawyer; b. Cleve., May 29, 1940; s. Robert Francis and Helen Cecelia (Freeman) C; children: Denise, Helene-Marie, Suzanne, James. Student, Sophia U., Tokyo, 1961; AB, Xavier U., 1962; JD, U. Cin., 1966; postgrad., Ohio State U., 1973-74; D. Tech. Letters, Cin. Tech. Coll., 1979. Bar: Ohio 1966, U.S. Dist. Ct. (so. dist.) Ohio 1967, U.S. Ct. Appeals (6th cir.) 1978, U.S. Supreme Ct. 1980, U.S. Dist. Ct. (ea. dist.) Ky. 1981. Pvt. practice law, 1966-78, 82—; asst. atty. gen. State of Ohio, 1971-74; first v.p. Cin. Bd. Park Commrs., 1973-74; vice mayor City of Cin., 1976-77; U.S. atty. So. Dist. Ohio, Cin., 1978-82. Adj. instr. law No. Ky. U., 1982-86; pres. Nat. Assn. Former U.S. attys., 2001—. Author: Oil and Gas Law in Ohio, 1964, Federal Criminal Trials, 5th edit., 1999; editor; Proving Federal Crimes. Gen. chmn. amateur pub. links championship U.S. Golf Assn., 1987; mem. coun. City of Cin., 1974-78, 85-87, 89-92; clk of cts., Hamilton County, 1992—, commr. Recreation Bd. Cin., 1974, Planning Bd. Cin., 1977; pres. Ohio Clk. of Cts. Assn., 1998; mem. Ohio Bicentennial Commn., 1998—; mem. Ohio Cts. Futures Commn., 1998-2000; mem. Ohio Supreme Ct. Adv. Com. on Tech. and the Cts., 2000—. Ford Found. fellow Ohio State U., 1973-74. Mem. Ohio Bar Assn., Cin. Bar Assn., Fed. Bar Assn., Former U.S. Attys. Assn. Avocations: golf, jogging. Federal civil litigation, Criminal, Probate. Home: 201B Belvedere 3900 Rose Hl Cincinnati OH 45229 Office: 602 Main St Ste 320 Cincinnati OH 45202-2521 E-mail: jcissell@cms.hamilton-co.org

CITREY, ERIC JEAN-PIERRE, lawyer; b. Lisieux, Calvados, France, May 24, 1955; s. André Jules-Louis and Micheline Marie Citrey; m. Annie Micheline Aleman, Dec. 14, 1984; children: Julie, Arnaud, Maxime, Aymeric, Charlotte. JD, Nice (France) U., 1977, Master's degree, 1978, PhD, 1983; LLM, Univ Miami, 1983. Pars Bar 1996. Trainee Shutts & Bowen PA, Miami, Fla., 1983-84; cons. IBC Inc., 1984-87; counselor at law Price Waterhouse, Paris, 1987-89; legal counsel GEC Alsthom, 1990-96; atty. Tinland, Evrard, PA, 1996, Ronseray, Tournois & Assocs., Paris, 1997; pvt. practice, 1997—. 1st class Alpin Infantry, 1978-79. Mem. Internat. C. of C. (French sect.). Antitrust, Private international, Mergers and acquisitions. Office: 25 Ave Pierre 1 de Serbie 75116 Paris France Fax: 330149528104. E-mail: eric.citrey@avocaweb.tm.fr

CITRON, BEATRICE SALLY, law librarian, lawyer, educator; b. Phila., May 19, 1929; d. Morris Meyer and Frances (Teplitsky) Levinson; m. Joel P. Citron, Aug. 7, 1955 (dec. Sept. 1977); children: Deborah Ann, Victor Ephraim. BA in Econs. with honors, U. Pa., 1950; MLS, Our Lady of the Lake U., 1978; JD, U. Tex., 1984. Bar: Tex. 1985; cert. all-level sch. libr., secondary level tchr., Tex. Claims examiner Social Security Adminstrn., Pa., Fla. and N.C., 1951-59; head libr. St. Mary's Hall, San Antonio, 1979-80; media, reference and rare book libr., asst. and assoc. prof. St. Mary's U. Law Libr., 1984-89; asst. dir. St. Thomas U. Law Libr., Miami, Fla., 1989-96, assoc. dir./head pub. svc., 1996-99, acting dir., 1997-98. Law libr. cons., 2000—. Mem. ABA, Am. Assn. Law Librs. (publs. com. 1987-88, com. on rels. with info. vendors 1991-93, bylaws com. 1994-96), S.W. Assn. Law Librs. (continuing edn. com. 1986-88, chmn. local arrangements 1987-88), S.E. Assn. Law Librs. (newsletter, program and edn. coms. 1991-98), South Fla. Assn. Law Librs. (treas. 1992-94, v.p. 1994-95, pres. 1995-96).

CLABAUGH, ELMER EUGENE, JR. retired lawyer; b. Anaheim, Calif., Sept. 18, 1927; s. Elmer Eugene and Eleanor Margaret (Heitshusen) C.; m. Donna Marie Organ, Dec. 19, 1960 (div.); children: Christopher C., Matthew M. BBA cum laude, Woodbury U.; BA summa cum laude, Claremont McKenna Coll., 1958; JD, Stanford U., 1961. Bar: Calif. 1961, U.S. Dist. Ct. (cen. dist.) Calif., U.S. Ct. Appeals (9th cir.) 1961, U.S. Supreme Ct. 1971. With fgn. svc. U.S. Dept. State, Jerusalem, Tel Aviv, 1951-53, Pub. Adminstrn. Svcs., El Salvador, Ethiopia, U.S., 1953-57; dep. dist. atty. Ventura County, Calif., 1961-62; pvt. practice, 1962-97; mem. Hathaway, Clabaugh, Perrett and Webster and predecessors, 1962-79, Clabaugh & Perfloff, Ventura, 1979-97; state inheritance tax referee, 1968-78; ret. Bd. dirs. San Antonio Water Conservation Dist., Ventura Cmty. Meml. Hosp., 1964-80; trustee Ojai Unified Sch. Dist., 1974-79; bd. dirs. Ventura County Found. for Parks and Harbors, 1982-96, Ventura County Maritime Mus., 1982-94. With USCGR, 1944-46, USMCR, 1946-48. Mem. NRA, Calif. Bar Assn., Safari Club Internat., Mason, Shriners, Phi Alpha Delta. Republican. Contracts commercial, Probate, Real property.

CLAGETT, BRICE MCADOO, lawyer, writer; b. Washington, July 6, 1933; s. Brice and Sarah Fleming (MaAdoo) C.; m. Virginia Lawrence Parker, Sept. 18, 1965 (div.); children: John Brice, Ann Calvert Brooke; m. Diana Wharton Singler Knop, July 26, 1987). AB summa cum laude, Princeton U., 1954; postgrad., U. Allanabad, India, 1954-55; JD magna cum laude, Harvard U., 1958. Bar: D.C. 1958, U.S. Supreme Ct. 1962. Assoc. Covington & Burling, Washington, 1958-67, ptnr., 1967-2000, sr. counsel, 2000—. Jud. counsellor Cambodian del. Internat. Ct. Justice, 1960-62; legal advisor Transition Team U.S. Dept. State, 1980-81; mem. nat. steering com. U.S. Iran Claimants Com., 1982-99; adv. bd. Inst. Transnat. Arbitration, 1989-2000; mem. lawyers com. Ctr. individual Rights, 1992—. Co-author: The Valuation of Property in International Law, vol. 4, 1987, An Illustrated History of St. Albans School, 1981; bd. editors Harvard Law Rev., 1956-58; contbr. articles to legal, geneal. and hist. jours. Bd. advisors Nat. Trust Hist. Preservation, 1978-81; Clagett family com. Chesapeake Bay Found., 1982—; trustee Md. Hist. Trust, 1971-78, chmn., 1972-78, Md. State House Trust, 1972-76, Md. Environ. Trust, 1978—, vice chmn., 1981-85, chmn., 1985-89; mem. Internat. Human Rights Law Group del. to Romania, 1990; bd. dirs. Chester-Sassafras Found., 1985-89; trustee New Eng. Hist. Geneal. Soc., 1989-92, 95-98, Tudor Place Found., 1992-96; counseloor to the Pres. Gen., Soc. Cin., 1988-89, solicitor, 1998—; mem. adv. coun. Accokeek Found., 1989-91, trustee, 1991-94; trustee Found. Preservation Hist. Georgetown, 2000—; comdr. Royal Order Cambodia, 1962. Recipient Cert. Disting. Citizens State Md., 1978. Mem. Am. Soc. Internat. Law, Am. Law Inst., Am. Arbitration Assn. (panel of arbitrators 1990—, large complex case panel arbitrators 1993—, internat. p anel arbitrators 1997—), Internat. Law Assn., Washington Inst. Fgn. Affairs, Federalist Soc., Sons Confederate Vets., Mil. Order Stars and Bars, So. Md. Soc., Met City Tavern Club, Harvard Club (N.Y.C.), Soc. Cin. Md. Club, Marlborough Hunt Club (Upper Marllboro, Md.), Radnor Club (Pa.), Hunt Club, Phi Beta Kappa. Republican. Episcopalian. Federal civil litigation, Private international, Public international. Home: Holly Hill PO Box 86 Friendship MD 20758-0086 also: 3331 O St NW Washington DC 20007-2814 Office: Covington & Burling PO Box 7566 1201 Pennsylvania Ave NW Washington DC 20044

CLAPMAN, PETER CARLYLE, lawyer, insurance company executive; b. N.Y.C., Mar. 11, 1936; s. Jack and Evelyn (Clapman); m. Barbara Posen, May 8, 1966; children: Leah, Alice. AB, Princeton U., 1957; JD, Harvard U., 1960. Bar: N.Y. 1961, Conn. 1972. Assoc. Sage, Gray, Todd & Sims, N.Y.C., 1961-63; asst. counsel Stichman Commn., 1964; legal cons. OEO, Washington, 1965; assoc. counsel Equitable Life, N.Y.C., 1965-72; sr. v.p., chief counsel investments Tchrs. Ins. and Annuity of Am., Coll. Ret. Equities Fund, 1972—. Author: Fiduciary Responsibilities of Institutional

Managers on Proxy Issues, Iowa Law Jour., 1994, SEC Market 2000 Report; co-author: Notre Dame U. Law Rev., 1981. Mem. ABA, Assn. Bar City N.Y. (com. on securities regulation special com. on mergers), Am. Law Inst., Assn. Life Ins. Counsel (bd. govs., chmn. investment sect.), Am. Coll. Investment Counsel (trustee), Am. Coun. Life Ins. (chmn. securities investment commn.). Administrative and regulatory, Contracts commercial, Private international. Home: 3 Valley Rd Scarsdale NY 10583-1123 Office: Tchrs Ins & Annuity Assn Am 730 3rd Ave New York NY 10017-3206

CLARE, ROBERT LINN, JR. lawyer; b. Perth Amboy, N.J., May 9, 1914; s. Robert Linn and Helen (Walsh) C.; m. Ruth Elizabeth Eyerkuss, Dec. 29, 1942 (dec. 1972); children: Robert L., Patricia Ruth (Mrs. J.J. O'Brien), Kathleen Clare Kelly, Michael K., Mark J., Timothy C.; m. Margaret Cross, Mar. 9, 1974. AB, Holy Cross Coll.; LLB, Harvard U., 1938. Bar: N.J. 1939, U.S. Dist. Ct. N.J. 1939, U.S. Ct. Appeals (1st cir.) 1939, U.S. Ct. Appeals (3d cir.) 1948, U.S. Ct. Appeals (2d cir.) 1949, U.S. Dist. Ct. (so. dist.) N.Y. 1949, U.S. Tax Ct. 1949, U.S. Dist Ct. (ea. dist.) N.Y. 1950, ICC 1951, U.S. Ct. Claims 1953, U.S. Supreme Ct. 1963, U.S. Dist. Ct. (we. dist.) N.Y. 1964. Assoc. Shearman & Sterling, N.Y.C., 1938-48, 52, ptnr., 1952-87, of counsel, 1987—, sr. ptnr., 1977-82. Assoc. Cronan, Kissell & Roseborough, N.Y.C., 1948-49. Contbr. chpts. to books, articles to profl. jours. Spl. mediator med. malpractice mediation part U.S. Supreme Ct., 1971—; mem. adv. bd. Project '87; mem. vol.'s masters' pilot program So. Dist. N.Y.; former trustee Found. on Commemoration of U.S. Constn., Nat. Inst. for Trial Advocacy (bd. dirs.); dir. So. Africa Legal Services and Legal Edn. Project Inc., Urban Found. USA Inc. Served to maj. JAGC U.S. Army, 1941-45. Mem. Practising Law Inst. (trustee), Am. Coll. Trial Lawyers (regent 1971-73, pres. 1973-74, trustee 1974—), Am. Judicature Soc., Guild Catholic Lawyers, Am. Bar Found., Fed. Bar Council, Supreme Ct. Hist. Soc., Harvard Law Sch. Assn. of N.Y.C. (trustee), Assn. Bar City N.Y., N.Y. State Bar Assn., N.Y. Law Inst. Roman Catholic. Antitrust. Home: 73 Sand Hill Rd # B Annandale NJ 08801-3111 Office: 153 E 53rd St New York NY 10022-4611

CLARK, BRUCE E. lawyer; b. N.Y.C., 1946; AB, Holy Cross, 1967; JD, Harvard U., 1970. Bar: N.Y. 1971. Mem. Sullivan & Cromwell, N.Y.C. General civil litigation. Office: Sullivan & Cromwell 125 Broad St Fl 28 New York NY 10004-2489

CLARK, CELIA RUE, lawyer; b. N.Y.C., Aug. 16, 1951; d. Edward Frank and Rosemary (Reddick) Clark, Jr.; m. Edgar Crawford Gentry, Jr., Aug. 11, 1979; children: Diana Marron, Carl Edgar. BA with distinction, U. Wis., 1974; JD, U. Chgo., 1979; LLM, NYU, 1988. Bar: N.Y. 1980. Mng. editor Heldref Publs., Washington, 1974-78; assoc. Rogers & Wells, N.Y.C., 1979-84; adj. asst. prof. law Yeshiva U., 1985; assoc. Weitzner, Levine & Hamburg, N.Y.C., 1988-92; counsel Pirro, Collier, Cohen, Crystal & Block, White Plains, N.Y., 1992-96; ptnr. Smith, Buss & Jacobs, L.L.P., N.Y.C., 1996—. Contbg. author: Asset-Based Financing, 1984, Jour. Taxation, 1998, Westchester County Bus. Jour., 1999, 2000. Bd. govs. Arthritis Found. (N.Y. chpt.); dir. Louis R. Cappelli Found. Mem. ABA, Westchester County Bar Assn. Democrat. General corporate, Estate planning, Taxation, general. Office: Smith Buss & Jacobs LLP 750 Lexington Ave New York NY 10022-1200 E-mail: cclark@sbjlaw.com

CLARK, DAVID KEITH, lawyer, real estate developer; b. Lakewood, Ohio, July 28, 1952; s. Don Roger and Patricia Ann (Hunt) C.; m. Beth Moore Malone, June 14, 1980; children: Blaire Megan, Shannon Elizabeth. BArch, BSBA, U. Ariz., 1977; JD, U. Houston, 1980. Bar: Tex. 1980, U.S. Dist. Ct. (no., so. and ea. dists.) Tex. 1980, U.S. Ct. Appeals (5th cir.) 1980. Law librarian, clk. Baker, Botts, Vinson & Elkins, Houston, 1977-78; assoc. Baker, Brown, et al, 1980-82; asst. gen. counsel, devel. officer Cadillac Fairview, Dallas, 1982-87; devel. officer Prentiss Properties Urban Devel., 1987-90; v.p. The Equity Group, Chgo., 1990-92; mng. dir. LaSalle Ptnrs., 1992-97, Tishman Speyer Properties, Chgo., 1997—. Bd. dirs. Don R. Clark M.D., P.C., Roswell, N.Mex., 1972—. Chmn. Dallas Urban Design Task Force, Mich. Ave. dist. task force, 1995; bd. dirs. Chgo. Devel. Coun., 1997—; chmn. Zoning Com., Chgo., 1998. Mem. Tex. Bar Assn. (real estate, probate and trust sects.), Urban Land Inst., Univ. Club Chgo., Leadership Dallas, Phi Delta Phi. Republican. Methodist. Home: 1184 Cedar Ln Northbrook IL 60062-3544 Office: Tishman Speyer Properties 500 W Monroe St Ste 2700 Chicago IL 60661-3630

CLARK, DAVID MCKENZIE, lawyer; b. Greenville, N.C., Sept. 1, 1929; s. David McKenzie and Myrtle Estelle (Brogdon) C.; m. Martha McKellar Early; children: David, Martha Dockery, Marietta Brogdon, Carolyn Elizabeth; m. Susan Summers Mullally; 1 child, McKenzie Lawrence. BA, Wake Forest Coll., 1951; LLD, NYU, 1957. Law clerk Chambers of Justice Black U.S. Supreme Court, Washington, 1957-59; assoc. Smith, Moore, Smith, Schell & Hunter, Greensboro, N.C., 1959-63; ptnr. Stern Rendleman & Clark, 1964-68, Clark & Wharton, Greensboro, 1968-98, Clark Bloss & McIver, Greensboro, 1999—. Mem. bd. dirs. Legal Svcs. of N.C., Raleigh, 1976-82; pres. Summit Rotary Club, Greensboro, 1967; mem. bd. trustees W. Market Street Methodist Ch., Greensboro; chmn., co-founder Greensboro Legal Aid Found., 1965-68. Mem. ABA, Am. Trial Lawyers Assn., Am. Bd. Trial Advocates, N.C. Bar Assn. (bd. govs. 1982-85), N.C. Acad. Trial Lawyers, Greensboro Bar Assn. (bd. dirs.). Avocations: golf, tennis. General civil litigation, Personal injury, Securities. Home: 328 E Greenway Dr N Greensboro NC 27403-1560 Office: Clark Bloss & McIver 125 S Elm St Ste 600 Greensboro NC 27401-2644

CLARK, DAVID WRIGHT, lawyer; b. West Point, Miss., May 19, 1948; s. Douglas Earl and Sarah Evelyn (Wright) C.; m. Victoria Baugher, Oct. 16, 1976; children: Alexander, Nicholas, Peter. BA with high honors, Millsaps Coll., 1970; MA, Harvard U., 1971; JD, U. Mich., 1974. Bar: Ill. 1974, Miss. 1978, U.S. Dist. Ct. (no. dist.) Ill. 1974, U.S. Ct. Appeals (7th cir.) 1974, U.S. Dist. Ct. (so. and no. dists.) Miss. 1978, U.S. Ct. Appeals (5th cir.) 1978. Adj. prof. Miss. Coll. Sch. Law, Jackson, 1978-82; assoc. Wildman, Harrold, Allen & Dixon, Chgo., Friedman & Koven, Chgo., 1974-78; shareholder Wise Carter Child & Caraway, P.A., Jackson, 1978-96; ptnr. Lake Tindall, LLP, 1996-2001, Bradley Arant Rose & White LLP, Jackson, 2001—. Pres. Miss. Bar Rev., 1979—. Mem. Miss. Constitution Study Commn., Jackson, 1985-87; bd. dirs. Miss. First, Inc., Jackson, 1983-87; pres. U.S.A. Internat. Ballet Competition, Jackson, 1990-98; mem. Leadership Jackson, 1989-90. Mem. ABA (sect. litigation, dir. divsn., com. chmn. and task force chmn. 1987-2001, chmn. gun violence coord. com. 1998—), Miss. Bar Assn. (chmn. litigation sect. 1994-95), Am. Law Inst., Charles Clark Am. Inn of Ct. Avocations: musicals, opera. Federal civil litigation, State civil litigation, General corporate. Home: 110 Olympia Fields Jackson MS 39211-2509 Office: Bradley Arant Rose & White LLP One Jackson Pl Ste 450 Jackson MS 39201 E-mail: dclark@barw.com

CLARK, DWIGHT WILLIAM, lawyer; b. Gothenburg, Nebr., Sept. 24, 1944; s. William Elwood Clark and Christina Antina Koster; m. Sharon Louise Anderson, Aug. 31, 1968; children: Andrea Christine, Nathan William. BS, U. Nebr., 1967; JD, Calif. Western Law Sch., 1974; MPA, U. So. Calif., 1976. Bar: Calif. 1975; cert. specialist in jud. adminstrn. Adminstrv. intern U.S. Probation Office, L.A., 1975-76; exec. asst. San Francisco Mcpl. Ct., 1976-84, clk.-adminstr., 1984-89; cons. justice systems IBM, 1989-95; chief dep. clk. U.S. Bankruptcy Ct., San Francisco, 1995-98; ct. exec. officer Humboldt County Superior Ct.; moot ct. judge U. San Francisco Sch. Anthropology, 1977; dir. Corp. Bus. Brokers No. Calif., Inc.; user rep. EDP priority com. City and County San Francisco, 1979, electronic info. steering com., 1983-86; assoc. faculty Nat. Judges Coll., Reno, 1985-88; lectr. in law and computer related fields. Mem. adv. bd. Coll. Bus. Adminstrn. U. Nebr., Lincoln, 1966, 67, chmn. placement bd. program, 1967; chmn. honor code revision com. Calif. Western Law Sch., San Diego, 1968, 69; trustee San Mateo Elem. Sch. Dist. (Calif.), 1983-91, San Mateo PTA; mem. adj. faculty Coll. Profl. Studies U. San Francisco, 1992-98. Recipient Am. Jurisprudence Scholastic award, 1969, Tech. Achievement award Fin. Pub. Tech., Inc., Washington, 1984, Hon. Svc. award PTA, 1986. Mem. ABA, Am. Judicature Soc., Calif. State Bar, Calif. Mcpl. Ct. Clks. Assn., San Mateo County Bar Assn., Nat. Assn. Ct. Mgrs., Nat. Conf. Bankruptcy Clerks, Fed. Ct. Clerks Assn., Western Internat. Law Soc. (founding mem.), Calif. Western Law Sch. Alumni Club, U. So. Calif. Alumni Club, Lawyers Club, Phi Delta Phi, Delta Sigma Pi (life), Trial Ct. Budget Commn., Calif. Ct. Exec. Com., Ct. Tech. Adv. Com., Calif. Trial Ct. Adminstrs. Assn., Calif. Ct. Clerks Assn., Humboldt County Bar Assn., Humboldt Law Enforcement Chief Assn. Contbg. author: (book) Handbook of Management Consulting Services, 1995. Democrat. Lutheran. Avocations: woodcrafts, music, reading. Home: 6000 Noe Ave Eureka CA 95503-6386 Office: Superior Ct Humboldt Cty Rm 226 825 5th St Eureka CA 95501-1153

CLARK, ELIAS, law educator; b. New Haven, Aug. 19, 1921; B.A., Yale U., 1943, LL.B., 1947, M.A., 1957. Bar: N.Y. 1948, Conn. 1950. Assoc. Cleary, Gottlieb, Friendly & Cox, N.Y.C., 1947-49; mem. faculty Law Sch., Yale U., New Haven, 1949—, prof., 1958—, Lafayette S. Foster prof., 1968-92, Lafayette S. Foster prof. emeritus, 1992—, Myres S. McDougal professorial lectr. law, 1992—. Master Silliman Coll., 1962-81. Co-author: Gratuitous Transfers, 1996, Cases and Materials on Federal Estate and Gift Taxation, 2000; contbr. articles to legal jours. Bd. dirs. Mental Health Conn., 1957-67; bd. dirs. New Haven Found., 1969-76. Mem. Conn. Bar Assn. (Disting. Pub. Service 1959) Home: 1179 Whitney Ave Apt B Hamden CT 06517-3434 Office: Yale U Sch Law SLB 336 127 Wall St New Haven CT 06511-6636

CLARK, GARY CARL, lawyer; b. Flippin, Ark., Mar. 4, 1947; m. Jane W. Clark; children: Ross, Lauren. BS in Agrl. Edn., Okla. State U., 1969, MS, 1972; JD with honors, U. Tex., 1975. Bar: Okla. 1975, U.S. Dist. Ct. (no. dist.) Okla. 1975, U.S. Ct. Appeals (10th cir.) 1979. Tchr. Laverne H.S., Okla., 1969-70; assoc. Conner, Winters, Ballaine, Barry & McGowen, 1975-81, ptnr., 1981, Baker & Hoster, Tulsa, 1981-97; dir. Crowe & Dunlevy, PC, 1997—. Lawyer-staffed Panel of Ct. Appeals, 1991; speaker in field. Vol. Legal Svcs. Ea. Okla., 1993—; trustee Okla. State Univ., Tulsa, 1999-2001; mem. bd. regents Okla. State Univ. and A&M Colls., 1993-2001, chmn., 1997-98; past v.p. Jane Addams Elem. Sch. PTA, sch. vol.; chair site adv.; mem. Okla. Jud. Evaluation Com., 1999—. Recipient Silver Beaver award Boy Scouts Am., 1996. Fellow Am. Bar Found., Okla. Bar Found. (trustee); mem. Okla. Bar Assn. (pres.-elect 2001, bd. govs. 1997-99, John Shipp Ethics award 1999, chair estate planning and probate sect. 1988-89, vice chair probate code com. 1991, bd. dirs. young lawyers divsn., mem. real property sect.), Tulsa County Bar Assn. (pres. 1993-94, Golden Rule award 1993, Outstanding Sr. Lawyer 1996), Tulsa County Bar Found. (pres. 1994-95, treas. 1995-99, charter fellow), Tulsa Title and Probate Lawyers Assn. (pres. 1989-90), Okla. State U. Alumni Assn. (life), FFA Alumni Assn. (life), Order of Coif, Alpha Gamma Rho Alumni Assn. (Okla. chpt. dir., past pres.), Phi Delta Phi. Bankruptcy, Estate planning, Probate. Home: 5505 S 97th West Ave Sand Springs OK 74063-4726 Office: Crowe & Dunlevy 500 Kennedy Bldg Tulsa OK 74103 E-mail: clarkg@crowedunlevy.com

CLARK, GLEN EDWARD, judge; b. Cedar Rapids, Iowa, Nov. 23, 1943; s. Robert M. and Georgia L. (Welch) C.; m. Deanna D. Thomas, July 16, 1966; children: Andrew Curtis, Carissa Jane. BA, U. Iowa, 1966; JD, U. Utah, 1971. Bar: Utah 1971, U.S. Dist. Ct. Utah 1971, U.S. Ct. Appeals (10th cir.) 1972. Assoc. Fabian & Clendenin, 1971-74, ptnr., 1975-81, dir., chmn. banking and comml. law sect., 1981-82; judge U.S. Bankruptcy Ct. Dist. Utah, Salt Lake City, 1982-86, chief judge, 1986—. Bd. govs. nat. Conf. Bankruptcy Judges, 1988-94; mem. com. on bankruptcy edn. Fed. Jud. Ctr., 1989-92; vis. prof. U. Utah, Salt Lake City, 1977-79, 83; pres. Nat. Conf. Bankruptcy Judges, 1992-93; chair bd. trustees Nat. Conf. Bankruptcy Judges Endowment for Edn., 1990-92; vis. assoc. prof. law Univ. Utah; instr. adv. bus. law Univ. Utah. Articles editor: Utah Law Review. With U.S. Army, 1966-68. Finkbine fellow U. Iowa. Fellow Am. Coll. Bnakruptcy (charter, mem. bd. regents 1995-2000); mem. Jud. Conf. U.S. (mem. com. jud. br. 1992-99, 10th cir. bankruptcy appellate panel 1996—), Utah Bar Assn., Order of Coif. Presbyterian. Office: 365 US Courthouse 350 S Main St Salt Lake City UT 84101-2106

CLARK, GRANT LAWRENCE, corporate lawyer; b. Syracuse, N.Y., Apr. 15, 1954; s. Robert William and Linda (Grant) C.; m. Diana Christine Baker, Aug. 5, 1983. BA, Framingham State Coll., 1979; JD, Suffolk U., 1983. Bar: Mass. 1983, Calif. 1992, U.S. Dist. Ct. Mass. 1983, U.S. Dist. Ct. (so. dist.) Calif. 1992, U.S. Ct. Appeals (D.C. cir.) 1995, U.S. Ct. Claims 1995, U.S. Ct. Mil. Appeals 1984. Staff judge advocate USAF, Washington, 1983-87; asst. gen. counsel GSA, 1987-88; assoc. Rivkin, Radler, Dunne & Bayh, 1988-91; assoc./ptnr. McKenna & Cuneo, 1991-94; asst. gen. counsel Sci. Applications Internat. Corp., San Diego, 1994-99; v.p.-gen. counsel Telcordia Tech., Inc., Morristown, N.J., 1999—. Instr. Fed. Publs., Inc., Washington, 1991—. Mem. pres.'s coun. Scripps Rsch. Found., LaJolla, Calif., 1998-99; mem. Founder's Soc., Morris Animal Found., Englewood, Colo., 1998-99. Capt., USAF, 1983-87. Mem. ABA, Fed. Bar Assn., Nat. Contracts Mgmt. Assn. Avocations: mountain biking, Latin dance, Medieval history. General civil litigation, Contracts commercial, Government contracts and claims. Home: 229 Mount Kemble Ave Morristown NJ 07960-6209 Office: Telcordia Tech Inc 445 South St Morristown NJ 07960-6454 E-mail: gclark@telcordia.com

CLARK, JAMES RICHARD, lawyer; b. Madison, Wis., Mar. 30, 1946; s. James F. and Gloria J. Clark; m. Martha C. Conrad, Mar. 18, 1950; children: Lindsey Kelley, Chad. BA, Ripon Coll., 1968; JD, U. Wis., 1971. Bar: Wis. 1971, U.S. Dist. Ct. (we. and ea. dists.) Wis. 1972, U.S. Ct. Appeals (7th cir.) 1973, U.S. Dist. Ct. (no. dist.) Ill. 1974, U.S. Supreme Ct. 1976. Assoc. Foley & Lardner, Milw., 1971-78, ptnr., 1978—. Editor-in-chief Wis. Law Rev., 1971. Trustee Ripon Coll., 1985—. 1st lt. U.S. Army, 1971. Mem. ABA, Am. Coll. Trial Lawyers, Am. Bd. Trial Advs., 7th Cir. Bar Assn., Wis. Bar Assn., Ripon Coll. Alumni Assn. (past pres.), Milw. Athletic Club; Tripoli Country Club, Order of Coif, Phi Beta Kappa. General civil litigation, Construction, Product liability. Home: 9719 N Dalewood Ln Mequon WI 53092-6210 Office: Foley & Lardner Firstar Ctr 777 E Wisc Ave Milwaukee WI 53202

CLARK, JONATHAN MONTGOMERY, lawyer; b. Bklyn., Oct. 20, 1937; s. Russell Inslee and Lillian (Longmore) C.; m. Priscilla M. Jorgensen, Sept. 24, 1960; children: Jonathan M. Jr., Christopher D. BA, Yale U., 1959; LLB, U. Va., 1964. Bar: N.Y. 1965. Assoc. Davis Polk & Wardwell, N.Y.C., 1964-71, ptnr., 1971-93; gen. counsel, mng. dir. Morgan Stanley & Co., Inc., 1993-97, sr. counsel, 1999—. Advisor mission to Poland, Fin. Svcs. Vol. Corps, 1990, 92; cons. Warren Commn., Washington, 1965; bd. dirs. Greenwich Hosp. Assn., 1990-98, Prentice Cup Com. bd. dirs. Caramoor Ctr. Music & the Arts. 1st lt. USMC, 1959-61. Mem. ABA, N.Y. State Bar Assn., Assn. Bar City N.Y., Securities Industry Assn. (bd. dirs., 1995-96), N.Y. Stock Exchange Legal Adv. Com. Republican. Episcopalian. Avocations: golf, fly fishing, birding. E-mail: jonathan.clark@dpw.com

CLARK, JOSEPH FRANCIS, JR. lawyer; b. Tulsa, Okla., Jan. 20, 1949; s. Joseph F. and Betty Sue C.; m. Carol J. Coleman, Nov. 2, 1974 (div. 1981); m. Cathy A. Baker, Jan. 6, 1989; children: Joseph F. Clark III, Thomas S. Clark, Joshua B. Baker. BA, Villanova U., 1971; JD, Tulsa U., 1973. Bar: Okla. 1974. Atty. Gibbon, Gladd, Clark et al, Tulsa, 1974-78; pvt. practice, 1979-80; atty. Williams, Clark et al, 1980-90; ptnr. Clark & Stainer, 1990-94, Layon, Cronin, Clark & Kaiser, P.L.L.C., Tulsa, 1994-99; pvt. practice, 1999—. Mem.: Am. Inns of Ct. (Council Oak chpt., term master 1996—98, master 1999—), Tulsa County Bar Assn. (fee dispute com. 1998—99, profl. responsibility com. 2001—). Democrat. Roman Catholic. Appellate, General civil litigation, Insurance. Home: 2922 E 39th St Tulsa OK 74105-3704 Office: 1605 S Denver Ave Tulsa OK 74119-4232 E-mail: joe@josephclarklaw.com

CLARK, LEROY D. legal educator, lawyer; b. 1934; BA, CCNY, 1956; LLB, Columbia U., 1961. Bar: N.Y. 1961. Staff atty. Office of N.Y. Atty. Gen., 1961-62; asst. counsel NAACP Legal Def. and Edn. Fund, Inc., N.Y.C., 1962-68; prof. law NYU Law Sch., 1969-79, Cath. U., 1981—. Gen. counsel EEOC, 1979-81; arbitrator Am. Arbitration Assn., Fed. Mediation and Conciliation Svc.; mem. Pub. Employee Rels. Bd. Author: The Grand Jury: The Use and Abuse of Political Power, 1975, Employment Discrimination Law--Cases and Materials, 5th edit., 2000. Office: Law School Catholic Univ Am 3600 John Mccormack Rd NE Washington DC 20064-0001 E-mail: clarkl@law.cua.edu

CLARK, MARK JEFFREY, paralegal, researcher; b. Alton, Ill., Nov. 2, 1953; s. William Alfred and Winifred May (Young) C.; m. Patricia Ann Newell, July 29, 1989; children: Jason William, Brandi Leigh. AS in Bus. Adminstrn., Lewis & Clark Coll., 1978; cert. paralegal, diploma in civil lit. and bus. law, Paralegal Inst., 1994. Commd. spl. officer Lake Ozark (Mo.) Police Dept., 1975-78; ind. paralegal J & B Enterprises, Woodriver, Ill., 1994—; criminal rschr. Pinkerton Svcs. Group, Charlotte, N.C., 1998—, MPC Legal Rsch. Consulting Svcs., Battle Creek, Mich., 1999—. Cons., rschr. Nationwide Corps., 1994—. With USN, 1972-75, Vietnam. Mem. Nat. Paralegal Assn., KC (4th degree), Am. Legion. Democrat. Roman Catholic. Avocations: scuba diving, golf, bowling. Home: Rt # 71 Box 272 Camdenton MO 65020

CLARK, MERRELL EDWARD, JR. lawyer; b. Bklyn., Apr. 30, 1922; s. Merrell Edward and Eleanor Everest (Wild) C.; m. Hollis Logan, May 22, 1943; children: Julie Clark Goodyear, Kenyon Wild. BA, Yale U., 1943, LLB, 1948. Bar: N.Y. 1948, U.S. Dist. Ct. (so. dist.) 1949, U.S. Ct. Appeals (2d cir.) 1949, U.S. Tax Ct. 1951, Conn. 1952, U.S. Dist. Ct. (ea. dist.) N.Y. 1952, U.S. Dist. Ct. (ea. dist.) N.Y. 1952, U.S. Supreme Ct. 1956, U.S. Ct. Appeals (6th cir.) 1965, U.S. Ct. Appeals (8th cir.) 1973, U.S. Ct. Appeals (4th cir.) 1974, U.S. Dist. Ct. (no. dist.) N.Y. 1982, U.S. Dist. Ct. (we. dist.) N.Y. 1982. Assoc. Winthrop, Stimson, Putnam & Roberts, N.Y.C., 1948-55, ptnr., 1956-91. Editor Yale Law Sch. Jour., 1947-48. Mem. Town Meeting, Greenwich, Conn., 1953-56, com. on jud. appointments (Appelate Div. 1st Dept.), 1978-82, 2d cir. jud. conf. evaluation com., 1980-87; dir.; trustee Perrot Meml. Library, Old Greenwich, Conn., 1956-63, Pomfret (Conn.) Sch., 1966-74, Richard Found., N.Y.C., 1965—, William Nelson Cromwell Found., N.Y.C., 1979—, Steep Rock Assn., Washinton, Conn., 1993-2000, Internat. Coll. Hospitality Mgmt., 1994-2000; adviser women's rights project ACLU, 1976-90; mem. N.Y.C. Bd. Ethics, 1987-89; chair N.Y.C. Conflicts of Interest Bd., 1989-90, N.Y.C. Hardship Appeals Bd., 1993-2001; bd. dirs. N.Y. Legal Aid Soc., 1985-88. Served to capt. AUS, 1943-46. Decorated Bronze Star with two battle stars. Mem. ABA (ho. of dels. 1985-89), Assn. of Bar of City of N.Y. (pres. 1978-80), Am. Law Inst., Am. Coll. Trial Lawyers, Conn. Bar Assn., N.Y. State Bar Assn. (ho. of dels. 1978-80), River Club (N.Y.C.), India House Club (N.Y.C.), Washington Club (Conn.). Antitrust, Federal civil litigation. Office: Winthrop Stimson Putnam Roberts 1 Battery Park Plz Fl 31 New York NY 10004-1490

CLARK, MORTON HUTCHINSON, lawyer; b. Norfolk, Va., Apr. 21, 1933; s. David Henderson and Catharine Angelica (Hutchinson) C.; m. Lynn Harrison Adams, Aug. 12, 1961; children: Allison Adams, David Henderson, Susan West, Julia Dixon. BA in English, U. Va., 1954, LLB, 1960. Bar: Va. 1960, U.S. Dist. Ct. (ea. dist.) Va. 1960, U.S. Ct. Appeals (4th cir.) 1976, U.S. Ct. Appeals (1st cir.) 1993, U.S. Supreme Ct. 1993. Assoc. Vandeventer Black LLP, Norfolk, 1960-65, ptnr., 1965—. Co-editor: The Virginia Lawyer, 1991-93. Chmn. Va. Commn. for Children and Youth, Richmond. Fellow Am. Coll. Trial Lawyers, Va. Law Found.; mem. Maritime Law Assn. (exec. com. 1984-87), Hoffman I'Anson Am. Inns of Ct. (exec. com. 1993-95), The Harbor Club (pres.), Town Point Club, Princess Anne Country Club, Farmington Country Club. Episcopalian. Avocations: off shore racing, cruising. Admiralty, Federal civil litigation. Home: 103 Rivers Edge Kingsmill Williamsburg VA 23185-8930 Office: Vandeventer Black LLP 500 World Trade Ctr Norfolk VA 23510-1679

CLARK, ROBERT CHARLES, dean, law educator; b. New Orleans, Feb. 26, 1944; s. William Vernon and Edwina Ellen (Nuessly) C.; m. Kathleen Margaret Tighe, June 1, 1968; children— Alexander Ian, Matthew Tighe. BA, Maryknoll Sem., 1966; PhD, Columbia U., 1971; JD, Harvard U., 1972. Bar: Mass. 1972. Assoc. firm Ropes & Gray, Boston, 1972-74; asst. prof. Yale U. Law Sch., New Haven, 1974-76, assoc. prof., 1976-77, prof., 1977-78; prof. law Harvard U., Cambridge, Mass., 1978—, dean of Law Sch., 1989—. Contbr. articles to profl. jours. Mem. Am. Bar Assn. Office: Harvard Law Sch Office of Dean 200 Griswold Hall 1525 Massachusetts Ave Cambridge MA 02138-2903*

CLARK, ROSS BERT, II, lawyer; b. Lafayette, Ind., Dec. 23, 1932; s. Ross Bert and Pauline Frances (Wilkinson) C.; m. Madge Logan, Dec. 27, 1959; 1 stepchild, George W. Johnson III. BA in History, U. of the South, 1954; JD, U. Tenn., 1960. Bar: Tenn. 1961, U.S. Dist. Ct. (we. dist.) Tenn. 1961, U.S. Dist. Ct. (no. dist.) Miss. 1981, U.S. Dist. Ct. (ea. dist.) Ark. 1996, U.S. Ct. Appeals (6th cir.) 1962. Law clk. to presiding judge U.S. Dist. Ct. (we. dist.) Tenn., Memphis, 1961-62; assoc. Rupert & Ewing, 1962-64, Laughlin, Watson, Garthright & Halle, Memphis, 1964-68; ptnr. Laughlin, Halle, Clark, Gibson, McBride, 1968-84, McKnight, Hudson, Lewis, Henderson & Clark, Memphis, 1985-91, Apperson, Crump, Duzane & Maxwell, Memphis, 1991-96, Armstrong Allen PLLC, Memphis, 1996—. Instr. med. and dental jurisprudence U. Tenn., Memphis, 1963-72; asst. city atty. City of Memphis, 1972-78. Chmn. bd. dirs. Memphis Heart Assn., 1971-72; mem. U. Tenn. Law Sch. Adv. Coun., 1983-90, chmn., 1986-88; trustee U. of The South, 1992-95, 98—. Fellow Am. Bar Found., Tenn. Bar Found. (trustee 1989-98, chmn. 1996-97); mem. ABA, Nat. Conf. Commrs. on Uniform State Laws (Tenn. commr. 1998—), Tenn. Bar Assn. (ho. of dels. 1986-88, bd. govs. 1988-94), Memphis Bar Assn. (treas. 1981, sec. 1982, v.p. 1983, pres. 1984), Rotary (sec. 1988, bd. dirs. 1988-90). Republican. Episcopalian. Federal civil litigation, Labor. Office: Armstrong Allen PLLC Brinkley Plz Ste 700 80 Monroe Ave Memphis TN 38103-2481

CLARK, R(UFUS) BRADBURY, lawyer, director; b. Des Moines, May 11, 1924; s. Rufus Bradbury and Gertrude Martha (Burns) C.; m. Polly Ann King, Sept. 6, 1949; children: Cynthia Clark Maxwell, Rufus Bradbury, John Atherton. BA, Harvard U., 1948, JD, 1951; diploma in law, Oxford U., Eng., 1952; D.H.L., Ch. Div. Sch. Pacific, San Francisco, 1983. Bar: Calif. 1952. Assoc. O'Melveny & Myers, L.A., 1952-62, sr. ptnr., 1961-93; mem. mgmt. com., 1983-90; of counsel O'Melveny & Myers LLP, L.A., 1993—. Bd. dirs. Econ. Resources Corp., Brown Internat. Corp., Brown Citrus Sys., Inc., Avoco Internat. Corp., John Tracy Clinic, also pres. 1982-88, Tracy Family Hearing Ctrs., Ch. Charitable Found. Episcopal Diocese L.A., 2000—. Editor: California Corporation Laws, 7 vols,

1976—. Chancellor Prot. Episcopal Ch. in the Diocese of L.A., 1967—, hon. canon, 1983—. Capt. U.S. Army, 1943-46. Decorated Bronze Star with oak leaf cluster, Purple Heart with oak leaf cluster; Fulbright grantee, 1952. Mem. ABA (com. law and acctg., task force on audit letters 1976-93, com. on opinions 1988-92), State Bar Calif. (chmn. drafting com. on gen. corp. law 1973-81, drafting com. on nonprofit corp. law 1980-84, mem. exec. com. bus. law sect. 1977-78, 84-87, sec. 1986-87, mem. com. nonprofit orgns. 1991—, mem. task force on opinions 1999—), L.A. County Bar Assn., Harvard Club, Chancery Club, Alamitos Bay Yacht Club (Long Beach, Calif.). Republican. Banking, General corporate, Public utilities. Office: O'Melveny & Myers LLP 400 S Hope St Los Angeles CA 90071-2899

CLARK, RUSSELL GENTRY, retired federal judge; b. Myrtle, Mo., July 27, 1925; s. William B. and Grace Frances (Jenkins) C.; m. Jerry Elaine Burrows, Apr. 30, 1959; children: Vincent A., Viki F. LLB, U. Mo., 1952. Bar: Mo. 1952. Mem. firm Woolsey, Fisher, Clark, Whiteaker & Stenger, Springfield, Mo., 1952-77; judge U.S. Dist. Ct. (we. dist.) Mo., Kansas City, 1977-91, sr. judge, 1991-2000; ret., 2000. 2d lt. U.S. Army, 1944-46. Fellow Am. Bar Found.; mem. ABA, Internat. Platform Soc., Mo. Bar Assn. (continuing legal edn. com. 1969), Greene County Bar Assn. (dir. 1968-71), Kiwanis (past pres. Springfield chpt.). Democrat. Methodist. Club: Kiwanis (past pres. Springfield chpt.).

CLARK, WILLIAM H., JR. lawyer; b. Phila., Apr. 10, 1951; s. William H. and Alice Kimes (Metts) C.; m. Cristine D. Merkel, Aug. 18, 1973; children: Matthew, Alison, Daniel. BA summa cum laude, Amherst Coll., 1973; MA in Religion, Westminster Sem., 1979; JD magna cum laude, Temple U., 1983. Bar: Pa. 1983. Assoc. Morgan, Lewis & Bockius, Phila., 1983-89; ptnr. Klett Lieber Rooney & Schorling, Pitts., 1989-98, Phila., 1998-99, Drinker Biddle & Reath LLP, Phila., 1999—. Chmn. corp. bur. advisory com. Pa. Dept of State, 1991—; cons. rules disciplinary bd. Supreme Ct. Pa., Harrisburg, 1983—. Fellow Am. Bar Found.; mem. ABA (com. on corp. laws, com. on bus. courts), Pa. Bar Assn. (draftsman, lobbyist, corp. law com. 1984—, coun. sect. corp. banking and bus. law 1989-93, officer 1993-2001), Allegheny County Bar Assn. (coun. sect. corp. banking and bus. law 1991-97, officer 1997-98), Phila. Bar Assn. (coun. bus. law sect. 1998—), Am. Law Inst., Phi Beta Kappa. Republican. Presbyterian. General corporate, Mergers and acquisitions, Securities. Office: Drinker Biddle & Reath LLP One Logan Sq Philadelphia PA 19103 E-mail: clarkwh@dbr.com

CLARKE, EDWARD OWEN, JR. lawyer; b. Balt., Dec. 19, 1929; s. Edward Owen and Agnes Oakford C.; m. P. Rhea Parker, Dec. 18, 1954; children: Deborah Jeanne, Catherine Ann, Carolyn Agnes, Edward Owen III. AB magna cum laude, Loyola Coll., Balt., 1950; JD with honors, U. Md., 1956. Bar: Md. 1956, U.S. Dist. Ct. Md. 1956. Law clk. U.S. Dist. Ct. Md., 1956-57; assoc. Smith, Somerville & Case, Balt., 1957-62, ptnr., 1962-71, Piper & Marbury, Balt., 1971-94, mem. policy and mgmt. com., 1981-94, mng. ptnr., 1987-90, co-chmn. bus. div., 1991-94. Mem. Gov.'s Com. to Study Blue Sky Law, 1961; mem. Md. Commn. on Revision Corp. Law, 1965-66. Bd. dirs. Bon Secours Hosp., 1964-73, sec., 1968-73; bd. dirs. Hosp. Cost Analysis Svc., 1966-81; bd. pres. mem. exec. coun. Md. Hosp. Assn., 1968-74, chmn. com. on legislation, 1971-73, treas., 1973; trustee St. Mary's Coll. Md., 1983-94, chmn. bd., 1988-94; trustee St. Mary's Sem., U. Balt., 1986-89, Loyola H.S., Balt., 1984-90, Hannah More Ctr., 1980-83; bd. dirs. Helix Health Sys., Inc., 1995-98, Med Star Health, 1998—; mem. Md. Higher Edn. Commn., 1994—, chmn. 1995-2000. Lt. USNR, 1952-55. Recipient Alumni Laureate award Loyola Coll. in Md., 2001. Mem. ABA, Md. State Bar Assn. (mem. sect. coun. corp., banking and bus. law sect. 1968-71, chmn. 1970-71), Wednesday Law Club (sec., treas. 1984-88, v.p. 1988-89, pres. 1990), Center Club (Balt., bd. govs. 1988-94), Order of Coif, Order of the Ark and the Dove, Phi Beta Kappa, Alpha Sigma Nu, Tau Kappa Alpha. General corporate, Municipal (including bonds).

CLARKE, J. CALVITT, JR. federal judge; b. Harrisburg, Pa., Aug. 9, 1920; s. Joseph Calvitt and Helen Caroline (Mattson) C.; m. Mary Jane Cromer, Feb. 1, 1943 (dec.1985); children: Joseph Calvitt III, Martha Tiffany; m. Betty Ann Holladay, May 29, 1986. BS in Commerce, JD, U. Va., 1945. Bar: Va. 1944. Practiced in Richmond, Va., 1944-74; partner firm Bowles, Anderson, Boyd, Clarke & Herod, 1944-60; firm Sands Anderson, Marks and Clarke, 1960-74; judge U.S. Dist. Ct. (ea. dist.) Va., 1975-91, sr. judge, 1991—. Mem. 4th Circuit Judicial Conf., 1963; hon. consul for Republic of Bolivia, 1959-75 Chmn. Citizen's Advisory Com. on Joint Water System for Henrico and Hanover counties, Va., 1968-69; mem. Mayor's Freedom Train Com., 1948-50; del. Young Republican Nat. Conv., Salt Lake City, 1949, Boston, 1951; chmn. Richmond (Va.) Republican Com., 1952-54; candidate for Congress, 1954; chmn. Va. 3d Dist. Rep. Com., 1955-58, 74-75, Va. State Rep. Conv., 1958— ; co-founder Young Rep. Fedn. of Va., 1950, nat. committeeman, 1950-54, chmn., 1955; chmn. 3d dist. Speakers Bur., Nixon-Lodge campaign, 1960, mem. fin. com., 1960-74; chmn. Henrico County Republican Com., 1956-58; fin. chmn. 1956; pres. Couples Sunday Sch. class Second Presbyn. Ch., Richmond, Va., 1948-50, mem. bd. deacons, 1948-61, elder, 1964-99, 1st Presbyn. Ch., Virginia Beach, 1999— ; bd. dirs. Family Service Children's Aid Soc., 1948-61, Gambles Hill Community Center, 1950-60, Christian Children's Fund, Inc., 1960-67, Children, Inc., 1967-75, Norfolk Forum, 1978-83; mem. bd. of chancellors Internat. Consular Acad., 1965-75; trustee Henrico County Pub. Library, chmn., 1971-73. Fellow Va. Law Found.; mem. Va. State Bar (mem. 3rd dist. com. 1967-70, chmn. 1969-70), Richmond Bar Assn., Norfolk-Portsmouth Bar Assn., Va. Bar Assn., Thomas Jefferson Soc. of Alumni U. Va. Lile Law Soc., McGuires U. Sch. Alumni (pres. 1995-96), Am. Judicature Soc., ABA, Va. Bar Assn. (vice chmn. com. on cooperation with fgn. bars 1960-61), Richmond Jr. C. of C. (dir. 1946-50), Windmill Point Yacht Club, Westwood Racquet Club (pres. 1961-62), Commonwealth Club, Delta Theta Phi. Office: US Dist Ct 600 Granby St Norfolk VA 23510-1915

CLARKE, MILTON CHARLES, lawyer; b. Chgo., Jan. 31, 1929; s. Gordon Robert and Senoria Josephine (Carlisa) C.; m. Dorothy Jane Brodie, Feb. 19, 1955; children: Laura, Virginia, Senoria K. BS, Northwestern U., 1950, JD, 1953. Bar: Ill. 1953, Mo. 1956, U.S. Dist. Ct. (we. dist.) Mo. 1961, U.S. Ct. Appeals (8th cir.) 1961. Assoc. Swanson, Midgley, Gangwere, Clarke & Kitchin, Kansas City, Mo., 1955-61, ptnr., 1961-91; of counsel Olsen & Talpers, P.C., 1994—. Served with U.S. Army, 1953-55. Mem. Rotary. State civil litigation, Probate. Office: Olsen and Talpers PC 2100 City Center Square 1100 Main St Kansas City MO 64105-2125 E-mail: miltonclarke@hotmail.com

CLARKSON, JULIAN DERIEUX, retired lawyer; b. Coral Gables, Fla., Mar. 12, 1929; s. Julian Livingston and Hazel (Lamar) C.; m. Joan Combs, Dec. 24, 1950, children— James L., Julian L., Joanna D., Melinda C.; m. 2d, Shirley Lazonby, Nov. 8, 1979; 1 child, Shirley Lamar. B.A., U. Fla., 1950, LL.B., 1955, J.D., 1967. Bar: Fla. 1955, U.S. Ct. Appeals (5th cir.) 1961, U.S. Supreme Ct. 1964, U.S. Ct. Appeals (11th cir.) 1981, D.C. 1983. Ptnr., Henderson, Franklin, Starnes & Holt, Ft. Myers, Fla., 1955-76; sole practice, Ft. Myers, 1976-77; ptnr. Holland & Knight, Ft. Myers, 1977-79, Tampa, 1979-82, Tallahassee, 1982—; ret., 1993; lectr. in field. Chmn. Fla. Supreme Ct. Jud. Nominating Commn., 1976-78. Served to 1st lt. U.S. Army, 1950-53. Decorated Purple Heart, 1951; named Outstanding Grad. Province V Phi Delta Phi, 1955. Mem. Am. Coll. Trial Lawyers, Am. Acad. Appellate Lawyers, Fla. Blue Key, Order of Coif, Phi Beta Kappa. Democrat. Episcopalian. Author: Let No Man Put Asunder— Story of a Football Rivalry, 1968, Golden Era II, 1994. Federal civil litigation, State civil litigation. Home: 17566 Osprey Inlet Ct Fort Myers FL 33908-6123

CLARKSON, STEPHEN BATCHELDER, lawyer; b. Hartford, Conn., July 1, 1937; s. Albert Batchelder and Elsie (Eden) C.; m. Nancy Lee Michelmore, Oct. 16, 1965; children: Janet, Leigh. BA, Yale U., 1959; LLB, U. Va., 1962. Bar: N.Y. 1963, D.C. 1969, U.S. Supreme Ct. 1967. Spl. asst. to gen. counsel and under-sec. U.S. Dept. Commerce, 1968-69; ptnr. Pierson, Ball & Dowd, Washington, 1982—. Adv. bd. Bur. Nat. Affairs Fed. Contracts Report, 1974-76; editorial cons., 1976—. Mem. ABA (antitrust litigation, corp. banking and bus. law, pub. contract law, ct. of claims com. sects.), Fed. Bar Assn., D.C. Bar Assn., Assn. Bar City N.Y. Antitrust, Government contracts and claims. Home: 3020 S Freeman Rd Williamsburg VA 23185-7661 Office: Newport News Shipbldg & Dry Dock Co 4101 Washington Ave Bldg 86 Newport News VA 23607-9700 E-mail: clarkson_sb@nns.com

CLARY, BRADLEY G. lawyer, educator; b. Richmond, Va., Sept. 7, 1950; s. Sidney G. and Jean B. Clary; m. Mary-Louise Hunt, July 31, 1982; children: Benjamin, Samuel. BA magna cum laude, Carleton Coll., 1972; JD cum laude, U. Minn., 1975. Bar: Minn. 1975, U.S. Dist. Ct. Minn. 1975, U.S. Ct. Appeals (10th cir.) 1977, U.S. Ct. Appeals (8th cir.) 1979, U.S. Ct. Appeals (6th cir.) 1980, U.S. Ct. Appeals (7th cir.) 1981, U.S. Supreme Ct. 1986, U.S. Ct. Appeals (4th cir.) 1989, U.S. Ct. Appeals (9th cir.) 1991. Assoc. Oppenheimer Wolff & Donnelly, St. Paul, 1975-81, ptnr., 1982-2000; legal writing dir. Law Sch. U. Minn., 1999—, clin. prof. Law Sch., 2000—. Adj. prof. Law Sch. U. Minn., Mpls., 1985-99; adj. instr. William Mitchell Coll. Law, St. Paul, 1995-96, 98, adj. prof., 1997, 99. Author: Primer on the Analysis and Presentation of Legal Argument, 1992; co-author: Advocacy on Appeal, 2001. Vestryman St. John Evangelist Ch., St. Paul, 1978-81, 98-00, pledge drive co-chmn., 1989-90, sr. warden, 2000—; mem. alumni bd. Breck Sch., Mpls., 1981-85, 89-96, exec. com., 1991-96, dir. emeritus, 1996—; mem. adv. bd. Glass Theatre Co., West St. Paul, Minn., 1982-87; mem. antitrust adv. panel dept. health State of Minn., 1992-93. Mem. ABA (adv. group antitrust sect. 1987-89, corp. counseling com.), Minn. Bar Assn. (program chmn. antitrust sect. 1986-87, treas. 1987-88, vice-chmn. 1989-90, co-chmn. 1990-92), Phi Beta Kappa. Avocations: tennis, sailing. Antitrust, General civil litigation. Office: U Minn Law Sch 229 19th Ave S Rm 444 Minneapolis MN 55455-0400

CLARY, RICHARD WAYLAND, lawyer; b. Tarboro, N.C., Oct. 10, 1953; s. S. Grayson and Jean (Beazley) C.; m. Suzanne Clerkin, July 21, 1991; children: Grayson Edward, Taryn Fenner. BA magna cum laude, Amherst Coll., 1975; JD magna cum laude, Harvard U., 1978. Bar: N.Y. 1981, U.S. Dist. Ct. (so. and ea. dists.) N.Y. 1981, U.S. Dist. Ct. (no. dist.) Calif., 1982, U.S. Ct. Appeals (9th cir.) 1983, U.S. Supreme Ct. 1989, U.S. Ct. Appeals (3d cir.) 1990, U.S. Ct. Appeals (2d cir.) 1994, U.S. Ct. Appeals (fed. cir.) 1995, U.S. Ct. Appeals (11th cir.) 1999, U.S. Ct. Appeals (6th cir.) 2000. Law clk. to judge U.S. Ct. Appeals (2d cir.), N.Y.C., 1978-79; law clk. to Justice Thurgood Marshall U.S. Supreme Ct., Washington, 1979-80; assoc. Cravath, Swaine & Moore, N.Y.C., 1980-85, ptnr., 1985—, mng. ptnr. litigation, 1997—. Bd. dirs. Legal Aid Soc., 1998—. John Woodruff Simpson fellow Amherst Coll., 1975-76. Mem. ABA, Fed. Bar Found. (bd. dirs. 1998-2001), N.Y. State Bar Assn., Assn. Bar City N.Y., Fed. Bar Coun., Phi Beta Kappa. Episcopalian. Antitrust, Federal civil litigation, Intellectual property. Office: Cravath Swaine & Moore Worldwide Pla 825 8th Ave New York NY 10019-7475 E-mail: rclary@cravath.com

CLAVELL, MARGA MONICA, lawyer; b. Buenos Aires, Argentina, Aug. 1, 1964; d. Miguel Mario and Filomena Perozziello Clavell; m. Jorge Antúnez Vega, Apr. 23, 1999; 1 child Jorge Gerardo. JD, Buenos Aires Law Sch., 1986; LLM, Harvard Law Sch., 1992. Jr. lawyer Klein & Mairal, Buenos Aires, Argentina, 1987-91; sr. lawyer Klein & Franco, Argentina, 1992-95, ptnr. Argentina, 1996—. Avocations: painting, literature. Office: Klein & Franco Av Cordoba 883 C1054AAH Buenos Aires Argentina E-mail: marga_clavell@kleinfranco.com

CLAVERIE, PHILIP DEVILLIERS, lawyer; b. New Orleans, June 29, 1941; s. Louis Barbot and Viola Aimee (Schlegel) C.; m. Laura Lynn McCampbell, Apr. 27, 1974; children: Philip deVilliers Jr., Stephanie McCampbell. A.B., Princeton U., 1963; J.D., Tulane U., 1966. Bar: La. 1966. Assoc. Phelps Dunbar, New Orleans, 1966-70, ptnr., 1970—. Contbr. articles to profl. jours. Pres. bd. trustees Children's Hosp. New Orleans, 1978-80; chmn. bd. govs. Isidore Newman Sch., 1995-98; mem. exec. bd. New Orleans Police Found., 1998—. Served to lt. comdr., JAGC, USNR, 1973-79. Fellow Am. Bar Found., La. Bar Found.; mem. ABA, La. State Bar Assn., New Orleans Bar Assn., Assn. Bar City N.Y., Am. Law Inst., Am. Judicature Soc., La. State Law Inst. Clubs: Pickwick, Stratford. Banking, Contracts commercial, Real property. Home: 14 Versailles Blvd New Orleans LA 70125-4114 Office: Phelps Dunbar LLP Ste 2000 365 Canal St New Orleans LA 70130-6534 E-mail: claverip@phelps.com

CLAY, ERIC L. judge; b. Durham, N.C., Jan. 18, 1948; BA, U. N.C., 1969; JD, Yale U., 1972. Bar: Mich. 1972, U.S. Dist. Ct. (ea. dist.) Mich. 1972, U.S. Supreme Ct. 1977, U.S. Ct. Appeals (6th cir.) 1978, U.S. Dist. Ct. (we. dist.) Mich. 1987, U.S. Ct. Appeals (D.C. cir.) 1994. Law clk. to Judge Damon J. Keith U.S. Dist. Ct. (ea. dist.) Mich., 1973-97; shareholder, dir. Lewis, White & Clay, P.C., Detroit, 1997; now judge U.S. Ct. Appeals (6th cir.), 1997—. John Hay Whitney fellow Yale U. Mem. ABA, Nat. Bar Assn., Nat. Assn. Railroad Trial Counsel, U.S. Sixth Jud. Conf. (life), Detroit Bar Assn., Wolverine Bar Assn., Phi Beta Kappa. Office: US Courthouse 231 W LafayetteRm 619 Detroit MI 48226-2700*

CLAYCOMB, HUGH MURRAY, lawyer, author; b. Joplin, Mo., May 19, 1931; s. Hugh and Fern (Murray) C.; m. Jeanne Cavin, May 6, 1956; children: Stephen H., Scott C. BS in Bus., U. Mo., 1953, JD, 1955; LLM, U. Miss., 1969. Bar: Mo. 1955, Ark. 1957, U.S. Tax Ct. 1956, U.S. Dist. Ct. (ea. dist.) Ark. 1957, U.S. Supreme Ct. 1979. Asst. staff judge advocate USAF, 1955-57; law clerk Ark. Supreme Ct., Little Rock, 1957-58; ptnr. Gregory & Claycomb, Pine Bluff, Ark., 1958-69; partner Haley, Claycomb, Roper & Anderson, Warren, 1969—. Dir. The Strong Co., Inc., Pine Bluff, Ark. Author: Arkansas Corporations, 1967, 82, 92. Pres. Jefferson County Bar Assn., Pine Bluff, 1969, Warren YMCA, 1973-75, S.E. Ark. Legal Inst., 1980-81, Ctrl. Ark. Estate Planning Coun., 1963-64; trustee Bradley County YMCA Found.; spl. assoc. justice Ark. Supreme Ct., 1978, 87. Lt. USAF, 1955-57. Recipient Pres.'s award Ark. Trial Lawyers Assn., 1985. Mem. Ark. Bar Found. (pres. 1990), Ark. Bar Assn. (sec.-treas. 1998-2000, C.E. Ransick award 1996, pres.-elect 2000-), Warren Rotary (pres. 1972, Paul Harris fellow). Episcopalian. General corporate, Estate planning, Probate. Home: 619 E Cedar St Warren AR 71671-3001 E-mail: paspin@ipa.net*

CLAYTON, CLAUDE F., JR. lawyer; b. Tupelo, Miss., June 15, 1948; s. Claude F. and Bronson (Munday) C.; children from a previous marriage: Frances, Claude III; m. Tacey Clark, July 25, 1997. Student, Stanton Mil. Acad., 1966; BA, Tulane U., 1971; JD, U. Miss., 1973. Bar: Miss. 1973. Mem. judiciary com. U.S. Senate, Washington, 1968; ptnr. Mitchell, Voge, Clayton and Beasley, Tupelo, 1973-85, Mitchell, McNutt & Sams, Tupelo, 1985—. Mem. complaints tribunal Supreme Ct. Miss., 1990-93; speaker Miss. Jud. Coll., also various trial practice and ethics seminars; special justice Miss. Supreme Ct., 2000. Mem. ABA (young lawyers div., chmn. justice dept. liaison com. 1978-79), Miss. State Bar (pres. fellows of young lawyers 1990-91, vice chmn. specialization com. 1990-92, chmn., 1980-82, lawyer econs. com. 1988-89, ethics com. 1982-85, vice chmn. continuing legal edn. com. 1980-81, law jour.-law sch. liaison com. 1974-76, various coms. young lawyers sect. 1985-90, bd. dirs. 1975-80), Miss. Def. Lawyers Assn. (bd. dirs. 1992-95), Def. Rsch. Inst., Internat. Assn. Def. Counsel. General civil litigation, Personal injury, Product liability. Office: Mitchell McNutt & Sams 105 S Front St Tupelo MS 38802-7120 E-mail: cclayton@mitchellmcnutt.com

CLAYTON, DANIEL LOUIS, lawyer; b. Chgo., Mar. 11, 1963; s. James D. and Betty (Brisendine) C.; m. Stacy Elizabeth Johnson, June 29, 1985; children: Amy Brooke, Hannah Margaret, Kay Ellen. BA, David Lipscomb Coll., Nashville, 1984; JD, U. Tenn., 1987. Bar: Tenn. 1987, U.S. Dist. Ct. (mid. and we. dists.) Tenn. 1987, U.S. Ct. Appeals (6th cir.) 1991. Ptnr. Kinnard & Clayton, Nashville, 1987—. Mem. faculty Law Seminars Internat., Seattle, 1991. Elected mem. Franklin Spl. Sch. Dist. Bd. Edn., 1994-97. Recipient Lewis F. Powell, Jr. medal for excellence in advocacy. Mem. Tenn. Bar Assn., Tenn. Trial Lawyers Assn. (bd. govs. 1998—), Nashville Bar Assn. Republican. Mem. Ch. of Christ. Avocations: golf, tennis. General civil litigation, Personal injury, Workers' compensation. Office: The Woodlawn 127 Woodmont Blvd Nashville TN 37205-2240

CLEAR, JOHN MICHAEL, lawyer; b. St. Louis, Dec. 16, 1948; s. Raymond H. and Marian (Clark) C.; m. Isabel Marie Bone, May 10, 1980. BA summa cum laude, Washington U., St. Louis, 1971; JD with honors, U. Chgo., 1974. Bar: Mo. 1974, D.C. 1975, U.S. Ct. Appeals (5th and D.C. cirs.) 1975, U.S. Supreme Ct. 1977, U.S. Ct. Appeals (3d cir.) 1978, U.S. Ct. Appeals (8th cir.) 1980, U.S. Ct. Appeals (9th cir.) 1990, U.S. Dist. Ct. (so. dist.) Ill. 1995, U.S. Ct. Appeals (7th cir.) 1997. Law clk. to judge U.S. Ct. Appeals (5th cir.), Atlanta, 1974-75; assoc. Covington & Burling, Washington, 1975-80; jr. ptnr. Bryan, Cave, McPheeters & McRoberts, St. Louis, 1980-81, ptnr., 1982—. Mem. ABA, Mo. Bar Assn., D.C. Bar Assn., St. Louis Met. Bar Assn., Am. Law Inst., Order of Coif., Racquet Club, Noonday Club, Fox Run Golf Club, Phi Beta Kappa. Antitrust, Federal civil litigation, Securities. Office: Bryan Cave LLP One Metropolitan Sq Saint Louis MO 63102-2750 E-mail: jmc@bryancave.com

CLEARY, DAVID LAURENCE, lawyer; b. Rochester, N.Y., Mar. 5, 1941; s. James W. and Margaret (Neary) C.; m. Valerie Claire Smith, July 27, 1968; children: Sean Michael, Megan Lynne. BS, St. John Fisher Coll., 1963; JD, Cornell U., 1970. Bar: Vt. 1970, U.S. Dist. Ct. Vt. 1970, U.S. Ct. Appeals (2d cir.) 1971, U.S. Ct. Appeals (1st cir.) 1974, U.S. Dist. Ct. N.H. 1974, U.S. Dist. Ct. Mass. 1975. Dep. stats atty. Chittenden County, Burlington, Vt., 1970-72; assoc. Wilson, Curtis, Bryan & Quinn, 1970-72; ptnr. R.E. Davis Assocs., Inc., Barre, 1972-78, Miller, Cleary & Faignant and predecessor firms, Rutland, 1978-91; pres. D.L. Cleary Assn. PC, 1991-98, Cleary-Shahi Assoc. PC, Rutland, 1998—. Spl. counsel Nat. Ski Areas Assn., Wilmington, Del., 1977—, United Ski Industries Assn., Fairfax, Va., 1989—; counsel Vt. Bd. Med. Practice, Montpelier, 1979-86. Capt. M.I., airborne inf. U.S. Army, 1964-68, Vietnam. Decorated Bronze Star. Mem. ABA, ATLA, Internat. Acad. Trial Lawyers, Am. Coll. Trial Lawyers, Fedn. Ins. and Corp. Counsel, Am. Arbitration Assn., Am. Bd. Trial Advocates (pres. Vt. chpt. 1993-94), Def. Rsch. Inst. (chmn. spl. ins. problems com. 1981-86), Vt. Bar Assn. (del. bd. govs. 1977-78, bd. profl. conduct 1979-89, chmn. tort reform commn. 1988—), Vt. Def. Trial Lawyers (pres. 1992-93), Chittenden County Bar Assn., Washington County Bar Assn., Rutland County Bar Assn., Ethan Allen Club, Lake George Yacht Club (bd. dirs., officer), Rutland Country Club, Smith Basin Club, Gooley Club. Republican. Roman Catholic. Avocations: scuba diving, hunting, fishing, boating, woodworking. General civil litigation, Construction, Personal injury. Office: DL Cleary Assoc PO Box 6740 110 Merchants Row Rutland VT 05701-5928

CLEAVER, DAVID CHARLES, lawyer, educator; b. Sunbury, Pa., Dec. 26, 1941; s. C. Perry and Gertrude Lillian (Clarke) C.; m. JoAnne Irene Sponenberg, Nov. 25, 2000; children: Lisa Eileen, David Clarke, Christopher Perry. Bar: Pa. 1967, U.S. Supreme Ct. 1971. Ptnr. Sharpe Cleaver, Wenger & Townsend, Chambersburg, Pa., 1967-84; sole practice, 1985—. Adj. prof. law Dickinson Sch. Law, Carlisle, Pa., 1971—. Author: Cases and Materials on Wills and Decedent's Estates, 1976, Probate and Estate Administration, The Law in Pennsylvania, 1983, 3d edit., 2000. Past pres., bd. dirs. Chambersburg YMCA; chmn. Franklin County (Pa.) Reps., 1986-92. Mem. ABA, Assn. Trial Lawyers Am., Pa. Trial Lawyers Assn. Lodges: Chambersburg Rotary, Elks, Moose. State civil litigation. Home: 455 Overhill Dr Chambersburg PA 17201-3161 Office: 1035 Wayne Ave Chambersburg PA 17201-2986 E-mail: dcleaver@cvn.net

CLEAVER, WILLIAM LEHN, lawyer; b. Harrisburg, Pa., Dec. 7, 1949; s. Gene Franklin and Goldie Jean (Haldeman) C.; children: Benjamin Neville, Valerie Anne. BA, Augustana Coll., 1971; JD, U. Iowa, 1974. Bar: Iowa 1974, Ill. 1975, U.S. Dist. Ct. (so. dist.) Iowa 1975, U.S. Dist. Ct. (so. dist.) Ill. 1975. Ptnr. Bozeman, Neighbour, Patton & Noe, Moline, Ill., 1991—. Chmn. bd. govs. BBB Ctrl. Ea. Iowa. Mem. adv. coun. Luth. Social Svcs. of Ill. Adult Day Care Ctr., Rock Island; v.p., bd. dirs. United Way of Quad Cities, Rock Island; pres. adv. coun. Ret. Sr. Vol. Program, Moline; bd. govs. Rock Island Cmty. Found.; commr., chmn. Rock Island Preservation Commn.; mem. Citizen's Adv. Com.; bd. dirs. Quad Cities chpt. ARC; mem. Rock Island/Milan Dist. 41 Sch. Bd. Col. USAR. Mem. ABA, Ill. State Bar Assn. (mem. assembly), Iowa State Bar Assn., Rock Island County Bar Assn., Scott County Bar Assn. Lutheran. Lodge: Kiwanis (pres. 1983-84, bd. dirs. 1984-85). Avocations: fine arts, racquet sports. Consumer commercial, Contracts commercial, Real property. Home: 8806 Ridgewood Rd Rock Island IL 61201-7655 Office: Bozeman Neighbour Patton & Noe 1630 5th Ave Moline IL 61265-7910 E-mail: wcleaver@bnpn.com

CLEMENS, RICHARD GLENN, lawyer; b. Chgo., Oct. 8, 1940; s. James Ralston and Jeanette Louise (Moellering) C.; m. Judith B. Clemens, Aug. 19, 1967; 1 child, Kathleen. BA, U. Va., 1962, JD, 1965. Bar: Ill. 1965. Assoc. Sidley & Austin, Chgo., 1965-66, Washington, 1968-71, Brussels, 1972-73; ptnr. Sidley Austin Brown & Wood, Chgo., 1973—. Served to capt. U.S. Army, 1966-68. Mem. ABA, Chgo. Bar Assn., Lawyers Club, Mid-Day Club. General corporate, Mergers and acquisitions, Securities. Office: Sidley Austin Brown & Wood 10 S Dearborn St Chicago IL 60603 E-mail: rclemens@sidley.com

CLEMENT, FRANCES ROBERTS, lawyer, mediator, nurse, consultant; b. Columbia, S.C., Oct. 1, 1945; d. Ralph Winfred and Frances Lucille (Harter) Roberts; m. Tom F. Clement; children: Everett Hudson Smith, Armenta Harter Smith. BS in Biology, U. Ala., 1967; MS in Counseling, Fla. State U., 1970; AA in Nursing, Victoria Coll., Tex., 1978; JD with honors, Jones Sch. Law, Montgomery, Ala., 1986. Bar: Ala. 1987, U.S. Supreme Ct. 1997. Staff nurse Citizen's Meml. Hosp., Victoria, Tex., 1978-81, DeTar Hosp., Victoria, 1981, Bapt. Med. Ctr., Montgomery, 1982-84; adminstr sch. nurse Bloomington (Tex.) Sch. Dist., 1981-82; supr. Humana Hosp., Montgomery, 1985; legal asst. Kaufman, Rothfeder & Blitz, 1985-87; assoc. Powers & Willis, 1987-88; pvt. practice, 1988-90; with Office of Atty. Gen., 1990-2001; mediator, 1999—. Adj. prof. U. Houston, Victoria, 1980, Auburn U., Montgomery, 1988-90, facilitator, mediator, 1999—. Mem. Montgomery County Bar Assn. Methodist. Avocation: computers. Home: 3502 Bankhead Ave Montgomery AL 36111-2018 Office: 312 Scott St Montgomery AL 36104 E-mail: FrClement@aol.com

CLEMENT, ROBERT LEBBY, JR. lawyer, director; b. Charleston, S.C., Dec. 14, 1928; s. Robert Lebby and Julia Axson (Thayer) C.; m. Helen Mathilda Lewis, Nov. 26, 1954; children: Jeanne Marie, Robert Lebby III, Thomas L.T. AB, The Citadel, 1948; JD, Duke U., 1951. Bar: N.C. 1951, S.C. 1954. Practiced in Charlotte, N.C., 1951-53; ptnr. Cornish, Clement & Horlbeck, Charleston, 1955-60, Hagood, Rivers & Young, 1960-65, Young, Clement, Rivers & Tisdale, LLP, 1965-93, of counsel, 1994—. Pres. Charleston Automotive Parts, Inc., 1969-84, Charleston Mus., 1980-83; mem. adv. bd. Bank of Am., 1960—; asst. city atty., Charleston, 1960; judge Mcpl. Ct., Charleston, 1961-63. Mem. Charleston County Coun., 1983-86, chmn., 1985-86. With JAGD, USAF, 1953-55. Mem. ABA, N.C. Bar Assn., S.C. Bar Assn., Charleston County Bar Assn. (pres. 1990-91), Rotary. Presbyterian. General corporate, General practice, Mergers and acquisitions. Office: Young Clement Rivers & Tisdale PO Box 993 Charleston SC 29402-0993

CLEMENTE, ROBERT STEPHEN, lawyer; b. Bklyn., May 5, 1956; s. Hugo and Mildred (Wilinsky) C.; m. Mary Martin, June 8, 1985. AA, St. John's U., 1976; BFA, NYU, 1978; JD, Southwestern U., 1981. Bar: N.Y. 1982, U.S. Dist. Ct. (ea. and so. dists.) N.Y. 1982, U.S. Supreme Ct. 1988, Calif. 1997, U.S. Dist. Ct. (ctrl. dist.) Calif. 1997. Counsel Composto & Longo, Bklyn., 1981-86; arbitration counsel N.Y. Stock Exch., N.Y.C., 1986-88, mgr. arbitration, 1988-91, dir. arbitration, 1991—. Arbitrator N.Y.C. Civil Ct., 1988—; adj. prof. securities arbitration NYU, 1999—. Mem. ABA, Am. Arbitration Assn., Am. Judges Assn., N.Y. Bar Assn., Assn. of Arbitrators, CPR Inst. Dispute Resolution. Avocations: reading, exercising, golf. Alternative dispute resolution, Finance, Securities. Office: NY Stock Exch Inc 20 Broad St Fl 5 New York NY 10005-2601 E-mail: rclemente@nyse.com

CLEMENTS, ALLEN, JR. retired lawyer; b. Macon, Ga., Jan. 15, 1924; s. Allen C. and Mamie F. (Vinson) C.; children: Mary, Jill, Byng, Allen. BBA, U. Miami, 1948, JD cum laude, 1951. Bar: Fla. 1951, U.S. Tax Ct. 1951, U.S. Dist. Ct. (so. dist.) Fla. 1951, U.S. Ct. Appeals (5th cir.) 1952, U.S. Ct. Appeals (11th cir.) 1981. Sr. assoc. Claude Pepper Law Offices, Miami Beach, Fla., 1953-72; ptnr. Pepper, Clements, Hopkins & Weaver, 1972-79; of counsel Tew, Critchlow, Sonberg, Traum & Friedbauer, Miami, Fla., 1979-82, Finley, Kumble, Wagner, Heinz, Underberg & Casey, Miami, 1982-87; pros. atty. City of West Miami, Fla., 1954-56, city atty., 1956-83; legal advisor Dade County Coun. Mayors, 1964-72; ret., 1987. Cons. atty. Dade County League of Cities, 1966-77; city atty. City of South Miami, 1969-72; atty. Miami Beach Tourist Devel. Authority, 1970-78, Village of Biscayne Park, 1972-75. Active West Miami Town Coun., 1952-53; bd. dirs. Claude Pepper Found., Tallahassee, 1992—, sec., 1994—. With U.S. Army, 1943-45. Decorated Bronze Star. Mem. ABA, Lake County Bar Assn., Dade County Bar Assn. (bd. dirs. 1984-86, grievance com., ethics com.). Democrat. Methodist. Home and Office: 2205 &th Ave Dr East Bradenton FL 34208 Fax: 352-753-7785

CLEMENTS, JAMIE HAGER, lawyer; b. Crockett, Tex., Dec. 9, 1930; s. Neal William and Alberta (Hager) C.; m. Ann Trigg, Apr. 28, 1962; children: Susan Clements Negley, Jamie Hager, Cynthia. BA with honors, U. Tex., 1952, JD, 1955. Bar: Tex. 1956. Gen. counsel Scott and White Med. Center, Temple, Tex., 1960—. Mem. Tex. Ho. of Reps., 1953-60; chmn. Tex. State Bd. Human Resources, 1977-78; chmn. Planning commn. City of Temple, 1969, mayor, 1970-74; pres. Temple United Fund, 1969; trustee Ralph Wilson Pub. Trust, Temple, 1980, 85; pres. Cultural Activities Ctr., Temple, 1981-82; mem. Tex. Bd. of Mental Health and Mental Retardation, 1986—; mem. State Commn. on Judicial Conduct, 1983-89, vice chmn. 1986-89. Served with USMC, 1956-58. Mem. ABA, Nat. Health Lawyers Assn. (pres. 1980-81), State Bar Tex. (chmn. com. on liaison with med. profession 1966-69), Bell-Lampasas-Mills Counties Bar Assn. (pres. 1966), Temple C. of C. (pres. 1975), East Tex. C. of C. (dir.). Democrat. Presbyterian. Health. Home: 2644 Marlandwood Cir Temple TX 76502-2503 Office: Scott & White Med Ctr 2401 S 31st St Temple TX 76508-0001

CLERMONT, KEVIN MICHAEL, law educator; b. N.Y.C., Oct. 25, 1945; s. William Theodore and Rita Ruth (Healy) C.; m. Emily Sherwin; 1 child, Adrienne Shaine. AB summa cum laude, Princeton U., 1967; postgrad., U. Nancy, France, 1967-68; JD magna cum laude, Harvard U., 1971. Bar: Mass. 1971, N.Y. 1974, U.S. Dist. Ct. (so. and ea. dists.) N.Y. 1974, U.S. Ct. Appeals (2d cir.) 1974. Law clk. to judge U.S. Dist. Ct. (so. dist.) N.Y., 1971-72; assoc. Cleary, Gottlieb, Steen & Hamilton, N.Y.C., 1972-74; asst. prof. Sch. Law Cornell U., Ithaca, N.Y., 1974-77, assoc. prof., 1977-80, prof., 1980-89, Flanagan prof. law, 1989—. Vis. prof. Sch. Law Harvard U., Cambridge, 1991. Author: (with another) Res Judicata: a Handbook on Its Theory, Doctrine, and Practice, 2001; Civil Procedure: Territorial Jurisdiction and Venue, 1999, (with others) Materials for a Basic Course in Civil Procedure, 7th edit., 1997, Civil Procedure, 6th edit., 2001, (with others) Law: Its Nature, Functions, and Limits, 3d edit., 1986; editor Harvard Law Rev., 1969-71. Fulbright scholar, 1967-68. Mem. ABA, Assn. Am. Law Schs., Order of Coif, Phi Beta Kappa, Sigma Xi. Home: 100 Iroquois Rd Ithaca NY 14850-2223 Office: Cornell U Sch Law Myron Taylor Hall Ithaca NY 14853 E-mail: kmc12@cornell.edu

CLEV, HEINRICH, lawyer; b. Cologne, Germany, Dec. 28, 1955; With Rechtsanwalte Clev & Pape, Dusseldorf, Germany. Mem. German Netherlands Jurists Assn. General corporate, Mergers and acquisitions, Estate taxation. Office: Rechtsanwalte Clev & Pape Konigsallee 70 40212 Dusseldorf Germany E-mail: heinrich.clev@clev-pape.de

CLEVENGER, RAYMOND C., III, federal judge; b. Topeka, Aug. 27, 1937; s. Raymond C. and Mary Margaret (Ramsey) C.; m. Celia Faulkner, Sept. 9, 1961 (div. Mar. 1987); children: Winthrop, Peter. BA, Yale U., 1959, LLB, 1966. Ptnr. Wilmer Cutler & Pickering, Washington, 1975-90; judge U.S. Ct. Appeals (Fed. Cir.), 1990—. Mem. ABA, D.C. Bar Assn. Office: Fed Cir Ct 717 Madison Pl NW Washington DC 20439-0002*

CLICK, DAVID FORREST, lawyer, investment advisor; b. Miami Beach, Fla., Dec. 17, 1947; s. David Gorman and Helen Margaret (McPhail) C.; m. Helaine London, June 2, 1974; children: Kenneth Randall, Adam Elliott. BA, Yale U., 1969, JD, 1973, MA, 1974. Bar: Conn. 1973, Md. 1983, U.S. Supreme Ct. 1983, Fla. 1984, Maine 1984. Asst. prof. Western New England Sch. Law, Springfield, Mass., 1974-77; assoc. prof. Ind. U., 1977-78, U. Md., Balt., 1978-84; assoc. Nixon, Hargrave, Devans and Doyle, Jupiter, Fla., 1984-86; pvt. practice, 1986—. Pres., dir. Click Farms, Inc., Clewiston, Fla.; pres. Click Capital Mgmt., LLC; vice chmn. adv. com. Palm Beach County Coop. Ext. Svc. Contbr. articles to profl. jours. Mem. Christmas Cove (Maine) Improvement Assn., Palm Beach-Martin County Estate Planning Coun., pres. 1988-89; participant Leadership Palm Beach County, 1991-92. Mem. ABA, Fla. Bar Assn., Palm Beach County Bar Assn. (cultural activities award 1992), Nat. Soc. Arts and Letters, Yale Club of the Palm Beaches (pres.), Kiwanis. Presbyterian. Estate planning, Probate, Real property. Home: 19216 Pinetree Dr Jupiter FL 33469-2002 Office: 810 Saturn St Ste 15 Jupiter FL 33477-4456

CLIFF, WALTER CONWAY, lawyer; b. Detroit, Jan. 2, 1932; s. Frank V. and Virginia L. (Conway) C.; m. Ursula McHugh, Nov. 5, 1960; children: Walter C., Mary F., Catherine C. B.S., LL.B., U. Detroit, 1955; LL.M., NYU, 1956. Bar: Mich. 1956, N.Y. 1958. Assoc. firm Cahill Gordon & Reindel, N.Y.C., 1958-66, ptnr., 1966-2000; sr. counsel, 2000—. Bd. dirs. Florence Gould Found., N.Y.C., 1983— ; bd. dirs. Austen Riggs Center, Stockbridge, Mass., 1983-89, Geoffrey Hughes Found., 1992—; mem. Collections com. Harvard U. Art Mus., 1992—. Served with U.S. Army, 1956-58. J.K. Lasser fellow NYU, 1955-56. Mem. ABA, Assn. of Bar of City of N.Y., N.Y. Bar Assn., Stockbridge Golf Club. Democrat. Roman Catholic. Corporate taxation. Office: Cahill Gordon & Reindel 80 Pine St Fl 17 New York NY 10005-1790 E-mail: wcliff@cahill.com

CLIFFORD, EUGENE THOMAS, lawyer; b. Utica, N.Y., July 15, 1941; s. James Anthony and Mary Margaret (Ellard) C.; m. Joyce Victoria Siwinski, Sept. 4, 1965; children: Michael Sean, Elizabeth Joyce, Thomas More. BA, Boston Coll., 1963, LLB, 1966. Bar: N.Y. 1967, U.S. Dist. Ct. (we. dist.) N.Y. 1967. Assoc. Chamberlain, D'Amanda, Bauman, Chatman & Oppenheimer, Rochester, N.Y., 1967-72, Lamb, Webster, Walz, Telesca & Donovan, Rochester, 1972-76; ptnr. Webster, Sullivan, Santoro & Clifford, 1976-86, Fulreader, Rosenthal, Sullivan, Clifford, Santoro & Kaul, Rochester, 1986-2001, Davidson, Fink, Cook, Kelly & Galbraith, 2001—. Bd. dirs. N.Y. state divsn. Am. Cancer Soc., Syracuse, 1972-78, 82-88, 90-97, chmn. bd. dirs., 1982-83, nat. bd. dirs., 1991-97; bd. dirs. Urban League of Rochester, 1988-91. Recipient Nat. Bronze award N.Y. state divsn. Am. Cancer Soc., 1984, Hope award Monroe County unit, 1983. Estate planning, Probate, Real property. Office: 28 Main St E Ste 1700 Rochester NY 14614 E-mail: eclifford@dfckg.com

CLIFFORD, ROBERT A. lawyer; b. Evergreen Park, Ill., Mar. 24, 1951; s. George Leonard and Shirley Marie (Meyer) C.; m. Joan Elizabeth Makowski, July 29, 1973; children— Erin Elizabeth, Tracy Ann. BS in Commerce, DePaul U., 1973, JD, 1976. Bar: Ill. 1976, U.S. Dist. Ct. (no. dist.) Ill. 1976, U.S. Supreme Ct. 1981. Assoc., Philip A. Corboy & Assocs., Chgo., 1974-82, Corboy & Demetrio, Chgo., 1982-84; ptnr. Clifford & Henely, Chgo., 1984-85, owner Robert A. Clifford and Assocs., 1985— ; cons. and lectr. in law; mediation panelist Endispute of Chgo., 1982— . Contbr. articles to profl. jours. Mem. exec. com., chmn. fin. aid com. DePaul U. Coll. Law, 1982— ; bd. dirs. exec. com. for U. Coll., Galway, Ireland, Chgo., 1983— ; bd. dirs. Access Living of Met. Chgo., 1982-84; trustee Deaul U. , 1987—; mem. coll. of law vis. com. DePaul U., 1982-85, chmn. fin. aid subcom. coll. of law vis., 1982-85, mem. exec. com. coll. of law vis. com., 1982-85, mem. Soc. of Fellows Found., 1976-83; mem. City of Hope Fund Raising Com. Mike Royko and James Roberts Jr. Benefits, 1981-82, products liability ADR devel. Ctr. for Pub. Resources, 1985-86, 1985-86; mediation panelist Endispute of Chgo., 1982-84. Mem. ABA (coun., sect. of litigation, tort and ins. practice), Assn. Trial Lawyers Am., Fed. Bar Assn., Am. Soc. Law and Medicine, N.W. Suburban Bar Assn., Ill. State Bar Assn. (gen. assembly, spl. com. on reduction of ct. costs, delays and involvement), Ill. Trial Lawyers Assn. (membership com., polit. action com., chmn. med. malpractice com.), Trial Lawyers Club of Chgo., Chgo. Bar Assn. (tort litigation, civil practice and health and hosp. care coms., com. on coms.), DePaul U. Alumni Assn. (pres. 1983—), Soc. Fellows Found. Roman Catholic. Clubs: Butler Nat. Golf (Oak Brook, Ill.); Inverness Golf (Ill.); Dairymen's Country (Boulder Junction, Wis.). Federal civil litigation, Libel, Personal injury. Office: Cifford Law Offices 33 N Dearborn St Fl 20 Chicago IL 60602-3102

CLIFFORD, ROBERT WILLIAM, state supreme court justice; b. Lewiston, Maine, May 2, 1937; s. William H. and Alice (Sughrue) C.; m. Clementina Radillo, Jan. 18, 1964; children: Laurence M., Matthew P. BA, Bowdoin Coll., 1959; LLB, Boston Coll., 1962; LLM, U. Va., 1998. Bar: Maine 1962, U.S. Dist. Ct. Maine 1965. Ptnr. Clifford & Clifford, Lewiston, 1964-79; justice Maine Superior Ct., Auburn, 1979-83, chief justice, 1984-86; assoc. justice Maine Supreme Jud. Ct., 1986—. Mem. Lewiston City Coun., 1968-70, mayor, 1971-72; mem. Maine State Senate, 1973-76; chmn. Lewiston Charter Commn., 1978-79; mem. Maine Probate Law Revision Commn., 1973-79; bd. overseers St. Joseph's Coll. Maine, 2000—. Mem. Maine Bar Assn., Androscoggin County Bar Assn., Am. Judicature Soc. Roman Catholic. Home: 14 Nelke Pl Lewiston ME 04240-5318 Office: Maine Supreme Jud Ct PO Box 3488 Auburn ME 04212-3488

CLIMAN, RICHARD ELLIOT, lawyer; b. N.Y.C., July 19, 1953; s. David Arthur and Mary (Vitale) C. AB cum laude, Harvard U., 1974, JD cum laude, 1977. Bar: Calif. 1977. Assoc. Pettit & Martin, San Francisco, 1977-83, ptnr., 1984-94; ptnr., head mergers and acquisitions group Cooley Godward LLP, Palo Alto, San Francisco, Calif., 1994—. Adv. bd. BNA Mergers & Acquisitions Law Report; lectr. and panelist in field; co chair Doing Deals Practising Law Inst., Mergers & Acquisitions Inst. Glasser Legal Works. Contbr. articles to profl. jours. Mem. ABA (sect. bus. law, vice chair com. on negotiated acquisitions). General corporate, Mergers and acquisitions, Securities. Home: 1 Tulip Ln San Carlos CA 94070-1551 Office: Cooley Godward LLP 5 Palo Alto Sq 3000 El Camino Real Palo Alto CA 94306-2120 E-mail: climanre@cooley.com

CLIMER, JAMES ALAN, lawyer; b. Chillicothe, Ohio, Dec. 17, 1954; s. James Parker and Jane Louise (Halsey) C.; m. Mary Ellen Murray, Oct. 17, 1981. BA in Polit. Sci., Miami U., Ohio, 1977; JD, U. Toledo, 1980. Bar: Ohio 1980, U.S. Dist. Ct. (no. and so. dists.) Ohio 1981. Assoc. Jones, Schell & Schaefer Co., Toledo, 1980-81; sole practice W. Carrollton, Ohio, 1981-83; asst. law dir. City of Parma, 1984-90; pvt. practice, Cleve., 1983-90; ptnr. Mazanec, Raskin & Ryder Co., LPA, Solon, Ohio, 1990—. Mem. Ohio State Bar Assn., Cuyahoga County Law Dirs. Assn. Presbyterian. Avocations: golf, skiing, reading. State civil litigation, Construction. Office: Mazanec Raskin & Ryder Co 34305 Solon Rd 100 Franklin's Row Cleveland OH 44139 E-mail: jclimer@mrrlaw.com

CLINE, RICHARD ALLEN, lawyer; b. Columbus, Ohio, Oct. 1, 1955; s. Ralph S. and Myrtle O. (Harrison) C.; m. Nora Jean Arth, Oct. 2. 1982; children: Caitlin, Patrick. BA in Polit. Sci., BS in Criminal Justice, Kent State U., 1977; JD, Ohio State U., 1981. Bar: Ohio 1981, U.S. Dist. Ct. (so. dist.) Ohio 1981, U.S. Ct. Appeals (6th cir.) 1983, U.S. Supreme Ct. 1985. Assoc. David Riebel, Columbus, 1981-84; ptnr. Riebel & Cline, 1984-85; ptnr., pres. Durkin, Cline and Co. L.P.A., 1985-88; pres. Richard Cline & Co. L.P.A., 1988-92; mem. Mitchell Allen Catalano & Boda Co. LPA, 1992—, ptnr., 1996—. Prosecutor City of Whitehall, Ohio, 1980-81, Village of Powell, Ohio, 1983-85, Powell Village Coun., 1996—; instr. Ohio Peace Officers Tng. Counsel, Columbus, 1985. Bd. dirs. Woodbridge Village Assn., Columbus, 1983-86. Served with JAGC, Ohio Nat. Guard, 1983—. Mem. Ohio Bar Assn., Jaycees (named one of Outstanding Young Men of Am., 1979), Phi Alpha Delta, Omicron Delta Kappa. Republican. Baptist. Avocations: martial arts, military history. State civil litigation, Criminal, General practice. Home: 290 Weatherburn Ct Powell OH 43065-9103 Office: Mitchell Allen Catalano & Boda 490 S High St Columbus OH 43215-5603

CLING, B. J. lawyer, psychologist; b. N.Y.C., Nov. 22, 1943; d. Isidore Irving and Josephine Jean (Friedman) Rosenbaum. BA, CUNY, 1966; PhD, NYU, 1980; postgrad. Inst. Psychiatry, Law and Behavioral Sci., U. So. Calif., 1982; JD, UCLA, 1985. Bar: Calif., N.Y.; lic. clin. psychologist, Calif. Instr. psychology Adelphi U., 1969-70; asst. prof. psychology La Guardia Coll., CUNY, 1970-71; editor Program Practices-Children CBS, Los Angeles, 1978; producer women's series Sta. KPFK, Los Angeles, 1980-81; pvt. practice clin. psychology, Los Angeles, 1980-86; instr. UCLA Extension, 1979-86; clin. instr. Inst. Psychiatry, Law and Behavioral Scis., U. So. Calif., 1982-85; clk., U.S. Ct. Appeals (9th cir.), 1985-86; assoc., Davis, Polk & Wardwell, N.Y.C., 1986-88, Debevoise and Plimpton, 1989—. Past bd. dirs. Women's Equal Rights Legal Def. and Edn. Fund. Mem. Screen Actor's Guild (past chmn. women's com.), Am. Psychol. Assn.

CLINTON, EDWARD XAVIER, lawyer; b. Chgo., July 13, 1930; s. Michael Xavier and Mary Agnes (Joyce) C.; m. Margaret Mary Clinton, May 1, 1965 (div. Oct. 1978); 1 child, Edward Xavier Jr. Student, DePaul U., 1949-50; JD, John Marshall U., 1953. Bar: Ill. 1953, U.S. Dist. Ct. (no. dist.) Ill. 1955, U.S. Ct. Appeals (7th cir.) 1955, U.S. Supreme Ct. 1995. Assoc. Schultz & Biro, Chgo., 1955-56; with securities dept. Ill. State Dept., Springfield, 1956-57; assoc. Hough, Young & Coale, Chgo., 1957-65, Keck, Mahin & Cate, Chgo., 1965-92; pvt. practice, 1992—; spl. counsel Bullwinkel Ptnrs., Ltd. Instr. John Marshall Law Sch., Chgo., 1965-74; arbitrator N.Y. Stock Exch. Contbr. articles to profl. jours.; speaker in field. Bd. dirs. Chgo. Opera Theatre, 1983-88, Children's Care Found., Records Mgmt. Svcs., 1966-97; pastoral coun. Holy Name Cathedral, 1989-94; mem. adv. bd. Steppenwolf Theatre, Chgo., 1988-89. With U.S. Army, 1953-55. Postgrad. scholar John Marshall Law Sch., 1953, John Jewell scholar, 1953. Mem. ABA, KC, Ill. Bar Assn., Chgo. Bar Assn., Bar. Assn. of 7th Cir., Rotary, Law Club, Union League Club, Execs. Club of Chgo. (bd. dirs. 1985-95), Evanston Golf Club, Am. Legion, KC. Roman Catholic. Avocations: golf, prisoner appeals (pro bono). General corporate, Real property, Securities. Home: 990 N Lake Shore Dr Chicago IL 60611-1366 Office: 19 S La Salle St Ste 1300 Chicago IL 60603-1406 E-mail: EClinton@aol.com

CLIPPARD, RICHARD F. prosecutor; Graduate, U. Miss., 1976; JD, U. Miss. Law Sch., 1980. Private practice Butler, Lackey, Holt and Snedeker; special asst. US atty. US Small Bus. Adminstrn.; asst. US atty. US Atty. Office, Nashville, chief of Civil Division; US atty. Middle Dist., 2001—. Office: US Attorney 800 Market St Ste 211 Knoxville TN 37902 Fax: 865-545-4176*

CLODFELTER, DANIEL GRAY, state legislator, lawyer; b. Thomasville, N.C., June 2, 1950; s. Billy G. and Marie Lorene (Wells) C.; m. Elizabeth Kay Bevan, Aug. 20, 1974; children: Julia Elizabeth, Catherine Gray. BA, Davidson Coll., 1972; AB, MA, Oxford U., Eng., 1974; JD, Yale U., 1977. Bar: N.C. 1977, U.S. Dist. Ct. (we. dist.) N.C. 1977, U.S. Dist. Ct. (ea. dist.) N.C. 1979, U.S. Ct. Appeals (4th cir.) 1984, U.S. Dist. Ct. (mid. dist.) N.C. 1985. Law clk. to presiding judge U.S. Dist. Ct., Charlotte, N.C., 1977-78; assoc. Moore & Van Allen, 1978-82, ptnr., 1983—. Mem. N.C. Senate, 1999—. Mem. Charlotte City Coun., 1987-93, Charlotte-Mecklenburg Planning Commn., 1984-87, chmn., 1986-87; state sec. Rhodes Scholarship Trust, N.C., 1986-97; trustee Z. Smith Reynolds Found., Inc., Winston-Salem, N.C., 1983—; bd. dirs. N.C. Ctr. for Pub. Policy Rsch., 1994-96. Rhodes scholar, 1972. Mem. N.C. Bar Assn. (antitrust law com., bankruptcy sect. coun.). Office: Moore & Van Allen 100 N Tryon St 4700 Charlotte NC 28202-4003*

CLORE, LAWRENCE HUBERT, lawyer; b. Tulsa, July 31, 1944; s. Hubert Charles and Jessie Louada (Fowler) C.; m. Carol Jean Roegelein, June 3, 1967 (div. 1981); children: Robert William, James Lawrence; m. Martha Jo Lawyer; children: Kathryn Denise, Michael Hubert. BBA, Tex. Christian U., 1966; JD, U. Tex., 1969. Bar: Tex. 1969. Assoc. Fulbright & Jaworski, Houston, 1971-77, ptnr., 1977—. Capt. U.S. Army, 1969-71, Vietnam. Mem. ABA, Tex. Bar Assn. (labor and employment sect., coun. 1990-93, vice chair 1993-94, chair 1994-95), Indsl. Rels. Rsch. Assn., Houston Mgmt. Lawyers Forum (chmn. 1976-77). Republican. Methodist. Avocations: hunting, fishing, golf. , Civil rights. Office: Fulbright & Jaworski 1301 Mckinney St Ste 5100 Houston TX 77010-3031 E-mail: lclore@fulbright.com

CLOSE, DAVID PALMER, lawyer; b. N.Y.C., Mar. 16, 1915; s. Walter Harvey and Louise De Arango (Palmer) C.; m. Margaret Howell Gordon, June 26, 1954 (dec. July 1992); children: Louise, Peter, Katharine, Barbara. B.A., Williams Coll., 1938; JD, Columbia U., 1942; LHD, Mount Vernon Coll., 1998. Bar: N.Y. State bar 1942. Practice law, Washington, 1946—; ptnr. Dahlgren & Close. Mem. adv. council Nat. Capital area Boy Scouts Am., 1961— ; bd. dirs. Nat. Soc. Prevention Blindness, 1961-63, Internat. Eye Found., 1965—, chmn., 1985-89; bd. dirs. D.C. Soc. Prevention of Blindness, 1957-63, pres., 1961-63; bd. dirs. Internat. Humanities, Inc., 1960—, pres., 1989—; bd. dirs. Marjorie Merriweather Post Found., 1974— , sec.-treas., 1974-76, sec., 1991—; trustee Williams Coll., 1963-68; trustee Hill Sch., 1965-85, chmn., 1973-85 ; trustee Mount Vernon Coll., 1963-75 , bd. pres., 1971-74; mem. Am. coun. UN U., 1980—. Served with O.N.I., USN, 1942-46. Mem. ABA, Inter-Am. Bar Assn., D.C. Bar Assn., Assn. Bar City of N.Y., Assn. Trial Lawyers Am., World Jurist Assn. of World Peace Through Law Ctr., Pilgrims, Order of St. John, Chevy Chase (Md.) Club, Fauquier Springs Country Club (Warrenton, Va.), Univ. Club (Washington). Administrative and regulatory, General practice, Probate. Home: 40 Hungry Run Farm Ln Amissville VA 20106-4017 Office: Dahlgren & Close 1000 Connecticut Ave NW Ste 204 Washington DC 20036-5337 E-mail: dahlgrenclose@cs.com

CLOSE, MICHAEL JOHN, lawyer; b. Sandusky, Ohio, Jan. 24, 1943; s. Robert J. and Mary Lee (Graefe) C.; m. Nancy L. Schelp, June 18, 1995; children: Christina C., Karen L. AB in History, Lafayette Coll., Easton, Pa., 1965; JD cum laude, U. Mich., 1968. Assoc. Dewey, Ballantine, Bushby, Palmer & Wood, N.Y.C., 1968-76; ptnr. Dewey Ballantine, 1976-96. Mem. Tax Exempt Bond Group; chmn. Tax Rev., N.Y.C. Author: Tax Aspects of Oil and Gas Drilling Funds, 1972, Drilling Funds: The 1977 Perspective, 1977, Special Allocations in Oil and Gas Ventures, 1982, The Final Section 704 (b) Regulations: Special Allocations Reach New Heights of Complexity, 1986, Fringe Benefit Regulation and the New York Law Firm Culture: A New Era, 1989, Off Balance Sheet Financings, 1994; contbr. articles to profl. jours. Bd. dirs., adminstrv. vice-chmn. Conn. Swimming, Inc., 1992-99; bd. dirs. Sharks Swim Team, Inc., 1991-94, pres., 1992-94. Mem. ABA (mem. tax sect. com. on partnerships), Assn. of Bar of City of N.Y., N.Y. Law Inst. (life mem.), N.Y. State Bar Assn. (mem. tax sect. com. partnerships, com. tax exempt financings), Ohio State Bar Assn., Nat. Assn. Bond Lawyers, India House (N.Y.C.), Burning Tree Country Club (Greenwich), Theta Chi. Republican. Congregationalist. Home: 4951 Windsor Pk Sarasota FL 34235-2610

CLOSEN, MICHAEL LEE, law educator; b. Peoria, Ill., Jan. 25, 1949; s. Stanley Paul and Dorothy Mae (Kendall) C. BS, MA, Bradley U., 1971; JD, U. Ill., 1974. Bar: Ill. 1974; notary pub., Ill. Instr. U. Ill., Champaign, 1974; jud. clk. Ill. Appellate Ct., Springfield, 1974-76, 77-78; asst. states atty. Cook County, Chgo., 1978; prof. law John Marshall Law Sch., 1976—. Vis. prof. No. Ill. U., 1985-86, adj. prof., 1990; adj. prof. St. Thomas U., 1991; vis. prof. U. Ark, 1993, 96; reporter Ill. Jud. Conf., Chgo., 1981—; arbitrator Am. Arbitration Assn., Chgo., 1981—; arbitrator Cook County Cir. Ct. Mandatory Arbitration Program, 1990—, Will County Cir. Ct. Mandatory Arbitration Program, 1996—; lectr. Ill. Inst. Continuing Legal Edn., Chgo., 1981—; dir. Ctr. for Legal Edn., Ltd., 1995-96. Author: (casebooks) Agency and Partnership Law, 1984, 3d edit., 2000, (with others) Contracts, 1984, 3d edit., 1992, AIDS Cases and Materials, 1989, 3d edit., 2001, Notary Law and Practice, 1997, Contract Law and Practice, 1998; co-author: The Shopping Bag: Portable Art, 1986, AIDS Law in a Nutshell, 1991, 2d edit., 1996, Legal Aspects of AIDS, 1991; contbr. articles to profl. jours. Recipient Svc. award Am. Arbitration Assn., 1984, 5-Yr. Comty. Achievement award Ill. Politics Mag., 1998; named one of Outstanding Young Men in Am., 1981. Mem. ABA, Ill. Bar Assn., Appellate Lawyers Assn., Chgo. Coun. Lawyers, Nat. Notary Assn. (Achievement award 1998), Am. Soc. Notaries, Notary Law Inst. Home: 17640 S Mccarron Rd Lockport IL 60441-9774 Office: John Marshall Law Sch 315 S Plymouth Ct Chicago IL 60604-3968

CLOSSEY, DAVID F. lawyer; b. Cleve., Jan. 31, 1944; s. William M. and Josephine Clossey; m. Jeanne Marie Ives, June 15, 1967; 1 child, Sarah Woodson. A.B., Georgetown U., 1965; J.D., Cornell U., 1968. Bar: Ohio 1968, Tex. 1981. Assoc. Jones, Day, Reavis & Pogue, Cleve., 1968-74, ptnr., 1974-81, ptnr.-in-charge, Dallas, 1981-84, regional mng. ptnr., 1984— ; dir. TBS Internat., Inc., Dallas. Trustee Dallas Ballet, 1982— ; bd. govs. Dallas Symphony Assn., 1983— ; mem. corp. council Dallas Mus. Art, 1983— . Recipient Fraser award Cornell U., 1968. Mem. ABA, Dallas Bar Assn., Order of Coif. General corporate, Private international. Home: 3727 Beverly Dr Dallas TX 75205-2805

CLOSSON, WALTER FRANKLIN, child support prosecutor; b. Phila., Dec. 24, 1944; s. David Mayard Jr. and Florence Louise (Anderson) C.; m. Irene Veronica Jones, Aug. 10, 1968; children: Forrest Troy, Carey-Walter Franklin. BS in Music Edn., West Chester U., 1967; JD, Potomac Sch. Law, Washington, 1981. Bar: Ga. 1983, Md. 1985. Tchr. music D.C. Pub. Schs., Washington, 1967-77; tchr. woodwinds D.C. Youth Orch. Program, 1969-71; dist. ct. commr. Dist. Ct. of Md., Ellicott City, 1978-89; supervising dist. ct. commr. Dist. Ct. of Howard County, 1984-89; asst. state's atty. State's Atty.'s Office, 1989-99, chief child support divsn. Md., 1999-2000; supervising atty. Bur. of Supoort Enforcement, Howard County Dept. Social Svcs., Columbia, 2000—. Mem.. Howard County Bar Assn., Waring-Mitchell Law Soc. (pres. 1992-94, Man of Yr. 1990), Masons (sr. deacon 1996-97, sr. warden 1997-98, worshipful master, 1998-99), Delta Theta Phi (v.p. 1979-80). Office: Howard County Dept Social Svcs 7121 Columbia Gateway Dr Columbia MD 21046 E-mail: wclosson@howard_dmH

CLOUES, EDWARD BLANCHARD, II, lawyer; b. Concord, N.H., Dec. 28, 1947; s. Alfred Samuel and H. Jeannette (Callas) C.; m. Mary Anne Matthews, Aug. 21, 1971; children: E. Matthew, M. Elizabeth. BA, Harvard U., 1969; JD, NYU, 1972. Bar: Pa. 1972, U.S. Dist. Ct. (ea. dist.) Pa. 1973. Law clk. to hon. judge James Hunter III U.S. Ct. Appeals (3d cir.), Phila. and Camden, N.J., 1972-73; assoc. Morgan, Lewis & Bockius, LLP, Phila., 1973-79, ptnr., 1979-98; chmn., CEO K-Tron Internat., Inc., Pitman, N.J., 1998—. Bd. dirs. K-Tron Internat., Pitman, N.J., vice chmn. bd., 1987-94; bd. dirs. Amrep Corp., chmn., 1995—; bd. dirs. AmeriQuest Tech., Inc. Republican. Lutheran. Avocations: travel, reading. Bankruptcy, General corporate, Mergers and acquisitions. Office: K-Tron Internat Inc PO Box 888 Rtes 55 & 553 Pitman NJ 08071

CLOUSE, JOHN DANIEL, lawyer; b. Evansville, Ind., Sept. 4, 1925; s. Frank Paul and Anna Lucille (Frank) C.; m. Georgia L. Ross, Dec. 7, 1978; 1 child, George Chauncey. AB, U. Evansville, 1950; JD, Ind. U., 1952. Bar: Ind. 1952, U.S. Supreme Ct. 1962, U.S. Ct. Appeals (7th cir.) 1965. Assoc. Firm of James D. Lopp, Evansville, 1952-56; pvt. practice law James D. Lopp, 1956—. Guest editorialist Viewpoint, Evansville Courier, 1978-86, Evansville Press, 1986-98, Focus, Radio Sta. WGBF, 1978-84; 2d asst. city atty. Evansville, 1954-55; mem. appellate rules sub-com. Ind. Supreme Ct. Com. on Rules of Practice and Procedure, 1980.. Pres. Civil Svc. Commn. Evansville Police Dept., 1961-62, v.p., 1988; pres. Ind. War Memls. Com., 1963-69; mem. jud. nominating com. Vanderburgh County, Ind., 1976-80; dir. Ind. Fed. Cmty. Defender Project, Inc., 1993-98. With inf. U.S. Army, 1943-46. Decorated Bronze Star; named one of World's Most travelled Man Guinness Book of Records, 1993, Most Travelled Man, 1995-2001. Fellow Ind. Bar Found.; mem. Evansville Bar Assn. (v.p. 1972, James Bethel Gresham Freedom award 1997), Ind. Bar Assn. (chmn. com. on civil rights 1991-92), Travelers Century Club (L.A.), Pi Gamma Mu. Republican. Methodist. State civil litigation, Criminal, Family and matrimonial. Office: 123 NW 4th St Ste 317 Evansville IN 47708-1712 E-mail: JDCMJS@aol.com

COAN, RICHARD MORTON, lawyer; b. N.Y.C., Sept. 17, 1948; s. Nelson W. and Phyllis (Tomashoff) C.; m. Kathleen M. Mitcheom, Sept. 5, 1983; children: Benjamin, Spencer, Eliza. AB, U. Rochester, 1969; JD, Yale U., 1974. Bar: Conn. 1974, U.S. Dist. Ct. Conn. 1981, U.S. Ct. Appeals (2d cir.) 1982. Ptnr. Belford, Belford & Coan, New Haven, 1977-81, Coan, Lewendon, Royston & Guliver, LLC, New Haven, 1981—. Mem. ABA (corp. banking and bus. law sects.), Conn. Bar Assn. (real estate and comml. law sects.). Bankruptcy, Family and matrimonial, Real property. Home: 17 E Haycock Point Rd Branford CT 06405-5301 Office: Coan Lewendon Royston & Gulliver LLC 495 Orange St New Haven CT 06511-3809 E-mail: richcoan@aol.com

COATES, BRADLEY ALLEN, lawyer; b. L.A., Mar. 27, 1951; s. Mark Edmund and Elizabeth (Allen) C.; m. Margaret Fife Bentley, Apr. 17, 1977 (div. Dec. 1980); m. Sachi Braden, Oct. 11, 1993. BA, U. So. Calif., 1973; JD, UCLA, 1976. Bar: Calif. 1977, Hawaii 1978, No. Marianas Islands 1978, Marshall Islands 1979, Federated States Micronesia 1981. Staff atty. Congress of Micronesia, Saipan, 1976-78; mng. ptnr. Rohlfing, Smith & Coates, Honolulu, 1978-85; prin. ptnr. Law Offices Bradley A. Coates, 1985-96; mng. ptnr. Coates and Frey, 1996—. Pres., exec. dir. Pacific Arbitration and Mediation, Honolulu, 1985—. Author: Divorce with Decency: The Complete How-To Handbook and Survivor's Guide to the Legal, Emotional, Economic and Social Issues. Chief counsel Hawaii State Rep. Party, Honolulu, 1981; founder, pres. Divorce with Decency Mediation Assn., Honolulu, 1985. Selected as Best Divorce Lawyer by Honolulu Weekly and Honolulu Mag. Mem. Hawaii Bar Assn. (family law sect.). Clubs: Outrigger Canoe, Honolulu. Avocations: all water sports, skiing, hiking. General corporate, Family and matrimonial, Probate. Home: 941 Kului Pl Honolulu HI 96821-1741 Office: 900 Fort Street Mall Honolulu HI 96813-3721

COATES, GLENN RICHARD, lawyer; b. Thorp, Wis., June 8, 1923; s. Richard and Alma (Borck) C.; m. Dolores Milburn, June 24, 1944; children— Richard Ward, Cristie Joan Student, Milw. State Tchrs. Coll., 1940-42, NMA and MA, 1943-44; LLB, U. Wis., 1949, SJD, 1953. Bar: Wis. 1949. Atty. Mil. Sea Transp. Service, Dept. Navy, 1951-52; pvt. practice law Racine, Wis., 1952—; of counsel Dye, Foley, Krohn, Shannon, S.E. Sec., gen. counsel Racine Federated Inc.; lectr. U. Wis. Law Sch., 1955-56. Author: Chattel Secured Farm Credit, 1953; contbr. articles to profl. publs. Chmn. bd. St. Luke's Meml. Hosp., 1973-76, bd. dirs., 1990-91; pres. Racine Area United Way, 1979-81; bd. curators State Hist. Soc. Wis., 1986-2001, pres., 1995-97; bd. dirs. Racine County Area Found., 1983-89; bd. dirs. Wis. History Found., Inc., 1983-99, Hist. Sites Found., Inc., 1987-89, St. Luke's Hosp./St. Mary's Med. Ctr. Healthcare Found., 1992-96. With U.S. Army, 1943-46. Fellow Am. Bar Found. (life); mem. ABA, State Bar Wis. (bd. govs. 1969-74, chmn. bd. 1973-74), Wis. Jud. Coun. (chmn. 1969-72), Am. Law Inst. (life), Racine Country Club, Masons, Order of Coif. Methodist (chmn. fin. com. 1961-67). General corporate, Estate planning, Mergers and acquisitions. Home: 2830 Michigan Blvd Racine WI 53402-4254 Office: 1300 S Green Bay Rd Racine WI 53406-4469

COATES, WILLIAM ALEXANDER, lawyer; b. Newberry, S.C., Oct. 8, 1949; s. William Floyd and Clara Monette (Alexander). B.S. in Bus. Administrn., U. S.C., 1971, J.D., 1974. Bar: S.C. 1974, U.S. Dist. Ct. S.C. 1976, U.S. Ct. Appeals (4th cir.) 1977. Asst. legis. asst. to senator Strom Thurmond, Washington, 1974-75; counsel to minority subcom. adminstrv. practice and procedure Com. on Judiciary U.S. Senate, 1975-76; asst. U.S. atty. Dept. of Justice, Greenville, S.C., 1976-80; ptnr. Love, Thornton, Arnold & Thomason, Greenville, 1980— ; instr. Atty. Gen. Adv. Inst. U.S. Dept. of Justice, Washington, 1979. Chmn. Citizens Adv. Council, Greenville Gen. Hosp., Greenville County Heart Fund, Easter Seal Soc. Greenville County; mem. S.C. State Ethics Commn., 1988-93, chmn. 1991-93. Served with Air N.G., 1970-76. Mem. ABA, S.C. Bar, S.C. Def. Trial Attys. Assn. (pres. 1994), Phi Delta Phi (magister 1973-74). Republican. Baptist. Clubs: Commerce, Heritage Sertoma Federal civil litigation, Criminal, Environmental. Office: Love Thornton Arnold & Thomason PO Box 10045 410 E Washington St Greenville SC 29603 E-mail: bcoates@ltatlaw.com

COATS, ANDREW MONTGOMERY, lawyer, former mayor, dean; b. Oklahoma City, Jan. 19, 1935; s. Sanford Clarence and Mary Ola (Young) C.; m. Linda M. Zimmerman; children— Andrew, Michael, Jennifer, Sanford B.A., U. Okla., 1957, J.D., 1963. Assoc. Crowe and Dunlevy, Oklahoma City, 1963-67, ptnr., 1967-76, sr. trial ptnr., 1980—; dist. atty. Oklahoma County, 1976-80; mayor City of Oklahoma City, 1983-87; dean U. Okla. Coll. Law. Pres. Okla. Young Lawyers Conf., 1968-69; dir. Local Okla. Bank, Oklahoma City. Democratic nominee U.S. Senate, 1980; pres. Oklahoma County Legal Aid Soc., 1972-73. Served to lt. USN, 1960-63 Named Outstanding Lawyer in Okla., Oklahoma City U., 1977 Fellow Am. Coll. Trial Lawyers (pres. 1996-97, 10th Cir. regent 1992-96), Am. Bd. Trial Advocates (charter pres. Okla. 1986); mem. ABA, U.S. Supreme Ct. Hist. Soc. (trustee), Okla. Bar Assn. (pres. 1992-93), Oklahoma County Bar Assn. (pres. 1976-77), Order of Coif, Oklahoma City Golf and Country Club (bd. dirs. 1977-80, 93-96), Petroleum Club (pres. 1995), Phi Beta Kappa (pres. 1975), Pi Kappa Alpha (pres. 1956), Phi Delta Phi (pres. 1962). Democrat. Episcopalian. Clubs: Oklahoma City Golf and Country, Petroleum. Avocations: music, golf. General civil litigation, Product liability. Office: Crowe and Dunlevy Mid-Am Tower 20 N Broadway Ave Ste 1800 Oklahoma City OK 73102-8273 also: U Okla Coll Law 300 Timber Dell Rd Norman OK 73019-5081 E-mail: acoats@ou.edu

COATS, NATHAN B. judge; m. Mary Ricketson; 1 child, Johanna. BA in Econs., U. Colo., 1971, JD, 1975. Assoc. Hough, Grant, McCarren and Bernard, 1977-78; asst. atty. gen. Appellate Sect., Colo., 1978-83, dep. atty. gen., 1983-86; adj. prof. U. Colo., 1990; chief appellate dep. dist. atty. 2d Jud. Dist., Denver, 1986-2000; justice Colo. Supreme Ct., 2000—. Chief reporter Erickson Commn. on Officer-Involved Shootings, 1996-97; lectr. Denver Police Acad., 1986-97; reporter Govs. Columbine Commn., 1999-2000; mem. Colo. Supreme Ct. Criminal Rules Com., 1983-2000, chmn., 1997-2000, Colo. Supreme Ct. Appellate Rules Com., 1985-2000, Colo. Supreme Ct. Civil Rules Com., Colo. Supreme Ct. Criminal Pattern Jury Instructions Com., 1987-2000, Colo. Supreme Ct. Jury Reform Pilot Project Com., 1998-2000, Colo. Dist. Attys. Coun. Legis. Com., 1990-2000. Office: Colo State Supreme Ct Judicial Bldg 2 E 14th Ave Denver CO 80203-2115*

COATS, WILLIAM SLOAN, III, lawyer; b. Fresno, Calif., Mar. 31, 1950; s. William Sloan Jr. and Willa (Macdonell) C.; m. Sherri Lee Young, Aug. 3, 1980; children: Devin Roseanne, Allyn Elizabeth. AB, U. San Francisco, 1972; JD, U. Calif., San Francisco, 1980. Bar: Calif. 1980, U.S. Dist. Ct. (no. dist.) Calif. 1980, U.S. Dist. Ct. (cen. and so. dists.) Calif. 1982. Assoc. Bancroft, Avery & McAlister, San Francisco, 1980-82, Hopkins, Mitchell & Carley, San Jose, Calif., 1982-84, Gibson, Dunn & Crutcher, San Francisco, 1984-93; ptnr. Brown & Bain, Palo Alto, Calif., 1993-96, Howrey Simon Arnold & White, Menlo Park, 1996—. Nat. Merit scholar, 1968. Mem. ABA (chair Internet and cyberspace com., councillor sect. on sci. and tech.), Calif. Bar Assn., Green and Gold Club, Univ. Club. Republican. Roman Catholic. General civil litigation, Computer, Intellectual property. Office: Howrey Simon Arnold & White 301 Ravenswood Ave Menlo Park CA 94025-3434

COBB, CHARLES KENCHE, lawyer, real estate broker; b. Canton, Ga., Aug. 23, 1934; s. Charlie Kench and Alice (Enloe) C.; m. Carolyn Webb, Aug. 31, 1963; children: Charlie Kenche, III, Catherine Elizabeth Fryman. BS, Ga. Tech., 1956; MBA, Harvard U., 1962; postgrad. Emory U., 1963, Georgetown U., 1959; LLD, Woodrow Wilson, 1968. Bar: Ga. 1969, Pres., C. Cobb Properties, Atlanta, 1969— , Sterling Land Co., Atlanta, 1973— , Bridgewood Properties, Stockbridge, Ga., 1983-91; dir. Canton Textile Mills, Inc., 1991—. Mem. Atlanta Area Coun.-Boy Scouts Am., 1979—; exec. com. Ga. Tech. Wesley Found., Atlanta, 1983—; former treas., sec., trustee Reinhardt Coll., Waleska, Ga., 1974—; lay leader Northside United Meth. Ch., Atlanta, 1978; bd. dirs. Ga. Tech. YMCA, Atlanta, 1976-89. Served to 1st lt. USAF, 1956-59, ETO. Mem. Ga Bar Assn., Atlanta Bd. Realtors (bd. dirs. 1983-90, Outstanding Transaction of Yr. award 1986), Ga. Assn. Exchangors (former pres.), Ga. Exchangor of Yr. 1971, 85, 90), Ga. Hist. Trust, Ga. Tech. Alumni Assn. (trustee 1976-79), Canton Golf Club, Buckhead 50 Club (v.p. 1996, pres. 1997), Mason, Shriner. Real property. Home: 2851 Howell Mill Rd NW Atlanta GA 30327-1333 Office: 1 Northside 75 NW Ste 102 Atlanta GA 30318-7715

COBB, ELIZABETH H. lawyer; b. Birmingham, Ala., Nov. 11, 1947; d. John Massey and Octavia Baird Sadler Cobb; m. Peter V. Maye. BS, La. State U., 1969, MLS, 1976, JD, 1981. Bar: La. 1981, N.Y. 1984, Minn. 1995. With U.S. Ct. Appeals 5th Cir., New Orleans, Skadden Arps, N.Y.C.; asst. gen. counsel N.Y. Life; with Mackall Crounse, Mpls.; sr. corp. counsel The St. Paul Cos., Inc. Office: The St Paul Companies Mail Code 515A 385 Washington St Saint Paul MN 55102-1396 E-mail: elizabeth.cobb@stpaul.com

COBB, HOWELL, federal judge; b. Atlanta, Dec. 7, 1922; s. Howell and Dorothy (Hart) C.; m. Torrance Chalmers (dec. 1963); children: Catherine Cobb Cook, Howell III, Mary Ann Cobb Walton; m. Amelie Suberbielle, July 3, 1965; children: Caroline Cobb Ervin, Thomas H., John L. Student, St. John's Coll., Annapolis, Md., 1940-42; LLB, U. Va., 1948. Assoc. Kelley & Ryan, Houston, 1949-51, Fountain, Cox & Gaines, Houston, 1951-54, Orgain, Bell & Tucker, Beaumont, 1954-57, ptnr., 1957-85; judge U.S. Dist. Ct. (ea. dist.) Tex., 1985—. Mem. jud. coun. U.S. Ct. Appeals (5th cir.), 1994-97; mem. adv. com. East Tex. Legal Svcs., Beaumont. Pres. Beaumont Art Mus., 1969, bd. dirs., 1967-68; mem. vestry St. Stephens Episcopal Ch., Beaumont, 1973; mem. bd. adjustment City of Beaumont, 1972-82; trustee All Saints Episcopal Sch., Beaumont, 1972-76. 1st lt. USMC, 1942-45, PTO. Mem. ABA, State Bar Tex. (grievance com. 1970-72, chmn. 1972, admissions com. 1974—, bd. dirs. 1993-94, adv. mem.), Jefferson County Bar Assn. (sec. 1960, bd. dirs. 1960-61, 67-68), Am. Judicature Soc., Am. Bd. Trial Advs., Maritime Law Assn. U.S., Beaumont Country Club. Office: US Dist Ct 118 US Courthouse PO Box 632 Beaumont TX 77704-0632 Business E-Mail: druann_wiley@txed.uscourts.gov

COBB, KAY BEEVERS, state supreme court justice, former state senator; m. Larry Cobb; children: Barbara Cobb Murphy, Elizabeth Cobb DeBusk. BS, Miss. U. Women; JD, U. Miss. Former spl. asst. atty. gen. North Miss.; assoc. justice Miss. Supreme Ct. Mem. Nat. Alliance/Model State Drug Laws, Vets. Aux., C. of C. Baptist. Office: Miss Supreme Ct PO Box 117 450 High St Jackson MS 39205

COBB, STEPHEN A. lawyer; b. Moline, Ill., Jan. 27, 1944; s. Archibald William and Lucile Bates C.; m. Nancy L. Hendrix, Dec. 18, 1972. AB cum laude, Harvard U., 1966; MA in Sociology, Vanderbilt U., 1968, PhD in Sociology, 1971, JD, 1977. Bar: Tenn. 1978, U.S. Dist. Ct. (mid. dist.) Tenn. 1978. Asst. prof. Tenn. State U., Nashville, 1970-74, dept. head, 1972-74; mem., chair edn. oversight com. Tenn. Ho. Reps., 1974-86; pvt, practice law, 1978-86; with Waller Lansden Dortch & Davis, 1986-90, ptnr., 1990—. Fullbright Jr. lectr. U. Caen, France, 1977-78; lectr. dept. sociology Fisk U., 1981-86. Former pres. Sister Cities of Nashville, Inc.; former vice chmn. commn. edn1. quality So. Regional Edn. Bd. Decorated officer Ordre des Palmes Academiques (France); recipient Paul Simon Internat. award, 1990, Edwin Cudeki Internat. Bus. award, 1992; NDEA fellow, NIMH fellow, 1966-70. Mem. ABA, Am. Immigration Lawyers Assn., Am. Sociol. Assn., So. Sociol. Soc., Tenn. Bar Assn., Tenn Fgn. Lang. Inst., Nashville Bar Assn., Fedn. Alliances Francaises (former pres.), Order of Coif. Family and matrimonial, Government contracts and claims, Immigration, naturalization, and customs. Home: 1929 Castleman Dr Nashville TN 37215-3901 Office: 511 Union St Ste 2100 Nashville TN 37219-1760

COBBS, NICHOLAS HAMMER, lawyer; b. N.Y.C., June 28, 1946; s. John Lewis and Phyllis Cobbs; m. Louise Bertram Stolman, Mar. 26, 1983; children: Robert White, Rebecca Ann. AB cum laude, Amherst (Mass.) Coll., 1968; JD, U. Pa., 1974. Bar: N.Y. 1975, D.C. 1982, Md. 1984, Va. 1990, U.S. Dist. Ct. (so. dist.) N.Y. 1975, U.S. Dist. Ct. D.C. 1982, U.S. Dist. Ct. (ea. dist.) Va. 1990, U.S. Dist. Ct. (we. dist.) Va. 1990, U.S. Dist. Ct. Md. 1989, U.S. Supreme Ct. 1984. Assoc. Burlingham Underwood & Lord, N.Y.C., 1974-77, Haight, Gardner, Poor & Havens, N.Y.C., 1977-83; ptnr., of counsel Tigert & Roberts, Washington, 1984-89; ptnr. Law Offices of Nicholas H. Cobbs, 1989—. Of counsel Klimck, Kolodnj & Casale, Washington, 1995-; mem. steering com. D.C. Bar Law Practice Mgmt., 2000-, litigation steering com., 2001-. Contbr. articles to profl. jours. Arbitrator, mediator D.C. Superior Ct., Washington, 1990—; instr. D.C. Bar Continuing Legal Edn., 1993—. Lt. USNR, 1969-73. Mem. ABA, Fed. Bar Assn., Lawyer-Pilot's Bar Assn., Maritime Law Assn. of the U.S. Episcopalian. Administrative and regulatory, Aviation, Government contracts and claims. Office: 1776 K St NW Ste 300 Washington DC 20006-2326 E-mail: ncobbs@erols.com

COCCOCCIA, AMY CHRISTINA, lawyer; b. Okinawa, Japan, Aug. 12, 1971; d. Christopher and Patricia Mary Coccoccia. BA in Internat. Rels., Tufts U., 1993; JD, Bklyn. Law Sch., 1998. Assoc. Fragomen, Del Rey, Bernsen & Loewy, P.C., N.Y.C., 1998—. Mem. Assn. Bar City N.Y. Immigration, naturalization, and customs. Office: Fragomen Del Rey Bernsen & Loewy 515 Madison Ave New York NY 10022

COCHEO, JOHN FRANK, lawyer; b. Hartford, Conn., Jan. 28, 1944; s. Frank and Olga Freida (Zotter) C. B.A., Quinnipiac Coll., 1969; J.D., New Eng. Sch. Law, 1973. Bar: Mass. 1974, Conn. 1975, U.S. Dist. Ct. Conn. 1975, U.S. Ct. Appeals (2d cir.) 1983, U.S. Supreme Ct. 1979; cert. Nat. Bd. Trial Advocacy; cert. Criminal Trial Specialist Am. Bd. Trial Advocacy. With Lach & Barron Rsch., Hartford, 1973; assoc. Deloreto & Karanian Assocs., New Britain, Conn., 1973-76; dep. asst. state's atty. New Britain, 1976-82, asst. state's atty., New London, 1982— . Rep. Victim-Witness Orgn., 1984. Mem. New Britain Bar Assn., New London Bar Assn. Continuing Legal Edn. Acad. Democrat. Roman Catholic. Lodge: K.C. Home: 201 Judson Ave Mystic CT 06355-2159 Office: O'Brien Shafner Stuart Baratnik 475 Bridge St Groton CT 06340-3723

COCHRAN, GEORGE MOFFETT, retired judge; b. Staunton, Va., Apr. 20, 1912; s. Peyton and Susie (Robertson) C.; m. Marion Lee Stuart, May 1, 1948; children— George Moffett, Harry Carter Stuart. BA, U. Va., 1934, LLB, 1936; LLD (hon.), James Madison U., 1991. Bar: Va. 1935, Md. 1936. Asso. law firm, Balt., 1936-38; partner firm Peyton Cochran and George M. Cochran, Staunton, 1938-64, Cochran, Lotz & Black, Staunton, 1964-69; justice Supreme Ct., Richmond, Va., 1969-87. Pres. Planters Bank & Trust Co., Staunton, 1963-69 Chmn. Woodrow Wilson Centennial Commn. Va., 1952-58, Va. Cultural Devel. Study Commn., 1966-68, Frontier Culture Mus. Va., 1986-98; mem. Va. Commn. Constl. Revisi on, 1968-69, Jud. Coun. Va., 1963-69, Va. Ho. Dels., 1948-66, Va. Senate, 1966-68; chmn. bd. dirs. Stuart Hall, 1971-86; mem. bd. visitors Va. Poly. Inst., 1960-68; trustee Mary Baldwin Coll., 1967-81, U. Va. Law Sch. Found., 1975-89, Woodrow Wilson Birthplace Found., 1955-93. Lt. comdr. USNR, 1942-46. Recipient Algernon Sydney Sullivan award Mary Baldwin Coll., 1981. Mem. ABA, Va. Bar Assn. (pres. 1965-66), Raven Soc., Soc. of Cin., Phi Beta Kappa, Phi Delta Phi, Beta Theta Pi. Episcopalian.

COCKRELL, RICHARD CARTER, retired lawyer; b. Denver, Oct. 9, 1925; s. Harold Arthur Sweet and Mary Lynne Cockrell. AB, U. Denver, 1949, JD cum laude, 1950. Bar: Colo. 1950, U.S. Supreme Ct. 1954. Supr. real estate, tax and claims Standard Oil, Denver, 1950-52; from assoc. to ptnr. Cockrell, Quinn & Creighton and predecessor firms, 1952-91; of counsel Cockrell, Quinn & Creighton, 1992-99, ret., 1999. Mem. law com. Colo. State Bd. Law Examiners, Denver, 1958-79; mem. bd. mgrs. Nat. Conf. Bar Examiners, Chgo., 1965-69. With U.S. Army, 1943-46, USAR, 1946-51, maj. USAFR, 1951-67, ret. 1985. Mem. Denver Bar Assn., Colo. Bar Assn., Denver Law Club (pres. 1963-64, Svc. to Bar and Cmty. Lifetime Achievement award 1996), University Club (bd. dirs. 1982-88), Phi Beta Kappa, Beta Theta Pi, Phi Delta Phi. Episcopalian. Home: 1155 Ash St Apt 1504 Denver CO 80220-3727

CODY, DANIEL SCHAFFNER, lawyer; b. Columbus, Ohio, Nov. 21, 1948; s. Ralph Eugene and Grace (Schaffner) C.; m. Susan Ragsdale, Mar. 27, 1992; 1 child, Sean. Student, Kent State U., 1977; BA, Ohio State U., 1970, BSEd, 1973; JD, U. Akron, 1990. Bar: Ohio 1990, U.S. Dist. Ct. (no. dist.) Ohio 1990, U.S. Ct. Appeals (6th cir.) 1990, U.S. Ct. Appeals (4th cir.) 1992. Tchg. Archbishop Hoban H.S., Akron, Ohio, 1973-88, athletic dir., 1980-84; rsch. asst. Hon. Arthur Goldberg (ret.) U.S. Supreme Ct., U. Akron, 1989, staff intern Appellate Rev. Office, 1990-91; jud. clk. Ohio Ct. Appeals (9th dist.), Akron, 1990-91; assoc. Jacobson, Maynard, Tuschman & Kalur, Cleve., 1991-93; pvt. practice Akron, 1993—. Trustee U. Akron Law Alumni Assn., 1992—, pres., 2000-01; trustee Archbishop Hoban H.S., 1995-2001. Mem. Ohio State Bar Assn., Akron Bar Assn. Democrat. Roman Catholic. Criminal, Personal injury. Office: 17 S Main St Ste 201 Akron OH 44308-1803

COE, ILSE G. retired lawyer; b. Koenigsberg, Germany, May 28, 1911; came to U.S., 1938; Referendar, U. Koenigsberg, 1935, JSD, 1936; JD, Bklyn. Law Sch., 1946. Bar: N.Y. 1946. Dir. econ. rsch. Internat. Gen. Electric Co., Berlin, 1936-38; asst. to sales promotion and advt. mgr. Ralph C. Coxhead Corp., N.Y.C., 1940-44; law clk. Mendes & Mount, 1944-46; assoc. Hill, Rivkins & Middleton, 1946-50, McNutt, Longcope & Proctor, N.Y.C., 1950-52, Chadbourne, Hunt, Jaeckel & Brown, N.Y.C., 1952-54; asst. v.p., asst. trust officer Schroder Trust Co. and J. Henry Schroder Banking Corp., 1954-76. Dir., sec., editor Fgn. Tax Law Assn., Inc., L.I., 1945-55; tchr. Drakes Bus. Sch., N.Y.C., 1946-49; lectr. on estate planning to ch., women's and bar assn. groups; tutor literacy vols., 1977-79; lectr. wills, trusts, estates, investment counseling and photography Pace U., St. Francis Coll. Rep. county com. woman, 1948-50; former deacon, past ruling elder, 1st Presbyn. Ch., Bklyn; exec. bd. Pace Adult Resource Ctr. (formerly Pace Active Retirement Ctr.) Pace U., 1977-79, v.p., 1980-81, pres. 1982-85, life mem. exec. bd., 1986—. Recipient Human Relations award NCCJ, 1979. Mem. Bklyn. Women's Bar Assn. (past treas., sec., bd. dirs. 1960-92, 93-94), Protestant Lawyers Assn. N.Y. Inc. (sec. 1960-75, 1st v.p. 1976-77, pres. 1978-88, lifetime pres. emeritus 1988—, bd. dirs. 1988—), Internat. Fedn. Women Lawyers, Bklyn. Heights Assn., Bklyn. Hist. Soc. (former mem. investment com.), N.Y. Color Slide Club (by-laws chmn. 1983—, bd. dirs. 1973-74), Bklyn. Jus., Bklyn. Botanic Garden, others. Home: Miller Bldg #A001 1925 W Turner St Allentown PA 18104-5551

COFFEE, MELVIN ARNOLD, retired lawyer; b. Chgo., July 8, 1934; s. Charles Hyman and Ida (Berson) C.; m. Beverly N. Segal, Aug. 26, 1956; children: Ronald M., Babette S. BS in Law, LLB, U. Denver, 1957; LLM, NYU, 1959. Bar: Colo. 1958. Ptnr. Drexler, Wald, Sobol & Coffee, Denver, 1959-63, Inman, Flynn & Coffee, Denver, 1963-78; sr. ptnr. Melvin Coffee & Assocs., 1978-2000; ret., 2000. Adj. prof. tax law U. Denver, 1974-83;

chmn. IRS liaison com. Southwest Bar, 1989. Author: Taxation for Accountants, 1970, Protecting Client in Tax Fraud Investigation, 1972, New Directions in Guarding Client Records, 1973, Criminal Tax Investigations, 1983, The Colorado Lawyer, 1983. Prin. draftsman statute Colo. Income Tax Act 1964; pres. Denver and Tri-County Respiratory Disease Assn., 1962; active Citizen Budget Rev., 1963; Dem. rep. Colo. Ho. of Reps., 1967-69. With U.S. Army, 1958-64. Mem. Colo. State Bd. Accountancy (bd. dirs., pres. 1981), Colo. Soc. CPAs (hon.), Colo. Bar Assn. (bd. govs. 1980-82, chmn. taxation sect. 1970, chmn. continuing legal edn. 1981), Arapahoe County Bar Assn. (trustee 1980-82), Nat. Assn. State Bds. Accountancy (v.p. 1981-84), Greater Denver Tax Counsel (pres., sec. 1963-65), Masons, Columbine. Criminal, Taxation, general, State and local taxation. Office: Melvin Coffee PC 4296 S Dahlia St Englewood CO 80110-5004

COFFEY, JOHN LOUIS, federal judge; b. Milw., Apr. 15, 1922; s. William Leo and Elizabeth Ann (Walsh) C.; m. Marion Kunzelmann, Feb. 3, 1951; children: Peter, Elizabeth Mary Coffey Robbins. BA, Marquette U., 1943, JD, 1948; MBA (hon.), Spencerian Coll., 1964. Bar: Wis. 1948, U.S. Dist. Ct. 1948, U.S. Supreme Ct. 1980. Asst. city atty. City of Milw., 1949-54; judge Civil Ct., Milw. County, 1954-60, Milw. County Mcpl. Ct., 1960-62; judge criminal divsn. Cir. Ct., Milw. County, 1962-72, sr. judge criminal divsn., 1972-75, chief presiding judge criminal divsn., 1976, judge civil divsn., 1976-78; justice Wis. Supreme Ct., Madison, 1978-82; cir. judge U.S. Ct. Appeals (7th cir.), Chgo., 1982—; mem. Wis. Bd. Criminal Ct. Judges, 1960-78, Wis. Bd. Circuit Ct. Judges, 1962-78. Chmn. adv. bd. St. Joseph's Home for Children, 1958-65; mem. adv. bd. St. Mary's Hosp., 1964-70; past bd. dirs., mem. exec. bd. Milw.-Waukesha chpt. ARC; past mem. Milwaukee County council Boy Scouts Am.; chmn. St. Eugene's Sch. Bd., 1967-70; pres. St. Eugene's Ch. Coun., 1974; mem. vol. svcs. adv. com. Milwaukee County Dept. Pub. Welfare. Served with USNR, 1943-46. Named Outstanding Man of Yr., Milw. Jr. C. of C., 1951, One of 5 Outstanding Men in State of Wis., 1957, Outstanding Law Alumnus of Yr., Marquette U., 1980, alumni merit award, 2001. Fellow Am. Bar Found.; mem. Wis. Bar Assn., 7th Cir. Bar Assn., Ill. State Bar Assn., Nat. Lawyers Club, Am. Legion (Disting. Svc. award 1973), Marquette U. Law Alumni Assn. (Disting. Profl. Achievement Merit award 1985), Marquette U. M Club (former dir.), Alpha Sigma Nu, Phi Alpha Delta (hon.) Roman Catholic.

COFFEY, LARRY B(RUCE), lawyer; BA, Wabash Coll., Crawfordsville, Ind., 1962; JD with honors, Ind. U., 1965; M of Comparative Law, U. Chgo., 1967. Bar: Ind. 1965, U.S. Dist. Ct. (so. dist.) Ind. 1965, N.Y. 1975, N.C. 1989, U.S. Dist. Ct. (we. dist.) N.C., 1989. Atty. European Union Commn., Brussels, 1967; assoc. Dewey Ballantine, N.Y.C. and Brussels, 1968-71; atty. GM, N.Y.C. and London, 1971-78; v.p. Revlon, Europe, Mid. East and Africa, Paris, 1978-83; pvt. practice, 1983-89; counsel Womble, Carlyle, Sandridge & Rice, Charlotte, N.C., 1989-91; pvt. practice, 1991—. Editor: The Common Market and Common Law, 1967. Wabash Coll. scholar 1958-62, Ind. U. Law Sch. fellow, 1962-65, U. Chgo. Law Sch. fellow, 1965-67. Mem. ABA, N.Y. State Bar Assn., N.C. Bar Assn. Contracts commercial, Immigration, naturalization, and customs, Private international. Office: 2449 Ardmore Manor Winston Salem NC 27103-4866 E-mail: coffeylaw@justice.com, coffeylaw@itgo.com

COFFEY, THOMAS WILLIAM, lawyer; b. Cin., Jan. 19, 1959; s. Joseph Paul and Doris June (Adams) C.; m. Shirley Ann Strode, July 24, 1982. MusB, U. Cin., 1981, JD, 1987. Bar: Pa. 1987, U.S. Dist. Ct. (we. dist.) Pa. 1987, U.S. Ct. Appeals (3d cir.) 1988, Ohio 1990, U.S. Dist. Ct. (so. dist.) Ohio 1990, U.S. Ct. Appeals (6th cir.) 1990. Dir. band Ea. Local Sch., Brown County, Ohio, 1981-83, Goshen (Ohio) High Sch., 1983-84; assoc. Buchanan Ingersoll, P.C., Pitts., 1987-90; chmn. bankruptcy group Cors & Bassett, Cin., 1990—. Mem. ABA, Ohio Bar Assn., Cin. Bar Assn., Am. Fedn. Musicians, Masons, Shriners. Avocations: symphonic and Dixieland jazz. Banking, Bankruptcy, Contracts commercial. Home: 933 Monastery St Cincinnati OH 45202-1510 Office: Cors & Bassett 537 E Pete Rose Way Ste 400 Cincinnati OH 45202-3578 E-mail: twc@cors.bassett.com

COFFIN, FRANK MOREY, federal judge; b. Lewiston, Maine, July 11, 1919; s. Herbert Rice and Ruth (Morey) C.; m. Ruth Ulrich, Dec. 19, 1942; children: Nancy, Douglas, Meredith, Susan. A.B., Bates Coll., 1940, LL.D., 1959; postgrad. indsl. adminstrn., Harvard U., 1943, LL.B., 1947; LL.D., Bates Coll., 1959, U. Maine, 1967, Bowdoin Coll., 1969; degree (hon.), Colby Coll., 1975. Bar: Maine 1947. Law clk. to fed. judge Dist. of Maine, 1947-49; engaged in practice Lewiston, 1947-52; Verrill, Dana, Walker, Philbrick & Whitehouse, Portland, Maine, 1952-56; mem. 85th-86th Congresses from 2d Dist. Maine, House Com. Fgn. Affairs; mng. dir. joint econ. com. Devel. Loan Fund, Dept. State, Washington, 1961; dep. adminstr. AID, 1961-64; U.S. rep. devel. assistance com. Orgn. Econ. Coop. and Devel., 1964-65; judge 1st circuit U.S. Ct. Appeals, 1965—, chief judge, 1972-83, sr. judge, 1989—; chmn. com. jud. br. U.S. Jud. Conf., 1984-90. Adj. prof. U. Maine Sch. Law, 1986-89. Author: Witness for Aid, 1964, The Ways of a Judge-Reflections from the Federal Appellate Bench, 1980, A Lexicon of Oral Advocacy, 1984, On Appeal, 1994. Emeritus Bates Coll.; dir. The Governance Inst., 1987—; mem. emeritus The Examiner; chair Maine Justice Action Group, 1996-2001. Lt. USNR, 1943-46. Recipient Edward J. Devitt Disting. Svc. to Justice award, Maine Justice Action Group, 2001. Mem. ABA (co chair com. on loan forgiveness and repayment 2001—), Am. Acad. Arts and Scis. Office: US Ct Appeals 156 Federal St Portland ME 04101-4152

COFFIN, MARY MCCARTHY, lawyer; b. Syracuse, N.Y., Oct. 15, 1920; m. Louis F. Coffin, Apr. 24, 1943; children: John, Sally, Laurie, Robert, Patricia, Deborah, Louis, Margaret. AB, Radcliffe Coll., 1942; postgrad., MIT, 1942-43; LLB, Albany Law Sch., 1967. Bar: N.Y. 1968, U.S. Supreme Ct. 1974. Rsch. tech. Children's Hosp., Boston, 1941-43; law clk. County Ct., Schenectady, N.Y., 1968-70; counsel Schenectady Urban Renewal Agy., 1970-72; pvt. practice Schenectady, 1972-79; ptnr. Antokol & Coffin, 1979-97, of counsel, 1990. County judge Schenectady County, 1968-70; legal counsel Sch. Urban Renewal Agy, Schenectady, 1970-73; past pres., incorporator Schenectady County Legal Aid; trustee, YWCA, 1975-90; mem. Schenectady Housing Code Commn., 1973-76, Hospice of Schenectady, 1982-88, Law, Order and Justice, 1975-82, Schenectady Family and Child Service, 1977-82; bd. dirs. Schenectady County Legal Aid, 1968-81, pres., 1970; bd. dirs. N.E. Legal Aid Soc., 1979-82. Recipient Susan B. Anthony award Schenectady County LWV, 1982; named Schenectady Jr. League Vol. of Yr., 1957; recipient Schenectady Law, Order and Justice award for Svc., 1982; Cmty. Svc. award YWCA, 1982. Mem. ABA, Schenectady Bar Assn., N.Y. Bar Assn. (Root/Stimson award), Torch Club. Democrat. Criminal, Family and matrimonial, Real property. Home: 235 Walker St Apt 172 Lenox MA 01240-2747 E-mail: marylouco@webtv.net

COFFINAS, ELENI, lawyer; b. Bklyn., Jan. 12, 1961; BA, Bklyn. Coll., 1982, JD, 1985. BAr: N.Y. 1985. Assoc. Sullivan & Liapakis, P.C., N.Y.C., 1986-93; ptnr. Sullivan, Papain, Block, McGrath & Cannavo, 1993—, ptnr., supr. med. malpractice dept., 1994—. Mem. ATLA, Assn. Bar City N.Y. (med. malpractice com. 1996—), N.Y. State Trial Lawyers Assn. (bd. dirs. 1997—). Greek Orthodox. Personal injury. Home: 9425 Shore Rd Brooklyn NY 11209-7259 Office: Sullivan Papain Block McGrath & Cannavo PC 120 Broadway New York NY 10271-0002

COFFMAN, CLAUDE T. law educator, lawyer; b. Robinsonville, Miss., Jan. 20, 1916; s. Tulus Jackson and Addie (Mick) C.; m. Ninna Carr Bailey, July 15, 1940; children: Mary, Margaret. AB, LLB, U. Miss., 1938; postgrad. Harvard U., 1939. Bar: Miss. 1938. Atty., U.S. Dept. Agr., Washington, 1939-51, dep. gen counsel, 1968-74; asst. legal counsel Tech. Corp. Adminstrn., Washington, 1951-53; prof. law Memphis State U., 1974-86; prof. emeritus and interim dean, 1986-87. Contbr. articles to profl. jours. Mem. ABA. Episcopalian. Home: 1028 Cresthaven Rd Ste 206 Memphis TN 38119-3871 Office: Dept Law Memphis State U Memphis TN 38152

COFFMAN, DANIEL RAY, JR. lawyer; b. Richmond, Va., Feb. 13, 1933; s. D. Ray and Clara (Noell) C.; m. Blanche Gray Coffman, Oct. 8, 1960; children— Elizabeth, Julia, Virginia, Emily. B.A., Vanderbilt U., 1954, J.D., 1960. Bar: Fla. 1960. Shareholder Coffman, Coleman, Andrews & Grogan, P.A., Jacksonville, Fla., 1971— ; labor counsel Fla. Jr. Coll., Jacksonville, 1975-88. Bd. dirs. Salvation Army; mem. adv. bd. Learn to Read, Jacksonville. Served to lt USNR, 1954-57. Mem. ABA, Jacksonville Bar Assn., Bar (chmn. labor and employment law com. 1969-70), Jacksonville Area C. of C. (gen. counsel 1985, v.p. 1987). Republican. Presbyterian Club: Exchange (past pres.). Labor. Home: 4061 Timuquana Rd Jacksonville FL 32210-8531 Office: Coffman Coleman Andrews & Grogan 2065 Herschel St Jacksonville FL 32204-3875

COFFMAN, JENNIFER BURCHAM, federal judge; b. 1948; BA, U. Ky., 1969, MA, 1971, JD, 1978. Ref. libr. Newport News (Va.) Pub. Libr., 1972-74, U. Ky., 1974-76; atty. Law Offices Arthur L. Brooks, Lexington, Ky., 1978-82; ptnr. Brooks, Coffman and Fitzpatrick, 1982-92, Newberry, Hargrove & Rambicure, Lexington, 1992-93; judge U.S. Dist. Ct. (ea. dist. and we. dist.) Ky., London, 1993—. Adj. prof. Coll. Law, U. Ky., 1979-81. Bd. dirs. YWCA Lexington, 1986-92; elder Second Presbyn. Ch., 1993-96. Mem. Ky. Bar Assn., Fayette County Bar Assn., U. Ky. Law Sch. Alumni Assn. Office: 207 US Courthouse 300 S Main St London KY 40741-1924

COGBURN, MAX OLIVER, lawyer; b. Canton, N.C., Mar. 21, 1927; s. Chester Amberg and Ruby Elizabeth (Davis) C.; m. Mary Heidt, Oct. 15, 1949; children: Max O. Jr., Michael David, Steven Douglas, Cynthia Diane. AB, U. N.C., 1948, LLB, 1950; LLM, Harvard U., 1951. Bar; N.C. 1950, U.S. Dist. Ct. (we. dist.) N.C. 1953, U.S. Ct. Appeals (4th cir.) 1984. Asst. dir. Inst. Govt., Chapel-Hill, N.C., 1951-52; staff mem. Atty. Gen. N.C., Raleigh, 1952-54; adminstr. asst. Chief Justice N.C., 1954-55; judge Gen. County Ct. Buncombe County, Asheville, N.C., 1968-70; sole practice Canton, Asheville, N.C., 1968, 1971—; ptnr. Roberts, Stevens & Cogburn, P.A., Asheville, 1986-95, Cogburn, Cogburn, Goosmann & Brazil, P.A., Ashville, 1995—. Chmn. Buncombe County Dem. Exec. Com., Asheville, 1974-76; mem. State Dem. Exec. Com., Raleigh, 1974-76. Mem. ABA, N.C. State Bar Assn., N.C. Bar Assn. (Gen. Practice Hall of Fame 1997), 28th Jud. Dist. Bar State of N.C., Buncombe County Bar Assn. (past pres.). Roman Catholic. Federal civil litigation, State civil litigation, General practice. Home: RR 1 Candler NC 28715-9801 Office: 77 Central Ave Ste H Asheville NC 28801-2451

COGGINS, PAUL EDWARD, JR. prosecutor; b. Hugo, Okla., May 21, 1951; s. Paul E. and Rebecca (Cates) C.; m. Regina T. Montoya, June 12, 1976; 1 child, Jessica Chandler. BA in Polit. Sci. summa cum laude, Yale U., 1973; BA with honors, Oxford U., 1975; JD cum laude, Harvard U., 1978. Bar: Tex. 1978. Tchr. Project New Gate N.Mex. State Penitentiary, 1973; law clk. Mass. Ct. Appeals, 1978-79; fed. prosecutor U.S. Attys. Office, Dallas, 1980-83; assoc. Johnson & Swanson, 1979-80, ptnr., 1983-86, Meadows, Owens, Collier, Reed & Coggins, Dallas, 1986-93; U.S. atty. U.S. Dept. of Justice, 1993-2001. Mem. adv. com. Magnet Sch. in Dallas, 1984—. Author: The Lady is the Tiger, 1987; co-author: Out of Bounds, 1992. Pres. bd. dirs. Dem. Forum, Dallas, 1985—. Rhodes scholar, 1973-76. Mem. ABA, Dallas Bar Assn. (mem. pro bono panel), Harvard Club (v.p. 1987—), Yale Club. Office: Fish & Richardson PC 5000 Bank One Ctr 1717 Main St Dallas TX 75201 Fax: (214) 747-2091. E-mail: Coggins@fr.com

COGHILL, WILLIAM THOMAS, JR. lawyer; b. St. Louis, July 20, 1927; s. William Thomas and Mildred Mary (Crenshaw) C.; m. Patricia Lee Hughes, Aug. 7, 1948; children: James Prentiss, Victoria Lynn, Cathryn Anne. JD, U. Mo., 1950, undergrad., 1944-45, 46-47. Bar: Mo. 1950, Ill. 1958. Pvt. practice, Farmington, Mo., 1950-51; spl. agt. FBI, 1951-52; ptnr. Smith, Smith & Coghill, Farmington, 1952-57; assoc. Coburn & Croft, St. Louis, 1957-58; ptnr. Thompson Coburn (formerly Thompson & Mitchell and predecessor firm), Belleville, Ill., 1958—. Co-author: Illinois Products Liability, 1991, Cavaliers, 1999. With USN, 1945-46. Fellow Am. Coll. Trial Lawyers; mem. ABA, Ill. State Bar Assn., Mo. State Bar Assn., Trial Attys. Am., Product Liability Adv. Coun. (sustaining mem.), Def. Rsch. Inst., Inc., Ill. Assn. Def. Counsel, Nat. Assn. R.R. Trial Counsel, Media Club, Elks. Federal civil litigation, State civil litigation, Insurance. Home: 715 W Moon Valley Dr Phoenix AZ 85023-6234 Office: Thompson Coburn 525 W Main St Belleville IL 62220-1534 E-mail: tcoghill@rni.net

COHEN, BARTON POLLOCK, lawyer; b. Kansas City, Kans., Dec. 11, 1930; s. Joseph Cohen and Margaret Pollock; m. Mary Davidson, Dec. 30, 1989; children: Thomas M., Margo, John. BA, Yale U., 1952; JD, Harvard U., 1955. Bar: Kans. 1955, U.S. Dist. Ct. Kans., U.S. Supreme Ct., U.S. Ct. Appeals (10th cir.). Assoc., ptnr. Cohen, Schnider, Shamberg, Kansas City, Kans., 1957-66; ptnr. Cohen, Benjamin, Comer, Overland Park, 1966-88, Blackwell Sanders Matheny Weary Lombardi, Overland Park, 1988-96; of counsel Blackwell Sanders Peper Martin LLP, 1997—. Pres. Metcalf BancShares Inc., Overland Park, 1980—; dir., vice-chmn., gen. counsel Metcalf Bank, Overland Park, 1968—, dir. Rosedale Bank, Kansas City, Kans., 1958-80. Councilman City of Prairie Village, Kans., 1964-69; bd. chmn. Johnson County Mental Health Ctr., Johnson County, 1974. With U.S. Army, 1955-57. Fellow Johnson County Bar Found. (treas.); mem. Nat. Assn. Security Dealers (arbitrator), Kans. State Hist. Soc. (bd. dirs.). Republican. Jewish. Avocations: golf, travel. Banking, Contracts commercial, Estate planning. Home: 12617 Briar Dr Leawood KS 66209-3169 Office: Blackwell Sanders Peper Martin LLP 9401 Indian Creek Pkwy Ste 1200 Overland Park KS 66210-2020 Fax: 913-696-7070. E-mail: bcohen@bspmlaw.com

COHEN, CAROL I. lawyer; b. Jersey City, Feb. 26, 1945; d. Harry and Sylvia Indursky; m. Burton David Cohen, June 18, 1967 (div.); children: Steven Corey, Richard Harris. BA, Douglass Coll., 1966; MA, NYU, 1967; JD, Seton Hall U., 1978. Bar: N.J. 1978, Calif. 1979, U.S. Ct. Appeals (3d cir.) 1978, U.S. Supreme Ct. 1999. Tchr. Jersey City Bd. Edn., 1966-67; social worker Monterey Welfare Dept., Salinas, Calif., 1967069; adoption caseworker DYFS, New Brunswick, N.J., 1969-71; supr. adoptions Adoption Svc. Ctr., Highland Park, 1971-73; legis. aide Sen. Anthony Russo, Union, 1980-82; atty. Union County Bd. Social Svcs., Elizabeth, 1984-88; asst. county counsel County of Union, 1988-94, freeholder, 1996-98, county counsel, 1998—; atty. in pvt. practice, Westfield, N.J., 1978-98. Vice chair Westfield Dem. Com., 1990—; mem. Union County Dem. Com., 1980—. Recipient award in govt. svc. N.J. Adv. Com. on Status of Women, 1998; NDEA fellow, 1966; NYU fellow, 1966. Mem. Women's Polit. Caucus (pres. 1999), N.J. County Counsel Assn., Union County Bar Assn. (trustee 1997—), N.J. Bar Assn., Phi Beta Kappa. Jewish. Home: 302 Roanoke Rd Westfield NJ 07090-2920 Office: Union County Counsel Adminstn Bldg Elizabeth NJ 07207 E-mail: ccohen@unioncountynj.org

COHEN, CYNTHIA MARYLYN, lawyer; b. Bklyn., Sept. 5, 1945; AB, Cornell U., 1967; JD cum laude, NYU, 1970. Bar: N.Y. 1971, U.S. Ct. Appeals (2nd cir.) 1972, U.S. Dist. Ct. (so. and ea. dists.) N.Y. 1972, U.S. Supreme Ct. 1975, U.S. Dist. Ct. (ctrl. and no. dists.) Calif. 1980, U.S. Ct. Appeals (9th cir.) 1980, U.S. Dist. Ct. (so. dist.) Calif. 1981, U.S. Dist. Ct. (ea. dist.) Calif. 1986. With Paul, Hastings, Janofsky & Walker, LLP, L.A., N.Y.C. Bd. dirs. N.Y. chpt. Am. Cancer Soc., 1977-80; active Pres.'s Coun. Cornell Women. Recipient Am. Jurisprudence award for evidence, torts and legal instns., 1968-69; John Norton Pomeroy scholar NYU, 1968-70, Founders Day Cert., 1969. Mem. ABA, Assn. Bar City N.Y. (trade regulation com. 1976-79), Assn. Bus. Trial Lawyers, Fin. Lawyers Conf., N.Y. State Bar Assn. (chmn. class-action com. 1979), State Bar Calif., Los Angeles County Bar Assn., Order of Coif, Delta Gamma. Avocations: tennis, bridge, rare books, wines. Antitrust, Bankruptcy, General civil litigation. Home: 4531 Dundee Dr Los Angeles CA 90027-1213 Office: Paul Hastings Janofsky & Walker LLP 555 S Flower St 23d Fl Los Angeles CA 90071 E-mail: cynthiacohen@paulhastings.com

COHEN, EDWARD HERSCHEL, lawyer; b. Lewistown, Pa., Sept. 30, 1938; s. Saul Allen and Barbara (Getz) C.; m. Arlene Greenbaum, Aug. 12, 1962; children: Fredrick, James, Paul. AB, U. Mich., 1960; JD, Harvard U., 1963. Bar: N.Y. 1964. Assoc. Rosenman and Colin, N.Y.C., 1963-72, ptnr., 1972-86, 88—, counsel, 1987; v.p., gen. counsel, sec. Phillips-Van Heusen Corp., 1987. Mem. Fenway Golf Club (Scarsdale, N.Y.), Ventana Golf and Racquet Club (Tucson). Republican. Jewish. Avocations: golf, travel. General corporate, Securities. Home: 21 Sycamore Rd Scarsdale NY 10583-7322 Office: Rosenman & Colin 575 Madison Ave Fl 26 New York NY 10022-2585

COHEN, EDWIN SAMUEL, lawyer, educator; b. Richmond, Va., Sept. 27, 1914; s. LeRoy S. and Miriam (Rosenheim) C.; m. Carlyn Labenberg, June 27, 1936 (dec. 1942); m. Helen Herz, Aug. 31, 1944; children: Edwin C., Roger, Wendy. B.A., U. Richmond, 1933; J.D., U. Va., 1936. Bar: Va. 1935, N.Y. 1937, D.C. 1973. Assoc. Sullivan & Cromwell, N.Y.C., 1936-49; ptnr. Root, Barrett, Cohen, Knapp & Smith (and predecessor firm), 1949-65; counsel Root, Barrett, Cohen, Knapp & Smith, 1965-69; prof. law U. Va., Charlottesville, 1965-68, Joseph M. Hartfield prof., 1968-69, 73-85, prof. emeritus, 1985—, professorial lectr. law, 1994—; asst. sec. treasury for tax policy, 1969-72; under sec. treasury, 1972-73; of counsel Covington & Burling, Washington, 1973-77, ptnr., 1977-86, sr. counsel, 1986—. Vis. prof. Benjamin N. Cardozo Sch. Law, Yeshiva U., 1987-92, U. Miami Law Sch., 1993, 95-99, chmn. grad. program in taxation and estate planning, 1995-98; mem., counsel adv. group on corp. taxes ways and means com. U.S. Ho. of Reps., 1956-58; spl. cons. on corps. fed. income tax project Am. Law Inst., 1949-54; mem. adv. group Fed. Estate and Gift Tax Project, 1964-68; mem. Va. Income Tax Conformity Study Commn., 1970-71; cons. Va. Income Tax Conformity Study Commn., 1966-68; mem. adv. group to commr. IRS, 1967-68. Author: A Lawyer's Life Deep in the Heart of Taxes, 1994. Recipient Alexander Hamilton award Treasury Dept. Mem. Am. Judicature Soc., ABA (chmn. com. on corporate stockholder relationships 1956-58, mem. council 1958-61, chmn. spl. com. on substantive tax reform 1962-63, chmn. spl. com. on formation tax policy 1977-80, Disting. Svc. award taxation sect. 1997), Va. Bar Assn., D.C. Bar Assn., N.Y. State Bar Assn., Va. Tax Conf. (planning com. 1965-68, 85-95, trustee emeritus 1995—), C. of C. of U.S. (bd. dirs., chmn. taxation com. 1979-84), Assn. Bar City N.Y., N.Y. County Lawyers Assn., Am. Law Inst., Am. Coll. Tax Counsel, Order Coif, Raven Soc., Colonnade Club, Boar's Head Club, Farmington Club, City Club, Phi Beta Kappa, Omicron Delta Kappa, Pi Delta Epsilon, Phi Epsilon Pi (Nat. Achievement award) Home: 104 Stuart Pl Ednam Forest Charlottesville VA 22903 E-mail: ecohen@law5.law.virginia.edu

COHEN, EZRA HARRY, lawyer; b. Macon, Ga., Mar. 13, 1942; s. Harry M. and Rena C. Cohen; m. Bonnie E. Cohen, Feb. 1, 1969 (div. Mar. 1988); children: Aaron M., Eileen R.; m. Katherine C. Meyers, June 18, 1989. BA, Columbia U., 1964; JD, Emory U., 1969. Bar: Ga. 1969. Ptnr. Troutman, Sanders, Lockerman & Ashmore, Atlanta, 1969-76, 79—; judge U.S. Bankruptcy Ct., U.S. Dist. Ct. (no. dist.) Ga., 1976-79. Dir. S.E. Bankruptcy Law Inst., Atlanta. Contbg. author: Cowan's Bankruptcy Laws & Practices, 1979. Mem. Emory U. Law Sch. Coun., Atlanta, 1988—. With U.S. Army, 1964-66, ETO. Fellow Am. Coll. Bankruptcy; mem. Ga. Bar Assn. (chmn. bankruptcy law sect.), Assn. Former Bankruptcy Judges (bd. dirs.), Nat. Assn. Bank Judges (assoc.), Atlanta Bar Assn. (bd. dirs. 1988-90), Lawyers Club of Atlanta. Bankruptcy. Home: 546 W Wesley Rd Atlanta GA 30305-3534 Office: Troutman Sanders 600 Peachtree St NE Ste 5200 Atlanta GA 30308-2216 E-mail: ezra.cohen@troutmansanders.com

COHEN, HARVEY, lawyer; b. Far Rockaway, N.Y., Sept. 20, 1918; s. Theodore Bernard and Gertrude (Gottlieb) C.; m. Norma Ruth Boiles, Nov. 2, 1947; children: Douglas Lee, Beth Cohen DeGrasse, Barry Scott. BA, Lafayette Coll., Easton, Pa., 1940; JD, Harvard U., 1947. Bar: N.Y. 1948. Atty. Bernhardt, Sahn, Shapiro & Epstein, N.Y.C., 1947-49; ptnr. Murtagh, Cohen & Byrne, 1950-77, Garden City, N.Y., 1977—. Bd. dirs., officer L.K. Comstock Co., Inc., N.Y.C., 1965-88, Electrospace Corp., Glen Cove, N.Y., 1963-81, Radiation Dynamics, Inc., Westbury, N.Y., 1958-83, Med. Sterilization, Inc., Syosset, N.Y., 1983-97. Mem. housing bd. dirs. Unitarian Universalist Congregation at Shelter Rock, 1970-72, chmn. bd. govs., 1978, trustee, 1966-75, 95-98, pres., 1974-75; trustee Mental Health Assn. Nassau County, 1984—, pres., 1990-91; active Port Washington Youth Activities. Recipient Wittelsburger award Heros, Inc., 1984, Good Guy award Nassau County Lacrosse Ofcls. Assn., 1985, Man of Yr. award Nassau County Lacrosse Coaches Assn., 1988, Bernie Ullman award Nat. Collegiate Lacrosse Ofcls. Assn., 1996, others; named to L.I. Met. Lacrosse Hall of Fame, 1986, Nat. Lacrosse Hall of Fame, 1988, Pt. Washington Youth Activities Hall of Fame, 1991. Mem. Nassau County Bar Assn., Phi Beta Kappa. Democrat. Avocations: youth sports, lacrosse, charitable work. Home: 125 Woodhill Ln Manhasset NY 11030-1716 Office: Murtagh Cohen & Byrne 1100 Franklin Ave Ste 303 Garden City NY 11530-1601

COHEN, HENRY RODGIN, lawyer; b. Charleston, W.Va, May 7, 1944; s. Louis W. and Bertie (Rodgin) C.; m. Barbara Latz, Aug. 31, 1969; children: Sarah Abigail, Jonathan David. BA, Harvard U., 1965, LLB, 1968; LLB (hon.), U. Charleston, 1998. Bar: W.Va. 1968, N.Y. 1970. Assoc. Sullivan & Cromwell, N.Y.C., 1970-77, ptnr., 1977—, vice chmn., 1999-2000, chmn., 2000—. Contbg. editor Fin. Svcs. Regulation Newsletter, 1985; bd. advisors Banking Law Rev.; mem. editorial adv. bd. Banking Expansion Reporter; mem. nat. bd. contbrs. Am. Lawyers Newspaper Group. Served with U.S. Army, 1968-70. Banking. Office: Sullivan & Cromwell 125 Broad St Fl 28 New York NY 10004-2489

COHEN, JAY LORING, lawyer; b. Erie, Pa., Oct. 26, 1953; s. Harold H. and Adelle (Stein) C.; children: Natanel M., Katrielle Z. BA cum laude, U. Rochester, 1974; JD, Georgetown U., 1977. Bar: Pa. 1977, U.S. Claims Ct. 1978, U.S. Ct. Appeals (D.C. cir.) 1978, D.C. 1979, U.S. Supreme Ct. 1981, U.S. Ct. Appeals (fed. cir.) 1982, Md. 1986. Mem. firm Israel, Raley & Cohen, Chartered (formerly Israel & Raley), Washington, 1977-87; pvt. practice, Washington and Bethesda, Md., 1988—. Editor Am. Criminal Law Rev., 1977. Vice-chmn. Montgomery County Ethics Commn., 1986-90, chmn., 1990—; bd. dirs. Hebrew Day Inst., 1984—, v.p., 1987-88, 90-91, treas. 1988—. Mem. Assn. Trial Lawyers Am. (comml. litigation sect.), ABA (pub. contract law sect.), Fed. Bar Assn. (fed. litigation sect.), Fed. Cir. Bar Assn. (gov. contract appeals sect.). General civil litigation, General corporate, Government contracts and claims. Office: 9007 Seneca Ln Bethesda MD 20817-3558

COHEN, JEFFREY, lawyer; b. Bklyn., Jan. 31, 1956; s. Fred and Ann (Piel) C. A.B. in Politics and Philosophy with depart mental honors magna cum laude, Brandeis U., 1977; J.D., Bklyn. Law Sch., 1980. Bar: N.Y. 1981, Colo. 1981. Assoc. Freedman & May, N.Y.C., 1980-81, Alter, Zall & Haligman, Denver, 1981-82; ptnr. Quiat & Dice, Denver, 1982-84, Koransky, Friedman & Cohen, P.C., Denver, 1984—. Mem. ABA (bus. bankruptcy com.), Colo. Bar Assn., Denver Bar Assn. Republican. Jewish. Clubs: Colo. Mountain, Denver Athletic. Bankruptcy, State civil litigation, General corporate. Office: Yates & Leal LLP 455 Sherman St Ste 455 Denver CO 80203-4405

COHEN, JEFFREY MICHAEL, lawyer; b. Dayton, Ohio, Nov. 13, 1940; s. H. Mort and Evelyn (Friedlob) C.; m. Betsy Z. Zimmerman, July 3, 1966; children: Meredith Sue, Seth Alan. AB, Colgate U., 1962; JD, Columbia U., 1965. Bar: Fla. 1965, U.S. Supreme Ct. 1969; cert. civil trial lawyer Fla. Bar Bd. Cert.; diplomate Nat. bd. Trial Advocacy. Asst. pub. defender Dade County (Fla.), 1968-70, asst. state's atty., 1970-72, spl. asst. state's atty., 1973; ptnr. Fromberg Fromberg Gross Cohen Shore & Berke, P.A., 1972-84, Cohen, Berke, Bernstein, Brodie & Kondell, P.A., Miami, Fla., 1984-2000, Carlton Fields, 2000—. Adj. prof. litigation skills U. Miami Sch. Law, 1989—, chmn. Fla. bar com. on civil trial cert.; Fla. bar bd. dirs. legal specialization and edn. Trustee Miami-Dade County Alliance for Ethical Govt. Mem. ABA, Dade County Bar Assn. (bd. dirs.), Acad. Fla. Trial Lawyers, Assn. Trial Lawyers Am., Am. Judicature Soc., Nat. Inst. Trial Advocacy (chair and faculty mem.), Fla. Criminal Def. Attys. Assn. Federal civil litigation, State civil litigation, Personal injury. Home: 3628 Saint Gaudens Rd Miami FL 33133-6533 Office: 4000 Internat Pl 100 SE 2d St Miami FL 33131 E-mail: jmcohen@carltonfields.com

COHEN, JOSHUA ROBERT, lawyer; b. East Patchogue, N.Y., Aug. 20, 1963; s. Abraham Cohen and Elizabeth Joan Caufield; m. Robin Renee Conlon, Feb. 28, 1967. BA, Hartwick Coll., 1985; JD, Fordham U., 1991. Bar: Conn. 1991, N.Y. 1992, U.S. Dist. Ct. (so. and ea. dists.) N.Y., 1992. Sr. assoc. Belair & Evans LLP, N.Y.C., 1991-99; ptnr. Garson, Gerspach, DeCorato & Cohen, LLP, 1999—. Health, Insurance, Personal injury. Office: Garson Gerspach De Corato & Cohen LLP One Whitehall St New York NY 10004

COHEN, LAURA, lawyer; b. Pitts., Feb. 26, 1958; d. Alfred and Rita K. Cohen; (div.); children: Sarah Hackney, Beth Hackney. BA in Polit. Sci. with honors, Chatham Coll., 1993; JD, U. Pitts., 1996. Bar: Pa. 1996, U.S. Dist. Ct. (we. dist.) Pa. 1996, U.S. Supreme Ct., 2000. Lawyer, owner Family Legal Ctr., Monroeville, Pa., 1996—. Mem.: ABA, Pa. Bar Assn., Allegheny County Bar Assn., Matrimonial Inns of Ct., Greater Pitts. Bus. Connection (v.p. 1997—99, pres. 2000—). Family and matrimonial, Juvenile, Probate. Office: Family Legal Ctr 3825 Northern Pike Monroeville PA 15146-2133 E-mail: lauraesq@ghplus.infi.net

COHEN, LOUIS RICHARD, lawyer; b. Washington, Nov. 28, 1940; s. Milton Howard and Rowna (Chaffetz) C.; m. Bonnie Rubenstein, Aug. 29, 1965; children: Amanda Carroll, Eli Augustus. AB, Harvard U., 1962, LLB, 1966; student, Wadham Coll., Oxford, Eng., 1962-63. Bar: D.C. Law clk. to Hon. John M. Harlan U.S. Supreme Ct., Washington, 1967-68; assoc. Wilmer, Cutler & Pickering, 1968-74, ptnr., 1974-86, 88—; dep. solicitor gen. U.S. Dept. Justice, 1986-88; ptnr. Wilmer, Cutler & Pickering, Wash., 1988—. Vis. prof. Stanford (Calif.) Law Sch., 1981; lectr. law Harvard Law Sch., Cambridge, Mass., 1986. Author: Book Review Michigan Law Review, 1993. Chair Harvard Law Sch. Fund, 1993-96; mem. overseers com. to Visit Harvard Law Sch., 1986-92; bd. dirs. Woolly Mammoth Theatre Co., Washington, 1988-91, 96—. Mem. Supreme Ct. Hist. Soc., Am. Acad. Appellate Lawyers, Am. Law Inst. Jewish. Avocation: hiking. Federal civil litigation, General corporate, Securities. Office: Wilmer Cutler & Pickering 2445 M St NW Ste 500 Washington DC 20037-1487 E-mail: lcohen@wilmer.com

COHEN, MARCY SHARON, lawyer; b. N.Y.C., Apr. 29, 1954; d. Morton Gilbert and Sue Cohen. AB, Lehman Coll., 1975; JD, N.Y. Law Sch., 1978. Bar: N.Y. 1979, U.S. Dist. Ct. (ea. and so. dists.) N.Y. 1979, U.S. Supreme Ct. 1982. Assoc. Marcus & Marcus, N.Y.C., 1978-80; v.p., assoc. gen. counsel Bank Leumi Trust Co. N.Y., 1980-84; sr. v.p., gen. counsel Atlantic Bank N.Y., 1984-93; 1st v.p., dep. gen. counsel Republic Nat. Bank N.Y., 1993-99; counsel for N.Am., Westdeutsche Landesbank Girozentrale, 1999—. Mem. faculty Am. Inst. Banking, N.Y.C., 1984-88. Mem. ABA (mem. corp. bankig and bus. law com.), Assn. of Bar of City of N.Y. (mem. banking law com.), N.Y. State Bar Assn. (chair corp. counsel sect.), Assn. Comml. Fin. Attys. Avocations: photography, art history, English and French literature. Banking, Consumer commercial, General corporate. Office: Westdeutsche Landesbank Girozentrale 1211 Ave of Americas New York NY 10036-8701

COHEN, MARY ANN, judge; b. Albuquerque, July 16, 1943; d. Gus R. and Mary Carolyn (Avriette) C. BS, UCLA, 1964; JD, U. So. Calif., 1967. Bar: Calif. 1967. Ptnr. Abbott & Cohen, P.C. and predecessors, L.A., 1967-82; judge U.S. Tax Ct., Washington, 1982—, chief judge, 1996-2000. Mem. ABA (sect. taxation), Legion Lex. Republican. Office: US Tax Ct 400 2nd St NW Washington DC 20217-0002

COHEN, MELANIE ROVNER, lawyer; b. Chgo., Aug. 9, 1944; d. Millard Jack and Sheila (Fox) Rovner; m. Arthur Wieber Cohen, Feb. 17, 1968; children: Mitchell Jay, Jennifer Sue. AB, Brandeis U., 1965; JD, DePaul U., 1977. Bar: Ill. 1977, U.S. Dist. Ct. (no. dist.) Ill., U.S. Ct. Appeals (7th cir.). Law clk. to Justice F.J. Hertz U.S. Bankruptcy Ct., 1976-77; ptnr. Altheimer & Gray, Chgo., 1977-89, 89—, Antonow & Fink, Chgo., 1977-89. Mem. Supreme Ct. of Ill. Atty. Registration and Disciplinary Commn. Inquiry Bd., 1982-86, hearing bd., 1986-94; instr. secured and consumer transactions creditor-debtor law DePaul U., Chgo., 1980-90; bd. dirs. Bankruptcy Arbitration and Mediation Svcs., 1994-96; instr. real estate and bankruptcy law John Marshall Law Sch., Chgo., 1996-98. Contbr. articles to profl. jours. Panelist, spkr., bd. dirs., v.p., fellow Brandeis U. Nat. Alumni Assn., 1981—; life mem. Nat. Women's Com., 1975—, pres. Chgo. chpt., 1975-82; mem. Glencoe (Ill.) Caucus, 1977-80; chair lawyers com. Ravinia Festival, 1990-91, chmn. sustaining com., 1991, mem. annual fund, 1991—. Mem. ABA (co-chair com. on enforcement of creditors' rights and bankruptcy), Ill. State Bar Assn., Chgo. Bar Assn. (chmn. bankruptcy reorganization com. 1983-85), Comml. Law League, Ill. Trial Lawyers Assn., Comml. Fin. Assn. Edn. Found. (bd. govs.), Turnaround Mgmt. Assn. (pres. Chgo./midwest chpt. 1990-92, nat. bd. dirs. 1990—, mem. mgmt. com. 1995—, pres. internat. bd. dirs. 1999-2000, chmn. internat. bd. dirs. 2000—). Banking, Bankruptcy, Contracts commercial. Home: 167 Park Ave Glencoe IL 60022-1351 Office: Altheimer & Gray 10 S Wacker Dr Ste 4000 Chicago IL 60606-7407 E-mail: cohenm@altheimer.com

COHEN, MYRON, lawyer, educator; b. Paterson, N.J., Feb. 4, 1927; s. Jacob B. and Rose (Stone) C.; m. Nancy Kamin, Nov. 4, 1951 (div. 1960); m. Barbara Levitov, May 12, 1963; children: Peter Fredric, Lee Susan. BEE, Cornell U., 1948; LLB, Columbia U., 1951. Bar: N.Y. 1951, U.S. Dist. Ct. (so., ea. dists.) N.Y. 1955, U.S. Ct. Appeals (2nd cir.) 1960, U.S. Ct. Appeals (Fed. cir.) 1984, U.S. Supreme Ct. 1974. Staff atty. Union Switch and Signal, Swissvale, Pa., 1952-54; assoc. Levisohn, Niner & Cohen, N.Y.C., 1954-56; sr. ptnr. Hubbell, Cohen, Stiefel & Gross, 1956-85, Cohen, Pontani, Lieberman & Pavane, N.Y.C., 1985—. Adj. prof. N.Y. Law Sch., 1970—; vis. lectr. Peking U. Law Sch., 2000—; bd. dirs. Tri Magna Corp.; sec. Medallion Funding Corp., N.Y.C., 1979-86, 86-96. Author: U.S. Patent Law and Practice, 1976, Recent Developments in U.S. Law of Intellectual Property, 1985. Chmn. Mayor's Subway Watchdog Commn., N.Y.C., 1974-76. Lt. j.g. USNR, 1944-57. Mem. ABA, N.Y. State Bar Assn., Assn. Bar City N.Y., N.Y. Intellectual Property Law Assn., Internat. Trademark Assn. Democrat. Jewish. Avocation: skiing. Intellectual property, Patent, Trademark and copyright. Home: Two Fifth Ave New York NY 10011 Office: Cohen Pontani Lieberman & Pavane 551 5th Ave Rm 1210 New York NY 10176-0091 E-mail: myron@cplplaw.com

COHEN, N. JEROLD, lawyer; b. Pine Bluff, Ark., June 13, 1935; s. Maurice and Gertrude L. Cohen; children: Pamela, Lindsey L., Giles T. BBA, Tulane U., 1957; LLB magna cum laude, Harvard U., 1961. Bar: N.Y. 1962, Ga. 1966, D.C. 1966. Assoc. Cleary, Gottlieb, Steen and Hamilton, N.Y.C., 1961-65, Sutherland, Asbill, and Brennan, Atlanta, Washington, 1965, ptnr., 1968-79, 81—; chief counsel IRS, 1979-81, adv. coun., 1999-2000, chmn. Former pres., former mem. nat. bd. dirs. ACLU Ga.; chmn. Atlanta Cmty. Rels. Commn., 1976-79. 1st lt. U.S. Army, 1958. Recipient Gen. Counsel's award U.S. Dept. Treasury, Commrs. award IRS. Fellow Am. Bar Found.; mem. ABA (past chair tax sect.), FBA, Am. Law Inst., Am. Coll. Tax Counsel (regent, chair). Corporate taxation, Estate taxation, Personal income taxation. Office: Sutherland Asbill & Brennan 999 Peachtree St NE Ste 2300 Atlanta GA 30309-3996 E-mail: njcohen@sablaw.com

COHEN, NELSON CRAIG, lawyer; b. Harrisburg, Pa., Nov. 8, 1947; s. Raymond and Rhea (Jaschik) C. BS in Acctg., Pa. State U., 1969; JD, George Washington U., 1973. Bar: Md. 1973, D.C. 1974. Assoc., ptnr. Levitan Ezrin West & Kerxton, Bethesda, Md., 1973-84; ptnr. Kerxton & Cohen Chartered, 1984-87, Zuckerman & Spaeder LLP, Washington, 1987—. Speaker on bankruptcy matters. Mem. ABA (bus. banking sec.), Bankruptcy Bar Assn. Md., Montgomery County Bar Assn., Md. State Bar Assn. Republican. Jewish. Avocation: golf. Bankruptcy, Consumer commercial. Office: Zuckerman Spaeder LLP 1201 Connecticut Ave NW Washington DC 20036-2605

COHEN, NORTON JACOB, lawyer; b. Detroit, Nov. 5, 1935; s. Norman and Molly Rose (Natinsky) C.; m. Lorelei Freda Schuman, June 16, 1957 (dec. Jan. 1998); children: Debrah Anne, Sander Ivan. Student, U. Mich., 1953-55, U. Detroit, 1955-56; JD, Wayne State U., 1959. Bar: Mich. 1959, Tex. 1962, U.S. Dist. Ct. (so. dist.) Mich. 1963, U.S. Ct. Appeals (6th cir.) 1966, U.S. Supreme Ct. 1970. Law clk. to presiding justice Mich. Supreme Ct., Lansing, 1959; assoc. Zwerdling, Miller, Klimist & Maurer, Detroit, 1963-68; legal dir. ACLU of Mich., 1968-69; sr. dir. Miller, Cohen, Martens, Ice & Geary, P.C., Southfield, Mich., 1969-97, Miller Cohen, P.L.C., Detroit, 1997—. Chmn. Southfield (Mich.) Dem. Party, 1965-67; co-chair Robert F. Kennedy for Pres., Oakland County, Mich., 1968; mem. exec. bd. Met. Detroit ACLU, 1969-93, chmn., 1972-74; vice chair Equal Justice Coun., Detroit, 1970-74; spl. counsel workers compensation Mich. AFL-CIO, 1983-86; mem. dir.'s adv. coun. Workers Compensation Bur., Mich. Dept. Labor, 1986-1999. Served to capt. U.S. Army, 1960-63. Recipient Spirit of Detroit award Detroit Common Coun., 1982; elected to Mich. Workers' Compensation Hall of Fame, 2000. Mem. ABA (labor co-chair workers compensation com. sect. labor and employment law 1989-96), Fed. Bar Assn., B'nai B'rith. Jewish. Labor, Workers' compensation.

COHEN, RICHARD PAUL, lawyer; b. Bklyn., Nov. 18, 1945; s. Morris T. and Ida (Tepletsky) C.; m. Laura Diane Keller, July 4, 1968; 1 child, Adam Morris. BME, CCNY, 1968; JD, Fordham U., 1973. Bar: N.Y. 1974, W.Va. 1979, U.S. Ct. Appeals (2d cir.) 1974, U.S. Dist. Ct. (so. dist.) N.Y. 1974, U.S. Dist. Ct. (so. and no. dists.) W.Va. 1979, U.S. Ct. Appeals (fed. cir.) 1994, U.S. Supreme Ct. 1977, U.S. Ct. Vets Appeals 1993. Asst. counsel Waterfront Commn. N.Y. Harbor, N.Y.C., 1973-78; asst. atty. Westchester County Atty's. Office, White Plains, N.Y., 1977-78; asst. prosecutor Wetzel County Atty's. Office, New Martinsville, W.Va., 1980-82; pvt. practice law Hundred and Fairmont, 1979-83; ptnr. Cohen, Abate & Cohen, L.C., Fairmont, 1984—. Named One of Oustanding Young Men of Am., Outstanding Young Men of Am., 1981; recipient Meritorious Svc. award Am. Assn. Mental Dificiency, 1987. Mem. ABA, Nat. Assn. Soc. Sect. Claimants Rep, Nat. Assn. Vets. Advocates, W.Va. State Bar Assn. Consumer commercial, Pension, profit-sharing, and employee benefits, Workers' compensation. Home: 116 Lincoln Ave Morgantown WV 26501-6512 Office: Cohen Abate & Cohen LC 114 High St PO Box 846 Fairmont WV 26507-0846

COHEN, ROBERT, medical device manufacturing and marketing executive; b. Glen Cove, N.Y., Sept. 23, 1957; s. Alan and Selma (Grossman) C.; m. Nancy A. Arey, Jan. 17, 1981. BA, Bates Coll., 1979; JD, U. Maine, 1982. Bar: N.Y. 1983, U.S. Dist. Ct. (so. and ea.) N.Y. 1983. Atty. Pfizer Inc., N.Y.C., 1982-86; asst. corp. counsel, asst. sec. Pfizer Hosp. Products Group, Inc., 1986-88; v.p. bus. devel., dir. for med. device mfr. and marketer Deknatel Inc., Fall River, Mass., 1988-92; pres., CEO GCI Med., Braintree, 1992-93; v.p. bus. devel. Sulzermedica USA, Inc., Angleton, Tex., 1993-94, group v.p., 1994-98; v.p. bus. & tech. devel. St. Jude Med., Inc., St. Paul, 1998—; dir. Horizon Med. Products, Inc., Atlanta, 1998-2001, CardioFocus, Inc., Boston, 1999-2000. Bd. dirs. Horizon Med. Products, Inc. Author: 19th Century Maine Authors, 1978. Mem. ABA, Am. Corp. Counsel Assn. Republican. Home: 18683 Bearpath Trl Eden Prairie MN 55347-3476 Office: St Jude Med Inc One Lillehei Plz Saint Paul MN 55117 E-mail: rcohen@sjm.com

COHEN, ROBERT (AVRAM), lawyer; b. Pitts., July 23, 1929; s. Max R. and Mollie (Segal) C.; m. Frances H. Steiner, Dec. 24, 1951 (div. Feb. 1974); children: Deborah E., David R.; m. Mary E. Connors, Mar. 11, 1974; children: Deborah A., Charles E., Chrisann (dec.). AB magna cum laude, Harvard U., 1951, JD, 1954. Bar: Pa. 1955, Fla. 1974, U.S. Dist. Ct. (we. dist.) Pa. 1955, U.S. Dist. Ct. (so. dist.) Fla. 1974, U.S. Tax Ct. 1983, U.S. Ct. Appeals (3d cir.) 1961, U.S. Supreme Ct. 1962. Assoc. Goldstock, Schwartz, Teitelbaum & Schwartz, Pitts., 1955-60; ptnr. Goldstock, Schwartz, Cohen & Schwartz, 1960-67, Fine, Perlow, Stone & Cohen, Pitts., 1967-70, Cohen & Goldstock, Pitts., 1970-73; assoc. Herring, Evans & Fulton, West Palm Beach, Fla., 1974; from assoc. to ptnr. Rothman, Gordon, Foreman and Groudine, P.A., Pitts., 1974-86; sole practice, 1986-2000; atty. Behrend & Ernsberger, 2000—. Trustee Western Allegheny Cmty. Libr., 1989-91, pres., 1991-98; pres. County Libr. Assn. Serving the People, 1993-94; mem. Zoning Bd. Borough of Oakdale, 1991—. Mem. ABA, Assn. Trial Lawyers Am. (pres. western Pa. chpt. 1972-73), Pa. Bar Assn. (com. on ethics and profl. responsibility 1988—, com. on professionalism 1990-94, civil rights com. 1995-97), Acad. Trial Lawyers Allegheny County, Pa. Trial Lawyers Assn., Allegheny County Bar Assn. (civil litigation coun. 1988-90, continuing legal edn. 1977—, profl. ethics com. 1996—), Golden Triangle Lodge (v.p. 1966-69), B'nai B'rith. Democrat. Jewish. Federal civil litigation, State civil litigation, Personal injury. Home: 205 Oak Heights Dr Oakdale PA 15071-1137 Office: Behrend & Ernsberger 306 4th Ave Pittsburgh PA 15222-2000

COHEN, ROBERT STEPHAN, lawyer; b. N.Y.C., Jan. 14, 1939; s. Abraham and Florence C.; children: Christopher, Ian, Nicholas; m. Stephanie J. Stiefel, Jan. 29, 1998. BA, Alfred U., 1959; LLB, Fordham U., 1962. Bar: N.Y. 1963, U.S. Dist. Ct. (so. and ea. dists.) N.Y. 1964, U.S. Ct. Appeals (2d cir.) 1965. Assoc. Saxe, Bacon & O'Shea, N.Y.C., 1963-68; mng. ptnr., chmn. Morrison, Cohen Singer and Weinstein and predecessor firms, 1968—. Lectr. in field; mem. faculty Am Acad. Psychiatry and the Law, 1984—. Contbr. articles to legal jours. Bd. dirs. N.Y. Pops, 1983—. 1st lt. JAG, USAR, 1965-67. Fellow Am. Coll. Family Trial Lawyers; mem. ABA, FBA, ATLA, N.Y. State Bar Assn., N.Y.C. Bar Assn., N.Y. Acad. Matrimonial Lawyers, Univ. Club (N.Y.C.). Federal civil litigation, State civil litigation, Family and matrimonial. Office: 750 Lexington Ave New York NY 10022-1200

COHEN, RONALD J. lawyer; b. Englewood, N.J., Dec. 16, 1950; s. Irwin and Shirley (Kushel) C.; m. Jeanne K. Houser, June 22, 1981; children: Shay, Emily. BA, U. Fla., 1973; JD, U. Miami, 1976. Asst. city atty. City of Miami, 1979-83; assoc. Paul, Landy, Bailey & Harper, Miami, 1983-87; ptnr. Klausner & Cohen, PA, Hollywood, Fla., 1987-97; pvt. practice Ronald J. Cohen, PA, Miami, 1997—. Civil rights, Labor, Pension, profit-sharing, and employee benefits. Office: 8100 Oak Ln Ste 403 Miami Lakes FL 33016-7051

COHEN, SHELDON IRWIN, lawyer; b. Newark, July 25, 1937; BS in Ceramic Engring., AB in Humanities, Rutgers U., 1959; LLB, Georgetown U., 1964. Bar: Va. 1964, D.C. 1964, U.S. Ct. Appeals (D.C. and 4th cirs.) 1964, U.S. Supreme Ct. 1967. Assoc. Chapman, Disalle & Friedman, Washington, 1964-70; pvt. practice law Washington, Arlington, Va., 1970—. Author: Security Clearances and the Protection of National Security Information, Law and Procedure, 2000. Vice chmn. Arlington Dem. Com., 1968-70; mem. Va. Dem. Cen. Com., 1969-70. Capt. USAR, 1959-67. Mem. ABA (chmn. govt. pers. com. 1986-89, chmn. nat. security interests com. 1990-95), D.C. Bar Assn. (chmn. civil svc. law com. 1984-86). Democrat. Administrative and regulatory, Labor, Military. Office: 2009 14th St N Ste 708 Arlington VA 22201-2514 E-mail: sicohen@sheldoncohen.com

COHEN, STANLEY DALE, lawyer; b. Nassau County, N.Y., Mar. 14, 1952; s. Lester and Eleanor (Mait) C.; m. Janis Wendrow, Sept. 11, 1976; children: Adam Benjamin, Heather Jill. JD, Western New Eng. Coll., 1976. Bar: N.Y. 1977, D.C. 1980, Fla. 1981, U.S. Dist. Ct. (so. and ea. dists.) N.Y. 1977, D.C. 1980, Fla. 1981, U.S. Ct. Appeals (9th cir.) 1982. Mem. firm Ruben, Schwartz & Silverberg, N.Y.C., 1977-78; sole practice, N.Y.C., 1978-83; mem. firm Cohen & Jaeger, 1984—; sec., bd. dirs. Manhattan Mag. Found. Corp. Mem. steering com. Fed. Hall Bill of Rights Bicentennial. Mem. N.Y. County Lawyers Assn. Contracts commercial, General corporate, Real property. Home: 83 Peachtree Ln Roslyn Heights NY 11577-2415 Office: 250 Old Country Rd Mineola NY 11501-4299

COHEN, STEPHEN BRUCE, lawyer; b. East Chicago, Ind., Mar. 14, 1939; s. Cecil Bernard and Ida Edith (Goldstein) Cohen; m. Lynn Sneider, Mar. 23, 1969; children: Debra Suzanne, Aaron Eliot, Sabrina Beth. AB, Harvard Coll., 1961; JD, Vanderbilt U., 1964; LLB in Internat. Law, Cambridge (Eng.) U., 1966, Diploma in Internat. Law, 1972. Bar: Ind. 1965, Ill. 1965, U.S. Dist. Ct. (no. dist.) Ill. 1967, U.S. Dist. Ct. (no. and so. dists.) Ind. 1965, U.S. Ct. Appeals (7th cir.) 1968, U.S. Tax Ct. 1981, U.S. Claims Ct. 1990, U.S. Supreme Ct. 1972. Assoc. Cohe, Foss, Schuman & Drake and predecessor firms, East Chicago, Foss, Schuman, Drake & Barnard, Chgo., 1965-69, ptnr., 1969-86, Cohen, Starck & Burchett, Northbrook, Ill., East Chicago, 1986-87, Cohen, Starck & Weiner, Skokie, Ill., East Chicago, 1987-88; pvt. practice Law Offices of Stephen B. Cohen, P.C., Northbrook, 1988-94; ptnr. Cohen & Pinsel, 1995-99, Kelly, Olson, Michod & Siepker, 2000; mem. Kelly, Olson, Michod, DeHaan & Richter, L.L.C., 2000—. Mediator Cohen Mediation Svcs., 1995—; arbitrator Cook County Mandatory Arbitration Program, 1993—; lectr. in field. Bd. dirs. U.S. Speedskating Charitable Found. Named to E. Chgo. (Ind.) Sports Hall of Fame, 2001; recipient Svc. award, Ill. Park Recreation Assn., 1986, Hall of Fame award, Northbrook Park Dist., 1992. Mem.: Ill. Bar Assn. (mem. ADR coun. 1998—), Ind. Bar Assn., Chgo. Bar Assn. (chmn. condominium subcom. 1980—82, exec. com. real property law com. 1980—90), Lake County/Ind. Bar Assn. (grievance com. 1990—91), East Chgo./Ind. Bar Assn. (pres. 1993—95), U.S. Internat. Speedskating Assn. (pres.'s adv. bd. 1988—2000, chmn. legal com. 1990—93, spl. counsel 1998—2001). Jewish. Avocations: weight lifting, racquetball, bicycling, masters track and field, fishing, reading. Personal injury, Real property, Sports. Office: Kelly Olsen et al 181 W Madison St Ste 4800 Chicago IL 60602 also: 3609 Main St East Chicago IN 46312-2107 E-mail: scohen@komdr.com, lawcp@aol.com

COHILL, MAURICE BLANCHARD, JR. federal judge; b. Pitts., Nov. 26, 1929; s. Maurice Blanchard and Florence (Clarke) C.; m. Suzanne Miller, June 27, 1952 (dec. May 1986); children: Cynthia Cohill Plattner, Jonathan, Jennifer Cohill O'Connor, Victoria. AB, Princeton U., 1951; LLB, U. Pitts., 1956. Bar: Pa. 1957. Judge family div. Common Pleas Ct., Allegheny County, Pitts., 1965-76; judge U.S. Dist. Ct. Pa. (we. dist.), 1976-94, chief judge, 1985-92, sr. judge, 1994—. Bd. dirs. Pa. George Jr. Republic, Grove City; bd. visitors Grad. Sch. Social Work, U. Pitts.; chmn. bd. fellows Nat. Center for Juvenile Justice. Served to capt. USMCR, 1951-53. Mem. Am., Pa., Allegheny County bar assns., Nat. Council Juvenile Ct. Judges (v.p.), Pa. Council Juvenile Ct. Judges (past pres.), Pa. Conf. State Trial Judges, Phi Delta Phi. Republican. Presbyterian. Office: US Dist Ct US Courthouse 8th Fl Rm 3 7th and Grant Sts Pittsburgh PA 15219

COHN, ALBERT LINN, lawyer, educator; b. Paterson, N.J., June 18, 1928; s. David and Rose (Yolken) C.; m. Sylvia J. Jacoby, June 14, 1959; children: Melissa Lynn, Joshua Peter, Priscilla Betsy, Liza-Faith Michaelis, Thaddeus Augustus David. BS, Georgetown U., 1948; JD, Harvard U., 1951. Bar: D.C. 1951, N.J. 1954; cert. civil trial atty. Supreme Ct. N.J. Bd. Trial Atty. Cert. Assoc. David Cohn, Paterson, 1954-59; ptnr. David & Albert L. Cohn, 1959-66; sr. ptnr. Cohn & Lifland, Saddle Brook, N.J., 1967—; adj. prof. law Rutgers U., Newark, 1979—, Inst. Continuing Legal Edn., 1980, 82—, chmn. curriculum adv. com., 1984-85; vis. instr. Mass. Continuing Legal Edn., Nat. Inst. Trial Attys., Harvard Law Sch., 1981; trustee N.J. Inst. Continuing Legal Edn., 1991—, chair, 1993—; master Arthur T. Vanderbilt Inn Ct., 1988-90; master Morris Pashman Inn of Ct., 1990-98, mem. coordinating com., 1992-98, fellow, Am. Bar Foundation, 2000—. Contbr. articles to profl. jours. Pres. Temple Shomrei Emunah, 1968-70. Served 1st lt. USAF, 1951-53. Mem. ABA, Passaic County Bar Assn. (trustee 1978-86), Bergen County Bar Assn., N.J. State Bar Assn., Soc. Med. Jurisprudence, Trial Attys. of N.J., Million Dollar Advs. Forum, Saddle Brook C. of C. (past pres., trustee). Clubs: Harvard (N.Y.C.), pres. Harvard Law Sch. Assn. fo N.J., 1999—; Hamilton (Paterson). E-mail: alc@njlawfirm.com. General civil litigation, Family and matrimonial, Personal injury. Home: Llewellyn Park West Orange NJ 07052 Office: Cohn & Lifland 1 Park 80 Plz W Ste 6A Saddle Brook NJ 07663-5830

COHN, ANDREW HOWARD, lawyer; b. N.Y.C., Jan. 17, 1945; s. Maurice John and Margaret Ethel (Gordon) C.; m. Marcia Bliss Leavitt, July 10, 1977; children: Marisa Leavitt, David Herman. BA, U. Pa., 1966; AM, Harvard U., 1970, PhD, 1972; JD, Yale U., 1975. Bar: Mass. 1975, U.S. Dist. Ct. Mass. 1976, U.S. Ct. Appeals (1st cir.) 1976. Law clk. to presiding justice U.S. Ct. Appeals (1st cir.), Providence and Boston, 1975-76; assoc. Hill & Barlow, Boston, 1976-80; sr. ptnr. Hale and Dorr, 1980—. Chmn. exec. com. Hale and Dorr, 1990-91, real estate dept., 1991-97, energy group, 1992—; cons. for juvenile justice standards project ABA and Inst. for Judicial Adminstrn., N.Y.C., 1973-74; rsch. fellow MIT-Harvard U. Joint Ctr. for Urban Studies, Cambridge, Mass., 1969-71, Univ. Coll., Nairobi, Kenya, 1968. Contbr. articles to profl. jours.; note and project editor Yale Law Jour., New Haven, 1974-75. Advisor Newton (Mass.) Community SChs. Found., 1987-88. Named Law and Social Sci.

fellow Russell Sage Found., 1972-74. Mem. ABA (environ.controls com., bus. law sect.), Am. Coll. Real Estate Lawyers, Boston Bar Assn. (chmn. real estate sect. 95-97), Yale Law Sch. Assn. Mass. (treas. 1985-87). Democrat. Jewish. Environmental, Finance, Real property. Office: Hale and Dorr 60 State St Ste 25 Boston MA 02109-1816

COHN, AVERN LEVIN, district judge; b. Detroit, July 23, 1924; s. Irwin I. and Sadie (Levin) C.; m. Joyce Hochman, Dec. 30, 1954 (dec. Dec. 1989); m. Lois Pincus Cohn, June 1992; children: Sheldon, Leslie Cohn Magy, Thomas. Student, John Tarleton Agrl. Coll., 1943, Stanford U., 1944; J.D., U. Mich., 1949. Bar: Mich. 1949. Practiced in, Detroit, 1949-79; mem. firm Honigman Miller Schwartz & Cohn, 1961-79; sr. judge U.S. Dist. Ct., 1979—. Mem. Mich. Civil Rights Commn., 1972-75, chmn., 1974-75; Mem. Detroit Bd. Police Commrs., 1975-79, chmn., 1979; bd. govs. Jewish Welfare Fedn., Detroit, 1972—. Served with AUS, 1943-46. Mem. ABA, Mich. Bar Assn., Am. Law Inst.

COHN, NATHAN, lawyer; b. Charleston, S.C., Jan. 20, 1918; s. Samuel and Rose (Baron) C.; 1 child, Norman; m. Carolyn Venturini, May 18, 1970. JD, San Francisco Law Sch., 1947. BAr: Calif. 1947, U.S. Supreme Ct. 1957. Pvt. practice law, San Francisco, 1947—. Judge pro tem Mcpl. Ct., Superior Ct. Columnist, San Francisco Progress, 1982-86; contr. and author seminars in field. Mem. Calif. State Recreation Commn., 1965-68; former mem. Dem. State Ctrl. Com. Served to 1st lt. USAF, 1950-55. Named to San Francisco Law Sch. Hall of Fame, 2000. Fellow Am. Bd. Criminal Lawyers (founder, past pres.), Am. Bd. Trial Advs. (diplomate; chpt. pres. 1984), Internat. Acad. Law and Sci., San Francisco Trial Lawyers (past pres., Lifetime Achievement award 2000), Criminal Trial Lawyers Assn. No. Calif., Irish-Israeli-Italian Soc. (co-founder, co-pres.), Internat. Footprinters Assn., Regular Vets. Assn., Calamari Club, Godfathers Club (past pres.), Press Club (life), Masons (32 deg.), Shriners, South of Market Boys (past pres.), Ancient Order Hibernians Am. (hon. life). Jewish. Criminal, General practice, Personal injury. Office: 2107 Van Ness Ave Ste 200 San Francisco CA 94109-2596

COKER, HOWARD C. lawyer; b. Jacksonville, Fla., Apr. 30, 1947; B in Journalism, U. Fla., 1969, JD, 1971. Bar: Fla. 1972. Asst. state atty. Fourth Jud. Cir., 1972; assoc. Howell, Kirby, Montgomery, D'Aiuto & Dean, P.A., 1973-76; pres., dir. Coker, Myers, Schickel, Sorenson, Higginbotham, & Green, Jacksonville, Fla., 1976—. Guest lectr. more than 40 CLE seminars on litig. and trial matters throughout Fla., for Fla. Bar Assn., Acad. Fla. Trial Lawyers; advisor mock trial team U. Fla. Law Sch., 1991-98; adj. prof. U. North Fla. Chair ednl. adv. coun. U. North Fla., 1992-94, chair adv. bd. for paralegals, 1990-92. Fellow Am. Bar Found., Internat. Soc. Barristers; mem. ABA, ATLA, Am. Arbitration Assn. (panel arbitrators 1983—), Fla. Bar Assn. (pres. 1998-99, bd. govs. 1994-99, exec. com. 1995-97, all bar fconf. del. 1990-92, 94, 96, 97, budget com. 1995-97, bd. rev. coml. on profl. ethics chair 1995-96, disciplinary rev. com. 1994-95, jud. qualification screen com. 1994-95, legis. com. 1994-95, profl. retreat chair 1996, program evaluation com. chair 1996-97, 4th jud. cir. grievance com. reviewer 1994-97, coun. sects. 1991-94, chair 1993-94, sect. leadership conf. chair 1995, trial lawyers sect. exec. coun. 1987-94, bd. govs. liaison 1996, chair 1992-93, exec. co. 1989-93, legis. com. 1988-93), Am. Bd. Trial Advocates (pres. Jacksonville chpt. 1988—, media rep. 1988, exec. com. 1988—, diplomate), Am. Judicature Soc., Chester Bedell Meml. Found. (trustee 1996-2001), First Coast Trial Lawyers Assn., Acad. Fla. Trial Lawyers (bd. dirs. 1995—, treas. 2000-2001, Eagle sponsor 1990—), Fla. Lawyers Assn. for Maintenance of Excellence (bd. dirs. 1995-97), So. Trial Lawyers, Nat. Conf. Bar Presidents, Fla. Supreme Ct. Hist. Soc., Jacksonville Bar Assn., Roscoe Pound Found., U.S. Supreme Ct. Hist. Soc., Fla. Conservation Assn. (pres. 1993-94), Fla. Ducks Unltd. (Sportsman of Yr. 1994), Fla. Wildlife Fedn., Seminole Club (bd. dirs. 1988, pres., 1989), U. Fla. Nat. Alumni Assn. (pres.'s coun. 1992-2001), Sigma Alpha Epsilon, Phi Delta Phi. General civil litigation, Consumer commercial, Personal injury. Office: PO Box 1860 136 E Bay St Jacksonville FL 32201 E-mail: hcoker@cokerlaw.com

COLAGIOVANNI, JOSEPH ALFRED, JR. lawyer; b. Providence, Dec. 26, 1956; s. Joseph Alfred Sr. and Rosemarie (Giordano) C.; m. Mary Jo Gagliardo, Aug. 9, 1980. AB in Polit. Sci. and Philosophy, Brown U., 1979; JD, Boston U., 1982. Bar: Mo. 1982, U.S. Dist. Ct. (ea. and we. dists.) Mo. 1982, U.S. Ct. Appeals (7th cir.) 1992. Asst. atty. gen. State of Mo., Jefferson City, 1982-84; ptnr., co-leader constrn. group Bryan, Cave, St. Louis, 1984—. Adj. prof. of law Wash. U. Sch. of Law, 1997—; hon. vice consul of Italy, 1997—. Mem. ABA, Mo. Bar Assn., Noonday Club. Avocations: tennis, music, collecting matchbooks. Construction. Office: Bryan Cave 211 N Broadway Ste 3600 Saint Louis MO 63102-2733 E-mail: jcolagiovanni@bryancave.com

COLBURN, STUART DALE, lawyer; b. Houston, July 3, 1969; s. Roy Dale and Sonda Gail (Peacock) C. BA cum laude, Southwestern U., 1991; JD, U. Tex., 1994. Bar: Tex. 1994. Mgr. hearings sect. Harris & Harris, Austin, 1994—. Recipient John Engalitcheff Jr. Outstanding Young Am. award Inst. Comparative Polit. and Econ. Sys., Georgetown U., 1989. Mem. Travis County Bar Assn., Def. Rsch. Inst., Am. Trial Lawyers Assn., Austin Young Lawyers Assn. (chmn. law related edn. for children com. 1996-98). Avocations: boating, golfing. Administrative and regulatory, State civil litigation, Workers' compensation. Office: Harris & Harris Ste 200 5300 Bee Caves Rd Bldg Iii Austin TX 78746-5225 E-mail: stuartcolburn@yahoo.com, stuart@harriswc.com

COLBY, WILLIAM MICHAEL, lawyer; b. Pontiac, Mich., Jan. 24, 1942; s. Orville Edgar and Jeannette (Nadon) C.; m. Brenda Schneckenburger, Nov. 28, 1964; children: Kathleen C. Scott, Thomas Brownell. AB, U. Mich., 1963, JD, 1966. Bar: N.Y. 1966, U.S. Tax Ct. 1969, U.S. Supreme Ct. 1972, Fla. 1982. Assoc. Harter, Secrest & Emery, Rochester, N.Y., 1966-74, ptnr., 1975-99, counsel, 2000—. Cons. various tax pubs. Contbr. articles to profl. jours.; editor various tax publs. Bd. dirs., hon. mem. Rochester Mus. and Sci. Ctr.; chmn. bd. dirs. Genesee Cmty. Charter Sch. Fellow Am. Bar Found.; mem. Monroe County Bar Found. (pres. 1980-81), Oak Hill Country Club. Avocations: golf, tennis, wine tasting, collecting ancient Greek coins, travel. Estate planning, Pension, profit-sharing, and employee benefits, Taxation, general. Home: 39 Granite Dr Penfield NY 14526-2851 Office: Harter Secrest & Emery 700 Midtown Tower Rochester NY 14604-2006 E-mail: bill@rochester.rr.com, colbyw@hselaw.com

COLDREN, IRA BURDETTE, JR. lawyer; b. Uniontown, Pa., June 15, 1924; s. Ira Burdette and Eleanor Clarke (Lincoln) C.; m. Phyllis Miles, Sept. 7 (div. Oct. 1970); children: Kathy, Lee Ellen, Janice, David; m. Frances Thomas, Aug. 27, 1971. BS, U.S. Mil. Acad., 1945; LLB, U. Pa., 1952; LLM in Estate Planning, U. Miami, 1982. Bar: Pa. 1952, U.S. Dist. Ct. (we. dist.) Pa. 1953, U.S. Ct. Appeals (3d cir.) 1983. Commd. 2d lt. U.S. Army, 1945, advanced through grades to lt. col., 1952, ret., 1956; assoc. Ray, Coldren & Buck, Uniontown, Pa., 1956-59; ptnr. Coldren & Coldren, 1959-62, Coldren & Adams, Uniontown, 1962-75, Coldren, DeHaas & Radcliffe, Uniontown, 1983-92, Coldren Adams, Uniontown, 1992—. Pres. Greater Uniontown United Fund, 1962, Fayette County Devel. Council, 1971-75. Fellow Am. Bar Found., Am. Coll. Trust and Estate Counsel; mem. Pa. Bar Assn. (ho. of dels. 1976-79, bd. govs. 1979-82, v.p. 1985-86, pres. 1986-87), Pa. Bar Inst. (pres. 1982-83), Fayette County Bar Assn. (pres. 1983), Am. Law Inst., Am. Judicature Soc., Internat. Assn. Ins. Counsel, Pa. Jaycees (pres. 1959), Club: Uniontown Country (pres. 1969-71). Lodges: Rotary (pres. Uniontown club 1964), Masons (master 1964, 69, mem. Scottish Rite Supreme Coun. 1991—). Democrat. Presbyterian. General corporate, Probate, Taxation, general. Home: 117 Belmont Cir Uniontown PA 15401-4759 Office: Coldren Adams 2 Main St Ste 700 Uniontown PA 15401 E-mail: CALawFirm@aol.com

COLE, CHARLES DEWEY, JR. lawyer; b. Lower Merion Twp., Pa., Aug. 12, 1952; s. Charles Dewey and Margaret Ann (Leach) C. AB, Columbia U., 1974; JD, St. John's U., Jamaica, N.Y., 1979; ML Info. Sci., U. Tex., 1982; LLM, NYU, 1988; LLM in Environ. Law, Pace U., 1993; LLM in Trial Advocacy, Temple U., 1999. Bar: N.Y. 1980, Tex. 1980, N.J. 1986, D.C. 1988, U.S. Dist. Ct. (we. and ea. dists.) Tex. 1980, U.S. Dist. Ct. (so. and ea. dists.) N.Y. 1980, U.S. Dist. Ct. (no. dist.) Tex. 1982, U.S. Dist. Ct. (no. dist.) N.Y. 1983, U.S. Dist. Ct. (we. dist.) N.Y. 1984, U.S. Dist. Ct. N.J. 1986, U.S. Dist. Ct. D.C. 1994, U.S. Ct. Internat. Trade 1980, U.S. Tax Ct. 1984, U.S. Ct. Appeals (5th and 11th cirs.) 1981, U.S. Ct. Appeals (Fed. cir.) 1982, U.S. Ct. Appeals (2d cir.) 1984, U.S. Ct. Appeals (D.C. cir.) 1987, U.S. Ct. Appeals (3d cir.) 1993, U.S. Supreme Ct. 1984; solicitor, Eng. and Wales, 1995. Law clk. to chief judge U.S. Dist. Ct. (ea. dist.), Beaumont, Tex., 1979-80, U.S. Ct. Appeals (5th cir.), Austin, 1981-82; assoc. Moore, Berson, Lifflander & Mewhinney, Garden City and N.Y.C., N.Y., 1982-85; assoc. and ptnr. Newman Schlau Fitch & Burns P.C., N.Y.C. and Mineola, 1985-88; assoc. Meyer, Suozzi, English & Klein, P.C., Mineola and N.Y.C., 1988-95; of counsel Newman Fitch Altheim Myers, P.C., N.Y.C. and Newark, 1995—. Instr. trial techniques program Hofstra Law Sch., 1994-2000; instr. intensive trial advocacy program Widener Law Sch., 1999—. Author: Law Books as a Charitable Contribution, 1975, The EPA Lender Liability Regulations: EPA's Questionable Authority to Promulgate the Regulations as Part of the National Contingency Plan, 1993; contbr. book revs. to profl. publs. Mem. The Law Soc., N.Y. State Bar Assn. (exec. and appellate practice coms. comml. and fed. litigation sect.), N.J. State Bar Assn., D.C. Bar, State Bar Tex., Assn. of Bar of City of N.Y., N.Y. County Lawyers Assn. (com. on fed. cts.), Maritime Law Assn. U.S. (proctor), Fed. Bar Coun., Bar Assn. 5th Fed. Cir., Am. Assn. Law Librs., Law Libr. Assn. Greater N.Y., Brit. and Irish Assn. Law Librs., Osgoode Soc., Am. Soc. for Legal History, Soc. Advanced Legal Studies, Supreme Ct. Hist. Soc., Selden Soc., Federalist Soc. for Law and Pub. Policy, Scribes (dir., chair brief-writing competition com.), Clarity. Republican. Appellate, Federal civil litigation, State civil litigation. Home: 16 94th St Apt 3B Brooklyn NY 11209-6643 Office: Newman Fitch Altheim Myers PC 14 Wall St New York NY 10005-2101 E-mail: dcole@nfam.com, cdc27@columbia.edu

COLE, GEORGE THOMAS, lawyer; b. Orlando, Fla., Mar. 14, 1946; s. Robert Bates and Frances (Arnold) C.; m. Peggy Ellen Stimson, May 23, 1981; children: Leslie Elizabeth, Ashley Ellen, Robert Warren. AB, Yale U., 1968; JD, U. Mich., 1975. Bar: Ariz. 1975, U.S. Dist. Ct. Ariz. 1975, U.S. Ct. Appeals (9th cir.) 1978; cert. real estate specialist Ariz. Bar. With Fennemore, Craig, von Ammon, Udall & Powers, Phoenix, 1975-81; ptnr. Fennemore Craig, P.C., 1981—. Mem. Ariz. State U. Coun. for Design Excellence. Served to lt. (j.g.) USN, 1968-71. Fellow Ariz. Bar Found. (founding); mem. Nat. and Ariz. Assns. Home Builders, Urban Land Inst. (cmty. devel. coun.), Community Assns. Inst., Nat. Golf Found (assoc.), Ariz. Bar Assn. (council Real Property sect. 1985-88, chmn. 1987-88), Maricopa Bar Assn., Yale Club (pres. 1984), Paradise Valley Country Club (Phoenix), White Mountain Country Club (Pinetop, Ariz.). Republican. Methodist. Real property. Home: 5102 E Desert Park Ln Paradise Valley AZ 85253-3054 Office: Fennemore Craig 3003 N Central Ave Ste 2600 Phoenix AZ 85012-2913 E-mail: gcole@fclaw.com

COLE, JAMES OTIS, lawyer; b. Florence, Ala., Feb. 6, 1941; s. Calloway and Eula (Reynolds) C.; m. Ada Dolores Cole, Dec. 16, 1961; children: James Otis Jr., Lerone Barrington. BA, Talladega Coll., 1963; JD, Harvard U., 1971. Bar: Ill. 1971, U.S. Dist. Ct. (no. dist.) Ill. 1971, Calif. 1977, U.S. Supreme Ct. 1981. Assoc. Kirkland & Ellis, Chgo., 1971-73; div. counsel The Clorox Co., Oakland, Calif., 1973—; now sr. v.p., gen. counsel, sec. AutoNation, Inc., Ft. Lauderdale. Arbitrator Contra Costa County Superior Ct., Martinez, Calif., 1980—. Counsel East Oakland Youth Devel. Ctr.; bd. dirs. Oakland Ballet, Bay Area Urban League, Oakland; bd. dirs. Black Filmmakers Hall of Fame, Oakland, pres. 1980-83. Mem. ABA, Nat. Bar Assn. (bd. govs. 1981—), Calif. Assn. Black Lawyers (pres.-elect 1986—), Charles Houston Bar Assn. (pres. 1985—), Calif. Bar Jud. Nominees Evaluation Commn. (commr. 1985—). Clubs: Oakland Athletic, Lakeview (Oakland). General corporate. Home: 10 Nurmi Dr Fort Lauderdale FL 33301-1403 Office: AutoNation Inc AutoNation Tower 110 SE 6th St Fort Lauderdale FL 33301-5000

COLE, JAMES YEAGER, foundation executive; b. Cleve., Sept. 20, 1957; s. Charles and Nancy C. JD, Blackstone Sch. Law, Dallas, 1980, U. N.C., 1989; MA, M.C.I., London, 1981; PhD, N.W. London U., 1981. CEO Cole Corp., Tallahassee, 1979-81; judge Inst. Advanced Law Study, Las Vegas, 1981-84; cons., sentencing advocate Cullowhee, N.C., 1984-2001. Recipient Presdl. medal of Merit Pres. Ronald Reagan, Washington, 1980; Knight Comdr. Royal Knights of Justice, London, 1981; Venerable Order of the Knights of Michael the Archangel Knight Chevalier, Disting. Leadership award ABA Jud. Divsn., 1997; lifetime dep. gov. Am. Biog. Rsch. Inst. Mem. Am. Judges Assn., World Judges Assn., Nat. Judges Assn., Internat. Bar Assn., Human Rights Inst., Island Found., Am. Fedn. of Police, Heirs, Inc., Nat. Sheriff's Assn., N.C. Sheriff's Assn., Haywood County C. of C., Maggie Valley C. of C., N.C. Fraternal Order of Police. Avocations: swimming, snow/water skiing, volleyball, tennis, cinema. Home and Office: PO Box 25 Chestnut Walk Waynesville NC 28786-0025 E-mail: drkanglf@bellsouth.net

COLE, JANICE MCKENZIE, former prosecutor; b. Feb. 16, 1947; m. James Carlton Cole. BA summa cum laude, John Jay Coll Criminal Justice, 1975, MPA, 1978; JD, Fordham U., 1979. Bar: N.Y. 1980, N.C. 1983. Asst. U.S. atty. Eastern Dist. N.Y., 1979-83; sole practitioner, 1983-89; with firm Cole & Cole, 1989-90; dist. ct. judge First Jud. Dist. N.C., 1990-94; U.S. atty. N.C. Eastern Dist., 1994—2001; sole practitioner, 2001—. Office: Ste 106 1034 Harvey Point Rd Hertford NC 27944-1461

COLE, PHILLIP ALLEN, lawyer; b. Washington, Mar. 3, 1940; s. Gordon Harding and Dorothy Barbara (Jugel) C.; m. Mary Jo Ruff, July 2, 1994; children: Jennifer Leigh, Christopher Harding, Catherine Anne. BA, U. Md., 1961; JD, Georgetown U., 1964. Bar: Md. 1964, Minn. 1968, U.S. Supreme Ct. 1967, U.S. Ct. Appeals (8th cir.) 1968, U.S. Dist. Ct. Minn. 1965, U.S. Ct. Mil. Appeals 1965; cert. civil trial specialist. Assoc. Beatty & McNamee, Hyattville, Md., 1968; founder, sr. mem. Lommen, Nelson, Cole & Stageberg, Mpls., 1969—. Spl. counsel Md. Ho. of Dels., 1968. Contbr. articles to profl. jours. Capt. USMC, 1965-67. Mem. Minn. Def. Lawyers, Am. Bd. Profl. Liability Attys., Internat. Assn. Def. Counsel. Avocations: golf, reading. General civil litigation, Professional liability, Securities. Office: Lommen Nelson Cole & Stageberg 1800 IDS Ctr Minneapolis MN 55402 E-mail: phil@lommen.com

COLE, RANSEY GUY, JR. judge; b. Birmingham, Ala., May 23, 1951; s. Ransey Guy and Sarah Nell (Coker) C.; m. Kathleine Kelley, Nov. 26, 1983; children: Justin Robert Jefferson, Jordan Paul, Alexandra Sarah. BA, Tufts U., 1972; JD, Yale U., 1975. Bar: Ohio 1975, D.C. 1982. Assoc. Vorys, Sater, Seymour and Pease, Columbus, Ohio, 1975-78, ptnr., 1980-87, 93—; trial atty. U.S. Dept. Justice, Washington, 1978-80; judge U.S. Bankruptcy Ct., Columbus, 1987-93; circuit judge U.S. Ct. Appeals (6th cir.) Ohio, Cinn., 1996—. Mem. ABA, Nat. Bar Assn., Columbus Bar Assn. Office: US Courthouse 85 Marconi BlvdRm 127 Columbus OH 43215-2823*

COLE, RICHARD A. lawyer; b. Syracuse, N.Y., Feb. 21, 1951; s. Victor and Marie (Pogacar) C.; m. Lois Hallonquist, Sept. 27, 1975. AB, Brown U., 1973; JD, Cornell U., 1976. Bar: Ill. 1976, U.S. Dist. Ct. (no. dist.) Ill. 1976. Assoc. Mayer, Brown & Platt, Chgo., 1976-82, ptnr., 1983—. Trustee U. Notre Dame, London, 1981—. Avocation: travel. Banking, General corporate, Private international. Home: 29 Beverley Rd London SW 13 England Office: Mayer Brown & Platt 3 Queen Victoria St London EC4 England

COLE, ROLAND JAY, lawyer; b. Seattle, Dec. 15, 1948; s. Robert J. and Josephine F. C.; m. Elsa Kircher, Aug. 16, 1975; children: Isabel Ashley, Madeline Aldis. AB in Econs. magna cum laude, Harvard U., 1970, M in Pub. Policy, 1972, PhD in Pub. Policy, JD, 1975. Bar: Wash. 1975, U.S. Supreme Ct. 1980, U.S. Dist. Ct. (we. dist.) Wash. 1984, Mich. 1989. Rsch. scientist Battelle Human Affairs Rsch. Ctrs., Seattle, 1975-83; assoc. Appel and Glueck, P.C., 1984-89; gen. counsel Indsl. Tech. Inst., Ann Arbor, Mich., 1990-94; founder, exec. dir. Software Patent Inst., Indpls., 1994—; of counsel Shughart Thomson & Kilroy PC, Overland Park, Kans., 1997-2000, Barnes & Thornburg, Indpls., 2000—. Founder, dir. MIS. Co-author: Government Requirements of Small Business, 1980, The Containment of Organized Crime, 1984; co-programmer Quadrant I software program, 1983. HUD fellow, 1970-71. Mem. Assn. Personal Computer User Groups (dir., founding pres. 1986), Wash. Athletic Club. Congregationalist. Avocations: squash, racquetball, volleyball, music. Computer, Non-profit and tax-exempt organizations, Trademark and copyright. Office: Barnes & Thornburg 11 S Meridian St Indianapolis IN 46204-3535 E-mail: rcole@btlaw.com

COLE, SEAN ANDREW BURKE, lawyer; b. Oakwood, Va., Apr. 29, 1971; s. Ronald Franklin and Sandra C. BA in History cum laude, King Coll., 1994; JD, Wake Forest U. Sch. of Law, 1997. Bar: N.C. 1997, U.S. Dist. Ct. (ea. dist.) N.C. 1997. Assoc. Patterson, Dilthey, Clay & Bryson, LLP, Raleigh, N.C., 1997—. Vol. advocate Project Together/Interact, Raleigh, N.C., 1997—. Recipient Eagle Scout Boy Scouts Am., 1989. Mem. ABA, Def. Rsch. Inst., N.C. Assn. of Def. Attys., N.C. Bar Assn., Order of Barristers (bd. govs. 1997). Presbyterian. Avocations: golf, chess, music. General civil litigation, Insurance, Professional liability. Office: Patterson Dilthey Clay & Bryson Ste 550 4020 West Chase Blvd Raleigh NC 27607

COLEMAN, JAMES H., JR. state supreme court justice; b. Lawrenceville, N.J., May 4, 1933; s. James H. Sr. and Neda (Rivers) C.; m. Sophia Coleman, May 12, 1962; 2 children. BA cum laude, Va. State U., 1956; JD, Howard U., 1959. Bar: N.J. 1960, U.S. Dist. Ct. N.J. 1960, U.S. Supreme Ct. 1963. Asst. and/or cons. various N.J. commns. and divs., 1960-64; pvt. practice law Elizabeth and Roselle, N.J., 1960-70; judge N.J. Workers' Compensation Ct., 1964-73, Union County Ct., 1973-78, Law div. N.J. Superior Ct., 1978-81; mem. spl. three-judge resentencing panel N.J. Superior Ct., 1979-81; judge Appellate div. N.J. Superior Ct., 1981-87, presiding judge, 1987-94; assoc. justice Supreme Ct. of N.J., Springfield, 1994—. Mem. various Supreme Ct. coms.; lectr. in field. Chmn. Elizabeth Good Neighbor Coun.; mem. Elizabeth Adv. Bd. on Urban Renewal; incorporator, bd. dirs. Union County Legal Svcs., Elizabeth Anti-Poverty Program; v.p., bd. dirs., counsel to Urban League of Union County; counsel to Elizabeth NAACP; v.p. Scotch Plains-Fanwood Human Rights Coun.; Mem. N.J. Com. on Hiring the Handicapped; mem. Union County Coordinating and Adv. Com. on Higher Edn.;mem. Essex County Coll. Equal Edn. Opportunity Fund Bd., others. Fellow ABA; mem. Nat. Bar Assn. (judicial coun.), N.J. Bar Assn., Union County Bar Assn., Am. Law Inst., Am. Judicature Soc., Garden State Bar Assn., Omega Psi Phi. Baptist. Avocations: tennis, gardening. Office: Supreme Ct of NJ 99 Mount Bethel Rd Warren NJ 07059-5126

COLEMAN, JAMES JULIAN, lawyer; b. New Orleans, May 5, 1915; s. William Ballin and Millie (Davis) C.; m. Dorothy Louise Jurisich, July 30, 1940; children: James Julian, Thomas Blaise, Peter Dee, Dian Judith. B.A., Tulane U., 1934, J.D., 1937; LL.D. (hon.), Hampden-Sydney Coll., 1982. Bar: La. 1937. Sr. ptnr. Coleman, Johnson, Artigues & Jurisich, New Orleans. Past pres. Internat. Trade Mart, New Orleans Philharmonic Symphony; hon. consul gen. Republic of Korea; vice-chmn. La. Jud. Compensation Commn. Past pres. New Orleans C. of C., Jr. Achievement New Orleans, Adult Edn. Ctr.; past bd. dirs. U.S. C. of C., Internat. House, Fed. Rels. Assn.; past chmn. New Orleans coordinating com. NASA; founder Peoples League; trustee emeritus Principia Coll.; past chmn. Tulane U. Bus. Sch. Coun.; chmn. bd. trustees Crimestoppers. Decorated Order of Oranje-Nassau Diplomatic Service Merit Republic Korea; recipient Nat. Achievement award Jr. Achievement, Loving Cup award New Orleans Times-Picayune, 1980, Joseph W. Simon, Jr. award, 1981, Disting. Alumnus award Tulane U., 1982, New Orleans Activist award, 1984, C. Alvin Bertel award, 1985; named to Bus. Hall of Fame, 1984; named Pres. Emeritus, World Trade Ctr., N.Y.C., Chmn. Emeritus, The City Energy Club, Humanitarian of Yr. ARC, 2000; recipient Benemerenti Papal Honor, 1989. Mem. ABA, Internat. Bar Assn., La. Bar Assn., New Orleans Bar Assn., Am. Judicature Soc. (past dir.), Beta Gamma Sigma (hon.) Christian Scientist (1st reader 1953-56). General practice, Probate, Real property. Home: 10 Audubon Pl New Orleans LA 70118-5526 Office: 321 Saint Charles Ave New Orleans LA 70130-3145

COLEMAN, JEROME P. lawyer; b. Washington, July 3, 1948; s. Francis Thomas and Helen Theresa (Hile) C. AB, Princeton U., 1970; JD, Georgetown U., 1973. Bar: D.C. 1973, N.Y. 1976, U.S. Dist. Ct. (so. and ea. dists.) N.Y. 1976, U.S. Ct. Appeals (2d cir.) 1976, U.S. Ct. Appeals (3d cir.) 1978, U.S. Supreme Ct. 1988. Atty., advisor Nat. Labor Rels. Bd., Washington, 1973-74; assoc. Townley & Updike, N.Y.C., 1974-81, ptnr., 1982-95, Nixon Peabody LLP, N.Y.C., 1995—. Steering com. Inner-City Schs. Laywers Com., N.Y.C., 1993—; mem. exec. com. Princeton Class of 1970, 1991-95, chmn. bd. govs., 1995-2000, co-chmn., 1998—, pres. 2000—. Mem. ABA, Federal Bar Assn. (chmn. labor law com. 1978-82), N.Y. State Bar Assn.(chmn. labor arbitration com. 1983-86), Univ. Club (governing coun. 1991-95, sec. 1996-99, v.p. 1999-2000, pres. 2000—). Federal civil litigation, Labor. Home: 124 E 84th St Apt 8B New York NY 10028-0917 Office: Nixon & Peabody LLP 437 Madison Ave New York NY 10022-7001

COLEMAN, JOHN MICHAEL, lawyer, consumer products executive; b. Boston, Dec. 28, 1949; s. John Royston Coleman and Mary Norrington Irwin; m. Susan Lee Lavine, Oct. 29, 1978; children: William L., Anne H. L. BA, Haverford (Pa.) Coll., 1975; JD, U. Chgo., 1978. Bar: N.Y. 1978, Pa. 1979, U.S. Ct. Appeals (3rd and 4th cirs.) 1979, U.S. Dist. Ct. (ea. dist.) Pa. 1979, U.S. Dist. Ct. (so. dist.) N.Y. 1981, U.S. Supreme Ct., 1982, N.J. 1988. Law clk. to judge U.S. Ct. Appeals, Richmond, Va., 1978-79; law clk. to chief justice Warren Burger U.S. Supreme Ct., Washington, 1980-81; assoc. Dechert Price & Rhoads, Phila., 1981-86, ptnr., 1986-89; v.p., gen. counsel Campbell Soup Co., Camden, N.J., 1989-90, sr. v.p. law and pub. affairs, 1990-97; sr. v.p., gen. counsel The Gillette Co., Boston, 1997-99; mng. dir., CEO, Cambridge (Mass.) Capital Ptnrs. LLP, 1999-2000, chmn., CEO, 2000—. Adj. prof. law U. Pa., Phila., 1985-88; bd. dirs. CDI Corp. Contbr. articles to profl. jours. Chmn. bd. trustees Campbell Soup Found., 1990-97; trustee N.J. State Aquarium, 1991-94, Food and Drug Law Inst., 1991-98, Inst. for Law and Econs., 1993-97, Am. Judicature Soc., 1995—; mem. vis. com. U. Chgo. Law Sch., 1993-95; mem. corp. Haverford Coll., 1994—; bd. dirs. The Guidance Ctr., treas., 2000—. Mem. Am. Law Inst., Order of the Coif, Phi Beta Kappa. Mem. Religious Soc. of Friends. General corporate.

COLEMAN, RICHARD WILLIAM, lawyer; b. Brookline, Mass., Dec. 9, 1935; s. Michael John and Mary Ellen (Motherway) C.; m. Mary M. Kilcommins, June 3, 1961; children: Lauren, Christopher. BS, Boston Coll., Newton, Mass., 1957; JD, Boston Coll., Brighton, Mass., 1960. Bar: Mass. 1960, U.S. Dist. Ct. Mass. 1961, U.S. Ct. Appeals (1st cir.) 1981. Field atty. NLRB, Newark, 1960-61; assoc. Segal & Flamm, Boston, 1961-69; labor rels. advisor Scott Paper Co., Phila., 1969-70; labor rels. mgr. Harvard U., Cambridge, Mass., 1970-72; ptnr. Segal, Roitman & Coleman, Boston, 1972-93; pres. Richard W. Coleman, P.C., Needham, 1994—. Contbg. editor Development of Law Under National Labor Relations Act, 1988. Bd. dirs. Little Bros. of St. Francis, 1998—. Recipient Cushing award Cath. Labor Guild Boston, 1976. Mem. ABA, Am. Prepaid Legal Svcs. Inst. (bd. dirs. 1997—), Indsl. Rels. Rsch. Assn., Mass. Bar Assn., Boston Bar Assn., AFL-CIO Lawyers Coord. Com. Democrat. Roman Catholic. Avocations: golf, reading, choir singing. Labor, Pension, profit-sharing, and employee benefits. Office: 214 Garden St Needham MA 02492-2398 E-mail: rcolegolf@aol.com

COLEMAN, ROBERT J. lawyer; b. Phila., Dec. 24, 1936; s. Francis Eugene and Mary Veronica (McCullough) C.; m. Mary Patricia Coleman, June 26, 1955; children: Debra, Robert P., Linda, Martin S. AB, Villanova U., 1959; JD, Temple U., 1964. Bar: Pa., U.S. Dist. Ct. (ea. dist.) Pa., U.S. Ct. Appeals (3d cir.), U.S. Supreme Ct. With First Pa. Bank, Phila., 1955-57; underwriter Employer's Mut. Co., 1957-59; claim adjuster Safeco Ins. Co., 1959-62; claim supr. Gen. Accident Ins., 1962-64; assoc. Rappaport & Lagakos, 1964; trial atty. Allstate Ins. Co., 1964-67; chmn., CEO Marshall, Dennehey, Warner, Coleman & Goggin, 1967—. Chmn. hearing com. Pa. Disciplinary Bd., Phila., 1986-94; mem. Pa. Bd. Law Examiners. Assoc. editor Phila. County Reporter, 1984-96; contbr. articles to legal publs. Bd. dirs. Ins. Soc. Phila.; dir. HERO Scholarship Fund Delaware County; bd. visitors Temple U. Law Sch. With USAR, 1954-62. Mem. ABA, Pa. Bar Assn., Phila. Bar Assn., Phila. Bar Found. (trustee), Pa. Def. Inst., Internat. Assn. Def. Lawyers, Def. Rsch. Inst. Republican. Roman Catholic. Avocations: tennis, boating, travel. Personal injury, Product liability. Home: 908 Penn Valley Rd Media PA 19063-1652 Office: Marshall Dennehey Warner Coleman & Goggin 1845 Walnut St Philadelphia PA 19103-4797

COLEMAN, ROBERT LEE, retired lawyer; b. Kansas City, June 14, 1929; s. William Houston and Edna Fay (Smith) C. BMus in Edn., Drake U., 1951; LLB, U. Mo., 1959. Bar: Mo. 1959, Fla. 1973. Law clk. to judge U.S. Dist. Ct. (we. dist.) Mo., Kansas City, 1959-60; assoc. Watson, Ess, Marshall & Engas, 1960-66; asst. gen. counsel Gas Svc. Co., 1966-74; v.p., corp. counsel H & R Block, Inc., 1974-94; retired, 1994. With U.S. Army, 1955-57. Mem. ABA. General corporate.

COLEMAN, ROBERT WINSTON, lawyer; b. Oklahoma City, Mar. 1, 1942; s. Clint Sheridan and Genevieve (Ross) C.; m. Judith Moore, Sept. 7, 1963; children: Robert Winston, Jr., Claire Elizabeth. BA, Abilene Christian Coll., 1964; JD with hons., U. Tex., 1968. Bar: Tex. 1968, Ga. 1970. Law clk. to presiding justice U.S. Ct. Appeals (5th cir.), Montgomery, Ala., 1968-69; assoc. Kilpatrick, Cody, Rogers, McClatchey & Regenstein, Atlanta, 1969-75; ptnr. Meyers, Miller, Middleton, Weiner & Warren and predecessor, Dallas, 1975-80, Jones, Day, Reavis & Pogue, Dallas, 1981-85; dir. Geary, Glast and Middleton, P.C., 1985-92; ptnr. Vial, Hamilton, Koch & Knox, LLP, 1992-2000, Brown McCarroll LLP, Dallas, 2000—. Mem. exec. com. Dallas County Dem. Com., 1980-87. Mem. ABA, Dallas Bar Found., Dallas Bar Assn., Tex. Bar Assn., Ga. Bar Assn., Am. Judicature Soc. Federal civil litigation, State civil litigation, Professional liability. Office: Brown McCarroll LLP 2000 Trammell Crow Ctr 2001 Ross Ave Dallas TX 75201 E-mail: RColeman@mailbmc.com

COLEMAN, VERONICA FREEMAN, prosecutor; U.S. atty. We. Dist. Tenn., U.S. Dept. Justice, Memphis, 1993—. Office: US Attys Office 800 Federal Office Bldg 167 N Main St Memphis TN 38103-1816

COLEN, FREDERICK HAAS, lawyer; b. Pitts., May 16, 1947; married, 1972. BSChemE, Tufts U., 1969; JD, Emory U., 1975. Bar: Pa. 1975, Ga. 1975, U.S. Patent Office 1976, U.S. Dist. Ct. (we. dist.) Pa. 1975, U.S. Dist. Ct. (no. dist.) Ga. 1975, U.S. Ct. Appeals (fed. and 3d cirs.) 1975, U.S. Supreme Ct. 1980. Chem. engr. Shell Oil Co., New Orleans, 1969-71; san. engr. USPHS, Morgantown, W.Va., 1971-73; patent atty. Mobay Chem. Corp., Pitts., 1975-79; assoc. Reed Smith, LLP, 1979-86, ptnr., 1986—. Contbr. articles to profl. jours. Mem. ABA, Allegheny County Bar Assn., Pa. Bar Assn., Ga. Bar Assn., Am. Intellectual Property Law Assn. Intellectual property, Patent, Trademark and copyright. Home: 4940 Ellsworth Ave Pittsburgh PA 15213-2807 Office: Reed Smith LLP 435 6th Ave Ste 2 Pittsburgh PA 15219-1886 E-mail: fcolen@reedsmith.com

COLETTA, RALPH JOHN, retired lawyer; b. Chillicothe, Ill., Dec. 13, 1921; s. Joseph and Assunta Maria (Aromatario) C.; m. Ethel Mary Meyers, Nov. 19, 1949; children: Jean, Marianne, Suzanne, Joseph, Robert, Michele, Renee. BS, Bradley U., 1943; JD, U. Chgo., 1949. Bar: Ill. 1949. Practice law, Peoria, Ill., 1949-99; gen. ptnr. Ralet Ltd. Partnership; now ret., 8/99. Pres. White Star Corp., Mark Tidd, Inc.; asst. state's atty. Peoria County. Chmn. United Fund. Served to 1st lt. AUS, 1943-46. Mem. ABA, Ill. State Bar Assn., Peoria County Bar Assn., Chgo. Bar Assn., Creve Coeur Club, Mt. Hawley Country Club, K.C., Union League Club. Republican. Roman Catholic. Estate planning, Probate, Real property. Home: 301 W Crestwood Dr Peoria IL 61614-7328

COLETTI, JOHN ANTHONY, lawyer, furniture and realty company executive; b. Cherry Point, N.C., Sept. 22, 1952; s. Joseph Nicholas and Gloria Lucy (Fusco) C.; m. Barbara Nancy Carlotti, July 20, 1975; children: Lisa M., Kristen B. Student, Biscayne Coll., 1970-72; BA summa cum laude, Boston Coll., 1974, JD, 1977. Bar; R.I. 1977, U.S. Dist. Ct. R.I. 1977. Assoc. Resmini, Fornaro, Colagiovanni & Angell, Providence, 1979-81; ptnr. Coletti & Tente, Cranston, R.I., 1981—. Pres. Coletti's Furniture, Inc., Johnston R.I., 1983-95, Coletti's Realty, Inc., Johnston, 1983-96. Legal counsel Cranston Housing Authority, 1988—; interviewer alumni admissions coun. Boston Coll., 1980—. Mem. ABA, R.I. Bar Assn., R.I. Conveyancers Assn., Nat. Assn. Retail Collection Attys., Phi Beta Kappa. Roman Catholic. Avocations: horseback riding, golf, figure skating. Consumer commercial, General practice, Real property. Office: Coletti & Tente 311 Doric Ave Cranston RI 02910-2903

COLFIN, BRUCE ELLIOTT, lawyer, video producer; b. Bklyn., June 9, 1951; s. Abraham and Sylvia (Laykin) C.; m. Virginia Mary Faszczewski, Sept. 27, 1981. BA, CUNY, 1977; JD, N.Y. Law Sch., 1980. Bar: N.Y. 1982, U.S. Dist. Ct. (so., ea. dists.) N.Y., 1987, U.S. Ct. Internat. Trade, 1990. Audio engr. Snowball Sound Systems, N. Bergen, N.J., 1974-77; producer, dir. cable TV program What's On, N.Y.C., 1976-84; stage mgr. Peter Tosh U.S. tour Rolling Stones Records, 1978; v.p., producer Upswing Artists Mgmt., N.Y.C., 1979-86; pres., producer, dir. LegalVision, Inc., 1982-87; ptnr. Jacobson & Colfin, N.Y.C. and Washington, 1985-90; mem. Jacobson & Colfin, P.C., 1990—; pres. Fifth Ave. Media, Ltd., N.Y.C., 1996—. Assoc. prof. music bus. and tech. Five Towns Coll., 1999—; spkr. Discovery Ctr., N.Y., 1st Ann. Musicians Seminar, L.I., N.Y. Law Sch. Media Law Soc., 1986; vis. lectr. SUNY, Oneonta, 1988—; panelist New Eng. Music Orgn. Conf., 1998, Emerging Artists and Talent in Music, 1999. Assoc. producer music video Blues Alive, 1982; exec. prodr., dir. video series Entertainment Law Video Primer, 1984; exec. prodr. (CD) Zen Tricksters, 1999; monthly columnist Ind. Music Producers Soc. Jour., NARAS N.Y. chpt. newsletter; contbr. articles to profl. jours.; columnist: Replication News, 1998, Medialine, 2000. Mem. ABA (com. on entertainment sports law, subcom. chmn. patent, trademark and copyright com. 1989, subcom. chmn. internat. law and practice, internat. intellectual property rights com., spl. subcom. on multimedia 1994—, editl. advisor pubs. com. internat. law sect. 1990-92, exec. com. entertainment law cir. 1989-91), NATAS (N.Y. chpt.), N.Y. State Bar Assn. (entertainment, arts and sports law sect., com. on talent agys. and talent mgmt., com. on rights of publicity 1994—), Nassau County Bar Assn., Speaker's Bureau (entertainment and sports law comm.), Copyright Soc. U.S.A. (editl. bd. 1986-88), Nat. Acad. of Recording Arts and Scis. (N.Y. chpt.). Jewish. Avocations: traveling, writing, stamp collecting, hockey. General civil litigation, Entertainment, Trademark and copyright. Office: Jacobson & Colfin PC 19 W 21st St Rm 603A New York NY 10010 E-mail: BRUCE@Thefirm.com

COLGAN, JEREMY SPENCER, lawyer; b. Belfast, Jan. 14, 1972; s. John Michael and Kathleen C. LLB with honors, Queens U., Belfast, 1995. Bar: Eng., Wales 1996, N.Y. 2001. Barrister Chambers of Michael Ashe Q.C., London, 1996-97, Queen Elizabeth Bldg. Chambers of Lindsey Burn, London, 1997-98; assoc. Gide Layrette Novel, Paris, 1998-99; sr. assoc. Beijing, 1999—. Contbr. articles to profl. jour. Key note spkr. All-China Fin. and Tax. Mgmt. Summit, Beijing, 2000. Accomodation scholar Honorable Soc. Inner Temple, 1996; named bursary Honorable Soc. Inner Temple, 1995. Mem. Honorable Soc. Knights Round Table (esquire, Sunley prize 1996). Communications, General corporate, Finance. Office: Gide Layrette Novel USS Tower 10 E 50th St New York NY 10022 Fax: (212) 644-1205, 008610 6597 4551. E-mail: jeremycolgan@hotmail.com, colgan@gide.fr

COLL, JOHN PETER, JR. lawyer; b. Pitts., Oct. 5, 1943; s. John Peter and Lelia (Nicolussi) C.; m. Nancy Kaye Swan; children: John Peter, Alexis S. AB in Polit. Sci., Duke U., 1965; JD, Georgetown U., 1968. Bar: N.Y. 1969, U.S. Dist. Ct. (so. dist.) N.Y. 1970, U.S. Dist. Ct. (ea. dist.) N.Y. 1974, U.S. Ct. Appeals (2d cir.) 1972, U.S. Supreme Ct. 1974, U.S. Ct. Appeals (5th cir.) 1981, U.S. Ct. Appeals (11th cir.) 1981, U.S. Ct. Appeals (8th cir.) 1980, U.S. Ct. Appeals (6th cir.) 1991, U.S. Ct. Appeals (1st cir.) 1993, U.S. Ct. Appeals (3d cir.) 1994, U.S. Ct. Appeals (9th cir.) 1994, U.S. Dist. Ct. (no. dist.) Calif. 1983, U.S. Dist. Ct. (no. dist.) N.Y. 1984, U.S. Dist. Ct. (we. dist.) N.Y. 1988, U.S. Tax Ct. 1990, U.S. Ct. Appeals (fed. cir.) 1999. Assoc. Donovan Leisure Newton & Irvine LLP, N.Y.C., 1968-76, ptnr., 1976-98, chmn. exec. com., 1989-98; ptnr. Orrick, Herington & Sutcliffe LLP, 1998—, mem. exec. com., 2000—. Bd. advisors product safety and liability rep. BNA, 1991-96; mem. litigation steering com. Def. Rsch. Inst., 1991-97. Contbg. author: Preparing for and Trying the Civil Law Suit, 1987, Supplement, 1997, Commercial Litigation in New York State Courts, 1995, Products Liability in New York, Strategy and Practice, 1997. Mem. ABA (litigation sect. 1983—), Fed. Bar Coun., N.Y. State Bar Assn., Assn. of Bar of City of N.Y., N.Y. Coun. Law Assocs. (mem. steering com. 1971-72), Lawrence Beach Club (bd. govs. 1991-2000), Cherry Valley Club, Univ. Club. Democrat. Roman Catholic. Federal civil litigation, General civil litigation, State civil litigation. Home: 385 Stewart Ave Garden City NY 11530-4615 Office: Orrick Herrington and Sutcliffe LLP 666 5th Ave New York NY 10103-1798

COLLAS, JUAN GARDUÑO, JR. lawyer; b. Manila, Apr. 25, 1932; s. Juan D. and Soledad (Garduño) C.; m. Maria L. Moreira, Aug. 1, 1959; children: Juan Jose, Elias Lopes, Cristina Maria, Daniel Benjamin. LLB, U. of Philippines, Quezon City, 1955; LLM, Yale U., 1958, JSD, 1959. Bar: Philippines 1956, Ill. 1960, Calif. 1971, U.S. Supreme Ct. 1967. Assoc., Sy Cip, Salazar & Assocs., Manila, 1956-57; atty. N.Y., N.H. & H. R.R., New Haven, 1959-60; assoc. Baker & McKenzie, Chgo., 1960-63, ptnr., Manila, 1963-70, San Francisco, 1970-95, Manila, 1995—. Contbr. articles to profl. jours. Trustee, sec. Friends of U. of Philippines Found. in Am., San Francisco, 1982—; co-chmn. San Francisco Lawyers for Better Govt., 1982—; chmn. San Francisco-Manila Sister City Com., 1986-92. Recipient Outstanding Filipino Overseas in Law award, Philippine Ministry Tourism Philippines Jaycees, 1979. Mem. ABA, Am. Arbitration Assn. (panelist), Ill. State Bar Assn., State Bar Calif., Integrated Bar of Philippines, Filipino-Am. C. of C. (bd. dirs. 1974-91, 94-96, pres. 1985-87, chmn. bd. dirs. 1987-89, 95-96). Republican. Roman Catholic. Clubs: World Trade, Villa Taverna (San Francisco). Contracts commercial, General corporate, Private international. Office: Baker & McKenzie 2 Embarcadero Ctr Ste 2400 San Francisco CA 94111-3909

COLLEN, JOHN, lawyer; b. Chgo., Dec. 26, 1954; s. Sheldon and Ann Collen; m. Lauren Kay Smulyan, Sept. 20, 1986; children: Joshua, Benjamin, Sarah, Joel. AB summa cum laude, Dartmouth Coll., 1977; JD, Georgetown U., 1980. Bar: Ill. 1980, U.S. Dist. Ct. (no. dist.) Ill. 1980, Trial 1982, U.S. Ct. Appeals (7th cir.) 1984, U.S. Supreme Ct. 1990. Ptnr. Duane & Morris LLP, Chgo. Mem. editl. adv. bd. Journal of Bankruptcy Law & Practice. Author: Buying and Selling Real Estate in Bankruptcy, 1997; contbr. articles to profl. jours.; lectr. in field. Mem. ABA, Chgo. Bar Assn., Am. Bankruptcy Inst. (chmn. com. real estate bankruptcy), Phi Beta Kappa. Avocations: water sports, magic, biographies. Bankruptcy, Real property. Office: Duane & Morris LLP 227 W Monroe St Chicago IL 60606-5016 Fax: 312-499-6701. E-mail: jcollen@duanemorris.com

COLLERAN, KEVIN, lawyer; b. Spalding, Nebr., July 16, 1941; s. James Edward and Helen Marcella (Vybiral) C.; m. Karen Ann Rooney, Aug. 1, 1964; children: Mary Jane, Patrick. BS, U. Nebr., 1964, JD with distinction, 1968. Bar: Nebr. 1968, U.S. Dist. Ct. Nebr. 1968, U.S. Dist. Ct. (we. dist.) La. 1975, U.S. Dist. Ct. (no. dist.) Tex. 1978, U.S. Supreme Ct. 1980, U.S. Ct. Appeals (8th cir.) 1981. Law. clk. U.S. Dist. Ct. Nebr., 1968-69; assoc. Cline, Williams, Wright, Johnson & Oldfather, LLP, Lincoln, Nebr., 1969-74, ptnr., 1975—, mng. ptnr., 1985-89, 96—. Bd. dirs. Lancaster County unit Am. Cancer Soc., 1972-83, pres., 1979. Fellow Am. Coll. Trial Lawyers; mem. ABA, Am. Bd. Trial Advocates, Nebr. Bar Assn. (chmn. worker's compensation com. 1980-82, chmn. civil practice & procedure com. 2001—), Internat. Assn. Def. Counsel, Nat. Assn. Trial Attys., Order of Coif. Democrat. Federal civil litigation, State civil litigation, Environmental. Office: Cline Williams Wright Johnson & Oldfather LLP US Bank Bldg Ste 1900 233 S 13th St Lincoln NE 68508 E-mail: kcolleran@cline-law.com

COLLI, BART JOSEPH, lawyer; b. Englewood, N.J., Feb. 13, 1948; s. Bart Joseph and Marie (Burns) C.; m. Mary Ellen Diemer, May 20, 1972; 1 son, Michael John. BA summa cum laude, Fordham Coll., 1968; JD cum laude, Harvard U., 1971. Bar: N.Y. 1972, Tex. 1975, N.J., 1988. Assoc. White & Case, N.Y.C., 1971-75; ptnr. Hughes & Luce, Dallas, 1976-85, McCarter & English, L.L.P., Newark, 1985—2000; exec. v.p., gen. counsel, sec. ARAMARK Corp., Phila. Judge Entrepreneur of the Yr. awards program, 1993, 95, 96, North Jersey Venture Fairs, 1993, 94, N.J. Family Bus. of Yr. awards program, 1997, 99; lectr. in field; mem. resources com. Edison Partnership Tech.; chmn. 1st annual Mergers and Acquisitions Conf., 1999, spkr. 2d annual Conf.; lectr. in field. Contbr. numerous articles to legal publs. Trustee Tri-County Scholarship Fund, No. N.J. chpt. Leukemia Soc. Am., Inc.; coun. Lincoln Ctr. Bus. Coun. of the Consol. Fund. Capt. M.I., USAR, 1968-76. Mem. ABA (fed. regulation of securities com., sect. on corp.k), N.J. State Bar Assn. (securities law com., chmn. bus. orgn. com. of the corp. and bus. law sect.), Phi Beta Kappa. General corporate, Mergers and acquisitions, Securities. Address: ARAMARK Corp ARAMARK Tower 1101 Market St Philadelphia PA 19107-2934 E-mail: colli-bart@aramark.com

COLLIN, THOMAS JAMES, lawyer; b. Windom, Minn., Jan. 6, 1949; s. Everett Earl and Genevieve May (Wilson) C.; m. Victoria Gatov, Oct. 11, 1985; children: Arielle, Elise, Sarah. BA, U. Minn., 1970; AM, Harvard U., 1972; JD, Georgetown U., 1974. Bar: Ohio 1975, U.S. Dist. Ct. (no. dist.) Ohio 1975, U.S. Ct. Appeals (10th cir.) 1977, U.S. Supreme Ct. 1980, U.S. Ct. Appeals (6th cir.) 1981, U.S. Ct. Appeals (8th cir.) 1982, U.S. Ct. Appeals (7th cir.) 1997, U.S. Ct. Appeals (11th cir.) 1999. Law clk. to Judge Myron Bright U.S. Ct. Appeals, 8th Cir., St. Louis, 1974-75; assoc. Thompson, Hine & Flory, LLP, Cleve., 1975-82, ptnr., 1982--. Author: Ohio Business Competition Law, 1994, (with others) Criminal Antitrust Litigation Manual, 1983; editor: Punitive Damages and Business Torts: A Practitioner's Handbook, 1998; contbr. articles to profl. jours. Active Citizens League, Cleve., bd. trustees, 1994-99, v.p., 1995-97, pres. 1997-99; bd. trustees Citizens League Rsch. Inst., Cleve., 1999—. Mem. ABA (chair bus. torts and unfair competition com., antitrust sect. 1995-98, chair annual mtg. com. antitrust sect., 2001-), Ohio State Bar Assn. (bd. govs. antitrust sect. 1988-98). Republican. Avocations: book collecting, music. Antitrust, Federal civil litigation, Intellectual property. Home: 7879 Oakhurst Dr Cleveland OH 44141-1123 Office: Thompson Hine LLP 127 Public Sq Cleveland OH 44114-1216

COLLINGS, KAY P. legal office administrator; b. Swansea, S.C., Dec. 18, 1944; d. Elvin Hampton and Sue D. Poole; m. Benny Lewis Collings, Apr. 25, 1992. AS, U. S.C., 1978, BS, 1987. Sec. Eastman Chem., Columbia, S.C., 1967-76, buyer, 1976-77, engring. records coord., 1978-87, staff asst., engring., 1987-89, purchasing rep., 1989-92, legal staff asst. Kingsport, Tenn., 1992-93, legal office adminstr., 1993-95, sr. office adminstr., 1995-98, prin. office adminstr., 1998—. Mem. family life ministries Mountain View United Meth. Ch., Kingsport, 1995—. Avocations: painting (oil and acrylic), eggery, stained glass, crafts, travel. Office: Eastman Chem Co 100 N Eastman Rd # B-75 Kingsport TN 37660-5299

COLLINGS, ROBERT L. lawyer; b. May 22, 1950; AB, Harvard U., 1972; JD, Boston Coll., 1977. Bar: Pa. 1977, U.S. Dist. Ct. (ea. and mid. dists.) Pa., U.S. Ct. Appeals (3d and D.C. cirs.). Atty. U.S. EPA, 1977-84, sect. chief, 1979-81, br. chief, 1981-84; ptnr., chair litigation dept. Schnader, Harrison, Segal & Lewis LLP, Phila., 1984—. Editor: Environmental Spill Reporting Handbook; contbr. Municipal Solicitors Handbook, 1994, 99, Brownfields: A Comprehensive Guide, 1997. Mem. Phila. Bar Assn. (chair environ. law com. 1986), Pa. Bar Assn. (nominating com. environ. mineral and natural resources law sect. 1992), Water Resources Assn. (sec. exec. com. 1990—). Administrative and regulatory, Environmental, Personal injury. Office: Schnader Harrison Segal & Lewis LLP 1600 Market St Ste 3600 Philadelphia PA 19103-7287

COLLINS, AUDREY B. judge; b. 1945; BA, Howard U., 1967; MA, Am. U., 1969; JD, UCLA, 1977. Asst. atty. Legal Aid Found. L.A., 1977-78; with Office L.A. County Dist. Atty., 1978-94, dept. dist. atty., 1978-94, head dep. Torrance br. office, 1987-88, asst. dir. burs. ctrl. ops. and spl. ops., 1988-92, asst. dir. atty., 1992-94; judge. U.S. Dist. Ct. (Ctrl. Dist.) Calif., 1994—. Dep. gen. counsel Office Spl. Acad. scholar Howard U.; named Lawyer of Yr., Langston Bar Assn., 1988; honoree Howard U. Alumni Club So. Calif., 1989; recipient Profl. Achievement award UCLA Alumni Assn., 1997, Ernestine Stahlhut award, Women Lawyers Assn., 1999. Mem. FBA, Nat. Assn. Women Judges, Nat. Bar Assn. (life), State Bar Calif. (com. bar examiners, chmn. subcom. on moral character 1992-93, co-chmn. 1993-94), Los Angeles County Bar Assn. (exec. com. litigation sect.), Assn. Los Angeles County Dist. Attys. (pres. 1983), Black Women Lawyers Los Angeles County, Women Lawyers L.A. (life, Ernestine Stahlhut award 1999), Calif. Women Lawyers (life), Order of Coif, Phi Beta Kappa. Office: US Dist Ct Edward R Roybal Fed Bldg 255 E Temple St Ste 670 Los Angeles CA 90012-3334

COLLINS, DANIEL FRANCIS, lawyer; b. N.Y.C., Mar. 5, 1942; s. Daniel Joseph and Madeline Elizabeth (Berger) C.; m. Margaret Mary Heyden, Jan. 15, 1966; children: Matthew C., Elizabeth C. BA in History and Polit. Sci., Hofstra U., 1964; JD, Am. U., 1967. Bar: D.C. 1968. Law clk. to E. Barrett Prettyman U.S. Ct. Appeals, Washington, 1967-68; assoc. Ross, Marsh & Foster, 1970-74, mem., 1974-78; ptnr. Brackett & Collins, P.C., 1978-87; v.p. regulatory law The Coastal Corp., 1987-2001; v.p., assoc. gen. counsel Pipelines El Paso Corp., 2001—. Administrative and regulatory, FERC practice, Public utilities. Office: El Paso Corp Ste 750 555 11th St NW Washington DC 20004 E-mail: daniel.collins@elpaso.com

COLLINS, DONNELL JAWAN, lawyer; b. Nov. 13, 1970; s. Artis Lee and Ruby Collins; m. Tonia Yvette Holloway, Nov. 28, 1998; 1 child, Demi Arnell. BA summa cum laude, Morehouse Coll., 1993; JD, Emory U., 1996. Bar: Ga. 1996, Supreme Ct. Ga. 1998, U.S. Dist. Ct. (no. dist.) Ga. 1998, U.S. Ct. Appeals (11th cir.) 1998. Atty. King & Spalding, Atlanta, 1996-97; assoc. Zirkle and Hoffman, LLP, 1997—2001, ptnr., 2001—. Mem.: ATLA, ABA, Atlanta Bar Assn., Ga. State Bar Assn., Phi Beta Kappa Soc., Phi Delta Phi. Avocations: geography, travel, philosophy. General civil litigation, State civil litigation, Insurance. Office: Zirkle and Hoffman LLP 5 Concourse Pkwy NE Ste 2900 Atlanta GA 30328-6104

COLLINS, J. BARCLAY, II, lawyer, oil company executive; b. Gettysburg, Pa., Oct. 21, 1944; s. Jennings Barclay and Golda Olevia (Hook) C.; m. Janna Claire Fall, June 25, 1966; children: J. Barclay III, L. Christian. AB magna cum laude, Harvard U., 1966; JD magna cum laude, Columbia U., 1969. Bar: N.Y. 1969. Law clk. to presiding judge U.S. Ct. Appeals (2d cir.), N.Y.C., 1969-70; assoc. Cravath, Swaine and Moore, 1970-78; v.p., asst. gen. counsel City Investing Co., 1978-84; exec. v.p., gen. counsel Amerada Hess Corp., 1984—, also bd. dirs. Bd. dirs. Dime Bancorp Inc. Trustee Bklyn. Hosp.-Caledonian Hosp., Plymouth Ch. of the Pilgrims, Bklyn.; bd. dirs. United Hosp. Fund N.Y., John Milton Soc. for Blind; past gov. Bklyn. Heights Assn. Mem. ABA, N.Y. Bar Assn., N.Y.C. Yacht Club. Clubs: Heights Casino (Bklyn.); Harvard N.Y.C. Office: Amerada Hess Corp Ste 810 1185 Avenue Of The Americas Fl 800 New York NY 10036-2601

COLLINS, JAMES SLADE, II, lawyer; b. St. Louis, June 9, 1937; s. James Slade and Dolma Ruby (Neilsen) C.; m. Neva Frances Guinn, June 27, 1959; children: Shari, Camala Ann. BSBA, Washington U., 1958, JD, 1961. Bar: Mo. 1961, U.S. Supreme Ct. 1969, U.S. Dist. Ct. (ea. dist.) Mo. 1972, U.S. Ct. Appeals (8th cir.) 1972. Assoc. Whalen, O'Connor, Grauel & Sarkisian, St. Louis, 1961-70, ptnr., 1970-72, Whalen, O'Connor, Collins & Danis, St. Louis, 1972-75; assoc. Hullverson, Hullverson & Frank, Inc., 1975-78; pvt. practice, 1979—. Trustee Village of Hanley Hills, Mo., 1966-69, mayor, 1967, mcpl. judge, 1967-68, 69-70. Mem. ABA, ATLA, Mo. Trial Lawyers Assn., Bar Assn. Met. St. Louis, Lawyers Assn. St. Louis, Phi Delta Phi. Republican. Baptist. Federal civil litigation, State civil litigation, Personal injury. Home: 916 Parkwatch Dr Ballwin MO 63011-3640 Office: 6654 Chippewa St Saint Louis MO 63109-2527 E-mail: jcollinslaw@aol.com

COLLINS, JOHN F. lawyer; b. N.Y.C., Dec. 15, 1948; AB, Fordham U., 1970; JD, U. Chgo., 1973. Bar: N.Y. 1974. Ptnr. Dewey Ballantine, N.Y.C. Mem. ABA, N.Y. State Bar Assn., Assn. Bar of City of N.Y., Phi Beta Kappa. Antitrust, General civil litigation, Securities. Office: Dewey Ballantine 1301 Avenue Of The Americas New York NY 10019-6022

COLLINS, JOHN TIMOTHY, lawyer; b. Springfield, Mass., Sept. 27; s. Edward T. and Elizabeth C.; m. Kathleen M. Collins, Nov. 25, 1972. A.B. in History, Holy Cross Coll., 1968; J.D., Georgetown U., 1971, LL.M. in Taxation, 1976. Bar: Mass. 1972, D.C. 1977. Atty., SEC, Washington, 1972-75; sr. atty. Fed. Res. Bd., Washington, 1975-77; gen. counsel U.S. Senate Banking Com., Washington, 1977-85; ptnr. Steptoe & Johnson, Washington, 1985— . Mem. covenants and code com. Woodacres Citizens Assn., Bethesda, Md., 1982-83. Served to 2d lt. U.S. Army, 1981-82, capt. USAR. John J. Cummings fellow Stonier Grad. Sch. Banking, Rutgers U., 1983. Mem. ABA (mem. banking law com. 1982—), Fed. Bar Assn. (mem. banking law com. 1982—). Banking, Securities. Office: 1330 Connecticut Ave NW Washington DC 20036-1704

COLLINS, MICHAEL HOMER, lawyer; b. Dallas, Apr. 26, 1949; s. William and Sheila (Peers) C.; m. Melissa Ringland, Aug. 11, 1956; children— Alexander, Valentina. B.A., Harvard U., 1971, J.D., 1977. Bar: Tex. 1977, U.S. Dist. Ct. (no. dist.) Tex. 1978, (so. dist.) Tex. 1993, (ea. dist.) Tex. 1989, U.S. Ct. Apls. (5th cir.) 1981. Briefing atty. Judge Robert Hill, U.S. Dist. Judge for No. Dist. Tex., Dallas, 1977-78; assoc. Locke, Purnell, Boren, Laney & Neely, Dallas, from 1978, now shareholder. Chmn. bd. mgmt. Town North YMCA, Dallas, 1983-85, bd. dirs. Dallas County Hist. Found., 1991—. Fellow ABA, Tex. Bar Found.; mem. Dallas Bar Assn. (chmn. legal ethics com. 1985). Federal civil litigation, State civil litigation, Oil, gas, and mineral. Home: 6207 Lakehurst Ave Dallas TX 75230-5126 Office: Locke Purnell Rain Harrell 2200 Ross Ave Ste 2200 Dallas TX 75201-6776

COLLINS, PHILIP REILLY, lawyer, educator; b. New Orleans, July 26, 1921; s. James Mark and Katherine (Gallaher) C.; m. Mary Catherine O'Leary, Feb. 9, 1946. BA, Loyola U., New Orleans, 1939, JD, 1942; MA in Govt. and Internat. Law and Rels., Georgetown U., 1948, PhD, 1950; LLM, George Washington U., 1952. Bar: La. 1942, Mass. 1948, D.C. 1953, Md. 1983, Va. 1986. Atty. Bur. Land Mgmt., Dept. Interior, Washington, 1946-47; asst. legis. counsel Office of Solicitor, P.O. Dept., 1947-48; pvt. practice Washington, 1954-77, 79—; ptnr. MacCracken, Collins & Hawes, 1960-69; chief counsel, staff dir. com. on rules U.S. Ho. of Reps., 1977-78. Spl. counsel Fed. Home Loan Bank Bd., 1961-69, Ky. Savs. and Loan League, 1967-68, State of Alaska, 1967-68; vis. prof., spl. asst. to pres. for labor rels. Queens Coll., 1969-70; lectr. pub. adminstrn. Sch. Social Scis. Cath. U. Am., 1954-56, lectr. Sch. Law, 1954-60. Mem. adv. com. on wills, trusts and other bequests Loyola U., New Orleans, 1966-69, charter mem. bd. visitors Law Sch., 1968-85, mem. pres.'s coun., 1976-85. Capt USAAF, 1942-46, PTO; maj. USAF, Korea; col. Res., ret. Mem. ABA, La. Bar Assn., Mass. Bar Assn., D.C. Bar Assn., Assn. of Bar of City of N.Y., Md. Bar Assn., Va. State Bar, KC, Mil. Order of Carabao, Univ. Club (Washington), Delta Theta Phi, Phi Alpha Theta. Democrat. Roman Catholic. Federal civil litigation, Legislative, Probate. Home: 1300 Crystal Dr Apt 209 Arlington VA 22202-3234

COLLINS, SAMUEL W., JR. judge; b. Caribou, Maine, Sept. 17, 1923; s. Samuel Wilson Collins & Elizabeth Black C; m. Dorothy Small, 1952; children: Edward, Elizabeth, Diane. BA, U. Maine; JD, Harvard U. Lawyer, Rockland, Maine, 1947—; justice Supreme Jud. Ct., Portland. Trustee Rockland Sch. Dist, 1949-61; Maine State Senate Dist. 21, 1975-84, majority leader, 1981-82, minority leader, 1983-84. Recipient Disting. Svc. award Jaycees, 1978. Mem. Maine Bar Assn., Rotary, Phi Beta Kappa, Phi Kappa Phi, Delta Tau Delta. Unitarian Universalist. Republican. Office: Knox County Courthouse 62 Union St Rockland ME 04841-2836

COLLINS, STEVEN M. lawyer; b. Atlanta, Oct. 22, 1952; s. E.B. and Judith (Morse) C.; divorced; 1 child, Erin M.; m. Anne Frances Garland, Oct. 31, 1987; 1 child, Timothy G. AB, Harvard U., 1974, JD, 1977. Bar: Ga. 1977, U.S. Dist. Ct. (no. dist.) Ga. 1977, U.S. Ct. Appeals (11th cir.) 1981, U.S. Dist. Ct. (mid. dist.) Ga. 1982, U.S. Tax Ct. 1984, U.S. Ct. Appeals (4th cir.) 1986, U.S. Ct. Appeals (6th cir.) 2001, U.S. Supreme Ct. 1994. Assoc. Alston & Bird, Atlanta, 1977-83, ptnr., 1983—. Editor-in-chief Ga. State Bar Journal, Atlanta, 1982-84. Mem. ABA, State Bar Ga., Atlanta Bar Assn. Banking, General civil litigation, Securities. Office: Alston & Bird One Atlantic Ctr 1201 W Peachtree St NW Atlanta GA 30309-3424 E-mail: scollins@alston.com

COLLINS, SUSAN ELLEN, lawyer; b. Mobridge, S.D., Oct. 20, 1950; d. Frank X. and Muriel (Culp) Sonnek; children: Elizabeth, John. BA, U. S.D., 1973, JD, 1976. Bar: S.D., Iowa, Wash., Tex. In-house counsel, trust officer Toy Nat. Bank, Sioux City, Iowa, 1976-78; trust officer Rainier Nat. Bank, Seattle, 1978-80; assoc. Finley, Kumble, Wagner, Heine, Underberg & Casey, Washington, 1980-81, Liddell, Sapp, Zivley, Hill & La Boon, Houston, 1981-87; v.p., assoc. gen. counsel Chase Bank of Tex., 1991—. Mem. State Bar Tex. (bus. law sect., UCC com., bd. cert. estate planning and probate, chair UCC article 9 subcom.), State Bar S.D., State Bar Iowa, State Bar Wash. Episcopal. Contracts commercial, Estate planning, Probate. Office: Chase Bank Tex PO Box 2558 Houston TX 77252-2558

COLLINS, THEODORE JOHN, lawyer; b. Walla Walla, Wash., Oct. 2, 1936; s. Robert Bonfield and Catherine Roselle (Snyder) C.; m. Patricia Spengler Pasieka, May 11, 1968; children: Jonathan, Caitlin, Matthew, Patrick, Flannary. BA, U. Notre Dame, 1958; postgrad., U. Bonn, Fed. Republic Germany, 1959; LLB, Harvard U., 1962. Bar: Wash. 1962, U.S. Supreme Ct. 1982, U.S. Ct. Appeals (fed. cir.) 1982, U.S. Dist. Ct. (ea. dist.) Wash. 1965, U.S. Dist. Ct. (we. dist.) Wash. 1962. Ptnr. Perkins Coie Law Firm, Seattle, 1962-86; v.p., gen. counsel The Boeing Co., 1986-98, sr. v.p., gen. counsel, 1998-2000; of counsel Perkins Coie Law Firm, 2001—. Adj. prof. Seattle U. Law Sch. Mem. ABA, Boeing Mgmt. Assn., Wash. State Bar Assn., King County Bar Assn., Wash. Athletic Club. General civil litigation, General corporate, Government contracts and claims. E-mail: tcoll10236@aol.com, colt@perkinscoie.com

COLLINS, WHITFIELD JAMES, lawyer; b. Dallas, Aug. 26, 1918; s. Jasper and Gertrude (James) C.; m. Beth Cooper, June 5, 1951 (dec. Aug. 1980); children: Whitfield James Jr., Kay, Cooper R. AA, Kemper Mil. Sch., 1936; BA, U. Tex., 1938, JD, 1940; LLM, Harvard U., 1941. Bar: Tex. 1940, U.S. Dist. Ct. (no. dist.) Tex. 1950, U.S. Ct. Claims 1978, U.S. Tax Ct. 1949, U.S. Ct. Appeals (5th cir.) 1981. Atty. Office Gen. Counsel Treasury Dept., Washington, 1941-42, Office Chief Counsel, IRS, Washington and N.Y.C., 1946-48; assoc. Cantey, Hanger, Johnson, Scarborough & Gooch, Ft. Worth, 1949-54; ptnr. Cantey & Hanger and predecessor firms, 1954-96, of counsel, 1996—. Sec., bd. dirs. Vol. Purchasing Groups, Inc., Bonham, Tex., 1968-95; pres. Fifth Ave. Found. and C.J. Wrightsman Ednl. Fund, 1980—; bd. dirs., sec.-treas. T.J. Brown and C.A. Lupton Found., Ft. Worth; bd. dirs. All Saints Health Found.; pro bono adv. bd. West Tex. Legal Svcs. Contbr. articles in field to profl. jours. Bd. dirs., past pres. Moncrief Radiation Ctr., Ft. Worth, Ft. Worth Art Assn., Arts Council Ft. Worth and Tarrant County, Ft. Worth Art Commn.; bd. dirs. Van Cliburn Found., Ft. Worth Opera Assn. Served to lt. commdr. USNR, 1942-46. Recipient Spl. Recognition award West Tex. Legal Svcs., 1999, Heritage award All Saints Health Found., 2001, Philanthropist award, 2001. Fellow ABA (life), State Bar Tex. (chmn. taxation sect. 1964-65), Tex. Bar Found. (life), Tarrant County Bar Found. (life); mem. Tarrant County Bar Assn. (Blackstone award 1995). Episcopalian. General corporate, Estate planning, Probate. Home: 6732 Brants Ln Fort Worth TX 76116-7202 Office: Cantey & Hanger 801 Cherry St Ste 2100 Fort Worth TX 76102-6898 E-mail: wcollins@canteyhanger.com

COLLINSON, DALE STANLEY, lawyer; b. Tulsa, Okla., Sept. 1, 1938; s. Harold Everett and Charlotte Elizabeth (Bonds) C.; m. Susan Waring Smith, June 7, 1969; children: Stuart, Eleanor. AB in Politics & Econs-.summa cum laude, Yale U., 1960; LLB, Columbia U., 1963. Bar: N.Y. 1963, U.S. Tax Ct. 1977. Law clk. U.S. Ct. Appeals (2d cir.), N.Y.C., 1963-64; law clk. to Justice Byron R. White U.S. Supreme Ct., Washington, 1964-66; asst. prof. Stanford (Calif.) Law Sch., 1966-68, assoc. prof., 1968-72; atty.-advisor Office of Tax Policy, U.S. Dept. Treasury, Washington, 1972-73, assoc. tax legis. counsel, 1973-74, dep. tax legis. counsel, 1974-75, tax legis. counsel, 1975-76; tax ptnr. Wilkie Farr & Gallagher, N.Y.C., 1976-2000; spl. counsel fin. instns. and products IRS, Washington, 2000—. Panel mem. Practising Law Inst. programs, 1981, 82, 84, 86, 88, Am. Law Inst.-ABA program, 1984, Investment Co. Inst. programs, 1992, 94, 97. Contbr. articles to legal jours. Fellow Am. Coll. Tax Counsel; mem. ABA, N.Y. State Bar (chmn. tax sect. 1985), Assn. of Bar of City of N.Y. (tax coun. 1990-93, vice chmn. taxation of corps. com. 1990-93), Nat. Assn. Bond Lawyers. Republican. Municipal (including bonds), Corporate taxation, Taxation, general. Home: 5480 Wisconsin Ave Apt 920 Chevy Chase MD 20815 Office: IRS 1111 Constitution Ave Washington DC 20224 E-mail: dale.collinson.td.60@aya.yale.edu

COLLOTON, STEVEN M. prosecutor; Grad., Princeton U., Yale Law Sch. Special asst. to Asst. Atty. Gen. Dept. Justice Office Legal Counsel, 1990—91; atty. Office Ind. Coun., 1995—96; asst. U.S. Atty. No. Dist. Iowa, 1991—99; ptnr. Belin, Lamson, McCormick, Zumbach & Flynn, DesMoines; U.S. Atty. so. dist. Iowa, 2001—. Office: US Courthouse Annex 110 E Couort Ave Ste 286 Des Moines IA 50309-2053 Office Fax: 515-284-6288*

COLLYER, MICHAEL, lawyer; b. N.Y.C., Feb. 5, 1942; s. Clayton Johnson and Heloise (Green) C.; m. Karen Machon, Nov. 4, 1963 (div. July 1979); m. Sandra Karen Schaum, July 28 1979 (div. Aug. 1999); m. Susan Catherine Bruyn, Nov. 13, 1999; children: Sophie Marie, Matthew Severyn; stepdaughter Shelley Malia. BA, Williams Coll., 1963; LLB, Columbia U., 1966. Bar: N.Y. 1966, Assoc., Becker & London, N.Y.C., 1966-70; ptnr. Kay Collyer & Boose and predecessors, N.Y.C., 1970—; legal adviser NATAS, N.Y.C., 1978—, trustee, 1982—, nat. officer, 1982—, chmn., 1990—; instr. bus. law Columbia U., N.Y.C., 1966-69; speaker conv. Practicing Law Inst., 1977, mem. chpt. motion pictures and TV under new copyright statute, 1978. Trustee George Heller Meml. Scholarship Fund; active N.Y.C. Mayor's Adv. Coun. Film and Broadcasting, 1993. With U.S. Army, 1966-71. Mem. Assn. of Bar of City of N.Y. (com. Entertainment Law 1992—), N.Y. Bar Assn. (author TV sect. entertainment law 1995), Internat. Radio and TV Soc., Internat. Coun. Nat. Acad. Arts and Scis. (bd. dirs.), N.Y. Yacht Club. Entertainment. Home: 25 Chester Ct Cortlandt Manor NY 10567-6361 Office: Kay Collyer & Boose LLP One Dag Hammarskjold Pla New York NY 10017-2299

COLMAN, RICHARD THOMAS, lawyer; b. Boston, Sept. 22, 1935; s. Albert Vincent and Marie Catherine (Henehan) C.; m. Marilyn Flavin, Dec. 1, 1962; children: Elizabeth B., Catherine B., Richard T. Jr., Patrick B. AB magna cum laude, U. Notre Dame, 1957; LLB cum laude, Boston Coll., 1962. Bar: Mass. 1962, D.C. 1966. Trial atty. Antitrust Div. U.S. Dept. Justice, Washington, 1962-66; ptnr. Howrey Simon Arnold & White LLP, 1970—. Trustee Indian Mountain Sch., Lakeville, Conn., 1992-98; regional del. Boston Coll. Law Sch. Alumni Assn., 1992-99; adv. bd. Georgetown U. Law Ctr., Corp. Counsel Inst., 1999—; bd. overseers Boston Coll. Law Sch., 2001—. Mem. ABA, Internat. Bar Assn., Fed. Bar Assn., D.C. Bar Assn., Wianno Club, Beach Club. Republican. Roman Catholic. Administrative and regulatory, Antitrust, Federal civil litigation. Office: Howrey Simon Arnold & White LLP 1299 Pennsylvania Ave NW Washington DC 20004-2420 E-mail: colmanr@howrey.com

COLMANT, ANDREW ROBERT, lawyer; b. Bklyn., Oct. 10, 1931; s. Edward J. and Mary Elizabeth (Byrne) C.; children: Stephen, Robert, Elizabeth, Carolyn. BBA, St. Johns U., Jamaica, N.Y., 1957, LLB, 1959. BAr: N.Y. 1959, U.S. Dist Ct. (so. and ea. dists.) N.Y. 1961, U.S. Ct. Appeals (2nd cir.) 1969, U.S. Ct. Appeals (4th cir.) 1977, U.S. Supreme Ct. 1991. Assoc. Hill, Rivkins, Carey, Loesberg O'Brien & Mulroy and predecessor firms, 1959-73, ptnr., 1973-87; of counsel Jerrold E. Hyams, 1988-97, Peter F. Broderick, 1992. Proctor in admiralty; active USMC amphibious reconnaissance Army Gen. Intelligence Sch. Author: Outline of General Average. Cpl. USMC, 1952-54. Mem. ABA, ATLA, N.Y. State Bar Assn., N.Y. County Lawyers Assn. (life), Maritime Law Assn. (life), Asia Pacific Law Assn., Pacific Rim Maritime Law Assn., Assn. Internat. de Droit des Assurances. Home: Bethany Manor 500 Broad St Apt 11Y Keyport NJ 07735-1640

COLTON, STERLING DON, lawyer, business executive, missionary; b. Vernal, Utah, Apr. 28, 1929; s. Hugh Wilkins and Marguerite (Maughan) C.; m. Eleanor Ricks, Aug. 6, 1954; children: Sterling David, Carolyn, Bradley Hugh, Steven Ricks. BS in Banking and Fin., U. Utah, 1951; JD, Stanford U., 1966. Bar: Calif. 1954, Utah 1954, D.C. 1967. Ptnr. Van Cott, Bagley, Cornwall & McCarthy, Salt Lake City, 1957-66; vice chair, sr. v.p., gen. counsel, bd. dirs. Marriott Corp. and Marriott Internat., 1954-95. Former pres. Can. Vancouver Mission Ch. of Jesus Christ of Latter Day Saints, 1995-98; pres. Washington DC Temple, Ch. of Jesus Christ of Latter Day Saints, 1999—; v.p. Colton Ranch Corp., Vernal, 1987—; former bd. dirs. Megaherz Corp. and Dyncorp; former chmn. bd. dirs. Nat. Chamber Litigation Ctr. Former bd. dirs. Polynesian Cultural Ctr.; former chmn. nat. adv. coun. U. Utah, Ballet West, nat. adv. counsel; mem. adv. coun. The Nat. Conservancy. Maj. JAG, U.S. Army, 1954-57. Mem. ABA, Calif. Bar Assn., Utah Bar Assn., D.C. Bar Assn., Washington Met. Corp. Counsel Assn. (former pres., dir.), Sigma Chi. Republican. Mem. LDS Ch. E-mial. General corporate, Finance, Real property. E-mail: sdercolton@aol.com

COLUMBUS, R. TIMOTHY, lawyer; b. West Bend, Wis., Mar. 17, 1949; s. Robert M. and Dena (Eggabean) C.; m. Penny G. Baker, June 16, 1979; children: Alexandra Baker, Robert Benjamin. BA, Harvard U., 1971; JD, U. Va., 1974. Bar: Va. 1974, D.C. 1975. Assoc. Collier Shannon Scott, PLLC, Washington, 1974-80, ptnr., 1980—. Administrative and regulatory, Legislative. Home: 6011 Nevada Ave NW Washington DC 20015-2527 Office: Collier Shannon Scott PLLC 3050 K St NW Washington DC 20007-5108

COLVILLE, ROBERT E. judge; b. Pitts., May 23, 1935; s. John and Mary M. (Goldbronn) C.; children: Michael C., Robert J., Molly. B.A. Duquesne U., 1963, J.D., 1969. Bar: Pa. 1969, U.S. Dist. Ct. (we. dist.) Pa. 1969. Tchr., coach North Catholic High Sch., Pitts., 1959-64; patrolman, detective Bur. of Police, Dept. Pub. Safety, Pitts., 1964-68, police legal adviser, 1969-70, asst. dir. Dept. Pub. Safety, 1970-71, supt. Bur. of Police, Pitts., 1971-75; clk., detective Dist. Atty.'s Office of Allegheny County, Pitts., 1968-69, dist. atty., 1976-97; judge Allegheny County Ct. Common Pleas, 1998—; adj. prof. law Duquesne U. Sch. of Law, Pitts., 1976-78; instr. in labor law LaRoche Coll., Pitts., 1983-84. Contbr. articles to profl. jours. Past chmn. Joint Allegheny County Narcotics Task Force; chmn. Allegheny County Drug Initiative; mem. Pa. Democratic Com. Served with USMC, 1953-56; foremr trustee Community Coll. of Allegheny County. Recipient Dapper Dan award Pitts. Post Gazette, 1963, Disting. Service award County Detectives Assn., 1977, Service Recognition award Pitts. Community Crime Prevention Coalition, 1980; Law Enforcement award Dep. Sheriff's Assn. of Pa., 1983; Outstanding Grad., Duquesne U., 1969; Jr. C. of C. Man of Yr. in Law, 1973; Phi Alpha Delta Law Alumni of Yr., 1976; Outstanding Grad., Duquesne U. Century Club, 1978; Outstanding Law Alumnus Duquesne U. Law Alumni Assn., 1985. Office: 436 Grant St Pittsburgh PA 15219-2400

COMAS, ALICE CUPRILL, lawyer; b. Weisbaden, Germany, Apr. 26, 1970; came to U.S., 1980; d. William M. Cuprill-Cuebas and Elsa Alicia Comas-Rivera; m. Richard M. Short, Aug. 12, 1994; 1 child, Alejandro Martin Comas Short. BA with honors, U. Tex., 1992; JD, Lewis and Clark Coll., 1995. Bar: Oreg. 1995, Tex. 1998. Atty. Tonkon Torp LLP, Portland, Oreg., 1995-98, Vinson & Elkins LLP, Austin, 1998—. Dir. Portland Creative Conf., 1997-98. Mem. Oreg. State Bar Assn. (affirmative action com. 1997-98), Tex. State Bar Assn., Hispanic Bar Assn. Office: Vinson & Elkins LLP 600 Congress Ave Ste 2700 Austin TX 78701-3248

COMBS, W(ILLIAM) HENRY, III, lawyer; b. Casper, Wyo., Mar. 18, 1949; s. William Henry and Ruth M. (Wooster) C.; divorced; 1 child, J. Bradley. Student, Northwestern U., 1967-70; BS, U. Wyo., 1972, JD, 1975. Bar: Wyo. 1975, U.S. Dist. Ct. Wyo. 1975, U.S. Ct. Appeals (10th cir.) 1990, U.S. Supreme Ct. 1990. Assoc. Murane & Bostwick, Casper, 1975-77, ptnr., 1978—. Mem. com. on resolution of fee disputes, 1990-92. Mem. ABA (tort and ins. practice, law office mgmt. sects.), Natrona County Bar Assn., Def. Rsch. Inst., Am. Judicature Soc., Def. Lawyers Assn. of Wyo., Assn. Ski Def. Attys., Nat. Bd. Trial Advocacy (cert.), U.S. Handball Assn., Waterski USA, Casper Boat Club, Porsche Club Am. Republican. Episcopalian. Avocations: handball, waterskiing, snow skiing, climbing, driving. Federal civil litigation, State civil litigation, Personal injury. Office: Murane & Bostwick 201 N Wolcott St Casper WY 82601-1922

COMERFORD, WALTER THOMPSON, JR. lawyer; b. May 27, 1949; s. Walter Thompson and Mary Lou (Phetteplace) C.; m. Joyce Faye Call; children: Callison Taylor, Erin Elizabeth, Kristen Nicole. Student, U. Tenn., 1968-70; BA magna cum laude, Wake Forest U., 1972; JD cum laude, 1974. Bar: N.C. 1974, U.S. Dist. Ct. (mid. and we. dists.) N.C. 1974, U.S. Ct. Appeals (4th cir.) 1977. Ptnr. Petree, Stockton & Robinson, Winston-Salem, N.C., 1980—. Contbr. articles to profl. jours. Chmn. Wake Forest Law ALumni Coun. (pres. 2000-01). Recipient Disting. Achievement award Internat. Acad. Trial Lawyers, 1974. Mem. Am. Trial lawyers Assn., N.C. Acad. Trial Lawyers, Am. Bd. Trial Lawyers, ABA (vice chmn), N.C. Bar Assn., N.C. State Bar, Forsyth County Bar Assn., Aviation Ins. Assn., Pilot's Bar Assn. Federal civil litigation, State civil litigation, Insurance. Home: 3500 Stonegate Ct Winston Salem NC 27104-1824 Office: Comerford & Brit 250 W First St Ste 300 Winston Salem NC 27101-2400 E-mail: wtc@comerfordbritt.com

COMINOS, THEODORE HARRY, JR. lawyer; b. Salinas, CA, July 12, 1969; s. Theodore Harry, Sr. and Philomena (Looij) C. BA, U. Calif., Davis, 1992; JD, Monterey Coll. of Law, Calif., 1996. Mem. State Bar of Calif. Paralegal Cominos & Biegel, Salinas, CA, 1992-95; assoc. Law Offices of THL, 1996-97, Burns Schwartz, Bucharest, Romania, 1997-2000, Linklaters & Alliance, Bucharest, Romania, 2000—. Mem. Am. Bar Assn., Monterey Bar Assn., Internat. Bar Assn. Avocations: fly fishing, sailing. General corporate, Private international. Office: Linklaters & Alliance 8 Nicolae Iorga St Sector 1 Bucharest Romania Fax: 00 401 310 4391. E-mail: theodore.cominos@linklaters.com

COMISKY, IAN MICHAEL, lawyer; b. Phila., Feb. 5, 1950; s. Marvin and Goldye (Elving) C. BS magna cum laude, U. Pa., 1971, JD, 1974; LLM in Taxation, U. Miami, 1984. Bar: Pa. 1974, Fla. 1976, D.C. 1976, U.S. Ct. Appeals (3rd and 11th cirs.), U.S. Ct. Claims, U.S. Tax Ct., U.S. Supreme Ct., U.S. Dist. Ct. (ea. dist.) Pa., U.S. Dist. Ct. (so. dist.) Fla., U.S. Dist. Ct. (mid. dist.) Fla. Law clk. to Hon. Alfred Luongo Jr. U.S. Dist. Ct. Pa., Phila., 1974-75; asst. dist. atty. Office of Dist. Atty., Philadelphia County, 1975-78; asst. U.S. atty. So. Dist. Fla., 1978-80; spl. asst. Office of Dist. Atty., So. Dist. Fla., 1980; ptnr. tax dept. Blank Rome Comisky & McCauley, Phila., 1980—. Presenter various profl. confs. seminars, 1981—; guest TV and radio programs, 1990. Co-author: Tax Fraud and Evasion (2 vols.); contbr. articles to profl. publs. Sec. Mann Music Ctr.; participant Fedn. Jewish Agys. Mem. ABA (past chmn. civil and criminal tax penalties com. tax sect., mem. CLE com. tax sect., cogs spl. projects, mem. various coms. criminal justice and litig. sect.), ATLA, Am. Law Inst., Am. Coll. Tax Counsel, Fed. Bar Assn., Pa. Bar Assn., Fla. Bar Assn. (bd. govs. 1998), D.C. Bar Assn., Phila. Bar Assn., Assn. Fellows and Legal Scholars or Ctr. for Internat. Legal Studies (hon.). Avocations: sailing, gardening, karate, jogging. Federal civil litigation, Criminal, Taxation, general.

COMISKY, MARVIN, retired lawyer; b. Phila., June 5, 1918; m. Goldie Elving; children: Ian M., Hope A., Matthew J. B.S.C. summa cum laude, Temple U., 1938; LL.B., U. Pa., 1941; LL.D., Dickinson Sch. Law, 1970. Bar: Pa. 1942. Law clk. Pa. Superior Ct., 1941-42; law clk. to presiding justice Pa. Supreme Ct., 1946; assoc. Lemuel B. Schofield, Phila., 1946-54; ptnr. Brumbelow & Comisky, 1954-59, Blank, Rome, Comisky & McCauley LLP, Phila., 1959-68, mng. ptnr., 1968-88; chmn. Blank, Rome, Comisky & McCauley, 1988-90, chmn. emeritus, 1991-99, ret., 1993. Mem. Pa. Bd. Law Examiners, 1974-75; former dir. Midlantic Bank. Co-author: Judicial Selection, Compensation, Ethics and Discipline, 1986 Gen. counsel Pa. Constl. Conv., 1967. Fellow Am. Bar Found., Am. Coll. Trial Lawyers, Internat. Acad. Trial Lawyers; mem. ABA (del. 1965, 70), Phila. Bar Assn. (chancellor 1965), Pa. Bar Assn. (past pres.), Order of Coif, Beta Gamma Sigma. Office: Blank Rome Comisky & McCauley LLP One Logan Square Philadelphia PA 19103

COMPTON, ALLEN T. retired state supreme court justice; b. Kansas City, Mo., Feb. 25, 1938; 3 children. B.A., U. Kans., 1960; LL.B., U. Colo., 1963. Pvt. practice, Colorado Springs, 1963-68; staff atty. Legal Svcs. Office, 1968-69, dir., 1969-71; supervising atty. Alaska Legal Svcs., Juneau, Alaska, 1971-73; pvt. practice, 1973-76; judge Superior Ct., Alaska, 1976-80; justice Alaska Supreme Ct., Anchorage, 1980-98, state supreme ct. chief justice, 1995-97, ret., 1998. Part-time judge Alaska Supreme Ct. Mem. 4 bar assns. including Juneau Bar Assn. (past pres.) Office: Alaska Supreme Ct 303 K St Anchorage AK 99501-2013

COMPTON, ASBURY CHRISTIAN, state supreme court justice; b. Portsmouth, Va., Oct. 24, 1929; BA, Washington and Lee U., 1950, LLB, 1953, LLD, 1975. Bar: Va. 1957. Mem. firm May, Garrett, Miller, Newman & Compton, Richmond, 1957-66; judge Law and Equity Ct., City of Richmond, 1966-74; justice Supreme Ct. Va., Richmond, 1974-2000, sr. justice, 2000—. Trustee Collegiate Schs., Richmond, 1972-89, chmn. bd., 1978-80; former chmn. adminstrv. bd. Ginter Park United Meth. Ch., Richmond; former mem. adminstrv. bd. Trinity United Meth. Ch., Richmond; trustee Washington and Lee U., 1978-90. With USN, 1953-56, USNR, 1956-62. Decorated Letter of Commendation. Mem. Va. Bar Assn., Va. State Bar, Bar Assn. City Richmond, Washington and Lee U. Alumni Assn. (past pres., dir.), Omicron Delta Kappa, Phi Kappa Sigma, Phi Alpha Delta. Club: Country of Va. Office: Va Supreme Ct 100 N 9th St Richmond VA 23219-2335

COMSTOCK, ROBERT FRANCIS, lawyer; b. Lincoln, Ill., June 4, 1936; s. William Bryan and Mary Euceba (Durham) C.; m. Jean Joyce Herring, May 9, 1970; children: James, Michael, Kelly, Jennifer, Margaret. AB, Cath. U., 1958, LLB, 1964. Bar: U.S. Dist. Ct. 1965, U.S. Ct. Appeals (D.C. cir.) 1965, U.S. Tax Ct. 1971. Ptnr. Comstock & Reilly LLP, Washington, 1965—. Chmn. bd. dirs. Balt. Bancorp, 1991, Met. Fed. Savs. & Loan, Bethesda, Md., 1986-87, Met Holding Co., Bethesda, 1985-87, First Continental Bank, Silver Spring, Md., 1983-86; dir. Nat. Captial Bank Washington, 1999—. Trustee, vice chmn. bd. trustees Cath. U. Am., Washington, 1987—; bd. dirs. Cath. Cemeteries Washington, 1986—, Cath. Youth Orgn. Capt. USAF, 1958-61. Named Knight of St. Gregory, Knight of Holy Sepulchre, Papal Award of Holy See, to Athletic Hall of

Fame, Cath. U., 1985. Mem. ABA, D.C. Bar Assn., Cath. U. Alumni Assn. (bd. govs.). Roman Catholic. Clubs: Columbia Country (Chevy Chase, Md.); Univ. Md. M. Avocation: sports. Banking, Probate, Real property. Home: 7707 Brookville Rd Bethesda MD 20815-3933 Office: Comstock & Reilly LLP Ste 300 5225 Wisconsin Ave NW Washington DC 20015-2014

CONABOY, RICHARD PAUL, federal judge; b. Scranton, Pa., June 12, 1925; m. Marion Hartnett; children: Mary Ann, Richard, Judith, Conan, Michele, Kathryn, Patrick, William, Margaret, Janet, John, Nancy. BA, U. Scranton, 1945; LLB, Cath. U. Am., 1950. Bar: Pa. 1951. Ptnr. firm Powell & Conaboy, Scranton, 1951-54; dep. atty. gen., 1953-62; assoc. firm Kennedy O'Brien & O'Brien, 1954-62; judge Pa. Ct. Common Pleas, 1962-79, pres. judge, 1978-79; judge U.S. Dist. Ct. (mid. dist.) Pa., Scranton, 1980—, chief judge, 1989-93, now sr. judge. Pres. Pa. Joint Council on Criminal Justice System, 1971-79; mem. Nat. Conf. Juvenile Justice, Nat. Conf. Corrections. Contbr. articles to legal jours. Bd. dirs. Marywood Coll., U. Scranton; apptd. chmn. U.S. States Sentencing Commn., 1994. Mem. Pa. Conf. State Trial Judges (pres. 1976-77, v.p. 1973-76, sec. 1968-73), ABA, Pa. Bar Assn., Am. Judicature Soc. Office: US Dist Courthouse & Post Office Bldg PO Box 189 Scranton PA 18501-0189

CONARD, FREDERICK UNDERWOOD, JR. lawyer; b. Bklyn., July 11, 1918; s. Frederick U. and Julia Ellmaker (Hand) C.; m. Annette Hall, June 19, 1943; children: Frederick U. III, Virginia H. BA with distinction in English, Wesleyan U., 1940; JD, Yale U., 1943. Bar: Conn. 1943, U.S. Dist. Ct. Conn. 1948, U.S. Dist. Ct. (no. dist.) N.Y. 1967, U.S. Dist. Ct. Vt. 1973, U.S. Ct. Appeals (2d cir.) 1960, U.S. Tax Ct. 1950, U.S. Supreme Ct. 1959. Assoc. Shipman & Goodwin, Hartford, Conn., 1943-49, ptnr., 1950-90, of counsel, 1990-93; justice of peace West Hartford, 1973-74, 77—. Mem. adv. com. to Waller Tenn. Trust, 1953-70, trustee, 1970-99; pres. Sunset Farm Corp., 1987-91; mem. panel Am. Arbitration Assn., 1992—, Stafed, Inc., 1993-95. Bd. dirs. YMCA of Met. Hartford, sec., 1944-50, bd. dirs., 1967-78, 79-85, pres., 1970-74, trustee, 1978-79, 85—, chmn. numerous coms., del. nat. coun. YMCA, 1981 83, bd. dirs. YMCA of USA, 1981-83; bd. dirs. Am. Sch. for the Deaf, Hartford, 1956-93, sec., 1956-68, 2d v.p., 1968-75, mem. exec. com., 1968-93; corporator Conn. Inst. for Blind, Inst. for Living, 1959-94; trustee Hartford Coll. for Women, 1954-84, 86-93, hon. trustee, 1993—; corporator Hartford Pub. Libr., 1963—; bd. dirs. Almada Lodge-Times Farm Corp., 1964-93; active Asylum Hill Congl. Ch., 1937—, elder, 1968—, mem. pastoral search com., 1974, deacon, 1962-68, 80-83; mem. Conn. Gen. Assembly, 1955-57, com. on judiciary, com. on rules, mem. interim rules com., 1955-57; mem. 10th Dist. Rep. Com., 1961-95; mem., vice chmn. charter revision commn. Town of West Hartford, 1963-64, chmn., 1964-65; del. Constl. Conv. of Conn., 1965; mem. jud. performance evaluation com. Conn. Staet Jud. Dept., 1983-84; mem. jud. adv. panel Jud. Performance Evaluation Program Conn. State Jud. Dept., 1984-90; state trial referee Jud. Dept., 1984—; spl. master U.S. Dist. Ct. Conn., parajud. U.S. Dist. Ct., 1992—. Recipient Greater Hartford Jaycees Disting. Svc. award, 1946, Robert C. Knox Jr. YMCA Disting. Leadership award, 1980, Am. Sch. for the Deaf awrd of Merit for Disting. Svc., 1982. Mem. ABA (ho. of dels. 1976-80, com. on prepaid legal svcs. 1980-81, com. on constn. and bylaws 1981-87, chmn. co. on sr. lawyers divsn., mem. coun. 1995-97, opthers), Conn. Bar Assn. (chmn. and mem. numerous coms., v.p. 1976-77, pres. 1978-79, bd. govs. 1976-80, ho. of dels. 1976-80, com. on jud. evaluation 1982-84), Hartford County Bar Assn. (com. on unauthorized practice of law 1961-80, chmn. 1969-80, chmn. com. on lawyer referral 1980-97), New Eng. Bar Assn. (bd. dirs. 1977-78, 80-82, v.p. 1984-85, pres. 1985-86), Am. Bar Found. (fellow, Conn. state chmn. 1990-95), Am. Law Inst., Marine Hist. Assn. of Mystic, Conn. River Watershed Coun., Wadsworth Atheneum Inc., Supreme Ct. Hist. Soc., Yale Law Sch. Assn. (exec. com. 1990—), Greater Hartford C. of C. (local govt. com. 1966-92), Yale Alumni Club of Hartford, Wesleyan U. Alumni Club (pres. 1948, 70, v.p. 1965-69), 20th Century Club, Hartford Club, Beta Theta Pi. Mem. United Ch. of Christ. Antitrust, Federal civil litigation, Contracts commercial, trust and estates. Home and Office: B519 The McAuley 275 Steele Rd West Hartford CT 06117-2716

CONBOY, KENNETH, lawyer, former federal judge; b. 1938; AB, Fordham Coll., 1961; JD, U. Va., 1964; MA in History, Columbia U., 1980. Asst. dist. atty., exec. asst. dist. atty. Manhattan Dist. Atty.'s Office, 1966-77; dep. commr., gen. counsel N.Y. Police, 1978-83; criminal justice dir. N.Y.C., 1984-86; N.Y.C. commr. of investigation, 1986-87; judge U.S. Dist. Ct. (so. dist.) N.Y, 1987-93; sr. litigation ptnr. Mudge, Rose, Guthrie, Alexander & Ferdon, N.Y.C., 1994-95; ptnr. Latham & Watkins, 1995—. Summer faculty Cornell Law Sch.; adj. prof. of law Fordham Law Sch. Author: Grand Jury Examination of the Recalcitrant Witness, 1977; contbr. articles to profl. jours. Mem. N.Y. State Crime Control Planning Bd., N.Y. Sovern Commn. Capt. U.S. Army, 1964-66. Mem. Am. Soc. Legal History, N.Y. State Bar Assn., Assn. of Bar of City of N.Y., Fed. Bar Coun. General civil litigation, Constitutional, Securities. Office: Latham & Watkins 885 3rd Ave Ste 1000 New York NY 10022-4834

CONCANNON, ANDREW DONNELLY, lawyer; b. Willoughby, Ohio, May 1, 1967; BA in History, Mich. State U., 1990; JD, U. Detroit, 1993. Bar: Mich. 1994, U.S. Dist. Ct. (ea. dist.) Mich. 1994. Sr. assoc. Kitch, Drutchas, Wagner & Kenney, Lansing, Mich., 1995-97; assoc. Smith, Bovill, Fisher, Meyer & Borchard, PC, Saginaw, 1997-2000, shareholder, 2001—. Mem. ABA, State Bar Mich., Saginaw Bar Assn., Am. Judicature Soc. Avocations: tennis, golf. General civil litigation, Personal injury, Professional liability. Office: Smith Bovill et al 200 Saint Andrews Rd Saginaw MI 48603-5938 E-mail: aconcannon@smithbovill.com

CONCANNON, JAMES M. law educator, university dean; b. Columbus, Ga., Oct. 2, 1947; s. James M. Jr. and Mary Jane (Crow) C.; m. Melissa P. Masoner, June 9, 1988. BS, U. Kans., 1968, JD, 1971. Law clk. Kans. Ins. Commn., Topeka, 1971; rsch. atty. Kans. Supreme Ct., 1971-73; asst. prof. law Washburn U., 1973-75, assoc. prof. law, 1976-81, prof., 1981—, dean, 1988-2001. Vis. prof. law Washington U., St. Louis, 1979; active Kans. Commn. on Pub. Understanding of Law, 1983-89, Task Force on Law Enforcement Consolidation, Topeka, 1991-92; mem. Nat. Conf. Commrs. on Uniform State Laws, 1998—; mem. Pattern Instrns. for Kans.-Civil Com., Kans. Jud. Coun., 2001—. Co-author: Kans. Appellate Practice Manual, 1978, Kansas Statutes of Limitations, 1988; sr. contbn. editor: Evidence in America-Federal Rules in the States, 1987. Coord. Citizens to Keep Politics Out of Our Courts, Topeka, 1984; co-reporter Citizens Justice Initiative, 1997-99; chmn. legal com. Concerned Citizens Topeka, 1995-99; bd. dirs. Mut. Funds Waddell and Reed, Inc., 1997—. Master: Topeka Am. Inn. of Ct.; fellow: Am. Bar Found., Kans. Bar Found.; mem.: Kans. Bar Assn. (CLE com. 1976—2001, Outstanding Svc. award 1982), Assn. Am. Law Schs. (com. on bar admission, lawyer performance 1994—97), Washburn Law Sch. Alumni Assn. (life)), Order of Coif. Office: Washburn U Law Sch 1700 SW College Ave Topeka KS 66621-0001

CONCANNON, THOMAS BERNARD, JR. lawyer; b. Newton, Mass., Nov. 10, 1939; s. Thomas Bernard and Anne Gertrude (Connolly) C.; m. Jeanne Ellen Twohig, Feb. 21, 1970; children— Kate Elizabeth, Maureen Anne. B.B.A., Boston Coll., 1961; M.Ed., State Coll. at Boston, 1962; J.D., Suffolk U., 1969. Bar: Mass. 1970, U.S. Dist. Ct. Mass. 1971. Assoc. Cohen & Concannon, Newton, 1970-76, Cohen, Concannon & Rosenberg, Newton, 1976-78, Concannon & Rosenberg, Newton, 1978-82, Concannon, Rosenberg & Freedman, Newton, 1982— ; sponsor Mass. Continuing Legal Edn., Inc. Mem. Newton Bd. Aldermen, 1970-78; chmn. Newton Democratic Citizens Com., 1978-82; bd. dirs. Newton Wellesley Weston Com. to Establish Residence for Retardates, 1983— . Named Outstanding Young Man in Newton, Jaycees, 1969. Mem. Mass. Bar Assn. (probate & family law sects.). Democrat. Roman Catholic. Estate planning, Family and matrimonial, General practice. Home: 8 Bacon Rd Newton MA 02460-1304 Office: Concannon Rosenberg & Freedman 93 Union St Newton MA 02159

CONDO, JAMES ROBERT, lawyer; b. Somerville, N.J., Mar. 2, 1952; s. Ralph Vincent and Betty Louise (MacQuaide) C. BS in Bus. and Econs., Lehigh U., 1974; JD, Boston Coll., 1979. Bar: Ariz. 1979, Colo. 2001, U.S. Dist. Ct. Ariz. 1979, U.S. Ct. Appeals (9th cir.) 1982, U.S. Supreme Ct. 1983, U.S. Ct. Appeals (D.C. cir.) 1989, U.S. Ct. Appeals (10th cir.) 1989, U.S. Ct. Appeals (6th cir.) 1991, U.S. Ct. Appeals (4th cir.) 1994. Assoc. Snell & Wilmer, Phoenix, 1979-84, ptnr., 1985—. Judge pro tem Ariz. Ct. Appeals. Active Ariz. Town Hall, 1985-2000. Fellow Ariz. Bar Found.; mem. ABA, State Bar Ariz., Maricopa County Bar Found., Defense Rsch. Inst. Federal civil litigation, State civil litigation, Product liability. Office: Snell & Wilmer One Arizona Ctr Phoenix AZ 85004-2202 E-mail: jcondo@swlaw.com

CONDON, CHARLES MOLONY, state attorney general; b. Charleston, S.C., May 2, 1953; s. James Joseph and Harriet (Molony) C.; m. Emily Yarbrough, June 21, 1980; children: Charles Molony Jr., Patrick Monaghan, Doreen Yarbrough, Emily Elliot. Student, Saltzburg (Austria) Summer Sch., 1972, U. Innsbruck, Austria, 1972-73; BA, U. Notre Dame, 1975; JD, Duke U., 1978. Bar: S.C. 1978, U.S. Dist. Ct. S.C. 1978, U.S. Ct. Appeals (4th cir.) 1987, U.S. Supreme Ct. 1988. Assoc. Nexsen, Pruet, Jacobs & Pollard, Columbus, S.C., 1978-79; asst. solicitor S.C. 9th Jud. Cir., Charleston, 1979-80, solicitor, 1980-92; atty. gen. State of S.C., Columbia, 1992—. Lectr. Med. U. S.C., 1982, U. S.C., 1983, Coll. Charleston, 1986, various confs.; bd. visitors com., Charleston, 1992—; panel mem. Nat. Inst. for Drug Abuse, Washington; prosecuter City of Isle Palms, S.C., 1993—; cons. Nat. Consortium for Justice Info. and Stats. profl. rep. So. Environ. Network, 1990-91. Profl. rep. So. Envion. Network., 1990-91. Mem. com. Charleston County Criminal Justice Task Force; sect. chmn. govtl. divsn. United Way; bd. dirs. com. for drug free soc. Charleston County Sch. Dist., 1989, Children's Ctr., Charleston, S.C., 1990-91, S.C. Commn. on Presecution Coord., 1991-92; ex-officio mem. Friends of Charleston County Courthouse. Mem. ABA, S.C. Bar Assn., Richland County Bar Assn., Charleston Lawyers Club, S.C. Cir. Solicitors Assn. (v.p. 1987-88, pres. 1988-89), S.C. Law Enforcement Assn., Notre Dame Club, Silver Elephant Club. Republican. Home: 835 Middle St Sullivans Island SC 29482-8726 Office: Office of Attorney General PO Box 11549 Columbia SC 29211-1549*

CONDRA, ALLEN LEE, lawyer, state official; b. Middlesboro, Ky., Apr. 11, 1950; s. Allen and Dorothy Dell (Douglas) C. BA, Western Ky. U., 1972; JD, No. Ky. U., 1978. Bar: Ky. 1979, U.S. Dist. Ct. (we. dist.) Ky. 1980. Staff atty. West Ky. Legal Services, Madisonville, 1979-81; dist. atty. Dept. Transp. Commonwealth of Ky., 1981—. Mem. Ky. Bar Assn., Hopkins County Bar Assn., Phi Alpha Delta. Democrat. Methodist. Lodge: Elks, Masons, K.T.

CONDRELL, WILLIAM KENNETH, lawyer; b. Buffalo, Sept. 19, 1926; s. Paul Kenneth and Celia Olga (Schinas) C.; m. Stacie J. Oliver, June 9, 1991; children: Paul, William, Alexander. B.S., Yale U., 1946; S.M., MIT, 1947; JD, Harvard U., 1950. Bar: N.Y. 1951, D.C. 1964, U.S. Ct. Appeals (4th cir.) 1974, U.S. Ct. Appeals (Fed. cir.) 1982, U.S. Ct. Appeals (D.C. cir.) 1984, U.S. Supreme Ct. 1965. Assoc. econ. adv. Exec. Office Pres., D.C., 1951-54; mgmt. cons. McKinsey and Co., Chgo., 1954-55; mgr. budgets Hotpoint div. Gen. Electric Co., 1955-59; sole practice, 1959-68; ptnr. Steptoe & Johnson, Washington, 1968-90, of counsel, 1990—. Lt. (j.g.) USNR, 1944-46. Mem. ABA. Club: Congressional Country (Bethesda, Md.) Home: 2510 Virginia Ave NW # 502 Washington DC 20037-1904 Office: 1330 Connecticut Ave NW Washington DC 20036-1704

CONE, GEORGE WALLIS, lawyer; b. Augusta, Ga., July 20, 1945; s. William Harry and Agnes M. (Hill) C.; student Clemson Coll., 1963-64; B.S. in Pharmacy, U. Ga., 1967, J.D., 1973; m. Patricia Ann Stabenow, Dec. 28, 1967; children— Jennifer Lee, Laura Katherine, David Wallis. Pharmacist-in-charge Walterboro Drug, Inc. (S.C.), 1967-76; admitted to Ga. bar, 1973, S.C. bar, 1974; atty. firm McLeod, Fraser & Unger, Walterboro, 1976-84, McLeod, Fraser & Cone, Walterboro, 1985— ; bd. dirs. Found. for Humans Svcs., Bank of Walterboro. Mem. S.C. Bd. Pharmacy, 1981-87, chmn. 1986-87; bd. dirs. S.C. Humane Assn., 1978— , treas., 1979-84, pres., 1984-85; bd. dirs. Colleton County SPCA, 1975— , pres., 1975-77; mem. Colleton County Alcohol and Drug Abuse Com., 1979-81, chmn., 1980-81; bd. dirs. Pub. Defender Corp. Colleton County, 1978— , sec., 1979— ; mem. Colleton County Bd. Voter Registration, 1982-84; bd. dirs. Nat. Assn. Bds. Pharm. Found./Bur. Voluntary Compliance, 1983-85; bd. dirs. Low Country Community Action Agy., Inc., 1980-85, sec., 1983-85. Served with S.C. Army N.G., 1970-76. Mem. Am. Pharm. Assn., Am. Soc. Pharm. Law, Nat. Assn. Retail Druggists, Am. Bar Assn., State Bar Ga., S.C. Bar Assn. (ho. of dels. 1985-89), S.C. Trial Lawyers Assn., S.C. Pharm. Assn. (ho. of dels. 1975-76, 77-78, 79-85), Colleton County Bar Assn., 14th Dist. Pharm. Assn. (pres. 1980-82), Sertoma (pres. Walterboro 1977-78), Delta Chi, Phi Alpha Delta. Democrat. Baptist. Notes editor Ga. Jour. Internat. and Comparative Law, 1971-72, revs. and comments editor, 1972-73. Office: PO Box 230 Walterboro SC 29488-0003

CONETTA, TAMI FOLEY, lawyer; b. Akron, Ohio, Aug. 29, 1965; d. Charles David and Roxanne (Onyett) Foley; m. Anthony Joseph Conetta, July 29, 1989; 1 child, Emory Elizabeth Conetta. BA in Polit. Sci., Furman U., 1987; JD with honors, U. Fla., 1990. Bar: Fla. 1991; bd. cert. estates, trusts and wills Fla. Bar Bd. Legal Specialization. Ptnr. Gassman & Conetta, PA, Clearwater, Fla., 1990-98, Ruden, McClosky, Smith, Schuster & Russell, PA, Sarasota, 1998—. Contbr. articles to profl. jours. Mem. planned giving com. All Children's Hosp. Found. Recipient Am. Jurisprudence awards in Estate Planning and Taxation of Gratuitous Transfers, 1990. Mem. Am. Bus. Womens Assn., Sarasota County Bar Assn. (chair probate and estate planning sect. 2000-01), Clearwater Bar Probate Com. (chair 1996-98), Southwest Fla. Estate Planning Coun., Fla. Bar Assn. (probate rules com.). Avocations: golf, reading. Estate planning, Probate, Estate taxation. Office: Ruden McClosky Smith Schuster & Russell PA 1549 Ringling Blvd Ste 600 Sarasota FL 34236-6772 also: PO Box 49017 Sarasota FL 34230-6017 E-mail: tami.conetta@ruden.com

CONGALTON, CHRISTOPHER WILLIAM, lawyer; b. N.Y.C., Apr. 8, 1946; s. William Alexander and Jacqueline Rose (Ryan) C.; m. Susan Tichenor, May 29, 1971. AB, Fairfield (Conn.) U., 1968; JD, Georgetown U., 1971. Bar: N.Y. 1972, U.S. Dist. Ct. (so. dist.) N.Y. 1974, U.S. Ct. Appeals (2d cir.) 1974, U.S. Supreme Ct. 1976, Ill. 1988, Colo. 1990. Assoc. Dunnington, Bartholow & Miller, N.Y.C., 1971-78; asst. gen. counsel Diamond Internat. Corp., 1978-82; gen. counsel, v.p. Children's TV Workshop, 1987-88; chmn. and ceo Moffitt Co., Schiller Park, Ill., 1988—. Mem. ABA, (corp. banking & bus. sect.), Am. Corp. Counsel Assn., N.Y. State Bar Assn., Assn. of Bar of City of N.Y., Chgo. Bar Assn., Eagle Springs Golf Club. General corporate, Securities. Home: 1500 N Lake Shore Dr Chicago IL 60610-6657 Office: Moffitt Co 9347 Seymour Ave Schiller Park IL 60176-2206

CONGLETON, CONLEY COLE, III, lawyer; b. N.Y.C., Sept. 17, 1945; s. Conley Cole and Gladys (Hale) C.; 1 child, Katharine Lindsay. BA, Eastern Ky. U., 1968; JD, U. Ky., 1971. Bar: Ky. 1973. Pvt. practice, Lexington, Ky., 1974-76, 88-89; with Begley Co., Richmond, Ky., 1976-88, v.p., sec., gen. counsel, 1980-88; asst. atty. gen. State of Ky., 1989—. Bd. dirs., treas. Bluegrass Boys' Ranch, Inc., Lexington, 1975-89, trustee, 1985-89. Capt. Transp. Corps, USAR, 1976. Democrat. Office: Capitol Bldg Ste 18 Frankfort KY 40601

CONGLETON, JOSEPH PATRICK, lawyer, conservationist; b. Barbourville, Ky., June 8, 1947; s. Isaac and B. (Johnson) C.; m. Rose Willingham Stewart; children: Isaac Tyler, Rosalie Mallary. Grad., McCallie Sch., Chattanooga; MA, Centre Coll., 1969; JD, U. Va., 1972. Bar: Tenn. 1972. Ptnr. Fowler & Rowntree, Knoxville, Tenn., 1972-83, Hunton & Williams, Knoxville, 1983—. Adv. editor Jour. Mineral Law and Policy, 1985—. Chmn. atty. divsn. United Way, Knoxville, 1985-87; bd. dirs. Tenn. Nature Conservancy, 1980-88, Knoxville Symphony, 1985—, pres., 1988-91; bd. dirs. Thompson Cancer Survival Ctr., 1987—, Gt. Smoky Mountain Conservation Assn., Knoxville, 1985—, pres., 1992—; sec. Webb Sch., Knoxville, 1986-2000; pres. Knoxville Watersports Festival, 1986-87; mem. Leadership Knoxville, 1986-87. Fellow Tenn. Bar Found.; mem. ABA, Tenn. Bar Assn., Knoxville Bar Assn. (bd. govs.), Nat. Assn. Bond Lawyers, Eastern Mineral Law Found. (trustee, exec. com. 1980—, pres. 1991-92), Trout Unltd. (nat. bd. dirs.), Knoxville Racquet Club (bd. dirs. 1980-82), Cherokee Country Club, Rotary (v.p. Knoxville 1985-87), Appalachian Club (Elkmont, Tenn.), Omciron Delta Kappa, Delta Kappa Epsilon. Avocations: upland and waterfowl hunting, fly fishing, Appalchian ecology. General corporate, FERC practice, Municipal (including bonds). Office: Hunton & Williams 2000 Riverview Twr 900 S Gay St Knoxville TN 37902-1810

CONINE, GARY BAINARD, lawyer, educator; b. Jackson, Miss., Nov. 26, 1947; s. Wallace Bainard and Mary Belle (Thompson) C.; m. Donna Sue Burnett, Sept. 2, 1982; 1 child, Joshua Wallace. B.A. in Econs., So. Meth. U., 1970; J.D., U. Okla., 1977. Bar: Tex. 1977. Assoc. Liddell, Sapp, Zivley & Brown, Houston, 1977-79; asst. prof. law U. Wyo., Laramie, 1979-80; assoc. Liddell, Sapp, Zivley, Brown & LaBoon, Houston, 1980-83; adj. prof. law South Tex. Coll. Law, Houston, 1982; ptnr. Liddell, Sapp & Zivley, Houston, 1984-87; adj. prof. law, advanced energy studies U. Houston Law Ctr., 1985-87. Contbr. articles to profl. jours. Served to 1st lt. USAF, 1970-74. Decorated Air Force Commendation medal; Leon J. York, Jr. scholar U. Okla., 1975, Rayburn L. Foster Meml. scholar 1975, George J. Fagin Mcpl. Law endowment scholar, 1976, William R. Bandy Meml. scholar 1977. Mem. ABA (vice chmn. oil com. 1981-83), Houston Bar Assn., State Bar Assn. Tex. (rsch. grantee 1987), Southwestern Legal Found. (planning com. annual inst. on oil and gas law and taxation 1985-88), Order of Barristers, Order of Coif, Houston C. of C. (govt. relations council 1983-87). Republican. Mem. Christian Ch. FERC practice, Oil, gas, and mineral, Real property.

CONINO, JOSEPH ALOYSIUS, lawyer; b. Hammond, La., Aug. 17, 1920; s. Dominic and Catherine (Tamborella) C.; m. Mae Evelyn Moragas, Feb. 27, 1943; children: Joseph Aloysius Jr., Robert Carl. BBA, Tulane U., 1950; JD, Loyola U., 1961; MBA, U. Pa., 1951. Bar: La. 1961, U.S. Dist. Ct. (ea. dist.) La. 1961, U.S. Ct. Appeals (5th cir.) 1972, U.S. Supreme Ct. 1989. Pvt. practice, Jefferson, La., 1961—. County judge State of La. Parish, Jefferson, 1970; del. State of La. Constnl. Conv., Baton Rouge, 1973-74; asst. atty. Parish of Jefferson, 1977—. With USN, 1942-45. Mem. La. Bar Assn. (ho. of dels. 1963-92, bd. dirs. 1981-83, 96-99), Jefferson Bar Assn. (pres.), New Orleans C. of C. (bd. dirs. 1974-77), Kiwanis (pres. Metairie, La. chpt.). Avocations: golf, swimming, tennis. General civil litigation, Estate planning, Real property. Office: 1920 Jefferson Hwy Jefferson LA 70121-3816

CONISON, JAY, lawyer; b. Cin., Oct. 21, 1953; s. Allan Abraham and Theresa (Yudofsky) C.; m. Nancy Jo Kelber, Sept. 7, 1980; children: Alexander, David. BA, Yale U., 1975; MA, U. Minn., 1978, JD, 1981. Bar: Ill. 1981, U.S. Dist. Ct. (no. dist.) Ill. 1980, U.S. Dist. Ct. (ea. dist.) Wis. 1984, U.S. Dist. Ct. (no. dist. trial) Ill. 1985, U.S. Ct. Appeals (7th cir.) 1986, U.S. Dist. Ct. (we. dist.) Okla. 1990, U.S. Supreme Ct. 1990. Atty. Sonnenschein, Carlin, Nath & Rosenthal, Chgo., 1981-90; asst. prof. Oklahoma City U. Sch. Law, 1990-92, assoc. prof., 1992-94, prof., assoc. dean, 1994-97, interim dean, 1997-98; dean, prof. Valparaiso (Ind.) U. Sch. Law, 1998—. Author: Employee Benefit Plans in a Nutshell, 1993, 2d edit., 1998. Mem. ABA (Forum com. franchising, sect. on legal edn. and admission to the bar). Federal civil litigation, Franchising, Pension, profit-sharing, and employee benefits. Home: 2103 Chandana Trl Valparaiso IN 46383-2295 Office: Valparaiso U Sch Law Wesemann Hall Valparaiso IN 46383 E-mail: jay.conison@valpo.edu

CONKEL, ROBERT DALE, lawyer, pension consultant; b. Oct. 13, 1936; s. Chester William and Marian Matilda (Ashton) Conkel; m. Elizabeth A. Cargill, June 15, 1958; children: Debra Lynn, Dale William, Douglas Alan; m. Brenda Jo Myers, Aug. 02, 1980; 1 child Chelsea Ashton. BA, Mt. Union Coll., 1958; JD cum laude, Cleve. Marshall Law Sch., 1965; LLM, Case Western Res. U., 1972. Bar: Ohio 1965, U.S. Ct. Appeals (5th cir.) 1979, U.S. Tax Ct. 1974, U.S. Supreme Ct. 1974. Supr. Social Security Adminstrn., Cleve., 1958—65; trust officer Harter Bank & Trust Co., Canton, 1965—70; exec. v.p. Am. Actuaries, Inc., Grand Rapids, Mich., 1970—73; mgr. plans and rsch. A.S. Hansen, Inc., Dallas, 1973—74; pvt. practice, 1973—; pension cons., southwest regional dir. Am. Actuaries, Inc., 1974—88. Sr. cons. Coopers & Lybrand, Dallas, 1989; pres. Robert D. Conkel, Inc., 1989—; mem. devel. bd. Met. Nat. Bank, Richardson, Tex.; instr. Am. Mgmt. Assn., 1975, Am. Coll. Advanced Pension Planning, 1975—76; enrolled actuary Joint Bd. Enrollment U.S. Depts. Labor and Treasury. Contbr. articles to legal publs.; mem. editl. adv. bd.: jour. Jour. Pension Planning and Compliance, 1974—83. Sustaining mem. Rep. Nat. Com., 1980—88. Mem.: ABA (employee benefit com. sect. taxation), Ohio State Bar Assn., Tex. Bar Assn., Dallas Bar Assn., Am. Soc. Pension Acutaries (dir. 1973—81), Am. Acad. Actuaries. Estate planning, Pension, profit-sharing, and employee benefits, Personal income taxation. Office: 100 N Central Expy # 519 Richardson TX 75080-5332

CONLIN, ROXANNE BARTON, lawyer; b. Huron, S.D., June 30, 1944; d. Marion William and Alyce Muraine (Madden) Barton; m. James Clyde Conlin, Mar. 21, 1964; children: Jacalyn Rae, James Barton, Deborah Ann, Douglas Benton BA, Drake U., 1964, JD, 1966, MPA, 1979; LLD (hon.), U. Dubuque, 1975. Bar: Iowa 1966. Assoc. Davis, Huebner, Johnson & Burt, Des Moines, 1966-67; dep. indsl. commr. State of Iowa, 1967-68, asst. atty. gen., 1969-76; U.S. atty. So. Dist. Iowa, 1977-81; ptnr. Conlin, P.C., Des Moines, 1983—. Adj. prof. law U. Iowa, 1977-79; chmn. Iowa Women's Polit. Caucus, 1973-75, del. nat. steering com., 1973-77; cons. U.S. Commn. on Internat. Women's Year, 1976-77; gen. counsel NOW Legal Def. and Edn. Fund, 1985-88, pres., 1986-88; lectr. in field. Contbr. articles to profl. jours. Nat. committeewoman Iowa Young Dems.; pres. Polk County Young Dems., 1965-66; del. Iowa Presdl. Conv., 1972; Dem. candidate for gov. of Iowa, 1982; bd. dirs. Riverhills Day Care Ctr., YWCA; chmn. Drake U. Law Sch. Endowment Trust, 1985-86; bd. counselors Drake U., 1982-86; pres. Civil Justice Found., 1986-88, Roscoe Pound Found., 1994-97; chair Iowa Dem. Party, 1998-99. Recipient award Iowa ACLU, 1974, Iowa Citizen's Action Network, 1987, Alumnus of Yr. award Drake U. Law Sch., 1989, ann. award Young Women's Resource Ctr., 1989, Verne Lawyer award as Outstanding Mem. Iowa Trial Lawyers Assn., 1994, Rosalie Wahl award Minn. Women Lawyers, 1998; named one of Top Ten Litigators Nat. Law Jour., 1989, 100 Most Influential Attys., 1991, 50 Most Powerful Women Attys. Nat. Law Jour., 1998, Marie

Lambert award, 2000, Mary Louise Smith award YWCA, 2001; Reader's Digest scholar, 1963-64, Fishcher Found., 1965-66; scholarship established in her honor Kansas City Women Lawyers, 1999. Mem. NOW (bd. dirs. 1986-88), ABA, ATLA (chmn. consumer and victims coalition com. 1985-87, chmn. edn. dept. 1987-88, parliamentarian 1988-89, sec. 1989-90, v.p. 1990-91, pres.-elect 1991-92, pres. 1992-93), Iowa Bar Assn., Assn. Trial Lawyers Iowa (bd. dirs.), Internat. Acad. Trial Lawyers, Iowa Acad. Trial Lawyers, Higher Edn. Commn. Iowa (co-chmn. 1988-90), Inner Circle of Advocates, Phi Beta Kappa, Alpha Lambda Delta, Chi Omega (Social Svc. award). Civil rights, General civil litigation, Personal injury. Office: Griffin Bldg 319 7th St Ste 600 Des Moines IA 50309-3826

CONLON, STEVEN DENIS, lawyer; b. Evanston, Ill., Aug. 17, 1957; s. Denis J. and Carolyn J. (Buck) C. BBA, Loyola U., Chgo., 1982, JD, 1986. CPA, Ill. Tax acct. Arthur Young & Co., Chgo., 1982-86; assoc., ptnr. Chapman and Cutler, 1986-95; ptnr. Baker & McKenzie, 1995-99, Katten, Muchin & Zavis, Chgo., 1999—. Adj. prof. law Kent Coll. Law, Chgo., 1988—; mem. adv. bd. Derivatives mag., N.Y.C., 1994—. Co-author: Principles of Financial Derivatives: U.S. and International Taxation, 1999; co-editor: Tax-Exempt Derivatives—A Guide to Legal Considerations for Lawyers, Finance Professionals and Municipal Issuers, 1994; co-author (chpt.) The Handbook of Derivatives and Synthetics, 1994; contbr. more than 20 articles to profl. jours. Mem. ABA (tax sect., chair fin. transactions com. 1994-95), Chgo. Bar Assn. (chair fed. tax com. 1997-98), Nat. Assn. Bond Lawyers (Bond Attys. Workshop steering com. 1993-95), Chgo. Fed. Tax Forum. Avocations: music, poetry, opera, karate. Banking, Securities, Taxation, general. Office: Katten Muchin & Zavis 525 W Monroe St Ste 1500 Chicago IL 60661-3693

CONLON, SUZANNE B. federal judge; b. 1939; AB, Mundelein Coll., 1963; JD, Loyola U., Chgo., 1968; postgrad., U. London, 1971. Law clk. to judge U.S. Dist. Ct. (no. dist.) Ill., 1968-71; assoc. Pattishall, McAuliffe & Hostetter, 1972-73, Schiff Hardin & Waite, 1973-75; asst. U.S. atty. U.S. Dist. Ct. (no. dist.) Ill., 1976-77, 82-86, U.S. Dist. Ct. (cen. dist.) Calif., 1978-82; exec. dir. U.S. Sentencing Commn., 1986-88; spl. counsel to assoc. atty. gen., 1988; judge U.S. Dist. Ct. (no. dist.) Ill., 1988—. Asst. prof. law De Paul U., Chgo., 1972-73, lectr., 1973-75; adj. prof. Northwestern U. Sch. Law, 1991-95; vice chmn. Chgo. Bar Assn. Internat. Inst., 1993—; vis. com. U. Chgo. Harris Grad. Sch. Pub. Policy, 1997—. Mem. ABA, FBA, Am. Judicature Soc., Internat. Bar Assn. Judges Forum, Lawyers Club Chgo. (pres. 1996-97). Office: US Dist Ct No Dist Everett McKinley Dirksen Bldg 219 S Dearborn St Ste 2356 Chicago IL 60604-1878

CONMY, PATRICK A. federal judge; b. 1934; BA, Harvard U., 1955; JD, Georgetown U., 1959. Bar: Va. 1959, N.D. 1959. Ptnr. Lundberg, Conmy et al, Bismarck, N.D., 1959-85; mem. Bismarck City Commn., 1968-76; state rep. N.D. House Reps., Bismarck, 1976-85; judge U.S. Dist. Ct. N.D., 1985—. Office: US Dist Ct Fed Bldg 220 E Rosser Ave Rm 411 PO Box 1578 Bismarck ND 58502-1578

CONNALLY, MICHAEL W. lawyer; b. Long Beach, Calif., July 8, 1957; s. Jack Walton and Melba June (Renfro) C.; m. Mary Kathleen Tubbiola, June 11, 1977; children: Steven William, Lisa Marie, Amber Lynn. BA in History, Loyola Marymount U., Los Angeles, 1978; JD, Loyola Law Sch., Los Angeles, 1981. Bar: Calif. 1981. Assoc. Wolf & Leo, L.A., 1981-84, sr. assoc., 1984-88, ptnr., 1987-91, Lewis, D'Amato, Brisbois & Bisgaard, Costa Mesa, Calif., 1991—. Faculty Calif. Mission Bapt. Inst., Bellflower, 1984-92. Youth assoc. Calif. Rep. State Cen. Com., 1976, assoc., 1977-86; deacon Hillcrest Missionary Bapt. Ch., Huntington Beach Calif., 1979-85, Grace Missionary Bapt. Ch., Anaheim, Calif., 1985-97; trustee Ctrl. Bapt. Ch., Huntington Beach, Calif., 1999—. Mem. Calif. State Bar, Orange County Bar Assn. Republican. Baptist. Avocations: white water rafting, bowling, chess, basketball, cooking. Appellate, General civil litigation, Insurance. Office: Lewis D'Amato Brisbois & Bisgaard 650 Town Center Dr Fl 14 Costa Mesa CA 92626-1989 E-mail: Connally@LDBB.com

CONNEEN, JAMES THOMAS, lawyer, management consultant; b. Orange, N.J., June 1, 1939; s. Thomas J. and Mary Elizabeth (Doyle) C.; B.S. (scholar), St. Peter's Coll., 1961; J.D. (scholar), N.Y. U., 1964; m. Maureen C. Rielly, Aug. 24, 1963; children— Elizabeth, Sheila, Martin. Admitted to Pa. bar, 1964, N.Y. bar, 1967; law clk. to chief justice Pa., 1964-65; asso. firm Breed, Abbott & Morgan, N.Y.C., 1967-69; v.p., gen. counsel, dir. Posi-Seal Internat., Inc., North Stonington, Conn., 1969-70; asso. counsel Union Camp Corp., Wayne, N.J., 1970-72; v.p. Syncronamics, Inc., Englewood Cliffs, N.J., 1972-75; chmn. bd. A. T. Hudson & Co., Inc., Paramus, N.J., 1975— , also dir. Served to capt., M.I., U.S. Army, 1965-67. Decorated Army Commendation medal. Mem. Am. Bar Assn., N.Y. Bar Assn., Pa. Bar Assn. Republican. Roman Catholic. Club: Ridgewood (N.J.) Country. Home: 299 Highland Ave Ridgewood NJ 07450-4003 Office: A T Hudson & Co Inc 299 Forest Ave Paramus NJ 07652

CONNELL, EDWARD PEACOCK, lawyer; b. Memphis, Apr. 8, 1936; s. Charles Willis, Sr., and Georgia (Peacock) C.; m. Ann Morris, Dec. 27, 1958 (div. 1966); m. Eva Badger, Nov. 23, 1968; 1 son, Edward P. Student Tulane U., 1954-55; B.B.A. with distinction, U. Miss., 1958, J.D. with distinction, 1961; postgrad, NYU, 1962. Bar: Miss. 1961, U.S. Supreme Ct. 1966. Part time adj. prof. law U. Miss., 1963-75; mem. Holcomb, Dunbar, Connell, Chaffin & Willard, Clarksdale, Miss., 1961— . Assoc. editor Miss. Law Jour., 1960-61. Fellow Am. Coll. Probate Csl. (state chmn. 1985-87); mem. ABA (exec. council young lawyers sect. 1966-68), Miss. State Bar (2d v.p. 1967-68, pres. young lawyers sect. 1966-67, chmn. com. on taxation 1973-74), Coahoma County Bar Assn. (pres. 1969-70), Lawyer Pilots Bar Assn., Phi Delta Phi, Phi Kappa Phi, Omicron Delta Kappa, Beta Gamma Sigma. Office: PO Box 368 Holcomb Dunbar Connell Chaffin & Willard 152 Delta Ave Clarksdale MS 38614

CONNELL, JANICE T. lawyer, author, arbitrator, business executive; BS in Fgn. Service, Georgetown U., 1961; M in Polit. and Internat. Adminstrn., U. Pitts., 1976; JD, Duquesne U., 1979. Bar: U.S. Dist. Ct. (we. dist.) Pa. 1979, U.S. Ct. Appeals (3d cir.) 1979, U.S. Supreme Ct. 1983. Pres. Regency Advertising, Jacksonville, Fla. and Pitts., 1968-74, Connell Leasing of Fla., Jacksonville and Pitts., 1970-80; v.p., sec. Nat. Motor Leasing Inc., Pitts., 1980-86; ptnr. Connell & Connell, 1980-1986. Arbitrator N.Y. Stock Exchange, 1981—, Am. Arbitration Assn., 1985—, Nat. Assn. Securities Dealers, 1983—. Author: Queen of the Cosmos, 1990, Visions of the Children, 1992, The Triumph, 1993, Angel Power, 1995, Meetings with Mary, 1996, Praying with Mary, 1997, Prayer Power, 1998, Queen of Angels, 1999. Founder Pitts. Ctr. for Peace, Inc., 1988—, Marion Ctr. World Peace, 1990—, Ctr. for Peace Ams., 1991; bd. dirs. Assn. Jr. Leagues Am., Wheeling, W.Va., Pitts., 1964—, Salvation Army, Wheeling, 1967-68, United Way, Jacksonville, 1971, YMCA, Jacksonville, 1992, Legal Aid Soc., Pitts., 1985—; bd. dirs. women's adv. bd. Duquesne U., Pitts., 1980—; founding dir. Inst. for World Concern, 1981—. Mem. ABA (real property sect.), Pa. Bar Assn., Allegheny County Bar Assn., Epiphany Assn. Estate planning, Probate, Securities. Office: 2 Gateway Ctr Ste 620 Pittsburgh PA 15222-1425

CONNELL, WILLIAM D. lawyer; b. Palo Alto, Calif., Apr. 1, 1955; s. Robert Charles and Audrey Elizabeth (Steele) C.; m. Kathy Lynn Mleko, Aug. 13, 1977; children: Hilary Anne, Andrew James. BA in Polit Sci. with honors, Stanford U., 1976; JD cum laude, Harvard U., 1979. Bar: Calif. 1979, U.S. Dist. Ct. (cen., no. and ea. dists.) Calif. 1979, U.S. Ct. Appeals (9th cir.) 1979. Assoc. Gibson, Dunn & Crutcher, L.A., 1979-80, San Jose, Calif., 1980-87, ptnr., 1988-97, Gen. Counsel Assocs. LLP, 1997—. Mem. Christian Legal Soc. Mem. Stanford Alumni Assn. (life), Commonwealth Club Calif., The Churchill Club, U.S. Golf Assn., The Federalist Soc., Phi Beta Kappa. Republican. Avocations: photography, golf. General civil litigation, Environmental, Product liability.

CONNELL, WILLIAM TERRENCE, lawyer, judge; b. Montclair, N.J., July 29, 1949; s. Raymond Charles and Kathryn (Hanley) C.; m. Honor Marilyn McMahon, July 19, 1975; children: Sean William, Heather Erin, Lauren Blythe. AB, Providence Coll., 1971; JD, Seton Hall U., 1976. Bar: N.J. 1977, D.C. 1979, U.S. Dist. Ct. N.J. 1977, U.S. Ct. Appeals (3d cir.) 1984; cert. trial atty. Investigator Comml. Union Ins. Co., West Orange, N.J., 1971, Essex County Prosecutors Office, Newark, 1971-77; mem. Dwyer, Connell & Lisbona, Montclair, 1977—, Fairfield, N.J., 1997—. Arbitrator Middlesex County Superior Ct., New Brunswick, N.J., 1984—; judge Mcpl. ct. Borough of Roseland, N.J., 1988—. Mem.: ABA, Assn. Trial Lawyers Am., Am. Bd. Trial Attys. (adv.), N.J. Bar Assn., Essex County Bar Assn., Middlesex County Bar Assn., Middlesex County Trial Lawyers Assn., Trucking Ind. Def. Assn., Def. Rsch. Inst., Essex Fells Country Club (N.J.). Roman Catholic. Civil rights, Federal civil litigation, Insurance. Home: 18 Ford Ln Roseland NJ 07068-1456 Office: Dwyer Connell & Lisbona Greenbrook Corp Ctr 100 Passaic Ave Fairfield NJ 07004-3508 E-mail: wconnell@dcllaw.com

CONNELLY, COLIN CHARLES, lawyer; b. Hopewell, Va., Nov. 1, 1956; s. Charles Bernell and Doris Louise (Beasley) C.; m. Stephanie Paige Lowder, May 9, 1981. AA, Richard Bland Coll., 1977; BA, Va. Commonwealth U., 1979; JD, U. Richmond, 1983. Bar: Va. 1983, U.S. Ct. Appeals (4th cir.) 1983. Assoc. Tuck, Freasier, & Herbig, Richmond, Va., 1984-87; ptnr. Tuck & Connelly Profl. Assocs., Inc., 1988-95, Connelly & Assocs., P.C., Chester, 1996—. Bd. dirs., v.p. Cen. Title Ins. Agy., Richmond, 1988—; agt. Chgo. Title Ins. Corp., Richmond, 1988—. Mem., assoc./counsel Home Builders Assn. South Side Va. Mem. ABA, Va. Bar Assn., Richmond Bar Assn., Southside Bd. Realtors (affiliate), Chester Jaycees, Omicron Delta Kappa, Phi Kappa Phi, Phi Alpha Delta (justice 1983-86). Baptist. Avocations: biking, racquetball, basketball. Construction, Real property. Home: 14206 Masada Ct Chesterfield VA 23838-8725 Office: Connelly & Assocs 4830 W Hundred Rd Chester VA 23831-1746

CONNELLY, GEORGE WILLIAM, lawyer; b. Charlottesville, Va., Nov. 27, 1945; s. George William and Margaret Mary (Shannon) C.; m. Elaine Helen Tylenda, Aug. 24, 1968; children— Allison Lynn, Devin Matthew. B.S.B.A., Northwestern U., 1967, J.D., 1971. Bar: Ill. 1971, U.S. Tax Ct. 1971, N.Y. 1979, U.S. Ct. Appeals (5th cir.) 1989, U.S. Supreme Ct. 1980. Spl. trial atty. Office of Chief Counsel, IRS, Buffalo, 1971-85; ptnr. Chamberlain, Hrdlicka, White, Williams & Martin, Houston, 1986—; instr. trial atty. tng., Washington, 1978-80, lectr. continuing profl. edn. North-Atlantic region, N.Y.C., 1981-85, cons. appeals tracking system, Washington, 1982-85. Moot ct. judge Albert R. Mugel Tax Competition, SUNY-Buffalo, 1974-85; brief grader, 1974-80; lectr. U. Rochester Tax Planning Inst., N.Y., 1981, Tex. Soc. CPA's, 1986—; Erie County Bar Assn., Buffalo, 1979; panel mem. N.Y. State Soc. of C.P.A.s, Buffalo, 1983. Served to sgt. USAR, 1969-75. Recipient James H. Markham, Jr. Meml. award, Chief Counsel IRS, 1980; named Atty. of Yr., North-Atlantic region IRS, 1983. Roman Catholic. Federal civil litigation, Corporate taxation, Personal income taxation. Office: Chamberlain Hrdlicka White Williams & Martin 1200 Smith St Ste 1400 Houston TX 77002-4401

CONNELLY, MARY JO, lawyer; b. Chgo., May 19, 1949; d. Joseph Anthony and Veronica Colette (Casey) C. BSN, Coll. St. Teresa, 1971; JD, DePaul U., 1980. Bar: Ill. 1980, U.S. Dist. Ct. (no. dist.) Ill. 1980, U.S. Dist. Ct. (ctrl. dist., no. dist.) Ill. 1990. Head nurse neurosurgery St. Mary's Hosp., Rochester, Minn., 1971-73; head nurse ambulatory care U. Calif., San Francisco, 1973-77; ptnr. Sweeney & Riman Ltd., Chgo., 1980-98. Mem. ABA, Women's Bar Assn. Ill., Ill. Bar Assn., Chgo. Bar Assn. (investigator hearing, bd. dirs. jud. evaluation com. 1984-89). General civil litigation, Personal injury. Home: 340 W Diversey Pky Apt 618 Chicago IL 60657-6242 E-mail: maryjo@21stcentury.net

CONNELLY, THOMAS JOSEPH, lawyer; b. Kansas City, Kans., Jan. 31, 1940; s. Edward J. and Mary (McCallum) C.; m. Barbara Helen Marciniak, Aug. 1, 1964; children: Catherine, Jennifer. AB, U. Detroit, 1963, JD, 1968. Bar: Mich. 1969, U.S. Dist. Ct. (so. and ea. dists.) Mich. 1969, U.S. Ct. Appeals (6th cir.) 1969. Sr. ptnr. Connelly, Crowley, Groth & Seglund, Walled Lake, Mich., 1975—. Exec. bd. dirs. Oakland County (Mich.) Reps., 1979-82. Mem. Mich. Bar Assn. (rep. assembly 1978—), Oakland County Bar Assn., Internat. Arabian Horse Assn. (pres.), Mich. Arabian Horse Assn. (pres. 1986—), Am. Horse Shows Assn. (bd. dirs., exec. com. 1996—). Roman Catholic. Personal injury, Real property. Home: 1635 S Garner Rd Milford MI 48380-4127 Office: Connelly Crowley Groth & Seglund 2410 S Commerce Rd Walled Lake MI 48390-2129 E-mail: ccgs@ismi.com

CONNELLY, WARREN E. lawyer; b. Mt. Vernon, N.Y., Nov. 18, 1946; BA cum laude, Dartmouth Coll., 1968; JD, Georgetown U., 1973. Bar: D.C. 1973. Atty. Cost of Living Coun., 1973-74; mem. Akin, Gump, Strauss, Hauer & Feld L.L.P., Washington. Active Georgetown U. Law Alumni Bd., 1986—, U.S./Canada Binat. Panel, 1989—. 1st lt. U.S. Army, 1968-70. Mem. D.C. Bar. Office: Akin Gump Strauss Hauer & Feld LLP 1333 New Hampshire Ave NW Washington DC 20036-1564

CONNER, JOHN SHULL, lawyer; b. Sioux City, Iowa, Jan. 9, 1954; s. Raymond Dudley and Sally Elizabeth (Shull) C.; m. Mary Ziemba, Aug. 16, 1980; children: Courtney, John, Margaret. BSBA, U. Nebr., 1976; JD, Drake U., 1979. Bar: Mo. 1979, U.S. Dist. Ct. (we. dist.) Mo. 1979,U.S. Dist. Ct. (no. dist.) Calif. 1984, U.S. Supreme Ct. 1988, U.S. Dist. Ct. Ariz. 1992, U.S. Ct. Appeals (10th cir.) 1992, U.S. Dist. Ct. Kans. 1998. Assoc. Shughart Thomson & Kilroy, P.C., Kansas City, Mo., 1979-83, dir., 1984—. Co-author: Kansas and Missouri Law for Design Professionals, 1997, Missouri Civil Actions, Vol. 1, 1989; contbr. articles to various publs. Coord. United Way, Kansas City, 1984—, loaned exec., 1998—; bd. dirs., pres. Pinehurst Estate, Overland Park, Kans., 1992-94; bd. dirs. Gillis Ctr., Kansas City, 1996—; com. mem. Valley View United Meth. Ch., Overland Park, 1998. Mem. ABA (constrn. forum), Mo. Bar Assn., Kansas City Bar Assn., Kansas City Club. General civil litigation, Construction, Insurance. Office: Shughart Thomson & Kilroy 120 W 12th St Ste 1500 Kansas City MO 64105-1929

CONNER, LEWIS HOMER, JR. lawyer; b. Chattanooga, Mar. 21, 1938; s. Lewis H. Sr. and Cleo (Johnson) C.; m. Ashley Whitsitt, June 1, 1960; children: Holland Ashley, Lewis Forrest. BA, Vanderbilt U., 1960, JD, 1963. Bar: Tenn. 1963, U.S. Dist. Ct. (all dists.) Tenn. 1963, U.S. Ct. Appeals (6th cir.) 1963, U.S. Ct. Mil. Appeals 1964, U.S. Supreme Ct. 1990; cert. mediator, Tenn. Founding ptnr., atty. Dearborn & Ewing, Nashville, 1972-80; judge Ct. Appeals Middle Dist., 1980-84; sr. ptnr., atty. Waller Lansden Dortch & Davis, 1985-89, Boult, Cummings, Conners & Berry, Nashville, 1989-96; of counsel Stokes & Bartholomew, 1997—. Chmn. Willis Coroon, Tenn., 1996-99; spl. chief justice Supreme Ct. Tenn., 1980-81; lectr. law Vanderbilt U. Sch. Law, Nashville, 1984-93; life del. Sixth Cir. Ct. Appeals Jud. Conf. Mng. editor Vanderbilt Law Rev. Elder Westminster Presbyn. Ch.; bd. dirs. Tenn. Golf Assn., Nashville, 1965—, pres., 1985, chmn. 1994-95, 98—; fin. co-chmn. Alexander for Gov., 1974-78; chmn. Tenn. Rep. Fin. Com., 1975, Tenn. Corrections Overcrowding Commn., 1985-86; bd. dirs. Boys & Girls Club Middle Tenn., 1980—, pres., 1991-92; bd. govs. Tenn. State Mus., 1987-91 Fellow Am. Acad. Matrimonial Lawyers, Am. Bar Found., Tenn. Bar Found., Nashville Bar Found.; mem. ABA, Am. Arbitration Assn. (bd. dirs. 1990-96, chmn. Tenn. large complex case panel 1992—, panel of arbitrators 1975—, panel of mediators 1995—), Tenn. Bar Assn., Tenn. Jud. Conf., Nashville Bar Assn. (pres. 1986-87, bd. dirs., 1984-87), Commn. on the Future of the Cts. in Tenn., Order of the Coif, PGA of Am. (hon. Tenn. sect.), The Golf Club Tenn. (founder, exec. com. 1991-97), Richland Country Club (bd. dirs. 1976-79, pres. 1978-79), Belle Meade Country Club, The Honors Course, Naples Grande Golf Club, Nashville City Club, Nashville Cumberland Club, Nashville Stadium Club, Tenn. Golf Assn. (amateur player of yr., 1973). Republican. Avocations: golf, basketball, softball, politics. Home: 163 Charleston Park Nashville TN 37205-4703 Office: Stokes & Bartholomew 424 Church St Ste 2800 Nashville TN 37219-2386 E-mail: lewconner@stokesbartholomew.com

CONNER, MICHAEL TIMOTHY, lawyer; b. Berkeley Heights, N.J., Oct. 6, 1947; s. Joseph H. and Marion C.; m. Carol Ann Mann, July 4, 1981; children: Kelly, Lindsay, David. BA in Polit. Sci., Am. U., 1969, JD, 1976. Bar: D.C. 1977, U.S. Ct. of Appeals (D.C. cir.) 1979, U.S. Ct. of Appeals (1st cir.) 1986, U.S. Ct. of Appeals (4th cir.) 1983. Staff atty. NOAA, Washington, 1977-81, U.S. Dept of Commerce, Washington, 1981-85, chief, gen. litig. divsn., 1985—. Named Atty. of the Year, Dept. Commerce Gen. Coun., 1989. E-mial. Home: 12588 Cross Hollow Ct Herndon VA 20170-5741 Office: US Dept Commerce Office Gen Counsel Rm 5890 Washington DC 20230-0001 E-mail: tconnerl@doc.gov

CONNER, WILLIAM CURTIS, judge; b. Wichita Falls, Tex., Mar. 27, 1920; s. D.H. and Mae (Weeks) C.; m. Janice Files, Mar. 22, 1944; children: William Curtis, Stephen, Christopher, Molly. BBA, U. Tex., 1941, LLB, 1942; student, Harvard, 1942-43, MIT, 1943. Bar: Tex. bar 1942, N.Y. State bar 1949. Asso., mem. firm Curtis, Morris & Safford (and predecessor firm), N.Y.C., 1946-73; judge U.S. Dist. Ct. (so. dist.) N.Y., White Plains, 1973—, now sr. judge. Editor Tex. Law Rev. Served to lt. USNR, 1942-45, PTO. Recipient Jefferson medal N.J. Patent Law Assn. Mem. Am. Judicature Soc., N.Y. Patent Law Assn. (pres. 1972-73) Presbyterian (elder). Club: St. Andrews Golf. Office: US Dist Ct US Courthouse 300 Quarropas St White Plains NY 10601-4140

CONNERS, PATRICIA A. lawyer; b. Patrick AFB, Fla., Nov. 10, 1958; d. Charles Patrick and Ella (Hardon) C. BS with distinction, U. Fla., 1979, JD, 1982. Bar: Fla., 1983. Law clerk Fifth Dist. Ct. Appeal, Daytona Beach, Fla., 1982-84; asst. atty. gen. criminal appeals Fla. Atty. Gen., Tallahassee, 1984-87, asst. atty. gen. antitrust, 1987-97, chief antitrust sect., 1997—. Southeast regional vice-chair Nat. Assn. Atty. Gen. Antitrust Task Force, Washington, 1996-98, nat.-vice-chair, 1999—. Mem. Fla. Supreme Ct. Com. on the Arts, Tallahassee, 1998—. Recipient Antitrust Sect. Davis Productivity award, Fla. Tax Watch, 1989, Economic Crimes Davis Productivity award Fla. Tax Watch, 1993. Mem. Am. Bar Assn. (antitrust sect., govt., pub. sector lawyers sect.), Fla. Bar (vice chair Antitrust Certification Comm. 2001—, govt. lawyers sect., bus. law sect., health law sect.), Fla. Assn. Women Lawyers, Tallahassee Womens Lawyers Assn., U.S. Supreme Ct., Eleventh Circuit Ct. Appeals, U.S. Dist. Ct. Northern Dist. Fla., U.S. Dist. Ct. Middle Dist. Fla., U.S. Dist. Ct. So. Dist. of Fla. Office: Atty Gen Office Antitrust Sect PL-01 The Capitol Tallahassee FL 32399-1050

CONNETTE, EDWARD GRANT, III, lawyer; b. Nashville, Sept. 23, 1952; s. Edward G. and Elizabeth (Stone) C.; m. Jane V. Harper, Feb. 10, 1990. BA, Davidson Coll., 1974; JD, U. N.C., 1977. Bar: N.C. 1980, Conn. 1977, U.S. Dist. Ct. Conn. 1979, U.S. Dist. Ct. (we. dist.) N.C. 1980, U.S. Dist. Ct. (mid. dist.) N.C. 1981, U.S. Ct. Appeals (4th cir.) 1981, U.S. Supreme Ct. 1986. Atty. United Ch. of Christ, N.Y.C., 1977-78, Legal Aid Soc. Hartford County, Hartford, Conn., 1978-80; mng. atty. Legal Svcs. of S-. Piedmont, Inc., Charlotte, N.C., 1980-84; ptnr. Lesesne & Connette, 1984—. Mem. N.C. Bar Assn., N.C. Acad. Trial Lawyers. Democrat. Presbyterian. Civil rights, Federal civil litigation, State civil litigation. Office: Lesesne & Connette 1001 Elizabeth Ave # D Charlotte NC 28204-2234

CONNOLLY, COLM F. prosecutor; BA, U. of Notre Dame; MA, London Sch. Econs.; JD, Duke U. Asst. U.S. Atty. Dist. of Del., 1992—99; ptnr. Morris, Nichols, Arsht and Tunnel, Wilmington, Del., 1999—2001; U.S. Atty. Dist. of Del., 2001—. Bd. mem. Wilmington Music Sch., Del. Hospice, St. Francis Healthcare Service. Recipient Director's award for Superior Performance as Asst. U.S. Atty., U.S. Atty. Gen., 1996. Office: US Attorney Chase Manhattan Ctr PO Box 2046 Wilmington DE 19899-2046 Fax: 302-573-6220*

CONNOLLY, JOSEPH THOMAS, lawyer, judge; b. Montclair, N.J., Mar. 22, 1938; s. Patrick Joseph and Ethelyn Marie (Dilkes) C.; m. Phyllis Jane Marturano, June 25, 1966; children: James V., Michael J., Victoria L. BS, St. Peter's Coll., Jersey City, 1959; JD, Fordham U., 1966. Bar: N.J. 1967, U.S. Dist. Ct. N.J. 1967, U.S. Supreme Ct. 1972. Claim adjuster Md. Am. Gen. Group, East Orange, N.J., 1962-66; jud. clk. Superior Ct. N.J., Newark, 1966-67; assoc. Feuerstein & Sachs, Newark, 1967-68, Donohue & Donohue, Nutley, N.J., 1969-71; trial lawyer Office Pub. Defender N.J., Newark, 1968-69; ptnr. Brown, Connolly & Karosen, Bloomfield, N.J., 1971-88; sole practitioner, Bloomfield, 1989—; judge Mcpl. Ct., Glen Ridge, N.J., 1980— ; instr. William Paterson Coll., Wayne, N.J., 1980; lectr. Inst. for Continuing Legal Edn., Trenton and Newark, 1975-82; moot ct. judge Seton Hall U. Sch. Law, Newark, 1980-94. Pres. Glen Ridge Community Fund, 1978-79, Bloomfield Jaycees, 1971-72; trustee League for Family Service Bloomfied and Glen Ridge. Served with U.S. Army, 1959-60. Mem. ABA, N.J. Bar Assn. (consultor 1979-84), Essex County Bar Assn. Republican. Roman Catholic. Clubs: Bloomfield Lawyers (pres. 1976-77, Outstanding Service award 1977); Glen Ridge Country. Lodge: Kiwanis (pres. 1979-80, sec., bd. dirs., Disting. Pres. award). Fax: 973-748-3167. General practice, Probate, Real property. Home: 13 Winsor Pl Glen Ridge NJ 07028-2124 Office: Office of JT Connolly P.O. Box 8273 13 Windsor Pl Glen Ridge NJ 07028

CONNOLLY, K. THOMAS, lawyer; b. Spokane, Wash., Jan. 23, 1940; s. Lawrence Francis and Kathleen Dorothea (Hallahan) C.; m. Laurie Samuel, June 24, 1967; children: Kevin, Megan, Amy, Matthew. BBA, Gonzaga U., Spokane, Wash., 1962; JD, Gonzaga U., 1966; LLM in Taxation, NYU, 1972. Bar: Wash. 1966, U.S. Ct. Mil. Appeals 1967, U.S. Tax Ct. 1973. Assoc. Witherspoon, Kelley, Davenport & Toole, Spokane, 1972-77, ptnr./prin., 1977—. Assoc. prof. law Gonzaga Sch. Law, 1973-77. Bd. overseers Gonzaga Prep. Sch., Spokane, 1988-89; bd. trustees Spokane Guild Sch. for the Handicapped, 1975-78, Wash. State U. Found. Bd., 1992-97, Whitman Coll. Planned Giving Coun., 1994—, Holy Family Adult Day Care Bd., 2001—. Capt. U.S. Army, 1966-70. Recipient Wall St. Jur. award, 1962; decorated Bronze Star medal. Mem. Wash. State Bar Assn. (founder, chmn. health law sect. 1989-92, health law coun. 1989-94, pres. tax sect. 1987-88, mem. tax coun. 1984—), ABA (chmn. health care subcom. 1990-94). Republican. Avocations: tennis, astronomy. Health, Pension, profit-sharing, and employee benefits, Corporate taxation. Office: Witherspoon Kelley Davenport & Toole 1100 Old National Bldg Spokane WA 99201 E-mail: ktc@wkdtlaw.com

CONNOLLY, KEVIN JUDE, lawyer; b. N.Y.C., May 25, 1954; s. John William and Beatrice Joan (Fallon) C.; m. Audrey Mason, May 25, 1995; children: Shea Alexander, Ciaran Jude. BA cum laude, Fordham Coll., 1976; JD, Fordham U., 1985. Bar: N.Y. 1990. Assoc. Stroock & Stroock & Lavan, N.Y.C., 1985-89, Shapiro & Byrne, P.C., Mineola, N.Y., 1989-92;

counsel Schreiber, Simmons, MacKnight & Tweedy, N.Y.C., 1992-94, Eaton & Van Winkle, N.Y.C., 1994-97; assoc. Robinson, Silverman, Pearce, Aronsohn & Berman LLP, 1998—. Vis. lectr. Sch. Visual Arts, N.Y.C., 1996-2000; dir. Internet Soc., N.Y.C. chpt., 1997-2000; outside counsel Internet Policy Adv. Body, Geneva, Switzerland, 1997-99, Internet Coun. Registrars, Geneva, 1997-98, Hatewatch, Inc., 1998—. Tactical field trainer U.S. Mil. Acad., West Point, 1989-99. Avocations: antiques, paintball. Computer, Construction, Intellectual property. Home: 205 Blackheath Rd Lido Beach NY 11561-4838 Office: Robinson Silverman Pearce Aronsohn & Berman 1290 Ave of Amers New York NY 10104 E-mail: jawz@cybersharque.com

CONNOLLY, THOMAS EDWARD, judge; b. Boston, Nov. 7, 1942; s. Thomas Francis and Catherine Elizabeth (Skehill) C. AB, St. John's Sem., Brighton, Mass., 1964; JD, Boston Coll., 1969. Bar: Mass., 1969. Assoc. Schneider & Reilly, Boston, 1969-73; ptnr. Schneider, Reilly, Zabin, Connolly & Costello, P.C., 1973-85, Connolly Leavis & Rest, Boston, 1986-90; judge Mass. Superior Ct., 1990—; regional adminstrv. justice Norfolk County, 2000—. Instr. law Northeastern Law Sch., Boston, 1975-76. Mem. governing coun. Boston Coll. Law Sch. Alumni Coun., 1980-82. Fellow Am. Coll. Trial Lawyers; mem. ABA (vice chmn. products liability sect. 1978-80), Trial Lawyers Assn. Am. (nat. gov. 1977-80), Mass. Acad. Trial Lawyers (gov. 1976-90), Univ. Club (Boston). Democrat. Roman Catholic. Home: 253 Marlborough St # 4 Boston MA 02116-1731 Office: The Superior Ct Dedham MA 02026

CONNOLLY, WILLIAM M. state supreme court justice; Former judge Nebr. Ct. of Appeals, Lincoln; assoc. justice Nebr. Supreme Ct. Office: Nebr Supreme Ct PO Box 98910 2413 State Capitol Bldg Lincoln NE 68509*

CONNOR, JOHN THOMAS, JR. lawyer; b. N.Y.C., June 16, 1941; s. John Thomas and Mary (O'Boyle) C.; m. Susan Scholle, Dec. 18, 1965; children: Seanna, Marin, John. BA cum laude, Williams Coll., 1963; JD, Harvard U., 1967. Bar: N.Y. 1968, D.C. 1980. Assoc. Cravath, Swaine & Moore, N.Y.C., 1967-71; dep. dir. Office Econ. Policy and Case Analysis, Pay Bd., Washington, 1971-72, Bur. East-West Trade, U.S. Dept. Commerce, Washington, 1972-73; sr. v.p. U.S.-USSR Trade and Econ. Coun., Moscow, 1973-76; assoc. Milbank, Tweed, Hadley & McCloy, N.Y.C., 1976-79; ptnr. Curtis, Mallet-Prevost, Colt and Mosle, Washington, 1980-82; v.p., gen. counsel, sec. PHH Corp., 1982-88; v.p., asst. gen. counsel Prudential Ins. Co. Am., Newark, 1988-90; ptnr. Sills Cummis, 1990-94; counsel Chadbourne & Parke, N.Y.C., 1994-96, Patterson, Belknap, Webb & Tyler, LLP, 1996-98; chmn. Great Am. Life Corp., 1993—, ROSGAL Group Fin Cos., Moscow, 1993—; portfolio mgr., chmn. Third Millennium Funds, 1998—. Exec. dir. Dem. Party N.J., 1969-70; pres., trustee Newark Boys Chorus Sch.; Fulbright tutor Ferguson Coll., Poona, India, 1963-64; chmn. Coun. on Econ. Priorities. Mem. N.Y. State Bar Assn., D.C. Bar Assn., Coun. Fgn. Rels., Am. Law Inst., Baltusrol Club N.J., Met. Club (Washington), Union Club (N.Y.C.), Chevy Chase Club (Md.), Wianno Club (Cape Cod), Mountain Lake Club (Fla.), Phi Beta Kappa. General corporate, Private international, Securities. Home: PO Box 832 Lake Wales FL 33859-0832 Office: Third Millennium Funds 32d Fl 1185 Ave of the Americas New York NY 10036

CONNOR, JOSEPH PATRICK, III, lawyer; b. Phila., Apr. 15, 1953; s. Joseph Patrick Jr. and Wanda Delores (Filipkowski) C.; m. Mary Margaret Kazanicka, Aug. 13, 1977; children: Cathleen Marie, Christopher Joseph, Christine Anne. BA in Polit. Sci., Villanova U., 1974; JD, St. Mary's U., San Antonio, 1974. Bar: Pa. 1977, U.S. Dist. Ct. (ea. dist.) Pa. 1977, U.S. Dist. Ct. (mid. dist.) Pa. 1997, U.S. Ct. Appeals (3d cir.) 1977, U.S Supreme Ct. 1982. Assoc. ptnr. Gibbons, Buckley, Smith, Palmer & Proud, Media, Pa., 1977-82; pres. Connor & Weber, P.C., Phila., Paoli, 1982—. Mem. ABA (tort & litigation sects.), Pa. Bar Assn., Pa. Def. Inst., Def. Research Inst., Pa. Trial Lawyers Assn., Chester County Bar Assn. Republican. Roman Catholic. Club: Overbrook County (Bryn Mawr). Avocations: flying, golf, swimming, traveling. General civil litigation, Insurance, Personal injury. Office: Connor & Weber PC 2401 Pennsylvania Ave Philadelphia PA 19130-3010

CONNOR, TERENCE GREGORY, lawyer; b. Chelsea, Mass., Dec. 28, 1942; s. Joseph Gerard Sr. and Rosalie Cecilia (Ryan) C.; m. Julie Kaye Berry, Dec. 18, 1971; children: Cormac, Kristin, Etain, Brendan. AB, Georgetown U., 1964; LLB, Seton Hall U., 1967; LLM, Georgetown U., 1975. Bar: D.C. 1968, U.S. Supreme Ct. 1976, Fla. 1980. Trial atty. U.S. Dept. Justice, Washington, 1973-76; labor counsel Nat. Airlines Inc., Miami, Fla., 1976-79; practicing atty. Morgan, Lewis & Bockius, 1979-96, mng. ptnr., 1996—. Mem. firm wide governing bd., 1996-2000. Chmn. Miami: Dade citizen com. for Observance Bicentennial of U.S. Constitution, 1986. Served to capt. JAG, USAF, 1968-73. Mem. Fla. Bar Assn. (chair labor and employment law sect. 1994-95, mem. exec. coun. 1986-93), Miami C. of C. (co-chair pers. and Labor mgmt. com. 1993-94) Roman Catholic. Civil rights, Federal civil litigation, Labor. Home: 1517 San Rafael Ave Miami FL 33134-6241 Office: Morgan Lewis & Bockius First Union Fin Ctr 200 S Biscayne Blvd Ste 5300 Miami FL 33131-2333

CONNORS, FRANK JOSEPH, lawyer; b. N.Y.C., Oct. 8, 1944; s. Frank Joseph and Nina Florence (Kirk) C.; m. Evelyn Noreen Mills, Oct. 14, 1983. BA, UCLA, 1965; MA, Columbia U., 1966; JD, Harvard U., 1969. Bar: N.Y. 1970, Fla. 1982, Mass. 1986, U.S. Supreme Ct. 1973. Assoc. Dewey, Ballantine, Bushby, Palmer & Wood, N.Y.C., 1969-75; asst. atty. gen. N.Y. State Spl. Prosecutor, 1975-77; gen. atty. Am. Broadcasting Cos., Inc., 1977-85; atty. Harvard U., Cambridge, Mass., 1985—; acting gen. counsel, 1992. Arbitrator N.Y.C. Civil Ct., 1980-85; comml. arbitrator Am. Arbitration Assn., N.Y.C., 1984-85. Bd. dirs. World Teach, Inc., 1992—. Mem. Am. Judicature Soc., N.Y. State Bar Assn. (copyright com. 1981-85), Assn. of Bar of City of N.Y. (profl. discipline com. 1983-85). Republican. Methodist. General corporate, Taxation, general. Office: Harvard U 1350 Massachusetts Ave Cambridge MA 02138-3846 E-mail: frank_connors@harvard.edu

CONNORS, JOSEPH ALOYSIUS, III, lawyer; b. Washington, June 24, 1946; s. Joseph Aloysius Jr. and Charlotte Rita (Fox) C.; m. Mary Louise Bucklin, June 14, 1969. BBA, U. Southwestern La., 1970; JD, U. Tex., 1973. Bar: Tex. 1973, U.S. Dist. Ct. (so. dist.) Tex. 1975, U.S. Supreme Ct. 1976, U.S. Ct. Appeals (5th cir.) 1976, U.S. Dist. Ct. (ea., we. and no. dists.) Tex. 1981, U.S. Ct. Appeals (11th cir.) 1981, U.S. Ct. Appeals (3d, 4th, 6th, 7th, 8th, 9th, 10th and D.C. cirs.) 1986. Law clk. to assoc. justice Tex. Ct. Civil Appeals, Amarillo, 1973-74; assoc. Rankin & Kern, McAllen, Tex., 1974-76; asst. criminal dist. atty. Hidalgo County, 1976-78; pvt. practice, McAllen, 1978—. Faculty Criminal Trial Advocacy Inst., Huntsville, Tex., 1981-84; speaker seminars State Bar Tex., 1980-81, 84; adj. prof. Reynaldo G. Garza Sch. Law, Edinburg, Tex., 1988-89. Contbg. editor Criminal Trial Manual, Tex., 1984-95; contbr. articles to profl. jours. Bd. dirs. Tex. Rural Legal Aid, 1991—, pres. bd. dirs., 1994-96. With USMCR, 1966-71. Mem. NACDL, State Bar Tex. (grievance com. 12B 1984-91, chmn. com. 1989-90, profl. enhancement program 1997-2000), Tex. Assn. Criminal Def. Lawyers (bd. dirs. 1982-89, Excellence award 1983, medal of honor 1987), Hidalgo County Bar Assn. (bd. dirs. 1981-83), Am. Soc. Writers on Legal Subjects, Hidalgo County Criminal Def. Lawyers Assn. (bd. dirs. 1991-98). Democrat. Roman Catholic. Criminal. Office: PO Box 5838 Mcallen TX 78502-5838

CONNORS, JOSEPH CONLIN, lawyer; b. Mineola, N.Y., Sept. 9, 1948; s. Gerard Edward and Mary Helen (Conlin) C.; m. Mary Napolitano, May 29, 1971; children: J.C., Ryan. BA, SUNY-Oneonta, 1970; JD, Fordham U., 1973. Bar: N.Y. 1974, Tenn. 1985. Confidential law sec. to judge N.Y. Supreme Ct., Cortland, 1973-75; atty. Chevron Corp., Perth Amboy, N.J., 1975-76, Schering-Plough Corp., Kenilworth, 1976-82, assoc. gen. counsel Memphis, 1982-87, staff v.p., planning and bus. devel. Kenilworth, N.J., 1987, dep. gen. counsel Madison, 1987-91, v.p., gen. counsel, 1991-92, sr. v.p., gen. counsel, 1992-96, exec. v.p. and gen. counsel, 1996—. Mem. adv. com. Met. Corp. Counsel; sr. advisor N.J. Corp. Counsel Assn. Mem. ABA (com. of corp. gen. counsel), N.Y. Bar Assn., Tenn. Bar Assn. (former chmn. corp. sect.), Assn. Nat. Advertisers (bd. dirs. 1987-90), N.J. Legal Aid and Defender Assn. (corp. adv. com.), N.J. Corp. Counsel Assn. (sr. advisor), N.J. Panel of the CPR Inst. for Dispute Resolution (bd. dirs.), Food and Drug Inst. (trustee, editl. adv. bd.), Pharm. Rsch. and Mfrs. Am. (exec. com. law sect. 1998). Roman Catholic. Avocations: travel, golf. Antitrust, General corporate. Office: Schering Plough Corp 2000 G Alloping Hill RD Kenilworth NJ 07033-0530

CONOUR, WILLIAM FREDERICK, lawyer; b. Indpls., June 21, 1947; s. William E. and Marian L. (Smith) C.; m. Jennifer Hentges; children: Tonja, Andrea, Erin, Rachel, Tyler, Elise. AB in History, Ind. U., 1970, JD cum laude, 1974. Bar: Ind. 1974, U.S. Dist. Ct. (so. dist.) Ind. 1974, U.S. Dist. Ct. (no. dist.) Ind. 1996, U.S. Ct. Appeals (7th cir.) 1975, U.S. Supreme Ct., 1982; cert. mediator Ind. Supreme Ct., 1992—. Dir. training Ind. Pros. Attys. Council, Indpls., 1974-82; ptnr. Conour & Davis, 1974-86; pvt. practice, 1986-88; ptnr. Conour Doehrman, 1988—. Assoc. prof., adj. faculty Ind. U. Purdue U. Indpls., 1976-86; lectr. Ind. Law Enforcement Acad.; rsch. analyst Ind. Criminal Law Study Commn., 1973-74. Contbg. author Indiana Criminal Procedure Sourcebook, 1974, Indiana Prosecuting Attorney's Deskbook; editor profl. bulletins; contbr. articles to profl. jours. Guarantor Butler U. Clowes Hall; patron Ind. Repertory Theatre, Indpls. Symphony Orch.; mem. Gov.'s club Ind. Dems., Conner Prairie Pioneer Settlement, Nat. Safety Coun., Hoosier Safety Coun. Recipient commendation Drug Enforcement Adminstrn. U.S. Dept. Justice, 1977, Commendation award Hoosier Safety Coun., 1989, Commendation award Ind. State Bar Assn. Criminal Justice Sect., 1990. Fellow Roscoe Pound Found. (life), Found. Am. Bd. Trial Advocates (sr. life), Indpls. Bar Found. (life); mem. ABA (litigation sect.), Am. Bd. Trial Advocates (pres. Ind. chpt.), Am. Soc. Safety, Ind. Bar Assn. (sec. litigation 1981-82, ad hoc com. on legal cert., mem. litigation sect., criminal justice sect., sec. 1977-78, treas. 1981-82), Indpls. Bar Assn. (grievance com. 1983-91, litigation sect.), Assn. Trial Lawyers Am. (cert. Nat. Coll. Advocacy 1979, Advanced Coll. Advocacy 1981, cons. site litigation group, M Club, lectr.), Coll. of Legal Medicine, Am. Coll. of Legal Medicine, Ind. Trial Lawyers Assn. (sustaining mem., bd. dirs., lectr., amicus curie com., rule of evidence com.), Ind. Lawyers Commn. (ad hoc com. on criminal justice standards and goals 1976-80), Am. Bd. Trial Advs., Ind. U. Alumni Assn. (life), Indpls. Law Club, Indpls. Athletic Club, US Equestrian Team (contbg. mem.), US Dressage Fedn. Ind. Dressage Soc. (dir.), Indpls. Mus. Art, Sagamore Am. Inn of Ct. (pres. 1999-2000), Phi Delta Phi (hon.). Democrat. Clubs: Inpls. Athletic; Ind. Soc. Chgo., Atla "M". Federal civil litigation, General civil litigation, Personal injury. Home: 10858 Sedgemoor Cir Carmel IN 46032-9189 Office: 10333 N Meridian St Ste 100 Indianapolis IN 46290-1074 E-mail: wfc@indianalaw.com

CONOVER, RICHARD CORRILL, lawyer; b. Bridgeport, Nebr., Jan. 12, 1942; s. John Cedric and Mildred (Dunn) C.; m. Cathy Harlan, Dec. 19, 1970; children— William Cedric, Theodore Cyril. B.S., U. Nebr., Lincoln, 1965, M.S., 1966; J.D., Cornell U., 1969. Bar: N.Y. 1970, Mont. 1982, U.S. Dist. Ct. (so. and ea. dists.) N.Y. 1971, U.S. Supreme Ct. 1977, U.S. Ct. Customs and Patent Appeals 1979, U.S. Ct. Claims 1980, U.S. Dist. Ct. Mont. 1984, U.S. Tax Ct. 1986. Assoc. Brumbaugh, Graves, Donohue & Raymond, N.Y.C., 1969-73; assoc. Townley, Updike, Carter & Rodgers, N.Y.C., 1974-75; assoc. gen. counsel legal office Automatic Data Processing, Inc., Clifton, N.J., 1975-77; assoc. Nims, Howes, Collison & Isner, N.Y.C., 1977-81; sole practice, Mont., 1981— ; lectr. indsl. and mech. engring. dept. Mont. State U., 1981-97. Mem. Mont. Gov.'s Bd. Sci. and Tech., 1985-87. Mem. ABA, Assn. Bar City N.Y., Mont. Bar Assn., Am. Pat. Law Assn. General civil litigation, Patent, Trademark and copyright. Home: PO Box 1329 Bozeman MT 59771-1329 Office: 104 E Main St Ste 404 Bozeman MT 59715-4787

CONRAD, ANNE MCGREW, lawyer; b. Cleve., Jan. 26, 1970; d. Frank Augustus III and Sharrel (Brown) M. BA, U. Va., 1992; JD, So. Meth. U., 1995. Bar: Tenn. 1995, U.S. Dist. Ct. (we. dist.) Tenn. Atty. Sofamor Danek Group, Inc., Memphis, 1995-96; sr. labor atty. Young & Perl PLC, 1996—. Bd. dirs. Memphis Arts Coun. Urban Art, 1998—; mem. Memphis Bot. Gardens, Jr. League of Memphis; active Young Reps., Memphis, 1995—. Mem. Assn. Women Attys., Memphis Bar Assn., Kiwanis of Memphis. Presbyterian. Avocation: antiques. Labor. Office: Young and Perl PLC One Commerce Sq Ste 2380 Memphis TN 38103

CONRAD, ROBERT J. prosecutor; BA Clemson U., JD U. Va. Pvt. practice Michie, Hamlett, Donato and Lowry, 1983—86, Horn and Conrad, 1986—87; aole practice, 1987—88; ptnr. Bush, Thurman and Conrad, 1988—89; asst. U.S. atty. We. Dist. N.C. U.S. Dept. Justice, 1989—2001, U.S. atty., 2001—. Office: Carillon Bldg Ste 1700 227 W Trade St Charlotte NC 28202*

CONRAD, WINTHROP BROWN, JR. lawyer; b. Detroit, May 26, 1945; s. Winthrop Brown and Dolores (Millard) C.; m. Ellen Rouse, May 12, 1973; children: Parker Rouse, Louisa Katherine, Frances Winthrop. AB, Yale U., 1967; JD, Harvard U., 1971. Bar: N.Y. 1972, U.S. Dist. Ct. (so. dist.) N.Y. 1975, U.S. Ct. Appeals (2d cir.) 1975. Ptnr. Davis, Polk & Wardwell, N.Y.C., 1979—, Paris Office, 1985-88. Bd. dirs. Found. for Joffrey Ballet, N.Y.C., 1985-86, British-Am. Ednl. Found.; trustee Episcopal Diocese of N.Y.; former trustee Estate and Property of the Conv. of the Diocese of N.Y., Ch. Pension Fund; trustee Vt. Studies Ctr.; dir., BAR Vermont Inc. Mem. ABA, Assn. of Bar of City of N.Y. Contracts commercial, General corporate, Securities. Home: 1120 5th Ave New York NY 10128-0144 Office: Davis Polk & Wardwell 450 Lexington Ave Fl 31 New York NY 10017-3982 also: 856 Old Post Rd Bedford NY 10506-1215

CONRAN, JOSEPH PALMER, lawyer; b. St. Louis, Oct. 4, 1945; s. Palmer and Theresa (Bussmann) C.; m. Daria D. Conran, June 8, 1968; children: Andrew, Lisabeth, Theresa. BA, St. Louis U., 1967, JD with honors, 1970. Bar: Mo. 1970, U.S. Ct. Mil. Appeals 1971, U.S. Ct. Appeals (8th cir.) 1974. Assoc. Husch and Eppenberger, St. Louis, 1974-78, ptnr., 1978—, chmn. litigation dept., 1980-95, chmn. mgmt. com., 1995—. Mem. faculty Trial Practice Inst. Capt., JAGC, USAF, 1970-74. Mem. Bar Assn. Met. St. Louis (Merit award 1976, 77), Mo. Bar Assn. (bd. govs. 1987-92), Mo. Athletic Club (pres. 1986-87), Norwood Hills Country Club. Roman Catholic. Federal civil litigation, State civil litigation, Securities. Home: 53 Hawthorne Est Saint Louis MO 63131-3035 Office: Husch & Eppenberger 100 N Broadway Ste 1300 Saint Louis MO 63102-2789 E-mail: joe.conran@husch.com

CONROY, ROBERT JOHN, lawyer; b. Newark, Feb. 17, 1953; s. Michael John and Frances (Goncalves) C.; m. Mary Catherine McGuire, June 7, 1975; children: Caitlin Michaela, Michael Colin. BS, St. Peter's Coll., 1977; M in Pub. Adminstrn., CUNY, 1981; JD, N.Y. Law Sch., 1981; MPH, Harvard U., 1985. Bar: N.Y. 1981, N.J. 1981, U.S. Dist. N.J. 1981, Calif. 1982, U.S. Dist. Ct. (so. and ea. dists.) N.Y. 1982, U.S. Dist. Ct. (we. dist.) Calif. 1990, U.S. Ct. Appeals (2d, 3d and 11th cirs.) 1982, Fla. 1984, D.C. 1984, U.S. Supreme Ct. 1984, Pa., 2000, U.S. Dist. Ct. (ea. dist.), Pa., 2001. Asst. corp. counsel City of N.Y., 1981-83, dep. chief med. malpractice unit, 1983, chief med. malpractice unit, 1984; assoc. Jones, Hirsch, Connors & Bull, N.Y.C., 1985-88; counsel Kern & Augustine, P.A., Morristown, N.J., 1988-90; prin. Kern Augustine Conroy & Schoppmann, P.C., Bridgewater, 1990—. Spl. counsel pro bono med. malpractice rsch. project, N.Y.C., 1985-88. Solomon scholar, N.Y. Law Sch., 1979; recipient Bronze Pelican award Roman Cath. Archdiocese, Newark, 2000. Fellow: Coll. Law Practice Mgmt.; mem.: ABA (chmn. govt. mgmt. com. 1984—86, mgr. products media bd. 1985—92, chmn. document retrieval com. 1985—86, vice-chmn. ins. and malpractice com. 1986—88, co-chmn. glass ceiling task force 1992—95, vice-chmn. law practice mgmt. phb. bd. 1992—95, coun. mem. 1989—95, co-chmn. law practice mgmt. pub. bd. 1995—98, Foonberg award 1998), N.J. Bar Assn. (dir., chmn. health hosp. sect. 1993—95, mem. com. health law litigation, mem. subcom. profl. licensing 1997—, del. gen. coun. adminstrn. sect. 1995—97), Soc. Health Care Risk Mgmt. N.J. (chmn. legis. com. 1987—96), Westfield Sr. Citizens Housing Corp., Inc. (trustee 1994—, v.p. 1996—98, pres. 1998—), Cmty. Health Law Project N.J., Inc. (trustee 1988—91), Am. Healthcare Lawyers Assn., Assn. of Bar of City of N.Y., N.Y. Bar Assn. (mem. health law sect. 1996—), Harvard Club, Mensa. Administrative and regulatory, General civil litigation, Health. Home: 905 Pennsylvania Ave Westfield NJ 07090-3433 Office: Kern Augustine Conroy & Schoppmann PC 1120 Rt 22 Bridgewater NJ 08807 E-mail: conroy@drlaw.com

CONTI, JOY FLOWERS, lawyer; b. Kane, Pa., Dec. 7, 1948; d. Bernard A. Flowers and Elizabeth (Tingley) Rodgers; m. Anthony T. Conti, Jan. 16, 1971; children: Andrew, Michael, Gregory. BA, Duquesne U., 1970, JD summa cum laude, 1973. Bar: Pa. 1973, U.S. Dist. Ct. (we. dist.) Pa. 1973, U.S. Ct. Appeals (3rd cir.) 1976, U.S. Supreme Ct. 1993. Law clk. Supreme Ct. Pa., Monessen, 1973-74; assoc. Kirkpatrick & Lockhart, Pitts., 1974-76, 82-83, ptnr., 1983-96; shareholder Buchanan, Ingersoll, P.C., 1996—. Prof. law Duquesne U., Pitts., 1976-82; hearing examiner Pa. Dept. State, Bur. Profl. Occupation and Affairs, 1978-82; chairperson search com. for judge U.S. Bankruptcy Ct. (we. dist.) Pa., 1987, 95; active Pa. Futures Commn. on Justice in 21st Century, 1995-97. Contbr. articles to profl. jours. Mem. disciplinary hearing com. Supreme Ct. Pa., 1982-88; v.p. Com. for Justice Edn., Pitts., 1983-84; mem. Leadership Pitts., 1987-88. Named One of Ten Outstanding Young Women in Am., 1981. Fellow Am. Bar Found. (Pa. state chair 1991-97); mem. ABA (ho. of dels. 1980-86, 91-97), Am. Law Inst., Am. Coll. Bankruptcy, Pa. Bar Assn. (gov. 1993-95, ho. of dels. 1978—, corp. banking and bus. law sect. coun. 1983-89, treas. 1991-93, v.p. 1993-95, chair-elect 1995-97, chmn. 1997-99, chmn. commn. comml. law 1990-93, co-chair 1995—, chairperson civil rights and responsibilities com. 1986-89, Achievement award 1982, 87, 99, Anne X. Alpern award 1995), Nat. Conf. Bar Pres. (exec. coun. 1993-96), Allegheny County Bar Assn. (adminstrv. v.p. 1984-86, 90, chairperson corp. banking and bus. law sect. 1987-89, treas. 1988-90, gov. 1991, pres.-elect 1992, pres. 1993), Internat. Women's Insolvency and Restructuring Confedn. (chair Tri-State Network 1996), Pa. Bar Inst. (dir. 1991-97), Duquesne Club, Treesdale Country Club. Roman Catholic. Bankruptcy, General corporate, Health. Home: 3469 Palomino Dr Gibsonia PA 15044-8965 Office: Buchanan Ingersoll PC 301 Grant St Fl 20 Pittsburgh PA 15219-1410 E-mail: conti@fobipc.com

CONTI, LEE ANN, lawyer; b. Astoria, Oreg. BA with honors, So. Ill. U., 1970; JD summa cum laude, De Paul U., 1976. Bar: Ill. 1976, U.S. Dist. Ct. (no. dist.) Ill. 1976. Ptnr. Mayer, Brown & Platt, Chgo., 1983-94; assoc. gen. counsel Citizens Comm. Co., Stamford, 1994—. Contbr. articles to profl. jours. Mem. Bd. Edn. Cmty. Consol. Sch. Dist. 89, Du Page County, 1987-93. Recipient Am. Jurisprudence awards in Torts, Remedies. Mem. ABA, Am. Corp. Counsel Assn., Ill. State Bar Assn., Du Page County Bar Assn., Chgo. Bar Assn., Phi Kappa Phi, Pi Sigma Alpha, Phi Lambda Pi. Office: Citizens Comm Co 1000 Internationale Pkwy Woodridge IL 60517-4924

CONTI, LOUIS THOMAS MOORE, lawyer; b. Phila., Aug. 31, 1949; s. Alexander and Yolanda (DiLorenzo) C.; m. Christina M.S. Moore, May 1, 1982; children: Charles Alexander, Whitney Caroline. BS, LaSalle Coll., 1971; MBA, Drexel U., 1972; JD, Creighton U., 1975; LLM, Temple U., 1981. Bar: Pa. 1975, U.S. Claims Ct. 1975, U.S. Tax Ct. 1975, U.S. Dist. Ct. (ea. dist.) Pa. 1978, U.S. Ct. Appeals (3d cir.) 1979, U.S. Supreme Ct. 1981, Fla. 1982, U.S. Dist. Ct. (mid. dist.) Fla. 1988. Tax atty. Office Chief Counsel IRS, Washington and Phila., 1975-81; tax mgr. Touche Ross & Co., Phila., 1981-84; assoc. Saul, Ewing, Remick & Saul, 1984-87; shareholder Swann & Haddock, P.A., Orlando, Fla., 1987-89; ptnr., chmn. corp. tax and securities dept. Holland & Knight, 1989—. Mem. fin. com. S.E. Pa. chpt. ARC, Phila., 1984-87; advisor Vol. Lawyers for Arts, Phila., 1984-87; bd. dirs. Fla. Hosp. Found., 1989—, Ctrl. Fla. Planned Giving Coun., 1989-97, Cmty. Found. Ctrl. Fla. Inc., 1993—, World Trade Ctr., Orlando, 1992-95; mem. internat. bus. adv. bd. Metro Orlando; grad. Leadership Orlando, 1994, Leadership Fla., 1996; chair recruiting com. East Ctrl. Region of Leadership Fla., 1997, bd. dirs. Orlando Performing Arts & Edn. Ctr., Inc., 1998-2001. Mem. ABA (tax and bus. law sect., chmn. task force on drafting prototype ltd. liability co. operating agreements 1998—, chmn. Fla. Bar drafting com. 1999), Fla. Bar Assn. (tax and bus. law sect., chmn. drafting com. ltd. liability co. act 1998—, chair corps. and securities com., bus. law sect. 1999-2001, chair long-range planning com. tax sect. 1999-2000, chair tax sect. 2001—), Orange County Bar Assn. (chmn. tax sect. 1990-91), Seminole County C. of C. (bd. dirs. 1994-97), Racquet Club, Alaqua Country Club, Citrus Club. Republican. Avocations: traveling, skiing, golfing, tennis, theatre. General corporate, Mergers and acquisitions, Corporate taxation. Home: 3003 Timpana Pt Longwood FL 32779-3108 Office: Holland & Knight PO Box 1526 Orlando FL 32802-1526 E-mail: lconti@hklaw.com

CONTI, SAMUEL, federal judge; b. L.A., July 16, 1922; s. Fred and Katie C.; m. Dolores Crosby, July 12, 1952; children: Richard, Robert, Cynthia. BS, U. Santa Clara, 1945; LLB, Stanford U., 1948, JD. Bar: Calif. 1948. Pvt. practice, San Francisco and Contra Costa County, 1948-60; city atty. City of Concord, Calif., 1960-69; judge Superior Ct. Contra Costa County, 1968-70, U.S. Dist. Ct. (no. dist.) Calif., San Francisco, 1970-88, sr. judge, 1988—. Mem. Ctrl. Contra Costa Bar Assn. (pres.), Concord C. of C. (pres.), Alpha Sigma Nu. Office: US Dist Ct 450 Golden Gate Ave Ste 36052 San Francisco CA 94102-3482

CONWAY, FRENCH HOGE, lawyer; b. Danville, Va., June 11, 1918; s. Lysander Broadus and Mildred (Hoge) C.; BS, U. Va., 1942, JD, 1946; m. Louise Throckmorton, Feb. 3, 1961; children: French Hoge, William Chenery, Helen (Mrs. Carlton Bedsole), Donna (Mrs. Michael Henderson). Starnes. Bar: Va. 1942. Sole practice, Danville, 1942—; mem. firm Clement, Conway & Winston, 1950-60. Sec., Danville City Bd. Rev., 1985— ; v.p. Va. Election Bd. Assn., 1974. Served with USNR, 1942-46. Mem. ABA, Va. Bar Assn., Danville Bar Assn. (pres. 1985-86), Am. Trial Lawyers Assn., Va. Trial Lawyers Assn., Soc. Cincinnati in State of Va., Ret. Officers Assn., Boat Owners Assn. U.S. Lodges: Kiwanis, Masons.

CONWAY, JOHN E. federal judge; b. 1934; BS, U.S. Naval Acad., 1956; LLB magna cum laude, Washburn U., 1963. Assoc. Matias A Zamora, Santa Fe, 1963-64; ptnr. Wilkinson, Durrett & Conway, Alamogordo, N.Mex., 1964-67, Durrett, Conway & Jordon, Alamogordo, 1967-80, Montgomery & Andrews, P.A., Albuquerque, 1980-86; city atty. Alamogordo, 1966-72; mem. N.Mex. State Senate, 1970-80, minority leader, 1972-80; chief fed. judge U.S. Dist. Ct. N.Mex., Albuquerque, 1986-2000, sr. fed. judge, 2000—. Mem. Jud. Resources Com., 1995-98. 1st lt. USAF,

1956-60. Mem. 10th Cir. Dist. Judges Assn. (pres. 1995-98), Fed. Judges Assn. (bd. dirs. 1996—), Nat. Commrs. on Uniform State Laws, N.Mex. Bar Assn., N.Mex. Jud. Coun. (vice chmn. 1973, chmn. 1973-75, disciplinary bd. of Supreme Ct. of N.Mex. vice chmn. 1980, chmn. 1981-84). Office: US Dist Ct Chambers #740 333 Lomas Blvd NW Albuquerque NM 87102-2272

CONWAY, JOHN K. lawyer; Gen. counsel Kemper Ins. Co., Long Grove, Ill. Office: Lumbermens Mutual Casualty Co 1 Kemper Dr Long Grove IL 60049-0001

CONWAY, NEIL JAMES, III, title company executive, lawyer, writer; b. Cleve., Feb. 15, 1950; s. Neil J. and Jeanne Louise (Gensert) C.; m. Maureen Dolan; children: Seanna, Neil James IV, Declan, Liam. BSBA, John Carroll U., 1972; MBA, Suffolk U., 1974; JD, Antioch Sch. Law (now U. D.C.), 1983. Bar: Ohio 1983, U.S. Dist. Ct. (no. dist.) Ohio 1983, U.S. Supreme Ct. 1987, D.C. 1988. Auditor U.S. Dept. Interior, Arlington, 1974-77; systems acct. Mil. Dist. Washington, 1978-79; legal intern Govt. Accountability Project, Washington, 1980-81; jud. intern for Hon. Ann Aldrich U.S. Dist. (no. dist.) Ct. Ohio, 1982; legal asst. Spiegel & McDiarmid, Washington, 1982-83; pvt. practice Painesville, Ohio, 1983—; from title examiner to pres. Conway Land Title Co., 1983—. Adj. prof. legal studies Lake Erie Coll., Painesville, Ohio; nat. press sec. Irish Am. Unity Conf., 2000-01. Editor in chief Antioch Law Jour., 1982-83; pub. The Ohio Irish Times, 1993—; contbr. articles to profl. jours. Active Lake County Econ. Devel. Coun., Lawyers Com. for Human Rights, N.Y.C. Capt. USAR, 1972-81. Mem. Am. Soc. Internat. Law (Dean Rusk award 1980), Ohio Bar Assn., Lake County Bar Assn. (co-author real estate symposium 1989), Brehon Law Soc. N.Y., Ohio Land Title Assn., Lake County Bd. Realtors (Affiliate of Yr. 1986, polit. affairs com.), Painesville Title Assn. (pres. 1985-86), Irish Am. Cultural Inst. (Editl. citation Ohio Irish Bull.), Lawyer Alliance for Justice in Ireland, Cleve. Skating Club. Democrat. Roman Catholic. Avocations: racquetball, youth hockey, traditional music. Home: 10930 Bradley Ct Concord OH 44077-2443

CONWAY, REBECCA ANN KOPPES, lawyer; b. Colorado Springs, Colo., May 18, 1952; d. Virgil Lee and Betty J. Koppes; children: Kelley, Kathrine; m. Sean P. Conway, Nov. 26, 1994. BA, U. Colo., 1975, JD, 1978. Bar: Colo. 1978, U.S. Dist. Ct. Colo. 1978. Atty. EEOC, Denver, 1978-79, Dist. Atty.'s Office, Adams County, Brighton, Colo., 1979-80; ptnr. Gutierrez & Koppes, Greeley, 1980-92; pvt. practice Law Office of Rebecca Koppes Conway, 1992—. Mem. Colo. Pub. Defenders Commn., 1985-95, chair, 1990-95; chair Civil Justice Task Force, State of Colo., 1999—. Chmn. Placement Alternatives Commn., Weld County, Colo., 1987-89; mem. Our Saviors Luth. Ch., Greeley, 1985, exec. dir., 1987-89; chmn. bd. dirs. Colo. Rural Legal Svcs., Denver, 1983-86, 93-96; mem. 19th Dist. Jud. Nominating Commn., 2000—; vice-chair Weld Child Care Network, 1988; chair transition com. jud. Gov. Owens Adminstrn., State of Colo., 1998; mem. state exec. com. Dem. Party, 1993-98, mem. ctrl. com., 1993-99; mem. Weld County Exec. Com., 1990-99, vice chair, 1991-92. Fellow ABA (ho. of dels. 1994-97), Colo. Bar Found. (dir. 1998, bd. dirs. 1999); mem. ABA (ho.of dels . 1994-97), Colo. Bar Assn. (com. mem., exec. coun. 1986-90, 94-98, bd. govs. 1983-90, 94-99, pres.-elect. 1996-97, pres. 1997-98, chair young lawyers divsn. 1988-89, Outstanding Young Lawyer 1988, v.p. 1989-90, litigation sect. coun. 1998, chair 1999-2000), Weld County Bar Assn. (pres. 1992-93). Avocation: reading. Personal injury, Workers' compensation. Home: 2595 56th Ave Greeley CO 80634-4503 Office: 912 8th Ave Greeley CO 80631-1112

CONWAY, ROBERT GEORGE, JR. lawyer; b. Albany, N.Y., Apr. 26, 1951; s. Robert George Sr. and Kathryn Ann (Kelly) C.; m. Lynda Rae Christenson, Dec. 15, 1979; 1 child, Phillip Christopher. AB, Dartmouth Coll., 1973; JD, Union U., 1976; diploma, U.S. Army JAGC Sch., 1986. Bar: Pa. 1978, U.S. Ct. Mil. Appeals 1978, N.C. 1983, U.S. Dist. Ct. (ea. dist.) N.C. 1983, U.S. Dist. Ct. (no. dist.) N.Y. 1998, U.S. Army Ct. Mil. Rev. 1986, U.S. Supreme Ct. 1986, U.S. Ct. Appeals (4th and fed. cirs.) 1987, N.Y. 1998; cert. USMC judge advocate. Commd. 2d lt. USMC, 1975, advanced through grades to maj., 1983, gen. staff sec. N.C., 1982-83, chief rev. officer, 1983-84, spl. asst. U.S. atty., 1984-85, dir. joint law ctr. air sta. Cherry Point, 1986-88, chief rsch. officer air sta., 1988, dep. asst. staff judge adv. to comdt. Washington, 1989; mil. justice officer Marine Corps Base, Quantico, Va., 1990-91; assoc. counsel for land use law Ea. Area Counsel Office USMC Dept. of Navy Office of Gen. Counsel, Camp Lejeune, N.C., 1991-96; ret. USMC, 1996; counsel, dep. commr. N.Y. State Divsn. Mil. and Naval Affairs, Latham, 1996—. Adj. faculty mem. Ga. Inst. Tech., 1993, Webster U., 1994-96; spkr. in field. Trustee Cath. student ctr. Aquinas House, Dartmouth Coll., Hanover, N.H., 1973-89, sec. Dartmouth class of 1973, 1994—. Recipient Legion of Merit, 1996. Mem.: ABA, Pa. Bar Assn., N.C. Bar Assn., N.Y. Bar Assn., U.S. Naval Inst., Marine Corps Assn., Fed. Bar Assn. (contbg. author assn. news and jour. 1990), Dartmouth Lawyers Assn., Dartmouth Club Ea. N.Y. (v.p. 1998—2001, pres. 2001—), Am. Legion, KC (adv. 1984—85). Roman Catholic. Home: 27 Manor Dr Glenmont NY 12077-3326 Office: NY State Divsn Mil and Naval Affairs Attn MNLA 330 Old Niskayuna Rd Latham NY 12110-3514

COOK, AUGUST JOSEPH, lawyer, accountant; b. Devine, Tex., Sept. 25, 1926; s. August E. and Mary H. (Schmidt) C.; m. Matie M. Brangan, July 12, 1952; children: Lisa Ann, Mary Beth, John J. BS, Trinity U., 1949; BBA, U. Tex., 1954; JD, St. Mary's U., 1960. Bar: Tex. 1960, Tenn. 1975. Bus. mgr., corp. sec. Life Enterprises, Inc. and affil. cos., San Antonio, 1950-58, also bd. dirs.; mgr. Ernst & Young, 1960-69, ptnr., Memphis, 1970-84; ptnr. McDonnel Boyd, 1984-91; of counsel Harris, Shelton, Dunlap and Cobb, 1991-97, Pietrangelo Cook, Memphis, 1997—. Author: A.J. $ Tax Court, 1987; author newspaper column A.J.'s Tax Fables, 1983—; contbr. articles to profl. jours. Alderman City of Castle Hills, Tex., 1961-63, mayor, 1963-69; chmn. Bexar County Coun. Mayors, 1967-69; v.p. Tex. Mcpl. League, 1968-69; bd. dirs. San Antonio Met. YMCA. With U.S. Army, 1945-46, PTO. Mem. AICPA, Tex. Soc. CPAs, Tex. Bar Assn., Estate Planning Coun. San Antonio (pres. 1967), Tenn. Soc. CPAs, Tenn. Bar Assn. (chmn. tax, probate and trust sect., 1993-95), Estate Planning Coun. Memphis (pres. 1983-84), Toastmasters (pres. 1963), Delta Theta Phi, Kappa Pi Sigma, University Club (Memphis), Canyon Creek Country Club (San Antonio, bd. dirs.), Chicksaw Country Club, Optimists (bd. dirs.), Rotary (treas. 1978, 99, bd. dirs. 1986-87, 96-97). Estate planning, Corporate taxation, Personal income taxation. Home: 6785 Slash Pine Cv Memphis TN 38119-5617 Office: Pietrangelo Cook PLC 6410 Poplar Ave Ste 190 Memphis TN 38119-4841

COOK, BARBARA ANN, lawyer; b. N.Y.C., Sept. 14, 1947; d. Paul J. and Mary (Doogan) McGuire; m. David S. Cook, Aug. 14, 1971; children: Peter James, Andrew David. AB, Manhattanville Coll., 1968; JD, Columbia U., 1971. Bar: N.Y. 1971, U.S. Dist. Ct. (so. and ea. dists.) N.Y. 1977. Assoc. Lynton, Klein, Opton & Saslow, N.Y.C., 1971-74; asst. gen. counsel McGraw-Hill, Inc., 1974-85; sr. counsel and asst. sec. Phelps Dodge Corp., 1986-87; regional counsel Cushman & Wakefield, Inc., 1987-90; sr. counsel Grow Group, Inc., 1990-92; asst. gen. counsel Rheem Mfg. Co., 1992—. Contbr. articles to profl. jours. Mem. Assn. of Bar of City of N.Y. (comm. law com., lib. com.), N.Y. County Lawyers Assn. (corp. law com., environ. law com.). General civil litigation, General corporate, Labor. Home: 2 Stuyvesant Oval Apt Mg New York NY 10009-2144 E-mail: cookba@nycorp.rheem.com

COOK, BRYSON LEITCH, lawyer; b. Balt., Apr. 17, 1948; s. A. Samuel Cook. BA magna cum laude, Princeton U., 1970; JD cum laude, MBA, U. Pa., 1973. Bar: Md. 1974, U.S. Dist. Ct. Md. 1976, U.S. Tax Ct. 1977. Assoc. Alex Brown & Sons, Balt., 1973-75, Venable, Baetjer & Howard, Balt., 1975-81, ptnr., 1981—. Adj. prof. U. Md. Law Sch., Balt., 1981, Loyola U. Bus. Sch., Balt., 1980-82. Contbr. articles to legal jours.; author tax mgmt. portfolios. Trustee Balt. Ballet, 1980-83, Keswick Home for the Incurables, Balt., 1983—; bd. dirs. Balt. City Jail, 1980-82; counsel Md. Hist. Soc., Balt., 1981—. Recipient Gordon A. Block award U. Pa. Law Sch., 1973. Mem. ABA, Bar Assn. Balt. City, Md. State Bar Assn., Internat. Fiscal Assn., Order of Coif, Elkridge Club (Balt.). Republican. Methodist. General corporate, Corporate taxation, Estate taxation. Home: 201 Woodbrook Ln Baltimore MD 21212-1037 Office: Venable Baetjer & Howard LLP Mercantile Bank Trust Bldg 2 Hopkins Plz Ste 1800 Baltimore MD 21201-2971 E-mail: blcook@venable.com

COOK, CHARLES ADDISON, lawyer; b. N.Y.C., Mar. 31, 1952; s. Hugh F. and Lurana (Higgins) C.; m. Barbara Edgar, June 10, 1973; children: Ian Hugh, Alexander Charles. BA, U. Conn., 1974; M in Pub. Adminstrn., Northeastern U., 1976; JD magna cum laude, New Eng. Sch. Law, 1980. Bar: Mass. 1980., U.S. Dist. Ct. Mass. 1980, U.S. Ct. Appeals (1st cir.) 1980, (D.C. cir.) 1992, U.S. Supreme Ct., 1991. With Colonial Gas Co., Lowell, Mass., 1978—, dir. human resources, 1978-80, counsel, 1980-82, v.p., 1982-88, v.p., counsel, 1988-89. Mem. ABA, Mass. Bar Assn., Am. Gas Assn., New England Gas Assn., Bristol Yacht Club (commodore R.I. 1985-87), Eastern Yacht Club. Republican. Avocation: yacht racing. General corporate, Labor, Public utilities. Home: 70 Amble Rd Chelmsford MA 01824-1959 Office: Colonial Gas Co 40 Market St Lowell MA 01852-1806

COOK, DEBORAH L. state supreme court justice; BA in English, U. Akron, 1974, JD, 1978, LLD (hon.), 1996. Ptnr. Roderick & Linton, Akron, 1976-91; judge 9th dist. Ohio Ct. Appeals, 1991-94; justice Ohio Supreme Ct., 1995—. Bd. trustees Summit County United Way, Vol. Ctr., Stan Hywet Hall and Gardens, Akron Sch. Law, Coll. Scholars, Inc.; bd. dirs. Women's Network; vol. Mobile Meals, Safe Landing Shelter. Named Woman of Yr., Women's Network, 1991. Fellow Am. Bar Found.; mem. Omicron Delta Kappa, Delta Gamma (pres., Nat. Shield award). Office: Ohio Supreme Ct 30 E Broad St Fl 3 Columbus OH 43266-0001

COOK, DONALD CHARLES, lawyer; b. Marshalltown, Iowa, Sept. 29, 1943; s. Gerald E. and Alma Mae (Johnson) C.; m. Mary Lou Schroeder, July 30, 1973; 1 dau., Caillin Alice. B.A., Calif. State U.-Long Beach, 1973; J.D., Whittier Coll., 1976. Bar: Calif. 1976, U.S. (cen. dist.) Calif. 1977, U.S. Ct. Appeals (9th cir.) 1978. Sole practice, Los Angeles, 1976-81; assoc. firm Cook & Symonds, Los Angeles, Westwood and Thousand Oaks, Calif., 1981-83, Glenn E. Stern A Law Corp., West Covina, Calif., 1983-84, Stern, Cook & Naiditch, 1984— . Atty., Olympic Classes Regattas Organizing Com., Long Beach, 1981. Served with U.S. Army, 1962-65. Mem. Los Angeles County Bar Assn. Democrat. Club: Seal Beach Yacht (judge advocate 1980-83) (Long Beach). Federal civil litigation, State civil litigation, Family and matrimonial.

COOK, JAMES CHRISTOPHER, lawyer; b. Quincy, Ill., Oct. 4, 1951; s. Waldo Fuller and Rita Cecilia (Kathmann) C.; m. Bernardeen Mary Kohler, Dec. 30, 1978; children: Christopher Aaron, Erin Leigh. Student, Quincy Coll., 1969-71; BA, U. Ill., 1973; JD, Loyola U., Chgo., 1976. Bar: Ill. 1976, Mo. 1984, U.S. Ct. Appeals (D.C. cir.) 1977, U.S. Ct. Appeals (7th cir.) 1978, U.S. Dist. Ct. (cen. dist.) Ill. 1978, U.S. Dist. Ct. (so. dist.) Ill. 1979, U.S. Supreme Ct. 1979. Clk. to justice Ill. Ct. Appeals 4th Cir., Springfield, 1976-78; assoc. Walker & Williams PC, Belleville, Ill., 1978-83, shareholder, 1983—. Pres. bd. trustees St. Clair County Law Libr., Belleville, 1982-85. Mem. Ill. State Bar Assn., Mo. Bar Assn., Chgo. Bar Assn., Bar Assn. Met. St. Louis, Inst. for Local Govt. Law, Nat. Assn. R.R. Trial Counsel, St. Clair County Bar Assn. (bd. dirs. 1999-2001). Roman Catholic. Federal civil litigation, State civil litigation, Personal injury. Office: Walker & Williams 4343 W Main St Belleville IL 62226-5597 also: 1115 Pine St Saint Louis MO 63101-1904 E-mail: wawpc@peaknet.net

COOK, JULIAN ABELE, JR. federal judge; b. Washington, June 22, 1930; s. Julian Abele and Ruth Elizabeth (McNeill) C.; m. Carol Annette Dibble, Dec. 22, 1957; children: Julian Abele III, Peter Dibble, Susan Annette. BA, Pa. State U., 1952; JD, Georgetown U., 1957, LLD (hon.), 1992; LLM, U. Va., 1988; LLD (hon.), U. Detroit, 1996, Wayne State U., 1997. Bar: Mich. 1957. Law clk. to judge, Pontiac, Mich., 1957-58; pvt. practice Detroit, 1958-78; judge U.S. Dist. Ct. (ea. dist.) Mich., 1978, chief judge, 1989-96, sr. judge, 1996—. Spl. asst. atty. gen. State of Mich., 1968-78; adj. prof. U. Detroit Sch. Law, 1971-74; gen. counsel pub. TV Sta. WTVS, 1973-78; labor arbitrator Am. Arbitration Assn. and Mich. Employment Rels. Commn., 1975-78; mem. Mich. State Bd. Ethics, 1977-78; instr. trial advocacy workshop Harvard U., 1988—, trial advocacy program U.S. Dept. Justice, 1989-90; com. on fin. disclosure Jud. Conf. U.S., 1988-93, chmn., 1990-93; screening panel NYU Root-Tilden-Snow Scholarship Program, 1991, 96—; mem. U.S. Sentencing Commn. Judicial Adv. Group, 1996-98; mem. nat. bd. trustees Am. Inn Ct., 1996—; mem. adv. com. Nat. Publs., 1994-96, chmn. nat. nominations and election com., 1994-95; pres. chpt. XI, Master of Bench, 1984-95. Contbr. articles to profl. jours. Exec. bd. dirs. Child and Family Svcs. Mich., 1968-89, past pres., 1975-76; bd. dirs. Am. Heart Assn. Mich., 1968-89, Hutzel Hosp., 1984-95; chmn. Mich. Civil Rights Commn., 1968-71; co-chair exec. com. Walter P. Reuther Libr. Labor and Urban Affairs, Wayne State U.; mem. bd. visitors Georgetown U. Law Ctr., 1992—. With Signal Corps, U.S. Army, 1952-54. Recipient Merit citation Pontiac Area Urban League, 1971, Pathfinders award Oakland U., 1977, Svc. award Todd-Phillips Home, Inc., 1978, Disting. Alumnus award Pa. State U., 1987, Georgetown U., 1989, Focus and Impact award Oakland U., 1985; resolution Mich. Ho. of Reps., 1971, Outstanding Community Svc. award Va. Park Community Investment Assocs., 1992, 1st Ann. Trailblazers award D. Augustus Straker Bar Assn., 1993, Renowned Jurist award Friends of African Art, 1993, Brotherhood award Jewish War Vets. U.S., 1994, Paul R. Dean award Georgetown U. Law Sch., 1997; named Boss of Yr., Oakland County Legal Secs. Assn., 1974, one of Mich. Most Respected Judges, Mich. Law Weekly, 1990-91; named one of the Best Judges, Detroit Monthly, 1991; named Disting. Citizen of Yr., NAACP Oakland County, Mich., 1970. Fellow Am. Bar Found., Mich. Bar Found. (vice-chmn. 1992-93, chmn. 1993—); mem. NAACP (mem. state constl. revision and legal redress com. 1963, Disting. Citizen of Yr. 1970, Presdl. award North Oakland County, Mich. chpt. 1987), ABA, Fed. Bar Assn. (fed.-state ct. seminar lectr. Detroit chpt. 1981—), Mich. Bar Assn. (chmn. constl. law com. 1969, vice-chmn. civil liberties com. 1970, co-chmn. profl. devel. task force 1984-87, U.S. cts. com. 1988-95, com. on professionalism 1991—, Champion of Justice 1994), Mich. Tribunal Assn. (bd. dirs. 3rd cir. 1992-98), Detroit Bar Assn. (Bench-Bar award 1987), Oakland County Bar Assn. (chmn. continuing legal edn. com. 1968-69, jud. liaison Dist. Ct. com. 1977, unauthorized practice law com. 1977), Wolverine Bar Assn. (Bench-Bar award 1987, D. Augustus Straker award 1988), Mich. Assn. Black Judges, Am. Inn of Ct. (founder Met. Detroit chpt., pres., master of bench, chmn. 6th cir. com. on standard jury instructions 1986—), Am. Law Inst., Union Black Episcopalians (Detroit chpt., Absalom Jones award 1988), Justice Frank Murphy Honor Soc.

COOK, MICHAEL HARRY, lawyer; b. June 9, 1947; s. Leonard James and Ethel (Shapiro) C.; m. Michele Anne Reday, Apr. 21, 1979; children: Noah Reday, Megan Rose. Student, U. Wis., Madison, 1965-66; BA with honors cum laude, Temple U., 1969; JD, Villanova U., 1973. Bar: Pa. 1973, D.C. 1979, U.S. Dist. Ct. (no. dist.) Ill. 1977, U.S. Dist. Ct. D.C. 1981, U.S. Ct. Claims 1982, U.S. Ct. Appeals (3d cir.) 1982, U.S. Ct. Appeals (5th cir.) 1981, U.S. Ct. Appeals (9th cir.) 1979, U.S. Ct. Appeals (11th cir.) 1981, U.S. Ct. Appeals (7th cir.) 1984, U.S. Ct. Appeals (10th cir.) 1984, U.S. Ct. Appeals (fed. cir.) 1984, U.S. Ct. Appeals (D.C. cir.) 1981, U.S. Supreme Ct. 1976. Atty. Gen. Counsel's Office U.S. Dept. Health and Human Svcs., Washington, 1973-80; assoc. Wood, Lucksinger & Epstein, 1981-85, ptnr., 1985-90, Katten, Muchin & Zavis, Washington, 1991-97; mem. Mintz, Levin, Cohn, Ferris, Glovsky and Popeo, P.C., 1997-98; shareholder Jenkens & Gilchrist, P.C., 1998—. Lectr. Am. Health Lawyers Assn., Aspen Sys., Inc., various state and nat. hosps. and long-term care assns. Contbg. author: Handbook of Subacute Health Care, 1994, Subacute Care: A Guide to Development, Implementation and Management, 1995, The Long Term Care Handbook: Regulatory, Operational, and Financial Guideposts, 2000; contbr. articles to profl. health care jours.; mem. editl. adv. bd. McKnight's Long Term Care News; briefings on subacute care and nat. report on subacute care, 1991-99. V.p. Taylor Run Citizens Assn., Alexandria, Va., 1982-84, pres., 1984-85, bd. dirs., 1985—. Named to 100 Most Influential People in Long Term Care, 1996; Pres.'s scholar Temple U., Phila., 1969. Mem. ABA (former mem. editl. bd. forum on health law), Am. Health Lawyers Assn., Nat. Subacute Care Assn. (mem. reimbursement task force), Assisted Living Fedn. Am. (former mem. task force on managed care, mem. pub. policy and legal task forces, leadership coun.), Nat. Assn. for Support of Long Term Care, Healthcare Fin. Mgmt. Assn. (former mem., nat. adv. task force on long-term care), Sword Soc., Phi Eta Sigma, Tau Epsilon Phi. Democrat. Jewish. Administrative and regulatory, Federal civil litigation, Health. Home: 2724 King St Alexandria VA 22302-4009 Office: Jenkens & Gilchrist a Profl Corp Ste 600 1919 Pennsylvania Ave NW Washington DC 20006-3404 E-mail: mhcook@jenkens.com

COOK, MICHAEL LEWIS, lawyer; b. Rochester, N.H., Mar. 5, 1944; s. Israel J. and Molly L. Cook; m. Roberta Tross, Feb. 25, 1995; children: Jonathan, Alexander. AB, Columbia U., 1965; JD, NYU, 1968. Bar: N.Y. 1968. Assoc. Weil, Gotshal & Manges, N.Y.C., 1970-75, ptnr., 1975-80, Skadden, Arps, Slate, Meagher & Flom, LLP, N.Y.C., 1980-2000; adj. prof. law NYU Sch. Law, 1975—; ptnr. Schulte Roth & Zabel LLP, N.Y.C., 2000—. Co-author: A Practical Guide to the Bankruptcy Reform Act, 1979, Creditors' Rights, Debtors' Protection and Bankruptcy, 1985, rev. edit., 1997; contbr.: Collier on Bankruptcy, 1979, rev. edit., 1999, Collier Bankruptcy Practice Guide, 1998; editor and contbg. author: Bankruptcy Litigation Manual, rev. edit., 2000. Bd. dirs. Goddard Riverside Cmty. Ctr.; bd. dirs., chair Lawyers Alliance for N.Y. Fellow Am. Coll. Bankruptcy; mem. ABA, Assn. of Bar of City of N.Y., Practicing Law Inst. (mem. bankruptcy law adv. com.), Columbia Coll. Alumni Assn. (bd. dirs., v.p.). Bankruptcy, Federal civil litigation, Contracts commercial. Home: 45 E 89th St New York NY 10128-1251 Office: Schulte Roth & Zabel LLP 919 3d Ave New York NY 10022

COOK, QUENTIN LAMAR, lawyer, healthcare executive, church leader; b. Sept. 8, 1940; s. J. Vernon and Bernice (Kimball) C.; m. Mary Gaddie, Nov. 30, 1962; children: Kathryn Cook Knight, Quentin Laurance, Joseph Vernon III. BS, Utah State U., 1963; JD, Stanford U., 1966. Bar: Calif. 1966. Assoc. Carr, McClellan, Ingersoll, Thompson & Horn, Burlingame, Calif., 1966-69, ptnr., 1969-93; interim pres., CEO Calif. Healthcare Sys., San Francisco, 1993-94, pres., CEO, 1994-95; vice chmn. Sutter Health/Calif. Healthcare Sys., 1996; gen. authority LDS Ch., 1996—. City atty. Town of Hillsborough, Calif., 1982-93; mem. adv. bd. Utah State U., Logan, 1985-95; mem. bd. visitors Brigham Young U. Law Sch., Provo, 1994-96.

COOK, ROBERT S., JR. lawyer; b. Syracuse, N.Y., Apr. 5, 1940; m. Sally Williams. BA, Amherst Coll., 1962; LLB, Yale U., 1965. Bar: N.Y. 1966. Assoc. Hancock, Ryan, Shove & Hust, Syracuse, N.Y., 1965-68; urban renewal rep. HUD, N.Y.C., 1968-71; exec. dir. The Parks Coun., Inc., 1972-73; v.p., co-founder Project for Pub. Spaces, Inc., 1974-77; cons., 1978-80; assoc. Tufo & Zuccotti, 1981-86; assoc., then ptnr. Brown and Wood, 1986-94; ptnr. DeForest & Duer, 1995—. Author: Zoning for Downtown urban Design, 1980. V.p., bd. dirs. Citizens Housing and Planning Coun., 1985; cons. The Denver Partnership, 1981; mem. N.Y. State Freshwater Wetlands Appeals Bd., 1991-94. Design project fellow Nat. Endowment for Arts, Washington, 1978-79; Graham Found. for Advanced Studies in the Fine Arts fellow, Chgo., 1979. Mem. N.Y. State Bar Assn., Assn. Bar City N.Y. (com. environ. law 1979-82, com. land use planning and zoning, 1994-2000, chmn. 1997-2000, com. N.Y.C. affairs 2000—). Environmental, Land use and zoning (including planning). Office: DeForest & Duer 90 Broad St Fl 18 New York NY 10004-2276

COOK, S. ALAN, lawyer, accountant; b. Bangor, Maine, Mar. 25, 1947; s. Harry George and Margaret (Black) C.; 1 child, Heather Alison. B.S., U. R.I., 1972; J.D., U. Ariz., 1978. Bar: Ariz. 1978, U.S. Dist. Ct. Ariz. 1978, U.S. Ct. Appeals (9th cir.) 1978, U.S. Supreme Ct., 1985; CPA, Ariz., R.I. Law clk. to chief judge U.S. Dist. Ct. Ariz., Phoenix, 1978-81; clk. of ct. Ariz. Supreme Ct., Phoenix, 1981-85; pvt. practice law Phoenix, 1985—; bd. visitors U. Ariz. Coll. Law, Tucson, 1983— . Editorial staff Appellate Ct. Adminstrn. Rev., 1982-83. Area chmn. Western region Nat. Eagle Scout Assn., 1983— . Served as chief warrant officer, U.S. Army, 1966-69, Vietnam; mem. Ariz. Army N.G. (capt. JAGC). Decorated Air medal with 29 clusters, Army Commendation medal. Mem. Nat. Conf. Appellate Ct. Clks. (chmn. various coms. 1981—), Am. Inst. C.P.A.s, U. Ariz. Law Coll. Assn. (exec. com. 1983—), Phi Kappa Phi, Beta Gamma Sigma, Beta Alpha Psi. Republican.

COOK, THOMAS ALFRED ASHLEY, lawyer; b. Merriam, Kans., Oct. 24, 1964; s. Alfred Harrison and Donna Rebecca Cook; m. Lisa Ann Kehr, Dec. 9, 1983; children: Ashley Alizabeth, Mackenzie Ann. BS in Act. and Bus. Adminstrn., U. Kans., 1985, MBA, 1987, JD, 1989. Bar: Mo. 1989, Ill. 1990. Assoc. Peper, Martin, Jensen, Maichel & Hetlage, St. Louis, 1989-97; ptnr. Peper, Martin Jensen, Maichel & Hetlage, 1997-98, Blackwell, Sanders, Peper, Martin, St. Louis, 1998—. Contracts commercial, General corporate, Mergers and acquisitions. Office: Blackwell Sanders Et Al 720 Olive St Fl 24 Saint Louis MO 63101-2338

COOK, WILLIAM LESLIE, JR. lawyer; b. July 1, 1949; s. William Leslie and Mary Elizabeth (Roberts) C.; m. Mary Jo Dorr, July 17, 1976; children: Leslie Patton, William Roberts, Maribeth Dorr. BA, U. Miss., 1971, JD, 1974. Bar: Miss. 1974, U.S. Dist. Ct. (no. dist.) Miss. 1974, U.S. Dist. Ct. (we. dist.) Tenn. 1986. Assoc. Bailey & Trusty, Batesville, Miss., 1974-79; ptnr. Bailey, Trusty & Cook, 1980-90, Bailey & Cook, Batesville, 1990-92, Bailey, Cook & Womble, Batesville, 1992—. Chmn., Miss. Coll. Rep. Clubs, 1973, Panola County March of Dimes, Batesville, 1976-78; Miss. chmn. Nat. Orgn. Social Security Claimants Reps., 1981-82; rep. Honor Coun., U. Miss. Sch. Law, 1974 King Batesville Jr. Aux. Charity Ball, 2000. Paul Harris fellow 1998—. Mem. ABA (torts and ins. practice sect. 1979—, vice chmn. com. on delivery of legal svcs. tothe disabled young lawyers divsn. 1983-85, gen. practice sect. 1985-86), ATLA, Miss. State Bar (state bd. bar admissions 1978-79, mem. ethics com. 1980-83, bd. dirs. Young Lawyers sect. 1980-83, chmn. com. on unauthorized practice of law 1983-86, workers compensation sect., mem. com. on Kid's Second Chance 1992), Panola County Bar Assn. (pres. 1979-80), Miss. Trial Lawyers Assn. (membership com. 1983-84), Ct. Practice Inst. (diplomate), Lawyer-Pilots Bar Assn., Lamar Soc. Internat. Law, Lamar Order-U. Miss., Batesville Jaycees (legal counsel 1975-77), Masons, Shriners, Rotary (pres. 1991-92, 96-97, asst. dist. gov. 1997-99, dist. gov. nominee 1999-2000, dist. gov. 2000-01, Paul Harris fellow, Four Aves. of Svc. Citation, Rotary Found. Dist. Svc. award), Omicron Delta Kappa, Pi Sigma Alpha, Delta Theta Pi. Methodist. Personal injury, Workers' compensation. Home: 110 Shagbark Dr Batesville MS 38606-8470 Office: Panola Plz 118 Highway 6 W Batesville MS 38606-2507 E-mail: wlcook@panola.com

COOKE, CHRISTOPHER ROBERT, former state judge, lawyer; b. Springfield, Ohio, Dec. 23, 1943; s. Warren and Margaret Louise (Martin) C.; m. Margaret (Nick), July 1, 1970; children— Karen, Anastasia, Nicholas. B.A., Yale U., 1965; J.D., U. Mich., 1968. Bar: Ohio 1968, Alaska 1970, U.S. Dist. Ct. Alaska 1970. Atty., Alaska Legal Services Corp., Anchorage, 1968-71, supervising atty., Bethel, 1971-73; mem. firm Rice, Hoppner & Hedland, Bethel, 1973-76; superior ct. judge State of Alaska, Bethel, 1976-86; ptnr. Hedland, Fleischer, Friedman, Brennan & Cooke, Bethel and Anchorage, 1986—. Composer, singer Chris Cooke's Tundra Music, 1981. Bd. regents U. Alaska-Fairbanks, 1975-77; mem. com. Alaska Humanities Forum, Anchorage, 1979-86; adv. bd. Bethel Sch. Bd., 1982-83. Mem. ABA, Alaska Bar Assn. State civil litigation, Criminal. Home and Office: PO Box 555 Bethel AK 99559-0555

COOKE, ROGER ANTHONY, retired lawyer; b. Bklyn., June 11, 1948; s. John J. and Virginia (Humphreys) C.; m. Joan J. Cirillo, June 19, 1976; children: Julia Cirillo, Elizabeth Cirillo. AB, Georgetown U., 1970, JD, 1973. Bar: N.Y. 1974. Assoc. Simpson, Thacher and Bartlett, 1973-80; dep. gen. counsel, sec. Pan Am. World Airways, N.Y.C., 1981-90; v.p., gen. counsel Fred Meyer Inc., 1990-2000. Mem. Assn. of Bar of City of N.Y. (aeros. com.). Office: Fred Meyer Incorporated 3800 SE 22nd Ave PO Box 42121 Portland OR 97242-0121

COOLEY, RICHARD EUGENE, lawyer; b. Flint, Mich., Apr. 28, 1935; s. Eugene J. and Helen Frances (Lumbert) C.; m. Wanda Lee Ford, Feb. 20, 1965; children: Scott Richard, Courtney Cooley Breaugh. AB, Albion Coll., 1957; JD, Duke U., 1960. Bar: Mich. 1960, U.S. Supreme Ct. 1970. Asst. pros. atty. Genesee County, Mich., 1962-64; ptnr. Bellairs, Dean, Cooley, Siler, Moulton & Smith, Flint, 1964—; spl. asst. atty. gen. State of Mich., 1975-81. City atty. City of Linden, Mich., 1964-89; twp. atty. Fenton (Mich.) Twp., 1970—; village atty. Village of Gaines, Mich., 1989-96. Past bd. dirs. Tall Pines coun. Boy Scouts Am., Fairwinds coun. Girl Scouts U.S.A.; past pres. Child and Family Svcs. Mich., Flint. Mem. State Bar Mich., Genesee County Bar Assn. (pres. 1977-78), Flint Estate Planning Coun. (pres. 1999-2000), Rotary, Masons. Republican. Presbyterian. Avocations: skiing, sailing, travel. Estate planning, Family and matrimonial, Municipal (including bonds). Home: 8292 Butternut Ct Grand Blanc MI 48439-2080 Office: Bellairs Dean Cooley Siler Moulton & Smith 412 S Saginaw St Ste 300 Flint MI 48502-1810

COOLIDGE, DANIEL SCOTT, lawyer; b. Portland, Maine, Sept. 20, 1948; s. John Walter and Mary Louise (Arnold) C.; m. Carolyn Stiles, Nov. 23, 1984; children: Lillian Mae, Lydia Stiles. BS summa cum laude, U. Bridgeport, 1976; JD, Harvard U., 1980. Bar: Conn. 1980, N.H. 1982, Mass. 2001, U.S. Ct. Appeals (1st cir.) 1983, U.S. Supreme Ct. 1985. Assoc. Cummings & Lockwood, Stamford, Conn., 1980-82, Sheehan, Phinney, Bass & Green PA, Manchester, N.H., 1982-87, ptnr., 1987—. Chmn. juvenile diversion com. Pittsfield (N.H.) Dist. Ct., 1982-85. Author: Survival Guide for Road Warriors, 1996; mem. editl. bd. Law Office Tech. Solutions; columnist Law Office Computing, 1997—; patentee tel. test equipment. Chmn. Bradford Constitution Bicentennial Com.; mem. Pittsfield Planning Bd., 1984-85; treas., trustee First Congl. Ch., Pittsfield, 1984-85, First Bapt. Ch. Bradford; pres. Pittsfield Arts Coun., 1985; del. N.H. Constl. Conv., Concord, 1984-94; founding bd. dirs., officer U.S. Found. for Inspiration and Recognition of Sci. and Tech. Mem. ABA (environ. law sect., intellectual property law sect., acting chmn., chmn. computer and tech. divsn., vice-chmn. sys. and tools law practice mgmt. sect. 1994—, governing coun. 1996—, advisor UCC article 2B drafting com. 1995-99), N.H. Bar Assn. (vice-chmn. tech. sect. 1993-96, chmn. lex mundi intellectual property sect. 1992-93), Manchester Bar Assn. Avocations: computers, physics, fly fishing, hiking, machining. Computer, Environmental, Intellectual property. Home: 106 Bible Hill Ln Warner NH 03278-3701 Office: Fish and Richardson 225 Franklin St Boston MA 02110 Personal E-mail: dancoolidge@yahoo.com; Business E-Mail: coolidge@fr.com

COOLIDGE, FRANCIS LOWELL, lawyer; b. Waltham, Mass., Aug. 4, 1945; s. Francis Lowell and Helen Read (Curtis) C.; m. Marylouise E. Redmond, July 7, 1984; children: Georgina Lowell, Lucy Read. BA cum laude, Harvard Coll., 1968; JD magna cum laude, Boston U., 1971. Bar: Mass. 1971. Assoc. Ropes & Gray, Boston, 1971-80, ptnr., 1980—. Sec., trustee Collage, Inc., Boston, 1974, Kodaly Musical Tng. Inst., Hartford, Conn., 1977, The Wayside Inn., 1989, sec., 1992—; trustee, adviser Colony Meml., Keene, N.H., 1977—; bd. dirs. Am. Cancer Soc., Inc., 1992—, sec., bd. dirs. Mass. Divsn. Am. Cancer Soc., 1981-86, 89—, chmn. bd. dirs., 1986-88; sec., bd. dirs. Boston Children's Service Assn., 1982, Bostonian Soc., 1984—, sec., 1991—; pres., bd. dirs. Ellis Meml. and Eldredge House, Boston, 1979—, The Hermes Found., Boston, 1984—; trustee Mus. Fine Arts, Boston, 1985-86, overseer, 1987-91; mem. bd. trustees Charity of Edward Hopkins, 1988—, sec.-treas., 1994—. Roman Catholic. Clubs: Somerset (sec. 1976—), Union Boat, Tavern, City Club Corp. (mgr. 1980-87, sec. 1987-94, pres. 1994—); Knickerbocker (N.Y.C.), Newport Reading Room (R.I.), Country Club (Brookline). Probate, Estate taxation. Home: 62 Beacon St Boston MA 02108-3542 Office: Ropes & Gray One International Pl Boston MA 02110

COOMBE, GEORGE WILLIAM, JR. lawyer, retired banker; b. Kearny, N.J., Oct. 1, 1925; s. George William and Laura (Montgomery) C.; A.B., Rutgers U., 1946; LL.B., Harvard, 1949; m. Marilyn V. Ross, June 4, 1949; children— Susan, Donald William, Nancy. Bar: N.Y. 1950, Mich. 1953, Calif. 1976, U.S. Supr. Ct. Practice in N.Y.C., 1949-53, Detroit, 1953-69; atty., mem. legal-staff Gen. Motors Corp., Detroit, 1953-69, asst. gen. counsel, sec., 1969-75; exec. v.p., gen. counsel Bank of Am., San Francisco, 1975-90; ptnr. Graham and James, San Francisco, 1991-95; sr. fellow Stanford Law Sch., 1995—. Served to lt. USNR, 1942-46. Mem. Am., Mich., Calif., San Francisco, Los Angeles, N.Y.C. bar assns., Phi Beta Kappa, Phi Gamma Delta. Presbyterian. Banking, State civil litigation, General corporate. Home: 2190 Broadway St Apt 2E San Francisco CA 94115-1312 Office: Am Arbitration Assn Asia Pacific Ctr 225 Bush St San Francisco CA 94104-4207

COOMBS, EUGENE G. lawyer; b. Hutchinson, Kans., Mar. 17, 1911; s. Albertus J. and Sarah (Dorth) C.; m. Nancy Elizabeth Wilcox, July 13, 1932 (div.); m. Mary Alice Johnson Goeney, July 12, 1965; children: Eugene G., Russell M., Judith Coombs Schreiber, Sheley Goemey Bush. A.B., Wichita State U., 1933; LL.B., U. Kans., 1936. Bar: Kans. 1936. Assoc., Cowan, McCorkie & Nelson, Wichita 1936-37; spl. agent FBI 1937-43; sole practice, Wichita; now ptnr. Coombs and Durrett, Chartered, Wichita. Mem. Wichita Met. Planning Commn. 1960-73; bd. dirs. United Fund, Community Planning Council; active YMCA, Salvation Army; trustee Herbert Hoover Library, West Branch, Iowa. Served with USNR 1943-46. Mem. ABA, Kans. State Bar Assn., Wichita Bar Assn., Am. Bd. Trial Advocates, Phi Delta Phi. Republican. Methodist. Clubs: Wichita Country, Rotary, Mason. General practice, Probate. Office: PO Box 405 421 E 3rd St N Wichita KS 67202-2509

COONEY, CHARLES HAYES, lawyer; b. Nashville, Apr. 25, 1937; s. Robert G. and Annie Lee (Hayes) C.; m. Patsy M. Cooney, Dec. 25, 1986; children: Susan, Hayes Jr. BA, Vanderbilt U., 1959, JD, 1963. Bar: Tenn. 1963. Pvt. practice Cornelius & Collins, Nashville, 1963-67; chief def. atty. gen. State of Tenn., 1967-80; ptnr. Watkins, McGugin, McNeilly & Rowan, 1980—. Staff mem. Vanderbilt U. Law Review, 1961-62. Capt. U.S. Army, 1959. Mem. ABA, Rotary, Tenn. Bar Assn. (pres. young lawyers sect., 1961), Nashville Bar Assn. (bd. dirs. 1985-87), Nashville Bar Found. Presbyterian. Avocations: golf, travel. General civil litigation, Personal injury, Workers' compensation. Office: Watkins McGugin McNeilly & Rowan 214 2nd Ave N Ste 300 Nashville TN 37201-1638

COONEY, J(OHN) GORDON, JR. lawyer; b. Alexandria, Va., Mar. 22, 1959; s. John Gordon Sr. and Patricia Ruth (McEwen) C.; m. Gretchen Smith Millspaugh, July 17, 1999. BA, Wesleyan U., 1981; JD magna cum laude, Villanova U., 1984. Bar: Pa. 1984, U.S. Dist. Ct. (ea. dist.) Pa. 1986, U.S. Ct. Appeals (5th cir.) 1997, U.S. Ct. Appeals (3d cir.) 1988. Law clk. to hon. judge J. William Ditter Jr. U.S. Dist. Ct. (ea. dist.) Pa., Phila., 1984-86; assoc. Morgan, Lewis & Bockius, LLP, 1986-92, ptnr., 1992—. Adj. lectr. Villanova U. Sch. of Law, 1993—, master Inn of Ct., 1999—; barrister U. Pa. Law Sch. Inn of Ct., 1994-96. Editor-in-chief Villanova U. Law Rev., 1983-84; mem. lawyer's editl. bd. The Legal Intelligencer, 1997—. Trustee Rosemont Sch. of the Holy Child, 1997—; alumni bd. mgrs. Episcopal Acad., 1996—. Mem. ABA (com. on class actions and derivative suits), Pa. Bar Assn., Phila. Bar Assn. (profl. guidance com., fed. cts. com.), Union League Phila., Merion Cricket Club, Pyramid Club, Wesleyan U. Alumni Assn. (pres. Phila. area 1993-96), Arthritis Found. (bd. dirs Ea. Pa. chpt. 1993-96), Order of Coif. Republican. Roman Catholic. Federal civil litigation, General civil litigation, State civil litigation. Office: Morgan Lewis & Bockius LLP 1701 Market St Philadelphia PA 19103-2903

COONEY, THOMAS EMMETT, lawyer; b. Portland, Oreg., July 16, 1931; s. Thomas M. and Ruth (Clune) C.; m. Janice Cooney; children: Jeff, Tom, Paul, Tracy, Eric. BA, U. Portland, 1953; JD, Willamette U., 1956. Bar: Oreg. 1956, U.S. Dist. Ct. Oreg. 1956, U.S. Ct. Appeals (9th cir.) 1956, U.S. Supreme Ct. 1980. Assoc. Maguire, Shields, Morrison, Bailey & Kester, Portland, 1956-60, ptnr., 1960-65, Morrison & Bailey, Portland, 1965-80, Cooney and Van Hoomissen, Portland, 1980-82, Cooney & Crew, Portland, 1982-88, 93—, Cooney, Moscato & Crew, Portland, 1988-93. Adj. instr. Coll. Law Lewis and Clark U., 1978-79. With USAF, 1951-52. Recipient Multnomal Bar Assn. Professionalism award, 1996; named Disting. Trial Lawyer of Yr. Fellow Am. Coll. Trial Lawyers, Nat. Health Lawyers Assn., Assn. Med. Soc. Attys., Oreg. Assn. Hosp. Attys.; mem. Oreg. Assn. Def. Counsel (past pres.), Am. Bd. Trial Advocates (diplomate), Internat. Assn. Def. Counsel, Def. Rsch. Inst., Oswego Lake Country Club, Elks. Health, Insurance, Professional liability. Address: 888 SW 5th Ave Ste 720 Portland OR 97204-2022

COONEY, WILLIAM J. lawyer; b. Augusta, Ga., July 31, 1929; s. John F. and Ellen (Joy) C.; m. Martha L. Whaley, May 1, 1971; children: William J. IV, Sarah C. BS, U. Notre Dame, 1951; JD, Georgetown U., 1954, LLM, 1955. Bar: Ga. 1963, Calif. 1961, D.C. 1954. Law clk. U.S. Ct. Appeals, Washington, 1954, U.S. Claims Ct., Washington, 1955; asst. U.S. atty., 1958-60, San Francisco, 1960-63; sole practice Augusta, 1963—. Capt. JAGC, U.S. Army, 1955-58. Mem. State Bar Ga., Spl. Master State Bar Ga., Augusta Bar Assn. (mem. exec. com.), Am. Arbitration Assn. (arbitrator). Roman Catholic. Civil litigation, general, Contracts commercial, Franchising. Office: 1 Habersham Sq 3602 Wheeler Rd Augusta GA 30909-1826 E-mail: cooney@knology.net

COONS, STEPHEN MERLE, lawyer; b. Indpls., May 27, 1941; s. Harold M. and Margaret L. (Richman) C.; children: Richard, Lori, Caroline. BA, Wabash Coll., 1963; JD, Ind. U., 1971. Bar: Ind. 1971, Ga. 1994, U.S. Dist. Ct. (so. dist.) Ind. 1971, U.S. Tax. Ct. 1971, U.S. Dist. Ct. (no. dist.) Ind. 1980, U.S. Dist. Ct. (no. dist.) Ga. 1994, U.S. Ct. Appeals (7th cir.) 1980, U.S. Supreme Ct. 1978. Ptnr. Bradford & Coons, Indpls., 1971-72; assoc. Yockey & Yockey, 1972-73; ptnr. Compton, Coons & Fetta, 1973-78, Coons & Saint, Indpls., 1979-92, Coons, Maddox & Koeller, Indpls., 1993-95; exec. v.p., gen. counsel, sec. Standard Mgmt. Corp., 1993—. Securities commr. State Ind., Indpls., 1978-83. Mem. ABA, State Bar Ga., Indpls. Bar Assn., Ind. State Bar Assn. General corporate, Real property, Securities. Office: 9100 Keystone Xing Ste 400 Indianapolis IN 46240-2159 also: 1135 Brookhaven Ct NE Atlanta GA 30319-2867

COOPER, ALAN SAMUEL, lawyer, educator; b. June 13, 1942; s. Rudey and Rosalie (Schwartz) C.; m. Maxine Jacobs, Aug. 13, 1966 (dec.); children: Lauren K., Jennifer D.; m. Linda Morguelan Klein, April 18, 1999. BA, Vanderbilt U., 1964, JD, 1968. Bar: Tenn. 1968, D.C. 1969, U.S. Dist. Ct. D.C. 1969, U.S. Supreme Ct. Appeals (Fed. cir.) 1975, U.S. Supremem Ct. 1980. Law clk. U.S. Dist. Ct. (mid. dist.), Tenn., 1967-68; assoc. Browne, Schuyler & Beveridge and Browne, Beveridge & DeGrand, Washington, Schyler, Birch, Swindler, McKie & Beckett, Washington, 1972-74; ptnr. Schyler, Banner, Birch, McKie & Beckett, 1974-94; mem. bd. dirs., shareholder Banner & Witcoff, Ltd., Washington, Chgo., Boston, 1995-97; ptnr. Shaw Pittman Potts & Trowbridge, Washington, N.Y.C., Londo, 1997—. Adj. prof. Georgetown U. Law Ctr., 1985—; adviser on trademark law to U.S. del. to Diplomatic Conf. on Revision of Paris Conv. for Protection of Indsl. Property, Nairobi, Kenya, 1981. Mem. ABA (faculty Nat. Insts. on Trademark Litigation 1978-79), Internat. Trademark Assn., D.C. Bar, Bar Assn. D.C., Tenn. Bar Assn., Bethesda Country Club. Jewish. Trademark and copyright. Office: 2300 N St NW Washington DC 20037-1122

COOPER, CLEMENT THEODORE, lawyer; b. Miami, Fla., Oct. 26, 1930; s. Benjamin Leon and Louise (Bethel) C.; m. Nan Coles Cooper; children: Patricia, Karen, Stephanie, Bridgette, Jessica (dec.), Stacy. AB, Lincoln U., 1952; student, Boston U., 1954-55; JD, Howard U., 1958; PhD in Bus. Adminstrn. (hon.), Colo. Christian Coll. Bar: D.C. 1960, Mich. 1960, U.S. Ct. Appeals (3rd, 4th, 6th, 9th and 10th cirs.), U.S. Supreme Ct. 1963. Pvt. practice, Washington, 1960—. Adj. prof. Strayer U., Washington, 1991-98; former legal cons. No. Calif. Mining Assn. Author: Sealed Verdict, 1964; contbr. articles to profl. jours. Adv. coun. D.C. Dept. Welfare, 1963-66; adv. bd. Com. on Irish Ethnicity, N.Y.C. Mem. ABA, ATLA, D.C. Bar Assn., Nat. Bar Assn., ACLU, Am. Judicature Soc., Rocky Mountain Mining Law Found., Internat. Platform Assn., Nat. Assn. Securities Dealers (arbitrator), Am. Legion, Knights Templar (Knights fellow), Alpha Phi Alpha (life). Episcopalian. Appellate, General civil litigation, Real property. Home: 728 Dahlia St NW Washington DC 20012-1844 Office: PO Box 76135 Washington DC 20013-6135

COOPER, CORINNE, communications consultant, lawyer; b. Albuquerque, July 12, 1952; d. David D. and Martha Lucille (Rosenblum) C. BA magna cum laude, U. Ariz., 1975, JD summa cum laude, 1978. Bar: Ariz. 1978, U.S. Dist. Ct. Ariz. 1978, Mo. 1985. Assoc. Streich, Lang, Weeks & Cardon, Phoenix, 1978-82; asst. prof. U. Mo., Kansas City, 1982-86, assoc. prof., 1986-94, prof., 1994-2000, prof. emerita, 2000—; pres. Profl. Presence, Comm. Cons., Mo., 2001—. Vis. prof. U. Wis., Madison, 1985, 91, U. Pa., Phila., 1988, U. Ariz., 1993, U. Colo., 1994. Author: (with Bruce Meyerson) A Drafter's Guide to Alternative Dispute Resolution, 1991; editor: The Portable UCC, 1993, 3d edit., 2001, Getting Graphic I and II, 1993, 94, The New Article 9, 1999, 2d edit., 2000; editor in chief Bus. Law Today, 1995-97; mem. editl. bd. ABA Jour., 1999—; contbr. articles to profl. jours., chpts. to books. Legal counsel Mo. for Hart campaign, 1984; dir. issues Goddard for Gov. campaign, 1990; bd. dirs. Com. for County Progress, Kansas City, 1985—. Mem. ABA (mem. coun. bus. sect. 1992-96, uniform comml. code com., chmn. membership com. 1992-94, editl. bd. Bus. Law Today, 1991-97, sect. of bus. law pubs. 1998—, jour. editorial bd. 1999—), Am. Assn. Law Schs. (comml. law 1982—, chair 1992-93, alternative dispute resolution com.), Am. Arbitration Assn. (arbitrator, mediator, mem. large complex case panel 1991-96), Mo. Bar Assn. (comml. law com.), Order of Coif, Phi Beta Kappa, Phi Kappa Phi. Democrat. Jewish. Office: Profl Presence 5100 Rockhill Rd 6412 Morningside Dr Kansas City MO 64113

COOPER, DOUGLAS KENNETH, lawyer; b. Ithaca, N.Y., June 6, 1947; s. Murray I. and Meta F. Cooper; m. Pamela A. Regan, Aug. 22, 1970; children: James, Sarah. BA, N.C. State U., 1970; JD, U. N.C., 1974. Bar: Ohio 1974, U.S. Dist. Ct. (no. dist.) Ohio 1974, U.S. Dist. Ct. (no. dist.) Mich. 1997. Assoc. Shapiro, Persky, Stone & Marken Co., L.P.A., Cleve., 1974-76; of counsel Leaseway Transp. Corp., 1976-78, assoc. corp. counsel, 1978-82, corp. counsel, 1982-88, asst. gen. counsel, 1988-92, v.p. opers. law, 1992-96; exec. v.p., gen. counse., sec. Peregrine Inc., Southfield, Mich., 1997—2001; v.p. law GDX Automotive, Farmington Hills, 2001—. Contbr. articles to law revs. Mem. Cleve. Citizens League, 1974—. Mem. ABA, Bar Assn. Greater Cleve., Ohio State Bar Assn., Mich. State Bar, Oakland County Bar Assn. General corporate, Mergers and acquisitions, Real property. Office: GDX Automotive 34975 W 12 Mile Rd Farmington MI 48331

COOPER, GARY ALLAN, lawyer; b. Bristol, Va., Feb. 3, 1947; s. Earl Clarence and Reba Evelyn (Jenkins) C.; chidlren: Drew Kelsey, Gavin Morgan. BS in Journalism, U. Tenn., 1969, JD, 1972. Bar: Tenn. 1972, U.S. Dist. Ct. (ea. dist.) Tenn. 1972, U.S. Supreme Ct. 1979, Fla. 1981. Assoc. Luther, Anderson & Ruth, Chattanooga, 1972-76; ptnr. Luther, Anderson, Cleary, Luhowiak & Cooper, 1976-79, Luther, Anderson, Cleary & Cooper, Chattanooga, 1979-80, Anderson, Cleary & Cooper, Chattanooga, 1981, Fleissner & Cooper, Chattanooga, 1982, Fleissner, Cooper & Marcus, Chattanooga, 1983-88, Fleissner Cooper Marcus & Steger, Chattanooga, 1988-89, Fleissner Cooper Marcus & Quinn, Chattanooga, 1990-97, Franklin, Cooper & Marcus, PLLC, Chattanooga, 1998—. Author: Tennessee Forms for Trial Practice, 1977, 5th edit., 1999, Tennessee Law Office Adminstration, 1977, Tenesee Forms for Trial Practice-Damages, 1997. With USAR, 1972-79. Recipient Herman Hickman Postgrad. scholarship for Athletes U. Tenn., 1969. Mem. ABA, Chattanooga Bar Assn. (bd. dirs. 1984-86), Fla. Bar Assn. (mem. out-of-state practitioners com. 1983-86), Tenn. Bar Assn., Tenn. Def. Lawyers Assn. (chmn. amicus curiae com. 1987-89), Phi Delta Phi. Republican. Methodist. Avocations: golf, reading, boating. Federal civil litigation, State civil litigation, Insurance. Home: 55 Carriage Hl Signal Mountain TN 37377-2331 Office: Franklin Cooper & Marcus PLLC 837 Fortwood St Chattanooga TN 37403-2313 E-mail: garyacooper@mindspring.com

COOPER, GEORGE, writer, consultant; b. Balt., May 31, 1937; s. Harry and Hilda C.; m. Jill Zimmerman, June 19, 1960 (div. 1972); 1 child, Amanda; m. Judy Blume, 1987. BS, U. Pa., 1958; LLB, Harvard U., 1961; cert. in celestial nav. Hayden Planetarium, 1972. Bar: D.C. 1961, N.Y. 1975, U.S. Supreme Ct. 1966. Assoc. Covington & Burling, Washington, 1963-66; faculty Columbia Law Sch., 1966-85, prof. law, 1969-85; writer, consultant, 1985—; vis. prof. Harvard U. Law Sch., 1975, U. Witwatersrand, Johannesburg, Republic South Africa, 1979. Author: A Voluntary Tax, 1979; (with Rabb and Rubin) Equal Employment Opportunity, 1975; editor: Law and Poverty, 1972. Home: 90 Riverside Dr New York NY 10024-5306

COOPER, JAMES RUSSELL, retired law educator; b. New Kensinston, Pa., July 21, 1928; s. John Edward and Isabella Bird (Bowen) C.; m. Carolyn Hocker, Sept. 21, 1953 (div. Dec. 1975); children: L. Rachel, Julia Anderoni, Evan Lloyd, Jennifer Meyer; m. Leigh Ann Brian, Feb. 25, 1995 (div. Nov. 1999). BS in Econs., U. Pa., 1952, JD, 1955. Bar: D.C., 1955, U.S. Supreme Ct., 1964; ordained to ministry Order of the Holy Spirit, Meeting House for Aspiring Spirits. Pres., chmn. Radio WKPA-AM, WYDD-FM, New Kensington, 1959-64; urban renewal dir. Redevelopment Authority, 1964-68; assoc. prof. U. Ill., Champaign-Urbana, 1968-74; prof. legal studies Ga. State U., Atlanta, 1974-94, emeritus prof., 1994—. Author: Twilights Last Gleaming, 1992, Real Estate Investments, 3d edit. 1992. Sgt. U.S. Army, 1946-48. Mem. Fed. Bar Assn., D.C. Bar Assn., Am. Real Estate Soc. (founder, dir.). Home: 4072 Lebanon Church Rd Athens GA 30607-2924 E-mail: jrcooper@randomc.com

COOPER, JOHN WEEKS, lawyer; b. Newark, Feb. 5, 1930; s. Ralph Emerson and Ann Elizabeth (Weeks) C.; m. Mary Kathryn Niles, Nov. 4, 1961; children: Sarah Elizabeth, Edward Niles. AB, Bowdoin Coll., 1952; LLB, Columbia U., 1955. Bar: N.J. 1955, U.S. Dist. Ct. N.J. 1955. Assoc. McCarter & English, Newark, 1955-57, Moser, Griffin & Kerby, Summit, N.J., 1957-63; ptnr. Kerby, Cooper, Schaul & Garvin, 1963-90, Cooper, Rose & English, LLP, Summit, 1990—. Sec., gen. counsel Anchorage Hotel, Antigua, West Indies, 1976-87. Pres. Summit First Aid Squad, 1967, Family Svc. Assn., Summit, 1978, Summit Area Pub. Found.; trustee Oak Knoll Sch., Summit, United Way, Summit; pres. United Way, 1985-87. Named United Way Citizen of Yr., 1990. Fellow Am. Coll. Trust and Estate Coun.; mem. Summit Bar Assn. (pres. 1975), Union County Bar Assn. (probate com. 1975—), N.J. Bar Assn. (bd. consultors, real property and probate sect., chmn. dist. XII supreme ct. fee arbitration panel, chmn. probate early settlement panel program Union County), No. N.J. Estate Planning Coun. (pres. 1985), Beacon Hill Club (pres. 1972-74), Shrewsbury Sailing and Yacht Club (Oceanport N.J.). Republican. Episcopalian. Estate planning, Probate, Estate taxation. Home: 80 Prospect St Summit NJ 07901-2406 Office: Cooper Rose & English LLP 480 Morris Ave Summit NJ 07901-1523

COOPER, LAWRENCE ALLEN, lawyer; b. San Antonio, Feb. 1, 1948; s. Elmer E. and Sally (Tempkin) C.; 1 child, Jonathan Alexander. BA, Tulane U., 1970; JD, St. Mary's U., San Antonio, 1974; LLM, Emory U., 1980. Bar: Ga. 1975, Tex. 1975. Ptnr. Cohen & Cohen, Atlanta, 1979-88; pvt. practice, 1989—. Arbitrator Fulton Superior Ct.; mem. Ga. Bar fee dispute com. Mem. ABA, ATLA, Atlanta Bar Assn., Ga. Trial Lawyers Assn., Tex. Bar Assn., Old War Horse Lawyers Club. Family and matrimonial, Personal injury, Product liability. Home: 2460 Peachtree Rd NW Apt 1704 Atlanta GA 30305-4159 Office: Cohen & Cooper LLC Ste 2220 3350 Riverwood Pkwy Atlanta GA 30339 E-mail: lacooperatty@mindspring.com

COOPER, MARY LITTLE, federal judge, former banking commissioner; b. Fond du Lac, Wis., Aug. 13, 1946; d. Ashley Jewell and Gertrude (McCoy) Little; m. John Francis Parell, May 28, 1972 (div. 1990); children: Christie, Morgan, Shawn, John Brady; m. John F. Cooper, Dec. 26, 1997. AB in Polit. Sci. cum laude, Bryn Mawr Coll., 1968; JD, Villanova U., 1972; LLD (hon.), Georgian Ct. Coll., 1987. Bar: N.J. 1972. Assoc. McCarter & English, Newark, 1972-80, ptnr., 1980-84; commr. N.J. Dept. Banking, Trenton, 1984-90; assoc. gen. counsel Prudential Property & Casualty Ins. Co., Holmdel, N.J., 1991-92; judge U.S. Dist. Ct. N.J., 1992—. Chmn. bd. Pinelands Devel. Credt Bank. Bd. trustees Exec. Commn. Ethical Standards, Trenton, 1984-90, Corp. Bus. Assistance, Trenton, 1984-91, N.J. Housing & Mortgage Fin. Agy., Trenton, 1984-90, N.J. Cemetery Bd. Assn., 1984-90, N.J. Hist. Soc., 1976-79., YMCA of Greater Newark, 1973-76; mem. Supreme Ct. N.J. Civil Practice Com., 1982-84, Supreme Ct. N.J. Dist. Ethics Com., 1982-84. Fellow Am. Bar Found.; mem. ABA, N.J. Bar Assn., Princeton Bar Assn., John J. Gibbons Am. Inn of Ct. Office: US Courthouse 402 E State St Ste 5000 Trenton NJ 08608-1507

COOPER, MICHAEL ANTHONY, lawyer; b. Passaic, N.J., Mar. 29, 1936; B.A., Harvard U., 1957, LL.B., 1960. Bar: N.Y. State 1961, U.S. Supreme Ct. 1969. With firm Sullivan & Cromwell, N.Y.C., 1960—, ptnr., 1968—. Pres. Legal Aid Soc., 1981-83; bd. fellows Inst. Jud. Adminstrn., chair, pro bono net, 2000—. Co-chair Lawyers Com. for Civil Rights Under Law, 1993-95; bd. dirs. Fund for Modern Cts., Vols. of Legal Svcs. Fellow Am. Coll. Trial Lawyers (bd. regents); mem. ABA, N.Y. State Bar Assn., Assn. Bar City N.Y. (chair exec. com. 1996-97, v.p. 1997-98, pres. 1998-2000, Fed. Bar Coun. (trustee 1994-2000), Am. Law Inst., Am. Judicature Soc. Antitrust, Federal civil litigation, Securities. Office: Sullivan & Cromwell 125 Broad St Fl 28 New York NY 10004-2489

COOPER, MICHAEL LEE, lawyer; b. Roseburg, Oreg., July 9, 1958; s. Leroy Everrett Cooper and Mattie Verline Orrell. BS with honors, U. Oreg., 1979, JD, 1984. Bar: Oreg. 1984, U.S. Dist. Ct. Oreg. 1986, U.S. Ct. Appeals (9th cir.) 1988, U.S. Supreme Ct. 1988. Pvt. practice, Eugene, Oreg., 1984—. Spkr. seminar Clergy and the Law, 1992-93. Deacon 1st Landmark Missionary Bapt. Ch., Springfield, Oreg., 1984—, treas. 1997—; trustee Union Roque Bapt. Camp, Springfield, 1985-98; tchr. Bapt. history Springfield Sch. of Bible, 1992-96, tchr. ancient history, 1984-96. Mem. Oreg. State Bar. Estate planning, General practice, Personal injury. Home: 1465 Cottonwood Ave Springfield OR 97477-7661 Office: 895 Country Club Rd Ste C175 Eugene OR 97401-6006

COOPER, MONIKA GOESCHEL, lawyer; b. Detroit, Aug. 31, 1968; m. May 18, 1997; children: Chad, Jennifer. BA, U. Tex., Arlington, 1992; JD, Tex. Wesleyan U., 1997. Bar: Tex. 1997, U.S. Dist. Ct. (no. dist.) Tex. 1997. Paralegal Shannon Gracey Ratliff & Miller, Ft. Worth, 1987-97, assoc., 1997—. Mem. Tex. Bar Assn., Tarrant County Bar Assn., Tarrant County Young Lawyers Assn. Avocations: horses, farming, sports, camping. General civil litigation, Criminal. Office: Shannon Gracey Ratliff Et Al Ste 1600 500 Throckmorton St Fort Worth TX 76102

COOPER, N. LEE, lawyer; m. Joy Clark; children: Clark, Catherine. BS, U. Ala., 1963, LLB, 1964. Pvt. practice, Birmingham, Ala., 1966—; founder Maynard, Cooper & Gale, P.C. Articles and Notes editor Ala. Law Rev., 1962-64. Nat. bd. dirs. U. Ala.; trustee Ala. Law Sch. Found.; bd. overseers Rand Inst. for Civil Jusice. 1st lt. U.S. Army, 1964-66, capt. USAR. Fellow Am. Bar Found.; mem. ABA (chair, litig. sect. 1985-86, sec. litig. sect. 1976-78, Birmingham bar del. to ho. of deps. 1979-80, Ala. del. to ho. of dels. 1980-89, mem. drafting com. on model rules of profl. conduct 1982-84, mem. commn. on professionalism 1985-87, chair select com. on ho. of dels. 1989-90, chair ho. of dels. 1990-92, pres.-elect 1995-96, pres. 1996-97), Am. Judicature Soc. (dir.), Am. Bar Endowment (dir.), Am. Law Inst. (council, advisor project on restatement of law governing lawyers), Ala. Bar Assn. (pres. young lawyers sect. 1974-75, Merit award 1976), Birmingham Bar Assn. (sec.-treas. 1972, vice chair congl. commn. on structural alts. for the fed. cts. of appeals, dir. lawyers com. for civil rights). Office: AmSouth Harbert Plz 1901 6th Ave N Ste 2400 Birmingham AL 35203-4604

COOPER, NANCY M. lawyer; b. Boulder, Colo., July 11, 1958; d. John Douglas and Betty Mae (Locke) McCullen; m. Neal David Cooper, July 29, 1984 (dec. Sept. 1998). BS in Pub. Adminstrn., U. Ariz., 1980; JD, Lewis and Clark Coll., 1995. Bar: Oreg. 1995. Juvenile probation officer Gila County, Globe, Ariz., 1980-82, State of Alaska, Anchorage, 1983-92; founding mem. Steinman, Cooper, Wiscarson, LLC, Portland, 1995—. Contbr. articles to profl. jours. Mem. progress bd. City of Gresham, Oreg., 1999—. Mem. ABA, Oreg. State Bar Assn. (chair legal ethics com. 2001, mem. svcs. com. new lawyer divsn. 1995-99, family law sect. 1995—, litig. sect. 1995—, employment law sect. 1995—), Multnomah County Bar Assn. (professionalsm com. 2000—), Gus Solomon Inns of Court. Family and matrimonial, Labor. Office: 317 SW Alder St 9t Fl Portland OR 97204-2532 E-mail: cooper@scwlawfirm.com

COOPER, PAUL DOUGLAS, lawyer; b. Kansas City, Mo., July 22, 1941; s. W.W. and Emma Marie (Ringo) C.; m. Elsa B. Shaw, June 15, 1963 (div. 1991); children: Richard, Dean; m. Kay J. Rice, Aug. 30, 1992; 1 child, Natanya. BA in English, U. Mich., 1963; LLB, U. Calif., 1966. Bar: Colo. 1966, U.S. Dist. Ct. Colo. 1966, U.S. Ct. Appeals (10th cir.) 1967, U.S. Supreme Ct. 1979. Dep. dist. atty., Denver, 1969-71; asst. U.S. atty. Dist. of Colo., 1971-73; ptnr. Yegge, Hall & Evans, Denver, 1973-80; pres., dir. Cooper & Kelley PC, 1980-94, Cooper & Clough PC, Denver, 1994—. Faculty trial practice seminar Denver U. Law Sch., 1982; spl. asst. U.S. atty. Dist. of Colo., 1973-75; spl. prosecutor Mar. 1977 term, Garfield County Grand Jury; pres. Bow Mar Owners, Inc., 1976-77; English adv. bd. U. Mich., 2000—. Recipient Spl. Commendation award for outstanding svc., 1972. Mem. ABA, Am. Bd. Trial Advocates, Colo. Bar Assn. (interprofl. com., bd. govs.), Denver Bar Assn. (trustee, 1st v.p. 1982-83), Colo. Med. Soc. (chmn. interprofl. com., Denver bar liaison com), Internat. Assn. Def. Counsel (exec. com. 1989-92), Denver Athletic Club. Republican. Insurance, Libel, Personal injury. Home: 1890 Bellaire St Denver CO 80220-1051 Office: 1512 Larimer St Ste 600 Denver CO 80202-1610 E-mail: pcooper@cooper-clough.com

COOPER, RICHARD ALAN, lawyer; b. Hattiesburg, Miss., July 19, 1953; s. H. Douglas and Elaine (Reece) C. BA, BS, U. Ark., Little Rock, 1976; JD, Washington U., St. Louis, 1979. Bar: Mo. 1979, Ill. 1980, U.S. Dist. Ct. (ea. dist.) Mo. 1980, U.S. Dist Ct. (so. dist.) Ill. 1988. Law clk. U.S. Dist. Ct., St. Louis, 1979-80; assoc. William R. Gartenberg, 1980-81, Danis, Reid, Murphy, Tobben & Cooper, St. Louis, 1983-87, ptnr., 1987-88, Law Office Terry Sharp, P.C., 1988-89; pvt. practice, 1989-90; ptnr. Danis & Boyce, 1990-93, Davis, Cooepr, Cavanagh & Hartweger, L.C., 1994-98; CFO MedCard Am., Inc., 1997-99. Liaison to Washington U. Sch. Law, Mo. Assn. Trial Attys., St. Louis, 1983-85; presenter in field. Bus. mgr. Urban Law Jour., 1978-79; editor Bankruptcy Law Reporter, 1983-88, co-mgr., editor, 1984-88; co-author seminars including Advanced Consumer Bankruptcy and Fair Debt Collection Practices, Collecting Judgments and Non UCC Liens, Advanced Consumer Bankruptcy. Recipient Milton F. Napier trial award Lawyers Assn. St. Lois, 1979, Outstanding Sr. Bus. Major award Wall St. Jour., 1976. Mem. Mo. Bar Assn., Boulder Yacht Club (commodore 1998-99), Commonwealth Yacht Club. Avocation: sailing. Bankruptcy, Federal civil litigation, Contracts commercial. Office: Law Offices Richard Alan Cooper 2379 Cedar Dale Ct Maryland Heights MO 63043 E-mail: rcooper@cableamericahsa.com

COOPER, RICHARD CASEY, lawyer; b. Tulsa, Jan. 20, 1942; s. Winston Churchill and Frances Margaret (Coppinger) C.; m. Ireen Lysbeth Evans, Nov. 24, 1965; children: Christopher Casey, Kimberly Ireen. BSBA, U. Tulsa, 1965, JD, 1967. Bar: Okla. 1967, U.S. Dist. Ct. (no., ea. and we. dists.) Okla. 1967, U.S. Ct. Mil. Appeals 1967, U.S. Ct. Appeals (10th cir.) 1972. Assoc. Boesche, McDermott & Eskridge, Tulsa, 1972-76, ptnr., 1977-92, mng. ptnr., 1990—. Editor in chief Tulsa Law Jour., 1967. Counsel Tulsa Philharm. Orch., 1990-92; trustee Mervin Bovaird Found., Tulsa, 1991—, pres., 1995—; trustee The Philbrook Mus. Art, 1997—, Tulsa Opera, 2000—, Bacone Coll., 2001—. Lt. USNR, 1967-71, mil. judge JAGC, 1970-71. Villard Martin scholar U. Tulsa, 1967; recipient Order of the Curule Chair, 1967. Mem. ABA, Okla. Bar Assn., Tulsa County Bar Assn., So. Hills Country Club. Republican. Avocations: family activities, fly fishing, travel. General civil litigation, General corporate, Environmental. Home: 2923 E 58th St Tulsa OK 74105-7453 Office: Boesche McDermott Eskridge 100 W 5th St Ste 800 Tulsa OK 74103-4291

COOPER, RICHARD MELVYN, lawyer; b. Phila., Nov. 13, 1942; s. Arthur Martin and Sophia Phyllis (Gottlieb) C.; m. Sabina Abbe Karp, June 12, 1965 (div. 1978); children: Alexander, Stephanie; m. Judith Carole Areen, Feb. 17, 1979; children: Benjamin, Jonathan. BA summa cum laude, Haverford Coll., 1964; BA 1st class, Oxford U., 1966, MA, 1970; JD summa cum laude, Harvard U., 1969. Bar: D.C. 1970, U.S. Ct. Appeals (5th, 6th and 9th cirs.) 1988, U.S. Ct. Appeals (10th cir.) 1982, U.S. Ct. Appeals (11th cir.) 1984, U.S. Ct. Appeals (fed. cir.) 1985, U.S. Ct. Appeals (4th cir.) 1997, U.S. Supreme Ct. 1973. Law clk. to Justice William J. Brennan, Jr. U.S. Supreme Ct., Washington, 1969-70; sr. lectr. Law Devel. Ctr., Kampala, Uganda, 1970-71; assoc. Williams, Connolly & Califano, Washington, 1971-77; chief counsel FDA, Rockville, Md., 1977-79; ptnr. Williams & Connolly, Washington, 1980—, mem. exec. com., 1983-84, 89-92. Sr. mem. Office Energy Policy and Planning, Exec. Office of Pres., Washington, 1977; adj. prof. Georgetown U. Law Ctr., Washington, 1987-92, 96; mem. Adminstrv. Conf. U.S., 1978-79, Jud. Conf. D.C., Washington, 1979; mem. Adv. Panel on Strategies for Med. Tech. Assessment, Washington, 1980-81; mem. coms. NAS, 1980-83, 87-90. Editor: Food and Drug Law, 1991; co-editor: Fundamentals of Law and Regulation, 1997; contbr. articles to profl. jours. Chief counsel credentials com. Dem. Nat. Conv., Washington and N.Y.C., 1976; bd. mgrs. Haverford Coll., 1997—. Rhodes Trust scholar 1964; recipient FDA Award of Merit, 1979. Jewish. Office: Williams & Connolly 725 12th St NW Washington DC 20005-5901 E-mail: rcooper@wc.com

COOPER, ROBERT ELBERT, state supreme court justice; b. Chattanooga, Oct. 14, 1920; s. John Thurman and Susie Inez (Hollingsworth) C.; m. Catherine Pauline Kelly, Nov. 24, 1949; children: Susan Florence Cooper Hodges, Bobbie Cooper Martin, Kelly Ann Smith, Robert Elbert Jr. BA, U. N.C., 1946; JD, Vanderbilt U., 1949. Bar: Tenn. 1948. Assoc. Kolwyck and Clark, 1949-51; ptnr. Cooper and Barger, 1951-53; asst. atty. gen. 6th Jud. Ct. Tenn., 1951-53; judge 6th Jud. Circuit Tenn., 1953-60, Tenn. Ct. Appeals, 1960-70, presiding judge Eastern divsn., 1970-74; justice Tenn. Supreme Ct., 1974-90, chief justice, 1976-77, 84-85. Chmn. Tenn. Jud. Coun., 1967-90; chmn. Tenn. Code Commn., 1976-77, 84-85; mem. Tenn. Jud. Standards Commn., 1971-77. Mem. exec. bd. Cherokee coun. Boy Scouts Am., 1960-64; bd. dirs. Met. YMCA, 1956-65, St. Barnabas Nursing Home and Apts. for Aged, 1966-69. With USNR, 1941-46. Recipient Nat. Heritage award Downtown Sertoma Club, Chattanooga, 1989. Mem. Am., Tenn., Chattanooga bar assns., Conf. Chief Justices, Phi Beta Kappa, Order of Coif, Kappa Sigma, Phi Alpha Delta. Democrat. Presbyterian. Clubs: Signal Mountain Golf and Country, Masons (33 deg.), Shriners. Home and Office: 196 Woodcliff Cir Signal Mountain TN 37377-3147

COOPER, ROY ASBERRY , III, lawyer; b. Rocky Mount, N.C., June 13, 1957; s. Roy Asberry Jr. and Beverly (Batchelor) C.; m. Kristin Bernhardt, Mar. 28, 1992; children: Hilary Godette, Natalie Rose, Claire Kristin. BA, U. N.C., 1979, JD, 1982. Bar: N.C. 1982. Ptnr. Fields and Cooper, Rocky Mount, 1982—2001; atty. gen. State of N.C., 2001—. Rep. N.C. Ho. of Reps., 1987-91, chmn. jud. com., 1989-91; senator N.C. Senate, 1991—, chmn. jud. com., 1991—. Morehead scholar U. N.C., 1975-79. Democrat. Presbyterian. Office: NC Dept Justice PO Box 629 Raleigh NC 27602*

COOPER, STEPHEN HERBERT, lawyer; b. N.Y.C., Mar. 29, 1939; s. Walter S. and Selma (Herbert) C.; m. Linda Cohen, Aug. 29, 1965 (dec.); m. Karen Gross, Sept. 6, 1981; 1 child, Zachary Noel. AB, Columbia U., 1960, JD cum laude, 1965. Bar: N.Y. 1965. Assoc. Breed, Abbott & Morgan, N.Y.C., 1965-66, Weil, Gotshal & Manges, N.Y.C., 1966-73, ptnr., 1973—. Lectr. Nat. Inst. Securities Regulation U. Colo., Boulder, 1985, Practicing Law Inst. 25th Annual Nat. Inst. Securities Regulation, N.Y.C., 1993, Law Jours. Seminars, 1997, 98. Served to lt. USNR, 1960-62. Fellow Am. Bar Found.; mem. ABA (com. fed. regulation securities, subcom. internat. securities matters, co-chmn. 1990—). General corporate, Private international, Securities. Home: 1125 Park Ave New York NY 10128-1243 Office: Weil Gotshal & Manges LLP 767 5th Ave New York NY 10153-0119 E-mail: stephen.cooper@weil.com

COOPER, THOMAS RANDOLPH, lawyer; b. Bath, Maine, July 8, 1953; s. Tommy Gene and Cecile Sunshine (Butler) C.; m. Twila Ann Pirkle, Sept. 15, 1984; 1 child, Kimberly Nicole. BS, U. Houston, 1975; JD, South Tex. Coll. Law, Houston, 1978. Bar: Tex. 1978, U.S. Dist. Ct. (so., no., ea. and we. dists.) Tex. 1987, U.S. Ct. Appeals (5th cir.) 1991. Gen. counsel Umm Al-Qaiwain Oil Consortium, United Arab Emirates, 1978-80; assoc. Hill & Spoliansky, Dubai, United Arab Emirates, 1979-81; gen. counsel, v.p. Unigulf Petroleum, Inc., 1981; legal cons. Azusa Internat., Ltd., Sharjah, United Arab Emirates, 1982; assoc. Shoemake & Selwyn, Houston, 1982-85, Law Offices of David N. Williams, Houston, 1987-92; sole practitioner, 1985-87, 92-00; gen. counsel, bd. dirs. Tramco Builders, Inc., 2000—, Cherokee Directional Drilling, Inc., 2000—. Bd. dirs. Hazard Assessment Leaders, Inc., Houston. Columnist What's On Mag., 1981-82. Sigma Nu endl. grantee, 1975. Mem. Coll. of State Bar of Tex., Nat. Assn. Eagle Scouts, Masons, Scottish Rite, Omicron Delta Kappa. Republican. Methodist. Avocations: woodworking, photography. Construction, General corporate, General practice. Home: 1158 Chantilly Ln Houston TX 77018-3240 Office: 1183 Brittmoore Rd Ste 300 Houston TX 77043 E-mail: tom@cherokeedd.com

COOPER, WENDY FEIN, lawyer; b. May 10, 1946; d. Jacob and Rose (Rothman) Fein; m. James C. Faltot, Apr. 4, 1971 (div. 1982); m. Leonard J. Cooper, June 19, 1983; children: Jennifer Regan, Ian Joshua. AB cum laude, Bryn Mawr Coll., 1968; JD, Temple U., 1973, LLM in Taxation, 1983. Assoc. Beitch & Block, Phila., 1973-76, ptnr., 1976-80; assoc. Narin & Chait, 1980-83, ptnr., 1983-85; assoc. Griffith & Burr P.C., 1985-87; shareholder Dolchin, Slotkin & Todd, P.C., 1987—. Bd. dirs., sec. Phila. Festival Theatre for New Plays, 1981-97. Mem. ABA, N.J. Bar Assn., Phila. Bar Assn. General corporate, Probate, Taxation, general. Home: 1603 Harris Rd Laverock PA 19038-7206 Office: Dolchin Slotkin & Todd PC 2005 Market St Fl 24 Philadelphia PA 19103-7042 also: Dolchin Slotkin & Todd 402 Park Blvd Cherry Hill NJ 08002-3317 E-mail: wcooper@dolchin.com

COOPER, WILLIAM LEWIS, research librarian, lawyer, consultant; b. Highland Park, Mich., Sept. 11, 1944; s. Frank Edward and Margaret Ellen (Hayes) C.; m. Linda Sue Leet, Mar. 5, 1977. AB, Dartmouth Coll., 1966; JD, U. Mich., 1972, AM in Library Sci., 1974. Bar: Mich. 1972, D.C. 1976. Assoc. Miller-Canfield, Detroit, 1972-74; reference libr. U. Pa., 1974-75; libr. Hogan & Hartson, Washington, 1975-77; dir. legal rsch. Dykema Gossett, Detroit, 1977-91, Williamsbury Assocs., Birmingham, Mich., 1991-95; rsch. libr. Coll. William and Mary, Williamsburg, Va., 1995—. Contbr. articles to law jours. Served with U.S. Army, 1967-69. Mem. Mich. State Bar Assn. (legal econs. sect.), Detroit Bar Found. (treas. 1980-82, trustee 1979-85). Episcopalian. Office: Coll William and Mary PO Box 651 Williamsburg VA 23187-0651

COOPER, WILLIAM S. state supreme court justice; BA, U. Ky., 1963, JD with high distinction, 1970. Ptnr. Collier, Arnett, Coleman & Cooper, 1970—79; judge Ky. 9th Judicial Cir., Div. 1, 1979—96; justice Ky. Supreme Ct., Frankfort, 1996—. Capt. USAF, 1963-67. Office: Hardin County Justice Ctr 120 E Dixie Ave Elizabethtown KY 42701-1487*

COOPERMAN, ROBERT N. lawyer; b. Bklyn., July 9, 1935; s. Albert J. and Edith (Seligman) C.; m. Barbara F. Burger, Mar. 22, 1959; children: M. James, Tod D., Nancy D. BBA, CCNY, 1956; LLB, Columbia U., 1959; LLM in Taxation, NYU, 1964. Bar: N.Y. 1959, U.S. Dist. Ct. (so. and ea. dists.) N.Y. 1959, U.S. Tax Ct. 1968, U.S. Supreme Ct. 1968. Assoc. Arthur Richenthal, N.Y.C., 1960-65; pres. Cooperman, Levitt, Winikoff, Lester & Newman and predecessor, 1966—. Pres. United Community Fund, Great Neck, N.Y., 1969; vice chmn. Great Neck Village Bd. Appeals, 1980-85; v.p. Temple Israel, Great Neck, 1975-81. Mem. ABA, N.Y. State Bar Assn., Tex. Homeowners Assn. (pres.). General corporate, Labor, Corporate taxation. Home: 25 Strathmore Rd Great Neck NY 11023-1035 Office: Cooperman Lester Miller LLP 800 3d Ave New York NY 10022-7604 also: 1129 Northern Blvd Manhasset NY 11030-3022 Address: 6 Mitchell Dunes Ln Amagansett NY 11930 E-mail: RCooperman@clmlaw.com

COOVER, ANN E. lawyer; b. Sparta, Wis., Aug. 23, 1948; d. Orlin H. Runde and Kathleen Ann Dwyer; m. David M. Coover, July 22, 1972; 1 child, D. Marshall. BS, U. Wis., 1971; JD magna cum laude, U. Houston, 1975. Bar: Tex. 1975, U.S. Dist. Ct. (fed. dist.) 1975, U.S. Supreme Ct. 1978; bd. cert. family law Tex. Bd. Legal Specialization. Sr. law clk. to dist. judge U.S. Dist. Ct., Corpus Christi, Tex., 1976-78; ptnr. Coover & Coover, 1978—. Chair Am. Cancer Soc. Cattlemen's Ball, Corpus Christi, 1998; chair Auction for Art Mus. Gala, Corpus Christi, 1997. Avocations: gardening, antiques, bridge. Alternative dispute resolution, Environmental. Office: Coover & Coover 921 N Chaparral St Corpus Christi TX 78401-2008

COPE, JOHN R(OBERT), lawyer; b. San Angelo, Tex., May 30, 1942; s. Robert Lloyd and Meta (Young) C.; m. Jeannette L. Naylor; 1 child, Lloyd Chapman. BBA, U. Tex., 1964, JD, 1966; MTS, Wesley Theol. Sem., Washington, 2001. Bar: Tex. 1966, D.C. 1976. Ptnr. Bracewell & Patterson, Attys., Houston, 1966-76, Washington, 1976—, mem. adv. mgmt. com., 1987-90; sr. ptnr., 1994—. Vice chmn. bd. dirs., gen. counsel Century Nat. Bank, Washington, 1982—; bd. dirs., gen. counsel Columbia Nat. Bank, Washington, 1987-90; bd. dirs., v.p., gen. counsel Century Bancshares, Washington, 1985—; mem. fed. savs. and loan adv. coun. Fed. Home Loan Bank Bd., Washington, 1980-81; chmn., lectr. Practicing Law Inst. Seminars on Energy Litigation, Washington, 1980, 81; chief judge Wake Island Ct., Wake Island, North Pacific Ocean, 1989. Bd. govs., mem. exec. com., chmn. personnel and acad. affairs com. Wesley Theol. Sem., Washington, 1997—; mem. devel. bd. Lon Morris Coll., Lake Jackson, Tex., 1974-76; mem. Southwest U. Spl. Edn. Found., San Marcos, Tex., 1973-76; v.p., dir. Harris County Easter Seal Soc., Houston, 1972-76; bd. dirs., sec. Nemours Wildlife Found., Yemassee, S.C., 1993—; treas. Dem. Party Harris County, Houston, 1976-77; mem. nat. fin. coun. Dem. Nat. Com., Washington, 1976-80; cert. lay spkr. United Meth. Ch., dist. dir. lay speaking dist. Washington-Columbia. Mem. ABA (mem. litigation sect.), D.C. Bar Assn. (mem. litigation and govt. contracts sect.), Tex. Bar Assn. (mem. litigation sect.), Houston Bar Assn. (mem. gen. litigation sect.), Orton Soc. Republican. Banking, General civil litigation, Government contracts and claims. Office: Bracewell & Patterson 2000 K St NW Ste 500 Washington DC 20006-1872 E-mail: jcope@bracepatt.com

COPE, THOM K. lawyer; b. Bremen, Fed. Republic Germany, Feb. 26, 1948; came to U.S., 1960; s. Ray and Gabriele E. (Meyer) C.; m. Melba D. Van Hemert, Nov. 8, 1980. BA with honors, Syracuse U., 1969; JD, U. Nebr., 1972. Bar: Nebr. 1972, U.S. Dist. Ct. Nebr. 1972, U.S. Ct. Appeals (8th cir.) 1972, Calif. 1976, U.S. Dist. Ct. (no. dist.) Calif. 1976, U.S. Ct. Appeals (9th cir.) 1976, U.S. Supreme Ct. 1987, U.S. Claims Ct. 1988, U.S. Ct. Appeals (D.C. cir.) 1990. Agy. legal counsel Nebr. Workers' Compensation Ct., Lincoln, 1972-73; assoc. counsel Fireman's Fund Ins. Co., San Francisco, 1973-76; asst. gen. counsel Argonaut Ins. Co., Menlo Park, Calif., 1976-78; assoc. counsel Ins. Svcs. Office, N.Y.C., 1978-82; assoc. atty. Tate & Assocs., Nebr., 1982-83, Bailey, Polsky, Cada & Todd, 1983-84; ptnr. Bailey, Polsky, Cope & Knapp, Lincoln, 1984-97, Polsky Cope Shiffermiller Coe and Monzon and predecessors, Lincoln, 1997—. Judge Nebr. Commn. of Indsl. Rels., 1986-91; mem. Nebr. Supreme Ct. Gender Bias Task Force; mem. Nebr. Motor Vehicle Industry Licensing Bd.; mem. Nebr. Atty. Gen. Odometer Fraud Task Force; mem. Fed. Practice Adv. Com.; lectr. in field. Author: Executive Guide to Employment Practices, 1985, 3d edit., 1999. Bd. dirs. Friends of Elderly Found., Lincoln, 1986-90, Capital Humane Soc., Planned Parenthood Lincoln, 1997—, v.p., 1998, pres. 1999—; bd. dirs. Child Advocacy Ctr., 1995-97; bd. trustees Lincoln Bar Assn. Fellow Coll. Employment and Labor Law; mem. Nat. Employment Lawyers Assn., Nebr. Bar Assn. (labor and employment sect., exec. com., sec.), Nebr. Trial Lawyers Assn., NOW (bd. dirs. 1999). Avocation: golf. Civil rights, State civil litigation, Labor. Home: 2244 Heritage Pines Ct Lincoln NE 68506-2874 Office: Polsky Cope Shiffermiller Coe and Monzon 3901 Normal Blvd Ste 102 Lincoln NE 68506-5200 Fax: (402) 484-7714. E-mail: epocgolf@aol.com

COPELAND, CHARLENE CAROLE, lawyer; b. Gloversville, N.Y., 22 July; d. Joseph Frank and Marion (Dye) Born; m. E. Allen Copeland, June 18; children: Christopher, Todd, Tiffani. BS in Polit Sci., Lamar U.; JD, John Marshall U. Bar: Ill. 1991, U.S. Dist. Ct. (no. dist.) Ill. 1991, U.S. Ct. Appeals (7th cir.) 1993, Fed. Trial Bar, 1993. Assoc. Brenner, Mavrias & Alm, New Lenox, Ill., 1992-96; assoc. civil divsn. Will County State's Attys. Office, Joliet, 1997-1999; with Lehrer, Flaherty & Canavan, Wheaton, 2000—. Mem. Will County Pro Bono Project; pres. Jaycettes, Port Authur, Tex., 1970-71; fin. chmn. League of Women Voters, 1971, pres. Joliet Region, 1979-81; area capt. March of Dimes Mothers' March, 1971; day chmn. George Bush for Senate Campaign, 1970; mem. Village of Shorewood Ad Hoc Com. on Ordinances, 1975, Fin. Com., 1976-78; pres. United Meth. Women of Grace Meth. Ch., 1980-81; crusade chmn. Shorewood Residential Cancer Crusade, 1982. Named Outstanding Pro Bono Vol., 1995. Mem. ATLA, Ill. State Bar Assn., Will County Bar Assn., Will County Arbitration Panel, Will County Women's Bar Assn. Federal civil litigation, State civil litigation, Environmental. Home: 516 Ca Crest Dr Shorewood IL 60431-9729 Office: Lehrer Flaherty & Canavan 429 W Wesley Wheaton IL 60187

COPELAND, EUGENE LEROY, lawyer, writer; b. Fairfield, Iowa, Mar. 5, 1939; BA, Parsons Coll., 1961; JD with distinction, U. Iowa, 1965. Admitted to Colo. bar, 1965, Iowa bar, 1965, U.S. Supreme Ct. bar, 1966. Individual practice law, Denver, 1965-66; sr. v.p., gen. counsel, sec. Security Life of Denver, 1966—; gen. counsel Nationale Nederlanden N.Am. Corp., 1986—. Lectr., speaker at legal and industry convs., seminars, meetings; participant contemporary issue program Today show NBC, 1980. Author: Preventive Law for Medical Directors and Underwriters, 1973; Underwriting in a New Age of Legal Accountability, 1978; Insurance Law, 1982; bd. editors Iowa Law Rev., 1965. Bd. dirs. Colo. Pub. Expenditures Coun., 1988—, Buffalo Mountain Met. Dist., Summit County, Colo., Friends Found. of Denver Pub. Libr., Denver Pub. Libr. Commn. Served with U.S. Army. Fulbright scholar (alt.). Mem. ABA, Colo. Bar Assn., Denver Bar Assn., Iowa Bar Assn., Assn. Life Ins. Council, Am. Council Life Ins. (state v.p. 1973-83, legis. com., reins. com., policyholder tax com., litigation com.), Colo. Life Conv. (pres. 1988-90, v.p. 1987-88, legis. chmn. 1973-86), Colo. Assn. Corp. Counsel, Denver Estate Planning Council, Colo. Assn. Life Underwriters (co-author learning guide 1978), Law Club Denver, Phi Kappa Phi. Unitarian. Office: Security Life Ctr 1290 Broadway Fl 6 Denver CO 80203-2122

COPELAND, JOHN DEWAYNE, law educator; b. Wichita Falls, Tex., Apr. 9, 1950; s. Howard R. and Lorene (Sharp) C.; m. Vannette Sue Thomas, July 2, 1970; children: Aaron, Seth, Sarah. BA, U. Tex., Arlington, 1971; JD, So. Meth. U., 1974; LLM, U. Ark., 1986, EdD, 1997. Bar: Tex. 1974, Ark. 1986, U.S. Dist. Ct. (no. dist.) Tex. 1974, U.S. Dist. Ct. (ea. and we. dists.) Ark. 1986, U.S. Ct. Appeals (5th cir.) 1975, U.S. Ct. Appeals (8th cir.) 1987, U.S. Supreme Ct. 1979. Ptnr. Short & Copeland, Wichita Falls, 1974-76, Helton, Copeland & Southard, Wichita Falls, 1976-78, Oldham, Copeland & Barnard, Wichita Falls, 1978-81; mem. Russell, Tate & Gowan, 1981-84; assoc. Roy & Lambert, Springdale, Ark., 1985-88; vis. asst. prof. U. Ark. Sch. Law, Fayetteville, 1988-89; dir. and rsch. prof. law Nat. Ctr. for Agrl. Law Rsch. and Info., 1989-98; exec. v.p. for ethics and environ. compliance Tyson Foods, Springdale, 1998—. Cons. environ. com. Nat. Pork Producers Coun., Des Moines, 1991-98, Am. Meat Inst., Washington, 1994-98, mem. environ. compliance com. Dairy Quality Assurance Bd. Author: Understanding the Farmers Comprehensive Personal Liability Policy, 1992, Recreational Access to Private Land: Liability Issues and Solutions, 1995; co-author: Food Safety: State and Federal Regulations, 1999; author book chpts.; contbr. articles to profl. jours. Legal advisor City Charter Revision Commn., Wichita Falls, 1976-77; bd. dirs. Wichita County Bar Assn., Wichita Falls, 1976-78, treas., 1978-79, dir. lawyer referral, 1982-84. Recipient grad. fellowship U. Ark. Sch. Law, 1984. Mem. ABA (vice chair agrl. law com. 1990-91), Am. Agrl. Law Assn. (bd. dirs. 1997—, Excellence in Profl. Scholarship award 1996, 99, Dissertation of Yr. award, U. Ark., 1998). Baptist. Home: 5059 Tall Pine Cir Springdale AR 72762-2577 Office: Univ Ark Leflar Law Ctr Fayetteville AR 72701 E-mail: copelandjo@tyson.com

COPELAND, ROY WILSON, lawyer; b. Ft. Knox, Ky., Jan. 2, 1957; s. George Wilson and Mary Lou Copeland; m. Cheryl LaFayne Smith, June 17, 1989; children: Roy II, Rachelle, Kelleigh, Kameron. AB, U. So. Calif., L.A., 1979; JD, U. Ga., 1983. Bar: Ga. 1984, U.S. Dist. Ct. (mid. dist.) Ga. 1984, U.S. Ct. Appeals (11th cir.) 1984. With Drew, Eckl & Farnham, Atlanta, 1983-84, Copeland & Haugabrook, Valdosta, Ga., 1985—. Adj. prof. bus. law Ga. State U.; prof. pub. law Valdosta State U., 1984-92. Contbr. articles to UCLA Black Law Rev., Howard Law Jour. Counsel NAACP, Valdosta, 1988-94; chmn. of bd. Georgians United, Atlanta, 1994-96; bd. dirs. Valdosta State Coll. Found., 1992-94; pres., bd. dirs. 100 Black Men of Valdosta, 1994-96; bd. dirs. 100 Black Men of Am.; v.p. Ga. Legal Svcs., Atlanta, 1996-98. Recipient Comty. Svc. award NAACP, 1993, Outstanding Svc. award 100 Black Men of Valdosta, 1997. Mem. Nat. Bar Assn., Ga. Assn. of African Am. Attys., State Bar Ga., Valdosta Bar Assn., Phi Beta Kappa. General civil litigation, Personal injury. Office: Copeland & Haugabrook 102 E Adair St Valdosta GA 31601-4506

COPENHAVER, JOHN THOMAS, JR. federal judge; b. Charleston, W.Va., Sept. 29, 1925; s. John Thomas and Ruth Cherrington (Roberts) C.; m. Camille Ruth Smith, Oct. 7, 1950; children: John Thomas III, James Smith, Brent Paul. AB, W.Va. U., 1947, LLB, 1950. Bar: W.Va., 1950. Law clerk to presiding judge U.S. Dist. Ct. (so. dist.) W.Va., 1950-51; mem. firm Copenhaver & Copenhaver, Charleston, 1951-58; U.S. bankruptcy judge So. Dist. W.Va., 1958-76; U.S. dist. judge, 1976—. Adj. prof. law W.Va. U. Coll. Law, 1970-76; mem. faculty Fed. Jud. Center, 1972-76; Pres. Legal Aid. Soc. Charleston, 1954; Chmn. Mcpl. Planning Commn. City of Charleston, 1964; chmn., pres. W.Va. Housing Devel. Fund, 1969-72; chmn. vis. com. W.Va. U. Coll. Law, 1980-83; mem. adv. com. on bankruptcy rules Jud. Conf. U.S., 1978-84. Contbr.: articles in fields of bankruptcy and comml. law to Bus. Lawyer, Am. Bankruptcy Law Jour., Personal Fin. Law Quar., W. Va. Law Rev., others. Served with U.S. Army, 1944-46. Recipient Gavel award W.Va. U. Coll. Law, 1971, Outstanding Judge award W. Va. Trial Lawyers Assn., 1983 Fellow Am. Bar Found.; mem. ABA, W.Va. Bar Assn., Kanawha County Bar Assn., Nat. Bankruptcy Conf., Nat. Conf. Bankruptcy Judges (past pres.), Phi Delta Phi, Beta Theta Pi. Republican. Presbyterian. Office: US Courthouse PO Box 2546 Charleston WV 25329-2546

COPLAN, DANIEL JONATHAN, lawyer, actor, writer, producer, director; s. Robert Saul and Constance Joan (Karl) C. BFA, NYU, 1977; JD, Southwestern U., Los Angeles, 1984. Bar: Calif., 1985. Exec. producer NCL Films, N.Y.C., 1975-77; ptnr. The Kizer/Coplan Co., 1977-78; agt. Daniel J. Coplan Entertainment Entrepreneur, 1979—; mgr., asst. film buyer Walter Reade Orgn., Inc., 1979-81; bus. affairs intern Paramount Pictures, Los Angeles, 1982-84; of counsel Raymond L. Asher PC, 1984-86; pvt. practice, 1986-97; mem. Sheldon & Mak, Inc., 1997—. Actor Madames Black Book, 1996, Man in the Iron Mask, 1997, Echos of Enlightenment, 2000; actor, writer, prodr. The Dragon Gate, 1994; actor in Hell Comes to Frogtown, 1987, Wish Man, 1991; exec. producer motion picture The Dream Factory, 1977; producer, writer motion picture Of Mirrors, The Mind and Time, 1973, The Incredibly Awful Dr. Sporgo, 1973 (Silver medal Atlanta Internat. Film Festival, 1974, Golden Image cert. L.I. Film Festival, 1975); agt. motion picture Just Before Dawn. Mem. Screen Actors Guild, State Bar Calif., ABA, Beverly Hills Bar Assn., So. Calif. Kendo Fedn. Avocations: Kendo, writing, music. General civil litigation, Entertainment, Intellectual property. Office: 330 Washington Blvd Ste 400 Marina Del Rey CA 90292-5141

COPLEY, EDWARD ALVIN, lawyer; b. Memphis, Jan. 17, 1936; s. Edward Alvin and Ethel Marie (Fooshee) C.; m. Connie James Patterson, Nov. 17, 1990; children: Julie, Ward, Drew, Kelly, Zeke. BA, So. Meth. U., 1957, JD, 1960. Bar: U.S. Dist. Ct. (no. dist.) Tex., U.S. Ct. Claims 1962, U.S. Supreme Ct. 1963, U.S. Tax Ct. 1966, U.S. Ct. Appeals (5th cir.) 1968. Atty. U.S. Dept. Justice, Washington, 1960-64, Ft. Worth, 1964-66; assoc. Akin, Gump, Strauss, Hauer & Feld, Dallas, 1966-67, ptnr., 1968—. Mem. ushering com. Highland Park Presbyn. Ch., Dallas, 1982. Fellow Am. Coll. Probate Counsel; mem. Internat. Acad. Estate Trust Law, Dallas Bar Assn. (tax sect.), Dallas Estate Coun. (pres. 1975-76), So. Meth. U. Law Sch. Alumni Assn. (pres. 1978-79), Salesmanship Club (legal counsel 1984), Order of Woolsac, Barristers, Dallas Petroleum Club, Dallas Country Club, Phi Alpha Delta. Avocations: racquetball, photography, hunting, fishing, reading. Corporate taxation, Estate taxation, Personal income taxation. Home: 3711 Shenandoah St Dallas TX 75205-2120 Office: Akin Gump Strauss Hauer & Feld Ste 4100 1700 Pacific Ave Dallas TX 75201-4675 E-mail: ecopley@akingump.com

COPLIN, MARK DAVID, lawyer; b. Balt., Dec. 1, 1928; m. Judith Charlotte Levinson, Jan. 27, 1991. BA, U. Md., 1949, LLB, 1952. Bar: Md. 1952. Law clk. presiding justice U.S. Ct. Appeals (4th cir.), 1952-53; assoc. Weinberg and Green, LLC, Balt., 1953-60, mem., 1960-98; sr. ptnr. Saul Ewing, 1998-2001, of counsel, 2001—. Pres. Md. chpt., Am. Jewish Congress, 1971-74, Balt. Jewish Coun., 1976-78; pres. HIAS of Balt., Inc., 1972-74; mem. adv. com. Md. Blue Sky, 1968-92; bd. dirs. Jewish Family Svc., 1992-98; chmn. bd. trustees Balt. Hebrew U., 1987-89; mem. bd. visitors Balt. City Coll., 1990-97, sec., 1992-97. Mem. ABA, Md. Bar Assn., Balt. City Bar Assn., Balt. Bar Found. (pres. 1991-93), Order of Coif, Omicron Delta Kappa, Jewish. General corporate, Franchising, Mergers and acquisitions. E-mail: mcoplin@saul.com, mdc12128@aol.com

COPPEL, LAWRENCE DAVID, lawyer; b. Washington, July 3, 1944; s. Albert and Anne (Gold) C.; m. Arlene Cohen, Aug. 10, 1968; children: Jennifer, Allison. BA, U. Md., 1966, JD, 1969. Bar: Md. 1969, U.S. Dist. Ct. Md. 1971, U.S. Ct. Appeals (4th cir.) 1976, U.S. Ct. Appeals (3d cir.) 1983. Law clk. Md. Ct. Appeals, Annapolis, 1969-70; assoc. Gordon, Feinblatt, Rothman, Hoffberger & Hollander, LLC, Balt., 1970-77, mem., 1977—. Fellow Am. Coll. Bankruptcy; mem. ABA, Md. State Bar Assn., Bankruptcy Bar Assn. Dist. Md. (pres. 1988-89), Balt. City Bar Assn. Jewish. Bankruptcy. Office: Gordon Feinblatt Rothman Hoffberger & Hollander LLC 233 E Redwood St Baltimore MD 21202-3332 E-mail: lcoppel@gfrlaw.com

COPPERSMITH, SAM, lawyer; b. Johnstown, Pa., May 22, 1955; m. Beth Schermer, Aug. 28, 1983; children: Sarah, Benjamin, Louis. AB in Econs. magna cum laude, Harvard U., 1976; JD, Yale Law Sch., 1982. Fgn. svc. officer U.S. Dept. State, Port of Spain, Trinidad, 1977-79; law clk. to Judge William C. Canby Jr. U.S. Ct. Appeals (9th cir.), Phoenix, 1982-83; atty. Sacks, Tierney & Kasen, P.A., 1983-86; asst. to Mayor Terry Goddard City of Phoenix, 1984; atty. Jones, Jury, Short & Mast P.C., Phoenix, 1986-88, Bonnett, Fairbourn & Friedman P.C., Phoenix, 1988-92; mem. 103d Congress from 1st Ariz. Dist., 1993-95; atty. Coppersmith Gordon Schermer Owens & Nelson PLC, 1995—. Former dir., pres. Planned Parenthood Ctrl. and No. Ariz.; former chair City of Phoenix Bd. of Adjustment; former dir. Ariz. Cmty. Svc. Legal Assistance Found., 1986-89; chair Ariz. Dem. Party, 1995-97; trustee Devereux Found., 1997—. Mem. ABA, State Bar of Ariz., State Bar of Calif., Maricopa County Bar Assn. Democrat. Contracts commercial, General corporate, Real property. Office: Coppersmith Gordon Schermer Owens & Nelson PLC 2633 E Indian School Rd Ste 300 Phoenix AZ 85016-6759 E-mail: sam@cgson.com

COPPIN, JONATHAN DAVID, lawyer; b. London, July 7, 1963; s. Michael Charles Coppin; m. Lucy Jane Williams, Apr. 30, 1969. Degree in Psychology and Philosophy, Leicester U., 1985. Solicitor of Supreme Ct., Eng. and Wales, 1989. Ptnr. Norton Rose, London, 1996—. Mem. Law Soc. Eng. and Wales (co. law com. 1999-2000). General corporate, Mergers and acquisitions, Securities. Office: Norton Rose Kempson House Camomile St London EC3A 7AN England Fax: 0207 283 6500. E-mail: coppinjds@nortonrose.com

COPPINGER, JOHN BAMPFIELD, lawyer; b. Edwardsville, Ill., Sept. 3, 1913; s. John Biggins and Clara (Bampfield) C.; m. Glenna Lou Edgington, Aug. 25, 1955 (div. 1979); children: John Brian, Elnora Anne. Student Shurtleff Coll., 1932-34; JD, St. Louis U., 1937. Bar: Mo. 1937, Ill. 1938, U.S. Dist. Ct. (so. dist.) Ill. 1939, Supreme Ct. Korea 1946, U.S. Ct. Mil. Appeals 1957, U.S. Supreme Ct. 1963. Atty. Travelers Ins. Co., St. Louis, 1937-39; practice, Alton, Ill., 1939— ; sole practice, 1949-55; ptnr. various firms, 1939-49, 55-64; ptnr. Coppinger, Carter, Schrempf & Blaine, P.C., Alton, 1964— ; atty. Village of Hartford, Ill., 1939-71; master in chancery Madison County Cir. Ct., Ill., 1956-60. Served with U.S. Army, 1943-46, lt. col. Res. ret. Mem. ABA, Ill. Bar Assn., Mo. Bar Assn., Met. St. Louis Bar Assn., Judge Advs. Assn., Madison County Bar Assn., Am. Judicature Assn., Alton C. of C. (pres. 1957-58). Republican. Roman Catholic. Probate, Real property. Home: PO Box 5310 Godfrey IL 62035-5310 Office: Coppinger Carter Schrempf & Blaine 307 Henry St Alton IL 62002-6326

COPSETTA, NORMAN GEORGE, real estate executive; b. Pennsauken, N.J., Mar. 11, 1932; s. Joseph J. and Mary P. (DeMello) C.; m. Patricia Fitzpatrick, Mar. 5, 1971; children: Gregory, Margaret, Andrew, Norman G. Jr.; stepchildren: Samuel Sassano, James Sassano. Cert. real estate, Rutgers U. Extension, Camden, N.J., 1952; AA, Internat. Accts. Soc. Schl. Acctg., Chgo., 1968. Lic. title insurance agent, N.J. Settlement clk. Market Street Title Abstract Co., Camden, 1949-53; settlement administrator West Jersey Title & Guaranty Co., 1953; title examiner, abstract adminstr. Realty Abstract Co., Cherry Hill, N.J., 1954-64; mcpl. treas., tax collector Borough of Somerdale, N.J., 1961-65; title examiner, legal adminstr. Davis, Reberkenny & Abramowitz, Cherry Hill, 1974-97; pres., title officer Cooper Abstract Co., 1974-99, chmn. bd., 1997—. N.J. fgn. commr. of deeds in and for Pa., 1959—2000; mem. faculty Title Acad. N.J. Custodian of funds Somerdale Bd. Edn., 1960-64. Mem. N.J. Title Ins. Agts. Assn., Haddonfield (N.J.) Hist. Soc., Camden County Hist. Soc. Avocation: local history. Office: Cooper Abstract Co 401 Cooper Landing Rd Ste C6 Cherry Hill NJ 08002-2598

COQUILLETTE, DANIEL ROBERT, lawyer, educator; b. Boston, May 23, 1944; s. Robert McTavish and Dagmar Alvida (Bistrup) C.; m. Judith Courtney Rogers, July 5, 1969; children: Anna, Sophia, Julia. AB, Williams Coll., 1966; MA Juris., U. Coll., Oxford U., Eng., 1969; JD, Harvard U., 1971. Bar: Mass. 1974, U.S. Dist. Ct. Mass. 1974, U.S. Ct. Appeals (1st cir.) 1974. Law clk. Mass. Supreme Ct., 1971-72; to chief justice Warren E. Burger U.S. Supreme Ct., 1972-73; assoc. Palmer & Dodge, Boston, 1973-75, ptnr., 1980-85; assoc. prof. law Boston U., 1975-78; dean, prof. Boston Coll. Law, 1985-93, prof., 1993-96, J. Donald Monan prof. law, 1996—. Vis. assoc. prof. law Cornell U., Ithaca, N.Y., 1977-78, 84; vis. prof. law Harvard U., 1978-79, 84-85, 94-2001, overseers com., Lester Kissel vis. prof., 2001—; reporter com. rules and procedures Jud. Conf. U.S.; mem. task force on rules of atty. conduct Supreme Jud. Ct. of Mass., 1996-97. Author: The Civilian Writers of Doctors Commons, London, 1988, Francis Bacon, 1993, Lawyers and Fundamental Moral Responsibility, 1995, Working Papers on Rules Governing Attorney Conduct, 1997, (with Basile, Beston, Donahue) Lex Mercatoria and Legal Pluralism, 1999, The Anglo-American Legal Heritage, 1999, (with McMorrow) Federal Law of Attorney Conduct, 2001; editor: Law in Colonial Massachusetts, 1985, Moore's Federal Practice, 3d edit., 1997; bd. dirs. New Eng. Quar., 1986—; contbr. articles to profl. jours. Trustee, sec.-treas. Ames Found; bd. overseers vis. com. Harvard Law Sch.; treas. Byron Meml. Fund; propr., trustee Boston Athenaeum. Recipient Kaufman prize in English Williams Coll., 1966, Sentinel of the Republic prize in polit. sci. Williams Coll., 1965; Hutchins scholar, 1966-67, Fulbright scholar, 1966-68 Mem. ABA (com. on profl. ethics 1990-93), Am. Law Inst., Mass. Bar Assn. (task force on model rules of profl. conduct), Boston Bar Assn., Am. Soc. Legal History (bd. dirs. 1985-89), Mass. Soc. Continuing Legal Edn. (bd. dirs. 1985-89), Selden Soc. (state corr.), Colonial Soc. Mass. (v.p., mem. coun.), Anglo-Am. Cathedral Soc. (bd. dirs.), Mass. Hist. Soc., Am. Antiquarian Soc., Phi Beta Kappa. Democrat. Quaker. Home: 12 Rutland St Cambridge MA 02138-2503 Office: Boston Coll Sch Law 885 Centre St Newton MA 02459-1148 E-mail: coquill@bc.edu

COQUILLETTE, WILLIAM HOLLIS, lawyer; b. Boston, Oct. 7, 1949; s. Robert McTavish and Dagmar (Bistrup) C.; m. Mary Katherine Templeton, June 19, 1971 (div. Oct. 1984); 1 child, Carolyn Patricia; m. Janet Marie Weiland, Dec. 8, 1984; children: Benjamin, Weiland, Madeline Marie, Elizabeth Charlotte. BA, Yale U., 1971, Oxford U., 1973; JD, Harvard U., 1975. Bar: Ohio 1976, Mass. 1976. Law clk. to presiding justice Mass. Supreme Ct., Boston, 1975-76; assoc. Jones, Day, Reavis & Pogue, Cleve., 1976-83, ptnr., 1984—. Trustee Cleve. Foodbank, Playhouse Sq. Found., Greater Cleve. Com. on Hunger. Mem. Kirtland Club, Yale Club (N.Y.C.), Union Club (Cleve.), Cleve. Skating Club, Rowfant Club, N.Y. Yacht Club. Banking, General corporate, Private international. Office: Jones Day Reavis & Pogue 901 Lakeside Ave E Cleveland OH 44114-1190

CORASH, MICHELE B. lawyer; b. May 6, 1945; BA, Mt. Holyoke Coll., 1967; JD cum laude, NYU, 1970. Legal advisor to chmn. FTC, 1970-72; dep. gen. counsel U.S. Dept. Energy, 1979; gen. counsel EPA, 1979-81; ptnr. Morrison & Foerster, San Francisco and L.A. Bd. editors Toxics Law Reporter; bd. advisors Jour. Environ. Law and Corporate Practice; mem. nat. editl. adv. bd. Prop 65 News. Bd. dirs. Calif. Counsel on Environ. and Econ. Balance, 1991—; mem. blue ribbon commn. Calif. Environ. Protection Agy. Unified Environ. Statute; mem. V.P. Bush Regulatory Task Force, 1981, mem. adv. council Environ. Curriculum Stanford Law Sch., bd. adv. Hastings WEst-Northwest Jour. Environmental Law & Practice. Mem. ABA (mem. standing com. on environ. 1988-91, chair com. environ. crimes 1990), Inter-Pacific Bar Assn. (chair environ. law com.). Environmental, Land use and zoning (including planning). Office: Morrison & Foerster 425 Market St San Francisco CA 94105-2482 Fax: 415-268-7522. E-mail: mcorash@mofo.com

CORASH, RICHARD, lawyer; b. N.Y.C., Mar. 31, 1938; s. Paul and Mildred (Spanier) C.; m. Carol A. McKevitt, Dec. 11, 1966; children: Richard Jr., Sharon, Peter, Amy. BA, Harpur Coll., SUNY, Bingamton, 1959; MA, Bklyn. Law Sch., 1966; JD, Rutgers U., 1963. Bar: N.Y. 1964, U.S. Dist. Ct. D.C. 1964, U.S. Supreme Ct. 1972. Pvt. practice, N.Y.C., 1964-77; pres. Corash & Hollender, P.C ., 1977—. Pres. Kobe Trading Co., N.Y.C.; chmn. North Eastern Fiscal Mgmt. Co., N.Y.C.; pres. North Eastern Abstract Assn.; counsel Caywood Homeowners Assn. Mem. N.Y. Bankruptcy Bar Assn. (chmn. grievance com.), Richmond County Bar Assn. Democrat. General corporate, Estate planning, Real property. Address: 81 Roxiticus Rd Far Hills NJ 07931-2225 E-mail: E-mailchlawnyc@aol.com

CORBETT, THOMAS WINGETT, JR. lawyer; b. Phila., June 17, 1949; s. Thomas Wingett and Mary Bernadine (Diskin) C.; m. Susan Jean Manbeck, Dec. 16, 1972; children: Thomas Wingett III, Katherine. BA, Lebanon Valley Coll., 1971; JD, St. Mary's U., 1975. Bar: Pa. 1976, U.S. Dist. Ct. (we. dist.) Pa. 1976, U.S. Ct. Mil. Appeals 1979, U.S. Supreme Ct. 1984. Asst. dist. atty. Allegheny County, Pitts., 1976-80; asst. U.S. atty. Office U.S. Atty. for Western Dist. Pa., 1980-83; assoc. Rose, Schmidt, Hasley & DiSalle, 1983-86, former ptnr., from 1986; U.S. atty. We. Dist. Pa., mem. U.S. atty. gen.'s adv. com., 1991—, chmn., 1993; Atty. Gen. State of Pa., Harrisburg, 1995-97; ptnr. Thorp, Reed & Armstrong, Pitts., 1993-95, 97-98; ast. gen. counsel for govt. affairs Waste Mgmt. Inc., 1998—. Pres. St. Mary's Parent-Tchr. Guild, Glenshaw, Pa., 1983-85; mem. Allegheny County Republican Com., 1985-89; mem. Shaler Twp. Bd. Commrs., 1988-89; chmn. Pa. Commn. on Crime and Delinquency, 1995—. Mem. ABA, Pa. Bar Assn., Allegheny County Bar Assn. (judiciary com.). Roman Catholic. Avocations: skiing, golf, reading. General civil litigation, Criminal. Office: Waste Mgmt Westpointe Corp Ctr One 1550 Coraopolis Heights Rd Moon Township PA 15108-2962 E-mail: tcorbett@wm.com

CORBIN, DONALD L. state supreme court justice; b. Hot Springs, Ark., Mar. 29, 1938; BA, U. Ark., 1964, JD, 1966. Bar: Ark. 1966, U.S. Dist. Ct. (we. dist.) Ark. 1966. Lawyer Lewisville and Stamps, 1967-80; judge Ark. Ct. Appeals, 1981-87, chief judge, 1987-90; assoc. justice Ark. Supreme Ct., Little Rock, 1991—. State rep. Ark. Gen. Assembly, 1971-80. Served with USMC, 1955-59. Mem. ABA, Ark. Bar Assn., SW Ark. Bar Assn., Sigma Alpha Epsilon. Democrat. Avocation: duck hunting. Office: Supreme Ct Justice Bldg 625 Marshall St Little Rock AR 72201-1054*

CORBIN, SOL NEIL, lawyer; b. N.Y.C., Apr. 16, 1927; s. Nathan I. and Sarah (Kaiser) C.; m. Tanya Jacobs, Aug. 7, 1963; 1 son, David J. BS, Columbia U., 1948; JD cum laude, Harvard U., 1951. Bar: N.Y. 1952. Practiced, N.Y.C., 1952—; law clk. Judge Charles D. Breitel, 1954-56; counsel Gov. of N.Y., 1962-65; ptnr. Corbin, Silverman & Sanseverino LLP, N.Y.C., 1970-96, sr. counsel, 1997—. Mem. N.Y. State Banking Bd., 1969-76; Chmn. N.Y. State Commn. Constl. Conv., 1966-67; mem. N.Y. State Commn. Local Govt. Powers, 1971-73; chmn. N.Y. State Crime Control Planning Bd., 1974-75; mem. Chief Judge's Com. to Recruit State Ct. Adminstr., 1973; trustee in bankruptcy Franklin N.Y. Corp., 1974-90; spl. counsel v.p. U.S., 1975 Trustee N.Y. Pub. Libr., 1977—; mem. Chief Judge's com. on Availability of Legal Svcs., 1988-90. With USNR, 1945-46. Mem. ABA, Assn. Br. City N.Y., New York County Bar Assn., Am. Law Inst., Lotos Club. Home: 1100 Park Ave New York NY 10128-1202 Office: 805 3rd Ave New York NY 10022-7513

CORBISIERO LOVE, ANGELA M. lawyer; b. N.Y.C., July 1964; d. Anthony and Mary Ann Corbisiero. BA in Polit. Sci., U. Pa., 1986, M in Govt. Adminstrn., 1992; JD, Rutgers U., Camden, 1989. Bar: N.J. 1989, Pa. 1989, D.C. 1991. Jud. law clk. to Hon. Martin L. Haines, Hon. Harold B. Wells, Mt. Holly, N.J., 1989-90; assoc. Parker, McCay & Criscuolo, Marlton, 1990-92, Archer & Greiner, Haddonfield, 1995-96; pvt. practice Sicklerville, 1996—; contract atty. Larrabe & Cunningham, Phila., 1997—. Mem. ABA, Am. Soc. Pub. Adminstrn., Nat. Italian-Am. Bar Assn., Order Sons Italy Am., N.J. State Bar Assn. Avocations: travel, foreign languages, cooking, politics. Contracts commercial, Real property. Home and Office: 62 Brearly Dr Sicklerville NJ 08081-4456

CORCORAN, ANDREW PATRICK, JR. lawyer; b. Fredrick, Md., Nov. 20, 1948; s. Andrew Patrick and Beatrice Josephine (Poletti) C.; m. Margaret Cecila Boyle, July 3, 1971; children: Maureen Meredith, Andrew Patrick III. BA, Villanova U., 1970; JD, Seton Hall U., 1973. Bar: Pa. 1973, U.S Dist. Ct. (ea. dist.) Pa. 1974, U.S. Ct. Appeals (7th cir.) 1976, U.S. Ct. Appeals (3d cir.) 1977, U.S. Supreme Ct. 1982. Atty. Pa. Cen. Transp. Co., Phila., 1973-75, sr. atty., 1975-79; asst. gen. atty. Consol. Rail Corp., 1979-82, gen. atty., 1982-85, sr. gen. atty., 1985-92, assoc. gen. counsel, 1992-99; gen. atty. Norfolk (Va.) So. Corp., 1999—. Mem. Conf. of Rwy. and Airline Labor Lawyers, Assn. of Am. R.R.'s (legal affairs com.). Republican. Roman Catholic. Administrative and regulatory, Federal civil litigation, Transportation. Home: 2433 Haversham Close Virginia Beach VA 23454-1157 Office: Norfolk So Corp Three Commercial Pl Norfolk VA 23510-9241 E-mail: andy.corcoran@nscorp.com

CORCORAN, CLEMENT TIMOTHY, III, judge; b. Kansas City, Mo., Dec. 18, 1945; s. Clement T. and Bette Lou (Hohl) C. BA, U. N.C., 1967; JD, U. Va., 1973. Bar: Fla. 1973, U.S. Dist. Ct. (mid. dist.) Fla. 1973, D.C. 1974, U.S. Dist. Ct. (no. and so. dists.) Fla. 1975, U.S. Supreme Ct. 1979, U.S. Ct. Appeals (11th cir.) 1981. Law clk. U.S. Dist. Ct., Tampa, Fla., 1973-75; assoc. Carlton, Fields, Ward, Emmanuel, Smith & Cutler, P.A., 1975-78, ptnr., 1978-89; judge Bankruptcy Ct. (mid. dist.) Fla., Orlando, 1989-93, Tampa, 1993—. Dir. Bay Area Legal Svcs., Inc., Tampa, 1983-89, v.p., 1987, pres., 1988; bd. dirs. Fla. Coun. Bar Pres., 1982-88, pres., 1986-87; arbitrator Ct. Annexed Arbitration Program, U.S. Dist. Ct. (mid. dist.) Fla., 1984-89; counselor U. Tampa, 1981-86, fellow, 1986-89. Co-author: Conflicts of Interest, 1984; contbr. articles to legal jours. Lt. USNR, 1967-70. Mem. ABA (litigation sect., coun. mem. 1999—, co-chair comm. com. 1990-92, chair book pub. bd. 1992-98, assoc. editor Litigation News 1982-87, mng. editor 1987, editor-in-chief 1988-90, Nat. Conf. of Lawyers and Reps. of Media 1992-95, mem. adv. com. on nominations 1994-95, chair media-law roundtable 1994, chair sect. officers conf. com. on non-dues revenue 1995-96, mem. working group on ABA bus. plan for pub. 1995-96, standing com. on pub. oversight 1996—), Fla. Bar (chmn. voluntary bar liaison com. 1985-86, chmn. grievance com. 13-D 1986-88, chmn. legal edn. com. 1981-82, Most Productive Young Lawyer award 1981), Am. Judicature Soc., Hillsborough County Bar Assn. (Red McEwen award 1980, pres. 1982-83), Am. Inns of Ct. (Master of the Bench 1990-93, 96—). Roman Catholic. Office: Sam M Gibbons US Courthouse 801 N Florida Ave Tampa FL 33602-3849

CORDY, ROBERT J. judge; b. Manchester, Conn., May 18, 1949; 4 children. AB cum laude, Dartmouth Coll., 1971; JD, Harvard U., 1974. Def. atty. Mass. Defenders Com., 1974—78; spl. asst. atty. gen. Mass. Dept. Revenue, 1978—79; assoc. gen. counsel in charge of enforcement Mass. State Ethics Commn., 1979—82; asst. U.S. atty., 1982—87; ptnr. Burns & Levinson, Boston, 1987—91; chief legal counsel to Gov. William F. Weld, 1991—93; mng. ptnr. McDermott, Will & Emery, 1993—2001; assoc. justice Mass. Supreme Judicial Ct., 2001—. Lectr. Harvard Law Sch., 1987—96. Office: 1300 New Courthouse Pemberton Sq Boston MA 02108*

CORKERY, GARVAN, lawyer; b. Dublin, Aug. 4, 1971; s. Michael and Eileen (Burke) C.; m. Elizabeth O'Connell, Dec. 28, 1998. B in Civil Laws, Nat. U. Ireland, Cork, 1992. Bar: solicitor Supreme Ct. Ireland 1995. Assoc. McCann Fitzgerald, Dublin, 1995-97, Ronan Daly Jermyn, Cork, 1997-99; ptnr., 1999—. Bd. dirs. Irotec Labs., Cork. Avocations: politics, literature, music, history, travel. Antitrust, General corporate, Intellectual property. Office: Ronan Daly Jermyn 12 South Mall Cork Ireland Fax: 353-21-4802790. E-mail: garvan.corkery@rdj.ie

CORLE, JAMES THOMAS, lawyer; b. Jay County, Ind., Dec. 28, 1927; s. Herbert R. and Mary M. (Reitenour) C.; m. Jean Polhemus, July 16, 1950; children— James Thomas, Sarah Corle Thomas, Kenneth D. B.S. in Engring. Law, Purdue U., 1955; J.D., Ind. U.-Bloomington, 1955. Bar: Ind. 1955, D.C. 1964. With E. I. duPont de Nemours & Co., Wilmington, Del., 1955— , patent counsel, Washington, 1967-70, sr. supervising patent counsel, legal dept., 1970-85, corp. counsel, legal dept., 1986-92, intellectual property cons., 1993—. Served to lt. col. U.S. Army, 1946-52. Mem. ABA, Am. Patent Law Assn., Phila. Patent Law Assn., Del. Bar Assn. Republican. Methodist. E-mail: jimcorle@aol.com. Patent.

CORLEW, JOHN GORDON, lawyer; b. Dyersburg, Tenn., July 13, 1943; s. Emmett Atkins and Margaret Elizabeth (Swann) C.; m. Elizabeth Lee Scott, July 8, 1967; children: John Scott, William Heath, Carey Elizabeth. BA, U. Miss., 1965; JD, Vanderbilt U., 1968. Bar: Miss. 1968. Clk. to judge U.S. Dist. Ct. (so. dist.) Miss., 1968-69; assoc., then ptnr. Megehee, Brown, Williams & Corlew, Pascagoula, Miss., 1969-74; sole practice, 1975-78; ptnr. Corlew, Krebs & Hammond, 1978-84, Watkins & Eager, Jackson, Miss., 1984. Mem. Miss. State Senate, 1974-80, chmn. appropriations com., 1979, chmn. constn. com., 1975-79, chmn. legis. audit com., 1978; chmn. Miss. State Bd. Pub. Welfare, 1980-84. Mem. ABA, Miss. Bar Assn., Hinds County Bar Assn., Miss. Bar Found., Order of Coif, Phi Delta Phi. Democrat. Methodist. General civil litigation, General corporate, Product liability. Home: 2124 Eastover Dr Jackson MS 39211-6719 Office: Emporium Bldg 400 E Capitol St Jackson MS 39201-2610

CORNABY, KAY STERLING, lawyer, former state senator; b. Spanish Fork, Utah, Jan. 14, 1936; s. Sterling A. and Hilda G. Cornaby; m. Linda Rasmussen, July 23, 1965; children: Alyse, Derek, Tara, Heather, Brandon. AB, Brigham Young U., 1960; postgrad. law, Heidelberg, Germany, 1961-63; JD, Harvard U., 1966. Bar: N.Y. 1967, Utah 1969, U.S. Patent and Trademark Office 1967. Assoc. Brumbaugh, Graves, Donahue & Raymond, N.Y.C., 1966-69; ptnr. Mallinckrodt & Cornaby, Salt Lake City, 1969-72; sole practice, 1972-85; mem. Utah State Senate, 1977-91, majority leader, 1983-84; shareholder Jones, Waldo, Holbrook & McDonough, Salt Lake City, 1985—. Mem. Nat. Commn. on Uniform State Laws, 1988-93; mem. adv. bd. U. Mich. Ctr. for Study of Youth Policy,1990-93; mem. Utah State Jud. Conduct Commn., 1983-91, chmn., 1984-85; bd. dirs. KUED-KUER Pub. TV and Radio, 1982-88; bd. dirs. Salt Lake Conv. and Visitors Bur., 1985—. Mem. N.Y. Bar Assn., Utah Bar Assn., Utah Harvard Alumni Assn. (pres. 1977-79), Harvard U. Law Sch. Alumni Assn. (pres. 1995—). Patent, Real property, Trademark and copyright. Office: Jones Waldo Holbrook & McDonough 1500 Wells Fargo Bank Plz 170 S Main St Salt Lake City UT 84101-1605

CORNELL, KENNETH LEE, lawyer; b. Palo Alto, Calif., Feb. 23, 1945; s. Clinton Burdette and Mildred Lucy (Sheafer) C.; m. Barbara J. Smith, June 26, 1966; children: Melinda Lee Van Hise, Geoffery Mark. BBA, BA in Social Sci., Pacific Union Coll., 1966; JD, U. Wash., 1971. Bar: Wash. 1971, U.S. Dist. Ct. (we. dist.) Wash. 1971, U.S. Supreme Ct. 1974. Ptnr. Keller & Rohrback, Seattle, 1971-75, Richard, Rossano & Cornell, Seattle, 1975-77, Moren, Lageschulte (now Cornell, Hansen, Bugni & McConnell), Seattle, 1978-87, Cornell, Hansen, Bugni & McConnell PS (firm name change), 1995-98; pvt. practice Seattle, 1998—. Cons. atty. Town of Clyde Hill, Wash. 1980-87. Editor Wash. U. Law Rev., 1970-71. Bd. dirs. Kirkland (Wash.) Seventh Day Adventist Sch., 1972-78, Auburn (Wash.) Acad., 1974-80, Western Wash. Corp. Seventh Day Adventists, Bothell, 1974-80. Mem. Wash. State Bar Assn., Wash. State Trial Lawyers Assn., Order of Coif. Democrat. Avocations: skiing, reading, gardening. State civil litigation, Personal injury, Real property. Office: 11320 Roosevelt Way NE Seattle WA 98125-6228 E-mail: kbcornell@yahoo.com

CORNELL, RICHARD FARNHAM, lawyer; b. Pitts., June 9, 1952; s. Paul Watson and Margaret Lucy (Boose) C.; m. Denise Vandevelde, May 24, 1975; children: Jonathan Watson, Julie Elizabeth, Benjamin Dunlap. BA in Polit Sci. and Econs., U. Calif., Irvine, 1974; JD, U. San Francisco, 1977. Bar: Calif. 1977, U.S. Dist. Ct. (no. dist.) Calif. 1977, Nev. 1979, U.S. Dist. Ct. Nev. 1979, U.S. Ct. Appeals (9th cir.) 1981, U.S. Supreme Ct. 1999. Law clk. to chief judge U.S. Dist. Ct. Nev., Las Vegas, 1978-80; dep. dist. atty. Washoe County Dist. Atty., Reno, 1980-81; assoc. Raggio, Wooster & Lindell, 1981-86; sole practice, 1986—. Pro-tem judge Reno Justice Ct., 1992—. Co-editor Nevada Civil Practice Manual, 1985-86. Bd. dirs. Drunk Drivers Inc. d/b/a Call-a-Ride, Reno, 1984-85, Assn. Excellence in Edn., Reno, 1986. Mem. Nev. Bar Assn. (criminal practice and procedures com. 1986, fee dispute com. 1998—). Club: Toastmasters (Reno). Appellate, Criminal, Family and matrimonial. Office: 150 Ridge St Reno NV 89501-1938 E-mail: Rcorn150@aol.com, Rcornlaw@a50.Reno.Nv.Us

CORNING, NICHOLAS F. lawyer; b. Seattle, Nov. 8, 1945; s. Frank C. and Jessie D. (Weeks) C.; m. Patricia A. Tomlinson, Dec. 14, 1968; children: Kristen Marie, Lauren Margaret. BCS cum laude, Seattle U., 1968; JD, U. Wash., 1972. Bar: Wash. 1972, U.S. Ct. Appeals (9th cir.) 1972, U.S. Dist. Ct. (we. dist.) Wash. 1973, U.S. Supreme Ct. 1976, U.S. Ct. Claims 1981. Assoc. Jennings P. Felix, Seattle, 1972-75; ptnr. Lagerquist, McConnell & Corning, 1975-77; pres., ptnr. Treece, Richdale, Malone, Corning & Abbott, Inc., P.S., 1977-99; atty. Corning Law Firm, 1999—. Pres. Windermere Corp., Seattle, 1988, also bd. dirs. Recipient Am. Jurisprudence award in Criminal Law U. Wash., 1971. Mem. Assn. Trial Lawyers Am., Nat. Inst. Trial Advocacy, Wash. State Bar Assn., Wash. State Trial Lawyers Assn. (pres. 1994-95, bd. dirs.), King County Bar Assn. (spkrs. bur. 1983-85, chmn. pub. info. com. 1985-87), Ballard C. of C. (bd. dirs., pres. 1989-92), Beta Gamma Sigma (Key award 1968). Federal civil litigation, State civil litigation, Personal injury. Home: 5640 NE 55th St Seattle WA 98105-2835 Office: The Corning Law Firm 5301 Ballard Ave NW Seattle WA 98107-4061 E-mail: corninglawfirm@seanet.com

CORNISH, JEANNETTE CARTER, lawyer; b. Steelton, Pa., Sept. 17, 1946; d. Ellis Pollard and Anna Elizabeth (Stannard) C.; m. Harry L. Cornish; children: Lee Jason, Geoffrey Charles. BA, Howard U., 1968, JD, 1971. Bar: N.J. 1976, U.S. Dist. Ct. N.J. 1976. Atty. Newark-Essex Law Reform, 1971-72; technician EEOC, Newark, 1972-73; atty., asst. sec. Inmont Corp., N.Y.C., 1974-82, sr. atty., asst. sec. Clifton, N.J., 1982-85; sr. atty. BASF Corp., Mt. Olive, 1986-99. Speaker on diversity in bus. Past mem., bd. dirs. YWCA, Paterson, N.J.; trustee Barnert Hosp., Paterson; bd. dirs. Lenni-Lenape coun. Girl Scouts Am. Mem. ABA (commn. on opportunities for minorities in the profession, minority in-house counsel group, diversity vice chair gen. practice sect. corp. counsel com.), Nat. Bar Assn., Assn. Black Women Lawyers, Am. Corp. Counsel Assn., Internat. Trademark Assn. (past mem. editorial bd. The Trademark Reporter, exec. commn. com., meetings com., program quality and evaluation subcom.). Contracts commercial, General corporate, Trademark and copyright. E-mail: jeannettecornish@law.com

CORNISH, LARRY BRIAN, lawyer, corporate executive; b. Kingston, N.Y., July 13, 1946; s. Harry Preston and Beverly Mae (Schmidt) C. B.A., George Washington U., 1968, J.D., 1973. Bar: Calif. 1974, N.Y. 1974. Mem. legis. counsel U.S. Ho. of Reps., Washington, 1973-74; dir. fed. affairs Am. Speech & Hearing Assn., Washington, 1974-76; asst. counsel Pres. Ford Com., Washington, 1975-76; exec. dir., gen. counsel Irwin Lehrhoff Ph.D. & Assocs., Beverly Hills, Calif., 1976-78; counsel, dir. legal affairs Beverly Enterprises, Inc., Pasadena, Calif., 1978-79, 79-82, v.p., gen. counsel, sec., 1982-84, sr. v.p., sec., chief legal officer, 1984—; sec., Beverly Investment Properties Inc., Pasadena, Calif., 1985-88; counsel Calif. Speech Pathologists and Audiologists in Pvt. Practice, San Jose, 1976-88. Served with U.S. Army, 1969-70; Vietnam. Decorated Bronze Star, Air medal. Mem. ABA, Nat. Health Lawyer's Assn. Republican. Mem. Dutch Reformed Ch.

CORNISH, RICHARD POOL, lawyer; b. Evanston, Ill., Sept. 9, 1942; s. William A. and Rita (Pool) C.; children: William Darby, Richard Gordon. BS, Okla. State U., 1964; LLB, U. Okla., 1966. Bar: Okla. 1966, U.S. Dist. Ct. (ea. dist.) Okla. 1969, U.S. Supreme Ct. 1979. Ptnr. Baumert & Cornish, McAlester, Okla., 1967-71, Cornish & Cornish, Inc., McAlester, 1971-77; magistrate U.S. Dist. Ct. for Ea. Dist. Okla., 1976—; prin. Richard P. Cornish, Inc., 1977—. Bd. dirs. McAlester Boys Club, 1970-80, pres., 1974. Capt. JAGC, USAR, 1966-78. Mem. Okla. Bar Assn. (legal aid to servicemen com., legal specialization com.), Pittsburg County Bar Assn., McAlester C. of C. (bd. dirs. 1973-75). Roman Catholic. General practice, Probate. Home: 611 E Creek Ave Mcalester OK 74501-6929 Office: PO Box 1106 Mcalester OK 74502-1106 E-mail: cornish@cwis.net

CORNYN, JOHN, state attorney general; b. Feb. 2, 1952; married; 2 children. BA, Trinity U., 1973; JD, St. Mary's U., 1977; postgrad., U. Va. Cert. personal injury trial law Tex. Bd. Legal Specialization. Assoc., ptnr. Groce, Locke & Hebdon, San Antonio, 1977-84; judge 37th Dist. Ct., Bexer County, 1985-90; presiding judge 4th Adminstrv. Jud. Region, 1989-92; justice Supreme Ct. Tex., Austin, 1991-98; atty. Thompson & Knight; atty. gen. State of Tex., Austin, 1999—. Tex. Supreme Ct. liaison Bd. LAw Examiners, 1991—, Gender Bias Task Force, 1993-95; lectr. CLE programs. Bd. vis. Trinity U., Pepperdine U. Sch. Law. Fellow Tex. Bar Found., San Antonio Bar Found.; mem. Am. Law Inst., William Sessions Inn of Ct. (master bencher 1988-90, pres. 1989-90), Robert W. Calvent Inn of Ct. (pres. 1994-95). Office: Office of Atty Gen PO Box 12548 Austin TX 78711-2548*

CORONADO, SANTIAGO SYBERT (JIM CORONADO), judge; b. Laredo, Tex., Nov. 12, 1951; s. Bill Gee and Lucía (Coronado) Sybert; m. Dawn Dittman, Apr. 27, 1996. BA cum laude, U. Tex., 1974, JD, 1978. Bar: Tex. 1978. Pvt. practice, Austin, Tex., 1979-89; mcpl. judge City of Austin, 1989-91, City of Kyle, Tex., 1989-91; magistrate judge Travis County Dist. Ct., 1991—. Bd. dirs. Am. Heart Assn., Austin, 1990; state pres. Mex. Am. Bar Assn., Tex., 1988-89; pres. Capital Area Mex. Am. Lawyers, Austin, 1986-87. Recipient Lifetime Achievement award Hispanic Issues Sect. State Bar of Tex., 1995, Presdl. citation for disting. svc., 1999. Mem. Hispanic Nat. Bar Assn. (regional pres. 1989-90, nat. v.p. 1991-92), Travis County Bar Assn. (dir. 1995—, pres-elect 2001, pres. 2001—). Democrat. Home: 5602 Palisade Ct Austin TX 78731-4508 Office: Travis County Ct House Austin TX 78701

CORPORON, MARY CAROLINE, lawyer; b. Oroville, Calif., May 9, 1956; d. Leonard and Leola (Seeds) C.; m. Gary W. Ott, May 8, 1983. B.A. in English, U. Utah, 1977, J.D., 1980. Bar: Utah 1980, U.S. Dist. Ct. Utah 1980, U.S. Ct. Appeals (10th cir.) 1983, U.S. Supreme Ct. 1984. Founder, ptnr. Corporon & Williams, Salt Lake City, 1980— . Tchr., BICEP, Salt Lake City, 1980— . Mem. Women Lawyers of Utah, Salt Lake C. of C., Mortar Bd. Office: Corporon & Williams 808 E South Temple Salt Lake City UT 84102-1305

CORRADA DEL RIO, BALTASAR, supreme court justice; b. Morovis, P.R., Apr. 10, 1935; s. Romulo and Ana Maria (del Rio) Corrada del R.; m. Beatrice Betances, Dec. 24, 1959; children: Ana Isabel, Francisco Javier, Juan Carlos, Jose Baltasar BA in Social Scis., U. P.R., 1956, JD, 1959. Bar: P.R., 1959. Ptnr. McConnell Valdes Sifre & Ruiz Suria, San Juan, 1959-75; atty., chmn. Civil Right Commn., P.R., 1970-72; mem., resident commr. from P.R. 95th-98th Congress; mayor City of San Juan, P.R., 1985-89; atty. Baltasar Corrada Law Office, 1989-92; sec. of state Govt. of P.R., 1993-95; assoc. justice P.R. Supreme Ct., 1995—. Pres. New Progressive Party, 1986-89. Pres. editorial bd. P.R. Human Rights Rev., 1971-72. Bd. dirs. P.R. Teleradial Inst. Ethics. Recipient Great Cross of Civil Merit of Spain King Juan Carlos I, 1987. Mem. ABA, Fed. Bar Assn., P.R. Bar Assn. Roman Catholic. Club: Exchange, San Juan Rotary. Office: P R Supreme Ct PO Box 9022392 San Juan PR 00902-2392

CORRIGAN, JAMES JOSEPH, II, lawyer; b. Providence, Feb. 17, 1943; s. Francis Vincent and Mary Catherine (Goggin) C.; m. Mary Katherine Fogle, Apr. 17, 1971 (div. Mar. 1984); children: Eileen, Leigh; m. Elaine Dennis, May 19, 1990 (div. June 1997). AB, Providence Coll., 1964; JD, Cath. U., 1968; LLM, George Washington U., 1974. Bar: Va. 1968, U.S. Supreme Ct. 1974. Mem. legis. office FDA, Washington, 1964-74; mem. consumer office White House, 1968; assoc. dir. Bur. Health Care Delivery Svc. and Assistance, 1968-86, dir. grants and procurement divsn., 1986-96, assoc. adminstr., 1996—. Lectr. George Mason U., Fairfax, Va., 1983-95, Keller Grad. Sch. Mgmt., 1996. Contbr. articles to profl. jours. Mem. ABA (subcom. govt. legislation and pub. interest food, drug and cosmetic law com. 1968-80). Roman Catholic. Home: 1450 E Ocean View Ave Norfolk VA 23503-2309 E-mail: jcorrigan@hrsa.gov

CORRIGAN, MAURA DENISE, judge; b. Cleve., June 14, 1948; d. Peter James and Mae Ardell (McCrone) C.; m. Joseph Dante Grano, July 11, 1976; children: Megan Elizabeth, Daniel Corrigan. BA with honors, Marygrove Coll., 1969; JD with honors, U. Detroit, 1973; LLD (hon.), No. Mich. U., 1999. Bar: Mich. 1974. Jud. clk. Mich. Ct. Appeals, Detroit, 1973-74; asst. prosecutor Wayne County, 1974-79, asst. U.S. atty., 1979-89, chief appellate divsn., 1979-86, chief asst. U.S. Atty., 1986-89; ptnr. Plunkett & Cooney PC, Detroit, 1989-92; judge Mich. Ct. Appeals, 1992-98, chief judge, 1997-98; justice Mich. Supreme Ct., Detroit, 1999-2001, chief justice, 2001—. Vice chmn. Mich. Com. to formulate Rules of Criminal Procedure, Mich. Supreme Ct., 1982-89; mem. Mich. Law Revision Commn., 1991-98; mem. com. on standard jury instrns., State Bar Mich., 1978-82; lectr. Mich. Jud. Inst., Sixth cir. Jud. Workshop, Inst. CLE, ABA-Cin. Bar Litigation Sects., Dept. Justice Advocacy Inst. Contbr. chpt. to book, articles to legal revs. Vice chmn. Project Transition, Detroit, 1976-92; mem. citizens Adv. Coun. Lafayette Clinic, Detroit, 1979-87; bd. dirs. Detroit Wayne County Criminal Advocacy Program, 1983-86; pres. Rep. Women's Bus. and Profl. Forum, 1991, bd. dirs. Recipient award of merit Detroit Commn. on Human Rels., 1974, Dir.'s award Dept. Justice, 1985, Outstanding Practitioner of Criminal Law award Fed. Bar Assn., 1989, award Mich. Women's Commn., 1998, Grano award, 2001. Mem. Mich. Bar Assn., Detroit Bar Assn., Fed. Bar Assn. (pres. Detroit chpt. 1990-91), Inc. Soc. Irish Am. Lawyers (pres. 1991-92, Achievment award 2001), Federalist Soc. (Mich. chpt.). Office: Mich Supreme Ct 500 Woodward Ave Fl 20 Detroit MI 48226-5498

CORSO, FRANK MITCHELL, lawyer; b. N.Y.C., July 28, 1928; s. Joseph and Jane (DeBenedetto) C.; m. Dorothy G. McVeety, Apr. 7, 1951; chldren: Frank, Elaine, Patricia, Dorothy. LLB, St. John's U., 1952. Bar: N.Y. 1944, D.C. 1981, U.S. Ct. Mil. Appeals 1954, U.S. Supreme Ct. 1960. Ptnr. Corso & FErtig, 1957-61, Corso & Petito, 1966-69, Corso & Landa, Jericho, N.Y., 1971-73, Corso & Engelberg, 1973-82; sr. ptnr. Frank Mitchell Corso, P.C., Westbury, N.Y., 1982—. Bd. dirs. UN Devel. Corp. by N.Y. Gov., N.Y. Mcpl. Bond Bank Agy.; lectr. St. John's U. Sch. of Law; U.S. congl. candidate, N.Y.; trustee WLIW pub. TV channel. Contbr. articles to legal jours.; TV commentator legal topics. With U.S. Army, 1951-53. Decorated Knight of Holy Sepulchre (Vatican City); named Man of Yr., Am.-Italians of L.I., 1966. Mem. ABA, ATLA, N.Y. State Bar Assn., Nassau Bar Assn., Internat. Bar Assn., World Assn. Lawyers (founding mem.). State civil litigation, General corporate, Personal injury. Home: 1 Southdown Ct Huntington NY 11743-2548 Office: 350 Jericho Tpke Jericho NY 11753-1317 E-mail: fmc28@aol.com

CORSON, KIMBALL JAY, lawyer; b. Mexico City, Sept. 17, 1941; came to U.S., 1942; s. Harland Jerry and Arleen Elizabeth (Jones) C.; m. Ann Dudley Wood, May 25, 1963 (div. Apr. 1978); 1 child, Claudia Ring; m. Joy Lorann Sligh, June 16, 1979; children: Bryce Manning, Jody Darlene. BA, Wayne State U., 1966; MA, U. Chgo., 1968, JD, 1971. Bar: Ariz. 1972, U.S. Dist. Ct. 1971, U.S. Supreme Ct. 1991. Assoc. Lewis & Roca, Phoenix, 1971-74, ptnr., 1974-90, Horne Kaplan & Bistrow, Phoenix, 1990-99; of counsel Shields and Andersen, 1999—. Co-author: Document Control: The Organization, Management and Production, 1988; co-author: Litigation Support Using Personal Computers, 1989. Co-founder Desert Hills Improvement Assn., Phoenix, 1988—. With U.S. Army, 1961-64. Fellow Woodrow Wilson Found., 1966-67. Mem. ABA (civil practice and procedures com. antitrust sect. 1988-2000), Ariz. Bar Assn. (spkr. 1991—), Maricopa County Bar Assn., Internat. Trademark Assn. (editl. bd. The Trademark Reporter 1993-94, 99-2000, mem. publs. com. 1995-96), INTA Speaker, Am. Sailing Assn., Phi Beta Kappa. Avocations: music, computers, sailing, photography, first century history. Appellate, Federal civil litigation, Intellectual property. Home: Summit Ranch 35808 N 15th Ave Phoenix AZ 85086-7228 Office: Shields and Andersen 7830 N 23rd Ave Phoenix AZ 85021-6808

CORTESE, ALFRED WILLIAM, JR. lawyer, consultant; b. Phila., Apr. 2, 1937; s. Alfred William and Marie Ann (Coccio) C.; m. Rosanna S. Zimmerman, Aug. 18, 1962 (div. Aug. 1981); children: Aline Elizabeth, Alfred William III, Christina Nicole. BA cum laude, Temple U., 1959; JD, U. Pa., 1962. Bar: Pa. 1963, U.S. Supreme Ct. 1972, D.C. 1977. Assoc., ptnr. Pepper, Hamilton & Scheetz, Phila., 1962-71; asst. exec. dir. FTC, Washington, 1972-73; assoc. Dechert, Price & Rhoads, Phila., 1974-76; ptnr. Clifford & Warnke, Washington, 1977-81; chmn., CEO Cortese & Loughran Inc., 1982-84; ptnr. Kirkland & Ellis, 1985-94, Pepper Hamilton, LLP, Washington, 1994-98; mng. mem. Cortese PLCC, 1999—. Cons. Gen. Motors Corp., Detroit, 1985—. Lt. U.S. Army, 1959-60. Mem. ABA, Am. Law Inst., Pa. Bar, D.C. Bar Assn., Def. Rsch. Inst., Lawyers for Civil Justice (mem. exec. com., bd. dirs.), Racquet Club (Phila.), Univ. Club, Capitol Hill Club. Avocations: vintage automobile racing and restoration, art & antique collecting, cooking. Administrative and regulatory, Federal civil litigation, Legislative. Home: 113 3rd St NE Washington DC 20002-7313 Fax: 202-637-9797. E-mail: awc@corteseplic.com

CORTESE, JOSEPH SAMUEL, II, lawyer; b. Des Moines, Aug. 17, 1955; s. Joseph Anthony and Kathryn Mary (Marasco) C.; m. Diane Caniglia, Aug. 5, 1978; children: Joseph III, James David, Kathryn Elizabeth. BA, Ind. U., 1977; JD with honors, Drake U., 1980. Bar: Iowa 1981, U.S. Dist. Ct. (no. and so. dists.) Iowa 1981, U.S. Ct. Appeals (8th cir.) 1984. Assoc. Jones, Hoffman & Huber, Des Moines, 1981-85; ptnr. Huber, Book, Cortese, Happe & Brown, P.L.C., 1985—. Mem. ABA, ATLA, Iowa State Bar Assn., Polk County Bar Assn., Def. Rsch. Inst., Iowa Trial Lawyers Assn. Roman Catholic. Personal injury, Product liability, Workers' compensation. Home: 2915 Sherry Ln Urbandale IA 50322-6813 Office: Huber Book Cortese Happe & Brown PLC 317 6th Ave Ste 200 Des Moines IA 50309-4127 Fax: 515-243-5481. E-mail: jcortese@desmoineslaw.com

CORWIN, GREGG MARLOWE, lawyer; b. Mpls., May 4, 1947; s. Gerald Sidney Corwin and Shirley Mae (Nathenson) Nadler; m. Frances Gail Shapiro, mar. 21, 1971; children: Mitchell, David. BA summa cum laude, U. Minn., 1969, JD cum laude, 1972. Bar: Minn. 1972, U.S. Dist. Ct. Minn. 1972, U.S. Ct. Appeals (8th cir.) 1976, U.S. Supreme Ct. 1977. Assoc. Fred Burstein Law Firm, Mpls., 1972-77; ptnr. Cortlen Cloutier, 1977-78; pvt. practice, 1978—. Capt. USAF. Mem. ABA, Minn. Bar Assn., Hennepin County Bar Assn., Phi Beta Kappa. Democrat. Jewish. Avocations: reading, music, sports. Civil Rights, Labor. Office: 1660 Hwy 100 Ste 508 E Minneapolis MN 55416-1534 E-mail: GCorwin@Mediaone.net, GCorwin@GCorwin.com

CORY, CHARLES JOHNSON, lawyer; b. Coulee Dam, Wash., Jan. 30, 1941; s. James Murdock and Margaret Mary (Johnson) C.; m. JoAnne Frances Freeman, 1965; children— Brian, Kevin. A.B. cum laude, Gonzaga U., 1963; J.D., Stanford U., 1966. Bar: Calif. 1970, U.S. Dist. Ct. (no. dist.) Calif. 1970. Atty., SBA, San Francisco, 1966; claims adjustor Allstate Ins. Co., San Jose, Calif., 1968-69, claims supr., 1969-70; assoc. Miller, Morton, Caillat & Nevis, San Jose, 1970-75, ptnr., 1975—; sec., dir. Mai Industries, Inc., San Jose, 1982-84; v.p., dir. Mai V, San Jose, 1982-83, Mai-Cory Devel. Co., San Jose, 1982-83; judge pro tem, arbitrator Santa Clara County Superior Ct., San Jose, 1975—; lectr. in field. Coach Little League, Babe Ruth, AYSO, Sunnyvale and Los Altos, Calif., 1976-82; planning commr. Sunnyvale Planning Commn., 1976-78; commr. Los Altos Cable TV Citizens' Adv. Com., 1984—. Served to capt. arty. U.S. Army, 1966-68. Mem. Assn. Trial Lawyers Am., Calif. Trial Lawyers Assn., ABA, Calif. Bar Assn., Santa Clara County Bar Assn., Phi Delta Phi. Democrat. Lutheran. Clubs: Mid-Peninsula Tennis Patrons (pres. 1981-82) (Los Altos); Sunnyvale Tennis (pres. 1978). Lodge: Masons. State civil litigation, Construction, Real property. Office: Miller Morton Caillat & Nevis 50 W San Fernando St Ste 1300 San Jose CA 95113-2434

COSS, ROCKY ALAN, lawyer; b. Dayton, Ohio, Apr. 6, 1951; s. Vernon F. and Necia Lea (Shaw) C.; m. Cheryl Sue Kelch, Sept. 9, 1972; children— : Tracey, Derek. B.A., Ohio State, 1973, J.D., 1976. Bar: Ohio, 1976, U.S. Supreme Ct., 1979, U.S. Dist. Ct. (so. dist.) Ohio 1982, U.S. Ct. Appeals (6th cir.) 1983. Sole practice, Hillsboro, Ohio, 1976-81; ptnr. Coss & Greer, Hillsboro, 1982— ; pros. atty. Highland County, Ohio, 1977— . Mem. Steering com. City of Hillsboro, 1980-85; county chmn. Highland County Fund Drive; pres. Highland County Soc. Crippled Children and Adults, 1985-86; mem. enrollment com. Highland County Boy Scouts Am., 1977-78. Fellow Ohio State Bar Found.; mem. Ohio State Bar Assn., Highland County Bar Assn. (pres. 1982), Ohio Pros. Atty's. Assn. (v.p.), Nat. Dist. Atty's. Assn., ABA, Ohio Council Sch. Bd. Attys., Nat. Council Sch. Bd. Attys., Hillsboro Jaycees (v.p. 1978-83). Democrat. Methodist. Lodges: Rotary (pres. 1983-84), Masons, Elks. Criminal, Probate, Other. Home: PO Box 258 Hillsboro OH 45133-0258 Office: 14612 E Main St Hillsboro OH 45133

COSSACK, JERILOU, labor arbitrator, mediator; b. Detroit, Apr. 11, 1944; d. Charles Minot and Betty Louise Hollis; divorced; children: Paul Kenneth, Rebecca Jean. BA, UCLA, 1965, MS, 1969. Rsch. asst. UCLA Inst. Indsl. Rels., 1966-68; asst. to pres. Engrs. & Scientists Guild, Burbank, Calif., 1968; field examiner NLRB, L.A., 1969-73, supr., 1973-76; mem. Calif. Pub. Employment Rels. Bd., Sacramento, 1976-79; arbitrator/mediator Lafayette, Calif., 1979—. Lectr. U. Louvain, Belgium, 1972; cons. Agrl. Labor Rels. Bd., Sacramento, 1975; chair Calif. Minimum Wage Bd., San Francisco, 1996; mem. Nat. Acad. Designating Liaison Com., 1998-2001, Nat. Acad. Pub. Employment Disputes Settlement, 2001—; spkr. in field, 1972—. Bd. mem. Futures Explored, Lafayette, 1997—; co-chair Com. to Re-elect Grodin; mem. various sch. dist. adv. coms. Mem. Nat. Acad. Arbitrators, Am. Arbitration Assn., Indsl. Rels. Rsch. Assn., Soc. Profls. In Dispute Resolution, Calif. Bar Assn. (labor and employment sect.), San Francisco Bar Assn. (labor and employment sect.). Democrat. Presbyterian. Avocations: reading, backpacking, music. Office: 3231 Quandt Rd Lafayette CA 94549-2638 E-mail: jcossack@bigfoot.com

COSTELLO, DANIEL BRIAN, lawyer, consultant; b. Arlington, Va., Apr. 23, 1950; s. James Russell and Hazel Virginia (Caudle) C.; m. Margaret Ruth Dow, June 13, 1970; children: James Brian, Rebecca Ruth, Kathleen Marie. BA, U. Va., 1972; JD, Coll. of William and Mary, 1975. Bar: Va. 1975, U.S. Dist. Ct. (ea. dist.) Va. 1979, U.S. Ct. Appeals (4th cir.) 1979, U.S. Bankruptcy Ct. (ea. dist.) Va. 1979, D.C. 1984. Reporter Globe Newspapers, Vienna, 1965-68; freelance journalist Williamsburg, 1972-73; news dir. Sta. WMBG, WBCI-FM, 1973-76; spl. asst. atty. gen. Commonwealth of Va., Suffolk, Va., 1976-78, asst. atty. gen. Richmond, 1978-80; ptnr. Dameron, Costello & Hubacher, Alexandria, 1980-89, Costello & Hubacher, Alexandria, 1989-99; pvt. practice Springfield, 1999—; corp. sec., gen. counsel Olivares U.S.A., Inc., Fairfax, Va., 1999-2000, pres., 2000—. Press rels. cons. Va. Bar Assn.; spl. commr. in chancery Alexandria Cir. Ct. Author: Land Use Planning and Eminent Domain, 1997, 2d edit. 1999, Foreclosure in Virginia, 1991; co-editor, co-author The Layman's Guide to Virginia Law, 1977; editor night news Sta. WINA, 1969-72; contbr. articles to profl. jours. Mem. Va. State Bar, D.C. Bar, Soc. Alumni Coll. of William and Mary, U. Va. Alumni Soc., Rolling Hills Club. Presbyterian. Avocations: hunting, fishing, coin collecting. General civil litigation, General practice, Real property. Office: Ste A-210 8136 Old Keene Mill Rd Springfield VA 22152-1843 E-mail: dbriancostello@att.net

COSTELLO, DONALD FREDRIC, lawyer; b. Tacoma, Wash., Nov. 8, 1948; s. Bernard Peter and Ada Harriet (Morrill) C.; 1 child, Don Eric. BA, Calif. State U.-San Francisco, 1970; JD, U. Calif.-Hastings Coll., 1974. Bar: Calif. 1974, U.S. Supreme Ct. 1980. Assoc. Frolik-Filley & Schey, San Francisco, 1974-78; mem. Salomon & Costello, 1978-80; mem. law offices Donald F. Costello, Palo Alto, Calif., 1980-84, Santa Cruz, Calif., 1984—; lectr. Stanford U., 1983, U. Santa Clara, 1980; faculty Hastings Coll. Trial Advocacy, 1988—; expert witness on medical malpractice law, Calif. Senate Jud. Com., 1987. Mem. Planning Commn., City of Belmont (Calif.), 1976. Mem. ABA, Assn. Trial Lawyers Am., Calif. Trial Lawyers Assn. (contbr. articles to Forum), Am. Soc. Law and Medicine, Million Dollar Advocates Forum. General civil litigation, State civil litigation, Personal injury. Office: 331 Soquel Ave Santa Cruz CA 95062-2323

COSTELLO, FRANCIS WILLIAM, lawyer; b. Cambridge, Mass., Apr. 16, 1946; s. Frank George and Anna M. (Sinnott) C. BA, Columbia U., 1968, JD, 1973. Bar: N.Y. 1974, Calif. 1977. Assoc. Whitman & Ransom, N.Y.C., 1973-74, L.A., 1976-82, ptnr., 1982-93, Whitman, Breed, Abbott & Morgan, L.A., 1993-2000, Holland & Knight, LLP, L.A., 2000—, mem. dirs. com., 2001—. Bd. dirs. Sunritz Corp., L.A., Japan Travel Bur. Internat., L.A. Served with U.S. Army, 1968-70, Vietnam. Mem. State Bar Calif., State Bar N.Y., L.A. County Bar Assn., Pumpkin Ridge Golf Club (Oreg.), Wilshire Country Club (L.A.), Calif. Club (L.A.). E-mial. General corporate, Private international. Home: 415 Knight Way La Canada Flintridge CA 91011-2725 E-mail: fcostell@hklaw.com

COSTELLO, JOHN WILLIAM, lawyer; b. Chgo., Apr. 16, 1947; s. William John and June Ester (O'Neill) C.; m. Maureen Grace Matthews, June 13, 1970; children— Colleen, William, Erin, Owen. BA, John Carroll U., 1969; JD, DePaul U., 1972. Bar: U.S. Dist. Ct. (no. dist.) Ill. 1982. Assoc. Arvey, Hodes, Costello & Burman, Chgo., 1972-76; ptnr., 1976-90, ptnr. Wildman, Harrold Allen & Dixon, 1990—. Co-author: (manual) The Bankrupcy Reform Act of 1978, 1981. Served to capt. U.S. Army, 1972-73. Mem. ABA (bus. bankruptcy com., jurisdiction and venue and secured creditors subcoms.), Ill. State Bar Assn. (former vice chmn., chmn. comml. banking and bankruptcy law sect. 1979-81), Am. Bankruptcy Inst., Turnaround Mgmt. Assn. (former bd. dirs. Midwest sect.). Democrat. Roman Catholic. Office: Wildman Harrold Aller & Dixon 225 W Wacker Dr Chicago IL 60606-1224

COSTELLO, JOSEPH MICHAEL, lawyer; b. N.Y.C., Feb. 28, 1925; s. Michael J. and Mary J. Costello; m. Marianne K. Costello, Oct. 26, 1957; children: Michael, Kelly, J. McGarry, Patrick, Irene, Brendan, Marianne. BBA, Iona Coll., 1948; LLD, Fordham U., 1951. Bar: N.Y. 1952, U.S. Dist. Ct. (ea. and so. dists.) N.Y. 1954, U.S. Supreme Ct. 1958. Assoc. William H. Morris, N.Y.C., 1952-55; ptnr. Hanrahan & Costello, 1955-60; sr. ptnr. Costello, Ward, Tirabasso & Shea, 1960-65, D'Amato, Costello & Shea, N.Y.C., 1965-78, Costello & Shea, N.Y.C., 1978-96, Costello, Shea and Caffney, N.Y.C., 1996—. With U.S. Army, 1943-45. Fellow Am. Coll. Trial Lawyers; mem. ABA, N.Y. County Lawyers Assn., N.Y. State Bar Assn. (chmn. trial lawyers sect. exec. com.). Admiralty, Personal injury, Product liability. Office: Costello Shea & Caffney 44 Wall St Fl 11 New York NY 10005-2401

COSTELLO, ROBERT JOSEPH, lawyer; b. N.Y.C., Jan. 4, 1948; s. Peter John and Barbara Theresa (Sheeran) C.; m. Alice Boyle, Aug. 31, 1975 (dec. 1990); children— Robert Ian, Maura Alison, Megan Ailish; m. Maureen Kearns, May 3, 1993. B.A., Fordham U., 1969, J.D., 1972. Bar: N.Y. 1973. Assoc., Dewey, Ballantine et al, N.Y.C., 1972-75; asst. U.S. atty. So. Dist. N.Y., N.Y.C., 1975-80, dep. chief criminal div., 1980-81; ptnr. Lumbard & Phelan, N.Y.C., 1981-82, Phelan & Costello, N.Y.C., 1982-94, Gibney, Anthony & Flaherty L.L.P., N.Y.C., 1994—. Mem. ABA, N.Y. State Bar Assn., Assn. Bar City of N.Y. Roman Catholic. Federal civil litigation, Criminal, Securities. Home: 233 Chapel Rd Manhasset NY 11030-3728 Office: Gibney Anthony & Flaherty LLP 665 5th Ave New York NY 10022-5305

COSTENBADER, CHARLES MICHAEL, lawyer; b. Jersey City, Dec. 9, 1935; s. Edward William and Marie Veronica (Danaher) C.; m. Barbara Ann Wilson, Aug. 1, 1959; children: Charles Michael Jr., William E., Mary E. BS in Acctg., Mt. St. Mary's Coll., 1957; JD, Seton Hall U., 1960; LLM in Taxation, NYU, 1968. Bar: N.J 1960; U.S. Tax Ct. 1961, U.S. Ct. Appeals (3d cir.) 1973, U.S. Supreme Ct. 1983. Trial atty. office regional counsel IRS, N.Y.C., 1961-69; tax assoc. Shanley & Fisher, Newark, 1969-76; tax ptnr. Stryker, Tams & Dill, 1976-98; spl. counsel McCarter & English, 1998—. Mem. N.J. State and Local Expenditure and Revenue Commn., 1985-88. Mem. ABA, N.J. Bar Assn. (chmn. taxation sect. 1984-85), N.J. State C. of C. (chmn. cost of govt. com. 1988—), Am. Coll. Tax Counsel. Republican. Roman Catholic. Avocations: gardening, reading, sports. Taxation, general, State and local taxation. Home: 8 Neptune Pl Colonia NJ 07067-2502 Office: McCarter & English Gateway Four Ctr 100 Mulberry St Newark NJ 07101-4096 E-mail: ccostenbader@mccarter.com

COSTIKYAN, EDWARD N. lawyer; b. Weehawken, N.J., Sept. 14, 1924; s. Mihran Nazar and Berthe (Muller) C.; m. Frances Holmgren, 1950 (div. 1975); chldren: Gregory, Emilie; m. Barbara Heine, Mar. 6, 1977. AB, Columbia U., 1947, LLB, 1949. Bar: N.Y. 1949, U.S. Dist. Ct. (so. dist.) N.Y. 1950, U.S. Ct. Appeals (2d cir.) 1950, U.S. Supreme Ct. 1964. Law sec. to judge Harold R. Medina U.S. Dist. Ct., N.Y.C., 1949-51; ptnr. Paul, Weiss, Rifkind, Wharton & Garrison, 1960-93, of counsel, 1994—. Spl. advisor to mayor on sch. and borough governance City of N.Y., 1994-96, chairperson mayor's investigative commn. on sch. safety, 1995-96; mem. Commn. on Integrity in Govt., N.Y.C., 1986, mem. joint com. on jud. adminstrn., 1985-92; adj. fellow Ctr. for Edn. Innovation, 1997—. Author: Behind Closed Doors: Politics in the Public Interest, 1966, How to Win Votes: The Politics of 1980, 1980; co-author: Re-Structuring the Government of New York City, 1972, New Strategies for Regional Cooperation, 1973; rsch. editor Columbia Law Rev.; mem. editl. bd. City Jour., 1992—; mem. bd. editors N.Y. Law Jour., 1976—; contbr. articles on legal and polit. subjects to profl. publs. Chmn. N.Y. State Task Force on N.Y.C. Juristiction and Structure, 1971-72; vice chmn. State Charter Revision for N.Y.C., 1972-77; county leader New York County Dem. Com., 1962-64; Dem. presdl. elector, 1964, 88; trustee, mem. exec. com., chmn. alumni adv. bd. Columbia U., 1981-93, trustee emeritus, 1993—; bd. dirs., mem. coun. Mcpl. Art Soc., 1993-98; chmn. bd. dirs. N.Y. Found. for Sr. Citizens, 1993—. 1st lt. inf. U.S. Army, 1943-46. Recipient William J. Brennan Jr. award for Outstanding Cont. to Pub. Discourse, 1997. Fellow Am. Coll. Trial Lawyers; mem. Assn. of Bar of City of N.Y. (mem. exec. com. 1986-90), Century Club. Unitarian. Home: 50 Sutton Pl S New York NY 10022-4167 Office: Paul Weiss Rifkind Wharton & Garrison Ste 12J 1285 Avenue Of The Americas Fl 21 New York NY 10019-6028

COTCHETT, JOSEPH WINTERS, lawyer, author; b. Chgo., Jan. 6, 1939; s. Joseph Winters and Jean (Renaud) C.; children— Leslie F., Charles P., Rachael E., Quinn Carlyle, Camilla E. BS in Engring., Calif. Poly. Coll., 1960; LLB, U. Calif. Hastings Coll. Law, 1964. Bar: Calif. 1965, D.C. 1980. Ptnr. Cotchett, Pitre & Simon, Burlingame, Calif., 1965—. Mem. Calif. Jud. Coun., 1975-77, Calif. Commn. on Jud. Performance, 1985-89, Commn. 2020 Jud. Coun., 1991-94; select com. on jud. retirement, 1992—. Author: (with R. Cartwright) California Products Liability Actions, 1970, (with F. Haight) California Courtroom Evidence, 1972, (with A. Elkind) Federal Courtroom Evidence, 1976, (with Frank Rothman) Persuasive Opening Statements and Closing Arguments, 1988, (with Stephen Pizzo) The Ethics Gap, 1991, (with Gerald Uelmen) California Courtroom Evidence Foundations, 1993; contbr. articles to profl. jours. Chmn. San Mateo County Heart Assn., 1967; pres. San Mateo Boys and Girls Club, 1971; bd. dirs. U. Calif. Hastings Law Sch., 1981-93. With Intelligence Corps, U.S. Army, 1960-61; col. JAGC, USAR, ret. Fellow Am. Bar Found., Am. Bd. Trial Advs., Am. Coll. Trial Lawyers, Internat. Acad. Trial Lawyers, Internat. Soc. of Barristers, Nat. Bd. Trial Advs. (diplomate civil trial adv.), State Bar Calif. (gov. 1972-75). Clubs: Commonwealth, Press (San Francisco) Federal civil litigation, State civil litigation. Office: 840 Malcolm Rd Burlingame CA 94010-1401 also: 12100 Wilshire Blvd Ste 1100 Los Angeles CA 90025-7124

COTTER, JAMES MICHAEL, lawyer; b. Providence, May 12, 1942; s. James Henry and Marguerite Louise (Clark) C.; m. Melinda Irene Tighe, Feb. 6, 1971; children: Elizabeth, Heather, Kathryn. AB, Fairfield U., 1964; LLB, U. Va., 1967. Bar: N.Y. 1967. Assoc. Simpson Thacher & Bartlett, N.Y.C., 1967-75, ptnr., 1975—. Trustee Fairfield U., 1995—; bd. dirs. M.G.A. Found., 1990—, chmn., 1990-92. Mem. ABA, N.Y. State Bar Assn., N.Y. Law Inst. (bd. dirs. 1984—, chmn. exec. com. 1993-98, pres. 1997—), Met. Golf Assn. (bd. dirs. 1974—, pres. 1990-92), Greenwich Conn. Country Club, Hudson Nat. Golf Club. General corporate, Mergers and acquisitions, Securities. Office: Simpson Thacher & Bartlett 425 Lexington Ave Fl 15 New York NY 10017-3954

COTTER, PATRICIA O'BRIEN, judge; b. South Bend, Ind., 1950; m. Michael W. Cotter, 1979; 2 children. BS in Polit. Sci. and History with honors, We. Mich. U, 1972; JD, Notre Dame, 1977. Pvt. practice, South Bend, 1977—83, Great Falls, Mont., 1984; ptnr. Cotter & Cotter, 1985—2000; justice Mont. Supreme Ct., 2001—. Office: PO Box 203001 Helena MT 59620*

COTTON, DEBRA ANNE, lawyer; b. Newport Beach, Calif., Jan. 16, 1968; d. Kenneth Wayne Stinnett and Beverly Anne Buchanan; m. David Gregory Cotton, Mar. 25, 1995; 1 child, Steven Donald. BA in Spanish, U. Calif., Irvine, 1990; JD, Western State U., 1996. Bar: Calif. 1997; cert. law clk.; lic. manicurist Calif. Bd. Cosmetology. Night mgr. Lucky Stores, Inc., Buena Park, Calif., 1986-91; sys. operation analyst McDonnell Douglas Aerospace, 1991-92, assoc. analyst program plans, 1992-94, analyst work definition, 1994, analyst fin. controls, 1994-96, cons. fin., 1996; law clk. Law Offices of Tammi L. Faulks, 1996-97, Law Offices of George W. Shaeffer, Jr., 1997; pvt. practice Law Offices of Debra A. Cotton, Foothill Ranch, Calif., 1997—. Active Pub. Law Ctr., 1997—, Stay in Sch. Program, 1998—, Orangewood Vol. Day, 1998. Leesfield/ATLA Law Student scholar, 1996. Mem. ATLA (family law sect. 1997-98, class rep. 1993-94, v.p. 1994-95, pres. 1995-96), Women's Law Assn., Consumer Attys. of Calif., Consumer Attys. Assn. L.A., Orange County Bar Assn. (family law sect. 1996—), Orange County Women's Lawyers (treas. 1998), Delta Theta Phi. Republican. Baptist. Family and matrimonial. Office: Law Offices of Debra A Cotton Ste 1E179 26741 Portola Pkwy Foothill Ranch CA 92610

COTTONGAME, W. BRICE, lawyer; b. Ft. Worth, June 4, 1958; s. William Robert and Nelda Ree Cottongame; m. Elizabeth Cramer, Jan. 9, 1992; children: Kate, Will. BA in Polit. Sci., U. Tex., 1980; JD, S. Tex. Coll. Law, 1984. Bar: Tex., 1984, U.S. Dist. Ct. (no. and so. dists.) Tex., U.S. Ct. Appeals (5th cir.), U.S. Supreme Ct.; bd. cert. personal injury trial law Tex. Bd. Legal Specialization. Atty. Wallace Craig & Assocs., Ft. Worth, 1980-95, Henderson Haksell & Cottongame, Ft. Worth, 1995-98, Law Office W. Brice Cottongame & Assocs., Ft. Worth, 1998—. Fellow State Bar Tex., Tarrant County Bar Found.; Mem. Tex. Trial Lawyers Assn. (assoc. dir. 1986-90, dir. 1990-95), Tarrant County Trial Lawyers Assn. (dir. 1989-93, pres. 1994), Tarrant County Bar Assn. Democrat. Methodist. General civil litigation, Insurance, Personal injury. Office: Law Office W Brice Cottongame PC 414 E Bluff St Ste 200 Fort Worth TX 76102-2254

COTTRELL, PAUL (WILLIAM COTTRELL), lawyer, educator; b. Penns Grove, N.J., Nov. 5, 1951; s. Arvil Earl and Gudbjorg (Gudmunsdottir) G.; m. Carolyn Anne Pokoyski, May 25, 1974; children: Jonathan Paul, Elizabeth Constance. BA magna cum laude, U. Del., 1975; JD, U. Chgo., 1978. Bar: Ill. 1978, U.S. Dist. Ct. (no. dist.) Ill. 1978, U.S. Ct. Appeals (7th cir.) 1980, U.S. Tax Ct. 1982, Pa. 1985, U.S. Dist. Ct. (ea. dist.) Pa. 1985, U.S. Ct. Appeals (3d cir.) 1985, Del. 1985, U.S. Dist. Ct. Del. 1986, Md. 1987. Assoc. Karon, Morrison & Savikas, Ltd., Chgo., 1978-81, Fohrman, Lurie, Sklar & Simon, Ltd., Chgo., 1981-84; assoc. dir. Constrn. Law Inst., Chgo., 1982-85; prin. Tighe, Cottrell & Logan, Wilmington, Phila., Balt., Woodstown, N.J., 1987—. Co-editor: Corporate Directors and Officers: Liability, Insurance and Risk Management, 1989; contbr. chpt. to Ill. Election Law, 1983, articles to profl. jours. Treas. Citizens Coalition, 1973-75; bd. dirs. Saxony Ct. Condominium Assn., Chgo., 1981-82. Named Outstanding Young Man of Am., Jaycees, 1983. Mem. Chgo. Bar Assn. (mem. exec. com. Young Lawyers sect. 1981-85, co-chmn. Fed. Trial Bar task force), ABA (vice chairperson com. on liaison Young Laywers Div., 1982-84, mem. exec. com., health care law com., 1982-84, del. ABA conv. 1983, editor-in-chief law practice notes Barrister 1985-88), Del. Alumni Assn. (Chgo. area coord. 1987-85), Phi Kappa Phi, Omicron Delta Kappa, Pi Sigma Alpha. Democrat. Unitarian. Construction, Environmental, Professional liability. Office: Tighe Cottrell & Logan P A First Fed Pla PO Box 1031 Wilmington DE 19899-1031

COUCH, MARK WOODWORTH, lawyer; b. Albany, N.Y., Sept. 5, 1956; s. Leslie Franklin and Joan Teresa (Dunham) C.; m. Mary Jane Bendon, Oct. 25, 1985; children: Braden Bendon, Dylan Bendon, Tucker Bendon. BA, Worcester State Coll., 1982; JD, Union U., 1985. Bar: N.Y. 1986, U.S. Dist. Ct. (no. dist.) N.Y. 1986, U.S. Dist. Ct. (we. dist.) N.Y. 1995. Prin. Couch & Howard, Albany, 1986-88; atty. Couch, White, Brenner, Howard & Feigenbaum, 1988-89; prin. Breakell & Couch, 1989—. Bd. dirs. Downtown Day Care Ctr. Inc., Albany, 1991-96. Mem. ABA, N.Y. State Bar Assn., Albany County Bar Assn., Schuyler Meadows Club. General civil litigation, Construction, Labor. Home: 27 Bergen Woods Dr Cohoes NY 12047-4951 Office: Breakell & Couch 11 N Pearl St Ste 1200 Albany NY 12207-2789

COUGHLAN, KENNETH L. lawyer; b. Chgo., July 8, 1940; s. Edward James and Mary Virginia (Lewis) C.; m. Therese Koziol, Oct. 11, 1981; 1 child, Kevin Edward. BA, U. Notre Dame, 1962; JD, Northwestern U., Chgo., 1966. Bar: Ill. 1967. Trust officer Am. Nat. Bank & Trust Co., Chgo., 1969-72; sec. bd., sr. v.p., gen. counsel, cashier Ctrl. Nat. Bank., 1972-82; sec., gen. counsel Ctrl. Nat. Chgo. Corp., 1976-82; sr. v.p., gen. counsel Exch. Nat. Bank, Chgo., 1982-83; gen. counsel Exch. Internat. Corp., 1982-83; chmn. bd., pres. Union Realty Mortgage Co., Inc., 1981-83; shareholder DeHaan & Richter P.C., 1983-2000; mem. Kelly, Olson, Michod, DeHaan & Richter, L.L.C. Capt. U.S. Army, 1966-68. Fellow Ill. Bar Found.; mem. ABA, Ill. State Bar Assn. (chmn. sect. on comml., banking and bankruptcy law 1981-82), Chgo. Bar Assn. (chmn. fin. instns. com. 1980-81, chmn. comml. fin. com. 1979-80), Lawyers Club (Chgo.). Bankruptcy, Contracts commercial, General corporate. Office: Kelly Olson Michod DeHaan & Richter LLC 181 W Madison St Ste 4800 Chicago IL 60602-4583 E-mail: kcoughlan@komdr.com

COULSON, ROBERT, retired association executive, arbitrator, author; b. New Rochelle, N.Y., July 24, 1924; s. Robert Earl and Abby (Stewart) C.; m. Cynthia Cunningham, Oct. 16, 1961; children: Cotton Richard, Dierdre, Crocker, Robert Cromwell, Christopher. BA, Yale U., 1949; LLB, Harvard U., 1953; DSc in Bus. Adminstrn. (hon.), Bryant U., 1985; LLD (hon.), Hofstra U., 1987. Bar: N.Y. 1954, Mass. 1954. Assoc. Whitman, Ransom & Coulson, N.Y.C., 1954-61; ptnr. Littlefield, Miller & Cleaves, 1961-63; exec. v.p. Am. Arbitration Assn., 1963-71, pres., 1971-94; ret., 1994. Cons. N.Y. State Div. Youth, 1961-63; pres. Youth Consultation Service of N.Y., 1970 Author: How to Stay Out of Court, 1968, Labor Arbitration: What You Need to Know, 1973, Business Arbitration: What You Need to Know, 1980, The Termination Handbook, 1981, Fighting Fair, 1983, Arbitration in Schools, 1985, Business Mediation, 1987, Alcohol and Drugs in Arbitration, 1988, Empowered at Forty, 1990, Police Under Pressure, 1993, ADR in America, 1994, Family Mediation, 1996; editor: Racing at Sea, 1958; contbr. articles to profl. jours. Bd. dirs. Fedn. Protestant Welfare Agys., pres., 1982-84, chmn. 1985-87; adv. com. Internat. Coun. for Comml. Arbitration. Mem. N.Y. Yacht Club, Cruising Club Am., Riverside Yacht Club. Avocations: sailing, travel, writing. Home: 9 Reginald St Riverside CT 06878-2522 E-mail: coulfamily@aol.com

COULSON, WILLIAM ROY, lawyer; b. Waukegan, Ill., Oct. 5, 1949; s. Robert E. and Rose (Stone) C.; m. Elizabeth A. Shafernich, Feb. 14, 1986. AB, Dartmouth Coll., 1969; JD, U. Ill., 1972. Bar: Ill. 1972, U.S. Dist. Ct. (no. dist.) Ill. 1974, U.S. Supreme Ct. 1976. Law clk. to judge U.S. Dist. Ct., East St. Louis, Ill., 1972-74, Chgo., 1975; asst. U.S. atty. U.S. Dept. Justice, 1975-88, supr. criminal divsn., 1980-88; mng. ptnr. Cherry & Flynn, 1988-99, Gold & Coulson, 1999—. Faculty Atty. Gens. Adv. Inst., Washington, 1980-88, Ill. Inst. for Continuing Legal Edn., Springfield, 1983-88, Fed. Law Enforcement Tng. Ctr., Glynco, Ga., 1983-86; co-chmn. U.S. Magistrate Merit Selection Panel, 1989-91. Author: Federal Juvenile Law, 1980; contbg. author Animation mag., 1993—. Served to 2d lt. Ill. N.G., 1965-66. Finalist U.S. Senate Jud. Selection Panel, 1996. Mem. ABA, Chgo. Bar Assn. (jud. evaluation com. 1987-89, vice chair 1990-91), Fed. Bar Assn. (pres. 1991-92), Dartmouth Club. Federal civil litigation, Criminal. Office: 30 N La Salle St Chicago IL 60602-2590

COULTAS, EDWARD OWEN, lawyer; b. Huntington Park, Calif., May 17, 1946; s. Stanley S. and Josephine E. (Buckley) C.; m. Wanda Jean Viebig, June 22, 1968; children— Amy, Todd, Mark. B.A., So. Meth. U., 1968, J.D., 1974; M.S., Ind. State U., 1971. Bar: Tex. 1974, Colo. 1975. Assoc., Gorsuch, Kirgis, Campbell, Walker & Grover, Denver, 1974-77, Strasburger & Price, Dallas, 1977-78; asst. dean So. Meth. U. Sch. Law, Dallas, 1978-80, assoc. dean, 1980-82; exec. dir. State Bar Tex., Austin, 1982-86; pres. Small, Craig & Werkenthin, P.C., Austin, 1986—. Office: Small Craig & Werkenthin PC 100 Congress Ave Ste 1100 Austin TX 78701-4042

COULTER, CHARLES ROY, lawyer; b. Webster City, Iowa, June 10, 1940; s. Harold L. Coulter and Eloise (Wheeler) Harrison; m. Elizabeth Bean, Dec. 16, 1961; 1 child, Anne Elizabeth. BA in Journalism, U. Iowa, 1962, JD, 1965. Bar: Iowa 1965. Assoc. Stanley, Bloom, Mealy & Lande, Muscatine, Iowa, 1965-68; v.p. Stanley, Lande & Hunter, 1969—, also bd. dirs. County fin. chmn. Leach for Congress, 1980-96; county coord. George Bush for Pres. , 1980, 88, Reagan-Bush Campaign, 1984. Fellow Coll. of Law Practice Mgmt., Am. Bar Found., Iowa State Bar Found., Am. Coll. Trust and Estate Counsel; mem. ABA (mem. coun. law practice mgmt. sect. 1984-88, sec. 1988-89, vice chair 1989-90, chair 1991-92, chair coord. commn. legal tech. 1994-97, mem. standing com. on tech. and info. sys. 1997-98), Iowa Bar Assn., Muscatine County Bar Assn., Thirty-Three Club (pres. 1981), Rotary, Order of Coif. Episcopalian. Avocation: tennis. General corporate, Probate, Real property. Office: Stanley Lande & Hunter 301 Iowa Ave Ste 400 Muscatine IA 52761-3881 E-mail: chuckcoulter@slhlaw.com

COUPE, JAMES WARNICK, lawyer; b. Utica, N.Y., Mar. 3, 1949; s. J. Leo and Helen Carbery (Brennan) C.; m. Andrea Jean Schaaf, Nov. 26, 1983; children: Helen Shriver, Benjamin Warnick, Charlotte Fitzgerald. AB, Hamilton Coll., 1971; JD, Vanderbilt U., 1974. Bar: N.Y. 1975, Calif. 1981, Tenn. 1995, U.S. Dist. Ct. (so. and ea. dists.) N.Y. 1975, U.S. Ct. Appeals (2d cir.) 1975. Law clk. to judge U.S. Dist. Ct. (so. dist.) N.Y., N.Y.C., 1974-75; assoc. Donovan, Leisure, Newton & Irvine, 1975-79, Phillips, Nizer, Benjamin, Krim & Ballon, N.Y.C., 1979-81; sr. atty. Atlantic Richfield Co., L.A., 1981-86; chief counsel Beverly Enterprises, Inc., Pasadena, Calif., 1986-88; gen. counsel Completion Bond Co., Inc., Century City, 1988-93; exec. Sullivan & Curtis Ins. Brokers, Pasadena, 1993-95; v.p. bus. & legal affairs Cinema Completions Internat. Inc., L.A., 1995-97; sr. v.p. bus. and legal affairs Cinema Completions Internat., 1997—. Mem. L.A. County Bar Assn., State Bar Calif. Republican. Roman Catholic. General corporate, Entertainment, Finance. Office: Cinema Completions Internat Inc 4040 Vineland Ave Ste 204 Studio City CA 91604-3350 E-mail: coupe.asst@cnacci.com

COURCHESNE, NYLES LEOPOLD, lawyer, educator; b. Boston, June 3, 1970; s. Richard Paul and Elaine Courchesne; m. Splendora Nicolina Pollack, Oct. 8, 1997; 1 child, Jacques Richard. BS in Comm., Boston U.; JD, Case Western Res. U. Bar: Mass. 1996. Assoc. Law Office Jeffery S. Bohnet, Palmer, Mass., 1996—. Instr. Elms Coll., Chicopee, Mass., 1996— Consumer commercial, Family and matrimonial, Real property. Office: Law Office Jeffery S Bohnet 16 King St Palmer MA 01069-1308

COURSEN, CHRISTOPHER DENNISON, lawyer; b. Mpls., Dec. 6, 1948; s. Richard Dennison and Helen Wilson (Stevens) C.; m. Pamela Elizabeth Lynch, June 3, 1978; children: Cameron Dennison, Matthew Ashbolt, Madeline Messurier. BA, Washington & Lee U., 1970; JD, George Washington U., 1975. Bar: D.C. 1975, U.S. Dist. Ct. D.C., 1976, U.S. Ct. Appeals (D.C. Cir.) 1976, U.S. Ct. Mil. Appeals 1976, U.S. Supreme Ct. 1978. Sole practice, Washington, 1975-78; assoc. Dempsey & Koplovitz, 1978-80; majority communications counsel U.S. Senate Com. Commerce, Sci., and Transp., 1980-83; ptnr. O'Connor & Hannan, 1983-87; pres. The Status Group, 1988-90, The Coursen Group, Washington, 1990—. Adj. prof. law The George Washington U., Washington, 1983. Team mem. Pres.-Elect Reagan's Transition Team, Washington, 1980; atty. adv. Reagan-Bush 1984, Washington; telecomms. advisor Bush/Quayle presdl. campaign, 1988; mem. Pres.' Adv. Bd. for Cuba Broadcasting, 1991, chmn., 1998—; mem. nat. fin. com. Bush-Quayle 1992; mem. adv. bd. Blue Ribbon Commn. on Reconstruction of Cuba; mem. bd. Children's Hosp. Found. Mem. D.C. Bar Assn., Chevy Chase Club, Chatham Beach and Tennis Club. Roman Catholic. Administrative and regulatory, Communications, Legislative. Home: 5006 Nahant St Bethesda MD 20816-2463 Office: The Coursen Group 1133 Connecticut Ave NW Ste 900 Washington DC 20036-4311

COURT, LEONARD, lawyer, educator; b. Ardmore, Okla., Jan. 11, 1947; s. Leonard and Margaret Janet (Harvey) C.; m. JoAnn Dilleshaw, Sept. 2, 1967; children: Chris, Todd, Brooke. BA, Okla. State U., 1969; JD, Harvard U., 1972. Bar: Okla. 1973, U.S. Dist. Ct. (we. dist.) Okla. 1973, U.S. Dist. Ct. (no. dist.) Okla., 1978, U.S. Dist. Ct. (ea. dist.) Okla. 1983, U.S. Ct. Appeals (10th cir.) 1980, U.S. Ct. Mil. Appeals 1973. Assoc. Crowe & Dunlevy, Oklahoma City, 1977-81, shareholder, dir., 1981—. Adj. prof. Okla. U. Law Sch., Norman, 1984-85, 88-89, 99—, Okla. City U. Law Sch., 1998—; planning com. Ann. Inst. Labor Law, S.W. Legal Found., Dallas, 1984—. Contbg. author: (supplement book) The Developing Labor Law, 1978, Corporate Counsel's Annual, 1974, Labor Law Developments, 1993, Employment Discrimination Law, Supplement, 1998, 2000. Chmn. bd. elders Meml. Christian Ch., Oklahoma City, 1980, 98-2000; cubmaster Last Frontier coun. Boy Scouts Am., 1984, co-chmn. sustaining fund raising drive Oklahoma City Downtown YMCA, 1989, mem. bd. mgmt., 1994-96; participant Leadership Oklahoma City, 1987-88, bd. govs. Okla. State U. Found., 1990—; Oklahoma City Ronald McDonald House, 1990-93, mem. exec. com. 1991-93; co-chmn. ann. teleparty fundraising drive Am. Heart Assn., Okla. City, 1996-98, bd. dirs., 1996-98. Capt. USAF, 1973-77. Fellow Am. Coll. Labor and Employment Lawyer; mem. Am. Employment Law Coun., U.S. C. of C. (mem. labor rels. com. 1997—, chmn. fair labor stds. act subcom. 1999—, mem. steering com. 1999—), Oklahoma City C. of C. (mem. sports and recreation com. 1982-85, indsl. devel. com. 1986), Okla. State U. Alumni Assn. (nat. bd. dirs. 1989—, nat. exec. com., 1992-97, pres. 1995-96, chmn. alumni ctr. task force 1998—, Disting. Alumni award 1998), Okla. County Alumni Assn. (bd. sec. 1987-88, treas. 1988-89, v.p. 1989-90, pres. 1990-91), Harvard Law Sch. Assn., ABA (labor and employment law sect. com. on devel. of law under Nat. Labor Rels. Act, com. on EEO law, lititgation sect./employment and labor rels. law com.), Okla. Bar Assn. (labor and employment law sect. coun. 1978-83, 85-87, chmn. 1986), Okla. County Bar Assn., Fed. Bar Assn., U.S. Tennis Assn. (life). Civil rights, Labor. Office: Crowe & Dunlevy Mid America Tower 20 N Broadway Ave Ste 1800 Oklahoma City OK 73102-8273

COURTEAU, GIRARD ROBERT, retired prosecutor; b. St. Paul, Aug. 21, 1942; s. Robert William and Laura Gertrude Courteau; m. Mary Linda Lucas, Apr. 3, 1964 (div. May 1997); m. Susan Frances DeBaca, Aug. 8, 1997; children: Steven, Girard, Devin, Heather. AA, Coll. Marin, 1965; BA, U. Calif., Berkeley, 1967; JD, U. Calif., 1970. Bar: Calif. 1971, U.S. Dist. Ct. (ctrl. dist.) Calif. 1971, U.S. Dist. Ct. (no. dist.) Calif. 1983. Dep. dist. atty. Monterey County, Calif., 1971, Marin County, San Rafael, 1972-2001; ret., 2001. Mem. editl. bd. Hasting's Law Jour., 1970; editor Marin Law Enforcement Newsletter, 1974-89. Named Prosecutor of the Yr., Marin County Dist. Attys. Office, San Rafael, Calif., 1987. Mem. Order of the Coif, Thurston Soc. Roman Catholic. Avocations: gardening, reading. Home: 1307 Park St Santa Rosa CA 95404-3542

COURTNEY WESTFALL, CONSTANCE, lawyer; b. Plainview, Tex., Nov. 29, 1960; d. M.H. and Carolyn Courtney; m. Monte Jay Westfall, Jan. 3, 1998; 1 child, William Henry Westfall. BS, U. Tex., 1982, JD, 1985. Bar: Tex., U.S. Dist. Ct. (so. dist.) Tex., U.S. Dist. Ct. (we. and ea. dists.) Ark., U.S. Dist. Ct. (we. dist.) Okla., U.S. Ct. Appeals (5th and 8th cirs.) Tex. Com. clk. Natural Resources Com., Tex. Ho. of Rep., 1979; legis. staff to hon. Buck Florence Tex. Ho. of Rep., 1980-82; law clk. to hon. Jerre Williams U.S. Ct. Appeals (5th cir.), 1985-86; assoc. Thompson & Knight, Dallas, 1986-92, Brown McCarroll, Dallas, 1992-94; ptnr. Hutcheson & Grundy, 1994-98, Strasburger & Price, Dallas, 1998—. Contbr. articles to profl. jours. Moderator So. Meth. U. Sch. Law Environ. Career Seminar, 1989-2000. Mem. ABA, State Bar Tex. (coll., chair outreach com. environ. sect. 1989-92, mem. law sch. com. 1988-97, chair law sch. com. 1997—, sec. environ. and natural resources sect. 2000—, State Bar Coll., 1995—). Administrative and regulatory, Environmental. Office: Strasburger & Price 901 Main St Ste 4300 Dallas TX 75202-3724

COUSINS, WILLIAM, JR. judge; b. Swiftown, Miss., Oct. 6, 1927; s. William and Drusilla (Harris) C.; m. Hiroko Ogawa, May 12, 1953; children: Cheryl Akiko, Noel William, Yul Vincent, Gail Yoshiko. BA, U. Ill., 1948; LLB, Harvard U., 1951. Bar: Ill. 1953, U.S. Dist. Ct. (no. dist.) Ill. 1961, U.S. Supreme Ct. 1975. Title examiner Chgo. Title & Trust Co., 1953-57; asst. state's atty. Cook County, Ill., 1957-61; sole practice Chgo., 1961-67; judge Circuit Ct. Cook County, 1976-92; justice Ill. Appeallate Ct., 1992—. Chair exec. com. 1st Dist. Appellate Ct., 1997—; lectr. DePaul Law Sch., Chgo.; bd. dirs. Nat. Ctr. State Cts., 1996—; faculty advisor Nat. Jud. Coll., 1987; mem. exec. com. Ill. Jud. Conf., 1983, former chmn. exec. com.; liaison assoc. judge coordinating com.; former chmn. Ill. Jud. Coun. Bd. dirs. Ind. Voters Ill., 1964-67, Ams. for Dem. Action, 1968, Operation PUSH, 1971-76, Nat. Ctr. for State Cts.; mem. Chgo. City Coun., 1967-76; del. Dem. Nat. Conv., 1972; asst. moderator United Ch. of Christ, N.Y.C., 1981. Served with U.S. Army, 1951-53. Decorated Army Commendation medal; named Judge of Yr., John Marshall Law Sch., Chgo., 1980; recipient Thurgood Marshall award Ill. Jud. Coun., 1992, Earl Burris Dickerson award Chgo. Bar Assn., 1998, C. Francis Stradford award, 2001. Mem. ABA, Nat. Bar Assn. (jud. coun., Raymond Pace Alexander award 1999, Hall of Fame 1994), Ill. Bar Assn., Cook County Bar Assn. (former bd. dirs., Edward N. Wright award 1968, William R. Ming award 1974, Hall of Fame 1997), Alpha Kappa Alpha (Monarch award for Statesmanship 1995), Kappa Alpha Psi, Sigma Pi Phi, Delta Sigma Rho. Home: 1745 E 83rd Pl Chicago IL 60617-1714 Office: Ill Appellate Ct 160 N La Salle St Rm 1905 Chicago IL 60601-3103

COUVILLION, DAVID IRVIN, federal judge; b. Simmesport, La., Oct. 27, 1934; s. J. Forest Couvillion and Leontine Rabalais. BS, La. State U., 1956, JD, 1959; LLM, Georgetown U., 1973. Bar: La. 1959. Pvt. practice, Marksville, La., 1959-67; adminstrv. asst. U.S. Congressman Speedy O. Long, Washington, 1967-72; assoc. McCollister, McCleary, Fazio and Holliday, Baton Rouge, 1974-85; spl. trial judge U.S. Tax Ct., Washington, 1985—. Mem. ABA, La. State Bar Assn. Office: US Tax Ct 400 2nd St NW Washington DC 20217-0002

COVINGTON, ANN K. former state supreme court justice; b. Fairmont, W.Va., Mar. 5, 1942; d. James R. and Elizabeth Ann (Hornor) Kettering; m. James E. Waddell, Aug. 17, 1963 (div. Aug. 1976); children: Mary Elizabeth Waddell, Paul Kettering Waddell; m. Joe E. Covington, May 14, 1977. BA, Duke U., 1963; JD, U. Mo., 1977. Bar: Mo. 1977, U.S. Dist. Ct. (we. dist.) Mo. 1977. Asst. atty. gen. State of Mo., Jefferson City, 1977-79; ptnr. Covington & Maier, Columbia, Mo., 1979-81, Butcher, Cline, Mallory & Covington, Columbia, 1981-87; justice Mo. Ct. Appeals (we. dist.), Kansas City, 1987-89, Mo. Supreme Ct., 1989—2001, chief justice, 1993-95. Bd. dirs. Mid Mo. Legal Services Corp., Columbia, 1983-87; chmn. Juvenile Justice Adv. Bd., Columbia, 1984-87. Bd. dirs. Ellis Fischel State Cancer Hosp., Columbia, 1982-83, Nat. Ctr. for State Cts., 1998—; chmn. Columbia Indsl. Revenue Bond Authority, 1984-87; trustee United Meth. Ch., Columbia, 1983-86, Am. Law Inst., 1998—. Recipient Citation of Merit, U. Mo. Law Sch., 1993, Faculty-Alumni award U. Mo., 1993; Coun. of State Govt. Toll fellow, 1988. Fellow Am. Bar Found.; mem. ABA (jud. adminstrv. divsn., mem. adv. com. on Evidence Rules, U.S. Cts.), Mo. Bar Assn., Boone County Bar Assn. (sec. 1981-82), Am. Law Inst., Acad. Mo. Squires, Order of Coif (hon.), Mortar Bd. (hon.), Phi Alpha Delta, Kappa Kappa Gamma. Home: 1201 Torrey Pines Dr Columbia MO 65203-4825 Office: Mo Supreme Ct 101 High St Jefferson City MO 65102-0150

COVINGTON, GEORGE MORSE, lawyer; b. Lake Forest, Ill., Oct. 4, 1942; s. William Slaughter and Elizabeth (Morse) C.; m. Shelagh Tait Hickey, Dec.28, 1966 (div. May 1995); children: Karen Morse, Jean Tait, Sarah Ingersoll Covington; m. Barbara Schilling Trentham, Dec. 19, 1998. AB, Yale U., 1964; JD, U. Chgo., 1967. Assoc. Gardner, Carton & Douglas, Chgo., 1970-75, ptnr., 1976-95; atty. pvt. practice, Lake Forest, Ill., 1995—. Lectr. in field. Contbr. articles to profl. jours. Active Grant Hosp. of Chgo., 1974-95, chmn. of bd. 1990-95; bd. dirs. Grant Healthcare Found., 1995—, chmn. 1999—; trustee Chgo. Acad. Sci., 1974-85, pres., 1980-82; trustee, chmn. Ill. chpt. Nature Conservancy, Chgo., 1974-88; bd. dirs. Latin Sch Chgo., 1979-80, Open Lands Project, Chgo., 1972-86, Chgo. Farmers, 1994-96; bd. dirs., sec. Lake Forest Open Lands Assn., 1984—; bd. dirs., sec., treas. Les Cheneaux Found., 1978—; bd. dirs. Student Conservation Assn., 1996—, Little Traverse Conservancy, 1998—, vice chmn., 1999—; mem. Bd. Fire and Police Commrs., Village of Lake Bluff, Ill., 1991—. With U.S. Army, 1967-69. Mem. ABA, Ill. Bar Assn., Lake County Bar Assn., Chgo. Bar Assn., Univ. Club (bd. dirs. 1985-88), Commonwealth Club, Legal Club, Shoreacres (Lake Bluff, Ill.), Les Cheneaux Club (Cedarville, Mich.), Lambda Alpha. Land use and zoning (including planning), Real property. Office: 500 N Western Ave Ste 204 Lake Forest IL 60045-1955*

COVINGTON, MARLOW STANLEY, retired lawyer; b. Langhorne, Pa., Apr. 25, 1937; s. Marlow O. and Madalyn L. (Johnson) C.; m. Laura Aline Wallace, Aug. 28, 1965; children: Lisa M., Scott, Eric (dec.). BS, Bloomsburg U., 1959; postgrad., Rutgers U., 1960; JD, Howard U., 1965. Bar: D.C. 1971, U.S. Dist. Ct. D.C. 1971, U.S. Supreme Ct. 1975, U.S. Dist. Ct. Md. 1981, Md. 1985. Tchr. Pub. Schs., Long Branch, N.J., 1959-62; referee N.J. Dept. Labor, Newark, 1965-66; claim examiner Allstate's Ins. Co., Verona, N.J., 1966-71, house counsel Washington, Greenbelt, Md., 1971-97; sr. trial atty. Allstate Ins. Co., Greenbelt, 1989-96; ret., 1996. Mem. adv. bd. Inverness Custom Plastics, Inc., Barrington, Ill., 1990—. Recipient cert. of recognition Balt.-Washington area Fellowship Christian Athletes, 1981. Mem. ABA (com. ins. negligence and compensation sect.), Md. Bar Assn., D.C. Bar Assn. (com. ins. and compensation sect.), Nat. Bar Assn., Bloomsburg U. Alumni Assn. (bd. dirs. 1977-80), Sigma Delta Tau, Gamma Theta Upsilon. Avocation: collecting antique pocket knives. General corporate, Insurance, Personal injury. Home: 16001 Amina Dr Burtonsville MD 20866-1039 Fax: 301-421-4329. E-mail: SCoving104@aol.com

COWAN, ALVIN RANDALL, lawyer; b. N.Y.C., Jan. 9, 1907; s. Meyer and Matilda (Abrams) C.; m. Shirley P. Cowan, June 27, 1932 (dec.); children— Michael N., Nancy E. A.B., Cornell U., 1927; J.D., Fordham U., 1930. Bar: N.Y. 1931, U.S. Dist. Ct. (ea. and no. dists.) N.Y., U.S. Ct. Appeals (2d cir.), U.S. Tax Ct., U.S. Ct. Appeals (9th cir.), U.S. Supreme Ct. Ptnr. Abrams and Cowan, N.Y.C., 1955— . Mem. N.Y. County Bar Assn. Democrat. Home: 2109 Broadway New York NY 10023-2106 Office: 66 W Lakeshore Dr Rockaway NJ 07866-1026

COWAN, FREDERIC JOSEPH, lawyer; b. N.Y.C., Oct. 11, 1945; s. Frederic Joseph Sr. and Mary Virginia (Wesley) C.; m. Linda Marshall Scholle, Apr. 28, 1974; children: Elizabeth, Caroline, Allison. AB, Dartmouth Coll., 1967; JD, Harvard U., 1978. Bar: Ky. 1978, U.S. Dist. Ct. (we. dist.) Ky. 1979, U.S. Ct. Appeals (6th cir.) 1984, U.S. Supreme Ct. 1989. Vol. Peace Corps, Ethiopia, 1967-69; assoc. Brown, Todd & Heyburn, Louisville, 1979-83; ptnr. Rice, Porter, Seiller & Price, 1983-87; atty. gen. Commonwealth of Ky., 1988-92; counsel Lynch, Cox, Gilman & Manan P.S.C., 1992—. Ky. State Rep., 32d legis. dist., 1982-87; chair Ky. Child Support Enforcement Commn., 1988-91, Ky. Sexual Abuse and Exploitation Prevention Bd., 1988-91; bd. dirs. Ky. Job Tng. Coordinating Council, Frankfort, Louisville Bar Found., 1986. Vice chmn. judiciary criminal com. Ky. Ho. of Reps., 1985-87; chmn. budget com. on justice Judiciary and Corrections Ky. Ho. of Reps., 1985-87, Leadership Ky., 1985; U.S. del. election mission to Namibia Nat. Dem. Inst. for Internat. Affairs, 1989; U.S. del. dem. instns. seminar Nat. Dem. Inst. for Internat. Affairs, Slovenia, 1992; electoral supr. Orgn. for Security and Cooperation in Europe, Bosnia and Herzogovina, 1996. Mem. ABA, Ky. Bar Assn., Louisville Bar Assn., Ky. Acad. Trial Attys. Methodist. Administrative and regulatory, General civil litigation, Communications. Home: 1747 Sulgrave Rd Louisville KY 40205-1643 Office: 400 W Market St Ste 2200 Louisville KY 40202-3354

COWAN, JOHN JOSEPH, retired lawyer; b. Chester, Pa., Nov. 14, 1932; s. John Joseph and Helen Marie (Frame) C.; m. Hilary Ann Gregory, Dec. 29, 1960; children: Daniel, Patrick, Meg, Jennifer. AB, LaSalle Coll., 1954; JD cum laude, U. Pa., 1959. Bar: D.C. 1960, Ohio 1964, W.Va. 1968, U.S. Supreme Ct. 1971. Tchg. fellow Stanford U., Palo Alto, Calif., 1959-60; trial atty. civil divsn. U.S. Dept. Justice, Washington, 1960-63; assoc. Taft, Stettinius & Hollister, Cin., 1963-67; gen. atty. Chesapeake & Potomac Tel. Co. of W.Va., Charleston, 1968-79; ptnr. Sullivan & Cowan, 1979-82; sole practice, 1982-98; ret. Sr. adv. editor U. Pa. Law Rev., 1958-59. Served to 1st lt. AUS, 1954-56. Mem. ABA. Federal civil litigation, State civil litigation, Criminal. Home and Office: 2326 Windham Rd Charleston WV 25303-3021

COWAN, MARTIN B. lawyer; b. N.Y.C., June 6, 1935; s. Joseph and Yetta (Wilkes) C.; m. Dorrit A. Blech, Dec. 20, 1959; children: Alison, Jillian, David. AB, Columbia U., 1957, JD, 1959. Bar: N.Y. 1960, Fla. 1976, U.S. Supreme Ct. 1963, U.S. Tax Ct. 1961. Assoc. Casey Lane & Mittendorf, N.Y.C., 1960-62, Reavis & McGrath, N.Y.C., 1966-68; tax atty. U.S. Dept. Justice, Washington, 1962-66; ptnr. Wien Lane & Malkin, N.Y.C., 1968-84, Milbank Tween Hadley & McCloy, N.Y.C., 1984-93. Adj. assoc. prof. NYU, 1977, Miami Law Sch., 1994; mem. adv. bd. real estate Bur. Nat. Affairs Tax Mgmt., 1972—; cert. review appraiser Nat. Assn. Rev. Appraisers; v.p. Nat. Jewish Commn. Law & Pub. Affairs, 1980—; vis. prof. Fla. State U. Coll. of Law, 1995, Quinnipiac Coll. Sch. of Law, 1995-96. Bd. advisors Jour. Real Estate Taxation. Mem. ABA (tax sect., council 1993-95), CM. Tax Counsel, Am. Law Inst., N.Y. Bar Assn. (tax sect., mem. exec. com. 1985-86). E-mail: mbcowan@aol.com

COWAN, WALLACE EDGAR, lawyer; b. Jersey City, Jan. 28, 1924; s. Benjamin and Dorothy (Zunz) C.; m. Ruth Daitzman, June 8, 1947; children: Laurie, Paul, Judith. BS magna cum laude, NYU, 1947; JD cum laude, Harvard U., 1950. Ptnr. Stroock, Stroock & Lavan, N.Y.C., 1950-93, of counsel, 1994—. Dir. Ametek, Inc., Paoli, Pa., 1982-93, sec., 1969-93, sec. H.S. Stuttman, Inc., Westport, Conn., to 1996; adv. bd. Hackensack River Greenway, Teaneck, N.J. Mem. Teaneck (N.J.) Adv. Bd. on Parks, Playgrounds and Recreation, 1966—, chmn., 1974—; pres. No. Valley Commuters Assn.; past pres., life trustee Congregation Beth Sholom, Teaneck; mem. Forum adv. bd. Sch.-Based Youth Svcs. Project, 1998—. 1st lt. USAF, 1942-45, ETO. Decorated Air medal with silver cluster; recipient Vol. in the Parks award Bergen County, N.J., 1993, Disting. Svc. award Bergen County, N.J., 1994, Disting. Achievement award Bergen County, N.J., 2001. Mem. Beta Gamma Sigma. Contracts commercial, General corporate, Securities. Home: 499 Emerson Ave Teaneck NJ 07666-1927 Office: Stroock Stroock & Lavan 180 Maiden Ln Fl 17 New York NY 10038-4937

COWART, T(HOMAS) DAVID, lawyer; b. San Benito, Tex., June 12, 1953; s. Thomas W. Jr. and Glenda Claire (Miller) C.; children: Thomas Kevin, Lauren Michelle, Megan Leigh; m. Greta E. Gerberding, Aug. 12, 1995. BBA, U. Miss., 1975, JD, 1978; LLM in Taxation, NYU, 1979. Bar: Miss. 1978, Tex. 1979; CPA Tex., Miss. Assoc. Dossett, Magruder & Montgomery, Jackson, Miss., 1978, Strasburger & Price, Dallas, 1979-87; ptnr., assoc., shareholder Johnson & Gibbs, 1988-90; shareholder Jenkens & Gilchrist, 1991—. Adj. prof. law So. Meth. U. Sch. Law, 1988; mem. key dist. adv. coun. IRA, Dallas, 1989-95, chmn., 1990-93; mem. Coll. State Bar Tex.; lectr. in field. Mem. editl. bd. Flexible Benefits, 1993—, 401k Advisor, 1994—, COBRA Adv., 1996—. Mem. adv. com. Goals for Dallas, 1984-85; vol. Children's Med. Ctr., 1992-96. Recipient Best Lawyer in Am. award. Mem.: ABA (sect. taxation, employee benefit com., vice-chmn. 1995—97, chmn. elect 1997—98, chmn. 1998—99, sect. 83 issues task force, chmn. health plan designs issues subcom. 1992—95, health care task force 1991—98, chmn.-designate joint com. on employee benefits 1997—99, chmn. joint com. employee benefits 1999—2000), Am. Coll. Employee Benefits Counsel (1st chair, charter mem.), State Bar Tex. (sect. taxation, com. compensation and employee benefits, fed. legislation, regulations and revenue rulings subcom. 1986—87, chmn. fiduciary stds. for trustees subcom. 1987—88), Dallas Bar Assn. (lectr. 1985—, coun. mem. employee benefits sect. 1989—92, treas. 1992, sec. 1993, v.p. 1994, pres. 1995), S.W. Benefits Assn. (bd. dirs. 1994—97), Phi Alpha Phi, Dallas Benefits Soc. (co-moderator 1991—92, bd. dirs. 1991—93), Omicron Delta Kappa, Beta Alpha Psi. Pension, profit-sharing, and employee benefits. Office: Jenkens & Gilchrist 1445 Ross Ave Ste 3200 Dallas TX 75202-2785 E-mail: dcowart@jenkens.com

COWELL, MARION AUBREY, JR. lawyer; b. Wilmington, N.C., Dec. 25, 1934; s. Marion Aubrey and Alice Saunders (Hargett) C.; m. Norma Hearne; children: Lindsay G., Mark P., Kathryn Huffman, Graham Shannonhouse, Elizabeth Shannonhouse, Mary Robbins Whisnant. BSBA, U. N.C., 1958, LLB, 1964. Bar: N.C. 1964. Pvt. practice law, Durham, N.C., 1964-72; assoc. Bryant, Lipton, Bryant and Battle, 1964-69, ptnr., 1971-72; pvt. practice law Durham, 1969-70; gen. counsel Cameron Brown Co., Raleigh, N.C., 1972-78; exec. v.p., gen. counsel, sec. First Union Corp., Charlotte, 1978-99, Kilpatrick-Stockton LLP, Charlotte, 1999—. Office: Kilpatrick Stockton LLP 1 First Union Ctr Charlotte NC 28288-6001

COWEN, EDWARD S. lawyer; b. N.Y.C., Mar. 3, 1936; s. Michael and Edith (Cohen) C.; m. Lesley J. Hoffman, Nov. 16, 1958; children: Adrienne, Justine. BS, Syracuse U., 1957; JD, NYU, 1961. Bar: N.Y. 1962, U.S. Dist. Ct. (so. dist.) N.Y. 1965, U.S. Ct. Appeals (2d cir.) 1965, U.S. Supreme Ct. 1967, U.S. Dist. Ct. (ea. dist.) N.Y. 1979. Law clk. to judge U.S. Dist. Ct. (so. dist.) N.Y., 1961-62; ptnr. Seligson & Morris, N.Y.C., 1963-69, Robinson, Silverman, Pearce, Aronsohn & Berman, N.Y.C., 1975-90, Kirkland & Ellis, N.Y.C., 1991-96; of counsel Pillsbury Winthrop, LLP, 1996—. Mem. faculty Practicing Law Inst. Author: Bankruptcy in Joint Venture Partnerships, Practicing Law Institute, 1985, Enforcing Liens Postpetition, Bankruptcy Strategist, 1998. With USAF, 1958. Named Honoree of Yr. Fedn. N.Y. Lawyers Divsn. Mem. ABA, N.Y. State Bar Assn., Assn. Bar City N.Y. (chmn. bankruptcy and corp. reorgn.), Harmonie Club. Bankruptcy, Contracts commercial, General corporate. Home: 860 Fifth Ave New York NY 10021-5856 Office: Pillsbury Winthrop LLP 34th Fl 1 Battery Park Plaza New York NY 10004 E-mail: ecowen@pillsburywinthrop.com

COWEN, ROBERT E. federal judge; b. Newark, Sept. 4, 1930; s. Saul and Lillie (Selzer) C.; m. Toby Cowen, Dec. 21, 1973; children: Shulie, Eve. BS, Drake U., 1952; LLB, Rutgers U., 1958. Assoc. Schreiber, Lancaster & Demos, Newark, 1959-61; asst. prosecutor Essex County, N.J., 1969-70; dep. atty. gen. organized crime Criminal Justice Dept., 1970-72, dir. Div. Ethics and Profl. Svcs., 1972-78; magistrate U.S. Dist. Ct. N.J., Newark, 1978-85, judge Trenton, 1985-87, U.S. Ct. Appeals (3d cir.), Trenton, 1987-98, sr. judge, 1998—. Pvt. practice, Newark, 1961-69. Office: US Ct Appeals 3d Cir US Courthouse Rm 207 402 E State St Trenton NJ 08608-1507*

COWEN, ROBERT NATHAN, lawyer; b. N.Y.C., July 6, 1948; s. Arthur S. and Elsie (Smerling) C.; m. Ann Barbara Goldberg, May 20, 1979; children: Elizabeth Rebecca, Alexandra Lee, Joanna Lindsay. AB, Cornell U., 1969, JD, 1972; LLM, NYU, 1979. Bar: N.Y. 1973. Law clk. Chief Judge State of N.Y., N.Y.C., 1972-74; assoc. Cleary, Gottlieb, Steen & Hamilton, N.Y.C., 1974-79, Proskauer, Rose, Goetz & Mendelsohn, N.Y.C., 1979; sec. Overseas Shipholding Group, Inc., N.Y.C., 1982—, gen. counsel, 1989-95, sr. v.p., 1993—, bd. dirs., 1993—; exec. v.p. Overseas Discount Corp., N.Y.C., 1979—. General corporate, Securities, Corporate taxation. Office: Overseas Discount Corp 511 5th Ave New York NY 10017-4903

COWEN, WILSON, federal judge; b. nr. Clifton, Tex., Dec. 20, 1905; s. John Rentz and Florence Juno (McFadden) C.; m. Florence Elizabeth Walker, Apr. 18, 1930; children: W. Walker, John E. LL.B., U. Tex., 1928. Bar: Tex. 1928. Pvt. practice, Dalhart, Tex., 1928-34; judge Dallam County, 1935-38; Tex. dir. Farm Security Adminstrn., 1938-40, regional dir., 1940-42; commr. U.S. Ct. Claims, Washington, 1942-43, 45-59, chief commr., 1959-64, chief judge, 1964-77, sr. judge, 1977-82; sr. judge fed. cir. U.S. Ct. Appeals, 1982—. Asst. adminstr. War Food Adminstrn., 1943-45; spl. asst. to sec. agr., 1945; mem. Jud. Conf. U.S., 1964-77. Mem. ABA, State Bar Tex., Fed. Bar Assn., Order of Coif, Cosmos Club (Washington), Delta Theta Phi. Presbyterian. Home: 2512 Q St NW Apt 205 Washington DC 20007-4310 Office: US Ct Appeals Federal Circuit 717 Madison Pl NW Washington DC 20439-0002

COWIN, JUDITH A. judge; m. William; 3 children. Grad., Wellesley Coll., Harvard U. Prosecutor, Norfolk County; judge Superior Ct., Newton, Mass.; assoc. justice Mass. Supreme Judicial Ct., Boston, 1999—. Office: Mass Supreme Judicial Ct 1300 New Courthouse Pemberton Sq Boston MA 02108*

COWLES, DOUGLAS MOODEY, lawyer; b. Painesville, Ohio, May 27, 1947; s. Charles Moodey and Marilyn (Greenwood) C.; children: Michael, Megan, Jessica, Victoria. BA, Miami U., Oxford, Ohio, 1971; JD, U. Calif., San Fransicso, 1975. Bar: Calif. 1975, Ohio 1976, U.S. Supreme Ct. 1980. Referee Franklin County Probate Ct., Columbus, Ohio, 1976-80; ptnr. Cowles & Boster, Gallipolis, 1980—; city solicitor City of Gallipolis, 1983—; spl. counsel Ohio Atty. Gen., Gallipolis, 1983—. Author, lectr. on wills. Adv. bd. Gallipolis Devel. Ctr., 1983—. With U.S. Army, 1968-70, Vietnam. Mem. ABA, Assn. Trial Lawyers Am., Calif. Bar Assn., Ohio State Bar Assn., Ohio Trial Lawyers Assn. Avocations: flying, tennis, running. Office: Cowles & Boster PO Box 969 435 2nd Ave Gallipolis OH 45631-0969

COWLES, FREDERICK OLIVER, lawyer; b. Steubenville, Ohio, Oct. 18, 1937; s. Oliver Howard and Cornelia Blanche (Regal) C.; m. Christina Monica Muller, Sept. 9, 1961; children: Randall, Eric, Gregory, Cornelius. AB magna cum laude, Yale U., 1959; JD, Harvard U., 1962. Bar: R.I. 1963, Mich. 1967, Ill. 1969, N.Y. 1998, Conn. 1998. Assoc. Hinckley, Allen, Salisbury & Parsons, Providence, 1962-67; internat. atty. Upjohn Co., Kalamazoo, 1967-69; chief internat. atty. Am. Hosp. Supply Crp., Evanston, Ill., 1969-71; internat. atty. Kendall Co., Boston, 1971-73; chief internat. counsel Colgate Palmolive Co., N.Y.C., 1973-86, assoc. gen. counsel, asst. sec., 1986-90, assoc. gen. counsel, asst. sec., v.p. legal ops., 1990-94, sr. assoc. gen. coun., asst. sec., v.p. legal ops., 1994-97, multinat. estate planning, 1997—. Dir. various cos. Deacon South Salem Presbyn. Ch.; mem. com. Lewisboro Boy Scouts; co-founder Internat. House R.I. Inc.; group leader Operation Crossroads Africa, Gambia. Mem. ABA, Am. Corp. Coun. Assn., Internat. Bar Assn., Westchester Fairfield Corp. Csl. Assn., Yale Alumni Assn. Westchester, Internat. Lawyers Assn., Phi Beta Kappa. Estate planning, Immigration, naturalization, and customs, Private international. Home: 111 Oscaleta Rd South Salem NY 10590-1003 Office: Multinational Estate Planning PLLC 358 Route 202 Somers NY 10589-3207 Fax: 914-276-7853. E-mail: focowles@bestweb.net

COWLES, ROBERT LAWRENCE, lawyer; b. Jacksonville, Fla., Feb. 5, 1942; m. Barbara Bearden; children: Robert L., Kelli R. McMullin. BS, U. N.C., 1964; JD, Emory U. Law Sch., 1969. Bar: Fla. 1969, Ga. 1969. Claims adjuster, supr. Travelers Ins. Co., Jacksonville, Atlanta, N.Y.C., 1964-68; assoc. Neely, Freeman & Hawkins, Atlanta, 1968-69, Swift, Currie, McGhee & Hiers, Atlanta, 1969-71; dir. Howell, Kirby, Montgomery, D'Aiuto, Dean & Hallowes PA, Jacksonville, 1971-76; pres. Cowles, Coker & Myers, 1976-83, Cowles, Coker, Myers, Schickel & Pierce PA, Atlanta, 1982-83, Cowles, Hayden, Facciolo, McMorrow & Barfield PA, Jacksonville, 1984-87; judge Fourth Judicial Cir. Ct., Atlanta, 1987-90; comdr. Legler, Werber, Dawes, Sadler & Howell PA, Jacksonville, 1990-91; pvt. practice Law Offices of Robert L. Cowles, 1991-93; ptnr. Cowles & Shaughnessy PA, Jacksonville, 1993-2000; pvt. practice The Cowles Law Firm, 2000—. Bd. dirs. Boys Home of Jacksonville, 19895. Mem. Am. Bd. Trial Advocacy, Fla. Bar Assn. (chmn. bd. cert. civil trial lawyers com. 1998-99), State Bar Ga. Avocations: golfing, gardening, travel. State civil litigation, Product liability, Professional liability. Office: The Cowles Law Firm 1930 San Marco Blvd Ste 203 Jacksonville FL 32207-1200 E-mail: rcowlesl@bellsouth.net

COWPERTHWAIT, LINDLEY MURRAY, retired lawyer; b. Abington, Pa., Mar. 13, 1933; s. Lindley Murray Cowperthwait and Ruth Bronde Nicholas; m. Suzanne Dewees, Nov. 26, 1955 (div. July 1976); children: Murray, Mary Ruth, Edward, Linda, Tom, Suzanne; m. Karin Schmid Cowperthwait, Apr. 1, 1989. BA, Calif. State U., 1957; LLB, U. Pa., 1960, JD, 1970. Assoc. Wisler, Pearlstine, Talone Craig & Garrity, Norristown, Pa., 1960-68, ptnr., 1968-80; pvt. practice, 1980-96; of counsel High, Swartz, Roberts & Seidel, LLP, 1997—. Prodr., author, dir. (video) Medicine for Lawyers, 1980-93; author: Damages-Delay and Punitive 1999, 2000, 2001, Scrivener Med-Leg Code of Ethics, 1960, 75, 94, 2001. Bd. dirs. ARC, Norristown, 1993-95, Big Bros./Big Sisters, Norristown, 1985-92. Recipient Citizenship award Big Bros./Big Sisters, 1992. Mem. Pa. Trial Lawyers Assn. (pres. 1974-75), Montgomery County Trial Lawyers (founder, sec. 1965-74), Assn. Trial Lawyers of Am., Pa. Bar Assn., Pa. Soc. Republican. Episcopalian. Avocation: sailing. Federal civil litigation, General civil litigation, State civil litigation. Office: High Swartz Roberts & Seidel LLP 40 E Airy St Norristown PA 19401-4803

COWSER, DANNY LEE, lawyer, mental health specialist; b. Peoria, Ill., July 7, 1948; s. Albert Paul Cowser and Shirley Mae (Donaldson) Chatten; m. Nancy Lynn Hatch, Nov. 11, 1976; children: Kimberly Catherine Hatch Cowser, Dustin Paul Hatch Cowser. BA, No. Ill. U., 1972, MS, 1975; JD, DePaul U., 1980. Bar: Ill. 1980, Wis. 1981, U.S. Dist. Ct. (no. dist.) Ill. 1981, U.S. Ct. Appeals (7th cir.) 1983, U.S. Dist. Ct. (ea. and we. dists.) Wis. 1984, U.S. Supreme Ct. 1984, Ariz. 1985, U.S. Ct. Appeals (9th cir.) 1987, U.S. Dist. Ct. Ariz. 1989, U.S. Tax Ct. 1990, U.S. Ct. Claims 1990, Colo. 2000. Adminstr. Ill. Dept. Mental Health, Elgin, 1972-76, psychotherapist, 1976-79; assoc. Slaby, Deda & Henderson, Phillips, Wis., 1982-83; ptnr. Slaby, Deda & Cowser, 1983-86; asst. atty. City of Flagstaff, Ariz., 1986-88; pub. defender Coconino County, Flagstaff, 1988-89; pvt. practice, 1989-97. Atty. City Park Falls, Wis., 1983-86; spl. dep. Mohave County capital def., 1989-90; instr. speech comms. No. Ariz. U., 1992-93; adminstrv. law judge Ariz. Dept. Econ. Security, 1997—. Bd. dirs. DeKalb County (Ill.) Drug Coun., 1973-75, Counseling and Personal Devel., Phillips, 1985-86, Northland YM-WYCA, 1990-91. Reginald Heber Smith fellow, 1980-81; C.J.S. legal scholar, 1979. Mem. ABA, NRA, Nat. Assn. Criminal Def. Lawyers, Ariz. Bar Assn., State Bar Ariz. (cert. specialist in criminal law 1993-98), State Bar Wis., Nat. Assn. of Criminal Def. Lawyers. Democrat. Avocations: skiing, photography, bicycling. Administrative and regulatory, Bankruptcy, Criminal. Office: PO Box 22329 Flagstaff AZ 86002-2329

COX, DALLAS WENDELL, JR. lawyer; b. Mar. 10, 1943; s. Dallas Wendell Cox and Fern (Maurer) Heidbreder; m. Lynn Barbre, Aug. 2, 1969 (div. Oct. 1982); children: Dallas Barbre, Ryan Ralph. BA, U. Ill., Champaign, 1964; JD, U. Mo., 1967; MLA, Washington U., 1991, MA, 1994. Bar: U.S. Supreme Ct. 1967, Mo. 1967, U.S. Dist. Ct. Mo. 1967. Ptnr. Cox, Moffitt & Cox, St. Louis, 1967-78; pvt. practice law, 1978—. Attendee global forum UN Conf. on Environ. and Devel., Rio de Janeiro, 1992. Editor Jour. Mo. Bar., Mo. Conservationist; contbr. articles to profl. jours. Asst. scoutmaster St. Louis area Boy Scouts Am., 1984-94; advocate Mo. Prairie Found., bd. dirs., 1993—; alderman City of Town and County, Mo., 1995-conservation commn. chmn., 1995-99. Lt. (j.g.) USNR, 1971. Mem. ATLA, Mo. Assn. Trial Lawyers (bd. govs. 1990-93), Lawyers Assn. St. Louis, Eagle Scouts Assn. (bd. dirs. 1988-91, vol. award of merit 1992), Greater Yellowstone Coalition, Windstar Found., Wilderness Soc., Nature Conservancy, Sigma Chi. Avocations: conservation, backpacking. Personal injury. Office: 111 Westport Plz Ste 610 Saint Louis MO 63146-3015 E-mail: dallaswcox@primary.net

COX, EMMETT RIPLEY, federal judge; b. Cottonwood, Ala., Feb. 13, 1935; s. Emmett M. Cox, Jr. and Myra E. (Ripley) Stewart; m. Ann MacKay Haas, May 16, 1964; children: John Haas, Catherine MacKay BA, U. Ala., 1957, JD, 1959. Bar: Ala. 1959, U.S. Ct. Appeal (5th, 8th and 11th cirs.), U.S. Supreme Ct. Assoc. Mead, Norman & Fitzpatrick, Birmingham, Ala., 1959-64; assoc. then ptnr. Gaillard, Wilkins, Smith & Cox, Mobile, 1964-69; ptnr. Nettles, Cox & Barker, 1969-81; judge U.S. Dist. Ct. (so. dist.) Ala., Mobile, 1981-88, U.S. Ct. Appeals (11th cir.), Mobile, 1988—. Mem. def. svcs. com. Jud. Conf. U.S., 1992-98, chair, 1995-98, mem. jud. br. com., 2001–. Mem. Ala. Bar Assn., Mobile Bar Assn., Fed. Bar Assn., Maritime Law Assn. of the U.S., Omicron Delta Kappa, Phi Delta Phi, Alpha Tau Omega (past pres.). Office: US Courthouse 11th Circuit 113 Saint Joseph St Ste 433 Mobile AL 36602-3624

COX, JOHN THOMAS, JR. lawyer; b. Shreveport, La., Feb. 9, 1943; s. John Thomas and Gladys Virginia (Canterbury) C.; m. Tracey L. Tanquary, Aug. 27, 1966; children: John Thomas, III, Stephen Lewis. BS, La. State U., 1965; JD, 1968. Bar: La. 1968, U.S. Dist. Ct. (we., mid. and ea. dist.) La., U.S. Dist. Ct. (ea. dist.) Tex., U.S. Ct. Appeals (5th and 8th cir.), U.S. Tax Ct., U.S. Supreme Ct. Assoc. Sanders, Miller, Downing & Keene, Baton Rouge, 1968-70, Blanchard, Walker, O'Quin & Roberts, Shreveport, La., 1970-71; ptnr., 1971—. Tchr. bus. law Centenary Coll. La. Served to lt. USAR, 1963-69. Lt. USAR, 1963-69. Recipient George Washington Honor medal Valley Forge Freedoms Found. Mem. ABA, La. Bar Assn., Caddo parish Bar Assn., Am. Assn. Def. Counsel, La. Assn. Def. Counsel, Shreveport Club. Presbyterian. Banking, General corporate, Labor. Address: 555 Dunmoreland Dr Shreveport LA 71106-6124 E-mail: jcox@bwor.com

COX, JOSEPH LAWRENCE, judge; b. Trenton, Mo., Dec. 7, 1932; s. Forrest Curtis and Lillian Judson (Ritzenthaler) C.; m. Lois Marie Hubble, May 20, 1956; children: Margaret Marie Cox Jarvis, Martha Mae Cox Anderson. BA, U. Mo., Kansas City, 1961, JD, 1965. Bar: Kans. 1965, U.S. Supreme Ct. 1970. Ptnr. Cox, Anderson & Covell, Mission, Kans., 1965-70; pvt. practice Tonganoxie, 1968-90; city atty., 1967-73, Linwood, Kans., 1972-78; mcpl. judge Mission, 1969-80, Tonganoxie, 1983-90, Topeka, 1990—. With USAF, 1952-54. Mem. Kans. Bar Assn., Kans. Mcpl. Judges Assn. (bd. dirs. 1975-79, pres. 1977-78), Topeka Bar Assn., Masons, Shriners, Sertoma (gov. Kans. dist. 1998-99, found. trustee), Topeka Evening Sertoma (pres. 1995-96), Jayhawk Sertoma (pres. 1973-76). Avocations: photography, boating, travel. Home: 910 SE 43rd St Topeka KS 66609-1620 Office: 214 E 8th St Topeka KS 66603 E-mail: jcox@topeka.org

COX, KENNETH ALLEN, lawyer, communications consultant; b. Topeka, Dec. 7, 1916; s. Seth Leroy and Jean (Sears) C.; m. Nona Beth Fumerton, Jan. 1, 1943; children— Gregory Allen, Jeffrey Neal, Douglas Randall. B.A., U. Wash., 1938, LL.B., 1940; LL.M., U. Mich., 1941; LL.D., Chgo. Theol. Sem., 1969. Bar: Wash. bar 1941. Law clk. Wash. Supreme Ct., 1941-42; asst. prof. U. Mich. Law Sch., 1946-48; with firm Little, Palmer, Scott & Slemmons (and predecessor), Seattle, 1948-61, partner, 1953-61; spl. counsel com. interstate and fgn. commerce charge TV inquiry U.S. Senate, 1956-57; chief broadcast bur. FCC, Washington, 1961-63, commr., 1963-70; counsel to comm. law firm Haley, Bader & Potts, 1970-99; sr. v.p., dir. MCI Comm. Corp., 1970-87; cons. MCI, 1987—. Lectr. U. Washington Law Sch., part-time 1954, 60; adj. prof. Georgetown U. Law Center, 1971, 72. Vice pres. Municipal League Seattle and King County, 1960, Seattle World Affairs Council, 1960; pres. Seattle chpt. Am. Assn. UN, 1957; chmn. one of five citizen subcoms. Legis. Interim Com. Edn., 1960; Bd. dirs. Nat. Pub. Radio, 1971-80; bd. dirs. Nat. Advt. Rev. Bd., 1971-74, chmn. bd., 1976-96 . Served to capt. Q.M.C. AUS, 1943-46, 51-52. Recipient Alfred I. duPont award in broadcast journalism Columbia U., 1970 Mem. Am., Fed. Communications, Wash. State, D.C. bar assns., Order of Coif, Phi Beta Kappa, Phi Delta Phi. Democrat. Conglist. Administrative and regulatory, Communications. Home: 5836 Marbury Rd Bethesda MD 20817-6076 Office: MCI Comm Corp 1133 19th St NW Washington DC 20036 E-mail: coxkio@cs.com, 1004689@mcimail.com

COX, MARSHALL, lawyer; b. Cleve., Nov. 17, 1932; s. Marshall H.C. and Mary (Bateman) Mills; m. Nancy Huntley, Aug. 3, 1957 (div. Oct. 1994); 1 child, Vanessa; m. Nathalie Menapace, Jan. 3, 1997. BA, Vanderbilt U., 1954; JD, Ohio State U., 1958. Bar: D.C. 1974, N.Y. 1959. Assoc. Cahill Gordon & Reindel, N.Y.C., 1959-67, ptnr., 1968-97. Served to 1st. lt. U.S. Army, 1955-57, Korea. Republican. Episcopalian. Antitrust, Federal civil litigation, State civil litigation.

COX, SANFORD CURTIS, JR. lawyer; b. El Paso, Tex., July 31, 1929; s. Sanford Curtis Sr. and Iva M. (Richardson) C.; m. Helen A. Thurston, Sept. 27, 1958; children: Sanford Curtis III, Christopher Thurston. BA, Tex. Western Coll., 1951, MA, 1952; LLB, U. Tex., 1957. Bar: Tex. 1957, U.S. Dist. Ct. (we. dist.) Tex. 1960, U.S. Ct. Appeals (5th cir.) 1964, U.S. Ct. Appeals (D.C. cir.) 1975. Assoc. Andress, Lipscomb, Peticolas & Fisk, El Paso, 1957-61; ptnr. Lipscomb, Fisk & Cox, 1961-74, Fisk & Cox, El Paso, 1974-79; sole practice, 1979-81; pres./shareholder Sanford C. Cox Jr. P.C., 1981-93, mem., 1993—. Mem. bd. editors U. Tex. Law Rev. Mem. adv. bd. Booth Meml. Home, 1963-79, Pleasant View Home, 1979-91. Served with U.S. Army, 1952-54. Mem. ABA, Tex. Bar Assn. (admissions com. 17th dist. 1976), El Paso Bar Assn. (ethics com. 1965-69, fee arbitration com. 1973-75), Order of Coif, Phi Delta Phi. Republican. Episcopalian. General civil litigation, Probate, Real property. Office: 6006 N Mesa St El Paso TX 79912-4659

COX, WILLIAM MARTIN, lawyer, educator; b. Bernardsville, N.J., Dec. 26, 1922; s. Martin John and Nellie (Fotens) C.; m. Julia Sebastian, June 14, 1952; children: Janice Cox Trautman, William Martin, Joann Cox Cahoon, Julieann Cox Allen. AB, Syracuse U., 1947; JD, Cornell U., 1950. Bar: N.J., U.S. Dist. Ct. Mem. Dolan & Dolan, Newton, N.J., 1950—; mem. faculty, tchr. zoning admintrn. Rutgers U., 1968-98. Gen. counsel emeritus N.J. Planning Ofcls.; pres. N.J. Inst. Mcpl. Attys., 1982-84, mem. Land Use Law Drafting Com., 1970— (chmn. 1993-98), dir., sec. Equip, Inc., Marion, N.C.; bd. dirs. Newton Cemetery Co., v.p., 2000—. Author: Zoning and Land Use Administration in New Jersey, 20th edit., 2001. With U.S. Army, 1943-45. Recipient Resolution of Appreciation award N.J. Senate and Gen. Assembly, 1994, Pres.'s Disting. Svc. award N.J. League Municipalities, 1999, N.J. Inst. Mcpl. Attys. Excellence in Land Use Law award, 1999. Mem. Am. Legion, VFW, N.J. Bar Assn., Sussex County Bar Assn., Am. Planning Assn., Monarchist League, Rotary (pres. 1978-79, Vocat. award 1996). Baptist. Land use and zoning (including planning). Office: 1 Legal Ln Newton NJ 07860-1827

COX, WILLIAM VAUGHAN, lawyer; b. Jersey City, Nov. 12, 1936; s. Walter Miles and Emily (McNenney); divorced; children: Millicent S., Jennifer V. BA, Princeton U., 1958; LLB, Yale U., 1964. Bar: Colo. 1965, Conn. 1972, N.Y. 1974. Law clk. Holland & Hart, Denver, 1963; atty. Conoco Inc., 1966-72, asst. to v.p., gen. counsel Stamford, Conn., 1972-73; v.p., gen. counsel Stromberg-Carlson Corp., Rochester, N.Y., 1974-78; mng. ptnr. Bader & Cox, Denver, 1979-86, of counsel, 1986-88; pres. William V. Cox, P.C., 1988—, also bd. dirs.; project and planning dir. Interwest Comm. Corp., 1995-97. Pres., bd. dirs. New West Indies Trading Co., Denver, 1984—; pres. Coll. Football Ltd., Denver, 1990—. Sportswriter/editor: Colorado Springs (Colo.) Free Press, 1960-61. Football coach Cheyenne Mountain H.S., Colorado Springs, 1961; founder, bd. dirs., v.p., com. chmn., editor Colo. chpt. Nat. Football Found., 1992-2001; mem. adv. bd. Downtown Denver Dist., 1991-93; bd. dirs., com. chmn. Downtown Denver Residents, 1990-93; pres., bd. dirs. Barclay Towers Condominiums, Denver, 1990-92, sec., bd. dirs., 1998-99, pres. bd. dirs., 1999-2001, sec. bd. dirs., 2001—; dist. capt. Rep. Com., Cherry Hills, Colo., 1980-85; bd. dirs. Monroe County Humane Soc., Rochester, 1975-78. Mem. Colo. Bar Assn., Denver Bar Assn., Am. Legion, Univ. Club Denver (bd. dirs. 1997-2000), Rocky Mountain Princeton Club (com. chmn. 1972), Law Club Denver (com. chmn. 1971), Corbey Ct., Phi Delta Phi. Roman Catholic. Avocations: running, politics, college football history, military history, animal rights. Alternative dispute resolution, State civil litigation, Contracts commercial. Office: 1625 Larimer St Ste 2707 Denver CO 80202-1538 E-mail: wvcsq@aol.com

COXE, TENCH CHARLES, lawyer; b. Asheville, N.C., Dec. 9, 1925; s. Tench Charles and Frances Kinloch (Huger) C.; m. Frances James Marbury, May 26, 1956; children— Tench, Molly. B.S., Yale U., 1949; J.D., U. N.C., 1953. Bar: Ga. 1954, U.S. Dist. Ct. (no. dist.) Ga. 1954, U.S. Ct. Appeals (5th cir.) 1956, U.S. Supreme Ct. 1960. Assoc. Troutman Sams Schroder & Lockerman, Atlanta, 1954-56, ptnr., 1956-71; ptnr. Troutman , Sanders, Lockerman & Ashmore, Atlanta, 1972-92; ptnr., Troutman, Sanders, (formerly Troutman, Sanders, Lockerman & Ashmore), Atlanta, 1992—; dir. Turner Broadcasting System, Atlanta, Munich Am. Reassurance Co., Atlanta. Served to 1st lt. AUS, 1944-53; ETO; Korea. Mem. Lawyers Club of Atlanta (pres. 1969), Atlanta Bar Assn., Ga. Bar Assn., ABA, Atlanta Lawyers Found. (treas. 1974—). Episcopalian. Clubs: Piedmont Driving, Commerce, Ashford (Atlanta). Communications, General corporate, Entertainment. Home: 600 Peachtree St NE Ste 5200 Atlanta GA 30308-2231 Office: Troutman Sanders 5200 NationsBank Plz 600 Peachtree St NE Ste 5200 Atlanta GA 30308-2216

COYLE, DENNIS PATRICK, lawyer; b. Detroit, Aug. 29, 1938; s. Myron Patrick and Vernice Beatrice (Smith) C.; children: Ian Patrick, Sean Patrick. B.A., Dartmouth Coll., 1960; J.D., Columbia U., 1964. Bar: N.Y. 1965, Fla. 1971. Assoc. Breed, Abbott & Morgan, N.Y.C., 1964-70; assoc. Courshon & Courshon, Miami Beach, Fla., 1970-74; mng. trustee First Mortgage Investors, Miami Beach, 1974-79; ptnr. Steel Hector & Davis, Miami, Fla., 1979-89; gen. counsel FPL Group, Inc., Fla. Power & Light Co., 1989—, dir. Fla. Power and Light Co., 1991—, Adelphia Comms. Corp., 1995—. Mem. ABA, Miami Beach C. of C. (hon. lifetime trustee). Contracts commercial, General corporate, Securities. Home: 405 Eagleton Cove Way Palm Beach Gardens FL 33418-8464 Office: FPL Group Inc PO Box 14000 700 Universe Blvd North Palm Beach FL 33408-2657

COYLE, MARTIN ADOLPHUS, JR. lawyer, consultant; b. Hamilton, Ohio, June 3, 1941; s. Martin Adolphus and Lucille (Baird) C.; m. Sharon Sullivan, Mar. 29, 1969 (div. Dec. 1991); children: Cynthia Ann, David Martin, Jennifer Ann; m. Linda J. O'Brien, July 31, 1993 (div. July 1996); m. Sandra C. Lund, July 1998. BA, Ohio Wesleyan U., 1963; JD summa cum laude, Ohio State U., 1966. Bar: N.Y. 1967, Ohio 1966. Assoc. Cravath, Swaine & Moore, N.Y.C., 1966-72; chief counsel securities and fin. TRW Inc., Cleve., 1972-73, sr. counsel, asst. sec., 1973-75, asst. gen. counsel, asst. sec., 1976, asst. gen. counsel, sec., 1976-80, v.p., gen. counsel, sec., 1980-89, exec. v.p., gen. counsel, sec., 1989-97, exec. v.p., 1997-99; sec. TRW Found., 1975-80, trustee, 1980-88. Sec. TRW Found., 1975-80, trustee, 1980-98. Co-inventor voting machine. Pres. Judson Retirement Cmty., 1986-88, trustee, 1986-90; chmn., sec. Martin A. Coyle Found.; trustee Berea Coll. 1989—, Chautauqua Inst., 1990-2000, Ohio Wesleyan U., 1992-2001. Mem. ABA, Am. Soc. Corp. Secs. (pres. Ohio regional group 1978-80, nat. dir. 1981-87, nat. chmn. 1985-86), Assn. Gen. Counsel (exec. com. 1992-99, pres. 1995-97), Harbour Club. General corporate. Home: 26 Cormorant Island Ln Kiawah Island SC 29455-5808 E-mail: coyle@cecomet.net

COYLE, MICHAEL LEE, lawyer; b. Mechanicsburg, Pa., Oct. 2, 1944; s. Patrick G. and Bertha M. (Wix) C.; m. Kathleen J. West, July 15, 1967; children: Patrick M., Darren W. BS in Acctg., Utica Coll., 1966; JD, Syracuse U., 1971; LLM in Taxation, Georgetown U., 1975. Bar: N.Y. 1972, Conn. 1975, U.S. Tax Ct. 1975. Acct. Peat, Marwick, Mitchell & Co., Syracuse, N.Y., 1966, tax acct., 1969-71; atty., adviser interpretive div. Office Chief Counsel IRS, Washington, 1971-73; atty. adviser to judge U.S. Tax Ct., 1973-75; mem. firm Reid & Riege, P.C., Hartford, Conn., 1975—. Trustee U. Hartford Tax Inst., 1982-86; bd. dirs. adv. coun. Nat. Inst. State & Local Taxation, Old Lyme, Conn., 1987—. Mem., v.p., pres. St. Paul's Luth. Ch. Coun., Wethersfield, Conn., 1976-82, 87-92, 97-2000; bd. dirs. Children's Home Cromwell, Inc., Conn., 1980-88; mem. leadership Greater Hartford, 1978, Conn. Task Force Corp. Taxation; pres. Wethersfield Bus. & Civic Assn., 1978-80. With U.S. Army, 1966-68. Mem. ABA (chmn. sales and fin. transaction com., tax sect. 1983-85), Conn. Bar Assn. (tax exec. com., ltd. liability subcom. 1991—), Conn. Bus. & Industry Assn. (tax com. 1987—), Hartford Tax Study Group, Tax Club Hartford (pres.). Avocations: tennis, reading. General corporate, Corporate taxation, State and local taxation. Home: 144 Stonehill Dr Rocky Hill CT 06067 Office: Reid & Riege PC 1 State St Ste 16 Hartford CT 06103-3185 E-mail: mcoyle@reidandriege.com

COYLE, ROBERT EVERETT, federal judge; b. Fresno, Calif., May 6, 1930; s. Everett LaJoya and Virginia Chandler C.; m. Faye Turnbaugh, June 11, 1953; children— Robert Allen, Richard Lee, Barbara Jean BA, Fresno State Coll., 1953; JD, U. Calif., 1956. Bar: Calif. Ptnr. McCormick, Barstow, Sheppard, Coyle & Wayte, 1958-82; chief judge U.S. Dist. Ct. (ea. dist.) Calif., 1990-96, sr. judge, 1996—. Former chair 9th Cir. Conf. of Chief Dist. Judges, chair 9th Cir. space and security com., mem. com. on state and fed. cts. Mem. Calif. Bar Assn. (exec. com. 1974-79, bd. govs. 1979-82, v.p. 1981), Fresno County Bar Assn. (pres. 1972). Office: US Dist Ct 5116 US Courthouse 1130 O St Fresno CA 93721-2201

COYNE, CHARLES COLE, lawyer; b. Abington, Pa., Dec. 3, 1948; s. James Kitchenman Jr. and Pearl (Black) C.; m. Paula J. Latta, May 15, 1976; 1 child, Anna Elizabeth. BS in Econs., U. Pa., 1970; JD, Temple U., 1973. Bar: Pa. 1973, U.S. Supreme Ct. 1982, N.J. 1985. Of counsel Hepburn, Willcox, Hamilton & Putnam, Phila., 1994—. Chmn. bd. dirs. George S. Coyne Chem. Co., Inc., Croydon, Pa. Assoc. editor Temple Law Review, 1972-73; columnist Life in the Country, Ledger Newspaper Group, 1993-99. Chester County (Pa.) rep. Delaware Valley Regional Planning Commn., 1982—; mem. Chester County Health and Edn. Facilities Authority, 1982—, chmn., 1996-2000; bd. suprs. East Fallowfield Twp., Chester County, 1982-83; mem. panel U.S. Bankruptcy Trustees, 1991-93; mem. Chester County Park and Recreation Bd., 1998—; mem. racing com. Pa. Hunt Cup, 1992—. Recipient Disting. Young Rep. award Greater Phila. Young Reps., 1976; Assn. Internat. Etudantes Scis. Econ. Comml. exch. fellow U. Melbourne, Australia, 1968. Mem. ABA, Pa. Bar Assn., Phila. Bar Assn., Temple Law Sch. Alumni Assn. (chmn. 10th reunion com.), U. Pa. Gen. Alumni Soc. (exec. bd. organized classes, pres. class of 1970), Nat. Steeplechase Assn., Pa. Soc., Union League Club (Phila.), Capitol Hill Club (Washington), Lawyer's Club Phila., Hartefeld Nat. Golf Club, Quaker City Farmers Club, Masons (master 1982), Kappa Alpha Soc., Sons Rev. (bd. mgrs. 2000—). Home: Sycamore Run Farm PO Box 155 Unionville PA 19375-0155 Office: Hepburn Willcox Hamilton & Putnam 1100 One Penn Ctr 1617 John F Kennedy Blvd Philadelphia PA 19103-1979 E-mail: cccoyne@aol.com

CRABB, BARBARA BRANDRIFF, federal judge; b. Green Bay, Wis., Mar. 17, 1939; d. Charles Edward and Mary (Forrest) Brandriff; m. Theodore E. Crabb, Jr., Aug. 29, 1959; children: Julia Forrest, Philip Elliott. A.B., U. Wis., 1960, J.D., 1962. Bar: Wis. 1963. Assoc. Roberts, Boardman, Suhr and Curry, Madison, Wis., 1962-64; legal rschr. Sch. Law, U. Wis., 1968-70, Am. Bar Assn., Madison, 1970-71; U.S. magistrate, 1971-79; judge U.S. Dist. Ct. (we. dist.) Wis., 1979—, chief judge, 1980-96, dist. judge, 1996—. Mem. Gov. Wis. Task Force Prison Reform, 1971-73 Membership chmn., v.p. Milw. LWV, 1966-68; mem. Milw. Jr. League, 1967-68. Mem. ABA, Nat. Assn. Women Judges, State Bar Wis., Dane County Bar Assn., U. Wis. Law Alumni Assn. Office: US Dist Ct PO Box 591 120 N Henry St Madison WI 53701-0591

CRADDOCK, ALLEN T. lawyer; b. Shelbyville, Ind., Aug. 27, 1968; s. James H. and Esther P. Craddock; m. Jacinda Carole Gruber, May 15, 1987 (div. June 1994); children: Erin L., Laruen M., Chelsea G.; m. Stacy L. Steinbrecher, Dec. 14, 1996. BS Computer Info. Sys. magna cum laude, Park Coll., 1992; JD cum laude, St. Mary's U., San Antonio, 1997. Bar: Tex. 1998, U.S. Dist. Ct. (we. dist.) Tex. 1998. Owner ACC Data Sys., San Antonio, 1992-95; legal asst. Law Office of Victoria Valerga, 1995-98; ptnr. Craddock & Rosier, PLLC, 1998—. Mem. bd. advocates St. Mary's U., 1997-98. With U.S. Army, 1986-92. Mem. ATLA, Fed. Bar Assn., Nat. Order of Barristers, John Jarlen Soc., Phi Delta Phi. Avocations: tennis, boating, camping. General civil litigation, Family and matrimonial, Workers' compensation. Office: Craddock & Rosier PLLC 7475 Callaghan Rd # 305 San Antonio TX 78229

CRAFT, ROBERT HOMAN, JR. lawyer; b. N.Y.C., Sept. 24, 1939; s. Robert Homan and Janet Marie (Sullivan) C.; m. Margaret Jamison Ford, Feb. 6, 1971; children: Robert H. III, Gerard Ford. AB, Princeton U., 1961; BA, Oxford U., 1963; LLB, Harvard U., 1966. Bar: N.Y. 1973, U.S. Dist. Ct. (so. and ea. dists.) N.Y. 1977, U.S. Ct. Appeals (D.C. cir.) 1977, U.S. Dist. Ct. D.C. 1978, U.S. Ct. Appeals (2nd cir.) 1974, U.S. Supreme Ct. 1977. Assoc. Sullivan & Cromwell, N.Y.C., 1966-74; spl. asst. to under sec. of state for security assistance U.S. Dept. State, Washington, 1974-76; exec. asst. to chmn. SEC, 1976; ptnr. Sullivan & Cromwell, 1977—. Bd. trustees Washington Opera, 1978—, pres. 1998—; dir. Coun. for Excellence in Govt., 1989—. Mem. ABA, D.C. Bar Assn., N.Y. State Bar Assn., Assn. Bar City of N.Y., Am. Soc. Internat. Law, Met. Club (Washington), Chevy Chase (Md.) Club. General corporate, Securities. Home: 5010 Millwood Ln NW Washington DC 20016-2620 Office: Sullivan & Cromwell 1701 Pennsylvania Ave NW Washington DC 20006-5866

CRAIG, C. YORK, III, lawyer; b. Oxford, Miss., Oct. 29, 1971; s. C. York Jr. and Helen W. C. BBA, U. Miss., 1994; JD, Sanford U., Birmingham, Ala., 1997. Bar: Miss. Atty. Armstrong, Allen, Prewitt Gentry Johnston & Holmes, Jackson, Miss., 1997—. Mem. Young Bus. Leaders, Jackson. Mem. Johnson Young Lawyers, Ctrl. Miss. Ole Miss Alumni Assn. (bd. dirs.). General civil litigation. Office: Armstron Allen et al 2525 Lakeward Dr Ste 200 Jackson MS 39216

CRAIG, ROBERT MARK, III, lawyer, educator; b. Mpls., Sept. 21, 1948; s. Robert Mark Jr. and Shirley A. (Collier) C.; m. Suzanne Bartlett, Aug. 22, 1970; children: Shannon Michelle, Scott Collier. BA in Journalism, Tex. Christian U., 1970; JD, U. Va., 1973. Bar: Va. 1973, U.S. Ct. Mil. Appeals 1974, Tex. 1975, U.S. Dist. Ct. (no. dist.) Tex. 1976, U.S. Dist. Ct. (so. dist.) Tex. 1980, U.S. Dist. Ct. (we. dist.) 1985, U.S. Ct. Appeals (5th and 11th cirs.) 1981, U.S. Supreme Ct. 1981, U.S. Ct. Appeals (9th and 10th cir.) 1984. Assoc. Judin, Ellis & Barron, McAllen, Tex., 1979-80, ptnr., 1980-81; sr. atty. Tenneco Oil Co., Houston, 1981-88; sr. v.p., assoc. gen. counsel First City, Tex., 1988-93; assoc. gen. counsel Am. Gen. Corp., 1993-99; v.p., gen. counsel A.G. Fin. Svc. Ctr., Inc., Evanville, Ind., 1999; assoc. gen. counsel Waste Mgmt., Inc., Houston, 1999—. Staff atty. Presdl. Clemency Bd., Washington, 1975; mem. faculty Vernon Regional Jr. Coll., Sheppard AFB, 1975-76; instr. paralegal tng., Houston, 1982-85; instr. USAF Acad., 1976-77, asst. prof. law, 1977-79; councilman City of Oak Ridge North, Tex., 1988-94, also mayor pro tem; dir. Oak Ridge Mcpl. Utility Dist., 1994-96; pres. Oak Ridge Econ. Devel. Corp., 1994-96. Vice pres. Upper Rio Grande Valley Heart Assn., McAllen, 1980-81; ruling elder Timber Ridge Presbyn. Ch., 1983-88; pres. Montgomery County Assn. for Gifted and Talented, Conroe, Tex., 1985; chmn. Permanent Jud. Commn., New Covenant Presbytery, 1986-92; legal counsel Tex. Jaycees, 1981-82. Capt. USAF, 1973-79. Mem. ABA (co-chair trial practice com. subcom. on corp. counsel of litigation sect.), Va. Bar Assn. (assoc.), Tex. Bar Assn. (coun. mem. antitrust and bus. litigation sect.), McAllen Jaycees (sec., bd. dirs. 1979-81). Republican. Avocation: golf. Federal civil litigation, State civil litigation, General corporate. Home: 27122 Wells Ln Conroe TX 77385-9080 Office: Waste Mgmt Inc 1001 Fannin St Ste 4000 Houston TX 77002-6711 E-mail: rcraig@wm.com, rmcraig@swbell.net

CRAIN, ALAN RAU, JR. lawyer, oil company executive; b. Washington, June 20, 1951; s. Alan Rau and Florence Carol (Clemmer) C. B.S., Rensselaer Poly. Inst., 1973, M.S., 1973; M.B.A., Syracuse U., 1976, J.D., 1976. Bar: D.C., Md., Tex. 1977, U.S. Dist. Ct. (so. dist.) Tex. 1980, U.S. Ct. Appeals (5th cir.) 1983, U.S. Ct. Internat. Trade 1983, U.S. Supreme Ct. 1983. Assoc. Glaser, Fletcher & Johnson, Washington, 1976; Successively counsel, sr. counsel, prin. counsel El Paso Co., Houston, 1976-81; chief counsel-internat. and research Pennzoil Co., Houston, 1981-88; successively counsel, asst. gen. counsel, v.p., gen. counsel Union Tex. Petroleum Holdings, Inc., Houston, 1988—; arbitrator N.Y. Stock Exchange, Houston, 1984— ; pres. Houston World Affairs Coun., 1997; mem. adv. bd. Inst. for Transnat. Arbitration, 1992—, South Tex. Coll. of Law, 1991—. Mem. Internat. Bar Assn., Tex. Bar Assn., Houston Bar Assn. (chmn. internat. law sect. 1987-88), State Bar of Tex. (chmn. 1989-90, corp. counsel 1996-97), Briar (Houston) Club. Contracts commercial, General corporate, Private international. Home: 411 N Rose Ln Haverford PA 19041-1923 Office: Union Tex Petroleum Holdings Inc 1330 Post Oak Blvd Houston TX 77056-3031

CRAMER, ALLAN P. lawyer; b. Norwich, Conn., Mar. 8, 1937; s. E.L. and Dorothy N. (Pasnik) C.; children: Peter Alden, Alison Jane. BA cum laude, U. Pa., 1958; JD, U. Conn., 1964. Bar: Conn. 1964, U.S. Dist. Ct. Conn. 1965, U.S. Ct. Appeals (2d cir.) 1965. Atty. HEW, Washington, 1964-65; ptnr. Cramer & Ahern, Westport, Conn., 1966— . Chmn. Westport Dem. Town Com., 1972-73; J.P., Town of Westport, 1973-77; bd. dirs. Westport Pub. Libr., 1975-82; mem. Westport Zoning Bd. Appeals, 1984-88 . Mem. Conn. Bar Assn., Westport Bar Assn. General practice, Personal injury, Real property. Home: Yankee Hill Rd Westport CT 06880 Office: Cramer & Ahern 38 Post Rd W Westport CT 06880-4207

CRAMER, HAROLD, lawyer; b. Phila., June 16, 1927; s. Aaron Harry and Blanche (Greenberg) C.; m. Geraldine Hassuk, July 14, 1957; 1 dau., Patricia Gail. AB, Temple U., 1948; JD cum laude, U. Pa., 1951. Bar: Pa. 1951. Law clk. to judge Common Pleas Ct. No. 2, 1953; mem. law faculty U. Pa., 1954; assoc. firm Shapiro, Rosenfeld, Stalberg & Cook, 1955-56, ptnr., 1956-67, Meslrov, Gelman, Jaffe & Levin, 1967-74, Mesirov, Gelman, Jaffe & Cramer, Phila., 1974-77, Mesirov, Gelman, Jaffe, Cramer & Jamieson, Phila., 1977-89, of counsel, 1996-2000; ret. ptnr. Schnader, Harison Segal & Levin, 2000—; CEO Grad. Health System, Phila., 1989-96. Instr. Nat. Inst. Trial Advocacy, 1970-78; pres. Jewish Exponent, 1987-89, Times., 1987-89. Co-author: Trial Advocacy, 1968; contbr. articles to profl. jours. Chmn. bd. Eastern Pa. Psychiat. Hosp., 1974-81, Grad. Hosp., 1975-91; trustee Fedn. Jewish Agys., Jewish Publ. Soc., pres., 1996-98, chmn., 1998-2001. 1st lt. U.S. Army, 1951-53. Decorated Bronze Star. Fellow Am. Bar Found.; mem. ABA, Am. Law Inst., Pa. Bar Assn. (ho. of dels. 1966-75, 78—, bd. govs. 1975-78), Phila. Bar Found. (pres. 1988, trustee, pres. elect), Phila. Bar Assn. (bd. govs. 1967-69, chmn. 1969, vice chancellor 1970, chancellor 1972, editor The Shingle 1970-72), U. Pa. Law Alumni Soc. (bd. mgrs. 1959-64, pres. 1968-70), Order of Coif (past chpt. pres., nat. exec. com. 1973-76), Tau Epsilon Rho (chancellor Phila. grad. chpt. 1960-62), Philmont Country Club, Pyramid Club, Greate Bay Golf Club. Federal civil litigation, General corporate, Health. Home: 728 Pine St Philadelphia PA 19106-4005 Office: Schnader Harrison Segal & Lewis 1735 Market St Ste #37 Philadelphia PA 19103-7501 E-mail: hcramer@schnader.com

CRAMP, JOHN FRANKLIN, lawyer; b. Ridley Park, Pa., Mar. 14, 1923; s. Alfred Charles and Mildred Frances (Cummins) C.; m. Suzanne Surrick, Sept. 15, 1951 (div.); children: John F., Catherine T., David B., Andrew H., Daniel E.; m. Gloria C. Maddox, Jan. 29, 1972. BS, Pa. Mil. Coll. (now Widener U.), 1943; LLB, Dickinson Sch. Law, 1948. Bar: Pa. 1949, U.S. Dist. Ct. (ea. dist.) Pa. 1951, U.S. Ct. Appeals (3d cir.) 1951. Assoc. Hodge, Hodge & Balderston, Chester, Pa., 1949-53; sr. ptnr. Cramp, D'Iorio, McConchie & Forbes, P.C., Media, 1954-75, pres., 1975-90; founding counsel Beatty, Cramp, Kauffman & Lincke, 1996—. Gen. counsel, bd. dirs. Bryn Mawr Group (name now Dixon Ticonderoga Inc.), 1965-79, pres. 1973-74; gen. counsel Widener U., 1968-91; bd. dirs. Phila. Subtransp. Co. Trustee Williamson Sch., 1968-91; bd. dirs., chmn. Crozer Chester Med. Ctr.; Elwyn Inst.; bd. dirs. Chester Hosp., Crozer-Keystone Health System; chmn. bd. dirs. Am. Inst. Mental Studies, Jerusalem Elwyn, Can. Friends of Elwyn; Rep. county chmn., 1957-61; del. Rep. Nat. Conv., 1960; state chmn. Citizens for Scranton, 1962. Mem. ABA, Del. County Bar Assn., Pa. Bar Assn., Internat. Soc. Barristers, Nat. Assn. Coll. and Univ. Attys., Def. Rsch. Inst., Wildcat Run Country Club, Masons. Episcopalian. State civil litigation, General corporate, Insurance. Office: 215 N Olive St Media PA 19063-2810

CRAMTON, ROGER CONANT, law educator, lawyer; b. Pittsfield, Mass., May 18, 1929; s. Edward Allen and Dorothy Stewart (Conant) C.; m. Harriet Cutter Haseltine, June 29, 1952; children: Ann, Charles, Peter, Cutter. AB, Harvard U., 1950; JD, U. Chgo., 1955; LLD, Nova U., 1980; MA (hon.), Oxford U., 1987. Bar: Vt. 1956, Mich. 1964, N.Y. State 1979. Law clk. to Hon. S.R. Waterman U.S. Ct. of Appeals (2d cir.), 1955-56; law clk. to assoc. justice Harold H. Burton U.S. Supreme Ct., 1956-57; asst. prof. U. Chgo., 1957-61; assoc. prof. U. Mich. Law Sch., 1961-64, prof., 1964-70; chmn. Adminstrv. Conf. of U.S., 1970-72; asst. atty. gen. Justice Dept., 1972-73; dean Cornell U. Law Sch., Ithaca, N.Y., 1973-80, Robert S. Stevens prof. emeritus, 1982—. Mem. U.S. Commn. on Revision Fed. Ct. Appellate Sys., 1973-75; bd. dirs. U.S. Legal Svcs. Corp., 1975-79, chmn. bd., 1975-78; mem. U.S. Commn. on Jud. Discipline and Removal, 1991-93. Co-author: Conflict of Laws, 5th rev. edition, 1993, Law and Ethics of Lawyering, 2d rev. edit., 1994; editor Jour. Legal Edn., 1981-87; contbr. articles to profl. jours. Guggenheim fellow, 1987-88; recipient Rsch. award Am. Bar Found., 2000. Mem. ABA, Am. Law Inst. (council mem.), Assn. Am. Law Schs. (pres. 1985), Am. Acad. Arts and Scis., Order of Coif, Phi Beta Kappa. Congregationalist. Home: 49 Highgate Cir Ithaca NY 14850-1486 Office: Cornell Law Sch Myron Taylor Hall Ithaca NY 14853-4901

CRANE, MARK, lawyer; b. Chgo., Aug. 27, 1930; s. Martin and Ruth (Bangs) C.; m. Constance Bird Wilson, Aug. 18, 1956; children: Christopher, Katherine, Stephanie. AB, Princeton U., 1952; LLB, Harvard U., 1957. Bar: U.S. Dist. Ct. (no. dist.) Ill. 1957, U.S. Ct. Appeals (7th cir.) 1968, U.S. Ct. Appeals (9th cir.) 1972, U.S. Supreme Ct. 1978, U.S. Ct. Appeals (10th cir.) 1982, U.S. Ct. Appeals (fed. cir.) 1983, U.S. Ct. Appeals (6th cir.) 1995, U.S. Ct. Appeals (8th cir.) 1998. Assoc. Hopkins & Sutter, Chgo., 1957-63, ptnr., 1963-2001; of counsel Foley & Lardner, 2001—, 2001—. Adj. prof. Loyola U. Law Sch., 2000—; comml. arbitrator, mediator complex case panel Am. Arbitration Assn., Chgo., 1997—. Served to lt. (j.g.) USNR, 1952-54. Fellow Am. Bar Found., Am. Coll. Trial Lawyers (chmn. upstate Ill. com. 1997-99); mem. ABA (chmn. antitrust sect. 1986-87), Ill. Bar Assn. (chmn. fed. jud. appointments com. 1978-79, chmn. antitrust sect. 1970), Chgo. Bar Assn., 7th Cir. Bar Assn. (pres. 1984-85). Republican. Episcopalian. Antitrust, Federal civil litigation, Criminal. Home: 520 Hoyt Ln Winnetka IL 60093-2623 Office: Foley & Lardner 3 1st National Plz Chicago IL 60602

CRANE, ROGER RYAN, JR. lawyer; b. Washington, Mar. 28, 1946; s. Roger Ryan Crane and Jeanette (Hurlbut) Rosar. AB, Coll. of Holy Cross, 1968; JD, Fordham U., 1973; LLM, NYU, 1980. Bar: N.Y. 1974; U.S. Dist. Ct. (so. and ea. dist.) N.Y. 1974; U.S. Ct. Appeals (2nd cir.) 1974, (1st cir.) 1994. Assoc. Dunnington Bartholow & Miller, N.Y.C., 1973-79, Trubin Sillcocks Edelman, N.Y.C., 1979-81, ptnr. 1981-84; ptnr., head litig. dept. Bachner Tally Polevoy & Misher, 1984-2000; co-mng. ptnr. N.Y. office McCarter & English, 2000—. Contbr. articles to profl. jours. Mem. N.Y.C. Bar Assn. (prof. discipline com. 1996-99), Univ. Club N.Y., Tuxedo Club. Avocations: golf, tennis, fly fishing, riding. General civil litigation, Intellectual property, Securities. Office: McCarter & English 300 Park Ave New York NY 10022-7402 E-mail: rcrane@mccarter.com

CRANMER, THOMAS WILLIAM, lawyer; b. Detroit, Jan. 13, 1951; s. William Eugene and Betty Lee (Orphal) C.; children: Jacqueline, Taylor, Chase. BA, U. Mich., 1972; JD, Ohio No. U., 1975. Bar: Mich. 1975, U.S. Dist. Ct. (ea. dist.) Mich. 1978, U.S. Ct. Appeals (6th cir.) 1978, U.S. Supreme Ct. 1982, U.S. Tax Ct. 1986. Asst. pros. atty. Oakland County, Mich., 1975-78; asst. atty. U.S. Dist. Ct. (ea. dist.) Mich., 1978-80, asst. chief criminal div., 1980-82; assoc. Miro, Miro & Weiner, Bloomfield Hills, Mich., 1982-84, ptnr., 1984—. Mem. faculty Atty. Gen's. Adv. Inst., Washington, 1980-82, Nat. Inst. Trial Adv., Northwestern Chicago, Ill., 1987—, trial adv. workshop Inst. Continuing Legal Edn., 1988—, local rules adv. com. U.S. Dist. Ct. (ea. dist.) Mich., 1989-92; hearing panelist Atty. Discipline Bd., 1987—. Fellow Am. Coll. Trial Lawyers, Oakland Bar-Adams Pratt Found. (charter, trustee 1994—), Mich. State Bar Found., Internat. Acad. Trial Lawyers; mem. ABA (chair litigation sect., Detroit graphic subcom. of com. on complex crimes litigation 1990), FBA (exec. bd. dirs. Detroit chpt. 1988—, pres. 1995—, Leonard R. Gilman award 1995), Am. Bd. Trial Advocates, Am. Arbitration Assn. (mem. hearing panel 1990), State Bar Mich. (rep. assembly 1986-92, mem. grievance com. 1990—, chair 1993-97, bd. commrs. 1998—), Oakland County Bar Assn. (chair CLE com. 1992, bd. dirs. 1994—, Disting. Svc. award 1996, chair membership com. 1997). Republican. Presbyterian. General civil litigation, Criminal, Labor. Home: 4249 Cherry Hill Dr Orchard Lake MI 48323-1607 Office: Miro Weiner & Kramer PC 38500 Woodward Ave Ste 100 Bloomfield Hills MI 48304-5047 E-mail: tcranmer@mirolaw.com

CRANNEY, MARILYN KANREK, lawyer; b. Bklyn., June 18, 1949; d. Sidney Paul and Aurelia (Valice) Kanrek; m. John William Cranney, Jan. 22, 1970 (div. June 1975); 1 child, David Julian. BA, Brandeis U., 1970; MA in History, Brigham Young U., 1975; JD, U. Utah, 1979; LLM in Tax Law, NYU, 1984. Bar: N.Y. 1980, U.S. Dist. Ct. (so. and ea. dists.) N.Y. 1992. Assoc. Cravath Swaine & Moore, N.Y.C., 1979-81; 1st v.p., asst. gen. counsel Morgan Stanley Investment Advisors Inc., 1981—. Mem. Order of the Coif. Democrat. Jewish. Avocations: travel, reading. General corporate, Securities. E-mail: marilyn.cranney@morganstanley.com

CRARY, MINER DUNHAM, JR. lawyer; b. Warren, Pa., Sept. 8, 1920; s. Miner D. and Edith (Ingraham) C.; m. Mary Chapman, Jan. 23, 1943; children: Edith Crary Howe, James G., Laura Crary Hall, Harriet Crary, Miner A. BA, Amherst Coll., 1942; MA, Harvard U., 1943, LLB, 1948. Bar: N.Y. 1949. Assoc. Curtis, Mallet-Prevost, 1949-61, ptnr., 1961-96, coun., 1996-2001. Trustee Am. U. in Cairo, 1959—, Heckscher Art Mus., Huntington, N.Y., 1968—; trustee Sterling and Francine Clark Art Inst., Williamstown, Mass., 1974—; bd. dirs. Robert Sterling Clark Found., N.Y.C., 1972—; chmn. exec. com. alumni coun. Amherst Coll., 1961-68; chmn. Huntington Bd. Edn. and Ctrl. Sch. Dist. 2, 1961-67; acting village justice Village of Asharoken, Northport, N.Y., 1987—. Lt. USNR, 1942-45. Mem. ABA (real property and probate com.), N.Y. State Bar Assn. (taxation and estate com. 1973), Assn. of Bar of City of N.Y. (surrogate ct. com. 1969-73), Union League Club, Century Assn. Club. (N.Y.C.), Huntington Country Club. Estate planning, Probate, Estate taxation. Office: Curtis Mallet-Prevost Colt 101 Park Ave Fl 34 New York NY 10178-0061 E-mail: mdcrary@aol.com, mcrary@cm-p.com

CRAVEN, CHARLES WARREN, lawyer; b. Johnstown, Pa., Dec. 5, 1947; s. Warren Grant and Constance (Galardie) C.; B.A. in Polit. Sci., St. Joseph's U., Phila., 1969; J.D., Temple U., 1973. Bar: Pa. 1973, U.S. Dist. Ct. (ea. dist.) Pa. 1973, U.S. Ct. Appeals (3d cir.) 1976, U.S. Supreme Ct. 1976. Assoc. Marshall, Dennehey, Warner, Coleman & Goggin, Phila., 1973-83; ptnr., 1983— . Mem. ABA, Pa. Bar Assn., Phila. Bar Assn. Federal civil litigation, State civil litigation, Insurance. Office: Marshall Dennehey Warner Coleman & Goggin 1845 Walnut St Philadelphia PA 19103-4708

CRAVEN, GEORGE W. lawyer; b. Louisville, Mar. 11, 1951; s. Mark Patrick and Doris Ann Craven; m. Jane A. Gallery, Aug. 16, 1980; children: Charles, Francis. Student, Sophia U., Tokyo, Japan, 1970-71; BA, U. Notre Dame, 1973; JD, Harvard U., 1976. Bar: Ill. 1976, U.S. Dist. Ct. (no. dist.) Ill. 1976, U.S. Tax Ct. 1977. Assoc. Sidley & Austin, Chgo., 1976-80; ptnr. Ogden & Robertson, Louisville, 1980-81; assoc. Mayer, Brown & Platt, Chgo., 1981-82, ptnr., 1983—. Sec., United Way/Crusade of Mercy, Inc., 1997—. Mem. ABA (sect. taxation), Coun. on Fgn. Rels. (Chgo. com. 1996—). Roman Catholic. General corporate, Corporate taxation, Taxation, general. Office: Mayer Brown & Platt 190 S La Salle St Ste 3100 Chicago IL 60603-3441 E-mail: gcraven@mayerbrown.com

CRAVER, CHARLES BRADFORD, legal educator; b. Detroit, July 27, 1944; s. Bradford North and Elena (Borikova) C.; m. Kathleen Mary Woods, June 9, 1967. BS, Cornell U., 1967, M Indsl. and Labor Rels., 1968; JD magna cum laude, U. Mich., 1971. Bar: Calif. 1973, U.S. Ct. Appeals (9th and D.C. cirs.) 1973, U.S. Supreme Ct. 1976. Law clk. U.S. Ct. Appeals (D.C. cir.) 1971-72; assoc. Morrison & Foerster, San Francisco, 1972-74; asst., then assoc. prof. U. Fla., Gainesville, 1974-76; vis. assoc. prof. U. Va., Charlottesville, 1976-77; prof. law U. Calif.-Davis, 1977-82; prof. U. Ill., Champaign, 1982-86; Leroy S. Merrifield rsch. prof. George Washington U., Washington, 1986—. Mem. labor arbitrator panel Fed. Mediation and Conciliation Service, Washington, 1976—, mem. labor arbitrator panel Am. Arbitration Assn., 1976—. Author: Effective Legal Negotiation and Settlement, 1986, 93, 97, 2001, Can Unions Survive?, rev. edit. 1993, The Rejuvination of the Am. Labor Movement, 1993; co-author: Labor Relations Law in Public Sector, 1979, 85, 91, Employment Discrimination Law, 1982, 88, 94, 2000, Labor Relations Law, 1984, 89, 94, 99, Collective Bargaining and Labor Arbitration, 1988, Individual Employment Rights Treatise (2 vols.), 1994, 99, Employment Law Hornbook, 1994, 99, Alternative Dispute Resolution: The Advocate's Perspective, 1997, 2001; contbr. articles to profl. jours. Mem. Am. Law Inst., Am. Arbitration Assn., Internat. Soc. for Labor Law and Social Security, ABA, Indsl. Rels. Rsch. Assn., Nat. Acad. Arbitrators. Home: 4056 Chancery Ct NW Washington DC 20007-2142 Office: George Washington U Nat Law Ctr 720 20th St NW Washington DC 20006-4306 E-mail: ccraver@main.nlc.gwu.edu

CRAWFORD, DEWEY BYERS, lawyer; b. Saginaw, Mich., Dec. 22, 1941; s. Edward Owen and Ruth (Wentworth) C.; m. Nancy Elizabeth Eck, Mar. 24, 1974. AB in Econs., Dartmouth Coll., 1963; JD with distinction, U. Mich., 1966. Bar: Ill. 1967, U.S. Dist. Ct. (no. dist.) Ill. 1969. Assoc. Gardner, Carton & Douglas, Chgo., 1969-74, ptnr., 1975—. Adj. prof. law, ITT, Kent Sch. Law, 1992—. Contbr. articles to profl. jours. Chmn. Winnetka (Ill.) Caucus Coun., 1988-89. With U.S. Army, 1966-68, Vietnam. Mem. ABA, Chgo. Bar Assn., Am. Coll. Investment Counsel, Law Club Chgo., Legal Club Chgo. Republican. Congregationalist. Avocations: running, reading, music. Finance, Mergers and acquisitions, Securities. Office: Gardner Carton & Douglas 321 N Clark St Ste 3000 Chicago IL 60610-4718 E-mail: dcrawford@ged.com*

CRAWFORD, DONALD MORSE, engineering, financial and legal consultant; b. Bklyn., June 4, 1908; s. John Fancher and Carrie Alida (Morse) C.; m. Edith May Lawrence, June 27, 1936 (dec. Apr. 2000); children: Douglas Lawrence, Donald Morse. AB, Colgate U., 1928; BSEE, Yale U., 1930; JD, NYU, 1941; postgrad., Heidelberg (Germany) U., 1930, Am. U., Cairo, 1977-78. Bar: N.Y. 1937-40, 1941; lic. prof. engr., N.Y. Corp. sec., house counsel J.G. White Engring. Corp., N.Y.C., 1940-46, 62-64; treas., asst. sec. Duplan Corp. (Can.) Textiles, Montreal, N.Y.C., 1946-53; mgr. fin. svcs. RCA Internat., N.Y.C., 1953-54; mgr. employee benefits Pepsi-Cola Internat., 1954-57; treas., controller ABC Vending Corp., 1957-58; dir. fin. Am. Mgmt. Assn., 1958-59; mgmt. cons. N.Y.C. and L.Am., 1959-68; devel. cons. UN, N.Y.C., 1968-74. Fin. services cons., engr. Sanderson & Porter, N.Y.C., World Bank, Nicaragua, Egypt, Ministry of Energy, 1975-79; cons. pension trust services Bankers Trust Co., N.Y.C., 1979-92. Editor Heat Engring., N.Y.C., 1937-40. Editor Heat Engring., N.Y.C., 1937-40. Mem. IEEE, Am. Mgmt. Assn., Soc. Internat. Devel., Soc. Mayflower Descendants, SAR, Yale Club (N.Y.C.), Apollo Club (Bklyn.). General corporate. Home: 4000 E Fletcher Ave Apt G-214 Tampa FL 33613-4818

CRAWFORD, LINDA SIBERY, lawyer, educator; b. Ann Arbor, Mich., Apr. 27, 1947; d. Donald Eugene and Verla Lillian (Schenck) Sibery; m. Leland Allardice Crawford, Apr. 4, 1970; children: Christina, Lillian, Leland. Student, Keele U., 1969; BA, U. Mich., 1969; postgrad., SUNY, Potsdam, 1971; JD, U. Maine, 1977. Bar: Maine 1977, U.S. Dist. Ct. Maine 1982, U.S. Ct. Appeals (1st cir.) 1983. Tchr. Pub. Sch., Tupper Lake, N.Y., 1970-71; asst. dist. atty. State of Maine, Farmington, 1977-79, asst. atty. gen. Augusta, Maine, 1979-95; prin. Litigation Consulting Firm, N.Y.C. & Hallowell, Maine, 1986—, Linda Crawford and Assoc. Law Firm, Hallowell, Maine, 1995-2000. Legal adv. U. Maine, Farmington, 1975; legal counsel Fire Marshall's Office, Maine, 1980-83, Warden Svc., Maine, 1981-83, Dept. Mental Health, 1983-90, litigation divsn. 1990-95; mem. tchg. team trial advocacy Law Sch., Harvard U., 1987—; lectr. Sch. Medicine Harvard U., 1991; counsel to Bd. of Registration in Medicine, 1994-95; chmn. editl. bd. Mental and Physical Disability Law Reporter, 1993-95; arbitrator Am. Arbitration Assn., 1995—; facilitator Nat. Constrn. Task Force, St. Louis, 1995. Contbg. editor Med. Malpractice Law and Strategy, 1997—, Managed Care Law Strategist, 1999—, Managed CAre Litigation Reporter, 2000—. Bd. dirs. Diocesan Human Rels. Coun., Maine, 1977-78, Arthritis Found., Maine, 1983-88; atty. expert commn. experts UN War Crime Investigation in the former Yugoslavia, 1994. Named one of Outstanding Young Women of Yr. Jaycees, 1981. Mem. ATLA, ABA (com. on disability 1992-95), Maine Bar Assn., Nat. Assn. State Mental Health Attys. (treas. 1984-86, vice chmn. 1987-89, chmn. 1989-91), Nat. Health Lawyers Assn. State civil litigation, Health, Personal injury. Home and Office: 1643 Cambridge #77 Cambridge MA 02138 also: 45 Rockefeller Plz Fl 20 New York NY 10111-2099 E-mail: lscrawford@aol.com

CRAWFORD, MURIEL LAURA, lawyer, author, educator; d. Mason Leland and Pauline Marie (DesIlets) Henderson; m. Barrett Matson Crawford, May 10, 1959; children: Laura Joanne, Janet Muriel, Barbara Elizabeth. BA with honors, U. Ill., 1973; JD with honors, Ill. Inst. Tech., 1977; cert. employee benefit splst., U. Pa., 1989. Bar: Ill. 1977, Calif. 1991, U.S. Dist. Ct. (no. dist.) Ill. 1977, U.S. Dist. Ct. (no. dist.) Calif. 1991, U.S. Ct. Appeals (7th cir.) 1977, U.S. Ct. Appeals (9th cir.) 1991; CLU; chartered fin. cons. Atty. Washington Nat. Ins. Co., Evanston, Ill., 1977-80; sr. atty., 1980-81; asst. counsel, 1982-83; asst. gen. counsel, 1984-87; assoc. gen. counsel, sec., 1987-89; cons. employee benefit splst., 1989-91; assoc. Hancock, Rothert & Bushoft, San Francisco, 1991-92. Author: (with Beadles) Law and the Life Insurance Contract, 1989, (sole author) 7th edit., 1994, Life and Health Insurance Law, 8th edit., 1998; co-author: Legal

Aspects of AIDS, 1990; contbr. articles to profl. jours. Recipient Am. Jurisprudence award Lawyer's Coop. Pub. Co., 1975, 2nd prize Internat. LeTourneau Student Med.-Legal Article Contest, 1976, LOMA FLMI Ins. Edn. award, 1999. Fellow Life Mgmt. Inst.; mem. Ill. Inst. Tech./Chgo.-Kent Alumni Assn. (bd. dirs. 1983-89, Bar and Gavel Soc. award 1977). Democrat.

CRAWFORD, SANDRA KAY, lawyer; b. Henderson, Tex., Sept 23, 1934; d. Obie Lee and Zilpha Elizabeth (Ash) Stalcup; m. William Walsh Crawford, Dec. 21, 1968; children: Bill, Jonathan, Constance, Amelia, Patrick. BA, Wellesley Coll., 1957; LLB, U. Tex., 1960. Bar: Tex. 1960, U.S. Supreme Ct. 1965, Colo. 1967, Ill. 1974. Asst. v.p.-legal Hamilton Mgmt. Corp., Denver, 1966-68; v.p., gen. counsel, sec. Transamerica Fund Mgmt. Corp., L.A., 1968; cons. to law dept. Met. Life Ins. Co., N.Y.C., 1969-71; counsel Touche Ross & Co., Chgo., 1972-75; v.p., assoc. gen. counsel Continental Ill. Bank, Chgo., 1975-83; sr. div. counsel Motorola, Inc., Schaumburg, Ill., 1984; sr. counsel, asst. sec. Sears Roebuck & Co., 1985-90. Mem. ABA, Ill. State Bar Assn., Colo. Bar Assn., Tex. Bar Assn., Everglades Club, Beach Club (Palm Beach), River Club (N.Y.C.). Federal civil litigation, General corporate, Securities. Home: 100 Royal Palm Way Apt G5 Palm Beach FL 33480-4270

CRAWFORD, SUSAN JEAN, federal judge; b. Pitts., Apr. 22, 1947; d. William Elmer Jr. and Joan Ruth (Bielau) C.; m. Roger W. Higgins; 1 child, Kelley S. BA, Bucknell U., 1969; JD, New Eng. Sch. Law, 1977. Bar: Md. 1977, D.C. 1980, U.S. Ct. Appeals for Armed Forces 1985, U.S. Supreme Ct. 1993. Tchr. history, coach Radnor (Pa.) H.S., 1969-74; assoc. Burnett & Eiswert, Oakland, Md., 1977-79; ptnr. Burnett, Eiswert and Crawford, 1979-81; prin. dep. gen. counsel U.S. Dept. Army, Washington, 1981-83, gen. counsel, 1983-89; insp. gen. U.S. Dept. Def., Arlington, Va., 1989-91; judge U.S. Ct. Appeals for the Armed Forces, Washington, 1991-99, chief judge, 1999—. Asst. states atty. Garrett County, Md., 1978-79; instr. Garrett County C.C., 1979-81. Del. Md. Forestry Adv. Commn., Garrett County, 1978-81, Md. Commn. for Women, Garrett County, 1980-83; chair Rep. State Cen. Com., Garrett County, 1978-81; trustee Bucknell U., 1988—, New England Sch. Law, 1989—. Mem. FBA, Md. Bar Assn., D.C. Bar Assn., Edward Bennett Williams Am. Inn of Ct. Presbyterian. Office: US Ct Appeals Armed Forces 450 E St NW Washington DC 20442-0001

CRAWFORD, WILLIAM WALSH, retired consumer products company executive; b. Clearwater, Fla., Oct. 7, 1927; s. Francis Marion and Frances Marie (Walsh) C. B.S., Georgetown U., 1950; LL.B., Harvard, 1954. Bar: N.Y. 1955, Ill. 1972. Assoc. Sullivan & Cromwell, N.Y.C., 1954-58; counsel Esso Standard Oil, 1958-60; ptnr. Alexander & Green, 1960-71; v.p., gen. counsel Internat. Harvester Co., Chgo., 1971-76, v.p., gen. counsel, sec., 1976-80; sr. v.p. gen. counsel Kraft, Inc., Glenview, Ill., 1980-81; sr. v.p., gen. counsel, sec. Dart & Kraft, Inc., 1981-86, Kraft, Inc., 1986-88, sr. v.p., sec., 1988-89, ret., 1989. Mem. ABA, Ill. Bar Assn., Assn. Bar City N.Y., Am. Judicature Soc., Am. Law Inst., Assn. Gen. Counsel, Chgo. Club, River Club (N.Y.C.), Beach Club, Everglades Club, Old Guard Soc. Palm Beach Golfers.

CRAYNE, LARRY RANDOLPH, lawyer; b. Waynesburg, Pa., Aug. 5, 1942; s. Robert Woodruff and Grace Louise (Ankrom) C.; m. Donna Lee Worley, Aug. 3, 1973; children: Jennifer, David, Stephanie. BA California U. Pa., 1967; JD, U. Pitts., 1971. Bar: Pa. 1971, U.S. Dist. Ct. (we. dist.) Pa. 1971, U.S. Supreme Ct. 1977. Assoc. atty. Duquesne Light Co., Pitts., 1971-72, atty., 1972-74, sr. atty., 1974-77, corp. atty., chief counsel, 1977—. Mem. Pa. Bar Assn., Allegheny County Bar Assn. Republican. Administrative and regulatory, General corporate, Public utilities. Home: 238 Johnston Rd Pittsburgh PA 15241-2556 Office: Duquesne Light Co 301 Grant St Pittsburgh PA 15219-1407

CREAMER, ROBERT ALLAN, lawyer; b. Peoria, Ill., Sept. 25, 1941; m. Joy A. Blakslee; BA, Northwestern U., 1963; LLB, Harvard U., 1967. Bar: Ill. 1967, U.S. Dist. Ct. (no. dist.) Ill. 1967, U.S. Ct. Appeals (7th cir.) 1969, U.S. Supreme Ct. 1976. Assoc. Keck, Mahin & Cate, Chgo., 1967-73, ptnr., 1974—; adj. prof. John Marshall Law Sch., Chgo., 1969-75. Mem. ABA, Chgo. Bar Assn., Ill. Bar Assn. (chari standing com. profl. conduct), Law Club Chgo., Legal Club Chgo., Northwestern U. Alumni Assn. (pres. 1990—). Democrat. Episcopalian. Club: Cliff Dwellers (Chgo.). General civil litigation, Insurance. Home: 1500 Oak Ave Evanston IL 60201-4279 Office: Attorney Liability Assessment Society 311 S Wacker Dr Ste 5700 Chicago IL 60606-6629

CREED, CHRISTIAN CARL, lawyer, investigator; b. Alexandria, La., Oct. 31, 1963; s. George Alton and Mickey (Svebek) C.; m. Catherine Campbell, Aug. 12, 1995. BA, La. State U., 1985; JD, Loyola U., New Orleans, 1995. Bar: La. 1995, U.S. Dist. Ct. (we., mid., and ea. dists.) La. 1995, U.S. Dist. Ct. (no. and so. dists.) Miss. 1998, U.S. Ct. Appeals (5th cir.) 1995. Assoc. Boles, Boles & Ryan, Monroe, La., 1995-98; mng. ptnr. Creed & Creed, 1998—. Author, contbg. editor (newsletter) Young Lawyers Newsletter, 1997-98. Mem. adv. bd. Salvation Army, Monroe, 1997—; mem. cabinet United Way, Monroe, 1998-99, bd. dirs., 2000—; mem. fundraising com. Boy Scouts Am. Mem. ABA, La. Bar Assn., 4th Jud. Dist. Ct. Bar Assn. (exec. com.), Baton Rouge Bar Assn., La. Trial Lawyers Assn. (bd. govs.), Am. Inns of Ct. (Fred Fudickar chpt. 1995—), Monroe C. of C. (state and fed. govt. com.), Kiwanis Internat., Ducks Unlimited (sponsorship com.), Rotary Internat., Phi Delta Phi (life mem.). Family and matrimonial, Personal injury, Real property. Office: Creed & Creed 1805 Tower Dr Monroe LA 71201-4964 E-mail: law@creedlaw.com

CREEKMORE, DAVID DICKASON, lawyer, educator; b. Knoxville, Tenn., Aug. 8, 1942; s. Frank Benson and Betsey (Beeler) C.; 1 child, Walton N.; m. Betty Jo Huffaker, May 1998; stepchildren: Seth Huffaker, Zach Hufaker, Christy White. LLB, U. Tenn., 1965, JD, 1966; grad, Judge Adv. Gen.'s Sch., 1979, Army Command Gen. Staff Sch., 1985. Bar: Tenn. 1966, U.S. Supreme Ct. 1970, U.S. Ct. Mil. Appeals 1985. Law clk. Gen. Session Ct. Knox County, Knoxville, Tenn., 1963-66; judge divsn. II, Gen. Sessions Ct. Knox County, 1972-86; asst. county atty. Knox County, 1966-70; ptnr. Creekmore, Thomson & Hollow, 1966-72, Walter, Regan & Creekmore, Knoxville, 1993-97; pvt. practice, 1986-93, 97-98; dep. law dir. Knox County, 1998—. Instr. criminal law and evidence Walters State Coll., Morristown, Tenn., 1974-80, U. Tenn., 1982-89. Committeeman Knox County Rep. Com., 1970—; active Tenn. Hist. Assn., Blount Mansion Assn. Lt. Col. JAGC, USAR, 1997. Mem. ABA, FBA, Tenn. Bar Assn., Tenn. Judges Conf. (v.p. 1976-78), Knox Bar Assn., Res. Officers Assn. (pres. 1989-91), Am. Legion (post judge adv. 1984-87), Studebaker Drivers Assn. (pres. 1992-97), Masons, Shriners, Elks, Eagles, Lions. Home: 11530 Midhurst Dr Knoxville TN 37922-4768 Office: Knox County Law Dept 612 City-County Bldg 400 W Main St Knoxville TN 37902-2405

CREEL, THOMAS LEONARD, lawyer; b. Kansas City, Mo., June 21, 1937; s. Thomas Howard and Elizabeth Alberta (Sharon) C.; m. Carol M. Plaisted, Nov. 26, 1992; children: Charles, Andrew, Andrea, Thomas. BS, U. Kans., 1960; LLB, U. Mich., 1963. Bar: Mich. 1963, N.Y. 1967, D.C. 1983, U.S. Supreme Ct. 1973, Ct. Mil. Appeals, 1964, U.S. Patent and Trademark Office 1965. Assoc. Kenyon and Kenyon, N.Y.C., 1966-74, ptnr., 1974-92, Kaye, Scholer, Fierman, Hayes & Handler, N.Y.C., 1992—. Faculty lectr. Columbia U. Sch. Law, N.Y.C., 1984—. Editor: Guide to Patent Arbitration, 1987. Capt., U.S. Army, 1963-66. Mem. ABA, Fed. Bar Coun., N.Y. Intellectual Property Law Assn. (past pres.), Am. Intellectual Property Assn. Federal civil litigation, Patent, Trademark and copyright. Home: 104 Cedar Cliff Rd Riverside CT 06878-2606 Office: Kaye Scholer Fierman Hayes & Handler 425 Park Ave New York NY 10022-3506

CREENAN, KATHERINE HERAS, lawyer; b. Elizabeth, N.J., Oct. 7, 1945; d. Victor Joseph and Katherine Regina (Lederer) Petervary; m. Edward James Creenan; 1 child, David Heras. BA, Kean Univ., 1968; JD, Rutgers U., 1984. Bar: N.J. 1984, Maine, 1996, U.S. Dist. Ct. N.J. 1984, U.S. Ct. Appeals (3d cir.), 1998. Various tchg. positions including, Union and Stanhope, N.J., 1968-81; law clk. to presiding judge Superior Ct. of N.J. Appellate Div., Newark, 1984-85; assoc. Lowenstein, Sandler, Kohl, Fisher & Boylan, Roseland, N.J., 1985-88, Kirsten, Simon, Friedman, Allen, Cherin & Linken, Newark, 1988-89, Whitman & Ranson, Newark, 1989-93; sr. atty. Whitman Breed Abbott & Morgan LLP, 1993-99; assoc. Skadden, Arps, Slate, Meagher & Flom LLP, 1999—. Mem. ABA, N.J. State Bar Assn. General civil litigation, General corporate. Office: Skadden Arps Slate Meaghar & Flom LLP 1 Newark Ctr Newark NJ 07102-5297 E-mail: kcreenan@skadden.com

CREHAN, JOSEPH EDWARD, lawyer; b. Detroit, Dec. 8, 1938; s. Owen Thomas and Marguerite (Dunn) C.; m. Sheila Anderson, Nov. 6, 1965; children: Kerry Marie, Christa Ellen. A.B., Wayne State U., Detroit, 1961; J.D., Ind. U., 1965. Bar: Ind. 1965, Mich. 1966, U.S. Supreme Ct. 1984. Pvt. practice, Detroit, 1966-68; assoc. Louisell & Barris (P.C.), 1968-72; ptnr. Fenton, Nederlander, Dodge, Barris & Crehan (P.C.), 1972-74, Barris & Crehan (P.C.), 1975-88; pvt. practice Bloomfield Hills, Mich. and Naples, Fla., 1977—. Mem. Am. Trial Lawyers Assn. Roman Catholic. Federal civil litigation, General practice, Personal injury. Home and Office: 827 Bentwood Dr Naples FL 34108-8204

CREHORE, CHARLES AARON, lawyer; b. Lorain, Ohio, Sept. 15, 1946; s. Charles Case and Catherine Elizabeth Crehore; 1 child Charles Case II. BA, Wittenberg U., 1968; postgrad., U. Mich., 1968-69, Cleve. State U., 1972-73; JD, U. Akron, 1976; diploma mgmt. mgrs. program, Pa. State U., 1983. Bar: US Patent Office 1975, Ohio 1976, US Dist Ct (no dist) Ohio 1976, US Ct Appeals (DC cir) 1977, US Tax Ct 1977, US Supreme Ct 1980, US Ct Appeals (fed cir) 1982. Assoc. chemist B.F. Goodrich Co., Akron, 1969-70, chemist, 1970-72, sr. chemist, 1972, patent atty. trainee, 1972-74, sr. patent atty. trainee, 1974-75, patent assoc., 1975-76, patent atty., 1976-79; atty. regulatory affairs The Lubrizol Corp., Wickliffe, Ohio, 1979-81, corp. counsel environment, health and safety, 1981-85, sr. corp. counsel, 1985-94, counsel, 1994-99; patent atty. Hudak and Shunk Co., L.P.A., 2000; of counsel Ulmer & Berne, LLP, 2000—. Guest lectr, moot ct judge Case Western Res Univ, 1983—; spkr environ regulations Calif Inst Bus Law, Ohio, 1991, Northeast Ohio Software Asn, 2001—; adv bd applied environ mgmt program Lake Erie Col, 1991—94. Grantee, Kennedy Found, 1968—69; scholar, Delta Sigma Phi Found, 1968—69. Mem.: ABA, Am Intellectual Property Law Asn, Environ Law Inst, Industry Coun Environ Safety and Health, Greater Cleveland Int Lawyers Group, Phi Alpha Delta. Intellectual property, Patent, Trademark and copyright. Home: PO Box 466 Wickliffe OH 44092-0466 Office: Penton Meda Bldg 1300 E 9th St Ste 900 Cleveland OH 44114 E-mail: ccrehore@aol.com

CREIM, WILLIAM BENJAMIN, lawyer; b. Seattle, May 12, 1954; s. Conrad Creim and Marjorie (Ross) Rosanoff; m. Linda Carol Denison, June 19, 1977; 1 child, Michael David. BA in Polit. Sci. summa cum laude, UCLA, 1976; JD, U. So. Calif., 1979. Bar: Calif. 1979, U.S. Dist. Ct. (cen. dist.) Calif. 1979, U.S. Ct. Appeals (9th cir.) 1980, U.S. Dist. Ct. (no. dist.) Calif. 1985, U.S. Supreme Ct. 1985, U.S. Dist. Ct. (ea. and so. dists.) Calif. 1987. Assoc. Fine, Perzik & Friedman, L.A., 1979-83; assoc. Dennis, Juarez, Reeser, Shafer & Young, 1983-85; ptnr. Dennis, Juarez, Shafer & Young, 1985-87; mng. ptnr. Dennis, Shafer, Fennelly & Creim, 1988-92, Bronson, Bronson & McKinnon, L.A., 1992-99; ptnr. Creim, Macias & Koeniz LLP, 1999—. Editor: Southern Calif. Law Rev., 1978-79, contbr., 1979; mem. editl. adv. bd. Credit Today. Recipient Am. Jurisprudence award, 1978. Mem. ABA (antitrust law sect., corp., banking and bus. law sects.), Calif. Bar Assn., L.A. County Bar Assn. (antitrust, bus. and corps. sect., comml. law and bankruptcy sect.), Century City Bar Assn. (bankruptcy and creditor's rights sect.), Conf. Fin. Lawyers, Order of Coif, Legion Lex (bd. dirs. 1992—), Phi Beta Kappa, Pi Gamma Mu, Phi Delta Phi. Democrat. Antitrust, Bankruptcy, Contracts commercial. Home: 26509 Sunbird Ct Valencia CA 91355-3505 Office: Creim Macias & Koeniz LLP 16th Flr 611 W 6th St Fl 16 Los Angeles CA 90017-3101

CREMER, LEON EARL, federal agent, lawyer; b. Cin., Dec. 30, 1945; s. Walter H. and Beatrice (Campbell) C. BS, Calif. State U., 1973; MA, George Washington U., 1976; JD, Rutgers U., 1982. Bar: Pa. 1982. Officer U.S. Secret Svc., Washington, 1975-77; spl. agt. U.S. Bur. Alcohol Tobacco and Firearms, U.S. Dept. Treasury, Phila., 1977-83, FBI, U.S. Dept. Justice, N.Y.C., 1983—. With U.S. Army, 1968-69. Mem. ABA, FBI Agts. Assn., Phila. Bar Assn., Pa. Bar Assn., Am. Trial Lawyers Assn., Internat. Platform Assn., Am. Mensa Soc. Avocations: yachting, aviation, skiing, tennis, long-distance running. Office: FBI 26 Federal Plz New York NY 10278-0127

CREMINS, JAMES SMYTH, political party official, lawyer; b. Washington, June 11, 1921; m. Mary Louise Gallagher (dec.); 5 children. AB with honors, U. Mo., Columbia, 1943; JD, U. Va., 1949. Asst. gen. counsel CSX Corp., Richmond, Va., 1980-85. Treas. Dem. Party Va., 1977-89. Contbr. articles to legal jours. Lay min., St. Mary's Ch., Richmond, 1968-85; bd. visitors, U. Va., 1984-88, Pres.'s Roundtable JMU, 1985-90; mem. adv. bd., St. Gertrude H.S., Richmond, 1984-88; past instnl. rep., Robert E. Lee coun. Boy Scouts Am.; me.m fin. coun., Richmond Cath. Diocese, 1978—; bd. dirs., Maymont Found., 1976-89; mem. State Dem. Steering Com., 1972-89, State Dem. Ctrl. Com., 1972-89. Lt., USNR, 1943-46. Mem. ABA, Va. Bar Assn., Richmond Bar Assn. (chmn. corp. counsel sect. 1964-65), Am. Judicature Soc. (dir. 1973-77), Nat. Soc. SAR (trustee 1989-90), Va. Soc. SAR (pres. 1988-89), Navy League U.S. (judge adv. Richmond coun. 1985-89), Ancient Order Hibernians Am. (charter mem. Maj. James Dooley Divsn. 1), KC (4th degree, knight equestrian order Holy Sepulchre of Jerusalem 1998), Alpha Tau Omega, Phi Delta Phi, Omicron Delta Kappa.

CREMINS, WILLIAM CARROLL, lawyer; b. Virginia Beach, Va., Nov. 13, 1957; s. James Smyth and Mary Louise (Gallagher) C.; m. Kelly Robin Knapp, July 6, 1985; children: William Carroll Jr., Robert Gallagher. BA, BJ, U. Mo., 1980; JD, St. John's U., 1984. Bar: Tenn. 1984, N.Y. 1985, U.S. Dist. Ct. (ea. dist.) Tenn., U.S. Ct. Appeals (6th cir.). Assoc. Law Offices of J.D. Lee, Knoxville, Tenn., 1984-85; pvt. practice, 1986—. Dep. nat. organizer Ancient Order of Hibernians in Am., Inc., Tenn., 1985, pres. James Dardis divsn., 1997, 98; bd. dirs. Florence Crittenton Agy. of Knoxville, Inc., 1989-96, pres., 1995; Little League baseball coach, 1993-97, football coach, 1987, 1993-94, soccer coach, 1992, 1995. Recipient Pro Bono award Knoxville Bar Assn. Vol. Legal Assistance Program, 1992. Mem. ATLA (Advocate recognition 1994), ABA, Tenn. Bar Assn., Knoxville Bar Assn., Tenn. Trial Lawyers Assn. Roman Catholic. General civil litigation, Family and matrimonial, Personal injury. Home: 710 Saint John Ct Knoxville TN 37922-1556 Office: 810 Henley St Knoxville TN 37902-2901 Fax: 865 546-7151. E-mail: wmcremins@aol.com

CREWS, WILLIAM EDWIN, lawyer; b. Cin., Oct. 29, 1944; s. Donald Luther and Mary Ruth (Gardiner) C. BA, Miami U., Oxford, Ohio, 1966; JD with honors, George Washington U., 1969. Bar: Ohio 1971, Ga. 1978, U.S. Dist. Ct. (no. dist.) Ga. 1978, U.S. Ct. Appeals (11th cir.) 1978. Assoc. Hausser & Atkinson, Marietta, Ohio, 1971-74; asst. counsel Union CommerceBank, Cleve., 1974-76; asst. corp. counsel Trust Co. Ga., Trust Co. Bank Atlanta, 1976-84; assoc. corp.counsel Trust Co. Ga., Trust Co. Bank, Atlanta, 1984-94; sr. atty. SunTrust Banks, Inc., 1994—. Mem. ABA, State Bar Ga. Banking, Contracts commercial, Finance. Home: 2460 Peachtree Rd NW Apt 1411 Atlanta GA 30305-4158 Office: SunTrust Banks Inc 25 Park Pl NE Atlanta GA 30303-2900

CRIGLER, B. WAUGH, federal judge; b. Charlottesville, Va., July 17, 1948; s. Bernard Weaver and Jayne (Waugh) C.; m. Anne Kendall, June 20, 1970; children: C. Kendall, Jason C., Anne Stuart. BA in History, Washington & Lee U., 1970; JD, U. Tenn., 1973. Bar: Tenn. 1973, U.S. Dist. Ct. (ea. dist.) Tenn. 1973, Va. 1974, D.C. 1974, U.S. Dist. Ct. (we. and ea. dists.) Va. 1975, U.S. Ct. Appeals (4th cir.) 1978, U.S. Supreme Ct. 1979. Law clk. to presiding judge U.S. Dist. Ct. Tenn., Knoxville, 1973-74; ptnr. Lea & Crigler, Culpeper, Va., 1974-75, Lea, Davies, Crigler & Barrell, Culpeper, 1975-79, Davies, Crigler, Barrell & Will, PC, Culpeper, 1979-81; magistrate judge U.S. Dist. Ct., Charlottesville, 1981—. Instr. trial practice Sch. Law, U. Va., 1986—; mem. criminal rules adv. com. Jud. Conf. U.S., 1992-97; mem. Fed.-State Jud. Coun., Va., 1992-2001. Mem. ABA (criminal law com. young lawyers divsn. 1974-80), Thomas Jefferson Inn of Ct. (pres. 1991-92), Va. State Bar (standing com. on professionalism 1997—), Va. Bar Assn. (chmn. criminal law corrections young lawyers divsn. 1979-80), Tenn. Bar Assn., Order of Coif, Phi Kappa Phi. Avocations: landscaping, swimming, Biblical studies. Home: 100 Peterson Pl Charlottesville VA 22901-3175 Office: US Magistrate Judge 255 W Main St Rm 328 Charlottesville VA 22902-5058

CRIST, PAUL GRANT, lawyer; b. Denver, Sept. 9, 1949; s. Max Warren and Marjorie Raymond (Catland) C.; m. Christine Faye Clements, June 4, 1972; children: Susan Christine, Benjamin Warren, John Willis. BA, U. Nebr., 1971; JD cum laude, NYU, 1974. Bar: Ohio 1974, U.S. Ct. Mil. Appeals 1975, Calif. 1976, U.S. Dist. Ct. (no. dist.) Ohio 1979, U.S. Ct. Appeals (6th cir.) 1982. Assoc. Jones, Day, Reavis & Pogue, Cleve., 1974, 78-83, ptnr., 1984—. Rsch. editor NYU Law Rev., 1972-74. Capt. JAGC, USAF, 1974-78. Decorated Meritorious Svc. medal. Fellow Am. Coll. Trial Lawyers; mem. Ohio State Bar Assn., Cleve. Bar Assn., Order of Coif, Am. Inns of Ct. Democrat. Presbyterian. Federal civil litigation, General civil litigation, State civil litigation. Home: 6565 Canterbury Dr Hudson OH 44236-3484 Office: Jones Day Reavis & Pogue N Point 901 Lakeside Ave E Cleveland OH 44114-1190

CRISTOL, A. JAY, federal judge; b. Fountain Hill, Pa., Feb. 25, 1929; s. Samuel and Mae (Stein) C.; m. Eleanor Rubin; children: Stephen Michael, David Alan. BA, U. Miami, 1958, LLB, 1959, PhD, 1997. Bar: Fla. 1959. Spl. asst. to Atty. Gen. of Fla., Tallahassee, 1959-65; sr. ptnr. Cristol, Mishan, Sloto, Miami, 1959-85; judge U.S. Bankruptcy Ct., 1985-93; chief judge, 1994-99; trustee U.S. Bankruptcy Ct., Miami, 1982-84. Adj. prof. U. Miami Law Sch.; bd. govs. 11th cir. Nat. Conf. Bankruptcy Judges; bankruptcy rules adv. com. Jud. Conf. of U.S., 1995; bankruptcy com. U.S. Ct. Appeals (11th cir.), 1996-98; tchr. bankruptcy law to judges in Czech Republic, Slovenia, Thailand, Russia, India, Malaysia, Hong Kong, South Africa. Bd. trustees U. Miami, 1988-90, Coral Gables; bd. dirs. ARC, Miami, 1989-97. Capt. USNR, 1951-89. Fellow Am. Coll. Bankruptcy; mem. ABA, Am. Bankruptcy Inst., Nat. Conf. Bankruptcy Judges, Bankruptcy Bar Assn. (S.D. and Fla. chpts.), Fla. Bar Assn., Dade County Bar Assn. Avocations: water skiing, windsurfing, flying, reading. Office: US Bankruptcy Ct 1412 Fed Bldg 51 SW 1st Ave Miami FL 33130-1669

CRITCHLOW, RICHARD H. lawyer; b. Pitts., Mar. 28, 1947; s. John Park and Ruth Lauderbaugh C.; m. Deirdre Lynn Flower, Feb. 18, 1979; children: Courtney Leigh, Caitlin Anne. BA in Polit. Sci., Union Coll., 1969; JD, U. Miami, 1973. Bar: Fla., 1973, U.S. Supreme Ct., 1976, U.S. Tax Ct., 1978, U.S. Dist. Ct. (ea. dist.) La. 1980, U.S. Dist. Ct. (so. dist.) Fla. 1973, U.S. Dist. Ct. (mid. dist.) Fla. 1978, U.S. Ct. Appeals (5th and 11th cirs.) 1973. Assoc. Tew, Tew, Rosen & Murray, Miami, Fla., 1973-76; ptnr. Tew & Tew, 1976-77, Tew, Critchlow, Sonberg, et al, Miami, 1977-82, Finley, Kumble, Wagner, Underberg, Manley & Casey, Miami, 1982-88; mng. ptnr. McDermott, Will & Emery, 1988-91; ptnr. Kenny, Nachwalter, Seymour, Arnold & Critchow, 1991—. Arbitrator Nat. Assn. Securities Dealers, Miami, 1988—. Active United Way of Miami, 1991. Mem. ABA (vice-chmn. TIPS 1985-87), Fla. Bar Assn. (chmn. grievance com. 1987-90). Republican. Congregational. General civil litigation, State civil litigation, Securities. Office: Kenny Nachwalter Seymour Arnold & Critchow 201 S Biscayne Blvd Miami FL 33131-4332

CRIVELLI, MARCELO, lawyer, consultant; b. Buenos Aires, Feb. 26, 1964; Diploma in Law, U. Buenos Aires, Argentina, 1987; M in Bus. Law, U. Austral, Buenos Aires, 1993. Clk. Assoc. & Ptnr., Estudio Cornejo, Argentina, 1987-91; ptnr. Estudio Casey, Buenos Aires, 1992-96; gen. counsel Grafica Ham S.A., 1987-96; asst. gen. counsel COTO CICSA, 1997-99; assoc. Klein & Franco Abogados, 1999—. Fellow Antiguos de la Univ. Austral; mem. Com. de Asuntos Juridicos (hon.), Camara Sociedades Anonimas de la Rep. Argentina, ABA. Antitrust, General corporate, Mergers and acquisitions. Office: Klein & Franco Abogados Av Cordoba 883 7th Flr Buenos Aires CP1054AA Argentina E-mail: mcrivel@kleinyfranco.com

CROCKER, PATRICK DAVID, lawyer, consultant; b. Kalamazoo, Sept. 21, 1964; s. David Gene and Doris Marie Crocker; m. Krista Kathleen Grabowski, Dec. 2, 1995; 1 child, Davis James. BA, U. Mich., 1986; JD, U. Detroit, 1989. Bar: Mich. 1989. Ptnr. Early, Lennon, Peters & Crocker, Kalamazoo, 1989—. Mem. Telecom. Resellers Assn., Kalamazoo Country Club. Communications. Office: Early Lennon Peters Et Al 900 Comerical Bldg Kalamazoo MI 49007-4719

CROCKER, SAMUEL SACKETT, lawyer; b. Washington, May 17, 1943; s. Reginald D. and Elizabeth (Sackett) C.; m. Dorothy Pamela Macdonald, Dec. 5, 1970; 1 child, Dorothy. BA, Williams Coll., 1965; LLB, U. Tex., 1968. Bar: Tex. 1968, Ohio 1969, Mich. 1973, N.Y. 1975. Atty., OEO/VISTA, Columbus, Ohio, 1968-69; atty. Schlumberger Ltd., Houston, 1969-73; gen. counsel Heath Co., Benton Harbor, Mich., 1973-75; corp. counsel, asst. sec. Schlumberger Ltd., N.Y.C., 1975-78; gen. counsel Schlumberger Well Services, Houston, 1978-80; v.p., sec., gen. counsel Moran Energy, Inc., Houston, 1980-84; v.p. legal affairs Baylor Coll. Medicine, 1984-97; ptnr. Gardere Wynne Sewell & Riggs, LLP, Houston, 1998-2000; v.p., gen. counsel Talent Tree, Inc., EESIS, Inc., 2000-. Mem. ABA, Forest Club. Republican. Episcopalian. Contracts commercial, Health, Intellectual property. Home: 3257 Huntingdon Pl Houston TX 77019-5925 Office: Talent Tree Inc 9703 Richmond Houston TX 77042 E-mail: samuel.crocker@talenttree.com

CROCKER, SAONE BARON, lawyer; b. Bulawayo, Zimbabwe, Jan. 11, 1943; came to U.S., 1963; d. Benjamin and Rachel (Joffe) Baron; m. Chester Arthur Crocker, Dec. 18, 1965; children: Bathsheba Nell, Karena Wynne, Rebecca Masten. BA, U. Cape Town, 1961, BA with honors, 1962; MA, Johns Hopkins U., 1966; JD cum laude, Georgetown U., 1983. Bar: D.C. 1983, U.S. Ct. Appeals (D.C. cir.) 1985, U.S. Dist. Ct. D.C. 1990, U.S. Supreme Ct. 1990, U.S. Ct. Appeals (7th cir.) 1991, U.S. Ct. Appeals (4th cir.) 1998. Adminstr. Guinea program African Am. Inst., Washington, 1965-66, author Africa Report, 1966; writer fgn. affairs div. Am. U.,

1967-68; freelance writer, 1968-80; atty. firm Wilmer, Cutler & Pickering, 1983-84; clk. to judge U.S. Ct. Appeals for D.C. Circuit, 1984-85; atty. firm O'Melveny & Myers, Washington, 1985-90, Beveridge & Diamond, Washington, 1990-92, Wright & Talisman, P.C., Washington, 1992-2001; pvt. practice, 2001—. Contbg. author: Zambia Handbook, 1967. AAUW fellow, 1963-65; Fulbright fellow, 1963; Johns Hopkins U. fellow, 1964-65; recipient Lawyers Coop. Pub. Co. awards, 1980. Mem. ABA, AAUW (state pres. 1992-94), Fulbright Assn. Environmental, Private international. E-mail: crocker@wrightlaw.com

CROFT, TERRENCE LEE, lawyer; b. St. Louis, Apr. 13, 1940; s. Thomas L. and Anita Belle (Brown) C.; m. Merry Patton, July 9, 1977; children: Michael, Shannon, Kimberly, Kristin, BethAnn, Katherine. AB, Yale U., 1962; JD with distinction, U. Mich., 1965. Bar: Mo. 1965, U.S. Dist. Ct. (ea. dist.) Mo. 1965, Ga. 1970, Fla. 1970, U.S. Ct. Appeals (5th, 8th and 11th cirs.) 1970, U.S. Supreme Ct. Assoc. Coburn, Croft & Kohn, St. Louis, 1965-69, Hansell, Post, Brandon & Dorsey, Atlanta, 1969-73; ptnr. Huie, Sterne & Ide, 1973-78, Kutak, Rock & Huie, Atlanta, 1978-83; shareholder Griffin, Cochrane & Marshall, 1983-93; ptnr. King & Croft LLP, 1994—. Mem. ABA (ho. of dels. 1993-99), ATLA, Atlanta Bar Assn. (pres., sec., treas. bd. dirs. 1986-99, chmn., bd. dirs. litigation sect. 1982-86, pres. Alt. Dispute Resolution Lawyers sect. 1996-97), Atlanta Bar Found. (pres. 1998—), Ga. Trial Lawyers Assn., Lawyers Club Atlanta, Old War Horse Lawyers Club. Episcopalian. Avocations: hiking, shooting, motorcycling, reading. Alternative dispute resolution, General civil litigation, Construction. Home: 2580 Westminster Heath NW Atlanta GA 30327-1449 Office: King & Croft LLP 707 The Candler Bldg 127 Peachtree St NE Atlanta GA 30303-1810 Fax: 404-577-8401. E-mail: tlc@king-croft.com

CROLAND, BARRY I. lawyer; b. Paterson, N.J., Jan. 11, 1938; s. Louis L. and Rae R. (Levine) C.; m. Joan Kohlreiter, Dec. 20, 1958; children: Richard, Heidi, Lizabeth, Jennifer. BA, Middlebury Coll., 1959; JD, Rutgers U., Newark, 1961. Bar: N.J. 1962, N.Y. 1983, U.S. Ct. Appeals (3d cir.) 1973. Law clk. to Hon. John Grimshaw N.J. Superior Ct., 1961, law clk. to Hon. Morris Pashman, 1961-62; assoc. Cole, Berman & Garth, Paterson, 1962-63, Shavick, Thevos, Stern, Schotz & Steiger, Paterson, 1963-68; ptnr. Shavick, Stern, Schotz, Steiger & Croland, 1968-79, Stern, Steiger, Croland, Tanenbaum & Schielke, Paterson, 1979-95, Shapiro & Croland, Hackensack, N.J., 1995—. Asst. bar examiner State of N.J., 1965-68; mem. Fed. Ethics Com., Dist. of N.J., 1975; lectr. Inst. for Continuing Legal Edn., Trial Advocacy and Family Law, 1975—. Mem. bd. editors Rutgers Law Rev., 1959-61, case editor, 1960-61; sr. editor N.J. Family Lawyer. Fellow Am. Bar Found., Am. Acad. Matrimonial Lawyers; mem. ABA (family law sect.), Am. Coll. Family Trial Lawyers (diplomate 1994—), Best Lawyers in U.S. (family law, 1987—), Am. Inns of Ct. (master Morris Pashman 1990-95, pres.-master N.J. family law 1995—), N.J. State Bar Assn. (mem. exec. com. family law sect. 1981-95), Bergen County Bar Assn. (chmn. jud. and prosecutorial appts. com. 1983-95, chmn. jud. performance com. 1999—). Family and matrimonial. Home: 243 Myrtle St Haworth NJ 07641-1137 Office: Shapiro & Croland 411 Hackensack Ave Fl 6 Hackensack NJ 07601-6365

CROMARTIE, ERIC ROSS, lawyer; b. Washington, Jan. 14, 1955; s. William Adrian and Dorothy Jane (Cann) C.; m. Lynn Prendergast, Sept. 12, 1981; children: William Ross, Morgan Nicole. BA, Amherst (Mass.) Coll., 1977; JD, Harvard U., 1980. Bar: Tex. 1980, U.S. Dist. Ct. (no. and ea. dists.) Tex. 1980, U.S. Tax. Ct. 1983, U.S. Ct. Appeals (5th and 11th cirs.) 1980, U.S. Ct. Appeals (8th and 10th cirs.) 1984, U.S. Supreme Ct. 1985. Assoc. Hughes and Luce, Dallas, 1980-85, ptnr., 1985-97. Mem. ABA, Dallas Bar Assn., Am. Law Inst. General civil litigation. Home: 4247 Brookview Dr Dallas TX 75220-3801

CROMLEY, BRENT REED, lawyer; b. Great Falls, Mont., June 12, 1941; s. Arthur and Louise Lilian (Hiebert) C.; m. Dorothea Mae Zamborini, Sept. 9, 1967; children: Brent Reed Jr., Giano Lorenzo, Taya Rose. AB in Math., Dartmouth Coll., 1963; JD with honors, U. Mont., 1968. Bar: Mont. 1968, U.S. Dist. Ct. Mont. 1968, U.S. Ct. Appeals (9th cir.) 1968, U.S. Supreme Ct. 1978, U.S. Ct. Claims 1988, U.S. Ct. Appeals (D.C. cir.) 1988. Law clk. to presiding justice U.S. Dist. Ct. Mont., Billings, 1968-69; assoc. Hutton & Sheehy and predecessor firms, 1969-77, ptnr., 1977-78, Moulton, Bellingham, Longo & Mather, P.C., Billings, 1979—, also bd. dirs.; mem. Montana Ho. Reps., 1991-92; pres. State Bar Mont., 1998-99. Contbr. articles to profl. jours. Mem. Yellowstone Bd. Health, Billings, 1972—; chmn. Mont. Bd. Pers. Appeals, 1974-80. Mem. ABA (appellate practice com.), ACLU, Internat. Assn. Def. Counsel, State Bar Mont. (chmn. bd. trustees 1995-97, trustee 1991—, pres. 1998-99), Yellowstone County Bar Assn. (various offices), Internat. Assn. Def. Counsel, Christian Legal Soc., Internat. Brotherhood of Magicians, Kiwanis. Avocations: running, magic, pub. speaking. General civil litigation, General practice. Home: 235 Parkhill Dr Billings MT 59101-0660 Office: Moulton Bellingham Longo & Mather PC 27 N 27th St Ste 1900 Billings MT 59101-2399 E-mail: Cromley@moultonlawfirm.com

CROMLEY, JON LOWELL, lawyer; b. Riverton, Ill., May 23, 1934; s. John Donald and Naomi M. (Mathews) C. JD, John Marshall Law Sch., 1966. Bar: Ill. 1966. Real estate title examiner Chgo. Title & Turst Co., 1966-70; pvt. practice Genoa, Ill., 1970—; mem. firm O'Grady & Crmoley, 1970-96. Bd. dirs. Citizen's First Nat. Bank, 1984-92, Kingston Mut. Ins. Co., Genoa Main St., Inc. Mem. ABA, Am. Judicature Soc., Ill. Stae Bar Assn., Chgo. Bar Assn., DeKalb County Bar Assn. General practice, Probate, Real property. Home: 130 Homewood Dr Genoa IL 60135-1260 E-mail: jcromley@msn.com

CRON, KEVIN RICHARD, lawyer; b. Vereeniging, Transvaal, South Africa, Feb. 25, 1956; m. Barbara Cron; children: Dylan, Erin. B in Commerce, U. Witwatersrand, South Africa, 1978, BL, 1980, ML, 1985. Ptnr., dir. Deneys Reitz, South Africa, 1982—, co. law com. South Africa, 1994—. Contbg. editor Trusts and Trustees; contbr. articles to profl. jours. including Internat. Fin. Law Rev., Profl. Mgmt. Rev., others; spkr. in field. Recipient Golden Arrow award Best Lawyer in S. Africa Profl. Mgmt. Rev, 1998. Mem. TVL Law Soc., Natal Law Soc., Cape Province Law Soc., Benoni Country Club, Rand Club. Avocations: reading, trout fishing, music. Banking, Contracts commercial, General corporate. Office: Deneys Reitz Inc Reitz Bldg 82 Maude St Sandton 2146 South Africa

CRONIN, GEORGE THOMAS, lawyer; b. San Francisco, May 18, 1913; s. Daniel W. and Florence (Brenzel) C.; m. Terese A. Mango, Feb. 6, 1943; children: Susan Cronin Laird, Thomas Michael, Terese A., Kevin Charles. BA, U. San Francisco, 1936, JD, 1939. Bar: Calif. 1939. Atty. City and County of San Francisco, 1940-42; assoc. Brobeck, Phleger & Harrison, San Francisco, 1942-52, ptnr., 1952—, of counsel, 1986—. Mem. adv. bd. St. Mary's Hosp. and Med. Ctr., San Francisco, 1970—; mem., chmn. St. Mary's Found.; regent U. San Francisco; mem. adv. bd. Marianist Province of the Pacific. Fellow Am. Coll. Probate Counsel; mem. Internat. Acad. Estate and Trust Law (academician), Am. Acad. Hosp. Attys., Calif. State Bar (mem. com. bar examiners 1956-61, chmn. 1960-61), ABA, Am. Judicature Soc., Nat. Conf. Bar Examiners (sec. 1961-62), Internat. Bar Assn. Clubs: Pacific-Union, San Francisco Golf, Olympic, Commonwealth. Home: 35 Santa Clara Ave San Francisco CA 94127-1517 Office: 2700 Spear St Tower One Market Plaza San Francisco CA 94105

CROOK, BETTY ROSS, lawyer; b. Shreveport, La., Aug. 16, 1927; d. John H. and Edna Allison (Wallette) Ross; m. Jack P.A. Crook, Sept. 25, 1966 (dec. 1976). BS, Centenary Coll., 1947; JD, Georgetown U. 1954. Bar: Tex. 1955. Claims examiner VA Regional Office, Waco, Tex., 1966-67; asst. fin. v.p. Baylor U., Waco, 1976-81, property mgmt. assoc. office bus. affairs, 1981-88, records rsch. coord., 1988—. Pres. Women's Guild St. Mary's Cath. Ch., Waco, 1982-84, 87-88, v.p., 1988-90, 95-96, chmn. liturgy commn., 1979-89, sec. parish bd., 1981-85, 88—, pres. parish bd., 1980-81, 87-88, mem. fin. com. 1987—; mem. legis. com. Regis-St. Elizabeth's Nursing Home, Waco, 1985; bd. trustees Reicher Cath. H.S., 1987-98, sec. bd., 1988-91, 94-96, pres. bd. trustees, 1991-93; parish historian St. Mary's Cath. Ch., 1991-95; bd. dirs. Holy Cross Cemetery Assn., 1991—. Mem. Tex. Bar Assn., Waco-McLennan County Bar Assn., Ctrl. Tex. Geneal. Soc. (bd. dirs. 1992—), Waco-McLennan County Libr. Commn. (chmn. 2001). Contbr. articles to numerous books. Avocations: reading, ch. choir singing. E-mail: Betty_Crook@baylor.edu. Real property. Home: 1810 Lyle Ave Waco TX 76708-2857 Office: Baylor U Bus Affairs Office PO Box 97086 Waco TX 76798-7086

CROOK, DONALD MARTIN, lawyer; b. Wichita, Kans., Dec. 18, 1947; s. Leroy R. and Audrey E. (Mattiason). BA in History/Polit. Sci. with honors, U. Kans., 1970; JD, U. Chgo., 1973. Bar: N.Y. 1974, Tex. 1982. Assoc. Kramer, Levin, Nessen, Kamin & Frankel, N.Y.C., 1973-75, Layton & Sherman, N.Y.C., 1975-80; counsel LTV Corp., Dallas, 1980-85; chief counsel corp. affairs Kimberly-Clark Corp., 1985-99, v.p., sec., 1986-99. Mem. ABA, Tex. Bar Assn., Dallas Bar Assn. (chmn. corp. counsel sect. 1986-87), Am. Soc. Corp. Secs. Banking, General corporate, Mergers and acquisitions.

CROOKS, N(EIL) PATRICK, state supreme court justice; b. Green Bay, Wis., May 16, 1938; s. George Merrill and Aurelia Ellen (O'Neill) C.; m. Kristin Marie Madson, Feb. 15, 1964; children: Michael, Molly, Kevin, Kathleen, Peggy, Eileen. BA magna cum laude, St. Norbert Coll., 1960; JD, U. Notre Dame, 1963. Bar: Wis. 1963, U.S. Supreme Ct. 1969. Assoc. Cohen and Parins, Green Bay, 1963; ptnr. Cohen, Grant, Crooks and Parins, 1966-70; sr. ptnr. Crooks, Jerry, Norman and Dilweg, 1970-77; judge Brown County (Wis.) Ct., 1977-78, Brown County (Wis.) Cir. Ct., 1978-96; justice Wis. Supreme Ct., Madison, 1996—. Instr. bus. law U. Wis., Green Bay, 1970-72; mem. faculty Wis. Jud. Coll., 1982. Editor Law Rev. Notre Dame, 1962-63. Pres. Brown County United Way, 1976-78; chmn. Brown County Legal Aid, 1971-73; mem. Northeast Criminal Justice Coord. Coun., 1973-85; pres. St. Joseph Acad. Sch. Bd., 1987-89. Capt. U.S. Army, 1963-66. Recipient Human Rights award Baha'i Community of Green Bay, 1971, Disting. Achievement award in Social Sci. St. Norbert Coll., 1977 award of Yr. U. Notre Dame, 1978, Brown County Vandalism Prevention Assn. award, 1982, W. Heraly MacDonald award Brown County United Way, 1983, Community Svc. award St. Joseph Acad., 1989, Alma Mater award St. Norbert Coll., 1992; named Wis. Trial Judge of the Year Wis. Chpt. Am. Bd. of Trial Advocates, 1994. Mem. ABA, FBA, State Bar Wis., Brown County Bar Assn. (pres. 1977), Wis. Acad. Trial Lawyers, Wis. Law Found. (bd. dirs., mem. exec. com.), Nat. Conf. of Appellate Ct. Judges, Assn. of Women Lawyers for Brown County, Dane County Bar Assn., James E. Doyle Am. Inn of Ct., Wis. Jud. Coun. Roman Catholic. Home: 5329 Lighthouse Bay Dr Madison WI 53704-1113 Office: PO Box 1688 State Capitol 16 E Madison WI 53701

CROSBY, WILLIAM DUNCAN, JR. lawyer; b. Louisville, Sept. 1, 1943; s. William Duncan and Lucille (Edwards) C.; m. Constance Elaine Frederick, June 2, 1973; children: William Duncan III, Lelia Margaret. BA, Yale U., 1965; JD, Columbia U., 1968. Bar: Ky. 1968, U.S. Dist. Ct. D.C. 1971, U.S. Supreme Ct. 1977. Minority chief counsel Com. on Rules U.S. Ho. of Reps., Washington, 1972-94, chief counsel Com. on Rules, 1995-99; v.p., COO The Solomon Group, 1999—. Chmn. Dranesville Dist., Fairfax County (Va.) Rep. Party, 1987-89; mem. Fairfax County Rep. Com., 1981—. Lt. (j.g.) USNR, 1968-71. Mem. ABA, FBA, Ky. Bar Assn., D.C. Bar, Columbia Law Sch. Alumni Assn. of Washington (pres. 1987-89). Baptist. Avocation: swimming. Home: 920 Mackall Ave Mc Lean VA 22101-1618 Office: The Solomon Group 801 Pennsylvania Ave NW Ste 750 Washington DC 20004-2670 E-mail: billcrosby@solomongroup.com, billcrosby1@aol.com

CROSS, CHESTER JOSEPH, lawyer, accountant; b. June 16, 1931; s. Chester Walter and Stephanie (Nowaczyk) Krzyzaniak. Student, Northwestern U., 1950-56, DePaul U., 1958-59; LLB, U. Ill., 1962. Bar: Ill. 1963, U.S. Dist. Ct. (no. dist.) Ill. 1963; CPA, Ill. 1957. Sr. acct. S.D. Leidesdorf & Co., Chgo., 1954-57, Hall, Penny, Jackson & Co., Chgo., 1957-58; contr. Comml. Discount Corp., 1958-59; pvt. practice Oak Park and Chgo., Ill., 1963—. Corp. dir. The Protectoseal Co. Mem. AICPA, Ill. State Bar Assn., Chgo. Bar Assn. (probate practice com., real property law com.), Ill. CPA Soc., East Bank Club (Al Lipman Black Shoe award 1989). General corporate, Probate, Estate taxation. Home: River's Edge at Sauganash 5320 N Lowell # 301 Chicago IL 60630 Office: PO Box 30339 Chicago IL 60630-0339

CROSS, JANIS ALEXANDER, lawyer; b. Plainview, Tex., Sept. 8, 1954; d. James Robert Alexander and Virginia May (Etter) Rech; m. Stephen Douglas Cross, Aug. 19, 1978; children: Beau Austin, Katherine Elizabeth. BA, Tex. Tech U., 1976, JD, 1979. Bar: Tex. 1979, U.S. Dist. Ct. (no. dist.) Tex. 1980. Pvt. practice, Amarillo, Tex., 1979-81; atty. Pioneer Corp., 1981-84, Cabot Corp., Amarillo, 1984-87; atty. (corp. counsel) Mason and Hanger, Silas Mason Co., Inc., 1987—. Instr. West Tex. State U., Canyon, 1983-87. Bd. dirs. March of Dimes, Amarillo, 1980-83, Campfire, Inc., Amarillo, 1980-83, women's programs Amarillo Coll., 1982-85, human relations com. Amarillo City Commn., 1984-86. Named one of Outstanding Young Women in Am., 1983. Mem. Tex. Bar Assn., Amarillo Bar Assn., Amarillo Area Young Lawyers Assn., Amarillo Women's Network (bd. dirs. 1980-83, pres.-elect 1987, pres. 1988), Delta Theta Phi, Gamma Phi Beta. Republican. Baptist. Avocations: bicycling, swimming, reading. Environmental, Government contracts and claims, Labor. Home: 5107 Emil Ave Amarillo TX 79106-4721 Office: Mason & Hanger Silas Mason Co Inc Pantex Plant PO Box 30020 Amarillo TX 79120-0020

CROSS, JOSEPH RUSSELL, JR. law librarian; b. Bennettsville, S.C., July 29, 1945; s. Joseph Russell and Julia Rogers C.; m. Inez Mary Robinson, May 12, 1973; children: David Sebastian, Sarah Harrington. BA, Wofford Coll., 1967; MLn, Emory U., 1972; JD, U. S.C., 1978. Bar: S.C. 1978. Tchr. Cross (S.C.) Schs., 1967-68, 70-71; reference librarian U. S.C., Columbia, 1972-75; head of pub. svcs. U. S.C. Law Library, 1978—, assoc. dir., 1997—, acting dir., 1983-84, 97-98. Served as staff sgt. U.S. Army, 1968-70, Vietnam. Mem. ABA, S.C. Bar Assn., Am. Assn. Law Libraries, S.C. Library Assn. Democrat. United Methodist. Home: PO Box 305 Cross SC 29436-0305 Office: U SC Coleman Karesh Law Library Columbia SC 29208-0001

CROSS, MILTON H. lawyer; b. Phila., July 28, 1942; s. Sidney B. and Edythe Cross; m. Joyce Volchok, June 4, 1966; children: Brian, Jonathon. BS, U. San Francisco, 1965; JD, Villanova U., 1968. Bar: Pa. 1968. Corp. counsel AEL, Inc., Phila., 1968-75; assoc. Cohen, Verlin, Sherzer & Porter, 1975-78; pvt. practice, 1978-79; ptnr. Monteverde & Hemphill, 1980-96, Spector, Gadon & Rosen, Phila., 1996—. Adj. prof. Phila. Coll. Textiles and Sci., 1970-73. Chmn. Cheltenham Twp. Sch. Bd. Authority. Mem. ABA (sect. corp., banking and bus. law), Pa. Bar Assn., Phila. Bar Assn. Contracts commercial, General corporate, Real property. Home: 251 Ironwood Cir Elkins Park PA 19027-1315 Office: Spector Gadon & Rosen 7 Penn Ctr Fl 7 Philadelphia PA 19103-2200

CROSS, ROBERT LEONARD, retired lawyer; b. Memphis, May 2, 1929; s. Earle Albright and Florence Irene (Hale) C.; m. Sharon Kay Fox, May 18, 1968; 1 child, Elizabeth. B.S., U. Ill., 1953; LL.B., DePaul U., 1955. Bar: Ill. 1956, U.S. Dist. Ct. (no. dist.) Ill. 1957, U.S. Dist. Ct. (so. dist.) Ill. 1959. Lawyer Chgo. Title & Trust Co., 1957-59; sole practice, Riverdale, Ill., 1959-64; ptnr. firm Cross, Pearcy & Burgess, Nashville, Ill., 1964-92. Bd. dirs. Nashville Pub. Library, 1965-84. Served with USMC, 1946-49. Mem. Washington County Bar Assn. (v.p. 1981-84), ABA, Ill. Bar Assn. Republican. Mem. United Ch. Christ. Lodge: Lions. Estate planning, Probate, Estate taxation. Home: 112 W Lebanon St Nashville IL 62263-1409

CROSS, WILLIAM DENNIS, lawyer; b. Tulsa, Nov. 7, 1940; s. John Howell and Virginia Grace (Ferrell) C.; m. Peggy Ruth Plapp, Jan. 30, 1982; children: William Dennis Jr., John Frederick. BS, U.S. Naval Acad., 1962; JD, NYU, 1969. Bar: N.Y. 1970, U.S. Dist. Ct. (so. and ea. dists.) N.Y. 1970, U.S. Ct. Appeals (2d cir.) 1970, U.S. Supreme Ct. 1974, Calif. 1977, U.S. Dist. Ct. (ctrl. dist.) Calif. 1977, U.S. Ct. Appeals (9th cir.) 1977, U.S. Ct. Appeals (5th, 10th and 11th cirs.) 1981, Mo. 1982, U.S. Dist. Ct. (we. dist.) Mo. 1982, U.S. Ct. Appeals (8th cir.) 1989, U.S. Ct. Appeals (fed. cir.) 1992, U.S. Dist. Ct. Ariz. 1997, U.S. Dist. Ct. Colo. 1997, U.S. Dist. Ct. Kans. 1998. Commd. ensign USN, 1962, advanced through ranks to lt., 1965, resigned, 1966; assoc. Cravath, Swaine & Moore, N.Y.C., 1969-76, Lillick, McHose & Charles, L.A., 1976-77; asst. gen. counsel FTC, Washington, 1977-82; of counsel Morrison & Hecker, Kansas City, Mo., 1982-83, ptnr., 1983—. Staff mem. NYU Law Rev., 1967-69, editor, 1968-69; assoc. editor Antitrust Mag. Mem. ABA, Calif. Bar Assn., Mo. Bar Assn., Assn. Bar City N.Y., Kansas City Bar Assn., Lawyers Assn. Kansas City. Administrative and regulatory, Antitrust, Federal civil litigation. Home: 1223 Huntington Rd Kansas City MO 64113-1347 Office: Morrison & Hecker 2600 Grand Blvd Kansas City MO 64108-4606 E-mail: wdcross@moheck.com

CROSSLAND, SAMUEL HESS, lawyer, heavy construction company executive; b. Tulsa, Aug. 30, 1929; s. Samuel Hess and Louise (Weaver) C.; student U. Tulsa, 1947-48, 52-53; B.A., U. Okla., 1955, LL.B., 1957; m. Yolonda Phillips, Sept. 18, 1958; 1 child, Julia Allison. Bar: Okla., D.C. Pros. atty., Tulsa County, Okla., 1957-59; chief legal counsel to gov. of Okla., 1959-62; ptnr. Stuart, Symington, Hollings & Crossland, Washington, 1962-64; atty. Morrison-Knudsen Co., Inc., 1964— , corp. sec., counsel, 1968-73, v.p., sec., gen. counsel, 1973-89, sr. v.p., spl. asst. to chmn., 1989— Served with USNR, 1948-52. Mem. ABA, Okla. Bar Assn., D.C. Bar Assn., Am. Soc. Corp. Secs., Phi Alpha Delta. Clubs: Hillcrest Country, Arid (Boise). General corporate. Office: Morrison Knudsen Corp PO Box 73 Boise ID 83729-0073

CROTHERS, DANIEL J. lawyer; b. Fargo, ND, Jan. 3, 1957; BA, U. ND, 1979, JD, 1982. Ptnr. Nilles, Hansen & Davies, Fargo. Adj. prof. Moorhead State U., 1984—90. Mem.: N.D. Bar Assn. (pres. 2001—). General civil litigation, Appellate. Office: Nilles Hansen & Davies 1800 Radisson Tower PO Box 2826 Fargo ND 58108*

CROTTY, ROBERT BELL, lawyer; b. Dallas, Aug. 16, 1951; s. Willard and Betty (Bell) C.; m. Sarah Smith, Mar. 8, 1980; children: Robert Edwin, Rebecca Bell. BA, Va. Mil. Inst, 1973; JD, U. Tex., 1976. Bar: Tex. 1976, U.S. Dist. Ct. (no. dist.) Tex. 1977, U.S. Ct. Appeals (5th cir.) 1978. Assoc. Akin, Gump, Strauss, Hauer & Feld, Dallas, 1976-82, ptnr., 1983-92, hiring ptnr., 1988-91; prin. McKool Smith, P.C., 1992-94; ptnr. Crotty & Johansen, L.L.P., 1995—. Bd. visitors Va. Mil. Inst., 1995-99. Mem. Leadership Dallas, 1981; dir. Salesmanship Club, 1989-90, 94-95, Va. Mil. Inst. Alumni Assn., 1991-95, Highland Park Ind. Sch. Dist. Edn. Found., 1991-97, pres. 1997-2000; chmn. GTE Byron Nelson Classic, 1995; pres. Dallas Bus. League, 1983, Big Bros./Big Sisters Met. Dallas, 1987-88; deacon North Dallas Bible Ch., 1989-95. 1st lt. U.S. Army, 1976, USAR, 1973-81. Fellow Tex. Bar Found. (life), Dallas Bar Found., Dallas Bar Found. Fellows (pres. 1999-2000); mem. Dallas Bar Assn., Tex. Law Rev. Assn. (life), State Bar Tex. Avocations: golf, reading, rock climbing, hiking. General civil litigation. Office: Crotty & Johansen LLP 2311 Cedar Springs Rd Ste 250 Dallas TX 75201-7810 E-mail: bcrotty@crojolaw.com

CROUCH, RICHARD EDELIN, lawyer; b. Arlington, Va., Dec. 3, 1940; s. Howard Fairfax and Helen Nora (Edelin) C.; m. Mary Blake French, Feb. 6, 1965; children: John Howard, Virginia Elizabeth. AB, Coll. William and Mary, 1962, JD, 1964. Bar: Va. 1964 (chmn. 10th dist. disciplinary comm. 1988-89), U.S. Ct. Mil. Appeals 1965, U.S. Dist. Ct. (ea. dist.) Va. 1970, U.S. Ct. Appeals (D.C. cir.) 1970, U.S. Supreme Ct. 1970, U.S. Ct. Appeals (4th cir.) 1972. Assoc. Crouch & Crouch, Arlington, 1964; editor U.S. Law Week & Criminal Law Reporter, Washington, 1968-74; prin. Crouch & Crouch, Arlington, 1974—. Mng. editor The Family Law Reporter, 1974-81; cons. editor for legal services Bur. Nat. Affairs, Inc., Washington, 1981-84. Author: The Rights of Homemakers in Virginia, 1977, Interstate Custody Litigation, 1981. Served as capt. U.S. Army, 1964-68. Mem. ABA, ACLU (legal dir. Va. 1972-76, nat. bd. dirs. 1977-80), Va. State Bar (bd. govs. family law sect. 1988-92), Internat. Acad. Matrimonial Lawyers, Am. Acad. Matrimonial Lawyers, Internat. Soc. Family Law, King and Queen County Hist. Soc., Arlington Hist. Soc., Fairfax County Hist. Soc., Loudoun County Preservation Soc. Episcopalian. Family and matrimonial, Professional liability. Home: 2624 18th St N Arlington VA 22201-4049 Office: 2111 Wilson Blvd Ste 550 Arlington VA 22201-3051

CROUCH, ROBERT P., JR. prosecutor; b. Mar. 28, 1948; s. Robert and Rosa Crouch; m. Clara Johnson Sept. 2, 1973; 1 child, Emily. BA, U. Md., 1971; MPA, U. N.C., 1982; JD, U. Va., 1988. Bar: Va. 1988. Aide to William B. Spong U.S. Senate, 1971-73; asst. mgr. employee benefits Fieldcrest Mills, 1973-75; adminstrv. asst. Patrick Henry Comm. Coll., 1975; adj. prof. Ferrum Coll., 1984-85; clerk circ. ct., 1976-85; assoc. McGuire, Woods, Battle & Boothe, 1988-89, Young, Haskins, Mann & Gregory, 1989-93; atty. U.S. Dept. Justice, Roanoke, Va., 1993—. Mem. bd. trustees Va. Mus. Nat. History, 1989-95, pres. bd. dirs., 1990-93; mem. edn. found. Patrick Henry C.C., 1984-93; mem. bd. visitors George Mason U., 1983-91; vice chmn. Dem. Party Va., 1989-93, state party sec., 1985-89, 5th dist. com. chmn., 1981-85; chmn. statewide Wilder-Beyer-Terry Campaign Com., 1989. Mem. Va. Bar Assn., Va. Trial Lawyers Assn. Democrat. Presbyterian. Office: Thomas B Mason Bldg PO Box 1709 105 Franklin Rd SW Ste 1 Roanoke VA 24011-2305

CROUSE, FARRELL R. lawyer; b. Portsmouth, Va., Dec. 23, 1963; s. Farrell Rondall and Grace Alice (Kenworthy) C. BA in History and Sociology, Bucknell U., Lewisburg, Pa., 1986; JD, Widener U., Wilmington, Del., 1989, LLM in Taxation, 1992. Bar: N.J. 1989, Pa. 1989, U.S. Dist. Ct. N.J. 1989. Assoc. Law Offices John William Neef, Carneys Point, N.J., 1990-91; pvt. practice Woodstown, 1991—. Mem. ABA, N.J. Bar Assn., Pa. Bar Assn. Avocations: auto racing, travel, collecting auto racing books and memorabilia. Family and matrimonial, General practice, Personal injury. Home and Office: 317 Auburn Rd # A Pilesgrove Township NJ 08098-2608

CROW, NANCY REBECCA, lawyer; b. Ridgecrest, Calif., Nov. 3, 1948; d. Edwin Louis and Eleanor Elizabeth (Gish) C.; 1 child, Rebecca Ann Carr; m. Mark A.A. Skrotzki, Apr. 4, 1987. BA, Antioch Coll., 1970; JD, U. Colo., 1974; LLM in Taxation, NYU, 1977. Bars: Colo. 1974, Calif. 1977. Atty., advisor IRS, N.Y.C., 1975-77; assoc. Brawerman & Kopple, Los Angeles, 1977-80; prof. Sch. Law, U. Denver, 1980-81; of counsel Krendl & Netzorg, Denver, 1981-84; shareholder Krendl & Krendl, 1984-92, Pendleton, Friedberg, Wilson & Hennessey, P.C., Denver,

1992—. Editor estate and trust forum Colorado Lawyer, 1992-93, bd. editors, 1993-2000; contbr. chpts. to books. Mem. alumni bd. Antioch Coll., 2000—; bd. dirs. Centennial Philharm. Orch., 1998-2001; bd. trustees, Centennial Philharmonic Found., 2001. Fellow Am. Coll. Trust and Estate Counsel; mem. ABA (chmn. Welfare Benefits subcom. of personal svcs. orgns. com. com., tax sect. 1987-92), Colo. Bar Assn. (exec. coun. tax sect. 1990-93, sec. tax sect. 1993-94, chair-elect 1994-95, chair 1995-96, bd. govs. 1996-98), Colo. Women's Bar Assn. (chair pub. policy com. 1982-83), Denver Bar Assn., Denver Tax Assn., Denver Tax Inst. Planning Com., Alliance of Profl. Women, Women's Estate Planning Coun. (bd. dirs. 1996-98), U.S.-Mex. C. of C. (bd. dirs. Rocky Mountain chpt., sec. 1998-2001), Sierra Club. Democrat. Unitarian. Avocations: skiing, backpacking, cello, running. Estate planning, Pension, profit-sharing, and employee benefits, Taxation, general. Home: 1031 Marion St Denver CO 80218-3016 Office: Pendleton Friedberg Wilson & Hennessey PC 303 E 17th Ave Ste 1000 Denver CO 80203-1263 E-mail: NCrow1@qwest.net, nrc@penberg.com

CROW, SAM ALFRED, federal judge; b. Topeka, May 5, 1926; s. Samuel Wheadon and Phyllis K. (Brown) C.; m. Ruth M. Rush, Jan. 30, 1948; children: Sam A., Dan W. BA, U. Kans., 1949; JD, Washburn U., 1952. Ptnr. Rooney, Dickinson, Prager & Crow, Topeka, 1953-63, Dickinson, Crow, Skoog & Honeyman, Topeka, 1963-70; sr. ptnr. Crow & Skoog, 1971-75; part-time U.S. magistrate, 1973-75; U.S. magistrate, 1975-81; judge U.S. Dist. Ct. Kans., Wichita, 1981-92, sr. judge Topeka, 1992—. Lectr. Washburn U. Sch. Law; participant adv. com. on criminal rules Jud. Conf., 1990-96; mem. 10th Cir. Jud. Coun., 1987-88; pres., 1992-94; criminal rules adv. com.'s liaison Ct. Adminstrn. and Case Mgmt. Com.'s Subcom. on Criminal Case Mgmt., 1994-96; bd. dirs. Riverside Hosp., Wichita, 1986-92; mem., founder The Honorable Sam A. Crow Am. Inn of Ct.; lectr. in field. Bd. rev. Boy Scouts Am., 1960-70, cubmaster, 1957-60; mem. vestry Grace Episcopal Ch., Topeka, 1960-65; chmn. Kans. March of Dimes, 1959, bd. dirs. 1960-65; bd. dirs. Topeka Coun. Chs., 1960-70; mem. Kans. Hist. Soc., 1960—; pres., v.p. PTA.; bd. govs. Washburn Law Sch. Alumni Assn., 1993-99. Col. JAGC, USAR, ret. Recipient Washburn U. Sch. Law Disting. Svc. award, 2000; named to Topeka H.S. Hall of Fame, 2000. Fellow Kans. Bar Found.; mem. ABA (del. Nat. Conf. Spl. Ct. Judges 1978, 19), Kans. Bar Assn. (trustee 1970-76, chmn. mil. law sect. 1965, 67, 70, 72, 74, 75), Kans. Trial Lawyers Assn. (sec. 1959-60, pres. 1960-61), Nat. Assn. U.S. Magistrates (com. discovery abuse), Topeka Bar Assn. (chmn. jud. reform com., chmn. bench and bar com., chmn. criminal law com., Disting. Svc. award 2000), Wichita Bar Assn., Topeka Lawyers Club (sec. 1964-65, pres. 1965-66), Am. Legion, Shawnee Country Club, Shriners, Delta Theta Phi, Sigma Alpha Epsilon. Office: US Dist Ct 444 SE Quincy St Topeka KS 66683

CROWDER, BARBARA LYNN, judge; b. Mattoon, Ill., Feb. 3, 1956; d. Robert Dale and Martha Elizabeth (Harrison) C.; m. Lawrence Owen Taliana, Apr. 17, 1982; children: Paul Joseph, Robert Lawrence, Benjamin Owen. BA, U. Ill., 1978, JD, 1981. Bar: Ill. 1981. Assoc. Louis E. Olivero, Peru, Ill., 1981-82; asst. state's atty. Madison County, Edwardsville, 1982-84; ptnr. Robbins & Crowder, 1985-87, Robbins, Crowder & Bader, Edwardsville, 1987-88, Crowder, Taliana, Rubin & Buckley, 1988-98; assoc. judge 3d Jud. Cir. of Madison County, Ill., 1999—, presiding judge family divsn., 2000—. Spkr. Continuing Legal Edn. Seminars Family Law Update, 1993-2001; co-chair 3d Jud. Cir. Family Violence Coord. Coun., 1999—, chair ct. com., 1999—. Co-editor ISBA Family Law Newsletter, 1993; co-author chpts. in ISBA Family Law Handbook, 1995, Maintenance Chapter Ill. Family Law IICLE, 1998, supplement, 2001; contbr. articles to profl. jours. Chmn. City of Edwardsville Zoning Bd. Appeals, 1986-87; committee woman Edwardsville De, Precinct 15, 1986-98; mem. City of Edwardsville Planning Commn., 1985-87; bd. dirs. Madison-Bond County Workforce Devel. Bd., 1995-96, 96-97. Named Best Oral Advocate, Moot Ct. Bd., 1979, Outstanding Young Career Woman, Dist. XIV, Ill. Bus. and Profl. Women, 1986; recipient Alice Paul award Alton-Edwardsville NOW, 1987, Outstanding Working Woman of Ill. Ill. Fed. of Bus. and Profl. Women, 1988-89, Woman of Achievement YWCA, 1996; recipient Athena award Edwardsville/Glen Carbon C. of C., 1991. Fellow Am. Acad. Matrimonial Lawyers; mem. Ill. Bar Assn. (family law coun. sect. 1990-99, chair 1997-98, co-editor family law newsletter 1993, vice chair 1996-97), Ill. Judges' Assn. (bd. dirs. 2000—), Am. Judicature Soc., Ill. Fedn. Bus. and Profl. Women (parliamentaria dist. XIV 1991-92), Women Lawyers Assn. Met. East (pres. 1986), Edwardsville Bus. and Profl Women's Club (pres. 1988-89, 95-96, treas. 1989-90, Woman of Achievement award 1985, Jr. Svc. award 1987), Ul Ill. Alumni Assn. (v.p. met.-east club 1994-95, bd. dirs. 1995-97). Democrat. Office: Madison County Courthouse 155 N Main St Edwardsville IL 62025-1955

CROWDER, MARJORIE BRIGGS, lawyer; b. Shreveport, La., Mar. 26, 1946; d. Rowland Edmund and Marjorie Ernestine (Biles) Crowder; m. Ronald J. Briggs, July 11, 1970 (div. Nov. 2000); children: Sarah, Andrew. BA, Carson-Newman Coll., 1968; MA, Ohio State U., 1969, JD, 1975. Bar: Ohio 1975, U.S. Ct. Appeals (6th cir.) 1983, U.S. Ct. Claims 1992. Asst. dean of women Albion Coll., Mich., 1969-70; dir. residence hall Ohio State U., Columbus, 1970-71, acad. counselor, 1971-72; assoc. Porter, Wright, Morris, Arthur, 1970-71, ptnr., 1983-2000; AmeriCorps atty. Southeastern Ohio Legal Svs., Portsmouth, 2000—. Legal aide Community Law Office, Columbus, 1973-74. Contbg. author: Going to Trial, A Step-By-Step Guide to Trial Practice and Procedure, 1989. Trustee, pres. Epilepsy Assn. Central Ohio, Columbus, 1977-84; bd. dirs. Columbus Speech & Hearing, 1977-82, Scioto County Somestic Violence Task Force, 2000—; mem. allocation com. United Way Franklin County, 1984-88. Fellow Am. Bar Found., Columbus Bar Found. (trustee 1993-95); mem. ABA (mem. gavel awards com. 1989-96, gen. practice sect. 1983—, chair litigation com. 1987-89, exec. coun. 1989-93, dir. bus. com. group 1990-91, chair program com. 1991-93, torts and ins. practice sect. 1993—, vice chair health ins. law com. 1993-96), Ohio Bar Assn. (Joint Task Force on Gender Fairness 1991-93), Columbus Bar Assn. (com. chmn. 1979-83, docket control task force 1989-91, editor 1981-83), Scioto County Bar Assn.; Women Lawyers Franklin County. Federal civil litigation, General civil litigation, Insurance. Home: 2106 Summit St Portsmouth OH 45662 Office: Southeastern Ohio Legal Svcs 800 Gallia St Ste 700 Portsmouth OH 45662-4035 E-mail: mcrowder@oslsa

CROWE, JAMES JOSEPH, lawyer; b. New Castle, Pa., June 9, 1935; s. William J. and Anna M. (Dickson) C.; m. Joan D. Verba, Dec. 26, 1959. BA, Youngstown State U., 1958; JD, Georgetown U., 1963. Bar: Va. 1963, Ohio 1966. Atty. SEC, Washington, 1964-65, Gen. Tire & Rubber Co., Akron, Ohio, 1965-68; sr. atty. Eaton Corp., Cleve., 1968-72; sec., gen. counsel U.S. Shoe Corp., Cin., 1972-95, v.p., 1975-95; ptnr. Kepley, Gilligan & Eyrich, 1996-2000; counsel Thompson Hine LLP, 2001—. Chmn. divsn. Fine Arts Fund, 1976; trustee Springer Ednl. Found., 1978-84, Cin. Music Festival Assn., 1980-86, 96—, Am. Music Scholarship Assn., 1999—; group chmn. United Appeal, 1980; mem. pres.'s coun. Coll. Mt. St. Joseph, 1985-88; trustee Tennis for Charity Inc., 1986—, Playhouse in the Park, 1990-96, Greater Cin. Ctr. for Econ. Edn., 1992-96, Leadership Cin., Class 1990-91; trustee Cin. Nature Ctr., 1993-2000, chmn. 1996-98; bd. visitors U. Cin. Coll. Law, 1993—; trustee Invest in Neighborhoods, 1982-89, pres. 1984-86; trustee Cin. Hort. Soc., 1996—, Am. Music Scholarship Assn., 1999—. 2d lt. U.S. Army, 1958-59. Mem. Ohio Bar Assn., Va. Bar, Cin. Bar Assn., Am. Soc. Corp. Secs., Cin. Country Club, Cin. Tennis Club, Met. Club. E-mila. General corporate. E-mail: jcrowe7246@aol.com

CROWE, JOHN T. lawyer; b. Cabin Cove, Calif., Aug. 14, 1938; s. J. Thomas and Wanda (Walston) C.; m. Marina Protopapa, Dec. 28, 1968; 1 child, Erin Aleka. BA, U. Santa Clara, 1960, JD, 1962. Bar: Calif. 1962, U.S. Dist. Ct. (ea. dist.) Calif. 1967. Lawyer, Visalia, Calif., 1964—; ptnr. Crowe, Mitchell & Crowe, 1971-85. Bd. dirs. World Parts Industries, 1993-98, Willson Ranch Co., pres. 1997—; referee State Bar Ct., 1976-82; gen. counsel Sierra Wine, 1986-96. Bd. dirs. Mt. Whitney Area coun. Boys Scouts Am., 1966-85, pres., 1971, 72; bd. dirs. Visalia Associated In-Group Donors (now United Way Tulare County), 1973-81, pres., 1978-79, Tulare County Libr. Found., 1997—; mem. Visalia Airport Commn., 1982-90; mem. Army Res. Forces Policy Com., 1995-99, chmn., 1997-99. 1st lt. U.S. Army, 1962-64, maj. gen. Res., 1964-99. Decorated Disting. Svc. Medal with oak leaf cluster, Legion of Merit with oak leaf cluster, Meritorious Svc. Medal with 3 oak leaf clusters, Army Commendation Medal; named Young Man of Yr., Visalia, 1973; Senator Jr. Chamber Internat., 1970; recipient Silver Beaver awrd Boy Scouts Am., 1983, Rudder medal Assn. U.S. Army, 1999. Mem. ABA, Tulare County Bar Assn., Nat. Assn. R.R. Trial Counsel, State Bar Calif., Assn. U.S. Army (bd. dirs. 2000—), Visalia C. of C. (pres. 1979-80), Rotary (pres. 1980-81), Visalia Country Club. Republican. Roman Catholic. General corporate, General practice. Home: 3939 W School Ave Visalia CA 93291-5514

CROWE, ROBERT ALAN, lawyer; b. N.Y.C., Feb. 20, 1950; s. John Thomas and Annette (Korall) C.; m. Carolyn Ann Kruse, Apr. 14, 1974; children: Emily, Andrew. AB, St. Louis U., 1971, JD, 1974. Bar: Mo. 1974, U.S. Dist. Ct. Mo. 1975, U.S. Ct. Appeals (8th cir.) 1976, U.S. Ct. Appeals (7th cir.) 1977, U.S. Supreme Ct. 1977. Assoc. Law Office of Harry J. Nichols, St. Louis, 1974-76; sole practice, 1976-83; ptnr. Kell, Kell, Custer, Weller & Crowe, 1983-85, Crowe & Shanahan, St. Louis, 1985—. Mem. editorial adv. bd. West's Social Security Reporting Service, 1983—; pres. U.S. Arbitration & Mediation Midwest, St. Louis, 1985—; midwest regional dir. U.S. Arbitration & Mediation, St. Louis, 1985-93. Mem. ABA, Mo. Bar Assn., Bar Assn. Met. St. Louis, Nat. Orgn. Social Security Claimants Reps. (exec. com. 1984-92, treas. 1986-87, sec. 1987-88, v.p. 1988-89, pres. 1989-90). Pension, profit-sharing, and employee benefits. Home: 1101 Hawken Pl Saint Louis MO 63119-3911 Office: Crowe & Shanahan 720 Olive St Ste 2020 Saint Louis MO 63101-2317 E-mail: racrowe@crowe-shanahan.com

CROWE, THOMAS LEONARD, lawyer; b. Amsterdam, N.Y., Aug. 3, 1944; s. Leonard Hoctor and Grace Agnes (O'Malley) C.; m. Barbara Ann Hauck, Aug. 2, 1969; children: Patrick, Brendan. AB, Georgetown U., 1966, JD, 1969. Law clk. to chief judge U.S. Dist. Ct. (no. dist.), Elkins, W.Va., 1969-70; trial atty. U.S. Dept. Justice, Washington, 1970-72; asst. U.S. atty. Balt., 1973-78; chief of criminal divsn. U.S. Atty.'s Office, 1977-78; ptnr. Cable, McDaniel, Bowie & Bond, 1979-91, McGuire, Woods, Battle & Boothe, Balt., 1991-95; of counsel Monshower & Miller, LLP, Columbia, Md., 1996-98; pvt. practice Balt., 1998—. Mem. jud. conf. U.S. Ct. Appeals for 4th Cir. Fellow Md. Bar Found.; mem. Fed. Bar Assn. (pres. Balt. chpt. 1981-82), Md. Bar Assn., Barristers Club (pres. 1990-91),. Democrat. Roman Catholic. Federal civil litigation, State civil litigation, Criminal. Home: 11 Osborne Ave Baltimore MD 21228-4935 Office: Law Offices of Thomas L Crowe 1622 The World Trade Ctr 401 E Pratt St Baltimore MD 21202-3117

CROWELL, ELDON HUBBARD, lawyer; b. Middletown, Conn., May 15, 1924; s. Eldon Lewis and Alice (Hubbard) C. A.B., Princeton U., 1948; LL.B., U. Va., 1951. Bar: D.C. 1951, Conn. 1951, U.S. Dist. Ct. D.C. 1951, U.S. Ct. Appeals (D.C. cir.) 1951, U.S. Ct. Appeals (3d cir.) 1956, U.S. Supreme Ct. 1958. Assoc. Cummings, Stanley et al Washington, 1951-52, ptnr., 1952-53; ptnr. Sellers, Conner & Cuneo, Washington, 1953-70, Jones, Day, Reavis, Washington, 1970-79, Crowell & Moring, Washington, 1979— ; lectr. U. Va. Law Sch., Charlottesville, 1967-80, Judge Adv. Gen. Sch., Charlottesville, 1975— , George Washington Nat. Law Sch., 1975— , Fed. Publs. Inc., Washington, 1975— . Contbr. articles to legal jours. Trustee Williston-Northampton Sch., Easthampton, Mass., 1965-75, Madeira Sch., Greenway, Va., 1970-75, Expt. in Internat. Living, Putney, Vt., 1950-60; chmn. law firm div. United Way Campaign for Met. Washington, 1983-85; bd. dirs. City Lights Sch., Washington, Procurement Round Table, 1993—. Served with U.S. Army, 1942-45. Fellow Am. Bar Found., Nat. Contract Mgmt. Assn.; mem. ABA, Internat. and Comparative Law Ctr. (bd. advisors), D.C. Bar Assn., Nat. Security Indsl. Assn. Democrat. Episcopalian. Clubs: Metropolitan, Chevy Chase. Administrative and regulatory, Government contracts and claims. Home: 2101 Connecticut Ave NW Washington DC 20008-1728 Office: Crowell & Moring 1001 Pennsylvania Ave NW Fl 10 Washington DC 20004-2595

CROWL, RODNEY KEITH, lawyer; b. Houston, July 23, 1948; s. Julian Charles and Joyce Hetty (Crump) C.; m. Linda Sue Wansbrough, May 17, 1974; children— Audrey, Blaire, Sarah, David. B.A. cum laude in Econs. and English, Rice U., 1970; J.D., U. Tex.-Austin, 1973. Bar: Tex. 1973, U.S. Dist. Ct. (so. dist.) Tex. 1974. Assoc. firm Woody & Rosen, Houston, 1973-74; atty. Pennzoil Co., Houston, 1974-77; oil and gas atty. Kaneb Services, Inc., Houston, 1977-80; sr. atty., asst. sec. Monsanto Oil Co., Houston, 1980-83; v.p. Instnl. Adv. U. Thomas, Houston, vice chief, 1990-98; devel. officer St. Joseph Hosp. Found.; guest speaker U. S.C. Coll. Internat. Bus. Adminstrn., Columbia, 1974, 76. Class chmn. Rice U. Ann. Fund., Houston, 1979-80. Mem. Assn. Internat. Petroleum Negotiators. Episcopalian. Clubs: Rice Owl (pres. 1984-86), Rice Rebounders (pres. 1981) (Houston). E-mail: rodcrowl@hotmail.com. General corporate, FERC practice, Oil, gas, and mineral. Home: 6016 Fordham St Houston TX 77005-3126

CROWLEY, JAMES MICHAEL, lawyer; b. Phila., Feb. 16, 1942; s. Joseph M. and Mary V. (McCall) C.; m. Beverly Ann Crystal, Mar. 28, 1987; children: David M., Benjamin T., Lauren R. PhB magna cum laude, Lateran U., Rome, 1965; STB magna cum laude, Lateran U., 1967, STL, 1969, JCB magna cum laude, 1970, JCL magna cum laude, 1973; JD, Notre Dame U., 1972. Bar: N.Y. 1973, U.S. Dist. Ct. (so. dist.) N.Y. 1973, U.S. Supreme Ct. 1976. Assoc. Shearman & Sterling, N.Y.C., 1972-78; resident Algiers, Algeria, 1976-78; sole practice N.Y.C., 1978-80; sr. counsel CIGNA Corp., Phila., 1980-84; v.p. CIGNA Internat. Holdings Ltd., Wilmington, Del., 1982-97; sr. v.p., chief counsel CIGNA Worldwide, Inc., Phila., 1984-96; sr. v.p. govt. affairs CIGNA Internat., 1996-97; mng. cons. Aon Religious Instns. Alliance, 1999—. Dir. CIGNA Worldwide Ins. Co., Wilmington. Mem. Archdiocesan Fin. Coun., Phila., 1984-87; exec. bd. Phila. coun. Boy Scouts Am., 1983-86; pro bono publico litig. Matter of Karen Ann Quinlan, N.J., 1976; trustee Country Day Sch. of the Sacred Heart, Bryn Mawr, Pa., 1999—. Recipient Cardinal Dougherty medal St. Charles Coll., Phila., 1963; Silver medal Pope Paul VI, Rome, 1967. Mem. Am. Soc. Internat. Law, ABA, Assn. Bar City N.Y., N.Y. State Bar Assn., N.Y. County Bar Assn., University Club (N.Y.C.). Roman Catholic. General corporate, Insurance, Private international. Home: 3503 Tall Oaks Ln Newtown Square PA 19073-2767 E-mail: jmcrowley@msn.com

CROWLEY, JAMES WORTHINGTON, retired lawyer, business consultant, investor; b. Cookville, Tenn., Feb. 18, 1930; s. Worth and Jessie (Officer) C.; m. Laura June Bauserman, Jan. 27, 1951; children: James Kenneth, Laura Cynthia; m. Joyce A. Goode, Jan. 15, 1966; children: John Worthington, Noelle Virginia; m. Carol Golden, Sept. 4, 1981. BA, George Washington U., 1950, LLB, 1953. Bar: D.C. 1954. Underwriter, spl. agt. Am. Surety Co. of N.Y., Washington, 1953-56; adminstrv. asst., contract adminstr. Atlantic Rsch. Corp., Alexandria, Va., 1956-59, mgr. legal dept., asst. sec., counsel, 1959-65, sec., legal mgr., counsel, 1965-67, Susquehanna Corp. (merger with Atlantic Rsch. Corp.), 1967-70; pres., dir. Gen. Communication Co., Boston, 1962-70; v.p., gen. counsel E-Systems, Inc., 1970-95, sec., 1976-95; ret., 1995; ind. cons. bus. and fin., investor Dallas, 1995—. V.p., asst. sec., dir. Cemco, Inc.; v.p., dir. TAI, Inc., Serv-air, Inc., Greenville, Tex., Engring. Rsch. Assocs., Inc., Vienna, Va., HRB Systems, Inc., State Coll., Pa.; mem. adv. bd. sec. Internat. and Comparative Law Ctr.; v.p., sec., dir. Advanced Video Products, 1992-95; v.p., sec., gen. counsel E-Systems Med. Electronics, Inc., 1992-95. Mem. Am. Soc. Corp. Secs. (pres. Dallas regional group 1988-89, nat. dir. 1989-92), Inf. Mus. Assn., Nat. Security Indsl. Assn., Mfrs.' Alliance for Productivity and Innovation (mem. law coun.), Omicron Delta Kappa, Alpha Chi Sigma, Phi Sigma Kappa. Republican. Baptist General corporate, Government contracts and claims, Pension, profit-sharing, and employee benefits. Home and Office: 16203 Spring Creek Rd Dallas TX 75248-3116 E-mail: jwcrowle@ix.netcom.com

CROWLEY, LAURENCE ANTHONY, lawyer; b. Cardiff, Glamorgan, Wales, Feb. 11, 1958; s. Anthony John Crowley and Joyce Lauretta Baskerville. BA (Jurisp) Oxon, U. Coll., Oxford, 1979. Cert. solicitor Supreme Ct., Eng., Wales. Trainee Durrant Piesse, London, 1981-83; lawyer Lovell White Durrant (merged with Durrant Piesse), 1983-91; ptnr. Lovells (formerly Lovell White Durrant), 1991—. Mem. Involvency Lawyers Assn. (dir. 1998—)., INSOL, AEPPC. Banking, Bankruptcy. Office: Lovells 65 Holborn Viaduct London EC1A 2DY England

CROWSON, JAMES LAWRENCE, lawyer, financial company executive, academic administrator; b. Duncan, Okla., Aug. 3, 1938; s. George L. and Emry Elifair (McKee) C.; children from previous marriage: James Lawrence Jr., Jason, Donna Kristan Nickel; m. Linda Sue Crowson, Mar. 2, 1986; stepchildren: Chadwick Lanier Johnson, Kim Johnson Osborn. BA in English Lit., U. Okla., 1960; LLB, So. Meth. U., 1963. Bar: Tex. 1963. Legis. counsel Tex. Legis. Coun., Austin, 1966-67; dir. hearings Tex. Water Quality Bd., 1967-68, chief legal officer, 1967-68, dir. hearings and enforcement, 1969-70; adminstrv. asst. Office of Gov., 1968-69; univ. atty. U. Tex. System, 1970; asst. to pres. U. Tex., 1970-71, Dallas, 1971-74, v.p., 1974-77, exec. v.p., 1977-80; vice chancellor, gen. counsel U. Tex. System, Austin, 1980-87; sr. v.p., gen. counsel Lomas Fin. Group, Dallas, 1987-94, exec. v.p., 1994-95; pvt. investment practice, 1995-96; dep. chancellor adminstrn. Tex. Tech. Univ. System, Lubbock, 1996—. Sec. Tex. Higher Edn. Found., 1988—, Higher Edn. Legis. Polit. Action Com., 1987—; vice chmn. HCB Enterprises Inc., 1995—; bd. dirs. KOHM Pub. Radio Sta., 1997-99, Tex. Univs. Health Plan, 1998—; bd. dirs. Market Lubbock, Inc., 1997-99, v.p. 1999. Trustee Alliance for Higher Edn., 1991-96, Dallas Edn. Ctr., 1995-96. Capt. U.S. Army, 1963-66. Mem. Mortgage Bankers Assn. Am. (mem. legal issues com., mem. legis. com.), U.S. C. of C. (mem. edn. employment and tng. com., mem. labor rels. com., mem. S.W. pub. affairs task force). Bankruptcy, General corporate, Legislative. Office: #258 PO Box 65600 Lubbock TX 79464 E-mail: jim.crowson@ttu.edu

CRUDEN, JOHN CHARLES, lawyer; b. Topeka, Feb. 23, 1946; s. George Harry and Agnes (Telban) C.; m. Sharon Lynn Holland, June 15, 1968; children: Kristen, Heather. BS, U.S. Mil. Acad., 1968; JD, U. Santa Clara, 1974; MA, U. Va., 1975; grad., Gen. Staff Coll., 1982; fellow, Army War Coll., 1988. Bar: Calif. 1975, D.C. 1979, U.S. Supreme Ct. 1979. Commd. 2d lt. U.S. Army, 1968, advanced through grades to col., 1987, with airborne, ranger, spl. forces Republic of Vietnam, 1968-71, clk. Calif. Supreme Ct., 1974, pros., 1975-76, chief litig. br. Hdqrs. Europe, 1976-78, sr. trial atty. comml. br. litig. divsn., 1978-79, gen. counsel Def. Nuclear Agy., 1979-80; prof., chief Adminstrv. and Civil Law divsn. Judge Adv. Gen.'s Sch., Charlottesville, Va., 1982-85; staff Judge Adv. Europe, 1985-87; spl. counsel to asst. atty. gen. civil divsn. U.S. Dept. Justice, 1987-88; chief legis. counsel Dept. Army, 1988-91; chief environ. enforcement sect. Environ. & Natural Resource divsn. U.S. Dept. Justice, Washington, 1991-95, dep. asst. atty. gen., 1995—. Contbr. articles to profl. jours. Mem. Fed. Bar Assn. (chpt. prse. 1984-85, Younger Fed. Lawyers award 1981), JAG Sch. Alumni Assn. (pres. 1982-85), D.C. Bar Assn. (bd. govs. 2001—), Calif. Bar Assn., ABA (vice chmn. adminstrv. law and gen. practice sect. 1985-88, vice chmn. fed. legis. com. 1989-92, adv. com., standing com. on law and nat. security 1988-94). Office: US Dept Justice 950 Pennsylvania Ave NW Washington DC 20530-0001 E-mail: john.cruden@usdoj.gov

CRUIKSHANK, DAVID EARL, lawyer; b. Painesville, Ohio, Apr. 23, 1945; s. Earl W. and Kathryn (Schlender) C.; m. Nancy Kathryn Heine, June 9, 1984. B.A., DePauw U., 1967; J.D., Case West Res. U., 1973. Bar: Ohio 1973, U.S. Dist. Ct. (so. dist.) Ohio 1973, U.S. Supreme Ct. 1980. Assoc. Turner & Badger, Mount Vernon, Ohio, 1973-75, Baker, Byron & Hackenberg, Painesville, 1975-76; assoc., ins. mgr. E.W. Cruikshank, Painesville, 1976-84; assoc. Byron & Ryan, Willoughby, Ohio, 1984— ; mem. faculty Ohio Legal Ctr. Inst., 1985, 86, U. Toledo Sch. of Law, CLE div., 1985. 1st lt. USMC, 1968-71, Vietnam. Mem. ABA, Ohio Bar Assn. (chmn. ins. law com. 1984-87, vice chmn. 1981-84), Lake County Bar Assn., Def. Research Inst., Ohio Bar Found, Ohio Acad. Civil Trial Attys. (lectr. 1984, 86), Masons. Insurance. Home: 30 Wintergreen Hill Dr Painesville OH 44077-5332 Office: Byron & Ryan 36100 Euclid Ave Willoughby OH 44094-4456

CRUMBLEY, R. ALEX, lawyer; b. McDonough, Ga., Jan. 31, 1942; s. Reuben Alexander and Lucy Margaret (Turner) C.; m. Claire Herd, Nov. 11, 1967; 1 child, Alexander Herd. BA in Journalism, U. Ga., 1964, JD, 1966; postgrad., Am. Acad. Jud. Adminstrn., 1980. Bar: Ga. 1965, U.S. Dist. Ct. (no. dist.) Ga. 1970, U.S. Supreme Ct. 1976. Asst. atty. gen. State of Ga., 1967-70; ptnr. Weltner, Kidd, Crumbley & Tate, Atlanta, 1970-76; pub. defender Flint Jud. Cir., 1976-77; judge Flin. Jud. Cir. Superior Ct., 1978-83; ptnr. Crumbley & Crumbley, McDonough, 1983—. Senator 17th dist. Ga. Senate, 1987-89; mem. bd. gov. state bar Ga., 1992-94; prof. Woodrow Wilson Coll. Law, Atlanta, 1971-75; counsel to com. on judiciary Ga. State Senate, 1970. Contbr. articles to profl. jours. With Ga. N.G., 1966-72. Mem. ABA, Henry County Bar Assn., State Bar Ga. (disciplinary bd. 1985-87), Lawyers Club Atlanta, Henry County Kiwanis (hon.). Democrat. Episcopalian. Alternative dispute resolution, State civil litigation, Family and matrimonial. Office: 80 Macon St McDonough GA 30253-3221 also: PO Box 2080 Mcdonough GA 30253 E-mail: alexwade@bellsouth.net

CRUMLEY, JOHN WALTER, lawyer; b. Ft. Worth, July 20, 1944; s. Frank E. and Mary Cecilia (Gaudin) C.; m. Paulette Gavin, July 25, 1970; children: John Gavin, Brian Christopher. BS, Springhill Coll., 1967; JD, So. Meth. U., 1970, M of Comparative Law, 1973. Bar: Tex. 1970, U.S. Dist. Ct. (no. dist.) Tex. 1976, U.S. Ct. Appeals (5th cir.) 1981, U.S. Tax Ct. 1988. Assoc. McBryde & Bogle, Ft. Worth, 1973-75; ptnr. Crumley, Murphy & Shrull, Inc., 1975-85, Tracy, Crumley & Holland, Ft. Worth, 1985-92; prin. John W. Crumley, P.C., 1992—. Mem. bd. dirs. Goodrich Ctr. for the Deaf, 1995—, pres., 1998—; vice chair Bingo Advisor Com., 1995-96. Mem. steering com. Tarrant County Vol. Guardianship, Ft. Worth, 1986-87; bd. dirs. Camp Fire, Ft. Worth, 1985-87, Cath. Social Svcs., Ft. Worth, 1985-86. Capt. U.S. Army, 1970-72. Mem. State Bar Tex., Tarrant County Bar Assn., Tex. Assn. Def. Counsel, Tex. Assn. Diocesan Attys., U.S. Conf. Diocesan Attys. Assn., Serra Club (pres. Ft. Worth club 1985-86), KC (state adv. 1986-91, 95-96). State civil litigation, Construction, Probate. Office: 316 University Ctr 1300 S University Dr Fort Worth TX 76107-5737 E-mail: crumley1@airmail.net

CRUMLISH, JOSEPH DOUGHERTY, lawyer; b. Phila., Aug. 19, 1922; s. James Charles and Ruth (Hardy) C.; m. Rebecca Kelley, Sept. 12, 1950 (div. 1979); 1 child, Rebecca Kelley. B.S.S., Georgetown U., 1946, PhD, 1954; MA, Cath. U. Am., 1948, JD, 1966. Bar: D.C. 1967, U.S. Ct. Appeals (D.C. cir.) 1968, U.S. Supreme Ct. 1975, U.S. Ct. Appeals (Fed. cir.) 1982,

U.S. Claims Ct. 1980. Rsch. coord. Ford Motor Co., Dearborn, Mich., 1953-61; fund dir. Georgetown U. Alumni Assn., Washington, 1961-62; econ. devel. adminstr. U.S. Dept. Commerce, Washington, 1962-64; rsch. program mgr., cons. Nat. Bur. Standards, Washington, 1964-77; counsel Casey, Scott & Canfield, Washington, 1977-88; counsel Dahlgren and Close, 1994—; dir., co-founder, former pres. and chmn., bd. mem. Thomas More Soc. Am., Washington, 1980—; adj. faculty Georgetown U., U. Md., George Washington U., 1973-79. Author: A City Finds Itself, 1950; author monographs; contbr. articles to profl. jours. Co-founder, First Friday Club of Phila., 1959; bd. dirs. Georgetown U. Alumni Assn., 1961-62, Cath. U. Am. Alumni Assn., 1962-65; sec., co-founder Men of Mercy, 1983—. With USAAF, 1943-46. Recipient Outstanding Cmty. Svc. award Ford Motor Co., 1959, High Quality Performance, Nat. Bur. Standards, 1966, Commendation, Presdl. Clemency Bd., 1975. Mem. Found. for Rsch. in Human Behavior (bd. advisors 1959-60), Ctr. for Applied Rsch. in the Apostolate (lay bd. advisors 1978-83), Pastoral Coun. Ch. Annunciation, D.C. Bar Assn., Fed. Bar Assn., John Carroll Soc., Sharswood Law Club, Friendly Sons of St. Patrick, Am. Legion (elected judge adv. of Washington dept., 2d vice comdr., comdr. Dept. of Justice Post). Home: 3900 Watson Pl NW # G-1eb Washington DC 20016-5416 Office: 1000 Connecticut Ave NW Ste 204 Washington DC 20036-5337

CRUMP, DAVID L. lawyer; b. Miami, Fla., Jan. 7, 1959; s. Edward III and Eileen M. Crump; m. Kathy J. Smith, Nov. 11, 1964. BA, Wash. State U., Pullman, 1981; JD, Calif. Western U., 1984; grad., Gerry Spence's Trial Lawyers Coll., Wyo., 1996. Prin. Law Office of David L. Crump, Seattle, 1989—. Former protem judge Seattle Mcp. Ct. and Seattle Bellevue Dist. Cts. Big brother Big Bros. King County, Kirkland, Wash., 1987-94. Mem. ATLA, Plantiff's Attorneys Legal Soc., Wash. State Bar Assn. (chmn. editl. adv. bd. Bar News 1998-99), Wash. State Trial Lawyers Assn. (Downtown Seattle roundtable 1998-2000, chmn. demonstrative evidence sect. 2000—, mem. editl. bd. Trial News, 1999-2001), Rotary (Paul Harris fellow). Avocations: musician, painting, SCUBA diving. Personal injury. Office: 701 5th Ave Ste 2420 Seattle WA 98104 Fax: 206-223-1099. E-mail: david@davidcrump.com

CRUMP, FRANCIS JEFFERSON, III, lawyer; b. Alexandria, Va., Dec. 4, 1942; s. Ross Gault and Pauline (DeVore) C.; m. Nancy Jo Burkle, Aug. 20, 1966; children: Tom, Laura, Elizabeth. BS in Math., Va. Mil. Inst., 1964; JD, Ind. U., 1967. Bar: Ind. 1967, U.S. Dist. Ct. (so. dist.) Ind. 1967. Gen. ptnr. Jewell, Crump & Angermeier, Columbus, Ind., 1971—. Pres. First Nat. Corp.; lectr. on estate planning and legal aspects of child abuse and neglect; bd. dirs., sec., treas. Hawpatch Corp. Past pres., bd. dirs. Columbus Boys' Club; past pres., bd. dirs., v.p., treas. Found. Youth, Inc., Babe Ruth Baseball, Inc., sr. v.p. 1983-88; past deacon First Presbyn. Ch. of Columbus, 1972-75, elder 1977-79, 2000—; bd. dirs. Ecumenical Assn. Barth County Chs., Inc., v.p., 2001. Mem. Ind. State Bar Assn., Bartholomew County Bar Assn., Inc. (pres. 1983, treas. 2001, dir. 2001), Rotary, Phi Alpha Delta. Republican. Estate planning, Probate, Real property. Home and Office: PO Box 1061 Columbus IN 47202-1061

CRUMPTON, CHARLES WHITMARSH, lawyer; b. Shreveport, La., May 29, 1946; s. Charles W. and Frances M. (McInnis) C.; m. Thu-Huong T. Cong-Huyen, Sept. 17, 1971; children: Francesca, Ian. BA, Carleton Coll., 1968; MA, U. Hawaii, 1974, JD, 1978. Bar: Hawaii 1978, U.S. Dist. Ct. Hawaii 1978, U.S. Ct. Appeals (9th cir.) 1982. Tchr. dept. edn. State of Hawaii, Honolulu, 1972-73, 75-77; Fulbright prof. U. Can Tho, Vietnam, 1973-75; assoc. John S. Edmunds, Honolulu, 1978-80, Ashford & Wriston, Honolulu, 1980-85, David W. Hall, Honolulu, 1985-88; dir. Hall & Crumpton, 1988-93; dir., shareholder Stanton Clay Chapman Crumpton & Iwamura, 1993—. Pres./dir. Internat. Law Found., 1996—; fellow Am. Coll. Civil Trial Mediators, 2000—; barrister Am. Inn of Ct. IV, Honolulu, 1985-87; arbitrator Court-Annexed Arbitration program 1st Cir. Ct. State of Hawaii, 1987—; arbitrator, mediator Am. Arbitration Assn., 1988—, Arbitration Forums, 1990—, Mediation Specialists, 1994—, Dispute Prevention & Resolution, 1995—; mem. com. on lawyer professionalism Hawaii State Jud. Conf., 1988-89; arbitrator/mediator com. fee disputes Hawaii Bar Assn., 1990—, mem. com. jud. adminstrn., 1990—, mem. com. jud. performance, 1992-94, chair sect. on alternative dispute resolution, 1997—; prof. Hawaii Pacific U., 1995—; faculty/spkr. on ins. law, employment law, alternative dispute resolution, civil litigation, 1993—. Asst. dir. youth vols. Am. Cancer Soc., Honolulu, 1972-73. Fulbright grantee U.S. Dept. State, 1973-75. Fellow Am. Coll Civil Trial Mediators; mem. ATLA, ABA (torts and ins. practice sect., litigation sect., alt. dispute resolution sec.), Am. Coll. Civil Trial Mediators, Hawaii Bar Assn., Inter-Pacific Bar Assn. Avocations: sports, guitar. Alternative dispute resolution, Insurance, Personal injury. Home: 47-538 Hui Iwa St Kaneohe HI 96744-4658 Office: Stanton Clay Chapman Crumpton & Iwamura 700 Bishop St Ste 2100 Honolulu HI 96813-4120 E-mail: crumpton@paclawteam.com

CRUSE, REX BEACH, JR. lawyer; b. Sherman, Tex., July 2, 1941; s. Rex Beach and Mary Ellen (Sim) C.; m. Maebeth Ann Brock, Mar. 19, 1958 (div. 1975); 1 child, Vicki Ann.; m. Carol A. Schaller, July 14, 1977 (div. 1983). BBA highest honors, U. Tex., 1962, PhD in Bus. Adminstrn., 1973; JD, St. Mary's U., San Antonio, 1988. Bar: Tex. 1989, N.Y. 1989, D.C. 1991, U.S. Dist. Ct. (we. dist.) Tex. 1990, U.S. Tax Ct. 1990, U.S. Bankruptcy Ct. 1990, U.S. Ct. Internat. Trade 1993, U.S. Ct. Fed. Claims 1996; CFP; CPA. Various Am. Inst. CPA's, N.Y., 1964-75, mng. dir., 1976-83; dean Sch. Accountancy U. Hawaii, Honolulu, 1983-84; pvt. practice acctg. San Antonio, 1985-89; pvt. practice law, 1989-96; assoc. Duncan, Weakley & Bressler, Inc., 1996—. Pres. San Antonio Coun. on Alcohol and Drug Abuse, 1994-96; bd. dirs. Unicorn Ctrs., Inc., 1994-96. Mem. ABA, AICPA (cert. spl. merit 1992), Am. Health Lawyers Assn., State Bar Tex. (The Coll. of the State of Bar of Tex.), Tex. Soc. CPAs (Outstanding com. chmn. 1993-94), San Antonio Bar Assn. Democrat. Methodist. Avocation: aerobics. Health, Taxation, general. Home: # 106 8401 N New Braunfels Ave San Antonio TX 78209-1110 Office: Duncan Weakley & Bressler 603 Navarro St Ste 1000 San Antonio TX 78205-1838 E-mail: rexcruse@duncanlaw.com

CSANK, PAUL LEWIS, lawyer, financial company executive; b. Cleve., Nov. 14, 1939; s. Frank P. and Marie (Palmer) C.; m. Carole J. Nicholson, Aug. 4, 1965; children— Melissa, Aaron. B.A., Ohio State U., 1963; J.D., Cleve.-Marshall Law Sch., 1967. Bar: Ohio 1967, U.S. Dist. Ct. (no. dist.) Ohio 1969, Fla. 1982. Pres. Csank Csank & Weiner, Cleve., 1967— , ptnr., Palm Beach, Fla., 1983— ; sec., gen. counsel, dir. Broadview Fin. Corp., Broadview Savs. and Loan, Cleve., 1974— ; Mem. Ohio Bar Assn., Fla. Bar Assn., Cleve. Bar Assn., ABA. Banking, Real property, Securities. Office: Broadview Fin Corp 1215 Superior Ave E Cleveland OH 44114-3249

CUBITTO, ROBERT J. lawyer; b. Globe, Ariz., Aug. 1, 1950; s. Claude A. and Arizona C. (DiMario) C. BA, U. Ariz., 1972, BSBA, 1974; JD, Harvard Law Sch., 1976. Bar: Mass. 1977, N.Y. 1979, U.S. Dist. Ct. (so. and ea. dists.) N.Y. 1979, U.S. Tax Ct. 1979. Cons. Boston Cons. Group, 1976-78; assoc. Debevoise & Plimpton, N.Y.C., 1978-84, ptnr., 1985—. Mem. ABA, N.Y. State Bar Assn. (exec. com. tax sect. 1987-88), Assn. of Bar of City of N.Y., Harvard Club N.Y.C. (asst. treas. 1985-89, bd. mgrs. 1990-93), The Club of Turtle Bay (treas. 1994-97, pres. 1998—). Corporate taxation, Taxation, general. Office: Debevoise & Plimpton 919 3rd Ave New York NY 10022-3904

CUDAHY, RICHARD D. federal judge; b. Milwaukee, Wisc., Feb. 2, 1926; s. Michael F. and Alice (Dickson) C.; m. Ann Featherston, July 14, 1956 (dec. 1974); m. Janet Stuart, July 17, 1976; children: Richard D., Norma K., Theresa E., Daniel M., Michaela A., Marguerite L., Patrick G. BS, U.S. Mil. Acad., 1948; JD, Yale U., 1955; LLD, Ripon Coll., 1981, DePaul U., 1995, Wabash Coll., 1996, Stetson U., 1998. Bar: Conn. 1955, D.C. 1957, Ill. 1957, Wis. 1961. Commd. 2d. lt. U.S. Army, 1948, advanced through grades to 1st lt., 1950; law clk. to presiding judge U.S. Ct. Appeals (2d cir.), 1955-56; asst. to legal adv. Dept. State, 1956-57; assoc. Isham, Lincoln & Beale, Chgo., 1957-60; pres. Patrick Cudahy, Inc., Wis., 1961-71, Patrick Cudahy Family Co., 1968-75; ptnr. firm Godfrey & Kahn, Milw., 1972; commr., chmn. Wis. Pub. Svc. Commn., 1972-75; ptnr. Isham, Lincoln & Beale, Chgo. and Washington, 1976-79; judge U.S. Ct Appeals (7th cir.), Chgo., 1979-94, sr. judge, 1994—. Lectr. law Marquette U. Law Sch., 1962; vis. prof. law U. Wis., 1966-67; prof. lectr. law George Washington U., Washington, 1978-79; adj. prof. DePaul U. Coll. Law, 1995—. Commr. Milw. Harbor, 1964-66; pres. Milw. Urban League, 1965-66; trustee Environ. Def. Fund, 1976-79; chmn. DePaul Human Rights Law Inst., 1990-98; mem. adv. com. Ctr. for Internat. Human Rights, Northwestern U., 2000—; chmn. Wis. Dem. party, 1967-68; Dem. candidate for Wis. atty. gen., 1968. Mem. ABA (spl. com. on Energy Law 1978-84, 90-96, pub. utility/sect. coun. group), Am. Law Inst., Wis. Bar Assn., Milw. Bar Assn., Chgo. Bar Assn., Fed. Judges' Assn. (bd. dirs.), Am. Inst. for Pub. Svc. (bd. selectors), Cath. Theol. Union (trustee), Lawyers Club Chgo. (pres. 1992-93, spl. divsn. D.C. cir. for appt. ind. counsel 1998—). Roman Catholic. Office: US Ct Appeals 219 S Dearborn St Ste 2722 Chicago IL 60604-1874

CUIFFO, FRANK WAYNE, lawyer; b. Houston, Oct. 13, 1943; s. Richard and Helen (Giaco) C.; m. Barbara Joyce Streeter, Nov. 26, 1966; children: Karen, Deborah, Richard, Steven. BS, U. Notre Dame, 1964; JD, Fordham U., 1967. Bar: N.Y. 1967. Assoc. Pennie & Edmonds (formerly Pennie, Edmonds, Morton, Taylor & Adams), N.Y.C., 1967-69; sr. assoc. Emmet, Marvin, & Martin, 1969-74, Golenbock & Barell, N.Y.C., 1974-78; mng. ptnr. Carro, Spanbock, Kaster & Cuiffo, 1978-93; chmn. real estate dept., exec. com. Donovan, Leisure, Newton & Irvine, 1993-98; ptnr. McDermott, Will & Emery, 1998—. Mem. ABA, U.S. Patent Bar, N.Y. State Bar, Siwanoy Country Club, South Seas Club. Real property. Office: McDermott Will & Emery 50 Rockefeller Plz Fl 12 New York NY 10020-1600

CULBERT, PETER V. lawyer; b. San Antonio, July 27, 1944; s. Robert William and Dorothy Fairfax (Kift) C.; m. Elizabeth Tamara Spagnola, July 12, 1980; children: Michael, Daniel, Robert, David, William. BA, Cornell U., 1966; MA, SUNY, Buffalo, 1969; JD, U. N.Mex., 1977. Bar: N.Mex. 1977, U.S. Dist. Ct. N.Mex. 1977, U.S. Ct. Appeals (10th cir.) 1977. Law clk. to Hon. Mack Easley N.Mex. Supreme Ct., Santa Fe, 1977-78; sr. ptnr. Jones, Snead, Wertheim, Wentworth & Jaramillo, 1978-98; pvt. practice, 1998—. Mem. adv. bd., legal counsel Desert Chorale, Santa Fe, 1991—, bd. dirs., 1986-91. Recipient hon. cert. Strathmore Registry Bus. Leaders, 1995-97. Mem. ABA, ATLA, N.Mex. Trial Lawyers Assn., Canyon Assn., Alpha Delta Phi (life). Avocations: flamenco guitarist, bicycling, horticulture, camping. General civil litigation, Insurance, Personal injury. Office: 911 Old Pecos Trl Santa Fe NM 87501-4566 E-mail: pvculbert@law-sf.com

CULLEN, JACK JOSEPH, lawyer; b. Sept. 20, 1951; s. Ray Brandes (stepfather) and Helen Cullen; m. Deborah L. Vick, Oct. 28, 1978; children: Cameron, Katherine. BA, Western Wash. State Coll., 1973; JD, U. Puget Sound, 1976. Bar: Wash. 1977, U.S. Dist. Ct. (we. dist.) Wash. 1977, U.S. Dist. Ct. (ea. dist.) Wash. 1977, U.S. Tax Ct. 1984, U.S. Ct. Appeals (9th cir.) 1980. Staff atty. Wash. State Bar Assn., Seattle, 1977-79; assoc. Hatch & Leslie, 1979-85, mng. ptnr., 1985-91; ptnr. Foster Pepper & Shefelman, 1991-96, mng. ptnr., 1996—, mng. chair, 1991—. Spkr. in field. Co-author: Prejudgment Attachment, 1986. Active Frank Lloyd Wright Bldg. Conservancy, 1989—; trustee Seattle Repertory Theater, 1999—. Mem. ABA (bus. law sect.), Am. Bankruptcy Inst., Wash. State Bar Assn. (creditor-debtor sect., chair exec. 1982-90, spl. dist. counsel 1988—, hearing officer 1990), Seattle-King County Bar Assn. (bankruptcy rules subcom. 1988-90), Vancouver-Seattle Involvency Group (charter mem. 1990—), U.S. Sport Parachuting Team (nat. and world champions 1976, instrument rated pilot). Bankruptcy, Contracts commercial, Real property. Office: Foster Pepper & Shefelman PLLC 1111 3rd Ave Ste 3400 Seattle WA 98101-3299 E-mail: jc@foster.com

CULLEN, JAMES D. lawyer; b. St. Louis, May 18, 1925; s. James and Frances C. Cullen; m. Joyce Marie Jackson, Aug. 19, 1950; children: Mary Lynn Cullen Walsh, James D., Michael Parnell, Carol Cullen Bernstein. LLD, St. Louis, 1948. Bar: Mo. 1948. Pvt. practice law, St. Louis. Bd. dirs. Marygrove, Gen. Protestant Children's Home; counsel Dismas House of St. Louis, Richard Greene Co. 1st lt. USAF, 1943-45. Mem. ABA, Mo. Bar Assn., St. Louis Bar Assn., Lawyers Assn. St. Louis, MAC Club. Roman Catholic. General corporate, Probate, Real property. Office: 16108 Wladen Pond La Saint Louis MO 63005

CULLEN, RAYMOND T. retired lawyer; b. June 26, 1937; AB, LaSalle Coll., 1959; JD, Temple U., 1969. Bar: Pa. 1969; U.S. Supreme Ct. 1977. Mem. Morgan, Lewis & Bockius, Phila. General civil litigation, Intellectual property, Product liability. Office: Morgan Lewis & Bockius 1701 Market St Philadelphia PA 19103-2903

CULLEN, RICHARD, lawyer, former state attorney general; b. N.Y.C., Mar. 10, 1948; m. Agnes Tullidge; children: Thomas, Anne Gray, Elizabeth, Richard. BS, Furman U., 1971; JD, U. Richmond, 1977. Bar: Va. Ptnr. McGuire, Woods, Battle and Boothe, Richmond, 1977-97, 98—; atty. gen. Commonwealth of Va., 1997-98. Spl. counsel Senate Iran-Contra Investigation, 1987; U.S. atty. for ea. dist. Va., 1991-93. Editor-in-chief U. Richmond Law Rev., 1976-77. Mem. Juvenile Criminal Commn.; mem. Va. Criminal Sentencing Commn.; co-chmn. Gov.'s Commn. on Parole Abolition and Sentencing Reform. Office: McGuire, Woods, Battle & Boothe One James Ctr 901 E Cary St Richmond VA 23219-4057

CULLEY, PETER WILLIAM, lawyer; b. Dover-Foxcroft, Maine, Oct. 17, 1943; s. William Redfern and Kathryn (Boyle) C.; children: Courtney Little, Jonathan Redfern. BA, U. Maine, 1965; JD, Boston U., 1968. Bar: Maine 1969, U.S. Dist. Ct. Maine 1969. Asst. atty. gen. Dept. of Atty. Gen. State of Maine, 1969-72, chief, criminal divsn., 1971-72; ptnr. Hewes, Culley and Beals, Portland, Maine, 1972-85, Pierce Atwood, Portland, 1985—. Chmn. Falmouth (Maine) Town Coun., 1986-87. Fellow Am. Coll. Trial Lawyers (state chmn. 1990-92), Am. Bar Found.; mem. ABA, Maine Bar Assn., Internat. Assn. Def. Counsel, Def. Rsch. Inst. (state chmn. 1978-87), No. New Eng. Def. Counsel (pres. 1985-86), Am. Bd. Trial Advocates. Federal civil litigation, General civil litigation, Product liability. Home: 406 Chandlers Wharf Portland ME 04101-4653 Office: Pierce Atwood One Monument Sq Portland ME 04101 E-mail: pculley@pierceatwood.com

CULLINA, WILLIAM MICHAEL, lawyer; b. Hartford, Conn., July 22, 1921; s. Michael Stephen and Margaret (Carroll) C.; m. Gertrude Evelyn Blasig, Apr. 29, 1961; children: William Gregory, Kevin Michael, John Stephen, Susan Margaret. AB, Catholic U. Am., 1942; LLB, Yale U., 1948. Bar: Conn. bar 1948. Assoc. Murtha Cullina LLP, Hartford, 1948—, ptnr., 1952-91, of counsel, 1992—. Bd. dirs. St. Francis Hosp. and Med. Ctr.; trustee St. Joseph Coll., 1986-98, trustee emeritus, 1998—; bd. govs. The Hartford Club, 1984-89, chair, 1987-88. Served with USNR, 1942-46. Fellow Am. Bar Found.; mem. ABA, Conn. Bar Assn., Hartford County Bar Assn., Hartford Tennis Club, Country Club of Farmington, Knight of St. Gregory, Phi Beta Kappa. Roman Catholic. Office: Murtha Cullina LLP City Pl 185 Asylum St Ste 29 Hartford CT 06103-3469

CULLUM, JAMES EDWARD, lawyer; b. Kingston, N.Y., Sept. 10, 1940; s. James Edward and Dorothy Ann (Donnelly) C.; m. Constance Mary Dyer, July 30, 1966; children— James Cullum, Kristin, Michael. B.S., Union U. Albany Coll. Pharmacy, 1962; LL.B., Albany Law Sch., 1967. Bar: N.Y. 1968, U.S. Dist. Ct. (no. dist.) N.Y. 1968, U.S. Ct. Apls. (2d cir.) 1971. Assoc. Wager, Taylor, Howd & Brearton, Troy, N.Y., 1967-69; adv. atty. N.Y. State Envron. Facilties Corp., Albany, 1969-71; asst. U.S. atty. U.S. Dept. Justice, Albany, 1971-76; ptnr. McPhillips, Fitzgerald, Meyer & McLenithan, Glens Falls, N.Y., 1976— . Lic. pharmacist, N.Y. Bd. dirs. United Cerebral Palsy Tri Counties, 1978— , chmn. bd., 1980-83; bd. dirs. Glens Falls YMCA, 1981-87, Tricounty United Way, 1988-94. Recipient Spl. Achievement award U.S. Atty. Gen., 1976. Mem. N.Y. State Bar Assn., Warren County Bar Assn. (bd. dirs. 1980-82, 94—, chmn. com. on ops. of ct. 1980-82, 84-85), Assn. Trial Lawyers Am. Republican. Roman Catholic. State civil litigation, General practice, Personal injury. Home: 19 Cedarwood Dr Queensbury NY 12804-1313 Office: McPhillips Fitzgerald Meyer & McLenithan 288 Glen St Glens Falls NY 12801-3501

CULMO, ELISABETH M. lawyer; b. Medford, Mass., Aug. 4, 1969; d. Robert Johnson and Kathleen Anne Francisca McCloskey; m. Thomas A. Culmo, Feb. 19, 2000. BA in Govt. and Law, Am. U., 1991; JD, U. Fla., Gainesville, 1994. Bar: Fla., U.S. Dist. Ct. (so. dist.) Fla. Assoc. Josephs, Jack & Gaebe, Miami, Fla., 1994—. Mem. AMA, Fla. Bar Assn., Dade County Bar Assn., Coral Gables Bar Assn., Acad. Fla. Trial Lawyers, Assn. Trial Lawyers Am. Democrat. Episcopalian. Avocations: running, cycling, guitar, piano, cooking. Office: Josephs Jack and Gaebe 2950 SW 27th Ave Ste 100 Miami FL 33133-3765

CULP, JAMES DAVID, lawyer, educator; b. Montgomery, Ala., June 12, 1951; s. Delos Poe and Martha Edwardine (Street) C.; m. Gretchen Ina Greene, Aug. 4, 1974; children: James Delos, Sarah Diana, Rebecca Caroline. B.S., East Tenn. State U., 1973, M.A., 1978; J.D., U. Tenn., 1977. Bar: Tenn. 1978, U.S. Dist. Ct. (ea. dist.) Tenn. 1978. Pvt. practice, Johnson City, Tenn., 1978-79; ptnr. Culp and Fleming, 1979-81, Thornton, Culp and Fleming, Johnson City, 1981-83; pvt. practice Jonesborough, Tenn., 1983-86; city staff atty. Johnson City, 1987—. Part-time instr. polit. sci. East Tenn. State U., 1980, Milligan Coll., 1994—; part-time instr. bus. law Draughons Jr. Coll., 1983-85 Active Johnson City Symphony Orch., 1969-74, Jr. Achievement, 1978-79; pres. Alcohol and Drug Counseling and Prevention Ctr., 1981-82; mem. East Tenn. State U. Wesley Found., 1979—, treas., 1981-82; mem. Upper East Tenn. Council on Alcoholism and Drug Dependence, 1981-83; mem. East Tenn. State U. Friends of Music, 1981-82, pres., 1982; mem. Johnson City Bd. Dwelling Standards and Rev., 1983-87, Washington County Election Commn., 1986-87. Served with USNR, 1971-73. Mem. Washington County Bar Assn., Tenn. Mcpl. Attys. Assn. (pres. 1992-93), Tenn. Trial Lawyers Assn., Mensa, Internat. Soc. for Philos. Enquiry, Am. Legion (judge adv. 1981-82), Johnson City Jaycees (state dir. 1979, named Spoke of Yr. 1978-79), Rotary. Democrat. Methodist. State civil litigation, Criminal, General practice. Home: 1634 Fairway Dr Johnson City TN 37601-2614 Office: 804 West Market St Johnson City TN 37604 E-mail: jcinjc@charter.net

CULP, NATHAN CRAIG, lawyer; b. Camden, Ark., 1965; s. Harold Lloyd and Carole Culp; m. Clara M. Graves, 1995. BA, La. Tech. U., 1988; JD, U. Ark., 1991. Bar: Ark. 1991, U.S. Dist. Ct. Ark. 1992. Law clk. Walker, Roaf, Campbell, Ivory and Dunklin, Little Rock, 1989-91, assoc., 1991-94; staff atty. Pub. Employee Claims divsn. Ark. Dept. Ins., 1994-99, Ark. Hwy. and Transp. Dept., 1999-2000; asst. dir. pub. employee claims div. Ark. Dept. Ins., Little Rock, 2000—. Mem. Ark. Bar Assn., Pulaski County Bar Assn. Methodist. Avocations: computers, reading. Office: Pub Employee Claims Div Ark Ins Dept 1200 West Third St Ste 201 Little Rock AR 72201

CUMBERLAND, WILLIAM EDWIN, lawyer; b. Washington, Sept. 11, 1938; m. Clare Hogan, Aug. 17, 1973; children: Lisa, Joseph, Kara. AB, Georgetown U., 1960; LLB, Harvard U., 1963. Bar: D.C. 1963, Va. 1963. Law clk. to judge U.S. Dist. Ct. D.C., Washington, 1963-64; from assoc. to ptnr. Cefaratti & Cumberland, 1964-71; atty. HUD, 1971-72; counsel Mortgage Bankers Assn. Am., 1972—, gen. counsel, sr. v.p., 1988-2000. Cons. Mortgage Banks Assn., 2000—. Banking, Finance, Real property.

CUMBOW, ROBERT CHARLES, lawyer, writer, educator; b. Columbus, Ohio, Oct. 22, 1946; s. Robert M. and Margaret Joan (O'Connor) C.; m. Grace Blond, Sept. 6, 1975; children: Rachel Elizabeth, Irena Alexis. BA in English, Seattle U., 1967, MA in English, 1969; JD, U. Puget Sound, 1991. News media rep. Puget Sound Power and Light, Bellevue, Wash., 1984-86, corp. communications coordinator, 1986-91; assoc. Perkins Coie, Seattle, 1991-99; shareholder Graham & Dunn, 1999—. Prof. law Seattle U. Law Sch., 1997—. Author: Pardon Me, Roy, 1983, Once Upon a Time: The Films of Sergio Leone, 1987, A Century of Service: The Puget Power Story, 1987, Order in the Universe: The Films of John Carpenter, 1990, 2d edit., 2000, West Pointers and Early Washington, 1992; contbr. articles on film to profl. jours. Bd. dirs. Wash. Lawyers for the Arts, 1994-2001, pres., 2000-01, Seattle Mime Theatre, 1996-99; vol. Bus. Vols. for the Arts, 1994-99. With U.S. Army, 1969-71. Recipient Copy Desk awards Dept. of Def., 1970-71, Army Commendation medal, 1971; George Boldt scholar, 1989, 90, 91, Wash. Superior Ct. Judges, 1989-90. Mem. Wash. State Bar Assn. (mem. editl. bd. 1993-97, internat. property sec., 1999-) Republican. Roman Catholic. Avocations: film, music, games, puzzles. Computer, Intellectual property, Trademark and copyright. Office: Graham & Dunn 1420 5th Ave Seattle WA 98101-2390 E-mail: rcumbow@grahamdunn.com

CUMMINGS, ANTHONY WILLIAM, lawyer, educator, banker; b. Port Jefferson, N.Y., Dec. 3, 1962; s. Leonard and Annie (Earl) C. Student, Tulane U., 1980-81; BS in Applied Econs., Hofstra U., 1985, JD, 1988; MBA, U. N.C., 1997. Bar: N.Y. 1988, D.C. 1990, U.S. Dist. Ct. (ea. and so. dists.) N.Y. 1990, U.S. Ct. Mil. Appeals 1990, U.S. Ct. Appeals (2d, 11th and fed. cirs.) 1991, U.S. Tax Ct. 1991, U.S. Supreme Ct. 1992, N.C. 1995. Assoc. Ronald J. Rosenberg, Garden City, N.Y., 1988-89; of counsel Costa & Bernsten, Hauppauge, 1989-92; contract atty. Bernsten & Newman, 1990-93; pvt. practice, Patchogue, N.Y., 1990-94, Raleigh, N.C., 1994-97; assoc. Fin. Instns. Group, 1995-97, First Union Securities, Inc., Charlotte, N.C., 1997-2000; v.p. Hales & Co., N.Y.C., 2000—. Adj. instr. law Suffolk County C.C., Selden, N.Y., 1992-94; coord. adminstrv. svcs. N.C. Biotech. Ctr., Research Triangle Park, N.C., 1994-95; adj. instr. bus. Wake Tech. C.C., Raleigh, 1995-97; coord., lectr. CLE programs Suffolk Acad. Law. 1989-94; co-chmn. appellate practice com. Suffolk County Bar Assn.; judge Jessup Internat. Law Moot Ct. Competition, 1990-91; pres. Cummings Capital Advisors LLC; adj. prof. law Hofstra U. Zarb Sch. Bus. Editor-in-chief Hofstra Property Law Jour., 1988; assoc. editor Jour. Suffolk Acad. Law, 1992-94. Pres. U. N.C. MBA Student Assn., 1996-97. Recipient award of recognition Suffolk County Bar Assn., 1991, cert. of disting. merit Suffolk Acad. Law, 1991. Mem. ABA, Am. Coll. Forensic

Examiners, N.C. State Bar Assn., D.C. Bar Assn., N.Y. State Bar Assn., Hofstra U. Alumni Orgn. (exec. coun. 1990-94), Scabbard and Blade, Phi Eta Sigma. Banking, General corporate, Finance. Office: Hales & Co 250 Park Ave New York NY 10177-0001 also: PO Box 672 Babylon NY 11702 E-mail: acummings@halesgroup.com, cummingsanthony @mindspring-.com

CUMMINGS, FRANK, lawyer; b. N.Y.C., Dec. 11, 1929; s. Louise and Florence (Levine) C.; m. Jill Schwartz, July 6, 1958; children: Peter Ian, Margaret Anne. BA, Hobart Coll., 1951; MA, Columbia U., 1955, LLB, 1958. Bar: N.Y. 1959, D.C. 1963. Adminstrv. asst. to U.S. Senator Jacob Javits, 1969-71; minority counsel com. labor and pub. welfare U.S. Senate, Washington, 1965-67, 71-72; assoc. Cravath, Swaine & Moore, N.Y.C., 1958-63, Gall, Lane & Powell, Washington, 1967-68, ptnr., 1972-75, Marshall, Bratter, Greene, Allison & Tucker, Washington, 1976-85, Nossaman, Keurger & Knox, 1982-83, Cummings & Cummings, P.C. and predecessor firm, 1983-86, LeBoeuf, Lamb, Greene & MacRae, LLP, Washington, 1986-2000, of counsel, 2000—. Lectr. law Columbia U. Law Sch., 1970-74, U. Va. Sch. Law, 2000—; adj. prof. Georgetown U. Law Sch., 1983-86; chmn. Am. Law Inst.-ABA Ann. Course Employee Benefits Litigation, 1989—, Employment and Labor Rels. Law for Corp. Coun. and Gen. Practitioner, 1978—; mem. pub. adv. coun. employee welfare and pension benefit plans Dept. Labor, 1972-74; mem. adv. bd. Pension Reporter Bur. Nat. Affairs. Author: Capitol Hill Manual, 1976, Capitol Hill Manual, 2d edit., 1984, Pension Plan Terminations-Single Employer Plans, 3rd edit., 2001, Multiemployer Plans, 2d edit., 1986; articles editor: Columbia U. Law Rev., 1957—58. Mem. ABA (chmn. com. pension, welfare and related plans 1976-79), Am. Law Inst., Bar Assn. D.C. (chmn. com. labor rels. law 1972-73), Cosmos Club, Phi Beta Kappa. Federal civil litigation, Insurance, Pension, profit-sharing, and employee benefits. Home: 4305 Bradley Ln Chevy Chase MD 20815-5232 Office: LeBoeuf Lamb Greene & MacRae LLP 1875 Connecticut Ave NW Washington DC 20009-5728 E-mail: fcumming@llgm.com

CUMMINGS, JOHN PATRICK, lawyer; b. Westfield, Mass., June 28, 1933; s. Daniel Thoams and Nora (Brick) C.; m. Dorothy June D'Ingianni, Dec. 27, 1957 (div. May 1978); children: John Patrick, Mary Catherine, Michael Brick, Kevin Andrew, Colleen Elise, Erin Christine, Christopher Gerald; m. Marilyn Ann Welch, May 23, 1980. BS, St. Michael's Coll., 1955; PhD, U. Tex., 1969; JD, U. Toledo, 1973, MCE, 1977. Bar: Ohio 1973, U.S. Mil. Appeals 1974, U.S. Dist. Ct. (no. dist.) Ohio 1979. Mgr. Hamilton Mgmt., Inc., Austin, Tex., 1962-68; scientist Owens Ill., Toledo, 1968-73, risk mgr., 1974-76, staff atty., 1977-80, mgr. legis. affairs, 1981-84; pres. Hansa World Cargo Svc., Inc., Oakland, Calif., 1984-86; in-house counsel Brown Vence & Assocs., San Francisco, 1987-88; gen. counsel Pacific Mgmt. Co., Sacramento, 1986-88; pres. John P. Cummings & Assoc., Fremont, Calif., 1988—. Cons. Glass Packaging Inst., Washington, 1970-83, EPA, Washington, 1970-74. Contbr. articles to profl. jours.; patentee in field. With USAF, 1955-62, 68-69, 75-76, 84-85, col. Res. ret. 1986. USPHS fellow, 1963-66. Fellow Royal Chem. Soc.; mem. ABA, VFW, Am. Chem. Soc., ASTM (chmn. 1979), Am. Ceramic Soc. (chpt. chmn. 1973), Res. Officers Assn. (legis. chmn. 1979-85), Am. Legion, KC (4th degree). Roman Catholic. Avocations: reading, travel, coin and stamp collecting. Environmental, Immigration, naturalization, and customs, Private international. Home: 843 Barcelona Dr Fremont CA 94536-2607 Office: PO Box 2847 Fremont CA 94536-0847 E-mail: epigeneint@aol.com

CUMMINGS, WILLIAM ROGER, international tax consultant, property management executive; b. Apr. 30, 1946; BBA, U. Miami, 1968, LLM, 1973; JD, Suffolk U., 1968; MBA, Fla. Atlantic U., 1978. Pvt. practice internat. tax mgmt., Palm Beach, Fla., 1971—. Mem.: Palm Beach C. of C., Mensa, English Spkg. Union, Phi Delta Theta. Republican. Episcopalian. Office: PO Box 7 Palm Beach FL 33480-0007

CUMMINS, CHARLES FITCH, JR. lawyer; b. Lansing, Mich., Aug. 19, 1939; s. Charles F. Sr. and Ruth M. Cummins; m. Anne Warner, Feb. 11, 1961; children: Michael, John, Mark. AB in Econs., U. Mich., 1961; LLB, U. Calif., Hastings, 1966. Bar: Calif. 1966, Mich. 1976. Assoc. Hall, Henry, Oliver & McReavy, San Francisco, 1966-70, ptnr., 1971-75, Cummins & Cummins, Lansing, Mich., 1976-82, Pitto & Ubhaus, San Jose, Calif., 1982-85; prin. Law Offices Charles F. Cummins Jr., 1985-87; ptnr. Cummins & Chandler, 1987-92; prin. Law Offices of Charles F. Cummins, Jr., 1992—. Bd. dirs., officer various civic orgns., chs. and pvt. shcs. Lt. (j.g.) USNR, 1961-63. Mem. Rotary. Alternative dispute resolution, General civil litigation, Estate planning. Office: 224 E Jackson St Ste B San Jose CA 95112 E-mail: cfclaw@ix.netcom.com

CUMMIS, CLIVE SANFORD, lawyer; b. Newark, Nov. 21, 1928; s. Joseph Jack and Lee (Berkie) C.; m. Ann Denburg, Mar. 24, 1956; children: Andrea, Deborah, Cynthia, Jessica. A.B., Tulane U., 1949; J.D., U. Pa., 1952; LL.M., N.Y. U., 1959. Bar: N.J. 1952. Law sec. Hon. Walter Freund, Appellate Div., Superior Ct., 1955-56; partner firm Cummis & Kroner, Newark, 1956-60; chief counsel County and Mcpl. Law Revision Commn., State of N.J., 1959-62; partner firm Schiff, Cummis & Kent, 1962-67, Cummis, Kent, Radin & Tischman, Newark, 1967-70; sr. v.p., dir. Cadence Industries, N.Y.C., 1967-70; dir. Plume & Atwood Industries, Stamford, Conn., 1969-71; chmn. Sills Cummis Radin Tischman Epstein & Gross, Newark, 1970—; exec. v.p. law and corp. affairs, sec., vice chmn. bd. dirs. Park Place Entertainment corp., Chatham, N.J. Dir. Essex County State Bank, Financial Resources Group; instr. Practising Law Inst. Chief counsel County and Mcpl. Revision Commn., 1959-62, N.J. Pub. Market Commn., 1961-63; counsel Bd. Edn. of South Orange and Maplewood, 1964-74, Town of Cedar Grove, 1966-70, Bd. Edn. of Dumont, 1968-72; mem. com. on rules and civil practice N.J. Supreme Ct., 1975-78. Assoc. editor NJ. Law Jour., 1961—. Trustee Newark Beth Israel Med. Ctr., 1965-75, Northfield YM-YWHA, 1968-70, U. Medicine and Dentistry N.J., 1980-84, Newark Mus., N.J. Performing Arts Ctr., Blue Cross and Blue Shield N.J.; gen. coun. N.J. Turnpike Authority, 1990-94; mem. bd. overseers U. Pa. Law Sch., 1991-96; mem. bd. govts. Daus. of Israel Home for Aged, 1968-70; mem. N.J. Commn. on Statue of Liberty; mem. pres.'s coun. Tulane U., 1992—; pres. bd. dirs. Tulane Assocs., 1994-96; mem. Pres.'s commn. on White House Fellows, 1993-2001; dir. N.J. Regional Planning Assn. Recipient 1st Ann. Judge Learned Hand award Am. Jewish Com., 1994. Fellow Am. Bar Found.; mem. ABA, Am. Law Inst., Am. Judicature Soc., U. Pa. Law Sch. Alumni Soc. (pres.), N.J. Bar Assn., Essex County Bar Assn., City Athletic Club (N.Y.C.), Greenbrook County Club (North Caldwell, N.J.), Stockbridge Golf Club (Mass.). Democrat. Jewish. Administrative and regulatory, Federal civil litigation, State civil litigation. Office: Sills Cummis Radin Tischman Epstein & Gross One Riverfront Pl Newark NJ 07102 also: Park Place Entertainment Corp Chatham NJ 07928 also: Park Place Entertainment Corp Las Vegas NV 89109 E-mail: ccummis@sillscummis.com, cummisc@ballys.com

CUNDIFF, JAMES NELSON, lawyer; b. Perkins, Okla., Dec. 18, 1954; s. Nelson A. and Meryl E. C. BSBA, Okla. State U., 1976; JD, U. Tulsa, 1979. Bar: Okla. 1979, U.S. Dist. Ct. (we. dist.) Okla. 1979, U.S. Dist. Ct. (no. dist.) Okla. 1980, U.S. Ct. Appeals (10th cir.) 1980. Asst. CLE dir. Okla. Bar Assn., Oklahoma City, 1979-80; contract coordinator Cities Svc. Co., Tulsa, 1980-81; atty. ETSI Pipeline Project, 1981-85, Mapco Inc., Tulsa, 1985-88, sr. atty., 1988-89, corp. sr. atty., asst. sec., 1989-91, asst. gen. counsel, asst. sec., 1991-97; gen. counsel, asst. sec. New Ventures & Corp. Svcs., 1997-98; sr. atty. internat. Williams Cos. Inc., 1998—. Continuing legal edn. resource bd. Tulsa U. Coll. Law, 1983-85, bd. dirs. Alumni Assn., 1993-98. Bd. dirs. Hyde Park Homeowners Assn., Tulsa, 1984-88, 89-97; bd. dirs. Downtown Tulsa, Unltd., 1990-91; mem. Leadership Tulsa, 1990-91; chmn. bd. trustees, pres. The Free Enterprise Found., Inc., 1989-93; oil and gas legal com. Ctr. for Pub. Resources, 1990-94, subcom. on environ. law, 1991-95; adv. bd. Jr. Divsn. of the Tulsa Philharmonic Soc., Inc., 1992-94. Mem. ABA, Okla. Bar Assn. (sec. house counsel sect. 1987, chmn. 1989-90), Tulsa County Bar Assn., Internat. Bar Assn., Am. Corp. Counsel Assn. (bd. dirs. Okla. chpt. 1986-88), Am. Soc. Corp. Secs. (securities law com. 1992-99, nat. mem. com. 1994-95, nat. bd. dirs. 1996-99, sec.-treas. Okla. Chpt. 1993-94, v.p. and mem. chmn. 1994-95, v.p. and program chmn. 1995-96, pres. 1996-97, adv. bd. 1997—), Phi Delta Phi, Phi Kappa Phi, Beta Gamma Sigma. Democrat. Baptist. Avocations: travel, swimming, oil painting. Contracts commercial, General corporate, Private international. Office: The Williams Cos Inc 1 Williams Ctr Ste 4100 Tulsa OK 74172-0140 E-mail: jim.cundiff@williams.com

CUNEO, DONALD LANE, lawyer, educator; b. Alameda, Calif., Apr. 19, 1944; s. Vernon Edmund and Dorothy (Lane) c.; m. Frances Susan Huze, Aug. 8, 1981; children: Kristen Marie, Lane Michael. BA, Lehigh U., 1966; JD, MBA, Columbia U., 1970. Bar: N.Y. 1971, D.C. 1992, U.S. Claims Ct. 1972, U.S. Tax Ct. 1972, U.S. Dist. Ct. (so. dist.) N.Y. 1973, U.S. Dist. Ct. (no. dist.) 1978, U.S. Dist. Ct. D.C. 1992, U.S. Ct. Appeals (2nd cir.) 1979, U.S. Ct. Appeals (D.C. cir.) 1992, U.S. Ct. Internat. Trade 1979, U.S. Ct. Appeals (fed. cir.) 1979, U.S. Supreme Ct. 1979. Assoc. Shearman & Sterling, N.Y.C., 1971-79, ptnr., 1979-93; pres., CEO Internat. House, 1993—. Sec./trustee Internat. House, N.Y.C., 1977-93; pres. Morningside Area Alliance, N.Y.C., 2000—. Author: (with others) Prevention and Prosecution of Computer and High Technology Crime, 1988; contbr. articles to profl. jours. Reginald Heber Smith Cmty. Lawyer fellow U.S. Govt., 1970-71. Mem. Coun. Fgn. Rels. Avocations: sports, travel. General civil litigation, Private international. Home and Office: Internat House 500 Riverside Dr New York NY 10027-3916

CUNHA, MARK GEOFFREY, lawyer; b. Lexington, Mass., Sept. 26, 1955; s. John Henry and Dolores (DeRosas) c.; m. Viviane Sirotto; children: Celine Yvonne, Nicholas Brian. AB magna cum laude, Cornell U., 1977; JD, Stanford U., 1980. Bar: N.Y. 1981, U.S. Dist. Ct. (so. and ea. dists.) N.Y. 1981, U.S. Ct. Appeals (2nd cir.) 1991, U.S. Tax Ct. 1992, U.S. Supreme Ct. 1996, U.S. Ct. Appeals (3d cir.) 2001. Intern The White House, Washington, 1979-80; assoc. Simpson Thacher & Bartlett, N.Y.C., 1980-88, ptnr., 1989—. Mediator comml. divsn. N.Y. State Supreme Ct., N.Y. County, 1996—; bd. dir. legal svcs. for N.Y.C., 1997—. Bd. dirs. N.Y. Lawyers for Pub. Interest, 1989—; trustee Inst. for Ednl. Achievement, 1995—, Lycee Francais N.Y., 1998—. Recipient Outstanding Vol. Lawyers award Legal Aid Soc., 1990, Pro Bono award N.Y. County Lawyers Assn., 1991. Mem.: ABA, Internat. Bar Assn., N.Y. State Bar Assn. (exec. com. on comml. and fed. litigation sect.), Assn. Bar City N.Y. (sec. exec. com., chmn. com. on legal assistance , chmn. del. to N.Y. State Bar Assn. Ho. of Dels., steering com. on legal assistance), Phi Beta Kappa. Democrat. Insurance, Product liability, Securities. Home: 1150 Fifth Ave Apt 3A New York NY 10128-0724 Office: Simpson Thacher & Bartlett 425 Lexington Ave New York NY 10017-3954 E-mail: mcunha@stblaw.com

CUNNINGHAM, ALICE WELT, lawyer, legal educator; b. Washington, Aug. 18, 1949; d. Samuel Louis and Beatrice (Boxer) Welt; m. Daniel Paul Cunningham, Aug. 10, 1975; adopted children: Stephen Paul, Philip James1 child Samuel Paul (dec.). BA summa cum laude, Yale U., 1971; JD, Harvard U., 1974; MA in Math. Edn., Columbia U., 2001, postgrad., 2001—. Bar: N.Y. 1975, Calif. 1975, U.S. Dist. Ct. (no. dist.) Calif. 1975, U.S. Ct. Appeals (fed. cir.) 1980, U.S. Tax Ct. 1976. Assoc. Shearman & Sterling, N.Y.C., 1974-75, Heller Ehrman, White & McAuliffe, San Francisco, 1975-78, Debevoise & Plimpton, N.Y.C., 1978-83; assoc. prof. N.Y. Law Sch., 1983-86. Contbr. articles to profl. jours. Mem.: ABA, N.Y. State Bar Assn., Assn. Bar City N.Y., Phi Beta Kappa, Kappa Delta Pi.

CUNNINGHAM, BRIAN C. lawyer, corporate executive; b. Sparta Ill., Oct. 17, 1943; s. Robert C. and Gail L. (McDill) C.; m. Martha Elizabeth Kerr; children: Laura, Scott, Colby. B.S. in Elec. Engring., Washington U., St. Louis, 1965, J.D., 1970. Bar: N.Y. 1971, Mo. 1980, Calif. 1983, U.S. Dist. Ct. (so. dist.) N.Y. 1974, U.S. Dist. Ct. (no. dist.) Calif. 1983. Vol., U.S. Peace Corps, Washington, 1965-67; assoc. Winthrop, Stimpson Putnam & Roberts, N.Y.C., 1970-79; assoc. corp. counsel Monsanto, St. Louis, 1979-82; v.p., sec., gen. counsel Genentech, South San Francisco, 1982—, also bd. dirs. General corporate, Patent, Securities. Home: 525 Pepper Ave Burlingame CA 94010-6437 Office: Cooley Godward et al 5 Palo Alto Sq Ste 400 Palo Alto CA 94306-2122

CUNNINGHAM, GARY H. lawyer; b. Grand Rapids, Mich., Jan. 11, 1953; s. Gordon H. and Marilyn J. (Lookabill) C.; children: Stephanie M., Gregory H. B.Gen. Studies, U. Mich., 1975, MA, 1977; JD, Detroit Coll. Law, 1980. Bar: Mich. 1980, U.S. Dist. Ct. Mich. 1983, U.S. Ct. Appeals (6th cir.) 1986, U.S. Ct. Appeals (Fed. cir.) 1990. Law clk. and estate adminstr. U.S. Bankruptcy Ct., Ea. Dist. Mich., Detroit, 1980-83; assoc./ptnr. Schlussel, Lifton, Simon, Rands, Galvin & Jackier, Southfield, Mich., 1983-90; ptnr./shareholder Kramer Mellen, P.C., 1990-95; prin. shareholder Strobl Cunningham Caretti & Sharp, P.C., Bloomfield Hills, 1995—. Sr. staff mem. Detroit Coll. of Law Rev., 1978-80; contbr. articles to profl. jours. Mem. ABA (bus. law sect.), Fed. Bar Assn. (chmn. bankruptcy sect. 1989-91), Oakland County Bar Assn. (bus. law com.), State Bar of Mich. (mem. corp., fin. and bus. law sect.), Am. Bankruptcy Inst. (sponsor), Comml. Law League of Am., Detroit Econ. Club, Detroit Inst. Arts, Delta Theta Phi. Avocations: sailing, skiing, tennis. Bankruptcy, General civil litigation, General corporate. Home: 3399 Roxbury Dr Troy MI 48084-2613 Office: Strobl Cunningham Caretti & Sharp PC 300 E Long Lake Rd Ste 200 Bloomfield Hills MI 48304-2376 E-mail: gcunningham@stroblpc.com

CUNNINGHAM, GUY HENRY, III, lawyer; b. Teaneck, N.J., Sept. 28, 1941; s. Guy Henry and Leonor (Lavedan) C.; m. Kathleen Schneider, June 11, 1966; children— Thomas, Douglas. B.A., Alfred U., 1964; J.D., Georgetown U., 1967; M.B.A., U. Pa., 1983. Bar: D.C. 1967, U.S. Ct. Appeals (D.C. cir.) 1970, U.S. Supreme Ct. 1972, Wash. 1991, Ohio, 1998. Asst. U.S. atty. Dept. Justice, Washington, 1969-72; atty. AEC, Washington, 1969-72; asst. gen. counsel Dept. Energy, Washington, 1975-78; atty. supr. Nuclear Regulatory Commn., Washington, 1978-82, exec. legal dir., 1982-86; gen. counsel Pacific N.W. div. Battelle Meml. Inst., Richland, Wash., 1986-97; assoc. gen. counsel Battelle Meml. Inst., Columbus, Ohio, 1997—. Served to capt. U.S. Army, 1967-69; Vietnam. Decorated Bronze Star medal. Republican. Roman Catholic. E-mail: cunninghamg@battelle.org. Home: 167 Green Springs Dr Columbus OH 43235-4644 Office: Battelle Meml Inst 505 King Ave Columbus OH 43201-2693

CUNNINGHAM, JAMES OWEN, lawyer; b. Janesville, Wis., Jan. 16, 1951; s. James A. and Mary E. (Owen) C.; m. Joyce Dickinson, Dec. 16, 1978; children: Emily, James A. BS, Fla. State U., 1973, JD, 1977; MS in Mgmt., Rollins Coll., Winter Park, Fla., 1975. Bar: Fla. 1977, U.S. Ct. Appeals (5th cir.); cert. civil trial adv. Nat. Bd. Trial Adv. Assoc. Fisher & Matthews, Altamonte Springs, Fla., 1970-77, Billings & Durie, Orlando, 1979, Billings & Durie & Morgan, Orlando, 1980; ptnr. Billings, Cunningham, Morgan & Boatwright, 1981—. Bd. dirs. Fla. State U. Coll. Law. Bd. dirs. Orange County Bar Found., 1998—. Mem. Fla. Bar Assn., Am. Trial Lawyers Assn., Fla. Trial Lawyers Assn., Orange County Bar Assn., Orange County Legal Aid Soc. (bd. dirs. 1996-99, pres. 1999—), Seminole County Bar Assn. Republican. Presbyterian. Personal injury. Home: 251 Rippling Ln Winter Park FL 32789-2841 Office: Billings, Cunningham Morgan & Boatwright 330 E Central Blvd Orlando FL 32801-1998 E-mail: jim@bcmb.com

CUNNINGHAM, JOEL DEAN, lawyer; b. Seattle, Feb. 19, 1948; s. Edgar Norwood and Florence (Burgunder) C.; m. Amy Jean Radewan, Oct. 1, 1970; children: Erin Jane, Rad Norwood. BA in Econs., U. Wash., 1971, JD with high honors, 1974. Lawyer, ptnr. Williams, Kastner & Gibbs, Seattle, 1974-95; ptnr. Luvera, Barnett, Brindley, Beninger & Cunningham, 1995—. Fellow Am. Coll. Trial Lawyers, Internat. Soc. Barristers; mem. Am. Bd. Trial Attys. (pres. Washington chpt. 1994), Damage Attys. Round Table, Order of Coif. Avocations: fishing, cycling, boating. General civil litigation, Personal injury, Product liability. Office: Luvera Barnett Brindley Beninger & Cunningham 6700 Columbia Ctr 701 5th Ave Seattle WA 98104-7097

CUNNINGHAM, JUDY MARIE, lawyer; b. Durant, Okla., Sept. 7, 1944; d. Rowe Edwin and Margaret (Arnott) C. BA, U. Tex., 1967, JD, 1971; postgrad., Schiller Coll., Heidelberg, Fed. Republic Germany, 1976. Bar: Tex. 1972. Quizmaster U. Tex. Law Sch., Austin, 1969-71; rschr. Tex. Law Rev., Washington, 1970; staff atty. Tex. Legis. Coun., Austin, 1972-75; adminstrv. law judge, dir. sales tax div., assoc. counsel Comptr. of Pub. Accounts, 1975-85; owner, editor J.C. Law Publs., 1986—; pvt. practice, 1986—. Author: (with others) Texas Tax Service, 1985; pub., editor, contbr. (newsletter) Tex. State Tax Update, 1986—; contbr. articles to Revenue Adminstrn.; assoc. editor Tex. Law Rev., 1968-71. State del. Dem. Party, Ft. Worth, 1990, county del., Austin, 1972, 88, 90, 92; vol. numerous Dem. campaigns, Austin, 1972-90. Mem. Industry Practitioners Liaison Group (comptr. pub. accts.), State Bar Tex. (taxation sect.), Travis County Bar (bus. corp. and taxation sect.), Tex. Taxpayers and Rsch. Assn. Avocations: traveling, cooking, reading mysteries, photography, swimming. Administrative and regulatory, Legislative, State and local taxation. Office: 4905 W Park Dr Austin TX 78731-5535

CUNNINGHAM, PIERCE EDWARD, lawyer, city planner; b. Cin., Aug. 18, 1934; s. Francis E. and Adelaide (Kraus) C.; m. Roberta Roche, Sept. 6, 1958; children: Pierce E., Jr. James M., Sarah Ellen, Anna C. BA, Coll. Holy Cross, 1956; LLB, Georgetown U., 1959. Bar: Ohio 1960, U.S. Supreme Ct. 1977. Atty. Hartford Accident and Indemnity Co., Cin., 1960-61; pvt. practice Hamilton, Ohio, 1961-62; asst. atty. gen. Ohio State Atty. Gen.'s Office, Columbus, 1963-70; prin. Pierce E. Cunningham and Assocs., Cin., 1964-75; ptnr. Clark & Eyrich, 1975-81, Frost & Jacobs, Cin., 1981-97; of counsel Baker Hostetler, Cleve., 1997—. Chmn. Riverfront Adv. Commn., Cin., 1970-72, Zoning Bd. Appeals, Cin., 1970-72; mem. Urban Design and Rev. Bd., Cin. 1970-72, City Planning Com., Cin., 1968-73, chmn. 1970-73. Contbr. articles to profl. jours. Mem. May Festival Com., Cin., 1972-74, Cin. Bar Assn. Vol. Lawyers for Poor. Named Lawyer of Yr. Cin. Bar Assn. Vol. Lawyers for Poor, 1982-83. Mem. Am. Bd. Trial Advs., Ohio Bar Assn. (faculty continuing legal edn.), Cin. Bar Assn. (panel of neutrals CPR 1998—), Am. Arbitration Assn. (midwest region adv. coun., large complex litigation panelist), Cin. Tennis Club (pres. 1976-78), Cin. Country Club (bd. govs. 1995—), Potter Stewart Inn of Ct., Inner Cir. U.S. Senate, 1999—. Avocations: tennis, sailing. Federal civil litigation, State civil litigation, Real property. Home: 8 Hill And Hollow Ln Cincinnati OH 45208-3317 Office: Baker & Hostetler 3200 312 Walnut St Cincinnati OH 45202 E-mail: pcunningham@fuse.net

CUNNINGHAM, ROBERT JAMES, lawyer; b. Kearney, Nebr., June 27, 1942; m. Sara Jean Dickson, July 22, 1967. BA, U. Nebr., 1964; JD, NYU, 1967, LLM in Taxation, 1969. Bar: N.Y. 1967, Ill. 1969, U.S. Dist. Ct. (no. dist.) Ill. 1969, U.S. Ct. Claims 1970, U.S. Tax Ct. 1970, U.S. Ct. Appeals (D.C. cir.) 1972, U.S. Ct. Appeals (9th cir.) 1975, U.S. Ct. Appeals (7th cir.) 1979, U.S. Ct. Appeals (fed. cir.) 1982. Instr. law NYU, N.Y.C., 1967-69; assoc. Baker & McKenzie, Chgo., 1969-74, ptnr., 1974—. Spkr. in field. Contbr. articles to profl. jours. Mem. ABA, Ill. Bar Assn., Chgo. Bar Assn. Private international, Corporate taxation, Taxation, general. Office: Baker & McKenzie One Prudential Plz 130 E Randolph Dr Ste 3700 Chicago IL 60601-6342 E-mail: robert.j.cunningham@bakernet.com

CUNNINGHAM, STANLEY LLOYD, lawyer; b. Durant, Okla., Feb. 7, 1938; s. Stanley Ryan and Hazel Dell (Dillingham) C.; m. Suzanne Yerger, Sept. 18, 1960; children: Stanley William, Ryan Yerger. BS in Geology, U. Okla., 1960, LLB, 1963. Bar: U.S. Dist. Ct. (we. dist.) Okla. 1963; U.S. Ct. Appeals (10th cir.) 1965; U.S. Supreme Ct. Okla. 1963. Atty. Phillips Petroleum Co., Oklahoma City, 1963-64, Bartlesville, Okla., 1964-71; counsel McAfee, Taft, et al., Oklahoma City, 1971—. Lectr. U. Okla. Coll. Law, Norman, 1977, 79, S.W. Legal Found., Dallas, 1986, 89. Contbr. articles to profl. jours. Layreader All Souls' Episcopal Ch., Oklahoma City, 1972-75. 1st lt. USAFR, 1963-72. Harry J. Brown scholar, U. Okla., 1960-63 Mem. ABA, Fed. Energy Bar Assn., Am. Soc. Internat. Law, Geological Soc. Am., Alumni Adv. Coun., U. Okla. Assoc., Oklahoma City Golf & Country Club, Order of Coif, Phi Alpha Delta, Sigma Gamma Epsilon. Republican. Episcopalian. Avocations: golf, reading. General civil litigation, Oil, gas, and mineral. Office: McAfee & Taft 2 Leadership Sq Fl 10 Oklahoma City OK 73102

CUNNINGHAM, THOMAS JUSTIN, lawyer; b. Hinsdale, Ill., Feb. 27, 1968; s. Thomas J. and Diane (Carlton) C.; m. Paula J. Friant, Sept. 9, 1989; children: Thomas Justin, Nicholas Joseph. BS, Ariz. State U., 1989; JD, DePaul U., 1993. Bar: Ill. 1993, U.S. Dist. Ct. (no. dist.) Ill. 1993, U.S. Ct. Appeals (7th cir.) 1993, U.S. Dist. Ct. (ctrl. dist.) Ill. 1996, U.S. Supreme Ct. 1996, Trial bar 1997. Dep. clk. U.S. Bankruptcy Ct., Chgo., 1989-90; law clk. Burke, Smith & Williams, 1990-93; assoc. Smith, Lodge & Schneider, 1993-98, Hopkins & Sutter, Chgo., 1998-2001, Lord, Bissell & Brook, Chgo., 2001. Contbr. articles to profl. jours. Pres. Ill. Dist. 58 Bd. Edn. Mem. Chgo. Bar Assn. (chair moot ct. com. 1995, co-editor in chief YLS jour.). Republican. Presbyterian. Avocations: hunting, fishing. Bankruptcy, Federal civil litigation, Contracts commercial. Home: 5135 Fairview Ave Downers Grove IL 60515-5211 Office: Lord Bissell & Brook 115 S LaSalle 31st Fl Chicago IL 60603 E-mail: tcunningham@lordbissell.com

CUNNINGHAM, TOM ALAN, lawyer; b. Houston, Nov. 5, 1946; s. Warren Peek and Ellen Ardelle (Benner) Cunningham; m. Jeanne Adrienne Moran, July 21, 1972; 1 child Christopher Alan. BA, U. Tex., 1968, JD, 1974. Bar: Tex. 1974, U.S. Dist. Ct. (so. dist.) Tex. 1976, U.S. Dist. Ct. (no. dist.) Tex. 1982, U.S. Dist. Ct. (we. dist.) Tex. 1984, U.S. Ct. Appeals (5th and 11th cirs.) 1981, U.S. Ct. Appeals (8th cir.) 1919. Ptnr. Fulbright & Jaworski L.L.P., Houston, 1974—98; founding ptnr. Cunningham, Darlow, Zook & Chapoton, L.L.P., 1998—. Bd. trustee Children's Charity Fund, Houston, 1983—88; active South Tex. Ctr. Legal Responsibility; mem. exec. com., bd. dirs. Assn. for Cmty. TV. Lt. (j.g.) USNR, 1969—72. Fellow: Am. Bar Found., Am. Coll. Trial Lawyers, Am. Bd. Trial Advs., Tex. Bar Found. (life; chmn. bd. trustees, adv. bd., chair 1995—, chair Lola Wright com., chair bd. trustees 1995—, adv. bd., mem. new fellows com., mem. awards com., mem. pub. com., bd. dirs., ct. ruels com.), Tex. Trial Lawyers Assn., Houston Bar Found.; mem.: ABA (litigation sect., discovery com., alternate dispute resolution com., forum com. constrn. industry, arbitration com. 1995—), Tex. Empowerment Network (bd. dirs.), CPR Inst. for Dispute Resolution, Resolution Forum, Inc. (pres.), Tex. Ctr. Legal Ethics and Professionalism, Am. Arbitration Assn. (panel of arbitrators), State Bar Tex. (chmn. dist.4H grievance com. 1982—88, chmn. spl. com. on lawyer adt. and solicitation 1982, bd. dirs. 1989—92, chair bd. dirs. exec. com. 1991—92, chair com. for lawyer discipline 1992—94, chair

gen. counsel adv. com., mem. exec. com., ct. rules com., Pres.'s award 1983, Pres.'s citation for meritorious svc. 1991, Pres.'s spl. recognition for meritorious svc. 1993, 1994, nominee Outstanding Young Lawyer 1981), Tex. Assn. Def. Counsel, Tex. Bd. Legal Specialization, Houston Bar Assn. (professionalism com., chmn. constn. bicentennial com., arbitration com., membership com., Pres.'s award 1988), Coronado Club, Houston Club, Lakeside Country Club, Phi Delta Phi. Federal civil litigation, State civil litigation. Home: 10811 Pine Bayou St Houston TX 77024-3018

CUPRILL, CHARLES, retired legal educator; b. 1919; JD, U. P.R., 1947. Bar: P.R. 1947. Prof. law, dean Sch. Law Cath. U. P.R., Santa Maria Ponce; ret., 1991. Pres. P.R. SSS Appeals Bd.; trustee Cath. U. P.R., pres. disciplinary bd., mem. acad. senate. Served to maj. U.S. Army, 1940-46; to lt. col., 1950-52; to brig. gen. P.R. NG, 1986-88; to commanding gen. P.R. State Guard, 1986-88. Club: Rotary Internat. (past gov.). Office: Cath U PR Sch Law Avenida de las Americas & Avenida San Jorge Santa Maria Ponce PR 00717 E-mail: derecho@pucpr.edu

CURE, CAROL CAMPBELL, lawyer; b. Phoenix, Dec. 16, 1944; d. Richard Converse Nowell and Nancy (Newcomb) Olson; m. Robert Norman Campbell, Jan. 2, 1965 (div. 1968); 1 child, Kelly Christine; m. Harding Briggs Cure, June 28, 1984. BA with distinction, Ariz. State U.-Tempe, 1972, JD, 1978. Bar: Ariz. 1979, Calif. 1979, U.S. Dist. Ct. Ariz. 1979, U.S. Ct. Appeals (9th cir.) 1981, U.S. Dist. Ct. (cen. dist.) Calif. 1984, White Mountain Apache Tribal Ct.; cert. specialist in personal injury and wrongful death litigation. Ptnr. O'Connor, Cavanagh, Anderson, Westover, Killingsworth & Beshears, Phoenix, 1978—; faculty mem. Pacific regional chpt. Nat. Inst. Trial Advocacy, 1985-86; faculty mem. Ariz. Trial Coll., 1988-92. Bd. dirs. Ariz. Coun. of the Blind, Social Svcs. and Rehab. Inc., 1980-85, Community Forum, 1994-95, Phoenix Childrens Theatre, 1981-83, Ariz. Cen. Credit Union, 1985-87; judge pro tem Ariz. Ct. Appeals, 1985; judge pro tem Maricopa County Superior Ct., 1988-95; mem. steering com. Pro Bono Juvenile Project, 1989-90; mem. Camelback East Village Planning Com., 1987-90; mem. coun. of the future Nat. Judicial Coll.; candidate U.S. Ho. Reps., Ariz., 1994. Fellow Am. Bar Found., Am Bd. Trial Advs.; mem. ABA (chair civil procedure and evidence com. tort and ins. practice sect., chair professionalism com. 1989-92, chair litigation sect. use of expert witness subcom. of com. trial practice 1982-90, mem. standing com. on professionalism, 1992—, del. ho. dels. 1993—), State Bar Ariz. (bd. govs. 1990-93, com. on rules of civil practice and procedure, chair trial practice sect.), Maricopa County Bar Assn. (bd. dirs. 1983-88, chair med./legal liaison com., 1987-89), Maricopa County Bar Found. (trustee 1984-88), Nucleus (chair membership com. 1984-85, chair 1986-87, bd. dirs. 1988—), AAUW (parliamentarian, bd. dirs. Ariz. State div. 1980-82, pres. elect 1994), Internat. Ins. Law Soc. (mem. presdl. coun.), Ariz. Epilepsy Assn. (bd. dirs. cmty. arts coun.), Ariz. State U. Coll. Law, Law Soc. (bd. dirs. 1995—), Ariz. State U. Coll. Law (bd. visitors), Ariz. State U. Alumni Assn. (bd. dirs. 1980-83), Kappa Delta Pi, Assn. Trial Lawyers Am., Phoenix Assn. Def. Counsel, Ariz. Women Lawyers Assn., Def. Rsch. Inst. (practice and procedure com.), Fedn. Ins. and Corp. Counsel. Democrat. Episcopalian. Insurance, Legislative, Personal injury. Office: O'Connor Cavanagh 1 E Camelback Rd Ste 1100 Phoenix AZ 85012-1691

CURLEY, ROBERT AMBROSE, JR. lawyer; b. Boston, June 5, 1949; s. Robert Ambrose and Terese M. (O'Hara) C.; m. Kathleen M. Foley, June 10, 1972; children: Christine, Elizabeth, Margaret. AB cum laude, Harvard U., 1971; JD, Cornell U., 1974. Bar: Mass. 1974, U.S. Dist. Ct. Mass. 1975, U.S. Ct. Appeals (1st. cir.) 1976. Prin. Curley & Curley, P.C., Boston, 1974—, pres. Lectr. Mass. Continuing Legal Edn., Mass. Def. Attys., Mass. Acad. Trial Attys., Flaschner Judicial Inst., Nat. Bus. Inst. Mem. ABA, ATLA (assoc.), Internat. Assn. Def. Counsel, Def. Trial Acad., Mass. Bar Assn. (lectr., chmn. civil trial practice sect., civil litig. com. 1990-91, Mass. Def. Lawyers Assn. (co-chmn. products liability sects. 1994-96, bd. dirs., sec. 1998-99, treas., v.p. 1999-2000, pres. 2001—), Nat. Bus. Inst., Def. Rsch. Inst., Harvard Club (Hingham, treas. 1983-84, v.p. 1984-85, pres. 1985-86), Clover (Boston). Roman Catholic. Federal civil litigation, State civil litigation, Personal injury. Office: Curley & Curley PC 27 School St Ste 600 Boston MA 02108-4391 E-mail: rae@curleylaw.com

CURRAN, BARBARA SANSON, lawyer; b. Wiesbaden, Fed. Republic of Germany, Jan. 25, 1955; came to U.S., 1973; d. Allan David and Gertrude Maria (Trendl) S.; m. Stephen P. Curran, Sept. 15, 1990; 1 child, Catherine L. Student, U. London, 1975-76; AB, Bryn Mawr Coll., 1977; JD, Dickinson Sch. Law, 1980. Bar: Pa. 1980, U.S. Dist. Ct. (ea. dist.) Pa. 1981. Law clk. Lehigh County Ct., Allentown, Pa., 1980-82; assoc. Duane Morris & Heckscher, Phila., 1982-84; atty. ICI Americas Inc., Wilmington, Del., 1984-90, corp. sec., 1991-2000, ICI American Holdings Inc., Wilmington, 2000—. Mem. ABA, Pa. Bar Assn. Avocation: ice skating. Home: 105 Montana Dr Chadds Ford PA 19317-9284 Office: ICI Ams Inc 3411 Silverside Rd Ste 101 Wilmington DE 19810-4837

CURRAN, J. JOSEPH, JR. state attorney general; b. West Palm Beach, Fla., July 7, 1931; s. J. Joseph Sr. and Catherine (Clark) C.; m. Barbara Marie Atkins, 1959; children: Mary Carole, Alice Ann, Catherine Marie, J. Joseph III, William A. (dec.). LLB, U. Balt., 1959. Bar: Md. 1959, U.S. Dist. Ct. Md., U.S. Supreme Ct. 1987. State senator from Md., 1963-83; lt. gov. State of Md., 1983-86, atty. gen., 1987—. Mem. Md. Regional Planning Coun., 1963-82 Mem. Md. Bar Assn., Balt. Bar Assn. Office: Office of Atty Gen 200 Saint Paul Pl Baltimore MD 21202-2004*

CURRAN, MARGARET E. prosecutor; M. Michel H. Feldhunhn; 1 child, Margee. BA in Biology; MS in Anthropology, Purdue U.; JD, U. Conn. Assoc. Wistow & Barylick, Providence; fed. prosecutor U.S. Atty.'s Office R.I. Dist., 1986—90, appellate chief, 1990—98, U.S. atty., 1998—. Editor-in-chief U. Conn. Law Rev. Democrat. Office: 50 Kennedy Plz Fleet Ctr 8th Floor Providence RI 02903-2018*

CURRAN, MAURICE FRANCIS, lawyer; b. Yonkers, N.Y., Feb. 20, 1931; s. James F. and Mary (O'Brien) C.; m. Deborah M. Dee, May 7, 1960; children: James, Maurice, Amy, Bridget, Ceara, Sara. Student, Cathedral Coll., 1950; BA in Philosophy, St. Joseph Coll. and Sem., 1952; LLB, Fordham U., 1958. Bar: N.Y. 1958, U.S. Dist. Ct. (so. and ea. dists.) N.Y. 1960, U.S. Ct. Appeals (2d cir.) 1982, U.S. Supreme Ct. Assoc. Kelley, Drye, Newhall & Maginnes, N.Y.C., 1958-60, Wilson & Bave, Yonkers, 1960-65; divsn. counsel Merck & Co., Rahway, N.J., 1965-67; asst. gen. counsel E.R. Squibb & Sons, Inc., N.Y.C., 1967-70; corp. counsel, chief law dept. City of Yonkers, 1970-72; ptnr. Bleakley, Platt, Schmidt & Fritz, White Plains, N.Y., 1972-83, Banks, Curran & Schwamm, LLP, Mt. Kisco, 1983—. Past trustee, vice chmn. Westchester C.C. Capt. USMC, 1952-58. Mem. Fed. Bar Coun., N.Y. State Bar Assn., Assn. Bar City N.Y. Roman Catholic. Federal civil litigation, State civil litigation, Education and schools. Home: 388 Bronxville Rd Bronxville NY 10708-1233 Office: 61 Smith Ave Mount Kisco NY 10549-2813

CURRAN, RICHARD EMERY, JR. lawyer; b. Portland, Maine, Jan. 31, 1950; s. Richard Emery and Catherine Margaret (Bunker) C.; m. Nancy Bokron, Aug. 16, 1975 (div. May 1982); m. Margaret Cary, Sept. 17, 1988. AB, Dartmouth Coll., 1972, MBA, 1973; JD, Harvard U., 1977; LLM, Boston U., 1983. Bar: Maine 1977, U.S. Dist. Ct. Maine 1977, U.S. Tax Ct. 1984. Assoc. Pierce, Atwood, Scribner, Allen, Smith & Lancaster, Portland, Maine, 1977-82, ptnr., 1983—. Mem. ABA, Maine Bar Assn. Republican. Congregationalist. Clubs: Portland Country, Falmouth Country, Yale (N.Y.C.). Avocations: skiing, sailing, art, running, reading. General corporate, Corporate taxation, Estate taxation. Home: 1 Winn Farm Ln Falmouth ME 04105-1195

CURRAN, ROBERT BRUCE, lawyer; b. Charleston, W.Va., July 2, 1948; s. Bruce Frederick and Hazel Viola (Hoy) C.; children: Michael Robert, Laura Elizabeth, Emily Ann. BA, U. Del., 1971; JD, U. Md., 1974. Bar: Md. 1974. Ptnr. Frank, Bernstein, Conaway & Goldman, Balt., 1974-92, Whiteford Taylor & Preston, Balt., 1992—. Co-author: Tax Planning Forms for Businesses and Individuals, 1985. Mem. Md. Bar Assn. (sec. and treas. taxation sect. 1985-86, chmn. taxation sect. 1987-88). General corporate, Pension, profit-sharing, and employee benefits, Corporate taxation. Office: Whiteford Taylor & Preston 7 Saint Paul St Baltimore MD 21202-1626 E-mail: rcurran@wtplaw.com

CURRAN, WILLIAM P. lawyer; b. Mpls., Feb. 27, 1946; s. William P. and Margaret L. (Killoren) C.; m. Jean L. Stabenow, Jan. 1, 1978; children: Patrick, Lisa, John. BA, U. Minn., 1969; JD, U. Calif., Berkeley, 1972. Law clk. Nev. Supreme Ct., Carson City, 1973-74, state ct. adminstr., 1973-74; assoc. Wiener, Goldwater & Galatz, Las Vegas, Nev., 1974-75; chief dept. dist. atty. Clark County Dist. Atty.'s Office, 1975-79; county counsel Clark County, 1979-89; pvt. practice, 1989-94; ptnr. Curran & Parry, 1994—. Co-author: Nevada Judicial Orientation Manual, 1974. Mem. Nev. Gaming Commn., Carson City, 1989-99, chmn., 1991-99. Recipient Educator Yr. award UNLV Internat. Gaming Inst., 1998. Mem. ABA (state del. 1994—), Internat. Assn. Gaming Regulators (chmn. 1992-94), Nat. Assn. County Civil Attys. (pres. 1984-85), State Bar Nev. (pres. 1988-89), Nev. Gaming Commn. (chmn. 1989-99). Democrat. Roman Catholic. Administrative and regulatory, Land use and zoning (including planning), Real property. Office: Curran & Parry 601 S Rancho Dr Ste C-23 Las Vegas NV 89106-4825 E-mail: curran_parry@msn.com

CURRIE, EDWARD JONES, JR. lawyer; b. Jackson, Miss., May 23, 1951; s. Edward J. and Nell (Branton) C.; m. Barbara Scott Miller, June 26, 1976; children: Morgan E., Scott E. BA, U. Miss., 1973, JD, 1976. Bar: Miss. 1976, U.S. Dist. Ct. (no. and so. dists.) Miss. 1976, U.S. Ct. Appeals (5th cir.) 1978, U.S. Supreme Ct. 1979. Assoc. Wise, Carter, Child, Steen & Caraway, Jackson, 1976-80; ptnr. Steen, Reynolds, Dalehite & Currie, 1980-94, Currie Johnson Griffin Gaines & Myers, Jackson, 1994—. Adj. prof. Miss. Coll. Sch. Law, Jackson, 1977-81, 84-86. Bd. dirs. Miss. chpt. Am. Diabetes Assn., Jackson, 1980-82. Mem. Fed. Bar Assn. (pres. Miss. chpt. 1989), Internat. Assn. Def. Coun. (trial acad. faculty 1992), Nat. Inst. Trial Advocacy, Nat. Lawyers Assn. (chmn. ins. sect. 1998-99), Nat. Lawyers Assn. Found. (bd. dirs. 1998-00), Miss. Jud. Coll. (model civil jury instrn. com. 1991), Miss. Def. Lawyers Assn. (bd. dirs. 2000—), Miss. Bar Assn. (bd. dirs. young lawyers sect. 1981-82, chmn. litigation/gen. practice sect. 1992, mem. MDP Task Force 2000), Miss. Bd. Bar Commrs., Jackson Young Lawyers (bd. dirs. 1980-81), Hinds County Bar Assn., Phi Delta Phi, Sigma Alpha Epsilon (pres. Ctrl. Miss. alumni 1981), Omicron Delta Kappa. Presbyterian. Federal civil litigation, State civil litigation, Insurance. Home: 50 Moss Forest Cir Jackson MS 39211-2905 Office: Currie Johnson Griffin Gaines & Myers PO Box 750 Jackson MS 39205-0750

CURRIVAN, JOHN DANIEL, lawyer; b. Paris; s. Gene and Rachel Currivan; m. Patrice Salley; children: Christopher, Melissa. BS with distinction, Cornell U.; MS , U Calif.-Berkeley; MS, U. West Fla.; JD summa cum laude, Cornell Law Sch., 1978. Bar: Ohio 1978. Mng. ptnr. S.W. Devel. Co., Kingsville, Tex., 1971-76; note editor Cornell Law Rev., Ithaca, N.Y., 1977-78; prosecutor Naval Legal Office, Norfolk, Va., 1978-79, chief prosecutor, 1979-81; sr. atty. USS Nimitz, 1981-83; trial judge Naval Base, Norfolk, 1983-84; tax atty. Jones, Day, Reavis & Pogue, Cleve., 1984-88, ptnr., 1989—. Adj. prof. law Case Western Res. U. Sch. Law, 1997—. Author: (with Rickert) Ohio Limited Liability Companies, 1999. Comdr. USN, 1969-84. Recipient Younger Fed. Lawyer award FBA, 1981. Mem. ABA, Nat. Assn. Bond Lawyers, Order of Coif, Tau Beta Pi, Eta Kappa Nu, Phi Kappa Phi. Municipal (including bonds), Corporate taxation, Taxation, general. Home: 12700 Lake Ave Ste 2105 Lakewood OH 44107-1506 Office: Jones Day Reavis & Pogue 901 Lakeside Ave E Cleveland OH 44114-1190

CURRY, DANIEL ARTHUR, judge; b. Phoenix, Mar. 28, 1937; s. John Joseph and Eva May (Wills) C.; m. Joy M. Shallenberger, Sept. 5, 1959; children: Elizabeth, Catherine, Peter, Jennifer, Julia , David. B.S., Loyola U., Los Angeles, 1957, LL.B., 1960; postgrad. exec. program, Grad. Sch. Bus., Stanford U., 1980. Bar: Calif. 1961, Hawaii 1972, N.Y. 1988, U.S. Dist. Ct. (cen. dist.) Calif. 1961, U.S. Ct. Appeals (9th cir.) 1961, U.S. Ct. Mil. Appeals 1963, U.S. Customs Ct. 1968, U.S. Dist. Ct. Hawaii 1972, U.S. Dist. Ct. (no. dist.) Calif. 1983 . Assoc. Wolford, Johnson, Pike & Covell, El Monte, Calif., 1964-65, Demetriou & Del Guercio, L.A., 1965-67; counsel, corporate staff divisional asst. Technicolor, Inc., Hollywood, Calif., 1967-70; v.p., sec., gen. counsel Amfac, Inc., Honolulu, 1970-78, sr. v.p., gen. counsel Honolulu and San Francisco, 1978-87; v.p., gen. counsel Times Mirror, L.A., 1987-92; judge Superior Ct. of State of Calif., 1992-98; assoc. justice Calif. Ct. Appeal 2d dist., L.A., 1998—. Served to capt. USAF, 1961-64. Mem. L.A. Country Club, Phi Delta Phi. Office: Calif Ct Appeal 2d Dist 4th Fl North Tower 300 S Spring St Los Angeles CA 90013-1230

CURRY, DONALD ROBERT, lawyer, oil company executive; b. Pampa, Tex., Aug. 7, 1943; s. Robert Ward and Alleith Elizabeth (Elliston) C.; m. Carolyn Sue Boland, Apr. 17, 1965; 1 son, James Ward. BS, West Tex. State U., 1965; JD, U. Tex., 1968. Bar: Tex. 1968, U.S. Dist. Ct. (no. dist.) Tex. 1970, U.S. Tax Ct. 1973. Assoc. Day & Gandy, Ft. Worth, 1968-69, ptnr., 1970-72; pvt. practice, 1972—; mng. ptnr. Curry & Thornton Oil, 1981—. Lectr. in field. Mem. bd. regents West Tex. State U., Canyon, 1969-77, sec., mem. exec. com., 1972-75; mem. exec. bd. Longhorn coun. Boy Scouts Am., 1970—, dist. chmn., 1970-75; precinct chmn. Tarrant County (Tex.) Dem. Party, 1982-88, election judge, 1982-94; mem. aviation adv. bd. City of Ft. Worth, 1990-95, vice chmn. bd., chmn. bd. dirs., 1994-95. Recipient Silver Beaver award Boy Scouts Am., 1995; James E. West fellow, 1997. Fellow Tex. Bar Found.; mem. ABA, State Bar Tex., Ft. Worth-Tarrant County Bar ASsn., Ft. Worth Bus. and Estate Coun., Ft. Worth Club, Petroleum Club of Ft. Worth, Phi Alpha Delta, Phi Delta Theta. Methodist. Estate planning, Probate, Real property. Home: 3800 Tulsa Way Fort Worth TX 76107-3346 Office: 905 Ft Worth Club Bldg Fort Worth TX 76102-4911

CURRY, ROBERT EMMET, JR. lawyer; b. N.Y.C., Jan. 18, 1946; s. Robert Emmet and Rose Ann (Mooney) C.; m. Margaret Courtney Kennedy, May 6, 1973; 1 child, Robert Emmet III. B.A. with honors, Georgetown U., 1967; J.D., Columbia U., 1970. Bar: N.Y. 1971, U.S. Supreme Ct. 1973. Assoc. Patterson, Belknap, Webb & Tyler, N.Y.C., 1971-73; sr. counsel Rouse Co., Columbia, Md., 1973-75; assoc. counsel Ogden Corp., N.Y.C., 1976-80, v.p., 1981-85, gen. counsel, 1983-87, sr. v.p., 1985-87; ptnr. Dickstein, Shapiro & Morin, 1987—. Mem. Assn. Bar City N.Y. (energy com.), N.Y. State Bar Assn. ABA, Am. Corp. Counsel Assn. (pres. Met. N.Y. chpt.). Roman Catholic. Club: Washington (Conn.). Office: Ogden Corp 277 Park Ave New York NY 10172-0003

CURRY, ROBERT LEE, III, lawyer; b. New Orleans, Sept. 29, 1931; s. Robert Lee Jr. and Lydia (Sporl) C.; m. Courtney Davis, June 11, 1955; children: Robert Lee IV, Cynthia Curry Alexander, Thomas Davis, Kevin Courtney. BS, JD, La. State U., 1954; LLM in Taxation, NYU, 1958. Bar: La. 1954, U.S. Ct. Appeals (5th cir.) 1961, U.S. Supreme Ct. 1958. Judge advocate USAF, Wichita, Kans., 1954-56; teaching fellow NYU Sch. of Law, 1956-57; atty. advisor U.S. Tax Ct., Washington, 1957-60; atty. Theus, Grisham, Davis & Leigh, Monroe, La., 1960—. Coun. mem. La. Law Inst. Coun., Baton Rouge, 1978—, pres., 1995-98. Fellow Am. Coll. Trust and Estate Counsel, Am. Coll. Tax Counsel; mem. Internat. Acad. Trust and Estate Law. Episcopalian. General corporate, Estate planning, Taxation, general. Office: Theus Grisham Davis & Leigh 1600 Lamy Ln Monroe LA 71201-3736 E-mail: rcurry@theuslaw.com

CURTIN, LAWRENCE N. lawyer; b. Glen Ridge, N.J., Apr. 29, 1950; BS with honors, Fla. State U., 1972, JD with honors, 1976. Bar: Fla. 1976, U.S. Dist. Ct. (no. dist.) Fla., U.S. Ct. Appeals (4th, 5th, 11th and D.C. cirs.). Law clerk to Hon. William Stafford U.S. Dist. Ct. (no. dist.) Fla., 1976-78; mem. Holland & Knight, Tallahassee. Co-author: Surface Water Pollution Control, vol. 1, 1986-96. Mem. ABA, Fla. Bar (chmn. energy law com. 1983-84), Tallahassee Bar Assn., Beta Gamma Sigma, Sigma Iota Epsilon. Administrative and regulatory, Environmental, Legislative. Office: Holland & Knight LLP PO Drawer 810 315 S Calhoun St Ste 600 Tallahassee FL 32301-1897 E-mail: lcurtin@hklaw.com

CURTIN, TIMOTHY JOHN, lawyer; b. Detroit, Sept. 21, 1942; s. James J. and Irma Alice (Sirotti) C.; m. B. Colleen Lindsey, July 11, 1964; children: Kathleen, Mary. BA, U. Mich., 1964, JD, 1967. Bar: Ohio 1968, Mich. 1970, U.S. Dist. Ct. (no. dist.) Ohio 1968, U.S. Dist. Ct. (we. dist.) Mich. 1970, U.S. Dist. Ct. (ea. dist.) Mich. 1980, U.S. Dist. Ct. Del. 1996, U.S. Dist. Ct. (no. dist.) Ill. 1999, U.S. Ct. Appeals (6th cir.) 1968. Assoc. Taft, Stettinius & Hollister, Cin., 1967-70, McCobb, Heaney & Van't Hof, Grand Rapids, Mich., 1970-72; ptnr. Schmidt, Howlett, Van't Hof, Snell & Vana, 1972-83, Varnum, Riddering, Schmidt & Howlett, Grand Rapids, 1983—. Contbr. articles to legal publs. Treas. Kent County Dem. Com., 1976-78, chmn. 3rd Dist. Dem. Com., 1993—. Mem. ABA, Mich. Bar Assn., Grand Rapids Bar Assn., Fed.. Bar Assn., Am. Bankruptcy Inst., Egypt Valley C.C. Roman Catholic. Avocations: travel, fishing. Bankruptcy, Contracts commercial. Office: Varnum Riddering Schmidt & Howlett Box 352 333 Bridge St SW Grand Rapids MI 49501-0352 E-mail: tjcurtin@varnumlaw.com

CURTIS, FRANK R. lawyer; b. Valley Stream, N.Y., Sept. 27, 1946; s. Frank and Rosalind (Vreeland) C.; m. Cynthia Mary Knapik, May 14, 1977; children: Lauren Josephine, Frank Edward, Michael Bennett. AB magna cum laude, Harvard Coll., 1968; JD, Yale U., 1971. Bar: N.Y. 1972, U.S. Dist. Cts. (so. and ea. dists.) N.Y. 1973, U.S. Ct. Appeals (2d cir.) 1975. Assoc. Hellerstein Rosier & Rembar, N.Y.C., 1971-73; ptnr. Rembar Wolf & Curtis, N.Y., 1974-77, Rembar & Curtis, N.Y.C., 1978—; lectr. PLI, N.Y.C., 1980, 88. Trustee, North Salem Free Library, N.Y., 1983-91. Mem. Assn. of Bar of City of N.Y. (sec. com. on copyright 1979-80), Copyright Soc. of the U.S.A., Harvard Club (N.Y.C.), Phi Beta Kappa. Entertainment, Libel, Trademark and copyright. Home: PO Box 108 2 Juengstville Rd Croton Falls NY 10519-0108 Office: Rembar & Curtis 19 W 44th St New York NY 10036-5902

CURTIS, GEORGE BARTLETT, lawyer; b. N.Y.C., June 27, 1947; s. George Bartlett and Rosemary Ann (Gaffney) C.; m. Marion Sugrue Golden, Aug. 13, 1976; children— Peter, Timothy. B.A., Fordham Coll., 1969; M.A., U. Va., 1971, Ph.D., 1973; J.D., U. Chgo., 1976. Bar: Calif. 1976, U.S. Dist. Ct. (cen. dist.) Calif. 1976, Colo. 1981, U.S. Ct. Appeals (9th cir.) 1976, U.S. Dist. Ct. Colo. 1981, U.S. Ct. Appeals (10th cir.) 1981, U.S. Supreme Ct. 1988. Teaching fellow U. Va., 1971-73; assoc. Gibson Dunn & Crutcher, Los Angeles, 1976-83, ptnr., Denver, 1984— . Contbr. articles to profl. jours. Russel Sage fellow, 1975-76. Mem. ABA, Colo. Bar Assn. (ethics com. 1984-86), Calif. Bar Assn., Denver Bar Assn. Federal civil litigation, State civil litigation, Insurance. Office: Gibson Dunn & Crutcher 1801 California St Ste 4100 Denver CO 80202-2641

CURTIS, GEORGE WARREN, lawyer; b. Merrill, Wis., Sept. 24, 1936; s. George Gregory and Rose E. (Zimmerman) C.; m. Judith Olson, 1956 (div. 1966); m. Mary Pelman, 1967 (dec. 1973); children: George, Catherine Edwall, Eric, Greg, Paul, David; m. Mary Ruth Kersztyn, Dec. 27, 1973 (div. 1999); children: Emily, Benjamin; m. Suzette Bigler Whyte, July 10, 1999. BA, U. Minn., 1959; JD, U. Wis., 1962. Bar: Wis. 1962, Fla. 1968. Assoc. Russell & Curtis, Merrill, 1962-68; ptnr. Nolan, Engler, Yakes & Curtis, Oshkosh, Wis., 1968-74, Curtis, MacKenzie, Haase & Brown, Oshkosh, 1974-83, Curtis, Wilde & Neal, Oshkosh, 1984-96, Curtis & Neal, Oshkosh, 1997-98; with Curtis Law Offices, 1999. Host TV program It's Your Environment. Host (TV show) It's Your Law. Mem. ATLA, Am. Coll. Trial Lawyers, Am. Bd. Trial Advocates (pres. Wis. chpt.), Wis. Acad. Trial Lawyers (bd. dirs. 1978-83, treas. 1984, sec. 1985, v.p. 1986, pres. 1987), Assn. Trial Lawyers Am. (bd. govs.), Internat. Soc. Barristers. Democrat. Avocations: conservationist, dog trainer. State civil litigation, Criminal, Personal injury. Home: 7361 Canary Rd Pickett WI 54964-9724 Office: Curtis Law Offices 2905 Universal St Oshkosh WI 54904-6341

CURTIS, JAMES THEODORE, lawyer; b. Lowell, Mass., July 8, 1923; s. Theodore D. and Maria (Souliotis) Koutras; m. Kleanthe D. Dusopol, June 25, 1950; children: Madelon Mary, Theodore James, Stephanie Diane, Gregory Theodosius, James Theodore Jr. BA, U. Mich., 1948; JD, Harvard U., 1951; ScD (hon.), U. Mass., 1972. Bar: Mass. 1951. Assoc. Adams & Blinn, Boston, 1951-52; legal asst., asst. atty. gen. Mass., 1952-53; pvt. practice law Lowell, 1953-57; sr. ptnr. firm Goldman & Curtis, and predecessors, Lowell and Boston, 1957—. Chmn. Lowell and Greater Lowell Heart Fund, 1967-68; mem. adv. bd. Salvation Army, sec., 1956-58; mem. Bd. Higher Edn. Mass., 1967-72; elected mem. Lowell charter Commn., 1969-71; del. Dem. Party State Convs., 1956-60; trustee U. Mass., Lowell, 1963-72, chmn. bd., 1968-72; bd. dirs. U. Mass. Rsch. Found., Lowell, 1965-72, Merrimack Valley Health Planning Coun., 1969-72. Served with U.S. Army, 1943-46, spl. agt. Counter Intelligence Corps., 1945-46. Decorated Knight Order Orthodox Crusade Holy Sepulcher. Mem. ABA, ATLA, Mass. Bar Assn., Middlesex County Bar Assn., Mass. Acad. Trial Lawyers, Am. Judicature Soc., Harvard Law Sch. Alumni Assn., U. Mich. Alumni Assn., Lowell Hist. Soc., DAV, Harvard Club of Lowell (pres. 1969-71, bd. dirs.), Masons, Delta Epsilon Pi. General corporate, General practice, Real property. Home: 111 Rivercliff Rd Lowell MA 01852-1471 Office: Goldman & Curtis PC 144 Merrimack St Ste 444 Lowell MA 01852-1789 E-mail: law@goldman-curtis.com

CURTIS, KAREN HAYNES, lawyer; b. Laurel, Miss., Sept. 15, 1951; d. John Travis Haynes Jr. and Jeannine Burkett Tanner; m. George Ware Cornell Jr., Nov. 10, 1978; children: Laurel Elizabeth Cornell, Jaime Rodriguez Cornell. BS in Biology, Tulane U., 1973; JD summa cum laude, Nova Law Ctr., 1978. Bar: Fla. 1978; U.S. Ct Appeals (5th cir.) Fla. 1980, U.S. Ct. Appeals (11th cir.) Fla. 1981; U.S. Dist Ct. (so. dist.) Fla. 1986, U.S. Dist Ct. (mid. dist.) Fla., 1986; U.S. Supreme Ct. 1994. Law clk. Steel, Hector & Davis, Miami, Fla., 1978; law clk. to Judge William M. Hoeveler U.S. Dist. Ct., 1978-80; assoc. Shutts & Bowen, 1980-84, ptnr., 1985-95; founding ptnr., pres. Gallwey, Gillman, Curtis, Vento & Horn P.A., 1995—. Treas., dir. Ch. by the Sea, 1994—. Listed in Leading Fla. Attys. for Civil Appellate Law. Mem. ABA, Fla. Assn. Women Lawyers, Fed. Bar Assn., Dade County Bar Assn. (ins. law com. 1990-91, banking and corp. litigation com. 1992-93, appellate ct. com. 1991—) Fla. Bar (appellate ct. rules com. 1993—, grievance com. 1988-91), Fla. Bar Bd. of Legal Specialization and Edn.(cert. in appellate practice), Acad. Fla. Trial

Lawyers, Assn. Trial Lawyers of Am., Supreme Ct. Historical Soc., Am. Judiciary Soc. United Ch. of Christ. Avocations: reading, piano, computer. Appellate, Federal civil litigation, General civil litigation. Home: 18720 SW 33rd Court Miramar FL 33029 Office: Gallwey Gillman Curtis Vento & Horn PA 200 SE 1st St Ste 1100 Miami FL 33131-1912

CURTIS, PHILIP JAMES, lawyer; b. Jackson, Mich., May 28, 1945; s. Robert N. and Marjorie Louise (Balyeat) C.; m. Denise R. Curtis; children: Laura Christina, Philip Campbell, Leslie Ann. BA, U. Mich., 1967; JD, Wayne State U., 1970. Bar: Mich., U.S. Dist. Ct. (ea. dist.) Mich. 1977. Atty. Curtis, Curtis & Thomson P.C., Jackson, Mich., 1970—. Former pres., dir. Family Svc. & Children's Aid, Jackson; dir. Jackson Bus. Indsl. Devel. Co., Ltd.; former trustee Ella Sharp Mus., Jackson; dir. Jackson Y Ctr., Inc., Jackson. General corporate, Pension, profit-sharing, and employee benefits, Probate. Office: Curtis Curtis & Thomson P C PO Box 594 Jackson MI 49204-0594

CURTIS, SUSAN GRACE, lawyer; b. N.Y.C., Apr. 24, 1950; d. Henry G. and Helen Curtis; m. Robert Y. Pelgrift Jr., June 8, 1974; children: Robert III, Henry, Victoria. A.B., Yale Coll., 1971; J.D., Columbia U., 1974. Bar: N.Y. 1975, U.S. Ct. Appeals (2d cir.) 1975. With Lord, Day & Lord, N.Y.C., 1974-79, Shearman & Sterling, N.Y.C., 1979-84, Proskauer, Rose, 1984-87, 93-98; ptnr. Epstein, Becker & Green, N.Y.C., 1987-93; of counsel White & Case, N.Y.C., 1998—; adj. asst. prof. law NYU Sch. Law, 1995-98; mem. faculty Practising Law Inst., 1990—. Contbg. editor: Jour. Pension Planning and Compliance, 1991—; mem. editl. adv. bd. BNA Pension Reporter, 1993—, tax mgmt. adv. bd., 1993—; contbr. articles to profl. jours. Mem. ABA (com. employee benefits), N.Y. State Bar Assn. (com. employee benefits), Assn. Bar City N.Y. (sec. com. employee benefits 1987-90). Pension, profit-sharing, and employee benefits. Office: White & Case Bldg Ll 1155 Avenue Of The Americas New York NY 10036-2787

CURTISS, THOMAS, JR. lawyer, educator; b. Buffalo, Nov. 4, 1941; s. Thomas and Hope (Middleton Plumb) C. BA, Yale U., 1963; JD, Harvard U., 1970. Bar: Calif. 1971. Assoc. Musick, Peeler & Garrett, L.A., 1970-72, Macdonald, Halsted & Laybourne, L.A., 1972-76, ptnr., 1976-88, Kindel & Anderson, L.A., 1992-96, McKenna & Cuneo, L.L.P., L.A., 1996—. Adj. prof. Loyola U., L.A. Law Sch., 1982-93, 99. Mem. editl. bd. L.A. Lawyer, 1992-93; contbr. articles to profl. jours. Mem. vestry Trinity Episc. Ch., L.A., sr. warden, 1982, 84-86; mem. Commn. on Ordained Ministry, Diocese of L.A., 1983-88; legal com. Music Ctr. Found., 1988-94, dir. Cath. Ctr. St. Paul, 1989-94, treas., 1989-95; mem. AIDS Interfaith Coun. So. Calif., Inc., 1989-91; Class of 1959 agt. Phillips Exeter Acad., 1994-98; dir. Mental Health Assn., L.A. County, 1996-97. Maj., USMCR, 1963-78. Fellow Am. Coll. Trust and Estate Counse; mem. ABA (mem. sect. real property, probate and trust law), L.A. County Bar Assn. (chmn. exec. com., probate and trust law sect. 1991-92), The Calif. Club, State Bar of Calif. (bd. of legal specialization, cert. specialist, estate planning, trust and probate law). Republican. Home: 2250 Micheltorena St Los Angeles CA 90039-3021

CURY, BRUCE PAUL, lawyer, magistrate, law educator; b. Englewood, N.J., Mar. 19, 1942; s. Beddy Galib and Violet (Maloof) C.; m. Orahdella Elizabeth Green, Oct. 14, 1972; 1 child, Lauren Elaine. BS, U. Ky., 1965; JD, U. Louisville, 1972. Bar: Fla. 1972, U.S. Dist. Ct. (mid. dist.) Fla. 1974, U.S. Ct. Appeals (5th cir.) 1980, U.S. Ct. Appeals (11th cir.) 1982, U.S. Supreme Ct. 1976. Assoc. George McDowell P.A., Tampa, Fla., 1972-73; sole practice, 1973-76; adj. prof. bus. law U. Tampa, 1977-85; adj. prof. criminal law U. South Fla., 1984-85, lectr., 1981-87; chief asst. pub. defender Office of Pub. Defender, Tampa, 1974-85; sole practice, 1985-90; gen. counsel Fla. Dept. Transportation, Bartow, 1990—. Magistrate traffic ct. Jud. 13 cir., Tampa, 1993—; chmn. Hills County Zoning Bd. Tampa, 1989-97; pres., dir. Bay Area Legal Svcs., Inc., Tampa, 1980-92; chmn. Hills County Land Use Appeals Bd. Tampa, 1997—. Legal counsel Big Bros./Big Sisters Greater Tampa, Inc., 1983-95; pres, bd. dirs. Rape Crisis Ctr., Tampa, 1982-84; bd. dirs. Hillsborough Edn. Found., Tampa, 1999—; mem. Hillsborough County City-County Planning Commn., Tampa, 1999—. Served to 1st lt. U.S. Army, 1966-69. Recipient Indigent Accused award Fla. Pub. Defender, 1985, Dirs. award Sexual Abuse Treatment Ctr. Tampa, 1986, Pres. and Dirs. award Bay Area Legal Svcs. Tampa, 1992, Sec. of Transp. Leadership award Fla. Dept. Transp., 2000. Mem. Criminal Def. Lawyers Assn. Hillsborough County, Fla. Bar Assn. (mem. several sects., chmn. 13th Jud. Circuit grievance com.), Hillsborough County Bar Assn. (mem. several coms., exec. counsel trial lawyers sect.), Fla. Leadership 2000, Am. Inn of Cts. Republican. Methodist. E-mial. Home: 4306 Carrollwood Village Dr Tampa FL 33624-4612 Office: Fla Dept Transportation 801 N Broadway Ave Bartow FL 33830-3809 E-mail: bruce.cury@dot.state.fl.us

CUSTER, BARBARA ANN, lawyer; b. Mineola, N.Y., Mar. 2, 1945; d. Merton Davis and Virginia Mary (Estabrook) C. B.A., Trinity Coll., 1966; J.D., Southwestern U., 1977. Bar: Calif. 1977, U.S. Dist. Ct. (cen. dist.) Calif. 1978, U.S. Ct. Appeals (D.C. cir) 1979. Adminstrv. asst. United Calif. Bank, N.Y.C., 1968-70; asst. to exec. dir. Am. Council for the Arts in Edn., N.Y.C., 1971-74; asst. to reference librarian Southwestern U., Los Angeles, 1975-78; atty. network anti-trust project Columbia Pictures, Burbank, Calif., 1979; sole practice, Los Angeles, 1980; atty. Orion Pictures Corp., Los Angeles, 1981— , now v.p. bus. and legal affairs. Entertainment. Home: 803 N La Jolla Ave Los Angeles CA 90046-6809 Office: Orion Pictures Corp 2500 Broadway Santa Monica CA 90404-3065

CUTCHIN, JAMES MCKENNEY, IV, lawyer, engineer; b. Whitakers, N.C., Oct. 11, 1933; s. James McKenney III and Helen Christine (Perkins) C.; m. Nancy Lucille Elks, June 12, 1955; children: James McKenney V, John William. BS, U.S. Mil. Acad., 1955; MS in Mech. Engring., N.C. State U., 1962; JD, George Washington U., 1975. Bar: Va. 1975, D.C. 1976, U.S. Dist. Ct. (ea. dist.) Va. 1976, U.S. Dist. Ct. D.C. 1976, U.S. Ct. Appeals (4th and D.C. cirs.) 1976, U.S. Supreme Ct. 1978. Engr., sr. engr. Babcock & Wilcox Co., Lynchburg, Va., 1962-68; licensing supr., 1968-71; sr. project mgr. U.S. Nuclear Regulatory Commn., Washington, 1971-76, atty., 1976-78, sr. litigation atty., 1978-83, legal adviser to commr., 1983-90; special counsel office of the General Counsel, 1990-95. Pres. Lynchburg Young Rep. Club, 1967-69; v.p. Sandusky Jr. High Sch. PTA, 1970; chmn. Lynchburg City Rep. Com., 1970-71. Served to 1st lt. USAF, 1955-59. Mem. Va. Bar, D.C. Bar, ASME (bd. dirs. Va. sect. 1970), Am. Nuclear Soc. (pres. N.C.-Va. sect. 1968), Lynchburg Jaycees (v.p. 1967-68), Sigma Xi, Westwood Country Club, Tau Beta Pi. Home: 11000 Devenish Dr Oakton VA 22124-1804

CUTCHINS, CLIFFORD ARMSTRONG, IV, lawyer; b. Norfolk, Va., May 13, 1948; s. Clifford Armstrong III and Ann (Woods) C.; m. Jane McKenzie, Aug. 14, 1971; children: Sarah Helen, Ann Woods. BA, Princeton U., 1971; JD, MBA, U. Va., 1975. Bar: Va. 1975, U.S. Dist. Ct. (ea. dist.) Va. 1975, U.S. Ct. Appeals (4th cir.) 1975. Ptnr. McGuire, Woods, Battle & Boothe, Richmond, Va., 1975-90; sr. v.p., gen. counsel, sec. James River Corp. Va., 1990-97, Ft. James Corp., Deerfield, Ill., 1997-2000; ptnr. McGuireWoods LLP, Richmond, 2001—. Bd. dirs. Ft. James Europe N.V., Ft. James Operating Co. Bd. dirs. Arts Coun. Richmond, 1980-86, Richmond Heart Assn., 1980-83, St. Catherine's Sch., Richmond, 1983-86, Richmond Ballet, 1986-88, Richmond Children's Mus., 1986-94, Richmond on the James, 1986-88, Henrico Drs. Hosp., 1986—, Hist. Richmond Found., 1990-94, Richmond Met. Blood Svc., 1995-97, Kohl Children's Mus., Wilmette, Ill., 1998-2000; chmn. Fort James Found., 1997-2000, Richmond First Tee. Mem. ABA, Va. Bar Assn., Country Club Va. (bd. dirs. 1990-93), Commonwealth Club (bd. dirs. 1983-86, 96-97), Kinloch Golf Clubs. Republican. Baptist. Avocations: golf, travel, photography. General corporate, Securities. Home: 118 Tempsford Ln Richmond VA 23226-2319 Office: McGuireWoods LLP 901 E Cary St Richmond VA 23219 E-mail: ccutchins@mcguirewoods.com

CUTLER, IRWIN HERBERT, lawyer; b. Mar. 28, 1943; s. Irwin Herbert Cutler and Eva Gloe (Thomas) Benedict; m. Carol Jean Smith, Dec. 28, 1965; children: Rachel, Alice. BA, Yale U., 1965; JD, Cornell U., 1968. Bar: Ky. 1968, U.S. Dist. Ct. (ea. dist.) Ky. 1969, U.S. Dist. Ct. (we. dist.) Ky. 1969, U.S. Ct. Appeals (6th cir.) 1970, U.S. Ct. Appeals (7th cir.) 1975. Mem.: Ky. Bar Assn., Louisville Bar Assn. (co-chmn. labor law sect. 1984, co-chmn. labor law sect. 1992). Democrat. Presbyterian. Labor. Home: 2249 Woodford Pl Louisville KY 40205-1651 Office: 1400 B Waterfront Plz 325 W Main St Louisville KY 40202-4251

CUTLER, LAURENCE JEFFREY, lawyer; b. Bklyn., May 23, 1945; s. Charles and Ruth (Grossman) C.; children: Rebecca L., Mitchell A. BA, Am. U., Washington, 1967; JD, U. Ky., 1970. Bar: N.J. 1970, U.S. Dist. Ct. N.J. 1970, U.S. Supreme Ct. 1974, U.S. Ct. Appeals (3rd cir.) 1982, N.Y. 1986; cert. matrimonial arbitrator and mediator Am. Acad. Matrimonial Lawyers. Pvt. practice, Morristown, N.J., 1970—. Mem. coms. civil practice N.J. Supreme Ct., 1976-79, matrimonial litigation, 1980-82, family part practice, 1985-87, 98—; guest lectr. Seton Hall U. Sch. Law, 1988-90, adj. prof. law, 1992—; lectr. Am. Acad. Matrimonial Lawyers, 1985, 93, N.J. Family Part Judges' Retreat, 1989, N.J. Jud. Coll., 1990, Nat. Bus. Inst., Inc., 1992, Inst. Continuing Legal Edn. N.J., 1978—, Morris County Bar Assn., 1986, 91, N.J. State Bar Assn., 1992, Am. Trial Lawyers Assn., 1993-96, 99—. Co-author: N.J. Family Law Practice (3 vol.); contbr. articles to profl. jours. Mem. Morris Plains Juvenile Conf. Com., 1973-82; bd. trustees Morris Plains Libr. Assn., 1982-87. Recipient Tishler award, 1993, Bar Register of Pre-Eminent Lawyers, 1994—; named to Best Lawyers in Am., 1995—, Best Lawyers in N.J., 1997—. Mem. AMA (litigation sect. 1987-90), Internat. Acad. Matrimonial Lawyers (bd. govs. U.S. chpt. 1994-98), Am. Acad. Matrimonial Lawyers (bd. govs. 1989-90, 91-94, arbitration com. 1993—, chmn. mktg. com. 1991-92, membership com. 1992-93, budget and fin. com. 1990-91, editl. bd. Law Jour. 1993—, chmn. SCUBA Network 1992-93, bd. mgrs. N.J. chpt. 1981—, pres. N.J. chpt. 1985-87, chmn. nominating com. 1992-93, chmn. scholarship com. 1991-94, membership com. 1991-94), Am. Coll. Family Trial Lawyers (exec. com. 1994—), N.J. Assn. Matrimonial Arbitrators (v.p. 1993—), N.J. State Bar Assn. (exec. com. 1975-93, appellate practice com. 1993-95, curriculum com. Inst. Continuing Legal Edn. 1982-91), Morris County Bar Assn. (mem. family law com. 1973-75, 80—, chmn. 1987, chmn. matrimonial early settlement program 1976), Inn of Ct. (N.J. master family law 1993—), N.J. Bd. of Atty. (cert. matrimonial). Avocations: computers, horses. Family and matrimonial. Office: 60 Washington St Morristown NJ 07960-6844 E-mail: LJC@Cutlaw.com

CUTNER, ROLANDE REGAT, lawyer; b. Paris, Sept. 6, 1934; came to U.S., 1963, naturalized, 1970; d. Luis Felipe and Marguerite (Thibault) Ibarra; m. Charles Yves Regat, Feb. 4, 1960 (dec. 1971); m. David Alan Cutner, June 25, 1977 (div. 1985). Diploma in Polit. Sci., U. Paris, 1959; Lic. in Law, Paris Faculty of Law, 1971; grad. Inst. Jud. Studies, 1972. Bar: Paris 1976, N.Y. 1978, U.S. Dist. Ct. (so. dist.) N.Y. 1978. Atty. Compagnie General d'Electricite, Paris, 1972-76, Usinor Steel Corp., N.Y.C., 1976-77; mem. firm Griggs, Baldwin & Baldwin, 1978-79, Regat-Cutner, 1980— . Mem. Internat. Bar Assn., ABA, Am. Fgn. Law Assn., Fed. Bar Council, Ordre des Avocats a la Cour de Paris, N.Y. County Lawyer Assn. (com. on immigration, nationality, and naturalization), Asia-Pacific Lawyers Assn. (com. on Customs and Internat. Trade Law). Federal civil litigation, General corporate, Private international. Office: Regat-Cutner 67 Park Ave Suite 12 D New York NY 10006

CUYPERS, CHARLES JAMES, lawyer; b. Dec. 11, 1949; s. Donald Charles and Hazel Charlotte (Hollingsworth) Cuypers; m. Judy Arlene Stutzman, Dec. 18, 1971; children: Christina Jean, Julie Anne. BS, Kearney State Coll., 1974; JD, Creighton U., 1976. Bar: Nebr. 1976, U.S. Dist. Ct. Nebr. 1976. Ptnr. Sherwood & Cuypers, Oxford, Cambridge, Nebr., 1976—86; pres. Oxford Devel. Corp., 1979—86; asst. city atty. Grand Island, 1986—89, city atty., 1995—; v.p., gen. mgr. 3-D Investment, Inc., Doniphan, 1989—95. Cons. Butler Meml. Libr. Found., Cambridge, Nebr., 1983—86; cons., lawyer Cambridge Mus. Found., Inc., 1983—86, Fairview Cemetary Found., 1983—86; village atty., Orleans, Nebr., 1976—81, Oxford, Nebr., 1976—86; city atty., Cambridge, 1982—86. Author (and narrator): (radio) Oxford Centennial Radio Series, 1980. Bd. dir. Oxford Pub. Libr. , 1978—86; mem. Hall County Regional Planning Commn.; county chmn. Gov. Thone Reelection Com., Oxford, Nebr., 1982. Mem.: Nebr. Bar Assn., 14th Jud. Dist. Bar Assn. (pres. 1980—81), Young Lawyers Study Group, Grand Island Indsl. Found. (trustee 1987—88, mem. Grand Island Civic Ctr. com. 1987—90), Oxford C. of C. Republican. Lutheran. Bankruptcy, State civil litigation, Private international. Home: 1508 Spruce Pl Grand Island NE 68801-7048 Office: City Hall 100 E 1st St Grand Island NE 68801-6023

CVETANOVICH, DANNY L. lawyer; b. Wheeling, W.Va., Oct. 2, 1952; s. Louis J. and Nila J. (Hall) C.; m. Sharon M. Smith, Sept. 8, 1979; children; Gregory L., Steven W. BA, West Liberty State Coll., 1974; JD, Harvard U., 1977. Bar: Ohio 1977, U.S. Dist. Ct. (so. dist.) Ohio 1978, U.S. Ct. Appeals (6th cir.) 1980, U.S. Dist. Ct. (no. dist.) Ohio 1984, W.Va. 1985, U.S. Dist. Ct. (so. dist.) W.Va. 1985, U.S. Ct. Appeals (4th cir.) 1986, U.S. Dist. Ct. (we. dist.) Tex. 1998, U.S. Dist. Ct. (no. dist.) W.Va. 2001. Assoc. Bricker & Eckler, Columbus, Ohio, 1977-82, ptnr., 1983-87, Arter & Hadden LLP, Columbus, 1987—. Mem. ABA, Ohio State Bar Assn., W.Va. State Bar Assn., Columbus Bar Assn. Republican. Avocations: hunting, fishing, golf. Appellate, Federal civil litigation, State civil litigation. Office: Arter & Hadden LLP One Columbus 10 W Broad St Columbus OH 43215-3422

CYMROT, MARK ALAN, lawyer; b. Queens, N.Y., Oct. 8, 1947; s. Irwin Maurice and Anne (Kipnis) C.; children: Isaac, Erin. BA, George Washington U., 1969; JD, Columbia U., 1972. Bar: D.C. 1973. Trial lawyer civil divsn. U.S. Dept. of Justice, Washington, 1972-77; sr. litigator Consumers Union of U.S. Inc., 1977-79; spl. litigation counsel civil divsn. U.S. Dept. of Justice, 1979-83; ptnr. Cole Corette & Abrutyn, 1983-91, Baker & Hostetler, Washington, 1991—. Contbr. articles to profl. jours. Named one of 50 Best Lawyers in Washington by Washingtonian Mag., 1992. Avocations: photography, golf, tennis. Federal civil litigation, Private international, Public international. Office: Baker & Hostetler 1050 Connecticut Ave NW Washington DC 20036-5304

CYR, CONRAD KEEFE, federal judge; b. Limestone, Maine, Dec. 9, 1931; s. Louis Emery and Kathleen Mary (Keefe) C.; m. Judith Ann Pirie, June 23, 1962 (dec. Mar. 1985); children: Keefe Clark, Jeffrey Louis Frederick; m. Diana Kathleen Sanborn, Sept. 25, 1987. BS cum laude, Holy Cross Coll., 1953; JD, Yale U., 1956; LLD (hon.), LLD (hon.), Husson Coll., 1991. Bar: Maine 1956. Pvt. practice, Limestone, 1956-59; asst. U.S. atty., Bangor, Maine, 1959-61; judge U.S. Bankruptcy Court, 1961-81, U.S. Dist. Ct., Bangor, 1981-83, chief judge, 1983-89; judge U.S. Fgn. Intelligence Surveillance Ct., 1987-89, U.S. Ct. Appeals (1st cir.), Boston, 1989-97, sr. judge, 1997—. Standing spl. master U.S. Dist. Ct., Maine, 1974-76; chief judge Bankruptcy Appellate Panel Dist., Mass., 1980-81; mem. Jud. Council for the 1st Circuit, 1987—, com. on adminstrn. of the bankruptcy system Jud. Conf. U.S., 1987—. Founder, editor-in-chief Am. Bankruptcy Law Jour., 1970-81; contbg. author, editor: Collier on Bankruptcy, Vol. 10. Treas. Limestone Republican Com., 1958; chmn. Town of Limestone Budget Com., 1959; mem. steering com. U.S. AID Project for Assisting Bankruptcy and Reorgn. Procedures in Ctr. and Ea. Europe. Recipient cert. of appreciation Kans. Bar Assn., 1979, U. Maine, 1983; Nat. Judge's Recognition award Nat. Conf. Bankruptcy Judges, 1979; Key to Town Limestone, 1983; named one of Outstanding Young Men of Maine, 1963. Fellow Maine Bar Found. (charter), Am. Coll. Bankruptcy; mem. Maine Bar Assn., Penobscot Bar Assn., Nat. Conf. Bankruptcy Judges (prs. 1976-77), Nat. Bankruptcy Conf. (exec. bd. 1974-77), Am. Juticature Soc., Limestone C. of C. (pres.). Roman Catholic.*

CZAJKOWSKI, FRANK HENRY, lawyer; b. Bklyn., Jan. 7, 1936; m. Cecilia J. Artowicz, Sept. 3, 1955. BA, St. John's U., Bklyn., 1957; JD, St. John's U., 1959; LLM, George Washington U., 1966. Bar: N.Y. 1960, Pa. 1970, Conn. 1974, U.S. Supreme Ct. 1964. Claims adjustor Hartford Accident & Indemnity Ins. Co., N.Y.C., 1959-60; agt. Equitable Life Assurance Soc., 1960; atty. Corp. Counsel's Office, 1960-62, Fgn. Claims Settlement Comm., Washington, 1962-68, Atlantic-Richfield Co., N.Y.C., 1968-70, Phila., 1970-72; assoc. gen. counsel Unilever U.S.A. Co., Greenwich, Conn., 1972-98; pvt. practice, 1998—. Instr. Fairfield U. Ctr. Lifetime Learning, 1976, Sacred Heart U., 1983; arbitrator Am. Arbitration Assn. Mem. ABA, Conn. Bar Assn., Westchester-Fairfield Corp. Counsel Assn. Labor, Pension, profit-sharing, and employee benefits, Product liability. Office: 7 Lafayette Dr Trumbull CT 06611-2751

CZARRA, EDGAR F., JR. lawyer; b. Langhorne, Pa., Oct. 4, 1928; s. Edgar F. and Mary Agnes (Copeland) C.; m. Doris Catharine Lane, June 14, 1952; children: Penelope L., Edgar F. III, Jonathan C., Melanie A. BS, Yale U., 1949, LLB, 1952. Bar: U.S. Dist. Ct. D.C. 1954, U.S. Ct. Appeals (D.C. cir.) 1954, U.S. Supreme Ct. 1959. Assoc. Covington & Burling, Washington, 1952, 55-63, ptnr., 1963-97, ret., 1997. Chmn. Global View Prodns., Inc. Served to lt. (j.g.) USN, 1952-55. Mem. ABA, D.C. Bar Assn., Fed. Communications Bar Assn. Administrative and regulatory, Federal civil litigation, Mergers and acquisitions. Office: Covington & Burling 1201 Pennsylvania Ave NW Washington DC 20004-2401

DADY, ROBERT EDWARD, lawyer; b. N.Y.C., Nov. 11, 1936; s. Edward Joseph and Florence (Scheidt) D.; m. Mollie D. Richman; children: Michael, Andrew, Rachel. BA, Queens Coll., 1958; LLB, Fordham U., 1961. Bar: N.Y. 1962, Fla. 1974. Asst. gen. counsel The Equity Corp., N.Y.C., 1962-66; gen. atty. ITT_Levitt and Sons, Inc., Washington, Lake Success, N.Y., 1966-70; sr. v.p.-legal First Realty Investment Corp., Miami Beach, Fla., 1970-71; v.p.-legal, sec. Cavanagh Cmtys. Corp., Miami, 1971-75; ptnr. Mann & Dady, P.A., 1975-80, Mann, Dady, Corrigan & Zelman, P.A., Miami, 1980-83, Dady, Siegfried & Kipnis, P.A., Miami, 1984-85; pvt. practice, 1985-87; ptnr. Kimbrell and Hamann, P.A., 1987-89; shareholder Popham, Haik, Schnobrich & Kaufman, Ltd., 1990-96; of counsel Fieldstone, Lester, Shear & Denberg, Coral Gables, Fla., 1996—. Past adj. prof. law U. Miami Sch. Law.; bd. dirs. Spectrum Programs, Inc., pres., 1984-86, Spectrum Found., Inc., pres. 1988—. Author: Land Acquistion and Development, 1975. Bd. dirs., exec. comm. Miami Coalition for a Safe and Drug Free Cmty., 1992-99; vice-chmn. Childrens Home Soc. Found. Miami, 1993-96, bd. dirs., 1993—; appointed to (by gov.) Fla. Jud. Nom. Com., 1995-98; bd. dirs. Wellness Cmty., Miami, 2001—. Mem. Nat. Land Coun. (pres. 1974-81, vice chmn. bd. dirs. 1973—), Builders Assn. So. Fla. (life dir., gen. counsel 1982-2001), ABA (environ. law com., timesharing and recreation law com., vice chmn.), Fla. Bar Assn. Republican. Consumer commercial, Contracts commercial, Real property. Home: 8440 SW 143rd St Miami FL 33158-1457 Office: Fieldstone Lester Shear & Denberg Sun Trust Plaza 201 Alhambra Cir Ste 601 Coral Gables FL 33134-5107

D'AGUSTO, KAREN ROSE, lawyer; b. Phila., Jan. 4, 1952; d. Les and Anne Heilenman; m. Stephen Joseph Bernasconi, Aug. 21, 1976; children: Lesley Anne D. Bernasconi, Stephanie Kalena D. Bernasconi. BA in History cum laude, Immaculata Coll., 1974; JD, U. San Diego, 1977; postgrad., U. So. Calif., 1983—. Bar: Conn. 1977, Hawaii 1978, S.C. 1986. Tng. coord. Protection and Advocacy, Honolulu, 1978, adv. coord., 1979, staff atty., 1980-81, assoc dir., 1982, project dir., 1983—; regional coord. S.C. Protection and Adv. Sys., 1986-88; dep. dir. Hawaii Protection and Advocacy, 1989-91; pvt. practice law Mililani, Hawaii, 1980—. Instr. Hawaii Pacific Coll., Honolulu, 1982-84; dir. Harmon-Johnson Inst., Honolulu, 1983-85; adj. prof. Immaculata Coll., 1998-2001; legal cons., 1999—. Author: Legal Rights of Handicapped, 1980; author, editor curriculum Vol. I Guardians Ad. Litem, 1983; editor Jour. Comparative Legis. Analysis of Protection and Advocacy System, 1991. Pres. Ctrl. Oahu Mental Health Ctr., Pearl City, Hawaii, 1981-82; officer Kings Grant Assn., Summerville, S.C., 1988; rep. St. Andrews Priory Parent-Tchr. Fellowship Bd., 1990-91; mem. John B. Dey PTA, mem. bd. dirs., chair legis. com.; leader Girl Scouts Am., svc. unit mgr., trainer, cons. Cape Henry Svc. unit, Colonial Coast coun.; mem. PTA legis. com.; vol. Great Neck Mid. Sch.; co-chair Tower Hill Camp Fair, 1998-2001; chair family appeal Brandywine Valley Girl Scout Svc. Unit, 1996-2001; mem. events com. Bayard Taylor Libr., 2000-01. Recipient Exceptional Achievement award, 1989-90, Disting. Contbn. to Civil Rights of Persons with Disabilities award, 1991, Outstanding Svc. to Hawaiis Disabled Citizens award, 1982, Outstanding Vol. of Yr. award Colonial Coast coun. Girl Scouts U.S., 1995, Vol. of Yr. award Great Neck Middle Sch., 1996; named Outstanding Adv., 1985. Mem. ABA, Hawaii State Bar Assn., S.C. Bar Assn., Conn. Bar Assn., Hawaii Lawyers Care, Am. Assn. Counsel for Children Counsel, Wimbledon on the Bay Homeowners Assn. (v.p. 1992-93, chair by-laws com. 1993-94). Civil rights, Education and schools, Personal injury. Fax: 610 793-4469. E-mail: kdagusto@aol.com

DAHL, LOREN SILVESTER, retired federal judge; b. East Fairview, N.D., Mar. 1, 1921; s. William T. and Maude (Silvester) D.; m. Pamela B. Miller, Mar. 16, 1995; children by previous marriage: Candy, Walter Ray. AA, Coll. of Pacific, 1940; LLB, JD, U. Calif., San Francisco, 1949. Bar: Calif., 1950, U.S. Supreme Ct., 1957. Pvt. practice law, Sacramento, 1950; sr. ptnr. Dahl, Hefner, Stark & Marois, 1950-80; chief judge U.S. Bankruptcy Ct. (ea. dist.) Calif., 1980, 86-94; chief judge emeritus, 1994—. Chmn. Conf. Chief Judges, 9th Cir., 1992. Pres. Golden Empire Coun. Boy Scouts Am., Sacramento, 1955-56, chmn. bd. trustees, 1956, exec. com. region 12, 1958, regional chmn. 1968-70, nat. exec. bd. 1968-70; Sacramento County Juvenile Justice Commn.; mem. bd. visitors McGeorge sch. law U. Pacific, 1987—; bd. dirs. Salvation Army, Sacramento, 1954-57; Sacramento Symphony Assn., 1958-59, Sacramento Safety Coun. With USAAF, 1942-46. Recipient Disting. Svc. award Jaycees, 1957, Silver Beaver award, Boy Scouts Am., 1957, Silver Antelope award, Boy Scouts Am., 1963, Disting. Eagle Scout award, Boy Scouts Am., Judge of Yr. award Sacramento County Bar Assn., 1993. Mem. U. of Pacific Alumni Assn. (pres. 1974-78, bd. regents 1980—, Disting. Alumnus award 1979), ABA, Calif. Bar Assn. (lectr. bankruptcy, continuing edn.), Am. Judicature Soc., Masons, Shriners, Lions (dir. Sacramento club 1952-53), Phi Delta Phi, Del Paso Country Club. Club: Del Paso Country. Lodge: Masons, Shriners, Lions (dir. Sacramento club 1952-53). Home: 842 Lake Oak Ct Sacramento CA 95864-6154

DAHLING, GERALD VERNON, lawyer; b. Red Wing, Minn., Jan. 11, 1947; s. Vernon and Lucille Alfrieda (Reuter) D.; m. Edell Marie Villella, July 26, 1969; children: David (dec.), Christopher, Elizabeth, Mary. BS, Winona (Minn.) State Coll., 1968; MS, U. Minn., 1970; PhD, Harvard U., 1974; JD, William Mitchell Coll. of Law, 1980. Bar: U.S. Patent Office 1979, Minn. 1980, Ind. 1980, Pa. 1997, U.S. Dist. Ct. (so. dist.) Ind. 1980. Patent atty. Eli Lilly and Co., Indpls., 1980-84, mgr. biotech. patents, 1984-86, asst. patent counsel biotech., 1986-89, asst. patent counsel biotech. and fermentation products, 1990, asst. gen. patent counsel,

1991-95; dir. intellectual property Pasteur Mérieux Connaught, Lyon, France and Swiftwater, Pa., 1995-97, corp. v.p., dir. intellectual property, 1997-98, sr. v.p. intellectual property France, 1998-99; Rhone Poulenc Rorer, Collegeville, Pa., 1998-99; sr. v.p. global patents Aventis Pharms., Bridgewater, N.J., 2000—. Mem. ABA, Ind. Bar Assn., Pa. Bar Assn., Am. Intellectual Property Law Assn., Intellectual Property Owners Assn. (bd. dirs.). Democrat. Roman Catholic. Federal civil litigation, Contracts commercial, Patent. Home: 501 Waterford Ct New Hope PA 18938 Office: Rt 202-206 PO Box 6800 Bridgewater NJ 08807-0800 also: Aventis Pasteur 13 Pont Pasteur 69348 Lyon France

DAIL, JOSEPH GARNER, JR. judge; b. Elloree, S.C., June 15, 1932; s. Joseph Garner and Esther Vernette (Harbort) D.; m. Martha E. MacReynolds; children: Edward Benjamin, Mary Holyoke. BS, U. N.C., 1953, JD with honors, 1955. Bar: N.C. 1955, Va. 1976. Pvt. practice, Washington, 1959-76, McLean, Va., 1976-87; ptnr. Croft, Dail & Vance (and predecessor), 1966-76; counsel Gabeler, Ward & Griggs, 1983-87; judge U.S. adminstrv. law Fresno, Calif., 1987-94, San Francisco, 1994-97, Tampa, 1997-99; sr. U.S. adminstrv. law judge, 1999—. Assoc. editor: N.C. Law Rev, 1954-55. Lt. USNR, 1955-59; capt. Res. (ret.). Mem. Fed. Bar Assn., N.C. Bar Assn., Va. Bar Assn., Transp. Lawyers Assn. (Disting. Svc. award 1976), Order of Coif, Phi Beta Kappa. Republican. Home: 103 Masters Ln Safety Harbor FL 34695-3722 Office: Times Bldg 1000 N Ashley Dr Ste 200 Tampa FL 33602-3719 E-mail: macdail@aol.com

DAILEY, COLEEN HALL, magistrate, lawyer; b. East Liverpool, Ohio, Aug. 10, 1955; d. David Lawrence and Deloris Mae (Rosensteel) Hall; m. Donald W. Dailey Jr., Aug. 16, 1980 (div. May 2001); children: Erin Elizabeth, Daniel Lester. Student, Wittenberg U., 1973-75; BA, Youngstown State U., 1977; JD, U. Cin., 1980. Bar: Ohio 1981, U.S. Dist. Ct. (no. dist.) Ohio 1981. Sr. libr. assoc. Marx Law Libr., Cin., 1979-80; law clk. Kapp Law Office, East Liverpool, 1979, 1980-81, assoc., 1981-85; pvt. practice, 1985-95; magistrate Columbiana County, Ohio, 1995—. Spl. counsel Atty. Gen. Ohio, 1985-92. Pres. Columbiana County Young Dems., 1985-87; bd. dirs. Big Bros./Big Sisters Columbiana County, Inc., Lisbon, Ohio, 1984-87, Planned Parenthood Mahoning Valley, Inc., 1993-97; trustee Ohio Women Inc., 1991-95; mem. Columbiana County Progress Coun., Inc. Mem. ABA, Ohio Bar Assn. (Ohio Supreme Ct. Joint Task Force on Gender Fairness, family law specialization bd.), Ohio Assn. Magistrates (chmn. domestic rels. sect. 1998-2000), Columbiana County Bar Assn., East Liverpool Bus. and Profl. Women's Assn., Ohio Women's Bar Assn. (trustee 1997-99). Democrat. Lutheran. Office: Columbia County Common Pleas Court 105 S Market St Lisbon OH 44432-1255 E-mail: cdailey@epohi.com

DAILEY, DIANNE K. lawyer; b. Great Falls, Mont., Oct. 10, 1950; d. Gilmore and Patricia Marie (Linnane) Halverson. BS, Portland State U., 1977; JD, Lewis & Clark Coll., 1982. Assoc. Bullivant, Houser, Bailey, et. al., Portland, Oreg., 1982-88, ptnr., 1988—. Contbr. articles to profl. jours. Mem.: ABA (vice chair tort and ins. practice sect. 1995—96, chair-elect tort and ins. practice sect. 1996—97, chair tort and ins. practice sect. 1997—98, governing coun. 1992—99, property ins. law com., ins. coverage litigation com., comm. com., chair task force on involvement of women 1990—93, liaison to commn. on women 1993—97, chair task force CERCLA reauthorization, litigation sect., standing com. environ. law 1996—99, chair sect. officers conf. 1998—2001), Wash. Bar Assn., Oreg. State Bar, Multnomah Bar Assn. (bd. dirs. 1994—95), Internat. Assn. Def. Counsel, Def. Rsch. Inst., Fedn. Ins. and Corp. Counsel. General civil litigation, Environmental, Insurance. Office: Bullivant Houser Bailey 300 Pioneer Tower 888 SW 5th Ave Ste 300 Portland OR 97204-2089

DAILEY, GARRETT CLARK, publisher, lawyer; b. Bethesda, Md., Mar. 22, 1947; s. Garrett Hobart Valentine and Margaret (Clark) Dailey; m. Carolynn Farrar, June 21, 1969; children: Patrick, Steven. AB, UCLA, 1969; MA, Ariz. State U., 1974; JD, U. Calif., Davis, 1977. Bar: Calif. 1977, U.S. Dist. Ct. (no. dist.) Calif. 1969. Assoc. Stark, Stewart, Simon & Sparrowe, Oakland, Calif., 1977-80; ptnr. Davies & Dailey, 1980-85, owner, 1986-90; ptnr. Blum, Davies & Dailey, 1985-86; pres., pub. Attys. Briefcase, Inc., 1989—, pres., CEO, 1989—. Lectr. U. Calif. Davis Sch. Law, 1988-90, Golden Gate U. Grad. Sch. Taxation, San Francisco, 1986—. Author: SupporTax, 2001; co-author: Attorney's Briefcase, Calif. Family Law, 1990—, Calif. Evidence, 1993—, Children and the Law, 1992—, Calif. Lawgic Marital Termination Agreements, 1996—, Calif. Divorce Guide, 1997—, Lawgic Premarital Agreements, 1997—. Bd. dirs. Amigos de las Americas, San Ramon Valley, Calif., 1980-85, Rotary 517 Found., Oakland, 1985, Kid's Turn, 1993. Recipient Hall of Fame award Calif. Assn. Cert. Family Law Specialists, 1995. Fellow Am. Acad. Matrimonial Lawyers; mem. Assn. Cert. Family Law Specialists (Hall of Fame award 1995). Democrat. Congregationalist. Home: 1651 W Livorna Rd Alamo CA 94507-1018 Office: Attys Briefcase Inc 2915 McClure St Oakland CA 94609 E-mail: briefcase@aol.com

DAILY, FRANK J(EROME), lawyer; b. Chgo., Mar. 22, 1942; s. Francis Jerome and Eileen Veronica (O'Toole) D.; m. Julianna Ebert, June 23, 1996; children: Catherine, Eileen, Frank, William, Michael. BA in Journalism, Marquette U., 1964, JD, 1968. Bar: Wis. 1968, U.S. Dist. Ct. (ea. dist.) Wis. 1968, U.S. Dist. Ct. (we. dist.) Wis. 1971, U.S. Dist. Ct. (ctrl. dist.) Ill. 1990, U.S. Dist. Ct. (ea. dist.) Mich. 1994, U.S. Ct. Appeals (7th cir.) 1977, U.S. Ct. Appeals (3d and 5th cirs.) 1985, U.S. Ct. Appeals (4th, 6th, 8th, 9th, 10th, 11th cirs.) 1990, U.S. Supreme Ct. 1998, U.S. Dist. Ct. (no. dist.) Ill. 1999. Assoc. Quarles & Brady, Milw., 1968-75, ptnr., 1975—. Lectr. in product liability law and trial techniques Marquette U. Law Sch., U. Wis., Harvard U.; lectr. seminars sponsored by ABA, State Bar Wis., State Bar S.D., State Bar S.C., Product Liability Adv. Coun., Chem. Mfrs. Assn., Wis. Acad. Trial Lawyers, Trial Attys. Am., Marquette U., Southeastern Corp. Law Inst., Risk Ins. Mgmt. Soc., Inc.; mem. bd. visitors Wake Forest U. Law Sch.; life mem. pres.'s coun. Marquette Univ., Wake Forest U., Breton Coll., Dayton Coll. Author: Your Product's Life Is in the Balance: Litigation Survival-Increasing the Odds for Success, 1986, Product Liability Litigation in the 80s: A Trial Lawyer's View from the Trenches, 1986, Discovery Available to the Litigator and Its Effective Use, 1986, The Future of Tort Litigation: The Continuing Validity of Jury Trials, 1991, How to Make an Impact in Opening Statements for the Defense in Automobile Product Liability Cases, 1992, How Much Reform Does Civil Jury System Need, 1992, Do Protective Orders Compromise Public's Right to Know, 1993, Developments in Chemical Exposure Cases: Challenging Expert Testimony, 1993, The Spoliation Doctrine: The Sword, The Shield and The Shadow, 1997, Trial Tested Techniques for Winning Opening Statements, 1997, Litigation in the Next Millennium -- A Trial Lawyer's Crystal Ball Report, 1998, What's Hot and What's Not in Non-Daubert Products Liability In the Seventh Circuit, 1998. Ct. commr. Milw. County, Wis., 2001; life mem. Pres.'s Coun., Marquette U., Pres.'s Cir., Boston Coll. Named Marquette U. Law Alumnus of Yr., 2000. Fellow Internat. Acad. Trial Lawyers; mem. ABA (past co-chair discovery com. litigation sect., vice chmn. products, gen. liability and consumer law com. of sect. tort and ins. practice, litigation sect. and mfrs. liability subcom.), ATLA, AAAS, Trial Atty. of Am., Wis. Bar Assn., Chgo. Bar Assn., Milw. Bar Assn., 7th Cir. Bar Assn., Am. Judicature Soc., Def. Rsch. Inst., Supreme Ct. Hist. Soc., Indsl. Truck Assn. (lawyers com.), Am. Law Inst., Product Liability Adv. Coun., Am. Agrl. Law Assn., Wis. Acad. Trial Lawyers, Assn. for Advancement of Automotive Medicine (life), Nat. I-Club U. Iowa, U. Ala. Nat. Alumni Assn., Circle of Champions. Roman Catholic. General civil litigation, Personal injury, Product liability. Office: Quarles & Brady 411 E Wisconsin Ave Ste 2550 Milwaukee WI 53202-4497 E-mail: fjd@quarles.com

DALE, ERWIN RANDOLPH, lawyer, author; b. Herrin, Ill., July 30, 1915; s. Henry and Lena Bell (Campbell) D.; m. Charline Vincent, Aug. 27, 1955; children: Allyson Ann (Mrs. Earl A. Samson III), Kristan Charline (Mrs. Victor L. Zimmermann). BA, U. Tex., El Paso, 1937; JD, U. Tex., 1943. Bar: Tex. 1943, D.C. 1953, Mich. 1956, N.Y. 1960. Atty. IRS, 1943-56, chief reorgn. and dividend br., 1954-56; legal staff Gen. Motors Corp., 1956-57; ptnr. firm Chapman, Walsh & O'Connell, N.Y.C. and Washington, 1957-59, Hawkins, Delafield & Wood, N.Y.C., 1959-84; of counsel Hutchison, Price, Boyle & Brooks, Dallas, 1985-86, Jenkens, Hutchison & Gilchrist, Dallas, 1986, Hutchison, Boyle, Brooks & Dansfield, Dallas, 1986-87. Lectr. tax matters; dir. Md. Electronics Mfg. Corp., 1948-58; dir., treas. The Renaissance Corp., 1968-72; dir., asst. treas. Shancom Reconstrn. Corp., 1968-72, Newhaven Corp., 1968-72 Author numerous articles on fed. tax matters; bd. editors: Tex. Law Rev., 1941-42, 42-43. Mem. ABA (chmn. com. consol. returns sect. taxation 1959-60), Tex. Bar Assn., Mich. Bar Assn., N.Y. State Bar Assn. (chmn. corp. tax com. tax sect. 1967-68, mem. exec. com. 1968-70), Tax Inst. Am. (bd. dirs. 1967-69, treas. 1966), Assn. of Bar of City of N.Y., Nat. Tax Assn., Nat. Assn. Bond Lawyers, Am. Coll. Tax Counsel, Ex-Students Assn. U. Tex., Ex-Students Assn. U. Tex., El Paso, Bronxville Field Club (N.Y.), Masons. Corporate taxation, Personal income taxation. Home: 10 Holly Ln Darien CT 06820-3303 Fax: 203-662-9386. E-mail: erdale@aol.com

D'ALEMBERTE, TALBOT (SANDY D'ALEMBERTE), academic administrator, lawyer; b. Tallahassee, June 1, 1933; m. Patsy Palmer; children: Gabrielle Lynn, Joshua Talbot. BA in Polit. Sci. with honors, U. South, 1955; postgrad., London Sch. Econs. and Polit. Sci., U. London, 1958-59; JD with honors, U. Fla., 1962. Bar: Fla. 1962, U.S. Ct. Appeals (5th cir.) 1962, U.S. Supreme Ct. 1970. Assoc. Steel Hector & Davis, Miami, Fla., 1962-65, ptnr., 1965-84, 89-93; prof. Fla. State U., 1984—, dean, 1984-89, pres., 1994—. Lectr. U. Miami Coll. Law, 1969-71, adj. prof., 1974-76; reader Fla. Bd. Bar Examiners, 1965-67; mem. jud. nominating commn. Fla. Supreme Ct., 1975-78; chief counsel Ho. Select Com. for Impeachment of Certain Justices, 1975; mem. Fla. Law Revision Coun., 1968-74; chmn. Fla. Constl. Revision Commn., 197-778. Contbr. articles to profl. jours.; articles editor U. Fla. Law Rev. Mem. Fla. Ho. Reps., 1966-72, chmn. com. on ad valorem taxation, 1969-70, chmn. judiciary com., 1971-72, mem. various coms.; chmn. Fla. Commn. on Ethics, 1974-75; trustee Miami-Dade Community Coll., 1976-84. Served with USN, 1955-58; to lt. USNR. Recipient award Fla. Acad. Trial Lawyers, 1972, 93, Fla. Patriots award Fla. Bicentennial Commn., 1976, Disting. Alumnus award U. Fla., 1977, Nelson Poynter award Fla. Civil Liberties Union, 1984, Gov.'s Emmy award Nat. Acad. TV Arts and Scis., 1985, 1st Amendment award Nat. Sigma Delta Chi/Soc. Profl. Journalists, 1986, Medal of Honor award Fla. Bar Found., 1987, Juris prudence award Anti-Defamation League of S. Fla., 1990, Fla. Acad. of Criminal Def. Lawyers Annual Justice award, 1993, Acad. of Fla. Trial Lawyers Perry Nichols award, 1993, Nat. Coun. of Jewish Women's Hannah G. Soloman award, 1996, Am. Judicature Soc. Justice award, 1996; named Outstanding First Term House Mem., 1967, Most Outstanding Mem. of House, Capital Press Corps; Rotary Found. fellowship. Mem. ABA (pres. 1991-92, chmn. spl. com. on election reform 1973-76, chmn. spl. com. on resolution of minor disputes 1976-79, chmn. spl. com. on med. malpractice 1985-86, state del. from Fla. 1980-89, commn. on governance 1983-84, rules and calender com. ho. of dels. 1982-84, commn. on women in profession 1987, chair com. rule of law project for Haiti 1993, chair nom. com. sect. dispute res. 1993, individual rights and responsibilities com., co-founder Ctrl. and East European Law Initiative, World Order Under Law award 1998, Robert J. Kutak award sect. legal edn. 1998), Fla. Bar Assn. (bd. govs. 1974-82), Dade County Bar Assn. (pres. young lawyers sect. 1965-66, bd. dirs.), Am. Judicature Soc. (pres. 1982-84), U. Fla. Law Ctr. Assn. (trustee 1967—), Order of Coif, Omicron Delta Kappa, Phi Beta Kappa. Office: Fla State U Office Pres 211 Westcott Bldg Tallahassee FL 32306-1470

D'ALESSANDRO, DANIEL ANTHONY, lawyer, educator; b. Jersey City, Oct. 10, 1949; s. Donato Marino D'Alessandro and Rose Teresa (Casamassimo) Drennan; m. Beth Anne Lill, Sept. 2, 1978; children: Daniel Patrick, Eric Charles. BA, St. Peter's Coll., 1971; JD, Seton Hall U., 1974; LLM in Criminal Justice, NYU, 1981. Bar: N.J. 1975, U.S. Dist. Ct. N.J. 1975, N.Y. 1982, U.S. Supreme Ct. 1985, U.S. Dist. Ct. (so. dist.) N.Y. 1989. Law clk. to presiding judge Juvenile and Domestic Relations Ct., Hudson County, N.J., 1974-75; pub. defender City of Jersey City, 1975-76; prosecutor Town of Secaucus, N.J., 1976-77; prin. D'Alessandro & Assocs., Jersey City, 1977-82; ptnr. D' Alessandro & Tutak, 1982-90; pres. D'Alessandro, Tutak & Aschoff, P.C., 1990-92; ptnr. D'Alessandro & Aschoff, P.C., 1993-94; pvt. practice, 1994—. Adj. prof. Middlesex County Coll., Edison, N.J., 1981-83, St. Peter's Prep., 1981-83; arbitrator automobile arbitration program N.J. Supreme Ct.; mem. ethics com. N.J. Supreme Ct. Dist. VI; counsel Employees Retirement System of Jersey City, 1985-89; vice-chair fee arbitration com. Supreme Ct. N.J. Vol. probation officer Hudson County Probation Dept., 1977; pro bono counsel Anthony R. Cucci Civic Assn., Jersey City, 1981—89, Battered Women's Shelter, Jersey City, 1982, Mayor's Task force for Handicapped, Jersey City, 1985—89; v.p. Jersey City Boys Club, 1991, pres., 1993—, also trustee; baseball coach Jersey Shore Thunderbirds, N.J. AAU, 1993—99, Mater Dei H.S., 2000—. Named Prof. of Yr., Secaucus (N.J.) Patrolmen's Benevolent Assn., 1980; recipient Disting. Svc. award Jersey City Police Dept., 1988, Cert. of Merit, N.J. Supreme Ct., Meritorious Pub. Svc. award, 1990, Outstanding Bd. Mem. award N.J. Boys Clubs Coun., 1991, Outstanding Bd. Mem. award Boys and Girls Clubs of Hudson County, 1998. Mem.: aba, N.J. State Bar Assn., Hudson County Bar Assn. (past chmn., mem. various coms., trustee, treas. 1991, sec. 1992, v.p. 1994, v.p. 1995, pres.-elect 1996, pres. 1997—, Outstanding Bd. Mem. award 1998, Cmty. Svc. award 2001). Democrat. Roman Catholic. Avocations: renovating old homes, sports, photography. State civil litigation, General practice, Real property. Office: 3279 John F Kennedy Blvd Jersey City NJ 07306-3418 E-mail: dadpclaw@aol.com

D'ALESSANDRO, DIANNE MARIE, public defender; b. N.Y.C., Apr. 20, 1952; d. Frank and Marie A. D'A.; m. John P. Foley, July 24, 1977; children: Maria, James. BA in Psychology, Upsala Coll., East Orange, N.J., 1974; JD, N.Y. Law Sch., 1981. Bar: N.J. 1981, N.Y. 1990, U.S. Dist. Ct. N.J. 1981. Staff atty. Bergen City Legal Svc., Hackensack, N.J., 1981-83; sr. trial atty. Office Pub. Defender, 1983—. Dist. II B ethics com., Office of Atty. Ethics of the Supreme Ct. of N.J., 1992-95; bd. dirs. Bergen County Legal Svc. Recipient citation from Susan Reisner, pub. advocate, for work done on State vs. Harris. Mem. Assn. Criminal Def. Lawyers, Women Lawyers in Bergen County. Avocations: reading, hiking, historic preservation. Office: Office of Pub Advocate/Pub Defender 60 State St Hackensack NJ 07601-5451 E-mail: dalessandro_d@opd.state.nj.us

DALEY, MICHAEL JOSEPH, lawyer; b. Phila., Aug. 9, 1955; s. Robert Charles and Agnes Theresa (Brophy) D. BA with honors, U. Denver, 1977; JD, Loyola U., Chgo., 1980. Bar: Ill. 1980, U.S. Dist. Ct. (no. dist.) Ill. 1980, Trial Bar (no. dist.) Ill. 1983, U.S. Ct. Appeals (7th cir.) 1985, U.S. Supreme Ct. 1985, U.S. Dist. Ct. (no. dist.) Ind. 1994, U.S. Tax Ct. 1994. Asst. state's atty. Cook County State Atty.'s Office, Chgo., 1981-83; assoc. Nisen & Elliott, 1983-86, ptnr., 1986—. Instr. trial advocacy Loyola U. of Chgo., 1986—. Recipient Lewis Powell Medal for Advocacy, Am. Coll. Trial Lawyers, 1980, Robert Bellarmine award Loyola U. Chgo., 1995. Mem. Bar Assn. of 7th Fed. Cir., Assn. of Transp. Practitioners, Nat. Assn. R.R. Trial Counsel, Union League Club of Chgo. (pub. affairs com. 1993—). Avocations: skiing, cycling, golf. Federal civil litigation, General civil litigation, Transportation. Office: Nisen & Elliott 200 W Adams St Ste 2500 Chicago IL 60606-5283

DALEY, SUSAN JEAN, lawyer; b. New Britain, Conn., May 27, 1959; d. George Joseph and Norma (Woods) D. BA, U. Conn., 1978; JD, Harvard U., 1981. Bar: Ill. 1981. Assoc. Altheimer & Gray, Chgo., 1981-86, ptnr., 1986—. Mem. ABA (real property, probate and trust law sect. 1983—, chmn. welfare plans com. real property, probate and trust law sect. 1989-95, employee benefits com. taxation sect. 1984—, chmn. EEOC issues subcom. employee benefits com. taxation sect. 1990—), Nat. Assn. Stock Plan Profls. (pres. Chgo. chpt. 1995—), Ill. Bar Assn. (chmn. employee benefits divsn. fed. taxation sect. 1984-86, chmn. employee benefits sect., 1995-96, mem. employee benefits sect. 1990-97), Chgo. Bar Assn. (chmn. employee benefits divsn. fed. taxation com. 1985-86, chmn. employee benefits com. 1990-91, chmn. fed. taxatin com. 1992-93), Chgo. Coun. on Fgn. Rels. Avocation: marathons. Pension, profit-sharing, and employee benefits. Home: 1636 N Wells St Apt 415 Chicago IL 60614-6009 Office: Altheimer & Gray 10 S Wacker Dr Ste 4000 Chicago IL 60606-7407 E-mail: daleys@altheimer.com

D'ALFONSO, MARIO JOSEPH, lawyer; b. Phila., Nov. 3, 1951; s. Albert Carmine and Yolanda (Zanfrisco) D'A.; m. Rita F. Borrelli, Apr. 26, 1975; 1 child, Mario C. BA, Villanova U., 1973; JD, Widener U., 1979. Bar: Pa. 1979, N.J. 1979, U.S. Dist. Ct. (ea. dist.) Pa. 1979, U.S. Dist. Ct. N.J. 1979, U.S. Ct. Appeals (3d cir.) 1980, U.S. Supreme Ct. 1983, U.S. Ct. Appeals (5th cir.) 1989. Assoc. Avena, Hendren & Friedman, Camden, N.J., 1979-81; ptnr. Avena, Hendren, Friedman & D'Alfonso, 1981-84, D'Alfonso & Camacho, P.A., Haddon Heights, N.J., 1984—. Cons. Marbert Construction, Haddon Heights, N.J., 1982—. Mem. Am. Arbitration Assn. (Svc. award 1984), Assn. Criminal Def. Lawyers, Camden County Bar Assn., N.J. Trial Lawyers Assn., Phi Delta Phi (pres. 1978), Phi Kappa Phi. Roman Catholic. Criminal, General practice, Personal injury. Home: 64 Lady Diana Cir Marlton NJ 08053-3705 Office: 200 Lake Dr E Ste 203 Cherry Hill NJ 08002

DALIANIS, LINDA, judge; B, Northeastern U.; law degree, Suffolk U. Pvt. law practice, Nashua, N.H., 1974-79; marital master N.H. Superior Ct., 1979-80, assoc. justice, 1980—2000, N.H. Supreme Ct., Concord, 2000—. Chair Interbranch Criminal and Juvenile Justice Com.; mem. edn. coms. N.H. Supreme and Superior Cts., Northern New Eng. Jud. Edn. Com.; mem. jud. adv. com. N.H. Dept. Corrections; mem. marital masters com., alternative dispute resolution com. N.H. Superior Ct. Office: Supreme Ct Bldg One Noble Dr Concord NH 03301-6160*

DALLAS, WILLIAM MOFFIT, JR. lawyer; b. Cedar Rapids, Iowa, May 7, 1949; s. William Moffit and Winifred Mae (Lillie) D.; m. Lynne Louise Russo, July 30, 1977 (div. July 1984); m. Janet Neustaetter, Apr. 19, 1985; children: Sarah Anne, Steven Kurt. AB, Oberlin Coll., 1971; JD, Harvard U., 1974. Bar: N.Y. 1975, U.S. Dist. Ct. (so. and ea. dists.) N.Y. 1975, U.S. Ct. Appeals (2d cir.) 1976, U.S. Ct. Appeals (3d cir.) 1983, U.S. Ct. Appeals (8th cir.) 1984. Assoc. Sullivan & Cromwell, N.Y.C., 1974-82, ptnr., 1982—. Fed. mediator U.S. Dist. Ct., 1995—. Contbr. articles on antitrust issues to law revs., 1978—, chpt. to book. Served to lt. USN, 1971-77. Mem. ABA, Assn. of Bar of City of N.Y. (chmn. com. on judicial admin., 1999—, sec. judiciary com. 1977-80, chmn. com. jud. adminstrn. 1999—), N.Y. County Lawyers' Assn. (chmn. com. on trade regulation 1978-81), India House Club (N.Y.C.). Antitrust, Federal civil litigation, State civil litigation. Office: Sullivan & Cromwell 125 Broad St Fl 28 New York NY 10004-2489

DAL SANTO, DIANE, writer, retired judge; b. East Chicago, Ind., Sept. 20, 1949; d. John Quentin Dal Santo and Helen (Koval) D.; m. Fred O'Cheskey, June 29, 1985. BA, U. N.Mex., 1971; cert., Inst. Internat. and Comparative Law, Guadalajara, Mex., 1978; JD, U. San Diego, 1980. Bar: N.Mex. 1980, U.S. Dist. Ct. N.Mex. 1980. Ct. planner Met. Criminal Justice Coordinating Coun., Albuquerque, 1973-75; planning coord. Dist. Atty.'s Office, 1975-76, exec. asst. to dist. atty., 1976-77, asst. dir. atty. for violent crimes, 1980-82; chief dep. city atty. City of Albuquerque, 1983; assoc. firm T.B. Keleher & Assocs., 1983-84; judge Met. Ct., 1985-89, chief judge, 1988-89; judge Dist. Ct., 1989-2000. Mem. faculty Nat. Jud. Coll., 1990-95, 97—, bd. trustees, 1995-96. Columnist Albuquerque Jour., 1996-98. Bd. dirs. Nat. Coun. Alcoholism, 1984, S.W. Ballet Co., Albuquerque, 1982-83; mem. Mayor's Task Force on Alcoholism and Crime, 1987-88, N.Mex. Coun. Crime and Delinquency, 1987-97, bd. dirs., 1992-94, Task Force Domestic Violence, 1987-94; pres. bench, bar, media com., 1987, pres. 1992, rules of evidence com. Supreme Ct., 1993-96, chair com. access to pub. records Supreme Ct., 1988; steering com. N.Mex. Buddy Awards, 1995—; mem. Metro. Criminal Justice Coordinating Coun., 1998—. U. San Diego scholar, 1978-79; recipient Women on the Move award YWCA, 1989, Disting. Woman award U. N.Mex. Alumni Assn., 1994, Outstanding Alumnus Dept. Sociology U. N.Mex., 1995; named Woman of Yr. award Duke City Bus. and Profl. Women, 1985. Mem. ABA (Nat. Conf. State Trial Judges Jud. Excellence award 1996), LWV, AAUW, Am. Judicature Soc., N.Mex. Women's Found., N.Mex. State Bar Assn. (silver gavel award 1997), N.Mex. Women's Bar Assn. (bd. dirs. 1991-92, Power and Caring award 2000), Albuquerque Bar Assn., Nat. Assn. Women Judges (bd. dist. dirs. 1999—), Greater Albuquerque C. of C. (steering com. 1989), N.Mex. Magistrate Judges Assn. (v.p. 1985-89), Dist. Judges Assn. (pres. 1994-95), Pennies for Homeless. Office: Dist Ct 415 Tijeras Ave NW Albuquerque NM 87102-3252 E-mail: dianedalsanto@hotmail.com

DALTON, ANNE, lawyer; b. Pitts., Dec. 6, 1951; d. Thomas John and Mary Olive (Paul) D.; m. Oliver E. Martin, Dec. 26, 1987. BA in Polit. Sci., NYU, 1973; JD, Fordham U., 1977. Bar: N.Y. 1978, U.S. Dist. Ct. (so. and ea. dists.) N.Y. 1979, Pa. 1987, Fla. 1990. Assoc. Mendes & Mount, N.Y.C., 1979-80; atty. news divsn. ABC, 1980-85; TV news prodr. ABC Network, 1985-86; sr. atty. Radio City Music Hall Prodns., Inc., 1986-87; pvt. practice Stroudsburg, Pa., 1987-91; asst. county att., asst. port authority atty. Lee County, Ft. Myers, Fla., 1991-94; pvt. practice, 1994—; family law mediator Fla., 1994—; cir. civil mediator, 1995—. Spl. hearing master 20th Jud. Cir., Fla., 1991—, ct. Commr., gen. master family civil and probate divsn., 1995—; adj. prof. Edison C.C., Ft. Myers, Barry U., Ft. Myers; family, cir. civil mediator, 1995. Recipient Clio award Internat. Clio Award Com., 1978. Mem. Pa. Bar Assn., Fla. Bar Assn., N.Y. Bar Assn., Lee County Bar Assn. Roman Catholic. Avocations: reading, gardening, swimming. Alternative dispute resolution, Computer, General practice. Office: 2044 Bayside Pkwy Fort Myers FL 33901-3102

DALTON, JOHN JOSEPH, lawyer; b. N.Y.C., Feb. 7, 1943; s. John Henry and Anna Veronica (Chiusano) D.; m. Martha E. Dalton, Feb. 24, 1968; children: Martha G., J. Michael, W. Brian. BBA, Fairfield U., 1964; JD, Northwestern U., 1967. Bar: Ill. 1967, Ga. 1970, U.S. Dist. Ct. (no. and mid. dists.) Ga., U.S. Dist. Ct. (no. dist.) Ill., U.S. Ct. Appeals (2d, 4th, 5th, 7th, 10th and 11th cirs.), U.S. Tax Ct., U.S. Supreme Ct. Atty. Clausen, Miller, Gorman, Caffrey & Witous, Chgo., 1967-69; ptnr. Troutman Sanders (formerly Troutman, Sanders, Lockerman & Ashmore), Atlanta, 1970—. Chmn. bd. Atlanta Vol. Lawyers Found., 1993. With U.S. Army, 1968-69. Fellow: Am. Coll. Trial Lawyers (regent), Am. Bar Found.; mem.: Atlanta Bar Assn. (dir.), Piedmont Driving Club, Peachtree Golf Club. Office: Troutman Sanders 600 Peachtree St NE Ste 5200 Atlanta GA 30308-2216

DALY, JOHN PAUL, lawyer; b. Pitts., Aug. 6, 1939; s. John Ambrose and Cora Evelyn (Faye) D.; m. Kathleen Ellen Paul, Dec. 21, 1961. AB, U. Calif., Riverside, 1961; JD, Loyola U., Los Angeles, 1971. Bar: Calif. 1972. Dep. dist. atty. San Luis Obispo, Calif., 1971-78, dep. county counsel, 1978—; judge pro tem Calif. Superior Ct., 1985—. Law prof. U. Calif. Polytech., 1979-81, lectr. Calif. Jud. Coll., 1982, post doctoral

forensic psychiatry curriculum U. Calif., Atascadero State Hosp., 1987—, chmn., 1996-98; lectr. probate/med. health specialists County Counsel's Assn. Calif., 1980—; lectr. for profl. credentials cert. Calif. Assn. Pub. Adminstrs., Pub. Guardians, Pub. Conservators, 1991. Speaker Mental Health Dept. Social Svcs., San Luis Obispo, 1975—. Mem. AMA, San Luis Obispo Govt. Attys. Union (founder, pres. 1977-82, chief negotiator 1977-79), Gold Wing Touring Assn., Gold Wing Road Riders Assn. Home: 10650 Colorado Rd Atascadero CA 93422-5706 Office: County Counsel Govt Ctr San Luis Obispo CA 93408

DALY, JOSEPH LEO, law educator; b. Phila., July 31, 1942; s. Leo Vincent and Genevieve Delores (McGinnis) D.; m. Kathleen Ann Dolan, July 24, 1965; children: Michael, Colleen. BA, U. Minn., 1964; JD, William Mitchell Coll. Law, 1969. Bar: Minn. 1969, U.S. Dist. Ct. Minn. 1970, U.S. Supreme Ct. 1972, U.S. Ct. Appeals (8th cir.) 1973, U.S. Ct. Appeals (D.C. cir.) 1974; cert. mediator and arbitrator alternative dispute rev. bd. Minn. Supreme Ct. Ptnr. Franke & Daly, Mpls., 1969-74; prof. law Hamline U. Sch. Law, St. Paul, 1974—. Arbitrator Am. Arbitration Assn., N.Y.C., 1980—, U.S. Fed. Mediation and Conciliation Svc., Washington, 1988—, for the states of Minn., Hawaii, Idaho, Ind., Mass., Mich., N.D., Pa., Oreg., Wisc., V.I and City of L.A.; arbitrator Bur. Mediation Svcs., St. Paul, 1978—; vis. scholar Ctr. for Dispute Resolution, Willamette U., Salem, Oreg., 1985; facilitator Minn. Internat. Health Vols., Kenya, 1985; observer Philippine Constl. Conv., Manila, 1986; participant European Arab Arbitration Congress, Bahrain, 1987; human rights investigator in the Philippines, 1989; vis. scholar U. Oslo, 1990, 91, 92, 96, 97; lectr. on trial skills for human rights lawyers, The Philippines, 1989; lectr. to leaders at Site 2 Cambodian Refugee Camp, Thai/Cambodian border, 1989; lectr. U. Cluj-NAPACA, Romania, 1991; vis. lectr. for developing countries Internat. Bar Assn., 1991-92; lectr. U. Tirana, Albania, 1992, London, 1993, Nat. Econs. U., Hanoi, Vietnam, 1993, 94, Danang (Vietnam) Poly. U., 1993, Ho Chi Minh Econs. U., Saigon, Vietnam, 1993, U. Hanoi Law Sch., 1994, U. Modena, Italy, 1994, Hanoi, Danang and Saigon, 1995, Phnom Penh, Cambodia, 1995, Hong Kong, 1996, Shenzhen, China, 1996, Oslo, Norway, 1996, Karolinska Inst., Stockholm, 1997; vis. prof. So. Cross U., Lismore, Australia, 1998, 99, U. Bergen, Norway, 1999, Tongji U., Shanghai, China, 1999, U. Saigon, Vietnam, 1999, 2000; cons. Chua U., Tokyo, 2001; team leader UN Devel. Programme mid-term evaluation of UN project, Vietnam, Hanoi, 2001; vis. prof. U. Queensland, Brisbane, Australia, 2001. Co-author: The Law, the Student and the Catholic School, 1981; co-author, editor: The Student Lawyer: A High School Handbook of Minnesota Law, 1981, rev. edit., 1986, Strategies and Exercises in Law Related Education, 1981, International Law, 1993, The American Trial System, 1994; contbr. more than 50 articles to profl. jours. Mem. Minn. Legislature Task Force on Sexual Exploitation by Counselors and Therapists, St. Paul, 1984-85, Nat. Adv. Com. on Citizen Edn. in Law, 1982-85; bd. dirs. Scenic Am., Washington, 1989-92. Recipient Spurgeon award Mayor and Citizens of St. Paul and Indianhead Scouting, 1983; named a Leading Am. Atty. in Alternative Dispute Resolution: Employment Law; fellow U. Miss. Law Sch. Mem. ABA (contbg. editor Preview of U.S. Supreme Ct. Cases mag. 1984—), Internat. Bar Assn. (London, vis. lectr. for devel. countries 1991—), Minn. State Bar Assn., Minn. Lawyers Internat. (human rights com., rep. to Philippine Constl. Conv. 1986), St. Paul Athletic Club, Phi Alpha Delta. Avocations: jogging, sailing. Office: Hamline U Sch Law 1536 Hewitt Ave Saint Paul MN 55104-1205 E-mail: jdaly@GW.hamline.edu

DALY, WILLIAM JOSEPH, lawyer; b. Bklyn., Mar. 19, 1928; s. William Bernard and Charlotte Marie (Saunders) D.; m. Barbara A. Longenecker, Nov. 19, 1955; children: Sharon, Nancy, Carol. B.A., St. John's U., 1951, J.D., 1953. Bar: N.Y. 1954, U.S. Dist. Ct. (so. and ea. dists.) N.Y. 1958, U.S. Ct. Mil. Appeals 1969, U.S. Ct. Claims 1969, U.S. Tax Ct. 1969, U.S. Supreme Ct. 1973. Assoc. Garvey & Conway, Esquires, N.Y.C., 1954-55, Wing & Wing, Esquires, N.Y.C., 1955-58; ptnr. Daly Lavery & Hall, Esquires and predecessors, Ossining, N.Y., 1958—. Adj. prof. law Mercy Coll., Dobbs Ferry, N.Y. V.p. Legal Aid Soc., Westchester County, N.Y., 1983—; mem. 9th Jud. Dist. Grievance Com., 1981-89, chmn. 1988-89; spl. referee in disciplinary procs.; trustee Supreme Ct. Libr. at White Plains, 1985—. With U.S. Army, 1946-48; ret. col. JA-AUS, 1978; mem. Hall of Fame U.S. Army Officer Cand. Sch., Ft. Benning, Ga. Fellow Am. Bar Found., N.Y. Bar Found.; mem. ABA, N.Y. State Bar Assn. (ho. of dels. 1977-89, 90-96, exec. com. 1983-89, 90-96, v.p. 1985-89, 90-96), Westchester County Bar Assn. (pres. 1979-81, dirs. coun. 1981—), Westchester County Bar Inst. (bd. dirs. 1982-98), Ossinging Bar Assn. (pres. 1966-67), Assn. Trial Lawyers Am., N.Y. State Trial Lawyers Assn., Res. Officers Assn. U.S., Assn. U.S. Army, Skull and Circle, Phi Delta Phi. Roman Catholic. Family and matrimonial, Personal injury, Probate. Home: 232 Hunter Ave Sleepy Hollow NY 10591-1317 Office: 73 Croton Ave Ste 209 Ossining NY 10562-4971

DAMASHEK, PHILIP MICHAEL, lawyer; b. N.Y.C., May 18, 1940; s. Jacob and Esther (Sassower) D.; m. Judith Ellen Gold, Dec. 3, 1967; children: Alan S., Jonathan S., Harris R. BBA, U. Miami, 1964. Bar: N.Y. 1969, U.S. Dist. Ct. (so. and ea. dists.) N.Y. 1977. Lawyer Cosmopolitan Mut. Ins. Co., N.Y.C., 1969-70, Schneider, Kleinick, Weitz & Damashek, 1971-73; sr. ptnr. Philip M. Damashek, P.C., N.Y.C., 1974-89; ptnr. Damashek, Godosky & Gentile, 1989-94; mng. ptnr. Schneider, Kleinick, Weitz, Damashek & Shoot, 1994-99, 1999-2000, mng. ptnr. The Cochran Firm, 2000—. Chmn. Combined Bar Assns. Jud. Screening Panel, N.Y.C., 1983-88; co-chair NYSTLA Law Pac, 1997—, trustee, 1989-91; legis. appointment mem. Com. to Rev. Audio-Visual Coverage of Ct. Procs., 1993-94; exec. apptd. to govs. N.Y. Jud. Screening Com., 1997—, adv. bd. N.Y. Israel Econ. Devel. Partnership, 1997—; apptd. Com. on Case Mgmt. Office of Ct. Adminstrn., Cts. of State of N.Y., 1993—, Task Force on Reducing Litigation Cost and Delay, 1st Judicial Dist., 1996—, Differentiated Case Mgmt. Project, Kings County, 1996—, Alt. Dispute Resolution Adv. Com. N.Y. State Unified Ct. Sys., 1999—, N.Y. State Jud. Salary Commn., 1997—, N.Y. State CLE Bd.(charter bd. mem.), 1997—; trustee N.Y. Law Sch., 1996—; mem. NYSTLA Designated Ind. Jud. Screening Panel, N.Y. County Dem. Commn., 1991—, malpractice panel Supreme Ct. of the State of N.Y., County of N.Y., 1990-91; dir. and v.p. for govt. rels. Respect for Law Alliance, Inc., 1995—; charter mem. N.Y. State CLE Bd. 1997-2000. Named Lawyer of Yr., Inst. Jewish Humanities, 1990, Lawyer of the Yr., UJA Fedn., 1993, N.Y. Law Schs. Lifetime Achievement award, 2000. Fellow Am. Bd. Trial Advs. (life), Am. Judicature Soc., Am. Bar Found., Roscoe Pound Found., Assn. Trial Lawyers Am. (Wiedemann Wysocki citation of excellence 1990, bd. govs. 1990-92, state rels. com. 1990-92, no-fault coordinating com. 1990-92); mem. ABA, N.Y. State Bar Assn. (ct. adminstrn. com., com. jud. adminstrn. 1990-94), Assn. of Bar of City of N.Y., N.Y. State Trial Lawyers Assn. (pres. 1990-91, bd. dirs., trustee), Assn. Trial Lawyers City N.Y. (bd. dirs.), N.Y. County Lawyers Assn., Trial Lawyers for Pub. Justice (sustaining), Jewish Lawyers Guild (bd. govs.). State civil litigation, Personal injury. Office: The Cochran Firm Schneider Kleinick Weitz Damashek & Shoot 233 Broadway Fl 5 New York NY 10279-0599

D'AMICO, ANDREW J. lawyer; b. Phila., Feb. 18, 1953; s. Joseph J. and Alice H. (Falotica) D'A.; m. Georgiana R. Etheridge, Feb. 25, 1978; children: Andrew J. Jr., Joseph W., Jennifer T., Theresa J. BA, St. Joseph's U., Phila., 1975; JD, Villanova U., 1978. Bar: Pa. Supreme Ct. 1978, U.S. Dist. Ct. (ea. dist.) Pa. 1979, U.S Ct. Appeals (3d Cir.) 1981, U.S Supreme Ct. 1982. Sole practitioner Law Offices Andrew J. D'Amico, Media, Pa., 1979—. Coach Llanerch Hills Little League, Drexel Hill, Pa., 1986-96, St. Bernadette CYO Basketball, 1996-2000. Mem. ATLA, Pa. Trial Lawyers Assn., Del. County Bar Assn. (bd. dirs. 1991-92, 97, 98), Guy G. deFuria Am. Inn of Ct. (pres. 1995-96), Alpha Sigma Nu. Roman Catholic. Avocations: music, coaching sports, reading. General civil litigation, Personal injury, Real property. Office: PO Box 605 115 N Monroe St Media PA 19063-3037

D'AMICO, JOHN, JR. judge; b. Long Branch, N.J., Jan. 24, 1941; s. John and Elvira (Caravello) D'A.; m. Sandra V. Vaccarelli, Nov. 25, 1967; 1 child, Kimberly Jean. AB cum laude, Harvard U., 1963, JD, 1966. Bar: N.J. 1966. Law clk. to presiding justice Monmouth County Ct., Freehold, N.J., 1966-67; assoc. Drazin, Warshaw, Auerbach & Rudnick, Red Bank, 1967-70; atty. Mut. Benefit Life Ins. Co., Newark, 1970-72, asst. counsel, 1972-74, assoc. counsel, 1974-77, counsel, 1978-81, 2d v.p., counsel, 1981-91; of counsel Shea & Gould, 1991; judge Superior Ct. of N.J., 1992—. Counsel Nat. Soc. to Prevent Blindness, New Brunswick, 1978-91, Partnership for N.J., New Brunswick, 1984-91; 1st vice chmn. N.J. Transp. Coordinating Coun.äa, Newark, 1984-89; mem. Monmouth County Bd. Social Services, Freehold, 1986; councilman Borough of Oceanport, N.J., 1979-84; freeholder Monmouth County, N.J., 1983-89; senator State of N.J., 1988-89; bd. dirs. Shore Commuter Coalition, Eatontown, N.J., 1982-91. Recipient Disting. Svc. award Nat. Soc. to Prevent Blindness, 1983. Mem. ABA, N.J. Bar Assn., Monmouth County Bar Assn., Assn. Life Ins. Counsel, Harvard U. Law Sch. Assn. Democrat. Avocations: reading, golf, tennis. Home: 53 Wittenberg Ct Oceanport NJ 07757-1027 Office: Monmouth County Courthouse Freehold NJ 07728 E-mail: jdamic@juno.com

DAMICO, NICHOLAS PETER, lawyer; b. Chester, Pa., June 29, 1937; s. Ralph A. and Mary C. (Ametrane) D.; m. Patricia Ann Swatek, Aug. 26, 1967; children: Christine, Gregory. BS in Acctg., St. Joseph's U., 1960; LLB, U. Pa., 1963; LLM, Georgetown U., 1967. Bar: Pa. 1963, D.C. 1967, Md. 1986. Tax law specialist IRS, Washington, 1963-66; assoc. Silverstein & Mullens, 1966-72, ptnr., 1972-76; prin. Damico & Assocs., 1976—. Adj. prof. Georgetown U. Law Ctr., Washington, 1973-75. Mem. ABA. Estate planning, Pension, profit-sharing, and employee benefits, Probate. Office: 1101 17th St NW Ste 820 Washington DC 20036-4731 E-mail: nicholas.damico@verizon.net

DAMPEER, JOHN LYELL, retired lawyer; b. Cleve., June 3, 1916; s. James W. and Felicia (Gressitt) D.; m. Lucie Augustin Kennerdell, June 30, 1950 (dec. July 1990); children: Lyell B., David K., G. Geoffrey. S.B., Harvard U., 1938, LL.B., 1942; student, New Coll., Oxford (Eng.) U., 1938-39. Bar: Ohio 1946. Since practiced in, Cleve.; ptnr. Thompson Hine & Flory LLP, 1955-97; ret., 1997. Trustee Family Svc. Assn. Cleve., 1951-70; trustee, chmn. bd. trustees Kelvin and Eleanor Smith Found., 1984-96; trustee, treas. Sea Rsch. Found., 1984-96. Henry fellow, 1938-39 Mem. ABA, Ohio Bar Assn. (chmn. corp. law com. 1960-62), Greater Cleve. Bar Assn. (exec. com. 1958-61), Phi Beta Kappa. Clubs: Union (Cleve.), Kirtland Country (Cleve.). General corporate, Non-profit and tax-exempt organizations, Securities. Home: 44 Laurel Lake Dr Hudson OH 44236-2159 Office: Thompson Hine LLP 3900 Key Ctr 127 Public Sq Cleveland OH 44114-1216

DAMSGAARD, KELL MARSH, lawyer; b. Darby, Pa., May 16, 1949; s. Kjeld and Dorothy (Fanck) D.; m. Katherine Elizabeth Stark, June 17, 1972; children: Peter Kjeld, Christopher William, David Zentner. BA cum laude, Yale U., 1971; JD, U. Pa., 1974. Bar: Pa. 1974, U.S. Dist. Ct. (ea. dist.) Pa. 1975, U.S. Ct. Appeals (3d cir.) 1984, U.S. Ct. Appeals (D.C. cir.) 1989, U.S. Ct. Appeals (8th cir.) 1990, U.S. Ct. Appeals (10th cir.), 1991, U.S. Supreme Ct. 1991. Law clk. to judge Superior Ct. of Pa., Phila., 1974-75; assoc. Morgan, Lewis & Bockius LLP, 1975-81; ptnr. Morgan, Lewis & Bockius, 1981—, firm adminstrv. ptnr., 1996—. Mem. ABA, Phila. Bar Assn. Avocations: skiing, jogging, tennis, antiques. General civil litigation, Computer, Product liability. Home: PO Box 141 Birchrunville PA 19421-0141 Office: Morgan Lewis & Bockius LLP 1701 Market St Philadelphia PA 19103-2903

DANA, HOWARD H., JR. state supreme court justice; Assoc. justice Supreme Jud. Ct. of Maine, Portland, 1993—. Office: Cumberland County Courthouse PO Box 368 142 Federal St Portland ME 04112-0368*

DANA, LAUREN ELIZABETH, lawyer; b. Hollywood, Calif., Sept. 30, 1950; d. Franklin Eugene and Margaret Elizabeth (Nixon) D.; m. Andrew Russell Willing, May 25, 1986; 1 child, Matthew Barkan Willing. BA cum laude, Calif. State U., Northridge, 1973; JD cum laude, Southwestern U., 1982. Bar: Calif. 1982, U.S. Dist. Ct. (cen. dist.) Calif. 1983, U.S. Ct. Appeals (9th cir.) 1983, U.S. Supreme Ct. 1987. Assoc. Law Office Andrew R. Willing, L.A., 1982-84; dep. atty. gen. Calif. Dept. Justice-Atty. Gen., 1984—. Temporary judge L.A. Mcpl. Ct. Assoc. editor legal update Police Officer Law Report, 1986-87. Recipient Am. Jurisprudence Book award Lawyers Coop. Pub. Co., 1980, Am. Jurisprudence Book award in Evidence, 1980. Mem. ABA, L.A. County Bar Assn. (conf. of dels., 1998, 99, 2000, 01), Am. Judicature Soc., Constitutional Rights Found., Selden Soc., U.S. Supreme Ct. Hist. Soc., Women Lawyers Assn. L.A., L.A. World Affairs Coun., Alliance for Children's Rights, Town Hall, Phi Alpha Delta, The Da Camera Soc. Avocations: reading, music, collecting books on English history, travel, French. Office: Calif Dept Justice 300 S Spring St Los Angeles CA 90013-1230

DANAHER, JOHN ANTHONY, III, prosecutor; b. New Haven, Aug. 22, 1950; s. John Anthony Jr. and Grace Elizabeth (Burkett) D.; m. Anne Elizabeth Morrison, May 11, 1985; children: Ceara Morrison Danaher, Brendan Ahearn, Austin Spellman, Mary Kate Shea. Awd, Fairfield U., 1972; MA, U. Hartford, 1977; JD, U. Conn., 1980. Bar: Conn. 1980; U.S. Dist. Ct. Conn. 1980; U.S. Ct. Appeals (2d cir.) 1982; U.S. Supreme Ct. 1987. Law clk. to hon. judge T. Emmet Clarie U.S. Dist. Ct. Conn., Hartford, Conn., 1980-81; trial atty. Day, Berry & Howard , 1981-86; prosecutor U.S. Atty.'s Office, 1986—, exec. asst., 1991—; U.S. atty. U.S. Atty.'s Office Ct. Dist. Editor Conn. Law Rev. 1978-80. Mem. Red Cross blood svcs. com., Hartford, 1981-85; active Long Rivers Coun., Boy Scouts Am., 1994—. Recipient Disting. Svc. award Atty. Gen. of U.S., Washington, 1990; 10 Superior Achievement awards Dept. of Justice, Hartford, 1988, 90-97. Mem. Fed. Bar Assn. (pres. Hartford County chpt. 1985-86). Office: US Attys Office Ct Fin Ctr 157 Church St PO Box 1824 New Haven CT 06508*

DANAS, ANDREW MICHAEL, lawyer; b. Redwood City, Calif., Apr. 25, 1955; s. Michael George and Marjorie Jean (Bailey) D. BA in Polit. Sci. and History, U. Conn., 1977; JD, George Washington U., 1982. Bar: D.C. 1982, U.S. Dist. Ct. (D.C. cir.) 1985, U.S. Dist. Ct. Md. 1987, U.S. Ct. Appeals (Fed. cir. 1984), U.S. Ct. Appeals (11th cir. 1987), U.S. Ct. Appeals (3d and 4th cirs.) 1988, U.S. Ct. Appeals (6th cir.) 1990, U.S. Ct. Appeals (2d cir.) 1998, U.S. Ct. of Claims 1984, U.S. Supreme Ct. 1994. Atty. Assn. Am. R.R.s, Washington, 1983-84; assoc. Grove Jaskiewicz & Cobert, 1984-90, Ptnr., 1991—. Contbg. author: Freewheeling; author legal column Intermodal Reporter, 1986-94; contbr. articles to profl. jours. Exec. com. Friends Assisting the Nat. Symphony, Washington, 1996-97. Mem. ABA, Internat. Bar Assn., Euro-Am. Lawyers Group (mgmt. com. 2000—), Transp. Law Inst. (chair 1993-94), Transp. Lawyers Assn. (chmn. legis. com. 1995-98, co-chmn. 1999-2000, Disting. Svc. award 1996), Phi Alpha Theta, Mensa, Univ. Club (Washington). Avocations: skiing, music, travel. Administrative and regulatory, Federal civil litigation, Private international. Home: 621 Tivoli Psge Alexandria VA 22314-1932 Office: Grove Jaskiewicz and Cobert 1730 M St NW Ste 400 Washington DC 20036-4579

DANE, STEPHEN MARK, lawyer; b. Chillicothe, Ohio, Mar. 27, 1956; s. Clyde and Rita M. (Murray) D.; m. Kim P. Piatt, July 7, 1979; children: Tara, Adam, Shannon, Alexandra, Courtney. BS with honors, U. Notre Dame, 1978; JD magna cum laude, U. Toledo, 1981. Bar: Ohio 1981, U.S. Ct. Appeals (6th and 10th cirs.) 1982, U.S. Dist. Ct. (no. dist.) Ohio 1983, U.S. Dist. Ct. (no. dist.) Tex. 1983, U.S. Ct. Appeals (5th cir.) 1984, U.S. Supreme Ct. 1985, U.S. Ct. Appeals (7th cir.) 1993. Law clk. U.S. Ct. Appeals (6th cir.), Cin., 1981-82; ptnr. Cooper, Walinski & Cramer, Toledo, 1986—. Judge pro tempore Perrysburg Mcpl. Ct., 1990—. Recipient Fair Housing award HUD, 1996, Spirit of Wood County award, 1988; named Lawyer of Yr. Lawyers Weekly, 1998; named to St. John's Jesuit H.S. Hall of Fame, 1991. Mem. ABA, Ohio State Bar Assn., Toledo Bar Assn. (chmn. fed. ct. com. 1987-89), Wood County Bar Assn.. Roman Catholic. Civil rights, Federal civil litigation, Labor. Home: 501 Hickory St Perrysburg OH 43551-2206 Office: Cooper Walinski & Cramer 900 Adams St Toledo OH 43624-1505

DANG, MARVIN S. C. lawyer; b. Honolulu, 1954; s. Brian K.T. and Flora Dang. BA with distinction, U. Hawaii, 1974; JD, George Washington U., 1978. Bar: Hawaii 1978, U.S. Dist. Ct. Hawaii 1978, U.S. Ct. Appeals (9th cir.) 1979. Atty. Gerson, Steiner & Anderson and predecessor firms, Honolulu, 1978-81; owner, atty. Law Offices of Marvin S.C. Dang, 1981—. Sr. v.p., bd. dirs. Rainbow Fin. Corp., Honolulu, 1984-95; bd. dirs. Foster Equipment Co. Ltd., Honolulu, Hawaii Cmty. Reinvestment Corp., 1994-96; bd. dirs. Hawaii Fin. Svcs. Assn., sec., 1991, treas., 1992, v.p., 1993, pres. 1994, lobbyist, 1996—; vice chmn. Hawaii Consumer Fin. Polit. Action Com., 1988-95, sec./treas., 1999—; hearings officer (per diem) Adminstrv. Drivers License Revocation Office, Honolulu, 1991-95. State rep., asst. minority floor leader Hawaii State Legislature, Honolulu, 1982-84; chmn., vice chmn., mem. Manoa Neighborhood Bd., Honolulu, 1979-82, 84-87; pres., v.p., mem. Hawaii Coun. on Legal Edn. for Youth, Honolulu, 1979-86; mem. Hawaii Bicentennial Commn. of U.S. Constn., Honolulu, 1986-88. Recipient Cert. of Appreciation award Hawaii Speech-Lang.-Hearing Assn., Honolulu, 1984; named one of Ten Outstanding Young Persons of Hawaii, Hawaii State Jaycees, 1983. Mem. ABA (standing com. on group and prepaid legal svcs. 2000—, coun. of fund for justice and edn. 1993-99, standing com. on law and electoral process 1985-89, spl. com. on youth edn. for citizenship 1979-85, 89-92, Hawaii membership chmn. 1981-93, exec. coun. young lawyers divsn. 1986-88), Hawaii State Bar Assn. (chair collection law sec. 1999—, bd. dirs. young lawyers divsn. 1990), Am. Prepaid Legal Svcs. Inst. (bd. dirs. 2000—). Avocations: family, law, politics. Consumer commercial, Probate, Real property. Office: PO Box 4109 Honolulu HI 96812-4109 E-mail: dangm@aloha.net

D'ANGELO, CHRISTOPHER SCOTT, lawyer; b. Phila., Aug. 30, 1953; s. George Anthony and Antonia Scott (Billett) D'A.; m. Betsy Hart Josephs, May 22, 1982; children: John Robert, Christopher Hart, Caroline Colt, Jennifer Scott. BA with honors and distinction, U. Va., 1975, JD, 1978. Bar: Pa. 1978, U.S. Dist. Ct. (ea. dist.) Pa. 1978, (mid. dist.) Pa. 1992, U.S. Ct. Appeals (3d cir.) 1978, U.S. Supreme Ct. 1981. From assoc. to ptnr. Montgomery, McCracken, Walker & Rhoads, LLP, Phila., 1978-96, chmn., product liability and toxic tort sect., 1996—. Sustaining mem. Products Liability Adv. Coun., 1985—, case selection com. 1988-91, experts com., 1993—, restatement project com., 1993-2000, exec. com. 1998—; mem. Am. Law. Inst., 1996—, mem. consultative group-products liability, mem. consultative group-Uniform Comml. Code, mem. consultative group-trusts, 1996—; lectr., writer in law internet and tech. matters. Co-founder The Declaration (U. Va. newsweekly), 1973-75; Editor: Counsel Table, 1990-94; contbr. articles to law jours. Mem. Internat. Vis. Ctr., Phila., 1982—, bd. dirs., 1987-90, chmn. long range fin. com., 1987-89, counsel for COMPASS (young profl. and spl. events div. of ctr.), 1982-89, exec. com., 1982-89; mem. selection com. Jefferson Scholars U. Va., Phila., 1980-84, chmn., 1981-82; fundraiser U.S. Ski Team, Phila., 1979-90, chmn., 1982-83, 87; fundraiser Acad. Natural Scis., Phila, 1979-88; trustee Episcopal Acad., Merion, Pa., 1988-91, 92—; chmn. ann. giving campaigns Episcopal Acad., 1983-88; bd. mgrs. Episc. Acad. Alumni Soc., Merion, Pa., 1983-92, treas., 1984-85, v.p. 1985-88, pres. 1988-91; treas., exec. com., bd. dirs. Phila. Art Alliance, 1980-86; bd. dirs. English Speaking Union U.S., 1979-82, chmn. young mem. group, 1980-83; bd. dirs. English Speaking Union Phila., 1980-88, chmn. fin. com., 1985-88; counsel honor com. and judiciary com. U. Va., 1976-78; mem. nominating com. St. Christopher's Ch., Gladwyne, Pa., 1989-91; fundraiser Friends Sch., Haverford, Pa., 1987-89; lay reader The Ch. of the Redeemer, Bryn Mawr, Pa., 1992—, mem. capital campaign, 1993—, head usher, 1993—, vestry, 1997—; mem. trophy com. Devon (Pa.) Horse Show, 1978—; mem. com. Benjamin Franklin Inst. Nat. Meml. Awards, 1995-98. Mem. ABA (mem. sect. litigation, products liability com., sect. internat. law, corp. counsel com.), Pa. Bar Assn. (exec. com. young lawyers divsn. 1979-85, probate sect. 1979—, litigation sect. 1979—), Phila. Bar Assn. (probate sect. 1979—), Products Liability Adv. Coun. (mem. Am. Law Inst. com., mem. experts com. 1991—, exec. com. 1998—), Def. Rsch. Inst. (products liability com., bus. litigation com., drug and med. device com., co-chmn European Corporate Outreach Com.), Fedn. of Ins. and Corp. Counsel (mem. computers and tech. com., products liability com., bus. litigation com.), Internat. Assn. Def. Counsel (mem. products liability com., mem. bus. litigation com., drug and med. device com., complex class action com., multi-nat. litigation com., computer and tech. com., author newsletters), Nat. Assn. Railroad Trial Counsel, Acad. Natural Scis., Anthenaeum, Phila. Mus. Art, Phila. Zoo, Please Touch Mus., Merion Cricket Club (Haverford), Penn Club, IV St. Club, The Assemblies, Phila. Club. Republican. Avocations: sailing, photography, travel, squash. General civil litigation, Private international, Product liability. Office: Montgomery McCracken Walker & Rhoads 123 S Broad St Fl 24 Philadelphia PA 19109-1099 E-mail: cdangelo@mmwr.com

DANIEL, J. REESE, lawyer; b. Sanford, N.C., Dec. 24, 1924; AB, U. S.C., 1949, JD cum laude, 1956. Bar: S.C. 1955, U.S. Dist. Ct. S.C. 1956, U.S. Tax Ct. 1959, U.S. Cr. Appeals (4th cir.) 1959. Sr. ptnr. Daniel & Daniel, Litchfield, S.C. Mem. S.C. Supreme Ct. Bd. Commrs. on Grievances and Discipline, 1970-73, Columbia Zoning Bd. of Adjustment, 1970-79. Contbg. author 7 South Carolina Law Quarterly; contbr. articles to profl. jours. With USNR, 1943-46. Mem. ABA, S.C. Bar Assn. (assoc. editor S.C. Bar Assn. News Bull. 1957, editor 1958-59), Phi Delta Phi. General civil litigation, Personal injury, Probate. Office: Daniel & Daniel PO Box 857 10B Pawleys Sta Hwy 17 S Pawleys Island SC 29585 E-mail: reesedaniel@email.msn.com

DANIEL, ROBERT MICHAEL, lawyer; b. Rocky Mount, N.C., Aug. 21, 1947; s. Harvey Derby and Edna Lois (McCullen) D.; m. Kaye Ruth Coates, Aug. 31, 1968; children: Robert M. Jr., John Matthew. AB in Econs., U. N.C., 1968, JD, 1971. Bar: N.C. 1971, Pa. 1976; U.S. Dist. Ct. (we. dist.) Pa. 1976; U.S. Tax Ct. 1979. Judge adv. U.S. Marine Corps., 1971-74; ptnr. Smith & Daniel, Pittsboro, N.C., 1974-75; trust officer Mellon Bank, N.A., Pitts., 1975-78; assoc. Buchanan Ingersoll, 1978-82, ptnr., 1982—. Pres. Greater Pitts. coun. Boy Scouts Am., 1996-99, bd. dirs. N.E. region. Col. USMCR, 1966-98, ret. Fellow Am. Coll. Trust and Estate

Coun.; mem. Pa. Bar Assn. (past chmn. real property, probate and trust law sect. 1998-99), Duquesne Club. Presbyterian. Avocations: travel, reading military history. Estate planning, Probate, Estate taxation. Home: 1491 Redfern Dr Pittsburgh PA 15241-2956 Office: Buchanan Ingersoll 301 Grant St Ste 20 Pittsburgh PA 15219-1410

DANIEL, SAMUEL PHILLIPS, lawyer; b. Tulsa, Okla., Dec. 20, 1932; s. Samuel P. and Mary (Rumley) D.; m. Mary Lou Lowe, Feb. 24, 1982; children: Sam P. III, Theodore W., John T. BS in Philosophy and Econs., Georgetown U., 1954; JD, U. Okla., 1959. Bar: Okla. 1959, U.S. Dist. Ct. (ea., we., no. dists.) Okla. 1960, U.S. Ct. Appeals (10th cir.) 1960, U.S. Supreme Ct. 1967. With Carlson, Lupardus, Holliman & Huffman, Tulsa, 1959-65; ptnr. Doerner, Saunders, Daniel & Anderson, L.L.P., 1965—. Adj. prof. U. Tulsa Law Sch., 1990, 92. Fellow Am. Acad. Matrimonial Lawyers, Am. Coll. Trial Lawyers; mem. Tulsa County Bar Assn. (pres. 1986-87), Am. Bar Found. (Okla. fellow), Tulsa County Bar Found. (trustee), Am. Inns of Ct. (master emeritus). Republican. Methodist. Avocations: hunting, fishing, golf. General civil litigation, Family and matrimonial. Office: Doerner Saunders Daniel & Anderson LLP 320 S Boston Ave Ste 500 Tulsa OK 74103-3725

DANIELS, JAMES WALTER, lawyer; b. Chgo., Oct. 13, 1945; s. Ben George and Delores L. (Wolanin) D.; m. Gail Anne Rihacek, June 14, 1969; children: Morgan, Abigail, Rachel. AB, Brown U., 1967; JD, U. Chgo., 1970. Bar: Calif. 1970, U.S. Dist. Ct. (ctrl. dist.) Calif. 1970, U.S. Tax Ct., 1972, U.S. Supreme Ct. 1979. Assoc. firm Latham & Watkins, L.A. and Newport Beach, Calif., 1970-77, ptnr., 1977-2000. Arbitrator Orange County Superior Ct., Santa Ana, Calif., 1978-88, judge pro tem, 1979-87. Fin. dir. St. Elizabeth Ann Seton Parish, Irvine, Calif., 1975-82; sec. Turtlerock Tennis Com., Irvine, 1981-83, 86—, pres., 1985-86; bd. dirs. Turtlerock Terr. Homeowners Assn., 1983-85, 87-89. Mem. ABA, Internat. Coun. Shopping Ctrs., Center club, Irvine Racquet Club, Palm Valley Country Club. Democrat. Roman Catholic. General corporate, Landlord-tenant, Real property. Home: 19241 Beckwith Ter Irvine CA 92612-3503 Office: Latham & Watkins 650 Town Center Dr Ste 2000 Costa Mesa CA 92626-7135

DANIELS, JOHN DRAPER, lawyer; b. Bklyn., Feb. 11, 1939; s. Draper L. and Louise Parker-Lux (Cort) D.; m. Sara Josephine Sears, Dec. 27, 1962; children: Stephen Draper, Elizabeth Marie, Rebecca Cort. AB, Princeton U., 1961; JD, U. Chgo., 1964. Bar: Ill. 1964, U.S. Dist. Ct. (no. dist.) Ill. 1967. Assoc. Jacobs & McKenna, Chgo., 1964-70, Law Offices Dale L. Schlafer, Chgo., 1970-73; assoc. then ptnr. Jacobs, Williams & Montgomery, 1973-87; ptnr. Sanchez & Daniels, 1987—. Arbitrator Cir. Ct. of Cook County. Mem. admissions screening panel Princeton Alumni Coun. Capt. U.S. Army, 1964-66. Mem. ABA, Ill. Bar Assn. (chmn. ins. sect. coun. 1985), Chgo. Bar Assn., Am. Arbitration Assn. (arbitrator 1977—), Internat. Assn. Def. Counsel, Soc. Trial Lawyers (bd. dirs. 1990, '92), Am. Bd. Trial Advs., Ill. Assn. Defense Trial Counsel, Trial Lawyers Club of Chgo., Tower of Chgo. Club (bd. trustees. 1985-87), East Bank Club. Roman Catholic. Avocations: guitar, musical composition, tennis, fishing, golf. General civil litigation, Insurance, Product liability. Home: 1611 Wilmette Ave Wilmette IL 60091-2424 Office: Sanchez & Daniels 333 W Wacker Dr Chicago IL 60606-1220 E-mail: jdaniels@sanchezdaniels.com

DANIELS, JOHN PETER, lawyer; b. N.Y.C., Feb. 5, 1937; s. Jack Brainard and Isabelle (McConachie) D.; m. Lynn Eldridge, Aug. 28, 1978 (div. Jan. 1980); m. Susan Gurley, Apr. 1, 1983. AB, Dartmouth Coll., 1959; JD, U. So. Calif., 1963. Bar: Calif. 1964; diplomate Am. Bd. Trial Advocates. Assoc. Bolton, Groff and Dunne, L.A., 1964-67, Jones and Daniels, L.A., 1967-70, Acret and Perrochet, L.A., 1971-81; ptnr. Daniels, Baratta and Fine, L.A.Angeles, 1982-99, Daniels, Fine, Israel & Schonbuch, L.A.Angeles, 1999—. Mem. Assn. So. Calif. Def. Counsel (bd. dirs. 1975-80), Fedn. Ins and Corp. Counsel. Club: Wilshire Country (Los Angeles). Avocations: scuba diving, golf, hunting. Federal civil litigation, State civil litigation. Office: Daniels Fine Israel & Schonbuch 1801 Century Park E Fl 9 Los Angeles CA 90067-2302

DANIELS, MICHAEL ALAN, lawyer; b. Cape Girardeau, Mo., Mar. 6, 1946; BS in Speech, Northwestern U., 1968, MA in Polit. Sci., 1969; JD, U. Mo., 1973. Bar: Fla. 1974, U. S. Supreme Ct. 1983. Spl. asst. for polit. sci. research Office Naval Research, Washington, 1969-71; legal aid Edwards, Seigfried, Runge and Hodge, Mexico, Mo., 1972-73; corp. atty. CACI, Inc., Washington, 1974-77; exec. v.p. gen. counsel Datex, Inc., 1977-78; chmn. bd., pres. Internat. Pub. Policy Research Corp., Falls Church, Va., 1978-86; sect. v.p. Sci. Applications Internat. Corp., Mc Lean, 1986—; pres. U.S. Global Strategy Council, Washington, 1986-94; chmn. bd. Network Solutions, Inc., 1995—. Chmn. No. Va. Tech. Coun., 1996-97. Mem. Republican Nat. Com., Internat. Affairs Council, Nat. Security Adv. Council; mem. investment policy adv. com. Office U.S. Trade Rep., 1982-87. Recipient Outstanding Fed. Securities Law Student award U. Mo., 1973. Mem. ABA (chmn. working group on law, nat. security and tech., standing com. law and nat. security 1984-92), Fla. Bar Assn., Fed. Bar Assn. (chmn. internat. law com. 1979-86), Internat. Studies Assn. General corporate, Private international. Office: SAIC 1710 Goodridge Dr # Ms1-125 Mc Lean VA 22102-3701

DANIELS, MICHAEL PAUL, retired lawyer; b. Maplewood, N.J., Apr. 22, 1930; s. Samuel and Lena E. (Oxman) D.; m. Lora Lee, June 23, 1949 (div. Aug. 1964); children: Lisa J., Rachel L., Aaron N.; m. Elaine Makris, Sept. 1, 1964; children: Anthony P., Maria, Alexander P. BA, U. Chgo., 1949, JD, 1952; student, U. Tokyo Sch. Law, 1958-59. Bar: U.S. Ct. Appeals (D.C. cir.) 1955, U.S. Supreme Ct., U.S. Ct. Internat. Trade; U.S. Ct. Appeals (fed. cir.). Atty. U.S. Congl. Reference Service, Washington, 1955-56; assoc. Becker & Maguire, 1956-57, Stitt & Hemendinger, Washington, 1958-63; ptnr. Stitt, Hemindinger & Daniels, 1963-67, Daniels, Houlihan & Palmeter, Washington, 1968-84; ptnr., internat. dept. head Mudge, Rose, Guthrie, Alexander & Ferdon, 1984-95; ptnr. Graham & James, 1995-97, Powell Goldstein Frazer & Murphy, Washington, 1997—2000; ret., 2000. Cons. Fasturn Inc., 2000—. Served with U.S. Army, 1952-54, Korea. Decorated Meritorious Bronze Star; fellow Fulbright fellow. Mem. ABA, D.C. Bar Assn. E-mial. Administrative and regulatory, Private international. Home: 5615 Bent Branch Rd Bethesda MD 20816-1049 E-mail: mpemd@erols.com

DANIELSON, GARY R. lawyer; b. Detroit, June 8, 1953; s. Ronald Gregory and Catherine (Gibson) D. BA in Psychology, Oakland U., Rochester, Mich., 1976; JD cum laude, Wayne State U., 1983. Bar: Mich. 1983, U.S. Dist. Ct. (ea. dist.) Mich., 1985, U.S. Supreme Ct. 1987. Sr. job placement counselor Ferndale (Mich.) Sch. Dist., 1976-79; employment and tng. adminstr. Oakland County Govt., Pontiac, Mich., 1979-82; sr. corp. labor rels. rep. Harper-Grace Hosps., Detroit, 1982-83; corp. labor rels. mgr. Vis. Nurse Assn., 1983-85; atty., v.p., cons. Indsl. Rels., Inc., 1985-90; pres. The Danielson Group, P.C., St. Clair Shores, 1989—. Pres., bd. dirs. St. Clair on Lake Condominium Assn., St. Clair Shores, Mich., 1987—. Mem. ABA, Mich. Bar Assn., Indsl. Rels. Rsch. Assn. Republican. Avocation: sailing. Civil rights, Labor. Office: Danielson Group PC 27735 Jefferson Ave Saint Clair Shores MI 48081-1309

DANIELSON, LUKE JEFFRIES, lawyer; b. Boulder, Colo., Aug. 8, 1948; s. Philip A. and Mildred S. (Page) D.; m. Rosa Venezia, Aug. 9, 1975. BA in Econ., Antioch Coll., 1971; JD, U. Calif.-Berkeley, 1975. Bar: Colo. 1975, U.S. Dist. Ct. Colo. 1975, U.S. Ct. Appeals (10th cir.) 1975, U.S. Dist. Ct. Nebr. 1984. Assoc. Holland & Hart, Denver, 1975-78; editor-in-chief Solar Law Reporter, Golden, Colo., 1978-79; counsel Nat. Wildlife Fedn., Boulder, Colo., 1979-81; ptnr. Danielson & Euser, Denver, 1982-85; Gersh & Danielson, Denver, 1985—; adj. asst. prof. U. Denver Coll. of Law, 1978, 85, 87, U. Denver, 1994, U. Colo. Sch. Law, Boulder, 1979-81, 82, 84, 94; arbitrator Am. Arbitration Assn., other orgns. Author articles on solar energy and law, energy policy, mediation and mediation of environ. disputes. Chmn. bd. dirs. Eco-Cycle, Inc., Boulder, 1985-86, bd. dirs., mem. 1983-86; bd. dirs. Colo. Conservation Found., Denver, 1985-94, Global Response, 1991—; vice chmn., mem. Nat. Wildlif Fedn. Action, Inc., 1992—; mem. Mined Land Reclamation Bd., 1987—, chair 1989, 91, 94; counsel Univ. Corp. Atmospheric Rsch. Found., 1987-89. Mem. ABA (sect. natural resources, energy and environ. law, vice chair internat. resources com. 1994—), Colo. Bar Assn. (bd. govs. 1992-94), Denver Bar Assn., Boulder Bar Assn., Wyo. Wildlife Fedn. (life), Colo. Wildlife Fedn., AAAS, Am. Solar Energy Soc. Federal civil litigation, State civil litigation, Environmental. Office: Gersh & Danielson 4747 Table Mesa Dr Boulder CO 80305-5573

DANIELSON, WALTER GEORGE, lawyer; b. Anaconda, Mont., July 3, 1903; s. John and Tekla Christina (Jonsson) D.; m. Beryl Marie Pearce, Aug. 17, 1935; children— Karin Lynn Godfrey, John Howard. LL.B., U. Mont., 1929, J.D. (hon.), 1970; diploma of honor Pepperdine U., 1980. Bar: Calif. 1929, pvt. practice, Los Angeles; vice consul for Sweden, Los Angeles, 1937-55, consul, 1955-69, consul gen., 1969-76, emeritus, 1976; sec. Los Angeles Consular Corps, 1976— . Trustee Luth. Hosp. Soc. So. Calif., Los Angeles; bd. dirs. Calif. Hosp. Decorated Knight Royal Order Vasa, comdr. Royal Order Vasa, comdr. Royal Order North Star (Sweden); officers cross (Hungary); Knight Royal Order St. Olav (Norway); Knight's cross 1st class Royal Order Dannebrog (Denmark). Mem. Calif. State Bar, Los Angeles Bar Assn. Clubs: California, Vasa Order Am., Swedish (Los Angeles). Home: 68 Fremont Pl Los Angeles CA 90005-3858 Office: Danielson & St Clair 68 Fremont Pl Los Angeles CA 90005-3858

DANILEK, DONALD J. lawyer; b. N.Y.C., Mar. 25, 1937; s. Joseph A. and Mary (Dedina) D.; m. Jane Till, Mar. 26, 1958; children: Christopher, Mary Jane, Gregory, Thomas. A.B., Princeton U., 1958; J.D., U. Va., 1961. Bar: Va. 1961, N.Y. 1961, U.S. Tax Ct. 1983. Asst. prof. law U.S. Mil. Acad., West Point, N.Y., 1961-65; assoc. firm Kirlin, Campbell & Keating, N.Y.C., 1965-70, ptnr., 1970-71, 75-88; mng. dir. Bank In Liechstein Trust Co., N.Y.C., 1988-90; sr. v.p. pvt. banking, sec. and gen. counsel trust div., Bank of Bermuda (N.Y.) Ltd., 1990—; ptnr. Gasser & Hayes, N.Y.C., 1971-74. Named Yachtsman of Yr, Port Washington Yacht Club, 1974, 77. Mem. Va. State Bar. Republican. Roman Catholic. Clubs: N.Y. Yacht (N.Y.C.); Manhasset Bay Yacht (Port Washington). Banking, General corporate, Probate. Office: Bank of Bermuda (NY) Ltd Pvt Banking Trust Div 350 Park Ave New York NY 10022-6022

DANKIN, PETER ALFRED, lawyer; b. Winsted, Conn., Oct. 23, 1942; s. Alexander Harry and Dorothy Barbara (Erfer) D. BA, Yale U., 1964; JD cum laude, U. Mich., 1967. Bar: N.Y. 1968, D.C. 1982, U.S. Dist. Ct. (so. and ea. dists.) N.Y. 1971, U.S. Ct. Appeals (2d cir.) 1972, U.S. Ct. Appeals (3d cir.) 1980, U.S. Ct. Appeals (D.C. cir.) 1980, U.S. Ct. Appeals (7th cir.) 1984, U.S. Supreme Ct. 1974, U.S. Ct. Appeals (5th cir.) 1985, U.S. Ct. Internat. Trade, 1987. Assoc. Chadbourne, Parke, Whiteside & Wolff, N.Y.C., 1968-71; assoc. Wender, Murase & White, N.Y.C., 1971-73, ptnr., 1973-86; ptnr. Shanely & Fisher, 1987-88; sole practitioner, 1988-93; prin. McPheters & Dankin, P.C., 1993—. Assoc. editor U. Mich. Law Rev., 1966-67. Served to 1st lt. U.S. Army, 1967-73. Mem. Am. Jurisprudence Soc. (book award 1965), N.Y. State Bar Assn., Order of Coif. Antitrust, Federal civil litigation, State civil litigation. Office: McPheters & Dankin 757 3rd Ave New York NY 10017-2013

DANKNER, JAY WARREN, lawyer; b. Bklyn., June 15, 1949; s. Morris and Frances Dankner; m. Iris Rose Terens, May 15, 1983; children: Danielle Renee, Nicole Beth. BA cum laude, Bklyn. Coll., 1970, JD cum laude, 1973. Bar: N.Y. 1974, Fla. 1974, U.S. Dist. Ct. (ea. and so. dists.) N.Y. 1974, U.S. Ct. Appeals (2d cir.) 1974, U.S. Supreme Ct. 1977, U.S. Dist. Ct. (no. dist.) N.Y. 1986. From assoc. to ptnr. Sullivan & Liapakis P.C., N.Y.C., 1974-94; ptnr. Dankner & Milstein, P.C., 1994—. Lectr. Practicing Law Inst., N.Y.C., 1983-87, N.Y. State Trial Lawyers Inst., 1985—, continuing legal edn. program Bklyn. Law Sch., 1986—, N.Y. State Bar Assn. CLE Programs, Nassau County Bar Assn., Queens Bar Assn.; mem. Bklyn. Law Rev., 1972-73; bd. dirs. Atty's Info. Exchange Group, Inc., 1981—. Author: Products Liability Practice Guide, 1988, Masters of Trial Practice, 1988, Deposing Corporate Defendants in Products Liability Actions, 1988, Trial Strategy - Plaintiffs View, 1988; contbr. articles to profl. jours. Named one of Best Trial Lawyers in the U.S., Town & Country, 1985. Mem. ABA, N.Y. State Bar Assn. (spl. com. on procedures for jud. discipline 1987-90), Assn. of Bar of City of N.Y. (mem. products liability com. 1993-94), Fla. Bar Assn., Assn. Trial Lawyers Am., N.Y. State Trial Lawyers Assn. (chair products liability com. 1991, 93-94), N.Y. County Lawyers Assn. General civil litigation, Personal injury, Product liability. Home: 524 E 72nd St New York NY 10021-9801 Office: Dankner & Milstein PC 41 E 57th St New York NY 10022-1908

DANNER, WILLIAM BEKURS, lawyer; b. Mobile, Ala., Aug. 18, 1944; s. John J. and Helen B. (Bekurs) D.; m. Eleanor E. Uehlinger; children: William B., Christina T. BS, Spring Hill Coll., 1967; JD, U. Louisville, 1978. Bar: Ky. 1979. Commd. ensign USN, 1967, advanced through grades to lt., 1972, ret., 1977; atty. U.S. Ecology Inc., Louisville, 1979-80, assoc. gen. counsel, 1980-81; staff atty. McDermott Internat., New Orleans, 1981-83, counsel Europe and Africa area Brussels, 1983-86, mgr. legal office for domestic, S.A., West Africa ops. New Orleans, 1987-91, sr. counsel corp. staff, 1991-97, corp. compliance atty., 1997—. Vice chmn. parish council, New Albany, Ind., 1980-81; bd. dirs. parish council, Brussels, 1984—. Mem. ABA (internat. law and practice sect.), Ky. Bar Assn., Phi Kappa Phi. Republican. Roman Catholic. Avocations: furniture refinishing, reading. Contracts commercial, Construction, Government contracts and claims. Home: 207 Driftwood Cir Slidell LA 70458-1437 Office: McDermott Legal Dept 1450 Poydras St New Orleans LA 70112-2401 E-mail: wdanner@bellsouth.net, wbdanner@mcdermott.com

DANNHAUSER, STEPHEN J. lawyer; b. N.Y.C., May 23, 1950; s. Frank A. and Irene (Tinney) D.; m. Mary Elizabeth Robinson, July 1, 1973; children: Benjamin, Todd, Jess. BA with honors, SUNY, Stonybrook, 1972; JD with honors, Bklyn. Law Sch., 1975. Bar: N.Y. 1976. Atty. Weil Gotshal & Manges LLP, N.Y.C., 1975—, exec. ptnr., 1989—. Decisions editor Bklyn. Law Rev., 1974-75. Pres. N.Y. Police and Fire Windows and Children's Fund, N.Y.C., 1985—; chmn. corp. steering com. Nat. Minority Bus. Coun., N.Y.C., 1993; bd. dirs. Boys and Girls Harbor, Inc., East Harlem, N.Y. Mem. ABA. Avocations: running, golf. Office: Weil Gotshal & Manges LLP 767 5th Ave Fl Conc1 New York NY 10153-0119

DANNREUTHER, DAVID ION, solicitor; b. London, Apr. 23, 1953; s. Lon Alexander and April Diana D.; m. Heather Mariel Clarke (div. 1998); children: Rupert John, Anna Olivia. Student, Winchester Coll., Eng., 1966-71; BA with honors, Oxford U., 1975. Solicitor Supreme Ct. Judicature. Trainee Herbert Smith, London, 1976-78; asst. solicitor Berwin Leigaiton, 1979-81, Sinclair Roche & Temperley, London, 1981-94, M.W. Cornish & Co., London, 1994-97; ptnr. Withers, 1997—. Chmn. L.I.N.C., London, 1993—. Co-editor Enforcement of Aircraft Mortgages in Europe. Avocations: tennis, squash, football, literature, art. Aviation, Banking, Finance. Home: 50 Handen Rd London SE12 8NR England Office: Withers 16 Old Bailey London EL4M 7EG England

DANOFF, ERIC MICHAEL, lawyer; b. Waukegan, Ill., June 30, 1949; m. Barbara Madsen, May 27, 1979; children: Nicholas Madsen Danoff, Alexander Madsen Danoff. AB, Dartmouth Coll., 1971; JD, U. Calif., Berkeley, 1974. Bar: Calif. 1974, U.S. Dist. Ct. (no., cen., ea. and so. dists.) Calif., U.S. Ct. Appeals (9th cir.), U.S. Supreme Ct. Assoc. Graham & James, San Francisco, 1974-80, ptnr., 1981-97, Kaye, Rose & Ptnrs., San Francisco, 1998-2001, Emard, Danoff, Port & Tamulski, LLP, San Francisco, 2001—. Contbr. articles to profl. publs. Mem. Maritime Law Assn. Admiralty, General civil litigation, Private international. Office: Emard Danoff Port & Tamulski LLP Ste 400 49 Stevenson St San Francisco CA 94105

D'ANTONIO, JAMES JOSEPH, lawyer; b. Tucson, Jan. 13, 1959; s. Lawrence Patrick and Rosemary Catherine (Kane) D'A. Student, Tufts U., 1978-79; BA, U. Ariz., 1981, JD, 1984. Bar: Ariz. 1984, U.S. Dist. Ct. Ariz. 1984, U.S. Ct. Appeals (9th cir.) 1993. Assoc. Law Office of D'Antonio and D'Antonio, Tucson, 1984-93; pvt. practice law Offices of James J. D'Antonio, 1993—. Chmn. bd. govs. U. Ariz. Coll. Law, 1983-84; mem. Pima County Teen Ct. Adv. Bd; mem. Health South Rehab. Inst., Tucson Cmty. Adv. Bd.; bd. dirs. Coyote Task Force. Named Outstanding Pro Bono Lawyer Pima County Vol. Lawyers Program, 1993. Fellow Ariz. Bar Found.; mem. ABA, Assn. Trial Lawyers Am., Ariz. Bar Assn., Ariz. Trial Lawyers Assn., Pima County Bar Assn. General civil litigation, Personal injury, Real property. Office: 2601 N Campbell Ave #202 Tucson AZ 85719

DANZIGER, PETER, lawyer; b. N.Y.C., Jan. 5, 1949; s. Herbert and Eleanor (Rosner) D.; m. Joan Nelick, Aug. 15, 1970; children: Lisa, Carrie, Beth. BA, U. Vt., 1970; JD, Albany Law Sch., 1973; MS, SUNY, Albany, 1977. Bar: N.Y. 1974, U.S. Dist. Ct. (no. dist.) N.Y. 1974. Assoc. O'Connell and Aronowitz, Albany, N.Y., 1973-79, sr. ptnr., 1979—. Instr. Albany Law Sch., 1972-73, SUNY at Albany, 1978-88. Author: (book) Special Education Litigation, 1989, Tapping Officials Secrets, 1989, 93, 97; author Albany Law Rev., 1972, (newspaper column) Legal Line, 1990-2000; contbr. Long Term Care Insurance in N.Y., 2000; editor: Representing People with Disabilities, 1989, 97, 2000. Legal counsel Jewish Family Svcs. of N.E. N.Y., Albany, 1977—. Named one of Best Lawyers in Am., Woodward/White Inc., 1991—. Mem. ABA, N.Y. State Trial Lawyers Assn., Am. Trial Lawyers Assn., Nat. Assn. of Elder Law Attys., N.Y. State Bar Assn. (chairperson com. on mental and phys. disabilities 1989-93). Education and schools, Libel, Product liability. Office: O'Connell and Aronowitz 100 State St Ste 800 Albany NY 12207-1897

DA PONTE, JOHN JOSEPH, JR. lawyer; b. Bristol, R.I., May 12, 1933; s. John J. and Mary Elizabeth (Ferris) DaP.; m. Gunilla Karen Tornhagen, Apr. 18, 1971; children— Karen, Karsten. B.A., Providence Coll., 1955; J.D., Boston U., 1962; LL.M., Georgetown U., 1966; cert. U. Muenster, W.Ger., 1967. Bar: Mass. 1962, D.C. 1964, U.S. Supreme Ct. 1976. Atty. U.S. Dept. Def., Washington, 1962, U.S. Treasury, Washington, 1962-67; atty. U.S. Dept. Commerce, Washington, 1968— , exec. sec. Fgn. Trade Zones Bd. Contbr. articles on law and internat. trade to profl. jours. Bd. dirs. Friendship Neighborhood Assn. Coalition, Washington, 1974-78; mem. Sumner Citizens Assn., Bethesda, Md., 1978— . Served to 1st. lt. U.S. Army, 1956-59. Recipient Am. Jurisprudence award Lawyers Coop Pub. Co., Rochester, N.Y., 1966, Bronze award U.S. Dept. Commerce, 1975, Silver medal, 1984. Mem. Am. Soc. Internat. Law, Fed. Bar Assn., Mass. Bar Assn., D.C. Bar Assn. Home: 5804 Madawaska Rd Bethesda MD 20816-2342 Office: Fgn Trade Zones Bd US Dept Commerce 14th and Pennsylvania Washington DC 20230

DARBY, KAREN SUE, legal education administrator; b. Columbus, Ohio, Sept. 15, 1947; d. Emerson Curtis and Kathryn Elizabeth (Bowers) Dum; m. R. Russell Darby, Dec. 21, 1974; children: David Randolph, Michael Emerson. BA magna cum laude, Capital U., Columbus, 1969; JD, Ohio State U., 1980. Bar: Ohio 1980, U.S. Dist. Ct. (so. dist.) Ohio 1981, Pa. 1998. High sch. English tchr. Columbus Pub. Schs., 1969-72; employee rels. specialist GE, Circleville, Ohio, 1972-74, mgr. EEO and manpower programs chem. met. div. Worthington, 1974-77; atty. Ohio Legal Rights Svc., Columbus, 1980-81; pvt. practice, 1981-90; assoc. dir. Ohio Continuing Legal Edn. Inst., 1989-95; dir. Phila. Bar Edn. Ctr., 1995-97; assoc. dir. Pa. Bar Inst., Phila., 1997—. Mem. rules adv. com. Supreme Ct. Ohio, Columbus, 1989-94. Author, editor: Civil Commitment in Ohio - A Manual for Respondents' Attorneys, 1980. Mem. divorce mediation panel Ohio State U. Commn. on Interprofl. Edn., Columbus, 1988-91; vol. Boy Scouts Am., Columbus, 1988-92, Columbus Pub. Schs., 1984-95. Mem. Pa. Bar Assn., Ohio State Bar Assn. (mem. family law com. 1991-95)., Assn. Continuing Legal Edn., Phila. Bar Assn. Democrat. Lutheran. Avocations: organ, piano, gardening. Office: PBI-PBEC Edn Ctr 100 Penn Sq E Philadelphia PA 19107-3322

DARDEN, MARSHALL TAYLOR, lawyer; b. Porstmouth, Va., Dec. 6, 1952; s. Arthur Dandridge and Marian (Mann) D.; m. Claudia Kay Golay, Feb. 11, 1978; 1 child, Brandon Taylor. BA, La. State U., 1974, JD, 1977. Bar: La. 1977. Assoc. Milling, Benson, Woodward, Hillyer, Pierson & Miller, New Orleans, 1977-82, ptnr., 1983—; speaker 31st Ann. Mineral Law Inst., Baton Rouge, Mar. 1984, 34th Ann. Mineral Law Inst., 1987; mem. adv. coun. La. Mineral Law Inst., 1988-92, chmn. adv. coun., 1990-92; mem. coun. La. Law Inst., 1991-92. Mem. ABA, La. State Bar Assn., Lambda Chi Alpha. Republican. Episcopalian. Federal civil litigation, State civil litigation, Oil, gas, and mineral. Home: 3517 Pin Oak Ave New Orleans LA 70131-8441 Office: Milling Benson Woodward Hillyer Pierson & Miller 909 Poydras St Ste 2300 New Orleans LA 70112-1010

DARIOTIS, TERRENCE THEODORE, lawyer; b. Chgo., Feb. 28, 1946; s. Theodore S. and Dorothy Mizzen (Thompson) D.; m. Jeanne Elizabeth Gibbons, Oct. 24, 1970; children: Sara Mizzen, Kristin Elizabeth, Jennifer Ann. BA in Philosophy, St. Joseph's Coll., Rensselaer, Ind., 1969; JD, Loyola U., Chgo., 1973. Bar: Ill. 1973, Fla. 1975, U.S. Tax Ct. 1993, U.S. Supreme Ct., 1978. Law clk. to presiding justice Appellate Ct. of Ill. (2d dist.), Waukegan, 1973-74; assoc. Keith Kinderman, Tallahassee, 1975-76; sole practitioner, 1976-82; ptnr. Kahn and Dariotis, P.A., 1982-96, Warfel, Goldberg, Dariotis, Waldoch & Olive, P.A., Tallahassee, 1996-00; sole practice, 2000—. Adj. prof. Fla. State U. Coll. Bus., 1987-93. Roman Catholic. Estate planning, Probate, Real property. Office: 1695 Metropolitan Cir Ste 6 Tallahassee FL 32308-3731

DARLING, ROBERT HOWARD, lawyer; b. Detroit, Oct. 29, 1947; s. George Beatson and Jeanne May (Mainville) D.; m. Cathy Lee Trygstad, Apr. 30, 1970; children: Bradley Howard, Brian Lee, Kara Kristine, Blake Robert. BS in Mech. Engring., U. Mich., 1969, MS in Mech. Engring., 1971; JD, Wayne State U., 1975. Bar: Mich. 1975, U.S. Dist. Ct. (ea. dist.) Mich. 1975, U.S. Ct. Appeals (6th cir.) 1975. Engr. Bendix Corp., Ann Arbor, Mich., 1970, Ford Motor Co., Dearborn, 1972-73; ptnr. Philo, Atkinson, Darling, Steinberg, Harper & Edwards, Detroit, 1975-81; sr. ptnr. Sommers, Schwartz, Silver & Schwartz, Southfield, Mich., 1981—. Assoc. editor Wayne State U. Law Review. Mem. ABA, Assn. Trial Lawyers Am., Mich. Trial Lawyers Assn. (exec. bd. 1981—, publs. chmn. 1981-85, products liability chmn. 1986—), Met. Detroit Trial Lawyers Assn., Oakland County Trial Lawyers Assn., State Bar Mich., Detroit Bar Assn., Plymouth Hist. Soc., Pi Tau Sigma. Avocations: golf. Federal civil litigation, State civil litigation, Personal injury. Home: 8785 Warren Rd Plymouth MI 48170-5119 Office: Sommers Schwartz Silver Schwartz 2000 Town Ctr Ste 900 Southfield MI 48075-1100 Address: 8785 Warren Rd Plymouth MI 48170-5119 E-mail: rdarling@s4online.com

DARLING, SCOTT EDWARD, lawyer; b. Los Angeles, Dec. 31, 1949; s. Dick R. and Marjorie Helen (Otto) D.; m. Cynthia Diane Harrah, June 1970 (div.); 1 child, Smokie; m. Deborah Lee Cochran, Aug. 22, 1981; children: Ryan, Jacob, Guinevere. BA, U. Redlands, 1972; JD, U.S.C., 1975. Bar: Calif. 1976, U.S. Dist. Ct. (cen. dist.) Calif. 1976. Assoc. atty. Elver, Falsetti, Boone & Crafts, Riverside, 1976-78; ptnr. Falsetti, Crafts, Pritchard & Darling, 1978-84; pres. Scott Edward Darling, A Profl. Corp., 1984—. Grant reviewer HHS, Washington, 1982-88; judge pro tem Riverside County Mcpl. Ct., 1980, Riverside County Superior Ct., 1987-88; bd. dirs. Tel Law Nat. Legal Pub. Info. System, Riverside, 1978-80. Author, editor: Small Law Office Computer Legal System, 1984. Bd. dirs. Youth Adv. Com. to Selective Svc., 1968-70, Am. Heart Assn. Riverside County, 1978-82, Survival Ministries, 1986-89; atty. panel Calif. Assn. Realtors, L.A., 1980—; pres. Calif. Young Reps., 1978-80; mem. GI Forum, Riverside, 1970-88; presdl. del. Nat. Rep. Party, 1980-84; asst. treas. Calif. Rep. Party, 1981-83; Rep. Congl. candidate, Riverside, 1982; treas. Riverside Sickle Cell Found., 1980-82, recipient Eddie D. Smith award; pres. Calif. Rep. Youth Caucus, 1980-82; v.p. Riverside County Red Cross, 1982-84; mem. Citizen's Univ. Com., Riverside, 1978-84, World Affairs Council, 1978-82, Urban League, Riverside, 1980-82. Calif. Scholarship Fedn. (life). Named one of Outstanding Young Men in Am., U.S. Jaycees, 1979-86. Mem. ABA, Riverside County Bar Assn., Speaker's Bur. Riverside County Bar Assn., Riverside Jaycees, Riverside C. of C. Lodge: Native Sons of Golden West. Avocations: skiing, swimming, reading. Personal injury, Real property, Estate taxation. Office: 3697 Arlington Ave Riverside CA 92506-3938

DARLINGTON, GAVIN, lawyer; b. Eng., June 27, 1949; s. Brook and Pamela Darlington; m. Pavla Kucek, Apr. 11, 1977; children: Nicholas, Georgina. MA with 1st class honors, Downing Coll., Cambridge, Eng., 1971. Cert. solicitor, Eng. and Wales. Assoc. Freshfields, Eng., 1972-76, 78-80; overseas assoc. Davis, Polk & Wardwell, N.Y.C., 1976-77; assoc. Freshfields, 1977-78, ptnr. Eng., 1980-99, Freshfields, Bruckhaus & Deringer, Paris, 1999—. Communications, Mergers and acquisitions, Securities. Office: Freshfield Bruckhaus Dering 69 Blvd Haussman 75008 Paris France

DARLOW, JULIA DONOVAN, lawyer; b. Detroit, Sept. 18, 1941; d. Frank William Donovan and Helen Adele Turner; m. George Anthony Gratton Darlow (div.); 1 child, Gillian; m. John Corbett O'Meara. AB, Vassar Coll., 1963; postgrad., Columbia U. Law Sch., 1964-65; J.D. cum laude, Wayne State U., 1971. Bar: Mich. 1971, U.S. Dist. Ct. (ea. dist.) Mich. 1971. Assoc. Dickinson, Wright, McKean, Cudlip & Moon, Detroit, 1971-78; ptnr. Dickinson, Wright, Moon, Van Dusen & Freeman and predecessor, 1978—; sr. v.p. Detroit Med. Ctr., 2001—. Adj. prof. Wayne State U. Law Sch., 1974-75, 96; commr. State Bar Mich., 1977-87, mem. exec. com., 1979-83, 84-87, sec. 1980-81, v.p., 1984-85, pres.-elect 1985-86, pres. 1986-87, coun. corp. fin. and bus. law sect. 1980-86, coun. computer law sect. 1985-88; mem. State Officers Compensation Commn., 1994-96; chair Mich. Supreme Ct. Task Force on Gender Issues in the Cts., 1987-89. Reporter: Mich. Nonprofit Corp. Act, 1977-82. Bd. dirs. Hutzel Hosp., 1984—, Mich. Opera Theater, 1985—, Mich. Women's Found., 1986-91, Detroit Med. Ctr., 1990—, Marygrove Coll., 1996—; trustee Internat. Inst. Met. Detroit, 1986-92, Mich. Met. coun. Girl Scouts U.S., 1988-91, Detroit coun. Boy Scouts Am., 1988—; mem. exec. com. Mich. Coun. for Humanities 1988-92; mem. Blue Cross-Blue Shield Prospective Reimbursement Com., Detroit, 1979-81; v.p., mem. exec. com. United Found., 1988-95; mem. Mich. Gov.'s Bilateral Trade Team for Germany, 1992-98. Fellow Am. Bar Found. (Mich. State chairperson 1990-96; mem. state officers compensation commn., 1994-96); mem. Detroit Bar Assn. Found. (treas. 1984-85, trustee 1982-85), Mich. Bar Found. (trustee 1987-94), Am. Judicature Soc. (bd. dirs. 1985-88), Internat. Women's Forum (global affairs com. 1994—), Women Lawyers Assn. (pres. 1977-78), Mich. Women's Campaign Fund (charter), Detroit Athletic Club. Democrat. Contracts commercial, General corporate, Private international. Office: Dickinson Wright PLLC 500 Woodward Ave Ste 4000 Detroit MI 48226-3416

DARNELL, ALAN MARK, lawyer; b. N.Y.C., Dec. 6, 1946; s. Sidney and Serene (Rackow) D.; m. Joan Silverman, Sept. 5, 1971. B.A., U. Rochester, 1968; J.D., U. Pa., 1971. Bar: N.J. 1971. Assoc. Wilentz, Goldman & Spitzer, Woodbridge, N.J., 1971-79, ptnr., 1980— . Named Trial Lawyer of the Yr., Trial Lawyers for Pub. Justice, 1983. Mem. Assn. Trial Lawyers Am., Def. Research Assn., Middlesex County Bar Assn., N.J. Bar Assn. Democrat. Jewish. Federal civil litigation, State civil litigation, Personal injury. Home: 8 Old Weathersfield Rd Asbury Park NJ 07712-3325

DARNELL, JAMES ORAL, lawyer; b. Oklahoma City, May 3, 1955; s. Victor Lee and Eileen (Bliss) D.; m. Susan Marie Cheslousky, Aug. 5, 1978; children: James Oral Jr., Jake Morris. AB cum laude, Dartmouth Coll.; JD cum laude, So. Meth. U. Bar: Tex. 1980, U.S. Dist. Ct. (we. dist.) Tex. 1982, U.S. Ct. Appeals (5th cir.) 1986, U.S. Dist. Ct. (no. dist.) Tex. 1987, U.S. Ct. Claims 1994, U.S. Supreme Ct. 1997. Ptnr. Grambling & Mounce, El Paso, Tex., 1980-90; pvt. practice, 1990-91; pntr. Grambling/Darnell, 1991-95; sole practitioner Jim Darnell P.C., 1995—. Worker Sun Bowl Assn., 1981-82; chmn. com. Southwestern Internat. Livestock Show and Rodeo, Inc., 1982-97, bd. dirs., 1987-97, asst. v.p., 1989-90, exec. v.p., 1990-91, vice chmn., 1991-94, CEO, 1994-97; bd. dirs. El Paso Svcs. for Children, 1982, pres., 1984-85; bd. dirs. YMCA, 1984-90; participant Leadership El Paso, 1985; mem. exec. com. Yucca coun. Boy Scouts Am., 1990-2000. Mem. ABA, Am. Bd. Trial Advocates (pres. El Paso chpt. 1998), Tex. Bar Assn., Tex. Young Lawyers Assn., Tex. Criminal Def. Lawyers Assn., (assoc. dir. 1992-94, exec. com. 1995-97), El Paso Criminal Def. Lawyers Assn. (bd. dirs. 1988, v.p. 1989-90), El Paso Young Lawyers Assn. (bd. dirs. 1983-85, treas. 1985-86), El Paso Legal Assistance Soc. (bd. dirs. 1982—, chmn. 1986-88), Tex. Trial Lawyers Assn., Tex. Bar Found., Nat. Assn. Criminal Def. Lawyers (State Bar of Tex. dist. 17 grievance com. 1986-92), El Paso Bar Assn. (bd. dirs. 1997-98). Democrat. Baptist. Avocations: basketball, baseball, horses, cattle, football. General civil litigation, Criminal, Personal injury. Home: 5 Paseo De Paz El Paso TX 79932-3501 Office: 310 N Mesa St Ste 212 El Paso TX 79901-1301 E-mail: jdarnell@jdarnell.com

DARR, CAROL C. lawyer; b. Apr. 24, 1951; d. Patt M. and Justine D.; m. Albert Louis May III Dec. 19, 1992. BA, U. Memphis, 1973, JD, 1976; M.Litt, Christ's Coll., Cambridge U., 1995. Bar: Tenn. 1977, D.C. 1981. Atty. Fed. Election Commn., 1976-77; asst. counsel U.S. Senate Com. on Rules & Adminstrn., 1977-79; dep. gen counsel Carter/Mondale Presidential Com., 1979-81; in house counsel Dem. Nat. Com., 1981-82; assoc. Skadden, Arps, Slate, Meagher & Flom, 1983-85; chief counsel Dukakis/Bentsen Com., Inc., 1987-91; gen. counsel Dem. Nat. Com., 1991-92; with Clinton/Gore Transition Com., 1992-93; actg. gen. counsel, dep. gen. counsel U.S. Dept. Commerce, 1993-94; assoc. Adminstrn. Nat. Telecom. and Info. Agy., Office Internat. Affairs, 1994-96; v.p. govt. affairs Info. Tech. Industry Coun., Washington, 1996-98; sr. v.p. bus. and pub. affairs Interactive Digital Software Assn., 1998-2001; dir. careers and external programs Grad. Sch. Polit. Mgmt. George Washington U., 2001—. Author: Political Parties, Presidential Campaigns, and National Party Conventions, 1992; Contributions and Expenditures by National, State, and Local Party Conventions, 1990; Active Corporate Participation, 1993; Candidates and Parties 1982, Registration and Reporting, 1981. Recipient U. Memphis Outstanding Young Alumnus award 1982. Mem. ABA, Fed. Bar Assn. (chair. com. on political campaigns and election laws 1983-85.

DARROW, MARY J. federal lawyer; b. Malone, N.Y. d. James William and Geraldine (Cosgrove) D.; m. Michael Ray Goebel, Dec. 30, 1982 (div. June 1990); 1 child, Jeanne Marie Darrow. BS, Clarkson U., 1979; JD, Loyola of New Orleans, 1985. CPA, 1984; Bar: La., 1985. Asst. controller Union Carbide Corp., Hahnville, La., 1979-82; tax. atty. Touche Ross, New Orleans, 1985; asst. dist. atty. Dept. Justice, 1990-99, asst. U.S. atty. Raleigh, N.C., 1999—; adj. prof. Tulane U. Sch. Law, New Orleans, 1994-99. Mem. United Cerebral Palsy of New Orleans, 1985-99, pres., 1989-90; mem. United Way New Orleans, 1987-99. Recipient Vol. Yr., United Cerebral Palsy N.O., 1985, Outstanding Vol. United Way, 1991. Mem. La. State Bar Assn. Office: US Attorney 301 New Bern Ave Fl 8 Raleigh NC 27601-1417

DAS, KALYAN, lawyer; b. Calcutta, India, June 23, 1956; s. Amulyaratan and Chaitaly (Mitra) D.; m. Pia Mukherjee, Feb. 18, 1986; children: Sabrina, Rahul. Barrister-at-Law, The Lincoln's Inn, London, 1979; diploma, Assoc. of the Chartered Inst. of Arbitrators, London, 1980; LLM, NYU, 1989. Bar: Eng. 1979, Wales 1979, N.Y. 1983; advocate Supreme Ct. India, 1981; barrister and solicitor Melbourne, Australia, 1984. Barrister-at-law Fountain Ct. Temple, London, 1980-81; assoc. Malcolm A. Hoffmann, N.Y.C., 1981-82, White & Case, LLP, N.Y.C., 1983-88, Milbank, Tweed, Hadley & McCloy, LLP, N.Y.C., 1988-90, Seward & Kissel, N.Y.C., 1990-93, ptnr., head global banking and instl. fin. restructuring/workout group, 1993—. Editor: Company Law, 1980. Internat. life v.p. Internat. Students' Trust, London, 1987—. Fellow Am. Coll. Investment Counsel (co-chair ann. meeting 1998); mem. ABA, N.Y. State Bar Assn., Assn. Bar City of N.Y., Am. Arbitration Assn. (panel mem.), Hon. Soc. Lincoln's Inn, Wine Soc. London, Met. Club (N.Y.C.). Avocations: sailing, tennis, travel. Banking, Contracts commercial, Finance. Home: 107 W 89th St +PhB New York NY 10024-1944 Office: Seward & Kissel LLP 1 Battery Park Plz Fl 21 New York NY 10004-1485 E-mail: das@sewkis.com

DAUER, EDWARD ARNOLD, law educator; b. Providence, Sept. 28, 1944; s. Marshall and Shirly (Moverman) D.; m. Carol Jean Egglestone, June 18, 1966; children: E. Craig, Rachel P. AB, Brown U., 1966; LLB cum laude, Yale U., 1969; MPH, Harvard U., 2001. Bar: Conn. 1978, Colo. 1986. Asst. prof. law sch. U. Toledo, 1969-72; assoc. prof. law U. So. Calif., L.A., 1972-74, Yale U., New Haven, 1975-85, assoc. dean, 1978-83, dep. dean law sch., 1983-85; dean, prof. law U. Denver, 1985-90, dean emeritus, prof. law, 1991—. Vis. scholar Harvard U. Sch. Pub. Health, 1996-97; of counsel Popham, Haik, Schnobrich and Kaufman, 1990-97; pres. CEJAD Aviation Corp.; sr. assn. Health Care Negotiation Assocs., Inc. Author: Materials on a Nonadversarial Legal Process, 1978, Conflict Resolution Strategies in Health Care, 1993, Manual of Dispute Resolution: ADR Law and Practice, 1994 (CPr Book award 1994), Health Care Dispute Resolution, 2000; contbr. articles to profl. jours. Bd. dirs. New Haven Cmty. Action Agy., 1978-81, Cerebral Palsy Found. Denver, 1989—, pres., 1992-95; founder, pres. Nat. Ctr. Preventive Law; mem. Colo. Commn. Higher Edn., 1987-91; commr. Colo. Advanced Tech. Inst., 1989-91. Recipient W. Quinn Jordan award Nat. Blood Found., 1994, Paella award Harvard Sch. Pub. Health, 1996, Sanbar award Am. Coll. Legal Medicine, 1999. Mem. Am. Law Inst., Order of Coif, Met. Club, Greenwood Athletic Club. Republican. Jewish. Home: 127 S Garfield St Denver CO 80209 Office: U Denver Coll Law 1900 Olive St Denver CO 80220 E-mail: edauer@du.edu, edauer@hcna.net

DAUGHERTY, FREDERICK ALVIN, federal judge; b. Oklahoma City, Aug. 18, 1914; s. Charles Lemuel and Felicia (Mitchell) D.; m. Marjorie E. Green, Mar. 15, 1947 (dec. Feb. 1964); m. Betsy F. Amis, Dec. 15, 1965. LL.B., Cumberland U., 1933; postgrad., Oklahoma City U., 1934-35, LL.B. (hon.), 1974; postgrad., Okla. U., 1936-37; HHD (hon.), Okla. Christian Coll., 1976. Bar: Okla. 1937. Practiced, Oklahoma City, 1937-40; mem. firm Ames, Ames & Daugherty, 1946-50, Ames, Daugherty, Bynum & Black, Oklahoma City, 1952-55; judge 7th Jud. Dist. Ct., 1955-61; U.S. dist. judge Western, Eastern and No. Dists. Okla., 1961—; chief judge Western Dist. Okla., 1972-82. Mem. Fgn. Intelligence Surveillance Ct., 1981-88, Temporary Emergency Ct. Appeals, 1983-93, Multi dist. Litigation panel, 1980-90; mem. codes of conduct com. U.S. Jud. Conf., 1980-87. Active local ARC, 1956—, chmn., 1958-60, nat. bd. govs., 1963-69, 3d nat. vice chmn., 1968-69; active United Fund Greater Oklahoma City, 1957—, pres., 1961, trustee, 1963—; pres. Community Coun. Oklahoma City and County, 1967-69; exec. com. Okla. Med. Rsch. Found., 1966-69. With AUS, 1940-45, 50-52. Decorated Legion of Merit with 2 oak leaf clusters, Bronze Star with oak leaf cluster, Combat Infantrymans badge; recipient award to mankind Okla. City Sertoma Club, 1962, Outstanding Citizen award Okla. City Jr. C. ofC., 1965, Disting. Alumni citation Samford U., 1974, Disting. Svc. citation Okla. U., 1973, Constn. award Rogers State Coll., 1988, Pathmakers award Oklahoma County Hist. Soc., 1991; named to Okla. Hall of Fame, 1969, Okla. Mil. Hall of Fame, 2000. Mem. Fed. Bar Assn., Okla. Bar Assn., Am. Bar Found., Sigma Alpha Epsilon, Phi Delta Phi, Men's Dinner Club (Oklahoma City) (pres. 1966-69), Kiwanis (pres. 1957, lt. gov. 1959), Masons (33 degree, sovereign grand insp. gen. in Okla. 1982-86), Shriners, Jesters, Order of Coif (hon. mem. Okla. chpt.). Episcopalian (sr. warden 1957).

DAUGHTREY, MARTHA CRAIG, federal judge; b. Covington, Ky., July 21, 1942; d. Spence E. Kerkow and Martha E. (Craig) Piatt; m. Larry G. Daughtrey, Dec. 28, 1962; 1 child, Carran. BA, Vanderbilt U., 1964, JD, 1968. Bar: Tenn. 1968. Pvt. practice, Nashville, 1968; asst. U.S. atty., 1968-69; asst. dist. atty., 1969-72; asst. prof. law Vanderbilt U., 1972-75; judge Tenn. Ct. Appeals, 1975-90; assoc. justice Tenn. Supreme Ct., 1990-93; circuit judge U.S. Ct. Appeals (6th cir.), 1993—. Lectr. law Vanderbilt Law Sch., Nashville, 1975-82, adj. prof., 1988-90; mem. faculty NYU Appellate Judges Seminar, N.Y.C., 1977-90, 94—. Mem. bd. editors ABA Jour., 1995—; contbr. articles to profl. jours. Pres. Women Judges Fund for Justice, 1984-85, 1986-87; active various civic orgns. Recipient Athena award Nat. Athena Program, 1991. Mem. ABA (chmn. appellate judges conf. 1985-86, chmn. jud. div. 1989-90, ho. of dels. 1988-91, standing com. on continuing edn. of bar 1992-94, commn. on women in the profession 1994-97, bd. editors ABA Jour. 1995—), Tenn. Bar Assn., Nashville Bar Assn. (bd. dirs. 1988-90), Am. Judicature Soc. (bd. dirs. 1988-92), Nat. Assn. Women Judges (pres. 1985-86), Lawyers Assn. for Women (pres. Nashville 1986-87). Office: US Ct Appeals 300 Customs House 701 Broadway Nashville TN 37203-3944*

DAUSTER, WILLIAM GARY, lawyer, economist; b. Sacramento, Nov. 25, 1957; s. William Joe and Marianne Dauster; m. Ellen Lisa Weintraub, May 10, 1986; children: Matthew Isaac, Natanya Miriam, Emma Sophia. BA in Econs., Polit. Sci. and Internat. Rels., U. So. Calif., 1978, MA in Econs., 1981; JD, Columbia U., 1984. Bar: N.Y. 1985, U.S. Dist. Ct. (so. and ea. dists.) N.Y. 1985, D.C. 1986, U.S. Supreme Ct. 1997. Assoc. Cravath, Swaine & Moore, N.Y.C., 1984-86; chief counsel com. on budget U.S. Senate, Washington, 1986-94, acting staff dir., chief counsel, 1994, Dem. chief of staff, chief counsel, 1995-97, Dem. dep. staff dir., gen. coun. com. labor/human resources, 1997, Dem. chief of staff, chief counsel, 1997-98; counselor Wellstone Pres. Exploratory Com., 1998-99; dep. asst. to the Pres. for econ. policy, dep. dir. Nat. Econ. Coun., The White House, 1999-2000; sr. counselor to Senator Russ Feingold U.S. Senate, 2000—01, legis. dir., 2001—. Author: Congressional Budget Act Annnotated, 1990, Budget Process Law Anntated, 1991, 1993; editor-in-chief Columbia Jour. Law and Social Problems, 1983-84; contbr. articles to profl. jours. Bd. visitors Columbia Law Sch., 1992-2000. Recipient Order of Palm, 1978; U. So. Calif. Trustee scholar, 1974, Harlan Fiske Stone scholar, 1982-84. Mem. D.C. Bar Assn., N.Y. Bar Assn. Democrat. Jewish. Home: 9713 Connecticut Ave Kensington MD 20895-3528 E-mail: bill_dauster@feingold.senate.gov, bill_dauster@yahoo.com

DAVENPORT, BRADFUTE WARWICK, JR. lawyer; b. Richmond, Va., Oct. 19, 1946; s. Bradfute Warwick and Martha (Orr) D.; m. Suzanne Jeannette Shepherd, May 3, 1987; children: Sarah Shepherd, Maria Byrd, John Sidney, Stephen Warwick, Kate Moore. BA, Yale U., 1969; JD, U. Va., 1972. Bar: Va. 1972, U.S. Supreme Ct. 1982, U.S. Ct. Appeals (4th cir.) 1975, U.S. Ct. Appeals (D.C. cir.) 1978, U.S. Dist. Ct. (ea. dist.) Va. 1973, U.S. Dist. Ct. (we. dist.) Va. 1982. Assoc. Mays & Valentine, Richmond, Va., 1972-78; ptnr. Troutman, Sanders, Mays & Valentine, LLP, 1978—. Mem. ABA, Va. Bar Assn., Va. State Bar, Def. Rsch. Inst., Va. Assn. Def. Attys., Va. Trial Lawyers Assn. Episcopalian. General civil litigation, Construction, Environmental. Home: 4 Kingsway Ct Richmond VA 23226-3131 Office: Troutman Sanders Mays & Valentine LLP PO Box 1122 1111 East Main St Richmond VA 23218-1122

DAVENPORT, GERALD BRUCE, lawyer; b. Adrian, Mich., May 17, 1949; s. Bruce Nelson and Mildred Louise (Avis) D.; m. RoxAnn Ferguson, Dec. 27, 1975; children: Jonathan Gerald, Christopher Bruce, Timothy Charles. AB, U. Mich., 1971; JD, U. Tex., 1975. Bar: Tex. 1975, Okla. 1993. Pvt. practice Law Office of Gerald B. Davenport, Cedar Park, Tex., 1975-77; atty. Milchem Inc., Houston, 1977-81, Baker Hughes Prodn. Tools Inc., Houston, 1981-87; sr. atty. Baker Hughes Inc., 1987-88; gen. atty. environ. law Tex. Ea. Corp., 1988; atty. Browning-Ferris Industries, 1988-89, mgr. environ. law sect., 1989-92; asst. gen. counsel environ. law Mapco Inc., Tulsa, 1992-94; of counsel McKinney, Stringer & Webster, P.C., 1994-95; dir. Davenport & Williams, P.C., 1995-96; shareholder Hall, Estill, Hardwick, Gable, Golden & Nelson, P.C., 1996-99; of counsel Shipley, Jennings & Champlin, P.C., Oklahoma City, 1999—. Contbr. articles to profl. jours. Mem. ABA, State Bar Tex. (environ. law sect.), Okla. Bar Assn. (environ. law sect.). Republican. Office: Shipley Jennings & Champlin Two Leadership Sq 211 N Robinson Ste 1300 Oklahoma City OK 73102-7114 Business E-Mail: GBDavenport@SWbell.net

DAVENPORT, JAMES KENT, lawyer; b. Dallas, Oct. 30, 1953; s. James R. and Betty Sue (Talbot) D.; m. Diana Gillingham, Aug. 16, 1980; children: Drew, Blake, Jennifer. BA, Emory U., Atlanta, 1975; MBA, Ga. State U., 1977; JD, So. Meth. U., Dallas, 1980. Bar: Tex. 1980, U.S. Dist. Ct. (no. dist.) Tex. 1980, U.S. Dist. Ct. (ea. dist.) Okla. 1988, U.S. Dist.Ct. (we. dist.) Tex. 1993, U.S. Ct. Appeals (5th cir.) 1985; bd. cert. civil trial law. Acct. Fox & Co., CPA, Dallas, 1980-81; asst. dist. atty. Dallas County Dist. Atty.'s Office, 1981-84; assoc. Pailet & Dekan, 1984-85, Newman, Shook & McManemin, Dallas, 1985-86; atty./shareholder Newman & Davenport, P.C., 1986—. Spkr. in field. Co-author: Bad Faith Litigation in Texas, 1996, also article in field. Mem. Tex. Bar Assn., Dallas Bar Assn. General civil litigation, Insurance. Home: 11135 Lawnhaven Rd Dallas TX 75230-3549 Office: Newman Davenport & Epstein PC Plaza of Americas Ste 1650 LB 314 700 N Pearl Dallas TX 75201-2628 Fax: (214) 754-0936

DAVEY, JOHN H. law librarian; b. Smyrna, Ga., Nov. 27, 1958; s. Kenneth Charles and Betty-Jo (Henderson) D. BM, Shorter Coll., Rome, Ga., 1980; MM, U. Mich., 1982. Law libr. Paul, Weiss, Rifkind Wharton & Garrison, N.Y.C., 1983-88, Dewey Ballantine, N.Y.C., 1988-90; asst. libr. Epstein Becker & Green, 1990-95; head libr. Dechert Price & Rhoads, 1995—. Law Lib. Assn. Greater N.Y. grant, 1995. Mem. Am. Assn. Law Librs. (social responsibilities chair 1997-98), Spl. Librs. Assn., Law Libr. Assn. Greater N.Y. (exec. bd. 1989-90, advt. chair 1991-96), Pvt. Law Libr. Assn. (advt. chair 1996-98). Democrat. Baptist. Home: 25 W 64th St Apt 7C New York NY 10023-6752 Office: Dechert 30 Rockefeller Plz Fl 22 New York NY 10112-2200

DAVID, CHRISTOPHER MARK, lawyer; b. Buffalo, Nov. 19, 1965; s. Thomas Leonard and Anne (Nickodemus) D.; m. Elizabeth Martina Wilson, Aug. 31, 1991; 1 child, Taylor Dawn. AA, Miami Dade C.C., 1989; BA, U. Fla., 1990; JD, U. Miami, 1993. Bar: Fla. 1993, U.S. Dist. Ct. (so. dist.) Fla. 1995. Ptnr. Hall, David and Joseph, P.A., Miami, Fla., 1993—, Hall, David and Joseph, PA, Miami, 1999—. Sgt. U.S. Army, 1983-87. Mem. ATLA, ABA, Acad. Fla. Trial Lawyers, Dade County Bar Assn. General practice. Office: Hall David and Joseph P A 1428 Brickell Ave Fl 8 Miami FL 33131-3438 E-mail: cdavid@hdjlaw.com

DAVID, GEORGE A. lawyer; b. Miami, Sept. 27, 1961; s. Alexander E. and Patricia Anne D. BA, U. Fla., 1985, JD, 1989. Bar: Fla. 1991, U.S. Dist. Ct. (so. dist.) Fla. 1993. Lawyer Charlip Delgado & Befeler, Miami, 1990-91, Parrillo Weiss & O'Halloran, Miami, 1991-96, Thornton, Mastrucci & Sinclair, Miami, 1996-98, Ligman, Martin & Evans, Miami, 1998—. Mem. ABA, Dade County Bar Assn. State civil litigation, Insurance, Personal injury. Office: Ligman Martin & Evans 230 Catalonia Ave Coral Gables FL 33134-6705

DAVID, JAMES P. lawyer; b. Kuala Lumpur, Malaysia, June 19, 1970; s. Nicholas Joshua and Joyce Pearl (Nathan) D. LLB, U. Sheffield, Eng., 1991; LLM, U. Cambridge, Eng., 1995. Bar: solicitor Supreme Ct. Eng. and Wales 1997, advocate and solicitor High Ct. of Malaya 2000. Solicitor Clyde & Co., Singapore and London, 1995-2000, Dibb Lupton Alsop, Singapore, 2000—. Spkr. in field. Fellow Cambridge Commonwealth Soc.; mem. Singapore Internat. Law Soc. Admiralty, Insurance, Private international. Office: Dibb Lupton Alsop 8 Robinson Rd #11-00 Cosco Bldg Singapore 048544 Singapore Fax: +65 236 0589. E-mail: james.david@dla.com

DAVID, REUBEN, lawyer; b. Baghdad, Iraq, June 12, 1928; came to U.S., 1951; s. Isaac Solomon David and Tefaha (Nisan) Solomon D.; m. Nesta Paley David; 1 child, Aram. License in Law, Iraq Law Coll., Baghdad, 1951; BA, NYU, 1958; JD, N. Y. Law Sch., 1962. Bar: Iraq 1951, N.Y. 1969. Asst. corp. counsel City of N.Y., 1970-76, chief legal unit dept. personnel, 1976-78; dep. dir. for legal affairs N.Y.C. Employees' Retirement System, 1978—. Mem. ABA, N.Y. State Bar Assn. Home: 30 Fifth Ave New York NY 10011-8812

DAVID, ROBERT JEFFERSON, lawyer; b. New Roads, La., Aug. 10, 1943; s. Joseph Jefferson and Doris Marie (Olinde) D.; m. Stella Marie Scott, Jan. 21, 1967; children: Robert J. Jr., Richard M. BA, Southeastern La. U., 1966; JD, Loyola U., New Orleans, 1969. Bar: U.S. Dist. Ct. (ea. dist.) La. 1969, U.S. Dist. Ct. (mid. dist.) La. 1969, U.S. Dist. Ct. (we. dist.) La. 1975. Assoc. Gainsburgh, Benjamin, Fallon, David, New Orleans, 1969-74; ptnr. Gainsburgh, Benjamin, David, 1974—. Adj. faculty mem. Tulane U. Sch. Law, New Orleans, 1982-84, law sch. Loyola U., New Orleans, 1996; lectr., speaker continuing legal edn. seminars. Staff mem. Loyola U. Law Rev., 1967-69; bd. dir Loyola Law Sch. Alumni Assn., 2001—. Reader, recorder for La. Blind and Handicapped, 1986-91; charter mem. Lawyers for Alliance for Nuclear Arms Control, New Orleans, 1986-1990; pres. Arden Hill Acad. Parent Tchr. League, 1979-80. Fellow Am. Coll. Trial Lawyers; mem. ABA, ATLA, Nat. Bd. Trial Advocacy, Am. Bd. Profl. Liability Attys., La. State Bar Assn. (asst. examiner commn. on bar admissions 1974-93, spl. ins. commn. 1974-82, med. legal interprof. com. 1987—, co-chmn. 1991-94, contbr. La. Bar Assn. Jour. column on Profl. Liability 1989—), La. Bar Found., La. Trial Lawyers Assn. (bd. govs.

1981-83, 95-96, exec. com. 1996-97, coun. of dirs. 1997—, contbg. editor Civil Trial Tactics manual 1981, chmn. sect. med. malpractice 92-94, legis. com.), Kappa Sigma, Phi Alpha Delta. Avocation: sports. General civil litigation, Health, Personal injury. Home: 21 Cypress Point Ln New Orleans LA 70131-3351 Office: Gainsburgh Benjamin David 2800 Energy Ctr New Orleans LA 70163

DAVIDOFF, RICHARD SAYLES, lawyer; b. N.Y.C., Nov. 3, 1932; s. Eli and Minnie Phyllis (Selesko) D.; children: Andrew M., Jennifer A. BA, Dartmouth Coll., 1954; JD, Harvard U., 1959. BAr: N.Y. 1960. Ptnr. Davidoff, Levinson & Davidoff, N.Y.C., 1960-74, Kantor, Davidoff, Wolfe, Mandelker & Kass, P.C., N.Y.C., 1974—. Class officer Class of 1954, Dartmouth Coll., 1964-68, 79-84; bd. dirs. Parents Assn. Trinity Coll., Hartford, Conn., 1982-86. Served to lt. (j.g.) USNR, 1954-56. Mem. N.Y. State Assn. General corporate, Probate. Home: 305 E 83d St New York NY 10028 Office: Kantor Davidoff Wolfe Mandelker & Kass PC 51 E 42nd St New York NY 10017-5404

DAVIDOW, JOEL, lawyer; b. N.J., July 24, 1938; s. Isadore Davidow; m. Katherine Davidow-Lucas (div.); children: Elizabeth, Judith; m. Debra Lynn Miller; children: Abigail, Molly. AB, Princeton U., 1960; LLB, Columbia U., 1963; postdoctoral, U. London, Stanford U. Bar: D.C. 1965, N.Y. 1981. Legal asst. to commr. U.S. Fed. Trade Commn., Washington, 1964-65; assoc. Freeman & Hanley, Chgo., 1969-70; trial atty. Antitrust divsn. U.S. Dept. Justice, Washington, 1966-69, evaluation atty. Antitrust divsn., 1970-73, chief fgn. commerce sect. Antitrust divsn., 1973-77, dir. policy planning antitrust div., 1978-81; ptnr. Mudge, Rose, Guthrie, Alexander & Ferdon, N.Y.C., 1981-87; ptnr., head internat. sect. Dickstein, Shapiro & Morin, Washington, 1987-93; ptnr., vice chmn. Ablondi, Foster, Sobin & Davidow, 1993-2001; ptnr. Miller & Chevalier, 2001—. Del. UN Conf. Restrictive Practice, Geneva, 1974-80; adj. prof. law Columbia U., N.Y.C., 1982-87, Am. U. 1987-91, George Mason U. 1992-99; arbitrator U.S.-Can. Free Trade Agreement, Washington, Ottowa, 1991-94. Author: Antitrust Rules for International Business (Bur. Nat. Affairs 1995); fgn. antitrust editor Antitrust Bulletin, 1981; adv. bd. Bur. Nat. Affairs Antitrust Bulletin, 1981; ocntbr. articles to profl. jours. Mem. ABA. Democrat. Avocation, tennis. Antitrust, Private international. Home: 3658 Upton St NW Washington DC 20008-3125 Office: Ablondi Foster Sobin & Davidow 1150 18th St NW # 9 Washington DC 20036-3816

DAVIDSON, DANIEL MORTON, lawyer; b. Lynbrook, N.Y., July 9, 1950; BA summa cum laude, Williams Coll., 1972; JD magna cum laude, Harvard U., 1975. Bar: D.C. 1975, Calif. 1977, U.S. Tax Ct. 1979, U.S. Supreme Ct. 1992. Law clk. Mass. Supreme Ct., 1975-76; ptnr. Sidley & Austin, Washington, 1985-98, Hogan & Hartson, L.L.P., Washington, 1998—. Contbr. articles to profl. jours. Mem. ABA, D.C. Bar Assn., State Bar Calif., Phi Beta Kappa. Corporate taxation, Taxation, general, Personal income taxation. Office: Hogan & Hartson LLP 555 13th St NW Ste 900W Washington DC 20004-1109 E-mail: dmdavidson@hhlaw.com

DAVIDSON, DAVID EDGAR, lawyer; b. Louisville, Aug. 24, 1954; s. William R. and Bernice Cline (Ashton) D.; m. Sally Anne Marguet, Dec. 27, 1975; children: Katherine Esther, Joseph William. BA, U. Louisville, 1976; JD, U. Cin., 1980. Bar: Ky. 1980, Ohio 1981, U.S. Dist. Ct. (ea. dist.) Ky. 1981, U.S. Dist. Ct. so. dist.) Ohio 1985, U.S. Ct. Appeals (6th cir.) 1981, U.S. Supreme Ct. 1985. Assoc. Cobb and Oldfield, Covington, Ky., 1980-85, ptnr., 1986—. Adv. bd. Welcome House No. Ky., exec. com., 1995—, chmn. bd. dirs., 2000—01; reader Radio Reading Svcs., Cin., 1982—99; trustee Covington Ladies Home, 1994—97; vestry mem. Trinity Episcopal Ch., Covington, 1988—95, 1997—99, sr. warden, 1985—87, 1990—91, 1993—95; vice-chancellor Episcopal Diocese Lexington, 1988—2001, chancellor, 2001—; bd. dirs. St. Paul's Child Care Ctr., Newport, Ky., 2000—. Mem. Ky. Bar Assn., Ohio Bar Assn., No. Ky. Bar Assn. (CLE com. 1986—, bd. dirs. 1998-2000, pres. 2001—), Ky. Assn. Criminal Def. Lawyers (bd. dirs.), Potter Stewart Inns of Ct. (so. dist. Ohio), Cin. Bar Assn. Democrat. Episcopalian. Criminal, Family and matrimonial, Personal injury. Home: 2446 Sheffiled Ct Covington KY 41017-4200 Office: Cobb and Oldfield PO Box 1078 213 E 4th St Covington KY 41012-1078 E-mail: ddavidson@cobbandoldfield.com

DAVIDSON, DAVID JOHN, lawyer, entertainer; b. Drexel Hill, Pa., Oct. 5, 1960; s. John Thomas and Eileen G. Davidson; m. Judith Duggan, Dec. 28, 1985; children: Cody T., Jocelyn C. BA, U. Fla., 1981, JD, 1987. Bar: Fla. 1988, U.S. Dist. Ct. (mid. dist.) Fla. 1988. Probation officer Fla. Dept. Corrections, West Palm Beach, 1981-84; assoc. atty. Mateer, Harbert & Bates, P.A., Orlando, Fla., 1988-91; entertainer Sports Magic Team, 1991—; gen. counsel Halifax Cmty. Health Sys., Daytona Beach, 1991—. Chmn. Volusia County Med.-Legal Liaison, Daytona Beach, 1995; spkr. in field. Mem. Tomoka Christian Ch., Ormond Beach, Fla., 1996—; bd. counselors Bethune Cookman Coll., Daytona Beach, 1997—. Mem. Am. Health Lawyers Assn., Leadership Daytona. Avocations: playing in a band since 1993, boating, camping, sports. General corporate, Health. Office: Halifax Cmty Health Sys 303 N Clyde Morris Blvd Daytona Beach FL 32114-2709

DAVIDSON, FRANK GASSAWAY, III, lawyer; b. Lynchburg, Va., Feb. 25, 1945; s. Frank Gassaway and Katherine (Graves) G.; children: Christian O., Frank G. BA, Hampden-Sydney Coll., 1969; JD, Washington and Lee U., 1971; LLM, NYU, 1975. Bar: Va. 1975. With trust dept. Morgan Guaranty Trust Co., N.Y.C., 1971-72; trust officer The Fiduciary Trust Co., 1973-75; pres. Davidson, Sakolosky & Moseley PC, Lynchburg, 1975—. Bd. dirs. Schewel Furniture Co., Inc.; past. pres. Central Va. Speech, Hearing Ctr., Inc. Bd. dirs. Greater Lynchburg Habitat for Humaity, Inc.; past chmn. Lynchburg Fine Arts Ctr.; chmn. United Way Annual Fund, 1997. With USMC, 1968-74. Mem. ABA, Va. Bar Assn., Lynchburg Bar Assn., Oakwood Country Club (Lynchburg). Episcopalian. General corporate, Estate planning, Pension, profit-sharing, and employee benefits. Home: 8340 Wards Rd Rustburg VA 24588-4283 Office: Davidson Sakolosky Moseley PO Box 798 Lynchburg VA 24505-0798 E-mail: davidsoniii@aol.com

DAVIDSON, FRANK PAUL, retired macroengineer, lawyer; b. N.Y.C., May 20, 1918; s. Maurice Philip and Blanche (Reinheimer) D.; m. Izaline Marguerite Doll, May 19, 1951; children: Roger Conrad, Nicholas Henry, Charles Geoffrey. BS, Harvard U., 1939, JD, 1948; DHL (hon.), Hawthorne Coll., 1987. Bar: N.Y. 1953, U.S. Dist. Ct. (so. dist.) N.Y. 1953. Dir. mil. affairs, gen. counsel Houston C. of C., 1948-50; contract analyst Am. Embassy, Paris, 1950-53; assoc. Carb, Luria, Glassner & Cook, N.Y.C., 1953-54; pvt. practice law, 1955-70; founding pres., counsel, bd. dirs. The Inst. for the Future, 1967-70; rsch. assoc. MIT, Cambridge, Mass., 1970-96, also chmn. system dynamics steering com. Sloan Sch. Mgmt., coord. macro-engrig. Sch. Engring.; ret., 1984. Pres. Tch. Studies Inc., N.Y.C., 1957-96, vice chmn. Inst. for Ednl. Svcs., Bedford, Mass., 1980-84, spl. lectr. Société des Ingénieurs et Scientifiques de France, 1991, NAS del. to Renewable Resources Workshop, Katmandu, Nepal, 1981, governing bd. Channel Tunnel Study Group, 1957-85, co-founder Channel Tunnel Study Group, London, Paris, 1957, apptd. to NASA Exploration Task Force, Washington, 1989, mem. internat. sci. and tech. com. Ocean Cities Symposium, Monaco, 1995. Author: Macro: A Clear Vision of How Science and Technology Will Shape Our Future, 1983, Macro: Big is Beautiful, 1986; editor: series of AAAS books on macroengring., Tunneling and Underground Transport, 1987; co-editor: Macro-Engineering, Global Infrastructure Solutions, 1992, Solar Power Satellites, 1993, 2nd edit., 1998, Festschrift, Macro-Engineering and The Earth: World Projects for the Year 2000 and Beyond, 1998; mem. editorial bd. Interdisciplinary Sci. Revs., 1985—; mem. adv. bd. Tech. in Soc., 1979—, Mountain R&D, 1981-2000, Project Appraisal, 1986-98. Bd. dirs. Internat. Mountain Soc., Boulder, Colo., 1981-2000, Assn. Prospective 2100, Paris, 1997; trustee Norwich (Vt.) Ctr., 1980-83, mem. steering com. Am. Trails Network, 1986-88, bd. dirs. Am. Trails Washington, 1988-90. RCAC, 1941-46, ETO; Troop Leader 10th Cdn., Armoured Rgt. (Fort Garry Horse), Intelligence Officer and Squadron Leader, GSO III (Intelligence) Second Armoured Brigade Group, maj. Tex. State Guard; apptd. to Senate Ft. Garry Horse, 1995. Decorated chevalier Legion of Honor (France), 1999, Bronze Star medal; recipient Key to City Osaka, Japan, 1987, Twice the Citizen award Royal Mil. Inst., Manitoba, Can., 1999, William James award Rensselaerville Inst., 2001; elected Mem. Honoraire, Pres. d'Honneur Assn. Louis Armand, Paris, 1996-99; Lewis Mumford Fellow Rensselaerville Inst., 1982, William James award, 2001. Mem. ABA, Internat. Assn. Macro-Engring. Socs. (bd. dirs. 1987—, hon.chmn. 1997-2000), Am. Soc. Macro-Engring. (bd. dirs. 1982—, vice chancellor 1983-97, pres. 1997-98, chmn. 1998), Assn. Bar of City of N.Y. (internat. law com. 1959-62), Major Projects Assn. (mem. overseas adv. com. U.K. 1995—), Knickerbocker (N.Y.C.) Club, St. Botolph (Boston) Club, MIT Quarter Century Club. Home: 26A Parker St Lexington MA 02421-4907

DAVIDSON, GEORGE ALLAN, lawyer; b. N.Y.C., Apr. 6, 1942; s. George Roger and Jean Allan (McKaig) D.; m. Annette L. Richter, Sept. 4, 1965; children: Emily, Charlotte. AB, Brown U., 1964; LLB, Columbia U., 1967. Bar: N.Y. 1967, U.S. Dist. Ct. (so. and ea. dists.) N.Y. 1969, U.S. Ct. Appeals (2d cir.) 1970, U.S. Supreme Ct. 1974, U.S. Tax Ct. 1974, U.S. Ct. Appeals (D.C. cir.) 1976, U.S. Dist. Ct. (no. dist.) Calif. 1980, U.S. Ct. Appeals (9th cir.) 1981, U.S. Ct. Appeals (5th cir.) 1982, U.S. Dist. Ct. (no. dist.) N.Y. 1982, U.S. Ct. Appeals (11th cir.) 1983, U.S. Ct. Appeals (1st cir.) 1986, U.S. Ct. Appeals (7th cir.) 1992. Law clk., 1967-68; assoc. Hughes Hubbard & Reed, N.Y.C., 1968-74, ptnr., 1974—; dir. P.R. Legal Def. and Edn. Fund, Inc., 1980-84. Dir. Legal Aid Soc., 1979-92, pres. 1987-89, N.Y. Lawyers for Pub. Interest, Inc., 1984-86, Columbia Law Sch. Alumni Assn., 1987-91, Practicing Attys. for Law Students, 1989—, VIP Cmty. Svcs., 1994—. Contbr. writings to legal publs. Fellow Am. Coll. Trial Laywers; mem. ABA, Internat. Bar Assn., Fed. Bar Coun., Am. Law Inst., N.Y. Sci. Policy Assn., N.Y. State Bar Assn., Assn. Bar City N.Y., Nat. Assn. Coll. and Univ. Attys., Union Internationale des Avocats, Century Assn. General civil litigation, Constitutional, Non-profit and tax-exempt organizations. Office: Hughes Hubbard & Reed LLP 1 Battery Park Plz Fl 12 New York NY 10004-1482 E-mail: davidson@hugheshubbard.com

DAVIDSON, GLEN HARRIS, federal judge; b. Pontotoc, Miss., Nov. 20, 1941; s. M. Glen and Lora (Harris) D.; m. Bonnie Payne, Apr. 25, 1973; children: Glen III, Gregory P. BA, U. Miss, 1962, JD, 1965. Bar: Miss. 1965, U.S. Ct. Appeals (5th cir.) 1965, U.S. Supreme Ct. 1971. Asst. dist. atty. First Jud. Dist., Tupelo, Miss., 1969-74, dist. atty., 1975; U.S. atty. U.S. Dist. Ct. (no. dist.) Miss., Oxford, 1981-85; U.S. district judge U.S. Ct. House, Aberdeen, Miss., 1985—; chief judge U.S. Dist. Ct. (no. dist.) Miss., 2000—. Atty. Lee County Sch. Bd., Miss., 1974-81. Bd. dirs. Community Devel. Found., Tupelo, 1976-81; exec. bd. Yocona Council Boy Scouts Am., 1972—. Maj. USAF, 1966-69. Mem. Fed. Bar Assn. (v.p. 1984), Miss. Bar Found., Lee County Bar Assn. (pres. 1974), Assn. Trial Lawyers Am., Miss. Prosecutors Assn., Kiwanis (pres. Tupelo 1978). Presbyterian. Office: US Dist Ct PO Box 767 Aberdeen MS 39730-0767 E-mail: Davidson@msnd.uscourts.gov

DAVIDSON, JAMES JOSEPH, III, lawyer; b. Lafayette, La., July 27, 1940; s. James Joseph and Virginia Lee (Dunham) D.; m. Kay Cecile Holloway, Aug. 7, 1962; children: Kimberly Kay, James Joseph IV, Lynda Leigh, Virginia Holland. BA, U. SW La., 1963; JD, Tulane U., 1964. Bar: La. 1964, U.S. Dist. Ct. (we. dist.) La. 1965, U.S. Dist. Ct. (ea. dist.) La. 1979, U.S. Dist. Ct. (mid. dist.) La. 1986, U.S. Ct. Appeals (5th cir.) 1972 Us. Supreme Ct. 1975, U.S. Ct. Appeals (11th cir.) 1981. Ptnr. Davidson, Meaux, Sonnier & McElligott, Lafayette, La., 1964—. Mem. exec. bd. Evangeline Area coun. Boy Scouts Am., 1969-80; trustee U. La. Lafayette Found., 1980—, pres., 1988-91. Fellow Am. Bar Found. (life); mem. La. State Bar Assn. (del. 1970-96), La. Bar Found., La. Assn. Def. Counsel (dir. 1975-77), Nat. Assn. R.R. Trial Counsel, Am. Bd. Trial Advocates (adv. bd.), Am. Counsel Assn., Internat. Assn. Def. Counsel, Assn. Def. Trial Attys., Assn. Transp. Practitioners. Republican. Baptist. Federal civil litigation, State civil litigation, Condemnation. Home: 539 Girard Park Dr Lafayette LA 70503-2601 Office: PO Box 2908 Lafayette LA 70502-2908

DAVIDSON, JOHN HENRY, legal educator; b. Washington, Pa., Dec. 9, 1942; s. John H. and Estous (Lee) D.; m. Cathy F. Beard, Oct. 14, 1967; children: Benjamin, Felix. BA, Wake Forest Coll., 1964; JD, U. Pitts., 1967; LLM, George Washington U., 1971. Bar: Pa. 1967, U.S. Dist. Ct. (we. dist.) Pa. 1967, S.D. 1974, U.S. Dist. Ct. S.D., 1972, U.S. Ct. Appeals (8th cir.) 1974. Sole practice, Pitts., 1967-69; staff atty. Neighborhood Legal Services, Pitts., 1969-71; lectr. in law George Washington U., Washington, 1971-72; prof. of law U. S.D., Vermillion, 1972—. Author: (with Delogu) Federal Environmental Regulations, 1989—; co-author, editor: Agricultural Law Treatise, 1981; Agricultural Law Cases, 1984. Mem. ABA (adv. com. forum on rural lawyers), Western Water Policy Rev. Com., Am. Trial Lawyers Assn., Am. Law Inst., Internat. Coun. Environ. Law, Am. Agrl. Law Assn. (bd. dirs. 1979-82), Dakota Plains Legal Services (bd. dirs. 1977—), Rocky Mountain Mineral Law Found. (trustee 1980-90). Democrat. Home: 31275 Saginaw Ave Vermillion SD 57069-6803 Office: U SD 414 E Clark St Vermillion SD 57069-2307 E-mail: jdavidso@usd.edu

DAVIDSON, KENNETH LAWRENCE, lawyer, educator; b. Tulsa, Feb. 4, 1945; s. Joe and Elsie (Hutchens) D.; m. Anne Devine; children: Rebecca Marie, Deborah Shannon. BSBA, U. Tulsa, 1968, JD, 1970; LLM, Georgetown U., 1975. Bar: Okla. 1970, U.S. Dist. Ct. (no. dist.) Okla. 1970, U.S. Ct. Mil. Appeals 1971, U.S. Supreme Ct. 1976, D.C. Ct. Appeals 1978, Ill. 1990. Assoc. CEO, assoc. legal counsel Bd. Regents Okla. State U. and A&M Colls., Stillwater, 1976-90; gen. counsel Regency Univs. System Ill. Bd. Regents, Springfield, 1990-96; parliamentarian, counsel, bd. trustees No. Ill. U., DeKalb. 1995-97, counsel for governance, risk mgmt., equity svcs., 1997-2000, corp. coun. & bd. parliamentarian, 2000—. Adj. assoc. prof. Coll. Edn. Okla. State U., 1986-90; adminstrv. law judge Okla. Dept. Edn., Oklahoma City, 1978-90. Bd. dirs. YMCA Aquatic Club, Stillwater, 1985-86, Judith Karman Hospice, Stillwater, 1987. Capt. JAGC, USAF, 1970-76. Decorated Meritorious Svc. medal, Commendation medal. Mem. AAUP, Ill. Bar Assn., DeKalb County Bar Assn., Okla. Bar Assn., D.C. Bar Assn., Nat. Assn. Coll. and Univ. Attys., Am. Soc. Parliamentarians, Univ. Risk Mgmt. Assn., Kappa Sigma. Democrat. Education and schools, Insurance, Labor. Office: No Ill U 302 Lowden Hall Dekalb IL 60115-3080 E-mail: kdavidso@niu.edu

DAVIDSON, ROBERT BRUCE, lawyer; b. N.Y.C., May 6, 1945; BS in Econs. cum laude, U. Pa., 1967; JD, Columbia U., 1972. Bar: N.Y. 1973, U.S. Dist. Ct. (so. and ea. dists.) N.Y. 1973, U.S. Ct. Appeals (2d cir.) 1975, U.S. Ct. Appeals (D.C. cir.) 1981, U.S. Supreme Ct. 1979, U.S. Tax Ct. 1984, U.S. Ct. Appeals (fed. cir.) 1989, U.S. Ct. Appeals (3d cir.) 1990. Assoc. Baker & McKenzie, N.Y.C., 1972-79, ptnr., 1979—. Mem. adv. bd. World Arbitration Inst., N.Y.C., 1984—. Author: (with others) Voting Laws and Procedures, 1973; also articles. Vol. U.S. Peace Corps, Philippines, 1968-70. Mem. ABA, Assn. of Bar of City of N.Y. (com. on internat. law 1986-89, com. on arbitration 1999—, chair 1982-85), Am. Fgn. Law Assn. (bd. dirs.), Maritime Law Assn. U.S., Fed. Bar Coun., Am. Arbitration Assn. (mem. internat. panel, 1997—, panel for large complex cases 1997—). Alternative dispute resolution, Federal civil litigation, Private international. Office: Baker & McKenzie 805 3d Ave New York NY 10022-7513 E-mail: robert.b.davidson@bakernet.com

DAVIDSON, SHEILA KEARNEY, lawyer; b. Paterson, N.J., Dec. 16, 1961; d. John James and Rita Barbara (Burke) Kearney; m. Anthony H. Davidson, Oct. 5, 1996; 1 child, Andrew John. BA cum laude, Fairfield U., 1983; JD, George Washington U., 1986. Bar: N.Y. 1987, U.S. Dist. Ct. (so. dist.) N.Y. 1987, D.C. 1989. Assoc. Shearson Lehman Bros., Inc., N.Y.C., 1986-87; staff atty. Nat. Assn. Securities Dealers, 1987-89, regional atty., 1989-90, sr. regional atty., 1990-91; regional counsel N.Y. Life Ins. Co., 1991-93, assoc. counsel, 1993-94, asst. gen. counsel, 1994-95, v.p., assoc. gen. counsel, 1995-97, sr. v.p. in charge of corp. compliance dept., 1998-00, sr. v.p./gen. counsel, 2000—. Mem. Securities Industry Assn., D.C. Bar Assn., Fairfield U. Alumni Club N.Y. (pres. 1988-90, exec. com. 2001—), Phi Delta Phi. Republican. Roman Catholic. Administrative and regulatory, General corporate, Securities. Office: NY Life Ins Co 51 Madison Ave New York NY 10010-1603

DAVIDSON, VAN MICHAEL, JR. lawyer; b. Baton Rouge, Nov. 26, 1945; s. Van Michael Sr. and Elizabeth Lamoine (Arnold) D.; m. Judith Ann Begue, Aug. 5, 1967; children: Van Michael III, Catherine Annette, Mary Elizabeth. BA in History, La. State U., 1968; JD, U. Miss., 1973; judge adv. gen.'s postgrad. course, 1978. Bar: Miss. 1973, U.S. Dist. Ct. (no. dist.) Miss. 1973, U.S. Ct. Mil. Appeals 1974, U.S. Supreme Ct. 1978, U.S. Ct. Claims 1979, U.S. Tax Ct. 1980, U.S. Ct. Appeals (5th cir.) 1981, La. 1982, U.S. Dist. Ct. (we. and mid. dists.) La. 1982, U.S. Dist. Ct. (no. dist.) Tex. 1982, U.S. Ct. Appeals (Fed. cir.) 1982, U.S. Dist. Ct. (so. dist.) Miss. 1985, U.S. Dist. Ct. (ea. dist.) La. 1985, D.C., 1987. Commd. 2d lt. U.S. Army, 1968, advanced through grades to maj., 1980, forward observer N.C., 1968, battery battalion officer Ft. Bliss, Tex., 1968-69, battery comdr., 1969-70, command spokesman IV Vietnam, 1970-71, trial counsel Fed. Republic Germany, 1974-77, trial atty. contact appeals divsn. Washington, 1978-81, resigned, 1981; ptnr. Carmouche, Gray & Hoffman, Lake Charles, La., 1981-87; sole practice, 1987-94; gen. counsel Stapp Towing Co. Inc., 1994-97; rsch. atty. 3d Cir. Ct. of Appeals, 1997—. Chmn. bd. dirs. Southwest Legl Services Agy., Lake Charles. Contbr. articles to profl. jours. Lt. col. USAR, 1987. Decorated Bronze Star, Army Commendation medal, Meritorious Svc. medal with one oak leaf cluster. Mem. ABA, Fed. Bar Assn., Assn. Trial Lawyers Am., Bd. of Contract Appeals Bar Assn., Phi Delta Phi. Republican. Presbyterian. Avocations: hunting, fishing, scuba diving, playing piano, writing novels. Federal civil litigation, Construction, Government contracts and claims. Home: 1525 N Greenfield Cir Lake Charles LA 70605-5307 E-mail: mike.judy@usunwired.net, mdavidso@la3circuit.org

DAVIES, CHARLES R. lawyer; BS, Duquesne U., 1964; JD, Georgetown U., 1967. Bar: D.C. 1968. Asst. v.p., asst. gen. counsel Geico Corp., Washington, 1978, v.p., gen. counsel, 1992—, group v.p., gen. counsel, 1999, sr. v.p., gen. counsel, 2000—. Office: Geico Corp Gelco Plz Washington DC 20076-0001

DAVIES, ISABEL MILNER, lawyer; b. Worksop, Eng., May 30, 1952; d. Eric and Janet Marjorie Brown. LLB, Leicester (Eng.) U., 1973. Cert. solicitor, Eng. Solicitor Alsop Stevens, London, 1976-78; from solicitor to ptnr. Wragge & Co., Birmingham, England, 1979-85; ptnr. Taylor, Johnson & Garrett, London, 1985-94; ptnr., head of intellectual property Eversheds, 1994—. Bd. dirs. INTA. Gen. editor Sweet & Maxwell European Trademark Litigation Handbook, 1998. Avocations: travel, exercise, theatre, food, wine. Intellectual property. Office: Eversheds Senator House 85 85 Queen Victoria St London EC4V 4JL England Fax: 02079194555. E-mail: daviesi@eversheds.com

DAVIES, PAUL LEWIS , JR. retired lawyer; b. San Jose, Calif., July 21, 1930; s. Paul Lewis and Faith (Crummey) D.; m. Barbara Bechtel, Dec. 22, 1955 (dec. June 2000); children: Laura (Mrs. Segundo Mateo), Paul Lewis III. AB, Stanford U., 1952; JD, Harvard U., 1957. Bar: Calif. 1957. Assoc. Pillsbury, Madison & Sutro, San Francisco, 1957-63, ptnr., 1963-89; gen. counsel Chevron Corp., 1984-89. Bd. dirs. FMC Corp. Hon. trustee Calif. Acad. Scis., trustee, 1970-83, chmn., 1973-80; pres. Herbert Hoover Found.; bd. overseers Hoover Instn., chmn., 1976-82, 91-93; hon. regent U. of Pacific, regent, 1959-90. Lt. U.S. Army, 1952-54. Mem. Bohemian Club, Pacific-Union Club, Villa Taverna, World Trade Club (San Francisco), Claremont Country Club, Cypress Point (Pebble Beach, Calif.), Sainte Claire (San Jose, Calif.), Collectors, Explorers, Links (N.Y.C.), Met. Club (Washington), Chgo. Club, Phi Beta Kappa, Pi Sigma Alpha. Republican. Office: 3470 Mt Diablo Blvd Ste A210 Lafayette CA 94549-3985 E-mail: pauldaviesjr@yahoo.com

DAVIES, THOMAS YOUNG, III, lawyer, law educator; b. Taylor, Pa., Mar. 10, 1946; s. Thomas Young, Jr. and Elizabeth (Robling) D.; m. Susan McCall, Mar. 8, 1969. B.A., U. Del., 1969; J.D., M.A., Northwestern U., 1975, Ph.D. in Polit. Sci., 1980. Bar: Ill. 1975, U.S. Dist. Ct. (no. dist.) Ill. 1976, U.S. Supreme Ct. 1983. Assoc. Kirkland & Ellis, Chgo., 1976-81; research atty. Am. Bar Found., Chgo., 1981-86, editor research jour., 1983-85; assoc. prof. U. Tenn. Coll. Law, Knoxville, 1986—. Contbr. articles to profl. jours.; articles editor Northwestern U. Law Rev., 1974. Russell Sage resident in law and social sci. U. Calif.-Berkeley, 1975-76. Served with U.S. Army, 1968-71. Mem. ABA, Law and Soc. Assn., Am. Judicature Soc., Am. Polit. Sci. Assn., Order Coif, Phi Beta Kappa. Democrat. Office: Univ of Tenn Coll of Law 1505 Cumberland Ave Knoxville TN 37916-3199

D'AVIGNON, ROY JOSEPH, lawyer; b. Dallas, July 20, 1942; s. Roy J. and Ann (Ham) D'A.; m. Tania M. Mychajlyshyn, Nov. 29, 1969; children: Larissa A., Markian W. BSS, Loyola U., New Orleans, 1964; LLB, Harvard U., 1967. Bar: Tex. 1967, Mass. 1969. Assoc. Hutchins & Wheeler, Boston, 1969-77; counsel Raytheon Co., Lexington, Mass., 1977-86, div. counsel, 1986-90, asst. gen. counsel, 1990-99; v.p., sect. and gen. counsel Simplex Time Recorder Co., Gardner, 1999—. Capt. M.I., U.S. Army, 1967-69. Mem. ABA, Mass. Bar Assn., Tex. Bar Assn., Boston Bar Assn. General corporate, Private international, Mergers and acquisitions.

DAVIS, ALAN JAY, lawyer; b. Phila., Feb. 4, 1937; s. Rudolph Alan and Adele (Saver) D.; m. Roslyn Kutcher, Oct. 4, 1939; children: Jennifer C., Michael R. BA, U. Pa., 1957; JSD, Harvard U., 1960. Bar: Pa. 1961, U.S. Dist. Ct. (ea. dist.) Pa. 1961, U.S. Ct. Appeals (3d cir.) 1961, U.S. Supreme Ct. 1979. Law clk. to chief judge U.S. Ct. Appeals (3d cir.), Phila., 1960-61; assoc. Wolf, Block, Schorr & Solis-Cohen, 1961-66; chief asst. dist. atty. Office Dist. Atty., 1966-68; ptnr. Wolf, Block, Schorr & Solis-Cohen, 1968-91, chmn. litigation dept., 1987-91; sr. litigation ptnr. Ballard Spahr Andrews & Ingersoll, 1991—. Spl. master to investigate prison system and sheriff's dept. Ct. of Common Pleas, Phila., 1968-70; lectr. law U. Pa. Sch. Law, Phila., 1973-77; City Solicitor Phila., 1980-82; chief labor negotiator Southeastern Pa. Transp. Authority, Phila., 1982, Sch. Dist. Phila., 1984, 96, City of Phila., 1991-93. Chmn. met. adv. bd. Anti-Defamation League of B'nai B'rith, Phila., 1986-88; mem. sch. com. Germantown Friends Sch., Phila., 1986-88; trustee Free Libr. of Phila., 1995-98; pres. U. Pa. Law Sch. Am. Inns of Ct., 1998—. Fellow Am. Coll. Trial Lawyers; mem. ABA, Pa. Bar Assn., Phila. Bar Assn., Am. Law Inst., Legal Club, Jr. Legal Club. Democrat. Jewish. Office: Ballard Spahr Andrews & Ingersoll 1735 Market St Fl 51 Philadelphia PA 19103-7599 E-mail: davis@ballardspahr.com

DAVIS, ANDREW HAMBLEY, JR. lawyer; b. Fall River, Mass., Feb. 10, 1937; s. Andrew Hambley and Doris (Baker) D.; m. Gail D. Perry, July 21, 1962; children: Andrew W., Katherine B., Joshua P. AB, Brown U., 1959; LLB, U. Va., 1962. Bar: R.I. 1963, Mass. 1962. Ptnr. Swan, Jenckes, Asquith & Davis, Providence, 1963-78, Davis, Jenckes, Kilmarx & Swan, Providence, 1979-2000, Davis, Kilmarx, Swan & Bowling LLP, Providence, 2000—. Sec., dir. Union Wadding Co., Uncas Mfg. Co. Pres. Bethany Home R.I., 1966; bd. dirs. Moses Brown Sch., R.I. Philharmonic Orch., 1967-90. Mem. ABA, R.I. Bar Assn., Boston Bar Assn., Estate Planning Coun., Am. Coll. Probate Coun., Acoaxet Golf Club, Agaqam Hunt Club, Elephant Rock Beach Club, Hope Club, Masons. General corporate, Estate planning, Probate. Home: 1 Quincy Adams Rd Barrington RI 02806-5030 Office: Davis Kilmarx Swan & Bowling LLP 1420 Hosp Trust Tower 101 Dyer St 2d Fl Providence RI 02903 E-mail: ahd@dksblaw.com

DAVIS, ANDREW NEIL, lawyer, educator; b. Boston, Nov. 7, 1959; s. Gerald Stanley and Sarah Lee D.; m. Suzanne Frances DiBenedetto, Oct. 11, 1992; children: David R. Bray, Hannah M., Zachary G. BS in Biology, Trinity Coll., 1981; MS in Botany, U. Mass., 1983, PhD in Botany, 1987; JD, George Washington U., 1990. Bar: Conn. 1990, U.S. Dist. Ct. Conn. 1991, Mass. 1998. Atty. Pepe & Hazard, Hartford, Conn., 1990-93, Brown, Rudnick, Freed & Gesmer, Hartford, 1993-94; ptnr. LeBoeuf, Lamb, Greene & MacRae LLP, 1994—. Adj. prof. environ. studies Conn. Coll., 1994—. Sr. author/co-author: The Home Environmental Sourcebook, 1996, ISO 14001: Meeting Business Goals Through An Effective Environmental Management System, 1998; contbr. articles to profl. jours. Mem. Leadership Greater Hartford, 1997; chmn. lake adv. commn. Town Marlborough, 1992—, zoning commn., 1993-95. Recipient Hon. Sci. award Bausch & Lomb, 1977; Albert L. Deslisle Botany fellow, 1982. Mem. Am. Arbitration Assn. (environ. adv. com. 1993-95), Conn. Bar Assn. (exec. com. environ. law sect. 1996—), Conn. Bus. and Industry Assn. (environ. policies coun. 1991—), Internat. Coun. Shopping Ctrs., Conn. Groundwater Assn. Avocations: photography, sailing, scuba diving, arctic travel, reading. Environmental, Land use and zoning (including planning), Mergers and acquisitions. Office: LeBoeuf Lamb Greene & MacRae LLP 225 Asylum St Fl 13 Hartford CT 06103-1529 E-mail: adavis@llgm.com

DAVIS, BONNIE CHRISTELL, judge; b. Petersburg, Va., July 13, 1949; d. Robert Madison and Margaret Elizabeth (Collier) D. BA, Longwood Coll., 1971; JD, U. Richmond, 1980. Bar: Va. 1980, U.S. DDist. Ct. (ea. dist.) Va. 1980, U.S. Ct. Appeals (4th cir.) 1982. Tchr. Chesterfield County Schs., Chesterfield, Va., 1971-77; pvt. practice, 1980-83; asst. commonwealth atty. Chesterfield County, 1983-93; judge Juvenile and Domestic Rels. Ct. for 12th Jud. Dist. Va., 1993—. Adviser Youth Svcs. Commn., Chesterfield, 1983-93; cons. Task Force on Child Abuse, 1983-93, Met. Richmond Multi-Discipline Team on Spouse Abuse, 1983-93, Va. Dept. of Children for handbook "Step by Step Through the Juvenile Justice System in Virginia, 1988; mem. nat. adv. com. for prodn. on missing and runaway children Theatre IV; mem. adv. group to set stds. and tng. for Guardians Ad Litem, Supreme Ct. Va., 1994; chmn. jud. adminstrn. com. Jud. Conf. Va. for Dist. Cts., 1995-97; mem. state adv. com. for CASA and children's Justice Act, 1998—. Co-author: Juvenile Law and Practice in Virginia, 1994. Mem. Chesterfield County Pub. Schs. Task Force on Core Values, 1999. Mem. State-Fed. Jud. Coun. Va., Va. State Bar (bd. govs. family law sect. 1997—), Va. Bar Assn., Va. Trial Lawyers Assn., Met. Richmond Women's Bar Assn., Chesterfield-Colonial Heights Bar Assn. Home: 415 Lyons Ave Colonial Heights VA 23834-3154 Office: Chesterfield Juvenile and Domestic Rels Dist Ct 7000 Lucy Corr Blvd Chesterfield VA 23832-6717

DAVIS, CHRISTOPHER PATRICK, lawyer; b. Allentown, Pa., July 12, 1954; s. Richard Arthur and Patricia Anne (Henry) D.; m. Carol Hecker, Aug. 19, 1978; children: Gregory Carl, Colin Stuart. AB summa cum laude, Dartmouth Coll., 1976; JD magna cum laude, Harvard U., 1980. Bar: Mass. 1981, U.S. Dist. Ct. Mass. 1981, U.S. Ct. Appeals (1st cir.) 1985, U.S. Dist. Ct. N.H. 1986. Law clk. to judge U.S. Dist. Ct., Boston, 1980-81; assoc. Goodwin Procter LLP, 1981-88, ptnr., 1988—, chair environ. dept., 1996-00. Editor Harvard Law Rev., 1978-80. Pres. Hamilton-Wenham Land Trust. Mem. ABA, Mass. Bar Assn., Boston Bar Assn., Phi Beta Kappa. Club: Dartmouth Lawyers Assn. (Hanover, N.H.). Avocations: skiing, tennis, bicycling, backpacking, gardening. Federal civil litigation, State civil litigation, Environmental. Office: Goodwin Procter LLP Exchange Pl Boston MA 02109-2803

DAVIS, CLARENCE CLINTON, JR. lawyer; b. Alexandria, La., Sept. 24, 1956; s. Clarence Clinton Sr. and Julia Isabel (Pace) D.; m. Lisa Cheryl Russell, Aug. 6, 1977 (div. Aug. 1978). BS, Northwestern State U., 1977; JD cum laude, So. Meth. U., 1980. Bar: Fla. 1980, U.S. Tax Ct. 1981, U.S. Ct. Appeals (5th cir.) 1981, Tex. 1982; cert. tax law Tex. Bd. Legal Specialization; CPA, Tex. Assoc. Trenam, Simmons, Kemker, Scharf, Barkin, Frye & O'Neill, Tampa, Fla., 1980-81, Moore & Peterson, Dallas, 1981-85, mem., 1986-89; ptnr. Krage & Jarvey, LLP, 1989—. Author: Partnership Taxation in Theory and Practice, 1991-95, Special Problems in Partnership Taxation, 1992—, Fundamentals of LLC and Partnership Taxation, 1996—, LLC and Partnership Allocations and Basis, 1996—, Real Estate and Tax Deferred Exchanges, 1996-99. Mem. ABA (taxation sect.), Tex. Bar Assn. (tax exempt orgn. subcom. taxation sect. 1986-87), Fla. Bar Assn., Dallas Bar Assn., Coll. State Bar Tex., Tex. Soc. CPAs, Order of Coif, Phi Kappa Phi. Republican. Episcopalian. Mergers and acquisitions, Corporate taxation, Taxation, general.

DAVIS, CLAUDE-LEONARD, lawyer, university official; b. Augusta, Ga., Feb. 16, 1944; s. James and Mary Davis; m. Margaret Earle Crowley, Dec. 30, 1965; 1 child, Margaret Michelle. BA in Journalism, U. Ga., 1966, JD, 1974. Bar: Ga. 1974. Broadcaster Sta. WKLE Radio, Washington, 1958-62; realtor Assocs. Realty, Athens, 1963-66; bus. cons. Palm Beach, Fla., 1970-71; asst. to dir. Ga. Coop. Extension Svc., Athens, 1974-81; atty. Office of Pres. U. Ga., 1981—; mem. faculty, regent Ga. Athletics Inst., 1988-98; broadcaster Leonard's Losers.com, Athens, Ga., 2000—. Cons. numerous agrl. chem. industry groups nationwide, 1977—, Congl. Office Tech. Assessment, Washington, 1978-79, USDA, Washington, 1979-80; del. Kellogg Nat. Leadership Conf., Pullman, Wash., 1980. Editor and contbr. Ga. Jour. of Internat. and Comparative Law, 1972-74; contbr. articles on agr. and fin. planning to profl. jours.; author and editor: DAWGFOOD: The Bulldog Cookbook, 1981, Touchdown Tailgates, 1986. Del. So. Leader Forum, Rock Eagle Ctr., Ga., 1976-99; trainer Ga. 4-H Vol. Leader Assn., 1979—; coordinator U. Ga. Equestrian Team, Athens, 1985-87; mem. Clarke County Sheriff's Posse, 1985-2000. Capt. U.S. Army, 1966-70. Chi Psi Scholar, 1965; Recipient Outstanding Alumnus award Chi Psi, 1972, Service to World Community award Chi Psi, 1975. Mem. Nat. Assn. Coll. and Univ. Attys., DAV, Poets Soc., Am. Legion, Rotary, The President's Club (Athens), Gridiron Secret Soc., Chi Psi (advisor 1974). Baptist. Avocations: martial arts, creative writing, music. General corporate, Education and schools, Labor. Home: 365 Westview Dr Athens GA 30606-4635 Office: U Ga Peabody Hall Ste 3 Athens GA 30602

DAVIS, DEBORAH LYNN, lawyer; b. N.Y.C., Apr. 23, 1948; d. Melvin Jerome and Beatrice (Greenapple) D. BS, Case Western Res. U., 1970, JD, 1973. Bar: N.Y. 1974, U.S. Dist. Ct. (ea. and so. dists.) N.Y. 1974. Staff atty., dir. litigation Community Action for Legal Svcs., Inc., Bklyn., 1974-77, 78-81; atty. BLS Legal Svcs., N.Y.C., 1977-78; assoc. Gallet & Dreyer, 1981-86; ptnr. Wagner, Davis & Gold, P.C., 1986-99, of counsel, 1999—; ptnr. El-Baz Gallery N.Y. Ltd., 1999-2000; pres., owner Deborah Davis Fine Art Inc., Hudson, N.Y., 2000—. Contbg. author chpts. in book. Incorporator, officer, bd. dirs. N.Y. Svc. Program for Older People, Inc., 1978-91; mem. Family Ct. Panel Screening and Oversight com. 1st Jud. Dept., 1985-88, vice-chair screening applicants, 1985-87. Mem. N.Y. State Bar Assn., N.Y. County Lawyers Assn., N.Y. Women's Bar Assn. General civil litigation, Landlord-tenant, Real property. Office: Deborah Davis Fine Art Inc 345 Warren St Hudson NY 12534 E-mail: deborahdavisfineart@earthlink.net

DAVIS, DONALD G(LENN), lawyer; b. San Gabriel, Calif., Sept. 15, 1949; s. Maurice G. and Elinore C. (Leigh) D.; m. Alex Davis; children: Christian Glenn, Alexandra, Donald Glenn Jr., Regina Ann Rogers, Katherine Ann, Andrew Glenn, Julia McLeod Davis. BS in Acctg., Calif. State U., Pomona, 1966; JD, U. So. Calif., 1969. Assoc. Adams, Duque & Hazeltine, L.A., 1968, O'Melveny & Meyers, L.A., 1969-72; prof. of law Southwestern U. Law Sch., 1972-80; gen. counsel Republic Corp., 1973; ptnr. Danielson, St. Clair & Davis, 1974-77; mng. ptnr. Davis & Assocs., 1980—, DGD Enterprises P.V., L.A., 1980—, DGD Investment Banking, L.A., 1980—. Exec. editor Law Rev. jour., U. So. Calif., 1968-69. Vice-pres. student body, Calif. State U., Pomona, 1964-65; candidate 42nd Congl. Dist., Calif., 1988. Mem. ABA, L.A. Bar Assn. (chmn. securities cooperative seminar 1988, chmn. bus. lawyers sect. 1986-87), Order of Coif, Calif. Club, L.A. Yacht Club. Entertainment, Public international, Securities. Address: 1900 Ave Of Stars Ste 2600 Century City CA 90067-4507

DAVIS, EDWARD BERTRAND, retired federal judge, lawyer; b. W. Palm Beach, Fla., Feb. 10, 1933; s. Edward Bertrand and Mattie Mae (Walker) D.; m. Patricia Lee Klein, Apr. 5, 1958; children: Diana Lee Davis, Traci Russell, Edward Bertrand, III. JD, U. Fla., 1960; LLM in Taxation, N.Y. U., 1961. Bar: Fla. 1960. Pvt. practice, Miami, 1961-79; counsel High, Stack, Lazenby & Bender, 1978-79; U.S. dist. judge So. Dist. Fla., 1979-2000; assoc. Ackerman Senterfitt, 2000; chair state wide litig. practice. Served with AUS, 1953-55. Mem. Fla. Bar Assn., Dade County Bar Assn. Office: Akerman Senterfitt Suntrust Internat Ctr One SE 3d Ave 28th Fl Miami FL 33131 Fax: 305-374-5095. E-mail: edavis@akerman.com

DAVIS, EMILY S. lawyer; m. Matthew I. Levine; 2 children. BA cum laude, U. Mass., 1978; JD cum laude, Boston Coll., 1982. Bar: Vt. 1982, N.H. 1990, U.S. Dist. Ct. Vt., U.S. Dist. Ct. N.H. Assoc. Downs, Rachlin & Martin, 1982-84; dep. state's atty. Windsor County State's Atty.'s Office, 1984-86; ptnr. Black Black & Davis, White River Junction, Vt., 1990-99, Davis & Steadman, White River Junction, 1999—. Adj. faculty Vt. Law Sch., 1991-94. Co-chair Citizens Justice Conf., 1998-99; mem. Commn. on the Future Vt.'s Justice Sys., 1998-99; bd. dirs. ProChoice Ct., 1982-92, co-chair, 1989-91. Mem. ABA (family law sect.), Vt. Bar Assn. (pres.-elect 1997-98, pres. 1998-99, bd. mgrs. 1993-2000, family law com. 1993—, long range/scope and program com. chair 1997-98, family ct. rev. com., chair rules and statutes subcom. 1997), Vt. Bar Found. (bd. dirs. 1995-98), New Eng. Bar Assn. (bd. dirs. 1995-98, 2000—), Vt. Trial Lawyers Assn. (bd. dirs. 1999—), Vt. Vol. Lawyers Project (Pro Bono Svc. award 1996), Windsor County Bar assn. (pres. 1991-92, v.p. 1989-91, sec.-treas. 1988-89), N.H. Bar Assn. Family and matrimonial. Office: Davis & Steadman PO Box 796 White River Junction VT 05001-0796 E-mail: Davis@WhiteRiverLawyers.com

DAVIS, EVAN ANDERSON, lawyer; b. N.Y.C., Jan. 18, 1944; s. Richard T. and Charlotte (Upham) D.; m. Mary Carroll Rothwell; children: Sara Mei-Ping, Charlotte Zhong Xue. BA, Harvard U., 1966; JD, Columbia U., 1969. Bar: N.Y. 1970, U.S. Dist. Ct. (so. dist.) N.Y. 1973, U.S. Ct. Appeals (2d cir.) 1973, U.S. Dist. Ct. (ea. dist.) N.Y., 1978, U.S. Supreme Ct. 1979. Law clk. to judge U.S. Ct. Appeals (D.C. cir.), 1969-70; law clk. to Justice Potter Stewart U.S. Supreme Ct., 1970-71; gen. counsel N.Y.C. Budget Bur., 1971-72; chief consumer protection div. N.Y.C. Law Dept., 1972-74; task force leader, impeachment inquiry staff U.S. Ho. of Reps., 1974; assoc. Cleary, Gottlieb, Steen & Hamilton, N.Y.C., 1975-78, ptnr., 1979-85, 91—; counsel to gov. of N.Y., 1985-90. Vice chmn., bd. dirs. Fund for N.Y.C., 1982-85; trustee Columbia U., 1993—, mem. exec. com., 1994—, vice-chair bd. Fin. com., vice chair bd., 2001—. Editor-in-chief Columbia Law Rev., 1968-69. Treas. Sch. for Field Studies, 1991-95; dir. Franklin and Eleanor Roosevelt Inst., 1993—, mem. exec. com., 1994—; dir. Mus. of Hudson Highlands, 1991—, Storm King Sch., 1991-98; bd. visitors Helen Hayes Hosp., 1992-98, mem. coun. fgn. rels.; co-chairperson N.Y. Fair Elections Project, 1998—. Recipient Hopkins medal St. David's Soc., N.Y., 1988, Bruckner medal Fed. Bar Coun., 1990, Aquarium Environ. award Wildlife Conservation Soc., 1995, Milton Gould award for outstanding advocacy Office Appellate Defender, 1998, award Brennan Ctr., 1999, Law and Soc. award N.Y. Lawyers for the Pub. Interest, 2000, 1844 award New York Correctional Assn, 2001. Mem. ABA (ho. of dels. 1983-85, 91-93, 2000—, chmn. spl. com. youth edn. for citizenship 1986-88, chmn. standing com. pub. edn.), Assn. Bar City N.Y. (chmn. exec. com. 1982-83, v.p. 1983-84, pres. 2000—), Legal Aid Soc. (v.p. 1983-85, 97-2000, exec. com. 1992-2000), Am. Law Inst., N.Y. State Bar Assn. (com. on stds. of atty. conduct 1992—, commn. on middle income access to legal svc. 1995—). Home: 1172 Park Ave New York NY 10128 Office: Cleary Gottlieb Steen & Hamilton 1 Liberty Plz Fl 38 New York NY 10006-1470

DAVIS, FERD LEARY, JR. law educator, lawyer, consultant; b. Zebulon, N.C., Dec. 4, 1941; s. Ferd L. and Selma Ann (Harris) D.; m. Joy Baker Davis, Jan. 25, 1963; children: Ferd Leary III, James Benjamin, Elizabeth Joy. BA, Wake Forest U., 1964, JD, 1967; LLM, Columbia U., 1984. Bar: N.C. 1967. Editor Zebulon (N.C.) Record, 1958; tchr. Davidson County Schs., Wallburg, N.C., 1966; ptnr. Davis & Davis and related law firms, Zebulon and Raleigh, 1967-76; asst. pros. Wake County Dist. Ct., Raleigh, 1968-69; town atty. Town of Zebulon, 1969-76; founding dean Campbell U. Sch. Law, Buies Creek, N.C., 1975-86, prof. law, 1975—. Dir. Inst. to Study Practice of Law and Socioecon. Devel., 1985—; chmn. The Davis Cons. Group, Inc., Buies Creek, 1987—; pres. LAWLEAD, 1995—, Nat. Inst. to Enhance Leadership and Law Practice, 1998—; cons. U. Charleston, W.Va., 1979; vis. scholar Ctr. for Creative Leadership, 1993. Assoc. editor Wake Forest U. Law Rev. Trustee Wake County Pub. Librs., 1971-75, Olivia Raney Trust, 1969-71; mem. N.C. State Dem. Exec. Com., 1970-72, N.C. Gen. Statutes Commn., 1977-79, Commn. on the Future of N.C., 1980-83. 1st Lt. USAR, 1959-66. Babcock scholar Wake Forest U., 1963-67; Dayton Hudson fellow Columbia U., 1982-83. Fellow Coll. Law Practice Mgmt.; mem. ABA, N.C. Bar Assn., N.C. State Bar, Rotary, Phi Delta Phi, Delta Theta Phi, Omicron Delta Kappa. Democrat. Office: Nat Inst to Enhance Leadership and Law Practice Campbell U Sch Law PO Box 4280 Buies Creek NC 27506-4280

DAVIS, FREDERICK BENJAMIN, law educator; b. Bklyn., Aug. 21, 1926; s. Clifford Howard and Anne Frances (Forbes) D.; m. Mary Ellen Saecker, Apr. 21, 1956; children: Judith, Robert, James, Mary. AB, Yale U., 1948; JD, Cornell U., 1953; LLM with honors, Victoria U. of Wellington, New Zealand, 1955. Bar: N.Y. 1953, Mo. 1970, Ohio 1981. Assoc. Engel Judge & Miller, N.Y.C., 1953-54; instr. U. Pa. Law Sch., 1955-56; asst. prof. NYU, 1956-57, U.S.D., 1957-60, assoc. prof., 1960-62, Emory U., 1962-63, prof., 1963-66, U. Mo.-Columbia, 1966-70, Edward W. Hinton prof. law, 1970-81, Edward W. Hinton prof. emeritus, 1981—; dean, prof. law U. Dayton Sch. Law, 1981-86; dean, prof. Memphis State U., 1987-92, prof., 1992-98, prof., dean emeritus, 1998—. Cons. adminstrv. procedure Mo. Senate, 1974-77; vis. prof. Wake Forest U. Sch. Law, 1980, 86-87, U. Wis., 1960, George Washington U., 1965, Tulane U., 1966, U. Mo.-Kansas City, 1973, U. Ky., 1977. Contbr. numerous articles, comments, revs., notes to profl. jours. Served with USNR, 1944-46. Mem. ABA (coun. sect. adminstrv. law 1969-75), Am. Law Inst., Rotary Club (Memphis So. chpt.), Summit Club. Republican. Episcopalian. Home: 2019 Quail Creek Cv Memphis TN 38119-6410 Office: U Memphis Sch Law Memphis TN 38152-0001 E-mail: FDavis@memphis.edu

DAVIS, G. REUBEN, lawyer; b. Muskogee, Okla., Nov. 5, 1943; s. Glenn Reuben and Margaret Elizabeth (Linebaugh) D.; m. D. Candace Jensen, June 17, 1967; children: Clay Reuben, Hayden Jensen. BA, Westminster Coll., 1966; JD, U. Okla., 1973. Bar: Okla. 1973, U.S. Dist. Ct. (no. dist.) Okla. 1973, U.S. Ct. Appeals (10th cir.) 1973, U.S. Supreme Ct. 1988, U.S. Tax Ct. Assoc. Boone, Smith, Davis, Hurst & Dickman, Tulsa, 1973-78, ptnr., 1978—. Past pres. Tulsa Cystic Fibrosis Found., bd. dirs., 1976—; trustee Hillcrest Med. Ctr., Inc., Tulsa, 1979, Alexander Trust, Tulsa Found.; v.p., bd. dirs. Indian Nations coun. Boy Scouts Am., 1987—, bd. dirs. so. region; bd. dirs. Philmont Ranch Com. Mem. ABA, Am. Inns Ct., Am. Bd. Trial Advocates, Okla. Bar Assn., Tulsa County Bar Assn. (v.p. 1986-87, pres. 1988-89), Order of Coif. Republican. Methodist. Avocations: running, tennis, golf. Federal civil litigation, General civil litigation, State civil litigation. Office: Boone Smith Davis Hurst & Dickman 100 W 5th St Ste 500 Tulsa OK 74103-4215

DAVIS, GLENN STUART, lawyer; b. Adelaide, Australia; LLB, B. Econs., U. Adelaide. Bar: High Ct. of Australia, Fed. Ct. Australia, Supreme Ct. South Australia, Supreme Ct. N.S.W., Supreme Ct. Victoria. Ptnr. Piper Alderman Lawyers, Adelaide, 1985—. Mem. Australian Law Coun., South Australian Law Soc., Law Soc. N.S.W., Australian Mining and Petroleum Law Assn. General corporate, Oil, gas, and mineral, Securities. Office: Piper Alderman Lawyers 167 Flinders St Adelaide SA 5000 Australia Fax: 618 82053300. E-mail: gdavis@piper-alderman.com.au

DAVIS, HENRY BARNARD, JR. lawyer; b. East Grand Rapids, Mich., June 3, 1923; s. Henry Barnard and Ethel Margaret (Turnbull) D.; m. Margaret Lees Wilson, Aug. 27, 1946; children: Caroline Dellenbusch, Laura Davis, George B. BA, Yale U., 1945; JD, U. Mich., 1950; LLD, Olivet Coll., 1983. Bar: MIch. 1951, U.S. Dist. Ct. (we. dist.) Mich. 1956, U.S. Ct. Appeals (6th cir.) 1971, U.S. Supreme Ct. 1978. Assoc. Allaben, Wiarda, Hayes & Hewitt, 1951-52; ptnr. Hayes, Davis & Dellenbusch PLC, Grand Rapids, Mich., 1952—. Mem. Kent County Bd. Commrs., 1968-72; mem. Cmty. Mental Health Bd., 1970-94, past chmn.; trustee, sec. bd. Olivet Coll., 1965-91, trustee emeritus, 1991—; bd. dirs. Jr. Achievement Grand Rapids, 1960-65; chair Grand Rapids Historic Preservation Com., 1977-79; trustee East Congregational Ch., 1979-81. Served with USAAF, 1943-46, Philippines. Mem. ABA, Mich. Bar Assn., Grand Rapids Round Table (pres. 1969), Masons. Republican. Estate planning, Probate, Real property. Home: 30 Mayfair Dr NE Grand Rapids MI 49503-3831 Office: 535 Fountain St NE Grand Rapids MI 49503-3421 E-mail: DavisHBdr@aol.com

DAVIS, HERBERT OWEN, lawyer; b. Washington, June 11, 1935; s. Owen Stier and Claudie Lea (Pointer) D.; children: Herbert O. Jr., Ann P., Paul B. BA, U. N.C., 1957; JD, Duke U., 1960. Bar: N.C. 1960, U.S. Dist. Ct. (mid. dist.) N.C. 1960. Assoc. Smith Moore Smith Schell & Hunter, Greensboro, N.C., 1960-66, ptnr., 1966-86, Smith Helms Mulliss & Moore, Greensboro, 1986—. Bd. dirs. Custom Industries, Inc., Greensboro. Editor in chief Duke Law Jour., 1959-60. Mem. ABA, N.C. Bar Assn., Greensboro Country Club, Greensboro City Club (bd. dirs.), The Carolina Club, Phi Beta Kappa. Banking, General corporate, Mergers and acquisitions. Home: 2303 Danbury Rd Greensboro NC 27408-5123 Office: Smith Helms Mulliss & Moore 300 N Greene St Ste 1400 Greensboro NC 27401-2171 E-mail: bert.davis@smithhelms.com

DAVIS, J. ALAN, lawyer, writer; b. N.Y.C., Nov. 7, 1961; Student, Marlborough Coll., Eng., 1979; BA with distinction, So. Meth. U., 1983; JD with honors, U. Tex., 1987. Bar: Calif. 1988. Assoc. O'Melveny & Myers, L.A., 1987-89, Rosenfeld, Meyer & Susman, Beverly Hills, Calif., 1989-90; pvt. practice L.A., 1990-94; ptnr. Davis & Benjamin, 1995-98, Garvin, Davis & Benjamin, LLP, L.A., 1998-99; pvt. practice, 1999-2000; head legal and bus. affairs Warner Bros. Internat. TV Prodn., Burbank, Calif., 2000—. Mem. Calif. Bar Assn., Beverly Hills Bar Assn. (entertainment law sect. exec. com.), Brit. Acad. Film and TV Arts, L.A. (mng. dir. 1998, bd. dirs.). Avocations: skiing, scuba diving, tennis. General corporate, Entertainment. Office: Bldg 170 Rm 3046 4000 Warner Blvd Burbank CA 91522-0001

DAVIS, J. MAC, lawyer, state judge; b. Washington, Apr. 5, 1952; s. Glenn Robert and Kathryn Janet (McFarlane) D.; m. Kristi Schuepp, June 5, 1976; children: Glenn Walter, Carl William, Ann Elizabeth. BA with honors, U. Wis., 1973; JD cum laude, U. Mich., 1976. Bar: Wis. 1976. Ptnr. Love, Brown, Love, Phillips & Davis Law Firm, Waukesha, Wis., 1976-82, Phillips & Davis Law Firm, Waukesha, 1982-90; mem. Wis. Senate, Madison, 1983-90; cir. ct. judge Waukesha, Wis., 1990—. Mem. faculty Nat. Jud. Coll., Reno, 1994—95, Wis. Jud. Coll.; parliamentarian, mem. legis. com. Wis. Jud. Conf. Mem. Nat. Conf. Commrs. on Uniform State Laws, 1983—90; chmn. Waukesha County Sheriff's Grievance Com., 1979—90; active Mental Health Assn. Waukesha County, 1976—, past pres.; pres. Glenn Davis Charitable Found., Waukesha, 1976—; bd. dirs. United Way in Waukesha County, 1993—96; mem. exec. com. Waukesha County Rep. Com., 1976—90. Recipient George Washington award Freedom's Found. at Valley Forge, 1970. Mem.: Wis. Bar Assn., Waukesha County Bar Assn. (bd. dirs. 2001—), Wis. Vol. Trial Judges Assn. (vice chair 2001—). Office: Waukesha County Courthouse 515 W Moreland Blvd Waukesha WI 53188-2428

DAVIS, JAMES FRANCIS, lawyer; b. Chester, Pa., Mar. 14, 1947; s. Paul Lamoyne and Kathryn Cora (Stump) D.; m. Patricia Ann Hewson, Aug. 7, 1971; children— Michael Brandon, Victoria Ashley. B.A., Columbia Coll., 1969; J.D., Villanova U., 1972. Bar: Del. 1973, Pa. 1973, U.S. Dist. Ct. Del. 1973, U.S. Ct. Appeals (3d cir.) 1983. Jud. law clk. Superior Ct. New Castle County, Wilmington, Del., 1972-73; assoc. Biondi & Babiarz, Wilmington, 1973-79, Morris, Nichols, Arsht & Tunnell, Wilmington, 1979-83; counsel I, Hercules, Inc., Wilmington, 1983— . Mem. ABA, Del. Bar Assn. (sec. comml. law sect. 1983-84). Republican. Roman Catholic. Federal civil litigation, State civil litigation, Product liability. Home: 138 Marcella Rd Wilmington DE 19803-3451 Office: Hercules Inc Hercules Plz Wilmington DE 19801-6101

DAVIS, JAMES THOMAS, lawyer; b. Uniontown, Pa., Oct. 17, 1951; s. Norman J. and Thelma (Solomon) D.; m. Martha Russin, Sept. 4, 1976; children: Cara Catherine, Jeremy James, Adina Ann, Jacob Jamail, Kalie Marie. BA, California (Pa.) State Coll., 1973; JD, Duquesne U., 1976. Bar: Pa. 1976, U.S. Dist. Ct. (we. dist.) Pa. 1976, U.S. Supreme Ct. 1984; cert. criminal and civil trial advocate Nat. Bd. Trial Advocacy. Asst. dist. atty. Fayette County, Pa., 1977-83; ptnr. firm Davis & Davis, Uniontown, 1976—. Adj. faculty California (Pa.) U. Mem. ATLA, Pa. Trial Lawyers Assn. Democrat. Eastern Orthodox. Criminal, Personal injury, Probate. Office: Davis & Davis PO Box 1163 Uniontown PA 15401-1163 E-mail: jdavis@davisanddavislaw.com

DAVIS, JIMMY FRANK, assistant attorney general; b. Lubbock, Tex., June 14, 1945; s. Jack and Fern Lisemby D.; M. Joyce Zelma Hart, Nov. 6, 1976; children: Jayme Leigh, Julee Ellen. BS in Edn., Tex. Tech. U., 1968; JD, U. Tex., 1972. Bar: Tex. 1972, U.S. Supreme Ct. 1975, U.S. Dist. (no dist.) Tex. 1976, U.S. Ct. Appeals (5th cir.) 1976, U.S. Ct. Appeals

(11cir.) 1981. Asst. criminal dist. atty. Lubbock County, 1973-74, adminstrv. asst., 1976-77; county and dist. atty. Castro County, Tex., 1977-92; asst. atty. gen. State of Tex., 1993—; mem. forms com. Atty. Gen. Office, 1999—. Mem. State Bar of Tex. (com. admissions dist. 16 1974-78, dist. 13 1983-92, govt. lawyers sect., coun. mem. 1991-92), Tex. Dist. and County Attys. Assn., Lubbock County Jr. Bar Assn. (pres. 1977), Tex. Tech. Ex Students Assn. (dist. rep. 1981-84, bd. dirs. 1985-90), Coll. of State Bar of Tex. (continuing legal edn. 1984-93), Kiwanis of Lubbock (pres. 1977), Kiwanis of Dimmitt (pres. 1981), Delta Theta Phi. Office: PO Box 2747 916 Main St Suite 900 Lubbock TX 79408

DAVIS, KENNETH BOONE, JR. dean, law educator; b. Louisville, Sept. 1, 1947; s. Kenneth Boone and Doris Edna (Gordon) D. m. Arrietta Evoline Hastings, June 2, 1984; children: Peter Hastings, Mary Elizabeth, Kenneth Boone III. AB, U. Mich., 1969; JD, Case Western Res. U., 1974. Bar: D.C. 1975, Ohio 1974. Law clk. to chief judge U.S. Ct. Appeals (9th cir.), San Francisco, 1974-75; assoc. Covington & Burling, Washington, 1975-78; prof. law U. Wis., Madison, 1978—, dean Law Sch., 1997—. Contbr. numerous articles on corp. and securities law to profl jours. Mem. ABA, Am. Fin. Assn., Am. Law Inst., Wis. Bar Assn. (reporter, corp. and bus. law com.). Office: U Wis Law Sch 975 Bascom Mall Madison WI 53706-1399

DAVIS, LANCE BARROW, lawyer, municipal judge; b. St. Joseph, Mo., May 3, 1954; s. William True, Jr. and Virginia (Motter) D.; divorced; 1 child, William Truett. Diploma, Cornell U., 1976; JD, Calif. Western U., San Diego, 1979. Bar: Mo. 1984, D.C. 1984, U.S. Supreme Ct. 1998. Staff mem. Sen. Thomas F. Eagleton, Washington, 1972, Ho. Judiciary Com./Impeachment Inquiry Staff, Washington, 1974, Sen. Stuart Symington, Washington, 1976; law clk. to presiding justice James H. Meredith U.S. Dist. Ct., St. Louis, 1979-80; ptnr. Bartlett Joint Ventures I & II, Wichita, Kans., 1980-85; assoc. Lamb & Ochs, Washington, 1986-87; asst. prosecuting atty. Buchanan County, St. Joseph, 1987-89; ptnr. Wilcox, Houts & Davis, 1989-94; pvt. practice law, 1994—; mcpl. judge 5th Jud. Dist., Easton, Mo., 1990—; city atty. Amazonia. Pres. Main St., St. Joseph, Inc., 1990-93, Buchanan County Dem. Club, 1988—; fin. coun. Mo. State Dem. Party, 1985; counsel Fed. Emergency Mgmt. Agy., Nat. Def. Exec. Res., Washington, 1989—. Recipient Progress award St. Joseph Devel. Corp., 1991. Mem. ABA, Mo. Bar Assn., D.C. Bar Assn., Masons. Episcopalian. Avocations: percussion, hist. preservation. Office: 510 N 4th St Saint Joseph MO 64501-1740

DAVIS, LOUIS POISSON, JR. lawyer, consultant; b. Washington, July 17, 1919; s. Louis Poisson and Edna (Shethar) D.; m. Emily Elizabeth Carl, Feb. 7, 1943; 1 child, Cynthia. BSc, U.S. Naval Acad., 1941; postgrad., Princeton U., 1947-48; JD, Rutgers U., 1953. Bar: N.Y. 1954, Ill. 1963, U.S. Dist. Ct. (so. dist.) N.Y. 1956, U.S. Dist. Ct. (no. dist.) Ill. 1965, U.S. Supreme Ct. 1964. Mgr. engring. Esso Std. Oil, Linden, N.J., 1946-57; sr. economist, head econs. and market rsch. dept. Internat. Petroleum Co., Lima, Peru, 1957-60; asst. overseas ops. AMF Internat. Abbott Labs., North Chicago, Ill., 1962-65; gen. mgr. Far East ops. Ralston Purina Co.; pres. Ralston Purina Eastern, Hong Kong, 1966-71; dir. internat. devel. Archer Daniels Midland Internat., Decatur, Ill., 1972-74. Lectr., rschr. internat. law and mgmt., N.Y.C., 1974-76; corp. rep. Europe, Mid East, Africa, Alexander & Baldwin Agribus, Inc., Abidjan, Ivory Coast, 1976, Madrid, Spain, 1977; internat. atty., cons., Sarasota, Fla., 1978-99; cons. Sarasota County Office of Sci. Advisor, 1985-86, Office of Gen. Counsel, 1989-91; vol. income tax assistance program IRS, 1983-00; cons., seminar leader Chipsoft, Inc., 1989-90; vol. atty. Gulfcoast Legal Svcs., 1987-91; instr. Sarasota Tech. Inst., 1990-98; cert. cons. Capsoft Devel. Corp. Legal Automation Software, 1991; gen. counsel Manasota Industry Coun., Inc., 1984-89; bd. dirs. Siesta Key Assn., v.p., 1993-94, 98-2001. Lt. comdr. USN, 1937-46. Mem. ABA, Hong Kong Country Club, Oaks Club (Sarasota). Republican. Episcopalian. Home and Office: 620 Mangrove Point Rd Sarasota FL 34242-1230 E-mail: loudavis@prodigy.net

DAVIS, M. G. lawyer; b. Concho County, Tex/, Nov. 11, 1930; s. Zack and Olive (Clifton) D.; m. Jeanne Focke, Feb. 7, 1959; children: Linda Jeanne, Lisbeth Dianne. BBA, Tex. Tech U., 1952; JD, U. Tex., 1958. Bar: Tex. 1957, U.S. Supreme Ct. 1964. Atty. Gen. Land Office, Austin, Tex., 1959-60; assoc. Smith, Porter & Caston, Longview, 1960-61; v.p. Am. Title Co., Dallas, 1961-67; owner, operator Security Land Title Co., Amarillo, Tex., 1967-69; pres. Dallas Title Co., Houston, 1969-70, Guardian Title, Houston, 1970-72, Collin County Title Co., Plano, Tex., 1972-87; pvt. practice, 1972-82; ptnr. Davis & Davis, Dallas, 1982-93, Davis & Sallinger, L.L.P., Dallas, 1993-98, Davis & Davis, Richardson, Tex., 1999—. Guest lectr. U. Houston, Richland Jr. Coll. Chmn. Slective Svc. bd. 46, 1982-92; mem. legis. task force, employer support guard and res. affairs Tex. N.G. Assn. 1st lt. USAF, 1952-54, Koera. Recipient Involved Citizen award Dallas Morning News, 1980. Fellow Coll. State Bar Tex.; mem. State Bar Tex., Dallas Bar Assn., Sons Republic Tex., Tex. Land Title Assn. (v.p. 1970-71), Tex. Tech. Ex-Students Assn. (dir. 1961-63), Collins County Title Assn. (pres. 1977), Dallas Mortgage Bankers Assn., Collin County U. Tex. Ex-Students Assn. (pres. 1980), U. Tex. Ex-Students (exec. coun. 1983-86), Alpha Tau Omega. Democrat. Episcopalian. Real property. Home: 8805 Clear Sky Dr Plano TX 75025-4128 Office: Davis & Davis 1701 N Greenville Ave Ste 900 Richardson TX 75081-1878 Fax: 972-690-8078

DAVIS, MARGUERITE HERR, judge; b. Washington, Nov. 12, 1947; d. Norman Phillip and Margaretha Joanna Herr; m. James Riley Davis, June 20, 1970; children: Amy Marguerite, Christine Riley. AA with honors, St. Petersburg J. Coll., Clearwater, Fla., 1966; BA with honors, U. of South Fla., 1968; JD with honors, Fla. State U., 1971. Bar: Fla. 1971, U.S. Dist. Ct. (no. dist.) Fla. 1971, U.S. Dist. Ct. (mid. dist.) Md. 1985, U.S. Ct. Appeals (11th cir.) 1985, U.S. Supreme Ct. 1986. Atty. workers compensation div. U.S. Dept. Labor, Tallahassee, 1971; sr. legal aide Fla. Supreme Ct., 1971-85, exec. asst. to Hon. Chief Justice Alderman, 1982-84; ptnr. Swann & Haddock, 1985-87, Katz, Kutler, Haigler, Alderman, Davis & Marks, Tallahassee, 1987-93; judge Dist. Ct. of Appeal (1st dist.) Fla., 1993—. Mem. editl. bd. Trial Advocate Quar., 1991-93; contbr. chpts. to books. Mem. ABA, Fla. Bar Assn. (Tallahassee chpt., appellate ct. rules com. 1995—, appellate ct. rules com. chair, 1995-97, grievance com., disciplinary rev. com., chmn. supreme ct. local rules adv. com., jud. cir. grievance com., rules of jud. adminstrn. 1995-99, chair 1997-98, chair jud. evaluation com. 1999-2000, chair 2001-02, exec. coun. appellate advocacy sect.), Fla. State Fed. Jud. Coun. (exec. dir. 1985—), Tallahassee Women Lawyers, Fla. Def. Lawyers Assn. (amicus curiae com.), Fla. Supreme Ct. Hist. Soc., Am. Arbitration Assn. (ad hoc com. stds. for appellate practice cert.), Altrusa Club of Tallahassee (treas. 1971-76), Fla. State U. Alumni Assn. (bd. dirs. 1975-76), Jud. Mgmt. Coun. (appellate ct. workload and jurisdiction com. 1996—, chair appellate rules liaison com., appellate practice and advocacy sect. 1996-98), Univ. So. Fla. (bd. dirs. Alumni Assn. 1999), Phi Theta Kappa. Methodist. Avocations: quilting, sewing, knitting, running, reading.

DAVIS, MATTIE BELLE EDWARDS, retired county judge; b. Ellabell, Ga., Feb. 28, 1910; d. Frank Pierce and Eddie (Morgan) Edwards; m. Troy Carson Davis, June 6, 1937 (dec. Aug. 1948); stepchildren: Jane (Mrs. Robert Gordon Potter), Betsy (Mrs. James W. Clark, Jr.). Student law in law office. Bar: Fla. 1936, U.S. Supreme Ct. 1950. Legal sec., 1927-36; practice with husband in Miami, 1936-48; pvt. practice, 1948-59; judge Met. Ct. County of Dade, Fla., 1959-72, judge County Ct., 1973-80, sr. judge County Ct., 1981-96. Mem. exec. com. Women's Conf. Nat. Safety Coun., 1960-80, chmn., 1968-70; bd. dirs. Nat. Safety Coun., 1972-80, v.p. women, 1973-80; mem. Fla. Gov.'s Hwy. Safety Com., 1970-81, Nat. Hwy. Safety Adv. Com., 1967-71; mem. registrants adv. bd. SSS, World War II. Pres. Dade County TB Assn., 1960-62; exec. com. Fla. TB and Respiratory Disease Assn., 1960-66; pres. Haven Sch. Mentally Retarded, 1958-60, sec., 1960-69; trustee Andrew Coll., Cuthbert, Ga., 1960-81; supt. Sunday sch. Meth. Ch., 1948-54, chmn. ofcl. bd., 1957-60, trustee, 1952-67, adminstrv. bd., 1968-98, 2000. Recipient Disting. Svc. to Safety award Nat. Safety Coun., 1988; first woman 50 yr. awardee Fellows of Am. Bar Found., 1987; inducted to Fla. Women's Hall of Fame Gov. Lawton Chiles, 1998. Mem. Nat. Assn. Women Lawyers (treas. 1961-62, corr. sec. 1962-63, v.p. 1963-64, pres. 1965-66, Appreciation award 1989), Fla. Assn. Women Lawyers (pres. 1957-58), ABA (ho. of dels. 1967-75, 77-81, resolutions com. 1973-75, com. on constn. and bylaws 1980-86), Dade County Bar Assn., Fla. Bar, Internat. Fedn. Women Lawyers, Nat. Assn. Women Judges (founder, life mem.), Miami Bus. and Profl. Women's Club (pres. 1952-54), Nat. Fedn. Bus. and Profl. Women's Clubs (dir. dist. Fla. 1956-57), Zonta Internat. Club, Kappa Beta Pi. Democrat. Methodist. Home: 402 Como Ave Coral Gables FL 33146-3508

DAVIS, MICHAEL J. judge; b. 1947; BA, Macalester Coll., 1969; JD, U. Minn., 1972; LLD (hon.) , Macalester Coll., 2001. Law clk. Legal Rights Ctr., 1971-73; with Office Gen. Counsel Dept. Health, Edn. and Welfare, Social Security Adminstrn., Balt., 1973; criminal def. atty. Neighborhood Justice Ctr., 1974, Legal Rights Ctr., 1975—78; pub. defender Hennepin County, 1978-83; judge Hennepin County Mcpl. Ct., 1983-84, Hennepin County Dist. Ct. (4th jud. dist.), 1984-94; atty., commr. Mpls. Civil Rights Commn., 1977-82; judge U.S. Dist. Ct. Minn., St. Paul, 1994—. Constnl. law instr. Antioch Mpls. C.C., 1974; criminal def. trial practice instr. Nat. Lawyer's Guild, 1977; trial practice instr. William Mitchell Coll. Law, 1977-81, Bemidji Trial Advocacy Course, 1992, 93; adj. prof. U. Minn. Law Sch., 1982—, Hubert H. Humphrey Sch. Pub. Affairs, 1990; instr. Minn. Inst. Legal Edn., Civil Trial Practice Inst., 1991-92; lectr. FBI Acad., 1991, 92. Mem. Minn. Superior Ct. Racial Bias Task Force, 1990—93, U.S. Dist. Ct.; chmn. Pretrial Release & Bail Evaluation Com., 1997—. Recipient Outstanding Alumni award Macalester Coll., 1989, Good Neighbor award WCCO Radio, 1989, Disting Svc. award William Mitchell Coll. of Law, 2000. Mem. ABA, Nat. Bar Assn., Minn. Minority Lawyers Assn., Am. Inns. of Ct., Fed. Bar Assn., Fed. Judges Assn., Hennepin County Bar Assn., Minn. State Bar Assn., Minn. Lawyers Internat. Human Rights Com. (past mem. bd. dirs.), Internat. Acad. Trial Judges, Nat. Assn. for Pub. Interest Law (bd. dirs.), 8th Cir. Jury Instruction Com., U.S. Assn. Constitutional Law. Office: US Dist Ct Minn 300 S 4th St Ste 14E Minneapolis MN 55415-2251 E-mail: mjdavis@mnd.uscourts.gov

DAVIS, MICHAEL STEVEN, lawyer; b. Brookline, Mass., Aug. 1, 1947; s. Ralph and Beatrice (Levy) D.; m. Madelyn O. Davis, Aug. 16, 1970; children: Gregory, Adam, Bethany. AB, U. Rochester, 1969; JD cum laude, Boston U., 1972. Bar: N.Y. 1973, U.S. Dist. Ct. (so. and ea. dists.) N.Y. 1974, U.S. Ct. Appeals (2d cir.) 1974, U.S. Supreme Ct. 1979, U.S. Ct. Claims, 1980. Assoc. Chadbourne & Parke, N.Y.C., 1972-82; sr. counsel corp. litigation Am. Internat. Group, 1982-88; ptnr. Zalkin, Rodin & Goodman, LLP, 1988-99, Zeichner, Ellman & Krause, LLP, N.Y.C., 1999—. Asst. adj. prof. C.W. Post Ctr., L.I. U., Glen Cove, N.Y., 1975-79. Editor Boston U. Law Rev., 1970-72. Mem. Citizens Ctr. for Children of N.Y., Inc., 1978-87; pres. Pelham (N.Y.) Jewish Ctr., 1986-88. Mem. ABA, Assn. Bar City of N.Y., Am. Arbitration Assn., Huguenot Bridge Club. Democrat. Bankruptcy, General civil litigation, Insurance. Office: Zeichner Ellman & Krause LLP 575 Lexington Ave New York NY 10022-6102 E-mail: mdavis@zeklaw.com

DAVIS, MULLER, lawyer; b. Chgo., Apr. 23, 1935; s. Benjamin B. and Janice (Muller) D.; m. Jane Lynn Strauss, Dec. 28, 1963 (div. July 1998); children: Melissa Davis Muller, Muller Jr., Joseph Jeffrey; m. Lynn Straus, Jan. 23, 1999. Grad. with honors, Phillips Exeter (N.H.) Acad., 1953; BA magna cum laude, Yale U., 1957; JD, Harvard U., 1960. Bar: Ill. 1960, U.S. Dist. Ct. (no. dist.) Ill. 1961. Practice law, Chgo., 1960—; assoc. Jenner & Block, 1960-67; ptnr. Davis, Friedman, Zavett, Kane, MacRae, Marcus & Rubens, 1967—. Lectr. continuing legal edn., matrimonial law and litigation; legal adviser Michael Reese Med. Research Inst. Council, 1967-82. Author: (with Sherman C. Feinstein) The Parental Couple in a Successful Divorce, Illinois Practice of Family Law, 1995, 97, 98-99, (with Jody Meyer Yazici) 4th edit., 2000-01; mem. editl. bd. Equitable Distbn. Jour., 1984—; contbr. articles to law jours. Bd. dirs. Infant Welfare Soc., 1975-96, hon. bd. dirs., 1996—, pres., 1978-82; co-chmn. gen. gifts 40th and 45th reunions Phillips Exeter Acad., chair class capital giving, 1994-98. Capt. U.S. Army, Ill. N.G., 1960-67. Fellow Am. Acad. Matrimonial Lawyers (bd. mgrs. Ill. chpt. 1996-99), Am. Bar Found.; mem. ABA, FBA, Ill. Bar Assn., Chgo. Bar Assn. (matrimonial com. 1968-83, sec. civil practice com. 1979-80, vice chmn. 1980-81, chmn. 1981-82), Am. Soc. Writers on Legal Subjects, Chgo. Estate Planning Coun., Legal Aid Soc. (vice chmn. matrimonial bar 1991-95, vice chmn. 1995-97, chmn. 1997-99), Lawyers Club Chgo., Tavern Club, Lake Shore Country Club, Chgo. Club. Republican. Jewish. Family and matrimonial. Home: 161 E Chicago Ave Apt 34 E Chicago IL 60611-2601 Office: Davis Friedman Zavett Kane MacRae Marcus & Rubens 140 S Dearborn St Ste 1600 Chicago IL 60603-5288 E-mail: mdavis@davisfriedman.com, lsmd@core.com

DAVIS, PRESTON LINDNER, lawyer; b. Danville, Pa., Jan. 22, 1936; s. Preston B. and M. Isabelle (Lindner) D.; m. Margaret E. Whitenight, Aug. 30, 1958; children: Kerry P. Davis, Kathy J. Hrenko, Kirk P. Davis, Kelly J. Farquhar. AB, Dartmouth Coll., 1957, LLB, JD, U. Pa., Phila., 1960. Bar: Pa. 1961, U.S. Ct. Appeals (3d cir.) 1961, U.S. Dist. Ct. (mid. dist.) Pa. 1962. Law clk. to Hon. Herbert F. Goodrich U.S. Ct. Appeals (3d cir.), Phila., 1960-61; ptnr. Davis Davis & Kaar, Milton, Pa., 1961—. Solicitor, Northumberland County, 1964-69, Milton Mcpl. Authority, 1980—; chmn. Milton Indsl. Authority, 1985—. Mem. exec. bd. Northumberland Rep. Party, Sunbury, Pa., 1964—. Mem. Northumberland County Bar Assn. (pres. 1984), Milton Rotary, Milton Elks Club, Milton Masons (past master), Moose, Milton Area C. of C. (past pres.). Lutheran. Avocations: sports, golf. General corporate, Estate planning, Probate. Office: Davis Davis & Kaar PO Box 319 Milton PA 17847-0319

DAVIS, RICHARD RALPH, lawyer; b. Houston, July 28, 1936; s. William Ralph and Virginia (Allison) D.; m. Christina R. Zelkoff, June 1, 1974; 1 child, Virginia Lee Allison. BA, Yale U., 1962, LLB, 1965; MBA, Columbia U., 1965. Bar: N.Y. 1966. Law clk. FAA, Washington, 1964; assoc. Chadbourne & Parke, N.Y.C., 1965-73, ptnr., 1974-83; sr. v.p., gen. counsel Inspiration Resources Corp., 1983-91; sr. v.p., sec., gen. counsel Bessemer Securities Corp./Bessemer Trust Co., NA, 1991—. With U.S. Army, 1956-59. Mem. ABA. Antitrust, Banking, General corporate. Home: 1185 Park Ave Apt 6-g New York NY 10128-1309 E-mail: davis@bessemer.com

DAVIS, RICHARD WATERS, lawyer; b. Rocky Mount, Va., July 9, 1931; s. Beverly Andrew and Julia (Waters) D.; m. Mary Alice Woods; children: Debra, Julie, Richard Jr., Bob, Bev. B, Hampden-Sydney Coll., 1951; LLB, U. Richmond, 1959. Bar: Va. 1959. Pvt. practice, Radford, Va., 1959—. Dist. judge City of Radford, 1962-80; mem. Pub. Defenders Commn. Va., 1993—; mem. Va. State Bar Coun., 1989-95; assoc. prof. bus. law Radford U.; lectr. Va. Trial Lawyers Assn. Fellow Am. Coll. Trial Lawyers, Am. Bar Found., Va. Law Found.; mem. ABA. Va. Bar Assn. State civil litigation, Insurance, Personal injury. Home: 101 5th St Radford VA 24141-2401 Office: PO Box 3448 Radford VA 24143-3448

DAVIS, ROBERT EDWARD, state supreme court justice; b. Topeka, Aug. 28, 1939; s. Thomas Homer and Emma Claire (Hund) D.; m. Jana Jones; children: Edward, Rachel, Patrick, Carolyn, Brian. BA in Polit. Sci., Creighton U., 1961; JD, Georgetown U., 1964. Bar: Kans. 1964, U.S. Dist. Ct. Kans. 1964, U.S. Tax Ct. 1974, U.S. Ct. Mil. Appeals 1965, U.S. Ct. Mil. Review, 1970, U.S. Ct. Appeals (10th cir.) 1974, U.S. Supreme Ct. 1982. Pvt. practice, Leavenworth, Kans., 1967-84; magistrate judge Leavenworth County, 1969-76, county atty., 1980-84, judge dist. ct., 1984-86; judge Kans. Ct. Appeals Jud. Br. Govt., Topeka, 1986-93; justice Kans. Supreme Ct., 1993—. Lectr. U. Kans. Law Sch., Lawrence, 1986-95. Capt. JAGC, U.S. Army, 1964-67, Korea. Mem. Am. Judges Assn., Kans. Bar Assn., Leavenworth County Bar Assn. (pres. 1977), Judge Hugh Means Am. Inn of Ct. Charter Orgn. Lawrence. Roman Catholic. Office: 301 W 10th Ave Topeka KS 66612

DAVIS, ROBERT LARRY, lawyer; b. Lubbock, Tex., June 6, 1942; s. R. H. and Bernice (Pray) D.; m. Peggy Saunders, Jan. 25, 1965; children: Lee Michael, Melissa Lynn. BA, Rice U., 1964; LLB (with honors), U. Tex., 1967. Bar: Tex. 1967, U.S. Dist. Ct. (We. dist.) Tex. 1969, U.S. Dist. Ct. (So. dist.) Tex. 1989. Assoc. Royston Rayzor & Cook, Houston, 1967-68; from assoc. to ptnr. Brown McCarroll & Oaks Hartline, Austin, Tex., 1968—. Bus. sect. coord., mem. mgmt. com.; parliamentarian, mem. exec. com. Downtown Revitalization Task Force, Austin, 1978-80. Mem., past pres. Boys Club of Austin and Travis County, 1981—; trustee Eanes Ind. Sch. Dist., Austin, 1986-93, pres., 1990-93. Mem. Assn. Atty. Mediators (pres. Cen. Tex. chpt. 1995). Methodist. Avocations: sports, music, reading. Alternative dispute resolution, Construction, Real property. Home: 3607-3 Pinnacle Rd Austin TX 78746 Office: Brown McCarroll 1400 One Congress Plz III Congress Austin TX 78701 E-mail: rdavis@mailbmc.com

DAVIS, ROBERT LAWRENCE, lawyer; b. Cin., Apr. 5, 1928; s. Bryan and Henrietta Elizabeth (Weber) D.; m. Mary Lee Schulte, June 14, 1952; children: Gregory, Randy, Jenny, Bradley. BA, U. Cin., 1952; JD with honors, Salmon P. Chase Coll. Law, 1958. Bar: Ohio, 1958, U.S. Supreme Ct. 1966. Assoc. Trabert & Gay, Cin., 1958-62; ptnr. Trabert, Gay & Davis, 1962-68, Gay, Davis & Kelly, Cin., 1969-71; pvt. practice, 1972—. Lectr. Mt. St. Joseph Coll, 1972-82; arbitrator Am. Arbitration Assn.; assoc. adj. prof. Salmon P. Chase Coll. Sch. Law, 1969-80; lectr. Good Samaritan Hosp. Sch. Nursing, 1960-71. Pres. bd. trustee Cmty. Ltd. Care Dialysis Ctr., 1978-86; mem. Hamilton County Ohio Hosp. Commn., 1986, Kidney Found. Greater Cin., 1989, 92. Capt. U.S. Army, 1946-48, 52-53. Decorated Bronze State medal. Fellow Am. Coll. Trial Lawyers (state chmn. 1994-95); mem. Ohio Bar Assn., Cin Bar Assn., Am. Bd. Trial Advs. (adv., pres. Cin. chpt. 1996), Lawyers Club (pres. 1962-63), Order of Curia, KC, Phi Delta Theta, Phi Alpha Delta, Sigma Sigma, Omicron Delta Kappa. State civil litigation, Personal injury, Probate. Home: 9969 Voyager Way Cincinnati OH 45252-1962 Office: 3600 Carew Tower Cincinnati OH 45202 E-mail: rdavis@choice.net

DAVIS, ROBIN JEAN, state supreme court justice; b. Boone County, W.Va., Apr. 6, 1956; m. Scott Segal; 1 child, Oliver. BS, W.Va. Wesleyan Coll., 1978; MA in Indsl. Rels., JD, W.Va. U., 1982. With Segal & Davis L.C., 1982-96; justice W.Va. Supreme Ct. of Appeals, 1996—, chief justice, 1998—. Mem. W.Va. U. Law Inst., W.Va. Bd. of Law Examiners, 1991—. Contbr. articles to W.Va. Law Rev. Mem. ABA, Assn. of Trial Lawyers of Am., Kanawha County Bar Assn., Am. Acad. Matrimonial Lawyers. Office: Supreme Ct of Appeals Bldg 1 Rm E 301 State Capitol Charleston WV 25305*

DAVIS, ROY WALTON, JR. lawyer; b. Marion, N.C., Jan. 15, 1930; s. Roy Walton and Mildred Gertrude (Wilson) D.; m. Madeline Burch Combs, Sept. 10, 1955; children: R. Walton III, Madeline Trent, Rebekah Wilson, Sally Fielding. BS, Davidson Coll., 1952; JD with honors, U. N.C., 1955. Bar: N.C. 1955, U.S. Dist. Ct. (we. dist.) N.C. 1960, U.S. Ct. Appeals (4th cir.) 1963. Ptnr. Davis & Davis, Marion, 1959-60; from assoc. to ptnr. and pres. Van Winkle, Buck, Wall, Starnes & Davis, Asheville, N.C., 1960—. Lectr. in field. Contbr. profl. publs. Chancellor Episc. Diocese of Western N.C., Black Mountain, 1980—. With U.S. Army, 1956-59. Fellow Am. Bar Found., Am. Coll. Trial Lawyers (state chair 1994-96), Internat. Soc. Barristers; mem. ABA (tort and ins. practice and litig. sects. Ho. of Dels. 1989-92), N.C. Bar Assn. (chmn. young lawyers divsn. 1965-66, chair adminstrn. of justice task force 1999—), N.C. State Bar (pres. 1985-86, trustee IOLTA 1987-93), N.C. Assn. Def. Attys., Order of Coif. Democrat. Federal civil litigation, State civil litigation, Insurance. Home: 359 Country Club Rd Asheville NC 28804-2639 Office: Van Winkle Buck Wall Starnes & Davis 11 N Market St Ste 300 Asheville NC 28801-2932

DAVIS, SCOTT JONATHAN, lawyer; b. Chgo., Jan. 8, 1952; s. Oscar and Doris (Koller) D.; m. Anne Megan, Jan. 4, 1981; children: William, James, Peter. BA, Yale U., 1972; JD, Harvard U., 1976. Bar: Ill. 1976, U.S. Dist. Ct. (no. dist.) Ill. 1976, U.S. Ct. Appeals (7th cir.) 1977, U.S. Ct. Appeals (8th cir.) 1986. Law clk. to judge U.S. Ct. Appeals (7th cir.), Chgo., 1976-77; assoc. Mayer, Brown & Platt, 1977-82, ptnr., 1983—. Bd. editors Harvard Law Rev., 1974-76; contbr. articles to profl. jours. V.p. Chgo. Police Bd. General civil litigation, General corporate, Mergers and acquisitions. Home: 838 W Belden Ave Chicago IL 60614-3236 Office: Mayer Brown & Platt 190 S La Salle St Ste 3100 Chicago IL 60603-3441

DAVIS, SUSAN RAE, lawyer; b. Salem, Oreg., July 15, 1948; d. William Ray and Pearl E. (Lundin) Catlin; m. Donald K. Davis, June 13, 1970. BA, U. Wash., 1969, JD, 1977. Bar: Wash. 1977, U.S. Dist. Ct. (we. dist.) Wash. 1977, U.S. Ct. Appeals (9th cir.) 1977, U.S. Dist. Ct. (ea. dist.) Wash. 1989. Writer, editor Associated Press, Seattle, 1969-70; news dir. Sta. KUUU, 1970-71; reporter, photographer Sta. KXLY-TV, Spokane, Wash., 1971-73, Sta. KHQ-TV, Spokane, 1973-74; ptnr. Burns, Schneiderman, Davis & Finkle P.S., Seattle, 1977-86, The Davis Firm, Seattle, 1987—. Instr. journalism Eastern Wash. State Coll., Spokane, 1973-74. Mem. tribunal Wash. State Human Rights Commn., Seattle, 1974-79; arbitrator King County Mandatory Arbitration Panel, Seattle, 1985—; bd. visitors U. Puget Sound, 1986-87. Mem. ATLA, Settlement Now (mediator 1988-97), Am. Bd. Trial Advs., Wash. State Bar Assn., Seattle-King County Bar Assn., Wash. State Trial Lawyers Assn. (leadership award 1984, bd. dirs. 1980-82, treas. 1982-83, v.p. west 1983-84, v.p. pub. affairs 1984-85, pres. elect 1985-86, pres. 1986-87), Wash. Women Lawyers. Democrat. Avocation: photography. Admiralty, Personal injury. Office: The Davis Firm 5301 Ballard Ave NW Seattle WA 98107-4061 E-mail: thedavisfirm@seanet.com

DAVIS, THOMAS HILL, JR. lawyer; b. Raleigh, N.C., June 11, 1951; s. Thomas Hill and Margie Wayne (Perry) D.; m. Julia Dee Wilson, May 31, 1980; children: Thomas Hill III, Alexander Erwin, Julia Hadley, Hunter McDowell. BA, N.C. State U., 1973; JD, Wake Forest U., 1976. Bar: N.C. 1976, U.S. Dist. Ct. (ea. and middle dist.) N.C. 1976, U.S. Ct. Appeals (11th cir.) 1982, U.S. Ct. Appeals (4th cir.) 1986, U.S. Supreme Ct. 1979. Reporter Winston-Salem (N.C.) Jour., 1974-76; asst. atty. N.C. Dept. Justice, Raleigh, 1976-88; gen. ptnr. Poyner & Spruill, 1988—. Arbitrator Am. Arbitration Assn., Charlotte, N.C., 1990—; lectr. Campbell U. Sch. Law, Buies Creek, N.C., 1992. Supplement editor: Construction Litigation, 1992; contbg. author: Public & Private Contracting in North Carolina, 1985, North Carolina Adminstrative Law, 1996; contbr. articles to profl. jours. Mem. N.C. R.R. Legis. Study Commn., Raleigh, 1985—87; legal counsel N.C. Aeronautics Coun., 1981; bd. dirs. Badger-Iredell Found. Mem. N.C. Bar Assn. (Appreciation award 1989), Wake County Bar Assn.

(VLP award 1995), North Hills Club, Lions. Democrat. Presbyterian. Avocations: fly fishing, wing shooting, photography, tennis. Condemnation, Construction, Labor. Home: 608 Blenheim Pl Raleigh NC 27612-4943 Office: Poyner & Spruill 3600 Glenwood Ave Raleigh NC 27612-4945 E-mail: thdavis@poynerspruill.com

DAVIS, VIRGINIA ESTELLE, lawyer; b. Orange, N.J., Mar. 23, 1947; d. A. Arthur and Mildred (Harr) D.; m. James C. Pitney Jr. Sept. 20, 1975; Children: Thaddeus, Alexandra, Kristian. BA, Skidmore Coll., 1969; MA, U. Denver, 1971; JD cum laude, Seton Hall U., 1974. Bar: N.J. 1974, U.S. Dist. Ct. N.J. 1974, Maine 1977, U.S. Dist. Ct. Maine 1978, U.S. Ct. Appeals (1st cir.), U.S. Ct. Appeals D.C. 1985. Law sec. Frederick Hall Assoc., N.J., 1974-75; assoc. Pitney, Hardin, Kipp, 1975-77; atty. AT&T, 1977-78; assoc. Verrill & Dana, Augusta, Maine, 1978-79; atty. Natural Resources Coun. Maine, 1979-84; gen. counsel Maine State Housing Authority, 1984-86; ptnr. Preti, Flaherty et al, 1986—. Bd. dirs. Maine Chamber and Bus. Alliance; bd. dirs. Literacy Vols. of Am., Augusta affiliate. Avocations: sailing, riding, skiing, gardening, rowing. Environmental. Office: Preti Flaherty 45 Meml Cir PO Box 1058 Augusta ME 04332-1058 E-mail: vdavis@preti.com

DAVIS, WANDA ROSE, lawyer; b. Lampasas, Tex., Oct. 4, 1937; d. Ellis DeWitt and Julia Doris (Rose) Cockrell; m. Richard Andrew Fulcher, May 09, 1959 (div. 1969); 1 child Greg Ellis ; m. Edwin Leon Davis, Jan. 14, 1973. BBA, U. Tex., 1959, JD, 1971. Bar: Tex. 1971, Colo. 1981, U.S. Dist. Ct. (no. dist.) Tex. 1972, U.S. Dist. Ct. Colo. 1981, U.S. Ct. Appeals (10th cir. 1981), U.S. Supreme Ct. 1976. Atty. Atlantic Richfield Co., Dallas, 1971; assoc. firm Crocker & Murphy, 1971-72; prin. Wanda Davis, Atty. at Law, 1972-73; ptnr. firm Davis & Davis Inc., 1973-75; atty. adviser HUD, 1974-75, Air Force Acctg. and Fin. Ctr., Danver, 1976-92; co-chmn. regional Profl. Devel. Inst. Am. Soc. Mil. Comptrollers, Colorado Springs, Colo., 1982; chmn. Lowry AFB Noontime Edn. Program, Exercise Program, Denver, 1977-83; mem. speakers bur. Colo. Women's Bar, 1995—, Lowry AFB, 1981-83. Mem. fed. ct. liaison com. U.S. Dist. Ct. Colo., 1983; mem. Leaders of the Fed. Bar Assn. People to People Del. to China, USSR and Finland, 1986. Contbr. numerous articles to profl. jours. Bd. dirs. Pres.'s Coun. Met. Denver, 1981-83; mem. Lowry AFB Alcohol Abuse Exec. Com., 1981-84. Recipient Spl. Achievement award USAF, 1978; Upward Mobility award Fed. Profl. and Adminstrv. Women Denver, 1979, Internat. Humanitarian award CARE, 1994. Mem. Fed. Bar Assn. (pres. Colo. 1982-83, mem. nat. coun. 1984—, Earl W. Kintner Disting. Svc. award 1983, 1st v.p. 10th cir. 1986-97, Internat. Hummanitarian award CARE, 1994), Zach Found. for Burned Children (award 1995), Colo. Trial Lawyers Assn., Bus. and Profl. Women's Club (dist. IV East dir. 1983-84, Colo. pres. 1988-89), Am. Soc. Mil. Comptrollers (pres. 1984-85), Denver south Met. Bus. and Profl. Women's Club (pres. 1982-83), Denver Silver Spruce Am. Bus. Women's Assn. (pres. 1981-82; Woman of Yr. award 1982), Colo. Jud. Inst., Colo. Concerned Lawyers, Profl. Mgrs. Assn., Fed. Women's Program (v.p. Denver 1980), Colo. Woman News Community adv. bd. 1988—), Dallas Bar Assn., Tex. Bar Assn., Denver Bar Assn., Altrusa, Zonta, Denver Nancy Langhorn Federally Employed Women (pres. 1979-80). Christian.

DAVIS, WILLIAM EUGENE, federal judge; b. Winfield, Ala., Aug. 18, 1936; s. A.L. and Addie Lee (Lenahan) D.; m. Celia Chalaron, Oct. 3, 1963 J.D., Tulane U., 1960. Bar: La. 1960. Assoc. Phelps Dunbar Marks Claverie & Sims, New Orleans, 1960-64; ptnr. Caffery Duhe & Davis, New Iberia, La., 1964-76; judge U.S. Dist. Ct., Lafayette, 1976-83, U.S. Ct. Appeals (5th Cir.), Lafayette, 1983—. Mem. ABA, La. Bar Assn., Maritime Assn. U.S. Republican Office: US Ct Appeals 800 Lafayette St Ste 5100 Lafayette LA 70501-6883

DAVIS, WILLIAM HOWARD, lawyer; b. Monmouth, Ill., May 24, 1951; s. Orville Francis and Alice Gertrude (Hennenfent) D.; m. Susan Claire Parris, April 11, 1981; children: Benjamin Patrick, Jackson Mitchell, Claire Marie. BA with honors, U. South Fla., 1974; JD with high honors, Fla. State U., 1977. Bar: Fla. 1977, U.S. Dist. Ct. (no. dist.) Fla. 1977, U.S. Dist. Ct. (mid. dist.) Fla. 1986, U.S. Ct. Appeals (11th cir.) 1986, U.S. Supreme Ct. 1993. Assoc. Thompson, Wadsworth, Messer & Rhodes, Tallahassee, 1977-80; ptnr. Wadsworth & Davis, P.A., 1980—. Instr. law Fla. State U., 1976-77. Editor notes and comments Fla. State U. Law Rev., 1976-77. Bd. dirs. Legal Aid Found., Inc., 1980-81, Fla. Legal Svcs., Inc., 1988-96, pres., 1993; pres. student govt., chmn., state coun. student body pres. State U. Sys. Fla., 1973-74. Mem. Acad. Fla. Trial Lawyers, Fla. Bar Assn. (2d cir. judge nominations comm. 1986-90, chmn. 2d cir. jud. grievance com. 1988-90), Fla. Bar Found. (bd. dirs. 1993-94, 97—, legal assistance to poor grant com. 1993—, chmn. exec. com. 2000—), Tallahassee Bar Assn. (bd. dirs. 1982-88, pres. 1986-87), Fla. Assn. Criminal Def. Lawyers, Am. Inns of Ct. (master of bench emeritus, exec. com. Tallahassee 1994-96), Cath. Charities (bd. dirs. Tallahassee region 1995—, pres. 1999-2001), Gulf Winds Track Club, Capital Tiger Bay Club, Omicron Delta Kappa, Phi Sigma Alpha. Democrat. General civil litigation, Criminal, Personal injury. Home: 914 Mimosa Dr Tallahassee FL 32312-3012 Office: Wadsworth & Davis PA 203 N Gadsden St Ste 1 Tallahassee FL 32301-7633

DAVISON, IRWIN STUART, lawyer; b. Hazelton, Pa., Feb. 17, 1942; s. Julius S. and Gertrude (Kempner) D.; m. Ilene F. Hershinson, Nov. 24, 1966; children— Jill, Joshua. B.A., Lafayette Coll., 1963; J.D., Bklyn. Law Sch., 1966. Bar: N.Y. 1967, U.S. Dist. Ct. (so. and ea. dist.) N.Y. 1969, U.S. Supreme Ct. 1971. Dir. criminal justice projects Addition Services Agy., N.Y.C., 1975, asst. commr., 1975-76, gen. counsel, 1976-77; counsel Office of Substance Abuse Services, City of N.Y., 1977-78; dep. gen. counsel Dept. Health, city of N.Y., 1978-80, gen. counsel, 1980— . Chmn. Zoning Bd. Appeals, Mt. Vernon, 1982— . Mem. N.Y. County Lawyers Bar Assn. Home: 92 Frederick Pl Mount Vernon NY 10552-2331

DAVIS-YANCEY, GWENDOLYN, lawyer; b. Jackson, Mich., Apr. 6, 1955; d. Wendell Norman Sr. and Jean Davis; children: Natosha, Michael, Nicole, Jennifer, Cyril; m. Kenneth Donald Yancey, Dec. 9, 1995. BS, Wayne State U., 1990; JD, U. Detroit-Mercy, 1994. Bar: Mich., U.S. Dist. Ct. (ea. dist.) Mich.; cert. tchr., Mich. Legal sec. Dykema, Gossett, Detroit; chemistry tchr. Detroit Bd. Edn., 1990-92; atty. Misdemeanor Def.'s Office, Detroit, 1994-95, Legal Aid and Def.'s Office, Detroit, 1995-96, Davis-Yancey Law Office P.L.L.C., Southfield, Mich., 1996—; ptnr., owner Men's Legal Svc., 1999—. Mem. ABA, State Bar of Mich. (family law sect., real estate sect., bus. law sect., litig. sect.), Wayne County Family Law Bar. Family and matrimonial, Real property. Office: Davis-Yancey Law Office PLLC # 703A W 15565 Northland Dr Southfield MI 48075

DAWE, JAMES ROBERT, lawyer; b. Bristol, Conn., Aug. 12, 1945; s. John Grosvenor and Madeline Rose (Pilbin) D.; m. Mary Gardner, July 5, 1970; children: Emily, Jeremy, Sarah. BA, Lehigh U., 1967; M City Planning, San Diego State U., 1974; JD, U. San Diego, 1976. Bar: Calif. 1976, U.S. Dist. Ct. (so. dist.) Calif. 1976. Atty. Seltzer Caplan McMahon Vitek, San Diego, 1976—. Chair Urban Librs. Coun., Evanston, Ill., 1993-94, San Diego Pub. Libr. Commn., 1986-94; chair Libr. Calif. Bd., Sacramento; past chair Downtown San Diego Partnership, San Diego City Mgr. Ballot com. Mem. ABA (real property sect.), Urban Land Inst., Calif. Bldg. Industry Assn. (legal action com.). Administrative and regulatory, Environmental, Land use and zoning (including planning). Office: Seltzer Caplan McMahon Vitek 750 B St Ste 2100 San Diego CA 92101-8177

DAWSON, CINDY MARIE, lawyer; b. Oklahoma City, May 3, 1960; d. Alva Glenn and Ethel Estelle Horner; m. Ronnie L. Dawson, July 14, 1977; children: Kristina Lee Ann, Kathryn DeeAnn, Shaunna Renee. AA, Rose State Coll., Midwest City, Okla., 1993; BBA, U. Ctrl. Okla., 1994, postgrad., 1997—; JD, Oklahoma City U., 1997. Bar: Okla. 1997. Leasing agt. Brentwood Apts., Shawnee, Okla., 1988; bus. advisor Triple H Constrn., Eufaula, 1989-96; pvt. practice atty. Edmond, 1997-2000; asst. dist. atty. Shawnee, 2000—. Mem. ATLA, Okla. Bar Assn., Okla. Trial Lawyers Assn., Legal Aid Western Okla., Eufaula Alumni Assn., Phi Delta Phi. Avocations: reading, cooking, sports, travel. Family and matrimonial, Criminal, Administrative and regulatory. Office: PO Box 3189 130 N Broadway Ste 300 Shawnee OK 74802

DAWSON, DENNIS RAY, lawyer, manufacturing company executive; b. Alma, Mich., June 19, 1948; s. Maurice L. and Virginia (Baker) D.; m. Marilynn S. Gordon, Nov. 26, 1971; children: Emily Lynn, Brett Thomas. AA, Gulf Coast Coll., 1968; AB, Duke U., 1970; JD, Wayne State U., 1973. Bar: Mich. 1973, U.S. Dist. Ct. (ea. dist.) Mich. 1973, U.S. Dist. Ct. (we. dist.) Mich. 1975. Assoc. Watson, Wunsch & Keidan, Detroit, 1973-75; mem. Coupe, Ophoff & Dawson, Holland, Mich., 1975-77; staff atty. Amway Corp., Ada, 1977-79; corp. counsel Meijer, Inc., Grand Rapids, 1979-82; sec., corp. counsel Tecumseh Products Co., 1982-92; corp. counsel, asst. sec. Holnam Inc., Dundee, Mich., 1992-93; v.p., gen. counsel, sec. Denso Internat. Am. Inc., Southfield, 1993-2000, sr. v.p., gen. counsel, sec., 2000—. Exec. com. Bank of Lenawee, Adrian, Mich., 1984-93, also bd. dirs.; adj. prof. Aquinas Coll., Grand Rapids, 1978-82; govt. regulation and litigation com. Outdoor Power Equipment Inst. Inc., Washington, 1982-92. Trustee Herrick Meml. Hosp., 1988-91, Tecumseh Civic Auditorium, 1986-89; mem. adv. coun. Montessori Children's House and Acad., Adrian, 1987-93. Mem. ABA, Mich. State Bar Assn., Am. Soc. Corp. Secs., Am. Corp. Counsel Assn., Mich. Mfrs. Assn. (lawyers com. 1987-92), Lenawee C. of C. (bd. dirs. 1988-92). General corporate. Office: Denso Internat America Inc PO Box 5133 24777 Denso Dr Southfield MI 48034-5244

DAWSON, KIMBERLI DAWN, lawyer; b. Broken Bow, Nebr., Apr. 8, 1970; d. Frederick Elroy and Alice Maureen Bindewald; m. Robert Doyle Dawson, Sept. 12, 1998. BS, U. Nebr., Lincoln, 1993, JD, 1997. Bar: Nebr. 1997. Jud. clk. Nebr. Supreme Ct., Lincoln, 1997-98; assoc. Kelley, Scritsmier & Byrne, North Platte, Nebr., 1998—. Democrat. Lutheran. Avocations: aerobics, water skiing, cooking. Family and matrimonial, Insurance. Office: Kelley Scritsmier & Byrne PC 221 W 2d St North Platte NE 69101

DAWSON, STEPHEN EVERETTE, lawyer; b. Detroit, May 14, 1946; s. Everette Ivan and Irene (Dresser) D.; m. Consiglia J. Bellisario, Sept. 20, 1974; children: Stephen Everette Jr., Gina C., Joseph J. BA, Mich. State U., 1968; MA, U. Mich., 1969, JD, 1972. Bar: Mich. 1972, U.S. Dist. Ct. (ea. dist.) Mich. 1972, U.S. Supreme Ct. 1978, U.S. Ct. Appeals (6th cir.) 1980. Assoc. Dickinson, Wright, Moon, Van Dusen & Freeman, Detroit, 1972-79; ptnr. Dickinson, Wright, PLLC, Bloomfield Hills, Mich., 1979—. Adj. prof. law U. Detroit, 1986-88. Mem. ABA, Am. Coll. Real Estate Lawyers, Mich. State Bar Assn. (mem. coun. real property law sect. 1986-93, chair 1992-93, land title stds. com. 1999—), Mich. State Bar Found., Phi Beta Kappa. Republican. Avocations: jogging, reading. Contracts commercial, Landlord-tenant, Real property. Office: Dickinson Wright PLLC 38525 Woodward Ave Ste 2000 Bloomfield Hills MI 48304-5092 E-mail: sdawson@dickinson-wright.com

DAY, CHRISTOPHER MARK, lawyer; b. Atlantic City, May 24, 1968; s. Frederick Nicholes and Judith Lee Day. BA in Polit. Sci., Stockton State U., 1990; JD, Widener U., 1994. Bar: N.J. 1994, Pa. 1994, U.S. Dist. Ct. N.J. 1994. Law clk. Hon. Richard J. Williams, Assignment Judge Superior Ct., Atlantic City, 1994-95; assoc. Cooper Perskie Law Firm, 1995-97; ptnr. Petro Cohen Day Law Firm, 1998—. Bd. dirs. Chief Arthur Brown Meml. Scholarship Found., 1992—, Chelsea Neighborhood Assn., 1995-97; chmn. Attys. Reaching Others, 1995—. Mem. Atlantic County Bar Assn. (trustee 1998—), N.J. Workers Compensation Am. Inns Ct., Jr. C. of C. Criminal, Personal injury, Workers' compensation. Home: 46 S Laclede Pl Atlantic City NJ 08401-5806 Office: Petro Cohen Day Law Firm 2111 New Rd Northfield NJ 08225-1512

DAY, EDWARD FRANCIS, JR. lawyer; b. Portland, Maine, Nov. 4, 1946; s. Edward Francis and Anne (Rague) D.; m. Claire Ann Nicholson, June 27, 1970; children: Kelley Ann, John Edward. BA, St. Anselm Coll., 1968; JD cum laude, U. Maine, 1973; LLM in Taxation, NYU, 1976. Bar: N.J. 1973, U.S. Dist. Ct. N.J. 1973, U.S. Tax Ct. 1974, N.Y. 1981. Assoc. Hannoch, Weisman, Stern & Besser, Newark, 1973-74, Carpenter, Bennett & Morrissey, Newark, 1974-78, ptnr., 1979-93, sr. ptnr., 1994-98, of counsel, 1999—. Instr. employee benefits and comml. law The Am. Coll., Valley Forge, Pa., 1981-82; bd. dirs. Weiss-Aug. Co., Inc., East Hanover, N.J., Main Tape Co., Tinton Falls, N.J., exec. v.p., gen. counsel, 1999—. Editor Maine Law Rev., 1972-73. Mem., vice-chmn. Allenhurst (N.J) Bd. Adjustment, 1983-85; mem., vice-chmn. Allenhurst Planning Bd., 1985-87; mem. Nat. Ski Patrol, Denver, 1985—; scoutmaster Monmouth coun. Boy Scouts Am., Ocean Twp., 1987-90; mem. 10th Mountain Divsn. Assn., Aspen, Colo., 1996—. Served in U.S. Army, 1968-70. Named One of Outstanding Young Men of Am., 1979; Ford Found. scholar, 1966-68. Mem.: ABA, N.J. Bar Assn., Essex County Bar Assn., Estate Planning Coun. No. N.J., Deal (N.J.) Golf and Country Club (bd. dirs. 1985—92, sec. 1991—92), Jersey Coast Club of Red Bank (v.p. 1976—77), Forsgate Country Club (Jamesburg, N.J.), Am. Legion. Roman Catholic. Avocations: golf, skiing, piano. Contracts commercial, Probate, Real property. Home: 225 Spier Ave Allenhurst NJ 07711-1120 Office: Carpenter Bennett & Morrissey 3 Gateway Ctr Newark NJ 07102-4079 also: Main Tape Co 2 Hance Ave Eatontown NJ 07724-2726

DAY, JAMES MCADAM, JR. lawyer; b. Detroit, Aug. 18, 1948; s. James McAdam and Mary Elizabeth (McGibbon) D.; m. Sally Marie Sterud; children: Cara McAdam, Brenna Marie, Michael James. AB, UCLA, 1970; JD magna cum laude, U. Pacific, 1973. Bar: Calif. 1973, U.S. Dist. Ct. (no. dist.) Calif. 1973, U.S. Ct. Appeals (9th cir.) 1975. Assoc. Downey, Brand, Seymour & Rohwer, Sacramento, 1973-78, ptnr., 1978—, chmn. natural resources dept., 1985-90; mng. ptnr. Downey, Brand, Seymour & Rohmer, 1990-94, 97—. Contbr. articles to profl. jours. Pres., bd. dirs. Sacramento Soc. for Prevention of Cruelty to Animals, 1976-79, Children's Home Soc. of Calif., Sacramento, 1979-85; bd. dirs. Sta. KXPR/KXJZ, Inc. Pub. Radio, Sacramento, 1984-94, chmn., 1990-93; bd. dirs. Calif. State Libr. Found., 1995—, chmn., 1995-2000. Mem. ABA (natural resources sect. 1998), Calif. Bar Assn. (exec. com. 1985-89, chmn. real property law sect. 1988), Rocky Mountain Mineral Law Found., Sacramento Petroleum Assn., Calif. Mining Assn., U. Pacific McGeorge Law Sch. Alumni Assn. (bd. dirs. 1980-83). Avocations: yacht racing and cruising, fishing. Office: Downey Brand Seymour & Rohwer 555 Capitol Mall Fl 10 Sacramento CA 95814-4504

DAY, JOHN ARTHUR, lawyer; b. Madison, Wis., Sept. 21, 1956; s. John Donald and Elinor Roletta (Heath) D. BS, U. Wis., Platteville, 1978; JD, U. N.C., 1981. Bar: Tenn. 1981, U.S. Dist. Ct. (mid. dist.) Tenn. 1981, U.S. Ct. Appeals (6th cir.) 1982; civil cert. Nat. Bd. Trial Advocacy 1991. Assoc. Boult Cummings Conners & Berry, Nashville, 1981-86, ptnr., 1987-92; shareholder Branham & Day, P.C., 1993—. Mem. Civil Justice Reform Act adv. group U.S. Dist. Ct. (mid. dist.) Tenn., 1991-95; bd. dirs. Nat. Bd. Trial Advocacy, 1998—; mem. Tenn. Supreme Ct. Commn. on Continuing Legal Edn. and Specialization, 2001—. Co-author: Tennessee Law of Comparative Fault, 1997; founder, editor Tenn. Tort Law Letter, 1995—; contbr. articles to profl. jours. Com. mem. Cohn Roundtable, Nashville, 1988; assoc. Harry Phillips Inn of Ct., 1990-92, Tenn. John Marshall Inn of Ct., 1999—. Mem. Tenn. Trial Lawyers Assn. (bd. govs. 1984-85, treas. 1985-89, v.p. 1989-93, pres. 1993-94, chair legal edn. com. 1985-86, chair legis. com. 1987-90, CLE com. 1984-97, pub. rels. com. 1986-88, long range planning com. 1991-93), Assn. Trial Lawyers Am. (Tenn. pub. rels. rep. 1986-87, people's law sch. com. co-chair 1986-88, pub. rels. com. 1986-91, chair 1988-89, edn. com. 1987-88, pub. affairs com. 1987-89, publs. com. 1990-93, vice chmn. 1991-93, co-chair 1992-93, key person com. 1987-89, nursing home litigation group 1985-89, chmn. 1987-89, mem. exec. com. 1994-95, chair pres.'s coun. 1994-95), Nashville Bar Assn. (bd. dirs. 1998-2000, circuit and chancery ct. com. chair 1989, fee disputes com. 1984-85, 87, vice chmn. 1988, chmn. 1989), Lawyers Involved for Tenn. (trustee 1988—), Tenn. Bar Assn. (mem. litigation sect. coun. 1989-90), Nat. Bd. Trial Advocacy (bd. dirs. 1998—, stds. com. 1998—, v.p. 2001-02), Tenn. Justice Ctr. (bd. dirs. 1999—). Democrat. Personal injury. Home: 5019 Country Club Dr Brentwood TN 37027-5173 Office: Branham & Day PC 5300 Maryland Way Ste 300 Brentwood TN 37027

DAY, MICHAEL GORDON, law educator; b. Madison, Wis., July 30, 1951; s. Lee Monroe and Joan (Meredith) D.; m. Donna Kay Corl, May 26, 1979 (div. Apr. 1986); children: Tomas Lee, Anne Elizabeth; m. Carol Ann Stefanko, Apr. 12, 1997. BA, Pa. State U., 1973; JD, George Washington U., 1976. Bar: Pa. 1976. Assoc. Alan Ellis, Esq., State College, Pa., 1976-77; pvt. practice, 1977-85; with Profl. Planning Cons., 1985-86, Century Fin. Svcs., State College, 1986-96; expert Netscape Solutions, 1996-99; dir. Info. Tech. Inst./Shepherd Coll., Shepherdstown, W.Va., 1999—. Instr. bus. law Pa. State U., University Park, 1978-79; counsel to Boccardo Law Firm, San Jose, Calif., 1983, Rees Law Firm, Washington, 1983; sr. v.p. Century Mortage Corp., 1991-96. Chmn. Com. to Elect Mel Hodes Senator, Pa., 1982, Dem. Com., State College, 1982-84; active Exec. Com. Centre County, 1982-84, United Pennsylvanians, 1982-83; gen. counsel CLEAN, 1982-85; v.p. Mt. Nittany Conservancy, 2000—; candidate for Pa. Ho. Reps., 1980; candidate for dist. justice 49th Dist. Pa., 1977. Mem. Sierra Club, Lions Paw Alumni Assn. (pres. 1999—), Parmi Nous, Omicron Delta Kappa, Delta Sigma Rho. Methodist. Office: 315 W Stephen St Martinsburg WV 25401 E-mail: lionspaw@psu.edu, mday@shepherd.edu

DAY, MICHAEL W. lawyer; b. Winner, S.D., July 26, 1958; BS, U. S.D., 1980, JD, 1983. Bar: S.D. 1983, U.S. Dist. Ct. S.D., U.S. Ct. Appeals (8th cir.). Mem. Day, Morris & Schreiber, Bell Fourche, SD. Mem.: ABA, ATLA, Am. Judicature Soc., Western Trial Lawyers Assn., S.D. Trial Lawyers Assn. (pres. 1992—93, bd. govs. 1984—94), State Bar S.D. (pres.-elect 2000—01, pres. 2001—), Butte County Bar Assn. (pres. 1996—97), Pennington County Bar Assn., Jackrabbit Bar Assn. Personal injury. Office: Day Morris & Schreiber 117 Fifth Ave PO Box 370 Belle Fourche SD 57717-0370*

DAY, RICHARD EARL, lawyer, educator; b. St. Joseph, Mo., Nov. 2, 1929; s. William E. and Geneva C. (Miller) D.; m. Melissa W. Blair, Feb. 2, 1951; children: William E., Thomas E. BS, U. Pa., 1951; JD with distinction, U. Mich., 1957. Bar: Ill. 1957, D.C. 1959, S.C. 1980. Assoc. Kirkland & Ellis, Chgo., 1957-58, Howrey Simon Baker & Murchison, Washington, 1958-61; asst. prof. law U. N.C., Chapel Hill, 1961-64; assoc. prof. Ohio State U., Columbus, 1964-66, prof., 1966-75, U. S.C., Columbia, 1975-76, 80-86, dean, 1977-80, John William Thurmond chair disting. prof. law, 1986-99, disting. prof. law emeritus, 1999—. Cons. U.S. Office Edn., 1964-66; course dir. Ohio Legal Ctr. Inst. Columbus, 1970-75; vis. prof. law U. Southampton (Eng.), fall 1988. Author: The Intensified Course in Antitrust Law, 1972, rev. edit., 1974; book rev. editor Antitrust Bull., 1968-71, adv. bd., 1971—; adv. bd. Antitrust and Trade Regulation Report, 1973-76, Jour. Reprints for Antitrust Law and Econs., 1974—. Ohio commr. Nat. Conf. on Uniform State Laws, 1967-75, S.C. commr., 1977-80; mem. Ohio Gov.'s Adv. Coun. Internat. Trade, 1972-74, S.C. Jud. Coun., 1977-80; chmn. S.C. Appellate Def. Coun., 1977-80, S.C. Com. Intellectual Property and Unfair Trade Practices Law, 1981-87. Lt. USNR, 1952-55. Named John William Thurmond Disting. Prof. Law. Mem. ABA, S.C. Bar Assn. (bd. govs. 1977-80), Am. Law Inst. Methodist. Home: 204 Saint James St Columbia SC 29205-3074 Office: U SC Law Ctr Main And Green Sts Columbia SC 29208-0001

DAY, ROLAND BERNARD, retired chief justice state supreme court; b. Oshkosh, Wis., June 11, 1919; s. Peter Oliver and Joanna King (Wescott) D.; m. Mary Jane Purcell, Dec. 18, 1948; 1 dau., Sarah Jane. B.A., U. Wis., 1942, J.D., 1947. Bar: Wis. 1947. Trainee Office Wis. Atty. Gen., 1947; assoc. mem. firm Maloney & Wheeler, Madison, Wis., 1947-49; 1st asst. dist. atty. Dane County, 1949-52; partner firm Day, Goodman, Madison, 1953-57; firm Wheeler, Van Sickle, Day & Anderson, Madison, 1959-74; legal counsel mem. staff Sen. William Proxmire, Washington, 1957-58; justice Wis. Supreme Ct., Madison, 1974-95, chief justice, 1995-96. Mem. Madison Housing Authority, 1960-64, chmn., 1961-63; regent U. Wis. System, 1972-74 Served with AUS, 1943-46. Mem. ABA, State Bar Wis., Am. Trial Lawyers Assn., Ygdrasil Lit. Soc. (pres. 1968), Madison Torske Klubben, Masons (33rd degree). Mem. United Ch. of Christ. Clubs: Madison, Madison Lit.

DAY, STUART REID, lawyer; b. Laramie, Wyo., July 2, 1959; s. Richard Erwin and Evelyn (Reid) D.; m. TimAnn Day, Jan. 18, 1980; children: Shelby Rochelle, Erica Rachel. BS, Ariz. State U., 1981; JD, U. Wyo., 1984. Assoc. Williams, Porter, Day & Neville, Casper, Wyo., 1984-87, ptnr., 1987—. Mem. unauthorized practice of law com. Wyo. State Bar. Mem. ABA, ATLA, Wyo. Bar Assn. (vice chmn., bd. CLE 1992-93, chmn. bd. CLE 1994-95, chmn. unauthorized practice of law com. 2001—), Colo. Bar Assn., Def. Rsch. Inst., Natrona County Bar Assn. (treas. 1989, v.p. 1990, pres. 1991), Casper C. of C. (bd. dirs. 1989-91, 97—). General civil litigation, Education and schools, Personal injury. Office: PO Box 10700 Casper WY 82602-3902 E-mail: sday@wpdn.net

DAYE, CHARLES EDWARD, law educator; b. Durham, N.C., May 14, 1944; s. Eccleasiastes and Addie Lula (Roberts) D.; m. Norma Lowery, Dec. 19, 1976; stepchildren: Clarence L. Hill, III, Tammy H. Roundtree. Student, N.C. Central U., 1966; JD, Columbia U., 1969. Bar: N.Y. 1970, D.C. 1971, N.C. 1975, U.S. Supreme Ct. 1979. Assoc. Dewey, Ballantine, Bushby, Palmer & Wood, N.Y.C., 1969; law clk. U.S. Ct. Appeals (6th cir.), 1969-70; assoc. Covington & Burling, Washington, 1970-72; prof. law Sch. Law U. N.C., Chapel Hill, 1972-81, 85—, Henry Brandis prof. law, 1991—. Dean, prof. law Sch. Law, N.C. Central U., Durham, 1981-85; cons. N.C. Dept. Adminstrn., 1975; mem. Triangle Housing Devel. Corp., 1973—, chmn. 1977-93; chair N.C. Poverty Project, 1990—; pres. Law Sch. Admission Coun., 1990-93. Author: (with Mandelker et al) Housing and Community Development, 1981, 2d edit., 1989, 3rd edit., 1999, (with Morris) N.C. Law of Torts, 2d edit., 1999; contbr. articles to profl. jours. Mem. ABA (mem. commn. on minorities in the profn. 1990-95), N.C. Assn. Black Lawyers (Lawyer of Yr. 1980, pres. 1976-78, exec. sec. 1979-99), N.C. Bar Assn. Democrat. Baptist. Home: 3400 Cambridge Rd Durham NC 27707-4508 Office: Univ NC Law Sch Chapel Hill NC 27599-0001 E-mail: cdaye@email.unc.edu

DAYNARD, RICHARD ALAN, law educator; b. N.Y.C., July 19, 1943; s. David M. and Sarah (Weidenbaum) D.; m. Carol S. Iskols, Aug. 9, 1975; children: David J., Gabriela C. BA, Columbia U., 1964, MA in Sociology, 1970; JD, Harvard U., 1967; PhD in Urban Studies and Planning, MIT, 1980. Bar: N.Y. 1967, U.S. Ct. Appeals (6th cir.) 1986, U.S. Supreme Ct. 1986, U.S. Ct. Appeals (11th cir.) 1987, U.S. Ct. Appeals (5th cir.) 1996.

Law clk. 2d cir. U.S. Ct. Appeals, N.Y.C., 1967-68; tchg. fellow Columbia U., 1968-69; asst. prof. law Northeastern U., Boston, 1969-71, assoc. prof. law, 1971-73, prof. law, 1973—. Lectr. Tufts Med. Sch., Boston, 1975-89; lectr. and cons. in field. Editor-in-chief Tobacco Products Litigation Reporter, 1985—; assoc. editor: Tobacco Control: An Internat. Jour., 1998—; contbr. articles to profl. jours. Chmn. Tobacco Products Liability Project, Boston, 1984—; pres. Group Against Smoking Pollution of Mass., Boston, 1983—, Clean Indoor Air Ednl. Found., Boston, 1983-92, Tobacco Control Resource Ctr., Inc., Boston, 1993—; pres. Stop Teenage Addiction to Tobacco, 1996-98. Mem. ABA, Am. Pub. Health Assn., Law and Soc. Assn., Phi Beta Kappa. Home: 90 Commonwealth Ave Boston MA 02116-3040 Office: Northeastern U Sch Law 400 Huntington Ave Boston MA 02115-5005 E-mail: r.daynard@neu.edu

DE, MEENA INDRAJIT, lawyer; b. Pune, India, Dec. 27, 1971; camd to U.S., 1990; d. Ramesh Chandra and Mamini Ramesh Goel; m. Indrajit De, Aug. 1995. BA, SUNY, Binghamton, 1993; JD, Fordham U., 1996; LLM in Taxation, U. Miami, 1999—. Bar: N.J. 1996, N.Y. 1997. Pvt. practice, Richmond Hill, N.Y., 1997-98. Mem. ABA, N.Y. State Bar Assn., N.Y. Women's Bar Assn., Assn. Bar City N.Y. Estate planning, General practice, Estate taxation. Home: 87-90 118th St Richmond Hill NY 11418

DEACON, JOHN C. lawyer; b. Newport, Ark., Sept. 26, 1920; BA, U. Ark., 1941, JD, 1948. Bar: Ark. 1948. Ptnr. Barrett & Deacon, Jonesboro, Ark. Commr. from Ark. to Nat. Conf. Commrs. on Uniform State Laws, 1966—, chmn. exec. com., 1977-79, pres. 1979-81. Recipient Ark. Outstanding Lawyer-Citizen award, 1973. Fellow Am. Coll. Trial Lawyers, Internat. Acad. Trial Lawyers (bd. d irs. 1978-84), Southwestern Legal Found. (trustee 1975-95, chmn. Research Fellows 1983-85); mem. Craighead County Bar Assn. (pres. 1968-69), N.E. Ark. Bar Assn. (pres. 1966-68), Ark. Bar Assn. (pres. 1970-71), ABA (chmn. sect. bar activities 1967-68, Ark. del. 1967-79, bd. govs. 1980-83, 92-93, chair sr. lawyers divsn. 1994-95), Am. Counsel Assn. (pres. 1974-75), Am. Bar Found. (pres. 1994-96), Internat. Assn. Def. Counsel, Nat. Assn. R.R. Trial Lawyers, Delta Theta Phi. General civil litigation, General practice. Office: PO Box 1700 Jonesboro AR 72403-1700 also: Barrett & Deacon PA Union Planters Bank Building 300 S Church St Jonesboro AR 72401-2911 E-mail: jdeacon@barrettdeacon.com

DEACY, THOMAS EDWARD, JR. lawyer; b. Kansas City, Mo., Oct. 14, 1918; s. Thomas Edward and Grace (Scales) D.; m. Jean Freeman, July 10, 1943 (div. 1988); children: Bennette Kay Deacy Kramer, Carolyn G., Margaret Deacy Vickrey, Thomas, Ann Deacy Krause; m. Jean Holmes McDonald, 1988. J.D., U. Mo., 1940; M.B.A., U. Chgo., 1949. Bar: Mo. 1940, Ill. 1946. Practice law, Kansas City, 1940-42; ptnr. Taylor, Miller, Busch & Magner, Chgo., 1946-55, Deacy & Deacy, Kansas City, 1955—. Lectr. Northwestern U., 1949-55, U. Chgo., 1950-55; dir., mem. exec. com. St. L.-S.F. Ry., 1962-80; dir. Burlington No. Inc., 1980-86; mem. U.S. team Anglo-Am. Legal Exchange, 1973, 77. Mem. Juv. Protective Assn. Chgo., 1947-55, pres., bd. dirs., 1950-53; mem. exec bd. Chgo. coun. Boy Scouts Am., 1952-55; pres. Kansas City Philharmonic Orch., 1961-63, chmn. bd. trustees, 1963-65; trustee Sunset Hill Sch., 1963-73; trustee, mem. exec. com. u. Kansas City, 1963—; trustee Mo. Law Sch. Found., pres., 1973-77, Kans. chpt. The Nature Conservancy, 1994-99. Capt. AUS, 1942-45. Fellow Am. Coll. Trial Lawyers (regent 1968— , treas. 1973-74, pres. 1975-76), Am. Bar Found; mem. Am. Law Inst., Jud. Conf. U.S. (implementation com. on admission of attys. to fed. practice 1979-86), ABA (commn. standards jud. adminstrn. 1972-74, standing com. fed. judiciary 1974-80), Ill. Bar Assn., Chgo. Bar Assn., Mo. Bar, Kansas City Bar Assn., Lawyers Assn. Kansas City, Chgo. Club, La Jolla (Calif.) Country Club, La Jolla Beach and Tennis Club, Kansas City Club, Kansas City Country Club, River Club, Q.E.B.H. Sr. Hon. Soc. of Mo. Univ., Beta Gamma Sigma, Sigma Chi. Appellate, Banking, General civil litigation. Home: 2724 Verona Cir Mission Hills KS 66208-1265 Office: 920 Main St Ste 1900 Kansas City MO 64105-2010 E-mail: ted@deacylaw.com

DEAKTOR, DARRYL BARNETT, lawyer; b. Pitts., Feb. 2, 1942; s. Harry and Edith (Barnett) D.; children: Rachael Alexandra, Hallie Sarah. BA, Brandeis U., 1963; LLB, U. Pa., 1966; MBA, Columbia U., 1968. Bar: Pa. 1966, Fla. 1980, N.Y. 1980. Assoc. firm Goodis, Greenfield & Mann, Phila., 1968-70, ptnr., 1971; gen. counsel Life of Pa. Fin. Corp., 1972; asst. prof. U. Fla. Coll. Law, Gainesville, 1972-74, assoc. prof., 1974-80; with Mershon, Sawyer, Johnston, Dunwody & Cole, Miami, Fla., 1980-81, ptnr., 1981-84, Walker Ellis Gragg & Deaktor, Miami, 1984-86, White & Case LLP, Miami, 1987-95, White & Case LLC, Johannesburg, South Africa, 1995-2000, Palo Alto, Calif., 2000—. Mem. Dist. III (Fla.) Human Rights Advocacy Com. for Mentally Retarded Citizens, 1974-78, chmn., 1978-80; mem. adv. bd. Childbirth Edn. Assn. Alachua County, Fla., 1974-80; mem. resource devel. bd. Mailman Ctr. for Child Devel., 1981-88. Mem. Fla. Bar. General corporate, Mergers and acquisitions, Securities. Office: White & Case LLP 3000 El Camino Real Five Palo Alto Sq 10th Fl Palo Alto CA 94306 E-mail: ddeaktor@whitecase.com

DEAN, BEALE, lawyer, director; b. Ft. Worth, Feb. 26, 1922; s. Ben J. and Helen (Beale) D.; m. Margaret Ann Webster, Sept. 3, 1948; children: Webster Beale, Giselle Liseanne. BA, U. Tex., Austin, 1943, LLB, 1947. Bar: Tex. 1946, U.S. Dist. Ct. (no., so, we. and ea. dists.), U.S. Cir. Ct. (5th and 11th cirs.) 1952, U.S. Supreme Ct. 1954. Asst. dist. atty., Dallas, 1947-48; assoc. Martin, Moore & Brewster, Ft. Worth, 1948-50; mem. Martin, Moore, Brewster & Dean, 1950-51, Pannell, Dean, Pannell & Kerry (and predecessor firms), 1951-65; ptnr. Brown, Herman, Scott, Young & Dean, Ft. Worth, 1965-71, Brown, Herman, Scott, Dean & Miles, Ft. Worth, 1971-98, Brown, Herman, Dean, Wiseman, Liser & Hart, LLP, Ft. Worth, 1998—. Spl. asst. Atty. Gen. Tex., 1959-61. Regent Nat. Coll. Dist. Attys., 1985—. With AUS, 1942-45, ETO. Mem. ABA, Bar Assn. Fifth Fed. Cir., Ft. Worth-Tarrant County Bar Assn. (past pres. 1971-72, Blackstone award 1991), Am. Coll. Trial Lawyers, State Bar Tex. (dir. 1973-75), Am. Bar Found., Tex. Bar Found. (charter mem.), Ft. Worth Boat Club, Ridglea Country Club, Ft. Worth Club. Presbyterian. Federal civil litigation, General civil litigation, State civil litigation. Office: 200 Ft Worth Club Bldg Fort Worth TX 76102-4905

DEAN, BILL VERLIN, JR. lawyer; b. Oklahoma City, Jan. 11, 1957; s. Bill V. and Mary Lou (Dorman) D.; m. Christine Potter; children: Bill V. III, Mary Megan. BS, Cen. State U., 1978; JD, Oklahoma City U., 1981. Bar: Okla. 1982, U.S. Dist. Ct. (we. dist.) Okla. 1983, (no. dist.) Okla. 1986, (ea. dist.) Okla. 1987, Tex. 1990, N.Y. 1992, U.S. Ct. Appeals (10th cir.) 1986; lic. real estate broker and ins. agt. Second dep. assessor Okla. County Assessor, Oklahoma City, 1978-80; atty. Struthers Oil and Gas Corp., 1980-82; cons. Bill Dean & Co., Jones, Okla., 1978—; ptnr. Dean & Assocs. P.C., 1982—; pres. Dean Ins. Agy. Ltd., 1986—, Casualty Corp. Am., Inc., 1999—. Bd. dirs. Union Mut. Ins. Co.; CEO Casualty Corp. of Am., Inc., 1999—. Mem. Okla. County Bar Assn., Okla. Bar Assn., Tex. Bar Assn., N.Y. Bar Assn., Shriners. Methodist. Banking, Insurance, Real property. Home: 200 Cherokee St Jones OK 73049-7709 Office: Dean & Assocs P C PO Box 1060 110 E Main St Jones OK 73049-7706 E-mail: bdean@deannet.com

DEAN, DAVID ALLEN, lawyer; b. Chattanooga, Tenn., Jan. 14, 1948; s. William Berry and Elizabeth (Connor) D.; 1 child, Hillary Diane. BBA, So. Meth. U., 1969; JD, U. Tex.-Austin, 1973. Bar: Tex. 1973. Asst. dir. Tex. Office Comprehensive Health Planning, Austin, 1973; adminstrv. asst. Gov. Tex., Austin, 1974; legal counsel Gov. Briscoe, State of Tex., Austin, 1975-78, to Gov. Clements, 1979-81; sec. state State of Tex., Austin, 1981-83; ptnr. Winstead, McGuire, Sechrest & Minick, Dallas, (now Winstead, Sechrest & Minick) 1983-93, chmn. pub. law sect., PAC com., bus. devel. com., also bd. dirs., 1994—; shareholder David A. Dean & Assocs., P.C., Dallas, 1994—; pres. Transp. Strategies, Inc., Dallas; pres., CEO Dean Internat., Inc., Dallas, 1994—, Innovative Transp. Strategies, Dallas, 1994—; lectr. in field. Editor: Texas Campaign and Financial Disclosure Manual, 1984; Election Study of Fifty States, 1982. Author: Gubernatorial Parole Policies, 1980. Contbr. articles to Tex. Bus. and Comml. Quar., 1981-83, Dallas Bus. and Profl. Rev. Exec. dir. Gov.'s Criminal Justice Div., Austin, 1980-81, Crime Stoppers Adv. Council, 1979-81; chmn. State Fed. Voter Fraud Task Force, 1982; chmn. Gov.'s Task Force on Health and Human Services, 1975-79, Nat. Gov.'s Health Consortium, 1977-78; trustee Dean Learning Ctr., Dallas, 1970—, mem. exec. com., chmn. nominating com., 1970—; bd. dirs. Girlstown U.S.A., 1973-85, Greater Dallas Crime Commn., 1983— , chmn., 1985-88, former mem. exec. com., past chmn. legis. com.; mem. Interstate Oil Compact Commn., Austin, 1979-83, State Bd. Canvassers, Austin, 1981-83; mem. spl. interim com. Criminal Justice System Tex., Austin, 1981; co-chmn., mem., chmn. subcom. pub. disclosure, polit. funds, and lobby regulations Pub. Servant Stds. Conduct Adv. Com., Austin, 1981-83; v.p., mem. Dallas Challenge Task Force, bd. dirs., 1983-88, mem. exec. com., 1983-88; mem. long-range planning com. St. Mark's Sch. Tex., Dallas, 1983-84; mem. exec. com. bd. dirs., chair pub. policy Nat. Crime Prevention Coun., Washington, 1984—; co-chmn., chmn. legis. com., mem. exec. com. Mayor's Criminal Justice Task Force, City of Dallas, 1985-88; mem. Greater Dallas Ahead, Inc., 1985-86, U.S Marshall Selection Com., 1986-87; mem. exec. com. Tex. Criminal Justice Task Force, Austin, 1986-90, vice-chmn., chmn. legis. com., 1986-90; mem. Citizen's Adv. Com. Long-Range Water Supply Study, City of Dallas, 1988-90; mem. Task Force Pub. Utility Regulation, State of Tex., Austin, 1989-90; mem. adv. bd. Dallas United, 1990-92; commr. Pres.'s Commn. Model State Drug Laws, Washington, 1992-93; co-chair Dallas host com. N.Am. Free Trade Agreement Negotiations, 1992; subcom. chmn. fin. com. Ursuline Acad. Dallas, 1992—, mem. bd. of dad's club, 1992—; co-chmn. Dallas Meml. Ctr. Holocaust Studies, Dallas, 1993; mem. mktg. com. Dallas/Ft. Worth Internat. Airport, 1994—; trustee Meth. Med. Ctr., Dallas, 1992, mem. quality rev. com., 1992, mem. long range planning com., 1992; bd. dirs. Swiss Ave. Ctr. Pastoral Care and Family Counseling, Dallas, 1983-88, Cotton Bowl Coun., Dallas, 1984-89, Tex. Bus. Hall of Fame, Dallas, 1988-90, Dallas Summer Musicals, 1992, Nat. Alliance Model State Drug Laws, 1993, mem. exec. com., 1993; sec. bd. dirs. St. Paul Hosp. Found., Dallas, 1985-88. Served with Tex. Air N.G., 1975. Recipient Spl. Recognition award Dallas City Coun., Mayor of Dallas, 1992. Mem. Am. Prosecutors Rsch. Inst., Tex. Bar Assn. (mem., chmn. spl. com. study Tex. election laws 1982-83), ABA, Dallas Bar Assn., Ctrl. Dallas Assn. (mem. exec. com. bd. dirs., mem. govtl. and legal affairs com.), Ducks Unltd., Am. Quarter Horse Assn., Greater Dallas C. of C. (chmn. N.Am. Free Trade Agreement initiatives, former chmn. pub. affairs divsn., past chmn. state govtl. affairs com., former bd. dirs., past mem. exec. com.), U. Tex. Ex-Students Assn. (life), Sigma Alpha Epsilon. Methodist. Clubs: Idlewild, Terpsichorean, Rainbo lake, Tower, Salesmanship Club (Dallas). Administrative and regulatory, Legislative. Office: David A Dean & Assocs PC 8080 Park Ln Ste 600 Dallas TX 75231-5911

DEAN, RONALD GLENN, lawyer; b. Milw., Feb. 18, 1944; children: Elizabeth Lucile, Joshua Henry. BA, Antioch Coll., 1967; JD, U. Wis., 1970. Bar: Wis. 1970, Calif. 1971. Assoc. Mink & Neiman, L.A., 1971; ptnr. Margolis, McTernan, Scope & Sacks, 1974-77; pvt. practice Pacific Palisades, 1977—. Mem. judge pro-tem program L.A. County Bar, 1978-91; judge pro tem Beverly Hills Mcpl. Ct., 1980-90; arbitrator L.A. Superior Ct., 1980—, L.A. County Fee Dispute Panel, 1979-86, 94—, Santa Monica Mcpl. Ct., 1980—; referee for disciplinary matters State Bar Ct., 1980-88, supervising referee, 1984-88, rev. dept. 1988-90, judge pro tem 1990-94. Bd. dirs. Pacific Palisades Residents Assn., 1983—, pres., 1985-88; counsel to Pacific Palisades Cmty. Coun., 1983-92, 2000—, C. of C. rep. to Cmty. Coun., 1995-2000; mem. Councilman's Citizen Adv. Com. to Develop Pacific Palisades Civic League, 1987-89; exec. bd. pacific Palisades Dem. Club, 1990—, pres., 1991, 96; mem. Palisades P.R.I.D.E., 1996—, pres., 1997-98, bd. dirs. Fellow Coll. Labor and Employment Lawyers, Am. Coll. Employee Benefit Counsel (charter, bd. dirs. 2000—); mem. Am. Arbitration Assn. (panel 1974-95), ABA (co-chmn. employee benefits com., labor sect., bd. sr. editors Employee Benefits Law 1995-98, plaintiff co-chair, nat. insts. subcom.), BNA Pension and Benefits Reporter (adv. bd. 1995—, co-chair sr. editors book Employee Benefits Law), Wis. Bar Assn., Calif. State Bar (chmn. pension and trust benefits com. of labor sect. 1984), L.A. County Bar Assn., Antioch Alumni Assn. (dir. 1982-88), Pacific Palisades (Calif.) C. of C. (bd. dirs. 1995—). Pension, profit-sharing, and employee benefits, Personal injury. Office: 15135 W Sunset Blvd Ste 280 Pacific Palisades CA 90272-3735 E-mail: rdean@74erisa.com

DEANE, ELAINE, lawyer; b. Washington, Sept. 10, 1958; d. William Francis Goode and Elizabeth Anne (Downes) Deane. AB, U. Calif., Berkeley, 1980; JD, U. San Francisco, 1986. Bar: Calif. 1986. Assoc. Parkinson, Wolf, Lazar & Leo, L.A., 1985-89, Peltit & Martin, San Francisco, 1989-91, Frandzel & Share, San Francisco, 1992-93, Arter & Haddon, San Francisco, 1994—. Mem. Calif. Bar Assn., L.A. County Bar Assn., Century City Bar Assn., Beverly Hills Bar Assn., San Francisco Bar Assn., Lawyers' Com. for Urban Affairs, Sierra Club, Amnesty Internat., Wilderness Soc., Greenpeace. Avocations: ballet, theatre, environment. Banking, General civil litigation, Insurance. Office: Arter & Haddon 2 Embarcadero Ctr Lbby 4 San Francisco CA 94111-3822

DEANE, RICHARD HUNTER, JR. federal judge; b. Oct. 18, 1952; BA, U. Ga., 1974, JD, 1977; LLM, U. Mich., 1979. Bar: Ga. 1977. Asst. U.S. atty. No. Dist. Ga., 1980-88; chief gen. crimes sect. U.S. Attys. Office, 1988-91, chief criminal divsn., 1991-94; magistrate judge U.S. Dist. Ct. (no. dist.) Ga., Atlanta, 1994-98; U.S. atty. No. Dist. Ga. , 1998—. Office: 1800 US Courthouse 75 Spring St SW Atlanta GA 30303-3331

DEASON, EDWARD JOSEPH, lawyer; b. Pasadena, Calif., July 5, 1955; s. Edward Patrick Deason and Marye Annette (Erramouspe) Kennedy; m. Charlotte Thunberg, Aug. 1, 1987; children: Keelin Marie, Erin Michelle. BA, Loyola Marymount U., 1977, JD, 1982. Bar: Calif. 1983, U.S. Dist. Ct. (ctrl. dist.) Calif. 1983, U.S. Dist. Ct. (ea. dist.) Calif. 1987, U.S. Ct. Appeals (9th cir.) 1993, U.S. Supreme Ct. 1994. Assoc. Law Offices Edwin C. Martin, L.A., 1983-86; ptnr. Martin & Deason, 1986-94; pvt. practice, 1994—. Mem. ATLA, Consumer Attys. of Calif., Trial Lawyers for Pub. Justice, L.A. Lawyers Club, Loyola Scott Moot Ct. Democrat. Roman Catholic. Personal injury. Office: 21515 Hawthorne Blvd Ste 1000 Torrance CA 90503-6505

DEASON, HEROLD MCCLURE, lawyer; b. Alton, Ill., July 24, 1942; s. Ernest Wilburn and Mildred Mary (McClure) D.; m. Wilma Lee Kaemmerle, June 18, 1966; children: Sean, Ian, Whitney. BA, Albion Coll., 1964; JD, Northwestern U., 1967. Bar: Mich. 1968. Assoc. Bodman, Longley & Dahling, LLP, Detroit, 1967-74, ptnr., 1975—. City atty. Grosse Pointe Pk., Mich., 1978—. Vice chmn. Detroit, Windsor Freedom Festival, 1978-92; bd. dirs. Spirit of Detroit Assn., 1980—. Recipient Spirit of Detroit award, Detroit City Coun., 1986. Mem. ABA, Mich. Assn. Mcpl. Attys. (pres. 1995-97), Detroit Bar Assn., Can.-U.S. Bus. Assn. (v.p. 1997—), Grosse Pointe Yacht Club (commodore 1992-93), Detroit Racquet Club, Windsor Club, Clinton River Boat Club. General corporate, Mergers and acquisitions, Municipal (including bonds). Home: 1044 Kensington Ave Grosse Pointe Park MI 48230-1437 Office: Bodman Longley & Dahling 100 Renaissance Ctr 34th Fl Detroit MI 48243-1001 E-mail: hdeason@bodmanlongley.com

DEATHERAGE, WILLIAM VERNON, lawyer; b. Drumright, Okla., Apr. 17, 1927; s. William Johnson and Pearl Mae (Watson) D.; m. Priscilla Ann Campbell, Sept. 16, 1932; children: Thomas William, Andrea Susan. BS, U. Oreg., 1952, LLB with honors, 1954. Bar: Oreg. 1954, U.S. Dist. Ct. Oreg. 1956. Ptnr. Frohnmayer, Deatherage, Pratt, Jamieson & Clarke & Moore, Medford, Oreg., 1954—. Bd. dirs. Oreg. Law Inst., U. Oreg. Found. With USN, 1945-48. Mem. Am. Coll. Trial Lawyers, Internat. Acad. Trial Lawyers, Delta Theta Phi, Rogue Valley Country Club (pres. 1988), Rogue River Valley Univ. Club. Democrat. Episcopalian. E-mail: fdfirm.com. Federal civil litigation, State civil litigation, Insurance. Address: 2592 E Barnett Rd Medford OR 97504-8345

DEAVER, PHILLIP LESTER, lawyer; b. Long Beach, Calif., July 21, 1952; s. Albert Lester and Eva Lucille (Welton) D. Student, USCG Acad., 1970-72; BA, UCLA, 1974; JD, U. So. Calif., 1977. Bar: Hawaii 1977, U.S. Dist. Ct. Hawaii 1977, U.S. Ct. Appeals (9th cir.) 1978, U.S. Supreme Ct. 1981. Assoc. Carlsmith, Wichman, Case, Mukai & Ichiki, Honolulu, 1977-83, ptnr., 1983-86, Bays, Deaver, Lung, Rose & Baba, Honolulu, 1986, mng. ptnr., 1986-95. Contbr. articles to profl. jours. Bd. dirs. Parents and Children Together, v.p. Mem. ABA (forum com. on the Constrn. Industry), AIA (affiliate Hawaii chpt.), Am. Arbitration Assn. (arbitrator). General civil litigation, Construction. Home: 2471 Pacific Heights Rd Honolulu HI 96813-1029 Office: Bays Deaver Lung Rose and Baba PO Box 1760 Honolulu HI 96806-1760 E-mail: pdeaver@legalhawaii.com

DEBAETS, TIMOTHY JOSEPH, lawyer, legal educator; b. South Bend, Ind., Aug. 16, 1949; s. Joseph H. and Dorothy (Marshall) DeB. BA, Columbia U., 1971; JD, Duke U., 1975. Bar: N.Y. 1976, U.S. Dist. Ct. (so. and ea. dists.) N.Y. 1976. Assoc. Simpson Thacher & Bartlett, N.Y.C., 1975-79, Pavia & Harcourt, N.Y.C., 1979-83, Stults & Marshall, N.Y.C., 1983-90, Cowan, DeBaets, Abrahams & Sheppard, N.Y.C., 1990-91, ptnr., 1991—. Asst. adj. prof. NYU Sch. of Arts, N.Y.C., 1984, Sch. of Continuing Film, Video & Edn. dept. of film and video and broadcasting, 1991. Mem. editl. bd. Duke Law Jour., 1974-75; contbr. articles to jours.; lectr., panelist in field. Bd. dirs. Dance Theatre Workshop, N.Y.C., 1981-91, Vol. Lawyers for the Arts. Served with USAR, 1971-77. Mem. ABA (forum com. on entertainment and sports industry 1980—), N.Y. State Bar Assn. (mem. spl. com. on copyright laaw 1981—, chmn. 1984-87, exec. com. sect. on entertainment and sports law 1988—, treas. 1994—, vice chmn. 1996—), Assn. Bar City N.Y. (mem. spl. com. on entertainment and sports law 1980-84, art law com. 1986-89, sports law 1993-95, entertainment law 1997-99), Copyright Soc. U.S. General corporate, Entertainment, Trademark and copyright. Office: Cowan DeBaets Abrahams & Sheppard 40 W 57th St New York NY 10019-4001

DEBDOUB, ALAN, lawyer; b. New Orleans, Sept. 1, 1972; s. Albert James and Flor de Maria Dabdoub. BA cum laude, La. State U., 1994, JD, 1997. Bar: La., U.S. Dist. (ea., we., mid. dists) La., U.S. Ct. Appeals (5th cir.). Assoc. Courtenay, Forstall, Hunger & Fontana, LLP, New Orleans, 1997-98, Montgomery, Barnett, Brown, Read, Hammond & Mintz, LLP, New Orleans, 1998—. Campaign vol. United Way, New Orleans, 1998; mem. Archbishop Cmty. Appeal, New Orleans, 1998. Mem. New Orleans Bar Assn. (mem. teaching law through sports com. 1998—). Avocations: reading, racquetball, travel, teaching. Home: 8721 26th St Metairie LA 70003 Office: Montgomery Barnett 3200 Energy Ctr 1100 Poydras St New Orleans LA 70163

DEBEAUBIEN, HUGO H. lawyer; b. Detroit, Sept. 20, 1948; s. Phillip Frances and June (Hesse) deB.; m. Mary Lazenby, Apr. 30, 1977; 1 child, Hugo Samuel. BS in Bus., Fla. State U., 1970; JD, Stetson U., 1973. Bar: Fla. 1973, U.S. Dist. Ct. (mid. dist.) Fla. 1974, U.S. Supreme Ct. 1978, U.S. Ct. Appeals (11th cir.) 1981. Asst. state atty. Fla. 9th Jud. Cir. Ct., Orlando, 1973-76; ptnr. Drage, deBeaubien, 1976-79; ptnr., pres. Drage, deBeaubien, Knight & Simmons, 1980-87, Drage, deBeaubien, Knight, Simmons, Romano and Neal, Orlando, 1987-98; ptnr. Drage, deBeaubien, Knight, Simmons, Mantzaris and Neal, 1999—. Lectr. Fla. Bar Assn., 1981-83; bd. dirs. Fla. Citrus Sports Assn., 1996—. Mem. ATLA, Nat. Assn. Criminal Def. Lawyers, Fla. State U. Alumni Assn. (bd. dirs. 1986-93, sec. 1993-94, treas. 1995-96, v.p. 1996-97, chmn.-elect 1997-98, chmn. 1998-99), Univ. Club Orlando, Country Club Orlando. Republican. Methodist. Avocations: golf, tennis. State civil litigation, Criminal, Family and matrimonial. Home: 1125 Belleaire Cir Orlando FL 32804-6703 Office: Drage deBeaubien Knight Simmons Mantzaris & Neal 322 N Magnolia Ave Orlando FL 32801-1609 E-mail: hdeBeaubien@dbksmn.com

DEBEVOISE, DICKINSON RICHARDS, federal judge; b. Orange, N.J., Apr. 23, 1924; s. Elliott and Josephine (Richards) D.; m. Katrina Stephenson Leeb, Feb. 24, 1951; children: Kate, Josephine Debevoise Davies, Mary Debevoise Rennie, Abigail D. Byrne. BA, Williams Coll., 1948; LLB, Columbia U., 1951. Bar: N.J. 1953, U.S. Supreme Ct. 1956. Law clk. to Hon. Phillip Forman, chief judge U.S. Dist. Ct. for Dist. N.J., 1952-53; assoc. firm Riker, Emery & Danzig, Newark, 1953-56; partner firm Riker, Danzig, Scherer, Debevoise & Hyland, 1957-79; judge U.S. Dist. Ct. for N.J., 1979—; adj. prof. constitutional law Seton Hall U., 1992-94. Pres. Newark Legal Services Project, 1965-70; chmn. N.J. Gov.'s Workmen's Compensation Study Commn., 1972-73; mem. N.J. Supreme Ct. Adv. Com. on Jud. Conduct, 1974-78; chmn. N.J. Disciplinary Rev. Bd., 1978-79; mem. Lawyers Adv. Com. for 3d Circuit, 1975-79, chmn., 1979; chmn. N.J. Legal Services Adv. Council, 1976-78 Asso. editor: N.J. Law Jour, 1959-79. Trustee Ramapo Coll., N.J., 1969-73, chmn. bd., 1971-73; trustee Williams Coll., 1969-74, Fund for N.J., 1985—; trustee Hosp. Ctr. at Orange, N.J., v.p., 1975-79; pres. Democrats for Good Govt., 1956-60, active various presdl., senatorial, gubernatorial campaigns, active St. Stephens Episcopal Ch. Sgt. U.S. Army, WWII, 1st lt. Korean War. Decorated Bronze Star. Fellow Am. Bar Found.; mem. ABA, N.J. Bar Assn., Fed. Bar Assn. (v.p. 1976), Assn. Fed. Bar State N.J. (v.p. 1977-79), Essex County Bar Assn. (treas. 1960-64, trustee 1968-71), Am. Law Inst., Judicature Soc., Columbia Law Sch. Assn. (bd. dirs., pres. 1992-94). Office: US Dist Ct PO Box 999 Newark NJ 07101-0999

DEBO, VINCENT JOSEPH, lawyer, manufacturing company executive; b. Bklyn., Feb. 14, 1940; s. George and Letitia (Ruggiero) D.; m. Linda Mellucci, June 25, 1966; 1 child, Jennifer Lynn. BS, Fordham U., 1961, JD, 1964. Bar: N.Y. 1965, U.S. Dist. Ct. (so. and ea. dists.) N.Y. 1967, U.S. Tax Ct. 1969, U.S. Ct. Appeals (2d cir.) 1967, U.S. Supreme Ct. 1969. Assoc. various law firms, N.Y.C., 1964-70; corp. counsel Bangor Punta Corp., Greenwich, Conn., 1970-73; from asst. gen. counsel, asst. sec. to v.p., gen. counsel Internat. Rheem Mfg. Co., N.Y.C., 1973—. Dir., officer various corp. subs. and joint ventures. Mem. ABA (subcoms.). Antitrust, Public international, Corporate taxation. Home: 4 Greenlea Ct Westport CT 06883-3016 Office: Rheem Mfg Co 405 Lexington Ave Fl 22D New York NY 10174-0307 E-mail: debovj@nycorp.rheem.com

DEBOIS, JAMES ADOLPHUS, lawyer; b. Oklahoma City, Dec. 23, 1929; s. James D. and Catherine (Bobo) DeB.; m. Mary Catherine Watkins, Aug. 4, 1951; children: James Adolphus Jr., Catherine Cecile, Annette Marie. B.A. in Liberal Arts, Okla. State U., 1951; LL.B., Okla., U., 1955. Bar: Okla. 1954, U.S. Dist. Ct. (ea. dist.) Okla. 1955, U.S. Dist. Ct. (we. dist.) Okla. 1959, Mo. 1963, N.Y. 1965, U.S. Ct. Appeals (8th cir.) 1969, Calif. 1971, U.S. Ct. Appeals (9th cir.) 1971, U.S. Ct. Appeals (D.C. cir.) 1975, U.S. Supreme Ct. 1976. Atty. Southwestern Bell Telephone Co., Oklahoma City, 1959-63, St. Louis, 1963-64, gen. atty., Oklahoma City, 1965-67, gen. solicitor, St. Louis, 1967-70; atty. AT&T, N.Y.C., 1964-65, gen. atty., 1976, gen. atty., Basking Ridge, N.J., 1976-78, assoc. gen. counsel, 1978-83, v.p. law, 1985-93; v.p. legal dept. Pacific Tel. and Tel.

Co., San Francisco, 1970-71, v.p., gen. counsel, 1971-76; v.p., gen. counsel, sec. AT&T Info. Systems Inc. (formerly Am. Bell Inc.), Morristown, N.J., 1983-85. Retired April, 1993. Lt. USAF, 1951-53, Korea. Mem. ABA (chmn. pub. utility law sect. 1985-86), Calif. Bar Assn., San Francisco Bar Assn. (sect. chmn. corp. law dept. 1975). Episcopalian. Club: Baltusrol (bd. govs. Springfield, N.J. 1982—). Administrative and regulatory, General corporate, General practice. Office: AT&T 131 Morristown Rd Rm 2014A Basking Ridge NJ 07920-1655

DE BRIER, DONALD PAUL, lawyer; b. Atlantic City, Mar. 20, 1940; s. Daniel and Ethel de B.; m. Nancy Lee McElroy, Aug. 1, 1964; children: Lesley Anne, Rachel Wynne, Danielle Verne. B.A. in History, Princeton U., 1962; LL.B. with honors, U. Pa., 1967. Bar: N.Y. 1967, Tex. 1977, Utah 1983, Ohio 1987. Assoc. firm Sullivan & Cromwell, N.Y.C., 1967-70, Patterson, Belknap, Webb & Tyler, N.Y.C., 1970-76; v.p., gen. counsel, dir. Gulf Resources & Chem. Corp., Houston, 1976-82; v.p. law Kennecott Corp. (former subs. BP America Inc.), Salt Lake City, 1983-89; assoc. gen. counsel BP America Inc., Cleve., 1987-89; gen. counsel BP Exploration Co. Ltd., London, 1989-93; exec. v.p., gen. counsel Occidental Petroleum Corp., L.A., 1993—. Bd. dirs. L.A. Philharm., 1995—. Served to lt. USNR, 1962-64. Mem. Calif. Club, Riviera Tennis Club. General corporate, General practice, Private international. Home: 699 Amalfi Dr Pacific Palisades CA 90272-4507 Office: Occidental Petroleum Corp 10889 Wilshire Blvd Los Angeles CA 90024-4201

DEBUNDA, SALVATORE MICHAEL, lawyer; b. Phila., June 17, 1943; s. Salvatore and Marie Ann (Carilli) DeB.; children: Lauren, David. BS in Econs., U. Pa., 1965, JD, 1968. Bar: Pa. 1968, U.S. Supreme Ct. 1977. Law clk. to justice Phila. Ct. of Common Pleas, 1968-69; asst. gen. counsel ARA Services, Inc., Phila., 1969-74; sr. assoc. Cohen, Verlin, Sherzer & Porter, 1974-75; v.p., sec., gen. counsel AEL Industries, Inc., Montgomeryville, Pa., 1975-80; v.p., gen. counsel Cooper Assocs., Inc., Marlton, N.J., 1980-81; v.p. cable TV devel. Greater Media, Inc., East Brunswick, 1981-85; ptnr., chmn. media/entertainment law group Fox, Rothschild, O'Brien & Frankel, Phila., 1985-91; shareholder, dir. Pelino & Lentz, PC, 1991—. Mem. ABA, Pa. Bar Assn., Phila. Bar Assn., Fed. Comm. Bar Assn. Avocations: sports, owning thoroughbred horses. Communications, General corporate, Entertainment. Office: Pelino & Lentz PC 1650 Market St One Liberty Pl 32d Fl Philadelphia PA 19103-7393

DECAMPS, CHARLES MICHAEL, lawyer; b. Arlington, Va., Oct. 14, 1950; s. Charles Modeste and Loraine (Seward) DeC.; children: Sarah Hopkins, Christopher Duff, William Michael. BA with honors, U. Va., 1972, JD, 1975. Bar: Va. 1975, U.S. Dist. Ct. (ea. dist.) Va. 1975, U.S. Dist. Ct. (we. dist.) Va. 1975, U.S. Ct. Appeals (4th cir.) 1975. Law clk. U.S. Dist. Ct. (we. dist.) Va., 1975; assoc. Cabell, Paris, Lowenstein & Bareford, Richmond, Va., 1976-86; ptnr., dir. Sands, Anderson, Marks & Miller, 1986—. Chmn. regional com. Young Lawyers Conf., Va. State Bar, 1978-84. Active Am. Cancer Soc., Richmond, 1978-81, United Givers Fund, Richmond, 1981-83; com. mem. St. James Ch., Richmond, 1980-82, vestryman, 1989-92, chmn. mission and outreach com., 1990, sr. warden, 1991; mem. Leadership Metro Richmond, 1991; bd. dirs. Richmond Ambulance Authority, Inc,. 1990—; bd. dirs. Historic Monument Ave. and Fan Dist. Found., Inc., Richmond, 1983-93; bd. dirs. Fan Dist. Assn., 1984-87; pres. West Richmond Little League, 1993-94. Mem. ABA, Richmond Bar Assn., Va. Bar Assn., Westwood Racquet Club (Richmond), Phi Beta Kappa, Omicron Delta Kappa. Episcopalian. Avocations: sports, running, tennis. General civil litigation, Labor, Personal injury. Home: 8963 Wishart Rd Richmond VA 23229-7158 Office: Sands Anderson Marks & Miller PO Box 1998 Richmond VA 23218-1998

DECARLO, DONALD THOMAS, lawyer, insurance company executive; BA in Econs., Iona Coll., 1960; JD, St. John's U., 1969. Bar: N.Y. 1970, U.S. Dist. Ct. (so. and ea. dists.) 1972, U.S. Supreme Ct. 1973; cert. reins. arbitrator. Asst. regional sales dir. Govt. Employees Ins. Co., 1962-71; lawyer, counsel Lee, McCarthy & Derosa, 1971-72; v.p., gen. counsel Nat. Coun. on Compensation Ins., 1972-86; sr. v.p. Am. Ins. Assn., N.Y.C., 1986-87; sr. v.p., gen. counsel Comml. Ins. Resources, Inc., 1987-96; dep. gen. counsel Travelers Corp., 1991-96; gen. counsel Travelers Ins. Cos., 1994-96; exec. v.p., gen. counsel Gulf Ins. Co., N.Y.C., 1987-97; ptnr. Lord, Bissell & Brook, 1997—. Apptd. master arbitrator N.Y. Inst. Supt.; adj. prof. NYU, Coll. Ins.; mem. Def. Rsch. Inst.; mem. N.Y. State commrs. N.Y. State Fund, 1997—. Author: (with D.J. Gruenfeld) Stress in the American Workplace--Alternatives for the Working Wounded, 1989, (with M. Minkowitz) Workers Compensation Insurance and Law Practice--The Next Generation, 1989; contbr. articles to profl. jours. Mem. ABA (past chmn. workers' compensation com., chair corp. counsel com. 1992-93), Assn. of Bar of City of N.Y. (ins. com.), Queens County Bar Assn. (past chmn. ins. com.), N.Y. State Bar Assn. (worker's compensation), N.Y. County Lawyers Assn. (chair workers' compensation com. 1993). Alternative dispute resolution, Insurance, Workers' compensation. Home: 200 Manor Rd Douglaston NY 11363-1130 Office: Lord Bissell & Brook 1 Penn Plz New York NY 10119-0002

DECKER, JOHN FRANCIS, lawyer, educator; b. Sherrill, Iowa, May 15, 1944; s. Lawrence and Loretta (Hefel) D. BA, U. Iowa, 1967; JD, Creighton U., 1970; LLM, NYU, 1971, JSD, 1979. Bar: Calif. 1973, U.S. Dist. Ct. (no. dist.) Calif. 1973, Ill. 1978, U.S. Dist. Ct. (no. dist.) Ill. 1980, U.S. Ct. Appeals (7th cir.) 1981. Asst. prof. law DePaul U. Coll. Law, Chgo., 1971-73, assoc. prof., 1974-79, prof. law, 1979—, coord. extern program, 1978—. Counsel R.E. Robbins Law Firm, Stockton, Ill., 1978-79; vis. prof. U. San Francisco Sch. Law, 1980; reporter Ill. Jud. Conf., Chgo., 1981—. Author: Prostitution: Regulation and Control, 1979, Revolution to the Right, 1982, The Investigation and Prosecution of Arson, 1999, Illinois Criminal Law: A Survey of Crimes and Defenses, 3d edit., 2000; contbr. articles to profl. jours.; staff editor Creighton Law Rev., 1969-70. Recipient award of Distinction, DePaul Law Rev., 1978, Excellence in Teaching, DePaul U., 1999. Mem. ABA, Assn. Trial Lawyers Am. Democrat. Roman Catholic. Home: 306 Maple Ave Elmhurst IL 60126-2333 Office: DePaul Univ Coll of Law 25 E Jackson Blvd Chicago IL 60604-2289 E-mail: jdecker1@depaul.edu

DECKER, MICHAEL LYNN, lawyer, judge; b. Oklahoma City, May 5, 1953; s. Leroy Melvin and Yvonne (Baird) D. BA, Oklahoma City U., 1975, JD, 1978; grad., Nat. Jud. Coll., U. Nev., Reno, 1990. Bar: Okla. 1978, U.S. Ct. Appeals (10th cir.) 1979, U.S. Dist. Ct. (we. dist.) Okla. 1985, U.S. Supreme Ct. 1994. Assoc. Bay, Hamilton, Lees, Spears, and Verity, Oklahoma City, 1978-80; assoc. dir. devel. Oklahoma City U., 1980-81, asst. dean, Sch. of Law, 1981-82; sr. oil and gas adminstrv. law judge Okla. Corp. Commn., Oklahoma City, 1982-92, sr. asst. gen. counsel oil and gas conservation, 1992-95, deputy gen. counsel oil and gas conservation, 1995—. Campaign staff intern U.S. Senator Henry Bellmon's Re-election Campaign, 1974; mem. Civil Arbitration Panel, U.S. Dist. Ct. (we. dist.) Okla., 1985—; seminar spkr. Am. Inst. Profl. Geologists (Okla. sect.), 1985, Conf. on Consumer Fin. Law, Oil and Gas Law Inst., 1999-2001; mem. dean's adv. com. Oklahoma City U. Law Sch., 1986; mem. sys. rev. bd. Okla. Corp. Commn., 1990-93, mem. process mgmt. rev. team, 1995-96; lectr. adminstrv. law Vanderbilt U. Sch. Law, 1993; mem. legal and regulatory affairs com. Interstate Oil and Gas Compact Commn., 2000— Trustee Oklahoma City U., 1989—91, mem. alumni bd. dirs., 1988—95; mem. com. of twenty Oklahoma City Art Mus., 1987—95, co-chair omelette party, 1990; vol. Contact Teleminister, Oklahoma City, 1986—91; Okla. Corp. Commn., 1990; mem. Class XI Leadership Oklahoma City, 1993; area rep. Okla. Mozart Festival, Bartlesville, 1988—; mem. adminstrv. bd. St. Luke's United Meth. Ch., 1988—92, chair missions com., 1993—94; mem. nat. alumni bd. dirs. Oklahoma City U., 2000—, also mem. devel. com., long range planning com. and adminstrv. liaison com.; bd. dirs. Eldercare Access Ctr., Inc., 2001—, Contact Teleminister, Oklahoma City, 1987—90, March of Dimes Western Okla., 1990—93. Mem.: Okla. Bar Assn. (mineral law sect., environ. law sect.), Okla. County Bar Assn. (exec. com. young lawyers sect. 1978—82, mem. law day com. 1979—88, chmn. law day luncheon spkr. com. 1979—88), Oklahoma City Mineral Lawyers Soc., Oklahoma City Dinner Club, Raymer Soc. for the Arts (bd. dirs., Lindsborg, Kans. 1999—), Lions, Phi Alpha Delta, Lambda Chi Alpha (treas. bldg. corp. 1984—89, pres. 1989—91, Outstanding Alumnus award 1983). Republican. Administrative and regulatory, Oil, gas, and mineral. Home: 2008 NW 44th St Oklahoma City OK 73118-1902 Office: Okla Corp Commn State Capitol Complex Jim Thorpe Bldg PO Box 52000 Oklahoma City OK 73152-2000

DEDMAN, ANNE GODDARD, lawyer; b. Dallas, Aug. 21, 1972; d. Thomas Curry Dedman and Elizabeth Dedman Alexander. 0BA, Ohio U., 1994; JD, U. Louisville, 1997. Bar: Ky. 1997, Ind. Assoc. Sheffer Hutchinson Kinney, Louisville, 1997—. Chmn. com. creative black tie fundraiser Am. Cancer Soc., Louisville, 1998—. Mem. ABA, Ky. Bar Assn., Ind. Bar Assn., Louisville Bar Assn. Presbyterian. Personal injury. Office: Sheffer Hutchinson Kinney Ste 1600 National City Tower Louisville KY 40202

DEENER, JEROME ALAN, lawyer; b. Newark, Jan. 23, 1943; s. Harry Simon and Ann Deener; m. Brenda Diane Appelbaum, June 28, 1965; children: Elisa Teri Deener-Agus, Shira Ann, Avi Michael. BS in Acctg., Pa. State U., 1965; JD, Bklyn. Law Sch., 1968; LLM in Taxation, NYU, 1971. Bar: N.Y. 1968, N.J. 1972, U.S. Dist. Ct. N.Y. 1971, U.S. Ct. Appeals 1981. Sr. tax acct. Arthur Andersen, N.Y.C., 1968-71; tax assoc. Herbert M. Gannet, Esq., Newark, 1971-72, Gruen, Sorkow & Sorkow, Hackensack, N.J., 1972-74; ptnr. Deener & Fond, 1974-79; sr. ptnr. Jerome A. Deener, P.C., 1980—, Deener Feingold & Stern, Hackensack, 1980—. Contbr. articles to profl. jours. Past pres. Solomon Schechter Day Sch., Cranford, N.J., 1983-84. Fellow Am. Coll. Trust and Estate Counsel; mem. Estate Planning Coun. Bergen County (pres. 1973). Jewish. Avocations: travel, tennis, photography, bike riding, hiking. Estate planning, Estate taxation, Taxation, general. Office: Deener Feingold & Stern PC Two University Plaza Hackensack NJ 07601

DEER, RICHARD ELLIOTT, lawyer; b. Indpls., Sept. 8, 1932; s. Leon Leslie and Mary Jane (Ostheimer) D.; m. Lee Todd, Feb. 22, 1958; children: William K., Laura A., Susannah T., Thomas E. A.B., DePauw U., 1954; LL.B. magna cum laude, Harvard U., 1957. Bar: Ind. 1957, U.S. Dist. Ct. (no. and so. dists.) Ind. 1957, U.S. Ct. Appeals (7th cir.) 1957, U.S. Ct. Appeals (9th cir.) 1990, U.S. Supreme Ct. 1962. Assoc. firm Barnes & Thornburg and predecessor firm, Indpls., 1957-65, ptnr., 1965—, chmn. mgmt. com., 1990-93; dir. Flagship Capital Corp., Indpls. Author: Indiana Corporation Law and Practice, 1990, Supplement, 1994; co-author: Indiana Limited Liability Company Forms and Practice Manual, 1996, Supplement, 1997; bd. editors Harvard Law Rev., 1956-57; contbr. articles to legal jours.; chief reporter: The Lawyer's Basic Corporate Practice Manual, 3d edit., 1984. Mem. Indpls. Coun. Fgn. Relations, Ind. Corps. Survey Commn., 1983—. Fellow Am. Bar Found., Ind. Bar Found.; mem. Indpls. Bar Assn., Ind. State Bar Assn. (past chmn. corp., banking and bus. law sect.), ABA (drafting com., exec. planning group of legal opinion project sect. bus. law, 3d party legal opinion report 1991), Am. Law Inst. Clubs: Hillcrest Country, Players, Columbia. General corporate, Mergers and acquisitions, Public utilities. Office: Barnes & Thornburg 11 S Meridian St Ste 1313 Indianapolis IN 46204-3535

DEFEIS, ELIZABETH FRANCES, law educator, lawyer; b. N.Y.C. d. Francis Paul and Lena (Amendola) D. BA, St. John's U., 1956, JD, 1958, JSD (hon.), 1984; LLM, NYU, 1971; postgrad., U. Milan, Italy, 1963-64, Inst. Internat. Human Rights, 1991. Bar: N.Y. 1959, U.S. Dist. Ct. (fed. dist.) 1960, U.S. Dist. Ct. (so. dist.) N.Y. 1961, U.S. Supreme Ct. 1965, U.S. Dist. Ct. (ea. dist.) N.Y. 1978, N.J. 1983. Asst. U. S. atty. So. Dist. N.Y., Dept. Justice, 1961-62; atty. RCA Corp., 1962-63; assoc. Carter, Ledyard & Milburn, N.Y.C., 1963-69; atty. Bedford Stuyvesant Legal Svcs. Corp., 1969-70; prof. law Seton Hall U., Newark, 1971—, dean Sch. Law, 1983-88. Vis. prof. St. Louis U. Sch. Law, 1988, St. John's U. Sch. Law, 1990, U. Milan, Italy, 1996; Fulbright-Hays lectr., Iran, India, 1977-79; lectr. Orgn. Security and Cooperation in Europe, Russia, Turkmenistan, Tajikistan, Azerbaijan; vis. scholar Ctr. Study of Human Rights, Columbia U., 1989; project dir. TV series Women and Law, 1974-80; narrator TV series Alternatives to Violence, 1981; mem. com. women and cts. N.J. Supreme Ct., 1982-95; trustee Legal Svcs. N.J., 1983-88; mem. 3rd Cir. Task Force on Equality in the Cts., 1995-98; tech. cons. on Constitution of Armenia, 1992-95; project dir. T.V. series Pub. Internat. Law.; legal expert Armenia election OSCE, 1998. Chair Albert Einstein Inst., Boston, 1995—. Fulbright-Hays scholar Milan, Italy, 1963-64, Fulbright-Hays, Orgn. for Security and Cooperation in Europe scholar, Armenia, Russia, Italy, 1996; Ford Found. fellow, 1970-71. Mem. ABA, Nat. Italian Am. Bar Assn., Columbian Lawyers Assn., Assn. of Bar of City of N.Y. (internat. law com., coun. internat. affairs), N.J. Bar Assn., Nat. Italian Am. Found. Office: Seton Hall U Law Sch One Newark Ctr Newark NJ 07102 E-mail: defeisel@shu.edu

DEFFINA, THOMAS VICTOR, lawyer, consultant; b. N.Y.C., Mar. 14, 1942; s. Philip Anthony and Antoinette (Napoli) D. BA, St. John's U., Jamaica, N.Y., 1964, JD, 1967. Bar: N.Y. 1967, U.S. Dist. Ct. (so. and ea. dists.) N.Y. 1968, U.S. Ct. Customs and Patent Appeals 1968. Assoc. Manton, Giaimo, P.C., N.Y.C., 1968-74; Anthony L. Schiavetti Law Practice, N.Y.C., 1974-77; ptnr. Deffina & Blau, P.C., N.Y.C., 1977-86, Deffina, Rosner & Nocera, N.Y.C., 1986—; trial cons. Employers Ins. Wausau, N.Y.C., 1977—, Aetna Casualty and Surety, N.Y.C., 1986; group coun. Mut. Ins. Co., N.Y.C.; talk show panelist Readers Digest Lifeline, Nat. Pub. Svc. TV, 1982. Mem. ABA, N.Y. State Bar Assn., N.Y. State Trial Lawyers Assn. Republican. Roman Catholic. Club: Downtown Athletic. Federal civil litigation, State civil litigation, Personal injury. Home: 8 Mountain Run Boonton NJ 07005-8709 Office: Deffina & Blau 377 Broadway New York NY 10013-3907

DEGALA, CESAR BUENAFE, lawyer; b. Bklyn., Nov. 16, 1972; BA, SUNY, Albany, 1994. Bar: N.Y. 1998. Assoc. Gary B. Pillerdorf & Assoc., N.Y.C., 1998—. Mem. N.Y. State Trial Lawyers Assn., Am. Trial Lawyers Assn., N.Y. County Lawyers Assn. Office: Gary B Pillersdorf & Assocs 225 Broadway New York NY 10007

DEGNAN, JOHN MICHAEL, lawyer; b. Mpls., Apr. 2, 1948; s. John F. and Lorraine A. D.; m. Barbara B. Degnan; children: John Patrick, Amy Marie, David Charles. BA, U. Minn., 1970; JD, William Mitchell Coll. Law, 1976. Bar: Minn. 1976, U.S. Dist. Ct. Minn. 1976, U.S. Ct. Appeals (8th cir.) Minn. 1976, U.S. Supreme Ct. 1976. Ins. underwriter Marsh & McLennan, Mpls., 1973-76; lawyer, pres. Bassford, Lockhart, Truesdell & Briggs, P.A., 1976—. Lectr. in field. Bd. dirs. Hennepin County Pub. Libraries, 1980-84, Storefront Youth Action, 1981-83, Mediation Ctr., 1991—. 1st lt. U.S. Army, 1971-72, Vietnam. Fellow Am. Coll. Trial Lawyers, Am. Bd. Trial Advs.; mem. ABA, Minn. State Bar Assn. (ins. com., lectr. convs. 1984-85, civil trial cert. governing coun., cert. trial specialist), Hennepin County Bar Assn. (mem. professionalism com.), Nat. Bd. Trial Advocacy (cert. civil trial specialist), Am. Bd. Trial Advocates, Minn. Def. Lawyers Assn (bd. dirs. 1986—, pres. 1990-91), Minn. Soc. Hosp. Attys., Def. Rsch. Inst., Am. Soc. Law and Medicine, Richfield Jaycees (past pres.). Avocations: running, tennis, golf, boating, sports. State civil litigation, Insurance, Personal injury. Office: Bassford Lockhart Truesdell & Briggs 3550 Multifoods Tower Minneapolis MN 55402

DE GOFF, VICTORIA JOAN, lawyer; b. San Francisco, Mar. 2, 1945; d. Sidney Francis and Jean Frances (Alexander) De G.; m. Peter D. Coppelman, May 2, 1971 (div. Dec. 1978); m. Richard Sherman, June 16, 1980. BA in Math. with great distinction, U. Calif., Berkeley, 1967, JD, 1972. Bar: Calif. 1972, U.S. Dist. Ct. (no. dist.) Calif. 1972, U.S. Ct. Appeals 1972, U.S. Supreme Ct. 1989; cert. appellate law specialist, 1996. Rsch. atty. Calif. Ct. Appeal, San Francisco, 1972-73; Reginald Heber Smith Found. fellow San Francisco Neighborhood Legal Assistance Found., 1973-74; assoc. Field, De Goff, Huppert & McGowan, San Francisco, 1974-77; pvt. practice Berkeley, Calif., 1977-80; ptnr. De Goff and Sherman, 1980—. Lectr. continuing edn. of bar, Calif., 1987, 90-92, U. Calif. Boalt Hall Sch. Law, Berkeley, 1981-85, dir. appellate advocacy, 1992; cons. Calif. Civil Practice Procedure, Bancroft Whitney, 1992; mem. Appellate Law Adv. Commn., 1995; apptd. applicant evaluation and nomination com. for State Bar Ct. by Calif. Supreme Ct., 1995, 2000; pvt. atty., clk. ct. com. Calif. Ct. Appeals, 1997-99; mem. com. on appellate practice ABA, 1997. Author: (with others) Matthew Bender's Treatise on California Torts, 1985. Apptd. to adv. com. Calif. Jud. Coun. on Implementing Proposition 32, 1984-85; mem. adv. bd. Hastings Coll. Trial and Appellate Adv., 1984-91; expert 20/20 vision project, commn. on future cts. Jud. Coun. Calif., 1993, apptd. to appellate standing adv. com., 1993-95; apptd. to Appellate Indigent Def. Oversight Adv. Com., State of Calif., 1995—; com. on appellate stds. of ABA Appellate Judges Conf., 1995-96; com. on appellate practice ABA, 1997; adv. bd. Witkin Legal Inst., Bancroft Whitney, 1996—; bd. dirs. Calif. Supreme Ct. Hist. Soc. (sec. 1999—), State Bar Calif., Appellate Law Cons. Group, 1994-95; appointee 9th Jud. Cir. Hist. Soc. Hon. Cecil Poole Biography Project, 1998. Fellow Woodrow Wilson Found., 1967-68. Mem. Calif. Trial Lawyers Assn. (bd. govs. 1980-88, amicus-curiae com. 1981-87, editor-in-chief assn. mag. 1980-81, Presdl. award of merit 1980, 81), Calif. Acad. Appellate Lawyers (sec.-treas. 1989-90, 2d v.p. 1990-91, 1st v.p. 1991-92, pres. 1992-93), Am. Acad. Appellate Lawyers, Edward J. McFetridge Am. Inn of Cts. (counsellor 1990-91, edn. chmn. 1991-92, social chmn. 1992-93, v.p. 1993-94, pres. 1994-95), Boalt Hall Sch. Law U. Calif. Alumni Assn. (bd. dirs. 1989-91), Order of Coif. Jewish. General civil litigation, Personal injury. Office: 1916 Los Angeles Ave Berkeley CA 94707-2419

DEGRANDPRE, CHARLES ALLYSON, lawyer; b. Manchester, N.H., July 7, 1936; s. Arthur Vital and Andrea Amanda (L'Etoile) DeG. AB, Clark U., 1958; JD, U. Mich., 1961. Bar: N.H. 1961, U.S. Dist. Ct. N.H. 1964, U.S. Supreme Ct. 1969. Dir. McLane, Graf, Raulerson & Middleton, P.A., Portsmouth, N.H., 1968—. Trustee, chair Smith Found., Manchester, 1986—; bd. dirs. Greater Piscataqua Cmty. Found., 1990-97. Author: Probate Law and Procedure, 1990, 2d edit., 1996, Wills, Trusts and Gifts, 1992, 3d edit., 1997. Chair bd. trustees Canterbury Shaker Village, 1992-97; trustee Strawbery Banke Mus., 1996—; bd. dirs. N.H. Bar Found., 1997—; trustee, chair Smith Found., Manchester, 1986-99; bd. dirs. Greater Piscataqua Cmty. Found., 1990-97, Seacoast Land Trust, 1997—. Recipient N.H. Vol. of Yr. award Office of Gov., Concord, N.H., 1982. Fellow Am. Coll. Trust and Estate Counsel; mem. N.H. Bar Assn. (Pres.'s award 1983). Avocations: hiking, reading, wine. General corporate, Estate planning, Probate. Home: 60 Pleasant Point Dr Portsmouth NH 03801-5265 Office: McLane Graf Raulerson & Middleton PO Box 4316 30 Penhallow St Portsmouth NH 03801-3816 E-mail: cdegrandpre@mclane.com

DE HAAN, KAREN L. lawyer, accountant; b. Long Beach, Calif., Mar. 24, 1968; d. John Maurice De Haan and Linda Louise Hanna. BS, N.E. Mo. State U., 1990; acctg. cert., Northwestern U., 1994; JD, U. Louisville, 1998. Bar: Ky. 1998. CPA, Ill. Sec. Lazar & Karasick, MD, Evanston, Ill., 1991-95; assoc. Golddberg & Simpson, Louisville, 1998—. Acct. Chilton & Medley, Louisville, part-time 1999. Mem. devel. bd. Actor's Theater, Louisville, 1998—. Mem. ABA, AICPA, Ky. Bar Assn., Ky. Soc. CPA's, Ill. CPA Soc., Louisville Bar Assn., Women Lawyers Assn., Jr. League Louisville (provisional), Bus. and Profl. Women River City, Brandeis Soc., Phi Beta Phi. Home: 5180 Charlestown Crossing Way New Albany IN 47150-9394 Office: Goldberg & Simpson 3000 National City Tower Louisville KY 40202

DE HOYOS, DEBORA M. lawyer; b. Monticello, N.Y., Aug. 10, 1953; d. Luis and Marion (Kinney) de H.; m. Walter C. Carlson, June 20, 1981; children: Amanda, Greta, Linnea. BA, Wellesley Coll., 1975; JD, Harvard U., 1978. Bar: Ill. 1978, U.S. Dist. Ct. (no. dist.) Ill. 1980. Assoc. Mayer, Brown & Platt, Chgo., 1978-84, ptnr., 1985—, mng. ptnr., 1991—. Bd. dirs. Evanston Northwestern Healthcare; bd. trustees Providence St. Mel. Sch. Contbr. chpt. to Securitization of Financial Assets, 1991. Trustee Chgo. Symphony Orch. Office: Mayer Brown & Platt 190 S La Salle St Ste 3100 Chicago IL 60603-3441

DE JONG, DAVID SAMUEL, lawyer, educator; b. Washington, Jan. 8, 1951; s. Samuel and Dorothy (Thomas) De J.; m. Tracy Ann Barger, Sept. 23, 1995; 1 child, Jacob Samuel. BA, U. Md., 1972; JD, Washington and Lee U., 1975; LLM in Taxation, Georgetown U., 1979. Bar: Md. 1975, U.S. Dist. Ct. Md. 1977, U.S. Tax Ct. 1977, U.S. Ct. Appeals (4th cir.) 1978, U.S. Supreme Ct. 1979, D.C. 1980, U.S. Dist. Ct. D.C. 1983, U.S. Ct. Claims, U.S. Ct. Appeals (fed. cir.) 1983; CPA, Md.; cert. valuation analyst. Atty. Gen. Bus. Svcs., Inc., Rockville, Md., 1975-80; ptnr. Stein Sperling Bennett De Jong Driscoll & Greenfeig, PC, 1980—. Adj. prof. Southea. U., Washington, 1979-85, Am. U., Washington, 1983—; instr. U. Md., College Park, 1986-87, Montgomery Coll., Rockville, 1983; mem. character com. 7th Appeals Cir. Md. Ct. of Appeals. Co-author: (ann. book) J.K. Lasser's Year-Round Tax Strategies, 1989—; editor Notes and Comments, Washington and Lee U. Law Rev., 1974-75. V.p. Seneca Whetstone Homeowners Assn., Gaithersburg, Md., 1981-82, pres. 1982-83. Mem. ABA, AICPA, Am. Assn. Atty.-CPAs (bd. dirs. 1997—, sec. 1998-99, treas. 1999-2000, v.p. 2000—), Md. Bar Assn., Montgomery County Bar Assn. (chmn. tax sect. 1991-92, treas. 1996-97), D.C. Bar Assn., Md. Assn. CPAs, D.C. Inst. CPAs, Nat. Assn. Cert. Valuation Analysts, Inst. Bus. Appraisers, Md. Soc. Accts., Phi Alpha Delta. Corporate taxation, Estate taxation, Personal income taxation. Office: 25 W Middle Ln Rockville MD 20850-2214

DEKIEFFER, DONALD EULETTE, lawyer; b. Newport, R.I., Nov. 8, 1945; s. Robert and Melissa (Hibberd) deK.; m. Nancy Kishida, June 27, 1970; 1 child, Nathan Hiroyuki. BA, U. Colo., 1968; JD, Georgetown U., 1971. Bar: U.S. Supreme Ct. 1982, U.S. Ct. Appeals (D.C. cir.) 1971, U.S. Dist. Ct. D.C. 1971, U.S. Ct. Claims 1971, U.S. Ct. Internat. Trade 1971. Mem. profl. staff Senate Rep. Policy Com., 1969-71; assoc. Collier, Shannon, Rill & Edwards, 1971-74; ptnr. Collier, Shannon, Rill, Edwards & Scott, 1974-80, deKieffer, Berg & Creskoff, 1980; gen. counsel U.S. Trade Rep., Washington, 1981-83; ptnr. Plaia, Schaumburg & deKieffer, Washington, 1983-84, Pillsbury, Madison & Sutro, Washington, 1984-92, deKieffer Dibble & Horgan, Washington, 1992—. Author: How to Lobby Congress, 1981, Doing Business with the USA, 1984, Doing Business with Romania, 1985, Doing Business in the United States, 1985, Doing Business With the New Romania, 1991, International Business Travellers Companion, 1992, How Lawyers Screw Their Clients, 1996, The Citizens Guide to Lobbying Congress, 1997. Mem. Presdl. Transition Team, 1980-81. Mem. ABA, D.C. Bar, Bar Assn. D.C., Fed. Bar Assn., Am. Soc. Internat. Law, Internat. Antitrust Soc. E-mail: ddekieffer@dhlaw.com. Antitrust, Private international, Public international. Office: deKieffer & Horgan 729 15th St NW Ste 800 Washington DC 20005-2105

DELA CRUZ, JOSE SANTOS, retired state supreme court justice; b. Saipan, Commonwealth No. Mariana Islands, July 18, 1948; s. Thomas Castro and Remedio Sablan (Santos) Dela C.; m. Rita Tenorio Sablan, Nov. 12, 1977; children: Roxanne, Renee, Rica Ann. BA, U. Guam, 1971; JD, U. Calif., Berkeley, 1974; cert., Nat. Jud. Coll., Reno, 1985. Bar: No. Mariana Islands, 1974, U.S. Dist. Ct. No. Mariana Islands 1978. Staff atty. Micro. Legal Svcs. Corp., Saipan, 1974-79; gen. counsel Marianas Pub. Land Corp., 1979-81; liaison atty. CNMI Fed. Laws Commn., 1981-83; ptnr. Borja & Dela Cruz, 1983-85; assoc. judge Commonwealth Trial Ct., 1985-89; state supreme ct. chief justice Supreme Ct. No. Mariana Islands, 1989-95; retired, 1995. Mem. Conf. of Chief Justices, 1989-95, Adv. Commn. on Judiciary, Saipan, 1980-82; chmn. Criminal Justice Planning Agy., Saipan, 1985-95. Mem. Coun. for Arts, Saipan, 1982-83; chmn. Bd. of Elections, Saipan, 1977-82; pres. Cath. Social Svcs., Saipan, 1982-85. Mem. No. Marianas Bar Assn. (pres. 1984-85). Roman Catholic. Avocations: golf, reading, walking.

DE LACY, RICHARD MICHAEL, arbitrator; b. Kingston upon Hull, Eng., Dec. 4, 1954; m. Sybil del Strother; children: Barbara, Edward, Philippa. MA, Clare Coll., Cambridge, 1975. Bar: Eng. 1976, Wales 1976. Comml. barrister Chambers of C. Symons QC & J.Jarvis QC, London, 1976—. Editor: Bullen & Leake & Jacob, Precedents of Pleading, 2000. Fellow Chartered Inst. of Arbitrators; mem. Queen's Counsel Eng. Avocations: music, equestrianism, wine. Office: Chambers C Symons & J Jarvi 3 Verulam Bldgs London WC1R 5NT England Office Fax: 44-2078318479. E-mail: rdelacy@vb.com

DELAFUENTE, CHARLES, lawyer, educator, journalist; b. N.Y.C., Oct. 6, 1945; s. Maurice and Rose (Schulder) De La F.; m. Jill Rosenfeld, Apr. 8, 1979; children: Marc, Carla. Student, Queens Coll., Flushing, N.Y., 1962-66; BA, SUNY, Albany, 1979; JD cum laude, Yeshiva U., N.Y.C., 1981. Bar: N.Y. 1982, D.C. 1985. Night city editor N.Y. Post, N.Y.C., 1969-78; assoc. Herzfeld & Rusin, 1981-83; atty. Fed. Jud. Ctr., Washington, 1984-85; fgn. desk editor UPI, 1985-87; asst. city editor Daily News, N.Y.C., 1987-90; asst. mng. editor Times Union, Albany, N.Y., 1990-94; dep. met. editor Daily News, N.Y.C., 1949-95; editor Record, Troy, N.Y., 1995-96; ptnr. Forman & De La Fuente, Latham, 1997-98; staff editor N.Y. Times, 1998—. Del. N.Y. State Fair Trial/Free Press Com., Albany, 1994-96; adj. prof. George Washington Coll. Law, Washington, 1985-87, Cardozo Law Sch. Yeshiva U., 1989-90. Mem. Order of Barristers. Appellate, Constitutional, Libel.

DELANEY, HERBERT WADE, JR. lawyer; b. Leadville, Colo., Mar. 30, 1925; s. Herbert Wade and Marie Ann (Garbarino) DeL.; m. Ramona Rae Ortiz, Aug. 6, 1953; children: Herbert Wade III, Paula Rae, Bonnie Marie. BSBA, U. Denver, 1949, LLB, 1951. Bar: Colo. 1951, U.S. Supreme Ct. 1959. Pvt. practice, Denver, 1953-64, 1965-91, 94—; mem. firm DeLaney and Sandven, P.C., 1992-94; faculty U. Denver, Colo., 1960-61, 89; ptnr. DeLaney & West, Denver, 1964-65. Capt. JAG's Dept., USAF, 1951-53. Mem. Colo. Bar Assn., Denver Bar Assn., Am. Legion, Masons, Elks, Phi Alpha Delta. Bankruptcy, State civil litigation, Personal injury. Office: 50 S Steele St Ste 660 Denver CO 80209

DELANEY, JOHN MARTIN, JR. lawyer; b. Alton, Ill., Aug. 14, 1956; s. John Martin and Joan Margaret (Galloway) D.; m. Julia Ann Spurgeon, Nov. 23, 1984; children: Margaret Louise, Victoria Jane, John M. III. BA, St. Louis U., 1978, JD, 1981. Bar: Ill. 1981, U.S. Dist. Ct. (so. dist.) Ill. 1985, Mo. 1990, U.S. Dist. Ct. (ea. dist.) Mo. 1990. Law clk. Madison County Cts., Edwardsville, Ill., 1978-79, Dunham Boman & Leskera, East St. Louis, 1980-81; asst. states atty. Madison County States Atty.'s Office, Edwardsville, 1981-84; assoc. Allen, Mendenhall & Assocs., Alton, Ill., 1985-89, Allen, Meyer, Mendenhall, Hackett & Delaney, 1989-90, Allen, Mendenhall, Delaney & Assocs., 1990-92, Smith, Allen, Mendenhall, Deleney & Assocs., 1992-96, Law Office of John Delaney, 1996—. Instr. criminal law and procedure Lewis and Clark C.C., Godfrey, Ill., 1986—. Bd. dirs. Cen. Bapt. Bd., Collinsville, Ill., 1982-83, Blue Knights Law Enforcement, Edwardsville, 1983-85; trustee Godfrey Village & Township, 1993-99. Named to Outstanding Young Men Am. U.S. Jaycees, 1983. Mem. Ill. State Bar Assn., Madison County Bar Assn., Alton-Wood River Bar Assn. Roman Catholic. Criminal, General practice, Pension, profit-sharing, and employee benefits. Office: Law Office of John Delaney 346 W Saint Louis Ave East Alton IL 62024-1148 E-mail: reywal@yahoo.com

DELANEY, MICHAEL FRANCIS, lawyer; b. Washington, Jan. 22, 1948; s. Donald J. and Evelyn A. (Edwards) D.; m. Sally E. Jenkins, July 30, 1977 (div. Nov. 1984); 1 child, Patrick Neal; m. Kathleen Lynette Gibbons, Feb. 22, 1986; children: Rebecca Marie, Laura Margaret. BA, U. Kans., 1969, JD, 1976. Bar: Mo. 1976, U.S. Dist. Ct. (we. dist.) Mo. 1976, U.S. Ct. Appeals (8th cir.) 1978, U.S. Ct. Appeals (10th cir.) 1979. Assoc. Spencer, Fane, Britt & Browne, Kansas City, Mo., 1976-81, ptnr., 1982—, mng. ptnr., 1992-93. Lectr. law U. Kans., Lawrence, 1977-78, 92-93. Articles editor U. Kans. Law Rev., 1975. Active Kansas City Tomorrow, 1982; mem. steering com. Kansas City Vets. Meml. Fund, 1984-88; vol. citizen rev. agy. rels. com. United Way, Kansas City, 1984—; co-chmn. Heartland Labor and Employment Conf., 1988—; bd. mem. Harwycke Homes Assn. Capt. U.S. Army, 1969-73, Vietnam. Mem. ABA, Mo. Bar Assn., Kans. City Met. Bar Assn., Lawyers Assn. Kansas City, Edn. Law Assn., Nat. Sch. Bds. Assn., Mo. Coun. Sch. Attys., U. Kans. Law Soc. (bd. govs. 1988-92), Kansas City Tomorrow Alumni Assn. (bd. dirs. 1990-94), Democrat. Roman Catholic. Federal civil litigation, Education and schools, Labor. Home: 5710 W 130th St Overland Park KS 66209-3645 Office: Spencer Fane Britt & Browne 1000 Walnut St Ste 1400 Kansas City MO 64106-2140 E-mail: mdelaney@speakerfone.com

DE LASA, JOSÉ M. lawyer; b. Havana, Cuba, Nov. 28, 1941; came to U.S., 1961; s. Miguel and Conchita de Lasa; m. Maria Teresa Figueroa, Nov. 23, 1963; children: Maria Teresa, José, Andrés, Carlos. BA, Yale U., 1968, JD, 1971. Bar: N.Y. 1973. Assoc. Cleary, Gottlieb, Steen & Hamilton, N.Y.C., 1971-76; legal dept. Bristol-Myers Squibb Co., 1976-94; sr. v.p., sec. and gen. counsel Abbott Labs., 1994—. Lectr. internat. law, various locations. Bd. dirs. Am. Arbitration Assn., Chgo. Children's Mus., The Resource Found., Chgo. Coun. Fgn. Rels., The Stovis Found. Mem. ABA, Assn. of Bar of City of N.Y., Assn. Gen. Counsel, North Shore Gen. Counsel Assn., Ill. State Bar Assn. Roman Catholic. General corporate, Health, Private international. Office: Abbott Laboratories D-364 AP6D-2 100 Abbott Park Rd North Chicago IL 60064-3500

(GUILD) DEL BONO, IRENE LILLIAN, attorney general; b. Milford, Mass., May 27, 1949; d. Roy Prescott and Sara Lucretia (Snyer) Stone; children: Gregory Howe Jr., Daniel David. BS in Criminal Justice, Westfield State Coll., 1989; JD, Boston U., 1991, MA in Hist. Preservation, 1992. Bar: Mass. 1991, U.S. Supreme Ct. 1996, U.S. Dist. Ct. Mass. 2000. Asst. atty. gen. Office Atty. Gen., Boston, 1992-2001; dir. land acquisition and protection State Mass. Dept. Environ. Mgmt., 2001—. Active Norwood Hist. Soc., Framingham Hist. Soc. Mem. ABA, Mass. Bar Assn. (property law sect. 1995—), Mass. Conveyancer's Assn., Nat. Trust Hist. Preservation, N.E. Legal Preservation Network, U.S. Supreme Ct. Hist. Soc., Boston Bar Assn., Danvers Alarm List Co. Avocations: writing, bicycling, hiking, Internet. Home: 9 Kimball Ct Natick MA 01760-4461 Office: State Mass Dept Environ Mgmt Land Acquisition/Protection 251 Causeway St Boston MA 02114 E-mail: idelbono@hotmail.com

DE LEON, JOHN LOUIS, public defender; b. North Miami, Fla., Feb. 14, 1962; s. Leon Juan and Lydia (Diaz Cruz) de L. AB cum laude, U. Miami, 1983; JD, Georgetown U., 1986; M in Internat. Affairs, Columbia U., 1992. Bar: Fla. 1987, U.S. Supreme Ct. 1993. V.p. Bristol Investment Group, Coral Gables, Fla., 1982-85; jud. intern to Judge Francis Bason Fed. Bankruptcy Ct., Washington, 1986; asst. pub. defender Office Pub. Defender for 11th Jud. Cir., Miami, 1987—; law clk. Geiger, Riggs & Freud, P.A., Fla., 1986-87; cons., adminstrn. Justice Specialist Checchi and Co., Bogota, Colombia, 2001—. Mem. bd. arbitrators Nat. Assn. Security Dealers, N.Y.C., 1989; press officer, intern. Delegation of the Commn. of the European Communities, UN, N.Y.C., 1990; mem. steering com. Georgetown Criminal Justice Clinic, Georgetown U. Law Ctr. Bd. dirs. Citykids, Inc., Miami, 1986; mem. adv. bd. Douglas MaCarthur Sr. H.S., Miami; mem. audience devel. commn. Mus. Contemporary Arts, North Miami, Fla.; bd. dirs. Urban Environment League, Miami. Named to 40 to Watch in New Millennium in South Fla., Miami Herald, Best Promoter of Cultural Diversity, Miami New Times, 2000. Mem. ABA, Cuban Am. Bar Assn., Nat. Assn. Criminal Def. Lawyers, Am. Civil Liberties Union, Fla. Assn. Pub. Defenders, ACLU (bd. mem. Dade County chpt., pres.), Amnesty Internat., Golden Key, Phi Delta Phi, Phi Kappa Phi, Pi Sigma Alpha. Roman Catholic. Avocations: reading, politics, arts. Home: 1805 Ixora Rd Miami FL 33181-2309 Office: Pub Defender Svc 1320 NW 14th St Miami FL 33125-1609

DELEON, PATRICK HENRY, lawyer; b. Waterbury, Conn., Jan. 6, 1943; s. Patrick and Catherine (Dzubay) D.; m. Jean Louise Murphy; children: Patrick Daniel Nainoa, Katherine Malia Malie. BA, Amherst Coll., 1964; MS, Purdue U., 1966, PhD in Clin. Psychology, 1969; MPH, U. Hawaii, 1973; JD, Catholic U., 1980. Bar: Hawaii 1981, U.S. Dist. Ct. Hawaii 1983, U.S. Ct. Appeals (9th cir.) 1983; diplomate Am. Bd. Profl. Psychology, Am. Bd. Forensic Psychology. Tng. psychologist Peace Corps Tng. Ctr., Hilo, Hawaii, 1969-70; staff psychologist Diamond Head Mental Health Ctr., Hawaii State Hosp., Honolulu and Kaneohe, 1970-73; adminstrv. asst. U.S. Senator Daniel K. Inouye, Washington, 1973—. Fellow APA (pres. 2000, assoc. editor Am. Psychologist Jour. 1981—, editor Profl. Psychology Rsch. and Practice 1995-2000), Hawaii Psychol. Assn. (Disting. Svc. award 1981), Hawaii Bar Assn. Democrat. Home: 5701 Wilson Ln Bethesda MD 20817 Office: care Senator D K Inouye Us Senate Washington DC 20510-0001

DELGADO, GRACIELA, court interpreter; b. Chihuahua, Mexico, Oct. 9, 1939; d. Francisco Rios and Adela Navarro; m. Tito Joel Delgado, Jan. 17, 1970; 1 child, Aixa. BA, U. Tex., El Paso, 1961, MEd, 1986. Tchr. h.s. El Paso Ind. Sch. dist., 1961-96; interpreter County of El Paso, 1998-99. Conf. interpreter, El Paso, 1993-99. Mem. AAUW (program pres. 1994-95, pres. 1998—), El Paso Interpreters and Translation Assn. (pres.-elect 1993-99), Am. Translators Assn. (cert.). Avocation: internat. travel. Home: 1003 Alethea Park Dr El Paso TX 79902-2136

DELHOMME, BEVERLY ANN, lawyer; b. New Orleans, Sept. 24, 1954; s. August Nevle and Shelby (Bourgeois) DelH.; m. Bertis Little. Cert. in radiologic tech., Charity Hosp. Sch., New Orleans, 1972-74; BS magna cum laude in Biology, William Carey Coll., 1980; JD, U. Houston, 1984. Bar: Tex. 1984, La. 1985, U.S. Dist. Ct. (no. dist.) Tex. 1985. X-ray technician VA Hosp., New Orleans, 1974-79; assoc. Richard Martin PC, Dallas, 1985, Paul A. Lockman PC, Dallas, 1986-88; ptnr. DelHomme & Skrepnek (name now DelHomme & Assocs.), 1986—, 1986—. Editor Houston Jour. Internat. Law, 1983-84. Vol. ARC, 1970-81. Prudential Life Ins. Health Law scholar U. Houston Law Ctr., 1983; recipient 10 Yrs. Svc. award ARC, Chalmette, La., 1980. Mem. ABA, Am. Trial Lawyers Assn., Tex. Trial Lawyers Assn., La. Bar Assn., Dallas Bar Assn., Dallas Trial Lawyers Assn. Episcopalian. Avocation: water skiing. Personal injury, Entertainment, Alternative dispute resolution. Office: DelHomme & Assocs 415 Oakwood Tower 3626 N Hall St Dallas TX 75219-5107 E-mail: tjtnsly@aol.com

DELIN, SYLVIA KAUFMAN, lawyer; b. Detroit, Nov. 10, 1945; d. Ira G. and Lillian (Farbman) Kaufman; m. Robert B. Smith, June 13, 1971 (div.); children: David, Mark, Barbara. Student, U. Sheffield, Eng., 1965-66; BA, U. Mich., 1967; JD, Loyola U., Chgo., 1973. Bar: Ill. 1973, U.S. Dist. Ct. (no. dist.) Ill. 1980, U.S. Ct. Appeals (7th cir.) 1981, U.S. Ct. Appeals (6th cir.) 1989, U.S. Supreme Ct. 1982. Pvt. practice, Flossmoor, Ill., 1975-86, Southfield, Mich., 1986-96, Birmingham, 1996—. Author: Two Against One, 1964, Out of the Slums, 1968. Mem. ABA, Mich. Bar Assn., Oakland County Bar Assn. (family law and juvenile law coms.), Women Lawyers Assn. of Mich. Republican. Jewish. General civil litigation, Family and matrimonial, General practice. Home: 1285 Ruffner Ave Birmingham MI 48009-7173 Office: Ste D 219 Elm St Ste D Birmingham MI 48009-6341 E-mail: sdelin@msn.com

DELL, MICHAEL JOHN, lawyer; b. N.Y.C., Aug. 18, 1954; Sidney Samuel and Ethel Rachel (Tannenholtz) D.; m. Lisa Ellen Rothschild, Aug. 24, 1980; children: Benjamin Reuben, Joshua Matthew, Rebecca Talia. BA, Oxford U., 1975; JD magna cum laude, Harvard U., 1978. Bar: N.Y. 1979, U.S. Dist. Ct. (no. so., ea., and we. dists.) N.Y., U.S. Ct. Appeals (2d, 3d, 7th, and 8th cirs.), U.S. Supreme Ct. Law clk. to judge Stanley A. Weigel U.S. Dist. Ct. Calif., San Francisco, 1978-79; assoc. Kramer, Levin, Nessen, Kamin & Frankel, N.Y.C., 1979-85, ptnr., 1986—. Editor and assoc. editorial dir. Harvard Law Rev., 1976-78. Mem. ABA, Bar Assn. of City of N.Y. Avocations: family, travel, swimming, writing. Federal civil litigation, State civil litigation, Pension, profit-sharing, and employee benefits. Office: Kramer Levin Naftalis & Frankel LLP 919 3rd Ave Rm 3803 New York NY 10022-3902 E-mail: mdell@kramerlevin.com

DELLAGLORIA, JOHN CASTLE, city attorney, educator; b. N.Y.C., June 29, 1952; s. Arthur A. and Marianne Dellagloria; divorced; 1 child, Rebecca; m. Marilyn Castle Dellagloria, Sept. 25, 1988; 1 child, Caitlin. BA in English Lit., SUNY, Binghamton, 1976; JD, U. Miami, 1979. Bar: Fla. 1979, N.Y. 1986, U.S. Ct. Appeals (11th cir.) 1981, U.S. Dist. Ct. (so. dist.) Fla. 1980, U.S. Supreme Ct. Rsch. asst. 3rd Dist. Ct. Appeal, Miami, Fla., 1980-81; assoc. Cassel & Cassel PA, 1981-82; dep. city atty. City of North Miami Beach, Fla., 1983-86; city atty. City of South Miami, 1986-90; chief dep. city atty. City of Miami Beach, 1990-96; city atty. City of North Miami, 1995—; gen. counsel Miami Beach Housing Authority, 1997-2000, South Miami Cmty. Redevel. Agy., 1998—. Instr. Sch. Profl. Devel., U. Miami, 1982-88, dir. paralegal program, 1984-86, instr. Sch. Bus., 1989—, lectr. real property program; lectr. govt. law sect. Fla. Bar; moderator Rachlin, Cohen & Holtz, Ann. Govt. Law Symposium, 1996—. Com. person Parrot Jungle Com., Pinecrest, Fla., 1998. Mem. Eugene P. Spellman Am. Inn of Ct., 1997—. Democrat. Jewish. Avocation: long distance running. Office: City of North Miami 776 NE 125th St North Miami FL 33161-5654 E-mail: catdel@hotmail.com

DELLA ROCCO, KENNETH ANTHONY, lawyer; b. Bridgeport, Conn., Sept. 5, 1952; BA, Sacred Heart U., Fairfield, Conn., 1974; JD, U. Bridgeport, 1982. Bar: Conn. 1983, U.S. Dist. Ct. Conn. 1985, N.Y. 1988, U.S. Supreme Ct. 1991. Assoc. Cummings & Lockwood, Stamford, Conn., 1982-88; asst. gen. counsel Melville Corp., Rye, N.Y., 1988-90, dir. legal affairs, counsel, 1990-94, asst. corp. sec., 1990-95, v.p. legal affairs, gen. counsel, 1994-95; counsel Cacace, Tusch & Santagata, Stamford, 1996—. Mem. Conn. Bar Assn., N.Y. State Bar, Regional Bar Assn. Office: Cacace Tusch and Santagata 777 Summer St Stamford CT 06901-1022

DELLINGER, ANNE MAXWELL, law educator; b. Omaha July 19, 1940; d. William Hampton and Margaret Mary (Jackson) Maxwell; m. Walter Estes Dellinger, June 12, 1965; children— Hampton Yeats, Andrew King. Student Randolph Macon Woman's Coll., 1958-60; B.A., U. N.C., 1962; M.A., Tulane U., 1964; J.D., Duke U., 1974. Bar: N.C. 1974, U.S. Supreme Ct. 1991. Tech. writer, editor Equitable Life Assurance Soc., N.Y.C., 1964-65; instr. English U. Miss., Oxford, 1966-68; assoc., asst. prof. pub. law and govt. U. N.C., Chapel Hill, Prof., 1974—; spl. asst. to dir. FBI, Washington, 1980-81; cons. health coms. N.C. Gen. Assembly, 1983. Author: North Carolina School Law: The Principal's Role, 1980; A Legal Guide for North Carolina School Board Members, 1978; editor Health Law Bull., Inst. Govt., 1982—; gen. editor. author chpt. Healthcare Facilities Law, 1991; counsel Hogan & Hartson, Washington, D.C., 1993-95; contbr. articles to profl. jours. Mem. Order Coif, Assn. Women Faculty U. N.C. (pres. 1984-85), N.C. Soc. Health Care Attys. (pres. 1984-85), Phi Beta Kappa. Democrat. Home: 604 E Franklin St Chapel Hill NC 27514-3822 Office: Inst Govt Univ NC Cb # 3330 Chapel Hill NC 27599-0001

DELLO IACONO, PAUL MICHAEL, lawyer; b. Brookline, Mass., July 26, 1957; s. John B. Jr. and Marie J.C. (Beaulieu) D.-I.; m. Donna M. Lynch, Jan. 10, 1981; children: Brad Michael, Andrea Marie. BA, St. Anselm Coll., 1979; JD, Suffolk U., 1982. Bar: Mass. 1982. V.p. Housing Dynamics, Boston, 1978-82; counsel DMC Energy Inc., 1982-85; exec. dir. Brockton (Mass.) Cen., Inc., 1985-89; Ea. regional counsel Proven Alternatives, Inc., Waltham, Mass., 1990-94; contracts mgr. Duke Solutions, Inc., Boston, 1995-98; asst. gen. counsel Duke Energy Corp., Boston/Charlotte, Mass./N.C., 1998—. Mem. devel. staff Vt. State Prison, 1978; apptd. mem. Citizens Adv. Commn., Boston, 1986-98; alt. atty. mem. Weymouth Zoning Bd. Appeals. Mem. Mass. Bar Assn., Delta Sigma Rho, Tau Kappa Alpha, Pi Gamma Mu. Democrat. Roman Catholic. Avocations: gardening, electronics, computers. Contracts commercial, General corporate. Home: 42 Weyfair Path Weymouth MA 02190-2638 Office: Duke Solutions Inc 1 Winthrop Sq Boston MA 02110-1209 E-mail: PMDELLOI@Duke-Ehersy.com

DEL NEGRO, JOHN THOMAS, lawyer; b. Springfield, Mass., Oct. 2, 1948; s. Angelo Antonio and Marguerite (Garofalo) Del N.; m. Linda Anne Mayberry, July 6, 1973. BA, George Washington U., 1970; JD, Cornell U., 1975. Bar: Conn. 1975, U.S. Dist. Ct. Conn. 1978, U.S. Tax Ct. 1981. Assoc. Murtha, Cullina, Richter & Pinney, Hartford, Conn., 1975-81, ptnr., 1982-95, Del Negro, Feldman & Volpe, LLC, Hartford, 1995—. Author: (with Levenson) Depreciation and Investment Tax Credits, 1983. Dir. Conn. Opera Assn., 1990—, Watkinson Sch., 1992-2000. Mem. ABA, Conn. Bar Assn. (tax exec. com. 1992—). General corporate, Health, Taxation, general. Office: Del Negro Feldman & Volpe LLC Goodwin Sq 225 Asylum St Hartford CT 06103-1524 E-mail: jdelnegro@hotmail.com

DELO, ELLEN SANDERSON, lawyer; b. Nassawadox, Va., Nov. 29, 1944; d. Robert G. and Daisy B. (Hitchens) Sanderson; m. Arthur C. Delo Jr., Mar. 20, 1971; 1 child, Marjorie Cotton Delo. BA, U. Richmond, 1966; JD, Rutgers U., 1977; LLM, NYU, 1985. Bar: N.J., 1977, U.S. Dist. Ct. N.J., 1977, U.S. Tax Ct., 1987, U.S. Ct. Appeals (2nd cir.) 1997, D.C. 1999, N.Y. 1999. Law clk. to Hon. John J. Geronimo N.J. Superior Ct., 1977-78; assoc. Lamb Hutchinson Chappell Ryan & Hartung, Jersey City, 1978-80, Chasan Leyner Holland & Tarrant, Jersey City, 1980-84, Stryker Tams & Dill, Newark, 1985-92, ptnr., 1993-98; exec. compensation assoc. Bachelder Law Offices, N.Y.C., 1998—. Lectr. on tax issues. Contbr. articles to profl. jours. Lay reader Ch. St. Andrew and Holy Communion, South Orange, N.J. Mem. ABA (tax sect., employee benefits com.). Democrat. Episcopalian. Avocation: animal welfare organizations and activities. Pension, profit-sharing, and employee benefits, Corporate taxation, Taxation, general. Home: 340 Montrose Ave South Orange NJ 07079-2439 E-mail: esd@jebachelder.com

DELONG, DEBORAH, lawyer; b. Louisville, Sept. 5, 1950; d. Henry F. and Lois Jean (Stepp) D.; children: Amelie DeLong, Samuel Prentice. BA, Vanderbilt U., 1972; JD, U. Cin., 1975. Bar: Ohio 1975, Ky. 1999, U.S. Dist. Ct. (so. dist.) Ohio 1975, U.S. Ct. Appeals (Fed. cir.) 1990, (11th cir.), 1995, U.S. Ct. Appeals (6th cir.) 1991, U.S. Supreme Ct. 1982. Assoc. Paxton & Seasongood, Cin., 1975-82, ptnr., 1982-88, Thompson, Hine & Flory, 1989—. Contbr. articles to profl. jours. Bd. dirs. Cin. Opera, People Working Cooperatively, Inc. Mem. ABA, Ohio State Bar Assn., Cin. Bar Assn., Arbitration Tribunal U.S. Dist. Ct., Ohio, 1984. Republican. Episcopalian. Federal civil litigation, State civil litigation, Labor. Office: Thompson Hine & Flory 312 Walnut St Ste 1400 Cincinnati OH 45202-4089

DEL PAPA, FRANKIE SUE, state attorney general; b. 1949; BA, U. Nev.; JD, George Washington U., 1974. Bar: Nev. 1974. Staff asst. U.S. Senator Alan Bible, Washington, 1971-74; assoc. Law Office of Leslie B. Grey, Reno, 1975-78; legis. asst. to U.S. Senator Howard Cannon, Washington, 1978-79; ptnr. Thornton & Del Papa, 1979-84; pvt. practice Reno, 1984-87; sec. of state State of Nev., Carson City, 1987-91, atty. gen., 1991—. Mem. Sierra Arts Found. (bd. dirs.), Trust for Pub. Land (adv. com.), Nev. Women's Fund. Democrat.*

DEL RASO, JOSEPH VINCENT, lawyer; b. Phila., Dec. 21, 1952; s. Vincent and Dolores Ann (D'Adamo) Del R.; m. Anne Marie McGloin, Apr. 17, 1982; children: Joseph Vincent Jr., Katherine Anne, Marianna. BS in Acctg., Villanova U., 1974, JD, 1983. Bar: Pa., 1983, Fla. 1988. Exec. v.p. Belgrade Constrn., Inc., Wayne, Pa., 1974-80; atty. SEC, Washington, 1983-85; assoc. Dechert, Price & Rhoads, 1986-88; ptnr. Holland & Knight, Ft. Lauderdale, Fla., 1988-92, Stradley, Ronon, Stevens & Young, Phila., 1992-98, Pepper Hamilton LLP, Phila., 1998—. Gen. counsel, bd. dirs. Nat. Italian-Am. Found., Am. U. Rome, Telespectrum Worldwide, Inc. Co-editor-in-chief Villanova Jour. Law and Investment Mgmt. Sec. of bd. consultors Villanova U. Sch. Law; bd. dirs. Justinian Found.; mem. exec. com. Rep. Eagles; trustee Am. U. Rome. Mem. ABA, Villanova U. Alumni Assn. (class agt. 1974-97), Aronimink Golf Club. Republican. Roman Catholic. General corporate, Securities. Office: Pepper Hamilton LLP 18th & Arch Sts 3000 Two Logan Sq Philadelphia PA 19103

DEL RUSSO, ALESSANDRA LUINI, retired law educator; b. Milan, Italy, Jan. 2, 1916; d. Avvocato Umberto and Candita (Recio) Luini; m. Carl R. del Russo, Apr. 12, 1947; children: Carl Luini, Alexander David. PhD in History with honors, Royal U., Milan, 1939; SJD summa cum laude, Royal U., Pavia, Italy, 1943; LLM in Comparative Law, George Washington U., Washington, 1949. Bar: Md. 1956, Md. Ct. Appeals, Ct. of Appeals (Milano) 1947, U.S. Ct. Appeals (D.C. cir.) 1950, U.S. Supreme Ct. 1955. Legal adviser Allied Mil. Govt. and Ct., Milan, 1945-46, U.S. Consulate Gen., Milan, 1946-47; pvt. practice Washington, Bethesda, Md., 1950-58; atty. adviser Legis. Ref. Libr. of Congress, Washington, 1958-59; atty. U.S. Commn. on Civil Rights, 1959-61; prof. Howard U. Sch. Law, 1961-81, dir. grad. program, 1972-74, prof. emerita, 1981—; adj. prof. Stetson U. Coll. Law, St. Petersburg, Fla., 1980-95, adj. prof. emerita, 1995—. Professorial lectr. George Washington U. Law Ctr., 1970-80; mem. legal cons. com. U.S. Commn. on Status of P.R., Washington, 1965-66; lectr. in field. Author: International Protection of Human Rights, 1971; editor and chmn. of symposium on International Law of Human Rights, Howard U. Sch. of Law, Washington, 1965; contbr. numerous articles to internat. and Am. profl. jours. Rsch. grant Howard U., 1963. Mem. ABA,

Brit. Inst. Internat. and Comparative Law, Am. Soc. Internat. Law. Republican. Roman Catholic. Achievements include 1st woman to receive LLM in Comparative Law from George Washington U. Avocations: travels, foreign languages, collecting antique books, genealogy. Home: 400 Ocean Trail Way Apt 908 Jupiter FL 33477-5527

DELSAUT, PHILIPPE PATRICK, lawyer; b. Veurne, West Vlaanderen, Belgium, Dec. 23, 1969; s. Jean-Luc and Erna (Coucke) D. Law Degree, Vrye U. Brussels, 1995, U. Fribourg, Switzerland, 1995; tax law, Fiscale Hogesch., Brussels, 1998'. Bar: Brussels. Assoc. Caestecker & Ptnrs., Brussels, 1995-98, McKenna & Cuneo LLP, Brussels, 1998-2000, Washington, 2000, Eversheds, Brussels, London, 2000—. Contbr. articles to profl. jour. Avocations: cooking, reading, sports. Contracts commercial, General corporate, Mergers and acquisitions. Office: Eversheds 75 Ave Cortenberg 1000 Brussels Belgium

DEL TUFO, ROBERT J. lawyer, former US attorney, former state attorney general; b. Newark, Nov. 18, 1933; s. Raymond and Mary (Pellecchia) Del T.; m. Katherine Nouri Hughes; children: Barbara, Ann, Robert, David. B.A. cum laude in English, Princeton U., 1955; J.D., Yale U., 1958. Bar: N.J. 1959. Law sec. to chief justice N.J. Supreme Ct., 1958-60; assoc. firm Dillon, Bitar & Luther, Morristown, N.J., 1960-62, ptnr., 1962-74; asst. prosecutor Morris County, 1963-65; 1st asst. prosecutor, 1965-67; 1st asst. atty. gen. State of N.J., 1974-77; dir. criminal justice, 1976-77; U.S. atty. Dist. of N.J., Newark, 1977-80; prof. Rutgers U. Sch. Criminal Justice, 1979-81; ptnr. firm Stryker, Tams & Dill, 1980-86, Hannoch Weisman, 1986-90; atty. gen. State of N.J., 1990-93; ptnr. Skadden, Arps, Slate, Meagher & Flom, N.Y.C. and Newark, 1993—; commr. N.J. State Commn. of Investigation, 1981-84. Instr. bus. law Fairleigh-Dickinson U., 1964; mem. N.J. State Bd. Bar Examiners, 1967-74; mem. criminal law drafting com. Nat. Conf. Bar Examiners, 1972—; bd. dirs. Nat. Ctr. for Victims of Crime, 1995—; Nat. Italian Am. Found., 1995—, Integrity Inc., 1995—, John Cabot U. in Rome, 1997—, Legal Svcs. N.J., 2000—, IOLTA, 1994-99, N.J. Pub. Interest Law Ctr., 1996-99, Daytop Village Found., 1998—, Planned Parenthood, 1998-99; mem. com. on character N.J. Supreme Ct., 1982-84; spl. master, fed. jail overcrowding litigation, Essex County, 1989-90; trustee Boys and Girls Clubs of Am., 2000—. Bd. editors Yale U Law Jour; contbr. articles to profl. jours. Mem. law enforcement adv. com. County Coll. of Morris, 1970-85; mem. Morris County Ethics Com., 1968-71, Morris County Jud. Selection Com., 1970-72, Essex County Jud. Selection Com., 1982-84; v.p., mem. exec. com. United Fund of Morris County, 1966-70; chmn. Morris Twp. Juvenile Conf. Com., 1963-74; bd. dirs. Nat. Found. March of Dimes, 1966-68, Vis. Nurse Assn. Morris County, 1963-70, Morristown YMCA, 1970-74, Boys & Girls Club Am., 16999—, Atty.'s Fund for Client Protection, 1999—; trustee Newark Acad., 1976-95, 97—, pres. bd. dirs. 1983-87; bd. regents St. Peter's Coll., 1979-85. Fellow Am. Bar Found.; mem. Am., N.J., Morris County bar assns., Nat. Dist. Attys. Assn., Yale Law Sch. Assn. (exec. com. 1978-84), Order of Coif. Home: 13 Ober Rd Princeton NJ 08540-4917 Office: Skadden Arts Slate Meagher & Flom One Newark Ctr Newark NJ 07102 also: 4 Times Sq New York NY 10036-6522 E-mail: rdeltufo@skadden.com

DE LUCA, THOMAS GEORGE, lawyer; b. Jersey City, Dec. 28, 1950; s. Michael Anthony and Estelle Theresa (Wickiewicz) De L.; m. Annette Catherine Pandolfo, Aug. 16, 1975; children: Michele, Thomas, Rachel. BS in Econs., St. Peters Coll., Jersey City, 1972; JD, Seton Hall U., 1978. Bar: N.J. 1978, U.S. Dist. Ct. 1978, N.Y. 1981, U.S. Dist. Ct. (so. and ea. dists.) N.Y. 1981, U.S. Ct. Appeals (2d cir.) 1986, U.S. Ct. Appeals (3d cir.) 1987, U.S. Claims Ct. 1989, U.S. Dist. Ct. (we. dist.) N.Y. 1990, U.S. Dist. Ct. (no. dist.) N.Y. 1991, U.S. Supreme Ct. 1987. Supervising underwriter Fireman's Fund Ins. Cos., Newark, 1972-77; assoc. Sellar, Richardson & Stuart, 1978-80, Postner & Rubin, N.Y.C., 1980-84, ptnr., 1985-93, De Luca & Forster, Cranford, N.J., 1994—. Mem. ABA, N.J. Bar Assn., N.Y. County Lawyers Assn. Roman Catholic. Federal civil litigation, State civil litigation, Construction. Home: 14 Kilmer Dr Colonia NJ 07067-1213 Office: De Luca and Forster 11 Commerce Dr Cranford NJ 07016-3501 also: 1 N Broadway White Plains NY 10601-2310 E-mail: delucafor@aol.com

DEMARIA, JOSEPH CARMINUS, lawyer; b. Phila., June 21, 1947; s. Joseph and Mary A. DeMaria. AB in Politics, St. Joseph's Coll., Phila., 1969; JD, Villanova U., 1972. Bar: Pa. 1972, U.S. Dist. Ct. (ea. dist.) Pa. 1972, U.S. Ct. Appeals (3rd cir.) 1982, U.S. Supreme Ct. 1982, Conn. 1988. Staff atty. Southeastern Pa. Transportation Authority, Phila., 1972-78; mng. atty. Aetna Life and Casualty, 1978-87, asst. v.p., staff counsel ops. Hartford, Conn., 1987-91; claim counsel Aetna Life & Casualty, Phila., 1991-96; pvt. practice, 1972—. Mem. Montgomery Bar Assn., Pa. Bar Assn., John Peter Zenger Law Soc., German Am. Police Assn., German Soc. Pa., FOP. Republican. Roman Catholic. Avocations: tennis, music, science fiction, classical automobile collecting. General civil litigation, Insurance, Probate. Home and Office: 237 Weadley Rd King Of Prussia PA 19406-3746

DE MARIE, ANTHONY JOSEPH, lawyer; b. Buffalo, May 10, 1928; s. Joseph and Josephine (Radice) DeM.; m. Rose Galluzzo, July 23, 1955; children— Michael, Janice, Gregory, Lynda. J.D., U. Buffalo, 1955. Bar: N.Y. 1956, U.S. Dist. Ct. (we. dist.) N.Y. 1960, U.S. Ct. Appeals (2d cir.) 1982. Ptnr., Dixon & De Marie, Buffalo, 1956— . Dir., Neighborhood Legal Services of Erie County, Buffalo, 1971-74. Served with AUS, 1946-48, 50-51. Mem. Erie County Bar Assn. (past bd. dirs.), Trial Lawyers Assn. Erie County (past pres., gov.) N.Y. State Bar Assn., Fla. Bar Assn., N.Y. State Trial Lawyers Assn., Assn. Trial Lawyers Am., Western N.Y. Trial Lawyers Assn. Republican. Roman Catholic. Club: Transit Valley Country. State civil litigation, Insurance, Personal injury. Office: De Marie & Schoenborn PC 930 Convention Tower Buffalo NY 14202-3174

DEMARTIN, CHARLES PETER, lawyer; b. N.Y.C., Aug. 21, 1952; s. Samuel Peter and Rose Marie (Parisi) DeM.; m. Frances Gloria Vitrano, Apr. 4, 1981; children: Stephen, Charles, Joseph. BS, SUNY, Binghamton, 1974; JD, St. John's U., Jamaica, N.Y., 1977. Bar: N.Y. 1978, D.C. 1978, U.S. Dist. Ct. (ea. and so. dists.) N.Y. 1978, U.S. Ct. Appeals (2d cir.) 1983; U.S. Dist. Ct. Ariz., 1993. Assoc. Hartman & Lerner, Mineola, N.Y., 1978-80; pvt. practice law Garden City, 1980, 85-87; counsel Curtis, Zaklukiewicz, Vasile & Devine, Merrick, 1980-82, 85-87; ptnr. DeMartin, Kranz, Davis & Hersh, Hauppauge, 1981-85, Damadeo & DeMartin, Hicksville, 1987-88; pvt. practice law Huntington, 1989-92; ptnr. McCarthy, McCarthy & DeMartin, 1992-94; pvt. practice law N.Y., 1994—. Mem. N.Y. State Bar Assn., Nassau County Bar Assn., D.C. Bar Assn., Brookville Country Club. Republican. Roman Catholic. Avocations: golf, sports, photography. General civil litigation, General corporate, Personal injury. Home: 2 Bluebird Ln Huntington NY 11743-6502 Office: 870 W Jericho Tpke Huntington NY 11743-6037

DEMBICER, EDWIN HERBERT, retired lawyer; b. June 12, 1928; s. Sam and Rose (Weinstein) Dembicer; m. Phyllis Rita Meyerowitz, Oct. 19, 1952; children: Leslye R. Geller, Tracy S. LLB, NYU, 1950. Bar: N.Y. 1950. Assoc. Louis L. Berko, N.Y.C., NY, 1950—51, Martin M. Kolbrener, N.Y.C., 1953—55; sole practice, 1955—57; ptnr. Dembicer & Lederer, Bklyn., 1957—92, ret., 1992. Assembly dist. leader Dem. Party, Hewlett, NY, 1965. With U.S. Army, 1951—53. Mem.: Am. Arbitration Assn. (arbitrator 1973—92), Am. Judges Assn., N.Y. State Trial Lawyers Assn., Masons (master 1966). Contracts commercial, Personal injury, Real property. Home: 11186 Green Lakes Dr Boynton Beach FL 33437-1470

DEMBLING, PAUL GERALD, lawyer, former government official; b. Rahway, N.J., Jan. 11, 1920; s. Simon and Fannie (Ellenbogen) D.; m. Florence Brotman, Nov. 22, 1947; children: Ross Wayne, Douglas Evan, Donna Stacy. BA, Rutgers U., 1940, MA, 1942; JD, George Washington U., 1951. Bar: D.C. 1952. Grad. asst., teaching fellow Rutgers U., 1940-42; economist Office Chief Transp., Dept. Army, 1942-45; since practiced in Washington; indsl. relations NACA, 1945-51, spl. counsel, legal adviser, gen. counsel, 1951-58; asst. gen. counsel NASA, 1958-61, dir. legis. affairs, 1961-63, dep. gen. counsel, 1963-67, gen. counsel, 1967-69, chmn. bd. contract appeals, 1958-61, vice chmn. inventions and contbns. bd., 1959-67; mem. and alt. rep. U.S. del. UN Legal Subcom. Com. on Outer Space, 1964-69; gen. counsel GAO, 1969-78; partner Schnader, Harrison, Segal & Lewis, Washington, 1978-93, sr. counsel, 1994—. Prin. author NASA Act, 1958; professorial lectr. George Washington U. Law Sch., 1965-86. Co-author: Federal Contract Management, 1988, Essentials of Grant Law Practice, 1991; editor in chief Fed. Bar Jour., 1962-69; contbr. articles to profl. jours. Recipient Meritorious Civilian Service award War Dept., 1945; Disting. Service medal NASA, 1968; Nat. Civil Service League award, 1973 Fellow: AIAA (chmn. com. law and sociology 1969—71), Nat. Contract Mgmt. Assn. (bd. advisers 1973—98), Nat. Acad. Pub. Adminstrn., Am. Bar Found. (life)); mem.: ABA (coun., pub. contract law sec. 1983—84, vice chmn. 1984—85, chmn. elect 1985—86, chmn. 1986—87), FBA (nat. coun. 1963—, pres. Capitol Hill chpt. 1977—78, nat. sec. 1978—79, pres.-elect 1981—82, nat. pres. 1983—84, bd. dirs. bldg. corp. 1989—), D.C. Bar (mem. steering com. govt. contracts and litigation sect. 1989—95), Procurement Roundtable (bd. dirs. 1984—, vice chmn. 1988—), Internat. Inst. Space Law (pres. Am. assn. 1970—72, Internat. Astronaut. Fedn. award 1992), Cosmos Club, Nat. Lawyers Club, Phi Delta Phi. Government contracts and claims, Public international. Home: 11625 Pamplona Blvd Boynton Beach FL 33437-4077 Office: Schnader Harrison Segal & Lewis 1300 I St NW Washington DC 20005-3314 E-mail: pfdemb@webtv.net

DEMBROW, DANA LEE, lawyer; b. Washington, Sept. 29, 1953; parents: Daniel William and Catherine Louise (Carder) D. BA, Duke U., 1975; JD, George Washington U., 1980. Bar: D.C., Md., W.Va. Law clk. D.C. Superior Ct., Washington, 1979-80; assoc. Smink & Scheuermann, 1980-81, Reback & Parsons, Washington, 1981-82, Howard M. Rensin, Hyattsville, Md., 1984-86; mem. com. on constitutional and adminstrv. law Md. Ho. of Dels., 1986-92; mem. jud. com. Md. State Legis., 1993—. Chair county affairs com., Montgomery Del., 1994—; can. for congress, Md.'s 4th Congl. Dist., 1992; chair subcom. on civil law and procedure House Judiciary Com., 1994—, chiar Intergovernmental Affairs Com., Southern Legis. Conference, 1999-2000. Chair Colesville Strawberry Festival, 1998, 99. Personal injury. Office: 220A Lowe House Office Bldg Annapolis MD 21401 E-mail: dana_dembrow@house.state.md.us, del.dem.@erols.com

DE MENT, IRA, judge; b. Birmingham, Ala., Dec. 21, 1931; s. Ira J. and Helen (Sparks) De M.; m. Ruth Lester Posey; 1 child, Charles Posey. AS, Marion Mil. Inst., 1951; AB, U. Ala., 1953, LLB, 1958, JD, 1969. Bar: Ala. 1958, U.S. Dist. Ct. (mid. dist.) Ala. 1958, U.S. Ct. Appeals (5th cir.) 1958, U.S. Supreme Ct. 1966, U.S. Dist. Ct. (so. dist.) Ala. 1967, U.S. Dist. Ct. D.C. 1972, U.S. Ct. Appeals (D.C.) 1972, U.S. Tax Ct. 1972, U.S. Customs and Patents Appeals 1976, U.S. Dist. Ct. (no. dist.) Ala. 1977, U.S. Ct. Appeals (11th cir.) 1981, U.S. Ct. Mil. Appeals 1972. Law clk. Sup. Ct. Ala., 1958-59; asst. atty. gen. State of Ala., 1959, spl. assty. atty. gen., 1966-69, 81-92; asst. U.S. atty. Montgomery, Ala., 1959-61; pvt. practice, 1961-69, 77-92; U.S. dist. judge (mid. dist.) Ala., 1992—. Acting U.S. atty. Mid. Dist. Ala. 1969, U.S. atty., 1969-77; asst. atty., legal advisor to police and fire depts. City of Montgomery, 1965-69; inst. Jones Law Sch., 1962-64; instr. Montgomery Police Acad., 1964-77; lect. constl. Ala. Police Acad., 1971-75; instr. law enforcement U. Ala., 1967, mem. adj. faculty New Coll., 1974-75, adj. prof. psychology, 1975-92; spl. counsel to Gov. State Ala., 1980-88, gen. counsel Commn. on Aging, 1980-82. Lt. col. USAR, 1953-74; maj. gen. USAFR ret. Recipient Disting. Svc. award Internat. Assn. Firefighters, 1975, Rockefeller Pub. Svc. award Woodrow Wilson Sch. Pub. and Internat. Affairs Princeton U., 1976; named Alumnus of Yr. Marion Mil. Inst., 1988, Significant Sig award Sigma Chi Fraternity, 1998, Judicial Award of Merit Ala. State Bar, 1998. Mem. ABA, Fed. Bar Assn., D.C. Bar Assn., Ala. Bar Assn. (mem. editl. adv. bd. The Alabama Lawyer 1966-72), Am. Judicature Soc., Nat. Assn. Former U.S. Attys., Phi Alpha Delta. Republican. United Methodist. Clubs: Masons, Shriners. Address: PO Box 2149 Montgomery AL 36102-2149 also: 15 Lee St Montgomery AL 36104 Fax: 334-223-7233. E-mail: Ira_DeMent@almd.uscourts.gov

DEMENT, JAMES ALDERSON, JR. lawyer; b. Clinton, Okla., Sept. 11, 1947; s. James Alderson and Ruby (Weaver) DeM.; m. Sally Anne Wylder, June 6, 1970; children: Stephen, Suzanne, Jonathan. BA summa cum laude, Tex. Christian U., 1969; JD in Internat. Affairs, Cornell U., 1972. Bar: N.Y. 1973, Tex. 1974. Assoc. Alexander & Green, N.Y.C., 1972-73, Baker Botts, LLP, Houston, 1977-85, ptnr., 1998—; ptnr., chmn. corp. tax and internat. sect. Butler & Binion, LLP, 1985-97. Adj. prof. U. Houston, 1987-88. Mem. edtl. rev. bd. The Internat. Lawyer, 1987-94. Trustee Houston Ballet Found., 1989-96, Brazos Presbyn. Homes, Inc., 1990-96. Capt. USAF, 1973-77. Fellow Tex. Bar Found.; mem. State Bar Tex. (internat. law sect., chmn. 1989-90), Internat. and Comparative Law Ctr. Southwestern Legal Found. (adv. coun. 1986—), Houston Bar Assn. (internat. law sect., pres. 1989-90). Presbyterian. Private international. Office: Baker Botts LLP 910 Louisiana St Houston TX 77002-4995 E-mail: james.dement@bakerbotts.com

DEMING, FRANK STOUT, lawyer; b. Oswego, Kans., Aug. 12, 1927; s. Robert Orin Jr. and Helen Josephine (Stout) D.; m. Carolyn Ruth Kauffman, June 24, 1950; children: Frank S. Jr., Christiana Deming Jacobsen, David M., Robert W. BS in Econs., U. Pa., 1949, LLB, 1952. Bar: Pa. 1953, U.S. Dist. Ct. (ea. dist.) Pa. 1953, U.S. Ct. Appeals (3d cir.) 1953, U.S. Ct. Appeals (9th cir.) 1965. Assoc., then ptnr., now of counsel Montgomery, McCracken, Walker & Rhoads, Phila., 1952—. Bd. dirs. New Covenant Trust co. Contbr. articles to profl. jours. Trustee Bricker Found., Phila., 1980—, Presbyn. Ch. (U.S.A.) Found., Jeffersonville, Ind., 1989-94, chmn., 1993, mem. gen. assembly coun., Louisville, 1990-91; dir. Presbyn. Children's Village, 1992-94. Sgt. U.S. Army, 1946-47. Fellow Am. Coll. Trust and Estate Counsel; mem. ABA, Pa. Bar Assn., Phila. Bar Assn., Mil. Figure Collectors Am., Phi Delta Theta, Beta Alpha Psi, Beta Gamma Sigma. Republican. Avocations: travel. Estate planning, Probate, Estate taxation. Home: Riddle Village 410 Hampton Media PA 19063-6009 Office: Montgomery McCracken Walker & Rhoads 123 S Broad St Fl 25 Philadelphia PA 19109-1029 Fax: 215-772-7620. E-mail: frankdeming@WebTV.net

DEMITCHELL, TERRI ANN, law educator; b. San Diego, Apr. 10, 1953; d. William Edward and Rose Annette (Carreras) Wheeler; m. Todd Allan DeMitchell, Aug. 14, 1982. AB in English with honors, San Diego State U., 1975; JD, U. San Diego, 1984; MA in Edn., U. Calif., Davis, 1990; EdM, Harvard U., 1997. Bar: Calif. 1985, U.S. Dist. Ct. (so. dist.) Calif. 1985; cert. elem. tchr., Calif. Tchr. Fallbrook (Calif.) Union Elem. Sch. Dist., 1976-86; adminstrv. asst. gen. counsel San Diego Unified Sch. Dist., 1984; assoc. Biddle and Hamilton, Sacramento, 1986-88; instr. U. N.H., 1990-93. Teaching asst. U. Calif., Davis, 1987. Author: The California Teacher and the Law, 1985, The Law in Relation to Teacher, Out of School Behavior, 1990, Censorship and the Public School Library: A Bicoastal View, 1991; contbr. chpt. to book: The Limits of Law-Based School Reform, 1997. Ava. Calif. Bar Assn., Internat. Reading Assn. Office: 2130 Bedford St Apt 307 Santa Rosa CA 95404-8051

DEMMLER, JOHN HENRY, retired lawyer; b. Pitts., June 20, 1932; s. Ralph Henry and Catherine (Hollinger) D.; m. Janet Rice, July 20, 1957; children: Richard H., Ralph W., Carol L. BA, Princeton U., 1954; LLB cum laude, Harvard U., 1959. Bar: Pa. 1960, U.S. Dist. Ct. (we. dist.) Pa. 1960. Assoc. Reed Smith Shaw & McClay, Pitts., 1959-65, ptnr., 1966-93, of counsel, 1994—. Dir. Duquesne Light Co., Pitts., 1977-90. Trustee Shady Side Acad., Pitts., 1969-75, 77—, vice chmn., 1980-84, chmn., 1984-87; chmn. Fox Chapel Borough Zoning Hearing Bd., 1993—. Mem. Pa. Bar Assn. (pub. utility law sect. 1976—), Duquesne Club, Fox Chapel Golf Club, HYP Pittsburgh Club. Republican. Episcopalian. General corporate, Municipal (including bonds), Public utilities. Home: 102 Foxtop Dr Pittsburgh PA 15238-2202 Office: Reed Smith LLP 435 6th Ave Pittsburgh PA 15219-1886

DEMOFF, MARVIN ALAN, lawyer; b. L.A., Oct. 28, 1942; s. Max and Mildred (Tweer) D.; m. Patricia Caryn Abelov, June 16, 1968; children: Allison Leigh, Kevin Andrew. BA, UCLA, 1964; JD, Loyola U., L.A., 1967. Bar: Calif. 1969. Asst. pub. defender Los Angeles County, 1968-72; ptnr. Steinberg & Demoff, L.A., 1973-83, Craighill, Fentress & Demoff, L.A. and Washington, 1983-86; of counsel Mitchell, Silberberg & Knupp, L.A., 1987—. Mem. citizens adv. bd. Olympic Organizing Com., L.A., 1982-84; bd. trustees Curtis Sch., L.A., 1985-94, chmn. bd. trustees, 1988-93; sports adv. bd. Constitution Rights Found., L.A., 1986—. Mem. ABA (mem. forum com. on entertainment and sports), Calif. Bar Assn., UCLA Alumni Assn., Phi Delta Phi. Avocations: sports, music, art. Entertainment, Sports. Office: Mitchell Silberberg Knupp 11377 W Olympic Blvd Los Angeles CA 90064-1625

DEMOND, WALTER EUGENE, lawyer; b. Sacramento, Oct. 15, 1947; s. Walter G. and Laura (Bartlett) D.; m. Kari Demond; 1 child, William. BA, U. Tex., 1969, JD with honors, 1976. Bar: Tex. 1976. With Clark, Thomas & Winters, Austin, 1976—, CFO, 1984—. Mem. mgmt. com. Clark, Thomas & Winters, 1984-94, 97-99, 01—. Capt. USAF, 1970-74. Fellow Am. Bar Found., Tex. Bar Found.; mem. ABA (vice chmn. gas com. pub. utility, comm. and transp. law sect. 1986-91, 97—, chmn. gas com. 1991-93, pub. utility comm. and transp. law sect.), State Bar of Tex. (adminstrv. law com. 1984-87). Avocations: sailing, jogging. Administrative and regulatory, Public utilities. Office: Clark Thomas & Winters Box 1148 Austin TX 78767

DEMOREST, MARK STUART, lawyer; b. Chambley, France, Mar. 14, 1957; came to U.S., 1960; s. Raymond Phillip and Maud Jane (Dahle) D.; m. Patricia Louise Button, July 28, 1979; children: Melissa, Matthew, Kristin, Kevin, Ryan. AB magna cum laude, Harvard U., 1979; JD magna cum laude, U. Mich., 1983. Bar: Mich. 1983, U.S Dist. Ct. (ea. dist.) Mich. 1983, U.S. Ct. Appeals (6th cir.) 1984, U.S. Ct. Appeals (7th cir.) 1986, U.S. Supreme Ct. 1993, U.S. Dist. Ct. (cen. dist.) Ill. 1995, U.S. Ct. Appeals (4th cir.) 1995, U.S. Dist. Ct. (we. dist.) Mich. 1996. Assoc. Dykema Gossett, Detroit, 1983-85, Simpson & Moran, Birmingham, Mich., 1985-87; ptnr. The Robert P. Ufer Partnership, Bloomfield Hills, 1987-92, Hainer, Demorest & Berman, P.C., Troy, 1993-98; pvt. practice, 1998—. Mem. ABA, State Bar Mich., Harvard Club of Ea. Mich. (schs. com.), Order of Coif. Methodist. Avocations: lacrosse, other sports. General civil litigation, General corporate, Labor. Office: Ste 100 19853 W Outer Dr Dearborn MI 48124-2066 E-mail: mdemorest@rileyhurley.com

DEMOSS, HAROLD RAYMOND, JR. federal judge; b. Houston, Dec. 30, 1930; s. Harold R. and Jessy May (Cox) DeM.; m. Judith Phelps; children: Harold R. III, Louise Holland. BA, Rice U., 1952; LLB, U. Tex., 1955. Bar: Tex. Assoc. Bracewell & Patterson, Houston, 1957-61, ptnr., 1961-91; judge U.S. Ct. of Appeals (5th cir.), 1991—. Area chmn. Bush Congl. Campaign, Houston, 1968; Harris County vice chmn. Tower Senate Campaign, Houston, 1972, Ford/Dale Campaign, 1976; Harris County chmn. Loeffler for Gov. Primary, 1986; Harris County co-chmn. Reagan/Bush Campaign, 1980, 84; Tex. State chmn. Bush for Pres. Primary, 1979-80, Tex. vice chmn., 1988; mem. platform group Bush for Pres., Washington, 1988; rsch. analyst Bush/Quayle Campaign, 1988; del. Rep. State Conv., Houston, 1968; dist. del. at large Rep. Nat. Conv., Houston, 1980, alternate del. at large, 1984, 88; vestryman St. Martin's Episcopal Ch., Houston, 1968-72; mem. exec. bd. Episcopal Diocese Tex., 1983-86, chmn. planning com., 1985-88, del. Diocesan Conv., 1976-88; chmn. bd. Tex. Bill Rights Found., Houston, 1969-70; bd. dirs. Amigos de las Americas, 1974-76; pres. Tanglewood Homeowners Assn., 1987. Sgt. U.S. Army, 1955-57. Fellow Tex. Bar Assn. (life); mem. ABA, Internat. Bar Assn., Am. Judicature Soc., Maritime Law Assn. U.S., Houston Bar Assn. (bd. dirs. 1969-71, 1st v.p. 1972-73), Tex. Assn. Def. Counsel (bd. dirs. 1972-74), The Houston Club, The Houstonian Club. Avocations: fishing, waterskiing. Office: US Courthouse 515 Rusk St Ste 12015 Houston TX 77002-2605*

DEMOSS, JON W. insurance company executive, lawyer; b. Kewanee, Ill., Aug. 9, 1947; s. Wendell and Virginia Beth DeMoss; m. Eleanor T. Thornley, Aug. 9, 1969; 1 child, Marc Alain. BS, U. Ill., 1969, JD, 1972. Bar: Ill. 1972, U.S. Dist. Ct. (cen. dist.) Ill. 1977, U.S. Supreme Ct. 1978, U.S. dist. Ct. (no. dist., trial bar) Ill. 1983. In house counsel Assn. Ill. Electric Coop., Springfield, 1972-74; registered lobbyist Ill. Gen. Assembly, 1972-74; asst. dir. Ill. Inst. for CLE, 1974-85; exec. dir. Ill. State Bar Assn., 1986-94; pres., CEO ISBA Mut. Ins. Co., Chgo., 1994—. Bd. dirs. Bar Plan Surety & Fidelity Co., St. Louis, 1999-. Bd. dirs. Springfield Symphony Orch., 1982-87, Ill. Inst. for CLE, 1986-89, Nat. Assn. of Bar Related Ins. Cos., 1989, pres., elect., 1998-99, pres. 1999—; bd. dirs. Lawyers Reins. Co., 1997—; bd. visitors John Marshall Law Sch., 1990—. Capt. U.S. Army, 1972. Fellow Am. Bar Found. (life, co-chmn. projects to prepare Appellate Handbook 1978, 90), Ill. Bar Found. (bd. dirs. 1983-85); mem. ABA (ho. of dels. 1979-85, 89, 91, 93-94), Nat. Conf. Bar Pres., Am. Judicature Soc. (bd. dirs. Ill. state chpt.), Ill. State Bar Assn. (pres. 1984-85, bd. govs. 1975-85, chmn. com. on scope and correlation of work 1982-83, chmn. budget com. 1983-85, chmn. legis. com. 1983-84, 85, chmn. com. on merit selection of judges 1977, del. long-range planning conf. 1972, 78, liaison to numerous coms. and sects.), Chgo. Bar Assn., Lake County Bar Assn., U. Ill. Coll. Dean's Club, La Chaine des Rotisseurs (Chgo.), Ordre Mondial des Gourmet Degustateurs (Chgo.), Les Gourmets (Chgo.). Home: 180 Norwich Ct Lake Bluff IL 60044-1914 Office: ISBA Mutual Ins Co 223 W Ohio St Chicago IL 60610-4101

DEMPSEY, ANDREW FRANCIS, JR. lawyer; b. Newark, Jan. 18, 1941; s. Andrew Francis and Veronica (White) D.; m. Mary Teresa McTague, Aug. 1, 1964; children—: Moira, Sheila, Andrew, Peter. B.A., St. Bonaventure U., 1962; J.D., Catholic U. Am., 1968. Bar: D.C. 1968, Md. 1974, U.S. Dist. Ct. Md. 1976, U.S. Ct. Claims, 1970, U.S. Ct. Appeals (4th cir.) 1976, U.S. Ct. Appeals (D.C. cir.) 1968, U.S. Supreme Ct. Ptnr. Hudson & Creyke, Washington, 1969-74; v.p., gen. counsel Intercounty Constrn., Balt. and Ft. Lauderdale, Fla., 1974-77; ptnr. Sullivan & Beauregard, Washington, 1977-82; chief exec. officer, mng. ptnr. Dempsey, Bastianelli, Brown and Touhey, Chartered, Washington, 1982— ; dir. Constructibility Cons., Washington; mem. NRC, Nat. Acad. Sci., U.S. Nat. Com on Tunneling Tech. Editor Catholic U. Law Rev., 1967-68. Served to capt. USMCR, 1962-65. Mem. ABA, D.C. Bar Assn., Md. State Bar Assn., Am. Arbitration Assn. (nat. panel arbitrators), Catholic U. Law Sch. Alumni Soc. (pres. 1982-85). Club: Army and Navy. Contracts commercial, Construction, Government contracts and claims. Home: 13304 Beall Creek Ct Rockville MD 20854-1117 Office: Dempsey Bastianelli Brown et al 2828 Pennsylvania Ave NW Washington DC 20007-3719

DEMPSEY, BERNARD HAYDEN, JR. lawyer; b. Evanston, Ill., Mar. 29, 1942; s. Bernard H. and Margaret C. (Gallagher) D.; m. Cynthia T. Dempsey; children: Bernard H. III, Matthew B., Kathleen N., Rose Maureen G., Alexandra C., Anastasia M. BS, Coll. Holy Cross, 1964; JD, Georgetown U., 1967. Bar: Fla. 1968, D.C. 1979. Law clk. to chief judge U.S. Dist. Ct. (mid. dist.) Fla., 1967-69; asst. U.S. Atty. Mid. Dist. Fla., 1969-73; pvt. practice Orlando, Fla., 1973—; spl. asst. to U.S. Atty. Mid. Dist. Fla., 1974. Lectr. in field. Contbr. articles to profl. jours. Recipient John Marshall award U.S. Dept. Justice, 1972, U.S. Atty's Outstanding Performance award 1970-73. Mem.: ABA, ATLA, Nat. Assn. Criminal Def. Lawyers, Fla. Assn. Criminal Def. Lawyers, U.S. Attys. Assn. for the Mid. Dist. Fla., Nat. Employment Lawyers Assn., Fla. Bar Assn., Am. Judicature Soc., Fla. Bar Found., Univ. Club (Orlando), Winter Park (Fla.) Racquet Club, Delta Theta Phi. Republican. Roman Catholic. Federal civil litigation, State civil litigation, Criminal. Office: Dempsey & Sasso Bank of America Ctr 390 N Orange Ave Ste 2700 Orlando FL 32801-1643 E-mail: demp-sas@magicnet.net

DEMPSEY, DAVID B. lawyer; b. Washington, June 26, 1949; s. James Raymon and Elizabeth (Barnes) D.; m. Elizabeth Carole Harwick, Oct. 9, 1982. BA cum laude, Amherst Coll., 1972; MPA, U. Tenn., 1973; JD, U. S.C., 1977. Bar: S.C. 1977, D.C. 1978, U.S. Dist. Ct. D.C. 1978, U.S. Ct. Appeals (D.C. cir.) 1979, U.S. Ct. Appeals (4th cir.) 1980, U.S. Supreme Ct. 1981, U.S. Claims Ct. 1981. Atty. advisor Def. Logistics Agy., Alexandria, Va., 1977-79, asst. counsel, 1980-82; asst. counsel Def. Fuel Supply Ctr., Alexandria, 1979-80; pvt. practice, Washington, 1982-84; ptnr. Whitney, Dempsey & Greif, Washington, 1984-86, Gardner, Carton & Douglas, 1986-88, Akin, Gump, Strauss, Hauer & Feld, 1988-96, Piper & Marbury, 1996—. Contbr. articles to legal jours. Mem. ABA, F ed. Bar Assn., D.C. Bar Assn., Burning Tree Club, Congl. Club (Bethesda). Government contracts and claims, Public international. Office: Akin Gump Strauss Hauer Feld Ste 400 1333 New Hampshire Ave NW Washington DC 20036-1564

DEMPSEY, EDWARD JOSEPH, lawyer; b. Lynn, Mass., Mar. 13, 1943; s. Timothy Finbar and Christine Margaret (Callahan) D.; m. Eileen Margaret McManus, Apr. 15, 1967; children: Kristen A. Stolfi, Katherine B. Aydin, Shelagh E., James P. AB, Boston Coll., 1964; JD, Cath. U. Am., 1970. Bar: D.C. 1970, Conn. 1982. Assoc. Arent, Fox, Kintner, Plotkin & Kahn, Washington, 1970-72, Akin, Gump, Strauss, Hauer & Feld, Washington, 1972-75; supervisory trial atty. EEOC, 1975-79; assoc. Whitman & Ransom, 1979-81, Farmer, Wells, McGuinn & Sibal, Washington, 1981-82; ptnr. Farmer, Wells, Sibal & Dempsey, Washington, Hartford, Conn., 1983-84; dir. indsl. rels. and labor counsel United Technologies Corp., Hartford, 1985—. Capt. USNR (ret.). Mem. ABA. Civil rights, Federal civil litigation, Labor. Office: United Techs Bldg Hartford CT 06101

DE MUNIZ, PAUL J. judge; Judge Oreg. Ct. Appeals, 1990—2001; justice Oreg. Supreme Ct., 2001—. Author (with others): Immigrants in Courts, 1999. Office: Supreme Ct 1163 State St Salem OR 97310*

DEMURO, PAUL ROBERT, lawyer; b. Aberdeen, Md., Mar. 21, 1954; s. Paul Robert and Amelia C. DeMuro; m. Susan Taylor, May 26, 1990; children: Melissa Taylor, Natalie Lauren, Alanna Leigh. BA summa cum laude, U. Md., 1976; JD, Washington U., 1979; MBA, U. Calif., Berkeley, 1986. Bar: Md. 1979, U.S. Dist. Ct. Md. 1979, D.C. 1980, U.S. Dist. Ct. D.C. 1980, U.S. Dist. Ct. (ea. dist.) Calif. 1986, U.S. Ct. Appeals (4th cir.) 1981, U.S. Tax Ct. 1981, Calif. 1982, U.S. Dist. Ct. (no. dist.) Calif. 1982; CPA, Md. Assoc. Ober, Grimes & Shriver, Balt., 1979-82; ptnr. Carpenter et al, San Francisco, 1982-89, McCutchen, Doyle, Brown & Enerson, San Francisco, 1989-93, Latham & Watkins, San Francisco, 1993—. Bd. dirs. HFMA Learning Solutions Inc. Author: The Financial Managers Guide to Managed Care and Integrated Delivery Systems, 1995, The Fundamentals of Managed Care and Network Development, 1999; co-author: Health Care Mergers and Acquisitions: The Transactional Perspective, 1996, Health Care Executives' Guide to Fraud and Abuse, 1998; editor, contbg. author Integrated Delivery Systems, 1994; article and book rev. editor Washington U. Law Qrtly., St. Louis, 1975-76. Mem. San Francisco Mus. Modern Art, 1985—. Fellow Healthcare Fin. Mgmt. Assn. (bd. dirs. No. Calif. chpt. 1990-93, 99—, sec. 1999-2001, pres.-elect 2001—, nat. principles and practices bd. 1992-95, vice chair 1993-95, nat. bd. dirs. 1995-97, exec. com. 1996-97, chair compliance officers forum adv. coun. 1998-2000); mem. ABA (health law sect., chair transactional and bus. health care interest group 1998-2000, chair programs com. 2000—, governing coun. 2000—),AICPA. L.A. County Bar Assn. (health law sect.), Calif. Bar Assn., San Francisco Bar Assn., Am. Health Lawyers Assn. (fraud and abuse and self-referral substantive law com. 1998—, task force on best practices in advising clients 1998-99), The IPA Assn. Am. (mem. legal adv. coun. 1996—), Med. Group Mgmt. Assn. Republican. Administrative and regulatory, Health, Mergers and acquisitions. Office: Latham & Watkins 505 Montgomery St Ste 1900 San Francisco CA 94111-2552 E-mail: paul.demuro@lw.com

DEMUTH, ALAN CORNELIUS, lawyer; b. Boulder, Colo., Apr. 29, 1935; s. Laurence Wheeler and Eugenia Augusta (Roach) DeM.; m. Susan McDermott; children: Scott Lewis, Evan Dale, Joel Millard. BA magna cum laude in Econs., U. Colo., 1958, LLB cum laude in Gen. Studies, 1961. Bar: Colo. 1961, U.S. Dist. Ct. Colo. 1961, U.S. Ct. Appeals (10th cir.) 1962. Assoc. Akolt, Turnquist, Shepherd & Dick, Denver, 1961-68; ptnr. DeMuth & DeMuth, 1968—. Conf. atty. Rocky Mountain Conf. United Ch. of Christ, 1970-95; bd. dirs. Friends of U. Colo. Libr., 1978-86; bd. dirs., sponsor Denver Boys Inc., 1987-93, sec., 1988-89, v.p., 1989-90, pres., 1992-93; bd. dirs. Denver Kids, Inc., 1993—, Children's Ctr. for Arts and Learning, 1995—; mem. bd. advisors Lambuth Family Ctr. of Salvation Army, 1994—, chmn., 1994—; bd. advisors Metro Denver Salvation Army, 1988—, vice chmn. 1994-96. Mem. ABA, Colo. Bar Assn., Denver Bar Assn., Denver Rotary (bd. dirs. 1996-98), Phi Beta Kappa, Sigma Alpha Epsilon, Phi Delta Phi. Republican. Mem. United Ch. of Christ. Bankruptcy, Consumer commercial, Real property. Office: DeMuth & DeMuth 990 S High St Denver CO 80209-4551

DENABURG, CHARLES L(EON), lawyer; b. Birmingham, Ala., June 5, 1934; s. Joe and Ethel (Levy) D.; m. Jan Barber, July, 1983; children: Lorraine, Edmond, David Todd. BS, U. Ala., 1954 JD, 1956. Bar: Ala. 1956. Sr. ptnr. Najjar Denaburg, P.C. and predessor firms, Birmingham, 1960—; panelist various seminars continuing legal edn. U. Ala., Tuscaloosa, 1965—. Capt. USAF, 1956-59. Fellow Am. Coll. of Bankruptcy (cert. creditors rights specialist); mem. ABA, Ala. State Bar Assn., Birmingham Bar Assn., Comml. Law League Am. Banking, Bankruptcy, Consumer commercial. Home: 3537 Mill Run Rd Birmingham AL 35223-1427 Office: Najjar Denaburg 2125 Morris Ave Birmingham AL 35203-4274

DENARO, GREGORY, lawyer; b. Rochester, N.Y., Dec. 10, 1954; m. Nancy Cardiff; children: Adrienne, Gregory, Madeline. BA, U. Rochester, 1976; JD, U. Miami, 1979. Bar: Fla. 1979, U.S. Dist. Ct. (so. dist.) Fla. 1979, U.S. Ct. Appeals (5th and 11th cirs.) 1981, U.S. Supreme Ct. 1984, N.Y. 1985, U.S. Dist. Ct. (mid. dist.) Fla. 1986, U.S. Ct. Appeals (D.C. cir.) 1989, U.S. Dist. Ct. (we. dist.) Tex. 1990, U.S. Ct. Appeals (4th cir.) 1992. Pub. defender Dade County, Miami, Fla., 1979-82; sr. ptnr. Gregory C. Denaro P.A., 1982—. Advisor nat. mock trial U. Miami Law Sch., 1984—. Mem. ABA (criminal law sect.), Dade County Bar Assn., Assn. Trial Attys., Nat. Assn. Criminal Def. Lawyers, Fla. Assn. Criminal Def. Lawyers (bd. dirs.). Criminal. Office: Coconut Grove Bank Bldg 2701 S Bayshore Dr Ste 605 Coconut Grove FL 33133-5360 E-mail: gdenaro@ix.netcom.com

DE NATALE, ANDREW PETER, lawyer; b. Bklyn., July 7, 1950; s. Peter E. and Mary (Tamberino) DeN.; m. Lynn Susan Kennedy, July 28, 1973; children: Andrew, Christopher. BS in Econs., U. Pa., 1972; JD, Fordham U., 1975. Bar: N.Y. 1976, U.S. Dist. Ct. (so. dist.) N.Y. 1976, U.S. Dist. Ct. (ea. dist.) N.Y. 1977, U.S. Ct. Appeals (2d cir.) 1978, U.S. Supreme Ct. 1979, U.S. Dist. Ct. (no. dist.) N.Y. 1982. Assoc. Krause, Hirsch & Gross, N.Y.C., 1975-79, Stroock & Stroock & Lavan, N.Y.C., 1980-83, ptnr., 1984-91, White & Case, N.Y.C., 1991—. Contbr. numerous articles to newspapers and profl. jours. Mem. ABA, N.Y. Yacht Club, Seawanhaka Corinthian Yacht Club. Bankruptcy, Contracts commercial. Office: White & Case Bldg Ll 1155 Avenue Of The Americas New York NY 10036-2787

DENGER, MICHAEL L. lawyer; b. Davenport, Iowa, Sept. 8, 1945; s. Ralph Henry and Bernice Marie (Cederberg) D.; m. Mary Elizabeth Colbert, Aug. 30, 1969; children: Lorna Marie, Mary Catherine, Rachel Anne. BS with highest distinction, Northwestern U., 1967; JD cum laude, Harvard U., 1970. Bar: D.C. 1970, U.S. Ct. Appeals (D.C. cir.) 1971, U.S. Supreme Ct. 1978. Assoc. atty. Sutherland, Asbill & Brennan, Washington, 1970-76, ptnr., 1976-92, Gibson, Dunn & Crutcher LLP, Washington, 1992—. Adj. prof. law Washington and Lee U., 2000—; speaker on antitrust, trade regulation numerous groups. Bd. editors Antitrust Report, 1992—; contbr. articles to profl. jours. Mem. nat. adv. coun. Northwestern U. Sch. Speech, Evanston, Ill., 1990—. 2d lt. USAR, 1970. Mem. ABA (vice chair antitrust law sect. 1985-86, sec. antitrust law sect. 1988-91, chair-elect antitrust law sect. 1991-92, chair antitrust law sect. 1992-93, chair edit. bd. antitrust sect. Federal and State Price Discrimination Law 1991, co-editor in chief antitrust sect. State Antitrust Practice and Statutes 3 vols. 1990, vice chair edit. bd. antitrust sect. Antitrust Law Devels. 2d edit. 1984), Columbia Country Club (Chevy Chase, Md.). Republican. Roman Catholic. Avocations: tennis, collecting military miniatures, military history, bridge. Antitrust, Federal civil litigation. Home: 5802 Kirkside Dr Chevy Chase MD 20815-7118 Office: Gibson Dunn & Crutcher LLP 1050 Connecticut Ave NW Ste 900 Washington DC 20036-5306 E-mail: mdenger@gibsondunn.com

DENHAM, EARL LAMAR, lawyer; b. Biloxi, Miss., July 1, 1947; s. Earl Lamar and Ruby (Young) D.; children: Katherine Elizabeth, Rachel Ann, Israel Anderson, Nathan Levi, Earl Lamar III; m. N.A. Hema Malini; children: Judith Jaya, Sachika Braka, Arya Tova. BS, U. Miss., 1969, JD, 1972. Bar: Miss. 1972, U.S. Dist. Ct. (no. and so. dists.) Miss. 1972, U.S. Ct. Appeals (5th cir.) 1978, U.S. Supreme Ct. 1978. Assoc. Hurlbert & O'Barr, Biloxi, 1972-73; ptnr. Levi & Denham, Ltd., Ocean Springs, Miss., 1973—. Capt. USAR, 1970-78. Mem. ABA, ATLA (sustaining), Nat. Assn. Criminal Def. Lawyers, Miss. Trial Lawyers Assn., Miss. Bar Assn., Ocean Springs Yacht Club (bd. govs. 1988). Democrat. Jewish. Avocations: sailing, hunting. Criminal, Family and matrimonial, Personal injury. Office: Levi & Denham Ltd 424 Washington Ave PO Box 596 Ocean Springs MS 39566-0596

DENHAM, VERNON ROBERT, JR. lawyer; b. Atlanta, Apr. 18, 1948; s. Vernon Robert and Sara Elizabeth (Robertson) D.; m. Susan Elizabeth Willis, Mar. 19, 1974; children: Whitney Willis, Tyler Willis. Student, Rensselaer Poly. Inst., 1966-68; BSE, U. Mich., 1970, MSE, 1972; JD with honors, U. Fla., 1979. Bar: Fla. 1979, Ga. 1979, U.S. Dist. Ct. (no. dist.) Ga. 1979, U.S. Ct. Appeals (11th cir.) 1981. Engr. Ford Motor Co., Dearborn, Mich., 1972-73; assoc. Powell, Goldstein, Frazer & Murphy, Atlanta, 1979-86, ptnr., 1986—. Mem. case notes com. U.S. Dist. Ct. (no. dist.) Ga., Atlanta, 1980-86, mem. magistrate merit selection panel, 1983. Lt. USNR, 1973-76. Mem. ABA (natural resources law sect., litigation sec., corp. and bus. sect.), Am. Chem. Soc., Internat. Soc. Regulatory Toxicology and Pharmacology, Fla. Bar (gen. practice trial sect., environ. and land use law sect.), State Bar Ga. (litigation and environ. sects.), Atlanta Bar Assn. (litigation, environ. sects., vice chair environ. sect. 1992-93, chair 1993-94), Order of Coif, Tau Beta Pi. General civil litigation, Environmental, Toxic tort. Home: 1433 Sheridan Walk NE Atlanta GA 30324-3253 Office: Powell Goldstein Frazer & Murphy 191 Peachtree St NE Fl 16 Atlanta GA 30303-1740 E-mail: bdenham@pgfm.com

DENKEWALTER, KIM RICHARD, lawyer; b. Chgo., May 7, 1948; s. Walter and Doris A. (Gast) D. BA, Loyola U., Chgo., 1971; JD, U. Ill., Chgo., 1974. Bar: Ill. 1974, U.S. Dist. Ct. (no. dist.) Ill. 1974, U.S. Ct. Appeals (7th cir.) 1977, U.S. Supreme Ct. 1979. Ptnr. Abramovic, Denkewalter & Ryan, Chgo., 1974-79; pres. Denkewalter & Assocs., 1979-85, Denkenwalter, Angelo & Minkow, 1986-97, Paramount Developers, Inc., 1997-98; real estate broker Chgo., 1978—. Mem. Hoopis Fin. Group, Northfield, Ill.; guest lectr. Am. Coll. Emergency Physicians, Rosemont, Ill., 1979-84. Served with USAR, 1970-76. Named hon. EMT-A, Ill. Dept. Pub. Health, 1983. Mem. ATLA, ABA, Ill. State Bar Assn., Chgo. Bar Assn., Ill. Real Estate Lawyers Assn., Mission Hills Country Club, The Men's Golf Assn. (bd. govs., v.p. 1997-98). General corporate, Estate planning, Real property. Home: 1762 Sienna Ct Wheeling IL 60090-6747 Office: Denkewalter & Angelo 790 W Frontage Rd Northfield IL 60093-1204 E-mail: krdlaw@aol.com

DENMAN, JAMES BURTON, lawyer; b. Brownwood, Tex., Nov. 15, 1947; s. James Burton and Margaret Gwendolyn D.; m. Donna Van Tuyle, Feb. 18, 1978; children— Tuyle, Lindsay. A.A., Porterville Jr. Coll., 1968; B.S., Calif. State U.-Fresno, 1970; J.D., Samford U., 1973. Bar: Fla. 1974. Ptnr., assoc. Dolan, Denman & Gramling, P.A., Fort Lauderdale, 1975-78; prin. James B. Denman & Assocs., P.A., Fort Lauderdale, 1978-80; ptnr. Bunnell, Denman & Woulfe, P.A., Fort Lauderdale, 1980— . Bd. dirs. Bethany Christian Sch., Fort Lauderdale, 1984. Mem. Assn. Trial Lawyers Am., Acad. Fla. Trial Lawyers. Democrat. Lutheran. Clubs: Lauderdale Yacht, Tower. Aviation, State civil litigation, Personal injury. Home: 1940 NE 59th St Fort Lauderdale FL 33308-2446 Office: Bunnell Denman & Woulfe PA 888 E Las Olas Blvd Fl 4 Fort Lauderdale FL 33301-2272

DENMARK, WILLIAM ADAM, lawyer; b. N.Y.C., July 30, 1957; s. Jerome and Frieda (Pollack) D.; m. Carol J. Sack, Apr. 20, 1986; children: Andrea K., Julie E. AB, Cornell U., 1979; JD, U. Pa., 1982. Bar: Pa. 1982, U.S. Dist. Ct. (ea. dist.) Pa. 1982. Assoc. Ballard, Spahr, Andrews & Ingersoll, Phila., 1982-86, Jacoby Donner, P.C., Phila., 1986-89, shareholder, 1989—. Contbr. articles to profl. jours. Mem. ABA, Nat. Assn. Demolition Contractors (assoc.), Phila. Bar Assn. (vice chair mergers and acquisitions com. bus. law sect. 1994-95, constrn. law and comml. leases com. real property sect.), Del. Valley Soc. Assn. Execs., Family Enterprise Inst., Phi Beta Kappa. Avocations: jogging, tennis, reading. Contracts commercial, Estate planning, Real property. Office: Jacoby Donner PC 1515 Market St Ste 2000 Philadelphia PA 19102-1920 E-mail: wdenmark@jacobydanner.com

DENNEEN, JOHN PAUL, lawyer; b. N.Y.C., Aug. 18, 1940; s. John Thomas Denneen and Pauline Jane Ludlow; m. Mary Veronica Murphy, July 3, 1965 (dec. Dec. 2000); children: John Edward, Thomas Michael, James Patrick, Robert Andrew, Daniel Joseph, Mary Elizabeth. BS, Fordham U., 1963; JD, Columbia U., 1966. Bar: N.Y. 1966, U.S. Ct. Appeals (2d cir.) 1974, U.S. Dist. Ct. (so. and ea. dists.) N.Y. 1975, Mo. 1987. Assoc. Seward & Kissel, N.Y.C., 1966-75; sr. v.p., gen counsel, sec. GK Techs., Inc., Greenwich, Conn., 1975-83; exec. v.p., gen. counsel, sec. Chromalloy Am. Corp., St. Louis, 1983-87; ptnr. Bryan Cave LLP, 1987-99; exec. v.p. corp. devel. and legal affairs, sec. and dir. NuVox, Inc., 1999—. Mem. ABA, Internat. Bar Assn., N.Y. State Bar Assn., N.Y.C. Bar Assn., Bar Assn. Met. St. Louis. Communications, Mergers and acquisitions, Securities. Office: NuVox Inc Ste 500 16090 Swingley Ridge Rd Chesterfield MO 63017-6029

DENNIS, ANTHONY JAMES, lawyer; b. Manchester, Conn., Feb. 11, 1963; s. Anthony James and Barbara Frances D. BA cum laude, Tufts U., 1985; JD, Northwestern U., Chgo., 1988. Bar: Conn. 1988, U.S. Dist. Ct. Conn. 1988, D.C. 1989. Assoc. Robinson & Cole, Hartford, Conn., 1988-89; atty. Aetna, Inc., 1989-92, counsel, 1992—. TV and radio talk show guest. Author: The Rise of the Islamic Empire and the Threat to the West, 1996, Letter to Khatami: A Reply to the Iranian President's Call for a Dialogue Among Civilizations, 2001; co-author: Healthcare Antitrust: Strategies for Changing Provider Organizations, 1994; contbr. articles to profl. jours. Mem. Conn. Bar Assn. (subcom. chmn. 1990-93, exec. com. 1990—, com. chmn. 1990—, treas. 1993-94, vice-chmn. 1994-95, chmn. 1995-99), D.C. Bar Assn., Am. Health Lawyers Assn., Wadsworth Atheneum, KC (past grand knight). Antitrust, General corporate, Health. Office: Aetna Inc 151 Farmington Ave Hartford CT 06156-0001 E-mail: dennisaj@aetna.com

DENNIS, EDWARD S(PENCER) G(ALE), JR. lawyer; b. Salisbury, Md., Jan. 24, 1945; s. Edward Spencer and Virginia (Monroe) D.; m. Lois Juliette Young, Dec. 27, 1969; 1 son, Edward Brookfield. BS, U.S. Mcht. Marine Acad., 1967; LLD, U. Pa., 1973. Bar: Pa. 1973. Law clk. Hon. A. Leon Higginbotham, Jr., U.S. Dist. Ct., Phila., 1973-75; asst. U.S. atty. U.S. Atty. Office, 1975-80, dep. chief. criminal div., 1978-80; chief narcotic and dangerous drug sect. U.S. Dept. Justice, Washington, 1980-83, asst. atty. gen. criminal div., 1988-90, acting dep. atty. gen., 1989; U.S. atty. Ea. Dist. Pa., Phila., 1983-88; ptnr., co-chair corp. investigations, criminal def. practice Morgan, Lewis & Bockius, 1990—. Adj. prof. Law Sch. U. Pa. Fellow Am. Coll. Trial Lawyers; mem. ABA, Nat. Bar Assn., Phila. Bar Assn., Internat. Soc. Barristers. Federal civil litigation, Criminal. Office: Morgan Lewis & Bockius 1701 Market St Philadelphia PA 19103-2903 also: 1800 M St NW Washington DC 20036-5802

DENNIS, JAMES LEON, federal judge; b. Monroe, La., Jan. 9, 1936; s. Jenner Leon and Hope (Taylo) D.; m. Gwen Nicolich; children: Stephen James, Gregory Leon, Mark Taylo, John Timothy. B.S. in Bus. Adminstrn, La. Tech. U., Ruston, 1959; J.D., La. State U., 1962; LL.M., U. Va., 1984. Bar: La. 1962. Assoc. firm Hudson, Potts & Bernstein, Monroe, 1962-65, ptnr., 1965-72; judge 4th Dist. Ct. La. for Morehouse and Ouachita Parishes, 1972-74, La. 2d Circuit Ct. Appeals, 1974-75; assoc. justice La. Supreme Ct., 1975-95; coord. La. Constnl. Revision Commn., 1970-72; del., chmn. judiciary com. La. Constnl. Conv., 1973; judge U.S. Ct. Appeals Fifth Cir., New Orleans, 1995—. Mem. La. Ho. of Reps., 1968-72; chmn. La. Commn. on Bicentennial U.S. Constn. With U.S. Army, 1955-57. Served with AUS, 1955-57. Mem. ABA (com. on appellate practice), La. Bar Assn., 4th Jud. Bar Assn. Methodist. Club: Rotary. Office: US Courthouse 600 Camp StRm 219 New Orleans LA 70130-3425*

DENNIS, SAMUEL SIBLEY, III, lawyer; b. Boston, June 23, 1910; s. Samuel Sibley and Helen M. (Ferguson) D.; m. Lillian Elena Williamson, Aug. 19, 1938; children: Nancy Anne (dec.), Ellen Ferguson Dennis Beck. AB, Harvard U., 1932, MBA, 1934, LLB, 1938. Bar: Mass. 1938. Sr. ptnr. Hale & Door, 1951—; v.p. Standex Internat. Corp., Andover, Mass., 1955—, also bd. dirs., mem. exec. com. and gen. counsel; bd. dirs.Augat, Inc., French River Industries; former mem. vis. com. of bd. overseers Law Sch., former co-chmn. bequest Com. Bus. Sch., Harvard U., past mem. com. on stockholder responsibility. Pres. Roxbury Latin Sch., 1972-84, life trustee, 1951—, vice chmn., 1984—; trustee corp. Jordan Hosp., Plymouth; bd. dirs. Montgomery Found., Fairchild Fellows; trustee, mem. exec. com. Plymouth Plantation, 1988—. Served to col. C.E., AUS, 1941-45, now col. Res. Decorated Legion of Merit. Mem. ABA, Mass. Bar Assn., Boston Bar Assn., Mil. Order World Wars, Harvard Bus. Sch. Assn., Harvard Law Sch. Assn. (former bd. govs.), World Affairs Council. Clubs: Harvard U. (Boston and Miami, Fla.); Duxbury Yacht; Country (Brookline, Mass.); Key Largo, Anglers, Coral Reef, Ocean Reef; Masons. Home: 42 Marina Dr RR 1 Box 262 Key Largo FL 33037 also: 175 Washington St PO Box 2565 Duxbury MA 02331-2565 Office: Hale and Dorr 60 State St Ste 25 Boston MA 02109-1816

DENNISON-LEONARD, SARAH, lawyer; b. Seattle, Oct. 6, 1962; d. David Christian III and Mary Louise (Dunker) Henny; m. Charles Edward Leonard, Oct. 22, 1988; children: Carlie, Gaela. BA, Smith Coll., 1986; JD, Stanford U., 1994. Bar: Oreg. 1994. Crew coach U. Mass., Amherst, 1987-88; dir. health svcs. Hampshire County chpt. ARC, Northampton, Mass., 1989-90; assoc. Stoel Rives LLP, Portland, Oreg., 1994-98; ptnr. Krogh & Leonard, 1998—. Spkr. in field. ECAC scholar-athlete, 1986. Mem. ABA, Oreg. State Bar Assn., Phi Beta Kappa. Avocations: parenting, sports, hiking. Office: Krogh & Leonard 506 SW 6th Ave Ste 750 Portland OR 97204-1555

DENNISTON, BRACKETT BADGER, III, lawyer; b. Oak Park, Ill., July 23, 1947; s. Brackett Bardger Jr. and Frances Ann (Jones) D.; m. Kathleen Foley, Aug. 2, 1975; children: Alexandra, Brackett Badger IV, Elizabeth. AB, Kenyon Coll., 1969; JD, Harvard U., 1973. Bar: Mass. 1974, U.S. Dist. Ct. Mass. 1975, U.S. Dist. Ct. (we. dist.) Tex. 1987, U.S. Ct. Appeals (1st cir.) 1975, U.S. Ct. Appeals (D.C. cir.) 1976, U.S. Ct. Appeals (7th cir.) 1978, U.S. Ct. Appeals (10th cir.) 1981, U.S. Supreme Ct. 1981. Law clk. to judge U.S. Ct. Appeals for 9th Cir., Honolulu, 1973-74; assoc. Goodwin, Procter & Hoar, Boston, 1974-81, ptnr., 1981-82, 86-93, mem. exec. com., 1990-93; chief major frauds unit U.S. Atty.'s Office, 1982-86; chief legal counsel Gov. of Mass., 1993-96; v.p., sr. counsel litigation GE, Fairfield, Conn., 1996—, also chmn. policy compliance rev. bd. Class chmn. Kenyon Coll., Gambier, Ohio, 1979-90, trustee, 2000—; mem. Duxbury (Mass.) Zoning Bd. Appeals, 1980-92, chmn., 1984-90. Recipient Dir.'s award for superior achievement U.S. Dept. Justice, 1986. Mem. Mass. Bar Assn. (chmn. coun. jud. adminstrn. sect. 1989-90, jud. adminstrv. coun. 1987-90, 95-96, criminal justice sect. 1986—, litig. sect. 1988—). General civil litigation, Criminal, Securities. Office: GE Co 3137 Easton Tpke Fairfield CT 06432-1008 E-mail: brackett.denniston@corporate.ge.com

DENNISTON, JEANNIE L. lawyer; b. Jackson, Miss., May 3, 1951; d. Verne Leroy Culbertson and Mabel Jean Bunge; m. Michael Edward Denniston, (div. Aug. 1999); 1 child, Sara Elizabeth. BS, U. Ozarks, 1973; JD, U. Ark., Little Rock, 1994. Office mgr. McGuire-Smith, Little Rock, 1976-79; mortgage banker Worthen Bank & Trust, 1979-84; constrn. loan officer City Nat. Bank, Ft. Smith, Ark., 1984; adminstrv. asst. ERC properties, 1984-91; pvt. practice law Morrilton, Ark., 1994-98; dep. prosecuting atty. Conway County, 1997-98; assoc. Gordon, Caruth & Virden, 1998—. Instr. 100 Proof Inc., Morrilton, 1997-2000. Mem. Morrilton Planning and Zoning Commn., 1996-99; bd. dirs. Safe Place Inc., Morrilton, 1995-96, Main St. Morrilton Inc., 1996-97. Mem. ABA, Ark. Bar Assn., Ark. Trial Lawyers Assn., Ark. Assn. Women Lawyers, Conway County Bar Assn., Morrilton Area C. of C. (treas. 1999, 2d v.p. 2000, 1st v.p. 2001, bd. dirs. 1997-98), Kiwanis. Baha'i. Avocations: SCUBA diving, needlework. Alternative dispute resolution, Criminal, Probate. Office: Gordon Caruth & Virden PLC PO Box 558 105 S Moose St Morrilton AR 72110-3425

DENNISTON, JOHN BAKER, lawyer; b. Cin., June 3, 1936; s. John B. Denniston and Edna (Gentile) Denniston Langlois Schrader; m. Susan Russell Loud, May 1990; children from previous marriage: Derek C., Lavinia H., Miles S. B.E. in Physics, Cornell U., 1958; LL.B., Harvard U., 1962; postgrad. Sydney U., Australia, 1962-63. Bar: U.S. Ct. Fed. Claims, U.S. Ct. Appeals (fed. cir.) 1963, U.S. Supreme Ct. 1964. Research engr. Rocketdyne div. N.Am. Aviation, 1958-59; research analyst Inst. for Def. Analysis, 1960-61; Teaching asst. MIT, 1960-61; assoc. Covington &

Burling, Washington, 1963-1971, ptnr., 1971— . Author: (with others) McGraw-Hill Construction Business Handbook. Mem. ABA, D.C. Bar Assn. (exec. council 1969-70, young lawyer of yr. 1971) Club: Metropolitan. Government contracts and claims, Immigration, naturalization, and customs, Public international. Home: 2800 Foxhall Rd NW Washington DC 20007-1129 Office: Covington & Burling PO Box 7566 1201 Pennsylvania Ave NW Washington DC 20004-2401

DENNY, COLLINS, III, lawyer; b. Richmond, Va., Dec. 5, 1933; s. Collins Jr. and Rebecca (Miller) D.; m. Anne Carples, June 28, 1957; children: Collins IV, William R., Katharine M. AB, Princeton U., 1956; LLB, U. Va., 1961. Bar: Va. 1961, U.S. Dist. Ct. (ea. dist.) Va. 1962, U.S. Ct. Appeals (4th cir.) 1962. U.S. Tax Ct. 1971, U.S. Ct. Claims 1976. Assoc. Denny, Valentine & Davenport, Richmond, 1961-67; ptnr. Mays & Valentine LLP, 1967-2000, mng. ptnr., 1992-93; ptnr. Troutman, Sanders, Mays & Valentine LLP, 2001—. Gen. counsel, corp. sec. Coastal Lumber Co., Weldon, NC, 1980—; gen. counsel Bear Island Timberlands Co., LLC, Ashland, Va., 1985—99, Bear Island Paper Co., LLC, 1989—2000. Contbr. chpt. to book, articles to profl. jours. Lt. USNR, 1956-66. Mem. ABA (chmn. exempt orgns. subcom., tax sect. 1971-86), Va. Bar Assn. (chmn. jr. bar 1965-66), Va. State Bar (com. chmn. 1981-83), Va. Tax Rev. (adv. bd. 1978—), Va. Forestry Assn., Richmond Feeder Cattle Assn. (pres. 1972-77), Princeton Alumni Assn. Va. (pres. 1974-78), Richmond-First Club (pres. 1969-70), Deep Run Hunt Club (pres. 1986-88), Va. Country Club. Episcopalian. Avocations: horse sports, tree farming, agriculture. General corporate, Natural resources, Taxation, general. Home: 1230 Millers Ln Manakin Sabot VA 23103-2720 Office: TroutmanSanders Mays & Valentine LLP 1111 E Main St PO Box 1122 Richmond VA 23218-1122

DENSMORE, DOUGLAS WARREN, lawyer; b. Jan. 30, 1948; s. Warren Orson and Lois Martha (Ery) D.; m. Janet Roberta Broadley, Oct. 26, 1973; children: Bradley Wythe, Andrew Fitz Douglas. AB, Coll. of William and Mary, Williamsburg, Va., 1970; JD cum laude, U. Toledo, 1975. Bar: Ohio 1976, U.S. Dist. Ct. (no. dist.) Ohio, Va. 1980, U.S. Dist. Ct. (ea. and we. dists.) Va. 1980, U.S. Ct. Appeals (4th cir.) 1980, U.S. Supreme Ct., 1997. Assoc. Gertner, Barkan & Robon, Toledo, 1975-77, Shumaker, Loop & Kendrick, Toledo, 1977-79; corp. counsel Dominion Bankshares Corp., Roanoke, Va., 1979-80; assoc. Woods, Rogers, Muse, Walker & Thornton, 1980-84; ptnr. Woods, Rogers & Hazlegrove, 1984-96, Flippin, Densmore, Morse and Jessee, Roanoke, 1996—. Co-author: Examining the Increase in Federal Regulatory Requirements and Penalties: Is Banking Facing Another Troubled Decade?, 1995; contbr. articles to profl. jours. Bd. dirs. New Century Tech. Coun. Decorated Venerable Order St. John (Eng.), Companion of the O'Conor Don (Ireland), knight grand cross Royal Order of Don Carlos I (Portugal), knight grand cross Order of St. Catherine, knight comdr. of justice Order of St. Lazarus, first class Order of Polonia Restituta (Poland), knight grand cross Order St. Stanislas (Poland), knight grand cross Order of the Temple, knight comdr. Order of Crown of Thorns, knight grand cross Order of St. Michael and St. George, knight grand cross Orthodox Order St. John, knight Order of St. John, Knights of Malta, knight grand cross Order of Holy Cross of Jerusalem, knight grand cross with collar Order of St. Gregory, knight grand cross Order of St. Stephen, Royal Ukranian Order of St. Vladimir the Great, knight grand cross Greek Order of St. Denis of Zante, Order of the White Eagle. Fellow Baskerville Soc. (U.K.); mem. ABA (banking law com. 1988—, uniform comml. code com. 1988—), Va. Bar Assn. (corp. code com. 1984—), Bar Assn. City of Roanoke (bd. dirs. 1998—; pres. 2001—), Am. Corp. Counsel Assn., Roanoke Regional C. of C. (bd. dirs. 1999—), Scottish Soc. Va. Highlands (bd. dirs. 1992—), Vet. Corps Art, Army-Navy Union, Brit. Manorial Soc. (Lord of Stratford St. Andrew), Augustan Soc., English Speaking Union (bd. dirs.), Soc. of St. George, Kiwanis Internat., Masons (32 degree, master, jr. deacon 1992), Shriners, Royal Order of Scotland, Shenandoah Club (Roanoke), Roanoke Country Club, Farmington Country Club (Charlottesville, Va.), Royal Overseas Club (London). Episcopalian. Avocations: golf, gardening, reading. Banking, General civil litigation, General corporate. Office: 2625 S Jefferson St Roanoke VA 24014-3315 E-mail: densmore@flippindensmore.com

DENSON, ALEXANDER BUNN, federal magistrate judge; b. Rocky Mount, N.C., Nov. 11, 1936; s. Samuel Leland and Elizabeth Pearl (Bunn) D.; children: Rebecca Anne Denson, Matthew Robert. BS, N.C. State U., 1959; LLB, Duke U., 1966. Bar: N.C. 1966. Assoc. Yarborough, Blanchard & Tucker, Raleigh, 1966-68; ptnr. Blanchard, Tucker, Twiggs & Denson, 1968-81; U.S. magistrate judge U.S. Dist. Ct. (ea. dist.), 1981—. OSHA adminstrv. law judge cons. N.C. Dept. Labor, Raleigh, 1978-81. 00536501Pres. Sir Walter Lions Club, 1982-83, Symphony Soc., Wake County chpt., 1975-76; founder Raleigh-Wake County Coalition for Homeless, 1987—; deacon Pullen Meml. Bapt. Ch., 1989-91; founding mem. Am. Shroud of Turin Assn., 1990-92; dir. Community Alternative Support Abodes for Mentally Ill Homeless, 1992-2000, chair 1996-2001; mem. initial bd. Next Step Housing, 2001—; elder Westminster Presbyn. Ch., 1998—. Lt. USNR, 1959-63. Recipient Outstanding Contbns. to Human Rels. and Human Svc. recognition, Gov., Raleigh Mayor, City Council, 1989. Mem. Wake County Duke Bar Assn. (past pres.). Republican. Avocations: gardening, chess. Office: US Dist Ct Po Box 25610 310 New Bern Ave Raleigh NC 27611-5610

DENT, EDWARD DWAIN, lawyer; b. Ft. Worth, Dec. 23, 1950; BA, Tex. Christian U., 1973; JD, St. Mary's U., Tex., 1976. Bar: Tex., U.S. Dist. Ct. (no. and so. dists.) Tex., U.S. Supreme Ct. Atty., ptnr. Kugle, Stewart, Dent, Frederick, Ft. Worth, 1979-89; founder Dent Law Firm, Ft. Worth, Dallas, 1990—. Bd. dirs. Greater Boys and Girls Clubs, Ft. Worth, West Side Little League. Recipient Hist. Preservation award, Tarrant County Hist. Soc., 1992. Mem. ATLA, U.S. Supreme Ct. Hist. Soc., Tex. Trial Lawyers (bd. dirs. 1989—), Tarrant County Trial Lawyers (bd. dirs. 1988-89, officer 1989), Trial Lawyers for Pub. Justice, Ft. Worth Club, Colonial Country Club, Million Dollar Advocacy Soc. (life). Democrat. Insurance, Personal injury. Office: Dent Law Firm 1120 Penn St Fort Worth TX 76102-3417

DENT, THOMAS AUGUSTINE, lawyer, educator; b. N.Y.C., Aug. 28, 1920; s. Darby Thomas and Mary Margaret (Goggins) D.; m. Virginia Michels, Apr. 21, 1951; children— Francis W. Koupash, Marie Dent Scofield, Marc Thomas. BA, Queens Coll., 1942; JD, Bklyn. Law Sch., 1948, LLM, 1957. Bar: N.Y. 1949, U.S. Dist. Ct. (so. dist.) N.Y. 1949, U.S. Dist. Ct. (ea. dist.) N.Y. 1980, U.S. Ct. Appeals (2d cir.) 1980. Assoc. Dayton & D'Amato, Bayside, N.Y., 1950-54; sole practice, Flushing, N.Y., 1954-55; ptnr. Dent & Witschieben and predecessor Dent, Goldblum & Witschieben, Flushing, 1955-78, Garden City, N.Y., 1978— ; adj. assoc. prof. bus. law Queens Coll., Flushing, 1962-88; asst. dist. atty. Queens County, Kew Gardens, 1964-66; arbitrator Civil Ct. City N.Y., Kew Gardens, 1981-91. Pres. Child Guidance Ctr. No. Queens, Flushing, 1959-62; counsel Udalls Cove Preservation Com., Inc., Douglaston, N.Y., 1979— . Lt. USN, 1943-46; PTO. Mem. Bar Assn. Nassau County, Queens County Bar Assn., Queens Coll. Alumni Assn. (pres. 1951-53, trustee 1974—). Democrat. Roman Catholic. Clubs: North Hills Country (Manhasset, N.Y.). Rotary (pres. local club 1955-56, dist. gov. 1976-77). Probate, Real property, Estate taxation. Home: 25025 41st Rd Flushing NY 11363-1712 Office: Dent & Witschieben 821 Franklin Ave Garden City NY 11530-4519

DENTEN, CHRISTOPHER PETER, lawyer; b. Oakland, Calif., Apr. 23, 1964; s. Richard and Waltraud Denten; m. Mary McLaughlin, May 18, 1996. BA, U. Calif., Berkeley, 1986; JD, U. San Francisco, 1990. Bar: Calif. 1991, U.S. Dist. Ct. (no. dist.) Calif. 1991, U.S. Ct. Appeals (9th cir.) 1991; CPA, Colo. Tax profl. KPMG Peat Marwick, Oakland, 1988-92; sr. tax analyst Cisco Sys., Inc., San Jose, Calif., 1992-97; dir. legal affairs and taxation Network Assocs., Inc. (formerly McAfee, Inc.), Santa Clara, 1997—. Bd. dirs. Network Assocs. fgn. subs., 2000—. Named to Outstanding Young Men of Am., 1982; Brother Gary Stone Meml. scholar, 1982. Mem. AICPA, Santa Clara Bar As, U. Calif. Berkeley Alumni Assn., U. San Francisco Law Sch. Alumni Assn., Network Assocs. Pres. Club. Republican. Roman Catholic. Avocations: marathons, golf, art, travel. General corporate, Mergers and acquisitions, Corporate taxation. Home: PO Box 117932 Burlingame CA 94011-7932 Office: Network Assocs Inc 3965 Freedom Cir Santa Clara CA 95054-1203

DENTON, DEBORAH S. lawyer; b. Kansas City, Mo., May 4, 1972; d. Ted L. and Mary R. Wills; m. Chuck C. Denton, June 14, 1997. BA in Polit. Sci., Westminster Coll., 1994; JD, U. Ark., 1997. Bar: Ark. 1997, U.S. Dist. Ct. Ark. 1998. Trial atty. Laser, Wilson, Bufford & Watts, Little Rock, 1997—. Mem. ABA, Ark. County Bar Assn., Pulaski County Bar Assn., William R. Overton Inns of Ct. Democrat. Methodist. General civil litigation, Insurance, Personal injury. Office: Laser Wilson Buford & Watts PA 101 S Spring St Ste 300 Little Rock AR 72201

DEORA, CHANDRA KUMAR, lawyer; b. Calcutta, India, July 1, 1950; s. Badri Prasad and Pana Devi Deora; m. Sudha Agarwal, Oct. 7, 1983. B in Comm. with honors, St. Xavier's Coll., Calcutta, 1969; M in Comm., Calcutta U., 1972; LLB, Univ. Coll. Law, Calcutta, 1973. Bar: West Bengal, India. Assoc. Leslie & Khettry, Solicitors, Calcutta, 1974-77, Himatsingica & Co., Calcutta, 1977-85; ptnr. S. Jalan & Co., Solicitors, 1985—. Bd. dirs. Jalan Cons. Pvt. Ltd., Calcutta. Mem. Bar Coun. West Bengal, Law Soc. Calcutta, Cosmopolitan Club Calcutta. Avocations: attending seminars, travel, social work, television, music. Office e-mail: 091-033-210-4641. Contracts commercial, Probate, Real property. Office: S Jalan & Co 10 Old Post Office St 700001 Calcutta India

DEORCHIS, VINCENT MOORE, lawyer; b. N.Y.C., Aug. 25, 1949; s. Mario E. and Frankie (Moore) DeO.; m. Donna B., July 24, 1971; children: Vincent Scott, Dana Lauren. BA, Fordham Coll., 1971, JD, 1974. Bar: N.Y. 1975, U.S. Dist. Ct. (so. and ea. dists.) N.Y. 1975, U.S. Ct. Appeals (2d cir.) 1975, U.S. Supreme Ct. 1985, U.S. Ct. Appeals (3d cir.) 1989, U.S. Dist. Ct. (so. dist.) Tex. 1992, U.S. Ct. Appeals (4th cir.) 1996. Assoc. Haight, Gardner, Poor & Havens, N.Y.C., 1974-84; ptnr. DeOrchis & Ptnrs., 1984-97, DeOrchis, Walker & Corsa, LLP, N.Y.C., 1997—. Co-author: Attorney's Practice Guide to Negotiations, 1985. Pres. North Stratmore Civic Assn., Manhasset, N.Y., 1978-82. Mem. ATLA, ABA (com. on maritime litig.), Inter-Pacific Bar Assn., Maritime Law Assn. (bd. dirs., rep. to Comite Maritime Internat.), Assn. Transp. Practitioners, N.Y. County Lawyers Assn. (com. on maritime and admiralty law), Propeller Club U.S. Avocation: sailing. Admiralty, Federal civil litigation, Insurance. Office: DeOrchis Walker & Corsa 61 Broadway Fl 26 New York NY 10006-2802

DEPEW, SPENCER LONG, lawyer; b. Wichita, Kans., June 6, 1933; s. Claude I. and Frances Ann (Bell) D.; m. Donna Wolever, Dec. 28, 1957; children: Clifford S., Sally F. AB, U. Wichita, 1955; LLB, U. Mich., 1960. Bar: Kans.; U.S. Dist. Ct. Kans.; U.S. Supreme Ct. Mem. Depew and Gillen, LLC, Wichita. Mem. Interstate Oil and Gas Compact Commn., Oklahoma City. With U.S. Army, 1955-57, Germany. Mem. IPAA, Kans. Ind. Oil and Gas Assn. General corporate, Oil, gas, and mineral, Estate planning. Home: 6322 E English St Wichita KS 67218-1802 Office: Depew and Gillen LLC 151 N Main St Ste 800 Wichita KS 67202-1409

DE PFYFFER, ANDRE, lawyer, director; b. Lucerne, Switzerland, Nov. 3, 1928; s. Leodegar and Anna (Carvalho) de P.; children by previous marriage: Corinne, Francois; m. Francoise Garnier del Campo, 1983. Baccalaureat, U. Berne, 1947; postgrad., U. Vienna, 1947-50. Admitted to Geneva Lawyers Assn., 1952; since practiced in Geneva; sr. ptnr. firm de Pfyffer & Assocs. Dir. Volvo Suisse S.A., Banque Paribas (Suisse) S.A.; vice chmn. Pargesa Holding, S.A.; past consul gen. of Sweden in Geneva. Decorated comdr. Royal Order of the Polar Star (Sweden). Mem. Internat. Law Assn., Circle de la Terrasse. Banking, Contracts commercial, General corporate. Home: 6 Rue Eynard Geneva Switzerland Office: 6 Rue Bellot Geneva Switzerland E-mail: andre.depfyffer@depfyffer.ch

DERBY, ERNEST STEPHEN, federal judge; b. Boston, July 10, 1938; s. Elmer Goodrich and Lucy (Davis) D.; m. Gretel Hanauer, June 10, 1961; children: Anne Gray, Michael Stephen. AB with distinction, Wesleyan U., 1960; LLB cum laude, Harvard U., 1965. Bar: Md. Ct. Appeals 1965, U.S. Dist. Ct. Md. 1966, U.S. Ct. Appeals (4th cir.) 1968, U.S. Supreme Ct. 1973. Law clk. to presiding justice U.S. Dist. Ct. Md. and U.S. Ct. of Appeals 4th cir., 1965-66; assoc. Piper & Marbury, Balt., 1966-71, ptnr., 1973-87; asst. atty. gen. Atty. Gen. Md., 1971-73; judge U.S. Bankruptcy Ct., Balt., 1987—. Adj. faculty U. Md. Sch. Law, 1987, 90-99. Pres. Dismas Ho., Balt. Inc., 1969—; trustee Enoch Pratt Free Libr., Balt., 1977-93. Fellow Am. Coll. Bankruptcy, Md. Bar Found.; mem. Md. State Bar Assn., Anne Arundel County Bar Assn., Paca/Brent Am. Inn of Ct. (pres. 1993-94). Office: US District Court US Courthouse 101 W Lombard St Ste 9442 Baltimore MD 21201-2906

DERBY, STEVEN LEO, lawyer; b. Lackawanna, N.Y., May 4, 1964; s. Leo Edward and Bernadette Muriel D.; m. Debbie Anuskiewicz, Oct. 17, 1992; children: Kevin Robert, Alison Bernadette. BA in French and Govt., St. Lawrence U ., Canton, N.Y., 1986; JD, Golden Gate U., 1990. Bar: Calif. 1990, U.S. Dist. Ct. (no. dist.) Calif. 1990. Law clk. Evans, Farber & Cipinko, San Francisco, 1988-90, 1990-92; assoc. Law Offices of Paul B. Engler, Walnut Creek, Calif., 1992—. Mock trial judge Golden Gate U., San Francisco, 1990—. Contbr. articles to profl. jours. Vol. Vol. Legal Svcs., San Francisco, 1992—, AIDS Action Legal Program, San Francisco, 1999, Atty.'s Reference Panel, Concord, 1992—; panel mem. KRON Action Com., Daly City, Concord, Calif., 1998-99. Mem. ATLA, Consumers Attys. Calif., Contra Costa City Bar Assn. (judge pro temp 1998, mediator 1998). Democrat. Roman Catholic. Avocations: baseball, carpentry, bowling, tennis. Home: 2460 Overlook Dr Walnut Creek CA 94596-3009 Office: Law Offices of Paul B Engler 961 Ygnacio Valley Rd Walnut Creek CA 94596-3825

DEROMA, NICHOLAS JOHN, lawyer, telecommunications company executive; b. Hartford, Connecticut, Mar. 1, 1946; s. Nicholas Rocco and Constance Marie (Rucci) D.; m. Sandra Marie Pergiovanni, Aug. 17, 1968. BS cum laude, U. Connecticut, Storrs, 1968; JD cum laude, COll. William and Mary, Williamsburg, Va., 1971. Bar: District of Columbia, 1972, Virginia, 1971. Editor William and Mary Law Review, Williamsburg, 1970-71; law clerk U.S. Court of Claims, Wahington D.C., 1971-72; regional counsel, staff lawyer IBM Corp., Atlanta, Washington D.C., 1972-81; general counsel, secretary IBM World Trade Asia Corp., Hong Kong, China, 1981-84; dvsn. counsel IBM Information Products Dvsn., New York, 1984-86; mng. atty. IBM Corp., 1986-87; assoc. general counsel IBM Application Business Systems, 1987-88, IBM Applications Solutions Line of Business, New York, 1989-91; v.p., general counsel, secretary IBM World Trade Europe, Middle East, Africa Corp., Paris, France, 1991-93; asst. general counsel, corporate law Internat. Business Machines Corp., New York, 1993-95; general counsel IBM North America, 1995-97; v.p., deputy general counsel Nortel Networks Corp., Brampton, Canada, 1998-99, chief legal officer Canada, 1999—. Mem. The Mentor Group, American Corporate Counsel Assn., Internat. Bar Assn., Canada-U.S. Law Inst. (adv. bd.), The Assn. of Canadian General Counsel, General Counsel Roundtable (corp. exec., chief legal officer), Canadian Bar Assn. Construction, General corporate. Office: Nortel Networks Corp 8200 Dixie Rd Ste 100 Brampton ON Canada L6T 5P6 Fax: 905-863-8544. E-mail: nderoma@nortelnetworks.com

DERON, EDWARD MICHAEL, lawyer; b. Detroit, Dec. 18, 1945; m. Jana Lene Berlenbach, Aug. 12, 1977. BS, Wayne State U., 1968, JD cum laude, 1972; LLM in Taxation, NYU, 1973. Bar: Mich. 1972, U.S. Ct. Appeals (6th cir.) 1973, U.S. Tax Ct. 1974. Assoc. Evans & Luptak, Detroit, 1973-79, ptnr., 1980—. Contbr. chpt. to book. With U.S. Army, 1969-71, ETO, Germany. Mem. ABA, Mich. Bar Assn. (taxation sect., chmn. estates and trusts com. 1994-96, taxation sect. coun. 1996-99, editor Mich. Tax Lawyer 1998-99, sec. 1999-2000, treas. 2000—) Detroit Met. Bar Assn. (co-chmn. taxation com. 1984-86), Fin. and Estate Planning Coun. Met. Detroit, Detroit Athletic Club, Rotary, KC. General corporate, Estate planning, Taxation, general. Office: Evans & Luptak 2500 Buhl Building Detroit MI 48226-3674 E-mail: ederon@evansluptak.com, ederon@aol.com

DE ROSSO, PABLO, lawyer; b. Buenos Aires, Dec. 20, 1965; Lawyer magna cum laude, Argentine Cath. U., 1989. Ptnr. Martelli Abogados, Buenos Aires, 1997—. Recipient Scholarship award for outstanding students of Japanese language Japanese Edn. Min., 1991. Mem. Internat. Bar Assn., Buenos Aires Bar Assn. Contracts commercial, General corporate, Oil, gas, and mineral. Office: Martelli Abogados San Martin 323 piso 13 C1004AAG Buenos Aires Argentina Fax: 54 11 4328 7557. E-mail: pablo.derosso@martelliabogados.com

DEROUIN, PHILIPPE, lawyer; b. Saint-Germain-En-Laye, France, Mar. 27, 1948; s. Daniel and Renee (Casse) Derouin; m: Dominique Dulieu, June 11, 1982; children: Alexandre, Beatrice, Frederic, Aurelie. Institut D' Etudes, Politiques, Paris, France, 1967; M in Economics, U. Paris, France, 1968, ML, 1973, LLD, 1976. Paris Bar, 1973. Auditor Arthur Andersen, Paris, 1970-71; assoc. Goldsmith, Chartier, Delvolve, 1971-75; counsel Cridon, 1975-77; assoc. barrister French Supreme Ct., 1977-87; ptnr. Gide, Loyrette, Nouel, 1987-99, Linklaters, Paris, 1999—. Author: La Taxe Sur La Valeur Ajoute Dans La Cee, 1976; En Impuesto Sobre El Valor Añadido El La Cee, 1981; co-author: Droit Penal De La Fiscalite, 1989; contbr. articles to profl. jours. Mem. Paris Bar Council, French Inst. of Tax Advisers (past pres.), Internat. Fiscal Assn., Internat. Bar Assn., American Bar Assn. Second lt. French Army, 1968-70. Avocations: jogging, gardening. Corporate taxation, Taxation, general, European and French Commercial & Corporate. Office: Linklaters Rue De Marignan 25 75008 Paris France Fax: 33 1 43 59 5095. E-mail: pderouin@linklaters.com

DEROUSIE, CHARLES STUART, lawyer; b. Adrian, Mich., May 24, 1947; s. Stuart J. and Helia I. (Juntunen) DeR.; m. Patricia Jean Fetzer, May 31, 1969; children: Jennifer, Jason. BA magna cum laude, Oakland U., 1969; JD magna cum laude, U. Mich., 1973. Bar: Ohio, 1973, U.S. Dist. Ct. (so. dist.) Ohio 1974. Ptnr. Vorys, Sater, Seymour and Pease, LLP, Columbus, Ohio, 1973—. Trustee Ballet Met., Inc., Columbus, 1978-90, pres., 1986-88; trustee Gladden Community House, Columbus, 1975-81, pres., 1979-81; mem. Children's Hosp. Devel. Bd., Columbus, 1987—, pres. 1995-96; trustee Elder Choices of Ctrl. Ohio, Columbus, 1989-95, Heritage Day Health Ctrs., Columbus, 1992-98. Fellow Columbus Bar Found.; mem. ABA, Am. Health Lawyers Assn., Columbus Bar Assn., Ohio Bar Assn., Order of Coif. Banking, General corporate, Health. Office: Vorys Sater Seymour and Pease LLP PO Box 1008 52 E Gay St Columbus OH 43215-3161

DERRICK, GARY WAYNE, lawyer; b. Enid, Okla., Nov. 3, 1953; s. John Henry and Leota Elaine (Glenn) D.; m. Susan Adele Goodwin, Dec. 22, 1979 (div. June 1981); m. Francys Hollis Johnson, May 3, 1986; children: Meghan, Drew, Jane. BA in History, English, Okla. State U., 1976; JD, U. Okla., 1979. Bar: Okla. 1979. Assoc. Andrews, Davis, Legg, Bixler, Milsten & Price, Oklahoma City, 1979-84, ptnr., 1985-90; of counsel McKinney, Stringer & Webster, P.C., 1990-93; ptnr. Derrick & Briggs, LLP, 1994—. Active Securities Law and Acctg. Group, Oklahoma City, 1979—; chmn. Gen. Corp. Act Commn., Okla., 1984—, chmn. Securities Liaison Com., Okla., 1985-86; lectr. sem. Okla. Corp. Act, 1986—. Conbg. author: Oklahoma Business Organizations. Mem. Okla. State U. Found., Stillwater, 1983-89, U. Okla. Found., Norman, 1982—; mem. condr.'s circle Okla. Symphony Orch., 1981-88; bd. dirs. Hist. Preservation, Inc., 1990—; chmn. constn. of canons com. Episcopal Diocese Okla. Mem. ABA (taxation and corp. sect., banking and bus. law sect.), Okla. Bar Assn. (chmn. bus. assn. sect. 1985-87, outstanding contbn. to continuing legal edn., Earl Sneed award 1997), Oklahoma County Bar Assn. (bd. govs. young lawyers div. 1981-82), Am. Soc. Corp. Secs. (pres. Okla.-Ark. chpt. 1994-95), Oklahoma City Boat Club. Republican. Episcopalian. Avocations: sailing, violin. Securities. Home: 500 NW 15th St Oklahoma City OK 73103-2102 Office: Derrick & Briggs LLP Bank One Ctr 20th Fl 100 N Broadway Ave Oklahoma City OK 73102-8606 E-mail: derrick@derrickandbriggs.com

DERSHOWITZ, ALAN MORTON, lawyer, educator; b. Bklyn., Sept. 1, 1938; s. Harry and Claire (Ringel) D.; m. Carolyn Cohen; children: Elon Marc, Jamin Seth, Ella Kaille Cohen Dershowitz. BA magna cum laude, Bklyn. Coll., 1959, LLD, 2001; LLB magna cum laude, Yale U., 1962; MA (hon.), Harvard Coll., 1967; LLD, Yeshiva U., 1989; PhD (hon.), Haifa U., 1993; LLD[,] Syracuse U., 1997; LLD, Hebrew Union Coll., Monmouth Coll. Bar: D.C. 1963, Mass. 1968, U.S. Supreme Ct. 1968. Law clk. to chief judge David L. Bazelon, U.S. Ct. Appeals, 1962-63; to justice Arthur J. Goldberg, U.S. Supreme Ct., 1963-64; mem. faculty Harvard Law Sch., 1964—, prof. law, 1967—, Felix Frankfurter Prof. of Law, 1993—; fellow Ctr. for Advanced Study of Behavioral Scis., 1971-72. Cons. to dir. NIMH, 1967-69, (Pres.'s Commn. Civil Disorders), 1967, (Pres.'s Com. Causes Violence), 1968, (NAACP Legal Def. Fund), 1967-68, NIMH Pres.'s Commn. Marijuana and Drug Abuse, 1972-73, Coun. on Drug Abuse, 1972—, Ford Found. Study on Law and Justice, 1973-76; rapporteur Twentieth Century Fund Study on Sentencing, 1975-76 Author: (with others) Psychoanalysis, Psychiatry and the Law, 1967, Criminal Law: Theory and Process, 1974, The Best Defense, 1982, Reversal of Fortune: Inside the von Bulow Case, 1986, Taking Liberties: A Decade of Hard Cases, Bad Laws and Bum Raps, 1988, Chutzpah, 1991, Contrary to Popular Opinion, 1992, The Abuse Excuse, 1994, The Advocate's Devil, 1994, Reasonable Doubts, 1996, The Vanishing American Jew, 1997, Sexual McCarthyism: Clinton, Starr and the Emerging Constitutional Crisis, 1998, Just Revenge, 1999, The Genesis of Justice, 2000, Supreme Injustice, 2001; contbr. articles to profl. jours.; editor-in-chief Yale Law Jour., 1961-62. Chmn. civil rights com. New England region Anti-Defamation League, B'nai B'rith, 1980-85; bd. dirs. ACLU, 1968-71, 72-75, Assembly Behavioral and Social Scis. at Nat. Acad. Scis., 1973-76. Guggenheim fellow, 1978-79. Mem. Order of Coif, Phi Beta Kappa. Jewish. Office: Harvard Law Sch 1575 Massachusetts Ave Cambridge MA 02138-2801

DERSHOWITZ, NATHAN ZEV, lawyer; b. Bklyn., May 5, 1942; s. Harry and Claire (Ringel) D.; m. Marilyn Barlach, Dec. 29, 1963; children— Adam, Rana. Grad. Bklyn. Coll., 1963; J.D., NYU, 1966. Bar: N.Y. 1966, U.S. Ct. Appeals (1st, 2d, 3d, 5th, 6th, 7th, 8th, 11th, D.C. and fed. cirs.), U.S. Supreme Ct. Atty., Legal Aid Soc., N.Y.C., 1966-69; assoc. Stroock & Stroock & Lavan, N.Y.C., 1969-73, Greenbaum, Wolff & Ernst, N.Y.C., 1974-77; bd. dirs. Commn. Law and Social Action, Am. Jewish Congress, N.Y.C., 1977-83; sr. ptnr. Dershowitz & Eiger, N.Y.C., 1983-86; gen. counsel Pearl, N.Y.C. and Washington, 1981— ; spl. prof. Hofstra U. Law Sch., Hempstead, N.Y., 1979. Contbr. articles to profl. jours. Mem. ch. state com. ACLU, N.Y., 1980-84. Civil rights, Federal civil litigation, Criminal. Home: 2 Tudor City Pl New York NY 10017-6800 Office: Dershowitz & Eiger 225 Broadway New York NY 10007-3001

DERWIN, JORDAN, lawyer, consultant, actor; b. N.Y.C., Sept. 15, 1931; s. Harry and Sadie (Baruch) D.; m. Barbara Joan Concool, July 4, 1956 (div. 1969); children: Susan Lee, Ellen; m. Joan Linda Wolfberg, May 6, 1973. BS, NYU, 1953, JD, 1959. Bar: N.Y. 1959, U.S. Dist. Ct. (so. and ea. dists.) N.Y. 1960, U.S. Ct. Appeals (2d. cir.) 1960, U.S. Supreme Ct. 1962. Arthur Garfield Hays rsch. fellow NYU, 1958-59, rsch. assoc. Duke U. Sch. of Law, Durham, N.C., 1959-60; assoc. Brennan, London, Buttenwieser, N.Y.C., 1960-64; sole practice Jordan Derwin, N.Y.C., 1964-70; gen. counsel N.Y.C. Off Track Betting Corp., 1970-74; assoc. gen. counsel Gen. Instrument Corp., N.Y.C., 1974-79; cons., 1980—; instr. basic life support, CPR and advanced 1st aid: ARC, 1988—, Am. Heart Assn., 1989—, Nat. Safety Coun., 1991—; instr. trainer basic cardiac lifesupport Am. Heart Assn., 1990—, mem. affiliate faculty, 1997—; emergency med. technician N.Y. State, 1990—; v.p., gen. counsel Cen. Park Med. Unit, Inc., N.Y.C., 1991—; del. N.Y.C. Ctrl. Labor Coun., 1996—. Author (with F. Hodge O'Neal), Expulsion or Oppression of Business Associates: Squeeze Outs in Small Business, 1960; actor in various films including Stardust Memories, 1980, Rollover, 1981, I'm Dancing as Fast as I Can, 1982, Hard Feelings, 1984, Cotton Club, 1984, One Down Two to Go, 1986, Cadillac Man, 1990, McBain 1991, Ambulance, 1992, Extreme Measures, 1996, Private Parts, 1997, TV programs including Nurse, Today's FBI, Another World, As The World Turns, Guiding Light, All My Children, One Life To Live, Loving, Saturday Night Live, Late Night and Late Show With David Letterman, Conan O'Brien Show, TV commls. 1980—; contbr. articles to prof. jours. Lt. j.g., USNR, 1953-56, Korea, Vietnam. Mem. SAG (dir. nat. bd. 1982—, nat. exec. com., 1983—, sec. N.Y. br. 1983-87, 12th nat. v.p. 1984-87, 4th nat. v.p. 1987-89, 1st v.p. N.Y. br. 1987-89, 2d v.p. N.Y. br. 1989-91, 95—, 3d v.p. N.Y. br. 1993-95), AFTRA (dir. N.Y. local bd. 1980-83, 87-90, dir. nat. bd. 1981-92, Ken Harvey award for outstanding svc. to the mem. 1998), Am. Soc. Mag. Photographers, Nat. Press Photographers Assn., Motion Picture Players Welfare Fund (trustee 1987—), Actors Equity Assn., Associated Actors and Artistes Am. AFL-CIO (del. internat. bd. 1984-94, 97—, ctrl. labor coun. N.Y.C. 1996—), Phi Delta Phi. Home and Office: 305 E 86th St New York NY 10028-4702

DERZAW, RICHARD LAWRENCE, lawyer; b. N.Y.C., Mar. 6, 1954; s. Ronald Murray and Diana (Diamond) D.; m. Susan Katz, 1993. BA magna cum laude, Fairleigh Dickinson U., 1976; JD, Ohio No. U., 1979. Bar: Fla. 1979, U.S. Dist. Ct. (so. dist.) Fla. 1981, U.S. Ct. Appeals (5th cir.) 1981, U.S. Ct. Appeals (11th cir.) 1981, U.S. Ct. Appeals (2d cir.), 1988, N.Y. 1982, N.C. 1995, U.S. Dist. Ct. (so. dist.) N.Y. 1985, U.S. Dist. Ct. (ea. dist.) N.Y., 1986, U.S. Tax Ct. 1986, U.S. Supreme Ct., 1988. Sole practice, Boca Raton, Fla., 1979-82, N.Y.C., 1982—. Mem. ABA, N.Y. State Bar Assn., N.C. Bar Assn., Fla. Bar Assn., Am. Arbitration Assn., Assn. of Bar of City of N.Y., Fed. Bar Coun., Lions of Boca Raton (treas. 1981-82), Phi Alpha Delta, Phi Zeta Kappa, Phi Omega Epsilon. General civil litigation, Contracts commercial, General corporate. Office: 708 3rd Ave New York NY 10017-4201 E-mail: derzlaw@aol.com

DESAI, AASHISH Y. lawyer; b. Chgo., Oct. 7, 1968; s. Yadvendra and Shradhha Desei. BA in Econs., U. Tex., 1991; JD, U. Houston, 1996. Bar: Calif. 1996, U.S. Dist. Ct. (ctrl. dist.) Calif. 1996, U.S. Dist. Ct. Colo. 1998. Tchg. asst. U. Houston Law Ctr., 1994-95; summer assoc. Thompson & Knight, Dallas, 1994-95; jud. clk. Hon. Judge Maloney U.S. Ct. Appeals (5th cir.), 1994-95; assoc. Law Offices of Alan Rubinstein, L.A., 1996-97, Mower, Koeller, Nebeker, Carlson & Haluck, Irvine, Calif., 1997—. Mem. ABA, Orange County Bar Assn. Avocations: golf, jazz, blues guitar, tennis, family. General civil litigation, Labor, Personal injury. Home: 9 Darlington Irvine CA 92620-0221 Office: Mower Koeller Nebeker Carlson & Haluck 108 Pacifica PO Box 19799 Irvine CA 92623-9799

DESAI, JIGNASA, lawyer; b. India, Dec. 12, 1969; came to U.S., 1971; d. Dinker and Bharti Desai. BA, Rutgers Coll., 1991; JD, Rutgers U., Camden, N.J., 1994; student, U. Exeter, Eng., 1989. Bar: N.J. 1994, U.S. Dist. Ct. N.J. 1995. Jud. clk. to two judges, New Brunswick, N.J., 1994-95; assoc. Lomurro, Davison, Eastman & Munoz, P.A., Freehold, 1995-98, sr. assoc., 1998-99; gen. counsel Dept. Def./Comms.-Electronics Command, Ft. Monmouth, 1999—. Mcpl. prosecutor Twp. of Millstone, N.J., 1997-99; asst. twp. atty. Twp. of Manalapan, N.J., 1996-99. Trustee Legal Aid Soc., Monmouth County, 1996—. Mem. N.J. State Bar Assn. (minorities sect.), Women Lawyers in Monmouth, Rutgers Law Alumni Assn. (bd. dirs. 1994—). Government contracts and claims, Labor. Office: Office of the Chief Counsel Dept of Def US Army Hdqrs CECOM AMSEL-LG-A Fort Monmouth NJ 07703-5000

DE SAINT PHALLE, PIERRE CLAUDE, lawyer; b. N.Y.C., July 21, 1948; s. Thibaut and Rosamonde (Frame) de Saint P. BA, Trinity Coll, 1970; JD, Columbia U., 1973. Bar: N.Y. 1974, U.S. Ct. Appeals (2d cir.) 1975, U.S. Dist. Ct. (so. and ea. dist.) N.Y. 1975, D.C. 1982. Assoc. Davis Polk & Wardwell, N.Y.C., 1973-82; European Office, 1976-77; ptnr. N.Y.C., 1983—. Asst. gen. counsel U.S. Synthetic Fuels Corp., Washington, 1980-81. Mem. ABA, N.Y.C. Bar Assn., Internat. Bar Assn. River Club, Quoque Field Club, Quoque Beach Club, Nat. Golf Links of Am. Roman Catholic. General corporate, Securities, Investment companies. Office: Davis Polk & Wardwell 450 Lexington Ave Fl 31 New York NY 10017-3982

DE SALVA, CHRISTOPHER JOSEPH, lawyer, consultant; b. Milw., June 16, 1950; s. Salvadore Joseph and Elaine Mae De S.; m. Erika Marie De Salva, May 24, 1975; 1 child, Jessica Anne. BA in Polit. Sci., St. Vincent Coll., 1972; JD summa cum laude, Am. Coll. Law, 1987; MBA, Calif. Coast U., 1993, postgrad., 1994. Bar: Calif. 1994, U.S. Dist. Ct. (ctrl. dist.) Calif. 1995, U.S. Ct. Fed. Claims 1995, U.S. Tax Ct. 1995. Founder, owner C.J. De Salva & Assocs. Investment and Mktg. Svcs. of La Quinta (now C.J. De Salva & Assocs., La Quinta, 1979—; pvt. practice Calif., 1994-98, Indio, 1994—, San Diego, 1996-98. Ceo, pres. The Kings Vault Gallery, Inc., 1985; adj. faculty property law Am. Coll. Law, Brea, Calif., 1989-90, 92-95; life and disability ins. agent C.J. De Salva Ins. Agency 1978—; real estate broker De Salva Realty Calif., 1980—, realtor, 1985-94; tax cons., preparer Christopher De Salva Tax Cons.; cons. Christopher De Salva Bus. and Mgmt. Cons.; lectr. property law. Am. Coll. Law. Author: NAFTA, The Hidden Agenda, 1995. 1st lt. USMC, 1974-77. Vietnam. Am. Jurisprudence award Am. Coll. Law. Mem. ABA, Assn. Trial Lawyers, Vietnam Era Vet., Vet. of Latin Am., Nat. Soc. Pub. Accts (cert. 1984). Calif. Bar Assn. Avocations: music, sports, writing songs, flying. General civil litigation, Criminal, Estate taxation. Office: 45-902 Oasis St Ste D Indio CA 92201

DE SAMPIGNY, GUILLAUME, lawyer; b. Paris, Dec. 7, 1972; s. Jean Marie and Chantal (Lacan) Husson de Sampigny. Maitrise, Paris-X, 1995; LLM, Widener U., 1996. Bar: Paris 1999, N.Y. 2000. Assoc. LeBoeuf, Lamb, Greene & MacRae LLP, Paris, 1998-2000, N.Y.C., 2000—. Served with French Army, 1997. Mem. ABA. Private international, Mergers and acquisitions, Securities. Office: LeBoeuf Lamb Greene MacRae 125 W 55th St New York NY 10019 E-mail: guillaume.de_sampigny@llgm.com

DESANTO, JAMES JOHN, lawyer; b. Chgo., Oct. 12, 1943; s. John Joseph and Erminia Asunda (Cassano) DeS.; m. Denise Clare Caneva, Feb. 3, 1968; children: Carrie Ann, James Thomas, John Joseph. BA, U. Ill., 1965; JD, DePaul U., 1969. Bar: Ill. 1969, U.S. Dist. Ct. (no. dist.) Ill. 1969, U.S. Ct. Appeals (7th cir.) 1972, U.S. Supreme Ct. 1974; cert. mediator 19th Jud. Circuit, Ill., 1996. Asst. state's atty., Waukegan, Ill., 1969-72; assoc. Finn, Geiger & Rafferty, 1972-74; ptnr. Rawles, Katz & DeSanto, 1975-80; pvt. practice, 1980-88; sr. ptnr. DeSanto & Bonamarte, 1988-91; pvt. practice, Libertyville, Ill., 1991—, James J. DeSanto and Assocs., 1992-99; ptnr. DeSanto, Morgan & Mittelman, Libertyville, 1999—. Lectr. in trial technique and practice Ill. Inst. for CLE and Ill. Bar Assn.; lectr. in bus. law Coll. of Lake County, 1974-84; bd. dirs. Ill. State Bar Assn. Mut. Ins. Co., 1989—, chairperson com. on finance and investment 1995-97, 2000-01, sec./treas., 1999—, 2nd v.p., 2001-02; mem. ad hoc com. on profl. quality in the practice of law State Bar Assn., 1995—. Co-editor Tort Trends newsletter, 1988-91. Trustee Village of Libertyville, 1991-93; chairperson parish pastoral coun. St. Joseph's Ch., Libertyville, 2000-02. Fellow Ill. Bar Inst.; mem. ATLA, Ill. Bar Assn. (chmn. fin. and budget com. of assembly 1988-89, chmn. tort law sect. coun. 1991-92, co-editor Tort Trends newsletter 1988-91, mem. standing com. on legislation 1995—, ins. law sect. coun. 2001—), Lake County Bar Assn. (sec. 1979-80, 2d v.p. 1991-92, pres. 1993-94), Lake County Trial Lawyers Assn. (sec. 1985—), Jefferson Inns of Ct., Libertyville Rotary (pres. 1990-91). Avocations: golf, fishing. Federal civil litigation, State civil litigation, Personal injury. Home: 1209 St William Dr Libertyville IL 60048-1275 Office: 712 Florsheim Dr Libertyville IL 60048-5270 E-mail: desanto@iconnect.net

DE SHIELDS-MINNIS, TARRA RAMIT, lawyer; b. Balt. d. Lawrence Franklin DeShields and Ramona Fleurette Brown. BA, U. Md., 1984; JD, U. Balt., 1987. Bar: Md. 1988, U.S. Dist. Ct. Md. 1990, U.S. Ct. Appeals (4th cir.), U.S. Supreme Ct. 1993. Jud. clk. Md. Ct. of Spl. Appeals, 1987-88; asst. state's atty. Office of the State's Atty., Montgomery County, 1988-90; asst. atty. gen. Office of the Atty. Gen., Balt., 1990-96; asst. U.S. atty. U.S. Atty.'s Office, 1996—. Recipient Am. Jurisprudence award Lawyer's Cooperative Pub. Co., 1988; Supreme Ct. fellow Nat. Assn. of Attys. Gens., 1993. Mem. Md. State Bar Assn., Nat. Bar Assn. Roman Catholic. Avocations: reading, antique shopping, racquetball. Office: US Attys Office 101 W Lombard St Baltimore MD 21201-2605

DESMOND, SUSAN FAHEY, lawyer; b. Greenville, Miss., Feb. 24, 1961; d. Richard Paul and Bonnie Jean (Williams) Fahey; m. John Michael Desmond; May 28, 1994; children: Meghan, Kelsey. BA in English and History, U. Miss., 1982; JD, U. Tenn., 1985. Bar: Miss. 1985, Colo. 1996, La. 1998. Assoc. Robertshaw, Terney & Noble, Greenville, Miss., 1985-86, Miller, Milam & Moeller, Jackson, 1986-89, Phelps Dunbar, Jackson, 1989-92, ptnr., 1992-97, New Orleans, 1998—. Author: Employment Issues for Hospital Supervisors, 1996; editor: Mississippi Pro Bono Material, 1989. Bd. dirs. Am. Cancer Soc. Hinds County Unit, Jackson, Miss., 1990-96. Mem. Jackson Young Lawyers (dir. 1991-93, merit award 1988), Am. Bar Assn./Young Lawyers (labor com. chmn., Chgo., 1990-92), Miss. Bar Assn. (dir. 1990-92, Outstanding Young Lawyer 1997). Republican. Roman Catholic. Avocations: tennis, reading. Civil rights, Immigration, naturalization, and customs, Labor. Office: Phelps Dunbar 365 Canal St Ste 2000 New Orleans LA 70130-6534 E-mail: desmonds@phelps.com

DE SOUSA, PAULA CRISTINA PACHECO, lawyer; b. Fremont, Calif., Apr. 3, 1969; d. Eliseu H. Sousa and Filomena Maria Perreira Pacheco. BA, U. Calif., Santa Barbara, 1992; JD, U. of the Pacific, 1997. Rsch. intern CNN Washington D.C. Bur., 1992; intern Campaign for a New Agenda (Jack Kemp), Washington, 1994; clk. Neilsen Merksamer Parinello, Mueller & Naylor, Mill Valley, Ohio, summer 1995; assoc. Best Best & Krieger LLP, San Diego, 1997—. Fundraising participant Komen Found., 1997—; participant in documentary A Healing Place. Vern Adrian & Annabel McGeorge Acad. Achievement scholar, 1995-96, Gary V. Schaber Meml. scholar McGeorge Sch. Law, 1996-97, Filomena Scalora scholar, 1996-97. Mem. ABA, Calif. Bar Assn., San Diego County Bar Assn., Federalist Soc., Lawyers Club. Roman Catholic. Municipal (including bonds), Real property. Office: Best Best & Krieger LLP Ste 1300 402 W Broadway San Diego CA 92101

DESSEN, STANLEY BENJAMIN, lawyer, cosmetic company executive; b. N.Y.C., Mar. 25, 1938; s. Irving and Edith (Nelson) D.; m. Mimi Lynne; children: Eric, Cheryl. BS in Acctg., Bklyn. Coll., 1959; JD, NYU, 1962, LLM, 1969; LLM, Bklyn. Law Sch., 1967. Bar: N.Y. 1962, U.S. Tax Ct. 1965, U.S. Supreme Ct. 1968. Staff mem. Arthur Andersen & Co., N.Y.C., 1962-64; assoc. Melvin Semel, N.Y.C., 1964-66; dir. taxes Pfizer, Inc., N.Y.C., 1966-74; v.p. taxation Revlon, Inc., N.Y.C., 1974-90, sr. v.p. taxation, 1990—. Mem. ABA, N.Y. State Bar Assn., Pharm. Mfrs. Assn. (tax com.), Tax Execs. Inst., Cosmetic, Toiletry and Fragrance Assn. (chmn. tax com.). Republican. Jewish. Corporate taxation, State and local taxation. Office: Revlon Inc 625 Madison Ave Fl 8 New York NY 10022-1894

DESUE, CHRISTINE L. lawyer; b. Pitts., Feb. 9, 1970; d. David Joseph and Linda Ann Desue; m. Scott Michael Verret, July 25, 1998. BA in Polit. Sci., Tulane U., 1992; JD in Civil and Common Law, Loyola U., New Orleans, 1995. Atty. Leger & Mestayer, New Orleans, 1994—. Mem., vol. The New Orleans Regional Chamber, 1999. Mem. ATLA, ABA, FBA, La. State Bar Assn., La. Trial Lawyers Assn., New Orleans Bar Assn. Avocations: reading, sports, working with Special Olympics. Admiralty, Personal injury, Product liability. Office: Leger & Mestayer 9th Fl 600 Carondelet St Fl 9 New Orleans LA 70130-3511

DETJEN, DAVID WHEELER, lawyer; b. St. Louis, Jan. 25, 1948; s. Don Wheeler and Shirley (Pence) D.; m. Barbara Louise Morgan, Jan. 6, 1973; children: Andrea Marlene, Erika Alexandra. AB magna cum laude, Washington U., 1970, JD with honors, 1973; postgrad., Eberhard-Karls-Universitaet, Tuebingen, Fed. Republic of Germany, 1969-70. Bar: Mo. 1973, U.S. Supreme Ct. 1976, U.S. Ct. Appeals (8th cir.) 1976, N.Y. 1981. Law clk. to chief judge U.S. Ct. Appeals (8th cir.), St. Louis, 1973-75; assoc. Lewis, Rice, Tucker, Allen & Chubb, 1975-80, Walter, Conston, Alexander & Green, P.C., N.Y.C., 1980-83; ptnr. Walter, Conston, Alexander & Green, 1983-2000, ptnr. N.Y. Office of Alston & Bird, LLP., affiliate resident Bangkok, 1991-92, ptnr. N.Y. Office of Alston & Bird LLP N.Y.C., 2001—. Lectr. in law Washington U., St. Louis, 1975-80. Author: Distributorship Agreements in the U.S., 1983, 2d edit., 1989, The Germans in Missouri, 1900-1918: Prohibition, Neutrality and Assimilation, 1985, Licensing Technology and Trademarks in the United States, 1988, 2d edit., 1997, Establishing a United States Joint Venture with a Foreign Partner, 1988, 3d edit., 1993, United States Joint Ventures with International Partners, 2000; bd. dirs. Felix Schoeller Tech. Papers Inc., 1998—. Mem. Wash. U. Law Sch. Nat. Coun., 1989—; sec. German Forum, N.Y.C., 1988—, bd. dirs. 1995—; mem. St. Louis County Repub. Cen. Com., 1976-83, Am. Coun. on Germany; co-pres. King-Merritt Comty. Assn., Greenwich, Conn., 1997—; trustee Am. Inst. Contemporary German Studies at Johns Hopkins U., 1999—, corp. sec., 2000—; mem. Rep. Town Meeting, Greenwich, Conn., 2000—. Recipient Disting. Alumnus award Wash. U. Law Sch., 1998. Mem. ABA, N.Y. State Bar Assn. (exec. editor Internat. Law Practicum 1988—, mem. exec. com. internat. law and practice sect. 1999—), Assn. Bar City N.Y., German Am. Law Assn., German Am. Round Table, William G. Eliot Soc. of Washington U. (N.Y. chmn. 1993—), Deutscher Verein Club N.Y.C. (bd. dirs. 1994-97, 99—, v.p., sec. 2000—), Order of Coif, Delta Phi Alpha. Presbyterian. General corporate, Private international, Mergers and acquisitions. Home: 35 Stonehedge Dr S Greenwich CT 06831-3220 Office: Walter Conston Alexander & Green NY Office Alston & Bird LLP 90 Park Ave Fl 14 New York NY 10016-1301 Fax: 212 210-9444. E-mail: ddetjen@alston.com

DETTINGER, WARREN WALTER, lawyer; b. Toledo, Feb. 13, 1954; s. Walter Henry and Elizabeth Mae (Zoll) D.; m. Patricia Marie Kasper, June 21, 1975; children: John Robert, Laura Marie. BS cum laude, U. Toledo, 1977, JD magna cum laude, 1980. Bar: Ohio 1980, U.S. Dist. Ct. (no. dist.) Ohio 1980, U.S. Ct. Appeals (6th cir.) 1980, U.S. Tax Ct. 1981. Law clk. to presiding judge U.S. Ct. Appeals (6th cir.), Grand Rapids, Mich., 1980-81; assoc. Fuller & Henry, Toledo, 1981-84; atty. Sheller-Globe Corp., 1984-87; v.p., gen. counsel Diebold, Inc., Canton, Ohio, 1987—. Mem. ABA, Ohio Bar Assn., Stark County Bar Assn., Am. Corp. Counsel Assn., Mfr.'s Alliance (law coun. II), Brookside Country Club, Phi Kappa Phi. Roman Catholic. Avocations: golf, travel, photography, tennis. General corporate, Private international, Mergers and acquisitions. Home: 5237 Birkdale St NW Canton OH 44708-1825 Office: Diebold Inc 5995 Mayfair Rd PO Box 3077 North Canton OH 44720-8077 E-mail: dettinw@diebold.com

DETTMER, MICHAEL HAYES, former prosecutor; b. Detroit, June 6, 1946; s. Frank Arthur and Mary Frances (Conway) D.; m. Teckla Ann Getts, Aug. 15, 1969; children: Bryn Patrick, Janna Hayes. BS, Mich. State U., 1968; JD, Wayne State U., 1971. Bar: Mich. 1971, U.S. Dist. Ct. (we. dist.) Mich. 1992. Atty. Dettmer Thompon Parsons, Traverse City, Mich., 1972-90; pres., CEO Mich. Lawyer Mutual Ins. Co., Southfield, Grand Rapids, 1990-93; U.S. atty. we. dist. Mich. U.S. Dept. Justice, Grand Rapids, 1994—2001. Lectr. in field. Contbr. articles to profl. jours. Pres. Traverse City Montessori Ctr., 1978-83; commr. Traverse City Human Rights Commn.; chmn. Grand Traverse County Dem. Party, 1986. Fellow Am. Bar Found., Mich. State Bar Found.; mem. ABA, State Bar of Mich. (pres. 1993-94, commr. No. Mich. and Upper Peninsula 1986-94, exec. com. bd. commrs. 1988-94, com. on legislation 1990-91, task force on professionalism 1988-90, co-chair standing com. on professionalism 1992—, chair Upper Mich. lawyers com. 1986-94, rep. assembly 1977-80, 88-94, atty. discipline bd. hearing panelist 1980-88), Am. Bd. Trial Advocates, Nat. Bd. Trial Advocacy (cert. 1981—). Democrat. Presbyterian.*

DE URIARTE, HORACIO MARIA, lawyer; b. Mexico City, Dec. 22, 1971; s. Ruben Maria de Uriarte adn Lorena Liliana Flores; m. Paola Alejandra Jimenez Pons, Jul. 25, 1998; 1 child, Maria del Pilar. Lic. Derecho, U. Iberoamericana, Mexico City, 1995; LLM, Harvard U., 1999. Bar: Mexico 1996, N.Y. 2000. Assoc. Mijares, Angoitia, Cortes y Fuentes SC, Mexico City, 1994-98, 2000—; fgn. assoc. Cleary, Gottlieb, Steen & Hamilton, N.Y.C., 1999-2000. Fulbright scholar, 1998. Mem. Barra Mexicana, Colegio Abogados. Roman Catholic. General corporate, Finance, Oil, gas, and mineral. Office: Montes Urales 505-3 Lomas de Chapultepe 11000 Mexico City Mexico Fax: 52 5520 1065. E-mail: hdeuriarte@macf.com.mx

DEUTSCH, HARVEY ELLIOT, lawyer; b. Bklyn., Aug. 18, 1940; s. Harry Deutsch and Beulah (Deutsch) Koft; m. Paula Kantor, Nov. 26, 1964; children— Stacia Francine, Steven Harold, Karen Gail. B.A., So. Methodist U., 1962; LL.B., U. Tex., 1966. Bar: U.S. Dist. Ct. Colo. 1967, U.S. Ct. Appeals (10th cir.) 1967. Assoc., Holland & Hart, Denver, 1967-69; ptnr. Isaacson, Rosenbaum, Spiegleman & Friedman, Denver, 1970-82; v.p., gen. counsel Bill L. Walters Cos., Englewood, Colo., 1982-84; ptnr. Deutsch & Sheldon, Englewood, 1984—; lectr. in field. Contbr. chpts. to books. Bd. dirs. Anti-Defamation League of B'nai B'rith, Denver, 1976—; commr. Colo. Civil Rights Commn., 1972-80, chmn., 1976-78. Served with USNR, 1962-70. Mem. Tex. Bar Assn., Colo. Bar Assn. Environmental, Land use and zoning (including planning), Real property. Home: 143 Monroe St Denver CO 80206-5503 Office: Deutsch Spillane & Reutzel PC 7951 E Maplewood Ave Ste 329 Englewood CO 80111-4723

DEUTSCH, JAMES BERNARD, lawyer; b. St. Louis, Aug. 24, 1948; s. William Joseph and Margaret (Klevorn) D.; m. Deborah Marie Hallenberg, June 26, 1976; children: Michael, Gabriel. BA, Southeast Mo. State U., 1974; JD, U. Mo., 1978. Bar: Mo. 1978, U.S. Dist. Ct. (we. dist.) Mo. 1978, U.S. Ct. Appeals (8th cir.), 1989, U.S. Supreme Ct., 1990. Assoc. Gt. Plains Legal Found., Kansas City, Mo., 1978-79; pvt. practice, 1979-81; gen. counsel Mo. Dept. Revenue, Jefferson City, Mo., 1981-83; commr. Mo. Adminstrv. Hearing Commn., 1983-89; dep. atty.-gen State of Mo., 1989-93; ptnr. Riezman & Blitz, P.C., Mo., 1993-99; Ptnr. Blitz Bardgett & Deutsch LC, 2000—. Served to lance cpl. USMC, 1968-70, Vietnam. Named one of Men of Yr. in Constrn. Industry, Engring. News, McGraw-Hill Pub., N.Y.C., 1985. Mem. ABA (jud. adminstrn. com.), ASCE (hon. fellow), Mo. Bar Assn. (council mem. taxation com. 1985—, adminstrn. law and jud. adminstrn. coms.), Mo. Inst. for Justice (bd. dirs. 1977—), VFW, Marine Corps League. Administrative and regulatory, State and local taxation. Office: Blitz Bardgett & Deutsch LC 308 E High St Jefferson City MO 65101-3237 E-mail: jdeutsch@blitzbardgett.com

DEUTSCH, STEPHEN B. lawyer; b. N.Y.C., Jan. 3, 1944; s. A. William and Rose (Berkowitz) D.; m. Jane M. Burnat, Nov. 23, 1986; children: Nancy, Jeffrey, Elizabeth. SB, MIT, 1965, PhD, 1969; JD, Harvard U., 1974. Bar: Mass. 1975, U.S. Dist. Mass., U.S. Ct. Appeals (1st cir.), U.S. Supreme Ct., U.S. Patent Office. Law clk. Supreme Judicial Ct. Mass., Boston, 1974-75; assoc. Foley, Hoag & Eliot, 1975-80, ptnr., 1981—. Mem. ABA, Mass. Bar Assn., Boston Bar Assn. Intellectual property, Labor, Patent. Office: Foley Hoag & Eliot 1 Post Office Sq Ste 1700 Boston MA 02109-2175

D'EVEGNEE, CHARLES PAUL, lawyer; b. Liege, Belgium, Aug. 4, 1939; came to U.S., 1959; s. Charles Clement and Fernande Francoise (Godet) Devignez; m. Marie-Therese L. Barnich, Apr. 17, 1962; children: Chantal E., Charles D. BA, Brigham Young U., 1966; MA, U. Conn., Storrs, 1969; JD, U. Conn., West Hartford, 1974. Bar: Va. 1991, U.S. Banktuptcy Ct. (ea. dist.-Richmond divsn.), U.S. Dist. Ct. 9ea. dist.) Va., U.S. Ct. Appeals (4th cir.), U.S. Supreme Ct. Group pension underwriter Conn. Gen. Life Ins. Co., Bloomfield, 1969-72; legal cons. Frank B. Hall & Co., N.Y.C., 1974-76; regional counsel Meidinger & Assocs., Richmond, Va., 1976-78; dir. Office Benefits Devel., Commonwealth of Va., 1978-91; pvt. practice, Ashland, Va., 1991—. Co-author: European Antitrust Law, 1976. Mem. Va. Gov.'s U.S. Savs. Bond Com., Richmond, 1986; rep. exec. bd. State's United Appeals of Greater Richmond Community Chest, 1989. With U.S. Army, 1960-63. Mem. ABA, Va. State Bar Assn., Hanover Bar Assn., Richmond Bar Assn. Avocations: travel, landscaping, sports. General practice, Private international, Workers' compensation. Home: 6034 Northfall Creek Pkwy Mechanicsville VA 23111-7522 Office: 6034 Northfall Creek Pkwy Mechanicsville VA 23111 E-mail: cdevegnee@aol.com

DEVENS, PAUL, lawyer; b. Gary, Ind., June 8, 1931; s. Zenove and Anna (Brilla) Dewenetz; m. Setsuko Sugihara, Aug. 14, 1955; children: Paula, Vladimir, Mignon. BA in Econs. cum laude, Ind. U., 1954; LLB, Columbia U., 1957. Bar: N.Y. 1958, U.S. Dist. Ct. Hawaii 1960, Hawaii 1961, U.S. Ct. Appeals (9th cir.) 1962, U.S. Ct. Internat. Trade 1963, U.S. Supreme Ct. 1970. Pvt. practice law, N.Y.C., 1958-60; ptnr. Lewis, Saunders & Key, Honolulu, 1960-69; corp. counsel City and County of Honolulu, 1969-72, mng. dir., 1973-75; ptnr. Devens, Nakano, Saito, Lee, Wong & Ching, Honolulu, 1975-94, of counsel, 1994—. Bd. dirs. Ctrl. Pacific Bank, Honolulu, CPB, Inc., Honolulu; judge Nuclear Claims Tribunal, Majuro, Republic of the Marshall Islands, 1988-90. Mem. Japan-Hawaii Econ. Coun., 1975-95, Honolulu Charter Reorgn. Com., 1979-80, Pacific and Asian Affairs Coun., 1983; trustee Japan-Am. Soc. Honolulu, 1981—, pres., 1987-89; chmn. bd. dirs. Nat. Assn. Japan-Am. Socs., 1989-91; mem. bd. govs. Japanese Cultural Ctr., Hawaii, 1989-94, mem. bd. dirs., v.p., 1994-96, chmn. bd. dirs., 1996-97. Decorated Imperial Order of the Sacred Treasure, Gold Rays with Neck ribbon Govt. of Japan, 1993. Democrat. Eastern Orthodox. Federal civil litigation, State civil litigation, Real property. Office: Devens Nakano Saito Lee Wong & Ching 220 S King St Ste 1600 Honolulu HI 96813-4597

DEVIENCE, ALEX, JR. law educator; b. Chgo., Nov. 18, 1940; s. Alex and Charlotte (Patelski) D. B.A., U. Md., 1964; J.D., Loyola U., Chgo., 1967. Bar: Ill. 1968, U.S. Dist. Ct. (no. dist.) Ill. 1968, U.S. Tax Ct. 1968, U.S. Ct. Appeals (7th cir.) 1970, Supreme Ct. 1971, U.S. Ct. Internat. Trade 1984, U.S. Ct. Appeals (9th and fed. cir.) 1984. Sole practice, Chgo., 1967-71; prof. bus. law DePaul U., Chgo., 1975—. Author: Legal and Social Obligations of Business Managers, 1986; contbr. numerous articles to profl. jours. Apptd. by Gov. to Small Bus. Adv. Council, 1985; mem. Fed. and State Legis. Implementation Task Force, 1985. Mem. Am. Bus. Law Profs., Chgo. Bar Assn. Home: 630 Sylviawood Ave Park Ridge IL 60068-2246

DEVINE, ANTOINE MAURICE, lawyer; b. Milw., Apr. 19, 1957; s. John and Marietta Elizabeth D. BS in Fin., Jackson State U., 1979; JD, U. Tex., 1991. Bar: Calif. 1993. Asst. auditor Trustmark Bank, Jackson, Miss., 1979-81; sr. compliance examiner NASD Regulation, Inc., Dallas, 1981-84; adminstr., pres. Hall Securities Corp./Funding Capital, Inc., 1985-86; pres. Devine Fin. Svcs., Bedford, Tex., 1987-88; assoc. Dennis & Coscia, San Diego, 1993-95; staff atty. San Diego Gas & Elec., 1995; corp. counsel Global Resource Investments, Ltd., Carlsbad, Calif., 1997-98; ptnr. Evers & Hendrickson, San Francisco, 1998-2000; pres. U.S. Pub. Shells, L.L.C., 1999—; spl. counsel Foley and Lardner, 2000—. Basketball coach Jackie Robinson YMCA, San Diego, 1994-97. Democrat. Avocations: golf, tennis, softball, jazz. General corporate, Private international, Securities. Home: 266 Lenox Ave Apt 301 Oakland CA 94610-4605 Office: Evers & Hendrickson LLP 155 Montgomery St Fl 12 San Francisco CA 94104-4105

DEVINE, DONN, lawyer, genealogist, former city official; b. South Amboy, N.J., Mar. 30, 1929; s. Frank Edward and Emily Theresa (DeRevere) D. m. Elizabeth Cecilia Baldwin, Nov. 23, 1951; children: Edward (dec.), Mary Elizabeth, Martin Joseph. BS, U. Del., 1949; JD with honors, Widener U., 1975. Bar: Del. 1975, U.S. Dist. Ct. Del. 1976, U.S. Supreme Ct. 1997; cert. genealogist and cert. genealogy instr. Bd. for Cert. Genealogists; cert. Am. Inst. Cert. Planners. Devel. chemist Allied Chem. Corp., Claymont, Del., 1950-52; newspaper writer, editor corp. publs. Atlas Powder Co., Wilmington, 1952-60; mgmt. cons., 1960-68; dir. renewal planning City of Wilmington, 1968-79, dep. dir. planning, 1979-80, dir. planning, 1981-85; cons. Wilmington City Coun., 1985-01; pvt. practice, 1985-00; archival cons. Cath. Diocese Wilmington, 1989—; of counsel City of Wilmington Law Dept., 2001—. Spl. counsel Del. Div. Alcoholism, Drug Abuse and Mental Health, 1990-93; trustee Bd. for Cert. Genealogists, 1992—; mediator Del. Superior Ct., 1998—. Author: Delaware National Guard, A Historical Sketch, 1968, DeRevere Family of Peekskill, New York, 1982; editor Del. Geneal. Soc. Jour., 1980-81, Cultural Resources Survey of Wilmington, Del., 1982-84; assoc. editor Del. Jour. Corp. Law, 1974-75; assoc editor Professional Genealogy: A Manual for Researchers, Writers, Editors, Lecturers and Librarians, 2001. Past bd. dirs. Wilmington Small Bus. Devel. Corp., Wilmington Econ. Devel. Corp.; past officer Delmarva Ecumenical Agy.; emeritus bd. dirs., past officer Generations Home Care (formerly Geriatric Svcs. Del.); past officer Christina Cultural Arts Ctr., Cath. Interracial Coun., Del. chpt. ACLU, Maplewood Housing for Elderly, St. Mary's-St. Patrick's Parish Coun. With USAR, 1950-54; brig. gen. Del. Army N.G., 1954-84, ret. Decorated Meritorious Svc. medal. Mem. Am. Planning Assn., Am. Chem. Soc., Del. Bar Assn., Del. Soc. SAR (past pres.), Nat. Geneal. Soc. (bd. dirs. 1994—), Assn. Cath. Diocesan Archivists (bd. dirs. 1993-95), Del. Geneal. Soc. (past pres.), Ft. Delaware Soc. (recognition award), Old Bohemia Hist. Soc. (bd. dirs. 1992—), Univ. and Whist Club, Chemists Club N.Y.C., Ancient Order Hibernians, Phi Kappa Phi, Delta Theta Phi. Democrat. Intellectual property, Land use and zoning (including planning). Home: 2004 Kentmere Pkwy Wilmington DE 19806-2014 E-mail: donndevine@aol.com

DEVINE, EDMOND FRANCIS, lawyer; b. Ann Arbor, Mich., Aug. 9, 1916; s. Frank B. and Elizabeth Catherine (Doherty) DeV.; m. Elizabeth Palmer Ward, Sept. 17, 1955; children: Elizabeth Palmer, Stephen Ward, Michael Edmond, Suzanne Lee. AB, U. Mich., 1937, JD, 1940; LLM, Cath. U. Am., 1941. Bar: Mich. 1940, U.S. Dist. Ct. (ea. dist.) Mich. 1940, U.S. Ct. Appeals (6th cir) 1974, U.S. Supreme Ct. 1975. Spl. agt. FBI, 1941-43; chief asst. prosecutor Washtenaw County (Mich.), Ann Arbor, 1947-53, prosecuting atty., 1953-58; ptnr. DeVine & DeVine, 1958-74, DeVine, DeVine, Kantor & Serr, Ann Arbor, 1974-84; sr. ptnr. Miller, Canfield, Paddock & Stone, 1984-92, of counsel, 1992—. Asst. prof., adj. prof. U. Mich. Law Sch., 1949-79. Co-author: Criminal Procedure, 1960. Bd. dirs. Youth for Understanding, Inc., Ann Arbor, 1966-70. Lt. USNR, 1943-46, PTO. Decorated Bronze Star with combat v. Fellow Am. Bar Found., Am. Coll. Trial Lawyers, Mich. Bar Found.; mem. ABA, State Bar Mich. (bd. commrs., chmn. judiciary com. 1976-85, mem. rep. assembly, chmn. rules and calendar com.1971-76, co-chair U.S. Cts. com. 1986-87), Internat. Assn. Def. Counsel, U.S. Supreme Ct. Hist. Soc., Ann Arbor C. of C. (chmn. bd. 1971), Detroit Athletic Club, Barton Hills Country Club, Pres.'s Club. U. Mich., Varsity M Club, Order of Coif, Barristers, Phi Delta Phi, Phi Kappa Psi. Republican. Roman Catholic. Avocations: golf, running, reading. Home: 101 Underdown Rd Ann Arbor MI 48105-1078 Office: Miller Canfield Paddock & Stone 101 N Main St Fl 7 Ann Arbor MI 48104-5507

DEVINE, EUGENE PETER, lawyer; b. Albany, N.Y., Oct. 14, 1948; s. Eugene Peter and Phyllis Jean (Albanese) D.; m. Debra Ann Ziamandanis, Apr. 11, 1992; children: Kimberly, Tracy, Adrianne, Madeline. JD, Union U., 1975. Bar: N.Y. 1975, U.S. Dist. Ct. (no. dist.) N.Y. 1975, U.S. Supreme Ct. 1980. Asst. N.Y. Pub. Defender, Albany County, 1976-85; ptnr. Cooper, Erving & Savage, Albany, 1975-85, Devine, Piedment & Rutnik, 1985-91; chief pub. defender Albany County, 1994—; of counsel Ruberti Girvin & Ferlazzo, 2000—; chief atty. Albany County Dept. Social Svcs., 1985-88. Bd. dirs. Ronald McDonald House, Albany, 1980—, founding mem.; committeman Albany County Dem. Com., 1979—; treas. com. to elect Jim Tully N.Y. State Compt., 1980, vice chmn. Albany Med. Ctr. Found., 1994—. Mem. Woolferts Roost Country Club, Steuben Athletic Club, Albany Sons of St. Patrick (pres. 1984). Criminal, General practice, Labor. Office: Carter Conboy Case Blackmore Napierski & Maloney 20 Corporate Woods Blvd Ste 8 Albany NY 12211-2362

DEVINE, MICHAEL BUXTON, lawyer; b. Des Moines, Oct. 25, 1953; s. Cleatie Hiram, Jr., and Katherine Ann (Buxton) D. Student, St. Peter's Coll., Oxford U., Eng., 1975; BA cum laude, St. Olaf Coll., 1976; MPA, JD, Drake U., 1980; diploma in Advanced Internat. Legal Studies, U. Pacific, Salzburg, Austria, 1986; LLM in Internat. Bus. Legal Studies, U. Exeter, Eng., 1988, postgrad., 1997—. Bar: Iowa 1980, U.S. Dist. Ct. (no. and so. dists.) Iowa 1980, U.S. Ct. Appeals (8th cir.) 1980, Nebr. 1985, Supreme Ct. 1985, Minn. 1986, D.C. 1986., N.Y. 1987, Wis. 1987, Colo. 1988, N.Y. 1990, U.S. Ct. Appeals (fed. cir.) 1990, U.S. Ct. Internat. Trade 1990, Eng. and Wales, 1995, U.K. Ho. of Lords, 1995, Ct. Justice of the European Com., 1995, No. Ireland, 2000. Assoc. Bump & Haesemeyer, P.C., Des Moines, 1980-85; jud. law clk. Jud. Dept. State of Iowa, 1987-88; assoc. Christianson, Hohnbaum & George, Des Moines, 1989, Pavelic & Levites, P.C., N.Y.C., 1989-92; with chambers Alan Tyrrell, Q.C., London, 1993-94; with legal dept. Philips Electronics U.K., Ltd., 1994; with Lafili, Van Crombrugghe & Ptnrs., Brussels, 1995; pvt. practice Des Moines/N.Y.C./London, 1997—; of counsel Pavelic & Levites, P.C., N.Y.C., 1997—. Internat. legal intern Herbert Oppenheimer, Nathan & Vandyk, London, 1986; lectr. in law U. Kent, Canterbury, Eng., 2000—. Contbr. articles to profl. jours. Nat. alt. U.S. Presdl. Mgmt. Intern Program, 1980. Scholar St. Olaf Coll., 1972-76 Mem. ABA (sect. internat. law), Fed. Bar Assn. (chmn. state of Iowa SBA export assistance program 1983-85, treas. Iowa chpt. 1984-85, exec. com. 1985-87), N.Y. State Bar Assn. (sec. internat. law), Assn. of Bar of City of N.Y. (coun. internat. affairs 1990-92), Phi Alpha Theta, Pi Alpha Alpha. Presbyterian. E-makl. Contracts commercial, General corporate, Private international. Home: 2611 40th St Des Moines IA 50310-3949 Office: Pavelic & Levites PC 865 3rd Ave New York NY 10017 E-mail: mde1009767@aol.com

DE VIVO, EDWARD CHARLES, lawyer; b. Newark, Dec. 10, 1953; s. Louis Joseph and Marian (Pistilli) De V. B.A. cum laude, NYU, 1975, M.A., 1982; J.D., U. Notre Dame, 1978. Bar: N.Y. 1979, U.S. Dist. Ct. (so. dist.) N.Y., U.S. Dist. Ct. (ea. dist.) N.Y. Assoc. Bigham Englar Jones & Houston, N.Y.C., 1978-82, Condon & Forsyth, N.Y.C., 1982-85, Catten, Muchin & Zavis, N.Y.C., 1990—; cons. Contbr. articles to legal publs. Mem. bd. spl. advisors Pres. Reagan's Phys. Fitness Commn., 1985—; active Big Bros. Program, United Way, 1985—; mem. Literacy Coun. Am. NYU scholar, 1971-75. Republican. Roman Catholic. Club: Bradford Pool and Raquet. Aviation, Federal civil litigation, Product liability. Home: 10 Kips Rdg Verona NJ 07044-2929 Office: 40 Broad St New York NY 10004-2315

DEVLIN, JAMES RICHARD, lawyer; b. Camden, N.J., July 7, 1950; s. Gerald William and Mary (Hand) D.; children: Grace, Jennifer, Kristen. BS in Indsl. Engring., N.J. Inst. Tech., 1972; JD, Fordham U., 1976. Bar: N.J. 1976, N.Y. 1977, U.S. Ct. Appeals (D.C. cir.) 1982. Various mgmt. positions in Long Lines Sect. AT&T, N.Y.C., 1972-76, counsel Long Lines Sect. Bedminster, N.J., 1976-82, counsel N.Y.C., 1982-83, gen. atty. comm. sect. Basking Ridge, N.J., 1983-86; v.p., gen. counsel telephone United Telecomm., Inc., Westwood, Kans., 1987-88; exec. v.p. gen. counsel and external affairs Sprint Corp., 1989—. Mem. bd. overseers N.J. Inst. Tech., 1997—. Past pres., bd. dirs. Ctr. for Mgmt. Assistance, Kansas City, Mo., 1993-96; bd. dirs. Heart of Am. United Way, Minority Supplier Coun., Kansas City; mem. bd. overseers N.J. Inst. Tech. Mem. ABA (past chmn. comm. com. pub. utility law sect.), Am. Arbitration Assn., Fed. Comm. Bar Assn. Administrative and regulatory, Communications, General corporate. Home: 4104 W 123rd St Leawood KS 66209-2220 Office: Sprint Corp 2330 Shawnee Mission Pkwy Westwood KS 66205-2090

DEVOTO, LOUIS JOSEPH, lawyer; b. Jersey City, July 27, 1965; s. Richard Louis and Concetta Ann DeVoto; m. Anne M. Hayes, June 1, 1991; children: Thomas, Emily, Caroline. BS in Mgmt., St. Joseph's U., Phila., 1987; JD, Ohio No. U., 1993. Bar: N.J. 1993, U.S. Dist. Ct. N.J. 1993, Pa. 1994, U.S. Ct. Appeals (3d cir.), 1995, U.S. Dist. Ct. (ea. dist.) Pa. 1998, U.S. Supreme Ct. 1999; cert. civil trial atty. Supreme Ct. N.J., cert. civil trial law Nat. Ab. Trial Advocacy. Jud. clk. to Hon. Marvin E. Schlosser, N.J. Superior Ct., Mt. Holly, 1993-94; assoc. Ferrara & Rossetti, P.A., Cherry Hill, N.J., 1994-97; ptnr. Ferrara, Rossetti & DeVoto, P.A., 1998—. Guest spkr. Gloucester County Coll., 1996. Exec. editor Ohio No. U. Law Rev., 1992-93. Mem. bldg. com. Our Lady Queen of Peach Ch., West Milford, N.J., 1987-88; sponsor annual fundraising banquet March of Dimes Found., Cherry Hill, N.J., 1994—, Bancroft Found., Phila., 1998; coach Marlton (N.J.) Rec. Coun.; trustee Bancroft Brain Injury Svcs. Corp., 1999—. Fellow Camden County Bar Found.; mem. ATLA (guest spkr. N.J. affiliate 1997), Am. Arbitration Assn. (adv. com.), N.J. Bar Assn., Trial Attys. N.J. (trustee 1999—), Trial Lawyers for Pub. Justice, Camden County Bar Assn. (personal injury law com.), Burlington County Bar Assn. (civil practice com.). Roman Catholic. Avocations: golf, ice hockey, rollerblading. General civil litigation, Personal injury, Product liability. Office: Ferrara Rossetti & DeVoto 601 Longwood Ave Cherry Hill NJ 08002-2856 Fax: 856-661-0369. E-mail: ldevoto@njinjurylaw.com

DEVRIES, DONALD LAWSON, JR. lawyer; b. Phila., May 1, 1947; s. Donald Lawson and Jeanne (Coleman) DeV.; m. Nancy Shafer, Aug. 10, 1977; children: Donald Lawson III, Emily Shafer; stepdaughter: Alison Brady Beale. BA with honors, Dartmouth Coll., 1969; JD with honors, U. Md., 1973. Bar: Md. 1973, U.S. Dist. Ct. Md. 1973, U.S. Ct. Appeals (4th cir.) 1976, U.S. Ct. Appeals (D.C. cir.) 1989, U.S. Dist. Ct. D.C. 1991. Assoc. Semmes, Bowen & Semmes, Balt., 1973-80, ptnr., chmn. med. malpractice dept., 1980-88; founding and mng. ptnr. Goodell, DeVries, Leech & Dann, 1988—. Chmn. dept. med. malpractice Semmes, Bowen & Semmes, 1980-88; mem. faculty Md. Inst. Continuing Profl. Edn. for Lawyers, 1984-95; gov.'s task force on Med. Malpractice Ins., 1985; master Am. Inns of Court, 1986-90. Contbr. Md. Law Rev., 1973. Trustee Roland Pk. Country Sch., 1987-94, Woodbourne Ctr., 1981-88; trustee, exec. com. South Balt. Gen. Hosp., 1983-88; mem. Canons and Other Bus. Coms. of Episcopal Diocese Md., 1984-95; vestryman St. David's Ch., 1982-85; bd. dirs. Md. affiliate Am. Heart Assn., 1986-90, co-chmn. Heart Ball, 1986, 87, 88, chmn. solicitation com. Shock Trauma Gala, 1988, 89, co-chmn., 1990, 91, bd. visitors Shock Trauma, 1989-93, chmn. 1990-93; chmn. Emergency Med. Svcs. Bd., Md., 1992—; mem. joint exec./legis. task force on med. malpractice ins., Md., 1985; mem. com. on uninsured persons Gov.'s Commn. on Health Care Policy and Financing, 1988-90. Fellow Am. Coll. Trial Lawyers; mem. ABA (spkr. ann. meeting 1984, moderator, program planner ann. meeting medicine and law com. 1986, 88, vice chmn. medicine and law com. torts and ins. practice sect. 1982-89, med. adv. panel medicine and law com. 1986-87, forum com. health law 1984—, faculty nat. inst. on med. malpractice 1987, 88, 89, 90, chmn. medicine and law com., torts and ins. practice sect. 1988-89), Internat. Assn. Ins. Counsel, Internat. Assn. Def. Counsel (faculty trial acad. 1991, moderator, program planner 1992, vice chmn. med. malpractice com. for newsletters 1989-90, program chmn. 1990-92, chmn. med. malpractice com. 1992-94, chmn. def. counsel com. 1997-99, exec. com. 1999—, George W. Yancey Meml. award 1998), Internat. Soc. Barristers, Assn. Def. Trial Attys., Am. Bd. Trial Advocates (pres. Md. chpt. 1993-95, nat. bd. dirs. 1993—), Md. State Bar Assn. (spl. com. on health claims arbitration 1983), Md. Trial Lawyers Assn. (faculty 1983, 85), Md. Assn. Def. Trial Counsel, Def. Rsch. Inst., Wednesday Law Club, Maryland Club, Chesapeake Bay Yacht Club, Center Club. Republican. Personal injury, Product liability, Professional liability. Office: Goodell DeVries Leech & Dann LLP 1 South St Ste 200 Baltimore MD 21202-7314

DEW, THOMAS EDWARD, lawyer; b. Detroit, Feb. 13, 1947; s. Albert Nelson and Irene Theresa (Morris) D.; m. Gail Ruth Tuesink, June 27, 1970. BA, U. Mich., 1969; JD, Detroit Coll. Law, 1974. Bar: Mich. 1974, U.S. Dist. Ct. (ea. dist.) Mich. 1974, U.S. Tax Ct. 1980. Agt. IRS, Detroit, 1969-74; trust officer Ann Arbor (Mich.) Trust Co., 1974-75, asst. v.p., 1975-78; ptnr. Conner, Harbour, Dew, Ann Arbor, 1978-83, Harris, Lax, Guenzel & Dew, Ann Arbor, 1983-87; private practice Thomas E. Dew Profl. Corp., 1987-88; prin. Dever and Dew Profl. Corp., 1988-99, Wise & Marsac, Detroit, 1999-2001, Berry Moorman, PC, Detroit, 2001—. Lectr. Am. Coll., Bryn Mawr, Pa., 1979-82, Am. Inst. Paralegal Studies, Detroit, 1982. Mem. Ann Harbor Housing Commn., 1979-81, pres. 1981; trustee Ann Arbor Area Cmty. Found. Named Law scholar, Sigma Nu Phi, 1974. Fellow Mich. State Bar Found.; mem. State Bar Mich., Washtenaw County Bar Assn., Washtenaw Estate Planning Coun. (pres. 1979-80), New Enterprise Forum. Republican. Presbyterian. General corporate, Probate, Estate taxation. Office: Berry Moorman PC 455 E Eisenhower Pky #210 Ann Arbor MI 48108 E-mail: tdew@berrymoorman.com

DEWEY, DENNIS JAMES, lawyer; b. Chgo., June 5, 1938; s. James Franklin and Dorothy Rose Dewey; m. Patricia Rees, Nov. 9, 1968; children: Joseph Arba, James Myron. BS, U. Evansville, 1963; LLB, Ind. U., 1966. Bar: Ind. 1966, U.S. Dist. Ct. (so. dist.) Ind. 1966, U.S. Ct. Appeals (7th cir.) 1968, U.S. Supreme Ct. 1976. Appellate staff mem. Ind. Atty. Gen.'s. Office, 1966-68; assoc. Early, Arnold & Ziemer, Evansville, Ind.; ptnr. Dewey & Feulner, Newburgh; chief dep. prosecuting atty. 2d Jud. Cir.; bankruptcy trustee U.S. Dist. Ct. (so. dist.) Ind., Evansville; ptnr. Weyerbacher, Dewey, Neff & Weyerbacher, Newburgh, 1982-86, Weyerbacher, Dewey and Weyerbacher, Newburgh, 1986—. Chmn. 8th div. Rep. Young Lawyers,1969-70. Past pres. Southwestern Ind. Easter Seal Soc. and Rehab. Ctr., Inc.; past bd. dirs. United Way Southwestern Ind., Inc. Mem. ABA, Ind. Bar Assn., Warrick County Bar Assn. (past pres.), Evansville Bar Assn., Phi Delta Phi, Sigma Phi. Bankruptcy, General corporate, General practice. Office: Weyerbacher Dewey & Weyerbacher 107 State St Newburgh IN 47630-1227

DEWEY, JOEL ALLEN, lawyer; b. Balt., Dec. 17, 1956; s. Allen Leonard and Mary Louise (Karcher) D.; m. Martha Dayle Nesbitt, Aug 25, 1979; children: Samuel Everett, Sarah Radcliffe. SBCE, MIT, 1977; JD, Harvard U., 1980. Bar: Calif. 1980, Md. 1981, D.C. 1981, U.S. Dist. Ct. Md. 1981, U.S. Ct. Appeals (4th cir.) 1981, N.Y. 1993, Va. 1994. Law clk. to presiding justice U.S. Dist. Ct. Md., Balt., 1980-81; assoc. Piper & Marbury, 1981-88, ptnr., 1989—. Mem. Chi Epsilon, Tau Beta Pi. Republican. Presbyterian. Avocation: running. Product liability, General civil litigation, Intellectual property. Home: 1428B W Joppa Rd Towson MD 21204-3618 Office: Piper Marbury 6225 Smith Ave Baltimore MD 21209-3600 E-mail: joel.dewey@piperrudnick.com

DEWHIRST, JOHN WARD, lawyer; b. Richmond, Va., Aug. 12, 1937; s. Howard Homer and Edith Rowland (Ward) D.; m. Virginia Dell Pound, Dec. 1, 1958; children: Kathy Lynn Dewhirst Wincheski, Suzanne Ward, John Ward Jr., Matthew Lee, Jeffrey Christopher. B of Indsl. Engring., Ga. Inst. Tech., 1960; JD, George Washington U., 1965. Bar: Va. 1966, D.C. 1971, U.S. Ct. Appeals (fed. cir.) 1970, U.S. Supreme Ct. 1972. Patent examiner Patent and Trademark Office, U.S. Dept. Commerce, Washington, 1960-70, asst. solicitor, 1970-72, assoc. solicitor, 1972-92, retired, 1992; pvt. practice Fairfax, Va., 1992—. Litig. cons. and expert witness in the field of patent law, patent and trademark office practice and procedures. Pres. Country Club View Civic Assn., Fairfax, Va., 1968. Mem. Patent Lawyer's Club Washington, Lions, Fed. Cir. Bar Assn. (intellectual property sect.), Va. State Bar. Episcopalian. Avocations: travel, cross-country skiing, camping, hiking, snorkeling. Federal civil litigation, Intellectual property, Patent. Home and Office: 5014 Portsmouth Rd Fairfax VA 22032-2225 also: 2812 Strategy Ct Williamsburg VA 23185

DEWITT, CHARLES BENJAMIN, III, lawyer, educator; b. Glendale, Calif., Nov. 29, 1952; s. Charles Benjamin Jr. and Lucille Ann (Johnston) deW.; m. Karen Denise Blackwood, Dec. 29, 1979. BA magna cum laude, Pacific Union Coll., 1973; JD, U. So. Calif., 1976; MA, U. Memphis, 1995. Bar: Tenn. 1984, U.S. Dist. Ct. (we. dist.) Tenn. 1984, D.C. 1989. Atty., agy. mgr., v.p. SAFECO/Chgo. Title Ins., Memphis, 1980-91; regional underwriting counsel Commonwealth Land Title Ins. Co., 1991-93. Asst. prof., instr. U. Memphis, 1986—, asst. dean paralegal, 1993-96., asst. dean law sch., 1996—; judge adv. U.S. Army Gen. Corps, ILT (Reserves). Contbr. articles to profl. jours. Registrar gen. Washington Family Descendants Mem. ABA, Memphis Bar Assn., Tenn. Land Title Assn. (sec.-treas. 1983-87), U. S.C. Alumni Assn. (life), Order Crown of Charlemagne, Kiwanis, Mensa, Phi Alpha Theta, Phi Kappa Phi, Phi Alpha Delta. Education and schools, Real property. Home: 2488 Cedarwood Dr Germantown TN 38138-5802 Office: U Memphis Sch Law 107 Law School Memphis TN 38152-0001 E-mail: cdewitt@memphis.edu

DEWOSKIN, ALAN ELLIS, lawyer; b. St. Louis, Sept. 10, 1940; s. Samuel S. and Lillian (Sachs) DeW.; m. Iris Lynn Shapiro, Aug. 15, 1942; children: Joseph, Henry, Franklin. BA, Washington U., St. Louis, 1962, JD, 1965; postgrad., U.S. Army Command & Gen. Staff Coll., 1978, U.S. Army War Coll., 1985. Bar: Mo. 1968, Ill. 1999, U.S. Dist. Ct. (ea. dist.) Mo. 1968, U.S. Ct. Appeals (8th cir.) 1969, U.S. Ct. Appeals (Armed Forces) 1976, U.S. Supreme Ct. 1990, U.S. Ct. Claims 1997. Pvt. practice, St. Louis, 1968-82; prin. Alan E. DeWoskin, PC, 1982—. Active Boy Scouts Am. Col. JAGC, USAR Ret. Recipient U.S. Legion of Merit, 1992. Fellow Am. Bar Found., Mo. Bar Found., St. Louis Bar Found. (disting.); mem. ABA (chmn., gen. practice sect. 1985-86, ho. of dels. 1986-87, assembly del., standing com. mil. law, standing com. assembly resolutions 1988-91, vice-chmn. task force solo and small firm practitioners), ATLA, Mo. Bar Assn. (chmn. gen. practice com. 1987-90, chmn. computer interest groups 1988-90), Bar Assn. Met. St. Louis (exec. com. 1993-94, bd. govts. 1994-95, chmn. solo and small firm sect. 1993-95), Mo. Assn. Trial Attys., Res. Officers Assn. (Mo. Dept. pres. 1979), Masons (past master, dir. 1972—), Am. Legion. Federal civil litigation, State civil litigation, General practice. Home: 14030 Deltona Dr Chesterfield MO 63017-3311 Office: 225 S Meramec Ave Ste 426 Saint Louis MO 63105-3511 E-mail: aedewoskin@cs.com

DHANASARNSOMBAT, PRAPAIPAN, lawyer; b. Thonburi, Bangkok, Thailand, Dec. 10, 1946; d. Sunghueng Khow and Kee Tieng Lim; m. Apichart Dhanasarnsombat, Nov. 17, 1975; children: Jarunan, Sansanee. B of Acctg., Thammasat U., Bangkok, 1971; LLB, 1997; MA in Econ. Law, Chulalongkorn U., Bangkok, 2000. CPA Thailand. Auditor, acctg. advisor Suthee & Co., Bangkok, 1971-79; fin. mgr. Chandler & Thong-Ek Law Offices, 1979—. Bd. dirs. Bio Data Co., Bangkok. Contbr. article to profl. jour. Dir. PTA Sai Nam Pheung Sch., Bangkok, 1997-99. Mem. Inst. Cert. Accts. and Auditors Thailand (life, dir. br. coordination 1997-99, dir. acctg. std. govt. sect. 1999—), Law Soc. Thailand (life), Bar Assn. Thailand (extraordinary). Avocations: reading, Japanese language, travel. Corporate taxation, Taxation, general, Personal income taxation. Home: 36/1 Soi Samarnchant Sukhumvit 42 Bangkok 10110 Thailand Office: Chandler & Thong-Ek Law Offices 20 N Sathorn Rd 7th Fl Bubhajit Bldg 10500 Bangkok Thailand Fax: (662) 266-6483-4. E-mail: prapaipan@ctlo.com

DIAMANT, AVIVA F. lawyer; b. N.Y.C., Mar. 13, 1949; d. Herman and Anni (Silbermann) D.; m. Steven Kaufman, May 31, 1976; 2 children. BS cum laude, CCNY, 1969; JD, Columbia U., 1972. Bar: N.Y. 1973, U.S. Ct. Appeals (2d cir.) 1975, U.S. Dist. Ct. (so. dist.) 1976. Assoc. Fried, Frank, Harris, Shriver & Jacobson, N.Y.C., 1972-79, ptnr., 1979—. James Kent scholar, 1972. Mem. Assn. of Bar of City of N.Y. (com. on corps. 1982-85), Phi Beta Kappa. Jewish. General corporate, Securities. Office: Fried Frank Harris Shriver & Jacobson 1 New York Plz Fl 22 New York NY 10004-1980

DIAMANT, MICHAEL HARLAN, lawyer; b. Cleve., July 30, 1946; s. Eugene and Rita June (Hausman) D.; m. Amy Sarah Bresnick, Nov. 23, 1969; children: Aaron Jeremy, Ethan Ari. BS in Engring. with high honors, Case Western Res. U., 1968; JD cum laude, Harvard U., 1971. Bar: Ohio 1971, U.S. Dist. Ct. Ohio 1973, U.S. Ct. Appeals (6th cir.) 1977, U.S. Ct. Appeals (fed. cir.) 1982, U.S. Supreme Ct. 1977. Prin. Kahn, Kleinman, Uanowitz & Arnson Co., Cleve., 1971-78, 1978—. Pres. Solomon Schecter Day Sch. Cleve., 1984-87; pres., Case Alumni Assn., 1995-96; mem. vis. com. undergrad. colls. Case Western Res. U., chmn. vis. com. Case Sch. Engring., 1993-99. Mem. ABA, Bar Assn. Greater Cleve. (chmn. computer law inst. 1983-85, chmn. jud. sel. com. 1985), Computer Law Assn., Case Alumni Assn. (pres. 1995-96). Democrat. Jewish. General civil litigation, Computer. Office: Kahn Kleinman Yanowitz & Arnson Co LPA 2600 Tower at Erieview Cleveland OH 44114-1824

DI AMATO, ASTOLFO, lawyer, law educator; b. Naples, Italy, Apr. 8, 1942; s. Stanislao Di Amato and Bice Laino; m. Ada Franchini, July 6, 1968; children: Stanislao, Alessio. Master's, U. La Sapienza, Rome, 1964. Bar: Supreme Ct. 1984. Judge Min. of Justice, Orvieto, Terni, Italy, 1967-84; mem. Superior Coun. Judiciary, Rome, 1978-82; sr. ptnr. Astolfo Di Amato e Associati. Avvocati, Rome, Naples, Milan, Italy, 1984—. Prof. bus. law Naples U. Federico II, 1984—; judge Basketball Fedn., Rome, 1981-91. Author: Il Segreto Bancario, 1978, Impresa e Nuovi Contratti,

1998, Diritto Penale Dell'impresa, 1999, L'interpretazione dei Contratti di Impresa, 2000, Italian Law on Business Crime, 2001; dir. treatise Diritto Penale dell'Impresa, 1990, Business Crimes under Italian Legislation, 2001. Mem. Circolo Nazionale dell'Unione. Consumer commercial, General corporate, Mergers and acquisitions. Office: Astolfo Di Amato e Assoc Avvocati via Nizza n 59 00198 Rome Italy also: via Carducci no 42 80121 Naples Italy also: Corso di Porta Vittoria u58 20122 Milan Italy Fax: 39.06.84242253. E-mail: diamatoeassociati@diamato.net

DIAMOND, ANN CYNTHIA, lawyer; b. Hollywood, Calif., Apr. 7, 1947; d. I.A.L. and Barbara Ann (Bentley) D.; m. Robert Sidney Pynoos, Mar. 31, 1969 (div. June 1977). BA, Sarah Lawrence Coll., 1968; JD, NYU, 1978. Bar: N.Y. 1979, U.S. Dist. Ct. (so. dist.) N.Y. 1979, U.S. Dist. Ct. (ea. dist.) N.Y. 1979, U.S. Ct. Appeals (9th cir.) 1983, U.S. Ct. Appeals (2d cir.) 1984. Jr. editor McCall's Mag., N.Y.C., 1968-69; copy and features editor Bride's Mag., 1969-73; copywriter Elizebeth Arden, Inc., 1973-75; assoc. Proskauer Rose Goetz & Mendelsohn, 1978-80, Finley, Kumble, Wanger, Heine, Underberg, Manley & Casey, N.Y.C., 1980-84, Bronstein, Van Veen & Bronstein, P.C., 1985—. Mentor Network for Women's Svcs., 1996-. Author: (with S.F. Enos) The Bride's Magazine Guide to the New Marriage, 1974; Bride's Book of Etiquette, 1972. Facilitator, presenter Parent Edn. and Custody Effectiveness Tng., 1999—; vol. counsel Assn. Bar City N.Y. Fund Shield Clinic; neutral evaluator Supreme Ct. State of N.Y., 1997—; staff counsel Gov. Jud. Nominating Com., 1980-82; del. Dem. Jud. Nominating Convs. N.Y., 1974-78; adminstrv. dir. N.Y. State Hdqrs., McGovern for Pres., N.Y.C., 1972; pres. Cmty. Free Dems. 1974, v.p. 1975-77; sec. N.Y. New Dem. Coalition, 1976-77; arbitrator matrimonial fee disputes Supreme Ct. of the State of N.Y., 1994—. Mem. ABA, Assn. Bar City N.Y., NYU Pub. Interest Law Found. (founding), N.Y. County Lawyers Assn. Family and matrimonial. Office: Carnegie Hall Tower 152 W 57th St New York NY 10019-3310

DIAMOND, BERNARD ROBIN, lawyer; b. Bronx, N.Y., July 3, 1944; m. Elizabeth Heimbuch, Oct. 20, 1976; children: Jessica, Carey, Erin. BA, Rutgers U., 1966; JD, Bklyn. Law Sch., 1972. Bar: N.Y. 1973, U.S. Dist. Ct. (so. and ea. dists.) N.Y. 1973, U.S. Ct. Appeals (2d cir.) 1974. Gen. counsel The Trump Orgn., N.Y.C., 1995—. Mem. Assn. of the Bar of the City of N.Y. Real property. Office: Trump Orgn 725 5th Ave Fl 26 New York NY 10022-2520

DIAMOND, DAVID ARTHUR, law educator; b. N.Y.C., May 8, 1937; s. Samuel and Ann (Kottick) D.; m. Shelley Sherman, Aug. 7, 1977; 1 child, Daniel. A.B., Harvard U., 1959, LL.B., 1962; LL.M., NYU, 1963. Bar: N.Y., 1963, U.S. Ct. Appeals (2d cir.), U.S. Ct. Appeals (5th cir.), U.S. Dist. Ct. (so. dist.) N.Y., U.S. Dist. Ct. (ea. dist.) N.Y. Assoc. Hughes, Hubbard & Reed, N.Y.C., 1963-68; dir. law reform unit MFY Legal Services, N.Y.C., 1968-72, also dir.; law prof. Syracuse Law Sch., N.Y., 1972-75, Hofstra Law Sch., Hempstead, N.Y., 1975— ; co-dir. North East Regional Program Nat. Inst. Trial Advocacy. Mem. due process com. ACLU. Mem. Assn. Bar City of N.Y. (mem. spl. com. on law and edn.). Home: 43 Jayson Ave Great Neck NY 11021-4239 Office: Hofstra Law Sch Rm 214 Hempstead NY 11550

DIAMOND, DAVID HOWARD, lawyer; b. N.Y.C., June 24, 1945; s. Philip and Betty (Resnikoff) D.; m. Barbara R. Jacobs, Sep. 6, 1969; children: John, Andrew, Jill. BA, SUNY, Binghamton, 1967; JD, Georgetown U., Washington, D.C., 1970. Bar: Va. 1970, D.C. 1971, N.J. 1972, N.Y. 1973, U.S. Supreme Ct. 1982, U.S. Dist. Ct. Asst. gen. counsel Nat. Treas. Employees Union, Washington, 1970-71; trial atty. Nat. Labor Relations Bd., Newark, 1971-73; assoc. Putney, Twombly, Hall & Hirson, N.Y.C., 1973-76; ptnr. Guggenheimer & Untermeyer, 1976-86, Summit, Rovins & Felderman, N.Y.C., 1986-89, Patterson, Belknap, Webb & Tyler, N.Y.C., 1989-91, Proskauer, Rose LLP, N.Y.C., 1991—. Contbg. editor: Developing Labor Law, 1975-82, The Fair Labor Standards Act, BNA, 2000. Pres., dir. Birchwood Civic Assn., Jericho, N.Y., 1985-95; trustee Jericho Libr. Bd., 1994—. Mem. ABA (sect. labor and employment law, com. fed. labor standards), N.Y. State Bar Assn. (com. on individual and employee rights). Avocations: biking, tennis, whitewater rafting. Civil rights, Health, Labor. Home: 18 Briar Ln Jericho NY 11753-2212 Office: Proskauer Rose LLP 1585 Broadway Fl 27 New York NY 10036-8299

DIAMOND, EUGENE CHRISTOPHER, lawyer, hospital administrator; b. Oceanside, Calif., Oct. 19, 1952; s. Eugene Francis and Rosemary (Wright) D.; m. Mary Theresa O'Donnell, Jan. 20, 1984; children: Eugene John, Kevin Seamus, Hannah Rosemary, Seamus Michael, Maeve Therese. BA, U. Notre Dame, 1974; MHA, St. Louis U., 1978, JD, 1979. Bar: Ill. 1979. Staff atty. AUL Legal Def. Fund, Chgo., 1979-80; adminstrv. asst. Holy Cross Hosp., 1980-81, asst. adminstr., 1981-82, v.p., 1982-83, counsel to adminstr., 1980—, exec. v.p., 1983-91; exec. v.p., COO, St. Margaret Mercy Healthcare Ctrs., Hammond, Ind., 1991-93, pres., CEO, 1993—, regional COO, 2001—. Cons. Birthright of Chgo., 1979—, mem. benefit com., 1981—; bd. dirs. Hammond C. of C., 1993, North West Ind. Forum. Mem. Ill. State Bar Assn., Chgo. Bar Assn. Roman Catholic. Health. Office: St Margaret Mercy Healthcare Ctrs 5454 Hohman Ave Hammond IN 46320-1999

DIAMOND, GUSTAVE, federal judge; b. Burgettstown, Pa., Jan. 29, 1928; s. George and Margaret (Solinsky) D.; m. Emma L. Scarton, Dec. 28, 1974; 1 dau., Margaret Ann; 1 stepdau., Joanne Yoney. A.B., Duke U., 1951; J.D., Duquesne U., 1956. Bar: Pa. bar 1958, U.S. Ct. Appeals bar 1962. Law clk. to judge U.S. Dist. Ct., Pitts., 1955-61; 1st asst. U.S. atty. Western Dist. Pa., 1961-62, U.S. atty., 1963-69; partner firm Cooper, Schwartz, Diamond & Reich, Pitts., 1969-75; formerly individual practice law Washington; former solicitor Washington County; judge U.S. Dist. Ct. Western Dist. Pa.; chief judge U.S. Dist. Ct. (we. dist.) Pa., 1992-94, sr. judge, 1994—. Chmn. Jud. Conf. Com. on Defender Svcs. Mem. ABA, Fed. Bar Assn., Pa. Bar Assn., Allegheny County Bar Assn., Washington County Bar Assn. Office: US Dist Ct 821 US Courthouse 7th St Rm 2 Pittsburgh PA 15219

DIAMOND, JOSEF, lawyer; b. L.A., Mar. 6, 1907; s. Michael and Ruby (Shifrin) D.; m. Violett Diamond, Apr. 2, 1933 (dec. 1979); children: Joel, Diane Foreman; m. Ann Dulien, Jan. 12, 1981 (dec. 1984); m. Muriel Bach, 1986. BBA, U. Wash., 1929, JD, 1931. Bar: Wash. 1931, U.S. Dist. Ct. (we. dist.) Wash. 1932, U.S. Ct. Appeals (9th cir.) 1934, U.S. Supreme Ct. 1944. Assoc. Caldwell & Lycette, Seattle, 1931-35; ptnr. Caldwell, Lycette & Diamond, 1935-45, Lycette, Diamond & Sylvester, Seattle, 1945-80, Diamond & Sylvester, Seattle, 1980-82, of counsel, 1982-88, Short, Cressman & Burgess, Seattle, 1988—. Chmn. bd. Diamond Parking Inc., Seattle, 1945-70; cons. various businesses. Bd. dirs. Am. Heart Assn., 1960; chmn. Wash. Heart Assn., 1962. Col. JAGC, U.S. Army, WWII. Decorated Legion of Merit. Mem. Wash. Bar Assn., Assn. Trial Lawyers Wash., Seattle Bar Assn., Mil. Engrs. Soc., Wash. Athletic Club, Bellevue Athletic Club, Harbor Club. Office: Diamond Bldg Ste 200 3161 Elliott Ave Seattle WA 98121

DIAMOND, MURRAY J. lawyer; b. N.Y.C., Dec. 25, 1923; s. Albert and Annie (Unger) D.; m. Beatrice Padwa, Apr. 4, 1955; children: Alayne, Lawrence. BA, Bklyn. Coll., 1947; JD, Bklyn. Law Sch., 1950, JSD, 1952. Bar: N.Y. 1950, U.S. Dist. Ct. (ea. and so. dists.) N.Y., U.S. Supreme Ct. 1956. Ptnr. firm Diamond & Dreifuss, N.Y.C., 1950-86; law lectr. N.Y.C. Tech. Coll., Bklyn., 1969-79; asst. prof. bus. law Hofstra U., Hempstead, N.Y., 1979-86; prof. St. Francis Coll., Bklyn., 1986-99, prof. emeritus, 1999—. Hearing officer N.Y. State Dept. Agr. and Markets; impartial hearing officer Bd. Edn., City of N.Y. Co-author manual; contbr. articles to profl. jours. Served to maj. USAR, 1947-67. Mem. Am. Bus. Law Assn. Office: 267 Whitman Dr Brooklyn NY 11234-6934 E-mail: bdmjd@aol.com

DIAMOND, PAUL STEVEN, lawyer, educator; b. Bklyn., Jan. 2, 1953; s. George and Anna (Jaeger) D.; m. Robin Nilon. BA magna cum laude, Columbia U., 1974; JD, U. Pa., 1977. Bar: Pa. 1977, U.S. Dist. Ct. (ea. dist.) Pa, 1979, U.S. Ct. Appeals (3d cir.) 1979, U.S. Supreme Ct. 1983. Asst. dist. atty. Phila. Dist. Atty. Office, 1977-83; law clk. Supreme Ct. Pa., Phila., 1980; assoc. Dilworth, Paxson, Kalish & Kauffman, 1983-85, ptnr., 1986-91, Obermayer, Rebmann, Maxwell & Hippel, Phila., 1992—. Lectr. Temple U. Sch. Law, Phila., 1990-92; mem. civil prodecural rules com. Supreme Ct. Pa., 1995-98, fed. judicial nominating commn., 1993, 95-2000; treas. Pa. lawyers fund for client security bd. Supreme Ct. Pa., 1999—; vice-chmn. Amicus Curiae Briefs Comm., 1995-99. Author: Federal Grand Jury Practice and Procedure, 1990, rev. 4d edit., 2001. Mem. ABA (criminal justice sect., Amicus Curiae briefs subcom. 1984-99, grand jury subcom. 1991-93), Am. Law Inst., Pa. Bar Assn., Phila. Bar Assn. Republican. Jewish. General civil litigation, Constitutional, Criminal.

DIAMOND, RICHARD S. lawyer; b. Newark, June 26, 1960; BA in Econs./Bus. Adminstrn., Rutgers U., 1981; JD, Seton Hall U., 1985. Bar: N.J. 1985, Fla. 1991, U.S. Dist. Ct. N.J. 1991; cert. matrimonial trial specialist, cert. divorce mediator; ct. apptd. econ. mediator N.J. Supreme Ct. Law sec. to Hon. Burton J. Ironson State of N.J., Union County, N.J., 1985-86; assoc. Law Firm of Robert Diamond, Springfield; ptnr. Diamond Hodes & Diamond, Gourvitz, Diamond, Hodes, Braun & Diamond, Springfield, Diamond & Diamond P.A., Millburn, N.J. Spkr., guest lectr. TV and radio broadcasts. Contbr. articles to profl. jours. Mem. Union County Bar Assn.), Essex County Bar (matrimonial practice), N.J. Bar Assn. (lectr., speaker). Avocations: racquetball, tennis, running. General civil litigation, Family and matrimonial. Office: Diamond & Diamond PA 225 Millburn Ave Ste 208 Millburn NJ 07041-1712 Fax: 973-379-9210. E-mail: njdivorcelawyer@aol.com

DIAMOND, STANLEY JAY, lawyer; b. Los Angeles, Nov. 27, 1927; s. Philip Alfred and Florence (Fadem) D.; m. Lois Jane Broida, June 22, 1969; children: Caryn Elaine, Diana Beth. B.A., UCLA, 1949; J.D., U. So. Calif., 1952. Bar: Calif. 1953. Practiced law, Los Angeles, 1953—; dep. Office of Calif. Atty. Gen., 1953; ptnr. Diamond & Tilem, 1957-60, Diamond, Tilem & Colden, Los Angeles, 1960-79, Diamond & Wilson, Los Angeles, 1979—. Lectr. music and entertainment law UCLA; Mem. nat. panel arbitrators Am. Arbitration Assn. Bd. dirs. Los Angeles Suicide Prevention Center, 1971-76. Served with 349th Engr. Constrn. Bn. AUS, 1945-47. Mem. ABA, Calif. Bar Assn., Los Angeles County Bar Assn., Beverly Hills Bar Assn., Am. Judicature Soc., Calif. Copyright Conf., Nat. Acad. Rec. Arts and Scis., Zeta Beta Tau, Nu Beta Epsilon. Entertainment. Office: 12304 Santa Monica Blvd Fl 3D Los Angeles CA 90025-2551

DIANA, RONALD SALVADOR, lawyer; b. Plainfield, N.J., May 9, 1930; s. Salvador and Catherine (Isolde) D.; m. Alix Clark, Nov. 21, 1963; children— Alexander, Christopher, Alix, Kate. A.B., Colgate U., 1952; LL.B., Columbia U., 1955. Bar: N.J. 1958, U.S. Dist. Ct. N.J. 1958, N.Y. 1960, U.S. Dist. Ct. (so. dist.) N.Y. 1960, U.S. Ct. Appeals (3d cir.) 1962, U.S. Ct. Appeals (2d cir.) 1962, U.S. Supreme Ct. 1964. Assoc. firm Shanley & Fisher, Newark, N.J., 1958-60, Lord, Day & Lord, N.Y.C., 1960-65; assoc. gen. counsel Curtis Pub. Co., N.Y.C., 1965-68, Cowles Communications, N.Y.C., 1968-71; spl. counsel State of N.J., Trenton, 1972-73; v.p. fin., gen. counsel Esquire Inc., N.Y.C., 1973-79; dep. gen. counsel Hearst Corp., N.Y.C., 1979— . Served with AUS, 1956-58. Clubs: University, Anglers, Essex Hunt. Administrative and regulatory, Federal civil litigation, General corporate. Home: 164 Talmage Rd Mendham NJ 07945-1513 Office: Hearst Corp 959 8th Ave New York NY 10019-3737

DIAZ, BENITO HUMBERTO, lawyer; b. Guines, Cuba, Dec. 6, 1950; came to U.S., 1962; s. Benito Marcos and Concepcion (Valdes) D.; m. Maria Adelaida Badenes, May 7, 1983; children: Ana Maria, Benito Ignacio, Patricia Maria. B.A., St. Peter's Coll., Jersey City, 1973; J.D., Duke U., 1976. Bar: Fla. 1976, U.S. Dist. Ct. (so. dist.) Fla. 1977, U.S. Ct. Appeals (5th cir.) 1977, U.S. Dist. Ct. (mid. dist.) Fla. 1979, U.S. Ct. Appeals (11th cir.) 1981. Assoc. Blackwell, Walker, Gray, Powers, Flick & Hoehl, Miami, Fla., 1976-82, Carroll & Halberg, Miami, 1982—. Vol. United Way of Dade County, Miami, 1982-83. Mem. ABA, Fla. Bar, Dade County Bar Assn., Cuban Am. Bar Assn. Roman Catholic. Federal civil litigation, State civil litigation, Personal injury. Office: Carroll & Halberg 2701 S Bayshore Dr Fl 5 Miami FL 33133-5337

DIAZ, OLIVER E., JR. lawyer, state representative; b. Biloxi, Miss., Dec. 16, 1959; s. Oliver E. Sr. and Sylvia (Fountain) D. AA, Miss. Gulf Coast Jr. Coll., 1979; BA, U. S. Ala., 1982; JD, U. Miss., 1985. Bar: Miss., U.S. Dist. Ct. (no. and so. dists.) Miss., U.S. Ct. Appeals (5th cir.). Assoc. Holkins Logan Vaughn & Anderson, Gulfport, Miss., 1985-86, Gerald R. Emil PA, Gulfport, 1986-88; ptnr. Diaz Davis & Emil, 1988—95; judge Miss. Ct. of Appeals, Jackson, 1995—2000; justice Miss. Supreme Court, 2000—. Miss. state rep., 1988-94; mem. Harrison County Rep. exec. com., 1987—; treas. Miss. State Young Reps., 1987-88; pres. Miss. Gulf Coast Young Reps., Harrison County, 1987-88. Mem. Assn. Trial Lawyers Am., Miss. Trial Lawyers Assn., Am. Legis. Exchange Com., Jaycees. Legislative, Libel, Personal injury. Office: Mississippi Supreme Ct Carroll Gartin Justice Bldg 450 High St Jackson MS 39201-1006 also: PO Box 117 Jackson MS 39205*

DIAZ-ARRASTIA, GEORGE RAVELO, lawyer; b. Havana, Cuba, Aug. 20, 1959; came to U.S., 1968; s. Ramon Fuentes and Elihut (Ravelo) D.-A.; m. Maria del Carmen Gomez, Aug. 6, 1983. BA in History, Rice U., 1980; JD, U. Chgo., 1983. Bar: Tex. 1983, U.S. Dist. Ct. (so. dist.) Tex. 1985, U.S. Ct. Appeals (5th and D.C. cirs.) 1985, U.S. Supreme Ct. 1992, U.S. Dist. Ct. (no., we. and ea. dists.) Tex. 1994. Assoc. Baker & Botts, Houston, 1983-88, Deaton & Briggs (formerly Deaton, Briggs & McCain), Houston, 1988-90; ptnr. Gilpin, Paxson & Bersch, LLP, 1991-98, Schirrmeister Ajamie LLP, Houston, 1998—. Fellow Tex. Bar Found., Houston Bar Found.; mem. ABA, Am. Judicature Soc., Am. Soc. Internat. Law, State Bar of Tex., Houston Bar Assn., Coll. of State Bar Tex. Republican. Roman Catholic. Consumer commercial, Construction, Education and schools. Home: 3794 Drake St Houston TX 77005-1118 Office: Schirrmeister Ajamie LLP 711 Louisiana St Ste 2150 Houston TX 77002-2720 E-mail: gdarrastia@salawfirm.com

DIBBLE, ROBERT KENNETH, lawyer; b. Leigh-on-Sea, Essex, Eng., Dec. 28, 1938; s. Herbert William and Irene Caroline D.; m. Teresa Frances MacDonnell, Aug. 26, 1972; children: William, Thomas, Edward, Matthew. Naval Officer, Naval Coll., Dartmouth, Eng., 1958; Russian Interpreter, Civil Svc., Eng., 1962; Telecomms. Specialist, Royal Navy, Eng., 1967. Bar: solicitor Supreme Ct. Eng. and Wales 1980. Commd. Brit. Royal Navy, 1958; advanced through grades to comdr., 1972; ret Royal Navy, 1977; lawyer Linklaters, Eng., 1978-81; ptnr. Wilde Sapte, Eng., 1982-98, LeBoeuf Lamb Greene & MacRae, London, 1998—. Dir. Dover Harbour Bd., Eng., 1998-2000, chmn., 2001—. Avocations: family life, music, reading, swimming, walking. Aviation, Banking, Transportation. Office: LeBoeuf Lamb Greene & MacRa 1 Minster Ct Mincing Ln EC3R 7AA London England Fax: 02074595099. E-mail: rdibble@llgm.com

DIBIAGIO, THOMAS M. prosecutor; BA, Dickinson Coll.; JD U. Richmond. Assoc. Semmes, Brown and Semmes, Balt., 1986—91; asst. U.S. atty. Dist. Md, U.S. Dept. Justice, 1991—2000, U.S. atty., 2001—; ptnr. Dyer, Ellis and Joseph, Washington, 2000—01. Office: 6625 US Courthouse 101 W Lombard St Baltimore MD 21201*

DIBLASI, GANDOLFO VINCENT, lawyer; b. Bklyn., July 7, 1953; s. Rudolph Francis and Theresa (Restivo) DiB.; m. Roberta Wilson, Sept. 13, 1980; children: Richard, William. BA, Yale Coll., 1975, JD, 1978. Bar: N.Y., 1979, U.S. Ct. Appeals (2d cir.), 1982, U.S. Ct. Appeals (4th cir.), 1991, U.S. Ct. Appeals (9th cir.), 1981, U.S. Supreme Ct., 1990, U.S. Dist. Ct. (so. dist.) N.Y., 1979, U.S. Dist. Ct. (ea. dist.) N.Y., 1982, U.S. Dist. Ct. (no. dist.) Calif., 1989. Assoc. Sullivan & Cromwell, N.Y.C., 1978-85, ptnr., 1985—. Antitrust, General civil litigation, Securities. Home: 200 E End Ave Apt 15I New York NY 10128-7887 Office: Sullivan & Cromwell 125 Broad St Fl 28 New York NY 10004-2489

DICHTER, BARRY JOEL, lawyer; b. Brookline, Mass., Feb. 19, 1950; s. Irving Melvin and Arlene Dichter; m. Judith Rand, Oct. 22, 1972; children: Rebecca Lynn, Jason Benjamin. AB magna cum laude, Harvard U., 1972, JD cum laude, 1975. Bar: Mass. 1975, N.Y. 1976, U.S. Dist. Ct. (so. and ea. dists.) N.Y. 1976, D.C. 1980, U.S. Dist. Ct. D.C. 1980, U.S. Ct. Appeals (D.C. cir.) 1985. Assoc. Webster & Sheffield, N.Y.C., 1975-82, Cadwalader, Wickersham & Taft, N.Y.C., 1983-84, ptnr., 1984—. Lectr. in field. Contbg. editor: Collier on Bankruptcy, 15th edit., rev. Vice chmn. Harvard Law Sch. Fund, Cambridge, Mass., 1984-88, class agt., 1988-99; bd. dirs. Children's Corner, Inc., 1990-95, treas., 1992-95; mem. exec. com., bankruptcy and reorgn. group of lawyers divsn. N.Y. United Jewish Appeal. Mem. ABA (mem. task force on Sect. 110 1991-92, mem. task force on emerging issues in the transp. industry 1992-96, mem. task force on Article 9 securitization issues), Assn. of Bar of City of N.Y. (mem. bankruptcy com. 1986-89, 91-94). Bankruptcy. Office: Cadwalader Wickersham & Taft 100 Maiden Ln New York NY 10038-4818

DICHTER, MARK S. lawyer; b. Phila., Jan. 22, 1943; s. Harry B. and Mollie (Silverstein) D.; m. Tobey Gordon, Aug. 17, 1969; children: Aliza, Melissa. BSEE, Drexel U., 1966; JD magna cum laude, Villanova U., 1969. Bar: Pa. 1969, U.S. Ct. Appeals (3d cir.) 1969, U.S. Supreme Ct. 1979. Assoc. Morgan, Lewis & Bockius, LLP, Phila., 1969-76, ptnr., 1976—, chmn. labor and employment law practice group. Co-author: Employee Dismissal Law: Forms and Procedures, 1986-91; editor-in-chief Ann. Supplement Employment Discrimination Law, 1984-89; co-editor: Employment-at-will, 1985, 86, State-by-State Survey, 1984-89; adv. bd. Disability Law Reporter. Bd. dirs. Urban League Phila.; bd. dirs., chmn. Wilma Theater; bd. consultors Villanova U. Sch. Law; bd. dirs. Pub. Interest Law Ctr. Phila. Mem. ABA (labor and employment law sect., chmn. 2000-01, mem. governing coun. 1991-2000, co-chmn. equal opportunity com. 1986-89, employment law com. litigation sect.), FBA (vice chmn. equal employment com. 1983-86), Nat. Employment Law Inst. (adv. bd. 1984—), Am. Employment Law Counsel (bd. dirs.), Am. Coll. Employment Lawyers, Def. Rsch. Inst. (chmn. employment law com. 1989-93). Labor. Home: 1017 Clinton St Philadelphia PA 19107-6016 Office: Morgan Lewis & Bockius LLP 1701 Market St Philadelphia PA 19103-2903 Fax: 215-963-5299. E-mail: mdichter@morganlewis.com

DICKERSON, CLAIRE MOORE, lawyer, educator; b. Boston, Apr. 1, 1950; d. Roger Cleveland and Ines Idelette (Roullet) Moore; m. Thomas Pasquali Dickerson, May 22, 1976; children: Caroline Anne, Susannah Moore. AB, Wellesley Coll., 1971; JD, Columbia U., 1974; LLM in Taxation, NYU, 1981. Bar: N.Y. 1975, U.S. Dist. Ct. (ea. and so. dists.) N.Y. 1975, U.S. Ct. Appeals (2d cir.) 1975, U.S. Supreme Ct. 1980. Assoc. Coudert Brothers, N.Y., 1974-82, ptnr., 1983-86, Schnader, Harrison, Segal & Lewis, N.Y., 1987-88, of counsel, 1988—; assoc. prof. law St. John's U., Jamaica, 1986-88, prof., 1989-2000; prof law Rutgers U., Newark, 2000—. Author: Partnership Law Adviser; contbr. articles to profl. jours. Trustee Rye (N.Y.) Presbyn. Nursery Sch., 1988-90. Mem. ABA, Assn. of Bar of City of N.Y., Union Internat. des Avocats, Shenorock Club. Democrat. E-mail: cmdckrsn@rci.rutgers.edu

DICKERT, NEAL WORKMAN, lawyer; b. Newberry, S.C., July 28, 1946; s. Elbert Jackson and Mary Elizabeth (Layton) D.; m. Floride Cantey Clarkson, June 4, 1969; 1 child, Neal Workman. BA, Wofford Coll., 1968; MBA, U. S.C., 1969, JD, 1974. Bar: S.C. 1974, Ga. 1975, U.S. Dist. Ct. S.C. 1975, U.S. Dist. Ct. (so. dist. Ga.) 1975, U.S. Ct. Appeals (11th cir.) 1981. With Hull, Towill, Norman and Barrett, Augusta, Ga., 1974— . Chmn., Richmond County Bd. Elections, Augusta, 1980-89; bd. dirs. Episcopal Day Sch., 1982. With AUS, 1969-71. Decorated Bronze Star medal. Mem. Ga. Bar Assn. (bd. govs. 1986—), Ga. Def. Lawyers Assn., Def. Rsch. Inst., Nat. Assn. R.R. Trial Counsel, Augusta Bar Assn. (past chmn. Law Day, past mem. exec. bd.), Wofford Coll. Nat. Alumni Assn. (dir. 1981-84), Rotary (bd. govs. Augusta 1986—, sec. 1988—). Episcopalian (sr. warden 1984). Federal civil litigation, State civil litigation, Personal injury. Office: Hull Towill Norman & Barrett PO Box 1564 Augusta GA 30903-1564

DICKEY, DENISE ANN, lawyer, arbitrator; b. L.A., Dec. 31, 1957; d. John W. and Virginia May (Giese) D. BA with high honors, U. Calif., Santa Barbara, 1979; JD, U. So. Calif., L.A., 1982. Bar: Calif. 1983, U.S. Dist. Ct. (ctrl. dist.) Calif. 1983, U.S. Ct. Appeals (9th cir.) 1983. Pvt. practice, L.A., 1983-84; dep. dist. atty. L.A. County Dist. Atty.'s Office, 1984-85; assoc. Shield & Smith, 1985-90, Tarkington, O'Connor and O'Neill, Ventura and L.A., 1990-91; pvt. practice Law Offices of Denise A. Dickey, Santa Barbara, Calif., 1991—. Arbitrator Ventura Superior Ct., Ventura Mcpl. Ct., Santa Barbara Superior Ct., 1991—; judge pro tem. Santa Barbara Mcpl. Ct., 1994—; cons. Inglewood (Calif.) Police Dept., 1986-92. Mem. Buy Santa Barbara Alliance, 1993-95. Mem. Santa Barbara Bar Assn. Episcopalian. Avocations: art, jewelry, photography, parrots, gardening. State civil litigation, Personal injury, Professional liability. Office: 2022 Cliff Dr # 292 Santa Barbara CA 93109-1506

DICKEY, JOHN HARWELL, lawyer; b. Huntsville, Ala., Feb. 22, 1944; s. Gilbert McClain and Marjorie Loucille (Harwell) D.; m. Nancy Margaret Eagar, Nov. 24, 1984; children: Marjorie Ruth, Gilbert Charles. BA, Samford U., 1966; JD, Cumberland Sch. of Law, 1969. Bar: Tenn. 1971, U.S. Dist. Ct. (ea. dist.) Tenn. 1972. Adminstrv. asst. Dist. Atty.'s Office, Huntsville, 1969-70; law clerk domestic and juvenille divsn. Cir. Ct., 1970-72; trial lawyer Legal Aid Soc., Chattanooga, 1972-75; pvt. practice, 1975-77, Fayetteville, Tenn., 1977-89; dist. pub. defender 17th jud. cir. State of Tenn., 1989-98; pvt. practice, Tenn., 1998—. Mem. continuing edn. com. Pub. Defenders Conf., Tenn., 1990-92, mem. long range planning com., 1991-93, mem. legis. com., 1990-93, mem. exec. com., Mid. Tenn. rep., 1993-94. Lectr. Fayetteville-Lincoln County Leadership Tng. Program, 1989—; mem. adv. bd. Community Correction South Ctrl. Tenn., Fayetteville, 1989—; mem. Bedford County Dem. Club, 1989—. Mem. Nat. Assn. Criminal Def. Lawyers, Tenn. Bar Assn., Tenn. Assn. Criminal Def. Lawyers (membership com. 1989—, juvenile law com. 1988—, Disting. Svc. award 1990, 91, 92), Marshall County Bar Assn., Fayetteville-Lincoln County Bar Assn. (treas. 1977, sec. 1978, v.p. 1979, pres. 1980), Fayetteville-Lincoln County C. of C., Elks, Masons (jr. steward 1991, sr. steward 1992, jr. deacon 1993, jr. warden 1994, sr. warden 1995, worshipful master 1996), York Rite Mason, Scottish Rite Mason (32d degree), Shriners (sgt.-at-arms 1993, v.p. 1994, dir. pub. rels.

1994, 96—, pres. 1995), Internat. Platform Assn., Order of Ea. Star (chaplain 1993-94), Tenn. 4-H Found., Gideons Internat. Democrat. Methodist. Avocations: hunting, fishing, canoeing, kayaking. Constitutional, Criminal, Juvenile. Home: 122 Brookmeade Dr Fayetteville TN 37334-2046 Office: 105 Main Ave S Fayetteville TN 37334-3057

DICKEY, JOHN W. lawyer; b. Springfield, Mo., 1927; AB, U. Mo., 1950; BA, Oxford (Eng.) U., 1952, MA, 1956; LLB, Harvard U., 1954. Bar: Mo. 1954, N.Y. 1955, Eng. and Wales 1999. Sr. counsel Sullivan & Cromwell, London. Mem. Am. Coll. Trial Lawyers. Appellate, General civil litigation, Private international. Office: Sullivan & Cromwell 9A Ironmonger Ln London EC2V 8EY England

DICKIE, ROBERT BENJAMIN, lawyer, consultant, educator; b. Glendale, Calif., Sept. 10, 1941; s. John A. and Dorothy C. (Merkel) D.; m. Susan J. Williams, Jan. 28, 1967 (div. 1987); children: Amy, John, Thomas. BA, Yale U., 1963; JD, U. Calif., Berkeley, 1967. BAr: Calif. 1967, N.Y. 1970, Mass. 1971. Assoc. Shearman & Sterling, N.Y.C., 1969-71, Sullivan & Worcester, Boston, 1971-77; asst. prof. mgmt. policy Boston U., 1977-83, tenured assoc. prof., 1983-94; prin The Dickie Group, 1994—. Cons. World Bank, Washington, Fortune 100 Cos., law firms. Author: Financial Statement Analysis and Business Valuation for the Practical Lawyer, 1999; contbr. numerous articles to Nat. Law Jour., Strategic Mgmt. Jour., Columbia Jour. World Bus., others. Mem. Boston Bar Assn., Calif. Bar Assn., N.Y. Bar Assn., Acad. Mgmt., Yale Club Boston, Longwood Cricket Club. Antitrust, General corporate, Securities. Home: 26 October Ln Weston MA 02493-1725

DICKSON, BRENT E(LLIS), state supreme court justice; b. July 18, 1941; m. Jan Aikman, June 8, 1963; children: Andrew, Kyle, Reed. BA, Purdue U., 1964; JD, Ind. U., Indpls., 1968; LittD, Purdue U., 1996. Bar: Ind. 1968, U.S. Ct. Appeals (7th cir.) 1972, U.S. Supreme Ct. 1975; cert. civil trial adv., NBTA. Pvt. practice, Lafayette, Ind., 1968-85; sr. ptnr. Dickson, Reiling, Teder & Withered, 1977-85; assoc. justice Ind. Supreme Ct., Indpls., 1986—. Adj. prof. Sch. of Law Ind. U., 1992-98. Past pres. Tippecanoe County Hist. Assn.; mem. dean's adv. coun. Sch. Liberal Arts Purdue U., 1990-94; mem. adv. bd. Heartland Film Festival, 1995—. Mem. Am. Inns Ct. (founding pres. Sagamore chpt.), Am. Law Inst. Office: Ind Supreme Ct 306 Statehouse Indianapolis IN 46204-2213

DICKSTEIN, SIDNEY, lawyer; b. Bklyn., May 13, 1925; s. Charles and Pearl (Stahl) D.; m. Barbara H. Duke, Sept. 20, 1953; children: Ellen Simeon, Matthew Howard, Nancy Joy. A.B., Franklin and Marshall Coll., Lancaster, Pa., 1947; J.D., Columbia U., 1949. Bar: N.Y. 1949, D.C. 1959. Law clk. to Joseph Richter, N.Y.C., 1949-50; assoc. law office Herman E. Cooper, 1950-53; founder Dickstein & Shapiro, N.Y.C., 1953; sr. ptnr. successor firm Dickstein, Shapiro, Morin & Oshinsky, Washington, 1953-97, sr. counsel, 1998—. Mem. bd. advisors Jour. of Wealth Mgmt. Trustee Franklin and Marshall Coll., 1978—. Served with AUS, 1943-44, USNR, 1944-46. Mem.: ABA, Bar Assn. D.C., Am. Jewish Com. (pres. Washington chpt. 1999-2001, mem. nat. bd. govs.)). Antitrust, General corporate, Securities. Office: 9050 Bradgrove Dr Bethesda MD 20817-3003 also: Dickstein Shapiro Morin & Oshinsky 2101 L St NW Washington DC 20037-1526 E-mail: dicksteins@dsmo.com

DICLERICO, JOSEPH ANTHONY, JR. federal judge; b. Lynn, Mass., Jan. 30, 1941; s. Joseph Anthony and Ruth Adel (Cummings) DiC.; m. Laurie Breed Thomson, July 27, 1975; 1 child, Devon Thomson. BA, Williams Coll., Williamstown, Mass., 1963; LLB, Yale U., 1966. Bar: N.H. 1967, U.S. Dist. Ct. N.H. 1967, U.S. Ct. Appeals (1st cir.) 1973, U.S. Supreme Ct. 1975. Law clk. to presiding justice U.S. Dist. Ct. N.H., Concord, 1966-67, N.H. Supreme Ct., Concord, 1967-68; assoc. Cleveland Waters & Bass, 1968-70; asst. atty. gen. State of N.H., 1970-77; assoc. justice N.H. Superior Ct., 1977-91, chief justice, 1991-92; chief judge U.S. Dist. Ct. N.H., 1992-97. Chmn. Superior Ct. sentence rev. disvn., 1987-92. Fellow Am. Bar Found. (life), N.H. Bar Found. (jud.); mem. N.H. Bar Assn (nat. conf. state trial judges 1986-92, nat. conf. fed. trial judges, 1992-96, mem. com. on codes of conduct jud. conf. of U.S. 1994—, dist. judge rep. from 1st cir. to Jud. Conf. of U.S. 1997-2000), Phi Beta Kappa. Republican. Roman Catholic. Avocation: gardening. Office: 55 Pleasant St Concord NH 03301-3954

DICUS, BRIAN GEORGE, lawyer; b. Kansas City, Mo., Oct. 29, 1961; s. Clarence Howard and Edith Helen (George) D.; m. Vali Ann Venner, Dec. 14, 1985; children: Brian George, Cady Alyssa. BA, So. Meth. U., 1984, JD, 1987. Bar: Tex. 1987, U.S. Dist. Ct. (no. dist.) Tex. 1988; bd. cert. estate planning and probate law Tex. Bd. Legal Specialization. Assoc. Thorp & Sorenson, Dallas, 1987-89, Joseph E. Ashmore Jr., P.C., Dallas, 1989-92; pvt. practice, 1992—. Chmn. local alumni student recruiting program So. Meth. U., Dallas, 1989-90. Fellow Tex. Bar Found.; mem. Tex. Bar Assn., Dallas Bar Assn., Phi Alpha Delta, Pi Sigma Alpha. General civil litigation, Estate planning, Probate. Home: 2336 Serenity Ln Heath TX 75032-1922 Office: 5910 N Central Expy Ste 920 Dallas TX 75206-5159

DIEFENBACH, DALE ALAN, law librarian, retired; b. Cleve., Aug. 14, 1933; s. Walter Ewald and Alice Naomi (Austin) D.; m. Olga Maspaitella, Jan. 20, 1973; 1 stepson, Andrew Ivan Ward. BA, Baldwin-Wallace Coll., 1955; MLS, U. Hawaii, 1970. Fgn. svc. officer U.S. Dept. State, 1961-68; reference libr. Cornell U. Law Libr., Ithaca, N.Y., 1970-87; sr. reference libr. Harvard U. Law Libr., Cambridge, Mass., 1987-97, ret., 1997; reference libr., adj. assoc. prof. law libr. Barry U. Sch. Law Euliano Law Libr., 1998—. Lt. (j.g.) USNR, 1956-60, Philippines. Recipient Ficken Meml. award Baldwin-Wallace Coll., Berea, Ohio, 1988. Mem. ALA, Am. Assn. Law Librs. Democrat. Home: 500 Windmeadows St Altamonte Springs FL 32701-3572 Office: Barry U Sch Law Euliano Law Libr 6441 E Colonial Dr Orlando FL 32807-3673 Fax: 407-275-3654. E-mail: adiefenbach@mail.barry.edu

DIEFFENBACH, CHARLES MAXWELL, emeritus law educator, lawyer; b. Westfield, N.Y., July 9, 1909; s. Arthur Warren and Mary Bertha (Meyer) D.; m. Gladys Ethel Gray, June 29, 1935; children— Gretchen Dieffenbach Gehlbach, Roxann Huschard. B.S. in Civil Engring., U. Ala., 1934; postgrad. Bus. Sch., Harvard U., 1934-35; M.A. in Econs., U. Cin., 1948; J.D., Ohio No. U., 1957. Bar: Ohio 1957. Meat packing exec. H.H. Meyer Packaging Co., Cin., 1935-55; from asst. prof. to prof. law Chase Coll. Law, Cin., 1957-65; prof. bus. adminstrn. N.Mex. State U., Las Cruces, 1965-68; prof. law Chase Coll. Law, No. Ky. U., Highland Heights, 1968-79, prof. law emeritus, 1980— ; vis. prof. law Detroit Coll. Law, 1979-80. Served to maj. U.S. Army, 1942-46, ETO. Republican. Episcopalian. Home: 7300 Dearwester Dr Apt 542 Cincinnati OH 45236-6127 Office: No Ky U Chase Coll Law 508 Nunn Hall Highland Heights KY 41076

DIEHL, RICHARD PAUL, lawyer; b. Toledo, Dec. 25, 1940; s. Clair Bertrand and Josephine Frances (Kwiatkowski) D.; m. Laura Gean Carpenter, Mar. 26, 1966; children: Michelle, Michael. BSME, U. Mich., 1963; MBA, Tulane U., 1972; JD, U. Detroit, 1983. Bar: Mich. 1983, U.S. Dist. Ct. (ea. dist.) Mich. 1983, U.S. Supreme Ct. 1988, U.S. Ct. Fed. Claims 1990, U.S. Ct. Appeals (6th cir.) 1991, U.S. Ct. Appeals (fed., D.C. cirs.) 1992), U.S. Dist. Ct. (we. dist.) Mich. 1996. Commd. 2d lt. U.S. Army, 1963, advanced through grades to col., ret., 1986; pres. Diehl & Sobczak, PC, Troy, Mich., 1986-99; with Inst. for Def. Analyses, Alexandria, Va., 1999—. Adj. prof. bus. Am. Tech. U., Killeen, Tex., 1977-78; adj. prof. law U. Detroit, 1987-89. Contbr. articles to profl. jours. Decorated 2 Silver stars, five Bronze stars, 2 Purple Hearts, 2 Legions of Merit Meritorious Svc. medal, Army Commendation medal, 3 Air medals, Cross of Gallantry. Mem. Am. Def. Preparedness Assn., Assn. U.S. Army, U. Mich. Alumni Assn., Elks. Avocations: hunting, fishing, sports. General practice, Government contracts and claims. Office: 1105 Kingsview Ave Rochester Hills MI 48309-2510 E-mail: rpdiehl@aol.com

DIEHM, JAMES WARREN, lawyer, educator; b. Lancaster, Pa., Nov. 6, 1944; s. Warren G. and Verna M. (Hertzler) D.; m. Cathleen M. Hohmeier; children: Elizabeth Ann, Rebecca Jane. B.A., Pa. State U., 1966; J.D., Georgetown U., 1969. Bar: D.C. 1969, V.I. 1975, Pa. 1988. Asst. U.S. atty., Washington, 1970-74; asst. atty. gen. Atty. Gen.'s Office U.S. V.I., St. Croix, 1974-76; from assoc. to ptnr. Isherwood, Hunter & Diehm, 1976-83; U.S. atty. U.S. V.I., 1983-87; prof. law Widener U., 1987—. Bar examiner U.S. V.I. Bar, 1979-87. Mem. ABA. Republican. Lutheran. Office: Widener U Sch Law 3800 Vartan Way PO Box 69382 Harrisburg PA 17106-9382

DIENSTAG, CYNTHIA JILL, lawyer; b. N.Y.C., Apr. 17, 1962; d. Jack Jacob Helman and Roni Helene (Turk) Setti; div.; children: Marissa, Allison. AA, Fla. State U., 1981; BS, Fla. Internat. U., 1983; JD, U. Miami, 1988. Bar: Fla. 1989; cert. family law mediator, Fla. Judicial asst. Cir. Judge Frederick N. Barad, Miami, Fla., 1982-85; assoc. Brenner & Dienstag, P.A., 1988-90, Weissman & Greenblatt, Ft. Lauderdale, 1990-91, Elser, Greene & Hodor, Miami, 1991-93; pvt. practice Coconut Grove, Fla., 1993—. Active lectr., participant Schs.; mem. professionalism and ethics com., family law com., Dade County Bar, 1992-97; mem. support issues and gen. masters com. Fla. Bar. Mem. ABA (family law sect.), Fla. Assn. Women Lawyers. Family and matrimonial. Home and Office: 2601 S Bayshore Dr Ste 1400 Miami FL 33133-5413

DIESELHORST, JOCHEN, lawyer; b. Hannover, Germany, Mar. 18, 1966; married. JD, U. Hamburg, Germany, 1992. Communications, Computer, Intellectual property. Office: Freshfields Bruckhaus Alsterakaden 27 20354 Hamburg Germany Fax: 49-40-36 90 61 55. E-mail: jochen.dieselhorst@freshfieldsbruckhaus.com

DIETEL, JAMES EDWIN, lawyer, consultant; b. Dallas, Sept. 14, 1941; s. Bernhard Herman and Gladys Ellen D.; m. Elizabeth Nathan, May 9, 1964; 1 child, Elizabeth Lindsay. BSME, So. Meth. U., 1964; JD, George Washington U., 1969; LLM in Internat. Trade, Georgetown U., 1977; MBA, U. Pa., 1992. Bar: D.C. 1971, U.S. Dist. Ct. D.C. 1971, U.S. Ct. Appeals (D.C. cir.) 1975, U.S. Supreme Ct. 1975, Va. 1990. Engr. CIA, Washington, 1964-70, program evaluation officer, 1970-73, assoc. gen. counsel, 1979-80, from assoc. dep. gen. counsel to insp., 1980-93, with office exec. dir., 1993-94; counsel for info. policy, 1994-95; pvt. practice, 1995—. Participant ann. jud. conf. U.S. Ct. Appeals (D.C. cir.), 1986; speaker, ltr. and presenter in field. Author: Leading a Law Practice to Excellence, 1992, Sustaining Law Practice Excellence, 1992, Designing Effective Records Retention Compliance Program, 1993, Leaders' Digest: A Review of the Best Books on Leadership, 1995; chmn. bd. Law Practice Quar.; contbr. articles to profl. jours. Mem. ABA (coun. mem. law practice mgmt. sect., chmn. govt. and pub. sector lawyers divsn.), Coll. Law Practice Mgmt., Cosmos Club, Pi Tau Sigma, Kappa Mu Epsilon, Kappa Alpha.

DIETRICH, DEAN RICHARD, lawyer; b. Milw., Sept. 22, 1952; s. Leon Martin and Enid Mary (Gamalski) D.; m. Cecelia Ann Frank, June 25, 1976; children; Sarah Elizabeth, Kathleen Ann, Michael Ryan. BS in Polit. Sci., Marquette U., 1974, JD, 1977. Bar: Wis., U.S. Dist. Ct. (ea. and we. dists.) Wis. Assoc. Kramer, Nelson, Kussmaul, Hawley, Fennimore, Wis., 1977-79, Mulcahy & Wherry, S.C., Wausau, 1979-90, Ruder, Ware & Michler, S.C., Wausau, 1990—. Mem. Wausau Area Cath. Schs. Edn. Com.; interim pres. North Ctrl. Tech. Coll., 1994-95. Mem. ABA (labor and local govt. sect.), Wis. Bar Assn. (labor and local govt. sect., young lawyers divsn. 1984-90, pres. young lawyers divsn. 1988-89, bd. govs. 1994-98, profl. ethics com. 1992—, chmn. 2000—), Marathon County Bar Assn., Wausau C. of C. (pres. 2001, bd. dirs., chmn. legislature action). Lodge: Rotary. Avocations: golf, ice hockey. Education and schools, Labor. Home: 3024 N 10th St Wausau WI 54403-3013 Office: Ruder Ware and Michler SC PO Box 8050 Wausau WI 54402-8050 E-mail: ddietrich@ruder.com

DIETZ, CHARLTON HENRY, lawyer; b. LeMars, Iowa, Jan. 8, 1931; s. Clifford Henry and Mildred Verna (Eggensperger) D.; m. Viola Ann Lange, Aug. 17, 1952; children: Susan (Mrs. Jay Kakuk), Robin (Mrs. Jack Mayfield), Craig. BA, Macalester Coll., 1953; JD, William Mitchell Coll. Law, 1957, LLD, 1993. Bar: Minn. 1957. Mem. pub. rels. staff 3M, St. Paul, 1952-58, atty., 1958-70, assoc. counsel, asst. sec., 1970-72, asst. gen. counsel, 1972-75, sec., 1972-76, gen. counsel, 1975-92, v.p. legal affairs, 1976-88, sr. v.p., 1988-93. Bd. dirs. Mairs & Power Mutual Funds, UFE, North Star Capital Markets; instr. William Mitchell Coll. Law, 1960-74, trustee, 1974-86, 87-96, pres., 1980-83. Bd. dirs. St. Paul Area YMCA, 1973-80, chmn. 1978-80, Minn. Citizens Coun. on Crime and Justice, 1976-88, pres., 1982-84, St. Paul United Way, 1980-95, Ramsey County Hist. Soc., 1979-86, St. Paul Lowertown Redevel. Corp., 1988-94, Minn. Hist. Soc., 1993—, Supreme Ct. Hist. Soc., 1991—, Children's Hosps. & Clins., 1994—; trustee United Theol. Sem., 1976-82, Macalester Coll., 1983-89, Wilder Found., 1989—, chmn., 1996-2000; mem. Conferees of Minn. Citizens Conf. on Cts.; bd. dirs. Masonic Cancer Ctr. Fund, 1984—, pres. 1994-97; exec. bd. Indianhead Coun., Boy Scouts Am., 1986—, pres., 1992-93; bd. dirs. North Star Capital Markets, 2000—. Fellow Am. Bar Found.; mem. ABA, Minn. Bar Assn., Ramsey County Bar Assn., Assn. Gen. Counsel, Am. Judicature Soc. (bd. dirs. 1989-95), Am. Law Inst., Masons, Shriners, Jesters. Republican. Mem. United Ch. of Christ. General corporate. Home: 1 Birch Ln Saint Paul MN 55127-6402*

DIETZ, ROBERT BARRON, lawyer; b. San Diego, May 14, 1942; s. J. Thomas and Mary Agnes (Barron) D.; m. Grace Louise Purcell, Aug. 19, 1967; children: Thomas E., Michael B., Denis P., M. Alison. AB, Coll. Holy Cross, 1964; JD, Cornell U., 1968. Bar: N.Y. 1968, U.S. Dist. Ct. (no. dist.) N.Y. 1968, U.S. Dist. Ct. (so. and ea. dists.) N.Y. 1973, U.S. Supreme Ct. 1974. Asst. dist. atty. County of Dutchess, Poughkeepsie, N.Y., 1969-70, confidential law clk. to surrogate of Dutchess County, 1970-73; corp. counsel City of Poughkeepsie, 1973-75; assoc. Garrity & Dietz, Poughkeepsie, 1969-73, ptnr., 1973-75; assoc. Gellert & Cutler, P.C. and predecessor firms, 1975-78, ptnr., 1978-86; pvt. practice law, 1986-94; ptnr. Dietz & Dietz LLP, 1995—. Lectr. Dutchess C.C., Poughkeepsie, 1985-98, practical skills course N.Y. State Bar Assn. Bd. dirs. Mid Hudson Workshop for Disabled; former mem. Sports Mus. Dutchess County; chmn. Mid Hudson adv. bd. Salvation Army, 1998-2000; bd. trustees Vassar-Warner Home, 1997—; bd. counsellors The Children's Home of Poughkeepsie, Inc., 1997—; past bd. dirs. Dutchess County coun. Boy Scouts Am., 1997; former mem. City of Poughkeepsie Recreation Commn.; bd. dirs. Greystone Programs, Inc., 1999—; mem. Pastoral Coun. Ch. Holy Trinity, 1999—. Fellow Dist. 721 Rotary, Poughkeepsie, 1964-65. Mem. ABA, N.Y. State Bar Assn. (lectr. practical skills course, probate, elder), Dutchess County Bar Assn., Poughkeepsie C. of C., Kiwanis (pres. Poughkeepsie club 1974-75). Republican. Roman Catholic. Avocations: golf, tennis, reading, baseball card collecting. General practice, Probate, Real property. Office: 2 Cannon St Poughkeepsie NY 12601-3229 E-mail: dietzattys@att.net

DIETZ, ROBERT SHELDON, lawyer; b. N.Y.C., Aug. 21, 1950; s. Sheldon and Annabel (Hagyard) D. Student, Harvard U., 1968-70; BA, Oxford U., 1974, MA, 1977; JD cum laude, U. Miami, 1982. Bar: Fla. 1983, La. 1983, D.C. 1987. Law clk. U.S. Dist. Ct. (ea. dist.) La., New Orleans, 1985-87; assoc. Milling, Bensen, Woodward, Pierson & Miller, 1983-85, Stroock & Stroock & Lavan, Washington, 1987-89; counsel merchant marine and fisheries com. Ho. Reps., 1989-90; assoc. LeBoeuf, Lamb, Leiby & MacRae, 1990-95, Dietz & Co., Washington, 1995—. Admiralty, Legislative. Home: Box 2245 Middleburg VA 20118 E-mail: rsd@lobsterville.com

DIGENOVA, JOSEPH E. lawyer; b. Wilmington, Del., Feb. 22, 1945; s. Egidio Joseph and Elizabeth (Castelline) diG.; m. Victoria Toensing, June 27, 1981; children: Todd, Brady, Amy. BA, U. Cinn., 1967; JD, Georgetown U., 1970. Bar: D.C. 1970, U.S. Dist. Ct. D.C. 1970, U.S. Ct. Appeals (D.C. cir.) 1972. Law clk. to assoc. judge D.C. Ct. Appeals, 1970-71; dir., gen. counsel U. Cinn., 1971-72; asst. U.S. atty. Office of U.S. Atty., Washington, 1972-75, prin. asst. U.S. atty., 1982-83; U.S. atty. D.C., 1983-88; counsel on intelligence matters Office of U.S. Atty. Gen., Washington, 1976; counsel for select com. on intelligence U.S. Senate, 1975-76, counsel for subcommittee on D.C., com. govt. affairs, 1976, counsel for com. on judiciary, 1978, chief counsel, staff advisor for com. on rules and adminstrn., 1981; adminstrv. asst., legis. counsel U.S. Senator Charles Mathias, 1979; U.S. Atty. for D.C., 1983-88; ptnr. Bishop, Cook, Purcell & Reynolds, 1988-90, Manatt Phelps & Phillips, 1991-95; founding ptnr. diGenova & Toensing, 1996—. Ind. counsel Clinton passport file search matter, 1992-95; apptd. grievance com. U.S. Dist. Ct. D.C., 1994. Contbr. articles to profl. jours. Mem. ABA (com. grand jury 1983-87, criminal justice sect. 1982—, white collar crime com. 1988—). Republican. Roman Catholic. Avocations: music, singing. Office: diGenova & Toensing 901 15th St NW Ste 430 Washington DC 20005-2327

DIGGES, EDWARD S(IMMS), JR. business management consultant; b. Pitts., June 30, 1946; AB, Princeton U., 1968; JD, U. Md., 1971. Bar: Md. 1972, U.S. Supreme Ct. 1975. With staff of gov. State of Md., Annapolis, 1973; ptnr. Piper & Marbury, Washington and Balt., 1977-84; founding ptnr. Digges, Wharton & Levin, Annapolis, 1984-89; corp. cons. various corps., Towson, Md., 1989—. Bd. dirs. Televest Comms., LLC, Corp. Comms. Mgmt. Group, LLC, Interlude, LLC, Spindrift, LLC, Plastic Print, LLC, Antiques News Group, LLC; instr. advanced bus. law Johns Hopkins U., 1975-78; lectr. civil procedure U. Balt. Law Sch., 1976-78; mem. govs. commn. to revise Md. code, 1978-90. Contbr. articles to profl. jours. Mem. Alumni Council Mercersburg Acad., 1982-88, pres. 1987-88; bd. advisors Indian Creek Sch., 1982-88, chmn. 1986-88; pres. Beacon Hill Community Assn., 1978-86. ROTC, U.S. Army, 1970-71. Mem. Md. State Bar Assn. (bd. govs. 1972-84), Am. Law Inst., Am. Bd. Trial Adv. (pres. Md. chpt. 1984-89), Inn XIII, Am. Inns of Ct. (Master of the Bench 1986-89), Scribes. Democrat. Roman Catholic. Clubs: So. Md. Soc. (bd. govs., pres. 1988), Mid Ocean (Bermuda), Princeton Club of N.Y. Home: PO Box 42737 Baltimore MD 21284-2737 E-mail: diggesy@home.com, diggesy@aol.com

DIGNAN, THOMAS GREGORY, JR. lawyer; b. Worcester, Mass., May 23, 1940; s. Thomas Gregory and Hester Clare (Sharkey) D.; m. Mary Anne Connor, Sept. 16, 1978; children: Kellyanne E., Maryclare E. BA, Yale U., 1961; JD, U. Mich., 1964. Bar: Mass. 1964, U.S. Supreme Ct. 1968. Assoc. firm Ropes & Gray, Boston, 1964-74, ptnr. firm, 1974-2000, of counsel, 2001—. Spl. asst. atty. gen. State of Mass., 1974-76; trustee NSTAR. Asst. editor: Mich. Law Rev., 1963-64; contbr. articles to profl. jours. Bd. dirs. Family Counseling and Guidance Ctrs., Inc., 1967-76, 78-94, v.p., 1983-87, pres., 1987-89; trustee Cath. Charitable Bur. of Boston, Inc., 1994-97, Dana Hall Sch., 1994—; bd. dirs. Gov.'s Mgmt. Task Force, 1979-81, Mass. Moderator's Assn., 1994-2000; mem. fin. com. Town of Sudbury, 1982-85, moderator, 1985—; bd. advisors Environ. Law Ctr., Vt. Law Sch., 1981—; mem. vis. com. U. Mich. Law Sch.; corporator Emerson Hosp., 1989—. Mem. Downtown Club, Nashawtuc Country Club, Order of the Coif, Phi Delta Phi. Republican. Roman Catholic. Federal civil litigation, Nuclear power, Environmental. Home: 8 Saddle Ridge Rd Sudbury MA 01776-2772 E-mail: tdignan@ropesgray.com

DIKTAS, CHRISTOS JAMES, lawyer; b. June 17, 1955; s. Christos James and Elpiniki (Angelou) D. Student, U. Salonika, Greece, 1976, U. Copenhagen, Denmark, 1976; BA, Montclair State U., 1977; JD, Calif. Western Sch. Law, 1981; diplomate, Rutgers U., 1992. Bar: N.J. 1982, U.S. Dist. Ct. N.J. 1982, N.Y. 1989, U.S. Supreme Ct. 1989. Law sec. to Hon. James F. Madden Superior Ct., Hackensack, N.J., 1981-82; sr. assoc. Klinger, Nicolette, Mavroudis & Honig, 1982-85; ptnr. Montecallo & Diktas, 1985-86, Biagiotti, Marino, Montecallo & Diktas, Hackensack, 1986-89, Diktas & Habeeb, North Bergen, N.J., 1989-94, Diktas Gillen, 1995-99; pvt. practice Diktas & Assocs., Cliffside Park, N.J., 2000—. Asst. counsel Bergen County, 1986-87; atty. zoning bd. adjustment Borough of Cliffside Park, 1986-94; atty. planning bd. Borough of Ridgefield, N.J., 1987-99, 2001—, borough atty., 2000-01; borough atty., Bogota, N.J., 1989-91, Fairview, N.J., 1994-95, Cliffside Park, 1994—; bd. edn. atty., Bogota, 1992-95; labor counsel Bergen County, N.J., 1990—; atty. planning bd. City of Garfield, N.J., 1994—; adj. prof. law Montclair (N.J.) State U., 1988—. Editor lead articles Calif. Western Internat. Law Jour., 1980-81. Campaign dir. Kingman for Senate Com., Bergen County, N.J., 1983; mcpl. coord. Kean for Gov. campaign, 1985; asst. treas. Arthur F. Jones for Congress, 9th Congl. Dist., 1986. Mem. ABA, N.J. Bar Assn., Bergen County Bar Assn., Order of Am. Hellenic Edn. Progressive Assn., Phi Alpha Delta (parliamentarian Campbell E. Beaumont chpt. 1978-81), Sons of Pericles (5th dist. gov. 1976-77, supreme gov. 1977-78). Greek Orthodox. Contracts commercial, General practice, Real property. Home: 445 Oncrest Ter Cliffside Park NJ 07010-2814 Office: Diktas & Assocs 596 Anderson Ave Cliffside Park NJ 07010-1831 E-mail: diktasesqs@aol.com

DILG, JOSEPH CARL, lawyer; b. Dallas, Apr. 1, 1951; s. Millard John and Helen Mary (Gill) D.; m. Alexandra Gregg, Aug. 5, 1972; children: Helen Lane, Mary Saunders. BA, So. Meth. U., 1973; JD with high honors, U. Tex., 1976. Bar: Tex. 1976. Assoc. Vinson & Elkins, Houston, 1976-83, ptnr., 1983—. Editor U. Tex. Law Rev., 1976. Named Outstanding Editor U. Tex. Law Rev., 1976. Mem. ABA, Tex. Bar Assn., Houston Bar Assn., Chancellors, Order of Coif. General corporate, Private international. Office: Vinson & Elkins 3401 First City Tower 1001 Fannin St Houston TX 77002-6760 E-mail: jdilg@velaw.com

DILLAHUNTY, WILBUR HARRIS, lawyer; b. Memphis, June 30, 1928; s. Joseph S. and Octavia M. (Jones) D.; 1 child, Sharon K. JD, U. Ark., 1954. Bar: Ark. 1954. City atty., West Memphis, Ark., 1958-68; U.S. atty. (ea. dist.) Little Rock, 1968-79; exec. asst. adminstr. SBA, Washington, 1979-80; prin. Dillahunty Law Firm, Little Rock, 1980—; chancery and probate judge 6th Jud. Dist., 6th Divsn., 1997—. Chmn. Ark. State Police Commn.; temp. assoc. justice Supreme Ct. Ark., 2000. Lt. U.S. Army, 1945-48, ETO. Mem. ABA, Pulaski Bar Assn., Nat. Assn. Former U.S. Attys. (pres. 1991X), Am. Inns of Ct. (pres. William R. Overton chpt. 1989-90). Federal civil litigation, State civil litigation. Home: 9710 Catskill Rd Little Rock AR 72227-5562

DILLARD, JOHN MARTIN, lawyer, pilot; b. Long Beach, Calif., Dec. 25, 1945; s. John Warren and Clara Leora (Livermore) D.; m. Patricia Anne Yeager, Aug. 10, 1968; children: Jason Robert, Jennifer Lee. Student, U. Calif., Berkeley, 1963-67; BA, UCLA, 1968; JD, Pepperdine U., 1976. Bar: Calif. 1976. Instr. pilot, Norton AFB, Calif., 1973-77; assoc. Magana, Cathcart & McCarthy, L.A., 1977-80, Lord, Bissell & Book, L.A., 1980-85; of counsel Finley, Kumble, Wagner, 1985-86, Schell & Delamer,

1986-94, Law Offices of John M. Dillard, 1986—; v.p., gen. counsel, dir. Resort Aviation Svcs., Inc., Calif., 1988-93; mng. ptnr. Natkin & Weisbach, So. Calif., 1988-89; arbitrator Orange County Superior Ct. Atty. settlement officer U.S. Dist. Ct. Ctrl. Dist. Calif.; trained mediator Straus Inst. Active Am. Cancer Soc.; bd. dirs. Placentia-Yorba Linda Ednl. Found., Inc. Capt. USAF, 1968-73, Vietnam. Mem. ATLA (aviation litigation com.), Am. Bar Assn. (aviation com.), Orange County Bar Assn., Fed. Bar Assn., L.A. County Bar Assn. (aviation com.), Century City Bar Assn., Internat. Platform Assn., Res. Officers Assn., Orange County Com. of 100, Sigma Nu. Home: 19621 Verona Ln Yorba Linda CA 92886-2858 Office: 313 N Birch St Santa Ana CA 92701-5263

DILLARD, STEPHEN C. lawyer; b. Tyler, Tex., Nov. 1, 1946; BA, Baylor U., 1968, JD, 1971. Bar: Tex. 1971. Mem. Fulbright & Jaworski L.L.P., Houston. Active Product Liability Adv. Coun., 1989—. Fellow Am. Coll. Trial Lawyers (life), Tex. Bar Found. (life), Internat. Assn. Def. Counsel, Am. Bd. Trial Advocates; mem. ABA, State Bar Tex., Tex. Assn. Def. Counsel, Houston Bar Assn., Phi Alpha Delta (v.p. 1984-87). Office: Fulbright & Jaworski LLP 1301 Mckinney St Ste 5100 Houston TX 77010-3031 E-mail: sdillard@fulbright.com

DILLIN, S. HUGH, federal judge; b. Petersburg, Ind., June 9, 1914; s. Samuel E. and Maude (Harrell) D.; m. Mary Eloise Humphreys, Nov. 24, 1940; 1 child, Patricia Wright. A.B. in Govt, Ind. U., 1936, LLB, 1938, LLD, 1992; D of Civil Law (hon.), Ind. State U., 1990. Bar: Ind. 1938. Ptnr. Dillin & Dillin, Petersburg, 1938-61; U.S. dist. judge So. Dist. Ind., 1961—, chief judge, 1982-84. Mem. Jud. Conf. U.S., 1979-82, mem. exec. com., 1980-82, mem. Jud. Conf. Com. on Ct. Adminstrn., 1983-89, chmn. subcom. on fed.-state rels., 1983-89; mem. Jud. Panel on Multidist. Litigation, 1983-92; sec. Pub. Svc. Commn. Ind., 1942; mem. Interstate Oil Compact Commn., 1949-52, 61. Mem. Ind. Ho. of Reps. from Pike and Knox Counties, 1937, 39, 41, 51, floor leader, 1951; mem. Ind. Senate from Pike and Gibson Counties, 1959-61, pres. pro tem, 1961. Capt. AUS, 1943-46. Recipient Disting. Alumnus award Ind. U. Coll. Arts and Scis., 1985, Ind. U. Sch. Law, 1987, 2001 Am. Inns of Ct. Professionalism award in the 7th Cir. Mem. Am. Bar Assn., Ind. State Bar Assn., Fed. Bar Assn., 7th Cir. Judges Assn. (pres. 1977-79), Am. Judicature Soc., Delta Tau Delta, Phi Delta Phi. Democrat. Presbyn. Club: Indianapolis Athletic. Office: US Dist Ct 255 US Courthouse 46 E Ohio St Indianapolis IN 46204-1903

DILLING, KIRKPATRICK WALLWICK, lawyer; b. Evanston, Ill., Apr. 11, 1920; s. Albert W. and Elizabeth (Kirkpatrick) D.; m. Betty Ellen Bronson, June, 1942 (div. July 1944); m. Elizabeth Ely Tilden, Dec. 11, 1948; children: Diana Jean, Eloise Tilden, Victoria Walgreen, Albert Kirkpatrick (dec.). Student, Cornell U., 1939-40; BS in Law, Northwestern U., 1942; postgrad., DePaul U., 1946-47, L'Ecole Vaubier, Montreux, Switzerland; Degré Normal, Sorbonne U., Paris. Bar: Ill. 1947, U.S. Dist. Ct. (no. dist.) Ill., Ind., Mich., Md., La., Tex., Okla., Wis., Idaho, U.S. Ct. Appeals (2nd, 3rd, 5th, 7th, 8th, 9th, 10th, 11th, fed. and D.C. cirs.), U.S. Supreme Ct. Ptnr. Dilling and Dilling, 1948—. Counsel Cancer Control Soc., Nat. Coun. for Improved Health; bd. dirs. Nutradelle Labs., Ltd., V.E. Irons, Inc.; v.p. Midwest Medic-Aide, Inc.; spl. counsel Herbalife (U.K.) Ltd., Herbalife Australasia Pty., Ltd.; lectr. on pub. health law. Contbr. articles to pub. health publs. Bd. dirs. Adelle Davis Found., Liberty Lobby. 1st lt. AUS, 1943-46. Recipient Humanitarian award Nat. Health Fedn. Mem. ABA, Ill. Bar Assn., Chgo. Bar Assn., Assn. Trial Lawyers Am., Stalwart Cornell Soc. Engrs., Am. Legion, Air Force Assn., Pharm. Advt. Club, Rolls Royce Owners' Club, Tower Club, Cornell U., Chicago Club, Delta Upsilon. Republican. Episcopalian. Administrative and regulatory, Federal civil litigation, Health. Home: 1120 Lee Rd Northbrook IL 60062-3816 E-mail: dilling1@juno.com

DILLOFF, NEIL JOEL, lawyer; b. Apr. 3, 1948; s. Marvin M. and Gertrude S. (Kraus) D.; m. Beverly A. Berd, June 6, 1971; children: Danielle, Shani, Scott. AB, U. N.C., 1970; JD, Georgetown U., 1973. Bar: Md. 1973, Pa. 1974, D.C. 1983, U.S. Dist. Ct. Md. 1977, U.S. Ct. Appeals (4th cir.) 1979, U.S. Supreme Ct. 1987. Assoc. Piper & Marbury, Balt., 1977-82, ptnr., 1982—. Head comml. lit. practice group, 1994-99, leader litigation sub-group, 1999—; instr. Md. Inst. for Continuing Legal Edn., Balt., 1983—. Author: Civil Pretrial Practice - Maryland Institute for Continuing Education in the Law; contbr. articles to profl. jours. Served to lt. JAGC, USN, 1973-77. Mem. ABA (assoc. editor litigation news 1980-82), Md. Bar Assn., Balt. City Bar Assn., Phi Beta Kappa, Balt. Ctr. Club. Democrat. Jewish. Federal civil litigation, State civil litigation. Office: Piper Marbury et al 6225 Smith Ave Baltimore MD 21209-3600

DILLON, CLIFFORD BRIEN, retired lawyer; b. Amarillo, Tex., Oct. 25, 1921; s. Clifford Newton and Leone (Brien) D.; m. Audrey Catherine Johnson, Jan. 16, 1945; children: Audrey Catherine Dillon Peters (dec. Nov. 1997), Robert Brien, Douglas Johnson. B.B.A., U. Tex., 1943, LL.B. with honors, 1947. Bar: Tex. 1947. Practiced in, Houston, 1947-87; ptnr. Baker & Botts, 1957-87, ret. ptnr., 1987—. Mem. faculty Southwestern Legal Found., 1968-87. Author articles in field. Life mem., bd. dirs. U. Tex. Health Sci. Ctr., Houston; past mem. antitrust adv. bd. Bur. Nat. Affairs; past bd. dirs. Houston Vis. Nurses Assn.; bd. visitors, life mem. Mc Donald Obs. and Astronomy, 1986—. Fellow ABA (chmn. sect. antitrust law 1975-76, Ho. of Dels. 1974-75, 85-87, bd. govs. 1985-87), State Bar Tex., Am. Judicature Soc., Tex. Bar Found., Houston Bar Found.; mem. Houston Bar Assn., Houston C. of C., U.S. C. of C. (past mem. adv. coun. antitrust policy), Phi Kappa Psi, Phi Delta Phi. Presbyterian. Clubs: Houston Country (Houston), Petroleum (Houston); Riverhill Country (Kerrville, Tex.), Old Baldy (Saratoga, Wyo.). Antitrust. E-mail: mardillon@compuserve.com

DILLON, JAMES JOSEPH, lawyer; b. Rockville Ctr., N.Y., June 18, 1948; s. James Martin and Rosemary (Peter) D.; m. Martha Stone Wiske, Mar. 19, 1977; 1 child, Eleanor. BA, Fordham U., 1970, Oxford U., 1972; JD, Harvard U., 1975; MA, Oxford U., 1982. Bar: Mass. 1975, U.S. Dist. Ct. Mass. 1976, N.Y. 2000, U.S. Ct. Appeals (1st cir.) 1978, U.S. Ct. Appeals (5th cir.) 1986, U.S. Ct. Appeals (6th cir.) 1996, U.S. Ct. Appeals (11th cir.) 1995, U.S. Supreme Ct. 1990. Assoc. Goodwin Procter LLP, Boston, 1975-83, ptnr., 1983—. Dir. Beth Israel Deaconess Med. Ctr. Obstetrics and Gynecology Found., Inc.; trustee Huntington Theatre Co. Mem. ABA, Mass. State Bar Assn., Boston Bar Assn. Democrat. Club: St. Botolph (Boston). Federal civil litigation, State civil litigation, Product liability. Office: Goodwin Procter LLP Exchange Pl Boston MA 02109-2881 E-mail: jjdillon@goodwinprocter.com

DILLON, JOSEPH FRANCIS, lawyer; b. Bklyn., Oct. 15, 1938; s. Joseph and Elizabeth (Sullivan) D.; m. Pamela Margaret Higbee, May 15, 1966 (div. Feb. 1972); children: Elizabeth Margaret, J. Alexander; m. Diane L. Long, Mar. 17, 1978. BBA, St. John's U., 1960; LLB, U. Va., 1963. Bar: Va. 1963, N.Y. 1964, U.S. Tax Ct. 1965, Mich. 1968, Ohio 1975, Fla. 1983. Tax trial atty. IRS, Washington and Detroit, 1963-68; mem. Raymond & Dillon, P.C., Detroit, 1969-93, Dykema Gossett PLC, Detroit, 1993-97, Cox, Hodgman & Giarmarco, P.C., Detroit, 1997—. Adj. prof. taxation U. Detroit Law Sch., 1977-87; spkr., planning chmn. Inst. CLE Programs; mem. magistrates merit selection panel and profl. assistance com. U.S. Dist. Ct. for Ea. Dist. Mich.; mem. U.S. Ct. Internat. Trade. Bd. dirs., mem. exec. com. Met. Ctr. for High Tech., Detroit, 1993-96. Cpl. USAR, 1958-64. Fellow Mich. State Bar Found.; mem. ABA (taxation and internat. sects. 1963—), FBA (officer, pres. Detroit chpt. 1978-82), Mich. Bar Assn. 1988—, (taxation counsel 1979-82, internat. sec. 1990—), Detroit Bar Assn. (taxation com. 1973—), Va. Bar Assn., N.Y. State Bar Assn., Ohio Bar Assn., Fla. Bar Assn., Am. Judicature Soc., Am. C. of C. in Japan, London Ct. of Internat. Arbitration, Inter-Pacific Bar Assn., Internat. Bar Assn., Greater Detroit-Windsor Japan Am. Soc. (bd. dirs. 1992—, exec. com. 1999—), Japanese Bus. Soc. Detroit Found. (v.p. 1992—), Detroit Regional Chamber (nominating com. for dirs.), French-Am. C. of C. of Detroit (bd. dirs. 1997-2000), Detroit Athletic Club, Lochmoor Club, Vineyards Country Club, World Trade Club, Econ. Club (Detroit). Republican. Roman Catholic. Avocations: golf, squash, skiing. General corporate, Private international, Taxation, general. Office: Cox Hodgman & Giarmarco PC 10th Fl Columbia Ctr 101 W Big Beaver Rd Troy MI 48084-5280 Fax: (248) 457-7001. E-mail: JDillon@CHGLAW.COM

DILORENZO, LOUIS PATRICK, lawyer; b. Waterloo, N.Y., Nov. 3, 1952; s.Luigi and Theresa Marie (Grieco) D.; m. Deborah Joan Boudreau, Aug. 18, 1973; children: Louis Patrick, Lisa Marie, Laura Gabriel. Student, U.S. Mil. Acad., West Point, 1970-72; BA, Syracuse U., 1973; JD, SUNY, Buffalo, 1976. Bar: N.Y. 1977, U.S. Dist. Ct. (no. dist.) N.Y. 1977, U.S. Supreme Ct. 1988. Assoc. Bond, Schoeneck & King, Syracuse, 1976-84, ptnr., 1985—, chair recruiting com., chair labor and employment law dept.; co-chair employment law litigation group, adj. prof. Syracuse U. Sch. Mgmt., 1988—. Participant NYU Ann. Conf. on Labor, 1989. Author: Syracuse Law Jour., 1978, Jour. of Coll. and U. Law Jour., 1980, N.Y. State Bar Jour., 1982; author: (with others) Corporate Counseling, 1988, Public Sector Labor Law, 1988, Duke Journal of Gender Law and Policy, 1999; mem. editl. bd. N.Y. State Bar Jour., 1998—; mem. editl. bd., N.Y. Civil Practice Before Trial, 2001. Bd. dirs. Syracuse Opera Co., 1986. Fellow Am. Coll. Employment and Labor Law; mem. ABA, Nat. Assn. Coll. and Univ. Attys., N.Y. State Bar Assn. (mem. ho. of dels. 1984-90, 99—, chmn. young lawyers sect. 1987, chmn. labor rels. com. 1988, chmn. CLE com. 1990-93, chmn. labor and employment law sect. 1994). Republican. Roman Catholic. Avocations: golf, gardening, reading. Federal civil litigation, Labor. Office: Bond Schoeneck & King 1 Lincoln Ctr Fl 18 Syracuse NY 13202-1324

DILTS, JON PAUL, law educator; b. Monterey, Ind., Sept. 7, 1945; s. Charles Albert and Janet Cecilia (Keitzer) D.; m. Anne Williams Avirett, Aug. 21, 1971; children: Christopher, Andrew. BA, Saint Meinrad Coll., 1967; MA, Ind. U., 1974; JD, Valparaiso U., 1981. Bar: Ind. 1981, U.S. Dist. Ct. (so. dist.) Ind. 1981, U.S. Supreme Ct. 2000. Reporter Peru (Ind.) Daily Tribune, 1972-73, wire editor, 1973-76, city editor, 1976-78; law clk. Ind. Ct. Appeals, Indpls., 1981-82; asst. prof. Ind. U., Bloomington, 1982-88, assoc. prof., 1988—, assoc. dean, 1985-2000. Author: The Magnificent 92 Indiana Courthouses, 1992; co-author: Media Law, 1994, 97; mem. editl. bd. Comms. Law & Policy, 1998—. Bd. overseers St. Meinrad Coll. Sch. Theology, 1992—, trustee 1996-98; exec. bd. dirs. Hoosier Trails Coun., Boy Scouts Am., Bloomington, 1992-93. With U.S. Army, 1968-71. Mem. Assn. for Edn. in Journalism and Mass Comm. (head law divsn. 1987-88), Internat. Comms. Assn., Soc. Profl. Journalists, AP Mng. Editors Assn., Rotary. Democrat. Roman Catholic. Avocations: skiing, hiking, backpacking, canoeing, sailing. Office: Ind U Sch Journalism 940 E 7th St Bloomington IN 47405-7108 E-mail: dilts@indiana.edu

DI MASCIO, JOHN PHILIP, lawyer; b. Bklyn., Feb. 4, 1944; s. Eugenio and Stella (Scheuermann) Di M.; m. Angela Piccininni, Apr. 2, 1967 (div. 1980); children: John Philip, Jr., Christine Pagano, Thomas; m. Linda Nick, Oct. 19, 1997. BA, C.W. Post Coll., 1975; MA, L.I. U., 1976; postgrad., NYU, 1976-79; JD, St. John's U., 1983. Bar: N.Y. 1984, U.S. Dist. Ct. (ea. and so. dists.) N.Y. 1984, U.S. Ct. Appeals (2d cir.) 1984, U.S. Supreme Ct. 1997, U.S. Ct. Appeals for Armed Forces 1997, U.S. Ct. of Fed. Claims, 1997, U.S. Ct. Appeals (fed. cir.) 1997. Sr. ct. officer N.Y. State Supreme Ct., Mineola, 1970-82; assoc. Joel R. Brandes, PC, Garden City, N.Y., 1984; pvt. practice, 1984-87; ptnr. Di Mascio, Meisner & Koopersmith, Carle Place, 1987-93; pvt. practice Garden City, 1993—. Lectr. Nassau Acad. Law. Contbg. author Ann. Survey. With USN, 1962-69. Recipient acad. awards. Mem. ABA (bus. law, health law and family law sects.), N.Y. State Bar Assn. (family law com. 1982), Nassau County Bar Assn. (vice-chmn. matrimonial com., ethics com., family ct. com. 1984, editor Recent Decisions), Am. Inns of Ct. (N.Y. family law chpt.). Avocations: photography, boating. General civil litigation, Family and matrimonial, General practice. Office: 300 Garden City Plz Garden City NY 11530-3302 E-mail: jpdlawoff@msn.com

DIMENTO, CAROL A.G. lawyer; b. Salem, Mass., Dec. 5, 1942; B in Edn., Salem State Coll., 1965, M in Edn., 1967; JD, Suffolk U., 1977. Bar: Mass. 1977. Tchr. Town of Hamilton, 1965—67, Town of Marblehead, 1967—74; ptnr. DiMento & DiMento, Swampscott, Mass., 1977—. Mem.: ABA (house of delegates 1995—), Mass. Bar Assn. (sec. 1996—97, v.p. 1997—98, treas. 1998—99, 1st v.p. 1999—2000, pres.-elect 2000—01, pres. 2001—), Essex County Bar Assn. (pres. 1992—94). Family and matrimonial. Office: 25 Pitman Rd Swampscott MA 01907*

DIMMICH, JEFFREY ROBERT, lawyer; b. Bethlehem, Pa., Mar. 13, 1948; s. Robert Carl and Barbara Sylvia (Worth) D.; m. Kathleen B. Brobst, Aug. 21, 1971. BA, Lehigh U., 1970; JD, Dickinson Sch. Law, 1973. Bar: Pa. 1973, U.S. Dist. Ct. (ea. dist.) Pa. 1974, U.S. Dist. Ct. (mid. dist.) Pa. 1974, U.S. Ct. Appeals (3d cir.) 1974. Assoc. Worth Law Offices, Allentown, Pa., 1973-78; sole practice, 1978-83; ptnr. Snyder & Dimmich, 1983-86, Snyder, Dimmich & Guldin, Allentown, 1986-97, Dimmich, Guldin, Dinkelacker & Brieza, P.C., Orefield, Pa., 1997—. Instr. Lehigh County C.C., Schnecksville, Pa., 1974-76; solicitor Borough of Catasauqua, Pa., 1977—, Upper Saucon Twp. Mcpl. Authority, 1991—, Salisbury Twp. Civil Svc. Commn., 1994—; mem. Borough of Emmays Civil Svc. Commn., 1996—; asst. solicitor County of Lehigh, Pa., 1978-86. Republican. Federal civil litigation, General civil litigation, Insurance. Office: Dimmich Guldin Dinkelacker & Brieza PC 2970 Corporate Ct Ste 1 Orefield PA 18069-3158 E-mail: dgdb.jeff@erols.com

DIMMICK, CAROLYN REABER, federal judge; b. Seattle, Oct. 24, 1929; d. Maurice C. and Margaret T. (Taylor) Reaber; m. Cyrus Allen Dimmick, Sept. 10, 1955; children: Taylor, Dana. BA, U. Wash., 1951, JD, 1963; LLD, Gonzaga U., 1982, CUNY, 1987. Bar: Wash. 1953. Asst. atty. gen. State of Wash., Seattle, 1953-55; pros. atty. King County, Wash., 1955-59, 60-62; sole practice Seattle, 1959-60, 62-65; judge N.E. Dist. Ct. Wash., 1965-75, King County Superior Ct., 1976-80; justice Wash. Supreme Ct., 1981-85; judge U.S. Dist. Ct. (we. dist.) Wash., Seattle, 1985-94, chief judge, 1994-97, sr. judge, 1997—. Chmn. Jud. Resources Com., 1991-94, active, 1987-94. Recipient Matrix Table award, 1981, World Plan Execs. Council award, 1981, Vanguard Honor award King County of Washington Women Lawyers, 1996, Honorable mention U. Wash. Law Rev., 1997, Disting. Alumni award U. Wash. Law Sch., 1997. Mem. ABA, Am. Judges Assn. (gov.), Nat. Assn. Women Judges, World Assn. Judges, Wash. Bar Assn., Am. Judicature Soc., Order of Coif (Wash. chpt.). E-mail: carolyn. Office: US Dist Ct 407 US Courthouse 1010 5th Ave Seattle WA 98104-1189 E-mail: dimmick@wawd.uscourts.gov

DIMMITT, LAWRENCE ANDREW, retired lawyer, educator; b. Kansas City, Kans., July 20, 1941; s. Herbert Andrew and Mary (Duncan) D.; m. Lois Kinney, Dec. 23, 1962; children: Cynthia Susan, Lawrence Michael. BA, Kans. State U., 1963, MA, 1967; JD, Washburn U., 1968. Bar: Kans. 1968, U.S. Dist. Ct. Kans. 1968, U.S. Ct. Appeals (10th cir.) 1969, Mo. 1973, N.Y. 1975, U.S. Supreme Ct. 1986. Atty. Southwestern Bell Telephone Co., Topeka, 1968-73, St. Louis, 1973-74, gen. atty. regulation, 1979; atty. AT&T, N.Y.C., 1974-79; gen. atty. Kans. Southwestern Bell Telephone Co., Topeka, 1979-94; ret., 1994. Adj. prof. telecom. law Washburn U. Sch. Law, 1996—. Bd. dirs. First United Meth. Ch., Topeka, 1979-84, mem. nominating com., 1985-87; bd. dirs. Sunflower Music Festival, 1993-94; mem. master planning com. Historic Ward-Meade Park, 1998—. Recipient commendation Legal Aid Soc. Topeka, 1986, 90, 93. Mem. Kans. Bar Assn. (pres. adminstrv. law sect. 1985-86, bd. editors newsletter), Topeka Bar Assn., Phi Alpha Delta (alumni bd. 1986-88, 1993-97), Rotary (bd. dirs., 1st v.p. 2000, pres. 2001). Administrative and regulatory, Federal civil litigation, Public utilities. Home: 3123 SW 15th St Topeka KS 66604-2515 E-mail: LLDimmitt@aol.com

DIMONTE, VINCENTE A. lawyer; b. Providence, Jan. 20, 1951; BA magna cum laude, Providence Coll., 1973; JD, Villanova U., 1976. Bar: R.I. 1976, U.S. Dist. Ct. R.I. 1977. Of counsel Lovett Schefrin Harnett, Providence. Master: R.I. Family Law Inns of Court; fellow: Am. Acad. Matrimonial Lawyers; mem.: R.I. Bar Assn. (sec. 1986—92, sec. 1999—2000, chair 1992—96, treas. 1998—99, pres. elect 2000—01). Family and matrimonial. Office: Lovett Schefrin Harnett 155 S Main St Providence RI 02903*

DINAN, DONALD ROBERT, lawyer; b. Nashua, N.H., Aug. 28, 1949; s. Robert J. and Jeanette F. (Farland) D.; m. Amy Littlepage, June 24, 1978; 1 child: Emma. BS in Econs., U. Pa., 1971; JD, Georgetown U., 1974; LLM, London Sch. Econs., 1975. Bar: Mass. 1976, D.C. 1977, N.Y. 1986, U.S. Supreme Ct. 1979, U.S. Ct. Internat. Trade 1982. Atty. advisor U.S. Internat. Trade Commn., Washington, 1976-81, chief patent br., 1981-82, chief unfair imports investigation div., 1981-82; ptnr. Adduci Dinan & Mastriani, 1982-88, Fitzpatrick, Cella, Harper & Scinto, Washington, 1988-90, O'Connor & Hannan, Washington, 1990-98, Hall Estill, 1998—. Prof. internat. trade Georgetown U., Wharton Econs. Soc.; prin. Coun. for Excellence in Govt. Mem. Mayor's Internat. Adv. Coun., Washington, D.C. Regulatory Reform Com.D.C., Washington Dem. State Com., gen. counsel, 1988-92, 94-2000. Mem. ABA, Fed. Bar Assn., ITC Trial Laywers Assn., Am. Intellectual Property Law Assn. (chmn. internat. trade com., export lic. com.). Democrat. Roman Catholic. Federal civil litigation, Intellectual property, Private international. Home: 221 9th St SE Washington DC 20003-2112 Office: Hall Estill Hardwick Gable Goldin & Nelson 1120 20th St NW Ste 700N Washington DC 20036-3485

DINARDO, JOSEPH, lawyer; b. Rochester, N.Y., Jan. 6, 1947; s. Carmen and Bertha Mascirelli DiN. B.A., SUNY, Buffalo, 1968, J.D., 1972. Bar: N.Y. 1973, U.S. Ct. Appeals (2d cir.) 1974, Pa., Ohio, Mich. Assoc. The DiNardo Law Firm. Recipient Outstanding Citizen award Erie County Coll., 1994. Statler trustee, 1992. Mem. Trial Lawyers Am., N.Y. State Bar Assn., Erie County Bar Assn., Brotherhood Locomotive Engrs. (counsel), United Transp. Union (counsel). Recipient Book award Bancroft-Whitney, 1969. Federal civil litigation, State civil litigation, Probate. Office: Dinardo Law Firm 2430 N Forest Rd Ste 195 Getzville NY 14068-1535

DINEEN, JOHN K. lawyer; b. Gardiner, Maine, Jan. 21, 1928; s. James J. and Eleanor (Kelley) D.; m. Carolyn Foley Reardon (dec. 1982); children: Jane, Martha, Louisa, Jessica, John; m. Susan Lowell Wales, Aug. 15, 1986; children: Theodore, Ralph, Andrew. BA, U. Maine, 1951; JD, Boston U., 1954. Bar: Maine 1954, Mass. 1954. Ptnr. Weston, Patrick & Stevens, Boston, 1954-67, Peabody & Arnold, Boston, 1967-70, 91—, Gaston & Snow, Boston, 1970-91. Spl. asst. atty. gen. Commonwealth of Mass., Boston, 1965-67; dir. Dingle Am. Properties Ltd., Dingle, County Kerry, Ireland, 1973—; pres., trustee Boston Local Devel. Corp., 1982—. Trustee emeritus Waring Sch., Beverley, Mass., 1981—, Cambridge (Mass.) Coll.; trustee U.S.S. Constn. Mus., 1993—; trustee, chmn. Nahant (Mass.) Pub. Libr., 1996—; former trustee Boston U. Med. Ctr., Winsor Sch. Emmanuel Coll., Boston, Hebron Acad., Maine; trustee Boston Aid to the Blind, 1994—. With U.S. Army, 1946-48. Mem. Boston Bar Assn., Mass. Bar Assn., Boston Law Sch. Alumni Assn. (exec. com. 1989-91), Marshall Street Hist. Soc., Tavern Club, Union Club, Cary Street Club, Apollo Club, Norway Weary Club. Republican. Roman Catholic. Real property. Home: 40 Pleasant St Nahant MA 01908-1632 Office: Peabody & Arnold 50 Rowes Wharf Fl 7 Boston MA 02110-3339

DINEEN, JOSEPH LAWRENCE, legal compliance professional, consultant; b. Jersey City, Sept. 25, 1942; s. Cornelius P. and Dolores (Fitzsimmons) D.; m. Andrea J. Manzone, Nov. 20, 1965; children: Jacqueline, Kimberley A. BA in Polit. Sci., Fordham U., 1964; MBA in Human Resources, St. John's U., Springfield, La., 1984, PhD in Indsl. Psychology, 1988. Tchr. Xavier H.S., N.Y.C., 1964-67; adminstrv. mgr. Royal Globe Ins., 1967-72; pers. mgr. U. Ga., Athens, 1972-74; v.p., dir. Fowler Products Co., 1974-85; sr. v.p. Scovill, Inc., Clarksville, Ga., 1985-88; dir. human resources Charter Med. Corp., Macon, 1988-93, G&O Mfg. Co., Jackson, Miss., 1993-96; chief compliance officer Union (S.C.) Hosp. Dist., 1996-2000, Spartanburg (S.C.) Regional Healthcare Sys., 2000—. Dir., chmn. bd. N.E. Ga. Employee Assistance Program, Athens, 1974-85, Employer Assistance Group-Dept. of Labor, Athens, 1988-93; mem., cert. tchr. Dept. Labor, 1986—; budget dir. United Way of N.E. Ga., Athens, 1985-88; cons. Gov.'s Com., Jackson, 1995-96. Author: Management in 21st Century, 1995, Management in the Twenty First Century - A Primer. Dir. United Way, Athens and Jackson, 1974-93, Employee Assistance Program, Athens, 1974-85; mem. Pres. Carter's Roundtable of Businessmen, Dept. of Commerce, 1978. Mem. Soc. Human Resource Mgmt. Avocations: teaching seminars, racquetball, tennis, reading. Home: 102 Rockport Way Pacolet SC 29372-3443

DINKES, WILLIAM, lawyer; b. N.Y.C., Apr. 24, 1942; s. Nathan and Estelle (Ludwig) D.; m. Linda Joan Plofsky, Aug. 15, 1965; children— Jill Ann, Jodi Allison, Jamie Alyse. J.D., Bklyn. Law Sch., 1965. Bar: N.Y. 1965, Ill. 1966, U.S. Dist. Ct. (so. and ea. dists.) N.Y. 1971; U.S. Ct. Appeals (2d cir.) 1981. Ptnr. Dinks Mandel & Dinkes, 1966-80, Dinkes Soll & Dinkes, Chgo., 1966— , Dinkes Mandel Dinkes & Morelli, N.Y.C., 1981— . Mem. N.Y. State Trial Lawyers Assn. (bd. dirs.), N.Y. State Bar Assn., Assn. Trial Lawyers N.Y.C., Met. Women's Bar Assn. Lodge: B'nai Brith (bd. dirs., past pres., Person of Yr. award 1982). Office: Dinkes Soll & Dinkes 179 W Washington St Chicago IL 60602-2305

DINKINS, CAROL EGGERT, lawyer; b. Corpus Christi, Tex., Nov. 9, 1945; d. Edgar H. Jr. and Evelyn S. (Scheel) Eggert; m. Bob Brown; children: Anne, Amy. BS, U. Tex., 1968; JD, U. Houston, 1971. Bar: Tex. 1971. Prin. assoc. Tex. Law Inst. Coastal and Marine Resources, Coll. Law U. Houston, Tex., 1971-73; assoc., ptnr. Vinson & Elkins, Houston, 1973-81, 83-84, 85—, mem. mgmt. com., 1991-96; asst. atty. gen. environ. and natural resources Dept. Justice, 1981-83, U.S. dep. atty. gen., 1984-85. Chmn. Pres.'s Task Force on Legal Equity for Women, 1981-83; mem. Hawaiian Native Study Commn., 1981-83; dir. Nat. Consumer Coop. Banks Bd., 1981, mem. Texas Parks Wildlife Com. Author articles in field. Chmn. Tex. Gov.'s Flood Control Action Group 1980-81; commr. Tex. Parks and Wildlife Dept., 1997—; bd. dirs. The Nature Conservancy, 1996—, Oryx Energy Co., 1990-95, U. Houston Law Ctr. Found., 1985-89, 96-98, Environ. and Energy Study Inst., 1986-98, Houston Mus. Natural Sci., 1986-98, 2000—, Tex. Nature Conservancy, 1985—, chair, 1996-99. Mem. ABA (ho. of dels., past chmn. state and local govt. sect., past chair sect. nat. resources, energy, and environ. law, standing com. on Fed. Judges 1997-98, bd. editors ABA Jour.), Fed. Bar Assn. (bd. dirs. Houston chpt. 1986), State Bar Tex., Houston Bar Assn., Tex. Water Conservation Assn., Houston Law Rev. Assn. (bd. dirs. 1978). Republican. Lutheran. Environmental. Office: Vinson & Elkins 2300 First City Tower 1001 Fannin St Ste 3300 Houston TX 77002-6706

DINNING, WOODFORD WYNDHAM, JR. lawyer; b. Demopolis, Ala., Aug. 15, 1954; s. Woodford W. and Gladys (Brown) D.; m. Tammy E. Cannon, May 27, 1994. AS, U. Ala., 1976, JD, 1979. Bar: Ala. 1979, U.S. Dist. Ct. (so. dist.) Ala. 1980. Mcpl. judge City of Demopolis, 1980-93, 98—; ptnr. Lloyd & Dinning, LLC, Demopolis, 1979—; mcpl. judge City of Linden, Ala., 1997—. Pres. and bd. dirs. Tenn. Tom Motel, Inc.; atty. Marengo County Commn. and City of Linden, Ala. Mem. U. Ala. Alumni Assn. (chmn. 1985-86). Avocations: water skiing, marathon running. State civil litigation, Contracts commercial, Family and matrimonial. Office: Lloyd & Dinning LLC PO Drawer Z Demopolis AL 36732

DINSMOOR, ROBERT DAVIDSON, judge; b. El Paso, Tex., May 19, 1955; s. William Bell Jr. and Mary (Higgins) D. BA in Polit. Sci., Brigham Young U., 1979, JD, 1982. Bar: Tex. 1983, U.S. Dist. Ct. (we. dist.) Tex. 1985, U.S. Ct. Appeals (5th cir.) 1986, U.S. Supreme Ct. 1987. Rsch. assoc. J. Reuben Clark Law Sch., Brigham Young U., Provo, Utah, 1981-82; asst. dist. atty. El Paso (Tex.) Dist. Atty., 1983-90; dist. ct. judge State of Tex., El Paso, 1991—. Spkr. Tex. County Judges Assn., 1992, Ann. Mex. Am. B ar Assn. of Tex. Conf., 1992, 97, 2001, St. Mary's U. Law Sch. Ethics Seminar, 1999, El Paso Bar Assn. Ethics Seminar, 1997—2001; spkr. various h.s. and mid. schs., El Paso, 1988—; co-founder El Paso Criminal Law Study Group. Contbr. articles to profl. jours. Bd. dirs. S.W. Repertory Orgn., El Paso, 1994-95; Sunday Sch. pres. Latter Day Saints Ch., 5th ward, El Paso, 1993-95; exec. sec. to bishop, 1995—. Recipient Outstanding Achievement award El Paso Young Lawyers Assn., 1990, Outstanding Jurist award, 1999, 2001. Mem. State Bar Tex. (mem. indigent representation com. 1994-98, 99—, victim/witness com. 1992-95, 97-98, 99—, chmn. 1999-00), El Paso Bar Assn. (mem. legal bar com., libr. com., criminal law com., others 1986—, bd. dirs. 1993-96, sec. 1996-97, treas. 1997-98, v.p. 1998-99, pres.-elect 1999-00, pres. 2000-01). Democrat. Avocations: playing piano, writing music, bicycle riding, basketball, accordion playing. Office: 120th Dist Ct County Bldg Rm 605 500 E San Antonio Ave El Paso TX 79901-2419

DINWIDDIE, BRUCE WAYLAND, lawyer; b. New Orleans, Aug. 24, 1943; s. George Summey and Augusta Rosser (Benners) D.; m. Judith Zatarain, May 7, 1966 (div. 1971); 1 child, Patrick; m. Kate Marie Crawford, Aug. 2, 1972 (div. 1987); children: Kate, Bruce, Wayland; Anita Rhea Cleaver, Dec. 5, 1987. B.S., Centenary Coll. of La., 1965; J.D., Tulane U., 1968. Bar: La. 1968, U.S. Dist. Ct. (ea. dist.) La. 1968, U.S. Dist. Ct. (we. dist.) La. 1978, U.S. Dist. Ct. (mid. dist.) La. 1970, U.S. Ct. Appeals (5th cir.) 1969, U.S. Supreme Ct. 1975. Law clk. to dist. atty. Orleans Parish, 1967-68; assoc. Terriberry, Carroll, Yancey & Farrell, New Orleans, 1968-72; ptnr. Ungar, Dulitz, Jacobs & Manuel, New Orleans, 1972-76; sole practice, Metairie, La., 1977-80; ptnr. Dinwiddie & Brandao, Metairie, 1981— . Mem. ABA, La. State Bar Assn., Assn. Trial Lawyers Am., La. Trial Lawyers Assn., Tulane Maritime Law Soc. (adv. editor 1976—). Republican. Methodist. Admiralty, General civil litigation, Personal injury. Office: Dinwiddie & Brandao 2313 N Hullen St Metairie LA 70001-6910

DIODOSIO, CHARLES JOSEPH, lawyer; b. Pueblo, Colo., Apr. 27, 1951; s. Warren Joseph and Lucille Julia Diodosio. BSChemE, U. Colo., 1973; JD, Northwestern U., 1976. Assoc. McDermott, Will & Emery, Chgo., 1976-80; internat. counsel Beatrice Co., 1980-84, v.p. Asia devel., 1984-88; chmn. TMGC Ltd., 1988—, Meadow Gold Investment Holding Co., Beijing, 1993—; chmn. L&D International Corp., 1993—. Chmn. L&D Internat. Corp., Beijing, China, 1993—. Mem. ABA, Ill. Bar. Home: 1387 Calle de Maria Palm Springs CA 92264-8503 Fax: 760-327-1200. E-mail: chardio@aol.com

DIOSEGY, ARLENE JAYNE, lawyer, consultant; b. Pitts., Sept. 13, 1949; d. William Cornelius and Rosemarie Arlene (Voivoda) D.; 1 child, Corey Redling. BA, Allegheny Coll., 1971; JD, Temple U., 1974. Bar: Pa. 1974, U.S. Dist. Ct. (mid. and ea. dists.) Pa. 1974, U.S. Supreme Ct. 1980, Colo. 1981, U.S. Dist. Ct. (ea. dist.) Colo. 1981, N.C. 1987, U.S. Cir. Ct. (4th cir.) 1987. Assoc. Smith & Roberts, Harrisburg, Pa., 1974-75; asst. atty. gen. Dept. of Edn., 1975-77; chief counsel Gov.'s Coun. on Drug and Alcohol Abuse, 1977-80; dir. legal affairs and risk mgmt. U. Colo. Health Scis. Ctr., Denver, 1980-81; asst. univ. counsel Duke U. Med. Ctr., Durham, N.C., 1981-85, adj. asst. prof. grad. dept. health adminstrn., 1983-87; v.p. legal svcs. Coastal Group Inc., 1985-87; assoc. Faison and Brown, 1987-90; gen. counsel N.C. Med. Soc., Raleigh, 1990-91; shareholder Maupin, Taylor & Ellis, P.A., 1992—. Cons. Colo. Dept. Health, Denver, 1980-81. Author, editor: Body Medical/Body Legal, A Look at Health Law in North Carolina, 1989—. Bd. dirs. YWCA, Durham, 1984-87, Durham County Advs. for the Mentally Ill, Inc., 1988-90; mem. Durham County Area Mental Health Authority, 1989-91. Mem. ABA, Am. Acad. Hosp. Attys., Nat. Health Lawyers Assn., N.C. Bar Assn. (sec. health law program com. 1983-84, vice chmn. 1984-85, chmn. 1985-86, 86-87, long range planning com., mem. bd. govs. 1989-92, trustee health benefit trust 1991-94), Wake and Durham County Bar Assns., N.C. Soc. Health Care Attys. (legis. com. 1983, program chmn. 1983, bd. dirs. 1985). Republican. Methodist. Avocations: fishing, reading. Office: Maupin Taylor & Ellis PA PO Box 13646 Research Triangle Park NC 27709 E-mail: adiosegy@maupintaylor.com

DIPIETRO, MARK JOSEPH, lawyer; b. Memphis, Aug. 25, 1947; s. Joseph Mark and Anne E. (Dorsey) DiP.; m. Kathleen Ann (Rafferty), June 22, 1968; children: Mark, Lora, Matthew. BA in Chemistry, So. Ill. U., 1969; JD, John Marshall Law Sch., 1976. Bar: Ill. 1976, Minn. 1983. Chemist Univ. Conn. Med. Sch., Hartford, 1969-70, VA Hosp., Indpls., 1970-71, U.S. Steel Corp., Gary, Ind., 1971-76; atty. Standard Oil of Ind. (now BP-Amoco), Chgo., 1976-81; from assoc. to ptnr. Merchant and Gould PA, Mpls., 1981-91; sr. v.p., sec. Merchant & Gould PA, St. Paul, 1992—. Mem. Met. Airport Sound Abatement Com., Mpls., 1984. Mem. ABA, AAAS, Internat. Bar Assn., Am. Intellectual Property Assn., Minn. Intellectual Property Assn., Ramsey County Bar Assn. Roman Catholic. Avocations: reading, bicycling, aerobics, piano. Intellectual property, Patent. Home: 815 Fairview Ave S Saint Paul MN 55116-2161 Office: Merchant & Gould 3100 Norwest Ctr 80 S 8th St Ste 3200 Minneapolis MN 55402-2215 Fax: 612 371-5323

DISCIULLO, ALAN MICHAEL, lawyer; b. Long Branch, N.J., Mar. 18, 1950; s. Peter Michael and Marion (Kaney) DiS.; m. Mary Jo Coppola, Oct. 13, 1979; children: Megan Eileen, Corinne Leigh. AB cum laude, Georgetown U., 1972, JD, 1977; MBA, NYU, 1986; M in Corp. Real Estate with honors, Nacore Inst., 1997. Bar: N.J. 1977; U.S. Dist. Ct. N.J. 1977, D.C. 1980, N.Y. 1980. Law clk. to presiding justice U.S. Tax Ct., Washington, 1975-76; assoc. Shanley & Fisher, Newark, 1977-78; asst. v.p. Paine Webber Jackson, N.Y.C., 1978-83; v.p., 1st v.p. Morgan Stanley Dean Witter Co., 1983—. V.p., dir. Wall St. Realty, N.Y.C., 1981-83; bd. dirs., gen. counsel, sec. Dean Witter polit. action com., N.Y.C., 1986-91; assoc. prof. masters real estate program NYU, 1991—; v.p. North Brunswick (N.J.) Tenants Assn., 1979-81; mem. task force Pres.'s Pvt. Sector Survey on Cost Control, Grace Commn., Washington, 1982-83; mem. land use adv. com. 12th Congrl. Dist., N.J., 1999—; spkr., panelist comml. real estate & planning issues; lectr. Practicing Law Inst., 1996—, Strategic Rsch. Inst., 1996—, Nacore Inst. for Corp. Real Estate; vice chmn. Negotiating Comml. Leases Panel, 2000—. Co-author: (treatise) Negotiating and Drafting Office Leases, 1995; co-editor: Met. Corp. Counsel Real Estate Corner column, corp. counsel adv. com. 1997-99; bd. editors Jour. of Corp. Real Estate Mgmt., 1998—; mem. editl. bd. Comml. Leasing Law and Strategy, 1999—; contbr. articles to profl. jours., book chpt. Advisor site plan rev. com. West Windsor Twp., 1987-88, mem. growth mgmt. planning com., 1988-90, mem. growth mgmt. adv. com. 1991-93; treas., dir., coach West Windsor Plainsboro Soccer Assn., 1990-97; mgr. West Windsor Little League, 1993-2000; coach West Windsor Wildcats Traveling ASA Team, 1998—; dir. Princeton Soccer Assn., 2001-; chmn. West Windsor Planning Bd., 1993-97; mem. West Windsor Plainsboro sch. redistricting com., 1995; trustee West Windsor Plainsboro Sch. Dist. Edn. Found., Inc., 1996—, v.p. 1999—; lectr. Sobelsohn Sch.; dir. N.J. Planning Ofcls., 1997—. Recipient O'Connor award for disting. legal writing, 1987, 89, 91, Individual Achievement in Planning award N.J. Planning Ofcls., 1996. Fellow Am. Bar Assn. Found.; mem. ABA (v.p. securities law divsn., chmn. young lawyers divsn. 1985-86, corp. banking and bus. law sect., comml. leasing subcom., exec. com. mem., chmn. coms. on tenant equity participation and subrogation and indemnification, chmn. task force bldg. safety 1995—, vice chair office lease sect. 1994-98, chair 1998—), Young Lawyers of N.Y.C. (treas. 1982-83, chmn. 1983-85), NACORE Internat. (dir. N.Y. chpt. 1996, pres. N.Y.C. chpt. 1997-98, pres.-elect 2001—, internat. bd. dirs. 1997—; dir. NACORE Inst. 1999—), Internat. Assn. Attys. in Corp. Real Estate, N.Y. County Lawyers Assn. (exec. com. corp. law sect. 1994-95, co-chair 1996-98), Practising Law Inst. (real estate adv. bd. mem. 1996—), Georgetown U. Wall Street Alliance, Princeton (N.J.) Athletic Rugby Club, Gavel Club, Mensa, Pi Sigma Alpha. Democrat. Roman Catholic. Avocations: athletics, photography, reading. General civil litigation, Contracts commercial, Real property. Home: 19 Taunton Ct Princeton Junction NJ 08550-2164 Office: Morgan Stanley Dean Witter & Co c/o Harburside Plaza II 7th Fl Jersey City NJ 07311-0002 E-mail: Adisciu9@aol.com, alan.disciullo@morganstanley.com

DISHER, DAVID ALAN, lawyer, consultant; b. Chgo., Apr. 15, 1944; s. Hugh George and Beatrice Rose (Selmanovitz) D.; children: Karl Theodore, Carol Ann; m. Clara Hoffman, Sept. 17, 1991. BS in Elec. Engring., MIT, 1965, MS in Elec. Engring., 1966; JD, U. Houston, 1983. Bar: Tex. 1984, U.S. Ct. Appeals (5th cir.) 1984, U.S. Tax Ct. 1984, U.S. Dist. Ct. (so. dist.) 1986, U.S. Supreme Ct. 1987. Mathematician Shell Devel., Houston, 1966-68; sr. engr. Tex. Instruments, Stafford, 1968; dir. rsch. GEOCOM, New Orleans, 1969-70; cons., inventor Disher Consulting Svc., Houston, 1970-73; pres., chmn. bd. Seismic Programming Internat., 1973-84, 1974-84; pvt. practice law LaMarque, Tex., 1984-99; pvt. practice Houston, 1999—. Ind. geophys. rsch. cons. Contbr. articles to Geophysics. Mem. ACLU, Coll. State Bar Tex., Harris County Bar Assn., Harris County Criminal Lawyers Assn., Houston Geophys. Soc., Houston Bar Assn., Coll. of State Bar of Tex. Criminal, Family and matrimonial, Personal income taxation. Office: 3318 Mercer St Houston TX 77027-6020 Fax: 713-961-9402. E-mail: disherdave@aol.com

DISSEN, JAMES HARDIMAN, lawyer; b. Pitts., Jan. 26, 1942; s. William Paul and Kathryn Grace (Reilly) D.; m. Shirley Ann Stark, Dec. 17, 1976; children: Elizabeth Ann, William Stark, Anna Kathryn. BS, Wheeling (W.Va.) Jesuit U., 1963; MBA, Xavier U., Cin., 1966; JD, Duquesne U., Pitts., 1972. Bar: Pa. 1972, U.S. Dist. Ct. (we. dist.) Pa. 1972, W.Va. 1973, U.S. Dist. Ct. (so. dist.) W.Va. 1973, U.S. Supreme Ct. 1976. Spl. agent Counter Intelligence U.S. Army Intelligence Corps, 1963-66; personnel mgr. Columbia Gas of Pa., Inc., Uniontown, 1969-73; dir. labor rels. Columbia Gas Transmission Corp., Charleston, W.Va., 1973-84, dir. personnel and labor rels., 1984-87, dir. employee rels., 1987-96; v.p. Columbia Nat. Resources, 1996-2001; v.p., ptnr. Triana Energy, 2001—. Bd. dirs. Fourth Venture Investment Group, Inc.; adj. prof. W.Va. Grad. Coll., 1996-97, Wheeling Jesuit U., 1997, U. Charleston, 1998; chmn., exec. com., bd. dirs. Star U.S.A. Fed. Credit Union. V.p., bd. trustees Highland Hosp., 1991—; chmn. bd. dirs. Inroads/W.Va., 1995—, Christmas in April, 2000-2001. Mem. ABA, W.Va. State Bar, Soc. Human Resource Mgmt., W.Va. C. of C. (chmn. human resource com.), St. Thomas Moore Soc., Berry Hills Country Club. Republican. Roman Catholic. Avocation: golf. Labor. Home: 1501 Brentwood Rd Charleston WV 25314-2307 Office: Triana Energy Ste 300 BB&T Bldg Charleston WV 25301 E-mail: jdissen@worldnet.att.net

DITKOWSKY, KENNETH K. lawyer; b. Chgo., July 12, 1936; s. Samuel J. and Lillian (Plavnik) D.; m. Judith Goodman, Aug. 9, 1959; children— Naomi, Deborah, R. Benjamin. B.S., U. Chgo.; J.D., Loyola U., Chgo. Bar: Ill. 1961, U.S. Dist. Ct. (no. dist.) Ill. 1962, U.S. Ct. Apls. (7th cir.) 1973, U.S. Tax Ct. 1973, U.S. Sup. Ct. 1975. Ptnr., Ditkowsky & Contorer, Chgo., 1961— . Mem. Ill. Bar Assn. Federal civil litigation, State civil litigation, General practice. Office: Ditkowsky & Contorer 2626 W Touhy Ave Chicago IL 60645-3110

DIVENERE, ANTHONY JOSEPH, lawyer; b. Bari, Italy, June 20, 1941; s. Joseph and Donna (Montini) DiV.; m. Sylvia Kathleen Scarnati, June 19, 1965; children: Anthony, Diana, John. AB, John Carroll U., 1964; JD, Ohio State U., 1967. BAr: Ohio 1967. Atty. in charge Cleve. Legal Aid Soc., 1967-70; prin., v.p. Burke Haber & Berick Co., L.P.A., Cleve., 1971; shareholder McDonald, Hopkins, Burke & Haber. Recipient Claude E. Clark award Cleve. Legal Aid. Soc., 1968, Cmty. Svc. aard North Olmsted Jaycees, 1972. Mem. ABA, Ohio Bar Assn., Cleve. Bar Assn. (Appreciation award 1979-80), Cleve. Assn. Trial Attys. (pres. 1979-80), Def. Rsch. Inst., Vermilion Yacht Club. Avocations: sailing, marathon running, squash, opera. Civil rights, General civil litigation, Personal injury. Home: 310 Rye Gate St Cleveland OH 44140-1272 Office: McDonald Hopkins Burke & Haber 2100 Bank One Center Cleveland OH 44114 E-mail: ajd@mhbh.com

DIXON, DANIEL ROBERTS, JR. retired tax lawyer; b. Rocky Mount, N.C., Feb. 22, 1911; s. Daniel Roberts and Ida Louise (Mason) D.; children: Daniel Roberts III, Carolyn Roy Dixon Dyess. AB, Coll. William and Mary, 1937; JD, Duke U., 1941; LLM in Taxation, NYU, 1951. CPA, N.C.; bar: N.C. Atty. Hamel, Park & Saunders, Washington, 1951-52; asst. prof. N.C. State U., Raleigh, 1954-76; pvt. practice, 1953—. Author: Graphic Guide Fundamental Accounting; inventor building block; contbr. articles to profl. jours. Mem. Internat. Visitors Coun., Raleigh, N.C. Capt. U.S. Air Corps., 1942-46. Mem. Navy League of U.S. (judge advocate 1990-96), N.C. Triangle Coun., N.C. Bar Assn., Wake County Bar Assn., Phi Beta Kappa (pres. Wake County), Omicron Delta Epsilon. Avocations: carpentry, organist. Home: 1022 Shelley Rd Raleigh NC 27609-4332 Office: Dixon & Hunt 7 N Bloodworth St Raleigh NC 27601-1101

DIXON, E. A., JR. lawyer; b. Bryn Mawr, Pa., Dec. 12, 1939; m. Margaret Kennedy Cortright; children: Thomas W.W., Abigail C., Marion W., Meghan. AB, Princeton U., 1962; JD with honors, George Washington U., 1967. Bar: Pa. 1968, U.S. Dist. Ct. (ea. dist.) 1968. Assoc. Montgomery, McCracken, Walker & Rhoads, Phila., 1967-69; assoc. resident counsel Industrial Valley Bank, 1970-73; ptnr. Hepburn, Ross, Wilcox & Putnam, 1974-78; owner wholesale nursery business, 1979-85; atty. Monumental Title Corp., Severna Park, Md., 1985-86; mgr. comml. divsn. The Sentinel Title Corp., Balt., 1987-89; regional underwriting counsel Nations Title Ins. (formerly Nat. Attys and TRW Title), Trevose, Pa., 1989-96; sr. title counsel Lawyers Title Ins. Corp., Phila., 1996, N.J. area counsel Iselin, 1997; counsel Stewart Title Guaranty Co., Wayne, Pa., 1998—. Seminar spkr. Nat. Bus. Inst., N.J., 1995-96, Title Acad. N.J., 1995—. Contbr. articles to co. publs., 1990—. Mem. Quaker City Farmers. 2d lt. USAF, 1963-64. Mem. Pa. Land Title Assn. (exec. com. 1993-96), Pa. Bar Assn., The Phila. Club, Princeton Club (Phila.), St. Andrew's Soc. (Phila.), Montrose Club. Libertarian. Episcopalian. Avocations: horticulture, sailing, fly fishing, tennis. Office: 900 W Valley Rd Wayne PA 19087-1830

DIXON, HARRY D., JR. (DONNIE DIXON), former prosecutor; b. Waycross, Ga., Nov. 6, 1953; s. Harry D. Sr. and Ruth (Starling) D.; m. Elizabeth Tonning, Apr. 19, 1980; 2 children. AB in History, Valdosta State Coll., 1974; JD, U. Ga., 1977. Bar: Ga. 1977, U.S. Dist. Ct. Ga. 1978, U.S. Ct. Appeals 1979. Law clk. to Hon. Marvin Hartley, Jr. Superior Ct. for Mid. Jud. Cir., 1977-78; asst. dist. atty. Waycross Jud. Cir, 1977-79, dist. atty., 1983-94; atty. Bennett, Pedrick and Bennett, 1979-83; U.S. atty. for so. dist. Ga. U.S. Dept. Justice, Savannah, 1994—2001.*

DIXON, JEROME WAYNE, lawyer; b. Shreveport, La., July 7, 1955; s. Huey P. Dixon and Myrtle Martin. BA, U. Calif., Santa Cruz, 1981; JD, So. U., Baton Rouge, La., 1986. Bar: La. 1988, U.S. Dist. Ct. (mid. dist.) La. 1988, U.S. Dist. Ct. (ea. dist.) La. 1989, U.S. Dist. Ct. (we. dist.) La. 1989, U.S. Dist. Ct. (no. dist.) Calif., 1989, U.S. Ct. Appeals (5th cir.) 1989. Pvt. practice, Baton Rouge, 1988—; staff atty. Legis. Bur. La. Senate, 1988-96. La. State Senate atty. for rsch. svcs., 1991-96. Coach Baker Brownfield Athletic Assn., Baton Rouge, 1990, Glen Oaks Athletics, Baton Rouge, 1989. Mem. ABA, ATLA, La. Trial Lawyers Assn., Baton Rouge Bar Assn. (v.p. 1997, pres. 1998), Kiwanis (v.p. 1989). Criminal, Insurance, Juvenile. Office: PO Box 44360 Baton Rouge LA 70804-4360

DIXON, PAUL EDWARD, lawyer, metal products and manufacturing company executive; b. Bklyn., Aug. 27, 1944; s. Paul Stewart and Bernice (Mathisen) D.; m. Kathleen Constance Kayser, Sept. 23, 1967; children: Jennifer Pyne, Paul Kayser, Meredith Stewart. BA, Villanova U., 1966; JD, St. Johns U., 1972. Bar: N.Y. 1972, U.S. Supreme Ct. 1976. Assoc. mem. firm Rogers & Wells, N.Y.C., 1972-77; sec., asst. gen. counsel Volvo of Am. Corp., Rockleigh, N.J., 1977-79, v.p., gen. counsel, 1979-81; v.p., gen. counsel, sec. Reichhold Chems. Inc., 1981-88; sr. v.p., gen. counsel, sec. The Warnaco Group Inc., 1988-91; v.p., gen. counsel, sec. Handy & Harman, Rye, N.Y., 1992-97, sr. v.p., gen. counsel, sec., 1997—. Chmn. Teeches Ltd., Bermuda. Mem. ABA, Assn. Bar City N.Y., N.Y. State Bar Assn., U.S. Supreme Ct. Hist. Soc., Am. Corp. Counsel Assn., Bedford Golf and Tennis Club. General corporate. Office: Handy & Harman 555 Theodore Fremd Ave Rye NY 10580-1451

DIXON, RICHARD DEAN, lawyer, educator; b. Columbus, Ohio, Nov. 6, 1944; s. Dean A. and Katherine L. (Currier) D.; m. Kathleen A. Manfrass, June 17, 1967; children: Jennifer, Lindsay. BSEE, Ohio State U., 1967, MSEE, 1968; MBA, Fla. State U., 1972, JD, 1974. Bar: Fla. 1975, Colo. 1985, Mich. 1992, U.S. Dist. Ct. (mid. dist.) Fla., U.S. Dist. Ct. Colo. 1985, U.S. Patent and Trademanrk Office 1975. Telemetry sys. engr. Pan Am. World Airways, Patrick AFB, Fla., 1968-72; sole practice Melbourne and Orlando, 1975-80; sr. counsel Harris Corp., Melbourne, 1980-85; corp. counsel, dir. strategic and bus. planning Ford Microelectronics, Inc., Colorado Springs, Colo., 1985-89; mgr. strategic alliances electronics divsn. Ford Motor Co., Dearborn, Mich., 1989-90, assoc. counsel intellectual property, 1991-93, dep. chief patent counsel, 1994—2000. Adj. prof. bus. law U. Cen. Fla., Cocoa, 1977, Fla. Inst. Tech., Melbourne, 1980-84. Cooper Industries Engring. scholar Ohio State U., 1964-67. Mem. ABA, Licensing Execs. Soc., Am. Intellectual Property Law Assn., Am. Corp. Counsel Assn., Sigma Iota Epsilon, Eta Kappa Nu, Phi Eta Sigma. Contracts commercial, Intellectual property, Patent. Home: 640 Jubilee St Melbourne FL 32940-7682 Office: Ford Motor Co 600 1 Parklane Blvd Dearborn MI 48126

DIXON, STEVEN BEDFORD, lawyer; b. San Bernardino, Calif., Dec. 25, 1945; s. Harold James Dixon and Jane Anna (Bedford) Kennedy; m. Lucy Pearson Dixon; children: Melanie Anne, Zachary David; stepchildren: Michael, Katherine. BA, U. Hawaii-Hilo, 1975; JD, Calif. Western Sch. Law, 1978; postgrad. Chaminade U. of Hawaii, Hawaii Tax Inst., 1978-82. Bar: Hawaii, U.S. Dist Ct. Hawaii, U.S. Tax Ct.; cert. continuing real estate edn. instr., Hawaii. Trial counsel, U. S. Army, 1969-70, Law clk. Linley, McDougal, Meloche & Murphy, El Cajon, Calif., 1976, D. Stephen Boner, San Diego, 1977, Tyson & Churchill, San Diego, 1977; law intern Legal Aid Soc. of Hawaii, 1978; law clk., investigator Stephen Christensen, Hawaii, 1978; gen. ptnr. Altman, Dicker & Dixon, tax attys., Hilo, 1978-79, Altman Dixon & Assocs., tax attys., Hilo, 1979-81; pvt. practice, Hilo, 1981-82; gen. ptnr. Dixon & Okura, Hilo, 1982-90; pvt. practice, 1990—; corp. counsel, broker Internat. Realty Corp., emphasizing Japan trade; arbitrator State of Hawaii Ct.; tchr. Hawaii Assn. Realtors, Grad. Realtor Inst., past Vitosek Real Estate Sch.; speaker, news columnist in field; writer; instr. bus. law U. Hawaii-Hilo, 1979-80 ; past bd. dirs. Elec. Co-operative Hawaii Inc. Columnist Money, Real Estate and You; radio show 50 Minutes with Steve Dixon. Past v.p. Hawaii Concert Soc.; counsel discharge Vets. Outreach, San Diego, 1976; bd. dirs. Big Island Substance Abuse Council; active community svcs. Served to 1st lt. 1967-70, Vietnam. Decorated Bronze Star. U. Hawaii-Hilo scholar, 1973. Mem. Hawaii County Bar Assn., Rotary. General corporate, Probate, Real property.

DIXON, WRIGHT TRACY, JR. retired lawyer; b. Raleigh, N.C., Oct. 7, 1921; s. Wright T. and Marion Jefferson (Homes) D.; m. Elizabeth Prince Nufer, June 3, 1950; children: Wright III, William N., Elizabeth Prince. AB, Duke U., 1947; LLB, U. N.C., 1951. Bar: N.C. 1951, U.S. Dsit. Ct. (ea., mid. and we. dists.), N.C. 1951, U.S. Ct. Appeals (4th cir.) 1956; cert. mediator, N.C. Ptnr. Bailey & Dixon, Raleigh, N.C., 1956-99; ret. Mem. Bd. of Adjustments, Raleigh, 1960-74, chmn., 1969-74. Jr. warden, sr. warden, mem. vestry St. Michael's Episcopal Ch., Raleigh; trustee So. Sem. Va., 1961-81, N.C. Client Security Fund, 1986-91. With USMC, 1943-59. Fellow Am. Bar Found.; mem. ABA (del. 1984-88), N.C. State Bar (counselor 1979-86, pres. 1985-86, Gen. Practice Hall of Fame 1997), Wake County Bar Assn. (pres. 1976, mem. N.C. commn. on code recodification 1979-81, hon. bd. mem. 1995, Joseph Branch professionalism award 1996), Raleigh Kiwanis Club (pres.), Sphinx Club (pres.), Carolina Country Club, Capital City Club. Avocations: golf, woodworking, genealogy, tennis, reading. Administrative and regulatory, General civil litigation, Insurance. Home: 414 Marlowe Rd Raleigh NC 27609-7018 Office: Bailey & Dixon PO Box 1351 2 Hannover Sq Raleigh NC 27602 E-mail: WDixon@BDixon.com

DLUGOFF, MARC ALAN, lawyer; b. N.Y.C., Oct. 6, 1955; s. Arnold M. and Ruth B. (Schnall) D. AB, Colgate U., 1976; JD, Hofstra U., 1980; LLM in Taxation, NYU, 1981. Bar: N.Y. 1981, D.C. 1985, Calif. 1988. Law clk. to presiding justice U.S. Tax Ct., Washington, 1981-83; assoc. Mudge, Rose, Guthrie, Alexander & Ferdon, N.Y.C., 1983-85, Milbank, Tweed, Hadley & McCloy, N.Y.C., 1985-89, ptnr., 1989-93; counsel Roberts & Holland, 1993-94; pres., CEO, Atlantic Adv. Corp., 1995—. Fundraiser lawyers divsn. United Jewish Appeal, N.Y.C. chpt., 1986-90. Charles Dana scholar Colgate U., 1976. Mem. ABA, N.Y. State Bar Assn., Assn. Bar City N.Y., State Bar Calif., Phi Beta Kappa. Jewish. General corporate, Private international, Taxation, general. Home and Office: 130 Water St New York NY 10005-1625 E-mail: marcnyc130@hotmail.com

DOAN, XUYEN VAN, lawyer; b. Hadong, Vietnam, Apr. 1, 1949; came to U.S., 1975; s. Quyet V. Doan and Binh T. Kieu; m. Binh Thanh Tran, 1980; children: Quy-Bao, Ky-Nam. Licence en droit, U. Saigon Law Sch., Vietnam, 1971; MBA, U. Ark., 1977; JD, U. Calif., Hastings, 1982. Bar: Saigon 1972, Calif. 1982. Sole practice, Costa Mesa and San Jose, Calif., 1982-84; ptnr. Doan & Vu, San Jose, 1984-90; prin. Law Offices of Xuyen V. Doan, 1990-95; ptnr. Doan & Tran, San Jose, 1995—. Founder, coord. VietLawyers Com., Calif. and Vietnam. Author: Of the Seas and Men, 1985, also other publs. in English and Vietnamese. Named Ark. Traveler Ambassador of Good Will, State of Ark., 1975. General corporate, Immigration, naturalization, and customs, Private international. Office: 2114 Senter Rd Ste 20 San Jose CA 95112-2608 E-mail: JD@VietLawyers.com

DOBBS, CARNEY H. retired lawyer and insurance company executive; b. Birmingham, Ala., Oct. 26, 1924; s. John Hoyt and Gertrude (Compton) D.; m. Josephine Philips, Aug. 18, 1956; children: John C., Philip G. JD, U. ala., 1949. Bar: Ala. 1949, U.S. Dist. Ct. (no. dist.) Ala. 1950; CPCU. Ptnr. Dobbs & Faulkner, Birmingham, 1949-51; asst. city atty. City of Birmingham, 1951-52; spl. agt., atty. U.S. Govt., Birmingham, 1952-53; atty., claim rep. State Farm Ins., 1954-60, claim supt., 1960-66, divsnl. claim supt., 1966—; ret. Semi-ret. arbitrator/ mediator; expert witness. Contbr. articles to profl. jours. Chmn., Spl. Arbitration com., Birmingham, 1965-74, Ala. Arson Prevention Task Force, 1979-83; mem. adv. com., Ala. State Fire Coll., 1979—; active Boy Scouts Am. Mem. ABA, Ala. Bar Assn. (task force on cmty. edn. 1985, 86—), Birmingham Bar Assn., Ala. Claims Assn. (pres. 1963), Internat. Assn. Arson Investigators (Carney Dobbs award for disting. svc. 1982), Mountain Brook Swim and Tennis Club, Downtown Club, Sigma Chi (Outstanding Alumnus U. Ala. 1981). Republican. Methodist. Insurance, Personal injury, Workers' compensation. Home and Office: 4009 Little Branch Rd Birmingham AL 35243-5815 E-mail: carneydobbs@webtv.net

DOBRANSKI, BERNARD, legal educator; b. Pitts., Sept. 3, 1939; s. Walter John and Helen Dolores (Rudnick) D.; m. Carroll Sue Wood, Aug. 31, 1963; children: Stephanie, Andrea, Christopher. BBA in Finance, U. Notre Dame, 1961; JD, U. Va., 1964. Bar: Va. 1964, U.S. Supreme Ct. 1968, U.S. Cir. Ct. (D.C. cir.) 1971. Legal advisor to bd. Nat. Labor Relations Bd., 1964-67; profl. staff mem. Pres.'s Adv. Commn. on Civil Disorders, 1967-68; adminstrv. asst. U.S. Ho. of Reps., 1968-71; gen. counsel Washington Met. Area Transit Commn., 1971-72; mem. faculty Creighton U. Sch. of Law, Omaha, 1972-77, U. Notre Dame, 1977-83; prof., dean U. Detroit Sch. of Law, 1983-95; dean Cath. U. Am. Sch. of Law, 1995—; labor arbitrator Fed. Mediation and Conciliation Svc.; active Mich. Commn. on Death and Dying. Contbr. articles to profl. jours. Mem. Am. Arbitration Assn., Am. Law Inst., ABA, Frank Murphy Honor Soc. Roman Catholic. Clubs: Hurlingham (London). Office: Cath U Am Columbus Sch Of Law Washington DC 20064-0001

DOBRONSKI, MARK WILLIAM, judge, justice of the peace; b. Detroit, Oct. 8, 1957; s. Clarence Robert and Jean (Shotey) D.; m. Susan Kay Roach, Sept. 12, 1980; children: Clarence Robert III, Juli E. AS, Henry Ford C.C., 1980. Cert. engr. Nat. Assn. Radio and Telecomm. Engrs. V.p. Mobilfone, Inc., Dearborn, Mich., 1977-79; asst. v.p. RAM Broadcasting Corp., N.Y.C., 1979-86; adminstr. State of Ariz., Phoenix, 1986-88, 89-97; divsn. comdr. City of Peoria (Ariz.) Police Dept., 1991; assoc. presiding justice of the peace Maricopa County, Ariz. Cons., expert witness Teletech, Inc., Dearborn, 1980-98. Mem., bd. dirs. Congl. Ch. of the Valley, United Ch. of Christ, Scottsdale, Ariz., 1994-98; mem. Maricopa County Sheriff's Exec. Posse, Phoenix, 1996-98. Mem. ABA, Am. Judicature Soc., Ariz. Justice of the Peace Assn., Maricopa County Bar Assn., Scottsdale Bar Assn., Am. Pvt. Radio Assn. (dir. 1989-98). Republican. Office: Scottsdale Justice Ct 3700 N 75th St Scottsdale AZ 85251-4544

DOBSON, ROBERT ALBERTUS, III, lawyer, executive, volunteer; b. Greenville, S.C., Nov. 27, 1938; s. Robert A. Jr. and Dorothy (Leonard) D.; m. Linda Josephine Bryant, Nov. 18, 1956; children: Robert, William, Michael, Daniel, Jonathan, Laura (dec.); m. Catherine Elizabeth Cornmesser, Sept. 17, 1983; children: Andrew, Thomas. BS in Acctg. summa cum laude, U. S.C., 1960, JD magna cum laude, 1962. Asst. dean of students U. S.C., 1960-62; pvt. practice pub. acctg. Greenville, 1962-64; ptnr. Dobson & Dobson, 1964-93. Chmn., bd. trustees Limestone Coll., 1987-89, founder Christian edn. and leadership program. Contbr. articles on tax and acctg. to profl. jours. Lay minister St. Francis Episcopal Ch., Greenville; chmn. bd. Dobson Tape Ministry, Homeless Children Internat., Inc.; bd. dirs. A Child's Haven, Inc., Found. for the Multihandicapped, Deaf and Blind, Spartanburg, S.C.; mem. adv. bd. Salvation Army, Greenville; chmn. bd. Sch. Ministries, Inc.; mem. History's Handful Campus Crusade for Christ; founder Dobson Vol. Svc. Program, U. S.C. Mem. ABA, S.C. Bar Assn., AICPAs, Am. Assn. Attys. and CPAs, S.C. Assn. Pub. Accts., Block C Assn. The Group, U. S.C. Alumni Assn. (cir. v.p.), Kappa Sigma (chmn. legal com. 1989-93, dist. grand master 1971—, Nat. Dist. Grand Master of the Yr. 1986, John G. Tower Disting. Alumni award 1997, Stephen Alonzo Jackson award 1998), Phi Beta Kappa. Episcopalian. Lodges: Sertoma Internat. (dist. treas.), Sertoma Sunrisers (pres. Greenville club). General corporate, Estate planning, Taxation, general. Home: 1207 Pelham Rd Greenville SC 29615-3643 Office: 1306 S Church St Greenville SC 29605-3814

DOCKRY, KATHLEEN A. lawyer; b. Denville, N.J., Nov. 6, 1953; d. Joseph M. and Margaret (McAndrew) D.; m. Peter N. Perretti, III, June 20, 1979. BA cum laude, Duke U., 1976; JD with honors, Rutgers U., 1982. Bar: N.J. 1983. Law clerk U.S. Ct. Appeals (3d cir.), Newark, 1982-83; assoc. Lowenstein, Sandler, Roseland, 1983-87; asst. gen. counsel Asarco, Inc., N.Y.C., 1987-93; gen. counsel Castrol North Am., Wayne, 1993-95, v.p., gen. counsel, 1995-96, sr. v.p. human resources, adminstrn. & law, 1996-98; pres. Burmah Castrol Holdings Inc., 1998—. Editor-in-Chief: Rutgers Law Review, 1981-82. Pres. Essex Youth Theater, Montclair, N.J., 1995—; trustee Bloomfield Coll. Mem. Am. Corp. Counsel Assn. General corporate. Office: Burmah Castrol Holdings Inc 1500 Valley Rd Wayne NJ 07470-8427

DODDS, MICHAEL BRUCE, lawyer; b. Spokane, Wash., June 27, 1952; s. Bruce Alison and Janet Lorraine (Swanbeck) D.; m. Karen Lynn Sifford, Jan. 5, 1972; children: Jennifer Ann, Stephanie Marie, Alexander Michael, Matthew Tyler. BA, Gonzaga U., 1974, JD, 1979. Bar: Wash. 1980, U.S. Dist. Ct. (ea. dist.) Wash. 1983, U.S. Dist. Ct. (we. dist.) Wash. 1987, U.S. Ct. Appeals (9th cir.) 1994, U.S. Supreme Ct. 1987. Dep. prosecutor Okanogan (Wash.) County, 1980-87, Clark (Wash.) County, 1987—. Served to 2d lt. U.S. Army, 1974-76. Recipient Excellence in Performance award Clark County, 1995. Mem. Clark County Bar Assn., Wash. State Bar Assn., Nat. Dist. Attys. Assn., Phi Alpha Delta. Republican. Lodge: Eagles, Moose. Home: 2104 NE Cranbrook Dr Vancouver WA 98664-2960 Office: Clark County Prosecuter's Office PO Box 5000 Vancouver WA 98666-5000

DODGE, DAVID A. lawyer; b. Grand Rapids, Mich., Mar. 3, 1946; s. Richard C. and Lorraine G. Dodge; m. Carol Ruth Longstreet, Apr. 27, 1968; children: David II, Brian, Julia, Mark, Emily. BA, U. Mich., 1968; JD, Ind. U., 1970. Bar: Ind., Mich., U.S. Dist. Ct. (we. dist.) Mich., U.S. Ct. Appeals (6th cir.), U.S. Supreme Ct. Asst. atty. Kent Prosecutor Office, Grand Rapids, 1973-74; ptnr. Dodge & Dodge, P.C., 1974-88; pvt. practice, 1988—. Served to capt. (judge advocate) USMC, 1970-73. Mem. Mich. Bar Assn. (chmn. prisons and corrections com. 1983-86), Grand Rapids Bar Assn. (trustee 1982-84). Roman Catholic. Clubs: Peninsular. Criminal. Office: 200 N Division Ave Grand Rapids MI 49503-2535

DODGE, JAMES WILLIAM, lawyer, educator; b. Springfield, Ill., Sept. 14, 1967; s. James U. and Nancy C. (Donaldson) D.; m. Cynthia Joy Selby, July 19, 1991; children: James A., Adrienne R.M. BS, U. Ill., 1989; JD, So. Ill. U., 1992. Bar: Ill. 1992, U.S. Dist. Ct. (ctrl. dist.) 1992, U.S. Ct. Appeals (7th cir.) 1993, U.S. Tax Ct. 1993. Pvt. practice, Springfield, 1992-93; asst. atty. gen. Ill. Atty. Gen.'s Office, 1993-97; first asst. state's atty. Christian County State's Atty.'s Office, Taylorville, Ill., 1997-99; legal counsel judiciary com. Ill. Senate Dem. Leader's Office, Springfield, 1999—; instr. MacMurry Coll., Jacksonville, 1998-99. Instr. Robert Morris Coll., Springfield, 1993—. Author: A Brief Survey of Limited Liability Partnership Law in Illinois, 1996; contbr. articles to profl. jours. Ky. Col., Commonwealth of Ky., 1994. Fellow Ill. Bar Found.; mem. ABA, Ill. State Bar Assn. (mem.law-related edn. to pub. com. 1994-97, Christian County Bar Assn. (v.p. 1998—), Ask a Lawyer Day vol. 1994—, h.s. mock trial evaluator 1994—), Sangamon County Bar Assn. (dir. Young Lawyer's divsn. 1993-98), Acad. Legal Studies in Bus., Sangamo Club, Masons, Phi Alpha Delta. Episcopalian. Office: Ill Senate Dem Leader's Office State Capitol Rm 309 Springfield IL 62706-0001

DODSON, CARR GLOVER, lawyer, director; b. Americus, Ga., Aug. 29, 1937; s. William A. Dodson Jr. and Mary (Crisp) Dodson Glover; m. Edith Katherine Pilcher; children: Mary Christine, Katherine, Carr Glover, Will. BA, U. Ga., 1959, JD, 1961. Bar: Ga. 1961, U.S. Dist. Ct. (mid. dist.) Ga. 1964, U.S. Ct. Appeals (11th cir.) 1984. Ptnr. Jones, Cork & Miller, Macon, Ga., 1966—. Dir. Glover Wholesale Co., Americus. Active Ga. Ho. of Reps., 1966-71, minority leader, 1968-71; chmn. Macon United Way, 1981—. Capt. USAF, 1961-64. Fellow Am. Coll. Trial Lawyers; mem. State Bar Ga. (sect. chmn. 1976-78), Bacon Bar Assn. (pres. 1976), Macon C. of C. (bd. dirs. 1976—), Macon Civic Club (bd. dirs.), Idle Hour Country Club (pres. 1980). Republican. Presbyterian. Banking, Federal civil litigation, State civil litigation. Home: 1168 Jackson Springs Rd Macon GA 31211-1435 Office: Jones Cork & Miller 500 Trust Co Bank Bldg Macon GA 31298

DOERNBERG, DONALD LANE, law educator; b. Chgo., May 21, 1945; s. Dudley David and Nanette (Lowenstern) D.; m. Cynthia A. Pope, July 31, 1983. B.A., Yale U., 1966; J.D., Columbia U., 1969. Bar: N.Y. 1969, U.S. Ct. Appeals (2d cir.) 1970, U.S. Ct. Appeals (3d cir.) 1971, U.S. Dist. Ct. (ea. and so. dists.) N.Y. 1971, U.S. Dist. Ct. (no. dist.) N.Y. 1972, U.S. Ct. Appeals (5th and 10th cirs.) 1972, U.S. Ct. Appeals (D.C. cir.) 1973, U.S. Dist. Ct. (we. dist.) 1973, U.S. Supreme Ct. 1974, U.S. Ct. Appeals (8th cir.) 1975, U.S. Ct. Appeals (9th cir.) 1984, Calif. 1985, U.S. Dist. Ct. (no. dist.) Calif. 1985. Tchr. League Sch. for Seriously Disturbed Children, Bklyn., 1969-70; assoc. Levy, Gutman et al, N.Y.C., 1970-74; Hofheimeret al, N.Y.C., 1974-75; staff atty. spl. litigation Legal Aid Soc., N.Y.C., 1975-78, dir. spl. litigation, 1978; prof. law Pace U., 1979— ; vis. prof. law Hastings Coll. Law, San Francisco, 1984-85, Santa Clara (Calif.) Sch. of Law, 1985-86. Contbr. articles to law revs. Mem. Westchester Civil Liberties Union (legal dir. 1978-84, vice chmn., 1974-77, 80-81, chmn. 1978-80). Office: Pace Univ Sch Law 78 N Broadway White Plains NY 10603-3710

DOERR, JOHN MAXWELL, lawyer; b. Pontiac, Mich., Oct. 3, 1939; s. Maxwell Hilberg and Jane (Park) D.; m. Eleanor Kilmon, Feb. 11, 1967 (div. Jan. 1989); children: Jennifer Anne, Julie Kristin. B.A., Coll. Wooster, 1961; postgrad., Johns Hopkins U., 1962-64; J.D., U. Md., 1973. Bar: Md. 1973, Pa. 1974, U.S. Dist. Ct. (ea. dist.) Pa. 1974. Various positions Acme Markets, Inc., Balt., 1961-73, dir. real estate, Phila., 1973-80, asst. sec., 1973— , counsel, 1980— . Del., Delaware County Bus. Task Force, Bryn Mawr, Pa., 1976-77. Recipient Freidlander award Coll. Wooster, 1961. Mem. ABA, Phila. Bar Assn. Republican. Presbyterian. General corporate, Landlord-tenant, Real property. Office: Acme Markets Inc 75 Valley Stream Pkwy Malvern PA 19355-1406

DOHERTY, ROBERT CHRISTOPHER, lawyer; b. Elizabeth, N.J., Sept. 3, 1943; s. Christopher Joseph and Marie Veronica (McLaughlin) D.; m. Sarajane Frances Doherty, June 12, 1965; children: Dennis Michael, Amy Elizabeth, Tracey Carolan. AB, St. Peter's Coll., 1965; JD, Seton Hall U., 1970. Bar: N.J. 1970, U.S. Ct. Appeals (3d cir.) 1982, U.S. Supreme Ct. 1977. Asst. prosecutor Union County, Elizabeth, 1971-72; mem. firm Schumann, Hession, Kennelly & Dorment, Jersey City, 1972-73, Robert D. Younghans, Westfield, N.J., 1973-76; ptnr. Doherty & Kopnicki, 9176-87; county counsel, Union County, 1981-88; assoc. Nelinson, Roche & Carter, East Orange, N.J., 1988-92, Stanley Marcus, Newark, 1992-98, Weiner Lesniak, Parsippany, N.J., 1998-2000; dep. atty. gen. N.J. Divsn. Law, Trenton, 2000—. Mem. ABA, N.J. Bar Assn., Union County Bar Assn., Essex County Bar Assn., N.J. Assn. County Counsels. Republican. Roman Catholic. State civil litigation, General practice, Personal injury. Home: 771 Fairacres Ave Westfield NJ 07090-2027 Office: RJ Hughes Justice Complex PO Box 112 Trenton NJ 08625-0112

DOHSE, ROBERTA SHELLUM, lawyer; b. Cin., Dec. 29, 1949; d. Harold and Ruth (Torgleson) Shellum; children: Gretchen, Kari, Christian. BA, U. Calif., Berkeley, 1971; JD with hons., U. Houston, 1991. Bar: Tex. 1992, U.S. Dist. Ct. (so. dist.) Tex. 1992, U.S. Dist. Ct. (no. dist.) Tex. 1997. Instr., program coord., legal support svcs. North Harris Coll., Houston, 1984-92; assoc. Bishop, Peterson & Sharp, 1992; lawyer pvt. practice, 1993-95; assoc. Wetzel & Herron, The Woodlands, Tex., 1995-96, Chaves Gonzales & Hoblit, L.L.P., Corpus Christi, 1997—. Mem. cutting horse com. Houston Livestock Show and Rodeo, 1988-93, legal adv. com. North Harris Coll., Houston. Mem. ABA, Tex. Bar Assn., Corpus Christi Bar Assn., U. Calif. Berkeley Alumni (life), Order of Coif, Phi Beta Kappa, Order of Barons, Phi Delta Phi. Presbyterian. Avocations: licensed commercial pilot, former flight instructor. Contracts commercial, Probate. Home: 4621 Hogan Dr Corpus Christi TX 78413-2136 Office: Chaves Gonzales & Hoblit 2000 Frost Bank Tower 802 N Carancahua St Corpus Christi TX 78470-0002 E-mail: rdohse@cghlaw.com

DOKE, MARSHALL J., JR. lawyer; b. Wichita Falls, Tex., June 9, 1934; s. Marshall J. and Mary Jane (Johnson) D.; m. Betty Marie Orsini, June 2, 1956; children: Gregory J., Michael J., Laetitia Marie. BA magna cum laude, Hardin-Simmons U., 1956; LLB magna cum laude, So. Meth. U., 1959. Bar: Tex. 1959. Founding ptnr. Rain Harrell Emery Young & Doke, Dallas, 1965-87; assoc. Thompson, Knight, Wright & Simmons, 1959, 62-65; founding ptnr. Doke & Riley, 1987-92; ptnr. McKenna & Cuneo, 1993-96, Gardere Wynne Sewell L.L.P., Dallas, 1996—. Gen. counsel Tex. Rep. Party, 1976-77; mem. adv. coun. U.S. Ct. Fed. Claims, 1982—. Author: Ann. Procurement Rev., Govt. Contractor Briefing Papers, Contract Changes, Fed. Contract Mgmt., 1982—, also articles; editor-in-chief: Southwestern Law Jour., 1958-59; editor: ABA Ann. Devels. in Govt. Contract Law, 1975-78 . Pres. Hope Cottage-Children's Bur., Inc., 1969-70, Hope Cottage Found., 1997—, pres., 1998—; mem. bd. visitors Law Sch., So. Meth. U., 1966-69, McDonald Obs., U. Tex., 1990—; dir. Tex. Hist. Found., 1993—, v.p., 1996-98, pres. 2000—; mem. law com., bd. trustees So. Meth. U., 1977-78; bd. dirs., pres. World Trade Assn., Dallas-Ft. Worth, 1979-80; chmn. bd. dirs. Internat. Trade Assn. Dallas/Ft. Worth, 1993-94; bd. dirs., sec. Theater Trustees Am., 1983-93; chmn. Mayor's Internat. Com., City of Dallas, 1984-87, mem. Judicial Nominating Commn., 1997—, vice chair, 1998—. 1st lt. JAGC, U.S. Army, 1959-62. Fellow Am. Bar Found., Tex. Bar Found.; mem. ABA (chmn. sect. pub. contract law 1969-70, ho. of dels. 1970-72, 74—, bd. govs. 1980-82, nominating com. 1988-91, 2000—, chmn. conf. sect. dels. 1991—), Tex. Bar Assn., U.S. Ct. of Fed. Claims Bar Assn. (bd. govs. 1987—, pres. 1996), Bd. of Contract Appeals Bar Assn. (pres. 1988-90, bd. govs. 1988—), Am. Bar Retirement Assn. (bd. dirs., trustee 1980-84, pres 1982-84), Nat. Conf. Lawyers and CPAs (co-chmn. 1983-85), Nat. Contract Mgmt. Assn. (nat. bd. advisors 1983—), Dallas C. of C. (chmn. internat. com. 1979-83). Construction, Government contracts and claims, Private international. Home: 6910 Dartbrook Dr Dallas TX 75240-7926 Office: Gardere Wynne Sewell LLP Thanksgiving Tower Ste 3000 Dallas TX 75201-7254 E-mail: mdoke@gardere.com

DOKURNO, ANTHONY DAVID, lawyer; b. Gardner, Mass., Mar. 14, 1957; s. Anthony Chester and Damey Anteena (Aleson) D. BA, Holy Cross Coll., 1979; JD, Vt. Law Sch., 1982; postgrad., Johns Hopkins U., 1993-94. Bar: Mass. 1982, U.S. Ct. Appeals for the Armed Forces 1986, U.S. Supreme Ct. 1987. Pvt. practice, Fitchburg, Mass., 1982-86; appellate counsel Navy-Marine Corps Appellate Rev. Activity, Navy JAG, Washington, 1986-88; atty. admiralty divsn. Navy JAG, 1988-90, atty. ops. and mgmt., 1991-93. Assoc. counsel, bd. vets. appeals Dept. Vets. Affairs, 1994-96; analyst Dept. of Def., 1996—. Comdr. USNR, 1998—. Mem.: Maritime Law Assn., Navy League, Nat. Cryptologic History Found., Am. Legion, Amnesty Internat., Naval Res. Assn., Mensa, Phi Beta Kappa. Home: 200 N Pickett St #1504 Alexandria VA 22304-2127

DOLAN, ANDREW KEVIN, lawyer; b. Chgo., Dec. 7, 1945; s. Andrew O. and Elsie (Grafner) D.; children: Andrew, Francesca, Melinda. BA, U. Ill., Chgo., 1967; JD, Columbia U., 1970, MPH, 1976, DPH, 1980. Bar: Wash. 1980. Asst. prof. law Rutgers-Camden Law Sch., N.J., 1970-72; assoc. prof. law U. So. Calif., L.A., 1972-75; assoc. prof. pub. health U. Wash., Seattle, 1977-81; ptnr. Bogle & Gates, 1988-93; pvt. practice law, 1993—. Commr. Civil Svc. Commn., Lake Forest Park, Wash., 1981; mcpl. judge City of Lake Forest Park, 1982-98. Russell Sage fellow, 1975. Mem. Order of Coif, Washington Athletic Club. Avocation: book collecting. Administrative and regulatory, Health, Legislative. Office: 5800 Columbia Ctr 701 5th Ave Seattle WA 98104-7097

DOLAN, BRIAN THOMAS, lawyer; b. Springfield, Ill., Dec. 27, 1940; s. William Stanley and Dorotha Caroline (Battles) D.; m. Kathleen Lois Smith, Sept. 14, 1963; children: Elizabeth Beaumont, Leslie Caroline. AB, Stanford U., 1963, JD, 1965. Bar: Calif. 1966, Colo. 1966, D.C. 1980. Capt. USAF, 1966-70; of counsel Davis, Graham & Stubbs LLP, Denver, 1970—; gen. counsel Resource Capital Funds, 2000—. Finance, Natural resources. Office: Resource Capital Funds 1400 16th St Ste 200 Denver CO 80202 E-mail: btd@rcflp.com

DOLAN, JAMES VINCENT, lawyer; b. Washington, Nov. 11, 1938; s. John Vincent and Philomena Theresa (Vance) D.; m. Anne McSherry Reilly, June 18, 1960; children: Caroline McSherry, James Reilly. AB, Georgetown U., 1960, LLB, 1963. Bar: U.S. Dist. Ct. 1963, U.S. Ct. Appeals (D.C.) cir. 1964, U.S. Ct. Appeals (4th cir.) 1976. Law clk. U.S. Ct. Appeals D.C., 1963-64; assoc. Steptoe & Johnson, Washington, 1964-71, ptnr., 1971-82; mem. Steptoe & Johnson Chartered, 1982-83; v.p. law Union Pacific R.R., Omaha, 1983—. Co-author: Construction Contract Law, 1981; contbr. articles to legal jours.; editor-in-chief: Georgetown Law Jour., 1962-63. Mem. ABA, Nebr. Bar Assn., D.C. Bar Assn., Barristers, Congl. Country Club (v.p. 1982, pres. 1983), Omaha Country Club. Republican. Roman Catholic. Federal civil litigation, General corporate, Public utilities. Home: 1909 County Road 8 Yutan NE 68073-5013 Office: Union Pacific RR 1416 Dodge St Omaha NE 68179-0002

DOLEAC, CHARLES BARTHOLOMEW, lawyer; b. New Orleans, Sept. 20, 1947; s. Cyril Bartholomew and Emma Elizabeth (St. Clair) D.; m. Denise Kilfoyle, Feb. 2, 1972; children: Keith Gabriel, Jessa Lee. BS cum laude, U. N.H., 1968; JD, NYU, 1971. Bar: Mass. 1972, N.H. 1972, Maine 1973. Law clk. to Justice Grimes N.H. Supreme Ct., Concord, 1972-73; assoc. Boynton, Waldron, Dill & Aeschliman, Portsmouth, N.H., 1973-76; ptnr. Boynton, Waldron, Doleac, Woodman & Scott, 1977—. Apptd. mediator N.H. Superior Ct., 1992—; del. to tour Chinese legal system Chinese Ministry Justice, 1982; del. to People's Republic of China/U.S. joint session on trade investments and econ. law Chinese Ministry Justice/U.S. Dept. Justice, Beijing, 1987; propr. Portsmouth Athenaeum; moderator seminars on ethics for Leaders & Comparative Cultures and Values/East & West and Exec. Seminar Aspen Inst., 1990-95; moderator exec. sem. Aspen Inst., 1997-2000; mem. faculty Southwestern Legal Found. Internat. & Comparative Law Ctr., 1997—; ofcl. guest Fgn. Ministry Japan, Tokyo, 1998; developed Asian Seminar, Aspen Inst., 2000; spkr. ethics Ann. Nat. Conf. Appellate Ct. Clks., 1999-2000. Contbr. articles to profl. jours. Mem. citizens adv. coun. Portsmouth Cmty. Devel. Program, 1976-77; incorporator N.H. Charitable Found.; pres., bd. dirs. Seacoast United Way; chmn. Portsmouth Bd. Bldg. Appeals, 1976-77; chmn. stewardship com. Soc. Preservation New Eng. Antiquities, 1980-84, also trustee; pres. bd. trustees Strawbery Banke Mus., 1985-88; founder Daniel Webster Inn of Ct., 1993, Charles C. Doe Inn of Ct., 1994, Portsmouth Peace Treaty Forums I-IV, 1994-2000; founder, pres. Japan-Am. Soc. N.H., 1988; develop Asian seminar, Aspen Inst., 2000. Named Citizen of Yr. Portsmouth, N.H., 1991. Fellow N.H. Bar Found; mem. ATLA, Mass. Bar Assn., Maine Bar Assn., N.H. Bar Assn., N.H. Trial Lawyers Assn., Maine Trial Lawyers Assn. Avocations: masters swimming. General civil litigation, Contracts commercial. Home: Little Harbor Rd Portsmouth NH 03801 Office: Boynton Waldron Doleac Woodman & Scott PA 82 Court St Portsmouth NH 03801-4414 E-mail: cdoleac@nhlawfirm.com

DOLIN, LONNY H. lawyer; b. Youngstown, Ohio, Jan. 24, 1954; d. Lawrence Joseph and Sonya (Sacks) Heselov; m. Gordon S. Black, Aug. 20, 1988; children: Nathaniel, Brooke, Aaron, Benjamin, Lindsay. AB, Georgetown U., 1976; JD, Cath. U., 1979. Bar: Vt. 1980, N.Y. State Bar 1984, U.S. Dist. Ct. (we. dist.) N.Y. 1984. Assoc. Downs, Rachlin & Martin, Burlington, Vt., 1979-81; pvt. practice, 1981-84; assoc., then ptnr. Harris, Beach, Wilcox, Rubin & Levey, Rochester, N.Y., 1984-90; ptnr. Harris, Beach & Wilcox, 1990-93; former of counsel to U.S. Congressman Fred J. Eckert; ptnr. Lonny H. Dolin and Assocs., Rochester, 1993—. Bd. dirs. Monroe County Legal Services Corp.; faculty mem. Nat. Adv. Inst.; co-chair 2d and 3d Ann. Nat. Inst. on Sexual Harassment; spkr. in field. Asst. editor ABA's Sect. of Labor and Employment Law Newsletter; contbr. chpts. and articles to profl. jours. Mem. Pittsford Town and County Com., N.Y., 1983—, Town of Pittsford Bd. of Zoning Appeals, N.Y., 1984—, vice chair 1990; chmn. Monroe County Comparable Worth Task Force, Rochester, 1985—, Fred J. Eckert Women's Adv. Council, Rochester, 1985—; del. The Jud. Dist. N.Y., Rochester, 1985—, chair 1990; bd. dirs. Nat. Council Jewish Women. Recipient Corpus Juris Secundum award West Pub. co., 1979. Fellow Coll. Labor and Employment Lawyers; mem. ABA (plaintiff's chair labor and amployment law sect., co-chair nat. CLE/Inst. and Meetings Com., nat. co-chair employee's rights and responsibilities ethics subcom., nat. vice chair tort and ins. practice sect., spkr. ann. meetings), Nat. Employment Law Assn. (co-chair disabilities rights com.), Vt. Bar Assn., N.Y. Bar Assn., Monroe County Bar Assn. (mem. practice and perf. com.), Greater Rochester Women's Bar Assn. (treas. 1986), Assn. Trial Lawyers Am., N.Y. State Trial Lawyers Assn., Genesee Valley Trial Lawyers Assn. (treas. 1990). Republican. Avocations: golf, skiing, tennis. Federal civil litigation, State civil litigation, Personal injury. Home: 9 Hidden Springs Dr Pittsford NY 14534-2897 Office: Ste 130 135 Corporate Wood St Rochester NY 14623 Fax: 716-272-0574. E-mail: ldolin@dts.esg.com

DOLINER, NATHANIEL LEE, lawyer; b. Daytona Beach, Fla., June 28, 1949; s. Joseph and Asia (Shaffer) D.; m. Debra Lynn Simon, June 5, 1983. BA, George Washington U., 1970; JD, Vanderbilt U., 1973; LLM in Taxation, U. Fla., 1977. Bar: Fla. 1973. Assoc. Smalbein, Eubank, Johnson, Rosier & Bussey, PA, Daytona Beach, Fla., 1973-76; vis. asst. prof. law U. Fla., Gainesville, 1977-78; assoc. Carlton, Fields, Ward, Emmanuel, Smith & Cutler, PA, Tampa, Fla., 1978-82, shareholder, 1982—, chmn. corp. and securities dept., 1984-96, treas., 1985-86, co-chair bus. transactions dept., 1996-98, chair bus. transactions practice group, 1998—. Spkr. NYU Real Estate Tax Inst., 1989, 94, Md. Advanced Tax Inst., Balt., 1994, ABA Presdl. Showcase Programs, 1993-96; co-chmn., spkr. ABA mergers and Acquisitions Inst., N.Y.C., 1996, ABA Nat., Inst. Negotiating Bus. Acquisitions, Chgo., 1997, New Orleans, 1998, Newport Beach, Calif., 1999, Boca Raton, 2000; spkr., Internat. mergers and acquisitions, Ctr. Internat. Legal Studies, Salzburg, Austria, 1999, ABA Nat. Inst., Internat. Ventures for Old and New Econ., 2000, others. Adv. bd. Mergers and Acquisitions Law Report, pub. Bur. Nat. Affairs. Bd. dirs. Big Bros./Big Sisters Greater Tampa, Inc., 1980-82, Child Abuse Coun., Inc., 1986-95, asst. treas., 1987-88, treas., 1988-89, pres.-elect 1989-90, pres., 1990-91; dist. commr. Gulf Ridge Coun. Boy Scouts Am., 1983; bd. dirs. Tampa Jewish Fedn.

Bd., 1988-91, Mus. Sci. and Industry, Tampa, 1994—, exec. com., 1994—, sec. 1995-97, first vice-chmn., 1997-99, chair, 1999—; alumni bd. Vanderbilt Law Sch., 1998-2000, bd. dirs., exec. com. Hillel Sch. Tampa, 1998—, first vice-chmn., 1999—, pres.-elect, 2000—. Fellow Am. Bar Found., Am. Coll. Tax Counsel; mem. ABA tax sect. (vice-chmn. continuing legal education com. 1986-88, chmn. 1988-90, bus. law sect. com. negotiated acquisitions, vice-chmn. 1997-98, chmn. 1998—, chmn. task force preliminary and ancillary agreements, 1992-95, mem. acquisition rev. subcom. 1992-95, chair program letters of intent in bus. transactions 1993, chmn. programs subcom. 1995-98, co-chmn. program mergers of for-profit and not-for-profit hosps. 1996), Am. Law Inst., Fla. Bar Assn. (exec. coun. tax sect. 1980-83, tax cert. com. 1987-88, vice-chmn. 1988-89, chmn. 1989-90), Greater Tampa C. of C. (chmn. Ambassadors Target Task Force of Com. of 100 1984-85, 87-88, chair geographic task force 1989-90, vice-chmn. govt. fin. and taxation coun. 1987-88, chmn. 1988-90, bd. govs. 1991-93, exec. com. 1992, chmn. govtl. affairs dept., 1992), Anti-Defamation League (regional bd. mem. 1986-90, exec. com. 1987-90), Tampa Club (bd. dirs. 1987-92, sec. 1987-89, pres. 1990-91). General corporate, Mergers and acquisitions, Taxation, general. Home: 13341 Golf Crest Cir Tampa FL 33624-4648 Office: Carlton Fields Ward Emmanuel Smith & Cutler PA Ste 500 777 S Harbour Island Blvd Tampa FL 33602-5729

DOLT, FREDERICK CORRANCE, lawyer; b. Louisville, Oct. 10, 1929; s. O. Frederick and Margaret A. (Corrance) D.; m. Lucy M. Voelker, Dec. 8, 1960; 1 child, Frederick C. Jr. JD, U. Louisville, 1952. Bar: Ky. 1952, U.S. Ct. Appeals (6th cir.) 1965, U.S. Supreme Ct. 1972, La. 1982. Assoc. Morris & Garlove, Louisville, 1955-59; sole practice, 1959-70, 79—; ptnr. Leibson, Dolt & McCarthy, 1970-73. Mem. Inner Circle Advocates, 1981. Served with U.S. Army, 1953-55. Mem. Ky. Bar Assn. (chmn. ins. negligence sect. 1968-70, mem. Ho. of Dels. 1970-80), Ky. Trial Lawyers Assn. (pres. 1970). Republican. Presbyterian. Avocation: golf. Federal civil litigation, State civil litigation. Home: 7216 Heatherly Sq Louisville KY 40242-2847 Office: 310 Starks Bldg Louisville KY 40202

DOMANSKIS, ALEXANDER RIMAS, lawyer; b. Chgo., June 3, 1952; s. Van and Alina Alexandra (Tamasauskas) Domanskis; m. Frances Laucka, May 06, 1978; children: Maria Laucka, John Joseph Laucka. AB, U. Mich, 1973; JD, U. Mich., 1977. Bar: Ill. 1977, U.S. Dist. Ct. (no. dist.) Ill. 1977, U.S. Ct. Appeals (7th cir.) 1978, U.S. Supreme Ct. 1985. Law clk. U.S. Dist. Ct. (no. dist.) Ill., Chgo., 1977—79; assoc. Ross & Hardies, 1979—84, ptnr., 1985—87, 1993—94, of counsel, 1987—92; ptnr. Shaw, Gussis, Domanskis, Fishman & Glantz, 1994—. Assoc. gen. counsel and v.p. Intercounty Title Co. of Ill., 1987—91, bd. dir., 1990—91. Editor (adminstrv.): (jour.) U. Mich Jour. Law Reform, 1976—77. Pres. Lithuanian World Ctr., 1988—92, bd. dir., 1988—95, chmn. bd., 1994—95; bd. dir. Intercounty Credit Corp., Chgo., 1988—91, Lithuanian Montessori Soc., Chgo., 1987—90. Mem.: ABA, Chgo. Bar Assn., Lithuanian Am. Coun. (bd. dir. Chgo. 1981—88), Lithuanian Roman Cath. Fedn. Am. (bd. dir. Chgo. 1980—87). General corporate, Land use and zoning (including planning), Real property. Home: 4236 Hampton Ave Western Springs IL 60558-1310 Office: Shaw Gussis Domanskis Fishmen & Glantz 1144 W Fulton Ste 200 Chicago IL 60607

DOMBROW, ANTHONY ERIC, lawyer; b. N.Y.C., Apr. 6, 1945; s. Oscar and Nettie (Maslow) D.; m. Penny McClurg, July 21, 1978; children: Joshua Alan, Ashley Smith. B.A., U. Wis., 1966, J.D., 1969. Bar: Wis. 1969, Ill. 1973, U.S. Ct. Apls. (8th cir.) 1974, U.S. Ct. Apls. (7th cir.) 1975, U.S. Sup. Ct. 1976, U.S. Ct. Appeals (9th cir.) 1987. Atty., Nat. Labor Relations Bd., Chgo., 1969-72; ptnr. Laner, Muchin, Dombrow & Becker Ltd., Chgo., 1972— . Labor, Pension, profit-sharing, and employee benefits. Office: Laner Muchin Dombrow & Becker Ltd 350 S Clark St Chicago IL 60604-3504

DOMIANO, JOSEPH CHARLES, lawyer; b. Cleve., Oct. 21, 1928; s. Charles Joseph and Mary Grace (Santora) D.; m. Julie Ann Birinyi, Sept. 9, 1950; children: Joseph, Jr., Laura, John. BBA, Case Western Reserve U., 1951; LLD, Cleve. State U., 1956. Bar: Ohio 1957. Ptnr. Mandanici & Domiano, Cleve., 1957-84, Sindell, Rubenstein, Cleve., 1984-87, Friedman, Domiano & Smith, Cleve., 1987—. Prosecutor City of Maple Heights (Ohio), 1963-65; solicitor Village of Bentleyville (Ohio), 1974-94; law dir. City of Olmsted Falls (Ohio), 1992-93; mem. (life) 8th Dist. Jud. Law Conf., Cleve., 1994—. Contbr. articles to law jours.;m presenter in field. Bd. dirs. Maple Heights Little Theatre, 1962-65, Transitional Housing, Cleve., 1994—; mem. parish coun. Ch. of Resurrection, Solon, Ohio, 1992-94, mem. fin. coun., 1996—. Mem. ATLA, Assn. Trial Lawyers, Ohio State Bar Assn., Ohio Acad. Trial Lawyers, Cleve. Bar Assn., Cleve. Acad. Trial Lawyers, Cuyahoga County Bar Assn. (pres. 1993-94), KC (mem. exec. com. 1985-86). Avocations: snow skiing, water skiing, sailing, golf, scuba diving. Personal injury, Product liability, Professional liability. Office: Friedman Domiano & Smith 600 Standard Bldg 1370 Ontario St Fl 6 Cleveland OH 44113-1701

DOMINA, DAVID ALAN, lawyer; b. Laurel, Nebr., Nov. 27, 1950; s. Marvin Everett and Jacqueline Mae (Hansen) D.; children from previous marriage: Thurston A., Salesia. J.D. with distinction, U. Nebr., 1972. Bar: Nebr. 1973, Mo. 1973, U.S. Tax Ct. 1973, U.S. Ct. Appeals (8th cir.) 1973. Assoc., Shook, Hardy & Bacon, Kansas City, Mo., 1973-74; ptnr. Jewell, Gatz & Domina, Norfolk, Nebr., 1974-82, Domina & Gerrard, P.C., Norfolk, 1982— ; gen. counsel Affiliated Foods Coop., Norfolk, 1982— ; dir. Farmers State Bank, Carroll, Nebr. Mem. state central com. Nebr. Democratic party, 1976-78; commr. Nebr. Econ. Devel. Commn., 1986—; trustee Nebr. Bd. Edn. Lands and Funds, Lincoln, 1983— ; spl. atty. gen. Nebr. Dept. Justice, Lincoln, 1983-84; counsel Nebr. Dept. Banking, Lincoln, 1983-84. Mem. ABA, Mo. Bar Assn., Nebr. Bar Assn. (vice chmn. young lawyers sect. 1982, chmn. corrections com. 1983), Assn. Trial Lawyers Am., U. Nebr. Coll. Law Alumni Assn. (bd. dirs.), Norfolk C. of C., Order of Coif, Order of Barristers. Lutheran. Federal civil litigation, State civil litigation, Contracts commercial. Office: Domina & Gerrard PC 2425 Taylor Ave Norfolk NE 68701-4511

DOMINIK, JACK EDWARD, lawyer; b. Chgo., July 9, 1924; s. Ewald Arthur and Gertrude Alene (Crotzer) D.; children: Paul, David, Georgia Lee, Elizabeth, Sarah, Clare. BSME with distinction, Purdue U., 1947; JD, Northwestern U., 1950. Bar: Ill. 1950, U.S. Patent Office 1953, Wis. 1959, Fla. 1964, U.S. Dist. Ct. (ea. dist.) Wis. 1959, U.S. Supreme Ct. 1965, U.S. Dist. Ct. (no. dist.) Ohio 1962, U.S. Dist. Ct. (so. dist.) Ill. 1965, U.S. Ct. Appeals (7th and 9th cirs.) 1965, U.S. Ct. Appeals (4th cir.) 1973, U.S. Dist. Ct. (so. dist.) Fla. 1974, U.S. Ct. Appeals (5th cir.) 1977, U.S. Dist. Ct. (mid. dist.) Fla. 1979, U.S. Ct. Appeals (fed. cir.) 1983, U.S. Ct. Appeals (11th cir.) 1984, U.S. Ct. Appeals (2d cir.) 1987. Assoc. Carlson, Pitzner, Hubbard & Wolfe, Chgo., 1950-54; ptnr. Ooms and Dominik, 1954-59, White & Hirshboeck, Milw., 1959-62, Dominik, Knechtel, DeMeur & Samlan, Chgo., 1962-78, Miami, Fla., 1978—. Served to 1st lt., C.E. AUS, 1943-46, ETO. Mil. govt. judge, 1945-46. Mem. ABA, Wis. Bar Assn., Fla. Bar Assn., Chgo. Bar Assn., Am. Patent Law Assn., Chgo. Patent Law Assn. (chmn. taxation com. 1966, 69-70), Milw. Patent Law Assn., Patent Law Assn. So. Fla. (founder, dir. 1982—, past pres.), Chgo. Yacht Club, Union League Club, Tau Beta Pi, Pi Tau Sigma, Tau Kappa Alpha. Avocation: flying. Federal civil litigation, Intellectual property, Private international. Home: 14751 Lewis Rd Miami Lakes FL 33014-2731 Office: 6175 NW 153rd St Miami Lakes FL 33014-2435

DONAHUE, CHARLOTTE MARY, lawyer; b. Columbus, Ohio, Sept. 29, 1954; d. Patrick Henry and Helen Dillon (Meany) D. AB, Holy Cross Coll., 1976; JD, U. Toledo, 1983. Bar: Pa. 1984, D.C. 1985, U.S. Dist. Ct. (ea. dist.) Pa. 1985, U.S. Ct. Appeals 3d cir.) 1985, U.S. Supreme Ct. 1990, Mass. 1992. Jud. clk. to presiding justice Commonwealth Ct. Pa., Phila., 1983-84; spl. asst. U.S. atty. U.S. Dist. Ct. (ea. dist.) Pa., 1987-90; atty. HUD, 1984-93, Boston, 1993—. Mem. Fed. Bar Assn., Pa. Bar Assn., Mass. Bar Assn., D.C. Bar Assn., Order of Barristers, Internat. Platform Assn., Supreme Ct. Hist. Soc. Home: 40 Meredith Cir Milton MA 02186-3916 Office: HUD Thomas P O'Neill Jr Fed Bldg 10 Causeway St Boston MA 02222-1092

DONAHUE, JOHN EDWARD, lawyer; b. Milw., Aug. 22, 1950; s. Joseph Robert and Helen Ann (Kelly) D.; m. Maureen Dolores Hart, Sept. 20, 1974; children: Timothy Robert Hart, Michael John Hart. BA with honors, Marquette U., 1972; JD, U. Wis., Madison, 1975. Bar: Wis. 1975, U.S. Dist. Ct. (we. and ea. dists.) Wis. 1975. Assoc. Weiss, Steuer, Berzowski and Kriger, Milw., 1975-80; ptnr. Weiss, Berzowski, Brady & Donahue LLP, 1981-2001; shareholder Godfrey & Kahn, S.C., 2001—. Guest lectr. Marquette U. Law Sch., Milw., 1976-90; presenter programs Wis. Inst. CPAs, 1984—, Minn. Soc. CPAs, 1992-97; expert witness The Best Lawyers in Am., 1995-96, 97-98, 99-2000, 01—. Past chmn. bd. trustees, past chmn. bd. dirs., past chmn. bd. govs., trustee, exec. com., com. chmn. Mt. Mary Coll., Milw., 1984—, past pres., bd. dirs. com. chmn. Met. Milw. Civic Alliance, 1980—, Children's Hosp. Found., Milw., 1984—; mem. steering com. Greater Milw. Initiative, 1989-92; v.p., bd. dirs. Future Milw., 1984-88; v.p., coun. bd., com. chmn., scoutmaster Boy Scouts Am., 1990—. Recipient citation Milw. County Bd. Suprs., 1990, spl. svc. award Met. Milw. Civil Alliance, 1990, silver beaver award Boy Scouts Am., 1995; named outstanding instr. AICPA, 1991. Mem. Wis. Bar Assn., Milw. Bar Assn., Wis. Retirement Plan Profls., Greater Milw. Employee Benefits Coun., Kiwanis Club (pres. Milw. unit 1989-90, Outstanding Kiwanian 1989-97, Kiwanian of Yr. 1993). General corporate, General practice, Pension, profit-sharing, and employee benefits. Office: Godfrey & Kahn SC 780 N Water St Milwaukee WI 53202-3590 Business E-Mail: jdonahue@gklaw.com

DONAHUE, MICHAEL CHRISTOPHER, lawyer; b. Norwood, Mass., Apr. 20, 1946; s. Michael Christopher and Helen (Joyce) D.; m. Erna Joyce Carrigan, Apr. 20, 1968; children: Kirsten, Michael, Brendan, Brian. AB, Boston Coll., 1968; JD, Boston U., 1972. Bar: Mass. 1972. Assoc., Klainer & Kappel, Boston, 1972-73, Sheridan, Garrahan & Lander, Framingham, Mass., 1981-88; asst. atty. gen. Mass. Atty. Gen., 1973-79; gen. counsel Mass. Dept. of Corrections, Boston, 1979-81; mem. Gov.'s Adv. Com. on Corrections, 1988—; spl. asst. atty. gen. Mass., Boston, 1979—; lectr. grad. criminal justice program Anna Maria Coll., Paxton, Mass., 1981-86. Contbr. articles to law review jours. Me.m Gov.'s Adv. Com. on Corrections, 1989. With USAR, 1968-72. Mem. ABA, Assn. Trial Lawyers Am., Mass. Bar Assn., Mass. Acad. Trial Attys. (author, editor), South Middlesex Bar Assn. Democrat. Roman Catholic. Civil rights, Federal civil litigation, State civil litigation. Home: 167 Depot St South Easton MA 02375-1537 Office: Gelerman and Cashman 270 Bridge St Ste 204 Dedham MA 02026-1798

DONAHUE, RIKER J. lawyer; b. Stamford, Conn., Mar. 28, 1968; d. Alphonsus Joseph III and Jane Riker Austin; m. Christopher M. Maceluch, July 22, 1995. BSSP cum laude, Emerson Coll., 1990; JD, Pace U., 1997. Bar: Conn. Clk. to presiding judge Stamford (Conn.) Superior Ct., 1997-98; assoc. Tooher & Wocl, Stamford, 1998—. Mem. Conn. Bar Assn., Stamford Regional Bar Assn. (chair law day com.), Am. Trial Lawyers Assn., Conn. Trial Lawyers Assn. Democrat. Roman Catholic.

DONAHUE, TIMOTHY PATRICK, lawyer; b. Phila., Sept. 7, 1955; s. Joseph Thomas and Margaret Teresa (Golden) D.; m. Diane Gilbert, June 26, 1982; children: Timothy Patrick Jr., Elizabeth O'Reilly. BA, U. Ala., 1977, JD, 1981. Bar: Ala. 1982. Assoc., then ptnr. Clark & Scott, P.A., Birmingham, Ala., 1982-87; assoc. then ptnr. Edmond & Vines, 1987-91; ptnr. Clark & Scott P.C., 1991—; shareholder Bradford & Donahue P.C., 1995—. Mem. Ala. Bar Assn., Ala. Trial Lawyers Assn., Birmingham Bar Assn. (exec. com. young lawyers sect. 1986-89). Roman Catholic. General civil litigation, Personal injury, Workers' compensation. Home: 2044 Magnolia Rdg Birmingham AL 35243-2018

DONALD, NORMAN HENDERSON, III, lawyer; b. Denver, Nov. 1, 1937; s. Norman Henderson Jr. and Angelene (Pell) D.; m. Alice Allen, Oct. 31, 1970 (div. Aug. 1980); children: Norman H. IV (dec.), Helen P.; m. Kathryn Akers, Sept. 26, 1981 (div. Jan. 1998). AB, Princeton U., 1959; LLB, Harvard U., 1962. Bar: N.Y. 1962. Assoc. Davis, Polk & Wardwell, N.Y.C., 1962-67, Skadden, Arps, Slate, Meagher & Flom, N.Y.C., 1967-68, ptnr., 1968-94. Chmn. bd. dirs. Norwil Holdings, Inc., N.Y.C., Atlanta and Sarasota. Mem. Assn. of Bar of City of N.Y., Practising Law Inst. (editor Reit Restructuring 1977—), St. Paul's Sch. Alumni Assn. (v.p., bd. dirs. 1984-86), Union Club (N.Y.C.), Rotary, Gold Creek Club (Dawsonville, Ga.). Republican. Episcopalian. General corporate. Home: Mistral Farms 1544 Bailey Waters Rd Dawsonville GA 30534-1807 Office: care Brock & Silverstein 800 3d Ave New York NY 10022 Fax: 706-265-2810. E-mail: mistral@syclone.net

DONALDSON, MICHAEL CLEAVES, lawyer; b. Montclair, N.J., Oct. 13, 1939; s. Wyman C. and Ernestine (Greenwood) D.; m. Diana D., Sept. 12, 1969 (div. 1979); children: Michelle, Amy, Wendy. BS, U. Fla., 1961; JD, U. Calif., Berkeley, 1967. Bar: Calif. 1967, U.S. Dist. Ct. (cen. dist.) Calif. 1967, U.S. Ct. Appeals (9th cir.) 1967. Assoc. Harris & Hollingsworth, L.A., 1969-72; ptnr. McCabe & Donaldson, 1972-79; pvt. practice Law Office of M.C. Donaldson, 1979-90; ptnr. Dern & Donaldson, 1990-94, Donaldson & Hart (formerly Berton & Donaldson), Beverly Hills, Calif., 1994—. Lectr. in field; judge, preliminary and finalist judge Internat. Emmys; preliminary judge Night Time Emmys; gen. counsel Ind. Feature Project West; pres. Internat. Documentary Assn. Author: EZ Legal Guide to Copyright and Trademark, 1995, (booklet) Something Funny Happened on the Way to Dinner, 1976; contg. author: Conversations with Michael Landon, 1992, Negotiating for Dummies, 1996, Clearance & Copyright What the Independent Filmmaker Needs to Know, 1997. Bd. dirs. Calif. Theatre Coun., L.A. 1st lt. USMC, 1961-64. Mem. ABA (entertainment and sports sect.), NATAS, Nat. Acad. Cable Broadcasting, Beverly Hills Bar Assn. (chmn. entertainment sect.), L.A. Copyright Soc. Republican. Avocations: photography, writing, gardening, hiking, skiing. Entertainment, Intellectual property. Home: 2074 Benedict Canyon Dr Beverly Hills CA 90210-1404 Office: Donaldson & Hart 9220 W Sunset Blvd Ste 224 Los Angeles CA 90069-3501 E-mail: mdonaldson@mdonaldsonlaw.com

DONALDSON, STEVEN BRYAN, lawyer; b. Vincennes, Ind., Sept. 23, 1963; s. Steve Donaldson and Lynne Raye (Wilson) Murray. BA, Ind. U., 1985, JD, 1988. Bar: Ind. 1988, U.S. Dist. Ct. (no. and so. dists.) Ind. 1988. Assoc. Berry Capper & Tulley, Crawfordsville, Ind., 1988-94; ptnr. Berry Capper Donaldson & Tulley, 1995-96; prin. S. Bryan Donaldson, 1997—. Judge teen ct. Youth Svc. Bur., Crawfordsville, 1993, 2001; mem. Montgomery County Cultural Found., 1994—; chmn. bd. trustees 1st United Meth. Ch., 1994—97, chmn. endowment com., 1999—2000, chmn. adminstrv. bd., 2001. Mem. Ind. Bar Assn., Montgomery County Bar Assn., Kiwanis (bd. dirs. Crawfordsville 1992-94, pres. 2001—). Republican. Avocations: bowling, golf, spectator sports, reading. Consumer commercial, Family and matrimonial, General practice. Home: 180 Shayne Dr Crawfordsville IN 47933-2149 Office: 134 W Main St Crawfordsville IN 47933-1718 E-mail: sbdlawoff@hotmail.com

DONDANVILLE, JOHN WALLACE, lawyer; b. Moline, Ill., Nov. 29, 1937; s. Laurence A. and Eva C. (Ender) D.; m. Maureen C. Ryan, Apr. 16, 1966; children: Edward John, Julie Ann. AB in History, Holy Cross Coll., 1959; JD, Northwestern U., 1962. Bar: Ill. 1962. Ptnr. Baker & McKenzie, Chgo., 1965-97; ret., 1997. Pres., mem. B&D Devel. LLC. Author: Product Liability Trends & Implications, 1970. Bd. advisors Marillac House, Chgo., 1986—. Mem. Ill. Bar Assn., Chgo. Bar Assn. Avocation: hiking. General civil litigation, Construction, Insurance.

DONEGAN, CHARLES EDWARD, lawyer, educator; b. Chgo., Apr. 10, 1933; s. Arthur C. and Odessa (Arnold) D.; m. Patty Lou Harris, June 15, 1963; 1 son, Carter Edward. B.S.C., Roosevelt U., 1954; M.S., Loyola U., 1959; J.D., Howard U., 1967; LL.M., Columbia, 1970. Bar: N.Y. 1968, D.C. 1968, Ill. 1979. Pub. sch. tchr., Chgo., 1956-59; with Office Internal Revenue, 1959-62; labor economist U.S. Dept. Labor, Washington, 1962-65; legal intern U.S. Commn. Civil Rights, summer 1966; asst. counsel NAACP Legal Def. Fund, N.Y.C., 1967-69; lectr. law Baruch Coll., 1969-70; asst. prof. law State U. N.Y. at Buffalo, 1970-73; assoc. prof. law Howard U., 1973-77; vis. assoc. prof. Ohio State U., Columbus, 1977-78; asst. regional counsel U.S. EPA, 1978-80; prof. law So. U., Baton Rouge, 1980—; sole practice law Chgo. and Washington, 1984—. Arbitrator steel industry, 1972, U.S. Postal Svc., New Orleans, D.C. Superior Ct., 1987—, Fed. Mediation and Conciliation Svc., 1985—, N.Y. Stock Exch.; vis. prof. law La. State U., summer 1981, N.C. Cen. U., Durham, 1988—, So. U., Baton Rouge, spring 1992; real estate broker; mem. bd. consumer claims Dist. D.C., 1988—; mem. Mayor's Transition Task Force, Washington, 1995; moot ct. judge Georgetown U. Law Sch., Washington, 1987—, Howard U. Law Sch., Washington, 1987—, Balsa, 1987—; spkr., participant nat. confs. on law, edn. and labor rels. Author: Discrimination in Public Employment, 1975; Contbr. articles to profl. jours., to Dictionary Am. Negro Biography. Active Ams. for Dem. Action; me. adv. com. D.C. Bd. of Edn. Named one of Top 42 Lawyers in Washington Area, Washington Afro-Am. Newspaper, 1993, 94, 95, 96' Ford Found. scholar, 1965-67. Columbia U., 1972-73, NEH Postdoctoral fellow in Afro-Am. studies Yale U., 1972-73. Mem. ABA (vice chmn. edn. and curriculum com. local govt. law sect. 1972-80, pub. edn. com. sect. local govt. 1974-84, chmn. liaison com. AALS, 1984, chair arbitration sect.), Nat. Bar Assn. (labor and employment law sect., steering com.), D.C. Bar Assn., Washington Bar Assn. (chmn. legal edn. com.), Chgo. Bar Assn., Fed. Bar Assn., Cook County Bar Assn., Am. Arbitration Assn. (arbitrator), D.C. Fee Arbitration Bd. (bd. govs. 1990—), Nat. Conf. Black Lawyers (bd. organizers), Nat. Futures Assn. (arbitrator), Nat. Assn. Securities Dealers (arbitrator), Assn. Henri Capitant, Roosevelt U. Alumni Assn. (rep. at George Washington U. 175th anniversary charter day convocation 1996), Loyola U. Alumni Assn. (v.p. Washington), Howard U. Alumni Assn. (rep. at Hunter Coll. Centennial 1970), Columbia U. Alumni Assn. (v.p. law Washington), Alpha Phi Alpha, Phi Alpha Kappa, Phi Alpha Delta. Alternative dispute resolution, General practice, Labor. Home: 4315 Argyle Ter NW Washington DC 20011-4243 Office: 601 Pennsylvania Ave NW Ste 900 Washington DC 20004-3615 also: 311 S Wacker Dr Ste 4550 Chicago IL 60606-6622

DONLEY, JERRY ALAN, lawyer; b. Denver, Feb. 17, 1930; s. Richard O. and Mildred K. (Bailey) D.; m. Dorothy Jean Mayhew, Sept. 5, 1953; children— Charles Alan, Jack Edward, David William. B.A., Beloit Coll., 1951; LL.B., U. Mich., 1954. Bar: Colo. 1954, U.S. Dist. Ct. Colo. 1954, U.S. Supreme Ct. 1977. Atty. Legal Aid Soc., Colorado Springs, Colo., 1957; dep. dist. atty. 4th Jud. Dist., Colorado Springs, 1957-60; sole practice, Colorado Springs, 1960-64; ptnr. Rector, Kane & Donley, 1964-68, Rector, Kane, Donley & Wills, 1968-71, Kane, Donley & Wills, 1971-83, Kane & Donley, 1983-90, Kane, Donley & Shaffer, 1990—. Active 1st Presbyterian Ch. of Colorado Springs; bd. dirs. Boys Club Colorado Springs and Vicinity, Colorado Springs Charter Assn., Pikes Peak Road Runners; mem. track and field com Colo. Assn. of Athletic Congress; chmn. masters track and field com. Athletics Congress U.S.A., 1984-85. Served to cpl. U.S. Army, 1954-56. Mem. Colorado Springs Estate Planning Council (sec. 1979), Colorado Springs Jaycees (bd. dirs.), El Paso County Bar Assn. Lodge: Kiwanis. General practice, Insurance, Probate. Home: 1715 Alamo Ave Colorado Springs CO 80907-7307

DONNALLY, ROBERT ANDREW, lawyer, real estate broker; b. Washington, July 10, 1953; s. Reaumur Stearnes and Katherine Ann (Sutliff) D.; m. Patricia Kane Broderick, Dec. 30, 1977; 1 child, Danielle Christine. BA in Psychology, U. Md., 1976; JD, U. Balt., 1980; cert. in bus., Stanford U., 1996. Bar: Md. 1980, Calif. 1986. Pvt. practice, Oxen Hill, Md., 1980-81; rsch. contract staff officer Dept. Def., Ft. Meade, 1981-85; with legal and contractual ops. ARGOSystems, Inc., Sunnyvale, Calif., 1985-90; asst. dir. Inst. Def. Analyses, San Diego, 1990-91; dep. chief counsel ARGOSystems, Inc., 1991-93, chief counsel, corp. sec., 1993-98; chief counsel comms. and infomanagement divsn. Boeing Co., 1997-98; gen. counsel, mng. ptnr. BT Comml. Real Estate, Palo Alto, Calif., 1998-99; assoc. gen. counsel Inhale Therapeutic Sys. Inc., San Carlos, 1999—. Editor-in-chief The Forum, 1979-80. Active The Pillars Soc./United Way, 1991-98. Waxter Legal scholar U. Baltimore, 1978. Mem. Am. Corp. Counsel, Nat. Contract Mgmt. Assn., Md. Bar Assn., Calif. Bar Assn., Assn. of Silicon Valley Brokers, Tae Kwon Do Assn. (Black Belt), Black Belt, Kukkiwon World Tae Kwon Do Assn. Avocations: martial arts, marathons, hiking, travel, reading. General corporate, General practice, Real property. E-mail: rdonnally@inhale.com

DONNELLA, MICHAEL ANDRE, lawyer, pharmaceutical company executive; b. Great Lakes, Ill., Oct. 16, 1954; s. Joseph Anthony and Jacqueline (Reddick) D. BA in Mathematics, Wesleyan U., Middletown, Conn., 1976; JD, U.Chgo., 1979. Bar: Ga. 1979, U.S. Ct. Appeals (D.C. and 11th cirs.) 1980, N.J. 1987. Assoc. Troutman, Sanders et al, Atlanta, 1979-83; atty. AT&T So. Region, 1983-86; sr. atty. AT&T Internat., Basking Ridge, N.J., 1986-95; asst. gen. counsel Am. Home Products Corp., St. Davids, PA, 1995—; v.p., counsel Wyeth-Ayerst Pharmaceuticals, 2000—. Vis. prof. Nat. Urban League Black Exec. Exchange Program, 1986, Huston-Tillotson Coll., Austin, Tex. Interviewer Wesleyan Schs. Com., Middletown, 1976—; counsel Ga. Legis. Black Caucus, Atlanta, 1982-86; mem. visitors com. U. Chgo. Law Sch., 1989-92. Named to 100 Black Men of N.J., Inc. Black Elected Ofcls. Found. Roman Catholic. Avocations: jazz, sports. General corporate, Private international, Public utilities. Office: Am Home Products Corp 170 N Radnor Chester Rd Wayne PA 19087-5221

DONNELLY, JAMES CORCORAN, JR. lawyer; b. Newton, Mass., June 10, 1946; s. James C. and Margery J. (MacNeil) D.; m. Carol R. Burns, June 28, 1968; children: James C. IV, Sarah Y. BA, Dartmouth Coll., 1968; JD, Boston Coll., 1973. Bar: Mass. 1973, U.S. Dist. Ct. Mass. 1974, U.S. Ct. Appeals (7th cir.) 1979, U.S. Ct. Appeals (1st cir.) 1983, U.S. Tax Ct. 1988, U.S. Dist. Ct. (no. dist.) Ohio 1991, U.S. Ct. Appeals (2d cir) 1994, U.S. Ct. Appeals (3d cir.) 1999. From assoc. to ptnr. Hale & Dorr, Boston, 1973-84; sr. ptnr. Mirick, O'Connell, DeMallie & Lougee, Worcester, Mass., 1985—, chmn. litigation dept., 1993-97. Bd. dirs. C.P. Bourg, Inc., New Bedford, Mass. Editor-in-chief 1972 Annual Survey of Mass. Law. Corporator Greater Worcester Cmty. Found., 1986—, mem. monitoring and evaluation com., 1997—; trustee Higgins Armory Mus., Worcester, 1985—, pres. 1994-97; corporator Worcester Art Mus., 1986—, pres., mem. coun., 1987-88; councilor Am. Antiquarian Soc., 1996—, treas., 1997—; mem. club officers exec. com. Dartmouth Coll., 1997—, pres., 1999—, mem. alumni coun., 2000—, mem. com. on alumni orgns., 2000—. Lt. U.S. Army, 1968-70. Decorated Army Commendation medal for meritorious svc., 1970. Fellow Mass. Bar Found., 1994; mem. ABA, Mass. Bar Assn., Worcester County Bar Assn. (co-chmn. fed. ct. com.

1995-98), Dartmouth Lawyers Assn., Worcester Club (bd. dirs. 1995-98), Dartmouth Club Ctrl. Mass. (exec. com. 1996—, pres. 1997—). Avocations: sailing, bicycling, hiking, history. General civil litigation, General corporate, Health. Home: 285 Salisbury St Worcester MA 01609-1661 Office: Mirick O'Connell 100 Front St Worcester MA 01608-1425

DONNELLY, KEVIN WILLIAM, lawyer; b. Rockville Centre, N.Y., Sept. 25, 1954; s. William Lorne and Marie Grace (Busch) D.; m. Judith Marcia Brier, July 19, 1986; children: Lisa, Jennifer. BS, Boston Coll., 1976, JD, 1979; MBA, Dartmouth Coll., 1982. Bar: N.Y. 1980, Mass. 1980, U.S. Supreme Ct. 1999. Tax atty. Exxon Corp., N.Y.C., 1979-80; assoc. Hemenway & Barnes, Boston, 1982-83; v.p., gen. counsel The Yankee Cos. Inc., 1983-88, Nortek, Inc., Providence, 1988—. Mem. ABA, Mass. Bar Assn. General civil litigation, General corporate, Mergers and acquisitions. Home: 11 Foxhunt Trl Walpole MA 02081-2270 Office: Nortek Inc 50 Kennedy Plz Ste 1700 Providence RI 02903-2393 E-mail: donnelly@nortek-inc.com

DONNEM, ROLAND WILLIAM, lawyer, hotel owner, developer; b. Seattle, Nov. 8, 1929; s. William Roland and Mary Louise (Hughes) D.; m. Sarah Brandon Lund, Feb. 18, 1961; children: Elizabeth Donnem Sigety, Sarah Madison. BA, Yale U., 1952; JD magna cum laude, Harvard U., 1957. Bar: N.Y. 1958, U.S. Dist. Ct. (ea. and so. dists.) N.Y. 1959, U.S. Ct. Appeals (2d cir.) 1959, U.S. Ct. Claims 1960, U.S. Tax Ct. 1960, U.S. Supreme Ct. 1963, U.S. Ct. Appeals (3d cir.) 1969, D.C. 1970, U.S. Ct. Appeals (D.C. cir.) 1970, Ohio 1976, U.S. Dist. Ct. (no. dist.) Ohio 1980, U.S. Ct. Appeals (7th cir.) 1980, U.S. Ct. Appeals (6th cir.) 1984. With Davis Polk & Wardwell, N.Y.C., 1957-63, 64-69; law sec. appellate divsn. N.Y. Supreme Ct., 1963-64; dir. policy planning antitrust divsn. Justice Dept., Washington, 1969-71; v.p., sec., gen. counsel Standard Brands Inc., N.Y.C., 1971-76; from v.p. law to sr. v.p. law and casualty prevention Chessie System, Cleve., 1976-86; ptnr. Meta Ptnrs., real estate devel., 1984-89, mng. ptnr., 1989—, registered security rep., 1985-90; bd. dirs., gen. counsel Acorn Properties, Inc., Cleve., 1985—, pres., 1989—; bd. dirs., gen. counsel Meta Devel. Corp., 1985—, pres., 1989—; bd. dirs., gen. counsel Meta Properties, Inc., 1988—, pres., 1989—. Founding mem., bd. dirs. Assn. Sheraton Franchisees N.Am., 1997—. Mem. editl. bd. Harvard Law Rev., 1955-57. Bd. dirs., fin. v.p. Presbyn. Home for Aged Women, N.Y.C., 1972-76; bd. dirs., treas. James Lenox Ho., Inc., 1972-76; trustee Food and Drug Law Inst., 1974-76; trustee, sec. Brick Presbyn. Ch., N.Y.C., 1974-76; sec. class of 1952, Yale U., 1992-97; bd. dirs. Yale Alumni Fund, 1990-95; chmn. Cleve. Area Yale Campaign, 1991-97. Lt. (j.g.) USNR, 1952-54. Fellow Timothy Dwight Coll., Yale U., 1987—. Mem. D.C. Bar Assn., Greater Cleve. Bar Assn., Am. Law Inst. (life), Am. Arbitration Assn. (nat. panel arbitrators), Def. Orientation Conf. Assn. (bd. dirs. 1996-99), Yale U. Alumni Assn. Cleve. (treas. 1982-84, del. 1984-87, trustee 1984-93, adv. coun. 1993—), Yale U. Alumni Assn. (bd. govs. 1987-90), Union Club (N.Y.C. and Cleve.), Capitol Hill Club (Washington), Washington Chevy Chase Club, Cleve. Racquet Club, Kirtland Club (Cleve.), Met. Club (Washington), Phi Beta Kappa. Republican. Presbyterian. Home: 2945 Fontenay Rd Shaker Heights OH 44120-1726 Office: Four Points by Sheraton 3619 Park East Dr Ste 214 Beachwood OH 44122 E-mail: acornp@yahoo.com

DONNER, HENRY JAY, lawyer; b. Atlantic City, Sept. 1, 1944; s. Harry and Sylvia (Payes) D.; m. Katherine Weiner, Dec. 20, 1969; children: Benjamin James, Melissa Faith. BA, Am. U., 1966; JD, Villanova U., 1969. Bar: Pa. 1969, U.S. Dist. Ct. (ea. dist.) Pa. 1969, U.S. Ct. Appeals (3d cir.) 1983. Staff mem. U.S. Senator Joseph A. Clark, Washington, 1965-68; assoc. Dilworth, Paxson, Kalish and Levy, Phila., 1969-74; ptnr. Jacoby, Donner & Jacoby, 1974-82; sr. mem. Jacoby Donner, P.C., 1982—. Lectr. Nat. Home Builders Assn., Pa. State U., State Coll., 1989-90. Author: West Legal Forms: Specialized Forms, Vol. 27, Chpt. 8, Building Agreements. Mem. sch. com. Germantown Friends Sch., 1993—; bd. dirs. Germantown Jewish Ctr., 1989-91. Mem. ABA, Phila. Bar Assn. (exec. com. real property sect. 1987-96, chmn. constrn. law com., real property sect. 1986-89, chmn. real property sect. 1993, bd. govs. 1993), Constrn. Fin. Mgmt. Assn. (bd. dirs. Phila. chpt. 1990-95), Union League Phila., Germantown Cricket Club. Construction, Estate planning, Pension, profit-sharing, and employee benefits. Office: Jacoby Donner PC 1515 Market St Ste 2000 Philadelphia PA 19102-1920 E-mail: hdonner@jacobydonner.com

DONNER, TED A. lawyer; b. N.Y.C., Nov. 22, 1960; s. Robert A. and Barbara (Wood) D.; m. Leslie Lynn Wasserman, Sept. 16, 1990; children: Alexandra Sofia, Samuel Joseph. BA, Roosevelt U., 1987; JD, Loyola U., 1990. Bar: U.S. Dist. Ct. Ill. 1990. Assoc. Rock, Fusco, Reynolds & Garvey, Chgo., 1990-94; of counsel Altheimer & Gray, 1994-2000; ptnr. Bisdoff & Swabowski Ltd., 2000—. Instr. Loyola U. Chgo. Sch. Law, 1990-96, lectr., 1996—. Author: Attorney's Practice Guide to Negotiations, 2d edit., 1995-99, Jury Selection Strategy & Science, 3d edit., 2000, Jury Selection Handbook, 1999. Mem. ATLA, ABA, Am. Soc. Trial Consultants, Am. Soc. Legal Writers, Internat. Platform Assn., DuPage County Bar Assn., Chgo. Bar Assn., Alpha Sigma Nu. Antitrust, General civil litigation, Insurance. Office: Bischoff & Swabowski 311 S Wacker Dr #2600 Chicago IL 60606 E-mail: tdonner@bis-law.com

DONOHOE, JAMES DAY, lawyer; b. Rochester, N.Y., Aug. 10, 1943; s. James Vincent and Constance Traganza (Day) D.; m. Laurel Andrews, Aug. 8, 1987; children by previous marriage: J. Douglas, Cynthia. BS, Cornell U., 1965; JD, Cath. U. Am., 1969; MBA, Case Western Res. U., 1979. Bar: N.Y. 1970, Ohio 1974, Pa. 1988. Assoc. Pennie & Edmonds, N.Y.C., 1967-73; house counsel Republic Steel Corp., Cleve., 1973-84, LTV Corp., Dallas, 1984-89, Republic Engineered Steels Inc., Marsillon, Ohio, 1989-98; with Squire, Sanders & Dempsey, Cleve., 1998-99; ret., 1999—. Active YMCA. Mem. Cleve. Bar Assn., Ohio Bar Assn., N.Y. State Bar Assn. Contracts commercial, General corporate, Environmental. Home: 2627 List St NW Massillon OH 44646-2723

DONOHOE, JEROME FRANCIS, lawyer; b. Yankton, S.D., Mar. 17, 1939; s. Francis A. and Ruth D.; m. Elaine Bush, Jan. 27, 1968; 1 child, Nicole Elaine. BA, St. John's U., 1961; JD cum laude, U. Minn., 1964. Bar: Ill. 1964, S.D. 1964. Atty. Atchison, Topeka & Santa Fe Ry. Co., Chgo., 1967-73, gen. atty., 1973-78; gen. counsel corp. affairs Santa Fe Industries Inc., 1978-84; v.p. law Santa Fe Industries, Inc., 1984-90, Santa Fe Pacific Corp., Chgo., 1984-94; ptnr. Mayer, Brown & Platt, 1990-99, sr. counsel, 1999—. Bd. dirs. Better Govt. Assn., 1989—, Evanston Cmty. Found., 2000—; Capt. JAGC. U.S. Army, 1964-67. Fellow: Ill. Bar Found.; mem.: ABA (sect. chair, pub. utility, comm. and transp. law sect.), Northwestern U. Assocs., Chgo. Club, Chgo. Athletic Assn., Mich. Shores Club (Wilmette, Ill.). Administrative and regulatory, General corporate, Securities. Office: Mayer Brown & Platt 190 S La Salle St Ste 3100 Chicago IL 60603-3441 E-mail: jdonohoe@mayerbrown.com

DONOHUE, JOHN PATRICK, lawyer; b. N.Y.C., Sept. 16, 1944; s. Joseph Francis and Catherine Elizabeth (Feeney) D.; m. Patricia Ann Holly, June 11, 1977; children: Eileen Mary, Anne Catherine. B.A., Providence Coll., 1966; J.D., Catholic U. Am., 1969. Bar: N.Y. 1973, U.S. Ct. Appeals (2d cir.) 1973, U.S. Ct. Appeals (fed. cir.) 1974, N.J. 1975, U.S. Dist. Ct. N.J. 1975, U.S. Dist. Ct. (so., ea. dists.) N.Y. 1975, U.S. Supreme Ct. 1978, D.C. 1981, Pa. 1986. Spl. agt. FBI, Washington, 1969-71; assoc. Donohue & Donohue, N.Y.C., 1971-74, ptnr., 1974—. Adj. prof. law internat. bus. transactions Seton Hall U. Sch. Law, Newark, 1986-94. Author book sect. Customs Fraud Section on Business Crimes, 1982; co-author: The Prevention and Prosecution of Computer and High Technology Crime. Bd. dirs. Maritime Exch. Delaware River and Bay, 1989—; mem. bd. regents Cath. U. Am., 1990-2000, chmn., 1997-2000; trustee Rosemont (Pa.) Sch., 1995-2001, chmn., 1996-2001; mem. bd. visitors Cath. U. Sch. Law, 1998—. Named Man of Yr., Phila. Customs, Brokers and Forwarders Assn., 1984. Mem. Customs and Internat. Trade Bar Assn., Pa. State Bar Assn. Republican. Roman Catholic. Federal civil litigation, Immigration, naturalization, and customs, Private international. Office: Donohue & Donohue 232 S 4th St Philadelphia PA 19106-3704 E-mail: jdonohue@donohueanddonohue.com

DONOVAN, CHARLES STEPHEN, lawyer; b. Boston, Feb. 28, 1951; s. Alfred Michael and Maureen (Murphy) D.; m. Lisa Marie Dicharry, Apr. 21, 1979; children: Yvette, Martine, Neal. BA, Haverford Coll., 1974; JD, Cornell U., 1977. Bar: Mass. 1977, La. 1977, Calif. 1982, U.S. Supreme Ct. 1988. Atty. Phelps, Dunbar, Marks, Claverie & Sims, New Orleans, 1977-81, Dorr, Cooper & Hays, San Francisco, 1981-84, Walsh, Donovan & Keech LLP, San Francisco, 1984-2000, Schnader Harrison Segal & Lewis, LLP, San Francisco, 2000—. Instr. maritime law Calif. Maritime Acad., Vallejo, 1982—; spl. advisor U.S. State Dept., 1993-96. Contbr. numerous articles to profl. jours. Recipient Gustavus H. Robinson prize Cornell Law Sch., 1977. Mem. ABA (chmn. admiralty and maritime law com. Chgo. 1989-90), Internat. Bar Assn., Maritime Law Assn. U.S. (chmn. com. on maritime criminal law 1998—, chmn. subcom. on maritime liens and mortgages 1994—), Tulane Admiralty Inst. (permanent adv. bd.), Marine Exch. (bd. dirs. San Francisco Bay region 1993-96). Avocations: skiing, hiking, mandolin, guitar, sailing. Admiralty, General civil litigation, Private international. Office: Schnader Harrison Segal & Lewis LLP Ste 1200 601 California St San Francisco CA 94108-2817 E-mail: cdonovan@schnader.com

DONOVAN, DENNIS FRANCIS, lawyer; b. Duluth, Minn., Jan. 29, 1925; s. Dennis Francis and Gertrude (Flaherty) D.; m. Lila Lindeman Munyon, Aug. 12, 1950; children: Kathleen Donovan Walsh, Theresa Donovan Brown, Dorothy Donovan; m. Marie Kendrick, Oct. 9, 1983. B.A., U. Minn., 1948, 1952, J.D., 1952. Bar: Minn. 1952, Calif. 1962. Ptnr. McCabe, VanEvera, et al, Duluth, 1952-61; assoc. U.S. atty. U.S. Dept. Justice, Los Angeles, 1961-64; assoc. Gendel, Raskoff, et al, Los Angeles, 1964-67; ptnr. Donovan & Somers, Los Angeles, 1967-82; v.p., sr. counsel Union Bank, Los Angeles, 1982; v.p., asst. gen. counsel Mitsui Mfrs. Bank, Los Angeles, 1983—; judge pro-tem Los Angeles Mcpl. Court, 1972-84; mem. exec. com. trial lawyer's sect. Los Angeles County Bar, 1977-80; dir. Legal Aid Soc., Duluth, 1957-59. Editor, contbr. to legal jours. Bd. dirs. Duluth Jr. C. of C., 1958, Duluth Playhouse, 1958; chmn. Duluth Port Authority Com., 1959. Served with USN, 1944-46, PTO. Mem. ABA, Los Angeles County Bar Assn. (exec. com. 1977-80), State Bar of Calif. (conf. of dels. 1977-78), U. Minn. Alumni Assn. (chmn. Los Angeles chpt. 1970). Club: Los Angeles Athletic. Home: 4047 Pala Mesa Oaks Dr Fallbrook CA 92028-8939 Office: 840 Union Bank Towers Torrance CA 90503

DOOLEY, JOHN AUGUSTINE, III, state supreme court justice; b. Nashua, N.H., Apr. 10, 1944; s. John A. and Edna Elizabeth (Elwell) D.; m. Sandra C. Sapp, Dec. 19, 1970 BS, Union Coll., 1965; LLB, Boston Coll., 1968. Bar: Vt. 1968. Law clk. to presiding judge U.S. Dist. Ct. Vt., 1968-69; asst. dir. Vt. Legal Aid, 1969-72, dir., 1972-78; legal counsel to gov. of Vt., 1985; sec. of adminstrn. State of Vt., 1985-87; assoc. justice Vt. Supreme Ct., 1987—. Part-time U.S. magistrate for Vt., from 1971. Co-author: Cases and Materials on Urban Poverty Law, 1974. Mem. Vt. Bar Assn. Office: Vt Supreme Ct 109 State St Montpelier VT 05609-0001*

DOPF, GLENN WILLIAM, lawyer; b. N.Y.C., June 6, 1953; s. William Bernard and Doris Virginia (Roxby) D. BS cum laude, Fordham Coll., 1975; JD, Fordham U., 1979; LLM, NYU, 1983. Bar: N.J. 1979, U.S. Dist. Ct. N.J. 1979, N.Y. 1980, U.S. Dist. Ct. (so. and ea. dists.) N.Y. 1980, U.S. Ct. Appeals (2d cir.) 1980, U.S. Ct. Internat. Trade 1981, U.S. Supreme Ct. 1983. Assoc. Martin, Clearwater & Bell, N.Y.C., 1980-81; ptnr. Kopff, Nardelli & Dopf, 1982—. Mem. ABA, Assn. Bar City N.Y. Federal civil litigation, State civil litigation, Insurance. Office: Kopff Nardelli & Dopf 440 9th Ave Fl 15 New York NY 10001-1688

DORADO, MARIANNE GAERTNER, lawyer; d. Wolfgang Wilhelm and Marianne L. Gaertner; m. Richard Manuel Dorado, Oct. 1, 1982; children: Marianne Christine, Kathleen Gina. BA, Yale U., 1978; JD, U. Mich., 1981. Bar: N.Y. 1982, U.S. Supreme Ct. 1993. Ptnr. The Dorado Law Group, N.Y.C., 1998—. Bd. dirs. Blue Heron Theater, N.Y.C. Contbr. articles to profl. jours. Extern office legal advisor U.S. Dept. State, Washington, 1980. Republican. Roman Catholic. General corporate, Mergers and acquisitions, Securities. Office: The Dorado Law Group Ste 1459 1180 Ave of Americas New York NY 10036 E-mail: mdorado@doradolaw.com

DORAN, KENNETH JOHN, lawyer; b. Janesville, Wis., Feb. 10, 1950; s. Henry James and Alice Elizabeth (Fanning) D.; m. Dianne Marie Carlson, Feb. 28, 1987; children: Taylor, Olivia. BA, U. Wis., 1974, JD, 1977. Atty. The Legal Clinic, Madison, Wis., 1978-79, Doran Law Offices, Madison, 1980-84, Smoler & Albert, S.C., Madison, 1984-88, Kassner Law Offices, Middleton, Wis., 1988-92, Doran Law Offices, 1993—. Author: Personal Bankruptcy and Debt Adjustment, 1991, 2d edit., 1996. Bd. dirs. Wis. Madison chpt. Civil Liberties Union, Wis., 1983-85. Mem. Dane County Bar Assn., Western Dist. Wis. Bankrutpcy Bar Assn. (pres. 2000-01). Democrat. Bankruptcy, General civil litigation, Consumer commercial. Home: 2101 Fox Ave Madison WI 53711-1920 E-mail: kendoran@execpc.com

DORAN, WILLIAM MICHAEL, lawyer; b. Albany, N.Y., May 26, 1940; s. James R. and Lorene Tinsley (Nees) D.; m. Susan Coryell Lloyd; children: Melissa, Heather, Leigh. BS in Journalism, Northwestern U., 1962; LLB, U. Pa., 1966. Assoc. Morgan, Lewis & Bockius, Phila., 1967-76, ptnr., 1976—. Dir. SEI Investments Co.; trustee SEI Liquid Asset Trust, SEI Daily Income Trust, SEI Tax Exempt Trust, SEI Instl. Managed Trust, SEI Index Funds, SEI Internat. Trust, The Advisors Inner Cir. Fund, The Arbor Fund, Inventor Funds, Incs.; chmns. adv. coun. Eisenhower Exchange Fellowships, Phila. Vice chmn. World Affairs Coun. Phila. Mem. ABA, Pa. Bar Assn., Phila. Bar Assn. General corporate, Finance, Private international. Home: 27 Druim Moir Ln Philadelphia PA 19118-4134 Office: Morgan Lewis & Bockius LLP 1701 Market St Philadelphia PA 19103-2903 E-mail: wdoran@morganlewis.com

DORE, FRANCIS CHRISTIAN MICHEL, lawyer, educator; b. Paris, France, May 4, 1933; s. Joseph and Madeline (Le Norcy) D.; m. Rashmi Sodhi, Jul. 25, 1973 (div.). Diplome de l'Institut d'etudes politiques de Paris, Sciences-Po, France; PhD in Political Sci., U. de Paris, France; Doctorate in Law, Faculte de droit de Paris, France. Prof. of Law South-East Asia, 1963-65; asst. to pres., French parliament Nat. Assembly, Paris, France, 1974-78; prof. U. Paris XII Sch. of Law, France, 1974; ambassador of France Seychelles, 1979-81; commissioner New Delhi, 1988-90; dir. mission Indian Ocean Countries French Ministry for Foreign Affairs, Paris, France, 1996-97; lawyer, 2001. Conseiller culturel, scientifique et de cooperation technique, French Embassy, New Delhi India, 1965-74; hon. prof. Nehru U., 1972. Author: Le Departement, 1963, Les Monarchies indoechinoises, 1967, La Republique indienne, 1970, Les regimes politiques en Asie, 1974, L'Inde d'aujourd'hui, 1974, La vie indienne, 1978, L'Europe retrouvee, 1978, L'Inde du Nord et le Nepal, 1979, L'Inde, l'hindouisme et l'egalite, 1990, contbr. articles to profl. jours. Nat. Sec., Republicans Independants, Paris, France (incl. Monaco), 1976-77; mem. mayor's office (Conseiller Municipal), Dampsmesnil, (Eure), France (incl. Monaco), 1995. Mem. Pen Club, Rotary Club of Paris, Master, Tagore Comm. Home and Office: 6 square du Croisic Paris 75015 France

DOREMUS, OGDEN, lawyer; b. Atlanta, Apr. 23, 1921; s. C. Estes and Mary (McAdory) D.; m. Carolyn Wooten Greene, Aug. 30, 1947 (dec. Aug. 1989); children: Celia Jane, Frank O., Dale Marie Doremus; m. Linda Parker, Dec. 4, 1992. BA, Emory U., 1946, JD, 1949. Bar: Ga. 1947; cert. U.S. postal mediator, 1999. Asst. solicitor gen., Atlanta, 1947-49; ptnr. firm Smith Field Doremus & Ringel, 1949-60, Falligant, Doremus and Karsman, Savannah, Ga., 1960-72, Doremus, Jones & Smith, P.C., Metter, 1972-94; of counsel Karsman, Brooks & Callaway, 1994—. Prof. Woodrow Wilson Sch. Law, Atlanta, 1948-50; judge State Ct. Candler County, Ga., 1985—, chair uniform rules com. Coun. State Cts., 1990—; pres. Ga. Coun. State Ct. Judges, 1990-91, chair legis. com., 1997-99; mem. Jud. Coun. State of Ga., 1989-91, Unified Trial Ct. Commn., 1997; mem. ct. futures com. State Bar Ga., 1996—; bd. dirs. Ctr. for Law in the Pub. Interest, 1996—; judge Mcpl. Ct., Metter, Ga., 1997—; mem. commn. on judiciary Supreme Ct. Ga., 1999—. Mem. editorial adv. bd. Environ. Law, Reporter, 1969-80. Scoutmaster Boy Scouts Am., Atlanta, 1951-60, commn., 1961-70; chmn. Ga. Day and Savannah Arts Festival, 1968-72; mem. Atlanta City Coun., 1950-53; mem. Savannah Govtl. Reorgn. Commn., 1960-61, Ga. Ct. Futures Commn., 1991-93, 97—; adv. com. Nat. Coastal Zone Mgmt. Coun., 1978-86; trustee Ga. Conservancy; bd. dirs. Legal Environ. Assistance Found., 1983-86, Ga. Hazardous Waste Authority, 1989—, Chatham Environ. Forum, 1990-93; mem. strategic planning com. Coun. State Cts. Ga., 1996—; bd. dirs. Coastal Environ. Orgn. Ga., 1998—. Served with USAAC, 1942-46, ETO. Named Young Man of Yr. Atlanta, 1951; recipient Thomas H. gignilliat award Cultural Progress of Savannah, 1969, Tradition of Excellence award Ga. State Bar, 1988, 1st Ann. Coun. of State Cts. award named Ogden Doremus in his honor, 1993. Mem.: ABA (chmn. environ law com., gen. practice 1976—77), State Bar Ga. (chmn. ins. law sect. 1963—67, chmn. ins. law sect. 1977—83, cert. mediator Ga. commn. on dispute resolution, mediator for U.S. Postal Svc. 1999—), Savannah Bar Assn., Atlanta Soc., Ga. Inst. Trial Advocacy (chmn. 1984—89), Izaak Walton League (founder Ga. chpt. 1950), Sierra Club (exec. com. Chattahoochee chpt. 1965—75, chair legal com. Ga. chpt. 1997—, Lifetime Achievement Ga. environ. coun. Citizenship award 1997, 1999, Conservation Leadership award Ga. chpt. 1999, Common Cause Citizenship award 1998), Chatham Club, Chatham Tennis Club, Willow Lake Country Club. Alternative dispute resolution, General civil litigation, Environmental. Home: RR 2 Box 188A Metter GA 30439-9570 Office: Doremus and Assocs Courthouse Sq PO Box 702 Metter GA 30439-0702 E-mail: odoremus@excite.com

DORF, ROBERT CLAY, lawyer, broadcaster; b. N.Y.C., Apr. 4, 1943; s. Irving and Jeanne (Hayflick) D.; m. Wendy Rappaport, Nov. 27, 1968; children— Andrew R., Jessica L. B.A. in History, U. Fla., 1964; student Alliance Francise, Paris, 1967; J.D., Bklyn. Law Sch., 1972. Bar: N.Y. 1973, U.S. Dist. Ct. (ea. and so. dists.) N.Y. 1974, U.S. Ct. Appeals (2d cir.) 1980. Announcer Sta. WIVI, V.I., 1964-65; office clk. Reuters News Service, Paris, 1967; film editor sta. WMAL-TV, Washington, 1968; asst. dist. atty. Bronx Dist. Atty.'s Office, 1972-76; practice law, N.Y.C., 1976-94; ptnr. law firm Dorf & Perlmutter, N.Y.C., 1984-94; prin. law clk. to Hon. James G. Starkey, Supreme Ct. State of N.Y., Kings County, 1995—; arbitrator U.S. Dist. Ct. (ea. dist.) N.Y., 1990-94; hearing officer Environ. Control Bd., N.Y.C., 1976-77; arbitrator N.Y. County Civil Ct., N.Y.C., 1981— ; adj. prof. geog. law hunter Coll./CUNY, 1997. Methadone counselor Beth Israel Hosp., 1969. Served with U.S. Army, 1965-67. Mem. Bklyn. Bar Assn. Democrat. Jewish. Criminal, Intellectual property, Personal injury. Home: 101 Clark St Brooklyn NY 11201-2746

DORFMAN, JOHN CHARLES, lawyer; b. Wilkinsburg, Pa., Feb. 3, 1925; s. Leo O. Dorfman; m. Ruth B. Davison; children: Beverly (Dorfman) Lenci, Laura, Carolyn, Bradley. BEE, Yale U., 1945; JD, Cornell U., 1949. Bar: N.Y. 1949, Conn. 1950, Pa., 1956, U.S. Dist. Ct. (ea. dist.) Pa. 1957, U.S. Ct. Appeals (fed. cir.) 1982, U.S. Supreme Ct. 1959, U.S. Patent & Trademark Office 1949. Patent counsel Machlett Labs. Inc., Springdale, Conn., 1950-54; assoc. Pennie & Edmonds, N.Y.C., 1949-55, Howson & Howson, Phila., 1955-59, ptnr., 1960-73; ptnr., chmn. Dann, Dorfman, Herrell & Skillman, 1974—. Elder Wayne Presbyn. Ch. Served to lt. (j.g.) USNR, 1943-46. Mem. ABA (chmn. sect. patent, trademark and copyright law 1984-85, hon. mem. coun.), Nat. Coun. Patent Law Assn. (chmn. 1978-79), Am. Intellectual Property Law Assn. (bd. dirs. 1973-76), Phila. Patent Law Assn. (pres. 1974-76), Nat. Inventors Hall of Fame Found. (pres. 1977-78, bd. dirs. 1979-99, hon. mem. coun., mem. joint bd. NIHF and Inventure Place 1979-2000), Union League Club (Phila.), St. David's Golf Club (Wayne, Pa.), Yale Club of Phila. (pres. 1980-81), Tau Beta Pi, Delta Tau Delta (bd. Cornell U. house corp. 1969—). Republican. Avocations: skiing, golf, travel. Patent, Trademark and copyright, Trade regulation, unfair competition. Home: 215 Midland Ave Wayne PA 19087-4108 Office: Dann Dorfman Herrell & Skillman 1601 Market St Ste 720 Philadelphia PA 19103-2307 E-mail: jdorfman@ddhs.com

DORIS, ALAN S(ANFORD), lawyer; b. Cleve., June 18, 1947; s. Sam E. and Rebecca (Sunshine) D.; m. Nancy Rose Spitzer, Jan. 10, 1976; children: Matthew, Lisa. AB and BS in Bus. cum laude, Miami U., Oxford U., 1969; JD cum laude, Harvard U., 1972. Bar: Ohio 1972, U.S. Dist. Ct. (no. dist.) Ohio 1972, U.S. Tax Ct. 1972, U.S. Ct. Appeals (6th cir.) 1972. Assoc. Stotter, Familo, Cavitch, Elden & Durkin, Cleve., 1972-77; ptnr. Elden & Ford, 1978-79, Benesch, Friedlander, Coplan & Aronoff, Cleve., 1980-2000, Squire, Sanders & Dempsey, 2000—. Editor: Ohio Transaction Guide. Treas. Hawthorne Valley Country Club, Cleve., 1984-85; chmn. Cleve. Tax Inst., 1994. Mem. ABA (chmn. capital recovery com. taxation sect. 1994-96). Avocation: golf. Corporate taxation, Taxation, general, Personal income taxation. Office: Squire Sanders & Dempsey LLP 4900 Key Tower Cleveland OH 44114*

DORN, TRILBY C. E. lawyer; b. Spokane, Wash., Aug. 20, 1970; d. Charles Stuart Dorn and Karen Dorn-Steele; m. Raymond Brent Walton, Aug. 8, 1996. BA with honors, Swarthmore Coll., 1992; JD cum laude, Tulane U., 1997. Bar: Wash. 1997, U.S. Dist. Ct. (we. dist.) Wash. 1997. Ea. Wash. field dir. Wash. Dem. Party Coordinated Campaign, Spokane, 1992, Wash. Environ. Coun., Spokane, 1992-94; law clk. Fed. Pub. Defender of Western Wash., Seattle, 1995, Wash. Environ. Coun., Seattle, 1995, Graham & James/Riddell Williams, Seattle, 1996, atty., 1997—. Mem. adv. bd. Tulane Environ. Law Jour., 1998-99, editor-in-chief, 1997. Ea. Wash. field organizer Clinton Campaign, Spokane, 1992; coop. atty. ACLU, Seattle, 1998—, mem., 1998-99; vol. N.W. Immigrants' Rights Project, Seattle, 1998—. Mem. Wash. Bar Assn., King County Bar Assn., King County Wash. Women Lawyers (bd. dirs. 1998-2000). Democrat. Avocations: reading, travel, hiking, dogs, cooking. General civil litigation, Environmental. Home: 4096 Lyttle Rd NE Bainbridge Island WA 98110 Office: Graham & James/Riddell Williams Ste 4500 1001 4th Ave Seattle WA 98154

DORNAN, DONALD C., JR. lawyer; b. Columbus, Miss., Oct. 26, 1952; s. Donald C. and Virginia (Shelley) D.; m. Jennieann Abel, Apr. 27, 1974; children: Gloria Diana, Donald Patrick. BA, Miss. State U., 1974; JD, U. Miss., 1976. Diplomate Nat. Coll. Trial Advocacy. Bar: Miss. 1977, U.S. Dist. Ct. (no. and so. dists.) Miss. 1977, U.S. Ct. Appeals (5th and 11th cirs.) 1981, cert. Civil Trial Advocate Nat. Bd. of Trial Advocacy. Atty. Page, Mannino & Peresich, Biloxi, Miss., 1976-80; ptnr. Denton, Persons,

Dornan & Bilbo, Biloxi, 1980-87; sole practice Biloxi, 1987—; asst. city prosecutor City of Biloxi, 1977-80, city judge pro tem, 1982—; bd. dirs. Gulf Law Inst., 1981—. Mem. ABA, Fed. Bar Assn., Miss. Bar Assn. (bd. dirs. young lawyers sect. 1985-86, pres. elect 2001-), Harrison County Bar Assn., Harrison County Young Lawyers (treas. 1980-81, v.p. 1981-82, pres. 1982-83), Miss. Trial Lawyers Assn., Assn. Trial Lawyers Am., Am. Judicature Soc., Southeastern Admiralty Law Inst., Phi Delta Phi. Methodist. General civil litigation, Insurance, Personal injury. Office: PO Box 154 771 Water St Biloxi MS 39530-4219*

DORNBUSCH, ARTHUR A., II, lawyer; b. Peru, Ill., Nov. 8, 1943; s. Arthur A. Sr. and Genevieve C. (Knudtson) D.; children: Kimberly, Brendan, Courtney, Eric; m. Jacqueline Bahrs Montanus, Feb. 10, 1996. BA, Yale U., 1966; LLB, U. Pa., 1969. Bar: N.Y. 1970, U.S. Ct. Appeals. (2d cir.) 1971, U.S. Dist. Ct. (so. and ea. dists.) N.Y. 1971. Assoc. Dewey, Ballantine, Bushby, Palmer & Wood, N.Y.C., 1969-72; asst. gen. counsel Boise Cascade Corp., 1972-75; asst. gen counsel Teleprompter Corp., 1975-76; asst. gen. counsel Engelhard Industries div. Engelhard Minerals and Chem. Corp., Edison, N.J., 1976-80; v.p., gen. counsel Minerals and Chems. divsn. Engelhard Corp., 1980-84, v.p., gen. counsel, sec. Iselin, N.J., 1984—. Mem. Pelham (N.Y.) Union Free Sch. Bd., 1979-82. Mem. ABA, N.Y. State Bar Assn., Assn. Bar City N.Y., Am. Corp. Counsel Assn., Am. Intellectual Property Law Assn., Am. Soc. Corp. Secs., Mfrs. Alliance for Productivity and Innovation. Antitrust, General corporate, Patent. Office: Engelhard Corp PO Box 770 101 Wood Ave S Iselin NJ 08830-0770 E-mail: arthur.dornbusch@engelhard.com

DORNE, DAVID J. lawyer; b. Chgo., Dec. 9, 1946; BS magna cum laude, U. Ill., 1969; MSc, London Sch. Econs., 1970; JD cum laude, Boston U., 1973. Bar: N.Y. 1973, U.S. Ct. Appeals (2d cir.) 1973, U.S. Tax Ct. 1973, U.S. Dist. Ct. (so. dist.) N.Y. 1975, Calif. 1978. Mem. Seltzer Caplan McMahon Vitek P.C., San Diego. Mem. City of San Diego Charter Rev. Commn., 1989—. Mem. ABA (taxation sect., corp., banking and bus. law sect.), State Bar Calif. (taxation sect., real property law sect., chmn. personal income tax subcom. 1982-84), San Diego County Bar Assn., Assn. of Bar of City of N.Y. (taxation sect.), Beta Gamma Sigma. General corporate, Real property, Taxation, general. Office: Seltzer Caplan McMahon Vitek PC 2100 Symphony Tower 750 B St San Diego CA 92101-8114

DORNETTE, W(ILLIAM) STUART, lawyer, educator; b. Washington, Mar. 2, 1951; s. William Henry Lueders and Frances Roberta (Hester) D.; m. Martha Louise Mehl, Nov. 19, 1983; children: Marjorie Frances, Anna Christine, David Paul. AB, Williams Coll., 1972; JD, U. Va., 1975. Bar: Va. 1975, Ohio 1975, U.S. Dist. Ct. (so. dist.) Ohio 1975, D.C. 1976, U.S. Ct. Appeals (6th cir.) 1977, U.S. Supreme Ct. 1980. Assoc. Taft, Stettinius & Hollister, Cin., 1975-83, ptnr., 1983—. Instr. law U. Cin., 1980-87, adj. prof., 1988-91. Co-author: Federal Judiciary Almanac, 1984-87. Mem. Ohio Bd. Bar Examiners, 1991-93, Hamilton County Rep. Exec. Com., 1982—; bd. dirs. Zool. Soc. Cin., 1983-94, Cin. Parks Found., 1995—. Mem. FBA, Ohio State Bar Assn., Cin. Bar Assn., Am. Phys. Soc. Methodist. Federal civil litigation, State civil litigation, Sports. Home: 329 Bishopsbridge Dr Cincinnati OH 45255-3948 Office: 1800 Firstar Tower 425 Walnut St Cincinnati OH 45202-3923 E-mail: dornette@taftlaw.com

DORNFELD, SHARON WICKS, lawyer; b. Detroit, Jan. 22, 1952; d. John Hoddard and Mary Catherine (Hogan) Wicks; m. William Harlan Dornfeld, Dec. 30, 1977; 2 children. BA, U. Mich., 1974, JD, 1981. Bar: Conn. 1982; U.S. Dist. Ct. Conn. 1983, U.S. Supreme Ct. 1996. Pvt. practice, Danbury, Conn., 1988—. Bd. dirs. A Better Chance in Ridgefield, Conn., 1985-91; parking violations hearing officer Town of Ridgefield, 1988—; mem. Office of Child Advocate Adv. Com., 1996-2000. Mem. ABA, Nat. Assn. Counsel Children, Conn. Bar Assn., Danbury Bar Assn. (pres. 1995). Democrat. Christian Scientist. General civil litigation, Family and matrimonial, Juvenile. Office: 70 North St Danbury CT 06810

DOROCKE, LAWRENCE FRANCIS, lawyer; b. Chgo., Oct. 4, 1946; s. Walter P. and Effie M. (Gillis) D.; m. Diane L. Roberts, June 22, 1968; children: Todd D., Rob L., Jill A. BS in Econs., Purdue U., 1968, MS in Indsl. Relations, 1970; JD magna cum laude, Ind. U., 1973. Bar: Ind. 1973, U.S. Dist. Ct. (so. dist.) Ind. 1973, Iowa 1974, U.S. Ct. Appeals (7th cir.). Asst. mgr. personnel Comml. Solvents Corp., Terre Haute, Ind., 1970-71; law clk. to chief justice U.S. Dist. Ct. (so. dist.) Iowa, Des Moines, 1973-75; ptnr. Dann, Pecar, Newman & Kleiman P.C., Indpls., 1975—. Mem. ABA, Ind. Bar Assn., Indpls. Bar Assn. Roman Catholic. General corporate, Landlord-tenant, Real property. Home: 308 W Haydn Dr Ste 1316 Carmel IN 46032-7047 Office: Dann Pecar Newman & Kleiman PO Box 82008 Indianapolis IN 46282-2008 E-mail: ldorocke@dannpecar.com

DORR, ROBERT CHARLES, lawyer; b. Denver, Jan. 7, 1946; s. Owen and Rose Esther (Tudek) D.; m. Sandra Leah Gehlsen, Feb. 26, 1972; children: Bryan, Aric. BSEE, Milw. Sch. Engring., 1968; MSEE, Northwestern U., 1970; JD, U. Denver, 1975. Bar: Colo. 1975, U.S. Dist. Ct. Colo. 1975, U.S. Patent Office 1975. Mem. tech. staff Bell Labs, Naperville, Ill., 1968-72, mem. patent staff Denver, 1975-76; ptnr. Dorr, Carson, Sloan & Birney, P.C., 1976-86, sr. ptnr., 1986—. Ptnr. Internat. Practicum Inst., Denver, 1979—; seminar speaker various profl. orgns. Co-author: Protecting Trade Secrets, Patents and Copyrights, 1995, 3d edit., 2000, Protecting Trade Dress, 1992, 2d edit., 1999; contbr. articles to profl. jours. Active Citizens Com. for Retention of Judges, Denver, 1984. Milw. Sch. Engring. scholar, 1964-68; named Outstanding Young Man Am., 1976. Mem. ABA, Colo. Bar Assn. (pres. patent, trademark, copyright sect.), Douglas-Elbert County Bar Assn. (pres. 1983), IEEE, AAAS, Sigma Xi. Roman Catholic. Computer, Patent, Trademark and copyright. Home: 6101 Muddy Creek Rd Pueblo CO 81004-9747 Office: Dorr Carson Sloan & Birney PC 3010 E 6th Ave Denver CO 80206-4328

DORSEN, DAVID M(ILTON), lawyer; b. N.Y.C., Oct. 10, 1935; s. Arthur and Tanya (Stone) D.; m. Harriet S. Stern, Mar. 5, 1969 (div. Feb. 1976); m. Kenna D. Peusner, Jan. 24, 1997. AB, Harvard U., 1956, JD, 1959. Bar: N.Y. 1960, D.C. 1960, U.S. Supreme Ct. 1977. Assoc. Kaye, Scholer, Fierman, Hays & Handler, N.Y.C., 1960-64; asst. U.S. atty. U.S. Dist. Ct. (so. dist.) N.Y., 1964-69; dep. commr. and 1st dep. commr. N.Y.C. Dept. Investigation, 1969-73; asst. chief counsel Senate Watergate Com., Washington, 1973-74; ptnr. Sachs, Greenebaum & Tayler, 1974-91; of counsel Hughes Hubbard & Reed, 1991-94; pvt. practice, 1994-98; of counsel Wallace King Marraro & Branson PLLC, 1998—. Vis. lectr. pub. policy studies Terry Sanford Inst. Pub. Policy, Duke U., Durham, N.C., 1995—; adj. prof. Georgetown U. Law Ctr., Washington, 2000—. Contbg. editor, wine and food editor The Washingtonian Mag., 1982—; assoc. prodr. Tolstoy, 1996; columnist The Hill, Washington, 1998-2000. Mem. D.C. Bar Assn. (chmn. arbitration bd. 1982-84), Internat. Club of Washington (chief counsel 1981-89). Home: 3501 Davis St NW Washington DC 20007-1426

DORSEN, NORMAN, lawyer, educator; b. N.Y.C., Sept. 4, 1930; s. Arthur and Tanya (Stone) D.; m. Harriette Koffler, Nov. 25, 1965; children: Jennifer, Caroline Gail, Anne. BA, Columbia U., 1950; LLB magna cum laude, Harvard U., 1953; postgrad., London Sch. Econs., 1955-56; LLD (hon.), Ripon Coll., 1981, John Jay Coll. Criminal Justice, 1992. Bar: D.C. 1953, N.Y. 1954. Law clk. to chief judge Calvert Magruder U.S. Ct. Appeals, Boston, 1956-57; law clk. to Justice John Marshall Harlan U.S. Supreme Ct., Washington, 1957-58; assoc. Dewey, Ballantine, Bushby, Palmer & Wood, N.Y.C., 1958-60; prof. law NYU Sch. Law, 1961-81, Stokes prof., 1981—, dir. Hays civil liberties program, 1961—, dir. global law sch. program, 1994-96, chmn., 1996—. Vis. prof. law London Sch. Econs., 1968, U. Calif., Berkeley, 1974-75, Harvard U., 1980, 83, 84; cons. U.S. Commn. on Violence, 1968-69, Random House, 1969-73, B.B.C., 1969-73, U.S. Commn. on Social Security, 1979-80, Native Am. Rights Fund, 1978-89; exec. dir. spl. com. on courtroom conduct Assn. Bar N.Y.C., 1970-73; chmn. Com. for Pub. Justice, 1972-74; vice chmn. HEW sec.'s rev. panel on new drug regulation, 1975-76, chmn., 1976-77; mem. N.Y.C. Commn. on Status of Women, 1978-80; chmn. Sec. of Treasury's Citizen Rev. Panel on Good O' Boy Round-up, 1995-96. Author (with others): Political and Civil Rights in U.S., 3rd edit., 1967, Political and Civil Rights in U.S., 4th edit., Vol. I, 1976, Political and Civil Rights in U.S., 4th edit., Vol. II, 1979, Frontiers of Civil Liberties, 1968, Discrimination and Civil Rights, 1969; author: (with L. Friedman) Disorder in the Court, 1973; author: (with S. Gillers) Regulation of Lawyers, 1985, Regulation of Lawyers, 2d edit., 1989; editor: The Rights of Americans, 1971; editor: (with S. Gillers) None of Your Business, 1974; editor: Our Endangered Rights, 1984, The Evolving Constitution, 1987; editor: (with others) Human Rights in Northern Ireland, 1991, The Unpredictable Constitution, 2001; author, editor(with P. Gifford): Democracy and the Rule of Law, 2001. 1st lt. JAGC, U.S. Army, 1953-55. Recipient medal French Minister of Justice, 1983, Eleanor Roosevelt Human Rights award 2000; Fulbright Disting. Prof., Argentina, 1987, 88. Fellow Am. Acad. Arts and Scis.; mem. ABA (chmn. com. free speech and press 1968-70), ACLU (gen. counsel 1969-76, pres. 1976-91), Am. Law Inst., Coun. on Fgn. Rels., Lawyers Com. Human Rights (chmn. bd. dirs. 1995-2000), Lawyer Com. Civil Rights, Internat. Assn. Constnl. Law (exec. com.), U.S. Assn. Constnl. Law (pres. 1996—), Soc. Am. Law Tchrs. (pres. 1972-74, Tchg. award 1997, Eleanor Roosevelt Human Rights award, 2000), Thomas Jefferson Ctr. for Free Expression (trustee). Home: 146 Central Park W New York NY 10023-2005 Office: NYU Sch Law 40 Washington Sq S New York NY 10012-1005 E-mail: norman.dorsen@nyu.edu

DORSEY, PETER COLLINS, federal judge; b. New London, Conn., Mar. 24, 1931; s. Thomas F., Jr. and Helen Mary (Collins) D.; m. Cornelia McEwen, June 26, 1954; children: Karen G., Peter C., Jennifer S., Christopher M. B.A., Yale U., 1953; J.D., Harvard U., 1959. Ptnr. Flanagan, Dorsey & Flanagan, New Haven, 1963-74; U.S. atty. Dept. Justice, 1974-77; ptnr. Flanagan, Dorsey & Mulvey, 1977-83; judge U.S. Dist. Ct. Conn., 1983-99, chief judge, 1994-98, now sr. judge. Mem. Jud. Conf. of U.S. Cts., 1995-98; adj. prof. Quinnipiac Coll. Sch. Law, 1999—. Councilman Town of Hamden, Conn., 1961-69; town atty., 1973-74; commr. Bd. of Police, Hamden, 1977-81. Served to lt. comdr., USNR, 1953-56 Fellow Am. Coll. Trial Lawyers; mem. ABA (mem. house of dels. 1974-78), Conn. Bar Assn. (bd. govs. 1968-70, 74-78, pres. 1978), Am. Coll. Trial Lawyers Assn., Conn. Def. Lawyers Assn. (pres. 1974), Am. Inns of Ct. Hartford (pres. 1991-93). Roman Catholic Office: US Dist Ct 141 Church St New Haven CT 06510-2030

DORWART, DONALD BRUCE, lawyer; b. Zanesville, Ohio, Dec. 12, 1949; s. Walter G. and Katherine (Kachmar) D.; children: Claire Lauren, Hillary Beth. BA, Vanderbilt U., 1971; JD, Washington U., St. Louis, 1974. Bar: Mo. 1974, U.S. Dist. Ct. (ea. dist.) Mo. 1974. Assoc. Thompson Coburn LLP, St. Louis, 1974-79, ptnr., 1980—; dir. New Energy Corp. Ind., 1992-95. Contbr. articles to profl. jours. Mem.: ABA, Maritime Law Assn. U.S. (proctor, mem. maritime fin. com. 1980—), Bar Assn. Met. St. Louis (chair securities regulation com. 1979), Focus St. Louis (mem. selection com. 1990—91, mem. fin. com. 1990—, chmn. 2001—, mem. cmty. police com. 2000—, bd. dirs. 2000—, treas. 2001—), Noonday Club. Admiralty, General corporate, Mergers and acquisitions. Office: Thompson Coburn LLP Firstar Plz Ste 3300 Saint Louis MO 63101-1643 E-mail: ddorwart@thompsoncoburn.com

DOSS, MARION KENNETH, lawyer; b. Wildwood, Fla., Sept. 25, 1939; s. Marion D. and Clide (Maxwell) D.; m. Addren Taylor, July 8, 1977; children— M. Kenneth Jr., Lisa Marie. B.S., Ga. Inst. Tech., 1961; LL.B., U. Ga., 1963. Bar: Ga. 1965, N.C. 1979, U.S. Dist. Ct. (no. dist.) Ga. 1977, U.S. Ct. Apls. (5th cir.) 1976, U.S. Sup. Ct. 1978. Ptnr., Northcutt, Edwards & Doss, Atlanta, 1963-71; v.p., gen. counsel Roy D. Warren, Atlanta, 1971-73; ptnr. Doss & Sturgeon, Atlanta, 1973-75; atty. Rollins, Inc., Atlanta, 1975-78; assoc. gen. counsel, asst. sec. Fieldcrest Mills, Inc., Eden, N.C., 1978-86; gen. counsel, sec., 1986—. Past pres., bd. dirs. Eden YMCA; past pres., bd. dirs. Rockingham County Arts Council. Mem. Assn. Trial Lawyers Am., Def. Research Inst., Ga. Assn. Plaintiffs Trial Attys., Corp. Counsel Assn. Greater Atlanta, Atlanta Bar Assn., N.C. Trial Lawyers Assn., ABA (corp. counsel com.), N.C. State Bar, Ga. Bar Assn., Rockingham County Bar Assn., Internat. Assn. of Ins. Counsel, Am. Textile Mfrs. Assn., N.C. C. of C. (past dir.). Democrat. Club: Meadow Greens Country. State civil litigation, General corporate, Workers' compensation. Office: Fieldcrest Mills Inc 326 E Stadium Dr Eden NC 27288-3523

DOST, MARK W. lawyer; b. Attleboro, Mass., May 22, 1955; s. Raymond and A. Louise (Fraser) D.; m. Karen M. Sullivan, Aug. 1976; children: Christopher, Stephen, Gregory, Isaac. AB summa cum laude, U. Mass., 1978; JD cum laude, Boston Coll., 1981. Bar: Conn. 1981, U.S. Dist. Ct. Conn. 1986, U.S. Tax Ct. 1985. Atty. Gager & Henry, Waterbury, Conn., 1981-95; ptnr. Tinley, Nastri, Renehan & Dost, 1995—. Author: (with John V. Galiette) Planning for Retirement Benefit Distributions, 1995, 2d revised edit., 1999. Fellow Am. Coll. Trust and Estate Counsel; mem. ABA, Conn. Bar Assn. (exec. com., elder law sect. 1991—, exec. com., estates and probate sect. 1991—, chair elder law sect. 1994-96, chair publs. com. 1997-2000), Nat. Acad. Elder Law Attys. Estate planning, Probate, Estate taxation. Office: Tinley Nastri Renehan Dost 60 N Main St Waterbury CT 06702-1403

DOTI, FRANK JOHN, law educator, consultant; b. Chgo., May 24, 1943; s. Roy and Carmelina Doti; m. Margaret Ann Elliott, Dec. 21, 1973; children: Matthew, Emily, Jillian. BS in Accountancy, U. Ill., Urbana, 1966; JD, Ill. Inst. Tech., 1969. Bar: Ill. 1969, U.S. Dist. Ct. (no. dist.) Ill. 1969, Calif. 1985, U.S. Tax Ct. 1987, Colo. 1992; cert. tax law specialist, Calif. Bd. Specialization; CPA, Ill. Assoc. McDermott, Will & Emory, Chgo., 1969-74; tax dir. CF Industries, Inc., Long Grove, Ill., 1974-77; v.p., tax dir. Leo Burnett Co., Inc., Chgo., 1977-82; prof. law Western State Law Sch., Fullerton, Calif., 1982-96, Chapman U. Sch. Law, Orange, 1996—. Contbr. articles to law revs. and legal jours. and mags. Bd. dirs., Ill. Inst. Tech.-Chgo. Kent Alumni Assn., 1979-83. Recipient 1st place award Moot Ct. Chgo.-Kent Law Sch., 1967, Corpus Juris award, 1969. Mem. ABA (com. on tchg. taxation), Calif. Bar Assn. Home: 7431 E Mill Stream Cir Anaheim CA 92808-1320 Office: Chapman U Sch Law Orange CA 92866

DOTTEN, MICHAEL CHESTER, lawyer; b. Marathon, Ont., Can., Feb. 23, 1952; came to U.S., 1957; s. William James and Ona Adelaide (Sheppard) D.; m. Kathleen Curtis, Aug. 17, 1974 (div. July 1991); children: Matthew Curtis, Tyler Ryan; m. Cheryl Calvin, Apr. 16, 1994. BS in Polit. Sci., U. Oreg., 1974, JD, 1977. Bar: Idaho 1977, Oreg. 1978, U.S. Dist. Ct. Idaho 1977, U.S. Dist. Ct. Oreg. 1978, U.S. Ct. Appeals (9th cir.), U.S. Ct. Appeals (D.C. cir.) 1987, U.S. Ct. Claims 1986, U.S. Supreme Ct. 1996. Staff asst. to Senator Bob Packwood, U.S. Senate, Washington, 1973-74; asst. atty. gen. State of Idaho, Boise, Idaho, 1977-78; chief rate counsel Bonneville Power Adminstrn., Portland, Oreg., 1978-83; spl. counsel Heller, Ehrman, White & McAuliffe, 1983-84, ptnr., 1985-98, 99—; gen. counsel PG&E Gas Transmission, N.W. Corp., 1998-99. Utility com. mem. Ctr. for Pub. Resources, N.Y.C., 1992—. Coun. Emanual Hosp. Assocs., Portland, 1988-92; bd. dirs. William Temple House, 1995-99, chmn. devel. com., 1996-98, v.p., 1997-98, pres., 1998-99; active Portland Interneighborhood Trans. Rev. Commn., 1986-88; vestryman Christ Episcopal Ch., Lake Oswego, Oreg., 1999—, sr. warden, 2001—. Hunter Leadership scholar U. Oreg., 1973, Oreg. scholar, 1970. Mem. ABA (chmn. electric power com. sect. natural resources 1985-88, coun. liaison energy com. 1990-93, coordinating group on energy law 1992-96), Fed. Bar Assn. (pres. Oreg. chpt. 1989-90, Chpt. Activity award 1990, Pres. award 1988-89), Oreg. State Bar (chmn. dispute resolution com. 1986-87), U. Oreg. Law Sch. Alumni Assn. (pres. 1989-92), Multnomah Athletic Club. Democrat. Episcopalian. Avocations: snow skiing, golf, hiking, travel, racquetball. Administrative and regulatory, FERC practice, Public utilities. Office: Heller Ehrman White & McAuliffe 200 SW Market St Ste 1750 Portland OR 97201-5722

DOTY, DAVID SINGLETON, federal judge; b. Anoka, Minn., June 30, 1929; BA, LLB, U. Minn., 1961; LLD (hon.), William Mitchell Coll. Law. Bar: Minn. 1961, U.S. Ct. Appeals (8th and 9th cirs.) 1976, U.S. Supreme Ct. 1982. V.p., dir. Popham, Haik, Schnobrich, Kaufman & Doty, Mpls., 1962-87, pres., 1977-79; instr. William Mitchell Coll. Law, 1963-64; judge U.S. Dist. Ct. for Minn., 1987—. Mem. Adv. Com. on Civil Rules, 1992-98, Adv. Com. on Evidence Rules, 1994-98; trustee Mpls. Libr. Bd., 1969-79, Mpls. Found., 1976-83. Fellow ABA Found.; mem. ABA, Minn. Bar Assn. (gov. 1976-87, sec. 1980-83, pres. 1984-85), Hennepin County Bar Assn. (pres. 1975-76), Am. Judicature Soc., Am. Law Inst. Home: 23 Greenway Gables Minneapolis MN 55403-2145 Office: US Dist Ct 14 W US Courthouse 300 S 4th St Minneapolis MN 55415-1320 E-mail: dsdoty@mnd.uscourts.gov

DOUCETTE, JODI LEAZOTT, lawyer; b. Eau Claire, Wis., June 5, 1962; d. Lawrence George and Sylvia Elaine Leazott; m. Dennis Joseph Doucette, March 26, 1988; children: Lauren E., Chanelle N., Lucas L. Cert. interpreter, U. Sampere, Madrid, 1983; BA, Pepperdine U., 1984; postgrad., Oxford U., 1985; JD, U. San Diego, 1987. Bar: Calif., U.S. Dist. Ct. (so. dist.) Calif. Dep. county counsel County San Diego, 1988-93; dep. city atty. City of Oceanside (Calif.), 1993—. Author: (model ordinance) League of California Cities Sign Ordinance, 1999; contbr. to handbook. Big sister Vol. in Parole, San Diego, 1988-93; chair, mem. Commn. Children & Youth, San Diego County, 1989-93; bd. dirs., treas. Hanna Fenichel Pre-Sch., 1994—; Sunday sch. tchr. St. James Ch., Solana Beach, Calif., 1995-97; bd. mem., com. chair U. San Diego Law Sch., 1995-99; classroom vol. Del Mar (Calif.) Heights Elem. Sch., 1995—. Mem. Bar Assn. No. San Diego (bd. dirs., com. chair, v.p., sec.). Roman Catholic. Avocations: running, skiing, reading, crafts. Office: City Attys Office 300 N Coast Hwy Oceanside CA 92054-2824

DOUCHKESS, GEORGE, lawyer; b. N.Y.C., Apr. 19, 1911; s. Frank A. and Dorothy (Grunberg) D.; m. Sonia Sloshay; children: Donald, Barbara. BBA in Acctg., CCNY, 1937; JD, Bklyn. Law Sch., 1939. Bar: N.Y. 1940, U.S. Dist. Ct. (ea. and so. dists.) N.Y. 1951, U.S. Supreme Ct. 1991. Claim supr. Aetna Casualty and Surety Co., N.Y.C., 1940-44; compensation hearing atty. Liberty Mut. Ins. Co., 1944-47; compensation atty. Preferred Accident and Ins. Co., 1947-51; U.S. supt. divsn. compensation claims, compensation atty. Gen. Fire and Casualty Co., 1951-65; compensation atty. Zurich Am. Ins. Co., 1965-96. Mem. Torch and Scroll. Republican. Administrative and regulatory, Workers' compensation. Home: 715 Park Ave New York NY 10021-5047

DOUGHERTY, JOHN CHRYSOSTOM, III, retired lawyer; b. Beeville, Tex., May 3, 1915; s. John Chrysostom and Mary V. (Henderson) D.; m. Mary Ireland Graves, Apr. 18, 1942 (dec. July 1977); children: Mary Ireland, John Chrysostom IV; m. Bea Ann Smith, June 1978 (div. 1981); m. Sarah B. Randle, 1981 (dec. June 1997). BA, U. Tex., 1937; LLB, Harvard U., 1940; diploma, Inter-Am. Acad. Internat. and Comparative Law, Havana, Cuba, 1948. Bar: Tex. 1940. Atty. Hewit & Dougherty, Beeville, 1940-41; ptnr. Graves & Dougherty, Austin, Tex., 1946-50, Graves, Dougherty & Greenhill, Austin, 1950-57, Graves, Dougherty & Gee, Austin, 1957-60, Graves, Dougherty, Gee & Hearon, Austin, 1961-66, Graves, Dougherty, Gee, Hearon, Moody & Garwood, Austin, 1966-73, Graves, Dougherty, Hearon, Moody & Garwood, Austin, 1973-79, Graves, Dougherty, Hearon & Moody, Austin, 1979-93, sr. counsel, 1993—; ret., 1997. Spl. asst. atty. gen., 1949-50; Hon. French Consul, Austin, 1971-86; lectr. on tax, estate planning, probate code, community property problems; mem. Tex. Submerged Lands Adv. Com., 1963-72, Tex. Bus. and Commerce Code Adv. Com., 1964-66, Gov.'s Com. on Marine Resources, 1970-71, Gov.'s Planning Com. on Colorado River asin Water Quality Mgmt. Study, 1972-73, Tex. Legis. Property Tax Com., 1973-75; bd. dirs. The Austin Project; adv. com. Mex. Ctr. Inst. of Latin-Am. Studies U. Tex., 1997—. Co-editor: Texas Appellate Practice, 1964, 2d edit., 1977; contbr. Bowe, Estate Planning and Taxation, 1957, 65; Texas Lawyers Practice Guide, 1967, 71, How to Live and Die with Texas Probate, 1968, 7th edit., 1995, Texas Estate Administration, 1975, 78; mem. bd. editors: Appellate Procedure in Tex., 1964, 2d edit., 1982; contbr. articles to legal jours. Bd. dirs. Tex. Beta Students Aid Fund, 1949-84, Grenville Clark Fund at Dartmouth Coll., 1976-90, Umlauf Sculpture Garden, Inc., 1990-91, New Life Inst., 1993—; past bd. dirs. Advanced Religious Study Found., Holy Cross Hosp., Sea Arama, Inc., Nat. Pollution Control Found., Austin Nat. Bank; trustee St. Stephen's Episcopal Sch., Austin, 1969-83, Tex. Equal Access to Justice Found., 1986-90, U. Tex. Law Sch. Found., 1974—; mem. adv. com. Legal Assts. Tng. Inst., U. Tex., 1990-98; mem. vis. com. Harvard Law Sch., 1983-87. Capt. C.I.C., AUS, 1941-44, JAGC, 1944-46, maj. USAR. Decorated Medaille Française, France, Medaille d'honneur en Argent des Affairs Etrangeres, France, chevalier l'Ordre Nat. du Merite; recipient Wm. Reece Smith Spl. Svcs. to Pro Bono award Nat. Assn. of Pro Bono Coords., 2000. Fellow Am. Bar Found., Tex. Bar Found., Am. Coll. Trust and Estate Counsel, Am. Coll. Tax Counsel; mem. ABA (ho. of dels. 1982-88, standing com. on lawyers pub. responsibility 1983-85, mem. spl. com. on delivery legal svcs. 1987-91, com. legal problems of the elderly 1997-2000, Sr. Lawyers divsn. Pro Bono Lawyer of 1999), Am. Arbitration Assn. (nat. panel arbitrators 1958-90), Travis County Bar Assn. (pres. 1979-80), Internat. Acad. Estate and Trust Law (exec. coun. 1988-90), State Bar Tex. (chmn. sect. taxation 1965-66, pres. 1979-80, com. legal svcs. to the poor 1986-94), Am. Judicature Soc. (bd. dirs. 1985-87), Am. Law Inst. (adv. com. project law governing lawyers 1990-97), Tex. Supreme Ct. Hist. Soc. (trustee 1997—, chmn. 1999—), Philos. Soc. Tex. (pres. 1989, bd. dirs. 1989—), Harvard Law Sch. Assn. (mem. com. on pub. svc. law 1990-95, chmn. 1990-95, coun. 1991-95, exec. com. 1992-95), Tex. Appleseed, Inc. (bd. dirs. 1996—), Rotary. Presbyterian. Office: Bank of America Center 515 Congress Ave Ste 2300 Austin TX 78701-3508 also: PO Box 98 Austin TX 78767-0098 E-mail: cdougherty@gdhm.com

DOUGHERTY, THOMAS JAMES, lawyer; b. Boston, Apr. 26, 1948; s. Thomas Lawlor and Mary (Morse) D.; m. Jessie d'Entremont Bourneuf, Sept. 25, 1971; children— Thomas McKean, Jennie d'Entremont. B.A., Holy Cross Coll., 1970; B.Phil., Oxford U., Eng., 1973; J.D., Harvard U., 1976. Bar: Mass. 1977, N.Y. 1977, U.S. Dist. Ct. Mass. 1977, U.S. Dist. Ct. (ea. and so. dists.) N.Y. 1977, U.S. Ct. Appeals (1st cir.) 1977, U.S. Ct. Appeals (6th cir.) 1981. Law clk. U.S. Ct. Appeals (1st cir.), 1980-81; assoc. Cravath, Swaine & Moore, N.Y.C., 1976-79; assoc. Skadden, Arps, Slate, Meagher & Flom, Boston, 1979-84, ptnr., 1984— . Author: Education at Holy Cross, 1970; Controlling the New Inflation, 1981. Marshall scholar Marshall Aid Commemoration Commn., London, 1970; Woodrow Wilson Found. fellow, 1970; Danforth Found. fellow, 1971. Mem. Acad. Polit. Sci., Soc. for Values in Higher Edn. Democrat. Roman Catholic. Federal civil litigation, State civil litigation, Libel. Office: Skadden Arps Slate Meagher et al 1 Beacon St Boston MA 02108-3107

DOUGHTY, ALEXANDER ROBERT, lawyer; b. Eng., Nov. 17, 1957; BDS, Birmingham (Eng.) U., 1980; MBA in Fin., City U., London, 1989; Common Profl. Exam, De Montfort U., Leics, Eng., 1990; Law Soc. Final Examination, 1991. Registered fgn. lawyer Budapest Bar Assn. Investment banker HSBC, London, 1985-87, Robert Fleming, London, 1987-88, Merril Lynch, London, 1988-89; trainee, lawyer Slaughter and May, 1989-94; sr. lawyer Clifford Chance, London and Budapest, 1995-98; ptnr. CMS Cameron McKenna, Budapest, Hungary, 1998—. Mem. Law Soc. Eng. and Wales. Avocations: family life, skiing, travel. Banking, Bankruptcy, Finance. Office: Ormai Es Tarsai CMS Cameron McKenna Fl 4 Bank Ctr Szabadsag Ter 7 H-1944 Budapest Hungary E-mail: alxd@cmck.com

DOUGHTY, MARK ANTHONY, lawyer; b. Pasadena, Calif., Aug. 18, 1951; s. Lawrence Richard and Bertha Lou D.; children: Matthew James, Luke Anthony. BA in Bus. Law, Calif. State U., Chico, 1976; JD, U. Pacific, Sacramento, Calif., 1979. Bar: Calif. 1979, U.S. Dist. Ct. (ea. dist.) Calif. 1979; lic. real estate broker. Law clk. Calif. Ct. Appeals (5th cir.), Fresno, Calif., 1979-80; assoc. Ashby and Guth, Yuba City, 1980-82; ptnr. Ashby, Guth and Doughty, 1982-86, Ashby & Doughty, Yuba City, 1986-92; prin. Law Offices of Mark A. Doughty, 1992—. Pres. Russian Radio Bible Inst. Mem. Sutter Buttes Rotary, Consumer Attys. of Calif. (bd. govs. 19th dist.), Fellowship of Christian Businessmen, Yuba Sutter Bar Assn. (pres. 2001), Consumer Attys. Gold Country (pres. 1999—). Republican. Avocations: fathering, golf, private pilot, hunting, boating. General civil litigation, Estate planning, Personal injury. Office: Law Offices of Mark A Doughty PO Box 3420 1528 Poole Blvd Ste A Yuba City CA 95992-3420 Fax: 530-674-1180. E-mail: mark@golaw.com

DOUGLAS, ANDREW, state supreme court justice; b. Toledo, July 5, 1932; 4 children J.D., U. Toledo, 1959. Bar: Ohio 1960, U.S. Dist. Ct. (no. dist.) Ohio 1960. Former ptnr. Winchester & Douglas; judge Ohio 6th Dist. Ct. Appeals, 1981-84; justice Ohio Supreme Ct., 1985—. Mem. nat. adv. bd. Ctr. for Informatics Law John Marshall Law Sch., Chgo.; former spl. counsel Atty. Gen. of Ohio; former instr. law Ohio Dominican Coll. Served with U.S. Army, 1952-54 Recipient award Maumee Valley council Girl Scouts U.S., 1976, Outstanding Service award Toledo Police Command Officers Assn., 1980, Toledo Soc. for Autistic Children and Adults, 1983, Extra-Spl. Person award Central Catholic High Sch., 1981, Disting. Service award Toledo Police Patrolman's Assn., 1982, award Ohio Hispanic Inst. Opportunity, 1985, Disting. Merit award Alpha Sigma Phi, 1988, Gold "T" award U. Toledo, First Amendment award Cen. Ohio Chpt. Soc. Profl. Journalists Sigma Delta Chi, 1989; named to Woodward High Sch. Hall of Fame. Mem. Toledo Bar Assn., Lucas County Bar Assn., Ohio Bar Assn., Toledo U. Alumni Assn., U. Toledo Coll. Law Alumni Assn. (Disting. Alumnus award 1991), Internat. Inst., North Toledo Old Timers Assn., Old Newsboys Goodfellow Assn., Pi Sigma Alpha, Delta Theta Phi. Office: Ohio Supreme Ct 30 E Broad St Fl 3 Columbus OH 43266-0001*

DOUGLAS, JAMES MATTHEW, law educator; b. Onalaska, Tex., Feb. 11, 1944; s. Desso D. and Mary L. (Durden) D.; div.; children: DeLicia, Renee. BA in Math., Tex. So. U., 1966, JD, 1970; MS Law, Stanford U., 1971. Bar: Tex. 1970. Programmer analyst Singer Gen. Precision Co., Houston, 1966-70, 71-72; asst. prof. law Tex. So. U., 1971-72; asst. prof. Cleve. State U., Cleve.-Marshall Coll. Law, 1972-75, asst. prof., asst. dean student affairs, 1974-75; assoc. prof. law, assoc. dean Coll. of Law Syracuse (N.Y.) U., 1975-80; prof. law Northea. U., Boston, 1980-81; dean, prof. law Tex. So. U., Houston, 1981-95, provost, v.p. acad. affairs, 1995, pres., 1995-99, prof., 1995—. Mem. Law Sch. Admissions Coun.; cons. computer law and computer contracts; bd. dirs. Civil Ct. Legal Svcs., Gulf Coast Legal Found.; bd. dirs. Boy Scouts Am., mem. exec. com., 1998—. Mem. editl. bd. The Tex. Lawyer. Mem. ABA (mem. affirmative action com.), Tex. Bar Assn., Houston Bar Assn., Hiscock Legal Soc. (dir.), Houston C. of C. (mem. chmns. club), Greater Houston Partnership (bd. dirs.). Home: 5318 Calhoun Rd Houston TX 77021-1714 Office: Tex U Thurgood Marshall Law Sch Bldg 3100 Cleburne St Houston TX 77004-4501

DOUGLAS, JAMES MCCRYSTAL, lawyer; b. Wantagh, N.Y., 1956; Student, Bucknell U.; BA, SUNY, Binghamton, 1978; JD cum laude, Fordham U., 1981. Bar: N.Y. 1982. Ptnr. Skadden, Arps, Slate, Meagher & Flom LLP, N.Y.C. Mem. Fordham Law Rev., 1980-81. E-mial. Office: Skadden Arps Slate Meagher & Flom LLP 4 Times Sq New York NY 10036-6595 E-mail: jdouglas@skadden.com

DOUGLAS, JOHN WOOLMAN, lawyer; b. Phila., Aug. 15, 1921; s. Paul H. and Dorothy S. (Wolff) D.; m. Mary Evans St. John, July 14, 1945; children: Katherine D. Torrey, Peter R. AB, Princeton U., 1943; LLB, Yale U., 1948; DPhil, Oxford U., 1950. Bar: N.Y. 1948, D.C. 1953. Law clk. to justice Harold H. Burton U.S. Supreme Ct., 1951-52; asst. atty. gen. U.S. Dept. Justice, 1963-66; assoc. Covington & Burling, Washington, 1950-51, 52-63, 1966—. Chmn. Carnegie Endowment for Internat. Peace, 1978-86. Served to lt. (j.g.) USNR, 1943-46, MTO, PTO. Trustee Deerfield Acad., 1972-77. Rhodes scholar, 1948-50. Fellow Am. Coll. Trial Lawyers; mem. ABA, D.C. Bar Assn. (pres. 1974-75), Practising Law Inst. (bd. trustees 1986—), Nat. Lawyers Com. for Civil Rights Under Law (co. chmn. 1969-71), Nat. Legal Aid Defender Assn. (pres. 1970-71), Yale Law Sch. Assn. (pres. 1975-77). Democrat. Presbyterian. Federal civil litigation. Home: 5700 Kirkside Dr Bethesda MD 20815-7116 Office: Covington & Burling 1201 Pennsylvania Ave NW PO Box 7566 Washington DC 20044-7566

DOUGLAS, PHILIP LE BRETON, lawyer; b. Paris, France, Apr. 18, 1950 (parents Am. citizens); s. Paul Wolff and Colette Marie Louise (Smith) D.; m. Elizabeth Kean, June 18, 1983; children: Eliza Shaw, Samuel Garrison. AB, Princeton U., 1972; JD, NYU, 1975. Bar: N.Y. 1976, U.S. Dist. Ct. (so. and ea. dists.) N.Y. 1977, D.C. 1980, U.S. Ct. Appeals (2d cir.) 1981, U.S. Ct. Appeals (5th cir.) 1976, U.S. Ct. Appeals (8th cir.) 1987. Law clk. to Hon. Robert A. Ainsworth U.S. Ct. Appeals (5th cir.), New Orleans, 1975-76; assoc., Davis Polk & Wardell, N.Y.C., 1977-79; asst. U.S. atty. U.S. Dist. Ct. (so. dist.) N.Y., 1979-84; ptnr. firm Hale Russell & Gray, N.Y.C., 1984-85, Winthrop, Stimson, Putnam & Roberts, N.Y.C., 1985—. Articles editor NYU Law Rev., 1974-75. Trustee Grace Ch. Sch., N.Y.C., 1986-92. Root-Tilden scholar NYU Law Sch., 1972-75. Mem. ABA, Assn. of Bar of City of N.Y., Fed. Bar Council. Federal civil litigation, State civil litigation, Criminal. Home: 76 Macdougal St New York NY 10012-2505 Office: Winthrop Stimson Putnam & Roberts 1 Battery Park Plz Fl 31 New York NY 10004-1490

DOUGLASS, JOHN JAY, lawyer, educator; b. Lincoln, Nebr., Mar. 9, 1922; s. Edward Lyman and Edna Marie (Ball) D.; m. Margaret Casteel Pickering, Aug. 31, 1946; children: Carrie Bess, Timothy Pickering, Margaret Marie. AB with distinction, U. Nebr., 1943; JD with distinction, U. Mich., 1952; MA, George Washington U., 1963; LLM, U. Va., 1973; postgrad., Army War Coll., 1963. Bar: Nebr. 1952, Mich. 1952, Tex. 1975. Infantry officer U.S. Army, 1943-52, advanced through grades to col., 1966, judge adv., 1952-74, Vietnam, 1968-69, mil. judge Ft. Riley, Kans., 1969-70; comdt. U.S. Army JAG Sch., Charlottesville, Va., 1970-74; ret. U.S. Army, 1974; dean emeritus Nat. Coll. Dist. Attys., Houston, 1974-94; prof., dir. trial advocacy U. Houston, 1974—. Advisor on criminal law to Albania, 1991; advisor on elections to Ukraine, 1993; advisor Russian procuracy, 1994, Ukraine procuracy, 1995; named dist. mem. JAGC, 1994. Author: Ethical Concerns in Prosecution, 1988, 93; contbr. articles to profl. jours. Judge Harris County Absentee Voting, Houston, 1980-92. Decorated D.S.C., Legion of Merit, Bronze Star. Fellow Am. Bar Found.; mem. ABA (ho. of dels. 1980-96, chmn. standing com. on law and electoral process 1987-90, Nelson award 2001), Tex. Bar Assn. (penal code and criminal process com. 1988-90), Houston City Club, Army andavy Club, Order of Coif, Alpha Tau Omega. Avocation: tennis. Home: 25 T 14 E Greenway Plz Houston TX 77046-1406 Office: Univ Houston Law Ctr 100 Law Center Houston TX 77204-6060 E-mail: jdouglass@UH.edu, johnjay5@juno.com

DOUMENGE, ARNAUD, lawyer; b. Sept. 10, 1970; M in Tax and Bus. Law, U. Paris II, 1992, KKN ub Kabir Kaw, 1993, Doctor of Law, 1996. Bar: France 1998. Bus. counsel CNPF, Paris, 1994-95, Fedn. Francaise des Courtiers d'Assurance, Paris, 1995-97; lawyer Coopers & Lybrand, CLC Juridique et Fiscal, 1997-99, Magellan, Paris, 1999—. Author: Droit Commercial, 1998. Labor, Labor Litigation. Office: Magellan 127 Rue de Montreuil 75011 Paris France

DOWD, EDWARD L., JR. lawyer, former prosecutor; s. Edward L. Dowd; m. Jill Goessling; 3 children. JD with distinction, St. Mary's Univ. With Dowd, Dowd & Dowd; from asst. U.S. atty. to chief narcotics sect. U.S. Atty.'s Office, 1979-84; pvt. practice, 1984-93; U.S. atty. ea. dist. of Mo. U.S. Dept. Justice, St. Louis, 1993-99; dep. spl. counsel to John C. Danforth Spl. Counsel Waco Investigation, 1999; ptnr. Bryan Cave, LLP, St. Louis, 1999—. Regional dir. south central region Pres.'s Organized Crime Drug Enforcement Task Force. Office: Bryan Cave LLP One Metropolitan Square 211 N Broadway Ste 3600 Saint Louis MO 63102-2733 Office Fax: 314-259-2020. E-mail: eldowd@bryancave.com*

DOWD, STEVEN MILTON, lawyer; b. Tyler, Tex., Feb. 1, 1951; s. Loyd Robertus and Roy Frances (Dickard) D.; m. Pamela Gayle Blacklock, Apr. 6, 1974; children: Anna Lisa, Lydia Caroline. BA, Austin Coll., 1973; JD, Baylor U., 1975; LLM, So. Meth. U., 1977. Bar: Tex. 1975, U.S. Dist. Ct. (so. dist.) Tex. 1983, U.S. Dist. Ct. (ea. dist.) Tex. 1985. Tax atty. Exxon Corp., Houston, 1977-79; assoc. Covington & Reese, 1982-84; pvt. practice Tyler, Tex., 1984-86; asst. gen. counsel Temple-Eastex, Inc., Diboll, 1986-92; co-owner Panola County Abstract and Title Co., 1992-99; pvt. practice, 1992—. Dist. judge 123rd Jud. Dist. Ct., Panola and Shelby Counties, 1995-97; pres. Lydianna Petroleum Co., Austin, Tex., 2000—. Bd. dirs. Noonday Holiness Camp, Hallsville, Tex. Baptist. General civil litigation, General corporate, Oil, gas, and mineral. Home and Office: 12404 Willow Bend Dr Austin TX 78758-2822

DOWDEY, LANDON GERALD, lawyer, writer; b. Washington, Aug. 2, 1923; s. Landon Ashton Dowdey and Dorothy M. Fogarty; m. Mary M. Shinners, June 7, 1947 (dec. June 1989); children: Patrick F., Kathleen M., Martin Joseph. BS in Econ., U. Pa., 1946; JD, Georgetown U., 1948. Bar: U.S. Ct. Appeals (D.C., fed., 2nd, 3rd, 4th, 6th, 7th and 9th cirs.), U.S. Supreme Ct. 1952. Assoc. Levi H. David & E.L. Sheehan, Washington, 1948-57; ptnr. Dowdey & Bartow, 1958-66, Dowdey, Levy & Cohen, Washington, 1966-72, Dowdey & Urbina, Washington, 1972-76; pvt. practice, 1977—. Editor: Journey to Freedom, 1969 (Nat. Book award 1969), The Four Zoas, 1983. Lawyer Dem. State Com. D.C., Washington, 1968-90. Pvt. U.S. Army, 1943-44. Roman Catholic. Appellate, Federal civil litigation, Constitutional. Office: 2000 L St NW Ste 200 Washington DC 20036-4924 E-mail: ldowdey@aol.com

DOWDLE, PATRICK DENNIS, lawyer; b. Denver, Dec. 8, 1948; s. William Robert and Helen (Schraeder) D.; m. Eleanor Pryor, Mar. 8, 1975; children: Jeffery William, Andrew Peter. BA, Cornell Coll., Mt. Vernon, Iowa, 1971; JD, Boston U., 1975. Bar: Colo. 1975, U.S. Dist. Ct. Colo. 1975, U.S. Ct. Appeals (10th cir.) 1976, U.S. Supreme Ct. 1978. Acad. dir. in Japan Sch. Internat. Tng., Putney, Vt., 1974; assoc. Decker & Miller, Denver, 1975-77; ptnr. Miller, Makkai & Dowdle, 1977—. Designated counsel criminal appeals Colo. Atty. Gens. Office, Denver, 1980-81; guardian ad litem Adams County Dist. Ct., Brighton, Colo., 1980-83; affiliated counsel ACLU, Denver, 1980—. Mem. Colo. Bar Assn., Denver Bar Assn. (various coms.), Porsche Club of Am. Avocations: scuba diving, photography, wine making, travel, skiing. Bankruptcy, General civil litigation, Real property. Home: 3254 Tabor Ct Wheat Ridge CO 80033-5367 Office: Miller Makkai & Dowdle 2325 W 72nd Ave Denver CO 80221-3101 E-mail: pdowdle@rmi.net

DOWDY, WILLIAM CLARENCE, JR. retired lawyer; b. McKinney, Tex., Feb. 27, 1925; s. William C. and Emily Harryette (Gilson) D.; m. Ann Atkinson, Aug. 31, 1947; children: William Clarence III, Jill Ann, Daniel Andrew. Student, North Tex. Agrl. Coll., Arlington, 1942-43; BBA, U. Tex., Austin, 1949, JD, 1951. Bar: Tex. 1951, U.S. Supreme Ct. 1957, U.S. Dist. Ct. (no. dist.) Tex. 1960, U.S. Ct. Appeals (5th cir.) 1974. Asst. dist. atty. Dallas County, 1951-54; atty. Tex. & Pacific Ry. Co., Dallas, 1954-59; gen. atty. Tex. & Pacific Ry. Co./Mo. Pacific R.R. Co., 1959-82; gen. solicitor Mo. Pacific R.R. Co./Union Pacific R.R. Co., 1982-86, sr. counsel, 1986-87; ret., 1987. Dir. Great S.W. R.R.; v.p., asst. sec., dir. Weatherford, Mineral Wells & Northwestern R.R. Elder, trustee Presbyn. Ch. With field arty. AUS, 1943-46; PTO. Mem. Nat. Assn. R.R. Trial Counsel (exec. com., regional v.p.), Tower Club (Dallas), Eldorado Club (McKinney, Tex.), Phi Alpha Delta, Kappa Sigma. Administrative and regulatory, General corporate, Personal injury. Home: 510 Tucker St Mc Kinney TX 75069-2714

DOWIS, LENORE, lawyer; b. N.Y., Nov. 7, 1934; d. Thomas and Julianna (Csitkovits) Esteves; children: Daniel, Lenore, Denise, Jonathan. AAS, Suffolk County Community Coll., 1981; BA, SUNY, Stony Brook, 1983; JD, Touro Coll., 1987. Bar: N.Y. 1988, N.J. 1988, U.S. Dist. Ct. N.J. 1988, U.S. Dist. Ct. (so. and ea. dists.) N.Y. 1992, U.S. Ct. Mil. Appeals 1993, U.S. Ct. Claims 1993, U.S. Ct. Appeals (fed. cir.) 1993, U.S. Supreme Ct. 1993. Tel. operator N.Y. Tel. Co., L.I., 1951-58; real estate sales agt. Gen. Devel. Corp., Hauppauge, N.Y, 1974-75; student law clk. to assoc. judge appellate div. U.S. Supreme Ct. N.Y., Bklyn., 1986; staff atty. Nassau/Suffolk Law Svcs., Bay Shore, N.Y., 1988; pvt. practice, Smithtown, 1988—. Mem. ABA, Suffolk County Bar Assn., N.Y. State Bar Assn., Phi Theta Kappa, Alpha Beta Gamma. Republican. Administrative and regulatory, Family and matrimonial, General practice. Home and Office: 33 Beverly Rd Smithtown NY 11787-5324

DOWLING, VINCENT JOHN, lawyer; b. N.Y.C., Dec. 20, 1927; s. Victor Hurlin and Joan Agnes (Reardon) D.; m. Jane Cooney, Apr. 16, 1958; children: Vincent John Jr., Douglas J., S. Colin, Joseph G. BS, Lehigh U., 1949; JD, U. Conn., 1957. Bar: Conn. 1957, Mass. 1985, Fla. 1986, U.S. Dist. Ct. Conn. 1958, U.S. Ct. Appeals (2d cir.) 1960, U.S. Ct. Claims 1986. Chief mfg. engr. Veeder-Root, Inc., Hartford, Conn., 1949-58; ptnr. Dowling & Dowling, 1958-65, Cooney, Scully & Dowling, Hartford, 1965—. Lectr. constrn. law. Capt. U.S. Army, 1951-53. Mem. ASME, ABA, Conn. Bar assn. (liaison com. with ctrs., constrn. law com., alt. dispute resolution com., chmn. specialization com.), Am. Arbitration Assn., Nat. Panel Constrn. Arbitrators and Mediators, Nat. Arbitration and Mediation (panel), Fed. Bar Assn., Mass. Bar Assn., Fla. Bar Assn., Internat. Bar Assn., Diocesan Attys. Assn., Hartford Golf Club, Hartford Club, John's Island Club (Vero Beach, Fla.), Kappa Alpha Soc. Roman Catholic. Alternative dispute resolution, Federal civil litigation, Construction. Address: 10 Columbus Blvd Hartford CT 06106-1976 E-mail: jvin@dowlingp.com, v.dowlingsr@att.net

DOWNER, ROBERT NELSON, lawyer; b. Newton, Iowa, July 15, 1939; s. Lowell William and Mabel Mary (Hannon) D.; m. Jane Alice Glafka, May 29, 1971; children: Elise Michele, Andrew Nelson. BA, U. Iowa, 1961, JD, 1963. Bar: Iowa 1963, U.S. Dist. Ct. (so. dist.) Iowa 1963, U.S. Dist. Ct. (no. dist.) Iowa 1964, U.S. Supreme Ct. 1995, U.S. Ct. Appeals (8th cir.) 2001. Assoc. Meardon Law Office, Iowa City, 1963-68; mem. Meardon, Sueppel & Downer PLC and predecessor firms, 1969—. Dir., sec. KZIA, Inc., Cedar Rapids, Iowa, 1975—, Iowa City Tennis & Fitness Ctr., 1987-93; trustee The Oaknoll Found., Iowa City, 1990-98, Herbert Hoover Presdl. Libr. Assn., West Branch, Iowa, 2000—; dir. Christian Retirement Svcs., Inc., Iowa City, 1967-82, Iowa State Bar Found., 1996—, Ill. Law Sch. Found., 2000—, Iowa Law Sch. Found., 2000—. Pres. Greater Iowa City Area C. of C., 1979; bd. trustees Iowa City Pub. Libr., 1971-75, chair, 1973-74; chair adminstrv. bd. First United Meth. Ch., Iowa City, 1985-87; del. Rep. Nat. Conv., New Orleans, 1988; mem. Iowa Supreme Ct. Commn. on Continuing Legal Edn., 1975-83, Task Force on Domestic Abuse, 1993-94; bd. dirs. Iowa City Area Devel. Group, 1993-2001, chmn., 1996-97, co-chair, 2000-01; dir., sec. Cmty. Found. Johnson County, Iowa, 2000—. Recipient Excellence in Svc. award Legal Svcs. Corp. Iowa, 1996. Fellow Am. Coll. Trust & Estate Counsel (state chair 2000—), Am. Bar Found., Iowa State Bar Found.; mem. ABA, Iowa State Bar Assn. (chair probate, property and trust law com. 1988-90, chair probate sect. 1990-93, v.p. 1993-94, pres.-elect 1994-95, pres. 1995-96), Johnson County Bar Assn. (pres. 1976), Rotary Club Iowa City (pres. 1988-89). Republican. Methodist. Banking, General corporate, Probate. Home: 2029 Rochester Ct Iowa City IA 52245-3246 Office: Meardon Sueppel & Downer PLC 122 S Linn St Iowa City IA 52240-1830 E-mail: bobd@meardonlaw.com

DOWNES, JAMES J. lawyer; b. La Crosse, Wis., Oct. 14, 1944; s. James Richard and Dorothy Elizabeth Downes; m. Susan Downes, Jan. 25, 1969; children: Ian, Kevin. AB, Mt. St. Mary's Coll., 1966; JD, N.Y. Law Sch., 1969. Bar: N.Y. 1969, U.S. Dist. Ct. (so. dist.) N.Y. 1973, U.S. Dist. Ct. (no. dist.) N.Y. 1998, U.S. Ct. Appeals (2d cir.) 1974, U.S. Supreme Ct. 1974. Asst. dist. atty. Westchester County Dist. Atty.'s Office, White Plains, N.Y., 1969-71; assoc. Clark, Gagliardi & Miller, 1971-82; founding ptnr. Rende, Ryan & Downes, 1982—. Spkr. Westchester County Bar Trial Lawyers, 1980—. Commr. Pound Ridge (N.Y.) Recreation Commn., 1987-94; pres. Bedford (N.Y.) Pound Ridge Little League, 1986-97. Mem. ATLA, N.Y. State Trial Lawyers, Westchester County Bar Assn., Lambda Iota Tau. Avocations: running, reading. General civil litigation, Personal injury. Office: Rende Ryan & Downes 202 Mamaroneck Ave Ste 601 White Plains NY 10601-5308

DOWNES, WILLIAM F. judge; b. 1946; BA, U. North Tex., 1968; JD, U. Houston, 1974. Ptnr. Clark and Downes, Green River, Wyo., 1976-78; mem. Brown & Drew, Casper, 1978-94; dist. judge U.S. Dist. Ct. Wyo., 1994—; chief judge. Capt. USMC, 1968-71. Mem. Wyo. State Bar, Natrona County Bar Assn., Casper Petroleum Club, Wyo. Athletic Club. Office: US Dist Ct 111 S Wolcott St Rm 210 Casper WY 82601-2534

DOWNEY, BRIAN PATRICK, lawyer; b. Pitts., Sept. 1, 1964; s. Edmond John and Mary Elizabeth (Wallace) D.; m. Linda Alice McKay, Oct. 9, 1993. BA, Dartmouth Coll., 1987; JD, Dickinson Sch. of Law, 1990. Bar: Pa. 1990, U.S. Dist. Ct. (we. dist.) Pa. 1991, U.S. Dist. Ct. (ea. and mid. dists.) Pa. 1994, U.S. Ct. Appeals (3rd cir.) 1994. Assoc. counsel Eckert Seamans Cherin & Mellott, Pitts., 1990-92; asst. counsel Pa. Dept. of Labor, Harrisburg, 1992-94; ptnr. Pepper Hamilton, LLP, 1994—. Mem. Friends of Tom Foley Com., Harrisburg, 1994; bd. dirs. Open Stage Harrisburg, 2001—. Mem. ABA, Pa. Bar Assn., Dauphin County Bar Assn. Democrat. Roman Catholic. Avocations: creative writing, golf, reading fiction. General civil litigation, Environmental, Product liability. Office: Pepper Hamilton LLP 200 One Keystone Plz Harrisburg PA 17108 E-mail: downeyb@pepperlaw.com

DOWNEY, RICHARD RALPH, lawyer, accountant, management consultant; b. Boston, Apr. 22, 1934; s. Paul Joseph and Evelyn Mae (Butler) D.; BS, Northeastern U., 1958; MBA, Harvard U., 1962; JD, Suffolk U., 1979; LLM, Boston U., 1981; children: Richard Ralph (dec.), Janice M., Erin C., Timothy M. Mem. audit staff Price Waterhouse & Co., Boston, 1962-64; assoc. Assos. for Internat. Rsch., Inc., Cambridge, Mass., 1964-68, v.p., 1968—, also dir.; admitted to Mass. bar, 1979, Fed. bar, 1980. Treas., 1580 House Condominium Trust, 1979-80. CPA, Mass., Mem. ABA, Am. Inst. CPAs, Mass. Soc. CPAs, Mass. Bar Assn., Assn. Trial Lawyers Am., Boston Bar Assn., Phi Delta Phi, Algonquin Club, Harvard Club (Boston, N.Y.C.). Pension, profit-sharing, and employee benefits, Taxation, general, Personal income taxation. Home: 25 Washington Ave Cambridge MA 02140-2834 Office: 1100 Massachusetts Ave Cambridge MA 02138-5241

DOWNS, BERNARD BOOZER, JR. lawyer; b. Montgomery, Ala., Mar. 15, 1950; s. Bernard B. and Sybil (King) D.; m. Carol Cain, May 27, 1972; children— Boozer Downs, III, Leah C. B.A., U. Ala. 1972, J.D., 1976. Bar: Ala. 1976, U.S. Dist. Ct. (no. dist.) Ala. 1976, U.S. Ct. Appeals (5th and 11th cirs.). Ptnr. Davies, Williams & Wallace, Birmingham, Ala., 1976-84, Harris, Evans & Downs, Birmingham, 1984-90; ptnr. Dominick, Fletcher, Yieldings, Wood & Lloyd. Vestryman, jr. warden All Saints Episcopal Ch., Homewood, Ala., 1981-84. Mem. ABA, Ala. Bar Assn., Birmingham Bar Assn. (exec. com., chmn. pub. relations com. 1983-84, chmn. social welfare com. 1981-83), pres.-elect young lawyers sect. 1984-85), Bench and Bar. Club: Magic City Civitan (bd. dirs. 1982-84, treas. 1981). State civil litigation, Insurance, Personal injury. Home: 2428 Kenvil Cir Birmingham AL 35243-2857 Office: 27447 Highway Five Woodstock AL 35188

DOWNS, CLARK EVANS, lawyer; b. Boston, July 30, 1946; s. Willis A. and Josephine Joyce (Evans) D.; m. Emilie Louise Hartnett, Aug. 17, 1968; children: Elizabeth Morgan, Julia Clark. AB in English Lit., Boston U., 1968, JD cum laude, 1973. Bar: Ill. 1973, D.C. 1981. Assoc. Isham Lincoln & Beale, Washington, 1973-80, ptnr., 1981-87, Jones Day Reavis & Pogue, Washington, 1988—. Bd. vistors Boston U. Sch. Law, 2000—. Trustee, sec. Found. Energy Law Jour., Washington, 1989-93; trustee Mt. Ida Coll., Newton Centre, Mass., 1989-98, chair, 1994-98; trustee Nat. Presbyn. Sch., Washington, 1986-90, Nat. Presbyn. Ch., Washington, 1991-93, Chevy Chase Presbyn. Ch., Washington, 1981-84; bd. visitors Boston U. Sch. Law, 2000—. Fellow Am. Bar Found.; mem. ABA (ho. of dels. 1995-97), Fed. Energy Bar Assn. (chmn. program com. 1985-86, bd. dirs. 1986-89), FERC (Practice Procedure Manual editl. adv. bd. 1996—), D.C. Bar (chmn. lawyers counseling com. 1989), Order St. John (serving brother 2000—). Avocations: cello, folk music, choral music. FERC practice, Finance, Public utilities. Office: Jones Day Reavis & Pogue 51 Louisiana Ave NW Washington DC 20001-2113

DOWNS, THOMAS EDWARD, IV, lawyer; b. South Amboy, N.J., Sept. 27, 1950; s. Thomas Edward III and Theresa Mary (Jaje) D.; m. Marie Popik, Oct. 6, 1979; children: Thomas Edward V, Lauren Ann. BA, St. Peter's Coll., 1972; JD, Seton Hall U., 1975. Bar: N.J. 1975, U.S. Dist. Ct. N.J. 1975, U.S. Dist. Cts. (so. and ea. dists.) N.Y. 1981. Law clk. to presiding judges Middlesex County, N.J., 1975; assoc. Irving Tabman, Old Bridge, 1975-76; ptnr. Tabman, Downs & McDonnell, 1976-77, Tabman & Downs, Old Bridge, 1978-82; pvt. practice, 1982—; South Amboy Mcpl. pros., 1977—; Sayreville Mcpl. pros., 1987-90, 94—, 2000. Sec. South Amboy Shade Tree com., 1974; co-chmn. South Amboy Blood Bank; pres. South Amboy Young Dem. Orgn.; dep. chmn. Sayreville Dem. Orgn., 1992—. Mem. Assn. Trial Lawyers Am., N.J. State Trial Lawyers Assn., Middlesex County Bar Assn., N.J. State Bar Assn., Lions (pres. South Amboy chpt. 1984). Roman Catholic. Criminal, Family and matrimonial, Real property. Home: 26 Carter Pl Sayreville PO Box Parlin NJ 08859 Office: PO Box 498 Old Bridge NJ 08857-0498

DOYLE, ANTHONY PETER, lawyer; b. Washington, July 13, 1953; s. Francis X. and Anna (Klekotka) D.; m. Maria H. Duda, Aug. 13, 1977; children: Jeffrey Anthony, Joseph Edward, Natalie Maria, Andrew Michael. AA, Berkshire Community Coll., Pittsfield, Mass., 1972-75; BS magna cum laude, Worcester State Coll., 1977; JD, Western New Eng. Coll., 1980. Bar: Mass. 1980; U.S. Dist. Ct. Mass. 1981; U.S. Ct. Appeals (1st cir.) 1981, U.S. Supreme Ct. 1999. Pvt. practice, Pittsfield, 1980-84; ptnr. Doyle & Cormier, 1985-88, Barry, Doyle & Cormier, Pittsfield, 1989, Barry & Doyle, Pittsfield, 1989—. Pres. Hospice of Cen. Berkshire, Pittsfield, 1988-90; v.p. HospiceCare of the Berkshires, Pittsfield, 1990-92, pres. 1992—; bd. dirs. Dalton (Mass.) Youth Ctr., 1986-89, Community Recreation Assn., Dalton, 1989-95; exec. com. Appalachian Trails Dist. Boy Scouts Am., Dalton, 1989-96; mem. Zoning Bd. Appeals, Dalton, 1995—, chmn., 1997—, Dalton Coun. Aging, 1997—. Recipient commendation Western Mass. Pro Bono Referral Svc., 1983-87. Mem. Mass. Bar Assn., Berkshire Bar Assn. (exec. com. 1989-91, v.p. 1997—, pres. 1999—). Roman Catholic. Avocations: skiing, tennis. General practice, Personal injury, Probate. Home: 108 Barton Hill Rd Dalton MA 01226-2005 Office: Barry & Doyle 8 Bank Row Ste 2 Pittsfield MA 01201-6224

DOYLE, GERARD FRANCIS, lawyer; b. Needham, Mass., Oct. 25, 1942; s. John Patrick and Catherine Mary (Lawler) D.; m. Paula Marie Dervay, may 14, 1983; children: Laura Dervay, Meredith Lawler, Philip John. BS in Indsl. Adminstrn., Yale U., 1966; JD, Georgetown U., 1972. Bar: D.C. 1973, U.S. Dist. Ct. D.C. 1973, U.S. Ct. Fed. Claims 1976, U.S. Ct. Appeals (fed. cir.) 1982, U.S. Supreme Ct. 1982, Va. 2000. Group head for operating submarine reactors and reactor tech Div. Naval Reactors AEC, Washington, 1970-72; atty. Morgan, Lewis & Bockius, 1972-76; legal counsel Am. Nuclear Energy Coun., 1975-76; ptnr. Cotten, Day & Doyle, 1976-87, Doyle & Savit, Doyle, Simmons & Bachman, Doyle & Bachman LLP, Washington, 1987-99, Arlington, Va., 1999—. Legal counsel Assn. Fed. Data Peripheral Suppliers, Washington, 1979; dir. M Internat., Inc.; author and lectr. in field; columnist Federal Computer Week, 1989. Served in USN, 1966-71. Recipient outstanding young man of yr. award, 1976. Mem. ABA (coun. publ. contract law sect. 1989-92), D.C. Bar Assn., Fed. Bar Assn., Am. Arbitration Assn. (panel arbitrators), Nat. Contract Mgmt. Assn., Met. Club (Washington), Yale Club (Washington), Washington Golf & Country Club. Republican. Roman Catholic. Computer, Government contracts and claims. Home: 901 Whann Ave Mc Lean VA 22101-1570 Office: Doyle & Bachman LLP 4245 Fairfax Dr Arlington VA 22203-1637 E-mail: gdoyle@doylebachman.com

DOYLE, JOHN ROBERT, lawyer; b. Chgo., May 12, 1950; s. Frank Edward and Dorothy (Bolton) D.; m. Kathleen Julius, June 14, 1974; children: Melissa, Maureen. BA magna cum laude, St. Louis U., 1971; JD summa cum laude, DePaul U., 1976. Bar: Ill. 1976, U.S. Dist. Ct. 1976, U.S. Dist. Ct. (no. dist.) Ill. 1982, Ill. Trial Bar 1982, U.S. Ct. Appeals (7th cir.) 1982. Ptnr. McDermott, Will & Emery, Chgo., 1976—. Mem. ABA, Chgo. Bar Assn. (jud. investigative hearing panel 1986-88), Phi Beta Kappa. Construction, Insurance, Personal injury. Office: McDermott Will & Emery 227 W Monroe St Ste 3100 Chicago IL 60606-5096

DOYLE, JUSTIN P, lawyer; b. Rochester, N.Y., Oct. 26, 1948; s. Justin Joseph and Jane Martha (Kreag) D.; m. Mary Elizabeth Mayer; children: Mary, Joe. BA, Dartmouth Coll., 1970; JD, Cornell U., 1974. Bar: N.Y. 1974. From assoc. to ptnr. Nixon, Hargrave, Devans & Doyle, Rochester, 1974-99; ptnr. Nixon Peabody LLP (formerly Nixon, Hargrave, Devans & Doyle), 1999—. Mem. N.Y. Bar Assn., Monroe County Bar Assn. General corporate, Mergers and acquisitions, Securities. Home: 252 Overbrook Rd Rochester NY 14618-3648 Office: Nixon Peabody LLP Clinton Sq PO Box 31051 Rochester NY 14603-1051

DOYLE, MICHAEL ANTHONY, lawyer; b. Atlanta, Nov. 4, 1937; s. James Alexander and Wilma (Summersgill) D.; children: John, David, Peter.; m. Bernice H. Winter, Nov. 12, 1977. BA, Yale U., 1959, LLB, 1962. Bar: Ga. 1961, D.C. 1967, U.S. Dist. Ct. D.C. 1967, U.S. Dist. Ct. (no. dist.) Ga. 1962, U.S. Ct. Appeals (5th cir.) 1962, U.S. Ct. Appeals (11th cir.) 1982, U.S. Ct. Appeals (D.C. cir.) 1968, U.S. Supreme Ct. 1972, U.S. Ct. Appeals (4th cir.) 1985. Assoc. Alston, Miller & Gaines, Atlanta, 1962-67; ptnr. Alston & Bird and predecessor, 1967—. Bd. dirs. Atlanta Legal Aid Soc., 1969-84, pres., 1975-76; bd. dirs. Ga. Legal Services Program; mem. Leadership Atlanta, 1974. Served to lt. USNR, 1964-69. Mem. ABA, State Bar Ga., Atlanta Lawyers Club, Master, Bleckley Inn of Court, Assn. Yale Alumni, Yale Law Sch. Assn. (nat. v.p. 1982-85, mem. exec. com. 1978-85, chmn. planning com. 1988-90, pres. 1991-92, chmn. exec. com. 1992-94). Piedmont Driving Club, Commerce Club, Yale Club Ga. (pres. 1982-84), Yale Club N.Y. Roman Catholic. Clubs: Peidmont Driving, Commerce, Yale of Ga. (pres. 1982-84), Yale of N.Y. Antitrust, Federal civil litigation, State civil litigation. Office: Alston & Bird 4200 One Atlantic Ctr 1201 W Peachtree St NW Atlanta GA 30309-3424

DOYLE, RICHARD HENRY, IV, lawyer; b. Elgin, Ill., Aug. 8, 1949; s. Richard Henry and Shirley Marian (Ohms) D.; m. Debbie Kay Cahalan, Aug. 2, 1975; children: John Richard, Kerry Jane. BA, Drake U., 1971, JD, 1976. Bar: Iowa 1976, U.S. Dist. Ct. (no. and so. dists.) Iowa 1977, U.S. Ct. Appeals (8th cir.) 1977, U.S. Supreme Ct. 1986. Asst. atty. gen. Iowa Dept. Justice, Des Moines, 1976-77; assoc. Lawyer, Lawyer & Jackson, 1977-79, Law Offices of Verne Lawyer & Assocs., Des Moines, 1979-93, Reavely, Shinkle, Bauer, Scism, Reavely & Doyle, Des Moines, 1993, Michael J. Galligan Law Firm, P.C., Des Moines, 1994-96, Galligan, Tully, Doyle & Reid, P.C., Des Moines, 1996—. Lawyer; b. Elgin, Ill., Aug. 8, 1949; s. Richard Henry and Shirley Marian (Ohms) D.; m. Debbie Kay Cahalan, Aug. 2, 1975; children: John Richard, Kerry Jane. BA, Drake U., 1971, JD, 1976. Bar: Iowa 1976, U.S. Dist. Ct. (no. and so. dists.) Iowa 1977, U.S. Ct. Appeals (8th cir.) 1977, U.S. Supreme Ct. 1986. Asst. atty. gen. Iowa Dept. Justice, Des Moines, 1976-77; assoc. Lawyer, Lawyer & Jackson, Des Moines, 1977-79; assoc. Law Offices of Verne Lawyer & Assocs., Des Moines, 1979-93, Reavely, Shinkle, Bauer, Scism, Reavely & Doyle, Des Moines, 1993, Michael J. Galligan Law Firm, P.C., Des Moines, 1994-96. Contbr. articles to profl. jours. With U.S. Army, 1971-73. Fellow Iowa Acad. Trial Lawyers; mem. ABA, ATLA, Iowa Trial Lawyers Assn., Iowa Bar Assn., Iowa State Bar Assn., Polk County Bar Assn., SAR (registrar Iowa 1983-94, v.p. 1994-97, chancellor 1997-99), Order of the Founders and Patriots of Am., Phi Alpha Delta (chpt. pres. 1975). Contbr. articles to profl. jours. With U.S. Army, 1971-73. Fellow Iowa Acad. Trial Lawyers; mem. ABA, ATLA, SAR (registrar Iowa 1983-94, 2001—, v.p. 1994-97, chancellor 1997-2001), Iowa Trial Lawyers Assn., Iowa Bar Assn., Iowa State Bar Assn., Polk County Bar Assn., Order of the Founders and Patriots of Am., Phi Alpha Delta (chpt. pres. 1975). E-mail;. State civil litigation, Personal injury. Home: 532 Waterbury Cir Des Moines IA 50312-1316 Office: Galligan Tully Doyle & Reid PC The Plaza 300 Walnut St Ste 5 Des Moines IA 50309-2233 E-mail: rdoyle@galliganlaw.com

DOZIER, DANIEL PRESTON, lawyer; b. Detroit, May 30, 1944; s. Daniel P. and Phyllis Ann D.; m. Martha S. Solt; children: Daniel P., William Robert, Rebecca Jane. BA, Wayne State U., 1968, JD, 1971. Bar: Mich. 1971, D.C. 1979. Asst. gen. counsel UAW, Detroit, 1971-74; exec. asst. to mayor City of Detroit, 1974-76; dir. congl. liaison HEW, Washington, 1977-79; legal counsel Fed. Mediation and Conciliation Svc., Washington, 1979-88; sr. mediator, Clean Sites, Inc., Alexandria, Va., 1988-93; mem. Adminstrv. Conf. of U.S, 1986-88. Ctr. Urban Studies fellow, 1970-71; v.p. TLI Sys., Inc., 1993—. Mem. D.C. Bar Assn., Soc. Profls. in Dispute Resolution (pres. D.C. chpt. 1988-89, mem. qualifications commn. 1988—), Little Falls Swim Club. Democrat. Mem. Soc. of Friends. Avocations: sailing, reading, camping, bicycling. E-mail: ddozier@tlisystems.com. Office: TLI Sys Inc 4340 E W Highway Ste 1120 Bethesda MD 20814

DRABKIN, MURRAY, lawyer; b. N.Y.C., Aug. 3, 1928; s. Max Drabkin and Minnie (Masin) Weiner; m. Mary Elizabeth Hooper, Nov. 27, 1971. AB, Hamilton Coll., 1950; LLB, Harvard U., 1953. Bar: D.C. 1953, U.S. Ct. Appeals (D.C. cir.) 1954, N.Y. 1966, U.S. Supreme Ct. 1972. Counsel com. on judiciary U.S. Ho. of Reps., Washington, 1957-66; spl. asst. to mayor City of N.Y., 1966-68; pvt. practice N.Y.C. and Washington, 1968-82; ptnr. Cadwalader, Wickersham & Taft, Washington, 1983-92; ret., 1992; of counsel Hopkins & Sutter, Washington, 1992-2000. Dir. Conn. State Revenue Task Force, 1969-71; mem. adv. com. FRS, Washington, 1970-71, D.C. Tax Revision Com., 1976-77; bd. dirs. Geneva Steel Corp. 2000—/ Contbr. articles to profl. jours. Served with USN, 1953-57, to lt. commdr. USNR. Mem. Nat. Bankruptcy Conf. (chmn. com. on RR reorgn. 1984-2000, chmn. com on bankruptcy crimes, 1994-98), D.C. Bar Assn., Harvard Club of Washington (pres. 2000—, bd. dirs. 1996—), Harvard Club of N.Y.C., Chesapeake Bay Bermuda 40 Assn., Nat. Press Club, Phi Beta Kappa (bd. dirs. 1998-, fellow, 1995—), Delta Sigma Rho. Bankruptcy, State and local taxation.

DRAKE, WILLIAM FRANK, JR. lawyer; b. St. Louis, Mar. 29, 1932; s. William Frank and Beatrice Drake; m. Martha Minohr Mockbee. BA, Principia Coll., 1954; LLB, Yale U., 1957. Bar: Pa. 1958. Practice, Phila., 1958-68, 84—; mem. firm Montgomery, McCracken, Walker & Rhoads, 1958-68, 87-96, of counsel, 1984-87, 96—; sr. v.p., gen. counsel Alco Std. Corp., 1968-79, 96-98, sr. v.p. adminstrn., 1979-83; chmn., CEO Alco Health Svcs. Corp., 1983-84, vice chmn., 1984-98, also bd. dirs.; vice chmn., gen. counsel Alco Standard Corp. (now Ikon Office Solutions Inc.), 1996-98. Trustee Peoples Light & Theatre Co., Malvern, Pa. With U.S. Army, 1957-58. Mem. ABA, Phila. Bar Assn., Union League (Phila.), Roaring Fork Club (Basalt, Colo.), Wilmington (Del.) Country Club, First Troop, Phila. City Calvary. General corporate, Pension, profit-sharing, and employee benefits, Securities. Office: Montgomery McCracken Walker & Rhoads 123 S Broad St Fl 24 Philadelphia PA 19109-1099

DRAPER, DANIEL CLAY, retired lawyer; b. Boston, June 7, 1920; s. John W. and Lulu H. (Clay) D.; m. Marcia Humphreys, Nov. 25, 1989. BA, W.Va. U., 1940, MA, 1941; LLB, Harvard U., 1947. Assoc. Kelly, Drye & Warren, N.Y.C., 1947-55; ptnr. Cadwalader, Wickersham & Taft, 1962-91, ret. Bd. dirs. Union Devel., Montclair, N.J.; adj. prof. history Bloomfield Coll., 1991. Contbr. articles to profl. jours. Mgr. campaign Montclair's Cmty. Com. Candidates, 1964; trustee Montclair Art Mus., 1966-71, Bloomfield Coll., 1974-81, 87-95. With USN, 1942-46. Decorated Bronze Star, European Service Ribbon (3 stars). Mem. N.Y. State Bar Assn. (chmn. banking com. 1981-85), N.Y. County Lawyers Assn. (sec. 1979-81, pres. 1984-87, chmn. banking com. 1968-78, housing and urban affairs and real property coms., chmn. investment com.), St. George Soc., Harvard Club, N.Y.C. Episcopalian. Home: 14 Houston Rd Little Falls NJ 07424-2406

DRAPER, GERALD LINDEN, lawyer; b. Oberlin, Ohio, July 14, 1941; s. Earl Linden and Mary Antoinette (Colloto) Draper; m. Barbara Jean Winter, Aug. 26, 1960; children: Melissa Leah Price, Stephen Edward. BA, Muskingum Coll., 1963; JD, Northwestern U., 1966. Bar: Ohio 1966, US Dist Ct (so dist) Ohio 1966, US Ct Appeals (6th cir) 1975, US Supreme Ct 1980, US Dist Ct (no dist) Ohio 2000. Ptnr. Bricker & Eckler, Columbus, Ohio, 1966-88, Thompson, Hine & Flory, Columbus, 1989-95, Draper, Hollenbaugh, Briscoe, Yashko & Carmany, Columbus, 1996-99, Roetzel & Andress, Columbus, 1999—. Trustee, pres Wesley Glen Retirement Ctr, Columbus, Ohio, 1979—95; trustee Meth Elder Care Servs, Inc, 1995—, Muskigum Col, New Concord, Ohio, 1988—92, 1993—, vice chair, 1994—; trustee, pres Wesley Ridge Retirement Ctr, 1995—2000, treas, 2001—. Fellow: Am Col Trial Lawyers, Am Bd Trial Advs (trustee Ohio chpt 2001—); mem.: ABA (House Dels 1991—97, House Dels 1999—2001), Ohio State Bar Asn (pres 1990—91), Ohio State Bar Found (trustee 1992—97), Columbus Bar Asn (pres 1982—83, Bar Serv Medal 1998), Columbus Bar Found (pres 1984—86), Nat Conf Bar Found (trustee 1987—90, trustee 1991—94), Ohio Continuing Legal Educ Inst (trustee 1992—98, chair 1997—98), Ohio Asn Hosp Attys, Def Research Inst. Avocations: travel, golf, photography. General civil litigation, Insurance, Professional liability. Office: Roetzel & Andress 155 E Broad St Columbus OH 43215-3609 E-mail: gdraper@ralaw.com

DRAY, MARK S. lawyer; b. Alliance, Ohio, Feb. 8, 1943; s. Dwight Leroy and N. Pauline (Clark) D.; m. Jonadell Pascoe, June 5, 1965; children: Melisa Louise, Justin Clark. BA, Mount Union Coll., Alliance, Ohio, 1965; JD, Coll. of William and Mary, 1968, M Law and Taxation, 1969. Bar: Va. 1968, U.S. Dist. Ct. (ea. dist.) Va. 1970, U.S. Tax Court 1971. Tax sr. Price Waterhouse, Washington, 1969-70; assoc. Hunton & Williams, Richmond, Va., 1970-77, ptnr., 1977—. Adv. coun. William and Mary Tax Conf., 1980-88; mem. So. Employee Benefits Conf., 1974—; trustee So. Fed. Tax Inst., 1989—, chair, 1997. Contbr. articles to profl. jours.; speaker in field. Fellow Am. Coll. Tax Counsel, Am. Coll. Employee Benefits Counsel (charter); mem. ABA (com. on employee benefits 1975—, chmn. 1989-90, joint com. on employee benefits 1988-91, chmn. 1990-91), Va. Bar Assn., Richmond Bar Assn., Country Club Va., Order of Coif, Blue Key. Episcopalian. Avocation: golf. Pension, profit-sharing, and employee benefits. Office: Hunton & Williams Riverfront Plz East Tower PO Box 1535 Richmond VA 23218-1535 E-mail: mdray@hunton.com

DRAYTON, V. MICHAEL, lawyer, educator; b. Evansville, Ind., Sept. 13, 1953; m. Janet L. Collings, Oct. 10, 1981; children: Christopher Michael, Phillip Arthur George. BA, Valparaiso U., 1976, JD, 1980. Bar: Ind. 1980, Ill. 1980, U.S. Dist. Ct. (so. and no. dists.) Ind. 1980, U.S. Ct. appeals (7th cir.) 1993, U.S. Supreme Ct. 1994; cert. mediator family law, civil litigation. Ptnr. Sallwasser & McCain, La Porte, Ind., 1980—. Adj. prof. law Ind. U., South Bend, 1985—. Mem. ATLA, ABA, Ind. Trial Lawyers Assn., Ind. Bar Assn., Ill. Bar Assn., LaPorte County Assn., La Porte City Bar Assn., Lions. General civil litigation, Criminal, Personal injury. Office: Sallwasser and McCain 820 Jefferson Ave La Porte IN 46350-3410

DREBSKY, DENNIS JAY, lawyer; b. N.Y.C., Sept. 28, 1946; s. Benjamin and Ronnie (Penso) D.; m. Norma Louise Linschitz, Aug. 16, 1970; children: Richard Michael, Joshua William Evan. BBA magna cum laude, CCNY, 1967; JD, Cornell U., 1970. Bar: N.Y. 1971, U.S. Dist. Ct. (so. dist.) N.Y. 1972, U.S. Ct. Appeals (2d cir.) 1971, U.S. Ct. Appeals (5th cir.) 1980, U.S. Ct. Appeals (9th cir.) 1982, U.S. Ct. Appeals (1st cir.) 1981, U.S. Ct. Appeals (10th cir.) 1984, U.S. Ct. Appeals (4th cir.) 1986, U.S. Ct. Appeals (D.C. cir.) 1998. Assoc. Skadden, Arps, Slate, Meagher & Flom, N.Y.C., 1970-77, ptnr., 1978-91, Clifford, Chance, Rogers & Wells, 1991—. Trustee Community Law Offices, N.Y.C., 1980—. Mem. Assn. of Bar of City of N.Y. (mem. com. on corp. reorgn. 1985—). Jewish. Avocations: reading, jogging, theater. Bankruptcy, General civil litigation, General corporate. Home: 7 Glen Hill Ct Dix Hills NY 11746-4819 Office: Clifford Chance Rogers & Wells 200 Park Ave Fl 8E New York NY 10166-0800 E-mail: dennis.drebsky@cliffordchance.com

DREIZE, LIVIA REBBEKA, lawyer; b. Jan. 14, 1964; BS in Hotel and Restaurant Mgmt., Fla. Internat. U., 1988; postgrad., U. Complutense de Madrid, 1990; JD summa cum laude, Pontifical Cath. U. P.R., Ponce, 1992. Bar: P.R. 1993, Fla. 1994, D.C. 1996, U.S. Dist. Ct. (so. dist.) Fla. 1995. Assoc. Law Offices of Nathan D. Clark, Miami, Fla., 1993-96; mng. ptnr. Damera & Dreize, P.A., 1996—. Lectr. Fla. Internat. U., Miami, 1998. Mem. Law Rev., Pontifical Cath. U. P.R., 1990-92. Recipient Acad. Excellence award P.R. Bar Assn., 1992. Mem. ATLA, Dade County Bar Assn. General corporate, Family and matrimonial, Immigration, naturalization, and customs. Office: Damera & Dreize PA 2701 S Le Jeune Rd Ste 406 Miami FL 33134-5821

DRENDEL, KEVIN GILBERT, lawyer; b. Boston, Dec. 29, 1959; s. Gilbert Xavier and Carol Katherine D.; m. Elizabeth Rosemary Caron, Feb. 24, 1961; childen: Nathan Xavier, Tyler Kevin, Jonathan David, Nicholas Raymond, Ryan Joseph, Julia Elizabeth. B Spl. Studies, Cornell Coll., 1982; JD, No. Ill. U., 1991. Bar: Ill. 1991, U.S. Dist. Ct. (no. dist. Ill.) 1992. With Drendel, Schanlaber, Horwitz, Tatnall & McCracken, Aurora, Ill., 1991-94, Drendel, Tatnall, Hoffman & McCracken, Batavia, 1994-96; ptnr. Drendel, Tatnall & Hoffman, 1996-97, Drendel, Tatnall, Batavia, 1998-2000, Drendel Tatnall Lonergan Drendel, 2000—. Trustee Am. Cancer Soc., Batavia, 1995-96. Recipient award for Outstanding Scholastic Achievement, West Pub., 1991. Mem. Ill. State Bar Assn., Kane County Bar Assn. (chmn. mem. com. 1995-98, dir. 1999-2000, sec./treas. 2000-01, second v.p. 2001—), Christian Legal Soc. Avocations: musky fishing, cigars. General practice, Municipal (including bonds), Probate. Office: Drendel Tatnall Lonergan Drendel 201 Houston St Ste 300 Batavia IL 60510-1980 E-mail: kgd@batavialaw.com

DRENGLER, WILLIAM ALLAN JOHN, lawyer; b. Shawano, Wis., Nov. 18, 1949; s. William J. and Vera J. (Simmonds) D.; m. Kathleen A. Hintz, June 18, 1983; children: Ryan, Jeffrey, Brittany. BA, Am. U., 1972; JD, Marquette U., 1976. Bar: Wis. 1976, U.S. Dist. Ct. (ea. and we. dists.) Wis. 1976. Assoc. Herrling, Swain & Drengler, Appleton, Wis., 1976-78; dist. atty. Outagamie County, 1979-81; corp. counsel Marathon County, Wausau, Wis., 1981-96, Drengler Law Firm, Wausau, 1997—. Vice chmn. Wis. Equal Rights Coun., 1978-83, Wis. Coun. on Criminal Justice, Madison, 1983-87. Nat. pres. Future Bus. Leaders Am., 1967-68; mem. nat. Dem. delegation, 1974-76; mem. adminstrv. com. Wis. Dems., Madison, 1977-81, 86-88; chmn. local Selective Svc. Bd., Wausau, 1982-89; mem. adv. bd. Wausau Salvation Army, 1986—; judge adv. officer Wis. Army N.G., 1989-96; bd. dirs. Wausau Youth/Little League Baseball, 1988—, team mgr., 1994—. Mem. ABA (chair com. on govt. lawyers, sect. state and local govt. 1991-93, bylaws com. govt. and pub. sect. lawyers divsn. 1993-98), KC, Nat. Assn. County Civil Attys. (dir. 1986-88, v.p. 1988-91, pres. 1991-92), Nat. Assn. Counties (bd. dirs. 1991-92, taxation and fin. steering com. 1991-93, deferred compensation adv. com. 1993-95, justice and pub. safety steering com. 1993-94), State Bar Wis. (govt. lawyers divsn., bd. dirs. 1982-86, sec. 1986-87, pres. 1989-91, professionalism com. 1987-91, 92-2000), Kiwanis (lt. gov. 1985-86, club pres. 1989-90, chair past lt. govs. coun. 1990-91), Wausau Elks (parliamentarian 2000—), Kiwanis Internat. Found. (Hixon Fellowship Award 2001). Roman Catholic. Avocations: baseball, camping, fishing, gardening, tennis. Criminal, Family and matrimonial, General practice. Office: PO Box 5152 609 Scott St Wausau WI 54402-5152

DRENNAN, JOSEPH PETER, lawyer; b. Albany, N.Y., Apr. 15, 1956; s. Richard Peter and Ann Marie (Conlon) D.; m. Adriana Sonia Miramontes, Sept. 26, 1987; children: Patricia Solange, Monica Adriana, Michael Robert II. BA in Polit. Sci., U. Richmond, 1978; JD, Cath. U. of Am., Washington, 1981. Bar: D.C. 1981, U.S. Dist. Ct. D.C. 1983, U.S. Ct. Appeals (fed. cir.) 1983, Va. 1984, U.S. Ct. Appeals (D.C. cir.) 1984, U.S. Dist. Ct. (no. dist.) Va. 1987, U.S. Ct. Appeals (4th cir.) 1987, U.S. Dist. Ct. (no. dist.) Miss. 1988, U.S. Dist. Ct. Md. 1990, U.S. Bankruptcy Ct. (ea. dist.) Va. 1991. Pvt. practice, Washington, 1981—. Adj. faculty mem. Germanna C.C., Fredericksburg, Va., 1995—. Mem. ATLA, Nat. Legal Aid & Def. Assn., Bar Assn. D.C., Am. Bankruptcy Inst., Alexandria Bar Assn., Va. Trial Lawyers Assn., Trial Lawyers Met. Washington. Republican. Roman Catholic. Federal civil litigation, Computer, Personal injury. Address: 218 N Lee St Fl 3 Alexandria VA 22314-2631 E-mail: joseph.drennan@ireland.net, j.drennan@gte.net

DRESCHER, JOHN WEBB, lawyer; b. Norfolk, Va., May 13, 1948; s. Otto Charles and Anne Best (Webb) D.; m. Dale McKeithan Moore, June 13, 1970; 1 child, Ryan. BA, Hampden-Sydney Coll., 1970; JD, U. Richmond, 1973. Bar: Va. 1973, U.S. Supreme Ct. 1980, U.S. Ct. Appeals (4th cir.) 1985, U.S. Dist. Ct. (ea. dist.) Va. 1976. Assoc. Brydges, Hammers & Hudgins, Virginia Beach, 1973-74; asst. atty. Office of Commonwealth Atty., 1974-75; assoc. Pickett, Spain & Lyle, P.C., 1976-78; ptnr. Pickett, Lyle , Siegel, Drescher & Croshaw P.C., 1979-87, Breit, Drescher & Breit, P.C., Norfolk, 1988—. Pres. Hampden-Sydney Alumni Assn., Tidewater, Va., 1970—. Named among best lawyers in Am. Naifch & Smith, 1995—. Fellow Am. Bd. Trial Advocates; mem. ATLA, Va. Trial Lawyers Assn. (bd. govs. 1990—), Am. Inns Ct., Norfolk-Portsmouth Bar Assn., U. Richmond Law Sch. Alumni Assn., Virginia Beach Bar Assn. (pres. 1990). Democrat. Episcopalian. Avocations: physical fitness, golf. Civil rights, Personal injury, Product liability. Home: 925 Holladay Pt Virginia Beach VA 23451-3912 Office: Breit Drescher & Breit 1000 Dominion Twr 999 Waterside Dr Ste 1000 Norfolk VA 23510-3304 E-mail: jdrescher@breitdrescherbreit.com

DRESCHER, KATHLEEN EBBEN, lawyer; b. Kaukauna, Wis., May 17, 1963; d. Willard Peter and Helen Mary (Joyce) Ebben; m. Park Morris Drescher, Aug. 12, 1989; children: John Park, William Morris. BA, Lawrence U., 1985; JD, Washington U. St. Louis, 1989. Bar: Mo. 1989, Wis. 1992. Assoc. Popkin & Stern, St. Louis, 1989-90; ptnr. Drescher & Drescher, 1990-92; shareholder Drescher & Drescher, S.C., Appleton, Wis., 1992—. Pres. bd. dirs. Emergency Shelters, Appleton, 1992—; bd. dirs. Child Care Resource and Referral, Appleton. Mem. ABA, Wis. Bar Assn., Mo. Bar Assn., Outagamie County Bar Assn. Avocation: tennis. Estate planning, General practice, Real property. Home: 14 Lamplighter Ct Appleton WI 54914-6519 Office: Drescher & Drescher SC 100 W Lawrence St Fl 3D Appleton WI 54911-5773

DRESCHER, PARK MORRIS, lawyer; b. St. Louis, Apr. 20, 1963; s. John Morris and Katherine (White) D.; m. Kathleen Ebben, Aug. 12, 1989; children: John Park, William Morris. BA, Lawrence U., 1985; JD, St. Louis U., 1988. Bar: Mo., 1989, Wis., 1992, U.S. Ct. of Appeals (8th cir.), 1989. Assoc. Biggs & Hensley, P.C., St. Louis, 1988-90; ptnr. Drescher & Drescher, S.C., Appleton, Wis., 1990—. Trustee The Mari Taniguchi Found., Appleton, 1997—; mem. small bus. sect. Appleton Area C. of C., 1997. Mem. ABA, Wis. Bar Assn., Mo. Bar Assn., Outagamie County Bar Assn. Avocation: tennis. Office: Drescher & Drescher SC 100 W Lawrence St Appleton WI 54911-5773

DREVVATNE, DAG, lawyer; b. Oslo, Norway, Oct. 10, 1955; s. Tor and Randi D.; m. Elizabeth Christensen Drevvatne, June 19, 1993; children: Catherine Elizabeth, Camilla Charlotte. JD, U. Oslo, Norway, 1983. Lawyer Tax Office, Barum, Norway, 1984-86; atty. Arthur Andersen, Oslo, Norway, 1986-88, Vogt & Co., Oslo, Norway, 1989-94, Sander, Truyen & Co., Oslo, Norway, 1994-99; lawyer pvt. practice Norway, 1999—. Avocations: boating, skiing, travel. General corporate, Franchising, General practice. Home: Asfaret 8 1362 Barum Norway Office: Advokat Dag Drevvatne Fossumveinen 70 1332 Osteras Norway

DREXLER, KENNETH, lawyer; b. Aug. 2, 1941; s. Fred and Martha Jane (Cunningham) D. BA, Stanford U., 1963; JD, UCLA, 1969. Bar: Calif. 1970. Assoc. David S. Smith, Beverly Hills, Calif., 1970, McCutchen, Doyle, Brown and Enersen, San Francisco, 1970-77, Chickering & Gregory, San Francisco, 1977-80, ptnr., 1980-82, Drexler & Leach, San Rafael, 1982—. Served with AUS, 1964-66. Mem. Calif. State Bar (resolutions com. conf. of dels. 1979-83, chmn. 1982-83, adminstrn. justice com. 1983-89, chmn. 1987-88, adv. mem. 1990-2000), Marin County Bar Assn. (bd. dirs. 1985-87), Bar Assn. San Francisco (bd. dirs. 1980-81), San Francisco Barristers Club (pres. 1976, dir. 1975-76), Marin Conservation League (bd. dirs. 1985-97, 98—, treas. 2001—). Estate planning, General practice. Office: 1330 Lincoln Ave Ste 300 San Rafael CA 94901-2143 E-mail: kdrexler@svn.net

DRIBIN, LELAND GEORGE, lawyer; b. Washington, Sept. 11, 1944; s. Daniel Macabeus and Tillie (Horowitz) D.; m. Eileen Wilansky, Sept. 28, 1969; 1 child, Julie Marie. B.A., George Washington U., 1965, J.D., 1968, LL.M., 1972. Bar: D.C. 1968, U.S. Ct. Appeals (D.C. cir.) 1969, U.S. Supreme Ct. 1972, Colo. 1973, U.S. Dist. Ct. Colo. 1973, Calif. 1976, U.S. Dist. Ct. (cen. dist.) Calif. 1981, U.S. Ct. Claims 1984, Ill. 1988. Asst. corp. counsel D.C. Govt., Washington, 1970-72; asst. counsel Martin Marietta Corp., Denver, 1972-74, regional counsel, Torrance, Calif., 1975-76; div. counsel Litton Industries, Van Nuys, Calif., 1976-81; assoc. McKenna, Conner & Cuneo, Los Angeles, 1981-83; v.p. legal affairs, aerospace group counsel Morton Thiokol, Chgo., 1983-87, Seyfarth, Shaw, Fairfeather & Geraldson, 1990—. Mem. ABA, Colo. Bar Assn., Los Angeles County Bar Assn., Nat. Contract Mgmt. Assn. Democrat. General corporate, Government contracts and claims. Home: 325 S Saltair Ave Los Angeles CA 90049-4128 Office: Seyfarth Shaw Fairweather & Geraldson 2029 Century Park E Ste 3300 Los Angeles CA 90067-3019

DRINKO, JOHN DEAVER, lawyer; b. St. Marys, W.Va., June 17, 1921; s. Emery J. and Hazel (White) D.; m. Elizabeth Gibson, May 14, 1946; children: Elizabeth Lee Sullivan, Diana Lynn Martin, John Randall, Jay Deaver. AB, Marshall U., 1942; JD, Ohio State U., 1944; postgrad., U. Tex. Sch. Law, 1944; LLD (hon.), Marshall U., 1980, Ohio State U., 1986, John Carroll U., 1987, Capital U., 1988, Cleve. State U., 1990; DHL (hon.), David N. Myers Coll., 1990, U. N.H., 1992, Baldwin-Wallace Coll., 1993, Ursuline Coll., 1994, Notre Dame Coll., 1997, U. Rio Grande, 1999, Marietta Coll., 2001. Bar: Ohio 1945, D.C 1946, U.S. Dist. Ct. (no. dist.) Ohio 1958. Assoc. Baker & Hostetler, Cleve., 1945-55, ptnr., 1955-69, mng. ptnr., from 1969, sr. adviser to mng. com. Chmn. bd. Cleve. Inst. Electronics Inc., Double D Ranch Inc., Ohio; bd. dirs. Cloyes Gear and Products Inc., McGean-Rohco Worldwide Inc., Orvis Co. Inc., Preformed Line Products Inc. Trustee Elizabeth G. and John D. Drinko Charitable Found., Orvis-Perkins Found., Thomas F. Peterson Found., Mellen Found., The Cloyes-Myers Found., Marshall U. Found.; founder Consortium of Multiple Sclerosis Ctrs., Mellen Conf. on Acute and Critical Care Nursing, Case Western Res. U. Disting. fellow Cleve. Clinc Found., 1991; Ohio State Law Sch. Bldg. named in his honor, 1995, libr. at Marshall U. named in his honor, 1997; inducted into Bus. Hall of Fame, Marshall Univ., 1996. Mem. ABA, Am. Jud. Assn., Bar Assn. Greater Cleve., Greater Cleve. Growth Assn., Ohio State Bar Assn., Jud. Conf. 8th Jud. Dist. (life), Soc. Benchers, Case Western Res. U. Law Sch. Assn., Cleve. Play House, Cleve. Civil War Round-table, Mayfield Country Club, Union Club, The Club at Soc. Ctr., O'Donnell Golf Club, Order of Coif, 33o Scottish Rite Mason, Knight Templar, York Rite, Euclid Blue Lodge No. 599 (Jesters, Shrine, Grotto). Republican. Presbyterian. Home: 4891 Middledale Rd Cleveland OH 44124-2522 also: 1245 Otono Dr Palm Springs CA 92264-8445 Office: Baker & Hostetler LLP 1900 E 9th St Ste 3200 Cleveland OH 44114-3475

DRISCOLL, DAWN-MARIE, lawyer; b. Framingham, Mass., Nov. 5, 1946; d. Paul Francis and Wanda Louise (Haznar) D.; m. Norman Marcus. BA, Regis Coll., 1968; JD, Suffolk U., 1973, DHL (hon.), 1989; DCS (hon.), Bentley Coll., 1994. Bar: Mass. 1973. Asst. counsel Mass. Senate, Boston, 1973-78; counsel William Filene's Sons Co., 1978-80, v.p. corp. affairs, gen. counsel, 1980-88; ptnr. Palmer & Dodge, 1988-90; pres. Driscoll Assocs., 1991—. Exec. fellow Ctr. Bus. Ethics Bentley Coll., 1995—; trustee Zurich, Scudder Funds, 1987—; dir. 1st Internat. Life Ins. Co., 199092, Premier Life Assurance Co. N.Y., 1991-92; mem. bd. govs. Investment Co. Inst., 1995-97, 99-2001; bd. dirs. Computer Rescue Squad; mem. adv. coun. divsn. employment security State of Mass., 1985-90; bd. dirs., mem. exec. com. Boston Mcpl. Rsch. Bur., 1978-92, chmn., 1988-90; lectr. Law Sch., Suffolk U., 1975, Law Sch., Boston Coll., 1976; bd. dirs. New Eng. Legal Found., Boston, 1980-85, United Way of Mass. Bay, 1989-91; overseer Sta. WGBH-TV, 1988-95, Children's Hosp., 1989-94; mem. adv. bd. Bentley Coll. Ctr. Bus. Ethics, 1991—; mem. adv. bd. Women's Equity Fund Colo., 1992-98; visitor in residence Bunting Inst. Radcliffe Coll., 1990-91. Co-author: Members of The Club: The Coming of Age of Executive Women, 1993, The Ethical Edge: Tales of Organizations That Have Faced Moral Crises, 1996, Ethics Matters: How to Implement Values-Driven Management, 2000. Trustee, mem. exec. com. Regis Coll., Weston, Mass., 1983-90; trustee, bd. dirs. Roxbury Cmty. Coll. Found., 1985-88; mem. Mass. Gov.'s Commn. on Mature Industries, 1983-84; bd. dirs. Downtown Crossing Assn., Boston, 1980-90, chmn., 1980-83; bd. dirs. Better Bus. Bur., 1984, Social Policy Rsch. Group, 1985-89, Mass. Assn. Mental Health, 1985-90. Mass. grad. legis. fellow, Boston, 1969-70. Mem. Nat. Assn. Corp. Dirs., Internat. Women's Forum, Soc. Bus. Ethics, Mass. Women's Forum, Boston Econ. Club. General corporate. Office: Driscoll Assocs 4909 SW 9th Pl Cape Coral FL 33914-7344

DRISCOLL, MICHAEL HARDEE, lawyer; b. Houston, Mar. 24, 1946; s. Victor Amadale and Inez Mildred (Hardee) D. B.B.A., U. Houston, 1969, J.D., 1972. Bar: Tex. 1972. Precinct judge Harris County, Tex., 1969-73; justice of peace Harris County, Tex., 1973-78; judge City of Friendswood, Tex., 1978-80; hearing judge Tex. Edn. Agy., 1978-80; ptnr. Burge, Shults & Driscoll, Houston, 1978-80; elected county atty. Harris County, Houston, 1980— . Bd. dirs. Bay Area Drug Abuse Com., 1975-80, Riverside Gen. Hosp., 1977-80; mem. Salvation Army Boys' Club Adv. Council. Mem. State Bar Tex., Houston Bar Assn., Tex. Dist. and County Attys. Assn. (bd. dirs.), Houston C. of C. Democrat. Baptist. Lodges: Rotary, Scottish Rite, Shriners (Houston.). Office: County Atty's Office 1001 Preston St Houston TX 77002-1839

DRONEY, CHRISTOPHER F. judge; b. June 22, 1954; m. Elizabeth Kelly, Oct. 13, 1979. BA, Coll. Holy Cross, 1976; JD, U. Conn., 1979. Ptnr. Reid & Riege, P.C., Hartford, Conn., 1983-93; U.S. atty. for dist. of Conn. U.S. Dept. Justice, New Haven, 1993-97; judge U.S. Dist. Ct., Conn., 1997—. Notes and comments editor Conn. Law Rev., 1978-79. Mem. U.S. atty. gen. adv. com., 1996-97. Office: 450 Main St Hartford CT 06103-3022

DROUGHT, JAMES L. lawyer; b. San Antonio, May 8, 1943; s. James L. and Juanita Herff Drought; m. Joane Bennett, Nov. 25, 1966; children: James L. III, Henry Patrick IV, Elizabeth H. BBA, U. Tex., 1966; JD, St. Mary's Sch. Law, San Antonio, 1969. Bar: Tex. 1969, U.S. Dist. Ct. (so. and we. dists.) Tex. 1975, U.S. Ct. Appeals (5th cir.) 1975, U.S. Supreme Ct. 1975; bd. cert. civil trial law Tex. Bd. Legal Specialization. Assoc. Law Office of Thomas Drought, San Antonio, 1969-73; ptnr. Brite Drought Bubbitt & Halter, 1973-88, Brite & Drought, San Antonio, 1988-93, Drought & Pipkin LLP, San Antonio, 1993-98, Drought, Drought, & Bobbitt, San Antonio, 1998—. Past pres. Sarah Roberts Fench Home, San Antonio, 1985-86, Boysville, Inc., San Antonio, 1994. Fellow Tex. Bar Found., San Antonio Bar Found.; mem. ABA, State Bar Tex. (mem. grievance com. 1996—). General civil litigation. Office: Drought Drought & Bobbit LLP 112 E Pecan St San Antonio TX 78205-1512

DROWOTA, FRANK F., III, state supreme court justice; b. Williamsburg, Ky., July 7, 1938; married; 2 children. B.A., Vanderbilt U., 1960, J.D., 1965. Bar: Tenn. 1965, U.S. Dist. Ct. Tenn. 1965. Pvt. practice, 1965-70; chancellor Tenn. Chancery Ct. Div. 7, 1970-74; judge Tenn. Ct. Appeals, Middle Tenn. Div., 1974-80; assoc. justice Tenn. Supreme Ct., Nashville, 1980-89, chief justice, 1989-93, assoc. justice, 1993-2001; chief justice, 2001—. Served with USN, 1960-62. Office: Tenn Supreme Ct 318 Supreme Ct Bldg 401 7th Ave N Nashville TN 37219-1406

DRUCKER, CHRISTINE MARIE, lawyer; b. Sioux City, Iowa, Apr. 16, 1947; d. Sigmund James and Paula Frances (Riedmann) Kulawik; m. John Joseph Drucker, Jr., June 19, 1971; children— Emily, Jeremy. B.A., Webster Coll., 1969; J.D., St. Louis U., 1972. Bar: Mo. 1972, Ill. 1973, Minn. 1977, U.S. Dist. Ct. (no. dist.) Ill. 1972, U.S. DIst. Ct. Minn. 1985. Law clk., Mo. Ct. Appeals, St. Louis, 1972-73; assoc. Walsh, Case & Coale, Chgo., 1973-74; atty. Ill. State's Attys. Assoc., Elgin, Ill., 1974-76; atty., adviser U.S. Dept. Interior, Mpls., 1979-81; sole practice, Mpls., 1983—. Mem. fin. com. Christ the King Parish, Mpls., 1979-81. Mem. ABA, Minn. State Bar Assn., Minn. Women Lawyers, Hennepin County Bar Assn., Minn. Women's Network. Democrat. Roman Catholic. General corporate, Entertainment. Home: 5121 Bryant Ave S Minneapolis MN 55419-1213 Office: 431 S 7th St Minneapolis MN 55415-1821

DRUCKER, JACQUELIN F. lawyer, arbitrator, mediator, educator, author; b. Celina, Ohio, Oct. 15, 1954; d. Jack Burton and Dorothea (Eckenstein) Davis; m. John H. Drucker, Sept. 8, 1990. BA with distinction and honors, Ohio State U., 1977, JD with honors, 1981. Bar: Ohio 1981, N.Y. 1992, U.S. Supreme Ct. 1989. Legis. asst. Speaker of Ohio Ho. of Reps., Columbus, 1974-78; rsch. asst., lobbyist United Auto Workers, 1978-81; labor atty. Porter, Wright, Morris & Arthur, 1981-84; gen. counsel Ohio Employment Rels. Bd., 1984-86, exec. dir., 1986-88, vice chmn., 1988-90; pvt. practice arbitration and mediation nationwide and the Caribbean, 1990—; dir. labor mgmt. programs sch. indsl. and labor rels. Cornell U., 1994-97. Dir. programs for neutrals Cornell U. Sch. of Indsl. and Labor Rels., 1996—; dir. for ednl. svcs. Cornell Inst. on Conflict Resolution, 1998—; cons. to W.J. Usery Ctr. for Workplace, Ga. State U.; counsel to Gov.'s Task Force on Collective Bargaining, Columbus, 1983-84; adj. prof. labor law Franklin U., Columbus, 1988-89; mem. panel of arbitrators Fed. Mediation and Conciliation Svc., Am. Arbitration Assn., Employment ADR Roster of Neutrals of Am. Arbitration Assn., N.Y. State Employment Rels. Bd.; mem. roster of neutrals N.Y.C. Office of Collective Bargaining; mem. panel V.I. Pub. Employment Rels. Bd., N.J. Pub. Employment Rels. Commn., N.Y. Pub. Employment Rels. Bd., Port Authority Employment Rels. Panel; mem. permanent arbitration panel United Mine Workers and Bituminous Coal Operators Assn., Am. Postal Workers Union, U.S. Postal Svc., Off-Track Betting Corp. and Local 32E, State of N.Y. and Pub. Employees Fedn., State of N.Y. and Civil Svc. Employees Assn., Consolidated Edison and Utility Workers Local 1-2, U. Cin. and Dist. 925, Beth Israel Med. Ctr. and 1199 Nat. Health and Human Svcs. Employees Union, Infineum and Teamsters Local 877; cons. labor mgmt. cooperation, 1996—; lectr., spkr. in field. Author: Collective Bargaining Law in Ohio, 1993; editor L.I. Indsl. Rels. Quar.; contbg. editor Pub. Sector Law and Employment Law supplement, 1995, Pub. Sector Labor and Employment Law, 2d edit.; assoc. editor Discipline and Discharge in Arbitration, 1998; contbg. editor: Public Sector Labor and Employment Law, 2nd edit., 1998; contbr. numerous articles to profl. jours. Mem. ABA (labor and employment law sect., co-chair tng. devel. sub-com. of ADR com., 1998-2001, dispute resolution sect., neutral chair, ADR employment and labor law com., 2001-), Nat. Acad. Arbitrators, Ohio State Bar Assn., Assn. of Bar of City of N.Y., N.Y. State Bar Assn. (labor and employment law sect. sec.-elect, sec. 1997-98, co-chair ADR in employment com. 1998-2001, continuing legal edu. chair, 2001-), N.Y. County Lawyers Assn. (employment law and labor rels. com., chmn.), Nassau County Bar Assn., Suffolk County Bar Assn., Indsl. Rels. Rsch. Assn. (N.Y. chpt., Cleve. chpt., L.I. chpt.), Soc. Fed. Labor Rels. Profls. Jewish. Alternative dispute resolution, Contracts commercial, Labor. Office: 432 E 58th St Suite 2 New York NY 10022-2331 E-mail: jd32@cornell.edu

DRUKE, WILLIAM ERWIN, lawyer, judge; b. Phoenix, Dec. 5, 1938; s. Erwin J. and Mary Nell (Hadden) D.; m. Shirley Jean Robinson, Aug. 12, 1978 (div. 1990); children: John E., Michael C.; m. Barbara L. Ross, Mar. 4, 1995. BS, Ariz. State U., 1961; JD, U. Ariz., 1969. Bar: Ariz. 1969, U.S. Dist. Ct. Ariz. 1969. Law clk. Ct. of Appeals, Phoenix, 1969-70; prosecutor Pima County Atty., Tucson, 1970-72; magistrate Tucson City Ct., 1972-74; judge Pima County Superior Ct., Tucson, 1975-85, presiding judge, 1980-85; ptnr. Druke, Feulner & Cornelio P.C., 1985-86; assoc. Fred R. Esser, P.C., Sedona, Ariz., 1986-88; pvt. practice Tucson, 1988-92; judge Ariz. Ct. Appeals, 1992—, chief judge, 1994-99. Mem. Commn. on Jud. Conduct, 1992-96; mem. Ariz. Jud. Coun., 1993-99; mem. Ariz. Supreme Ct. Appellate Study Com., 1994-95; chair bench/bar ad hoc criminal com., 1994-95; chair Ariz. Supreme Ct. Ct. Reporters Com., 1995-97; dean Ariz. Jud. Coll., 1999—. Mem. Juvenile Pro Bon Task Force, Tucson, 1991-92; bd. dirs. The Haven, Am. Heart Assn., Tucson, 1984-85, Alcoholism Counsel of Tucson, 1980-83; mem. Ariz. Criminal Justice Commn., Phoenix, 1983-85; judge Teen Ct.; vol. U. Med. Ctr. With Ariz. Air N.G., 1961-67. Fellow Ariz. Bar Found.; mem. Ariz. Judges Assn. (pres. 1984), Pima County Bar Assn. (bd. dirs. 1981-85). Avocations: roller blading, skiing, travel, reading, tap dancing. Office: Ariz Ct of Appeals 400 W Congress St Tucson AZ 85701-1352 E-mail: druke@alptwo.ct.state.az.us

DRUMMOND, ERIC HUBERT, lawyer; b. Alamogordo, N.Mex., Nov. 16, 1959; s. Howard and Rosaline Drummond; m. Elizabeth Ann Bruch, May 19, 1990; children: Jordan Eric, Natalie rose. BA, U. Tex., 1989, JD, 1992. Bar: Tex. 1993. Assoc. Bickerstaff, Heath & Smiley, LLP, Austin, Tex., 1992-98; ptnr. Casey, Gentz & Sifuentes, LLP, 1998—. Judge mock trial and moot ct. Bd. Advs., Austin, 1992—. Bd. dirs. Legal Aid Ctrl. Tex., Austin, 1996—, Big Bros.-Big Sisters, Austin, 1998-99. Mem. Fed. Comm. Bar Assn., Travis County Bar Assn. Avocations: running, backpacking, mountain climbing. Administrative and regulatory, Communications, Public utilities. Office: Casey Gentz & Sifuentes LLP 919 Congress Ave Ste 1060 Austin TX 78701-2157

DRURY, STEPHEN PATRICK, solicitor; b. London, May 20, 1954; s. Patrick Keith and Anne Rosemary Drury; m. Deborah Swain, June 25, 1983; 3 children. BA in Jurisprudence, Oxford U., 1976, MA in Jurisprudence, 1980. Bar: Eng., Wales 1980, Hong Kong 1984. Ptnr. Holman Fenwick & Willan, London, 1985—. Author: The Arrest of Ships, 1987. Chmn. law fellowship appeal Oxford U.; lic. umpire Amateur Rowing Assn.; trustee Oriel Coll. Devel. Fund. Mem. Kingston Rowing Club, Effingham Golf Club, Merchant Taylors Co. (liveryman). Avocations: rowing, sculling, golf. Banking, Contracts commercial, Transportation. Office: Holman Fenwick & Willan Marlow House 1A Lloyds Ave London EC3N 3AL England

DRYDEN, ROBERT EUGENE, lawyer; b. Chanute, Kans., Aug. 20, 1927; s. Calvin William and Mary Alfreda (Foley) D.; m. Jetta Rae Burger, Dec. 19, 1953; children: Lynn Marie, Thomas Calvin. AA, City Coll., San Francisco, 1947; BS, U. San Francisco, 1951, JD, 1954. Bar: Calif. 1955; diplomate Am. Bd. Trial Advocates (pres. San Francisco chpt. 1997). Assoc. Barfield, Dryden & Ruane (and predecessor firm), San Francisco, 1954-60, jr. ptnr., 1960-65, gen. ptnr., 1965-89; sr. ptnr. Dryden, Margoles, Schimaneck & Wertz, 1989—. Lectr. continuing edn. of the bar, 1971-77; evaluator U.S. Dist. Ct. (no. dist.) Calif. Early Neutral Evaluation Program; master atty. San Francisco Am. Inn of Ct. Mem. bd. counsellors U. San Francisco, 1993—. With USMCR, 1945-46. Fellow Am. Coll. Trial Lawyers, Am. Bar Found., Internat. Acad. Trial Lawyers; mem. ABA, San Francisco Bar Assn., Assn. Def. Counsel (bd. dirs. 1968-71), Def. Rsch. Inst., Internat. Assn. Ins. Counsel, Fedn. Ins. Counsel, U. San Francisco Law Soc. (mem. exec. com. 1970-72), U. San Francisco Alumni Assn. (mem. bd. govs. 1977), Phi Alpha Delta. Insurance, Personal injury, Product liability. Home: 1320 Lasuen Dr Millbrae CA 94030-2846 Office: Dryden Margoles Schimaneck & Wertz 1 California St Ste 2600 San Francisco CA 94111-5427

DRYMALSKI, RAYMOND HIBNER, lawyer, banker; b. Chgo., June 1, 1936; s. Raymond P. and Alice H. (Hibner) D.; m. Sarah Fickes, Apr. 1, 1967; children: Robert, Paige. BA, Georgetown U., 1958; JD, U. Mich., 1961. Bar: Ill. 1962. Lawyer Chgo. Title & Trust Co., 1963-65; asst. sec., atty. No. Trust Co., Chgo., 1965-68; ptnr. Boodell, Sears, Giambalvo & Crowley, 1968-87; mem. Bell Boyd & Lloyd LLC, 1987—. Contbr. articles to profl. jours. Bd. dirs. Northwestern Meml. Hosp., Chgo., 1978—, Northwestern Meml. Healthcare, 1987—, vice chmn., sec., 1998—99, chmn., 2000—; bd. dirs. McGaw Med. Ctr. of Northwestern U., 2000—, Lincoln Park Zool. Soc., 1972—, pres., 1980—84; bd. dirs., officer Offield Family Found., 1990—; mem. coun. govs. Northwestern Healthcare Network, 1990—, bd. dirs., 1999. Mem. ABA, Econ. Club Chgo. Roman Catholic. General corporate, Corporate taxation. Home: 443 W Eugenie St Chicago IL 60614-5674 Office: Bell Boyd & Lloyd LLC 70 W Madison St Ste 3300 Chicago IL 60602-4244 E-mail: rdrymalski@bellboyd.com

DUBBS, JOHN WILLIAM, III, lawyer, accountant; b. Chgo., July 2, 1951; s. John William, Jr. and Rita Jean (Kucharski) D. B.S. in Fin., U. Ill., 1973; J.D., Northwestern U., 1976; M.B.A. in Fin., U. Chgo., 1981. Bar: Ill. 1976, Fla. 1977, U.S. Dist. Ct. (no. dist.) Ill. 1976; C.P.A., Ill. Tax acct. Arthur Young & Co., Chgo., 1976-80; ptnr. firm Hinshaw, Culbertson, Moelmann, Hoban & Fuller, Chgo., 1980— . Mem. ABA, Ill. Bar Assn., Fla. Bar Assn., Chgo. Bar Assn. Roman Catholic. Pension, profit-sharing, and employee benefits, Corporate taxation, Personal income taxation. Office: Hinshaw & Culbertson 222 N La Salle St Ste 300 Chicago IL 60601-1081

DUBÉ, LAWRENCE EDWARD, JR. lawyer; b. Chgo., Sept. 25, 1948; s. Lawrence Edward and Rosemary Nora (Cooney) D.; m. Paula Ann Googal, Jan. 10, 1982; 1 child, Charles Bernard. BA in Polit. Sci. cum laude, Knox Coll., 1970; JD with distinction, U. Iowa, 1973. Bar: Ill. 1973, Md. 1982, Pa. 1982, D.C. 1983, U.S. Supreme Ct., 1987. Field atty. NLRB, Chgo., 1973-80, supr. atty., 1980-81; sole practice Balt., 1981-85; assoc. Grove, Jaskiewicz, Gilliam & Cobert, Washington, 1985-87; ptnr. Dubé & Googal, P.C., Balt., 1987—. Author: Management on Trial-The Law of Wrongful Discharge, 1987, New Employment Issues: How to Shield your Business from Costly Lawsuits, 1988, Employment References and the Law, 1989; co-author: The Maryland Employer's Guide, 1984. Mem. Nat. Assn. Securities Dealers (arbitrator). Federal civil litigation, Labor, Pension, profit-sharing, and employee benefits. Home: 622 W University Pky Baltimore MD 21210-2908 Office: Dubé & Googal PC 2400 Boston St Ste 407 Baltimore MD 21224-4787

DUBIN, JAMES MICHAEL, lawyer; b. N.Y.C., Aug. 20, 1946; s. Benjamin and Irene (Wasserman) D.; m. Susan Hope Schraub, Mar. 15, 1981; children: Alexander Philip, Elizabeth Joy. BA, U. Pa., 1968; JD, Columbia U., 1974. BAr: N.Y. 1975, D.C. 1984, U.S. Dist. Ct. (so. and ea. dists.) N.Y. 1975, U.S. Ct. Appeals (2d cir.) 1975. Assoc. Paul, Weiss, Rifkind, Wharton & Garrison, N.Y.C., 1974-82, ptnr., 1982—, chmn. corp. dept., 1995—. Bd. dirs. FOJP Svc. Corp., Conair Corp., Carnival Corp., CTPI Group, Inc., European Capital Ventures, NV. Mem. bd. editors Columbia Law Rev., 1973-74. Bd. dirs. YM-YWHA of Mid-Westchester, Scarsdale, N.Y., 1983-86, chmn. budget and fin. com., 1984-85; bd. dirs., mem. exec. com. Nat. Found. Advancement in Arts, 1991—, vice chmn., 1994-99, sec., 1999-2001; trustee Solomon Schechter Sch. Westchester, 1991—, vice chmn., 1997—, chmn. ann. fund, 1993-96, chmn. devel. com., 1994-97, v.p., sec., 1996-97; bd. dirs. Jewish Guild for the Blind, 1989—, mem. exec. com., 1991—, chmn., 1995-99, chmn. exec. com., 2000—; trustee Jewish Cmty. Ctr. of Harrison, 1994-97, mem. bd. edn., 1987-90; chmn. Cable Oversight Com., Harrison, NY., 1983-85. With U.S. Army, 1969-71. Mem. ABA, Assn. Bar City N.Y., Am. Arbitration Assn. (comml. panel arbitrators 1989—), Sunningdale Country Club (bd. govs. 1989—, pres. 2000—), Queenwood Golf Club, The Dukes Golf Club, Colony Club, Phi Delta Phi. General corporate, Mergers and acquisitions, Securities. Office: Paul Weiss Rifkind Wharton & Garrison Ste 3700 1285 Avenue Of The Americas New York NY 10019-6064 E-mail: jdubin@paulweiss.com

DUBIN, STEPHEN VICTOR, lawyer, holding company executive; b. Bklyn., June 17, 1938; s. Herman E. and Rhoda (Fogel) D.; m. Paula L. Dubin, June 28, 1959; children: Jeffrey D., Michelle L. BA, CUNY, 1961; JD, Boston U., 1961. Bar: N.Y. 1961, Ill. 1975, Pa. 1984, U.S. Dist. Ct. (so. and ea. dists.) N.Y. 1966, U.S. Dist. Ct. (no. dist.) Ill. 1975, U.S. Ct. Appeals (2d cir.) 1975, U.S. Supreme Ct. 1970, U.S. Dist. Ct. (ea. dist.) Pa. 1993, U.S. Ct. Appeals (3d cir.) 1993. Assoc. Kronish, Lieb, Weiner & Hellman, N.Y.C., 1965-67; counsel corp. sec Seligman & Latz, 1967-72; gen. atty. Montgomery Ward & Co., Inc., 1972-75, regional counsel, asst. sec. Chgo., 1975-78; gen. counsel, exec. v.p., sec. dir. CSS Industries, Inc., Phila., 1978—. Lectr. consumer law Am. Mgmt. Assn., 1974, 79, 81, Practicing Law Inst., 1982, 88. Nassau County Dem. committeeman, 1967-75, mem. county jud. screening com., 1972-75, del. Nat. Dem. Issues Conv., 1974; pres. Phila. chpt. Am. Jewish Com., 1995-97, chmn. 1997-99, nat bd. govs., 1997—. Capt. JAGC AUS, 1961-65. Mem. ABA, N.Y. State Bar Assn., Pa. Bar Assn., Ill. Bar Assn., Chgo. Bar Assn., Phila. Bar Assn., Bar Assn. Nassau County, N.Y. County Lawyers Assn., Am. Soc. Corp. Secs., Masons (master 1982). General corporate, Mergers and acquisitions, Real property. Office: CSS Industries Inc 1845 Walnut St Philadelphia PA 19103-4708 E-mail: stephen.dubin@cssindustries.com

DUBINA, JOEL FREDRICK, federal judge; b. 1947; BS, U. Ala., 1970; JD, Cumberland Sch. Law, 1973. Pvt. practice law Jones, Murray, Stewart & Yarbrough, 1974-83; law clk. to presiding judge U.S. Dist. Ct. (mid. dist.) Ala., Montgomery, 1973-74, U.S. magistrate, 1983-86, U.S. Dist. judge, 1986-90; judge U.S. Ct. Appeals (11th cir.), 1990—. Mem. FBA (pres. Montgomery chpt. 1982-83), Nat. Coun. U.S. Magistrate Judges, Fed. Judges Assn., Supreme Ct. Hist. Soc., Ala. State Bar Assn., 11th Cir. Hist. Soc., Montgomery County Bar Assn. (chmn. Law Day com. 1975, constrn. and bylaws com. 1977-80, grievance com. 1981-83), Cumberland Sch. Law Alumni Assn., Lions, Am. Inn of Cts. (pres. Montgomery chpt. 1993-94), Phi Delta Phi. Office: US Cir Ct Appeals 11th Cir PO Box 867 Montgomery AL 36101-0867

DUBOFF, LEONARD DAVID, lawyer; b. Bklyn., Oct. 3, 1941; s. Rubin Robert and Millicent Barbara (Pollach) DuB.; m. Mary Ann Crawford, June 4, 1967; children: Colleen Rose, Robert Courtney, Sabrina Ashley. JD summa cum laude, Bklyn. Law Sch., 1971. Bars: N.Y. 1974, Oreg. 1977, U.S. Dist. Cts. (so. and ea. dists.) N.Y. 1974, U.S. Ct. Appeals (2d cir.) 1974, U.S. Ct. Appeals (9th cir.) 1990, U.S. Customs Ct. 1975, U.S. Supreme Ct. 1977, U.S. Fed. Dist. Ct. 1990. Teaching fellow Stanford (Calif.) U. Law Sch., 1971-72; mem. faculty Lewis & Clark Coll. Northwestern Sch. Law, Portland, Oreg., 1972-94, prof. law, 1977-94; ptnr. DuBoff & Ross, PLLC, Portland, 1994—; instr. Hastings Coll. Law Coll. Civil Advocacy, San Francisco, summers 1978, 79. Founder, past pres. Oreg. Vol. Lawyers for Arts; mem. lawyers' com. ACLU, 1973-78, bd. dirs. Oreg., 1974-76; mem. Mayor's Adv. Com. Security and Privacy, 1974; bd. dirs. Portland Art Mus. Asian Art Council, 1976-77, Internat. Assn. Art Security, N.Y.C., 1976-80; pres. Arts Commn. of Tigard Tualatin and Sherwood, 1990-92; Gov. Oreg. Com. Employment of Handicapped,

1978-81; cons., panelist spl. projects Nat. Endowment for Arts, 1978-79; mem. Mayor's Adv. Com. on Handicapped, 1979-81; mem. Wash. State Atty. Gen.'s Com. to Reorganize Maryhill Mus.; Oreg. Commn. for Blind, 1987-93; Oreg. Com. for Humanities, 1981-87. Recipient Bklyn. Law Sch. Stuart Hirschman Property, Jerome Prince Evidence, Donald W. Matheson Meml. awards, 1st scholarship prize; Hofstra U. Lighthouse scholar 1965-71; recipient Hauser award, 1967, Howard Brown Pickard award, 1967-69, Oreg. Govs. Arts award, 1990, Dist. award of merit Pioneer Dist., Boy Scouts Am., 1995, Silver Beaver award Boy Scouts Am., 1996, Vigil mem. Order of the Arrow, 1996. Mem. Am. Soc. Internat. Law, Assn. Alumni and Attenders of Hague Acad. Internat. Law, Assn. Am. Law Schs. (standing com. sect. activities 1975, chmn. sect. law and arts 1974-80, 91-93, spl. com. on disabilities 1989-91), ABA, N.Y. State Bar Assn., Oreg. Bar Assn., Delta Kappa Phi, Sigma Pi Sigma, Sigma Alpha. Spl. columnist on craft law, The Crafts Report, 1973-87; editor, contbr. materials to legal and art textbooks; author textbooks and articles for legal and art jours. General corporate, Securities, Art. Office: DuBoff & Ross PLLC Hampton Oaks 2nd Fl 6665 SW Hampton St Portland OR 97223-8357

DU BOFF, MICHAEL H(AROLD), lawyer; b. N.Y.C., June 27, 1945; s. Rubin Robert and Millicent Barbara (Pollack) Du B.; widow; children: Jill Bonnie, Robert Evan. BBA, Pace U., 1967; JD, Bklyn. Law Sch., 1970. Bar: N.Y. 1971, U.S. Dist. Ct. (so. and ea. dists.) N.Y. 1972, U.S. Supreme Ct. 1974, U.S. Tax Ct. 1973, U.S. Ct. Internat. Trade 1973. Sr. trial asst. dist. atty. Bronx County, N.Y.C., 1970-78; ptnr. Gainesburg, Gottlieb, Levitan & Cole, 1978-81; counsel Hahn & Hessen, 1981-84; ptnr. Salon, Marrow & Dyckman, 1985-97, Kavidoff & Malito LLP, N.Y.C., 1997—. Dir., cons. Harwell Group, Inc., N.Y.C., 1982— ; v.p. Classic Antique & Restored Spls., Ltd., N.Y.C., 1980—; bd. trustees, gen. coun. Soundview Preporatory Acad., 1993—; bd. trustees The Harvey Sch. 1997—. Contbr. article to Bklyn. Law Sch. Law Review, 1969, Patron Children's Art Workshop, Mamaroneck, N.Y., 1979—. Sponsor Children's Med. Ctr., Lake Success, N.Y., 1979—; mem. Westchester Coun. Arts., N.Y., 1980—; assoc. chmn. fin. industries div. Nat. Asthma Ctr., Denver, 1981. Recipient award for disting. svc. Bronx Dist. Atty., 1973. Mem. ABA, Am. Arbitration Assn. (panel of arbitrators 1979—, guest spkr. 1983), Assn. Bar City of N.Y. (com. uniform state laws 1972-81), Fed. Bar Coun., N.Y. State Bar Assn. (arbitration com.), Lawyers Assn. Textile and Apparel Industries (pres.), Alpha Phi Omega (v.p. N.Y.C. chpt. 1964-67). Contracts commercial, General practice, Securities. Home: 7 Mckenna Pl Mamaroneck NY 10543-2112

DUBUC, CARROLL EDWARD, lawyer; b. Burlington, Vt., May 6, 1933; s. Jerome Joachim and Rose (Bessette) D.; m. Mary Jane Lowe, Aug. 3, 1963; children: Andrew, Steven, Matthew. BS in Acctg., Cornell U., 1955; LLB, Boston Coll., 1962; postgrad., NYU, 1963-64. Bar: N.Y. 1963, D.C. 1972, Va. 1999; U.S. Dist. Ct. (so. and ea. dists.) N.Y. 1964, U.S. Ct. Appeals (2d cir.) 1965, U.S. Supreme Ct. 1970, D.C. 1972, U.S. Ct. Appeals (D.C. cir.) 1972, U.S. Dist. Ct. D.C. 1973, U.S. Ct. Claims 1975, U.S. Ct. Appeals (4th cir.) 1977, U.S. Ct. Appeals (7th cir.) 1984, U.S. Ct. Appeals (9th cir.) 1985, U.S. Ct. Appeals (5th cir.) 1986, U.S. Ct. Appeals (fed. cir.) 1988, U.S. Ct. Internat. Trade 1988, U.S. Ct. Appeals (6th cir.) 1989, Va. 1999; cert. ct. mediator 1998. Assoc. Haight, Gardner, Poor & Havens, N.Y.C., 1962-70, ptnr., 1970-75; resident ptnr. Finley Kumble Wagner Heine Underberg Manley Myerson & Casey, Washington, 1983-87, Laxalt, Washington, Perito & Dubuc, Washington, 1988-90, Washington, Perito & Dubuc, 1990-91; ptnr. Graham & James, 1991-95, of counsel, 1996-98, Cohen Gettings & Dunham, 1998—; exec. dir. Aviation Mediation & Arbitration Providers LLC, 2000—. Capt. AC USN, 1954-59. Mem. AIAA, ABA (chmn. aviation and space law com. 1985-86, subcom. aviation ins., subcom. internat. practice 1985-87, vice chmn. alternative resolution com., mktg. legal svcs. com. 1991-92, vice chmn. ins. com. 1982-84), N.Y. State Bar Assn. (past chmn. aviation law com.), D.C. Bar Assn., Va. Bar Assn., Assn. of Bar of City of N.Y. (aeroav. com.), Fed. Cir. Bar Assn., Fed. Bar Coun., Nat. Transp. Safety Bd. Bar Assn., Maritime Law Assn. U.S., Naval Aviation Command (vice comdr.), Internat. Assn. Def. Counsel (chmn. ADR com. 2001—), Fed. Ins. and Corp. Counsel (chmn. alternate dispute resolution sect. 1996-99, aviation transp. 1996—), Helicopter Assn. Internat., Transp. Lawyers Assn., Assn. Trial Lawyers Am., Def. Assn. N.Y., Boston Coll. Law Sch. Alumni (pres. Washington chpt. 1992-96), Internat. & Bar Assn. (vice chmn. travel and tourism com. 1998—), Internat. Soc. Air Safety Investigators, Soc. Sr. Aerospace Execs., Internat. Aviation Club, Washington chpt. Aero Club, Nat. Aeronautic Assn., French-Am. C. of C., Cornell Club, Wings Club, Congrl. Country Club, Sigma Chi. Alternative dispute resolution, Aviation, Federal civil litigation.

DUCANTO, JOSEPH NUNZIO, lawyer, educator; b. Utica, N.Y., Mar. 18, 1927; s. Joseph and Martha (Purchine) D'Acunto; m. Connie Davis (div. May 1990); children: Anthony D. DuCanto, James C. DuCanto; m. Patricia Naegle; children: 1 adopted child, William P. Heiman-DuCanto. BA, Antioch Coll., 1952; JD, U. Chgo., 1955. Bar: Ill. 1955, U.S. Tax Ct. 1960, U.S. Ct. Mil. Appeals 1960, U.S. Supreme Ct. 1960. Rsch. asst. Law and Behavioral Sci. Rsch. Project U. Chgo., 1954-55; assoc. Cotton, Fruchtman & Watt, Chgo., 1955-62; ptnr. Bentley, Campbell, DuCanto & Silvestri, 1962-80; prin. Schiller, DuCanto & Fleck, Ltd., 1981—; chmn., CEO Securatex, 1982—. Adj. prof. family law Loyola U., Chgo., 1968-2001, vis. prof., 2001; frequent lect r. on family law, taxation, fin. planning and estate planning in connection with divorce. Author: Tax Aspects of Litigation, 1979; contbr. articles, essays on family law and fed. taxation, trusts and estates to profl. publs.; editor, pub. Tax, Fin. and Estate Planning Devels. in Connection with Divorce and Family Law, 1970-85; mem. editorial bd. Fair Share, 1981—, Equitable Distbn. Reporter, 1981—, Matrimonial Lawyer Strategist, 1982—. Served with USMCR, 1944-47, PTO, Guam, Iwo Jima, China. Fellow Am. Acad. Matrimonial Lawyers (nat. pres. 1977-79, chmn.-dir. Inst. Matrimonial Law 1976-85), Am. Coll. Trust and Estate Counsel; mem. Ill. State Bar As sn. (bd. g ovs. 1983-89), Scribes, Cliff Dwellers Club, Union League Club. Republican. Unitarian. Family and matrimonial. Office: 200 N LaSalle 27th Floor Chicago IL 60601-1089 E-mail: jducanto@sdflaw.com

DUCKETT, JOAN, law librarian; b. Bklyn., Oct. 21, 1934; d. Stephen and Mary (Wehrum) Kearney; m. Richard Duckett, Aug. 25, 1956; children: Richard, David, Daniel, Deirdre. BA, Kean Coll., 1974; MLS, Rutgers U., 1977; JD, Suffolk U., 1983; postgrad., Oxford (Eng.) U., 1986. Bar: Mass. 1983, U.S. Ct. Appeals (fed. cir.) 1984. Media specialist Oak Knoll Sch., Summit, N.J., 1976-80; law clk. Dist. Atty. Suffolk County, Boston, 1982; vol. atty. Cambridgeport Problem Ctr., Cambridge, Mass., 1984-85; reference libr. Harvard Law Sch. Libr., 1982-84, coord. The New Eng. Law Libr. Consortium, 1984-87, head reference svcs., 1987—, profl. devel. com., chmn. Bryant fellowship award panel, 1987—. Contbr. articles to profl. jours. Protocol hostess L.A. Olympic Com., 1984. Fellow Mass. Bar Found.; mem. Mass. Bar Assn., Boston Bar Assn., Am. Assn. Law Libr., Law Librs. New Eng., Assn. Boston Law Librs., Alpha Sigma Lambda, Beta Phi Mu. Office: Harvard Law Sch Libr Langdell Hall Cambridge MA 02138

DUCKETT, WARREN BIRD, JR. state's attorney; b. Annapolis, Md., Aug. 28, 1939; s. Warren B. Sr. and Mary Knight (Linthicum) D.; m. Judith Livingstone, Mar. 25, 1961; children— Pamela, Stephanie, Warren. A.B., U. Md., 1962, J.D., 1966. Bar: Md. 1967, U.S. Ct. Appeals (4th cir.) 1967, U.S. Supreme Ct. 1972. Asst. state's atty. Anne Arundel County, Annapolis, Md., 1967-69, state's atty., 1973— ; ptnr. Turk, Manis & Duckett, Annapolis, 1968-75; prof. law and evidence Anne Arundel Community Coll.; mem. Anne Arundel County Council, Annapolis, 1970-73. Del. Democratic Nat. Conv., 1972; pres. Anne Arundel County YMCA, 1985-87. Named Outstanding Young Annapolitan, Jaycees, Annapolis, 1970; Prosecutor of Yr., Washington Bd. Trade, 1978; recipient Human Relations award Frontiers Internat., Annapolis, 1981, Exceptional Service award HHS, 1986. Mem. Nat. Dist. Attys. Assn. (dir. 1975-77, 82-86), Md. State's Attys. Assn. (dir. 1973— , pres. 1975-77, 82-86), Md. Bar Assn., Anne Arundel County Bar Assn. Episcopalian. Club: Touchdown (sec. 1985—) (Annapolis). Lodges: Lions (sec. Annapolis 1968-70), Rotary. Home: 208 Wardour Dr Annapolis MD 21401-1249 Office: State Attys Office Anne Arundel County 101 South St Annapolis MD 21401-2635

DUCKWORTH, MARVIN E. lawyer, educator; b. Aug. 16, 1942; s. Marvin E. and Maryann Duckworth; children: Matthew, Brian, Jennifer, Jeffrey. BS in Indsl. Engring., Iowa State U., 1964; JD, Drake U., 1968. Bar: Iowa 1968, U.S. Dist. Ct. (no. and so. dists.) Iowa 1969. Assoc. Davis, Huebner, Johnson & Burt, Des Moines, 1968-70; asst. prof. Drake U., 1970-71, lectr. law, 1971-85, assoc. dean clin. programs, 1986-87, adj. prof., 1987—; shareholder Hopkins & Huebner, P.C., Des Moines, 1971—. Spkr. in field. Pres. Drake Law Bd. Counselors, 1991-92, Drake Law Endowment Trust, 1995-96. Named Alumnus of Yr. Drake Law Sch., 1997. Fellow Iowa Bar Found.; mem. ABA (chmn. workers compensation and employers liability law 1986-87, vice hmn. toxic and hazardous substances and environ. law com. 1989-93), Iowa Bar Assn. (pres. young lawyers sect. 1977-78, Merit award 1982, chair workers compensation sect. 1992-93), Def. Rsch. Inst., Fedn. Ins. and Corp. Counsel (workers compensation com.), Iowa Assn. Workers Compensation Lawyers (pres. 1988-89), Iowa Acad. Trial Lawyers, Order of Coif. State civil litigation, Insurance, Workers' compensation. Office: 2700 Grand Ave Ste 111 Des Moines IA 50312-5215

DUDGEON, THOMAS CARL, judge; b. Oak Park, Ill., Oct. 3, 1952; s. Harold Arthur and Elizabeth Ann (Bode) D.; m. Britt Lin Gilbertz, Sept. 12, 1981; children: Elizabeth Lin, Grant Arthur. Student, Am. U., 1972; BA summa cum laude, Augustan Coll., 1974; JD, Drake U., 1977. Bar: Ill. 1977, U.S. Dist. Ct. (no. dist.) Ill. 1977, U.S. Ct. Appeals (7th cir.) 1988. Assoc. O'Reilly & Cunningham, Wheaton, Ill., 1977-85; ptnr. O'Reilly, Cunningham, Duncan & Huck, 1985-87, Richter, Jaros & Dudgeon, Oak Brook, Ill., 1987-92; assoc. judge 18th Jud. Cir. Ct., DuPage County, 1992—. Mem. Ill. Bar Assn., DuPage County Bar Assn., Phi Beta Kappa, Omicron Delta Kappa. Lutheran. Avocations: bicycling, reading, backpacking, photography. State civil litigation, Insurance, Personal injury. Office: 505 N County Farm Rd Wheaton IL 60187-5112

DUDLEY, GEORGE ELLSWORTH, lawyer; b. Earlington, Ky., July 14, 1922; s. Ralph Emerson and Camille (Lackey) D.; m. Barbara J. Muir, June 28, 1950 (dec. Feb. 1995); children: Bruce K., Camille Dudley McNutt, Nancy S., Elizabeth Dudley Stephens. BS in Commerce, U. Ky., 1947; JD, U. Mich., 1950. Bar: Ky. 1950, D.C. 1951, U.S. Dist. Ct. (we. dist.) Ky. 1962, U.S. Ct. Appeals (6th cir.) 1987. Assoc. Gordon, Gordon & Moore, Madisonville, Ky., 1950-51; pvt. practice law Louisville, 1952-59; ptnr. Brown, Ardery, Todd & Dudley, 1959-72, Brown, Todd & Heyburn, Louisville, 1972-92, of counsel, 1992—, mem. mgmt. com., 1972-90, chmn., 1989-90. Pres. Ky. Easter Seal Soc., Louisville, 1971-72; treas. Ky. Dem. Party, Frankfort, 1971-74; bd. dirs. Alliant Adult Health Svcs., Louisville, 1976—; 1st v.p. Nat. Easter Seal Soc., Chgo., 1981. Capt. inf. U.S. Army, 1943-46, ETO; capt. JAGC, U.S. Army, 1951-52. Mem. ABA, Ky. Bar Assn., Louisville Bar Assn., U.S. 6th Cir. Jud. Conf. (life), Harmony Landing Country Club (pres. 1978-79), Tavern Club, Barristers Soc., Omicron Delta Kappa. Presbyterian. Avocations: golf, tennis, travel, sports spectator. Home: 1905 Crossgate Ln Louisville KY 40222-6405 Office: Brown Todd & Heyburn 3200 Providian Louisville KY 40202

DUE, DANFORD ROYCE, lawyer; b. Louisville, Sept. 28, 1948; s. Victor T. and Betty (Duffy) D.; m. Susan L. Landrum, Aug. 14, 1971; children: Stephen L., Michael R. BA, Vanderbilt U., 1970; JD cum laude, Ind. U., 1973. Bar: Ind. 1973, U.S. Dist. Ct. (so. dist.) Ind. 1973, U.S. Dist. Ct. (no. dist.) Ind. 1980, U.S. Ct. Appeals (7th cir.) 1986. Assoc. Stewart, Irwin, Gilliom, Fuller & Meyer, Indpls., 1973-79, ptnr., 1979-84, Stewart, Due, Doyle & Pugh, Indpls., 1984—. Contbg. author (Continuing Legal Edn. series) Uninsured/Underinsured Motorist Coverage in Indiana, 1988, The Wrongful Death Case in Indiana, 1989, Successful Handling of Wrongful Death Cases: The Experts Share Their Secrets, 1998. Bd. mgrs. Baxter YMCA, Indpls., 1983—. Mem. ABA, Def. Rsch. Inst., Ind. State Bar Assn., Ind. Def. Lawyers Assn., Johnson County Bar Assn. Avocations: golf, reading, mountain hiking, fishing. General civil litigation, Insurance, Personal injury. Home: 524 Ho Hum Ct Greenwood IN 46142 Office: Stewart Due Miller & Pugh 55 Monument Circle 900 Circle Tower Indianapolis IN 46204

DUERBECK, HEIDI BARBARA, lawyer; b. Duisburg, Fed. Republic of Germany, July 19, 1947; came to U.S., 1956; d. Kurt and Irmgard (Gottsche) D.; m. Jenik R. Radon, June 10, 1971; 1 child, Kaara. BA cum laude, UCLA, 1968, MA, 1969; student Gottingen U., Fed. Republic Germany, 1967-68; JD, Stanford U., 1972. Bar: Calif. 1973, N.Y. 1975, U.S. Dist. Ct. (so. dist.) N.Y. 1975. Atty. Sullivan & Cromwell, N.Y.C., 1972-77; ptnr. Walter, Conston, Alexander & Green, P.C., N.Y.C., 1980—. contbr. articles to German legal bus. jours.; Bd. dirs. Hugh O'Brien Youth Found., N.Y.C., 1984—; mem. N.Y. State Trade Mission, Europe, 1982, N.Y.C. Trade Mission, Europe, 1983; mem. Am. Council on Germany, N.Y.C., German Forum, N.Y.C. Soroptimist fellow, 1970. Mem. German-Am. Law Assn. (bd. dirs. 1982-86, pres. 1982—), ABA, Assn. of Bar of City of N.Y. Lutheran. General corporate, Private international, Securities. Home: 269 W 71st St New York NY 10023-3701 Office: Walter Conston Alexander & Green PC 90 Park Ave Fl 14 New York NY 10016-1301

DUESENBERG, RICHARD WILLIAM, lawyer; b. St. Louis, Dec. 10, 1930; s. (John August) Hugo and Edna Marie (Warmann) D.; m. Phyllis Evelyn Buehner, Aug. 7, 1955; children: Karen, Daryl, Mark, David. BA, Valparaiso U., 1951, JD, 1953, LLD, Valparaiso U., 2001; LLM, Yale U., 1956. Bar: Mo. 1953. Prof. law NYU, N.Y.C., 1956-62, dir. law ctr. publs., 1960-62; sr. atty. Monsanto Co., St. Louis, 1963-70, asst. gen. counsel, asst. sec., 1975-77, sr. v.p., sec., gen. counsel, 1977-96. Dir. law Monsanto Textiles Co., St. Louis, 1971-75; corp. sec. Fisher Controls Co., Marshalltown, Iowa, 1969-71, Olympia Industries, Spartanburg, S.C., 1974-75; vis. prof. law U. Mo., 1970-71; faculty Banking Sch. South, La. State U., 1967-83; vis. scholar Cambridge U., England, 1996; vis. prof. law St. Louis U., 1997-98. Author: (with Lawrence P. King) Sales and Bulk Transfers Under the Uniform Commercial Code, 2 vols, 1966, rev., 1984, New York Law of Contracts, 3 vols, 1964, Missouri Forms and Practice Under the Uniform Commercial Code, 2 vols, 1966; editor: Ann. Survey of Am. Law, NYU, 1961-62; mem. bd. contbg. editors and advisors: Corp. Law Rev, 1977-86; contbr. articles to law revs., jours. Mem. lawyers adv. coun. NAM, Washington, 1980, Adminstrv. Conf. U.S., 1980-86, legal adv. com. N.Y. Stock Exch., 1983-87, corp. law dept. adv. coun. Practising Law Inst., 1982; bd. dirs. Bach Soc., St. Louis, 1985-86, pres., 1973-77; bd. dirs. Valparaiso U., 1977—, chmn. bd. visitors law sch., 1966—, Luth. Charities Assn., 1984-87, vice chmn., 1986-87; bd. dirs. Luth. Med. Ctr., St. Louis, 1973-82, vice chmn., 1975-80; bd. dirs. Nat. Jud. Coll., 1984-90, St. Louis Symphony, 1988—, Opera Theatre St. Louis, 1988—, Luth. Brotherhood, Mpls., 1992-2000, Liberty Fund, Inc., Indpls., 1997—. Served with U.S. Army, 1953-55. Decorated officer's cross Order of Merit (Germany); named Disting. Alumnus, Valparaiso U., 1976. Fellow Am. Bar Found.; mem. ABA (chmn. com. uniform comml. code 1976-79, coun. sect. corp., banking and bus. law 1979-83, sec. 1983-84, chmn. 1986-87), Mo. Bar Assn., Am. Law Inst., Mont Pelerin Soc., Nat. Jud. Coll. (bd. dirs. 1984-90), Order of Coif, Bach Soc., Am. Soc. Corp. Sec. (bd. chmn. 1987-88), Assn. Gen. Coun., Am. Arbitration Assn., St. Louis Club. Contracts commercial, General corporate, General practice. Home: 1 Indian Creek Ln Saint Louis MO 63131-3333 E-mail: rwduesenberg@worldnet.att.net

DUESENBERG, ROBERT H. retired lawyer; b. St. Louis, Dec. 10, 1930; s. Hugo John August and Edna Marie (Warmann) D.; m. Lorraine Freda Hall, July 23, 1938; children: Lynda Renee, Kirsten Lynn, John Robert. BA, Valparaiso (Ind.) U., 1951, LLB, 1953; LLM, Harvard U., 1956. Bar: Mo. 1953, U.S. Supreme Ct. 1981, Va. 1993. Pvt. practice, St. Louis, 1956-58; atty. Wabash R.R. Co., 1958-65, Norfolk & Western Ry. Co., St. Louis, 1962-65; atty., assoc. gen. counsel Pet Inc., 1965-77, v.p., assoc. gen. counsel, 1977-80, v.p., gen. counsel, 1980-83, Gen. Dynamics Corp., Falls Church, Va., 1984-91, sr. v.p. and gen. counsel, 1991-93; ret., 1993. Bd. dirs. Valparaiso (Ind.) U.; adv. bd. ELawForum, Inc., Washington. Contbr. numerous articles to profl. jours. Sec., treas., legal advisor Am. Kantorei, St. Louis, 1970-75; mem. Coun. on World Affairs, St. Louis, 1975—, Mo. Coordinating Bd. for Higher Edn., Jefferson City, 1976-83, chmn., 1978-81; mem. pres.'s coun. Valparaiso (Ind.) U., 1979—, bd. dirs., 1995—; bd. dirs. Higher Edn. Loan Authority, 1982-84; mem. adv. bd. Northwestern U. Corp. Counsel Ctr., 1988—, chmn. adv. bd., 1992; bd. dirs. Opera Theatre of St. Louis, 1988—; bd. dirs. Luther Inst., Washington, 1999—, chair, 2000—; mem. adv. bd. ELawForum, Washington. Cpl. U.S. Army, 195355. Recipient Disting. Alumnus award Valparaiso U., 1982. Mem. ABA, Va. Bar Assn., Mo. Bar Assn., St. Louis Bar Assn. (chmn. antitrust com. 1971-73, v.p. bus. law sect. 1972-73, chmn. 1973-74), Am. Law Inst., Gen. Counsels Assn., Machine and Allied Products Inst. (legal counsel 1986—), Am. Corp. Counsel Assn., S.W. Legal Found. (adv. bd.), Aerospace Industry Assn. (legal com. 1981-88), Bach Soc. of St. Louis (bd. dirs.). Republican. Lutheran. General corporate, Government contracts and claims. Home: 10171 Castlewood Ln Oakton VA 22124-3027

DUETSCH, JOHN EDWIN, lawyer; b. Newark, Sept. 25, 1915; s. John J. and Barbara A. (Nickl) D.; m. Gertrude A. Stewart, Aug. 31, 1940; children: John E., Karen A. Duetsch Gammond, Thomas F. LLB, Fordham U., 1941. Bar: N.Y. 1941. Clk. Ira Haupt & Co., N.Y.C., 1933-34; with Morris & McVeigh, N.Y.C., 1934—, ptnr., 1961-85, of counsel, 1985-90. Mem. planning bd. Township of Livingston, N.J., 1955-56, mayor, councilman, 1957-64; bd. dirs. Jacaranda Homeowners Assn. With U.S. Army, 1945. Mem. ABA, N.Y. Bar Assn., Am. Arbitration Assn. (panel), Guild Cath. Lawyers, N.J. State Srs. Golf Assn. (assoc., v.p., bd. dirs.), Am. Legion, Spring Brook Country Club (hon. life, pres. 1970-77) (Morristown, N.J.), Country Club of Jacaranda West (Venice, Fla.), KC (hon., life). Probate, Real property. Home: 900 N Doral Ln Venice FL 34293-3805 Office: Morris & McVeigh 767 3rd Ave New York NY 10017-2023

DUFFEY, WILLIAM SIMON, JR. lawyer; b. Phila., May 9, 1952; s. William Simon and Elinor (Daniluk) D.; m. Betsy Byars, Dec. 17, 1977; children: Charles, Scott. BA in English, honors, Drake U., 1973; JD cum laude, U. S.C., 1977. Bar: S.C. 1977, Ga. 1982, U.S. Dist. Ct. (no., mid. and so. dists.) Ga. 1982, U.S. Ct. Appeals (llth cir.) 1983, U.S. Supreme Ct., 1992. Atty. Nexson, Pruet, Jacobs & Pollard, Columbia, S.C., 1977-78, King & Spalding, Atlanta, 1982-94; dep. ind. counsel Office of the Ind. Counsel, Little Rock, 1994-95; ptnr. King & Spalding, Atlanta, 1995—; adj. prof. U. S.C. Adj. prof. U. S.C. Law Sch., 2000—. Articles editor S.C. Lawyer, 1990-94. Pres. Pine Hills Civic Assn., Atlanta, 1984-88; trustee Drake U.; mem. Atlanta Task Force Neighborhood Buyouts, 1986, Ga. Rep. Found., Leadership Atlanta; bd. dirs. Ga. Wilderness Inst., 1992—; mem. Peachtree Rd. Race Com., 1993—, chmn. Ga. Good Govt. Com.; chmn. bd. advisors Coverdell Leadership Inst., 1995—; coun. mem. Chastain Fellowship; bd. mem. North Ga. Walk to Emmaus, Camp Hope. Mem. Altanta Bar Assn. (chmn. alt. dispute resolution com. 1984-88), Lawyers Club, Atlanta Track Club (gen. counsel 1993—), Nat. Practitioners Advisory Coun. The Fed. Soc. Republican. Avocation: running. Federal civil litigation, State civil litigation, Criminal. Home: 4825 Franklin Pond NE Atlanta GA 30342-2765 Office: King & Spalding 191 Peachtree St NE Ste 40 Atlanta GA 30303-1763 E-mail: bduffey@kslaw.com

DUFFY, DONNA JAN, law educator, lawyer; b. Wichita, Kans., Apr. 27, 1950; d. Dwight C. and Helen J. Hornberger; AB, Stanford U., 1972; JD, Case Western Res. U., 1976. Bar: Ohio 1976, Calif. 1978. Assoc. Jones Day Reavis & Pogue, Cleve., 1976-77, Orrick, Herrington & Sutcliffe, San Francisco, 1978-80; assoc. prof. Calif. Poly. State U., San Luis Obispo, 1980-84, prof., 1984— ; of counsel Sinsheimer, Schiebelhut & Baggett, San Luis Obispo, 1983-91; prin. Jan Duffy Assocs., 1992—. Contbr. articles to legal jours. Chair Calif. Minimum Wage Bd., 1984. Mem. ABA (co-chair workplace privacy subcom. 1981-94, co-chair employee rights and responsibilities com. 1994-97, co-chair continuing legal edn. technology subcom.), Calif. Women Lawyers. Democrat. Office: Jan Duffy Assocs 530 Jackson St # 3rd-fl San Francisco CA 94133-5105

DUFFY, JAMES EARL, JR. lawyer; b. St. Paul, June 4, 1942; s. James Earl and Mary Elizabeth (Westbrook) D.; m. Jeanne Marie Ghiardi, June 7, 1969; children— Jennifer, Jessica. B.A., Coll. St. Thomas, 1965; J.D., Marquette U., 1968. Bar: Wis. 1968, Hawaii 1969. Assoc. Cobb & Gould, Honolulu, 1968-71, Chuck & Fujiyama, Honolulu, 1972-74; ptnr. Fujiyama, Duffy & Fujiyama, Honolulu, 1975— ; mem. Am. Bd. Trial Advocates. ; mem. med. ethical resources com. Kapiolani Children's Med. Ctr., 1984— . Mem. Hawaii Bar Found. (bd. dirs. 1984—), Hawaii Bar Assn. (pres. 1982), Hawaii Trial Lawyers Assn. (pres. 1981), Hawaii Supreme Ct. Jud. Coun., Trial Lawyers Assn. Am. (bd. govs. 1982-85), Hawaii Acad. Plaintiff's Attys. (pres. 1986-93), Am. Inns of Court IV. Roman Catholic. Federal civil litigation, State civil litigation, Personal injury. Home: 1567 Ulueo St Kailua HI 96734-4408 Office: Fujiyama Duffy & Fujiyama 1001 Bishop St Honolulu HI 96813-3429

DUFFY, MARTIN PATRICK, lawyer; b. Louisville, Feb. 2, 1942; s. Martin Joseph and Elsie (Shrader) D.; m. Virginia Schoo, Mar. 20, 1970; children: Timothy Brian, Kathleen Kelly. AB in English, U. Notre Dame, 1964; JD, U. Louisville, 1975. Bar: Ky. 1975, U.S. Tax Ct. 1980. Ptnr. Olson, Baker, Henriksen & Duffy, Louisville, 1978-79, Wyatt, Tarrant & Combs, Louisville, 1979--. Bd. dirs. Bellarmine Coll. Overseers, Louisville, 1974-80; trustee St. Mary & Elizabeth Hosp., Louisville, 1980-86, chmn. bd. 1982-85. With U.S. Army, 1964-65, 68-69. Mem. ABA, Ky. Bar Assn., Louisville Bar Assn. Democrat. Roman Catholic. Avocations: running, golf. Estate planning, Probate, Estate taxation. Office: Wyatt Tarrant & Combs 2700 Citizens Plz Louisville KY 40202 Fax: 502-589-0309. E-mail: pduffy@wyattfirm.com

DUFFY, W. LESLIE, lawyer; b. N.Y.C., Dec. 31, 1939; s. William L. and Edna (Torseillo) D.; 1 child, Alexander Durand. BA, U. Notre Dame, 1961; LLB, Columbia U., 1964; LLM, NYU, 1967. Assoc. Cahill, Gordon & Reindel, N.Y.C., 1965-73, ptnr., 1973—. Bd. dirs. various pub. cos. Contbr. articles to profl. jours. Served to lt. USNR. Mem. ABA, N.Y. State Bar Assn. General corporate, Mergers and acquisitions. Office: Cahill Gordon & Reindel 80 Pine St Fl 17 New York NY 10005-1790

DUFLOS, JEAN-JACQUES, lawyer; b. Neuilly sur Seine, France, Dec. 14, 1950; s. Jacques and Janine (Chapsal) D.; m. Beatrice Delabre, Mar. 21, 1993; children: Charline, Cyrielle, Esther. Law Degree, U. Paris-X, Nanterre, 1973, Postgrad. Diploma, Law Doctorate, 1975. Bar: Lyon France 1985. Lawyer Lanière de Roubaix, France, 1977-79; legal mgr. Castorama, Lille, France, 1979-85; atty., ptnr. Cabinet Ratheaux, Lyon, France, 1985-90, Ernst & Young, France, 1990-98; atty., ptnr., leader of Lyon legal and tax office Deloitte & Touche Juridique et Fiscal, Lyon-Villeurbanne, France, 1998—. Author: Workers Committee Guide, 1992. Dep. mayor Ville de Roncz, France, 1982-85. Served with French Army, 1975-77, Cameroun. Recipient Diploma of Honor, French Social Ct., 1994. Avocation: classical organ. General corporate, Labor, Pension, profit-sharing, and employee benefits. Office: Deloitte & Touche Juridique 81 Blvd Stalingrad Lyon-Villeurbanne 69100 France Fax: (0)4.72.43.39.94. E-mail: jduflos@deloitte.fr

DUGAN, JOHN F. lawyer; b. Phila., May 25, 1935; s. Albert C. and Helen Josephine (Pritchard) D.; m. Colette Gregory, Jan. 18, 1987. AB, U. Pa., 1956, LLD, 1960. Bar: Pa. 1961, U.S. Ct. Appeals (3d cir.) 1961, Va. 1966, U.S. Supreme Ct. 1967. Assoc. Obermayer Rebmann Maxwell & Hippel, Phila., 1960-66; of counsel Reynolds Metals Co., Richmond, Va., 1966-69, Pennwalt Corp., Phila., 1969-71; ptnr. Berkman Ruslander, Pitts., 1971-85, Kirkpatrick & Lockhart, Pitts., 1985—. Labor rels. law rep. mgmt., Kirkpatrick & Lockhart. Mem. Pitts. Field Club, Duquesne Club, Order of the Coif, Phi Beta Kappa. Republican. Labor. Office: Kirkpatrick & Lockhart 1500 Oliver Building Pittsburgh PA 15222-2312

DUGAN, KEVIN F. lawyer; b. Kingston, N.Y., Oct. 30, 1959; s. Owen F. and Helen A. (Frost) D.; m. Diane Tremaine, Dec. 30, 1988; children: Molly, Brighid, Owen. BS, Fla. State U., 1981; JD, Stetson Coll. Law, 1985. Bar: Fla. 1985, U.S. Dist. Ct. (mid. dist.), Fla., 1986, U.S. Ct. Appeals (11th cir.) 1987, N.H. 1991, U.S. Supreme Ct. 1991. Lawyer Woodworth & Dugan, St. Petersburg, Fla., 1985-90, Abramson, Brown & Dugan, Manchester, N.H., 1990—, Masterson, Rogers, Masterson & Gustafson, St. Petersburg, 1998—. Mem. ATLA, N.H. Trial Lawyers Assn. (Bd. Govs. award 1997, bd. govs. 1995—, pres. 1999-2000, chair legis. com. 1999—), N.H. Bar Found., Inns of Ct. Democrat. Roman Catholic. Personal injury. Office: Abramson Brown & Dugan 1819 Elm St Manchester NH 03104-2910 E-mail: kdugan@arbd.com

DUGAN, SEAN FRANCIS XAVIER, lawyer; b. Bklyn., June 21, 1951; s. Thomas Joseph and Maureen (Brett) D.; m. Martha S. Dones, 1981; children: Vanessa, Shivaun, Brandon, Ann Veronica. BA, SUNY, Oneonta, 1973; JD, Bklyn. Law Sch., 1977; LLM in Environ. Law, Pace U., 1991. Bar: N.Y. 1978, U.S. Dist. Ct. (so. and ea. dists.) N.Y. 1979, U.S. Ct. Appeals (2d cir.) 1993, U.S. Supreme Ct. 1988. Assoc. Martin, Clearwater & Bell, N.Y.C., 1978-84, ptnr., 1985—. Co-author: (book chpt.) Automated Cervical Cancer Screening, 1994; contbr. articles to profl. jours. Mem. Environ. Council Village Sleepy Hollow, N.Y., 1987; pro bono mediator U.S. Dist. Ct. (so. dist.), N.Y. Mem. ABA (com. toxic and hazardous substances and environ. law), N.Y. State Bar Assn. (mpcl. law sect., solid and hazardous waste mgmt. com., com. product liability ins.), Assn. of Bar of City of N.Y., Nat. Inst. Trial Advocacy, Westchester County Bar Assn. (mpcl. law com.), Defense Rsch. Inst., Soc. Friendly Sons of St. Patrick. Civil rights, Government contracts and claims, Professional liability. Home: 9 Birch Close Sleepy Hollow NY 10591-1001 Office: Martin Clearwater & Bell 220 E 42nd St New York NY 10017-5806 E-mail: DuganS@MCBlaw.com

DUGAS, LOUIS, JR. lawyer; b. Beaumont, Tex., Dec. 12, 1928; s. Louis and Loney (Duron) D.; m. Frances Elizabeth Tuley, Feb. 3, 1956; children: Mary Hester Dugas Koch, Kerry Beth Dugas Davidson, Louis Claiborne, Evin Garner, Reagan Taylor. AA, Lamar Jr. Coll., 1950; BBA in Banking and Fin., U. Tex., 1956, LLB, 1960. Bar: Tex. 1960, U.S. Ct. Appeals (5th cir.) 1972, U.S. Ct. Appeals (11th cir.) 1984, U.S. Supreme Ct. 1967. Pvt. practice, 1960—. Mem. Tex. Ho. of Reps., 1954-60; justice of the peace, Orange County, Tex., 1963; spl. counsel D.C. com. U.S. Ho. of Reps., 1967; dist. and county atty., Orange County, 1968-72; former tchr. Tex. history and govt., Lamar U. Former columnist The Opportunity Valley News; columnist Orange County Record, 1993—. Regent Nat. Criminal Def. Coll., Mercer Law Sch., Macon, Ga.; explorer leader Boy Scouts Am., 1963; comdr. Am. Legion Post, 1967; mem. Bd. Adjustments, City of Orange, 1967; founder "Les Acadiens du Texas"; pres. Orange County Hist. Soc., 1974-76; active Orange Art League; bd. dirs. Orange Cmty. Players, 1977-82; tchr. Cajun French Orange City Parks and Recreation Dept., 1980-81; nominee Rep. Party for 2d Congl. Dist., Tex., 1984; pres. Lamar U. Friends of Arts, 1985-86; mem. adminstrv. bd. 1st United Meth. Ch., Orange, 1983, 84, 85, also trustee; pres. S.E. Tex. Vets. Coalition, 1999—. Sgt. USMC, 1950-52, Korea. Mem. Tex. Bar Assn. (sec. criminal law sect. 1969, 72), Orange County Bar Assn. (pres. 1979), Nat. Assn. Criminal Def. Lawyers (bd. dirs. 1982-88), Tex. Criminal Def. Lawyers Assn. (bd. dirs. 1976-88, pres. 1985-86, contbr. to pub. The Voice), Tex. Criminal Def. Lawyers Inst. (pres. 1986), Tex. Assn. Bd. Cert. Specialists in Criminal Law (pres. 1983), Tex. Criminal Def. Lawyers (sec.-treas. 1981), VFW, Gulf Coast Leathernecks (founder 1995), Optimists Club, Phi Alpha Delta Avocations: historical research, bird watching, photography, conchology, writing. Civil rights, General civil litigation, Criminal. Home: 1802 16th St Orange TX 77630-3309 Office: 1804 16th St Orange TX 77630-3309 E-mail: lugas@pnx.com

DUGGAN, JAMES E., JR. judge; b. 1942; Prof. Franklin Pierce Law Ctr., 1977—2001, interim dean, 1992—93; chief appellate defender State of NH, 1981—2001; assoc. justice NH Supreme Ct., 2001—. Office: Supreme Ct Bldg One Noble Dr Concord NH 03301-6160*

DUGGAN, PATRICK JAMES, federal judge; b. 1933; BS in Econs., Xavier U., 1955; LLB, U. Detroit, 1958. Pvt. practice Brashear, Duggan & Tangora, 1959-76; judge Wayne County Cir. Ct., 1977-86, U.S. Dist. Ct. (ea. dist.) Mich., Detroit, 1987—. Adj. prof. Madonna U., Livonia, Mich., 1975-93. Chmn. Livonia Family YMCA, 1970-71; bd. trustees Madonna U., 1970-79. Mem. Mich. Jaycees (pres. 1967-68). Office: US Dist Ct 867 Theodore Levin Cthouse 231 W Lafayette Blvd Detroit MI 48226-2700

DUGHI, LOUIS JOHN, JR. lawyer; b. Westfield, N.J., June 22, 1946; s. Louis John and Maybelle Helen (Albano) D.; m. Virginia Kiss, Aug. 9, 1974; stepchildren: Christopher Polek, David Polek; 1 child, Christina Blair. BA, Cornell U., 1969, JD, 1972. Bar: N.J. 1972, U.S. Dist. Ct. N.J. 1972. Assoc. Shanley & Fisher, Newark, 1972-79; ptnr. Dughi & Hewit, Cranford, Mt. Laurel, N.J., 1979—. Lectr. Inst. Continuing Legal Edn., Newark, 1973—. Trustee, Blair Acad., Blairstown, N.J., 1975-85, Kent Place Sch., Summit, N.J., 1986—. Mem. ABA, N.J. State Bar Assn., Fed. Bar Assn., Am. Bd. Trial Advocates, Def. Rsch. Inst., Echo Lake Country Club (Westfield), Bayhead Yacht Club, Beacon Hill Club (Summit). Episcopalian. Federal civil litigation, State civil litigation. Home: 921 Kimball Ave Westfield NJ 07090-1938

DUHE, JOHN MALCOLM, JR. judge; b. Iberia Parish, La., Apr. 7, 1933; s. J. Malcolm and Rita (Arnandez) D.; children: Kim Duhe Holleman, Jeanne Duhe Sinitier, Edward M., M. Bofill. Student Washington and Lee U., 1951-53, BBA, Tulane U., 1955, LLB, 1957. Atty. Helm, Simon, Caffery & Duhe, New Iberia, La., 1957-78; dist. judge State of La., New Iberia, 1979-84; judge U.S. Dist. Ct. (we. dist.) La., Lafayette, 1984-88; cir. judge, U.S. Ct. Appeals (5th cir.), Lafayette, 1988-99, sr. judge, 1999—. Assoc. editor Tulane Law Rev., 1956, editor-in-chief, 1967. Mem. Order Coif, Omicron delta Kappa, Kappa Delta Phi. Office: US Ct Appeals 800 Lafayette St Ste 5200 Lafayette LA 70501-6865*

DUKES, JAMES OTIS, lawyer; b. Quitman, Miss., Aug. 4, 1946; s. James O. and Helen (Carlson) D.; m. Leslie Ann McIntyre, Jan. 24, 1970; children: Leslie Macon, William James. BS in Math., U. Miss., 1968, MS in Math., 1970, JD, 1975. Bar: Miss. 1975, U.S. Dist. Ct. (no. and so. dists. Miss.) 1975, U.S. Ct. Appeals (5th cir.) 1981, U.S. Supreme Ct. 1993. Law clk. to chief judge U.S. Dist. Ct. (so. dist.) Miss., Biloxi, 1975-77; assoc. Bryant, Stennis & Colingo, Gulfport, Miss., 1977-79; ptnr. Bryant, Clark, Dukes, Blakeslee, Ramsay & Hammond, PLLC, 1979—. Vestry, jr. warden, sr. warden St. Peters Episc. Ch., Gulfport, 1976-83, 94-95; pres. standing com. Episcopal Diocese Miss., Jackson, 1989, exec. com., 1990-92, v.p., 1992. 1st lt. U.S. Army, 1969-71. Fellow Miss. Bar Found. (trustee 1995-98); mem. ABA, Fed. Bar Assn., Def. Rsch. Inst., Assn. Def. Trial Attys., Southeastern Admirality Inst., Am. Coll. Trial Lawyers, Am. Bd. Trial Advocates, Miss. Bar Assn. (pres. 1999-2000), Miss. Def. Lawyers Assn. (bd. dirs. 1991-94, v.p. 1995, pres.-elect 2001), Harrison County Bar Assn. (sec. 1979-80, v.p. 1991-91, pres. 1992-93), Harrison County Jr. Bar Assn. (pres. 1981-82), Am. Inns. of Ct., Rotary. Insurance, Personal injury, Professional liability. Home: 149 Bayou Cir Gulfport MS 39507-4623 Office: Bryant Clark Dukes Blakeslee Ramsay & Hammond 2223 14th St Gulfport MS 39501-2006 E-mail: jodukes@datasync.com

DULA, ARTHUR MCKEE, III, lawyer; b. Arlington, Va., Feb. 6, 1947; s. Arthur McKee D.; m. Tamea A. Smith, Dec. 27, 1970. BS, Eastern N.Mex. U., 1970; JD, Tulane U., 1975. Bar: Tex. 1975. Assoc. Butler & Binion, Houston, 1975-79; mem. Dula & Assocs., 1979—. Faculty law U. Houston, 1977-97, South Tex. Coll. Law, 1985-97; vis. disting. prof. law U. Akron, 1992-93. Mem. editl. bd. U. Houston Law Rev., 1978-84; contbr. articles to profl. jours. Fellow AIAA (assoc.), Brit. Interplanetary Soc.; mem. ABA (sci. and tech. sect. chmn. 1982-83, award 1982), Internat. Inst. Space Law (Paris). Private international, Patent. Home: 3102 Beauchamp St Houston TX 77009-7206 Office: 3106 Beauchamp St Houston TX 77009-7206

DULANEY, RICHARD ALVIN, lawyer; b. Charlottesville, Va., Oct. 18, 1948; s. Alvin Tandy and Susie Lucille (Sims) D. BA, Yale U., 1971; JD, Coll. William and Mary, 1977. Bar: Va. 1977, U.S. Dist. Ct. (ea. dist.) Va. 1978. V.p. Christian Ctr., Charlottesville, Va., 1972-73; rsch. asst. Marshall-Wythe Sch. Law, Williamsburg, 1975; assoc. Niles & Chapman, Remington, 1977-79; gen. ptnr. Niles, Dulaney & Parker, Culpeper, 1980-92; of counsel Chandler, Franklin, and O'Bryan, 1988—; ptnr. Niles Dulaney Parker and Lauer LLP, 1992-98, Dulaney, Parker, Lauer & Thomas LLP, Culpeper, 1999-2001, Dulaney, Lauer & Thomas LLP, Culpeper, 2001—. Bd. dirs. Rappahanock Legal Svcs., Fredericksburg, Va., 1981-83. Bd. dirs. Christian Ctr., Syria, Va., 1974-89, U. Sci. and Philosophy Swannanoa, Waynesboro, Va., 1985—, The Quest Inst., Charlottesville, Va., 1986-87; mem. Bd. Zoning Appeals, Culpeper County, Culpeper, Va., 1983-90. Mem. Piedmont Bar Assn., Va. Bar Assn., Va. Trial Lawyers, Assn., Am. Trial Lawyers Assn., Culpeper Bar Assn. (pres. 1985-86), New Haven chpt. Pierson Fellowship Club, Omicron Delta Kappa. Home: PO Box 511 Culpeper VA 22701-0511 Office: Dulaney Lauer & Thomas LLP PO Box 190 Culpeper VA 22701-0190 E-mail: dulaneylaw@aol.com

DULAUX, RUSSELL FREDERICK, lawyer; b. West New York, N.J., Dec. 30, 1918; s. Frederick and Theresa A. (Noble) L.; m. Ann deFriedberg, Aug. 22, 1962 (dec.); m. Eva DeLuca, Dec. 24, 1985. Student, Drake's Bus. Sch., 1937, Pace Inst., 1938-40, Fordham U., 1946-48; LLB summa cum laude, N.Y. Law Sch., 1950; postgrad., Pace Coll., 1951, Columbia U., 1955; DBA (hon.), Adam Smith U. Am., 2001. Bar: N.Y. 1951, U.S. Dist. (so. dist.) N.Y. 1951, U.S. Ct. Appeals (2d cir.) 1951, U.S. Ct. Claims 1952, U.S. Tax Ct. 1952, U.S. Dist. Ct. (ea. dist.) N.Y. 1953, U.S. Ct. Customs and Patent Appeals 1963, U.S. Ct. Mil. Appeals 1963, U.S. Supreme Ct. 1963. Mem. staff N.Y. State Dept. Law, Richmond County Investigations, 1951-54, N.Y. State Exec. Dept. Office of Commr. of Investigations, 1954-57; comptroller-counsel Odyssey Productions, Inc., 1957-59; ptnr. Fyn, Murray & Laux, N.Y.C., 1951-61, Ryan & Laux, N.Y.C., 1961; pvt. practice, 1961—. Served with AUS, 1940-46; capt. JAG, vet. corps. of arty. State of N.Y., 1975-92, maj., 1992—; spl. agt. counter intelligence corps and security intelligence corps; col. U.S. Army. Recipient Eloy Alfaro Grand Cross Republic of Panama, Cert. of World Leadership for Leadership and Achievement, 1987, Cert. of Merit for Disting Achievement, 1984, Cert. for Internt. Contemporary Achievement for Outstanding Contbr. to Soc., 1984, Disting. Leadership award for Contbns. to the Legal Profession, Award of Merit for Outstanding Profl. and Pub. Svc., Guglielono Marconi Bronze award, 1987, 1st Century award for achievements in bus. adminstrn. and law, 2001; inducted Hall of Fame for Contbn. to Legal Profession. Mem. NATAS, Bronx County Bar Assn. (Townsend Wandell Gold medal), Met. Opera Guild, Internat. Platform Assn., VFW (adjutant Floyd Gibbons Post 500, Cert. of Recognition and Appreciation Polit. Action Com. 1990, Cert. of Svc. on Pres. Rehab. Com. Vets. sect.), Order of Lafayette, Am. Def. Preparedness Assn., Sons Union Vets. Civil War, Soc. Am. Wars, Nat. Sojourners, Heroes of '76, Navy League, St. Andrews Soc. N.Y., St. George Soc. N.Y., Soc. Friendly Sons St. Patrick, English Speaking Union, Asia Soc., China Inst. Am., Army and Navy Union USA, Am. Legion (past post comdr. admen's post 209), Mid Manhattan C. of C., Res. Officers Assn. U.S. (col.), Humanity Against Hatred, Delta Theta Phi, Lambs Club, Knights Hospitaller of St. John of Jerusalem, Grand St. Boys' Club, Soldiers' Club, Sailors' and Airmen's Club, Order Ea. Star, Masons (past comdr. N.Y. Masonic War Vets), Shriners, Knights of Malta, Knights of St. George, Sovereign Mil. Order of Temple of Jerusalem. Probate, Real property, Estate taxation. Office: FDR Station PO Box 477 New York NY 10150-0477

DULCHINOS, PETER, lawyer; b. Chicopee Falls, Mass., Feb. 2, 1935; s. George and Angeline D.; children: Matthew George, Paul Constantine, Gregory Peter. BSEE, MIT, 1956, MSEE, 1957; MS in Engring. Mgmt., Northeastern U., 1965; JD, Suffolk U., 1984. Bar: Mass. 1984, U.S. Dist. Ct. (Mass.) 1984, U.S. Ct. Appeals (1st cir.) 1985, U.S. Supreme Ct. 1988, U.S. Patent and Trademark Office 1989, U.S. Claims Ct. 1989. With Sylvania Co., Waltham, Mass., 1957-61, Needham, 1963-66, Tech Ops, Burlington, 1961, RCA, Burlington, 1962-63, Raytheon Co., Lexington, Mass., 1966—. Computer ops. mgr. tactical software devel. facility Patriot Ground Computer System, 1977-86, intellectual property mgr., 1986—; lectr. Fitchburg State Coll., 1985-90; corporator Ctrl. Savs. Bank, Lowell, Mass., 1980-92; sec.-treas. U. Lowell Bldg. Authority, 1974-85; mem. statewide adv. coun. Dept. Mental Health, 1996—. Mem. statewide adv. coun. Dept. Mental Retardation, 1993-96; mem. human studies subcom. Bedford VA Hosp., 1987-90; pres. Chelmsford Rep. Club, 1964-70; chmn. Chelmsford Rep. Town Com., 1972-76, 80—, chmn., 2000—; assoc. town counsel Tyngsborough, Mass., 1985-87; mem., chmn. Chelmsford Bd. Health, 1972-87, 93—; mem. Nashoba Tech. High Sch. Com., 1970-71; trustee, chmn. Medfield State Hosp., 1993—; v.p. Greater Lowell Comprehensive Cmty. Support Systems Bd. Dept. Mental Health, 1994-99; mem. State Mental Health Planning Coun., 1999—. 2d lt. U.S. Army, 1957-58. Mem. Mass. Bar Assn., Boston Patent Law Assn., Raytheon Employees Profl. Assn. (treas. 1998, pres. 1999). Republican. Greek Orthodox. Intellectual property, Probate, Trademark and copyright. Home: 17 Spaulding Rd Chelmsford MA 01824-1021 Office: Raytheon Co 141 Spring St Lexington MA 02421-7899 E-mail: peter_dulchinos@raytheon.com

DULIN, THOMAS N. lawyer; b. Albany, N.Y., May 26, 1949; s. Joseph Paul and Mary Carol (Keane) D.; m. Pamela Lee Kendall, May 14, 1983; 1 children: Chelsea K., Danielle Y. Boshea, Amanda L. Boshea, Thomas M. Boshea. BA, Siena Coll., 1972; JD, Western New England U., 1976. Bar: N.Y. 1977, U.S. Dist. Ct. (no. dist.) N.Y. 1977, U.S. Supreme Ct. 1984. Asst. dist. atty. Albany County, 1977-81; assoc. McCarthy & Evanick, Albany, 1981-83; sole practice, 1983-88; sr. ptnr. Dulin, Harris & Bixby, 1988-92; ptnr. Gerstenzang, Weiner & Gerstenzang, 1992-93, The Dulin Law Firm, Albany, 1993—. Staff atty. Albany County Pub. Defender's Office, 1983—. Bd. dirs. Big Bros. and Sisters of Albany County, Inc., 1983-92, pres., bd. dirs. , 1988-90. Mem. ABA, N.Y. State Bar Assn. (lectr. criminal justice sect.), Nat. Assn. Criminal Def. Lawyers, N.Y. State Assn. Criminal Def. Lawyers, Capital Dist. Trial Lawyers Assn., Albany County Bar Assn., Assn. Trial Lawyers Am., N.Y. State Trial Lawyers Assn. Democrat. Avocations: skiing, golfing, swimming. Criminal, Personal injury. Home: 2 Country Rdg Schenectady NY 12304-2531 Office: 4 Tower Pl Exec Park Tower Albany NY 12203

DUMVILLE, S(AMUEL) LAWRENCE, lawyer; b. Richmond, Va., Mar. 14, 1953; m. Frances Adair Davis, Oct. 24, 1981; 2 children. BA, Washington and Lee U., 1975; JD, Coll. William and Mary, 1978. Bar: Va. 1978, U.S. Dist. Ct. (ea. dist.) Va. 1978, U.S. Ct. Appeals (4th cir.) 1979, U.S. Dist. Ct. (we. dist.) Va. 1981. Assoc. Breeden, Howard & MacMillan, Norfolk, Va., 1978-85; ptnr. Breeden, MacMillan & Green, PLC, 1985-95. Bd. dirs. Breeden Adams Found., 1992-95. Mem. adv. bd. Back Bay Restoration Found., Virginia Beach, 1982-87; fin. chair, mem. adminstrn. bd. St. Andrew's United Meth. Ch., Virginia Beach, 1992—, del. to ann. conf., 1989-92, pres., 1995-97; treas., bd. dirs. Larkspur Civic League, 1989-92, 94-2000; pres. Norfolk Law Libr. Found., 1989; bd. dirs. Norfolk Law Libr., 1986-91; mem., chaplain troop com. Boy Scouts Am., 1998—. Mem. ATLA, Va. Bar Assn., Norfolk-Portsmouth Bar Assn. (bd. dirs. 1988-89), Virginia Beach Bar Assn., Va. Assn. Def. Counsel. Republican. Avocations: deep sea sport fishing, sporting clays. Federal civil litigation, General civil litigation, Insurance. Office: Independence Law Ctr 4356 Bonney Rd Ste 2-102 Virginia Beach VA 23452-1200 E-mail: bch-law@exis.net

DUNAGAN, WALTER BENTON, lawyer, educator; b. Midland, Tex., Dec. 11, 1937; s. Clinton McCormick and Allie Mae (Stout) D.; m. Tera Childress, Feb. 1, 1969; children: Elysha, Sandi. BA, U. Tex., 1963, JD, 1965, postgrad., 1965-68. Bar: Tex. 1965, Fla. 1970, U.S. Dist. Ct. (mid. dist.) Fla. 1971, U.S. Ct. Appeals (11th cir.) 1982. Corp. atty. Gulf Oil, New Orleans, 1966-69, Getty Oil Co., L.A., 1969—, Westinghouse/Econocar, Internat., Daytona Beach, Fla., 1969-72; assoc. Becks & Becks, 1973-75; prin. Walter B. Dunagan, 1975—. Cons. Bermuda Villas Motel, Daytona Beach, Buccanneer Motel, Daytona Beach, Pelican Cove West Homeowners Assn., Edgewater, Fla. Organizer Interfaith Coffee House, New Orleans; tchr., song leader various chs.; chief Indian guide/princess program YMCA, Daytona Beach; bd. dirs. Legal Aid, Daytona Beach. Lance cpl. USMC. Mem. Volusia County Bar Assn., Lawyers Title Guaranty Fund, Phi Delta Phi. Avocations: reading, languages. Consumer commercial, Contracts commercial, General corporate. Home and Office: 714 Egret Ct Edgewater FL 32141-4120 Fax: 386-409-3710. E-mail: wbdunfla@aol.com

DUNAU, ANASTASIA THANNHAUSER, retired administrative law judge; b. Munich, Germany, July 16, 1919; came to U.S., 1935; d. Siegfried Joseph and Franziska (Reiner) Thannhauser; m. Bernard Dunau, July 10, 1950 (dec. Mar. 1975); children: Mark, Frank, Miriam, Andrew. BA, Smith Coll., 1941; LLB, Yale U., 1943. Bar: N.Y. 1945, D.C. 1958, U.S. Supreme Ct. 1958. Assoc. Hughes, Hubbard & Ewing, N.Y.C., 1943-47; atty. advisor NLRB, Washington, 1947-52; pvt. practice, 1952-63; atty. U.S. Dept. Labor, 1963-79, adminstrv. law judge, 1979-85, ret., 1985. Mediator U.S. Dist. Ct., Washington, 1992—; vol. atty. LCE-AARP, Washingtno, 1993—. Mem. Nat. Assn. Women Judges (life, chair resolutions com. 1985, 86). Democrat.

DUNCAN, ED EUGENE, lawyer; b. Gary, Ind., Dec. 10, 1948; s. Attwood and Freddie Leon (Ballard) D.; m. Patricia Louise Revado, Sept. 8, 1973 (div.); children: Kristin, Anika, Gregory. BA, Oberlin Coll., 1970; JD, Northwestern U., 1974. Bar: Ohio 1974, U.S. Dist. Ct. (no. dist.) Ohio 1977, U.S. Supreme Ct. 1977. Assoc. Arter & Hadden, Cleve., 1974-82, ptnr., 1982—. Bd. mem. Glenville br. YMCA, Cleve., 1979—, Ohio Bd. of Bldg. Standards, Columbus, 1986-89; trustee Legal Aid Soc., Cleve., 1990-91. Mem. Ohio Bar Assn., Cleve. Bar Assn., Minority Ptnrs. in Majority Corp. Law Firms, Internat. Assn. Def. Counsel. Avocations: writing, reading. General civil litigation, Insurance, Personal injury. Home: 935 Roland Rd Cleveland OH 44124-1033 Office: Arter & Hadden 925 Euclid Ave Ste 1100 Cleveland OH 44115-1475 E-mail: eduncan1@arterhadden.com

DUNCAN, JOHN DEAN, JR. lawyer; b. Detroit, Nov. 25, 1950; s. John Dean Duncan and Ann Marie (Bruton) Bridges; m. Vickie Renee Olafson, May 10, 1986; children: Katherine Lund, John Dean III. Student, USAF Acad., 1969-71; BA, Cath. U., 1973, JD, 1976; MPA, Harvard U., 1991. Bar: U.S. Ct. Appeals Md. 1976, U.S. Ct. Appeals D.C. 1978, U.S. Supreme Ct. 1980. Law clk. to presiding justice 6th Jud. Ct., Rockville, Md., 1976-77; sr. asst. state's atty. Montgomery County, 1977-81; sr. trial atty. pub. integrity sect., criminal divsn. Dept. Justice, Washington, 1981-87; chief counsel to Inspector Gen. Dept. State, 1987-98, sr. seminar, 1998-99; dir. Office Internat. Econ. Policy Nat. Security Coun., 1999; vice-chmn. Nat. Security Coun. Task Force on Internat. Trade, Washington, 1999-2000; spl. advisor for internat. econ. policy and counselor Nat. Security Coun. and Nat. Econ. Coun. The White Ho., 2000—. Career mem. Sr. Exec. Svc. U.S., 1987—; fin. com. chair Samaritan Min. of Greater Washington. Admissions com. J.F. Kennedy Sch. of Govt., Harvard U., Cambridge, Mass., 1991. Named one of Outstanding Young Men Am., 1980. Mem. D.C. Bar Assn., Mountgomery County Bar Assn. Avocations: skiing, squash, jogging. office phone. Office: Dept State Nat Sec Council The White House Washington DC 20520-0001 E-mail: brushway@aol.com, jduncanj@nsc.eop.gov

DUNCAN, JOHN PATRICK CAVANAUGH, lawyer; b. Kalamazoo, Jan. 25, 1949; s. James H. and Colleen Patricia (Cloney) D.; children: Sarah Ellen, James Patrick Cloney. BA cum laude, Yale U., 1971; JD, U. Chgo., 1974. Bar: Ill. 1974, U.S. Dist. Ct. (no. dist.) Ill. 1974, U.S. Ct. Appeals (7th cir.) 1975, U.S. Supreme Ct. 1979. Assoc. firm Holleb & Coff, Chgo., 1974-79; mem., 1979-87; ptnr. Jones, Day, Reavis & Pogue, Chgo., 1987-99; leader banking and investment practice area, 1996-99; prin. Duncan Assocs., LLC, 2000—. Adj. prof. IIT Chgo.-Kent Coll. Law Fin. Svcs. LLM Program, 1988—; mem. Fulbright Vis. Scholar Adv. Bd., 1995-98; mem. Chgo. com. Chgo. Coun. on Fgn. Rels., 1998—. Contbr. articles to profl. jours. Fellow NSF, 1970. Fellow Ill. Bar Found.; mem. ABA (bus. and banking sect., chmn. securities activities banks subcom. 1995-98, privacy task force 1998-2001), Chgo. Bar Assn. (chmn., fin. insts. coms. 1985-86), Ill. Bankers Assn. (legal affairs com. 1986-87), Yale Club (Chgo., N.Y.), Met. Club (Chgo.). Banking, Finance, Mergers and acquisitions. Home: 3814 N Paulina St Chicago IL 60613-2716 Office: Duncan Assocs LLC 180 N LaSalle Ste 2410 Chicago IL 60601-2704 E-mail: jpcd@jpcdlaw.com

DUNCOMBE, RAYNOR BAILEY, lawyer; b. Washington, July 17, 1942; s. Raynor Lockwood and Avis Ethel (Bailey) D.; m. Janice Assunta Rini, Apr. 12, 1969; children: Christina Luccioni, Raynor Luccioni. AB, Franklin and Marshall Coll., 1965; JD, Syracuse U., 1968. Bar: N.Y. 1972, U.S. Dist. Ct. (no. dist.) N.Y. 1972. Staff atty. State of N.Y., Albany,

1968-70; mgmt. trainee State Bank Albany, 1970-72; staff atty. Vibbard, Donaghy & Wright, Schoharie, N.Y., 1972-73, F. Walter Bliss, Esq., Schoharie, 1973-74; pvt. practice, 1974—. Chmn. bd. dirs. Fulmont Mut. Ins. co., Mohawk Minden Ins. Co.; town atty. seven towns, one village and one water dist. in Schoharie County, 1975—; adminstr. Assigned Counsel Program, 1975—; sch. atty. Middleburgh (N.Y.) Schs., 1981-85, 97—; atty. Schoharie County, 1982-87, 90-91, Schoharie County Hist. Soc., 1975—; mem. Tax Cons. Tech. Adv. Group, Catskill Watershed Corp., 1998—. Rep. committeeman Schoharie county, 1984-92; dist. commr. Boy Scouts Am., 1987-92, asst. scoutmaster, 1988-91, Explorer advisor, 1991-99, dist. chmn., 1992-95, asst. coun. commr., 1995-96, coun. commr. 1996-99, coun. pres. 1999—; elder Presbyn. Ch., 1992-98, mem. pers. com. Albany Presbytery of Presbyn. Ch., 1998—; chmn. Middleburgh Rep. Town Com., 1995—. Mem. ABA, N.Y. State Bar Assn., Schoharie County Bar Assn. (sec.-treas. 1975—), Rotary (past pres.), Masons (past master), Lions. Avocations: camping, cross country skiing, collecting stamps. General practice. Home: RR 2 Box 360 Middleburgh NY 12122-9415 Office: PO Box 490 319 Main St Schoharie NY 12157

DUNDAS, PHILIP BLAIR, JR. lawyer; b. Middletown, Conn., Apr. 29, 1948; s. Philip Blair and Madolyn Margaret Dundas; m. Elizabeth Anne Adorno, Aug. 9, 1969; children: Philip Blair III, Chapman P. BA, Wesleyan U., Conn., 1970; JD, Washington and Lee U., 1973. Bar: N.Y. 1974. Assoc. Shearman & Sterling, N.Y.C., 1973-81, ptnr., 1981—, ptnr. in charge of Abu Dhabi, United Arab Emirates Office, 1981—. Mem. ABA, Internat. Bar Assn., N.Y. State Bar Assn., Assn. Bar City N.Y., Union Internationale des Avocats, Clinton Country Club. General corporate, Finance, Private international. Home: 288 Old Kelsey Point Rd Westbrook CT 06498-2132

DUNE, STEVE CHARLES, lawyer; b. Vithkuqi, Korca, Albania, June 15, 1931; s. Costa Pappas and Evanthia (Vangel) D.; m. Irene Duff Boudreau, Sept. 4, 1955; children: Michelle Dune Gesky, Christopher Michael. AB, Clark U., 1953; JD, NYU, 1956. Bar: N.Y. 1957. Law clk. U.S. Ct. Appeals 1st Cir., 1956-57; from assoc. to ptnr. Cadwalader, Wickersham & Taft, N.Y.C., 1957-95; counsel Albanian-Am. Enterprise Fund, 1995-96. Trustee Clark U., Worcester, Mass., 1974-86, 93-97, hon. trustee, 1997-2001, vice-chmn. bd. dirs., 1980-84, chmn. bd. dirs., 1984-86, chmn. presdl. search com., 1983-84, mem. pres.'s coun., 1987-90; dir. Albanian Children Fund, 1998—, chmn. Albanian-Am. C. of C., 1995-96; mem. Natl. Albanian Am. Coun., 2000—. Root-Tilden scholar, 1953-56 Mem. ABA (divsn. sr. lawyers), N.Y. State Bar Assn., Assn. Bar City N.Y. (com. on Ea. European affairs 1992-95, admiralty com. 1976-79, 87-90), Maritime Law Assn. U.S. (marine fin. com. 1980-95), Internat. Bar Assn. (bus. and law sect. Ea. European Forum), India House, Phi Beta Kappa. Admiralty, Contracts commercial, General corporate. Home and Office: PO Box 456 98 Barrett Hill Rd Brooklyn CT 06234-1500 E-mail: scdune@snet.net

DUNFEE, THOMAS WYLIE, law educator; b. Huntington, W.Va., Nov. 15, 1941; s. Wylie Ray and Chloe Edith (Wylie) D.; m. Dorothy Jane Taylor, Aug. 26, 1967; children: John Wylie, Jennifer Sue, Shannon Elizabeth. AB, Marshall U., 1963; JD, NYU, 1966, LLM, 1969. Instr. N.Y. Inst. Tech., 1965-68; asst. prof. Ill. State U., Normal, 1968-70, Ohio State U., Columbus, 1970-72, assoc. prof., 1972-74; assoc. prof. legal studies Wharton Sch., U. Pa., Phila., 1974-79, prof., 1979—, Kolodny prof. social responsiblity, 1982—, chmn. dept. legal studies, 1980-84, 87-91, dir. Wharton ethics program, 1995-96, dir. Zicklin Ctr. for Bus. Ethics Rsch., 1997-2000, vice dean, 2000—. Vis. prof. U. Fla., 1989, U. Newcastle, Australia, 1981, 85, Georgetown U., 1994, U. Mich., 2000; cons. United Way of Am., McGraw-Hill, Ind. Stds. Bd., Citibank, GM, Honda, Glaxo, SmithKline, AT&T. Author: Business and Its Legal Environment, 1992, Modern Business Law, 1996; editor: Business Ethics: Japan and the Global Economy, 1993, (with Thomas Donaldson) Ethics in Business and Economics, 2 vols., 1997, Ties That Bind: A Social Contracts Approach to Business Ethics, 1999; editor-in-chief Am. Bus. Law Jour., 1976-79; contbr. articles to profl. jours. Grantee Exxon Found., 1985-86, Kemper Found., 1993. Mem. Acad. Legal Studies in Bus. (pres. 1989-90, Disting. Sr. Faculty award for Excellence 1991), Soc. Bus. Ethics (pres. 1995-96). E-mail: dunfeet@wharton.upcnn.edu

DUNHAM, CHRISTOPHER COOPER, b. N.Y.C., Jan. 29, 1937; s. Robert Secrest and Elizabeth Walls (Cooper) D.; m. Marjorie Jean Corliss, June 14, 1958; children: Douglas Webber, William Sigler, Anne Corliss. BA, Wesleyan U., 1958; JD, Columbia U., 1961. Bar: N.Y. 1961, U.S. Dist. Cts. (so. and ea. dists.) N.Y. 1963, U.S. Patent and Trademark Office 1964, U.S. Ct. Appeals (2d cir.) 1964. Assoc. Cooper, Dunham, Dearborn & Henninger, N.Y.C., 1961-68; ptnr. Cooper & Dunham LLP and predecessor firms, 1968—. Chmn. Westport Democratic Town Com., Conn., 1965-66, 67-70, 80-86; mem. Conn. Dem. Ctrl. Com., 1978-80; del. Conn. Dem. Conv., Conn., 1966, 68, 74, 80, 82, 84, 90, 98; alt. Westport Planning and Zoning Com., 1965; mem. Westprot Bd. Fin., 1975, Conn. Safety Commn., 1977-78, Westport Rep. Town Meeting, 1986-93. Mem. N.Y. Intellectual Property Law Assn., Gamma Psi, Phi Beta Kappa. Congregationalist. Patent. Home: 277 Compo Rd S Westport CT 06880-6513

DUNHAM, WOLCOTT BALESTIER, JR. lawyer; b. N.Y.C., Sept. 14, 1943; s. Wolcott Balestier and Isabel Caroline (Bosworth) D.; m. Joan Scott Findlay, Jan. 26, 1974; children: Mary Findlay, James Wolcott. AB magna cum laude, Harvard U., 1965, LLB cum laude, 1968. Bar: N.Y. 1969. Vol. VISTA, 1968-69; assoc. Debevoise & Plimpton and predecessor Debevoise, Plimpton, Lyons & Gates, N.Y.C., 1969-76, ptnr., 1977—. Exec. dir. N.Y. State Exec. Adv. Commn. on Ins. Industry Regulatory Reform, 1982; spkr. in field. Co-author: Insurance M&A, 1997—; contbr. articles to profl. jours.; gen. editor and chpt. author, New York Insurance Law, 1991, and ann. supplements. Treas., trustee Fund for Astrophys. Rsch., N.Y.C., 1970—, sec., 1970-84, pres., 1984—; bd. dirs. UN Assn., N.Y.C., 1973-79, vice chmn., 1975-79, adv. coun., 1992—; vestry mem. St. James Ch., N.Y.C., 1987-93, clk., 1988-93, jr. warden, 1993-94, sr. warden, 1994-95, chancellor, 1994—; bd. dirs. Neighborhood Coalition for Shelter, Inc., 1983—; pres., bd. dirs. East Side Cmty. Ctr., Inc., 1988—; bd. dirs. Dutchess Land Conservancy, 1996—; bd. mgrs. Shekomeko Valley Farm Assn., LLC, 1996—. Fellow Am. Coll. Investment Counsel; mem. ABA (chmn. com. on ins. sect. adminstrv. law 1979-83), Assn. Bar City N.Y. (com. on ins. 1981-87, chmn. com. 1984-87), Union Internationale des Avocats, Am. Soc. Internat. Law, Harvard Law Sch. Assn. N.Y.C. (dir. 1978-81) Episcopalian. General corporate, Insurance, Securities. Office: Debevoise & Plimpton 919 3rd Ave New York NY 10022-3904

DUNIPACE, IAN DOUGLAS, lawyer; b. Tucson, Dec. 18, 1939; s. William Smith and Esther Morvyth (McGeorge) D.; m. Janet Mae Dailey, June 9, 1963; children: Kenneth Mark, Leslie Amanda. BA magna cum laude, U. Ariz., 1961, JD cum laude, 1966. Bar: Ariz. 1966, U.S. Supreme Ct. 1972, Nev. 1994, Colo. 1996. Reporter, critic Long Branch (N.J.) Daily Record, 1963; assoc. firm Jennings, Strouss, Salmon & Trask, Phoenix, 1966-69; assoc. Jennings, Strouss & Salmon, PLC, 1969-70, ptnr., 1971-93, mem., 1993—, chmn. comml. practice dept., 1998—. Comments editor Ariz. Law Rev., 1965-66. Reporter Phoenix Forward Edn. Com., 1969-70; mem. Phoenix Arts Commn., 1990-93, chmn., 1992-93; bd. mgmt. Downtown Phoenix YMCA, 1973-80, chmn. 1977-78; bd. dirs. Phoenix Met. YMCA, 1976-87, 88—, chmn. 1984-85; bd. mgmt. Paradise Valley YMCA, 1979-82, chmn. 1980-81; bd. mgmt. Scottsdale/Paradise Valley YMCA, 1983, mem. legal affairs com. Pacific Region YMCA, 1978-81; chmn. YMCA Ariz. State Youth and Govt. Com., 1989-95; bd. dirs. The Schoolhouse Found. 1990-96, pres. 1990-94, Kids Voting, 1990-94, Beaver Valley Improvement Assn. 1977-79, Pi Kappa Alpha Holding Corp., 1968-72, The Heard Mus. 1993-94, Ariz. Bar Found., 1996—, pres., 2001—, Phoenix Kiwanis Charitable Found, 2001—; trustee Paradise Valley Unified Dist. Employee Benefit Trust, 1980-93, chmn. 1987-93, Sch. Theology, Claremont, Calif. 1994—; trustee First Meth. Found. of Phoenix, 1984-93, 99—, v.p., 2001—; mem. Greater Paradise Valley Cmty. Coun., 1985-87; bd. dir. Heard Mus. Coun., 1990-95, pres. 1993-94; mem. Ariz. Venture Capital Conf. Planning Com., 1994—, mem. exec. com. 1997—, chmn., 2000; mem. Assn. for Corp. Growth, 1995-96, Ariz. Bus. Leadership Assn., 1996—, bd. dirs., 2001—; bd. visitors U. Ariz. Law Coll., 1996—. Capt. AUS, 1961-63. Mem. State Bar Ariz. (securities regulation sect. 1970—, chmn. 1991-92, mem. com. unauthorized practice of law 1972-84, chmn. 1975-83, mem. bus. law sect. 1981—, chmn. 1984-85), State Bar Nev., State Bar Colo., Am., Fed. (pres. Ariz. chpt. 1980-81), Maricopa County Bar Assns. (bd. dirs. Corp. Coun. divsn. 1996-99), Ariz. Zool. Soc., U. Ariz. Law Coll. Assn. (bd. dirs. 1983-90, pres. 1985-86, bd. visitors 1996—), Smithsonian Assn., U. Ariz. Alumni Assn. (bd. dirs. 1985-86), Ariz. Club, Renaissance Club, Orange Tree Club, Masons, Kiwanis (pres. Phoenix 1984-85, disting. lt. gov. 1986-87, S.W. dist. cmty. svc. chmn. 1987-88, dist. activity com. coord. 1988-89, dist. laws and regulation chmn. 1989-90, 92-93, 95-96, asst. to dist. gov. for club svcs. 1990-91, field dir. 1991-92, dist. conv. chmn. 1993-94, pub. rels. chmn. 1996-98, mem. internat. com. on Project 39, 1988-89, internat. com. On to Anaheim 1990-91, internat. com. on leadership tng. and devel. 1991-92, 93-94, trustee SW dist. found. 1987-92, 1st v.p. 1990-92), Phi Beta Kappa, Phi Kappa Phi, Phi Delta Phi, Phi Alpha Theta, Sigma Delta Pi, Phi Eta Sigma, Pi Kappa Alpha (nat. counsel 1968-72). Democrat. Methodist (mem. met. Phoenix commn. 1968-71, lay leader 1975-78, trustee 1979-81, pres. 1981; mem. Pacific S.W. ann. conf. 1969-79, lawyer commn. 1980-85, chancellor Desert S.W. ann. conf. 1985—). General corporate, Non-profit and tax-exempt organizations, Securities. Home: 2527 E Vogel Ave Phoenix AZ 85028-4729 Office: Jennings Strouss & Salmon PLC 201 E Washington Ste 1100 Phoenix AZ 85004-2383 E-mail: dunipace@jsslaw.com

DUNLAY, CATHERINE TELLES, lawyer; b. Cin., Apr. 5, 1958; d. Paul Albert and Donna Mae Telles; m. Thomas Vincent Dunlay, July 10, 1981; children: Christine Jennifer, Thomas Paul, Brian Patrick. Student, Ind. U., 1976-78; BA in English Lit. summa cum laude, U. Cin., 1981; JD summa cum laude, Ohio State U., 1984. Bar: Ohio 1984. Teaching asst., legal rsch. and writing Ohio State U. Coll. of Law, Columbus, 1982; law clk. Brownfield, Bowen & Bally, 1983; assoc. Schottenstein, Zox & Dunn, LPA, 1984-91, atty., principal, 1991—. Mng. editor Ohio State Law Jour., 1983-84; co-author Health Span, 1993, Akron Law Rev., Fall 1993; co-editor Health Law Jour. of Ohio, 1994-95. Grad. Columbus Leadership Program, 1991; mem. admissions/inclusiveness com. United Way of Franklin County, Columbus, 1991-94, 96. Recipient C. Simeral Bunch award for Acad. Excellence, Ohio State U., 1984, Law Jour. Past Editors award, 1984. Mem. ABA, Ohio State Bar Assn. (chair healthcare law com. 2000—), Columbus Bar Assn., Ohio Women's Bar Assn., Women Lawyers of Franklin County (trustee, treas. 1990-93, 91-92), Am. Health Lawyers Assn., Soc. of Ohio Hosp. Attys., Order of the Coif. Roman Catholic. Avocations: cooking, hiking, camping, reading. General corporate, Health, Securities. Office: Schottenstein Zox & Dunn 41 S High St Ste 2600 Columbus OH 43215-6109 E-mail: cdunlay@szd.com

DUNLEVY, WILLIAM SARGENT, lawyer; b. Burbank, Calif., June 5, 1952; s. Roy William and Zella LaVerne (Singleton) D.; m. Margaret Joy Lehman Dunlevy, June 22, 1974; children: Thomas William, Gregory Michael. BA, U. Calif., Davis, 1974; JD, UCLA, 1977. Bar: Calif. 1977. Lawyer Law office of Robert Silver, Ventura, Calif., 1977-80, Taylor, Churchman & Lingl, Camarillo, 1980-84, Liebmann & Dunlevy, Camarillo, 1984-88, James P. Lingl & Assoc., Camarillo, 1988-97, Knopfler & Robertson, Camarillo, 1998-2001; pvt. practice, 2001—. Editor Inst. Channel Islands chpt. Cmty. Assn., Ventura, Calif., 1984—, pres., 1986-87. Pres. Ventura (Calif.) Downtown Lions Club, 1985-86; bd. mem. Am. Youth Soccer Orgn., Ventura, Calif., 1986-88, 90-96. Mem. Community Assn. Inst., Poinsetta Lodge. Republican. Baptist. Avocations: photography, hiking. Estate planning, Real property. Office: Law Offices William S Dunlevy 1200 Paseo Camarillo Ste 165 Camarillo CA 93010-6085 Fax: 805-383-6227. E-mail: dunlevylaw@aol.com

DUNN, DONALD JACK, law librarian, law educator, dean, lawyer; b. Tyler, Tex., Nov. 9, 1945; s. Loren Jack and Clara Inez (Milam) D.; m. Cheryl Jean Sims, Nov. 24, 1967; 1 child, Kevin. BA., U. Tex.-Austin, 1969, MLS, 1972; JD, Western New Eng. Coll., 1983. Asst. to law libr. U. Tex., 1969-72, supervising libr. Criminal Justice Reference Libr., 1972-73; law libr., prof. law Western New Eng. Coll., Springfield, Mass., 1973-96, interim dean, 1996-98, dean, 1998—2001, assoc. dean for info. resources, prof. law Miss., 2002—. Editor: Immigration and Nationality Law Rev., vols. 3-7, 1979—84; editor: (with Mersky) Fundamentals of Legal Research, 8th edit., 2002. Bd. dirs. Pioneer Valley chpt. ARC; pres. Scribes, 2001—. Mem. ALA, ABA (chair law librs. com. 1988-92), Am. Assn. Law Librs. (chair acad. law librs. spl. interest sect. 1989-90), Spl. Libr. Assn., Law Librs. New Eng. (pres. 1982-83). Democrat. Episcopalian. Office: Western New Eng Coll Sch Law 1215 Wilbraham Rd Springfield MA 01119-2612 E-mail: ddwunn@law.wnec.edu

DUNN, HERBERT IRVIN, lawyer; b. Balt., July 19, 1946; s. Albert M. and Hilda F. (Winakur) D.; m. Marsha Edith Greenfield, Apr. 1, 1979; children: Marla Phyllis, Jonathan Howard. BS with high honors, U. Md., 1969, JD, 1971. Bar: Md. 1971, D.C. 1971, U.S. Ct. Claims 1972, U.S. Tax Ct. 1972, U.S. Dist. Ct. D.C. 1971, U.S. Ct. Appeals (D.C. cir.) 1971, U.S. Supreme Ct. 1975. Atty.-adviser Office of Gen. Counsel U.S. Gen. Acctg. Office, Washington, 1971-83, sr. atty., 1983—. Served with USAR, 1968-74. Fellow: Found. of the FBA (advisor 1999—); mem.: FBA (treas. younger lawyers divsn. 1977—79, nat. coun. 1978—79, nat. coun. 1991—, Capitol Hill chpt. exec. coun. 1975—83, v.p. 1990—91, pres. 1992—93, v.p. D.C. cir. 1994—, nat. exec. com. 1999—2000, v.p. for the cirs. chmn. 1999—2000), Md. Bar Assn., Northwest Br. Citizens Assn. (sec. 1988—95, 1st v.p. 1995—99), Omicron Delta Epsilon. Office: 441 G St NW Washington DC 20548-0001

DUNN, JACKSON THOMAS, JR. lawyer, legal educator; b. Charlotte, N.C., Nov. 30, 1943; s. Jackson Thomas and Dorothy Holland (Schweiger) D.; m. Mary Louise Miller, Apr. 23, 1944; children: Jackson Thomas, Michael Lansing, Mary Katharine Holland. AB, Belmont Abbey Coll., 1965; JD, U. N.C., 1968. Bar: N.C. 1968, U.S. Dist. Ct. (mid. dist.) N.C. 1977, U.S. Dist. Ct. (we. dist.) N.C. 1974, U.S. Supreme Ct. 1982. Asst. prof. East Carolina U., Greenville, N.C., 1968-69, U. Ga., Athens, 1969-75; ptnr. Edwards & Dunn, Charlotte, N.C., 1975; counsel The Ervin Co., 1976; v.p., sr. counsel Northwestern Fin. Corp./Northwestern Bank, North Wilkesboro, 1976-85; sr. v.p., dep. gen. counsel 1st Union Corp./1st Union Nat. Bank, Charlotte, 1985-2000; ptnr. Moore & Van Allen PLLC, 2000—. Instr. N.C. Bankers Assn. Seminars. Contbr. articles to profl. jours. Bd. govs. U. N.C. Law Sch. Alumni Assn. Mem. ABA, N.C. Bar Assn. (chmn. fin. Instns. com.), N.C. Carolina Bar, Am. Law Inst., N.C. Bankers Assn. (chmn. N.C. bank counsel com.). Democrat. Banking, Bankruptcy, Contracts commercial. Office: Moore & Van Allen PLLC LEG 100 N Tryon St Ste 4700 Charlotte NC 28202 E-mail: tomdunn@mualaw.com

DUNN, JAMES EDWARD, JR. corporate consultant, lawyer; b. Pitts., May 31, 1947; s. James Edward and Anne Elizabeth (O'Connor) D.; m. Sally Skeehan, June 6, 1970; children: Meghan, Mark. BS, St. Joseph's Coll., 1969; JD, Duquesne U., 1972. Bar: Pa. 1972, Ohio 1973, Fla. 1981, Ga. 1999. Assoc. atty. IRS, Cleve., 1972-76; asst. gen. atty. Chessie System, 1976-79; asst. to treas. Harris Corp., Melbourne, Fla., 1979-83; treas. Harris Graphics, 1983-86; prin. Ernst & Whinney, Atlanta, 1986—. Mem. Estate Planning Council Brevard County; bd. dirs. Space Coast Sci. Ctr., Melbourne, 1986; vice chmn. devel. council Holmes Regional Med. Ctr., Melbourne, 1986. Mem. ABA, So. Pension Conf. Home: 8360 Greensboro Dr Apt 603 Mc Lean VA 22102 Office: Ernst & Whinney 225 Peachtree Ctr South Tower 8484 Westpark Dr Mc Lean VA 22102

DUNN, M(ORRIS) DOUGLAS, lawyer; b. Ionia, Mich., Nov. 1, 1944; s. Morris Frederick and Lola Adella (Gee) D.; m. Jill Lynn Fasbender, July 22, 1967; children: Brooks, Gillian, Joshua. BSME, U. Mich., 1967; JD, Vanderbilt U., 1970. Bar: U.S. Dist. Ct. (so. dist.) N.Y. 1972, U.S. Ct. Appeals (2d cir.) 1973, U.S. Supreme Ct. 1978. Assoc. Winthrop Stimson, Putnam & Roberts, N.Y.C., 1970-78, ptnr., 1978-84; sr. v.p., mng. dir. Shearson Lehman Bros., Inc., 1984-85; ptnr. Milbank, Tweed, Hadley & McCloy, N.Y.C, 1985—. Contbr. articles to profl. jours. Fellow ABA (fed. regulation of securities com. bus. law sect. mem. 1981—, chair pub. utility, comms. and transp. law sect. 1997-98, bd. govs. 1998-2001), Am. Bar Found.; mem. Assn. Bar City N.Y. (chmn. nuclear tech. and law com. 1976-77), Internat. Bar Assn. (com. chmn. 1990-94), Alumni Bd. Vanderbilt U. Law Sch., Down Town Club (N.Y.C.), Canoe Brook Country Club (Summit, N.J.). Mergers and acquisitions, Public utilities, Securities. Office: Milbank Tweed Hadley & McCloy LLP 1 Chase Manhattan Plz Fl 47 New York NY 10005-1413

DUNN, RANDY EDWIN, lawyer; b. Hutchinson, Kans., Oct. 8, 1954; s. Roy Edwin and Joan Irene (Farney) D.; m. Michelle Renee Sandwith, Dec. 18, 1976 (div. Aug. 1979); 1 child, Brandi Dawn Sandwith; m. Rosalind O'Nita Heiman, Dec. 22, 1990. BA magna cum laude, Wichita State U., 1977; JD, U. Colo., 1983. Bar: Colo. 1983, U.S. Dist. Ct. Colo. 1986. Store and sales mgr. Pop Shoppe, Inc., Wichita, Kans., 1976-77; sales rep. Lifesavers, Inc., 1977-80; asst. mgr. Quik Trip, Inc., 1980; assoc. McIntyre & Varallo, P.C., Greeley, Colo., 1983-85; pvt. practice law Denver, 1985-87; ptnr. Dean & Dunn, P.C., 1987-89; assoc. Lau & Choi, P.C., 1989-90, Baker & Hostetler, Denver, 1991, Hopper & Kanouff, P.C., Denver, 1991-95; pvt. practice law, 1995—. Mem. ABA, Colo. Bar Assn., Denver Bar Assn., Masons. Democrat. General civil litigation, Contracts commercial, General corporate. Office: Clanahan Tanner Downing and Knowlton PC 730 17th St Ste 500 Denver CO 80202-3580

DUNN, WILLIAM BRADLEY, lawyer; b. Newark, Dec. 2, 1939; s. Ernest William and Ruth Harriet (Bradley) D.; m. Judy Ann Shepherd, Aug. 2, 1988; children: John, Peter, Brian, Kelly. AB, Muskingum Coll., 1961; JD, U. Mich., 1964. Bar: Mich. 1964. Mem. Clark Hill PLC (formerly Clark, Klein & Beaumont), Detroit, 1964—. Lectr. in field. Contbr. articles to legal jours. Mem.: ABA (chair sect. real property, probate and trust law 1989—90, mem. ho. of dels. 1990—98, mem. standing com. on professionalism 1993—96, mem. standing com. on ethics and profl. responsibility 1998—2001, spl. adv. standing com. on ethics and profl. responsibility 2001—02), Am. Coll. Real Estate Lawyers (pres. 1983—84), Urban Land Inst., Internat. Assn. Attys. and Exec. Corporate Real Estate. Episcopalian. Contracts commercial, Real property. Home: 6398 Catalpa Ct Troy MI 48098-2231 Office: Clark Hill PLC 500 Woodward Ave Ste 3500 Detroit MI 48226-3435 E-mail: wdunn@clarkhill.com

DUNN, WILLIAM WYLY, corporate lawyer; b. N.Y.C., Mar. 7, 1925; s. Beverly Charles and Helen Ward (Fay) D.; m. Rosemarie Boehme, Sept. 4, 1947; 1 child, Fred Wyly. BA cum laude, Harvard U., 1947, JD cum laude, 1950. Bar: D.C. 1950, U.S. Cir. Ct. D.C. 1958, N.Y. 1982. Atty., advisor USAF, Wiesbaden, Fed. Republic of Germany, 1951-58; mng. dir. Collins Radio GmbH, Frankfurt, 1958-61; dir. contracts Litton Industries GmbH, Hamburg and Bonn, 1962-64; mgr. Paris office LTV, Inc., 1964-68, dir. European affairs, 1969-70; gen. counsel Mobil Oil Francaise, 1970-81; sr. counsel Mobil Oil Corp., N.Y.C., 1981-86. Exec. v.p. Assn. of Ams. Resident Overseas, Paris, 1980-81; co-chmn, corp. counsel subcom. Am. C. of C., Paris, 1981. Served to 1st lt. U.S. Army, 1944-47. Recipient Saltonstall prize Harvard U., Cambridge, Mass., 1947, Sheldon prize Harvard U., Cambridge, 1948. Mem. ABA, N.Y. Bar Assn., D.C. Bar Assn., Farmington County Club (Charlottesville, Va.). Republican. Avocations: golf, dancing, classical music. General corporate, Oil, gas, and mineral, Private international. Home: 116 Shasta Ct Charlottesville VA 22903-4216 E-mail: wwd5t@earthlink.net

DUNNAN, WEAVER WHITE, retired lawyer; b. Paxton, Ill., Sept. 23, 1923; s. J. Wallace and Mabel (White) D.; m. Diana Barrett Baldwin, Feb. 14, 1953; children— Bruce B., Douglas M., Donald S., Winifred B., John M. A.B., Harvard U., 1947, LL.B., 1949. Bar: D.C. 1951, U.S. Supreme Ct. 1954, U.S. Tax Ct. 1957, U.S. Ct. Appeals (D.C. cir.) 1960. Law clk. U.S. Ct. Appeals 2d cir., N.Y.C., 1949-50; law clk. to justice Felix Frankfurter, U.S. Supreme Ct., Washington, 1950-51; assoc., ptnr., sr. counsel firm Covington & Burling, Washington, 1960-94; retired ptnr. 1994—. Bd. govs. St. Albans Sch., Washington, 1974-80; bd. dirs. Beauvoir Sch., Nat. Cathedral, Washington, 1969-74. Served to sgt. U.S. Army, 1943-46; PTO. Decorated 2 Overseas Service bars, Am. Campaign medal, Asiatic Pacific Theater ribbon with 3 bronze battle stars, Phillippine Liberation ribbon with 2 bronze stars. Mem. ABA. Republican. Clubs: Metropolitan (Washington); Chevy Chase. General corporate, Government contracts and claims, Corporate taxation. Home: 5110 Cammack Dr Bethesda MD 20816-2902 Office: Covington & Burling 1201 Pennsylvania Ave NW PO Box 7566 Washington DC 20044-7566

DUNNE, FREDERICK R., JR. b. Kearny, N.J., Mar. 27, 1944; s. Frederick R. and Agnes M. (Lynch) D.; m. Donna M. Polc, Nov. 17, 1973; children: Kelly Anne, Jaime Elizabeth, Frederick R. III. BA, Niagara U., 1966; JD, Seton Hall U., 1970. Bar: N.J. 1972, U.S. Dist. Ct. N.J. 1972, N.Y. 1984, U.S. Dist. Ct. Colo. 1997, U.S. Ct. Appeals (3rd cir.) 1998, U.S. Dist. Ct. (so. and ea. dists.) N.Y. 2000. Tchr. St. Benedict's Prep. Sch., 1966-68, Essex Coll. Bus., 1968-69, East Orange (N.J.) H.S., 1969-73; atty. N.J. Office Pub. Defender, 1973; ptnr. Harrington & Dunne, Kearny, 1973-77; sole practice, 1977-81; ptnr. Dunne & Waller, 1981-86, Dunne & Thompson PC, 1987—. Examining atty. Chgo. Title Ins. Co., 1973—, Chelsea Title & Guaranty Co., 1973—; atty. Kearny Bd. Edn., 1978-95; pub. defender Borough of North Arlington, 1984—, spl. prosecutor ABC violations, 1985—; alpine official USSA Ski Racing, 1994—. V.p. Immaculate Heart of Mary Sch. Bd., Wayne, N.J., 1981-82; bd. trustees Pioneer Boys Am., 1976-78; chmn. St. Benedict's Alumni Fund, 1978-92. Recipient Svc. and Citizenship award, Pioneer Boys Am., 1978, Outstanding Performance Resolution, Kearny Bd. Edn., 1980, Cert. of Appreciation, Supreme Ct. N.J., 1985, 1986, 1989, 1990, 1991, 1992, 1999, 2000, 2001. Mem. ABA, N.J. Bar Assn., West Hudson Bar Assn., Hudson County Bar Assn. Family and matrimonial, General practice, Real property. Home: 81 Hemlock Ter Wayne NJ 07470-4341 Office: 683 Kearny Ave Kearny NJ 07032-3004 Address: 304 Lincoln Ave Avon By The Sea NJ 07717

DUNNE, GERARD FRANCIS, lawyer; b. Huntington, N.Y., Aug. 23, 1947; s. Frank and Adele A. (Malerba) D.; m. Judith Ellen Gordon, Dec. 5, 1976; 1 child, Heather Chelsey. B in Engring., Manhattan Coll., 1969; JD, U. Balt., 1974. Bar: D.C. 1974, N.Y. 1974, U.S. Patent Office, U.S. Dist. Ct. (ea. and so. dists.) N.Y. 1976, U.S. Ct. Appeals (fed. cir.) 1982, U.S. Ct. Appeals (2d and 8th cirs.) 1985, U.S. Supreme Ct. 1987. Examiner patents U.S. Patent Office, Washington, 1969-74; assoc. Law Offices of Albert C. Johnston P.C., N.Y.C., 1974-76, Wyatt, Gerber, Burke & Badie, N.Y.C., 1976-82, ptnr., 1982-94; sole practice law, 1995—. Mem. ABA, Assn. of Bar of City of N.Y., Fed. Bar Council, Am. Intellectual Property Law Assn. Federal civil litigation, Patent, Trademark and copyright. Home: 89-04 63rd Ave Flushing NY 11374-2815 Office: 156 5th Ave Ste 1223 New York NY 10010-7002 E-mail: gfdunne@rcn.com

DUNST, ISABEL PAULA, lawyer; b. N.Y.C., Feb. 21, 1947; d. Philip R. and Mae F. Dunst. BS, U. Wis., 1967; JD, NYU, 1971; MPH, Harvard U., 1979. Bar: N.Y. 1971, D.C. 1973. Staff atty. Office Gen. Counsel HEW, Washington, 1971-75, sr. aggy., 1975-79, assoc. gen. counsel, 1979—. Dep. gen. counsel, 1987-90; ptnr. Hogan & Hartson, Washington, 1990—. Bd. dirs. Women's Legal Def. Fund, 1973—, pres., 1973-74. Mem. ABA, Nat. Health Lawyers Assn., Fed. Bar Assn. (Sr. Exec. Svc. award 1980-87). E-mail: ipdunst@hhlaw.com

DUPLANTIER, ADRIAN GUY, federal judge; b. New Orleans, Mar. 5, 1929; s. F. Robert and Amelie (Rivet) D.; m. Sally Thomas, July 15, 1951; children: Adrian G., David L., Thomas, Jeanne M., Louise M., John C. JD cum laude, Loyola U., New Orleans, 1949; LLD, Loyola U., 1993; LLM, U. Va., 1988. Bar: La. 1950, U.S. Supreme Ct. 1954. Pvt. practice law, New Orleans, 1950-74; judge Civil Dist. Ct. Parish of Orleans, 1974-78, U.S. Dist. Ct., New Orleans, 1978-94, sr. judge, 1994—. Part-time prof. code of civil procedure Loyola U., 1951—, lectr. dental jurisprudence, 1960-67, lectr. English dept., 1948-50, chmn. law sch. vis. com., 1995-97, adj. prof. law, 1952—; prof. summer sch. abroad Tulane Law Sch., Rhodes, Greece, 1992, Cambridge, England, 1993, Loyola Law Sch., Vienna, Austria, 1996; mem. La. State Senate, 1960-74; 1st asst. dist. atty. New Orleans, 1954-56; mem. Jud. Conf. of U.S. Bankruptcy Rules Adv. Com., 1994-96, chmn. 1997—; elected La. State Senate, 1960-74; 5th cir. dist. judge rep. Jud. Conf. U.S., 1993-94, com. bicentennial of constn., 1986-91; chmn. Bill of Rights Bicentennial Conf. Fed. Judges, 1991. Editorial bd.: Loyola Law Rev, 1947-48; editor-in-chief, 1948-49. Del. Democratic Nat. Conv., 1964; pres. Associated Cath. Charities New Orleans, Social Welfare Planning Council Greater New Orleans; mem. adv. bd. St. Mary's Dominican Coll., 1970-71, Ursuline Acad., 1968-73, Mt. Carmel Acad., 1965-69; chmn. pres.'s adv. coun. Jesuit H.S., 1980-81, mem., 1976—; chmn. bd. dirs. Boys Hope, 1980—, nat. bd. dirs., 1982-92, coun., 1992—; active Assn. Retarded Children. Recipient Meritorious award New Orleans Assn. Retarded Children, 1965, Gov.'s Cert. of Merit, 1970, Outstanding Alumnus award Loyola U., 1985, Vol. Activist award Outstanding Vol. Svc., 1986. Mem. ABA (award 1960), La. Bar Assn., New Orleans Bar Assn., Loyola Law Sch. Vis. Com. (chmn. 1993-96), Jud. Conf. of U.S., Loyola Law Sch. Alumni Assn. (St. Ives award 1998), U.S. Adv. Com. (jud. conf. on bankruptcy rules 1993—, chmn. 1996—), Order of Coif, Alpha Sigma Nu. Office: US Dist Ct C-205 US Courthouse 500 Camp St New Orleans LA 70130-3313

DUPLECHIN, D. JAMES, lawyer; b. Rayne, La., Aug. 1, 1967; s. Kermit Joseph and Neva (Boudreaux) D.; m. Deborah Lynn McEachern, Oct. 13, 1990; children: Ryan James, Andrew David. BS, Troy State U., 1990, MPA, 1991; JD, Birmingham U. Sch. Law, 1996. Bar: Ala. 1997, U.S. Dist. Ct. (mid. dist.) Ala. 1997, U.S. Dist. Ct. (so. dist.) Ala. 2001. Case mgr. Norris & Assocs., Birmingham, 1991-95; intern McCallum & Assocs., 1996; from law clk. to assoc. Powell, Powell & Powell, Crestview, Fla., 1996—. Adv. coun. USAF Tactical Air Warfare Ctr., Eglin AFB, Fla., 1988-91, 8th Tactical Fighter Wing, Kunsan Air Base, South Korea, 1987-88. Mem. ABA, Ala. State Bar Assn., ATLA, Acad. Fla. Trial Lawyers. Roman Catholic. State civil litigation, Personal injury, Workers' compensation. Office: Powell Powell & Powell 422 N Main St Crestview FL 32536-3540

DUPONT, RALPH PAUL, lawyer, educator; b. Fall River, Mass., May 21, 1929; s. Michael William and Gertrude (Murphy) D.; children: Ellen O'Neill, Antonia Chafee, William Albert. AB cum laude with highest honors in Am. Civilization, Brown U., 1951; JD cum laude, Harvard U., 1956. Bar: Conn. 1956, U.S. Supreme Ct. 1967; diplomate Nat. Bd. Trial Advocacy; cert. civil trial specialist, Conn. Assoc. Davies, Hardy & Schenck, N.Y.C., 1956-57; ptnr. Copp & Dupont, New London, Conn., 1957-60; mem. Suisman, Shapiro & Wool, 1961-63; ptnr. Dupont & Dupont (and successor firms), 1963-91; of counsel Durant, Nichols, Houston, Mitchell & Sheahan, Bridgeport, Conn., 1992-97; ptnr. Dupont and Radlauer LLP, New London, 1997—. Instr. Am. history and bus. law Mitchell Coll., New London, 1955, 57-58, trustee, 1991-94; instr. bus. law U. New Haven, 1998; vis. prof. Northeastern U. Sch. Law, 1977-78; vis. prof. law Bridgeport Law Sch. Quinnipiac Coll., 1991-92, We. New Eng. Coll. Law, 1992-94; lectr.-on-law U. Conn. Sch. Law, 1980-86; mem. exec. bd., adj. prof. Quinnipiac Coll. Sch. Law, Hamden, Conn., 1994-96; trustee Anne S.K. Brown Mil. Collection, Brown U., 1988-94, presiding trustee, 1990-92; mem. Conn. Legal Svcs. Adv. Coun., 1980-82; pres. Conn. Acad. Cert. Trial Lawyers, 1998-2000. Author: Litigation in 1 Attorney's Desk Library, 1994, Dupont On Connecticut Civil Practice, 2001. Mem. bd. edn. New London, Conn., 1959-61; Dem. candidate for Conn. Senate, 1960; trustee U.S. Atlantic Tuna Tournament, 1984-85, pres. 1988-90. Lt. (j.g.) USNR, 1951-53. Named Outstanding Young Man of Yr. Conn. Jr. C. of C., 1960; recipient Disting. Svc. award Greater New London Jr. C. of C., 1960. Fellow Am. Coll. Trust and Estate Counsel; mem. ABA, Nat. Bd. Trial Advocacy, Conn. Bar Assn., Conn. Bar Found. (bd. dirs. 1975-79), Internat. Acad. Trust and Estate Law, Harvard U. Law Sch. Assn., Harvard Club, Delta Sigma Rho, Kappa Sigma. Roman Catholic. Home: PO Box 710 New London CT 06320-0710 Office: Dupont and Radlauer LLP PO Box 710 165 State St New London CT 06320-6397 E-mail: Radlaw@Snet.net

DUPONT, WESLEY DAVID, lawyer; b. Putnam, Conn., Nov. 1, 1968; s. Thomas Edward Sr. and Patricia Fay Dupont. BA magna cum laude, Brown U., 1992; JD with honors, U. Conn., 1995. Bar: Conn. 1995, N.Y. 1995, U.S. Dist. Ct. Conn. 1995. Assoc. Kelley Drye & Warren LLP, Stamford, Conn., 1995—. Sec. Fano Securities LLC, Greenwich, Conn., 1997—, Fano Holdings Corp., 1998—. Contbr. articles to profl. jours. Atty., Stamford Symphony, 1998—. Mem. ABA, Conn. Bar Assn., N.Y. State Bar Assn., The Corp. Bar, Phi Delta Phi. Avocations: fly-fishing, running, golf. General corporate, Mergers and acquisitions, Securities. Office: Kelley Drye & Warren LLP 281 Tresser Blvd Stamford CT 06901-3229

DUPRIEST, DOUGLAS MILLHOLLEN, lawyer; b. Ft. Riley, Kans., Dec. 28, 1951; s. Robert White and Barbara Nadine (Millhollen) DuP. AB in Philosophy with high honors, Oberlin Coll., 1974; JD, U. Oreg., 1977. Bar: Oreg. 1977, U.S. Dist. Ct. Oreg. 1977, U.S. Ct. Appeals (9th cir.) 1977. Assoc. Coons & Anderson and predecessors, Eugene, Oreg., 1977-81, Hutchinson, Harrell et al, 1981; ptnr. Hutchinson, Cox, Coons & DuPriest and predecessors, 1982—. Adj. prof. sch. law U. Oreg., 1986; mem. task forces Wetlands Mgmt., 1988-89, 92-93. Author: (with others) Land Use, 1982, 2000, Administrative Law, 1985; contbg. editor Real Estate & Land Use Digest, 1983-86; articles editor, mng. bd. mem. U. Oreg. Law Rev., 1976-77. Bd. dirs. Home Health Agy., Eugene, 1977-79, pres., 1978-79; bd. dirs. Oreg. Environ. Coun., Portland, 1979-84, pres., 1980-81; mem. Lane Econ. Com., 1989-91; chair voters pamphlet com. Eugene City Club, 1993. Recipient Disting. Svc. award Oreg. Environ. Coun., 1988. Mem. Oreg. Bar Assn. (exec. com. real estate and land use sect. 1978-81). General practice, Land use and zoning (including planning), Real property. Home: 225 Dartmoor Dr Eugene OR 97401-6620 Office: Hutchinson Cox Coons & DuPriest 777 High St Ste 200 Eugene OR 97401-2750

DUPRIEST, JOANNA G. lawyer; b. Wilkes-Barre, Pa., June 5, 1972; d. Anthony and Joan Garbush; m. Read T. DuPriest, Aug. 9, 1997. AB, Bryn Mawr Coll., 1994; JD, Temple U., 1997. Bar: N.J., Pa., U.S. Dist. Ct. (ea. dist.) Pa., U.S. Ct. Appeals (3d cir.). Assoc. Fox, Rothschild, O'Brien & Frankel, LLP, Phila., 1997—. Mem. ABA, Pa. Bar Assn., N.J. Bar Assn., Phila. Bar Assn. Labor. Office: Fox Rothschild O'Brien & Frankel LLP 10th Fl 2000 Market St Philadelphia PA 19103

DUQUETTE, DONALD NORMAN, law educator; b. Manistique, Mich., Apr. 3, 1947; s. Donald Francis and Martha Adeline (Rice) D.; m. Kathy Jo Loudenbeck, June 17, 1967; 1 child, Gail Jean. BA, Mich. State U., 1969; JD, U. Mich., 1974. Bar: Mich. 1975. Children's caseworker Mich. Dept. Social Svcs., Muskegon, 1969-72; asst. prof. pediatrics and human devel. Mich. State U. Coll. Human Medicine, East Lansing, 1975-76; clin. prof., dir. child advocacy law clinic U. Mich., Ann Arbor, 1976—, co-dir. interdisciplinary project on child abuse and neglect, 1979-89, dir. permanency planning legal svcs., 1984—, dir. interdisciplinary grad. edn. in child abuse-neglect, 1986-92, dir. Kellogg child welfare law program, 1995-98. Bd. visitors U. Ariz. Sch. of Law, 1995-99; legal cons. U.S. Children's Bur., Pres. Clinton's Initiative on Adoption and Foster Care, 1997-98; bd. dirs. Nat. Assn. Counsel for Children, 1999—. Author: (non-fiction) Advocating for the Child, 1990, Michigan Child Welfare Law, 1990, Michigan Child Welfare Law, rev. edit., 2000; editor (mem. editl. bd.): (jour.) Child Abuse and Neglect Internat. Jour., 1985—90; contbr.: articles to profl. jours. Commr. Washtenaw County Bd. Commrs., 1981-88; bd. dirs. Children's Trust Fund for Prevention of Child Abuse, 1983-85; mem. Permanency Planning Com. Mich. Supreme Ct., 1982-85, Probate Ct. Task Force, 1986-87, Govs. Task Force on Children's Justice, 1992—. Named Citizen of Yr. Huron Valley NASW, Ann Arbor, 1985; recipient Rsch. in Advocacy award Nat. Ct. Apptd. Spl. Advocate Assn., Seattle, 1985, Outstanding Legal Advocacy award Nat. Assn. of Counsel for Children, 1996, Hicks Child Welfare Leadership award Mich. Fedn. Children's Agys., 1998. Mem. Am. Profl. Soc. on Abuse of Children, Mich. State Bar (co-chair Children's Task Force 1993-95). Democrat. Unitarian. Avocations: piano, sailing. Home: 1510 Linwood Ave Ann Arbor MI 48103-3659 Office: U Mich Sch Law Child Advocacy Law Clinic 625 S State St Ann Arbor MI 48109-1215 E-mail: duquette@umich.edu

DURANT, MARC, lawyer; b. N.Y.C., Jan. 17, 1947; s. Sidney Irwin and Estelle (Haas) D.; m. Karen Rose Baker, June 9, 1968 (div. 1975); children: Lauren, Elyssa; m. Rita Mary Tatar, Dec. 31, 1979; children: David, Alexander. BS, Cornell U., 1968; JD, Harvard U., 1968-71. Bar: Pa. 1972, U.S. Dist. Ct. (ea. dist.) Pa. 1972, U.S. Supreme Ct. 1980, U.S. Ct. Appeals (3d cir.) 1981, N.Y. 1991. Law clk. U.S. Dist. Ct., Wilmington, Del., 1971-72; assoc. Schnader, Harrison, Segal & Lewis, Phila., 1972-75; asst. U.S. Atty. U.S. Dept. Justice, 1975-77; dep. chief criminal divsn.v. U.S. Atty.'s Office, 1977-81; ptnr. Durant and Durant, 1981—. Mem. ABA, FBA, Nat. Assn. Criminal Def. Lawyers, Pa. Bar Assn., Phila. Bar Assn. Federal civil litigation, Criminal. Office: Durant & Durant 325 Chestnut St Philadelphia PA 19106-2614 E-mail: durantlaw@aol.com

DURBIN, RICHARD LOUIS, JR. lawyer; b. Gary, Ind., Dec. 23, 1955; s. Richard Louis and Carolyn Martha (Bohrer) D.; m. Diana Cabaza Durbin, June 2, 1979; children: Louis Eloy, Laura Elena. Student, Rutgers U., 1973-75; BA, U. Chgo., 1977; JD, U. Tex., 1980. Bar: Tex. 1980. Law clk. to presiding judge U.S. Dist. Ct. (we. dist.) Tex., San Antonio, 1980-82; assoc. Susman, Godfrey & McGowan, Houston, 1982-83; asst. U.S. atty. U.S. Atty.'s Office (we. dist.), San Antonio, 1983—, chief criminal sect., 1988-90, 98—, chief narcotics sect., 1990-92, 97-98, chief appellate sect., 1992-98; adj. prof. law St. Mary's U. Sch. of Law, 1995—. Instr. U.S. Atty. Gen. Adv. Inst., Washington, 1987—; Dept. of Justice Nat. Advocacy Ctr., 1998—; speaker San Antonio Bar Assn. Criminal Law Inst. 1999— Editor Tex. U. Law Rev., 1979-80. Interviewer U. Chgo. Alumni Schs. Com., San Antonio, 1984—. Recipient Dir.'s award Tex. Dept. Pub. Safety, Austin, 1985. Mem. Tex. State Bar, Coll. State Bar Tex., Order of Coif, Phi Beta Kappa. Office: US Attys Office 601 NW Loop 410 Ste 600 San Antonio TX 78216-5512 E-mail: richard.durbin@usdoj.gov

DURCHSLAG, STEPHEN P. lawyer; b. Chgo., May 20, 1940; s. Milton Lewis and Elizabeth (Potovsky) D.; m. Ruth Florence Mayer, Nov. 21, 1976; children: Rachel Beth, Danielle Leah. BS, U. Wis., 1963; LLB, Harvard U., 1966. Bar: Ill. 1966. Assoc. Sidley & Austin, Chgo., 1966-72, ptnr., 1972-89, Winston & Strawn, Chgo., 1989—. Contbr. articles to numerous publs. Bd. dirs., pres. Anshe Emet, Chgo., 1983—; bd. trustee Nathan Cummings Found., 1996—. Mem. ABA (AAF legal com.), Promotion Mktg. Assn. (bd. dirs.), Am. Standard Club, East Bank Club. Jewish. Avocations: skiing, running, tennis, rare books. Administrative and regulatory, General corporate, Entertainment. Office: Winston & Strawn 35 W Wacker Dr Ste 3600 Chicago IL 60601-1695 E-mail: sdurchsl@winston.com

DURHAM, CHRISTINE MEADERS, state supreme court justice; b. L.A., Aug. 3, 1945; d. William Anderson and Louise (Christensen) Meaders; m. George Homer Durham II, Dec. 29, 1966; children: Jennifer, Meghan, Troy, Melinda, Isaac. A.B., Wellesley Coll., 1967; J.D., Duke U., 1971. Bar: N.C. 1971, Utah 1974. Sole practice law, Durham, N.C., 1971-73; instr. legal medicine Duke U., 1971-73; adj. prof. law Brigham Young U., Provo, Utah, 1973-78; ptnr. Johnson, Durham & Moxley, Salt Lake City, 1974-78; judge Utah Dist. Ct., 1978-82; assoc. justice Utah Supreme Ct., 1982—. Pres. Women Judges Fund for Justice, 1987-88. Fellow Am. Bar Found.; mem. ABA (edn. com. appellate judges' conf.), Nat. Assn. Women Judges (pres. 1986-87), Utah Bar Assn., Am. Law Inst. (coun. mem.), Nat. Ctr. State Courts (bd. dirs.), Am. Inns of Ct. Found. (trustee). Office: Utah Supreme Ct PO Box 140210 Salt Lake City UT 84114-0210*

DURHAM, DREW TAYLOR, lawyer; b. Big Spring, Tex., July 3, 1949; s. Worth Barton and Mary Jo (Nance) D.; m. Patricia Enright, May 29, 1976; children— Alexis, Benjamin. B.A., U. Tex., 1971; J.D., St. Mary's U., San Antonio, 1975. Bar: Tex. 1976. Briefing atty. Fed. Dist. Judge, Lubbock, Tex., 1976-77; asst. county atty. Sterling County (Tex.), 1977-78, county atty., 1978— ; owner Durham & Durham, Sterling City, 1977— . Mem. ABA, Tex. Bar Assn., Phi Alpha Delta. Democrat. Methodist. Oil, gas, and mineral, Environmental, Real property. Home: PO Box 900 Sterling City TX 76951-0900 Office: Durham & Durham PO Box 7 Sterling City TX 76951-0007

DURHAM, JAMES W. lawyer; b. Nov. 18, 1937; m. Kathleen B. Wollman; children: Linda, Cynthia, Andrea. BSBA, Pa. State U., 1959; MBA in Bus. Adminstrn., U. Portland, 1962; JD, Dickinson Coll., 1965. Bar: Oreg. 1965, U.S. Dist. Ct. Oreg., U.S. Ct. Appeals (9th cir.), U.S. Supreme Ct. Assoc. Davies, Biggs, Strayer, Stoel & Boley, Portland, Oreg., 1965—68; ptnr. Durham, Smith, Todd & Ball, 1968—70; atty. Oreg. Dept. Justice, Salem, 1970—78; sr. v.p., gen. counsel, sec. Portland Gen. Electric Co., 1978—87; sr. v.p., gen. counsel Phila. Electric Co. (now Exelon Corp.), 1988—. Chmn. bd. dir. Oreg. Pub. Broadcasting Found., 1984—88; chmn. Oreg. Pub. Defender Com., 1984—85. Chmn., bd. dir. Columbia-Willamette YMCA; bd. dir., trustee Franklin Inst., 1991—; bd. dir. Del. Valley Citizens Crime Commn.; mem. legal adv. com. Rep. Com. Oreg., 1984—86. Mem.: ABA, Oreg. State Bar (bd. govs. 1983—86, pres. 1985—86), Oreg. Law Found. (bd. dir. 1986—88, pres. 1988), Pa. Bar Assn., Pa. Electric Assn. (chmn. 1993—94), Phila. Bar Found. (trustee 1991—), Phila. Bar Assn., Del. Valley Corp. Counsel Assn. (bd. dir. 1989—), Rotary, Tau Kappa Epsilon (fraternity alumnus of yr. 1987). General practice. Office: Mediation & Arbitration Svcs 121 Woodgate Lane Paoli PA 19301

DURHAM, J(OSEPH) PORTER, JR. lawyer, educator; b. Nashville, May 11, 1961; AB in Polit. Sci. and History cum laude, Duke U., 1982, JD, 1985. Bar: Tenn. 1985, Md. 1988. Ptnr. Miller & Martin, Chattanooga, 1990-96, Baker, Donelson, Bearman & Caldwell, Chattanooga, 1997—, chmn. corp. dept., 1998—. Adj. prof. dept. acctg. and fin. U. Tenn., Chattanooga, 1992-98; participant Russian tax code adv. group, 1999. Editor Duke Law Mag., 1984-85; contbr. articles to legal publs. Mem. Balt. Citizens Planning and Housing Assn., 1988-90; career edn. spkr. Explorer Scout program Boy Scouts Am., 1985, 88, 90-92; mem., v.p. bd. dirs., chmn. fin. com. Waxter Ctr. Found., 1989-91; mem., sec. bd. dirs. Assn. for Visual Artists, 1993-96; trustee Good Shepherd Sch., 1992-93; chmn. spl. mgmt. com. Nashville Rehab. Hosp., 1995; trail maintenance vol. U.S. Pk. Svc., 1993-95; mem. adv. com. Chattanooga State Tech. C.C.; bd. dirs. Sr. Neighbors, Inc., 2001—. Recipient Outstanding Svc. award Waxter Ctr. Found., 1991. Mem. ABA, Tenn. Bar Assn., Md. Bar Assn., Duke U. Law Sch. Alumni Assn. (bd. dirs. 1994-97), Duke U. Gen. Alumni Assn. (bd. dirs. 1986-92, exec. com. 1989-92). General corporate, Mergers and acquisitions, Securities. Home: 600 W Brow Rd Lookout Mountain TN 37350-1118 Office: Baker Donelson Bearman & Caldwell 1800 Republic Ctr 633 Chestnut St Chattanooga TN 37450-4000

DURHAM, ROBERT DONALD, JR. state supreme court justice; b. Lynwood, Calif., May 10, 1947; s. Robert Donald Durham and Rosemary Constance (Brennan) McKelvey; m. Linda Jo Rollins, Aug. 29, 1970; children: Melissa Brennan, Amy Elizabeth. BA, Whittier Coll., 1969; JD, U. Santa Clara, 1972; LLM in the Judicial Process, U. Va., 1998. Bar: Oreg. 1972, Calif. 1973, U.S. Dist. Ct. Oreg. 1974, U.S. Ct. Appeals (9th cir.) 1980, U.S. Supreme Ct. 1987. Law clk. Oreg. Supreme Ct., Salem, 1972-74; ptnr. Bennett & Durham, Portland, Oreg., 1974-91; assoc. judge Oreg. Ct. Appeals, Salem, 1991-94; state supreme ct. assoc. justice Oreg. Supreme Ct., 1994—. Mem. adv. com. to Joint Interim Judiciary Com., 1984-86; chair Oreg. Commn. on Adminstrv. Hearings, 1988-89; faculty Nat. Jud. Coll., Reno, Nev., 1992; mem. Case Disposition Benchmarks Com., 1992-93, Coun. on Ct. Procedures, 1992-93, 95—; mem. Oreg. Rules of Appellate Procedure Com., 1998—; bd. dirs. Oreg. Law Inst., 2001—. Mem. ACLU Lawyer's Com., Eugene and Portland, Oreg., 1978-91. Recipient award for civil rights litigation ACLU of Oreg., 1988, Ed Elliott Human Rights award Oreg. Edn. Assn., Portland, 1990. Mem. Am. Acad. Appellate Lawyers (ninth cir. screening com. 1991—, rules com. 1994, co-chair appellate cts. liaison com. 1994), Oreg. Appellate Judges Assn. (pres. 1996-97), Oreg. State Bar (chair labor law sect. 1983-84, adminstrv. law com. govt. law sect. 1986), Willamette Valley Inns of Ct. (master of bench, team leader 1994—). Office: Oreg Supreme Ct 1163 State St Salem OR 97310-1331

DURIO, WILLIAM HENRY, lawyer; b. Crowley, La., May 15, 1947; s. Lennard Edwin and Helen Hazel (Miller) D.; m. Rita Jane Putch, June 6, 1971; children: Matthew, Caroline. BS, U. La., Lafayette, 1970; JD, La. State U., 1975. Pvt. practice, Lafayette, La., 1976-78, 83-89; ptnr. Hughes Durio & Grant, 1978-83; gen. counsel Global Industries Ltd., Maurice, La., 1990-91; pvt. practice. Lafayette, 1991—. Adj. prof. mineral law U. La., Lafayette, 1983-84. With U.S. Army, 1970-72. Mem. La. Bar Assn., Lafayette Town House Club, Order of Troubadours. Avocations: running, fishing, scuba diving, hunting, traveling. Oil, gas, and mineral, Natural resources, Probate. Home: 608 Claymore Dr Lafayette LA 70503-4020

DURN, RAYMOND JOSEPH, lawyer; b. Cleve., Nov. 28, 1925; s. Joseph Frank and Mary (Spenko) D.; m. Emmy Reboly, June 5, 1954; children: David, Sarah, Tamara. B.A., Harvard U., 1950, LL.B., 1953. Bar: Ohio 1953, U.S. Dist. Ct. Ohio 1954, U.S. Ct. Appeals 6th cir. 1974. Assoc. Jones, Day, Reavis & Pogue, Cleve., 1953-60, ptnr., 1960-89; acting gen. counsel Univ. Hosps., 1989-91, sr. counsel, 1991-93. Trustee Cleve. Neighborhood Health Svcs., Inc., 1969-93, pres., 1987-89; trustee Chester Twp., Ohio, 1972-75; mem. Chester Twp. Bd. Zoning Appeals, 1969-72, Chester Twp. Zoning Commn., 1985-91. Served with USAAF, 1944-46. Mem. Ohio Bar Assn., Cleve. Bar Assn. Democrat. Unitarian. Health, Land use and zoning (including planning), Real property. Home: 13088 W Geauga Trl Chesterland OH 44026-2830 E-mail: raydurn@earthlink.net

DURNYA, LOUIS RICHARD, lawyer; b. Plainfield, N.J., July 24, 1950; s. Louis and Mary Ann (Pellegrino) D.; m. Elizabeth Trabue Shelton, July 16, 1977; children: Cameron, Sarah. BBA, Seton Hall U., 1972; JD, U. Richmond, 1975; postgrad. Command and Gen. Staff Coll., 1990. Bar: N.J. 1975, U.S. Dist. Ct. N.J. 1975, U.S. Supreme Ct. 1979, U.S. Ct. Claims 1981, Ct. Appeals (Fed. cir.) 84. Assoc. Orlando & McGimpsey, Esquires, New Brunswick, N.J., 1975-76; atty. Office of Chief Counsel Kennedy Space Ctr., Fla., 1979-82; assoc. chief counsel Marshall Space Flight Ctr., Ala., 1982-96, asst. chief counsel, 1996—. Lt. col. JAGC, USAR, 1994—. Recipient Superior Achievement award NASA, 1982, Merit award, 1989, Exceptional svc. medal, 1996, Silver Snoopy award U.S. Astronaut Corps., 1988; named an Outstanding Young Man of Am., Jaycees, 1977. Mem. Fed. Bar Assn. (past pres. North Ala. chpt.), Ky. Col. Assn., Delta Theta Phi (scholarship key 1973-74). Government contracts and claims. Home: 1005 Appalachee Dr SE Huntsville AL 35801-2202 Office: Office of Chief Counsel Marshall Space Flight Ctr Huntsville AL 35812

DU ROCHER, JAMES HOWARD, lawyer; b. Racine, Wis., Aug. 4, 1945; s. Howard James and Frances Ann (Rasmussen) Du R.; m. Rosalyn Ann, Sept. 2, 1972; children: Jessica Lynn, James Howard, Emily Rosalyn. Student, U.S. Mil. Acad., 1963-65, Ripon Coll., 1965-66; JD, U. Wis., 1969. Bar: Wis. Assoc. Stewart, Peyton, Crawford & Josten, Racine, 1969-78; pres. Du Rocher, Murphy, Murphy & Schroeder, S.C., Racine, 1978-96, Du Rocher Law Offices, S.C., 1996—. Bd. dirs., Careers Industries, Inc., pres., 1988-89. Bd. dirs. Racine Area United Way, 1973-79, v.p., 1977-79; chmn. Park Trails Dist. Boy Scouts Am., 1979-82; bd. dirs. Careers for Retarded Adults, Inc., 1982, pres., 1983, 90; bd. dirs. A-Center of Racine, Inc., 1978-85, pres., 1985; bd. dirs. Careers Industries Support Found., Inc., 1993-2000; deacon Atonement Luth. Ch., Racine, 1978-81; mem. adv. bd. Children's Svc. Soc. Wis. Capt. JAGC, U.S. Army, 1969-73. Decorated Bronze Star. Mem. State Bar Wis., Mason, Rotary (pres. Racine-West club 1998-99). General corporate, Probate, Real property. Home: 5531 Whirlaway Ln Racine WI 53402-1865 Office: 827 Main St PO Box 1406 Racine WI 53401-1406 E-mail: durlaw@execpc.com

DURONI, CHARLES EUGENE, retired lawyer, food products executive; b. McCune, Kans., Apr. 9, 1933; s. Charley S. and Dorothy M. D.; m. Charlene D. White, Feb. 18, 1978; children: Renee, Ashley, Michele, Lance. B.S., U. Kans., 1955; LL.B., U. Wis., 1962. Bar: Wis. 1962, Pa. 1979, U.S. Supreme Ct. 1979, U.S. Dist. Ct. (mid. dist.) Pa. 1980, U.S. Ct. Appeals (3d cir.) 1982. Staff atty. FTC, 1962-64; staff counsel Rockwell Internat. Co., Pitts., 1964-68; sr. atty. H.J. Heinz Co., 1968-77; sr. assoc. counsel, asst. gen. counsel Hershey (Pa.) Foods Corp., 1977-79, v.p., gen. counsel, 1979-93; ret., 1993. Bd. dirs. U.S. Trademark Assn., 1972-76; trustee Food & Drug Law Inst. Served with USAF, 1955-59. Mem. ABA (com. corp. law depts., com. corp. counsel), Wis. Bar Assn., Pa. Bar Assn., Lancaster County Bar Assn., Am. Law Inst., Atlantic Legal Found., The Bus. Roundtable (lawyers steering com.), Cen. Pa. Corp. Lawyers Group, Grocery Mfrs. Am. (legal com.), Sigma Chi, Phi Delta Phi, Met. Club (N.Y.C.). General corporate, General practice. Home: 928 Forest Rd Lancaster PA 17601-2203

DURRANT, MATTHEW B. state judge; JD, Harvard U., 1984. Adj. prof. Brigham Young U., Salt Lake City; law clerk U.S. Supreme Ct. Appeals (10th cir.); shareholder Parr, Waddoups, Brown & Gee; judge Third Dist. Ct., 1997-2000; justice Utah Supreme Ct., 2000—. Office: Utah Supreme Ct PO Box 140210 Salt Lake City UT 84114-0210*

DURRETT, JAMES FRAZER, JR. retired lawyer; b. Atlanta, Mar. 23, 1931; s. James Frazer and Cora Frazer (Morton) D.; m. Lucretia McPherson, June 9, 1956; children: James Frazer III, William McPherson, Lucretia Heston Miller, Thomas Ratcliffe. AB, Emory U., 1952; postgrad., Princeton U., 1952-53; LLB cum laude, Harvard U., 1956. Bar: Ga. 1955. Ptnr.

Alston & Bird (and predecessor firm), Atlanta, 1956-97, retired, 1997. Adj. prof. Emory U. Law Sch., 1961-77. Trustee emeritus Student Aid Found., The Howard Sch. Mem. Am. Law Inst. (life, adv. estate and gift tax project, restatement, second. property, Fed. Income Tax project), Capital City Club, Harvard Club (Atlanta). Presbyterian. General corporate, Estate planning, Taxation, general. Home: 3483 Ridgewood Rd NW Atlanta GA 30327-2417 Office: Alston & Bird 1 Atlantic Ctr Atlanta GA 30309-3400

DURST, ROBERT JOSEPH, II, lawyer; b. Pitts., Jan. 23, 1943; s. Robert J. and Catherine (Thomas) D.; m. Sandra A. Cattani; children: Thomas Sandberg, Eric Francis. BA, Gettysburg Coll., 1964; JD, Villanova U., 1967. Bar: Pa. 1967, N.J. 1968, U.S. Dist. Ct. (we. dist.) Pa. 1967, U.S. Dist. Ct. (N.J.) 1968, U.S. Supreme Ct. 1973. Corp. staff atty. Alcoa, Pitts., 1967; assoc. Herr & Fisher, Flemington, N.J., 1967-76; ptnr. Bernhard, Durst & Dilts, 1976-89, Stark & Stark, Princeton, N.J., 1989—. Board cert. matrimonial atty. N.J. Supreme Ct., 1982— ; lectr., author on divorce and family law. With USMC, 1960-64. Fellow Am. Acad. Matrimonial Lawyers (pres. N.J. chpt. 1998-99); mem. ABA, Am. Trial Lawyers Assn., N.J. Bar Assn. (mem. exec. com. family law sect.), Hunterdon County Bar Assn., Mercer County Bar Assns., Am. Coll. Family Trial Lawyers (diplomate). Family and matrimonial. Home: 28 Marvin Ct Lawrenceville NJ 08648-2112 Office: Stark & Stark PO Box 5315 Princeton NJ 08543-5315

DUTILE, FERNAND NEVILLE, law educator; b. Lewiston, Maine, Feb. 15, 1940; s. Wilfred Joseph and Lauretta Blanche (Cote) D.; m. Brigid Dooley, Apr. 4, 1964; children: Daniel, Patricia. AB, Assumption Coll., 1962; JD, U. Notre Dame, 1965. Bar: Maine 1965. Atty. U.S. Dept. Justice, Washington, 1965-66; prof. law Cath. U. Am., 1966-71, U. Notre Dame Law Sch., Ind., 1971—. Bd. dirs. Ind. Lawyers Commn., Indpls., 1975-85, Legal Svcs. No. Ind., South Bend, 1975-83; dir. South Bend Work Release Ctr., 1973-75, Ind. Criminal Law Study Commn., 1991-99. Editor: Legal Education and Lawyer Competency, 1981; author: Sex, Schools and the Law, 1986; co-editor: Early Childhood Intervention and Juvenile Delinquency, 1982, The Prediction of Criminal Violence, 1987; co-author: State and Campus, 1984. Democrat. Roman Catholic.

DUTKO, MICHAEL EDWARD, lawyer; b. Memphis, Jan. 18, 1954; s. Edward James and Norma Dean (Sparks) D.; m. Bettie Ballowe, Mar. 14, 1981; children: Michael, Christina, Ashley. BA, Biscayne Coll., 1978; JD, Nova U., 1984. Police officer, detective Ft. Lauderdale (Fla.) Police Dept., 1976-81; pros., asst. state atty. Broward State Atty.'s Office, Ft. Lauderdale, 1984-86; assoc. Kay & Bogenschutz, P.A., 1986-90; ptnr. Kay, Bogenschutz & Dutko, 1990-92, Bogenschutz & Dutko, P.A., Ft. Lauderdale, 1992—. Mem. Broward Assn. Criminal Def. Lawyers. Democrat. Roman Catholic. Avocations: golf, boxing, motorcycles. Criminal. Office: Bogenschutz & Dutko PA 600 S Andrews Ave Ste 500 Fort Lauderdale FL 33301-2851

D'UTRA VAZ, MARCO ANTONIO, lawyer; b. Sao Paulo, Mar. 3, 1941; s. Eduardo and Olga P. d'U.; m. Hilda Haydu, Nov. 28, 1987. B, U. Sao Paulo, 1964; postgrad., Columbia U., 1970. Bar: Brazil 1965. Trainee Pinheiro Neto Adviogadis, Sao Paulo, 1963-66; assoc. Moura Teiceira Adviogadis, 1967-77; ptnr. Campos Salles, Portugal e Vaz Advogades, 1977-88, Vaz e Rolim Advogados, Sao Paulo, 1991—. Mem. Am. C. of C., Swedish=Brazilian C. of C., Deutsch-Brazilian C. of C., Brazil-Israel C. of C. Avocations: reading, travel, classical music. General corporate, Private international, Corporate taxation. Office: Vaz e Rolim Advagados Rua Funchal 573 9th Fl Sao Paulo 04551060 Brazil Fax: 55-11 3845-9228. E-mail: vradvagados@vazrolim.com.br

DUTTERER, DENNIS ALTON, lawyer; b. Hanover, Pa., July 12, 1944; s. Alton J. and Garma S. (Barnhart) D.; m. Judith Barnett, Nov. 11, 1972; children: Andrew, Emily. BS, U. Md., 1967; JD, Am. U., 1970; LLM, George Washington U., 1971. Bar: D.C. 1970, N.Y. 1984, U.S. Ct. Claims 1974, U.S. Ct. Appeals (D.C. cir.) 1974, U.S. Ct. Appeals (7th cir.) 1982, U.S. Ct. Appeals (9th cir.) 1981, U.S. Ct. Appeals (10th cir.) 1979, U.S. Supreme Ct. 1973. Trial atty. lands and natural resources divsn. Dept. Justice, Washington, 1972-77, asst. U.S. atty., 1977-81; dep. chief civil divsn. U.S. Attys. Office, 1979-81; gen. counsel Commodity Futures Trading Commn., 1981-83; ptnr. Wiley & Rein, 1983-85; v.p., gen. counsel Bd. Trade Clearing Corp., Chgo., 1985-87; from sr. v.p., gen. counsel to exec. v.p., gen. counsel Bd. of Trade Clearing Corp., 1987-98, pres., CEO, 1998—. Interim pres., CEO Chgo. Bd. Trade, 2000-2001. Mem. ABA, D.C. Bar Assn., N.Y. Bar Assn., Ill. Bar Assn., Chgo. Bar Assn. Home: 21 Woodley Rd Winnetka IL 60093-3738 Office: 141 W Jackson Blvd Chicago IL 60604-2992 E-mail: dennis.dutterer@botcc.com

DUTTON, CLARENCE BENJAMIN, lawyer, director; b. Pitts., May 31, 1917; s. Clarence Benjamin and Lillian (King) D.; m. Marian Jane Stevens, June 21, 1941; children: Victoria Lynn Dutton Sheehan, Barbara King Dutton Morgan. BS with distinction, Ind. U., 1938, JD with high distinction, 1940, LLD, 1970. Bar: Ind. 1940. Instr. bus. law Ind. U. Sch. Bus., 1940-41; atty. E.I. duPont de Nemours & Co., Inc., Wilmington, Del., 1941-43; asst. prof. law Ind. U. Sch. Law, 1946-47; pvt. practice, Indpls., 1947—. Bd. dirs. Sarkes Tarzian, Inc.; mem. Ind. Jud. Study Commn., 1965-74; regional adv. group Ind. U. Sch. Medicine, 1966-75; mem., sec. Ind. Civil Code Study Commn., 1967-73; mem. Ind. Commn. on Uniform State Laws, 1970—, chmn., 1980-91, life mem., 1991. Author: (bus. law sect.) Chemical Business Handbook, 1954; contbr. articles to profl. jours. Bd. dirs. Found. Ind. U. Sch. Bus., Found. Econ. and Bus. Studies; mem. bd. visitors Ind. U. Sch. Law, 1971—, chmn., 1974-75; bd. dirs. Soc. for Advanced Study, Ind. U., 1984—, pres., 1985-87; mem. Acad. Alumni Fellows, Ind. U. Sch. Law, 1988. Comdr. USNR, 1943-45. Recipient Ind. Bar Found. 50-Yr. award, 1992, Ind. U. Disting. Alumni Svc. award, 1995. Mem. ABA (ho. of dels. 1960-62, state del. 1967-72, bd. govs. 1971-74, chmn. gen. practice sect. 1971-72), Ind. State Bar Assn. (bd. mgrs. 1957-63, pres. 1961-62), Indpls. Bar Assn. (v.p. 1957), Ind. Soc. Chgo., Lawyers Club (pres. 1959-60), Indpls. Country Club (pres. 1955), Columbia Club, Woodstock Club, Wilderness Country Club (Naples, Fla., dir. 1991-94). Republican. Presbyterian. Construction, General corporate, Probate. Home: 1402 W 52d St Indianapolis IN 46228-2317

DUTTON, DIANA CHERYL, lawyer; b. Sherman, Tex., June 27, 1944; d. Roy G. and Monett (Smith) D.; m. Anthony R. Grindl, July 8, 1974; children: Christopher, Bellamy. BS, Georgetown U., 1967; JD, U. Tex., 1971. Bar: Tex. 1971. Regional counsel U.S. EPA, Dallas, 1975-79, dir. enforcement div., 1979-81; ptnr., head firm-wide environ. practice, mem. Dallas practice com. Akin, Gump, Strauss, Hauer & Feld, L.L.P., 1981—. Bd. dirs. Dallas Nature Ctr., 2001—; chair Greater Dallas Chamber Environ. Com., 2001. Mem. ABA, Tex. Bar Assn. (chmn. environ. and natural resources law sect. 1985-86), Dallas Bar Assn. (chmn. environ. law sect. 1984). Episcopalian. Administrative and regulatory, Environmental. Office: Akin Gump Strauss Hauer & Feld LLP 1700 Pacific Ave Ste 4100 Dallas TX 75201-4675 E-mail: ddutton@akingump.com

DUTTON, DOMINIC EDWARD, lawyer; b. New Orleans, Aug. 21, 1944; s. Lee M. and Fara C. (Cusimano) D. B.S., Lamar Coll. Tech., 1968; J.D., U. Houston, 1973. Bar: Tex. 1973, N.Mex. 1973, U.S. Dist. Ct. (we. dist.) Tex., U.S. Dist. Ct. N.Mex., U.S. Tax Ct., U.S. Ct. Appeals (10th cir.). Assoc. Bivins, Wienbrenner P.A., Las Cruces, N.Mex., 1973-76; ptnr. Dutton, Winchester, Las Cruces, 1976-81, Underwood & Dutton Ltd., Ruidoso, N.Mex., 1982-85, Underwood, Dutton & Giffin, Ltd., Ruidoso, 1985—, Dutton, Griffin & Hakanson, Ltd., 1991-94, Dutton & Hakanson, Ltd., 1994-96, The Dutton Firm,Ltd., 1997—; village atty. Ruidoso Downs, N.Mex., 1982-86, Carrizozo, N.Mex., 1983-85, Capitan, N.Mex., 1987—. Bd. dirs. Open Door Ctr., Inc., Las Cruces, 1976-80; del. Democratic State Conv., 1980, 84. Mem. Tex. State Bar Assn., Doña Ana County Bar Assn., Lincoln County Bar Assn. (sec.-treas. 1983-84, pres. 1985-87), N.Mex. State Bar Assn. (chmn. ethics 1976-77). Clubs: Cree Meadows Country (Rui, N.Mex.); Alto Lakes Country (Alto, N.Mex.). Lodge: Lions (past bd. dirs. Las Cruces club). Banking, Personal injury, Real property. Home: 200 Racquet Ct Ruidoso NM 88345-1668 Office: The Dutton Firm Ltd 1096 Mechem Dr Ste 229 Ruidoso NM 88345-7068

DUTTON, STEPHEN JAMES, lawyer; b. Chgo., Sept. 20, 1942; S. James H. and Marjorie C. (Smith) D.; m. Ellen W. Lee; children: Patrick, Mark. BS, Ill. Inst. Tech., 1965; JD, Ind. U., 1969. Bar: Ind. 1969, U.S. Dist. Ct. (so. dist.) Ind. 1969, U.S. Ct. Appeals (7th cir.) 1972, U.S. Ct. Appeals (D.C. cir.) 1980, U.S. Supreme Ct. 1978. With McHale, Cook & Welch, P.C., Indpls., 1969-86, Dutton & Overman, P.C., 1986-91, Dutton & Bailey, P.C., 1991-94, Locke, Reynolds, Boyd & Weisell, 1994-99, Leagre Chandler & Millard LLP, Indpls., 1999—. Mem. Com. on Law of Cyberspace Bus. Law Sect. Mem. ABA. Computer, General corporate, Securities. Home: 3705 Spring Hollow Rd Indianapolis IN 46208-4169 Address: 135 N Pennsylvania St Ste 1400 Indianapolis IN 46204-2489 E-mail: sdutton@lcmlaw.com

DUUS, GORDON COCHRAN, lawyer; b. Ridley Park, Pa., Oct. 17, 1954; s. Frank Martin and Shirley (Cochran) D.; m. Mary Ellen Moses, Nov. 9, 1985; children: Alexander, Hannah, Julianne. BA magna cum laude, U. Pa., 1977; JD with honors, George Washington U., 1981. Bar: D.C. 1981, N.J. 1982, Calif. 1987, U.S. Dist. Ct. N.J. 1982, U.S. Supreme Ct. 1989. Assoc. Previti, Todd, Gemmel, Fitzgerald & Nugent, Linwood, N.J., 1982-87; ptnr., chmn. environ. law dept. Margolis, Chase, Kosicki, Aboyoun & Hartman, Verona, 1987-90, Cole, Schotz, Meisel, Forman & Leonard, Hackensack, 1990—. Mem. faculty Cook Coll. of Rutgers U., New Brunswick, N.J., 1991—, Nat. Bus. Insts., Saddlebrook, N.J., 1992, Govt. Inst., Atlantic City, 1995; spkr. in field. Contbr. articles to profl. jours. Mem. ABA, N.J. Bar Assn., Bergen County Bar Assn. Environmental, Land use and zoning (including planning), Real property. Office: Cole Schotz Meisel Forman & Leonard 25 Main St Hackensack NJ 07601-7015 E-mail: gduus@coleschotz.com

DUVAL, STANWOOD RICHARDSON, JR. judge; b. New Orleans, Feb. 8, 1942; m. Deborah Barnes, Jan. 20, 1979. BA, La. State U., 1964, JD, 1966. Assoc. Duval, Arceneaux & Lewis, 1966-94; ptnr. Duval, Funderburk, Sundberry & Lovell, L.L.P., 1966-94; asst. city atty. Terrebonne Parish Consol. Govt., 1970-72, parish atty., 1988-92; dist. judge U.S. Dist. Ct. (ea. dist.), New Orleans, 1994—. Mem. Indigent Def. Bd., 1976-82; elected La. Constnl. Conv., 1973, mem. exec. br. com., com. to write rules of procedure. Mem. Terrebone Parish. Mem. ABA (adv. com. appellate rules 1997-2003), La. Law Inst. (coun. 1996-2001), La. State Bar Assn., Terrebonne Parish Bar Assn., Tulane Inns of Ct. Avocations: traveling, scuba diving, fishing, performing arts. Office: US Dist Ct Ea Dist 500 Camp St Rm C-368 New Orleans LA 70130-3313

DUVALL, RICHARD OSGOOD, lawyer; b. Washington, Sept. 25, 1942; s. Charles F. and Edith (Osgood) D.; m. Donna Morris; children: Julianne T., Tyler D., Nicholas C., Jacqueline L. BA, U. Ill., 1964; LLB, U. Va., 1967. Bar: Md. 1967, D.C. 1970, Va. 1998, U.S. Supreme Ct., U.S. Ct. Appeals (D.C. cir.), U.S. Ct. Appeals (4th cir.), U.S. Ct. Appeals (fed. cir.), U.S. Ct. Fed. Claims. Assoc. Pierson, Ball & Dowd, Washington, 1970-73, Dunnells & Duvall, 1973-94, mgn. ptnr., 1980-84, mem. exec. com., 1986-93; dir. Holland & Knight LLP, 1994—. Exec. ptnr., No. Va., mem. dirs. com., chair govt. contracts nat. practice group, dir. H&K Cons. LLC, chair lit. practice group, D.C., 1994-96. Gen. counsel Fairfax County C. of C., 2000—; bd. dirs. No. Va. Cmty. Found., 1999—. Lt. U.S Navy, JAGC, 1968-70. Fellow Am. Bar Found.; mem. Bar Assn. D.C. (bd. dirs. 1988-89), Bd. Contract Appeals Bar Assn. (bd. dirs. 1998-99). Administrative and regulatory, Federal civil litigation, Government contracts and claims. Home: 5811 Westchester St Alexandria VA 22310-1149 also: Suite 100 2099 Pennsylvania Ave NW Washington DC 20006-6801 E-mail: rduval@hklaw.com

DUVIN, ROBERT PHILLIP, lawyer; b. Evansville, Ind., May 18, 1937; s. Louis and Henrietta (Hamburg) D.; m. Darlene Chmiel, Aug. 23, 1961; children: Scott A., Marc A., Louis A. BA with honors, Ind. U., 1958, JD with highest honors, 1961; LLM with highest honors, Columbia U., 1963. Bar: Ohio 1964. Since practiced in, Cleve.; pres. Duvin, Cahn & Hutton, 1972—. Lectr. law schs.; labor adviser corps., cities and hosps. Contbr. to books and legal jours.; bd. editors: Ind. Law Jour., 1961, Columbia Law Rev., 1963. Served with AUS, 1961-62. Mem. ABA, FBA, Ohio Bar Assn., Cleve. Bar Assn., Cleve. Racquet Club, Beechmont Country Club, Soc. Club, Canterbury Golf Club, Sanctuary Golf Club. Jewish. Labor. Home: 2775 S Park Blvd Cleveland OH 44120-1669 Office: Duvin Cahn & Hutton Erieview Tower 1301 E 9th St Ste 2000 Cleveland OH 44114-1886 E-mail: rduvin@duvin.com

DUVIVIER, KATHARINE KEYES, lawyer, educator; b. Alton, Ill., Jan. 1, 1953; d. Edward Keyes and Marjorie (Attebery) DuV.; m. James Wesley Perl, Mar. 30, 1985 (div. Aug. 1997); 2 children: Alice Katharine Perl, Emmett Edward Perl. BA in Geology and English cum laude, Williams Coll., 1975; JD, U. Denver, 1982. Bar: Colo. 1982, U.S. Dist. Ct. Colo. 1982, U.S. Ct. Appeals (10th cir.) 1982. Intern-curator Hudson River Mus., Yonkers, N.Y., 1975; geologist French Am. Metals Corp., Lakewood, Colo., 1976-79; assoc. Sherman & Howard, Denver, 1982-84, Arnold & Porter, Denver, 1984-87; atty. Office of City Atty., 1987-90; sr. instr. sch. law Univ. Colo., 1990-00; reporter of decisions Colo. Ct. of Appeals, Denver, 2000; asst. prof., dir. lawyering process program U. Denver Coll. Law, 2000—. Chair Appellate Practice Subcommittee, 1998-2000, vice-chmn. 1996-98, 2000—. Contbr. articles to profl. jours. Mem. Denver Botanic Garden, 1981-88; vol. Outdoor Colo., Denver, 1985-87, 1998—. Mem. ABA (vice chmn. subcom. 1985-91), Colo. Bar Assn., Boulder Bar Assn., Boulder Women's Bar Assn. (pres. 1991-93), Alliance Profl. Women (bd. dirs. 1985-90, pres. 1988-89), Work and Family Consortium (bd. dirs. 1988-90), St. Ives, William Coll. Alumni Assn. (co-pres. Colo. chpt. 1984-86), Phi Beta Kappa. Avocations: geology, hiking, skiing, dancing, swimming. Home: 4761 Mckinley Dr Boulder CO 80303-1142 E-mail: kkduvivier@law.du.edu

DUZEY, ROBERT LINDSEY, lawyer; b. Long Beach, Calif., Nov. 15, 1960; s. Donald Bohdan and Noreen (Rosen) D.; m. Susan Misook Yoon, Mar. 14, 1987; children: Dylan Grey, Zenon Drake. BA, U. Calif., Irvine, 1984; JD, Western State U., Fullerton, Calif., 1994. Bar: Calif. 1994., U.S. Dist. Ct. (so., ctrl., ea. and no. dists.) Calif., U.S. Ct. Appeals (9th cir.), U.S. Supreme Ct. Claims rep., mgr. Farmers Ins. Group, Santa Ana, Calif., 1985-89; risk mgr. Dollar Rent A Car, Irvine, 1989-93; law clk. Callahan, McCune & Willis, Tustin, Calif., 1994-96; atty. Madigan, Evans & Boyer, Costa Mesa, 1996-98, Law Offices of Robert Lindsey Duzey, Downey, 1998—. Recipient Am. Jurisprudence award, 1993. Mem. ATLA, ABA, Orange County Bar Assn., Fed. Bar Assn., Orange County Barristers, Def. Rsch. Inst., Am. Inns of Ct., Peter M. Elliot Inn, L.A. County Bar Assn., Delta Theta Phi. Avocations: gardening, badminton, home decorating. Consumer commercial, Contracts commercial, Insurance. Office: Law Offices Robert Lindsey Duzey 9900 Lakewood Blvd Ste 250 Downey CA 90240-4038 Fax: (562) 862-7721. E-mail: RDuzey@earthlink.net

DWORKIN, MICHAEL LEONARD, lawyer; b. Bridgeport, Conn., Oct. 10, 1947; s. Samuel and Frances (Stein) D.; m. Christina Lyn Hildreth, Sept. 25, 1977; children: Jennifer Hildreth, Amanda Hildreth. BA in Govt. with honors, Clark U., 1969; JD with honors, George Washington U., 1973. Bar: D.C. 1973, Calif. 1975, U.S. Supreme Ct. 1978, U.S. Ct. Appeals (9th cir.) 1982, U.S. Claims Ct. 1983. Atty. FAA, Washington, L.A., 1973-77, United Airlines, San Francisco, 1977-81; pvt. practice, 1981-95, San Mateo, Calif., 1995—. Instr. Embry Riddle Aeronautical U., San Francisco, 1980-81; dir. Poplar Ctr., San Mateo, Calif., 1979-86. Benefactor Hiller No. Calif. Aviation Mus. Jonas Clark scholar Clark U., 1966-69. Mem. ABA, Lawyer Pilot's Bar Assn., Nat. Transp. Safety Bd. Bar Assn. (regional v.p. 1986-87, 90-99, chmn. rules com. 1985-99, pres. 2000—), Aircraft Owners and Pilots Assn., Conn. Aviation Hist. Assn., Benefactor-Hiller Aviation Mus., San Mateo County Bar Assn., Bar Assn. San Francisco, Internat. Soc. Air Safety Investigators (bd. dirs. San Francisco regional chpt. 1988-89), State Bar Calif., D.C. Bar Assn., Regional Airline Assn., Commonwealth Club of Calif., New England Air Mus. Jewish. Aviation, Contracts commercial, Insurance. Office: 465 California St Ste 210 San Francisco CA 94104 E-mail: law@avialex.com

DWORKIN, RONALD MYLES, legal educator; b. Worcester, Mass., Dec. 11, 1931; s. David and Madeline (Taber) D.; m. Betsy Ross, July 18, 1958; children; Anthony Ross, Jennifer. BA, Harvard U., 1953, LLB, 1957; BA, Oxford U., 1955; MA; LLB (hon.), Yale U., 1965. Bar: N.Y. 1959. Law clk. to Judge Learned Hand, 1957-58; assoc. firm Sullivan & Cromwell, 1958-62; faculty Yale Law Sch., 1962-69, master Trumbull Coll., 1966-69, Hohfeld prof. jurisprudence, 1968-69, Oxford, Eng., 1969-98; Quain prof. jurisprudence Univ. Coll., London, 1998—; prof. law NYU, 1975—. Prof.-at-large Cornell U., 1976—; vis. prof. philosophy Princeton (N.J.) U., 1963, 74-75, Gauss seminarian, 1966; vis. prof. law Stanford U., 1967; vis. prof. law and philosophy Harvard U., Cambridge, Mass., 1977, vis. prof. philosophy, 1979; acad. freedom lectr. U. Witwatersrand, 1976. Author: Taking Rights Seriously, 1977, A Matter of Principle, 1985, Law's Empire, 1986, A Bill of Rights for Britain, 1990, Life's Domain, 1993, Freedom's Law, 1996, Sovereign Virtue, 2000; editor: Philosophy of Law, 1977; contbr. articles to profl. jours. Chmn. Dems. Abroad, 1972-74; del. Dem. Nat. Conv., 1972, 76; mem. Dem. Charter Commn., 1974. Fellow Brit. Acad., Am. Acad. Arts and Scis. Office: NYU Law Sch 40 Washington Sq S New York NY 10012-1099

DWORSKY, CLARA WEINER, lawyer, former merchandise brokerage executive; b. N.Y.C., Apr. 28, 1918; d. Charles and Rebecca (Becker) Weiner; m. Bernard Ezra Dworsky, Jan. 2, 1944; 1 child, Barbara G. Goodman. BS, St. John's U., N.Y.C., 1937, LLB, 1939, JD, 1968. Bar: N.Y. 1939, U.S. Dist. Ct. (ea. dist.) N.Y. 1942, U.S. Dist. Ct. (so. dist.) Tex. 1993, U.S. Ct. Appeals (9th cir.) 1994, U.S. Ct. Appeals (5th cir.) 1995. Pvt. practice, N.Y.C., 1939-51; assoc. Bessie Farberman, 1942; clk., sec. U.S. Armed Forces, Camp Carson, Colo., Camp Claiborne, La., 1944-45; abstractor, dir. Realty Title, Rockville, Md., 1954-55; v.p. Kelley & Dworsky Inc., Houston, 1960—. Appeals agt. Gasoline Rationing Apls. Bd., N.Y.C., 1942; bd. dirs. Southlan Sales Assocs., Houston. Vol. ARC, N.Y.C.; vice chmn. War Bond pledge drive, Bklyn.; vol. Houston Legal Found., 1972-73; pres. Women's Aux. Washington Hebrew Acad., 1958-60, v.p. bd. trustees, 1959-60; co-founder, v.p. S. Tex. Hebrew Acad. (now Hebrew Acad.), Houston, 1970-75, hon. pres. women's divsn., 1973. Recipient Cert. award Treas. of U.S., 1943; Commendation Office of Chief Magistrate of City N.Y., 1948; Pietas medal St. Johns U., 1985. Mem. ABA (chmn. social security com., sr. lawyers divsn. 1989-93, 95—, chairsub-com. 1993-95, mem. sr. lawyers divsn. coun. 1989-95, mem. editl. bd. sr. lawyers divsn. pub. Experience), N.Y. State Bar Assn., Fed. Bar Assn. (vice chair for programs, sr. lawyers divsn. 1994-96, dep. chair 1996-97, chmn. 1997-98, chmn. soc. sec. com., sen. lawyers divsn. rep. south Tex. chpt. bd. 1998—), Houston Bar Assn. (sec. social security sect. 1995-96), Nat. Assn. Women Lawyers (chmn. organizer Juvenile Delinquency Clinic N.Y. 1948-51), St. Johns U. Alumni Assn. (coord. Houston chpt. 1983—, pres. 1986), Delphians Past Pres.'s Club, Amit Women Club, Hadassah. Jewish. Pension, profit-sharing, and employee benefits. Home: 9726 Cliffwood Dr Houston TX 77096-4406

DWYER, CORNELIUS J., JR. lawyer; b. New Rochelle, N.Y., Sept. 3, 1943; s. Cornelius John and Mary Cecelia (McDonough) D.; m. June Forsythe Sonnekalb, Sept. 14, 1968; children: Cornelius William, Colin Micheal. BA, Yale U., 1965; LLB, Harvard U., 1968. Bar: N.Y. 1968, U.S. Dist. Ct. N.Y. 1969. Assoc. ptnr. Shearman & Sterling, N.Y.C., 1968-76, ptnr., 1976—. Democrat. Roman Catholic. Banking, Contracts commercial, General corporate. Office: Shearman & Sterling 599 Lexington Ave Fl C2 New York NY 10022-6069 E-mail: cdwyer@sharman.com

DWYER, JOHN P. law educator, dean; b. 1951; BA DePauw U.; PhD, Calif. Inst. Tech., 1978; JD, U. Calif., Berkeley, 1980. Bar: D.C. 1981, Calif. 1982. Law clk. to Hon. Harry T. Edwards U.S. Ct. Appeals (D.C. cir.), Washington, 1980-81; law clk. to Hon. Sandra O'Connor U.S. Supreme Ct., 1981-82; staff atty. D.C. Pub. Defender Svc. , 1982-84; prof. U. Calif., Berkeley, 1984—, dean, 2000—. Editor in chief Ecology Law Quarterly. Office: U Calif Sch Law 215 Boalt Hall Berkeley CA 94720*

DWYER, WILLIAM L. federal judge; b. Olympia, Wash., Mar. 26, 1929; s. William E. and Ila (Williams) D.; m. Vasiliki Asimakopulos, Oct. 5, 1952; chldren: Joanna, Anthony, Charles. BS in Law, U. Wash., 1951; JD, NYU, 1953; LLD (hon.), Gonzaga U., 1994. Bar: Wash. 1953, U.S. Ct. Appeals (9th cir.) 1959, U.S. Supreme Ct. 1968. Law clk. Supreme Ct. Wash., Olympia, 1957; ptnr. Culp, Dwyer, Guterson & Grader, Seattle, 1957-87; judge U.S. Dist. Ct. (we. dist.) Wash., 1987—, now sr. judge. Author: The Goldmark Case, 1984 (Gavel award ABA 1985, Gov.'s award Wash. 1985). 1st lt. U.S. Army, 1953-56. Recipient Outstanding Svc. award U. Wash. Law Rev., 1985, Helen Geisness disting. Svc. award Seattle-King County Bar Assn., 1985, Disting. Alumnus award U. Wash. Sch. of Law, 1994, W.G. Magnuson award King County Mcpl. League, 1994, Judge of Yr. Wash. State Trial Lawyers, 1994, Outstanding Jurist award Am. Bd. Trial Advocates, Washington, 1998, William L. Dwyer Lifetime Achievement award, King County Bar Assn., 1998, Civil Rights award Anti-Defamation League, 1999, Ahepa Periclean award, 2000, William L. Dwyer endowed chair U. Wash. Sch. Law, 2001. Fellow Am. Coll. Trial Lawyers, Am. Bar Found., Hon. Order of Coif; mem. ABA, Inter-Am. Bar Assn., Am. Judicature Soc., Supreme Ct. Hist. Soc., 9th Cir. Hist. Assn. Office: US Dist Ct 713 US Courthouse Seattle WA 98104-1189

DYE, WILLIAM ELLSWORTH, lawyer; b. Detroit, Oct. 15, 1926; s. Edward Ellsworth and Elizabeth Esther (Bloom) D.; m. Joy Ann Kuehneman, Apr. 28, 1956 (div.); children: Constance, Elizabeth, William. BA, U. Wis., 1948, LLB, 1951. Bar: Wis. 1951. Assoc. John F. Thompson, Racine, Wis., 1951-75; ptnr. Heft, Dye, Paulson & Nichols, 1975-87, Foley, Dye, Foley and Tollaksen, S.C., Racine, 1987-92, Coates, Dye, Foley & Shannon, S.C., Racine, 1993-98, Dye, Foley, Krohn & Shannon, S.C., Racine, 1998—. Instr. U. Wis. Law Sch., 1970-71. Bd. visitors U. Wis., 1982-85. With U.S. Army, 1946-47. Mem. ABA, State Bar Wis. (bd. govs. 1972-78), Racine County Bar Assn. (pres. 1985-86), Racine Country Club, U. Milw. Club, Somerset of Racine Club. Republican. Episcopalian. Banking, Consumer commercial, General corporate. Home: 111 11th St Racine WI 53403-1966 Office: Dye Foley Krohn & Shannon 1300 S Green Bay Rd Racine WI 53406-4469 E-mail: dfkssc@amerilynk.com

DYER, CHARLES ARNOLD, lawyer; b. Blairstown, Mo., Aug. 29, 1940; s. Arnold and Mary Charlotte (West) D.; children: Kristine, Erin, Kathleen, Kerry. BJ, U. Mo., 1962; JD, U. Calif., 1970. Bar: Calif. 1971, U.S. Supreme Ct. 1976. Ptnr. Dyer & White, Menlo Park, Calif.; judge Pro

Tem Mcpl. and SuperiorCt., San Mateo County, Pro Tem Superior Ct., Santa Clara County, arbitrator, mediator. Lectr. in field. Bd. dirs. Boys Club of San Mateo, 1971-83, pres., 1975; mem. exec. coun. Boys Clubs of Bay Area, 1977-83; mem. Dem. Nat. Fin. Com., 1978. Served to capt. USNR, 1963-93, ret. Mem. Calif. Bar Assn., San Mateo County Bar Assn., Santa Clara County Bar Assn., Palo Alto Bar Assn., Consumer Attys. Calif., Consumer Attys. San Mateo County, Assn. Atty. Mediators, Trial Lawyers Pub. Justice, Am. Bd. Trial Advs., Nat. Bd. Trial Advocacy. Roman Catholic. Federal civil litigation, State civil litigation. Office: Dyer & White 800 Oak Grove Ave Menlo Park CA 94025-4477

DYER, CROMWELL ADAIR, JR. lawyer, international organization official; b. St. Louis, Sept. 9, 1932; came to The Netherlands, 1973; s. Adair and Tompie Leora (Giles) D.; m. Margaret Copeland Peickert, June 12, 1958 (div. Aug. 1976); children: Gretchen, Jack, Julie, Stephen; m. Susan Aynesworth, Aug. 20, 1977; stepchildren: Carol Godso, Amanda McDonough, Donne Brown. BA, U. Tex., 1954; JD, 1961; LLM, Harvard U., 1971. Bar: Tex. 1961, U.S. Dist. Ct. (no dist.) Tex. 1965, U.S. Dist. Ct. (ea. dist.) Tex. 1966, U.S. Ct. Appeals (5th cir.) 1965, U.S. Ct. Appeals (11th cir.) 1982, U.S. Ct. Appeals (9th cir.) 1999. Law clk. FTC, Washington, 1960; assoc. Branscomb, Gary, Thomasson & Hall, Corpus Christi, Tex., 1961-62; staff atty. So. Union Gas Co., Dallas, 1962-64; assoc. Dedman & May, 1964-65, White, McElroy & White, Dallas, 1965-67; sole practice, 1967-73; sec. Hague Conf. on Pvt. Internat. Law, The Hague, The Netherlands, 1973-78; 1st sec., 1978-93; dep. sec. gen., 1993-97; observer, cons. to intergovtl. orgns., 1976-97. Lectr. Asser Coll. Europe, 1992-96, Davis Sch. Law U. Calif. Davis, 1996, Brigitte M. Bodenheimer Meml. Lecture on the Family, 1996; ; moderator Common Law Jud. Conf. on Internat. Child Custody, Washington, 2000; condr. seminars. Honoree of symposium: Globalization of Child Law The Role of the Hague Conventions, 1999; co-author: Report on Trusts and Analogous Institutions, 1982; contbr. articles to profl. jours. Mem. jury for award of Diploma in Internat. Law Hague Acad., 1980, 84, 85, 86, 87, 91, 94, 95, 96, dir. studies, 1985, course on Unfair Competition in Pvt. Internat. Law, 1988. Lt. (j.g.) USN, 1954-57. Mem.: ABA (law sect. internat. law and practice 2000, Leonard J. Theberge award for pvt. internat. law), ATLA, Am. Soc. Internat. Law, Am. Fgn. Law Assn., Travis County Bar Assn., Dallas Bar Assn., Internat. Soc. Family Law, Assn. Louis Chatin pour la Def. des Droits de l'Enfant (Paris), Club du jeudi (The Hague) (pres. 1983—85). Private international, Public international. Office: PO Box 30020 Austin TX 78705-4206 Fax: 512 476-6683. E-mail: adyer@jump.net

DYER, JAMES HARRISON, lawyer; b. Phoenix, Oct. 25, 1952; s. Harvey L. and Nonavie (Harman) D. BA, U. Ariz., 1975, JD, 1978. Bar: Ariz. 1978, U.S. Dist. Ct. Ariz. 1980. Assoc., Healy & Beal, P.C., Tucson, 1978-86; sole practice, Tucson, 1986—; instr. Ariz. State Bar, 1984-85; arbitrator Am. Arbitration Assn., 1980—; host monthly legal radio show Sta. KNST, Tucson. Chmn. for So. Ariz., Republican Commitment '80 campaign; mem. Ariz. Town Hall, 1981; pres. Tucson Sport Fishing Festival, 1983-85; surrogate speaker Reagan/Bush Campaign, 1984; founding mem., bd. dirs., sgt. at arms, chmn. environ. impact com. Tucson Horizons; sponsor Project Hospitality Homeless Shelter. Mem. ABA, Ariz. Bar Assn., Pima County Bar Assn., Assn. Trial Lawyers Am., Ariz. Trial Lawyers Assn., Blue Key, Phi Gamma Delta. Club: U. Ariz. Pres.'s, 20/30 Internat. Tucson (charter, bd. dirs. 1986-87, chmn. polo tournament 1986-87). Home: 2020 N Soldier Trl Tucson AZ 85749-9000 Office: 5255 E Williams Cir Ste 6000 Tucson AZ 85711-7717

DYK, TIMOTHY BELCHER, federal judge, educator; b. Boston, Feb. 14, 1937; s. Walter and Ruth (Belcher) D.; m. Inga Shirer, June 18, 1960 (div. 1970); children: Deirdre, Caitlin; m. Sally Katzen, Oct. 31, 1981; 1 child, Abraham Benjamin AB, Harvard U., 1958, LLB magna cum laude, 1961. Bar: D.C., N.Y. Law clk. to Justices Reed and Burton U.S. Supreme Ct., Washington, 1961-62, law clk. to Chief Justice Earl Warren, 1962-63; spl. asst. to asst. atty. gen. U.S. Dept. Justice, Washington, 1963-64; assoc. Wilmer Cutler & Pickering, 1964-69, ptnr., 1969-90, Jones, Day, Reavis and Pogue, Washington, 1990-2000; circuit ct. judge U.S. Court of Appeals Fed. Circuit, 2000—. Adj. prof. Georgetown U. Law Ctr., Washington, 1983, 86, 89, 91, U. Va. Law Sch., Charlottesville, 1984-85, 87-88, Yale U. Law Sch., 1986-87, 89. Mem. Harvard Law Rev., 1959-61; contbr. articles to profl. jours. Office: US Court Appeals Fed Cir 717 Madison Pl NW Ste 808 Washington DC 20439

DYKES, OSBORNE JEFFERSON, III, lawyer; b. L.A., Dec. 3, 1944; s. Osborne J. Jr. and Frances (Fox) D.; m. Ann Dennis, Dec. 29, 1973; children: Barbara Nell, Osborne J. IV. BA, Stanford U., 1966, MA, 1968; JD, U. Tex., 1972. Bar: Tex. 1973, U.S. Supreme Ct. 1977, U.S. Ct. Appeals (5th cir.) 1973, U.S. Ct. Appeals (11th cir.) 1981, U.S. Dist. Ct. (so. dist.) Tex. 1975, U.S. Dist. Ct. (ea. dist.) Tex. 1976, U.S. Dist. Ct. (no. dist.) Tex. 1994. Law clk. to Hon. Homer Thornberry U.S. Ct. Appeals 5th Cir., Austin, Tex., 1972-73; ptnr. Fulbright & Jaworski, Houston, 1973—. Contbr. articles to profl. publs. With U.S. Army, 1969-71. Fellow Am. Bar Found., Tex. Bar Found. (life), Houston Bar Found. (life); mem. ABA (chmn. property ins. law com. 1983-84, tort and ins. practice sect.), Energy Bar Assn., Bar Assn. of Fifth Fed. Cir., Am. Bd. Trial Advs., Tex. Assn. Civil Trial Specialists (pres. 1982-83, bd. dirs. 1984—). Republican. Episcopalian. Avocations: tennis, bicycling. General civil litigation, Oil, gas, and mineral, Insurance. Home: 5135 Holly Terrace Dr Houston TX 77056-2125 Office: Fulbright & Jaworski 1301 Mckinney St Houston TX 77010-3031 E-mail: jdykes@fulbright.com

DYKHOUSE, DAVID WAYNE, lawyer; b. Paterson, N.J., Sept. 21, 1949; s. Garret J. and Raeanna L. Dykhouse; m. Barbara D. Kooy, Aug. 1, 1970; children: Rebecca, Christopher, Laura, Julia. AB Calvin Coll., 1971; JD magna cum laude U. Pa., 1974. Bar: Pa. 1974, N.Y. 1976, U.S. Dist. Ct. (so. dist.) N.Y. 1976, U.S. Dist. Ct. (ea. dist.) N.Y. 1985, U.S. Dist. Ct. (no. dist.) N.Y. 1988, U.S. Ct. Appeals (2nd cir.) 1991. Law clk. to assoc. justice Supreme Ct. of Pa., 1974-75; assoc. Patterson, Belknap, Webb & Tyler LLP Attys., N.Y.C., 1975-82, ptnr., 1982—. Bd. dirs. Ea. Christian Sch. Assn., 1986-89, 90-93, v.p., 1987-88, 91-92, pres., 1988-89, 92-93. Recipient The Peter McCall, Oscar Milton Davis, and Bernard A. Chertcoff prizes, Faculty of the U. Pa. Law Sch., 1974. Mem. ABA (subcom. secured transactions of com. on uniform comml. code sect. bus. law 1985—, com. internat. comml. transactions sect. internat. law and practice, 1989—, mem. bus. bankruptcy com. of bus. law sect. 1995—), N.Y. State Bar Assn. (multinat. reorgns. and insolvencies com. of internat. law and practice section, 1987—), Assn. of Bar of City of N.Y. (mem. com. on bankruptcy and corp. reorgn. 1980-85), Internat. Bar Assn. (com. on insolvency and creditors rights, com. on internat. sales and related comml. transactions 1990—). Democrat. Mem. Christian Reformed Ch. Bankruptcy, Contracts commercial, General corporate. Home: 741 Smoke Hollow Trl Franklin Lakes NJ 07417-1733 Office: Patterson Belknap Webb & Tyler LLP Ste 1700 1133 Avenue Of The Americas Fl 22 New York NY 10036-6731

DYTRYCH, DENISE DISTEL, lawyer; b. Chgo., June 20, 1961; d. Melvin John Distel and Patricia Loretta Blake. AA, Broward C.C., Coconut Creek, Fla., 1979; B in Associated Arts, Fla. Atlantic U., 1982; JD, Nova U., 1986. Bar: Fla. 1987; cert. Am. Coun. on Exercise, Lifestyle and Weight Mgmt. Cons.; cert. personal trainer, weight room instr. and advanced fitness practitioner Aerobic Fitness Assn. Am. Law clk. Panza, Maurer, Maynard, Ft. Lauderdale, Fla., 1984-86; asst. county atty. Palm Beach County Atty., West Palm Beach, 1986-94, exec. asst. county atty., 1994-96, county atty., 1996—. Author: Christmas Party Celebrations: 71 New and Exciting Party Plans for Holiday Fun, 1998. Auction com. mem. Am. Heart Assn., 1998—, advt. chmn. Heart Ball, 1999—. Recipient Up & Comers award Price Waterhouse, 1994; named Outstanding Young Women of Am., 1987. Mem. Fla. Bar (15th jud. at-large rep. govt. lawyer sect.), Palm Beach County Bar (com. mem. govt. lawyer sect.), Fla. Guild Cath. Lawyers, 15th Jud. Cir. Pro Bono Com. Roman Catholic. Avocations: reading, writing, health and fitness, golf. Address: Ofc Bd Cty Commrs PO Box 1989 West Palm Beach FL 33402-1989

DYWAN, JEFFERY JOSEPH, judge; b. Hammond, Ind., Apr. 26, 1949; s. Joseph Michael and Florence Marie (Buda) D.; m. Jacque Ann Shulmistras, June 20, 1971; children: Dina, Abigail, Kathryn. BS in Indsl. Engring., Purdue U., 1971; JD, Valparaiso U., 1974. Bar: Ind. 1974, U.S. Dist. Ct. (no. and so. dists.) Ind. 1974, U.S. Ct. Appeals (7th cir.) 1975, Ill. 1984, U.S. Dist. Ct. (no. dist.) Ill. 1986. Assoc. Breclaw & Dywan, Griffith, Ind., 1974-77; sole practice, 1977-81; dep. prosecuting atty. Lake County, Crown Point, Ind., 1978-80, pub. defender, 1981-83; assoc. Chudom & Meyer, Schererville, 1981-89; ptnr. O'Drobinak, Dywan & Austgen, Crown Point, 1989-91; judge Lake Superior Ct., 1991—, chief judge, 1998-2000. Instr. Calumet Coll., Hammond, Ind., 1974-76, Ind. Vocat. and Tech. Coll., Gary, Ind., 1978-79. Mem. Ind. State Bar Assn., Lake County Bar Assn., Am. Judicature Soc., KC. Roman Catholic. Office: Lake Superior Ct 2293 N Main St Crown Point IN 46307

EABY, CHRISTIAN EARL, lawyer, small business owner; b. Reading, Pa., June 16, 1945; s. David Russell and Pearl Haller (Root) E.; m. Dace Rekis, Jan. 4, 1986. BA in Univ. Studies, U. N.Mex., 1976, JD, 1980. Bar: N.Mex. 1980, Pa. 1990, U.S. Dist. Ct. (ea. dist.) Pa. 1992. Tchr. Albuquerque Pub. Schs., 1976; ednl. dir. N.Mex. Pub. Employees Coun., 1977; tutor Am. Indian Law Ctr. U. N.Mex., 1978-79; pvt. practice Albuquerque, 1980-90; owner Eby Clock Co., New Holland, Pa., 1990-95; pvt. practice, 1990—. Past legal coun. N.Mex. Vietnam Vets. of Am. Contbr. articles to profl. jours. Bd. dirs. U. N.Mex. Cancer Ctr., 1984-92, Albuquerque United Artists Downtown Ctr. for Arts, Ea. Lancaster County Sch., 1990-93; pres. Coalition Albuquerque Neighborhoods, 1983-85, Nob Hill Neighborhood Assn., 1980-86; mem. task force Albuquerque Goals Com.; founding dir., sec. Nob Hill Main St., 1987; founding dir. Casa Esperanza Cancer Patients Homes, 1987. Mem. ABA, ATLA (product liability sect.), Am. Arbitration Assn., Am. Numismatic Assn., N.Mex. Bar Assn., N.Mex. Trial Lawyers Assn., Albuquerque Bar Assn., Pa. Bar Assn. (workers' compensation sect.), Lancaster Bar Assn., Pa. Trial Lawyers Assn., Nat. Assn. Watch and Clock Collectors, Nat. Trust Hist. Preservation, Hist. Preservation Trust of Lancaster County, Lancaster Mennonite Hist. Soc., Lancaster Hist. Soc., Hist. Soc. of Cocalico Valley, Eby Family Assn. (pres. 1992—). Avocations: geneology, numismatics, horology, restoring 1727 family home. Personal injury, Product liability, Workers' compensation. Home: 405 Peters Rd New Holland PA 17557-9389 Office: 352 E Main St Ste 230 Leola PA 17540-1961 Fax: 717-656-3434. E-mail: cee@eabylaw.com

EADES, RONALD WAYNE, law educator; b. Lexington, Ky., Sept. 6, 1948; s. Thomas William and Evelyn Louise (Smith) E.; m. Lillian Arpi Aivazian, July 2, 1971; children: Matthew Adrian, Emily Rachael. BA in English, Rhodes Coll., 1970; JD, U. Memphis, 1973; LLM, Harvard U., 1977. Bar: Tenn. 1974, Ky. 1984. Staff atty. Tenn. Valley Authority, Knoxville, Tenn., 1974-76; asst. prof. law U. Louisville, 1977-80, assoc. prof., 1980-82, prof. law, 1982—, disting. tchg. prof., 1991. Vis. prof. U. Leeds, Eng., 1993, Johannes Gutenburg U., Mainz, Germany, 1994, U. Turku (Finland), 2000. Author: Wrongful Death Actions—The Law in Kentucky and supplements, 1981, (with Gramham Douthwaite) Jury Instructions in Automobile Negligence Action, 2d edit., 1991, 3d edit., 1996, Workers Compensation—The Law in Kentucky, 1989, (with John Palmore) Kentucky Jury Instructions, 1989, Products Liability Actions—The Law in Kentucky and supplements, 1981, Watson vs. Jones—The Walnut Street Presbyterian Church and the First Amendment, 1982, Kentucky Damages Law and supplement, 1985, Products Liability, Actions and Remedies, 1985, Kentucky Jurisprudence Evidence, 1987, Law for Asphalt Athletes, 1983, Jury Instructions on Products Liability, 3d edit., 1999, Jury Instructions on Damages in Tort Actions, 3d edit., 1993, Kentucky Wrongful Death Actions, 1994, Kentucky Products Liability Law, 1994, Kentucky Law of Damages, 3d edit., 1998, Jury Instructions in Automobile Actions, 3d edit., 1996, Jury Instructions in Commercial Litigation, 1996, Jury Instructions on Medical Issues, 5th edit., 1997, Fights For Rights, 2000. James R. Merritt fellow for disting. tchg., 1994-95; Disting. Univ. scholar, 1996—; CALI fellow in tort law, 2001. Mem. ABA, Ky. Bar Assn., Assn. Trial Lawyers Am. Democrat. Presbyterian. Avocation: jogging, amateur radio. Office: U Louisville Sch Of Law Louisville KY 40292-0001

EAGAN, CLAIRE VERONICA, magistrate judge; b. Bronx, N.Y., Oct. 9, 1950; d. Joseph Thomas and Margaret (Lynch) E.; m. M. Stephen Barrett, Aug. 25, 1978 (div. 1984); m. Anthony J. Loretti, Jr., Feb. 13, 1988. Student, U. Fribourg, Switzerland, 1970-71; BA, Trinity Coll., Washington, 1972; postgrad., U. Paris, 1972-73; JD, Fordham U., 1976. Bar: N.Y. 1977, Okla. 1977, U.S. Dist. Ct. (no. dist.) Okla. 1977, U.S. Ct. Appeals (10th cir.) 1978, U.S. Supreme Ct. 1980, U.S. Dist. Ct. (we. dist.) Okla. 1981, U.S. Ct. Appeals (5th cir.) 1982, U.S. Dist. Ct. (ea. dist.) Okla. 1988, U.S. Ct. Appeals (Fed. cir.) 1990. Mem. Hall, Estill, Hardwick, Gable, Golden & Nelson, Tulsa, 1978-98, shareholder, 1981-98, also bd. dirs., exec. com.; magistrate judge U.S. Dist. Ct. (no. dist.) Okla., 1998—. Editor Fordham Law Rev., 1975-76. Bd. dirs. Cath. Charities, Tulsa, 1983-98, Cystic Fibrosis Found., Tulsa, 1982-84; mem. Jr. League Tulsa, Inc., 1983—; trustee Gannon U., Erie, Pa., 1995-98; bd. dirs. Okla. Sinfonia, Tulsa, 1982-86; adj. settlement judge, Tulsa County, 1990-97. Fellow Am. Bar Found.; mem. Tulsa County Bar Assn., 10th Cir. Jud. Conf., Am. Inns of Ct. (chpt. pres. 1999-2000). Republican. Roman Catholic. Federal civil litigation, General civil litigation, State civil litigation. Office: US Dist Ct No Dist Okla 333 W 4th St Ste 411 Tulsa OK 74103-3819 E-mail: ceagan@oknd.uscourts.gov

EAGAN, WILLIAM LEON, lawyer; b. Tampa, Fla., Feb. 10, 1928; s. John Robert and Margaret (Williams) E.; m. Marjorie Young, Mar. 6, 1959; children: Barbara Anne, Rebecca Elizabeth, Laurel Lea. Student, U. Tampa, 1959; LLB, U. Fla., 1961. Bar: Fla. 1961, U.S. Dist. Ct. (mid. dist.) Fla. 1959, U.S. Dist. Ct. (so. dist.) Fla. 1962, U.S. Ct. Appeals (5th cir.) 1972; bd. cert. civil trial lawyer, Fla. Assoc. Dexter, Conlee & Bissell, Sarasota, Fla., 1961-62; ptnr., v.p. Arnold, Matheny & Eagan, P.A., Orlando, 1962—. Mem. Fla. Bar Ninth Circuit Grievance Com., 1982-84; mediator Family Law Mediation Program. Articles editor U. Fla. Law Rev., 1961. Chmn. bd. trustees First Bapt. Ch., Winter Park, Fla., 1970-72, chmn. bd. deacons, 1967-69; active Indsl. Devel. Commn. Mid-Fla., Orlando, 1979-84. Served to seaman 2d class USN, 1945-46. Mem. ATLA, Acad. Fla. Trial Lawyers, Lawyers Title Guaranty Assn., Orange County Bar Assn. (exec. coun.), Univ. Club, Citrus Club (Orlando), Order of Coif, Phi Alpha Delta, Phi Kappa Phi. Republican. Baptist and Methodist. Federal civil litigation, State civil litigation, Real property. Office: Arnold Matheny & Eagan PA 801 N Magnolia Ave Ste 201 Orlando FL 32803-3842 E-mail: Weagan@ameorl.com

EAGLES, SIDNEY SMITH, JR. judge; b. Asheville, N.C., Aug. 5, 1939; s. Sidney Smith Sr. and Mildred Truman (Brite) E.; m. Rachel Phillips, May 22, 1965; children: Virginia Brite, Margaret Phillips. BA, Wake Forest U., 1961, JD, 1964. Bar: N.C. 1964. Revisor Gen. Statutes Commn., Raleigh, N.C., 1967-70; asst. atty. gen. legis. drafting service Office Atty. Gen. N.C., 1970-74, dep. atty. gen. spl. prosecution divsn., 1974-76; counsel to speaker N.C. State Legislature, 1976-80; ptnr. Eagles Hafer & Hall, 1977-82; judge N.C. Ct. Appeals, 1983—, chief judge, 1998—. Adj. prof. Campbell U. Sch. Law, 1977; chmn. N.C. Jud. Stds. Commn., 1994—96; mem. faculty Appellate Judges Sch. Law Sch. NYU, N.Y.C., 1993—99; mem. Uniform Laws Conf., 1968—83, 1992—99, 2001—. Co-author: North Carolina Criminal Procedure Forms, 1975, 3d edit., 1989; contbr. articles to profl. jours. V.p. Raleigh Jaycees, 1972-73; mem. Senatorial Dist. Dem. Com., 1979-81; bd. dirs. Wake County (N.C.) Symphony Soc., 1980-81, Women's Aid of Wake County, 1978—; bd. elders, bd. deacons, trustee, tchr. Sunday sch. Hillyer Meml. Christian Ch., 1980—, chmn bd., 1989; bd. visitors Wake Forest U. Sch. Law; vice chair bd. trustees Barton Coll. Served to capt. USAF, 1964-67; col., ret. 1991. Named Disting. Law Alumnus, Wake Forest U., 1981; N.C. Justice Found. fellow, 1972. Mem. ABA (chmn. appellate judges conf. 1993-94, mem. appellate jud. edn. com. 1994-98, ho. of dels. 1992—), Am. Law Inst. (life), N.C. Bar Assn. (v.p. 1989-90), Wake county Bar Assn. (chmn. exec. com. 1975), N.C. State Bar, Execs. Club (pres. 1985), Kiwanis (disting. pres. Raleigh 1986-87, disting. lt. gov. 1995, Kiwanian of Yr. award 1989), Phi Delta Phi, Phi Alpha Delta (James Iredell award 1990). Avocations: politics, reading. Office: NC Ct of Appeals PO Box 888 Raleigh NC 27602-0888

EAGLETON, EDWARD JOHN, lawyer; b. Tulsa, Jan. 22, 1932; s. William L. and Pauline (Dellinger) E.; m. Norma Lee, Oct. 6, 1956; children: Courtney Jean, Richard John. BA, Okla. U., 1954, JD, 1956. Bar: Okla. 1955, U.S. Dist. Ct. (ea., we. and no. dists.) Okla. 1956, U.S. Tax Ct. 1958, U.S. Supreme Ct. 1964; CPA, Tex., Okla. Acct. Peat Marwick Mitchell, Dallas, 1956-58; with IRS, Dallas and New Orleans, 1958-62; assoc. Houston & Klein, Tulsa, 1962-65; ptnr. Kothe & Eagleton, 1965-74, Houston & Klein Inc., Tulsa, 1974-94, Eagleton Eagleton & Harrison Inc., Tulsa, 1994—. Served with U.S. Army, 1956. Named one of Best Tax Lawyers in Am., Bar Register of Preeminent Lawyers, 1983—2001. Republican. Unitarian. General civil litigation, General corporate, Estate planning. Home: 3210 E 65th St Tulsa OK 74136-1225 Office: Eagleton, Eagleton & Harrison Inc 320 S Boston Ave Ste 1700 Tulsa OK 74103-4706

EAKEN, BRUCE WEBB, JR. lawyer; b. Cleve., Mar. 23, 1938; s. Bruce Webb and Kathryn (Peacock) E.; m. Wilhelmina Murray Martin, Oct. 23, 1971; children: Amanda, Webb. BA, Dartmouth Coll., 1960; JD, U. Mich., 1964. BAr: Ohio 1964, N.Y. 1965. Atty. Allied Chem. Co., N.Y.C., 1966-72; assoc. counsel U.S. Filter Corp., 1972-81; prin. atty. N.Y. Power Authority, 1981—. Bd. dirs. East Harlem Little League, N.Y.C., 1970-73; pres. St. Bartholomews Players, N.Y.C., 1972-74; bd. dirs., treas. Media Ctr. for Children, N.Y.C., 1982-90. Mem. Assn. Bar City N.Y. (adminstrv. law com. 1983-86, inter-Am. Affairs com. 1986-88, 98—, corp. law dept. com. 1989-92, second century com. 1990-94), UN Assn. N.Y.C. (treas.), Dartmouth Alumni Assn. N.Y.C. (pres. 2000—), Lincoln Racquet Club (N.Y.). Nuclear power, Public utilities, Real property. E-mail: eaken@aol.com

EAKIN, MARGARETTA MORGAN, lawyer; b. Ft. Smith, Ark., Aug. 27, 1941; d. Ariel Thomas and Oma (Thomas) Morgan; m. Harry D. Eakin, June 7, 1959; 1 child, Margaretta E. BA with honors, U. Oreg., 1969, JD, 1971. Bar: Oreg. 1971, U.S. Dist. Ct. Oreg. 1973, U.S. Ct. Appeals (9th cir.) 1977. Law clk. to chief justice Oreg. Supreme Ct, Salem, 1971-72; Reginald Heber Smith Law Reform fellow, 1962-73; house counsel Hyster Co., 1973-75; assoc. N. Robert Stoll, 1975-77; pvt. practice, Margaretta Eakin, P.C., Portland, Oreg., 1977—. Tchr. bus. law Portland State U., 1979-80; spkr.; mem. bd. profl. responsibility Oreg. State Bar, 1979-82; mem. bd. visitors U. Oreg. Sch. Law, 1986-93, vice chair, 1989-91, chair, 1992-93; mem. Oreg. State. Bar Com. on Uniform State Laws, 1989-93; vol. lawyer Fed. Emergency Mgmt. Assn., 1995—. Mem. ann. fund com. Oreg. Episcopal Sch., 1981; chmn. subcom county fair, 1981; sec. bd. Parent Club St. Mary's Acad., 1987. Paul Patterson fellow. Mem. ABA, ATLA, Oreg. Trial Lawyers Assn., Oreg. Bar Assn., Multnomah County Bar Assn. (jud. selection com. 1992-94), 1000 Friends of Oreg., City Club. Federal civil litigation, State civil litigation, Contracts commercial. Office: 1001 SW 5th Ave 13th Fl Portland OR 97204 E-mail: ME71051@aol.com

EARLY, ALEXANDER RIEMAN, III, judge; b. Phila., Sept. 22, 1917; s. A.R. Jr. and Elizabeth Frances (Dence) E.; m. Marjory Celeste Worland, Aug. 15, 1959; children: A.R. IV, Lucia C. Stroh, Elizabeth V., John Drennan V. BA, Cornell U., 1938; LLB, Harvard U., 1941. Bar: Calif. 1946. Pvt. law practice, L.A., 1946-50; sr. atty. Divsn. of Hwys., State of Calif., 1950-55; asst. U.S. atty. Lands divsn. U.S. Dept. Justice, L.A., 1955-57; asst. county counsel Los Angeles County, Calif., 1957-72; judge Superior Ct., L.A., 1972-87, chmn. exec. com. Rules Com., BAJI Com.; judge by assignment, 1987—; ret., 1987. Adj. prof. Southwestern Law Sch., L.A., 1970-79. Contbr. articles to profl. jours. Mgr. internat. fedn. rels. boxing venue 1984 Olympics. Comdr. USNR, 1941-46. Served U.S. Navy in Destroyers, Pacific (earned nine battle stars); dir. sinking I.J.N. sub. RO-38, 1943. Decorated comdr. Order Polonia Restituta (Poland); knight grand cross Order of Holy Sepulchre (Vatican), Law Enforcement medal SAR, 1981. Mem. Am. Bd. Trial Adv., Nat. Conf. State Tax Judges, Calif. Soc. Sons of Revolution (pres., Disting. Svc. award), Calif. Soc. Colonial Wars (Disting. Svc. medal), Soc. War of 1812 (vice pres. gen., Disting. Svc. award), Soc. Cincinnati, Md. Hist. Soc., U.S. Naval Inst., Aztec Club, Navy League. Roman Catholic. Avocations: American history, genealogy, camellia seedlings. Home: 3017 Kirkham Dr Glendale CA 91206-1127

EARLY, BERT HYLTON, lawyer, consultant; b. Kimball, W.Va., July 17, 1922; s. Robert Terry and Sue Keister (Hylton) E.; m. Elizabeth Henry, June 24, 1950; children— Bert Hylton, Robert Christian, Mark Randolph, Philip Henry, Peter St. Clair Student, Marshall U., 1940-42; A.B., Duke U., 1946; J.D., Harvard U., 1949. Bar: W.Va. 1949, Ill. 1963, Fla. 1981. Assoc. Fitzpatrick, Marshall, Huddleston & Bolen, Huntington, W.Va., 1949-57; asst. counsel Island Creek Coal Co., 1957-60, assoc. gen. counsel, 1960-62; dep. exec. dir. ABA, Chgo., 1962-64, exec. dir., 1964-81; sr. v.p. Wells Internat., 1981-83, pres., 1983-85, Bert H. Early Assocs. Inc., Chgo., 1985-94, Early Cochran & Olson, Chgo., 1994-98, of counsel, 1999—. Dir. Am. Bar Found., Chgo., 1993-95; instr. Marshall U., Huntington, W.Va., 1950-53; legal search cons. and lectr. in field. Bd. dirs. Morris Meml. Hosp. for Crippled Children, 1954-60, Huntington Pub. Libr., 1951-60, W.Va. Tax Inst., 1961-62, Huntington Mus. Art, 1961-62; mem. W.Va. Jud. Coun., 1960-62, Huntington City Coun., 1961-62; bd. dirs. Cmty. Renewal Soc., Chgo., 1965-76, United Charities Chgo., 1972-80, Hinsdale (Ill.) Hosp. Found., 1987-93, Internat. Bar Assn. Found., 1987-89; bd. dirs. Am. Bar Endowment, 1983-95, sec., 1987-89, treas., 1989-91, v.p., 1991-93, pres., 1993-95, dir. emeritus, 1995-2000; mem. vis. com. U. Chgo. Law Sch., 1975-78; trustee Davis and Elkins Coll., 1960-63; mem. Hinsdale Plan Commn., 1982-85. 1st lt. AC, U.S. Army, 1943-45. Fellow Am. Bar Found., Ill. Bar Found. (charter); mem. ABA (ho. of dels. 1958-59, 84-93, chmn. young lawyers divsn. 1957-58, Disting. Svc. award young lawyers divsn. 1983), Am. Law Inst. (life), Internat. Bar Assn. (asst. sec. gen. 1967-82), Nat. Legal Aid and Defender Assn., Legal Aid Soc. Chgo., Am. Judicature Soc. (bd. dirs. 1981-84), Fla. Bar, W.Va. Bar Assn., Chgo. Bar Assn. Presbyterian. Office: Early Cochran & Olson LLC 401 N Michigan Ave Ste 2010 Chicago IL 46061-4206

EARLY, JAMES H., JR. lawyer; b. Henderson, N.C., May 6, 1939; s. James Howard and Nettie Anna (Hicks) E.; children from previous marriage: James H. III, Anna Elizabeth, Mary Elizabeth. AA, Mars Hill Coll., 1960; BA, Wake Forest U., 1962, LLB, 1964, JD, 1970. Bar: N.C. 1964, U.S. Dist. Ct. (mid. dist.) N.C. 1970, U.S. Ct. Appeals (4th cir.) 1995; cert. mediator Superior Cts. of N.C., 1992. Pvt. practice, Winston-Salem, 1964—; mediator Adminstrv. Office of the Cts. of N.C., 1992—. Mediator Am. Arbitration Assn., 1992—. Contbr. articles to profl. jours. With U.S. Army, 1957. Chmn. fundraising Cub Scouts/Boy Scouts Am., Little League, Pop Warner, Indian Guides, March of Dimes, others. With U.S.

Army. Mem. ABA, ATLA, N.C. Bar Assn. (chmn. continuing legal edn. subcom., mem. effectiveness and quality of life com., moderator skills course com.), , Forsyth County Bar Assn. (sec. 1970-71), N.C. Acad. Trial Lawyers, Phi Alpha Delta (alumni advisor 1969-84, Outstanding Alumnus award 1967), Kiwanis (pres. 1989-90, 91-92), Masons. Baptist. Avocations: hunting, fishing, walking horses, bird dogs, racing. General corporate, Labor, Personal injury. Home: 144 Sterling Pt Ct Winston Salem NC 27104 Office: 1320 Westgate Center Dr Winston Salem NC 27103-2933

EARLY, STEPHEN BARRY, lawyer; b. South Gate, Calif., Apr. 8, 1945; s. Charles Nelson and Hilma Mae (Mumaw) E.; m. Janice Ann Webb, Aug. 20, 1966 (div. Feb. 1978); m. Susan Lippert Buzzotta, Dec. 28, 1996; children— Christian Webb, Jana Kay. B.A., Tex. Christian U., 1967; M.B.A., U. Dayton, 1970; J.D., So. Meth. U., 1975. Bar: Tex. 1975, Ky. 1982, U.S. Supreme Ct., various fed. cts. appeal and dist. cts.; CLU. Assoc. atty. Roberts, Harbour Smith, Harris, French & Ritter, Longview, Tex., 1975-77; sole practice, Longview, 1977-80; gen. counsel, sec., dir. Shakey's Inc., Dallas, 1980-81; v.p., gen. counsel Ky. Fried Chichken Corp., Louisville, 1981— . Served to capt. USAF, 1968-72. Mem. ABA, Tex. Bar Assn., Ky. Bar Assn., Soc. Mayflower Descs., SAR. Republican. Mem. Christian Ch. Avocations: running, flying. Home: 7608 Woodridge Dr Pewee Valley KY 40056-9027 Office: Ky Fried Chicken Corp 1441 Gardiner Ln Louisville KY 40213-1914

EARNHEART, FRANK JONES, lawyer; b. Salisbury, N.C., June 14, 1924; s. Hilbert F. and Fannie (Jones) E.; B.A. in Chemistry, U. N.C., 1947; postgrad. Duke U. Law Sch., 1947-48; J.D., George Washington U., 1951; m. Mildred Schulken, Aug. 15, 1946 (div. 1965); children— Laurie Jeanne, Gregory Steven, Barbara Susan; m. 2d, Sonia Keeble, May 6, 1967; 1 stepson, Christopher Keeble. Admitted to D.C. bar, 1951, Ark. bar, 1956, Ohio bar, 1958, Pa. bar, 1975; asso. firm Cushman, Darby & Cushman, Washington, 1948-52; asst. patent counsel Beaunit Mills Inc., N.Y.C., 1952-54; patent counsel Lion Oil div. Monsanto Chem. Co., El Dorado, Ark., 1954-56; chief patent counsel Gen. Tire & Rubber Co., Akron, Ohio, 1956-67; gen. mgr. Gen. Tire Internat. Co., 1967-69; chmn. bd. and spl. patent counsel Genitiruco, Zug, Switzerland, 1967-69; v.p. adminstrn. Interpace Corp., Parsippany, N.J., 1969-71; pres., dir. Interpace Found., 1969-71; asst. to pres., sec., corp. counsel Selas Corp. Am., Dresher, Pa., 1971-80, v.p., sec., gen. counsel, 1980— . Trustee, N.J. Citizens Hwy. Com., 1969-71; pres., counsel Plumstead Civic Assn., 1975-80. Served to lt. (j.g.) USNR, 1943-46. Fellow Internat. Acad. Law and Sci.; mem. Am. Bar Assn., Am. Patent Law Assn., Phila. Patent Law Assn., Delta Theta Phi. Republican. Lutheran. Home: Tall Trees Bergstrom Rd Doylestown PA 18901 Office: Selas Corp America Dresher PA 19025

EASLEY, CHARLES D., JR. judge; b. Port of Spain, Trinidad, Apr. 8, 1949; , parents Am. citizens; s. Charles D. and Doris B. Easley; m. Pamela Robinson; children: Christopher, Lindsey, Ali Mara. BBA, U. Miss., 1972, JD, 1979; MBA, Miss. State U., 1976. Asst. dist. atty. 3d Judicial Circuit Ct. Dist., 1980—83; pvt. practice Columbus, Miss., 1983—2000; assoc. justice Miss. Supreme Ct., 2001—. Mem.: ATLA, ABA, Miss. Trial Lawyer's Assn., Miss. Mcpl. Judge's Assn., Lowndes County Bar Assn., NRA, Shriners, Masons. Office: Miss Supreme Ct Carroll Gartin Justice Bldg 450 High St Jackson MS 39201 also: PO Box 117 Jackson MS 39205*

EASLEY, MICHAEL F. governor; b. Rocky Mount, N.C., 1950; m. Mary Pipines; 1 child, Michael F. Jr. BA in Polit. Sci. cum laude, U. N.C., 1972; JD cum laude, N.C. Ctrl. U. Dist. atty. 13th Dist., N.C., 1982-91; pvt. practice Southport, 1991-93; atty. gen., 1993-2000; gov. State of N.C., 2000—. Contbr. numerous articles in field. Recipient Pub. Svc. award U.S. Dept. Justice, 1984. Pres. N.C. Conf. Dist. Attys.; mem. N.C. Dist. Attys. Assn. (past pres., legis. chmn.). Avocations: hunting, sailing, woodworking. Office: Office of the Gov 20301 Mail Service Ctr Raleigh NC 27699-0303

EASTAUGH, FREDERICK ORLEBAR, lawyer; b. Nome, Alaska, June 12, 1913; s. Edward Orlebar and Lucy Evelyn (Ladd) E.; m. Carol Benning Robertson, Aug. 8, 1942; children: Robert Ladd, Alison Benning Eastaugh Farnan. BA, U. Wash., 1937; D Humanities (hon.), U. Alaska, 1982. Bar: Alaska 1948, U.S. Ct. Appeals (9th cir.) 1956, U.S. Supreme Ct. 1958. With Alaska Steamship Co., Seattle, 1934-39; acct. Pan Am. Airways, Juneau, Fairbanks, Seattle and San Francisco, 1940-46; clk. Robertson, Monagle & Eastaugh , Juneau, 1946-48, ptnr., 1948-88, ret., 1988; Royal Norwegian Consul for Alaska, 1951-87; commr. Nat. Conf. Uniform State Laws, 1962-69; mem. Alaska Land Use Adv. Com., 1984-86; pres. Alaska-Dano Mines Co. Founder, bd. dirs. Develop Juneau, Inc.; pres. U. Alaska Found., Fairbanks, 1981-82; bd. dirs. Alaska Resource Devel. Council; trustee Pacific Legal Found., 1983-86. Named Citizen of Yr., Juneau C. of C., 1977. Fellow ABA Found.; mem. ABA, Alaska Bar Assn., Rocky Mt. Mineral Law Found., Alaska C. of C. (pres. 1955-56, named Outstanding Alaskan 1978). Republican. Episcopalian. Home: 12555 Auke Nu Dr PO Box 20589 Juneau AK 99802-0589

EASTAUGH, ROBERT L. state supreme court justice; b. Seattle, Nov. 12, 1943; BA, Yale U., 1965; JD, U. Mich., 1968. Bar: Alaska 1968. Asst. atty. gen. State of Alaska, 1968-69, asst. dist. atty., 1969-72; lawyer Delaney, Wiles, Hayes, Reitman & Brubaker, Inc., 1972-94; assoc. justice Alaska Supreme Ct., 1994—. Office: Alaska Supreme Ct 303 K St Anchorage AK 99501-2013*

EASTERBROOK, FRANK HOOVER, federal judge; b. Buffalo, Sept. 3, 1948; s. George Edmund and Vimy (Hoover) E. B.A., Swarthmore Coll., 1970; J.D., U. Chgo., 1973. Bar: D.C. Law clk. to judge U.S. Ct. Appeals, Boston, 1973-74; asst. to solicitor gen. U.S. Dept. Justice, Washington, 1974-77, dep. solicitor gen. of U.S., 1978-79; asst. prof. law U. Chgo., 1978-81, prof. law, 1981-84, Lee & Brena Freeman prof., 1984-85; prin. employee Lexecon Inc., Chgo., 1980-85; sr. lectr. U. Chgo., 1985—; judge U.S. Ct. Appeals (7th cir.), Chgo., 1985—. Mem. adv. com. on tender offers SEC, Washington, 1983 Author: (with Richard A. Posner) Antitrust, 1981, (with Daniel R. Fischel) The Economic Structure of Corporate Law, 1991; editor Jour. Law and Econs., Chgo., 1982-91; contbr. articles to profl. jours. Trustee James Madison Meml. Fellowship Found., 1988—. Recipient Prize for Disting. scholarship Emory U., Atlanta, 1981 Mem. AAAS, Am. Law Inst., Mont Pelerin Soc., Order of Coif, Phi Beta Kappa. Office: US Ct Appeals Everett McKinley Dirksen Fed Bldg 219 S Dearborn St Ste 2746 Chicago IL 60604-1803*

EASTERLING, CHARLES ARMO, lawyer; b. Hamilton, Tex., July 22, 1920; s. William Hamby and Jennie (Arilla) E.; m. Irene A. Easterling, Apr. 25, 1943; children: Charles David, Danny Karl, Jan Easterling Petty. BBA, LLB, Baylor U., 1951, JD, 1969. Bar: Tex. 1950, U.S. Supreme Ct. 1954. Sr. asst. city atty. City of Houston, 1952-64; pvt. practice Houston, 1964-70; city atty. Pasadena, Tex., 1970-82; of counsel Easterling and Easterling, Houston, 1982—. Instr. So. Tex. Coll. Law, 1954-69. Lt. col. (ret.) USAFR. Mem. Houston-Harris County Bar Assn., Masons (33d degree, inspector gen. hon.), Shriners, Jesters, Arabia Temple Shrine (past potentate), Red Cross Constantine (past sovereign) Phi Alpha Delta. Democrat. Medthodist. Estate planning, General practice, Probate. Fax: 713-228-4072. E-mail: eaepc@swbell.net

EASTLAND, S. STACY, lawyer; b. Houston, Oct. 27, 1948; s. Seaborn and Anne (Stacy) E.; m. Tara Gardner, Mar. 24, 1972; children: Tara Doran, Seaborn Gardner. BS, Washington & Lee U, 1971; JD, U. Tex., 1974. Assoc. Baker & Botts, Houston, 1974-81, ptnr., 1982—. Bd. dirs. Houston Estate and Fin. Forum, Camp Mystic, Inc.; mem. Tex. Bd. Legal Specialization in Estate Planning and Probate Law. Bd. dirs. Oscar Neuhaus Found., St. John Meml. Endowment Fund, Houston chpt. Ortin Soc., DePelchin Children's Ctr., Inst. Child and Family Svcs.; trustee Kelsey-Seabold Found. Fellow Am. Coll. Probate Counsel; mem. ABA (coun. 1990—, publs. coord. probate and trust divsn. 1992-93, bylaws and handbook com. 1992—, sec. adv. Revision Uniform Partnership Act 1987—, publs. com. 1992-93, budget and fin. com. 1991-92, chair divsn. coord. ann. meeting programs 1987-89), Am. Coll. Trust and Estate Counsel (bd. regents, chmn. transfer tax study com. 1988-93), Tex. State Bar Assn., Houston Bar Assn., Houston Country Club, Tex. Allegro Club. Episcopalian. Avocations: tennis, golf. Estate planning, Probate, Estate taxation. Home: 3730 Piping Rock Ln Houston TX 77027-4032

EASTMENT, THOMAS JAMES, lawyer; b. N.Y.C., Mar. 3, 1950; s. George Thomas and Grace Anne (Manning) E. BChemE, Manhattan Coll., 1972; JD, U. Mich., 1975. Bar: N.Y. 1976, D.C. 1977. Assoc. Morton, Bernard, Brown, Washington, 1975-77, Baker & Botts, Washington, 1977-84, ptnr., 1985—. Mem. D.C. Bar Assn., Fed. Energy Bar Assn. Republican. Roman Catholic. General civil litigation, FERC practice, Oil, gas, and mineral, Administrative and regulatory. Office: Baker & Botts The Warner 1299 Pennsylvania Ave NW Washington DC 20004-2400 E-mail: Tom.Eastment@BakerBotts.com

EATON, J(AMES) TIMOTHY, lawyer; b. Decatur, Ill., Sept. 2, 1951; s. Edward Loftus and Helen Christine (Carlson) E.; m. Jane Katzenberg, Dec. 10, 1983. BA, Miami U., Oxford, Ohio, 1973; JD, So. Ill. U., 1977; LLM, Washington U., 1979. Bar: Ill. 1977. Law clk. to presiding justice Ill. Supreme Ct., Decatur, Ill., 1977-79; ptnr. Baird, Latendresse, McCarthy & Rowden, 1979-83, Hinshaw, Culbertson, Moelmann, Hoban & Fuller, Chgo., 1983-86, Ungaretti & Harris and predecessor firms, Chgo., 1986—. Contbr. articles to profl. jours. Dept. legal counsel Ill. campaign Mondale for Pres., 1983-84; mem. St. Matthews Episc. Ch., Evanston. Fellow Ill. Bar Found.; mem. Ill. Bar Assn. (active various coms., pres. 2001-), Lawyers Trust Fund Ill., Appellate Lawyers Assn. (bd. dirs. 1982-84), Miami U. Alumni Assn. (pres. elect 1986—). State civil litigation, Product liability. Home: 1029 Chestnut Ave Wilmette IL 60091-1731 Office: Ungaretti & Harris 3500 3 First Nat Plaza Chicago IL 60602*

EATON, JANET RUTH, lawyer, mediator; b. Cin., Dec. 25, 1947; d. Stanley Lee and Pettrila Grace (Ochs) E.; BMus Edn., Ind. U., 1969; JD, U. Cin., 1975. Bar: Ohio 1975, U.S. Dist. Ct. (so. dist.) Ohio 1975, U.S. Ct. Appeals (6th cir.) 1980; cert. master practitioner neurolinguistic programming. Staff atty. Legal Aid Soc., Cin., 1975-81; assoc. Dinsmore & Shohl, Cin., 1981-85; sole practice Cin., 1985—; assoc. Ctr. for Resolution Disputes, 1988—; adj. faculty Chase Law Sch. No. Ky. U., 1992—. Author: Your Day In Court and How To Prepare For It: Mental Health Professionals as Expert Witnesses, 1985. Trustee Mental Health Assn. Cin., 1976-87; mem. bus. relations com. Cin. Symphony Orch., 1983-86; active Cin. Symphony Assn., 1983-89. Am. Bar Found. grantee, 1972. Mem. Cin. Bar Assn., Acad. Family Mediators (practitioner). Democrat. Family and matrimonial, General practice, Mental health. Office: 2250 Kroger Bldg 1014 Vine St Cincinnati OH 45202-1141

EATON, JOE OSCAR, federal judge; b. Monticello, Fla., Apr. 2, 1920; s. Robert Lewis and Mamie (Gireadeau) E. AB, Presbyn. Coll., 1941, LLD (hon.), 1979; LLB, U. Fla., 1948. Pvt. practice law, Miami, Fla., 1948-51, 55-59; asst. state atty. Dade County, 1953; circuit judge Miami, 1954-55, 59-67; mem. Fla. Senate, 1956-59; mem. law firm Eaton & Achor, Miami, 1955-58, Sams, Anderson, Eaton & Alper, Miami, 1958-59; judge U.S. Dist. Ct. (so. dist.) Fla., 1967-83, chief judge, 1983-85, sr. judge, 1985—. Instr. law U. Miami Coll. Law, 1954-56 Served with USAAF, 1941-45; Served with USAF, 1951-52. Decorated D.F.C., Air medal. Methodist. Club: Kiwanian.

EATON, JOEL DOUGLAS, lawyer; b. Miami, Fla., Oct. 31, 1943; s. Joe Oscar and Patricia (MacVicar) E.; m. Mary Benson, June 24, 1967; children: Douglas, Darryl, David. BA, Yale U., 1965; JD, Harvard U., 1975. Bar: Fla. 1975, U.S. Dist. Ct. (so. dist.) Fla. 1976, U.S. Ct. Appeals (5th cir.) 1976, U.S. Supreme Ct. 1978, U.S. Ct. Appeals (11th cir.) 1981, U.S. Ct. Appeals (Fed. cir.) 1996. Ptnr. Podhurst, Orseck, Josefsberg, Eaton, Meadow, Olin & Perwin, P.A. and predecessors, Miami, 1975—. With USN, 1965-71. Decorated Air medal with Bronze Star and numeral 14, Navy Commendation medal with 2 gold stars, Cross of Gallantry (Viet Nam). Mem. ABA, ATLA, Am. Law Inst., Acad. Fla. Trial Lawyers, Fla. Bar Assn. (appellate rules com. 1981—, chmn. 1989-90, jud. evaluation com. 1995-98, Fla. std. jury instn. com. 1998—), Am. Acad. Appellate Lawyers. Democrat. Appellate, Federal civil litigation, State civil litigation. Office: Podhurst Orseck Josefsberg Eaton Meadow Olin & Perwin PA 25 W Flagler St Ste 800 Miami FL 33130-1720 E-mail: jeaton@podhurst.com

EATON, LARRY RALPH, lawyer; b. Quincy, Ill., Aug. 18, 1944; s. Roscoe Ralph and Velma Marie (Beckett) E.; m. Janet Claire Rosen, Oct. 28, 1978. BA, Western Ill. U., 1965; JD, U. Mich., 1968. Bar: Ill. 1968, U.S. Dist. Ct. (no. dist.) Ill. 1978, U.S. Ct. Appeals (D.C. cir.) 1984, U.S. Ct. Appeals (7th cir.) 1989, N.Y. 1997. Vol., instr. law U. Liberia Sch. Law, U.S. Peace Corps, Monrovia, 1968-70; lawyer Forest Park Found., Peoria Heights, Ill., 1970-71; asst. atty. gen. State of Ill., Springfield, 1971-75; ptnr. Peterson & Ross and predecessors, Chgo., 1975-94; founder Blatt, Hammesfahr & Eaton, 1994-2000; sr. mem. Cozen O'Connor, 2000—. Instr. environ. law Quincy Coll., Ill., 1973-75. Mem. Young Men's Jewish Council, Chgo., 1974—84; trustee Edgewater Cmty. Coun., 2000—; pres. Lakewood Balmoral Residents' Coun., 2000—01; bd. dirs. Near North Montessori Sch., 1989—95, vice chmn., 1992—95; bd. dirs. Edgewater Devel. Corp., 0200—. Contbg. writer Chgo. Daily Law Bull., 1975-77; field editor Pollution Engrng., 1976. Fellow: Ill. Bar Found. (charter); mem.: ABA (environ. ins. litig. task force 1990—), Atticus Finch Inn of Ct., Ill. Bar Assn. (chmn. environ. control law sect. 1976—77, coun. 1973—77, coun. 1990—94, editor sect. newsletter 1972—77, assembly 1980—86, assembly 1989—92, coun. jud. evaluation Cook County 2000—), Chgo. Bar Assn., Bar Assn. for 7th Jud. Cir., Law Club Chgo., Lawyers Club Chgo. Federal civil litigation, Environmental, Insurance.

EATON, RICHARD KENYON, judge; b. Walton, N.Y., Aug. 22, 1948; s. Paul Francis and Frances Emmaretta E.; m. Susan Henshaw Jones, Sept. 26, 1981; children; Alice, Elizabeth. BA, Ithaca Coll., 1970; JD, Union U., N.Y., 1974. Bar: N.Y. 1975. Judge U.S. Ct. Internat. Trade, N.Y.C., 2000-01. Office: US Ct of Internat Trade 1 Federal Plaza New York NY 10278

EBEL, DAVID M. federal judge; b. 1940; BA, Northwestern U., 1962; JD, U. Mich., 1965. Law clk. assoc. justice Byron White U.S. Supreme Ct., 1965-66; pvt. practice Davis, Graham & Stubbs, Denver, 1966-88; judge U.S. Ct. Appeals (10th cir.), 1988—. Adj. prof. law U. Denver Law Sch., 1987-89; sr. lectr. fellow Duke U. Sch. Law, 1992-94. Mem. Am. Coll. Trial Lawyers, Colo. Bar Assn. (v.p. 1982), Jud. Conf. U.S. (com. on codes of conduct 1991-98, co-chair 10th cir. gender bias task force 1994-99). Office: US Ct Appeals 1823 Stout St Rm 109L Denver CO 80257-1823 E-mail: david_m._ebel@ca10.uscourts.gov

EBERHARDT, DANIEL HUGO, lawyer; b. Milw., Feb. 19, 1938; s. Erwin M. and Hazel M. (Daley) E.; m. Josephine E. Jeka, Sept. 10, 1960; children: Daniel Hugo Jr., Mark John. BS, Colo. State U., 1962; JD, Marquette U., 1968. Bar: Wis. 1968, U.S. Dist. Ct. (ea. dist.) Wis. 1968. Assoc. Morrissy, Morrissy, Sweet & Race, Elkhorn, Wis., 1968-70; ptnr. Sweet & Eberhardt, 1970-76; sole practice, 1976—. Commr. Walworth County Cir. Cts., 1975—. Served to 1st lt. U.S. Army, 1962-65, AUS. Mem. ABA, Wis. Bar Assn., Walworth County Bar Assn. (sec., treas. 1983-85, v.p. 1985-86, pres. 1986-87), VFW (comdr. 1980-81). Republican. Roman Catholic. Lodge: Rotary (pres. 1980-81). Family and matrimonial, Probate, Real property. Home: N6601 Peck Station Rd Elkhorn WI 53121-3247 Office: 18 S Broad St PO Box 258 Elkhorn WI 53121-0258

EBERLE, DONALD CRAMER, lawyer, governmental relations consultant; b. Balt., Dec. 29, 1948; s. William Cramer and Margaret Elizabeth (Mullaney) E.; m. Patricia Ann Gorman Barry, Aug. 14, 1971. BA, U. Colo., 1970, JD, 1974; advanced studies Harvard, 1984. Bar: Colo., 1974. Asst. dean students U. Colo., Denver, 1970-72; dep. dist. atty., Denver, 1974-77; chief counsel Met. Econ. Crime Office, Denver, 1977-79; sr. appellate atty. Office of Denver Dist. Atty., 1979-80; state rep. Color. House of Reps., 1980-82; dir. legis. affairs gov. Colo., 1982-84; dir. external affairs regional gen. counsel MCI Telecomms. Corp., Denver, 1984-90; prin. Eberle & Assocs., 1991—; lectr. in field; chmn. State Bd. Equalization, 1985-93; bd. dirs. Capitol Complex Commn., 1983-85, Denver Civic Ventures, 1985-93, Colo. Dance Festival, 1986-89; chmn. exec. bd. U. Colo. Internat. Telecom Program, 1989—. Mem. DRCOG Clean Air Task Force, Colo., 1980-82; mem. adv. com. on Crime Reclassification, Colo., 1981-83; bd. dirs. Capitol Hill Community Ctr., Denver, 1981-82; chmn. Gov's. Task Force on the Homeless; chmn. The Denver Ptnrship. Com. on Homeless. Harvard scholar Gates Found., 1984; mem. Colo. Coun. on the Arts, 1993-96; bd. dirs., sec. CA:RE; chmn. Colo. Homeless Youth Adv. Com., 1992-96. Mem. ABA, Colo. Bar Assn., Nat. Dist. Attys. Assn., Colo. Dist. Attys. Assn. Democrat. Home: 379 Dahlia St Denver CO 80220-5713 Office: MCI Telecomms Corp 1760 Lafayette St Denver CO 80218-1117

EBERLY, RUSSELL ALBERT, lawyer, manufacturing company executive; b. Dover, Ohio, July 27, 1922; s. Herbert Lamoyne and Meta Charlotte (Bimeler) E.; B.S., Washington and Jefferson Coll., 1944; J.D., Akron U., 1950; m. Jean McWilliams Fisher, Jan. 19, 1946; children— Ann Eberly Calvert, James Allen. Bar: Ohio 1950, Pa. 1977. Patent atty. B.F. Goodrich Co., Akron, 1946-52; with PPG Industries, Inc., 1952— , asst. patent counsel, then corp. patent counsel, Pitts., 1970-77, corp. counsel, 1977-78, v.p. law, 1978-79, v.p., gen. counsel, 1979— ; dir. PPG Industries Found. Mem. devel. council Washington and Jefferson Coll., 1979— , trustee, 1981— . Served with USNR, 1943-46. Mem. ABA, Am. Patent Law Assn., Assn. Gen. Counsel, Patent Law Assn. Pitts. Republican. Methodist. Clubs: Duquesne (Pitts.); South Hills Country. General corporate. Office: PPG Industries Inc 3503 Wagon Wheel Wichita Falls TX 76310-1423

EBERSOLE, JODI KAY, lawyer; b. Pitts., Mar. 15, 1966; d. Denver J. Weigel and JoAnn Ramsey; m. Gary R. Ebersole, Nov. 3, 1990. BA in Social Work, Elizabethtown Coll., 1987; JD, Widener U., 1990. Bar: Md. 1990, D.C. 1991, U. S. Dist. Ct. Md. 1991, U.S. Ct. Appeals (4th cir.) 1991, U.S. Ct. Appeals (3d cir.) 1994. Assoc. Thieblot, Ryan, Martin & Ferguson, Balt., 1990-96, Ferguson, Schetelich & Heffernan, Balt., 1996-97, ptnr., 1997-99; sr. claim counsel St. Paul Fire & Marine Ins. Co., 1999-2000, regional group counsel, 2000—. Fellow Md. Bar Found., Balt. Bar Found. (trustee 1999—); mem. Md. State Bar Assn. (bd. govs. 2001—), Def. Rsch. Inst., Bar Assn. Balt. City (chair young lawyers divsn. 2000—). Insurance, Personal injury, Product liability. Office: St Paul Fire & Marine Ins Co MC-31 Claim Legal Exposure Mgmt 5801 Smith Ave Baltimore MD 21209-3611 E-mail: jodi.ebersole@stpaul.com

EBERT, DARLENE MARIE, lawyer; b. Milw., Dec. 29, 1951; d. Frank James and Marie Antoinette (Ermenc) Leban; m. Lee Arthur Ebert, Dec. 30, 1972; children: Kristen Ann, Mark Alan. BA, U. Wis., 1973, MS, 1974, JD, 1977. Bar: Wis. 1977, Colo. 1977. Assoc. Lobato-Bleidt, Bleidt & Haight, Lakewood, Colo., 1978-79; asst. city atty. City of Denver, 1979-96; gen. counsel Denver Health and Hosp. Authority, 1997—. Mem. ABA, Colo. Bar Assn. (chmn. pub. coun. com.), Denver Bar Assn., Colo. Women's Bar Assn., Nat. Health Lawyers Assn., Nat. Inst. Mcpl. Law Officers (chmn. pers. com. 1990-93), City Club (bd. dirs. 1991-94, pres. 1993), Beta Sigma Phi (pres. 1981-82, v.p. 1986-87, 89-90). Democrat. Roman Catholic. Home: 4015 S Niagara Way Denver CO 80237-2004 Office: Denver Health & Hosp Auth 660 Bannock St Fl 5 Denver CO 80204-4506

EBINER, ROBERT MAURICE, lawyer; b. L.A., Sept. 2, 1927; s. Maurice and Virginia (Grand) E.; m. Paula H. Van Sluyters, June 16, 1951; children: John, Lawrence, Marie, Michael, Christopher, Joseph, Francis, Matthew, Therese, Kathleen, Eileen, Brian, Patricia, Elizabeth, Ann. JD, Loyola U., L.A., 1953. Bar: Calif. 1954, U.S. Dist. Ct. (cen. dist.) Calif. 1954. Pvt. practice, West Covina, Calif., 1954—. Judge pro tem L.A. Superior Ct., 1964-66, 90—, arbitrator, 1979—; arbitrator San Bernardino Superior Ct., 1990—; judge pro tem Citrus Mcpl. Ct., 1966-70, 1990—, El Monte Mcpl. Ct., 1998—, Whittier Mcpl. Ct., 2001—; mem. disciplinary hearing panel Calif. State Bar, 1968-75. Bd. dirs. West Covina United Fund, 1958-61, chmn. budget com., 1960-61; organizer Joint United Funds East San Gabriel Valley, 1962, bd. dirs., 1961-68; bd. dirs. San Gabriel Valley Cath. Social Svcs., 1969—, pres., 1969-72; bd. dirs. Region II Cath. Social Svc., 1970—, pres., 1970-74; trustee L.A. Cath. Welfare Bur. (now Cath. Charities), 1978—; charter bd. dirs. East San Gabriel Valley Hot Line, 1969-74, sec., 1969-72; charter bd. dirs. N.E. L.A. County unit Am. Cancer Soc., 1973-78, chmn. by-laws com., 1973-78; bd. dirs. Queen of the Valley Hosp. Found., 1983-89; organizer West Covina Hist. Soc., 1982—; active Calif. State Dem. Cen. Com., 1963-68; mng. meet dir. Greater La Puente Valley Spl. Olympics, 1985-88, Bishop Amat Relays, 1981-96; mem. MSAC Relays Com., 1978—; campaign mgr. Congressman Ronald B. Cameron, 1964. With U.S. Army, 1945-47. Recipient L.A. County Human Rels. Commn. Disting. Svc. award, 1978, Thomas A. Kiefer Humanitarian award, 1993; named West Covina Citizen of Yr., 1986, San Gabriel Valley Daily Tribune's Father of Yr., 1986. Mem. ABA, Calif. Bar Assn., L.A. County Bar Assn. (arbitrator 1975—), Fed. Ct. So. Dist. Calif. Assn., L.A. Trial Lawyers Assn., Ea. Bar Assn. L.A. County (pres. Pomona Valley 1965-66), West Covina C. of C. (pres. 1960), Am. Arbitration Assn. (arbitrator 1965-98), KC, Bishop Amat H.S. Booster Club (bd. dirs. 1973-96, pres. 1978-80), Kiwanis (charter West Covina, pres. 1976-77, lt. gov. divsn. 35 1980-81, Kiwanian of Yr. 1978, 82, Disting. Lt. Gov. 1980-81, bd. dirs. Cal-Nev-Ha Found. 1986-98, pres. 1994-96). Avocation: collector of historical Olympic and political memorabilia. State civil litigation, Personal injury, Probate. Office: 100 N Citrus St Ste 520 West Covina CA 91791-1694

EBITZ, ELIZABETH KELLY, lawyer; b. LaPorte, Ind., June 9, 1950; d. Joseph Monahan and Ann Mary (Barrett) Kelly; m. David MacKinnon Ebitz, Jan. 23, 1971 (div. 1981). AB with honors, Smith Coll., 1972; JD cum laude, Boston U., 1975. BAr: Maine 1979, Mass. 1975, U.S. Dist. Ct. Mass. 1976, U.S. Dist. Ct. Maine 1979, U.S. Ct. Appeals (1st cir.) 1976, U.S. Supreme Ct. 1982. Law clk. Boston Legal Assistance Project, 1973-75; law clk., assoc. Law Offices of John J. Thornton, Boston, 1974-76; ptnr. Ebitz & Zurn, Northampton, Mass., 1976-79; assoc. Gross, Minsky, Mogul & Singal, Bangor, Maine, 1979-80; pres. Elizabeth Kelly Ebitz P.A., 1980-92, Ebitz & Thornton, P.A., 1993—. Pres. Greater Bangor Rape Crisis Bd., 1983-85; bd. dirs. Bangor Area Homeless Shelter, 1985-92, 93-99, Maine Women's Lobby, 1986-89, No. Maine Bread for the World, 1987-90, Machias River Clinic for Mental Health and Substance

Abuse, 2000—; bd. dirs. Am. Heart Assn., Maine, 1989—, chair, 1993-95, chmn., 1995-97; mem. various peace, feminist and hunger orgns., Bangor, 1982—. Named Young Career Woman of Hampshire County, Nat. Bus. and Profl. Women, Northampton, 1979. Mem. ABA, ATLA, Nat. Orgn. Social Security Claimant (rep. 1994—), Sigma Xi. Democrat. Roman Catholic. Family and matrimonial, Pension, profit-sharing, and employee benefits, Personal injury. Home: 111 Maple St Bangor ME 04401-4031 Office: 329 Wilson St Brewer ME 04412-1504 E-mail: bgrlegal@aol.com

ECHOLS, ROBERT L. federal judge; b. 1941; BA, Rhodes Coll., 1962; JD, U. Tenn., 1964. Law clk. to Hon. Marion S. Boyd U.S. Dist. Ct. (we. dist.) Tenn., Nashville, 1965-66; legis. asst. Congressman Dan Kuykendall, 1967-69; ptnr. Baily, Ewing, Dale & Conner, Nashville, 1969-72, Dearborn & Ewing, Nashville, 1972-92; fed. judge U.S. Dist. Ct. (mid. dist.) Tenn., 1992—, chief judge, 1998—. Mem. exec. com. 6th Cir. Jud. Coun.; mem libr. com. 6th Cir. Ct. Appeals; mem. ann. conf. planning com. 6th Cir. With U.S. Army, 1966; brig. gen. Tenn. Army N.G., 1969-2001 Mem. ABA, Am. Bar Found., Fed. Judges Assn., Tenn. State-Fed. Jud. Coun., Tenn. Bar Found., Tenn. Bar Assn., Nashville Bar Assn., Nashville Found., Harry Phillips Am. Inn of Ct., Jud. Br. Com. U.S. Jud. Conf. Office: US Dist Ct 801 Broadway Ste 824 Nashville TN 37203-3868 E-mail: robert.l._echols@tnmd.uscourts.gov

ECKER, HOWARD, lawyer; b. N.Y.C., June 10, 1946; s. David and Sylvia (Goldstein) E.; children: David, Ashley. BA, U. Mich., 1967; JD, NYU, 1971. Bar: Nev. 1973, U.S. Dist. Ct. Nev. 1974, U.S. Ct. Appeals (9th cir.) 1976, U.S. Supreme Ct. 1976. Pub. defender Clark County Pub. Defender's Office, Nev., 1973-77; ptnr. Ecker & Standish, Chtd., Clark County, 1977—. Apptd. settlement judge in appeals Nev. Supreme Ct., 1997—; guest lectr. in field. Mem. Nev. Employee Mgmt. Rels. Bd., Las Vegas, 1990-94. Mem.: ATLA, State Bar Nev. (bd. govs. 1984—90), Clark County Bar Assn., Nev. Trial Lawyers Assn. (bd. govs. 1977—89, pres. 1985—86), Am. Inns of Ct. (barrister 1990—93, master 1993—), Am. Acad. Matrimonial Lawyers. Avocations: travel, golf, reading. Family and matrimonial. Office: Ecker & Standish Chtd 300 S 4th St Ste 901 Las Vegas NV 89101-6025

ECKHARDT, WILLIAM RUDOLF, III, lawyer; b. Houston, Dec. 14, 1915; s. William Rudolf and Ura (Link) E.; m. Elra Hodges, Oct. 11, 1940; 1 son, Donald Kent. B.A., Rice Inst., 1937; LL.B., U. Tex., 1940. Bar: Tex. 1940. Asst. U.S. atty. Dept. Justice, So. Dist. Tex., 1940-44, 46-52; assoc. McGregor & Sewell, Houston, 1952-56, Vinson & Elkins, Houston, 1956—91. Served to lt. (j.g.) USN, 1944-46. Fellow Am. Coll. Trial Lawyers; mem. ABA, Tex. Bar Assn., Maritime Law Assn., Tex. Def. Attys. Assn., Chancellors, Order of Coif, Phi Delta Phi, Chi Phi Republican. Baptist. Club: Houst. Admiralty, General civil litigation, Insurance. Home: 25 Robinlake Ln Houston TX 77024-7121 Office: Ste 111 7880 San Felipe Houston TX 77063 Fax: 713-781-2573

ECKOLS, THOMAS AUD, lawyer, educator; b. Springfield, Ill., Oct. 3, 1950; s. Aud L. and Jean (Sutton) E.; m. Cynthia Marie Yontz, Aug. 19, 1973; children: Molly, Cally. BA, U. Iowa, 1972; JD, U. Ill., 1975. Bar: Ill. 1975, U.S. Dist. Ct. (cen. dist.) Ill. 1975, U.S. Supreme Ct., 1998. Assoc. Fleming, Messman & O'Connor, Bloomington, Ill., 1975-80; ptnr. Fleming, Messman, O'Connor & Eckols, 1980-81; sr. atty. State Farm Ins. Cos., 1981-85, asst. counsel, 1985-87, counsel, 1987—. Asst. prof. legal studies Ill. State U., Normal, 1984-92. Chmn. issues com. Sen. John Maitland, Ill., 1980-92; program chmn. McLean County Lincoln Club, Bloomington, 1978-80; legis. aid Rep. John Hirschfeld, Champaign, Ill., 1972-75; precinct committeeman, 1994—. Mem. ABA (commerce, banking and bus. subcom. 1985—, litigation sect. 1984—), Ill. Bar Assn., McLean County Bar Assn. (sec. 1977-78). Republican. Presbyterian. Avocations: swimming, running, golf. Federal civil litigation, General corporate, Insurance. Home: RR 13 Bloomington IL 61704-9813 Office: State Farm Ins Cos Corp Law Dept One State Farm Plaza Bloomington IL 61710

ECKSTEIN, JOHN ALAN, lawyer; b. Iowa City, Aug. 11, 1948; s. John William and Imogene B. (O'Brien) E.; m. Ledy R. Garcia, June 10, 1972; children: Cody Brien, Maria Alejandra. Student Grinnell Coll., 1966-67; BA, Iowa U., 1970; MA, Johns Hopkins U., 1972; JD, U. Va., 1975. Bar: Ind. 1975, U.S. Dist. Ct. (so. dist.) Ind. 1975, U.S. Tax Ct. 1975, Colo. 1981, U.S. Dist. Ct. Colo. 1981. Assoc. Ice, Miller, Donadio & Ryan, Indpls., 1975-81; assoc. Calkins, Kramer, Grimshaw & Harring, Denver, 1981-83, ptnr., 1983-89; ptnr. Kelly, Stansfield & O'Donnelly, 1989; ptnr., officer, dir. Jensen Byrne Parsons Ruh & Tilton, P.C., 1990—; lectr. internat. fin. Contbr. articles to profl. jours. Mem. Gov.'s Edn./Industry Mobilization Coun., 1987-90; mem. adv. com. Colo. Sec. Commr., 1987—; mem. Millenium Club Colo. Dems., 1984-88; chmn. elect Colo. Advanced Tech. Inst., 1990—. Mem. ABA, Fed. Bar Assn. (bd. dirs. 1982—, pres. Colo. chpt. 1986-87), Colo. Bar Assn., Denver Bar Assn., Denver C. of C., Colo. Assn. Commerce and Industry, Serra, Denver Athletic Club, Phi Delta Phi. Democrat. Roman Catholic. General corporate, Finance, Securities. Home: 1737 Glencoe St Denver CO 80220-1342

EDDS, STEPHEN CHARLES, lawyer; b. Lexington, Ky., Apr. 28, 1949; s. William Harold and Ann Louise (Fisher) E.; m. Carole Brand. BA, U. Miss., 1971, JD, 1973. Bar: Miss. 1973, U.S. Dist. Ct. (no. and so. dists.) Miss. 1973, U.S. Ct. of Appeals (5th cir.) 1973, U.S. Supreme Ct. 1977. Ptnr. Gholson, Hicks and Nichols, Columbus, Miss., 1973-86, Heidelberg, Woodliff & Franks, Jackson, Miss., 1986-90, Ott, Purdy & Scott, Jackson, 1991—. Mem. editorial bd. Mag. Barrister, 1979-83, editor, 1981-83. Pres. Lowndes County Heart Assn., Columbus, 1981, Columbus Civic Arts Coun., 1984; v.p. Lowndes County Red Cross, Columbus, 1982; mem. Miss. Art Commn., Jackson, 1983—, chmn., 1985-88; mem. Leadership Jackson, 1990. Mem. Miss. Bar Assn. (young lawyers sect., sec. 1981, pres. 1984), ABA (young lawyers div. exec. coun. coord. 1983, budget dir. 1984, coun. mem. litigation sect. 1985-87, pres. fellows Miss. young lawyers sect. 1992), Golden Triangle Young Lawyers (pres. 1982), Am. Judicature Soc. (bd., dirs. 1984), Nat. Assn. Bond Lawyers, Miss. State Bar Assn. (chmn. ethics com. 1981, bd. bar commrs. 1985, 2d v.p. 1986), Omicron Delta Kappa, Phi Delta Phi. Banking, Bankruptcy, Municipal (including bonds). Home: 300 Sherborne Pl Flowood MS 39208-8959 Office: Ott Purdy & Scott PO Box 1079 Jackson MS 39215-1079

EDELMAN, ALAN IRWIN, lawyer; b. Poughkeepsie, N.Y., June 14, 1958; s. Edwyn Herman and Shirley Frances (Kandel) E.; m. Erica Joy Schwartz, Aug. 16, 1981; children: Leah Hanit, Avram Natan, Samuel Aaron. BA, Cornell U., 1980; JD, Boston U., 1983. Bar: D.C. 1983, U.S. Dist. Ct. D.C. 1985, U.S. Supreme Ct. 1991. Atty. enforcement div. SEC, Washington, 1983-86, atty. Office of Gen. Counsel, 1986-87; counsel U.S. Senate Permanent Subcom. on Investigations, 1987-97, U.S. Senate Com. on Govtl. Affairs, 1997-99; trial atty. divsn. enforcement Commodity Futures Trading Commn., Washington, 1999—. Edward F. Hennessy scholar Boston U., 1983. Mem. ABA, Fed. Bar Assn. Office: Commodity Futures Trading Commn Three Lafayette Centre 1155 21st St NW Washington DC 20581-0001

EDELMAN, PAUL STERLING, lawyer; b. Bklyn., Jan. 2, 1926; s. Joseph S. and Rose (Kaminsky) E.; m. Rosemary Jacobs, June 15, 1951; children: Peter, Jeffrey. AB, Harvard U., 1946, JD, 1950. Bar: N.Y. 1951, U.S. Dist. Ct. (so. and ea. dists.) N.Y. 1954, U.S. Ct. Appeals (2d cir.) 1965, U.S. Supreme Ct. 1967. Ptnr. Kreindler & Kreindler, N.Y.C., 1953-95, counsel, 1996—. Legal advisor Andrea Doria TV show, 1984, QE2 TV show, 1995; cons. Slave Ship TV Program, April, 2001. Author: Maritime Injury and Death, 1960; editor: Maritime Law Reporter, 1987-99, Marine Laws, 1993, 94; columnist N.Y. Law Jour. With U.S. Army, 1944-46. Fellow N.Y. Bar Found.; mem. ABA (past chmn. admiralty com., toxic and hazardous substances litigation com., mem. long range planning com. 1982-84, mem. TIPS coun. 1984-88, Soviet-Am. lawyers conf. Moscow 1987, 94, TIPS lawyer conf. Russia 1993), ATLA (past chmn. admiralty coms.), Maritime Law Assn. (rep. to law of the sea seminar Moscow 1994), N.Y. State Bar Assn. (INCL award 1980, 90, 93, chmn. INCL sect. 1982-83, editor Ins. Jour. 1973—), Maritime Law Assn., World Peace Through Law Ctr., Hudson Valley Tennis Club, Hastings on Hudson (past chmn., planning bd.). Democrat. Jewish. Admiralty, Private international, Personal injury. Home: 57 Buena Vista Dr Hastings On Hudson NY 10706-1103 Office: 100 Park Ave New York NY 10017-5516 E-mail: pedelman@kreindler.com

EDEN, NATHAN E. lawyer; b. Key West, Fla., Mar. 24, 1944; s. Delmar M. and Lois (Archer) E.; m. Cindy Pike, Jan. 4, 1964 (div. Mar. 1984); 1 child, Jennifer S. BA, U. Fla., 1966; JD magna cum laude, Stetson U., 1969. Bar: Fla. 1969, U.S. Dist. Ct. (so. and mid. dists.) Fla. 1969, U.S. Ct. Appeals (5th cir.) 1969, U.S. Ct. Appeals (11th cir.) 1982. Assoc. Nelson, Stinnett, Surfus, et al, Sarasota, Fla., 1969; ptnr. Feldman & Eden & predecessors, Key West, 1970-84; sole practice, 1984-99; of counsel Lazzara and Paul, P.A., Tampa, 1982—; ptnr. Browning, Eden, Sireci & Klitenick, 1999—. Bd. atty. Utility Bd. of Key West, 1974—; asst. pub. defender State of Fla., Key West, 1970, county solicitor State of Fla., Key West, 1970-72; chief asst. state atty State of Fla., Key West, 1972-74; U.S. magistrate, U.S. Dist. Ct. (so. dist.) Fla., 1974-78. Mem. jud. nominating com. 16th Jud. Cir. State of Fla., 1995, bd. dirs. Hospice Monroe County, Hospice-VNA of Fla. Keys, 1998—. Mem. Acad. Trial Lawyers, Fla. Acad. Trial Lawyers, Nat. Assn. Criminal Def. Lawyers, Fla. Bar Assn. (bd. govs. 1976-80), North Am. Hunt Club, NRA. Democrat. Avocations: hunting, softball, jogging, basketball. Office: 402 Applerouth Ln Key West FL 33040-6535 also: Lazzara and Paul PA 606 E Madison St Ste 2001 Tampa FL 33602-4017

EDEN, ROBERT ELWOOD, lawyer; b. Freeport, Ill., Mar. 8, 1947; s. Bert Richard and Glades Kathryn (Randecker) E.; m. Kathryn Sue Martin, Aug. 7, 1976; children: Angela, Rebecca, Andrew. BA, Luther Coll., 1969; MA, U. Iowa, 1976, JD, 1979. Bar: Iowa 1979, Ill. 1979, U.S. Dist. Ct. (no. dist.) Ill. 1980. Tchr. Kee H.S., Lansing, Iowa, 1969-75; tchr. supr. U. Iowa, Iowa City, 1975-76; prin. Plager, Hasting & Krug, Freeport, Ill., 1979-83, dir., asst. sec., 1984-88; pvt. practice, 1989—. Mem. ATLA, Ill. Trial Lawyers Assn., Iowa State Bar Assn., Ill. State Bar Assn., Stephenson County Bar Assn. (sec. 1980-81, pres. 1995), Shannon C. of C., Lena Bus. & Profl. Club, Lions, Phi Delta Kappa. Lutheran. State civil litigation, Probate, Real property. Office: 722 Santa Fe Dr Freeport IL 61032-2924 also: 156 W Main St Lena IL 61048-7906 also: 106 E Market St Shannon IL 61078-9340

EDENFIELD, BERRY AVANT, federal judge; b. Bulloch County, Ga., Aug. 2, 1934; s. Perry and Vera E.; m. Vida Melvis Bryant, Aug. 3, 1963. B.B.A. U. Ga, 1956, LL.B., 1958. Bar: Ga. 1958. Partner firm Allen, Edenfield, Brown & Wright (and predecessors), Statesboro, Ga., 1958-78; judge U.S. Dist. Ct. (so. dist.) Ga., Savannah, 1978-90, chief judge, 1990-97, judge, 1997—. Mem. Ga. Senate, 1965-66. Office: US Dist Ct PO Box 9865 Savannah GA 31412-0065

EDGAR, R(OBERT) ALLAN, federal judge; b. Munising, Mich., Oct. 6, 1940; s. Robert Richard and Jean Lillian (Hansen) E.; m. Frances Gail Martin, Mar. 30, 1968; children: Amy Elizabeth, Laura Anne. BA, Davidson Coll., 1962; LLB, Duke U., 1965. Bar: Tenn. 1965. From assoc. to ptnr. Miller & Martin, Chattanooga, 1967-85; judge U.S. Dist. Ct. (ea. dist.) Tenn., 1985—. Mem. com. ct. adminstrn. and case mgmt. Jud. Conf. of the U.S. Mem. Tenn. Ho. of Reps., Nashville, 1970-72, Tenn. Wildlife Resources Commn., Nashville, 1979-85. Served to capt. U.S. Army, 1966-67, Vietnam. Decorated Bronze Star, 1967. Mem. Fed. Bar Assn., Chattanooga Bar Assn. Episcopalian. Office: US Dist Ct PO Box 1748 960 Georgia Ave Chattanooga TN 37402-2220

EDGE, J(ULIAN) DEXTER, JR. lawyer; b. Newport News, Va., June 7, 1942; s. Julian Dexter and Mildred (Castellow) E.; m. Carol Kinsley Browning, May 30, 1964; children— Julian Dexter III, Kinsley, Richard. B.S.I.M., Ga. Inst. Tech., 1964; J.D., Emory U., 1973; M.B.A., Ga. State U., 1977. Bar: Ga. 1973, D.C. 1977. Assoc., Henkel & Lamon, Atlanta, 1973-77, ptnr., 1977-81; ptnr. Henkel, Hackett, Edge, & Fleming, Atlanta, 1981-85, Troutman Sanders, Atlanta, 1985—, lectr. to bus., profl. meetings. Mng. editor Emory Law Jour., 1972-73. Co-chmn. DeKalb County Govt. Study Com., Ga., 1977; mem. DeKalb County Govt. Reorgn. Commn., 1979; chmn. DeKalb County Select Com. on Property Appraisals, 1982; mem. Ga. Republican Exec. Com., 1977-79; Ga. Rep. fin. chmn., 1977-79; treas. Bob Bell for Gov. Ga., 1981-82; Ga. Rep. counsel for Fourth Dist., 1981-86; mem. Mattingly Fin. Com., 1983-86; mem. adv. bd. DeKalb Community Coll., 1982-88. Served to lt. USN, 1964-70; Vietnam. Decorated Air medal, Navy Commendation medal. Mem. State Bar Ga. (sect. taxation), D.C. Bar (div. taxation), ABA (sect. taxation), Atlanta Bar Assn., Decatur DeKalb Bar, Lawyers Club Atlanta, Nat. Assn. Bond Lawyers, Order of Coif, Omicron Delta Kappa. General corporate, Real property, Corporate taxation. Home: 1775 Redd Rd Alpharetta GA 30004-3146 Office: Troutman Sanders 600 Peachtree St NE Ste 5200 Atlanta GA 30308-2216

EDGELL, GEORGE PAUL, lawyer; b. Dallas, Mar. 9, 1937; s. George Paul and Sarah Elizabeth (McDonald) E.; m. Karin Jane Williams; 1 child, Scott Rickard. BS in Aero. Engring., U. Ill., 1960; JD, Georgetown U., 1967; MBA, Roosevelt U., 1983, BGS in Computer Sci., 1986. Bar: Va. 1967, D.C. 1968, Ill. 1980. Patent examiner U.S. Patent Office, Washington, 1963-65; assoc. Schuyler, Birch, McKie & Beckett, 1965-69, ptnr., 1969-80; group patent counsel Gould, Inc., Rolling Meadows, Ill., 1980-86, asst. chief patent counsel, 1986—88, chief patent counsel, 1988—89; of counsel Pillsbury Winthrop LLP, Washington, 1989-93, ptnr., 1994—. Vol. tutor Hopkins Ho., 1968-69; officer St. Stephens Dads Club, 1975-77. With USMC, 1960-63. Mem. ABA, D.C. Bar Assn., Ill. Bar Assn., Va. Bar Assn., Am. Intellectual Property Law Assn., Army Navy Country Club. Republican. Presbyterian. Intellectual property, Patent, Trademark and copyright. Home: 6275 Chaucer View Cir Alexandria VA 22304-3546 Office: Pillsbury Winthrop LLP 1600 Tysons Blvd Mc Lean VA 22102-4865 E-mail: gpedgell@pillsburywinthrop.com

EDH, STAFFAN, lawyer; b. Uppsala, Sweden, Dec. 16, 1959; s. Thorolf and Ulla Edh; m. Veronica Wingstedt, July 12, 1986; children; Rebecka, Mathilda. LLM, U. Uppsala, Sweden, 1986. Chief clk. dist. ct. Gothenburg Dist. Ct., Sweden, 1986-88; chmn. bd. Facit AB (publs.), Stockholm, 1997-98; bd. mem. Hamilton & Co., 1999—. With Swedish Mil., 1978-79. Mem. Bd. Mems. Acad. Western Sweden. General corporate, Mergers and acquisitions. Office: Hamilton & Co Lawfirm Stora Nygatan 33 S-411 08 Gothenburg Sweden Fax: 46 31 743 20 61. E-mail: staffan.edh@hamilton-adv.se

EDIN, CHARLES THOMAS, lawyer; b. Williston, N.D., Mar. 23, 1955; s. Charles Crane and A. Borgni (Skorpen) E.; children: Charles, Taylor Marie. BA summa cum laude, Concordia Coll., 1978; JD with honors, U.N.D., 1983. Bar: N.D. 1984, U.S. Dist. Ct. N.D. 1984, U.S. Ct. Appeals (8th cir.) 1984. With Landman Westex Petroleum Corp., Bismarck, N.D., 1980-82; ptnr. Zuger Kirmis & Smith, 1984-94; pvt. practice, 1995—; spl. asst. atty. gen. State of N.D., 1998—. Precinct committeman Rep. Party, Bismarck, 1990. Burtness scholar U. N.D., 1983. Mem. N.D. Bar Assn. (mineral title stds. com. real property sect.), Burleigh County Bar Assn., Rocky Mountain Mineral Law Found. (N.D. case law reporter Mineral Law Newsletter 1988-96). Lutheran. General civil litigation, Insurance, Real property. Office: PO Box 2391 Bismarck ND 58502-2391

EDLES, GARY JOEL, lawyer; b. N.Y.C., Feb. 27, 1941; s. Allen Irving and Helen (Hurowitz) E.; m. Nadine Cohen, Feb. 15, 1973. BA, Queens Coll., 1962; JD, NYU, 1965; LLM, George Washington U., 1966, DJuridical Sci., 1975. Bar: N.Y. 1966, U.S. Ct. Appeals (D.C. cir.) 1970. Staff atty. Civil Aeronautics Bd., Washington, 1967-75, assoc. gen. coun., 1975-77, dep. gen. coun., 1977-80; dir. office of procs. Interstate Commerce Commn., 1980-81; adminstrv. appeals judge Nuclear Regulatory Commn., 1981-87; gen. coun. Administrv. Conf. U.S., 1987-95; fellow Am. U., 1995—. Faculty Dept. Justice Legal Edn. Inst., 1982-97; vis. prof. U. Sheffield, Eng., 1994, U. Hull, Eng., 1997—. Co-author: Federal Regulatory Process, 2d edit., 1989; contbr. articles to profl. jours. Mem. ABA, Fed. Bar Assn. (chmn. administrv. law sect. (1989-91). Home: 10 Keldgate Beverley HU17 8HY England E-mail: G.J.Edles@law.hull.ac.uk, Gedles@wcl.american.edu

EDMONDS, ELIZABETH A. lawyer; b. Carlsbad, N.Mex., Dec. 17, 1945; d. Byron P. and Eugenia E. Edmonds BA, U. N.D., 1966; MA, U. Denver, 1967; JD, Am. U., 1973. Bar: Wash. 1974, D.C. 1988. Asst. city atty. City of Seattle, 1974-86; atty. advisor U.S. EPA, Washington, 1987-88; trial atty. U.S. Dept. Justice, 1988—. Pres., bd. dirs. Evergreen Legal Svcs., Washington, 1985-86. Sec., bd. dirs. Capitol Hill Housing Improvement Program, Seattle, 1984-86. Named 1st Citizen of Seattle, Mayor of Seattle, 1983; recipient Spl. Achievement award U.S. Dept. Justice, 1991, 97, Spl. Commendation, 1998. Mem. Wash. Bar (ct. rules com. 1982-86), Wash. Women Lawyers (co-pres. 1981). Office: US Dept Justice Environ Enforcement Sect PO Box 7611 Washington DC 20044-7611 E-mail: elizabeth.edmonds@usdoj.gov

EDMONDS, THOMAS ANDREW, legal association administrator; b. Jackson, Miss., July 5, 1938; B.A., Miss. Coll., 1962; LL.B., Duke U., 1965. Bar: Fla. 1965, Va. 1981. Pvt. practice law, Orlando, Fla., 1965-66; assoc. prof. law U. Miss., Oxford, 1966-70; assoc. prof.law Fla. State U., Tallahassee, 1970-74, prof., 1974-77; dean Sch. Law, U. Richmond (Va.), 1977-87, U. Miss. Sch. Law, University, 1987-89; exec. dir. Va. State Bar, Richmond, 1989—. Vis. assoc. prof. Duke U., 1968-69; vis. prof. McGeorge Sch. Law of the Univ. of the Pacific, 1975-76. Served with USMC, 1957-60. Office: VA State Bar 707 E Main St Ste 1500 Richmond VA 23219-2800

EDMONDS, THOMAS LEON, lawyer, management consultant; b. Borger, Tex., May 10, 1932; s. Cline Azel and Flora (Love) E.; m. Virginia Marguerite Leon, June 20, 1960; 1 child, Stephanie Lynn. BSChemE, Tex. Tech. U., 1953, JD, 1973. Bar: Tex. 1974, U.S. Tax Ct. 1975, U.S. Ct. Appeals (5th cir.) 1975, U.S. Dist. Ct. (no. dist.) Tex. 1976, U.S. Supreme Ct. 1996; registered profl. engr., Tex. Engr. computers-exec. dept. Phillips Petroleum, Bartlesville, Okla., 1953-67; mktg. specialist Control Data, Dallas, 1967-68; exec. v.p. CUI, Austin, Tex., 1968-70; mgmt. cons. Mcauto, St. Louis, 1970-71; sr. ptnr. Edmonds & Assocs., Borger, 1973—. City atty. City of Borger, 1991—; treas., dir. Ram Biochems., Inc. Mem. chancellor's coun. Tex. Tech. U.; bd. dirs. Can. River Mcpl. Water Authority, Hutchinson County Tex. Hist. Commn., chmn. 1992-00. Mem. 5th Cir. Bar Assn. (charter), Borger Bar Assn. (pres. 1998—). Oil, gas, and mineral, Estate planning, Intellectual property. Home: 210 Broadmoor St Borger TX 79007-8210 Office: PO Box 985 Borger TX 79008-0985

EDMONDSON, FRANK KELLEY, lawyer, legal administrator; b. Newport, R.I., Aug. 27, 1936; s. Frank Kelley Sr. and Margaret (Russell) E.; m. Christiane Semirot, Mar. 5, 1959 (div. Sept. 1969); children: Mylene Anne, Yvonne Marie, Catherine May; m. Elaine Sueko Kaneshiro, Aug. 17, 1970 (div. June 1992); m. Karen Louise Bishop, Feb. 27, 1993 (div. Feb. 1996). BBA, Ind. U., 1958; MBA, So. Ill. U., 1978; JD, U. Puget Sound, 1982. Bar: Wash. 1982, U.S. Dist. Ct. (we. dist.) Wash. 1983. Commd. 2d lt. USAF, 1959, advanced through grades to maj., 1969, ret., 1979; contracts specialist Wash. State Lottery, Olympia, 1982-85, asst. contracts adminstr., 1985-87; contracts officer 1989 Washington Centennial Commn., 1987-90; fin. svc. officer Office of the Adminstr. for the Cts., 1990-92; contracts officer, office of adminstr. for the cts. State of Wash. Supreme Ct., Olympia, 1992-99. Mem. Seattle U. Sch. Law, Law Alumni Soc. Nat. Coun., 1997—, scholarship com. Wash. State Employees Credit Union, 1995-2001. Bd. dirs. Friends of Chambers Creek, Tacoma, 1981-90; mem. pro bono panel Puget Sound Legal Assistance Found., Olympia, 1985-90; mock trial program com. Youth and Govt. YMCA, 1994-96. Mem. Wash. State Bar Assn. (spl. dist. counsel 1993-95), Thurston County Bar Assn., Govt. Lawyers Bar Assn. (sec. 1985-86, 1st v.p. 1986-87, pres. 1987-89, liaison to Wash. State Bar Assn. 1989-93), Beta Gamma Sigma, Coll. Club. Home: 6600 Miner Dr SW Tumwater WA 98512-7282 E-mail: fkedmon@aol.com

EDMONDSON, JAMES LARRY, federal judge; b. Jasper, Ga., July 14, 1947; s. James George and Betty Ruth (Holcomb) E.; m. Eugenia Dettelbach (div. 1992); children: Kelley Eugenia, Alexandra Lisa. BA, Emory U., 1968; JD, U. Ga., 1971; LLM in Jud. Process, U. Va., 1989. Bar: Ga. 1971. Law clk. to dist. judge U.S. Dist. Ct. (no. dist.) Ga., Gainesville, 1971-73; instr. in trial practice U. Ga. Sch. Law, Athens, 1975-84; assoc. Webb, Fowler, Tanner & Edmondson, Lawrenceville, Ga., 1973-76, ptnr., 1976-81; mem. firm Tennant, Davidson & Edmondson, P.C., 1982-86; judge U.S. Ct. Appeals (11th cir.), Atlanta, 1986—. Instr. U. Ga. Sch. Law, 1975-84. Contbr. articles to legal jours. Trustee Inst. Continuing Legal Edn., 1980-84. Mem. State Bar Ga. (bd. govs. 1982-86), Gwinnett County Bar Assn. (pres. 1980-81), Fellows Ga. Bar Found. (charter), Old War Horse Lawyers Club, Order of Barristers, Pi Sigma Alpha. Episcopalian. Office: US Ct Appeals 11th Circuit 56 Forsyth St NW Atlanta GA 30303-2205*

EDMONDSON, WILLIAM ANDREW, state attorney general; b. Washington, D.C., Oct. 12, 1946; m. Linda Larason; children: Mary Elizabeth, Robert Andrew. BA in Speech Edn., Northeastern State U., Tahlequah, Okla., 1968; JD, U. Tulsa, 1978. Mem. Okla. Legislature, 1974-76; intern Office Dist. Atty., Muskogee, Okla., 1978—, asst. dist. atty., 1979, chief prosecutor, 1982—, dist. attorney, 1982-92; pvt. practice atty., 1979-82, Green & Edmondson, 1992-94; atty. gen. State of Okla., 1994—. With U.S. Navy, 1968-72. Named Outstanding Dist. Atty., State of Okla., 1985. Mem. Okla. Bar Assn., Okla. Dist. Attys. Assn. (pres. 1983-85). Office: Office Atty Gen 2300 N Lincoln Blvd Rm 112 Oklahoma City OK 73105-4894

EDMUNDS, NANCY GARLOCK, federal judge; b. Detroit, July 10, 1947; m. William C. Edmunds, 1977. BA cum laude, Cornell U., 1969; MA in Teaching, U. Chgo., 1971; JD summa cum laude, Wayne U., 1976. Bar: Mich. 1976. With Plymouth Canton Public Schools, 1971-73; law clk. Barris, Sott, Denn & Driker, 1973-75; law clk. to Hon. Ralph Freeman U.S. Dist. Ct. (ea. dist.) Mich., 1976-78; with Dykema Gossett, Detroit, 1978-84, ptnr. litigation sect., 1984-92; apptd. judge U.S. Dist. Ct. (ea. dist.) Mich., 1992—. Commr. 21st Century Comm. on Cts., 1990; mem. faculty, bd. mem. Fed. Advocacy Inst., 1983-91. Editor in chief Wayne Law Review. Mem. com. of visitors Wayne Law Sch., Detroit; mem. com. on defender svcs. Nat. Jud. Conf.; mem. Nat. Coun. Jewish Women; bd. gov.'s Cranbrook Schs.; bd. dirs. Mich. Mems. of Stratford Festival; bd. trustees Stratford Shakespearean Festival of Am., Temple Beth El, 1990-97, Hist.

Soc. U.S. Dist. Ct. (ea. dist.) Mich., 1993-98. Mem. ABA, Fed. Bar Assn. (exec. bd. dirs. 1989-92), Am. Judicature Soc., Fed. Judges Assn., State Bar Mich. (chair U.S. cts. com. 1990-91). Avocations: skiing, reading. Office: US Dist Ct US Courthouse #211 231 W Lafayette Blvd Detroit MI 48226-2700 E-mail: khillebrand@ckb.uscourts.gov

EDMUNDS, ROBERT H., JR. judge; Student, Williams Coll., Williamstown, Mass., 1967—69; BA in English, Vassar Coll., 1971; JD, U. N.C., Chapel Hill, 1975. Bar: NC 1975, Va. 1977. Asst. dist. atty. 18th Judicial Dist., Guilford County, NC, 1978—82; asst. U.S. atty. Mid. Dist. N.C. U.S. Dept. Justice, Asheville, 1982—86, U.S. atty. Mid. Dist. N.C., 1986—93; ptnr. Stern & Klepfer, 1993—98; assoc. judge N.C. Ct. Appeals, 1999—2001; assoc. justice N.C. Supreme Ct., 2001—. Contbr. articles to profl. jours. Office: PO Box 1841 Raleigh NC 27602*

EDWARDS, BLAINE DOUGLASS, lawyer; b. Borger, Tex., Sept. 30, 1961; s. Charles Afton and Harriett (Hauser) E.; m. Jill Summers Hendrickson. Sept. 1, 1984; children: Audrey Summers, Cole Douglass. BBA in Acctg. and Fin., Tex. A&M U., 1984; JD magna cum laude, St. Mary's U., 1990. Bar: Tex. 1990, U.S. Dist. Ct. (so., no., and ea. dists.) Tex. 1991, 96, U.S. Ct. Appeals (5th cir.) 1992. Oil and gas/real estate lending officer InterFirst Bank, San Antonio, 1984-87; participating assoc. Fulbright & Jaworski, LLP, Houston, 1990-95; ptnr. Shook, Hardy & Bacon, LLP, 1995—. Adj. prof. law South Tex. Coll. of Law Tex. A&M U., Houston. Co-author: Texas Environmental Law Handbook, 1990, 92; editor St. Mary's Law Jour., 1989-90; contbr. articles to profl. jours. Mem. Phi Delta Phi. Avocations: reading, snow skiing, golfing. General civil litigation, Environmental, Toxic tort. Office: Shook Hardy & Bacon Ste 1600 600 Travis St Houston TX 77002

EDWARDS, DANIEL WALDEN, lawyer; b. Vancouver, Wash., Aug. 7, 1950; s. Chester W. Edwards and Marilyn E. Russell; m. Joan S. Heller, Oct. 18, 1987; children: Nathaniel, Matthew, Stephen, Alexander. BA in Psychology magna cum laude, Met. State Coll., Denver, 1973, BA in Philosophy, 1974; JD, U. Colo., 1976. Bar: Colo. 1977, U.S. Dist. Ct. Colo. 1977. Dep. pub. defender State of Colo., Denver, 1977-79, Littleton, 1979-81, Pueblo, 1981-86, head office pub. defender Brighton, 1987-89, mem. jud. faculty, 1988-91; sole practitioner Denver, 1991-93; magistrate Denver Juvenile Ct., 1993-99; sole practice law Denver, 1999—. Instr. sch. of law U. Denver, 1988-91, adj. prof., 1991—, coach appellate advocacy team, 1991-99; adv. coun. Colo. Legal Svcs., 1989—; adj. mem. Colo. Supreme Ct. Grievance Com., 1991-95. Author: Basic Trial Practice: An Introduction to Persuasive Trial Techniques, 1995, Principles of Persuasion: Basic Appellate Advocacy Techniques, 1999. Mem. visual arts com. City Arts III, 1989-90, com. chmn., mem. adv. coun., 1991; bd. dirs. Metropolitan State Coll., Alumni Assn., 1991-92; vol. lectr. CSE Thursday Night Bar Pro Se Divorce Clinic, 1991-95. Named Pub. Defender of Yr. Colo. State Pub. Defender's Office, 1985, Outstanding Colo. Criminal Def. Atty., 1989. Mem. ABA, Assn. Trial Lawyers Am., Colo. Bar Assn., Adams County Bar Assn., Denver Bar Assn., Met. State Coll. Alumni Assn. (bd. dirs. 1991-94). Home: 2335 Clermont St Denver CO 80207-3134 Office: 1733 High St Denver CO 80218-1320 E-mail: edwards_dan_atty@msn.com

EDWARDS, HARRY LAFOY, lawyer; b. Greenville, S.C., July 29, 1936; s. George Belton and Mary Olive (Jones) E.; m. Suzanne Copeland, June 16, 1956; 1 child, Margaret Peden. LLB, U. S.C., 1963, JD, 1970. Bar: S.C. 1963, U.S. dist. Ct. S.C. 1975, U.S. Ct. Apls. (4th cir.) 1974. Assoc. Edwards and Edmunds, Greenville, 1963; v.p., sec., dir. Edwards Co., Inc., 1963-65; atty. investment legal dept. Liberty Life Ins. Co., 1965-67, asst. sec., asst. v.p., head investment legal dept., 1967-70; asst. sec. Liberty Corp., 1970-75; asst. v.p. Liberty Life Ins. Co., 1970-75; sec. Bent Tree Corp., CEL, Inc., 1970-75; sec., dir. Westchester Mall, Inc., 1970-75; asst. sect. Libco, Inc., Liberty Properties, Inc., 1970-75; pvt. practice, Greenville, 1975—. Editor U. S.C. Law Rev., 1963. Com. mem. Hipp Fund Spl. Edn., Greenville County Sch. System; mem. Boyd C. Hipp II Scholarship Com., Wofford Coll. Spartanburg, S.C.; mem. scholarship com. Liberty Scholars, U. S.C., 1984, 86-2001. With USAFR, 1957-63. Mem. ABA, S.C. Bar Assn., Greenville County Bar Assn., Phi Delta Phi, Greenville Lawyers, Poinsett Club (Greenville). Baptist. General corporate, Estate planning, Real property. Home: 106 Ridgeland Dr Greenville SC 29601-3017 Office: PO Box 10350 Greenville SC 29603-0350 E-mail: hle106@aol.com

EDWARDS, HARRY T. federal judge; b. N.Y.C., Nov. 3, 1940; s. George H. E. and Arline (Ross) Lyle; m. Pamela Carrington; children: Brent, Michelle. BS, Cornell U., 1962; JD, U. Mich., 1965. Assoc. firm Seyfarth, Shaw, Fairweather & Geraldson, Chgo., 1965-70; prof. law U. Mich., 1970—75; vis. prof. law Harvard U., 1975-76, prof., 1976-77; now judge U.S. Ct. Appeals, Washington, 1980—; vis. prof. Free U. Brussels, 1974; dir. AMTRAK, 1977-80, chmn. bd., 1979-80; disting. lectr. law Duke U., 1983-89; lectr. law Georgetown Law Ctr., 1985—86; chief judge U.S. Ct. Appeals (D.C. cir.), Washington, 1994-2001; prof. law U. Mich., 1977—80. Adj. prof. law NYU Law Sch., 1989—; lectr. Harvard Law Sch., 1982—88, Mich. Law Sch., 1988—89; mem. Adminstrv. Conf. of U.S., 1976—80. Co-author: Labor Relations Law in the Public Sector, 1974, 79, 85, Lawyer as a Negotiator, 1977, Collective Bargaining and Labor Arbitration, 1979, Higher Education and the Law, 1979. Mem. Nat. Acad. Arbitrators (dir. 1975-80, v.p. 1978-80), Am. Acad. Arts and Scis., Am. Arbitration Assn. (dir. 1979-80), Am. Bar Assn. (sec. sect. labor law 1976-77), Am. Law Inst., Order of Coif. Office: US Ct Appeals 333 Constitution Ave NW Washington DC 20001-2866

EDWARDS, JAMES ALFRED, lawyer; b. Orlando, Fla., Feb. 18, 1954; BA in Psychology with high honors, Auburn U., 1976; JD with high honors, U. Fla., 1979. Bar: Fla. 1979, U.S. Dist. Ct. (no. dist.) Fla. 1979, U.S. Dist. Ct. (mid. and so. dists.) Fla. 1981, U.S. Ct. Appeals (5th cir.) 1979, U.S. Ct. Appeals (11th cir.) 1982, U.S. Supreme Ct. 1984; bd. cert. civil trial lawyer Fla. Bar Assn. Ptnr. Rumberger, Kirk & Caldwell, Orlando, Fla., 1979-89, Roth, Edwards & Smith, P.A., Orlando, 1989-2000, Cabaniss, Conroy & McDonald, LLP, Orlando, 2000, Law Office James A. Edwards, PA, Maitland, Fla., 2001—. Sustaining mem. Product Liability Adv. Coun., Detroit, 1989—. Mem. Fla. Bar Assn. (cert. civil trial lawyer, mem. trial lawyers, appellate practice sects., equal opportunity law sector), Orange County Bar Assn. (mem. professonalism com.). Avocations: fishing, water skiing, snow skiing. Federal civil litigation, State civil litigation, Product liability. Office: 100 E Sybelia Ave # 375 Maitland FL 32751 Fax: 407-647-9735. E-mail: JEdwards@bigfishlaw.com

EDWARDS, JAMES EDWIN, lawyer; b. Clarkesville, Ga., July 29, 1914; s. Gus Calloway and Mary Clara (McKinney) E.; m. Frances Lillian Stanley, Nov. 22, 1948; children: Robin Anne Edwards Kahler, James Christopher, Clare Edwards Weber. Student, U. Tex., 1931-33; BA, George Washington U., 1935, JD cum laude, 1946. Bar: Fla. 1938, Va. 1987. Practice law, Cocoa, Fla., 1938-42; hearing and exam. officer USCG, 1943-45; divsn. asst. State Dept., Washington, 1945-50; practice law Ft. Lauderdale, Fla., 1951-55, 59-77; mem. firm Bell, Edwards, Cocker, Carlon & Amsden, 1956-59; sole practice Coral Springs, Fla., 1977-81, 84-85; asst. city atty. Ft. Lauderdale, 1961, 63-65; mem. firm Edwards & Leary, Coral Springs, 1981-84; mem. panel Am. Arbitration Assn., 1984—; sole practice Albemarle County, Va., 1987-88, Charlottesville, 1988—. Author: Myths About Guns, 1978. Commr., Coral Springs, 1970-76, mayor, 1972-74; mem. bd. suprs. Sunshine Water Mgmt. Dist., 1976-80; chmn. Ft. Lauderdale for Eisenhower, 1952; pres. Fla. Conservative Union, Broward County, 1976. Lt. USCGR, 1943-45, lt. col. JAG, USAFR, 1950-68. Recipient 50 Yr. award Fla. Bar, 1988. Mem. SAR, English Speaking Union Club (Charlottesville), The Ret. Officers Assn., Air Force Assn., Rotary. Estate planning, Probate, Estate taxation. Office: Commonwealth Ctr 300 Preston Ave Ste 312 Charlottesville VA 22902-5044

EDWARDS, JAMES MALONE, lawyer; b. Champaign, Ill., Aug. 15, 1931; s. Harold Mortimer and Marion Bell (Scarlett) E.; m. Veronica Marianne Greeven, Mar. 2, 1968; children: Nina Scarlett, Philip Mortimer. BA, U. Ill., 1953; postgrad., Inst. des Sci. Politiques, 1955; LLB, Yale U., 1960. Bar: N.Y. 1961. Law clk. to justice Charles E. Whittaker U.S. Supreme Ct., Washington, 1960-61; assoc. Cravath, Swaine & Moore, N.Y.C., 1961-69, ptnr., 1969—. 1st lt. USAF, 1955-56. General corporate, Private international, Mergers and acquisitions. Office: Cravath Swaine & Moore 721 Darby St Raleigh NC 27610-4015

EDWARDS, JAMES RICHARD, lawyer; b. Long Beach, Calif., Apr. 14, 1951; s. Nelson James and Dorotny June (Harris) E.; m. Joan Marie Carriveau, Sept. 24, 1988. BS, Colo. State U., 1973; JD, U. San Diego, 1977. Bar: Calif. 1977, U.S. Dist. Ct. (so. dist.) Calif. 1977, U.S. Dist. Ct. (cen. dist.) Calif. 1978. Atty. Downtown Sr. Ctr., San Diego, 1977-78, Getty Oil Co., L.A., 1978-80, Logicon Inc., Torrance, Calif., 1980-85, sec., 1982-85, gen. counsel, 1981-85; ptnr. Mirassou, Nyznyk & Edwards, 1985-87; v.p., gen. counsel, sec. Gen. Atomics, San Diego, 1987-2000, Vapotronics Inc., 2000—. Lawyer; b. Long Beach, Calif., Apr. 14, 1951; s. Nelson James and Dorothy June (Harris) E.; m. Joan Marie Carriveau, Sept. 24, 1988, BS, Colo. State U., 1973; JD, U. San Diego, 1977. Bar: Calif. 1977, U.S. Dist. Ct. (so. dist.) Calif., 1977, U.S. Dist. Ct. (cen. dist.) 1978. Atty., Downtown Sr. Ctr., San Diego, 1977-78, Getty Oil Co., Los Angeles, 1978-80; atty. Logicon, Inc., Torrance, Calif., 1980-85, sec., 1982-85, gen. counsel, 1981-85; ptnr. Mirassou, Nyznyk & Edwards, 1985-87; v.p., gen. counsel, sec. Gen. Atomics, San Diego, 1987—. Recipient championship medals U.S. Parachute Assn., 1977, 79, 80. Mem. ABA, State Bar Calif., San Diego County Bar Assn., Am. Corp. Counsel Assn. Recipient championship medals U.S. parachute Assn., 1977, 79, 80. Mem. ABA, State Bar Calif., San Diego County Bar Assn., Am. Corp. Counsel Assn. General corporate, Private international, Mergers and acquisitions. Office: Vapotronics Inc 12555 High Bluff Dr Ste 330 San Diego CA 92130

EDWARDS, JOHN DUNCAN, law educator, librarian; b. Louisiana, Mo., Sept. 15, 1953; s. Harold Wenkle and Mary Elizabeth (Duncan) E.; m. Beth Ann Rahm, May 21, 1977; children: Craig, Martha, Brooks. BA, Southeast Mo. State U., 1975; JD, U. Mo., Kansas City, 1977; MALS, U. Mo., Columbia, 1979. Bar: Mo. 1978, U.S. Dist. Ct. (we. dist.) Mo. 1978. Instr. legal research and writing U. Mo., Columbia, 1978, dir. legal research and writing, librarian, 1979-80; pub. svcs. librarian Law Sch., U. Okla., Norman, 1980-81, assoc. librarian, 1981-84, adj. instr. sch. library sci., 1983-84; prof. law, dir. law library law sch. Drake U., Des Moines, 1984—. Adj. instr. Columbia Coll., 1979-80; cons. Cleveland County Bar Assn., 1984. Contbr. articles to profl. jours. Cons. Friends Drake U. Libr., 1985—; coach, mgr. Westminster Softball Team. Des Moines, 1987-94; pres. Crestview Parent-Tchr. Coun., Des Moines, 1988-90; trustee Westminster Presbyn. Ch., Des Moines, 1988-89, treas., 1990, pres., 1991; mem. Clive City Coun., 1995—, mayor pro tem, 1998—; trustee Des Moines Metro Transit Authority, 1996—, chmn. bd. dirs., 1997-98, sec.-treas., 1996, 2001. Recipient Presdl. award Drake U. Student Bar Assn., 1987; named Outstanding Vol., Crestview Elem. Sch., 1989-90. Mem. Am. Assn. Law Librs. (chmn. awards com. 1987-88, chmn. grants com. 1996-97, chmn. scholarship com. 1998-99), Mid-Am. Assn. Law Librs. (chmn. resource sharing 1986-93, v.p. 1994-95, pres. 1995-96), Mid-Am. Law Sch. Librs. Consortium (pres. 1986-88), Delta Theta Phi, Beta Phi Mu. Avocations: softball, tennis. Office: Drake U Libr Law Sch 27th & Carpenter Sts Des Moines IA 50311

EDWARDS, MARGARET A. lawyer; b. Lake Charles, La., Aug. 24, 1951; d. John and Catherine V. Edwards; m. Elisha A. Wattly, Sept. 1977 (div. May 1986). BA in Govt., BA in Liberal Arts, McNeese State U., 1991; JD cum laude, Southern U., 1995; LLB in Taxation, So. Meth. U., 1996. Bar: La. Sole practice, Lake Charles, La., 1997—. Instr. tax paralegal McNeese State U., Lake Charles, 1998—; ct. apptd. spl. advocate CASA, Lake Charles, 1998. Bd. dirs. YMCA, Lake Charles, 1998; mem. adv. bd. dirs., corp. atty. Home Health 2000, Lake Charles, 1997—; religion instr. St. Henry Cath. Ch., Lake Charles, 1997. Recipient Lady of Yr. award, Profl. Lawyer of Yr., Negro Bus. and Profl. Women, 1998. Mem. ABA, La. Trial Lawyers Assn., La. Bar Assn., S.W. Bar Assn. Avocations: reading, writing articles, bowling. General practice. Home: 2014 Winterhalter St Lake Charles LA 70601 Office: 830 Moss St Lake Charles LA 70601

EDWARDS, NINIAN MURRY, judge; b. St. Louis, Jan. 11, 1922; s. N. Murry and Mabel E. (Dailey) E.; m. Mary Catherine McKeown, May 12, 1944; children: Katherine S. Edwards Burckhalter, Barbara Edwards Perkins. JD, U. Mo., 1947. Trial lawyer, St. Louis area, 1947-65; cir. judge St. Louis County, Clayton, Mo., 1965-66, 70-88, sr. judge, arbitrator, mediator, 1988—. Coun. mem. City of Kirkwood, Mo., atty., 1968-70. Maj. USAFR, 1950-69, ret. Mem. Mo. Bar Assn. (past bd. govs.), Bar Assn. Met. St. Louis, St. Louis County Bar Assn. (Disting. Svc. award 1970), Nat. Coun. Juvenile and Family Ct. Judges (bd. trustees, past sec., treas., v.p., pres. elect 1990, pres. 1991-92), Phi Delta Phi. Democrat.

EDWARDS, PRISCILLA ANN, paralegal, business owner; b. Orlando, Fla., Sept. 28, 1947; d. William Granville and Bernice Royster; m. Charles R. King, Apr. 2, 1981. Paralegal cert., U. Calif., Berkeley, 1994. Paralegal Charles R. Garry Esquire, San Francisco, 1989-90, Marvin Cahn Esquire, San Francisco, 1990-91; owner, mgr. Fed. Legal Resources, 1991—. Speaker Sonoma State U., Santa Rosa, Calif., 1993. Publisher: (book) Zero Weather, 1981. Recipient Wiley W. Manuel award for pro bono legal svcs. Bd. Govs. State Bar of Calif., 1994, 95, 96, 97, 98. Episcopalian. Avocations: horseback riding, mountain biking.

EDWARDS, RICHARD LANSING, lawyer; b. Wilmington, Del., Apr. 16, 1944; s. Robert Wilson Jr. and Eleanor (Inscho) E.; m. Betsey Ann Barney, Aug. 24, 1980; children: Beth, Melissa, Jeffrey, Jason, Karen. BS in Indsl. Engring., Lehigh U., 1966; JD, Northeastern U., 1980. Bar: Mass. 1980, U.S. Dist. Ct. Mass. 1981, U.S. Ct. Appeals (1st cir.) 1983, U.S. Supreme Ct. 1985, U.S. Dist. Ct. Conn. 1998. Lawyer Craig & Macauley, Boston, 1980-83; lawyer, shareholder Campbell, Campbell, Edwards & Conroy P.C., 1983—. Faculty Internat. Assn. Def. Counsel Trial Acad., 1994, ABA TIPS Nat. Trial Acad., 2000. Contbr. articles to profl. jours. Capt. USAF, 1966-70. Decorated Bronze star. Mem. ABA (tort and ins. practice and litigation sect. 1984—, faculty torts and ins. sect. Nat. Trial Acad. 2000), Mass. Bar Assn. (civil litigation sect. 1983—), Def. Rsch. Inst. (bd. dirs. 1999—, products liability com., chmn. 1997-99, chmn. duty to warn and labeling subcom. 1985-88, steering com. 1988—), Internat. Assn. of Def. Counsel (chmn. advocacy practice and procedure com. 1993-95, faculty Trial Acad. 1994), Mass. Def. Lawyers Assn., Product Liability Adv. Coun., Boston Bar Assn. Construction, Personal injury, Product liability. Office: Campbell Campbell Edwards & Conroy PC One Constitution Plaza Boston MA 02129 E-mail: redwards@campbell-trial-lawyers.com

EFFEL, LAURA, lawyer; b. Dallas, May 9, 1945; d. Louis E. and Fay (Lee) Ray; m. Marc J. Patterson, Sept. 19, 1992; 1 child, Stephen. BA, U. Calif., Berkeley, 1971; JD, U. Md., 1975. Bar: N.Y. 1976, U.S. Dist. Ct. (so. and ea. dists.) N.Y. 1976, U.S. Ct. Appeals (2d cir.) 1980, U.S. Supreme Ct. 1980, D.C. 1993, N.C. 1998, Va. 2001. Assoc. Burns Jackson Miller Summit & Jacoby, N.Y.C., 1975-78, Pincus Munzer Bizar & D'Alessandro, N.Y.C., 1978-80; v.p., sr. assoc. counsel Chase Manhattan Bank, N.A., 1980-96; counsel Baker & McKenzie, 1996-99; gen. counsel Garban Cos., 1999-2000; counsel Flippin Densmore Morse & Jessee, Roanoke, Va., 2000—. Bd. dirs. Bklyn. Legal Svcs. Corp. A. Treas. Workforce Devel. Com., New Century Tech. Coun.; bd. dirs. Bklyn. Legal Svcs. Corp. A, 1992-2000. Mem. ABA (litig. sect. co-chair, subcom. atty. client privilege, com. pretrial practive 2000-2001), Am. Corp. Counsel Assn. (dir. emeritus, pro bono svc. award 1989), Assn. of Bar of City of N.Y. (com. on lectures and continuing edn. 1991-96, com. on banking law 1997-99, com. on arbitration 1999-2000), N.C. Bar Assn., Va. Bar Assn., Roakoke Bar Assn. General civil litigation, Labor, Alternative dispute resolution. Office: Flippin Densmore Morse & Jessee Drawer 1200 Roanoke VA 24006 E-mail: effel@flippindensmore.com

EFROS, ELLEN ANN, lawyer; b. N.Y.C., Jan. 18, 1950; d. Edwin David and Judith (Breitman) E.; m. Fritz R. Kahn, June 26, 1983. BA, Case Western Res. U., 1971; MA, St. John's U., 1973; JD, Hofstra U., 1978. Bar: D.C. 1978, N.Y. 1979, Md. 1990, U.S. Ct. Appeals (5th cir.) 1978, U.S. Ct. Appeals (2d, 7th and D.C. cirs.) 1979, U.S. Ct. Appeals (Fed. cir.) 1993, U.S. Dist. Ct. D.C. 1981, U.S. Ct. Claims 1986, U.S. Supreme Ct. 1989. Trial atty. ICC Gen. Counsel, Washington, 1978-79; assoc. Verner & Liipfert, 1979-81; ptnr. Vorys, Sater, Seymour & Pease, 1981-97; hearing officer, office dispute resolution NASD Regulation, Inc., 1997-2000; ptnr. Rader, Fishman & Grauer, 2000—. Asst. editor Antitrust Law Jour., 1987-90. Mem. ABA (sects. intellectual property and litigation), D.C. Bar Assn., N.Y. Bar Assn., Md. Bar Assn. Federal civil litigation, General civil litigation, Intellectual property. Office: Rader Fishman & Grauer 1233 20th St NW Ste 501 Washington DC 20036-2365 E-mail: eae@raderfishman.com

EGAN, CHARLES JOSEPH, JR. lawyer, greeting card company executive; b. Cambridge, Mass., Aug. 11, 1932; s. Charles Joseph and Alice Claire (Ball) E.; m. Mary Bowersox, Aug. 6, 1955; children: Timothy, Sean, Peter, James. AB, Harvard U., 1954; LLB, Columbia U., 1959. Bar: N.Y. 1960, Mo. 1973. Assoc. Donovan, Leisure, Newton & Irvine, N.Y.C., 1959-62; ptnr. Hall, McNicol, Marett & Hamilton, 1962-68; v.p., gen. counsel Thomson & McKinnon Securities, 1969-70, Hallmark Cards, Inc., Kansas City, Mo., 1972—. Bd. dirs. Am. Multi Cinema, Inc., Kansas City, Mo. Trustee Notre Dame de Sion Sch., Kansas City, 1973-77, Pembroke Country Day Sch., Kansas City, 1976-82, Kansas City Art Inst., 1995—; bd. dirs. Kansas City YMCA, 1976-80; mem. dean's coun. Columbia Law Sch., 1991—; vice chmn. Harvard Coll. Fund, 1994-99, co-chmn., 2000—. Served to 1st lt. USMC, 1954-56. Mem. Mo. Bar Assn., Kansas City Lawyers Assn., Harvard Alumni Assn. (pres. 1989-90, exec. com. 1987—), Century Assn., Somerset Club, Harvard Club of N.Y., Harvard Club of Kansas City (pres. 1985-87). Roman Catholic. Antitrust, General corporate, Taxation, general. Office: Hallmark Cards Inc 2501 Mcgee St Kansas City MO 64108-2600

EGENOLF, ROBERT F. lawyer; b. San Francisco, Jan. 23, 1946; s. John D. and Virginia (Kirkland) Butler; m. Judy Wish, Jan. 23, 1970; children: Cristi Michelle, Jonah Wish. BA, U.S. Internat. U., San Diego, 1970; JD, Calif. Western U., San Diego, 1973; LLM, U. Miami, Fla., 1974. Bar: Calif. 1973, U.S. Tax Ct. 1974. Assoc. Blum & Blum, Oakland, Calif., 1974-75; ptnr. Westwick & Collison, Santa Barbara, 1976-80, Egenolf & Moore, Santa Barbara, 1980-94. Pres., founder Calif. Exchange Corp., Santa Barbara, 1984-90, Santa Barbara Exch. Corp., 1984-90, 97—, First Exch. Corp., Santa Barbara, 1988-90, Amherst Exch. Corp., Santa Barbara, 1989—; instr., lectr. Santa Barbara City Coll., 1987—; lectr. in real estate exch. seminars Lawyers Throughout the U.S., 1987—. Bd. dirs. Tri Counties Devel. Disabilities Bd., Santa Barbara, 1977-78, Child Abuse Listening Mediation, Santa Barbara, 1979-80, Ensemble Theatre Project, Santa Barbara, 1981-83, Santa Barbara City Coll. Theatre Group, 1983-84; trustee Laguna Blanca Sch., 1997—; dir. Am. Inst. Food and Wine, 1991-93, Santa Barbara Wine Auction, 1993-94, Semana Nautica Masters Volleyball Tournament, 1993-97; mem. polit. action com. Planned Parenthood, 1995; mem. fin. devel. steering com. Santa Barbara Contemporary Arts Forum, 1995-96. With USN, 1963-69. Mem. Calif. Bar Assn. (co-chair joint tax subsect. 1990-95), Santa Barbara Bar Assn. (bd. dirs. 1978, 95—, pres. 2000), Barristers Santa Barbara (pres. 1976-77). Avocations: pilot, volleyball, sailing. Estate planning, Real property, Taxation, general. Office: Egenolf Assocs LLP 130 E Carrillo St Santa Barbara CA 93101-2111 E-mail: egenolf@egenolf.com

EGGERT, RUSSELL RAYMOND, lawyer; b. Chgo., July 28, 1948; s. Ralph A. and Alice M. (Nischwitz) E.; m. Patricia Anne Alegre, 1998. AB, U. Ill., 1970, JD, 1973; postgrad., Hague Acad. Internat. Law, The Netherlands, 1972. Bar: Ill. 1973, U.S. Supreme Ct. 1979. Assoc. U. Ill., Champaign, 1973-74; asst. atty. gen. State of Ill., Chgo., 1974-79; assoc. O'Conor, Karaganis & Gail, 1979-83; legal counsel to Ill. atty. gen., 1983-87; ptnr. Mayer, Brown & Platt, 1987—. Contbr. articles to profl. jours. Mem. ABA. Democrat. Administrative and regulatory, General civil litigation, Environmental. Office: Mayer Brown & Platt 190 S La Salle St Ste 3100 Chicago IL 60603-3441 E-mail: reggert@mayerbrown.com

EGINTON, WARREN WILLIAM, federal judge; b. Bklyn., Feb. 16, 1924; AB, Princeton U., 1948; LLB, Yale U., 1951. Bar: N.Y. 1952, Conn. 1954. Assoc. Davis Polk & Wardwell, N.Y.C., 1951-53; ptnr. Cummings & Lockwood, Stamford, Conn., 1954-79; judge U.S. Dist. Ct., Bridgeport, 1979—. Editor-in-chief Products Liability Law Jour., 1988-93. Mem. ABA, Am. Judicature Soc., Am. Bar Found., Am. Law Inst., Conn. Bar Assn., Fed. Bar Coun., Fed. Bar Assn., Ins. Jud. Adminstrn., Jud. Leadership Devel. Coun., Internat. Jud. Acad., Fgn. Policy Assn. Office: US Dist Ct 915 Lafayette Blvd Ste 335 Bridgeport CT 06604-4765

EGLIT, HOWARD CHARLES, educator, lawyer, arbitrator; b. Chgo., Sept. 20, 1942; s. Nathan Norman and Grace (Wiener) E.; m. Barbara Weiner, July 1, 1973; children: Daniel, Michael, Susan. BA, U. Mich., 1963, JD, 1967. Bar: Ill. 1967, D.C. 1971, U.S. Dist. Ct. (no. dist.) Ill. 1973, U.S. Ct. Appeals (7th cir.) 1973, U.S. Supreme Ct. 1973. With office of gen. counsel U.S. Office Econ. Opportunity, Washington, 1968-69; legis. asst. rep. William F. Ryan, Washington, 1969-71; counsel Com. on Judiciary, U.S. Ho. of Reps., Washington, 1971-73; legal dir. ACLU, Chgo., 1973-75; prof. Ill. Inst. Tech./Chgo.-Kent Coll. Law, 1975—; dir. Nat. Conf. on Constl. and Legal Issues Relating to Age Discrimination, Chgo., 1981; adv. com. Buehler Ctr. on Aging, Mcgaw Sch. Medicine, Northwestern Univ., 1991—. Author: Age Discrimination, vols. 1-3, 1982, ann. supplements 1983—, 2d edit., 1994. Contbr. articles to profl. jours. Order of Coif, Phi Beta Kappa, Phi Kappa Phi. Office: Ill Inst Tech Chgo Kent Coll Law 565 W Adams St Chicago IL 60661-3613 E-mail: heglit@kentlaw.edu

EHLINGER, RALPH JEROME, lawyer; b. Oconto, Wis., Mar. 22, 1941; s. Jerome Nicholas and Margaret Ann (Otradovec) E.; m. Nancy L. McKinley, Dec. 26, 1966 (div. Oct. 1986); children: Nicholas Joseph, Martha Johanna; m. Mary Verstegen, Sept. 25, 1987; children: Autumn V., Andrea V., Jessa V., Jenna V. BA in Philosophy, St. Paul Sem., 1963; JD, Georgetown U., 1968. Bar: Wis. 1968, U.S. Dist. Ct. (ea. dist.) Wis. 1969, U.S. Dist. Ct. (we. dist.) Wis. 1977, U.S. Ct. Appeals (7th cir.) 1983, U.S. Supreme Ct. 1986, D.C. 1988, U.S. Ct. Appeals (4th cir.) 1988. Ptnr.

Meissner, Tierney, Ehlinger & Whipp, Milw., 1968-86; pvt. practice, 1986-87; counsel Casson, Harkins & LaPallo, Washington, 1987-88; pres. Ehlinger & Krill, SC, Milw., 1988-99, Ehlinger Law Office, Milw., 2000—; adj. prof. law Marquette U. Law Sch., 1999—. Dir. Milw. Bar Assn., 1990-93. Articles editor: The Georgetown Law Jour., 1967-68 (Outstanding Editor 1968); editor-in-chief: The Milwaukee Lawyer, 1982-84. Trustee Wis. Sch. Profl. Psychology, Milw., 1990-93; bd. pres. Grand Ave Club, Milw., 1990-92, Mental Health Assn., Milw., 1992-93; dir. Centro Legal Por Derechos Humanos, 1996-2001. Mem. Am. Judicature Soc., Milw. Bar Assn. Found. (pres. 1994-97), Nordic Ski Club (life), Milw. Bar Assn. (Lawyer of Yr. award 1997). Democrat. Roman Catholic. Avocations: instrumental and vocal music, cross-country skiing, backpacking, canoeing, poetry. General civil litigation, General corporate, Health. Office: Ehlinger Law Office W175 N 11117 Stonewood Dr Germantown WI 53022 E-mail: ehlinger@execpc.com

EHLKE, BRUCE FREDERIC, lawyer; b. Two Rivers, Wis., Aug. 31, 1942; s. Roland W. and Mary E. (Mueller) E.; m. Darlene Carol Erickson (div.); children— Stephen, Kara, Christopher; m. Jacqualine Caren Andersen, Aug. 20,. 1977; 1 son, John. BA, U. Wis.-Milw., 1965; JD, U. Wis., 1968. Bar: Wis. 1968, U.S. Dist. Ct. (we. dist.) Wis. 1968, U.S. Dist. Ct. (ea. dist.) Wis. 1971, U.S. Tax Ct. 1978, U.S. Ct. Appeals (7th cir.) 1971, U.S. Supreme Ct. 1979, U.S. Ct. Vets. Appeals 1993. With Wis. Local Affairs and Devel. Dept., Madison, 1968; shareholder Lawton & Cates S.C., Madison, 1968-94, Shneidman, Myers, Dowling, Blumfield, Ehlke, Hawks & Domer, Madison, 1995—. Mem. Wis. State Bar, Wis. Acad. Trial Lawyers, Dane County Bar Assn. (pres. 1995-96). Lutheran. Administrative and regulatory, Labor, Workers' compensation. Home: 605 Hilltop Dr Madison WI 53711-1358 Office: Shneidman Myers Dowling Blumfield Ehlke Hawkes & Domer PO Box 2155 Madison WI 53701-2155

EHMANN, ANTHONY VALENTINE, lawyer; b. Chgo., Sept. 5, 1935; s. Anthony E. and Frances (Verweil) E.; m. Alice A. Avina, Nov. 27, 1959; children: Ann, Thomas, Jerome, Gregory, Rose, Robert. BS, Ariz. State U., 1957; JD, U. Ariz., 1960. Bar: Ariz. 1960, U.S. Tax Ct. 1960, U.S. Supreme Ct. 1968; CPA, Ariz.; cert. tax specialist, trusts and estates specialist. Spl. asst. atty. gen., 1961-68; mem. Ehmann and Hiller, Phoenix, 1969—. Rep. dist. chmn. Ariz., 1964; pres. Grand Canyon coun. Boy Scouts Am., 1987-89, mem. exec. com., 1981—, v.p. western region, 1991-99; bd. dirs. Nat. Cath. Com. on Scouting, 1995—. Recipient Silver Beaver award Boy Scouts Am., 1982, Bronze Pelican award Cath. Com. on Scouting, 1981, Silver Antelope award Boy Scouts Am., 1994. Fellow Am. Coll. Trusts and Estate Counsel; mem. State Bar Ariz. (chmn. tax sect. 1968, 69), Ctrl. Ariz. Estate Planning Coun. (pres. 1968, 69), KC (grand knight Glendale, Ariz. 1964, 65), Serra Internat. (pres. Phoenix 1992-93, dist. gov. ariz. 1993-95), Knight of Holy Sepulchre, Knight of Malta, Legatus. Republican. Roman Catholic. Estate planning, Pension, profit-sharing, and employee benefits, Corporate taxation. Office: Ehmann & Hiller 2525 E Camelback Rd Ste 720 Phoenix AZ 85016-4229 E-mail: ehmann@ehpclaw.com

EHRENBARD, ROBERT, lawyer; b. N.Y.C., Aug. 20, 1925; m. Lila T. Ehrenbard, Apr. 17, 1949; children— Richard, Dan. LL.B. cum laude, Harvard U., 1951. Bar: N.Y. 1951, U.S. Dist. Ct. (so. dist.) N.Y. 1952, U.S. Ct. Appeals (2d cir.) 1952, U.S. Ct. Appeals (3d cir.) 1971, U.S. Ct. Appeals (7th cir.) 1976, U.S. Ct. Appeals (D.C. cir.) 1982, U.S. Ct. Appeals (11th cir.) 1982, U.S. Ct. Appeals (9th cir.) 1984, U.S. Supreme Ct. 1969. Law clk. U.S. Dist. Ct. (so. dist.) N.Y. 1951-53, U.S. Dist. Ct. (so. dist.) N.Y. 1954; sr. litigation ptnr. Kelley Drye & Warren, N.Y.C., 1961— . Author: Interrogatories And Document Requests, 1983. Served to lt. (j.g.) USN, 1943-46; PTO. Mem. Lawyer's Com. for Civil Rights Under Law, ABA, N.Y. State Bar Assn., Assn. Bar City N.Y. Federal civil litigation, State civil litigation, Private international. Home: 239 Central Park W New York NY 10024-6038 Office: Kelley Drye & Warren 101 Park Ave Fl 30 New York NY 10178-0062

EHRENWERTH, DAVID HARRY, lawyer; b. Pitts., Apr. 22, 1947; s. Ben and Beatrice Lee (Schwartz) E.; m. Judith B. Ehrenwerth; children: Justin Reid, Lindsey Royce. BA, U. Pitts., 1969; JD, Harvard U., 1972. Bar: Pa. 1972, U.S. Dist. Ct. (we. dist.) Pa. 1972, U.S. Ct. Appeals (3d cir.) 1976. Asst. atty. gen. Commonwealth of Pa., Pitts., 1972-74; assoc. Kirkpatrick & Lockhart, 1974-79, ptnr., 1979—. Pres. Pitts. chpt. Am. Jewish Com., 1988-90, nat. bd. govs., 1991-95, 2001—, chmn. Pitts. chpt., 1996-98; mem. nat. adv. coun. Fed. Nat. Mortgage Assn., 1984-85; bd. dirs. Pa. Bd. Vocat. Rehab., Harrisburg, 1983-88, United Jewish Fedn., Pitts., 1991-93, Presbyn. U. Hosp., Pitts., 1993-94, Riverview Ctr. for Jewish Srs., 1991-93, U. Pitts. Cancer Inst., 1995-99; mem. Am. Israel Pub. Affairs Com., 1995-99; bd. dirs. Montefiore Hosp., Pitts., 1985-93, treas., 1989, vice chmn., 1990-92, chmn., 1992-93; bd. govs. Pa. Econ. League, Western Region, 1999—. Recipient Human Rels. award Am. Jewish Com., 1999; named Pittsburgher to Watch Pitts. Mag., 1980. Mem. Pa. Bar Assn. (chmn. real estate fin. com. 1985-87), Allegheny County Bar Assn. (chmn. real property sect. 1989), Harvard U. Law Alumni Assn. Western Pa. (pres. 1986-87), Concordia Club, Westmoreland Country Club, Heinz Fifty-Seven Club (chmn. 1974-91), Duquesne Club, Phi Beta Kappa. Republican. Jewish. Avocations: tennis, golf. Finance, Real property, Securities. Home: 413 Windmere Dr Pittsburgh PA 15238-2440 Office: Kirkpatrick & Lockhart 1500 Oliver Building Bldg Pittsburgh PA 15222-2312 E-mail: dehrenwerth@kl.com

EHRLE, WILLIAM LAWRENCE, lawyer, association executive; b. Colorado City, Tex., Dec. 11, 1932; s. Frank Lawrence and Mary Elma (Hinds) E.; m. Sandra Faye Luckey, Aug. 3, 1963; children— Sharon Elaine, William Lawrence, Rhonda Kay. B.A., McMurry Coll., 1953; J.D., U. Tex., 1961. Bar: Tex. 1961. Asst. gen. counsel Lone Star Gas Co., Dallas, 1961-67; pres. Coaches Life Ins. Co., El Paso, Tex., 1967-70; sole practice, Austin, Tex., 1970-78; pres., gen. counsel Tex. Manufactured Housing Assn., Austin, 1978— ; dir. Nat. Manufactured Housing Fedn., Washington, 1978— ; mem. adv. council Fed. Nat. Mortgage Assn., Dallas, 1983-84. Mem. Tex. Ho. of Reps., 1957-63. Served as 1st lt. USMC, 1953-56. Office: Tex Manufactured Housing Assn PO Box 14428 Austin TX 78761-4428

EICHENBERGER, JERRY ALAN, lawyer; b. Columbus, Ohio, Apr. 16, 1947; m. Candace R. Roberson, Jan. 17, 1971; 1 child, Sara Marie. BS, Ohio State U., 1970; JD, Capital U., 1975. Bar: Ohio 1975, U.S. Supreme Ct. 1978, U.S. Dist. Ct. (no. and so. dists.) Ohio 175, U.S. Ct. Appeals (6th cir.) 1976. Ptnr. Martin & Eichenberger, Columbus, 1975-90, Crabbe, Brown, Jones, Potts & Schmidt, Columbus, 1990-2000, Eichenberger & Hoehn, Columbus, 2001—. Adj. prof. aviation law Ohio State U., Columbus, 1988-90. Author: General Aviation Law, 1990, 2d edit., 1998, Your Pilot's License, 1998, Cross Country Flying, 1996, Handling In-Flight Emergencies, 2001; contbr. articles to bus. and comml. aviation jours. Lt. col. CAP, chief check pilot 1980-84, legal officer, 1986-90. Named Ky. Col. Commonwelath Ky., 1972. Mem. ABA, Lawyer-Pilots Bar Assn., Ohio State Bar Assn., Aviation Ins. Assn., Aircraft Owners and Pilots Assn., Exptl. Aircraft Assn., Gen. Aviation Operators Assn., Columbus Maennerchor Club, Masons, Shriners. Republican. Baptist. Avocations: aviation, bicycling. Aviation, Construction, Product liability. Office: Eichenberger & Hoehn 6099 Frantz Rd Columbus OH 43017 E-mail: JEichenberger@ehlawyers.com

EICHLER, BURTON LAWRENCE, lawyer; b. Newark, Mar. 1, 1933; s. Philip and Anna (Kessler) E.; children— Betsy, Peter, Thomas. B.S., Ohio State U., 1954; LL.B., Rutgers U.-Newark, 1957. Bar: N.J. 1958, N.Y. 1983, U.S. Dist. Ct. N.J. 1958, U.S. Ct. Appeals (3d cir.) 1981. Assoc., Zucker, Brach & Eichler and predecessor, Newark, 1958-59, ptnr., 1959-67; ptnr. Eichler, Rosenberg & Silver, Newark, 1967-69, Brach, Eichler, Rosenberg, Silver, Newark, 1969-72, Brach, Eichler, Rosenberg, Silver, Bernstein & Hammer P.A., East Orange, N.J., 1972-81, Brach, Eichler, Rosenberg, Silver, Bernstein, Hammer & Gladstone P.C., Roseland, N.J., 1981— ; chmn. dist. fee arbitration com. for Essex County, Dist. V-C, N.J. Sup. Ct., 1983-86. Pres., chmn. bd. United Cerebral Palsy, East Oarnge, 1967-69; bd. dirs. South Orange/Maplewood Bd. Edn., 1979-83, v.p., 1981-83; bd. dirs. YM-YWHA Met. N.J., West Orange, 1970-74; former trustee Congregation B'nai Jeshurun, Short Hills, N.J. Recipient J. H. Cohn Outstanding Young Leadership award Jewish Community Fedn. Met. N.J., East Orange, 1961. Mem. Eseex County Bar Assn. (chmn. med.-legal affairs com. 1985-86), N.J. Bar Assn., ABA, Am. Health Lawyers Assn. Administrative and regulatory, Health, Real property. Office: Brach Eichler Rosenberg Silver Bernstein Hammer & Gladstone PC 101 Eisenhower Pkwy Roseland NJ 07068

EICHSTADT, CRAIG MARTIN, lawyer; b. Huron, S.D., Aug. 1, 1951; s. Martin Edward and Edith Marie (Scheibe) E.; m. Gail Lynn Carlson, June 1, 1975; children: Anne Elizabeth, Neil Craig, Carl Martin. BA, S.D. State U., 1973; postgrad., Ohio U., 1973-74; JD, U. S.D., 1978. Bar: S.D. 1978, U.S. Dist. Ct. S.D. 1979, U.S. Ct. Appeals (8th cir.) 1984, U.S. Supreme Ct. 1986, U.S. Ct. Appeals (D.C. cir.) 1987. Law clk. S.D. Supreme Ct., Pierre, 1978-79, U.S. Dist. Ct. S.D., Pierre, 1979-80; assoc. Bantz, Gosch & Cremer, Aberdeen, S.D., 1980-81; ptnr. Steele & Eichstadt, Plankinton, 1981-84; asst. atty. gen. State of S.D., Pierre, 1984-90; dep. atty. gen., head appellate div. Office Atty. Gen. State of S.D., 1991—. W.W. French scholar U. S.D., 1977-78, Dean Marshall, Alice and Frances McCusick scholar U. S.D., 1976-77. Mem. S.D. Bar Assn. (com. criminal pattern jury instructions 1983-88, com. on adminstrv. law 1988-91, 92—), Phi Kappa Phi, Delta Phi Alpha. Lutheran. Avocations: furniture refinishing, coin collecting, reading. Home: 412 N Van Buren Ave Pierre SD 57501-2665 Office: Office Atty Gen State Capitol Bldg 500 E Capitol Ave Pierre SD 57501-5070 E-mail: cmeace1@home.com, craig.eichstadt@state.sd.us

EIGNER, RICHARD MARTIN, lawyer; b. Swampscott, Mass., July 7, 1929; s. Israel and Bessie (Polansky) E.; m. Beverly Israel, Dec. 26, 1964; children: David, Danielle. AB, Dartmouth Coll., 1951; LLB, Harvard U., 1954. Bar: Calif. 1955, Mass. 1956. Ptnr. Pillsbury Winthrop, San Francisco, 1965—. Cons. Internat. Tax Project, Am. Law Inst., 1981-86. Mem. Internat. Tax Planning Assn., Internat. Fiscal Assn., Phi Beta Kappa. Jewish. Home: 2955 Piedmont Ave Berkeley CA 94705-2342 Office: Pillsbury Winthrop 50 Fremont St Fl 9 San Francisco CA 94105 E-mail: reigner@pillsburywinthrop.com

EILAND, GARY WAYNE, lawyer; b. Houston, Apr. 25, 1951; s. William N. and Louise A. (Foltin) E.; m. Sandra K. Streetman, Aug. 4, 1973; children; Trina L. Wuensche, Peter T. BBA, U. Tex., 1973, JD, 1976. Bar: Tex. 1976, U.S. Ct. Claims 1977, U.S. Ct. Appeals (5th cir.) 1978, U.S. Ct. Appeals (11th cir.) 1981, U.S. Supreme Ct. 1989. Assoc. Wood, Lucksinger & Epstein, Houston, 1976-81, ptnr., 1981-91, Vinson & Elkins L.L.P., Houston, 1991—; co-chair health industry group, 1996—. Lectr. Aspen Health Care Industry seminars, Aspen Pubs., Inc., Rockville, Md., 1978-89, HLO Health Care seminars, 1990-91. Mem. Tex. Bar Assn. (chmn. health law sect. 1991-92), Am. Acad. Healthcare Attys. (bd. dirs. 1991-97, pres. 1996-97), Am. Health Lawyers Assn. (past pres., exec. com. 1997-98), Healthcare Fin. Mgmt. Assn. (pres. Texas Gulf Coast chpt. 1992-93, Region 9 chpt. liaison rep. 1994-95, compliance officers forum adv. coun. 2000—, Founders medal of honor 1999), Assn. Am. Med. Colls., Houston Ctr. Club, Bentwater Yacht and Country Club. Administrative and regulatory, Government contracts and claims, Health. Home: 23319 Holly Hollow Tomball TX 77375-3684 Office: Vinson & Elkins LLP 1001 Fannin St Ste 2300 Houston TX 77002-6760 E-mail: geiland@velaw.com

EILEN, HOWARD SCOTT, lawyer, mediator; b. N.Y.C., Mar. 28, 1954; m. Sharon R. Kornbluth, Oct. 21, 1979; children: Michael, Jeffrey. BA summa cum laude, MA, CUNY, 1975; JD, St. John's U., 1979. Bar: N.Y. 1980, U.S. Tax Ct. 1980, U.S. Dist. Ct. (so., ea. dists.) N.Y. 1980, U.S. Dist. Ct. (ea. dist.) Mich. 1982. Assoc. Bloom & Tese, N.Y.C., 1980-83; ptnr. Bloom & Eilen, 1983-86, 87-94; of counsel Spengler, Carlson, Gubar, Brodsky & Frischling, 1986-87; ptnr. Lehman & Eilen, Uniondale, N.Y., 1994—. Arbitrator Nat. Assn. Securities Dealers, Inc., Nat. Futures Assn., Am. Arbitration Assn., U.S. Arbitration and Mediation, Inc.; mediator Nat. Assn. Securities Dealers, Inc.; spl. master N.Y. Supreme Ct.; mem. faculty securities arbitration program Practising Law Inst.; lectr. securities arbitration program Nassau Acad. Law. Contbg. editor Futures Tribune Mag., Japan. Mem. N.Y. County Lawyers Assn. (com. on securities and exchs. 1983—, chmn. subcom. on commodities regulation, com. on arbitration and conciliation 1990—), Nassau County Bar Assn. (securities law com.). Alternative dispute resolution, General civil litigation, Securities. Office: Lehman & Eilen LLP Ste 505 50 Charles Lindbergh Blvd Uniondale NY 11553-3650 E-mail: heilen@lehmaneilen.com

EIMER, NATHAN PHILIP, lawyer; b. Chgo., June 26, 1949; s. Irving A. and Charlotte Eimer; m. Kathleen L. Roach; children: Micah Jacob, Noah Joseph, Daniel Jordan, Anna Beatrice. AB in Econs. magna cum laude, U. Ill., 1970; JD cum laude, Northwestern U., 1973. Bar: Ill. 1973, U.S. Supreme Ct. 1978, N.Y. 1985, Tex. 1998. Assoc. Sidley & Austin, Chgo., 1973-80, ptnr., 1980-2000; founding ptnr. Eimer Stahl Klevorn & Solberg, 2000—. Adj. prof. Law Sch., Northwestern U., Chgo., 1989-96. Note and comment editor Northwestern U. Law Rev., 1972-73. Bd. dirs. Chgo. Lawyers Com. for Civil Rights, 1991—, pres., 1993-94; bd. dirs. UNICEF, 1992-93, Infant Welfare Soc., Chgo., exec. v.p., 1992-96, pres., 1996-98; mem. adv. bd. Children & Family Justice Ctr., Northwestern U. Legal Clinic, 1996—. Mem. ABA, Univ. Club. Antitrust, General civil litigation. Office: Eimer Stahl Klevorn & Solberg 122 S Michigan Ave Ste 1776 Chicago IL 60603 E-mail: neimer@eimerstahl.com

EINHORN, DAVID ALLEN, lawyer; b. Bklyn., Dec. 11, 1961; s. Harold and Jane Ellen (Weiner) E. BA in Computer Sci. magna cum laude, Columbia U., 1983, JD, 1986. Bar: N.Y. 1987, D.C. 1988, U.S. Dist. Ct. (so. and ea. dists.) N.Y. 1989, U.S. Ct. Appeals (fed. cir.) 1992, U.S. Dist. Ct. (no. dist.) Calif. 1994. Assoc. Kaye, Scholer, Fierman, Hays & Handler, N.Y.C., 1986-89; ptnr. Anderson Kill & Olick, PC, 1989—. Columnist Grapevine; lectr. Am. Conf. Inst. Co-author: (2-vol. treatise) Patent Licensing Transactions; editor-in-chief Intellectual Property for the New Millenium, 1997—; contbr. articles to profl. jours. Lt. Col. N.Y. Guard, 1987—. Harlan Fiske Stone scholar Columbia U., 1985; recipient Nat. prize Nathan Burkan Copyright Essay Competition, 1985; named to Order of Merit, Les Amis du Vin, 1982. Mem. ABA (chmn. software patent subcom. 1988-91, software licensing subcom. 1991-95, software copyright subcom. 1995-96, chmn. broadcasting, sound recordings, and performing artists com. 2000—), Am. Israel Pub. Affairs Com., Am. Intellectual Property Law Assn. (chmn. software copyright subcom. 1999—), N.Y. Intellectual Property Law Assn., Internat. Trademark Assn., D.C. Bar Assn. (computer law sect.), Columbia Soc. Law and Tech. (pres. 1985-86), Licensing Execs. Soc. (lectr.), N.Y. Soc. Mil. and Naval Officers (v.p. 1995—), Wine Lovers Internat. (v.p., bd. dirs. 1994—, Order of Merit 1997), Tasters Guild (v.p., bd. dirs. 1997—), Untitled Theater Co. #61, Ltd. (chmn. bd. dirs., producing dir., treas. 1994—). Jewish. Democrat. Avocations: tennis, racquetball, wine tasting, theater. Computer, Patent, Trademark and copyright. Home: 2373 Broadway Apt 802 New York NY 10024-2835 Office: Anderson Kill & Olick PC 1251 Ave of the Americas New York NY 10020-1182 E-mail: deinhorn@andersonkill.com

EINSTEIN, STEVEN HENRY, investment banker, lawyer, accountant; b. N.Y.C., Aug. 14, 1954; s. Ralph Gunther and Beatrice (Katz) E. BS, Lehigh U., 1976; JD, Seton Hall U., 1979; LLM in Taxation, NYU, 1985. Bar: N.J. 1979, N.Y. 1985, U.S. Dist. Ct. N.J. 1979, U.S. Tax Ct. 1982, U.S. Ct. Appeals (3d cir.) 1983, U.S. Supreme Ct. 1985. Judicial law clk. to presiding justice Superior Ct., Hackensack, N.J., 1979-80; assoc. Wacks, Hirsch, Ramsey & Berman Esqs., Morristown, 1980-81; sr. tax mgr. Touche Ross, Newark, 1981-86; v.p., investment banking, mergers-acquistions dept. Paine Webber Capital Mkts., N.Y.C., 1986-88; v.p. Kluge, Subotnick, Perkowski & Co., 1988-90; mng. dir. Price Waterhouse Corp. Fin. Group, 1991-99; ptnr., chmn. global corp. devel. group Pricewaterhouse Coopers LLP, 1999—. Mem. editl. bd. Corp. Taxation Mag.; contbr. articles to profl. jours. Mem. ABA, AICPAs, N.J. State Bar Assn., N.Y. State Bar Assn., Essex County Bar Assn. (taxation divsn.), N.J. Soc. CPAs, Beta Gamma Sigma, Phi Eta Sigma. Jewish. Corporate taxation, Estate taxation, Personal income taxation. Home: 174 Carter St New Canaan CT 06840-5007 Office: Pricewaterhouse Coopers LLP 1177 Avenue Of The Americas New York NY 10036-2714

EISELE, JOHN EUGENE, lawyer; b. Mpls., Apr. 22, 1938; s. James William and Fayloa Geneva E.; m. Patricia Anne Thornburg, Mar. 2, 1962 (div. Feb. 1981); children: John Michael, William Todd. BA, Ind. U., 1961, JD, 1968. Bar: Ind. 1968, U.S. Dist. Ct. Ind. 1968, U.S. Supreme Ct. 1990. Personnel, foreman GM, Anderson, Ind., 1964-68; hearing officer Ind. Pub. Svc. Commn., Indpls., 1968-70; deputy prosecutor Madison County, Anderson, 1970, pub. defender, 1971-76, atty., 1968—. Mem. Anderson Police Merit Commn., 1997—. 1st lt. U.S. Army, 1962-64. Mem. Ind. Bar Assn., Ind. Trial Lawyers Assn., Madison County Bar Assn. (pres. 1989), Am. Legion, Anderson Country Club (sec./bd, dirs. 1991-94), Exch. Club. Avocations: fishing, jogging, weightlifting. Home: 514 Ironwood Ln Anderson IN 46011-1650 Office: Eisele Lockwood & Eisele 200 E 11th St Ste 100 Anderson IN 46016-1779

EISEN, EDWIN ROY, lawyer; b. Bklyn., May 25, 1932; s. Edward and Cecile (Kurland) E.; m. Elaine Sollar, Feb. 15, 1963; 1 child, Marc. A.B., Colby Coll., 1954; LL.B., Cornell U., 1957. Bar: N.Y. 1958, U.S. Dist. Ct. (ea. and so. dists.) N.Y. 1963, U.S. Ct. Appeals (2d cir.) 1963. Ptnr., Tenzer, Greenblatt, Fallen & Kaplan, N.Y.C., 1973-74, Eisen & Fishman, N.Y.C., 1979-81; ptnr. Eisen & Schulman, P.C., 1974-78, 81— . Clubs: Brae Burn Country (exec. com.) (Purchase, N.Y.); City Athletic (bd. dirs) (N.Y.C.). Estate planning, Real property, Estate taxation. Office: Eisen & Schulman PC 575 5th Ave New York NY 10017-2422

EISEN, ERIC ANSHEL, lawyer; b. N.Y.C., Apr. 9, 1950; s. Morton and Victoria (Goldstein) E.; m. Claire L. Shapiro, Jan. 6, 1979; children: Rebecca, Jennifer, Melissa. AB, U. Mich., 1971, JD magna cum laude, 1975. Bar: Alaska 1976, D.C. 1977, Md. 1988. Law clk. to presiding justice Alaska Supreme Ct., Fairbanks, 1975-76; assoc. Covington & Burling, Washington, 1976-81, Birch, Horton, Bittner, Washington, 1981-85, ptnr., 1985-93, Eisen Law Offices, Bethesda, Md., 1993—. Speaker various seminars and colloquia on energy and bus. matters. Contbr. articles legal publs. Pres. Wildwood Hills Citizens Assn., Bethesda, Md., 1987—; sec. N. Bethesda Cong. Citizens Assns., 1989-90. Mem. ATLA, Energy Bar Assn. (antitrust com.), D.C. Bar Assn., Montgomery County Bar Assn. (intellectual property, bus. and litigation sects.), Toastmasters, Order of Coif. Avocation: woodworking. Administrative and regulatory, General civil litigation, FERC practice. Office: Eisen Law Offices 10028 Woodhill Rd Bethesda MD 20817-1218 also: 1101 30th St NW Ste 500 Washington DC 20007-3708

EISENBERG, ANDREW LEWIS, lawyer; b. Nov. 28, 1949; s. Eugene Robert and Shirley (Helman) Eisenberg; m. Sheryl Diane Fox, June 03, 1973; children: Benjamin Samuel, Lauren Beth. AB, Brown U., 1971; JD, Columbia U., 1974. Bar: Mass. 1974, U.S. Dist. Ct. Mass. 1975, U.S. Ct. Appeals (1st cir.) 1979, U.S. Supreme Ct. 1980. Assoc. Herrick & Smith, Boston, 1974—81, ptnr., 1982—84, Goldstein & Manello, Boston, 1984—89, Palmer & Dodge, Boston, 1989—. Clk., mem. CASE Engring. LLC; pres. Suncor Corp.; chmn. ASA Engring. Co., LLC; dir. LEA Group, Inc., Boston, 1983—95. Dir., mem. exec. bd. Combined Jewish Philanthropies, Boston, 1983—94, vice chmn., 1987—89; trustee, dir. Hebrew Coll., Brookline, 1983—2001, vice chmn., 1987—89; pres. Jewish Cmty. Ctr. Greater Boston, 1991—94; dir. Jewish Cmty. Ctrs. Assn. of N.Am., 1987—; bd. dir. Jewish Cmty. Rels. Coun., Boston, 1985—87, Jewish Cmty. Ctr., Newton, 1985—, v.p., 1986—87, pres., 1987—89; dir. Jewish Vocat. Svc., Boston, 1983—87. Recipient Young Leadership award, Combined Jewish Philanthropies, 1986. Mem.: ABA, Boston Bar Assn. Labor. Home: 131 Pembroke Street Apt 2 Boston MA 02118 Office: Palmer & Dodge LLP 111 Huntington Ave Boston MA 02199-7613

EISENBERG, HOWARD BRUCE, law educator; b. Chgo., Dec. 9, 1946; s. Herman Levy and Margie M. (Meyers) E.; m. Phyllis Terry Borenstein, Aug. 25, 1968; children: Nathan, Adam, Leah. BA, Northwestern U., 1968; JD, U. Wis., 1971. Bar: Wis. 1971, D.C. 1980, Ill. 1983, U.S. Dist. Ct. (ea. and we. dists.) Wis. 1971, U.S. Ct. Appeals (8th cir.) 1983, U.S. Supreme Ct. 1974, U.S. Ct. Appeals (D.C. cir.) 1978, U.S. Dist. Ct. (ea. and we. dists.) Ark. 1991. Mem. staff Wis. Judicare Legal Svcs. Agy. OEO, Madison, 1968-71; law clk. to justice Wis. Supreme Ct., 1971-72; asst. state pub. defender State of Wis., 1972, state pub. defender, 1972-78; dir. defender divsn. Nat. Legal Aid and Defender Assn., Washington, 1978-79, exec. dir., 1979-83; assoc. prof. law, dir. clin. edn. So. Ill. U., Carbondale, 1983-91, assoc. prof., 1983-87, prof., 1987-91; dean Sch. Law, prof. law U. Ark., Little Rock, 1991-95; dean, prof. law Law Sch. Marquette U., 1995—. Mem. Wis. Bd. Bar Examiners, 1996—, chmn., 2001; bd. dirs. appellate practice sect. Bar of Wis., 1999—, chmn., 2001—; dir. Coalition for Legal Assn., 1981—82, Ill. Guardianship and Protective Svcs. Assn., 1990—91, Ark. CLE Bd., 1991—95, Pulaski County Bar Assn., 1991—95, Ark. Inst. CLE, Assn. Religiously Affiliated Law Schs.; chair Fed. Jud. Nominating Commn., Ea. Dist., Wis., 1995—. Contbr. articles to profl. jours. Bd. dirs. Hospice So. Ill., 1988-91, Milw. Legal Aid Soc., 1997—. Ill. State scholar, 1964-68; NDEA grantee, 1967. Mem. ABA, Am. Acad. Appellate Lawyers, Nat. Acad. Elder Law Attys., State Bar Wis., Wis. Assn. Criminal Attys., Ark. State Bar Assn., 7th Cir. Bar Assn., Ill. State Bar Assn., Milw. Bar Assn., Milw. Bar Assn. Found. (bd. 1997—), Equal Justice Coalition (bd. mem. 1998—), Nat. Assn. Criminal Def. Lawyers, Northwestern U. Alumni Assn., Wis. U. Alumni Assn., Phi Beta Kappa. Democrat. Jewish. Office: Marquette U Sch of Law PO Box 1881 Milwaukee WI 53201-1881

EISENBERG, JONATHAN LEE, lawyer; b. Hornell, N.Y., Jan. 10, 1955; s. Louis and Marcia E.; m. Jill Levenson, May 22, 1976; children: Samuel David, William Mayer. BA summa cum laude, Macalester Coll., 1976; JD, Yale U., 1979. BAr: Minn. 1979, U.S.Ct. Appeals (8th cir.) 1979, U.S. Dist. Ct. Minn. 1980. Law clk. to assoc. justice Minn. Supreme Ct., St. Paul, 1979-80; assoc. Pepin, Dayton, Herman, Graham & Getts, Mpls., 1980-84, ptnr., 1985-86; litigation atty. Pillsbury Co., 1986-90; shareholder Briggs & Morgan, 1990-95; sr. legal counsel Medtronic, Inc., 1995—. Mem. ABA, Am. Corp. Counsel Assn., Minn. State Bar Assn., Hennepin County Bar Assn., Macalester Coll. Alumni Assn. (bd. dirs. 1982-84). Antitrust, Federal civil litigation, Patent. Office: Medtronic Inc 710 Medtronic Pky NE Minneapolis MN 55432-3576

EISENBERG, MEYER, lawyer; b. Bklyn., Dec. 15, 1931; s. Samuel and Bella (Fishman) E.; m. Carolyn Schoen, Dec. 26, 1954; children— Julie S., Ellen M. BA, Bklyn. Coll., 1953; LLB, Columbia U., 1958. Bar: N.Y. 1960, D.C. 1970, U.S. Supreme Ct. 1963. Law clk. to Chief Justice William McAllister Supreme Ct. Oreg., Salem, 1958-59; atty. SEC, Washington,

1959-70, counsel spl. study securities markets, 1962-64, asst. gen. counsel, 1966-68, exec. asst. to chmn., 1968-69, assoc. gen. counsel, 1969-70; with firm Lawler, Kent & Eisenberg, Washington, 1970-79, Rosenman, Colin, Freund, Lewis & Cohen, Washington, 1980-87, Ballard, Spahr, Andrews & Ingersoll, Washington, 1987-93, Kramer, Levin, Naftalis & Frankel, Washington, 1994-98; dep. gen. coun. sec. SEC, 1998—. Adj. prof. law George Washington U., 1972-75, Georgetown U. Law Sch., 1988-90; vis. prof. law U. Calif., Berkeley; dir. Nat. Ctr. Fin. Svcs., 1985-86; mem. exec. com. Calif. Securities Regulation Inst.; cons. in field. Contbr. articles to profl. publs. Mem. internat. bd. govs. B'nai B'rith, 1978-92; mem. nat. exec. com. Anti-Defamation League, 1980—, nat. vice chmn., 1994—, chmn. Nat. Civil Rights Com., 1992-94, Nat. Legal Affairs Com., 1980-92. Mem. ABA (chmn. com. on devels. in investment svcs. 1981-86, chmn. com. on long-range issues affecting bus. law practice 1986-90, coun. sect. bus. law 1990-94, chmn. com. on internat. tech. assistance 1994—, sec. bus. law), Fed. Bar Assn. (chmn. securities law com. 1984-85). Banking, General corporate, Securities. Home: 8216 Lakenheath Way Potomac MD 20854-2740 Office: SEC Office of Gen Counsel 450 5th St NW Washington DC 20549-0001 E-mail: eisenbergm@sec.gov

EISENBERG, THEODORE, law educator; b. Bklyn., Oct. 26, 1947; s. Abraham Louis and Esther (Waldman) E.; m. Lisa Wright, Nov. 27, 1971; children: Katherine Wright, Ann Marie, Thomas Peter. BA, Swarthmore Coll., 1969; JD, U. Pa., 1972. Bar: Pa. 1972, N.Y. 1974, U.S. Ct. Appeals (2d cir.) 1974, Calif. 1977. Law clk. U.S. Ct. Appeals, D.C. Cir., 1972-73; law clk. to U.S. Supreme Ct. Justice Earl Warren, 1973; assoc. Debevoise & Plimpton, N.Y.C., 1974-77; prof. law UCLA Law Sch., 1977-81, Cornell U. Law Sch., Ithaca, N.Y., 1981-96, Henry Allen Mark prof. law, 1996—. Vis. prof. law Harvard U. Law Sch., 1984-85; vis. prof. Law, Stanford U. Law Sch., 1987. Author: Civil Rights Legislation, 1981, 4th edit., 1996, Bankruptcy and Debtor-Creditor Law, 1984, 2d edit., 1988; mem. adv. bd. Law and Soc. Rev., Am. Law and Econ. Rev.; contbr. articles to profl. jours. Am. Bar Found grantee, NSF grantee. Fellow Royal Statis. Soc.; mem. ABA, Assn. Bar City N.Y., Law and Soc. Assn., Am. Law and Econ. Assn., Am. Bankruptcy Inst. Office: Cornell U Law Sch Myron Taylor Hall Ithaca NY 14853 E-mail: te13@cornell.edu

EISENMANN, CARL D. lawyer; b. Bridgeport, Conn., Mar. 20, 1928; s. Victor F. and Marietta (Barnes) E.; m. Nancy Koenig, May 9, 1956; children: Robert, William. AB, Georgetown U., 1948, JD, 1951. Bar: Conn. 1952, U.S. Dist. Ct. D.C. 1951, U.S. Ct. Appeals for Armed Forces 1956. Assoc. Louis L. Buccanelli, New Canaan, Conn., 1952, Kenny & Ritenband, Hartford, 1957-59; asst. atty. gen. State of Conn., 1959-75; pub. defender Superior Ct., 1975-87, Jud. Dist. of Litchfield, 1987-95; sec. Johnson Gage Co., Bloomfield, Conn., 1979—. Bd. dirs. Simsbury Ctr. for Arts Edn., Conn.; chmn. Simsbury Police Commn., 1995-96, clk., 2001—, Justice of the Peace, 1995—; bd. parole State of Conn., 2000—. Lt. col. USAF, 1952-57. Mem. Conn. Bar Assn. (exec. com., com. on criminal justice), Hartford County Bar Assn., Pub. Defender Svcs. Commn./State of Conn. (chmn. 1995—), Conn. Criminal Def. Lawyers Assn. (bd. govs. 1996—), Litchfield County Bar Assn., Rotary (bd. dirs. 1974). Republican. Universalist. Home: 34 Lincoln Ln Simsbury CT 06070-3014

EISMANN, DANIEL T. judge; b. Eugene, Oreg. m. Sheila Wood, 1982; 1 child Matthew stepchildren: Catherine Richardson, Christine Putz. Grad. cum laude, U. Idaho, 1976. Magistrate judge Owyheee County, 1986—95; dist. judge Fourth Jud. Dist., 1995—98; adminstrv. dist. judge Id. State Supreme Ct., Boise, 1998—2000, Supreme Ct. justice, 2001—. Mem. Ada County Domestic Violence Task Force, Region III Coun. for Children and Youth; judge Ada County Drug Ct. With USAR. Decorated 2 Purple Hearts. Mem.: Id. Bar Assn. (mem. Bar Exam Preparation Com.), Inns of Ct. (Boise Chpt.). Office: Supreme Ct Bldg Rm 207 451 W State St Boise ID 83720*

EISNER, LAWRENCE BRAND, lawyer, real estate developer; b. New Haven, Sept. 27, 1951; s. Robert Raphael and Anita Stanton (Brand) E.; m. Karen Marie Menne, Nov. 11, 1979; children: Benjamin, Anna, Julia. B.A., Union Coll., 1973; J.D., Georgetown U., 1976. Bar: Conn. 1976, D.C. 1978, Mass. 1982. Atty., adviser Commodity Futures Trading Commn., Washington, 1977-79; treas. Continental Lumber Co., West Haven, Conn., 1979-85; pres. Eisner Devel. Group, Hamden, Conn., 1985—. Mem. Conn. Bar Assn., D.C. Bar Assn., Phi Beta Kappa. Democrat. Jewish. Private international. Home: 44 Valley Rd Bethany CT 06524-3410 Office: Eisner Devel Group 2911 Dixwell Ave Hamden CT 06518-3195

EISNER, NEIL ROBERT, lawyer; b. Syracuse, N.Y., Feb. 19, 1943; s. Martin Bert and Bertha Martha (Roniger) E.; m. Joan Merle Stock, Sept. 11, 1966; children: David Jeffrey, Jennifer Lauren; m. Janis Lynn Paushter, Feb. 8, 1981 (div. Mar. 2000). AB, Syracuse U., 1964; JD, Columbia U., 1967. Bar: N.Y. 1967, D.C. 1972. Trial atty. FAA, Washington, 1967-72, chief accident counsel br., 1972-76, dep. asst. chief counsel, 1976, asst. chief counsel, 1976-78; asst. gen. counsel U.S. Dept. Transp., 1978—. Mem. Adminstrv. Conf. U.S., Washington, 1982-95. Mem. ABA (coun. mem. sect. on adminstrv. law & regulatory practice 1989-92, vice chair 2000-01), D.C. Bar Assn., Pi Sigma Alpha (chpt. pres. 1963-64). Jewish. Home: 6356 Lakeview Dr Falls Church VA 22041-1333 Office: US Dept Transp 7th And D Sts SW Washington DC 20590-0001 E-mail: neil.eisner@ost.dot.gov

EITTREIM, RICHARD MACNUTT, lawyer; b. Neptune, N.J., Feb. 10, 1945; s. Wilbur Lawrence and Leta Blanch (MacNutt) E.; m. Margaret Anne Nolan, June 11, 1967; children: Theodore Scott, Elisabeth Marie, Samantha Leta. AB, Yale U., 1967; JD, U. Va., 1973. Bar: N.J. 1973, U.S. Dist. Ct. N.J. 1973, U.S. Ct. Appeals (3d cir.) 1984, U.S. Supreme Ct. 1998. Assoc. McCarter & English, Newark, 1973-80, ptnr., 1980—. Trustee Children's Psychiat. Ctr., Eatontown, N.J., 1977-87, Riverview Hosp. Found., Red Bank, N.J., 1988-93. Mem. ABA, N.J. State Bar Assn., Essex County Bar Assn., Phi Alpha Delta, Sea Bright Lawn Tennis and Cricket Club (pres. 2000—, bd. govs. 1994—), Monmouth Boat Club (treas. 1983-86), Essex Club, Yale Club (pres. 1986-87). Democrat. Presbyterian. Federal civil litigation, Insurance, Libel. Home: Windmill Ln Rumson NJ 07760 Office: McCarter & English 4 Gateway Ctr 100 Mulberry St Newark NJ 07102-4004 E-mail: reittreim@mccarter.com

EKLUND, CARL ANDREW, lawyer; b. Aug. 12, 1943; s. John M. and Zara (Zerbst) E.; m. Nancy Jane Griggs, Sept. 7, 1968; children: Kristin, Jessica, Peter. BA, U. Colo., 1967, JD, 1971. Bar: Colo. 1971, U.S. Dist. Ct. Colo. 1971, U.S. Ct. Appeals (9th cir.) 1975, U.S. Ct. Appeals (10th cir.) 1978, U.S. Supreme Ct. 1978. Dep. dist. atty. Denver Dist. Attys. Office, 1971-73; ptnr. DiManna, Eklund, Ciancio & Jackson, Denver, 1975-81, Smart, DeFurio, Brooks & Eklund, Denver, 1982-84, Roath & Brega, P.C., Denver, 1984-88, Faegre & Benson, Denver, 1988-94, LeBoeuf, Lamb, Greene & MacRae LLP, Denver, 1994—. Mem. local rules com. Bankruptcy Ct. D.C., 1979-80; reporter Nat. Bankruptcy Conf., 1981-82; lectr. ann. spring meeting Am. Bankruptcy Inst., Rocky Mountain Bankruptcy Conf., Continuing Legal Edn. Colo., Inc., Colo. Practice Inst., Colo. Bar Assn., Nat. Ctr. Continuing Legal Edn., Inc., Profl. Edn. Sys., Inc., Comml. Law Inst. Am., Law Edn. Inst., Inc., Bur. Nat. Affairs, Inc., Practising Law Inst., So. Meth. U. Sch. Law, Continuing Edn. Svcs., Lorman Bus. Ctr., Inc. Author: The Problem with Creditors' Committees in Chapter 11: How to Manage the Inherent Conflicts without Loss of Function; contbg. author: Collier's Bankruptcy Practice Guide, Representing Debtors in Bankruptcy, Letters Formbook and Legal Opinion, Advanced Chapter 11 Bankruptcy Practice, mem. adv. bd. ABI Law Rev., 1993-2000; contbr. to law jours. Fellow Am. Coll. Bankruptcy; mem. ABA (bus. law and corp. banking sect. 1977—, bus. bankruptcy com. 1982—, subcom. on rules 1981—), Colo. Bar Assn. (bd. govs. 1980-82, corp. banking and bus. law sect. 1977—, ethics com. 1981-82, subcom. bankruptcy cts.), Am. Bankruptcy Inst. (dir. Rocky Mountain Bankruptcy Conf.), Denver Bar Assn. (trustee 1983-86). Bankruptcy. Office: LeBoeuf Lamb Greene & MacRae LLP 633 17th St Ste 2000 Denver CO 80202-3620

EKLUND-EASLEY, MOLLY SUE, lawyer; b. Benton Harbor, Mich., Aug. 17, 1953; d. Robert Gordon and Arlene Ann Eklund; m. Herman Easley, Jr., July 8, 1981; 1 child, Rachel Nicole. BA, Grand Valley State Coll., 1975; JD, U. Detroit, 1979. Bar: Mich. 1979, U.S. Dist. Ct. (ea. dist.) Mich. 1979. Assoc. Stalburg, Fisher & Weberman, Detroit, 1989-87; ptnr. Goodman & Eklund-Easley, 1988-94, Goodman, Eklund-Easley & Davis, 1994-99, Eklund-Easley & Assocs., Southfield, Mich., 1999—. Mem. ABA, Women Lawyer's Assn. Mich., Assn. Trial Lawyers Am., Mich. Trial Lawyers Assn., Mich. Bar Assn. Lutheran. Criminal, Family and matrimonial, Probate. Office: 19111 W Ten Mile #106 Southfield MI 48075 E-mail: scionmee@msn.com

ELAM, JOHN CARLTON, lawyer; b. Ft. Wayne, Ind., Mar. 6, 1924; s. Bernard C. and Eunice (Gawthrop) E.; m. Virginia Mayberry, July 14, 1945; children: Nancy Lee, Patricia Scott, Mary Jane, John William. B.A., U. Mich., 1948, J.D. with distinction, 1949. Bar: Mich. 1949, Ohio 1950. Assoc. Vorys, Sater, Seymour & Pease, Columbus, Ohio, 1949-54, ptnr., 1954—, presiding ptnr., 1964-94, of counsel, 1995—. Trustee Columbus Coll. Art and Design, 1981-88. Fellow Am. Coll. Trial Lawyers (pres. 1980-81); mem. ABA (standing com. on fed. judiciary and ho. of dels.), Ohio Bar Assn., Columbus Bar Assn. (pres. 1964), 6th Cir. Jud. Conf. Federal civil litigation, General civil litigation. Home: 5000 Squirrel Bnd Columbus OH 43220-2278 Office: Vorys Sater Seymour & Pease 52 E Gay St Columbus OH 43215-3161

EL AZAR, SHEIKH SAMIR FARID, lawyer; b. Amyoun, Lebanon, Mar. 30, 1966; s. Sheikh Farid Ishak El Azar and Sara Georges Jeha. Lic. in law, St. Joseph U., Beiirut, Lebanon, 1988. Traniee atty. Edde & Baroudi Law Firm, Beirut, Lebanon, 1988-92; atty. pvt. practice, Lebanon, 1992-95; sr. atty. Al Tamimi & Co., Sharjah, United Arab Emirates, 1995—. Home: St Georges Amyoun Lebanon Office: Al Tamimi & Co Mina 00971 Sharjah United Arab Emirates Fax: 00971 6 5727258. E-mail: azar@tamimi.com

ELBERGER, RONALD EDWARD, lawyer; b. Newark, Mar. 13, 1945; s. Morris and Clara (Denes) E.; m. Rena Ann Brodey, Feb. 15, 1975; children: Seth, Rebecca. AA, George Washington U., 1964, BA, 1966; JD, Am. U., 1969. Bar: Md. 1969, D.C. 1970, Ind. 1971, U.S. Ct. Appeals (7th cir.) 1971, U.S. Supreme Ct. 1973. Atty. Balt. Legal Aid Bur., 1969-70; chief counsel Legal Services Orgn., Indpls., 1970-72; ptnr. Elberger & Stanton, 1974-76, Bose, McKinney & Evans, LLP, Indpls., 1976—. Asst. sec., v.p., litigation counsel Emmis Comm. Corp., 1986—; v.p. Cardboard Shoe Prodns., Inc., 1989—, Worldwide Slacks, Inc., 1984—. Mem., v.p. Med. Licensing Bd. Ind., 1982-98; pres., chmn. bd. dirs. Ind. Civil Liberties Union, Indpls., 1972-77, bd. dirs., 1972, 80-82; bd. dirs. ACLU, N.Y.C., 1972-77, Jewish Cmty. Rels. Coun., 1997-2000; trustee Children's Mus. of Indpls., 1994—; mem. Nat. Coun. on Media and Pub. Affairs, George Washington U., 2000—; bd. dirs. Flanner House of Indpls., Inc., 1999—. Reginald Heber Smith fellow U. Pa., 1969-71. Fellow Indpls. Bar Found.; mem. ABA, Ind. Bar Assn., Md. Bar Assn., D.C. Bar Assn., Indpls. Bar Assn. Democrat. Jewish. Avocations: fishing, music, gardening. Federal civil litigation, State civil litigation, Entertainment. Office: Bose McKinney & Evans LLP 2700 First Indiana Pla 135 N Pennsylvania St Indianapolis IN 46204-2400

ELCANO, MARY S. lawyer; BA cum laude, Lynchburg Coll., 1971; JD, Cath. U., Washington, 1976. Litigation atty. Balt. Legal Aide Bur., 1976; staff atty. Office Solicitor Dept. Labor, 1979; gen. trial and appellate atty. Office Labor Law U.S. Postal Svc., 1982, exec. dir. Office EEO, 1984, regional dir. human resources N.E. region, 1987, sr. v.p., gen. counsel, 1992-99, exec. v.p., gen. counsel, 1999-2000; ptnr. Sidley Austin Brown & Wood LLP, Washington, 2000—. Alternative dispute resolution, General corporate, Labor. Office: Sidley Austin Brown & Wood LLP 1666 K St NW Fl 7 Washington DC 20006-2803 E-mail: melcano@sidley.com

ELDEN, GARY MICHAEL, lawyer; b. Chgo., Dec. 11, 1944; s. E. Harold and Sylvia Arlene (Diamond) E.; m. Phyllis Deborah Mandler, Apr. 20, 1975; children: Roxanna Mandler, Erica Mandler. BA, U. Ill., 1966; JD, Harvard U., 1969. Bar: Ill. 1969, U.S. Dist. Ct. (no. dist.) Ill. 1969, U.S. Ct. Appeals (7th cir.) 1973, U.S. Supreme Ct. 1973, U.S. Dist. Ct. (ea. dist.) Mich. 1985, U.S. Ct. Appeals (8th cir.) 1988, U.S. Ct. Appeals (6th and 10th cirs.) 1990, U.S. Dist. Ct. (ea. dist.) Wis. 1992. Ptnr. Kirkland & Ellis, Chgo., 1969-78, Reuben & Proctor, Chgo., 1978-86, Isham, Lincoln & Beale, Chgo., 1986-88, Grippo & Elden, Chgo., 1988—. Contbr. articles to profl. jours. Fellow Am. Coll. Trial Lawyers; mem. ABA, Chgo. Bar Assn. (sec. com. appellate procedures 1975-77), Chgo. Coun. Lawyers, Appellate Lawyers Assn. (bd. dirs. 1975-77), Met. Club. Federal civil litigation, General civil litigation, Insurance. Home: 3750 N Lake Shore Dr Chicago IL 60613-4238 Office: Grippo & Elden 227 W Monroe St Ste 3600 Chicago IL 60606-5098

ELDER, JAMES CARL, lawyer; b. Detroit, Mar. 11, 1947; s. Carl W. and Alta M. (Bradley) E.; m. Margaret Ford, Apr. 6, 1974; children: James B., William J., Michael L., Samuel F. BA, U. Okla, 1969, JD, 1972. Bar: Okla. 1972, U.S. Dist. Ct. (we. dist.) Okla. 1972. Ptnr., dir. Crowe & Dunlevy, Oklahoma City, 1972-82; dir., mem. Mock, Schwabe, Waldo, et. al., 1982-96, 98—; ptnr. Gable Gotwals Mock Schwabe Kihle Gaberino, 1996-98. Nat. coun. rep. Last Frontier Coun. Boy Scouts Am., 1989—, pres., 1997-99; trustee Norman (Okla.) Pub. Sch. Found., 1989-98, pres., 1995-97; elder Meml. Presbyn. Ch., Norman, clk. of session, 1992-95; dir. Cmty. Coun. Ctrl. Okla., 1999—. Recipient Silver Beaver award Boy Scouts Am., Oklahoma City, 1988, Silver Antelope award, 1999. Fellow Okla. Bar Found. (life), Baden Powell World Fellowship; mem. ABA (mem. title ins. com. real property, probate and trust law sect. 1993—, chmn. closing issues subcom. 1995—), Rotary, Beta Theta Pi Corp. of Okla. (trustee, v.p., chpt. counselor 1975-85, pres. 1995—). Avocations: scouting, skiing, reading. Banking, Contracts commercial, Real property. Office: Mock Schwabe Waldo et al 211 N Robinson 2 Leadership Sq 14th Fl Oklahoma City OK 73102

ELDERKIN, E(DWIN) JUDGE, retired lawyer; b. Missoula, Mont., Oct. 25, 1932; s. Emerson Winston and Valma Agnes (Judge) E.; m. Marie Jane Fletcher, June 20, 1954; children: Susan Marie, Michael Judge. BS in History, U. Oregon, 1954; LLB, U. Calif., Berkeley, 1959. Bar: Calif. 1960, U.S. Ct. Appeals (9th crct.) Calif. 1960, U.S. Supreme Ct. 1967. Assoc. Brobeck, Phleger & Harrison, San Francisco, 1959-66, ptnr., 1966-92, mng. ptnr., 1984-88, ret., 1992. Pvt. judge Pvt. Adjudication Ctr., Inc.; advisor Ctr. Pub. Resources; lectr. in field; bd. dirs. MPC Ins. Ltd., The Renewal Project; mem. policy com. Aetna dental. Pscyhol. lay counsel for low income families. Named Counselor of the Yr. 1996. Fellow Am. Coll. Trial Lawyers, Am. Bar Found.; mem. Am. Cancer Soc. (driver, Driver of Yr. 1996). Mem. Evangel. Covenant Ch. Avocations: hiking, swimming, golf, tennis. Antitrust, Federal civil litigation, State civil litigation.

ELDRIDGE, DOUGLAS ALAN, lawyer; b. Boulder, Colo., Mar. 15, 1944; s. Douglas Hilton and Clara Effie (Young) E.; m. Benna June Germann, June 24, 1967; children: Heather Dana, Ethan Douglas, Hilary Beca. BA, Yale U., 1966; LLB, U. Pa., 1969; cert., Nat. Inst. Trial Advocacy, Boulder, 1973. Bar: N.Y. 1972, U.S. Dist. Ct. (no. dist.) N.Y. 1973, U.S. Supreme Ct. 1975. Staff atty. Onondaga Neighborhood Legal Svcs., Syracuse, N.Y., 1971-74, exec. dir., 1974-76; counsel N.Y. State Divsn. of Substance Abuse Svcs., Albany, 1976-79; dep. counsel N.Y. State Health Dept., 1979-80, N.Y. State Energy Office, Albany, 1980-82, asst. counsel, 1982-87; gen. counsel Commn. for Siting Low-Level Radioactive Waste Disposal Facilities, Troy, N.Y., 1987-95; sole practice, 1995—. Govt. affairs counsel N.Y. Rehab. Assn., Inc., 1995-2000. Contbr. articles to legal jours. Bd. dirs. Coun. Cmty. Svcs. United Way of Northeastern N.Y., Albany, 1980-90, pres., 1986-88; bd. dirs. United Way Ea. N.Y., 1986-88, Mohawk-Hudson Found., 1986-89; law guardian Schenectady County, 1996—. Recipient Reginald Heber Smith Cmty. Lawyer fellowship OEO, 1969-71. Mem. N.Y. State Bar Assn., Albany County Bar Assn. (chair legis. com. 1998—), Onondaga County Bar Assn., Assn. of Bar of City of N.Y., Yale Alumni Schs. Com., Yale Alumni Assn. Northeastern N.Y., Assn. of Yale Alumni (rep. 1985-88, 94-97), University Club (bd. dirs. 1998—). Home: 9 Pinedale Ave Delmar NY 12054-3012 E-mail: eldesq@nycap.rr.com

ELDRIDGE, JOHN COLE, judge; b. Balt., Nov. 13, 1933; s. Arthur Clement and Bertha Jean (Klitch) E.; m. Dayne S. Worsham, July 15, 1961; children: Kathryn Chandler, John Cole. B.A., Harvard U., 1955; LL.B., U. Md., 1959. Bar: Md. 1960, D.C. 1961. Law clk. to chief judge U.S. Ct. Appeals 4th Circuit, 1959-61; trial atty. appellate sect., civil div. Dept. Justice, 1961-67, asst. chief appellate sect., 1967-69; chief legis. officer, counsel Staff of Gov. of Md., 1969-74; judge Ct. Appeals Md, Annapolis, Md., 1974—. Chmn. Md. Adv. Bd. Correction, 1969-70; dir. Annapolis Fine Arts Found., 1974-77 Mem. Anne Arundel County Bar Assn., Annapolis Yacht Club. Democrat. Methodist. Office: Ct Appeals Md Robert Murphy Cts Appeal Bldg 361 Rowe Blvd Annapolis MD 21401-1672*

ELDRIDGE, RICHARD MARK, lawyer; b. Okmulgee, Okla., June 20, 1951; s. H.G. and Marcheta (Barnes) E.; m. Nellene Jane Mark, Aug. 20, 1971; children: Richard Mark Jr. (dec.), Christopher Bryan, Ryan Matthew, Michael Jonathan. BA, Okla. State U., 1973; JD, U. Tulsa, 1975. Bar: Okla. 1976, U.S. Dist. Ct. (no. dist.) Okla. 1976, U.S. Dist. Ct. (ea. dist.) Okla. 1989; U.S. Ct. Appeals (10th cir.) 1977, U.S. Dist. Ct. (we. dist.) Okla. 1991. Ptnr. Jacobus, Green & Eldridge, Tulsa, 1976-78; spl. judge Dist. Ct., 1979-81; ptnr. Rhodes, Hieronymus, Jones, Tucker & Gable, 1981—. Adj. prof. Oral Roberts U., Tulsa, 1985. Tchr. Couples for Christ, Asbury United Meth. Ch., Tulsa, 1979—; pres., sec. Christian Businessmen's Com., Tulsa, 1981-93; chmn. Asbury Presch. Bd., Tulsa, 1985-95; trustee Metro. Christian Acad., 1998—, 1st v.p., 2001—. Recipient Cert. of Achievement, Am. Acad. Jud. Edn., 1979. Mem.: ABA, Okla. Bar Assn., Tulsa County Bar Assn., Def. Rsch. Inst., Am. Judicature Soc. Republican. Republican. Avocation: coaching baseball and basketball. Federal civil litigation, State civil litigation, Product liability. Home: 2916 E 88th St Tulsa OK 74137-2507 Office: Rhodes Hieronymus et al 100 W 5th St Ste 400 Tulsa OK 74103-4287

ELDRIDGE, TRUMAN KERMIT, JR. lawyer; b. Kansas City, Mo., July 27, 1944; s. Truman Kermit and Nell Marie (Dennis) E.; m. Joan Ellen Jurgeson, Feb. 9, 1965; children: Christina Joanne, Gregory Truman. AB, Rockhurst Coll., 1966; JD, U. Mo., Kansas City, 1969. Bar: Mo. 1969, U.S. Dist. Ct. (we. dist.) Mo. 1969, U.S. Ct. Appeals (8th cir.) 1977, (10th cir.) 1995, U.S. S. Ct., 1992, U.S. Dist. Ct. Kans. 1998. Assoc. Morris, Foust, Moudy & Beckett, Kansas City, 1969-70, Dietrich, Davis, Dicus, Rowlands & Schmitt, Kansas City, 1971-74, ptnr., 1975, Armstrong, Teasdale, LLP, Kansas City, 1989-2000; sr. counsel Schlee, Huber McMullen & Krause, 2001—. Author: (with othrs) Missouri Environmental Law Handbook, 1990, 2d edit., 1993, 3d edit., 1997; contbr. articles to profl. jours. Chmn. bd. dirs. Loretto Sch., Kansas City, 1981-83; mem. Friends of Art, Nelson Atkins Gallery, Kansas City, 1980—; mem. Energy and Environ. Commn. City of Kansas City, 1990-91, 1994, bd. dirs. Sheffield Pl., 1997—, vice chair, 1998-99, chair, 1999-2000. Master Ross T. Roberts Inn of Ct.; mem. ABA, Def. Rsch. Inst., Mo. Bar Assn., Kansas City Met. Bar Assn. (fed. ct. com., vice chair 1989-90, chair 1990-91), Mo. Orgn. Def. Lawyers, Internat. Trademark Assn., Greater Kansas City C. of C. (mem. environ. com. 1989—), Kansas City Club (athletic com. 1990—, chair 1995—, house com. 1993-96, 98-99, long range planning com. 1993-97, bd. dirs. 1997—). Roman Catholic. Avocations: sailing, reading, photography, raquetball. General civil litigation, Environmental, Product liability. Home: 448 W 68th Ter Kansas City MO 64113-1933 Office: 4050 Pennsylvania Ste 300 Kansas City MO 64111 E-mail: truman_eldridge@hotmail.com, teldridge@schleehuber.com

ELDRIDGE, WILLIAM BUTLER, lawyer; b. Greensboro, N.C., Jan. 26, 1931; s. James Eiffel and Clara Mae (Butler) E.; m. Barbara Jeanette Galloway, June 15, 1957; children— David Mark, Julia Claire. A.B., Duke U., 1953, J.D., 1956. Bar: Mo. 1956. Assoc., Coburn & Croft, St. Louis, 1956-57; research adminstratr. Am. Bar Found., Chgo., 1960-65, asst. exec., 1966-68; dir. research Fed. Jud. Ctr., Washington, 1969— . Author: Narcotics and the Law, 1967; co-author: Second Circuit Sentencing Study, 1974; contbr. articles to chptrs. in books and profl. jours. Served to cpt. U.S. Army, 1957-60. Home: 11209 Old Post Rd Rockville MD 20854-2533 Office: Fed Jud Ctr Rsch Thurgood Marshall Fed Jud Bldg 1 Columbus Cir NE Washington DC 20002-8000

ELEY, RANDALL ROBBI, lawyer; b. Portsmouth, Va., Jan. 29, 1952; s. Melvin Clyde and Florence Beatrice (Lomax) E.; m. Beverly Joyce Gibson, Feb. 5, 2000. BA, Yale U., 1974; JD, U. Chgo., 1977. Bar: U.S. Dist. Ct. Nebr. 1977, D.C. 1986. Ptnr. Kutak, Rock & Campbell, Omaha, 1977-86, The Edgar Lomax Co., Springfield, Va., 1986—. Avocation: stock investments. General corporate, Municipal (including bonds), Securities. Office: The Edgar Lomax Co Ste 310 6564 Loisdale Court Springfield VA 22150-1812

ELFAKI, MOHAMED AHMED MOHAMED, lawyer, consultant; b. Meroe, No. State, Sudan, Jan. 1, 1957; s. MOhamed Abdalla and Fatima (Abdalla) H.; m. Hanan, Nov. 17, 1987; children: Tasneem, Rayan. LLB, U. Khartoum, Sudan, 1984. Legal advisor atty. gen. chambers, Khartoum, Sudan, 1986-89, Alsafa Cons., Muscut, Central Oman, 1989-90, Law Office Dr. M. Hoshan, Riyadh, Central Province, Saudi Arabia, 1990—. Avocations: reading, swimming. General practice, Intellectual property, Patent. Office: Law Offices Dr Mohamed Hoshan 4547 Olaya Rd Olaya Bldg Riyadh Central Province 2626 Saudi Arabia Fax: 966-1-4632083

ELFMAN, ERIC MICHAEL, lawyer; b. Phila., Oct. 24, 1954; s. Isaac Selig and Mae (Kline) E.; m. Barbara Cecile Feldstein, Oct. 9, 1982; children: Elizabeth, Bradley, Todd. BS in Econs., U. Pa., 1975, MS in Acctg., 1976; JD, George Washington U., 1980. Bar: Calif. 1980, U.S. Tax Ct. 1981, Mass. 1986; CPA, Pa. Acct. Peat, Marwick, Mitchell and Co., Phila., 1976-77; assoc. Pettit & Martin, San Francisco, 1980-83; assoc. office of tax legis. counsel U.S. Dept. of Treas., Washington, 1983-85; ptnr. Ropes & Gray, Boston, 1985—. Mem. ABA (chair corporate tax com. 1996-97, taxation sect.), AICPA, Mass. Soc. CPAs, Boston Bar Assn. General corporate, Corporate taxation, Personal income taxation. Home: 19 Gypsy Trl Weston MA 02493-1607 Office: Ropes & Gray One Internat Pl Boston MA 02110-2624 E-mail: eelfman@ropesgray.com

ELFVIN, JOHN THOMAS, federal judge; b. Montour Falls, N.Y., June 30, 1917; s. John Arthur and Lillian Ruth (Dorning) E.; m. Peggy Pierce, Oct. 1, 1949. B.E.E., Cornell U., 1942; J.D., Georgetown U., 1947. Bar: D.C. 1948, N.Y. 1949. Confidential clk. to U.S. Circuit Ct. Judge E. Barrett Prettyman, 1947-48; asst. U.S. atty., Buffalo, 1955-58; U.S. atty. Western

Dist. N.Y., 1972-75; with firm Cravath, Swaine & Moore, N.Y.C., 1948-51, Dudley, Stowe & Sawyer, Buffalo, 1951-55, Lansdowne, Horning & Elfvin, Buffalo, 1958-69, 70-72; justice N.Y. Supreme Ct., 1969; judge U.S. Dist. Ct., Buffalo, 1975—, now sr. judge. Mem. bd. suprs. Erie County, N.Y., 1962-65, mem. bd. ethics, 1971-74, chmn., 1971-72; mem., minority leader Buffalo Common Council Delaware Dist., 1966-69. Mem. Am. Judicature Soc., Erie County Bar Assn., Engring. Soc. Buffalo (pres. 1958-59), Tech. Socs. Niagara Frontier (pres. 1960-61), Phi Kappa Tau, Delta Sigma Chi. Republican. Clubs: Cornell (pres. 1957-58); City (Buffalo), Buffalo Country, Saturn. Office: US Dist Ct 716 US Courthouse 68 Court St Buffalo NY 14202-3405

ELIAS, JOHN SAMUEL, lawyer; b. Lawrence, Mass., May 2, 1951; s. Fred G. and Evon (Erban) E.; m. Cynthia Lee Eppley, Jan. 29, 1979; children: Daniel, Allison. AB summa cum laude, Dartmouth Coll., 1973; MA, Oxford U., Eng., 1975; JD, Harvard U., 1979; LLM in Taxation, NYU, 1982. Bar: Ill. 1979, Ohio 1980, U.S. Tax Ct. 1980, N.Y. 1981, Mass. 1982. Law clk. Ohio Supreme Ct., Columbus, 1979-81; assoc. Goodwin, Proctor & Hoar, Boston, 1982-84; ptnr. Sutkowski & Washkuhn Assocs., Peoria, Ill., 1984-89, Keck, Mahin & Cate, Peoria, 1989-96, Elias, Meginnes, Riffle & Seghetti, P.C., Peoria, 1996—. Lectr. Ill. Inst. CLE, Springfield, 1984—; lectr. law edn., 1990—. Contbr. articles to legal jours. Reynolds Meml. scholar Oxford U., 1974. Mem. ABA, Ill. State Bar Assn. (chmn. fed. tax sect. coun. 1991, corp. and securities law sect. coun.), Peoria County Bar Assn., Peoria Country Club, Rotary, Phi Beta Kappa. Roman Catholic. General corporate, Real property, Taxation, general. Office: Elias Meginnes Riffle & Seghetti PC 416 Main St Ste 1400 Peoria IL 61602-1168 E-mail: jelias@emrslaw.com

ELIASON, RUSSELL ALLEN, judge; b. Mpls., Jan. 28, 1944; s. Walter Joseph and Hazel Agnes Pearl (Jensen) E.; m. Karen L. Stevens; children: Nathaniel, Heidi, Justine, Danielle. Student U. Minn., 1964-65, JD, 1970; BA, Yale U., 1967; student Wake Forest U. Sch. Law, 1967-68. Bar: Minn. 1970, Iowa 1971, N.C. 1973, Nebr. 1975, U.S. Dist. Ct. (no. dist.) Iowa 1971, U.S. Dist. Ct. (mid. dist.) N.C. 1974, U.S. Dist. Ct. Nebr. 1975, U.S. Ct. Appeals (8th cir.) 1971, U.S. Ct. Appeals (4th cir.) 1976. Law clk. to judge U.S. Ct. Appeals 8th Cir., 1970-71; asst. U.S. atty. Dept. Justice, Sioux City, Iowa, 1971-72; law clk. to judge U.S. Dist. Ct. Mid. Dist. N.C., 1972-74; assoc. Ryan, Scoville & Uhlir, South Sioux City, Nebr., 1974-75; asst. U.S. atty. Dept. Justice, Greensboro, N.C., 1975-76; U.S. magistrate judge U.S. Dist. Ct. Mid. Dist. N.C., Winston-Salem, 1976—; lectr. in field; active law-sch. skills programs. Trumpeter Salem Band, Old Salem Band. Mem. ABA, N.C. Bar Assn., Forsyth County Bar, Minn. Bar Assn., Nebr. Bar Assn., Sons of Norway, Phi Alpha Alpha Delta. Mem. Moravian Ch. Office: 224 Fed Bldg 251 N Main St Winston Salem NC 27101-3914

ELICKER, GORDON LEONARD, lawyer; b. Cleve., May 27, 1940; BA in Math., U. Mich., 1962, JD, 1965; postdoctoral, U. Aix-Marseille, Aix-En Provence, France, 1965-66. Bar: Mich. 1967, N.Y. 1968, U.S. Dist. Ct. (so. dist.) N.Y. 1973. Stagiaire EEC, Brussels, 1966-67; assoc. Shearman & Sterling, N.Y.C., 1967-77, ptnr., 1977-91, Nixon Peabody LLP, N.Y.C., 1991—. Speaker in field. Contbr. articles to profl. jours. Mem. legal com. U.S.-U.S.S.R. Trade and Econ. Coun., N.Y.C., 1978-91; chmn. legis. com. N.Y. Dist. Export Coun., N.Y.C., 1980-86; mem. Dem. Town Com., New Canaan, 1985-87; mem. bd. edn., New Canaan, Conn., 1986-90, chmn., 1989-90. Fulbright scholar, 1965. Mem. ABA, Internat. Bar Assn., Assn. of Bar of City of N.Y. Democrat. Banking, Oil, gas, and mineral, Private international. Office: Nixon Peabody LLP 437 Madison Ave New York NY 10022-7001

ELKINS, S. GORDON, lawyer; b. Phila., Dec. 21, 1930; m. Ethel Bronstein, June 16, 1957; children: Tod, Adam, Peter, Douglas. BS, Temple U., 1952; LLB, Yale U., 1955. Bar: Pa. 1956, U.S. Dist. Ct. (ea. dist.) Pa. 1956, U.S. Ct. Appeals (3d cir.) 1956, U.S. Ct. Appeals (6th cir.) 1979, U.S. Supreme Ct. Assoc. Stradley, Ronon, Stevens & Young, Phila., 1955-62, ptnr., 1962—. Speaker on surety and fidelity matters to ABA, Practicing Law Inst., Internat. Assn. Def. Counsel, also others, on antitrust matters to Wood Machinery Mfrs. Assn., Fluid Power Distbr. Assn., Am. Brush Mfrs. Assn., Nat. Welding Supply Assn.; former trial cons. Cmty. Legal Svcs. Phila.; bd. dirs. Entertainment Comm., Inc. Contbr. articles to legal publs. Past pres. Melrose Park Improvement Assn.; former panel mem. Philadelphians for Equal Justice; bd. dirs. Phila. and Pa. chpts. ACLU, pres. Greater Phila. chpt., 1976-81; frequent speaker at meetings, participant various TV and radio panels on civil liberties matters; mem. Cheltenham Twp. Govt. Study Commn., 1974-76. Mem. ABA (fidelity and surety law com. tort ins. practice sect., past vice chair), Phila. Bar Assn., Internat. Assn. Def. Counsel (fidelity and surety law com.), Fedn. Ins. and Corp. Counsel (fidelity com.), Forum Com. for Constrn. Industry, Def. Rsch. Inst., Defenders Assn. Phila. (past bd. dirs.). Civil rights, Federal civil litigation, General civil litigation. Office: Stradley Ronon Stevens & Young 2600 One Commerce Sq Philadelphia PA 19103 Fax: 215-635-0207. E-mail: patchhead@aol.com

ELKINS-ELLIOTT, KAY, law educator; b. Dallas, Nov. 21, 1938; d. William Hardin and Maxidine (Sadler) E.; m. Michael Gail Hodgson, July 7, 1960 (div. Dec. 1974); children: Michael Brett, Ashley Kim, Samantha; m. Frank Wallace Elliott, Aug. 15, 1983. AA with honors, Stephens Coll., 1958; JD, U. Okla., 1964; LLM, So. Meth. U., 1984; MA, U. Tex., Dallas, 1990. Bar: Okla. 1964, Tex. 1982, U.S. Dist. Ct. (no. dist.) Tex. 1982, U.S. Supreme Ct. 1984, U.S. Dist. Ct. (we. dist.) Okla. 1989. Assoc. Ben Hatcher and Assocs., Oklahoma City, 1964-65; dir., gen. counsel Take-A-Tour Swaziland, Mbabane, Swaziland, 1966-74; atty. Dept. Health and Human Svcs., Dallas, 1975-80; hearing officer EEOC, 1980-84; atty. pvt. practice, 1984-92; vis. assoc. prof. Tex. Wesleyan U. Sch. Law, 1992-95; arbitrator State Farm Ins., 1991-96. Adj. prof. Wesleyan U. Sch. Law, 1995—, coach nat. ABA champion negotiation team, 1998; mediator pvt. practice, Dallas, Granbury, 1991—; coord. cert. in conflict resolution program Tex. Woman's U., 1996—; cons. in field. Author: (with others) West Texas Practice, 1995, (with Frank Elliott) State Bar of Texas ADR Handbook, 2001. Mem. ABA (peer mediation and cmty. com. 1997—, alternative dispute resolution sect.), Tex. Bar Assn. (ADR sect. coun. mem. 1998-2001, chair publs. com.), Tex. Bar Found., Tex. Initiatives for Mediation in Edn. (founder, planning com. 1993-95), Soc. for Profls. in Dispute Resolution (pres. Dallas region 1995-97), Tex. Assn. Mediators, Assn. Atty. Mediators, Dallas Bar Assn. (coun. mem. 1993-94), Inst. for Responsible Dispute Resolution (charter), Acad. Family Mediators, Toastmasters (v.p. 1993-94, pres. 1996-97), AIM for Peacepath. Avocations: singing, public speaking, peer mediation training. Home: 2120 N Rough Creek Ct Granbury TX 76048-2903 Office: 2401 Turtle Creek Blvd Dallas TX 75219-4712 E-mail: k4mede8@flash.net

ELLETT, JOHN SPEARS, II, retired taxation educator, accountant, lawyer; b. Richmond, Va., Sept. 17, 1923; s. Henry Guerrant and Elizabeth Firmstone (Maxwell) E.; m. Mary Ball Ruffin, Apr. 15, 1950; children: John, Mary Ball, Elizabeth, Martha, Henry. BA, U. Va., 1948, JD, 1957, MA, 1961; PhD, U. N.C., 1969. CPA, Va., La.; bar: Va. 1957. Lab. instr. U. Va., Charlottesville, 1953-58; instr. Washington and Lee U., 1958-60; asst. prof. U. Fla., 1967-71; assoc. prof. U. New Orleans, 1971-76, prof. taxation, 1976-94, prof. emeritus, 1994—. Trainee Va. Carolina Hardware Co., Richmond, 1948-51; acct. Equitable Life Assurance Soc., Richmond, 1951-52; staff acct. Musselman & Drysdale, Charlottesville, 1952-54; staff acct. R.M. Musselman, Charlottesville, 1957-58; mem. U. New Orleans Oil and Gas Acctg. Conf., 1973-92; bd. dirs., publicity chmn. U. New Orleans Energy Acctg. and Tax Conf., 1993-94, bd. dirs. publicity com.; pres. Maxwelton Farm and Timber Corp., 1994—; treas. U. New Orleans Estate Planning Seminar, 1975-78, lectr. continuing edn.; CPCU instr. New Orleans Ins. Inst., 1975-78. Author books; contbr. articles to profl. jours. Served with AUS, 1943-46. Mem. AICPA (40 yr. hon. mem. 2000—), Am. Acctg. Assn., Am. Assn. Atty.-CPAs (chmn. ptnrship. taxation continuing edn. com. 1989, ptnrship. taxation com. 1990, organized La. chpt., v.p. 1991-93), Va. Soc. CPAs, Soc. La. CPAs, Va. Bar Assn. (40 yr. hon. mem. 2000—). Democrat. Episcopalian. Home: 177 Maxwelton Rd Charlottesville VA 22903-7859

ELLICKSON, ROBERT CHESTER, law educator; b. Washington, Aug. 4, 1941; s. John Chester and Katherine Heilprin (Pollak) E.; m. Ellen Zachariasen, Dec. 19, 1971; children: Jenny, Owen. AB, Oberlin Coll., 1963; LLB, Yale U., 1966. Bar: D.C. 1967, Calif. 1971. Atty. adviser Pres.'s Com. on Urban Housing, Washington, 1967-68; mgr. urban affairs Levitt & Sons Inc., Lake Success, N.Y., 1968-70; prof. law U. So. Calif., L.A., 1970-81, Stanford U., Calif., 1981-85, Robert E. Paradise prof. natural resources law, 1985-88; Walter E. Meyer prof. of property and urban law Yale U., New Haven, 1988—, dep. dean, 1991-92. Author: (with Tarlock) Land-Use Controls, 1981, Order Without Law, 1991 (Triennial award Order of the Coif), (with Rose & Ackerman) Perspectives on Property Law, 2d edit., 1995, (with Been) Land Use Controls, 2d edit., 2000. Mem. Am. Acad. Arts and Scis., Am. Law and Econs. Assn. (pres. 2000-01), Am. Law Inst. Office: Yale U Law Sch PO Box 208215 New Haven CT 06520-8215 E-mail: robert.ellickson@yale.edu

ELLICOTT, JOHN LEMOYNE, lawyer; b. Balt., May 26, 1929; s. Valcoulon LeMoyne and Mary Purnell (Gould) E.; m. Mary Lou Ulery, June 19, 1954 (dec. Jan. 1995); children: Valcoulon, Ann; m. Beatrice Berle Meyerson, Sept. 14, 1996. AB summa cum laude, Princeton U., 1951; LLB cum laude, Harvard U., 1954. Bar: D.C. 1957, U.S. Supreme Ct. 1959. Assoc. Covington & Burling, Washington, 1958-65, ptnr., 1965-98, chmn. mgmt. com., 1986-90, sr. counsel, 1998—. Pres. Fairfax County Fedn. Citizens Assn., Va., 1964; mem. governing bd. Nat. Cathedral Sch., Washington, 1973-80, 85-90, chmn., 1978-79; trustee Landon Sch., Bethesda, Md., 1972-76; bd. dirs. Protestant Episc. Cathedral Found., Washington, 1980-88. Mem. ABA (counselor, sect. internat. law and practice), Washington Inst. Fgn. Affairs, Phi Beta Kappa. Democrat. Administrative and regulatory, General corporate, Private international. Home: 5117 Macomb St NW Washington DC 20016-2611 Office: Covington & Burling 1201 Pennsylvania Ave NW Washington DC 20004 E-mail: jellicott@cov.com

ELLIN, MARVIN, lawyer; b. Balt., Mar. 6, 1923; s. Morris and Goldie (Rosen) E.; m. Stella J. Granto, Aug. 2, 1948; children: Morris, Raymond, Elisa. JD, U. Balt., 1953. Bar: Md. 1953, U.S. Supreme Ct. 1978; diplomate Am. Bd. Forensic Examiners. Practice law, Balt., 1953—; mem. firm Ellin & Baker, 1957—; specialist in med. malpractice law. Cons. on med. and legal trial matters; lectr. ACS, U. Md. Law Sch., U. Balt. City, Yale U. Sch. Medicine, Johns Hopkins Hosp., U. Calif., San Francisco, U. N.J.; former mem.'s adv. coun. com. on judiciary U.S. Senate. Mem. editl. adv. bd.: Ob/Gyn Malpractice Prevention; contbr. chpts. on med. malpractice to various profl. publs. including Radiation Therapy of Benign Diseases. Fellow Internat. Acad. Trial Lawyers; mem. ABA, Am. Soc. Law and Medicine. General civil litigation, Personal injury. Home: 13414 Longnecker Rd Glyndon MD 21071-4805 Office: 1101 Saint Paul St Baltimore MD 21202-2662

ELLINSON, DEAN AVRAHAM, lawyer; b. Tel Aviv, Israel, Apr. 3, 1961; arrived in Australia, 1966; s. Ya'akov and Varda Ellinson; m. Megan Ruth Ehrmann, Aug. 18, 1986; children: Nadav, Tal, Rebecca. B of Econs., Monash U., Melbourne, Australia, 1982, LLB, 1983, LLM, 1992. Articled clk. Joseph Lynch & Window, Melbourne, 1984-85; solicitor John McDonald Smith Box & Royston, 1985-86, Dunhill Madden Butler, Melbourne, 1986-89, sr. assoc., 1989-92, ptnr., 1992-93; gen. counsel Ferntree Computer Corp. Ltd., 1993-96, GE Capital Info. Tech. Solutions Pty. Ltd., Melbourne, 1996-97; cons. Clayton Utz, 1998-2000; spl. counsel Blake Dawson Waldron, 2001—. Contbr. articles to profl. jours. Mem. internat. humanitarian law com. Red Cross, Melbourne, 1993; pres. 15th Brighton Scout Group, Melbourne, 2000—; vol. lawyer Prahran Free Legal Svc., Melbourne, 1993; mem. Monash U. Patents Com., Melbourne, 1987-91; chmn. intellectual property, info. tech. and trade practices com. Law Inst. of Victoria, Melbourne, 1999—; mem. comml. law sect. exec. Law Inst., Melbourne, 1999—; rep. of Australian Corp. Lawyers Assn. on Coun. of Law Inst. of Victoria, 1995-96. Mem. Intellectual Property Soc. Australia and New Zealand, Licensing and Exec. Soc. of Australia and New Zealand, Victorian Soc. for Computers and Law. Avocations: swimming, Israeli folk dancing, current affairs. Computer, Intellectual property, Trademark and copyright. Office: Blake Dawson Waldron Level 39 101 Collins St Melbourne Victoria 3000 Australia

ELLIOT, CAMERON ROBERT, lawyer; b. Portland, Oreg., Jan. 6, 1966; s. James Addison and Dianne Louise (Youngblood) E. BS, Yale U., 1987; JD, Harvard U., 1996. Bar: Calif. 1996, D.C. 1999. Jud. clk. U.S. Dist. Ct., Reno, 1996-98; atty. civil divsn. U.S. Dept. Justice, Washington, 1998—. Editor-in-chief: (jour.) Harvard Environ. Law Rev., 1995-96. Mem. Reno Environ. Bd., 1996-97. Lt. USN, 1987-92. Home: 1725 17th St NW Apt 112 Washington DC 20009-2414 Office: US Dept Justice Civil Divsn Washington DC 20530-0001 E-mail: cameron@justice.com

ELLIOT, RALPH GREGORY, lawyer; b. Hartford, Conn., Oct. 20, 1936; s. K. Gregory and Zarou (Manoukian) E. BA, Yale U., 1958, LLB, 1961. Bar: Conn. 1961, U.S. Dist. Ct. Conn. 1963, U.S. Ct. Appeals (2d cir.) 1966, U.S. Ct. Appeals (Fed. cir.) 1993, U.S. Ct. Appeals (1st cir.) 1997, U.S. Supreme Ct. 1967. Law clk. to assoc. justice Conn. Supreme Ct., Hartford, 1961-62; assoc. Alcorn, Bakewell & Smith, 1962-67, ptnr., 1967-83, Tyler, Cooper & Alcorn, Hartford, 1983—. Adj. prof. law U. Conn., Hartford, 1973—; sec. Superior Ct. Legal Internship Com., Conn., 1971—; chmn. Superior Ct. Legal Specialization Screening Com., Conn., 1981—, U.S. Dist. Ct. Panel Spl. Masters, Hartford, 1983-88. Chmn. bd. editors Conn. Law Tribune, 1986-87. Chmn. Constn. Bicentennial Commn., Conn., 1986-91; mem. Criminal Justice Commn. Conn., 1991-95. Recipient Fenton P. Futtner award Conn. Reps., 1993. Fellow Am. Bar Found.; mem. ABA (standing com. on ethics and profl. responsibility 1989-95, standing com. on profl. discipline 1998-2001, ho. of dels. 1983-87), Conn. Bar Assn. (officer, bd. govs. 1971-79, 83-87, pres. 1985-86, John Eldred Shields Disting. Profl. Svc. award 1993), Am. Law Inst., Yale Law Sch. Assn. (pres. 1988-90, chmn. exec. com. 1990-92), Yale Club (pres. 1977-79, Nathan Hale award 1984, Betty McCallip Meml. award 1991), Hartford, Grad. Club (New Haven), Phi Beta Kappa. Republican. Episcopalian. Federal civil litigation, State civil litigation, Libel. Home: 27 Brookline Dr West Hartford CT 06107-1265

ELLIOTT, BRADY GIFFORD, judge; b. Harlingen, Tex., Nov. 26, 1943; s. Clyde Andres Elliott and Mildred (Parker) Bounds; m. Rhea Elizabeth Ricks, May 15, 1967; children: Adrian Winthrope, Jason Lawrence. BBA, McMurray Coll., 1970; JD, South Tex. Coll. Law, 1973. Bar: Tex. 1973, U.S. Dist. Ct. (so. dist.) Tex. 1974, U.S. Tax Ct. 1974, U.S. Ct. Appeals (5th cir.) 1974, U.S. Supreme Ct. 1979, U.S. Ct. Appeals (11th cir.) 1981. Asst. sec., asst. treas., asst. gen. counsel Gordon Jewelry Corp., Houston, 1970-79; sec., gen. counsel Oshman's Sporting Goods, Inc., Houston, 1979-82; sole practice, Sugar Land, Tex., 1982-88; legal counsel Ft. Bend C. of C., Sugar Land, Tex., 1982-88; mcpl. judge Missouri City, Tex., 1983-88; judge 268th Dist. Ct., Fort Bend County, Tex., 1988—. Bd. dirs. Ft. Bend chpt. Texans' War on Drugs, Sugar Land, 1981-94; bd. dirs. Ft. Bend Boys Choir, 1984-94. Mem. ABA, Houston Bar Assn., Fort Bend County Bar Assn., Masons, Rotary (treas. 1983-85). Republican. Methodist. Office: County Ct House Richmond TX 77469

ELLIOTT, FRANCES CARANO, lawyer, educator; b. Carovilli, Italy, Aug. 17, 1950; d. Remo Marino and Angelia (Elia) Carano; m. G. Mark Elliott, Sept. 23, 1972; children: Cara, Adrienne. BS in Phys. Therapy, Ohio State U., 1972; JD cum laude, U. Akron, 1983; postgrad., John Marshall Sch. Law, Chgo., 1998—. Bar: Ohio, U.S. Dist. Ct. Ohio; cert. phys. therapist. Dir. phys. therapy Ohio Rehab. Clinic, Columbus, 1972-76; rsch. asst. U. Akron Sch. Law, 1980, adj. prof., 1984-85; prodr., legal advisor Feedback Series: Legal Questions, WEAO Pub. TV, Kent, Ohio, 1989-94; ind. contractor West Group, Inc., 1998—; sole practitioner Hudson, Ohio, 1983—. Legal advisor WEAO Pub. TV, 1989-94; lectr. in field. Pres., Hudson Music Assn., 1990-94; mem. cabinet, legal divsn. United Way, Akron, 1987; publicity dir. Hudson Bicentennial Commn., 1995-97. Mem. Ohio State Bar Assn., Ohio Bar Coll., Akron Bar Assn. (publicity dir.), Hudson C. of C. (bd. dirs. 1986-88). Republican. Roman Catholic. Avocations: gardening, trading in the stock market, reading, travel. Home: 83 Sussex Rd Hudson OH 44236-1650 Office: Law Offices of Frances Elliott 118 W Streetsboro St # 140 Hudson OH 44236-2711 E-mail: eeefce@yahoo.com

ELLIOTT, FRANK WALLACE, lawyer, educator; b. Cotulla, Tex., June 25, 1930; s. Frank Wallace and Eunice Marie (Akin) E.; m. Winona Trent, July 3, 1954 (dec. 1981); 1 child, Harriet Lindsey; m. Kay Elkins, Aug. 15, 1983. Student, N.Mex. Mil. Inst., 1947-49; BA, U. Tex., 1951, LLB, 1957. Bar: Tex. 1957, U.S. Supreme Ct. 1962, U.S. Ct. Mil. Appeals 1974, U.S. Dist. Ct. (no. dist.) Tex. 1987, U.S. Ct. Appeals (5th cir.) 1988. Asst. atty. gen. State of Tex., 1957; briefing atty. Supreme Ct. Tex., 1957-58; prof. U. Tex. Law Sch., 1958-77; dean, prof. law Tex. Tech U. Sch. Law, 1977-80; pres. Southwestern Legal Found., 1980-86; ptnr. Baker, Mills & Glast, Dallas, 1987-88; of counsel Ramirez & Assocs., 1988—; dean Dallas/Ft. Worth Sch. Law, 1989-92; dean Sch. Law Tex. Wesleyan U., 1992-94, prof., dean emeritus, 1994—. Parliamentarian Tex. Senate, 1969-73; dir. rsch. Tex. Constl. Revision Commn., 1973 Author: Texas Judicial Process, 2d edit., 1977, Texas Trial and Appellate Practice, 2d edit., 1974, Cases on Evidence, 1980, West's Texas Forms, 20 vols., 1977—, West's Texas Practice, vol. 11, 1990, vol. 14, 1996. Served with U.S. Army, 1951-53, 73-74. Decorated Purple Heart. Mem. ABA, Judge Advs. Assn., Am. Judicature Soc., Am. Bar Found., Tex. Bar Found., Dallas Bar Found., Am. Law Inst., N.Mex. Mil. Inst. Alumni Hall of Fame. Federal civil litigation, State civil litigation, Private international. Home: 2120 N Rough Creek Ct Granbury TX 76048-2903 Office: 1515 Commerce St Fort Worth TX 76102-6572 E-mail: felliott@law.txwes.edu

ELLIOTT, HOMER LEE, lawyer; b. Madison, Ind., Aug. 3, 1938; s. William A. and Mabel E. (Talbot) E.; children: Homer, Charles, Jane. AB, Ind. U., 1960; postgrad., Princeton U., 1960-61; JD, Coll. William and Mary, 1969. Bar: Va. 1969, D.C. 1970, Pa. 1977, U.S. Supreme Ct. 1973, U.S. Tax Ct. 1971. Assoc. Steptoe & Johnson, Washington, 1969-77; ptnr. Drinker, Biddle & Reath, Phila., 1977-98, Duane, Morris & Heckscher, Phila., 1998—. Contbr. articles to profl. jours. With U.S. Army, 1961-65. Mem. ABA, Pa. Bar Assn., D.C. Bar Assn., VA State Bar, Princeton Club (Phila.), Phi Beta Kappa. Pension, profit-sharing, and employee benefits, Corporate taxation, Personal income taxation. Home: 1326 Spruce St Unit 2701 Philadelphia PA 19107 Office: Duane Morris & Heckscher LLP One Liberty Pl Philadelphia PA 19103-7396 E-mail: elliothl@aol.com, hlelliott@duanemorris.com

ELLIOTT, NICHOLAS BLETHYN, barrister; b. Nicosea, Cyprus, Dec. 11, 1949; s. Blethyn William and Zara E.; m. Nemmy Margaret Browne Elliott; children: Max Blethyn, George Hugh. LLB, Bristol, 1971. Queens counsel Grays Inn, Eng., 1995—. Joint editor Warne & Elliott, 1999. Asst. boundary commr., 2000. Avocations: tennis, cycling, skiing, bridge. Office: 3 Verulam Bldgs. Gray's Inn London WC1R 5NT England E-mail: nelliott@3verulam.co.uk

ELLIOTT, RICHARD HOWARD, lawyer; b. Astoria, N.Y., Apr. 30, 1933; m. Judith A. Kessler, Dec. 26, 1956; children: Marc Evan, Jonathan Hugh, Eve; m. 2d, Diane S. Schaefer, Nov. 18, 1978; children: Alexis, Sara Jane, Benjamin, David. BS, Lehigh U., 1954; JD cum laude, U. Pa., 1962. Bar: U.S. Dist. Ct. (ea. dist.) Pa. 1962, Pa. Supreme Ct. 1962, U.S. Ct. Appeals (3d cir.) 1963, U.S. Dist. Ct. (mid. dist.) Pa. 1976. Assoc. Clark, Ladner, Fortenbaugh & Young, Phila., 1962-69, ptnr., 1970-75, Elliott & Magee, Doylestown, Pa., 1976—. Moderator Permanent Jud. Commn., Presbytery of Phila.; v.p., dir. Bucks County Soc. Prevention Cruelty to Animals; former pres., dir. Pa. Soc. for Prevention of Cruelty to Animals; gen. counsel, dir. Pa. Fedn. Humane Socs., adj. faculty Bucks County Cmty. Coll.; mem. Pa. Navigation Commn., 1977-80. Lt. USN, 1954-59. Mem. ABA, Pa. Bar Assn., Phila. Bar Assn., Bucks County Bar Assn. Democrat. General civil litigation, General practice, Probate. Home: 1205 Victoria Rd Warminster PA 18974-3923 Office: Elliott & Magee 1795 S Easton Rd Doylestown PA 18901-2837 E-mail: relli59360@aol.com

ELLIOTT, ROBERT LLOYD, lawyer, educator; b. Lexington, Ky., Oct. 22, 1949; s. James Nathan and Lloyd (Lanier) E.; m. Jane Webb Higgins, June 25, 1971; children: James Kenneth, Lloyd Blair. BA, Centre Coll., Danville, Ky., 1971; JD, U. Ky., 1974. Bar: Ky. 1974, U.S. Dist. Ct. (ea. dist.) Ky. 1974, U.S. Ct. Appeals (6th cir.) 1982. Assoc. Harbison, Kessinger, Lisle & Bush, Lexington, 1974-78; ptnr. Harbison, Kessinger, Lyle & Bush, Lexington, 1978-82; assoc. Turley, Savage & Moore, Lexington, 1982-84; ptnr. Savage, Garmer & Elliott, P.S.C., Lexington, 1984— ; adj. prof. litigation skills U. Ky. Coll. Law, Lexington, 1981— ; dir. Central Ky. Legal Services, Inc., Lexington. Mem. Mayor's Adv. Com. on Cable TV, 1978— ; bd. dirs. Lexington Humane Soc., Metro Group Homes. Mem. ABA, Ky. Bar Assn. (Continuing Legal Edn. Commn. 1984— , admissions com. 1983—), Fayette County Bar Assn. (sec. 1975-76, bd. dirs. 1976-78, 83-84, v.p. 1985), Centre Coll. Alumni Assn. (bd. dirs.). Democrat. Episcopalian. Lodge: Optimists. Avocations: coaching youth baseball, basketball, tennis, jogging. Federal civil litigation, State civil litigation, Personal injury. Home: 4711 Iron Works Rd Georgetown KY 40324-9490 Office: Savage Garmer & Elliott PSC 141 N Broadway Lexington KY 40507-1240

ELLIOTT, SCOTT, lawyer, theater artistic director, critic; b. San Jose, July 26, 1957; s. Roland Meredith and Sandra Gale (Deem) E.; m. Nancy Marie Oller, Apr. 6, 1979; children: Tristan Robin, Jordan Brook, Robin Sage, Forest Dream. BA in Drama magna cum laude, Calif. State U. Stanislaus, Turlock, 1979; JD, U. Oreg., 1987. Bar: Oreg. 1987, U.S. Dist. Ct. Oreg. 1988, U.S. Ct. Appeals (9th cir.) 1992. Assoc. Larry O. Gildea, Eugene, Oreg., 1987-88, Thorp, Dennet, Purdy & Golden, Springfield, 1988; law clk. U.S. Dist. Ct. Nev., Las Vegas, 1988-89; ptnr. Green & Elliott, Lincoln City, Oreg., 1989-95; assoc. Thorp, Purdy, Jewett, Urness & Wilkinson, Springfield, 1995-96, Wine, Weller, Ehrlich and Green, Lincoln City, 1996-98; pvt. practice, 1998—. Theatre critic: Lincoln City News Guard. Choir Congl. Ch., 1997—; founder, artistic dir. Cmty. Family Players, 1997—. Recipient Commitment to Excellence in Art award, YCS, 2001; U. Oreg. Theatre grad. tchg. fellow, 1979-80. Mem. Kiwanis. Avocations: family, gardening, theatre, singing. Civil rights, General civil litigation, Consumer commercial. Office: 2137 NW Highway 101 Ste B Lincoln City OR 97367-4214 also: Lincoln City Congl Ch 1760 NW 25th St Lincoln City OR 97367-4151 E-mail: lawyer_elliott@yahoo.com

ELLIS, ALFRED WRIGHT (AL ELLIS), lawyer; b. Cleve., Aug. 26, 1943; s. Donald Porter and Louise (Wright) E.; m. Kay Genseke, June 1965 (div. 1976); 1 child, Joshua Kyle; m. Sandra Lee Fahey, Feb. 11, 1989. BA with honors, U. Tex., Arlington, 1965; JD, So. Meth. U., 1971. Bar: Tex., U.S. Dist. Ct. (no., so., ea. and we. dists.) Tex., U.S. Ct. Appeals (5th cir.), U.S. Supreme Ct.; cert. personal injury and civil trial lawyer. Atty.

Woodruff, Kendall & Smith, Dallas, 1972; ptnr. Woodruff & Ellis; pvt. practice, 1983-96; of counsel Howie & Sweeney, 1996—. Instr. So. Meth. U. Law Sch. Trial Advocacy; past pres. Law Focused Edn., Inc. Past mem. City of Dallas Urban Rehab. Standards Bd., Dallas Assembly, Salesmanship Club, Dallas; bd. dirs. Dallas Habitat for Humanity, 1998—; trustee Hist. Preservation League, 1992-94; tournament dir. Dallas Regional Golden Gloves Tournament, 1976-96; pres., bd. dirs. Dallas Coun. on Alcoholism, 1980. Capt. U.S. Army, 1965-69. Fellow Roscoe Pound Found.; named one of Outstanding Young Mem of Am., 1977, named Boss of Yr. Dallas Assn. Legal Secs., 1978; recipient Certs. of Recognition (8) D.I.S.D., 1971-83, Wall St. Jour. award So. Meth. U. Law Sch., 1972, Hayward McMurray award Dallas Jaycees, 1975-76, Spl. Recognition award All Sports Assn., 1977, Cert. of Appreciation for Exceptional and Disting. Vol. Svc. Gov. Mark White, 1983, Community Spirit award Dallas Bus. Jour., 1993, Disting. Svc. award Dallas All Sports Assn., 1993,award Nancy Garms Meml. for outstanding Contr. to Law Focus Edn., 1996-Leon Jaworski award. Fellow Tex. Bar Found. (sustaining life), Dallas Bar Found. (trustee); mem. ATLA, Am. Bd. Trial Advocates (diplomate, sec.-treas. Dallas chpt. 1998, pres. 1999), Am. Coll. Legal Medicine (assoc.), Legal Svcs. of North Tex. (bd. dirs., Outstanding Svc. award 1990), State Bar Tex. (lectr. seminars, bd. dirs. 1991-94, 95, Excellence in Diversity award 1994, Outstanding 3d Yr. Dir. award, Judge Sam Williams Local Bar Leadership award), Dallas Bar Assn. (bd. dirs. 1978, chmn. bd. dirs. 1986, v.p. 1987-88, pres. 1990), Dallas Trial Lawyers Assn. (pres. 1977, Disting. Cmty. Svc. award 1990), Tex. Trial Lawyers Assn., Tex. Equal Access to Justice Found. (bd. dirs. 1994-96), Coll. State Bar of Tex. (bd. dirs. 1997—), Dallas All Sports Assn. (pres.-1980), Tex. Commn. for Lawyer Discipline, Tex. Ctr. for Legal Ethics and Professionalism (bd. dirs. 1999—), Tex. Legal Svcs. Ctr. (bd. dirs. 1999—). Avocations: tennis, skiing. General civil litigation, Insurance, Personal injury. Office: 2911 Turtle Creek Blvd Ste 1400 Dallas TX 75219-6258

ELLIS, ANDREW JACKSON, JR. lawyer; b. Ashland, Va., June 23, 1930; m. Dorothy L. Lichliter, Apr. 24, 1954; children: Elizabeth E. Attkisson, Andrew C., William D. AB, Washington and Lee U., 1951, LLB, 1953. Bar: Va. 1952. Ptnr. Campbell, Ellis & Campbell, Ashland, 1955-70, Mays, Valentine, Davenport & Moore, Richmond, Va., 1970-88, Mays & Valentine, Richmond, 1988-96, sr. counsel, 1998—. Substitute judge County of Hanover (Va.) Ct., 1958-63, commonwealth atty., 1963-70, county atty., 1970-78; substitute judge 15th jud. dist., 1990-96; judge 15th dist Juvenile and Domestic Rels. Ct., 1996-98; mem. capital adv. bd. NationsBank of Va., 1960-93. Mem. Ashland Town Coun., 1956-63, mayor, 1958-63; trustee J. Sargent Reynolds C.C., 1972-80. 1st lt. U.S. Army, 1953-55. Fellow Am. Coll. Trial Lawyers, Va. Law Found.; mem. Am. Judicature Soc., Va. Bar Assn., Va. State Bar (coun. 1968-74), Va. Trial Lawyers Assn., S.R., Kiwanis. Episcopalian. General civil litigation, Condemnation, Insurance. Home: 15293 Old Ridge Rd Beaverdam VA 23015-1610 Office: PO Box 1122 Richmond VA 23218-1122

ELLIS, BARNES HUMPHREYS, lawyer; b. Boston, Jan. 21, 1940; s. Raymond Walleser and Eleanor (Gwin) E.; m. Beatrice Cleland, Aug. 25, 1962; children: Cynthia, Barnes, Mary, Joy, Heidi, Curtis. BA, Yale U., 1961; postgrad., Stanford U., 1962; LLB, Harvard U., 1964. Bar: Oreg. 1964, Wash. 1983, U.S. Dist. Ct. Oreg. 1964, U.S. Dist. Ct. (we. dist.) Wash. 1983, U.S. Ct. Appeals (1st cir.) 1968, U.S. Ct. Appeals (9th cir.) 1971, U.S. Supreme Ct. 1968. Assoc. Stoel, Rives, Boley, Jones & Grey, Portland, Oreg., 1964-70, ptnr., 19770—. White House fellow U.S. Dept. Justice, Washington, 1967-68. Chmn. Met. Pub. Defender Svcs. Inc., Portland, 1975—; chmn. Oreg. Commn. on Jud. Br., Salem, 1979-83; chmn. Oreg. Pub. Def. Svcs. Commn., 2000—. Fellow Am. Coll. Trial Lawyers; mem. ABA, Oreg. State Bar Assn., Wash. State Bar Assn., Multnomah Bar Assn. Republican. E-mal. Antitrust, Federal civil litigation, State civil litigation. Home: 410 Bergis Rd Lake Oswego OR 97034-6250 Office: Stoel Rives LLP 900 SW 5th Ave Ste 2300 Portland OR 97204-1229 E-mail: bhellis@stoel.com

ELLIS, COURTENAY, lawyer; b. Cottingham, Eng., Jan. 4, 1946; came to the U.S., 1970; BA, Oxford U., Eng., 1967, MA, 1974; LLM, George Washington U., 1972. Bar: D.C. 1973; cert. solicitor, Eng. Solicitor's articled clk. Field, Fisher & Co., London, 1968-69; solicitor Farrer & Co., 1970; assoc. atty. Covington & Burling, Washington, 1972-76, Akin, Gump, Strauss, Hauer & Feld, 1976-78, ptnr., 1979-98, Oppenheimer Wolff Donnelly Bayh, Washington, 1998-99, Murphy Ellis Weber, 2000—. Bd. dirs. The Episcopal Ctr. for Children, Washington, 1986-92. Mem. ABA, Law, Law Soc. London, Brit. Am. Bus. Assn. (bd. dirs., program chair 1997-98, pres. 1999-2001), Washington Fgn. Law Soc. (bd. govs., membership coord. 1993-95, program coord. 1995-96, pres. 1997-98), Fed. Bar Assn. (internat. law sect., chair 1996-98), The Law Soc., London, Met. Club, Annapolis Yacht Club. General civil litigation, Oil, gas, and mineral, Private international. Office: Murphy Ellis Weber Ste 700 818 Connecticut Ave NW Washington DC 20006 E-mail: cellis@murphyellisweber.com

ELLIS, DAVID DALE, lawyer; b. Columbus, Ga., Dec. 22, 1952; s. Audie Stammattee and Eva Grace (Thomas) E. BA cum laude Mercer U., Macon, Ga., 1974; JD, Drake U., 1976, MPA, 1977. Bar: Iowa 1977, Ga. 1978, U.S. Dist. Ct. (no. dist.) Ga. 1979, U.S. Ct. Appeals (11th cir.) 1979, U.S. Supreme Ct. 1983, U.S. Dist. Ct. (so. dist.) 1985, Tex. 1986. Instr. Grad. Sch., Drake U., Des Moines, 1977; claims adjuster Farm Bur. Ins. Co., Des Moines, 1977; assoc. firm Cotton, White & Palmer, Atlanta, 1978-82; mng. atty. Hyatt Legal Svcs., Marietta and Smyrna, Ga., 1982-84, regional ptnr., Houston, 1984-86; sr. ptnr. Hughes & Hilbert P.C., 1986-87; sr. ptnr. Jeffers & Ellis, P.C., Houston, 1987-88; pvt. practice, 1988—. Contbr. articles to profl. jours. Career awareness chmn. Houston coun. Boy Scouts Am., 1984-85; instr. project bus., legal advisor Jr. Achievement, Houston, 1984-85; mem. Houston Bankruptcy Conf. Mem. Iowa Bar Assn., Ga. Bar Assn., State Bar Tex., Am. Soc. Tng. and Devel., Atlanta Jaycees (chmn. Empty Stockings Fund 1982, v.p. individual devel. 1983-84; Officer of Yr. 1984), U.S. Jaycees (life, ambassador award 1985, named JCI senator), Houston Jaycees (exec. v.p. 1986—, chmn. govt. affairs 1984-85, pres. 1987—), Tex. Jaycees (legal counsel 1985-87), ABA (chmn. bankruptcy com. 1985-87, co-chmn. 1987, chmn. 1987—), Atlanta Bar Assn., Houston Bar Assn., Houston Young Lawyers Assn., Tex. Young Lawyers Assn., Assn. Trial Lawyers of Am., Ga. Trial Lawyers Assn., Fed. Bar Assn., Masons. Bankruptcy, General practice. Office: PO Box 130447 Houston TX 77219-0447

ELLIS, DONALD LEE, lawyer; b. Oct. 2, 1950; s. Truett T. and Rosemary (Tarrant) Ellis; children: Angela Nicole, Laura Elizabeth, Natalie Dawn, Donald Lee II. BS, U. Tulsa, 1973; JD, Okla. City U., 1976. Bar: Tex. 1979, Okla. 1977, U.S. Dist. Ct. (ea. dist.) Tex. 1978, U.S. Dist. Ct. (we. dist.) Okla. 1978, U.S. Ct. Appeals (5th cir.) 1984, U.S. Ct. Appeals (11th cir.), U.S. Supreme Ct. 1984. Spl. agt. FBI, Washington, 1976—78; asst. dist. atty. Smith County, Tyler, Tex., 1979—80; mem. firm Barron & Ellis, 1985—. Bd. dir. Mental Health Assn. Mem.: Assn. Trial Lawyers Am., Tex. Bar Assn., Okla. Bar Assn., Smith County Bar Assn., Soc. Former Spl. Agts. FBI, Tex. Trial Lawyers Assn., FBI Agents Assn., Lawyers-Pilot Bar Assn. Personal injury. Home: PO Box 131221 Tyler TX 75713-1221 Office: 217 W Houston St Tyler TX 75702-8137

ELLIS, DORSEY DANIEL, JR. lawyer, educator; b. Cape Girardeau, Mo., May 18, 1938; s. Dorsey D. and Anne (Stanaland) E.; m. Sondra Wagner, Dec. 27, 1962; children: Laura Elizabeth, Geoffrey Earl. BA, Maryville Coll., 1960; JD, U. Chgo., 1963; LLD, Maryville Coll., 1998. Bar: N.Y. 1967, U.S. Ct. Appeals (2d cir.) 1967, Iowa 1976, U.S. Ct. Appeals (8th cir.) 1976. Assoc. Cravath, Swaine & Moore, N.Y.C., 1963-68; assoc. prof. U. Iowa, Iowa City, 1968-71, prof., 1971-87, v.p. fin. and univ. svcs., 1984-87, spl. asst. to pres., 1974-75; dean Washington U. Sch. Law, St. Louis, 1987-98, prof. law, 1998-99; disting. prof. law, 1999—. Vis. mem. sr. common room Mansfield Coll., Oxford U., Eng., 1972-73, 75; vis. prof. law Emory U., Atlanta, 1981-82, Victoria U., New Zealand, 1999; vis. sr. rsch. fellow Jesus Coll. Oxford U., Eng., 1998; bd. dirs. Maryville Coll., 1989-98, 99—. Contbr. articles to profl. jours. Trustee Mo. Hist. Soc., St. Louis, 1995-2000. Nat. Honor scholar U. Chgo., 1960-63; recipient Joseph Henry Beale prize, 1961, Alumni award Maryville Coll., 1988. Mem. ABA, Am. Law Inst., Bar Assn. Metro St. Louis, Mound City Bar Assn., Iowa Bar Assn., AALS Acad. Resource Corps., Order of Coif. Home: 6901 Kingsbury Blvd Saint Louis MO 63130 E-mail: ellis@wulaw.wustl.edu

ELLIS, FREDRIC LEE, lawyer; b. Springfield, Mass., Nov. 21, 1957; s. Irving Donald and Evelyn Gladys (Melnick) Ellis; m. Wendy J. Murphy, Oct. 21, 1988; children: Grant, Taylor, Reed, Cameron, Brit. BA, Hampshire Coll., Amherst, Mass., 1979; JD cum laude, Harvard U., 1983. Bar: Mass. 1983, U.S. Dist. Ct. Mass. 1983, U.S. Ct. Appeals (1st cir.) 1983, U.S. Ct. Appeals (11th cir.) 1994. Law clk. to Justice Raya Dreben Mass. Appellate Cr., Boston, 1983-84; asst. dist. atty. Dist. Atty.'s Office, Cambridge, Mass., 1984-86, dep. chief Appeals and Tng. Bur., 1986-87; ptnr. Gilman, McLaughlin & Hanrahan, Boston, 1987-96; founding ptnr. Ellis & Rapacki, 1996—. Mem. bd. editors med./Legal Aspects of Breast Implants, 1996—. Named Lawyer of Yr., Mass. Lawyers Weekly, 1996, Outstanding Civil Trial Atty., Middlesex Bar Assn., 1998. Mem. ATLA, Mass. Bar Assn., Mass. Assn. Trial Attys. General civil litigation, Personal injury, Product liability. Office: Ellis & Rapacki 85 Merrimac St Ste 500 Boston MA 02114-4715 E-mail: rellis@ellisrapacki.com

ELLIS, JAMES ALVIS, JR. lawyer; b. Lubbock, Tex., Mar. 19, 1943; s. James Alvis and Myrle Alice (Peden) E.; m. Sandra Gay Gillespie, June 18, 1966; children: Claire Ellis Gentry, James Alvis III. BA, Tex. Tech U., 1965; JD, U. Tex., 1968. Bar: Tex. 1968, U.S. Dist. Ct. (no., so., ea. and we. dists.) Tex. 1969, U.S. Ct. Appeals 1970, U.S. Supreme Ct. 1980; cert. in civil trial law Tex. Bd. Legal Specialization. Law clk. to presiding judge U.S. Dist. Ct. (we. dist.) Tex., 1968-69; assoc. Carrington, Coleman Sloman & Blumenthal, Dallas, 1970-74, ptnr., 1975—. Pres. Dallas Jr. Bar Assn., 1972. Fellow Tex. Bar Found., Dallas Bar Found.; mem. ABA, State Bar Tex., Dallas Bar Assn. Presbyterian. Club: Crescent. Federal civil litigation, General civil litigation, State civil litigation. Office: Carrington Coleman Sloman & Blumenthal 200 Crescent Ct Ste 1500 Dallas TX 75201-1848 E-mail: Jellis@CCSB.com

ELLIS, JAMES HENRY, lawyer, management consultant; b. Hartford, Conn., May 6, 1933; s. Robert Isaac and Eve (Alperin) E.; m. Linda Abess, Feb. 22, 1959; children: James Arthur, Nancy Jean, Arthur Ungar. BS, U. Conn., 1955; MBA, Harvard U., 1957; JD, U. Miami, 1968. Bar: Fla. 1968, D.C. 1969, N.Y. 1975. V.p., sec. Fed. Fire & Casualty Co., Miami, Fla., 1959-68; atty. SEC, Washington, 1968-70; exec. v.p., sec., gen. counsel CNA Mgmt. Corp. and 5 related mut. funds, N.Y.C., 1970-79; pres., gen. counsel Mut. Fund Cons. Group, Scarsdale, N.Y., 1979—. Founder, pres. Sentry Savs. and Loan Assn., Stamford, Conn., 1983-90; chmn. edn. com., assocs. div. No. Load Mut. Fund Assn., 1986-89. Contbr. numerous articles to profl. jours.; prodr. of several off-broadway shows; prodr. (short film) Italian Lessons (best narrative short film Westchester N.Y. Film Festival 2000). Bd. dirs., v.p. White Plains (N.Y.) Symphony Orch., 1975-87; bd. dirs. Stanford Ctr. for the Arts, 1994—; pres., bd. dirs. Parsons Dance Found., 1998—. Mem. ABA, N.Y. State Bar Assn., Harvard Club (N.Y.C.). Democrat. Jewish. General corporate, Entertainment, Securities. Home: 36 Butler Rd Scarsdale NY 10583-2214 E-mail: jhellis@cyburban.com

ELLIS, JAMES REED, lawyer; b. Oakland, Calif., Aug. 5, 1921; s. Floyd E. and Hazel (Reed) E.; m. Mary Lou Earling, Nov. 18, 1944 (dec.); children: Robert Lee, Judith Ann (dec.), Lynn Earling, Steven Reed. B.S., Yale, 1942; J.D., U. Wash., 1948; LL.D., Lewis and Clark U., 1968, Seattle U., 1981, Whitman Coll., 1992. Bar: Wash. 1949, D.C. 1971. Ptnr. Preston, Thorgrimson, Horowitz, Starin & Ellis, Seattle, 1952-69, Preston, Thorgrimson, Starin, Ellis & Holman, Seattle, 1969-72, Preston, Thorgrimson, Ellis, Holman & Fletcher, Seattle, 1972-79; sr. ptnr. Preston, Thorgrimson, Ellis & Holman, 1979-90, Preston, Thorgrimson, Shidler, Gates & Ellis, Seattle, 1990-92; ret., of counsel Preston, Gates & Ellis, 1992—; chmn., CEO Wash. State Convention and Trade Ctr., 1986—. Dep. pros. atty. King County, 1952; gen. counsel Municipality of Met. Seattle, 1958-79; dir., mem. exec. com. Key Bank of Wash., 1969-94, KIRO, Inc., 1965-95; dir. Blue Cross of Wash. and Alaska, 1989-98. Mem. Nat. Water Commn., 1970-73; mem. urban transp. adv. council U.S. Dept. Transp., 1970-71; mem. Wash. Planning Adv. Council, 1965-72; mem. Washington State Growth Strategies Commn., 1989-90; pres. Forward Thrust Inc., 1966-73; chmn. Mayors Com. on Rapid Transit, 1964-65; trustee Ford Found., 1970-82, mem. exec. com., 1978-82; bd. regents U. Wash., 1965-77, pres., 1972-73; trustee Resources for the Future, 1983-92; mem. council Nat. Mcpl. League, 1968-76, v.p., 1972-76; chmn. Save our Local Farmlands Com., 1978-79, King County Farmlands Adv. Commn., 1980-82; pres. Friends of Freeway Park, 1976-99; bd. dirs. Nat. Park and Recreation Assn., 1979-82; trustee Lewis and Clark U., 1988-94; pres. Mountains to Sound Greenway Trust, Inc., 1991—; trustee Henry M. Jackson Found., 1992—. 1st lt. USAAF, 1943-46. Recipient Bellevue First Citizen award, 1968, Seattle First Citizen award, 1968, Nat. Conservation award Am. Motors, 1968, Distinguished Service award Wash. State Dept. Parks and Recreation, 1968, Distinguished Citizen award Nat. Municipal League, 1969, King County Distinguished Citizen award, 1970, La Guardia award Center N.Y.C. Affairs, 1975, Environ. Quality award EPA, 1977, Am. Inst. for Public Service Nat. Jefferson award, 1974, State Merit medal State of Wash., 1990, Nat. Founders award Local Initiatives Support Corp., 1992, Henry M. Jackson Disting. Pub. Svc. medal, 1998, U. Wash. Alumnus Summa Laude Dignatus award, 1999. Fellow Am. Bar Found.; mem. ABA (ho. dels. 1978-82, past chmn. urban, state and local govt. law sect.), Nat. Assn. Bond Lawyers (com. standards of practice), Wash. Bar Assn., Seattle Bar Assn. (Pres.'s award 1993), D.C. Bar Assn., Am. Judicature Soc., Acad. Pub. Adminstrn., Coun. on Fgn. Rels., Mcpl. League Seattle and King County (past pres.), Order of Hosp. of St. John of Jerusalem, AIA (hon.), Order of Coif (hon.), Phi Delta Phi, Phi Gamma Delta, Rainier Club (Seattle). General practice, Municipal (including bonds). Home: 903 Shoreland Dr SE Bellevue WA 98004-6738 Office: 5000 Bank of America Tower 701 5th Ave Seattle WA 98104-7097 Fax: (206) 623-7022. E-mail: jamese@prestongates.com

ELLIS, JEFFREY ORVILLE, lawyer; b. Parsons, Kans., Mar. 9, 1944; s. Orman Carl Ellis and Esther Jane (Landreth) Ellis-Hett; m. Carol Lynne Byington, Aug. 6, 1966; children: Robert James, Jeffrey Todd. BS, U. Kans., 1966; JD, Washburn U., 1977. Bar: Kans. 1977, U.S. Dist. Ct. Kans. 1977, Mo. 1993. Tchr. Shawnee Mission (Kans.) Dist. Schs., 1966-68; atty., ptnr. Holbrook, Ellis & Heaven, Shawnee Mission, 1977-91, Lathrop & Gage, L.C., Kansas City, Mo., 1991—. Bd. dirs. United Cmty. Svcs., Johnson County, Johnson County Health Partnership, Mid-Am. chpt. MS Soc., United Way of Johnson County; spkr. in field. Author, editor: Handbook for Peer Review, 1992. Chmn. task force Gov.'s Commn. on Health Care, Topeka, 1989-90; mem. Legis.'s Commn. on Health Care Svcs., Topeka, 1987-90; chmn. Kans. Rep. Party, 3d Congl. Dist., 1990-92. Capt. U.S. Army, 1966-74, Vietnam. Mem. Am. Health Lawyers Assn., Kans. Assn. Hosp. Attys. (bd. dirs. 1987-90, pres. 1992-93), Kansas Head Injury Assn. (bd. dirs. 1987-91), Greater Kansas City C. of C. (chmn. task force 1991-93), Rotary (pres. Overland Park 1992). Republican. Episcopalian. Avocations: golf, bicycling. General corporate, Health, Insurance. Home: 183 Hillcrest Rd W Shawnee Mission KS 66217-8731 Office: Lathrop & Gage LC 1050 Corporate Woods Overland Park KS 66210-2019

ELLIS, LESTER NEAL, JR. lawyer; b. Washington, Aug. 1, 1948; s. Lester Neal and Marie (Brooks) E. BS, U.s. Mil. Acad., 1970; JD, U. Va., 1975. Bar: Va. 1975, U.S. Ct. Appeals (5th cir.) 1977, D.C. 1978, U.S. Ct. Appeals (4th and D.C. cirs.) 1979, U.S. Ct. Appeals (11th cir.) 1982, N.C. 1985, U.S. Supreme Ct. 2000, U.S. Dist. Ct. (ea., mid., we. dists.) N.C., U.S. Dist. Ct. (ea., we. dists.) Va., U.S. Ct. Claims. Trial atty. litigation divsn. Office of JAG, U.S. Dept. Army, Washington, 1975-78; assoc. Hunton & Williams, Richmond, Va., 1978-84, ptnr. Raleigh, 1984—. Maj. U.S. Army, 1970-78, col. USAR, 1993-99. Recipient Judge Paul Brosman award U.S. Ct. Mil. Appeals, 1975. Mem.: ABA (chair tort and trial practice steering com., editor-in-chief Tort Source, chair comml. torts commn., chair trial techniques com., tort and ins. practice sect., editor-in-chief Tort and Ins. Law Jour.), Va. Bar Assn. (spl. issues com. 1982), D.C. Bar Assn. (ct. rules com., Wake County bd. elections 1986—93, chmn. 1987—93), Phi Kappa Phi. Republican. Episcopalian. General civil litigation, Environmental. Home: 2608 Dover Rd Raleigh NC 27608-2032 Office: Hunton & Williams One Hanover Sq PO Box 109 Raleigh NC 27602-0109

ELLIS, WILLIAM R. lawyer; b. Pitts., Aug. 14, 1949; s. Edwin Francis and Mary Jane Ellis; m. Deborah L. Ellis, Mar. 14, 1981; children: Catherine, Deborah, Jennifer, Jillian. BA, U. Dayton, 1970; JD, Duquesne U., 1975. Assoc. Leventon & Leventon, Pitts., 1975-79, Waite, Schneider, Bayless & Chesley, Cin., 1979-84; ptnr. Wood & Lamping LLP, 1984—. Office: Wood & Lamping LLP 600 Vine St Cincinnati OH 45202-2400

ELLISON, NONI LOIS, lawyer; b. Jennings, La., Sept. 7, 1971; d. Grant Ellison Jr. and Gloria (McZeal) E. BA, Howard U., 1993; MBA, JD, U. Chgo., 1997. Cert. in health adminstrn. and policy. Assoc. Vinson & Elkins LLP, Houston, 1997—. Bar: Tex. Mem. Houston Bar Assn. (com. 1998-99). General corporate, Mergers and acquisitions, Securities. Fax: 713-615-5536. E-mail: nellison@velaw.com

ELLMANN, DOUGLAS STANLEY, lawyer; b. Detroit, July 15, 1956; s. William Marshall and Sheila Estelle E.; m. Claudia Joan Roberts, Feb. 16, 1985; children: Ben Bosworth, Liam Roberts. AB, Occidental Coll., 1978; JD, U. Mich., 1982. Bar: Mich. 1982, U.S. Dist. Ct. (ea. dist.) Mich. 1982, U.S. Ct. Appeals (6th cir.) 1982. Assoc. Butzel, Keidan, Simon, Myers & Graham, Detroit, 1982-84; ptnr. Ellmann & Ellmann, 1984-86; atty. Wise & Marsac, 1987-89; U.S. panel trustee, 1989—; prin. Ellmann & Ellmann, P.C., Ann Arbor, Mich., 1989—. Spl. asst. atty. gen., 1986; sec. bankruptcy trustees U.S. Bankruptcy Ct. (ea. dist.) Mich., 1993—, mem. bench bar com., 1994—. Author: Selected Issues in Asset Protection, 1994, My Advice: Next Time Go Solo, 1994, LWUSA; co-author: Winning Labor Arbitrations, 1987. Founder Amnesty Internat., Detroit, Lawyer's Support Network; mem. nat. com. U. Mich. Law Sch. Fund, 1986—. Mem. ABA (vice chair bankruptcy com. 1995—), Mich. Bar Assn. (rep. assembly 1983-89, 90-92, 98—, exec. counsel young lawyers sect. 1985-87, mem. client security fund com. 1987-95), State Bar Mich. (mem. manditory CLE com. 1989-96, chmn. 1995-96, judicial qualifications com. 2000—), Washtenaw County Bar Assn. (chmn. banking, bus., bankruptcy com. 1995—). Bankruptcy, General civil litigation, Contracts commercial. Office: 308 W Huron St Ann Arbor MI 48103-4204

ELLMANN, WILLIAM MARSHALL, lawyer, mediator, arbitrator, researcher; b. Highland Park, Mich., Mar. 23, 1921; s. James I. and Jeannette (Barsook) E.; m. Sheila Estelle Frenkel, Nov. 1, 1953; children: Douglas S., Carol E., Robert L. Student, Occidental Coll., 1939-40; AB, U. Mich., 1946; LLB, Wayne State U., 1951. Bar: Mich. 1951. Pvt. practice law, Detroit, 1951—; ptnr. Ellmann & Ellmann, 1970—. Spl. com. atty. gen. Mich. to study use state troops in emergencies, 1964-65; mem. exec. Inst. Continuing Legal Edn., 1964-68; mem. Mich. Employment Rels. Commn., 1973—, chmn., 1983-86; commr. Mackinac Island State Park Commn., 1979-85, chmn., 1983-86; panel mem. numerous orgns. Author: Of Hemingway, Toscanni and Arbitration: Practical Considerations for Preparing Winning Cases, 1985, A Reply to the Ambassador on Russia, 1991, (with Douglas S. Ellmann) Winning Labor Arbitrations, 1987; contbr. articles to profl. jours. With USAAF, 1942-46. Fellow Am. Bar Found.; mem. ABA (ho. of dels. 1969-72), Am. Arbitration Assn. (mem. adv. council), Nat. Acad. Arbitrators, Detroit Bar Assn. (vice chmn. pub. relations com. 1959), State Bar Mich. (commr. 1959-69, pres. 1966-67, co-chmn. com. on qualification jud. candidates 1970-78, mem. Detroit News secret witness panel 1983), Practicing Law Inst. (adv. council 1969-70, spl. asst. atty. gen. 1970-78), Sigma Nu Phi. General practice, Labor, Probate. Home: 28000 Weymouth Ct Farmington Hills MI 48334-3267 Office: Ellmann & Ellmann 308 W Huron St Ann Arbor MI 48103-4204

ELLWANGER, THOMAS JOHN, lawyer; b. Summit, N.J., Feb. 26, 1949; s. James Warren and Lorean (Nicholson) E.; children: James Hunter, Margaret Lorean. BA, Northwestern U., 1970; JD, U. Fla., 1974. Bar: Fla. 1975, U.S. Dist. Ct. (mid. dist.) Fla. 1976, U.S. Ct. Appeals (11th cir.) 1976, U.S. Dist. Ct. (so. dist.) Fla. 1977, U.S. Tax Ct. Mem. Fowler, White, Gillen, Boggs, Villareal & Banker P.A., Tampa, Fla., 1975—. Instr. law U. Fla., Gainesville, 1975; adj. prof. Stetson U. Coll. Law, 1997-2000. Editor: Gadsden County Times, 1970-72. Pres. Neighborhood Housing Services Hyde Park, Tampa, 1978. Fellow Am. Coll. Trust and Estate Counsel, Fla. Bar (cert. tax lawyer), Hillsborough County Bar Assn. (chmn. com. probate liaison 1985-86, real property probate and trust law sect. 1987-89), Tampa Bay Estate Planning Counsel (pres. 1994-95). Democrat. Avocations: music. lit., sports. Estate planning, Probate, Estate taxation. Office: Fowler White Gillen Boggs Villareal & Banker PA 501 E Kennedy Blvd Ste 1700 Tampa FL 33602-5239 E-mail: tellwang@fowlerwhite.com

ELLWOOD, SCOTT, lawyer; b. Boston, July 8, 1936; s. William Prescott and Doris (Cook) E.; m. Suzanne M. Timble; children: Victoria, William Prescott II, Marjorie. Student, Williams Coll., 1954-56; AB, Eastern Mich. U., 1958; LLB, Harvard U., 1961. Bar: Iowa 1961, Ill. 1961, U.S. Dist. Ct. (no. dist.) Ill., 1961. Assoc. McBride & Baker, Chgo., 1961-67, ptnr., 1968-84, McDermott, Will & Emery, Chgo., 1984-99. Pres. Miller Investment Co., 1973-93, bd. dirs.; pres. SMI Investment Corp., 1978—. Pres., bd. dirs. 110 N Wacker Dr Found., 1974-84, Northfield Found., 1978-84, Leadership Found., 1979-84, Woodbine Found., 1980-84, The Cannon River Found., 1982-84, L.M. McBride Found., 1982-84, Bellarmine Found., 1982-84, Mark Morton Meml. Fund, 1982—. Mem. Iowa Bar Assn., Ill. State Bar Assn., Harvard Law Soc. Ill. (bd. dirs. 1983-98, treas. 1987-88, sec. 1988-89, v.p. 1989-93, pres. 1993-95), Harvard Club Chgo. (bd. dirs. 1993-95), Monroe Club (bd. dirs. 1988-98), Skokie Country Club (Glencoe, Ill.). Republican. Episcopalian. Estate planning, Corporate taxation, Personal income taxation. Home: 1296 Hackberry Ln Winnetka IL 60093-1606 Office: McDermott Will & Emery 227 W Monroe St Ste 3100 Chicago IL 60606-5096

ELMAN, GERRY JAY, lawyer; b. Chgo., Oct. 7, 1942; s. Earl Samuel and Lucille Paulyne Elman; m. Lois Suzanne Bermet Levine; children: Jason Farrel, Floren Haley. BS, U. Chgo., 1963; MS in Chemistry, Stanford U., 1964; JD, Columbia U., 1967. Bar: N.Y. 1967, Pa. 1969, U.S. Dist. Ct. (so. and ea. dists.) N.Y. 1971, U.S. Dist. Ct. (ea. dist.) Pa. 1973, U.S. Dist. Ct. (mid. dist.) Pa. 1974, U.S. Ct. Appeals (Fed. cir.) 1987, U.S. Ct. Appeals (3d cir.) 1989, U.S. Patent Office, 1967, U.S. Supreme Ct. 1973. Assoc. Hubbell, Cohen & Stiefel, N.Y.C., 1967-68; patent atty., enzymes and health products Rohm and Haas Co., Phila., 1968-72; dep. atty. gen. Pa. Dept. Justice, Harrisburg, 1972-76; trial atty. Mid. Atlantic office antitrust divsn. U.S. Dept. Justice, Phila., 1976-82; pvt. practice, 1982-83; mem. Elman Assocs., 1984-88, Lipton, Famiglio & Elman, Media, Pa., 1988-89, Elman Wilf & Fried, Media, 1990-95, Elman & Fried, Media,

1995-96, Elman & Assocs., Media, 1996—. Instr. short course in computer law Temple U., Phila., 1984; mem. faculty in intellectual property mgmt. U. Phoenix Online Campus, 1995-98. Contbg. author: Lawyers' Microcomputer Users Group Jour., 1985-88; editor: Columbia Jour. Transnat. Law, 1966-67; mem. adv. bd. Jour. Computer Law Reporter, 1983-90; mem. editl. bd. Jour. Trademark Reporter, 1968; founder, editor in chief legal jour. Biotech. Law Report, 1982—; mem. adv. bd. BNA Spl. Reports Biotech., 1989-90, The LIcensing Jour., 1998—; mem. bd. advisors Santa Clara Computer and High Tech. Law Jour., 1994—; mem. Global Cyber-Law Network, 1997—. Chmn. Three Steps Nursery Sch., Phila., 1977; arbitrator Phila. Ct. Common Pleas, 1971-72, 83-88, U.S. Dist. Ct. (ea. dist.) Pa. 1983—, Am. Arbitration Assn., 1987-96, Delaware County Ct. Common Pleas, Pa., 1993—, Forum Sysop, CompuSErve online svc., 1994—. Mem. ABA, Am. Chem. Soc., Licensing Execs. Soc., Am. Intellectual Property Law Assn., Phila. Bar Assn. (chmn. jurimetrics com. 1975-77), Phila. Intellectual Property Law Assn. (chmn. biotech. subcom. 1982-86, continguing legal edn. com. 1995-97), Delaware County Bar Assn., Computer Law Assn., Benjamin Franklin Am. Inn of Ct. Computer, Intellectual property, Patent. Home: 406 Yale Ave Swarthmore PA 19081-2024 Office: Elman & Assocs 20 W Third St Media PA 19063-2824 E-mail: elman@elman.com

ELMORE, EDWARD WHITEHEAD, lawyer; b. Lawrenceville, Va., July 15, 1938; s. Thomas Milton and Mary Norfleet (Whitehead) E.; m. Gail Harmon, Aug. 10, 1968; children: Mary Jennifer, Edward Whitehead Jr. B.A., U. Va.-Charlottesville, 1959, J.D., 1962. Bar: Va. 1962. Assoc. firm Hunton & Williams, Richmond, Va., 1965-69; staff atty. Ethyl Corp., 1969-78, asst. gen. counsel, 1978-79, gen. counsel, 1979-80, gen. counsel., sec., 1980-83, v.p., gen. counsel, sec., 1983-94, spl. counsel to exec. com., corp. sec., 1994-97; sr. v.p., gen. counsel, sec. Albemarle Corp., 1994-2001, exec. v.p., sec., 2001—. Served to capt. AUS, 1962-65. Decorated Army Commendation medal Mem. ABA, Va. Bar Assn., Internat. Bar Assn., Va. State Bar, Am. Corp. Counsel Assn., Bar Assn. Richmond, Am. Soc. Corp. Secs., Raven Soc., Phi Beta Kappa General corporate. Office: Albemarle Corp 330 S 4th St Richmond VA 23219-4350

ELROD, EUGENE RICHARD, lawyer; b. Roanoke, Ala., May 14, 1949; s. James Woodrow and Selma Fromer (Steinbach) E. AB, Dartmouth Coll., 1971; JD, Emory U., 1974. Bar: Ga. 1974, D.C. 1976, U.S. Ct. Appeals (D.C. cir.) 1985, U.S. Ct. Appeals (5th cir.) 1987, U.S. Dist. Ct. D.C. 1987, U.S. Ct. Appeals (11th cir.) 1987, U.S. Supreme Ct. 1987, U.S. Ct. Appeals (10th cir.) 1997. Trial atty. Fed. Power Com., Washington, 1974-76; atty.-advisor Fed. Energy Adminstrn., 1977; assoc. Sidley & Austin, 1977-80, ptnr., 1981—. Mem. adv. bd. The Keplinger Cos., Houston. Mem. selection com. for Woodruff scholars Emory U. Law Sch., Dartmouth '71 Exec. Com. Mem. ABA, D.C. Bar Assn., Ga. Bar Assn., Energy Bar Assn. (chmn. oil pipeline com. 1982-83, tax com. 1980-81, 92-95, liaison with adminstrv. law judges 1986-87, ethics com. 1997-2001, bd. dirs. 2000—), Dartmouth Club (exec. com. class of 1971), Book Club of Calif. Avocations: running, book collecting, gardening. Administrative and regulatory, FERC practice. Home: 4300 Hawthorne St NW Washington DC 20016-3571 Office: Sidley Austin Brown & Wood 1501 K St NW Washington DC 20005

ELROD, LINDA DIANE HENRY, lawyer, educator; b. Topeka, Mar. 6, 1947; d. Lyndus Arthur Henry and Marjorie Jane (Hammel) Allen; divorced; children: Carson Douglas, Bree Elizabeth. BA in English with honors, Washburn U., 1969, JD cum laude, 1971. Bar: Kans. 1972. Instr. U. S.D., Topeka, 1970-71; research atty. Kans. Jud. Council, 1972-74; asst. prof. Washburn U., 1974-78, assoc. prof., 1978-82, prof. law, 1982-93; disting. prof., 1993—. Vis. prof. law U. San Diego, Paris Summer Inst., 1988, 90, Washington U. Sch. Law, St. Louis, 1990, 98, summer 1991, 93, Fla. State U. Law Sch., spring, 2000. Author: Kansas Family Law Handbook, 1983, rev. edit., 1990, supplement, 1993, Child Custody Practice and Procedure, 1993, supplements, 1994-97, 99, 2000, 2001; co-author: Principle of Family Law, 1999, supplement, 2000, Kansas Family Law Guide, 1999, supplement, 2000, 2001; editor Family Law Quar., 1992—; contbr. articles to profl. jours. Pres. YWCA, Topeka, 1982-83; vice-chair Kans. Commn. on Child Support, 1984-87, Supreme Ct. Com. on Child Support, 1989—; chair Kans. Cmty. Svc. Orgn., 1986-87; adv. bd. CASA, 1997—. Recipient Disting. Service award Washburn Law Sch. Assn., 1986; named woman of distinction Appleseed Bd. Dirs., 1997. Mem. ABA (coun. family law sect. 1988-92, sec. 1998, vice-chair, 1999, chair-elect 1999-2000, chair 2000—, chair Schwab Meml. Grant Implementation 1984-87, co-chair Amicus Curiae com. 1987-92), Topeka Bar Assn. (sec. 1981-85, v.p. 1985-86, pres. 1986-87), Kans. Child Support Enforcement Assn. (bd. dirs. 1988—, Child Support Hall of Fame 1990), Kans. Bar Assn. (sec.-treas. 1988-89, com. ops. and fin. 1988, pres. family law sect. 1984-86, Disting. Svc. award 1985), NONOSO, Phi Kappa Phi, Phi Alpha Delta Alumni Assn. (justice 1976-77), Phi Beta Delta, Kappa Alpha Theta (pres. alumnae chpt. 1995-97). Presbyterian. Avocations: bridge, reading, quilting. Office: Washburn U Law Sch 17th and College Topeka KS 66621 E-mail: Zzelro@washburn.edu

ELSEN, SHELDON HOWARD, lawyer; b. Pitts., May 12, 1928; m. Gerri Sharfman, 1952; children: Susan Rachel, Jonathan Charles. AB, Princeton U., 1950; AM, Harvard U., 1952, JD, 1958. Bar: N.Y. 1959, U.S. Supreme Ct. 1971. Ptnr. Orans, Elsen & Lupert, N.Y.C., 1965—. Adj. prof. law Columbia U. Law Sch., 1969—; chief counsel N.Y. Moreland Act Commn. on UDC, 1975-76; asst. U.S. atty. So. Dist. N.Y., 1960-64; cons. Pres.'s Commn. Law Enforcement Adminstrn. Justice, 1967; mem. faculty Nat. Inst. Trial Advocacy, 1973; panel chair 1st dept. disciplinary com. N.Y., 1992-96. Contbr. articles to profl. jours. Fellow Am. Coll. Trial Lawyers; mem. Assn. of Bar of City of N.Y. (v.p. 1988-89, chmn. com. on fed. legislation 1969-72, chmn. com. on fed. cts. 1983-86, chmn. nominating com. 1986-87, chmn. com. amenities in land use process for N.Y.C. 1987-88), Am. Law Inst. (adviser Transnat. Rules of Civil Procedure 1999—), Phi Beta Kappa. Federal civil litigation, State civil litigation, Criminal. Home: 50 Fenimore Rd Scarsdale NY 10583-2251 Office: 1 Rockefeller Plz New York NY 10020-2102 E-mail: selsen@oellaw.com

ELSMAN, JAMES LEONARD, JR. lawyer; b. Kalamazoo, Sept. 10, 1936; s. James Leonard and Dorothy Isabell (Pierce) E.; m. Janice Marie Wilczewski, Aug. 6, 1960; children— Stephanie, James Leonard III. B.A., U. Mich., 1958, J.D., 1962; postgrad., Harvard Div. Sch., 1958-59. Bar: Mich. 1963. Clk. Mich. Atty. Gen.'s Office, Lansing, 1961; atty. legal dept. Chrysler Corp., Detroit, 1962-64; founding ptnr. Elsman, Young, O'Rourke, Bruno & Bunn, Birmingham, Mich., 1964-72; pvt. practice Elsman Law Firm, 1972—. Owner Radio Sta. WOLY, Battle Creek, Mich. Author: The Seekers, 1962; screenplay, 1976, 200 Candles to Whom?, 1973; contbr. articles to profl. jours.; Composer, 1974, 76; talk show host Citizen's Court, TV-48, Detroit. Mem. Regional Export Expansion Coun., 1966-73, Mich. Ptnrs. for Alliance for Progress, 1969-80; cand. U.S. Senate, 1966, 76, 94, 96, U.S. Ho. of Reps., 1970. Rockefeller Bros. Found. fellow Harvard Div. Sch., 1959. Mem. ABA, Am. Soc. Internat. Law, Econ. Club Detroit, World Peace Through Law Center, Full Gospel Businessmen, Bloomfield Open Hunt Club, Pres. Club (U. Mich.), Circumnavigators Club, Naples Bath and Tennis, Rotary. Republican. Mem. Christian Ch. Private international, Personal injury, Product liability. Home: 4811 Burnley Dr Bloomfield Hills MI 48304-3781 Office: 635 Elm St Birmingham MI 48009-6768

ELSON, CHARLES MYER, law educator; b. Atlanta, Nov. 12, 1959; s. Edward Elliott and Suzanne (Goodman) E.; m. Aimee F. Kemker, Dec. 18, 1993; 1 child, Caroline Kemker. AB magna cum laude, Harvard U., 1981, postgrad., 1981-82; JD, U. Va., 1985. Bar: N.Y. 1987, D.C. 1988, U.S. Dist. Ct. (so. and ea. dists.) N.Y. 1987, U.S. Ct. Appeals (11th cir.) 1987. Law clk. to judge U.S. Ct. Appeals (11th cir.), Atlanta, 1985-86; assoc. Sullivan & Cromwell, N.Y.C., 1986-90; asst. prof. Stetson U. Coll. Law, St. Petersburg, Fla., 1990-93, assoc. prof., 1993-96, prof., 1996-2001; Edgar S. Woolard Jr. prof. corp. governance U. Del., 2000—, dir. Ctr. for Corp. Governance, 2000—. Vis. prof. law U. Ill., Champaign-Urbana, 1995, Cornell U. Law Sch., Ithaca, N.Y., 1996, U. Md. Law Sch., Balt., 1998; cons. Holland & Knight, 1995—, Towers, Perrin, 1998; bd. dirs. Auto Zone, Inc., Nuevo Energy Co., Sunbeam Corp., Investor Responsiblity Rsch. Ctr., Gulfcoast Legal Svcs. Corp., 1991-99. Bd. dirs. Big Apple Circus, Ltd., N.Y.C., 1987-93, Circon Corp., 1997-99 ; trustee Talladega Coll., 1994-2001, Tampa Bay Performing Arts Ctr., 2000—, Tampa Mus. Art, 1993-99. Salvatori fellow Heritage Found., 1993-94. Mem.: ABA (vice chair com.on corp. governance, mem. com.on corp. laws), Am. Law Inst., Assn. of Bar of City of N.Y., Nat. Assn. Corp. Dirs. (adv. coun. 1997—, commn. dir. compensation 1995, commn.dir. professionalism 1996, com.on securities litig. reform and fraud detection 1997, com.on succession planning 1998, com. on audit coms. 1999, com on role of bd. in strategic planning 2000, com. on dir. evaluation 2001), Chevaliers du Tastevin, Harvard Club N.Y.C., Down Town Assn., Univ. Club N.Y.C. Home: 906 Cecil Rd Wilmington DE 19807 Office: U Del Coll Bus and Econs 104 MBNA America Hall Newark DE 19716 E-mail: elson@be.udel.edu

ELWIN, JAMES WILLIAM, JR. lawyer; b. Everett, Wash., June 28, 1950; s. James William Elwin and Jeannette Georgette (Zichy-Litscheff) Sherman; m. Regina K. McCabe, Oct. 25, 1986. BA, U. Denver, 1971, MA, 1972; JD, Northwestern U., 1975. Bar: Ill. 1975, U.S. Dist. Ct. (no. dist.) Ill. 1975, U.S. Ct. Appeals (7th cir.) 1977, U.S. Supreme Ct. 1980, U.S. Ct. Fed. Claims 1989. Trial atty. antitrust divsn. U.S. Dept. Justice, Chgo., 1975-77; asst. dean Sch. Law Northwestern U., 1977-82, assoc. dean, 1982-2000; dir. profl. devel. and tng. Shearman & Sterling, N.Y.C., 2000—. Exec. dir. Corp. Counsel Ctr., 1984-2000; planning dir. Corp. Counsel Inst., Garrett Corp. and Securities Law Inst., Chgo., 1983-2000; dir. Short Course for Pros. Attys., 1981-2000, Short Course for Def. Lawyers in Criminal Cases, Chgo., 1979-2000. Bd. dirs. Legal Assistance Found. of Chgo., 1985-97; vice chmn. Gov.'s Adv. Coun. on Criminal Justice Legis., 1986-91. Fellow German Acad. Exch. Svc., 1986; Fulbright scholar, Germany, 1990. Mem. Chgo. Coun. Fgn. Rels. (mem. Chgo. com.), Chgo. Bar Assn. (bd. mgrs. 1983-85), Chgo. Bar Found. (bd. dirs. 1985-93, pres. 1989-91), Ill. Inst. Continuing Legal Edn. (bd. dirs. 1978-90, chmn. 1987-88), Am. Law Inst., Legal Club (pres. 1991-92), Univ. Club, Law Club City of Chgo., Phi Beta Kappa, Pi Gamma Mu. Antitrust, General corporate. Office: Shearman & Sterling 599 Lexington Ave Ste N721 New York NY 10022-6030

ELY, HIRAM, III, lawyer; b. Lexington, Ky., May 14, 1951; s. Hiram and Buena E. (Wright) E.; m. Deborah A. Johnson, Oct. 22, 1977. B.A., Centre Coll. Ky., 1973; J.D., Washington and Lee U., 1976. Bar: Ky. 1976, U.S. Dist. Ct. (we. dist.) Ky. 1976, U.S. Dist. Ct. (ea. dist.) Ky. 1979, U.S. Supreme Ct. 1979, U.S. Ct. Appeals (6th cir.) 1979, U.S. Ct. Claims, 1979, U.S. Tax Ct. 1984. Clk. to presiding justice U.S. Dist. Ct. Va., Roanoke, 1976-77; assoc. Ewen, MacKenzie & Peden, P.S.C., Louisville, 1977-81; assoc. Greenebaum, Doll & McDonald, Louisville, 1981-84, ptnr., 1984—. Chmn. Ky. Atty. Gen.'s Task Force on Election Reform, 1987-88; vice-chmn. policy com. Downtown Action Plan for Louisville; fund raiser profl. div. Metro United Way, Louisville, 1983-85; bd. dirs. Goodwill Industries, 1985—, Louisville C. of C., 1985—. Legal Research Assn. grantee, 1974; named among Top Ten Outstanding Kentuckians, Ky. Jaycees, 1969. Mem. Young Lawyers Club (v.p. 1982-83, pres. 1983-84), Louisville Bar Found. (chmn. continuing legal edn. sect. 1985—, bd. dirs. 1986—), Louisville Bar Assn. (mem. litigation, internat. law, fed. practice sects.) Ky. Bar Assn., ABA (discovery com. litigation sect. 1981-84), Ky. Acad. Trial Atty's., Ky. Def. Counsel, Def. Research Inst., Sigma Chi. Club: Jefferson, Harmony Landing Country (Louisville). Federal civil litigation, State civil litigation. Office: Greenebaum Doll & McDonald 3300 First Nat Towers Louisville KY 40202

ELY, JAMES WALLACE, JR. law educator; b. Rochester, N.Y., Jan. 20, 1938; s. James Wallace and Edythe (Farnham) E.; m. Ruth Buell MacCameron, Aug. 27, 1960; children: A. Elizabeth, Kimberly Farnham, Suzanne B., James W. AB, Princeton U., 1959; LLB, Harvard U., 1962; PhD, U. Va., 1971. Bar: N.Y. 1962, U.S. Dist. Ct. (we. dist.) N.Y. 1963. Assoc. Harris, Beach and Wilcox, Rochester, 1962-67; instr. U. Va., 1970; from instr. to asst. prof. U. Richmond, Va., 1970-73; asst. prof. law Vanderbilt U., Nashville, 1973-75, assoc. prof., 1975-78, prof., 1978—, Milton R. Underwood prof. law, 1999—. Vis. prof. law. U. Leeds, Eng., 1981-82; Chapman disting. vis. prof. U. Tulsa, 1985. Author: The Crisis of Conservative Virginia: The Byrd Organization and the Politics of Massive Resistance, 1976, The Guardian of Every Other Right: A Constitutional History of Property Rights, 1992, 2d edit., 1998, The Chief Justiceship of Melville W. Fuller 1888-1910, 1995; co-author: (with Bruce) Modern Property Law: Cases and Materials, 1984, 4th edit., 1999, (with Bodenhamer) Ambivalent Legacy: A Legal History of the South, 1984 (with Brown) Legal Papers of Andrew Jackson, 1987, (with Bruce), The Law of Easements and Licenses in Land, 1988, rev. edit., 1995, (with Hall) An Uncertain Tradition: Constitutionalism and the History of the South, 1989, (with Hall, Grossman, Wiecek) The Oxford Companion to the Supreme Court, 1992, (with Bodenhamer) The Bill of Rights in Modern America: After 200 Years, 1993; asst. editor Am. Jour. Legal History, 1987—; series editor Property Rights in American History, 6 vols., 1997. Mem. Am. Soc. Legal History (treas. 1980-81, 82-83, 84-85), Orgn. Am. Historians, So. History Assn. Office: Vanderbilt U Sch Law 21st Ave S Nashville TN 37240-0001

ELY, ROBERT EUGENE, lawyer, author, educator; b. Ft. Wayne, Ind., Aug. 18, 1949; s. Virgil Eugene and Alberta Irene (Steiner) E.; m. Jackline Sue Meyer, Apr. 14, 1973; 1 child, Elizabeth Vanessa. BA, Manchester Coll., 1971, MA, 1975; JD, Ind. U., 1983. Bar: Ala. 1985, U.S. Dist. Ct. (mid. dist.) Ala. 1988. Sales promotion cons. Lincoln Nat. Corp., Ft. Wayne, 1971-73; asst. dir. humanities Manchester Coll., North Manchester, Ind., 1973-75; assoc. instr. English Purdue U., West Lafayette, 1975-77; instr. English Ala. State U., Montgomery, 1977-81, dir. honors, 1984-86, asst. v.p., 1984-85, assoc. prof. English, 1986—; pvt. practice law, 1985—. Communications cons. Cummins Internat., Columbus, Ind., 1982; adj. prof. paralegalism Auburn (Ala.) U., 1990-95. Author: The Humanities, 1979, Mose T.'s Slapout Family Album (children's verse), 1996 (Shaw-Montgomery prize for poetry 1985), Encanchata, 2001; contbr. articles to profl. jours. Summer inst. fellow NEH, 1981; rsch. fellow Ala. State U., 1978; Mobil Found. fellow for Islamic studies in Turkey, 1999; Henry Luce Found. fellow for East-West studies U. Hawaii, 2000; named to Order of Reyes del Monte do Gozo. Mem. ABA, Ala. Bar Assn., Montgomery County Bar Assn., Am. Acad. Poets, Nat. Coun. Tchrs. English, Lower Audubon Brook Soc., Coventry Motoring and Aviation Soc., The Writs. Democrat. Presbyterian. Avocations: serious and light verse, fishing, folk art, sports cars. General practice, Personal injury, Workers' compensation. Home: 3212 LeBron Rd Montgomery AL 36106-2334 Office: 659 S Hull St Montgomery AL 36104-5807 E-mail: relylaw@juno.com

ELZUFON, JOHN A. lawyer; b. Newark, N.Y., Nov. 1, 1946; s. Milton Harold and Muriel (Albert) E.; m. Lena Janis Jacobs, Mar. 22, 1981. B.S.Ch.E., Rose Hulman Inst. Tech., 1968; J.D., Georgetown U., 1974. Bar: Del. 1974, U.S. Dist. Ct. Del. 1975, U.S. Ct. Appeals (3d cir.) 1977. Assoc., Killoran & Van Brunt, Wilmington, Del., 1974-76; assoc. Tybout, Redfearn, Casarino & Pell, Wilmington, 1976-82; sole practice, Wilmington, 1982-83; ptnr. Elzufon & Bailey, Wilmington, 1983-84, dir. Elzufon & Bailey, P.A., 1984— ; of counsel Del. Claims Assn., 1984. Co-author: New Member's Manual to U.S. Ho. of Reps., 1974. Served to 1st lt. U.S. Army, 1969-70, Vietnam. Decorated Bronze Star. Mem. Am. Trial Lawyers Assn. (assoc.), Def. Research Inst., Del. Trial Lawyers Assn. Democrat. Jewish. Club: Toastmasters (Wilmington, pres. 1984). Computer, Insurance, Personal injury. Home: 512 Ruxton Dr Wilmington DE 19809-2830

EMANUEL, WILLIAM JOSEPH, lawyer; b. Hawthorne, Calif., Oct. 31, 1938; s. Lawrence John and Henrietta (Moser) E.; m. Elizabeth Wolfe, Mar. 14, 1964; children— Christina, Michael, Steven. A.B., Marquette U., 1960; J.D., Georgetown U., 1963. Bar: Nebr. 1963, Calif. 1965, U.S. Supreme Ct. 1976. Assoc. Musick, Peeler & Garrett, L.A., 1963-70, ptnr., 1970-76; ptnr. Morgan, Lewis & Bockius, L.A., 1976-97; ptnr. Jones, Day, Reavis & Pogue, L.A., 1998—; mem. labor rels.. com. Am. Hosp. Assn., also mem. spl. subcom. to analyze report of Nat. Commn. on Nursing, Comparable Worth Task Force; mem. adv. com. NLRB, 1994—. Author: (with Michael L. Wolfram) California Employment Law, A Guide to California Laws Regulating Employment in the Private Sector, 1989. Mem. ABA (mem. com. on devel. of law under Nat. Labor Relations Act sect. on labor and employment law), State Bar Calif. (labor and employment law sect.), Los Angeles County Bar Assn. (chmn. labor law sect. 1983-84, mem. exec. com. 1974-86), So. Calif. Labor Law Symposium (founding chmn. 1980, 81), Am. Soc. Hosp. Attys., State Bar Nebr. Contbr. articles to profl. jours. Labor. Office: Jones Day Reavis & Pogue 555 W 5th St Ste 4600 Los Angeles CA 90013-1025

EMBRY, STEPHEN CRESTON, lawyer; b. Key West, Fla., Feb. 13, 1949; s. Jewell Creston and Julia Martine (Taylor) E.; m. Priscilla Mary Brown, Aug. 21, 1971; children: Nathaniel, Julia, Jessamyn. BA, Am. U., 1971; JD, U. Conn., 1976. Bar: Conn. 1976, U.S. Dist. Ct. Conn. 1976, U.S. Ct. Appeals (2d, 5th and 9th cirs.). Staff aide to Pres. The White House, Washington, 1969-72; assoc. Turner & Hensley, Great Bend, Kans., 1976, O'Brien, Shafner, Bartinik, & Stuart, Groton, Conn., 1976-85, Embry and Neusner, Groton, 1985—. Editor: Longshore and Harborworkers Textbook; mem. editl. bd. Matthew Bender, BRB Reporter; contbr. articles to profl. publs. Mem. Groton Rep. com., 1976-83, North Stonington Rep. com., 1984-88; chmn. Groton Housing Authority, 1979-80. Mem. ATLA (chair workers compensation sect. 1984-85, bd. dirs. workplace injury litigation group, sec. 1999-2000, pres.-elect 2001—), Maritime Claimants Attys. Assn. (bd. dirs. 1980—), Conn. Trial Lawyers, Conn. Bar Assn. (exec. bd.), Thames Club, Grange. Democrat. Personal injury, Product liability, Workers' compensation.

EMERSON, JOHN WILLIAMS, II, lawyer; b. Greeneville, Tenn., Nov. 9, 1929; s. John Williams and Dorothy Mae (Moore) E.; m. Carolyn Rose Buchanan, Dec. 21, 1956; children: John Williams III, Amy Elizabeth, Emily Alicia. JD, Vanderbilt U., 1960. Bar: Fla. 1960, Tenn. 1960, U.S. Dist. Ct. (so. dist.) Fla. 1961, U.S. Ct. Appeals (5th cir.) 1961, U.S. Supreme Ct. 1968, U.S. Dist. Ct. (ea. dist.) Tenn. 1982, U.S. Ct. Appeals (6th cir.) 1983, U.S. Dist. Ct. (mid. dist.) Tenn. 1988, U.S. Dist. Ct. (mid. dist.) Fla. 1990. Ins. agt. Emerson Ins. Agy., Greeneville, 1949-56; instr. Peabody Coll., Nashville, 1958-59; assoc. Henderson, Franklin, Starnes & Holt, Ft. Myers, Fla., 1960-63; ptnr. Parks & Emerson, Naples, 1963-72, Treadwell, Emerson & Elkins, Naples, 1972-79, Emerson & Emerson P.C., Johnson City, Tenn., 1979-83, Emerson & Emerson P.A., Naples, 1983—. Judge Small Claims Ct., Collier County, Naples, Fla., 1963-64. Col. aide de camp gov.'s staff State of Tenn., 1963-66; lt. gov. dist. 11 Fla. Dist. of Kiwanis, 1970-71. Capt. U.S. Army, 1950-54, Korea. Fellow Fla. Kiwanis Found. (life); mem. ABA, The Fla. Bar (bd. govs. young lawyers sect. 1963-66), Fla. Acad. Trial Lawyers, Assn. Trial Lawyers Am., Araba Temple (Ft. Myers, Fla.), Masons (32 Degree). Democrat. Presbyterian. Avocations: boating, travel. Contracts commercial, Private international, Real property. Home: 1935 Seville Blvd Apt 112 Naples FL 34109-3367 Office: Emerson & Emerson PA PO Box 1675 Naples FL 34106-1675

EMERSON, STERLING JONATHAN, lawyer; b. Pasadena, Calif., July 2, 1929; s. Sterling H. and Mary Foote (Randall) E.; m. Virginia Beabes, July 3, 1954; children: Margaret Ellen, Henry Rollins, Peter Randall. BA in Econs. with honors, U. Calif., Berkeley, 1955; JD, U. Mich., 1957. Bar: Pa. 1958, U.S. Dist. Ct. (ea. dist.) Pa. 1958, U.S. Ct. Appeals (3d cir.) 1958. Assoc. Montgomery, McCracken, Walker & Rhoads, Phila., 1958, ptnr., 1966-97; pvt. practice Media, Pa., 1998—. Asst. editor Law Rev. U. Mich., 1957. With U.S. Army, 1950-52. Fellow Am. Coll. Trust and Estate Counsel; mem. ABA, Fiduciary Law Soc., Pa. Bar Assn., Phila. Bar Assn. (former bd. govs., former chmn. sect. on probate and trust law), Delaware County Bar Assn. Republican. Avocations: tennis, gardening, travel. Estate planning, Probate, Estate taxation. Home: 16 Oberlin Ave Swarthmore PA 19081-1512 Office: Monroe Profl Bldg 117 N Monroe St Media PA 19063-3037

EMERSON, WILLIAM HARRY, lawyer, retired, oil company executive; b. Rochester, N.Y., Jan. 13, 1928; s. William Canfield and Alice Sarah (Adams) E.; m. Jane Anne Epple, Dec. 27, 1956; children: Elizabeth Anne, Carolyn Jane. BA, Cornell U., 1951, LLB, 1956. Bar: Ill. 1974. Atty. Amoco Corp., 1956-91; sec., dir. Amoco Gas Co., 1979-91. Pres., dir. Undercroft Montessori Sch., Tulsa, 1965-67, Tulsa Figure Skating Club, 1969; bd. dirs. Lake Forest (Ill.) Found. for Hist. Preservation, 1983-2001; mem. vestry Ch. Holy Spirit, Lake Forest, 1988-91. Federal civil litigation, State civil litigation, FERC practice. Home: 593 Greenvale Rd Lake Forest IL 60045-1526

EMERTON, ROBERT WALTER, III, lawyer; b. Hanover, Pa., Feb. 4, 1950; s. James Leonard and Dorothy (Davenport) E.; m. Sharon Whitaker, June 9, 1973 (div. Mar. 1982); children: Chad, Ryan. BA, U. Fla., 1972, JD, 1975. Bar: Fla. 1975, U.S. Dist. Ct. (mid. dist.) Fla. 1976, U.S. Ct. Appeals (11th cir.) 1981, U.S. Supreme Ct. 1982. Asst. pub. defender State of Fla., Tampa, 1975-76; litigation counsel Jim Walter Corp., Tampa, 1976-79, sr. litigation counsel, 1979-82, asst. v.p., 1982-88, v.p., gen. counsel, sec., 1988—; bd. dirs. Asbestos Claims Facility, Inc., Celotex Corp.; legal cons. Com. for Equitable Compensation, Washington, 1982—. Spl. award Ctr. for Pub. Resources, 1985. Mem. Hillsborough County Bar Assn. (corp. counsel subcom. 1977—). Republican. General corporate, Insurance, Personal injury. Home: 928 W Cimmeron Dr Tampa FL 33603-1728 Office: Jim Walter Corp 4010 W Boy Scout Blvd Tampa FL 33607-5727

EMGE, DEREK JOHN, lawyer; b. Glendale, Calif., Aug. 27, 1967; s. Carl Richard and Heather Anne Emge; m. Suzanne Katleman, Aug. 5, 1989; children: Zachary Brayton, Allison Leigh. BA, Claremont McKenna Coll., Claremont, Calif., 1989; JD, U. San Diego, 1992. Bar: Calif. 1992, U.S. Dist. Ct. (so. dist.) Calif. 1992. Atty. Edwards, White & Sooy, San Diego, 1992-96, Booth, Mitchel & Strange, San Diego, 1996-99; prin. Gilliland & Emge, LLP, 1999-2000, Emge & Assocs., San Diego, 2000—. Author: Hidden Trails of San Diego, 1994. Mem. Consumer Lawyers of San Diego. Avocations: cycling, running, backpacking. General civil litigation, Contracts commercial, Professional liability. Office: Emge & Assocs 550 W C St #1770 San Diego CA 92101

EMHARDT, CHARLES DAVID, lawyer; b. Indpls., Feb. 13, 1931; s. John William and Martha Jack (Macdougall) E.; m. Ann Devaney, Nov. 12, 1954; children— John D., Carol A., Frederick D., Martha A., Lucy E. B.S. in Engring. Mechanics, Purdue U., 1952, A.S. in Elec. Engring. Tech., 1966; LL.B., Harvard U., 1955. Bar: D.C. 1955, Ind. 1958, U.S. Patent Office 1955. Patent atty. Western Electric Co., Washington, Balt., 1955-57; assoc. Harold B. Hood, Indpls., 1957-59, Lockwood, Woodard, Smith & Weikart, Indpls., 1959-64; ptnr. Woodard, Emhardt, Naughton, Moriarty & McNett and previous firm Woodard, Weikart, Emhardt & Naughton, Indpls., 1964— . Republican precinct committeeman, 1965-70. Served with Army NG, 1955-66. Mem. ABA, Ind. State Bar Assn. (chmn. pat. sect. 1967-68), Indpls. Bar Assn. (bd. 1979-81, chmn. ethics com. 1982-83). Presbyterian. Clubs: Woodstock, Indpls. Athletic, Masons, Shriners. E-mail: demhardt@uspatent.com; emhardts@msn.com. Federal civil litigation, Patent, Trademark and copyright. Home: 4801 Fauna Ln Indianapolis IN 46234 Office: Woodard Emhardt Naughton Moriarty & McNett 3700 Bank One Ctr 111 Monument Cir Indianapolis IN 46204-5137

EMRICH, EDMUND MICHAEL, lawyer; b. N.Y.C., Apr. 12, 1956; s. Edmund and Mary Ann (Picarella) E. BA, SUNY, Albany, 1978; JD, Hofstra U., 1981. Bar: N.Y. 1982, U.S. Dist. Ct. (so. and ea. dists.) N.Y. 1982, U.S. Ct. Appeals (2d cir.) 1987. Law clk. to presiding justice U.S. Bankruptcy Ct. (ea. dist.) N.Y., Westbury, 1982-83; assoc. Levin & Weintraub & Crames, N.Y.C., 1983-90, Kaye, Scholer, Fierman, Hays & Handler, N.Y.C., 1990-92, ptnr., 1993—. Local rules com. U.S. Bankruptcy Ct. (ea. dist.) N.Y., 1985-86; mem. local rules drafting subcom. U.S. Bankruptcy Ct. (so. dist.) N.Y., 1985-86, 95-98. Mem. Hofstra U. Law Rev., 1981-82. Mem. ABA, N.Y. State Bar Assn., Am. Bankruptcy Inst. Avocations: golf, tennis, wine collecting. Bankruptcy. Home: 300 E 85th St New York NY 10028-4500 Office: Kaye Scholer LLP 425 Park Ave New York NY 10022-3506 E-mail: eemrich@kayescholer.com

ENDSLEY, MEREDITH NELSON, lawyer; b. Jan. 28, 1946; d. Kenneth Meredith and Margaret (Ihling) N.; m. Harry Barclay, May 28, 1971; children: Slexis Christine, Victoria Caroline. BA, Duke U., 1968; JD, U. Mich, 1971. Bar: Calif. 1972, D.C. 1987. Fgn. assoc. Anderson,Mori & Rabinowitz, Tokyo, 1973-75; assoc. Thelen, Marrin, Johnson & Bridges, San Francisco, 1971-72, 76-78; sr. counsel Matson Nav. Co., 1978-81; asst. gen. counsel, 1983—. Panelist 15th Inst. of Law Office Mgmt. and 17th Denver, Mpls. dir. Community Disputes Service, Am. Arbitration Assn., San Francisco, 1980-82. Mem. ABA, San Francisco Bar Assn. (chmn. corp. law dept. sect. 1983, exec. com. 1980-84, exec. com. law office mgmt. com. 1994—), Am. Corp. Counsel Assn. General corporate, Finance. Office: Matson Nav Co PO Box 7452 San Francisco CA 94120-7452

ENERSEN, BURNHAM, lawyer; b. Lamberton, Minn., Nov. 17, 1905; s. Albert H. and Ethel (Rice) E.; m. Nina H. Wallace, July 21, 1935; children: Richard W., Elizabeth. A.B., Carleton Coll., 1927, L.H.D., 1974; LL.B., Harvard U., 1930. Bar: Calif. 1931. Assoc. McCutchen, Doyle, Brown & Enersen, San Francisco, 1930-43, ptnr., 1943-78, counsel, 1978—. Dir. Pomfret Estates, Inc., Calif. Student Loan Fin. Corp., 1981-90; chmn. Gov.'s Com. Water Lawyers, 1957; mem. Calif. Jud. Coun., 1960-64; vice chmn. Calif. Constn. Revision Commn., 1964-75; mem. com. to rev. Calif. Master Plan for Higher Edn., 1971-72. Mem. Calif. Citizens Commn. for Tort Reform, 1976-77; bd. dirs. Assn. Calif. Tort Reform, 1979-93, chmn., 1979-80; mem. Calif. Postsecondary Edn. Com., 1974-78; bd. dirs. Criminal Justice Legal Found., 1982-94, chmn. bd. trustees, 1985-86; bd. dirs. Fine Arts Mus. Found., 1983-94, pres. bd. trustees, 1987-92; pres. United Bay Area Area Crusade, 1962, United Crusades of Calif., 1969-71; trustee Mills Coll., 1972-82, chmn., 1976-80. Fellow Am. Bar Found.; mem. ABA (ho. of dels. 1970-76), State Bar Calif. (pres. 1960), Bar Assn. San Francisco (pres. 1955), Assn. of Bar of City of N.Y., Am. Judicature Soc., Am. Law Inst., Calif. C. of C. (dir. 1962-78, pres. 1971), Calif. Hist. Soc. (bd. trustees 1976-78, 83-89), Bohemian Club, Pacific-Union Club, Commercial Club (pres. 1966), Commonwealth Club Calif., San Francisco Golf Club, Cypress Point Club. Home: 1661 Pine St Apt 1111 San Francisco CA 94109-0413 Office: 3 Embarcadero Ctr San Francisco CA 94111-4003

ENGBERS, JAMES AREND, lawyer; b. Grand Rapids, Mich., Dec. 11, 1938; s. Martin Hoffius and Harriet Jean (Riddering) E.; m. Harriet M. Wissink, Sept. 13, 1960; children: Charles M., James A., Nancy L. Falk, David W. LLB, Hope Coll., Holland, Mich., 1960; JD, Wayne U., 1963. Bar: Mich. 1963, U.S. Dist. Ct. (we. dist.) Mich. 1963. Mem. firm Miller, Johnson, Snell & Cummiskey, P.L.C., Grand Rapids, Mich., 1963—. Mem. State Bar Mich. (standing com. on character and fitness 1993-97), Grand Rapids Bar Assn. (trustee 1972-73), Rotary Club. Republican. Presbyterian. Avocations: golf, tennis, reading, photography. Bankruptcy, Contracts commercial, General corporate. Office: Miller Johnson Snell & Cummiskey PLC 800 Calder Plaza Bldg Grand Rapids MI 49503-2250 E-mail: engbers@mjsc.com

ENGEL, ALBERT JOSEPH, federal judge; b. Lake City, Mich., Mar. 21, 1924; s. Albert Joseph and Bertha (Bielby) E.; m. Eloise Ruth Bull, Oct. 18, 1952; children: Albert Joseph III, Katherine Ann, James Robert, Mary Elizabeth. Student, U. Md., 1941-42; A.B., U. Mich., 1948, LL.B., 1950. Bar: Mich. 1951. Ptnr. firm Engle & Engel, Muskegon, Mich., 1952-67; judge Mich. Circuit Ct., 1967-71; judge U.S. Dist. Ct. Western Dist. Mich., 1971-74; circuit judge U.S. Ct. Appeals, 6th Circuit, Grand Rapids, Mich., 1974-88, chief judge, 1988-89, sr. judge, 1989—. Served with AUS, 1943-46, ETO. Fellow Am. Bar Found.; mem. ABA, Fed. Bar Assn., Mich. Bar Assn., Cin. Bar Assn., Grand Rapids Bar Assn., Am. Judicature Soc., Am. Legion, Phi Sigma Kappa, Phi Delta Phi. Episcopalian. Club: Grand Rapids Torch. Home: 5497 Forest Bend Dr SE Ada MI 49301-9079 Office: US Ct Appeals 100 E 5th St Ste 418 Cincinnati OH 45202-3911 also: 640 Federal Bldg 110 Michigan St NW Grand Rapids MI 49503-2313

ENGEL, DAVID ANTHONY, lawyer; b. Albany, N.Y., Mar. 5, 1951; s. Herbert and Rose Helen (Fink) E.; m. Cynthia Ann White, Nov. 2, 1975; children: Leslie Ruth, Jeffrey Aaron. BA, Union Coll., Schenectady, N.Y., 1972; JD, Albany Law Sch., 1975. Bar: N.Y. 1976, U.S. Dist. Ct. (no. dist.) N.Y. 1976, U.S. Ct. Appeals D.C. 1984. Asst. atty. N.Y. State Dept. Agr. and Markets, Albany, 1975-77, staff atty., 1977; sr. atty. N.Y. State Dept. Environ. Conservation, Albany, 1977-79, energy counsel, 1979-84, asst. counsel for enforcement, 1984-86, dep. dir. Environ. Enforcement Div., 1986-87, dir., 1987-88; atty. Herzog, Engstrom, Burke, Koplovitz & Cavalier, P.C., Albany, 1988-90; ptnr. Burke, Cavalier, Lindy & Engel, P.C., Albany, 1990-92, Harris, Beach & Wilcox, Albany, 1992—. Mem. Chmn.'s Com. Handgun Control, Inc., Washington, 1983-84, County Dem. Com., Schenectady, 1983-87. Recipient Merit award Catskill Ctr., Arkville, N.Y., 1988. Mem. ABA (nat. resources, pub. utility law sects.), N.Y. State Bar Assn. (exec. com. environ. law sect.), Fed. Energy Bar Assn., Sierra Club (wilderness guardian 1983), So. Poverty Law Ctr . Democrat. Jewish. Avocations: skiing, travel, reading. Home: 1246 Viewmont Dr Niskayuna NY 12309-1220 Office: Harris Beach & Wilcox 20 Corporate Woods Blvd Ste 2 Albany NY 12211-2349

ENGEL, DAVID LEWIS, lawyer; b. N.Y.C., Mar. 31, 1947; s. Benjamin and Selma (Fruchtman) E.; m. Edith Greetham Smith, June 9, 1973; children: Richard William, Jonathan Martin. AB in Gen. Studies in Econ. cum laude, Harvard U., 1967, JD magna cum laude, 1973; Disting. Naval grad., U.S. Naval Officer Candidate Sch., 1969. Bar: Mass. 1975. Law clk. to Judge Henry J. Friendly U.S. Ct. Appeals (2nd cir.), N.Y.C., 1973-74; assoc. Goodwin, Procter & Hoar, Boston, 1974-76, 79-80; asst. prof. law Stanford U., Calif., 1976-79; ptnr. Berman, Dittmar & Engel, P.C., Boston, 1980-84, Bingham Dana LLP, Boston, 1984—. Contbr. article to Stanford Law Rev., 1979; pres. Harvard Law Rev., 1972-73. Mem. bd. visitors Stanford U. Law Sch., 1982-84; bd. dirs. Project Joy, 1995-2001. Lt. (j.g.) USNR, 1969-71. Named John Harvard scholar, Harvard Coll. scholar, Nat. Merit scholar, 1964-67; recipient Sears prize, 1968, John Bingham Hurlbut award, 1979. Mem. ABA, Boston Bar Assn. (working group of task force on revision of Mass. corp. statute 1987-2001), Phi Beta Kappa. General corporate, Securities. Office: Bingham Dana LLP 150 Federal St Boston MA 02110-1713 E-mail: dlengel@bingham.com

ENGEL, DAVID WAYNE, lawyer, federal official; b. Salisbury, Md., Nov. 29, 1956; s. Robert Peter Engel and Joan (King) Bradshaw; m. Laura Marie Tuck, June 25, 1983; children: Michael Andrew, Jennifer Lynn, Matthew Alan. AB, William & Mary Coll., 1978; JD, Washington & Lee U., 1981; LLM, Judge Advocate Gen.'s Sch., Charlottesville, Va., 1988. Bar: Va. 1981, U.S. Dist. Ct. (ea. and we. dists.) Va. 1981, U.S. Ct. Mil. Appeals 1981, U.S. Ct. Appeals (4th cir.) 1981, U.S. Tax Ct. 1982, U.S. Ct. Appeals (5th cir.) 1985, Tex. 1985, U.S. Dist. Ct. (we. dist.) Tex. 1985, U.S. Supreme Ct. 1988, U.S. Ct. Appeals Vets. Claims 1990, U.S. Ct. Appeals (Fed. cir.) 1991, U.S. Ct. Appeals (10th cir.) 1998, U.S. Dist. Ct. (no. dist.) Okla. 1998. Capt. U.S. Army, 1981-89, active duty, 1989, USAR, 1989-97; appellate litigation atty. U.S. Dept. Vets. Affairs, Washington, 1989-92, spl. asst. to acting asst. gen. counsel, 1992-93; deputy asst. Gen. Coun., 1993-97; U.S. adminstrv. law judge Social Security Adminstrn., Office Hearings & Appeals, Tulsa, Okla, 1997—; col. USAF Res., 1997—. Lt. col. USAFR, 1997—. Office: Office of Hearings & Appeals Social Security Adminstrv 5110 South Yale Ste 204 Tulsa OK 74135-7481 E-mail: david.engel@ssa.gov

ENGEL, RALPH MANUEL, lawyer; b. N.Y.C., May 13, 1944; s. Werner Herman and Ruth Fredericke (Friedlander) E.; m. Diane Linda Weinberg, Aug. 10, 1968; children— Eric M., Daniel C., Julie R. BA in Econs. with highest honors, NYU, 1965, JD, 1968. Bar: N.Y. 1968, U.S. Supreme Ct. 1972. Assoc. Gilbert, Segall and Young, N.Y.C., 1968-71, Trubin Sillcocks Edelman & Knapp, N.Y.C., 1971-76; assoc., then ptnr. Summit Rovins & Feldesman and predecessor firms, 1976-91; ptnr. Rosen & Reade, LLP, 1991-2001, Sonnenshein, Nath & Rosenthal, N.Y.C., 2001—. Lectr. Sch. Law, Fordham U., 1990-91. Contbr. articles to legal and other publs.; editor-in-chief The Commentator, NYU, 1968 Mem. Planning Com., Larchmont, N.Y., 1992—. Fellow Am. Coll. Trust and Estate Counsel; mem. N.Y. State Bar Assn. (trust and estate law sect. com. on practice and ethics 1991—, elder law sect., com. on guardianships and fiduciaries 1991-97, com. on estates and tax planning 1997—), Assn. Bar City of N.Y. (com. on estate and gift taxation 1992-95, chmn. subcom. on splitting and combining trusts 1994-95, chmn., subcom. on spousal rights 1994-95, com. on trusts, estates and surrogate's cts. 1997-2000), Estate Planning Coun. Westchester County (bd. dirs. 1985-91). Estate planning, Probate, Estate taxation. Home and Office: 6 Rockwood Dr Larchmont NY 10538-2537 Office: 1221 Ave of the Americas New York NY 10020 E-mail: engelesq@aol.com, rengel@sonnenschein.com

ENGEL, RICHARD LEE, lawyer, educator; b. Syracuse, N.Y., Sept. 19, 1936; s. S. Sanford and Eleanor M. (Gallop) E.; m. Karen K. Engel, Dec. 26, 1965; children: Todd Sanford, Gregg Matthew. BA, Yale U., 1958, JD, 1981. Bar: N.Y. 1961. Law asst. justices Appellate Divsn. N.Y. 4th Jud. Dist., 1961-63; law clk. judge N.Y. Supreme Ct., 1963-65; sr. ptnr. Nottingham, Engel, Gordon & Kerr LLP, Syracuse, 1970—. Adj. prof. law Syracuse U. Coll. of Law; arbitrator, mediator law and medicine, equine law Coll. Law trial practice Am. Arbitration Assn., AP Com. reviewer Prudential Class Action; lectr. in field. Contbr. articles to profl. jours. Pres. Temple Soc. Concord, 1985-87; bd. dirs. Am. Field Svcs. Intercultural Programs, Inc., 1974-81. Mem. ABA, Am. Coll. Legal Medicine, N.Y. State Bar Assn., Onondaga Bar Asn. (mem. trial lawyers com. 1978-80, chmn. med. legal liaison com. 1976-77, chmn. spl. ins. com. 1988, Bench and Bar com. 1991, found. bd. 1992-98, grievance com. 1998—), N.Y. State Trial Attys. Assn., Upstate Trial Attys. Assn. (pres. 1973-74, chmn. bd. 1974-77), Thoroughbred Owners and Breeders Assn. (owners coun.), Def. Rsch. Inst., Inc., Cavalry Country, Saratoga Reading Rooms, Inc., Yale (pres. Ctrl. N.Y.). General civil litigation, General corporate, General practice. Home: 603 Kimry Moor Fayetteville NY 13066-1832 Office: Nottingham Engel Gordon & Kerr LLP One Lincoln Ctr 8th Flr Syracuse NY 13202 E-mail: equineesq@aol.com

ENGEL, TALA, lawyer; b. N.Y.C. d. Volodia Vladimir Boris and Risia (Modelevska) E.; m. James Colias, Nov. 22, 1981 (dec. Nov. 1989). AA, U. Fla., 1952; BA in Russian and Spanish, U. Miami, 1954; JD, U. Miami, Coral Gables, 1957; postgrad., Middlebury Coll., 1953. Bar: Fla. 1957, D.C. 1982, U.S. Dist. Ct. (so. dist.) Fla. 1957, Ill. 1962, U.S. Dist. Ct. (no. dist.) Ill. 1962, U.S. Supreme Ct., 1965. Pvt. practice, Miami, Fla., 1957-61, Chgo., 1966-86, 90-93, Washington, 1987-89, 93—. Atty. Immigration and Naturalization Service, Chgo., 1961-62; parole agt. Ill. Youth Commn., Chgo., 1963-66. Editor The Lawyer, 1956; mem. editl. bd. Miami Law Quar., 1955-57, 10 ML Q 110 Criminal Law, 10 ML Q 608 Ins. Law, 1955-56. Bd. dirs. Cordi-Marian Settlement, Chgo., 1977-93. Named One of 2000 Outstanding Women of 20th Century, Dictionary Internat. Biography, 2000. Mem.: Ill. Bar Assn. (gen. assembly 1984—86), Chgo. Bar Assn. (devel. of law com. 1985—87, entertainment com. 1971—72), Chgo. Bar Found. (life)), Fed. Bar Assn., Fla. Bar Assn., Alpha Lambda Delta, Nu Beta Epsilon. Avocations: travel, theater, singing, writing, Russian and Spanish languages. Immigration, naturalization, and customs. Home and Office: 2800 Quebec St NW Apt 1027 Washington DC 20008-1237 E-mail: talaengel@aol.com

ENGEL, TODD SANFORD, lawyer; b. Syracuse, N.Y., Mar. 28, 1967; s. Richard Lee and Karen Kutner E.; m. Dawn Allison Susskind, July 8, 1995; 1 child, Geoffrey Adam. BS, Syracuse U., 1990, JD, 1996. Bar: N.Y. 1998, U.S. Dist. Ct. (no. dist.) N.Y. 1998. Atty. Nottingham, Engel, Gordon & Kerr LLP, Syracuse, 1998—. Arbitrator, small claims ct. Syracuse City Cts., 1998—. Bd. dirs. Syracuse Jewish Family Svcs., Syracuse, 1998—, Temple Soc., Concord, 1999—; candidate N.Y. State Assembly 121st Dist., Onondaga County, 1998; mem. Manlius Town Dem. Com., Onondaga County Dem. Com., 1998—, exec. com., 1998-2000, lawyer's com., 1998—, rules com., 2001—; vol. coord. Assemblywoman Joan Christensen 1996 campaign. Mem. ABA, ATLA, N.Y. State Bar Assn., N.Y. State Trial Lawyer's Assn., Onondga County Bar Assn. (CLE com. 1998—, chair newly admitted atty. program 1999, family law). Democrat. Jewish. Environmental, General practice, Juvenile. Home: 8247 Drinkwater Ln Manlius NY 13104 Office: Nottingham Engel Gordon & Kerr LLP One Lincoln Ctr Syracuse NY 13202

ENGELHARDT, JOHN HUGO, lawyer, banker; b. Houston, Feb. 3, 1946; s. Hugo Tristram and Beulah Lillie (Karbach) E.; m. Jasmin Inge Nestler, Nov. 12, 1976; children: Angelique D., Sabrina N. BA, U. Tex., 1968; JD, St. Marys U., San Antonio, 1973. Tchr. history Pearsall H.S., Tex., 1968-69; pvt. practice New Braunfels, 1973-75, 82—; examining atty. Comml. Title Co., San Antonio, 1975-78, San Antonio Title Co., 1978-82. Adv. dir. M Bank Brenham, Tex., 1983-89. Fellow Coll. State Bar Tex.; mem. ABA, Pi Gamma Mu. Republican. Roman Catholic. Probate, Real property, Estate taxation.

ENGLAND, JOHN MELVIN, lawyer, clergyman; b. June 29, 1932; s. John Marcus and Frances Dorothy (Brown) E.; m. Jane Cantrell, Aug. 2, 1953; children: Kathryn Elizabeth, Janette Evelyn, John William, Kenneth Paul, James Andrew, Samuel Robert. Student, Ga. State U., 1951-53; JD, U. Ga., 1956; BD magna cum laude with honors Theology, Columbia Theol. Sem., Decatur, Ga., 1964. Bar: Ga. 1959, U.S. Dist. Ct. (no. dist.) Ga. 1967, U.S. Ct. Mil. Appeals 1976, U.S. Ct. Appeals (5th cir.) 1967, U.S. Ct. Appeals (11th cir.) 1981, U.S. Supreme Ct. 1977, U.S. Dist. Ct. (mid. dist.) Ga. 1986, U.S. Dist. Ct. (so. dist.) Ga. 1991, U.S. Dist. Ct. (no. dist.) Tex. 1991; ordained to ministry Presbyn. Ch., 1964. Spl. agt. FBI, Washington, 1956-57, Indpls., 1957-59, Charlotte, N.C., 1959, Greenville, S.C., 1959-60; student supply pastor Bethel and Buford Presbyn. Chs., Atlanta, 1960-63; pastor Mullins (S.C.) Presbyn. Ch., 1964-67; asst. dist. atty. Fulton County, Ga., 1967-75; sr. ptnr. England and Weller, Atlanta, 1975-88, England, Weaver & Kytle, 1988-94, England & McKnight, 1994-2000, England & England, 2000—. Legal seminar lectr. and spkr. throughout the country under auspices of Christian orgns.; spl. pros. for gov. Ga., 1976-79; spl. cons. on appellate reform Supreme Ct. Ga., 1979-80; state bar rep. to Superior Ct. Uniform Rules Com. Coun. Superior Ct. Judges, 1984, Uniform Rules Com. State Bar Ga., 1993—. Elder, tchr., evangelism coord. Presbyn. Ch. USA; chmn. Christian Bus. Men's Coms. of U.S.A., Atlanta, 1971-73, chmn. internat. conv., Atlanta, 1979, bd. dirs., 1971-81. Mem. ABA, ATLA, State Bar Ga., Atlanta Bar Assn., Lawyers Club Atlanta, Ga. Trial Lawyers Assn., Nat. Assn. Criminal Def. Lawyers, Ga. Assn. Criminal Def. Lawyers, North Fulton Bar Assn. E-mail: england engl. General civil litigation, Criminal, Personal injury. Office: England & England 201 Bombay Ln Roswell GA 30076 E-mail: 11p@hotmail.com

ENGLAND, LYNNE LIPTON, lawyer, speech pathologist, audiologist; b. Youngstown, Ohio, Apr. 11, 1949; d. Sanford Y. and Sally (Kentor) Lipton; m. Richard E. England, Mar. 5, 1977. BA, U. Mich., 1970; MA, Temple U., 1972; JD, Tulane U., 1981. Bar: Fla. 1982, U.S. Dist. Ct. (mid. dist.) Fla. 1982, U.S. Ct. Appeals (11th cir.) 1982; cert. clin. competence in speech pathology and audiology. Speech pathologist Rockland Children's Hosp., N.Y., 1972-74, Jefferson Parish Sch., Gretna, La., 1977-81; audiologist Rehab. Inst. Chgo., 1974-76; assoc. Trenam, Simmons, Kemker, Scharf, Barkin, Frye & O'Neill, Tampa, Fla., 1981-84; asst. U.S. atty. for Middle Dist. Fla., 1984-87; asst. U.S. trustee, 1987-91; ptnr. Stearns, Weaver, Miller, Weissler, Alhadeff & Sitterson, P.A., 1991-94, Prevatt, England & Taylor, Tampa, Fla., 1994-99; pvt. practice Brandon, 1999—. Editor Fla. Bankruptcy Casenotes, 1983. Recipient clin. assistantship Temple U., 1972-74. Mem. ATLA, Comml. Law League, Am. Speech and Hearing Assn., Tampa Bay Bankruptcy Bar Assn. (dir. 1990-95), Am. Bankruptcy Inst., Fla. Bar Assn., Hillsborough County Bar Assn., Order of Coif. Jewish. Avocations: tennis, golf, playing French horn and piano. Bankruptcy. Office: 1463 Oakfield Dr Ste 125 Brandon FL 33511-0802 E-mail: englandlawoffice@aol.com

ENGLAND, RUDY ALAN, lawyer; b. Snyder, Tex., Sept. 29, 1959; s. Bud and Imo D. (Witcher) E.; m. Zenda Cherie Ball, Mar. 24, 1978 (div. June 1988); children: Aaron, Kyle; m. Susan Ann Steadman, Mar. 10, 1990 (div. Dec. 1998); m. De'Anne Hudson, Apr. 27, 2001. AA summa cum laude, Western Tex. Coll., 1979; BS summa cum laude, U. Houston, 1986, JD, 1989. Bar: Tex. 1990, U.S. Dist. Ct. (so. dist.) Tex. 1990, U.S. Dist. Ct. (no., ea. and we. dists.) Tex. 1994, U.S. Ct. Appeals (5th cir.) 1990. Adminstrv. asst. Tartan Oil & Gas, Houston, 1981-82; div. order analyst Moran Exploration, Inc., 1982-83; sr. lease analyst Integrated Energy Inc., 1983-84; landman Cambridge Royalty Co., 1984-85; supr. div. orders MCO Resources Inc., 1985-87; assoc. Hutcheson & Grundy, L.L.P., 1989-96, ptnr., 1997-98; of counsel Haynes and Boone LLP, 1998-2000, ptnr., 2001—. Mem. Houston Law Rev., 1988-89, bd. dirs. Houston Law Rev. Alumni Assn., 1996-97, v.p. 1997-98, pres., 1998-99. Mem. taxi squad U. Houston, 1991; mgr. Little League Baseball, 1993-96; bd. dirs. Braeburn Little League, 1995-96; mgr., coach basketball and softball E.A. Smith YMCA, 1999—. Mem. Am. Assn. Profl. Landmen, Coll. of State Bar, State Bar Tex. (professionalism com. 1996-99), Houston Bar Assn. (lawyers for literacy com. 1991-92, lawyers in pub. schs. com. 1995-98), Tex. Young Lawyers Assn. (bd. dirs. 1993-95, liaison to Tex. lawyer's creed com. of State Bar 1994-95, co-chmn. profl. and grievance awareness com. 1994-95, chmn. profl. com. 1993-94, mem. legis. com. 1990-93, vice chmn. legis. com. 1993-94, mem. local affiliates com. 1991-92, dropout prevention com. 1991-92, Tex. Young Lawyer Assn. sect. Tex. Bar Jour. com., 1991-93, profl. and ethics com. 1995-96, outstanding young lawyer com. 1995-96), Houston Young Lawyers Assn. (bd. dirs. 1991-93, sec. 1993-94, chmn. professionalism com. 1991-92, chmn. Law Day com. 1992-93, award achievement com. 1993-94, chmn. ops. com. 1993-94, outstanding young lawyers com. 1991-92, Liberty Bell award com. 1992-93), Houston Prodrs.' Forum, U. Houston Law Ctr. Alumni Assn. (bd. dirs. 1997-98), Cougar Cager Club. Mem. Unity Ch. of Christianity. Avocations: golf, snow skiing. General civil litigation, Oil, gas, and mineral, Securities. Office: Haynes & Boone LLP 1000 Louisiana St Ste 4300 Houston TX 77002-5020 E-mail: englandr@haynesboone.com

ENGLERT, ROY THEODORE, JR. lawyer; b. Alexandria, Va., Dec. 5, 1958; s. Roy Theodore and Helen Frances (Wiggs) E. AB, Princeton U., 1978; JD, Harvard U., 1981. Ct. law clk. U.S. Ct. Appeals-D.C. Cir., Washington, 1981-82; assoc. Wilmer, Cutler & Pickering, 1982-86; asst. to solicitor gen. U.S. Dept. Justice, 1986-89; assoc. Mayer, Brown & Platt, 1989-90, ptnr., 1991-2001, Robbins, Russell, Englert, Orseck & Untereiner LLP, Washington, 2001—. Tech. official judo Centennial Olympic Games, Atlanta, 1996. Presbyterian. Avocation: judo. Administrative and regulatory, Antitrust, Appellate. Home: 411 S Pitt St Alexandria VA 22314-3713 Office: Robbins Russell Englert et al Ste 411 1801 K St NW Washington DC 20006 E-mail: royenglert@aol.com, renglert@robbinsrussell.com

ENGLISH, DALE LOWELL, circuit court judge; b. Madison, Wis., Nov. 12, 1956; s. Richard Dale and Grace Elaine (Piehler) E.; m. Patricia Kay Becker, Sept. 11, 1982; children: Kristopher Scott, Shane Patrick. BA cum laude, Luther Coll., 1979; JD, Marquette U., 1982. Bar: Wis. Supreme Ct. 1982, U.S. Dist. Ct. (ea. and we. dist.) Wis. 1982, U.S. Ct. Appeals (7th cir.) 1986, U.S. Supreme Ct. 1988. Ptnr. Colwin & English Svc. Corp., Fond du Lac, Wis., 1982-94; atty. Wausau Ins. Cos., Appleton, 1994-96; judge Br. I Fond du Lac County Circuit Ct., 1996—. Bd. dirs. Brooke Industries, vice chmn., 1990. Mem. Fond du Lac Planning Commn., 1986-95; mem. adv. com. Legal Sec. Assocs. Degree Program, Fond du Lac, 1986; bd. dirs. Fond du Lac YMCA, 1988-95, 97-2001, sec., 1989, v.p., 1990-91, pres.-elect, 1992, pres., 1993, past pres., 1994; bd. dirs. Drug Awareness Resistance Edn. of Fond du Lac, Inc., 1989-96; bd. dirs. Fond du Lac Festivals, Inc., 1996-99. Mem. ABA, Nat. Conf. of State Trial Judges, Am. Judges Assn., Wis. Bar Assn., Wis. Trial Judges Assn., Fond du Lac County Bar Assn. (pres. 2001, treas. 1984-85), Jaycees (legal counsel 1983-85, state dir. 1983-84, bd. dirs. 1983-85), Omicron Delta Epsilon. Avocations: weight lifting, sports. Insurance, Personal injury, Workers' compensation. Home: 16 Country Ct Fond Du Lac WI 54935-9612 Office: 160 S Macy St Fond Du Lac WI 54935-4241

ENGLISH, GREGORY BRUCE, lawyer; b. Lynchburg, Va., Nov. 8, 1946; s. Edgar George and Mavis Clark (Daniel) E.; m. Elaine Coleman Patton, Sept. 18, 1971; 1 child, Erik Todd. B.A., Lynchburg Coll., 1969; J.D., U. Va., 1973; LL.M., George Washington U., 1979. Bar: Pa. 1973, U.S. Supreme Ct. 1977, U.S. Dist. Ct. (no. dist.) Ohio 1981, U.S. Ct. Mil. Appeals 1976, U.S. Ct. Appeals (6th cir.) 1981, Va. 1986, D.C. 1986, U.S. Dist. Ct. (ea. dist.) Va. 1986, U.S. Ct. Appeals (4th and D.C. cirs.) 1986. Atty., Navy Gen. Counsel, 1977-78; sr. trial atty. U.S. Dept. Justice, narcotic and dangerous drug sect., criminal div., Washington, 1978-86; ptnr. English & Smith, 1988—; staff judge advocate, maj. JAGC D.C. Army Nat. Guard, Washington, 1977— . Contbr. articles to profl. jours. Bd. dirs. ACLU, Lynchburg, Va., 1969; dir. Democratic Central Com., Lynchburg, 1969. Served to capt. JAGC, U.S. Army, 1973-77. Recipient Atty. Gen.'s Spl. Commendation award, 1981; Commr.'s Meritorious Service

award IRS, 1982, Meritorious award Justice Dept., 1982, Outstanding Contbns. award Drug Enforcement Adminstrn., 1983, Meritorious Contbns. award, 1984; Carey Brewer Alumni award Lynchburg Coll., 1983. Mem. ABA. Republican. Unitarian. Clubs: U. Va. Student Aid Found. (Washington) (dir. 1977—), Lee Dist. Basketball Assn. (Alexandria, Va.) (commr. 1984-86). Criminal.

ENGLISH, JERRY FITZGERALD, lawyer, educator; b. Houston, Dec. 18, 1934; d. William Edward Michael and Viola Catherine (Christopherson) Fitzgerald; m. Alan Taylour English, July 23, 1955; children: Holly, Christopher, Anderson, Eric. BA, Stanford U., 1956; JD, Boston Coll., 1963. Bar: N.J. 1965, U.S. Dist. Ct. N.J. 1965. Clk., assoc., ptnr. Moser, Griffin, Kerby & Cooper, Summit, N.J., 1964-74; mem. N.J. Senate, 1971-72, asst. counsel to, 1972-74; legis. counsel Gov. N.J., Trenton, 1974-79; commr. N.J. Dept. Environ. Protection, 1979-82; of counsel Kerby, Copper, English, Schaul & Garvin, Summit, 1982-86, ptnr., 1986—. Adj. prof. N.J. Inst. Tech., 1983—; lectr. nationally for many orgns. Assoc. editor, vice chmn., editl. bd. N.J. Law Jour. Commr. Port Authority of N.Y. and N.J., 1979-88; bd. trustees N.J. Ctr. for Visual Arts, N.J. Harvard Law Sch. Assn., 1973; bd. dirs. Friendship Amb., Regional Plan Assn.; mem. Gateway Nat. Recreation Area Adv. Commn., 1981; mem. exec. coum. Democratic Nat. Com., 1978-84. Mem. ABA (co-chair subcom. hazardous waste & CERCLA), ATLA (gov. 9th circuit 1967-72, 1976-77, chmn. midwinter convs. 1964, 68, 71, 73, 76, 85, student advocacy program, 1973-74, legal inst. program, 1969, 71, citation for outstanding leadership 1971), Internat. Acad. Trial Lawyers (bd. dirs.), Am. Bd. Trial Advs., Western Trial Lawyers Assn. (pres. 1964-65, bd.dirs.), Internat. Soc. Barristers, Million Dollar Advs. Forum, Nat. Bd. Trial Advocacy (cert. trial law), Nev. State Bar Assns. (bd. govs. 1990—), Nev. Supremem Ct. (settlement conf. judge 1997—, ADR com. 1983-84, Nev. Rules Civil Procedure 1970-80, Nev. State Bar Study 1989, Lawyer Adv. Study 1989-1990), Ninth Circuit Ct. Appeals (lawyer rep. 1992-94), U. Nev. Sch. Medicine (dean's counsel 1995-97), Nev. Legis. Com. (spl. advisor, evidence code 1970-71), Plaintiffs' Lead Counsel Com. (co-chmn. MGM Multi-Dist. fire litig. 1980-82), Hilton Fire Litig. (co-chmn. 1981-86), PEPCON Explosion Plaintiff's Com. (chmn. 1988-92), Internat. Bar Assn., N.J. Bar Assn., Summit Bar Assn., Am. Bd. Profl. Liability Attys. (cert. specialists med. malparactice bd. dirs. 1996-98), Essex Club. Unitarian. Environmental, Private international. Home: 4 Drum Hill Rd Summit NJ 07901-3107

ENGLISH, JOHN DWIGHT, lawyer; b. Evanston, Ill., Mar. 28, 1949; s. John Francis English and Mary Faye (Taylor) Butler; m. Claranne Kay Lundeen, Apr. 22, 1972; children: Jennifer A., Katharine V., Margaret E. BA, Drake U., 1971; JD, Loyola U., 1976. Bar: Ill. 1976, U.S. Dist. Ct. (no. dist.) Ill. 1976, U.S. Tax Ct. 1977. Assoc. Bentley DuCanto Silvestri & Forkins, Chgo., 1976-79; ptnr. Silvestri Mahoney English & Zdeb, 1979-81; assoc. Ungaretti & Harris, 1981-83; ptnr. Coffield Ungaretti & Harris, 1983—. Instr. estate planning Loyola U., Chgo., 1982-87; instr. Ill. Inst. Continuing Edn. Estate Planning Short Course, 1998, 2001. Bd. dirs. Prince of Peace Luth. Sch., Chgo., 1977-83, Bethesda Home for the Aged, Chgo., 1981-89, 2000—, Luth. Family Mission, Chgo., 1985-91; alderman Park Ridge (Ill.) City Coun., 1991-95. Mem. Ill. State Bar Assn., Chgo. Bar Assn. (chmn. div. II probate practice com.), Phi Beta Kappa. Lutheran. Estate planning, Probate, Estate taxation. Home: 631 Wisner St Park Ridge IL 60068-3428 Office: Ungaretti & Harris 3500 Three 1st Nat Bank Plz Chicago IL 60602

ENGLISH, MARK GREGORY, lawyer; b. Mpls., Oct. 14, 1951; s. Earl Mark and Georgia Corrine (Lastrange) E.; m. Renee Ann Thielen, Aug. 31, 1979; children— Janelle, Brandon. B.E.E. with high distinction, U. Minn., 1973, J.D. magna cum laude, 1976. Bar: Minn. 1976, Mo. 1981. Assoc. Arvesen, Donoho, Lundeen, Hoff, Svingen & English and predecessor Arvesen Donoho Lundeen, Hoff & Svingen, Fergus Falls, Minn., 1976-77, ptnr., 1978-80; atty. Kansas City Power & Light Co., Mo., 1981-82, staff atty., 1982-86, sr. atty., 1986-88, dep. gen. counsel, 1988—. Gen. counsel Minn. Jaycees, Mpls., 1978-79. Recipient Silver medal Royal Soc. Arts, London, 1973. Mem. Mo. Bar Assn., Mensa. General corporate, Environmental, Public utilities. Home: 11101 W 120th St Overland Park KS 66213-2045 Office: Kansas City Power & Light Co 1330 Baltimore Ave Kansas City MO 64105-1910

ENGLISH, R(OBERT) BRADFORD, marshal; b. Jefferson City, Mo. BS in Criminal Justice, Lincoln U., 1982; MPA, U. Mo., 1984. Residential juvenile counselor Cole County Juvenile Ctr., Jefferson City, Mo., 1972-74; patrolman Jefferson City Police Dept., 1975-76, detective, 1976-78; comdr. Mo. Capitol Police, Jefferson City, 1978-79, police chief, 1979-94; marshal U.S. Marshal Svc., Kansas City, Mo., 1994—. Chmn. ct. security com. U.S. Dist. Ct. (we. dist.) Mo., Kansas City, 1995—; mem. dirs. adv. and leadership coun. U.S. Marshall Svc., 1996—. Chmn. bd. dirs. Capitol Area Cmty. Svc. Agy., Jefferson City, 1994. Named Statesman of Month, News Tribune Co., 1994. Mem. Internat. Assn. Chiefs of Police (life), Masons. Democrat. Avocations: golf, scuba diving, walking, weight lifting. Office: US Marshal Svc 400 E 9th St Ste 3740 Kansas City MO 64106-2635

ENGLISH, WILLIAM DESHAY, lawyer, director; b. Piedmont, Calif., Dec. 25, 1924; s. Munro and Mabel (Michener) E.; m. Nancy Ames, Apr. 7, 1956; children: Catherine, Barbara, Susan, Stephen. AB in Econs., U. Calif., Berkeley, 1948, JD, 1951. Bar: Calif. 1952, D.C. 1972. Trial atty., spl. asst. to atty. gen. U.S. Dept. Justice, Washington, 1953-55; sr. atty. AEC, 1955-62; legal advisor U.S. Mission to European Communities, Brussels, 1962-64; asst. gen. counsel internat. matters COMSAT, Washington, 1965-73; counsel Internat. Telecomm. Satellite Orgn., 1965-73; v.p., gen. counsel, dir. COMSAT Gen. Corp., 1973-76; sr. v.p. legal and govtl. affairs Satellite Bus. Sys., McLean, Va., 1976-86; v.p., gen. counsel Satellite Transponder Leasing Corp. (IBM), 1986-87; pvt. practice Washington, 1987—; counsel Am. Space Transp. Assn., 1987-93, Washington Space Bus. Roundtable; gen. counsel Iridium, LLC, 1992-96, spl. counsel, 1996-2000. With USAAF, 1943-45. Decorated Air medal. Fellow Coun. on Econ. Regulation, 1985-91; mem. ABA, AIAA (chmn. com. legal aspects aeronautics and astronautics,1993-2000, chmn. allocation space launch risks subcom. 1987, chmn. orbital debris legal subcom.), Am. Competitive Telecomm. Assn. (bd. dirs. 1976-84, pres. 1983), D.C. Bar Assn., Fed. Comm. Bar Assn., State Bar Calif., Fgn. Policy Discussion Group, Met. Club, Chevy Chase Club. Administrative and regulatory, Private international, Legislative. Home: 7420 Exeter Rd Bethesda MD 20814-2352

ENNIS, BRUCE CLIFFORD, lawyer; b. Dover, Del., Mar. 22, 1941; s. Clifford Morgan and Mary Elizabeth (Jones) E.; m. Diane Wallace, July 19, 1969; 1 child, Heather Diane. BA, W.Va. Wesleyan Coll., 1963; JD, Dickinson Law Sch., 1966. Bar: Del. 1969, U.S. Dist. Ct. Del. 1971. Ptnr. Schmittinger & Rodriguez, P.A., Dover, 1969—. Instr. Wesley Coll., Dover, 1970-78, Del. Tech. and C.C., Dover, 1978-98. Active United Meth. Ch., Dover. With U.S. Army, 1966-68. Mem. Del. State Bar Assn., Kent County Bar Assn. Real property. Office: Schmittinger & Rodriguez PA PO Box 497 Dover DE 19903-0497

ENNIS, EDGAR WILLIAM, JR. lawyer; b. Macon, Ga., May 20, 1945; s. Edgar W. and Nelle (Branan) E.; m. Judith Anne Godfrey, June 29, 1974; children: William, Branan. BS in Engring. Sci., USAF Acad., Colorado Springs, Colo., 1967; JD, U. Ga., 1971. Bar: Ga. 1971. Commd. 2d lt. USAF, 1967, advanced through ranks to capt., 1970, resigned, 1975; asst. U.S. atty. U.S. Atty.'s Office-Mid. Dist. of Ga., Macon, 1975-88; U.S. atty. U.S. Dept. Justice, 1988-93; of counsel Haynsworth, Baldwin, Johnson & Harper, 1993-97; ptnr. Haynsworth, Baldwin, Johnson & Greaves LLC, 1998-99, Constangy, Brooks & Smith LLC, Macon, 1999—. Federal civil litigation, Environmental, Labor. Office: Constangy Brooks & Smith LLC 577 Mulberry St Ste 710 Macon GA 31201-8588 E-mail: eennis@constangy.com

ENOCH, CRAIG TRIVELY, state supreme court justice; b. Wichita, Kans., Apr. 3, 1950; s. Donald Kirk and Margery (Trively) E.; m. Kathryn Stafford Barker, Aug. 2, 1975. BA, So. Meth. U., 1972, JD, 1975; LLM, U. Va., 1992. Bar: Tex. 1975, U.S. Dist. Ct. (no. dist.) Tex. 1976, U.S. Ct. Appeals (5th cir.) 1979. Assoc. Burford, Ryburn & Ford, Dallas, 1975-77; ptnr. Moseley, Jones, Enoch & Martin, 1977-81; judge 101st Dist. Ct., 1981-87; chief justice Tex. Ct. Appeals (5th dist.), 1987-92; justice Tex. Supreme Ct., Austin, 1993—. Mem. exec. bd. Dedman Sch. Law So. Meth. U., 1990—. Capt. USAFR, 1973-81. Recipient Disting. Alumni award for judicial svc. So. Meth. U. Dedman Sch. Law, 1999. Fellow Am. Bar Found., Tex. State Bar Found., Dallas Bar Found.; mem. ABA (vice chair exec. bd. appellate judges conf. jud. divsn.), Am. Law Inst. Episcopalian.

ENSENAT, DONALD BURNHAM, lawyer, former ambassador; b. New Orleans, Feb. 4, 1946; s. A.G. and Genevieve (Burnham) E.; m. Taylor Harding, June 5, 1976; children: Farish, Will. BA, Yale U., 1968; JD, Tulane U., 1973. Bar: La. 1973, U.S. Ct. Appeals (5th cir.) 1974, U.S. Supreme Ct. 1975, U.S. Ct. Appeals (11th cir.) 1982, Tex. 1991. Legis. asst. Congressman Hale Boggs, U.S. Ho. of Reps., Washington, 1969-70, legis asst. Congresswoman Lindy Boggs, 1973-74; personal aide Hon. George Bush, Houston, 1970; asst. atty gen. State of La., New Orleans, 1975-80; assoc., dir., mng. dir. Carmouche, Gray, & Hoffman, A.P.L.C., 1981-89; mng. dir. Hoffman Sutterfield Ensenat, A.P.L.C., 1989-92, sr. dir., 1994-97; of counsel Locke Liddell & Sapp, PC, 1997-2001; U.S. Chief of Protocol Washington, 2001—. U.S. amb. to Brunei, 1992-93. Bd. dirs. World Trade Ctr., New Orleans, chmn. fin. com., 1990-92, exec. com., 1993—, pres.-elect, 1995, pres., 1996, chmn. bd. dirs., 1997. With USAR, 1968-74. Mem. State Bar Tex., La. State Bar Assn., Maritime Law Assn. U.S., Yale Alumni Assn. La. (bd. dirs. 1976-92, 94—, pres. 1980-82), Assn. Yale Alumni (rep. 1976-79). Republican. Roman Catholic. Avocation: sports. Home: 1233 Harmony St New Orleans LA 70115-3422 Office: US State Dept S/CPR 2201 C St NW Washington DC 20520 E-mail: dbe@ensenat.com

ENSIGN, GREGORY MOORE, lawyer; b. Cleve., June 3, 1949; s. Gerald Edward and Patricia Mae (Komlos) E.; m. Nancy Beth Udelson, Jan. 9, 1977 (div.); children: Julie Ann, Jennifer Brooke; m. Cathryn Rae Halas, Oct. 24, 1987. BA, Ohio Wesleyan U., 1971; JD, Capital U., 1975. Bar: Ohio 1975, U.S. Dist. Ct. (so. dist.) Ohio 1975, U.S. Dist. Ct. (no. dist.) Ohio 1978, U.S. Ct. Appeals (6th cir.) 1984. Mgr. legal sect. Dept. Mental Health and Mental Retardation, Columbus, Ohio, 1972-77, chief counsel, 1977-78; assoc. Weltman, Strachan and Green Co., L.P.A., Cleve., 1978-79; ptnr. Sindell, Sindell & Rubenstein, Cleve., 1979-86; v.p. adminstrn., gen. counsel, sec. Kirkwood Industries, Inc., Cleve., 1986—. Contbr. articles to profl. jours. Mem. University Heights Communications and Devel. Commn., Ohio, 1981-84. Mem. ABA, Ohio State Bar Assn., Cleve. Bar Assn., Rotary. Republican. General corporate, Environmental, Labor. Office: Kirkwood Industries Inc 4855 W 130th St Cleveland OH 44135-5182

ENSLEN, PAMELA CHAPMAN, lawyer; b. Detroit, Dec. 29, 1953; d. Ralph Nicholas Chapman and Roberta Margaret Clarke McLaughlin; m. Richard Alan Enslen, Nov. 2, 1985; 1 child, Alan Gennady Robert. BMus, U. Mich., 1976, MMus, 1977; JD, Wayne State U., 1981. Bar: Mich. 1981, U.S. Dist. Ct. (ea. and we. dist.) Mich., U.S. Ct. Appeals (6th cir.), U.S. Supreme Ct. Pre-hearing atty. Mich. Ct. Appeals, Detroit, 1981-83; fed. law clk. U.S. Dist. Ct., We. Dist. Mich., Kalamazoo, 1983-85; sr. ptnr. Miller, Canfield, Paddock & Stone, 1985-2001; fed. pub. defender We. Dist. Mich., 2001—. Lectr., cons., arbitrator, author and mediator in field. Co-founder, bd. dirs. Community Dispute Resolution Ctr. of Kalamazoo County, 1988—; bd. dirs. Am. Cancer Soc., Kalamazoo, 1991—. Named Mich. Lawyer of Yr., Mich. Lawyers Weekly, 1998. Mem.: ABA (standing com. on dispute resolution 1990—93, governing coun. dispute resolution sect. 1994—97, chair dispute resolution sect. 1997—, sect. del. Ho. of Dels. 1999—, standing com. on fed. jud. improvements 2001—), ATLA, MENSA, Mich. Bar Assn. (counsel sect. on arbitration and alternative dispute resolution 1985—), Nat. Order of Barristers, Kalamazoo County Bar Assn. (chair law day com. 1989, bd. dirs. 1996—), Kalamazoo Trial Lawyers Assn., Women Lawyers of Mich. (regional rep. 1989—90), Pi Kappa Lambda. Democrat. Avocations: reading, music. Alternative dispute resolution, Federal civil litigation, Labor. Office: Ste 500 50 Louis NW Grand Rapids MI 49503

ENSLEN, RICHARD ALAN, federal judge; b. Kalamazoo, May 28, 1931; s. Ehrman Thrasher and Pauline Mabel (Dragoo) E.; m. Pamela Gayle Chapman, Nov. 2, 1985; children— David, Susan, Sandra, Thomas, Janet, Joseph, Gennady. Student, Kalamazoo Coll., 1949-51, Western Mich. U., 1955; LL.B., Wayne State U., 1958; LL.M., U. Va., 1986. Bar: Mich. 1958, U.S. Dist. Ct. (we. dist.) Mich. 1960, U.S. Ct. Appeals (6th cir.) 1971, U.S. Ct. Appeals (4th cir.) 1975, U.S. Supreme Ct 1975. Mem. firm Stratton, Wise, Early & Starbuck, Kalamazoo, 1958-60, Bauckham & Enslen, Kalamazoo, 1960-64, Howard & Howard, Kalamazoo, 1970-76, Enslen & Schma, Kalamazoo, 1977-79; dir. Peace Corps, Costa Rica, 1965-67; judge Mich. Dist. Ct., 1968-70; U.S. dist. judge Kalamazoo, 1979—; chief judge, 1995-2001. Mem. faculty Western Mich. U., 1961-62, Nazareth Coll., 1974-75; adj. prof. polit. sci. Western Mich. U., 1982— Co-author: The Constitution Law Dictionary: Volume One, Individual Rights, 1985; Volume Two, Governmental Powers, 1987, Constitutional Deskbook: Individual Rights, 1987, (with Mary Bedikian and Pamela Enslen) Michigan Practice, Alternative Dispute Resolution, 1998. Served with USAF, 1951-54. Named Person of the Century-Law and Courts, The Kalamazoo Gazette, 1999; recipient Disting. Alumni award, Wayne State Law Sch., 1980, Western Mich. U., 1982, Outstanding Practical Achievement award, Ctr. Pub. Resources, 1984, award for Excellence and Innovation in Alternative Dispute Resolution and Dispute Mgmt., Legal Program; scholar, Jewel Corp., 1956—57, Lampson McElhorne, 1957. Mem. ABA (standing com. on dispute resolution 1983-90), Mich. Bar Assn., Am. Judicature Soc. (bd. dirs. 1983-85), Sixth Cir. Jud. Coun. Office: US Dist Ct 410 W Michigan Ave Kalamazoo MI 49007-3757

ENTENMAN, JOHN ALFRED, lawyer; b. White Plains, N.Y., Apr. 14, 1948; s. Alfred Morris and Mae Muriel (Hamilton) E. B.A., U. Mich., 1970, J.D., Harvard U., 1973. Bar: Mich. 1973, U.S. Dist. Ct. (ea. dist.) Mich. 1973, U.S. Ct. Appeals (6th cir.) 1974, U.S. Supreme Ct. 1974. Assoc. Dykema Gossett et al., Detroit, 1973-80, ptnr. 1980— ; adj. prof. labor law U. Detroit Sch. Law, 1975-78. Mem. State Bar Assn. Mich., ABA, Indsl. Relations Research Assn., Theta Delta Chi (sr. exec. 1969-70). Club: Renaissance (Detroit). Labor. Home: 638 Westchester Rd Grosse Pointe MI 48230-1824 Office: Dykema Gossett 400 Renaissance Ctr Ste 35 Detroit MI 48243-1501

EPISCOPE, PAUL BRYAN, b. Chgo., Nov. 27, 1939; s. Paul J. and Loretta (Gibbons-Coleman) E. BS, DePaul U., 1965, JD magna cum laude, 1969. Bar: Ill. 1969, U.S. Dist. Ct. (no. dist.) Ill. 1969. Assoc. McDermott, Will & Emery, Chgo., 1969, Philip H. Corboy & Assocs., Chgo., 1970-74; ptnr. Paul B. Episcope, Ltd., 1974—. Instr. trial techniques Ill. Inst. Tech. Chgo.-Kent Coll. Law, 1976-77; Ill. Supreme Ct. Com., Pattern Jury Instructions, Civil. Contbr. writings in field to legal publs. Mem. ABA, Internat. Acad. Trial Lawyers, Ill. State Bar Assn., Chgo. Bar Assn., Assn. Trial Lawyers Am., Ill. Trial Lawyers Assn. (bd. mgrs.), Am. Judicature Soc., Justinian Soc., Soc. Trial Lawyers, Pi Gamma Mu, Abota. State civil litigation, Personal injury, Workers' compensation. Office: 77 W Washington St Chicago IL 60602-2801

EPPERSON, KRAETTLI QUYNTON, lawyer, educator; b. Ft. Eustis, Va., May 2, 1949; s. Dimpster Eugene Sr. and Helen Walter (Davidson) E.; m. Kay Lawrence, Aug. 22, 1970; children: Kraettli L., Kristin J., Kevin Q., Keith W. BA in Polit. Sci., U. Okla., 1971; MS in Urban and Policy Scis., SUNY, Stony Brook, 1974; JD, Oklahoma City U., 1978. Bar: Okla. 1979, U.S. Dist. Ct. (we. dist.) Okla. 1984, Fed. Claims Ct. 1997. Urban planner Gov.'s Office of Community Affairs and Planning, Oklahoma City, 1974-75; adminstr. of pub. transp. planning Okla. Dept. of Transp., 1975-79; title examiner Lawyers Title of Oklahoma City, Inc., 1979-80; gen. counsel, v.p. Am. First Land Title Ins. Co., Oklahoma City, 1980-82; assoc. Ferguson & Litchfield, 1982-85, Ames & Ashabranner, Oklahoma City, 1986-88, ptnr., 1989-93, Cook & Epperson, Oklahoma City, 1994-97; pvt. practice, 1997—. Adj. prof. law Okla. land titles Oklahoma City U., 1982—; instr. real property Okla. Bar Rev., 1998—; instr. real property titles Grad. Realtors Inst., 1998-99. Author: Basye Clearing Land Titles, 1998; contbg. author, editor: Vernon's Oklahoma Forms 2d-Real Estate, 2000—; contbr. articles to profl. jours. Asst. scoutmaster Boy Scouts Am., Oklahoma City, 1984-88, 93—, asst. cubmaster, 1989-90, cubmaster, 1990-91, webelos leader, 1991-95, dist. vice-chair, 2000-01, dist. chair, 2001—. 2d lt. USAR, 1971. Mem. ABA (vice-chmn. conveyancing com. 1987-88, 93-94, chmn. 1991-93, chmn. state customs and practice subcom. 1987-88, project chmn. title exam. standards nat. survey 1988—), Am. Land Title Assn. (legis. com. 1981-82, jud. com. 1981-82), Okla. Bar Assn. (real property sect. 1979—, dir. 1982-88, 94-95, chmn. 1985-86, project chmn. Okla. Title Exam. Standards Handbook project 1982-85, mem. title exam. standards com. 1980—, chmn. 1992—, legis. liaison com. 1986-92, co-chmn. abstracting standards com. 1982-84), Oklahoma City Real Property Lawyers Assn. (dir. 1985-91, pres. 1990-91), Oklahoma City Commml. Law Attys. Assn. Republican. Episcopalian. Avocations: skeet, storytelling, camping. State civil litigation, Land use and zoning (including planning), Real property. Home: 3029 Rock Ridge Ct Oklahoma City OK 73120-5731 Office: 4334 NW Expressway St Ste 174 Oklahoma City OK 73116-1574 E-mail: kqelaw@aol.com

EPPS, JAMES HAWS, III, lawyer; b. Johnson City, Tenn., Sept. 15, 1936; s. James Haws and Anne Lafayette (Sessoms) E.; m. Jane Mahoney, Oct. 9, 1976; children from previous marriage--James Haws IV, Sara Stuart. B.A., U.N.C., 1955-59; J.D., Vanderbilt U., 1962. Bar: Tenn. 1962, U.S. Dist. Ct. Tenn. 1962, U.S. Ct. Appeals (6th cir.) 1971, Interstate Commerce Commn. Bar 1962, U.S. Supreme Ct. 1967. Prin. Epps & Epps, Johnson City, Tenn. City atty. Johnson City, 1967—, Johnson City Bd. Edn., 1967-86; spl. counsel State of Tenn., 1966-70; former gen. counsel Appalachian Flying Svc. Inc., ET&WNC Transp. Co., Inc. First bd. govs. Transp. Law Jour. Past bd. dirs. Washington County Mental Health Assn., East Tenn. and Western N.C. Transp. Co., East Tenn. and Western N.C. R.R., Tennolina Corp., Appalachian Air Lines, Inc., Appalachian Flying Svc., Inc., Farmers and Mchts. Bank, Limestone, Tenn., Tenn. Mental Health Assn., budget com. United Fund of Johnson City, 1964-68, Assault Crime Counsel Early Support Svcs. Inc., Safe Passage Inc., Johnson City Homeless Coalition, Home Base Adv. Coun.; former legal adviser Appalachian Council Girl Scouts U.S.A.; mem. Tenn. Law Revision Commn., 1970-71; legal counsel Salvation Army, mem. adv. bd. 1974—, exec. com. 1977—, 1st v.p. adv. bd. 1991, pres. adv. bd. 1993, 94, mem. property com.; chmn. Family Violence Coun.; mem. Civil Def., 1967—; chmn. Washington County for Tenn. Leukemia Soc., 1991; mem. exec. com. Washington County Dem. Party, Tenn. Bicentennial Commn., exec. and fin. coms. Fellow Tenn. Bar Found.; mem. ABA, Fed. Bar Assn., Nat. Orgn. Legal Problems Edn., Am. Counsel Assn., Nat. Assn. R.R. Trial Counsel, Internat. Mcpl. Lawyers Assn., (state chmn. Tenn. 1988-89, ethics and environ. coms. 1989—, regional v.p. 1989-92, chmn. resolutions com. 1989-90, chmn. dues and alternatives revenue 1996-97, budget and fin. 1996—, mem. federalism com. 1996—, state league counsel rev. com. 1997, awards com., 1999—, lectr., trustee, 1992—, 2d v.p. 2000, bd. mem. policy adv. com. 2000), Nat. Legal Aid Defender Assn., Tenn. Bar Assn., Am. Judicature Soc., Washington County Bar Assn. (past pres.), Tenn. Mcpl. Attys. Assn., Assn. ICC Practitioners (past com. profl. ethics and grievences), Transp. Lawyers Assn., Motor Carrier Lawyers Assn., Johnson City C. of C. (Disting. Service award 1968), Internat. Platform Assn., Lawyers Com. for Civil Rights Under Law, World Peace Through Law Ctr., Tenn. Lung Assn., Tenn. Correctional Assn., Tenn. Taxpayers Assn. (past bd. dirs.), Tennesseans for Better Transp., U.S. Supreme Ct. Hist. Soc., Def. Research Inst., Tipton Haynes Hist. Assn. (past dir.); Clubs: Hurstleigh, J.C. Country, Unaka Rd. and Gun, Highland Stable, North Johnson City Bus. (dir., past pres. 1966-67), Nat. Lawyers, East Tenn. State U. Centry, Boys'Club (charter) (Johnson City/Washington County), Masons, Elks (legal counsel 1963-67), Phi Delta Phi, Phi Delta Theta. Episcopalian. Administrative and regulatory, General practice. Office: 115 E Unaka Ave Johnson City TN 37601-4623 also: PO Box 2288 Johnson City TN 37605-2288

EPSTEIN, ALAN BRUCE, lawyer; b. Passaic, N.J., Sept. 20, 1944; s. Jerome P. and Stella M. (Goldfinger) E.; m. Eve Teichholz, June 21, 1966; children: Jason, Dylan. BA, Temple U., 1967, JD, 1969. Bar: Pa. 1970, U.S. Dist. Ct. (ea. dist.) Pa. 1970, U.S. Ct. Appeals (3d cir.) 1972, U.S. Ct. Appeals (5th cir.) 1977, U.S. Dist. Ct. (cen. and we. dists.) Pa. 1987, U.S. Supreme Ct. 1988, U.S. Ct. Appeals (9th cir.) 2000. Assoc. firm Freedman, Borowsky & Lorry, Phila., 1969-77; ptnr. firm Jablon, Epstein, Wolf & Drucker, 1977-99; shareholder Spector, Gadon & Rosen, 1999—. Pres. Judicate Nat. Pvt. Ct. System, Phila., 1983-88. Fellow Pa. Bar Found., Coll. Labor and Employement Lawyers; mem. ABA, ATLA, Pa. Trial Lawyers Assn. (bd. govs. 1984-86), Phila. Trial Lawyers Assn., Pa. Bar Assn., Phila. Bar Assn., Temple Am. Inn Ct. (bd. dirs. 1994—, pres. 2001—, nat. edn. chair 2000—). Jewish. Civil rights, Federal civil litigation, Labor. Home: 404 S Camac St Philadelphia PA 19147-1112 Office: Spector Gadon & Rosen PC Seven Penn Ctr 1635 Market St Fl 7 Philadelphia PA 19103-2217 E-mail: aepstein@lawsgr.com

EPSTEIN, ELAINE MAY, lawyer; b. Phila., May 29, 1947; d. Sidney and Helen (Brill) Epstein; m. James A. Krachey, July 25, 1987; stepchildren: Ross Krachey, Anna Krachey. BA, U. Pa., 1968; MA, Yale U., 1971; JD, Northeastern U., 1976. Assoc. Law Offices of P.J. Piscitelli, Brockton, Mass., 1975-78; ptnr. LoDolce & Epstein, 1978-94, Todd & Weld, Boston, 1994—. Mem. Bd. Bar Overseers, Boston, 1984-88; trustee Mass. Continuing Legal Edn., Boston, 1991-93. Mem. editl. bd. Mass. Lawyers Weekly, 1993-98. Fellow Mass. Bar Found. (trustee 1993-98); mem. ABA, Mass. Bar Assn. (pres. 1992-93), Women's Bar Assn. (pres. 1979-80). Democrat. Jewish. Appellate, General civil litigation, Family and matrimonial. Home: 4 Manns Hill Cres Sharon MA 02067-2267 Office: Todd & Weld 28 State St Fl 31 Boston MA 02109-1775

EPSTEIN, JEREMY G. lawyer; b. Chgo., Sept. 28, 1946; s. Joseph and Gayola (Goldman) E.; m. Amy Kallman, Sept. 15, 1968; children: Joshua, Abigail. BA summa cum laude, Columbia U., 1967; BA, Cambridge U., Eng., 1969, MA, 1973; JD, Yale U., 1972. Bar: N.Y. 1973. Law clk. to judge Arnold Bauman U.S. Dist. Ct. (so. dist.) N.Y., 1972-74; asst. U.S. atty. so. dist. N.Y. U.S. Dist. Ct., 1974-78; ptnr. Shearman & Sterling, N.Y.C., 1982—. Bd. dirs. Fund for Modern Cts., Legal Aid Soc.; vol. Lawyers for the Arts. Fellow Am. Coll. Trial Lawyers, Phi Beta Kappa. Office: 599 Lexington Ave Fl C2 New York NY 10022-6030

EPSTEIN, JOEL DONALD, lawyer; b. N.Y.C., July 3, 1947; s. Samuel B. and Estelle (LeBas) E.; m. Janet Chall, Sept. 27, 1981; children: Joshua Lee, Jenny Leigh. BA, CCNY, 1970; JD, Syracuse U., 1973. Assoc. Viscardi & Steinman, P.C., N.Y.C., 1973-79, Samuel A. Almon, N.Y.C., 1979-92, Law Offices John Guglielmo, 1992-97, Law Offices Anne D. Pope, N.Y.C., 1997-2001. Bar: N.Y. 1974. Small claims arbitrator N.Y.C. Civil Ct., 1982—; arbitrator Am. Arbitration Assn., N.Y.C., 1979—. Mem. N.Y. State Bar Assn. Federal civil litigation, State civil litigation, General practice. Home: 6 Hillside Ave Great Neck NY 11021-3236 Office: McDonnell Adels & Goodstein 5 Dakota Dr Lake Sucess NY 11042

EPSTEIN, JOSEPH MARC, lawyer; b. Phila., Oct. 31, 1944; s. Arthur and Shirley (Rubenstone) E.; m. Susan Nancy Landerson, June 25, 1967; children: Daniel, Samara. BA, SUNY, Buffalo, 1966; JD, NYU, 1969. Bar: N.J. 1969, U.S. Dist. Ct. N.J. 1969, U.S. Ct. Appeals (3d cir.) 1971, U.S. Dist. Ct. Colo. 1973, U.S. Ct. Appeals (10th cir.) 1980, U.S. Supreme Ct. 1973, Nebr. 1993, Wyo. 1993. Assoc. Neville & Pendleton, Denville, N.J., 1970-71; asst. U.S. Atty. Newark, 1971-73; assoc. Kripke, Carrigan & Bragg, Denver, 1973-75; ptnr. Epstein & Gilbert, 1975-78; pvt. practice, 1978-80; ptnr. Kripke, Epstein & Lawrence, P.C., 1980-95; ADR specialist JAMS/Endispute n/k/a JAMS, 1995-2000, Conflict Resolution Svcs., Inc., Denver, 2000—. Lectr. in field. Contbr. articles to profl. jours. Bd. dirs. Colo. Assn. Retarded Citizens, 1976-80, Theodore Herzl Day Sch., 1981-84. Recipient Leadership award Denver C. of C., 1978-79. Fellow Internat. Acad. Mediators (founder 1997); mem. ATLA (bd. govs. 1990-92), Colo. Bar Assn., Denver Bar Assn., Colo. Trial Lawyers Assn. (past v.p., pres.-elect, pres.), Trial Lawyers for Public Justice (bd. dirs.). Republican. Jewish. Federal civil litigation, State civil litigation, Personal injury. Office: Kripke Epstein & Lawrence PC 4710 El Camino Dr Englewood CO 80111-1152

EPSTEIN, MELVIN, lawyer; b. Passaic, N.J., Jan. 4, 1938; s. Hyman and Lillian (Rozenblum) E.; m. Rachel Judith Stein, Dec. 20, 1964; children: Jonathan Andrew, Emily E. Landau. AB, Harvard U., 1959, LLB, 1962. Bar: N.Y. 1963. Assoc. Stroock & Stroock & Lavan, L.L.P., N.Y.C., 1962-71, ptnr., 1972—. Bd. dirs. Hillel of N.Y.C.; mem. schs. com. Harvard U., 1984—. Mem. N.Y. State Bar Assn., Assn. of Bar of City of N.Y. Democrat. Jewish. General corporate, Private international, Securities. Office: Stroock & Stroock & Lavan LLP 180 Maiden Ln New York NY 10038-4925 E-mail: mepstein@stroock.com

EPSTEIN, MICHAEL ALAN, lawyer; b. N.Y.C., June 26, 1954; s. Herman and Lillian (King) E. BA, Lehigh U., 1975; JD, NYU, 1979. Bar: N.Y., 1980, US. Dist. Ct. (so., ea. dists.) N.Y., 1980. Ptnr. Weil, Gotshal & Manges, N.Y.C., 1979—. Lectr. in field. Author: Modern Intellectual Property, 1984, 3d edit., 1994, International Intellectual Property, 1992; editor: Corporate Counsellors Deskbook, 1982, 3d edit., 1990, Biotechnology Law, 1988, The Trademark Law Revision Act, 1989, Trade Secrets, Restrictive Covenants and Other Safeguards, 1986, Online-Internet Law, 1997, Epstein on Intellectual Property, 1998; co-editor, mem. editl. bd. Jour. Proprietary Rights, The Computer Lawyer, The Intellectual Property Strategist, The Cyberspace Lawyer; contbr. articles to profl. jours. Trustee Jonas Salk Found., Am. Health Found. Donald L. Brown fellow in trade regulation NYU Sch. Law, 1978-79. Mem. ABA, N.Y. State Bar Assn. Antitrust, Computer, Trademark and copyright. Home: 1020 Park Ave New York NY 10028-0913 Office: Weil Gotshal & Manges 767 5th Ave Fl Concl New York NY 10153-0119

ERBS, THOMAS J. lawyer, arbitrator; b. St. Louis, Aug. 31, 1936; s. Harry G. and Jeanne (Tinsley) E.; m. Mary Anne Gansmann, Aug. 23, 1958; children: Scott, Michelle, Todd, Jeanne. BS in Acctg., U. Notre Dame, 1958, JD, 1960. Bar: Mo. 1960, Ill. 1963. Ptnr. Erbs & Erbs P.C., St. Louis, 1960—, pres., 1973—. Arbitrator Fed. Mediation Service, 1974— ; adv. dir. Firstar Bank, St. Louis. Mem. Nat. Acad. Arbitrators, ABA, St. Louis Bar Assn., Am. Arbitration Assn. Estate planning, Probate, Real property. Office: Erbs & Erbs PC 1650 Des Peres Rd Ste 135 Saint Louis MO 63131-1899

ERCKLENTZ, ENNO WILHELM, JR. lawyer; b. N.Y.C., Jan. 27, 1931; s. Enno Wilhelm and Hildegard (Schlubach) E.; m. Mai A. Vilms, Sept. 20, 1969; children: Cornelia, Stephanie. AB, Columbia U., 1954; JD, Harvard U., 1957. Bar: N.Y. 1958. Assoc. Curtis, Mallet-Prevost, Colt & Mosle, N.Y.C., 1957-60; sec., gen. counsel Channing Fin. Corp., 1960-69; v.p., sec., gen. counsel Inverness Mgmt. Corp., 1969-75; pvt. practice, 1975-78; ptnr. Whitman & Ransom, 1978-87, Greeven & Ercklentz, N.Y.C., 1987-98; pvt. practice, 1998—. Author: Modern German Corporation Law, 1979. Mem. ABA, N.Y. State Bar Assn., Assn. of Bar City of N.Y., Am. Fgn. Law Assn. Republican. Roman Catholic. General corporate, Private international, Securities. Office: Enno W Ercklentz Jr PC 630 5th Ave Ste 1905 New York NY 10111-0100 E-mail: ennoerck@aol.com

ERICKSON, PHILLIP ARTHUR, lawyer, corporate executive; b. Duluth, Minn., June 27, 1941; s. Carl Edward and Velma Cecilia (Pera) E.; BA, U. Minn., 1967, JD, 1970; children: Michael Phillip, Amy Diane. Bar: Minn. 1970, U.S. Supreme Ct. 1981, U.S. Ct. Appeals (fed. cir.) 1989. Gen. counsel and sec. North Cen. Cos., Inc., St. Paul, 1970-73; gen. atty. JFP Enterprises, Duluth, 1973-74; corp. atty., The Cornelius Co., Anoka, Minn., sr. v.p. law and corp. sec., 1974-86; sr. v.p., corp. sec. IMI Cornelius (Americas) Inc., 1986-88, sr. v.p. legal and regulatory affairs IMI Group Inc., Mpls., 1988—. Mem. adv. com., legal assistance for people with devel. disabilities, mem. facilities com. Christian Edn. Com. Social Ministry, Singles Fellowship Com.; Luth. Ch. St. Philip Deacon; usher social ministry com., stewardship com. Prince of Peace Luth. Ch., coach Plymouth Athletic Assn., mem. parents adv. com. and mem. acad. com. Wayzata W. Jr. High Sch., program evaluation & review com. Bklyn. Park Elem. Sch.; bd. dirs., past pres. Homeward Bound, Inc., 1981-83; past dir. Mpls. Assn. Retarded Citizens. Mem. ABA, Minn. State Bar Assn., Hennepin County Bar Assn., Rotary (Mpls., City Lakes chpt.). Contracts commercial, General corporate, General practice. Home: 14605 34th Ave N Minneapolis MN 55447-5229 Office: IMI Group Inc 1 Cornelius Pl Anoka MN 55303-1583

ERICKSON, ROBERT STANLEY, lawyer; b. Kemmerer, Wyo., Apr. 17, 1944; s. Stanley W. and Dorothy Marie (Johnson) E.; m. Alice Norman, Dec. 27, 1972; children: Robert Badger, Erin Elizabeth, Andrew Carl, Scott Stanley, Courtney Ellen, Brennan Marie. BS in Bus., U. Idaho, 1966; JD, U. Utah, 1969; LLM in Taxation, George Washington U., 1973. Bar: U.S. Supreme Ct. 1973, U.S. Ct. Appeals (9th cir.) 1980, U.S. Dist. Ct. Idaho 1973, U.S. Tax Ct. 1969, Idaho 1973, Utah 1969. Assoc. atty. Office of Chief Counsel, Dept. Treasury, Washington, 1969-73; assoc. Elam, Burke, Jeppesen, Evans & Boyd, Boise, Idaho, 1973-77; ptnr. Elam, Burke, Evans, Boyd & Koontz, 1977-81; spl. counsel Holme Roberts & Owen, Salt Lake City, 1981-83; ptnr. Hansen & Erickson, Boise, 1983-85, Hawley Troxell Ennis & Hawley, Boise, 1985—. Contbr. articles to profl. jours. Named Citizen of Yr., Boise Exch. Club, 1980. Fellow Am. Coll. of Trust and Estate Counsel (past Idaho chmn. 1993—); mem. ABA (sect. on taxation, com. state and local taxes), IRS/Western Region Bar Assn. (mem., past chmn. liaison com. Idaho co-chair local task force IRS non-filer program 1993), Idaho State Bar (founding chmn. taxation, probate and trust law sect.), Utah State Bar (tax and estate planning sect.), Boise Estate Planning Council, Idaho State Tax Inst. (exec. com., numerous other local and nat. coms.). Mem. LDS Ch. Estate planning, Probate, Corporate taxation. Office: Hawley Troxell Ennis & Hawley First Interstate Ctr 877 Main St Ste 1000 Boise ID 83702-5884

ERICKSON, WILLIAM HURT, retired state supreme court justice; b. Denver, May 11, 1924; s. Arthur Xavier and Virginia (Hurt) E.; m. Doris Rogers, Dec. 24, 1953; children: Barbara Ann, Virginia Lee, Stephen Arthur, William Taylor. Degree in petroleum engring., Colo. Sch. Mines, 1947; student, U. Mich., 1949; LLB, U. Va., 1950. Bar: Colo. 1951. Pvt. practice, Denver; state supreme ct. justice Colo. Supreme Ct., 1971-96, state supreme ct. chief justice, 1983-86; faculty NYU Appellate Judges Sch., 1972-85. Mem. exec. Commn. on Accreditation of Law Enforcement Agys., 1980-83; chmn. Pres.'s Nat. Commn. for Rev. of Fed. and State Laws Relating to Wiretapping and Electronic Surveillance, 1976. Chmn. Erickson Commn., 1997, Owens Columbine Rev. Commn., 2000-01; chmn. gov.'s Columbine Rev. Commn., 1999-2001. With USAAF, 1943. Recipient Disting. Achievement medal Colo. Sch. Mines, 1990. Fellow Internat. Acad. Trial Lawyers (former sec.), Am. Coll. Trial Lawyers, Am. Bar Found. (chmn. 1985), Internat. Soc. Barristers (pres. 1971); mem. ABA, (bd. govs. 1975-79, former chmn. com. on standards criminal justice, former chmn. coun. criminal law sect., former chmn. com. to implement standards criminal justice, mem. long-range planning com., action com. to reduce ct. cost and delay), Colo. Bar Assn. (award of merit 1989), Denver Bar Assn. (past pres., trustee), Am. Law Inst. (coun. 1973—), Practising Law Inst. (nat. adv. coun., bd. govs. Colo.), Freedoms Found. at Valley Forge (nat. coun. trustees, 1986—), Order of Coif, Scribes (pres. 1978). Home: 10 Martin Ln Englewood CO 80110-4821

ERICSON, JAMES DONALD, lawyer, insurance executive; b. Hawarden, Iowa, Oct. 12, 1935; s. Elmer H. and Martha (Sydness) E.; children: Linda Jean, James Robert. B.A. in History, State U. Iowa, 1958, J.D., 1962. Bar: Wis. 1965. Assoc. Fitzgerald, Brown, Leahy, McGill & Strom, Omaha, 1962-65; with Northwestern Mut. Life Ins. Co., Milw., 1965—, asst. to pres., 1972-75, dir. policy benefits, 1975-76, v.p., gen. counsel, sec., 1976-80, sr. v.p., 1980, exec. v.p., 1987, pres., 1990, chief operating officer, 1991-93, pres., CEO, 1993-2000, chmn., CEO, 2000-2001. Dir. MGIC Investment Corp., Green Bay Packaging Inc., Kohl's Corp., Marcus Corp., Northwestern Mut. Investment Svcs., Frank Russell Co.; immediate past chmn. Am. Coun. Life Ins. Bd. dirs. Wis. Taxpayers Alliance, Competitive Wis., Inc., Greater Milw. Com., Milw. Redevel. Com., United Way, Met. Milw. Assn. Commerce, Med. Coll. Wis., Milw. Sch. Engring.; trustee Lawrence U., Com. for Econ. Devel., Boys and Girls Club Greater Milw., Lyric Opera Chgo. Mem. ABA, Assn. Life Ins. Counsel (hon.), Wis. Bar Assn., Milw. Club (bd. dirs.), Phi Beta Kappa. Republican. Presbyterian. General corporate. Office: Northwestern Mut 720 E Wisconsin Ave Milwaukee WI 53202-4703

ERICSON, ROGER DELWIN, lawyer, forest resource company executive; b. Moline, Ill, Dec. 21, 1934; s. Carl D. and Linnea E. (Challman) E.; m. Norma F. Brown, Aug. 1, 1957; children: Catherine Lynn, David. AB, JD, Stetson U., 1958; MBA, U. Chgo., 1971. Bar: Fla. 1958, Ill. 1959, Ind. 1974. Atty. Brunswick Corp., Skokie, Ill., 1959-62; asst. sec., asst. gen. counsel Chemetron Corp., Chgo., 1962-73; asst. v.p. Inland Container Corp., Indpls., 1973-75, v.p., gen. counsel, sec., 1975-83, Temple-Inland, Inc., 1983-94, of counsel, 1994—. V.p., sec. bd. dirs. Inland Container Corp.; dir., pres., co-CEO Kraft Land Svcs., Inc., Atlanta, 1978-88; bd. dirs., v.p. Guaranty Holdings Inc., Dallas; v.p. Temple-Inland Fin. Svcs., Inc., Austin, 1990-94; bd. dirs. Temple-Inland Forest Products, Temple-Inland Real Estate Investment, Inc., Temple-Inland Realty Inc. Trustee Chgo. Homes for Children, 1971-74; mem. alumni coun. U. Chgo., 1972-76; mem. Palatine Twp. Youth Commn., 1969-72; sect. chmn. Chgo. Heart Assn., 1972, 73; alumni bd. dirs. Stetson U.; bd. dirs. Temple-Inland Found; mem. Safe and Drug-Free Comm. Collier County Sch. Bd., 1996—. Mem. ABA, Am. Arbitration Assn. (nat. panel comml. arbitrators), Am. Soc. Corp. Secs., Am. Forest Products Assn. (past mem. govt. affairs com. and legal com.), Am. Corp. Counsel Assn., Ind. Bar Assn., Fla. Bar Assn., Chgo. Bar Assn., Indpls. Bar Assn. (chmn. corp. counsel sect., mem. profl. responsibility com. 1982), Collier County Bar Assn., Indpls. C. of C. (govt. affairs com.), Plum Grove Club (pres. 1967), The Club at Olde Cypress, Omicron Delta Kappa, Phi Delta Phi. Administrative and regulatory, Antitrust, General corporate. Home: PO Box 110218 Naples FL 34108-0104 Office: Temple-Inland Inc Drawer N Diboll TX 75941

ERLANDSSON, ASA, lawyer; b. Sollentuna, Stockholm, Sweden, Aug. 13, 1968; d. David and Monika Carlsson; m. Hans Erlandsson, Aug. 23, 1997. LLM, U. Uppsala, Sweden, 1993; LLM in European Law, Amsterdam Sch. Internat. Rels., 1997. Law clk. Dist. Ct. of Stockholm, 1994-96; jr. judge Svea Appeal Ct., Stockholm, 1997-98; assoc. Setterwalls Law Firm, 1998—. Prof.'s asst. U. Uppsala, 1991-93. Contbr. chpt. to book, articles to profl. jours. General civil litigation, General corporate, Labor. Office: Setterwalls Law Firm Arsenalsgatan 6 Stockholm SE-11147 Sweden Fax: 46 8 598 890 90. E-mail: asa.erlandsson@setterwalls.se

ERLEBACHER, ARLENE CERNIK, retired lawyer; b. Chgo., Oct. 3, 1946; d. Laddie J. and Gertrude V. (Kurdys) Cernik; m. Albert Erlebacher, June 14, 1968; children: Annette Doherty, Jacqueline. BA, Northwestern U., 1967, JD, 1973. Bar: Ill. 1974, U.S. Dist. Ct. (no. dist.) Ill. 1974, U.S. Ct. Appeals (7th cir.) 1974, Fed. Trial Bar 1983, U.S. Supreme Ct. 1985. Assoc. Sidley & Austin, Chgo., 1974-80, ptnr., 1980-95, ret., 1996. Fellow Am. Bar Found.; mem. Order of Coif. Federal civil litigation, State civil litigation, Product liability. E-mail: Erlebacher@home.com

ERNST, DANIEL PEARSON, lawyer; b. Des Moines, Sept. 30, 1931; s. Daniel Ward and Thea Elaine (Pearson) E.; m. Ann Robinson, April 14, 1956; children: Ellen, Daniel R., Ruth Ann. BA, Dartmouth Coll., 1953; JD, U. Mich., 1956. Bar: Iowa 1956, Ill. 1964, Mich. 1980. Assoc. Clewell Cooney & Fuerste, 1960-64; ptnr. Nelson Stapleton & Ernst, Stapleton & Ernst, Stapleton Ernst & Sprengelmeyer, East Dubuque, Ill., Nelson Stapleton & Ernst & Sprengelmeyer, Dubuque, Iowa, 1964-79; pvt. practice, 1979-80; ptnr. Ernst & Cody, 1981-84, Daniel P. Ernst, P.C., Dubuque, 1984-90, Vincent Roth & Ernst, P.C., Galena, Ill., 1991; pub. defender State of Iowa, Dubuque, 1991-96; pvt. practice, 1997—. U.S. trustee 1979-91. Capt. USAF, 1957-60, U.S. Coast Guard Aux. Mem. ABA, Iowa State Bar Assn. (bd. govs. 1985-89), Dubuque County Bar Assn. (2d v.p. 1979-80, 1st v.p. 1980-81, pres. 1981-82), Ill. State Bar Assn., Jo Daviess County Bar Assn., State Bar Assn. Mich., Grand Traverse-Leelanau-Antrim Bar Assn. Democrat. Avocations: swimming, boating. Office: Attorney-at-Law 899 Mount Carmel Rd Dubuque IA 52003-7946 Fax: 563-582-0324. E-mail: ernstdan@home.com

ERSEK, GREGORY JOSEPH MARK, lawyer, business administrator; b. Cleve., Aug. 30, 1956; s. Joseph Francis and Mary H. (Hurchanik) E. AB, Columbia U., 1977; MBA, U. Pa., 1979; JD, U. Fla., 1984; cert. cir. civil mediator, Fla. Internat. U., 1998. Bar: Fla. 1986, U.S. Dist. Ct. (so. dist.) Fla. 1987. Cons. fin. valuation Am. Appraisal Co., Princeton, N.J., 1979-80; mgr. import-export Marie L. Veslie Co., Coral Gables, Fla., 1980-85; assoc. Lunny, Tucker, Karns & Brescher, Ft. Lauderdale, 1986; dir. legal dept. Horizons Rsch. Labs. Inc., 1986-89, sr. corp. planner, 1988-89; gen. counsel Unisco Corp., 1989-93, TRICORD Corp., Ft. Lauderdale, 1990-93, Irish Times, Inc., Ft. Lauderdale, 1993-97; dir. corp. fin. dept. & sr. corp. counsel Canton Fin. Svcs. Corp., subs. Cyber Am. Corp., Salt Lake City, 1995-96; gen. counsel Greenstreet Capital Corp., Investment Bankers, Las Vegas, 1996-99, Gaelic Pub. Devel., Inc., Ft. Lauderdale, 1998—, Premier Fin. Corp., Jacksonville, 1998—. Sec.-treas., dir. Sorkar Group, Inc., Ft. Lauderdale, 1987-89; CEO Am. CompuShopper, Inc., 1989-98; with legal dept. Pfizer Inc., N.Y.C., 1983; co-founder, mgr. Poland/U.S. Trade and Mktg. Consortium, 1989—; mem. Philip C. Jessup Internat. Moot Ct. team, 1983; gen. counsel Biltmore Vacation Resorts, Inc., f/k/a Cyber Information, Inc., Las Vegas, 1997-99, Avalon Group, Inc., Cedar Rapids, Iowa, 1997-99. Editor Medscanner, med. industry newsletter, 1987-89. Mem. venture coun. forum. Mem. Fla. Bar Assn., Nat. Assn. Securities Dealers (nat. arbitration com. 1991-98), Coun. on Fgn. Rels. (local com.), Wharton Club South Fla. Muslim. Avocations: travel, books, internat. bus. ventures, mergers and acquisitions. Private international, Mergers and acquisitions, Securities. Home and Office: 17820 NW 18th Ave Miami FL 33056-4949

ERSTAD, LEON ROBERT, lawyer; b. Tyler, Minn., Aug. 3, 1947; s. Clifford and Josie (Dellberg) E.; m. Nancy Youel, July 19, 1969; children: Eric, Andrew, Jonathan. BSBA, U. Minn., 1969; JD cum laude, Temple U., 1976. Bar: Minn. 1976, U.S. Dist. Ct. Minn. 1976, U.S. Ct. Appeals (8th cir.) 1992, U.S. Supreme Ct. 1994; cert. ct. mediator. Ptnr. Chadwick, Johnson & Condon, P.A., Mpls., 1976-90, Erstad & Riemer P.A., 1990—. Adj. instr. law William Mitchell Coll., St. Paul, 1985-94; spkr. at profl. seminars. Contbr. articles to profl. jours. Bd. dirs. Loring Nicollet Cmty. Ctr., Mpls., 1981-91, Minn. Returned Peace Corps Vols., Mpls., 1980-86, pres., 1980-81; trustee Lynnhurst Congrl. Ch., 1997—, deacon, 1994-97. Named alumni of notable achievement U. Minn. Mem. ABA, Minn. State Bar Assn., Minn. Def. Lawyers Assn. (bd. dirs. 1999-2000, sec. 2000-01, treas. 2001—), Def. Rsch. Inst., Def. Lawyers Assn. General civil litigation, Environmental, Insurance. Home: 4700 Dupont Ave S Minneapolis MN 55409-2324 Office: Erstad & Riemer PA 8009 34th Ave S 200 Riverview Office Tower Minneapolis MN 55425 E-mail: lerstad@erstad.com

ERTEL, RUTH ROBINSON, lawyer, government official; b. Feb. 9, 1943; BA, George Mason U., Fairfax, Va., 1974; JD, George Washington U., 1983. Bar: D.C. Program analyst/writer U.S. Women's Bur., Washington, 1975-84; atty. U.S. Dept. Labor, 1984-87, OSC, Washington, 1987-96; assoc. spl. counsel for investigation Office of Spl. Counsel, 1996—. Mem. D.C. Bar Assn. Office: Office of Spl Counsel 1730 M St NW Ste 300 Washington DC 20036-4531

ERVIN, SPENCER, lawyer; b. Bala, Pa., Nov. 25, 1932; s. Spencer and Miriam Williams (Roberts) E.; m. Florence Wetherill Schroeder, Sept. 12, 1964; children: Margaret, Mary, Miriam, Helen. AB, Harvard U., 1954, JD, 1959. Bar: Pa. 1960, Maine 1995, U.S. Supreme Ct. 1963. Staff counsel Philco Corp., Phila., 1959-62; assoc. Ringe & Dewey, 1962-64; ptnr. Ringe, Tate & Ervin, 1964-72, Gratz, Tate, Spiegel, Ervin & Ruthrauff, Phila., 1972-92, Hepburn, Willcox, Hamilton & Putnam, Phila., 1992-96, Largay Law Offices, Bangor, Maine, 1996-97; pvt. practice, Bass Harbor, 1998—. Bd. dirs. Mt. Desert Island Biol. Lab. Bd. dirs., officer Neighborhood Club, Bala Cynwyd, Pa., 1969-89. Lt. USNR, 1954-56. Republican. Episcopal. Bankruptcy, General civil litigation, General practice. Home and Office: PO Box 383 Bass Harbor ME 04653-0383 E-mail: law@spencerervin.com

ERVIN, SUSAN CHADWICK, lawyer; b. Aberdeen, Md., May 16, 1951; d. A.R. and Ellyn (Wiegert) E. BA, Mt. Holyoke Coll., 1973; JD, Rutgers U., 1976. Bar: N.Y. 1977, D.C. 1985. Assoc. Kronish, Lieb, Shainswit, Weiner & Hellman, N.Y.C., 1976-78, Kramer, Levin, Nessen, Kamin & Frankel, N.Y.C., 1978-83; asst. gen. counsel Commodity Futures Trading Commn., Washington, 1983-86, assoc. dir. div. of trading and markets, 1986-87, dep. dir., chief counsel div. of trading and markets, 1987-97; counsel Dechert, Price & Rhoads, 1998-2000; ptnr. Dechert, 2001—. Mem. ABA, Assn. Bar of City Of N.Y. (chair com. futures regulation). Office: Dechert 1775 Eye St NW Washington DC 20006 E-mail: susan.ervin@dechert.com

ERWIN, H. ROBERT, lawyer; b. L.A., May 19, 1945; s. Howard R. and Nina B. Erwin; m. Nancy Smick, Sept. 9, 1967; children: Meghan, Kate, Benson, Carter. BA, Purdue U., 1967; JD, Georgetown U., 1972. Bar: Md. 1973, D.C. 1972, U.S. Dist. Ct. Md. 1973, U.S. Ct. Appeals (4th cir.) 1985. Dir. Consumer Law Ctr. Legal Aid Bur., Balt., 1972-78; cons., Office of Consumer Affairs U.S. Dept. Energy, Washington, 1978; chief Consumer Protections Divsn. Office of Atty. Gen., Balt., 1979-82; ptnr. Pretl & Erwin, P.A., 1983-95, The Erwin Law Firm, P.A., Balt., 1996—. Guest lectr., moot ct. judge U. Md. Sch. Law, Balt., 1988, 91-94; adv. bd. St. Ambrose Legal Svcs., Balt., 1994—. Contbr. chpt. to book. Pres., bd. mem. League for the Disabled, Balt., 1989-98; chpt. mem. Cathedral of the Incarnation, Balt., 1987-89. With U.S. Army, 1969-71. Mem. Am. Trial Lawyers Assn., Md. Trial Lawyers Assn., Md. State Bar Assn., Nat. Assn. Consumer Advocates, Engring. Soc. Consumer commercial, Product liability. Office: The Erwin Law Firm PA 8 W Madison St Baltimore MD 21201-5221

ERWIN, JAMES WALTER, lawyer; b. Carthage, Mo., Nov. 18, 1946; s. Charles Max and Juanita Carmen (Adams) E.; m. Vicki Berger, Dec. 30, 1972; children: Elizabeth Susan, James Bryan. B.A., Southwest Mo. State U., 1968; M.A., U. Mo., 1972, J.D., 1976. Bar: Mo. 1976, Ill. 1977, U.S. Dist. Ct. (ea. and we. dists.) Mo. 1976, U.S. Ct. Appeals (8th cir.) 1976, U.S. Supreme Ct. 1979, U.S. Dist. Ct. (so. dist.) Ill. 1984, U.S. Ct. Appeals (7th, 10th and fed. cirs.) 1990. Assoc. firm Thompson Coburn, St. Louis, 1976-83, ptnr., 1984—; adj. lectr. Washington U., St. Louis, 1980-84. Lead articles editor Mo. Law Rev., 1976. Pres. Nursery Found. St. Louis, 1989-92. Served to 1st lt. U.S. Army, 1968-70. Mem. ABA, Bar Assn. Met. St. Louis, Ill. State Bar Assn., Order of Coif. Democrat. Roman Catholic. Federal civil litigation, State civil litigation. Home: 532 W Jewel Ave Saint Louis MO 63122-2515 Office: Thompson Coburn 1 Mercantile Ctr Ste 3400 Saint Louis MO 63101-1643

ERXLEBEN, WILLIAM CHARLES, lawyer, consultant; b. Chgo., Dec. 18, 1942; s. Walter Oscar and Sarah Louise (Githens) E.; m. Gayle Amelia Reichmuth, Aaug. 28, 1965; children: David William, Jennifer Renée. BS in Bus., Miami U., Oxford, Ohio, 1963; JD, Stanford U., 1966. Bar: Wash. 1969. Asst. state atty. gen. Wash. State Atty. Gen.'s Office, Olympia, 1968-70; exec. asst. U.S. atty. Dept. Justice, Seattle, 1970-72; regional dir. FTC, 1972-79; lectr. Grad. Sch. Bus., U. Wash., 1979-85; ptnr. Foster, Pepper & Shefelman, Bellevue, Wash., 1985-91, Lane Powell Spears Lubersky, Olympia, 1991-93; pres., CEO, Data I/O Corp., Redmond, Wash., 1993-98, bd. dirs., 1979-98, cons., 1998- . Chmn., dir. Advanced Digital Tech., Bellevue, 1983-85. Contbr. articles to law revs. Counsel Wash. Assn. for Children and Adults with Learning Disabilities, Seattle, 1985-93; chmn. Portwatch, Seattle, 1985; mem. advt. rev. com. BBB, Seattle, 1982; bd. dirs. Wash. Citizens for Recycling, Seattle, 1980-84; Dem. nominee for Wash. State Atty. Gen., 1988; mem. Newcastle City Planning Commn., 2001—. Recipient Excellence in Supervision award FTC, 1975, Disting. Svc. award, 1979; Sloan exec. fellow Stanford U. Grad. Sch. Bus., 1975-76. Mem. ABA, Wash. State Bar Assn. (sec.-treas. antitrust subcom 1981-83). Home: 7625 120th Pl SE Newcastle WA 98056-1791

ESCARRAZ, ENRIQUE, III, lawyer; b. Evergreen Park, Ill., Aug. 30, 1944; s. Enrique Jr. and Mary Ellen (Bandy) E.; children from previous marriage; Erin Christine, Martina Mary; m. Patricia Jane Escarraz; children: Sarah Ellen, James Lee, Jason F. BA, U. Fla., 1966, JD, 1968. Bar: Fla. 1969, U.S. Dist. Ct. (so. and mid. dists.) Fla. 1969, U.S. Ct. Appeals (5th cir.) 1971, U.S. Ct. Appeals (11th cir.) 1981. VISTA atty. Community Legal Counsel, Chgo., 1968-69; mng. atty. Fla. Rural Legal Services, Ft. Myers, 1969-71; pvt. practice law St. Petersburg, Fla., 1971-82, 85-87, 88—; ptnr. Anderson & Escarraz, 1982-85; asst. gen. counsel U. South Fla., 1987-88; assoc. James L. Eskald Law Office, Largo, Fla., 1988. Part-time atty. Pub. Defender's Office Fla. 6th Cir., St. Petersburg, 1973-74; bd. dirs. Gulf Coast Legal Svcs., Inc., 1989—, pres., 1994-96. Vol. Cmty. Law Prog., Inc.; coord. James B. Sanderlin for Judge, Pinellas County, Fla., 1972-76; mem. ACLU Legal Panel, St. Petersburg, 1972—; cooperating

atty. NAACP Legal Panel, St. Petersburg, 1972—; cooperating atty. NAACP Legal Def. Edn. Funds, Inc., N.Y.C., 1973—; pres. Creative Care, Inc., Clearwater, Fla., 1974-80; mem. allocations com. United Way, Pinellas County, 1976, 1978-81; pres., treas. Cmty. Youth Svcs., Inc., St. Petersburg, 1977-82; co-chmn. Blue Ribbon Com. Pinellas County Dem. Exec. Com., 1977-82; mem. Fla. HRS Dist. V Adv. Coun., Pinellas County, 1982, St. Petersburg Human Rels. Rev. Bd., 1984, 90—, St. Petersburg Adult Cmty. Band, 1989—, Greater St. Petersburg Second Time Around Marching Band, 1990-92; mem. adv. bd. Jacquelyn Elvera Hodges Johnson Fund, 1990—. Mem. ABA, ATLA, FBA, Nat. Assn. Social Security Claimant Reps., Pinellas County Trial Lawyers Assn., St. Petersburg Bar Assn. (pro bono com. 1988, 95-2001, diversity com., 2000-), Greater Pinellas County Dem. Club (sec.-treas. 1989-97, bd. dirs. 1997—). Civil rights, Pension, profit-sharing, and employee benefits, Workers' compensation. Office: 2121 5th Ave N Saint Petersburg FL 33713-8013 also: PO Box 847 Saint Petersburg FL 33731-0847

ESCHBACH, JESSE ERNEST, federal judge; b. Warsaw, Oct. 26, 1920; S. Jesse Ernest and Mary W. (Stout) E.; m. Sara Ann Walker, Mar. 15, 1947; children: Jesse Ernest III, Virginia. BS, Ind. U., 1943, JD with distinction, 1949, LLD (hon.), 1986. Bar: Ind. 1949. Ptnr. Graham, Rasor, Eschbach & Harris, Warsaw, 1949-62; city atty., 1952-53; dep. pros. atty. 54th Jud. Circuit Ct. Ind., 1952-1954; judge U.S. Dist. Ct. Ind., 1962-81, chief judge, 1974-81; judge U.S. Ct. Appeals (7th cir.), W. Palm Beach, Fla., 1981-85, sr. judge, 1985—. Pres. Endicott Church Furniture, Inc., 1960-62; sec., gen. counsel Dalton Foundries, Inc., 1957-62 Editorial staff: Ind. Law Jour., 1947-49. Trustee Ind. U., 1965-70. Served with USNR, 1943-46. Hastings scholar, 1949; Recipient U.S. Law Week award, 1949 Mem. U.S. C. of C. (labor relations com. 1960-62), Warsaw C. of C. (pres. 1955-56), Nat. Assn. Furniture Mfrs. (dir. 1962), Ind. Mfrs. Assn. (dir. 1962), ABA, Ind. Bar Assn. (bd. mgrs. 1953-54, ho. dels. 1950-60), Fed. Bar Assn., Am. Judicature Soc., Order of Coif. Presbyn. Club: Rotarian (pres. Warsaw 1956-57). Home: 1712 Homewood Blvd # 486 Delray Beach FL 33445 Office: US Ct Appeals 7th Cir 253 US Courthouse 701 Clematis St West Palm Beach FL 33401-5101

ESKEW, BENTON, judge; b. Bastrop, Tex., Sept. 2, 1961; s. Charles Allen and Vina M. (Sims) E. BBA, Baylor U., 1984, JD, 1986. Bar: Tex., U.S. Dist. Ct. (no. and we. dists.) Tex.; ordained Bapt. minister. Assoc. McCamish, Ingram, Martin & Brown, Austin, Tex., 1986-88, Naman, Howell, Smith & Lee, Austin, 1989-91; ptnr. Eskew & Goertz, Bastrop, Tex., 1992-94; judge Bastrop County, 1994—. Bd. dirs. Child Protective Svcs. Bd., Bastrop, 1994—, Bastrop Boys and Girls Club, 1998—. Mem. Bastrop C. of C., Masons, York Rite, Scottish Rite, Shriners, Lions Club, Kiwanis Club. Home: PO Box 1120 Bastrop TX 78602-1120 Office: Bastrop County Ct Law 804 Pecan St Bastrop TX 78602-3846

ESKIN, BARRY SANFORD, court investigator; b. Pitts., Mar. 6, 1943; s. Saul and Dorothy (Zaron) E.; m. M. Joyce Rosalind, Sept. 12, 1965; 1 child, David. AA, L.A. City Coll., 1963; BA, Calif. State U., L.A., 1965; JD, Citrus Belt Law Sch., 1976. Bar: Calif. 1976. Social service worker San Bernardino (Calif.) Dept. Pub. Social Services, 1965-77; assoc. Law Office of Lawrence Novack, San Bernardino, 1978; ct. investigator San Bernardino Superior Ct., 1978, supervising investigator, 1978—. Pro bono atty. Mex. Am. Commn., 1977-78. Mem. ARC Svc. Ctr. Advising Bd., San Bernardino, 1980-82; bd. dirs. Golden Valley Civ. Assn., San Bernardino, 1978-81, Congregation Emanuel, San Bernardino, 1984-87, bd. dirs. 1994-96. Mem. ABA, Calif. Assn. of Superior Ct. Investigators (pres. 1980-81, treas. 1984-85, bd. dirs., chmn. guardianship legis. com.), San Bernardino County Bar Assn., B'nai B'rith (pres. Paradise Lodge 1988), Alpha Phi Omega. Democrat. Jewish. Avocations: reading, photgraphy, baseball. Office: San Bernardino Superior Ct 351 N Arrowhead Ave Rm 200 San Bernardino CA 92415-0240

ESPOSITO, CHERYL LYNNE, lawyer; b. Cleve., Dec. 13, 1964; d. John N. and Patricia A. (Manilla) E.; m. John J. Nebel III, Oct. 20, 1990; children: Deanna Teresa, Dominic Franklyn. BA in Polit. Sci., cert. in East Asian studies, U. Pitts., 1986, JD, 1989. Bar: Pa. 1989, U.S. Dist. Ct. Pa. 1989, U.S. Ct. Appeals (3rd cir.) 1995, W.Va. 1999. Assoc. Riley & DeFalice, P.C., Pitts., 1989-93, Cauley & Conflenti, Pitts., 1993-94; Marshall, Dennehey, Warner, Coleman & Goggin, 1994-97; atty. Warner, Coleman & Goggin, 1994-97, Gigler & Joyal, Pitts., 1997—. Soprano U. Pitts. Choral Soc., 1986-91; cantor St. James Ch., Wilkinsburg, Pa., 1991-92, St. Maurice Ch., Forest Hills, Pa., 1992—; mem. steering com. Tribute for First 100 Women Lawyers in Allegheny County, 1992, Tribute to the Female Judiciary of Pa., 1993-94. Mem. Pa. Bar Assn., Allegheny County Bar Assn., Westmoreland County Bar Assn., Am. Inn of Ct. (charter), Japan-Am. Soc. Pitts., St. Thomas More Soc. Roman Catholic. General civil litigation, Personal injury. Office: Gigler & Joyal 437 Grant St Ste 612 Pittsburgh PA 15219-6003 E-mail: cheryl.esposito@stpaul.com

ESPOSITO, DENNIS HARRY, lawyer; b. Providence, June 30, 1947; s. Harry Victor and Irene Rose (Radoccia) E.; m. Susan Audrey Cohen, Sept. 28, 1985; children: Matthew Perry, Lauren Elizabeth, Adam Aarons. BS, Boston Coll., 1969; JD, Boston U., 1974. Bar: R.I. 1974, U.S. Dist. Ct. R.I. 1974, Mass. 1984. Assoc. Goldman & Biafore, Providence, 1974-81; ptnr. Vrana, Cunha & Esposito, Providence, 1981-84; pvt. practice, Providence, 1984-91; of counsel McGregor, Shea & Doliner, Boston, 1987-91; ptnr., chmn. environ. practice group Adler Pollock and Sheehan, 1991—; legal counsel Coastal Resources Mgmt., Providence, 1974-81, Narragansett Bay Water Quality Mgmt. Dist. Commn., Providence, 1980-85; adj. prof. environ. law Sch. Law Roger Williams U. Alt. designee R.I. State Planning Council, 1980; legal advisor R.I. Constl. Conv. Commr., 1986-87, R.I. Environ. Quality Study Commn., 1988-90; administrv. hearing officer R.I. Dept. of Environ. Mgmt., 1987-89; gov.'s task force for Statutory Reorgn. R.I. Dept. Environ. Mgmt. and Coastal Resources Mgmt. Coun., 1989-90; mem. Gov.'s Commn. on Individual Sewage Disposal Systems and Freshwater Wetlands, 1995. Maj. USAFR, ret. Mem. ABA, R.I. Bar Assn. (chmn. environ. law com. 1985-95), R.I. Trial Assn. General civil litigation, Environmental, General practice. Office: Adler Pollock & Sheehan 2300 Hospital Trust Tower Providence RI 02903-2443

ESPOSITO, MARK MARIO, lawyer; b. Petersburg, Va., Nov. 27, 1958; s. Marion Francis and Mary Josephine (Straccioni) E.; m. Suzanne Marie Daley, Apr. 1988; children: Mark Francis, David Anthony. BS, James Madison U., 1980; JD, U. Richmond, 1984. Bar: Va. 1984, U.S. Dist. Ct. (ea. dist.) Va. 1984, U.S. Ct. Appeals (4th cir.) 1984, U.S. Supreme Ct. 1994. Assoc. Eliades & Eliades, Hopewell, Va., 1984-87; ptnr., dir. Hundley & Johnson, Richmond, 1987—. Insurance, Personal injury. Office: Hundley & Johnson 5501 Staples Mill Rd Richmond VA 23228-5440

ESRICK, JERALD PAUL, lawyer; b. Moline, Ill., Oct. 1, 1941; s. Reuben and Nancy (Parson) E.; m. Ellen Feinstein, June 18, 1966; children: Sara Elizabeth, Daniel Michael. BA, Northwestern U., 1963; JD, Harvard U., 1966. Bar: Ill. 1966, U.S. Dist. Ct. (no. dist.) Ill. 1967, U.S. Supreme Ct. 1974, U.S. Ct. Appeals (9th cir.) 1985, U.S. Ct. Appeals (7th cir.) 1967. Law clk. U.S. Dist. Ct. (no. dist.) Ill., 1966-68; assoc. Wildman, Harrold, Allen & Dixon, Chgo., 1968-73, ptnr., 1973—, also chmn. firm mgmt. com., 1987-90. Lectr. Northwestern U., 1984-93, Coll. Arts and Scis. bd. advs., 1993—, Nat. Panel Comml. Arbitrators, Am. Arbitration Assn. Pres. bd. trustees Nat. Lekotek Ctr., Evanston, Ill., 1989-93, U.S. Toy Libr. Assn., 1987-88; bd. dirs. Evanston Mental Health Assn., 1984-86, Fund for Justice, 1969-95, Lawyers' Com. for Civil Rights, 1974-84. Fellow Am. Coll. Trial Lawyers; mem. ABA, Ill. State Bar Assn., Chgo. Coun. Lawyers (bd. dirs., sec., founding mem.), Chgo. Bar Assn., Legal Club Chgo. Avocations: running, skiing, sailing, windsurfing, classical music. Antitrust, General civil litigation, General corporate. Home: 1326 Judson Ave Evanston IL 60201-4720 Office: Wildman Harrold Allen & Dixon 225 W Wacker Dr Ste 3000 Chicago IL 60606-1229 E-mail: esrick@wildmanharrold.com

ESSER, CARL ERIC, lawyer; b. Montclair, N.J., Feb. 12, 1942; s. Josef and Elly (Graber) E.; m. Barbara A. B. Stelzer, Oct. 12, 1968; children: Jennifer, Eric, Brian. AB, Princeton U., 1964; JD, U. Mich., 1967. Bar: Pa. 1967. Assoc. Reed Smith LLP, Phila., 1967-72, ptnr., 1973—. With USMCR, 1960-66. Mem. ABA, Pa. Bar Assn., Phila. Bar Assn., Pa. Soc. Healthcare Attys. (bd. dirs.), Pa. Lawyers Fund for Client Security (bd. dirs., chmn.), Octavia Hill Assn. (bd. dirs., asst. sec.), Racquet Club, Penllyn Club (bd. govs.), Mfrs. Golf and Country Club. Republican. Banking, Health, Securities. Office: Reed Smith LLP 2500 One Liberty Pl Philadelphia PA 19103 E-mail: cesser@reedsmith.com

ESSLINGER, JOHN THOMAS, lawyer; b. Ephrata, Pa., Aug. 11, 1943; s. Doster Alvin and Lucy Mildred (Ream) E.; m. Patricia Lynn Smith, Aug. 15, 1970; 1 child, John David. BA, Yale U., 1965; JD, Georgetown U., 1973. Bar: D.C. 1973, U.S. Dist. Ct. D.C. 1974, U.S. Supreme Ct. 1974, U.S. Ct. Appeals (D.C. cir.) 1974. Assoc. Morgan, Lewis & Bockius, Washington, 1973-76; ptnr. Schmeltzer, Aptaker & Shepard, P.C., 1976—. Capt. USMC, 1966-70, Vietnam. Decorated Purple Heart, Bronze Star, Gold Star. Mem. ABA, Bar Assn. D.C., D.C. Bar Assn., Maritime Adminstrv. Bar Assn. Episcopalian. Avocations: golf, wine, baseball. Federal civil litigation, Labor, Transportation. Home: 9102 Brierly Rd Chevy Chase MD 20815-5655 Office: Schmeltzer Aptaker & Shepard PC 2600 Virginia Ave NW Ste 1000 Washington DC 20037-1922

ESSMYER, MICHAEL MARTIN, lawyer; b. Abilene, Tex., Dec. 6, 1949; s. Lytle Martin Essmyer and Roberta N. Essmyer Nicholson; m. Cynthia Rose Piccolo, Dec. 27, 1970; children: Deanna, Mike, Brent Austin. BS in Geology, Tex. A&M U., 1972; postgrad., Tex. Christian U., 1976; JD summa cum laude, South Tex. Coll. Law, 1980. Bar: Tex. 1980, U.S. Dist. Ct. (no., so., ea. we. dists) Tex. 1982, U.S. Ct. Appeals (5th cir.) 1981, U.S. Ct. Appeals (9th cir.) 1990, U.S. Ct. Appeals (1st cir.) 1993, U.S. Ct. Appeals (7th cir.) 1995, U.S. Ct. Appeals (fed. cir.) 1985, U.S. Ct. Claims, 1981, U.S. Supreme Ct. 1991. Briefing atty. Supreme Ct. Tex., Austin, 1980-81, Haynes & Fullenweider, Houston, 1981-89, Essmyer & Hanby, Houston, 1989-92; atty. Essmyer & Assocs., 1992-94; pres. Essmyer & Tritco, LLP, 1994-95, Essmyer, Tritco & Clary, LLP, Houston, 1995-99, Essmyer & Tritco, LLP, Houston, 1999—. Lead article editor South Tex. Law Jour., 1979. Dem. candidate for state rep., Bryan, Tex., 1972; del. Dem. Party, Houston, 1982, 84; precinct chmn. Harris County Dem. Exec. Com., Houston, 1983-86. Capt. USAF, 1972-78. Nat. Merit Scholar, 1968-72. Mem. ABA, Houston Bar Assn., Tex. Trial Lawyers Assn. (assoc. dir. 1996—), Harris County Trial Lawyers Assn. (dir. 1997—), Assn. Trial Lawyers Am., Tex. Criminal Def. Lawyers Assn., Tex. Bar Found., Harris County Criminal Lawyers Assn. (dir. 1986-87), Fed. Bar Assn., Houstonian Club, The Doctor's Club of Houston. Roman Catholic. Federal civil litigation, Criminal, Personal injury. Home: 1122 Glourie Dr Houston TX 77055-7506 Office: Essmyer & Tritico LLP 4300 Scotland St Houston TX 77007-7328 E-mail: essmyer@flash.net

ESTEP, ROBERT LLOYD, lawyer; b. Marion, Va., Dec. 20, 1939; s. Lanson Eugene and Clara Nell (White) E.; m. Elizabeth Grayson Werth, July 10, 1971; 1 child, Laura White. BA with Honors, U. Va., 1962, JD, 1973. Bar: Ill. 1973, U.S. Dist. Ct. (no. dist.) Ill. 1973, Tex. 1984. From assoc. to ptnr. Isham, Lincoln & Beale, Chgo., 1973-83; ptnr. Jones, Day, Reavis & Pogue, Dallas, 1983—. Served to capt. U.S. Army, 1966-70, Vietnam.. Woodrow Wilson fellow, U. Va., 1962. Mem. Tex. Bar Assn., Law Club Chgo., Spl. Forces Assn., Phi Beta Kappa. Republican. Lutheran. General corporate, Securities. Home: 6331 Park Ln Dallas TX 75225-2108 Office: Jones Day Reavis & Pogue 2727 N Harwood St Dallas TX 75201-1515

ESTES, ANDREW HARPER, lawyer; b. Pecos, Tex., Dec. 16, 1956; s. Bobby Frank and Gayle (Harper) E.; m. Deidre Dement, Mar. 19, 1976; children: Andrew Kimble, Jada Catherine. BA, Tex. Tech U., 1977; JD, Baylor Sch. Law, 1979. Bar: Tex. 1980, U.S. Dist. Ct. (no. dist.) Tex. 1980, U.S. Dist. Ct. (we. dist.) Tex. 1981, U.S. Ct. Appeals (5th cir.) 1982, U.S. Supreme Ct. 1983, U.S. Tax Ct., U.S. Ct. Appeals (10th cir.) 1987. Ptnr. Lynch, Chappell & Alsup P.C., Midland, Tex., 1980—. Mem. admissions com. Dist. 16, State Bar Tex., 1982-85, bd. dirs., 1999—. Mem. Tex. Tech. U. Coll. Edn. Devel. Coun., Lubbock, 1986-87; vol. Big Bros., Midland, 1983—, bd. dirs., 1985-89; bd. dirs. Hearthstone Temporary Children's Shelter, 1988-92. Named Big Brother of Yr., Big Bros./Big Sisters of Midland, 1985; recipient Trimble Vol. Svc. award, Leadership Midland Alumni, 1986, Pro Bono Atty. award West Tex. Legal Svcs., 1991. Mem. ABA, Midland County Young Lawyers Assn. (sec., treas. 1987-88, Outstanding Young Lawyer of Midland County 1992), Midland County Bar Assn. (sec., treas. 1987-88, v.p. 1992-93, pres. elect. 1993-94, pres. 1995-96), State Bar Tex. (Dist. 16B grievance com. 1990-93, chmn. 1992-93, bd. dirs. 1999—), Tex. Young Lawyers Assn. (bd. dirs. 1987-89), Tex. Bd. Legal Specialization (cert.), Phi Delta Phi. Presbyterian. Federal civil litigation, State civil litigation. Home: 1404 Princeton Ave Midland TX 79701-5760 Office: Lynch Chappell & Alsup PC The Summit Bldg 300 N Marienfeld St Fl 7 Midland TX 79701-4345

ESTES, CARL LEWIS, II, lawyer; b. Ft. Worth, Feb. 9, 1936; s. Joe E. and Carroll E.; m. Gay Gooch, Aug. 29, 1959; children: Adrienne Virginia, Margaret Ellen. B.S., U. Tex., 1957, LL.B., 1960. Bar: Tex. 1960. Law clk. U.S. Supreme Ct., 1960-61; assoc. firm Vinson & Elkins, Houston, 1961-69, ptnr., 1970—. Bd. dirs. Houston Grand Opera Assn., Houston Arboretum. Fellow Am. Bar Found., Tex. Bar Found.; mem. ABA, Internat. Bar Assn., Am. Law Inst., Am. Coll. Probate Counsel, Tex. Bar Assn., Internat. Fiscal Assn., Internat. Acad. Estate and Trust Law. Fellow Am. Bar Found., Tex. Bar Found.; mem. ABA, Internat. Bar Assn., Am. Law Inst., Am. Coll. Probate Counsel, Tex. Bar Assn., Internat. Fiscal Assn., Internat. Acad. Estate and Trust Law, Asia Soc. (bd. dirs.). Private international, Corporate taxation, Personal income taxation. Office: Vinson & Elkins 1900 First City Towers Houston TX 77002

ESTES, MARK ERNEST, law librarian; b. Topeka, July 18, 1950; s. Jack E. and Bonnita A. (Hatfield) E.; m. Elizabeth M. Stever Wrenn, Jan. 16, 1978. BA, magna cum laude, Ottawa U., Kans., 1972; JD, MLL, U. Denver, 1977. Law librarian, asst. prof. law U. LaVerne, Calif., 1978-80; librarian Holme Roberts & Owen LLP, Denver, 1980—; cons. Calif. Inst. for Women, Frontera, 1979-80. Bd. dirs. U.S. Cycling Fedn., 1981-83; exec. dir., legis. lobbyist Bicycles Now, Denver, 1973-74; bd. chair Colo. Lir. Resource Sharing and Info. Access, 1994-95, active, 1995—; pres. Bicycle Racing Assn. Colo., 1976-77. Mem. Am. Assn. Law Libraries (constn. and membership com. 1980—, pres. 1992-93, fin. long range planning com. 1993-94, chair govt. rels. com., task force on value of law librs. 1995-96, ann. meeting program selection com. 1997—), Pvt. Law Libraries (exec. bd. 1982-83), Colo. Bar Assn. (law and tech. com. 1981-82), Colo. Consortium Law Libraries (v.p. 1980-81, sec.-treas. 1976-77), Southwestern Assn. Law Libraries (pvt. libraries com. 1981-82). Home: 2374 Glencoe St Denver CO 80207-3248 Office: Holme Roberts & Owen LLP 1700 Lincoln St Ste 4100 Denver CO 80203-4541

ESTILL, JOHN STAPLES, JR. lawyer; b. Grapevine, Tex., Jan. 20, 1919; s. John Staples and Ada Beauchamp (Chambers) E.; m. Dorothy Finlayson, Nov. 27, 1940; children: John S. III, James Calloway, Sally Finlayson Muhlbach. BS in Commerce, Tex. Christian U., 1940; JD, So. Meth. U., 1948. Bar: Tex. 1948, U.S. Dist. Ct. (no. dist.) Tex. 1948, Kans. 1958, Okla. 1966, U.S. Ct. Appeals (5th cir.) 1973, D.C. 1978, U.S. Supreme Ct. 1978. Pvt. practice law, Ft. Worth, 1948-50; asst. atty. U.S. Dept. Justice, 1950-53; atty. Sinclair Oil & Gas Co., 1953-57, Tulsa, 1965-66; atty., gen. atty. Sinclair Pipe Line Co., Independence, Kans., 1957-65; atty. Hall, Estill, Hardwick, Gable, Golden & Nelson, P.C., Tulsa, 1966-76, pres., 1976-90, of counsel, 1990—. Sec. Sinclair Pipe Line Co., Independence, 1964-65, Williams Pipe Line Co., Tulsa, 1969-87. Served to lt. USNR, 1942-46. Mem. ABA, Okla. Bar Found. (trustee 1984-87), D.C. Bar Assn., Kans. Bar Assn., Tex. Bar. Assn., Tulsa County Bar Assn., Colonial Country Club. Republican. Methodist. Avocation: golf. Address: 320 S Boston Ave Ste 400 Tulsa OK 74103-3704

ESTREICHER, SAMUEL, lawyer, educator; b. Bergen, Democratic Republic Germany, Sept. 29, 1948; came to U.S., 1951; s. David and Rose (Abramowicz) E.; m. Aleta Glaseroff, Aug. 10, 1969; children: Michael, Hannah. BA, Columbia U., 1970, JD, 1975; MS in Labor Rels., Cornell U., 1974. Bar: N.Y. 1976, D.C. 1978, U.S. Dist. Ct. (so. and ea. dists.) N.Y., U.S. Ct. Appeals (2d and 11th cirs.), U.S. Supreme Ct. Law clk. to assoc. judge U.S. Ct. Appeals (D.C. cir.), 1975-76; assoc. Cohn, Glickstein, Lurie, Ostrin & Lubell, N.Y.C., 1976-77; law clk. to assoc. justice Lewis F. Powell Jr. U.S. Supreme Ct., Washington, 1977-78; prof. law NYU, 1978—; of counsel Cahill, Gordon & Reindel, N.Y.C., 1984-98; labor and employment counsel O'Melveny & Myers LLP, 1998—. Vis. prof. law Columbia U., 1984-85; dir. NYU-Inst. Jud. Adminstrn., 1991—, Ctr. for Labor and Employment Law at NYU Sch. Law, 1996—. Author: Redefining the Supreme Court, 1986, Labor Law and Business Change, 1988, The Law Governing the Employment Relationship,1990, 2d edit., 1992, Labor Law: Text and Materials, 4th edit., 1996, Procs. of 49th NYU Annual Conference on Labor, 1997, Employee Representation in the Emerging Workplace: Alternatives/Supplements to Collective Bargaining, 1999, Sexual Harassment in the Workplace, 1999, Foundations of Labor and Employment Law, 2000, Employment Discrimination and Employment Law, 2000, Global Competition and The American Employment Landscape, 2000; contbr. articles to profl. jours.; editor-in-chief Columbia U. Law Rev., 1974-75. Pulitzer Fund scholar, 1966-70; Herbert H. Lehman fellow, 1970-72. Mem. ABA (labor and employment law sect. 1978—), N.Y. State Bar Assn. (labor and employment law sect. 1980—), Assn. Bar City N.Y. (chmn. labor and employment law com. 1984-87), Am. Law Inst. (reporter Restatement of Employment Law 2000—). Office: O'Melveny & Myers LLP 153 E 53d St New York NY 10022-4611

ETHRIDGE, LARRY CLAYTON, lawyer; b. Houston, Feb. 27, 1946; s. Robert Pike and Gladys Jeannette (Grant) E.; m. Edith Kirkbride Gilbert, May 21, 1977; children: Elizabeth Kirkbride, Grant Harbin. BA, Duke U., 1968; JD cum laude, U. Louisville, 1975. Bar: Ky. 1975, U.S. Dist. Ct. (we. dist.) Ky. 1980, U.S. Ct. Appeals (6th cir.) 1981. Intern Adv. Commn. on Intergovtl. Rels., Washington, 1975-76; asst. dir. model procurement code project ABA, 1976-80; ptnr. Mosley, Clare & Townes, Louisville, 1980-97, Ackerson Mosley & Yann, 1998—. Cons. ABA model procurement code project, Washington, 1980-82; panel mem. N.Y. State Procurement Rev., 1984—. Co-author: Supplement to Annotations on the Model Procurement Code, 1991, Annotations, 3d edit., 1996. Elder Highland Presbyn. Ch., Louisville, clk. of session, 1989-90, 96-2001; vol. Am. Cancer Soc.; gen. counsel Mobile Riverine Force Assn., 1995—. Lt. USNR, 1969, Vietnam, Cambodia, and Japan. Recipient Disting. Svc. award Nat. Inst. Govtl. Purchasing, 1987. Fellow Am. Bar Found. (life); mem. ABA (chmn. coord. com. on a model procurement code 1985-96, co-chmn. model procurement code revision project steering com. 1997—, coun. mem., state and local govt. law sect. 1988—, sect. publs. dir. 1990-93, comms. dir. 1993-95, sec. 1995-96, vice-chmn. 1996-97, chmn. elect 1997-98, chmn. 1998-99, Donald M. Davidson award), AAA Ky. (bd. dirs. 1990-96, sec., gen. counsel 1996—) , Ky. Bar Assn., Louisville Bar Assn. (co-chmn. golf com.), Jefferson Fordham Soc., U. Louisville Law Alumni Assn. (pres. 1990-92), U. Louisville Alumni Assn. (exec. com., bicentennial history com. 1994—, Alumni Svc. award), Duke Club Ky. (pres. 1992-94), Waggener H.S. Alumni Assn. (pres. 1996-97), Univ. of Louisville Club (bd. dirs. 1997—, treas. 2000—). Republican. Presbyterian. Avocations: gardening, travel, golf, bicycling, reading. General civil litigation, Construction, Government contracts and claims. Home: 2402 Longest Ave Louisville KY 40204-2125 E-mail: lethridge@amy_law.com

ETRA, BLANCHE GOLDMAN, lawyer; b. N.Y.C., Mar. 8, 1915; d. Jack and Anna (Simon) Goldman; m. Harry Etra, Apr. 19, 1939; children: Aaron, Marshall, Donald, Jonathan. BA, Barnard Coll., 1937; LLB, Columbia U., 1939; DHL (hon.) Yeshiva U., 1988. Bar: N.Y. 1939, U.S. Supreme Ct. 1960. Assoc. Hautman, Sheridan & Tekulsky, N.Y.C., 1938-39; assoc. Etra & Etra, N.Y.C., 1939-77, ptnr., 1977—. Bd. dirs. Cardozo Sch. Law, N.Y.C., 1978—; bd. overseers Albert Einstein Coll. Medicine, N.Y.C. Recipient Louise Waterman Wise award Am. Jewish Congress, N.Y.C., 1975; Disting. Service award Albert Einstein Coll. Medicine, 1978. Mem. Assn. of Bar of City of N.Y., N.Y. Women's Bar Assn. Jewish. General corporate, Estate planning, Probate. Office: Etra & Etra 331 Madison Ave New York NY 10017-5102

ETRA, DONALD, lawyer; b. N.Y.C., July 23, 1947; s. Harry and Blanche (Goldman) E.; m. Paula Renee Wiener, Dec. 28, 1985; children: Harry, Dorothy, Anna, Jonathan. BA, Yale U., 1968; MBA, JD, Columbia U., 1971. Atty. to Ralph Nader, Washington, 1971-73; trial atty. U.S. Dept. Justice, 1973-77, asst. U.S. atty. L.A., 1978-81; ptnr. Sidley & Austin, 1983-95, Law Offices of Donald Etra, L.A., 1995—. Co-author: Citibank, 1973. Office: Law Offices of Donald Etra 2029 Century Park East Ste 1020 Los Angeles CA 90067 E-mail: etralaw@aol.com

ETTER, JOHN KARL, lawyer; b. Portland, Oreg., Feb. 16, 1957; s. Richard F. and M. Eloise Etter; m. Carol Louise Shapley, Aug. 31, 1980; children: Darryl W., Vanessa R.E. BS in Engring., Swarthmore Coll., 1979; JD, Tulane U., 1997. Bar: La. 1997, U.S. Dist. Ct. (we., mid. and ea. dists.) La. 1997, U.S. Patent and Trademark Office 1997, U.S. Ct. Appeals (5th cir.), 1997, U.S. Ct. Appeals (6th cir.), 2001; cert. profl. engr., Colo. Mfg. engr. Storage Tech. Corp., Louisville, 1979-81; quality engr. Synthemed Corp., Boulder, Colo., 1981-82; reliability engr. Valleylab Corp., 1982-89; product mgr. Imex, Golden, Colo., 1989-90; mgr. quality assurance Beacon Labs., Broomfield, 1990-92; mgr. regulatory affairs Mountain Med., Lakewood, 1992-94; atty. Rodney, Bordenave, Boykin & Ehret, New Orleans, 1997—. Mem. ABA, La. Bar Assn., Order of Coif (award 1997). Avocations: skiing, sailing, reading, hiking and camping. Administrative and regulatory, General civil litigation, Intellectual property. Office: Rodney Bordenave Boykin & Ehret 400 Poydras St Ste 2450 New Orleans LA 70130

ETTERS, RONALD MILTON, lawyer, government official; b. San Antonio, Nov. 6, 1948; s. Milton William and Ilse Charlotte (Ostler) E.; m. Anna Colleen Wesson, Feb. 12, 1977; children: William Lawrence, Elizabeth Charlotte, Margaret Lawreen. BA magna cum laude, Am. U., 1971, JD, 1976. Bar: Va. 1976, U.S. Ct. Appeals (D.C. cir.) 1977, U.S. Dist. Ct. (ea. dist.) Va. 1978, U.S. Ct. Appeals (4th and 9th cirs.) 1978, U.S. Supreme Ct. 1979, D.C. 1980, U.S. Dist. Ct. D.C. 1980, U.S. Ct. Appeals (1st and 2d cirs.) 1980, U.S. Ct. Appeals (7th cir.) 1981, U.S. Ct. Appeals (3rd, 11th and fed. cirs.) 1982, U.S. Ct. Appeals (5th cir.) 1983. Intern to gen. counsel Adminstrv. Office of U.S. Cts., Washington, 1970-71; fed. mgmt. intern IRS, 1971-72, labor rels. officer, 1972-75; ptnr. Nusbaum &

Etters, Burke, Va., 1976-80; gen. counsel Nat. Mediation Bd., Washington, 1980—. With Sigma Alpha, 1971; justice Phi Alpha Delta, 1975; professorial lectr. Am. U., Washington, 1978-83; adj. prof. law Georgetown U., Washington, 1985-88; vis. prof. George Mason U. Sch. Law, Arlington, Va., 1999—, dir. Ctr. Advanced Study of Law and Dispute Resolution Processes, Arlington, 2000—. Sr. bd. editors The Railway Labor Act, 1991—. Mem. ABA (co-chmn. com. on railway and airline labor law 1987-93, 99—), Christian Legal Soc., Nat. Lawyers Assn., Fed. Bar Assn. Home: PO Box 2374 Centreville VA 20122-2374 Office: George Mason U Sch Law 3401 N Fairfax Dr Arlington VA 22201-4498 E-mail: etters5@etters.net, retters@gmu.edu

ETTINGER, JOSEPH ALAN, lawyer; b. N.Y.C., July 21, 1931; s. Max and Frances E.; children: Amy Beth, Ellen Jane. BA, Tulane U., 1954, JD with honors, 1956. Bar: La. 1956, Ill. 1959. Asst. corp. counsel City of Chgo., 1959-62; pvt. practice, Chgo., 1962-73, 76-80; sr. ptnr. Ettinger & Schoenfield, 1980-92; pvt. practice, 1993—. Assoc. prof. law Chgo.-Kent Coll., 1973-76; chmn. Village of Olympia Fields (Ill.) Zoning Bd. Appeals, 1969-76; chmn. panel on corrections Welfare Coun. Met. Chgo., 1969-76; spl. state appellate defender State of Ill., 1997-98. Contbr. articles to profl. publs. Capt. JAGC, U.S.Army, 1956-59. Recipient svc. award Village of Olympia Fields, 1976. Mem. Chgo. Bar Assn., Assn. Criminal Def. Lawyers (gov. 1970-72). Federal civil litigation, Criminal, Personal injury. E-mail: joeett@aol.com

EUBANKS, GARY LEROY, SR. lawyer; b. North Little Rock, Ark., Nov. 22, 1933; s. Herman and Gertrude (Carmack) E.; m. Mary Joyce Gathright, 1955 (div. 1966); children: Gary Leroy Jr., Bobby Ray; m. Beverly Gayle Mauldin, Apr. 21, 1971 (div. 1983); 1 child, Shane Mauldin; m. Elizabeth Duncan, Dec. 18, 1987. JD, U. Ark., 1960. Bar: Ark. 1960, U.S. Dist. Ct. Ark. 1960, U.S. Supreme Ct. 1970. Ptnr. Bailey, Jones, and Eubanks, Little Rock, 1960-63, Eubanks and Deane, Little Rock, 1963-65, Eubanks, Hood, and Files, Little Rock, 1965-69, Eubanks, Files and Hurley, Little Rock, 1969-76, Haskins Eubanks and Wilson, Little Rock, 1976-79, Gary Eubanks and Assocs., Little Rock, 1979—. Mem. Ark. Ho. of Reps., 1963-66, Pulaski County (Ark.) Sch. Bd., 1967. Served with USN, 1952-54. Mem. ABA, Ark. State Bar Assn., Pulaski County Bar Assn., Ark. Trial Lawyers Assn., Assn. Trial Lawyers Am., Am. Bd. Trial Advocacy (civil trial advocate). Democrat. Methodist. Personal injury. Home: 211 Scenic Dr Hot Springs National Park AR 71913-7729 Office: PO Box 3887 Little Rock AR 72203-3887

EUBANKS, PATRICE D. court administrator; b. Dallas; d. Wilbur Howard and B. Lucille (Beaver) Cupp; m. Terry Lynn Eubanks, Aug. 7, 1976 (div. Feb. 1996); children: Jennifer Suzanne, Misty Lynn. Cert. trial ct. mgmt., Tex. Ctr. Judiciary, Austin. Dep. county clk. Collin County, McKinney, Tex., 1976-79; chief dep./courts divsn. Collin Co., 1979-86, court adminstr., 1986—. Mem./chair Marquette Booster Team, 1993-99; treas. Caldwell PTA, 1993-94; sec. McKinney H.S. PTO, 1998-99. Mem. Nat. Assn. Court Mgmt., Tex. Assn. Court Adminstrn. (bd. dirs. 1994-98, Charles W. Barrow award 1997). Republican. Disciples of Christ. Avocations: antiques, travel, reading. Office: Co Court at Law #1 210 S Mcdonald St Ste 524 Mc Kinney TX 75069-5666 E-mail: trieubanks@hotmail.com

EULAU, PETER H. lawyer; b. Basel, Switzerland, June 17, 1946; s. Werner and Marlise (Levaillant) E.; m. Miriam J. Bachner; children: Thomas M., Liliane A., Florence R. Lic. iur., U. Basel, 1970, dr. iur. magna cum laude, 1976; student, Harvard Law Sch., 1976-77, postgrad., 1977—78. Bar: Basel 1972; cert. notary public 1973. Asst. to prof. Basel U., 1973-74; trainee A. Sarasin & Cie., Banquiers, 1976; assoc. Csaplar & Bok, Boston, 1977-78; ptnr. Eulau Kaufmann Giavarini & Recher, Basel, 1978—. Bd. dirs. numerous cos. Author: Verleitung zum Vertragsbruch und Ausnutzung fremden Vertragsbruches, Zurich, 1976, Inducing Breach of Contract, 1978, A Comparison of Laws of the United States, France, the Federal Republic of Germany and Switzerland, 1978. Mem. parliament Canton Basel-Stadt, 1980-91; vicechair Freisinnig-Demokratische Partei, Basel-Stadt, 1988-92; with constl. coun. Canton of Basel-Stadt, 1999—. Scholar Swiss Nationalfonds, 1976-77. Mem. ABA (internat. assoc.), Bar Assn. Basel-Stadt, Internat. Bar Assn., Internat. Fiscal Assn., Harvard Law Sch. Assn. General corporate, Finance, Mergers and acquisitions. Office: Eulau Kaufmann Giavarini Recher Marktplatz 18 CH-4001 Basel Switzerland

EUSTICE, FRANCIS JOSEPH, lawyer; b. LaCrosse, Wis., Feb. 2, 1951; s. Frank R. and Cecelia T. (Babler) E.; m. Mary J. McCormick, July 28, 1971; children: Cristen L., Tara L. BS in Chemistry, Kansas Newman Coll., 1976; JD, U. Wis., 1980. Bar: Wis. 1980, U.S. Dist. Ct. (ea. and we. dists.) Wis. 1980, U.S. Tax Ct. 1981, U.S. Ct. Appeals (7th cir.) 1990, U.S. Dist. Ct. (no. dist.) Ill. 1993. With Eustice, Laffey & Shellander, S.C. and predecessor firms, Sun Prairie, Wis., 1980—. Bd. dirs., pres. Sun Prairie Devel. Corp., 1989—. Bd. dirs. Exch. Ctr. for Prevention of Child Abuse, Inc., Dane County, Wis., 1984-95. Sgt. USAF, 1973-77. Mem. Wis. Bar Assn., Dane County Bar Assn., Sun Prairie C. of C. (bd. dirs., pres., amb. 1987—), Sun Prairie Exch. Club (sec., pres., bd. dirs. 1980—). Roman Catholic. Alternative dispute resolution, Banking, Contracts commercial. Office: PO Box 590 100 Wilburn Rd Ste 202 Sun Prairie WI 53590-1478 E-mail: f.eustice@els-law.com

EUSTICE, JAMES SAMUEL, legal educator, lawyer; b. Chgo., June 9, 1932; s. Burt C. and Julia (Bohon) E.; m. LaVaun Schild, Jan. 29, 1956 (dec. 1994); m. Carol Fonda, Nov. 1995; children: Cynthia, James M. BS, U. Ill., 1954, LLB, 1956; LLM in Taxation, NYU, 1958. Bar: Ill. 1956, N.Y. 1958. Assoc. White & Case, N.Y.C., 1958-60; prof. law NYU, 1960—; counsel Kronish Lieb, N.Y.C., 1970—. Author: (with Kuntz) Federal Income Taxation of Subchapter S Corporations, 2001, (with Bittker) Federal Income Taxation of Corporations and Shareholders, 2000. Mem. ABA, N.Y. State Bar Assn., Am. Coll. Tax Counsel, Order of Coif. Club: University (N.Y.C.). Republican. Presbyterian. Office: NYU Sch Law 40 Washington Sq S New York NY 10012-1005

EUSTIS, RICHMOND MINOR, lawyer; b. New Orleans, Nov. 24, 1945; s. David and Molly Cox (Minor) E.; m. Catherine Luise Baños, Apr. 15, 1971; children: Richmond Minor Jr., Julie Bransford, Joshua Leeds, Molly Minor. BA in Econs., U. Va., 1967; JD, Tulane U., 1970. Bar: La. 1970. Assoc. Phelps Dunbar, New Orleans, 1970-75; ptnr. Monroe and Lemann, 1975-96; founder, ptnr. Eustis, O'Keefe & Gleason LLC, 1996—. Bd. dirs. New Orleans Bd. of Trade. Bd. dirs. Children's Bur., 1976-88, treas., 1984. Mem. ABA, La. Bar Assn., New Orleans Bar Assn. (chmn. torts and ins. com. 1992-95), Maritime Law Assn., S.E. Admiralty Law Inst., Boston Club, La. Club. Republican. Episcopalian. Avocation: fishing. Admiralty, General civil litigation, Insurance. Home: 289 Audubon St New Orleans LA 70118-4841 Office: Eustis & O'Keefe 228 Saint Charles Ave Ste 1010 New Orleans LA 70130-2686

EVANGELISTA, DONATO A. retired lawyer, computer and infosystems manufacturing company executive; b. Port Chester, N.Y., 1932. BS, U. Rochester, 1954; LLB, Cornell U., 1957. With IBM Corp., Armonk, N.Y., 1961—, atty., 1961-64, area counsel fed. systems div., Owego, 1964-66, regional counsel data processing div., Washington, 1966-69, counsel data processing product group, 1969-75, corp. asst. gen. counsel, 1975-83, v.p. & deputy gen. counsel, 1983-85, v.p. & gen. counsel, 1985-89, sr. v.p., gen counsel, 1989-96, ret. 1996. Home: 2911 Winding Oak Ln Wellington FL 33414-7044

EVANS, ALLENE DELORIES, lawyer; b. Cin., Oct. 4, 1951; d. Allen Douglas and Margaret (Spradley) E. Student, U. Ams., Cholula, Mex., 1971; BA, Adams State Coll., 1972; JD cum laude, U. Minn., 1977. Bar: Minn. 1977, Tex. 1983, U.S. Dist. Ct. (no., so., ea., we. dists.) Tex. 1983, U.S. Dist. Ct. Minn. 1977, U.S. Ct. Appeals (5th and 9th cirs.), U.S. Supreme Ct. Assoc. Broeker, Hardfelt, Mpls., 1977-80; assoc. counsel Northwestern Nat. Life Ins. Co., 1980-82; asst. city atty. City of Corpus Christi, Tex., 1983-84; asst. dist. atty. Nueces County, Corpus Christi, 1984-85; asst. atty. gen. Atty Gen.'s Office, Austin, 1985-91; mem. bd. dirs. Tex. State Bd. Ins., 1991-94; ptnr. Perry & Haas, LLP, Austin, Corpus Christi, 1994—. Expert witness on NAFTA Tex. Legislature and U.S. Congress; speaker to bar, industry and govt. groups on ins. regulations, anti-trust issues. Recipient Tex. Outstanding Pub. Svc. award Consumers' Union, Tex. Consumer Assn., Tex. Gray Ptnrs. Mem. Tex. Bar Assn. (chair anti-trust and bus. litigation sect. 1993-94), Tex.-Mex. Bar Assn (treas. 2000—). Democrat. Presbyterian. Antitrust, Insurance, Product liability. Office: Perry & Haas LLP 2100 Frost Bank Plz Corpus Christi TX 78403

EVANS, DANIEL FRALEY, JR. lawyer; b. Indpls., Apr. 19, 1949; s. Daniel Fraley and Julie (Sloan) E.; m. Marilyn Schultz, Aug. 11, 1973; children: Meredith, Benjamin, Suzannah, Theodore. BA, Ind. U., 1971, JD, 1976. Bar: Ind. 1976, U.S. Dist. Ct. (so. dist.) Ind. 1976, U.S. Ct. Appeals (7th cir.) 1983, U.S. Supreme Ct. 1983. Assoc. Sparrenberger, Duvall, Tabbert, Lalley & Newton, Indpls., 1976-77; ptnr. Duvall, Tabbert, Lalley & Newton, 1977-81, Bayh, Tabbert & Capehart, Indpls., 1981-85, Baker & Daniels, Indpls., 1985—. Chmn. Ind. Bd. Correction, Indpls., 1976-88, Qyaule for Senate Com., 1980, 86, Quayle for v.p. com.; mem. Fed. Jud. Merit Sel. Com., Indpls., 1981-88, Adminstrv. Conf. U.S., 1983-88; chmn. Indpls. Dist. Fed. Home Loan Bank Bd., 1987-90, Fed. Housing Fin. Bd., 1990-93; vice chmn. Methodist Health Group, Inc., 1996—, Cir. Investors, Inc., 1997—; vice chmn. Hudson Inst., Inc., 1996—, Cir. Investors, 1994-99; chancellor South Ind. Conf. United Meth. Ch., 1998—; gen. coun. Citizens Gas Utility, 1999—; bd. dirs. Clarian Health Ptnrs., Inc., Indpls., Downtown, Inc., 1992-96, Meth. Hosp. Ind. Mem. Ind. Bar Assn., Indpls. Bar Assn., Woodstock Club, Indpls. Club. Republican. Methodist. Administrative and regulatory, General corporate. Office: Baker & Daniels 300 N Meridian St Ste 2700 Indianapolis IN 46204-1782

EVANS, DONALD CHARLES, JR. lawyer; b. New London, Conn., Nov. 1, 1938; s. Donald Charles and Henrietta Agnes (Perkins) E.; m. Magda Anna Wehr, Apr. 30, 1966; children: Donald Charles III, Sean Thomas. BA, U. Miami, 1961; JD, U. Fla., Gainesville, 1967; LLM, NYU, 1968. Bar: Fla. 1967, D.C. 1974, U.S. Tax Ct. 1974. Legis.-adminstrv. asst. Fla. State Senate, 1967; atty.-adviser legis. and regulations divsn. Office Chief Csl., IRS, 1968-71; legis. latty. U.S. Congress Joint Com. on Internal Revenue Taxation, Washington, 1971-74; mem. Williams & Jensen PC, 1974-83, Evans & Assocs., Washington, 1983—. 1st lt. AUS, 1963-65. Mem. ABA, Fla. Bar Assn. (gov. 1979-83), D.C. Bar Assn., U. Fla. Alumni Assn. (pres. D.C. chpt. 1974-75), Fla. State Soc. (dir. 1972-77). Legislative, Corporate taxation, Personal income taxation. Home: 9315 Winbourne Rd Burke VA 22015-1755 Office: Evans & Assocs Ste 300 1201 Pennsylvania Ave NW Washington DC 20004

EVANS, DOUGLAS HAYWARD, lawyer; b. Providence, July 21, 1950; s. Jerrold Merton and Gladys Jean (Snelgrove) E.; m. Sarah Edwards Cogan, May 28, 1983; children: Anne Morrill, Thomas Taylor Seelye, Elizabeth Hayward. AB, Franklin and Marshall Coll., 1972; JD, Cornell U., 1975. Bar: N.J. 1975, U.S. Dist. Ct. N.J. 1975, N.Y. 1976, U.S. Dist Ct. (so. dist.) N.Y. 1991. Assoc. Windels, Marx, Davies & Ives, N.Y.C., 1975-85, Sullivan & Cromwell, N.Y.C., 1985-90, spl. counsel, 1990—. Faculty NYU Inst. Fed. Taxation, N.Y.C., 1984; counsel, treas., pres. St. David's Soc. State of N.Y., N.Y.C., 1985—; bd. dirs. Friends of Washington Sq. Park, 1989—, Washington Sq. Assn., 1992—, 1st Presbyn. Ch. Nursery Sch., 1999-2001. Co-Author: Estate Accounting, 1980, Probate and Estate Administration, 1982, Administration of Estates, 1985, Settling An Estate, 1989; editor-in-chief, co-author: Probate and Administration of New York Estates, 1995, 2d edit., 2001; also articles. Trustee Franklin and Marshall Coll., 1994—. Grace Ch. Sch., N.Y.C., 1997—, vice chmn., 2000-01, chmn., 2001—; mem. Ch. Club of N.Y., Salmagundi Club, N.Y.C. Fellow Am. Coll. of Trust and Estate Coun.; mem. ABA, N.J. Bar Assn., N.Y. State Bar Assn. (estate litig. and adminstrn. of trusts and estates com., com. on Cont. Legal Edn.; chmn. 1991-94), N.Y. County Lawyers Assn. (not-for-profit com.), Phi Beta Kappa, Phi Delta Phi, Phi Alpha Theta, Pi Gamma Mu. Episcopalian. Estate planning, Probate, Estate taxation. Home: 43 Fifth Ave New York NY 10003-4368 Office: Sullivan & Cromwell 125 Broad St Fl 28 New York NY 10004-2489

EVANS, LAWRENCE E. lawyer, educator; b. Houston, Mar. 30, 1950; s. Lawrence Edgar and Edith (Kinzy) E.; m. Nancy Campbell, Aug. 20, 1977; children: Christopher, Laura. BA, Washington & Lee U., 1973; JD, South Tex. Coll., 1977. Bar: Tex. 1977, Mo. 1989; registered patent atty. Lawyer Gunn, Lee & Miller, Houston, 1977-88, Herzog, Crebs & McGhee, St. Louis, 1988-2000, Blackwell, Sanders, Peper, Martin LLP, St. Louis, 2000—. Adj. prof. Washington Univ. Sch. of Law, St. Louis. Mem. Metro. Bar Assn. St. Louis (chmn. Patent, Trademark and Copyright sect. 1994), Internat. Trademark Assn., Am. Intellectual Property Law Assn. Intellectual property, Patent, Trademark and copyright. Office: Blackwell Sanders Peper Martin LLP 720 Olive St Ste 2400 Saint Louis MO 63101 E-mail: levans@bspmlaw.com

EVANS, MARTIN FREDERIC, lawyer; b. Nashville, June 12, 1947; s. Robert Clements and Adelaide Hawkins (Roberts) E.; m. Margaret Carroll Kidder, Apr. 17, 1982. BA, U. Va., 1969; JD, Yale U., 1972. Bar: N.Y. 1973, U.S. Dist. Ct. (so. dist.) N.Y. 1973, U.S. Ct. Appeals (2d cir.) 1974, U.S. Ct. Appeals (D.C. cir.) 1981, U.S. Supreme Ct. 1981, D.C. 1982. Assoc. Debevoise & Plimpton, N.Y.C., 1972-80, ptnr., 1981—. Researcher Nat. Commn. for Rev. of Antitrust Laws and Procedure, Washington, 1978. Mem. ABA (sect. for antitrust law), Assn. of Bar of City of N.Y., Phi Beta Kappa. Antitrust, Federal civil litigation, Insurance. Office: Debevoise & Plimpton 875 3rd Ave Fl 23 New York NY 10022-6225

EVANS, PAUL VERNON, lawyer; b. Colorado Springs, Colo., June 19, 1926; s. Fred Harrison and Emma Hooper (Austin) E.; m. Patricia Gwyn Davis, July 27, 1964; children: Bruce, Mike, Mark, Paul. B.A. cum laude, Colo. Coll., 1953; J.D., Duke U., 1956. Bar: Colo. 1956, U.S. Dist. Ct. Colo. 1956, U.S. Supreme Ct. 1971, U.S. Ct. Appeals (10th cir.) 1974. Field mgr. Keystone Readers Service, Dallas, 1946-50; sole practice Colorado Springs, 1956-60; ptnr. Goodbar, Evans & Goodbar, 1960-63; sr. ptnr. Evans & Briggs Attys., Colorado Springs, 1963-95. City atty. City of Fountain, Colo., 1958-62, City of Woodland Park, Colo., 1962-78; atty. Rock Creek Mesa Water Dist., Colorado Springs, 1963—. Author instruction materials. Precinct com. man Republican Com., Colorado Springs, 1956-72. Served with USNR, 1944-46, PTO. Recipient Jr. C. of C. Outstanding Achievement award, 1957. Mem. Colo. Mining Assn., Am. Jud. Soc., ABA, Colo. Bar Assn. (com. chmn. 1966-67, 84), El Paso County Bar Assn. (com. chmn. 1956—0, Assn. Trial Lawyers Am., Colo. and Local Trial Lawyers, Tau Kappa Alpha (pres.), Phi Beta Kappa. Republican. Club: Optimist (pres. 1966-67). E-mial. Family and matrimonial, General practice, Personal injury. Home: 244 Cobblestone Dr Colorado Springs CO 80906-7624 Office: 227 E Costilla St Colorado Springs CO 80903-2103 E-mail: pvevansesq@msn.com

EVANS, ROBERT DAVID, legal association executive; b. Vergennes, Vt., Mar. 1, 1945; BA, Yale U., 1966; JD, U. Mich., 1969. Bar: Ill. 1969. Assoc. Sachnoff Schrager Jones & Weaver, Chgo., 1969-72; asst. dir. divsn. pub. svc. activities ABA, 1972-73, asst. dir. govtl. rels. office Washington, 1973-78, assoc. dir. govtl. rels. office, 1978-82, dir. govtl. affairs office, 1982—, assoc. dir., dir. Washington Office, 1988—. Mem. Washington Grove (Md.) Town Coun., 1977-81, 98—, Washington Grove Town Planning Commn., 1977-81, 98—; mayor Washington Grove, 1981-83; vice chmn. assns. divsn. Nat. Capital Area United Way, 1986, chmn., 1987. Recipient Spl. Achievement award Nat. Legal Aid and Defender Assn., 1990. Fellow ABA, Am. Bar Found.; mem. Am. Law Inst. Home: PO Box 332 Washington Grove MD 20880-0332 Office: ABA 740 15th St NW Fl 8 Washington DC 20005-1019

EVANS, TERENCE THOMAS, federal judge; b. Milwaukee, Wisc., Mar. 25, 1940; s. Robert Hansen and Jeanette (Walters) E.; m. Joan Marie Witte, July 24, 1965; children: Kelly Elizabeth, Christine Marie, David Rourke. BA, Marquette U., 1962, JD, 1967. Bar: Wis. 1967. Law clk. to justice Wis. Supreme Ct., 1967-68; dist. atty. Milw. County, 1968-70; pvt. practice law Milw., 1970-74; cir. judge State of Wis., 1974-80; judge U.S. Dist. Ct. (ea. dist) Wis., Milw., 1980-95, U.S. Ct. Appeals (7th cir.), 1995—. Mem. ABA, State Bar Wis., Milw. Bar Assn. Roman Catholic. Office: US Courthouse & Federal Bldg 517 E Wisconsin Ave Rm 721 Milwaukee WI 53202-4504*

EVANS, THOMAS WILLIAM, lawyer; b. N.Y.C., Dec. 9, 1930; s. William J. and R. Helen (Stenvall) E.; m. Lois deBaun Logan, Dec. 22, 1956; children: Heather, Logan, Paige. BA, Williams Coll., 1952; JD, Columbia U., 1958; EdD, Piedmont Coll., 1993. Bar: N.Y. 1958, U.S. Supreme Ct. 1961. Assoc. Simpson, Thacher & Bartlett, N.Y.C., 1958-64; asst. coun. to spl. state commn. of investigation, spl. dep. asst. N.Y. Atty. Gen., 1964-65; assoc. Mudge Rose Guthrie Alexander & Ferdon, 1965-66, ptnr., 1967-93, of counsel, 1993-94. Founder MENTOR, nat. law-related edn. program for pub. sch. students, 1983. Author: The School in the Home, 1973, Admissions Practices (Center for Public Resources), 1986, Mentors, 1992. Chmn. Nat. Symposium on Partnerships in Edn., 1983-90; chmn. bd. trustees Columbia U. Tchrs. Coll., 1991-98, trustee, 1985—, adj. prof. of ednl. adminstrn., 1992-95; co-chmn. N.Y. Korean Vets. Meml. Commn.; chmn. The Mentor Ctr., L.C., 1998—. With USMC, 1952-54. Mem. ABA, Fed. Bar Coun. (pres. 1989-90, trustee 1981—), Century Assn. Republican. Episcopalian. Federal civil litigation, State civil litigation. Home: 10245 Collins Ave Apt 9A Bal Harbour FL 33154-1407 E-mail: thoswevans@aol.com

EVANS, WAYNE LEWIS, lawyer; b. Bluefield, W.Va., Mar. 30, 1954; s. Douglas Evan and Wanda (Shrewsberry) E.; m. Cheryl Jane Richardson, June 28, 1980; children: Lisa Marie, Jason Lloyd. BA summa cum laude, U. N.C., Greensboro, 1976; MS, Radford U., 1978; diploma, Roanoke Police Acad., 1980; JD, Wake Forest U., 1984. Bar: W.Va. 1984, U.S. Dist. Ct. (so. dist.) W.Va. 1984, U.S. Ct. Appeals (4th cir. 1989); cert. Va. Cert. Bds. Zoning Appeals Programs. Probation/parole officer Va. Dept. Corrections, Tazewell, Va., 1976-77; dep. sheriff Roanoke County Sheriff Dept., Salem, 1979-81; summer assoc. Katz Kantor & Perkins, Bluefield, W.Va., 1982; ptnr. Katz, Kantor & Perkins, 1985—; summer assoc. Gardner, Moss, Brown & Rocovich, Roanoke, 1983; assoc. Law Office of John H. Shott, Bluefield, 1984-85. V.p., sec. WELD Enterprises, 1989-95; mem. Campaigning With Lee-Civil War Roundtable, Va. Tech., 1994, 95, 96, 97; speaker at seminars. Mem. Bd. Zoning Appeals, Bluefield, 1991—, chmn., 2000—; participant Career Awareness, Mercer County (W.Va.) Schs., 1989, 92; coach Odyssey of the Mind, Tazewell County (Va.) Schs., 1994, 95, 96, 97, judge, 1999; vol. United Way, Mercer and Tazewell Counties, 1989; chmn. com. PTA, Dudley Primary Sch; leader Boy Scouts Am., Bluefield, Va., 1996-99, 2000—; pres. Graham Middle Sch. PTA, Bluefield, 1997-98; pres. Graham H.S. Band Boosters, 1999-00. Mem. ATLA, W.Va. Trial Lawyers Assn., Fincastle Country Club, Phi Beta Kappa, Psi Chi, Phi Kappa Phi. Avocations: golf, tennis, Civil War history. General civil litigation, Health, Personal injury. Home: 45 College Dr Bluefield VA 24605-1736 Office: Katz Kantor and Perkins 307 Federal St Bluefield WV 24701-3005

EVANS, WILLIAM DAVIDSON, JR. lawyer; b. Memphis, Jan. 20, 1943; s. William D. and Maxey (Carter) E.; m. Eileen McKenna, June 19, 1971; children: William D., Carter M., Alexander B. BA, Vanderbilt U., 1965; JD, U. Tenn., 1968; LLM, Georgetown U., 1985. Bar: Tenn. 1968, D.C. 1988, Md. 1996. Spl. agt. FBI, N.Y.C., 1968-72; ptnr. Glankler, Brown, Gilliland, Chase, Robinson & Raines, Memphis, 1972-82; trial atty. environ. enforcement sect. U.S. Dept. of Justice, Washington, 1982-86; of counsel Washington, Perito & Dubuc, 1986-91, Graham & James, Washington, 1991-93; ptnr. Rich and Henderson, P.C., Annapolis, Md., 1993-98; sr. asst. county atty. Anne Arundel County Office of Law, 1998—. Editor Digest Environ. Law of Real Property, 1986-90, Environ. Hazards, 1989-90; contbr. articles to profl. jours. Mem. environ. issues group George Bush for Pres. Campaign, Washington, 1987-88, Robert Dole for Pres. Campaign, Washington, 1995-96. Mem. ABA, D.C. Bar Assn., Md. Bar Assn., Environ. Law Inst. Republican. Roman Catholic. Home: 4701 Willard Ave Apt 1633 Chevy Chase MD 20815-4634 Office: Anne Arundel County Office Law 2660 Riva Rd Annapolis MD 21401-7305 E-mail: billevansjr@hotmail.com

EVELETH, JANET STIDMAN, law association administrator; b. Balt., Sept. 6, 1950; d. John Charles and Edith Janet (Scales) Stidman; m. Donald P. Eveleth, May 11, 1974. BA, Washington Coll., 1972; MS, Johns Hopkins U., 1973. Counselor Office of Mayor, Balt., 1973-75; asst. dir. Gov. Commn. on Children, 1975-78; lobbyist, 1978-80; comm. specialist Med. Soc., 1980-81; dir. pub. affairs Mid-Atlantic Food Dealers, 1981-84; dir. comm. Home Builders Assn., 1984-87, Md. Bar Assn., Balt., 1987—. Contbr. articles to profl. jours. Recipient Gov. citation State of Md., 1993, Citizen citation City of Balt., 1993. Mem. NAFE, Am. Soc. Profl. Women, Md. Soc. Assn. Execs. (pres. 1992-93), Nat. Assn. Bar Execs. (chmn. pub. rels. sect. 1994-95, achievement award 1995, ABA's E.A. Wally Richter award 1997, Luminary award 1999), Alpha Chi Omega, Pi Lambda Theta. Office: Md Bar Assn 520 W Fayette St Baltimore MD 21201 1781 E mail: jeveleth@msba.org

EVERARD, GERALD WILFRED, lawyer, trust company executive; b. Green Bay, Wis., Sept. 25, 1952; s. Wilfred A. and Regina P. (Arendt) E.; m. Paula M. Devroy, Sept. 17, 1977. BA, St. Norbert Coll., 1974; JD, U. Wis., 1977. Bar: Wis. 1977. Assoc. Boaroman, Suhr, Curry & Field, Madison, Wis., 1977-81; trust officer 1st Wis. Nat. Bank, 1981—. Law instr. U. Wis., Madison, 1985. Bd. dirs. Cen. YMCA, Madison, 1983-86. Mem. Wis. Bar Assn., Dane County Bar Assn., ABA. Probate. Office: Firstar Bank PO Box 7900 Madison WI 53707-7900 E-mail: jay.everard@firstar.com

EVERBACH, OTTO GEORGE, lawyer; b. New Albany, Ind., Aug. 27, 1938; s. Otto G. and Zelda Marie (Hilt) E.; m. Nancy Lee Stern, June 3, 1961; children: Tracy Ellen, Stephen George. BS, U.S. Mil. Acad., 1960; LLB, U. Va., 1966. Bar: Va. 1967, Ind. 1967, Calif. 1975, Mass. 1978. Counsel CIA, Langley, Va., 1966-67; corp. counsel Bristol-Meyers Co., Evansville, Ind., 1967-74, Alza Corp., Palo Alto, Calif., 1974-75; sec., gen. counsel Am. Optical Corp., Southbridge, Mass., 1976-81; assoc. gen. counsel Warner-Lambert Co., Morris Plains, N.J., 1981-83; v.p. Kimberly-Clark Corp., Neenah, Wis., 1984-86, sr. v.p., gen. counsel, 1986—, sr. v.p. law & govt. affairs, 1988—. Served with U.S. Army, 1960-63. Mem. Am. Bar Assn., Mass. Bar Assn., Ind. Bar Assn., Calif. Bar Assn. Office: Kimberly-Clark Corp DFW Airport Sta PO Box 619100 Dallas TX 75261-9100

EVERDELL, WILLIAM, retired lawyer; b. N.Y.C., May 29, 1915; s. William and Rosalind (Romeyn) E.; m. Eleanore Darling, July 2, 1940; children: William Romeyn, Coburn Darling, Preston. BA, Williams Coll., 1937; LLB, Yale U., 1940. Bar: N.Y. 1941. Assoc. Debevoise & Plimpton, N.Y.C., 1940-49, ptnr., 1949-85, of counsel, 1986-88. Contbr. articles to profl. jours. Trustee Woods Hole Oceanographic Instn., Mass., 1978-86; mem. exec. com., 1981-86, hon. trustee, 1987—; trustee, mem. exec. com. Cold Spring Harbor Lab., N.Y., 1987-93. Served to lt. comdr. USNR, 1942-45, PTO, ATO. Fellow Am. Bar Found.; mem. ABA, Assn. of Bar of City of N.Y. (mem. exec. com. 1960-64), N.Y. State Bar Assn. (chmn. com. corp. law 1971-73). Episcopalian. Club: The Links (gov. 1959-62) (N.Y.C.) Avocations: sailing; golf.

EVERETT, C(HARLES) CURTIS, retired lawyer; b. Omaha, Aug. 9, 1930; s. Charles Edgar and Rosalie (Cook) E.; m. Joan Rose Bader, Sept. 7, 1951; children: Jeffrey, Ellen, Amy, Jennifer. BA cum laude, Beloit Coll., 1952; JD, U. Chgo., 1957. Bar: Ill. 1957. Pvt. practice, Chgo., 1957-91; ptnr. Bell, Boyd, Lloyd, Haddad & Burns, 1965-81, successor firm Bell, Boyd & Lloyd, 1981-91; v.p. law, sec., gen. counsel AMRE, Inc., Dallas, 1991-96; v.p. law, sec., gen. counsel, bd. dirs. Am. Remodeling, Inc., 1992-96; v.p. Canre Remodelling, Inc., 1992-94. V.p., sec. Hans Bader, Cons., Inc., Clearwater, Fla., 1954-99, also bd. dirs.; vis. com. U. Chgo. Law Sch., 1986-89; lectr. Ill. Inst. CLE. Mem. editl. bd. U. Chgo. Law Rev., 1956-57; contbr. articles to profl. jours. Chmn. So. Suburban area Beloit Coll. Ford Found. challange program, 1964-65; pres. The Players, Flossmoor, 1970-71; bd. govs. Lake Shore Dr. Condominium Assn., 1986-91. With AUS, 1952-54. Mem. ABA, Ill. Bar Assn., Chgo. Bar Assn. (mem. securities law com. 1960-91), U. Chgo. Law Sch. Alumni Assn. (dir. 1973-76, pres. Chgo. chpt. 1979-80), Legal Club, Law Club, Monroe Club (bd. govs. 1976-97), Univ. Club Chgo., Order of DeMolay (past master counselor Rock River chpt.), Order of Coif, Sigma Chi, Phi Alpha Delta. Mem. Cmty. Ch. (deacon). General corporate, Mergers and acquisitions, Securities. Home: 532 Long Reach Dr Salem SC 29676-4214

EVERETT, JAMES JOSEPH, lawyer; b. San Antonio, May 7, 1955; BA, St. Mary's U., San Antonio, 1976; JD, Tex. So. U., 1980. Bar: U.S. Dist. Ct. Ariz. 1987, U.S. Tax Ct. 1980, U.S. Ct. Appeals (9th cir.) 1988. Sr. trial atty. IRS, Phoenix, 1980-87; ptnr. Brnilovich & Everett, 1987-89; owner Law Offices of James J. Everett, 1989—; of counsel Broadbent, Walker & Wales, 1991-95. Mem. ATLA, ABA (bus. and tax sects.), Fed. Bar Assn., Tex. Bar Assn., Ariz. Bar Assn., State Bar Ariz. (cert. tax specialist), Maricopa County Bar Assn., Ariz. Tax Controversy Group, Valley Estate Planners (Phoenix), Ctrl. Ariz. Estate Planners, Ariz. Soc. Boutiques, St. Thomas Moore Soc. Corporate taxation, Estate taxation, Personal income taxation. Office: Ste 225 2999 N 44th St Phoenix AZ 85018 E-mail: james.everett@azbar.com

EVERETT, JAMES WILLIAM, JR. lawyer; b. Buffalo, Oct. 26, 1957; s. James William and Esther (Kratzer) E.; m. Christine L. Johnson. BA in Polit. Sci., Coll. Wooster (Ohio), 1979; JD, SUNY, Buffalo, 1984; LLM in Banking Law with honor, Boston U., 1985. Bar: N.Y. 1985, U.S. Dist. Ct. (we. dist.) N.Y. 1989, U.S. Dist. Ct. (no. dist.) N.Y. 1990, U.S. Supreme Ct. 1991. Officer Emil A. Kratzer Co., Inc., Buffalo, 1980-95; assoc. John C. Peters, P.C., Hartford, Conn., 1986-87; assoc. counsel for banks, corps., ins. and sml. bus. N.Y. State Assembly, Albany, N.Y., 1987-88; asst. counsel for banks, commerce, real property, fin. N.Y. State Senate Majority, 1988-94; v.p., counsel for state proceedings and taxation Securities Industry Assn., 1995-98; gen. ptnr. Everett Law, 1998—. Speechwriter for chair policy com. for nat. adv. counsel on women's edn. programs. Observer Nat. Conf. Commr. on Uniformed State Laws Trust Act Drafting Com.; spkr fin. svcs. Nat. Com. State Legislators, Exec. Enterprises. Author N.Y. Law Revision Commn. Review on Leasing Remedies, Forward to Securities Regulation Compilations; contbg. editor Barnert Reports; contbr. to Buffalo News, Bus. Ins., Corp. Fin. Week, The Bank Letter, The Bond Buyer, Compliance Reporter. Mem. judicial nominating com. Erie County (N.Y.) Rep. Com., 1979—; deacon N. Presbyn. Ch., Amherst, N.Y. Recipient Cummings-Rumbaugh prize Coll. of Wooster, Harmony Heights Sch. Pub. Svc. award. Mem. ABA (com. on state regulation of securities), Am. Corp. Counsel Assn., N.Y. State Bar Assn. (banking law com.), Assn. Bar City N.Y., Nat. Assn. Life Cos., Nat. Assn. for Variable Annuities. Republican. Avocations: hiking, cycling, travel. Estate planning, Finance, Mergers and acquisitions. Home: 304 Fisher Blvd Ste L Delmar NY 12054 Office: Securities Industry Assn 120 Broadway Fl 35 New York NY 10271-3599 E-mail: jeverett@abanet.org, everettlaw@msn.com

EVERETT, PAMELA IRENE, legal management company executive, educator; b. L.A., Dec. 31, 1947; d. Richard Weldon and Alta Irene (Tuttle) Bunnell; m. James E. Everett, Sept. 2, 1967 (div. 1973); 1 child, Richard Earl. Cert. Paralegal, Rancho Santago Coll., Santa Ana, Calif., 1977; BA, Calif. State U.-Long Beach, 1985; MA, U. Redlands, 1988. Owner, mgr. Orange County Paralegal Svc., Santa Ana, 1979—; pres. Gem Legal Mgmt. Inc., Fullerton, Calif., 1986—; co-owner Bunnell Publs., 1992-96. Instr. Rancho Santiago Coll., 1979-96, chmn. adv. bd., 1980-85; instr. Fullerton Coll., 1989—, Rio Hondo Coll., Whittier, Calif., 1992-94; advisor Saddle-back Coll., 1985—, North Orange County Regional Occupational Program, Fullerton, 1986—, Fullerton Coll. So. Calif. Coll. Bus. and Law; bd. dirs. Nat. Profl. Legal Assts. Inc., editor PLA News. Author: Legal Secretary Federal Litigation, 1986, Bankruptcy Courts and Procedure, 1987, Going Independent--Business Planning Guide, Fundamentals of Law Office Management, 1994. Republican. Avocation: reading. Office: 940 Manor Way Corona CA 92882 E-mail: Peverett@home.com

EVERITT, ALICE LUBIN, labor arbitrator; b. Dec. 13, 1936; d. Isador and Alice (Berliner) Lubin. BA, Columbia U., 1968, JD, 1971. Assoc. Amen, Weisman & Butler, N.Y.C., 1971-78; spl. asst. to dir. Fed. Mediation and Conciliation Svc., Washington, 1978-81; pvt. practice labor arbitration Washington, N.Y.C., 1981-87, Petersburg, Va., 1987—. Mem. various nat. mediation and arbitration panels including Fed. Mediation and Conciliation Svc., U.S. Steel and United Steelworkers, Am. Arbitration Assn. Editor Dept. Labor publ., 1979. Mem. Am. Arbitration Assn., Soc. Profls. Dispute Resolution, Indsl. Rels. Rsch. Assn., Civil War Roundtable of Richmond, Petersburg Planning Commn. Office: 541 High St Petersburg VA 23803-3859 E-mail: aloffice@techcom.net

EVERSON, STEVEN LEE, lawyer, real estate executive; b. Philippi, W.Va., June 16, 1950; s. Billie Lee and Mildred Ann (Hill) E.; m. Donna Janine Chmielarz, May 29, 1976; 1 child, Michael. BA in Math. magna cum laude, W. Va. U., 1972; JD, Northwestern U., 1979. Bar: Colo. 1979. Tax sr. acct. Deloitte, Haskins & Sells, Colorado Springs, Colo., 1979-82; v.p., sec., treas. The Schuck Corp., 1982—. Instr. real estate U. Colo. Bd. dirs., past chmn. Pikes Peak Found. for Mental Health, Colorado Springs, 1986—, Silver Key Sr. Svcs., Inc., Boys and Girls Club of Pikes Peak Region, Colorado Springs, 1987-90; mem. UCCS Exec. Club, Colorado Springs, 1988-90; treas. Steve Schuck for Gov. Com., 1988-98; project bus. instr. Jr. Achievement, 1985-87. Capt. USAF, 1972-76. Named Vol. of Yr. Pikes Peak Mental Health Ctr., 1999. Mem. Phi Beta Kappa. Republican. Mem. Ch. of Christ. Avocations: racquetball, skiing, softball, golf, tennis, vol. coaching youth sports teams. Real property, Taxation, general, Personal income taxation. Home: 1690 Colgate Dr Colorado Springs CO 80918-8106 Office: The Schuck Corp 2 N Cascade Ave Ste 1280 Colorado Springs CO 80903-1601

EVEY, MERLE KENTON, lawyer; b. Altoona, Pa., Oct. 9, 1930; s. Merle Houser and Dorothy Ellen (Miller) E.; m. Veronica Nuala Moran, Sept. 1, 1962; children: Eileen Veronica, Kathleen Marie. BA, Pa. State U., 1952; JD, Dickinson Sch. of Law, 1955. Bar: Pa. 1956, U.S. Dist. Ct. (we. dist.) Pa. 1959, U.S. Supreme Ct. 1959. Ptnr. Evey, Routch, Black, Dorezas, Magee & Levine, Hollidaysburg, Pa., 1957—. Bd. dirs. Hollidaysburg Trust Co., Omega Fin. Corp., State College, Pa. Chmn. adv. bd. Pa. State U., Altoona; bd. dirs., solicitor Home Nursing Affiliates, 1978—; solicitor County of Blair, 1978—, Blair County Hosp. Authority, Hollidaysburg, 1978—. Served with U.S. Army, 1955—57. Mem. ABA, Blair County Bar Assn. (bd. govs. 1964-67, pres. 1982-83), Pa. Bar Assn. (ho. of dels. 1980-83, bd. govs. 1983-86). Republican. Methodist. Club: Spruce Creek (Pa.) Rod & Gun. Lodge: Masons. Avocation: golf. State civil litigation, General corporate, Probate. Home: PO Box 16 Elm St Sylvan Hills Hollidaysburg PA 16648 Office: Evey Routch Black et al 401 Allegheny St Hollidaysburg PA 16648-2011 E-mail: mevey@evayroutch.com

EWAN, DAVID E. lawyer; b. Camden, N.J., June 23, 1959; s. Eugene H. and Catherine T. (Stannard) E.; m. Lisa J. Draves, Sept. 12, 1998. BA, Dickinson Coll., 1981; JD, Rutgers U., 1991. Bar: N.J. 1991, Pa. 1991, Fla. 1992, Colo. 1994, U.S. Dist. Ct. N.J. 1991, U.S. Ct. Appeals (3d cir.) 1992. Legal intern Camden County Prosecutor, 1989; law clk. U.S. Ct. Appeals (3d cir.), Phila., 1990-91; assoc. Begley, McCloskey & Gaskill, Moorestown, N.J., 1991—. Sr. adj. prof. paralegal program Burlington County Coll., Pemberton, N.J., 1996—. Mem. Am. Ednl. Rsch. Assn. Real property. Home: 400 N Haddon Ave Unit 50 Haddonfield NJ 08033-1731 Office: Begley McCloskey & Gaskill 40 E Main St Moorestown NJ 08057-3310

EWBANK, THOMAS PETERS, lawyer, retired banker; b. Indpls., Dec. 29, 1943; s. William Curtis and Maxine Stuart (Peters) E.; m. Alice Ann Shelton, June 8, 1968; children: William Curtis, Ann Shelton. Student, Stanford U., 1961-62; AB, Ind. U., 1965, JD, 1969. Bar: Ind. 1969, U.S. Tax Ct. 1969, U.S. Dist. Ct. (so. dist.) Ind. 1969, U.S. Supreme Ct. 1974; cert. trust & fin. advisor. Legis. asst. Ind. Legis. Coun., 1966-67; estate and inheritance tax adminstr. mchts. Nat. Bank, Indpls., 1967-69; assoc. Hilgedag, Johnson, Secrest and Murphy, 1969-71; asst. gen. counsel Everett I. Brown Co., 1971-72; with Mchts. Nat. Bank & Trust Co. (now Nat. City Bank), 1972-95; from probate adminstr. to pres. Mechants Capital Mgmt., Inc., Ind., 1990-93; ptnr. Krieg DeVault LLP, Indpls., 1995—. Contbr. articles to profl. jours. Asst. treas. Ruckelshaus for U.S. Senator Com., 1968; candidate for Ind. Legislature, 1970, 74; bd. dirs. Noble Found. Ind., 1997-99, Indpls. Art Ctr., 1997—, Ruth Lilly Found., 1997—, Ctr. Philanthropy, Ind. U., Indpls., 1998—, Benjamin Harrison Home Found., 1994—, v.p., 1996-98, pres., 1998-2000; chmn. adv. com. ARC, 1987—. Fellow Ind. Bar Found. (life patron); mem. Estate Planning Coun. Indpls. (pres. 1982-83), Indpls. Bar Assn., Ind. Bar Assn., Indpls. Bar Found. (treas 1976-81), Blue Key, Meridian Hills Country Club, Kiwanis (Circle K Internat. trustee 1963-64, pres. 1964-65, chmn. internat. com. 1988-90, George Hixson Diamond fellow 6th level, treas. Indpls. club 1980-81, 84-85 designated maj. builder 1983, Pres. Career award 2001), English Speaking Union Indpls. Republican. Baptist. Estate planning, Probate, Estate taxation. Office: One Indiana Sq Ste 2800 Indianapolis IN 46204-2017 E-mail: tpe@kdlegal.com

EWELL, A. BEN, JR. lawyer, businessman; b. Elyria, Ohio, Sept. 10, 1941; s. Austin Bert and Mary Rebecca (Thompson) E.; m. Suzanne E.; children: Austin Bert III, Brice Ballantyne, Harrison Dale, Jonathan Eli. BA, Miami U., Oxford, Ohio, 1963; JD, Hasting Coll. Law, U. Calif., San Francisco, 1966. Bar: Calif. 1966, U.S. Dist. Ct. (ea. dist.) Calif. 1967, U.S. Supreme Ct. 1982, U.S. Ct. Appeals (9th cir.) 1967. Pres. A.B. Ewell, Jr., A. Profl. Corp., Fresno, 1984-98, The Clarksfield Co., Inc., Fresno, 1989—; formerly gen. counsel to various water dists. and assn.; gen. counsel, chmn. San Joaquin River Flood Control Assn., 1984-88; CEO Millerton New Town Devel. Co., 1988-94, chmn., 1994-96; pres. Millerton Open Space and Natural Resource Plan, 1999—; regional v.p. Western Water Co., Fresno, 2001—. Mem. task force on prosecution, cts. and law reform Calif. Coun. Criminal Justice, 1971-74; mem. Fresno Bulldog Found., Calif. State U.; mem. San Joaquin Valley Agrl. Water commn., 1979-88; co-chmn. nat. adv. coun. SBA, 1981, 82, mem. 1981-87; bd. dirs. Fresno East Cmty. Ctr., 1971-73; mem. Fresno County Water Adv. Com., 1989; chmn. various area polit. campaigns and orgns., including Reagan/Bush, 1984, Deukmejian for Gov., 1986; mem. adv. com. St. Agnes Med. Ctr. Found., 1983-89; trustee U. Calif. Med. Edn. Found., 1989-90, Fresno Met. Mus. Art, History and Sci., active, 1989—, mem. adv. coun., 1993-94; bd. dirs. Citizens for Cmty. Enrichment, Fresno, 1990-93; mem. Police Activities League, 1995—; bd. dir. Fresno Conv. and Visitors Bur., 1997—; bd. dirs. Fresno Volleyball Club, 1998—, pres. 1999-2000. Columnist The Wellington Enterprise. Bd. dirs. fresno Volleyball Club, 1998—, pres., 1999—. Mem. Millerton Lake C. of C., Brighton Crest Country Club (pres. 1989-96), Cooper River Country Club, Phi Alpha Delta, Brighton Crest Golf and Country Club, Sigma Nu. Congregationalist. General corporate, Public utilities, Real property. Office: 410 W Fallbrook Ave Ste 102 Fresno CA 93711-5830

EWEN, PAMELA BINNINGS, lawyer; b. Phila., Mar. 22, 1944; d. Walter James and Barbara (Perkins) Binnings; m. Jerome Francis Ayers, Aug. 22, 1965 (div. July 1974); 1 child, Scott Dylan; m. John Alexander Ewen, Dec. 13, 1974. BA, Tulane U., 1977; JD cum laude, U. Houston, 1979. Bar: Tex. 1979, U.S. Dist. Ct. (so. dist.) Tex. 1981, U.S. Ct. Appeals (5th cir.) 1981. Law clk. Harris, Cook, Browning & Barker, Corpus Christi, Tex., 1977-79; assoc. Kleberg, Dyer, Redford & Weil, Corpus Christi, 1979-80; atty. law dept. Gulf Oil Corp., Houston, 1980-84; assoc. Baker & Botts, L.L.P., Houston, 1984-88, ptnr., 1988—. Author: Faith On Trial, 1999. La. Legis. scholar, New Orleans, 1976-77. Mem. ABA (forum com. on franchising 1983-85, corp., banking, bus. law sect., 1984—, law practice mgmt. sect., subcom. Women Rainmakers Assn.), Am. Petroleum Inst. (spl. subcom. to gen. com. on law, com. on product liability 1982-85), Tex. State Bar (com. on uniform communal code 1988—), Tex. Assn. Bank Coun. (bd. dirs. 1994-97), Jr. Achievement S.E. Tex. (bd. dirs. 1997—), Order of Barons. Contracts commercial, General corporate, Finance. Office: Baker & Botts 3000 1 Shell Plz Houston TX 77002

EWERT, QUENTIN ALBERT, lawyer, consultant; b. Griggsville, Ill., Aug. 19, 1915; s. Albert Merritt and Anna Mabel (Beard) E.; m. Frances Norfleet, Dec. 25, 1941; children: David Norfleet, Gregory Albert, Catherine Ann, Mary Frances, Jane Cranston; m. Arlayne Joy Brown, May 1973 (div. June 1981). BA, Mich. State U., 1938; JD, U. Mich., 1946. Bar: Mich. 1946. Atty. Auto Owners Ins. Co., Lansing, Mich., 1946-47; ptnr. Ewert and Fagan, 1947-48; sole practice, 1948-53; pres., bd. chmn. Guardsman Ins. Co., Pasadena, Calif., 1953-55; ptnr. Loomis, Ewert, Ederer, Parsley, Davis & Gotting, P.C., Lansing, 1955-87, of counsel, 1988—. Owner, bd. chmn. Communications, Inc., Grand Rapids, Mich., 1972-87; cons. TIE/communications, Inc., Shelton, Conn., 1988-91. Met. area chmn. Rep. party, Lansing, 1952. Served to lt. cmdr. USNR, 1941-45. Mem. The Springs Country Club. Home: 11 Mount Holyoke Dr Rancho Mirage CA 92270-3667 Office: Loomis Ewert Parsley Davis & Gotting 232 S Capitol Ave Ste 1000 Lansing MI 48933-1526

EWIN, GORDON OVERTON, retired lawyer, farmer; b. New Orleans, June 1, 1923; s. James Perkins and Lucille Havard (Scott) E.; m. Katharine Elise Keller, Sept. 6, 1947; 1 dau., Katharine Adair. BA, Tulane U., 1943, JD, 1948; postgrad. Faculté de Droit, U. Paris, 1948-49. Bar: La. 1948, U.S. Dist. Ct. (ea. dist.) La. 1949, U.S. Ct. Appeals (5th cir.) 1949. Assoc. Milling, Saal, Saunders, Benson & Woodward, New Orleans, 1949-52; ptnr. Ewin & Robertson, New Orleans, 1952-55; staff atty. Humble Oil & Refining Co., New Orleans, 1955-59; ptnr. Chaffe, McCall, Phillips, Toler & Sarpy, New Orleans, 1959-93; pres. Greenwood Planting Co., 1979-89; ptnr. Green Field Farms, 1984-91; dir. Farmers Bank & Trust of Cheneyville (La.), Prodrs. Mut. Gin. Bd. dirs. New Orleans Philharm. Orch., 1961; mem. Young Life Adv. Coun., 1972; bd. dirs. Garden Dist. Assn., 1967-74, pres., 1973-74; bd. dirs. Friends of the Cabildo, 1976-82, pres., 1981-82. Lt. (j.g.) USNR, 1943-46; PTO. Mem. New Orleans Bar Assn. (treas.), La. Bar Assn., La. Club, Boston Club, Soc. Colonial Wars (past La. gov.). Episcopalian. (vestryman Trinity Ch. 1976-80). Oil, gas, and mineral, Probate, Real property. Home: Greenwood Plantation PO Box 403 Cheneyville LA 71325-0403

EWING, KY PEPPER, JR. lawyer; b. Victoria, Tex., Jan. 7, 1935; s. Ky Pepper and Sallie (Dixon) E.; m. Almuth Rott, Apr. 6, 1963; children: Kenneth Patrick, Kevin Andrew, Kathryn Diana. B.A. cum laude, Baylor U., 1956; LL.B. cum laude, Harvard U., 1959. Bar: D.C. 1959, U.S. Supreme Ct 1963. Assoc. firm Covington & Burling, Washington, 1959-64; partner firm Prather, Seeger, Doolittle, Farmer & Ewing, 1964-77; dep. asst. atty. gen. antitrust div. Dept. Justice, 1978-80; ptnr. Vinson & Elkins, 1980—. Dir. Washington Inst. Fgn. Affairs. Co-editor-in-chief: State Antitrust Practice and Statutes, 3 Vols., 1990; mem. antitrust adv. bd. Antitrust and Trade Regulation Report Bur. Nat. Affairs, 1990—; mem. edit. bd. Antitrust Report Matthew Bender & Co., 1993—. Pres. Potomac Valley League, 1977, Carderock Springs Citizens Assn., 1975-78. Fellow: Am. Bar Found. (life); mem.: ABA (chmn. legis. com. antitrust sect. 1987—91, coun. antitrust sect. 1991—94, fin. officer antitrust sect. 1994—96, chmn. FTC/Dept. Justice working group 1994—97, mem. Ho. of Dels. 1996—98, vice chair antitrust sect. 1998—99, chair-elect antitrust sect. 1999—2000, chair antitrust sect. 2000—01), Am. Soc. Internat. Law, Internat. Bar Assn. (editl. bd. Bus. Law Internat.), Inter-Am. Bar Assn., D.C. Bar Assn., Met. Club. Democrat. Episcopalian. Antitrust, Federal civil litigation, Environmental. Home: 8317 Comanche Ct Bethesda MD 20817-4561 Office: Vinson & Elkins 1455 Pennsylvania Ave NW Washington DC 20004-1013 E-mail: kewing@velaw.com

EWING, ROBERT CLARK, lawyer; b. Lower Merion, Pa., Nov. 26, 1957; m. Cheralynn Kennedy, Mar. 22, 1986; children: Edward, Jaesun; stepchildren: Kristin, Shannon. BS in Fin., Pa. State U., 1980; JD, Villanova U., 1983. Bar: Pa. 1983, U.S. Dist. Ct. (ea. dist.) Pa. 1985, U.S. Ct. Appeals (3rd cir.) 1987, U.S. Supreme Ct. 1987. Ranger Pa. State Park Svc., 1976-78, Valley Forge Nat. Park, 1979; police officer Ocean City (Md.) Police Dept., 1980-81, Springfield Twp. Delaware County, 1992-99; assoc. Lagoy & Lyons, West Chester, Pa., 1983-86, Ronald H. Silverman, P.C., King of Prussia, 1986-88, Anthony J. McNulty & Assocs., Media, 1988-91; pvt. practice, 1991—. Contbr. articles to profl. jours. Mem. Lima (Pa.) Fire Co., 1973—, bd. dirs., 1981-88; mem. Media (Pa.) Fire Co., 1988—; bd. dirs. Hank Nacrelli Scholarship Fund, 1988-97, Delaware County Emergency Health Svcs. Coun., 1986-93; active Delaware County Critical Incident Stress Mgmt. Program, Media, 1987—. Mem. Delaware County Bar Assn., Delaware County Firemen's Assn., Assn. Trial Lawyers Am., Pa. Trial Lawyers Assn. General civil litigation, Family and matrimonial, Real property. Office: 115 N Monroe St PO Box 1468 Media PA 19063-8468

EWING, ROBERT CRAIG, lawyer, educator; b. Glen Ridge, N.J., May 9, 1953; s. Donald Graham and Barbara (Hansen) E.; m. Mary Arnold Hengy, Aug. 30, 1981; 1 child, Kyle Ross. BA, Middlebury Coll., 1976; JD, Denver U., 1980. Bar: Colo. 1980, Mass. 1981, U.S. Dist. Ct. Colo. 1980, U.S. Ct. Appeals (10th cir.) 1984, Maine 1997. Assoc. Hall & Evans, Denver, 1981-84; part-time prof. Metro. State Coll., Denver, 1983-88; ptnr. Holme, Roberts & Owen, Denver, 1984-95; CEO, founder skifreestyle-.com; shareholder EWing & Ewing, PC; bd. dirs. State Adv. Council on Emergency Med. Services, Denver, 1981-83; emergency med technician Am. Coll. Surgeons, Colo. Dept. Health, Denver, 1979— ; bd. dirs. McArthur Ranch Homeowners Assn., 1981-85; mem. Am. Trakehner Assn., Columbus, Ohio, 1983— . Author: Emergency Medical Personnel and the Law, 1982, Electromagnetic Fields at the Millenium-Should We Tresspass Against Us, 1991; editor Legal Information Rev., 1983; Trends in Law Report newsletter, 1983-84. Named Charles A. Dana Scholar Middlebury Coll., Vt., 1975. Mem. Colo. Bar Assn., Denver Bar Assn., Am. Trial Lawyers Assn., Colo. Trial Lawyers Assn. Republican. Presbyterian. Clubs: Araphaoe Hunt (Littleton); Greenwood Athletic. General civil litigation, Insurance, Personal injury. Home: 4256 S Perry Park Rd Sedalia CO 80135-8207

EWING, WILLIAM HICKMAN, JR. lawyer; b. Memphis, June 11, 1942; s. William Hickman and Addie Carolyn (Young) E.; m. Mary Clair Deyling, May 13, 1972; children: Jessica, Adam, Abigail. B.A., Vanderbilt U., 1964; J.D., Memphis State U., 1972. Bar: Tenn. 1972, U.S. Supreme Ct. 1978, U.S. Ct. Appeals, 6th cir. 1974. Asst. U.S. atty. Dept. Justice, Memphis, 1972-77, 1st asst. U.S. atty., 1977-81; U.S. atty. (we. dist.) Tenn., 1981-91; individual practice Germantown, Tenn., 1991—; dep. ind. counsel Office of the Ind. Counsel (Whitewater), 1994-2001. Served with USN, 1964-69, to capt. USNR. Mem. Memphis Bar Assn., Fed. Bar Assn., Tenn. Bar Assn. E-mial. Office: 1500 Cobblestone Cv Germantown TN 38138-1707 E-mail: 102745.2760@compuserve.com

EYMANN, RICHARD CHARLES, lawyer; b. Hanover, N.H., June 6, 1945; BS, U. Oreg., 1968; JD, Gonzaga U., 1976. Bar: Wash. 1976, U.S. Dist. Ct. (ea. dist.) Wash. 1978, U.S. Ct. Appeals (9th cir.) 1987, U.S. Dist. Ct. (we. dist.) Wash. 1989, U.S. Supreme Ct. 1995. Ptnr. Eymann, Allison, Fennessy, Hunter & Jones, P.S., Spokane, Wash. Mem. ABA (founder, chmn. nat. appellate advocacy competition 1975-84, bd. advs. 1985-93), ATLA, Wash. State Bar Assn. (bd. govs. 1997-98, pres. elect 1998-99, pres. 1999-2000), Wash. State Trial Lawyers Assn. (bd. govs. 1984-86, 88-95, legis. steering com. 1990-96, membership chair 1984-85, v.p. East 1991-92, fin. com. 1994-95, Trial Lawyer of Yr. 1995, pres. 1996-97), Wash. Trial Lawyers for Pub. Justice (bd. dirs. 1994-98), Spokane County Bar Assn., Am. Inns of Ct. (barrister 1986, master of the bench 1990, Charles L. Powell & Inn pres. 1991-93). Personal injury, General civil litigation. Office: Eymann Allison Fennessy Hunter & Jones PS 601 W Main Ave Ste 801 Spokane WA 99201 E-mail: eymann@eahjlaw.com

FABE, DANA ANDERSON, state supreme court chief justice; b. Cin., Mar. 29, 1951; d. George and Mary Lawrence (Van Antwerp) F.; m. Randall Gene Simpson, Jan. 1, 1983; 1 child, Amelia Fabe Simpson. BA, Cornell U., 1973; JD, Northeastern U., 1976. Bar: Alaska 1977, U.S. Supreme Ct. 1981. Law clk. to justice Alaska Supreme Ct., 1976-77; staff atty. pub. defenders State Alaska, 1977-81; dir. Alaska Pub. Defender Agy., Anchorage, 1981—. Judge Superior Ct., Anchorage; justice Alaska Supreme Ct., Anchorage, 1996—, chief justice, 2000—. Named alumna of yr. Northeastern Sch. Law, 1983, alumni pub. svc. award, 1991. Office: Alaska Supreme Ct 303 K St Fl 5 Anchorage AK 99501-2013

FABER, DAVID ALAN, federal judge; b. Charleston, W.Va., Oct. 21, 1942; s. John Smith and Wilda Elaine (Melton) F.; m. Deborah Ellayne Anderson, Aug. 24, 1968; 1 dau., Katherine Peyton. B.A., W.Va. U., 1964; J.D., Yale U., 1967; LLM, U. Va., 1998. Bar: W.Va. 1967, U.S. Ct. Mil. Appeals 1970, U.S. Supreme Ct. 1974. Assoc. Dayton, Campbell & Love, Charleston, W.Va., 1967-68, Campbell, Love, Woodroe, 1972-74; ptnr. Campbell, Love, Woodroe & Kizer, Charleston, 1974-77, Love, Wise, Robinson & Woodroe, Charleston, 1977-81; U.S. atty. U.S. Dept. Justice, 1982-86; ptnr. Spilman, Thomas, Battle & Klostermeyer, 1987-91; judge U.S. Dist. Ct. (so. dist.) W.Va., Bluefield, 1991—. Counsel to ethics commn. W.Va. State Bar, Charleston, 1974-76 Served to capt. USAF,

1968-72, to col. W.Va. Air N.G., 1978-92. Nat. law scholar Yale Law Sch. New Haven, 1964-65 Mem. W.Va. State Bar, W.Va. Bar Assn., Phi beta Kappa. Republican. Episcopalian. Office: US Dist Ct PO Box 5009 110 N Heber St Beckley WV 25801 Fax: (304) 253-6811

FABER, ROBERT CHARLES, lawyer; b. N.Y.C., June 26, 1941; s. Sidney G. and Beatrice (Siebert) F.; m. Carol Z. Zimmerman, Aug. 15, 1965; 1 child, Susan Faber. BA, Cornell U., 1962; JD, Harvard Law Sch., 1965. Bar: N.Y. 1966; U.S. Dist. Ct. (so. dist.) N.Y. 1967; U.S. Ct. Appeals (2nd cir.); U.S. Ct. Appeals (fed. cir.) 1982; U.S. Supreme Ct. 1971; U.S. Patent and trademark Office 1967. Atty., ptnr. Ostrolenk, Faber, Gerb & Soffen, LLP, N.Y.C., 1965—. Lecturer Practicing Law Inst., N.Y.C., 1974—. Author: Landis on Mechanics of Patent Claim Drafting, 3d edit. 1990, 4th edit. 1996. Mem. Am. Intellectual Property Law Assn., N.Y. Intellectual Property Law Assn., Harvard Club of N.Y. Intellectual property, Patent, Trademark and copyright. Office: Ostrolenk Faber Gerb & Soffen LLP 1180 Ave of Americas New York NY 10036-8401

FACTOR, MAX, III, mediator, arbitrator; b. L.A., Sept. 25, 1945; s. Sidney B. and Dorothy (Levinson) F.; BA in Econs. magna cum laude, Harvard Coll., 1966; JD, Yale U., 1969. Bar: Calif. 1970, U.S. Ct. Appeals (6th cir.) 1971, U.S. Dist. Ct. (cen. dist.) Calif. 1971. Law clk. U.S. Ct. Appeals (6th cir.), 1969-71; exec. dir. Calif. Law Ctr., Los Angeles, 1973-74; dir. Consumer Protection Sect., Los Angeles City Atty., 1974-77; pvt. practice Factor & Agay, Beverly Hills, Calif, 1978—. expert witness numerous state and fed. bds., 1974-78; guest lectr. UCLA, U. So. Calif., Los Angeles County Bar Assn., Calif. Dept. Consumer Affairs, 1974-76; hearing examiner City of Los Angeles, 1975. Contbr. articles to profl. jours. Bd. dirs. Western Law Ctr. for the Handicapped, Los Angeles, 1977-79, Beverly Hills Unified Sch. Dist., 1979-83; pres. Beverly Hills Bd. Edn., 1983; bd. councilors U. So. Calif. Law Ctr., Los Angeles, 1983— ; chmn. Beverly Hills Visitors Bur., 1989-90. Recipient scholarship award Harvard Coll., 1965; Max Factor III Day proclaimed in his honor Beverly Hills City Council, 1979; recipient Disting. Service to Pub. Edn. award Beverly Hills Bd. Edn., 1979. Mem. Los Angeles County Bar Assn. (chmn. various coms. 1976-78), Beverly Hills C. of C. (pres. 1987-88), Beverly Hills Edn. Found. (pres. 1977-79). Office: 345 N Maple Dr Ste 294 Beverly Hills CA 90210-3878

FADELEY, EDWARD NORMAN, retired state supreme court justice; b. Williamsville, Mo., Dec. 13, 1929; m. Nancie Peacocke, June 11, 1953; children: Charles, Shira; m. Darian Cyr, Sept. 12, 1992. A.B., U. Mo., 1951; J.D. cum laude, U. Oreg., 1957. Bar: Oreg. 1957, U.S. Supreme Ct. 1968. Practice law, Eugene, Oreg., 1957-88; mem. Oreg. Ho. of Reps., 1961-63, Oreg. Senate, 1963-87, pres., 1983-85; justice Oregon Supreme Ct., 1989-98; ret., 1998. Mem. jud. working group Internat. Water Tribunal, Amsterdam, The Netherlands 1991-95; invitee Rio Environ. Conf., 1992, Indigenous Peoples of World Conf., New Zealand, 1993; adj. prof. law U. Oreg.; formerly gen. couns., bd. officer for rsch. corp., fin. instn.; founder, dir. N. Am. Hollis Internat. Law Ctr., 2001—. Advisor to past Pres.; chmn. Oreg. Dem. party, 1966-68; chmn. law and justice com. Nat. Conf. Legislators, 1977-78; adv. com. to State and Local Law Ctr., Washington; participants com. Washington Pub. Power Supply System, 1982-88; candidate for nomination for gov., 1986; bd. dirs. Wayne Morse Hist. Park; mgr. Stille Nacht Found., 1990—. Lt. USNR, 1951-54. Recipient First Pioneer award U. Oreg., 1980, Assn. Oreg. Counties award for leadership in the reform of state ct. system, 1982. Mem. ABA (internat. law, pub. utility law), Oreg. State Bar Assn. (chmn. uniform laws com. 1962-64), Order of Coif, Alpha Pi Zeta, Phi Alpha Delta. Democrat. Methodist. Avocations: canoeing, backpacking, hunting, riding, poetry.

FAGERBERG, ROGER RICHARD, lawyer; b. Chgo., Dec. 11, 1935; s. Richard Emil and Evelyn (Thor) F.; m. Virginia Fuller Vaughan, June 20, 1959; children: Steven Roger, Susan Vaughan, James Thor, Laura Craft. B.S. in Bus. Adminstrn., Washington U., St. Louis, 1958, J.D., 1961, postgrad., 1961-62. Bar: Mo. 1961. Grad. teaching asst. Washington U., St. Louis, 1961-62; assoc. firm Rassieur, Long & Yawitz, 1962-64; ptnr. Rassieur, Long, Yawitz & Schneider and predecessor firms, 1965-91; pvt. practice, 1991—. Mem. exec. com. Citizens' Adv. Council Pkwy. Sch. Dist., 1974—, pres.-elect, 1976-77, pres., 1977-78; bd. dirs. Parkway Residents Orgn., 1969—, v.p., 1970-73, pres., 1973—; scoutmaster Boy Scouts Am., 1979-83; Presbyn. elder, 1976—, pres. three local congs. 1968-70, 77-78, 83-84. Mem. ABA, Mo. Bar Assn., St. Louis Bar Assn., Christian Bus. Men's Com. (bd. dirs. 1975-78, 87-91), Full Gospel Bus. Men's Fellowship, Order of Coif, Omicron Delta Kappa, Beta Gamma Sigma, Pi Sigma Alpha, Phi Eta Sigma, Phi Delta Phi, Kappa Sigma. Republican. Lodges: Kiwanis (bd. dirs. 1988-91), Masons, Shriners. General corporate, Probate, Taxation, general. Home and Office: 13812 Clayton Rd Chesterfield MO 63017-8407

FAGG, GEORGE GARDNER, federal judge; b. Eldora, Iowa, Apr. 30, 1934; s. Ned and Arleene (Gardner) F.; m. Jane E. Wood, Aug. 19, 1956; children: Martha, Thomas, Ned, Susan, George, Sarah. BS in Bus. Adminstrn., Drake U., 1965, JD, 1956. Bar: Iowa 1958. Ptnr. Cartwright, Druker, Ryden & Fagg, Marshalltown, Iowa, 1958-72; judge Iowa Dist. Ct., 1972-82, U.S. Ct. Appeals (8th cir.), 1982-99, sr. judge, 1999-. Mem. faculty Nat. Jud. Coll., 1979 Mem. ABA, Iowa Bar Assn., Order of Coif. Office: US Ct Appeals US Courthouse Annex 110 E Court Ave Ste 455 Des Moines IA 50309-2044

FAHEY, RICHARD PAUL, lawyer; b. Oakland, Calif., Nov. 2, 1944; s. John Joseph and Helene Goldie (Whetstone) F.; m. Suzanne Dawson, June 8, 1968; children: Eamon, Aaron Chad. AA, Meritt Coll., 1964; BA, San Francisco State Univ., 1966; JD, Northwestern U., 1971. Bar: N. Mex., 1971, U.S. Dist. Ct., N. Mex., 1972, U.S. Ct. Appeals (10th cir.) 1972, Ohio 1973, U.S. Dist. Ct. (no. and so. dists.), U.S. Supreme Ct. 1975. Atty. in charge Dinebeiina Nahiilna Be Agaditahe, Shiprock, New Mexico, 1971-73; asst. atty. genl. State of Ohio, Columbus, OH, 1973-76; ptnr. Fahey & Schraff, 1976-80; atty. Sanford, Fisher, Fahey, Boyland & Schwarzwalder, 1980-84; of counsel Knepper, White, Arter & Hadden, 1984-85; ptnr. Arter & Hadden, 1985-99; of counsel Vorys Sater Seymour and Pease LLP, 2000—; adj. prof.law Capital U., 1976-86; adj. prof. law Ohio State Univ., 1986-87; chmn. Ohio Oil and Gas Regulatory Rev. Commn., 1986-87. Author: Underground Storage Tanks A Primer of the Federal Regulatory Program, 2nd edit., 1995; contbr. articles to profl. jours. Vol. Peace Corps, Liberia, 1966-68. Mem. Columbus Pub. Schs. Bd. Edn., 1986-93, pres. 1989; trustee Godman Guild Settlement House, Columbus, 1976-82, Ohio Environ. Coun., 1981-83, Downtown Columbus, Inc., 1989, Pilot Dogs, Inc., 1993—, pres. 2001; adv. bd. WCBE Pub. Radio; pres. Ohio Audubon, 1999—, City in Schools, 2000—. Russell Sage Found. grantee, 1969; mem. bd. dirs. Nat.; mem. exec. com. Dem. Party, 1996-; mem. Charter rev. com. Columbus City, 1998-99. Mem. ABA (vice chair Sonreel water quality com. 1993-97), Ohio Bar Assn., N. Mex. Bar Assn., Columbus Bar Assn., Columbus Bar Found. Democrat. Unitarian. Avocations: travel, fishing, reading, jogging, skiing. Administrative and regulatory, General corporate, Environmental. Home: 449 E Dominion Blvd Columbus OH 43214-2216 Office: Vorys Sater Seymour and Pease LLP 52 E Gay St Columbus OH 43215

FAIGNANT, JOHN PAUL, lawyer, educator; b. Proctor, Vt., Mar. 24, 1953; s. Joseph Paul and Ann (DeBlasio) F.; children: Janelle, Melissa. BA, U. New Haven, 1974; JD, George Mason U., 1978. Bar: Va. 1978, Vt. 1979, U.S. Dist. Ct. Vt. 1979, U.S. Ct. Appeals (4th cir.) 1979, U.S. Supreme Ct. 1992. Assoc. Griffin & Griffin, Rutland, Vt., 1978-79, Miller, Norton & Cleary, Rutland, 1979-84, ptnr., 1984-87, Miller, Cleary and Faignant PC, Rutland, 1988-91, Miller & Fiagnant, Ltd., Rutland, 1991-97, Miller Faignant & Whelton PC (now Miller Faignant & Behrens), Rutland, 1997—. Adj. prof. Coll. St. Joseph, Rutland, 1982-90. Mem. Rutland Town Fire Dept., 1989—; mem., pres. No. New England Def. Counsel, 1995-96. Mem. Va. Bar Assn., Vt. Bar Assn., Assn. Trial Lawyers Am., Def. Rsch. Inst., Am. Bd. Trial Advocates. Roman Catholic. Avocation: antique trucks. General civil litigation, Insurance, Personal injury. Home: RR 1 Box 3762 Rutland VT 05701-9214 Office: Miller Faignant & Behrens PC 36 Merchants Row PO Box 6688 Rutland VT 05702-6688

FAIN, JOEL MAURICE, lawyer; b. Miami Beach, Fla., Dec. 11, 1953; s. William Maurice and Carolyn Genievive (Baggett) F.; m. Moira Joan Slocum, June 15, 1974; children: Hannah Ruth, Dylan Michael, Rachel Joan. BA, Yale U., 1975; JD, U. Conn., 1978. Bar: Conn. 1978, U.S. Dist. Ct. Conn. 1978, U.S. Ct. Appeals (2d cir.) 1989, U.S. Supreme Ct. 1999. Assoc. Kahan, Kerensky, Capossela, Levine & Breslau, Vernon, Conn., 1978-83, ptnr., 1984-90, mng. ptnr., 1990-91; ptnr. Morrison, Mahoney & Miller, Hartford, Conn., 1992—. Chmn. Youth Adv. Bd., Tolland, Conn., 1983-92; chmn. Tolland Town Coun., 1995-97. Mem. ABA, Conn. Bar Assn., Tolland County Bar Assn. (pres. 1991-92), Assn. Trial Lawyers Am., Conn. Trial Lawyers Assn., Lions (pres. 1987-88). Democrat. Congregationalist. Federal civil litigation, State civil litigation, Personal injury. Home: 140 Huyshope Ave Hartford CT 06106-2857 Office: Morrison Mahoney & Miller 1 Constitution Plaza Hartford CT 06103-4506

FAIRBANK, ROBERT HAROLD, lawyer; b. Northampton, Mass., Mar. 4, 1948; s. William Martin and Jane (Davenport) F.; m. Gail Lees, Feb. 16, 1992; children: Sarah Julia, David Kivy; stepchildren: Kristin Burdge, Lindsay Burdge. AB in Polit. Sci., Stanford U., 1972; MLS, U. Calif.-Berkeley, 1973; JD, NYU, 1977. Bar: Calif. 1977, U.S. Dist. Ct. (cen. and no. dists.) Calif. 1978, U.S. Dist. Ct. (so. dist.) Calif. 1993. Assoc. Gibson, Dunn & Crutcher, L.A., 1977-84, ptnr., 1985-96; co-founding ptnr. Fairbank & Vincent, 1996—. Lawyer rep., co-chair 9th circuit Jud. Conf. Ctrl. Dist., 2000-2002. Author: Effective Pretrial and Trial Motions, 1983, California Practice Guide: Civil Trials and Evidence (The Rutter Group 1993, with yearly updates); mem. editl. bd. NYU Law Rev., 1975-76. Named One of Top 100 Bus. Lawyers in L.A., L.A. Bus. Jour., 1995. Mem. Assn. Bus. Trial Lawyers (co-founder San Francisco and Orange County chpts., bd. govs. 1984-85, treas. 1986-87, sec. 1987-88, v.p. 1988-89, pres. 1989-90), L.A. County Bar Assn. (fed. cts. com. 1983-85), Jud. Coun. Calif. Adv. Com. on Local Rules (subcom. chair on civil trial rules). Federal civil litigation, State civil litigation, Securities. Office: Fairbank & Vincent 11755 Wilshire Blvd Ste 2320 Los Angeles CA 90025-1501 E-mail: rhf@fvlaw.com

FAIRBANKS, ROBERT ALVIN, lawyer; b. Oklahoma City, July 9, 1944; s. Albert Edward and Lucille Imogene (Scherer) F.; m. Linda Gayle Geer, Aug. 26, 1967; children: Chele Lyn, Kimberly Jo, Robert Alvin II, Michael Albert, Richard Alan, Joseph Alexander. BS in Math., U. Okla., 1967, JD, 1973; MBA, Oklahoma City U., 1970, MCJA, 1975; LLM, Columbia U., 1976; MA, Stanford U., 1984; MEd, Harvard U., 1993. Bar: Okla. 1974, U.S. Dist. Ct. (we. dist.) Okla. 1974, U.S. Ct. Customs and Patent Appeals 1974, U.S. Ct. Mil. Appeals, 1974, U.S. Tax Ct. 1974, U.S. Claims Ct. 1975, U.S. Customs Ct. 1975, U.S. Ct. Appeals (10th cir.) 1975, U.S. Supreme Ct. 1977, U.S. Dist. Ct. (ea. dist.) Okla. 1984, Minn. 1993. Commd. 2d lt. USAF, 1967, advanced through grades to capt., 1970; col. USAFR, 1986; asst. staff judge adv., chief of claims div. Office of Staff Judge Adv., Tinker AFB, Okla., 1974-75; legal asst. to Justice William A. Berry, Okla. Supreme Ct., 1977; pvt. practice Norman, Okla., 1974—; v.p. St. Gregory's U., Shawnee, 1997—. Instr. bus. adminstrn. U. Md. Far East div., Nha Trang, Viet Nam, 1970-71, Rose State Coll., Midwest City, Okla., 1974; rsch. assoc. in law U. Okla., Norman, 1974, spl. lectr., 1974-75, vis. asst. prof., 1976-77, adj. prof. law, 1984—; vis. asst. prof. law Oklahoma City U., 1977; asst. prof. law U. Ark., Fayetteville, Arks., 1977-81; assoc. prof. law La. State U., Baton Rouge, 1981; rsch. asst. dept. family, community and preventative medicine Stanford (Calif.) Med. Sch., 1981-82; adj. asst. prof. govt. contract law Air Force Inst. Tech., Wright-Patterson AFB, Ohio, 1985—; v.p. St. Gregory's U., Shawnee, Okla.; prof. bus. adminstrn. U. Phoenix; adj. prof. law and mgmt. Okla. Christian U. Coll. Bus.; cons. Cheyenne Tribe, Clinton, Okla., 1977-81, 90, Citizens Band of Pottawatomie Tribe, Shawnee, Okla., 1977-79, Inst. for Devel. of Indian Law, Washington, 1976-81; dir. Native Am. Coll. Prep. Ctr. Bemidji State U., Minn., 1993—. Editor-in-chief Am. Indian Law Rev., 1973; editor Okla. Law Rev., 1971-73; producer, dir.: (with Barbara P. Ettinger) "Aa-Niin" film, 1994; author book revs.; contbr. articles to profl. jours. Mem. bd. control Fayetteville (Ark.) City Hosp., 1977-81; cubmaster Boy Scouts Am., Norman, 1982-83, asst. scoutmaster, Stanford, 1981, scoutmaster, Norman, 1990-91, com. mem., den leader, 1988; softball coach Jr. High Girls League, Fayetteville, 1977-81; mem. adv. bd. Native Am. Prep. Sch., Santa Fe; pres., chmn. bd. Native Am. Coll. Prep. Ctr., Bemidji, Minn.; mem. exec. adv. bd. Aerospace Sci. and Tech. Edn. Ctr. of Okla., Okla. City Univ.; mem. legal edn. com., Okla. Bar Assn. U.S. Dept. Edn. fellow Stanford U. Med. Sch.; Charles Evans Hughes fellow Columbia U. Law Sch., 1976; Sequoyah fellow Assn. Am. Indian Affairs, 1975-76; Mellon fellow Harvard U. Sch. Edn., 1993; nominee Pulitzer prize for Disting. Commentary, 1997. Mem. ABA, Okla. Bar Assn., Fed. Bar Assn., Am. Trial Lawyers Assn., Okla. Trial Lawyers Assn., Okla. Indian Bar Assn., Oklahoma County Bar Assn., Assn. Am. Law Schs., N.G. Assn. U.S., Air Force Assn. (life), Res. Officers Assn. (life), Nat. Contract Mgmt. Assn., Soc. Logistics Engrs., Phi Alpha Delta, Phi Delta Epsilon, Phi Delta Kappa. Republican. Roman Catholic. Entertainment, Personal injury. Office: 2212 Westpark Dr Norman OK 73069-4012 E-mail: ojibuwve@oklahoma.net, robert.fairbanks@oc.edu

FAIRCHILD, THOMAS E. federal judge; b. Milw., Dec. 25, 1912; s. Edward Thomas and Helen (Edwards) F.; m. Eleanor E. Dahl, July 24, 1937; children: Edward, Susan, Jennifer, Andrew. Student, Princeton, 1931-33; A.B., Cornell U., 1934; LL.B., U. Wis., 1938. Bar: Wis. 1938. Practiced, Portage, Wis., 1938-41, Milw., 1945-48, 53-56; atty. OPA, Chgo., Milw., 1941-45; hearing commr. Chgo. Region, 1945; atty. gen. Wis., 1948-51; U.S. atty. for Western Dist. Wis., 1951-52; justice Supreme Ct. Wis., 1957-66, U.S. Ct. Appeals for 7th Circuit, 1966—. Dem. candidate Senator from Wis., 1950, 52. Mem. ABA, Wis. Bar Assn., Fed. Bar Assn., Milw. Bar Assn., 7th Cir. Bar Assn., Dane County Bar Assn., Am. Judicature Soc., Am. Law Inst., Phi Delta Phi, KP. Democrat. Mem. United Ch. of Christ. Office: US Courthouse Rm 2764 219 S Dearborn St Chicago IL 60604-1702

FAISS, ROBERT DEAN, lawyer; b. Centralia, Ill., Sept. 19, 1934; s. Wilbur and Theresa Ella (Watts) F.; m. Linda Louise Chambers, Mar. 30, 1991; children: Michael Dean Faiss, Marcy Faiss Ayres, Robert Mitchell Faiss, Philip Grant Faiss, Justin Cooper. BA in Journalism, Am. U., 1969, JD, 1972. Bar: Nev. 1972, D.C. 1972, U.S. Dist. Ct. Nev. 1973, U.S. Supreme Ct. 1977, U.S. Ct. Appeals (9th cir.) 1978. City editor Las Vegas (Nev.) Sun, 1957-59; pub. info. officer Nev. Dept. Employment Security, 1959-61; asst. exec. sec. Nev. Gaming Commn., Carson City, 1961-63; exec. asst. to gov. State of Nev., 1963-67; staff asst. U.S. Pres. Lyndon B. Johnson, White House, Washington, 1968-69; asst. to exec. dir. U.S. Travel Adminstrn., 1969-72; ptnr., chmn. adminstrv. law dept. Lionel, Sawyer & Collins, Las Vegas, 1973—. Mem. bank secrecy Act Adv. Group U.S. Treasury. Co-author: Legalized Gaming in Nevada, 1961, Nevada Gaming License Guide, 1988, Nevada Gaming Law, 1991, 95, 98. Recipient Bronze medal Dept. Commerce, 1972, Chris Schaller award We Can, Las Vegas, 1995, Lifetime Achievement award Nev. Gaming Attys. Assn., 1997; named One of 100 Most Influential Lawyers in Am. and premier U.S. gaming atty., Nat. Law Jour., 1997. Mem. ABA (chmn. gaming law com. 1985-86), Internat. Assn. Gaming Attys. (founding, pres. 1980), Nev. Gaming Attys. Administrative and regulatory, Legislative, Libel. Office: Lionel Sawyer & Collins 300 S 4th St Ste 1700 Las Vegas NV 89101-6053

FALBAUM, BERTRAM SEYMOUR, law educator, investigator; b. N.Y.C., July 28, 1934; s. Abraham and Shari (Greenfield) F.; m. Roberta Jessie Oberstone, Sept. 1, 1957; children: Vance Leonard, Stacy Lynn. AA, L.A. City Coll., 1961; BS with honors, Calif., State U.-L.A., 1962; postgrad. George Washington U., 1966-68; MPA, Syracuse U., 1972. Lic. pvt. investigator Va., Washington DC, Ariz. Agt., U.S. Customs Service, Los Angeles and Nogales, Ariz., 1961-66; instr. Treasury Law Enforcement Sch., Washington, 1966-69; spl. agt. U.S. Customs Service, Washington, 1969-73; dep. chief law enforcement U.S. Fish & Wildlife Service, Washington, 1973-78, spl. projects officer, Washington, 1978-79; sr. criminal investigator U.S. Dept. Justice (office spl. investigations), Washington, 1979-86; v.p. The Investigative Group, Inc., Washington, 1986-92; pres. Investigative Dynamics, Inc., Tucson, 1992—; adj. prof. Am. U., 1977-78, 1990-91; bd. dirs. Forensic Scis. Corp., adv. bd. Found. Genetic Medicine, Inc.; bd. dirs. Crime, 1988—; Author: Basic Investigative Photography, 1967; Marksmanship, 1969. Contbr. articles to profl. jours. Chmn. troop com. Nat. Capital Area council Boy Scouts Am., Centreville, Va., 1974-77. Served with USAF, 1953-57. Recipient commendations U.S. Customs Svc., U.S. Dept. Justice. Fellow Am. Bd. Forensic Examiners; mem. Am. Criminal Justice Assn. (life, chpt. pres. 1959-61), Assn. Fed. Investigators (bd. dirs. 1979-86 , cert. profl. investigator), Am. Judicature Soc., Fed. Criminal Investigators Assn., Am. Fedn. Police, Am. Law Enforcement Officers Assn., Internat. Assn. Chiefs of Police (life), Assn. Cert. Fraud Examiners (cert. fraud examiner), Am. Soc. Indsl. Security (cert. protection profl.), Nat. Dist. Attys. Assn., Coun. Internat. Investigators (cert.), World Assn. Detectives, Nat. Assn. Legal Investigators, Internat. Narcotic Enforcement Officers Assn., Soc. Competitive Intelligence Profls., So. Ariz. Counter Intelligence Corps Assn., Assn. of Former Intelligence Officers, Nat. Coun. Investigation and Security Svcs. (bd. dirs. 1998), Ariz. Assn. of Lic. Pvt. Investigators (bd. dirs. 1994-96, pres. 1997), Fed. Law Enforcement Officers Assn., Fraternal Order of Border Agents, Fraternal Order of Police, Nat. Assn. Chiefs of Police, Pvt. Investigators and Security Assn., Pvt. Investigators Assn. of Va., Calif. Assn. Licensed Investigations, World Investigators Network, Global Investigators Network, Internat. Assn. Law Enforcement Intelligence Analysts, Customs Special Agent Assn. (pres. 1994—), Vidocq Soc., Am. Coll. Forensic Examiners (life, cert.), INTELNET (mem. adv. bd. 1997—), Global Investigators Network, World Investigators Network, Sunrise Territory Village Homeowners Assn. (v.p. 1994, pres. 1995-98), Lambda Alpha Epsilon. Jewish. Clubs: Chantilly Country (v.p. for golf 1978, 80, 81, 83, bd. dirs. 1984, chmn. bd. 1985-89), La Paloma Country (golf com. and handicap chmn. 1994—). Home: 4921 N Fort Verde Trl Tucson AZ 85750-5903

FALCON, RAYMOND JESUS, JR. lawyer; b. N.Y.C., Nov. 17, 1953; s. Raymond J. and Lolin (Lopez) F.; m. Debra Mary Bomeisl, June 4, 1977; children: Victoria Marie, Mark Daniel. BA, Columbia U., 1975; JD, Yale U., 1978. Bar: N.Y. 1979, U.S. Dist. Ct. (so. and ea. dist.) N.Y. 1979, U.S. Ct. Appeals (D.C. and 2d cirs.) 1983, Fla. 1987, N.J. 1988, U.S. Dist. Ct. N.J. 1988. Assoc. Webster and Sheffield, N.Y.C., 1978-82; ptnr. Falcon and Hom, 1982-85; sr. atty. Degussa Corp., Ridgefield Park, N.J., 1985-88, v.p., sec., gen. counsel, 1989-94; pvt. practice Woodcliff Lake, 1994-95; prin. Falcon & Singer PC, 1995—. Contbr. articles to profl. jours. Dem. candidate Town Justice, Town of Rye, N.Y., 1983; Dem. jud. del., Westchester, N.Y., 1984-89. Mem. ABA, N.J. State Bar Assn., Fla. Bar Assn., Bergen County Bar Assn., Nat. Acad. Elder Law Attys., Park Ridge Rotary (bd. dirs. 1997-2001, officer 2001—), Columbia Alumni of Westchester County (v.p., bd. dirs. 1983-90, 97—). Contracts commercial, General corporate, Estate planning. Home: 582 Colonial Rd River Vale NJ 07675-6107 Office: 172 Broadway Woodcliff Lake NJ 07677-8077 also: 14 Harwood Ct Scarsdale NY 10583-4121 E-mail: rfalcon@falconsinger.com

FALEY, R(ICHARD) SCOTT, lawyer; b. Trenton, N.J., Aug. 18, 1947; s. Henry and Winifred (Goeke) F.; m. Josepha Ann Bartlett, Aug. 29, 1970; children: Scott Joseph, Zachary Lorin, Katherine Winifred. BA, Georgetown U., 1969, JD, 1972; LLM, George Washington U., 1975. Bar: D.C. 1973, U.S. Tax Ct. 1973, U.S. Dist. Ct. D.C. 1973, Mont. 1996. Assoc., ptnr. Danzansky, Dickey, Tydings, Quint & Gordon, Washington, 1972-78; prin. R. Scott Faley, P.C., 1978—. Bd. dir. Fed. Employees News Digest, Inc., Fairfax, Va., 1980—; bd. dir., pres. NCC Trout Unltd., 1985—; del. Mid Atlantic Coun. Trout Unltd., 1985—, v.p., 1992—; bd. dirs. Falling Springs Greenway, Inc., Chambersburg, Pa. Inst. for Safety Analysis, Inc., Rockville, Md., 1980-89. Contbr. articles to profl. jours. Mem. instnl. rev. com. Sibley Meml. Hosp., Washington, 1980—. Capt. USAF, 1974. Mem. ABA, FBA, Univ. Club, Boca Bay Pass Club, The Williams Club, Alpha Phi Omega, Phi Alpha Delta. Roman Catholic. Estate planning, Pension, profit-sharing, and employee benefits, Estate taxation. Home: 25 Primrose St Chevy Chase MD 20815-4228 Office: Ste 401 5100 Wisconsin Ave NW Washington DC 20016-4119 Fax: 202-363-7355. E-mail: faleyfish@aol.com

FALK, JAMES HARVEY, SR. lawyer; b. Tucson, Aug. 17, 1938; s. George W. and Elsie L. (Higgins) F.; m. Bobbie Jo Vest, July 8, 1960; children: James H. Jr., John Mansfield, Kathryn Colleen. BS, BA, U. Ariz., 1960, LLB, JD, U. Ariz., 1965. Bar: Ariz. 1965, U.S. Dist. Ct. Ariz. 1968, U.S. Dist. Ct. D.C. 1971, U.S. Dist. Ct. Md., 1990, U.S. Ct. Appeals (fed., 4th, 6th and 9th cirs.) 1981, U.S. Ct. Claims 1985, U.S. Supreme Ct. 1972. Counsel El Paso (Tex.) Natural Gas Co., 1965-66, The Anaconda Co., Tucson, 1967-68; ptnr. Waterfall Economidis, Falk & Caldwell, 1968-71; staff asst. to pres. Office of the Pres., Washington, 1971-73; assoc. dir. Domestic Coun., The White House, 1973-76; assoc. Touche Ross & Co., 1976-78; ptnr. Coffey, McGovern, Noel & Novogroski, 1978-81, Larkin, Noel & Falk, Washington, 1981-86, Thompson & Mitchell, Washington, 1986-87, McGovern, Noel & Falk, Ltd., Washington, 1987-90, Falk & Causey, Washington, 1991-92; prin. Falk Law Firm, 1993—. Rep. of U.S. Pres. to state and local govts., D.C., U.S. ters., 1974-75, U.S. Govs. Conf., 1974-75, U.S. Conf. Mayors, 1974-75, U.S. Del. Peoples Republic of China, 1974; asst. city prosecutor, city atty., Tucson, 1966-67; chmn. Tucson Transit Authority, 1971-72; apptd. D.C. Bar Jud. Evaluation Com., 1992-95, 95-98. Mem. ABA. Republican. Congregationalist. Federal civil litigation, General corporate, Government contracts and claims. Home: 9430 Cornwell Farm Rd Great Falls VA 22066-2702 Office: Falk Law Firm 2445 M St NW Washington DC 20037-1435

FALKIEWICZ, CHRISTINA L. lawyer; b. Houston, June 17, 1971; d. Ronald James and Edna Katherine Fraser; m. Adam M. Falkiewicz, Dec. 30, 1994. BA in English, St. Mary's U., 1993; JD, U. Tex., 1996. Bar: Tex. 1997. Assoc. Barker & Barker, Attys., San Antonio. Atty., mediator Bexar County Dispute Resolution Ctr., San Antonio, 1998—. Roman Catholic. Avocations: oil painting, creative writing. General practice, Probate, Real property.

FALKNER, WILLIAM CARROLL, lawyer; b. Baird, Tex., Mar. 26, 1954; s. Vernon Lee and Eunice Vera (Fore) F.; m. Linda May (Tilley), May 23, 1987; children: Heather Lynn, Holly Ann. BA in Govt., Tarleton State U., Stephenville, Tex., 1976; JD, Stetson U., Gulfport, Fla., 1984. Bar: Fla. 1984, U.S. Dist. Ct. (mid. dist.) Fla. 1985, U.S. Ct. Appeals (11th cir.) 1985. Asst. co. atty., sr. asst. co. atty. Pinellas County Atty.'s Office,

Clearwater, Fla., 1985—. Editor Res Ipsa, Clearwater, Fla., 1992-93; contbr. articles to profl. jours. Col. U.S. Army Res., 1976—. Mem. ABA, Fla. Bar Assoc., Clearwater Bar Assoc. Baptist. Avocations: reading, writing, sports, biblical studies. Office: Pinellas County Atty's Office 315 Court St Clearwater FL 33756-5165 E-mail: bfalkner@co.pinellas.fl.us

FALLEK, ANDREW MICHAEL, lawyer; b. Bklyn., Aug. 15, 1956; m. Elaine Friedman, June 4, 1984. BA, U. Pa., 1978; JD, Vanderbilt U., 1981. Bar: N.Y. 1982, U.S. Dist. Ct. (so. and ea. dists.) N.Y. 1985, U.S. Ct. Appeals (2d cir.) 1991, U.S. Ct. Appeals (D.C. cir.) 1993. Assoc. Belson, Connolly & Belson, N.Y.C., 1981-84; pvt. practice Bklyn., 1984—2001, N.Y.C., 2001—. Dir. Bklyn. Bar Found. Editor in-chief Bklyn. Barrister. Mem. N.Y. State Bar Assn., Bklyn. Bar Assn. (judiciary com., continuing legal edn. com., trustee), Def. Rsch. Inst. General civil litigation, Labor, Product liability. Office: One Whitehall St 16th Flr New York NY 10004

FALLER, RHODA DIANNE GROSSBERG, lawyer; b. N.Y.C., Dec. 21, 1946; d. Benjamin and Marion (Mediasky) Sragg; m. Stanley Grossberg, Apr. 12, 1973 (div. Oct. 1983); children: Joseph Seth, Daniel Benjamin; m. Bernard Martin Faller, May 31, 1987. BS, SUNY, Stony Brook, 1967; MS, Pace U., 1973; JD, N.Y. Law Sch., 1978. Bar: N.Y. 1979, N.J. 1979, U.S. Dist. Ct. N.J. 1979, Fla. 1980, U.S. Dist. Ct. (ea. and so. dists.) N.Y. 1982, Ky. 1996, U.S. Dist. Ct. (ea. dist.) Ky. 1997. Assoc. Fuchsberg & Fuchsberg, N.Y.C., 1982-91, DeBlasio & Alton, P.C., N.Y.C., 1991-95, Rhoda Grossberg Faller, Esq., Teaneck, 1995-96, Becker Law Office, Louisville, 1997-2000; pvt. practice, 2000—. Mem. Assn. Trial Lawyers Am., Nat. Assn. Women Bus. Owners, Ky. Acad. Trial Attys., Ky. Bar Assn., N.Y. State Trial Lawyers Assn., N.Y. State Bar Assn., Fla. Bar Assn., Louisville Bar Assn., Women Lawyers Assn. Democrat. Jewish. Personal injury. Home: 213 Mockingbird Gardens Dr Louisville KY 40207-5718 Office: Law Office of Rhoda Faller PLLC 500 W Jefferson St Louisville KY 40202-2823

FALLER, SUSAN GROGAN, lawyer; b. Cin., Mar. 1, 1950; d. William M. and Jane (Eagen) Grogan; m. Kenneth R. Faller, June 8, 1973; children: Susan Elisabeth, Maura Christine, Julie Kathleen. BA, U. Cin., 1972; JD, U. Mich., 1975. Bar: Ohio 1975, Ky. 1989, U.S. Dist. Ct. (so. dist.) Ohio 1975, U.S. Ct. Claims 1982, U.S. Ct. Appeals (6th cir.) 1982, U.S. Supreme Ct. 1982, U.S. Tax Ct. 1984, U.S. Dist. Ct. (ea. dist.) Ky., 1991. Assoc. Frost & Jacobs, Cin., 1975-82; ptnr. Frost & Jacobs LLP, 1982-2000; mem. Frost Brown Todd LLC, 2000—. Assoc. editor Mich. Law Rev., 1974-75; contbg. author: LDRC 50-State Survey of Media Libel and Privacy Law, 1982—. Bd. dirs. Summit Alumni Coun., Cin., 1983-85; trustee Newman Found., Cin., 1980-86, Cath. Social Svc., Cin., 1984-93, nominating com., 1985-88, sec., 1990; mem. Class XVII Leadership Cin., 1993-94; pres., mem. exec. com., def. counsel sect. Libel Def. Resource Ctr., 2001; parish coun. St. Monica-St. George Ch., 1996-2000. Recipient Career Women of Achievement award YWCA, 1990. Mem. ABA (co-editor newsletter media litigation 1993-97), FBA, Ky. Bar Assn., No. Ky. Bar Assn., No. Ky. Women's Bar Assn., Ohio Bar Assn. (chair media law com.), Cin. Bar Assn. (com. mem.), Potter Stewart Inn of Ct., U. Cin. Alumni Assn., Arts & Scis. Alumni Assn. (bd. govs. U. Cin. Coll. 1988—), U. Mich. Alumni Assn., Mortar Bd., Women Entrepreneurs (pres. 1988-89), Leland Yacht Club, Lawyers Club, Coll. Club, Clifton Meadows Club, Phi Beta Kappa, Theta Phi Alpha. Roman Catholic. Appellate, General civil litigation, Libel. Home: 5 Belsaw Pl Cincinnati OH 45220-1104 Office: Frost Jacobs Todd LLC 2200 PNC Ctr 201 E 5th St Cincinnati OH 45202-4182

FALLON, FRANCIS E(DWARD), lawyer, corporation executive; b. N.Y.C., Jan. 19, 1926; s. Francis Patrick and Mary Nora (Curry) F.; m. Adelaide Monica Haley, Dec. 26, 1953; children: Joseph F., Stephen F., Francis P., Donna Marie, Louise C., James C.. BA, St. John's U., 1950; LLB, Columbia U., 1953. Bar: N.Y. 1953. Atty. New Haven and Hartford R.R., N.Y.C., 1954-56, GAF Corp., N.Y.C., 1956-58, Curtiss-Wright Corp., Lyndhurst, N.J., 1958-61, corp. sec., 1961—. Mem. Planning Bd. Clarkstown, New City, N.Y., 1976-83. Served with USN, 1944-46, PTO. Mem. Am. Soc. Corp. Secs., Assn. Corp. Counsel N.J. (sec. 1983-84). Democrat. Roman Catholic. Avocation: golf. Home: 26 Concord Dr New City NY 10956-4037 Office: Curtiss-Wright Corp 1200 Wall St W Lyndhurst NJ 07071-3680

FALSGRAF, WILLIAM WENDELL, lawyer; b. Cleve., Nov. 10, 1933; s. Wendell A. and Catherine J. F.; children: Carl Douglas, Jeffrey Price, Catherine Louise. AB cum laude, Amherst Coll., 1955, LLD (hon.), 1986; JD, Case Western Res. U., 1958. Bar: Ohio 1958, U.S. Supreme Ct. 1972. Ptnr. Baker & Hostetler, Cleve., 1971—. Chmn. vis. com. Case Western Res. U. Law Sch., 1973-76; trustee Case Western Reserve U., 1978-90, chmn. bd. overseers, 1977-78; trustee Cleve. Health Mus., 1975-90, Hirom Coll., 1989—; chmn. bd. trustees Hiram Coll., 1990-99. Recipient Disting. Service award; named Outstanding Young Man of Year Cleve. Jr. C. of C., 1962. Fellow Am. Bar Found., Ohio Bar Found.; mem. ABA (chmn. young lawyers sect. 1966-67, mem. ho. of dels. 1967-68, 70—, bd. govs. 1971-75, pres. 1985-86, bd. dirs. Am. Bar Endowment 1974-84, 87-97), Am. Bar Ins. Plans Cons. (pres. 1991—), Ohio Bar Assn. (mem. coun. of dels. 1968-70), Cleve. Bar Assn. (trustee 1979-82), Amherst Alumni Assn. (pres. N.E. Ohio 1964), Union Club, The Country Club. General corporate, Environmental, Probate. Home: 616 North St Chagrin Falls OH 44022-2514 Office: Baker & Hostetler LLP 3200 National City Ctr Cleveland OH 44114-3485 E-mail: wfalsgraf@bakerlaw.com

FALSTROM, KENNETH EDWARD, lawyer; b. San Luis Obispo, Calif., June 25, 1946; s. William and Irene (Carroll) F.; children: Kenneth Todd, Tricia Karen. BA, UCLA, 1967; JD, U. Calif., Berkeley, 1970. Bar: Calif. 1971, U.S. Dist. Ct. (cen. dist.) Calif. 1977. Rsch. asst. Ctr. Study Dem. Insts., Santa Barbara, Calif., 1971; atty. Law Office Christopher Zayic, 1972; pvt. practice, 1973—. Bd. dirs. Hope Sch. Dist. Santa Barbara, 1972-80. General practice. Office: 1530 Chapala St Santa Barbara CA 93101-3017

FALVEY, PATRICK JOSEPH, lawyer; b. Yonkers, N.Y., June 29, 1927; s. Patrick J. Falvey and Nora Rowley Falvey; m. Eileen Ryan, June 29, 1963; 1 child, Patrick James. Student, Iona Coll., 1944-47; JD cum laude, St. John's U., Jamaica, N.Y., 1950. Bar: N.Y. 1951, U.S. Supreme Ct. 1972. Law asst. Port Authority of N.Y. and N.J., 1951, atty., 1951-65, chief condemnation and litigation, 1965-67, asst. gen. counsel, 1967-72, gen. counsel, 1972-91, gen. counsel, asst. exec. dir., 1979-87, dep. exec. dir., 1987-91, spl. counsel, 1991—. Advisor U.S. del. to UN Com. on Internat. Trade Law, U.S. State Dept. Pvt. Trade Law; advisor to U.S. del. UN diplomatic confs. on treaty on liability of ops. of transport terminals, N.Y. County Lawyers Assn., 1992—. With USN, 1945-46. Recipient Howard S. Cullman Disting. Svc. medal Port Authority of N.Y. and N.J., 1982, 91; Loftus award and Trustee's Honoree Iona Coll., 1982. Fellow Am. Bar Found.; mem. ABA (chmn. urban state and local govt. law sect. 1983-84, vice-chmn. model procurement code project 1979—, sect. del. 1987-90, Award for Lifetime Achievement in Local Law 2000), Assn. Bar City N.Y., N.Y. County Lawyers Assn., Internat. Assn. Ports and Harbors (hon., legal counsellors com., arbitrator, mediator trade and comml. matters, cons. transp. and trade studies). Address: PMB 81 Pondfield Rd Ste 338 Bronxville NY 10708-3818 E-mail: woodlawnfalvey@aol.com

FALVEY, W(ILLIAM) PATRICK, judge; b. Penn Yan, N.Y., Aug. 31, 1946; s. William Jennings and Thelma Rosetta (Hall) F.; m. Suzanne G. Christensen, Sept. 14, 1968; children: Scott P., Jennifer G. BA, Hobart Coll., 1968; JD, John Marshall Law Sch., 1975; postgrad., U. Nev., 1994. Bar: N.Y. 1976, U.S. Dist. Ct. (we. dist.) N.Y. 1979, U.S. Supreme Ct. 1984. Confidential law clerk N.Y. State Supreme Justice, Penn Yan, 1976-77; atty. Dept. Social Svcs. Yates County, 1976-77, pvt. practice, 1976-88, asst. pub. defender, 1977-80, acting dist. atty., 1980-81, dist. atty., 1981-88, judge surrogate and family ct., acting Supreme Ct. Justice, 1988—. Mem. alternatives to incarceration com. Yates County; mem. Yates County Custody and Visitation Mediation Bd., 1995—; adv. com. Finger Lakes Vol. Lawyer's Svc., Geneva, N.Y., 1989-91; chair bd. trustees Yates County Law Libr.; jud. adv. coun. Seventh Jud. Dist. Mem., sec. Yates County Republican Com., Penn Yan, 1977-81; mem. Yates County Coop. Farm & Craft Market, Penn Yan, 1976-79; bd. dirs. Lit. Vols., Penn Yan, 1979-83; mem., pres. Yates County Profl. & Health Adv. Com., Penn Yan, 1980-88. 1st lt. U.S. Army, 1969-71, Vietnam. Recipient N.Y. State Conspicuous Svc. Cross, Hon. Hugh R. Carey Gov. N.Y., 1979. Ctr. for Dispute Settlement's Disting. Jurist award, 1996. Mem. Am. Judges Assn., Am. Judicature Soc., Ontario/Yates Magistrates Assn., N.Y. Bar Assn., N.Y. State, County, Family and Surrogate Judges Assn., Yates County Bar Assn. (past pres.), VFW, Am. Legion (post comdr. 1981). Office: Yates County Cts 108 Court St Penn Yan NY 14527-1102 Fax: 315 536-5190

FALVO, MARK ANTHONY, lawyer; b. Boston, June 11, 1960; s. Carl Albert and Thelma Ann (Evans) F. BA in Polit. Sci., Pa. State U., 1982; JD, Ohio No. U., 1988. Bar: Pa. 1990, U.S. Supreme Ct. 1997; cert. solicitor County Treas.'s Office 1993. Account exec., pub. rels. staff, broadcaster Clearfield (Pa.) Broadcasters, Inc., 1975-82, 91; account exec., pub. rels. staff Ctr. Comm., Inc., State College, Pa., 1982-83, Gilcom Comm., Inc., Altoona, 1983-84, State College Broadcasters, Inc., 1984-85; pub. rels. mgr. dept. arts and comm. Ohio No. U., Ada, 1985-88; law clk., atty. Ct. Common Pleas of Clearfield County-Pa. 46th Jud. Dist., 1988-93; pvt. practice Clearfield, 1993—. Intern Hill, Morgan & Africa, Warren, Pa., summer 1986, Dist. Atty.'s Office Clearfield County, summer 1987; county coord. Clearfield County Statewide Mock Trial Competition, 1989-96; dist. coord. Pa. Statewide Mock Trial Competition, 1991-95, regional coord., 1993-94; dir. Boy Scouts of Am., Law and Law Enforcement Explorers Post, 1992-94; coord. Teen Ct. Program, Clearfield County, 1992—; law clk., atty. Ct. Common Pleas of Clearfield County, Pa., 46th Jud. Dist., 1998—; others. Campaign staff Congressman William F. Clinger, Jr., State College, 1984; bd. dirs., vice-chmn. ARC/Clearfield Chpt., 1989-95; bd. dirs., mem. Am. Cancer Soc./Clearfield County, 1989-93; bd. dirs., treas. Pa. State Alumni Assn., DuBois, 1989-95; vol. Clearfield Sr. Little League Baseball, 1975-82, Clearfield Little League Baseball, 1999—; mem. Clearfield County Crimestoppers, 1998. Recipient Spl. Recognition award Pa. Ho. of Reps., Harrisburg, 1988, Spl. Recognition award Pa. Senate, Harrisburg, 1988, Spl. Recognition award U.S. Congress, 1988, Law Mentoring Program award Conf. of County Bar Leaders, Harrisburg, 1991, Street Law Program award Conf. of County Bar Leaders, Harrisburg, 1991, Outstanding Young Alumni award Pa. State U., DuBois, 1992, Spl. Recognition award Teen Ct. Program Clearfield County, 1996. Mem. ABA (Pub. Svc. award 1990, 91, 98), Pa. Bar Assn., Clearfield County Bar Assn. (v.p. 1998—, rep. under 35 1989-98, chmn. young lawyers divsn. 1989-98, exec. com. 1989—, chmn. Law Day 1989, 90, 91, 92, 97, 98, mem. Law Day com. 1993, 94, 95, 96, 98), Sports, Art and Entertainment Law Com., The Forum on Entertainment and Sports Industries, Clearfield County Pa. Bar Inst. (chmn. CLE 1998—). Democrat. Methodist/Roman Catholic. Avocations: painting, tennis, golf, music, skiing. Communications, Entertainment, General practice. Home and Office: 7 Bigler Rd Clearfield PA 16830-1762

FANCHER, RICK, lawyer; b. Tucson, July 27, 1953; s. James Richard and Margaret Mae (Gum) F.; m. Cecelia Francis Baney, July 12, 1975; children: Jeffery Reed, Ashley Kristin. BA, Trinity U., 1975; JD, U. Tex., 1978. Bar: Tex. 1979, U.S. Dist. Ct. (we. and so. dists.) Tex. 1981, U.S. Ct. Appeals (5th cir.) 1981. Law clk. U.S. Dist. Ct., Corpus Christi, Tex., 1978-80; asst. atty. City of Corpus Christi, 1980; assoc. Gibbins, Burrow & Bratton, Austin, Tex., 1981, John L. Johnson, Corpus Christi, 1982-85; ptnr. Thornton, Summers, Biechlin, Dunham & Brown, 1985-99, Barker, Leon, Fancher & Matthys, Corpus Christi, 2000—. Mem. Tex. Bar Assn., Tex. Bd. Legal Specialization (cert. personal injury trial law). Democrat. Avocations: jogging, bicycling, hunting, golf. Insurance, Personal injury, Product liability. Home: 4502 Lake Bistineau Dr Corpus Christi TX 78413-5261 Office: Barker Leon Fancher & Matthys 1200 First City Tower II 555 N Carancahua St Corpus Christi TX 78478-0002 E-mail: rfancher@blfmlaw.com

FANGANELLO, JOSEPH MICHAEL, lawyer; b. Denver, Nov. 16, 1941; s. Anthony and Imogene (Baskett) F.; m. JoAnne Craig, Aug. 13, 1966; children: Joseph Duffy, Anne, Joan. BA, Regis Coll., 1963; JD, U. Colo., 1968. Bar: Colo. 1968. Law clk. Denver Dist. Ct., 1968-69; sole practice Denver, 1968-82; ptnr. Joseph M. Fanganello, P.C., 1982—. Officer, dir. numerous Colo. cos., 1968—. Bd. dirs., counsel Denver Opera Co., 1977-80. Mem. Denver Bar Assn., Colo. Bar Assn. General corporate, General practice, Real property. Office: Joseph M Fanganello PC 1650 Washington St Denver CO 80203-1407

FANONE, JOSEPH ANTHONY, lawyer; b. Sharon, Pa., Apr. 14, 1949; s. Anthony and Nancy Fanone; children: Michael, Kathleen, Peter. AB, Georgetown U., 1971, JD, 1974. Bar: Pa. 1974, D.C. 1980. Asst. atty. gen. Pa. Dept. of Justice, 1974-77; assoc. Squire, Sanders & Dempsey, Washington, 1977-81, Ballard, Spahr, Andrews & Ingersoll, Washington, 1981-83, ptnr., 1983-94, Piper & Marbury, Washington, 1994-95, Ballard, Spahr, Andrews & Ingersoll, Washington, 1996—. Mem. ABA. Finance. Office: Ballard Spahr Andrews & Ingersoll 601 13th St NW Ste 1000 Washington DC 20005-3807

FAPPIANO, TARA C. lawyer; b. New Haven, Mar. 9, 1973; d. Anthony Bernard and Christine (Shrude) Fappiano; m. Charles Turner Zegers, Oct. 3, 1998. BA, Fordham U., 1995; JD, St. John's Sch. Law, Jamaica, N.Y., 1998. Bar: N.J. 1998, N.Y. 1999, Conn. 1999; notary pub., N.Y. Paralegal Law Offices of Kevin J. Quaranta, Bronx, N.Y., 1993-95; law clk. Law Offices of Anthony D. Perri, N.Y.C., 1996-97; assoc. Verner Simon, LLP, 1997-00, Ohrenstein & Brown, LLP, N.Y.C., 2000—. Articles editor St. John's Jour. Legal Commentary, 1997-98. Mem. N.Y. State Bar Assn., N.Y. County Lawyers Assn. Roman Catholic. Avocations: travel, cooking, wine, reading. E-mail: tara.fappiano@oandb.com

FARBER, BERNARD JOHN, lawyer; b. London, Feb. 27, 1948; came to U.S., 1949; s. Solomon and Regina (Wachter) F.; m. Mary Lee Mueller, Feb. 14, 1987; children: Zachary, Anne. BS, U. of State of N.Y., Albany, 1978; JD, Ill. Inst. Tech., 1983. Bar: Ill. 1983, U.S. Dist. Ct. (no. dist.) Ill. 1983, U.S. Ct. Appeals (7th cir.) 1985, U.S. Tax Ct. 1986, U.S. Ct. Mil. Appeals 1986, U.S. Supreme Ct. 1987, U.S. Ct. Appeals (6th cir.) 1988, U.S. Ct. Appeals (4th cir.) 1989, U.S. Ct. Appeals (11th cir.) 1990. Instr. legal writing Chgo.-Kent Law Sch. Ill. Inst. Tech., 1983-85, computer rsch. atty., 1985-86, adj. prof. law, 1987—; legal editor Longman Fin. Svcs., Chgo., 1986-87; rsch. counsel publs. Ams. for Effective Law Enforcement, 1987—. Instr. Law Scholastic Aptitude Test; preparation course BAR/BRI, Chgo., 1984-88; v.p. Brickton Montessori Sch., Chgo., 1992-93; sec. bd. dirs., 1993-95. Mng. editor: Chgo.-Kent Law Rev., 1981-82, editor-in-chief, 1982-83; co-author: Protective Security Law, 1996; editor: (with others) Dow Jones-Irwin Handbook of Micro Computer Applications in Law, 1987, Illinois Law of Criminal Investigation, 1986; contbr. articles to profl. jours. Elected mem. Local Sch. Coun., Agassiz Elem. Sch., Chgo., 1996—, chmn., 1999—. Mem. ABA, Ill. State Bar Assn., Chgo. Bar Assn., Sci. Fiction Rsch. Assn., Mensa. Avocations: history, computers, science fiction. Civil rights, Criminal, General practice. Home and Office: 1126 W Wolfram St Rear Chicago IL 60657-4330 E-mail: bernfarber@aol.com, bernardjfarber@voyager.net

FARBER, DONALD CLIFFORD, lawyer, educator; b. Columbus, Nebr., Oct. 19, 1923; s. Charles and Sarah (Epstein) F.; m. Ann Eis, Dec. 28, 1947; children: Seth, Patricia. BS in Law, U. Nebr., 1948, JD, 1950. Bar: N.Y. 1950. Assoc. Newman, Hauser & Teitler, N.Y.C., 1950-58; pvt. practice, 1958-80; of counsel Conboy, Hewitt, O'Brien & Boardman, 1980-84; ptnr. Tanner Propp Fersko & Sterner, 1984-95, Farber & Rich LLP, N.Y.C., 1995-98; of counsel Hartman & Craven LLP, 1998—, Jacob Medinger & Finnegan LLP, N.Y.C., 1998—. Prof. law York U., Toronto, Ont., Can., 1970, 72-73; prof. theatre law Hofstra Law Sch., Hempstead, N.Y., 1974-75; prof. New Sch. for Social Rsch., N.Y.C., 1972—, Hunter Coll., 1978. Author: From Option to Opening, 1968, 4th edit., 1st Limelight edit., 1988, Producing on Broadway, 1969, Actor's Guide: What You Should Know About the Contracts You Sign, 1971, Producing, Financing and Distributing Film, 1973, 2d edit., 1991, The Amazing Story of the Fantasticks: America's Longest Running Play, 1991, Producing Theatre: A Comprehensive Legal and Business Guide, 1981, 3d Limelight edit., 1997, Common Sense Negotiation-The Art of Winning Gracefully, 1996; gen. editor (10 vol. series, author theatre vol.) Entertainment Industry Contracts-Negotiating and Drafting Guide. With AUS, 1941-44, ETO. Mem. Order of Coif. Home: 14 E 75th St New York NY 10021-2657 Office: Jacob Medinger & Finnegan LLP 1270 Ave of Americas New York NY 10020 Fax: (212) 332-7235 . E-mail: donaldc14@aol.com

FARBER, JOSEPH, lawyer; b. Bklyn., Jan. 31, 1944; s. David and Hanna (Beckhoff) F.; children: Leslie Farber Tayne, Dana, Douglas, Andrew; m. Ellen Morris Tiegerman, Aug. 19, 1993; children: Jeremy Tiegerman, Jonathan Tiegerman. BS, L.I. U., 1965; JD, Bklyn. Law Sch., 1986. Bar: N.Y. 1969, U.S. Ct. Appeals (2d cir.) 1969, U.S. Dist. Ct. (ea. and so. dists.) N.Y. 1970, U.S. Supreme Ct. 1972. Mng. atty. Queens Legal Svcs. Corp., N.Y., 1969-72, chmn. bd. dirs., 1975—; ptnr. Previte, Farber & Rosen PC, Queens, 1972—. Trustees panel U.S. Bankruptcy Ct. (ea. dist.) N.Y. Trustee ARC, Greater N.Y., 1997-98, Queens Mus. Art, 1997-99, pres.; dist. gov. Lions Club Internat., 1992-93. Named Man of Yr., Jackson Hts. Lions, 1979; recipient Disting. Alumni award L.I. U., 1997. Mem. Queens County Bar Assn., N.Y. State Bar Assn., Queens C. of C. (bd. dirs.), Elks. Contracts commercial, Family and matrimonial, General practice. Office: Previte Farber & Rosen 97-77 Queens Blvd Ste 1004 Rego Park NY 11374

FARBER, STEVEN GLENN, lawyer; b. Phila., July 20, 1946; s. Isadore Irving and Sylvia (Galperin) F.; children: Jamie, Daniel, Zoey, Avi. BBA, Temple U., 1968, JD, 1972. Bar: Pa. 1972, U.S. Dist. Ct. (ea. dist.) Pa. 1972, U.S. Dist. Ct. Appeals (3d cir.) 1972, N.Mex. 1975, U.S. Dist. Ct. N.Mex. 1975, U.S. Ct. Appeals (10th cir.) 1979, U.S. Supreme Ct. 1980. Asst. defender Pub. Defender Assn. Phila., 1972-74; acting dist. pub. defender State of N.Mex., Santa Fe, 1975-76, asst. atty. gen., 1976-78; pvt. practice, 1978—. Mem. N.Mex. Bd. Legal Specialization, 1986-90, chmn., 1991-93. Elected city councilor City of Santa Fe, 1992-96, mem. Santa Fe Mcpl. Home Rule Charter Commn., 1997; bd. dirs. Ptnrs. in Edn., 1997—, Temple Beth Shalom, 1997—, v.p., 2000-01; bd. dirs. Santa Fe County United Way, 1998—. Mem. Nat. Assn. Criminal Def. Lawyers (vice-chmn. continuing legal edn. com. 1990-91), N.Mex. Lawyers Guild (pres. 1980-81), N.Mex. State Bar Assn. (bd. dirs. criminal law sect. 1980-83, chmn. 1981-82), N.Mex. Criminal Def. Lawyers Assn. (bd. dirs. 1991, treas. 1996), First Jud. Dist. Criminal Def. Lawyers Assn. (sec. 1999). Democrat. Jewish. Civil rights, Criminal, Personal injury. Office: PO Box 2473 306 Catron St Santa Fe NM 87504-2473 E-mail: sgfsaf@aol.com

FARICY, JOHN HARTNETT, JR. lawyer; b. Augsburg, Germany, Nov. 5, 1955; came to U.S., 1956; s. John Hartnett and Mary Helen Sarah (Bowe) F. BA, Tulane U., 1977; JD, William Mitchell Coll. Law, St. Paul, 1982. Bar: Minn. 1982, U.S. Dist. Ct. Minn. 1983, U.S. Ct. Appeals (2d cir.) 1987, U.S. Supreme Ct. 1988. Ptnr. Faricy & Roen, P.A., Mpls., 1996—. Mem. Univ. Club of St. Paul. General civil litigation, Insurance, Toxic tort. Office: Faricy & Roen PA 150 S 5th St Minneapolis MN 55402-4200

FARINA, JOHN, lawyer; b. Rockville Center, N.Y., Oct. 20, 1959; s. Joseph P. Farina and Marilyn A. Echkoff; m. Julia Pressly, May 30, 1987; children: Matthew, Timothy, Nicholas. BA, Villanova U., 1981; JD, Suffolk U., 1985. Bar: Mass. 1985, Fla. 1986. Law clk. U.S. Ct. Appeals (4th dist.), West Palm Beach, Fla., 1985-86; assoc. Winthrop Stimson Putnam & Roberts, Palm Beach, 1986-90, Edwards & Angell, Palm Beach, 1990-94; ptnr. Boyes & Farina, West Palm Beach, 1994—. Mem. Fla. Probate Rules Com., Fla. Bar Greivance Com., 1998—. Mem. Palm Beach County Bar Assn. Avocations: trap and skeet shooting, running, tennis. State civil litigation, Probate. Home: 131 Thornton Dr Palm Beach Gardens FL 33418-8089 Office: Boyes & Farina PA 1601 Forum Pl Ste 900 West Palm Beach FL 33401-8105

FARLEY, BARBARA L. lawyer; b. Abington, Pa., Nov. 13, 1949; d. Vincent Lanza Jr. and Noreen Marie Cathcart; m. David Allen Farley, July 8, 1972. BS in Fin. and Acctg., Drexel U., 1970; JD, Rutgers U., 1973; LLM in Taxation, Villanova U., 1988. Bar: N.J. 1974, Pa. 1974, U.S. Tax Ct. 1975. Pres. Barbara Lanza Farley, A Profl. Corp., Phila., Haddonfield, N.J., 1975—. Contracts commercial, Estate planning, Probate. Office: 325 Chestnut St Ste 915 Philadelphia PA 19106-2609 Also: 13 Wilkins Avenue Haddonfield NJ 08033

FARLEY, BARBARA SUZANNE, lawyer; b. Salt Lake City, Dec. 13, 1949; d. Ross Edward Farley and Barbara Ann (Edwards) Farley Swanson; m. Arthur Hoffman Ferris, Apr. 9, 1982 (div. 1995); children: Barbara Whitney, Taylor Edwards; m. Michael L. Levine, Aug. 7, 1999. BA with honors, Mills Coll., 1972; JD, U. Calif.-Hastings, San Francisco, 1976. Bar: Calif. 1976. Extern law clk. to justice Calif. Supreme Ct., San Francisco, 1975; assoc. Pillsbury, Madison & Sutro, 1976-78, Bronson, Bronson & McKinnon, San Francisco, 1978-80, Goldstein & Phillips, San Francisco, 1980-84; ptnr., head litigation Rosen, Wachtell & Gilbert, 1984-89; of counsel Lempres & Wulfsberg, Oakkland, Calif., 1989-99; pvt. practice, 2000—. Arbitrator U.S. Dist. Ct. (no. dist.) Calif., San Francisco, 1981—, Calif. Superior Ct., San Francisco, 1984-89; judge pro tem San Francisco Mcpl. Ct., 1983—; probation monitor Calif. State Bar, 1990-97; spkr. Nat. Bus. Inst. Estate Adminstrn. 2000, Lorman Edn. Svcs. Tax Exempt Orgns. Contbg. author Calif. Continuing Edn. of the Bar, Nat. Bus. Inst., Lorman Edn. Svcs.; mng. editor Hastings Coll. of Law-U. Calif.-San Francisco Constl. Law Quar., 1975-76; civil litigation reporter. Mills Coll. scholar, 1970-72, U. Calif.-Hastings, San Francisco scholar, 1973-76. Mem. ATLA, San Francisco Bar Assn., Calif. Trial Lawyers Assn., San Francisco Trial Lawyers Assn., Alameda Bar Assn. General civil litigation, Probate.

FARLEY, JAN EDWIN, lawyer; b. Bartlesville, Okla., Dec. 4, 1948; s. Earl Franklin Farley and Martha Lynn Crisp; m. Sybil Anne Bova, Aug. 3, 1974; children: Elizabeth Anne, Christopher George. BA magna cum laude, Midwestern U., Wichita Falls, Tex., 1971; cert. Inst. Advanced Internat. Studies, U. Paris, 1973; JD with honors, U. Tex., 1975. Bar: Tex. 1975. Assoc. Baker & Botts, Houston, 1975-81; asst. sec., asst. gen. counsel Weatherford Internat. Inc., Houston, 1981-85 ; asst. gen. counsel ARA Services, Inc., Houston, 1986-87, v.p., gen. counsel health and edn. svcs. sector, 1987—; lectr. in internat. comml. trans. U. Houston Law Sch., 1976. Sec. Houston-Nice Sister City Assn., 1977-78. Rotary Found. fellow U. Paris, 1972-73. Mem. ABA, Tex. Bar Assn., Houston Bar Assn. (treas. internat. law sect. 1981, exec. council 1982-85, chmn.-elect 1985-86,

chmn. 1986-87), Petroleum Equipment Suppliers Assn. (corp. counsel com., steering com. 1983-85), U. Tex. Internat. Law Jour. Alumni Assn. (pres. 1980-81), Houston Athletic Club. Presbyterian. General civil litigation, General corporate, Health. Home: 2927 Deer Creek Dr Sugar Land TX 77478-4267 Office: ARA Services Inc 10205 Westheimer Rd # 1142 Houston TX 77042-3115

FARLEY, JOHN JOSEPH, III, federal judge; b. Hackensack, N.J., July 30, 1942; s. John Joseph and Patricia (Earle) F.; m. Kathleen Mary Wells, June 27, 1970; children: Maura, Brendan, Thomas, Caitlin. AB in Econs., Holy Cross Coll., 1964; MBA, Columbia, 1966; JD cum laude, Hofstra U., 1973. Bar: N.Y. 1974, D.C. 1975, U.S. Supreme Ct. 1977. Trial atty. torts sect. civil div. U.S. Dept. Justice, Washington, 1973-78, asst. dir. torts br. civil div., 1978-80, dir. torts br. civil div., 1980-89; judge U.S. Ct. of Appeals for Vets. Claims, 1989—. Mem. faculty OPM Exec. Seminar Ctrs., Denver, 1980—; lectr. Atty. Gen's. Advocacy Inst., Washington, 1976-89, FBI Acad., Quantico, Va., 1978-88. Editor-in-chief Hofstra Law Rev., 1971-73; contbr. articles to profl. jours. Vice-chmn. bd. dirs. Amputee Coalition of Am., 1997—. Served to capt. U.S. Army, 1966-70, Vietnam. Decorated Bronze Star with V device and 3 oak leaf clusters, Purple Heart with oak leaf cluster; recipient Sr. Exec. Service Spl. Achievement award U.S. Dept. Justice, 1984, Civil Div. Spl award U.S. Dept. Justice, 1980; Samuel Bronfman fellow, 1964-65, Dean's award for Disting. Hofstra Law Sch. Alumni, 1995, Disting. Alumni medal Hofstra U. Sch. of Law, 1986; inducted into Massapequa H.S. Hall of Fame, 1999. Mem. Fed. Bar Assn. (1st chmn. vets. law sec. 1990-91). Roman Catholic. Avocations: skiing, tennis, bicycling, reading. Office: US Court Of Appeals for Vets Claims 625 Indiana Ave NW Ste 900 Washington DC 20004-2917

FARLEY, THOMAS T. lawyer; b. Pueblo, Colo., Nov. 10, 1934; s. John Baron and Mary (Tancred) F.; m. Kathleen Maybelle Murphy, May 14, 1960; children: John, Michael, Kelly, Anne. BS, U. Santa Clara, 1956; LLB, U. Colo., 1959. Bar: Colo. 1959, U.S. Dist. Ct. Colo. 1959, U.S. Ct. Appeals (10th cir.) 1988. Dep. dist. atty. County of Pueblo, 1960-62; pvt. practice Pueblo, 1963-69; ptnr. Phelps, Fonda & Hays, 1970-75, Petersen & Fonda, P.C., Pueblo, 1975—. Bd. dirs. Pub. Svc. Co. Colo., Denver, Wells Fargo Pueblo, Wells Fargo Sunset, Health Net, Inc., Colo. Pub. Radio. Minority leader Colo. Ho. of Reps., 1967-75; chmn. Colo. Wildlife Commn., 1975-79, Colo. Bd. Agr., 1979-87; bd. regents Santa Clara U., 1987—; commr. Colo. State Fair; trustee Cath. Found. Diocese of Pueblo, Great Outdoors Colo. Trust Fund. Recipient Disting. Svc. award U. So. Colo., 1987, 93, Bd. of Regents, U. Colo., 1993. Mem. ABA, Colo. Bar Assn., Pueblo C. of C. (bd. dirs. 1991-93), Rotary. Democrat. Roman Catholic. Administrative and regulatory, Education and schools, Health. Office: Petersen & Fonda PC 215 W 2d St Pueblo CO 81003-3251

FARMER, CORNELIA GRIFFIN, lawyer, consultant, hearings official; b. N.Y.C., Mar. 3, 1945; d. John Bastin and Elizabeth (McCue) Griffin; m. William Paul Farmer, Jan. 8, 1972; children: Suzanne Elizabeth, John Paul. BA, Mt. Holyoke Coll., 1967; M in Regional Planning, Cornell U., 1970; JD, Marquette U., 1978. Bar: Wis. 1978, Pa. 1981, Minn. 1996, Oreg. 1999. Planner Frederick P. Clark Assoc., Rye, N.Y., 1970-71, Tri State Regional Planning Com., N.Y.C., 1971-72, State of Wis. and City of Milw., 1973-75; assoc. Friebert & Finerty, Milw., 1978-80, Baskin & Sears, Pitts., 1981-82; adj. faculty U. Pitts., 1986-94; jud. law clk. Commonwealth Pa., Pitts., 1992-95; sole practice Mpls., 1996-99; staff atty., hearings ofcl. Lane Coun. Govts., Eugene, Oreg., 1999—. Cons. County of Allegheny, Pitts., 1983; mem., vice chmn. loan monitoring com. Pitts. Countywide Corp., 1981-87; child adv. Allegheny County Pro Bono Program, Pitts., 1986-92; mediator Dispute Resolution Ctr., St. Paul, 1998-99; Lane Coun. Govts., Eugene, Oreg., 1999-2001. Book rev., referee books, articles. Vol. polit. campaigns, Pitts. and Mpls., 1972-96; bd. dirs., trustee, v.p. PTA Falk Lab. Sch. U. Pitts., 1987-89; ct. monitor abuse cases WATCH, Mpls., 1996-99; pres. Class of 1967 Mt. Holyoke Coll., 1992-97, reunion co-chair, 1987, 2000—; vol. SMART reading program, Eugene, Oreg. Mem. ABA, Silver Bay Assn. Coun., Mt. Holyoke Coll. Alumnae Assn. (alumnae vol., officer). Mt. Holyoke Club Pitts. (pres., treas.). Home: # 148 655 Goodpasture Island Rd Eugene OR 97401

FARMER, JOHN J. state attorney general, prosecutor; b. June 24, 1957; m. Beth Gates. BA, Georgetown U., 1979, JD, 1986. Law clk. hon. Alan B. Handler N.J. Supreme Ct. Justice; assoc. Riker, Danzig, Scherer, Hyland and Perretti, Morristown, 1988-90; asst. U.S. atty. Dist. N.J., 1990-94; dep. chief counsel, asst. counsel to the Gov.; chief counsel, chief law enforcement officer State N.J., Trenton, 1997-99, atty. gen., 1999—. Adj. prof. law Seton Hall U. Law Sch.; chmn. Juvenile Justice Commn. Mem. Nat. Assn. Attys. Gen. (co-chair health care fraud, abuse and adv. com.). Office: Office Atty Gen Hughes Justice Complex PO Box 80 Trenton NJ 08625-0080*

FARNHAM, CLAYTON HENSON, lawyer; b. New Brunswick, N.J., Aug. 18, 1938; s. Richard Bayles and Naomi Shropshire (Henson) F.; m. Katharine Gross, Sept. 16, 1967; children: Julia Kernan, Richard Bayles II. BA, U. of the South, 1961; LLB, U. Ga., 1967. Bar: Ga. 1968, U.S. Dist. Ct. (no., so. and mid. dists.) Ga. 1968, U.S. Supreme Ct. 1978, U.S. Dist. Ct. (no. dist.) Miss. 1978, U.S. Ct. Appeals (5th. cir., 11th cir.) 1968, (4th cir.) 1980, U.S. Ct. Appeals (8th cir.) 1992. Law clk. to judge U.S. Dist. Ct., Atlanta, 1967-69; from assoc., to ptnr. Swift, Currie, McGhee & Hiers, 1969-82; ptnr. Drew, Eckl & Farnham, 1982—. Contbr. articles to profl. jours. Lt. (j.g.) USNR, 1961-64. Mem. ABA (coun. TIPS sect. 1989-92), Internat. Assn. Def. Counsel (com. chmn. 1987-89), Ansley Golf Club, Lawyer's Club Atlanta, Old War Horse Lawyer's Club. Federal civil litigation, State civil litigation, Insurance. Home: 30 Inman Cir NE Atlanta GA 30309 Office: Drew Eckl & Farnham 800 W Peachtree St NW PO Box 7600 Atlanta GA 30357 E-mail: cfarnham@deflaw.com

FARNHAM, DAVID ALEXANDER, lawyer, banker; b. Washington, Sept. 7, 1946; s. Waller and Leslie (Thompson) F. BA, Yale U., 1969; JD, Columbia U., 1975. Bar: Md. 1977, Va. 1981, U.S. Dist. Ct. Md. 1979, U.S. Dist. Ct. (we. dist.) Va. 1981, U.S. Ct. Appeals (4th cir.) 1981. Asst. counsel Bankers Trust Co., N.Y.C., 1975-76; assoc. Weinberg & Green, Balt., 1976-80; legal compliance officer Dominion Bankshares Corp., Roanoke, Va., 1980-82, v.p., corp. counsel, 1983-89, sr. v.p. corp. counsel, 1989—. Author: (with Earl E. McGuire, Jr.) A Banker's Guide to IRAs, 1982. With U.S. Army, 1969-72. Mem. ABA, Md. Bar Assn., Va. State Bar, Roanoke City Bar Assn. Episcopalian. Club: Yale (N.Y.C.); Jefferson (Roanoke). Bankruptcy, Contracts commercial, General corporate. Home: PO Box 8682 Roanoke VA 24014-0682 Office: Dominion Bankshares Corp 10 S Jefferson St Roanoke VA 24011-1331

FARNSWORTH, E(DWARD) ALLAN, lawyer, educator; b. Providence, June 30, 1928; s. Harrison Edward and Gertrude (Romig) F.; m. Patricia Ann Nordstrom, May 30, 1952; children: Jeanne Scott, Karen Ladd, Edward Allan (dec.), Pamela Ann. BS, U. Mich., 1948; MA, Yale U., 1949; JD (Ordronaux prize 1952), Columbia U., 1952; LLD (hon.), Dickenson Law Sch., 1988; Docteur en Droit (hon.), U. Paris, 1988, U. Louvain, 1989. Bar: D.C 1952, N.Y. 1956. Mem. faculty Columbia U., N.Y.C., 1954—, prof. law, 1959—, Alfred McCormack prof. law, 1970—. Vis. prof. U. Istanbul, U. Dakar, 1964, U. Paris, 1974-75, 90, 93, Harvard Law S ch., 1970-71, Stetson Coll. Law, 1991, 94, U. Mich., 1994; mem. faculty Salzburg Seminar Am. Law, 1963, Columbia-Leyden-Amsterdam program on Am. law, 1964, 69, 73, 85, San Diego Inst. Internat. and Comparative Law, Paris, 1982, 94, Tulane Summer Inst., Paris, 1995, 98, 99, 00, Rhodes, 1996, China Ctr. for Am. Law Study, Beijing, 1986; dir. orientation program on Am. law Assn. Am. Law Schs., 1965-68; U.S. rep. UN Commn. on Internat. Trade Law, 1970-81; reporter Restatement of Contracts 2nd, 1971-80; cons. N.Y. State Law Revision Commn., 1956, 58, 59, 61, P.R. comml. code revision, 1988-91; mem. coms. validity and agy. internat. sales contracts Internat. Inst. Unification Pvt. Law, Rome, 1966-72, mem. governing coun., 1978-98; mem. adv. com. on pvt. internat. law Sec. of State, 1985-89; spl. counsel city reorgn. N.Y.C. Coun., 1966-68; U.S. del. Vienna Conf. on Internat. Sales Law, 1980, Bucharest and Geneva Conf. on Internat. Agy., 1979, 83. Author: Changing Your Mind: The Law of Regretted Decisions, 1998, An Introduction to the Legal System of the United States, 3d edit., 1993; (with J. Honnold, S. Harris, C. Mooney, and C. Reitz) Cases and Materials on Commercial Law, 5th edit., 1993; (with W.F. Young and C. Sanger) Cases and Materials on Contracts, 6th edit., 2001, Cases and Materials on Negotiable Instruments, 4th edit., 1993, Treatise on Contracts, 1982, 3d edit., 1999; (with V. Mozolin) Contract Law in the USSR and the United States, 1987, Farnsworth on Contracts, 3 vols., 1990, 2nd edit., 1998, United States Contract Law, 1992, 2d revised edit, 1999. Capt. USAAF, 1952-54. Fellow British Acad.; mem. ABA (Theberge award for pvt. internat. law 1996), Am. Philos. Soc., Am. Law Inst., Assn. of Bar of City of N.Y. (chmn. com. on fgn. and comparative law 1967-70, chmn. spl. com. on products liability 1979-82), Phi Beta Kappa, Phi Delta Phi. Unitarian. Home: 201 Lincoln St Englewood NJ 07631-3158 Office: Columbia U 435 W 116th St New York NY 10027-7201

FARNSWORTH, T BROOKE, lawyer; b. Grand Rapids, Mich., Mar. 16, 1945; s. George Llelwyn and Gladys Fern (Kennedy) F.; children: Leslie Erin, T. Brooke. BS in Bus., Ind. U., 1967; JD, Ind. U., Indpls., 1971. Bar: Tex. 1971, U.S. Dist. Ct. (so. dist.) Tex. 1972, U.S. Tax Ct. 1972, U.S. Ct. Appeals (5th cir.) 1977, U.S. Ct. Appeals D.C. Cir. 1977, U.S. Supreme Ct. 1978, U.S. Ct. Appeals (11th cir.) 1982, U.S. Dist. Ct. (we. dist.) Tex. 1988, U.S. Dist. Ct. (no. dist.) Tex. 1994. Adminstrv. asst. to treas. of State of Ind., Indpls., 1968-71; assoc. Butler, Binion, Rice, Cook & Knapp, Houston, 1971-74; counsel Damson Oil Corp., 1974-78; prin. Farnsworth & Assocs., 1978-90, Farnsworth & von Berg, Houston, 1990—. Contbr. articles on law to profl. jours. Mem. ABA, Fed. Bar Assn., State Bar Tex., Houston Bar Assn., Fed. Energy Bar Assn., Assn. Trial Lawyers Am., Tex. Trial Lawyers Assn., Comml. Law League Am., Olympic Club, Loch Lomond Golf Club, Champions Golf Club. Democrat. Christian. General civil litigation, Contracts commercial, Oil, gas, and mineral. Home: 6606 Oakland Hills Houston TX 77069 Office: Farnsworth and von Berg 333 N Sam Houston Pkwy E Ste 300 Houston TX 77060-2414

FARQUHAR, ROBERT MICHAEL, lawyer; b. Chelsea, Mass., Apr. 28, 1954; s. Robert Vociel and Helen Margaret (Stevens) F.; m. Carol Elizabeth Auch, Dec. 16, 1978; children: Stephanie Elizabeth, Andrew Michael. BS, So. Meth. U., 1977, JD, 1980. Bar: Tex. 1980, U.S. Dist. Ct. (no. and ea. dists.) Tex. 1980, U.S. Ct. Appeals (5th and 11th cirs.) 1980, U.S. Supreme Ct. 1990; cert. bus. bankruptcy law Tex. Bd. Legal Specialization. Assoc. Carter Jones MaGee Rudberg Moss & Mayes, Dallas, 1980-82; ptnr. Johnson & Cravens, 1982-88; shareholder Winstead Sechrest & Minick, P.C., 1988—. Mem. ABA, Dallas Bar Assn. Republican. Episcopalian. Avocations: bicycling, computers. Bankruptcy, Computer. Office: Winstead Sechrest Minick PC 1201 Elm St Ste 5400 Dallas TX 75270-2199

FARQUHAR, ROBERT NICHOLS, lawyer; b. Dayton, Ohio, Apr. 23, 1936; s. Robert Lawrence and Mary Frances (Nichols) F.; m. Elizabeth Lynn Bryan, Aug. 29, 1959 (div. 1971); children: Robert Nichols, Laura Ann; m. Carol A. Smith, Dec. 27, 1975. AB, Kenyon Coll., 1958; JD, Cornell U., 1961. Bar: Ohio 1961, U.S. Dist. Ct. (so. dist.) Ohio 1962, U.S. Ct. Appeals (6th cir.) 1966, U.S. Supreme Ct., 1978. Assoc. Altick & McDaniel, Dayton, 1961-69; ptnr. Gould, Bailey & Farquhar and predecessor firms, 1969-78, Brumbaugh, Corwin & Gould, Dayton, 1978-80, Altick & Corwin, Dayton, 1981—, pres., 1996—. Bd. dirs. Ohio Law Abstract Pub., Columbus; city atty., Centerville, Ohio, 1969—, Oakwood, Ohio, 1997—; sec., gen. counsel Miami Conservancy Dist., 1990—; bd. commrs. character and fitness Ohio Supreme Ct., 1988-94, 97—, chair, 2000—. Mem. Montgomery County Rep. Ctrl. Com, 1965-69, exec. com., 1968-69; bd. dirs. Centerville Hist. Soc., 1971-75, pres. 1973-74; trustee Montgomery County Legal Aid Soc., 1972-76; trustee Dayton Law Libr. Assn., 1972—, pres., 1980-86; mem. governing bd.äv. bdä Carillon Hist. Park, Dayton, chair, 1999-2001; mem. congressional screening com. U.S. Naval Acad., 1979-83. Mem. ABA (ho. of dels. 2001—), Ohio State Bar Assn. (chmn. legal ethics and profl. conduct com. 1982-86, exec. com. 1988-91, coun. of dels. 1988—), Dayton Bar Assn. Found. (pres. 1984-85), Dayton Bicycle Club, Dayton Lawyers Club, Delta Phi, Phi Delta Phi. Episcopalian. General practice, Land use and zoning (including planning). Home: 1731 Ladera Trl Dayton OH 45459-1403 Office: Altick & Corwin 1700 One Dayton Ctr 1 S Main St Dayton OH 45402-2024 E-mail: nikfar@aol.com, farquhar@altickcorwin.com

FARR, CHARLES SIMS, lawyer; b. Hewlett, N.Y., June 29, 1920; s. John Farr and Hazel (Zealy) Sims; m. Mary Randolph Rue, Dec. 21, 1946 (dec. Dec. 1980); children: Charles Sims, Virginia Farr Ramsey, Randolph Rue, John II; m. Muriel Tobin Byrnes, Oct. 13, 1990. Student, Princeton U., 1938-40; LLB, Columbia U., 1948. Bar: N.Y. 1949, Fla. 1984. Assoc. White & Case, N.Y.C., 1948-58, ptnr., 1959-88, of counsel, 1989-92, ret. Mem. bd. visitors Columbia U. Sch. Law. Contbr. articles to profl. publs. Lt. comdr. USN, 1941—45, ETO, MTO, PTO. Recipient medal Columbia U. Alumni Assn., 1977. Fellow Am. Coll. Probate Counsel (regent 1960-75), Am. Bar Found.; mem. Assn. of Bar of City of N.Y., Century Club (trustee 1992-95), Links Club, River Club, Pilgrims Club, Yeamen's Hall (S.C.). Democrat. Family and matrimonial, Probate. Home: PO Box 9455 900 Yeomans Hall Rd Charleston SC 29410 also: 200 E 66th St Apt E802 New York NY 10021-9192

FARR, G(ARDNER) NEIL, lawyer; b. L.A., Jan. 9, 1932; s. Gardner and Elsie M. (Schuster) F.; m. Lorna Jean, Oct. 26, 1957; children: Marshall Clay, Jennifer T., Thomas M. BA, U. Calif., Berkeley, 1957; JD, U. Calif., San Francisco, 1960. Bar: Calif. 1961, U.S. Supreme Ct. 1977; cert. specialist family law Calif. Bd. Specialization. Dep. dist. atty. Solano County, 1961-66; recreation commr. City of Fairfield, 1964-66; dep. dist. atty. Kern County, 1966-69; ptnr. Law Offices Young Wooldridge, Bakersfield, Calif., 1969—. Dir. Cen. Calif. Appellate Program, Inc.; judge protem Kern County Superior Ct. Chmn. Kern County Juvenile Justice Commn. With USNR, 1949-53. Mem. ABA, Calif. Bar Assn., Kern County Bar Assn. (pres. 1984, past pres. family law sect.). Family and matrimonial. Office: Young Wooldridge 1800 30th St Fl 4 Bakersfield CA 93301-1919 Fax: 805-327-1087

FARRAR, STANLEY F. lawyer; b. Santa Ana, Calif., 1943; BS, U. Calif., Berkeley, 1964, JD, 1967. Bar: Calif. 1968, N.Y. 1969. Mem. Sullivan & Cromwell, L.A. Mem. ABA (chmn. subcom. on bank holding cos. and nonbank activities banking law com. 1980-85, chmn. letters credit subcom. uniform comml. code com. 1982-88, sect. bus. law), State Bar Calif. (chmn. fin. instns. com. 1981-82). E-mila. Banking, Mergers and acquisitions, Securities. Office: Sullivan & Cromwell 1888 Century Park E Los Angeles CA 90067-1710 E-mail: farrars@sullcrom.com

FARRELL, CLIFFORD MICHAEL, lawyer; b. Gallup, N.Mex., Jan. 17, 1956; s. Francis and Carolyn Louise (Evans) F.; m. Mary E. Moore, Oct. 22, 1994. BA, Moravian Coll., 1978; JD, Capital U., 1982. Bar: Ohio 1982, Pa. 1983, U.S. Dist. Ct. (we. dist.) Pa. 1983, U.S. Ct. Appeals (3d cir.) 1983, U.S. Dist. Ct. (so. dist.) Ohio 1984, U.S. Ct. Appeals (6th cir.) 1984, U.S. Ct. Appeals (4th and 11th cirs.) 1985. Staff atty. HHS, Columbus, Ohio, 1982-83; mem. firm Robert N. Peirce, Jr., P.C., Pitts., 1983-84, Barkan & Neff Co., L.P.A., Columbus, 1984-88; ptnr. Farrell & Golian, 1988-91, Mauring & Farell, Columbus, 1991—. Mem. Ohio Mock Trial Program, N.W. Civic Assn. Mem. ABA, Assn. Trial Lawyers Am., Ohio Bar Assn., Ohio Acad. Trial Lawyers (chair social security sect. 2000—), Franklin County Trial Lawyers Assn., Pa. Bar Assn., Allegheny County Bar Assn., Columbus Bar Assn. Administrative and regulatory, State civil litigation, Personal injury. Home: 3199 Martin Rd Dublin OH 43017-1451

FARRELL, JOHN BRENDAN, lawyer; b. Gary, Ind., Jan. 26, 1946; s. Edward Lawrence and Margaret (Byrnes) F.; m. Sue Ann Schulte, June 8, 1974; children: Sean Edward, Brian Patrick, Joseph Brendan. BA Marquette U., 1968; JD Thomas F. Cooley Law Sch., Lansing, Mich., 1977. Bar: Mich. 1977, U.S. Dist. Ct. (we. dist.) Mich. 1977. Midwest div. claims supt. Foremost Ins. Co., Grand Rapids, 1974-77 (sr. litigation counsel 1986—), claims atty., 1978-81, claims counsel, 1981-84, asst. v.p. claims, 1984—, assoc. Seth Barsky, Southfield, 1977-78; ptnr. Hibbs, Welch & MacAlpine P.C., Grand Rapids. Sec., Kentwood Zoning Bd. Appeals, 1982—; mem. Kentwood Citizens Safety Commn., 1983; adviser Jr. Achievement, Grand Rapids, 1980. Mem. Def. Research Inst., Mich. Def. Trial lawyers Assn., Assn. Trial Lawyers Am., ABA, Fedn. Ins. Defense Counsel (assoc.), Macomb County Bar Assn. Republican. Roman Catholic. Club: Charlevoix. State civil litigation, Insurance, Personal injury. Home: 660 Ten Point Dr Rochester Hills MI 48309-2549 Office: Hibbs Welch & MacAlpine PC 71 North Ave Mount Clemens MI 48043-5543

FARRELL, MICHAEL W. state supreme court justice; Grad., U. Notre Dame; MA, Columbia U.; JD, Am. U. Law clerk to Assoc. Judge John P. Moore Md. Ct. Spl. Appeals, 1973; atty. criminal divsn. U.S. Dept. Justice; chief appellate divsn. Office U.S. Atty. D.C., 1982-89; assoc. judge Ct. Appeals, 1989—. Chmn. Eng. dept. Georgetown Prep. Sch. Office: Ct Appeals 500 Indiana Ave NW Rm 6000 Washington DC 20001-2131*

FARRELL, TERESA JOANNING, lawyer; b. L.A., Sept. 17, 1958; d. Harold T. and Helen Dolores Joanning; m. Michael P. Farrell, Oct. 18, 1986. BA, U. Calif., San Diego, 1980; JD, U. Calif., 1986. Bar: Calif. 1986, U.S. Dist. Ct. (ctrl. dist.) Calif. 1987. Assoc., spl. counsel Gibson, Dunn & Crutcher LLP, Irvine, Calif., 1986-98, ptnr., 1999—. Bd. dirs. Second Harvest Food Bank, Orange, Calif., 1993—, The Harvesters, Newport Beach, Calif., 1993—, Pretend City--The Children's Mus. of Orange County, Newport Beach, Calif., 2001—. Mem. Calif. State Bar Assn. (real property sect.), Internat. Coun. Shopping Ctrs. Finance, Landlord-tenant, Real property. Office: Gibson Dunn & Crutcher LLP 4 Park Plz Ste 1400 Irvine CA 92614-8557

FARRIS, JEROME, federal judge; b. Birmingham, Ala., Mar. 4, 1930; s. William J. and Elizabeth (White) F.; widower; 2 children. BS, Morehouse Coll., 1951, LLD, 1978; MSW, Atlanta U., 1955; JD, U. Wash., 1958. Bar: Wash. 1958. Mem. Weyer, Roderick, Schroeter and Sterne, Seattle, 1958-59; ptnr. Weyer, Schroeter, Sterne & Farris and successor firms, 1959-61, Schroeter & Farris, Seattle, 1961-63, Schroeter, Farris, Bangs & Horowitz, Seattle, 1963-65, Farris, Bangs & Horowitz, Seattle, 1965-69; judge Wash. State Ct. of Appeals, 1969-79, U.S. Ct. of Appeals (9th cir.), Seattle, 1979-95, sr. judge, 1995—. Lectr. U. Wash. Law Sch. and Sch. of Social Work, 1976— ; mem. faculty Nat. Coll. State Judiciary, U. Nev., 1973; adv. bd. Nat. Ctr. for State Cts. Appellate Justice Project, 1978-81; founder First Union Nat. Bank, Seattle, 1965, dir., 1965-69; mem. U.S. Supreme Ct. Jud. Fellows Commn., 1997—; mem. Jud. Conf. Com. on Internat. Jud. Rels., 1997-2000. Del. The White House Conf. on Children and Youth, 1970; mem. King County (Wash.) Youth Commn., 1969-70; vis. com. U. Wash. Sch. Social Work, 1977-90; mem. King County Mental Health-Mental Retardation Bd., 1967-69; past bd. dirs. Seattle United Way; mem. Tyee Bd. Advisers, U. Wash., 1984-88, bd. regents, 1985-97, pres., 1990-91; trustee U. Law Sch. Found., 1978-84, Morehouse Coll., 1999—; mem. vis. com. Harvard Law Sch., 1996—. With Signal Corps, U.S. Army, 1952-53. Recipient Disting. Service award Seattle Jaycees, 1965, Clayton Frost award, 1966 Fellow Am. Bar Found. (chair of fellows 2000); mem. ABA (exec. com. appellate judges conf. 1978-84, 87-88, chmn. conf. 1982-83, del. jud. adminstrn. coun. 1987-88, sr. lawyers divsn. coun. 1998—), Wash. Council on Crime and Delinquency (chmn. 1970-72), Am. Bar Found. (bd. dirs. 1987, exec. com. 1989-97), State-Fed. Jud. Council of State of Wash. (vice-chmn. 1977-78, chmn. 1983-87), Order of Coif (mem. law rev.), U. Wash. Law Sch. Office: US Ct Appeals 9th Cir 1030 US Courthouse 1010 5th Ave Seattle WA 98104-1181

FARUKI, CHARLES JOSEPH, lawyer; b. Bay Shore, N.Y., July 3, 1949; s. Mahmud Taji and Rita (Trownsell) F.; m. Nancy Louise Glock, June 5, 1971 (div. Oct. 1995); children: Brian Andrew, Jason Allen, Charles Joseph Jr.; m. Michelle F. Zalar, June 15, 1996. BA summa cum laude, U. Cin., 1971; JD cum laude, Ohio State U., 1973. Bar: Ohio 1974, U.S. Dist. Ct. (no. and so. dists.) Ohio 1975, U.S. Ct. Appeals (9th cir.) 1977, U.S. Tax Ct. 1977, U.S. Supreme Ct. 1977, U.S. Ct. Appeals (6th cir.) 1978, U.S. Dist. Ct. (no. dist.) Tex. 1979, U.S. Dist. Ct. (ea. dist.) Ky. 1982, U.S. Ct. Appeals (D.C. cir.) 1982, U.S. Ct. Customs and Patent Appeals 1982, U.S. Ct. Appeals (4th cir.) 1986, U.S. Ct. Appeals (2d cir.) 1989, U.S. Ct. Appeals (fed. cir.), 1991, U.S. Ct. Appeals (8th cir.) 1997. Assoc. Smith & Schnacke, Dayton, Ohio, 1974-78, ptnr., 1979-89; founder, mng. ptnr. Faruki Gilliam & Ireland, PLL, 1989—. Lectr. in field. Contbr. articles in field. Served to capt. U.S. Army Res., 1971-79. Fellow Am. Bar Found., Am. Coll. Trial Lawyers (complex litigation com. 1993-98); mem. ABA, Fed. Bar Assn. (officer and exec. com. Dayton chpt. 1988-93, pres. 1991-92), Ohio State Bar Assn. (bd. govs. Antitrust sect. 1992—), Dayton Bar Assn. (officer 1992-94, pres. 1994-95), Def. Rsch. Inst., Human Factors and Ergonomics Soc. (affiliate mem.), Fed. Cir. Bar Assn. Avocation: numismatics. Antitrust, Federal civil litigation, General civil litigation. Home: 300 Fairforest Cir Dayton OH 45419-1308 Office: Faruki Gilliam & Ireland PLL 500 Courthouse Plz SW Dayton OH 45402 E-mail: cfaruki@fgilaw.com

FASS, PETER MICHAEL, lawyer, educator; b. Bklyn., Apr. 11, 1937; s. Irving and Bess (Fordin) F.; m. Deborah K. Orshan, May 6, 1989; 1 child, Olivia Jae; children from previous marriage: Brian Samuel, Lyle Williams. BS in Econs. with honors, U. Pa., 1958; JD cum laude, Harvard U., 1961; LLM, NYU, 1964. Bar: N.Y. 1965; CPA. From assoc. to ptnr. Carro, Spanbock, Fass, Geller, Kaster & Cuiffo, N.Y.C., 1968-86; ptnr. Kaye, Scholer, Fierman, Hayes & Handler, 1988-95, Battle Fowler LLP, N.Y.C., 1995-2000, Proskauer Rose LLP, N.Y.C., 2000—. Adj. asst. prof. real estate NYU; lectr. Practising Law Inst., N.Y. Law Jour., Instl. mag., Ill. Inst. Continuing Legal Edn.; spl. cons. Calif. Commr. of Corps Real Estate Adv. Com.; mem. ad hoc com. Real Estate Securities and Syndication Inst., chmn. regulatory legis and taxation com., 1975-76; mem., dir. participant/real estate com. NASD, 1991-94. Co-author: Tax Advantaged Securities, 1977—, Real Estate Syndication Handbook, 1985-87, Tax Aspects of Real Estate Investments, 1988—, Blue Sky Practice Handbook, 1987—, Real Estate Investment Trusts Handbook, 1987—, S Corporation Handbook, 1985—, Tax Advantaged Securities Handbook, 1979—; contbr. articles to profl. jours. Recipient Haskins award for outstanding achievement in N.Y. State C.P.A.s exam., 1964 Mem. ABA (chmn. real estate investment com., real property, probate and trust sect.), N.Y. State Bar Assn., Am. Inst. CPA's, N.Y. State Soc. CPA's, Pi Lambda Phi, Beta Gamma Sigma, Beta Alpha Psi. Securities, Taxation, general, General corporate. Home: 115 Central Park W New York NY 10023-4153 Office: Proskauer Rose LLP 1585 Broadway New York NY 10036-8299 E-mail: p.fass@proskauer.com, reitman411@aol.com

FASSETT, STEPHANIE A. lawyer; b. Monte Vista, Colo., Feb. 28, 1968; d. Robert Charles Fassett and Karen Fassett Herbold. BS, U. Idaho, 1990, JD, 1994. Law clk. Twin Falls County, Twin Falls, Idaho, 1994-96; assoc. Benoit, Alexander, Sinclair, Harwood & High, 1996—. Cons. to various

orgns. on employment law issues, 1996—. Editor Idaho Law Rev., 1994; contbr. articles to profl. jours. Bd. dirs. United Way, Twin Falls, 1996-97. Mem. PEO, Order of DeMolay (adv. staff 1984—, Cross of Honor for Adult Leadership 1999). Office: Benoit Alexander et al 126 2d Ave N Twin Falls ID 83301

FATO, GILDO E. lawyer, chemical engineer; b. Chgo., Mar. 27, 1928; s. Frank and Mary Louise (Phillipi) F.; m. Marie A. Matz, Sept. 18, 1954; children: Barbara Ann, Debra R., Karen M. BS in Chem. Engring., Ill. Inst. Tech., 1950; JD, DePaul U., 1960; postgrad., John Marshall Law Sch., 1960-63. Sr. chemist, patent asst. Ditto, Inc., Chgo., 1950-61; patent counsel Fansteel Metall. Corp., North Chicago, Ill., 1961-64; divsn. patent counsel Abbott Labs., 1964-83; asst. patent counsel Am. Hosp. Supply Corp., Evanston, 1983-86; sr. counsel E.I. duPont de Nemours & Co., 1986-89; pvt. practice Libertyville, 1989—. Co-inventor transfer sheet. Served with U.S. Army, 1946-47, PTO. Mem. ABA, Ill. Bar Assn., Patent Law Assn.. Chgo., Toastmasters Bicycle Club (v.p., sec. 1977-80, Lake County, Ill.). Intellectual property, Patent, Trademark and copyright. Home and Office: 515 Ash St Libertyville IL 60048-2706

FAURI, ERIC JOSEPH, lawyer; b. Lansing, Mich., Feb. 16, 1942; s. Fedele Fauri and Iris M. Petersen; m. Sherrill Lynn Nurenberg, July 15, 1969; children— Lauren, Nadia, Kirk. B.A., U. Del., 1963; J.D. with distinction, U. Mich., 1966. Bar: Mich. 1967, U.S. Dist. Ct. (ea. dist.) Mich. 1967, U.S. Dist. Ct. (we. dist.) Mich. 1972, U.S. Ct. Appeals (6th cir.) 1974. Assoc. Dykema, Gossett, Spencer, Goodnow & Trigg, Detroit, 1966-71; Parmenter Forsythe, Rude et al, Muskegon, Mich., 1971-73; ptnr. Parmenter, Forsythe, Rude et al, Muskegon, 1973—; Parmenter O'Toole, 1992—. Served to capt. U.S. Army, 1967-68. Mem. ABA, State Bar Mich. Banking, Contracts commercial. Office: Parmenter O'Toole 175 W Apple Ave PO Box 786 Muskegon MI 49443-0786

FAUST, ANNE SONIA, lawyer; b. Aug. 27, 1936; d. Alfred and Geneva Dora (Barnett) F. BA, U. Hawaii, 1960; cert. in Pub. Affairs, Coro Found. Internship, 1961; JD, Harvard U., 1964. Bar: Hawaii, 1964. Dept. corp. counsel City and County of Honolulu, 1964-66; asst. rschr. Legis, Ref. Bur., Honolulu, 1966-69; assoc. counsel Legal Aid Soc., 1969-70; dep. atty. gen. State of Hawaii, 1970-72; atty., exec. officer Hawaii Pub. Employment Rels. Bd., 1972-80; 1st dep. corp. counsel County of Maui, Wailuku, Hawaii, 1980-81; chief antitrust div. Dep. Atty. Gen. State of Hawaii, Honolulu, 1981-86; chief regulatory Hawaiin Homelands Hawaii Housing Authority Div. Dept., Hawaii, 1986-95. Supervising dep. atty. gen., land and transp. divsn. Dept. Atty. Gn. State of Hawaii; ex-officio mem. Gov.'s Com. Status of Women, Hawaii, 1971-72; mem. Hawaii Bd. Bar Examiners, 1975-79. Mem. ABA (membership chmn. Hawaii 1965), Phi Beta Kappa, Phi Kappa Phi. Mem. Ch. of Christ. Club: Obedience Tng. of Hawaii (Honolulu) (treas. 1982-87). Home: 47-415 A Kapehe St Kaneohe HI 96744-4845 Office: Dept Atty Gen 465 S King St Honolulu HI 96813-2911

FAWELL, REED MARQUETTE, III, lawyer; b. Miami Beach, Fla., Nov. 29, 1944; s. Reed Marquette Jr. and Betsy Page (McLean) F.; m. Anna Catherine Ikenberry, Dec. 27, 1969; children— Reed Marquette IV, Henry Pendleton. B.A., U. Va., 1967; J.D., U. Md., 1970. Bar: D.C. 1970, Md. 1970. Assoc. firm Glassie, Pewett, Dudley, Beebe & Shanks, P.C., Washington, 1970-75, ptnr., 1975-85, pres., 1982-85, of counsel, 1985-88; lawyer, real estate developer Rouse & Assocs., McLean, Va., 1985— ; of counsel McGuire, Woods, Battle & Boothe, McLean, Va., 1989—; pres. The Pendleton Adv. Group Ltd. Ptnrship., McLean, 1989—. Contracts commercial, Construction, Real property. Home: 4429 Garrison St NW Washington DC 20016-4055

FAWSETT, PATRICIA COMBS, federal judge; b. 1943; BA, U. Fla., 1965, MAT, 1966, JD, 1973. Pvt. practice law Akerman, Senterfitt & Edison, Orlando, Fla., 1973-86; commr. 9th Cir. Jud. Nominating Commn, 1973-75, Greater Orlando Crime Prevention Assn., 1983-86; judge U.S. Dist. Ct. (mid. dist.) Fla., Orlando, 1986—. Trustee Legal Aid Soc., 1977-81, Loch Haven Art Ctr., Inc., Orlando, 1980-84, U. Fla. Law Sch., 2001—; hon. trustee Reago Spiritual Scholarship Found., 1999—; commr. Orlando Housing Authority, 1976-80, Winter Park (Fla.) Sidewalk Festival, 1973-75; bd. dirs. Greater Orlando Area C. of C., 1982-85. Mem. ABA (trial lawyers sect., real estate probate sect.), Am. Judicaturs Soc., Assn. Trial Lawyers Am., Fla. Bar Found. (bd. dirs. grants com.), Commn. on Access to Cts., Fla. Coun. Bar Assn. Pres.'s (pres., bd. dirs. 9th cir. grievance com.) Osceola County Bar Assn., Fla. Bar (bd. govs. 1983-86, budget com., disciplinary rev. com., integration rule and bylaws com., com. on access to legal system, bd. of cert., designation and advt., jud. adminstrn., selection and tenure com., jud. nominating procedures com., pub. rels. com., ann. meeting com., appellate rules com., spl. com. on judiciary-trial lawyer rels., chairperson midyr. conv. com., bd. dirs. trial lawyers sect.), Orange County Bar Assn. (exec. coun. 1977-83, pres. 1981-82), Order of Coif, Phi Beta Kappa. Office: US Dist Ct Federal Bldg 80 N Hughey Ave Ste 611 Orlando FL 32801-2231

FAY, PETER THORP, federal judge; b. Rochester, N.Y., Jan. 18, 1929; s. Lester Thorp and Jane (Baumler) F.; m. Claudia Pat Zimmerman, Oct. 1, 1958; children: Michael Thorp, William, Darcy. B.A., Rollins Coll., 1951, LL.D., 1971; J.D., U. Fla., 1956; LL.D., Biscayne Coll., 1975. Bar: Fla. 1956, U.S. Supreme Ct. 1961. Ptnr. firm Nichols, Gaither Green, Frates & Beckham, Miami, Fla., 1956-61, Frates, Fay, Floyd & Pearson (and predecessors), Miami, 1961-70; prof. Fla. Jr. Bar Practical Legal Inst., 1959-65; judge U.S. Dist. Ct. for So. Fla., Miami, 1970-76, U.S. Ct. Appeals (5th cir.), 1976-81, U.S. Ct. Appeals (11th cir.), 1981-94, sr. judge, 1994—; lectr. Fla. Bar Legal Inst., 1959—; faculty Fed. Jud. Center, Washington, 1974-94. Mem. Jud. Conf. Com. for Implementation Criminal Justice Act, 1974-82, Adv. Com. on Codes of Conduct, 1980-87, Adv. Com. on Appellate Rules, 1987-90; co-chmn. Nat. Jud. Coun. for State and Fed. Cts., 1990—. Mem. Orange Bowl Com., 1974—; dist. collector United Fund, 1957-70; mem. adminstrv. bd. St. Thomas U., 1970—; trustee U. Miami, Fla., 1989—; mem., supr. Ind. Counsel, 1994—. With USAF, 1951-53. Mem. Law Sci. Acad., Fla. Acad. Trial Attys., Am., Fla., Dade County, John Marshall (past pres.) bar assns., Fla. Council of 100, U. Fla. Alumni Assn. (dir.), Miami C. of C., Medico Legal Inst., Order of Coif, Phi Delta Phi (past pres.), Omicron Delta Kappa (past pres.), Pi Gamma Mu (past pres.), Phi Kappa Phi, Phi Delta Theta (past sec.) Republican. Roman Catholic. Clubs: Wildcat Cliffs (N.C.); Snapper Creek Lakes (Miami), Coral Oaks (Miami), Miami. Home: 99 NE 4th St Rm 1255 Miami FL 33132-2140*

FAYETTE, KATHLEEN OWENS, lawyer; b. N.Y.C., Feb. 28, 1939; d. Edward Francis and Margaret Grace (Quigley) Owens; m. Alan Gerard Fayette, June 15, 1963; children: Stephen, Suzanne, Christopher. AB, Marymount Coll., N.Y.C., 1960; JD, Pace U., White Plains, N.Y., 1979. Asst. MHLS atty. Appellate divsn. N.Y. State Supreme Ct., N.Y.C., 1979-82; instr. law Interboro Inst., 1983-84; ct. liaison Project Greenhope, N.Y.C., 1985-87; dir. alternative to incarceration N.W. Bronx Cmty. and Clergy Coalition, 1987-89; ct. liaison Children's Village, Dobbs Ferry, N.Y., 1989-91; pvt. practice, 1998—. Lectr., cons. on the legal rights of the mentally disabled; cons. alternative incarceration. Author: The Bar is Closed, 1986; columnist You and the Law, 1982-83. Cons., dir. Bishop-Browne Project, Fla., 1994—; pro bono child welfare advocate Guardian ad Litem Program, Fla., 1992—. Mem. ATLA, ABA, Fla. Bar Assn., Pace U. Sch. Law Alumni Assn., Marymount Coll. Alumni Assn. Roman Catholic. Avocations: curling, skeet shooting, scuba diving. Bankruptcy, Environmental, Family and matrimonial. Office: 1515 N Federal Hwy Ste 300 Boca Raton FL 33432-1994 Fax: 561-451-3035

FAZIO, PETER VICTOR, JR. lawyer; b. Chgo., Jan. 22, 1940; s. Peter Victor and Marie Rose (LaMantia) F.; m. Patti Ann Campbell, Jan. 3, 1966; children: Patti-Marie, Catherine, Peter. AB, Coll. of Holy Cross, Worcester, Mass., 1961; JD, U. Mich., 1964. Bar: Ill. 1964, U.S. Dist. Ct. (no. dist.) Ill. 1965, U.S. Ct. Appeals (7th cir.) 1972, U.S. Supreme Ct. 1977, D.C. 1981, U.S. Ct. Appeals (D.C. cir.) 1988, Ind. 1993. Assoc. Schiff, Hardin & Waite, Chgo., 1964-70, ptnr., 1970-82, 84-95, mng. ptnr., 1995—2000; exec. v.p. Internat. Capital Equipment, 1982-83, also bd. dirs., 1982-85, sec., 1982-87; exec. v.p., gen. counsel NiSource Inc., 2000—. Bd. dirs. Planmetrics Inc., Chgo., 1984-92, Chgo. Lawyers Commn. for Civil Rights Under Law, 1976-82, co-chmn., 1978-80; bd. dirs. Seton Health Corp. No. Ill., Chgo 1987-90, vice chmn., 1989-90. Trustee Barat Coll., Lake Forest, Ill., 1977-82; bd. dirs. St. Joseph Hosp., Chgo., 1990-95, mem. exec. adv. bd., 1984-89, chmn., 1986-89; vice chmn. bd. dirs. Cath. Health Ptnrs., 1995-99, chmn., 1999—; dir. exec. com. Ill. Coalition, 1994—, N.W. Ind. Forum, 1994-98. Mem. ABA (coun. 1991-94, chmn. sect. pub. utility, transp. and comm. law 2000-01), FBA, Ill. Bar Assn., Chgo. Bar Assn., Fed. Energy Bar Assn., Edison Electric Inst. (chmn. legal com. 1999-2001), Am. Gas Assn. (legal com.), Am. Soc. Corp. Secs., Met. Club, Econ. Club Chgo., Comml. Club Chgo. Contracts commercial, FERC practice, Public utilities. Office: Schiff Hardin & Waite 6600 Sears Tower 233 S Wacker Dr Chicago IL 60606-6473

FEAGLEY, MICHAEL ROWE, lawyer, educator; b. Exeter, N.H., Feb. 1, 1945; s. Walter Charles and Laura (Rowe) F. BA, Wesleyan U., 1967; JD, Harvard U., 1973. Bar: Mass., Ill., U.S. Dist. Ct. (no. dist.) Ill., U.S. Dist. Ct. (ctrl. dist.) Ill., U.S. Ct. Appeals (6th, 7th, 8th and 10th cirs.), U.S. Supreme Ct. Assoc. Mayer Brown & Platt, Chgo., 1973-79, ptnr., 1980—. Instr. Nat. Inst. Trial Advocacy, Chgo., 1977--, John Marshall Law Sch., Chgo., 1980-85. Served to 1st lt. U.S. Army, 1968-71, Vietnam. Fellow Am. Coll. Trial Lawyers; mem. ABA, Chgo. Coun. Lawyers, Chgo. Bar Assn., Union League Club (Chgo.). Federal civil litigation, General civil litigation, State civil litigation. Office: Mayer Brown & Platt 190 S La Salle St Ste 3100 Chicago IL 60603-3441

FEATHERSTONE, BRUCE ALAN, lawyer; b. Detroit, Mar. 2, 1953; s. Ronald A. and Lois R. (Bosshart) F.; children: Leigh Allison, Edward Alan. BA cum laude with distinction in Econs., Yale U., 1974; JD magna cum laude, U. Mich., 1977. Bar: Ill. 1977, Colo. 1983, U.S. Dist. Ct. (no. dist.) Ill. 1978, U.S. Dist. Ct. Colo. 1983, U.S. Ct. Appeals (5th cir.) 1980, U.S. Ct. Appeals (7th cir.) 1981, U.S. Ct. Appeals (10th cir.) 1983, U.S. Ct. Appeals (9th cir.) 1991, U.S. Ct. Appeals (fed. cir.), U.S. Supreme Ct. 1984. Assoc. Kirkland & Ellis, Denver, 1977-83, ptnr., 1983-96, Featherstone & Shea, LLP, Denver, 1996-99, Featherstone DeSisto LLP, Denver, 1999—. Articles editor U. Mich. Law Rev., 1976-77. Mem. ABA (litigation sect.), Assn. Trial Lawyers Am., Colo. Bar Assn., Colo. Trial Lawyers Assn., Colo. Def. Lawyers Assn., Denver Bar Assn., Order of Coif. Avocations: swimming, biking, running. Federal civil litigation, State civil litigation, Appellate. Home: 725 Saint Paul St Denver CO 80206-3912 also: PO Box 1467 Denver CO 80201-1467 Office: Featherstone DeSisto LLP 600-17th St Ste 2400 Denver CO 80202-5402 E-mail: bfeatherstone@featherstonelaw.com

FEAVEL, PATRICK MCGEE, lawyer, mediator; b. Appleton, Wis., Dec. 15, 1949; s. Norman William and Lillian Estelle (Bucklew) F.; m. Kathleen Sonoe Thompson, Feb. 11, 1989; 1 child, Justin Michael. AA, Long Beach City Coll., 1973; BA, Northeast La. U., 1978; JD with honors, Loyola U., 1982. Bar: Calif., U.S. Dist. Ct. (ctrl. dist.) Calif. 1983, U.S. Dist. Ct. (ea. dist.) Calif. 1988. Assoc. Law Offices of Ron Minkin, L.A., 1981-83, Long & Levitt, L.A., 1983-84, Parkinson, Wolf & Leo, Century City, Calif., 1984-85; ptnr. Dunnion Law Firm, Monterey, 1985-2000; pvt. practice Feavel Law Firm, Visalia, 2000—. Assoc. editor Internat. and Comparative Law Jour., 1981. Mem. bd. dirs. Transp. Agy. of Monterey County, 1994. Mem. Monterey County Bar Assn., Velo Club Monterey, Phi Beta Kappa. Republican. Roman Catholic. Avocations: competitive bicyclist (U.S. Cycling Fedn.), debate. State civil litigation, Insurance, Personal injury. Home: 1111 S Rio Vista St Visalia CA 93292-9296 Office: Feavel Law Firm 1111 S Rio Vista St Visalia CA 93292-9296 E-mail: pfeavel@aol.com

FEAZELL, VIC, lawyer; b. Monroe, La., June 8, 1951; 1 child, Gregory Victor. BA, Mary Hardin Baylor Coll., 1972; JD, Baylor U., 1979. Bar: Tex. 1979, U.S. Dist. Ct. (5th cir.) 1988, U.S. Dist. Ct. (no. dist) 1988, U.S. Dist. Ct. (so. dist), 1989. Dir. drug abuse treatment program Mental Health-Mental Retardation, Waco, Tex., 1975-79; pvt. practice, 1979-82; dist. atty. McLennan County, Tex., 1983-88; pvt. practice Austin, 1989-94; of counsel Rosenthal and Watson, 1995-2000; ptnr. Feazell, Rosenthal and Watson, 2001—. Pres. McLennan County Peace Officers Assn., Waco, 1984-87; pro bono def. counsel Henry Lee Lucas, 1989-94; expert legal corr. O.J. Simpson Trial, KTBC TV. Primary character: Careless Whispers, 1986 (Edgar award 1986); exec. prodr. Rhinos the Movie, Natural Selection, Blood Sweat and Teeth, Rage in the Cage; pres. One Horn Prodns.; contbr. articles to profl. jours. Del. State Dem. Conv., Houston, 1988. Named Outstanding Young Alumni, U. Mary Hardin Baylor, Belton, Tex., 1985, Peace Officer of Yr., Waco JC's, 1986. Mem. Nat. Assn. Criminal Def. Lawyers (life), Tex. Trial Laywers Assn., Tex. Criminal Def. Lawyers Assn., State Bar Tex., Bar of U.S. Fifth Cir., life fellow, Tex. Bar. Found. Avocation: flim making. General civil litigation, Criminal, Personal injury. E-mail: vic@vicfeazell.com

FECHTEL, EDWARD RAY, retired lawyer, educator; b. Pocatello, Idaho, Apr. 20, 1926; s. Edward Joseph and Frances Lucille (Myers) F.; m. Jewell Reagan, Apr. 7, 1950 (div.); children: Scot Gerald, Mark Edward, Kim; m. 2d Mary K. Milligan, Dec. 1983. BA in Bus., Idaho State U., 1949; JD, U. Oreg., 1967; MBA in Fin., 1968. Bar: Oreg. 1967, U.S. Dist. Ct. Oreg. 1967, U.S. Tax Ct. 1967, U.S. Ct. Appeals (9th cir.) 1968, U.S. Ct. Appeals (11th cir.) 1985, U.S. Ct. Appeals (10th cir.) 1986, U.S. Ct. Appeals (8th cir.) 1987, U.S. Supreme Ct. 1988. Sales rep. Genesco, 1950-59; gen. mdse. mgr. Fargo Wilson Wells Co., Pocatello, 1960-64; ptnr. Husband, Johnson & Fechtel, Eugene, Oreg., 1967-83, Ray Fechtel, P.C., 1984-96, ret., 1997; prof. bus. law U. Oreg.; lectr. Oreg. State Bar. Bd. dirs. Legal Aid Soc., Lane County, Oreg., Oreg. Citizens for Fair Land Planning. With USN, 1944-46. Mem. ABA, ATLA, Oreg. State Bar Assn., Phi Alpha Delta. Republican. Antitrust, Federal civil litigation, State civil litigation. Home: 1498 Quaker St Eugene OR 97402-6603 Office: PO Box 2654 Eugene OR 97402-0222

FECHTEL, VINCENT JOHN, legal administrator; b. Leesburg, Fla., Aug. 10, 1936; s. Vincent John and Annie Jo (Hayman) F.; m. Dixie Davenport, Feb. 1992; children: John, Katherine, Elizabeth D., MaryKatherine. BSBA, U. Fla., 1959. Mem. Fla. Ho. of Reps., 1972-78, Fla. Senate, 1978-80; parole commr. U.S. Dept. Justice, Chevy Chase, Md., 1983-96. Served with USNR and Fla. Nat. Guard. Mem. Alpha Tau Omega. Republican. Methodist. Home: 609 Cascade Ave Leesburg FL 34748-6323

FECTEAU, FRANCIS ROGER, judge; b. Worcester, Mass., July 8, 1947; s. Arthur F. and Rita F. (Jubinville) F.; m. Margaret M. Sharry, Mar. 26, 1972; children: Mary, Matthew, Daniel. BA, Holy Cross Coll., 1969; JD, Boston Coll., 1972. Bar: Mass. 1972, U.S. Dist. Ct. Mass. 1973, U.S. Ct. Appeals (1st cir.) 1973. Asst. dist. atty. Worcester County Dist. Attys. Office, Worcester, 1973-79; assoc. Lawrence H. Fisher, 1979-82, Healy & Rocheleau, Worcester, 1982-84, ptnr., 1984-2000; judge, 2000. Instr. Anna Maria Coll., 1976—. Mem. Worcester County Bar Assn. (exec. com. 1981-83), Mass. Bar Assn., Mass. Def. Lawyers Assn., Mass. Acad. Trial Lawyers, Am. Arbitration Assn., Am. Soc. Law and Medicine.

FEDER, ARTHUR A. lawyer, business executive; b. N.Y.C., Mar. 23, 1927; s. Leo and Bertha (Franklin) F.; m. Ruth Musicant, Sept. 4, 1949; children: Gwen Lisabeth, Leslie Margaret, Andrew Michael. BA, Columbia Coll., 1949; LLB, Columbia U., 1951. Bar: N.Y. 1951. Assoc. Fulton Walter & Halley, 1951-53; rsch. asst. Am. Law Inst. Fed. Income, Estate and Gift Tax Project, 1953-54; assoc., ptnr. Roberts & Holland, N.Y.C., 1954-66; ptnr. Willkie, Farr & Gallagher, 1966-69, Fried, Frank, Harris, Shriver & Jacobson, N.Y.C., 1970-94, of counsel, 1994—; sr. adv. to exec. com. Herzog, Heine, Geduld Inc., 1996—. Lectr. in law Columbia U., 1961-63; lectr. Am. Law Inst., NYU Inst. on Fed. Taxation, Practicing Law Inst., various profl. groups. Editor Columbia Law Rev., 1949-51; contbr. articles to profl. jours. With USN, 1945-46. Fellow Am. Coll. Tax Counsel; mem. ABA (taxation sect., chmn. com. on real property tax problems 1964-66, com. on legis. drafting 1968-84), Assn. of Bar of City of N.Y. (various coms.), N.Y. State Bar Assn. (taxation sect., co-chmn. various coms. 1982-86, sec. 1987-88, 2d vice chmn. 1988-89, vice chmn. 1989-90, chmn. 1990-91), Internat. Fiscal Assn. (coun. U.S.A. br. 1984-91), Am. Law Inst. (tax adv. group fed. income tax project), Univ. Club, Phi Beta Kappa. Democrat. Corporate taxation, Estate taxation, Taxation, general. Home: 25 W 81st St New York NY 10024-6023 Office: Herzog Heine Geduld Inc 525 Washington Blvd Jersey City NJ 07310-1690 Fax: 201-418-5293. E-mail: afeder@herzog.com

FEDER, DAVID L. lawyer; b. Mar. 13, 1949; s. Aaron A. and Edith (Forman) Feder; m. Deborah Kuzman, Nov. 01, 1980. BA, SUNY, 1971; JD, Northeastern U., 1974; LLM in Labor Law, NYU, 1975. Bar: Pa. 1975, U.S. Supreme Ct. 1977. Atty., adv. Fed. Labor Rels. Coun., Washington, 1975—79; dep. asst. gen. counsel Fed. Labor Rels. Authority, 1979—81, asst. gen counsel field mgmt. and legal policy, 1981—94, aging gen. counsel, 1994—. Home: 29 Shadow Point Ct Edgewater MD 21037-1212 Office: Fed Labor Relations Authority 607 17th St NW Washington DC 20424

FEDER, ROBERT, lawyer; b. N.Y.C., Nov. 29, 1930; BA cum laude, CCNY, 1953; LLB, Columbia U., 1953. Bar: N.Y. 1953, U.S. Tax Ct. 1956, U.S. Dist. Ct. (so. dist.) N.Y. 1973. V.p., gen. counsel Presdl. Realty Corp., White Plains, N.Y., 1953-71; ptnr. Cuddy & Feder & Worby, 1971—. Bd. dirs. Westchester County (N.Y.) Legal Aid Soc., 1972—, pres., 1974-78; adj. prof. sch. bus. Columbia U., 1988-89; bd. dirs. Presdl. Realty Corp. (Amex), Interplex Industries, Inc., Healthstar Network, Inc., vice-chmn., 2001—; pres., White Plains Community Action Program, 1967-69; bd. dirs. White Plains Hosp. Ctr., 1978—, also sec., treas., chmn. 1992-97; commr. White Plains Housing Authority, 1984—; trustee SUNY-Purchase Coll. Found., 1988—, vice-chmn., 1995—; adj. prof. Pace U. Law Sch., 1985-87. Mem. ABA, N.Y. State Bar Assn., White Plains Bar Assn., Westchester County Bar Assn., Am. Coll. Real Estate Lawyers. General corporate, Environmental, Real property. Home: 9 Oxford Rd White Plains NY 10605-3602 Office: Cuddy & Feder & Worby 90 Maple Ave White Plains NY 10601-5105 E-mail: rfeder@pipeline.com, rfeder@cfwlaw.com

FEDER, SAUL E. lawyer; b. Bklyn., Oct. 8, 1943; s. Joseph Robert and Toby Feder; m. Marcia Carrie Weinblatt, Feb. 25, 1968; children: Howard Avram, Fayge Miriam, Tamar Miriam, Michael Elon, David Ben-Zion Aaron, Alexandra Rachel, Evan Daniel. BS, NYU, 1965; JD, Bklyn. Law Sch., 1968. Bar: N.Y. 1969, U.S. Ct. Appeals (2d cir.) 1969, U.S. Ct. Claims 1970, U.S. Customs Ct. 1972, U.S. Supreme Ct. 1972, U.S. Ct. Customs and Patent Appeals 1974. Mng. lawyer Queens Legal Svcs., Jamaica, N.Y., 1970-71; ptnr. Previte-Glasser-Feder & Farber, Jackson Heights, 1972-73, Hein-Waters-Klein & Feder, Far Rockaway, 1973-78, Regosin-Edwards-Stone & Feder, N.Y.C., 1979—. Spl. investigator Bur. Election Frauds, Atty. Gen.'s Office, N.Y.C., 1976-77, spl. dep. atty. gen., 1969-70; arbitrator, consumer counsel small claims div. Civil Ct. City of N.Y., 1974—. Pres. Young Israel Briarwood, Queens, N.Y., 1978; chmn. polit. affairs com. Young Israel Staten Island, 1985—; rep. candidate State of N.Y. Assembly, Queens, 1976; chmn. Stat Pac Polit. Action Com. Mem. N.Y. Bar Assn., Queens County Bar Assn., Nassau County Bar Assn., Am. Judges Assn., N.Y. Trial Lawyers Assn., Richmond County Bar Assn., Com. on Law and Pub. Affairs, Internat. Acad. Law & Sci., Am. Jud. Soc., Soc. Med. Jurisprudence, Am. Arbitration Assn. Republican. State civil litigation, Contracts commercial, General practice. Home: 259 Ardmore Ave Staten Island NY 10314-4349 Office: Regosin Edwards Stone & Feder 225 Broadway Ste 613 New York NY 10007-3059 E-mail: sfeder@everestbn.com

FEDOR, ALLAN JOHN, lawyer; b. Erie, Pa., Jan. 2, 1947; s. Alexander Joseph and Janet Joan (Moraski) F.; m. Franell Prhne, Mar. 18, 1977. BS cum laude, Gannon U., 1973; JD, U. Akron, 1976; MBA, Pepperdine U., 1979. Bar: Ohio 1976, Hawaii 1978, Calif. 1981, Fla., 1990. mfg. mgr. GE Co., Erie, 1965-73; gen. counsel, Trilogy Ltd., Cupertino, Calif., 1985-86; Big Bros. of Hawaii, Honolulu, 1977-80. Author: (with others) Drafting Agreements for the Sale of Businesses, 2nd edit., 1988, California Business Incorporations, 1988. Served with JAGC, Capt. U.S. Army, 1977-80. Mem. Blue Key Bracton's Inn (pres. 1975). Republican. Roman Catholic. General practice, Securities. Office: Fedor & Fedor 10225 Ulmerton Rd Ste 8A Largo FL 33771-3522

FEEGEL, JOHN RICHARD, pathologist; b. Middletown, Conn., Nov. 16, 1932; s. Fred Benjamin and Eva Lilian (Kane) Feegel; m. Elaine Antoinette Blanchet, Feb. 1968; children: John R., Mark, Catherine, Elizabeth, Thomas. BS, Holy Cross Coll., 1954; MD, U. Ottawa, Ont., Can., 1960; JD, U. Denver, 1964; MPH, U. So. Fla., 1991. Bar: Colo. 1964, Fla. 1967, U.S. Dist. Ct. (mid. dist.) Fla. 1983; diplomate Am. Bd. Pathology (AP, FP). Intern St. Mary's Hosp., West Palm Beach, Fla., 1960—61; resident in pathology and forensic pathology Denver Gen. Hosp., Denver Coroner's Office, 1961—65; chief med. examiner Tampa, Fla., 1973—76; assoc. chief med. examiner State of N.C., 1976—77, Fulton County, Atlanta, 1977—83; ptnr. Mitzel, Mitzel & Feegel, Tampa, 1983—86; adj. assoc. prof. pathology U. N.C., Chapel Hill, 1976—77; assoc. prof. pathology Emory U., Atlanta, 1977—81; pvt. practice Tampa. Author: (novels) Autopsy, 1976 (Edgar award, 1977), Dance Card, 1980. Fellow: Coll. Am. Pathologists, Am. Acad. Forensic Scis., Am. Coll. Legal Medicine; mem.: ATLA. Republican. Roman Catholic. Criminal, Personal injury. Home: 3002 W Waverly Ave Tampa FL 33629-8912 Office: Law Office of John R FeegelPA 401 S Albany Ave Tampa FL 33606-2019

FEENEY, DAVID WESLEY, lawyer; b. Phila., Nov. 1, 1938; s. William James McKay and Mary Catherine (Watkins) Feeney; m. Elizabeth Butler Shamel, Aug. 15, 1959; children: Shawn, Shari, David, Darryl. BS, Cornell U., 1960, LLB with distinction, 1963. Bar: U.S. Tax Ct. 1966, U.S. Dist. Ct. (so. dist.) N.Y. 1976, U.S. Ct. Claims 1976, U.S. Ct. Appeals (2d cir.) 1976. Assoc. Cadwalader, Wickersham & Taft, N.Y.C., 1963-64, 66-71, ptnr., 1971—. Served to 1st lt. U.S. Army, 1964-66. Mem. N.Y. State Bar Assn. (tax sect.), Cornell Club of N.Y.C. Republican. Presbyterian. Corporate taxation. Home: 1 Black Point Horseshoe Rumson NJ 07760-1500 Office: Cadwalader Wickersham et al 100 Maiden Ln New York NY 10038-4818

FEERICK, JOHN DAVID, dean, lawyer; b. N.Y.C., July 12, 1936; s. John D. and Mary J. F.; m. Emalie Platt, Aug. 25, 1962; children: Maureen, Margaret, Jean, Rosemary, John, William. B.S., Fordham U., 1958, LL.B., 1961; hon. degree, Coll. New Rochelle, 1991. Bar: N.Y. 1961. Assoc. Skadden, Arps, Slate, Meagher & Flom, N.Y.C., 1961-68, partner, 1968-82; dean Fordham U. Sch. Law, 1982—. Author: From Failing Hands: The Story of Presidential Succession, 1965, The 25th Amendment, 1976; co-author: The Vice Presidents of the United States, 1967, NLRB Representation Elections-Law, Practice and Procedure, 1980; also articles;

editor-in-chief Fordham Law Rev., 1960-61. Chmn. N.Y. State Commn. Govt. Integrity, 1987-90. Recipient Eugene J. Keefe award Fordham U. Law Sch., 1975, 85, spl. award Fordham U. Law Rev. Assn., 1977 Fellow Am. Bar Found.; mem. ABA (chmn. spl. com. election law and voter participation 1976-79, spl. award 1966), N.Y. State Bar Assn. (chmn. com. fed. constrn. 1979-83, exec. com. 1985-87), Assn. Bar City N.Y. (v.p. 1986-87, pres. 1992-94), Am. Arbitration Assn. (chair exec. com. 1995, chair Fund for Modern Cts. 1995—), Fordham U. Law Sch. Alumni Assn. (dir. 1972—, medal of achievement 1980), Phi Beta Kappa. Office: Fordham U Sch Law 140 W 62nd St New York NY 10023-7407*

FEFFER, GERALD ALAN, lawyer; b. Washington, Apr. 24, 1942; s. Louis Charles and Elsie (Glick) F.; children: Andrew, John, Keith. BA with honors, Lehigh U., 1964; JD, U. Va., 1967. Bar: N.Y. 1968, D.C. 1980. Assoc. Mudge, Rose, Guthrie & Alexander, N.Y.C., 1967-71; asst. U.S. atty. So. Dist. N.Y., 1971-76, asst. chief criminal div., 1975-76; ptnr. Kostelanetz & Ritholz, N.Y.C., 1976-79; dep. asst. atty. gen. tax div. Dept. Justice, Washington, 1979-81; ptnr. Steptoe & Johnson, 1981-86, Williams & Connolly, Washington, 1986—. Mem. editl. bd. Busniess Crimes Bulletin: Compliance and Litigation; contbr. articles to profl. jours. Fellow Am. Coll. Tax Counsel, Am. Coll. Trial Lawyers; mem. ABA (criminal justice litigation and taxation sects.), Nat. Assn. Criminal Def. Lawyers, Nat. Inst. on Criminal Tax Fraud (chmn.). Criminal. Home: 3000 Garrison St NW Washington DC 20008-1032 Office: Williams & Connolly 725 12th St NW Washington DC 20005-5901

FEHELEY, LAWRENCE FRANCIS, lawyer; b. Phila., Oct. 9, 1946; s. Francis Edward and Dorothy May (Greenhalgh) F.; divorced; 1 child, Matthew Francis; m. Janet Kay Douglass, Apr. 6, 1979; children: Brendan Patrick, Lawren Kaitlin, Tyne Brielle. BA, Cornell U., 1969, JD with distinction, 1973. Bar: Ohio 1973, U.S. Dist. Ct. (so. dist.) Ohio 1974, U.S. Ct. Appeals (6th cir.) 1980, U.S. Supreme Ct. 1993. Assoc. Emens, Kegler, Brown, Hill & Ritter, Columbus, Ohio, 1973-77; ptnr. Emens, Hurd, Kegler & Ritter, 1977—, also bd. dirs., mng. dir., 1986. Bd. dirs. Netcare Corp., Youth Achievement Camps, Inc., Columbus. Mem. ABA, Ohio Bar Assn. (bd. govs. labor law sect.), Columbus Bar Assn. Republican. Episcopalian. Avocations: art, soccer. Administrative and regulatory, Labor. Office: Emens Kegler Brown Hill & Ritter 65 E State St Ste 1800 Columbus OH 43215-4213

FEIBLEMAN, GILBERT BRUCE, lawyer; b. Portland, Oreg., Jan. 29, 1951; s. Herbert Frank and Bernice (Kaplan) F.; m. Ellen M. McDowell, June 20, 1981; 1 child, Benjamin David. BS, U. Oreg., 1972; JD, U. Pacific, 1976. Bar: Oreg. 1976, U.S. Dist. Ct. Oreg. 1976, U.S. Ct. Appeals (9th cir.). Assoc. Goodenough & Pierson, Salem, Oreg., 1976-78; mng. ptnr. Ramsay, Stein, Feibleman & Myers P.C., 1978-89, Ramsay, Stein & Feibleman P.C., Salem, 1989-94, Feibleman & Assocs. P.C., 1995—. Adj. prof. trial law and negotiation skills Willamette U.; adj. prof. bus. law Chemeketa Community Coll., Marion County, Oreg., 1977; arbitrator Marion County Ct., Salem, 1985—; referee juvenile ct., 1985; judge pro tem Oreg. Dist. Cts., 1982—, Oreg. Cir. Cts., 1987—; reference judge Marion County, 1989—. Fellow Am. Acad. Matrimonial Lawyers; mem. Assn. Trial Lawyers Am., Oreg. Trial Lawyers Assn., Oreg. Bar Assn. (arbitrator), Oreg. State Bar Assn. (bar counsel 1989—, sec. joint chiropractic com. 1989—, chair family juvenile law sect). Democrat. Avocations: skiing, gourmet cooking. State civil litigation, Family and matrimonial, Personal injury. Home: 552 Stagecoach Way SE Salem OR 97302-3925 Office: 1815 Commercial St SE Salem OR 97302-5203 E-mail: gil@feibleman-law.com

FEIGENBAUM, EDWARD D. legal editor, publisher, consultant; b. Rochester, N.Y., Mar. 16, 1958; s. Samuel and Norma Feigenbaum; m. Ann Elizabeth Andrews, Aug. 6, 1983; children: Edward Andrews, Breanna Layne. BA with honors, Ind. U., 1978, MBA, JD, 1982. Bar: Ind. 1983, U.S. Dist. Ct. (no. and so. dists.) Ind. 1983. Sr. staff assoc. Inst. for Rsch. in Pub. Safety, Bloomington, Ind., 1977-83; dir. legal affairs Coun. State Govts., Lexington, Ky., 1983-87; legal counsel, dir. mktg. Hudson Inst., Indpls., 1987-89; editor, pub. Ind. Legislative Insight, 1989—, Ind. Gaming Insight, Indpls., 1993—, Ind. Edn. Insight, Indpls., 1997—. Researcher D.T. Skelton Svc. Assocs. Inc., Bloomington, 1983-88. Contbr. numerous articles to profl. jours. Chmn. City of Bloomington Environ. Quality & Conservation Commn., 1982, mem. Redistricting Com., 1982-83, City of Noblesville (Ind.) Planning Commn., 1989-96; co-chair election subcom. of urban, state and local govt. law govt. ops. com. 1994-96. Mem. ABA (vice chmn. com. election law adminstrv. law sect. 1984-90), Coun. on Govtl. Ethics Laws (steering com. 1987-90), Am. Polit. Sci. Assn., Midwest Polit. Sci. Assn., Ind. State Bar Assn. (chair govtl. practice sect. 1991-92), Columbia Club. Avocation: collecting polit. memorabilia. Home: 5537 Salem Dr N Carmel IN 46033-8582 Office: INGroup PO Box 383 Noblesville IN 46061-0383

FEIKENS, JOHN, federal judge; b. Clifton, N.J., Dec. 3, 1917; s. Sipke and Corine (Wisse) F.; m. Henriette Dorothy Schulthouse, Nov. 4, 1939; children: Jon, Susan Corine, Barbara Edith, Julie Anne, Robert H. A.B., Calvin Coll., Grand Rapids, Mich., 1938; J.D., U. Mich., 1941; LL.D., U. Detroit, 1979, Detroit Coll. Law, 1981. Bar: Mich. 1942. Gen. practice law, Detroit; dist. judge Ea. Dist. Mich., 1960-61, 70-79, chief judge, 1979-86, sr. judge, 1986—. Past co-chmn. Mich. Civil Rights Commn.; past chmn. Rep. State Central Com.; past mem. Rep. Nat. Com.; mem. com. visitors U. Mich. Law Sch. Past bd. trustees Calvin Coll. Fellow Am. Coll. Trial Lawyers; mem. ABA, Detroit Bar Assn. (dir. 1962, past pres.), State Bar Mich. (commr. 1965-71), U. Mich. Club (com. visitors). Office: US Dist Ct 851 Theodore Levin US Ct 231 W Lafayette Blvd Detroit MI 48226-2700

FEIMAN, RONALD MARK, lawyer; b. N.Y.C., Feb. 28, 1951; s. Richard and Patricia Feiman; m. Hilary J. Ronner, Jan. 7, 1984. BA, Yale U., 1972; JD, MBA, NYU, 1977. Bar: N.Y. 1978., CPA, N.Y. Assoc. Gordon Altman Butowsky Weitzen Shalov & Wein, N.Y.C., 1977-85, ptnr., 1985-99, Mayer, Brown & Platt, 1999—. Mem. ABA (intellectual property law com., bus. law com.), AICPA (appointed to fin. svcs. industry taxation com.), Assn. Bar City N.Y., Yale Club. General corporate, Entertainment, Securities. Office: Mayer Brown & Platt 1675 Broadway New York NY 10019-5889 E-mail: rfeiman@mayerbrown.com, ronald.feiman.es.72@aya.yale.edu

FEIN, ROGER GARY, lawyer; b. St. Louis, Mar. 12, 1940; s. Albert and Fanny (Levinson) F.; m. Susanne M. Cohen, Dec. 18, 1965; children: David I., Lisa J. Student, Washington U., St. Louis, 1959, NYU, 1960; BS, UCLA, 1962; JD, Northwestern U., 1965; MBA, Am. U., 1967. Bar: Ill. 1965, U.S. Dist. Ct. (no. dist.) Ill. 1968, U.S. Ct. Appeals (7th cir.) 1968, U.S. Supreme Ct. 1970. Atty. divsn. corp. fin. SEC, Washington, 1965-67; ptnr. Arvey, Hodes, Costello & Burman, Chgo., 1967-91, Wildman, Harrold, Allen and Dixon, Chgo., 1992—. Co-chair Corp., Securities and Tax Practice Group, 1992-99; mem. Securities Adv. Com. to Sec. State Ill., 1973—, chmn., 1973-79, 87-93, vice-chmn., 1983-87, chmn. emeritus, 1994—; spl. asst. atty. gen. State of Ill., 1974-83, 85-99; spl. asst. state's atty. Cook County, Ill., 1989-90; mem. Appeal Bd., Ill. Law Enforcement Commn., 1980-83; mem. lawyer's adv. bd. So. Ill. Law Jour., 1980-83; mem. adv. bd. securities regulation and law report Bur. Nat. Affairs Inc., 1985—; lectr., author on land trust financing, consumer credit and securities law. Mem. Bd. Edn., Sch. Dist. No. 29, Northfield, Ill., 1977-83, pres., 1981-83; mem. Pub. Vehicle Ops. Citizens Adv. coun. City Chgo., 1985-86; mem. Anti-Defamation League of B'nai B'rith, mem. Anti-Defamation League Greater Chgo./Upper Midwest Region, Chgo. regional bd., 1975-91, vice chmn., 1980-88, mem. exec. com., 1996—, assoc. nat. commr., 2000—; chmn. lawyers' com. for ann. telethon Muscular Dystrophy Assn., 1983; past bd. dirs. Jewish Nat. Fund, Am. Friends Hebrew U., Northfield Comty. Fund. Recipient Sec. State Ill. Pub. Svc. award, 1976, Citation of Merit, WAIT Radio, 1976, Sunset Ridge Sch. Comty. Svc. award, 1984, City of Chgo. Citizen's award, 1986; named one of Leading Ill. Attys., Am. Rsch. Corp., 1997. Fellow Am. Bar Found., Ill. Bar Found. (bd. dirs. 1978-88, v.p. 1982-84, pres. 1984-86, chmn. Fellows 1983-84, chmn., past pres. adv. com. 1988-90, Cert. of Appreciation 1985, 86, Stalwart fellow 1997), Chgo. Bar Found; mem. ABA (ho. of dels. 1981-85, state regulation of securities com. 1982—, Ill. liaison of com., chmn. subcom. liaison with securities adminstrs. and NASD 1998—), Ill. State Bar Assn. (bd. govs. 1976-80, del. assembly 1976-88, sec. 1977-78, cert. of appreciation 1980, 88, chmn. Bench and Bar com. 1982-83, chmn. Bench and Bar sect. coun., 1983-84, chmn. bar elections supervision com. 1986-87, chmn. assembly com. on hearings 1987-88, mem. com. on jud. appointments 1987-90), Chgo. Bar Assn. (mem. task force delivery legal svcs. 1978-80, cert. of appreciation 1976, chmn. land trusts com. 1978-79, chmn. consumer credit com. 1977-78, chmn. state securities law subcom. 1977-79), Decalogue Soc. Lawyers, Northwestern U. Sch. of Law Alumni Assn. (dir.), Standard Club, The Law Club of the City of Chgo., Tau Epsilon Phi, Alpha Kappa Psi, Phi Delta Phi. General corporate, Mergers and acquisitions, Securities. Office: Wildman Harrold Allen & Dixon 225 W Wacker Dr Ste 2800 Chicago IL 60606-1224 E-mail: fein@wildmanharrold.com

FEIN, SCOTT NORRIS, lawyer; b. N.Y.C., Oct. 22, 1949; s. Sidney and Charlotte (Blaustein) F.; m. Patricia Martinelli, Oct. 16, 1983. BA, Am. U., 1971; JD, Georgetown U., 1975; LLM, NYU, 1979. Bar: N.Y. 1976, U.S. Dist. Ct. (ea. dist.) N.Y. 1978, U.S. Dist. Ct. (no. dist.) N.Y. 1982, U.S. Dist. Ct. (so. dist.) N.Y. 1978, U.S. Dist. Ct. (we. dist.) N.Y. 1985. Asst. dist. atty. Nassau County, Mineola, N.Y., 1975-79; asst. counsel to Gov. Hugh Carey of N.Y., Albany, 1979-82, Gov. Mario Cuomo, 1982-83; ptnr. Whiteman Osterman & Hanna, Albany, 1983—; litigation counsel N.Y. State Civil Liberties Union, 1984—. Co-author: The Defense of Environmental Offenses. Trustee The Nature Conservancy. Mem. Assn. Trial Lawyers Am., ABA, N.Y. State Bar Assn. (co-chmn. environ. sect. criminal litigation com.). Environmental. Office: Whiteman Osterman & Hanna 99 Washington Ave Ste 1930 Albany NY 12210-2886 E-mail: snf@wolf.com

FEIN, SHERMAN EDWARD, lawyer, psychologist; b. June 17, 1928; s. Samuel L. and Mildred B. (Sherman) F.; m. Myra N. Becker, Nov. 13, 1955; children: Dina, Julia, Sara. BA, Bowdoin Coll., 1949; J.D., Boston U., 1953; MS, Springfield Coll., 1962; EdD, U. Mass., 1969; Sc.M.D., Sch, Medicine, Ross U., Portsmouth, Dominica, West Indies, 1983; PhD, Kensington U., 1993. Bar: Maine 1952, Mass. 1953, U.S. Dist. Ct. Mass., 1957, U.S. Supreme Ct. 1965; diplomate Am. Bd. Med. Psychotherapists. Ptnr. Fein, Pearson & Edmond, P.C., Springfield, 1953—; pvt. practice psychology, 1962—; hon. consul Republic of Nicaragua, 1999—. Author: Selected Cases on Shoplifting, 1975; Divorce Handbook, 1978. Sgt. USAF, 1950-52; to lt. col. CAP, 1953-77. Mem. ABA, Hampden County Bar Assn., Mass. Bar Assn., Assn. Trial Lawyers Am., N.Y. Acad. Scis., Am. Psychology-Law Assn., Masons, Shriners. Republican. Jewish. Health, Personal injury, Workers' compensation. Home: 224 Longmeadow St Longmeadow MA 01106 Office: Fein Pearson Emond & Fein 52 Mulberry St Springfield MA 01105-1410

FEINBERG, GARY H. lawyer, retail company executive; b. Buffalo, Oct. 19, 1942; s. Harold and Edna (Kaufman) F.; BA, U. Pa., 1964; JD, SUNY, Buffalo, 1968; m. Ellen Talles, Mar. 5, 1977; 1 child, Kevin M. Admitted to N.Y. State bar, 1968. Various positions with NLRB, Washington, Phila., Buffalo, 1968-73; atty. labor relations dept. Montgomery Ward, Balt., 1973-81, asst. labor relations dir., 1981-86, asst. dir. labor relations, Chgo., 1986—. Mem. ABA, U.S. Golf Assn. Labor. Home: 601 E Palo Verde Dr Apt 23 Phoenix AZ 85012-1344 Office: Montgomery Ward 1 Montgomery Ward Plz Chicago IL 60671-0001

FEINBERG, PAUL H. lawyer; b. Yonkers, N.Y., Nov. 24, 1938; AB, U. Pa., 1960; LLB cum laude, Harvard U., 1963; LLM, NYU, 1970. Bar: N.Y. 1965, Ohio 1979. Asst. gen. counsel The Ford Found., 1971-77; ptnr. Baker & Hostetler LLP, Cleve. Speaker in field. Contbr. articles to profl. jours. Mem. ABA (mem. sect. taxation, mem. tax exempt orgns. com., co-chair subcom. non C3 organs. 1993-94, co-chair subcom. pvt. founds. 1995—), N.Y. State Bar Assn., Ohio State Bar Assn., Cleve. Bar Assn. (treas. 1996-99). Office: Baker & Hostetler LLP 3200 Nat City Ctr 1900 E 9th St Cleveland OH 44114-3475

FEINBERG, WILFRED, federal judge; b. N.Y.C., June 22, 1920; s. Jac and Eva (Wolin) F.; m. Shirley Marcus, June 23, 1946; children: Susan Stelk, Jack Feinberg, Jessica Twedt. BA, Columbia U., 1940, LLB, 1946, LLD (hon.), 1985, Syracuse U., 1985, Bklyn. Law Sch., 1998. Bar: N.Y. 1947. Law clk. Hon. James P. McGranery U.S. Dist. Ct. (ea. dist.) Pa., 1947-49; assoc. Kaye, Scholer, Fierman & Hays, N.Y.C., 1949-53; ptnr. McGoldrick, Dannett, Horowitz & Golub, 1953-61; dep. supt. N.Y. State Banking Dept., 1958; judge U.S. Dist Ct. (so. dist.), N.Y., 1961-66, U.S. Ct. Appeals (2nd cir.), N.Y.C., 1966—, chief judge, 1980-88, sr. judge, 1991—. Mem. U.S. Jud. Conf. U.S., 1980-88, chmn. exec. com., 1987-88, mem. Devitt award com., 1989, 90, mem. long-range planning com., 1991-96; Madison lectr. NYU Law Sch., 1983; Sonnett lectr. Fordham U. Law Sch., 1984; Inaugural Howard Kaplan Meml. lectr. Hofstra U. Law Sch., 1986; The Future of Justice lectr. Inst. of Comparative Law, Chuo U., Japan, 1991. Editor-in-chief Columbia Law Rev, 1946; contbr. to profl. jours. and mags. With AUS, 1942-45. Recipient Learned Hand medal for excellence in fed. jurisprudence, 1982, Gold medal, award for disting. svc. in the law N.Y. State Bar Assn., 1990, medal for excellence Columbia Law Alumni Assn., 1990, Pursuit of Justice award Internat. Assn. Jewish Lawyers and Jurists, 1993, Disting. Pub. Svc. award N.Y. County Lawyers Assn., 1994, Edward Weinfeld award N.Y. County Lawyers Assn., 1995; Ann. Wilfred Feinberg Prize named in his honor for best student work at Columbia Law Sch. related to fed. cts., 1998. Mem. ABA, Assn. of Bar of City of N.Y., N.Y. County Lawyers Assn., Am. Judicature Soc., Am. Law Inst., Phi Beta Kappa. Office: US Ct Appeals 2nd Cir Room 2004 US Court House Foley Sq New York NY 10007-1501

FEINOUR, JOHN STEPHEN, lawyer; b. Kingston, Pa., July 30, 1951; s. John Gouger and Ethel Cooke (Peterson) F.; m. Bernadette Barattini, Apr. 16 1977; children— J. Stephen, Kathleen M. B.A., Dickinson Coll., 1973; J.D., Temple U., 1976. Bar: Pa. 1976, U.S. Dist. Ct. (mid. dist.) Pa. 1979, U.S. Supreme Ct. 1983. Law clk. to presiding justice Dauphin County Ct. Common Pleas, Harrisburg, Pa., 1976-77; assoc. Nauman, Smith, Shissler & Hall, Harrisburg, 1977-82, ptnr., 1982— ; arbitrator Dauphin County Ct. Common Pleas, 1982-84, chmn. arbitration bd., 1984— . Co-editor Dauphin County Young Lawyers Handbook. Bd. dirs. Camp Shikellimy br. Harrisburg Area YMCA, 1979-84, sec. 1988—, bd. dirs. Harrisburg Area, 1985—; moderator, bd. deacons, ruling elder Paxton Presbyterian Ch., Pa., 1982-83. Mem. ABA, Assn. Trial Lawyers Am., Pa. Bar Assn. (litigation and workmen's compensation sects.), Dauphin County Bar Assn. (ct. relations, ct. rules and arbitration coms.), Kappa Sigma (alumnus advisor 1982). Republican. Federal civil litigation, State civil litigation, Insurance. Home: 333 Willow Ave Camp Hill PA 17011-3655 Office: Nauman Smith Shissler & Hall 6 N 3rd St Harrisburg PA 17113-2306

FEINSTEIN, FRED IRA, lawyer; b. Chgo., Apr. 6, 1945; s. Bernard and Beatrice (Mines) F.; m. Judy Cutler, Aug. 25, 1968; children: Karen, Donald. BSC, DePaul U., 1967, JD, 1970. Bar: Ill. 1970, U.S. Supreme Ct. 1977. Ptnr. McDermott, Will & Emery, Chgo., 1976—; lectr. in field. Pres., Skokie/Evanston (Ill.) Action Council, 1981-84; bd. dirs. Temple Judea Mizpah, Skokie, 1982-84, 2000—, Deborah Goldfine Meml. Cancer Research, 1968—, YMCA of Chgo., 1985—. Mem. Ill. Bar Assn., Am. Coll. Real Estate Lawyers, Union League, Blue Key, Beta Gamma Sigma, Beta Alpha Psi, Pi Gamma Mu, Lambda Alpha. Contbr. articles to profl. jours. Bankruptcy, Environmental, Real property. Office: McDermott Will & Emery 227 W Monroe St Ste 3100 Chicago IL 60606-5096

FEINSTEIN, MILES ROGER, lawyer; b. Camden, N.J., June 25, 1941; s. Louis Emory and Sylvia K. (Jacobs) F.; m. Margaret Bott, Oct. 3, 2000; children: Bari, Matthew, Elizabeth. BA, Rutgers U., 1963; JD, Duke U., 1966. Bar: N.J. 1966, U.S. Dist. Ct. N.J. 1966, U.S. Ct. Appeals (3d cir.) 1967, U.S. Ct. Appeals (2d cir.) 1971. Pvt. practice, Clifton, N.J., 1967—. Mem. Passaic Criminal Justice commn.; mem. com. on drugs and cts. N.J. Supreme Ct.; mem. speedy trial com. N.J. Supreme Ct.; expert commentator Nat. Courtroom TV; lectr. N.J. Inst. of Continuing Legal Edn., Trial Lawyers Assn. Author: Historical Development of Pineys of Southern New Jersey. Trustee Passaic County Heart Fund, 1970-93, Passaic County Cancer Soc.; chmn. Passaic County March of Dimes, 1989. Named Man of Yr., Passaic County Heart Fund, 1976, Passaic County Cancer Soc., 1978, Passaic County coun. Boy Scouts Am., 1978, Passaic County Bad Guys Charitable Orgn., 1974; recipient award Passaic Civic Orgn., Humanitarian award Unico, 1976, Nationwide Bail Bonds award Policeman's Benevolent Assn., Disting. Svc. award, 1980, 84, 85, History prize Soc. Colonial Wars; subject of numerous legal articles. Mem. ABA, Assn. Trial Lawyers Am., Nat. Assn. Criminal Def. Lawyers, Fed. Bar Assn., N.J. Bar Assn., N.J. Assn. Criminal Def. Lawyers (former trustee, treas., v.p., pres. 1990-91; lectr.), N.J. Assn. of Trial Lawyers (bd. govs. 1992-93), Passaic County Bar Assn. (chmn. criminal law com. 1990-93), Phi Beta Kappa, Phi Delta Phi, Phi Alpha Theta (Henry Rutgers scholar). Avocations: sports, theatre, collecting stamps. Criminal. Office: 1135 Clifton Ave Clifton NJ 07013-3642

FEINSTEIN, STEPHEN MICHAEL, lawyer; b. Stamford, Conn., Jan. 19, 1959; s. Norton Perry and Phyllis Marilyn (Fabel) F.; m. Bonnie Helene Litsky, Aug. 27, 1989; children: Shayna Justine, Maxwell Benjamin, Sydney Ilana. BA, U. Conn., 1981; JD, Quninnipiac Coll., 1984. Bar: Conn. 1984, U.S. Dist. Ct. Conn. 1985. Assoc. Feinstein & Hermann, Norwalk, Conn., 1984-91; ptnr. Feinstein & Hermann, P.C., 1991—. Instr. Conn. Inst. Paralegal Studies, Stamford, 1994-98; bd. dirs. Conn. State Law Libr. Adv. Com., Hartford, Conn., 1993—. Commr. 3d taxing dist. City of Norwalk, Conn., 1999; chmn. adult adv. bd. B'nai B'rith Youth Orgn., New Haven, 1994-96. Mem. Assn. Trial Lawyers Am., Conn. Bar Assn., Conn. Trial Lawyers Assn., Friends of Stamford Law Libr. (pres. 1992-94, v.p. 1994). Republican. Jewish. General civil litigation, Criminal, General practice. Home: 21 Ludlow Mnr Norwalk CT 06855-2010 Office: Feinstein and Hermann PC 5 Myrtle St Norwalk CT 06855-1315

FEISEL, LYLE DEAN, lawyer; b. Boston, Dec. 14, 1918; s. Edward Barton and Jeannette (Thomas) C.; m. Elizabeth Ann Parker, Sept. 6, 1940; children: Allan M., Elizabeth M. B.A., Yale U., 1940; J.D., Harvard U., 1943. Bar: Mass. 1943. Of counsel Warner & Stackpole LLP now Kirkpatrick & Lockhart LLP, Boston, 1954—. Chmn. bd. dirs. H.B. Smith Co., Inc.; pres., trustee emeritus Phillips Acad.; chmn. emeritus, trustee Mass. Eye and Ear Infirmary and Found. Hon. dir. Chewonki Found. Inc.; chmn. Yale U. Planned Giving; trustee Sturbridge Village; mem. leadership coun. New Bedford Whaling Mus.; mem. state adv. com. Salvation Army; v.p. Polly Hill Found. Fellow Am. Bar Found., Mass. Bar Found.; mem. ABA, Boston Bar Assn., Mass. Bar Assn., Internat. Bar Assn., Edgartown Yacht Club. Home: 15 Traill St Cambridge MA 02138-4738 Office: 75 State St Fl 6 Boston MA 02109-1808 E-mail: mchapin@kl.com

FEIT, GLENN M. lawyer; b. Elizabeth, N.J., Oct. 16, 1929; s. Charles Theodore and Beatrice (Esther) F.; m. Rona F. Gottlieb, June 14, 1953 (div. 1974); children: Glenn M., John Paul, Adam Gibbs (dec.); m. Barberi Platt Paull. BS in Econ., U. Pa., 1951; JD magna cum laude, Harvard U., 1957. Bar: N.Y. 1958, U.S. Dist. Ct. (2d dist.) 1959). Assoc. Cravath, Swaine & Moore, N.Y.C., 1957-64; ptnr. London, Buttenwieser & Chalif, 1965-70, Feit & Ahrens, N.Y.C., 1970-88, Feit & Shor, N.Y.C., 1988-89, Proskauer Rose LLP, N.Y.C., 1989—. Bd. dirs. C&D Techs., Inc., Blue Bell, Pa., Blair Industries, Inc., Scott City, Mo.; sec. Charterhouse Group Internat., Inc., N.Y.C. Mem. editl. bd. Harvard Law Rev., 1955-57. Bd. dirs. Friends of the IDF, N.Y.C. Lt. USN, 1951-54. Mem. ABA, Assn. Bar City N.Y., Aircraft Owners and Pilots Assn., Exptl. Aircraft Assn., Tailhook Assn., Harvard Club, Seaplane Pilots Assn., N.Y. Yacht Club, Doubles. General corporate, Mergers and acquisitions, Securities. Office: Proskauer Rose LLP 1585 Broadway Fl 22 New York NY 10036-8299 E-mail: gfeit@proskauer.com

FEKETE, GEORGE OTTO, judge, lawyer, pharmacist; b. Budapest, Hungary; s. Bela and Ilona (Meer) F.; m. Amy Zheng; children: Jacqueline Kim, Jeanette Lee. BS in Psychology, Wayne State U., 1954; PhD, U. So. Calif., 1960; postgrad. in psychology, Calif. State U., Long Beach; JD, Pepperdine U., 1973. Bar: Calif. 1973, U.S. Dist. Ct. (so. dist.) Calif. 1973, U.S. Supreme Ct. 1980, U.S. Dist Ct. (no. dist.) Calif. 1986. Chief pharmacist Hylo Drug Co., Huntington Beach, Calif., 1970; pres. G.O. Fekete Law Corp., Anaheim, 1973-86; lead trial lawyer Melvin Belli Law Offices, San Francisco, 1986-88; ind. trial specialist, superior ct. apptd. arbitrator San Francisco and Bay Area, 1988—; judge pro tem. Served to maj. USAF, 1954-59. Mem. ABA, Assn. Trial Lawyers Am., Calif. Trial Lawyers Assn. (legis. com. 1976-78), Orange County Trial Lawyers Assn (bd. dirs. 1977). State civil litigation, Insurance, Personal injury. Fax: 707-552-4672. E-mail: GOFesg@earthlink.net

FELD, ALAN DAVID, lawyer; b. Dallas, Nov. 13, 1936; s. Henry R. and Rose (Scissors) F.; m. Anne Sanger, June 1, 1957; children: Alan David, Elizabeth S., John L. B.A., So. Methodist U., 1957, LL.B., 1960. Bar: Tex. 1960. Since practiced in Dallas; from ptnr. to chmn. bd. Akin, Gump, Hauer, Strauss & Feld, Dallas, 1960-96, sr. exec. ptnr., 1996—. Lectr. Southwestern U. Med. Sch.; chmn. Tex. State Securities Bd.; bd. dirs. Clear Channel Comms., Inc., Ctr. Point Properties, Inc. Contbr. articles to legal jours. Bd. trustees Brandeis U., AMR Advantage Funds, So. Meth. U.; bd. dirs. Dallas Day Nursery Assn., Timberlawn Found., Dallas Symphony Orch. Mem. Am., Tex., D.C., Dallas bar assns., Salesmanship Club, Dallas Club, Royal Oaks Country Club, Phi Delta Phi. General corporate, Mergers and acquisitions, Securities. Home: 4235 Bordeaux Ave Dallas TX 75205-3717 Office: Akin Gump Strauss Hauer & Feld 1700 Pacific Ave Ste 4100 Dallas TX 75201-4675

FELDBERG, MICHAEL SVETKEY, lawyer; b. Boston, May 21, 1951; s. Sumner Lee Feldberg and Eunice (Svetkey) Cohen; m. Ruth Lazarus, Sept. 23, 1978; children: Rachel, Jesse, Ben. BA, Harvard U., 1973, JD, 1977. Bar: N.Y. 1978, U.S. Dist. Ct. (ea. and so. dists.) N.Y. 1978, U.S. Ct. Appeals (2d cir.) 1983, U.S. Supreme Ct. 1994. Assoc. Orans, Elsen, Polstein & Naftalis, N.Y.C., 1977-80; asst. U.S. atty. So. Dist. of N.Y., 1981-84; ptnr. Shea & Gould, 1985-91, Schulte Roth & Zabel, N.Y.C., 1991—. Bd. dirs. 92d St. YMCA, N.Y.C., Child Devel. Rsch., N.Y.C., 1988—. Mem. Assn. Bar City N.Y. (criminal law com., com. on the judiciary, com. on profl. responsibility). Federal civil litigation, State civil litigation, Criminal. Office: Schulte Roth & Zabel 919 3rd Ave Fl 19 New York NY 10022-4774 E-mail: michael.feldberg@srz.com

FELDER, MONICA LEE, lawyer; b. Vallejo, Calif., Aug. 20, 1968; d. Kenneth Doyle Allen and Barbara Jean Felder. BA in Internat. Rels., Tulane U., 1989; JD, Duke U., 1992, LLM in Internat. Law, 1995. Bar: Fla. 1993. Sr. atty. Agy. for Health Care Adminstrn., State of Fla., Tallahassee, 1993-96; asst. atty. gen. Fla. Office Atty. Gen., Ft. Lauderdale, 1996-98; assoc. Dresnick & Ellsworth, PA, Miami, Fla., 1998—; ptnr. Dresnick, Ellsworth & Felder, P.A. Mem. Am. Health Lawyers Assn., Fla. Bar Assn., Fla. Hosp. Assn., Dade County Bar Assn. Administrative and regulatory, Health. Office: Dresnick Ellsworth Felder PA 201 Alhambra Cir Ste 701 Coral Gables FL 33134-5108

FELDER, MYRNA, lawyer; b. N.Y.C., Apr. 19, 1941; BA magna cum laude, Brown U., 1961; JD cum laude, NYU, 1971. Bar: N.Y. 1971, U.S. Dist. Ct. (so. and ea. dists.) N.Y. 1974, U.S. Ct. Appeals (2nd cir.) 1977, U.S. Supreme Ct. 1978. Ptnr. Raoul Lionel Felder P.C., N.Y.C., 1972—. Lectr., cons. in field; mem. N.Y. State Civil Practice Adv. Com., chair subcom. on matrimonial procedures, 1983—. Editor-in-chief: The Matrimonial Strategist, 1985-89; bimonthly columnist New York Law Jour.; contbr. chpts. to books. Mem. ABA, N.Y. State Bar Assn. (chair cts. of appellate jursidiction com. 1988-92), Assn. Bar City of N.Y., Women's Bar Assn., State N.Y. (dir. 1980-85, chmn. com. on matrimonial law 1984-85, pres. 1986-87), N.Y. Women's Bar Assn. (pres. 1976-77), Order of the Coif, Phi Beta Kappa. Family and matrimonial. Home: 60 Sutton Pl S Apt 19as New York NY 10022-4168 Office: Raoul Lionel Felder PC 437 Madison Ave New York NY 10022-7001

FELDER, RAOUL LIONEL, lawyer; b. N.Y.C., May 13, 1934; s. Morris and Millie (Goldstein) F.; m. Myrna Felder, May 26, 1963; children: Rachel, James. BA, NYU, 1955; JD, NYU, Switzerland, 1959; postgrad., U. Bern, Switzerland, 1955-56; hon. degree of fellow in jurisprudence, Oxford U., 1995. Bar: N.Y. 1959, U.S. Dist. Ct. (so. and ea. dists.) N.Y. 1962, U.S. Ct. Appeals (2d cir.) 1962, U.S. Supreme Ct. 1970. Pvt. practice, N.Y.C., 1959-61, 64—; asst. U.S. atty., 1961-64. Mem. faculty Practicing Law Inst., 1979, Marymount Coll., 1982-85, Ethical Culture Sch., 1981, 82; moderator Nat. Conf. on Child Abuse, 1989; apptd. to N.Y.C. Cultural Affairs Adv. Commn., 1995—, State Commn. on Child Abuse, 1996. Author: Divorce: The Way Things Are, Not the Way Things Should Be, 1971, Lawyers Practical Handbook to the New Divorce Law, 1981, Raoul Felder's Encyclopedia of Matrimonial Clauses, 1990, updated, 1991—, Getting Away with Murder, 1996, Restaurant Guide to Los Angeles and New York, 1996, Survival Guide to New York, 1997; columnist Fame mag., 1988-92, Am. Women Mag., 1994, N.Y. Daily News Sundays, 1995; contbr. articles on law to profl. jours. and N.Y. Times; editorials to Newsweek mag., Harper's Bazaar mag., Newsday newspaper, N.Y. Post, The Guardian (London),Jerusalem Post, Penthouse mag., Cosmopolitan mag., N.Y. Times; columnist Am.Spectator Mag, 1999—, Washington Times, 1999—; commentator Cable News Network, 1989, BBC World Wide, 1994, 95, 97, Crossing the Line, 1997-99, The Felder Report, 1998-99, guest commentator Court TV, 1992, bd. advisors, 1992-95, editl. contbr.; (documentary) Survival Guide to New York, 1998; host (TV series) Metrolaw, 1995-97; host (radio talk show) The Felder Report, 1997—, TalkAmerica. Chmn. Nat. Kidney Found. Auction, also N.Y. Fund; chmn. Dinner Jerusalem Reclamation Project; grand marshall U.S.A. Day Washington, Israel Day Parade, N.Y.C.; bd. dirs. Big Apple Greeters, 1997-99, Cop Care, Hosp. Audiences Inc., Nat. Kidney Found., N.Y.C. Econ. Devel. Corp., 2000—; mem. Govs. Commn. on Child Abuse, 1989; hon. N.Y. City Police Comms., 2000, 2001; appointed to Cultural Adv. Commn., N.Y.C., 2001—. Named Man of Yr. Bklyn. Sch. for Spl. Children, Met. Geriatric Ctr., Shield Inst., 1997; recipient Defender of Jerusalem medal, 1990, Crimebusters award Take Back N.Y., 1996. Mem. ABA (judge nat. finals client counseling competition), Assn. of Bar of City of N.Y. (spl. com. matrimonial law 1975-77), N.Y. State Trial Lawyers Assn. (past chmn. matrimonial law 1974-75), Am. Arbitration Assn., N.Y. Women's Bar Assn., Minion of the Stars (chmn. bd. 1993). Appellate, Family and matrimonial, General practice. Home: 60 Sutton Pl S New York NY 10022-4168 Office: 437 Madison Ave New York NY 10022-7001 E-mail: raoulfelder@raoulfelder.com

FELDERSTEIN, STEVEN HOWARD, lawyer; b. Rochester, N.Y., Oct. 28, 1946; s. Lester and Ruth (Tatelbaum) F.; m. Sandra Lynn Goldman, Aug. 26, 1969; 1 child, Janis. BA, SUNY, 1968; JD, U. Calif., San Francisco, 1973. Bar: Calif. Law clk. U.S. Dist. Ct., Sacramento, 1973-75; ptnr. Felderstein Rosenberg & McManus, 1978-86, Diepenbrock, Wulff, Plant & Hanmegan, LLP, Sacramento, 1986-98, Felderstein Fitzgerald Willoughby & Pascuzzi LLP, Sacramento, 1999—. Contbr. articles to profl. jours. Bd. trustees Jewish Fedn. Sacramento Region, 1990-95. Mem.: Calif. Bar Assn. (uniform comml.code com. bus. sect. 1983—85, insolvency com. bus. sect. 1999—), Calif. Continuing Edn. of Bar (lectr. 1987—), Practicing Law Inst. (lectr. 1995—), Am. Coll. Bankruptcy, Bankruptcy Forum (v.p. 1998, pres. 1998—99), Anthony M. Kennedy Inn of Ct. (master of the Bar 1999—2001). Bankruptcy, Contracts commercial. Office: Felderstein Willoughby & Pascuzzi LLP 400 Capitol Mall Ste 1450 Sacramento CA 95814-4434 Fax: 916-329-7435. E-mail: sfelderstein@ffwplaw.com

FELDHAUS, STEPHEN MARTIN, lawyer; b. Lawrenceburg, Tenn., Jan. 12, 1945; s. Lawrence Bernard and Margaret Martha (Holthouse) F.; m. Allis Rennie, Aug. 18, 1968 (div. 1980); 1 child, Rennie Elizabeth; m. Marcia Virginia Hughes, Dec. 30, 1980; stepchildren: Matthew Rankin FitzSimmons, Ryan Ford FitzSimmons. AB, U. Notre Dame, 1967; JD, Stanford U., 1973. Bar: Tex. 1973, D.C. 1984, U.S. Tax Ct. Law clk. to Hon. Eugene A. Wright U.S. Ct. Appeals (9th cir.), Seattle, 1972-73; assoc. Fulbright & Jaworski, Houston, 1973-76, London, 1976-79, ptnr., 1979-81, Washington, 1981—. Bd. dirs. Foundation, Vaduz, Liechtenstein. Bd. dirs. D.C. Downtown Partnership, Washington, 1988-92 Mem.: ABA, Internat. Bar Assn., Internat. Fiscal Assn., D.C. Bar, City Club of Washington. Republican. Avocations: tennis, squash, skiing, chess, reading. General corporate, Private international, Taxation, general. Office: Fulbright & Jaworski 801 Pennsylvania Ave NW Fl 3-5 Washington DC 20004-2623 E-mail: sfeldhaus@fulbright.com

FELDKAMP, JOHN CALVIN, lawyer, educational administrator; b. Milw., Sept. 5, 1939; s. Leroy Lyle and Dorothea Arpke (Reineking) F.; m. Barbara Joan Condon, June 30, 1962; children: John Calvin, Stephen Patrick, Amy Genevieve. BA, U. Mich., 1961, JD, 1965. Bar: Mich. 1970, N.J. 1980, D.C. 1983. Asst. to v.p. U. MIch., Ann Arbor. 1964-66, dir. housing, 1966-77; gen. mgr. svcs. Princeton U., N.J., 1977-82; pvt. practice law Ann Arbor, 1970-77, Princeton, 1977-82; assoc. Caplin & Drysdale, Washington, 1982-85; assoc., exec. dir. Brown & Wood, N.Y.C., 1985—. Councilman, City of Ann Arbor, 1967-69; hearing referee Mich. Civil Rights Commn., Lansing, 1975-77. Mem. Rotary (bd. dirs. Ann Arbor 1970-77, Princeton 1978-82). General practice. E-mail: jfeldkamp@brownwoodlaw.com

FELDMAN, JEFFREY MARC, lawyer; b. Providence, Nov. 8, 1949; s. Samuel and Shirley (Halpern) F.; m. Marjorie Burrows, Aug. 15, 1971; children: Peter, James. BA, Northeastern U., Boston, 1972, JD, 1975. Bar: Alaska 1976, U.S. Dist. Ct. Alaska 1976, R.I. 1976, U.S. Dist. Ct. R.I. 1976, U.S. Ct. Appeals (9th cir.) 1976, U.S. Supreme Ct. 1980. Law clk. Alaska Supreme Ct., Anchorage, 1975-76; asst. pub. defender Alaska Pub. Defender Office, Anchorage, 1976-78; mem. Gilmore & Feldman, Anchorage, 1978-90, Young, Sanders & Feldman, 1991—; mem. Supreme Ct. Com. on Pattern Jury Instrns., 1979-85, Alaska Com. Bar Examiners, 1981-86; chmn. Supreme Ct. on Criminal Rules, 1984-90; atty. rep. Jud. Conf. 9th Cir. Ct. Appeals, 1983-87; reporter Dist. of Alaska Adv. Group for Civil Justice Reform Act of 1990, 1991—. Contbr. articles to profl. jours. Mem. ABA, Am. Judicature Soc., Assn. Trial Lawyers Am., Am. Bd. Trial Advocates, Nat. Assn. Criminal Def. Lawyers, Alaska Acad. Trial Lawyers, R.I. Bar Assn., Alaska Bar Assn. (mem. bd. govs. 1986-92, pres. 1989-90), Anchorage Bar Assn. Federal civil litigation, State civil litigation, Criminal. Home: 1014 H St Anchorage AK 99501-3431 Office: Young Sanders & Feldman 500 L St Ste 400 Anchorage AK 99501-5911

FELDMAN, MARTIN L. C. federal judge; b. St. Louis, Jan. 28, 1934; s. Joseph and Zelma (Bosse) F.; m. Melanie Pulitzer, Nov. 26, 1958; children: Jennifer Pulitzer, Martin L.C. Jr. B.A., Tulane U., 1955, J.D., 1957. Bar: La., Mo. 1957. Law clk. to Hon. J.M. Wisdom, U.S. Ct. Appeals, 1958-59; assoc. Bronfin, Heller, Feldman & Steinberg, New Orleans, 1959-60, ptnr., 1960-83; judge U.S. Dist. Ct., New Orleans, 1983—. Trustee, former chmn. Sta. WYES-TV; spl. counsel to Gov. of La., 1979-83. Contbr. articles to profl. jours. Former nat. sec. Anti-Defamation League; former pres. bd. mgrs. Touro Infirmary; bd. dirs. Public Broadcasting Service, 1978-84, Fed. Jud. Ctr., 1991-95; bd. dirs. Fed. Jud. Ctr., 1991-95. Mem. ABA (chair nat. conf. of fed. trial judges 1996-97), La. Bar Assn. (chmn. law reform com. 1981-82), Mo. Bar Assn., Am. Law Inst., Order of Coif. Republican. Jewish. Home: 12 Rosa Park New Orleans LA 70115-5044 Office: US Dist Ct Chambers of Judge Feldman 500 Camp St New Orleans LA 70130-3313

FELDMAN, ROGER DAVID, lawyer; b. N.Y.C., Apr. 7, 1943; s. Louis and Dora (Goldsmith) F.; m. Gail Steg, May 31, 1969; children: Rebecca, Seth. AB, Brown U., 1962; LLB, Yale U.; MBA, Harvard U. Bar: N.Y. 1966, D.C. 1977. Ops. rsch. analyst Office Asst. Sec. Def., Washington, 1967-68; staff asst. Office of Pres. U. S., 1968-69; assoc. LeBoeuf Lamb Leiby & MacRae, 1969-75; ptnr. Le Boeuf Lamb Leiby & MacRae, 1977-83; dep. asst. adminstr. FEA, Washington, 1975-77; mng. ptnr. project fin. group Nixon Hargrave Devans & Doyle, 1983-89; head ptnr. project fin. group McDermott Will & Emery, 1989-97; chair project fin. group Bingham Dana LLP, 1997—. Mem. fin. adv. bd. EPA, 1989-92; bd. dirs. R.J. Rudden & Assocs. Inc., Cogeneration Inst., pub.-pvt. venture divsn. Am. Road and Transp. Builders, 1991-93, N.E. Energy and Commerce Assn., Water Industry Coun.; pres. Nat. Coun. for Pub. and Pvt. Partnerships, 1983-98, chair, 1998—. Author: (with others) Infrastructure Finance: Tools for the Future, 1988, Public-Private Ventures in Transportation, 1990, Comprehensive Guide to Water and Wastewater Finance, 1991, Privatization of Public Utilities, 1995, Privatization, 1995; mem. bd. editors Yale Law Jour., 1964-65, Jour. Project Fin., 1995—, Constrn. Bus. Rev., 1992—; Washington editor Cogeneration Monthly Letter, 1987-98, Mcht. Power Monthly, 1998—, Strategic Planning for Energy and the Environment, 1992— (Author of the Yr. 1998), Power Marketers Assn. On Line Mag., 1999—; contbr. articles to profl. jours. Mem. ABA (chmn. energy law com. 1980-83, alt. energy sources com. 1981-84, 86-90, chmn. environ. values com. 1983-89, com. on privatization 1985-90, chmn. energy fin. 1990-91), Fed. Energy Bar Assn. (chmn. cogeneration com. 1981-82), Nat. Coun. for Pub.-Pvt. Partnerships (Outstanding Contbn. to Privatization award), N.Y. Bar Assn., D.C. Bar Assn. (chair internat. fin. and investment com. 1998—), Assn. Energy Engrs. (Cogeneration Profl. of Yr. 1990), Phi Beta Kappa. FERC practice, Finance, Transportation. Office: Bingham Dana LLP 1120 20th St NW Ste 800 Washington DC 20036-3406 E-mail: feldmanr@bingham.com

FELDMAN, STANLEY GEORGE, state supreme court justice; b. N.Y.C., N.Y., Mar. 9, 1933; s. Meyer and Esther Betty (Golden) F.; m. Norma Arambula; 1 dau., Elizabeth L. Student, U. Calif., Los Angeles, 1950-51; LL.B., U. Ariz., 1956. Bar: Ariz. 1956. Practiced in, Tucson, 1956-81; ptnr. Miller, Pitt & Feldman, 1968-81; justice Ariz. Supreme Ct., Phoenix, 1982—, chief justice, 1992-97. Lectr. Coll. Law, U. Ariz., 1965-76, adj. prof., 1976-81. Bd. dirs. Tucson Jewish Community Council, U. Ariz. Found., 1999—. Mem. ABA, Am. Bd. Trial Advocates (past pres. So. Ariz. chpt.), Ariz. Bar Assn. (pres. 1974-75, bd. govs. 1967-76), Pima County Bar Assn. (past pres.), Am. Trial Lawyers Assn. (dir. chpt. 1967-76). Democrat. Jewish. Office: Ariz Supreme Ct 1501 W Washington St Phoenix AZ 85007-3222

FELDSTEIN, JAY HARRIS, lawyer; b. Elizabeth, Pa., June 23, 1937; s. Norman George and Gladys Shirley (Goldstein) F.; m. Judith Mae Stern, Sept. 8, 1963; children: Wendy Shawn, David Eric, Marc Howard. BA, Pa. State U., 1959; JD, Yale U., 1962. Bar: Fla. 1963, Pa. 1963, U.S. Dist. Ct. (we. dist.) Pa. 1963, U.S. Supreme Ct. 1967. Sole practice, Pitts., 1963-65; ptnr. Feldstein, Grinberg, Stein & McKee and predecessors, Pitts., 1965—. Chmn. Pa. Lottery Commn., Harrisburg, 1980-82; pres. Southview Apts. for Sr. Citizen Housing, Mt. Lebanon, 1980-84, State U. Nat. Alumni Assn., 1979-81; v.p. Am. Jewish Com., Pitts., 1984—. Served with USAF, 1963-69. Recipient Outstanding Young Man in Pitts. Area award Jr. C. of C., 1969. Mem. Pa. Trial Lawyers Assn. (bd. govs. 1984—), Allegheny County Acad. Trial Lawyers, Nat. Bd. Trial Advocacy (cert.). Democrat. Jewish. Club: Harvard, Yale, Princeton. Lodge: Masons (master 1972). State civil litigation, Personal injury. Home: 592 Sandrae Dr Pittsburgh PA 15243-1733 Office: Feldstein Grinberg Stein & McKee 428 Blvd of Allies Pittsburgh PA 15219

FELICIANO, JOSÉ CELSO, lawyer; b. Yauco, P.R., Mar. 7, 1950; s. Santiago and Cielo (Rodríguez) F.; m. Mary Colleen Dempsey; children: José, Rebecca, Marisa. BA, John Carroll U., 1972; JD, Cleve. State U., 1975; MBA, 1984. Bar: Ohio 1975, U.S. Dist. Ct. (no. dist.) Ohio 1975, U.S. Supreme Ct. 1979, U.S. Ct. Appeals (6th cir.) 1981, Staff atty. Legal Aid Soc., Cleve., 1975-78; asst. county pub. defender Cuyahoga County, Cleve., 1978-80; chief police prosecutor City of Cleve., 1980-84; White House fellow, Washington, 1984-85, ptnr. Baker & Hostetler, Cleve., 1985—. Contbr. articles to legal jours. V.p., gen. counsel Neighborhood Housing Svc., Cleve., 1977-80; v.p. United Way Svcs., Cleve., 1981-84, Fedn. for Community Planning, Cleve., 1981-84; bd. dirs. ARC, Cleve., 1981-84; chmn. vis. com. Case Western Res. U. Law Sch., Cleve., 1983-84; pres., founder Hispanic Community Forum, Cleve., 1984; bd. dirs. St. John's Hosp., 1986—; trustee Cleve. Ballet, 1986—. Book reviewer for Cleve. Plain Dealer. Recipient Disting. Svc. award Cleve. Jaycees, 1982, Disting. Alumni award Cleve. State U., 1990; named One of Outstanding Young Men of Ohio Ohio Jaycees, 1983, One of Outstanding Young Men of Am. U.S. Jaycees, 1985; named Pub. Adminstr. of Yr. Am. Soc. Pub. Adminstrn., 1983. Mem. ABA (sec. alternate dispute resolution sect.), Am. Bar Found., Ohio State Bar Assn. (mem. del. assembly), Ohio Hispanic Bar Assn. (founder, trustee, v.p. 1983-84), Cleve. Bar Assn. (trustee 1982-84). Democrat. Roman Catholic. Avocations: travel, reading, sports. General civil litigation, Public international. Home: 46 Wolfpen Dr Chagrin Falls OH 44022-4268 Office: Baker & Hostetler 3200 Nat City Ctr 1900 E 9th St Ste 3200 Cleveland OH 44114-3475

FELIX, ROBERT LOUIS, law educator; b. Detroit, Apr. 7, 1934; s. Camille Auguste and Rosalie (Le Floch) F.; m. Judith Joan Grossman, Aug. 25, 1962; children: Marie, Bridget, Robert, Conan. AB, U. Cin., 1956, LLB, 1959; MA, U. B.C., 1962; postgrad. Oxford U. 1962-63; LLM, Harvard U., 1967. Asst., assoc. prof. law Duquesne U., Pitts., 1963-67; assoc. prof. law U. S.C., 1967-72, prof., 1973—; chair James P. Mozingo III prof., 1984—; faculty assoc. U.S.C. Inst. Internat. Studies. With U.S. Army, 1960. Ford fellow Harvard Law Sch., 1966-67; Fulbright vis. lectr. U. Clermont-Ferrand, France, 1975-76; lectr. Program on Internat. Legal Coop., Free U., Brussels, Belgium, 1976. Mem. Assn. Am. Law Schs. (sect. on Conflict of Laws), S.C. Fulbright Alumni Assn. Roman Catholic. Author: (with R. Leflar, L. McDougal) Cases and Materials on American Conflicts Law, 1982, 2d edit., 1989, 3d edit., 1998, American Conflicts Law, 4th ed., 1986, 5th ed, 2001; (with F.P. Hubbard) The South Carolina Law of Torts, 1990, 2d edit., 1997; (with others) New Directions in Legal Education, 1969, (with others), The Vanity Fair Gallery, 1979. Contbr. articles to profl. jours. Home: 6233 Macon Rd Columbia SC 29209-2016 Office: U SC Law Sch Main & Greene St Columbia SC 29208-0001

FELL, RILEY BROWN, lawyer; b. New Orleans, Apr. 28, 1921; s. William Riley Brown and Lucy Agnes (Alcantara) F.; m. Mildred Elizabeth Gause, Aug. 21, 1947 (dec. July 1995); children: Damon, Martha, Mark, Michael, Brigid, James (dec.), Monica, Mary, Grace, Gerard. BSME, La. Poly. Inst., Ruston, 1943; LLB, Tulane U., 1947. Bar: La. 1947, Okla. 1961, U.S. Ct. Appeals (5th and 10th cirs.), U.S. Supreme Ct. 1957, U.S. Dist. Ct. (we. and ea. dists.) La., U.S. Dist. Ct. (no. and ea. dists.) Okla., U.S. Dist. Ct. (so. dist.) Ill., U.S. Dist. Ct. (so. dist.) Miss., others. Lawyer Hunt Oil Co., Shreveport, 1947-55, The Ohio Oil Co., Shreveport, Tulsa, 1955-63; divsn. atty. Marathon Oil Co., Tulsa, 1963-72; gen. counsel Loop Inc., New Orleans, 1972-79; ptnr. Barham & Churchill, 1979-82; sole practice law New Orleans, Tulsa, 1982—. Legal com. Interstate Oil Compact Commn., Tulsa, 1966-70, New Orleans, 1973-81. Served in U.S. Navy, 1944-45. Mem. ABA, Am. Petroleum Inst. (chmn. subcom. 1969-81), Serra Club. Republican. Roman Catholic. Avocations: church choir, cooking, aerobics, mentoring, tutoring. Alternative dispute resolution, Oil, gas, and mineral, Environmental. Home: 4231 S Sandusky Ave Tulsa OK 74135-2860

FELLER, LLOYD HARRIS, lawyer; b. New Brunswick, N.J., Aug. 27, 1942; s. Alexander and Freda (Kaminsky) F.; m. Susan Sydney Weinberg, Aug. 6, 1967; children: Jennifer, Andrew. BS in Econs., U. Pa., 1964; LLB, NYU, 1967. Bar: N.Y. 1967, D.C. 1980. Assoc. Rubin, Wachtel, Baum & Levin, 1967-70; trial atty. organized crime sect., divsn. enforcement SEC, Washington, 1970-72, legal asst. Commr. A. Sydney Herlong, Jr., 1972-73, legal asst. Commr. A.A. Sommer, Jr., 1973-76; chief counsel Office of the Chief Acct., 1976-77; assoc. dif. divsn. market regulation Office of Market Structure and Trading Practices, 1977-79, of counsel, 1979-81; ptnr. Morgan, Lewis & Bockius LLP, Washington, 1981-99, mem. governing bd., 1996-99, mem. exec. com., 1998-99, mem. allocations com., 1999—; sr. v.p., co-gen. counsel Wit Capital Group, Inc., N.Y.C., 1999—2001; sr. v.p., gen. counsel SoundView Tech. Group, Inc. General corporate, Mergers and acquisitions, Securities. Home: 3448 Clay St San Francisco CA 94118 Office: Wit SoundView Tech Group Steuart Twr One Market Plaza San Francisco CA

FELLERS, RHONDA GAY, lawyer; b. Gainesville, Tex., July 20, 1955; d. James Norman and Gaytha Ann (Sanders) F.; m. Bruce C. Hinton, Oct. 15, 1981 (div. Oct. 1985). BA, U. Tex., 1977, JD, 1980; LLM in Taxation, U. Denver, 1987. Bar: Tex. 1981, Colo. 1981, U.S. Dist. Ct. (no. dist.) Tex. 1982, U.S. Dist. Ct. Colo. 1985, U.S. Tax Ct. 1985, U.S. Ct. Appeals (5th cir.) 1986, U.S. Ct. Appeals (10th cir.) 1989, U.S. Supreme Ct. 1993, U.S. Ct. Claims 1993. Assoc. Walters & Assocs., Lubbock, Tex., 1981-83; gen. counsel Security Nat. Bank, 1983; sole practice, 1983-87; assoc. Melvin Coffee & Assocs., P.C., Denver, 1984-85, 87-90; atty. adviser U.S. Tax Ct., Washington, 1990-94; pvt. practice Pinehurst, Tex., 1994-98; with Andersen LLP, Houston, 1998—. Mem. ABA, State Bar Tex., Colo. Bar Assn., Houston Bar Assn. Avocations: golf, tennis, photography. Office: 711 Louisiana St Ste 1300 Houston TX 77002-2716 E-mail: rhonda.g.fellers@us.andersen.com, rgfellers@email.com

FELLOWS, HENRY DAVID, JR. lawyer; b. N.Y.C., Dec. 17, 1954; s. Henry D. Sr. and Mary (Stecko) F.; m. Pam Neal Fellows, May 15, 1982; children: Christopher, Suzanne, Thomas. BSBA, Bucknell U., 1975; JD, Georgetown U., 1978. Bar: Ga. 1978, U.S. Dist. Ct. (no. dist.) Ga. 1978, U.S. Ct. Appeals (11th cir.) 1978, U.S. Supreme Ct. 1997. Law clk. to hon. judge Charles A. Moye Jr. U.S. Dist. Ct. (no. dist.) Ga., Atlanta, 1978-80; assoc. Hurt, Richardson, Garner, Todd & Cadenhead, 1981-87, ptnr., 1987-92, Fellows, Johnson & LaBriola, LLP (and predecessor firm), Atlanta, 1993—. Mem. ABA, Ga. Bar Assn., Atlanta Bar Assn. (chmn. ct. com. 1992-98, bd. dirs. litigation sect. 1999—), Lawyers Club of Atlanta, Indsl. Rels. Rsch. Assn. (bd. dirs. Atlanta chpt.), Futton Indsl. Bus. Assn. (gen. counsel). Avocations: tennis, piano. Federal civil litigation, General civil litigation. Office: Fellows Johnson & LaBriola LLP Peachtree Ctr # 2300 South 225 Peachtree St NE Atlanta GA 30303-1701 E-mail: hfellows@fjl-law.com

FELLOWS, JERRY KENNETH, lawyer; b. Madison, Wis., Mar. 19, 1946; s. Forrest Garner and Virginia (Witte) F.; m. Patricia Lynn Graves, June 28, 1970; children: Jonathon, Aaron, Daniel. BA in Econs., U. Wis., 1968; JD, U. Minn., 1971. Bar: U.S. Dist. Ct. (no. dist.) Ill. 1971. Ptnr. McDermott, Will & Emery, Chgo., 1971—. Speaker Bur. Nat. Affairs, Washington, 1985—. Contbr. articles to profl. jours. Bd. dirs. Midwest Benefits Coun., 1998. Mem. U. Minn. Law Alumni Assn. (bd. visitors), Gamma Eta Gamma. Avocations: coaching track, basketball, baseball. Administrative and regulatory, Pension, profit-sharing, and employee benefits, Personal income taxation. Home: 4541 Middaugh Ave Downers Grove IL 60515-2761 Office: McDermott Will & Emery 227 W Monroe St Ste 3100 Chicago IL 60606-5096 E-mail: jfellows@mwe.com, jpfellows@msn.com

FELPER, DAVID MICHAEL, lawyer; b. Springfield, Mass., Dec. 17, 1954; s. Lawrence Allen and Edith Charlotte (Flesher) F.; m. Kimberlee White, May 19, 1979; children: Andrew Martin, Evan Matthew, Scott Tyler. BA in Polit. Sci., George Washington U., 1976; JD cum laude, Western New Eng. Coll., 1980. Bar: Mass. 1980, U.S. Dist. Ct. Mass. 1981, U.S. Ct. Appeals (1st cir.) 1987. Assoc. Michelman & Feinstein, Springfield, 1980-82; asst. regional counsel Dept. Social Services, Commonwealth of Mass., 1982-83; labor relations counsel Sprague Electric Co., Lexington, Mass., 1983-87; assoc. Bowditch & Dewey, Framingham, 1987-92, ptnr., 1992—. Lectr. various human resource orgns. throughout U.S., 1984—; pres. Valley Tech. Ednl. Found. Inc., 1998—; corporator Milford-Whitinsville Regional Hosp. Dir. United Way Tri County; pres. Hopedale Youth Baseball Assn.; chmn. bd. Horace Mann Ednl. Assocs., Inc. Mem. Mass. Bar Assn. (labor law com., labor and employment sect. coun.), Worcester County Bar Assn. (labor and employment law com.), Blackstone Valley C. of C. (dir.). Avocations: golf, running, reading. Labor, Pension, profit-sharing, and employee benefits, Workers' compensation. Office: Bowditch & Dewey 311 Main St Worcester MA 01608 E-mail: DFelper@bowditch.com

FELS, JAMES ALEXANDER, lawyer; b. Chgo., Nov. 13, 1944; s. William Frederick and Rosemary (Budasi) F.; m. Nancy Ann Dugan, July 15, 1967; children: Jeffery Scott, Scott Thomas, Thomas Jeffery. BS, Butler U., 1970; JD magna cum laude, Ind. U., 1974. Assoc. atty. Wilson & Tabor, Indpls., 1974-76, Wilson, Tabor & Holland, Indpls., 1976-81; mng. atty. Holland & Tabor, 1981-87; ptnr. Tabor, Fels & Tabor, 1987-2000, The Mediation Group LLC, Indpls., 2000—. With U.S. Army, 1967-72. Mem. ABA, Assn. Trial Lawyers Am., Lawyer-Pilots Bar Assn., Ind. trial Lawyers Assn., Ind. Bar Assn. Republican. Roman Catholic. Alternative dispute resolution, Insurance, Personal injury. Home: 8136 Rush Pl Indianapolis IN 46250-4266 Office: The Mediation Group LLC Ste 640 8888 Keystone Crossing Indianapolis IN 46204-4614 E-mail: felsjim@iquest.net, jfels@mede8.com

FELS, NICHOLAS WOLFF, lawyer; b. White Plains, N.Y., Mar. 19, 1943; s. Lawrence P. and Fredericka (Gaines) F.; m. Susan T. McEwan, Dec. 28, 1968; 1 child, Sarah. BA, Harvard U., 1964; MA, U. Calif., Berkeley, 1965; LLB, Harvard U., 1968. Bar: N.Y. 1968, Calif. 1970, U.S. Dist. Ct. (cen. dist.) Calif. 1970, D.C. 1971, U.S. Dist. Ct. D.C. 1971, U.S. Ct. Appeals (10th cir.) 1976, U.S. Ct. Appeals (D.C. cir.) 1977, U.S. Supreme Ct. 1978, U.S. Ct. Appeals (4th cir.) 1979, U.S. Ct. Appeals (8th cir.) 1981, U.S. Ct. Appeals (5th cir.) 1982. Law clk. to Hon. John Minor Wisdom U.S. Ct. Appeals, New Orleans, 1968-69; atty. OEO Legal Services, Los Angeles, 1969-70; assoc. Covington & Burling, Washington, 1970-76, ptnr., 1976—. Mem. Nat. Com. on U.S.-China Relations, N.Y.C., 1982—. Contbr. articles to profl. jours. Mem. Fed. Energy Bar Assn., D.C. Appleseed Ctr. (bd. dirs. 1994—, pres. 1996-2000). FERC practice. Home: 3534 Edmunds St NW Washington DC 20007-1431 Office: Covington & Burling 1201 Pennsylvania Ave NW Washington DC 20004-2401 E-mail: nfels@cov.com

FELSENTHAL, STEVEN ALTUS, lawyer, educator; b. Chgo., May 21, 1949; s. Jerome and Eve (Altus) F.; m. Carol Judith Greenberg, June 14, 1970; children: Rebecca Elizabeth, Julia Alison, Daniel Louis Altus. AB, U. Ill., 1971; JD, Harvard U., 1974. Bar: Ill. 1974, U.S. Dist. Ct. (no. dist.) Ill. 1974, U.S. Ct. Claims 1975, U.S. Tax Ct. 1975, U.S. Ct. Appeals (7th cir.) 1981. Assoc. Levenfeld, Kanter, Baskes & Lippitz, Chgo., 1974-78; ptnr. Levenfeld & Kanter, 1978-80, Levenfeld, Eisenberg, Janger, Glassberg & Lippitz, Chgo., 1980-84; sr. ptnr. Sugar, Friedberg & Felsenthal, 1984—. Lectr. Kent Coll. Law, Ill. Inst. Tech., Chgo., 1978-80. Mem. ABA, Ill. Bar Assn., Chgo. Bar Assn., Chgo. Coun. Lawyers, Harvard Law Soc. Ill., Standard Club, Harvard Club, Phi Beta Kappa. General corporate, Estate planning, Taxation, general. Office: Sugar Friedberg & Felsenthal 30 N La Salle St Ste 2600 Chicago IL 60602-2506 E-mail: saf@sff-law.com

FELT, JULIA KAY, lawyer; b. Wooster, Ohio, Apr. 8, 1941; d. George Willard and Betty Virginia F.; m. Lawrence Roger Van Til, May 31, 1969. BA, Northwestern U., 1963; JD, U. Mich., 1967. Bar: Ohio 1967, Mich. 1968. Tchr. Triway Local H.S.s, Wooster, Ohio, 1963-64; assoc. Dykema, Gossett, Detroit, 1967-75, ptnr., 1975—; adj. asst. prof. dept. cmty. medicine Wayne State U., Detroit, 1974—. Contbr. articles to profl. jours., chpts. to books. Trustee Rehab. Inst., Detroit, 1971—, sec., 1974-77, 91—, vice chmn., 1978-83, 85-90, chmn. bd., 1983-85; trustee Detroit Med. Ctr. Corp. 1984-85; bd. dirs. Travelers Aid Soc., Detroit, 1974—, v.p., 1978-81, United Way Southeastern Mich., Detroit, bd. dirs., 1981—; vis. com. U. Mich. Law Sch., Ann Arbor, 1972—, nat. vice chmn. law sch. fund, 1984-86, bd. dirs. Detroit Assn. U. Mich. Women, 1968-72, pres., 1971-72, Mich. Women's Found., trustee, 1993—, Planned Giving Round table Southeatern Mich., chmn., 1993-94; chmn. Leave a Legacy Southeastern Mich., 1996-98. Campbell Competition winner U. Mich. Law Sch., 1967; recipient Svc. award Mich. League Nursing, 1977, Alumna-in-Residence U. Mich. Alumnae Coun., 1986, Disting. Svc. award Mich. Bus. and Profl. Assn., 1998. Fellow Am. Bar Found., Mich. Bar Found.; mem. Am. Acad. Health Care Attys. of Am. Hosp. Assn. (pres. 1985-86, bd. dirs. 1980-87), Mich. Soc. Hosp. Attys. (pres. 1975-76, bd. dirs. 1975-77), Cath. Health Assn. U.S. (legal services adv. com. 1980-84), Gov's. Commn. on End Life Case, Adv. Com. Pain and Symptom Mgmt. , ABA, Ohio State Bar Assn., State Bar Mich. (com. medicolegal problems 1973-81, adminstrv. rule making com. 1978-79, awards com. chmn. 1989-99, disabilities com. Open Justice Commn., 1999—), Am. Hosp. Assn., Detroit Bar Assn., Women Lawyers Mich., Am. Soc. Law and Medicine, Am. Health Lawyers Assn. Presbyterian. E-mail: kfeet@dykema.com. General corporate, Health. Office: Dykema Gossett 400 Renaissance Ctr Ste 35 Detroit MI 48243-1501

FELTER, EDWIN LESTER, JR. judge; b. Washington, Aug. 11, 1941; s. Edwin L. Felter and Bertha (Peters) Brekke; m. Yoko Yamauchi-Koito, Dec. 26, 1969. BA, U. Tex., 1964; JD, Cath. U. of Am., 1967. Bar: Colo. 1970, U.S. Dist. Ct. Colo. 1970, U.S. Ct. Appeals (10th cir.) 1971, U.S. Supreme Ct. 1973, U.S. Tax Ct. 1979, U.S. Ct. Claims 1979, U.S. Ct. Internat. Trade 1979. Dep. pub. defender State of Colo., Ft. Collins, 1971-75; asst. atty. gen. Office of the Atty. Gen., Denver, 1975-80; state adminstrv. law judge Colo. Divsn. of Adminstrv. Hearings, 1980-83, chief adminstrv. law judge, 1983-98, sr. adminstr., law judge, 1998—. Disciplinary prosecutor Supreme Ct. Grievance Com., 1975-78; mem. faculty Nat. Jud. Coll., 1999—. Contbg. editor Internat. Franchising, 1970. Mem. Colo. State Mgmt. Cert. Steering Com., 1983-86; No. Colo. Criminal Justice Planning Coun., Ft. Collins, 1973-75; bd. dirs., vice chmn. The Point Cmty. Crisis Ctr., Ft. Collins, 1971-73; mem. Denver County Dem. Party Steering Com., 1978-79, chmn. 12th legis. dist., 1978-79; bd. dirs., pres. Denver Internat. Program, 1989-90. Mem.: ABA, Nat. Conf. Adminstrv. Law Judges (chair 2000—01), Arapahoe County Bar Assn., Denver Bar Assn., Colo. Bar Assn. (chmn. grievance policy com. 1991—94, interprofl. com. 1995—), Nat. Assn. Adminstrv. Law Judges (pres. Colo. chpt. 1982—84, Fellowship winner 1994), Am. Inns of Ct. (master level 1996—). Office: Colo Divsn Adminstrv Hearings 1120 Lincoln St Ste 1400 Denver CO 80203-2140

FELTY, KRISS DELBERT, lawyer; b. Cleve., May 5, 1954; s. John Gilbert and Stephanie (Kriss) F. BA in Psychology, Case Western Res. U., 1976; postgrad., Cleve. State U., 1977-79; JD, U. Akron, Ohio, 1983. Bar: Ohio 1983, Tex.1988, Wis. 1989, U.S. Dist. Ct. Ohio 1983, U.S. Ct. Appeals (6th cir.) 1984, Fla. 1985, U.S. Supreme Ct. 1986. Assoc. Dennis Reimer Co., LPA, Twinsburg, Ohio, 1983-87; mng. ptnr. Shapiro & Felty, Independence, 1987--. Mem. ABA, Fla. Bar Assn., Ohio Bar Assn., Greater Cleve. Bar Assn., Cuyahoga County Bar Assn., Mortgage Bankers Assn. Am., Ohio Mortgage Bankers Assn., Mortgage Bankers Assn. Met. Cleve., Phi Kappa Theta (trustee 1973-74). Avocations: golf, swimming, reading, music, leaded glass lamps. Bankruptcy, Consumer commercial, Real property. Office: Shapiro & Felty 800 W Saint Clair Ave Fl 2 Cleveland OH 44113-1266

FENDLER, OSCAR, lawyer; b. Blytheville, Ark., Mar. 22, 1909; s. Alfred and Rae (Sattler) F.; m. Patricia Shane, Oct. 26, 1946; children: Tilden P. Wright III (stepson), Frances Shane. B.A., U. Ark., 1930; LL.B., Harvard, 1933. Bar: Ark. bar 1933. Practice in, Blytheville, 1933-41, 46—. Spl. justice Ark. Supreme Ct., 1965; Mem. Ark. Jud. Council, 1959- 60; pres. Conf. Local Bar Assn., 1958-60; pres. bd. dirs. Ark. Law Rev., 1961-67; mem. Ark. Bd. Pardons and Paroles, 1970-71 Mem. Miss. County Democratic Central Com., 1948— . Served with USNR, 1941-45. Fellow Am. Coll. Trust and Estate Counsel, Am. Bar Found.; mem. ABA (chmn. gen. practice sect. 1966-67, mem. council sect. gen. practice 1964—, ho. dels. 1968-80, mem. com. edn. about Communism 1966-70, com. legal aid and indigent defendants 1970-73, chmn. com. law lists 1973-76, Founders award 1992), Ark. Bar Assn. (chmn. exec. com. 1956-57, pres. 1962-63), Am. Judicature Soc. (dir. 1964-68), Scribes, Nat. Conf. Bar Presidents (exec. council 1963-65), Blytheville C. of C. (past v.p., dir.), Navy League, Am. Legion. Club: Blytheville Rotary (past pres.). General civil litigation, General practice, Probate. Home: 1062 Hearn St Blytheville AR 72315-2659 Office: PO Box 548 104 N 6th St Blytheville AR 72315-3315

FENDLER, SHERMAN GENE, lawyer; b. Alexandria, La., Jan. 22, 1947; s. Ben and Rae (Kaplan) F.; m. Sarah Linda Dantzler, Dec. 26, 1976; children: Julia Kathleen, Abigail Leigh, Benjamin Brooks. BA, U. Va.-Charlottesville, 1969; JD, La. State U., 1973. Bar: La. 1973, U.S. Dist. Ct. La. 1974, U.S. Ct. Appeals (5th and 11th cirs.) 1975, U.S. Supreme Ct. 1980. Law clk. U.S. Dist. Ct., Ea. Dist. La., New Orleans, 1973-74; ptnr. law firm Liskow & Lewis, New Orleans, 1974—. Served to capt. AUS, 1973-79. Mem. La. Bar Assn., ABA, Maritime Law Assn., Order of Coif. Admiralty, Aviation, Federal civil litigation. Home: 1102 Metairie Rd Metairie LA 70005-3301 Office: Liskow & Lewis One Shell Sq 50th Fl New Orleans LA 70139

FENECH, JOSEPH CHARLES, lawyer; b. London, May 28, 1950; came to U.S., 1953; s. Carmel John and Elizabeth Frances (Borg) F.; m. Cynthia A. Rennie, June 14, 1980 (div. 1998); children: Paul C., Peter J., Elizabeth F. BA with honors, Mich. State U., 1972; JD, U. Mich., 1975. Bar: Mich. 1975, U.S. Dist. Ct. (ea. dist.) Mich. 1975, U.S. Ct. Appeals (6th cir.) 1977, Ill. 1980, U.S. Dist. Ct. (no. dist.) Ill. 1980, U.S. Dist. Ct. (ctrl. dist.) Ill. 1993, U.S. Dist. Ct. (ea. dist.) Wis. 1993, U.S. Ct. Appeals (7th cir.) 1980, U.S. Supreme Ct. 1993, U.S. Tax Ct. 1993. Law clk. Washtenaw Cir. Ct., Ann Arbor, Mich., 1975-76; asst. atty. gen. State of Mich., Detroit, 1976-80; labor rels. counsel McDonald's Corp., Oak Brook, Ill., 1980-82, sr. internat. atty., 1982-84; sr. mem. Fenech & Assoc., 1985—. Contbr. articles to profl. jours. Bd. dirs. Cath. Charities Diocese of Joliet, Ill.; active Family Focus, Mich., 1979-80, Internat. Found. Employee Benefit Plans, Brookfield, Wis., 1980-83, Chmns. Club Ctrl.; mem. bd. govs. DuPage Hosp., Ctrl. DuPage Hosp. Tree Life, Ctrl., Glen Oaks Med. Ctr., Tree of Life, Rep. Campaign Coun., 1995; supt. adv. com. Naperville Cmty. Sch. Dist. 203; improvement com. Mill St. Sch., Naperville; charter mem. Marklund Children's Home Endowment; bd. govs. Ctrl. DuPage Hosp. Named Regents scholar U. Mich., 1973, 74, 75, Trustees scholar Mich. State U., 1969-72. Mem. ABA, Ill. State Bar Assn., Mich. Bar assn., DuPage Estate Planning Coun., U. Mich. Lawyers Club, Ill. Bankers Assn., Ill. Mortgage Bankers Assn., Internat. Platform Assn. Am. Hosp. Assn. (sr. mem.), Am. Acad. Healthcare Attys. (sr. mem.). Contracts commercial, General corporate, Private international. Office: Fenech & Pachulski PC 1 Lincoln Ctr Ste 840 Oakbrook Terrace IL 60181-4265

FENNER, SUZAN ELLEN, lawyer; b. Grand Junction, Colo., Dec. 5, 1947; d. Harry J. and Louise (Bain) Shaw; m. Michael Lee Riddle, Apr. 24, 1969 (div. Feb. 1976); m. Peter R. Fenner, Nov. 24, 1978; children: Laura Elizabeth, Adam Kyle. BA, Tex. Tech U., 1969, JD, 1971. Bar: Tex. 1972, U.S. Dist. Ct. (no. dist.) Tex. 1972. Assoc. Smith & Baker, Lubbock, Tex., 1971-72; law clk. to presiding judge U.S. Dist. Ct., Dallas, 1972-73; assoc. Gardere, Wynne & Sewell, L.L.P., 1973-78, ptnr., 1978—, also mem. ptnrs. bd., 1991-94. Chair retirement com. Gardere, Wynne & Sewell, L.L.P., , 1990—, chair recruiting com. 1992-94, mem. ptnrs. compensation com., 1999—, chair tax practice group, 2001—; bd. dirs. Tex. Lawyers Ins. Exch., 1985—; bd. dirs. S.W. Benefits Assn. (formerly S.W. Pension Conf.), 1987-92, pres. 1990-91. Bd. dirs. East Dallas Devel. Ctr., 1982-91; Lone Star coun. Camp Fire Boys and Girls, Inc., 1995-2001, v.p. outdoor programs, 1996-98, pres.-elect, 1997, pres., 1998-2000; bd. dirs. Episcopal Ch. Women of the Diocese of Dallas, 1992—, pres. 1996-2000; del. to triennial nat. conv. Episcopal Diocese of Dallas, 1994, 97, 2000; asst. chancellor, 1994—, exec. coun., 1995-00; pres. Episcopal Ch. Women for Episcopal Ch. of Ascension, 1992, bd. dirs. 1992-94; pres. Province VII Episcopal Ch. Women, bd. dirs. 1999—; exec. coun. Province VII of the Episcopal Ch., 1999—. Mem. ABA, Tex. Bar Assn. (chmn. bar. jour. com. 1982-88), Dallas Bar Assn. (treas. employee benefits com. 1998, sec. 1999, v.p. 2000, pres. 2001), Dallas Bus. League (pres. 1986), 500 Club. Episcopalian. Avocation: sailing. Pension, profit-sharing, and employee benefits. Home: 600 Goodwin Dr Richardson TX 75081-5603 Office: Gardere Wynne Sewell LLP 1601 Elm St Ste 3000 Dallas TX 75201-4761 E-mail: sfenner@gardere.com

FENNING, LISA HILL, lawyer, mediator, former federal judge; b. Chgo., Feb. 22, 1952; d. Ivan Byron and Joan (Hennigar) Hill; m. Alan Mark Fenning, Apr. 3, 1977; 4 children. BA with honors, Wellesley Coll., 1971; JD, Yale U., 1974. Bar: Ill. 1975, Calif. 1979, U.S. Dist. Ct. (no. dist.) Ill., U.S. Dist. Ct. (no., ea., so. & cen. dists.) Calif., U.S. Ct. Appeals (6th, 7th & 9th cirs.), U.S. Supreme Ct. 1989. Law clk. U.S. Ct. Appeals 7th cir., Chgo., 1974-75; assoc. Jenner and Block, 1975-77, O'Melveny and Myers, L.A., 1977-85; judge U.S. Bankruptcy Ct. Cen. Dist. Calif., 1985-2000; mediator JAMS, Orange, Calif., 2000-01; ptnr. Dewey Ballantine LLP, L.A., 2001—. Bd. govs. Nat. Conf. Bankruptcy Judges, 1989-92; pres. Nat. Conf. of Women's Bar Assns., N.C., 1987-88, pres.-elect, 1986-87, v.p., 1985-86, bd. dirs.; lectr., program coord. in field; bd. govs. Nat. Conf. Bankruptcy Judges Endowment for Edn., 1992-97, Am. Bankruptcy Inst., 1994-2000; mem., bd. advisors Nat. Jud. Edn. Program to Promote Equality for Women and Men in the Cts., 1994—. Mem., bd. advisors: Lawyer Hiring & Training Report, 1985-87; contbr. articles to profl. jours. Durant scholar Wellesley Coll., 1971; named one of Am's. 100 Most Important Women Ladies Home Jour., 1988, one of L.A.'s 50 Most Powerful Women Lawyers, L.A. Bus. Jour., 1998. Fellow Am. Bar Found., Am. Coll. Bankruptcy (bd. regents 1995-98); mem. ABA (standing com. on fed. jud. improvements 1995-98, mem. commn. on women in the profession 1987-91, Women's Caucus 1987—, Individual Rights and Responsibilities sect. 1984—, bus. law sect. 1986—, bus. bankruptcy com.), Nat. Assn. Women Judges (nat. task force gender bias in the cts. 1986-87, 93-94), Nat. Conf. Bankruptcy Judges (chair endowment edn. bd. 1994-95), Am. Bankruptcy Inst. (nominating com. 1994-95, bd. steering com. stats. project 1994-96), Calif. State Bar Assn. (chair com. on women in law 1986-87), Women Lawyers' Assn. L.A. (ex officio mem., bd. dirs., chmn., founder com. on status of women lawyers 1984-85, officer nominating com. 1986, founder, mem. Do-It-Yourself Mentor Network 1986-96), Phi Beta Kappa. Democrat. Office: Dewey Ballantine LLP 333 S Grand Ave 26th Fl Los Angeles CA 90071 E-mail: Lfenning@deweyballantine.com

FENSTER, FRED A. lawyer, educator; b. Hartford, Conn., Oct. 8, 1946; s. Albert J. and Eleanor S. (Meyers) F.; m. Andrea Reifman, Jan. 2, 1972; children: Amanda Susanne, Monica Danielle. BA, U. So. Calif., 1968, JD, 1971. Bar: Calif. 1972, U.S. Dist. Ct. (cen. and so. dists.) Calif. 1972. Assoc. Richards, Watson & Gershon, L.A., 1971-76, ptnr., 1977-94, Heenan Blaikie, 1995—; adj. prof. U. So. Calif., L.A., 1977—. Campaign organizer Democratic Party, L.A.. Recipient 4 Am. Jurisprudence awards U. So. Calif., 1968-71; Asso. Men's Student's Scroll of Honor, 1968; scholar Cambridge U., Eng., 1967. Mem. Los Angeles County Bar Assn., Calif. Bar Assn., ABA, Order of Coif, Phi Beta Kappa, Phi Kappa Phi, Phi Eta Sigma, Pi Sigma Alpha. State civil litigation. Office: Richards Watson & Gershon 333 S Hope St Bldg 38 Los Angeles CA 90071-1406

FENSTER, HERBERT LAWRENCE, lawyer; b. N.Y.C., Mar. 29, 1935; s. Oscar Samuel and Bessie Estelle (Schafran) F.; m. Gail Frances Meier, Apr. 18, 1964; children— Christopher Lawrence, Jennifer Gail, Jonathan Adam; m. Jane Porter Elam Allen, Dec. 31, 1993. A.B., U. Pa., 1957, M.A., 1958; J.D., U. Va., 1961. Bar: Va. 1961, D.C. 1962, U.S. Supreme Ct. 1967, Colo., 1993. Assoc., Sellers, Conner & Cuneo, Washington, 1961-66, ptnr., 1967-78, sr. ptnr., 1978-80; sr. ptnr. McKenna, Conner & Cuneo, 1980-90, McKenna & Cuneo, 1990—. Author treatise Anti Deficiency Act, ABA, 1979. Litigation counsel Reagan-Bush Campaign Com., Washington, 1980-83, pres.'s pvt. sector survey Grace Commn., 1982— ; bd. dirs. Nat. Chamber Litigation Ctr., Washington, 1983— ; bd. dirs. Keewaydin Found., Middlebury Vermont, 1982—, also trustee, corp. dir. Fellow Assn. Trial Lawyers Am.; mem. ABA, Fed. Bar Assn., D.C. Bar Assn., Am. Law Inst. Republican. Episcopalian. Clubs: Metropolitan, University. Environmental, Government contracts and claims, Product liability. Home: 845 6th St Boulder CO 80302-7418 Address: 370 17th St Denver CO 80202-1370

FENSTER, MARVIN, lawyer, department store executive; b. Bklyn., Jan. 19, 1918; s. Isaac and Anna (Greenman) F.; m. Louise Rapoport, Nov. 13, 1953; children: Julie, Mark. AB, Cornell U., 1938; LLB, Columbia U., 1941. Bar: N.Y. 1942. Assoc. Lauterstein, Spiller, Bergerman & Dannett, N.Y.C., 1941-42, 46-48; atty., asst. gen. atty. R.H. Macy & Co., Inc., N.Y.C., 1948-60, sr. v.p., gen. counsel, sec., 1960-84, sr. v.p. spl. counsel, sec., 1984-87, dir., sr. v.p., spl. counsel, sec., 1987—; pres., dir. Macy's Bank, 1981—; sr. v.p., sec. Macy Credit Corp., N.Y.C., 1961-86, pres., dir., chief exec. officer, 1986—; pres., chief exec. officer Macy Receivables Funding Corp., N.Y.C., 1989—. 1st lt. U.S. Army, 1943-46. Mem. Assn. of Bar, City of New York (corp. law depts. post-admission legal edn., council jud. adminstrn. 1983), Am. Coll. Real Estate Lawyers, Harmonie Club, Beach Point Club, Phi Epsilon Pi. Jewish. Finance, Landlord-tenant, Real property. Office: R H Macy & Co Inc 151 W 34th St New York NY 10001-2180

FENSTER, ROBERT DAVID, lawyer; b. N.Y.C., Sept. 25, 1946; s. Alfred Howard and Esther (Eisenberg) F.; m. Janet Lynne Shanes, July 27, 1969; children: Lori Beth, Eric Steven. BA, CUNY, 1968; JD, Bklyn. Law Sch., 1973. Bar: N.Y. 1974, U.S. Dist. Ct. (so. and ea. dists.) N.Y. 1974, U.S. Supreme Ct. 1977. Investigator, prosecutor N.Y. Stock Exch., N.Y.C., 1972-73; ptnr. law firm various law firms, Rockland County, N.Y., 1974-80; ptnr. Fenster & Weiss, New City, 1980-2000, Robert D. Fenster, Atty. at Law, P.C., New City, 2001—. Bd. dirs. Brit. Pub. Corp., various other corps. Advisor Clarkstown Youth Ct., New City, N.Y., 1982; bd. dirs. Legal Aid Soc., Rockland County, 1974-78, Nyack Hosp. Found., Good Samaritan Hosp. Found. Mem. ABA, N.Y. State Bar Assn., Rockland County Bar Assn., Am. Arbitration Assn. (arbitrator), Police Chiefs Found., Internat. Bus. Network of Greater N.Y. General civil litigation, General corporate, Real property. Office: Office of Robert D Fenster PC Attorney at Law PC 337 N Main St Ste 11 New City NY 10956-4310 Fax: 845-638-4767

FENSTERSTOCK, BLAIR COURTNEY, lawyer; b. N.Y.C., Aug. 20, 1950; s. Nathaniel and Gertrude (Isaacson) F.; children: Michael Bayard, Evan Steele, Laurel Sage. AB summa cum laude, Bowdoin Coll., 1972; JD, Columbia U., 1975. Bar: Ind. 1976, N.Y. 1976, U.S. Dist. Ct. (so., ea. and no. dists.) 1976, U.S. Ct. Appeals (2d cir.) 1976, U.S. Customs Ct. 1976, U.S. Ct. Internat. Trade 1976, U.S. Supreme Ct. 1980. Assoc. Simpson, Thacher & Bartlett, N.Y.C., 1975-79, Dewey, Ballantine, Bushby, Palmer & Wood, N.Y.C., 1979-83; v.p., assoc. gen. counsel, asst. sec. Reliance Group Holdings, Inc., 1983-91; sr. v.p., gen. counsel, sec. Frank B. Hall & Co., Inc., 1987-92; ptnr. Sutherland, Asbill & Brennan, 1993-95, Brock, Fensterstock, Silverstein & McAuliffe, LLC, N.Y.C., 1995-98, Fensterstock & Ptnrs., LLP, N.Y.C., 1998—. Mem. bd. visitors Columbia U. Sch. Law, 1988—. Bd. dirs. Safety Nat. Casualty Corp., 1990-93. Harlan Fiske Stone scholar Columbia U., 1975. Mem. ABA, N.Y. State Bar Assn., Assn. Bar City N.Y., Coun. N.Y. Law Assocs. (bd. dirs. 1979-82), Lawyers Com. for Internat. Human Rights (bd. dirs. 1979-80), Am. Arbitration Assn. (panel of arbitrators), Internat. Peace Acad. (sec. 1977-79), Univ. Club (N.Y.C.), Aspetuck Valley Country Club (Weston, Conn.) (bd. govs. 1993-97), Palmas del Mar Country Club (Porto Rico), Phi Beta Kappa. Republican. Jewish. Federal civil litigation, State civil litigation, Securities. Home: 799 Park Ave New York NY 10021-3275 Office: Fensterstock & Ptnrs LLP 30 Wall St New York NY 10005-2201

FENTON, ELLIOTT CLAYTON, lawyer; b. Oklahoma City, Nov. 26, 1914; s. Edgar R. and Mary (Gaddo) F.; m. LeNoir Massey, July 6, 1939; children: Mike, Ann Wallis. BA, U. Okla., 1935, LLB, 1937. Bar: Okla. 1937, U.S. Dist. Ct. (no., ea. and we. dists.) Okla., U.S. Ct. Appeals (10th cir.), U.S. Supreme Ct., U.S. Ct. Mil. Appeals. Atty. Looney & Fenton, Oklahoma City, 1937-38; atty., claims rep. Nat. Mut. Casualty Co., Tulsa, 1938-40, Hartford Ins. Group, Oklahoma City, 1940-47; atty. Fenton & Fenton, 1947—. Chmn. bd. trustees United Meth. Found., Oklahoma City, 1973-83; chancellor United Meth. Found., Oklahoma City, 1983-89. Fellow Am. Bar Found; mem. Def. Research Inst. (state chmn. 1978-83), Okla. Assn. Def. Counsel (pres. 1972), Okla. County Bar Assn. (bd. dirs.). Republican. United Methodist. Avocations: golf. Federal civil litigation, State civil litigation, Personal injury. Home: 14901 N Penn Ave Apt 139 Oklahoma City OK 73134-5958 Office: Fenton Fenton Smith et al 1 Leadership Sq Ste 800 Oklahoma City OK 73102 E-mail: Pokyoky@home.com, Fenton@ionet.net

FENTON, HOWARD NATHAN, III, lawyer, educator; b. Toledo, May 6, 1950; s. Howard Nathan, Jr. and Maxine Claire (LaFountaine) F.; children: William Carl, Margaret Claire, Andrew Scimeca, Julie Marie, Christopher Howard. BS with honors, U. Tex., 1971, JD with honors, 1975. Bar: Tex. 1975, D.C. 1976, Ohio 1990, U.S. Dist. Ct. D.C. 1976, U.S. Ct. Appeals (D.C. cir.) 1976. Assoc. Williams & Jensen PC, Washington, 1975-77; ptnr. Swift & Swift PC, 1978; supervisory compliance officer office antiboycott compliance Internat. Trade Adminstrn./U.S. Dept. Commerce, 1979-80, dir. compliance policy, 1981-84; assoc. prof. Miss. Coll. Sch. Law, Jackson, 1984-87, prof., 1987-88, Ohio Northern U. Coll. Law, Ada, 1988—, assoc. dean, 1988-93. Cons. adminstrv. law reform to govts. of Ukraine, Georgia, Armenia, 1996—; interim dean 1995-96; cons. Adminstrv. Conf. U.S., 1989-91, 93-94; fellow Nat. Ctr. for Export/Import Studies, Georgetown U., Washington, 1983-86; adj. faculty Cath. U. Law Sch., Washington, spring 1984; mem. U.S.-Can. Free Trade Agreement Dispute Panel, 1993-94, N.Am. Free Trade Agreement Dispute Panel, 1994-01. Cons. editor Boycott Law Bull., 1984-92. Mem. ABA, Am. Soc. Internat. Law. Democrat. Office: Pettit Coll of Law Ohio Northern U Ada OH 45810

FENTON, THOMAS CONNER, lawyer; b. Cin., Feb. 9, 1954; S. William Conner and Virginia (Rawnsley) F.; m. Karen Lois Haswell, Oct. 20, 1979; children: Margaret Lois, Rebecca Conner, Robert Ellis. BA, Centre Coll., 1976; JD, Ohio State U., 1979. Bar: Ky. 1979, U.S. Dist. Ct. (we. dist.) Ky. 1979, U.S. Ct. Appeals (D.C. cir.) 1981, U.S. Dist. Ct. (ea. dist.) Ky. 1985, U.S. Ct. Appeals (6th cir.) 1986. Assoc. Greenebaum, Treitz, Brown & Marshall, Louisville, 1979-85, ptnr., 1985-88; v.p., counsel Nat. City Bank Ky., 1989-93; counsel Nat. City Corp., Cleve., 1989-93; v.p. human resources Nat. City Processing Co., Louisville, 1993-95; of counsel Morgan & Pottinger PSC, 1996-2001, mem., 2001—. Lectr. Ohio Bankers Assn. Sch. of Human Resources Adminstrn., 1989-91. Author: Affirmative Action Relevant to Bankers, 1996. Bd. dirs. Elder Serve Inc., Louisville, 1983-91, 95—, sec. 1984-86, v.p., 1986-87, pres., 1987-90; bd. dirs. Louisville Youth Choir, Inc., 1996—, chmn., 1997—. Mem. Ky. Bar Assn. (chmn. labor rels. law sect. 1981-83), Louisville Bar Assn. Methodist. Banking, Contracts commercial, Labor. Home: 11003 Fox Moore Ct Louisville KY 40223-5531 Office: Morgan & Pottinger PSC 601 W Main St Louisville KY 40202-2976

FENWICK, LYNDA BECK, lawyer, writer; b. Great Bend, Kans., Oct. 24, 1944; d. Ralph George and Margaret Pauline (Hawk) Beck; m. Larry Dean Fenwick, Dec. 23, 1962. BS with distinction, Fort Hays State U., 1966; JD, Baylor U., 1975. Bar: Tex. 1975, Ga. 1989, N.C. 1993, U.S. Dist. Ct. (we. dist.) Tex. 1980, U.S. Dist. Ct. (no. dist.) Tex. 1986. Atty. VA, Waco, Tex., 1975-79; assoc. Pakis, Cherry, Beard & Giotes, 1979-81; sole practice Dallas, 1981-85; assoc. Taylor & Mizell P.C., 1985-88. Adj. faculty law Baylor U., Waco, 1979-81; grader exams Supreme Ct. of Tex., 1981-85. Author: Should the Children Pray? Historical, Judicial, Political Examination of Public School Prayer, 1989, Private Choices, Public

Consequences; Reproductive Technology and the New Ethics of Conception, Pregnancy, and Family, 1998; assoc. editor Baylor U. Law Rev., 1974-75. Docent Dallas Mus. Art., 1982-85. Named Ga. Author of Yr. for Nonfiction, 1990. Mem. ABA, Tex. Bar Assn., Ga. Bar Assn., Portrait Soc. Atlanta, Southeastern Pastel Soc., Phi Delta Phi. Federal civil litigation, State civil litigation, Real property.

FERGUS, GARY SCOTT, lawyer; b. Racine, Wis., Apr. 20, 1954; s. Russell Malcolm and Phyl Rose (Muratore) F.; m. Isabelle Sabina Beekman, Sept. 28, 1985; children: Mary Marckwald Beekman Fergus, Kirkpatrick Russell Beekman Fergus. SB, Stanford U., 1976; JD, U. Wis., 1979; LLM, NYU, 1981. Bar: Wis. 1979, Calif. 1980. Assoc. Brobeck, Phleger & Harrison, San Francisco, 1980-86, ptnr., 1986-2000, mng. ptnr. products liability, ins. coverage, environ. and antitrust/appellate practices, 1996-2000, ptnr. internet and E-commerce team, 2000—, sr. ptnr. e-commerce anti-trust group, 2000—. Energy Arch. computerized case mgmt. sys. Vol. San Francisco Leadership. Mem. ABA. Product liability, Toxic tort, Transportation. Home: 3024 Washington St San Francisco CA 94115-1618 Office: Brobeck Phleger & Harrison 1 Market Plz Ste 341 San Francisco CA 94105-1420

FERGUSON, CHARLES ALAN, lawyer; b. Fulton, Mo., Jan. 7, 1940; s. Charles Milton and Hazel A. (Jackson) F.; m. Janill Florene; children: Stacy Christine, Scot Alan. BA, So. Meth. U., 1962, JD, 1965. Bar: Tex. 1965, U.S. Dist. Ct. (we. dist.) Tex. 1967, U.S. Supreme Ct. 1976; CLU. Assoc. McGown, McClanahan & Hamner, San Antonio, 1965-69; atty. Govt. Personnel Mut. Life Ins. Co., 1969—, assoc. gen. counsel, asst. sec., 1970-79, v.p., gen. counsel and sec., 1979-88, sr. v.p., gen. counsel, sec., 1988—, also bd. dirs.; pres., bd. dirs. G.P.M. Fed. Credit Union, 1971-80; sec., bd. dirs. Greenwood Life Ins. Co., 1970-76. Mem. adv. com. on replacement, Tex. State Bd. Ins., 1981-82; mem. legis. com. Tex. Life Ins. Assn.; com. chmn. aero. med. divsn. and Wilford Hall USAF Hosp., San Antonio, 1972-73, Joint Jr. Officers Council, San Antonio, 1974, Brooks AFB, 1980-81; chmn. PAC com. Tex. Assn. Life and Health Insurers, 1997—. Bd. dirs. Scenic Oaks Property Owners Assn., 1986—, pres. 1986-94. Fellow Life Mgmt. Inst.; mem. ABA, San Antonio Bar Assn., San Antonio Jr. Bar Assn. (v.p. 1973), State Bar Tex. (Coll.), Fiesta Men (v.p. 1974-76), Assn. Life Ins. Counsel, San Antonio C. of C., Phi Gamma Delta, Phi Alpha Delta. Clubs: Turtle Creek Country (bd. govs.), Diez y Seis Handball (sec.-treas. 1975), The Dominion. General corporate, Insurance. Home: 8601 Barn Swallow San Antonio TX 78255-3623 Office: 800 NW Loop 410 San Antonio TX 78216-5619

FERGUSON, CLEVE ROBERT, lawyer, educator; b. Long Beach, Calif., Dec. 31, 1938; s. Frank H and Ruth S Ferguson; m. Kathryn Jane Weaver, Apr. 10, 1965 (div. June 25, 1995); children: Sharon Anne, Robert Timothy; m. Peggy Burke Daniell, Nov. 19. 1995. AB in Econs., U. So. Calif., 1961, JD, 1965. Bar: Calif 1966, US Dist Ct (cent dist) Calif 1966, US Ct Appeals (9th cir) 1987, US Supreme Ct 1975. Assoc. Musick, Peeler & Garrett, L.A., 1965-69, Hayes & Hume, Beverly Hills, Calif., 1969-74; pvt. practice Pasadena/Claremont, 1974—; adj. prof. physics and astronomy U. La Verne (Calif.), 1993—, adj. prof. civil procedure and law and motion Coll. Law, 1994-2000; pres., CEO Mars Manned Mission Corp. Mem alcohol and drug abuse comt Calif State Bar, 1990—91; instr astronomy and bus law Chapman Univ, 1992—93; arbitrator Am Arbit Asn, Nat Arbit Forum. Editor: (book) Tall Tales and Memories, 1987. Mem. Stony Ridge Obs., 1985—, pres., 1994—97; co-founder, bd. govs. Mt. Wilson (Calif.) Inst., 1987—; lectr., cons. Californians for Redevel. Edn., South Gate, 1996—; mem. L.A. Opera League; bd. dirs. Clan Fergusson Soc. N.Am., 1987—2000. With U.S. Army, 1961—62. Decorated Knight Knights Templar of Jerusalem, Grand Priory of the Scots. Fellow: Soc Antiquaries Scotland; mem.: Los Angeles Copyright Asn, Univ Club Pasadnea, Univ Club Claremont, Beta Theta Pi (past pres). Avocations: astronomy, mountaineering, dry fly fishing, skiing. General civil litigation, General corporate, Land use and zoning (including planning). Office: C Robert Ferguson Atty at Law 237 W 4th St Claremont CA 91711-4710

FERGUSON, DALLAS EUGENE, lawyer; b. Blackwell, Okla., Dec. 20, 1945; s. Clyde L. and Agnes Loree (Humphrey) F.; m. Christine Joslin, Sept. 5, 1970; children: Erin Nicole, Dallas Scott, Robert Brent. BA, Cornell Coll., Mt. Vernon, Iowa, 1968; JD, Columbia U., 1971. Bar: Okla. 1971, U.S. Ct. Appeals (10th cir.) 1971, U.S. Dist. Ct. (we. dist.) Okla. 1971, U.S. Dist. Ct. (no. dist.) Okla. 1973, U.S. Dist. Ct. (ea. dist.) Okla. 1978. Law clk. to judge U.S. Ct. Appeals (10th cir.), Oklahoma City, 1971-72; assoc. Doerner, Saunders, Daniel & Anderson LLP, Tulsa, 1973-78, ptnr., 1978—. Mem. ABA, Okla. Bar Assn., Tulsa County Bar Assn. (Outstanding Young Lawyer 1980). Democrat. Unitarian. Federal civil litigation, Communications, Administrative and regulatory. Home: 1225 E 25th St Tulsa OK 74114-2615 Office: Doerner Saunders Daniel & Anderson LLP 320 S Boston Ave Ste 500 Tulsa OK 74103-3725 E-mail: dferguson@dsda.com

FERGUSON, GERALD PAUL, lawyer; b. Teaneck, N.J., Oct. 17, 1951; s. James Richard and Ilene Veronica (Meyer) F.; m. Nancy Ivers, Aug. 20, 1977; 1 child, James Ralph. BA, Fairleigh Dickinson U., 1974; JD, Capital U., 1979. Bar: Ohio 1979, U.S. Dist. Ct. (so. dist.) Ohio 1980, U.S. Ct. Appeals (6th cir.) 1986, U.S. Supreme Ct. 1990. Ptnr. Vorys, Sater, Seymour and Pease, Columbus, 1979—; mem. rules adv. com. Ohio Supreme Ct., 1993. Mem. ABA (litigation sect., mem. trial evidence subcom. 1985-86), Ohio State Bar Assn. (mem. jud. adv. and legal reform com., unauthorized practice law com. 1985-90), Columbus Bar Assn. (chmn. juror subcom. 1979-86). Republican. Roman Catholic. Avocations: tennis, golf, fishing. Federal civil litigation, State civil litigation, Intellectual property. Office: Vorys Sater Seymour & Pease 52 E Gay St Columbus OH 43215-3161 E-mail: gpferguson@ussp.com

FERGUSON, HAROLD LAVERNE, JR. lawyer; b. Cleveland, Miss., Dec. 3, 1938; s. Harold Laverne and Allene Thompson (Burford) F.; m. Jamie Frances Flemming, Nov. 20, 1965; children: Harold Laverne III, Samuel Christopher, Julie Allene. BA in Pub. Adminstrn., U. Miss., 1960; JD, Samford U., 1973. Bar: Ala. 1973. Ptnr. Spain, Gillon, Riley, Tate & Etheredge, Birmingham, Ala., 1973-80, Dominick, Fletcher, Yeilding, Wood & Lloyd P.A., Birmingham, 1980-98, Ferguson, Frost & Dodson LLP, Birmingham, 1998—. Served with Miss. and Tenn. N.G., 1955-63. Mem. ABA, Ala. Bar Assn., Tenn. Bar Assn., Birmingham Bar Assn., Ala. Def. Lawyers Assn., Def. Research Inst., Birmingham Ole Miss. Alumni Club (pres. 1985-86). Republican. Baptist. Lodge: Rotary. E-mila. Insurance, Personal injury, Workers' compensation. Home: 440 Hillwood Dr Birmingham AL 35209-5346 E-mail: hlf@ffdlaw.com

FERGUSON, JOHN MARSHALL, retired federal judge; b. Marion, Ill., Oct. 14, 1921; s. John Marshall and Vessie (Widdows) F.; m. Jeanne Harmon, Sept. 23, 1950; children: Marcia Ferguson Velde, Mark Harmon, John Scott, Mary Sue Holkey. Student, So. Ill. U., 1939-41, S.E. Mo. Tchrs. Coll., 1941; LLB, JD, Washington U., St. Louis, 1948. Bar: Ill. 1949, U.S. Ct. Appeals (7th cir.) 1956, U.S. Supreme Ct. 1960. Asst. mgr. I.W. Rogers Theaters, Inc., Anna, Ill., 1934-42; atty. U.S. Fidelity & Guaranty Co., St. Louis, 1948-51; assoc. Baker, Kagy & Wagner, East St. Louis, Ill., 1951-56, ptnr., 1956-59, Wagner, Conner, Ferguson, Bertrand & Baker, East St. Louis and Belleville, Ill., 1959-72; magistrate judge U.S. Dist. Ct. (so. dist.) Ill., 1990-94. Pres. bd. Arch Aircraft, Inc., 1966-68; disciplinary commr. Ill. Supreme Ct., 1957-90, mem. joint com. on revision disciplinary rules, 1972-74; mem. hearing bd. Ill. Registration and Disciplinary Commn., 1974-90; pres. 1st Dist. Fedn. Bar Assns. Precinct committeeman Stookey Twp., St. Clair County (Ill.) Republican Com., 1958-62; Bd. dirs., v.p. East St. Louis chpt. ARC. Capt. AUS, 1942-45. Mem. ABA, Ill. Bar Assn. (prof. responsibility com. 1975-86, chmn. 1983-84), St. Clair County Bar Assn., 7th Fed. Cir. Bar Assn. (bd. govs.), Ill. Club (govs., pres. 1966-67), East St. Louis City Club (pres. 1960-61), Ill. Club (gov. pres. 1966-67), St. Clair Country Club (Belleville, pres. 1972-73), Masons, Elks, Delta Theta Phi. Home: 12 Oak Knoll Pl Belleville IL 62223-1817 E-mail: jferg7@juno.com

FERGUSON, MILTON CARR, JR. lawyer; b. Washington, Feb. 10, 1931; s. Milton Carr and Gladys (Emery) F.; m. Marian Evelyn Nelson, Aug. 21, 1954; children: Laura, Sharon, Marcia, Sandra. B.A., Cornell U., 1952; LL.B., 1954; LL.M., N.Y. U., 1960. Bar: N.Y. State 1954. Trial atty. tax div. Dept. Justice, Washington, 1954-60, asst. atty. gen., 1977-81; asst. prof. law U. Iowa, 1960-62; assoc. prof. N.Y.U., 1962-65; prof. N.Y. U., 1965-77; vis. prof. law Stanford (Calif.) U., 1972-73; of counsel Wachtell, Lipton, Rosen & Katz, N.Y.C., 1969-76; ptnr. Davis Polk & Wardwell, 1981—. Spl. cons. to Treasury Dept., Commonwealth P.R., 1974 Author: (with others) Federal Income Taxation Legislation in Perspective, 1965, Federal Income Taxation of Estates and Beneficiaries, 1970, 2d edit., 1994. Trustee NYU Law Ctr. Found., Lewis and Clark Coll. Mem. ABA (chmn. tax sect. 1993-94), N.Y. State Bar Assn., Soc. Illustrators. Corporate taxation, Taxation, general. Home: 32 Washington Sq W New York NY 10011-9156 Office: Davis Polk & Wardwell 450 Lexington Ave Fl 31 New York NY 10017-3982

FERGUSON, THOMAS CROOKS, lawyer; b. Nov. 27, 1933; s. Thomas C. and Grace (Crooks) F.; children: Leslie Mead, Ian Thomas. AB, Vanderbilt U., 1955, JD, 1959; cert., Hague Acad. Internat. Law, 1958; postgrad., Kenney Sch. Govt., Harvard U., 1985. Bar: Ill. 1960, Ky. 1961, D.C. 1993. Bd. mem. Mead Johnson Found., 1960-70, Taylor Energy, Taylor Found.; mktg. mgr. Pharmaseal Labs., 1962-75; pres. Atlantic Salvage Corp., 1975-78, Brevard Marina, 1977-82; dir. Eastern Caribbean Peace Corps, 1982-84; dep. commr. Immigration and Naturalization Service Dept. Justice, 1984-87; U.S. amb. to Brunei Darussalam, 1987-89; pres. Airscan Internat., Indialantic, Fla., 1989-91; pvt. practice Washington, 1991—. With U.S. Army, 1955-56. Recipient Comdr.'s medal for civilian svc. Grenada, 1983. Mem. ABA, Fed. Bar Assn. Clubs: Offshore Cruising of Calif., Eau Gallie Yacht. Avocations: sailing, tennis, diving. Home: 6781 Linford Ln Jacksonville FL 32217-2660 Office: 336 S Carolina Ave SE Washington DC 20003-4223 E-mail: hetf@aol.com

FERGUSON, WARREN JOHN, federal judge; b. Eureka, Nev., Oct. 31, 1920; s. Ralph and Marian (Damele) F.; m. E. Laura Keyes, June 5, 1948; children: Faye F., Warren John, Teresa M., Peter J. B.A., U. Nev., 1942; LL.B., U. So. Calif., 1949; LL.D. (hon.), Western State U., San Fernando Valley Coll. Law. Bar: Calif. 1950. Mem. firm Ferguson & Judge, Fullerton, Calif., 1950-59; city atty. for cities of Buena Park, Placentia, La Puente, Baldwin Park, Santa Fe Springs, Walnut and Rosemead, 1953-59; mcpl. ct. judge Anaheim, 1959-60; judge Superior Ct., Santa Ana, 1961-66, Juvenile Ct., 1963-64, Appellate Dept., 1965-66; U.S. dist. judge Los Angeles, 1966-79; judge U.S. Circuit Ct. (9th cir.), 1979-86; sr. judge U.S. Ct. Appeals (9th cir.), Santa Ana, 1986—; faculty Fed. Jud. Ctr., Practising Law Inst., U. Iowa Coll. Law, N.Y. Law Jour. Assoc. prof. psychiatry (law) Sch. Medicine, U. So. Calif.; assoc. prof. Loyola Law Sch. Served with AUS, 1942-46. Decorated Bronze Star. Mem. Phi Kappa Phi, Theta Chi. Democrat. Roman Catholic. Office: US Courthouse 411 W 4th St Ste 10-80 Santa Ana CA 92701-4500 E-mail: judge_ferguson@ca9.uscourts.gov

FERNANDEZ, CANI, lawyer; b. Cartagena, Spain, Apr. 21, 1963; arrived in Belgium, 1998. d. Jose Luis Sambeat and Conception Vicien; widowed, Oct. 10, 1991; children: Borja, Pablo. LLB, Faculty Law, Zaragoza, Spain, 1986; M in European Law, ULB, Brussels, Belgium, 1987. Bar: Zaragoza, 1986; Barcelona, 1989. Lawyer BAE, Brussels, 1987-88, Sancho-Vallet, Barcelona, Spain, 1988-89, Cuatrecasas, Barcelona, Spain, 1989-94; sr. clerk European Ct. of Justice, Luxemberg, Spain, 1994-97; ptnr. Cuatrecasas, Barcelona, Spain, 1997-98, dir. Brussels Office Spain, 1998. Prof. U. Barcelona, 1994-96, prof. U. Autonoma, Barcelona, 1997-99, prof. Internat. programs McGeroge U. Pacific, 1991-2000. Contbg. Author: European Telecommunications Liberalisation, 1998, European Franchising, 1991, European Legal Order and Protection of Individuals, 1995. Fellow NATO, Brussels, 1987. Mem. IBA, FIDE. Office: Cuatrecasas Avenue Cortenbergh 60 B-1000 Brussels Belgium Fax: 02 743 3901. E-mail: canifernandez@cuatrecases.com

FERNANDEZ, DENNIS SUNGA, lawyer, electrical engineer, entrepreneur; b. Manila, June 3, 1961; came to U.S., 1972; s. Gil Conui and Imelda Sunga (Miller) F.; m. Irene Y. Hu, Aug. 26, 1989; children: Megan H., Jared R. BSEE, Northwestern U., 1983; JD, Suffolk U., 1989. Bar: Mass. 1989, U.S. Dist. Ct. Mass. 1989, D.C. 1990, U.S. Ct. Appeals (Fed. cir.) 1990, Calif, 1991. Engr. NCR, Ft. Collins, Colo., 1983-84; product mgr. Digital Equipment Corp., Hudson, Mass., 1984-86; program mgr. Raytheon, Andover, 1986-88; engr. Racal, Westford, 1988-89; assoc. Nutter, McClennen & Fish, Boston, 1989-91, Fenwick & West, Palo Alto, Calif., 1991-94; v.p. Walden Internat. Investment Group, San Francisco, 1995-96, Singapore Techs./Vertex Mgmt., 1996-97, Neo Paradigm Labs., Inc., 1997-98; ptnr. Fernandez & Assocs., LLP, 1998—. Contbr. articles to profl. jours. Mem. IEEE, Sci. and Tech. Adv. Coun. (dir.). Computer, Patent.

FERNANDEZ, FERDINAND FRANCIS, federal judge; b. 1937; BS, U. So. Calif., 1958, JD, 1963; LLM, Harvard U., 1963. Bar: Calif. 1963, U.S. Dist. Ct. (cen. dist.) Calif. 1963, U.S. Ct. Appeals (9th cir.) 1963, U.S. Supreme Ct. 1967. Elec. engr. Hughes Aircraft Co., Culver City, Calif., 1958-62; law clk. to dist. judge U.S. Dist. Ct. (cen. dist.) Calif., 1963-64; pvt. practice law Allard, Shelton & O'Connor, Pomona, Calif., 1964-80; judge Calif. Superior Ct. San Bernardino County, 1980-85, U.S. Dist. Ct. (cen. dist.) Calif., L.A., 1985-89, U.S. Ct. Appeals (9th cir.), L.A., 1989—. Lester Roth lectr. U. So. Calif. Law Sch., 1992. Contbr. articles to profl. jours. Vice chmn. City of La Verne Commn. on Environ. Quality, 1971-73; chmn. City of Claremont Environ. Quality Bd., 1972-73; bd. trustees Pomona Coll., 1990—. Fellow Am. Coll. Trust and Estate Counsel; mem. ABA, State Bar of Calif. (fed. cts. com. 1966-69, ad hoc com. on attachments 1971-85, chmn. com. on adminstrn. of justice 1976-77, exec. com. taxation sect. 1977-80, spl. com. on mandatory fee arbitration 1978-79), Calif. Judges Assn. (chmn. juvenile cts. com. 1983-84, faculty mem. Calif. Jud. Coll. 1982-83, faculty mem. jurisprudence and humanities course 1983-85), Hispanic Nat. Bar Assn., L.A. County Bar Assn. (bull. com. 1974-75), San Bernardino County Bar Assn., Pomona Valley Bar Assn. (co-editor Newsletter 1970-72, trustee 1971-78, sec.-treas. 1973-74, 2d v.p. 1974-75, 1st v.p. 1975-76, pres. 1976-77), Estate Planning Coun. Pomona Valley (sec. 1966-76), Order of Coif, Phi Kappa Phi, Tau Beta Pi. Office: US Ct Appeals 9th Cir 125 S Grand Ave Ste 602 Pasadena CA 91105-1621

FERNANDEZ, JOSE WALFREDO, lawyer; b. Cienfuegos, Cuba, Sept. 19, 1955; came to U.S., 1967; s. Jose Rigoberto and Flora (Gomez) F.; m. Andrea Gabor, June 22, 1985. BA, Dartmouth Coll., 1977; JD, Columbia U., 1980. Bar: N.Y. 1981, N.J. 1981, U.S. Dist. Ct. (so. dist.) N.Y. 1981, U.S. Dist. Ct. N.J. 1981. Assoc. Curtis, Mallet, Prevost, Colt & Mosle, N.Y.C., 1981-84, Baker & McKenzie, N.Y.C., 1984-89, ptnr., 1989-96, O'Melveny & Myers, L.L.P., N.Y.C., 1996—, chair global practice group. Adj. prof. N.Y. Law Sch., 1984-87. Contbr. articles to profl. jours. Bd. dirs. Ballet Hispanico, Ceiba Prodns., WBGO-FM Newark Pub. Radio. Mem. ABA (com. Inter-Am. law 1985—, Ctrl. Am. task force 1985-92, presdl. commn. L.Am. 1986-91), N.Y.C. Bar Assn. (com. fgn. and comparative law, chmn. Inter-A m. affairs com. 1996-98, city bar fund 1999—), U.S.-Spain C. of C. (bd. dirs. 1999—), Brazilian-U.S. C. of C. (bd. dirs. 1994-99, 2001—). Avocations: sports, non-fiction writing, travel. Banking, Contracts commercial, Private international. Home: 508 E 87th St New York NY 10128-7602 Office: O'Melveny & Myers LLP Citicorp Ctr 153 E 53rd St Fl 53D New York NY 10022-4611

FERNANDEZ, RODOLFO, lawyer; b. Barcelona, Spain, Jan. 9, 1964; s. Alvaro and Juana Fernandez; m: Diana Marly; children: Sandra, Rodolfo. LLB, U. Barcelona, Spain, 1988, postgraduate E-Commerce Law, 2000. Assoc. Marti and Assoc., Barcelona, Spain, 1994-98, Pedro Brosa and Assoc., Barcelona, Spain, 1998—. Lctr. U. Barcelona, 1995-2001. Contr. articles to profl. jours. Avocations: skiing, diving. Communications, Computer, General corporate. Office: Pedro Borsa & Associates A V Diagonal 598 08021 Barcelona Lata Lunya Spain Fax: 93-2022907. E-mail: rodolfo.fernandez@ben.brosa-assiados.com

FERNÁNDEZ-GONZÁLEZ, JUSTO, lawyer, legal assistance director; b. San Gaspar, Jalisco, Mexico, Oct. 18, 1952; came to U.S., 1966; s. Feliciano and Paula (González) Fernández; m. Bernice Armijo-Fernández, Feb. 1984 (div.); children: Justo, Natalia, Maclovio, Rene. AA, Reedley Coll., 1973; BA, UCLA, 1976, student, 1978; JD, U. Calif. Hastings, San Francisco, 1981. Bar: Tex. 1983, U.S. Ct. Appeals (5th cir.) 1984, U.S. Dist. Ct. (no. and we. dists.) Tex. 1986, U.S. Supreme Ct. 1990. Staff atty. North Ctrl. Tex. Legal Aid, Dallas, 1984-86, El Paso (Tex.) Legal Assistance, 1986, supr., 1986-87, dep. dir., 1987-89, exec. dir., 1989—. Bd. dirs. Tex. Legal Svcs. Ctr., Austin, 1986—, Ctr. de Medico Del Valle, El Paso, 1990—, Alternative Dispute Resolution, El Paso, 1989—, Project Adv. Group region 7, Washington, 1985—; adv. com. United Way, El Paso, 1990. Reginald Heber Smith fellow Legal Svcs. Corp., Washington, 1981-84; named Most Outstanding Atty. North Cen. Legal Svcs., Dallas, 1985, Atty. of Yr., Tex. Clients Coun., 1992. Mem. Tex. Bar Assn., Fed. Bar Assn., Mexican-Am. Bar, Coll. of the State Bar. Avocations: jogging, swiming, reading, raising pigeons. Home: 2325 San Diego Ave El Paso TX 79930-1322 Office: El Paso Legal Assistance 1301 N Oregon St El Paso TX 79902-4025

FERRANTI, THOMAS, JR. lawyer; b. S.I., N.Y., Mar. 14, 1969; s. Thomas and Janet Rose (Giordano) F.; m. Renée Esposito, July 11, 1998. BA, St. John's U., N.Y.C., 1991, JD, 1994. Bar: N.Y. 1995, N.J. 1995, D.C. 1995. Dietary aide S.I. (N.Y.) U. Hosp., 1987-1993; intern Dept. of Investigation, N.Y.C., 1990, Justice Finnegan, N.Y. State Supreme Ct., Queens, 1990; legal intern Macy's Northeast, N.Y.C., 1991, N.Y.C. Coun., S.I., 1992; intern Supreme Ct. trial divsn. Richmond County Dist. Atty., 1993-94; tchr. law Monsignor Farrell H.S., 1994-95; pvt. practice, 1995—. Lawyer, witness Criminal Trial Inst., St. John's U., 1991-94, Civil Trial Inst., 1991-94; tutor, counselor Student Network Accessing Counselor Program, 1991-94; fire fighter N.Y.C. Fire Dept., 1993—. Gen. mgr., pres. Sta. WMOC, S.I., 1989-91. St. John's U. scholar, 1988-91. Mem. ABA, N.Y. State Bar Assn., Nat. Italian-Am. Bar Assn., Golden Key, Lambda Kappa Phi, Kappa Gamma Pi, Iota Alpha Sigma (pres. 1990-91). Roman Catholic. Avocations: aquarium hobbyist, weight training, science fiction, coin collecting, travel. General practice, Probate, Real property. Home and Office: 99 Pitney Ave Staten Island NY 10309-1918 Fax: 718-317-5294. E-mail: tofesq@aol.com

FERRARA, RALPH C. lawyer; b. Gloversville, N.Y., June 16, 1945; s. Rufus Ferrara and Clara F. Riccitiello. BSBA, Georgetown U., 1967; JD, U. Cin., 1970; LLM in Corp. Law summa cum laude, George Washington U., 1972. Bar: D.C. 1970, U.S. Ct. Appeals, U.S. Supreme Ct.; cert. ind. assessor Ins. Marketplace Stds. Assn. Profl. asst. to law libr. Nat. Law Ctr., Washington, 1970-72; mem. faculty George Washington U. Nat. Law Ctr.; atty. divsn. enforcement SEC, 1971-72, trial atty. divsn. trading and markets, 1972-73, spl. counsel to chief enforcement atty., 1973-74, supervisory trial atty., 1974-75, spl. counsel to chmn., 1975, asst. gen. counsel, 1975-76, exec. asst. to legal counsel, 1976-77, exec. asst., 1977-78, gen. counsel, 1978-81; ptnr. Debevoise & Plimpton, 1981—. Co-chmn. PLI Ann. Inst. on Securities Law, 1994-98; bd. advisor The Ctr. for Corp. Law, U. Cin. Coll. Law, 1995—; bd. visitors U. Cin. Coll. Law, 1995—. Author: Takeovers II: A Strategists' Manual for Business Combinations in the 1990s, 1993, Shareholder Derivative Litigation: Beseiging the Board, 1995, Ferrara on Insider Trading the Wall, 1995, Managing Marketeers: Supervisory Responsibilities of Broker-Dealers and Investment Advisors, 2000, Takeovers: A Strategic Guide to Mergers and Acquisitions, 2001;contbr. articles on topics related to fed. securities law to profl. jours. With USAR. Recipient John L. Sayler award, Am. Jurisprudence award, Judge Alfred Mack award. Mem. ABA (planning rev. com. sect. on corp. and banking bus. law, fed. regulation of securities com.), FBA (exe. coun. securities law com., nat. coun., gen. counsels' com.), Southwestern Legal Found. (adv. com.). Administrative and regulatory, Federal civil litigation, General corporate. Office: Debevoise & Plimpton 555 13th St NW Ste 1100E Washington DC 20004-1163 also: Debevoise & Plimpton 875 3rd Ave New York NY 10022-6225

FERRARL, ALEXANDER DOMONICO, lawyer; b. London, June 21, 1964; s. John Ferrarl and Miceala Donner; m. Sarah Jane Nichols; 1 child, Amelia. Grad., London U., 1994. Asst. underwriter Westminster Aviation Ins. Group, 1985-89. Admiralty, Aviation, Consumer commercial. Office: Beaumont & Son 1 Portsoren St London E18 AW England

FERRELL, MILTON MORGAN, JR. lawyer; b. Coral Gables, Fla., Nov. 6, 1951; s. Milton M. and Annie (Blanche) Bradley; m. Lori R. Sanders, May 22, 1982; children: Milton Morgan III, Whitney Connolly. BA, Mercer U., 1973, JD, 1975. Bar: Fla. 1975. Asst. state's atty. State's Atty.'s Office, Miami, 1975-77; ptnr. Ferrell & Ferrell, 1977-84; sole practice, 1985-87; ptnr. Ferrell & Williams, P.A., 1987-90, Ferrell & Fertel, P.A., Miami, 1990-98, Ferrell Schultz Carter & Fertel P.A., 1999-2000, Ferrell Schultz Carter Zumpano & Fertel, P.A., 2000—. Bd. dirs. Isotag Tech., Inc. Trustee Mus. Sci. and Space Transit Planetarium, 1977-82; mem. Ambs. of Mercy, Mercy Hosp. Found., Inc., 1985-94; trustee, mem. legal com., chair com. U. Miami Project to Cure Paralysis, 1985-94; trustee Eaglebrook Sch., 1995-98, Robinson Charitable Found., 1993—, United Way of Miami-Dade, 2000—; bd. dirs. Jackson Meml. Found., 2000—. Fellow Nat. Assn. Criminal Def. Lawyers, Am. Bd. Criminal Lawyers (bd. govs. 1981-82, sec. 1983-84, v.p. 1984-86, pres. 1987-88); mem. ABA (grantee 1975), Fla. Bar Assn. (jury instrns. com. 1987-88, chmn. grievance com. 11-L 1989-91), Dade County Bar Assn. (bd. dirs. 1977-80), Assn. Trial Lawyers Am., mem. Performing Arts Ctr. Found. Greater Miami, Bath Club (bd. govs. 1992-95), Miami City Club, Univ. Club, Banker's Club, Cat Cay Yacht Club, Inc. (bd. dirs. 1997-2000, treas. 1998-99, pres. 1999-2000), Indian Creek Country Club, LaGorce Country Club, Fisher Island Club, U. Club. Federal civil litigation, State civil litigation, Criminal. Home: Bay Point 4511 Lake Rd Miami FL 33137-3372 Office: Ferrell Schultz Carter Zumpano & Fertel PA 201 S Biscayne Blvd Fl 34 Miami FL 33131-4332 E-mail: mmf@ferrellschultz.com

FERREN, JOHN MAXWELL, lawyer; b. Kansas City, Mo., July 21, 1937; s. Jack Maxwell and Elizabeth Anne (Hansen) F.; m. Ann Elizabeth Speidel, Sept. 4, 1961 (div.); children: Andrew John, Peter Maxwell; m. Linda Jane Finkelstein, June 17, 1994. AB magna cum laude, Harvard U., 1959, LLB, 1962. Bar: Ill. 1962, Mass. 1967, D.C. 1970. Assoc. Kirkland, Ellis, Hodson, Chaffetz & Masters, Chgo., 1962-66; dir. Neighborhood Law Office Program, Harvard U. Law Sch., Cambridge, Mass., 1966-68; teaching fellow, dir. Neighborhood Law Office Program, Harvard Law Sch. (Legal Svcs. Program), 1968-69, lectr. law, dir., 1969-70; ptnr. Hogan & Hartson, Washington, 1970-77; assoc. judge D.C. Ct. Appeals, 1977-97, Corp. Counsel, Washington, 1997-99; sr. judge D.C. Ct. Appeals, 1999—; fellow Woodrow Wilson Internat. Ctr. for Scholars, 2000-2001; mem.

disciplinary bd. D.C. Ct. Appeals, 1972-76; mem. exec. com., bd. dirs. Council on Legal Edn. for Profl. Responsibility, 1970-80; sr. judge D.C. Ct. Appeals, 1999—. Exec. com. Washington Lawyers Com. for Civil Rights Under Law, 1970-77 Contbr. articles to profl. jours. Treas., bd. dirs. Firman Neighborhood House, Chgo., 1964-66; legis. subcom. on consumer credit Chgo. Commn. on Human Rels. Com. on New Residents, 1964-66; bd. dirs. Frederick B. Abramson Meml. Found., 1991-97, People's Devel. Corp., Washington, 1970-74, George A. Wiley Meml. Fund, 1974-84, Nat. Resource Ctr. for Consumers of Legal Svcs., 1973-77, Ctr. for Law and Edn., Cambridge, Mass., 1989-94; originator, chmn. Neighborhood Legal Advice Clinics, Ch. Fedn. Greater Chgo., 1964-66; exec. com. of legal adv. com. Nat. Com. Against Discrimination in Housing, 1974-77; steering com. Nat. Prison Project of ACLU Found., 1975-77. Woodrow Wilson Internat. Ctr. for Scholars fellow, 2000-01. Fellow Am. Bar Found., Woodrow Wilson Internat. Ctr. Scholars; mem. ABA (Commn. on Nat. Inst. Justice 1972-80, mem. consortium on legal svcs. and pub. 1972-73, 76-79, chmn. 1979-82, chmn. spl. com. on pub. interest practice 1976-78), Am. Law Inst., Phi Beta Kappa. Presbyterian. Office: Dist Columbia Ct Appeals 500 Indiana Ave NW Washington DC 20001-2131

FERRIS, WILLIAM MICHAEL, lawyer; b. Jackson, Mich., May 1, 1948; s. Franklyn C. and Betty J. (Dickerson) F.; m. Cynthia L. Muffitt, June 26, 1970 (div.); 1 child, Christina M.; m. Kathleen S. Santacroce, Mar. 21, 1987; stepchildren: Michael W. Santacroce, Megan D. Santacroce. BS with distinction, U.S. Naval Acad., 1970; JD summa cum laude, U. Balt., 1978, LLM in Taxation, 1994. Commd. ensign USN, 1970, advanced through grades to lt., 1974, resigned active duty, 1977; staff atty. Md. Legis., Annapolis, 1977-78, 80-81; assoc. Semmes, Bowen & Semmes, Balt., 1978-80; ptnr. Ferris & Robin, Annapolis, 1981-83, Krause & Ferris, Annapolis, 1983-87, Michaelson, Krause & Ferris, PA, Annapolis, 1987-91, Krause & Ferris, Annapolis, 1991—. Adj. faculty Anne Arundel C.C., 1988—, U. Balt. Sch. Law, 1997—. Author: Maryland Style Manual for Statutory Law, 1985; article supr. Md. Annotated Code, 1981-84. Elder Woods Meml. Presbyn. Ch., Severna Park, Md., 1980—; chmn. Com. to rev. Anne Arundel County Code, Annapolis, 1985-86; temporary zoning hearing officer, Anne Arundel County, Annapolis, 1984-87; hearing officer Anne Arundel County Bd. Edn., Annapolis, 1990-98; pres. Md. Bd. Dental Examiners, Balt., 1987-88; mem. inquiry com. Md. Atty. Grievance Commn., 1987—; mem. Md. Commn. on Jud. Disabilities, 1995—; treas. Bay Hills Cmty. Assn., 1990-96. Comdr. USNR, 1984-91, ret. Mem. ABA, Md. State Bar Assn., Maritime Law Assn., Anne Arundel County Bar Assn. Republican. Avocations: golfing, running, tennis. General civil litigation, Family and matrimonial, Military. Home: 606 Bay Green Dr Arnold MD 21012-2009 Office: Krause & Ferris 196 Duke Of Gloucester St Annapolis MD 21401-2515 E-mail: wferris@krauseferris.com

FERSHTMAN, JULIE ILENE, lawyer; b. Detroit, Apr. 3, 1961; d. Sidney and Judith Joyce (Stoll) F.; m. Robert S. Bick, Mar. 4, 1990. Student, Mich. State U., 1979-81, James Madison Coll., 1979-81; BA in Philosophy and Polit. Sci., Emory U., 1983, JD, 1986. Bar: Mich. 1986, U.S. Dist. Ct. (ea. dist.) Mich. 1986, U.S. Ct. Appeals (6th cir.) 1987, U.S. Dist. Ct. (we. dist.) Mich. 1993. Assoc. Miller, Canfield, Paddock and Stone, Detroit, 1986-89; assoc. Miro, Miro & Weiner P.C., Bloomfield Hills, Mich., 1989-92; pvt. practice, Bingham Farms, 1992—. Adj. prof. Schoolcraft Coll., Livonia, Mich., 1994—; lectr. in field. Author: Equine Law & Horse Sense, 1996, More Equine Law and Horse Sense, 2000; contbr. article to Barrister Mag. Bd. dirs. Franklin Cmty. Assn., 1989-92, sec., 1991-92; mem. Franklin Planning Commn., 1993-94. Recipient Nat. Ptnr. in Safety award Assn. for Horsemanship Safety and Edn., 1997, Outstanding Achievement award Am. Riding Instrs. Assn., 1998; named one of Crain's Detroit Bus. "40 Bus. Leaders Under 40", 1996. Mem. ABA (planning bd. litigation sect. young lawyers divsn., honoree Barrister mag., 1995, FBA (courthouse tours com. Detroit chpt., featured in Barrister mag. in 21 Young Lawyers Leading US and the 21st Century 1995), State Bar Mich. (exec. coun. young lawyers sect. 1989-96, bd. commrs. 1994-96, 99—, chmn. 1995-96, professionalism com. 1997-, grievance com. 1997-99, structure and governance com. 1997-98, strategic planning action group 2001, rep. assn. 1997—, chmn. 2001-2002, chair rep. assembly 2001—), Oakland County Bar Assn. (prof. com. 1995—, Inns of Ct. com. 1995—, chair 1998—, Professionalism award 2000), Markel Equestrian Safety Bd., Women Lawyers Assn., Mich. Soc. Coll. Journalists, Phi Alpha Delta, Omicron Delta Kappa, Phi Sigma Tau, Pi Sigma Alpha. Avocations: horse showing, writing, music, art. Bus. General civil litigation, Insurance, Labor. Home: 31700 Briarcliff Rd Franklin MI 48025-1273 Office: 30700 Telegraph Rd Ste 3475 Bingham Farms MI 48025-4571 E-mail: fershtman@aol.com

FERSKO, RAYMOND STUART, lawyer; b. Newark, Dec. 6, 1947; s. Seymoure Arnold and Hannah Judith (Geffner) F.; children: Stacey Michelle, Madeline Poses. BA, Am. U., 1969; JD, 1972. Bar: N.Y. 1973, U.S. Ct. Appeals (D.C. cir.) 1973, U.S. Dist. Ct. (so., ea. and we. dists.) N.Y. 1975, U.S. Ct. Appeals (2nd cir.) 1975, U.S. Supreme Ct. 1982. Trial atty. CAB, Washington, 1972-75; assoc. Demov Morris Levin & Shein, N.Y.C., 1975-76; assoc. Walsh & Levine, N.Y.C., 1976-80, ptnr., 1980-82; ptnr. Shapiro Shiff Beilly Rosenberg and Fox, N.Y.C., 1982-84, Tanner Propp Fersko & Sterner, N.Y.C., 1984— ; cons. World Aviation Services, Ltd., London, 1982— , Internat. Joint Ventures, Ltd., London, 1983— ; sec. Tradewinds Express Inc., N.Y.C., 1982-86; pres. Cornwell Corp., N.Y.C., 1986-88. Treas., Paine Heights Orgn., New Rochelle, N.Y., 1978—; dir. conservation of chimpanzees com., Sierre Leore, West Africa, 1988, Austria, 1987, U.S., 1989—. Mem. Assn. of Bar of City of N.Y. (mem. com. on state legis. 1976-78), N.Y. County Bar Assn., ABA (mem. anti-trust sect. civil practice and procedure com. 1973— , mem. adminstrv. law sect. aviation com. 1973-77), N.Y. State Bar Assn., Internat. Bar Assn., Argentine U.S.C. of C., Spain U.S.C. of C., Phi Alpha Delta. Jewish. Club: Harmonie (N.Y.C.). Aviation, Federal civil litigation, Private international. Office: Tanner Propp Fersko & Sterner 99 Park Ave Ste 25th New York NY 10016

FETTERMAN, JAMES CHARLES, lawyer; b. Charleston, W.Va., Apr. 13, 1947; s. Kenneth Lee and Sara Jane (Shaffer) F.; children: Janet, Paula, Kenneth, David. BA, Miss. State U., 1969, MA, 1970; JD, U. Miss., Oxford, 1972; MBA, St. Louis U., 1985. Bar: Miss. 1972, Sarasota County, U.S. Dist. Ct. (no. dist.) Miss. 1972, U.S. Ct. Mil. Appeals 1972, U.S. Dist. Ct. (mid. dist.) Fla. 1986, U.S. Tax Ct. 1986, U.S. Ct. Appeals (11th cir.) 1986. Staff atty. First Miss. Corp., Jackson, 1976-77; cert. of need adminstr. Office of Gov. State of Miss., 1977-78; adminstrator, prin. investigator Miss. Bd. Nursing, 1978-79; asst. prof., head dept. fin. Jackson State U., 1979-82; asst. prof. dept. mgmt sci. St. Louis U., Mo., 1982-86; ptnr. Borza Fetterman, Sardelis, Chartered, Sarasota, 1986-89, James C. Fetterman, P.A., Sarasota, Fla., 1989-2000; pres., ptnr. Fetterman & Zitani, P.A., 2001—. Sr. res. adviser to gen. counsel and assoc. gen. counsel Def. Lobistics Agy., 1993-94; assoc. prof. U. Sarasota, 1987—; judge advocate I.M.A. USAF, 1987; spl. master for zoning and code enforcement Sarasota County, 1991-2000; vol. counsel Am. Radio Relay League, 1995—; legal advisor Family Forum, CompuServe, 1996—. Editor Midwest Law Review U. Kans., 1984-86, also textbooks. Active Incarnation Ch. Folk Group, 1986-90, 2000—; bd. dirs., v.p., chaperone Sarasota Boy's Choir, 1992-93; asst. scoutmaster Boy Scouts Am., 1991-95, 99—, scoutmaster, 1995-98, scoutmaster nat. jamboree troop, 1998, dist. com., 1998—; bd. dirs. Fla. Inst. Traditional Chinese Medicine, 1998—, chmn. bd. dirs., 1998—; mem. sch. adv. coun. McIntosh Mid. Sch., 1999-2000; mem. Eagles Club, 1999—. Capt. USAF, 1972-76, ETO; col. res. 1972—, chaplain, 1991—. Named one of Outstanding Young Men of Am., Jaycees, 1982; recipient award of merit Boy Scouts Am., 1998, Order of the Bronze Pelican, Nat. Cath. Com. on Scouting, 2001. Mem. Am. Bus. Law Assn., Res. Officer Assn. (Sarasota chpt. pres. 1989-91, v.p. 1991-92), Fla. Bar (vice chmn. mil. law com. 1991-94, chmn. 1994-95), Ret. Officer's Assn. (bd. dirs. Sarasota chpt. 1991-93), Am. Legion, Nat. Eagle Scout Assn. Republican. Roman Catholic. Avocations: running, swimming, ham radio. Bankruptcy, General corporate, Education and schools. Office: 4521A Bee Ridge Rd Sarasota FL 34233-2517 E-mail: jfetterman@compuserve.com

FETZER, MARK STEPHEN, lawyer; b. Louisville, Oct. 10, 1950; s. Sherrill Lee and Betty Ann (Meyer) F.; m. Pamela Ferrell, May 8, 1982; children: Martha Meyer, John Mark. Student, Purdue U., 1968-70; BA, U. Ky., 1973; JD, U. Denver, 1976. Bar: Colo. 1979, U.S. Dist. Ct. Colo. 1979. Sr. landman Minerals Svc. Co., Grand Junction, Colo., 1976-79; mgr. land & pub. affairs Marline Oil Corp., Danville, Va., 1980-85; mgr. R.R., utility & govtl. acquisition Dallas Area Rapid Transit, 1986-88; environ. counsel Cura, Inc., Dallas, 1989-91; dir., environ. counsel Terra-Mar, Inc., 1991-92; environ. counsel Infodata Systems, Inc., Falls Church, Va., 1992-94; project mgr. Walcoff & Assocs., Inc., Fairfax, 1994; sr. regulatory analyst Ecology and Environment, Inc., Idaho Falls, Idaho, 1995-99, Portage Environ., Inc., Idaho Falls, 2000—. Mem. ABA, Colo. Bar Assn., Rocky Mountain Mineral Law Found., Air and Waste Mgmt. Assn. Evangelist. Avocation: bicycling. Nuclear power, Environmental, Real property. E-mail: msfetzer@hotmail.com

FEUERSTEIN, ALAN RICKY, lawyer; b. Buffalo, Oct. 24, 1950; s. Aaron Irving and Doris Jean (Davis) F.; m. June, 1973 (div. Jan. 1984); children: Marni Lauren, Jami Lynn; m. Susan T. Skop, Dec. 31, 1986; children: Christopher Borkowski, Philip Borkowski. BS cum laude, SUNY, Buffalo, 1974; LLB, U. Toledo, 1977. Bar: N.Y. 1978, Territorial and Dist. Ct. V.I. 1989, U.S. Supreme Ct. 1991, Fed. Ct. Puerto Rico 1993. Assoc. Law Offices of Salvatore Martoche, Buffalo, 1977-79; ptnr. Martoche & Feuerstein, 1979-81; lectr. Erie County Cen. Police Svcs. Acad., 1981-82; pvt. practice, 1981-93; ptnr. Feuerstein & Santapia, 1993-94; prin. Law Offices of Alan R. Feuerstein, 1994-97; ptnr. Feuerstein & Smith, LLP, 1998—. Lectr. Daemen Coll. Consortium, Buffalo, 1980-81; cons. in field. Mem. Erie County Reps., Buffalo, 1979—. Mem. Niagara Club, St.Thomas Yacht Club, The Buffalo Launch Club, Confrérie de la Châne des Rôtisseurs (chevalier). Republican. Jewish. Civil rights, General civil litigation, Personal injury. Office: 17 St Louis Pl Buffalo NY 14202-1502 also: Woods & Woods 1 Comptroller Plz San Juan PR 00917 also: PO Box 502008 Saint Thomas VI 00805-2008

FEUERSTEIN, DONALD MARTIN, lawyer; b. Chgo., May 30, 1937; s. Morris Martin and Pauline Jean (Zagel) F.; m. Dorothy Rosalind Sokolsky, June 3, 1962 (dec. Mar. 1978); children: Eliza Carol, Anthony David; m. Summer Donna Berben, May 25, 1987; 1 child, Ashley Paul. BA magna cum laude, Yale U., 1959; JD magna cum laude, Harvard U., 1962. Bar: N.Y. 1962. Assoc. firm Cleary, Gottlieb, Steen & Hamilton, N.Y.C., 1962-63; law clk. to U.S. dist. judge, 1963-65; assoc. firm Saxe, Bacon & Bolan, 1965; asst. gen. counsel, chief counsel instl. investor study SEC, Washington, 1966-71; ptnr., counsel Salomon Bros., N.Y.C., 1971-81, mng. dir., sec., 1981-91; exec. v.p., chief legal officer Salomon, Inc., 1991; spl. asst. U.S. Dept. Edn., Washington, 1993-94, sr. advisor, 1994-99; pres. New Am. Schs., Arlington, Va., 1999-2000, sr. advisor, 2000-2001, Imaging Acceptance Corp., 2001—. Spl. cons. Intersch. Group, N.Y.C., 1991-93; mem. bus. policy coun. com. on excellence in edn. Nat. Alliance of Bus., 2000-2001. Editor Harvard Law Rev., 1960-62; mem. editl. adv. bd. Securities Regulation Law Jour., 1973-90; bd. editors Nat. Law Jour., 1978-90. Mem. vis. com. Northwestern U. Law Sch., 1975-78; bd. dirs. 1st All Children's Theatre, 1976-85, chmn., 1976-82; mem. long-range planning and capital campaign coms. Brearley Sch., N.Y.C., 1981-83; mem. adv. bd. Solomon R. Guggenheim Mus., N.Y.C., 1984-91, chmn. bus. com., 1988-91, mem. internat. coun., 1991—; bd. dirs. Arts and Bus. Coun., 1980-85, v.p., 1985-88; trustee, v.p., mem. exec. com. Dalton Sch., 1983-89, 90-93; mem. dean's adv. coun. Harvard U. Law Sch., 1988-95, mem. steering com. and capital campaign, 1991-95; mem. com. on univ. resources Harvard U., 1988—; mem. vis. com. Harvard Grad. Sch. Edn., 1993-99; mem. tech. adv. coun., 1996—; chmn. tech. com. Georgetown Day Sch., 1997—, trustee, 1997—; mem. Brookings Coun., 1998-2001. Mem. ABA, Phi Beta Kappa, Pi Sigma Alpha. General corporate, General practice, Securities. Home: 6430 Bradley Blvd Bethesda MD 20817-3246 E-mail: dfeuer13@cs.com

FEVURLY, KEITH ROBERT, educational administrator; b. Leavenworth, Kans., Oct. 30, 1951; s. James R. Fevurly and Anne (McDade) Barrett; m. Peggy L. Vosburg, Aug. 4, 1978; children: Rebecca Dawn, Grant Robert. BA in Polit. Sci., U. Kans., 1973; JD, Washburn U. of Topeka Sch. Law, 1976; postgrad., U. Mo. Sch. Law, 1984; MBA, Regis U., 1988; LLM, U. Denver, 1992. Bar: Kans. 1977, Colo. 1986; cert. fin. planner. Pvt. practice, Leavenworth, 1977; atty. estate and gift tax IRS, Wichita and Salina, Kans., Austin, Tex., 1977-83; atty., acad. assoc. Coll. for Fin. Planning, Denver, 1984-91, program dir., 1991-95, v.p. edn., 1995-98; COO, U. St. Augustine (Fla.) for Health Scis., 1998-2000; exec. dir. fin. planning edn. program Kaplan Coll., Denver, 2000—. Adj. prof. taxation Met. State Coll., Denver; adj. faculty in retirement planning and estate planning Coll. Fin. Planning. Contbg. author tng. modules, articles on tax mgmt., estate planning. Mem. Colo. Bar Assn., Toastmasters Internat., Rotary Internat., Delta Theta Phi, Pi Sigma Alpha. Republican. Presbyterian. Avocations: softball, racquetball. Home: 3007 E Otero Pl Littleton CO 80122-3666 Office: Kaplan Coll 1401 19th St Denver CO 80202 E-mail: Keith_Fevurly@kaplan.com

FEWELL, CHARLES KENNETH, JR. lawyer; b. Washington, Jan. 26, 1943; s. Charles Kenneth and Mary Amanda (Hunt) F.; m. Christine Baker Huff, Jan. 23, 1971; children: Anna Catherine, John Maenner. BA magna cum laude, Dartmouth Coll., 1964; JD, Harvard U., 1967. Bar: N.Y. 1968, U.S. Dist. Ct. (so. dist.) N.Y. 1970, U.S. Ct. Appeals (2d cir.) 1975. Law clk. U.S. Dist. Ct. (so. dist.) N.Y., N.Y.C., 1967-68; assoc. White & Case, 1968-75; v.p., counsel Nat. Westminster Bank, 1975-80; sr. counsel, sr. v.p. Deutsche Bank AG, 1980-92; chief counsel, mng. dir. Deutsche Bank N.Am., 1992-97; ptnr. Eaton & Van Winkle, N.Y.C., 1998—. Bd. dirs. Deutsche Bank Trust Co., Deutsche Fin. Svcs. Can. Corp.; v.p., sec. Deutsche Bank Fin., Inc., N.Y.C., 1980-97. Mem. mediation panel U.S. Dist. Ct. (so. dist.) N.Y., 2001—; mem. vestry Grace Episc. Ch., Hastings-on-Hudson, N.Y., 2000—. Mem. ABA (banking com. 1980—, co-chair internat. banking and fin. com. 1995-98), Am. Fgn. Law Assn. (v.p. 2000—), Inst. Internat. Bankers (legis. and regulatory com. 1988-97), German Am. Law Assn. (dir. 1982—), N.Y. State Bar Assn. (internat. banking and securities markets 1987—, internat. employment law 1992—, publ. com., editl. bd. 2001—), Assn. Bar City N.Y. (banking law sect. 1992-95), Phi Beta Kappa. Banking, General corporate, Private international. Office: Eaton & Van Winkle Three Park Ave New York NY 10016-2078 E-mail: cfewell@evw.com

FICKLER, ARLENE, lawyer; b. Phila., Apr. 21, 1951; BA cum laude, U. Pa., 1971, JD cum laude, 1974. Bar: Pa. 1974, D.C. 1980, U.S. Supreme Ct. 1989. Ptnr. Hoyle Morris & Kerr LLP, Phila. Staff atty. Commn. on Revision of Fed. Ct. Appellate System, 1974-75; exec. asst. Bicentennial Com. Jud. Conf. of U.S., 1975-76. Comment editor U. Pa. Law Rev., 1973-74; contbr. articles to law jours. Pres. U. Pa. Law Sch. Alumni Bd. Mgrs., 1997-99; trustee Jewish Fedn. of Greater Phila., 1981-88, 89-93, 94-98, 99—, Phila. Bar Found., 1993-98, Jewish Cmty. Rels. Coun. Greater Phila., 1983-94, 98—; trustee Jewish Cmty. Ctrs. of Phila., 1997—, asst. treas., 1999-2000, v.p., 2000—; trustee HIAS Immigration Svcs. Phila., 1998—, treas., 1999—; mem. United Jewish Appeal Nat. Young Women's Leadership Cabinet, 1982-87; v.p. Phila. chpt. Am. Jewish Congress, 1995—. Recipient Mrs. Isidore Kohn Young Leadership award Jewish Fedn. Greater Phila., 1981, Next Generation Leadership award Jewish Cmty. Ctrs. Assn., 2000, award of merit U. Pa. Law Sch. Alumni, 2001. Mem. ABA, Am. Law Inst., Am. Bar Found., Pa. Bar Assn., D.C. Bar, Phila. Bar Assn. (chmn. fed. cts. com. 1992), Fed. Bar Coun. of Second Cir. General civil litigation, Product liability, Toxic tort. Office: Hoyle Morris & Kerr LLP 1650 Market St Ste 1 Philadelphia PA 19103-7301 E-mail: afickler@hoylemk.com

FIEBACH, H. ROBERT, lawyer; b. Paterson, N.J., June 7, 1939; s. Michael M. and Silvia Irene (Nadler) F.; m. Elizabeth D. Carlton, Mar. 17, 1984; children: Michael, Emma; children by previous marriage: Jonathan, Rachel. BS, U. Pa., 1961, LLB cum laude, 1964. Bar: Pa. 1965, U.S. Supreme Ct. 1971. Law clk. to Chief Judge Biggs U.S. Ct. Appeals for 3d Cir., 1964-65; assoc. Wolf, Block, Schorr and Solis-Cohen, Phila., 1965-71, ptnr., 1971-79, sr. ptnr., 1979-95; sr. mem. Cozen & O'Connor, 1995—. Permanent mem. U.S. Jud. Conf. for 3d cir., 1967—; mem. Pa. Supreme Ct. Adv. Com. on Appellate Rules, 1987-93, Commn. on Jud. Elections, 1997-98; arbitrator, mediator U.S. Dist. Ct. (ea. dist.) Pa., Am. Arbitration Assn., 1966—; bd. dirs. Pa. Capital Case Resource Ctr. Contbg. author: Business and Commercial Litigation in the Federal Courts, 1998; rsch. editor U. Pa. Law Rev., 1964-65; contbr. articles to legal jours. Past mem. Phila. adv. bd. Anti-Defamation League of B'nai Brith, Greater Phila. Regional Commn. on Law and Social Action, Am. Jewish Congress; bd. dirs. Greater Phila. chpt. ACLU, past chmn. criminal justice and police practices com.; past bd. dirs. Pa. chpt. ACLU; bd. dirs. Pa. Bar Trust and Ins. Fund, 1996—, pres., 2001—. Fellow: Am. Coll. Trial Lawyers (Pres.'s award 2001); mem.: ABA (bd. govs. 1997—2000, ho. of dels. 1991—2000, ho. of dels. 2001—, pres. nat. caucus state bar assns. 1994—95, nat. conf. bar pres. 1991—95, chmn. standing com. on lawyers profl. liability 1994—95, past chmn. jud. performance and conduct com., jud. adminstrn. divsn. 1986—91, litigation sect., 1988 midyear meeting host com., state del. 2001—), Pa. Bar Assn. (pres.-elect 1992—93, pres. 1993—94, bd. govs. 1987—95, ho. of dels. 1983—, Pa. Bar Trust 1996—, past vice-chmn. jud. selection com., chmn. jud. retention election com 1980—83, chmn. com. on profl. liability 1984—87, chmn. polit. action com. for merit retention of judges 1980—83, Spl. Achievement award 1986), Phila. Bar Assn. (bd. govs. 1983—87, past chmn. fed. cts. com., past vice-chmn. arbitration com., past mem. spl. com. to study appellate cts., chmn. spl. com. on ins. 1983—84, civil jud. procedures com., spkr. various panels), Pa. Bar Inst. (pres. bd. dirs. 1984—90, pres. bd. dirs. 2000—), Pa. Bar Trust and Ins. Fund (bd. dirs. 1996—, pres. 2001—), Defender Assn. Phila. (bd. dirs.), Am. Judicature Soc. (state membership chmn. 1988), Phila. Trial Lawyers Assn. (past chmn. bus. litig. com., bd. dirs. 1989—90), Soc. of Fellows, Am. Bar Foun.d, Order of Coif (past dir. U. Pa. chpt.). Federal civil litigation, State civil litigation. Home: 301 Delancey St Philadelphia PA 19106-4208 Office: Cozen & O'Conner 1900 Market St Fl 3 Philadelphia PA 19103-3572 E-mail: rfiebach@cozen.com

FIEDEROWICZ, WALTER MICHAEL, lawyer; b. Hartford, Conn., Aug. 23, 1946; s. Michael and Sylvia Christine (Ramunno) F.; m. Gerry Prattson, June 1, 1968; children: Michael, Catherine. B.A., Yale U., 1968; J.D. (DuPont fellow), U. Va., 1971. Bar: Conn. 1971, U.S. Supreme Ct. 1977. Mem. firm Cummings & Lockwood, Stamford, Conn., 1971-76, ptnr. firm, 1979-88, of counsel, 1989-91; pres. Covenant Mut. Ins. Co., Hartford, 1985-92; White House fellow U.S. Dept. Justice, Washington, 1976-77; spl. asst. to Atty. Gen., Dept. Justice, 1976-77; assoc. dep. Atty. Gen., 1977-79. Bd. dirs. Photronics, Inc., First Albany Corp., Hematech; chmn. CDT Corp., Meacock Capital, Heritage Underwriting Agy. Mem. editorial bd.: Va. Law Review, 1969-71. Mem. grad. coun. Loomis-Chaffee Sch. Bd.; trustee Conn. Trust for Hist. Preservation. Mem. ABA, Conn. Bar Assn., Order of the Coif, Hartford Golf Club, Citrus Club, Univ. Club. Roman Catholic. Banking, Contracts commercial, General corporate. Home: 102 North St PO Box 939 Litchfield CT 06759-0939 E-mail: fiederowicz@juno.com

FIEGER, GEOFFREY NELS, lawyer; b. Detroit, Dec. 23, 1950; s. Bernard Julian and June Beth (Oberer) F.; m. Kathleen Janice Podwoiski, June 25, 1983. BA, U. Mich., 1974, MA, 1976; JD, Detroit Coll. Law, 1979. Bar: Mich. 1979, U.S. Dist. Ct. (ea. dist.) Mich. 1979, Fla. 1980, U.S. Dist. Ct. (mid. dist.) Fla. 1980, Ariz. 1980. Ptnr. Fieger Fieger Kenney & Johnson, P.C., Southfield, Mich., 1979—. V.p. Orgns. United to Save Twp., West Bloomfield, Mich., 1987. Mem. ABA, Detroit Bar Assn., Assn. Trial Lawyers Am. Unitarian. Avocations: running, swimming. Federal civil litigation, State civil litigation, Personal injury. Office: Fieger Fieger Kenney & Johnson PC 19390 W 10 Mile Rd Southfield MI 48075-2463

FIELD, HAROLD GREGORY, lawyer; b. Sept. 27, 1923; s. Harold Gregory and Catherine (Crowley) F.; m. Nancy L. Kesecker, Sept. 30, 1977. BS, Ariz. State U., 1948; LLB, Chgo. Kent Coll. Law, 1952. Bar: Ill. 1953. Ptnr. Burek & Field, Wheaton, Ill., 1960-86; pvt. practice, 1986-96; ptnr. Schiller, DeCarto & Fleck, 1996—. Family and matrimonial. Home: 979 Creekside Cir Naperville IL 60563-2472 Office: 311 S County Farm Rd Ste G Wheaton IL 60187-2438

FIELD, RICHARD CLARK, lawyer; b. Stanford, Calif., July 13, 1940; s. John and Sally Field; m. Barbara Faith Butler, May 22, 1967 (dec. Apr. 1984); 1 child, Amanda Katherine; m. Eva Sara Halbreich, Dec. 1, 1985. BA, U. Calif., Riverside, 1962; JD, Harvard U., 1965. Bar: Calif. 1966, U.S. Supreme Ct., 1971, U.S. Ct. Appeals (9th cir.) 1979. Assoc. Thompson & Colegate, Riverside, 1965-69; ptnr. Adams, Duque & Hazeltine, Los Angeles, 1970-89, mem. mgmt. com., 1981-84, chmn. litigation dept., 1985-89; ptnr. Cadwalader, Wickersham & Taft, 1989-97, McCutchen, Doyle, Brown & Enersen, LLP, Los Angeles, 1997—. Bd. dirs. ARC, L.A., 1984-93, 97—. Mem. ABA (litigation, torts and ins. practice sects., bus. torts com., products, gen. liability and consumer law com.), Los Angeles County Bar Assn. (trial lawyers sect.), Assn. Bus. Trial Lawyers (bd. govs. 1978-82), Am. Arbitration Assn. (comml. arbitration panel). Episcopalian. General civil litigation, Insurance, Product liability. Office: McCutchen Doyle Brown & Enersen LLP 355 S Grand Ave Ste 4400 Los Angeles CA 90071-3106

FIELD, ROBERT EDWARD, lawyer; b. Chgo., Aug. 21, 1945; s. Robert Edward and Florence Elizabeth (Aiken) F.; m. Jenny Lee Hill, Aug. 5, 1967; children: Jennifer Kay, Kimberly Anne, Amanda Brooke. BA, Ill. Wesleyan U., 1967; MA, Northwestern U., 1969, JD, 1973. Bar: Ill. 1973, U.S. Dist. Ct. (no. dist.) Ill. 1974, U.S. Supreme Ct. 1979. Exec. dir. Winnetka (Ill.) Youth Orgn., 1969-73; assoc. Seyfarth, Shaw, Fairweather & Geraldson, Chgo., 1973-79, ptnr., 1979-93, Field & Golan, Chgo., 1993—. Bd. dirs. Gt. Lakes Fin. Resources, Matteson, Ill., 1983—, vice chmn., 1988-91, chmn. 1991—; bd. dirs. Chgo. chpt. Ill. Wesleyan U. Assocs.; chmn. bd. dirs. 1st Nat. Bank of Blue Island, 1989-2001, Great Lake Bank, 2001—, Bank of Homewood, 1988-2001; bd. dirs. Winchester Mfg. Co., Wood Dale, Ill., Ludell Mfg. Co., Milw., Comml. Resources Corp., Naperville, Ill., 1984-93; dir., sec. Ellis Corp., Itasca, Ill., 1980—; chmn. bd. dirs. Cmty. Bank of Homewood-Flossmoor, Ill., 1983-92, Bank of Matteson, Ill., 1992-99; mem. State Banking Bd. Ill., 1993-97. Bd. dirs. Ctr. for New Beginnings, 1997—, Svcs. Exch., 1998—, Family Svc. Ctrs. Cook County, Matteson, 1979—, treas., 1981-82, pres., 1986-88, chmn., 1988-93; pres. Lakes of Olympia Condominium Assn., 1987-89; trustee Village of Olympia Fields, Ill., 1981-89, pres., 1991-97; trustee Ill. Wesleyan U., 1990—, treas., 1994—; bd. dirs. Northwestern U. Sch. Law Alumni Assn., 1990-94. Mem. ABA, Ill. Bar Assn., Am. Bankers Assn., Ill.

Bankers Assn., United Meth. Bar Assn. (v.p. Chgo. chpt. 1989), Chgo. Bar Assn., Bankers Club Chgo., Union League Club Chgo., Calumet Country Club. Banking, Contracts commercial, Real property. Home: 3424 Parthenon Way Olympia Fields IL 60461-1321 Office: Field & Golan 3 1st National Plz Ste 1500 Chicago IL 60602 E-mail: refield@fieldgolan.com

FIELDS, RICHARD LAWRENCE, lawyer, consultant; b. Washington, May 3, 1948; s. Robert Arthur and Helen Elizabeth (Hasty) F.; m. Michele McDowell, Apr. 17, 1971; children— Lauren Michele, Lindsey Suzanne. A.B., Columbia U., 1970; disting. grad. Officers Tng. Sch., U.S. Air Force, 1971; honor grad. Criminal Investigator Sch., U.S. Treasury, 1973; M.A., U. Md., 1974, J.D., 1977. Bar: Md. 1977, U.S. Dist. Ct. D.C. 1978, U.S. Dist. Ct. Md. 1978, U.S. Ct. Appeals (D.C. and 4th cirs.) 1978, Position classification specialist U.S. Geol. Survey, Washington, 1971-73; chief position mgmt. Bur. Alcohol, Tobacco, and Firearms, 1973-78; sole practice, Md. and Washington, 1978-82; ptnr. Fields & Fields, Oxon Hill, Md., and Washington, 1982— ; cons. mgmt. and personnel adminstrn., 1978-80. Served to 1st lt. USAFR, 1971-72. Mem. ABA, Assn. Trial Lawyers Am., Md. Bar Assn., Prince Georges County Bar Assn. Democrat. State civil litigation, Probate, Real property. Office: Fields & Fields Ste LL500 5620 Saint Barnabas Rd Oxon Hill MD 20745

FIENBERG, LINDA DORIS, lawyer; b. Albany, July 7, 1942; d. Chester Leonard Fienberg and Marcia Shirley Doris Kartzman; m. Jeffrey D. Bauman, Mar. 2, 1980; children by previous marriage; Lane Blumenfeld, Shawn Blumenfeld. B.A., Cornell U., 1964; M.A.T., Wesleyan U., 1966; J.D.; Georgetown U., 1973. Bar: D.C. 1973, U.S. Supreme Ct., U.S. Ct. Appeals (various cirs.), U.S. Dist. Ct. D.C. 1974. Research analyst EEOC, Washington, 1968-69, U.S. Commn. on Civil Rights, Washington, 1969-70; assoc. Arnold and Porter, Washington, 1973-78; spl. counsel SEC, Washington, 1979-80, asst. gen. counsel, 1980-82, assoc. gen. counsel, 1982— . Mem. ABA, Women's Legal Def. Fund, Phi Beta Kappa. Office: SEC 450 5th St NW Washington DC 20001-2739

FIERKE, THOMAS GARNER, lawyer; b. Boone, Iowa, Nov. 12, 1948; s. Norman Garner and Mary Margaret (Mullen) F.; m. Susan Marie Butler, July 17, 1976 (div. Mar. 1983); m. Debra Lynn Clayton, Sept. 17, 1988; children: Veronica Helen, Caroline Margaret. BSMetE, Iowa State U., 1971; JD, U. Minn., 1974; LLM, Boston U., 1978. Bar: Ill. 1974, U.S. Dist. Ct. Mass. 1976, U.S. Dist. Ct. (no. dist.) Ill. 1976, U.S. Ct. Appeals (1st cir.) 1976, U.S. Tax Ct. 1978, U.S. Supreme Ct. 1978, Mass. 1980, N.Y. 1981, U.S. Ct. Appeals (fed. cir.) 1989. Commd. 2nd lt. U.S. Army, 1971, advanced through grades to capt., resigned, 1980; trial ct. prosecutor Ft. Devens, Mass., 1974-77; group judge adv. 10th Spl. Forces Group, 1975-78; chief adminstrv. law sect. Ft. Devens, 1977-78; chief legal counsel, contracting officer U.S. Def. Rep., Am. Embassy, Tehran, Iran, 1979; chief adminstrv. law Ft. Devens, 1979-80; judge adv. gen. corps, 1974-80; atty.-advisor Army Materiel Command, 1980-82; mgr. contracts policy and review Martin Marietta Michoud Aerospace, Martin Marietta Corp., New Orleans, 1982; gen. counsel Lockheed Martin Manned Space Sys., Lockheed Martin Corp., 1984—. Apptd. to La. Gov.'s Mil. Adv. Commn., 1991—; bd. dirs. La. Orgn. for Jud. Excellence, 1988—; mem. La. state com. Employer Support of Guard and Res., 1988—, regional ombudsman, 1989-92, dep. state ombudsman, 1992-94, state ombudsman, 1994—, chmn. New Orleans sect., 1992-94. Col. USAR, 1995. Recipient Most Valuable Employer Support for the Guard and Res. award, NASA Pub. Svc. medal, 1992, La. Cross Merit award State of La., 1994, 5 Outstanding Vol. Svc. medals Dept. Def., 1994, 96, 97, 99, 2001, Legion of Merit, 1998, USN Superior Pub. Svc. medal, 1999, USCG commendation, 2001. Mem. Am. Corp. Counsel Assn. (bd. dirs. New Orleans chpt. 1987—, v.p. 1989-90), Internat. Assn. Def. Counsel. Republican. Episcopalian. Avocations: snow skiing, reading, running. General civil litigation, General corporate, Government contracts and claims. Office: Lockheed Martin Michoud Space Sys PO Box 29304 New Orleans LA 70189-0304 E-mail: tom.fierke@lmco.com

FIERST, BRUCE PHILIP, lawyer; b. Chgo., Jan. 26, 1951; s. Robert Jay and Esther Toby (Kaplan) F. BA with honors, Tulane U., 1973; JD, U. Denver, 1975. Bar: Colo. 1976, U.S. Dist. Ct. Colo. 1976. Assoc. Epstein, Lozow & Preblud, P.C., Denver, 1976-79; pres. Bruce P. Fierst, P.C., 1979—. Co-author manual Handling the DUI case, 1981. Big Brother, Big Bros. of Colo., Denver, 1975-81. Mem. ABA, Colo. Bar Assn., Denver Bar Assn., Am. Trial Lawyers Assn., Colo. Trial Lawyers Assn. (lectr., bd. dirs. 1986-94). Democrat. Jewish. Avocations: sports. Criminal, Personal injury. Home: 5431 S Dayton Ct Greenwood Vlg CO 80111-3633 E-mail: bruce1st@qwest.net

FIFIELD, GUY, lawyer; LLB, U. West England, 1981. Ptnr. Denton Wilde Sapte, London, 1984—. Mem. City of London Solicitors Co., Inst. Dirs. I.B.A. Labor. Office: Denton Wilde Sapte 1 Fleet Place London EC4M 7WS England Office Fax: 02072467777

FIFIELD, WILLIAM O. lawyer; b. Crown Point, Ind., May 25, 1946; BS with honors, Purdue U., 1968; JD cum laude, Harvard U., 1971. Bar: Ill. 1971, Tex. 1998. Assoc. Sidley & Austin, Dallas, 1971-77, ptnr., 1977—, mng. ptnr. Dallas office, 1996—. Bd. dirs. Kimberly-Clark Corp. Office: Sidley & Austin 717 N Harwood St Ste 3400 Dallas TX 75201-6534

FIFLIS, TED JAMES, lawyer, educator; b. Chgo., Feb. 20, 1933; s. James P. and Christine (Karakitsos) F.; m. Vasilike Pantelakos, July 3, 1955; children: Christina Eason, Antonia Fowler, Andreanna Lawson. BS, Northwestern U., 1954; LLB, Harvard U., 1957. Bar: Ill. 1957, Colo. 1975, U.S. Supreme Ct. 1984. Pvt. practice law, Chgo., 1957-65; mem. faculty U. Colo. Law Sch., Boulder, 1965—, prof., 1968—. Vis. prof. NYU, 1968, U. Calif., Davis, 1973, U. Chgo., 1976, U. Va., 1979, Duke U., 1980, Georgetown U., 1982, U. Pa., 1983, Am. U., 1983, Harvard U., 1988; Lehmann disting. vis. prof. Washington U., St. Louis, 1991; cons. Rice U.; arbitrator AT&T divesture disputes, 1984-87. Author: (with Homer Kripke, Paul Foster) Accounting for Business Lawyers, 1970, 3rd edit., 1984, Accounting Issues for Lawyers, 1991; editor-in-chief Corp. Law Rev., 1977-88; contbr. articles to profl. jours. Mem. ABA, Am. Assn. Law Schs. (past chmn. bus. law sect.), Colo. Bar Assn. (mem. coun. sect. of corp., banking and bus. law 1974-75), Am. Law Inst. (chmn. com. on rsch. proposed fed. securities code), Colo. Assn. Corp. Counsel (pres. 1998-99). Greek Orthodox. Home: 1340 Bluebell Ave Boulder CO 80302-7832 Office: Univ Of Colo Law Sch Boulder CO 80309-0001

FIGA, PHILLIP SAM, lawyer; b. Chgo., July 27, 1951; s. Leon and Sarah Figa; m. Candace Cole, Aug. 19, 1973; children: Benjamin Todd, Elizabeth Dawn. BA, Northwestern U., 1973; JD, Cornell U., 1976. Bar: Colo. 1976, U.S. Dist. Ct. Colo. 1976, U.S. Ct. Appeals (10th cir.) 1980, U.S. Supreme Ct. 1980. Assoc. Sherman & Howard, Denver, 1976-80; ptnr. Burns & Figa, P.C., 1980-90, pres., 1988-90; pres., shareholder Burns, Figa & Will, P.C., Englewood, Colo., 1991—. Instr. U. Denver Law Sch., 1984, 86, Nat. Inst. Trial Advocacy, Rocky Mountain Region, 1992, 94; bd. dirs. Colo. Lawyers Com., Denver, 1984-89, vice chair 1987-88, treas. 1988-89; mem. model rules of profl. conduct Colo. Supreme Ct., 1987-92, com. lawyer regulation to revise Colo. discipline rules, 1997-98, com. group legal svcs. and advt., 1982-86; mem. U.S. Dist. Ct. Justice Reform Act. Adv. Com., 1994-97; active Colo. Commn. on Jud. Discipline, 1995—; chair nominating com. Faculty Fed. Advs., 1999, 2000; spl. dir. Colo. Jud. Inst., 1999—. Articles editor Cornell Internat. Law Rev., 1975-76; contbr. articles to legal jours. Bd. dirs. B'nai B'rith Anti-Defamation League, 1984—, regional bd. chair, 1996-98; trustee Rose Med. Ctr., 1987-95, exec. com., 1990-95, AMC Cancer Rsch. Ctr., 1993-95; co-chair Civil Rights Com., 1988-90, Rose Cmty. Found., Jewish Life Com., 2001—. Evans scholar, 1969-73. Fellow Internat. Soc. Barristers, Am. Bar Found., Colo. Bar Found. (trustee 1999—, pres. Colo. Bar. Fellows 2001—); mem. ABA (standing com. on profl. discipline 1997-99), Am. Judicature Soc., Colo. Bar Assn. (mem. ethics com. 1978-93, chair ethics com. 1984-85, bd. govs. 1986-88, 89-91, pres. 1995-96, chair awards com. 1998-99, chair nominating com. 1999-2000), Denver Bar Assn., Arapahoe County Bar Assn., Phi Beta Kappa, Phi Eta Sigma. Antitrust, Federal civil litigation, State civil litigation. Home: 9928 E Ida Ave Greenwood Vlg CO 80111-3743 Office: Burns Figa & Will PC Ste 1030 6400 S Fiddlers Green Cir Englewood CO 80111-4950 E-mail: pfiga@burnsfigawill.com

FIGNAR, EUGENE MICHAEL, financial company executive, lawyer; b. Hazleton, Pa. s. Basil W. and Helen (Hannock) F.; m. Rosemary Casey. BBA, King's Coll., Wilkes-Barre, Pa., 1967; JD, Duquesne U., 1972. Bar: Pa. 1972, U.S. Dist. Ct. (we. dist.) Pa. 1972, Conn. 1988, N.Y. 1998; lic. real estate broker, N.Y., Conn. Counsel Westinghouse Electric Corp., Pitts., 1972-80; asst. gen. counsel Champion Internat. Corp., Stamford, Conn., 1980-81; v.p., gen. counsel, sec. Merrill Lynch Realty, 1981-82, Merrill Lynch Mortgage, Stamford, 1982-84, v.p. quality, product devel., 1985-88, also bd. dirs.; sr. v.p., sr. lending officer The Bank Mart, Bridgeport, 1988-90; pres., CEO TDS Fin., Inc., Stamford, 1990-97; of counsel Pryor, Cashman Sherman & Flynn, N.Y.C., 1997-99; ptnr. Kronish Lieb Weiner & Hellman, 1999—. Mem. bus. adv. coun. King's Coll., Wilkes-Barre, 1985—; bd. dirs. Ea. Fairfield County United Way, 1988—94; bd. dirs., vice chmn. Bridgeport Regional Counsel for Homeless, 1989—94. Sgt. U.S. Army, 1969—71. Mem.: Am. Arbitration Assn. (mem. panel of arbitrators), Real Estate Fin. Assn., N.Y. State Bar Assn., West End Yacht Club (commodore). Democrat. Catholic. Avocations: sailing, bicycling, model railroading, gardening. Home: 21 West End Ave Old Greenwich CT 06870-1611 Office: Kronish Lieb et al 1114 Avenue Of The Americas New York NY 10036-7703

FILLER, RONALD HOWARD, lawyer; b. St. Louis, Apr. 11, 1948; s. Leon Isaac and Jeanette Frances (Sanofsky) F.; m. Paula; children: Stephen Paul, Lindsay Ann. BS, U. Ill., 1970; JD, George Washington U., 1973; LLM in Taxation, Georgetown U., 1976. Bar: D.C. 1973, Ill. 1976, N.Y. 1993. Atty. SEC, Washington, 1973-76; assoc. Abramson & Fox, Chgo., 1976-77; assoc. counsel Conti Cmty. Svc., 1977-78, dir. mgmt. accounts, 1978-80; mng. ptnr. Filler Zaner & Assocs., 1980-85; ptnr. Vedder, Price, Kaufman & Kammholz, 1985-93, corp. practice leader, 1989-91, mem. exec. com., 1991-93; dir. futures adminstrn. Lehman Bros., Inc., 1993—. Dir. Commodities Law Inst., Ill. Inst. Tech./Chgo-Kent Law Sch., 1978-97, adj. prof. law, 1977-93, bd. overseers, 1982-97; lectr. Commodities Ednl. Inst., 1977-89; adj. prof. law Bklyn. Law Sch., 1994-96. Contbr. articles to jours. and futures mags. Named one of top 315 lawyers State of Ill., 1991. Mem. ABA (chmn. sub futures commn. mchts. 1986—), Nat. Futures Assn. (bd. dirs. 1984-87), Am. Arbitration Assn. (arbitrator), Mid Am. Commodity Exch. (bd. dirs. 1984-86), Chgo. Bar Assn. (chmn. commodities law com. 1981-82, vice chmn. fin. and legal svcs. com. 1988-89, co-vice chmn. large law firm com. 1991-92), Nat. Assn. Futures Traders Assn., Futures Industry Assn. (bd. dirs. 1990-92, exec. com. Chgo. divsn. 1986-88, exec. com. Law and Comp. divsn. 1985-90, 92—, sec. 1995-98, pres. 1998—), N.Y. State Bar Assn., Ill. State Bar Assn. Democrat. Jewish. Contracts commercial, Securities, Commodities. Home: 54 Collinwood Rd Maplewood NJ 07040-1038 Office: Lehman Bros Inc Am Exp Tower 3 World Fin Ctr Fl 8 New York NY 10285-0001 Fax: 212 526-6193. E-mail: RFiller@LEHMAN.com

FILPI, ROBERT ALAN, lawyer; b. Chgo., Oct. 8, 1945; s. John Andrew and Eunice Lorraine (Taylor) F.; m. Janice Elizabeth Crusoe, June 24, 1967; children: Jennifer Anne, Christopher Alan, Emily Elizabeth. BA in History, magna cum laude, Harvard U., 1967; JD, Northwestern U., 1970. Bar: Ill. 1970, U.S. Dist. Ct. (no. dist.) Ill. 1971, U.S. Ct. Appeals (7th cir.) 1971, U.S. Supreme Ct. 1975. Asst. U.S. atty. No. Dist. Ill., Chgo., 1971-75; dep. chief U.S. atty. No. Dist. Ill., Civil Divsn., 1975-76; ptnr. Stack & Filpi, 1976—. Assoc. editor Jour. Criminal Law, Criminology and Police Sci., 1969-70. Coach, Spring Lake Sports League, Lincolnshire, Ill. 1984-91; mem. Village of Lincolnshire Plan Commn., 1984-94. Recipient Hyde prize Northwestern U. Sch. Law, 1967. Mem. ABA, Chgo. Bar Assn., Union League, Harvard Club. General civil litigation, General corporate, General practice. Office: 140 S Dearborn St Ste 411 Chicago IL 60603-5201

FILSON, MARGUERITE B. lawyer; b. N.Y.C., Feb. 22, 1935; d. Bernard and Ruth (Wallerstein) Berger; m. Daniel H. Filson, June 20, 1954 (dec.); children: Paul Eliot, Adele Janet; m. Abraham Spector, May 27, 1983. BA, UCLA, 1956; MA, Brandeis U., 1965; JD, Harvard U., 1969. Bar: N.Y. 1971, U.S. Dist. Ct. (so. and ea. dists.) N.Y. 1973, U.S. Ct. Appeals (2d cir.) 1974, U.S. Supreme Ct. 1976. Law clk. to presiding judge U.S. Dist. Ct., Balt., 1969-70; assoc. Paul, Weiss, Rifkind, Wharton & Garrison, N.Y.C., 1970-73; sr. assoc. Patterson, Belknap, Webb & Tyler, N.Y.C., 1973-76, Schulte, Roth & Zabel, N.Y.C., 1976-77; atty. AT&T Technologies Inc., N.Y.C., 1977-84; counsel Internat. Paper Co.; counsel land utilization, 1984-86; v.p. Bader Research Corp., N.Y.C., 1986-92; adj. instr. New York Law Sch., N.Y.C., 1978-79; adminstrv. law judge N.Y.C. Dept. Health, Parking Violations Bureau; arbitrator N.Y. Stock Exchange, NASD, Am. Arbitration Assn., 1991—. Vol. atty. NAACP Legal Def. Fund, N.Y.C., 1979-81. Mem. Assn. Bar City N.Y., Harvard Law Sch. Assn. Administrative and regulatory, Alternative dispute resolution, General civil litigation. Office: 808 Broadway Ph 612 New York NY 10003-4809

FINA, PAUL JOSEPH, lawyer; b. Chgo., Mar. 1, 1959; s. Paul Emil and Vera Christiane (Mutzbauer) F.; m. Robyn Leann Hughes, May 24, 1986; 1 child, Paul George. BA in Econs., U. Ill., 1982, MA, 1983; JD, DePaul U., Chgo., 1987. Bar: Ill. 1988, U.S. Dist. Ct. (no. dist.) Ill. 1990, U.S. Ct. Appeals (7th cir.) 1990, U.S. Supreme Ct. 1991. Assoc. Haskin, Taylor & McDonough, Wheaton, Ill., 1988-90, Komessar & Wintroub, Chgo., 1990-94; pvt. practice Law Office of Paul J. Fina, 1994—. Mem. bus. faculty Coll. of DuPage, Glen Ellyn, Ill., 1986—, Aurora (Ill.) U., 1997—. Gen. counsel Housing Helpers, Inc., Riverside, Ill., 1991—. DePaul law grantee, 1985. Mem. ABA, Ill. Bar Assn., Assn. Trial Lawyers Am., DuPage County Bar Assn. (civil practice com.), Million Dollar Advocates Forum (life), Phi Alpha Delta. Roman Catholic. Avocations: music performance, athletics. State civil litigation, Personal injury. Home: 509 Bent Tree Ct Oswego IL 60543-8734 Office: 30 N La Salle St Ste 1530 Chicago IL 60602-2503 E-mail: pjflawyer@aol.com

FINBERG, JAMES MICHAEL, lawyer; b. Balt., Sept. 6, 1958; s. Laurence and Harriet (Levinson) Finberg; m. Melanie Piech; 1 child Joseph. BA, Brown U., 1980; JD, U. Chgo., 1983. Bar: Calif. 1984, U.S. Dist. Ct. (no. dist.) Calif. 1984, U.S. Dist. Ct. (ea. dist.) Calif. 1987, U.S. Ct. Appeals (9th and fed. cirs.) 1987, U.S. Dist. Ct. Hawaii, 1988, U.S. Supreme Ct. 1994. Law clk. to assoc. justice Mich. Supreme Ct., 1983-84; assoc. Feldman, Waldman and Kline, San Francisco, 1984-87, Morrison and Foerster, 1987-90; ptnr. Lieff, Cabraser, Heimann & Bernstein, L.L.P., San Francisco, 1991—. Lawyer rep. to 9th Jud. Conf., 1999-2001 (chair No. Calif. del. 2000-01); adv. com. local rules for securities cases U.S. Dist. Ct., Calif., 1996. Exec. editor U. Chgo. Law Rev., 1982-83. Mem.: ABA (chmn. securities subcom. class and derivative action com. 1998—, plaintiff's program chair equal employment opportunity com. 1999—2001), ACLU (bd. dirs. No. Calif. chpt. 1995), Bar Assn. San Francisco (jud. evaluation com. 1994, bd. dirs. 1999—2000, sec. 2001—), Calif. Bar Assn. (mem. standing com. on legal svcs. to poor 1990—94, vice-chmn. 1993—94), Lawyers Com. for Civil Rights of San Francisco Bay Area (bd. dirs. 1992—98, fin. chmn. 1992—95, sec. 1996, co-chmn. 1997—98). Federal civil litigation, Securities. Office: Lieff Cabraser Heimann & Bernstein LL 275 Battery St Fl 30 San Francisco CA 94111-3305

FINCH, EDWARD RIDLEY, JR. lawyer, diplomat, author, lecturer; b. Westhampton Beach, N.Y., Aug. 31, 1919; AB with Atwater honors, Princeton U., 1941; JD, NYU, 1947; LLD (hon.), Mo. Valley Coll., 1963; DSc (hon.), Cumberland Coll., 1985. Bar: N.Y. 1948, U.S. Supreme Ct. 1953, D.C. 1978, Fla. 1980, Pa. 1992. Ptnr. Finch & Schaefler, N.Y.C., 1950-85; of counsel Le Boeuf, Lamb, Leiby & MacRae, 1986-88; commr. City of N.Y., 1955-58. V.p. gen. counsel, dir. St. Giles Found., 1994—, Am. Internat. Petroleum Corp., 1988-92; U.S. del. 4th UN Congress, Geneva, 1970, 5th UN Congress, Japan, 1975; U.S. spl. ambassador to Panama, 1972; legal advisor, mem. U.S. Del. UNISPACE II, 1982, UNISPACE III, Vienna, Austria, 1999; lectr. in field. Author: Holes in Your Pockets, 3rd edit., Astro Business-A Guide to Commerce and Law of Outer Space, Judicial Politics; contbr. articles to profl. jours. Pres., bd. dirs. St. Nicholas Soc. N.Y., 1948—; past pres. N.Y. Inst. Spl. Edn., 1950—; bd. govs. Nat. Space Soc., 1984—; mem. faculty adv. com. dept. politics Princeton U.; treas. Jessie Ridley Found., N.Y.C., Finch Trusts; pres. Adams Meml. Fund Inc.; v.p. St. Giles Found.; trustee St. Andrew's Dune Ch., Southampton, Cathedral of St. John the Divine, 1989-92, Whittell Trust; bd. dirs. Am. Found. Cancer Rsch.; life trustee Met. Mus. of Art, N.Y.C.; mem. Coun. Am. Ambs. Col. JAG, USAFR, 1941-72. Decorated U.S. Legion of Merit with oak leaf cluster; order Brit. Empire; Knight Order St. John; officer French Legion of Honor, Disting. Eagle Scout, Coun. of Am. Ambassadors. Fellow Am. Bar Found. (chmn. aerospace coun. sect. sci. and tech 1986-92); mem. ABA (ho. of dels. 1971-72, chmn. corp. lawyers sr. lawyer divsn., chmn. aerospace law divsn. internat. law sect.1973-79), AIAA (sr.), Fed. Bar Assn., Inter-Am. Bar Assn. (Hallgartern telecommunications award 1991), N.Y. State Bar Assn. (internat. law and practice sec., chmn. arms control and nat. security com.), Pa. Bar Assn., Fla. Bar Assn., Assn., Bar City of N.Y., Internat. Bar Assn., Judge Advs. Assn. U.S. (past pres.), Am. Law Inst., Am. Judicature Soc. (sr.), Internat. Astronautical Acad. (full elected mem.), Internat. Inst. Space Law (Lifetim Disting. Svc. award 1997), Am. Arbitration Assn. (panelist), Univ. Clubs of Wash. and N.Y., Union League Club, Union Club, Princeton Club (bd. govs. 1982—), L.I. Club, Bathing Corp. of Southampton, Westhampton Country Club, Hillsboro Club (sr.). Non-profit and tax-exempt organizations, Securities, Estate taxation. Office: 862 Park Ave New York NY 10021-1831 Fax: 212-327-0593. E-mail: erfinchjr@aol.com

FINCH, FRANK HERSCHEL, JR. lawyer; b. Mpls., Mar. 13, 1933; s. Frank H. and Louise A. (Henry) F.; children: Frank H. III, Lani D.L. BA, Harvard U., 1953; LLB, Harvard U. Law Sch., 1959. Bar: Conn. 1959, U.S. Supreme Ct. 1967, U.S. Dist. Ct. Conn. 1997. Assoc. Howd & Lavieri, Winsted, Conn., 1959-61; ptnr. Howd, Lavieri & Finch, 1961—. Pros. atty. Conn. Cir. Ct., 1961-78; bd. dirs. Northwest Conn. Health Corp. Chmn., bd. dirs. Winsted Meml. Hosp., 1975-77; mem. regional adv. coun. N.W. Conn. C.C.; chmn. bd. trustees N.W. Conn. YMCA. Lt. USNR, 1953-59. Mem. ABA, Conn. Bar Assn. (bd. govs. 1985-99, pres. 1998-99), Litchfield County Bar Assn. (pres. 1974-76, grievance com. 1982-86, state trial referee 1984—), Am. Arbitration Assn. (arbitrator 1975—), Nat. Assn. Dist. Attys., N.W. Conn. C. of C. (bd. dirs. 1978-93, chmn. 1980-81, sec. 1985-89, v.p. 1989—), Rotary (pres. Winsted club 1967-68), Univ. Club (exec. com. 1985—, v.p. 1998—). General corporate, General practice, Real property. Office: Howd Lavieri & Finch LLP PO Box 1080 682 Main St Winsted CT 06098-1515

FINCH, MICHAEL PAUL, lawyer; b. Galveston, Tex., Jan. 4, 1946; s. Albert Lynn and Ila Belle (Robertson) F.; m. Rebecca Jean Minnear, Dec. 27, 1969; children: Michael Paul, Rachelle Jean. BEE cum laude, MEE, Rice U., 1969; JD magna cum laude, U. Houston, 1972. Bar: Tex. 1973. Petroleum engr. Exxon Corp., Houston, 1969-72; assoc. Vinson & Elkins, 1972-79, ptnr., 1980—. Dir. Houston Pops Orch., 1988-89; bd. dirs. Rice Engring. Alumni, 1994-98. Mem. ABA, Tex. Bar Assn., Houston Bar Assn., Am. Contact Bridge League (life master 1964—). Republican. Methodist. Clubs: Houston Ctr., Rice U. (founder). Avocations: electronics, woodworking, snow skiing, piano. General corporate, Mergers and acquisitions, Securities. Home: 12531 Overcup Dr Houston TX 77024-4915 Office: Vinson & Elkins 2300 First City Tower 1001 Fannin St Ste 3300 Houston TX 77002-6706

FINCH, RAYMOND LAWRENCE, judge; b. Christiansted, St. Croix, V.I., Oct. 4, 1940; s. Wilfred Christopher and Beryl Elaine (Bough) F.; m. Anne Marie Mohammed, May 8, 1996; children: Allison, Mark, Jennifer. A.B., Howard U., 1962, J.D., 1965. Bar: V.I. 1971, Third Circuit Ct. of Appeals 1976. Law clk. Judge's Municipal Ct. of V.I., 1965-66; partner firm Hodge, Sheen, Finch & Ross, Christiansted, 1970-75; judge Territorial Ct. of V.I., Charlotte Amalie, 1975-86, Ct. of Appeals, V.I., Charlotte Amalie, 1986-94, U.S. Dist. Ct. of V.I., 1994—, chief judge, 1999—. Instr. Grad. div., Coll. of V.I., Am. Inst. Banking, 1976— Bd. dirs. Boy Scouts Am., Boys Club Am. Served to capt. U.S. Army, 1966-69. Decorated Army Commendation medal, Bronze Star medal. Mem. Am. Judges Assn., Am., Nat. bar assns., Internat. Assn. Chiefs of Police. Democrat. Lutheran. Office: PO Box 24051 Christiansted VI 00824-0051

FINCK, KEVIN WILLIAM, lawyer; b. Whittier, Calif., Dec. 14, 1954; s. William Albert and Ester (Gutbub) F.; m. Kathleen A. Miller, Oct. 7, 1989. BA in History, U. Calif., Santa Barbara, 1977; JD, U. Calif., San Francisco, 1980. Bar: Calif. 1980. Lectr. Internat. Bar Assn., Learning Annex. Author: California Corporation Start Up Package and Minute Book, 1982, 9th edit., 1998; contbr. articles to various profl. jours. Avocations: hiking, golf, skiing. Contracts commercial, General corporate, Private international. Office: Ste 1670 Two Embarcadero Ctr San Francisco CA 94111 E-mail: kevin@kevinfinck.com

FINE, A(RTHUR) KENNETH, lawyer; b. N.Y.C., June 29, 1937; s. Aaron Harry and Rose (Levin) F.; m. Ellen Marie Jensen, July 11, 1964; children: Craig Jensen, Ricki-Barie, Desiree-Ellen. AB, Hunter Coll., 1959; JD, Columbia U., 1963; CLU, Coll. Ins., 1973; diploma, Command and Gen. Staff Coll., 1978. Bar: N.Y. 1974; registered rep. and limited prin. Nat. Assn. Securities Dealers, Inc. Joined U.S. Army N.G., 1955, advanced through grades to maj., 1973, ret., 1980. Cons. U.S. Life Ins. Co., N.Y.C., 1970-74, atty., 1975-78, asst. gen. counsel, 1978; asst. counsel USLIFE Corp., N.Y.C., 1978-79, assoc. counsel, 1979-93; v.p., sr. counsel Western Res. Life Assurance Co. Ohio, Clearwater, Fla. Mem. ABA, Soc. Fin. Svc. Profls., N.Y. State Bar Assn., N.G. Assn. U.S., Militia Assn. N.Y. (chmn. vet. officers com. 1981-90), Am. Legion (7th regt. post), Ret. Officers Club St. Petersburg, Fla. Republican. Lutheran. Administrative and regulatory, General corporate, Insurance. Home: 5953 36th Ave N Saint Petersburg FL 33710-1835 Office: Western Res Life Assurance Co of Ohio PO Box 5068 Clearwater FL 33758-5068 E-mail: kfine@aegonusa.com

FINE, J. DAVID, lawyer; b. N.Y.C., Jan. 30, 1951; s. Phillip and Irma (Miller) F.; m. Judith Lynn McMillan, June 6, 1984. BSFS, Georgetown U., 1970; LLB, McGill U., Montreal, Que., 1973, BCL, 1974; LLM, Columbia U., 1978. Bar: We. Australia, 1987, High Ct. Australia, 1987, Oreg., 1992, U.S. Dist. Ct. Oreg., 1994. Asst. prof. U. Melbourne, Australia, 1974-76; clin. instr. Osgoode Hall Law Sch., Toronto, Ont., Can., 1976-77; Jervey fellow comp. law Columbia U., N.Y.C., 1977-79; assoc. prof. Loyola U., New Orleans, 1979-84, Macquarie U., Sydney, Australia, 1984-86; prof. U. Western Australia, Perth, 1986-91; pvt. practice Ashland, Oreg., 1992—.

Traffic safety commr., City of Ashland, 1997-99. Contbr. articles to profl. jours. City councilman City of Ashland, 1999—; bd. dirs. Rogue Valley Coun. Govts., 2001—. Mem. Internat. Trademark Assn., So. Oreg. Internat. Trade Coun. (charter mem.), Oreg. State Bar Assn. (continuing legal edn. com. 1995-98), Jackson County Bar Assn. (pres. 2001), Ashland Gun Club. Jewish. Avocations: reading, shooting, cooking, fly fishing. Intellectual property, Private international, Municipal (including bonds). Home: PO Box 66 Ashland OR 97520-0166 Office: 50 3rd St PO Box 66 Ashland OR 97520-0166

FINE, RICHARD ISAAC, lawyer; b. Milw., Jan. 22, 1940; s. Jack and Frieda F.; m. Maryellen Olman, Nov. 25, 1982; 1 child, Victoria Elizabeth. BS, U. Wis., 1961; JD, U. Chgo., 1964; PhD in Internat. Law, U. London, 1967, cert., 1965, 66; cert. comparative law, Internat. U. Comparative Sci., Luxembourg, 1966; diplôme supérieur, Faculté Internat. pour l'Enseignment du Droit Comparé, Strasbourg, France, 1967. Bar: Ill. 1964, D.C. 1972, Calif. 1973. Trial atty. fgn. commerce sect. antitrust divsn. U.S. Dept. Justice, 1968-72; chief antitrust divsn. L.A. City Atty.'s Office, also spl. counsel gov. efficiency com., 1973-74; prof. internat., comparative and EEC antitrust law U. Syracuse (N.Y.) Law Sch. (overseas program), 1970-72; individual practice Richard I. Fine and Assocs., L.A., 1974—; mem. antitrust adv. bd. Bur. Nat. Affairs, 1981—. Bd. dirs. Citizens Island Bridge Co., Ltd., 1992—; vis. com. U. Chgo. Law Sch., 1992-95; hon. consul gen. Kingdom of Norway, 1995—. Contbr. articles to legal publs. Bd. dirs. Retinitis Pigmentosa Internat., 1985-90. Mem. ABA (chmn. subcom. internat. antitrust and trade regulation, internat. law sect. 1972-77, co-chmn. com. internat. econ. orgn. 1977-79), ATLA, Am. Soc. Internat. Law (co-chmn. com. corp. membership 1978-83, exec. coun. 1984-87, budget com. 1992-97, regional coord. for L.A. 1994—, 1995 ann. program com. 1994-95, corr. editor Internat. Legal Materials 1983—), Am. Fgn. Law Assn., Internat. Law Assn., Brit. Inst. Internat. and Comparative Law, State Bar Calif. (chmn. antitrust and trade regulation law sect. 1981-84, exec. com. 1981-87), L.A. County Bar Assn. (chmn. antitrust sect. 1977-78, exec. com. sect. internat. law 1993—, treas. 1997), Ill. Bar Assn., Am. Friends London Sch. Econs. and Polit. Sci. (bd. dirs. 1984—, chmn. So. Calif. chpt. 1984—, chmn. L.A. adv. com.), L.A. World Affairs Coun. (internat. cir. 1990—), Phi Delta Phi. Antitrust, Federal civil litigation, State civil litigation. Office: Ste 200 468 N Camden Dr Beverly Hills CA 90210 E-mail: rifinelaw@earthlink.net

FINE, ROBERT PAUL, lawyer; b. Buffalo, June 10, 1943; s. Leonard and Sylvia (Wagner) Finkelstein; m. Eileen Joyce Levitsky, Nov. 26, 1967; children: Lisa Robin, Julie Beth. BA, SUNY, Buffalo, 1965, JD, 1968. Bar: N.Y. 1968, U.S. Dist. Ct. (we. dist.) N.Y. 1969, U.S. Tax Ct. 1973, Fla. 1985. Intern U.S. Dept. Justice, Washington, 1967; law asst. appellate divsn. 4th jud. dept. N.Y. Superior Ct., Rochester, 1968-69, chief law asst., 1969-70; assoc. Williams, Stevens, McCarville & Frizzell, P.C., Buffalo, 1970-74, ptnr., 1974-77; co-founder, sr. ptnr. Hurwitz & Fine, P.C., 1977—. Participant, panelist Fed. Tax Inst. Western N.Y., 1976—85, chmn. inst., 1978—81; adj. prof. SUNY Buffalo Sch. Law, 1996—; vice chmn. Buffalo and Erie County Pvt. Industry Coun., 1988—95; exec. com., counsel local organizing com. to bring 1993 World Univ. Games to Buffalo; bd. dirs. Roswell Park Cancer Inst., 1998—, chair fin. com. Bd. dirs. United Jewish Fedn., 1979-84, treas., 1982-84, v.p., 1986-88; chmn. exec. bd. We. N.Y. Israel Bonds Orgn., 1980-82; mem. Dean's Adv. Coun., SUNY Buffalo Law Sch., mem. dean search com., 1986-87; mem. dept. jud. screening com. 4th dept. appellate divsn. state of N.Y., 1999—, Magistrate Judge, merit selection panel we. dist. N.Y., 1990—, chair, 2000—. Mem. ABA, N.Y. State Bar Assn. (exec. com. bus. law sect.), Fla. Bar Assn., Erie County Bar Assn. (chmn. tax com. 1978-81, chmn. corp. law com. 1981-84, bd. dirs. 1985-88), Fin. Planning Counselors We. N.Y. (pres. 1986-87), Estate Analysts We. N.Y., Nat. Health Lawyers Assn., SUNy Sch. Law Alumni Assn. (pres. 1976-77), Mid-Day of Buffalo Club, Westwood Country Club (Williamsville, N.Y.), Buffalo Club. General corporate, Health, Estate planning. E-mail: rpf@hurwitzfine.com

FINELSEN, LIBBI JUNE, lawyer; b. Encino, Calif., Apr. 14, 1968; BA in Polit. Sci. summa cum laude, U. Nev., 1990; JD magna cum laude, Lewis and Clark Coll., 1993. Bar: D.C. 1996, U.S. Ct. Appeals (9th, 11th and D.C. cirs.) 1996, U.S. Ct. Appeals (4th cir.) 1999, U.S. Ct. Appeals (fedl. cir.) 2001. Jud. law clk. Gen. Svcs. Bd. Contract Appeals, Washington, 1993-94; assoc. McAleese & Assocs. P.C., McLean, Va., 1994-96; atty. USDA, Washington, 1996-99; trial atty. U.S. Dept. Air Force, Wright Patterson AFB, Ohio, 2000—. V.p. edn. Hadassah Young Profls. Group, Washington, 1998-99; mem. hospitality com. Kesher Israel Synagogue, Washington, 1998-99. Mem. ABA, Phi Alpha Delta, Phi Kappa Phi. Avocations: cooking, handicrafts, travel, art exhibitions.

FINEMAN, S. DAVID, lawyer; b. Phila., Oct. 23, 1945; BA, Am. U., 1967; JD with honors, George Washington U., 1970. Bar: Pa. 1971, U.S. Dist. Ct. (ea. dist.) Pa., U.S. Ct. Appeals (3d cir.) Pa. 1980. Trial atty. Defender Assn., Phila., 1971-72; law clk. Superior Ct. Commonwealth, Pa., 1972-73; mng. ptnr. Fineman & Bach, P.A., Phila., 1981—, Fineman & Bach, Phila., 1987—. Instr. bus. law Temple U., 1974-83; mem. Phila. Planning Commn., 1989-91; mem. Industry Policy Adv. Com. to Advise Sec. of Commerce on Internat. Trade Issues, 1994-98. Bd. govs. U.S. Postal Svc., 1995—, chmn. compensation com., 1997-2000, v. chmn., 2001—, chmn. strategic planning com., 2001— Mem. ABA, Phila. Bar Assn., Pa. Bar Assn., Pa. State Trial Lawyers Assn., Def. Rsch. Inst. Administrative and regulatory, General civil litigation, Insurance. Home: 335 Woodley Rd Merion Station PA 19066-1430 Office: 1608 Walnut St Ste 19 Philadelphia PA 19103-5443 E-mail: sdfineman@finemanbach.com

FINK, EDWARD MURRAY, lawyer, educator; b. N.Y.C., Mar. 11, 1934; s. Nathaniel and Elsa Charlotte (Lenrow) F.; divorced; children: Jeffrey Neil, Andrea Sue; m. Rita Toby Cohen, Aug. 11, 1985. BS in Chemistry, CCNY, 1955; JD, Georgetown U., 1959. Bar: D.C. 1960, U.S. Dist. Ct. D.C. 1960, U.S. Ct. Appeals (D.C. cir.) 1960, N.Y. 1962, N.J. 1970, U.S. Dist. Ct. N.J. 1970, U.S. Patent and Trademark Office 1960. Patent examiner U.S. Patent Office, Washington, 1955-60; atty. Bell Labs., Murray Hill, N.J., 1960-83, Bell Comm. Rsch. Inc., Livingston, 1984-91, Edward M. Fink, P.A., Edison, 1991—; v.p., gen. counsel Eastern R.R. Investment Corp., Bridgewater, 2000—, chmn. bd. dirs., 2001—, Somerset Terminal R.R. Corp., 2001—. Adj. prof. torts, bus. law and civil litigation Middlesex County Coll., Edison, N.J., 1980-2000; adj. prof. partnerships and corps, contract law Montclair State U., Upper Montclair, N.J., 1984-2000. Mem. ABA, Am. Intellectual Property Assn., N.J. Patent Law Assn., N.J. State Bar Assn., Middlesex County Bar Assn., D.C. Bar Assn., N.Y. State Bar Assn. Democrat. Jewish. General practice, Patent, Real property. Home and Office: 51 Jamaica St Edison NJ 08820-3726 E-mail: patemf@aol.com

FINK, JOSEPH ALLEN, lawyer; b. Lexington, Ky., Oct. 4, 1942; s. Allen Medford and Margaret Ruth (Draper) F.; m. Marcia L. Horton; children: Alexander Mentzer, Justin McGranahan. Student, Wayne State U., 1960-61; BA, Oberlin Coll., 1964; JD, Duke U., 1967. Bar: Mich. 1968, U.S. Dist Ct. (ea. dist.) Mich. 1968, U.S. Dist. Ct. (we. dist.) Mich. 1974, U.S. Ct. Appeals (6th cir.) 1987, U.S. Supreme Ct. 1998. Assoc. Dickinson, Wright, McKean & Cudlip, Detroit, 1972-75, Lansing, Mich., 1968-75; ptnr. Dickinson Wright PLLC, 1976—. Instr. U.S. Internat. U. Grad. Sch. Bus., San Diego, 1971; adj. prof. trial advocacy Thomas M. Cooley Law Sch., Lansing, 1984-85; mem. com. on local rules U.S. Dist. Cts., 1985; chmn. trial experience subcom. U.S. Dist. Ct. (we. dist.) Mich., 1981. Contbg. author: Construction Litigation, 1979, Legal Considerations in Managing Problem Employees, 1988, Michigan Civil Procedure During Trial, 2d edit., 1989; contbr. articles to profl. jours. Bd. dirs. Lansing 2000 Inc., 1985-92; bd. trustees Olivet (Mich.) Coll., 1985-94; mem. bd. advisors Mich. State U. Press, 1993-96. Lt. JAGC, USNR, 1968-72. Fellow Mich. State Bar Found.; mem. Fed. Bar Assn., State Bar of Mich. (chmn. local disciplinary com. 1983—, mem. com. for U.S. Cts. 1984), Mich. Def. Trial Counsel Assn. Episcopalian. Avocations: writing, reading, golf. Federal civil litigation, General civil litigation, Insurance. Home: 6302 W Lake Dr Haslett MI 48840-8930 Office: Dickinson Wright PLLC 215 S Washington Sq Ste 200 Lansing MI 48933-1816

FINK, NORMAN STILES, lawyer, educational administrator, fundraising consultant; b. Easton, Pa., Aug. 13, 1926; s. Herman and Yetta (Hyman) F.; m. Helen Mullen, Sept. 1, 1956; children: Hayden Michael, Patricia Carol. AB, Dartmouth Coll., 1947; JD, Harvard U., 1950. Bar: N.Y. 1951, U.S. Dist. Ct. (ea. and so. dists.) N.Y. 1954, U.S. Supreme Ct. 1964. Mem. legal staff Remington Rand, Inc., N.Y.C., Washington, 1949-54; ptnr. Lans & Fink, N.Y.C., 1954-68; counsel devel. program U. Pa., Phila., 1969-80; v.p. devel. and univ. rels. Brandeis U., Waltham, Mass., 1980-81; dep. v.p. devel., alumni rels., assoc. gen. counsel devel. Columbia U., N.Y.C., 1981-89; sr. counsel John Grenzebach & Assocs., Inc., Chgo., 1989-91. Cons. v.p. Engle Consulting Group, Inc., Chgo. Editor: Deferred Giving Handbook, 1977; author: (with Howard C. Metzler) The Costs and Benefits of Deferred Giving, 1982. V.p. Am. Australian Studies Found.; mem. bd. visitors Brevard (N.C.) Coll., 1995-99, life trustee, 1999, Warren Wilson Coll., 1997—. With U.S. Army, 1945-46. Recipient Alice Beeman award for excellence in devel. writing Coun. Advancement and Support of Edn., 1984, Silver medal for fundraising comms., Coun. Advancement and Support of Edn., 1988; Lilly Endowment grantee, 1979-80. Master Mason; mem. ABA (mem. com. on exempt orgns. sect. taxation and com. estate planning and drafting, charitable givint), Coun. Advancement and support of Edn. (various coms.), Am. Arbitration Assn. (panelist), Assn. of Bar of City of N.Y.C. (com. on tax-exempt orgns. 1987-90), Dartmouth Lawyers Assn., Harvard Law Sch. Assn., Nat. Soc. Fund Raising Execs (Contbn. to Knowledge award 1985), Harvard Club Western N.C., Elks. Democrat. Jewish.

FINK, ROBERT STEVEN, lawyer, writer, educator; b. Bklyn., Dec. 7, 1943; s. Samuel Miles and Helen Leah (bogen) F.; m. Abby Deutsch, Mar. 20, 1980; children: Juliet Leah, Robin Rachel. Diploma, U. Vienna, 1962; BA, Bklyn. Coll., 1965; JD, NYU, 1968, LLM, 1973. Bar: N.Y. 1969, U.S. Dist. Ct. (so. and ea. dists.) N.Y. 1970, U.S. Tax Ct. 1970, U.S. Ct. Appeals (2d cir.) 1970, U.S. Supreme Ct. 1972, U.S. Dist. Ct. (we. dist.) N.Y. 1975, U.S. Ct. Claims 1984, U.S. Dist. Ct. (no. dist.) N.Y. 1985, U.S. Ct. Appeals (fed. cir.) 1990, U.S. Ct. Internat. Trade 1998. Assoc. Kostelanetz & Ritholz, N.Y.C., 1968-75, ptnr., 1975-87, Kostelanetez, Ritholz, Tigue and Fink, N.Y.C., 1987-94, Kostelanetz & Fink LLP, N.Y.C., 1994—. Lectr. in field; expert witness IRS; mem. adv. com. tax divsn. Dept. Justice; chmn. IRS/Bar Liaison Com. N.E. Region, 1996-99; adj. prof. law NYU. Author: Tax Fraud: Audits, Investigations, Prosecutions, 2 vols., 1980, 20th rev. edit., 2001; co-author: How to Defend Yourself Against the IRS, 1985, You Can Protect Yourself from the IRS, 1987, 2d rev. edit., 1988; dept. editor Jour. of Taxation; contbr. numerous articles in field to profl. jours. Fellow Am. Coll. Tax Counsel; mem. ABA (chmn. com. civil and criminal tax penalties 1983-85, chmn. task force for revision of tax penalties 1982), N.Y. State Bar Assn. (chmn. com. criminal and civil tax penalties 1982-85, 88-90, chmn. compliance and unreported income 1985-87, chmn. commodities and fin. futures 1987-88, chmn. com. compliance and penalties 1991-93, chmn. com. compliance practice and procedure 1993—, mem. house of dels. 1995-97), Fed. Bar Assn., N.Y. County Lawyers Assn. (chmn. com. taxation 1988-92, 96-97, bd. dirs. 1989-95), Assn. of Bar of City of N.Y., Am. Arbitration Assn. (arbitrator). Federal civil litigation, Criminal, Taxation, general. Office: Kostelanetz & Fink LLP 530 5th Ave New York NY 10036-5101 E-mail: rfink@kflaw.com

FINK, ROSALIND SUE, lawyer; b. Cleve., May 24, 1946; d. Sanford and Bess (Tiktin) F.; m. Robert Cannel Herz, Feb. 4, 1979; 1 child, Zachary Robert. AB, Barnard Coll., 1968; JD, Yale U., 1972. Bar: N.Y. 1973, U.S. Ct. Appeals (2d cir.) 1975, U.S. Supreme Ct., 1977, U.S. Dist. Ct. (ea. dist.) N.Y., 1993. Assoc. Proskauer Rose Goetz & Mendelsohn, N.Y.C., 1972-74, Dretzin & Kauff PC, N.Y.C., 1974-75; asst. atty. gen. N.Y. State Dept. Law, 1975-80; dir. Office Equal Opportunity and Affirmative Action-Columbia U., 1980-94; of counsel Brill & Meisel, 1994—. Adj. assoc. prof. polit. sci. Barnard Coll., N.Y.C., 1991-94, mem. departmental discipline com., appellate divsn. Supreme Ct., 1st jud. dept., 1990-95, 99—, def. adv. com. on women in the svcs. U.S. Dept. Def., 1994-97. Exec. bd. Barnard Coll. Womens Ctr., N.Y.C., 1980-84; active Am. Coun. Edn. Task Force on Affirmative Action, Washington, 1981-83. Named to YWCA Acad. Women Achievers, 1997. Mem. N.Y. County Lawyers Assn. (bd. dirs. 1982-88, 90-92, 95—, com. womens rights 1973—, chair 1981-84, v.p. 1996-97, pres. 1997-98), Assn. Bar City of N.Y., Nat. Assn. Coll. and Univ. Attys. (vice-chair. affirmative action and nondiscrimination section 1983-84, co-chair 1984-90), N.Y. State Bar Assn. (ho. of dels. 1991—), Assn. Yale Alumni, Yale Law Sch. Alumni Assn. (exec. com. 1996—, v.p., 2000—). Democrat. Jewish. Office: Brill & Meisel 488 Madison Ave Rm 504 New York NY 10022-5702 E-mail: rozfink@nela.org

FINK, THOMAS MICHAEL, lawyer; b. Huntington, Ind., Oct. 6, 1947; s. Francis Anthony and Helen Elizabeth (Hartman) F.; m. Sheila Ann Jeffers, Aug. 11, 1973; children: Mark, Matthew, Megan. BBA, U. Notre Dame, 1970; JD, Northwestern U., 1973. Bar: Ind. 1973, U.S. Dist. Ct. (no. dist.) Ind. 1973. Assoc. Barrett & McNagny, Ft. Wayne, Ind., 1973-78, ptnr., 1979—. Speaker Estate Planning Coun., Ft. Wayne, 1987—. Pres. Bishop Luers H.S. Bd. Edn., Ft. Wayne, 1992-93; bd. dirs. Ft. Wayne Cmty. Found. Bus. Edn. Fund, 1990—; bd. dirs., treas. Planned Giving Coun. N.E. Ind., 1995—. Mem. Am. Coll. Trust and Estate Counsel, Ft. Wayne Country Club, Notre Dame Club of Ft. Wayne, Beta Gamma Sigma. Roman Catholic. Avocations: coaching basketball, golf, tennis, travel. Estate planning, Probate, Estate taxation. Home: 1302 Sunset Dr Fort Wayne IN 46807-2952 Office: Barrett & McNagny 215 E Berry St Fort Wayne IN 46802-2705 E-mail: tmf@barrettlaw.com

FINKBOHNER, GEORGE WHEELER, JR. lawyer; b. Mobile, Ala., Mar. 30, 1935; s. George Wheeler Finkbohner and Rachel Elizabeth Norville; m. Beverly Ryan Finkbohner, Feb. 6, 1960; children: George W., Patricia, Patrick Ryan, Elizabeth F. Sayler. BA, U. Ala., 1957, LLB, 1960. Bar: Ala. 1960, U.S. Dist. Ct. (so. dist.) Ala. 1960, U.S. Ct. Appeals (5th and 11th cirs.) 1981. Assoc. Howell, Johnston, and Langford, Mobile, 1960-63; ptnr. Howell, Johnston, Langford, Finkbohner & Lawler, 1964-82, Finkbohner, Lawler & Olen, Mobile, 1982-92; ptnr., mem. Finkbohner & Lawler, LLC, 1993—. Spkr. Cath. Charities for Archdiocese, Mobile, 1973-97; seminar spkr. Cath. Archdiocese of Mobile, 1970-71. Pres. St. Thomas Moore Cath. Lawyers Guild, Mobile, 1965; mem., pres. Bd. Cath. Edn., Mobile, 1974-76, Archdiocesan Bd. Cath. Edn., 1976-78; dist. chmn. Cath. Charities, Mobile, 1973-75, deanery chmn., 1976, archdiocesan chmn., 1978; rep. Diocesan Pastoral Coun., Evergreen, Ala., 1974-76; coun. pres. St. Mary's Parish. Mobile, 1970-71, 83-84, fin. coun., 1994—; bd. dirs., author of constitution Vol. Mobile, 1976-78, Jr. Tennis Patrons Assn., Mobile, 1976-78; mem., chmn. Mattei Meml. Endowment Fund, St. Mary's Sch., Mobile, 1994—; lector St. Mary's Parish, Mobile; bd. dirs. Little Sisters of the Poor, Mobile, 1979-86; mem. maj. gifts com. McGill-Toolen H.S., Mobile, 1994-95. Named Outstanding Cath. Alumnus, St. Mary's Sch./Nat. Cath. Edn. Assn. Cath. Social Svcs., Mobile, 1994; Recipient Valentine award Cath. Social Svcs., 1996. Mem. KC (3d and 4th deg., advocate 1967-74, knight of quar. 1964—), ABA, Ala. Bar Assn. (founding mem. bankruptcy and comml. law sect. 1983—, pres. bankruptcy sect. 1984), Mobile Bar Assn. (pres. young lawyer's sect. 1967-68, pres. 1990, nominating com. 1995—, constn. com. 1999, spkr.), Athelstan Downtown Men's Club (bd. dirs. 1987-89), Mardi Gras Orgns., KC (3rd, 4th degree, bd. advisors 1967-74, Knight of Quarter 1969). Roman Catholic. Avocations: tennis, golf, aerobic exercise, gardening, hunting. Home: 116 Ryan Ave Mobile AL 36607-3228

FINKE, ROBERT FORGE, lawyer; b. Chgo., Mar. 11, 1941; s. Robert Frank and Helen Theodora (Forge) F. AB, U. Mich., 1963; JD, Harvard U., 1966. Bar: Ill. 1966, U.S. Dist. Ct. (no. dist.) Ill. 1966, U.S. Ct. Appeals (7th cir.) 1966, U.S. Supreme Ct. 1970, U.S. Ct. Appeals (9th cir.) 1980, U.S. Ct. Appeals (4th and 6th cirs.) 1982. Law clk., 1966-67; assoc. Mayer, Brown & Platt, Chgo., 1967-71, ptnr., 1972—. Bd. dirs. Lyric Opera Guild; trustee Rush Presbyn. St. Luke's Med. Ctr. Mem. ABA (sects. litigation, bus., antitrust, legal edn. and admissions to the bar, vice chmn. 1974-75), Lawyers Club Chgo., Univ. Club, Econ. Club. Antitrust, General civil litigation, General corporate. Office: Mayer Brown & Platt 190 S La Salle St Ste 3100 Chicago IL 60603-3441

FINKEL, SANFORD NORMAN, lawyer; b. Troy, N.Y., Oct. 19, 1946; s. Max and Mildred (Fares) F.; m. Amy Lynn Gordon, Oct. 13, 1974 (div. July 1984); children: Marcy Jennifer, Melanie Gordon. BA, SUNY, Buffalo, 1968; JD, Union U., 1974. Bar: N.Y 1975, U.S. Dist. Ct. (no. dist.) N.Y. 1975. Tchr. sci. Enlarged City Sch. Dist. of Troy, N.Y., 1968-71; pvt. practice Troy, 1975—; counsel to dem. study group N.Y. State Assembly, Albany, 1977-78; instr. paralegal studies Jr. Coll. Albany divsn. Russell Sage Coll., 1977-81; dep. corp. counsel City of Troy, 1990-94. Mem. Rensselaer County Bar Assn. Avocations: reading, numismatics, philately, travel. General civil litigation, Family and matrimonial, Personal injury. Home: 19 Capitol Pl Rensselaer NY 12144-9658 Office: 68 2nd St Troy NY 12180-3932

FINKELSTEIN, ALLEN LEWIS, lawyer; b. N.Y.C., Mar. 19, 1943; s. David and Ella (Miller) F.; m. Judith Elaine Stutman, June 20, 1964 (div. Mar. 1980); children: Jill, Jennifer; m. Shelley Gail Barone, June 15, 1980; 1 child, Amanda. BS, NYU, 1964; JD, Bklyn. Law Sch., 1967; MBA, L.I. U., 1969. Bar: N.Y. 1968, U.S. Dist. Ct. (ea. and so. dists.) N.Y. 1973, U.S. Ct. Appeals (2d cir.) 1973, U.S. Supreme Ct. 1976, U.S. Tax Ct. 1979. Ptnr. Finkelstein, Bruckman, Wohl, Most & Rothman, N.Y.C., 1974-97; sr. ptnr. Pressman Finkelstein, 1997-99; ptnr. Ganfer & Shore LLP, 1999—. Asst. prof. L.I. U., N.Y.C., 1969-73, adj. assoc. prof., 1973-74; bd. dirs. Amotrophic Lateral Sclerosis Assn. Mem. ABA (bus. law and family law sect.), N.Y. State Bar Assn., Assn. of Bar of City of N.Y., Queens County Bar Assn. Jewish. Lodge: Masons. General corporate, Family and matrimonial, Real property. Home: 425 E 63rd St New York NY 10021-7804 Office: Ganfer & Shore LLP 360 Lexington Ave New York NY 10017-6502 E-mail: afinkelstein@ganshore.com

FINKELSTEIN, IRA ALLEN, lawyer; b. N.Y.C., Oct. 7, 1946; s. Louis and Lillian (Reiser) F.; m. Madelyn Kay Hoffman, May 30, 1982; 1 child, Sarah Rebekah. BA, CCNY, 1967; JD, Harvard U., 1973. Bar: N.Y. 1974, U.S. Dist. Ct. (ea. and so. dists.) N.Y. 1974, U.S. Ct. Appeals (2d cir.) 1976, U.S. Supreme Ct. 1978. Assoc. firm Cahill, Gordon & Reindel, N.Y.C., 1972-81, Tenzer, Greenblatt, Fallon & Kaplan, N.Y.C., 1981-83, ptnr., 1983-99, Blank Rome Tenzer Greenblatt LLP, N.Y.C., 2000—. Mem. Harvard Law Rev., 1970-72. Mem. ABA, Fed. Bar Coun., N.Y. State Bar Assn., Assn. Bar City N.Y. General civil litigation, Securities, Sports. Office: Blank Rome Tenzer Greenblatt LLP 405 Lexington Ave New York NY 10174-0002 E-mail: ifinkelstein@blankrome.com

FINKELSTEIN, JOSEPH SIMON, lawyer; b. Vineland, N.J., Feb. 28, 1952; s. Absalom and Goldie (Cukier) F.; m. Sara M. Green, May 30, 1976; children: Adam, Julia, Seth. BA, Rutgers U., 1973; JD, U. Pa., 1976. Bar: Pa. 1976, N.J. 1976, U.S. Supreme Ct. 1982. Assoc. Wolf, Block, Schorr and Solis-Cohen, Phila., 1976-85, ptnr., 1985—. Exec. bd. young leadership coun. bd. Fedn. Jewish Agys., Phila., 1986-88; mem. Nat. Young Leadership cabinet United Jewish Appeal, 1987-91; pres. Perelman Jewish Day Sch., 1996-99; bd. dirs. Temple Beth Hillel Beth El, Beth Am Israel, State of Israel Bonds, Phila., Beth Am Israel; mem. Wexner Heritage Found., 1991-95; exec. com., bd. dirs., chair funds. distbn. United Way of Southeastern Pa., 1997-99; trustee Jewish Fedn. of Greater Phila., 1996-2000. Recipient New Life/New Leadership award State of Israel, 1989, Hearts of Gold award United Way, Southeastern Pa., 1999. Mem. ABA, Internat. Coun. Shopping Ctrs., Pa. Bar Assn., N.J. Bar Assn., Phila. Bar Assn., Pa. Land Title Assoc. Contracts commercial, Real property. Home: 716 Oxford Rd Bala Cynwyd PA 19004-2112 Office: Wolf Block Schorr & Solis-Cohen LLP 1650 Arch St Fl 22D Philadelphia PA 19103-2097 E-mail: jfinkelstein@wolfblock.com

FINKELSTEIN, STUART M. lawyer; b. N.Y., 1960; BBA with distinction, U. Mich., 1982, JD cum laude, 1985. Bar: N.Y. 1986. Assoc. Skadden, Arps, Slate, Meagher & Flom LLP, N.Y.C., 1985-93, ptnr., 1993—. Corporate taxation, Taxation, general. Office: Skadden Arps Slate Meagher & Flom LLP 4 Times Sq New York NY 10036-6595

FINLEY, KERRY A. lawyer; b. Iowa CIty, Iowa, June 15, 1965; d. Thomas A. and Diane Deckard F.; m. Roger A. Dahl, Dec. 14, 1996; children: Beckett, Deckard. BA, Dartmouth Coll., 1987; JD, U. Iowa, 1990. Bar: N.Y. 1991, Iowa 1993. Assoc. Willkie, Farr & Gallagher, N.Y.C., 1990-93, ptnr., shareholder Finley, Alt, Smith, Scharnberg, Craig, Hilmes & Gaffey, Des Moines, 1993—. Mem. ABA, Iowa Bar Assn., Polk County Bar Assn., C. Edwin Moore Am. Inn of Ct. (barrister). Democrat. Appellate, General civil litigation, Professional liability. Home: 712 50th St Des Moines IA 50312-1810 Office: Finley Alt Smith Scharnberg Craig Hilmes & Gaffey 604 Locust St Des Moines IA 50309-3705

FINN, ANNE-MARIE, lawyer; b. Providence; d. James and Elizabeth (McDole) Hultquist; m. S. Michael Finn, May 29, 1982. BA, Providence (R.I.) Coll., 1979; JD, Boston U., 1983. Bar: Mass. 1983, R.I. 1989, U.S. Dist. Ct. Mass. 1984, U.S. Dist. Ct. R.I. 1990. Attorney Lynch & Lynch, Easton, Mass., 1984 . Mem. Am. Bar Assn. General civil litigation, Insurance, Personal injury. Office: Lynch & Lynch 45 Bristol Dr South Easton MA 02375-1916

FINN, MARVIN RUVEN, lawyer; b. Boston, Sept. 9, 1938; s. Max and Edith N. (Goldstein) F.; m. Norma R. Cadiff, July 4, 1965; children—Jonathan, Andrew. B.S. cum laude, Babson Coll., 1959; J.D., Boston Coll., 1962. Bar: Mass. 1962, U.S. Dist. Ct. Mass. 1964, U.S. Ct. Appeals (1st cir.) 1980. Assoc. Fox, Orlov & Cowin, Boston, 1962-63; atty. Mass. Crime Commn., Boston, 1963-65; spl. asst. atty. gen. Mass., Boston, 1965-69; ptnr. Spencer & Stone, Boston, 1969-82; chief trial dept. Fulman & Fulman, Malden, Mass., 1982— ; cons. civil litigation; rep. extradition proc. U.S. State Dept., Israel, 1968; speaker WBZ Radio, 1966. Coach, Youth Basketball Team, North Shore Jewish Community Ctr., 1976-81; mem. sch. com. Temple Beth El Sch., Swampscott, Mass., 1980. Mem. ABA, Mass. Bar Assn. (civil litigation com.), Boston Bar Assn., Assn. Trial Lawyers Am., Mass. Acad. Trial Lawyers, Am. Judicature Soc., Boston Coll. Alumni Assn., Babson Coll. Alumni Assn. Jewish. Lodges: K.P., Masons. State civil litigation, Personal injury, Workers' compensation. Office: Fulman & Fulman 7 Dartmouth St Malden MA 02148-5103

FINNEY, ERNEST ADOLPHUS, JR. retired state supreme court chief justice; b. Smithfield, Va., Mar. 23, 1931; s. Ernest A. Sr. and Collen (Godwin) F.; m. Frances Davenport, Aug. 20, 1955; children: Ernest A. III, Lynn Carol (Nikky) Finney, Jerry Leo. BA, Claflin Coll., 1952; JD, S.C. State U., 1954, LHD (hon.), 1996; HHD (hon.), Claflin Coll., 1977; LLD,

U. S.C., 1991, The Citadel, 1995, Johnson C. Smith U., 1995, Morris Coll., 1996; LHD (hon.), Coll. of Charleston, 1995; LLD, Morris Coll., 1996. Bar: S.C. 1954, U.S. Dist. Ct. S.C. 1957, U.S. Ct. Appeals (4th cir.) 1964. Pvt. practice law, Conway, S.C., 1954-60, Sumter, 1960-66; with Finney and Gray, Attys. at Law, 1966-76; mem. S.C. Ho. of Reps., Columbia, 1973-76; judge S.C. Cir. Ct., 1976-85; assoc. justice S.C. Supreme Ct., 1985-94, chief justice, 1994-2000. Chmn. S.C. Legis. Black Caucus, Columbia, 1973-75; chmn. bd. dirs. Buena Vista Devel. Corp., Sumter, 1967—; mem. S.C. State Elections Commn., Columbia, 1968-72; trustee Claflin Coll., Orangeburg, S.C., 1986—, chmn. bd. trustees, 1987-95; sch. law minority adv. com. U. S.C., 1988—. Recipient Disting. Alumni of Yr. award Nat. Assn. Equal Opportunity Edn., 1986, Achievement award C. of C., Sumter, 1986, Presdl. Citation Morris Coll., Sumter, 1986, Wiley A. Branton award NBA, 1998, Afro Am. Achievement award Turner Broadcasting Sys., 1998, Pub. Servant of Yr. S.C. C. of C., 1999, David P. Richardson Jr. Nation Builder award The Nat. Black Caucus of State Legislators, 1999; named 1987 Citizen of Yr. Charleston (S.C.) Med. Soc., 1987; inductee Nat. Black Coll. Alumni Hall of Fame, 1988. Mem. ABA, Am. Judges Assn., Am. Law Inst. (bd. dirs.), Conf. Chief Justices (bd. dirs.), Sumter County Bar, S.C. Bar, Assn. Trial Lawyers Am., Nat. Bar Assn. (appellate com.), S.C. Trial Lawyers Assn. (hon.), Masons, Shriners. Methodist. Avocations: reading, fishing, golf. Home: 24 Runnymede Blvd Sumter SC 29153-8742 Office: PO Box 1309 Sumter SC 29151-1309

FINO, TERESA CRISTINA, legal secretary, business owner; b. Serra do Bouro, Portugal, Aug. 6, 1972; d. Antonio Jose Fino and Maria Rosa Jeronimo. AS, Ocean County Coll., Toms River, N.J., 1993; BS, St Peters U., Jersey City, 1995. CEO AmPort Constrn., Bayville, N.J., 1987-97; ins. coord. W. Hudson Chiropractic Ctr., Kearny, 1994-96; bus. owner Europa Constrn., 1997—; legal sec. Cynthia M. Russo, Esq., Newark, 1996—. Mem. PALCUS, Washington, 1998—.

FINSTAD, SUZANNE ELAINE, writer, producer, lawyer; b. Mpls., Sept. 14, 1955; d. Harold Martin and Elaine Lois (Strom) F. Student, U. Tex., 1973-74; BA in French, U. Houston, 1976, JD, 1980; postgrad., London Sch. Econs., 1980, U. Grenoble, France, 1979. Bar: Tex. 1981. Legal asst. Butler & Binion, Houston, 1976-78, law clk., 1978-81, assoc., 1982; spl. counsel Ad Litem in the Estate of Howard Hughes Jr., 1981; mng. ptnr. Finstad & Assoc., 1990—. Author: Heir Not Apparent, 1984 (Frank Wardlaw award 1984), Ulterior Motives, 1987, Child Bride, 1997, Sleeping With the Devil, 1991, co-prodr. (TV), 1997; collaborator Queen Noor biography and cons. CBS miniseries; Natasha: The Biography of Natalie Wood, 2001. Named to Order of Barons, Bates Coll. Law, 1979-80. Mem. Order of Barons. Office: Joel Gotler AMG Renaissance Agy 9465 Wilshire Blvd Beverly Hills CA 90212-2612

FIORENTINO, CARMINE, lawyer; b. Bklyn., Sept. 11, 1932; s. Pasquale and Lucy (Coppola) F. LLB, Blackstone Sch. Law, Chgo., 1954, John Marshall Law Sch., Atlanta, 1957. Bar: Ga., D.C., U.S. Supreme Ct., U.S. Dist. Ct. D.C., U.S. Ct. Appeals (2d cir.), U.S. Dist. Ct. (no. dist.) Ga., U.S. Ct. Appeals (5th cir.), U.S. Ct. Claims. Mem. N.Y. State Workmen's Compensation Bd., N.Y. State Dept. Labor, 1950-53; ct. reporter, hearing stenographer N.Y. State Com. State Counsel and Attys., 1953; pub. rels. sec. Indsl. Home for Blind, Bklyn., 1953-55; legal stenographer, rschr., law clk. Atlanta, 1955, 57-59; sec. import-export firm, 1956; sole practice, 1959-63, 73—. Atty., advisor, trial atty. HUD, Atlanta and Washington, also legal counsel Peachtree Fed. Credit Union, 1963-74; acting dir. Elmira (N.Y.) Disaster Field Office, HUD, 1973; former candidate U.S. Adminstrv. Law Judge. Writer nonfiction and poetry; composer songs and hymns. Mem. Smithsonian Instn., pres., dir., gen. counsel The Hexagon Corp., Rep. Nat. Com., Rep. Presdl. Task Force, Nat. Hist. Soc.; mem. Atlanta Hist. Soc., Atlanta Bot. Gardens, Am. Mus. Natural History, Mus. Heritage Soc. Recipient State of Victory World Culture prize; inducted into Rep. Presdl. Legion Merit, 1993; Life Dynamics fellow; named Eminent Wisdom fellow to Wisdom Hall of Fame, 2000. Mem. ABA, ATLA, AAAS, Internat. Platform Soc., Nat. Audubon Soc., Fed. Bar Assn., Atlanta Bar Assn., Decatur-DeKalb Bar Assn., Am. Judicature Soc., Old War Horse Lawyers Club, Toastmasters, Gaslight Club, Sierra Club. General corporate, General practice, Personal injury. Home and Office: 4717 Roswell Rd NE Apt R4 Atlanta GA 30342-2915

FIORETTI, MICHAEL D. lawyer; b. Phila., Mar. 25, 1946; s. Michael R. and Mafalda (Fala) F. BS, St. Joseph's U., Phila., 1967; JD, Villanova U., 1972. Bar: Pa. 1972, N.J. 1981. Sr. ptnr. Law Offices of Michael D. Fioretti, Phila., 1972—, sole propietor Cherry Hill, N.J., 1981—. Author: Divorce Rules and Practice Manual. With U.S. Army, 1968-70, Vietnam. Roman Catholic. Family and matrimonial. Office: Bourse Bldg Ste 790 111 S Independence Mall E Philadelphia PA 19106-2515 also: 1765 Springdale Rd Ste B1 Cherry Hill NJ 08003-2177 E-mail: mdfioretti@aol.com

FIORETTI, ROBERT WILLIAM, lawyer; b. Chgo., Mar. 8, 1953; s. Edward E. and Helene (Krypcio) F. BA, U. Ill., 1975; JD, No. Ill. U., 1978. Bar: Ill. 1978, U.S. Dist. Ill. 1978, N.Y. 1981, U.S. Supreme Ct. 1981. Asst. corp. counsel City of Chgo., 1978-82, sr. supervising atty., 1982-86; litigation chief Shain, Firsel & Burney, Chgo., 1986-88; ptnr. Fioretti & Des Jardins Ltd., 1989—. Adj. prof. law No. Ill. U., 2000—; appointed Ill. Supreme Ct. com. on character and fitness, 2000—; mem. bus. adv. com. Sec. of STate, 1999—. Contbr. articles to law rev. Bd. dirs. Historic Pullman Found. (exec. bd. 1995—), Chgo., 1992-00, pres., 1995—; mem. pres.'s coun. U. Ill. Found., Champaign, 1993—; mem. bd. visitors No. Ill. U., DeKalb, 1992—, mem. alumni coun. Coll. law, 1991-00, pres. alumni coun., 1994-98; bd. dirs. Chgo. Vol. Legal Svcs., 1997—, v.p. devel., 1999—; mem. adv. bd. St. Mary Nazareth Hosp., 1998—; bd. dirs. One Historic Blvd., treas., 1999-2000, pres., 2000—; mem. Friends of 5 Hosp.; appointed spl. asst. states atty. of Cook County, 1992-95, spl. asst. atty. gen., 1990—; pres. Historic Pullman Found., 1995-2000; alumni mem. search com. for pres. No. Ill. U., 1999-00; bd. visitors No. Ill. Coll. Law, 1996—; appointed ethics commns. vice-chair State of Ill. Office of Treas., 2000—; mem. Bus. Adv. Coun., Sec. of State, 1999—. Named Outstanding Young Alumni No. Ill. U., 1994, Outstanding Alumni, 1999, Disting. Svc. award, 1999. Mem. FBA (bd. dirs.), Chgo. Bar Assn. (mem. jud. evaluation com. 1996—), Chgo. Athletic Assn. (bd. dirs. 1993-97, v.p. 1995-97), No. Ill. U. Alumni Assn. (bd. dirs. 1997—, v.p. 1999, pres. 2000—). Office: Fioretti & Des Jardins Ltd 8 S Michigan Ave Chicago IL 60603-3357

FIORITO, EDWARD GERALD, lawyer; b. Irvington, N.J., Oct. 20, 1936; s. Edward and Emma (DePascale) F.; m. Charlotte H. Longo; children— Jeanne C., Kathryn M., Thomas E., Lynn M., Patricia A. BSEE, Rutgers U., 1958; JD, Georgetown U., 1963. Bar: U.S. Patent and Trademark Office 1960, Va. 1963, N.Y. 1964, Mich. 1970, Ohio 1975, Tex. 1984. Patent staff atty. IBM, Armonk, N.Y., 1958-69; v.p. patent and comml. relations Energy Conversion Devices, Troy, Mich., 1969-71; mng. patent prosecution Burroughs Corp., Detroit, 1971-75; gen. patent counsel B.F. Goodrich Corp., Akron, Ohio, 1975-83; dir. patents and licensing Dresser Industries, Inc., Dallas, 1983-93. Alt. mem. Dept. Commerce Adv. Commn. on Patent Law Reform, 1991-92; spl. master, arbitrator, neutral evaluator, expert providing opinion testimony in intellectual property litigation, 1986—; U.S. del. to World Intellectual Property Orgn. Diplomatic Conf., 1991. Bd. dirs. Akron's House Extending Aid on Drugs, 1976. Mem. ABA (chmn. sci. and tech. sect. 1984-85, chair intellectual property law sect. 2000-2001), IEEE, Tex. Bar Assn. (chmn. intellectual property law sect. 1990-91), Internat. Assn. for Protection Indsl. Property (exec. bd. 1989—), Assn. Corp. Patent Counsel (exec. com. 1982-84), Tau Beta Pi. Roman Catholic. Avocations: music, running. Intellectual property, Patent, Trademark and copyright. E-mail: ipconsulting@msn.com

FIRESTONE, RICHARD BARTLETT, lawyer; b. Jackson, Mich., July 13, 1934; s. Hubert M. and Elizabeth (Bartlett) F.; m. Isabelle Sherman, Oct. 9, 1985; children— Suzanne Lynne, Kathryn Jean. B.A., U. Mich., 1957; J.D., Detroit Coll. Law, 1960. Bar: Mich. 1960; mem. firm McInally, Rosenfeld & Firestone, Jackson, Mich., 1960-67; chmn. bd., pres. Camp Internat., Inc., Jackson, 1967— ; dir. Camp Ltd., Winchester, Eng., Camp Scandinavia AB, Helsingborg, Sweden, Camp Internat. Ltd., Trenton, Ont., Can., Comerical Bank-Jackson. Trustee Jackson Found., 1984, Ella Sharp Mus. Assn., 1984; mem. bd. edn. Jackson Pub. Schs., 1970-73. Mem. Jackson County Bar Assn., Mich. Bar Assn., Greater Jackson C. of C. (pres. 1984), LWV. Republican. Episcopalian. Clubs: Country of Jackson, Town. Home: 1004 Browns Lake Rd Jackson MI 49203-5669 Office: Camp Internat Inc 744 W Michigan Ave Jackson MI 49201-1909

FIRETOG, THEODORE WARREN, lawyer; b. Bklyn., Sept. 18, 1950; s. Max E. and Ilene (Volk) F.; m. Kathleen Ann Neudecker, Feb. 21, 1980; children: Heather, Philip, Trevor. BS in Natural Resources, U. Mich., 1974, MS in Natural Resources, 1976; JD, SUNY, Buffalo, 1979. Bar: N.Y. 1980, U.S. Dist. Ct. (ea. dist.) N.Y. 1986, U.S. Dist. Ct. (so. dist.) N.Y. 1986. Dir. nature and conservation Nassau County coun. Boy Scouts Am., N.Y., 1967-73; teaching fellow dept. natural resources U. Mich., Ann Arbor, 1975-76; staff atty. Environ. Law Inst., Washington, 1979-80; atty., advisor EPA, 1980-85; sr. assoc. Rivkin, Radler, Dunne & Bayh, Uniondale, N.Y., 1985-87; environ. counsel Shea & Gould, N.Y.C., 1987-94; with Jaspen, Ginsberg, Schlesinger, Silverman & Hoffman, Garden City, N.Y., 1994-95; pvt. practice Farmingdale, 1995—. Lectr. various environ. seminars. Contbr. articles to profl. jours. Mem. com. Nassau County Dem. Com., 1987—. Sea Grant Law fellow U. Buffalo, 1977; recipient Cert. of award EPA, 1985. Mem. ABA (natural resources divsn.), Environ. Law Inst. (assoc.), N.Y. Bar Assn., Suffolk County Bar Assn. Jewish. Environmental. Office: 111 Thomas Powell Blvd Farmingdale NY 11735-2251

FIRST, HARRY, law educator; b. 1945; BA, U. Pa., 1966, JD, 1969. Bar: Pa. 1969, N.Y. 1979. Law clk. to justice Supreme Ct. Pa., 1969-70; atty. U.S. Dept. Justice, Washington, 1970-72; asst. prof. U. Toledo Coll. Law, 1972-76; vis. assoc. prof. NYU Law Sch., N.Y.C., 1976-77, assoc. prof., 1977-79, prof., 1979—; counsel Loeb & Loeb, N.Y.C. and Los Angeles, 1985-99; chief antitrust bur. N.Y. State Office of Atty. Gen., 1999-2001. Mem. editl. bd. Pa. Law Rev. Mem. Pa. Law Rev., Order of Coif, Phi Beta Kappa. Office: NYU Law Sch 40 Washington Sq S New York NY 10012-1099

FIRTH, PETER ALAN, lawyer; b. Rockville Center, N.Y., Jan. 7, 1943; s. Richard V. and Patricia (Gilmour) F.; m. Carol A. Smith, Aug. 21, 1965; children: Andrew, Marysusan, Patrick, James, William. AB in Econs., Georgetown U., 1964; LLB, Albany Law Sch., 1967. Bar: N.Y. 1967, U.S. Dist. Ct. (no. dist.) N.Y. 1967, U.S. Tax Ct. 1971, U.S. Ct. Appeals (2d cir.) 1985. Assoc. LaPann & Reardon, Glens Falls, N.Y., 1967-71; ptnr. LaPann, Reardon, FitzGerald & Firth, 1971-86, LaPann, Reardon, Morris, Fitzgerald & Firth P.C., Glens Falls, 1986-90, Fitzgerald Morris Baker Firth PC, 1990—; asst. dist. atty. Warren County, Lake George, N.Y., 1972-74. V.p. Queensbury Econ. Devel. Corp., 1989-92. Assoc. editor Albany Law Rev., 1966-67. Mem. Albany Diocese Sch. Bd., 1989-91. Mem. ABA, N.Y. State Bar Assn., Warren County Bar Assn. (sec. 1969-72, treas. 1985-89, pres. 1993-94), Assn. Trial Lawyers Am., N.Y. State Trial Lawyers Assn., Am. Arbitration Assn. (arbitrator 1977-2000). Republican. Roman Catholic. General civil litigation, Insurance, Personal injury. Office: Fitzgerald Morris Baker Firth PC PO Box 2017 Glens Falls NY 12801-2017 E-mail: paf@fmbf-law.com

FISCHER, DAVID CHARLES, lawyer; b. Columbia, S.C., Oct. 10, 1952; s. Emeric and Bernice (Cooper) F.; m. Vicki Joyce Stoller, Nov. 9, 1985; children: Adam, Jeremy. BA, Vanderbilt U., 1975; JD, Coll. William & Mary, 1978. Bar: Mich. 1978, N.Y. 1980. Lawyer GM, Detroit, 1978-79, N.Y.C., 1979-80; assoc. Finley Kumble Wagner Heine Underberg & Casey, 1980-82, Burns Summit Rovins & Feldesman, N.Y.C., 1982-86; ptnr. Summit Rovins & Feldesman, 1986-90, Loeb & Loeb, LLP, N.Y.C., 1990—. General corporate, Mergers and acquisitions, Securities. E-mail: dfischer@loeb.com

FISCHER, DAVID JON, lawyer; b. Danville, Ill., July 27, 1952; s. Oscar Ralph and Sarah Pauline (Pomerantz) F. BA, U. Miami, 1974, JD, 1977. Bar: Fla. 1977, Iowa 1978, (mid. dist.) Fla. 1993, U.S. Ct. Appeals (8th cir.) 1978, U.S. Ct. Appeals (D.C. cir.) 1979, U.S. Ct. Appeals (llth cir.) 1984, U.S. Tax Ct. 1987, Ga. 1989, U.S. Dist. Ct. (no. dist.) Ga. 1990, U.S. Supreme Ct. 1990, U.S. Dist. Ct. (mid. dist.) Fla., 1993. Atty. Iowa Dept. Social Svcs., Des Moines, 1978; assoc. Parrish & Del Gallo P.C., 1978-79, Donald M. Murtha & Assocs., Washington, 1979-80; assoc. editor Lawyers Coop. Pub. Co., 1980-82; pvt. practice law, 1982-83, Des Moines, 1983-84, Atlanta, 1984-93; pvt. practice Tampa, Fla., 1993; asst. dist. legal counsel Fla. Dept. Health and Rehab. Svcs., Largo, 1993-95; pvt. practice law Atlanta, 1995-2000; case law editor LexisNexis Group, 2001—. Part-time atty. Fla. Dept. of Children and Families, 1996-2000; prof. John Marshall Law Sch., Atlanta, 1986-88; instr. legal studies program dept. ins. and risk mgmt. Ga. State U., 1988-93, instr. aviation adminstrn. program Coll. Pub. and Urban Affairs, 1989-93; apptd. gen. counsel Techwerks, Inc., Mo., 1990-92; instr. Bridge the Gap seminar, Inst. CLE in Ga., 1993; presenter State of Fla. Dept. Health and Rehabilitative Svcs. Dist. Legal Counsel Workshop, 1994, 96, 97; spkr. Clearwater Bar Assn., 1993, 94, 95. Author: The Aeronaut's Law Handbook, 1986, (with others) Georgia Corporate Practice Forms for the Small Business Attorney, 1992; contbg. editor Balloon Life mag., 1986-96; editor: (suppl.) Georgia Corporate Forms, 1993—, Florida Criminal Sentencing, 1997-99; editor: Georgia Corporate Forms, 2d edit., 1999. Vol. liaison Atlanta Com. for the Olympic Games, 1991-92. Mem. ABA (ect. com. 1980-82), Fed. Bar Assn., Iowa Bar Assn., State Bar Ga., Atlanta Bar Assn., Fla. Bar Assn., D.C. Bar Assn., Polk County Bar Assn., Pros. Attys. Coun. Ga. (tech. editor Computer Crime Jour.), U. of Miami Alumni Assn., Balloon Fedn. Am. (chmn. com. 1986-91), Carolinas Balloon Assn., Ga. Balloon Assn. (chmn. com. 1985-90), Chesapeake Balloon Assn., Great Ea. Balloon Assn., Alpha Epsilon Pi (hon., faculty advisor). Jewish. Avocations: hot air balloon pilot, writing, competitive sports. General civil litigation, Computer, General corporate. E-mail: schnauzers@mindspring.com, davidjon.fischer@lexisnexis.com

FISCHER, ERIC ROBERT, lawyer, educator; b. N.Y.C., Aug. 22, 1945; s. Maurice and Pauline (Pilcer) F.; m. Anita Ellen Cohen, July 31, 1977; children: Joshua, Lauren BA, U. Pa., 1967; MBA, JD, Stanford U., 1971; LLM in Taxation, Boston U., 1982. Bar: N.Y. 1975, Mass. 1977. Assoc. Fried, Frank, Harris, Shriver & Jacobson, N.Y.C., 1971-76; v.p., asst. gen. counsel, asst. sec. First Nat. Bank of Boston, 1976-86; exec. v.p., gen. counsel, corp. sec. UST Corp., Boston, 1986-2000; sr. counsel Goodwin Procter (formerly Goodwin, Procter & Hoar), 2000—. Lectr. on law Boston U. Law Sch., 1984— Trustee Boston Lyric Opera, Inc., 1989-2001; bd. dirs. Boston Area Youth Soccer, 1989-90, Spirit of Mass. Boys Soccer Club, 1991-97. Mem. ABA (banking law com., chmn. cmty. banking subcom., banking law com.), Bank Capital Markets Assn. (chmn. banking law subcom. 1984-90), UN Assn. Boston (treas. 1978-91), New Eng. Legal Found. (bd. dirs. 1990-92). Jewish. Banking, General corporate, Securities. Home: 205 Waban Ave Waban MA 02468-2101 Office: Goodwin Procter Exchange Pl Boston MA 02109 E-mail: efischer@goodwinprocter.com

FISCHER, THOMAS COVELL, law educator, consultant, writer, lawyer; b. May 2, 1938; s. Vilas Uber and Elizabeth Mary (Holland) F.; m. Katherine Brenda Andrew, Sept. 29, 1972. AB, U. Cin., 1960; postgrad., U. Wash., 1960-62, Loyola U., Chgo., 1964-66; JD, Georgetown U., 1966. Asst. dir. U. Ill.-Chgo., 1964-66; asst. dean Georgetown U. Law Ctr., 1966-72; cons. Antioch Sch. Law, 1972-73; asst. exec. dir. Am. bar Found., Chgo., 1974-76; assoc. dean, prof. law U. Dayton, 1976-78, 1978-81; prof., 1981—. Vis. scholar, Cambridge, 1991, Exeter, 91, Edinburgh, 91, Konstanz U., 1993, Muenster U., 1993; fellow Inst. Advanced Legal Studies, U. London; Lincolns fellow Inns of Ct.; vis. fellow Wolfson Coll., Cambridge, England, 1997; sr. vis. fellow U. Southampton Law Faculty, 2001; cons. in field. Author: Due Process in the Student/Institutional Relationship, 1970; author: (with Duscha) The Campus Press: Freedom and Responsibility, 1973; author: (with Zenhle) Introduction to Law and Legal Reasoning, 1977, Legal Education, Law Practice and the Economy: A New England Study, 1990, The Europeanization of America: What Americans Need to Know About the European Union, 1996, The United States, the European Union, and the Globilization of World Trade: Allies or Adversaries?, 2000; author: (with Cox) Quick Review of Conflict of Laws, 4th edit., 2001. Project dir. Commn. on Legal Edn. and Practice and the Economy of New Eng. Recipient Eliane R. Maham award U. Cin., 1960; Pi Kappa Alpha Meml. scholar 1960-62. Mem. Delta Theta Phi, Pi Delta Epsilon, Phi Alpha Theta. Roman Catholic. Office: New Eng Sch Law 154 Stuart St Boston MA 02116-5616

FISCHMAN, BERNARD D. lawyer; b. N.Y.C., Feb. 26, 1915; s. Isidor and Rose Josephine F.; m. Hilda Schlang, June 10, 1937; children: Judith Fischman Johnson, Robert W. Student CCNY, 1931-33, Yeshiva U., 1931-34; LLB, NYU, 1936. Ptnr. Shea & Gould, N.Y.C., 1950-94; of counsel Le Boeuf, Lamb, Greene & MacRae, N.Y.C., 1994—. bd. dirs. Lechters, Inc., Apple Bank for Savs., N.Y. Water Svc. Corp. Mem. privacy com. ACLU, N.Y.C.; bd. govs. High Point Hosp.; adv. bd. CUNY Law Sch. at Queens Coll. Fellow Am. Orthopsychiat Assn. (atty.); mem. Century Assn. (N.Y.C.). Condemnation, General corporate, Public utilities. Home: 115 Central Park W New York NY 10023-4153 Office: Le Boeuf Lamb Greene & MacRae 125 W 55th St New York NY 10019-5369

FISCHOFF, GARY CHARLES, lawyer; b. Manhasset, N.Y., Nov. 23, 1954; s. Harold and Ann (Yablon) F.; m. Linda Lee Sacca, Nov. 22, 1985; 1 child, Lisa Frances. BA, U. Buffalo, 1976; JD, St. John's U., Jamaica, N.Y., 1983. Bar: N.J. 1983, U.S. Dist. Ct. N.J. 1983, N.Y. 1984, U.S. Dist. Ct. (so. and ea. dists.) N.Y. 1985, U.S. Dist. Ct. (no. and we. dist.) N.Y., U.S. Ct. Appeals (2d cir.) 1988. Asst. treas. IAP, Inc., Lyndhurst, N.J., 1980-82; assoc. Hannoch Weisman, Roseland, 1983-85; ptnr. Fischoff Gelberg & Director, Garden City, N.Y., 1985-96, Fischoff & Assocs., Garden City, 1996—. Lectr. seminar Nat. Bus. Inst., Westbury, N.Y., 1990, 91, Practicing Law Inst., 1992, 93, N.Y. State Bar Assn., 1995. Rep. Greentree Homeowners Assn., Northport, N.Y., 1988-89; trustee Suffolk County Vanderbilt Mus., 1994—, corp. sec., 1995-97, treas. 1997-99, 1st v.p., 1999—. Mem. Am. Bankruptcy Bd. Cert. (cert. bus. bankruptcy and consumer bankruptcy), N.Y. State Bar Assn. (real property sect., seminar lectr. 1995, Practicing Law Inst., continuing legal edn. lectr. 1992, 93), Nassau County Bar Assn. (mem. bankruptcy com., jud. liaison 1988-89). Jewish. Avocation: bicycling. Bankruptcy, General civil litigation, Real property. Office: Fischoff & Assocs 600 Old Country Rd Garden City NY 11530-2001

FISH, DONALD WINSTON, lawyer, healthcare company executive; b. Nashville, Nov. 21, 1930; s. Walter Howard and Sarah (Hassell) F.; m. Sarah Evelyn Leaver, June 12, 1953; children: Debra, Donald. BS, U. Tenn., 1957; JD, Vanderbilt U., 1966. Bar: Ga. 1966, Tenn. 1966. Freight rate analyst Lehigh Portland Cement Co., Allentown, Pa., 1957-63; assoc. Fisher & Phillips, Atlanta, 1966-67; asst. gen. counsel Life Ins. Co., Ga., 1967-70; sr. v.p., gen. counsel, sec. Hosp. Corp. Am., Nashville, 1970—. Commr. Williamson County (Tenn.), 1980-82. Served with USN, 1951-55. Mem. ABA (lectr. forum com. health law 1980, sec. corp. banking and bus. law), Tenn. Bar Assn., State Bar Ga., Nashville Bar Assn., Am. Acad. Hosp. Attys., Soc. Corp. Secs. General corporate. Home: 108 Sheffield Ct Nashville TN 37215-3245 Office: Waller Lansden Dortch & Davis 511 Union St Ste 2100 Nashville TN 37219-1760

FISHBACK, DAVID SIMON, lawyer; b. Oct. 20, 1947; s. Sam and Hilda (Barcan) F.; m. Barbara Helene Lewell, June 19, 1977; children: Michael Lawrence, Daniel Ross. BA with distinction, George Washington U., 1969; JD cum laude, Harvard U., 1973. Bar: D.C. 1973, U.S Supreme Ct. 1977, U.S. Ct. Appeals (1st, end. 3rd, 4th, 5th, 7th, 9th, 10th, 11th, and D.C. cirs.). VISTA vol. Shelby County Penal Farm, Memphis, 1969-70; cons. Ctr. for Polit. Reform, Washington, 1971-72; atty. Appellate Ct. br. NLRB, 1973-83, Supreme Ct. br., 1977-79; sr. trial counsel., environ. and occupational disease lit., 1983—; asst. dir. Environ. Torts Sect. Torts Br. Civil Divsn., 1983—. Adj. prof. law Georgetown U. Law Ctr., 1989—90. Mem. nat. bd. dirs. Am.for Democratic Action, Washington 1984-90; pres. Rosemary Hills Primary Sch. PTA, Silver Spring, Md., 1984-86; mem. Montgomery County Martin Luther King Commemorative Com., 1986-92; bd. trustees Temple Emanuel, Kensington, Md., 1986-90; pub. affairs dir., Gifted and Talented Assn. Montgomery County, 1991-94; exec. com. Richard Montgomery H.S. PTSA, 1996-99; mem. bd. dirs. Northeast Montgomery County Polit. Action Com., 2000-; mem. bd. dirs. Parnership Edn. Policy, 2001-. Mem. Phi Beta Kappa. Office: Dept Justice Civil Div Box 340 Ben Franklin Sta Washington DC 20044

FISHBERG, GERARD, lawyer; b. Bronx, N.Y., May 23, 1946; s. Alfred and Sarah (Goldberg) F.; m. Eileen Taubman, Dec. 23, 1972; children: David, Dana. BA, Hofstra U., 1968; JD, St. John's U., Bklyn., 1971. Bar: N.Y. 1972, U.S. Dist. Ct. (ea. and so. dists.) N.Y. 1973, U.S. Ct. Appeals (2d cir.) 1975, U.S. Supreme Ct. 1976. Assoc. Cullen & Dykman, Garden City, N.Y., 1972-79, ptnr., 1980—. Assoc. editor St. John's U. Law Rev., 1970-71. Mem. legis. com. N.Y. Conf. of Mayors and Mcpl. Ofcls., Albany, 1976—; bd. dirs. Am. Heart Assn. L.I. region, 1995—, treas. 1997-98, vice chair, 1998-2000, chair, 2000—; bd. dirs. Heritage Affiliate 1999—. Capt. USAR, 1968-77. St. Thomas Moore scholar St. John's U. Sch. Law, 1969-71. Mem.: N.Y. State Bar Assn. (labor law sect. 1985, sec. 1985—87, 1st vice chmn. 1989—91, chmn. 1991—93, mem. ho. of dels. 1993—2001, mem. exec. com. 1978—, mcpl. law 1985—), Nassau County Bar Assn. (chmn. mcpl. law com. 1981—83, chmn. mcpl. law com. 1985—87, chmn. labor law com. 1991-92 1991—92, bd. dirs. 1999—), Garden City C. of C., Rotary (bd. dirs. 1988—94, treas. 1990—91, pres. 1992—93), Rotacare (bd. dirs. 1992—, pres. 1993—99). Jewish. Labor. Home: 1 Bucknell Dr Plainview NY 11803-1801 Office: Cullen & Dykman Ste 102 100 Quentin Roosevelt Blvd Garden City NY 11530-4850

FISHBURNE, BENJAMIN P., III, lawyer; b. South Bend, Ind., Nov. 14, 1943; s. Benjamin Postell and Peggy (Gahan) F.; m. Edith E., Aug. 5, 1983. BA cum laude, U. Notre Dame, 1965; JD, U. Va., 1968. Bar: U.S. Ct. Mil. Appeals 1968, U.S. Army Ct. Mil. Rev. 1968, D.C. 19. Capt. Judge Advocate gen's. corps. US Army, 1968-72; atty. Surrey & Morse, Washington, 1968, ptnr., 1975, mng. ptnr., 1981-84; ptnr. Jones, Day, Reavis & Pogue, 1986, ptnr.-in-charge Hong Kong office, 1986-91, ptnr., 1991-93, Winston & Strawn, Washington, 1993—. Gen. counsel. Nat. Coun. U.S.-China Trade, 1981-87, assoc. coun. 1987-89, chmn. legal com. 1994-2001; mem. nat. coun. U.S.-China Trade Investment Delegation to China, 1986; alt. mem. U. Assn's. Nat. Policy panel study U.S.-China Rels., 1979; spkr. in field. Contbr. articles to profl. jours. Co-chmn. Am. C. of C. Hong Kong legal com., 1990, mem. bd. govs., 1991; mem. bd. advisors Johns Hopkins Nanjing Ctr., 1986-97. Mem. ABA (mem. Mid. East law com. internat. sect. 1979-81), Am. Arbitration Assn. (mem.

China-U.S. Conciliation Ctr. adv. com. 1993—, mem. spl. corp. com. East-West trade arbitration 1973-79), Order of Coif. Alternative dispute resolution, Private international, Mergers and acquisitions. Home: 5535 Nevada Ave NW Washington DC 20015-1768 Office: Winston & Strawn 1400 L St NW Washington DC 20005-3508 E-mail: bfishbur@winston.com

FISHER, ANN LEWIS, judge; b. Reading, Pa., Mar. 31, 1948; d. William E. and Florence (Makowiecki) Lewis; m. Donald E. Fisher, Dec. 27, 1965 (div. July 1986); children: Caroline E., Catherine E., John Michael (dec.); m. David H. DeBlasio, May 28, 1988; 1 child, Michael Joseph DeBlasio. BS in Liberal Studies, Oreg. State U., 1975; JD, Willamette U., 1983. Bar: Oreg. 1984, U.S. Dist. Ct. Oreg. 1984, U.S. Ct. Appeals (9th cir.) 1984, Wash. 1987, U.S. Dist. Ct. (we. dist.) Wash. 1987, U.S. Dist. Ct. (ea. dist.) Wash. 1996, U.S. Ct. Appeals (fed. cir.) 1996. Atty. Spears, Lubersky, Portland, Oreg., 1983-85, Greene & Markley, Portland, 1985-89; asst. gen. counsel Portland GE, 1988-93; atty. Schwabe, Williamson & Wyatt, Portland, 1993-96; founder Ann L. Fisher Legal and Consulting Svcs., 1996—. Pro tem judge Multnomah County Cir. Ct., Portland, 1995—; spkr. on corp. ethics, 1993-95; spkr. on energy issues, 1997—. Contbg. author: (treatise) ABA Year in Review, 1994, 95, Fed. Energy Bar Yr. Rev., 1997, 2000. Mem. ABA, FBA (vice chmn. electric power com. sect. natural resources, energy and environ. law, vice chmn. gas pipelines com. 1994-96), Wash. State Bar Assn., Oreg. State Bar (legis. exec. com. of adminstrv. law sect. 2000—), Oreg. Bar Assn. (ins. and bar sponsored program com. 1985-87, sec. 1986-87, chmn. 1987-88, MCLE bd. 1991-94, sec. 1992-93, chmn. 1993-94, Disciplinary Bd. Region 5 1991-97, chair 1996, 97, ethics com. 1998-2001), Multnomah Bar Assn. (membership com. 1987-89, Multnomah Lawyer publ. com. 1994-96, chair 1995-96, professionalism com. 1997-99, ct. liason com. 2001-), Fed. Energy Bar Assn. (electric utility regulation com. 1996-99, ethics com. 1999—), NW Energy Assn. (sec., treas. 1999-2000). Avocations: reading, writing, computers, golf, family activities. Office: Ann L Fisher Legal and Cons Svcs 1425 SW 20th Ave Ste 202 Portland OR 97201-2485 Fax: (503) 223-2305. E-mail: afisher1@quest.net

FISHER, BART STEVEN, lawyer, educator, investment banker; b. St. Louis, Feb. 16, 1943; s. Irvin and Orene (Moskow) F.; m. Margaret Cottony, Mar. 1, 1969; 1 child, Ross Alan. AB, Washington U., 1963; MA, Johns Hopkins Sch. Advanced Internat. Studies, 1967, PhD, 1970; JD, Harvard U., 1972. Bar: D.C. 1972. Assoc. Patton, Boggs & Blow, Washington, 1972-78, ptnr., 1978-94, Arent Fox Kintner Plotkin & Kahn, Washington, 1994-95; mng. ptnr. Capital House, LLC, 1995—. Adj. prof. internat. rels. Georgetown U. Sch. Fgn. Svc., Washington, 1974-82, 97; profl. lectr. internat. rels. Johns Hopkins U. Sch. Advanced Internat. Studies, 1983-96, George Mason U., 1991, 93; chmn., bd. dirs., CBQ, Inc., exec. br. Webcasting Corp, The Energy Bar Co., The Ctr. for Democracy. Author: The International Coffee Agreement, 1972, (with John H. Barton) International Trade and Investment: Regulating International Business, 1986; editor: Regulating the Multinational Enterprise, 1983, Barter in the World Economy, 1985. Pres. Aplastic Anemia Found. Am. Inc., Balt., 1983-92, pres. emeritus, 1993; bd. dirs. The Ctr. for Democracy, Marrow Found., Aplastic Anemia Found., The Inst. at Mars Hill Coll.; program com. Georgetown Leadership Sem., Washington, 1981—; pres. Capital Baseball, Inc.; ex-officio bd. govs. Internat. Practice sect. Bar Va.; participating mem. Internat. Trade Working Group, Pres. Coun. on Year 2000 Conversion. Recipient Dean's Cert. Appreciation Georgetown U. Sch. Fgn. Svc., Washington, 1984. Mem. ABA, Internat. Bar Assn., Am. Soc. Internat. Law (rapporteur, panel trade policy and insts. 1974-77), Va. State Bar (bd. govs. internat. law sect.), Wash. Fgn. Law Soc., Parkville Post Am. Legion, Great Falls Swim and Tennis Club Va. Jewish. Administrative and regulatory, Private international, Public international. Home: 9009 Potomac Forest Dr Great Falls VA 22066-4110 Office: Porter Wright Morris & Arthur 1919 Pennsylvania Ave NW Washington DC 20006-3434 E-mail: bfisher@porterwright.com

FISHER, BERTRAM DORE, lawyer; b. N.Y.C., July 10, 1928; s. Samuel and Dorothy (Eisman) F.; m. Barbara Marks, Aug. 23, 1959; children—Beth Carlyle Cutler, Priscilla Brooke. Student Johns Hopkins U.; B.A., U. Miami, Fla., 1949; LL.B., Bklyn. Law Sch., 1951; postgrad. NYU Grad. Sch. Law. Bar: N.Y. 1951, D.C. 1981, U.S. Dist. Ct. (so. and ea. dists.) N.Y., U.S. Ct. Appeals (2d cir.), U.S. Supreme Ct. Sr. ptnr. Queller, Fisher & Wisotsky, N.Y.C.; mem. Supreme Ct. Com., 1985—, Med. Malpractice Jud. Panel, N.Y. State Supreme Ct., N.Y. County and Kings County, 1987—; Ind. Jud. Screening com., 1982—; lectr. N.Y. Acad. Trial Lawyers; frequent lectr. to profession on trial techniques, evidence, cross-examination. Bd. govs. Nat. Conf. for Furtherance of Jewish Edn., 1985—. With U.S. Army, 1951-53, Korea. Decorated Bronze Star. Recipient Man of Year award Nat. Com. for Furtherance of Jewish Edn., 1984. Mem. ABA, N.Y. State Trial Lawyers Assn. (bd. dirs. 1983—, mem. jud. screening com. 1978—), N.Y. State Bar Assn. (mem. ethics com. 1979-80, toxic waste com., negligence com. 1984—), Assn. of Bar of City of N.Y. (mem. judiciary com. Bklyn. chpt., 1987—, ethics com. 1978-80, Supreme Ct. com. 1985-86, tort com.), D.C. Bar Assn., N.Y. County Lawyers Assn. (com. on Supreme Ct. 1978—, forum com. 1983—), Assn. Trial Lawyers of City of N.Y., N.Y. Criminal and Civil Bar Assn., Bklyn. and Manhattan Trial Counsel Assn., Bklyn. Bar Assn. (mem. ethics com. 1978-80), Met. Women's Bar Assn., Jewish Lawyers Guild (corr. sec. 1979-81, 1st v.p. 1982-83, pres. 1984-87, chmn. bd. govs. 1988—), Assn. Trial Lawyers Am. (Roscoe Pound Found., M Club), Joint Bar Assn. (jud. screening com. 1983—), Internat. Assn. Jewish Lawyers and Jurists (bd. dirs. 1986, Merit award 1986), Bklyn. Law Sch. Alumni Assn., Am. Coll. Legal Medicine (assoc. in law 1986—), Network of Bar Leaders (com. of 26 N.Y. bar assns. 1982-88). Clubs: Downtown Athletic (N.Y.C.), Iota Theta; Dunes Racquet (Ammagamset, N.Y.). Personal injury. Office: Queller Fisher & Wisotsky 110 Wall St New York NY 10005-3801

FISHER, CHERYL SMITH, lawyer; b. Corning, N.Y., Sept. 4, 1951; d. Norman Albert and Betty (Manzella) Smith; 1 child: Daniel Terence. BA cum laude, SUNY, Oswego, 1973; JD cum laude, SUNY, Buffalo, 1976. Bar: N.Y. 1977, U.S. dist. Ct. (we. dist.) N.Y. 1977, U.S. Ct. Appeals (2d cir.) 1980, U.S. Supreme Ct. 1992. Assoc. Runfola, Birzon & Renda, Buffalo, 1976-77, Kavinoky Cook et al, Buffalo, 1977-79; asst. to U.S. Atty. Western Dist. N.Y., 1979-84; assoc. Cohen Swados Wright Hanifin Bradford & Brett, 1984-86, Magavern & Magavern, Buffalo, 1986-87; ptnr. Magavern, Magavern & Grimm, 1988—. Spl. asst. U.S. atty. Dept. Justice, Buffalo, 1984. Pres. Cathedral Park Counseling Svc., Inc., Buffalo, 1979-83; bd. dirs. Child and Family Service Erie County, Buffalo, 1982—; chmn. bd. dirs. Civil Justice Reform Act, 1993-96, adv. panel, 1993-98; mem. vestry St. Paul's Cathedral, Buffalo, 1979-82, 84-87. Recipient Trial Practice award Trial Lawyers Assn. Erie County, 1976, Bishop Lauriston Scaife award Episcopal Cmty. Svcs., 1999, John N. Walsh Jr. award Chico & Family Svcs. of Erie County, 2000. Mem. N.Y. State Bar Assn. (com. on profl. ethics), Erie County Bar Assn. (bd. dirs. 1996-99), N.Y. State Women's Bar Assn., Women Lawyers Assn., Alpha Psi Omega. Democrat. Episcopalian. Bankruptcy, Federal civil litigation, General civil litigation. Home: 306 Highland Ave Buffalo NY 14222-1751 Office: Law Offices 1100 Rand Building Bldg Buffalo NY 14203-1911 E-mail: cfisher@magavern.com

FISHER, D. MICHAEL, state attorney general; b. Pitts., Nov. 7, 1944; s. C. Francis and Dolores (Darby) F.; m. Carol Hudak, Aug. 15, 1973 (dec.); children: Michelle Lynn, Brett Michael. AB, Georgetown U., 1966; JD, Georgetown Law Ctr., 1969. Bar: Pa. 1970. Asst. dist. atty. Allegheny County, Pitts., 1970-74; rep. Pa. Ho. of Reps., Harrisburg, 1974-80; mem. Pa. Senate, 1980-97; ptnr. Houston Harbaugh, Pitts., 1984-97; atty. gen. Commonwealth of Pa., Harrisburg, 1997—. Chmn. House Subcom. on Crime and Corrections, 1979-80, Senate Environ. Resources & Energy, 1981-90, Senate Majority Policy Com., 1988-90, Senate Rep. Caucus, 1992—; vice-chmn. Senate Jud. Com., 1981-90; Majority Whip, 1990-96. Author numerous reports. Rep. candidate for lt. gov. Pa., 1986; mem. Pa. Gov.'s Energy Coun., 1981-86, Pa. Energy Devel. Authority, 1984-86, Environ. Quality Bd., 1980-90, Pa. Commn. on Crime and Delinquency, 1979—; del. Rep. Nat. Conv., 1988, 92. Named Man of Yr. Upper St. Clair Rep. Club, 1980, Outstanding Young Man Am., 1977-79, Man of Yr. Vector's Law & Govt., 1991. Mem. Pa. Bar Assn., Elks, Am. Legion, Bethel Park Chamber, Rotary. Roman Catholic. Avocations: golf, hockey, football. Office: Atty Gen 16 Strawberry Sq Harrisburg PA 17101-1800*

FISHER, FREDRICK LEE, lawyer; b. Charleston, W.Va., Nov. 12, 1952; s. Ahaz and Lois Mildred (O'Dell) F.; m. Roberta Lee Lane, Sept. 16, 1972; children: Jamie Elizabeth, John Fredrick, Jennifer Katherine. BA in Econs., Ohio State U., 1973; JD, Harvard U., 1976. Bar: Ohio 1976, U.S. Dist. Ct. (no. dist.) Ohio 1976, U.S. Claims Ct. 1978, U.S. Tax Ct. 1978. Assoc. Squire, Sanders & Dempsey, Cleve., 1976-80, Columbus, Ohio, 1981-85, ptnr., 1985-87, Schottenstein, Zox & Dunn, Columbus, 1987—. Trustee Players Theatre Columbus, 1982-93, pres., 1987-88; sec., treas., trustee The Bill and Edith Walter Found., Columbus, 1982—; trustee Meadow Park Ch., Columbus, 1985-88, 95-97, ctrl. Ohio chpt. Arthritis Found., 1988-89, Directions for Youth, Columbus, 1992-94. Mem. ABA, Ohio Bar Assn., Columbus Bar Assn., Phi Beta Kappa, Capital Club (Columbus). Republican. Avocations: reading, swimming, skiing, biking. General corporate, Estate planning, Health. Home: 6711 Elmers Ct Columbus OH 43085-2976 Office: Schottenstein Zox & Dunn 41 S High St Columbus OH 43215-6101 Fax: (614) 462-5135. E-mail: rfisher671@aol.com, ffisher@szd.com

FISHER, JAMES CRAIG, lawyer; b. Cin., Dec. 23, 1942; s. James Donald and Helen Francis (Lineback) F.; m. Sara S. Godfrey, Apr. 21, 1964; children: Alicia Lynn, Bart Harry; m. Cynthia Hardy, Aug. 30, 1996. BA, Fla. State U., 1964; JD, Stetson U., 1967. Bar: Fla. Assoc. Billings, Frederick & Rumberger, 1967-69, Russell Troutman, 1969-70; ptnr. Mairs, Wood, Miller, Dorroughs & Fisher, 1970-72; prosecutor City of Longwood, 1971-76; pvt. practice Fisher & Matthews, P.A., Altamonte Springs, Fla., 1972-76, ptnr., 1976—. Counsel AFL-CIO, Seminole and Orange County, Fla., 1989-90; mem. bd. cert. commn. Fla. Bar; mem. unauthorized practice of law com. 18th Jud. Cir., 1988, vice chmn. grievance com., 1992-95. Co-author: Chapter 81 Liability of Attorneys Fla. Forms of Jury Instruction, 1989. Mem. ABA, ATLA (workers compensation sect.), Fla. Bar Assn., Nat. Bd. Trial Advocacy, Seminole County Bar Assn. (25 Yr. Outstanding Svc. award 1992). Democrat. Avocations: fishing, racquetball, reading. General civil litigation, Personal injury, Workers' compensation. Office: 377 Maitland Ave Ste 107 Altamonte Springs FL 32701-5442

FISHER, JAMES R. lawyer; b. South Bend, Ind., Apr. 15, 1947; s. Russell Humphries and Virginia Opal (Maple) F.; m. Cynthia Ann Winters, Aug. 14, 1971; children: Gabriel Christopher, Cory Andrew. AB in Psychology, Ind. U., 1969, JD summa cum laude, 1972. Bar: Ind. 1972, U.S. Dist. Ct. (so. dist.) Ind. 1972. Ptnr. Ice Miller, Indpls., 1971—. Co-author: Personal Injury Law and Practicesol. 23 of Indiana Practico series; contbr. articles to legal publs. Mem. ABA, Am. Trial Lawyers Assn., Am. Bd. Trial Advs., Ind. Bar Assn., Ind. Trial Lawyers Assn., Indpls. Bar Assn., Order of Coif. Federal civil litigation, State civil litigation, Personal injury. Office: Ice Miller 1 Am Sq PO Box 82001 Indianapolis IN 46282

FISHER, JOHN WELTON, II, law educator, magistrate judge, university official; b. Fisher, W.Va., Dec. 11, 1942; s. John Welton and Orrie (Shobe) F.; m. Susan Carol Vass, June 6, 1964; children: John Welton III, Jennifer Lynn. BA, W.Va. U., 1964, JD, 1967. Bar: W.Va. 1967, U.S. Dist. Ct. (no. and so. dists.) W.Va. 1967, U.S. Ct. Appeals (4th cir.) 1969. Law clk. to chief judge U.S. Dist. Ct. (no. dist.) W.Va., 1967-68; assoc. Farmer & Farmer, Morgantown, W.Va., 1968-71; mem. faculty W.Va. U. Coll. Law, 1971—, prof. law, 1977—, acting dean, 1981-82, 92-93, 97-98, dean, 1998—, exec. officer univ., 1982-86; magistrate judge U.S. Dist. Ct. No. Dist. W.Va., 1977-98. Reporter Speedy Trial Planning Group, No. Dist. W.Va. Reporter: Local Rules of Practice, Northern District of West Virginia, 1980. Mem. ABA, W.Va. State Bar, W.Va. Bar Assn., Fourth Cir. Jud. Conf., Order of Coif. Office: PO Box 6130 Morgantown WV 26506-6130 E-mail: jfisher4@wvu.edu

FISHER, MORTON POE, JR. lawyer; b. Balt., Aug. 17, 1936; s. Morton Poe Sr. and Adelaide (Block) F.; m. Ann P. Fisher, Aug. 12, 1962; children: Stephen N., Marjorie P. AB, Dartmouth Coll., Hanover, N.H., 1958; LLB, Yale U., 1961. Bar: Md. 1961, D.C. 1961. Law clk. to presiding justice U.S. Dist. Ct. Md., Balt., 1961-62; assoc. Piper & Marbury, 1962-68; asst. gen. counsel Rouse Co., 1968-73; ptnr. Frank, Bernstein, Conaway & Goldman, Balt., 1973-92; mng. ptnr. Balt. office Ballard Spahr Andrews & Ingersoll, 1992—. Faculty mem. U. Md. Law Sch., 1978-87. Mem. Balt. County Econ. Devel. Commn., 1988-90, Mayor's Adv. Commn., Balt. City, Risk Mgmt. Com. Balto City, 1999; bd. dirs. Balt. Downtown Partnership, 1998-2000; dean U. of Shopping ctrs., 1998-99. Mem. ABA (vice chmn. real property divsn 1990-92, chmn. sect. real property, probate and trust law 1993-94), Am. Coll. Real Estate Lawyers (pres. 1988-89), Am. Coll. Constrn. Lawyers, Am. Law Inst., Anglo-Am. Real Property Inst., Internat. Coun. Shopping Ctrs. (co-chmn. law conf. 1995-97). Environmental, Real property. Office: Ballard Spahr Andrews & Ingersoll 300 E Lombard St Ste 1900 Baltimore MD 21202-6739 E-mail: fisher@ballardspahr.com

FISHER, MYRON R. lawyer; b. Chgo., Aug. 13, 1935; BA, Calif. State U., Long Beach, 1964; JD, Southwestern U., 1969. Bar: Calif. 1970, U.S. Dist. Ct. (cen. dist.) Calif. 1970, U.S. Supreme Ct. 1974. Dep. pub. defender San Bernardino County (Calif.), 1970-71; assoc. Anderson, Adams & Bacon, Rosemead, Calif., 1971-74; sole practice San Clemente, 1974—. Judge pro tem South Orange County Mcpl. Ct., 1978— . Mem. State Bar Calif., South Orange County Bar Assn. (bd. dirs. 1978-83), Orange County Bar Assn., Los Angeles Trial Lawyers Assn., Orange County Trial Lawyers Assn., Calif. Trial Lawyers Assn., Assn. Trial Lawyers Am. Insurance, Personal injury, Probate. Office: Fisher Profl Bldg 630 S El Camino Real San Clemente CA 92672-4200 Fax: 949-498-2673. E-mail: mrfesq@fea.net

FISHER, RAYMOND CORLEY, judge, lawyer; b. Oakland, Calif., July 12, 1939; s. Raymond Henry and Mary Elizabeth (Corley) F.; m. Nancy Leigh Fairchilds, Jan. 22, 1961; children: Jeffrey Scott, Amy Fisher Ahlers. BA, U. Calif., Santa Barbara, 1961; LLB, Stanford U., 1966. Bar: Calif. 1967, U.S. Ct. Appeals (9th cir.) 1967, U.S. Dist. Ct. (no. and cen. dists.) Calif. 1967, U.S. Ct. Claims 1967, U.S. Supreme Ct. 1967. Law clk. to Hon. J. Skelly Wright U.S. Ct. Appeals (D.C. cir.), Washington, 1966-67; law clk. to Hon. William J. Brennan U.S. Supreme Ct., 1967-68; ptnr. Tuttle & Taylor, L.A., L.A., 1968-88; sr. litigation ptnr. Heller, Ehrman, White & McAuliffe, 1988-97; assoc. atty. gen. U.S. Dept. of Justice, Washington, 1997-99; judge U.S. Ct. Appeals (9th cir.), 1999—. Exec. com. 9th Cir. Jud. Conf., 1989-91; mem. Am. Law Inst., So. Calif. ADR Panel, CPR Inst. for Dispute Resolution. Pres. Stanford Law Rev., 1965-66. Spl. asst. to Gov. of Calif., Sacramento and L.A., 1978—; dir. Constl. Rights Found., L.A., 1978-97, pres., 1983-87; pres. L.A. City Bd. Civil Svc. Commn., 1987-88; dep. gen. counsel Christopher Commn., L.A., 1991-92; pres. L.A. City Bd. Police Commrs., 1996-97. With USAR, 1957. Fellow Am. Coll. Trial Lawyers, Am. Bar Found.; mem. ABA, Fed. Bar Assn. (exec. com. 1990-96), Calif. State Bar, L.A. County Bar Assn., Chancery Club, Order of Coif. Office: US Ct Appeals 125 S grand Ave Rm 402 Pasadena CA 91105*

FISHER, RICHARD N. lawyer; b. L.A., Oct. 28, 1943; BA, U. Redlands, 1965; MA, U. Wis., 1966; JD, U. Calif., Berkeley, 1969. Bar: Calif. 1970. Mem. O'Melveny & Myers, L.A. Editor, Calif. Law Rev., 1967-69. Mem. and chmn. bd. trustees U. Redlands. Mem. ABA, L.A. County Bar Assn. (labor and employment law sects.). Labor, Alternative dispute resolution. Office: O'Melveny & Myers 400 S Hope St Los Angeles CA 90071-2899 E-mail: Dick.Fisher@OMM.com

FISHER, ROBERT I. lawyer; b. Bklyn., July 10, 1939; s. Sidney B. and Jeanette (Talisman) F.; m. Debra Kram Fisher, June 30, 1974; children: Daniel I., Elizabeth R. BA, Columbia U., 1960; JD cum laude, Harvard U., 1963; LLM, N.Y.U., 1967. Bar: N.Y. 1964. Assoc. Dewey, Ballantine, Bushby, Palmer & Wood, N.Y.C., 1964-67, Sullivan & Cromwell, N.Y.C., 1967-72; ptnr. Greenbaum, Wolff & Ernst, 1972—82, Rosenman & Colin, N.Y.C., 1982—. Lectr. Practicing Law Inst. Fulbright fellow, Israel, 1963-64. Mem. ABA, N.Y. State Assn., Assn. Bar. City of N.Y., General corporate, Private international, Securities. Home: 150 Factory Pond Rd Locust Valley NY 11560-1416 Office: Rosenman & Colin LLP 575 Madison Ave Fl 11 New York NY 10022-2585 E-mail: rifisher@rosenman.com

FISHER, ROBERT SCOTT, lawyer; b. Detroit, July 16, 1960; s. Alvin Fisher and Beverly (Raider) Levin. BA, U. Mich., 1982; JD, U. Colo., 1985. Bar: Colo. 1985, U.S. Dist. Ct. Colo. 1985, Mich. 1987, U.S. Ct. Appeals (10th cir.) 1989, U.S. Supreme Ct. 1989, U.S. Ct. Appeals (D.C. cir.) 1999. Prin. Law Office of Robert S. Fisher, Colorado Springs, Colo., 1985—. Mem. Colo. Bar Assn., El Paso County Bar Assn., Criminal Def. Bar Assn., Phi Delta Phi. Avocations: scuba diving, ice hockey, skiing, racquetball. Criminal, Family and matrimonial, Personal injury. Home: 508 N Sheridan Ave Colorado Springs CO 80909-4518 Office: 924 N Wahsatch Ave Colorado Springs CO 80903-2915

FISHER, ROGER DUMMER, lawyer, educator, negotiation expert; b. Winnetka, Ill., May 28, 1922; s. Walter Taylor and Katharine (Dummer) F.; m. Caroline Speer, Sept. 18, 1948; children: Elliott Speer, Peter Ryerson. AB, Harvard U., 1943, LLB magna cum laude, 1948; LHD, Conn. Coll., 1994; DHL, Bay Path Coll., 1999. Bar: Mass. 1948, D.C. 1950. Asst. to gen. counsel, then asst. to dep. U.S. spl. rep. ECA, Paris, 1948-49; with firm Covington & Burling, Washington, 1950-56; asst. to solicitor gen. U.S., 1956-58; lectr. law Harvard Law Sch., Cambridge, Mass., 1958-60, prof. law, 1960-76, Samuel Williston prof. law, 1976-92, prof. emeritus, 1992—, dir. Harvard negotiation project Mass., 1980—. Vis. prof. internat. rels. dept. London Sch. Econs., 1965-66; cons. pub. affairs editor WGBH-TV, Cambridge, 1969; tech. adivsor Found. for Internat. Conciliation, Geneva, 1984-87. Originator, 1st exec. editor: (pub. TV series) The Advocates, 1969-70, moderator, 1970-71; co-originator, exec. editor: (pub. TV series) Arabs and Israelis, 1975; author: International Conflict for Beginners, 1969, Dear Israelis, Dear Arabs, 1972, International Mediation: A Working Guide, 1978, International Crises and the Role of Law: Points of Choice, 1978, Improving Compliance with International Law, 1981; co-author: Getting to Yes: Negotiating Agreement Without Giving In, 1981, 2d edit., 1991, Getting Together: Building Relationships as We Negotiate, 1988, Beyond Machiavelli: Tools for Coping with Conflict, 1994, Getting Ready to Negotiate: The Getting to Yes Workbook, 1995, Coping with International Conflict: A Systematic Approach to Influence in International Negotiation, 1997, Getting It Done: How to Lead When You're Not in Charge, 1998; co-author, editor: International Conflict and Behavioral Science--The Craigville Papers, 1964; lectr., contbr. articles on internat. rels., negotiation, internat. law and TV. Bd. dirs. Coun. for Livable World; trustee Hudson Inst., 1962-95. 1st lt. USAF, 1942-46. Recipient Sziland Peace award 1981, Peace Advocate award Lawyers Alliance for Nuclear Arms Control, 1988, Spl. Contbn. award Ctr. Pub. Resources, 1993, Steve Brutschè award Assn. Atty. Mediators, 1994, D'Alemberte-Raven Outstanding Achievements and Contributions to Dispute Resolution award, 1995, Honorato Vasquez Nat. Order Insignia Great Cross Republic Ecuador, 1999, Lifetime Achievement award Am. Coll. Civil Trial Mediators, 1999, Pioneer award New Eng. Soc. Profls. Dispute Reolution, 1999, St. Thomas More award St. Mary's U. Law Sch., 1999; named Guggenheim fellow 1965-66. Fellow Am. Acad. Arts and Scis.; mem. ABA (sect. dispute resolution), Am. Soc. Internat. Law (exec. coun. 1961-64, 66-69, v.p. 1982-84), Mass. Bar Assn., Commn. to Study Orgn. of Peace, Coun. Fgn. Rels., Phi Beta Kappa. Clubs: Metropolitan (Washington); Harvard (N.Y.C.). Office: Harvard U Law Sch Harvard Negotiation Project Pound Hall # 524 Cambridge MA 02138 also: Conflict Mgmt Group 9 Waterhouse St Cambridge MA 02138-3607

FISHER, STEWART WAYNE, lawyer; b. Phila., Mar. 5, 1950; s. Frederick and Evalyn (Wilson) F.; m. Melinda Ruley, Oct. 1, 1994; children: Henry J., Isabel Rose; children from previous marriage: Kira H., Amos N., Emily E. BA magna cum laude, Duke U., 1972; MA, Yale U., 1974; JD with honors, U. N.C., 1982. Bar: N.C. 1982, U.S. Dist. Ct. (ea. and mid. dists.) N.C. 1982, U.S. Ct. Appeals (4th cir.) 1993, U.S. Dist. Ct. (west dist.) N.C. 1997, U.S. Supreme Ct. 1997; bd. cert. Civil Trial Advocate Nat. Bd. Trial Advocacy, 1998. Atty. Haywood, Denny & Miller, Durham, N.C., 1982-85; ptnr. Glenn, Mills & Fisher, PA, 1985—. Faculty Nat. Inst. for Trial Advocacy, Durham, 1988—. Coop. atty. ACLU, Raleigh, 1992—. Mem. ABA, ATLA, Nat. Employment Lawyers, N.C. Acad. Trial Lawyers, N.C. Bar Assn., Phi Beta Kappa. Democrat. Avocations: fishing, gardening. Civil rights, Labor, Personal injury. Office: Glenn Mills & Fisher PA PO Box 3865 Durham NC 27702-3865

FISHER, THOMAS EDWARD, lawyer; b. Cleve., Sept. 29, 1926; s. McArthur and Ruth Morgan (Dissette) F.; m. Virginia Moore, June 29, 1957; children: Laura, Linda, John. BS in Naval Sci. and Tactics, Purdue U., 1947, BS in Engring. Law, 1950; JD, Ind. U., 1950. Bar: Ohio 1951, U.S. Dist. Ct. (no. dist.) Ohio 1954, U.S. Supreme Ct. 1955, U.S. Ct. Appeals (Fed. cir.) 1973. Asst. to v.p. Lempco Products, Bedford, Ohio, 1950-51; house counsel Willard Storage Battery Co., Cleve., 1951-54; assoc. Schram & Knowles, 1954-55; ptnr. Watts, Hoffmann, Fisher & Heinke Co. (predecessor firms), 1955—. Mem. adv. bd. BNA Patent Trademark and Copyright Jour., 1972—; mem. adv. panel Franklin Pierce Law Sch., 1987—. Councilman Mentor (Ohio) on the Lake, 1955-57; chmn. ARC, Painesville, Ohio, 1956. Lt. USN, 1944. Mem. ABA (divsn. chair), Cleve. Bar Assn. (trustee), Am. Intellectual Property Law Assn. (chair com., bd. dirs.), Cleve. Intellectual Property Law Assn. (pres.), Cleve. World Trade Assn., Nat. Inventors Hall of Fame (pres.), Nat. Coun. Patent Law Assns. (chair). Avocations: woodworking, fishing, travel, gardening. Federal civil litigation, Patent, Trademark and copyright. Home: 617 Falls Rd Chagrin Falls OH 44022-2560 Office: Watts Hoffmann Fisher & Heinke Co 1100 Superior Ave Ste 1750 Cleveland OH 44114-2518 E-mail: iplaw@wattshoff.com

FISHER, THOMAS GEORGE, JR. lawyer; b. Washington, June 1, 1961; s. Thomas George and Rita (Knisley) F.; m. Susan Jane Koenig, June 23, 1990. BA, Iowa State U., 1983; JD with high distinction, U. Iowa, 1986. Bar: Iowa 1986, U.S. Dist. Ct. (so. dist.) Iowa 1987, U.S. Ct. Appeals (8th cir.) 1987, U.S. Dist. Ct. (no. dist.) Iowa 1993. Jud. clk. Iowa Supreme Ct., Davenport, 1986-87; assoc. Duncan, Jones, Riley & Finley, P.C., Des Moines, 1987-91; asst. atty. gen. State of Iowa, Justice Dept., 1991-95; counsel Am. Mut. Life Ins. Co., 1995-96; ptnr. Hogan & Fisher, PLC, 1997—. Precinct chair Polk County Dem. Party, Des Moines, 1988-90, 94-96, 98-2000; candidate Iowa Ho. of Reps. Dists. 73, 1994;

mem. Des Moines Leadership Inst., 1998-99; bd. dirs. Anawim Housing; bd. dirs., mem. exec. com. Metro Arts Alliance of Greater Des Moines. Mem. Blackstone Inn of Ct. Democrat. Roman Catholic. Communications, Public utilities, Real property. Office: Hogan & Fisher PLC 3101 Ingersoll Ave Des Moines IA 50312-3918 E-mail: Tom@Hogan-Fisher.com

FISHER, THOMAS GEORGE, lawyer, retired media company executive; b. Debrecen, Hungary, Oct. 2, 1931; came to U.S., 1951; s. Eugene J. and Viola Elizabeth (Rittersporn) F.; m. Rita Knisley, Feb. 14, 1960; children: Thomas G. Jr., Katherine F. Vaaler. B.S., Am. U., 1957, J.D., 1959; postgrad., Harvard U., 1956. Bar: D.C. 1959, Iowa 1977. Atty. FCC, Washington, 1959-61, 65-66; pvt. law practice, 1961-65, 66-69; asst. counsel Meredith Corp., N.Y.C., 1969-72, assoc. gen. counsel Des Moines, 1972-76, gen. counsel, 1976-80, v.p. gen. counsel, 1980-94, corp. sec., 1988-94. Comml. law liaison ABA Ctr. and East European Law Initiative, Krakow, Poland, 1994-95; atty. Legal Aid Soc. Polk County, 1996—. Contbr. articles to profl. jours. Bd. dirs. Des Moines Met. Opera Co., Indianola, 1980-94, pres., 1990-91; bd. dirs. Civic Music Assn., Des Moines, 1982-92, pres., 1987-88; chmn. legis. com. Greater Des Moines C. of C., 1976-77; bd. dirs. Legal Aid Soc. Polk County, 1986-93, pres., 1993; bd. dirs., sec., treas. Friends of Benedictine Edn. in Hungary Found., 1999—. With U.S. Army, 1952-54. Mem. ABA, Iowa State Bar Assn. (chmn. corp. counsel subcom. 1979-82), Polk County Bar Assn., Embassy Club. Communications, Intellectual property. Office: Legal Aid Assn Polk County 1111 9th St Ste 380 Des Moines IA 50314-2527

FISHER, THOMAS GRAHAM, judge; b. Flint, Mich., May 15, 1940; s. John Corwin and Bonnie Decou (Graham) F.; m. Barbara Alden Molnar, June 2, 1963; children: Anne Corwin, Thomas Molnar. AB, Earlham Coll., 1962; JD, Ind. U., 1965. Bar: Ind. 1965, U.S. Dist. Ct. (no. dist.) Ind. 1965, U.S. Supreme Ct. 1969. Assoc. John R. Nesbitt, Remington and Rensselaer, Ind., 1965-68; ptnr. Nesbitt & Fisher, 1968-73, Nesbitt, Fisher & Daugherty, Remington and Rensselaer, 1973-78, Nesbitt, Fisher, Daugherty & Nesbitt, Remington and Rensselaer, 1978-82, Nesbitt, Fisher & Nesbitt, Remington and Rensselaer, 1982-83, Fisher & Nesbitt, Remington and Rensselaer, 1983-86; judge Ind. Tax Ct., Indpls., 1986—. Pros. atty. Jasper County, Ind., 1967-86; lectr. bus. law St. Joseph's Coll., Rensselaer, 1970-86; trustee Earlham Coll., 1995—. Recipient Eugene Feller award Ind. Pros. Attys. Assn., Indpls., 1986. Mem. ABA, Ind. Bar Assn., Jasper County Bar Assn., Nat. Conf. State Tax Judges, Ind. Soc. Chgo., Columbia Club (bd. dirs. 1991-99, sec. 1992, treas. 1993, pres. 1997), Rotary (v.p. Indpls. chpt. 1998-99, pres. 2000-2001), Jaycees (Outstanding Young Man Am. 1975). Republican. Mem. Soc. of Friends. Home: 4702 Mallard View Dr Indianapolis IN 46226-2187 Office: Ind Tax Ct 115 W Washington St Ste 1160S Indianapolis IN 46204-3418 E-mail: tfisher@courts.state.in.us

FISHMAN, BARRY STUART, lawyer; b. Chgo., June 14, 1943; s. Jacob M. and Anita (Epstein) F.; m. Meredith Porte, Mar. 27, 1976; 1 child, Janna. BA, U. Wis., 1965; JD, DePaul U., 1968. Bar: Ill. 1968, Fla. 1969, Calif. 1969. Ptnr. firm Fishman & Fishman, Chgo., 1968-72; counsel real estate fin. dept. Baird & Warner, Inc., 1972-75; counsel Biscayne Fed. Savs. and Loan Assn., Miami, Fla., 1976-79; mem. firm, Ea. regional counsel Logs Nationwide Representation of Lenders; mem. firm Pallott, Poppell, Goodman & Slotnick, Miami, 1977-80; sr. ptnr. Shapiro & Fishman, Aventura, Tampa, Orlando, Deerfield Beach, Fla., 1984—. Dir. investment divsn. Cushman and Wakefield of Fla., 1978—. Mem. big gifts com. Greater Miami Jewish Fedn., 1977—; dir. Neighborhood Housing Svcs., Dade County, Fla., 1977—. Mem. Fla. Bar Assn., Calif. Bar Assn., Ill. Bar Assn., Chgo. Bar Assn., Dade county Bar Assn., Nat. Assn. Realtors, Real Estate Securities and Syndication Inst., Mortgage Bankers Assn., Fla. Mortgage Bankers Assn., Comml. Law League, Turnberry Isle Yacht and Racquet Club, Turnberry Country Club. Jewish. Home: 912 Captiva Dr Hollywood FL 33019-5045 Office: 20803 Biscayne Blvd Ste 300 Aventura FL 33180-1429 E-mail: barryf.mia@logs.com

FISHMAN, EDWARD MARC, lawyer; b. Cambridge, Mass., Apr. 28, 1946; s. Eli Manuel and Marian (Goldberg) F.; m. Barbara Ellen Stern, June 29, 1969 (div. Sept. 1982); children: Andrea Stern, Bradley Craig; m. Tracy Ann Lind, July 13, 1985; children: Alison Leigh, Kendall Paige. AB, Bowdoin Coll., 1968; JD, Columbia U., 1972. Bar: Tex. 1972. Assoc. Akin, Gump, Strauss, Hauer & Feld, Dallas, 1972-73, Luce, Hennessy, Smith & Castle, Dallas, 1973-76; corp. counsel Centex Corp., 1976-78; from assoc. to ptnr. Brice & Barron, 1978-82; v.p. Baker, Smith & Mills, 1982-86; pres. Fishman, Jones, Walsh & Gray, 1986-99; v.p. Clements, Allen, Fishman, Woods & Walsh, P.C., 1999-2000; with Glast, Phillips & Murray, P.C., 2000—. Bd. dirs. Space Found. Roundtable, Dallas, 1985-87, Hope Cottage, Dallas, 1990-96; officer local pub. TV sta., Dallas, 1976—. Mem. ABA, Tex. Bar Assn., Dallas Bar Assn. Avocations: reading, bicycling, swimming, running, skiing. General corporate, Landlord-tenant, Real property. Home: 4723 Stonehollow Way Dallas TX 75287-7525 Office: Glast Phillips & Murray PC Ste 2200 13355 Noel Rd Dallas TX 75240-6657 E-mail: efishman@gpm-law.com

FISHMAN, FRED NORMAN, lawyer; b. N.Y.C., Aug. 21, 1925; s. Arthur Elihu and Frederica (Greenspan) F.; m. Claire S. Powsner, Sept. 19, 1948; children: Robert J., Nancy K. S.B. summa cum laude, Harvard U., 1946, LL.B. magna cum laude, 1948; postgrad., Yale U., 1945-46. Bar: N.Y. State 1950, U.S. Supreme Ct. 1954. Law clk. to Chief Judge Calvert Magruder, U.S. Ct. Appeals, 1st Circuit, Boston, 1948-49; to Asso. Justice Felix Frankfurter, Supreme Ct. U.S., 1949-50; assoc. firm Dewey Ballantine (and predecessors), N.Y.C., 1950-57; with Freeport Minerals Co., 1957-61, asst. sec., 1958-59, asst. v.p., 1959-61; partner firm Kaye Scholer LLP, N.Y.C., 1962-92, mem. exec. com., 1970-87, chmn. exec. com., 1981-83, spl. counsel, 1993-95. Editor, officer: Harvard Law Rev. Chmn. Harvard Law Sch. Fund, 1977-79; mem. bd. overseers' com. to visit Harvard Law Sch., 1975-81, 88-94; chmn. com. Harvard Law Sch. Class of 1948 Twenty-Fifth Anniversary Gift, Forty-Fifth Anniversary Gift; mem. bd. overseers' com. to visit Grad. Sch. Edn., Harvard U., 1971-77, bd. overseers' Com. on Univ. Resources, 1991—, permanent class com. Harvard Coll. Class of 1946; bd. overseers' com. to visit Med. Sch. and Sch. of Dental Medicine Harvard U., 1997—; trustee Public Edn. Assn., N.Y.C., 1956-73, chmn. bd., 1970-71; dir. Harvard Alumni Assn., 1981-83; trustee Hosp. for Joint Diseases and Med. Center, N.Y.C., 1971-73; trustee Lawyers' Com. for Civil Rights under Law, 1979—, bd. dirs., 1983—, co-chmn., 1983-85; mem. steering com. Campaign for Harvard Law Sch., 1991-95; mem. dean's adv. bd. Harvard Law Sch., 2001-. Fellow Am. Bar Found.; mem. ABA, Assn. of Bar of City of N.Y. (chmn. com. fed. legis. 1963-66, exec. com. 1966-70, chmn. com. corp. law 1980-82, treas. 1993-94), Am. Law Inst. (adviser corp. governance project 1980-92), Legal Aid Soc. (bd. dirs. 1991-94), Harvard Law Sch. Assn. (pres. 1986-88, 1st v.p. 1984-86, coun. 1978-82, exec. com. 1980-82, 88-90, trustee N.Y.C. assn. 1966-69, v.p. N.Y.C. assn. 1974-75, pres. 1988-89), Phi Beta Kappa, Harvard Club N.Y.C. Home: 650 Park Ave Apt 3D New York NY 10021-6115 Office: Kaye Scholer LLP 425 Park Ave New York NY 10022-3598 E-mail: ffishman@kayescholer.com

FISHMAN, LEWIS WARREN, lawyer, educator; b. Bklyn., Dec. 19, 1951; BA in Polit. Sci., Syracuse U., 1972; MPA, Maxwell-Syracuse U., 1973; JD, U. Miami, 1976. Bar: Fla. 1976, U.S. Dist. Ct. (so. dist.) Fla. 1977, U.S. Dist. Ct. D.C. 1978, U.S. Ct. Appeals (5th and 11th cirs.) 1981. Assoc. Simons & Fishman P.A. (and predecessor firm), Miami, 1976-80; ptnr., 1980-81; assoc. Wood, Lucksinger & Epstein, Miami, 1982—. Adj. prof. law Fla. Internat. U., 1981, 83, 84, 91; mem. bd. legal specialization and edn. Fla. Bar, 1999—. Mem. Fla. Acad. Healthcare Attys. (bd. dirs., sec. 1986-88, pres. 1990-92), Nat. Health Lawyers Assn. (lectr. 1983, 88-89), Fla. Hosp. Assn. (lectr. 1983, 88-89), Fla. Hosp. Assn. (lectr.), Fla.Med. Record Assn. (lectr. 1982, 83, 84), Am. Acad. Hosp. Attys. (lectr. 1989, 90, 91), Nat. Health Lawyers Assn., Cath. Health Assn., Fla. Bar Assn. (mem. exec. coun. health law sect. 1988-97, chmn. health law sect. 1988-97, chmn. health law sect. 1995-96, cert. health law atty., mem. health law cert. com. 1994-99, vice chmn. 1995-96, chmn. 1996-98, bd. legal specialization and edn. 1999—). Jewish. General corporate, Health, Insurance. Home: 14140 SW 104th Ave Miami FL 33176-7064 Office: 9130 S Dadeland Blvd Miami FL 33156-7818 E-mail: lwfpa@aol.com

FISHMAN, MITCHELL STEVEN, lawyer; b. N.Y.C., July 27, 1948; s. Abraham and Sylvia (Sher) F.; children: Danielle, Matthew, Jeremy. BA cum laude, Harvard U., 1970, JD cum laude, 1973. Bar: N.Y. 1974, D.C. 1984. Assoc. Breed, Abbott & Morgan, N.Y.C., 1973-74, Paul, Weiss, Rifkind, Wharton & Garrison, N.Y.C., 1975-81, ptnr., 1981-99. Exec. dir. Temp. State Commn. on Banking, Ins. and Fin. Svcs., N.Y., 1983-84; cons. Sirius Satellite Radio, Inc., N.Y.C., 2000—. Mem. ABA, Assn. of Bar of City of N.Y. (com. on corp. law 1976-79, mem. com. on securities regulation 1998-01). Democrat. Banking, General corporate, Securities. Home: 200 E 57th St Apt 18L New York NY 10022-2869 E-mail: mfishman@siriusradio.com, mshishman@excite.com

FISHMAN, RICHARD GLENN, lawyer, accountant; b. Orange, N.J., June 2, 1952; s. Irving and Eleanor (Tanenbaum) F.; m. Jean Goldhammer, Aug. 11, 1974; children: Neil Samuel, Peter Lawrence, Ellen Melissa. BA in Econs. with highest honors and highest distinction, Rutgers U., 1974; JD, Yale U., 1977; LLM in Taxation, NYU, 1980. Bar: N.Y. 1978, N.J. 1978, U.S. Dist. Ct. N.J. 1978, U.S. Ct. Claims 1978, U.S. Tax Ct. 1978, U.S. Dist. Ct. (so. dist.) N.Y. 1979, U.S. Ct. Appeals (3d cir.) 1994. Assoc. Stroock & Stroock & Lavan, N.Y.C., 1977-80, Roberts & Holland, N.Y.C., 1980-85; tax mgr. Spicer & Oppenheim (formerly Oppenheim, Appel, Dixon & Co.), 1985-87, ptnr., 1987-88; sr. tax. counsel AlliedSignal Inc., Morristown, N.J., 1988-94, dir. internat. taxes and sr. tax counsel, 1994-96, sector tax dir., engineered materials sector, 1996-97, assoc. gen. tax counsel, 1997-99; dir. tax planning for bus. units, assoc. gen. tax counsel Honeywell Internat., Inc., 1999—. Contbr. articles to profl. jours. Mem. ABA, AICPA, N.Y. State Bar Assn., N.J. State Bar Assn. Public international, Corporate taxation, Taxation, general. Home: 6 Tilden Ct Livingston NJ 07039-2419 Office: Honeywell Internat Inc PO Box 1057 Morristown NJ 07962-1057 E-mail: richard.fishman@honeywell.com

FISHMAN, ROBERT MICHAEL, lawyer; b. Bloomington, Ill., Dec. 28, 1953; s. Hank and Lucy (Moscovitch) F.; m. Victoria M. Swan, Aug. 12, 1979; children: Eric B., Samuel C., Matthew A. BA, U. Ill., 1972-76; JD, George Washington U., 1979. Bar: Ill. 1979, U.S. Dist. Ct. (no. dist.) Ill. 1979, (ea. dist.) Wis. 1998, U.S. Ct. Appeals (7th circuit) 1994. Atty. Office of Ill. Atty. Gen., Chgo., 1979-80; ptnr. Levit, Mason and Fishman, Ltd., 1980-89, Ross & Hardies, Chgo., 1990-98; mem. Shaw, Gussis, Domanskis, Fishman & Glantz LLC, 1998—. Mem. adv. bd. BNA Bankruptcy Law Reporter. Mem. ABA (bus. bankruptcy sect.), Chgo. Bar Assn., Am. Bankruptcy Inst. (chmn., pres., bd. dirs., exec. com., mgmt. com.). Banking, Bankruptcy, Contracts commercial. Office: Shaw Gussis Domanskis Fishman & Glantz LLC 1144 W Fulton St Ste 200 Chicago IL 60607-1204 E-mail: rfishman@shawgussis.com

FISHMAN, SHANTI ALICE, lawyer; b. Lafayette, Ind., Mar. 1, 1968; d. Theodore Fishman and Ernestine Stevenson. BA, U. Mass., 1991; JD, U. Va., 1995. Bar: N.Y. 1995, Calif. 1998. Assoc. Cadwalader, Wickersham and Taft, N.Y.C., 1995-97, Brobeck, Phleger and Harrison, San Francisco, 1997-98; mng. atty., assoc. gen. counsel E*Trade Group, Inc., Menlo Park, Calif., 1998-2000; sr. dir. legal afffairs Logicter, Inc., 2000—. Mem. Israeli Def. Forces, 1986-88. Mem. ABA. Jewish. Contracts commercial, Computer, Intellectual property. Office: Logic Tier Inc 2 Waters Park Dr San Mateo CA 94403-1148

FISKE, JORDAN JAY, prosecutor; b. Bklyn., Apr. 4, 1943; s. George Vlatofe and Pearl (Kalker) F.; m. Sandra Joyce Rappaport, June 22, 1974. BA, Brandeis U., 1963; JD, Fordham U., 1966. Bar: N.Y. 1967. Spl. agt. USAF Office of Spl. Investigations, Washington, 1966-71; trial atty. Dept. of Justice, N.Y.C., 1971-73; spl. asst. atty. gen. N.Y. State Office of the Spl. Prosecutor, 1973-76; chief asst. dist. atty. Onondaga County Dist. Attys. Office, Syracuse, N.Y., 1976—. Adviser Dist. Attys. Adv. Coun., Syracuse, 1976—; mem. Criminal Justice Adv. Bd., Syracuse, 1991. Capt. USAF, 1970-71, Vietnam. Mem. Jewish War Vets., Disabled War Vets., Vietnam Vets. Am. Office: Onondaga County Dist Attys Office Civic Ctr 12th Fl Syracuse NY 13202

FISKE, ROBERT BISHOP, JR. lawyer; b. N.Y.C., Dec. 28, 1930; s. Robert Bishop and Lenore (Seymour) F.; m. Janet Tinsley, Aug. 21, 1954; children: Linda Goucher, Robert Bishop, Susan Williams. BA, Yale U., 1952; JD, U. Mich., 1955, LLD (hon.), 1997. Bar: Mich. 1955, N.Y. 1956, U.S. Ct. Appeals (2nd cir.) 1957, U.S. Supreme Ct. 1961. Assoc. Davis, Polk, Wardwell, Sunderland & Kiendl, 1955-57; asst. U.S. atty. So. Dist. N.Y., 1957-61; assoc. Davis Polk & Wardwell, 1961-64, ptnr., 1964-76, 80-00; U.S. atty. So. Dist. N.Y., N.Y.C., 1976-80; ind. counsel for Whitewater, Little Rock, 1994. Fellow Am. Coll. Trial Lawyers (pres. 1991-92); mem. ABA (chmn. standing com. on fed. judiciary 1984-87), Assn. of Bar of City of N.Y., Fed. Bar Coun. (pres. 1982-84), N.Y. State Bar Assn., Noroton Yacht Club, Wee Burn Country Club. Republican. Congregationalist. Federal civil litigation, State civil litigation, Criminal. Office: 450 Lexington Ave New York NY 10017-3911

FISS, OWEN M. law educator; b. 1938. BA, Dartmouth Coll., 1959; BPhil, Oxford U., 1961; LLB, Harvard U., 1964. Bar: N.Y. 1965. Law clk. to Judge Thurgood Marshall, U.S. Ct. Appeals 2d Cir., 1964-65, to Justice Brennan, U.S. Supreme Ct., 1965; spl. asst. to asst. atty. gen., civil rights div. U.S. Dept. Justice, Washington, 1966-67, acting dir. Office of Planning Coordination, 1968; prof. U. Chgo. Law Sch., 1968-74; prof. Yale U. Law Sch., New Haven, 1974-84, Alexander M. Bickel prof. pub. law, 1984-92, Sterling prof., 1992—; vis. prof. Stanford U., 1973. Mem. Harvard Law Rev.; author: Injunctions, 1972; The Civil Rights Injunction, 1978; (with R.M. Cover) The Structure of Procedure, 1979; (with D. Rendleman) Injunctions, 2d edit., 1984; (with Cover and J. Resnik) Procedure, 1988; (with Cover and Resnik) The Federal Procedural System, 1988, 3d edit., 1991, Holmes Devise History of the Supreme Ct. :Troubled Beginnings of the Modern State, 1888-1910, 1993, Liberalism Divided, 1996, The Irony of Free Speech, 1996, A Community of Equals, 1999; mem. editl. bd. Philosophy and Pub. Affairs and Found. Press, Yale Jour. Criticisim, Yale Jour. Law and Humanities, Law, Econs. and Orgns. Office: Yale Law Sch PO Box 401A New Haven CT 06520

FITTS, MICHAEL ANDREW, law educator, dean; b. Phila., Mar. 1, 1953; s. William Thomas Jr. and Barbara Kinsey (Willits) F.; m. Renee Judith Sobel, Jan. 2, 1982; children: Alexis, Whitney. AB, Harvard Coll., 1975; JD, Yale U., 1979; MA (hon.), U. Pa., 1991. Law clk. Hon. A. Leon Higginbotham, Jr., U.S. Ct. Appeals (3d cir.), Phila., 1979-81; atty. office legal counsel Dept. of Justice, Washington, 1981-85; asst. prof. law U. Pa., Phila., 1985-90, assoc. prof., 1990-92, prof., 1992—, assoc. dean acad. affairs, 1996-98, Robert G. Fuller Jr. prof. law, 1996-2000, Bernard G. Segal prof. law, 2000—, dean Sch. of Law, 2000—. Vis. prof. dept. polit. sci. Swarthmore Coll., 1999. Editor Yale Law Jour., 1978-79; contbr. articles to profl. jours. and chpts. to books. Harvard U. scholar, 1971. Mem. Am. Polit. Sci. Assn. (law and polit. process working group), Pa. Bar Assn., Phi Beta Kappa. Mem. Soc. of Friends. Office: U Pa Law Sch 3400 Chestnut St Philadelphia PA 19104-6204 Office Fax: 215-573-2025. Business E-Mail: mfitts@law.upenn.edu*

FITZGERALD, EITHNE MARGARET, lawyer; b. London, England, June 22, 1960; d. Eamonn and Joan Fitzgerald; m: Kilian Thomas McGrogan, Aug. 29,1989; children: Matthew, Michael. BA Legal Science, Trinity College, Dublin, Ireland, 1982; Diploma in European Law, U. College, Dublin, Ireland, 1985. Mem. Rolls of Solicitors, Ireland, 1986. Partner A & L Goodbody, Dublin, Ireland, 1991—. Co-author (chpt.): A Practitioner's Guide to Take-Overs and Mergers in the European Union, 1999. Mem. Incorp. Law Soc. of Ireland. General corporate, Mergers and acquisitions, Insurance. Office: A&L Goodbody Internat Financial Svcs Ctr North Wall Quay Dublin 1 Ireland Fax: 00353 1649 2649. E-mail: ehtzgerald@algoodybody.ie

FITZGERALD, JAMES PATRICK, lawyer; b. Omaha, Nov. 30, 1946; s. James Joseph and Lorraine (Hickey) F.; m. Dianne Fager, Dec. 27, 1968; 1 child, James Timothy. BA, U. Nebr., 1968; JD, Creighton U., 1974. Bar: Nebr. 1974, U.S. Dist. Ct. Nebr. 1974, U.S. Ct. Appeals (8th cir.) 1974. Law clk. U.S. Dist. Ct. Nebr., Omaha, 1974-76; atty. McGrath, North, Mullin & Kratz, P.C., 1976—. Sgt. U.S. Army, 1968-71. Mem. ABA, Nebr. Bar Assn., Assn. Trial Lawyers Am., Nebr. Assn. Trial Attys., Def. Rsch. Inst. General civil litigation, Contracts commercial. Home: 16728 Jones Cir Omaha NE 68118-2711 Office: McGrath North Mullin & Kratz 1 Central Park Plz Ste 1400 Omaha NE 68102-1638

FITZGERALD, JOHN EDWARD, III, lawyer; b. Cambridge, Mass., Jan. 12, 1945; s. John Edward Jr. and Kathleen (Sullivan) FitzG. BCE, U.S. Mil. Acad., West Point, N.Y., 1969; JD, M in Pub. Policy Analysis, U. Pa., 1975. Bar: Pa. 1975, N.Y. 1978, Calif. 1983, U.S. Supreme Ct. 1991. Commd. 2d lt. U.S. Army, 1969, advanced through grades to capt., 1971, resigned, 1972; assoc. Saul Ewing Remick & Saul, Phila., 1975-77, Shearman & Sterling, N.Y.C., 1977-78; atty., dir. govt. rels. and pub. affairs Pepsico, Inc., Purchase, N.Y., 1978-82; sr. v.p., dept. head Security Pacific Corp., Los Angeles, 1982-83; ptnr. Schlesinger, FitzGerald & Johnson, Palm Springs, Calif., 1983-87; mng. ptnr. FitzGerald & Mulé, 1987—. Judge pro tem Desert Jud. Dist.; lectr. Calif. Continuing Edn. of the Bar; trustee Nat. Coun. Freedom Found., Valley Forge, Pa. Bd. dirs., chmn. Palm Sprngs Boys and Girls Club, Desert Youth Found.; chmn., pres. United Way of the Desert; mem. Com. of 25, Palm Springs; trustee, v.p., Palm Springs Desert Mus.; pres. exec. bd. Coachella Valley coun. Boy Scouts Am. Named Palm Springs Disting. Citizen of Yr., 1999; recipient Friend of Youth award Boys and Girls Clubs, 1998, Disting. Eagle award Boy Scouts Am., 1999. Mem.: ABA, ATLA, Calif. Bar Assn., Desert Bar Assn. (trustee, treas.), Am. Arbitration Assn. (arbitrator), Calif. Trial Lawyers Assn. (lectr.), World Affairs Coun., Riverside County Bar Assn., Orange County Bar Assn., O'Donnell Golf Club, Desert Bus. Roundtable, Lincoln Club of the Coachella Valley (vice chmn. bd. dirs., jud. nomination com.). General civil litigation, Contracts commercial, Labor. Office: Ste 105 3001 Tahquitz Canyon Way Palm Springs CA 92262-6900 E-mail: jackfitzgerald3@aol.com

FITZGERALD, JUDITH KLASWICK, federal judge; b. Spangler, Pa., May 10, 1948; d. Julius Francis and Regina Marie (Pregno) Klaswick; m. June 5, 1971 (div. Dec. 1982); 1 child; m. Barry Robert Fitzgerald, Sept. 20, 1986; 1 child. BSBA, U. Pitts., 1970, JD, 1973. Legal rschr. Assocs. Fin., Pitts., 1972-73; law clk. to pres. judge Beaver County (Pa.) Ct. Common Pleas, 1973-74; law clk. to judge Pa. Superior Ct., Pitts., 1974-75; asst. U.S. atty. U.S. Dist. Ct. (we. dist.) Pa., Pitts. and Erie, 1976-87, U.S. bankruptcy judge Pitts., Erie and Johnstown, 1987—, U.S. Dist. Ct. (ea. dist.) Pa., U.S. Dist. Ct. Del., 1997. Adj. prof. law U. Pitts., 1997. Co-author: Bankruptcy and Divorce, Support and Property Division, 1991; editor: Pennsylvania Law of Juvenile Delinquency and Deprivation, 1976; contbr. articles to profl. jours. Mem. Pitts. Camerata, 1978-80, Allegheny County Polit.-Legal Edn. Project, 1980, Mendelssohn Choir Pitts., 1982—; mem. coun. Program to Aid Citizen Enterprise, 1985-87. Recipient Spl. Achievement awards Dept. Justice, Spl. Recognition award Pittsburgh mag., Operation Exodus Outstanding Performance award Dept. Commerce, 1986. Mem. Internat. Women's Insolvency and Restructuring Conf., Allegheny County Bar Assn., Women's Bar Assn. of Western Pa., Nat. Conf. Bankruptcy Judges, Am. Bankruptcy Inst., Nat. Conf. Bankruptcy Clks., Comml. Law League of Am., Fed. Criminal Investigators Assn. (Spl. Svc. award 1988), Zonta. Republican. Lutheran. Avocations: singing, reading, traveling. Office: US Bankruptcy Ct 600 Grant St Ste 5490 Pittsburgh PA 15219-2805

FITZGERALD, KEVIN MICHAEL, lawyer, mediator; b. Kansas City, Kans., May 10, 1956; s. Thomas Francis and Theresa Ann (Grosdidier) FitzG.; m. Susan Patricia Parker, June 21, 1980; children: Kathryn Ann, Shannon Elizabeth, Erin Parker. BBA, U. Tex., Arlington, 1981; JD, U. Ark., 1985. Bar: Mo. 1985, U.S. Dist. Ct. Mo. 1985, U.S. Ct. Appeals (8th cir.) 1985. Assoc. Taylor, Stafford, Woody, Cowherd and Clithero, Springfield, Mo., 1985-90; ptnr. Taylor, Stafford, Woody, Clithero and FitzGerald, 1990-2000, Taylor, Stafford, Clithero, FitzGerlad & Harris, Springfield, 2001—. Mediator, neutral U.S. Dist. Ct. (we. dist.) Mo. Atty. Roman Cath. Diocese of Springfield-Cape Girardeau. Mem. Mo. Bar Assn., Springfield Met. Bar Assn. (sec. 1997, chmn. alternative dispute com. 2000), Legal Aid Southwest Mo. (bd. dirs. 1993-96), Nat. Diocesan Attys. Assn. General civil litigation, Personal injury, Product liability. Office: Taylor Stafford et al 3315 E Ridgeview St Ste 1000 Springfield MO 65804-4083

FITZGERALD, MICHAEL EDWARD, barrister, solicitor; b. London, May 13, 1958; s. John and Maureen (Kennedy) F.; m. Robyn Erica Coltman; children: Alexandra, Tara. LLB, London U., 1978; LLM, Boston U., 1992. Barrister Lincoln's Inn, London; barrister and solicitor, Victoria; solicitor, NSW. Pvt. practice, London, 1978-80; legal counsel Orion Royal Bank, 1980-82; assoc. dir. Wardley Australia Ltd. (now HSBC), Sydney, 1982-86; sr. legal counsel Alliance Investments, SAM, Monaco, 1986-92; chmn. Cloverleaf Holdings Ltd., 1992—, Gemini Holdings, Plc, Cambridge, Eng., 1995—. Dir. Cypress Internat. Ptnrs. Ltd., Jersey, 1993—. Contbr. articles on banking and co. law to internat. fin. publs. Office: Cloverleaf Holdings Ltd 13-15 Blvd des Moulins MC 98000 Monaco Monaco

FITZGERALD, PATRICK J. prosecutor; BA, Amherst Coll.; JD, Harvard U. Asst. U.S. atty. So. Dist. N.Y., 1988—2001; U.S. atty. No. Dist. Ill. U.S. Dept. Justice, 2001—. Office: 219 S Dearborn St 5th Fl Chicago IL 60604*

FITZGERALD, THOMAS ROBERT, judge; b. Chgo., July 10, 1941; s. Thomas Henry and Kathryn (Touhy) F.; m. Gayle Ann Aubry, July 1, 1967; children: Maura, Kathryn, Jean, Thomas., Ann. Student Loyola U., Chgo., 1959-63; J.D., John Marshall Law Sch., Chgo., 1968. Bar: Ill. 1968, U.S. Dist. Ct. (no. dist.) Ill. 1968. Asst. state's atty. State's Atty. Cook County, Chgo., 1968-76, trial asst., 1968-72, felony trial supr., 1973-76; judge criminal div. Circuit Ct. Cook County, 1976—2000, justice Ill. State Supreme Ct., 2000-; adj. prof. law Chgo., Kent Coll. Law, 1977— , asst. coor. trial ad program, 1989-96, instr. Einstein Inst. for Sci., Health and Cts.; mem. faculty Nat. Inst. Trial Advs., Boulder, Colo., 1982, Ill. Jud. Conf., Chgo., 1982— . Pres. Sch. Bd. Queen of Universe Parish, Chgo., 1974-75. Served with USN. Recipient Outstanding Jud. Performance award Chgo. Crime Commn., Herman Kogan Media award for excellence in broadcast jour.; named Celtic Man of Yr. Celtic Legal Soc. Fellow Ill. Bar Found.; mem. Chgo. Bar Assn., Ill. Bar Assn., Ill. Judges Assn. (bd. dirs. 1981-84, treas. 1985, sec. 1986, 3d v.p. 1987, pres.). Office: 160 N LaSalle St Rm N-2013 Chicago IL 60601 Fax: 312-793-4579*

FITZGIBBON, DANIEL HARVEY, lawyer; b. Columbus, Ind., July 7, 1942; s. Joseph Bales and Margaret Lenore (Harvey) FitzG.; m. Joan Helen Meltzer, Aug. 12, 1973; children: Katherine Lenore, Thomas Bernard. BS in Engring., U.S. Mil. Acad., 1964; JD cum laude, Harvard U., 1972. Bar: Ind. 1972; U.S. Dist. Ct. (so. dist.) Ind. 1972, U.S. Tax Ct. 1977. Commd. 2d lt. U.S. Army, 1964, advanced through grades to capt., 1967, served with inf. Vietnam, resigned, 1969; assoc. Barnes & Thornburg, Indpls., 1972-79, ptnr., 1979-99, mem. mgmt. com., 1983-95, of counsel, 2000—. Speaker various insts; comml. law liaison, ABA-CEELI, Moscow, 1998-99. Mem. Sch. Bd. Met. Sch. Dist. Lawrence Twp., 1988-96, pres., 1990-91, 94-95; bd. advs. Eiteljorg Mus. Am. Indian and Western Art. Capt. U.S. Army, 1964-69, Vietnam. Fellow Am. Coll. Tax Counsel, Am. Bar Found.; mem. ABA (internat. law sect.), Am. Law Inst., Ind. State Bar Assn. (tax sect.), Indpls. Bar Assn. (chmn. tax sect. 1982-83, coun. 1982-86), Indpls. Athletic Club, Lawyers Club, Woodstock Club. Contracts commercial, General corporate, Private international. Home: 6460 Lawrence Dr Indianapolis IN 46226-1035 Office: Barnes & Thornburg 1313 Merchants Bank Bldg Indianapolis IN 46204-3506

FITZHUGH, DAVID MICHAEL, lawyer; b. San Francisco, Nov. 24, 1946; s. William DeHart and Betty Jean (Jeffries) F.; m. Jenny Lu Conner, Dec. 22, 1967; children: Ross DeHart, Cameron Hyatt, Michael Jeffries. Student, Carleton Coll., 1964-67; BA, Coll. William and Mary, 1972; JD, U. Va., 1975. Bar: D.C. 1975, U.S. Dist. Ct. D.C. 1979, U.S. Dist. Ct. Md. 1987, U.S. Ct. Claims 1980, U.S. Ct. Appeals (fed. cir.) 1982, U.S. Ct. Appeals (D.C. cir.) 1987, U.S. Ct. Appeals (4th cir.) 1989, U.S. Supreme Ct. 1982. Assoc. McKenna & Cuneo, Washington, 1975-80, ptnr., 1980-98, chmn. litigation dept., 1984-94; assoc. counsel Office of Counsel Naval Air Systems Command, 1999—. Mem. editl. bd. Nat. Contract Mgmt. Assn. Jour., 1975-2000; contbr. articles to legal pubs. Capt. USMC, 1967-71, Vietnam. Mem. ABA (litigation sect., discovery com. pub. contracts sect.). Federal civil litigation, Government contracts and claims. Home: 11140 Beacon Way Lusby MD 20657-2442 Office: Office of Counsel AIR 7.7 Bldg 2272 Ste 257 47123 Buse Rd Unit IPT Patuxent River MD 20670-1547 E-mail: fitzhughdm@navair.navy.mil

FITZPATRICK, DUROSS, federal judge; b. Macon, Ga., Oct. 19, 1934; s. Mark W. and Jane L. (Duross) F.; m. Beverly O'Connor, Mar. 17, 1963; children: Mark O'Connor, Devon Hart. BS in Forestry, U. Ga., 1961, LLB, 1966. Bar: Ga. 1965. Assoc. Elliott & Davis, Macon, 1966-67; sole practice Cochran, Ga., 1967-83; ptnr. Fitzpatrick & Mullis, 1983-86; judge U.S. Dist. Ct. (mid. dist.) Ga., Macon, 1986-95, chief judge, 1995-2001. Bd. govs. State Bar Ga., 1976-83, mem. exec. com., 1979-84, pres., 1984-85; mem. Ga. Chief Justice's Commn. on Professionalism. Legal counsel Rep. del. Gen. Assembly Ga., 1969. Served with USMC, 1954-57. Fellow Am. Bar Found., Ga. Bar Found.; mem. Oconee Bar Assn. (pres. 1970), Am. Inns Ct. (Master of the Bench, W.A. Bootle chpt. 1999—), Macon Bar Assn. Republican. Episcopalian. Home: RR 1 Box 1525 Jeffersonville GA 31044-9768

FITZPATRICK, GARRETT JOSEPH, lawyer; b. N.Y.C., Aug. 11, 1949; s. Daniel Edward and Lillian (Brown) F.; m. Karen Ann Chenault, Jan. 27, 1979; children— Michael, Brian. B.S., U. Dayton, 1970; J.D., St. John's U., 1973. Bar: N.Y. 1974. Sr. ptnr. Mendes & Mount, N.Y.C., 1973— . Mem. ABA (aviation and space law com.), Internat. Assn. Ins. Counsel. Roman Catholic. Insurance, Personal injury. Home: 360 West St Harrison NY 10528-2509 Office: Mendea & Mount 750 7th Ave New York NY 10019-6834

FITZPATRICK, HAROLD FRANCIS, lawyer; b. Jersey City, Oct. 16, 1947; s. Harold G. and Anne Marie F.; m. Joanne M. Merry, Sept. 22, 1973; children: Elizabeth, Kevin, Matthew, Christopher. AB, Boston Coll., 1969; MBA, NYU, 1971; JD, Harvard U., 1974. Bar: N.J. 1974, U.S. Dist. Ct. N.J. 1974, U.S. Ct. Internat. Trade, 1986, U.S. Supreme Ct. 1994. Securities analyst Chase Manhattan Bank, N.Y.C., 1970-71, Brown Bros., Harriman & Co., N.Y.C., 1971; staff asst. U.S. Senate, Washington, 1972; law clk. to assoc. justice N.J. Supreme Ct., Trenton, 1974-75; assoc. Cleary, Gottlieb, Steen & Hamilton, N.Y.C., 1975-78; mng. ptnr. Fitzpatrick & Waterman, Secaucus, N.J., 1978—, Bayonne, 1978—. Gen. counsel Housing Authority City of Bayonne, 1976—, Color Pigments Mfrs. Assn., Alexandria, Va., 1978—, N.J. Assn. Housing and Redevel. Authorities, Brick, N.J., 1979—, Housing Authority Town of Secaucus, N.J., 1980-88, Rahway (N.J.) Geriatrics Ctr. Inc., 1981-92, Housing Authority City of Englewood, N.J., 1985-91, Housing Authority City of Rahway, 1986-2000, Edgewater Mcpl. Utilities Authority, 1986-93, Housing Authority City of Woodbridge, N.J., 1988-94, Housing Authority City of Asbury Pk., N.J., 1991-94, Bd. Edn. City of Rahway, 1994-97, N.J. Pub. Housing Authority Joint Ins. Fund, 1995-2001. Mem. ABA, N.J. Bar Assn., Hudson County Bar Assn. (trustee, officer 1984-92, pres. 1993), Beta Gamma Sigma. General corporate, Environmental, Municipal (including bonds). Office: Fitzpatrick & Waterman 333 Meadowlands Pkwy Secaucus NJ 07096-3159

FITZPATRICK, JAMES DAVID, lawyer; b. Syracuse, N.Y., Oct. 21, 1938; s. William Francis and Margaret Mary (Shortt) F. BS, Holy Cross Coll., Worcester, Mass., 1960; JD, Syracuse U., 1963. Bar: N.Y. 1963, U.S. Dist. Ct. (no. dist.) N.Y. 1965. Assoc. Bond, Schoeneck & King, Syracuse, N.Y., 1963-76, mem., 1976-88, ptnr., 1988—. Pres. Hiscock Legal Aid Soc., Syracuse, 1975-76; faculty Nat. Bus. Inst., Eau Claire, Wis., 1990—; del. Russian Conf. on Banking-The Kremlin, Moscow, 1992, 93. Mem. presdl. Roundtable, Washington, 1991-92; founding mem. pres.'s task force Nat. Coalition Against Pornography, Common Cause; chmn. adv. bd. Rep. Nat. Coms., 1994; mem. The Studio Mus. in Harlem, Am. Mus. Nat. History; founding mem. Am. Air Mus.; nat. adv. coun. USN Meml. Found. Recipient Afghanistan Freedom Fighter award Afghan Mercy Fund, 1989, Rep. Senatorial Medal of Freedom, Honored Friend of El Salvador award, 1991, Wisdom award of Honor, Wisdom Soc. for Advancement of Knowledge, Learning and Rsch. in Edn., named to Wisdom Hall of Fame, 1999. Mem. ABA, NAACP, N.Y. State Bar Assn., Onondaga County Bar Assn. (chmn. real estate com. 1990-96), Internat. Bar Assn., Am. Land Title Assn., UN Assn. of U.S.A., Habitat for Humanity Internat., Amnesty Internat. U.S.A., Nat. Audubon Soc., Ctr. for Nat. Independence in Politics, Smithsonian Nat. Assocs., Nat. Trust for Hist. Preservation, Navy League U.S., World Future Soc., Ams. Guild, Internat. Platform Assn. (spkr. Internat. Youth Ctr., New Delhi), Inst. Global Ethics, World Jurist Assn. Republican. Roman Catholic. Avocations: housing education, reading, walking. Private international, Real property. Home: 201 Croyden Rd Syracuse NY 13224-1917 Office: Bond Schoeneck & King 1 Lincoln Ctr Fl 18 Syracuse NY 13202-1324 E-mail: fitzpaj@bsk.com

FITZPATRICK, JOSEPH MARK, lawyer; b. Jersey City, May 27, 1925; s. Joseph Francis Stephen and Meave (Wilson) F.; m. Elizabeth Anne Keane, June 18, 1949; children: Elizabeth A., Susan E., Christopher M., Stephen R. ME, Stevens Inst. Tech., 1945; JD, Georgetown U., 1951. Bar: Va. 1950, U.S. Patent Office 1950, N.Y. 1954. Trial atty. anti-trust divsn. Dept. Justice, 1951-53; mem. firm Ward, McElhannon, Brooks & Fitzpatrick, N.Y.C., 1954-70, Fitzpatrick, Cella, Harper & Scinto, N.Y.C., 1970—. With USNR, 1943-46. Fellow Am. Coll. Trial Lawyers; mem. ABA, Va. Bar Assn., N.Y. Bar Assn., Assn. of Bar of City of N.Y., Am. Intellectual Property Law Assn., N.Y. Intellectual Property Law Assn., Manasquan River Yacht Club. Federal civil litigation, Patent, Trademark and copyright. Home: 17 Oak Ln Scarsdale NY 10583-1628 Office: Fitzpatrick Cella Harper Scinto 30 Rockefeller Plz Fl 38 New York NY 10112-3800

FITZSIMMONS, B. JOSEPH, JR. lawyer; b. Weymouth, Mass., Oct. 18, 1940; s. B. Joseph Sr. and Rita M. (Mitchell) F. AB in History cum laude, Boston Coll., 1963; JD, New Eng. Sch. Law, 1967. Cert. U.S. Profl. Tennis Registry instr.; PGA golf profl. Pvt. practice, Weymouth, 1967-77, 93—; spl. assst. atty. gen., asst. dist. atty. Commonwealth of Mass., Boston and Dedham, 1970-73; equity clk. Norfolk County/Commonwealth of Mass., Dedham, 1972-80; trial judge Mass. Trial Ct., Boston, 1980-93. Author: Representing the Plaintiff, 1980; contbr. articles to profl. jours. Pers. officer Town of Weymouth, 1970-73, selectman, 1973-77, chmn., 1976, chair Nike site acquisition task force. Mem. Mass. Bar Found., Mass. Bar Assn., Bar Assn. Norfolk County, Quincy Bar Assn. (bd. govs. 1967—, Alfred P. Malaney award for leadership in legal field 1991). Roman Catholic. Avocations: tennis, golf, reading. Alternative dispute resolution, General civil litigation, Federal civil litigation. Office: Fitzsimmons Law Offices 255 Main St Weymouth MA 02188-2000 E-mail: fitzlaw@xpres.net

FIX, BRIAN DAVID, lawyer; b. Rochester, N.Y., May 31, 1944; s. Meyer and Elizabeth (Goldsmith) F. AB cum laude, Columbia U., 1965, LLB, 1968. Bar: N.Y. 1968, D.C. 1969, conseil juridique Paris, France 1974, France 1992. Ptnr. Surrey & Morse, Beirut, Lebanon, 1975, Washington, 1976-78, Paris, 1974-75, 78-81, N.Y.C., 1981-85, Jones, Day, Reavis & Pogue, N.Y.C., 1986-90, Cole, Corette & Abrutyn, London, 1991-92, Salans Hertzfeld & Heilbrom, London, 1992—. Served to cpl. USAR, 1968-76. Mem. ABA, Internat. Bar Assn. Clubs: University, 29 (N.Y.C.); Circle de l'Union Interalliée (Paris). Avocations: tennis, skiing. Private international, Mergers and acquisitions. Office: Salans Hertzfeld & Heilbrom 9 Rue Boissy d'Anglas 75008 Paris France

FLADUNG, RICHARD DENIS, lawyer; b. Kansas City, Mo., Aug. 1, 1953; s. Jerome Francis and Rosemary (Voeste) F.; m. Leslie Lynn Cox, June 1, 1985; children: Daniel Edwin, Erica Anne, Derek Richard. BSCE, U. Kans., 1976, postgrad., 1977; JD, Washburn U., 1980. Bar: Kans. 1980, U.S. Dist. Ct. Kans. 1980, Ind. 1981, U.S. Dist. Ct. (so. dist.) Ind. 1981, U.S. Patent and Trademark Office 1982, Mo. 1983, Tex. 1984, U.S. Dist. Ct. (we. dist.) Mo. 1983, U.S. Dist. Ct. (so. dist.) Tex. 1984, U.S. Ct. Appeals (fed. cir.) 1984, U.S. Ct. Appeals (5th cir.) 1987, U.S. Supreme Ct. 1987, U.S. Dist. Ct. (we. dist.) Tex. 1988, U.S. Dist. Ct. (ea. and no. dists.) Tex. 2000. Engr. Black and Veatch Cons. Engrs., Kansas City, 1975-80; corp. counsel CTB Inc., Milford, Ind., 1980-82; patent atty. Chase & Yakimo and predecessor firm, Kansas City, 1982-83, Bush, Moseley, Riddle and Jackson and predecessor firm, Houston, 1983-87, Pravel, Hewitt & Kimball, Houston, 1987-98, Akin, Gump, Strauss, Hauer & Feld LLP, Houston, 1999—. Contbr. articles on patent matters and ins. coverage for intellectual property matters to profl. edn. programs. Legal aide to spkr. of Kans. Ho. of Reps., Topeka, 1980; com. chmn. Troop 1089, BSA, Houston, 2000—. Named One of Outstanding Young Men of Am., 1985. Fellow Houston Bar Found., Houston Young Lawyers Found.; mem. ABA (vice chmn. patent, trademark sect. young lawyer div. 1988-89), ASCE, Houston Bar Assn. (ex officio bd. dirs. 1987-88, vice chmn. profl. responsibility com. 1991—), Am. Intellectual Property Law Assn., Tex. Young Lawyers Assn. (bd. dirs. 1988), Mo. Bar Assn., Ind. Bar Assn., Houston Young Lawyers Assn. (pres. 1987-88, exec. mem. bd. dirs. 1987-88, Outstanding Com. Chmn. award 1984-86), Kansas City Bar Assn., Houston Intellectual Property Law Assn., Pi Alpha Kappa (treas. 1974-75). Roman Catholic. Avocations: tennis, jogging, biking, golf. Federal civil litigation, Intellectual property, Patent. Office: Akin Gump Strauss Hauer & Feld LLP 1900 Pennzoil Pl S Tower 711 Louisiana St Houston TX 77002-2716 E-mail: rfladung@akingump.com

FLAGG, RONALD SIMON, lawyer; b. Milw., Dec. 3, 1953; s. Arnold and Marian (Levy) F.; m. Patricia Sharin, June 20, 1982; children: Laura Sharon, Emily Rachel, Naomi Erica. AB, U. Chgo., 1975; JD, Harvard U., 1978. Bar: Wis. 1978, U.S. Dist. Ct. (ea. dist.) Wis. 1978, U.S. Ct. Appeals (7th cir.) 1979, D.C. 1980, U.S. Dist. Ct. D.C. 1980, U.S. Ct. Appeals (D.C. cir.) 1980, U.S. Ct. Appeals (3d cir.) 1984, U.S. Supreme Ct. 1986, U.S. Ct. Appeals (5th cir.) 1987, U.S. Ct. Appeals (8th cir.) 1989. Law clk. to presiding judge U.S. Dist. Ct. (ea. dist.) Wis., Milw., 1978-80; atty., adv. office of intelligence policy and rev. U.S. Dept. Justice, Washington, 1980-82; assoc. Sidley & Austin, 1982-85, ptnr., 1986—. Bd. dirs. Nat. Vets. Legal Svcs. Program, Legal Counsel for the Elderly. Mem. ABA, D.C. Bar Assn. (pro bono program com.). Administrative and regulatory, Federal civil litigation, Securities. Home: 3909 Garrison St NW Washington DC 20016-4219 Office: Sidley & Austin 1722 I St NW Fl 7 Washington DC 20006-3705

FLAHERTY, JOHN PAUL, JR. state supreme court chief justice; b. Pitts., Nov. 19, 1931; s. John Paul and Mary G. (McLaughlin) F.; m. Linet Flaherty; 7 children, 2 stepchildren. BA, Duquesne U., 1953; JD, U. Pitts., 1958; LLD (hon.), Widener U., 1993. Bar: Pa. 1958. Pvt. practice, Pitts., 1958-73; mem. faculty Carnegie-Mellon U., 1958-73; judge Ct. Common Pleas Allegheny County, 1973-79, pres. judge civil divsn., 1978-79; justice Supreme Ct. Pa., 1979-96, chief justice, 1996—. USIA speaker in Far East, 1985-86. Mem. Pa. Hist. Soc.; bd. visitors U. Pitts. Sch. Law; chair Pa. County Records Com. Recipient Medallion of Distinction U. Pitts., 1987, Judicial award Pa. Bar Assn., 1993, Pres. award Pa. Bar Assn., 1999; Chief Justice John P. Flaherty award, Pa. Bar Assn. Conf. of Bar Leaders, 2001; named Man of Yr. in law and govt., Greater Pitts. Jaycees, 1978, named to Century Club of Disting. Alumni, Duquesne U., 1994. Mem. Pa. Acad. Sci. (chmn. hon. exec. bd. 1978-89, Disting. Alumnus award 1977), Am. Law Inst., Pa. Soc., Pa. Bar Assn. (award 2001), Mil. History Soc. Ireland, Friendly Sons St. Patrick, Am. Legion. Office: Pa Supreme Ct 6 Gateway Ctr Pittsburgh PA 15222-1318

FLAHERTY, THOMAS JOSEPH, lawyer; b. Berwick, Pa., Oct. 1, 1943; s. Edward A. and Lucy (Simon) F.; m. Margaret Ann Broxton, Oct. 3, 1970; children— Jenifer, Thomas. B.S., St. Louis U., 1967, J.D., 1973. Bar: Mo. 1974, Oreg. 1974, U.S. Dist. Ct. Oreg. 1974, U.S. Ct. Appeals (9th cir.) 1977. Assoc., Lachman & Henninger, Portland, Oreg., 1974-78; sole practice, Lake Oswego, Oreg., 1979-84, Portland, 1986—; ptnr. Flaherty & Hall, Portland, 1984-86; staff Judge Advocate Marine Air Group-42, 4th Marine Aircraft Wing, U.S. Marine Corps Res., Naval Air Sta. Whidbey Island, Oak Harbor, Wash., 1982-85, asst. regional def. counsel, Pacific region, 1986-90, dep. chief def. counsel to the USMC, 1990-93. Scoutmaster Columbia council Boy Scouts Am., 1975; mem. parish council St. Matthews Ch., Hillsboro, Oreg., 1980— . Served to 1st lt. USMC, 1967-70, col. Res.; Vietnam. Decorated Purple Heart (2), Vietnamese Cross of Gallantry. Mem. Assn. Trial Lawyers Am., Oreg. Trial Lawyers Assn., Oreg. State Bar Assn. Republican. Roman Catholic. Federal civil litigation, State civil litigation, Personal injury. Office: 10300 SW Greenburg Rd Suite 490 Portland OR 97223

FLAIG, DONALD WILLIAM, lawyer; b. Panorama City, Calif., Apr. 19, 1972; s. Robert Bruce and Carol Ann F. BA, U. So. Calif., 1994; JD, Southwestern U., 1997. Bar: Calif., U.S. Dist. Ct. (so. dist., ctrl. dist., ea. dist.) Calif., U.S. Ct. Appeals (9th cir.). Atty. Knopfler & Robertson, Woodland Hills, Calif., 1997—. Mem. ABA, L.A. County Bar Assn. General civil litigation, Construction, Insurance. Home: 5410 Las Virgenes Rd Calabasas CA 91302 Office: Knopfler & Robertson 21650 Oxnard St Woodland Hills CA 91367

FLAMM, LEONARD N(ATHAN), lawyer; b. Newark, May 23, 1943; s. Sydney Lewis and Lillian (Schreiber) F. Cert., London Sch. Econs., 1964; BA, Dartmouth Coll., 1965; JD, Harvard U., 1968. Bar: N.J. 1968, N.Y. 1970, U.S. Ct. Appeals (2d cir.) 1970, Fla. 1976, U.S. Dist. Ct. (so. and ea. dists.) N.Y. 1976, U.S. Ct. Appeals (7th cir.) 1986, U.S. Ct. Appeals (3d cir.) 1987, U.S. Supreme Ct. 1989. Assoc. Marshall, Bratter, Greene, Allison & Tucker, N.Y.C., 1968-70, Donovan, Leisure, Newton & Irvine, N.Y.C., 1970-72, Glass, Greenberg & Irwin, N.Y.C., 1972-75; ptnr. Hockert & Flamm, 1975-90; pvt. practice, 1990—. Contbg. author Employee Rights Litigation: Pleadings and Practice, 1991. Named one of Best Lawyers in U.S., Town & Country Mag., 1985. Mem. Assn. Bar City N.Y. (legal referral panel 1975—), Nat. Employment Lawyers Assn. (v.p. N.Y. chpt., nat. co-chmn. Age Discrimination in Employment Act com.) Civil rights, Federal civil litigation, Labor. Home: 80 Roosevelt St Closter NJ 07624-2711 Office: 880 3rd Ave Ste 1300 New York NY 10022-4730 E-mail: adealnf@aol.com

FLANAGAN, CHRISTIE STEPHEN, lawyer; b. Port Arthur, Tex., June 28, 1938; s. Christie John and Rita Catherine (Hancock) F.; m. Gretchen Dowling Neuhoff; children: Mary Eileen, Margaret, Christopher, Michael. BBA, U. Notre Dame, 1960; LLB, U. Tex., Austin, 1962. Bar: Tex. 1962. Assoc. Hutchenson & Grundy, Houston, 1962-68; ptnr. Jenkens & Gilchrist, Dallas, 1968-88, mgr. ptnr., 1982-87, mem., 1988—; dir. Calif. preferred Capital Corp., 1997—. Active Dallas Citizens Coun., 1982-92; trustee Hockaday Sch., 1980-86, St. Marks Sch. Tex., 1986-92, Sierra Internat. Found., 1984-88. Mem. ABA, Tex. Bar Assn., Dallas Bar Assn., Salesmanship Club, Serra Club Dallas, Fishers Island Club, Brook Hollow Gold Club, Coon Creek Club. Banking, General corporate, Securities. Office: Jenkens & Gilchrist PC 1445 Ross Ave Ste 3200 Dallas TX 75202-2785

FLANAGAN, JAMES HENRY, JR. lawyer, business educator; b. San Francisco, Sept. 11, 1934; s. James Henry Sr. and Mary Patricia (Gleason) F.; m. Charlotte Anne Nevins, June 11, 1960; children: Nancy, Christopher, Christina, Alexis, Victoria, Grace. AB in Polit. Sci., Stanford U., 1956, JD, 1961. Bar: Calif. 1962, U.S. Dist. Ct. (no. dist.) Calif. 1962, U.S. Ct. Appeals (9th cir.) 1962, U.S. Dist. Co. (so. dist.) Calif. 1964, U.S. Dist. Ct. (ea. dist.) Calif. 1967, Oreg. 1984. Assoc. Creede, Dawson & McElrath, Fresno, Calif., 1962-64; ptnr. Pettitt, Blumberg & Sherr and successor firms, 1964-75; pvt. practice, Clovis, Calif., 1975-92, North Fork, 1992-98. Instr. Humprey's Coll. Law, Fresno, 1964-69; instr. bus. Calif. State U., Fresno, 1986—; instr. MBA program Coll. of Notre Dame, Belmont, 1990-91; instr. Nat. U., 1991—, Emerson Inst., 1998—; judge pro tem Fresno County Superior Ct., 1974-77; gen. counsel Kings River Water Assn., 1976-79. Author: California Water District Laws, 1962; Sierra Star columnist and corr. Mem. choir, Our Lady of Sierra, 1998—; exec. com. parish coun. St. Helen's Ch., 1982-85, chmn. exec. com., 1985; pres. parish coun. St. John's Cathedral, 1974-82; pres. bd. dirs. 3d Floor Ctrl. Calif.; bd. dirs. Fresno Facts Found., 1969-70, Fresno Dance Repertory Assn., St. Anthony's Retreat Ctr., Three Rivers, Calif.; pres. Inst. for Interactive Edn., Inc. (formerly Bus. & Nonprofit Devel. Ctr. Ea. Madera County, Inc. Dispute Resolution Ctr. Ctrl. Calif.), 1988—; pres. Am. Benefit Devel. Corp., 1995-98; co-founder Am. Benefit Trust; active Clovis Big Dry Creek Hist. Soc.; co-chmn., sec. Sierra Vista Nat. Scenic Byway Assn., Byway Assn. rep. on bd. dirs. North Fork Cmty. Devel. Coun. Recipient President award Fresno Jaycees, 1964. Mem. ATLA, Calif. Bar Assn., Oreg. Bar Assn. (inactive), Fresno County Bar Assn., Calif. Trial Lawyers Assn. (chpt. pres. 1975, 83, mem. state bd. govs. 1990-94), Fresno Trial Lawyers Assn., Am. Arbitration Assn., Stanford Alumni Assn. (life, svc. award), Fresno Region Stanford Club (pres. 1979-80), Celtic Cultural Soc. Ctrl. Calif. (pres. 1977-78), Fresno county and City C. of C. (chmn. natural resources com. 1977-78), Clovis C. of C., North Fork C. of C. (pres. 1993-96, sec. 1998-2000, exec. dir. 2000—), Sierra Club (pres. Fresno chpt. 1980-81, v.p. 1986-87), Rotary, Elks, KC (3d degree chancellor), Yosemite / Sequoia RC&D (1st v.p.), Superchex, Western Assn. Chamber Exec. Republican. Roman Catholic. Avocations: writing, music, gardening, sailing, fishing. Office: PO Box 1555 North Fork CA 93643-1555 E-mail: jayflanagan@netptc.net

FLANAGAN, JOANNA SCARLATA, lawyer; b. Pitts., Oct. 10, 1967; d. Charles Francis and Antonia (Lynch) Scarlata; m. Michael Joseph Flanagan, Aug. 10, 1996; 1 child, Madelyn. BA in English, Cath. U. Am., 1989; JD, Duquesne U., 1994. Bar: Pa. 1994. Jud. law clk. to Hon. Bernard L. McGinley Commonwealth Ct. of Pa., Pitts., 1994-97; assoc. atty. Burns, White & Hickton, 1997-98, Houston Harbaugh, Pitts., 1999—. Treas. young leadership bd. Girls Hope, Pitts., 1996—2001. Avocations: skiing, biking, walking, aerobics. Estate planning, Probate. Office: Houston Harbaugh 2 Chatham Ctr Fl 12 Pittsburgh PA 15219-3465

FLANAGAN, JOHN ANTHONY, lawyer, educator; b. Sioux City, Iowa, Nov. 29, 1942; s. J. Maurice and Lorna K. (Fowler) F.; m. Martha Lang, May 8, 1982; children: Sean, Kathryn, Molly. BA, State U. of Iowa, 1964; JD, Georgetown U., 1968. Bar: Iowa 1968, D.C. 1975, Ohio 1977. Law clk. to judge U.S. Tax Ct., Washington, 1968-70; trial atty. U.S. Dept. Justice, 1970-74; prof. law U. Cin., 1974-78; sr. tax ptnr. Graydon, Head & Ritchey, Cin., 1978—. Adj. prof. U. Cin., 1978--. Contbr. articles to profl. jours. Corp. mgr. United Way, Cin., 1988; head lawyers' div. Fine Arts Fund, Cin., 1987-88; mem. Downtown Cin. Inc., 1995-2000. Mem. D.C. Bar Assn., Cin. Bar Assn., Order of Coif. Roman Catholic. Avocations: gardening, golf, fly fishing. General corporate, Corporate taxation, Taxation, general. Home: 5 Walsh Ln Cincinnati OH 45208-3435 Office: Graydon Head & Ritchey 1900 Fifth-Third Ctr PO Box 6464 Cincinnati OH 45202

FLANAGAN, JOSEPH PATRICK, JR. lawyer; b. Wilkes-Barre, Pa., Sept. 18, 1924; s. Joseph P. and Grace B. F.; m. Mary Elizabeth Mayock, Aug. 5, 1950; children: Maureen Elizabeth, Joseph P. III. B.S., U.S. Naval Acad., 1947; J.D., U. Pa., 1952. Bar: Pa. 1953, U.S. Dist. Ct. (ea. dist.) Pa. 1953, U.S. Ct. Appeals (3d cir.) 1953, U.S. Supreme Ct. 1997. Assoc. Saul, Ewing, Remick & Saul, Phila., 1952-56; ptnr. Ballard, Spahr, Andrews & Ingersoll, 1956-94, chmn. pub. fin. dept., 1961-90. Editor: Practicing Law Inst., Health Facilities Financing, 1976; co-author: In Search of Capital-A Trustee's Guide to Hospital Financing; reviewing editor Disclosure Roles of Counsel in State and Local Government Securities Offerings. editor-in-chief: U. Pa. Law Rev., 1951-52; contbr. articles to profl. jours. Bd. dirs. Phila. Com. of 70, 1952-56; former trustee Wyoming Sem., Kingston, Pa.; former mem. bd. visitors U. Pa. Law Sch.; bd. dirs. John Bartram Assn.; adv. coun. of federalism Nat. Govs. Assn., 1988. Served to lt. (j.g.) USN, 1946-49. Fellow Am. Bar Found.; mem. ABA (past chmn. urban, state and local govt. sect.), Nat. Assn. Securities Dealers (regulation arbitrator 1998—), Phila. Bar Assn. (past chmn. bus. law sect., bd. govs., past founding chmn. tax exempt fin. com., past chmn. profl. edn. com., client's security fund com., fee disputes com.), Pa. Bar Assn., Pa. Bar Inst. (pres. 1983, chmn. curriculum and course planning com. 1976-88), Phila. Club, Racquet Club, Phila. Cricket Club, Chesapeake Bay Yacht Club, Army Navy Country Club of Va. Republican. Roman Catholic. Finance, Health. Home: 401 E Mill Rd Flourtown PA 19031-1631 Office: Ballard Spahr Andrews & Ingersoll 1735 Market St Fl 49 Philadelphia PA 19103-7501 E-mail: flanagen@ballardspahr.com

FLANARY, DONALD HERBERT, JR. lawyer; b. Texarkana, Ark., July 27, 1949; s. Donald Herbert and Tenney-Margaret (Webb) F.; m. Gina Lynn Rexrod; children: Donald Herbert III, Shannon Gail, Lauren Paige, David Tyerr, John Paul, Noah Toliver. BS with honors, Tex. A&M U., 1971; JD, U. Houston, 1974. Bar: Tex. 1974, U.S. Dist. Ct. (no. dist.) Tex. 1975, U.S. Dist. Ct. (ea. dist.) Tex. 1976, U.S. Dist. Ct. (so. dist.) Tex. 1982, U.S. Tax Ct. 1982, U.S. Ct. Appeals (5th cir.) 1976, U.S. Ct. Appeals (11th cir.) 1984, U.S. Supreme Ct. 1983. Law clk. Hon. Mary Lou Robinson, U.S. Dist. Ct., Amarillo, Tex., 1974-75; asst. dist. atty. Dallas County, Tex., 1975-76; ptnr. Henderson Bryant & Wolfe, Sherman, Tex., 1976-87; ptnr. Vial Hamiton Koch & Knox, Dallas, 1988-99, Arter and Hadden, 1999—; lectr. for bar assns. on tort law, 1981-84. Bd. dirs. Texoma Valley council

Boy Scouts Am., Cancer Soc., Sherman. Named one of Outstanding Young Men Am., U.S. Jaycees, 1981; Eagle Scout, Boy Scouts Am., 1963. Fellow Tex. Bar Found. (life); mem. Tex. Assn. Def. Counsel (bd. dirs. 1981-84, 86-88), Grayson County Bar Assn. (pres. 1983-84), Internat. Assn. Ins. Counsel (bd. cert. personal jury trial law), Bd. Legal Specialization (civil trial law), Nat. Bd. Trial Adv., State Bar Assn. Tex. (bd. dirs. 1986-89, pres.-elect 1999), Am. Bd. Profl. Liability Attys. (cert.), Am. Bd. Trial Advocates (cert.). Democrat. Roman Catholic. Federal civil litigation, State civil litigation, Insurance.

FLANDERS, LAURENCE BURDETTE, JR. retired lawyer; b. Longmont, Colo., Feb. 7, 1917; s. Laurence Burdette and Harriet (Secor) F.; m. Eleanor Carlson, June 6, 1941; children— Laurel Flanders Umile, John C., Lynette Flanders Moyer, Paul L. B.S. with honors, U. Colo., 1938; J.D., 1940. Bar: Colo. 1940, U.S. Dist. Ct. Colo. 1965. Dep. dist. atty. Boulder County, Colo., 1948-52; ptnr. Flanders, Wood, Sonnesyn & Steinkamp, Longmont, Colo., 1946-89; pres., trustee Flanders Found., Inc. Bd. trustees Colo. Bar Found., 1967-87; mem. Longmont Charter Conv., 1961; mem. Longmont Water Bd., 1952-85; chmn. Longmont Long Range Planning Commn., 1971-72. Served with USNR, 1942-45. Fellow Am. Coll. Probate Counsel, Am. Bar Found.; mem. Colo. Bar Assn. (bd. of govs. 1963-67, v.p. bd. govs. 1967-68, chmn. probate and trust law sect. 1965-66), Boulder County Bar Assn., Am. Judicature Soc., Delta Sigma Pi, Order of Coif. Republican. Mem. United Ch. of Christ. Clubs: Rotary Internat., Boulder Country, Masons. Probate, Estate taxation. Home: 917 3rd Ave Longmont CO 80501-5413

FLANDERS, ROBERT G., JR. state supreme court justice; b. Freeport, N.Y., July 9, 1949; m. Ann I. Walls, May 29, 1971; children: Danielle, Heather, Zachary. AB magna cum laude, Brown U., 1971; JD, Harvard Law Sch., 1974. Bar: N.Y. 1975, Mass. 1976, R.I. 1976, U.S. Ct. of Appeals (1st and 2d. cir.), U.S. Dist. Ct. (so. dist., ea. dist.) N.Y., R.I., Mass. Assoc. Paul, Weiss, Rifkind, Wharton & Garrison, N.Y.C., 1974-75; ptnr., chmn. litig. dept. Edwards & Angell, Providence, 1975-87; founding ptnr. Flanders & Medeiros Inc., 1987-96; assoc. justice R.I. Supreme Ct., 1996—. Mem. Am. Law Inst., 2000—; bd. dirs. Rsch. Engring. and Mfg., Inc. Contbr. articles to profl. publ. Bd. dirs. Brown Sports Found., 2000, Greater Providence YMCA, 1995—, Providence Performing Arts Ctr., 1997—, Vets. Meml. Auditorium, 1999—, Women and Infants Hosp., 1996—. Mem. ABA, Phi Beta Kappa. Avocations: tennis, clarinet, jazz, poetry, cigars. Office: Rhode Island Supreme Ct 250 Benefit St Providence RI 02903-2719 E-mail: rflanders@courts.state.ri.us

FLANNERY, ELLEN JOANNE, lawyer; b. Bklyn., Dec. 13, 1951; d. William Rowan and Mary Jane (Hamilla) Flannery. AB cum laude, Mount Holyoke Coll., 1973; JD cum laude, Boston U., 1978. Bar: Mass. 1978, D.C. 1979, U.S. Ct. Appeals (D.C. cir.) 1979, U.S. Ct. Appeals (4th cir.) 1981, U.S. Ct. Appeals (6th cir.) 1983, U.S. Ct. Appeals (3d cir.) 1987, U.S. Dist. Ct. D.C. 1980, U.S. Dist. Ct. Md. 1985, U.S. Supreme Ct. 1983. Spl. asst. to commr. of health Mass. Dept. Pub. Health, Boston, 1973-75; law clk. U.S. Ct. Appeals D.C. cir., Washington, 1978-79; assoc. Covington & Burling, 1979-86, ptnr., 1986—. Lectr. ins. U. Va. Sch. Law, 1984-90, Boston U. Sch. Law, 1993, U. Md. Sch. Law, 1994; mem. Nat. Conf. Lawyers and Scientists, AAAS-ABA, 1989-92. Contbr. to articles to profl. jours. Fellow Am. Bar Found.; mem. ABA (chmn. com. med. practice 1987-88, chmn. life scis div. 1982-84, 88-91, vice chair food and drug law com. 1991-97, chmn. sect. sci. and tech. 1992-93, del. of sci. and tech. sect. to ho. of dels. 1993—, chmn. coordinating group on bioethics and the law 1998-2000), Cosmos Club. Administrative and regulatory, Health, Product liability. Office: Covington & Burling 1201 Pennsylvania Ave NW Washington DC 20004-2401

FLANNERY, HARRY AUDLEY, lawyer; b. New Castle, Pa., June 11, 1947; s. Wilbur Eugene and Ruth (Donaldson) F.; m. Maureen Louise Flaherty, June 28, 1969; children: Preston Wilbur, Courtney Lilyan. BA, Wesleyan U., 1969; JD, Ohio No. U., 1972; LLM in Taxation, Boston U., 1973. Bar: Pa. 1972, U.S. Tax Ct. 1973, U.S. Dist. Ct. (we. dist.) Pa. 1975, U.S. Supreme Ct. 1976, U.S. Ct. Appeals 1984, Ohio 2000. Sr. gen. svcs. specialist Pitts. Nat. Bank, 1973, asst. trust officer, 1974-75, trust legal officer, 1976; atty. Pa. Power Co., New Castle, 1977-98, FirstEnergy Corp., 1998—; sec. fed. and state polit. coms. Pa. Power Co., New Castle, 1983-2000. V.p. Euclid Manor Corp.; mem. panel arbitrators Bur. Mediation Dept. Labor and Industry. Assoc. editor Pitts. Legal Jour., 1981-99; contbr. numerous articles to legal publs. Bd. dirs. Lawrence County chpt. Pa. Assn. for Blind, 1st v.p., 1994-96, pres. 1996-98; mem. Highland Presbyn. Ch., New Castle, Estate Planning Coun. of Pitts., 1975-77; sec. Lil Maur Found., 1989—, v.p., 1999—; elected mem. sch. bd. dirs. Neshannock Twp. Sch. Bd., Pa., 1993—, v.p., 1997-99, pres., 1999—; mem. Pearson Park Commn., 1993-95; v.p. Neshannock Twp. Sch. Bd., Lawrence County, Pa., 1997-99, pres., 1999—; elected mem. Rep. Com., 3d Dist. Neshannock Twp., 2000. Mem. ABA (labor and employment law sect. com. on labor arbitration and law of collective bargaining agreements, tax sect. 1973-92, com. excise and employment taxes, subcom. payroll tax issues 1978-80), Pa. Bar Assn. (workmen's compensation sect., adminstrv. law sect., labor and employment law sect., pub. utility law sect., in house counsel com. 1995-98, 99-2000, dispute resolution com. 1989-91, 99-2000), Allegheny County Bar Assn. (coun., taxation sect. 1975-77, labor law sect., workmen's compensation sect., coun. labor and employment law sect. 2000—), Pitts. Legal Jour. Com., Lawrence County Bar Assn., Allegheny Tax Soc., Pennsylvania Soc. (life), Am. Arbitration Assn., The Supreme Ct. Pa. Hist. Soc. (life, trustee 1994—, sec. 1995—, v.p. 1999—), Pa. Sch. Bd. Assn., Duquesne Club, Lawrence Club, New Castle Country Club, Lions (bd. dirs. 1982-91, tailtwister 1983-84, 3rd v.p. 1984-85, 2nd v.p. 1985, 1st v.p. 1986-87, pres. 1987-88), New Castle Lions Charities, Inc. (Lion of Yr. 1988-89), Iroquois Boating and Fishing Club, Phi Alpha Delta (life). Republican. Avocations: family, writing, tennis, boating. Labor, Public utilities, Workers' compensation. Home: 116 Valhalla Dr New Castle PA 16105-1037 Office: Pa Power Co 1 E Washington St New Castle PA 16101-3814 also: FirstEnergy Corp 76 S Main St Akron OH 44308-1425 E-mail: flanneryh@firstenergycorp.com

FLANNERY, JAMES PATRICK, lawyer; b. Shenandoah, Pa., May 15, 1943; s. Anthony Joseph and Helen (Dorning) F.; m. Carol Lee Haddaway, July 12, 1970; children— Karen, Erin. B.A., St. Francis Coll., 1965; M.P.A., Am. U., 1967; J.D., Georgetown U., 1972. Bar: D.C. 1974, Pa. 1974, Minn. 1976. Mgr. Supreme Ct., Washington, 1970-73; cons. Arthur Young & Co., Washington, 1973-75, U.S. Dist. Ct., St. Paul, 1975-76; atty. Hugo Law Office, Minn., 1976— . Author: Speedy Trial, 1976. Chmn. Charter Commn., Lino Lakes, 1982— ; mem. Park Bd., Lino Lakes, 1981— ; chmn. Lino Lake Republican Com., 1984. Mem. ABA, Minn. Trial Lawyers (bd. govs. 1980), C. of C. (bd. dirs.). Republican. Roman Catholic. State civil litigation, Criminal, Personal injury. Office: 5669 147th St N Hugo MN 55038-9256

FLANNERY, JOHN FRANCIS, lawyer; b. Oct. 15, 1928; s. Edward J. and Ellie (Brennan) Flannery; m. Catherine E. Barden, Nov. 29, 1991; children: Colleen, John F., Erin, Kevin(dec.) , Brian, Patrick, Michael. BSEE, U. Ill., 1950; postgrad., Northwestern U., 1953—55; JD, Loyola U., Chgo., Ill., 1959. Bar: Ill. 1959. Assoc. Fitch, Even, Tabin & Flannery, Chgo., 1957—61, ptnr., 1961—. Trustee Village of Lincolnwood, 1978—83. Mem.: ABA, Chgo. Bar Assn., Chgo. Patent Law Assn., Am. Coll. Trial Lawyers, Am. Trial Lawyers Assn., Am. Legion, Eta Kappa Nu. Federal civil litigation, Patent, Trademark and copyright. Office: Fl 1600 120 S La Salle St Ste 1600 Chicago IL 60603-3402

FLANNERY, JOHN PHILIP, lawyer; b. N.Y.C., May 15, 1946; s. John Philip and Agnes Geraldine (Applegate) F.; m. Bettina Gregory, Nov. 14, 1981; 1 child, Diana Elizabeth. BS in Physics, Fordham Coll., 1967; BS in Engring., Columbia U., 1969, JD, 1972; student, Art Students League, 1972-73. Bar: N.Y. 1973, U.S. Dist. Ct. (so. dist.) N.Y. 1973, U.S. Ct. Appeals (2d cir.) 1973, Va. 1983, U.S. Ct. Appeals (4th cir.) 1985, U.S. Ct. Appeals (D.C. cir.) 1985, U.S. Dist. Ct. (ea. dist.) Va. 1985, U.S. Supreme Ct. 1985. Mem. staff Ford Found. Project to Restructure Columbia U., N.Y.C., 1968; news rep. nat. press rels. IBM, 1970; law clk. Adminstrv. Conf. U.S., 1971, U.S. Ct. Appeals (2d cir.), 1972-74; asst. U.S. atty. Narcotics and Ofcl. Corruption units, So. Dist. N.Y., N.Y.C., 1974-79; sr. assoc. Poletti Freidin Prashker Feldman & Gartner, 1979-82; spl. counsel U.S. Senate Judiciary Com., 1982, U.S. Senate Labor Com., 1982-83; Dem. candidate U.S. Congress from Va. 10th Dist., 1983-84; pvt. practice in civil and criminal litigation, 1984—. Spl. counsel Sen. Howard Metzenbaum, 1985-87; asst. dist. atty., Bronx, N.Y., 1986-87; counsel, bd. dirs. Washington Internat. Horse Show Assn., 1989-91; legal expert "Crime in D.C.", Fox TV, 1993, "Crime Bill" Wis. Pub. Radio, 1994, "People vs. O.J. Simpson" ABC Network Radio, 1994-95, "Va.'s No Parole" Larry King Live CNN, 1994, "Imprisonment" CBS Morning Show, 1994, Habeas Reform Court TV, 1996, Terrorism, 1996; spl. counsel U.S. House Judiciary Com., 1996-97; project dir., spl. counsel U.S. Edn. and Work Force Com., 1997-98; spl. counsel (impeachment proceedings) U.S. Rep. Zoe Lofgren, 1998-99, Washington staff chief, spl. counsel, 1999—; lectr. in field. Author: Commercial Information Brokers, 1973, Habeas Corpus Bores Hole in Prisoners' Civil Rights Action, 1975, Pro Se Litigation, 1975, Prison Corruption: A Mockery of Justice, 1980, Conspiracy: A Primer, 1988, Is Innocence Relevant to Execution? If Not, Isn't that Murder?, 1994, Equal Justice For All, 1995, Virginia Governor Allen's No-Parole Plan: A Billion Dollar Wasteland of Prisons, 1995. Committeeman Dem. Party N.Y. County, 1979-80; mem. legis. commn. Citizen's Union, 1971-72; mem. Arlington Transp. Commn., 1983-85; chmn. bus. coun. Va. Gov.'s War on Drugs Task Force, 1983-84; committeeman Dem. Party Arlington County, 1983-84; coord. N.Y. State Lawyers Com. for Senatory Edward M. Kennedy, 1979-80; dir. Citizens for Senator M. Kennedy, 1980; pres. Franklin Soc., 1979-80; del. Dem. Nat. Conf., 1988, Va. Assembly U. W.Va., 1990; committeeman Loudoun County Dem. Com., 1995—, sec. 1995—, chmn., 1995-97; del. 10th Congress and Dist. Com., 1997—; mem. Ctrl. State (Va.) Com., 1997—; del. Dem. Nat. Conv., 2000. Recipient U.S. Justice Dept. award for Outstanding Contbns. in Field of Drug Law Enforcement, 1977, U.S. Atty. Gen.'s Spl. Commendation for Outstanding Svc., 1979, FLEOA award, Fed. Law Enforcement Officer's Assn., 1984, NACDL's Marshall Stern award Outstanding Legis. Achievement, 1997. Mem. ABA, Bar Assn. of City of N.Y., N.Y. County Lawyers Assn., Arlington County Bar Assn., Loudon County Bar Assn., Nat. Assn. Criminal Def. Lawyers (chair briefbank com. 1990-91, legis. co-chair 1991—, dir. 1993—, President's commendation 1991, 92, 95), Acad. Polit. Sic., Va. Coll. Criminal Def. Attys. (bd. dirs. 1993-96). Democrat. Home: Shamrock Farm 38138 Forest Mills Rd Leesburg VA 20175-9146 Office: Rep Zoe Lofgren 227 Cannon House Off Bldg Washington DC 20515-0001 E-mail: jonflan@aol.com

FLANNERY, THOMAS AQUINAS, federal judge; b. Washington, May 10, 1918; s. John J. and Mary (Sullivan) C.; m. Rita Sullivan, Mar. 3, 1951; children: Thomas Aquinas, Irene M. LL.B., Cath. U., 1940. Bar: D.C. 1940. Practice in, Washington, 1940-42, 45-48; trial atty. Dept. Justice, 1948-50; asst. U.S. Atty., 1950-62; ptnr. Hamilton and Hamilton Washington, 1962-69; U.S. atty for D.C. Washington, 1969-71; U.S. dist. judge for D.C., 1971-85; now sr. judge U.S. Dist. Ct. for D.C., 1985-99. Served as combat intelligence officer USAF, 1942-45, ETO. Fellow Am. Coll. Trial Lawyers; Mem. Am., D.C. bar assns. Office: US Dist Ct US Courthouse 333 Constitution Ave NW Washington DC 20001-2802

FLATTERY, THOMAS LONG, lawyer, legal administrator; b. Detroit, Nov. 14, 1922; s. Thomas J. and Rosemary (Long) F.; m. Gloria M. Hughes, June 10, 1947 (dec.); children: Constance Marie, Carol Dianne Lee, Michael Patrick, Thomas Hughes, Dennis Jerome, Betsy Ann Sprecher; m. Barbara J. Balfour, Oct. 4, 1986. BS, U.S. Mil. Acad., 1947; JD, UCLA, 1955; LLM, U. So. Calif., 1965. Bar: Calif. 1955, U.S. Patent and Trademark Office 1957, U.S. Customs Ct. 1968, U.S. Supreme Ct. 1974, Conn. 1983, N.Y. 1984. With Motor Products Corp., Detroit, 1950, Equitable Life Assurance Soc., Detroit, 1951, Bohn Aluminum & Brass Co., Hamtramck, Mich., 1952; mem. legal staff, asst. contract adminstr. Radioplane Co. (divsn. Northrop Corp.), Van Nuys, Calif., 1955-57; successively corp. counsel, gen. counsel, asst. sec. McCulloch Corp., L.A., 1957-64; sec., corp. counsel Technicolor, Inc., Hollywood, Calif., 1964-70; successively corp. counsel, asst. sec., v.p., sec. and gen. counsel Amcord, Inc., Newport Beach, 1970-72; v.p., sec., gen. counsel Schick Inc., L.A., 1972-75; counsel, asst. sec. C.F. Braun & Co., Alhambra, Calif., 1975-76; sr. v.p., sec., gen. counsel Automation Industries, Inc. (now PCC Tech. Industries Inc. a unit of Penn Cen. Corp.), Greenwich, Conn., 1976-86; v.p., gen. counsel G&H Tech., Inc. (a unit of Penn Cen. Corp.), Santa Monica, Calif., 1986-93; temp. judge Mcpl. Ct. Calif. L.A. Jud. Dist. and Santa Monica Unified Cts., 1987—; settlement officer L.A. Superior and Mcpl. Cts., 1991—; pvt. practice, 1993—. Panelist Am. Arbitration Assn., 1991—; jud. arbitrator and mediator Alternative Dispute Resolution Programs L.A. Superior and Mcpl. Cts, 1993—, Calif. Ct. Appeals 2d Appellate Dist., 1999—; mem. L.A. Supr. Ct. Alternative Dispute Resolution com., 2001—. Contbr. articles to various legal jours. Served to 1st lt. AUS, 1942-50. Mem. ABA, Nat. Assn. Secs. Dealers, Inc (bd. arbitrators 1996, mediators 1997), State Bar Calif. (co-chmn. corp. law dept. com. 1978-79, lectr. continuing legal edn. program), L.A. County Bar Assn. (chmn. corp. law dept. com. 1966-67), Century City Bar Assn. (chmn. corp. law dept. com. 1979-80), Conn. Bar Assn., Santa Monica Bar Assn. (trustee 1999—, chmn. alt. dispute resolution sect. 2000—), N.Y. State Bar Assn., Am. Soc. Corp. Secs. (L.A. regional group pres. 1973-74), L.A. Intellectual Property Law Assn., Am. Ednl. League (trustee 1988—, sec. 1998—), West Point Alumni Assn., Army Athletic Assn., Friendly Sons St. Patrick, Jonathan Club (dir. 1996-99), Braemar Country Club, Phi Alpha Delta. Roman Catholic. Alternative dispute resolution, General corporate, Intellectual property. Home and Office: 439 Via De La Paz Pacific Palisades CA 90272-4633 E-mail: flatterytl@earthlink.net

FLAUM, JOEL MARTIN, federal judge; b. Hudson, N.Y., Nov. 26, 1936; s. Louis and Sally (Berger) F.; m. Delilah Brummet, June 4, 1989; children from previous marriage: Jonathan, Alison. BA, Union Coll., Schenectady, 1958; JD, Northwestern U., 1963, LLM, 1964. Bar: Ill. 1963. Asst. state's atty. Cook County, Ill., 1965-69, 1st asst. atty. gen. Ill., 1969-72; 1st asst. U.S. atty. Chgo., 1972-75; judge U.S. Dist. Ct. (no. dist.) Ill., 1975-83, U.S. Ct. Appeals (7th cir.), 1983—. Adj. prof. Northwestern U. Sch. Law, 1993—; lectr. DePaul U. Coll. of Law, 1987-88; mem. Ill. Law Enforcement Commn., 1970-72; cons. U.S. Dept. Justice, Law Enforcement Assistance Adminstrn., 1970-71. Mem.: Northwestern U. Law Rev., 1962-63; contbr. articles to legal jours. Mem. vis. com. U. Chgo. Law Sch., 1983-86, Northwestern U. Sch. Law, 1983—; mem. adv. com. USCG Acad., 1990-93. Lt. comdr. JAGC, USNR, 1981-92. Ford Found. fellow, 1963-64. Fellow Am. Bar Found. (life); mem. ABA, Fed. Bar Assn., Ill. Bar Assn., Chgo. Bar Found. (life), 7th Cir. Bar Assn., Chgo. Inn of Ct., Chgo. Bar Assn., Maritime Law Assn., Navy-Marine Corps Ret. Judge Advs. Assn., Am. Judicature Soc., Naval Res. Assn., Legal Club Chgo., Law Club Chgo. Jewish. Office: US Ct Appeals 7th Ct 219 S Dearborn St Chicago IL 60604-1702

FLECHAS, EDUARDO A. lawyer; b. New Orleans, Sept. 30, 1964; s. Enrique J. and Judith P. F.; m. Anna Lynn Beach, Mar. 24, 1990. BS in History, Miss. Coll., 1994; JD, U. Miss., 1997. Bar: Miss., U.S. Dist. Ct. (no. and so. dists.) Miss., U.S. Ct. Appeals (5th cir.), U.S. Ct. Vets. Appeals. Atty. Bell & Assocs., P.A., Madison, Miss., 1997—. Contbr. articles to profl. jours. Mem. ABA, Charles Clark Am. Inns of Ct. Republican. Catholic. Avocations: running, golf, reading. Appellate, Contracts commercial, Personal injury. Office: Bell & Assoc PA 967 Madison Ave Madison MS 39110

FLECK, JOHN R. lawyer; b. Huntington, Ind., Oct. 9, 1944; s. Ford Bloom and Deloris (Morrison) F.; m. Susan E., Dec. 31, 1975; children: Todd., Heather Fleck Erekson, Jeremy W. BA, Purdue U., 1966; JD, Ind. U., 1971. Bar: Ind. 1971, U.S. Supreme Ct. 1976, U.S. Dist. Ct. (no. and so. dists.) Ind. 1971. Law clk. Allen Superior Ct., Ft. Wayne, Ind., 1971-72; pvt. practice, 1972—. Adj. prof. Ind. U., Ft. Wayne, 1972-75; assoc. city atty. City of Ft. Wayne, 1972-75; atty. Town of Markle, Ind., 1975-80; city atty. City of New Haven, 1998—. Bd. dirs. Canterbury Sch., Ft. Wayne, 1988—; pres., bd. dirs. United Cerebral Palsy, Ft. Wayne, 1972—, Sagamore of the Wabash, 1995. Criminal. Office: 625 Lincoln Tower Fort Wayne IN 46802

FLEDDERMAN, HARRY L. lawyer; Sr. v.p., gen. counsel, sec. Crown Zellerbach Corp., San Francisco. General corporate. Office: James River Corp Nev 1 Bush St San Francisco CA 94104-4425

FLEER, KEITH GEORGE, lawyer, former motion picture executive; b. Bklyn., Feb. 28, 1943; s. Samuel Robert and Sophia M. (Scherer) F.; BA in Govt., Am. U., 1964, JD, 1967. Bar: N.Y. 1968, D.C. 1968, Calif. 1976. Asst. dir. athletics Fordham U., 1967-68; assoc. Gettinger, Gettinger & Manheimer, N.Y.C., 1968-72, Kaye, Scholer, Fierman, Hays & Handler, N.Y.C., 1972-75; sr. counsel Avco-Embassy Pictures, Hollywood, Calif., 1976; assoc. Schiff, Hirsch & Schreiber, Beverly Hills, Calif., 1977; sr. v.p. bus. and legal affairs Melvin Simon Prodn., Inc., Beverly Hills, 1978-81; exec. v.p. Simon, Reeves, Landsburg Prodns., Beverly Hills, 1982-84; v.p. bus. affairs Warner Bros., 1984-88, ptnr. Denton Hall Burgin and Warrens, 1987-88; ptnr. Sinclair Tenenbaum & Emanuel & Fleer, Beverly Hills, 1989—; guest lectr. U. West Los Angeles Law Sch., 1979-80; legis. counsel N.Y. State Assemblyman, 1969-70; adj. prof. Law Ctr. U. So. Calif., 1995. Bus. editor Am. U. Law Rev., 1966-67. Bd. trustees Am. U., 1991—. Recipient Bruce Hughes award Am. U., 1964, Alumni award Am. U. Law Sch., 1967, Stafford H. Cassell award, 1979. Mem. ABA, Beverly Hills Bar Assn., L.A. Copyright Soc. (trustee 1983-90, pres. 1988-89), Acad. of Motion Picture Arts and Scis. Banking, Entertainment, Trademark and copyright. Office: The Ice House 9348 Civic Center Dr Beverly Hills CA 90210-3624

FLEISCHAKER, MARC L. lawyer; b. Cin., Feb. 22, 1945; s. Leopold and Betty Jane (Spritz) F.; m. Phyllis S. Schmidt, June 16, 1969; children: Deborah, Julia. BS in Econs., Wharton Sch. U. Pa., 1967; JD, George Washington U., 1971. Bar: D.C. 1971, U.S. Dist. Ct. D.C. 1971, U.S. Supreme Ct. 1974, U.S. Ct. Mil. Appeals, U.S. Ct. Appeals D.C., U.S. Ct. Appeals (3d cir.) 1986, U.S. Ct. Appeals (4th, 5th and 11th cirs.). Assoc. Arent, Fox, Kintner, Plotkin & Kahn, Washington, 1971-78, ptnr., head environ. practice, 1978-2000, exec. com., 1983—, vice chmn., 1989-96, chmn., 1997—, interim mng. ptnr., 1993. Mem. exec. com. Washington Lawyers Com. for Civil Rights and Urban Affairs, 1989—, co-chmn., 1990-91, 99—, chair fin. com. 1992-93; bd. dirs. Nat. Lawyers Com. Civil Rights Under Law, 1995—, co-chmn. 1996-98; chmn. tech. com. legal sect. Am. Soc. Assn. Execs., 1995-96, bd. dirs. tchg., learning and tech. group; gen. counsel to 10 nat. trade assns. Contbr. articles to legal publs. Mem. Fed. City Coun., 2000—. With USNG, 1969-75. Recipient Triangle award Motor and Equipment Mfrs. Assn., 1976. Mem. ABA, Fed. Bar Assn., Univ. Club Washington, Econ. Club Washington. Avocations: politics, competitive running, golf, tennis. Administrative and regulatory, Antitrust, Environmental. Home: 6308 Broad Branch Rd Bethesda MD 20815-3342 Office: Arent Fox Kintner Et Al 1050 Connecticut Ave NW Washington DC 20036-5339 E-mail: FLEISCHM@ARENTFOX.com

FLEISCHER, ARTHUR, JR. lawyer; b. Hartford, Conn., Jan. 27, 1933; s. Arthur and Clare Lillian (Katzenstein) F.; m. Susan Abby Levin, July 6, 1958; children: Elizabeth, Katherine. BA, Yale U., 1953, LLB, 1958. Bar: N.Y. 1959. Assoc. Strasser, Spiegelberg, Fried & Frank, N.Y.C., 1958-61; legal asst. SEC, Washington, 1961-62, exec. asst. to chmn., 1962-64; assoc. Fried, Frank, Harris, Shriver & Jacobson, N.Y.C., 1964-67, ptnr., 1967—, chmn., 1989-97, sr. ptnr., 1997—. Vis. lectr. law Columbia U., N.Y.C., 1972-73; adviser to adv. com. Fed. Securities Code Project, Am. Law Inst., 1970-78; adviser to com. to consider new issue proposals Nat. Assn. Securities Dealers, 1973-75, mem. com. corp. financing, 1976-80; bd. dirs. Haleakala, Inc. (The Kitchen), N.Y.; chmn. Ann. Inst. on Securities Regulation, Practising Law Inst., 1969-81; mem. indsl. issuers adv. com. SEC, 1972-73; mem. adv. com. corp. disclosure, 1976-77; bd. govs. Am. Stock Exch., 1977-83; legal adv. com, bd. dirs. N.Y. Stock Exch., 1987-91; mem. adv. bd. J. Ira Harris Ctr. Mich. Bus. Sch. Co-author: Tender Offers, 1978, 5th edit., 1995, Board Games, 1988; co-editor: Annual Institute on Securities Regulation, 1970-81; contbr. articles to profl. jours. Mem. adv. coun. Ctr. for study of fin. instns. U. Pa., 1969—; trustee, mem. photography com. of Whitney Mus.; trustee Ind. Curators, Internat. Recipient Disting. Cmty. Svc. award Brandeis U., 1983, Judge Learned Hand Human Rels. award Am. Jewish Com., 1983, Harold P. Seligson award Practicing Law Inst., 1988, Judge Joseph W. Proskauer award UJA Fedn., 1994. Mem. ABA (mem. com. on fed. regulation of securities regulation 1969—), Assn. Bar City N.Y. (mem. spl. com. on lawyers role in securities transactions 1973-77, chmn. com. securities regulation 1972-74), Century Country Club (N.Y.C.). Home: 1050 Park Ave New York NY 10028-1031 Office: Fried Frank Harris 1 New York Plz Fl 27 New York NY 10004-1980

FLEISCHMAN, EDWARD HIRSH, lawyer, consultant; b. Cambridge, Mass., June 25, 1932; s. Louis Isaac and Jean (Grossman) F.; m. Joan Barbara Walden, Dec. 27, 1953 (dec. 1993), m. Judy Vernon, Sept. 27, 1998. BA, Harvard U.; LLB, Columbia U., 1959. Bar: N.Y. 1959, U.S. Supreme Ct. 1980. Assoc. Beekman & Bogue, N.Y.C., 1959-67, ptnr., 1968-86; commr. SEC, Washington, 1986-92; ptnr. Rosenman & Colin, 1992-94; sr. counsel Linklaters, N.Y.C., 1994—. Adj. prof. NYU Law Sch., 1976—2000; bd. dirs. Soundview Tech. Group, Inc. (formerly Wit Capital Corp.). Served with U.S. Army, 1952-55. Mem. ABA (co-chmn. internat. law com. on internat. securities transactions 1999—, bus. law com. on counsel responsibility 1995-99, com. on devels. in bus. financing 1987-91, subcom. model simplified indenture 1980-83, adminstrv. law com. on securities, commodities and exchs. 1981-84, bus. law subcom. broker-dealer matters 1973-78, subcom. rule 144 1970-72), Am. Law Inst., Am. Coll. Investment Counsel (pres. 1990-91), Am. Soc. Corp. Secs., Internat. Bar Assn., Internat. Law Assn. (chmn. com. on internat. securities regulation 1998—), Security Traders Assn. (bd. govs. 1997-2000). Republican. Jewish. Administrative and regulatory, Private international, Securities. Office: Linklaters 1345 6th Ave New York NY 10105-0302 Home: 897 Franklin Lake Rd Franklin Lakes NJ 07417-2115 E-mail: edward.fleischman@linklaters.com, edwardhf@aol.com

FLEISCHMAN, HERMAN ISRAEL, lawyer; b. Bklyn., Aug. 30, 1950; s. Boris and Bella (Weisbrot) F.; m. Francine Moskowitz, Feb. 3, 1973; children: Meredith, Brandon, Gary. BA, Bklyn. Coll., 1972; JD, Bklyn. Sch. Law, 1976; MPA, NYU, 1974. Bar: N.Y. 1977, U.S. Dist. Ct. (ea., so., we. and no. dists.) N.Y. 1977, U.S. Ct. Appeals (D.C. cir.) 1979, U.S. Tax Ct. 1982. Asst. counsel Amalgamated Ins. Co., N.Y.C., 1976; asst. spl. atty. gen. State of N.Y., 1977-79; asst. counsel N.Y. State Dept. Mental Hygiene,

Staten Island, N.Y., 1979; assoc. Ackerman, Salwen & Glass, N.Y.C., 1979-80; sole practice, 1980—. Mem. Thomas Jefferson Dem. Club, Bklyn., 1983-85; chmn. B'nai Brith Youth Orgn., 1980-82; bd. dirs. Big Apple Region, vice chmn., 1986-88, bd. dirs. Nassau and Suffolk Counties, N.Y., 1990-98. Recipient Citation, Town of Hempstead, 1986, Dist. Key award, B'nai B'rith Youth Org., 1979, Man of Yr. award, B'nai B'rith Youth Org., 1980; named Coach of Yr., North Merrick-North Bellmore Basketball League, 1998. Mem. ABA, ATLA, N.Y. State Bar Assn., Bklyn. Bar Assn., United Mut. Industries, Inc. (pres. 1983—). General civil litigation, General practice, Personal injury. E-mail: HFleischma@aol.com

FLEISCHMAN, KEITH MARTIN, lawyer; b. Newark, June 13, 1958; BA, U. Vt., 1980; JD, Calif. Western U., 1984. Bar: N.Y. 1985, U.S. Dist. Ct. (so. dist.) N.Y. 1986, U.S. Ct. Appeals (2d cir.) 1989, U.S. Ct. Appeals (11th cir.) 1995, U.S. Ct. Appeals (4th cir.) 1999, U.S. Supreme Ct. 2000. Asst. dist. atty. Bronx (N.Y.) County Dist. Atty., Rackets and Maj. Offense, 1984-88; trial atty. U.S. Dept. Justice, Dallas Bank Fraud Task Force, Washington, 1988-90; asst. U.S. atty. U.S. Atty. Office, Dist. Conn., 1990-92; trial lawyer, ptnr. Milberg Weiss Bershad Hynes & Lerach LLP, N.Y.C., 1992—. Inst., lectr. trial practice U.S. Dept. Justice, Washington, 1990-91. Coord. com. mem. New England Bank Fraud Task Force, Dist. Conn., 1990-92. Avocations: skiing, climbing. Civil rights, General civil litigation, Securities. Office: Milberg Weiss Bershad Hynes & Lerach LLP One Pennsylvania Plaza New York NY 10119

FLEMING, JOSEPH CLIFTON, JR. dean, law educator; b. Atlanta, July 24, 1942; s. Joseph Clifton Sr. and Claudia Leola (Duncan) F.; m. Linda Wightman, May 27, 1964; children: Allison, Erin, Anne, Matthew Clifton, Stephen Joseph, Michael Grant. BS, Brigham Young U., 1964; JD, George Washington U., 1967. Bar: Wash. 1967, U.S. Dist. Ct. (we. dist.) Wash. 1967, U.S. Tax Ct. 1969, U.S. Ct. Appeals (9th cir.) 1970, Utah 1979. Assoc. Bogle & Gates, Seattle, 1967-73; assoc. prof. Law Sch. U. of Puget Sound, Tacoma, 1973-74, Brigham Young U., Provo, Utah, 1974-76, prof. Law sch., 1976-98, assoc. dean Law Sch., 1986—, Ernest L. Wilkinson prof. Law Sch., 1998—; Fulbright prof. faculty law U. Nairobi, Kenya, 1977-78; prof. in residence Office of Chief Counsel IRS, Washington, 1985-86. Vis. prof. U. Queensland, Brisbane, Australia, 1997, 99, Central European U., Budapest, 2001. Author: Estate and Gift Tax, 1975, Tax Aspects of Buying and Selling Corporate Businesses, 1984, Tax Aspects of Forming and Operating Closely Held Corporations, 1992, Federal Income Tax: Doctrine, Structure and Policy, 1995, 2nd edit., 1999; notes editor George Washington U. Law Rev., 1966-67; contbr. numerous articles to profl. jours. Bishop Ch. of Jesus Christ of LDS, Orem, Utah, 1981-85. Mem. ABA (subcom. chair tax sect. corp. tax com. 1979-83, chair tax sect. com. on teaching taxation 1992-94), Am. Law Inst. (tax adv. group 1988-94, 98-2001). Office: Brigham Young U J Reuben Clark Law Sch PO Box 28000 Provo UT 84602-8000

FLEMING, JOSEPH Z. lawyer; b. Miami, Fla., Jan. 30, 1941; s. Richard Marion and Lenore C. Fleming; m. Betty Corcoran, Feb. 12, 1947; 1 child, Katherine Anne. BA in English, U. Fla., 1958; postgrad., U. Chgo., 1959, Hague Acad. Internat. Law, 1966; JD, U. Va., 1965; LLM in Labor Law, NYU, 1966. Bar: Fla. 1965, D.C. 1981. Assoc. Paul & Thomson, Miami, 1966-72, ptnr., 1972-74, fleming & Neuman, 1974-81, Fleming & Huck, Miami, 1981-86; sole practice, 1986-87, Fleming & Klink, 1987-88; pvt. practice, 1988-96, 96—, Ford & Harrison. Lectr. profl. programs, seminars. Author: Airline and Railroad Labor Law, 1981-2000; editor, contbg. author Environmental Regulation and Litigation in Florida, 1980, 82, 84, 85, 87, 88, 90, 91, 93-95, 97, 99, 2000; editor, contbg. author: Environmental Pollution and Individual Rights, 1978, Reporter's Handbook, 1979—, Historic Preservation Law, 1984-87, 89, 99, 2001, Entertainment Arts and Sports Law, 1989-91, 97-99, 2001. Trustee Met. Dade County Ctr. for Fine Arts, 1982-86; mem. Biscayne Bay Environ. Task Force Subcom., 1982-83, well field protection adv. com. Dade County Task Force, 1984-87; mem. Noguchi-Bayfront Park Trust, Miami, 1983-89; pres., bd. dirs. Fla. Rural Legal Svcs., 1967-78, Pres.'s Water Policy Implementation Workshops, Dept. of Interior Water Task Force, 1979; bd. dirs. Miami chpt. Am. Jewish Com. Recipient conservation award Fla. Audubon Soc., 1981, 89, Tropical Audubon Soc., 1979, award Dade County Mental Health Assn., 1974, award Miami Design Preservation League, 1982, 83, award Progressive Architecture, 1982, Am. Jewish Com. award. Mem. Am. Law Inst., ABA (continuing profl. edn. com. 1985—), Fla. Bar Assn. (past chmn. environ. and land use law sect., labor law and employment discrimination law sect., entertainment, arts and sports law sect., cert. labor and employment law). Administrative and regulatory, Environmental, Labor. Home: 34 LaGorce Cir Miami Beach FL 33141-4520 Office: 516 Ingraham Bldg 25 SE 2nd Ave Miami FL 33131-1506 E-mail: jzfleming@fordharrison.com

FLEMING, JULIAN DENVER, JR. lawyer; b. Rome, Jan. 12, 1934; s. Julian D. and Margaret Madison (Mangham) F.; m. Sidney Howell, June 28, 1960; 1 dau., Julie Adrianne. Student, U. Pa., 1951-53; BChemE, Ga. Inst. Tech., 1955, PhD, 1959; JD, Emory U., 1967. Bar: Ga. 1966, D.C. 1967; registered profl. engr., Ga., Calif. Rsch. engr., prof. chem. engring. Ga. Inst. Tech., 1955-67; ptnr. Sutherland, Asbill & Brennan, Atlanta, 1967—. Contbr. articles to profl. jours.; patentee in field. Bd. dirs. Mental Health Assn. Ga., 1970-80; bd. dirs. Mental Health Assn. Met. Atlanta, 1970-80, pres., 1974-75; mem. coun. legal advisors Rep. Nat. Com., 1981-85. Fellow Am. Inst. Chemists, Am. Coll. Trial Lawyers, Am. Bar Found.; mem. AAAS, ABA (coun. sect. sci. and tech. 1980-82, vice chmn. 1982-84, chmn. 1985-86, ho. dels. 1990, 94-96, bd. govs. 1994-95, chmn. spl. citation issues com. 1995-96, coord. commn. on legal tech. 1995-97, standing com. on tech. and info. sys. 1997—), AIChE, Nat. Conf. Lawyers and Scientists (chmn. ABA del. 1988-90, ABA liaison 1990-93, standing com. on nat. conf. groups 1990, chmn. 1992-93), Bleckley Inn of Ct. (master of bench). Achievements include patent for data apparatus. Federal civil litigation, State civil litigation, Intellectual property. Home: 1248 Oxford Rd NE Atlanta GA 30306-2610 Office: Sutherland Asbill & Brennan 999 Peachtree St NE Ste 2300 Atlanta GA 30309-3996

FLEMING, MACK GERALD, lawyer; b. Hartwell, Ga., May 3, 1932; s. Mack Judson and Dessie Leola (Vickery) F.; m. Elizabeth McClellan, Mar. 30, 1963; children: Katharine Lee, John McClellan. B.S., Clemson (S.C.) U., 1956; J.D., Am. U., Washington, 1966. Asst. dir. prodn. control Woodside Mills, Simpsonville, S.C., 1959-60; adminstrv. asst. to mem. Congress, 1960-64; dir. Congressional Liaison Office, VA, Washington, 1965-68, spl. asst. to adminstr., 1968-69; adminstrv. asst., counsel to mem. congress, 1969-70; pvt. practice law Washington, 1970-74; chief counsel Com. on Vets. Affairs, U.S. Ho. of Reps., 1974-80, staff dir. and chief counsel, 1980-95; pvt. practice Seneca, S.C., 1997—. Served to 1st lt. U.S. Army, 1956-58. Mem. D.C., S.C. Bar Assns. Democrat. Methodist. Home: 3023 Lake Keowee Ln Seneca SC 29672-6747

FLEMING, MICHAEL PAUL, lawyer; b. Orlando, Fla., June 25, 1963; s. Joseph Patrick and Therese (Eccles); m. Natalie Jackson, Oct. 15, 1988; children: Shannon Isabel, Nicholas Patrick, Patrick Edward, Michael Paul, Eamon John, Celeste Natalie. BA, U. St. Thomas, 1984; JD, U. Houston, 1987. Bar: Tex. 1987; U.S. Dist. Ct. (so. dist.) Tex. 1988; U.S. Ct. Appeals (5th cir.) 1988, U.S. Supreme Ct. 1991; cert. personal injury. Ptnr. Fleming & Fleming, Houston, 1987-91; asst. county atty. Harris County, 1991-96, elected Harris county atty., 1996-2001; ptnr. Bracewell & Patterson, 2001—. Named Irish Person of Yr., 2000. Mem. State Bar of Tex., Houston Bar Assn., Ancient Order of Hibernians, KC, Phi Delta Phi (Jameson Irish Person of Yr. 2000), 1000 Club of Houston, Irish Soc. Roman Catholic. Avocation: genealogy, Castlemahon history. Home: 6106 Lymbar Dr Houston TX 77096-4619 Office: 711 Louisiana Ste 2900 Houston TX 77002-1102

FLEMING, TOMMY WAYNE, lawyer; b. Canyon, Tex., Nov. 13, 1941; s. Benjamin Dalby and Willie Mildred (Vineyard) F.; m. Sally Ann Moore, Nov. 30, 1968; children: Benjamin Dalby II, Hunter Leah. Student, West Tex. State U., 1960-61; BBA, U. Tex., 1964, JD, 1966. Bar: Tex. 1969, U.S. Dist. Ct. (so. dist.) Tex. 1971, U.S. Supreme Ct. 1978, U.S. Ct. Appeals (5th cir.) 1983. Asst. dist. atty. Office Dist. Atty., Amarillo, Tex., 1969-70; asst. criminal dist. atty. Cameron County Criminal Dist. Atty.'s Office, Brownsville, 1970-72; ptnr. Wiech, Lewis & Fleming, 1972-74, Wiech, Fleming, Hamilton & Uribe, Brownsville, 1974-82, Wiech & Black, Brownsville, 1982-89, Atlas & Hall, Brownsville, 1989-94, Fleming, Hewitt & Olvera, Brownsville, 1994-98, Fleming & Olvera, Brownsville, 1998-2001, Fleming & Hernandez, Brownsville, 2001—. Mem. Supreme Ct. Grievance Oversight Com., 1983-2000. Chmn. Brownsville Cmty. Health Clinic, 1978-79. 1st lt. U.S. Army, 1966-69. Fellow Tex. Bar Found. (life, bd. dirs. 1984-87); mem. Tex. Assn. Bank Counsel, State Bar Tex. (bd. dirs. 1981-84), Cameron County bar Assn. (bd. dirs. 1972-79, pres. 1979-80), Brownsville Hist. Assn. (bd. dirs. 1977-80). Banking, Contracts commercial, General practice. Home: 915 Santa Ana Ave Rancho Viejo TX 78575-9749 Office: Fleming & Hernandez 1650 Paredes Line Rd Ste 102 Brownsville TX 78521-1665

FLETCHER, ANTHONY L. lawyer; b. Washington, Dec. 12, 1935; s. Robert J. and Lyndell (Pickett) F.; m. Juliana Schump, Sept. 3, 1960 (div. 1977); children: Leigh Anne Grinstead, Kristine Marie Giffin, Julie Bowen Cimino; m. Zelda L. Fletcher, Mar. 30, 1986. BA, Princeton U., 1957; JD, Harvard U., 1962. Bar: N.Y. 1963, U.S. Ct. Appeals (2d cir.) 1966, U.S. Ct. Appeals (7th cir.) 1966, U.S. Supreme Ct. 1966, U.S. Ct. Appeals (3d cir.) 1969, U.S. Ct. Appeals (5th cir.) 1973, U.S. Ct. Appeals (1st cir.) 1981, U.S. Ct. Appeals (9th cir.) 1983. Assoc. Simpson Thacher & Bartlett, N.Y.C., 1962-71, Conboy, Hewitt, O-Brien & Boardman, N.Y.C., 1971-74, ptnr., 1974-86, Hunton & Williams, N.Y.C., 1986-97; prin. Fish & Richardson P.C., 1997—. Editor-in-chief Trademark Reporter, 1982-84; contbr. articles to profl. jours. With U.S. Army, 1957-59. Mem. Internat. Trademark Assn. (bd. dirs. 1983-85), Princeton Club. Episcopalian. Federal civil litigation, State civil litigation, Trademark and copyright. Office: Fish & Richardson PC 45 Rockefeller Plz Fl 28 New York NY 10111-2889

FLETCHER, BETTY BINNS, federal judge; b. Tacoma, Mar. 29, 1923; B.A., Stanford U., 1943; LL.B., U. Wash., 1956. Bar: Wash. 1956. Mem. firm Preston, Thorgrimson, Ellis, Holman & Fletcher, Seattle, 1956-1979; judge U.S. Ct. Appeals (9th cir.), 1979—, sr. judge, 1998-. Mem. ABA (Margaret Brent award 1992), Wash. State Bar Assn., Am. Law Inst., Fed. Judges Assn. (past pres.), Order of Coif, Phi Beta Kappa. Office: US Ct Appeals 9th Cir 1010 5th Ave Ste 1000 Seattle WA 98104-1196*

FLETCHER, NORMAN S. state supreme court justice; b. July 10, 1934; s. Frank Pickett and Hattie Sears Fletcher; m. Dorothy Johnson, 1957; children: Mary Kiker, Elizabeth Coan. BA, U. Ga., 1956, LLB, 1958; LLM, U. Va., 1995. Assoc. Matthews, Maddox, Walton and Smith, Rome, 1958-63; pvt. practice LaFayette, 1963-90; city atty. City of LaFayette, 1965-89; county atty. County of Walker, 1973-88; spl. asst. atty. gen. State of Ga., Atlanta, 1979-89; justice Supreme Ct. of Ga., 1990—, now presiding justice. Mem. State Disciplinary Bd., 1984-87, chair investigative panel, 1986-87. Ruling elder Peachtree Presbyn. Ch., Atlanta; former officer First Presbyn. Ch. of Rome, Ga., LaFayette Presbyn. Ch., Cherokee Presbytery; former commr. Presbyn. Ch. USA Gen. Assembly, 1984, 85; bd. visitors U. Ga. Sch. Law, 1992-95, chmn., 1994-95. Master Joseph Henry Lumpkin Inn of Ct.; fellow Am. Bar Found., Ga. Bar Found.; mem. State Bar Ga. (chair local govt. sect. 1977-78), U. Ga. Law Sch. Alumni Assn. (pres. 1977), Rotary. Office: Supreme Ct Ga 244 Washington St SW Rm 572 Atlanta GA 30334-9007*

FLETCHER, RICHARD ROYCE, lawyer; b. Garden City, Kans., Aug. 3, 1959; s. Dick Royce and Betty Sue (Rabun) F.; m. Rhonda Denise Pacanowski, Aug. 10, 1979; children: Chelsie N., Christin D., Catherine M. BS, Lubbock Christian U., 1981; MBA, Abilene Christian U., 1985; JD, Tex. Tech. U., 1989. Bar: Tex. 1989, N.Mex. 1990, U.S. Dist. Ct. (we. dist.) Tex. 1991, U.S. Ct. Appeals (5th cir.) 1992, U.S. Dist. Ct. (so. dist.) Tex. 1993, U.S. Supreme Ct. 1993, U.S. Dist. Ct. N.Mex. 1995, U.S. Ct. Appeals (10th cir.) 1996, U.S. Dist. Ct. (no. dist.) Tex. 1997, U.S. Tax Ct. 2000; cert. personal injury and civil trial law, Tex. Bd. Legal Specialization. Ptnr., shareholder Cotton, Bledsoe, Tighe & Dawson, Midland, Tex., 1989—. Mem. Tex. Assn. of Def. Counsel, Order of Barristers, Midland County Bar Assn., Phi Delta Phi. Mem. Church of Christ. Avocations: backpacking, fly fishing, racquetball. General civil litigation, Insurance, Personal injury. Office: Cotton Bledsoe Tighe & Dawson 500 W Illinois Ave Ste 300 Midland TX 79701-4337 E-mail: rfletcher@cbtd.com

FLETCHER, WILLIAM A. federal judge, law educator; b. 1945; BA, Harvard U., 1968, Oxford U., 1970; JD, Yale U., 1975. Law clk. to presiding justice U.S. Dist. Ct. Calif., San Francisco, 1975-76; law clk. to Justice J. Brennan U.S. Supreme Ct., D.C., 1976-77; acting prof. law U. Calif., Berkeley, 1977-84, prof. law, 1984—; judge U.S. Ct. Appeals (9th cir.), San Francisco, 1998—. Office: 95 7th St San Francisco CA 94103*

FLICKINGER, DON JACOB, patent agent; b. Massillon, Ohio, Dec. 31, 1933; s. John Jacob and Elizabeth Ann (Slinger) F.; m. Sonja Loy Jersild (dec. Aug. 1987); 1 child, Packy J. Flickinger. Student, Kent (Ohio) State U., 1951-54, U. Ariz., 1958; BA, Ariz. State U., 1963, MA, 1964. Bar: U.S. Patent and Trademark Office, 1973. Apprentice tool and die maker Spun Steel Corp., Canton, Ohio, 1951-54; staff Ariz. State U., Tempe, 1963-65; law clerk, paralegal Drummond, Cahill & Phillips, Phoenix, 1966-73; reg. patent agent Drummond, Nelson & Ptak, 1973-77, self employed, Phoenix, 1977-94; counsel Parsons & Goltry, 1995—2001. Lectr., instr. Patent Seminars & Courses, Phoenix, 1977—; staff Rio Salado C.C., Phoenix, 1982-84; intellectual property counselor SCORE Phoenix Chpt. 105, 2001. Patentee Collapsible Dust Pan, Hort. Growing Unit. Comdg. officer Poolee Enrichment Program, Family Marine Force, Poolee Assistance Co., Phoenix; sponsor Thunderbird Little League, Phoenix, 1985, 86, 87; big brother Valley Big Brothers, Phoenix, 1968-70; participant, staff Valley Big Bros./Big Sisters Fish-a-Ree, 1984-87; judge Crown Royal Kinetic Contraption Compeition, 1990. With USMC, 1954-57. Am. Soc. Tool. scholar, Tucson, 1960; recipient Disting. Svc. cert. Valley Big Brothers, Phoenix,1970, Honor award Westside Area Career Project, Glendale, 1981. Mem. BBB, NRA (endowment), Nat. Wildlife Fedn. (leaders club), Am. Legion, Ariz. Heritage Alliance, Phoenix Symphony Guild, Sundome Performing Arts Assn., Wilderness Soc., Nature Conservancy, Sea Shepard Conservation Soc., Legal Defense Fund, Defenders of Wildlife, Am. Legion, Mensa, Svc. Corps. of Ret. Exec. (intellectual property counselor Phoenix chpt. 105 2001—), Kappa Delta Pi. Republican. Buddhist. Avocations: philosophy, reading, woodworking, arts and crafts. Patent. Office: Phoenix Score Chpt 105 2828 N Central Ave Ste 800 Phoenix AZ 85004

FLICKINGER, HARRY HARNER, organization and business executive, management consultant; b. Hanover, Pa., July 27, 1936; s. Harry Roosevelt and Goldie Anna (Harner) F.; m. Hsin Yang, May 30, 1961; children: Audrey Mae, Deborah Lynn. B.S. in Psychology, U. Md., 1958. Investigator U.S. Civil Service Commn., Washington, 1962-64; personnel specialist U.S. Naval Ordinance Lab., Silver Spring., Md., 1964-66; from asst. dir. to dir. personnel U.S. OMB, Washington, 1966-73; asst. dir. personnel AEC and Dept. Energy, 1973-78; dir. personnel U.S. Dept. Justice, 1978-79, dep. asst. atty. gen. adminstrn., 1979-85, assoc. asst. atty. gen., 1985-87, asst. atty. gen., 1987-92; exec. dir. Am. Consortium for Internat. Pub. Adminstrn., 1993; pres. Flickinger Enterprises, Gaithersburg, Md., 1994—. Recipient Presdl. Disting. Exec. Rank award, 1988. Office: 8730 Lochaven Dr Gaithersburg MD 20882-4464

FLIPPEN, EDWARD L. lawyer; b. Richmond, Va., Dec. 2, 1939; s. Hannie Thomas Flippen; m. Pearcy light, Feb. 14, 1970; children: Elizabeth Hunter, Margaret Harlan. BS, Va. Commonwealth U., 1965; MBA, Coll. of William and Mary, 1967, JD, 1974. Bar: Va. 1974, N.C. 1981. Gen. atty. Va. State Corp. Commn., Richmond, 1975-78, assoc. gen. counsel, 1978-80, dep. gen. counsel, 1980; asst. gen. counsel Duke Power Co., Charlotte, N.C., 1980-81, assoc., 1981-83; ptnr. Mays & Valentine, LLP, Richmond, 1983-99, McGuireWoods, LLP, Richmond, 1999—. Lectr., U. Va. Sch. Law, 1978-82; adj. law prof. Coll. of William and Mary, 1996—, Washington and Lee U., 1997—, U. Richmond, 2000—; vis. prof. George Mason Sch. Law, 2001—; vis. fellow U. London, 1998-99; chmn. Gov's. Blue Ribbon Commn. Higher Edn., 1998-2000. Author: Practical Networking: How to Give and Get Help with Jobs, 2001. Bd. visitors Va. Commonwealth U., Richmond, 1994, rector, 2000—; adv. bd. Va. Ctr. on Aging, Richmond, 1994-98; trustee River Rd. United Meth. ch., Richmond, 1995-98; bd. VCU Health Sys., 2000—. With U.S. Army, 1958-61. Mem. Va. State Bar (chmn. adminstrv. law sect., 1986-87), Soc. for Advanced Legal Studies (assoc. fellow). Republican. Avocations: writing, teaching, assisting others in job placements. Public utilities. Office: McGuireWoods LLP One James Ctr 901 E Cary St Richmond VA 23219-4057 E-mail: eflippen@mcguirewoods.com

FLOM, JOSEPH HAROLD, lawyer, director; b. Balt., Dec. 20, 1923; s. Isadore and Fannie (Fishman) F.; m. Claire Cohen, Nov. 14, 1958; children: Peter Leslie, Jason Robert. Student, Coll. City N.Y.; LLB cum laude, Harvard U., 1948; LHD (hon.), Queens Coll., 1984; LLD (hon.), Fordham U., 1990. Practice of law, N.Y.C., 1949—. Spl. counsel subcom. on adminstrn. of internal revenue laws House Ways and Means Com., 1951-52; mem. com. on tender offers SEC, 1983. Editor Harvard Law Rev., 1947-48; co-editor: Disclosure Requirements of Public Corporations and Insiders, 1967, Texas Gulf Sulphur-Insider Disclosure Problems, 1968, Lawyer's Conflicts-The Evolving Case Law, 1991. Mem. N.Y.C. Mayor's Commn. on Status of Women, 1976-77; mem. Mayor's Coun. Econ. Advisors, 1990-93; co-chmn. task force on capital fin. and constrn. N.Y.C. Bd. Edn., 1987-89; co-chmn. N.Y.C. Operation Welcome Home Commn., 1991; chmn. N.Y.C. Commn. on Bicentennial of Constn., 1986-89; trustee Fedn. Jewish Philanthropies N.Y., 1977-86, Barnard Coll., 1983-93, N.Y. Hist. Soc., 1989-94; chair adv. com. Export-Import Bank of U.S., 1995; trustee Mt. Sinai-NYU Health Sys., 1978-99; trustee Petrie Stores Liquidating Trust; mem. Archdiocesan Task Force on Crime Prevention and Youth, 1982-87; trustee Skadden Fellowship Found., Constl. Edn. Found., 1989-93, United Way N.Y.C., 1991-97; mayor's rep. Met. Mus. of Art, 1990-93; mem. Mayor's Mgmt. Adv. Task Force, 1991-93; chair Woodrow Wilson Internat. Ctr. for Scholars, 1994-98. Fellow ABA; mem. Assn. Bar City N.Y. Office: Skadden Arps Slate 4 Times Sq Fl 41 New York NY 10036-6522

FLOOD, JOAN MOORE, paralegal; b. Hampton, Va., Oct. 10, 1941; d. Harold W. and Estalena (Fancher) M.; 1 child by former marriage, Angelique. B.Mus., North Tex. State U., 1963; postgrad., So. Meth. U., 1967-68, Tex. Women's U., 1978-79, U. Dallas, 1985-86. Clk. Criminal Dist. Ct. Number 2, Dallas County, Tex., 1972-75; reins. libr. Scor Reins. Co., Dallas, 1975-80; corp. ins. paralegal Assocs. Inc. Group, 1980-83; corp. securities paralegal Akin, Gump, Strauss, Hauer & Feld, 1983-89; asst. sec. Knoll Internat. Holdings Inc., Saddle Brook, N.J., 1989-90, 21 Internat. Holdings, Inc., N.Y.C., 1990-92; dir. compliance Am. Svc. Life Ins. Co., Ft. Worth, 1992-93; v.p., sec. Express Comm., Inc., Dallas, 1993-94; fin. transactions paralegal Thompson & Knight, 1994-96; corp. transactions paralegal Jones, Day, Reavis & Pogue, 1996-97, Weil, Gotshal & Manges, LLP, 1998; corp. paralegal PennCorp. Fin. Group, Inc., Dallas, 1999-2001; debt trade mgr. Patton Boggs LLP, 2001—. Mem. ABA, Tex. Bar Assn. Home: PO Box 190165 Dallas TX 75219-0165 E-mail: jflood@pattongobbs.com

FLORENCE, KENNETH JAMES, lawyer; b. Hanford, Calif., July 31, 1943; s. Ivy Owen and louella (Dobson) F.; m. Verena Magdalena Demuth, Dec. 10, 1967. BA, Whittier Coll., 1965; JD, Hastings Coll. Law U. Calif., San Francisco, 1974. Bar: Calif. 1974, U.S. Dist. Ct. (ctrl. dist.) Calif. 1974, U.S. Dist. Ct. (ea. and so. dists.) Calif. 1976, U.S. Dist. Ct. (no. dist.) Calif. 1980, U.S. Ct. Appeals (9th cir.) 1975, U.S. Supreme Ct. 1984. Dist. mgr. Pacific T&T, Calif., 1969-71; assoc. Parker, Milliken, et al, L.A., 1974-78; ptnr. Dern, Mason, et al, 1978-84, Swerdlow Florence Sanchez & Rathbun A Law Corp., Beverly Hills, 1984—. Pres. Westside Legal Services, Inc., Santa Monica, Calif., 1982-83. Served to lt. USNR, 1966-69, Vietnam. Col. J.G. Boswell scholar, 1961. Mem. ABA (co-chmn. state labor law com. 1988-91). Democrat. Labor. Office: Swerdlow Florence Sanchez & Rathbun 9401 Wilshire Blvd Ste 828 Beverly Hills CA 90212-2921 E-mail: kjflaw@aol.com

FLORY, JAMES E. prosecutor; U.S. Atty., Kans. Office: 1200 Epic Ctr 301 N Main Wichita KS 67202-4812 Office Fax: 316-269-6484*

FLOWE, BENJAMIN HUGH, JR. lawyer; b. Durham, N.C., Feb. 8, 1956; s. Benjamin H. and Dorothy Amelia (Bell) F.; children: Samantha Kathleen, Andrew Benjamin. AB in Sociology and Psychology cum laude, Duke U., 1978; JD with high honors, N.C. U., 1981. Bar: U.S. Ct. Appeals (D.C. cir.) 1981, U.S. Supreme Ct. 1990. Assoc. Arent, Fox et al, Washington, 1981-84, Bowman, Conner & Touhey P.C., Washington, 1984-87, Verner, Liipfert, Bernhard, McPherson & Hand, Washington, 1987-89, ptnr., 1990-96; pvt. practice, 1996-97; ptnr. Berliner, Corcoran & Rowe, L.L.P., 1997—. Contbr. congrl. testimony on export controls Ctr. for Strategic and Internat. Studies; mem. tech. adv. com. Commerce Dept. Author: Export Compliance Guide, 1995; contbr. articles to profl. jours. Mem. ABA (vice chair export controls and econ. sanctions com.), Am. Electronics Assn., Am. Soc. Internat. Law, Order of the Coif. Democrat. Presbyterian. Avocations: skiing, writing, golf, tennis. Admiralty, Contracts commercial, Private international. Home: 8120 Paisley Pl Potomac MD 20854-2748 Office: Berliner Corcoran & Rowe LLP 1101 17th St NW Ste 1100 Washington DC 20036-4798

FLOWE, CAROL CONNOR, lawyer; b. Owensboro, Ky., Jan. 3, 1950; d. Marvin C. Connor and Ethel Marie (Thorn) Smith; children: Samantha Kathleen, Andrew Benjamin. BME magna cum laude, Murray State U., 1972; JD summa cum laude, Ind. U., 1976. Bar: Ohio 1977, D.C. 1981, U.S. Dist. Ct. (so. dist.) Ohio 1977, U.S. Dist. Ct. Md. 1983, U.S. Dist. Ct. D.C. 1981, U.S. Supreme Ct. 1987, U.S. Ct. Appeals (2d, 3d, 4th, 5th, 7th and D.C. cirs.). Assoc. Baker & Hostetler, Columbus, Ohio, 1976-80, Arent Fox Kintner Plotkin & Kahn, Washington, 1980-87; deputy gen. counsel Pension Benefit Guaranty Corp., 1987-89, gen. counsel, 1989-95; ptnr. Arent, Fox, Kintner, Plotkin & Kahn, 1995—. Mem. ABA, D.C. Bar Assn., Order of Coif, Alpha Chi, Phi Alpha Delta. Avocations: computers, reading. Federal civil litigation, Labor, Pension, profit-sharing, and employee benefits. Home: 8608 Aqueduct Rd Potomac MD 20854-6249 Office: Arent Fox Kintner Plotkin & Kahn 1050 Connecticut Ave NW Ste 500 Washington DC 20036-5303 E-mail: flowec@arentfox.com

FLOWERS, KENT GORDON, JR. lawyer; b. Aurora, N.C., Apr. 29, 1955; s. Kent Gordon Sr. and Shirley Temple (Deal); m. Debra Ann Henries, Aug. 21, 1981; children: Kent Gordon III, Rachel Ann. BA in Social Sci., U. N.C., Wilmington, 1976, BA in Secondary Edn., 1977; postgrad., Emmanuel Coll., 1977-78; JD, U. Ark., Little Rock, 1981. Bar: N.C. 1982, U.S. Dist. Ct. (ea. dist.) N.C. 1986. Staff atty. Craven County, New Bern, N.C., 1982—. Cons. Craven County Foster Parents, New Bern, 1982-92; com. chairperson Craven County Council for Children, New Bern, 1982-86; bd. dirs. Smart Start, 1999—; dist. comdr. Royal Rangers, 1994—. Mem. N.C. Bar Assn., N.C. Coll. of Advocacy, N.C. Assn. Social Service Attys. (sec. 1984-85). Democrat. Avocations: collecting antiques, home restoration. Home: PO Box 593 New Bern NC 28563-0593 Office: PO Box 12039 New Bern NC 28561-2039 E-mail: jr.flowers@ncmail.net

FLOWERS, WILLIAM HAROLD, JR. lawyer; b. Chgo., Mar. 22, 1946; s. William Harold and Ruth Lolita (Cave) F.; m. Pamela Mays, Sept. 13, 1980. BA, U. Colo., 1967, JD, 1971. Bar: Colo. 1973, U.S. Dist. Ct. Colo. 1973, U.S. Ct. Appeals (10th cir.) 1978, U.S. Supreme Ct. 1985, U.S. Ct. Appeals (4th cir.) 1994. Atty. Pikes Peak Legal Svcs., Colorado Springs, Colo., 1973; ptnr. Tate, Tate & Flowers, Denver, 1973-76; dep. dist. atty. Office Adams County Dist. Atty., Brighton, Colo., 1977-78; ptnr. Taussig & Flowers, Boulder, 1978-81; pvt. practice, 1981-89; ptnr. Holland & Hart, LLP, Denver, 1989-97, Hurth Yeager & Sisk, LLP, 1997—. Mem. Boulder County Cmty. Corrections Bd., 1985-90. Mem. Boulder Bd. Zoning Adjustment, 1973-78, chmn., 1977-78; mem. Boulder Growth Task Force, 1980-82; mem. exec. bd. Longs Peak coun. Boy Scouts Am., 1983-98; bd. dirs. Sta. KGNU, Boulder County Broadcasting, 1981-84. Mem.: ATLA (creative com. 2001—, chair-elect state dels. 2001—, pres. Coun. of Presidents 2001—), Nat. Bar Assn. (regional dir. 1983—86, bd. govs. 1983—96, v.p. 1990—91), Colo. Criminal Def. Bar (bd. dirs. 1982—83), Colo. Trial Lawyers Assn. (past pres. 1999—2000, exec. com. 2001—, bd. dirs. 1989—), Boulder County Bar Assn. (civil litigation com. 1978—, criminal law com. 1979—), Sam Cary Bar Assn. (pres. 1987), U. Colo. Boulder Alumni Assn. (bd. dirs. 1987—96, pres. 1994—95), U. Colo. Found. (bd. dirs. 1995—). Democrat. Methodist. Criminal, Personal injury, Professional liability. Office: Hurth Yeager & Sisk LLP PO Box 17850 4860 Riverbend Rd Boulder CO 80308

FLOYD, WALTER LEO, lawyer; b. St. Louis, May 29, 1933; s. Walter L. Sr. and Estelle E. (Kiess) F.; children: Michael W., Mary Ann, Mark L.; m. Patricia A. Knapko, Sept. 3, 1994. BS, St. Louis U., 1955, LLD, 1959. Bar: Mo. 1959, Ill. 1959, U.S. Dist. (ea. dist.) Mo. 1959. Owner The Floyd Law Firm P.C., St. Louis, 1959—. Contbr. articles to profl. jours. Fellow: Orgn. Nat. Bd. Trial Advocacy; mem. Mo. Assn. Trial Attys. (sec. 1961, v.p. 1962, 85), Am. Trial Lawyers Assn. (lectr.), Mo. Bar Assn., Ill. Assn., Phi Delta Phi. Democrat. Unitarian. Federal civil litigation, General civil litigation, State civil litigation. Address: Floyd Law Firm 8151 Clayton Rd Ste 202 Saint Louis MO 63117-1111

FLUHARTY, JESSE ERNEST, lawyer, judge; b. San Antonio, Tex., July 25, 1916; s. Jesse Ernest and Gwendolyn (Elder) F.; m. Ernestine Gertrude Corlies, Oct. 25, 1945; 1 son, Stephen Robert. Student Calif. State U.-San Diego, 1935-36, Art Ctr. Sch. Design Los Angeles, 1938-39; J.D. with distinction, U. Pacific, 1951; grad. Nat. Jud. Coll. Adminstrv. Law 1982. Bar: Calif. 1952, U.S. Dist. Ct. (no. dist.) Calif. 1952, U.S. Ct. appeals (9th cir.) 1952, U.S. Dist. Ct. (cen. dist.) Calif. 1979, U.S. Supreme Ct. 1983. Sole practice, Sacramento, 1952-60; referee in charge Indsl. Accident Commn., Stockton, Calif., 1960-67; presiding referee so. Calif. Workers Compensation Appeals Bd., Los Angeles, 1967-71, workers compensation Judge, Los Angeles, 1971-79; presiding judge, Los Angeles, 1979-81, Long Beach, 1981-83; of counsel Law Office of Stephen Fluharty, Glendale, Calif., 1984-87; workers compensation judge., Van Nuys, Calif., 1987—. Pres. Family Service Agy., Sacramento, 1958, 59, Community Council Stockton and San Joaquin County, 1965, Service Club Council Los Angeles, 1973-74, Glendale Hills Coordinating Council, 1976-78, Chevy Chase Estates Assn., 1971-77; chmn. San Joaquin County Recreation and Park Commn., 1963-67. Served with U.S. Army, 1943-45. Decorated Bronze Star, Philippine Liberation medal; recipient Meritorious citation Calif. Recreation Soc., 1967. Mem. Calif. State Bar, Los Angeles County Bar Assn., Glendale Bar Assn., Lawyers Club Los Angeles (pres. 1980, Judge of Yr. 1982). Republican. Congregationalist. Clubs: Chevy Chase Country, Verdugo. Lodges: Lions (pres. Los Angeles 1971-72), Masons. Home: 3330 Emerald Isle Dr Glendale CA 91206-1112

FLYNN, MICHAEL, lawyer; b. Bklyn., Sept. 20, 1952; s. James Thomas and Catherine Marie (Fratello) F.; m. Janet Marie DiPaolo, Jan. 11, 1975; chldren: Michael Sean, Ashley Brooke, Thomas James. BA, Bklyn. Coll., 1970; JD, N.Y. Law Sch., 1978. Bar: N.Y. 1979, U.S. Dist. Ct. (so., ea., we. and no. dists.) N.Y. 1979, U.S. Ct. Appeals (2d cir.) 1979, U.S. Supreme Ct. 1985. Assoc. firm Elkind & Lampson, N.Y.C., 1979-83; sr. ptnr. Elkind, Flynn & Maurer, P.C., 1983—. Cons. counsel United Transp. Union, Cleve., Brotherhood R.R. Signalmen, Cleve., Transport Workers Union N.Y., Brotherhood Locomotive Engrs. N.Y., Sheetmetal Workers N.Y., Internat. Brotherhood Elec. Workers, N.Y.; judge (arbitration) Civil Ct., N.Y.C., 1980— ; cons. atty. Oceanside civil counsel (N.Y.), 1984; judge N.Y. Law Sch., N.Y.C., 1978. Recipient Am. Jurisprudence award, 1976; Goodrich award Western New Eng. Sch. Law, Springfield, Mass., 1977. Mem. ATLA, N.Y. State Bar Assn., Civil Justice Found. (founding sponsor 1987), N.Y. State Trial Lawyers Assn., Acad. Rail Labor Attys. Federal civil litigation, State civil litigation, Personal injury. E-mail: efmlaw1@aol.com

FLYNN, PETER ANTHONY, judge; b. Bronxville, N.Y., July 23, 1942; s. Ralph Harold and Caroline (Lindberg) F. BA magna cum laude, Harvard U., 1963; LLB, Yale U., 1966. Bar: Ill. 1969, U.S. Dist. Ct. (no. and so. dists.) Ill. 1969, U.S. Ct. Appeals (7th cir.) 1969, U.S. Supreme Ct. 1976, U.S. Dist. Ct. (ea. dist.) Wis. 1980, U.S. Ct. Appeals (2d and 5th cirs.) 1980, U.S. Ct. Appeals (9th cir.) 1987. Asst. lect. law U. Ife, 1967-69; assoc. Jenner & Block, Chgo., 1969-75; ptnr. Cherry & Flynn, 1976-99; judge Cir. Ct. of Cook County, Ill., 1999—. Mem. Olympia Fields Plan Commn., Ill., 1979-83, chmn., 1983-85; trustee Village of Olympia Fields, 1985-89; pres. Touchstone Theatre, 1990-93; active U.S. Peace Corps, 1967-69. Mem. ABA, Ill. Bar Assn., Am. Law Inst., Chgo. Lincoln Inn of Ct. Roman Catholic. Avocations: theater, piano, poetry, guitar, choral music, sailing, history. E-mail: laotze100@prodigy.net

FOCHT, THEODORE HAROLD, lawyer, educator; b. Reading, Pa., Aug. 20, 1934; s. Harold Edwin and Ruth Naomi (Boyer) F.; m. Joyce Gundy, Aug. 11, 1956; children: David Scott, Eric Steven. AB in Philosophy, Franklin and Marshall Coll., 1956; JD, Coll. of William and Mary, 1959. Bar: Va. 1959. Teaching assoc. Columbia U. Sch. Law, N.Y.C., 1959-60; atty. Office of Gen. Counsel SEC, Washington, 1960-61, legal asst. to Commr., Washington, 1961-63; mem. faculty U. Conn. Sch. Law, Hartford, 1963-71 (leave of absence, 1969-71); spl. counsel on securities legislation Interstate and Fgn. Commerce Com., U.S. Ho. of Reps., Washington, 1969-71; gen. counsel Securities Investor Protection Corp., Washington, 1971-94, pres., 1984-94; adj. prof. law American U. Sch. Law, Washington, 1979-84; mem. Fla. State Comptroller's Task Force on Regulatory DeCoupling, 1995. Mem. Va. State Bar, Phi Beta Kappa. Bankruptcy, General corporate, Securities. Home: 8436 Pinafore Dr New Port Richey FL 34653-6739

FODERA, LEONARD V. lawyer; b. Bklyn., Sept. 9, 1956; s. Vito Leonard and Nancy Rose (Calderola) F.; m. Kathleen M. Scanlon, Sept. 4, 1981; children: Leonard, Nancy. BA, LaSalle Coll., Phila., 1978; JD, Temple U., Phila., 1989. Bar: Pa. 1989, U.S. Dist. Ct. (ea. dist.) Pa. 1989. Gen. counsel Plymouth Risk Mgmt., Plymouth Meeting, Pa., 1990-92; assoc. Sheller Ludwig & Badey, Phila., 1992-95; ptnr. Monheit, Monheit, Silverman & Fodera, PC, 1995—. Legal counsel Roosevelt Adv. Counsel, 1989—; mem. Cinnaminson Curriculum Com., N.J., 1992-93, Cinnaminson planning bd., 1998—; advisor Com. of 70, Phila., 1986—. Mem. ABA, Assn. Trial Lawyers Am., Phila. Bar Assn., Million Dollar Advocates Forum, Phila. Trial Lawyers Assn. Roman Catholic. Civil rights, State civil litigation, Professional liability. Office: Mongheit Monheit Silverman Fodera 2010 Chestnut St Philadelphia PA 19103-4411 E-mail: civil@civilrights.com

FOERSTER, BARRETT JONATHAN, lawyer; b. Charleston, S.C., Oct. 20, 1942; S. Donald Madison Foerster and Margaret Jean (Barrett) Foerster Harkins; m. Susan Ruth Sibert, June 17, 1967; children: Andrea B., Bryn E. BA, U. Pa., 1964; JD, UCLA, 1967; LLM, U. San Diego, 2000. Bar: Calif. 1970, U.S. Dist. Ct. (so. and cen. dists.) Calif. 1970. Ptnr. Greer, Popko, Miller and Foerster, San Diego, 1970-75, Olins, Foerster and Hayes, San Diego, 1975—. Contbr. articles to legal jours. Served to capt. U.S. Army, 1967-69, Vietnam. Recipient Preservation award Save Our Heritage Orgn., 1983. Mem. Calif. Bar Assn., San Diego County Bar Assn., Calif. State Probate Referees Assn. (bd. dirs. 1984-85). Episcopalian. Avocation: jogging. Family and matrimonial, General practice, Labor. Home: 4476 Ampudia St San Diego CA 92103-1046 Office: 2214 2nd Ave San Diego CA 92101-2020 E-mail: BFoerster@ofh.com

FOGARTY, JAMES ROBERT, lawyer; b. Norwalk, Conn., Jan. 24, 1943; s. James R. and Alice (Henshon) F.; m. Frances Sclafani, Dec. 12, 1975; children: Brendan John, Brian Henshon. B.A., Fordham U., 1964, LL.B., 1967; LL.M., NYU, 1972. Bar: N.Y. 1967, Conn. 1968, U.S. Supreme Ct. 1973, U.S. Ct. Appeals (2d cir.) 1975. Law clk. Honorable Howard Alcorn, Conn. Supreme Ct., Hartford, Conn., 1968-69; ptnr. Durey & Pierson, Stamford, Conn., 1969-79, Epstein & Fogarty, Stamford, 1969-95; prin. Fogarty, Cohen, Selby & Nemiroff, LLC, 1995—. Editor Conn. Bar Jour., 1976-82. Mem. Rep. Town Meeting, Greenwich, Conn., 1969-73; mem. Inland Wetlands and Water Courses Agy., Greenwich, 1973-80; bd. dirs. YMCA, Stamford, Conn., 1982-84. Mem. Conn. Bar Assn., Am. Coll. Trial Lawyers, Am. Bd. Trial Advocates (assoc.). Roman Catholic. Clubs: Greenwich Country, Indian Harbor Yacht (Greenwich, Conn.). Federal civil litigation, State civil litigation. Office: Fogarty Cohen Selby & Nemiroff LLC 88 Field Point Rd Greenwich CT 06830-6468

FOGEL, RICHARD, lawyer, educator; m. Sheila Feldman; children: Bruce, Lori Ellen. BA, York Coll., CUNY, 1971; JD, N.Y. Law Sch., 1974. Bar: N.J. 1976, U.S. Dist. Ct. N.J. 1976, N.Y. 1981, U.S. Dist. Ct. (so. dist.) N.Y. 2000, U.S. Tax. Ct. 1977. Tax law specialist IRS, Newark, 1975-77; sr. pension cons., atty. N.Y. Life, N.Y.C., 1977-81; pvt. practice Franklin, N.J., 1981-85, Wayne, 1985-88, McAfee, 1988—. Lectr. Inst. for Continuing Legal Edn., Newark, 1977—; mem. adj. faculty Upsala Coll., East Orange, N.J., 1978-88; presenter 34th ann. meeting. Internat. Soc. for Systems Scis., Portland State U., 1990. Recipient Certs. of Appreciation, IRS, Newark, 1977, Inst. Continuing Legal Edn., Newark, 1981-82, 84, Cert. in Recognition of Accomplishments, Coop. Extension Cook Coll., Rutgers U., 1982, Disting. Grad. award York Coll., 1984, Founder's Day Dist. Alumni award, 1992. Estate planning, Pension, profit-sharing, and employee benefits, Real property. Home: 28 Elizabeth Dr Sussex NJ 07461-3402 Office: Vernon Colonial Pla PO Box 737 Rt 94 Mc Afee NJ 07428

FOGELMAN, MARTIN, lawyer, law educator; b. N.Y.C., Mar. 16, 1928; s. Herman and Fanny (Abramowitz) F.; m. Suzanne Stern, Dec. 21, 1952; children: Henry Jonathan, Jeffrey Scott, Martin, Jr., Douglas Edmund. AB cum laude, Syracuse U., 1948, JD magna cum laude, 1950. Bar: N.Y. 1950, U.S. Dist. Ct. (no. dist.) N.Y. 1953, U.S. Supreme Ct. 1956, U.S. Dist. Ct. (so. dist.) N.Y. 1957, U.S. Dist. Ct. (ea. dist.) N.Y. 1958. Confidential law clk. to chief judge N.Y. Ct. Appeals, Albany, 1950-54; assoc. Saxe, Bacon, O'Shea & Bryan, N.Y.C., 1955-58; adj. prof. Fordham Law Sch., 1956-58, prof. law, 1958-62, Arthur A. McGivney prof. law, 1982—. Pres. univ. senate, 1980-83, chmn. athletic bd., 1980-93, bd. dirs. Univ. Press, 1978—, chmn. 1987—, also mem. univ. trustees acad. affairs com.; arbitrator Nat. Assn. Security Dealers, 1981—, Chgo. Bd. Trade, 1986—; mem. complaint mediation panel appellate div., 1st dept. N.Y. Supreme Ct. Co-author: Cases and Materials on Mortgages, 1963; author: West's Forms and Text, New York Business Corporation Law, 1965, 2d edit., 1984 and ann. supplements; West's Forms and Text, New York Not-For-Profit Corporation Law, 1972, 2nd edit., 1990, and ann. supplements. Mem. ABA, N.Y. State Bar Assn., Assn. of Bar of City of N.Y. (com. on profl. discipline), Assn. Trial Lawyers Am., N.Y. State Trial Lawyers Assn., Assn. Am. Law Schs. (ho. of dels. 1969-91), Phi Delta Phi. Home: 21 Brookside Dr Huntington NY 11743-2642 Office: Fordham U Sch Law 140 W 62nd St New York NY 10023-7407

FOGGAN, LAURA ANNE, lawyer; b. Lake Forest, Ill., Sept. 21, 1958; d. John and Sherry Hope West F. BA, MSEd, U. Pa., 1980; JD, George Washington U., 1983. Bar: D.C. 1983, U.S. Supreme Ct. 1987. Assoc. Wald, Harkrader & Ross, Washington, 1983-85, Piper & Marbury, Washington, 1985-87; ptnr. Wiley, Rein & Fielding, 1988—. Bd. dirs. Aynda, Washington, 1994-2000. Contbr. articles to profl. jours. Named Vol. of Yr. Women's Legal Def. Fund, 1990, Top 100 Women Bus. Ins. Mag., 2000; recipient Hugh Johnson , Jr. award, AYUDA, 1993, pro bono award DC Coalition Against Domestic Violence, 1988. Mem. ABA (mem. ins. litigation issues, subcom. chair), Women's Bar Assn., Def. Rsch. Inst. Appellate, General civil litigation, Insurance. Office: Wiley Rein & Fielding 1776 K St NW Washington DC 20006

FOHRMAN, BURTON H. lawyer; b. Chgo., July 9, 1939; s. Max and Helen (Naparty) F.; m. Raleigh S. Newman, Dec. 12, 1975. AB cum laude, U. So. Calif., Los Angeles, 1960; JD, UCLA, 1963. Bar: Calif. 1964. Pvt. practice, Riverside, Calif., 1964-66; mng. ptnr. Redwine and Sherrill, 1966-83; ptnr. Jones, Day, Reavis and Pogue, L.A., 1983-92, former chmn. gen. real estate sect.; ptnr. White & Case, 1992—. Editor Calif. Real Property Jour., 1978-83. Mem. State Bar Calif. (chmn. real property sect. 1983), Los Angeles County Bar Assn. (chmn. real property fin. com. 1979-80, exec. com. real property sect. 1980-83), Daini Bar Assn. Office: 1-19-1 Kanda-Nishikicho Chiyoda-ku Tokyo 101-0054 Japan E-mail: bfohrman@whitecase.com

FOLBERG, HAROLD JAY, lawyer, mediator, educator, university dean; b. East St. Louis, Ill., July 7, 1941; s. Louis and Matilda (Ross) F.; m. Diana L. Taylor, May 1, 1983; children: Lisa, Rachel, Ross. BA, San Francisco State U., 1963; JD, U. Calif., Berkeley, 1968. Bar: Oreg. 1968. Assoc. Rives & Schwab, Portland, Oreg., 1968-69; dir. Legal Aid Service, 1970-72; exec. dir. Assn. Family and Conciliation Cts., 1974-80; prof. law Lewis and Clark Law Sch., 1972-89; clin. asst. prof. child psychiatry U. Oreg. Med. Sch., 1976-89; judge pro-tem Oreg. Trial Cts., 1974-89; dean, prof. U. San Francisco Sch. Law, 1989-99, prof. law, 1999—. Chair jud. coun. Calif. Task Force on Alternative Dispute Resolution and the Jud. Sys., 1998-99; Rockefeller Found. scholar in residence Bellagio, Italy, 1996; vis. prof. U. Wash. Sch. Law, 1985-86; mem. vis. faculty Nat. Jud. Coll., 1975-88; mem. Nat. Commn. on Accreditation for Marriage and Family Therapists, 1984-90; cons. Calif. Jud. Coun., U.S. Dist. Ct. (no. dist.) Calif. Author: Joint Custody and Shared Parenting, 1984, 2d edit., 1991; (with Taylor) Mediation-A Comprehensive Guide to Resolving Conflicts without Litigation, 1984; (with Milne) Divorce Mediation-Theory and Practice, 1988; mem. editorial bd.Family Counts Rev., Jour. of Divorce, Conflict Resolution Quar.; contbr. articles to profl. jours. Bd. dirs. Internat. Bioethics Inst., 1989-95, Oreg. Dispute Resolution Adv. Coun., 1988-89. Mem. ABA (chmn. mediation and arbitration com. family law sect. 1980-82), Oreg. State Bar Assn. (chmn. family and juvenile law sect. 1979-80), Am. Bd. Trial Advs., Multnomah Bar Assn. (chmn. bd. dirs. legal aid svc. 1973-76), Am. Arbitration Assn. (mem. panel of arbitrators), Internat. Soc. Family Law, Assn. Family and Conciliation Cts. (pres. 1983-84), Assn. Marriage and Family Therapists (disting. mem.), Am. Assn. Law Schs. (chmn. alternative dispute resolution sect. 1988), Acad. Family Mediators (bd. dirs., pres. 1988), Assn. Conflict Resolution, World Assn. Law Profs. (sec.-gen. 1995-2000). Office: U San Francisco Sch Law 2130 Fulton St San Francisco CA 94117-1080 E-mail: folbergj@usfca.edu

FOLEY, JOHN FRANCIS, retired judge, lawyer; b. Detroit, Feb. 10, 1928; s. Henry Michael and Rosemary (O'Neill) F.; m. Joan Marlow, Aug. 17, 1957; children: Sean, Patrick, Rosemary, Joan, Margaret, Ella. BS, Georgetown U., 1948; JD, U. Mich., 1957. Bar: Mich. 1957, U.S. Dist. Ct. (ea. dist.) Mich. 1961, U.S. Dist. Ct. (we. dist.) Mich. 1969, U.S. Ct. Appeals (6th cir.) 1983. Assoc. firm Wilson, Ingraham and Kavanagh, Birmingham, Mich., 1957-59; atty. NLRB, Detroit, 1959-61; ptnr. firm Swartz, O'Hare, Sharples & Foley, 1961-66, Gergely & Foley, P.C., Vicksburg , 1969-85; judge Kalamazoo County Cir. Ct., 1985-98; ret. Commr. Mich. Ct. Appeals, Lansing, 1966-68. Mem. Dem. Exec. Com., Oakland City, Mich., 1961-64, Kalamazoo, 1980; bd. dirs. Kalamazoo ACLU, 1971-83. Lt. (j.g.) USN, 1951-55. Mem. ABA, Mich. Bar Assn., Kalamazoo County Bar Assn. Alternative dispute resolution. Home: 2846 W Y Z Ave Schoolcraft MI 49087-9744

FOLEY, RION DUBOSE, tax lawyer; b. Durham, N.C., Apr. 7, 1970; s. David Michael Floey and Kay Doran Clamp. BS in Econs., U. S.C., 1994, JD, 1997; LLM in Tax Law, NYU, 1998. Bar: S.C. Assoc. McNair Law Firm, P.A., Charleston, S.C., 1998—. Ind. Ins. Agt.'s scholar, 1993, Towne Meml. scholar, 1994. Mem. ABA, S.C. Bar Assn. (tax and estate planning sect.), Golden Key Nat. Honor Soc., Omicron Delta Epsilon. Corporate taxation, Estate taxation, Taxation, general. Office: McNair Law Firm PO Box 1431 Charleston SC 29402-1431

FOLEY, THOMAS JOHN, lawyer; b. Detroit, July 3, 1954; s. Thomas John and Mary Catherine (Gluekert) F.; m. Virginia Lee, Aug. 20, 1977; 1 child, Kaitlin Shea. BA, Mich. State U., 1976, JD, 1979. Bar: Mich. 1980, Ohio 1992, U.S. Dist. Ct. (ea. and we. dists.) Mich. 1980, U.S.Ct. Appeals (6th cir.) 1980. Assoc. Kitch, Drutchas, Wagner, Denardis & Valitutti, Detroit, 1980-84, assoc. prin., 1984-87, prin., shareholder, 1987—. Contbr. articles to profl. jours. Mem. FBA, Internat. Assn. Def. Counsel, Def. Rsch. Inst., Food and Drug Law Inst., Greater Detroit C. of C. Avocations: swimming, private pilot. General civil litigation, Personal injury, Product liability. Office: Kitch Drutchas et al 1 Woodward Ave Fl 10 Detroit MI 48226-3402 E-mail: folet1@kitch.com

FOLLICK, EDWIN DUANE, law educator, chiropractic physician; b. Glendale, Calif., Feb. 4, 1935; s. Edwin Fulfford and Esther Agnes (Catherwood) F.; m. Marilyn K. Sherk, Mar. 24, 1986 BA, Calif. State U., L.A., 1956, MA, 1961, Pepperdine U., 1957, MPA, 1977; PhD, DTh, St. Andrews Theol. Coll., Sem. of Free Prot. Episc. Ch., London, 1958; MS in Libr. Sci., U. So. Calif., 1963, MEd in Instructional Materials, 1964, AdvMEd in Edn. Adminstrn., 1969; postgrad., Calif. Coll. Law, 1965; LLB, Blackstone Law Sch., 1966, JD, 1967; DC, Cleve. Chiropractic Coll., L.A., 1972; PhD, Academia Theatina, Pescara, 1978; MA in Organizational Mgmt., Antioch U., L.A., 1990. Tchr., libr. adminstr. L.A. City Schs., 1957-68; law librarian Glendale U. Coll. Law, 1968-69; coll. librarian Cleve. Chiropractic Coll., L.A., 1969-74, dir. edn. and admissions, 1974-84, prof. jurisprudence, 1975—, dean student affairs, 1976-92, chaplain, 1985—, dean of edn., 1989—; assoc. prof. Newport U., 1982; extern prof. St. Andrews Theol. Coll., London, 1961; dir. West Valley Chiropractic Health Ctr., 1972-2000, West Valley Chiropractic Consulting, 2001—. Contbr. articles to profl. jours. Chaplain's asst. U.S. Army, 1958-60. Decorated cavaliere Internat. Order Legion of Honor of Immaculata (Italy); Knight of Malta, Sovereign Order of St. John of Jerusalem; Knight Grand Prelate, comdr. with star, Order of Signum Fidei; comdr. chevalier Byzantine Imperial Order of Constantine the Gt.; comdr. ritter Order St. Gereon; chevalier Mil. and Hospitaller Order of St. Lazarus of Jerusalem (Malta); numerous others. Mem. ALA, NEA, Am. Assn. Sch. Librarians, L.A. Sch. Libr. Assn., Calif. Sch. Libr. Assn., Assn. Coll. and Rsch. Librarians, Am. Assn. Law Librarians, Am. Chiropractic Assn., Internat. Chiropractors Assn., Nat. Geog. Soc., Internat. Platform Assn., Phi Delta Kappa, Sigma Chi Psi, Delta Tau Alpha. Democrat. Episcopalian. Home: 6435 Jumilla Ave Woodland Hills CA 91367-2833 Office: 590 N Vermont Ave Los Angeles CA 90004-2115 also: 7022 Owensmouth Ave Canoga Park CA 91303-2005 E-mail: follicke@cleveland.edu

FONG, PETER C. K. lawyer, judge, company executive; b. Honolulu, Oct. 28, 1955; s. Arthur S.K. and Victoria K.Y. (Chun) F. BBA with honors, U. Hawaii, 1977; JD, Boston Coll., 1980. Bar: Hawaii 1980, U.S. Dist. Ct. Hawaii 1980, U.S. Ct. Appeals (9th cir.) 1980, U.S. Supreme Ct. 1983. Law clk. to presiding justice Supreme Ct. Hawaii, Honolulu, 1980-81; dep. pros. atty. Pros. Atty.'s Office, 1981-84; with Davis, Reid & Richards, 1984-89; chief legal counsel, chief clk. Senate jud. com. Hawaii State Legislature, 1989—; judge per diem Dist./Family Ct., Hawaii, 1989—; ptnr. Hong, Kwock & Fong, Honolulu, 1990-91, Fong & Fong, Honolulu, 1989—; pres., CEO, dir. Chun Kim Chow, Ltd., 1998—. Gen. legal counsel Hawaii Jr. C. of C., 1983-84; pres., bd. dirs. Legal Aid Soc. Hawaii, 1984-90; pres., 1986-87; arbitrator Hawaiian Cir. Ct., 1986—, Am. Arbitration Assn., 1989—; mediator Arbitration Forums, Inc., 1989—. Editorial staff Boston Coll. Internat. and Comp. Law Rev., 1978-80. Mem. City and County Honolulu Neighborhood Bd., 1981-83; campaign treas. for Hawaii state senator, 1981-89; mem. aux. admissions com. Boston Coll. Law Sch., 1982—, major gifts com. and sustaining membership fundraising drive com. YMCA, 1988; del. Gov.'s Congress on Hawaii's internat. role, 1988; del. Hawaii Jud. Forsight Congress, 1991; mem. hearings com. Hawaii State Atty.'s Disciplinary Bd., 1991—. Recipient Pres.'s award Hawaii Jr. C. of C., 1984; named one of ten Outstanding Persons of Hawaii, 1990, 92. Mem. ABA, ATLA, Hawaii State Bar Assn. (co-chmn. and vice-chmn., jud. salary com., mem. legis. com., coord. legis. resource bank, mem. task force on disciplinary counsel), Hawaii Developer's Coun., Am. Judicature Soc., Hawaii Supreme Ct. Hist. Soc., Hawaii Trial Judges Assn., Nat. Coun. Juvenile and Family Ct. Judges, Rsch. Bd. of Advisors, Nat. Assn. Dist. Attys., U.S. Supreme Ct. Hist. Soc., Mortar Bd., Tu Chiang Shen (past pres.), Waialae Country Club. General civil litigation, General practice, Insurance. Home: 5255 Makalena St Honolulu HI 96821-1808 Office: Fong & Fong Grosvener Ctr Makai Tower 733 Bishop St Ste 1550 Honolulu HI 96813-4003

FONG, PHYLLIS KAMOI, lawyer; b. Phila., Oct. 16, 1953; d. Bernard W.D. and Roberta (Wat) F.; m. Paul E. Tellier, Nov. 25, 1978. BA, Pomona Coll., 1975; JD, Vanderbilt U., 1978. Bar: Tenn. 1978, D.C. 1982. Atty. U.S. Commn. on Civil Rights, Washington, 1978-81; asst. gen. counsel Legal Svcs. Corp., 1981-83; assoc. counsel to the insp. gen. Office of Insp. Gen, U.S. Small Bus. Adminstrn., 1983-88, asst. insp. gen. for mgmt. and policy, 1988-94, asst. insp. gen. for mgmt. and legal counsel, 1994-99, insp. gen., 1999—. Mem. ABA, Tenn. Bar Assn., D.C. Bar Assn. Office: 409 3rd St SW Ste 7100 Washington DC 20024-3212

FONTES, J. MARIO F., JR. lawyer; b. São Paulo, Brazil, Jan. 17, 1964; m. Gladys Fontes, Jan. 7, 1995. BA cum laude in Econs. and Internat. Studies, Am. U., Washington, 1987; JD, Cath. U., Washington, 1992. Bar: Pa. 1993, Fla. 1995, U.S. Ct. Claims 1993, U.S. Ct. Internat. Trade 1993. Assoc. Porter, Wright, Morris & Arthur, Washington, 1992-93, Hughes Hubbard & Reed, Miami, Fla., 1993-96, Baker & McKenzie, Miami, 1996-2000, ptnr., 2000—. Mem. ABA, Brazilian-Am. Chamber (mem. program com. 1994-95), Phi Kappa Phi. General corporate, Private international, Securities. Office: Baker & McKenzie 1200 Brickell Ave Miami FL 33131-3214

FONVIELLE, CHARLES DAVID, lawyer; b. Melbourne, Fla., Dec. 28, 1944; s. Charles David Fonvielle Jr. and Margaret Jordan Palmer; m. Deborah Konas, July 25, 1970; children: C. Caulley, D. Jordan. BA, U. Fla., 1968; JD, Fla. State U., 1972. Bar: Fla. 1972, U.S. Dist. Ct. (no., mid. and so. dists.) Fla. Asst. pub. defender Fla. Pub. Defender Assn., Tallahassee, 1972-74; pvt. practice, 1974-77; ptnr. Thompson, Wadsworth, Messer, Turner & Rhodes, 1977-80, Green & Fonvielle, Tallahassee, 1980-84, Green, Fonvielle & Hinkle, Tallahassee, 1984-85, Fonvielle Hinkle & Lewis, Tallahassee, 1985—. Bd. dirs. Fla. State U. Coll. Law, endowed prof. litigation. Mem. ALTA (sustaining), Tallahassee Bar Assn. (bd. dirs. 1978-79), Acad. Fla. Trial Lawyers (Eagle sponsor 1990—), Nat. Bd. Trial Advocacy (cert.), Fla. Bar Assn. (bd. legal specialization and edn. 1991—), Fla. State U. Pres.'s Club (bd. visitors). Avocations: physical fitness, flying, spearfishing, sports cars. Personal injury, Product liability, Professional liability. Office: Fonvielle Hinkle & Lewis 3375 Capital Cir NE Ste A Tallahassee FL 32308-3778 E-mail: david@fonhink.com

FOOTE, RICHARD CHARLES, lawyer; b. July 4, 1951; s. George Harry and Arlene Marie Foote; 1 child Elizabeth Ann. BA, Harvard U., 1973; JD, Case Western Reserve U., 1976. Bar: Ohio 1976, U.S. dist. Ct. (no. dist.) Ohio 1976, U.S. Ct. Appeals (6th cir.) 1982. Ptnr. Law Offices of Mark L. Hoffman and Richard C. Foote, Shaker Heights, Ohio, 1983—. Mem.: Cuyahoga County Bar Assn., Bar Assn. Greater Cleve. Methodist. Bankruptcy, Probate. Office: Ohio Savs Bldg 20133 Farnsleigh Rd Cleveland OH 44122-3613

FOOTE, RICHARD VAN, lawyer; b. Feb. 5, 1930; s. Ernest Edward and Luva Gladys Foote; m. Lois Earlene Moore, Jan. 28, 1956; children: John Kevin, Christopher Lee. BS in Bus., Wichita State U., 1955; LLB, Washburn U., Topeka, 1958. Bar: Kans. 1958, U.S. Dist. Ct. Kans. 1958, U.S. Ct. Appeals (10th cir.) 1966. IBM operator Wichita, Kans., 1954—55, Kans. State Treasury, Topeka, 1955—57; law clk. Glen Cogswell, 1957—58; sole practice Wichita, 1958—64; ptnr. Matlack & Foote, 1965—95. Dir. Bank Whitewater; Kans. bd. dir. Wichita Area Builders Assn., 1970—72. Sgt. USMC, 1951—54. Mem.: ABA, Kans. Bar Assn., Wichita Bar Assn. Republican. Episcopalian. Banking, Contracts commercial, Real property. Home: 7506 Norfolk Cir Wichita KS 67206-2108

FORBES, ARTHUR LEE, III, lawyer; b. Houston, Sept. 3, 1928; s. Arthur Lee Jr. and Corinne (Mayfield) F.; m. Nita R. Harrison, Mar. 25, 1957; children: Dana, Tricia, Kim, Arthur Lee. BSCE, U. Tex., Austin, 1952; JD, So. Tex. Coll. Law, 1959. Bar: Tex. 1959, U.S. Ct. Appeals (5th cir.) 1960, U.S. Supreme Ct. 1967. Ptnr. Lee & Forbes, Houston, 1960-73, Shapiro, Forbes & Cox, Houston, 1974-88; gen. counsel Bay Houston Towing Co., 1989—. Lt. USMC, 1952-54. Mem. ABA, Tex. Bar Assn., Houston Bar Assn., Assn. Trial Lawyers Am., Houston Racquet Club, Sigma Chi, Phi Delta Phi. Unitarian. General corporate, Environmental, General practice. Home: 5 Leisure Ln Houston TX 77024-5123 E-mail: artf165@earthlink.net

FORBES, FRANKLIN SIM, lawyer, educator; b. Kingsport, Tenn., Sept. 21, 1936; s. Harvey Sim and Virginia Smith (Pooler) F.; m. Suzanne Marie Willard, June 30, 1962; children— Franklin Sim, Anne Marie. BA, U. Hawaii, 1959; JD, U. Iowa, 1963. Bar: Hawaii 1963, Nebr. 1964. Law clk. Hawaii Supreme Ct., 1963; mem. faculty U. Nebr. Coll. Bus. Adminstrn., Omaha, 1965—, prof. law, 1965—, chmn. dept. law and society, 1970-97, acting chmn. dept. profl. acctg., 1986-87, Peter Keweit disting. prof. law, 1987-93; pvt. practice, 1964—. Author: Going Into Business in Nebraska: The Legal Aspects, 1983, Instructor's Resource Guide-Business Law, 1983-88, Starting and Operating a Business in Nebraska, 1995, Debtors and Creditors Rights, 1988, Legal Environment of Telemarketing, 1991; contbr. articles to legal pubs. Mem. integration com. Omaha Sch. Bd., 1974; mem. St. James Bd. Edn., Omaha, 1974; pres. parish coun. St. James Roman Cath. Ch., 1975, St. Elizabeth Ann Ch., 1983-84, 90-91. Recipient Real Dean award U. Hawaii, 1959, Gt. Tchr. award U. Nebr., 1978, 81, Chancellor's medal U. Nebr., 1977, Outstanding Achievement award U. Nebr. Coll. Bus. Adminstrn., 1983, 84, 85, 87, 88; Rotary Found. grantee Australia, 1972 Mem. ABA, Am. Arbitration Assn., Am. Judicature Soc., Midwest Bus. Adminstrs. Assn., Midwest Bus. Law Assn. (pres. 1975), Nebr. Bar Assn., Omaha Bar Assn. (del. conf. Future Law 1979), Hawaii Bar Assn., Nat. Golden Key Soc., Alpha Phi Omega, Phi Alpha Delta, Beta Gamma Sigma, Phi Theta Chi. Democrat. Club: Rotary. Office: Univ Nebr Coll Bus Adminstrn Omaha NE 68182-0001

FORBES, MORTON GERALD, lawyer; b. Atlanta, July 12, 1938; s. Arthur Mark and Mary Dean (Power) F.; m. Eunice Lee Haynesworth, Jan. 25, 1963; children: John, Ashley, Sarah. AB, Wofford Coll., 1962; JD, U. Ga., 1965. Bar: Ga. 1965, U.s. Dist. Ct. (mid. dist.) Ga. 1965, U.S. Dist. Ct. (so. dist.) Ga. 1968, U.S. Dist. Ct. (no. dist.) Ga. 1993, U.S. Ct. Appeals (5th cir.) 1974, U.S. Ct. Appeals (4th cir.) 1972, U.S. Ct. Appeals (11th cir.) 1981. Assoc. Pierce, Ranitz, Lee, Berry & Mahoney, 1967-70; ptnr. Pierce, Ranitz, Berry, Mahoney & Forbes, 1970-76, Pierce, Ranitz, Mahoney, Forbes & Coolidge, 1976-81; ptnr., sec. Ranitz, Mahoney, Forbes & Coolidge, P.C., 1981-91, Forbes & Bowman, Savannah, Ga., 1991—. Gen. counsel Ga. Fed. Young Rep. Clubs, 1971-72; guest lectr. dept. dental hygiene Armstrong State Coll., 1970-72. Mem. Savannah Armstrong State Coll., 1973—, chmn., 1979-81; mem. Chatham County Devel. Authority, 1973-80; mem. nat. com. Nat. Fedn. Young Reps., 1973; mem. econ. adv. coun. Coastal Area Planning and Devel. Authority, 1980—; bd. dirs. Savannah Symphony Soc., 1971-75; Ga. del. to Japan/Southeast Trade Mission, Kyoto, Japan, 1983, S.E. Asia U.S.A./Japan Assn. meeting, Birmingham, Ala., 1984. Served with USN, 1965-67. Recipient Outstanding Service award Savannah Port Authority, 1981. Mem. ABA, Internat. Assn. Defense Counsel, State Bar Ga., Am. Judicature Soc., Nat. Assn. Bond Counsel, Ga. Def. Lawyers Assn. (v.p. 1987—, mem. exec. com. 1988, bd. dirs., exec. v.p. 1990-91, pres. 1991-92), Savannah Bar Assn. (exec. com. 1989-94, pres. 1992-93), Libel Def. Resource Ctr., Def. Rsch. Inst. (state chmn. 1992-99, bd. dirs. 1999-2002), Savannah Econ. Devel. Action Coun. (founding), Savannah Area Wofford Coll. Alumni Club (past pres.), Soc. of the Cincinnati (Va.), St. Andrews Soc., Soc. Colonial Wars, Sons of Revolution (sec. 1988-92), Chatham Club, Savannah Yacht Club, 1st City Club, The Landings Club. Republican. Presbyterian. Federal civil litigation, Insurance, Product liability. Office: Forbes & Bowman PO Box 13929 Savannah GA 31416-0929

FORD, ASHLEY LLOYD, lawyer, retired consumer products company executive; b. Cin., Mar. 10, 1939; s. Starr MacLeod and Mary Lloyd (Mills) F.; m. Barbara Hill, Apr. 23, 1965; children: Christopher Ashley, Elizabeth Hill. AB, Princeton U., 1960; JD, Yale U., 1963. Bar: Ohio 1963. Assoc. Dinsmore & Shohl, Cin., 1965-69; counsel Procter & Gamble Co., 1969-71, divsn. counsel, 1971-89, sec., 1979-94; ret., 1994. Shareholder Cin. Mus. Assn.; dir. Hist. S.W. Ohio; mem. Cin. History Mus. Adv. Bd. Lt. USNR, 1966-72. Mem. Soc. Col. Wars, Cin. Country Club, Queen City Club, Univ. Club, Sailfish Pt. Country Club, Order of Coif, Phi Beta Kappa. Episcopalian. Antitrust, General corporate.

FORD, DIANE, lawyer; b. Salem, Ill., Mar. 2, 1953; d. Robert Edwin and Mary Evelyn Ford; m. Zack Stamp, Oct. 23, 1983; children: Perry Ford Stamp, Nathan Ford Stamp. BA, Eastern Ill. U., 1975; JD, U. Ill., 1979. Bar: Ill. 1979. Legal counsel Ill. State Senate Republicans, Springfield, 1979-87, Gov. of Ill., Springfield, 1987-95; chief counsel Ill. Sec. of State, 1995-99, Gov. of Ill., Springfield, 1999—. Republican. Methodist. Office: Chief Counsel to Gov 204 State House Springfield IL 62706-0001 E-mail: diane_ford@gov.state.il.us

FORD, MICHAEL W. lawyer; b. Peoria, Ill., Dec. 9, 1938; s. Benjamin W. and Charlene (Oder) F.; m. Kristine L. Ford; children from a previous marriage: Sarah, Scott, Amy, Michael B. BA, U. Chgo., 1960; JD, Loyola U., 1965. Bar: Ill. 1965, Tex. 1997, U.S. Dist. Ct. (no. dist.) Ill. 1965, U.S. Dist. Ct. (ea. dist.) Wis. 1974, U.S. Dist. Ct. (mid. dist.) Ill. 1986, U.S. Dist. Ct. Nebr. 1987, U.S. Dist. Ct. (so. dist.) Tex. 1999, U.S. Ct. Appeals (7th cir.) 1965, U.S. Ct. Appeals (3d cir.) 1988, U.S. Ct. Appeals (6th dist.) 1989, U.S. Ct. Appeals (5th cir.) 1999, U.S. Supreme Ct. 1977. Mng. ptnr., sr. ptnr. in charge of gen. and corp. litigation Chapman and Cutler, Chgo., 1965-96; of counsel Jones, Day, Reavis & Pogue, Houston, 1996—. Contbr. numerous articles to profl. jours.; spkr. many seminars for legal or ednl. groups. Mem. nominating com. Riverwoods, Ill. Caucus, 1992-93. Mem. ABA (mem. trial evidence com. and other coms.), Tex. Bar Assn. General civil litigation, Environmental, Toxic tort. Home: 4 Timberwood Ln Riverwoods IL 60015-2400 Fax: (713) 223-0042

FORD, ROBERT DAVID, lawyer; b. New Orleans, Oct. 30, 1956; s. Thomas Paul and Inez Mary (Rodriguez) F.; m. Jean Ann Burg, May 5, 1979; children: Robert David Jr., Charlene Elizabeth, Timothy Michael. BA, U. New Orleans, 1978; JD, Loyola U., 1983. Bar: La. 1983, U.S. Dist. Ct. (ea. dist.) La. 1983, U.S. Dist. Ct. (mid. dist.) La. 1997, U.S. Ct. Appeals (5th cir.) 1985. Claims rep. State Farm Mut. Auto Ins. Co., Metairie, La., 1978-80; assoc. Hammett, Leake & Hammett, New Orleans, 1983-86; ptnr. Thomas, Hayes, Beahm & Buckley, 1986-95; mem. Chehardy, Sherman, Ellis, Breslin & Murray, Metairie, La., 1995-96; ptnr. Hailey, McNamara, Hall, Larmann & Papale, 1996—. Mem. ABA (coms. on health law, profl. liability and products liability litigation 1992, subcoms. on hosp. and clinic med. devices and med. malpractice liability 1992), La. Bar Assn., La. Assn. Def. Counsel, Am. Soc. Law and Medicine, La. Soc. Hosp. Attys. of La. Hosp. Assn., Def. Rsch. Inst., Phi Kappa Theta, Pi Alpha Delta. Republican. Roman Catholic. Avocations: golf, softball. Health, Insurance, Product liability. Home: 8 Caney Ct Kenner LA 70065-3944 Office: Hailey McNamara Hall Larmann & Papale 1 Galleria Blvd Ste 1400 Metairie LA 70001-7543 E-mail: rford@hmhlp.com

FOREMAN, EDWARD RAWSON, retired lawyer; b. Atlanta, May 15, 1939; s. Robert Langdon and Mary (Shedden) F.; m. Margaret Reeves, Oct. 19, 1968; children: Margaret Langdon, Mary Rawson BA, Washington & Lee U., 1962; JD, Emory U., 1965. Bar: Ga. 1965. Assoc. Jones, Bird & Howell, Atlanta, 1965-70, ptnr., 1970-82, Alston & Bird, Atlanta, 1982-99; ret., 1999. Chmn. McAliley Endowment Trust, 1978—; lectr. Inst. for Continuing Legal Edn. in Ga., 1989; panelist, moderator Bus. Atlanta's Office Leasing and Tenant Opportunities in 1990s. Bd. editors Comml. Leasing Law and Strategy, 1996—. Bd. dirs. Ansley Park Beautification Found., Atlanta, 1984—; bd. dirs. Midtown Alliance, Atlanta, 1988-96, sec., chmn. fundraising com., 1989-91, v.p., 1991, pres., 1992; trustee Paidela Sch. Endowment Fund, Atlanta, 1980—, Woodruff Arts Ctr., Atlanta, 1985-90; chmn. Emory U. Law Fund, Atlanta, 1981; chmn. legal divsn. United Way Met. Atlanta, 1984; chmn. strategic planning com. High Mus. Art, 1986-95, chmn., bd. dirs. 1998—, chmn. nominating com., 1993-95; vestryman, sr. warden St. Luke's Episc. Ch., 1975, 94, 2001, mem. com., 1975—; pres. Atlanta Legal Aid Soc., 1975-76, Atlanta Preservation Ctr., 1986-91; trustee Miss Hall's Sch., Pittsfield, Mass., 1990-2001. Recipient Cmty. Svc. award Martin Luther King Jr. Ctr. Nonviolent Social Change, 1980, Outstanding Svc. award Atlanta Preservation Ctr., Inc., 1983. Mem. ABA (mem. comml. leasing com. 1987—), State Bar Ga. (chmn., panelist, moderator comml. leasing seminars 1979-86), Atlanta Bar Assn. (chmn., panelist, moderator leasing seminars 1979-86, chmn. hdqrs. search com. 1988-96), Lawyers Club Atlanta (chmn. long-range planning com. 1989-90), Atlanta Bar Found. (bd. dirs.), Old War Horse Lawyers Club, Nine O'Clocks Club (mem. centennial com. 1983), Highlands Country Club N.C. Democrat. Episcopalian. Landlord-tenant, Real property. Home: 238 15th St NE House 16 Atlanta GA 30309-3594 Office: Alston & Bird One Atlantic Ctr 1201 W Peachtree St NW Ste 4000 Atlanta GA 30309-3424 E-mail: mccoy10@mindspring.com

FOREMAN, JAMES LOUIS, retired judge; b. Metropolis, Ill., May 12, 1927; s. James C. and Anna Elizabeth (Henne) F.; m. Mabel Inez Dunn, June 16, 1948; children: Beth Foreman Banks, Rhonda Foreman Wittig, Nanette Foreman Love. BS in Commerce and Law, U. Ill., 1950, JD, 1952. Bar: Ill. Ind. practice law, Metropolis, Ill.; ptnr. Chase and Foreman, until 1972; state's atty. State of Ill., Massac County, asst. atty. gen.; chief judge U.S. Dist. Ct. (so. dist.) Ill., Benton, 1979-92, sr. status, 1992—. Pres. Bd. of Edn., Metropolis. With USN, 1945-46. Mem. Ill. State Bar Assn., Metropolic C. of C. (past pres.). Republican. Home: 38 Hilanoa-East Dr Metropolis IL 62960-2533 Office: US Dist Ct 301 W Main St Benton IL 62812-1362

FOREMAN, MICHAEL LOREN, lawyer; b. Sarasota, Fla., Mar. 13, 1944; s. Alexander Maynard and Edith Frances (Beck) F.; m. Alice Lynne Rodgers, Aug. 31, 1969; children: Laurie Kay, Gregory Michael. BSBA, U. Fla., 1966, JD, 1969. Bar: Fla. 1969, U.S. Dist. Ct. (mid. dist.) Fla. 1973, U.S. Ct. Appeals (5th and 11th cirs.) 1983. Assoc. Icard, Merrill, Cullis, Timm, Furen & Ginsburg, PA, Sarasota, 1969-78, sr. ptnr., 1978—. Contbr. articles to law revs. Bd. dirs. Big Bros./Big Sisters Found. of Sarasota, 1984-93, Fame Charities Inc., Sarasota. Mem. Fla. Bar (realtor-atty. jt. com. 1978088, cir. rep. real property, probate and trust law sect. 1980-93, econs. of law practice sect. 1980-83, vice chmn. guardianship law com. 1990-91, chmn. 1992-97, chmn. guardianship law and durable powers of atty. com., 1992-2001, Real Property, Probate and Trust Law Sec. Ann. Svc. award 1995), Sarasota Countly Bar Assn. (econs. law practice sect. 1980-93, treas. 1981-84, v.p. 1984-85, pres. 1986-87), Kiwanis of Sarasota-Sunrise (pres. 1984). Contracts commercial, Probate, Real property. Home: 4917 Leatha Ln Sarasota FL 34232-2651 Office: Icard Merrill Cullis Timm Furen & Ginsburg PA 2033 Main St Ste 600 Sarasota FL 34237-6056 E-mail: mforeman@icardmerrill.com

FORESTER, JOHN GORDON, JR. lawyer; b. Wilkesboro, N.C., Jan. 14, 1933; s. John Gordon and Mary Hope (Hendren) F.; m. Georgina Ramirez, June 26, 1957; children: John Gordon III, Robert Raoul, Georgina Yasué, Richard Alexander. B.S.; in Indsl. Relations, U. N.C., 1955; LL.B., George Washington U., 1962. Bar: D.C. 1962, Md. 1993. Internat. economist Dept. Commerce, 1958-62; confidential asst. to dep. asst. sec. commerce, 1962-63; law clk. to U.S. Dist. Judge L.P. Walsh, 1963-64; pvt. practice Washington, 1964-80; ptnr. Pohoryles & Greenstein, P.C., 1980-89, Greenstein Delorme & Luchs, P.C., Washington, 1989-95; pvt. practice, 1995—. Mem. Jud. Conf. D.C. Cir., 1981, 82, 92, adv. com. Civil Justice Reform Act, U.S. Dist. Ct., 1991-93; pres. Lawyers Mut. Ins. Co. of D.C., 1990-92. Contbr. articles to profl. jour. Pres. Friendly Citizens Assn., 1963, Gonzaga Fathers Club, 1974-76; chmn. bd. dirs. Henson Valley Montessori Sch.; bd. dirs. Sursum Corda Neighborhood Center, 1975-77. Lt. comdr. USNR, 1955-58. Mem. ABA, D.C. Bar Assn. (pres. 2001—), Md. Bar Assn., Coun. for Ct. Excellence (chmn. ct. improvement com.), George Washington U. Law Alumni Assn. (pres. D.C. chpt. 1988-89), Counsellors (pres. 1984-85), Barrister Inn (pres. 1976-77), Order Golden Fleece, Kappa Alpha Order, Phi Delta Phi. Roman Catholic. Home: 10701 Laurel Leaf Pl Potomac MD 20854-1770 Office: 1742 N St NW Washington DC 20036-2907 E-mail: jgfcadence@aol.com

FORESTER, KARL S. district court judge; b. 1940; BA, U. Ky., 1962, JD, 1966. With Eugene Goss Esp., 1966-68; mem. firm Goss & Forester, 1968-75, Forester, Forester, Buttermore & Turner, P.S.C., 1975-88; judge U.S. Dist. Ct. (ea. dist.) Ky., Lexington, 1988—. Mem. Ky. Bar Assn., Harlan County Bar Assn., Fayette County Bar Assn. Office: US Dist Ct PO Box 2165 Lexington KY 40588-2165

FORGER, ALEXANDER DARROW, lawyer; b. N.Y.C., Feb. 19, 1923; BA with honors, Princeton U., 1947; JD, Yale U., 1950. Assoc. Milbank, Tweed, Hadley & McCloy, N.Y.C., 1950-57, ptnr., 1958—, chmn., 1986-92, spl. counsel, 1993—. Pres., Legal Svcs. Corp., 1994-97. Trustee Rockefeller U.; chmn. bd., Legal Aid Soc., 1984-92; v.p., Dorotha Leonhardt Found., Gerard B. Lambert Meml. Found., Inc. Fellow Am. Bar Found., N.Y. Bar Found., Am. Coll. Trust and Real Estate Counsel; mem. ABA (past state del. to ho. of dels.), N.Y. State Bar Assn. (past pres. ho. of dels.), Assn. Bar City of N.Y., Lawyers; Com. for Civil Rights Under Law (dir. Children's Advocacy Ctr.). Estate planning, Family and matrimonial. Office: Milbank Tweed Hadley & McCloy 1 Chase Manhattan Plz Fl 47 New York NY 10005-1413 E-mail: aforger@milbank.com

FORKAS, ROBERT JASON, lawyer; b. Ottawa, Ont., Can., July 5, 1973; s. Andrew and Judith Maria Farkas. BA, George Washington U., 1994; JD, Harvard U., 1997. Bar: N.J. 1997, U.S. Dist. Ct. N.J. 1997, N.Y. 1998. Assoc. Sills Cummis et al, Newark, 1997—. General civil litigation. Office: Sills Cummis Et Al One Riverfront Plz Newark NJ 07102

FORMELLER, DANIEL RICHARD, lawyer; b. Chgo., Aug. 15, 1949; s. Vernon Richard and Shirley Mae (Gruber) F.; m. Ann M. Paa, Aug. 17, 1974; children: Matthew Daniel, Kathryn Ann, Christina Marie. BA with honors, U. Ill., 1970; JD cum laude, DePaul U., 1976. Bar: Ill. 1976, U.S. Dist. Ct. (no. and cen. dists.) Ill. 1976, U.S. Ct. Appeals (7th cir.) 1976, U.S. Ct. Appeals (D.C. cir.) 1995. Assoc. McKenna, Storer, Rowe, White & Farrug, Chgo., 1976-82, ptnr., 1982-86, Tressler, Soderstrom, Maloney & Priess, Chgo., 1986—. Exec. editor DePaul U. Law Rev., 1975-76. With USN, 1970-72, Vietnam. Mem. ABA, Ill. Bar Assn., Ill. Assn. Def. Trial Counsel (pres. 1994-95), Chgo. Bar Assn., Assn. Def. Trial Attys. Federal civil litigation, General civil litigation, Product liability. Office: Tressler Soderstrom et al 233 S Wacker Dr Chicago IL 60606-6306 E-mail: dformeller@mail.tsmp.com

FORREST, HERBERT EMERSON, lawyer; b. N.Y.C., Sept. 20, 1923; s. Jacob K. and Rose (Fried) F.; m. Marilyn Lefsky, Jan. 12, 1952; children: Glenn Clifford, Andrew Matthew. Student, CCNY, 1941, Ohio U., 1943-44; BA with distinction, George Washington U., 1948, JD with highest honors, 1952. Bar: Va. 1952, D.C. 1952, U.S. Supreme Ct. 1956, Md. 1959, U.S. Ct. Appeals (D.C. cir.) 1953, U.S. Ct. Appeals (1st cir.) 1992, U.S. Ct. Appeals (2d cir.) 1971, U.S. Ct. Appeals (3d cir.) 1957, U.S. Ct. Appeals (4th cir.) 1956, U.S. Ct. Appels (5th cir.) 1981, U.S. Ct. Appeals (7th cir.) 1996, U.S. Ct. Appeals (8th cir.) 1991, U.S. Ct. Appeals (9th cir.) 1994, U.S. Ct. Appeals (11th cir.) 1981. Plate printer Bur. Engraving and Printing, Washington, 1942-43, 1946-52; law clk. to chief judge Bolitha J. Laws U.S. Dist. Ct., 1952-55; pvt. practice, 1952-87; with Welch & Morgan, 1955-65, Steptoe & Johnson, 1965-85, of counsel, 1986-87; trial atty. fed. programs br. civil divsn. U.S. Dept. Justice, Washington, 1987—; chmn. adv. bd. D.C. Criminal Justice Act, 1971-74; sec. com. admissions and grievances U.S. Ct. Appeals, D.C., 1973-79; title-1 audit hearing bd. U.S. Office Edn. HEW, 1976-79; edn. appeals bd. U.S. Dept. Edn., 1979-82. Mem. Lawyer's Support Com. for Visitors Service Center, 1975-87 Contbr. articles to profl. jours.; mem. editl. bd. Duke Law Jour, 1969-75. Pres. Whittier Woods PTA, 1970-71. With F.A., Signal Corps U.S. Army, 1943-46. Recipient Walsh award in Irish history, 1952, Goddard award in commerce, 1952. Fellow Am. Bar Found. (life), ABA (council 1972-75, 1981-84, budget officer 1985-88, vice chmn. task force on sect. devel. 1987-89, chmn. com. on agy. rule making 1968-72, 1976-81, chmn. membership com. 1984-85, editor ann. reports 1973-88, adminstrv. law sect., fellow adminstrv. law and regulatory practice, mem. comm. com. public utilities law sect., vice chmn. industry regulation com. 1985-86, chmn. comm. subcom. 1983-85, antitrust law sect., internat. law sect., sec. judicial adminstrn., sect. sci. and tech., comm. forum); mem. George Washington Law Assn., Am. Judicature Soc., Va. State Bar Assn., Fed. Bar Assn. (chmn. jud. rev. com. 1981-85, vice chmn. adminstrv. law sect. 1985-87), Fed. Comm. Bar Assn. (del. to ABA Ho. Dels. 1979-81, exec. com. 1967-71, 76-84, v.p. 1981-82, pres. 1982-83, chmn. telecomm. com. 1983-87), D.C. Bar Assn. (past sec., exec. com.), NAM, Nat. Conf. Bar Pres., Washington Council Lawyers, Legal Aid and Pub. Defender Assn., Am. Arbitration Assn. (comml. panel 1976-87), D.C. Unified Bar (bd. govs. 1976-79, chmn. com. on employment discrimination complaint service 1973-79, chmn. task force on services to public 1974-78, chmn. com. on appointment counsel in criminal cases 1978-88, co-chmn. com. on participation govt. employees in pro bono activities 1977-79), Broadcast Pioneers, Order of Coif, B'nai Brith, Phi Beta Kappa, Pi Gamma Mu., Artus, Phi Eta Sigma, Phi Delta Phi. Democrat. Home: 8706 Bellwood Rd Bethesda MD 20817-3033 Office: US Dept Justice 901 E St NW Rm 1050 Fed Washington DC 20004-2037

FORRESTER, J. OWEN, federal judge; b. 1939; B.S., Ga. Inst. Tech., 1961; LL.B., Emory U., 1966. Bar: Ga. 1966. Assoc. Fisher & Phillips, Atlanta, 1967-69; asst. U.S. Atty., 1969-76; magistrate U.S. Dist. Ct. (no. dist.) Ga., 1976-81, judge, 1981—. Office: US Dist Ct 1921 US Courthouse 75 Spring St SW Atlanta GA 30303-3309

FORRY, JOHN INGRAM, lawyer; b. Washington, Feb. 9, 1945; s. John Emerson and Marion Carlotta (MacArthur) F.; m. Carol Ann Micken, Jan. 12, 1980; children: Alicia Ann, Camilla Lorraine. BA, Amherst Coll., 1966; JD, Harvard U., 1969. Bar: Calif. 1970, D.C. 1998, N.Y. 1998, U.S. Tax Ct. 1977, U.S. Supreme Ct. 1975. Founding ptnr. Forry Golbert Singer & Gelles, L.A., 1973-80; sr. ptnr. Morgan, Lewis & Bockius, 1980-97, McDermott, Will & Emery, N.Y.C., 1997-98, Ernst & Young LLP, N.Y.C., 1999—. Co-author, editor: A Practical Guide to Foreign Investment in the United States, 1979, 3d edit., 1989, Joint Ventures in the United States, 1988, Differences in Tax Treatment of Foreign Investors, 1989, others; contbr. more than 40 articles to profl. jours. Co-founder Forry Fund in Philosophy and Sci., Amherst (Mass.) Coll., 1984—; mem. adv. group to U.S. Commr. of Internal Revenue, Washington, 1985-86. Mem. Internat. Bar Assn., Internat. Fiscal Assn., other bar assns. Republican. Roman Catholic. Avocations: philosophical implications of scientific developments, automobile racing, mountain climbing, scuba diving. Finance, Private international, Corporate taxation. Office: Ernst & Young LLP 787 7th Ave Fl 22 New York NY 10019-6018 Fax: 212-773-5116. E-mail: john.forry@ey.com

FORSCH, THOMAS, lawyer, consultant; b. Wiesbaden, Hessen, Germany, Oct. 6, 1964; s. Friedrich Willy Hugo and Gertrud Forsch; m. Souher Dassoum, Feb. 10, 1999; 1 child, Yasmina. Bar: Germany 1994, France 1995. Atty. Law Offices Fritz Ranke, Paris, Ile de Paris, Monaco, 1994-95, Fingerhut Karg Maul, Dresden, Germany, 1995-96, Cabinet Emil Epp, Strasbourg, Monaco, France, 1996-97, Alem & Assocs., Beirut, Lebanon,

1997-99, Al Suwaidi Advs., Dubai, United Arab Emirates, 1999-2001, Galardi & Assocs., Dubai, France, Monaco, 2001—. Lectr. U. Burgundy, Dijon, France, Monaco, 1990-91; ind. cons. Dubai, 2001—. Editor: (On-line mag.) DUBAI INVEST, 2001. Mem. Social Democratic Party. Communications, Computer, Intellectual property. Office: Galardi & Assocs Bur Dubai PO Box 7992 Dubai United Arab Emirates Office Fax: 971-4 393 77 55. E-mail: itlawconsultant@hotmail.com

FORSMAN, ALPHEUS EDWIN, lawyer; b. Montgomery, Ala., May 12, 1941; m. Greta Friedman, July 5, 1964; children: Ellen E., Jennifer Ann. BA with distinction, George Washington U., 1963, JD, 1967. Bar: Va. 1968, D.C. 1969, U.S. Supreme Ct. 1973, Mo. 1979; cert. trademark agt. Can. Trademark examiner U.S. Patent Office, Washington, 1967-69; atty. Marriott Corp., 1969-72; assoc. Roylance, Abrams, Berdo and Kaul, 1972-75, ptnr., 1975-78; trademark atty. Ralston Purina Co., St. Louis, 1978-81, trademark counsel, 1981-91, v.p., sr. trademark counsel, 1991-96; asst. v.p. Eveready Battery Co., Inc., 1986-98; asst. sec. Ralston Purina Co., 1990—, v.p., sr. counsel, 1996—; v.p. Eveready Battery Co., 1998-2000. Asst. sec. Continental Baking Co., 1990-95; adj. prof. law Washington U., 2000. Mem. ABA, Bar. Assn. Met. St. Louis, Inst. Trade Mark Attys., London. Republican. Episcopalian. Trademark and copyright. Home: 417 Glan Tai Dr Manchester MO 63011-4067 Office: Ralston Purina Co Checkerboard Sq Saint Louis MO 63164-0001 E-mail: aforsman@purina.com

FORSTADT, JOSEPH LAWRENCE, lawyer; b. Bklyn., Feb. 21, 1940; BA, CCNY, 1961; LLB, NYU, 1964. Bar: N.Y. 1965, U.S. Supreme Ct. 1968. Spl. legal counsel to bd. justices Supreme Ct. N.Y. County, 1965-67; dep. commr. N.Y.C. Dept. Licenses, 1967-68, acting commr., 1968-69, N.Y.C. Dept. Consumer Affairs, 1969; asst. adminstr. Econ. Devel. Adminstrn., 1969; assoc. Stroock & Stroock & Lavan, N.Y.C., 1969-75, ptnr., 1976—. Lectr. trial practice N.Y. County Lawyers Assn., Practising Law Inst., 1993; mem. N.Y.C. Rent Guidelines Bd., 1984-97; arbitrator U.S. Dist. Ct. (ea. dist.) N.Y.; spl. counsel Appellate div. First Dept., Disciplinary Com.; mem. Housing Ct. Adv. Bd., 2001—. Contbr. articles to profl. jours. Dist. campaign mgr. John V. Lindsay for Mayor of N.Y.C., 1965; campaign mgr. Congressman Theodore Kupferman, 1966; chmn. N.Y.C. Young People for Nixon, 1968, pres. N.Y. State Assn. Young Rep. Clubs, 1970-72; pres. N.Y. Young Rep. Club, 1969-71; vice-chmn. N.Y. Com. to Re-elect Pres. Nixon, 1972. Judge Jacob Markowitz scholar NYU Law Sch., N.Y.C., 1964; recipient Brotherhood award NCCJ, 1987. Mem. Fed. Bar Coun., Am. Judicature Soc., Phi Alpha Delta. Federal civil litigation, State civil litigation. Office: Stroock Stroock & Lavan 180 Maiden Ln Suite 32108 New York NY 10038-4937 E-mail: jforstadt@stroock.com

FORSTMOSER, PETER BRUNO, lawyer, educator; b. Zurich, Switzerland, Jan. 22, 1943; s, Alois and Ida (Locher) F.; divorced; children: Marco, Stefan. Lic. Juris, Zurich Law Sch., 1967, JD, 1970; LLM, Harvard U., 1972. Asst. prof. Zurich Law Sch., 1971-74, prof., 1974— ; assoc., Zurich, 1970-74; chief editor Swiss Lawyers Rev., 1973-2000; ptnr. Niederer Kraft & Frey, Zurich, 1974—; dir. Mikron Holding AG, Biel, Switzerland, 1976, Swiss Reins. Co., Zurich, 1990, chmn., 2000, Hesla AG, Zug, Switzerland, 1993; chmn. Commn. Inquiry on Misuse Inside Info., 1982-89, chmn. and mem. various legis. commns., 1976—; hon. prof. Beijing Normal U. Author: Schweiz. Genossenschaftsrecht, 1972-74, Schweiz. Aktienrecht, Aktienrechtliche Verantuortlikeit, 2d edit., 1987, Swiss Corporation Law, 1996; contbr. articles to profl. jours. Pres. Liberales I nst., Zurich, 1979-2000. Maj. inf. Swiss Army, 1981-98. Mem. Zivilrechtslehrervereinigung, Schweiz. Anwaltsverband. Office: Niederer Kraft & Frey Bahnhofstrasse 13 8001 Zürich Switzerland

FORSYTHE, RANDALL NEWMAN, paralegal, educator; b. Hammond, Ind., Mar. 24, 1959; s. Perry Newman and Elwanda (Cox) F.; children: Kenneth Newman, Keith Randall. AA in Law Enforcement, Calumet Coll., Whiting, Ind., 1979, BA in Criminal Justice magna cum laude, BS in Mgmt. magna cum laude, Calumet Coll., 1982; Lawyer's Asst. Cert., Roosevelt U., Chgo., 1986. Labor leader/painter Inland Steel Co., East Chicago, Ind., 1978-86; ins. and securities rep. Primerica, Portage, 1984-91; paralegal Katz, Brenman & Angel, Merrillville, 1987-91, Komyatte & Freeland, P.C., Highland, 1991—; coord. paralegal divsn. Sawyer Coll., Merrillville, 1989-92, paralegal instr., 1989—. Ct. apptd. spl. advocate Juvenile divsn. Lake County Superior Ct., Gary, Ind., 1987—. Manuscript/book reviewer West Pub. Co., St. Paul, 1991—. Parliamentarian Orchard Dr. Bapt. Ch., Hammond, Ind., 1981-91. Mem. Assn. Trial Lawyers Am., Nat. Assn. Legal Assts., Ind. Legal Assts. (Ind. Legal Asst. of Yr. 1990, liaison to nat. orgn. 1989-92, 97). Avocations: coaching children's Little League baseball, basketball, football teams, adult softball, hunting, fishing, camping. Office: Komyatte & Freeland PC 9650 Gordon Dr Highland IN 46322-2909

FORT, DENISE DOUGLAS, law educator, former state official; b. Lexington, Ky., July 24, 1951; d. John Porter and Ruth (Chapin) Fort. BA, St. John's Coll., 1972; JD, Cath. U. Am., 1975. Bar: N.Mex. 1976, U.S. Supreme Ct. 1976, U.S. Ct. Appeals (9th and 10th cirs.) 1976. Atty. N.Mex. Pub. Interest Rsch. Group, Albuquerque, 1976-77, S.W. Rsch. and Info. Ctr., Albuquerque, 1977-79, Taxation and Revenue Dept., Santa Fe, 1979-83; sec. gov.'s cabinet Dept. Fin. and Adminstrn., 1983-84, Environ. Improvement Dept., Santa Fe, 1979-83; asst. prof. law U. N.Mex., Albuquerque, 1991—. Past mem. State Investment Council, Santa Fe, 1983-84; exec. sec. N.Mex. Bd. Fin., Santa Fe, 1983-84; dir. water resources adminstrn. program, U. N.Mex., 1991—; chair We. Water Policy Rev. Adv. Com., 1995—; mem. water, sci. and tech. bd., Nat. Rsch. Coun., 1997-2000. Democrat.

FORTENBAUGH, SAMUEL BYROD, III, lawyer; b. Phila., Nov. 6, 1933; s. Samuel Byrod Jr. and Katherine Francisca (Wall) F.; children: Samuel Byrod IV, Cristina Fortenbaugh Alemany, Katherine Dooley, Francesca Cowden. BA, Williams Coll., 1955; LLB, Harvard U., 1960. Bar: N.Y. 1961, U.S. Dist. Ct. (so. dist.) N.Y. 1961. Assoc. Kelley Drye & Warren, N.Y.C., 1960-69, ptnr., 1970-79, Morgan, Lewis & Bockius, N.Y.C., 1980—. Bd. dirs. Baldwin Tech. Co., Inc., Shelton, Conn., Security Capital Corp., Greenwich, Conn., Goodman Equipment Corp., Chgo.; bd. dirs., sec. Furgueson Capital Mgmt. Inc., N.Y.C.; chmn. bd. dirs., sec. Wall Industries, Inc., Kannapolis, N.C.; chmn. bd. dirs. Knight Textile Corp, Saluda, S.C.; trustee Patroni Scholastici, New Brunswick, N.J., 1978—, sec. 1985—; lectr. profl. seminars. Contbr. articles to profl. jours. Mem. ABA, Assn. of Bar of City of N.Y. (mem. Young Lawyers com. 1962-65, corp. law com. 1976-79, com. on securities regulation 1982-85, chmn. com. on issue distbn. of securities 1984-85), Racquet and Tennis Club, N.Y. Yacht Club, Bay Head (N.J.) Yacht Club, Indian Harbor Yacht Club (Greenwich, Conn.) (bd. dirs.), Phi Beta Kappa. General corporate, Mergers and acquisitions, Securities. Office: Morgan Lewis & Bockius LLP 101 Park Ave Fl 45 New York NY 10178-0002

FORTIER, ALBERT MARK, JR. lawyer; b. Cambridge, Mass., July 22, 1936; s. Albert M. and Marie R. (Tagney) F.; m. Bente Mortensen, Nov. 10, 1964; children: John, Mark. AB, U. Chgo., 1955; LLB, Harvard U., 1958. Bar: Mass. 1958. Assoc. Richard S. Bowers, Boston, 1958-65; ptnr. Bowers, Fortier & Lakin, 1966-76, Rackemann, Sawyer & Brewster, Boston, 1976—. Contbr. articles to profl. jours. Mem. ABA, Am. Bar Found., Boston Bar Assn. (probate sect. former chair), Am. Coll. Trust and Estate Counsel (past state chair), Union Club (Boston, past bd. govs.). Republican. Methodist. Estate planning, Probate, Estate taxation. Home: 90 Craftsland Rd Chestnut Hill MA 02467-2632 Office: Rackemann Sawyer & Brewster One Financial Ctr Boston MA 02111 E-mail: amf@rackemann.com

FORTIER, SAMUEL JOHN, lawyer; b. Spokane, Wash., Mar. 30, 1952; s. Charles Henry and Mary (Petersen) F.; m. Dagmar Christine Mikko, Sept. 15, 1983; children: Nova Marie, Matthew Theodore. BA cum laude, Boston U., 1974; JD magna cum laude, Gonzaga U., 1982. Bar: Alaska 1982, U.S. Dist. Ct. Alaska 1983, U.S. Ct. Appeals (9th cir.) 1987, U.S. Ct. Claims 1999, U.S. Ct. Appeals (fed. cir.) 2000. Acting exec. dir. manpower Vista Bristol Bay Native Assn., Dillingham, Alaska, 1974-76; fin. analyst Alaska Fedn. of Natives, Anchorage, 1976-78; loan analyst State of Alaska, 1978-79; law clk. consumer protection div., atty. gen.'s office State of Wash., Spokane, 1980-82; assoc. Cummings & Routh P.C., Anchorage, 1982-84; ptnr. Fortier & Mikko, 1984—. Adj. prof. U. Alaska, Anchorage, 1982-85; speaker workshop Small Bus. Adminstrn., Anchorage, 1982-85. Mem. ABA, Alaska Bar Assn. (Native law sect.), Anchorage Bar Assn. Democrat. Avocations: reading, writing, camping, skiing. Federal civil litigation, General corporate, Native American. Home: 6800 Sequoia Cir Anchorage AK 99516-3755 Office: Fortier & Mikko 101 W Benson Blvd Ste 304 Anchorage AK 99503-3936 E-mail: sfortier@fortmikk.alaska.com

FORTMAN, MARVIN, law educator, consultant; b. Bklyn., Oct. 20, 1930; s. Herman and Bess (Smith) F.; m. Sorale Esther Elpern, Aug. 3, 1958; children: Brian E., Anita J., Deborah J. BS in Acctg., U. Ariz., 1957, JD magna cum laude, 1960; LLM, NYU, 1961. Bar: Ariz. 1960, N.Y. 1961, U.S. Tax Ct. 1962, U.S. Ct. Appeals 1962, U.S. Supreme Ct. 1962. Assoc. Aranow, Brodsky, Bolinger, Einhorn & Dann, N.Y.C., 1961-63, O'Connor, Cavanaugh, Anderson, Westover & Beshears, Phoenix, 1963-65; prof. bus. law, bus. and pub. adminstrn. U. Ariz., Tucson, 1965—. Legal cons. various corps., 1963—. Author: Legal Aspects of Doing Business in Arizona, 1970; contbr. articles to profl. jours. Mem. legal com. Ariz. Coun. on Econ. Edn., Tucson, 1975—, Sabbar Shrine Temple, Tucson, 1978—, legal advisor, chmn. wills and gifts, 1981-84, 1990—. With U.S. Army, 1951-53; ETO. Kenneson fellow NYU, 1960-61. Mem. N.Y. State Bar Assn., Ariz. Bar Assn. (wills, trusts, estates sect.), Phi Kappa Phi, Beta Gamma Sigma (v.p., treas. 1972—), Beta Alpha Psi, Alpha Kappa Psi. Home: 5844 E 15th St Tucson AZ 85711-4508 Office: U Ariz Coll Of Bus And Pub Adminstr Tucson AZ 85721-0001

FORTUNO, VICTOR M. lawyer; b. N.Y.C., Jan. 24, 1952; s. Victor M. Fortuno and Ceda Aguayo; m. Vicki Ann Clark; children: Adam R., Victor III, Scott, Erica, Bryce. AB in Econs., Columbia U., 1974, JD, 1977. Bar: Pa. 1977, U.S. Dist. Ct. (ea. dist.) Pa. 1977, U.S. Ct. Appeals (3d cir.) 1977, U.S. Supreme Ct. 1980, U.S. Ct. Appeals (D.C. cir.) 1987, D.C. 1988, U.S. Dist. Ct. D.C. 1988, U.S. Ct. Appeals (4th cir.) 1988, U.S. Dist. Ct. Ariz. 1991. Staff atty. Cmty. Legal Svcs., Inc., Phila., 1977-78; asst. dist. atty. Office Dist. Atty., 1978-83; staff atty. Legal Svcs. Corp., Washington, 1983-85, acting dir. compliance divsn., 1985-86, asst. gen. counsel, 1986, sr. litigation counsel, 1986-88, acting gen. counsel, 1987, 91, dep. gen. counsel, 1988-91, gen. counsel, 1991—, corp. sec., 1995—, v.p. legal affairs, 1999—. Adj. faculty Grantham Coll. Engring., 2001—. Bd. dirs. Friends of Legal Svcs. Corp., 2001—, Columbia Coll. Alumni Assn., 1981-83, Phila. Health Plan, 1980-83. Pulitzer Found. scholar, 1970-74, Assn. of Bar of City of N.Y. C. Bainbridge Smith scholar, 1974-77. Mem. ABA, D.C. Bar Assn., Fed. Small Agy. Coun. Home: 7479 Thorncliff Ln Springfield VA 22153-2153 Office: Legal Svcs Corp 750 1st St NE Ste 1000 Washington DC 20002-4250 Fax: 202-336-3954. E-mail: vfortuno@lsc.gov

FOSCHIO, LESLIE GEORGE, lawyer; b. Oct. 29, 1940; s. Frank George and Sonia (Kaczynski) F.; m. Virginia Rose Kostur, June 27, 1964; children: John, Michael, Amy, Robert, Christa. BA cum laude, U. Buffalo, 1962; LLB cum laude, SUNY, Buffalo, 1965. Bar: N.Y. 1966, U.S. Dist. Ct. (we. dist.) N.Y. 1975, U.S. Tax Ct. 1980, U.S. Ct. Appeals (7th cir.) 1973, U.S. Ct. Appeals (2d cir.) 1977, U.S. Ct. Appeals (D.C. cir.) 1977, U.S. Supreme Ct. 1975. Law clk. to Hon. William B. Lawless, Jr. N.Y. State Supreme Ct., 1965; atty. Counsel's Office, SUNY, 1965-66; asst. dist. atty. Erie County, Buffalo, 1966-69; assoc. prof., asst. dean U. Notre Dame Law Sch., Ind., 1969-74; corp. counsel City of Buffalo, 1975-77; ptnr. Cohen Swados Wright Hanifin Bradford & Brett, Buffalo, 1978-80; commr. Dept. Motor Vehicles, State of N.Y., Albany, 1981-83; gen. counsel, sec., v.p. Barrister Info. Sys. Corp., Buffalo, 1983-91; U.S. magistrate judge U.S. Dist. Ct. (we. dist.) N.Y., 1991—. Lectr. law SUNY, Buffalo, 1966-68, 78-80. Comment editor Buffalo Law Rev., 1964-65; contbr. articles to profl. jours. Dem. candidate for N.Y. State Assembly from Erie County, 1968; Dem. primary candidate for mayor, Buffalo, 1977; pres. Theodore Roosevelt Inaugural Nat. Hist. Site Found., Buffalo, 1978-87, trustee, 1978—; trustee Theodore Roosevelt Assn., 1981-98; dist. chmn. Greater Niagara Frontier coun. Boy Scouts Am., Buffalo, 1980-82. Recipient T. R. McConnell Leadership, Scholarship and Character award U. Buffalo, 1962, Disting. Pub. Svc. award N.Y. Jaycees, Buffalo, 1976, Outstanding Svc. to Hwy. Safety award N.Y. State Assn. Traffic Safety, 1982, Disting. Alumnus award U. Buffalo Alumnus Assn., 1983, Alumnus of Yr. award H. C. Tech. H.S., 1997. Fellow N.Y. State Bar Found. (life), Am. Bar Found. (life); mem. Fed. Magistrate Judges Assn., N.Y. State Bar Assn. (Action Unit 5 1980-83), Bar Assn. Erie County (dir. 1988-91), U. Buffalo Alumni Assn. (dir. 1995-99, v.p. membership 1988-99), U. Buffalo Law Sch. Alumni Assn. (pres. 1980-81, Disting. Alumnus award for pub. svc. 1987), Phi Alpha Delta (hon.). Roman Catholic. Computer, General corporate. Home: 46 Woodley Rd Buffalo NY 14215-1321 Office: 424 US Courthouse 68 Court St Buffalo NY 14202-3405 E-mail: lesliefoschio@nywd.uscourts.gov

FOSTER, ARTHUR KEY, JR. retired lawyer; b. Birmingham, Ala., Nov. 22, 1933; s. Arthur Key and Vonceil (Oden) F.; m. Jean Lyles Foster, Jan. 7, 1967; children: Arthur Key III, Brooke Oden. BSE, Princeton U., 1955; JD, U. Va., 1960. Bar: Ala. 1960. Ptnr. Balch & Bingham, Birmingham, 1965-99. Trustee Episcopal Found. Jefferson County; bd. dirs. Met. YMCA, Downtown Club, Highlands Day Sch., Altamont Sch. Served to lt., USN, 1955-60. Mem. ABA, Ala. Bar Assn., Birmingham Bar Assn., Estate Planning Coun. of Birmingham, Nat. Assn. Bond Lawyers, Newcomen Soc. of U.S., Kiwanis (bd. dirs.). Republican. Estate planning, Municipal (including bonds), Probate. Office: Balch & Bingham PO Box 306 Birmingham AL 35201-0306

FOSTER, C(HARLES) ALLEN, lawyer; b. Aug. 26, 1941; s. Charles Shearer and Bessie Lea (Long) F.; m. Susan Coomes; children: Charles Shearer Sanders II, Susan Elizabeth Coomes, Charles Henry Edward. BA summa cum laude, Princeton U., 1963; BA in Jurisprudence 1st class honors, Oxford (Eng.) U., 1965, MA in Jurisprudence, 1971; JD magna cum laude, Harvard U., 1967. Bar: N.C. 1967, D.C. 1994, U.S. Dist. Ct. (mid. dist.) N.C. 1968, U.S. Dist. Ct. (we. dist.) N.C. 1968, U.S. Dist. Ct. (ea. dist.) N.C. 1968, U.S. Tax Ct. 1970, U.S. Ct. Appeals (4th cir.), U.S. Ct. Appeals (5th cir.) 1970, U.S. Ct. Appeals (11th cir.) 1991, U.S. Ct. Appeals (10th cir.) 1993, U.S. Ct. Appeals (fed. cir.) 1995, U.S. Supreme Ct. 1971, U.S. Dist. Ct. D.C. 1985, U.S. Dist. Ct. (no. dist.) Tex. 1990, U.S. Dist. Ct. (so. dist.) Tex. 1991, U.S. Ct. Fed. Claims 1994. Assoc. McLendon, Brim, Brooks, Pierce & Daniels, Greensboro, N.C., 1967-72, ptnr., 1972-73; sec., dir., gen. counsel Spanco Industries, Inc., Greensboro and Sanford, 1973-75, Conestee, S.C., 1973-75; ptnr. Turner, Enochs, Foster, Sparrow & Burnley, Greensboro, 1975-81, Foster, Conner & Robson, 1983-88, Patton, Boggs LLP, 1988-99, Greenberg Traurig, Washington, 1999—. Sr. lectr. law Duke U., 1981-88; arbitrator Am. Arbitration Assn., mem. nat. panels of labor, constrn. and internat. comml. arbitrators; mem. Nat. Acad. Arbitrators; pub. mem. N.C. Tax Rev. Bd., 1972-76; mem. N.C. Judicial Selection Study Commn., 1987-88; U.S. rep. Internat. Energy Agy. Dispute Resolution Ctr., Paris, 1984—; permanent panel arbitrator Martin Marietta and Atomic Trades and Labor Coun.; others. Author: Construction and Design Law, 1984—, Construction and Design Law Digest, 1981—, Law and Practice of Commercial Arbitration in North Carolina, 1984; contbr. articles to profl. jours. Co-founder, sec., bd. dirs. Greensboro Day Sch.; exec. com. Princeton U. Alumni Assn.; exec. com. Harvard Law Sch. Assn. N.C., 1970; Rep. candidate for atty.-gen. N.C., 1984; spl. counsel Rep. Nat. Com., 1989—; spl. litigation counsel N.C. Rep. Cen. Com., 1987—. Mem. ABA (litigation sect., labor and employment discrimination law sect., forum com. on constrn. industry), Am. Law Inst., Am. Arbitration Assn. (bd. dirs. 1980-83, nat. panels labor, constrn., internat. comml. arbitrators 1975—, chmn. N.C. regional adv. coun. 1979-83), Am. Coll. Constrn. Arbitrators (pres. 1983-84), Princeton U. Alumni Assn. (pres. alumni coun., exec. com. 1978-79, pres. mid. N.C. chpt. 1968-80), Phi Beta Kappa, Cap and Gown Club. Federal civil litigation, Labor. Home: 3846 Cathedral Ave NW Washington DC 20016 E-mail: fostera@gtlaw.com

FOSTER, CHARLES CRAWFORD, lawyer, educator; b. Galveston, Tex., Aug. 1, 1941; s. Louie Brown and Helen (Hall) F.; m. Marta Brito, Sept. 7, 1967 (div. Apr. 1986); children: John, Ruth; m. Lily Chen, Jan. 7, 1989; children: Zachary, Anthony. AA, Del Mar Jr. Coll., 1961; BA, U. Tex., 1963, JD, 1967. Bar: Tex. 1967, N.Y. 1969. Assoc. Reid & Priest, N.Y.C., 1967-69, Butler & Binion, Houston, 1969-73; ptnr. Tindall & Foster, 1973—. Hon. consul gen. Kingdom of Thailand, 1996—; adj. prof. immigration law U. Houston, 1985-89; bd. dirs. Greater Houston Partnership, 1997, chmn. econ. devel. adv. bd., 2000; chmn. Asia Soc.-Tex., bd. trustees, 1990—; bd. dirs. Houston World Affairs Coun., 1990—; chmn. Inst. Internat. Edn., The Houston Club, 1999—, Houston Ballet Found., Assn. of Cmty. TV, Houston Holocaust Mus.; chmn. World Trade Adv. Bd., 1997; mem. Mayoral Adv. Bd. for Internat. Affairs and Devel./Asia, 1999—. Contbr. articles to profl. jours. Chmn. Immigration Reform Gov.'s Task Force on Tex., 1984-87. Decorated comdr. 3d class Order of the Crown (Thailand); Rotary Internat. fellow U. Concepción, Chile, 1964; recipient Houston Internat. Svc. award Houston Jaycees, 1996, Disting. Friend of China award U.S. China Friendship Found., 2000; honoree Am. Immigration Law Found., 1998. Mem. ABA (chmn. immigration com. internat. law and practice sect. 1982-90, chmn. coordinating com. on immigration and law 1987-89, fgn. rels. com. 2000—), Am. Immigration Lawyers Assn. (pres. 1981-82, Outstanding Svc. award 1985), Tex. Bar Assn. (chmn. com. law on immigration and nationality 1984-86), Tex. Bd. Legal Specialization (chmn. immigration adv. commn. 1979—), Houston Bar Assn., Asia Soc. (trustee 1992—, chmn. Houston Ctr. 1992—), Rotary, Houston Club (pres. 2001). Methodist. Avocations: mountain climbing, photography, travel. Immigration, naturalization, and customs. Home: 17 Courtlandt Pl Houston TX 77006-4013 Office: Tindall & Foster 2800 Chase Tower 600 Travis St Ste 2800 Houston TX 77002-3094

FOSTER, DAVID LEE, lawyer; b. Des Moines, Dec. 13, 1933; s. Carl Dewitt and Dorothy Jo (Bell) F.; m. Marilyn Lee Bokemeier, Aug. 12, 1957 (div. June 1978); children: Gwendolyn Foster Reed, Cynthia Foster Curry, David Lee Jr.; m. Kathleen Carol Walsh, Mar. 24, 1979; 1 child, John Wickersham. Student, Simpson Coll., 1951-52; BA, U. Iowa, 1954, JD, 1957. Bar: Iowa 1957, N.Y. 1958, Ohio 1964, U.S. Supreme Ct. 1975. Assoc. Cravath, Swaine & Moore, N.Y.C., 1957-63; from assoc. to ptnr. Jones, Day, Cockley & Reavis, Cleve., 1963-72; ptnr. Willkie Farr & Gallagher, N.Y.C., 1972—. Lectr. So. Meth. U., 1979-84, U. Pitts., 1984, Practicing Law Inst., N.Y.C., 1984-85; mem. adv. bd. Civil RICO Report LRP Publs., 1988—; bd. govs. N.Y. Ins. Exch., 1987-96. Contbr. chpts. to book, articles to legal jours. Mem., bd. trustees Cardigan Mountain Sch., 1995—. Served with USNR, 1952-60. Fellow Am. Coll. Trial Lawyers, Internat. Acad. Trial Lawyers (bd. dirs. 1987-92); mem. Am. Counsel Assn. (pres. 1994-95, bd. dirs. 1992-98), River Club, Order of Coif, Phi Beta Kappa. Antitrust, Federal civil litigation, Insurance. Office: Willkie Farr & Gallagher 787 7th Ave New York NY 10019-6099 E-mail: dfoster@willkie.com

FOSTER, DAVID SCOTT, lawyer; b. White Plains, N.Y., July 13, 1938; s. William James and Ruth Elizabeth (Seltzer) F.; m. Eleanore Stalker, Dec. 21, 1959; children: David Scott, Robert McEachron. BA, Amherst Coll., 1960; LLB, Harvard U., 1963. Bar: N.Y. 1963, D.C. 1977, Calif. 1978. Jud. law clk. U.S. Dist. Ct. (so. dist.) N.Y., 1963-64; assoc. Debevoise & Plimpton, N.Y.C., 1964-72; internat. tax counsel U.S. Treasury Dept., Washington, 1972-77; ptnr. Brobeck, Phleger & Harrison, San Francisco, 1978-90, Coudert Bros., San Francisco, 1990-91, Thelen, Reid & Priest LLP, San Francisco, 1991—. Mem. ABA, San Francisco Bar Assn., Internat. Fiscal Assn., Western Pension and Benefits Confs., St. Francis Yacht Club (San Francisco). Presbyterian. Pension, profit-sharing, and employee benefits, Taxation, general. Office: Thelen Reid & Priest LLP 101 2nd St Ste 1800 San Francisco CA 94105-3659

FOSTER, DAVID SMITH, lawyer, arbitrator, private adjudicator; b. Wilmington, Del., May 20, 1927; s. David Smith and Mary Jeannette (Johnson) F.; m. Marie Elise Labbe, Nov. 10, 1956; children— Elise L., Chadford W., Donald Patch. B.A., U. Va., 1951; J.D., Tulane U., 1964. Bar: La. 1964. Landman Continental Oil Co., Lafayette, La., 1953-56, lease broker DS Foster Oil Proprs., Lafayette, 1956-61; ptnr. Voorhies & Labbe, Lafayette, 1964-71; pres. David S. Foster, P.C., Lafayette, 1971— ; judge pro tem 15th Jud. Dist. Ct., La., Lafayette Cir. Ct.; bd. dirs. Offshore Logistics, Lafayette, Billeaud Cos., Lafayette, Billead Marshlands, Lafayette. Past pres. Lafayette Parish Youth Council; past youth counselor Lafayette Juvenile and Young Adult Program; past bd. dirs. ADAPT Inc., Lafayette Mus. Natural History and Planetarium Assn.; past adv. bd. Mt. Carmel Cath. Sch., Acad. of Sacred Heart, Ascension Day Sch.; v.p. Faith House; past sec. Hamilton Sch. PTA; past mem. external services funding adv. council City of Lafayette, traffic planning commn.; Served as sgt. USAF, 1945-46, ETO. Mem. ABA, La. State Bar Assn., Lafayette Parish Bar Assn. (pres. 1977-78). Oil, gas, and mineral, General practice. Home: 242 Girard Park Cir Lafayette LA 70503-2043 Office: 242 Girard Park Cir Lafayette LA 70503-2043

FOSTER, DOUGLAS TAYLOR, lawyer, investor; b. L.A., Oct. 30, 1927; s. James Taylor Foster and Irene Eve Ericksen; m. Nita Burt Peterson, July 3, 1951 (div. May, 1975); children: Jane Taylor Dickson, Stephanie Foster Abram. BA in Econ. and Bus., U. Wash., 1950; JD, Stanford U., 1956. Bar: Calif. 1957, U.S. Dist. Ct. (so. dist.) Calif. 1957, U.S. Ct. Appeals (9th cir.) 1959, U.S. Dist. Ct. (no. dist.) Calif. 1969, U.S. Supreme Ct. 1971, U.S. Dist. Ct. (ea. dist.) Calif. 1985. From assoc. to ptnr. Farrand, Fisher & Farrand, L.A., 1956-66; legal counsel McClatchy Newspapers and Broadcasting, Sacramento, 1967-81; ptnr. Diepenbrock, Wulff, Plant & Hannegan, 1981-84; pvt. practice, 1985—. Sec. bus. and corp. sect. L.A. County Bar Assn., 1966. Candidate L.A. County Rep. Ctrl. Com., San Marino, Calif., 1965. Lt. USN, 1950-53, Korean War. Mem. ABA, ATLA, Calif. State Bar, Sacramento County Bar Assn., Calif. Trial Lawyers Assn., Consumer Attys. of Calif., Capital City Trial Lawyers Corp., Consumer Attys. of Sacramento County, Rotary Club Arden-Arcade, Seattle Yacht Club, Sacramento Yacht Club, Sutter Club, Am. Trial Lawyers Am. Presbyterian. Achievements include succesful defense of cable television license, Lake of the Pines Development, No. Calif., involving first judicial interpretation and ruling under the Cable TV Act of 1984 in U.S. Dist. Ct. (ea. dist.) Calif., 1986. Avocations: boating, tennis, golf, bridge, other sports. General civil litigation, Communications, General corporate. Office: 2625 Fair Oaks Blvd Ste 1 Sacramento CA 95864-4936

FOSTER, GEORGE WILLIAM, JR. lawyer, educator; b. Boston, Nov. 23, 1919; s. George William and Marguerite (Werner) F.; m. Jeanette Raymond, May 26, 1950; children— Susan, Bill, Fred. Student, Antioch Coll., 1937-40; B.S. in Chemistry, Stanford U., 1947; LL.B., Georgetown U., 1951; LL.M., Yale U., 1952. Bar: Wis. bar 1972. Exec. asst. to U.S.

Senator, 1949-50; spl. asst. to Sec. of State Dean Acheson, 1951; asst. prof. law U. Wis., Madison, 1952-56, assoc. prof., 1956-59, prof., 1959-86, assoc. dean, 1969-72, prof. emeritus, 1986—. Reporter Wis. Long-Arm Process Statute, 1955-59; cons. sch. desegregation guidelines HEW, 1965; legal advisor Ministry of Justice, Kabul, Afghanistan, 1976 Served to lt. (j.g.) USN, 1942-46. Mem. Am. Orthithologists Union, Am. Law Inst. Democrat. Home: 5616 Lake Mendota Dr Madison WI 53705-1036 Office: U Wis N Lawn Ave Bldg Madison WI 53704-5034

FOSTER, JOHN ROBERT, lawyer; b. Long Beach, Calif., Feb. 13, 1940; s. Orlon c. and Catherine Rose Foster; m. Nancy Crandall, June 17, 1962; children: John Crandall, Christopher Peter, Blayney Robert, Courtland William. BA in History, San Jose State U., 1961; LLB, U. Calif., Berkeley, 1964. Bar: Calif. 1965, U.S. Dist. Ct. (no. dist.) Calif. 1965, U.S. Ct. Appeals (9th cir.) 1965; cert. specialist in probate, estate planning, and trust law. Dep. legis. counsel State of Calif., Sacramento, 1964-65; pres. Rusconi, Foster, Thomas & Wilson, APC, Morgan Hill, Calif., 1965—; asst. dist. atty. San Benito County, Hollister, 1967. Mem. Morgan Hill Unified Sch. Dist. Bd. Edn., 1967-74, 79-83, chmn. bd., 1969-71; councilman City of Morgan Hill, 1984-88, 97-98, mayor, 1984. Named Citizen of Yr., City of Morgan Hill. Mem. Calif. State Bar (past state bar exec. com. on estate planning, probate and trusts), Santa Clara County Bar Assn., Gilroy-Morgan Hill Bar Assn. (past pres.), Morgan Hill C. of C. (past pres.), Masons, Rotary (past pres. Morgan Hill). Republican. Methodist. Avocations: skiing, fly fishing, backpacking, camping. General corporate, Estate planning, Probate. Home: 17630 Black Oak Ct Morgan Hill CA 95037-9442 Office: Rusconi Foster Thomas & Wilson 30 Keystone Ave Morgan Hill CA 95037-4325 E-mail: bob@rftw.com

FOSTER, LLOYD BENNETT, lawyer, musician; b. Wellman, Iowa, May 6, 1911; s. George Elliott and Lulu Nettie (Bennett) F.; m. Rowene Stevens, Sept. 1, 1940. BA cum laude in Commerce and Fin., Coe Coll., 1937; MS in Econs., Iowa State U., 1939; JD, De Paul U., 1952. Bar: Ill. 1952, U.S. Supreme Ct. 1980. Instr. Shenandoah Coll., Va., 1939-41; acct. McGladrey, Hansen, Dunn and Co., Cedar Rapids, Iowa, 1941-42; agt. Office of Dist. Dir., IRS, Chgo., 1946-52, pension plan reviewer, 1952-53, tech. advisor Appellate div., 1953-60; atty. Office of Chief Counsel, Washington, 1961-67; dep. asst. chief counsel Bur. of Pub. Debt, Chgo., 1967-71, atty., Washington, 1967; atty., income tax hearing officer, supr. regulations legis. rulings sect., litigation counsel, adminstrv. law judge Ill. Dept. Revenue, Chgo., 1971-87; of counsel McDermott, Will & Emery, Chgo., 1988. Mem., Chgo. Met. Symphony Orch., 1969—, Deerfield Park Dist. Community Band, 1968—. Served to comdr. USN, 1942-46. Mem. Fed. Bar Assn., Hammond Musicians Guild, Chgo. Fedn. Musicians, D.C. Fedn. Musicians, Naval Res. Assn., Retired Officers Assn.

FOSTER, MARK STEPHEN, lawyer; b. Edgerton, Mo., Feb. 6, 1948; s. George Elliott and Annabel Lee (Bradshaw) F.; m. Camille Pepper, June 27, 1970; children: Natalie Ashley, Stephanie Ann. BS, U. Mo., 1970; JD, Duke U., 1973. Bar: Mo. 1973, U.S. Ct. Mil. Appeals 1974, Hawaii 1975, U.S. Dist. Ct. Hawaii 1975, U.S. Dist. Ct. (we. dist.) Mo. 1977, U.S. Ct. Appeals (8th cir.) 1986, U.S. Supreme Ct. 1994. Assoc. Stinson, Mag & Fizzell, Kansas City, 1977-80, ptnr., 1980—, mng. ptnr., 1987-90, also bd. dirs., 1991—, chmn. bd. dirs., 1998—. Arbitration panelist Nat. Assn. Securities Dealers, N.Y.C., 1985—, Pvt. Adjudication Found., Durham, N.C., 1988—. Active Citizens Assn., Kansas City, 1982-92; pres. Spelman Med. Found., Smithville, Mo., 1984-88; bd. dirs. Alzheimers Assn. Metro. Kansas City, 1997—, 1st v.p., 1998, pres., 1999. Lt. comdr. USNR, ret. Mem. ABA, Hawaii Bar Assn., Mo. Bar Assn., Kansas City Met. Bar Assn., Am. Arbitration Assn. (panelist 1990—, large complex case adv. com. 1993—), Carriage Club (bd. dirs. 2000—, 2d v.p. 2001), Lawyers Edn. Assistance Program (bd. dirs. 2000—), Masons. Bankruptcy, General civil litigation, Labor. Home: 1035 W 65th St Kansas City MO 64113-1813 Office: Stinson Mag & Fizzell PC PO Box 419251 1201 Walnut St Ste 2800 Kansas City MO 64106-2117

FOSTER, MARK WINGATE, lawyer; b. Bryn Mawr, Pa., Dec. 10, 1942; s. Frank Brisbon and Marion Reed (Keator) F.; m. Hope Schwarz, June 7, 1971; children— Victoria Reed, Noah Cary. B.A., Yale U., 1965; J.D., Harvard U., 1971. Bar: Conn. 1971, D.C. 1972, U.S. Supreme Ct. 1975, Md. 1985. Staff atty. Pub. Defender's Service, Washington, 1971-74, chief criminal trial div., 1974-75; assoc. Bierbower & Rockefeller, Washington, 1975-76; ptnr. Moore & Foster, P.C., Washington, 1976-83; ptnr., Zuckerman, Spaeder, Goldstein, Taylor & Kolker, Washington, 1983— ; mem. Bd. Profl. Responsibility, D.C. Ct. Appeals, 1982-88, chmn., 1984-88. Contbr. articles to Dist. Lawyer, 1977-82. Bankruptcy, Federal civil litigation, Contracts commercial. Home: 5068 Sedgewick St NW Washington DC 20016-1940 Office: Zuckerman Spaeder Goldstein Taylor & Kolker 1201 Connecticut Ave NW Washington DC 20036-2638

FOULKE, EDWIN GERHART, JR. lawyer; b. Perkasie, Pa., Oct. 30, 1952; s. Edwin G. and Mary Claire (Keller) F. BA, N.C. State U., 1974; JD, Loyola U., New Orleans, 1978; LLM, Georgetown U., 1993. Bar: S.C. 1979, U.S. Dist. Ct. S.C. 1979, U.S. Ct. Appeals (4th cir.) 1979, Ga. 1986, U.S. Ct. Appeals (11th cir.) 1986, D.C. 1989, U.S. Ct. Appeals (D.C. cir.) 1989, U.S. Supreme Ct. 1990, N.C. 1997. Assoc. Thompson, Mann & Hutson, Greenville, S.C., 1978-83, Rainey, Britton, Gibbes & Clarkson, Greenville, 1983-85; ptnr. Constangy, Brooks & Smith, Columbia, S.C., 1985-90; chmn. Occupational Safety and Health Rev. Commn., Washington, 1990-95; ptnr. Jackson Lewis, Greenville, S.C., 1995—. Instr. St. Mary's Dominican Coll., New Orleans, 1977-78. Field rep. Reagan/Bush Campaign, Columbia, 1980, S.C. state coord., 1984; sec., treas. Employment Labor Law Sect., Columbia, 1981-82. Mem. ABA, S.C. Bar Assn., Ga. Bar Assn., Greenville County Bar Assn. (chmn. pub. rels. com. 1984-85), SAR, Rotary. Roman Catholic. Avocations: swimming, tennis, skiing, golf. Office: Jackson Lewis & Krupman 301 N Main St Ste 2100 Greenville SC 29601-2122

FOURNIE, RAYMOND RICHARD, lawyer; b. Belleville, Ill., Jan. 3, 1951; s. Raymond Victor and Gladys M. (Muskopf) F.; m. Mary Lindeman, Sept. 2, 1978; children: Sarah Dozier, John David, Anne Gerard, David Raymond. BS, U. Ill., 1973; JD, St. Louis U., 1979. Bar: Mo. 1979, Ill. 1980. Assoc. Moser, Marsalek, et al., St. Louis, 1979-80, Brown, James & Rabbitt, P.C., St. Louis, 1981-82, Shepherd, Sandberg & Phoenix, P.C., St. Louis, 1982-86; shareholder Shepherd, Sandberg & Phoenix, 1986-88; ptnr. Armstrong Teasdale LLP, 1988—. U. Ill. fellow, 1974. Mem. Mo. Bar Assn., Ill. Bar Assn., St. Louis Bar Assn. (sec. trial sect.), Lawyers Assn. (v.p. 1987-88, pres. 1990-91), Actors Equity Assn. Roman Catholic. Avocations: professional singer and actor, baseball, golf. General civil litigation, Personal injury, Product liability. Home: 4 Ridgetop St Saint Louis MO 63117-1021 Office: Armstrong Teasdale LLP One Metropolitan Sq Ste 2600 Saint Louis MO 63102-2740

FOUST, CHARLES WILLIAM, lawyer; b. Bethlehem, Pa., May 27, 1952; s. Alan Shivers and Helen Elizabeth (Aigler) F.; m. Melissa A. Cherney, July 31, 1982; children: Kyle Cherney, James Terrell. BA, U. Wis., 1974, JD, 1978. Bar: Wis. Bar, U.S. Dist. Ct. (we. dist.) Wis. 1978. Asst. dist. atty. Dane County Dist. Atty.'s Office, Madison, 1979-82; asst. pub. defender State Pub. Defender's Office, Milw., 1982-83; assoc. Smoler & Albert SC, Madison, 1983-88; dist. atty. Dane County, 1988-97; judge Dane County Circuit Ct., 1997—, presiding judge criminal divsn., 2001—. Mem. govs. adv. bd., Dane County adv. bd. Treatment Alternatives Program; chair coordinated commun. response task force on domestic violence Dane County Commn. on Sensitive Crimes; mem. Dane County Jail/Space Needs, Dane County Long Range Jud. Planning; mem. Dane County Jury Selection, Wis. Jud. Coun. Commn. on Criminal Procedure; mem. Wis. Working Group on Sentencing and Corrections. Mem. State Bar Wis., Dane County Bar Assn. (bd. dirs. criminal law sect. 1985-89, chmn. 1985-89), Wis. Dist. Attys. Assn. (exec. bd., 1st v.p., com. on DNA evidence, dir. state cts. criminal benchbook com. 2000—). Criminal. Home: 2105 Madison St Madison WI 53711-2131 Office: Dane County Circuit Ct Br 14 210 Martin Luther King Jr Blvd Madison WI 53709-0002 E-mail: william.foust@dane.courts.state.wi.us

FOUSTE, DONNA H. association executive; b. N.Y.C., Feb. 26, 1944; d. Donald Lynn and Edna (Parker) Ham; m. James Edward Fouste, Nov. 2, 1980. AA in Mgmt. and Supervision, Coastline Community Coll., Fountain Valley, Calif., 1980; BS in Organizational Behavior, U. San Francisco, 1985, MS in Orgnl. Devel., 1988. Officer mgr., bus. mgr. Fulwider, Patton, Rieber, Lee & Utecht, L.A., 1971-79, 89-91; patent adminstrn. specialist Discovision Assocs., Costa Mesa, Calif., 1979-82; law office mgr. City of Anaheim, 1982-89; exec. dir. Orange County Bar Assn., Santa Ana, 1992—. Instr. Rancho Santiago Coll., Santa Ana, with legal asst. program, 1987—; instr. U. Calif., Irvine, 1997; mem. adv. bd. Pub. Svc. Inst., Santa Ana, 1986-88. Patron Friends of South Coase Repertory, Costa Mesa, Calif., 1985; mem. applause chpt. Performing Arts Ctr., Costa Mesa, 1986-87. Recipient Silver medal in Chess Corp. Challenge, 1988, Tribute to Women award YWCA, 1997, Spirit of Volunteerism award Vol. Ctr. of Greater Orange County, 1996. Mem. Assn. Legal Adminstrs., Nat. Assn. Bar Execs. (membership chair 1999), State Bar Calif. (minimum continuing legal edn. com.), Am. Soc. Assn. Execs., So. Calif. Soc. Assn. Execs., Execs. of Calif. Law Assns. Avocations: gourmet cooking, skiing, gardening. Office: Orange County Bar Assn PO Box 17777 Irvine CA 92623-7777

FOWLER, DANIEL MCKAY, lawyer; b. Chgo., Mar. 25, 1950; m. Julia M. Duffy, Apr. 20, 1990; children: Douglas M., Peter M. BA, Monmouth Coll., 1972; JD, U. Denver, 1975. Bar: Colo. 1975, Wyo. 1994, U.S. Dist. Ct. Colo. 1975, U.S. Ct. Appeals (10th cir.) 1975. Shareholder Wood, Ris & Hames, P.C., Denver, 1975-87; pres. Fowler, Schimberg & Flanagan, P.C., 1987—. Mem. ABA, Colo. Bar Assn., Denver Bar Assn., Def. Rsch. Inst., Fedn. Ins. and Corp. Counsel, Colo. Def. Lawyers Assn., Denver Athletic Club, Lakewood Country Club. Avocations: motorcycle touring, skiing, boating, travel. General civil litigation, Insurance, Personal injury. Office: Fowler Schimberg & Flanagan PC 1640 Grant St Ste 300 Denver CO 80203-1640 E-mail: d_fowler@fsf-law.com

FOWLER, DAVID LUCAS, corporate lawyer; b. Heidelberg, Germany, Sept. 26, 1952; s. James Daniel and Nannie Romay (Lucas) F.; m. Cynthia Lou Smith, Aug. 19, 1989. BS, U.S. Mil. Acad., 1974; JD, Georgetown U., 1981. Bar: N.J. 1982, Calif. 1990, U.S. Ct. Fed. Claims 1990, U.S. Dist. Ct. (cen. dist.) Calif. 1990. 2d lt. U.S. Army, 1974, advanced through grades to maj., infantry platoon leader, 1975-76, asst. protocol officer, 1976-77, aide-de-campe U.S. Commander, 1977-78; minority augmentation recruit officer U.S. Mil. Acad., 1978; chief adminstrv. law sect. U.S. Army Tng. Ctr., Ft. Dix, N.J., 1983-86; command judge advocate U.S. Army Field Sta., Sinop, Turkey, 1985-86; trial atty. U.S. Army Legal Svcs. Agy., Falls Church, Va., 1986-89; resigned U.S. Army, 1989; corp. staff counsel Hughes Aircraft Co., L.A., 1989-94, sr. sgt. counsel Electro-Optical Sys. El Segundo, Calif., 1994-95, asst. gen. counsel Arlington, Va., 1996-97; v.p., dep. gen. counsel Raytheon Sys. Co., 1998-99; v.p. legal, Washington ops. Raytheon Co., 2000—; v.p., gen. counsel, sec. Raytheon Internat. Inc., 2000—. Mem. Armed Svcs. Bds. of Contract Appeals Assn. (bd. govs.), Army Sci. Bd., Bd. Contract Appeals Bar Assn. (bd. govs.). Avocations: reading, weightlifting, golf. General civil litigation, General corporate, Government contracts and claims. Office: Raytheon Co 1100 Wilson Blvd Ste 2000 Arlington VA 22209-2297

FOWLER, DON WALL, lawyer; b. Apr. 19, 1944; s. Slayden Grimes and Dorothy Lavenia (Wall) Fowler; m. Ruthann Arneson, Sept. 16, 1968 (div.); 1 child ; m. Deborah Dewar, Sept. 15, 1984 (dec. Feb. 1986); m. Patricia Petlin, Oct. 01, 1988. BA, Emory U., 1966; JD, U. Chgo., 1969. Bar: Ill. 1969, U.S. Dist. Ct. (no. dist.) Ill. 1969, U.S. Ct. Appeals (7th cir.) 1980. Assoc. Lord Bissell & Brook, Chgo., 1969—77, ptnr., 1977—. Mem.: Chgo. Bar Assn., Ill. Bar Assn., ABA, Ill. Assn. Def. Trial Counsel, Def. Rsch. Inst. Unitarian. Federal civil litigation, State civil litigation, Insurance. Office: Lord Bissell & Brook 115 S La Salle St Chicago IL 60603-3902

FOWLER, DONALD RAYMOND, retired lawyer, educator; b. Raton, N.Mex., June 2, 1926; s. Homer F. and Grace B. (Honeyfield) F.; m. Anna M. Averyt, Feb. 6, 1960; children: Mark D., Kelly A. BA, U. N.Mex., 1950; JD, 1951; MA, Claremont Grad. Sch., 1979, PhD, 1983. Bar: N.Mex. 1951, Calif. 1964, U.S. Supreme Ct. 1980. Atty. AEC, Los Alamos and Albuquerque, 1951-61, chief counsel Nev. Ops., 1962-63; pvt. practice, Albuquerque, 1961-62; asst., then dep. staff counsel Calif. Inst. Tech., Pasadena, 1963-72, staff counsel, 1972-75, gen. counsel, 1975-90; lectr. exec. mgmt. program Claremont Grad. Sch., Calif., 1981-84. Contbr. articles to profl. publs. Served with USAAF, 1944-46. Recipient NASA Pub. Svc. award, 1981. Mem. Calif. State Bar Assn., Fed. Bar Assn., Nat. Assn. Coll. and Univ. Attys. (exec. bd. 1979-82, 84-90, chmn. publs. com. 1982-84, pres. 1987-88, chmn. nominations com. 1988-89, chmn. honors and awards com. 1989-90, Life Mem. award 1991, Disting. Svc. award 1992), Calif. Assn. for Rsch. in Astronomy (sec. 1985-90).

FOWLER, FLORA DAUN, retired lawyer; b. Washington , Aug. 11, 1923; d. Herman Hartwell and Flora Elizabeth (Adams) Sanford; m. Kenneth Leo Fowler, Aug. 22, 1941; children: Kenneth Jr., Michael, Kathleen, Daun, Jonathan, Colin, Kevin, James, Shawn, Maureen, Wendelyn, Liam, Tobias, Melanie. Student, Wilson Tchrs. Coll., 1940-41; AA, U. Md., 1973; JD, U. Balt., 1976. Bar: Fla. 1977, U.S. Dist. Ct. (mid. dist.) Fla. 1979, U.S. Ct. Appeals (5th and 11th cirs.) 1981. Staff atty. Cen. Fla. Legal Services Inc., Daytona Beach, 1978-80, mng. atty., 1980-81; pvt. practice, 1981-93; ret., 2001. Past editor Seabrook Acres Citizens' League Newsletter; columnist Bowie Express & Community Times; contbr. poems to New Voices in American Poetry, 1974. V.p. Seabrook (Md.) Acres Citizens League, 1970; past v.p. Prince Georges County Civic Fedn., Md.; past unit chmn. League of Women Voters, Prince Georges County; past pres., v.p., publicity chmn. Lanham-Bowie Dem. Club, Seabrook. Recipient Evening Star Trophy award Prince Georges County Civic Fedn., 1969. Mem. Fla. S. Ct. Hist. Soc. Democrat. Roman Catholic. Avocations: swimming, creative writing, Cursillo. E-mail: daunfowler@msn.com

FOWLER, J. EDWARD, lawyer; AB, Princeton U., 1953; LLB, Yale U., 1959. Bar: N.Y. 1960. Atty. Debevoise, Plimpton, Lyons & Gates, 1959-68; gen. counsel internat. divsn. Mobil Oil Corp., 1974-77, asst. gen. counsel, 1977-78, assoc. gen. counsel, 1979-83, gen. counsel mktg. and refining divsn., 1983-86; gen. counsel Mobil Corp., Fairfax, Va., 1986-95; sr. ptnr. Holland & Knight, Washington, 1995-98. Bd. editors Yale Law Jour., 1958-59. Bd. dirs. Nat. Symphony Orch. Assn., 1991—, pres., 1995-98; trustee Shakespeare Theatre, 1993-2000; bd. dirs. Adirondack Nature Conservancy, 1998—, vice-chmn., 2000—; bd. dirs. Adirondack Coun., 1998—. Office: 10 Kalorama Cir NW Washington DC 20008-1616

FOWLER, JOHN WELLINGTON, lawyer; b. Waterbury, Conn., May 26, 1935; s. Donald Eugene and Elsie (Paige) F.; m. Judith Seymour, July 27, 1957; children— Stephen, Jeannine, Suzanne. A.B., Harvard U., 1957; J.D., U. Calif.-Berkeley, 1965. Bar: Calif. 1965, U.S. Dist. Ct. (no. dist.) Calif. Assoc. McCutchen, Doyle, Brown, and Enersen, San Francisco, 1965-72, ptnr. 1972— , mng. ptnr., San Jose, 1981— ; lectr. Calif. Continuing Edn. of Bar, 1980-81, 84. Pres. Santa Clara Bar Found., San Jose, 1984, Moraga Park and Recreation Commn., Calif. 1972, Moraga Parks Found., 1974; pres. Moraga Community Assn., 1971; councilman, mayor Town of Moraga, 1977-81. Served to capt. USMC, 1957-62. Mem. ABA, Santa Clara County Bar Assn. Fax: 650-849-4800. E-mail: jwfowler@mdbe.com. Federal civil litigation, State civil litigation, Environmental. Office: McCutchen Doyle Brown & Enersen 3150 Porter Dr Palo Alto CA 94304-1212

FOX, DONALD THOMAS, lawyer; b. Council Bluffs, Iowa, June 12, 1929; s. Donald and Genevieve (Tinley) F.; m. Ana Clemencia Tercero-Graham; children: Mark, Matthew, Genevieve, Melissa. AB magna cum laude, Harvard U., 1951; LLB, N.Y. U., 1956; Brevet de Traduction et de Terminologie Juridiques, U. Paris, 1957, Diplôme de Droit Comparé, 1961. Bar: N.Y. 1957, U.S. Ct. Claims 1960, U.S. Dist. Ct. (so. and ea. dists.) N.Y. 1960, U.S. Ct. Appeals (2nd cir.) 1960, D.C. 1968, U.S. Tax Ct. 1973. Instr. Inst. Comparative Law, NYU, 1957-59; assoc. Davis, Polk, Wardwell, Sunderland & Kiendl, N.Y.C., 1958-67; ptnr. Fox Horan & Camerini, LLP and predecessor firms, 1968—. Bd. dirs. Washington Sq. Legal Svcs., Inc., N.Y.C., 1974-85, Uniroyal Goodrich Tire Co., 1990-96, Michelin Licensing Svcs. Inc., Globalstar do Brazil, 1995-99; mem. adv. com. on history and theory Harvard U. Grad. Sch. Design, 1990—. Author: Conciliation of International Economic Disputes, 1964, Human Rights in Guatemala, 1979, Report on Contra Activity in Nicaragua, 1985, Violence in Colombia, 1989, Hungarian Constitutional Reform and the Rule of Law, 1993, Elections in Ethiopia, 1995, Elections in Nicaragua, 1996, Elections in Mexico, 1997; editor: The Cambodian Incursion: Legal Issues, 1971; mem. panel advisors Jour. Internat. Law and Politics, 1968-99; contbr. articles to legal jours. Trustee Law Ctr. Found., N.Y.U., 1975-86, chmn. campaign fund , 1980; mem. Am. Soc., 1975—; Coun. on Fgn. Rels., 1973—; Pres.'s assocs. Harvard U., 2000—. 1st lt. USAF, 1951-53. Named to Com. of Honor, Giulio Romano Exhbn., Mantova, Italy, 1989; Albert Gallatin fellow, 1978; Nat. scholar Harvard U., Root-Tilden scholar NYU, Fulbright scholar U. Paris. Fellow: Am. Bar Found. (life); mem.: Am. Law Inst. (sustaining life), Am. Assn. Internat. Commn. Jurists (exec. com., bd. dirs. 1970—, chmn. 1991—), Am. Arbitration Assn. (panel arbitrators 1970—), Assn. of Bar of City of N.Y. (chmn. com. lawyers role in search for peace 1969—71, chmn. com. audit 1978—80, treas. 1982—84, chmn. com. profl. responsibility 1971—74, chmn. fin. com. 1982—84), NYU Law Alumni Assn. (pres. 1971—73), NYU Alumni Fedn. (pres. 1983—85), Humanitarian Found. for Nicaragua (exec. com. bd. dirs. 1991—96), The Century Assn. (chmn. wine com.), Harvard Club of N.Y.C. Federal civil litigation, General corporate, Private international. Office: Fox Horan & Camerini LLP 825 3rd Ave New York NY 10022-7519 Fax: 212 269-2383. E-mail: dtfox@foxlex.com, dtfoxny@aol.com

FOX, EDWARD HANTON, lawyer; b. Oil City, Pa., June 3, 1945; s. Harry Hanton and Elizabeth Belle (Amsler) F.; children: Michael, Joseph, Katherine. AB, Cornell U., 1967, JD, 1971. Bar: N.Y. 1971, U.S. Dist. Ct. (we. and no. dists.) N.Y. 1971, U.S. Ct. Appeals (2d cir.) 1972, U.S. Supreme Ct. 1975. Staff atty. Monroe County Legal Assistance Corp., Rochester, N.Y., 1971-73; assoc. Harris, Beach & Wilcox, 1973-79, ptnr., 1980—. Counsel N.Y. Civil Liberties Union, 1972-83. Bd. dirs., Rochester Metnal Health Ctr., 1983-2001, Health Assn. Rochester and Monroe County, 1983—, Monroe County Legal Assistance Corp., 1993-2000, Rochester Health Care, 1993-96; pres. Park-Oxford Neighborhood Assn., 1977-83. Served with USAR, 1969-74. Recipient cert. of Appreciation, ACLU, 1982, Am. Arbitration Assn., 1984. Mem. Am. Bd. Trial Advocates, N.Y. Bar Assn., Monroe County Bar Assn. (trustee). Roman Catholic. State civil litigation, Condemnation, Health. Home: 10 Whitestone Ln Rochester NY 14618-4118 Office: Harris Beach Wilcox 130 Main St E Rochester NY 14604-1687

FOX, ELAINE SAPHIER, lawyer; b. Chgo., Nov. 18, 1934; d. Nathan Abraham and Rhoda M. (Schneidman) Saphier; m. Alan A. Fox, Apr. 25, 1954; children: Susan Fox Lorge, Wendy Fox Schneider, Mimi. BS, Northwestern U., 1955; JD, Ill. Inst. Tech., 1975. Bar: Ill., 1975, U.S. Dist. Ct. (no. dist.) Ill., 1975, U.S. Ct. Appeals (7th cir.) 1975, U.S. Ct. Appeals (fed. cir.) 1985. Trial atty. NLRB, Chgo., 1975-80; assoc. Hirsh & Schwartzman, 1980-81, Gottlieb & Schwartz, Chgo., 1981-84, ptnr., 1984-90, D'Ancona & Pflaum, Chgo., 1990—. Co-editor in chief How to Take a Case to the NLRB, 7th edit.; contbr. articles to profl. jours. and mags. Bd. dirs., exec. com. Am. Cancer Soc., Chgo., 1993—; mem. nat. and local governing coun. Am. Jewish Congress, Chgo., 1991—; bd. dirs. Jewish Vocat. Svc. Mem. ABA (subcom. NLRB practice and procedures, employment and labor rels. law, labor and employment law com., Women Rainmakers, midwest regional mgmt. chair NLRB practice and procedure com.), Women's Bar Assn., Chgo. Bar Assn. (labor and employment rels. vice chmn. 1989-90, chmn. 1990-91, co-chmn. Alliance for Women 1994-95, co-chair bd. mgrs. 1996-98), Decalogue Assn. Avocations: swimming, walking, reading, theater, art. General civil litigation, Labor. Office: Dancona and Pflaum 11 E Wacker Dr Ste 2800 Chicago IL 60601-2101 E-mail: efox@dancona.com

FOX, ELEANOR MAE COHEN, lawyer, educator, writer; b. Trenton, N.J., Jan. 18, 1936; d. Herman and Elizabeth (Stein) Cohen; children: Douglas Anthony, Margot Alison, Randall Matthew. BA, Vassar Coll., 1956; LLB, NYU, 1961. Bar: N.Y. 1961, U.S. Dist. Ct. N.Y. 1964, U.S. Supreme Ct. 1965. Editor high sch. textbooks Cambridge Book Co., N.Y.C., 1956-57; editor labor service publ. Bur. Nat. Affairs, Washington, 1957-58; assoc. Simpson Thacher & Bartlett, 1962-70, partner, 1970-76, of counsel, 1976—; assoc. prof. law NYU, 1976-78, prof., 1978—, dir. Root-Tilden program, 1979-81, assoc. dean Law Sch., 1987-90, Walter Derenberg prof. trade regulation, 1994—. Lectr. on antitrust and competition policy, domestic, internat. and comparative; mem. Pres. Carter's Nat. Commn. Rev. Antitrust Laws and Procedures, 1978-79; mem. adv. bd. Bur. Nat. Affairs Antitrust and Trade Regulation Reporter, 1977—; trustee NYU Law Ctr. Found., 1974-92; trustee Lawyers' Com. Civil Rights Under Law, 1988—; mem. Coun. Fgn. Rels., 1993—; mem. Pres. Clinton's internat. competition policy adv. com. to advise the U.S. Atty. Gen., 1997-2000. Author: (with Byron E. Fox) Corporate Acquisitions and Mergers, Vol. 1, 1968, Vol. 2, 1970, Vol. 3, 1973, Vol. 4, 1981, rev. edit., 2000; (novel) W.L., Esquire, 1977, (with G. Bermann, R. Goebel, W. Davey) European Community Law, Cases and Materials, 1993, supplement, 1998; (with Lawrence A. Sullivan) Antitrust—Cases and Materials, 1989, supplement, 1995; (with J. Fingleton, D. Neven, P. Seabright) Competition Policy and the Transformation of Central Europe, 1996; bd. editors N.Y. Law Jour., 1976-99, Antitrust Bull., 1986—; mem. adv. bd. Antitrust Law and Econs. Rev., 1988—, Rev. Indsl. Orgn., 1990—, EEC Merger Control Reporter, 1992—, Gaceta Juridica de la CE y de la Competencia, 1992—, World Competition: Law and Economics Review, 1999—; contbr. articles to legal jours. Fellow Am. Bar Found., N.Y. Bar Found.; mem. ABA (chmn. merger com. antitrust sect. 1974-77, chmn. publs. com. 1977-78, chmn. Sherman Act com. 1978-79, mem. council antitrust sect. 1979-83, 90-94, vice chmn. antitrust sect. 1992-94, chair NAFTA Task Force, 1993-99), N.Y. State Bar Assn. (chmn. antitrust sect. 1978-79, mem. exec. com. antitrust sect. 1979-83), Fed. Bar Council (trustee 1974-76, v.p. 1976-78), Assn. of Bar of City of N.Y. (v.p. 1989-90, exec. com. 1977-81, chmn. trade regulation com. 1973-76, lawyer advt. com. 1976-77, chmn. com. on U.S. in a global economy, 1991-94), Am. Law Inst., Assn. Am. Law Schs. (chmn. sect. antitrust and econ. regulation 1981-83), NYU Law Alumni Assn. (bd. dirs. 1974-79, 87-91), Am. Fgn. Law Assn. (v.p. 1979-82, 98—). E-mail: eleanor.fox@nyu.edu

FOX, GARY DEVENOW, lawyer; b. Detroit, Sept. 8, 1951; s. Edward J. Fox. BA in Polit. Sci. and Drama, Drury Coll., 1973; JD, U. Fla., 1976. Bar: Fla. 1976, U.S. Dist. Ct. (so. and mid. dists.) Fla. 1977, U.S. Ct. Appeals (5th and 11th cirs.) 1977, U.S. Supreme Ct. 1981. From assoc. to ptnr. Frates, Floyd, Pearson, Stewart, Richman & Greer, Miami, 1976-84; ptnr. Stewart, Tilghman, Fox & Bianchi, PA, 1984—. Exec. editor U. Fla. Law Rev.; contbr. articles to profl. jours. Mem. ABA, Fla. Bar (cert. civil trial advocacy 1983, chmn. code and rules of evidence com. 1997—, civil procedure rules com.), Fla. Bd. Bar Examiners, Dade County Bar Assn., Assn. Trial Lawyers Am. (substaining, lectr.), Acad. Fla. Trial Lawyers (diplomate, lectr.), Dade County Trial Lawyers Assn. (bd. dirs. 1986-89), Am. Bd. Trial Advocates (pres. Miami chpt. and Fla. fedn.), Bankers Club. Avocations: tennis, skiing. Personal injury, Product liability, Professional liability. Office: 1 SE 3rd Ave Ste 3000 Miami FL 33131-1715

FOX, JAMES CARROLL, federal judge; b. Atchison, Kans., Nov. 6, 1928; s. Jared Copeland and Ethel (Carroll) F.; m. Katharine deRosset Rhett, Dec. 30, 1950; children: James Carroll, Jr., Jane Fox Brown, Ruth Fox Jordan. BSBA, U. N.C., 1950, JD with honors, 1957. Bar: N.C. 1957. Law clk. U.S. Dist. Ct. (ea. dist.) N.C., Wilmington, 1957-58; assoc. Carter & Murchison, N.C., 1958-59; ptnr. Murchison, Fox & Newton, 1960-82; sr. fed. judge U.S. Dist. Ct. (ea. dist.) N.C., 1982—. Lectr. in field. Contbr. articles to profl. jours. Vestryman, St. James Episcopal Ch., 1973-75, 79-82. Mem. Hew Hanover County Bar Assn. (pres. 1967-68), Fifth Jud. Dist. Bar Assn. (sec. 1960-62). Office: US Dist Ct Alton Lennon Fed Bldg PO Box 2143 Wilmington NC 28402-2143

FOX, KATHY PINKSTAFF, lawyer; b. Indpls., Mar. 8, 1942; d. Kenneth Ellsworth and Mary Margaret (Spence) Pinkstaff; m. Richard T. Fox; chidlren: Amy, Michael, John Saxton. BA, DePauw U., 1964; JD, Northwestern U., 1979. Bar: Ill. 1979, U.S. Dist. Ct. (no. dist.) Ill. 1979, U.S. Ct. Appeals (7th cir.) 1989, U.S. Dist. Ct. (cen. dist.) 1990, U.S. Ct. Appeals (5th cir.) 1993, U.S. Supreme Ct. 1996. Ptnr. Wildman, Harrold, Allen & Dixon, Chgo., 1979—. Mem. ABA, Phi Beta Kappa. General civil litigation, Government contracts and claims, Personal injury. Home: 661 Sheridan Rd Winnetka IL 60093-2323 Office: Wildman Harrold Allen & Dixon 225 W Wacker Dr Chicago IL 60606-1224

FOX, MICHAEL EDWARD, lawyer; b. Chgo., Apr. 14, 1938; s. Charles and Beatrice (Chazin) F.; children— William Bradley, Elizabeth Rachel; m. Karen A. Fox; stepchildren: Christopher S. Riback, Melissa J. Riback, L. Brandon Liss; B.S., U. Ill., 1959; J.D., Harvard U., 1962. Bar: Ill. 1962, U.S. Dist. Ct. (no. dist.) Ill. 1963, U.S. Supreme Ct. 1967. Assoc. firm Rusnak, Deutsch & Gilbert, Chgo., 1963-65; staff atty. Joint Com. on Internal Revenue Taxation, U.S. Congress, Washington, 1965-68; assoc. firm Seyfarth, Shaw, Fairweather & Geraldson, Chgo., 1968-72, ptnr., 1972-74; ptnr. firm Adams, Fox, Adelstein & Rosen, Chgo., 1974—89; ptnr. Jenner & Block, 1989-92; ptnr. Aronbers, Goldsehn, Davis & Garmisa, 1992-94; ptnr. Michael E. Fox & Assocs., 1994-95; ptnr. Fox, Swibel & Lewis, 1995-99; ptnr. Fox, hefter, Swibel, Lewis & Carroll, 1999-. Contbr. articles to Jour. of Taxation. Bd. dirs., trustee Goodwill Industries of Chgo. and Cook County, 1973-83. Mem. Chgo. Bar Assn., Ill. Bar Assn., ABA. Home e-mail: MEFox@home.com; office e-mail: MFox@FHSLC.com. General corporate, Real property, Corporate taxation. Home: 529 Voltz Rd Northbrook IL 60062-4709

FOX, PATRICK JOSEPH, lawyer; b. Atlanta, May 30, 1950; s. Joseph M. and Betty J. (Garvey) F.; m. Martha Ann Adams, June 12, 1976; children: Meredith Ashley, Patrick Joseph Jr. AB, U. Ga., 1972, JD, 1975. Bar: U.S. Dist. Ct. (no. dist.) Ga. 1976, U.S. Ct. Appeals (11th cir.) 1981, U.S. Supreme Ct. 1979. Assoc. Thomas K. McWhorter, Jonesboro, Ga., 1975-78, Glaze McNally & Glaze, Jonesboro, 1978-80; ptnr. Glaze & McNally P.C., Jonesboro, 1980-86, McNally, Fox, Mahler, Cameron and Stephens, P.C. (formerly McNally, Fox, Mahler & Cameron, P.C.), Fayetteville, Ga., 1986—. Mem. Ga. Trial Lawyers Assn. (v.p. 1986—), Assn. Trial Lawyers Am., State Bar Assn. Ga., Clayton Bar Assn., Fayette County Bar Assn., Lawyers Club Atlanta, Atlanta Bar Assn. Family and matrimonial, Personal injury, Workers' compensation. Home: 135 Stable Creek Rd Fayetteville GA 30215-7408 Office: McNally Fox Mahler & Cameron PC 100 Habersham Dr Fayetteville GA 30214-1381

FOX, PAUL WALTER, lawyer; b. Temple, Tex., June 22, 1949; s. Robert Bryan and Geraldine (Davis) F.; m. Dana Hendricks, Mar. 15, 1975. A.B. cum laude, Harvard U., 1970; J.D., U. Tex., 1972. Bar: Tex. 1973, D.C. 1975, U.S. Ct. Appeals (D.C. cir.) 1975, U.S. Ct. Appeals (5th cir.) 1974, U.S. Ct. Appeals (10th cir.) 1984, U.S. Supreme Ct. 1976. Assoc. Ashton & Fox, Austin, Tex., 1973-75, Glendening & Schmid, Washington, 1975-77; ptnr. Bracewell & Patterson, Washington, 1977— . Mem. ABA, Fed. Energy Bar Assn., U. Tex. Law Sch. Alumni Assn. (dist. bd. dirs. 1981—). Democrat. Episcopalian. Clubs: Gibson Island, International, Harvard (Washington). General corporate, FERC practice, Private international. Home: Stillwater Rd Gibson Island MD 21056 Office: Bracewell & Patterson 2000 K St NW Ste 500 Washington DC 20006-1872

FOX, REEDER RODMAN, lawyer; b. Easton, Pa., Oct. 18, 1934; s. Louis Rodman and Mary Catherine (Cannon) F.; m. Marion Laffey, May 12, 1962; children: Rodman R., Drew D., Vanessa S. BA, Yale U., 1956; LLB, Harvard U., 1959. Bar: Pa. 1960, U.S. Dist. Ct. (ea. dist.) Pa. 1960, U.S. Ct. Appeals (3d cir.) 1960. Assoc. Duane, Morris & Heckscher, Phila., 1960-65, ptnr., 1965—. Served with Pa. N.G., 1959-60. Mem. ABA, Pa. Bar Assn., Phila. Bar Assn. Republican. Roman Catholic. General civil litigation, Construction, Product liability. Office: Duane Morris & Heckscher Ste 4200 1 Liberty Pl Philadelphia PA 19103 E-mail: fox@duanemorris.com

FOXHOVEN, JERRY RAY, lawyer; b. Yankton, N.D., July 24, 1952; s. Elmer William and Ida Elizabeth (Lubbers) F.; m. Julie Ann Greco, Apr. 6, 1985; children: Anthony Michael, Peter Joseph. BS summa cum laude, Morningside Coll., 1974; JD, Drake U., 1977. Bar: Iowa 1977, U.S. Dist. Ct. (so. and no. dists.) Iowa 1977, U.S. Ct. Appeals (8th cir.) 1977, U.S. Supreme Ct. 1981, Nebr. 1985, U.S. Dist. Ct. Nebr. 1985, Wis. 1986. Assoc. Critelli & Pille, Des Moines, 1977-79, ptnr., 1979-82, Foxhoven & McCann, Des Moines, 1982-88, Peddicord, Wharton, Thune, Foxhoven & Spencer, P.C., 1988-91; pvt. practice, 1991-2000; adminstr. Iowa Citizen Foster Care Rev. Bd., Des Moines, 2000—. Instr. criminaljustice dept. Des Moines Area Community Coll., Ankeny, Iowa, 197 8-81, Am. Inst. Banking, 1982-85. Mem. steering con. Culver for U.S. Senate, Des Moines, 1980; chmn. Iowa State Foster Care Rev. Bd., 1986-99; bd. dirs., nat. pres. Nat. Assn. Foster Care Reviewers, 1988-01; mem. parish coun. Sacred Heart Roman Cath. Ch., West Des Moines, 1982. Lodge: Masons (master 1990). Democrat. State civil litigation, Criminal, Personal injury. Home: 1608 NW 101st St Clive IA 50325-6716 Office: Lucas Bldg 321 E 12th St 3d Fl Des Moines IA 50319-0083 E-mail: jfoxhoven@dia.state.ia.us

FOY, HERBERT MILES, III, lawyer, educator; b. Statesville, N.C., Mar. 22, 1945; s. Herbert Miles Jr. and Perci Aileen (Lazenby) F.; m. Eleanor Jane Meschan, June 27, 1970; children: Anna Meschan, Sarah Aileen. AB, U. N.C., 1967; MA, Harvard U., 1968; JD, U. Va., 1972. Bar: N.C. 1973, U.S. Dist. Ct. (mid. and we. dists.) N.C., U.S. Ct. Appeals (4th cir.). Jud. clk. U.S. Ct. Appeals (5th cir.), Atlanta, 1972-73; assoc. Smith, Moore, Smith, Schell & Hunter, Greensboro, N.C., 1973-77, 81-83, ptnr., 1983-84; sr. atty. advisor office legal counsel U.S. Dept. Justice, Washington, 1977-81; assoc. prof. Sch. Law Wake Forest U., Winston-Salem, N.C., 1984-87, prof., 1987—, assoc. dean acad. affairs, 1990-95, Law Sch., Wake Forest U., Winston-Salem, 2000—. Contbr. articles to legal jours. Morehead scholar, 1963; Woodrow Wilson fellow, 1968. Mem. ABA, N.C. Bar Assn., N.C. State Bar Assn., Fosythe County Bar Assn., Order of Coif, Phi Beta Kappa. Democrat. Methodist. Avocations: banjo playing, gardening, athletics, poetry. Home: 2328 Oak Ridge Rd Oak Ridge NC 27310-9701 Office: Wake Forest U Sch Law PO Box 7206U Winston Salem NC 27109-7206

FRADELLA, HENRY F. law educator; b. N.Y.C., Feb. 11, 1969; s. Diana Dressel and Anthony Peter F. BA, Clark U., 1990; M Forensic Sci., JD, The George Washington U., 1993; PhD, Ariz. State U., 1997. Bar: Ariz. 1995; U.S. Dist. Ct. Ariz., 1995. Jud. law clk. U.S. Dist. Ct., Phoenix, 1993-94; instr. Ariz. State U., Tempe, 1994-97; law clk./summer assoc. Squire, Sanders & Dempsey, Washington, 1991; prof. of law and justice The Coll. of N.J., Ewing, N.J., 1997; assoc. Kaye, Scholar, Fineman, Hays & Handler, 1990. Dir. Fradella Forensic Cons., Yardley, Pa., 1997. Author: (books) Key Cases, Comments, and Questions on Substantive Criminal Law, 2000, Forensic Psychology: The Use of Behavioral Sciences in the Civil and Criminal Justice Systems, 2002, others. Trustee Samuel DeWitt Proctor Acad. Charter Sch., West Trenton, N.J., 1999-2000. Mem. Am. Soc. Criminology, Acad. Criminal Justice Scis., ABA, Am. Judicature Soc., N.E. Assn. Criminal Justice Scis., N.J. Assn. Criminal Justice Educators, Lambda Legal Def. and Edn. Fund/U.S., Human Rights Campaign/Phila., Phi Beta Kappa. Avocations: movies, music, singing, travel, cooking.

FRAIBERG, MATTHEW AARON, lawyer; b. Detroit, Aug. 13, 1971; s. Allan David and Nancy Ellen F.; m. Karen Beth Pierce, Sept. 27, 1997. BA, Mich. State U., 1994; JD, U. Toledo, 1997. Lawyer Guardian Alarm Corp., Southfield, Mich., 1997-98, Sommers, Schwartz Silver and Schwartz, Southfield, 1998—. Avocations: sports, flying. Personal injury, Product liability. Office: Sommers Schwartz Silver & Schwartz 2000 Town Center Ste 900 Southfield MI 48075

FRAME, NANCY DAVIS, lawyer; b. Brookings, S.D., Dec. 13, 1944; m. J. Davidson Frame, Mar. 28, 1970 (div. Oct. 1994); 1 child, Katherine Adele; m. Kelly C. Kammerer, Oct. 2, 1999. BS, S.D. State U., 1966; MA, Georgetown U., 1968, JD, 1976. Bar: D.C. 1976. Atty., advisor AID, Washington, 1976-81, asst. gen. counsel, 1981-86; dep. dir. Trade and Devel. Agy., 1986-99. Bd. dirs. Daktronics, Inc. Recipient Superior Honor award AID, 1984, Presdl. Meritorious Rank award, 1993, Disting. Alumnus award S.D. State U., 1998, Presdl. Disting. Rank award, 1998; Fulbright fellow , 1966, NDEA fellow, 1967. Home: Psc 116 Box Oecd APO AE 09777-5000 also: 11 bis Boulevard Jules Sandeau 75016 Paris France

FRAME, TED RONALD, lawyer; b. Milw., June 27, 1929; s. Morris and Jean (Lee) F.; m. Lois Elaine Pilgaim, Aug. 15, 1954; children: Kent, Lori, Nancy, Owen. Student, UCLA, 1946-49; AB, Stanford U., 1950; LLB, 1952. Bar: Calif. 1953. Gen. agri-bus. practice, Coalinga, Calif., 1953—; sr. pntr. Frame & Matsumoto and predecessor , 1965—. Trustee Baker Mus.; dir. West Hills Coll. Found. Mem. ABA, Calif. Bar Assn., Fresno County Bar Assn., Kings Co. Bar Assn., Am. Agrl. Law Assn., Coalinga C. of C. (past pres.), Masons, Shriners, Elks. Avocations: bicycling, hiking. Contracts commercial. Home: 1222 Nevada St Coalinga CA 93210-1239 Office: 201 Washington St Coalinga CA 93210-0895 E-mail: lawriam@lightspeed.net

FRAMME, LAWRENCE HENRY, III, lawyer; b. Louisville, Oct. 8, 1949; s. Lawrence Henry and Margaret Gertrude (Hayes) F.; m. Frances Claire Schwacke, Dec. 27, 1969; children: Jessica Marie, Lawrence Henry IV, Benjamin Hayes. BA, Centre Coll., 1971; JD cum laude, Washington and Lee U., 1974. Bar: Va. 1974, U.S. Dist. Ct. Va., 1974, U.S. Ct. Appeals (4th cir.) 1974. Assoc. McGuire, Woods & Battle, Richmond, Va., 1974-81, Lacy & Baliles, Richmond, 1981-82; mem. firm, dir. Mezzullo, McCandlish & Framme, Richmond, 1982-90; sec. econ. devel. (gov's. cabinet) Commonwealth of Va., 1990-92; chmn. Virginians for Progress Found., 1992; v.p. LeClair, Ryan, Joynes, Epps & Framme, Richmond, 1992-95; prin. Framme Law Firm, 1995—; co-chmn. gov's. adv. coun. Workforce 2000, 1990-91. Chmn. Dem. Party Va., 1986-90, 2001-. Va. State Bd. Community Colls., mem. 1987-90, chmn. 1989-90; bd. visitors Va. Commonwealth U., 1992-96; mem. bd. dirs. Downtown YMCA, 1986-95, chmn. 1992-94; bd. dirs., sec. Va. Biotech. Rsch. Park Authority, 1991-92, 93-95, Va. Biotech. Rsch. Park Corp., 1994—, Leadership Metro Richmond, 1991-94; bd. dirs., legal advisor Richmond Urban League, 1985-86; mem. bd. dirs. Metro Richmond YMCA, 1995—. Recipient Legal award Housing Opportunities Made Equal, Richmond, 1983; named Alumni of Yr., Leadership Metro Richmond, 1990. Mem. ABA, VSB, Va. Bar Assn., Richmond Bar Assn., Omicron Delta Kappa. Roman Catholic. General civil litigation, General corporate, Finance. Home: 2906 Douglasdale Rd Richmond VA 23221-3614 Office: Framme Law Firm PC One Capital Square 830 E Main St 19th Fl Richmond VA 23219-3539 Business E-Mail: lframme@frammelaw.com

FRANCESCHI, ERNEST JOSEPH, JR. lawyer; b. L.A., Feb. 1, 1957; s. Ernest Joseph and Doris Cecilia (Beluche) F. BS, U. So. Calif., 1978; JD, Southwestern U., L.A., 1980. Bar: Calif. 1984, U.S. Dist. Ct. (cen. dist.) Calif. 1984, U.S. Dist. Ct. (ea. dist.) Calif. 1986, U.S. Dist. Ct. (no. and so. dists.) Calif. 1987, U.S. Ct. Appeals (9th cir.) 1984, U.S. Supreme Ct. 1989. Pvt. practice law, L.A., 1984—; judge pro tem L.A. Superior Ct., 1999—. Mem. Assn. Trial Lawyers Am., Calif. Trial Lawyers Assn., L.A. Trial Lawyers Assn., Trial Lawyers for Pub. Justice, Fed. Bar Assn. Federal civil litigation, Personal injury. Office: 445 S Figueroa St Ste 2600 Los Angeles CA 90071-1630

FRANCH, RICHARD THOMAS, lawyer; b. Melrose Park, Ill., Sept. 23, 1942; s. Robert and Julia (Martino) F.; m. Patricia Staufenberg, Apr. 18, 1971 (dec. Apr. 1994); children: Richard T. Jr., Katherine J.; m. Susan L. Rice, Sept. 1, 1995. B.A. cum laude, U. Notre Dame, 1964; J.D., U. Chgo., 1967. Bar: Ill. 1967, U.S. Dist. Ct. (no. dist.) Ill. 1967, U.S. Supreme Ct. 1980, U.S. Ct. Appeals (2d cir.) 1984, U.S. Ct. Appeals (3d cir.) 1981, U.S. Ct. Appeals (6th cir.) 1991, U.S. Ct. Appeals (7th cir.) 1971, U.S. Ct. Appeals (8th cir.) 1981, U.S. Ct. Appeals (9th cir.) 1997, U.S. Dist. Ct. (no. dist.) Wis. 1989, U.S. Tax Ct. 1994. Assoc. Jenner & Block, Chgo., 1967-68, 70-74, ptnr., 1975—. Former mem. Ill. Supreme Ct. Rules Com. Served to capt. U.S. Army, 1968-70 Decorated Bronze star, Army Commendation medal. Fellow Am. Coll. Trial Lawyers; mem. Am. Law Inst. Antitrust, Federal civil litigation, State civil litigation. Office: Jenner & Block Ste 4700 One IBM Plz Chicago IL 60611 E-mail: dickfranch@aol.com, rfranch@jenner.com

FRANCHINI, GENE EDWARD, state supreme court justice; b. Albuquerque, May 19, 1935; s. Mario and Lena (Vaio) F.; m. Glynn Hatchell, Mar. 22, 1969; children: Pamela, Lori (dec.), Gina, Joseph James, Nancy. BBA, Loyola U., 1955; degree in adminstrn., U. N.Mex., 1957; JD, Georgetown U., 1960; LLM, U. Va., 1995. Bar: N.Mex. 1960, U.S. Dist. Ct. N.Mex. 1961, U.S. Ct. Appeals (10th cir.) 1970, U.S. Supreme Ct. 1973. Ptnr. Matteucci, Gutierrez & Franchini, Albuquerque, 1960-70, Matteucci, Franchini & Calkins, Albuquerque, 1970-75; judge State of N.Mex. 2d Jud. Dist., 1975-81; atty.-at-large Franchini, Wagner, Oliver, Franchini & Curtis, 1982-90; chief justice N.Mex. Supreme Ct., Santa Fe, 1990-99, justice, 1999—. V.p. bd. dirs. Conf. Chief Justices, 1997-98. Chmn. Albuquerque Pers. Bd., 1972, Albuquerque Labor Rels. Bd., 1972, Albuquerque Interim Bd. Ethics, 1972. Capt. USAF, 1960-66. Recipient Highest award Albuquerque Human Rights Bd., 1999. Mem. Am. Bd. Trial Advocates, N.Mex. Trial Lawyers (pres. 1967-68), N.Mex. Bar Assn. (bd. dirs. 1976-78), Albuquerque Bar Assn. (bd. dirs. 1976-78, Outstanding Judge award 1997). Democrat. Roman Catholic. Avocations: fishing, hunting, golf, mushroom hunting. Home: 4901 Laurene Ct NW Albuquerque NM 87120-1026 Office: NMex Supreme Ct PO Box 848 Santa Fe NM 87504-0848*

FRANCIS, CLINTON WILLIAM, legal educator; b. Wanganui, New Zealand, Aug. 29, 1951; s. Raymond and Jean (Dickie) F.; m. Steffani Weiss, May 29, 1982. LL.B. with honors, Victoria U., Wellington, New Zealand, 1973, LL.M. with honors, 1978; S.J.D., U. Va., 1982. Bar: New Zealand 1975. Jr. lectr. Victoria U. Law Sch., 1974-75; assoc. in law U. Calif., Berkeley, 1977-78; asst. prof. Northwestern U. Sch. Law, Chgo., 1978-82, assoc. prof., 1982-84, prof., 1984— . Contbr. articles to profl. jours. Victoria U. sr. scholar, 1974; DuPont fellow U. Va., 1975-77; Fulbright grantee, 1975-78; recipient Robert Childres award for teaching excellence Northwestern U., 1984; Walter Meyer Research grantee Am. Bar Found., 1984. Home: 415 W Surf St Chicago IL 60657-6142 Office: Northwestern U Sch Law 357 E Chicago Ave Chicago IL 60611-3059

FRANCIS, JEROME LESLIE, lawyer; b. Seattle, May 25, 1941; s. Leslie J. and Phyllis G. (Pike) F.; m. Jen H. Hough, Nov. 2, 1968; children: David S., Catherine E. BA in Bus. Adminstrn., U. WAsh., 1963; JD, San Francisco Law Sch., 1968. Bar: Mass. 1970. Sole practice, Sudbury, Mass., 1970-74; atty. legal dept. Texaco Inc., Boston, 1974-76, Cherry Hill, N.J., 1976-84, Denver, 1984-89; sr. atty. Star Enterprise (Texaco-SRI), Houston, 1989-98; atty. legal dept. Equiva Svcs. (Texaco-Shell-SRI), 1998—. Mem. ABA, Mass. Bar Assn. Republican. Episcopalian. General corporate, Environmental, Real property.

FRANCIS, MERRILL RICHARD, lawyer; b. Iowa City; children: Kerry L., David M., Robin A. B.A. magna cum laude, Pomona Coll., 1954; J.D., Stanford U., 1959. Bar: Calif. 1960, Supreme Ct. 1970. Ptnr. Sheppard, Mullin, Richter & Hampton, L.A., 1959-00, of counsel, 2001—. Mem. Fellows of Contemporary Art, 1980—. Served to lt. (j.g.) U.S. Navy, 1954-56. Fellow Am. Bar Found., Am. Coll. Bankruptcy (chmn. 9th cir. admissions coun. 1992-95, 2001—, bd. dirs. 1995—, chair bd. regents 1995-01); mem. ABA (bus. law sect., chmn. secured creditors com. 1981-85, chmn. bus. bankruptcy com. 1986-89, chmn. Task Force on Fed. Ct. Structure 1990-93, mem. Coun. Bus. Law sect. 1991-95, chmn. ad hoc com. on brown bag programs 1994-97, chmn. ad hoc com. bankruptcy ct. structure and insolvency process com. 2001-, sr. lawyers divsn., chmn. sr. housing and real estate practice com. 2001—), State Bar of Calif. (mem. debtor/creditor and bankruptcy com. of bus. law sect. 1978-79), L.A. County Bar Assn. (mem. real property sect., exec. com. 1970-80, mem. comml. law and bankruptcy sect., sect. chmn. 1976-77), Fin. Lawyers Conf. (bd. govs. 1970—, pres. 1972-73), La Canada-Flintridge C. of C. and Cmty. Assn. (pres. 1971-72), Order of the Coif, Jonathan Club, Phi Beta Kappa. Banking, Bankruptcy, Contracts commercial. Office: Sheppard Mullin Richter & Hampton 333 S Hope St Fl 48 Los Angeles CA 90071-1406 E-mail: mfrancis@smrh.com

FRANCK, BRIGITTE BRODERICK, lawyer; b. Vereeniging, South Africa; d. David John and Penelope Anne Brady; m. Bruce Edward Franck, Mar. 5, 1999. B of Commerce, U. Stellenbosch, South Africa, 1993, LLB, 1995. Candidate atty. Cliffe Dekker & Todd, Inc., Johannesburg, South Africa, 1996-97, profl. asst. South Africa, 1998; assoc. Cliffe Dekker Fuller Moore, Inc., South Africa, 1999, dir. South Africa, 2000—. Mem. Law Soc. Transvaal, Law Soc. Cape. General corporate, Mergers and acquisitions, Taxation, general. Office: Cliffe Dekker Fuller Moore Private Bag X7 Johannesburg 2010 South Africa Fax: 27 11 290 7300. E-mail: franck@cdfm.co.za

FRANK, ALIX, lawyer; b. Klagenfurt, Austria, Dec. 5, 1959; d. Otto Dkfm and Beatrix F.; m. Gunther Mag Thomasser. M, U. Salzburg, PhD, 1982. Ex ho. gen. counsel Wienerberger Baustoffindustrie, Vienna, 1989—. Mem. Austrian Bar Assn. (bd. dirs.), MacIntyre Straiter, EureseaU (v.p.). Computer, Mergers and acquisitions, Personal injury. Office: Schottengasse 10 1010 Vienna Austria Fax: 0043 1 523 33 15. E-mail: austrolaw@alix-frank.co.at

FRANK, BARRY H. lawyer; b. Nov. 19, 1938; s. David and Rose (Pearl) F.; divorced; children: Toby L., S. Kenneth, Gary A. BS, Pa. State U., 1960; LLB, Temple U., 1963. Bar: Pa. 1964. Staff atty. IRS, Phila., 1963-66; tax mgr. Ernst & Whinney, 1966-74; exec. v.p., gen. counsel N.F.I. Industries, Inc., Vineland, N.J., 1974-75; ptnr. Pechner, Dorman, Wolffe, Rounick & Cabot, Phila., 1975-87, Schnader, Harrison, Segal & Lewis, LLP, Phila., 1987—. Instr. Temple U. Tax Inst., Phila., 1976—. Co-author: Alimony, Child Support and Counsel Fees; mem. editl. bd. The Practical Acct.; contbr. more than 60 articles to profl. jours. Mem. exec. com. Mayor's Small Bus. Adv. Coun., Phila., 1981-83. Mem. ABA, AICPA, Phila. Bar Assn., Pa. Inst. CPAs. Republican. Jewish. Corporate taxation, Estate taxation, Taxation, general. Office: Schnader Harrison Segal & Lewis LLP & Jamieson 1735 Market St Ste 3800 Philadelphia PA 19103-7503 E-mail: bprank@schnader.com

FRANK, BERNARD, lawyer; b. Wilkes-Barre, Pa., June 11, 1913; s. Abraham and Fanny F.; m. Muriel I. Levy, June 19, 1938; children: Roberta R. Penn, Allan R. PhB, Muhlenberg Coll., Allentown, Pa., 1935, LHD, 1987; JD, U. Pa., 1938; postgrad., NYU, 1940-42. Bar: Pa. 1939. Since practiced in, Allentown; asst. U.S. atty. Eastern Dist. Pa., 1950-51; asst. city solicitor Allentown, 1956-60. Author articles on ombudsmen in profl. jours. Vice chmn. B'nai B'rith Nat. Commn. Adult Jewish Edn., 1959-61, chmn., 1961-63; bd. dirs. Muhlenberg Coll., 1987-93. With AUS, 1943-46. Decorated comdr. Order of North Star Sweden; recipient Disting. Service award Internat. Ombudsman Inst., 1980 Mem. ABA (chmn. com. ombudsman 1970-76, vice chmn. com. on pub. advs. and pub. representation adminstrv. law sect. 1984-92, fellow adminstrv. law and regulatory procedure sect. 2000), Internat. Bar Assn. (chmn. com. ombudsman 1973-80), Fed. Bar Assn. (chmn. com. ombudsman 1973-80), Pa. Bar Assn., Lehigh Bar Assn., Inter-Am. Bar Assn., World Assn. Lawyers, U.S. Assn. Ombudsmen (hon.), Internat. Ombudsman Inst. (hon. life mem., bd. dirs. 1978-89, pres. 1984-88), Jewish Pub. Soc. Am. (bd. dirs. 1982-99, v.p. 1986-89, 94-98, life trustee 1999—), 94th Inf. Div. (pres. 1953-54). Estate planning, Non-profit and tax-exempt organizations, Probate. Home: 3203 W Cedar St Allentown PA 18104-3407 Office: 640 Hamilton Mall Allentown PA 18101-2110

FRANK, BERNARD ALAN, lawyer; b. Rochester, N.Y., Nov. 12, 1931; s. Mark Louis and Ella Mildred Frank; m. Barbara L. Wilan, June 14, 1952; children: Jeffrey, Glenn, Lauren. BSL, Northwester U., 1953, JD, 1955. Bar: N.Y. 1955, Ill. 1955, U.S. Dist. Ct. (we. dist.) N.Y. Ptnr. Frank, Garrity & Tiernan, Rochester, 1966—78, Weldman Williams Jordan Angeloff & Frank, Rochester, 1979-83, Underberg & Kessler LLP, Rochester, 1983—. Bd. dirs. Monroe Title Co. Mem. N.Y. Bar Assn., Monroe County Bar Assn., U.S. Tennis Assn. General corporate, Probate, Real property. Address: 25 San Rafael Dr Rochester NY 14618-3754 E-mail: bfrank@underberg-kessler.com

FRANK, FREDERICK NEWMAN, lawyer; b. Pitts., Jan. 10, 1947; s. Abraham C. and Nancy (Newman) F. BA, U. Pitts., 1967, JD, 1970. Bar: Pa. 1970, U.S. Dist. Ct. (we. dist.) Pa. 1970, U.S. Ct. Appeals (3d cir.) 1972. Law clk. Pa. Ct. of Common Pleas, Pitts., 1970-71; asst. atty. gen. Pa. Dept. of Justice, 1971-73; ptnr. Raphael-Sheinberg & Barmen, 1973-79, Baskin, Flaherty, Elliott & Mannino, P.C., Pitts., 1979— ; solicitor

Allegheny County Treas., 1974-94. Contbr. articles to law revs. Chmn. Urban Affairs Found., Pitts., 1976-79; treas. Allegheny County Democratic Com., 1980— ; bd. dirs. United Jewish Fedn. Recipient Stark Young Leadership award 1976, Levinson Human Relations award, 1984 (both United Jewish Fedn.). Mem. Pa. Bar Assn. (council family law sect. 1985—, editor newsletter, 1975-77), Allegheny County Bar Assn. (sec. family law sect. 1987—, vice chmn. council young lawyers div. 1978-79). Democrat. Jewish. Clubs: Concordia, Pitts. Athletic Assn. General civil litigation, Family and matrimonial, Election. Office: Gulf Towers Fl 34 Pittsburgh PA 15219

FRANK, GEORGE ANDREW, lawyer; b. Budapest, Hungary, Apr. 6, 1938; came to U.S., 1957; s. Alex and Ilona (Weiss) F.; m. Carole Shames, Feb. 14, 1979; children: Cheryl, Charles. BS, Colo. State U., 1960; PhD in Organic Chemistry, MIT, 1965; JD, Temple U., 1977. Bar: Pa. 1977, U.S. Dist. Ct. (ea. dist.) Pa. 1977, D.C. 1980, U.S. Ct. Appeals (fed. cir.) 1982, U.S. Supreme Ct. 1984. Sr. chemist Rohm & Haas Co., Phila., 1965-69; lab. head Borden Chem., 1969-73; sr. scientist Thiokol Corp., Trenton, N.J., 1973-74; counsel Du Pont Corp., Wilmington, Del., 1974-85, sr. counsel, 1986-92, corp. counsel, 1992-2001, intellectual property law group leader, 2000-2001; of counsel Drinker Biddle & Reath LLP, Philadelphia, 2001—. External adv. com. Colo. State U. Coll. Natural Scis., 1996—. Contbr. articles to profl. jours; patentee in field. Recipient Merck award Merck & Co., 1960; Sun Oil Co. grantee, 1964; fellow NIH. Mem. ABA (chair divsn. biotech. 1993-94, coun. 1994-98, chair chem. practice com. 1998-2000, chair divsn. biotech. and chem. practice 2000—), Phila. Patent Lawyers Assn. (chair bioscis. com. 1983-87, bd. govs. 1987-92, pres. 1992-93), Am. Intellectual Property Law Assn. (chair task force 1986), Benjamin Franklin Am. Inn of Cts. (v.p. 1996-97, pres. 1997-98). Republican. Avocations: tennis, squash, travel, books, opera. Intellectual property, Patent. Home: 520 Lindy Ln Bala Cynwyd PA 19004-1331 Office: Drinker Biddle & Reath LLP 1 Logan Square 18th & Cherry St Philadelphia PA 19103 E-mail: frankga@dbr.com

FRANK, JACOB, lawyer; b. Albany, Apr. 4, 1936; s. Isidore and Sara F.; m. Yoelith Frank, Aug. 26, 1936; children: Eytan, Michael, Adam, Orly. BEE, Rensselaer Poly. Inst., 1957; LLB, Am. U., 1963; postgrad., George Washington U. Coll. Law, 1964-67, NYU Law Sch., 1969-73. Bar: D.C. 1963, Mass. 1979, Va. 2001, U.S. Patent Office. Of counsel Alliance Law Group, Tysons Corner, Va., 2000—. General corporate. Home: 17040 Thousand Oaks Dr Haymarket VA 20169 Office: Alliance Law Group Tysons Corner VA 22182 E-mail: JYFRANK8@aol.com

FRANK, JOHN LEROY, lawyer, government executive, educator; b. Eau Claire, Wis., Mar. 13, 1952; s. George LeRoy and Frances Elaine (Torgerson) F. BS summa cum laude, U. Wis., Eau Claire, 1974; JD cum laude, U. Wis., Madison, 1977. Bar: Wis. 1977, U.S. Dist. Ct. (we. dist.) Wis. 1977, U.S. Supreme Ct. 1982. Instr. law U. Wis., Madison, 1976-77; assoc. Garvey, Anderson, Kelly & Ryberg, S.C., Eau Claire, 1977-81; legis dir., counsel Congressman Steve Gunderson, Washington, 1981-85, chief of staff, counsel, 1985-89; staff coord. 92 Group, 1987-89; instr. Chippewa Valley Tech. Coll., 1989-93, 97—, paralegal program dir., 1992-93, 97-01, pvt. practice Wis., 1990-93, 97—; counsel, minority cons. House Subcommittee on Livestock, Washington, 1993-95; counsel Congressman Steve Gunderson, 1993-97; dep. minority counsel House Com. on Agr., 1993-95, dep. chief counsel, 1995-97; commr. W. Ctrl. Wis. Regional Planning Commn., Eau Claire, 1998—, W. Ctrl. Wis Regional Planning Commn., Eau Claire, 1998—. Pol. analyst, commentator WEAU-TV, Eau Claire, Wis., 1998—; mem. Bush-Cheney Transition Adv. Com., 2001. Named One of Outstanding Young Men in Am., U.S. Jaycees, 1977. Mem. ABA, FBA, Wis. Bar Assn., The Presto Found. (v.p. 1992-93, 2000—, bd. dirs. 1992-93, 2000-01, pres. elect 2001-02), Wis. Assn. for Career and Tech. Edn. (bd. dirs. 2000—, legis. com. chair 2000-01, pres.-elect 2001—), U. Wis. Alumni Assn. (outstanding sr. arts & scis. 1974), Phi Delta Phi, Phi Gamma Delta (Durrance award 1978). Republican. Lutheran. Address: 2113 Meadow Ln Eau Claire WI 54701-7965

FRANK, JOSEPH ELIHU, lawyer; b. Burlington, Vt., Jan. 28, 1934; s. Max and Sara Ruth (Bramson) F.; m. Catherine Hartman Layne, Aug. 28, 1971; chldren: Sara Rebecca, Cheryl Elizabeth. AB, Harvard U., 1956, JD, 1959. Bar: Vt. 1960, U.S. Dist. Ct. Vt. 1960, U.S. Ct. Appeals (2d cir.) 1961. U.S. Supreme Ct. 1954. Law clk. to judge U.S. Dist. Ct. Vt., 1960; asst. U.S. atty. Dist. of Vt., 1961; sole practice Burlington, 1961-68; mem. Paul, Frank & Collins, Inc., 1968-96, of counsel, 1996—. Spl. counsel to Vt. Hwy. Bd., 1962-75, to Pub. Service Bd., 1965-69; chmn. adv. com. civil rules Vt. Supreme Ct., 1983-89. Alderman, City of Burlington, 1971-73; trustee Med. Ctr. Hosp. of Vt., Burlington, 1977-86. Mem. ABA, Vt. Bar Assn. (pres. 1983-84), Chittenden County Bar Assn., Am. Judicature Soc. Alternative dispute resolution, General civil litigation, Condemnation. Home: 8 Bay Crest Dr South Burlington VT 05403-7758 Office: Paul Frank & Collins, Inc 1 Church St Burlington VT 05402-1307 E-mail: w1sov@earthlink.net

FRANK, LLOYD, lawyer, retired chemical company executive; b. N.Y.C., Aug. 9, 1925; s. Herman and Selma (Lowenstein) F.; m. Beatrice Silverstein, Dec. 26, 1954; children: Margaret Lois, Frederick. B.A., Oberlin Coll., 1947; J.D., Cornell U., 1950. Bar: N.Y. 1950, U.S. Supreme Ct. 1973. Practiced law, N.Y.C., 1950—; sr. ptnr., exec. com., chmn. corp. dept. Parker Chapin LLP, 1985-99; sec., dir. Grow Group, Inc., 1964-95. Bd. dirs. Volt Info. Scis. Inc., (NYSE) N.Y.C., Madison Industries, Inc., N.Y.C., Dryclean, USA, Inc., Miami, Fla., AMEX, Pub. Art Fund, Inc., N.Y.C., Park Electrochem. Corp., (NYSE) Lake Success, N.Y., Internat. Longevity Ctr. U.S.A. Ltd., N.Y.C., Kulite Semicondr., Inc., Leonia, N.J.; sec. Esquire Radio & Electronics, Inc., Bklyn.; lectr. Am. Mgmt. Assn., 1967-77, Probe Internat., Inc., 1975-77, Corp. Seminars, Inc., 1968-71. Mem. ABA (com. negotiated acquisitions), Assn. Bar City of N.Y. (com. on internat. environ. law com. on product liability, com. on lawyers in transition, com. on securities law), N.Y. County Lawyers Assn. (com. on corp. law depts.), General corporate, Public international, Securities. Home: 25 Central Park W Apt 17Q New York NY 10023-7211 Office: Jenkins & Gilchrest Parker Chapin LLP Chrysler Bldg 405 Lexington Ave New York NY 10174-0002 E-mail: lfrank@jenkens.com

FRANK, RONALD WILLIAM, lawyer, financier; b. Greensburg, Pa., Mar. 11, 1947; s. William John and Louise (Mautino) F.; m. Marsha Ann Kolesar, Aug. 30, 1969. BSChemE, Carnegie Mellon U., 1969; JD, Duke U., 1972. Bar: Pa. 1972. Ptnr. Buchanan Ingersoll P.C., Pitts., 1972-93, Babst, Calland, Clements & Zomnir, P.C., Pitts., 1993-99, Reed Smith LLP, Pitts., 2000—. Sec. Nat. Roll Co. Contbr. articles to profl. jours. Chmn. nat. fund raising com., Carnegie-Mellon U., Pitts., 1983-88, bd. advisors Sch. Engring. and Sci., Carnegie Mellon U.; mem. bd. visitors sch. law Duke U., Durham, N.C. Mem. ABA, Pa. Bar Assn. (chmn. Internat. and Comparative law sect. 1992—), Allegheny County Bar Assn., Internat. Bar Assn., Duquesne Club, Shannopin Country Club. Avocations: golf, skiing, computers, amateur radio. General corporate, Private international, Mergers and acquisitions. Home: 1675 Gloucester Ct Sewickley PA 15143-8518 Office: Reed Smith 435 6th Ave Pittsburgh PA 15219-1886 E-mail: rfrank@reedsmith.com

FRANK, SARAH MYERS, lawyer; b. Indpls., Jan. 19, 1937; s. Dewey Everett and Minnie Estelle (Mitchell) M.; m. Ronald Marsh, Aug. 25, 1956; children: James, John, Janet. Student Principia Coll., Elsah, Ill., 1954-56; BS with Distinction, Purdue U., 1958; JD, Ind. U., 1977. Bar: Ind. 1977, U.S. Dist. Ct. (so. dist.) Ind. 1977, U.S. Ct. Appeals (7th cir.) 1984. Tchr. Colfax High Sch. (Ind.), 1958-59, Washington Twp. Schs., Indpls., 1973-74; sr. law clk. Ind. Supreme Ct., Indpls., 1977-85; staff atty. Hyatt Legal Svcs., Indpls., 1985-86, UAW Legal Svcs. Plan, Indpls., 1986-92; pvt. practice, 1992—. V.p. bd. dirs. Camp Fire, Inc., Indpls., 1983-85; bd. dirs. Dela. Trails Sch., Indpls., 1967-69, Ind. State Mus. Soc., 1992—. Mem. Ind. Bar Assn., Indpls. Bar Assn. (co-chmn. spl. projects women's div., family law sect., probate law sect.), AAUW (bd. dirs. 1981-82). Republican. Club: Pincipia (pres. 1983-84). Office: UAW-Ford Legal Svcs Plan 320 N Meridian St Ste 628 Indianapolis IN 46204-1725

FRANK, WILLIAM NELSON, lawyer, accountant; b. Cin., June 3, 1953; s. Nelson A. and Marion A. (Kirbert) F.; m. Brenda L. Norwood, Sept. 30, 1995. Student, Capital U., 1971-74; BS in Edn., Bowling Green State U., 1975; JD, U. Toledo, 1978; postgrad., U. Cin., 1980-82. Bar: Ohio, 1978, U.S. Dist. Ct., U.S. Tax Ct., U.S. Supreme Ct.; CPA, Ohio; cert. tchr., Ohio.. Asst. city prosecutor City of Columbus, Ohio, 1978-80; asst. pub. defender Hamilton (Ohio) County, 1981-84; sole practice William N. Frank, Columbus, 1978-85; regional fin. mktg. mgr. Primerica Fin. Svcs., 1984-90, Cin., 1990-92; atty., acct. Tyirin, Benvie & Co., 1990-92; atty. Hyatt Legal Svcs., 1992-93; pvt. practice, 1993—; spl. counsel to Ohio Atty. Gen., 1996—. Auditor Phillip Willeke, Inc., Columbus, 1985-87; securities rep. 1st Am. Nat. Securities, Columbus, 1985-92; lectr. in law Hondros Career Ctr., 1993—, special council to the Ohio Attorney Gen., 1996—; regional dir. Excel Comm., 2000—. Mem. Hamilton County Rep. Club, Cin., 1981—. Named to Hon. Order Ky. Cols. Commonwealth of Ky., 1978. Mem. AICPA, Cin. Bar Assn., Ohio Soc. CPAs, Cheviot Masons (worshipful master, master 1999), Royal Order of Scotland, Knights Templar, Royal Arch Mason, Order of Eastern Star, Shriners, Cin. Hist. Soc. (tour dir.), Order of DeMolay (gov. 7th dist. Ohio coun., chevalier degree 1972, Legion of Honor 1994), Delta Tau Upsilon, Phi Alpha Delta. Republican. Mem. Ch. of Christ. Avocations: tennis, Scottish Bagpipe musician, martial arts. Criminal, Probate, Taxation, general. Home: 3260 Milverton Ct Cincinnati OH 45248-2857 Office: 3050 Harrison Ave Cincinnati OH 45211-5752 E-mail: wfrank@myexcel.com, wmfrank@zoomtown.com

FRANKE, LINDA FREDERICK, lawyer; b. Mankato, Minn., Aug. 28, 1947; d. Cletus and Valeria (Haefner) Frederick; m. Willis L. Franke, Dec. 17, 1966; children: Paul W., Gregory J. BA, U. Mo., 1981, JD, 1984. Bar: Mo. 1985, U.S. Dist. Ct. (we. dist.) Mo. 1985. Rsch. assoc. Koenigsdorf, Kusnetzky and Wyrsch, Kansas City, Mo., 1984-85; asst. gen. counsel dept. revenue State of Mo., Independence, 1985-86; claims rep. workers' compensation Cigna Ins. Co., Overland Park, Kans., 1986-87; sr. claims rep. workers' compensation Gulf Ins. Co., Kansas City, Mo., 1987-88; worker's compensation atty. Fireman's Fund Ins. Co., 1988—. Mem. Mo. Worker's Compensation Com. U. Mo. scholar, 1980, 81. Mem. Platte County Bar Assn., Kansas City Met. Bar Assn. (adv. bd. workers' compensation com.). Administrative and regulatory, Insurance, Workers' compensation. Home: 8117 NW Eastside Dr Weatherby Lake MO 64152-1666 Office: Bren Przybeck & Stotler 1100 Walnut St Kansas City MO 64106-2109

FRANKEL, JAMES BURTON, lawyer; b. Chgo., Feb. 25, 1924; s. Louis and Thelma (Cohn) F.; m. Louise Untermyer, Jan. 22, 1956; children: Nina, Sara, Simon. Student, U. Chgo., 1940-42; BS, U.S. Naval Acad., 1945; LLB, Yale U., 1952; MPA, Harvard U., 1990. Bar: Calif. 1953. Mem. Steinhart, Goldberg, Feigenbaum & Ladar, San Francisco, 1954-72; of counsel Cooper, White & Cooper, 1972-97. Sr. fellow, lectr. in law Yale U., 1971-72; lectr. Stanford U. Law Sch., 1973-75; vis. prof. U. Calif. Law Sch., 1975-76, lectr. 1992—; lectr. U. San Francisco Law Sch., 1994—; adj. asst. prof. Hastings Coll. Law, 1996—. Pres. Coun. Civic Unity of San Francisco Bay Area, 1964-66; chmn. San Francisco Citizens Charter Revision Com., 1968-70; mem. San Francisco Pub. Schs. Commn., 1975-76; trustee Natural Resources Def. Coun., 1972-77, 79-92, staff atty., 1977-79, hon. trustee, 1992—; chmn. San Francisco Citizens Energy Policy Adv. Com., 1981-82. Mem. ABA, Calif. Bar Assn.

FRANKENA, KARL ROELOFS, lawyer; b. Ann Arbor, Mich., June 9, 1939; s. William K. and Sadie R. Frankena; m. Gloria D. Sauer, June 04, 1966; children: Jason T., Lara K. Student, Internat. Sch. Geneva, U. Wash., U. Grenoble; BA with honors, U. Mich., 1961, JD, 1964. Bar: Mich. 1964. Law clk. Mich. Ct. Appeals, Lansing, 1965-66; assoc. Conlin, Kenney & Green, Ann Arbor, 1966-68; ptnr. Conlin, McKenney & Philbrick, 1968—. Chmn. Ann Arbor Twp. Planning Commn., 1978—83; dir. Washtenaw Land Trust, Ann Arbor, 1978—2001. Mem. ABA, Washtenaw County Bar Assn., Mich. Bar Assn. (com. mem. young lawyers sect. 1966-70). Avocations: travelling, skiing. Real property. Home: 3632 Creekside Dr Ann Arbor MI 48105-9308 Office: Conlin McKenney & Philbrick 350 S Main St Ste 400 Ann Arbor MI 48104-2131

FRANKENHEIM, SAMUEL, retired lawyer; b. N.Y.C., Dec. 20, 1932; s. Samuel and Mary Emma (Ward) F.; m. Nina Barbara Mennerich, Sept. 2, 1960; children: Robert Mennerich, John Frederick. BA, Cornell U., 1954, LLB, 1959. Bar: N.Y. 1959, Mass. 1976. Law clk. N.Y. Ct. Appeals, 1959-61; assoc. Shearman & Sterling, attys., N.Y.C., 1961-68, ptnr., 1968-69; sr. v.p., dir. Damon Corp., Needham Heights, Mass., 1969-78; sr. v.p., gen. counsel mem. Office of Chmn. Gen. Cinema Corp., Chestnut Hill, 1979-92; counsel Ropes & Gray, Boston, 1992-2000. Mem. corp. Ptnrs. Healthcare Sys., Inc., 1999—. Overseer Newton-Wellesley Hosp., Newton, Mass., 1973-85, pres., 1980-82; bd. givs. Newell Health Care Sys., 1983-93; overseer Wang Ctr. for Performing Arts, Boston, 1985-87, trustee, 1987-97; trustee Huntington Theatre Co., Boston, 1993—; assoc. First Night, Inc., 1988, chmn. bd., 1991-93; chmn. bd. Internat. Alliance of First Night Celebrations, 1994-99, treas., 1999-2000. 1st lt. USAF, 1955-57. Mem. ABA. General corporate. Home: 115 Shornecliffe Rd Newton MA 02458-2420

FRANKINO, STEVEN P. lawyer, law educator; b. 1936; AB, Cath. U. Am., 1959, JD, 1962. Bar: D.C. 1963, Nebr. 1977. Tchg. fellow Northwestern U. Sch. Law, Chgo.; asst. prof. Cath. U. Am., Washington, 1963-65, dean sch. law, gen. counsel, 1979-86; prof. law Villanova U., 1965-71; dean Creighton U. Sch. Law, Omaha, 1971-77; ptnr. Kutak, Rock & Huie, 1977-79; dean Villanova (Pa.) U. Law Sch., 1987-97, prof. law, 1997—. Rsch. editor Cath. U. Law Jour. Mem. Am. Law Inst., Am. Bar Found., Pa. Bar Found., Knight of Malta, Order of Coif. Office: Villanova U Law Sch Garey Hall Villanova PA 19085 E-mail: frankino@law.villanova.edu

FRANKL, KENNETH RICHARD, retired lawyer; b. N.Y.C., May 23, 1924; s. Hugo Joseph and Sydney (Miller) F.; m. Jeanne Ritchie Silver, Aug. 6, 1972; 1 child, Kathryn; 1 son by previous marriage, Keith E. AB cum laude, Harvard U., 1945, LLB, 1950. Bar: N.Y. 1951, U.S. Ct. Appeals (2d cir.) 1956. Asst. dist. atty. N.Y. County, 1951-56; assoc. firm Liebman Eulau & Robinson, N.Y.C., 1959-60; asst. gen. atty. CBS, 1960-69; gen. counsel, asst. sec. Bishop Industries, Inc., 1969-70; v.p., gen. counsel, sec. RKO Gen., Inc. and Subs., 1970-84, cons.; ptnr. Law Offices of Ronald Kahn, N.Y.C., 1986; v.p. Charles H. Greenthal Comml. Co., 1989-91. Dir. staff Spl. Com. to Study Defender Sys. of N.Y.C. Assn. of the Bar, 1957-58. Co-author: (report) Equal Justice for the Accused, 1959. Mem. East Hampton Jewish Ctr., Amateur Chamber Music Soc.; mem. Amagansett Citizen Adv. Com. Served with Signal Corps, U.S. Army, 1943-46, PTO. Received Okinaua Invasion Ary Unit Commendation medal. Mem. Harvard Club N.Y. Home: PO Box 955 67 Old Montauk Hwy Amagansett NY 11930

FRANKLE, EDWARD ALAN, lawyer; b. N.Y.C., Dec. 14, 1946; m. Myrna Elaine Friedman, Feb. 22, 1986. BSE, Cath. U. Am., 1968, MSE, 1971; JD, Georgetown U., 1974. Bar: Md. 1974, D.C. 1980, U.S. Ct. Claims, 1976, U.S. Supreme Ct. 1978. Aerospace engr. Naval Ordnance Sta., Indian Head, Md., 1968-71; trial atty. Navy Gen. Counsel, Washington, 1974-78, asst. to gen. counsel, 1978-79, assoc. chief trial atty., 1979-80; assoc. dir. for policy SSS, 1980-82; chief counsel Goddard Space Flight Ctr., NASA, Greenbelt, Md., 1982-85; dep. gen. counsel NASA, Washington, 1985-88, gen. counsel, 1988—. Recipient Presdl. Rank, Meritorious Exec., 1988, Disting. Exec., 1992, NASA Disting. Svc. medal, 1993, 2001. Mem. ABA, AIAA (legal aspects com.), Internat. Inst. Space Law. Office: NASA Gen Counsel 300 E St SW Washington DC 20546-0005

FRANKLIN, BRUCE WALTER, lawyer; b. Ellendale, N.D., Feb. 26, 1936; s. Wallace Henry and Frances (Webb) F.; m. Kristy Ann Jones, Feb. 7, 1944; children: Kevin, Monica, Taylor. Student, U. Mich., 1954-56; LLB, Detroit Coll. Law, 1962. Bar: Mich. 1963. Sole practice, Troy, Mich., 1962-90; mng. ptnr. Franklin, Bigler, Berry & Johnston, P.C., 1991-98, Franklin & Davis, Troy, 1998—. Bd. dirs. First Union-Newnan Bank; pres., CEO Landward III Devel. Corp. (Arbor Springs Plantation). Past chmn. Mich. Young Reps., United Meth. Retirement Cmtys.; bd. dirs. Peachtree Hosp., Wesley Woods. Served with U.S. Army. State civil litigation, Personal injury, Product liability. Office: Landward III 250 Arbor Springs Plantation Dr Newnan GA 30265 E-mail: BWf@arborsprings.com

FRANKLIN, FREDERICK RUSSELL, retired legal association executive; b. Mar. 20, 1929; s. Ernest James and Frances (Price) F.; m. Barbara Ann Donovan, Jan. 26, 1952; children: Katherine Elizabeth, Frederick Russell. AB, Ind. U., 1951, JD with high distinction, 1956. Bar: Ind. 1956. Trial atty. criminal div. and ct. of claims sect. civil div. U.S. Dept. Justice, Washington, 1956-60; gen. counsel Ind. State Bar Assn., Indpls., 1960-67; dir. continuing legal edn. for Ind., adj. prof. law Ind. U., 1965-68; staff dir. profl. standards ABA, Chgo., 1968-70, legal edn. and admissions to the bar, 1972-92, sr. lawyers divsn., 1985-93; ret., 1993. Exec. v.p. Nat. Attys. Title Assurance Fund, Inc., Indpls., 1970-72. Trustee Olympia Fields (Ill.) United Meth. Ch., 1980-84; treas. bd. dirs. Olympia Fields Pub. Libr., 1984-91; mem. Olympia Fields Pub. Safety Bd., 1983-92. Capt. USAF, 1951-53. Named to Honorable Order Ky. Cols., 1967, 74, Adm. Tex. Navy, 1967, Adm. Nebr. Navy, 1972, 74, Sagamore of Wabash, 1972. Fellow Ind. Bar Found. (life); mem. ABA (coun. sr. lawyers divsn. 1993—, mem. com. bar admissions 1993-97, 99—, vice chair affiliate outreach com. divsn. sr. lawyers 1995—, vice-chmn. membership com. sr. lawyers divsn. 1995—, vice-chmn. pub. com. 1995—, vice-historian 1995-96, historian 1996—, long range planning com. 1995—, vice-chmn. social security com. 1998—, vice-chmn. real estate com. 1999—), Ind. State Bar Assn. (sec.-treas. sr. lawyers sect. 1998—, coun. sr. lawyers sect. 1996—, editor sr. lawyers sect. newsletter 1996-98, coun. profl. legal edn. sect. 2000—, vice-chmn. articles and bylaws com. 1994—, legal edn. and bar admissions com. 1990—, chmn. articles and bylaws com. 1999—, ho. of dels. 1999—, coun., profl. edn. sect.), Fed. Bar Assn. (officer, found. bd. dirs. 1974—, historian 1979—, life fellow 1976—, treas. sr. lawyers divsn. 1993-95, sec. 1995-97, dep. chmn. 1997-98, chmn. 1998-99, nat. coun. 1961-93, 97—, nat. v.p 1967-69, chpt. pres. 1965-66, chmn. admission to practice and recert. com. 1980-82, bd. dirs. Chgo. chpt. 1984-93), Nat. Orgn. Bar Counsel (pres. 1967), Ind. U. Air Force ROTC Alumni Assn. (pres. 1997-98), Lakeview Hills Homeowners Assn. (pres. 1997-99), Kiwanis, Elks, Order of Coif, Am. Legion (life), Phi Delta Phi. Home: 712 Romans Ct Bloomington IN 47401-8676

FRANKLIN, JAMES BURKE, lawyer; b. Statesboro, Ga., Mar. 11, 1938; s. Sam J. and Eva Claire (Burke) F.; m. Fay Foy Smith, Mar. 20, 1976; children— Julie Foy, Rebecca Claire. B.S., Ga. Inst. Tech.; J.D., U. Ga. Bar: Ga. U.S. Dist. Ct. (so. dist.) Ga. 1966. Assoc., Allen Edenfield, Brown & Franklin and predecessor Allen & Edenfield, 1966-69, ptnr., 1969-74; ptnr. Franklin, Taulbee, Rushing & Brogdon and predecessor firms, Statesboro, Ga., 1974— ; magistrate U.S. Dist. Ct. (so. dist.) Ga., 1979-81. Chmn. Devel. Authority Bulloch County; pres. Bulloch County (Ga.) C. of C.; candidate for Republican nomination for Congress, 1st Dist. Ga., 1982. Served to 1st lt. U.S. Army, 1964-66. Mem. State Bar Ga. (bd. govs., pres. 2001-), Ga. Trial Lawyers Assn. (v.p. 1986—). Methodist. Club: Rotary (pres.) (Statesboro). State civil litigation, General practice, Personal injury. Address: PO Box 327 Statesboro GA 30459-0327*

FRANKLIN, JEANNE F. lawyer; b. N.Y.C., July 22, 1946; BA cum laude, Vassar Coll., 1968; JD, U. Va., 1971. Bar: Mich. 1971, U.S. Dist. Ct. Mich. (ea. dist.) 1975, U.S. Ct. Appeals (10th cir.) 1975, N.Mex. 1977, D.C. 1977, Va. 1981, U.S. Dist. Ct. Va. (ea. dist.) 1984. Sole practice, Alexandria, Va. Fellow: Am. Bar Found.; mem.: ABA, Va. Bar Assn. (mem. exec. com. 1997—, pres.), Alexandria Bar Assn., Am. Health Lawyers Assn., Va. State Bar (mem. health law sect.), D.C. Bar (mem. health law sect.). Health, Labor. Office: 604 Cameron St Alexandria VA 22314*

FRANKLIN, JONI JEANETTE, lawyer; b. Council Grove, Kans., Jan. 26, 1971; d. Jerry P. and Sonja Jeanette F. BA, Kans. State U., 1993; JD, Kans. U., 1996; cert., Nairobi (Kenya) Law Sch., 1994. Bar: Kans. 1996, U.S. Dist. Ct. Kans. 1996. Assoc. Prochaska & Scott, Wichita, Kans., 1996-97, Render Kamas L.C., Wichita, 1998—. Pro bono atty. Wichita Lawyers That Care, 1997—; vol. atty. Sedgwick County Protection from Abuse, Wichita, 1997—; vol. Cystic Fibrosis Assn., 1997-98, Katelyn's Hope, 1998; active East Hts. United Meth. Ch., 1998—. Named Woman of the Yr. Leukemia Soc., 1999. Mem. ABA, Kans. Bar Assn., Wichita Bar Assn., Wichita Young Lawyer's Assn. (pres. elect 1999), Wichita Womens Atty. Assn. Democrat. Avocations: theater, softball, volleyball. General civil litigation, Personal injury, Workers' compensation. Office: Render Kamas LC PO Box 700 Wichita KS 67201-0700

FRANKLIN, RANDY WAYNE, lawyer; b. Chgo., Mar. 28, 1945; s. Sidney Aaron and Hilda (Goldstein) Franklin Skora; m. Danette Penny Siegel, Dec. 21, 1974; children: Jennifer Rose, Jason Adam, Seth Peter. BS., Bradley U., 1967; JD, Massey U., 1971. Bar: Ga. 1972, Ill. 1973, Wis. 1987. Tchr. high sch., Chgo. Bd. Edn., 1968-70; asst. pub. defender Cook County, Chgo., 1973-79; assoc. McLennon, Nelson, Gabriele & Nudo, Park Ridge, Ill., 1979-81; ptnr. Gabriele & Franklin, Park Ridge, 1981— . Bd. dirs. Young Men's Jewish Council, Chgo., 1974-76, Main Family and Mental Health Ctr., Little Mexico Convent Holy Spirit, Mt. Prospect, Ill., 1980— ; advisor Northeastern Ill. U. Sch. of Bus. Mem. ABA, Ill. Bar Assn., Ga. Bar Assn., No. Suburban Bar Assn. (bd. of mgrs.), Nat. Assn. Criminal Def. Lawyers, Assn. Trial Lawyers Am. State civil litigation, Family and matrimonial, General practice. Home: 330 Landis Ln Deerfield IL 60015-3422 Office: Randy W Franklin & Assocs 1550 N Northwest Hwy Sute 308 Park Ridge IL 60068 also: 151 N Michigan Ave Suite 3314 Chicago IL 60601

FRANKLIN, RICHARD MARK, lawyer; b. Chgo., Dec. 13, 1947; s. Henry W. and Gertrude (Gross) F.; m. Marguerite June Wesle, Sept. 2, 1973; children: Justin Wesley, Elizabeth Cecilia, Catherine Helena, Caroline Lucinda. BA, U. Wis., 1970; postgrad., U. Freiburg, Fed. Republic Germany, 1968-69; JD, Columbia U., 1973. Bar: Ill. 1973, U.S. Dist. Ct. (no. dist.) Ill. 1973, U.S. Ct. Appeals (7th cir.) 1973. Assoc. Baker & McKenzie, Chgo., 1973-79, Frankfurt, Fed. Republic Germany, 1979-80, ptnr. Chgo., 1980—. Mem. ABA, Ill. Bar Assn., Chgo. Bar Assn. Mem.

United Ch. Christ. Avocations: music, literature, theatre, outdoor activities. Federal civil litigation, State civil litigation, Private international. Home: 1161 Oakley Ave Winnetka IL 60093-1437 Office: Baker & McKenzie 1 Prudential Plz 130 E Randolph St Ste 3700 Chicago IL 60601-6342 E-mail: rmfwim@aol.com, richard.m.franklin@bakenet.com

FRANKLIN, ROBERT DRURY, oil company executive, lawyer; b. Mead, Okla., June 6, 1935; s. Sam Wesley and Frankie Marjorie (Gooding) F.; m. Barbara Jean Bellis, May 30, 1958 (div. 1973); children: Philip Foster, Elizabeth Jean. BS in Petroleum Engring., U. Okla., 1957; JD, So. Methodist U., 1964. Registered profl. engr., Tex. Petroleum engr. Mobil Oil Corp., Denver City, Tex., 1957-59; prodn. mgr. Bayview Oil Corp., Dallas, 1959-65; sec., dir. Siboney Corp., 1965-70; pres., dir. Northland Oils Ltd., 1970-89, Costa Resources, Inc., Dallas, 1972—; v.p., dir. Internat. Oil & Gas Corp., 1979-84; pvt. practice, Canyon Lake, Tex. Mem. Rep. Eagles, Washington. Mem. State Bar Tex., Ind. Petroleum Assn. Am., Soc. Petroleum Engrs., Am. Petroleum Inst., Energy Club of Dallas, Mensa. Presbyterian. Clubs: Willow Bend Polo, Midland Country, Beverly Hills Avocations: polo, tennis, skiing. Home and Office: Costa Resources Inc 2293 Common St Apt 85 New Braunfels TX 78130-3184 Office: 1395 Sattler Rd Canyon Lake TX 78130

FRANKLIN, ROBERT STAMBAUGH, lawyer; b. N.Y.C., Jan. 28, 1942; s. John Edward and Bernice (Stambaugh) F.; m. Eva Johanna D'Addario, July 22, 1967 (div. 1984); children— David, Kathryn; m. Patricia Lee Posner, Jan. 2, 1986. B.A., Harvard U., 1963, J.D., 1966; LL.M., NYU, 1973. Bar: N.Y. 1966, U.S. Tax Ct. 1982. Clk. N.Y. County Dist. Atty.'s Office, N.Y.C., 1964; assoc. Milbank, Tweed, Hadley & McCloy, N.Y.C., 1969-72, Debevoise, Plimpton, Lyons & Gates, N.Y.C., 1973-75; assoc. Coudert Bros., N.Y.C., 1975-78, ptnr., 1978— ; lectr. NYU Sch. Continuing Edn., 1981. Served to 1st. lt. U.S. Army, 1966-69. Mem. ABA, N.Y. State Bar Assn. Roman Catholic. Private international, Corporate taxation. Home: 392 South Ave New Canaan CT 06840-6313 Office: Coudert Bros 1114 Avenue Of The Americas Fl 4 New York NY 10036-7710

FRANKLIN, WILLIAM JAY, lawyer; b. Logansport, Ind., Mar. 1, 1945; s. Frederick Arthur and Ferne (Friskney) F.; m. Kathleen Killette, Feb. 5, 1988; 1 child, James Frederick. BSME with highest distinction, Purdue U., 1968, MS in Computer Sci., 1970; JD, Georgetown U., 1977. Bar: D.C. 1977, U.S. Dist. Ct. D.C. 1978, U.S. Ct. Appeals (D.C. cir.) 1977, U.S. Supreme Ct. 1981. Computer specialist antitrust div. U.S. Dept. Justice, Washington, 1976-77; assoc. Lowenstein, Newman Reis & Axelrad, 1977-80, Becker, Gurman, Lukas, Meyers & O'Brien, Washington, 1980-82; prin. Mahn, Franklin & Goldenberg, P.C., 1982-85; ptnr. Bell, Boyd & Lloyd, 1985-87, Pepper & Corazzini, Washington, 1988—. Guest lectr. Brookings Instn., Washington, 1982. Author monthly column: Legal Briefs, 1984—. Mem. ABA, Fed. Communications Bar Assn., Tau Beta Pi. Administrative and regulatory, Communications, Computer. Home: 6300 Stratford Rd Bethesda MD 20815-5321

FRANKS, HERBERT HOOVER, lawyer; b. Joliet, Ill., Jan. 25, 1934; s. Carol and Lottie (Dermer) F.; m. Eileen Pepper, June 22, 1957; children: David, Jack, Eli. BS, Roosevelt U., 1954; postgrad., Am. U., 1960. Bar: Ill. 1961, U.S. Dist. Ct. (no. dist.) Ill. 1961, U.S. Supreme Ct. 1967. Ptnr. Franks, Gerkin & McKenna, 1985—. Chmn. Wonder Lake State Bank, Ill., 1979—, First Nat. Bank, Marengo, Ill., 1976-84, mem. exec. com., 1976—; vice-chmn. hotel mgmt. orgn. Bricton Group, Park Ridge, Ill., 1992-98. Bus. editor Am. U. Law Rev., 1959, 60. State pres. Young Dems. of Ill., 1970-72; trustee Hebrew Theol. Coll., Skokie, Ill., 1974—; trustee, sec. Forest Inst. Profl. Psychology, Springfield, Mo., 1979-91; chmn. Forest Hosp., Des Plaines, 1980-88. With U.S. Army, 1956-58. Fellow Ill. State Bar Assn. (bd. govs. 1994-97, treas. 1996-97, 3d v.p. 1997-98, 2d v.p. 1998-99, pres.-elect 1999-2000, pres. 2000—); mem. Ill. Trial Lawyers (mng. bd. 1975-92, treas. 1985-87), Masons (33d degree), Shriners, Sigma Nu Phi (pres. 1980-82). Banking, Workers' compensation. Home: 19324 E Grant Hwy Marengo IL 60152-9438 Office: Franks Gerkin & McKenna 19333 E Grant Hwy Marengo IL 60152-8234 E-mail: franklaw@mc.net

FRANKS, HERSCHEL PICKENS, judge; b. Savannah, Tenn., May 28, 1930; s. Herschel R. and Vada (Pickens) F.; m. Judy Black; 1 child, Ramona. Student U. Tenn.-Martin, U. Md.; JD, U. Tenn.-Knoxville; grad. Nat. Jud. Coll. of U. Nev. Bar: Tenn. 1959, U.S. Supreme Ct. 1968. Claims atty. U.S. Fidelity & Guaranty Co., Knoxville, 1958; ptnr. Harris, Moon, Meacham & Franks, Chattanooga, 1959-70; chancellor 3d Chancery div. of Hamilton County, 1970-78; judge Tenn. Ct. Appeals, Chattanooga, 1978—; spl. justice Tenn. Supreme Ct., 1979, 86, 87; presiding judge Hamilton County Trial Cts., 1977-78; spl. judge Tenn. Ct. of Criminal Appeals, 1990-92; mem. commn. to study appellate cts., 1990-92. Served with USNG, 1949-50, USAF, 1950-54. Mem. ABA (award of merit), Tenn. Bar Assn. (award of merit 1968-69), Tenn. Bar Found., Chattanooga Bar Found., Chattanooga Bar Assn. (pres. 1968-69, Founds. of Freedom award 1986), Am. Judicature Soc., Inst. Jud. Adminstrn., Optimists (pres. 1965-66), Community Service award 1971), Mountain City Club, City Farmers Club, Phi Alpha Delta. Mem. United Ch. of Christ. Address: 540 Mccallie Ave Ste 562 Chattanooga TN 37402-2039

FRANO, ANDREW JOSEPH, lawyer, civil engineer; b. Chgo., July 14, 1953; s. Joseph Neil Frano and Lorraine Rose (Jeczalik) Patchett; children: Alaina Marie, Jacqueline Elyse. BSCE, Bradley U., 1975, MSCE, 1976; JD, Ill. Inst. Tech., 1982. Registered profl. engr., Ill., Ind., Nebr., Wis., lic. gen. engring. constrn. contractor, Fla., Utah; bar: Ill. 1982, Nebr. 1986, U.S. Dist. Ct. (no. dist.) Ill. 1982, U.S. Dist. Ct. Nebr. 1992, U.S. Dist. Ct. Ariz. 1993, U.S. Dist. Ct. Tex. 1997. Soils lab. instr. and residence hall dir. Bradley U., Peoria, Ill., 1975-76; civil engr. Harza Engring. Co., Chgo., 1976-85; pvt. practice, 1982-85; pres. GEC Engring. Co. Inc., 1985-86; corp. constrn. atty. Peter Kiewit Sons Inc., Omaha, 1986-92; asst. gen. counsel Harza Engring. Co., Chgo., 1992-95; owner The Law and Engring. Office of Andrew J. Frano, 1996—. Adj. asst. prof. dept. civil and architectural engring., Ill. Inst. Tech., Chgo., 1993—; corp. atty., civil engr. T.J. Lambrecht Constrn., Inc., Joliet, Ill., 1996-98; prin. engr. RSV Engring., Inc., Schaumburg, Ill., 1998—. Chmn. San. Improvement Dist. 111, Sarpy County, Nebr., 1987-92; vol. atty. Chgo. Vol. Legal Svcs., 1983-85; bd. dirs., treas. Trails Assn. Inc., Roselle, Ill., 1983-86. Mem. ASCE, Tau Beta Pi, Chi Epsilon. Roman Catholic. Avocations: basketball, tennis. Construction, General practice. Home: 2 N Dee Rd Apt 107 Park Ridge IL 60068-2871 Office: RSV Engring Inc 1870 N Roselle Rd Ste 101 Schaumburg IL 60195-3100 Fax: 847-843-3047. E-mail: ajfrsvil@rsv-engineering.com

FRANTZ, ROBERT WESLEY, lawyer; b. Long Branch, N.J., Dec. 31, 1950; BS, Rutgers U., New Brunswick, N.J., 1973; JD, Rutgers U., Newark, 1977. Bar: N.J. 1977, U.S. Dist. Ct. N.J. 1977, U.S. Ct. Appeals (4th and 10th cirs.) 1978, U.S. Ct. Appeals (6th, 7th and 8th cirs.) 1979, D.C. 1980, U.S. Ct. Appeals (9th cir.) 1980, U.S. Dist. Ct. D.C. 1981. Trial atty. U.S. Dept. Justice, Washington, 1977-80; assoc. Hamel and Park, 1980-82; asst. gen. counsel Chem. Mfrs. Assn., 1982-85; counsel, environ. protection GE, Fairfield, Conn., 1985-88, Pittsfield, Mass., 1988-89; mgr. and counsel Environ. Remediation Program, Fairfield, Conn., 1989-95; mgr., sr. counsel Environ. Ops. Program, 1995-98; gen. mgr., counsel GE Engines Svcs., Cin., 1998—. Mem. sci. adv. bd. subcom. on risk reduction options U.S. EPA, 1996—. Contbr. articles to profl. publs.; editorial bd. Rutgers Law Rev., 1976. Mem. Newtown (Conn.) Charter Revision Commn., 1986-87, Glendale Planning Commn., 2000—. Mem. ABA (exec. editor Natural Resources and Environment 1986-93, coun. mem. sect. natural resources 1993-96). Avocations: sailing, golf, skiing, bicycling, woodworking. Federal civil litigation, General civil litigation, Environmental. Office: GE Engine Svcs 1 Neumann Way # Md-t164 Cincinnati OH 45215-1915

FRANTZE, DAVID WAYNE, lawyer; b. Kansas City, Mo., Jan. 28, 1955; s. James W. and Margaret M. (Pursley) F.; m. Geri L. Sexton, July 28, 1979; children: Kevin, Lisa, Christopher, Timothy. BA, Avila Coll., 1976; JD, U. Mo., Kansas City, 1981. V.p. Stinson, Mag & Fizzell, P.C., Kansas City, 1981—. Bd. dirs. Kansas City Spirit, Inc., 1986-88, pres., 1988, mem. adv. coun., 1989—; bd. dirs. Kansas City Neighborhood Alliance, 1987—, chmn., 1994-96, Kansas City Riverfront, Inc., 1991-94; bd. counselors Avila Coll., 1989—; trustee Mid-Am. chpt. Leukemia and Lymphoma Soc., 1992—, chpt. pres. 1998-2000, nat. bd. trustees, 2001—; trustee Victor and Caroline Schutte Found., 2000—; trustee U. Mo.-Kansas City Law Found., 1996—, exec. com., 2000—; mem. Civic Coun. Kansas City, 1995—, urban core com. 1996—. Mem. ABA, Mo. Bar Assn., Kansas City Met. Bar Assn. (chmn. real estate law com. 1992), Lawyers Assn. Kansas City, Am. Coll. of Real Estate Lawyers. Roman Catholic. Condemnation, Landlord-tenant, Real property. Home: 11812 Central St Kansas City MO 64114-5536 Office: Stinson Mag & Fizzell 1201 Walnut St Ste 2600 Kansas City MO 64106-2150 E-mail: dfrantze@stinson.com

FRANZKE, RICHARD ALBERT, lawyer; b. Lewistown, Mont., Mar. 7, 1935; s. Arthur A. and Senta (Clark) F.; divorced; children: Mark, Jean, Robert. BA in Polit. Sci., Willamette U., 1958, JD with honors, 1960. Bar: Oreg. 1960, U.S. Dist. Ct. Oreg., 1960, U.S. Supreme Ct., 1961. Ptnr. Stoel, Rives, Portland, 1960—. Bd. dirs., chmn. various coms. Assn. Gen. Contractors Am., Portland, 1972-79; mem. com. on legis. affairs Assn. Builders & Contractors, Portland, 1983—. Author: A Study of the Construct by Contract Issue, 1979. Mem. Gov.'s Task Force on Reform of Worker's Compensation, Salem, Oreg., 1980-81; atty. gen.'s com. on Pub. Contracting. Recipient SIR award Assn. Gen. Contractors, 1979, Nat. Winner Outstanding Oral Argument award U.S. Moot Ct., 1959. Mem. ABA (sect. pub. contract law), Oreg. Bar (law sch. liaison, com. on practice and procedure specialization), Multnomah County Bar Assn. Republican. Avocations: antique autos, antique furniture, boating. Construction. Home: 14980 SW 133rd Ave Tigard OR 97224-1646 Office: Stoel Rives 900 SW 5th Ave Ste 2300 Portland OR 97204-1229 E-mail: rafranzke@stoel.com

FRASER, BRIAN SCOTT, lawyer; b. Bronxville, N.Y., Oct. 14, 1956; BA, Manhattanville Coll., 1978; JD, Fordham U., 1984. Bar: N.Y. 1987, U.S. Dist. Ct. (so. and ea. dists.) N.Y. 1991. Law clk. hon. William H. Timbers U.S. Ct. Appeals 2nd Cir., Bridgeport, Conn., 1984-85; assoc. Cravath, Swaine & Moore, N.Y.C., 1985-91; ptnr. Richard Spears Kibbe & Orbe, 1991—. Active Scarsdale (N.Y.) Town and Village Civic Assn. Mem. ABA (sects. litigation and intellectual property), Fed. Bar Coun., Bar Assn. City of N.Y. (mem. antitrust com. 1991-94. Antitrust, Federal civil litigation, Securities. Office: Richards Spears Kibbe & Orbe One Chase Manhattan Plaza New York NY 10005

FRASER, DAVID A. retired lawyer; b. Syracuse, N.Y., Dec. 30, 1911; s. Hector Alexander and Minnie (Salmon) F.; m. Marion Ford, Sept. 17, 1938; children: David, Robert, Frederick, Janet. BA, Hamilton Coll., 1934; JD, Cornell U., 1937. Bar: N.Y.; U.S. Ct. of Appeals (2d cir.). Ptnr. Fraser Brothers, Syracuse, N.Y., 1938-58, Coulter, Fraser, Bolton, Bird and Ventre, Syracuse, 1958-87, counsel, 1987-2000; retired. Past pres., mem. life adv. bd. Salvation Army, Syracuse, 1960—; pres. Hiscock Legal Aid Soc., Syracuse, 1969-70, Onondaga Co. Bar. Assn., 1968-69, Onondaga Co. Libr. Sys., Syracuse, 1966; dir. Syracuse C. of C., 1957-62; chmn. Greater Syracuse Safety Coun., 1963-64; chmn. libr. trustees Syracuse U., 1963-70; trustee Hamilton coll., 1969-75. Mem. N.Y. State Bar Assn., Grolier Club, Phi Beta Kappa. Republican. Episcopal. Home: 300 Carlton Rd Syracuse NY 13207-1529

FRASER, ORLANDO, barrister; b. London, May 9, 1967; s. Hugh and Antonia (Pinter) F. Degree in History, Cambridge U., Eng., 1989; degree in Law, Inns Ct. Sch. Law, London, 1994. Asst. to M.P. European Parliament, 1989-90; intern European Commn., 1990; mgr. spl. projects GEC Plessey Telecomm., 1990-92; barrister London, 1994—. Chmn. Bosnia Winter Appeal, 1992. Mem. MCC. Avocations: country sports, tennis, cricket, politics, chess. Office: Lincolns Inn Stone Bldg 4 London UC2 AXT England

FRASIER, RALPH KENNEDY, lawyer, banker; b. Winston-Salem, N.C., Sept. 16, 1938; s. LeRoy Benjamin and Kathryn O. (Kennedy) F.; m. Jeannine Quick, Aug. 1981; children: Karen D. Frasier Alston, Gail S. Frasier Cox, Ralph Kennedy Jr., Keith Lowery, Marie Kennedy, Rochelle Doar. BS, N.C. Cen. U., Durham, 1963, JD, 1965. Bar: N.C. 1965, Ohio 1976. With Wachovia Bank and Trust Co., N.A., Winston-Salem, N.C., 1965-70, v.p., counsel, 1969-70; asst. counsel, v.p. parent co. Wachovia Corp., 1970-75; v.p., gen. counsel Huntington Nat. Bank, Columbus, Ohio, 1975-76, sr. v.p., 1976-83, sec., 1981-98, exec. v.p., 1983-98, cashier, 1983-98. V.p. Huntington Bancshares Inc., 1976-86, gen. counsel, 1976-98, sec., 1981-98; sec., dir. Huntington Mortgage Co., Huntington State Bank, Huntington Leasing Co., Huntington Bancshares Fin. Corp., Huntington Investment Mgmt. Co., Huntington Nat. Life Ins. Co., Huntington Co., 1976-88; v.p., asst. sec. Huntington Bank N.E. Ohio, 1982-84; asst. sec. Huntington Bancshares Ky., 1985-97; sec. Huntington Trust Co., N.A., 1987-97, Huntington Bancshares Ind., Inc., 1986-97, Huntington Fin. Services Co., 1987-98; dir. The Huntington Nat. Bank, Columbus, Ohio, 1998—; of counsel Porter Wright Morris & Arthur LLP, Columbus, 1998—; trustee OCLC Online Computer Libr. Ctr., Inc., Dublin, Ohio, 1999—, mem. fin. com., 2000—, mem. audit com., 2000—; dir. ADATOM.COM, Inc., Milpitas, Calif., 1999-2001, mem. compensation com., 1999-2001, chair audit com., 1999-2001. Bd. dirs. Family Svcs. Winston-Salem, 1966-74, sec., 1966-71, 74, v.p., 1974; chmn. Winston-Salem Transit Authority, 1974-75; bd. dirs. Rsch. for Advancement of Personalities, 1968-71, Winston-Salem Citizens for Fair Housing, 1970-74, N.C. United Community Svcs., 1970-74; treas. Forsyth County (N.C.) Citizens Com. Adequate Justice Bldg., 1968; trustee Appalachian State U., Boone, N.C., 1973-83, endowment fund, 1973-83, Columbus Drug Edn. and Prevention Fund, Inc., 1989-92; trustee, vice chmn. employment and Edn. Commn. Franklin County, 1982-85; mem. Winston-Salem Forsyth County Sch. Bd. Adv. Coun., 1973-74, Atty. Gen's Ohio Task Force Minorities in Bus., 1977-78; bd. dirs. Inroads Columbus, Inc., 1986-95, Greater Columbus Arts Coun., 1986-94, Columbus Urban League Inc., 1987-94, vice chmn., 1990-94; trustee Riverside Meth. Hosp. Found., 1989-90, Grant Med. Ctr., 1990-95, Grant/Riverside Meth. Hosps., 1995-97; trustee Ohio Health Corp., 1997—, treas., chair Fin./Audit Com., 2001—; dir. Cmty. Mutual Ins. Co., 1989-92, mem. audit com., 1989-92; trustee N.C. Ctrl. U., Durham, N.C., 1993-2001, vice-chmn., 1993-94, chmn. 1995, chair ednl. planning and acad. affairs com., 1995-98, audit, devel. and personnel coms., 1998-2001, chair audit com., 1999-2001; mem. Ohio Bd. Regents, 1987-96, vice-chmn., 1993-95, chmn., 1995-96; trustee Nat. Jud. Coll., Reno, Nevada, 1996—, fin. and audit com., 1997—, treas., chair, 1999—, Columbus Bar Found., 1998— (fellows com. 1998—, grants com., 1998—); AEFC Pension Adminstrn. Com. defined benefit plan of the ABA, Am. Bar Endowment, Am. Bar Found., and Nat. Jud. Coll., Chgo, Ill., 1998—. With AUS, 1958-64. Mem. ABA, Nat. Bar Assn., Ohio Bar Assn., Columbus Bar Assn. Banking, Consumer commercial, General corporate. Office: Porter Wright Morris & Arthur LLP 41 S High St Ste 3100 Columbus OH 43215-6194 E-mail: rfrasier@porterwright.com, rfrasier@columbus.rr.com

FRAZEN, MITCHELL HALE, lawyer; b. Great Lakes, Ill., Sept. 19, 1955; s. Sidney Joseph and Norma Ileane (Solomon) F.; m. Mary Elizabeth Huelsbusch, Sept. 14, 1974; children: Daniel Joseph, Christina Elizabeth. BA, U. Ill., 1977; JD, U. Mich., 1980. Bar: Ill. 1980, U.S. Dist. Ct. (no. dist.) Ill. 1980, U.S. Ct. Appeals (7th cir.) 1987, U.S. Dist. Ct. (ea. dist.) Wis. 1994, U.S. Ct. Appeals (8th cir.) 1995, U.S. Dist. Ct. (ea. dist.) Mich. 1995. Assoc. Phelan, Pope & John, Ltd., Chgo., 1980-87; shareholder Burditt & Radzius, Chartered, 1987-98, dir., 1989-98; ptnr. Litchfield Cavo, 1998—. Arbitrator, chairperson mandatory ct.-annexed arbitration program Cook County Cir. Ct., Chgo., 1990—, mediator vol. mediation program, 1992—. Bd. govs. Chgo. Coun. Lawyers, 1992-95; chair State Ct. Practices Com., 1995—. Mem. ABA, Chgo. Bar Assn., Phi Beta Kappa, Order of Coif. Democrat. Lutheran. General civil litigation, Insurance, Personal injury. Home: 4050 Hudson Dr Hoffman Estates IL 60195-1717 Office: Litchfield Cavo 303 W Madison St Ste 200 Chicago IL 60606-3309 E-mail: frazen@litchfieldcavo.com

FRAZIER, DANA SUE, lawyer; b. Danville, Fla., Sept. 24, 1963; d. James L. and Shirley A. Norman; m. Philip M. Frazier. BS, U. Ill., 1985; MBA, So. Ill. U., 1989. Bar: Ill. 1997, U.S. Dist. Ct. (so. dist.) Ill. 1997. Fin. counselor Germania, Mt. Vernon, Ill., 1985-87; asst. v.p. brokerage First Bank & Trust, 1987-89; coord. cmty. svcs. Rend Lake Coll., Ina, Ill., 1989-94; assoc. Barrett, Twomey, Morris, Broom & Hughes, Carbondale, 1997—. Part-time instr. Rend Lake Coll., 1990-94. Mem. Ill. State Bar Assn., Jackson County Bar Assn., Phi Kappa Phi, Beta Sigma Gamma. Avocations: running, tennis, golf, reading. Bankruptcy, Civil rights, State civil litigation. Office: Barrett Twomey Morris Broom & Hughes 100 N Illinois Ave Carbondale IL 62902

FRAZIER, WILLIAM SUMPTER, lawyer, pharmacist; b. Mexia, Tex., Aug. 8, 1941; s. William Sumpter and Johnnie Ione (Archer) F.; m. Carolyn Casey, July 26, 1946; children: Casey Rene, Kelley Shea. AA with honors, Navarro Jr. Coll.; BS in Pharmacy, U. Tex.; JD with honors, South Tex. Coll. Law. Bar: Tex. 1972, U.S. Dist. Ct. (so. dist.) Fla. 1982, U.S. Supreme Ct. 1973. Pharmacist Tidelands Hosp., Channelview, Tex., 1967-69; chief pharmacist San Jacinto Meth. Hosp., Baytown, 1969-71; sole practice law Houston, 1971—. Mem. ABA, Tex. Bar Assn., Tex. Pharm. Assn., Am. Pharm. Assn. Mem. Ch. of Christ. General civil litigation, Criminal, Personal injury. Home: 27127 Glencreek Dr Huffman TX 77336-3712 Office: PO Box 968 Huffman TX 77336

FREDERICI, C. CARLETON, lawyer; b. Jan. 17, 1938; s. Cecil Carleton and Lois Alida (Selzer) F.; m. Virginia A. Gregori, Oct. 14, 1961 (div.); m. Susan A. Low, Oct. 1, 1983; children: Gloria M., Carleton J., Charles W., Seth L. Student, Iowa State U., 1956; BA, U. Iowa, 1960, JD with high distinction, 1965. Bar: Iowa 1965, N.Y. 1966, U.S. Dist. Ct. (no. dist.) Iowa 1968, U.S. Dist. Ct. (so. dist.) Iowa 1969, U.S. Supreme Ct. 1970, U.S. Ct. Appeals (8th cir.) 1970, U.S. Ct. Appeals (3d cir.) 1973. Assoc. Willkie, Farr & Gallagher, N.Y.C., 1965-68, Shull, Marshall & Marks, Sioux City, Iowa, 1968-69, Davis, Brown, Koehn, Shors & Roberts, P.C., Des Moines, 1969-71, jr. ptnr., 1971-73, sr. ptnr., 1973-90, shareholder, 1990-95, counsel, 1996—. Spkr. Supreme Ct. Day, Law Sch. Drake U., 1973. Contbr. articles to legal publs. Vestryman St. Luke's Ch., bd. dirs., 1976-78, 82-85; mem. Polk County Rep. Cen. Com., 1969-71. 1st lt. U.S. Army, 1961-62. Mem. ABA (chmn. 8th cir. commn. on class actions and derivative suits), Iowa Bar Assn. (chmn. prison reform com., adv. mem. fed. practice commn., litigation sect. bench and bar com.), Polk County Bar Assn. (bench and bar com.), Assn. Bar City of N.Y., Am. Judicature Soc. (bd. dirs. Iowa 1990-96), Order of Coif, Wakonda Club. Federal civil litigation, State civil litigation. Office: Davis Brown Koehn Shors & Roberts PC 666 Walnut St Ste 2500 Des Moines IA 50309-3904 E-mail: ccf@lawiowa.com

FREDERICKS, WESLEY CHARLES, JR. lawyer; b. N.Y.C., Mar. 31, 1948; s. Wesley Charles and Dionysia W. (Bitsanis) F.; m. Jeanne Maria Judson, May 19, 1973; children: Carolyn Anne, Wesley Charles III. BA, Johns Hopkins U., 1970; JD, Columbia U., 1973. Bar: N.Y. 1974, Conn. 1976, U.S. Supreme Ct. 1979. Assoc. Shearman & Sterling, N.Y.C., 1973-83, Cummings & Lockwood, Stamford, Conn., 1976; chmn. bd. Lotus Performance Cars, L.P., Norwood, N.J., 1983-87; group exec. cons. Group Lotus PLC, 1987; automotive industry cons., 1988-90; pres., CEO Mfrs. Products Co., 1990-94; counsel Gersten, Savage, Kaplowitz & Fredericks, LLP, N.Y.C., 1994, ptnr., 1995-98, Dorsey & Whitney LLP, N.Y.C., 1998—. Lawyer; b. N.Y.C., Mar. 31, 1948; s. Wesley Charles and Dionysia W. (Bitsanis) F.; m. Jeanne Maria Judson, May 19, 1973; children: Carolyn Anne, Wesley C. III. BA Johns Hopkins U., 1970; JD, Columbia U., 1973. Bar: N.Y. 1974, Conn. 1976, U.S. Supreme Ct. 1979. Assoc. Shearman & Sterling, N.Y.C., 1973-83, Cummings & Lockwood, Stamford, Conn., 1976; chmn. bd. Lotus Performance Cars, L.P., Norwood, N.J., 1983-87; group exec. cons. Group Lotus PLC, 1987; automotive industry cons., 1988-90; pres, CEO Mfrs. Products Co., 1990-94; counsel Gersten, Savage, Kaplowitz & Fredericks, LLP, N.Y.C., 1994, ptnr., 1995-98, Dorsey & Whitney LLP, N.Y.C., 1998—. Mem. Johns Hopkins U. Alumni Schs. Com. With USMC, 1968-69. Mem. ABA (co-chmn. bus. law sect. subcom. multinat. mergers and acquisitions 1996—, mem. com. on negotiated acquisitions 1997—), Mashomack Fish and Game Preserve, Campfire Am. Club (N.Y.), Weston Gun Club (Conn.), Sigma Phi Epsilon. Republican. Congregationalist. Mem. Johns Hopkins U. Alumni Schs. Com. With USMC, 1968-69. Mem. ABA (co-chmn. bus. law sect. subcom. multinat. mergers and acquisitions 1996—, mem. com. on negotiated acquisitions 1997—), Mashomack Fish and Game Preserve, Campfire Am. Club (N.Y.), Weston Gun Club (Conn.), Columbia Club of New York, Sigma Phi Epsilon. Republican. Congregationalist. General corporate, Private international, Mergers and acquisitions. Home: 221 Benedict Hill Rd New Canaan CT 06840-2913 Office: Dorsey & Whitney LLP 250 Park Ave New York NY 10177-0001

FREDERICKS, WILLIAM CURTIS, lawyer; b. Washington, July 3, 1961; s. J. Wayne and Anne Curtis Fredericks; m. Ivy Lindstrom, Jan. 21, 1995; children: Charlotte Lindstrom, Thomas Curtis. BA in Polit. Sci., Swarthmore Coll., 1983; MLitt in Internat. Rels., Oxford (Eng.) U., 1988; JD, Columbia U., 1988. Bar: N.Y. 1990, U.S. Dist. Ct. (so. and ea. dists.) N.Y. 1990, U.S. Ct. Appeals (2nd cir.) 1991, U.S. Ct. Appeals (10th cir.) 1997, U.S. Ct. Appeals (6th cir.) 1998. Law clk. hon. Robert S. Gawthrop U.S. Dist. Ct. Pa., Phila., 1988-89; assoc. Simpson Thacher & Bartlett, N.Y.C., 1989-93, Willkie Farr & Gallagher, N.Y.C., 1993-97, Milberg Weiss Bershad Hynes & Lerach LLP, N.Y.C., 1997-98, ptnr., 1999—. Articles editor Columbia Jour. Transnational Law, 1987-88. V.p. Swarthmore Coll. Alumni Assn., 1988-90. Mem. Assn. of the Bar of the City of N.Y. (chair com. on mil. affairs and justice 1997-99). Democrat. Federal civil litigation, General civil litigation, Securities. Office: Milberg Weiss Bershad Hynes & Lerach LLP One Pennsylvania Plaza New York NY 10119-0165

FREDMAN, HOWARD S, lawyer; b. St. Louis, Feb. 1, 1944; s. Manuel and Sydine Fredman; children: Jocelyn Bly, Amber Alexandra, Cameron Penn. BA, Princeton U., 1966; JD, Columbia U., 1969. Bar: Calif. 1970, U.S. Dist. Ct. (no. dist.) Calif. 1970, U.S. Ct. Appeals (9th cir.) 1970, U.S. Dist. Ct. (so. dist.) Calif. 1974, U.S. Dist. Ct. (ctrl. dist.) Calif. 1975, U.S. Dist. Ct. (ea. dist.) Calif. 1996, U.S. Dist. Ct. Colo. 2000. Law clk. to Hon. Milton Pollack U.S. Dist. Ct. (so. dist.) N.Y., 1969-70; assoc. McCutchen, Doyle, Brown & Enersen, San Francisco, 1970-75; counsel, sr. atty., atty. legal divsn. Atlantic Richfield Co., L.A., 1975-87; assoc. Frandzel & Share, 1987-90, ptnr., 1991-99; pvt. practice, 1999—. Mem. faculty Practicing Law Inst., 1982, 86-88; lectr. in field. Mem. editl. adv. bd. Calif. Causes of Action, 1998. Mem. com. to nominate alumni trustees

Princeton Alumni Coun., 1998—2001, treas., 2001—, mem. strategic planning com., 1997—98; chair alumni schs. com. L.A. area Princeton, 1992—94. Mem. ABA, Assn. Bus. Trial Lawyers, Fed. Bar Assn., L.A. County Bar Assn. (chmn. antitrust sect. 1986-87, exec. com. antitrust sect. 1982—, nominating com. 1986-87, del. state bar conf. dels. 1987, 88), Princeton Club So. Calif. (pres. 1994-96). Democrat. Jewish. Antitrust, Banking, Antitrust. Office: 1875 Century Park E Ste 2200 Los Angeles CA 90067-2523 E-mail: hsflawyer@aol.com

FREE, E. LEBRON, lawyer; b. Cleveland, Tenn., Jan. 27, 1940; s. James D. and Mary Kathleen (Hunt) F.; children: Jason LeBron, Ryan Edward. BA, Berea Coll., 1963; ThM, So. Meth. U., 1966; JD, Okla. City U., 1974. Bar: Ga. 1974, Fla. 1975, U.S. Dist. Ct. (mid. dist.) Fla. 1975, U.S. Supreme Ct. 1975. Litigation atty. Jim Walter Corp., Tampa, Fla., 1975-79; prin. E. Lebron Free, P.A., Clearwater, 1980—. Editor Res. IPSA Loquitur, 1996—. Bd. dirs. Ye Mystice Krewe of Neptune, Pinellas County, Fla., 1980-90, capt., 1984; bd. dirs. Hospice of the Fla. Suncoast, 1981-91; chmn., 1984; mem. Met. Planning Orgn., Pinellas County, 1984, Zoning Bd., Clearwater, 1984; bd. dirs. Family Svc. Ctrs., 1993—. Mem. ABA, ATLA, Canakaris Inns of Ct. (bd. dirs. 1997—), Fla. Bar Assn. (family law sect., chmn. fee arbitration com. 1991), Fla. Acad. Trial Lawyers, Clearwater Bar Assn., Rotary (Paul Harris fellow 1992), Masons. Avocation: sailing. Family and matrimonial, Personal injury, Probate. Office: 2725 Park Dr Ste 3 Clearwater FL 33763-1023 Fax: 727-726-4677

FREEBERG, EDWARD RONALD, lawyer; b. Omaha, Nov. 26, 1943; s. Edward Frederic and Janice Ellen (Miller) F.; m. Norena Marie Anderson, Aug. 23, 1969; children: Edward Miller, Gregory Trent. BS, U. Nebr., 1970; JD, Creighton U., 1973. Bar: Nebr. 1973, Mich. 1977, U.S. Dist. Ct. Nebr. 1973, U.S. Ct. Appeals (8th cir.) 1974, U.S. Dist. Ct. (we. dist.) Mich. 1980, U.S. Dist. Ct. (ea. dist.) Mich. 1984, U.S. Ct. Appeals (6th cir.) 1985. Labor counsel Midwest Employers Council, Omaha, 1973-76; corp. labor relations atty. Whirlpool Corp., Benton Harbor, Mich., 1976-80; ptnr. Gemrich Moser, Dombrowski, Bowser and Fette, Kalamazoo, 1980-88; ptnr. Durant, Freeberg, Schanz & Connelly, Kalamazoo, 1988—. Contbr. chpts. to legal publs. Mem. ABA (equal employment opportunity law com. 1977—), Internat. Found. Employee Benefit Plans. Republican. Lutheran. Labor, Pension, profit-sharing, and employee benefits. Home: 7689 N 14th St Kalamazoo MI 49009-6391 Office: Durant Freeberg Schanz & Connelly 5955 W Main St Kalamazoo MI 49009-8700

FREEBORN, MICHAEL D. lawyer; b. Mpls., June 30, 1946; s. Andrew W. and Verena M. (Keller) F.; m. Nancie L. Siebel, Oct. 19, 1947; children: Christopher A., Nathan M., Joel C., Paul K. BS, USAF Acad., 1968; MBA, U. Chgo., 1975; JD, Ind. U., 1972. Bar: Ill. 1972, Ind. 1972. Assoc., ptnr. Rooks, Pitts & Poust, Chgo., 1972-83; ptnr. Freeborn & Peters, 1983—. Writer, lectr. in field. Assoc. editor Ind. Law Rev., 1970-71. Vice chmn. Voices for Ill. Children, 1993—; bd. dirs. Constnl. Rights Found. Chgo., 1996—, Chgo. Youth Ctrs., 1998—; chmn. citizens adv. coun. Ill. Coastal Zone Mgmt. Program, Chgo., 1979. Capt. USAF, 1968-72. Recipient Founders Day award Ind. U. Law Sch., 1972. Mem. Ill. Bar Assn., Ind. Bar Assn., Union League, Legal (Chgo.). Lutheran. Antitrust, Environmental, Labor. Office: Freeborn & Peters 311 S Wacker Dr Ste 3000 Chicago IL 60606-6679

FREED, DANIEL JOSEF, law educator; b. New York, May 12, 1927; s. Julius L. and Sara (Lobel) F.; m. Judith Darrow, June 30, 1967; children: Peter Jacob, Emily Sara; children from previous marriage: Jonathan Michael, Amy. BS, Yale U., 1948, LLB, 1951; LLD (hon.), New England Coll., 1994. Bar: N.Y. 1952, D.C. 1953, U.S. Supreme Ct. 1955. Atty.-investigator, preparedness subcom., com. on armed svcs., U.S. Senate, Washington, 1951-52; assoc. Ford, Bergson, Adams & Borkland, 1952-59; sr. trial atty. antitrust divsn. U.S. Dept. Justice, 1959-64, assoc. dir. office of criminal justice, 1964-66, acting dir., 1966-68, dir., 1968-69; prof. law and its adminstrn. Yale U., New Haven, 1969-75, clin. prof., 1975-94, clin. prof. emeritus, profl. lectr. in law, 1994—. Dir. clin. program law Yale U., 1969-72, dir. Daniel and Florence Guggenheim program in criminal justice, 1972-87, dir. criminal sentencing program, 1988-96. Co-author: (with Wald) Bail in the United States: 1964, publ.1964; editor (periodical) Fed. Sentencing Reporter, 1988—; contbr. articles to profl. jours. Trustee Vera Inst. Justice, N.Y., 1970—; pres. Yale Law Sch. Assn. Washington, 1968. With USN, 1945-46. Recipient Glenn R. Winters award Am. Judges Assn., 1992. Democrat. Jewish. Avocations: metal sculpture, swimming. Home: 164 Linden St New Haven CT 06511-2400 Office: Yale Law Sch 127 Wall St PO Box 208215 New Haven CT 06520-8215 E-mail: daniel.freed@yale.edu

FREED, KENNETH ALAN, lawyer; b. Buffalo, Apr. 28, 1957; s. Sherwood E. and Renee (Liebesman) F.; m. Odette Ashley Freed; children: David Benjamin, Daniel Lawrence, Lauren Allyssa. BA in Econs. magna cum laude, Boston U., 1979; JD, U. Chgo., 1982. Bar: Calif. 1982, U.S. Dist. Ct. (no. dist.) Calif., 1982. Prin., shareholder Feldman, Waldman & Kline, San Francisco, 1982-95; sr. v.p., gen. counsel Sydran Svcs., LLC, San Ramon, Calif., 1995—. Mem. ABA, Calif. Bar Assn. Contracts commercial, Franchising, Mergers and acquisitions. Office: 3000 Executive Pkwy Ste 515 San Ramon CA 94583-4254 E-mail: kfreed@sydran.com

FREEDMAN, BART JOSEPH, lawyer; b. New Haven, Sept. 27, 1955; s. Lawrence Zelic and Dorothy (Robinson) F.; m. Esme Detweiler, Sept. 28, 1985; children: Luke Edward, Samuel Meade, Benjamin Zelic. BA, Carleton Coll., 1977; JD, U. Pa., 1982. Bar: Wash. 1984, U.S. Dist. Ct. (we. dist.) Wash. 1984, U.S. Ct. Appeals (9th cir.) 1985, U.S. Dist. Ct. (ea. dist.) Wash. 1988. Law clk. to chief justice Samuel Roberts Supreme Ct. Pa., Erie, 1982-83; asst. city solicitor City of Phila., 1984; assoc. Perkins Coie, Seattle, 1984-90; ptnr. Preston Gates & Ellis, 1990—. Editor: Natural Resource Damages, 1993. Bd. dirs. Seattle Metrocenter YMCA, 1988-97, chmn. 1993-97; bd. dirs. Leadership Tomorrow, 1996-97; chair Sierra Club Inner City Outings Program, Seattle, 1986-90; chmn. bd. advisors Earth Svc. Corps/YMCA, Seattle, 1990-97. Mem. ABA (com. on corp. counsel 1985-95), Wash. State Bar Assn., Seattle-King County Bar Assn. (participant neighborhood legal clinics 1985-94). Federal civil litigation, General civil litigation, Environmental. Office: Preston Gates & Ellis 701 5th Ave Ste 5000 Seattle WA 98104-7078 E-mail: bartf@prestongates.com

FREEDMAN, GERALD M. lawyer; b. Hampton, Va., July 26, 1943; s. Henry and Arlene L.; m. Kristin King; 1 child, Eliza King. BA, Columbia U., 1964, JD, 1967. Bar: N.Y. 1968, U.S. Dist. Ct. (so. and ea. dists.) N.Y. 1970, U.S. Ct. Appeals (2d cir.) 1976. Adminstr. Columbia U., N.Y.C., 1967-69; assoc. Kelley, Drye & Warren, 1969-71, Trubin Sillcocks Edelman & Knapp, N.Y.C., 1971-76, ptnr., 1976-84, Morgan, Lewis & Bockius, N.Y.C., 1984—. Contbr. articles to profl. jours. Ptnr., N.Y.C. Partnership, 2001—. Mem. ABA, Assn. of Bar of City of N.Y., Am. Bankruptcy Inst., Univ. Club. Banking, Bankruptcy, Finance. Office: Morgan Lewis & Bockius 101 Park Ave Fl 44 New York NY 10178-0060 E-mail: gfreedman@morganlewis.com

FREEDMAN, HELEN E. justice; b. New York, N.Y., Dec. 15, 1942; d. David Simeon and Frances (Fisher) Edelstein; m. Henry A. Freedman, June 7, 1964; children: Katherine Eleanor, Elizabeth Sarah. BA, Smith Coll., 1963; JD, NYU, 1967. Bar: N.Y. 1970, U.S. Dist. Ct. (so. and ea. dists.), U.S. Supreme Ct. 1979. Staff atty. office of gen. counsel Am. Arbitration Assn., N.Y.C., 1967-69; assoc. Hubbel, Cohen & Stiefel, 1970-71, Shaw, Bernstein, Scheuer, Boyden & Sarnoff, N.Y.C., 1971-74; law sec. Civil Ct., 1974-76; sr. atty. housing litigation bur. N.Y.C. Dept. Housing Preservation and Devel., 1976; supervising atty. Dist. Coun. 37 Legal Svcs. Plan, N.Y.C., 1976-78; judge Civil Ct., 1979-88; acting justice Supreme Ct., 1984-88, justice, 1989-95; apptd. to appellate term 1st dept. NY Supreme Ct., 1995-99, apptd. to comml. divsn., 2000—. Co-chair State Judges Mass Tort Litigation Com.; mem. pattern jury instrns. com., Supreme Ct. Justices; adj. prof. N.Y. Law Sch., 1999, 2000; lectr. in field. Author: New York Objections, 1999, rev. edit., 2000; contbr. articles to profl. jours. Recipient Disting. Alumna award Smith Coll., 2000. Fellow Am. Bar Found., N.Y. State Bar Found.; mem. ABA (chair small claims ct. com. 1986-89, bioethics com. nat. conf. spl. ct. judges, N.Y. State Ct. del. to ann. meetings, nat. conf. spl. ct. judges, 1987, 88, Spl. Cts. Conf. award 1987, 88, 93, Jud. Excellence award 1998), Nat. Assn. Women Judges, N.Y. State Bar Assn. (del.), N.Y. Fed. State Jud. Coun., N.Y. Women's Bar Assn., N.Y. State Assn. Women Judges (pres. 1995-97), Assn. of Bar of City of N.Y. (mem. various coms., chair com. med. malpractice, v.p. 1994-95), Judges and Lawyers Breast Cancer Alert (pres.). Home: 150 W 96th St New York NY 10025-6469 Office: NY Supreme Ct 60 Centre New York NY 10007-1488

FREEDMAN, HOWARD JOEL, lawyer; b. Cleve., Jan. 30, 1945; s. Samuel Brooks and Marian (Kirschner) Freedman; m. Terry Jay Greene, Dec. 22, 1966 (div.); children: Randall Greene, Jonathan Jay; m. Rita Bialosky, June 20, 1981. BA, Tulane U., 1967; JD, Case-Western Res. U., 1970. Bar: Ohio 1970. Assoc. Benesch, Friedlander, Coplan & Aronoff and predecessor firms, Cleve., 1970-75; founding ptnr. Friedman, Freedman & Kurdland and predecessor firms, 1975-85, Goodman Weiss Miller adn predecessor firms, Cleve., 1986-88, of counsel, 1988-95; founding partner Weiss & Freedman LLP, Chagrin Falls, 1997—. Bd dirs Archit Research Found. Trustee, pres Spaces, 1993—. Mem.: ABA, Ohio Bar Asn, Bar Asn Greater Cleveland, Cleveland Film Soc (trustee 1995—), Ohio-Israel CofC (trustee, secy 1996—), Cleveland Raquet Club (Pepper Pike, Ohio). Home: 2951 Montgomery Rd Cleveland OH 44122-2828 Office: 35 River St Chagrin Falls OH 44022-3031 E-mail: hjf@weissfreedman.com

FREEDMAN, JAY WEIL, lawyer; b. Washington, May 19, 1942; s. Walter and Maxine (Weil) F.; m. Linda Newman, Aug. 7, 1966; children: Courteney, Spencer. BA, Williams Coll., 1964; JD, Yale U., 1967. Bar: D.C. 1968, U.S. Supreme Ct. 1973. Atty. office of gen. counsel FCC, 1967-68; assoc. Freedman, Levy, Kroll & Simonds, Washington, 1968-72, ptnr., 1972-2001, Foley & Lardner (formerly Freedman, Levy, Kroll & Simonds), Washington, 2001—. Pres. Am. Jewish Com., Washington, 1987—89; bd. dirs. Smithsonian Instn. Librs., 2001—; pres. Washington Hebrew Cong., 1982—84. Mem. ABA, D.C. Bar Assn., Woodmont Country Club (pres. 1997-99), Yale Law Sch. Alumni Assn. (exec. com. 1999—), Econ. Club. Washington, Phi Delta Phi. General corporate, Probate, Securities. Office: Foley & Lardner 3000 K Street NW Ste 500 Washington DC 20007 E-mail: jfreedman@foleylaw.com

FREEDMAN, MONROE HENRY, lawyer, educator, columnist; b. Mt. Vernon, N.Y., Apr. 10, 1928; s. Chauncey and Dorothea (Kornblum) F.; m. Audrey Willock, Sept. 24, 1950 (dec. 1998); children: Alice Freedman Korngold, Sarah Freedman Izquierdo, Caleb (dec. 1998), Judah. AB cum laude, Harvard U., 1951, LLB, 1954, LLM, 1956. Bar: Mass. 1954, Pa. 1957, D.C. 1960, U.S. Dist. Ct. (ea. dist. N.Y.), U.S. Ct. Appeals (D.C. cir.) 1960, U.S. Supreme Ct. 1960, U.S. Ct. Appeals (2d cir.) 1968, N.Y. 1978, U.S. Ct. Appeals (9th cir.) 1982, U.S. Ct. Appeals (11th cir.) 1986, U.S. Ct. Appeals (Fed. cir.) 1987. Assoc. Wolf, Block, Schorr & Solis-Cohen, Phila., 1956-58; ptnr. Freedman & Temple, Washington, 1969-73; dir. Stern Community Law Firm, 1970-71; prof. law George Washington U., 1958-73; dean Hofstra Law Sch., Hempstead, N.Y., 1973-77, prof. law, 1973—, Howard Lichtenstein Disting. prof. legal ethics, 1989—; Drinko-Baker & Hostetler chair in law Cleve. State U., 1992; CFO Olive Tree Mktg. Internat., 1998—. Faculty asst. Harvard U. Law Sch., 1954-56, instr. trial advocacy and legal ethics, 1978—; lectr. on lawyers' ethics; exec. dir. U.S. Holocaust Meml. Coun., 1980-82, gen. counsel, 1982-83, sr. adviser to chmn., 1982-87; cons. U.S. Commn. on Civil Rights, 1960-64, Neighborhood Legal Services Program, 1970; legis. cons. to Senator John L. McClellan, 1959; spl. com. on courtroom conduct N.Y.C. Bar Assn., 1972; exec. dir. Criminal Trial Inst., 1965-66; expert witness on legal ethics state and fed. ct. proceedings, U.S. Senate and House Coms., U.S. Dept. Justice, FDIC; spl. investigator Rochester Inst. Tech., 1991; reporter Am. Lawyer's Code of Conduct, 1979-81; mem. Arbitration panel U.S. Dist. Ct. (ea. dist.) N.Y., 1986—; Inaugural Wickwire lectr. Dalhousie Law Sch., N.S., 1992; lectr. S.C. Bar Found., 1993, numerous profl. confs; adv. subgroup on ethics U.S. Dist. Ct. (ea. dist.) N.Y., 1994-96. Author: Contracts, 1973, Lawyers' Ethics in an Adversary System, 1975 (ABA gavel award, cert. of merit 1976), Teacher's Manual Contracts, 1978, American Lawyer's Code of Conduct, 1981, Understanding Lawyers' Ethics, 1990, Group Defamation and Freedom of Speech—The Relationship Between Language and Violence, 1995; co-editor; columnist Cases and Controversies, Am. Lawyer Media, 1990-96, (with Supreme Ct. Justice Ruth Bader Ginsburg) Freedom, Life, & Death: Materials on Comparative Constitutional Law, 1997; television appearances include Donohue, CNN Money Line, CBS 60 Minutes, CNN Late Edition, Court TV, and others; contbr. articles to profl. jours. Recipient Martin Luther King Jr. Humanitarian award, 1987, The Lehman-LaGuardia Award for Civic Achievement, 1996. Fellow Am. Bar Found. (life); mem. ABA (ethics adv. to chair criminal justice sect. 1993-95, Michael Franck award 1998), ACLU (nat. bd. dirs. 1970-80, nat. adv. coun. 1980—, spl. litigation counsel 1971-73), Am. Law Inst. (consultative group on the law governing lawyers, 1990-99, consultative group on Uniform Comml. Code art. 2 1990—), Soc. Am. Law Tchrs. (mem. governing bd. 1974-79, exec. com. 1976-79, chmn. com. on profl. responsibility 1974-79, 87-90), ABA (vice chmn. ethical considerations com. criminal justice sect. 1989-90, ethics advisor to chmn. criminal justice sect., 1993-96), N.Y. State Bar Assn. (com. on legal edn. and admission to bar 1988-92, criminal justice sect. com. on profl. responsibility, 1990-92, award for Dedication to Scholarship and pub. svc. 1997), Assn. Bar City N.Y. (com. on profl. responsibility 1987-90, com. on profl. and jud. ethics 1991-92), Fed. Bar Assn. (chmn. com. on profl. disciplinary standards and procedures 1970-71), Am. Soc. Writers on Legal Subjects (mem. com. on constitution and bylaws 1999—) Am. Jewish Congress (nat. governing coun. 1984-86), Am. Arbitration Assn. (arbitrator, nat. panel arbitrators 1964—, cert. svc. award 1986), Nat. Network on Right to Counsel (exec. bd., exec. com. 1986-90), Nat. Prison Project (steering com. 1970-90), Nat. Assn. Criminal Def. Lawyers (vice chmn. ethics adv. com. 1991-93, co-chmn., 1994). Democrat. Jewish.

FREEDMAN, STUART JOEL, lawyer; b. Oct. 14, 1939; s. Hyman J. and Lillian G. (Ruby) Freedman; m. Nancy Nathanson, Dec. 17, 1972; children: Lauren H., Jacqueline D. BA, Rutgers U., 1962; JD, Columbia U., 1965. Bar: N.J. 1965, N.Y. 1982, U.S. Supreme Ct. 1975. Law sec. to sr. presiding judge appellate divsn. N.J. Superior Ct., 1965—66; assoc. Sills Cummis Radin & tischman, Newark, 1966—69; asst. gen counsel Cadence Industries Corp., West Caldwell, 1969—70, v.p., sec., counsel, 1970—84; sr. v.p. law, sec. Sedgwick James, Inc., N.Y.C., NY, 1984—89; ptnr. Greenberg, Margolis, P.C., Roseland, NJ, 1989—93; sr. v.p., gen. counsel and sec. DiGiorgio Corp., Somerset, 1993—95; ptnr. Norris, McLaughlin & Marcus, Somerville, 1993—. Decorated Bronze Star; scholar Henry Rutgers, 1961—62, Harlan Fiske Stone, 1964—65. Mem.: ABA, N.J. Bar Assn., Assn. of Bar of City of N.Y. (chmn. workshops subcom. of com. corp. law depts.), Am. Soc. Corp. Secs. (pres. N.Y. regional group 1984—85), N.J. Gen. Counsel Group (chmn. 1982—84), Assn. Corp. Counsel of N.J. (pres. 1982—84), Phi Beta Kappa. Antitrust, General corporate, Insurance. Office: Norris McLaughlin & Marcus PO Box 1018 Somerville NJ 08876-1018

FREEDMAN, WALTER, lawyer; b. St. Louis, Oct. 30, 1914; s. Sam and Sophie (Gordon) F.; m. Maxine Weil, June 23, 1940; children— Jay W., Sandra Freedman Sabel. AB, JD, Washington U., 1937; LLM, Harvard, 1938. Bar: Mo., Ill., D.C. Atty. SEC, Washington, 1938-40, U.S. Dept. Interior, Washington, 1940-42; chief counsel Office Export Control, Foreign Econ. Adminstrn., 1942-44, dir., 1944-45; ptnr. Freedman, Levy, Kroll & Simonds (and predecessor firm), Washington, 1946-2001, Foley & Lardner, Washington, 2001—. Fairchild fellow Harvard U. Law Sch., 1937-38 Editor-in-chief: Washington U. Law Quarterly, 1936-37; Contbr. articles to profl. jours. Decorated chevalier de l'Order de la Couronne (Belgium); recipient Disting. Alumni award Washington U. Sch. Law, 1995. Mem. Am. Law Inst., ABA, Fed. Bar Assn., D.C. Bar Assn., Woodmont Country Club (bd. mgrs.), Cosmos Club, Phi Beta Kappa, Omicron Delta Kappa, Phi Sigma Alpha. Jewish (trustee temple). Administrative and regulatory, General corporate, Probate. Home: 4545 W St NW Washington DC 20007-1513 Office: 3000 K St NW Washington DC 20007-5109 E-mail: wfreedman@foleylaw.com

FREEHLING, DANIEL JOSEPH, law educator, law library director; b. Montgomery, Ala., Nov. 13, 1950; s. Saul Irving and Grace (Lieberman) L. BS, Huntingdon Coll., 1972; JD, U. Ala., 1975, MLS, 1977. Ref. libr., asst. to assoc. dean U. Ala. Sch. Law, Tuscaloosa, 1975-77; assoc. law libr. U. Md., Balt., 1977-79, Cornell U., Ithaca, N.Y., 1979-82; law libr. dir., assoc. prof. U. Maine, Portland, 1982-86; law libr. dir., assoc. prof. law Boston U., 1986-92, prof., 1992—, assoc. dean for adminstrn., 1993-97, assoc. dean for info. svcs., 1999—. Mem. steering com., law program com. Rsch. Librs. Group, 1989-91; treas. New Eng. Law Libr. Consortium, 1989-91; vice chair, chair-elect sect. on law librs. Assn. Am. Law Schs., 1990-91, chair, 1992. Mem.: ABA (accreditation com. 1995—2001), Am. Assn. Law Librs. (chair acad. law librs. spl. interest sect. 1981—82, edn. com. 1982—83, membership com. 1983—84, program chair 1987—88, local arrangements co-chair 1992—93, chair mentoring and retention com. 1995—96). Home: 21A Lakeshore Rd Boxford MA 01921-1113 Office: Boston U Law Sch Pappas Law Libr 765 Commonwealth Ave Boston MA 02215-1401

FREEHLING, PAUL EDWARD, lawyer; b. Chgo., June 10, 1938; s. Norman and Edna (Wilhartz) F.; m. Susan Seder, June 27, 1961; children: Daniel, Joel. AB, Harvard U., 1959, LLB, 1962. Bar: Ill. 1962, U.S. Dist. Ct. (no. dist.) Ill. 1962, U.S. Ct. Appeals (7th cir.) 1973, U.S. Ct. Appeals (6th cir.) 1980, U.S. Ct. Appeals (D.C. cir.) 1983, U.S. Supreme Ct. 1974. Law clk. to judge U.S. Dist. Ct. No. Dist. Ill., Chgo., 1962-64; assoc. Pope, Ballard, Shepard & Fowle, 1964-70, ptnr., 1970-82, dir., mem., 1982-93; ptnr.l D'Ancona & Pflaum, 1994—. Fellow: Am. Coll. Trial Lawyers; mem.: Am. Law Inst. (appointee, roster of disting. neutrals CPR Inst. for Dispute Resolutio), Fed. Bar Assn., Am. Judicature Soc., Ill. Bar Assn., Chgo. Bar Assn., Chgo. Coun. Lawyers, 7th Cir. Bar Assn., Northmoor Country Club (Highland Park, Ill.), Std. Club (Chgo.). Jewish. Administrative and regulatory, Federal civil litigation, State civil litigation. Office: D'Ancona & Pflaum 111 E Wacker Dr Ste 2800 Chicago IL 60601-4209 E-mail: pFreehli@dancona.com

FREELAND, CHARLES, lawyer, accountant; b. Balt., July 18, 1940; s. Benjamin and Beatrice (Polakoff) F.; m. Beverly Klaff, July 15, 1965; children— Stephen Jason, Jennifer Jill, Gwen Nicole, Kimberly Suzanne. B.S., U. Md., 1962, LL.B., 1965; diploma U.S. Naval Justice Sch., 1966. Bar: Md. 1965, U.S. Dist. Ct. Md. 1965, U.S. Tax Ct. 1966, U.S. Ct. Mil. Apls. 1966, U.S. Ct. Claims 1968, U.S. Supreme Ct. 1969, U.S. Ct. Appeals (4th cir.) 1974. Fin. v.p. Collins Electronics Mfg. Co.; dir. fin. planning Cellu-Craft, Inc., Stevensville, Md., 1963-65; controller Braun-Crystal Mfg. Co., Inc., Middle Village, N.Y., 1969-70, BCN Design Products, Inc., Bayshore, N.Y., 1969-70; asst. city solicitor City of Balt., 1972-82; pvt. practice law and acctg., Balt., 1971-93; ptnr. Kaplan, Freeland & Schwartz, Balt., 1982-86; pres. Charles Freeland, PC, 1986—. Served to lt. USNR, 1965-68. Mem. Am. Judicature Soc., Am. Assn. Attys.-CPA's, ABA, Md. Bar Assn., Balt. County Bar Assn., Am. Assn. CPA's, Md. Assn. CPA's, Am. Arbitration Assn. (nat. panel 1970—). Democrat. Jewish. Club: Woodholme Country. General corporate, Corporate taxation, Personal income taxation. Home: PO Box 422 4 Timothys Green Ct Brooklandville MD 21022 Office: 1300 York Rd Ste 180 Lutherville Timonium MD 21093-6806

FREEMAN, ANTOINETTE ROSEFELDT, lawyer; b. Atlantic City, Oct. 7, 1937; d. Bernard Paul and Fannie (Levin) Rosefeldt; m. Alan Richard Freeman, June 22, 1958 (div. Apr. 1979); children: Barry David, Robin Lisa. BA, Rutgers U., 1972; JD, Ind. U., 1975; LLM, Temple U., 1979. Bar: Pa. 1975, Wash. 1992, U.S. Dist. Ct. (ea. dist.) Pa. 1976, U.S. Ct. Appeals (3d cir.) 1982. Substitute tchr. Washington Twp. Sch. Dist., Indpls., 1972; dep. prosecutor intern Marion County Prosecutor, 1974-75; asst. dist. atty. City of Phila., 1975-76; mgr. EEO Wyeth Labs., Radnor, Pa., 1976-80, SmithKline & French Labs., Phila., 1980-82; sr. counsel SmithKline Beecham Corp., 1982-91; assoc. gen. counsel Immunex Corp., 1991—; arbitrator Am. Arbitration Assn., 1976—. Counsel Regional Interests Developing Efficient Transp., 1983-85; adv. bd. Family Svc. Phila., 1980-81, Greater Phila. C. of C., 1983; pres. Croskey Ct. Condominium Assn., 1983-87; bd. dirs. Logan Sq. Neighborhood Assn., 1983-91, pres., 1985-87; v.p., sec. Friends of Logan Sq. Found., 1985-91; counsel Hapoel Games USA; chairperson Ctr. City Coalition for Quality of Life; atty. Vol. Lawyers for the Arts, Phila., 1985-91; bd. dirs. Sr. Employment and Ednl. Svc., BathHouse Theater, 1991-99, v.p. 1994-96; bd. dirs. Bellini preview group Seattle Opera Guild, 1994-96 ; mem. Assoc. Corp. Coun. for Arts., 1992-93; mem. adv. bd. regulatory affairs cert. program U. Wash. Mem. ABA, Pa. Bar Assn., Phila. Bar Assn., Wash. State Bar Assn., Merit Employers Coun. (1st v.p. 1978-79), Phila. Women's Network, Phila. Lawyers Club, Phila. King County Med. Soc./King County Bar Assn. (med.-legal com.). Democrat. Jewish. Administrative and regulatory, Government contracts and claims, Labor. Office: Immunex Corp 51 University St Seattle WA 98101-2936

FREEMAN, CHARLES E. state supreme court justice; b. Richmond, Va., Dec. 12, 1933; m. Marylee Voelker; 1 child, Kevin. BA in Liberal Arts, Va. Union U., 1954; JD, John Marshall Law Sch., 1962, LLD (hon.), 1992. Bar: Ill. 1962. Pvt. practice, 1962-76; pvt. practice, Cook County, Chgo., 1962-76, asst. state's atty., 1964; asst. atty. Bd. Election Commrs., Chgo., 1964-65; mem. Ill. Indsl. Commn., 1965-73, Ill. Commerce Commn., Chgo., 1973-76; judge law and chancery divsns. Cook County Circuit Ct., 1976-86; judge Appellate Ct. Ill., 1986-90; supr. of justice Ill. Supreme Ct., 1990-2000, chief justice, 1997-2000, retained, 2000—. First African-Am. to swear in a Mayor city Chgo., to serve on Ill. Supreme Ct., 1990; leader in case disposition by published opinion, 1988, 89; recipient Cert. Achievement, Internat. Christian Fellowship Missions, Earl B. Dickerson award Chgo. Bar Assn., Merit award Habilative Systems, award Statesmanship, Monarch Awards Found. of Alpha Kappa Alpha, Freedom award John Marshall Law Sch. Mem. ABA (cert. Recognition, task force opportunities minorities in jud. adminstrn. divsn. and coms. opportunities minorities in profession), Am. Judges' Assn., Am. Judicature Soc., Ill. State Bar Assn., Ill. Jud. Coun. (Kenneth Wilson Meml. award, Meritorious Svc. award), Ill. Judges' Assn., Cook County Bar Assn. (Kenneth E. Wilson award, Cert. Merit, Ida Platt award, Presdl. award, Jud. award), Du Page County Bar Assn. Office: Supreme Ct Ill 160 N La Salle St Fl 20 Chicago IL 60601-3119

FREEMAN, DAVID JOHN, lawyer; b. N.Y.C., Aug. 9, 1948; s. John L. and Josephine F. (Wilding) F.; m. Ellen Gogolick, Dec. 29, 1974; children: Matthew, Julie. B.A., Harvard U., 1970; J.D., 1975. Bar: Mass. 1975, D.C. 1977, N.Y. 1982, U.S. Dist. Ct. D.C. 1981, N.Y. 1982, U.S. Dist. Ct. D.C. 1981, U.S. Dist. Ct. (so. and ea. dists.) N.Y. 1982, U.S. Ct. Appeals (D.C. cir.) 1979, U.S. Ct. Appeals (2nd cir.) 1982, U.S. Supreme Ct. 1988. Spl. asst. to U.S. Senator Frank E. Moss, 1970-72; trial atty. FTC, Washington, 1975-77; assoc. Ginsburg, Feldman & Bress, 1977-81, Holtzmann, Wise & Shepard, N.Y.C., 1981-84; ptnr., 1984-94; ptnr., chmn. environ. dept. Battle Fowler, 1994-2000; head N.Y. environ. practice group Paul, Hastings, Janofsky & Walker, N.Y.C., 2000—. Spl. legal counsel N.Am. Environ. Affairs, UN Environ. Programme; co-chair emeritus ISO 14000 Legal Issues Forum, U.S. Tech. Com. to TC-207, Internat. Com. Standardization. Editor-in-chief: Jour. Environ Law Practice (West), 1998-2000. Mem. ABA (environment, energy and resources sect.), Assn. Bar City of N.Y., Harvard Law Sch. Assn., N.Y. State Bar Assn. (environ. law sect., co-chair hazardous waste com., co-chair task force on superfund reform). E-mail: david. Federal civil litigation, Environmental. Office: Paul Hastings Janofsky & Walker LLP 75 E 55th St New York NY 10022-3205 E-mail: freeman@paulhastings.com

FREEMAN, FLORENCE ELEANOR, lawyer; b. Cambridge, Mass., Feb. 25, 1921; s. Elbern and Olive Blanche (Rice) F.; AB, Wellesley Coll., 1942; JD, U. Pa., 1945. Bar: Del. 1947, U.S. Dist. Ct. Del. 1948, U.S. Ct. Appeals (3d cir.) 1950, Mass. 1954, U.S. Dist. Ct. Mass. 1960. Assoc., Lynch & Hermann, Wilmington, Del., 1946-53; sole practice, Weston, Mass., 1954-69; ptnr. Freeman & Conceison, Weston, 1970-83, Freeman & White, Weston, 1984— ; town counsel Town of Weston, 1968-86, spl. counsel, 1986-89. Author: (play) Portrait of a Prince, 1965. Pres. Weston LWV, 1960-62, Weston Drama Workshop, 1963-71; mem. bd. selectmen Town of Weston, 1964-68; sec., trustee So. New Eng. Conf. United Meth. Ch., Boston, 1971-74, chancellor, 1976-86 ; bd. visitors Boston U. Sch. Theology, 1978—; chmn. bd. advisors Anna Howard Shaw Ctr., 1988—; mem. council fin. and adminstrn. United Meth. Ch., Chgo., 1980-88, alt. jud. council, 1980-88, chmn. legal responsibilities com. 1980-88. Mem. ABA, Bar Assn. Club: Footlight (Boston) (pres. 1962-64); Wellesley Coll., Eastern Point Yacht. Probate, Church law. Office: Freeman & White 483 Boston Post Rd Weston MA 02493-1553

FREEMAN, FRANKLIN EDWARD, JR. state governmental assistant; b. Dobson, N.C., May 5, 1945; s. Franklin Edward and Clara E. (Smith) F.; m. Margaret Carson McKnight, 1966 (div. 1974); children: Margaret Elizabeth, Nancy Lorrin; m. Katherine Lynn Lloyd, Aug. 12, 1978; children: Katherine Ann, Franklin Edward III, Alexander Lloyd, May Clare. BA, U. N.C., 1967, JD, 1970. Bar: N.C. 1970. Rsch. asst. Assoc. Justice Dan K. Moore, Raleigh, N.C., 1970-71; asst. dist. atty. 17th jud. dist. N.C. Ct. System, 1971-73; exec. sec. Jud. Coun., 1973-78; asst. dir. Adminstrv. Office of Cts., Raleigh, 1973-78, dir., 1981-93; dist. atty. 17th jud. dist. N.C. Ct. System, 1979-81; sec. N.C. Dept. Correction, Raleigh, 1993-97; chief staff Gov. James B. Hunt, Jr., 1997-99; assoc. justice N.C. Supreme Ct., 1999-2001; sr. asst. for govt. affairs Gov. of N.C., 2001—. Contbr. articles to profl. jours. Tchr. Sunday sch. Main Street United Meth. Ch., Reidsville, 1996—, chmn. every mem. canvas, 1980, chmn. adminstrv. bd., 1981; mem. Hayes Barton Meth. Ch., Raleigh; pres. Raleigh Host Lions Club, 1992—. Recipient Svc. award Conf. Superior Ct. Judges, Svc. award Conf. Dist. Ct. Judges, Svc. award N.C. Clks. Superior Ct. Assn., Svc. award N.C. Magistrates Assn. Mem. N.C. State Bar, N.C. Correctional Assn., Surry County Bar Assn., Rockingham County Bar Assn., 10th Dist. Bar Assn., 17th Dist. Bar Assn., State Correctional Adminstrs., Conf. State Ct. Adminstrs. (pres-elect 1992-93, bd. dirs. 1987-90, 94-95), Lions Club (pres. Raleigh Host club 1994), Delta Upsilon. Democrat. Avocations: horses, history, reading. Office: Gov's Office 20301 Mail Svc Ctr Raleigh NC 27699-0301

FREEMAN, GEORGE CLEMON, JR. lawyer; b. Birmingham, Ala., Jan. 3, 1929; s. George Clemon and Annie Laura (Gill) F.; m. Anne Colston Hobson, Dec. 6, 1958; children: Anne Colston McEvoy, George Clemon III, Joseph Reid Anderson. BA magna cum laude, Vanderbilt U., 1950; LLB, Yale U., 1956. Bar: Ala. 1956, Va. 1958, D.C. 1974. Law clk. to Justice Hugo L. Black U.S. Supreme Ct., 1956; assoc. Hunton & Williams, Richmond, Va., 1957-63, ptnr., 1963-95, sr. counsel, 1995—. Contbr. articles to profl. jours. Pres. Va. chpt. Nature Conservancy, 1962-63; counsel Va. Outdoors Recreation Study Com. Va. Legis., 1963-65; mem. sect. 301 Superfund Act Study Group Congl. Adv. Com., 1981-82; mem. Falls James Com., 1973-89; chmn. Richmond City Dem. Com., 1969-71; chmn. adv. coun. Energy Policy Studies Ctr. U. Va., 1981-85; chmn. legal adv. com. to Va. Commn. on Transp. in the 21st Century, 1986-87; mem. Va. Gov.'s Commn. to Study Historic Preservation, 1987-88, Va. Coun. on the Environment, 1989-91; chmn. Va. Bd. Hist. Resources, 1989-91; mem. The Atlantic Coun., 1986-95; bd. dirs. Nat. Mus. Am. History, 1997—. Lt. (j.g.) USN, 1951-54. Ctr. for Pub. Resources fellow, 1990—. Fellow Am. Bar Found. (Va. state chmn. 1986-90); mem. ABA (chmn. standing com. on facilities of Law Libr. of Congress 1967-73, coordinating group on regulatory reform 1981-85, nominating com. 1984-87, chmn. civil justice coordinating com. 1990-92, sect. bus. law, sect. coun. 1976-79, chmn. ad hoc com. on Fed. Criminal Code 1979-81, chmn. program com. 1981-82, chmn. ad hoc com. on tort law reform 1986-87, sect. del. to ho. of dels. 1983-87, sec. 1987-88, vice-chmn. and ed. The Business Lawyer 1988-89, chmn.-elect 1989-90, chmn. 1990-91), Richmond Bar Assn., Va. Bar Assn., Am. Law Inst. (coun. 1980—, advisor to coun. on project on compensation and liability for product and process injuries 1986-91, advisor restatement of law, THRD, torts apportionment 1993-97, advisor restatement law THRD torts gen. prins. 1997—), Am. Judicature Soc., Country Club of Va., Knickerbocker Club, Met. Club, Phi Beta Kappa, Phi Delta Phi, Omicron Delta Kappa, Alpha Tau Omega. Democrat. Episcopalian. Avocation: gardening. Administrative and regulatory, Constitutional, Environmental. Home: Oyster Shell Point Farm 314 Oyster Shell Rd Callao VA 22435 Office: Hunton & Williams 951 E Byrd St Richmond VA 23219-0005 E-mail: gfreeman@hunton.com

FREEMAN, GILL SHERRYL, judge; b. N.Y.C., June 24, 1949; d. Norman and Arlene (Vigdor) Jacovitz. BS in Edn. cum laude, Temple U., 1970; student, U. Wis., 1966-68; MEd, U. Miami, Miami, Fla., 1973; JD cum laude, U. Miami, 1977. Bar: Fla. 1977, U.S. Dist. Ct. (so. dist.) 1977, U.S. Dist. Ct. (mid. dist.) Fla. 1984, U.S. Ct. Appeals (5th cir.) 1977. Tchr. Dade County Pub. Schs., Miami, 1970-76; assoc. Walton, Lantaff, Schroeder & Carson, 1977-82, Ruden, McClosky, Smith, Schuster & Russell, Miami, 1982—, ptnr., 1983-97; apptd. cir. ct. judge Dade County Fla., 1997—. Vice chair Fla. Supreme Ct. Gender Bias Commn., 1987-90; chair Fla. Supreme Ct. Gender Bias Study Implementation Commn., 1991-94; mem. Supreme Ct. Commn. on Fairness, 1997, chair, 1999—; chmn. bd. dirs. Journey Inst., 1997-01. Trustee Dade County Law Libr., 1996—. Elected Fellow of the ABA, 1993; Master, Family Law Inns. of Ct., 1992. Mem. Fla. Bar Assn. (pres. 1984-85), Fla. Assn. Women Lawyers. Avocations: alpine skiing, travel, tennis. Office: R E Geistein Bldg 1351 NW 12th St Miami FL 33125

FREEMAN, RICHARD LYONS, lawyer; b. Chgo., Oct. 29, 1932; s. Reuben L. and Bernice (Green) F.; m. Mary Leopold, May 2, 1959; children: Thomas R., Richard Lyons. AB cum laude, Harvard U., 1954; LLB, Yale U., 1957. Bar: Ill. 1958. Assoc. Friedman, Zoline & Rosenfield, Chgo., 1958-60; investment analyst Robert J. Levy & Co., 1960-62; assoc. Schwartz & Freeman, 1962-68, ptnr., 1968-91, of counsel, 1991—2001, Michael Best & Friedrich L.L.C., Chgo., 2001—. Bd. dirs. Chgo. Hearing Soc., pres., 1972-74. Served with Air N.G., 1957-63. Fellow Am. Coll. Trust and Estate Counsel; mem. ABA, Chgo. Bar Assn., Ill. Bar Assn., Lake Shore Country Club (Glencoe, Ill.). Pension, profit-sharing, and employee benefits, Probate, Real property. Office: Suite 1900 401 N Michigan Ave Chicago IL 60611-4274 E-mail: rundick@aol.com

FREEMAN, TODD IRA, lawyer; b. Mpls., Nov. 24, 1953; s. Earl Stanley and Gretta Lois (Rudick) F.; m. Judy Lynn Sigel, June 15, 1975; children: Jennifer, Katie, Zachary. BS in Mktg., U. Colo., 1974; JD, U. Minn., 1978. Bar: Minn. 1978, U.S. Dist. Ct. Minn. 1978, U.S. Tax Ct. 1980; CPA, Minn. Acct. Coopers & Lybrand, Mpls., 1978-80; shareholder Larkin, Hoffman, Daly & Lindgren, 1980—, treas., 1990—, also bd. dirs., 1990-93. Bd. dirs. Temple of Aaron, St. Paul, 1983—, Sholom Home, Inc., St. Paul, 1983-89. Mem. ABA (tax sect., past chmn. personal svc. orgns.), AICPA, Minn. Soc. CPAs (tax conf. com. 1987—), Minn. State Bar Assn., Hennepin County Bar Assn. Avocations: tennis, racquetball, football. General corporate, Estate planning, Pension, profit-sharing, and employee benefits. Office: Larkin Hoffman Daly & Lindgren 7900 Xerxes Ave S Ste 1500 Minneapolis MN 55431-1128

FREERKSEN, GREGORY NATHAN, lawyer; b. Washington, Iowa, June 4, 1951; s. Floyd and Betty Jo (Frederick) F.; m. Patricia A. Menges, Mar. 21, 1981; children: Suzanna, Andrea, Paul, Timothy. B.S., No. Ill. U., 1973; J.D., DePaul U., 1976. Bar: Ill. 1976, U.S. Dist. Ct. (no. dist.) Ill. 1976, U.S. Supreme Ct. 1980, U.S. Ct. Appeals (D.C. cir.) 1983. Ptnr. Witwer, Burlage, Poltrock & Giampietro, 1988—; arbitrator in court annexed arbitration proceedings 18th Jud. Cir. and Cook County Cir. Cts. Author: (annotated bibliography) Children in the Legal Literature, 1976; Non-Salary Provisions in Negotiated Teacher Agreements, 1975. Editor Ill. law issue DePaul U. Law Rev., 1975-76. Mem. ABA, Ill. State Bar Assn., Chgo. Bar Assn., Appellate Lawyers Assn., DuPage Bar Assn. Democrat. General civil litigation. Home: 645 Hill Ave Glen Ellyn IL 60137-5077 Office: Witwer Burlage Poltrock & Giampietro 125 S Wacker Dr Ste 2700 Chicago IL 60606-4401

FREIJE, PHILIP CHARLES, lawyer; b. Princeton, N.J., July 27, 1944; s. Brahim K. and Evelyn M. (Haddad) F.; m. Karen Mae Janovic, Oct. 18, 1969; children: Michael P., James C., Christine L. BA, U. Conn., 1966, JD, 1969; LLM, George Washington U., 1972. Bar: Conn. 1970, D.C. 1970, U.S. Supreme Ct. 1973. Assoc. Conway, Londregan, Leuba & McNamara, New London, Conn., 1969; atty.-advisor Office of Fgn. Direct Investment, U.S. Dept. Commerce, Washington, 1970-73, asst. dir. litigation, 1974; legal advisor Social & Econ. Statistics Adminstrn., U.S. Dept. Commerce, 1974-75; dep. asst. gen. counsel adminstrn./econ. affairs Office of Gen. Counsel, U.S. Dept. Commerce, 1975-81, dep. asst. gen. counsel econ. affairs/regulation, 1981-85, dep. chief counsel for econ. affairs, 1985-92, chief counsel for econ. affairs, 1992-98; bureau coun. U.S. Census Bureau U.S. Dept. Commerce, 1998—. Dir. Lake Barcroft Community Assn., Falls Church, Va., 1980-82. Mem. ABA, Fed. Bar Assn., Conn. Bar Assn., D.C. Bar Assn., Am. Judicature Soc. Home: 6212 Beachway Dr Falls Church VA 22041-1423 Office: US Dept Commerce 14th & Constitution Ave NW Washington DC 20230-0001

FREILICH, IRVIN MAYER, lawyer; b. Ulm, Germany, Mar. 3, 1949; arrived in U.S., 1949; s. Charles J. and Sylvia (Schaengold) F.; m. Judith Ellen Pines, June 20, 1971; children: Jared P., Emily R. BA, U. Cin., 1971; JD, Georgetown U., 1974. Bar: N.Y. 1975, N.J. 1977, U.S. Dist. Ct. (so. and ea. dist.) N.Y. 1975, U.S. Dist. Ct. (no. dist.) N.Y. 1985, U.S. Dist. Ct. N.J. 1975, U.S. Ct. Appeals (3d cir.) 1983, U.S. Ct. Appeals (2d cir.) 1975, U.S. Ct. Appeals (D.C. cir.) 1996, U.S. Supreme Ct. 1987. Assoc. Kaye, Scholer, Fierman, Hayes & Handler, N.Y.C., 1974-77; from assoc. to ptnr. Hannoch Weisman, Roseland, N.J., 1977-90, 94-99; ptnr. Edwards & Angell, Newark, 1990-94, Robertson, Freilich, Bruno & Cohen, LLC, Newark, 1999—. Federal civil litigation, Environmental. Office: Robertson Freilich Bruno & Cohen LLC One Riverfront Plz Newark NJ 07102 E-mail: ifreilich@rfbclaw.com

FREILICH, ROBERT H. lawyer, law educator, legal consultant; b. N.Y.C., Mar. 10, 1936; s. Julius and Evelyn R. (Ravitt) F.; m. Carole S. Traktman, Dec. 25, 1958; children— Amy Elizabeth, Bradley Lawrence. A.B., U. Chgo., 1954; LL.B., Yale U., 1957; M.I.A., Columbia U., 1958, LL.M., 1969, J.S.D., 1974. Bar: N.Y. 1958, Mo. 1968, Calif. 1989; U.S. Ct. Appeals (2d cir.) 1958, U.S. Ct. Appeals (4th cir.) 1974, U.S. Ct. Appeals (8th cir.) 1968, U.S. Ct. Appeals (9th cir.) 1976, U.S. Supreme Ct. 1960. prof. law in urban affairs Sch. Law, U. Mo., Kansas City, 1968— ; ptnr. Freilich, Leitner & Carlisle, P.C., Kansas City, 1972—; ptnr. Freilich, Kaufman, Fox & Sohagi, L.A., Calif.; cons. mcpl. law zoning, litigation and real estate devel.; vis. prof. Sch. Law, London Sch. Econs. and Reading U., 1974, Harvard U. Law Sch. 1984-85. Author: Cases and Materials on Land Use, 1993, Model Subdivision Regulations, 1993; Urban Growth Management Systems, 1978; The Land Use Awakening, 1982; The Sword and The Shield, 1983 . Dir. Mcpl. Legal Studies Ctr., Southwestern Legal Found., Rocky Mountain Land Use Inst. Mem. ABA (mem. council of sect. urban, state and local govt., editor Urban Lawyer jour.), Am. Planning Assn. (chair-elect, planning and law div.), Am. Coll. Real Estate Lawyers, Assn. Am. Law Schs. (chmn. sect. local govt. law). Home: 400 W 49th Ter Apt 2048 Kansas City MO 64112-2532 Office: Freilich, Leitner & Carlisle 1000 Plaza West 4600 Madison Ave Kansas City MO 64112-1277

FREIMUTH, MARC WILLIAM, lawyer; b. Duluth, Minn., Sept. 23, 1946; s. Edgar and Marcia (Zuckerman) F.; m. Sharon Rae Sager, Feb. 7, 1946 (dec.); children: Ladeene Asher, Kyle Gregory, Joel Todd. BA, U. Minn., 1968, JD magna cum laude, 1971. Bar: Ohio 1971. Assoc. Squire, Sanders, Dempsey, Cleve., 1971-78; sr. v.p., gen. counsel, sec. Ohio Savs. Fin. Corp., 1978—. Sec. Superior Flux & Mfg. Co., Cleve., 1979-89, Solid Sound Inc., Chgo., 1982-92. Trustee Bur. Jewish Edn., Cleve., 1980-90, Jewish Cmty. Fed., Cleve., 1986-91, 2000—; pres., trustee The Agnon Sch., Cleve., 1984—; trustee, v.p. Park Synagogue, 1984-94; assoc. v.p. United Way, Cleve., 1986-89; active Leadership Cleve., 1985; trustee, pres. Jewish Cmty. Ctr., Cleve., 1995—; lawyers com. Cleve. Opera, 1996-2000. Mem. ABA, Ohio State Bar Assn., Greater Cleve. Bar Assn. Avocations: golf, tennis, softball. Banking, General corporate, Real property. Office: Ohio Savs Fin Corp 1801 E 9th St Cleveland OH 44114-3103

FREMONT-SMITH, MARION R. lawyer; b. Boston, Oct. 29, 1926; d. Max and Frances (Davis) Ritvo; m. Joseph Miller, Sept. 12, 1948 (div.); children: Beth Miller Johnsey, Keith Lane Miller, E. Bradley Miller; m. Paul Fremont-Smith, July 6, 1961 (dec. July 2000). BA with high honors, Wellesley (Mass.) Coll., 1948; LLB cum laude, Boston U., 1951. Bar: Mass. 1951, U.S. Supreme Ct. 1979. Instr. dept. polit. sci. Wellesley Coll., 1958=59; asst. atty. gen. Commonwealth Mass., Boston, 1961-62; project dir. Russell Sage Found., 1963-65; assoc. Choate, Hall & Stewart, 1964-71, ptnr., 1971-96, sr. counsel, 1997—. Sr. rsch. fellow Hauses Ctr. for Nonprofit Orgns., Harvard U., 1998—; dir. Fed. Tax Inst. New Eng., Mount Auburn Cemetery, Aid to Artisans. Author: Foundations and Government: State and Federal Law and Supervision, 1965, Philanthropy and the Business Corporation, 1972; contbr. articles to profl. jours. Past dir. Ind. Sector, Washington; hon. trustee Carnegie Endowment for Internat. Peace, Washington; trustee Mass. Environ. Trust. Fellow Am. Acad. Arts and Scis., Am. Bar Found., Am. Coll. Tax Counsel, Internat. Acad. Estate and Trust Law; mem. ABA (past chmn. com. on exempt orgns. tax sect.), Am. Law Inst. Estate planning, Probate, Personal income taxation. Office: Exchange Pl 53 State St Boston MA 02109-2804

FRENCH, BRUCE COMLY, lawyer, educator; b. Phila., June 22, 1947; s. Paul Comly French and Dorothy (Felten) Boothertone; m. Diane Wortman, July 19, 1987. B.A., Am. U., 1969, M.A., 1970; J.D., Antioch Sch. Law, 1975. Bar: Pa. 1975, D.C. 1976, Ohio 1985, U.S. Tax Ct. 1984, U.S. Dist. Ct. D.C. 1976, (ea. dist.) Pa. 1976, (no. dist.) Ohio 1979, U.S. Supreme Ct. 1979, U.S. Ct. Appeals (D.C. cir.) 1976, (fed. cir. 1984), (6th cir. 1985), Internat. Trade (9th cir.) 1997. Campus coordinator CARE, Washington, 1966-69; community relations dir. Met. Washington Planning and Housing Assn., 1969-70; research assoc., pres. adv. council on exec. orgns., White House, 1970; project dir. Inst. for Study Health and Soc., Washington, 1970-72; staff dir., counsel D.C. Council, 1975-78, legis. counsel, 1979-83; asst. prof. law Ohio No. U., Ada, 1978-79, assoc. prof. law, 1983-87, prof. law 1987—; trustee U.S. Bankruptcy Ct., Toledo; assoc. mem. Nat. Conf. Commrs. on Uniform State Laws. Washington, 1981-84; mem. D.C. Law Revision Com., Washington, 1980-85; hearing examiner D.C. Com. on Human Rights, 1980-83; acting genl. counsel, D.C. Taxicab Commn., 1987; neutral, Ohio State Employees Relations Bd., 1985-88. Contbr. articles to profl. jours. Treas. Neighbors, Inc., Washington, 1982-83; treas., counsel Allen County Citizens for the Environ., Lima. Democrat. Mem. Society of Friends. Office: Ohio Northern Coll Law Ada OH 45810

FRENCH, DANIEL J. prosecutor; JD, Syracuse U. Law clk. to Judge Rosemary Pooler U.S. 2d Cir.; aide to U.S. Senator Daniel Patrick Moynihan; atty. U.S. Dept. Justice (no. dist.) N.Y., 1999—. Democrat. Office: 100 S Clinton St Rm 900 Syracuse NY 13261-6100

FRENCH, JOHN, III, lawyer, director; b. Boston, July 12, 1932; s. John and Rhoda (Walker) F.; m. Leslie Ten Eyck, Jan. 11, 1957 (div. 1961); children: John B., Lawrence C.; m. Anne Hubbell, Jan. 9, 1965 (div. 1983); children: Daniel J., Susanna H.; m. Marina Kellen, Nov. 21, 1987. BA, Dartmouth Coll., 1955; JD, Harvard U., 1958. Bar: N.Y. 1959, D.C. 1988. Assoc. Milbank, Tweed, Hadley & McCloy, N.Y.C., 1961-68, Satterlee & Stephens, N.Y.C., 1968-73; asst. gen. counsel Continental Group, Inc., Stamford, Conn., 1973-81; v.p., gen. counsel, sec. Peabody Internat. Corp., 1981-82; ptnr. Appleton, Rice & Perrin, N.Y.C., 1982-84, Beveridge and Diamond, N.Y.C., 1985-93, counsel, 1993-99; chmn. Tudor Assocs., LLC, 1999—. Lectr. Practising Law Inst., 1979-83, Am. Law Inst., 1978; bd. dirs. Resorts Mgmt., Inc., Tudor Assocs., LLC, N.Y.C. Contbr. articles to profl. jours. Trustee Hudson River Found., YMCA-YWCA Camping Svcs. of Greater N.Y., Inc.; bd. dirs. Third St. Music Sch. Settlement House, Inc., N.Y.C., Internat. House, Inc., N.Y.C., Young Concert Artists, Inc., 33 E. 70th St. Corp., Teatro alla Scala Found.; mem. Westchester County Planning Bd., 1974-85; mem. N.Y. State Environ. Bd., 1976-88. Capt. JAGC, USAF, 1958-61. Mem. ABA, N.Y. State Bar Assn. (lectr.), Assn. of Bar of City of N.Y. (lectr.), Environ. Law Inst., Am. Soc. Corp. Secs., Met. Opera, Soc. Mayflower Descs., River Club, Harvard Club, Knickerbocker Club, The Pilgrims, Century Assn. Republican. General corporate, Environmental. Office: Tudor Assocs LLC 33 E 70th St New York NY 10021-4941 E-mail: tudor33@aol.com, tudorassoc@aol.com

FRENCH, JOHN DWYER, lawyer; b. Berkeley, Calif., June 26, 1933; s. Horton Irving and Gertrude Margery (Ritzen) F.; m. Annette Richard, 1955; m. Berna Jo Mahling, 1986. BA summa cum laude, U. Minn., 1955; postgrad, Oxford U., Eng., 1955-56; LLB magna cum laude, Harvard U., 1960. Bar: D.C. 1960, Minn. 1963. Law clk. Justice Felix Frankfurter, U.S. Supreme Ct., 1960-61; legal asst. to commr. FTC, 1961-62; assoc. Ropes & Gray, Boston, 1962-63, Faegre & Benson, Mpls., 1963-66, ptnr., 1967-75, mng. ptnr., 1975-94, chmn. mgmt. com., 1989-94. Mem. adj. faculty Law Sch. U. Minn., 1965-70, mem. search com. for dean of Coll. of Liberal Arts, 1996; mem. exec. com. Lawyers Com. for Civil Rights Under Law, 1978—; co-chmn. U.S. Dist. Judge Nominating Commn., 1979; vice chmn. adv. com., mem. dir. search com., chmn. devel. office search com. Hubert Humphrey Inst., 1979-87. Contbr. numerous articles and revs. to legal jours. Chmn. or co-chmn. Minn. State Dem. Farm Labor Party Conv., 1970-90, 94, chmn. Mondale Vol. Com., 1972, treas., 1974; assoc. chmn. Minn. Dem.-Farmer-Labor Party, 1985-86; mem. Dem. Nat. Com., 1985-86; mem. Dem. Nat. Conv., 1976, 78, 80, 84, 88; trustee Twin Cities Public TV, Inc., 1980-86, mem. overseers com. to visit Harvard U. Law Sch., 1970-75, 77-82; chmn. Minn. steering com. Dukakis for Pres., 1987-88; mem. Sec. of State's Commn. on Electoral Reform, Minn., 1994; mem. Mayor's Commn. on Regulatory Reform, Mpls., 1995. With U.S. Army, 1955-56. Rotary Found. fellow, 1955-56 Mem. ABA (editorial bd. jour. 1976-79, commn. to study fed. trade 1969—), Minn. Bar Assn., Hennepin County Bar Assn., Jud. Coun. Minn., Lawyers Alliance for Nuclear Arms Control (nat. bd. dirs. 1982-84), U. Minn. Alumni Assn. (exec. com. 1985-87, v.p. 1989-91, pres. 1991-92, Vol. of Yr. award 1988), Phi Beta Kappa. Episcopalian. Administrative and regulatory, Antitrust, Federal civil litigation. Office: Faegre & Benson 2200 Wells Fargo Ctr 90 S 7th St Ste 2200 Minneapolis MN 55402-3901

FRENKEL, HERBERT MILTON, lawyer, judge; b. N.Y.C., July 28, 1924; s. Herman and Renee (Roth) F.; m. Beverly Vivian Rosenberg, Apr. 2, 1967; 1 child, Charles Robert. LLB, N.Y. Law Sch., 1952; LLD (hon.), Philathea Coll., London, Ont., Can., 1969. Bar: N.Y. 1972, U.S. Dist. Ct. (so. and ea. dists.) N.Y. 1974. Investigator, tech. analyst writer EEOC, Newark 1972-74, dist. counsel, 1974-80, sr. trial atty., N.Y.C., 1979-81, adminstrv. judge, 1981-88, adminstrv. law judge, 1988—; ptnr. Telecommunications Rsch. Assocs., Scarsdale, N.Y. Contbr. in field. Served with M.C., U.S. Army, 1943-45, ETO. Lodge: Masons. Home: 205 E 78th St Apt 6H New York NY 10021-1232 Office: Social Security Adminstrv Office Hearings & Appeals 26 Federal Plz Ste 2909 New York NY 10278-0004

FRESCH, MARIE BETH, court reporting company executive; b. Norwalk, Ohio, Jan. 16, 1957; d. Ralph Roy and Vonda Mae (Brunkhorst) Spiegel; m. James R. Fresch, Aug. 5, 1978; 1 child, Alexandra Jane. AS in Bus., Tiffin U., 1977; cert. in ct. reporting, Acad. Ct. Reporting, 1979. Registered profl. reporter, Ohio. Ofcl. reporter Seneca County Common Pleas Ct., Tiffin, Ohio, 1979-80; owner, operator Marie B. Fresch & Assocs., Norwalk, 1980—. Coach indoor & outdoor Soccer teams, 1994-99, summer softball teams, 1994—; leader Girl Scouts Am., 1998—, sch. organizer, team leader, 1997-99, parade organizer, 1998—. Recipient Cert. of Merit, Nat. Ct. Reporters Assn., 1990; named Outstanding Leader, Girl Scout Coun., 1998, Outstanding Vol., 2000. Mem. Nat. Ct. Reporters Assn., Ohio Ct. Reporters Assn. (student promotions and pub. rels. coms. 1986-90, dist. rep. 1994-95, fundraising com. 1993-96), NOW (sec. Port Clinton chpt. 1984-86, treas. 1986-87, 91), Am. Legion Aux., Kappa Delta Kappa. Democrat. Methodist. Lodge: Order of Eastern Star (esther 1979-81). Avocations: target shooting, swimming, biking, gardening, hiking. Home and Office: 47 Warren Dr Norwalk OH 44857-2447 E-mail: MBF1@AccNORWALK.com

FREUD, NICHOLAS S. lawyer; b. N.Y.C., Feb. 6, 1942; s. Frederick and Fredericka (von Rothenburg) F.; m. Elsa Doskow, July 23, 1966; 1 child, Christopher. AB, Yale U., 1963, JD, 1966. Bar: N.Y. 1968, Calif. 1970, U.S. Tax Ct. 1973. Ptnr. Chickering & Gregory, San Francisco, 1978-85, Russin & Vecchi, San Francisco, 1986-93, Jeffer, Mangels, Butler & Marmaro, LLP, San Francisco, 1993—. Mem. joint adv. bd. Calif. Continuing Edn. of Bar, chair taxation subcom. 1987-87; mem. fgn. income adv. bd. Tax Management Internat. Jour., mem. bd. advs. The Jour. of Internat. Taxation; mem. adv. bd. NYU Inst. on Fed. Taxation; academician Internat. Acad. Estate and Tax Law. Author: (with Charles G. Stephenson and K. Bruce Friedman) International Estate Planning, rev. edit., 1997; contbr. articles to profl. jours. Fellow Am. Coll. of Tax Counsel (cert. specialist in taxation law) mem. ABA (tax sect. vice chair adminstrn.

2000—, vice-chair coun. dir. 1995-97, chair com. on U.S. activities of foreigners and tax treaties 1989-91, vice chair 1987-89, chair subcom. on tax treaties 1981-87), Calif. State Bar Assn. (taxation sect. exec. com. 1981-85, vice chair 1982-83, chair 1983-84, vice chair income tax com. 1981-82, chair 1982-83, vice chair personal income tax subcom. 1979-80, chair 1980-81, co-chair fgn. tax subcom. 1978-79), N.Y. State Bar Assn. (taxation sect., mem. com. on U.S. activities of fgn. taxpayers and fgn. activities of U.S. taxpayers), Bar Assn. of San Francisco, Bar Assn. of City of N.Y., San Francisco Tax Club (pres. 1988), San Francisco Internat. Tax Group. Private international, Taxation, general. Office: Jeffer Mangels Butler & Marmaro LLP 1 Sansome St Fl 12 San Francisco CA 94104-4430 E-mail: nsf@jmbm.com

FREUND, FRED A. retired lawyer; b. N.Y.C., June 18, 1928; s. Sidney J. and Cora (Strasser) F.; m. Rosalie Sampo, Nov. 18, 1975 (div. Apr. 1983); m. Patricia A. Gardner, Mar. 13, 1957 (div. Jan. 1967); children: Gregory G., K. Bailey A.B., Columbia U., 1948, J.D., 1949. Bar: N.Y. 1949, U.S. Supreme Ct. 1968. Law clk. to chief judge U.S. Dist. Ct. So. Dist. N.Y., N.Y.C., 1949-51; assoc. Kaye, Scholer, Fierman, Hays & Handler, 1953-58, ptnr., 1959-93, ret., 1993. Served to 1st lt. USAF, 1951-53. Mem. ABA, Assn. Bar City N.Y., Phi Beta Kappa Home: 1085 Park Ave Apt 4C New York NY 10128-1179

FREUND, SAMUEL J. lawyer; b. Forenwald, Germany, Jan. 3, 1949; came to U.S., 1949; s. Abraham and Syma (Skop) F.; m. Barbara Susan Sasmor, July 1, 1979; children: Alexandra, Stefanie. BSc in Acctg., Bklyn. Coll., 1971; JD, Bklyn. Law Sch., 1974; LLM in Taxation, NYU, 1980. Bar: N.Y. 1975, U.S. Dist. Ct. (so. and ea. dists.) N.Y. 1978, U.S. Tax Ct. 1981, Fla. 1981, N.J. 1988. Tax acct. Oppenheim, Appel and Dixon, N.Y.C., 1974-75, assoc., 1975; atty./advisor Bur. Hearing and Appeals, Dept. HEW, Johnstown, Pa., 1976-77; atty. Tax Dept. N.Y. State, N.Y.C., 1977-82; assoc. tax counsel CBS Inc., 1982-84; sr. tax assoc. Am. Brands, Inc., Friedman & Shaftan, P.C., 1986-89, Hugh Janow & Irwin Meyer, Pearl River, NY, 1990-96; pvt. practice Montclair, NJ, 1989-90, 96-97; v.p. taxation The Halpern Group, Springfield, 1998-99; of counsel Keenan Powers & Andrews, Hauppauge, NY, 2000—; adminstrv. law judge N.Y.C. Dept. Fin., 2001—. Mem. ABA, Fla. Bar Assn., N.J. State Bar Assn. Avocations: computers, photography, music. Taxation, general, Personal income taxation, State and local taxation. E-mail: sfreund@lycosmail.com

FREY, A. JOHN, JR. lawyer; b. Little Falls, Minn., Dec. 2, 1944; s. Arnold John and Mae A. (Monk) F.; m. Cheryl Ann McCoy, June 11, 1966; children— Deborah Lynn, Robert Christopher, Laura Kathleen. B.A. in Polit. Sci., U. Iowa, 1967, J.D. with distinction, 1969. Bar: Iowa 1969, U.S. Dist. Ct. (no. and so. dists.) Iowa 1973. Spl. agt. FBI, Washington, 1969-73; assoc. Jurgemeyer & Eddy, Clinton, Iowa, 1973-74; ptnr. Jurgemeyer & Frey, Clinton, 1974-75, Jurgemeyer, Frey & Haufe, Clinton, 1975— ; speaker Bridge-the-Gap Seminar, Des Moines, 1977; mem. faculty Clinton Community Coll., 1979-80. Bd. dirs. Eagle Point Nature Soc., Clinton, 1974-75, Clinton County Legal Aid, Inc., 1978-80, Clinton Y's Mens Club, 1978, Arch, Inc., Clinton, 1984, past pres. Clinton YMCA, 1984, Gateway United Way, Clinton, 1981-84; pres. Seton Sch. Bd. Edn., Clinton, 1982-84; councilman City of Clinton, 1984—. Recipient letters of commendation FBI, 1970-73. Mem. Clinton County Bar Assn. (pres. 1977-78), Iowa State Bar Assn., Assn. Trial Lawyers Am., Clinton C. of C. (past pres.) Republican. Roman Catholic. Lodge: K.C. (adv. 1979—). General practice, Personal injury, Real property. Home: 3221 Mckinley St Clinton IA 52732-1436 Office: Jurgemeyer Frey & Haufe 601 S 3rd St Clinton IA 52732-4313

FREY, ANDREW LEWIS, lawyer; b. N.Y.C., Aug. 11, 1938; s. Daniel B. and Ruth J. Frey; children: Matthew S., Alexandra S. BA with high honors, Swarthmore Coll., 1959; LLB, Columbia U., 1962. Bar: N.Y. 1962, D.C. 1966, U.S. Supreme Ct. 1972. Law clk. to judge U.S. Ct. Appeals (D.C. cir.), 1963-64; spl. counsel to Gov. U.S. V.I., 1963-65; assoc. Koteen & Burt, Washington, 1965-70; ptnr. Dutton, Gwirtzman, Zumas, Wise & Frey, 1970-72; dep. solicitor gen. Office U.S. Solicitor Gen., 1972-86; ptnr. Mayer Brown & Platt, Washington, N.Y.C., 1986—. Notes editor Columbia Law Rev., 1961-62. Recipient John Marshall award Dept. Justice, 1975, Disting. Svc. award Atty. Gen., 1980, Presdl. award for Meritorious Svc., 1985. Mem. Am. Law Inst., Am. Acad. Appellate Lawyers, D.C. Bar Assn., Phi Beta Kappa. Office: Mayer Brown & Platt 1675 Broadway Fl 19 New York NY 10019-5820 E-mail: afrey@mayerbrown.com

FREY, LOUIS, JR. lawyer, federal and state government official; b. Jan. 11, 1934; m. Marcia Turner, 1956; children: Julie, Lynn, Louis III, Lauren, Christine. BA cum laude, Colgate U., 1955; JD, U. Mich., 1961. Bar: Fla. 1961, U.S. Supreme Ct. 1969. Asst. county solictor Orange County, Fla., 1961-63; gen. counsel Fla. State Turnpike Authority, 1966-67; congressman U.S. Ho. of Reps., 1969-79, Rep. leader, 1973-76, mem. interstate and fgn. commerce com., sci. and tech. com., select com. on narcotics, sub-com. on communications, sub-com. on energy research; ptnr. Lowndes, Drosdick, Doster, Kantor & Reed, P.A., Orlando, Fla., 1987—; commr. Dept. of Lottery State of Fla., 1987-88. Chmn. Fla. Fedn. of Young Reps., 1965-66; treas. Rep. Party Fla., mem. state exec. com., 1966; past chmn., mem. exec. com. Fla. Coun. on Econ. Edn., 1991—; chmn. Former Mems. Congress, 1992-94, bd. dirs., 1992—. Served with USN, 1955-58, capt. Res. ret. Recipient Watchdog of Yr. Treasury award, 1970, 72, 74, 76, 78, Guardian of Small Bus. award, Disting. Service award Ams. for Constitutional Action, Man of Yr. award Fla. Assn. Broadcasters, 1977, Masada award; elected to Sr. Citizen's Hall of Fame. Mem. Order of the Coif, Phi Gamma Delta, Phi Delta Phi. Lutheran. Communications, General corporate, Municipal (including bonds). Home: 139 Genius Dr Winter Park FL 32789-5103 Office: Lowndes Drosdick Doster Kantor & Reed PA 215 N Eola Dr # 2809 Orlando FL 32801-2095 E-mail: Lou.Frey@Lowndes-law.com

FREY, MARTIN ALAN, lawyer, educator; b. Rochester, N.Y., Feb. 26, 1939; s. Morrey and Betty (Weinstein) F.; m. Phyllis Sue Hurley, Apr. 19, 1966; 1 child, David Andrew. BS in Mech. Engring., Northwestern U., 1962; JD, Washington U., St. Louis, 1965; LLM, George Washington U., 1966. Bar: Mo. 1965, Okla. 1976, U.S. Dist. Ct. (no. dist.) Okla. 1983. Asst. prof. law Drake U., Des Moines, 1966-67; prof. law Tex. Tech. U., Lubbock, 1967-76, U. Tulsa, 1976—, assoc. dean, 1981-84. Vis. prof. law U. Maine, Portland, 1974-75, Washington U., St. Louis, 1986-87; adj. settlement judge U.S. Dist Ct. and U.S. Bankruptcy Ct. (no. dist.) Okla., 1988—; reporter adv. group Civil Justice Reform Act, U.S. Dist. Ct. (no. dist) Okla. 1991-97; dir. Ctr. Dispute Resolution U. Tulsa Coll. Law, 1994—. Author: (with T. Bitting) An Introduction to Contracts and Restitution, 1988, (with T. Bitting and P.H. Frey) 2d edit., 1993, study guide, 1994, (with McConnico and Frey) An Introduction to Bankruptcy Law, 1990, 2d edit., 1992, 3d edit., 1997, (with Bitting and Frey) An Introduction to the Law of Contracts, 3d edit., 1999, (with Frey) Essentials of Contract Law, 2000; contbg. author (with McConnico and Frey) West's Bankruptcy Practice Systems, 1991, 95, 97; founder, advisor, Tex. Tech. Law Rev., 1967-71; contbr. articles to legal jours. Mem. ABA (accreditation site evaluation teams 1978—), Tulsa County Bar Assn., Am. Inns of Ct. (master W. Lee Johnson chpt.). Democrat. Jewish. Office: U Tulsa Coll Law 3120 E 4th Pl Tulsa OK 74104-2418

FREYER, DANA HARTMAN, lawyer; b. Pitts., Apr. 17, 1944; m. Bruce M. Freyer, Dec. 21, 1969. Student, L' Institut De Hautes Etudes Internationales, Geneva, 1963-64; BA, Conn. Coll., 1965; postgrad., Columbia U., 1968, JD, 1971. Bar: N.Y. 1972, Ill. 1974, U.S. Dist. Ct. (no. dist.) Ill. 1974, U.S. Ct. Appeals (7th cir.) 1976, U.S. Supreme Ct. 1977, U.S. Dist. Ct. (so. dist.) N.Y. 1978, U.S. Dist. Ct. (ea. dist.) N.Y. 1981, U.S. Ct. Appeals (2d cir.) 1982. Staff atty. Legal Aid Soc. Westchester County, Mt. Vernon, N.Y., 1971-72; assoc. Friedman & Koven, Chgo., 1973-77, Skadden, Arps, Slate, Meagher & Flom, LLP, N.Y.C., 1977-88; spl. counsel Skadden, Arps, Slate, Meagher & Flom, 1988-93, ptnr., 1994—. Pres. Westchester Legal Services, Inc., White Plains, N.Y., 1985-87, bd. dirs., 1978-98; mem. governing coun. Comml. Arbitration and Mediation Ctr. for Ams., rules rev. task force; U.S. Coun. for Internat. Bus. Arbitration Com.; London Ct. of Internat. Arbitration; adv. bd. World Arbitration and Mediation Report. Mem. editl. bd. ADR Currents. Mem. ABA, Bar Assn. of City of N.Y., Internat. Bar Assn. Alternative dispute resolution, General civil litigation, Private international. Office: Skadden Arps Slate Meagher & Flom LLP 4 Times Sq Fl 48 New York NY 10036-6522

FREYTAG, SHARON NELSON, lawyer; b. May 11, 1943; d. John Seldon and Ruth Marie (Herbel) Nelson; children: Kurt David, Hillary Lee. BS with highest distinction, U. Kans., Lawrence, 1965; MA, U. Mich., 1966; JD cum laude, So. Meth. U., 1981. Bar: Tex. 1981, U.S. Dist. Ct. (no. dist.) Tex. 1981, U.S. Ct. Appeals (5th cir.) 1982, U.S. Ct. Appeals (8th cir.) 2001, U.S. Supreme Ct. 1993. Tchr. English Gaithersburg (Md.) H.S., 1966-70; instr. English Eastfield Coll., 1974-78; law clk. U.S. Dist. Ct. (no. dist.) Tex., 1981-82, U.S. Ct. Appeals (5th cir.), 1982; ptnr. Haynes and Boone, Dallas, 1989—. Vis. prof. law Southern Meth. U., 1985-86; faculty Appellate Adv. program NITA. Editor-in-chief Southwestern Law Jour., 1980-81; contbr. articles to law jours. Woodrow Wilson fellow; recipient John Marshall Constl. Law award, Baird Cmty. Spirit award, 1995. Mem. ABA (litigation sect., former chair subcom. on local rules), Fed. Bar Assn. (co-chmn. appellate practice and adv. sect. 1990-91), Tex Bar Assn. (appellate coun. 1995-98, former barrister), State Bar Tex. (bd. dirs., exec. com. 1997-2001), Dallas Bar Assn. (appellate coun.), Barristers, Order of Coif, Phi Beta Kappa. Lutheran. Appellate, Federal civil litigation, State civil litigation. Office: Haynes & Boone 3100 Bank of America Plz Dallas TX 75202 E-mail: freytags@haynesboone.com

FRICK, BENJAMIN CHARLES, lawyer; b. Overbrook, Pa., Feb. 23, 1960; s. Sidney Wanning and Marie Pauline Frick; m. Stephanie Ann Sears, June 1, 1991; children: Sarah Marie, Anna Elizabeth, Charles Andrew. BA, Cornell U., 1982; JD, U. Richmond, 1985; LLM in Taxation, Villanova U., 1994. Bar: Pa. 1985. Clerk to Hon. John B. Hannum U.S. dist. court, 1984; trust officer Provident Nat. Bank, Phila., 1985-89; sole practice Bryn Mawr, Pa., 1989—. Deacon, elder, Ardmore (Pa.) Presbyn. Ch. Mem. ABA, S.R. (bd. dirs. Pa. Soc. 1987—, sec. 1991-95, treas. 1995-97, v.p. 1997—), Pa. Bar Assn., Phila. Bar Assn., Soc. Mayflower Descs., Colonial Soc. Pa. (treas. 2000—), Soc. Colonial Wars (bd. dirs. Pa. chpt. 1999—), St. Andrew's Soc. Phila., Mil. Order Loyal Legion U.S. (sec. 1993-95, v.p. 1995-97, comdr. 1997-99, judge adv.-in-chief 1997—), The Union League of Phila., Athenaeum of Phila., The Phila. Club, Phi Alpha Delta (pres. local chpt. 1984-85), Alpha Delta Phi. Republican. Presbyterian. Estate planning, Probate, Estate taxation. Office: Bldg 1 Ste 303 919 Conestoga Rd Bryn Mawr PA 19010-1352

FRICKE, RICHARD JOHN, lawyer; b. Ithaca, N.Y., Apr. 17, 1945; s. Richard I. and Jeanne L. (Hines) F.; m. Carol A. Borelli, June 17, 1967 (div. 1990); children: Laura, Richard, Amanda; m. Penny Yrizarry, Dec. 29, 1990 (div. 1999); children: Stephanie, Matthew, Tyler. BA, Cornell U., 1967, JD, 1970. Bar: Conn. 1970. Assoc. Gregory & Adams, Wilton, Conn., 1970-73; ptnr. Crehan & Fricke, Ridgefield, 1973-90; gen. counsel Connex Internat. Inc.; corp. counsel, pres. Safe Alternatives Corp. of Am., Inc.; pres., gen. counsel, dir. T.F.I. Industries, Inc.; gen. counsel, dir. Gold Mustache Pub. Corp., Inc.; sec., dir. DXTC.COM, Inc.; dir. Village Bank & Trust Co.; town atty. Town of Ridgefield, 1973-81. Bd. dirs. Gold Mustache Pub. Corp., Inc.; mem. Closing Mgmt. Svcs. LLC. Co-patentee low reactive pressure foam, polyurethane foam for cellulostic products. Bd. dirs. Ridgefield Community Ctr., Ridgefield Montessori, Ridgefield Community Kindergarten; founder, pres. Ridgefield Lacross League; constable Town of Wilton, Conn.; mem. Conn. Bar Commn. on Women, 1976. Mem. ABA, Conn. Bar Assn., Danbury Bar Assn. Democrat. Roman Catholic. Family and matrimonial, General practice, Real property. Address: 440 Main St Ridgefield CT 06877-4525 E-mail: rickfricke@aol.com

FRIEBERT, ROBERT HOWARD, lawyer; b. Milw., Aug. 24, 1938; s. Lewis and Erna F.; m. Susan Frances Sweed, Aug. 11, 1968; children: Jonathan, Ellen, Leslie. BBA, LLB, U. Wis., 1962. Bar: Wis. 1962, U.S. Dist. Ct. (we. dist.) Wis. 1962, U.S. Ct. Appeals (7th cir.) 1964, U.S. Supreme Ct. 1967, U.S. Dist. Ct. (ea. dist.) Wis. 1968, U.S. Ct. Appeals (9th cir.) 1977, U.S. Ct. Appeals (D.C. cir.) 1998. Asst. U.S. atty. U.S. Justice Dept., Madison, Wis., 1962-64; assoc. LaFollette, Sinykin, Doyle & Abrahamson, 1964-66; state pub. defender Wis. Supreme Ct., 1966-68; assoc. Shellow, Shellow & Coffey, Milw., 1968-71; ptnr. Friebert, Finerty & St. John, 1971—. Treas. campaign fund Wis. Gov. Pat Lucey, 1971; co-chmn. Pres. Carter Re-election Campaign, Wis., 1980, Gary Hart Campaign for Pres., Wis., 1984; chmn. Al Gore Campaign for Pres., Wis., 1988; trustee Med. Coll. Wis., 1993—. Recipient Human Rels. award, Am. Jewish Com., Milw., 1996. Fellow Am Acad. Appellate Lawyers; mem. Wis. Bar Assn. Administrative and regulatory, General civil litigation, General practice. Office: Friebert Finerty & St John 330 E Kilbourn Ave Ste 1250 Milwaukee WI 53202-3158 E-mail: rhf@ffsj.com

FRIED, ARTHUR, lawyer; m. Kym Vanderbilt. JD magna cum laude, Cornell U., 1975. Bar: N.Y. Law clk. to Hon. John M. Cannella U.S. Dist. Ct. (so. dist.) N.Y., 1975-77; with The Legal Aid Soc. N.Y.C., 1977-90; acting gen. counsel, dep. gen. counsel N.Y.C. Human Resources Adminstrn.; gen. counsel N.Y.C. Dept. Housing Preservation and Devel., to 1995, Social Security Adminstrn., Balt., 1995—2000; exec. dir. NYU Ctr. Excellence in N.Y.C. Governance. Mem. Order of Coif. Office: NYU 269 Mercer St Rm 203 New York NY 10003 Business E-Mail: arthur.fried@nyu.edu.

FRIED, CHARLES, law educator; b. Prague, Czechoslovakia, Apr. 15, 1935; came to U.S., 1941, naturalized, 1948; s. Anthony and Marta (Winterstein) F.; m. Anne Sumerscale, June 13, 1959; children: Gregory, Antonia. AB, Princeton U., 1956; BA, Oxford (Eng.) U., 1958, MA, 1961; LLB, Columbia U., 1960; LLD (hon.), New Eng. Sch. of Law, 1987, Pepperdine U., 1994, Suffolk U., 1996. Bar: D.C. 1961, Mass. 1966. Law clk. to Hon. John M. Harlan U.S. Supreme Ct., 1960; from asst. prof. to prof. law Harvard U., Cambridge, 1961-85, Carter prof. gen. jurisprudence, 1981-85, 89-95, Carter prof. emeritus, disting. lectr. Law Sch., 1995-99, Beneficial prof. law, 1999—; retired assoc. justice Supreme Jud. Ct. Mass., Boston, 1995-99. Spl. cons. Treasury Dept., 1961-62; cons. White House office Policy Devel., 1982, Dept. Transp., 1081-82, Dept. Justice, 1983; solicitor gen. U.S., 1985-89. Author: An Anatomy of Values, 1970, Medical Experimentation: Personal Integrity and Social Policy, 1974, Right and Wrong, 1978, Contract as Promise: A Theory of Contractual Obligation, 1981, Order and Law: Arguing the Reagan Revolution, 1991; contbr. legal and philos. jours. Guggenheim fellow, 1971-72 Fellow Am. Acad. Arts and Scis.; mem. Inst. Medicine, Am. Law Inst., Century Assn., Mass. Hist. Soc., Phi Beta Kappa. E-mail: fried@law.harvard.edu

FRIED, DONALD DAVID, lawyer; b. N.Y.C., Feb. 28, 1936; s. Fred and Sylvia (Falk) F.; m. Joan Hilbert, Sept. 15, 1963; children: Neil, Derek. BA, CCNY, 1956; JD, Harvard U., 1959. Bar: N.Y. 1959. Assoc. Conboy, Hewitt, O'Brien & Boardman, N.Y.C., 1960-68, ptnr., 1968-86, Hunton & Williams, N.Y.C., 1986-88, 92-96; sr. counsel, 1996—; v.p., sec., assoc. gen. counsel Philip Morris Cos., Inc., N.Y.C., 1988-91. General corporate, Mergers and acquisitions, Securities. Home: 37 W 12th St New York NY 10011-8502 Office: Hunton & Williams 200 Park Ave Rm 4400 New York NY 10166-0091 E-mail: dfried@hunton.com

FRIED, L. RICHARD, JR. lawyer; b. N.Y.C., Apr. 3, 1941; s. L. Richard and Jane (Kent) Wick F.; 1 child, Paula Suzanne. BS, U. Ariz., 1963, JD, 1966. Bar: Ariz. 1966, Hawaii 1968, U.S. Dist. Ct. No. Mariana Islands 1978, U.S. Ct. Claims 1978, U.S. Ct. Internat. Trade 1977, U.S. Tax Ct. 1977, U.S. Ct. Appeals (9th cir.) 1969, U.S. Supreme Ct. 1977. Assoc. Case, Kay & Lynch, Honolulu, 1967-72; ptnr., pres. Cronin, Fried, Sekiya, Kekina & Fairbanks, 1974—. Lawyer rep. 9th Cir. Jud. Conf., Hawaii, 1991-93, 2001. Mem. ABA, Assn. Trial Lawyers Am. (nat. committeeman 1980-82), Am. Bd. Trial Advocates (v.p. 1986-94), Hawaii Trial Lawyers Assn. (pres. 1981-82, 84—, Hawaii Trial Lawyer of Yr. 1994), Hawaii State Bar Assn. (bd. dirs. 1995-97), Ariz. State Bar Assn., Hawaii Acad. Plaintiffs Attys. (bd. dirs. 1994-96), Consumer Lawyers Hawaii (pres.-elect 2001), Exch. of Honolulu Club. Episcopalian. Aviation, Personal injury, Product liability. Office: Cronin Fried Sekiya Kekina & Fairbanks 841 Bishop St Ste 1900 Honolulu HI 96813-3962 E-mail: rfried@croninfried.com

FRIED, WILLIAM C. lawyer; b. Saginaw, Mich., Apr. 7, 1938; m. Barbara J. Benham, June 20, 1965; children: Marcus W., Kristina L., Jason A., Rebecca E. BBA in Acctg., U. Mich., 1960, LLB, 1963, MBA in Fin., 1964. Bar: Mich. 1964, U.S. Dist. Ct. (ea. dist.) Mich. 1981, U.S. Ct. Appeals (6th cir.) 1982, U.S. Tax Ct. 1979, U.S. Claims Ct. 1987. With tax dept. Arthur Young & Co., Detroit, 1964-74; tax assoc., ptnr. R.J. Dickshott & Co., Livonia, Mich., 1974-79; assoc. Robert Heritier, Detroit, 1979-80; ptnr. Fried & Mies, P.C., Livonia, 1980-92. Sec. Livonia Spree-51 com., Livonia Cmty. Found., Livonia Heart Fund,; bd. dirs. Livonia Bldg. Authority; v.p. Livonia Symphony Orch. Mem.: ABA, Mich. Bar Assn., Detroit Bar Assn., AICPA, Mich. Soc. CPA's, Livonia Bar Assn., Livonia C. of C., Rotary (pres. elect 2001—). Corporate taxation, Estate taxation, Personal income taxation. Home: 16009 Riverside St Livonia MI 48154-2460 Office: Fried & Assocs 32900 5 Mile Rd Ste 204 Livonia MI 48154-3083

FRIEDEN, CLIFFORD E. lawyer; b. L.A., Mar. 8, 1949; s. Sidney S. and Norma (Stern) F.; m. Dinah S. Baumring, June 20, 1971; children: Jamie, Kari, Curtis. BA, UCLA, 1971; JD, U. Calif., Berkeley, 1974. Bar: Calif. 1974, U.S. Dist. Ct. (so. dist.) Calif. 1974, U.S. Dist. Ct. (cen. dist.) Calif. 1977. Ptnr. Rutan & Tucker, Costa Mesa, Calif., 1974—. Active Orange County chpt. ARC, 1995-2001. Mem. Orange County Bar Assn. (del. state conv. 1983-95, chair judiciary com. 1987-88, bd. dirs. 1989-91), Phi Beta Kappa. Avocations: basketball, jogging. State civil litigation, Consumer commercial, Real property. Office: Rutan & Tucker PO Box 1950 611 Anton Blvd Ste 1400 Costa Mesa CA 92626-1931

FRIEDEN, JONATHAN DAVID, lawyer; b. Albemarle County, Va., May 3, 1971; s. David Ralph and Katherine Louise (Pennington) F. BS in Sys. Engring., U. Va., 1994; JD, U. Richmond, 1997. Bar: Va. 1997, U.S. Dist. Ct. (ea. dist.) Va. 1998. Assoc. Odin, Feldman, and Pittleman, P.C., Fairfax, Va., 1997—. Adj. prof. bus. adminstrn. Marymount U., 1999—. Author: Medicaid Eligibility Planning for Aged Clients in Virginia, 1997. Midshipman U.S.N., 1989-90. Recipient Lewis F. Powell Medal for Excellence in Advocacy, Am. Coll. of Trial Lawyers, 1996. Avocation: martial arts. Home: 3800 Lyndhurst Dr Apt 103 Fairfax VA 22031-3728 Office: Odin Feldman and Pittleman PC 9302 Lee Hwy Ste 1100 Fairfax VA 22031-1215 Fax: 703-218-2160. E-mail: jdf@ofplaw.com

FRIEDERICHS, NORMAN PAUL, lawyer; b. Ft. Dodge, Iowa, Sept. 13, 1936; s. Norman Paul and Dorothy Mae (Vinsant) F.; m. Marjorie Darlene Farrand, Aug. 23, 1959; children: Laurie Lynne, Norman Paul, Stacie Lynne. AA, Ft. Dodge Community Coll., 1956; BA, Wartburg Coll., 1959, JD, U. Iowa, 1966. Bar: Iowa 1966, Mich. 1968, Minn. 1974, U.S. Ct. Appeals (2nd, 7th, 8th and fed. cirs.) 1978, Wis. 1993. Tchr. chemistry Janesville Sch. Dist., Iowa, 1960-63; mem. Woodhams, Blanchard & Flynn, Kalamazoo, 1966-68; atty. PPG Industries, Pitts., 1968-69, Gen. Mills, Inc., Mpls., 1969-76; mem. Merchant, Gould, Smith, Edell, Welter & Schmidt, Mpls., 1976-90, Kinney & Lange P.A., Mpls., 1990-93, pres., bd. dirs. Friederichs Law Firm PLC Mpls., 1993—; pres., bd. dirs. AdSatNet, Inc., JB2 Inc. Editor: (booklet) Report of Economic Survey, 1983. Mem. Minn. Rep. Cen. Com.; chmn. St. Louis Park Sch. Dist., Minn., 1973; mem. Suburban Hennepin Vocat.-Tech. Bd., 1980-84, chmn. 1982-84. Mem. ABA, Acad. Trial Lawyers, Eden Prairie C. of C. (bd. dirs. 1979-88, pres. 1989), Am. Trial Lawyers Assn. (advocate), Am. Patent Law Assn. (com. chmn. 1980-84), Minn. Patent Law Assn. (chmn. small bus. com.), Optimists (pres. 1971-72, lt. gov. 1976-77), Masons. Baptist. Federal civil litigation, Patent, Trademark and copyright. Home: 6421 Kurtz Ln Eden Prairie MN 55346-1609

FRIEDLANDER, JEROME PEYSER, II, lawyer; b. Washington, Feb. 7, 1944; s. Mark Peyser and Helen (Finkel) F.; m. Irene Bluethenthal, Apr. 23, 1972; children: Jennifer R., Tyler Weil. BS, Georgetown U., 1965; LLB, U. Va., 1968. Bar: Va. 1968, U.S. Dist. Ct. (ea. dist.) Va. 1968, U.S. Ct. Appeals (4th and D.C. cirs.) 1978, U.S. Supreme Ct. 1978. Ptnr. Friedlander & Friedlander, P.C., McLean, Va., 1971—. Substitute judge Arlington (Va.) Gen. Dist. Ct., 1985-2000, Fairfax, Va., 2000— Author: Virginia Landlord-Tenant Law, 1992, 2nd edit., 1998, The Limited Liability Company, 1994; co-author: Legal Aspects of Doing Business in North America, 1987; contbr. articles to profl. jours. With U.S. Army, 1969-71. Mem. ABA, FBA (past pres. No. Va. chpt.). Contracts commercial, General practice, Personal injury. Office: Friedlander & Friedlander PC 1364 Beverly Rd Ste 201 Mc Lean VA 22101-3645 E-mail: friedlander@friedlander.com

FRIEDLI, GEORG, lawyer; b. Solothurn, Switzerland, Jan. 1, 1952; s. Rudolf and Agatha F.; m. ruth Elisabeth Duebendorfer; children: Lukas, peter, Fabio. M Comparative Law, George Washington U., 1981. Bar: Switzerland. Lawyer Justice Dept., Bern, 1978-80; fgn. assoc. Arnold and Porter, Washington, 1980-81; with Swiss Bank Corp., bern, 1981-83; lawyer von Graffenried, Bratschi, Emch, Bern, 1983-88; sr. ptnr. Friedli & Schnidrig, 1988—. Expert on revision of the law in criminal matters, Internat. legal Coop.; sec. Agreement on the Swiss Bank's Code of Conduct. Contbr. articles to profl. jours. and publs. Mem. Bernese Bar Assn., Swiss Bar Assn. Banking, Contracts commercial, Estate planning. Home: Max Buristrasse 17 3400 Burgdorf Switzerland Office: Friedli & Schnidrig Bahnhofplatz 5 PO Box 6233 3001 Bern Switzerland

FRIEDMAN, BART, lawyer; b. N.Y.C., Dec. 5, 1944; s. Philip and Florence (Beckerman) F.; m. Wendy Alpern Stein, Jan. 11, 1986; children: Benjamin Alpern, Jacob Stein. AB, L.I. U., 1966; JD, Harvard U., 1969. Bar: N.Y. 1970, Mass. 1972. Rsch. fellow Harvard U. Bus. Sch., Cambridge, Mass., 1969-70; assoc. Cahill, Gordon & Reindel, N.Y.C., 1970-72, 77-80, ptnr., 1980—; spl. counsel SEC, Washington, 1974-75, asst. dir., 1975-77. Lectr. internat. tax program Harvard U. Sch. Law, 1971, 85. Vis. com. Harvard U. Grad. Sch. Edn., 1995-2001, com. on univ. resources, 1996—; trustee Julliard Sch., 1988—, vice-chmn., 1994-2001; trustee Brookings Inst., 1997—, chmn. N.Y. adv. com., 1997—, coun. fgn. rels., 1995—, jt. task force on resources for fgn. affairs; mem. ind. task force on non-lethal weapons; del. to NATO Hdqrs. and Field, 1998; adv. bd. Remarque Inst. NYU, 1997—, Internat. Inst. for Strategic Studies, 2000; mem. to assess enterprise effectiveness of CIA IN-Q tel venture Bus. Execs. for Nat. Security and Independent Panel. Mem. Assn. Bar City of N.Y., Coun. Fgn. Rels., Explorers Club, Down Town Assn. (N.Y.C.), The River Club, The Tuxedo Club, Century Assn., The Metro. Club (Washington). General corporate, Securities. Home: 1172 Park Ave Apt 5B New York NY 10128-1213 Office: Cahill Gordon & Reindel 80 Pine St Fl 17 New York NY 10005-1790

FRIEDMAN, BERNARD ALVIN, federal judge; b. Detroit, Sept. 23, 1943; s. David and Rae (Garber) F.; m. Rozanne Golston, Aug. 16, 1970; children: Matthew, Megan. Student, Detroit Inst. Tech., 1962-65; JD, Detroit Coll. Law, 1968. Bar: Mich. 1968, Fla. 1968, U.S. Dist. Ct. (ea. dist.) Mich. 1968, U.S. Ct. Mil. Appeals 1972. Asst. prosecutor Wayne County, Detroit, 1968-71; ptnr. Harrison & Friedman, Southfield, Mich., 1971-78, Lippitt, Harrison, Friedman & Whitefield, Southfield, 1978-82; judge Mich. Dist. Ct. 48th dist., Bloomfield Hills, 1982-88; U.S. dist. judge Ea. Dist. Mich., Detroit, 1988—. Lt. U.S. Army, 1967-74. Recipient Disting. Service award Oakland County Bar Assn., 1986. Avocation: running. Office: US Dist Ct US Courthouse Rm 238 231 W Lafayette Blvd Detroit MI 48226-2700

FRIEDMAN, DANIEL MORTIMER, federal judge; b. N.Y.C., Feb. 8, 1916; s. Henry Michael F. and Julia (Freedman) Friedman; m. Leah Lipson, Jan. 16, 1955 (dec. Dec. 1969), m. Elizabeth Ellis, Oct. 19, 1975. AB, Columbia U., 1937, LLB, 1940. Bar: N.Y. 1941. Practice law, N.Y.C., 1940-42; with SEC, Washington, 1942-51, Justice Dept., Washington, 1951-78, asst. to solicitor gen., 1959-62, 2d asst. to solicitor gen., 1962-68, 1st dep. solicitor gen., 1968-78; chief judge Ct. Claims and U.S. Ct. Appeals, 1978-89, sr. judge, 1989—. Served with AUS, 1942-46. Recipient Exceptional Service award Atty. Gen., 1969 Office: US Ct Appeals Federal Circuit 717 Madison Pl NW Washington DC 20439-0002

FRIEDMAN, ELAINE FLORENCE, lawyer; b. N.Y.C., Aug. 22, 1924; d. Henry J. and Charlotte Leah (Youdelman) F.; m. Louis Schwartz, Apr. 10, 1949; 1 child, James Evan. BA, Hunter Coll., 1944; JD, Columbia U., 1946. Bar: N.Y. 1947, U.S. Dist. Ct. (so. and ea. dists.) N.Y., U.S. Ct. Appeals (2d cir.), U.S. Supreme Ct. 1954. Assoc. Oseas, Pepper & Siegel, N.Y.C., 1947-48, Bernstein & Benton, N.Y.C., 1948-51, Copeland & Elkins, N.Y.C., 1951-53; sole practice, 1953—. Bd. dirs. Health Ins. Plan of Greater N.Y. Mem. Fedn. Internat. des Femmes Juristes (v.p. U.S. chpt. 1993-95), N.Y. State Bar Assn., Hunter Coll. Alumni Assn., Columbia Law Sch. Assn. Jewish. Avocation: poetry. Family and matrimonial, General practice, Probate. Home: 2 Agnes Cir Ardsley NY 10502-1709 Office: 60 E 42nd St New York NY 10165-0006

FRIEDMAN, EUGENE STUART, lawyer; b. N.Y.C., Apr. 5, 1941; s. Abe and Etta (Fischer) F.; m. Karin L. Mehlem, Feb. 3, 1968; children: Gabrielle, Douglas, Jason. AB, NYU, 1961; LLB, Columbia U., 1964. Bar: N.Y. 1965, U.S. Supreme Ct. 1979. Atty. NLRB, San Francisco, 1965-67; assoc., ptnr. Cohen, Weiss & Simon, N.Y.C., 1968-86; sr. ptnr. Friedman Wolf & Grisi, 1987—. Lectr. Ill. Inst. Continuing Legal Edn., Chgo., 1982-84, NYU Conf. Labor & Practicing Law Inst., N.Y.C., 1983-85; adv. bd. for labor and employment law ctr. NYU Law Sch. Contbr. articles to profl. jours. Active N.Y. State Task Force Plant Closings, N.Y.C., 1984. With USN, 1964-65. Mem. N.Y. State Bar Assn., Assn. of Bar of City of N.Y. (chmn. labor & employment law com. 1987-90), Am. Arbitration Assn. (law com.). Democrat. Jewish. Avocations: scuba diving, tennis. Labor, Pension, profit-sharing, and employee benefits. Home: 277 W End Ave New York NY 10023-2604 Office: Friedman Wolf & Grisi 1500 Broadway Ste 2300 New York NY 10036-4056

FRIEDMAN, FRANK BENNETT, lawyer; b. Newark, May 1, 1940; s. Martin and Gertrude (Tow) F.; m. Esta Kossack, June 2, 1962; children: Amy, Emily. AB, Columbia U., 1962, JD, 1965. Bar: D.C., Pa., Colo., Calif. Atty. FCC, Washington, 1965-67, Dept. Justice, Washington, 1967-70; counsel ATlantic Richfield Co., Phila., 1970-71, Denver, 1971-73, L.A., 1973-78; dir. environ. health and safety ARCO Chem. Co., Phila., 1978-79, mgr. external affairs occupation and environ. protection L.A., 1979-81; v.p. health, environ. and safety Occidental Petroleum Corp., 1981-93; ptnr. McClintock, Weston, Benshoff, Rocheford, Rubalcava &MacCuish, 1993-94; sr. v.p. health, environ. and safety Elf Atochem N.Am., Phila., 1994—; v.p. health safety and environ. Elf Aquitaine, Inc., Washington, 1998—. Mem. exec. com., bd. dirs. Environ. Law Inst., 1979-95, 99—, adv. bd., 1996—. Author: Practical Guide to Environmental Management, 3d edit., 1991, 5th edit., 1993, 6th edit., 1995, 7th edit., 1997. Mem. ABA (natural resources sect. energy and environ. law, chmn. air quality commn. 1975-78, coun. nat. resource energy and environ. law sect. 1978-81, 91-94, internat. environ. law 1989-91), Am. Law Inst., Nat. Environ Devel. Assn. (bd. dirs. 1984-93, 96—), Nat. Safety Coun. (bd. dirs. 1991-93). Office: Elf Aquitaine Inc 910 17th St NW Ste 800 Washington DC 20006-2606

FRIEDMAN, HOWARD MARTIN, law educator; b. Springfield, Ohio, Sept. 26, 1941; s. Sam and Ida (Rubinoff) F.; m. Sharon Eve Kaufman, June 15, 1969; 1 child, Leah. BA, Ohio State U., 1962; JD, Harvard U., 1965; LLM, Georgetown U., 1967. Bar: Ohio 1965, .S. Supreme Ct. 1970, U.S. Dist. Ct. (no. dist.) Ohio 1973. Atty. SEC, Washington, 1965-67; asst. prof. U. N.D., Grand Forks, 1967-69; atty. U.S. Indian Claims, Washington, 1969-70; assoc. prof. law U. Toledo, 1970-74, prof. law, 1974—, dir. Cybersecurities Law Inst., 2000—. Of counsel Eastman and Smith, Toledo; vis. prof. Case Western Res. U., spring 1990, St. John's U., fall 1995, Notre Dame U., fall 1999; mem. Supreme Ct. Commn. on Cert. of Specialists, 1994-99. Author: Securities and Commodities Enforcement, 1981, Ohio Securities Law and Practice, 1987, 2d edit., 1996, Securities Regulation in Cyberspace, 1997, 2d edit., 1998; contbr. articles to profl. jours. Trustee ACLU of N.W. Ohio, 1982-89, pres. Toledo Bd. Jewish Edn., 1984-86, Temple B'Nai Israel, Toledo, 1991-93; v.p. govt. affairs com., Ohio Jewish Cmtys., 1993-96, pres., 1996-98; exec. com. Nat. Jewish Cmty. Rels. Adv. Coun., 1993-95. Mem. ABA, Ohio State Bar Assn. (chmn. specialization com. 1991-94), Toledo Bar Assn. (chmn. corp. and securities law com. 1991-92). Democrat. Jewish. Home: 3715 Sylvanwood Dr Sylvania OH 43560-3925 Office: U Toledo Coll Law Toledo OH 43606 E-mail: howard.friedman@utoledo.edu

FRIEDMAN, HYMAN, lawyer, accountant; b. Bklyn., Mar. 25, 1923; s. Sam and Regina (Meltzer) F.; m. Shirley Bernard, Mar. 15, 1946; 1 child, Dana B. B.S. in Acct., L.I. U., 1952; J.D., Bklyn. Law Sch., 1956. Bar: N.Y. 1957, U.S. Dist. Ct. (so. and ea. dist.) N.Y. 1959, U.S. Supreme Ct. 1971. Ptnr. Kleinberg & Friedman, N.Y.C., 1957— . Chmn. Selective Service Bd., Bklyn., 1965— . Served with USAF, 1943-46; ETO. Personal injury. Office: 1200 Ontario St Cleveland OH 44113-1604

FRIEDMAN, J. KENT, lawyer; b. Columbia, S.C., Feb. 12, 1944; s. Earl B. and Rose (Frolich) F.; m. Barbara Robins, July 25, 1965 (div. Dec. 1989); children: Elizabeth, Alison, Brent, Andrew; m. Ann Loretson, Oct. 11, 1992; 1 child, Ryan. BBA, Tulane U., 1966, LLB, 1967; LLM, Boston U., 1968. Bar: Tex. 1968. Assoc. Sullivan & Worcester, Boston, 1967-68, Butler, Binion, Rice, Cook & Knapp, Houston, 1968-74, ptnr., 1974-82; mng. ptnr. Mayor, Day, Caldwell & Keeton, 1982-92, sr. ptnr., 1992—. Bd. dirs. Sam Houston Race Park, Pacific Lumber Co. Bd. govs. Am. Jewish Com., N.Y.C., 1984-94; mem. exec. com. bd. dirs. Houston Symphony, 1985-99; bd. regents Tex. So. U., Houston, 1987-90; chmn. cmty. rels. coun. Jewish Fedn. Greater Houston, 1988-89; co-pres. Found. for Jones Hall, Houston, 1988-97; pres. Friends of Hermann Park, Houston, 1996-97; co-chair Greater Houston Inner City Games, 1997—. Recipient Max Nathan award Am. Jewish Com., Houston, 1990, Leon Jaworski award Houston Bar Assn. Auxilliary, 1999. Mem. Houston Club, Houston City Club. Administrative and regulatory, Estate planning, Estate taxation. Office: Mayor Day Caldwell & Keeton 700 Louisiana St Ste 1900 Houston TX 77002-2725

FRIEDMAN, JAMES DENNIS, lawyer; b. Dubuque, Iowa, Jan. 11, 1947; s. Elmer J. and Rosemary Catherine (Stillmunkes) F.; m. Kathleen Marie Maersch, Aug. 16, 1969; children: Scott, Ryan, Andrea, Sean. AB in Polit. Sci., Marquette U., 1969; JD, U. Notre Dame, 1972. Bar: Wis. 1972, U.S. U.S. Ct. Appeals (D.C. cir.) 1973, U.S. Ct. Appeals (7th ci (7th cir.) 1976, U.S. Supreme Ct. 1978, U.S. Ct. Appeals (6th cir.) 1989, Ill. 1996, U.S. Tax Ct. 1997. Pvt. practice, Milw., 1972-81; ptnr. Quarles & Brady, 1981—. Presenter in field; mem. legis. coun. spl. study com. on regulation of fin. instns. State of Wis., 1986-87; bd. dirs. Am. Paper and Packaging Corp., Concours Motors, Inc., Equal Justice Coalition, Inc.; mem. dept. fin. instns. task force on fin. competitiveness 2005, State of Wis., 2000; mem., vice chair State of Wis. Supreme Ct., Office Lawyer Regulation Preliminary Rev. Com., 2000—. Mng. Editor: Notre Dame Law Review, 1971-72; contbr. articles to profl. jours. Alderman 4th and 7th dists. Mequon, Wis., 1979-85, pres. common coun., 1980-82, bd. ethics 1996-98, 2000—, chair blue ribbon visioning com. 1998-99; bd. dirs. Weyenrg, Pub. Libr. Found. Inc., 1983—, pres., 1984—; bd. dirs. Ptnrs. Advancing Values in Edn. Inc., 1987—, Wis. Law Found., 1998—; bd. visitors Marquette U. Ctr. for Study of Entrepreneurship, Milw., 1987-95; bd. dirs. Ozaukee Family Svcs., 1983-99, sec., 1993-98; bd. dirs. Notre Dame Club of Milw., 1984-88, sec., 1978, v.p., 1986-88; bd. dirs. Marquette Club of Milw., 1987-88; chair attys. unit United Way Fund Dr. Greater Milw., 1987; mem. St. James Ch., Mequon. Named Outstanding Sr., Coll. of Liberal Arts, Marquette U. Fellow Wis. Law Found.; mem. ABA (banking law com. sect. bus. law), State Bar Wis. (chair bd. govs. 1999-2000, chair exec. com. 1999-2000, fin. com. 1997-98, strategic planning task force 1997-98, bd. govs. 1996-2000, exec. com. 1998-2000, internat. transactions sect. bd. dirs. 1984-99, sec. and chair-elect 1988-89, chair 1989-90, del. to ABA Ho. of Dels. 1980-82, standing com. on adminstrn. justice and judiciary 1979-81, legal edn. and bar admissions com. 1984-89, com. on minority lawyers 1992-99, chmn. 1997-1999, bd. dirs. young lawyers divsn. 1978-82, chmn. bar admission stds. and requirements com. 1979, So. Regional chair capital fund campaign 1998-99), Milw. Bar Assn., Wis. Acad. Trial Lawyers (bd. dirs. 1980-82), Wis. Bankers Assn., Milw. Country Club, Sigma Phi Epsilon. Roman Catholic. Avocations: tennis, golf. Banking, General corporate, Health. Office: Quarles & Brady LLP 411 E Wisconsin Ave Ste 2550 Milwaukee WI 53202-4497 E-mail: jdf@quarles.com

FRIEDMAN, JOEL WILLIAM, law educator; b. Mar. 16, 1951; s. Max Aaron and Muriel (Yudien) F.; m. Vivian Stoleru, Apr. 5, 1987; children: Alexa Erica, Chloe Gabriella, Max Aaron. BS, Cornell U., 1972; JD, Yale U., 1975. Bar: Calif. 1975, U.S. Dist. Ct. (cen. dist.) Calif. 1975. Asst. prof. Tulane U., New Orleans, 1976-79, assoc. prof., 1979-82, prof. law, 1982—, C.J. Morrow prof. law, 1985-86, dir. tech., 1996—, dir. ITESM PhD program, 2000—. Vis. prof. law U. Tel Aviv, Israel, 1983, U. Tex. Law Sch., 1985-86, Chuo Law Sch., Tokyo, 1988, Hebrew U. of Jerusalem Law Sch., 1990; lectr. Fed. Jud. Ctr., Washington, 1987—; cons. La. Ho. of Reps., Baton Rouge, 1982-85, West Group, 1996—; bd. dirs. Ctr. for Computer-Assisted Legal Instrn., 1996-99; spl. master Pasadena Ind. Sch. Dist., Houston, 1987-93. Editor: Cases and Materials on Law of Employment Discrimination, 1983, 4th edit., 1997, 5th edit., 2001; contbr. articles to law revs. Pres., bd. dirs. Woldenberg Village, Inc., 1995-97; pres., bd. dirs., Jewish Fedn. Greater New Orleans, 2001—. Recipient Felix Frankfurter Faculty award for disting. tchg. Tulane Law Sch., 1989; Fulbright scholar, Israel, 1990. Mem. Am. Assn. Law Schs. (chair sect. on employment discrimination law 1987-88), Am. Law Inst., B'nai B'rith Hillel Found. (pres. New Orleans 1987-91), Internat. Assn. of Jewish Lawyers and Jurists La. Br. (pres. 1994-95). Democrat. Avocations: running, squash, scuba diving, skiing. Home: 1230 State St New Orleans LA 70118-6027 Office: Tulane Law Sch 6329 Freret St New Orleans LA 70118-6231 E-mail: jfriedman@law.tulane.edu

FRIEDMAN, JOHN MAXWELL, JR. lawyer; b. N.Y.C., Oct. 31, 1944; s. John M. and Jane (Blum) F.; m. Laurie Suzanne Nevin, July 8, 1973 (div. 1988); children: David, Michael; m. Judith Zuckerman, Mar. 5, 1989; 1 child, Julia. AB, Princeton U., 1966; MA, U. Sussex, Brighton, Eng., 1967; JD, U. Chgo., 1970. Bar: N.Y. 1971, U.S. Ct. Appeals (2d cir.) 1971, U.S. Dist. Ct. (so. and ea. dist.) N.Y. 1972, U.S. Supreme Ct. 1974. Assoc. Dewey Ballantine, N.Y.C., 1970-78, ptnr., 1978-96. Bankruptcy, Federal civil litigation, State civil litigation. Home: 80 Rocky Mountain Rd Roxbury CT 06783-1623 E-mail: jmfriedman@mindspring.com

FRIEDMAN, JULIAN RICHARD, lawyer; b. Savannah, Ga., Oct. 9, 1936; s. W. Leon and Evelyn B. F.; m. Deborah I. Shaw, Sept. 12, 1963; m. Em Olivia Bevis, Dec. 27, 1974; children: Sheldon A., Esther B. AA cum laude, Armstrong State Coll., 1954; BA, Emory U., 1956; JD cum laude, U. Ga., 1959; LLM in Taxation, NYU, 1964. Bar: Ga. 1958, S.C. 1980. Assoc. W. Leon Friedman, Savannah, 1959, 61-63, Cheatham, Bergen & Sparkman, Savannah, 1960, Adams, Adams, Brennan & Gardner, Savannah, 1965-68, ptnr., 1968-82, Oliver Maner & Gray, LLP, Savannah, 1982-2000, of counsel, 2000—. Mem. Ga. del. S.E. Liaison Tax Com., 1971-73, chmn. Ga. del., 1972-73; mem. Ga. Fiduciary Law Revision Study Com., 1976-81, Ga. Probate Code Revision Com., 1992—. Contbr. articles to profl. publs.; asst. editor-in-chief student editl. bd. Ga. Bar Jour., 1958-59. Pres. Congregation, Mickve Israel Synagogue, Savannah, 1998-2001; pres. Ga. Pub. Radio, 1984-86. Served to capt. USAFR, 1961-68. Recipient Outstanding Grad. award Phi Delta Phi, 1959, Henry Shinn Meml. award Phi Alpha Delta, 1959. Mem. ABA, Am. Coll. Trust and Estate Counsel, Am. Coll. Tax Counsel, Savannah Estate Planning Coun. (pres. 1972-73), Fed. Bar Assn. (pres. Savannah chpt. 1971-72), State Bar Ga. (chmn. sect. taxation 1971-72, chmn. fiduciary law sect. 1975-76), State Bar S.C., Savannah Bar Assn., Phi Beta Kappa, Phi Kappa Phi, Omicron Delta Kappa, Pi Sigma Alpha. Club: B'nai B'rith (pres. Savannah lodge 1968-69). General corporate, Probate, State and local taxation. Home: 7 Rose Dhu Dr Bluffton SC 29910-6801 Office: Oliver Maner & Gray 218 W State St Savannah GA 31401-3232 E-mail: jfriedlaw@aol.com

FRIEDMAN, RICHARD LLOYD, lawyer; b. Bklyn., Feb. 17, 1943; s. H. Martin and Naomi (Ortman) F.; m. Carole Anne Greenhause, Aug. 28, 1966; children: Melissa Joy, Jonathan Scott. BA, Rutgers U., 1964; JD, U. Calif., Berkeley, 1967; LLM, NYU, 1972. Bar: N.Y. 1968, U.S. Dist. Ct. (so. and ea. dists.) N.Y. 1968, U.S. Ct. Appeals (2d cir.) 1968, U.S. Supreme Ct. 1971, N.J. 1972, U.S. Dist. Ct. N.J. 1972, U.S. Ct. Appeals (3d cir.) 1982, U.S. Ct. Appeals (11th cir.), 1986; cert. criminal trial atty., civil trial atty. Asst. dist. atty. Office N.Y. County Dist. Atty., N.Y.C., 1967-71; ct. planner Appellate Divsn., 1971-72; exec. dir. Dist. Atty.'s Assn., 1972-74, Office Prosecutorial Svcs., N.Y.C., 1974-75; asst. U.S. atty., Newark, 1975-82; officer Giordano, Halleran & Ciesla, Middletown, N.J., 1982—. Lectr., advisor Inst. for Continuing Legal Edn., 1982—; lectr. Nat. Inst. Trial Advocacy; mem. Supreme Ct. Criminal Practice Com., Trenton, 1983-86, Supreme Ct. Women in Cts. com., 1994—, Mayor's Anti-Rape Task Force, N.Y.C., 1973-75; adj. assoc. prof. John Jay Coll. Criminal Justice, N.Y.C., 1973-74. Editor Dist. Atty. Newsletter, 1972-75, Criminal Law Sect. Newsletter, 1978-81. Recipient Dir.'s award Dept. Justice, 1982, spl. commendation award, 1983, spl. achievement awards, 1978, 80. Mem. NACDL, N.J. Bar Assn. (chmn. criminal law sect. 1983=84), Monmouth County Bar Assn., N.Y. State Bar Assn. (sec. criminal justice sect. 1974-75), N.J. Assn. Criminal Def. Lawyers (v.p., trustee, editor newsletter). Federal civil litigation, State civil litigation, Criminal. Office: Giordano Halleran & Ciesla PC PO Box 190 Middletown NJ 07748-0190 E-mail: carrich21@aol.com, rfriedman@ghclaw.com

FRIEDMAN, ROBERT LAURENCE, lawyer; b. Mt. Vernon, N.Y., Mar. 19, 1943; s. Alvin S. and Frances (Feinsod) F.; m. Barbara Lander, Dec. 25, 1964; children: Lisa, Andrew. AB, Columbia Coll., 1964; JD, U. Pa., 1967. Bar: N.Y. 1968. Assoc. Simpson, Thacher & Bartlett, N.Y.C., 1967-74, ptnr., 1974-99; sr. mng. dir. The Blackstone Group LP, 1999—. General corporate, Mergers and acquisitions, Securities. Office: The Blackstone Group LP 345 Park Ave Fl 31 New York NY 10154-0004

FRIEDMAN, ROBERT MICHAEL, lawyer; b. Memphis, June 19, 1950; s. Harold Samuel and Margaret (Siegel) F.; m. Elaine Freda Burson, Dec. 21, 1975; children: Daniel Justin, Jonathan Aaron. B.S., U. Tenn., 1973, J.D., 1975; postgrad., Exeter U., Eng., 1974, Nat. Coll. Trial Advocacy, 1985. Bar: Tenn. 1976, U.S. Dist. Ct. (we. dist.) Tenn. 1977, U.S. Dist Ct. (no. dist.) Miss. 1979, U.S. Ct. Appeals (5th cir.) 1979, U.S. Supreme Ct. 1983, U.S. Dist. Ct. (so. dist.) Tex. 1986, U.S. Ct. Appeals (6th cir.) 1986. Assoc. Cassell & Fink, Memphis, 1976-78; pres., sr. ptnr. Friedman & Sissman, P.C., 1978-91, Friedman, Sissman & Heaton, P.C., Memphis, 1991—; commr. State of Tenn. Jud. Selection Commn., 1994—. Corp. legal/litigation counsel, dir. Tenn. Interpreting Svc. for Deaf, Memphis, 1981-89, Mid-South Hospitality Mgmt. Ctr., Inc., Memphis, 1984-88; legal counsel Moss Hotel Co., Inc., 1986-89, Helena Hotel Co., 1986-89, Charlestown Hotel Co., 1986-89, Jackson Hotel Co., 1986-89, Murfreesboro Hotel Co., 1986-89, Santee Hotel Co., 1986-89, Kingsport Hotel Co., 1986-89, Raleigh Hotel Assocs., Ltd., 1986-89, Ozark Regional Eye Ctr., 1986-90, Brookfield Mortgage Co., Inc., 1987—, Mt. Pleasant Hotel Co., 1987-89, Hattiesburg Hotel Assocs. Ltd., 1987-89, Wright and Assocs. Constrn. Co. Inc., 1987-90, Pro Billiards Tour Assn. Inc., 1996—; legal counsel, pres. Biloxi Hotel Co., Inc., 1986-89; litigation counsel Independence Fed. Bank Batesville, Ark., 1987-88; legal counsel Autorama, Inc., 1988—; bd. dirs./legal counsel Evan R. Harwood Day Tng. Ctr., 1989—; legal/litigation counsel Super D Drugs, Inc., 1989-93, So. Comm. Vols., Inc., WEVL FM Cmty. Radio, 1990-92; mem. staff, contbr. Tenn. Law Rev., 1974-75, recipient cert., 1975; corp. gen., litigation counsel U.S. for Inversiones Tesmo, Sociedad Anonima, Republic of Costa Rica, 1990—; rep. of Tenn. Bar Assn. and State of Tenn. to Nat. Summit Crime and Violence, 1994; legal counsel Pro Billiards Tour Assn., Inc., 1996—. Bd. dirs. Project 1st Offenders, Shelby County, Tenn., 1976-78; bd. dirs., legal counsel Memphis Community Ctr. for Deaf and Hearing Impaired, 1980-81; bd. dirs. Eagle Scout Day, Chickasaw coun. Boy Scouts Am., 1978—, Ea. Dist. committeeman, 1991-93, mem. adv. bd., 1993—, chmn. Eagle Scout recognition day, 1993-98, chaair Silver Beaver Com., 1999; scoutmaster Boy Scouts Am., Memphis, 1991—, mem. nat. bd. dirs. Nat. Eagle Scout Assn., 1998—; mem. U. Tenn. Coll. Law Alumni Adv. Coun., Dean's Cir., 1992—; rep. of Tenn. Bar Assn. and State of Tenn. Nat. Summit Crime and Violence, 1994. With USCG, 1971-77. James E. West fellow, 1996; A.S. Graves Meml. scholar, 1974-75; recipient Outstanding Svc. award and Key, Alpha Phi Omega, 1972, Am. Jurisprudence award Lawyers Co-op. Pub. Co. and Bancroft-Whitney Co., 1973-74, Chancellor's Honor award George C. Taylor Sch. Law, U. Tenn., 1975, Robert W. Richie Outstanding Svc. award Tenn. Assn. Criminal Def. Lawyers, 1993, Order of Arrow, Vigil of Honor, 1994, Nat. award Boy Scouts Am., 1996, Silver Beaver award, 1998. Mem. ABA, ATLA, Tenn. Bar Assn. (ho. dels. 1991-94, bd. dirs. criminal justice sect. 1998—, chmn. criminal justice sect. 1991-94, exec. bd. criminal justice sect. 1998-99, atty./solicitor Tenn Supreme Ct. 1994), Tenn. Jud. Selection Commn. (Tenn. state commr. 1994—), Tenn. Trial Lawyers Assn., Tenn. Assn. Criminal Defense Lawyers (bd. dirs. 1994), Nat. Assn. Criminal Def. Lawyers (vice chmn. law practice mgmt. com. 1990-93, co-chmn. forfeiture abuse task force 1991-93), Memphis and Shelby County Bar Assn., Fed. Bar Assn., Nat. Criminal Justice Assn. (charter 1984—), Alpha Phi Omega, Delta Theta Phi. Democrat. Jewish. General corporate, Criminal, Personal injury. Home: 3303 Spencer Dr Memphis TN 38115-3000 Office: Friedman Sissman & Heaton PC 100 N Main St Ste 3400 Memphis TN 38103-0534 Fax: 901-527-3633

FRIEDMAN, ROSELYN L. lawyer; b. Cleve., Dec. 9, 1942; d. Charles and Lillian Edith (Zalzneck) F. BS, U. Pitts., 1964; MA, Case Western Res. U., 1967; JD cum laude, Loyola U., Chgo., 1977. Bar: Ill. 1977, U.S. Dist. Ct. (no. dist.) Ill. 1977. Mem. legal dept. No. Trust Co., Chgo., 1977-79; assoc. Rudnick & Wolfe, 1979-84, ptnr., 1984-95, Sachnoff & Weaver, Ltd., Chgo., 1995—. Mem. Loyola U., Chgo. law rev.; mem. profl. adv. com. Chgo. Jewish Fedn., chmn., 1999-2001; mem. profl. adv. com. Chgo. Cmty. Trust. Trustee Jewish Women's Found., 1997—; vol. mediator Ctr. for Conflict Resolution, 2000—. Fellow Am. Coll. Trust and Estate Counsel; mem. ABA, Am. Jewish Congress (gov. coun. Midwest region 1995-97), Chgo. Bar Assn. (cert. appreciation continuing legal edn. program 1984, chmn. trust law com. 1989-90), Chgo. Estate Planning Coun. (program com. 1992-94, 98-2000, membership com. 1997-98, bd. dirs. 2001—), Chgo. Fin. Exch. (bd. dirs. 1995-97, sec. 1996-97). Estate planning, Probate, Estate taxation. Office: Sachnoff & Weaver Ltd 30 S Wacker Dr Ste 2900 Chicago IL 60606-7413 E-mail: rfriedman@sachnoff.com

FRIEDMAN, SAMUEL SELIG, lawyer; b. N.Y.C., July 25, 1935; s. Nathan and Anne M. (Sobel) F.; m. Maxine E. Goldfarb, Jan. 7, 1961; 1 child, Alison J. BS, MIT, 1956; MBA, U. Pa., 1959; LLB, Columbia U., 1965. Bar: N.Y. 1965, U.S. Dist. Ct. (so. and ea. dists.) N.Y. 1967, U.S. Supreme Ct. 1984. Assoc. Lord, Day & Lord, N.Y.C., 1965-72; ptnr., mem. exec. com. Lord Day & Lord, Barrett Smith and predecessor firm, 1972-94; ptnr. Morgan, Lewis & Bockius, LLP, 1994—. Vice chmn., dir., mem. exec. com. Times Square Bus. Improvement Dist., 1992-95. 1st lt. U.S. Army, 1959-62. Mem. ABA, N.Y. State Bar Assn., Assn. of Bar of City of N.Y., MIT Club N.Y., The Penn Club, Phi Delta Phi. Avocations: travel, wine, sports. General corporate, Mergers and acquisitions, Securities. Office: Morgan Lewis & Bockius LLP 101 Park Ave New York NY 10178-0060

FRIEDMAN, SARI MARTIN, lawyer; b. Bklyn., Nov. 17, 1956; d. David and Sylvia (Friedman) Martin; m. Kenneth L. Friedman, Aug. 10, 1980; children: Andrea, Deborah. BA, Hofstra U., N.Y., 1977; JD, Hofstra Law Sch., 1980. Bar: U.S. Dist. Ct. (ea. and so. dists.) N.Y., 1981, U.S. Supreme Ct. 1993. Law clk. appellate divsn. Supreme Ct., Bklyn., 1980-84; pvt. practice pvt. practice, Garden City, N.Y., 1985—. Gen. counsel Father's Rights Assn. N.Y., L.I., 1990—; counsel. Nat. Ctr. for Men, 1994—, Dad's Advocacy Group, Bklyn., 1993—. Author: Monthly Father's Rights Newsletter; mem. Hofstra U. Law Rev. Mem. Nassau Bar Assn. Office: 666 Old Country Rd Ste 704 Garden City NY 11530-2018

FRIEDMAN, STEPHEN JAMES, lawyer; b. Mar. 19, 1938; s. A.E. Robert and Janice Clara (Miller) F.; m. Fredrica L. Schwab, June 25, 1961; children: Vanessa V., Alexander S. AB magna cum laude, Princeton U., 1959; LLB magna cum laude, Harvard U., 1962. Bar: N.Y. 1962, D.C. 1982. Law clk. to justice William J. Brennan Jr. U.S. Supreme Ct., 1963-64; spl. asst. to maritime adminstr. Maritime Adminstrn., Dept. Commerce, 1964-65; assoc. Debevoise & Plimpton, N.Y.C., 1965-70, ptnr., 1970-77, 81-86, 93—; dep. asst. sec. for capital markets policy Dept. Treasury, Washington, 1977-79; commr. SEC, 1980-81; exec. v.p., gen. counsel E.F. Hutton Group Inc., N.Y.C., 1986-88, Equitable Life Assurance Soc., N.Y.C., 1988-93; ptnr. Debevoise & Plimpton, 1994—. Lectr. law Columbia U., N.Y.C., 1974-77, 82-85; bd. dirs. CCL Industries Inc. Author: An Affair With Freedom, the Opinions and Speeches of William J. Brennan, Jr., 1967; contbr. articles on legal and policy aspects of fin. inst.

to profl. jours. Active Coun. on Fgn. Rels.; trustee, chmn. emeritus Am. Ballet Theatre, N.Y.C.; dir. United Way N.Y.C.; mem. bd. govs. NASD, 1991-94, Chgo. Bd. Options Exch., 1982-88. With USAR, 1962-68. Mem. ABA, Assn. of Bar of the City of N.Y. (chmn. com. on securities regulation), Univ. Club. Office: Debevoise & Plimpton 875 3rd Ave Fl 23 New York NY 10022-6225

FRIEDRICH, CRAIG WILLIAM, lawyer; b. Oshkosh, Wis., Oct. 25, 1946; s. William Harold and Lorraine June (Pugh) F. AB, U. Wis., Madison, 1968; JD cum laude, Harvard U., 1972. Bar: N.Y. 1973, U.S. Tax Ct. 1973, U.S. Dist. Ct. (so., ea. dists.) N.Y. 1979, U.S. Ct. Internat. Trade 1980, Maine 1986. Atty., advisor Office Tax Legis. Counsel U.S. Treasury Dept., Washington, 1974-76; assoc. Weil, Gotshal and Manges, N.Y.C., 1972-74, 1976-77, Debevoise and Plimpton, N.Y.C., 1977-81; assoc. prof. N.Y. Law Sch., N.Y.C., 1981-83; counsel Schoeman, Marsh, Updike and Welt, 1982-83, ptnr., 1983-86, Bernstein, Shur, Sawyer & Nelson, Portland, Maine, 1986—. Cons. Bank Tax Inst., 1981-83; subject specialist Council Non Collegiate Continuing Edn., 1982. Mem. bd. contbg. editors, advisors Jour. Corp. Taxation, 1980—, author column, 1980—; contbr. articles to profl. jours. Mem. N.Y. State Bar Assn., Maine Bar Assn., Am. Soc. Internat. Law, N.Y.C. Bar Assn., Cumberland Club, Purpoodock Club, Phi Beta Kappa, Phi Kappa Phi, Phi Eta Sigma. Republican. Congregationalist. General corporate, Corporate taxation, Taxation, general. Home: 1 Ellie Ave Scarborough ME 04074-8549 Office: Bernstein Shur Sawyer & Nelson PO Box 9729 Portland ME 04104-5029

FRIES, KENNETH EUGENE, lawyer; m. Janet Martin; 1 child, Clint. BA, Stanford U., 1963; JD, U. Calif., Berkeley, 1966; M in Comparative Lit., U. Chgo., 1968. Atty. adviser U.S. Agy. for Internat. Devel., Washington, 1969-77, asst. gen. counsel for contract and commodity mgmt., 1977-93, dep. gen. counsel, 1994; gen. counsel U.S. Trade and Devel. Agy., 1995-2000; dir. Ctr. for Pub. Procurement and Policy, Internat. Law Inst., 2000. Vis. instr. Internat. Devel. Law Inst., Rome; negotiation adviser Internat. Law Inst., Washington; U.S. del. devel. assistance com./fin. aspects Orgn. for Econ. Coop. and Devel., Paris; U.S. del. UN Commn. on Internat. Trade Law, Model Procurement Law; cons. and instr. in internat. procurement. Office: 1621 N Kent St Ste 300 Arlington VA 22209-2131 E-mail: kfries@ili.org

FRIESE, ROBERT CHARLES, lawyer; b. Chgo., Apr. 29, 1943; s. Earl Matthew and Laura Barbara (Mayer) F.; m. Chandra Ullom; children: Matthew Robert, Mark Earl, Laura Moore. AB in Internat. Rels., Stanford U., 1964; JD, Northwestern U., 1970. Bar: Calif. 1972. Dir. Tutor Applied Linguistics Ctr., Geneva, 1964-66; atty. Bronson, Bronson & McKinnon, San Francisco, 1970-71, SEC, San Francisco, 1971-75; ptnr. Shartsis, Friese & Ginsburg, 1975—. Pres., bd. dirs. Custom Diversification Fund Mgmt., Inc., 1993—; dir.-co-founder Internat. Plant Rsch. Inst., Inc., San Carlos, Calif., 1978-86. Chmn. bd. suprs. Task Force on Noise Control, 1972-78; chmn. San Franciscans for Cleaner City, 1977; exec. dir. Nob Hill Neighbors, 1972-81; bd. dirs. Nob Hill Assn., 1976-78, Palace Fine Arts, 1992-94, San Francisco Beautiful, 1986—, pres., 1988-2000; chmn. Citizens Adv. Com. for Embarcadero Project, 1991—; mem. major gifts com. Stanford U.; bd. dirs. Presidio Heights Neighborhood Assn., 1993—, pres., 1996-98; bd. dirs. Inst. of Range and the American Mustang, 1990—. Mem. ABA, Assn. Bus. Trial Lawyers (bd. dirs.), Calif. Bar Assn., Bar Assn. San Francisco (bd. dirs. 1982-85, chmn. bus. litigation com. 1978-79, chmn. state ct. civil litigation com. 1983-90, new courthouse com. 1993—), Lawyers Club of San Francisco, Mensa, Calif. Hist. Soc., Commonwealth Club, Swiss-Am. Friendship League (chmn. 1971-79). General civil litigation, Securities. Office: Shartsis Friese & Ginsburg 1 Maritime Plz Fl 18 San Francisco CA 94111-3404 E-mail: rcf@sfglaw.com

FRIEZE, H(AROLD) DELBERT, lawyer; b. Tulsa, Feb. 15, 1943; s. Harold William and Violet Izenna (Schnelle) F.; m. Connie Dixon, Dec. 28, 1966; 1 child, Todd William. BBA, U. Okla., 1966; JD, U. Tulsa, 1975. Bar: Okla. 1975, U.S. Dist. Ct. (no. dist.) Okla. 1975, U.S. Dist. Ct. (ea. dist.) Okla. 1976. Ptnr. Petrik & Frieze, Broken Arrow, Okla., 1975—. Bd. dirs. 1st Nat. Bank & Trust Co., Broken Arrow. Bd. mem. Broken Arrow Bd. Adjustment, 1976-78; asst. city atty. City Broken Arrow, 1978-81; bd. dirs. Broken Arrow Community Found., 1999—, bd. dirs. Angel Flight of Oklahoma, 1997—, Broken Arrow Public Schs. Adv. Council, 2001—. Mem. Tulsa County Bar Assn. Republican. Methodist. Lodge: Rotary (past pres. Broken Arrow club, Paul Harris fellow 1983). State civil litigation, Contracts commercial, Real property. Office: Petrik & Frieze 121 E College St Broken Arrow OK 74012-3910

FRIGERIO, CHARLES STRAITH, lawyer; b. Detroit, Mar. 8, 1957; s. Louie John and LaVern (Straith) F.; m. Annette Angela Russo, Oct. 18, 1985; 1 child, Charles Anthony. BA, St. Mary's U., 1979, JD, 1982. Bar: Tex. 1982, U.S. Ct. Appeals (5th cir.) 1987, U.S. Supreme Ct. 1987; cert. in personal injury trial law. Pros. atty. City Attys. Office, San Antonio, 1982-84; trial atty. City Atty's. Office, 1984—; litigation chief and chief prosecutor City Atty.'s Office, 1995; pvt. practice law enforcement litigation, 1995—. Mem. Dem. Nat. Com., San Antonio, 1976; asst. mgr. local campaigns, San Antonio, 1976-84. Mem. ABA, Tex. Bar Assn., Fed. Bar Assn., San Antonio Bar Assn., Assn. Trial Lawyers Am., Cath. Lawyers Assn., Delta Epsilom Sigma. Democrat. Roman Catholic. Home: 317 Cleveland Ct San Antonio TX 78209-5862 Office: Riverview Towers 111 Soledad St Ste 840 San Antonio TX 78205-2219

FRII, JONAS ERIK WERNER, lawyer; b. Karlskrona, Sweden, Aug. 16, 1972; s. Lennart and Agneta (Tegler) F. LLM, U. Lund, Sweden, 1998. Author: The Criminalisation of Insider-Trading, 1998 (award Swedish Inst. of Stock Exch. 1998). St. Swedish Navy, 1993-94. Computer, Mergers and acquisitions. Office: Setterwalls Advokatbyr in Malmo KB, Stortorget 23 Malmo 21134 Sweden Fax: 46406900470. E-mail: jonas.frii@setterwals.se

FRISBIE, CURTIS LYNN, JR. lawyer; b. Greenville, Miss., Sept. 13, 1943; s. Curtis Lynn and Edith L. (Brantley) F.; m. Gena F. Johnson, May 30, 1965; children: Curtis L. III, Mark A. BSBA, U. Ala., 1966; JD, St. Mary's U., San Antonio, 1971. Bar: Tex. 1971; U.S. Dist. Ct. (no. dist.) Ga. 1974, U.S. Dist. Ct. (no. dist.) Tex. 1978, U.S. Dist. Ct. (we. dist.) Tex. 1985, U.S. Dist. Ct. (ea. and so. dists.) Tex. 1986, U.S. Dist. Ct. (ea. dist.) Wis. 1986; U.S. Tax Ct. 1986; U.S. Ct. Appeals (5th cir.) 1975, U.S. Ct. Appeals (10th cir.) 1982, U.S. Ct. Appeals (8th cir.) 1987; U.S. Supreme Ct. 1977. Trial atty. Antitrust divsn. U.S. Dept. Justice, Atlanta, 1971-73; assoc. King & Spalding, 1974-77; ptnr. Gardere Wynne Sewell LLP (formerly Gardere & Wynne LLP), Dallas, 1978—. Assoc. editor St. Mary's Law Jour., 1970-71. Capt. USMC, 1966-69, Vietnam. Fellow Tex. Bar Found. (life), Dallas Bar Assn. (life); mem. ABA (antitrust and bus. law sect.), Tex. Bar Assn. (antitrust sect., mem. coun. 1995—, vice chair, chair elect 2000-01, chair 2001—), Dallas Bar Assn. (pres. antitrust and trade regulation sect.), Phi Alpha Delta. Avocations: scuba diving, fishing, hunting. Antitrust, Federal civil litigation, Trademark and copyright. Home: 5605 Palomar Ln Dallas TX 75229-6417 Office: Gardere Wynne Sewell LLP Thanksgiving Tower 1601 Elm St Ste 3000 Dallas TX 75201-4761

FRISCH, HARRY DAVID, lawyer, consultant; b. N.Y.C., June 5, 1954; s. Isaac and Regina (Rottenberg) F.; m. Sherry Beth Bannerman, 1992; children:, Rachel Michele, Michael Elliot. BS, CCNY, 1976; postgrad., Rutgers U., 1976-77; JD, Pace U., 1980. Bar: N.Y 1981, U.S. Dist. Ct. (so. and ea. dists.) N.Y. 1981, U.S. Ct. Appeals (2d cir.) 1984, U.S. Supreme Ct. 1986, U.S. Ct. Appeals (5th cir.) 1987. Law clk. Shearson Hayden Stone, Inc., N.Y.C., 1977-80; assoc. gen. counsel Shearson Loeb Rhoades, Inc., 1980-82; asst. v.p., asst. corp. sec., assoc. gen. counsel Shearson/Am. Express, Inc., 1982-85; v.p., sr. litigator, assoc. gen. counsel Shearson Lehman Bros., Inc., 1985-88; 1st v.p., sr. litigator, assoc. gen. counsel Shearson Lehman Hutton, Inc., 1988-90, Shearson Lehman Bros., Inc., N.Y.C., 1990-93; 1st v.p., sr. litigator, asst. gen. counsel Smith Barney Shearson Inc., 1993-94; asst. gen. counsel Gruntal & Co. Inc., 1994-97, Gruntal & Co., L.L.C., N.Y.C., 1997-99; spl. counsel Lubiner & Schmidt, 1999; sr. v.p., compliance mgr. Datek Online Holdings Corp., Jersey City, 1999—. Contbr. articles to profl. jours. Mem. ABA, N.Y. State Bar Assn., Assn. of Bar of City of N.Y., N.Y. County Lawyers Assn., Fed. Bar Council. Democrat. Jewish. E-mial. Home: 49 Hudson Watch Dr Ossining NY 10562-2442 Office: Datek Online Holdings Corp 70 Hudson St 7th Fl Jersey City NJ 07302 E-mail: hfrisch@datek.com

FRISCH, SIDNEY, JR. lawyer, real estate developer; b. Evanston, Ill., Oct. 25, 1940; s. Sidney and Helen (Hunter) F.; m. Deborah A. King, Aug. 27, 1988. BS in Fin., U. Ill., 1962, JD, 1965. Bar: Ill. 1966, U.S. Dist. Ct. (no. dist.) Ill. 1966, U.S. Ct. Appeals (7th cir.) 1968, Colo. 1977, U.S. Dist. Ct. (mid. dist.) Ga. 1974, U.S. Supreme Ct. 1986. Ptnr. Frisch & Frisch, Chartered, Chgo., 1977—; v.p., gen. counsel Weber-Stephen Products Co., Palatine, Ill., 1966—. Gen. ptnr. Locks Landing Residential Devel., Stuart, Fla.; lectr. seminars in field; mem. sec. of state's adv. com. to revise Ill. Bus. Corp. Act, 1984. Author: Illinois Mechanic's Liens, 1972; Attorney's Guide to Negotiation, 1979. Asst. editlr Ill. Law Forum, U. Ill. Coll. Law, 1964, 65; mem. editorial com. Illinois Business Act Annotated, 1978. Assoc. bd. mem. U. Chgo. Cancer Research Found., 1982, v.p. 1984. Served to lt. USNR, 1962-69. Recipient cert. of appreciation Ill. Inst. for Continuing Legal Edn., 1983. Mem. ABA, Ill. Bar Assn., Chgo. Bar Assn. (chmn. corp. law com. 1983-84, cert. of appreciation 1978, 83), Order of Coif. Club: Deans (U. Ill. Coll. Law). General corporate, Real property. Office: Frisch & Frisch Chartered 312 W Randolph St Chicago IL 60606-1721

FRITH, DOUGLAS KYLE, retired lawyer; b. Henry County, Va., Sept. 2, 1931; s. Jacob and Sally Ada (Nunn) F.; m. Ella Margaret Tuck, Sept. 10, 1960; children: Margaret Frith Ringers, Susan Elaine Lonkevich. AB, Roanoke Coll., 1952; JD, Washington and Lee U., 1957. Bar: Va. 1957. Pvt. practice, 1957-58; assoc. Taylor & Young, Martinsville, Va., 1957-58; ptnr. Young, Kiser & Frith, 1960-71, Frith, Gardner & Gardner, 1973-78; pres. Douglas K. Frith & Assocs., P.C., Martinsville, 1979-99; ret., 1999. Bd. dirs. Frith Constrn. Co., Inc., Frith Equipment Corp.; substitute judge 21st Gen. Dist. Ct., 21st Juvenile and Domestic Relations Dist. Ct., 1969-80. Chmn. March of Dimes, 1960, Brotherhood Week, 1960; capt. profl. div. United Fund, 1971. With U.S. Army, 1952-54. Mem. ABA, Am. Bd. Trial Advocates, Va. Bar Assn., Martinsville-Henry County Bar Assn. (pres. 1970-71), Va. Trial Lawyers Assn. (dis. v.p. 1970-71, del. at large 1971-77), Kiwanis. Republican. Baptist. Estate planning, Personal injury, Real property. Address: 1409 Whittle Rd Martinsville VA 24112

FRITTON, KARL ANDREW, lawyer; b. Olean, N.Y., Mar. 29, 1955; s. William John and Margaret (O'Brian) F.; m. Christine Evelyn Councill, June 9, 1984; children: Katherine Evelyn, Jessica Claire, Rebecca Lee. BS in Econs., SUNY, Albany, 1977; JD, Rutgers U., 1980. Bar: Pa. 1981, N.Y. 1981, U.S. Supreme Ct. 1985. Assoc. Bond, Schoeneck & King, Syracuse, N.Y., 1980-81, Obermayer, Rebmann, Maxwell & Hippel, Phila., 1981-84, Sprecher, Felix, Visco, Hutchinson & Young, Phila., 1984-86, ptnr., 1987-91, Montgomery, McCracken, Walker & Rhoads, Phila., 1991-96, Reed, Smith, Shaw & McLay LLP, Phila., 1996—. Contbr. articles to profl. jours. Active Phila. Vol. Lawyers For Arts, 1981—, Big Brs. Phila., 1981—. Mem ABA (labor law sect.). Democrat. Roman Catholic. Labor. Home: 53 Cedarbrook Rd Ardmore PA 19003-1617 Office: Reed Smith Shaw & McLay 2500 One Liberty Pl Philadelphia PA 19103

FRIZELL, DAVID J. lawyer; b. National Park, N.J., Sept. 13, 1948; s. Robert E. and Kathleen S. (Ford) F.; m. Aurelia M. Wright, Aug. 5, 1989; children: Brigid, St. John, Catherine. AB, Rutgers U., 1970, JD (with honors), 1973. Bar: N.J. 1973, U.S. Dist. Ct. N.J. 1973, U.S. Supreme Ct. 1986. Counsel Levin Affiliates, Plainfield, N.J., 1975-77; ptnr. Frizell & Pozycki, Metuchen, 1977-93, Frizell Goldman Jaffe & Samuels, 1993—. Mem. N.J. Legislature Adv. Com. Land Use Law Revisions, 1979-86; lectr. Inst. for CLE, 1983—; pres. Frizell Real Estate Devel. Group, 1994—. Author: New Jersey Land Use Law, 2000; contbr. articles to profl. jours.; editor Land Use Law Newsletter, 1983-92; mem. editl. bd. Housing N.J. Mag., 1990-96. Bd. Govs. Raritan Yacht Club; bd. dirs. First Concern, Inc., 1998—. Mem. ABA, N.J. State Bar Assn. (dir., chmn. land use sect. 1983, dir. 1984-96, Outstanding Svc. award 1983), Metuchen C. of C. Democrat. Avocations: sailing, hiking. State civil litigation, Health, Real property. Office: PO Box 474 Metuchen NJ 08840-0474 E-mail: djfrizell@aol.com

FRIZELL, SAMUEL, law educator; b. Buena Vista, Colo., Aug. 30, 1933; s. Franklin Guy and Ruth Wilma (Noel) F.; m. Donna Mae Knowlton, Dec. 26, 1955 (div. June 1973); children: Franklin Guy III, LaVerne Anne; m. Linda Moncure, Jul. 3, 1973 (div. June 1996); m. Jeannette Graham, Jan. 1997. AA cum laude, Ft. Lewis Coll., 1957; BA cum laude, Adams State Coll., 1959, EdM, 1960; JD, Hastings U. Calif., 1964. Bar: Calif. 1965. Assoc. atty. McCutcheon, Black, Verleger & Shea, Calif., L.A., 1964-67; atty. Law Offices Samuel Frizell, Santa Ana, Calif., 1967-82; adj. prof. Cerritos Coll., Norwalk, 1977-81, Western State U., Fullerton, 1982-84, assoc. prof., 1984-90, prof., 1990-98, prof. emeritus, 1998—; cons. Law Offices Samuel Frizell, Mira Loma, Calif., 1982-98. Author: Frizell's Torts Tips, 1992; contbr. articles to profl. jours.; editor law jour. Mem. Main St. Adv. Panel, Garden Grove, Calif., 1975-76; judge pro-tem Orange County Superior Ct., Santa Ana, 1979-80; chair, com. atty. advertising Orange County Bar Assn., 1975; bd. dirs. Orange County Trial Lawyers Assn., 1972-75; adv. panel to legal assts. Cerritos Coll., Norwalk, 1982-86. Fellow Soc. Antiquaries; mem. Order of the Coif. Avocations: history, reloading and target shooting, saddle making. Office: Western State U 1111 N State College Blvd Fullerton CA 92831-3000 E-mail: SJFrizell@Earthlink.net

FRIZZELL, GREGORY KENT, judge; b. Wichita, Kans., Dec. 13, 1956; s. D. Kent and Shirley Elaine (Piatt) F.; m. Kelly Susan Nash, Mar. 9, 1991; children: Benjamin Newcomb, Hannah Kirsten, Robert Nash, David Gregory, Elizabeth Piatt, Jubilee Kathryn. BA, U. Tulsa, 1981; JD, U. Mich., 1984. Bar: Okla. 1985, U.S. Dist. Ct. (no., ea. and we. dists.) Okla. 1985, U.S. Ct. Appeals (10th cir.) 1985, U.S. Supreme Ct. 1990. Jud. clk. to judge U.S. Dist. Ct. for No. Dist. Okla., Tulsa, 1984-86; pvt. practice, 1986-95; gen. counsel Okla. Tax Commn., 1995-97; dist. judge Tulsa County, 1997—. Counsel bd. dirs. Tulsa Speech and Hearing Assn., 1987-95, pres., 1994-95. Mem. Okla. Bar Assn., Am. Inns of Ct. (past pres. local chpt.), Rotary, Federalist Soc. Avocations: duck hunting, flying. Office: Tulsa County Courthouse 500 S Denver Ave Tulsa OK 74103-3838

FROEBE, GERALD ALLEN, lawyer; b. The Dalles, Oreg., Feb. 16, 1935; s. Earl Wayne and Ethelene Alvina (Ogle) F.; m. Olivia Ann Tharaldson, Aug. 31, 1958; children: Dana Lynn, Heidi Ann. BBA, U. Oreg., 1956, LLB, 1961; LLM, NYU, 1962. Bar: N.Y. 1962, Oreg. 1962, U.S. Dist. Ct. Oreg. 1962. Auditor Arthur Andersen & Co., Seattle, 1956-58; lawyer, ptnr. Miller, Nash, Wiener, Hager & Carlsen, Portland, Oreg., 1962—. Editor-in-chief Oreg. Law Rev., Eugene, 1960-61. Republican. Christian. Avocations: hiking, travel. Estate planning, Pension, profit-sharing, and employee benefits, Taxation, general. Home: 1109 SW Ardmore Ave Portland OR 97205-1004 Office: 1109 SW Ardriove Ave Portland OR 97205

FROHLICH, ANTHONY WILLIAM, lawyer, master commissioner; b. Covington, Ky., Dec. 8, 1954; s. Kenneth Raymond and Joan Jude (Laake) F.; m. Candace Powell Robbins, May 31, 1975; children: Kenneth Zane, Matthew Andrew. BS, No. Ky. U., 1976, JD, 1980. Bar: Ky. 1980, U.S. Dist. Ct. (ea. dist.) Ky. 1981. Staff atty. Boone County (Ky.) Child Support Program, 1980-97; city atty. City of Walton, 1980-89; master commr. Boone County Cir. Ct., Burlington, Ky., 1989—; asst. commonwealth atty. 54th Jud. Dist., 1984-89; ptnr. Mathis, Dallas & Frohlich, Florence, 1980-96, Law Office of Anthony W. Frohlich, Florence, 1996—. Pres. Soccer Tech., Union, Ky., 1994. Bd. dirs. No. Ky. Soccer Club, Florence, 1994; state coach Ky. Youth Soccer, 1994-96; coaching dir. Ky. Olympic Devel. Program Dist. One, Florence, 1992-94; active Union Town Plan Steering Com., 1999; bd. dirs. Greater Cin. Consumer Credit Counseling, 1999—; nominating chmn. Boy Scout Am., 1999—; mem. steering com. Boone County Parks & Recreation, 2000—. Named Coach of Yr., No. Ky. Soccer Club, 1992. Mem. ATLA, Ky. Bar Assn., Boone County Bar Assn. (treas. 1980), Ky. Acad. Trial Lawyers. Roman Catholic. Avocations: coaching soccer, basketball. General practice. Home: 9253 Us Highway 42 Union KY 41091-9470 Office: Law Office Anthony Frohlich PO Box 396 Florence KY 41022-0396 E-mail: awfpsc42@fuse.net

FROHNMAYER, DAVID BRADEN, academic administrator; b. Medford, Oreg., July 9, 1940; s. Otto J. and MarAbel (Fisher) B. F.; m. Lynn Diane Johnson, Dec. 30, 1970; children: Kirsten (dec.), Mark, Kathryn (dec.), Jonathan, Amy. AB magna cum laude, Harvard U., 1962; BA, Oxford (Eng.) U., 1964, MA (Rhodes scholar), 1971; JD, U. Calif., Berkeley, 1967; LLD (hon.), Willamette U., 1988; D Pub. Svc. (hon.), U. Portland, 1989. Bar: Calif. 1967, U.S. Dist. Ct. (no. dist.) Calif. 1967, Oreg. 1971, U.S. Dist. Ct. Oreg. 1971, U.S. Supreme Ct. 1981. Assoc. Pillsbury, Madison & Sutro, San Francisco, 1967-69; asst. to sec. Dept. HEW, 1969-70; prof. law U. Oreg., 1971-81, spl. asst. to univ. pres., 1971-79; atty. gen. State of Oreg., 1981-91; dean Sch. Law U. Oreg., 1992-94, pres., 1994—. Chmn. Conf. Western Attys. Gen., 1985-86; chmn. Am. Coun. Edn. Govtl. Rels. commn, 1996-98; bd. dirs. Umpqua Holding Co. Mem. Oreg. Ho. of Reps, 1975-81; mem. coun. pub. reps. NIH, 1999-2000; bd. dirs. Fred Hutchinson Cancer Rsch. Ctr., 1994-2000, Nat. Marrow Donor Program, 1987-99, Fanconi Anemia Rsch. Fund, Inc., Tax Free Trust of Oreg. Fund; active Oreg. Progress Bd. Recipient awards Weaver Constl. Law Essay competition Am. Bar Found., 1972, 74, Advocacy award Research!Am., 1999, Albert B. Sabin Heroes of Sci. award Ams. for Med. Progress Ednl. Found., 2000; Rhodes scholar, 1962. Mem. ABA (Ross essay winner 1980), Oreg. Bar Assn., Calif. Bar Assn., Nat. Assn. Attys. Gen. (pres. 1987, Wyman award 1987), Round Table Eugene, Order of Coif, Phi Beta Kappa, Rotary. Republican. Presbyterian. Home: 2315 McMorran St Eugene OR 97403-1750 Office: U Oreg Johnson Hall Office Pres Eugene OR 97403 E-mail: pres@oregon.uoregon.edu

FROLIK, LAWRENCE ANTON, law educator, lawyer, consultant; b. Lincoln, Nebr., Jan. 10, 1944; s. Elvin F. and Rita K. (Haley) F.; m. Ellen M. Doyle, Sept. 25, 1973; children: Winnefred, Cornelius. BA with distinction, U. Nebr., 1966; JD cum laude, Harvard U., 1969, LLM cum laude, 1972. Asst. prof. U. Pitts., 1975-78, assoc. prof., 1978-81, prof., 1981—; dir. Pitts. office programing Grater Inst. for Law & Behavioral Rsch. Bd. dirs. Kendal Corp. Author: Federal Tax Aspects of Injury, 1993, Loss and Damage, 1987; co-author: Pennsylvania Elder Law Manual, 1988, Advising the Elderly and Disabled Client, 1991, 2d edit., 1999, The Elderly and the Law: Cases and Materials, 1991, 2d edit., 1999, Elder Law in a Nutshell, 1995, 2d edit., 1998, Residence Options for Older or Disabled Clients, 1997, Aging and the Law: An Interdisciplinary Reader, 1999. Mem. exec. com. Gruter Inst. Law and Behavioral Rsch. Capt. U.S. Army, 1969-71. Fellow Am. Bar Found., Am. Coll. Trust and Estate Counsel; mem. Phi Beta Kappa. Home: 4345 Schenley Farms Ter Pittsburgh PA 15213-1206 Office: U Pitts Sch Law Pittsburgh PA 15260 E-mail: frolik@law.pitt.edu

FROMM, FREDERICK ANDREW, JR. lawyer; b. Grosse Pointe Farms, Mich., Aug. 2, 1951; s. Frederick Andrew and Jeanette (Sellars) F.; m. Kathleen Ann Lewis, Sept. 25, 1976; children; Andrew Blair, Jennifer Kathleen. BS, Mich. State U., 1973; JD, U. Detroit, 1976. Bar: Mich. 1976, U.S. Dist. Ct. (ea. dist.) Mich. 1976. Law clk. to J.m.M. kelly Mich. Ct. Appeals, Detroit, 1976-77; atty. legal staff GM, 1977-92, sr. counsel, atty., practice area mgr., 1997—. V.p., gen. counsel, sec. Delco Electronics Corp., 1992-96. Mem. Mich. Bar Assn., Ind. Bar Assn. Contracts commercial, Environmental. Home: 2887 Chestnut Run Dr Bloomfield Hills MI 48302-1105 Office: GM Corp MC 482-C23-D24 300 Renaissance Ctr Detroit MI 48265-3000

FROMM, JEFFERY BERNARD, lawyer; b. Washington, Oct. 9, 1947; s. Seymour Morris and Frances Sylvia (Goldstein) F.; m. Mary Ellen Sommer, Sept. 11, 1971; children: Aaron M., David P. BS in Elec. Engring., BA in Physics, U. Pa., 1970; JD, Widener U., 1981. Bar: Pa. 1982, Calif. 1982, U.S. Ct. Appeals (9th and fed. cirs.) 1982, Colo. 1988. Patent atty. Hewlett-Packard Co., Palo Alto, Calif., 1981-83, sr. patent atty., 1983-85, mng. patent counsel Andover, Mass., 1985-87, sr. mng. counsel intellectual property Ft. Collins, Colo., 1987—. Asst. scout master Boy Scouts Am., Ft. Collins, 1988-96; asst. coach-umpire Little League, Andover and San Jose, Calif., 1983-87. Mem. ABA, Pa. Bar Assn., Calif. Bar Assn., Colo. Bar Assn., IEEE, Am. Corp. Counsel Assn. Avocations: skiing, golf. Computer, Patent, Trademark and copyright. Office: Hewlett-Packard Co 3404 E Harmony Rd Fort Collins CO 80528-9599 E-mail: jeff_fromm@hp.com

FROST, BRIAN STANDISH, lawyer; b. Kansas City, Mo., Feb. 24, 1958; s. Hugh Lathan and Sharon Duayne Frost; m. Kathy L. Whittington, Mar. 7, 1992. Student, Okla. State U., 1978-80; BBA, Washburn U., 1982, JD, 1985. Bar: Kans. 1985, U.S. Dist. Ct. Kans. 1985, U.S. Ct. Appeals (10th cir.) 1986. Assoc. Law Office Brock R. Snyder, Topeka, 1985-90, Florez and Frost, Topeka, 1990-98; Brian Frost, Atty. at Law, 1998-99; of counsel Alderson, Alderson, Weiler, Conklin, Burchart & Crow, LLC, 1999—. Counsel CASA of Shawnee County; guardian ad litem Domestic Divsn., Shawnee County; Family Law Com., Shawnee County. Bd. dirs. Safe Visit of Shawnee County, 1994—. Mem. Topeka Bar Assn., Kans. Trial Lawyers Assn., Sigma Phi Epsilon. Democrat. Methodist. Avocations: music, computers, golf. General civil litigation, General corporate, Family and matrimonial. Home: 8001 SW 21st Ter Topeka KS 66614-4832

FROST, CHARLES ESTES, JR. lawyer; b. Houston, Aug. 17, 1950; s. Charles Estes and Lucille Fourmey (DeGravelles) F. BS, U.S. Mil. Acad., 1972; MBA, Armstrong State Coll., 1979; JD, U. Tex., 1981. Bar: Tex. 1982, U.S. Dist. Ct. (no. and so. dists.) Tex. Commd. 2d lt. U.S. Army, 1972, advanced through grades to capt., 1979; resigned from active duty, 1979; assoc. Strasburger & Price, Dallas, 1982-84, Chamberlain, Hrdlicka et al, Houston, 1985-88; shareholder Chamberlain Hrdlicka et al, 1989—. Mem. bd. advocates U. Tex. Law Sch. Note editor: Tex. Law Rev., U. Tex. Law Sch.1981-82. Mem. ethics com. Haris County Rep. Party, 2000. Lt. col. USAR, 1979-98. Mem. Houston Bar Assn. (dir. litigation sect. 2000—). Republican. Avocations: running, church. Federal civil litigation, State civil litigation, Intellectual property, Oil, gas, and mineral, Contracts commercial, Probate, Securities. Office: Chamberlain Hrdlicka et al 1200 Smith St Ste 1400 Houston TX 77002-4401

FROST, EDMUND BOWEN, lawyer; b. Pueblo, Colo., Dec. 5, 1942; s. Hildreth and Doris (Bowen) F.; m. Molly Spitzer; children: Julia A., Elizabeth E., Edmund N., Luette S. BA, Dartmouth Coll., 1964; JD magna cum laude, U. Mich., 1967. Bar: Colo. 1967, D.C. 1970, U.S. Supreme Ct. 1980. Assoc. Steptoe & Johnson, Washington, 1969-75; chief legal advisor

to commr. ICC, 1975-76; asst. dir. for gen. litigation Bur. Competition, FTC, 1976-77; v.p., gen. counsel Chem. Mfrs. Assn., 1978-82; ptnr. Kirkland & Ellis, 1982-88, Davis, Graham & Stubbs, Washington, 1988-94; sr. v.p. and gen. counsel Clean Sites, Inc., Alexandria, Va., 1994-99. Bd. dirs., exec. dir., sec. Ctr. for Land Renewal, Inc., Alexandria, 1996—; shareholder, dir. Leonard Hurt Frost, Lilly & Levin, P.C., Washington, 1998—; adv. coun. Environtl. Law Inst., 1998—; bd. dirs., exec. com., sec. Comty. Coun. for Homeless, Washington, 1993—; chair corp. governance, environ. and nominating com., bd. dirs. Philip Svcs. Corp., 2000—. Contbr. articles to profl. jours. Participant pub. policy dialogs on environ. issues Keystone (Colo.) Ctr., 1980—;guest artisan Washington Nat. Cathedral, 1997—. Capt. U.S. Army, 1967-69. Mem. Cosmos Club Washington. Avocations: sculpture and stone carving, skiing, mountain climbing, tuba and euphonium. Federal civil litigation, Environmental, Non-profit and tax-exempt organizations. Home: 3309 35th St NW Washington DC 20016-3141 E-mail: ebfrost@leonardhurt.com

FROST, WINSTON LYLE, lawyer, educator; b. Washington, June 26, 1958; s. Lyle Gooden and Elizabeth Caddell (McLennan) F. BA in Social Sci., U. Calif., Irvine, 1979; JD, O.W. Coburn Sch. of Law, 1982; MBA, Pepperdine U., 1989; LLM in Taxation, Washington U., 1993; MA in Internat. Human Rights, Simon Greenleaf U., 1994; Diplomé Internat. Human Rights, Internat. Human Rights Inst., Strasbourg, France, 1995; MA in Faith and Culture, Trinity Internat. U., 1998, MA in Bioethics, 2001. Bar: Ill. 1982, Calif. 1986, U.S. Dist. Ct. (cen. dist.) Calif. 1987, U.S. Supreme Ct. 1987, D.C. 1989. Pvt. practice, Carthage, Ill., 1982-84; adjunct faculty Carl Sandburg Coll., 1982-84; legal editor James Pub. Co., Costa Mesa, Calif., 1985-86; assoc. Law Offices of John Ford, Irvine, 1986-89, Hunt and Colaw, Inc., Santa Ana, 1989, Cassidy, Warner, Brown, Combs and Thurber, Santa Ana, 1989-90; ptnr. Harbin and Frost, 1990—2000. Prof. Simon Greenleaf U., Anaheim, Calif., 1987-97, asst. dean Sch. Internat. Human Rights, 1994-96; acad. dean Trinity Sch. Law, 1996-98, dean, 1999-2000; regional pres. Calif. campus Trinity Internat. U., 2000-2001; arbitrator Orange County Superior Ct., 1992—; judge pro tem Orange County Mcpl. Ct., 1992—; mediator Christian Conciliation Svc., 1995—; columnist Brokers and Agents mag., 1997-2001 Editor Jour. Christian Juris, 1980-81; editorial staff Athletes in Action mag., 1986-87; columnist Orange County Reporter, 1989-91; editor Orange County Bar Jour., 1991-93. Mem. campaign staff Reagan for Pres., 1980; bd. dirs. Religioius Freedom Internat., 1995-2000, Alliance for Life, 1998—, Conciliators Inc., 2000—. Recipient Outstanding Achievement award The Travelers, 1987, 88. Mem. ABA, Orange County Bar Assn. (bd. dir. 1988-90, 92-95), Orange County Bar Found. (bd. dirs. 1992-95), Orange County Barristers (bd. dirs. 1989, pres. 1990), Orange County Ins. Def. Assn. (pres. 1991), Christian Legal Soc., Peter M. Elliot Inn of Ct., Kiwanis, Toastmasters, Univ. Faculty for Life. Republican. Avocations: collecting books, sports, community theater, travel. General civil litigation, Real property. Office: Trinity Law Sch 2200 N Grand Ave Santa Ana CA 92705-7016 E-mail: wfrost@tiu.edu

FRUE, WILLIAM CALHOUN, lawyer; b. Pontiac, Mich., Dec. 29, 1934; s. William Calhoun and Evelyn Laura Frue; m. Eloise Saunders, June 22, 1956 (div. Dec. 1989); m. Jane Torres Fletcher, Dec. 30, 1989; children: William C. III, John C., Michael C., Victoria. BA, Washington & Lee U., 1956; LLB, U. N.C., 1960. Bar: N.C. 1960, U.S. Dist. Ct. (we. dist.) N.C. 1961, U.S. Tax Ct. 1968, U.S. Ct. Appeals (4th cir.) 1988. Rsch. asst. Inst. of Govt., Chapel Hill, N.C., 1958-60; assoc. Wright & Shuford, Asheville, 1961-69; ptnr. Shuford, Frue & Sluder, 1969-72, Shuford, Frue & Best, Asheville, 1973-84, The Frue Law Firm, Asheville, 1984—. Editor Popular Govt. mag., 1958-60. Chmn. Asheville Police Retirement Fund, 1973-83, Morehead Scholarship Selectincom., 1965-90, Asheville Planning and Zoning Commn., 1982-92. Mem. N.C. Bar Assn., Buncombe County Bar Assn., (sec., v.p. 1978-92), Trout Unl d. (N.C. coun. 1965). Democrat. Episcopalian. Avocations: fishing, camping. State civil litigation, Probate, Real property. Office: PO Box 7627 Asheville NC 28802-7627

FRUG, GERALD E. law educator; b. 1939; AB, U. Calif.-Berkeley, 1960; JD, Harvard U., 1963. Bar: Calif. 1964, N.Y. 1969. Frank Knox fellow London Sch. Econs., 1963-64; law clk. to chief justice Supreme Ct. Calif., 1964-65; assoc. Heller, Ehrman, White & McAuliffe, San Francisco, 1965-66; spl. asst. to chmn. EEOC, 1966-69; assoc. Cravath, Swaine & Moore, N.Y.C., 1969-70; gen. counsel Health Services Adminstrn., 1970-72, 1st dep. adminstr., 1972-73, adminstr., 1973-74; assoc. prof. U. Pa. Law Sch., Phila., 1974-78, prof., 1978-81, Harvard U. Law Sch., 1981-94, Samuel R. Rosenthal prof. law, 1994-2000, Louis D. Brandeis prof., 2000—. Mem. Phi Beta Kappa. Office: Law Sch Harvard U Cambridge MA 02138

FRUIN, ROGER JOSEPH, lawyer; b. El Paso, Ill., July 27, 1915; s. William Mark and Ella (Hayes) F.; m. Mary Frances Barth, June 18, 1940; children: Nancy Fluss, Karen Todd, Jeanne Cooper. AB, U. Ill., 1936, JD, 1938. Bar: Ill. 1938, U.S. Dist. Ct. (ea. dist.) Ill. 1943. Assoc. Hannah & Figenbaum, Mattoon, Ill., 1938-41; pvt. practice Paris, 1941-43, 46; ptnr. Lauher & Fruin, 1947-63; pvt. practice, 1963-66; ptnr. Fruin & Lund, 1967-72; pvt. practice, 1972-75; ptnr. Fruin, Andrews & Hoff, 1975-87, Fruin & Garst, Paris, 1987-91, 93-97, Fruin Garst Piper, Paris, Paris, 1991-93, Fruin, Garst & Kash, Paris, 1997, of counsel, 1997—. Asst. atty. gen. State of Ill., Paris, 1946-70; chmn. Inst. on Continuing Legal Edn., Ill. Bar Assn., Springfield, 1973-74. Contbr. articles to profl. jours. Bd. dirs. Paris Community YMCA, 1987-93; sec., treas. Paris YMCA Spl. Endowment Trust, 1982-2000; mem. St. Mary's Cath. Ch., Paris, former mem. ch. sch. bldg. com.; former mem. deanery and diocesan bds. Confraternity of Christian Doctrine, Diocese of Springfield, Ill. Sgt. U.S. Army, 1943-46, ETO. Recipient Addis E. Hull award IICLE, 1990; named Ill. Tree Farmer of Yr., 1994. Fellow Am. Coll. Trust & Estate Counsel; mem. ABA, Ill. State Bar Assn. (life), Paris C. of C. (bd. dirs.), U. Ill. Alumni Assn. (life), KC (grand knight 1942-43), VFW, Elks, Am. Legion. Democrat. Roman Catholic. Avocations: American Walnut Council, Illinois Walnut Council. Estate planning, Probate. Office: Fruin Garst & Kash 129 N Central Ave Paris IL 61944-1704

FRY, MORTON HARRISON, II, lawyer; b. N.Y.C., May 15, 1946; s. George Thomas Clark and Louise Magdalen (Cronin) F.; m. Patricia Laylin Coffin, May 29, 1971. AB, Princeton U., 1968; JD, Yale U., 1971. Bar: N.Y. 1973, U.S. Ct. Mil. Appeals 1973, U.S. Dist. Ct. (so. and ea. dists.) N.Y. 1975, U.S. Ct. Appeals (2d cir.) 1975. Assoc. Cravath, Swaine & Moore, N.Y.C., 1971-72, 75-79; dep. gen. counsel Columbia Pictures Industries, Inc., 1979-81; v.p., gen. counsel Warner Home Video Inc., 1982-83; exec.v.p. Warner Electronic Home Svcs., 1983-84; sr. counsel corp. and new techs. Warner Comms. Inc., 1984-85; pres., CEO, bd. dirs. The Congress Video Group, Inc., 1985-87; pres., cons. Fry Assocs., 1987-89; ptnr. Marshall, Morris, Bomser & Fry, N.Y.C., 1990-94, Rubin, Bailin, Ortoli, Mayer, Baker & Fry, N.Y.C., 1995-2000; of counsel Stairs, Dillenbeck, Finley & Rendon, 2000—. Mem. Dem. Nat. Fin. Com. Capt. USMC, 1966-75. Democrat. Congregationalist. Communications, Entertainment, Public international. Home: 382 Lafayette St New York NY 10003-6907 E-mail: frylaw@mindspring.com

FRYE, EDWARD MOSES, law educator; b. Sallisaw, Okla., Jan. 28, 1920; s. Edward Moses and Mattie Lucille (Watts) F.; m. Mary Lois Rulifson, Aug. 15, 1953; children— Lynette, Camille, Renee. Student Muskogee Jr. Coll., 1937-39; B.A., U. Okla., 1941; J.D., Oklahoma City U., 1957. Bar: Okla. 1957, U.S. Dist. Ct. (we., no. and so. dists.) Okla. 1957, U.S. Ct. Appeals (10th cir.) 1960, U.S. Supreme Ct. 1962. Tax agt. Okla. Tax Commn., Oklahoma City, 1954-57, legal counsel, 1957-62; legal counsel bd. regents A&M Colls., Stillwater, Okla., 1962-75; prof. law Okla. State U., Stillwater, 1975— . Author: Oklahoma Higher Education Law, 1976; Oklahoma Public School Law, 1976; Teacher and the Law, 1977. Bd. dirs. Okla. Hist. Soc., 1972-81; dep. chief Cherokee Nation of Okla., Tahlequah, 1976, Cherokee Council, 1978— , mem. supreme ct., 1980, mem. council, 1982. Served to brig. gen. AUS (Ret.). Mem. ABA, Okla. Bar Assn., Payne County Bar Assn. Republican. Presbyterian. Home: 702 W Lakeshore Dr Stillwater OK 74075-1335 Office: Coll Edn Okla State U Rm 309 Stillwater OK 74078-0001

FRYE, HELEN JACKSON, federal judge; b. Klamath Falls, Oreg., Dec. 10, 1930; d. Earl and Elizabeth (Kirkpatrick) Jackson; m. William Frye, Sept. 7, 1952; children: Eric, Karen, Heidi; 1 adopted child, Hedy; m. Perry Holloman, July 10, 1980 (dec. Sept. 1991). BA in English with honors, U. Oreg., 1953, MA, 1960, JD, 1966. Bar: Oreg. 1966. Public sch. tchr., Oreg., 1956-63; with Riddlesberger, Pederson, Brownhill & Young, 1966-67, Husband & Johnson, Eugene, 1968-71; trial judge State of Oreg., 1971-80; U.S. dist judge Dist. Oreg. Portland, 1980-95; sr. judge U.S. Dist. Ct., 1995—. Mem. Phi Beta Kappa. Office: 1107 US Courthouse 1000 SW 3rd Ave Portland OR 97204-2930

FRYE, MARY CATHERINE, prosecutor; b. Amarillo, Tex., Feb. 9, 1950; d. John Gristy and Estelle Angelina (Ashton) F.; m. Irwin Allen Popowsky, Dec. 18, 1977; children: Matthew Frye, Rebecca Susan. AB, Oberlin Coll., 1972; JD, U. Pa., 1977. Bar: Pa. 1977. Law clk. Phila. Orphans' Ct., 1977-79; assoc. Reager, Selkowitz & Adler, Harrisburg, Pa., 1980-89; staff atty. Pa. State Edn. Assn., 1989-92; chief counsel Pa. Assn. Elem. and Secondary Sch. Prins., 1992-94; chief civil divsn./asst. U.S. atty. U.S. Atty.'s Office (mid. dist.) Pa., 1994—. Adj. prof. law Widener U., Harrisburg, 1994-94. Author: Sexual Harassment: A Guide for Administrators, 1993. Democrat. Home: 4218 Kirkwood Rd Harrisburg PA 17110-3122 Office: US Atty's Office 228 Walnut St Harrisburg PA 17101-1714

FRYE, ROLAND MUSHAT, JR. lawyer; b. Princeton, N.J., Feb. 8, 1950; s. Roland Mushat and Jean (Steiner) F.; m. Susan Marie Pettey, Jan. 23, 1988. AB cum laude, Princeton U., 1972; JD, Cornell U., 1975. Bar: Pa. 1975, D.C. 1978, U.S. Ct. Appeals (D.C. cir.) 1991, U.S. Supreme Ct. 1991. Litigation assoc. White and Williams, Phila., 1975-77; litigation atty. U.S. Dept. Energy, Washington, 1977-79, asst. solicitor, 1979-80; presiding officer Fed. Energy Regulatory Commn., 1980-83, chief presiding officer, 1983-85, supervisory atty., 1985-88, adv. atty., 1988-91; energy atty. Pepper, Hamilton & Scheetz, 1991-92; sr. atty. Office Commn. Appellate Adjudication U.S. Nuclear Regulatory Commn., 1992—. Mediator Ctr. for Community Justice, D.C. Superior Ct., 1984-86; bd. editors alumni mag. Sidwell Friends Sch., 1994—. Editor Cornell Law Rev., 1974-75; mem. editl. bd. Sidwell Friends Sch. Alumni Mag., 1994—; contbr. articles to profl. jours. Mem. schs. and ann. giving coms. Princeton U., Washington and Phila., 1978-91; arbitrator Better Bus. Bur. Greater Washington, 1983-86, Phila. Ct. Common Pleas, 1975-77; mem. Sidwell Friends Sch. Parents Assn., treas. 2001—. Capt. USAR. Recipient Outstanding Young Man Am. award U.S. Jaycees, 1979. Mem. ABA, D.C. Bar Assn. (fee arbitration panel 1983-89, com. on alt. dispute resolution 1983-87), Fed. Bar Assn., Fed. Energy Bar Assn. (adminstrv. practice com. 1991-92), Sidwell Friends Sch. Alumni Assn. (exec. com. 1985-93, 94—, v.p. 1987-89, pres. 1989-93, Newmyer award), Soc. Cin., St. Andrews Soc., Prettyman-Leventhal Am. Inn of Ct. (barrister 1989-92, master 1992-99, exec. com. 1992-99, program chmn. 1993-95, counsellor 1995-96, pres.-elect 1996-97, pres. 1997-98, nat./emeritus mem. 1999—), Cosmos Club. Presbyterian. Avocations: trout fishing, singing, travel. Home: 207 S Royal St Alexandria VA 22314-3329 Office: US Nuclear Regulatory Commn 11555 Rockville Pike Rockville MD 20852-2739 E-mail: rmf@nrc.gov

FRYMAN, VIRGIL THOMAS, JR. lawyer; b. Maysville, Ky., Apr. 9, 1940; s. Virgil Thomas and Elizabeth Louis (Marshall) F. AB cum laude, Harvard U., 1962, LLB, 1966. Bar: N.Y. 1967, U.S. Ct. Appeals (2d cir.) 1967, U.S. Dist. Ct. (so. and ea. dists.) N.Y. 1968, U.S. Supreme Ct. 1970, U.S. Ct. Appeals (6th cir.) 1988, U.S. Dist. Ct. (ea. and we. dists.) Ky. 1988. Assoc. Cravath, Swaine & Moore, N.Y.C., 1966-73; asst. U.S. atty. U.S. Dist. Ct. (so. dist.) N.Y., 1973-78; assoc. gen. counsel Price Waterhouse, 1978-86; staff counsel select com. to investigate covert arms transactions with Iran, U.S. Ho. Reps., 1987; mem. Greenebaum, Doll & McDonald PLLC, Lexington, Ky., 1988—. Contbr. to Proving Federal Crimes, 6th edit., 1976. Mem. ABA, Assn. Bar City of N.Y., Ky. Bar Assn., Fayette County Bar Assn., Harvard Club, Idle hour Country Club. Democrat. Episcopalian. Federal civil litigation, State civil litigation, Criminal. Home: Fed Hill Washington KY 41096-0173 Office: Greenebaum Doll & McDonald PLLC 333 W Vine St Ste 1400 Lexington KY 40507-1635

FUCHS, OLIVIA ANNE MORRIS, lawyer; b. Louisville, May 2, 1949; d. H.H. Morris Jr. and Betty Jean Wills Saltkill; m. Robert Edward Fuchs, Dec. 27, 1969. BA, U. Louisville, 1977; JD cum laude, 1980. Bar: Ky. 1980, Ind. 1987, U.S. Dist. Ct. (we. dist.) Ky. 1985, U.S. Tax Ct. 1987. Assoc. Brown, Todd & Heyburn, Louisville, 1981-87; mem. Conliffe, Sandmann & Sullivan PLLC, 1987-97; pvt. practice, 1997—. Notes editor Jour. Family Law, 1979-80. Vol. advocate R.A.P.E. Relief Ctr. YWCA, Louisville, 1981-87. Mem. ABA, Ind. Bar Assn., Ky. Bar Assn., Louisville Bar Assn. (probate sect. chmn. 1990, profl. responsibility com., com. chmn. 1988), U. Louisville Law Alumni Coun. (bd. dirs., pres. 1997-98), Exec. Club Louisville (pres. 1996-97), Jefferson Club, Citizens for Better Judges, Phi Alpha Delta. Democrat. Presbyterian. Family and matrimonial, Probate, Estate taxation. Office: 745 W Main St Ste 250 Louisville KY 40202-2647

FUENTES, JULIO M. federal judge; b. 1946; BA, So. Ill. U.; JD, SUNY, Buffalo. Superior ct. judge State N.J. Essex County; judge U.S. Ct. Appeals 3rd Cir., 2000—. Office: US Ct Appeals Third Cir M L King Jr Fed Bldg & Cthse 50 Walnut St ROOM 5032 Newark NJ 07102*

FUERST, STEVEN BERNARD, lawyer; b. Somerville, N.J., Sept. 18, 1945; s. Ernest S. and Else (Loewengart) F.; m. Elizabeth Yusem, Aug. 2, 1970; 1 dau., Emma. B.S. in Econs., U. Pa., 1967, J.D., 1970. Bar: N.J. 1970, U.S. Dist. Ct. N.J. 1970. Law clk. to judge N.J. Appellate Ct., Somerville, 1970-71; sr. mem. Fuerst, Yusem & Boehmer and predecessor firms, Somerville, N.J., 1973— ; sec. FCS Industries, Inc., N.J. and Ariz., 1981— ; mem. N.J. Supreme Ct. Dist. 7 ethics com. 1978-81. Bd. dirs. Somerset City Spl. Olympics Com., 1978-83. Served to maj. USAR, 1970— . Mem. Somerset County Bar Assn. (pres. 1984). Jewish. Bankruptcy, Contracts commercial, General corporate. Office: Lowenstein Sandler Kohl Fisher & Boylan PO Box 1113 Somerville NJ 08876-1113

FUGATE, WILBUR LINDSAY, lawyer; b. Pulaski, Va., Mar. 27, 1913; s. Jesse Honaker and Elizabeth Gertrude (Brown) F.; m. Barbara Louise Brown, Sept. 19, 1942; m. Cornelia Wolfolk Alfriend, Jan. 2, 1971; children— William, Richard, Barbara, Elizabeth B.A. cum. laude, Davidson Coll., 1934; LL.B., U. Va., 1937; LL.M., George Washington U., 1951, S.J.D., 1954. Bar: Va. 1937, W.Va. 1938, U.S. Supreme Ct. 1949, D.C. 1971, U.S. Dist. Ct. D.C. 1971, U.S. Ct. Appeals (D.C. cir.) 1971, U.S. Dist. Ct. (ea. dist.) Va. 1979, U.S. Ct. Appeals (5th and 8th cirs.) 1980. Assoc. Campbell & McNeer, Huntington, W.Va., 1937-38; counsel Kanawha Banking & Trust Co., Charleston, 1938-42; with antitrust div. Dept. Justice, 1947-73, asst. chief trial sect., 1951-53, chief Honolulu office, 1960-61, chief fgn. commerce sect., 1962-73; of counsel Glassie, Pewitt, Beebe & Shanks, 1974-77, Baker & Hostetler, Washington, 1977—. U.S. del. OECD Restrictive Bus. Practices Commn., 1962-73 Author: Foreign Commerce and the Antitrust Laws, 1958, 5th edit., 1997; contbr. articles to legal jours., chpts. to books; bd. advisors Va. Jour. Internat. Law, 1976—. Served to lt. USCG, 1942-45 Mem. ABA (chmn. Antitrust com. internat. law sect. 1975-76, chmn. subcoms. in patents, fgn. antitrust laws sect. antitrust law 1971-77), Fed. Bar Assn., Internat. Bar Assn., Inter-Am. Bar Assn., Cosmos Club, Univ. Club, Army-Navy Country Club. Democrat. Presbyterian. Home: 4800 Fillmore Ave Apt 1152 Alexandria VA 22311-5054 Office: 437 N Lee St Alexandria VA 22314-2301

FUJIYAMA, WALLACE SACHIO, lawyer; b. Honolulu, Aug. 8, 1925; s. George Susumu and Cornelia (Matsumoto) F.; m. Mildred Hatsue Morita, Jan. 24, 1959; children— Rodney Michio, Susan Misao, Keith Susumu. B.A., U. Hawaii, 1950; J.D., U. Cin., 1953. Bar: Hawaii 1954. Dep. atty. gen. State of Hawaii, Honolulu, 1954-56, examiner employment relations bd., 1956-59; ptnr. Chuck & Fujiyama, 1959-74; pres. Fujiyama, Duffy & Fujiyama, Honolulu, 1974— ; dir. 1st Hawaiian Bank; chmn. adv. bd. Duty Free Shoppers Ltd., 1982— , lectr. William S. Richard Sch. Law, Honolulu, 1981— . Mem. Hawaii Statehood Commn., Honolulu, 1957-59; regent U. Hawaii, 1974-82; bd. dirs. Honolulu Symphony, 1983— , Hawaii Imin Centennial Corp., 1983— ; mem. Palama Settlement Exec. Campaign Com., 1981— , Stadium Authority, 1982— . Served to pvt. U.S. Army, 1944-46. Mem. Hawaii Bar Assn. (bd. bar examiners 1962-82, pres. 1973, jud. appointments com. 1975), ABA mem. ho. of dels. 1973, active com. mem.), Hawaii Trial Lawyers Assn. (pres. 1971-79), Assn. Trial Lawyers Am., Calif. Trial Lawyers Assn., Fedn. Ins. Counsel, Def. Research Inst., Am. Judicature Soc., Trial Attys. Am., Am. Bd. Trial Advocates (pres. Hawaii chpt. 1980—), Am. Inn of Ct. (bencher 1982—), Hastings Ctr. Trial and Appellate Advocacy (bd. dirs. 1977—), Order of Coif, Phi Alpha Delta. Clubs: Honolulu Internat. Country (dir., gen. counsel), Waialae Country, Plaza (bd. dirs. 1985—). Banking, Federal civil litigation, State civil litigation. Home: 1803 Laukahi St Honolulu HI 96821-1333 Office: Fujiyama Duffy & Fujiyama 1001 Bishop St 2700 Pauahi Tower Honolulu HI 96813

FUKUMOTO, LESLIE SATSUKI, lawyer; b. L.A., Mar. 10, 1955; parents: Robert Fukumoto and Florence Teruko Kodama Kuroda. BA, U. Hawaii, 1977; JD, William S. Richard Sch. Law, 1980. Bar: Hawaii 1980, U.S. Dist. Ct. Hawaii 1980, U.S. Ct. Appeals (9th cir.) 1981. Dep. pub. defender State of Hawaii, Honolulu, 1980-81; assoc. Pyun, Kim & Okimoto, 1981-83; ptnr. Pyun, Okimoto & Fukumoto, 1983-84; sole practice, 1984-85; ptnr. Fukumoto & Wong, 1985-93, Tanaka & Fukumoto, Honolulu, 1993-94; prin. Fukumoto Law Corp., 1994—. Bd. dirs. Ichiryo Enterprises, Inc., Honolulu. Assoc. editor U. Hawaii Law Rev., 1979-80. Mem. ATLA, Honolulu Club. Federal civil litigation, State civil litigation, Personal injury. Office: 841 Bishop St Ste 1711 Honolulu HI 96813-3924 E-mail: fukulaw@mail.com

FULLAM, JOHN P. federal judge; b. Gardenville, Pa., Dec. 10, 1921; s. Thomas L. and Mary Nolan F.; m. Alice Hilliar Freiheit, Apr. 15, 1950; children: Nancy, Sally, Thomas, Jeffrey. B.S., Villanova U., 1942; J.D., Harvard U., 1948. Atty., Bristol, Pa., 1948-60; judge Pa. Ct. Common Pleas, 7th Jud. Dist., 1960-66, U.S. Dist. Ct. (ea. dist.) Pa., Phila., 1966—, chief judge, 1986-90; now sr. judge. Lectr. in law U. Pa. Law Sch., Phila., Temple U. Law Sch., Phila.; mem. adv. com. Codes of Conduct of Jud. Conf. U.S., mem. adminstrn. magistrates sys., mem. com. to rev. jud. coun. disciplinary and disability orders. Democratic candidate for U.S. Congress, 1954, 56 Mem. Am. Law Inst., Pa. Bar Assn., Bucks County Bar Assn., Phila. Bar Assn. Office: 15614 US Courthouse Ind Mall W 601 Market St Philadelphia PA 19106-1713

FULLENWEIDER, DONN CHARLES, lawyer; b. Milw., Jan. 25, 1935; s. Russell Charles and Anne Mae (Murphy) F.; m. Wendy Lattimer; 1 child, Keith Rabon. B.S., U. Houston, 1957, J.D., 1958. Bar: Tex. bar 1958; Cert. in family law and civil trials Tex. Bd. Legal Specialization. Assoc. Fred Parks, Houston, 1958-65; partner Haynes & Fullenweider, 1965-89; pvt. practice, 1989-93; ptnr. Fullenweider and Wardell L.L.P., 1993-97, Fullenweider & Assocs., 1997—. Adj. assoc. prof. law U. Houston Bates Coll. Law, 1972-74 Mem. 43d Joint Civilian Orientation Conf., 1973; mem. Tex. Bd. Legal Specialization, 1977-98. Recipient Emison award Tex. Acad. Family Specialists, 1993. Fellow Am. Bar Found., Houston Bar Found., Tex. Bar Found. (dir. 1973-76), Am. Acad. Matrimonial Lawyers (pres. Tex. chpt. 1979-81, bd. dirs. 1981-84, treas. 1985-88, pres.-elect 1988-89, pres. 1990-91); mem. ABA, Am. Bd. Trial Advocacy (advocate), Houston Bar Assn. (treas. 1961-62, 2d v.p. 1962-63, dir. 1971, 73, 1st v.p. 1970-73, Outstanding Svc. award 1974), Am. Coll. Family Trial Lawyers (diplomate 1994—), State Bar Tex. (dir. 1973-76, chmn. bd. 1975-76, exec. com. 1976-77, chmn. litigation sect. 1979-81), Am. Trial Lawyers Assn., Houston Trial Lawyers Assn. (v.p. 1971), Def. Orientation Conf. Assn., Houston C. of C., River Oaks Country Club, Sigma Chi, Phi Delta Phi. State civil litigation, Family and matrimonial. Home: 5502 Fieldwood Dr Houston TX 77056-2719 Office: 4265 San Felipe St Ste 1400 Houston TX 77027-2999

FULLER, CHARLES ROBERT SAUNDERS, lawyer; b. Middlesbrough, North Yorkshire, England, Jan. 7, 1967; s. Robert Saunders and Brenda F. LLB with honors, Birmingham U., Eng., 1988; Law Soc. Finals, Guildford Law Sch., Eng., 1989. Assoc. Simmons & Simmons, London, 1989-93, 95-99; ptnr., 1999—; assoc. Nagashima & Ohno, Tokyo, 1995. Mem. Law Soc. Eng. and Wales. Communications, General corporate, Mergers and acquisitions. Office: Simmons & Simmons City Pt 1 Ropemaker St EC24 2S5 London England E-mail: charles.fuller@simmons-simmons.com

FULLER, DAVID OTIS, JR. lawyer; b. Grand Rapids, Mich., May 28, 1939; s. David Otis and Virginia Chapin (Emery) F.; m. Isabelle Patrice Gigout, July 5, 1968; children: Thomas Andrew, Christian Scott, Pierre Emery, Margaret Isabelle. BA, Wheaton Coll., 1961; JD, Harvard U., 1964; postgrad., George Washington U., 1963, U. Paris, 1966. Bar: Mich., 1964, N.Y., 1967, U.S. Supreme Ct., 1968. Law clk. U.S. Ho. of Reps. Judiciary Com., 1963; assoc. Amberg, Law & Fallon, Grand Rapids, 1964-65; asst. dist. atty. N.Y. County, 1966-72, law sec. to justice, 1972-73; corp. atty. Pan Am. World Airways, Inc., 1973-74; dep. gen. counsel Reader's Digest Assn., Inc., 1974-84; pvt. practice N.Y.C., 1984-87; ptnr. Baker, Nelson & Williams, N.Y.C., 1987-94, Bosworth, Gray & Fuller, Bronxville, N.Y., 1994—; justice Tuckahoe Village, 1986—. Lectr. Am. Bar Assn., Practicing Law Inst., Bronx C.C. Editor: Harvard Jour. on Legislation, 1962-64; contbr. articles to profl. jours. Warden Episc. Ch., 1991-97. Mem. ABA, Internat. Bar Assn., N.Y. State Bar Assn. (chmn. privacy com. 1982-84), Assn. Bar City N.Y. (comms. law com. 1984-87), Am. Arbitration Assn. (arbitrator 1983-96), N.Y. State Magistrates Assn. (dir. 1998—), Westchester County Bar Assn., Westchester County Magistrates Assn. (pres. 1993-94), Harvard Club (N.Y.C.). Republican. Avocations: fishing, skiing, coins, racquet sports, French. General civil litigation, General practice, Intellectual property. Office: Bosworth Gray & Fuller 116 Kraft Ave Bronxville NY 10708-3810 E-mail: dofjr@aol.com

FULLER, DIANA CLARE, lawyer; b. Omaha, Jan. 26, 1953; d. William Thomas and Dorothy Louise (Gallen) F.; m. James E. O'Connor, 1984; 1 child, Elizabeth Rose. BA, U. Nebr., Omaha, 1974; JD, Creighton U., 1977. Bar: Nebr. 1977, U.S. Dist. Ct. Nebr. 1977. Law clk. to presiding justice Nebr. 4th Jud. Dist., Omaha, 1978-79; atty. United Omaha subs. Mut. Omaha, 1979-83; assoc. corp. counsel Mut. of Omaha, 1983-85; asst. v.p. Actuarial United of Omaha subs. Mut. of Omaha, 1985—. Explorers leader Boy Scouts Am., 1978-84; mem. membership com. bd. dirs. Campfire, Inc., Omaha, 1982-83; trustee Cen. Presby. Ch., Omaha, 1984-87; mem. Leadership Omaha Program, 1986. Recipient award Boy Scouts Am.,

1984, Merit award Boy Scouts Am., 1986; named one of 10 Outstanding Young Omahans, 1985. Mem. Omaha Fin. Planners (pres. 1982-83), Omaha Bar Assn. (pub. service com. 1983—), Nebr. Bar Assn., Urban Housing Found. (bd. dirs.), Rotary. Democrat. Insurance, Legislative. Office: Mut Omaha Law Div Mutual Of Omaha Plz Omaha NE 68175-0001

FULLER, DIANA LYNN, lawyer; b. Morgantown, W.Va., Nov. 16, 1952; d. William Fleming and Amelia Marie (Lattanzi) F.; m. Robert Deeb Batey, July 21, 1979. B.S., W.Va. U., 1972, J.D., 1977. Bar: W.Va. 1977, U.S. Dist. Ct. (so. dist.) W.Va. 1977, Fla. 1978, U.S. Dist. Ct. (no., mid. and so. dists.) Fla., U.S. Ct. Appeals (5th and 11th cirs.). Law clk., ct. crier to chief judge U.S. Dist. Ct. (mid. dist.) Fla., Tampa, 1977-79, arbitrator arbitration program; ptnr. Fowler, White, Gillen, Boggs, Villareal & Banker, P.A., Tampa, 1979-85; ptnr. Smith & Fuller, P.A., Tampa, 1985—; lectr. in area of constrn. law. Contbr. articles to profl. jours. Mem. ABA (del. gen. assembly 1984, litigation sect., construction litigation com.), Forum on the Construction Industry, Am. Judicature Soc., Fed. Bar Assn., Hillsborough County Bar Assn., W.Va. Trial Lawyers Assn., Greater Tampa C. of C., Nat. Coun. of W.Va. U. Coll. of Law, Phi Alpha Delta. Federal civil litigation, Construction. Home: 2418 W Palm Dr Tampa FL 33629-7312 Office: 101 E Kennedy Blvd Ste 1800 Tampa FL 33602-5148

FULLER, G. M. lawyer; b. Anadarko, Okla., Aug. 6, 1920; s. G.M. and Alma (Tabor) F.; m. Alta Duncan, June 18, 1948; 1 dau., Teresa Ann. AB, Okla. U., 1941, LLB, 1946. Bar: Okla. 1942, U.S. Tax Ct. 1957, U.S. Supreme Ct. 1961. Pvt. practice law, Oklahoma City, 1946-64; ptnr. Fuller, Tubb & Pomeroy, Oklahoma City, 1964-74, pres., 1974-97, ptnr. Fuller, Tubb, Pomeroy, Kirschner, Bickford & Stokes, 1997—. State rep. Okla. Legislature, 1952-60; state chmn. YMCA Youth and Govt. Com., Oklahoma City, 1960-90; commr. Nat. Conf. Commrs. Uniform State Laws, 1961-67. Maj. USAF, 1942-45. Recipient Jour. Record award, 1991. Fellow Am. Bar Found. (life); mem. ABA, Oklahoma County Bar Assn. (pres. 1959-60), Okla. Bar Assn., Okla. Bar Found., Am. Judicature Soc., Order of Coif, Oklahoma City Golf and Country Club, Beacon Club. Democrat. Methodist. General corporate, Probate, Real property. Home: 6429 Grandmark Dr Oklahoma City OK 73116-6534 Office: Fuller Tubb Pomeroy et al 3300 Bank One Tower 100 N Broadway Ave Oklahoma City OK 73102-8606

FULLER, ROBERT L(EANDER), lawyer; b. N.Y.C., Sept. 8, 1943; s. Robert L. and Elsie V. Fuller; m. Barbara Braverman, Dec. 5, 1973. BS cum laude, SUNY, Stony Brook, 1971; MBA, Columbia U., 1972; JD, Cath. U., Washington, 1977; LLM in Taxation, Georgetown U., 1981. Bar: Md. 1977, D.C. 1978; CPA, N.Y., D.C. Acct. Ernst & Ernst, N.Y.C., 1972-74; contr. Warner-Jenkinson East Inc., 1974-75, Atomic Indsl. Forum, Inc., N.Y.C., Washington, 1975-76; tax analyst So. Ry. Co., 1976-78; asst. tax counsel CACI, Inc., Arlington, Va., 1978-84; tax counsel, mgr. VSE Corp., Alexandria, 1984-87; exec. dir. taxes Ciba Corning Diagnistics Corp., Medfield, Mass., 1988-96; sr. mgr. KPMG Pear Marwick, LLP, Boston, 1997-98; dir. taxes Instron Corp., Canton, Mass., 1998-2000; tax prin. Spector Abbott & Co., Inc., Wellesley, 2000—. With USN, 1961-67. Mem. ABA (tax sect.), AICPA, Mayflower Descs., SAR, Sigma Pi Sigma. Private international, Corporate taxation, State and local taxation. Home: 151 Grove St Wellesley MA 02482-7001 Office: 36 Washington St Wellesley MA 02481 E-mail: rfuller@spectorabbott.com

FULLER, SAMUEL ASHBY, lawyer, mining company executive; b. Indpls., Sept. 2, 1924; s. John L.H. and Mary (Ashby) F.; m. Betty Winn Hamilton, June 10, 1948; children— Mary Cheryl Fuller Hargrove, Karen E. Fuller Wolfe, Deborah R. BS in Gen. Engring, U. Cin., 1946, JD, 1947; cert. fin. planner, Coll. for Fin. Planning, 1989. Bar: Ohio 1948, Ind. 1951, Fla. 1984; cert. fin. planner, 1989. Cleve. claims rep. Mfrs. and Mchts. Indemnity Co., 1947-48; claims supr. Indemnity Ins. Co. N.Am., 1948-50; with firm Stewart, Irwin, Gilliom, Fuller & Meyer (formerly Murray, Mannon, Fairchild & Stewart), Indpls., 1950-85, Lewis Kappes Fuller & Eads (name changed to Lewis & Kappes), Indpls., 1985-89, of counsel, 1990—; pres., dir. Irsugo Consol. Mines, Ltd., 1953-80. Dir. Ind. Pub. Health Found., Inc., 1972-84; staff instr. Purdue U. Life Ins. and Mktg. Inst., 1954-61; instr. Am. Coll. Life Underwriters, Indpls., 1964-74; mem. Ind. State Bd. Law Examiners, 1984-96, treas. 1987-88. Bd. dirs. Southwest Social Centre, Inc., 1965-70; pres., dir. Westminster Village North, Inc., 1981-89. Fellow Indpls. Bar Found.; mem. Ind. State Bar Assn. (bd. mgrs. 1986-88), 7th Cir. Bar Assn., Fla. Bar, Sun City Ctr. Golf and Racquet Club, Lincoln Hills Golf Club, Caloosa Golf and Country Club, Masons, Beta Theta Pi. Republican. Roman Catholic. Home: 306 Thornhill Pl Sun City Center FL 33573-5842

FULLERTON, ROBERT VICTOR, lawyer; b. Lakewood, Ohio, Mar. 30, 1918; s. Victor G. and Gertrude H. (Horsley) F.; m. Frances Riebel Aug. 23, 1941 (dec. Mar. 1989); children: Susan Anne, Thomas George; m. Margaret Paver Van Voorhis, Feb., 1991. BS in Bus., Miami U., Oxford, Ohio, 1939; LL.B., JD, Case Western Res. U., 1941. Bar: Ohio 1941, Calif. 1945, U.S. Dist. Ct. (ctrl. dist.) Calif. 1945, U.S. Dist. Ct. (so. dist.) Calif. 1974, U.S. Ct. Appeals (9th cir.) 1974, U.S. Tax Ct. 1952, U.S. Supreme Ct. 1974. Spl. agt. FBI, 1941-46; dep. dist. atty. San Bernardino County (Calif.), 1946; asst. dist. atty., 1946-47; individual practice law San Bernardino, 1947—. Chmn. San Bernardino County U.S. Savs. Bond Com. Dept. Treasury, 1963— Pres. United Fund, San Bernardino, 1961-62; trustee Found. for Calif. State U., San Bernardino, 1981—, v.p., 1986—; bd. dirs. Inland Action, 1974-90; trustee Inland Area Symphony Assn., 1983—, v.p. endowments, 1986; bd. dirs. Estate Planning Coun. San Bernadino County, 1984-92, pres., 1990-91; chmn. planning divsn. United Cmty. Svcs., San Bernardino, 1966-69; mem. adv. bd. Auto. Club So. Calif., 1969-80. Recipient Citizens of Yr. award San Bernardion Realtors, 1967. Mem. ABA, State Bar Calif. (asst. sec. San Bernardino County 1953-56, conf. coord. com. on fed. rules 1954-57), Am. Judicature Soc., Air Force Assn. (pres. local chpt. 1969-70), San Bernardino C. of C. (pres. 1968-69), Kiwanis (pres. local club 1959-60), Arrowhead Country. Republican. Home: 3255 Valencia Ave San Bernardino CA 92404-2418 Office: 215 N D St San Bernardino CA 92401-1733 E-mail: rfullerton@inlandbusinesslaw.com

FULSHER, ALLAN ARTHUR, lawyer; b. Portland, Oreg., July 5, 1952; s. Rémy Walter and Barbara Lee (French) F.; m. Karen Louise Schmid, Dec. 28, 1974 (dec. Sept. 1990); children: Brian Rémy, Louise Katherine, Elizabeth Alane. BA in Biology, U. Oreg., 1974, BA in Econs., 1976; JD, U. of Pacific, 1979. Bar: Oreg. 1979, Calif. 1980, U.S. Dist. Ct. Oreg. 1980, U.S. Dist. Ct. (ea. dist.) Calif. 1981, U.S. Ct. Appeals (9th cir.) 1982, U.S. Dist. Ct. (no. dist.) Calif. 1985, U.S. Dist. Ct. (so. dist.) Calif. 1986. Assoc. Law Offices of Jacques B. Nichols PC, Portland, 1979-82, Ragen, Roberts, O'Scannlain, Robertson & Neill, Portland, 1982-83; shareholder Bauer, Hermann, Fountain & Rhoades PC, 1983-87, v.p., 1984-87; shareholder, v.p. Fulsher and Weatherhead PC, 1987-88, pres., 1988—; gen. counsel Peregrine Holdings, Ltd., Beaverton, Oreg., 1993-97, Peregrine Capital, Inc., Beaverton, 1993-2000; mgr. Stamford Bridge, LLC, 1995—; gen. counsel Redfire, Inc., 2000—. Pres., mgr. ProSoccer, L.L.C., Tigard, Oreg., 1998-2001; gen. counsel World Indoor Soccer League, L.L.C., Dallas, 1998-2000. Mem. Audi Quattro Club U.S.A. Republican. Roman Catholic. Avocations: basketball, automobile racing and restoration, coaching youth and adult sports. Communications, Finance, Mergers and acquisitions. Home: 16399 SE Sager Rd Portland OR 97236-5509 Office: Redfire Inc 9725 SW Beaverton Hillsdale Hw Beaverton OR 97005-3305

FULTZ, ROBERT EDWARD, lawyer; b. Columbus, Ohio, May 24, 1941; s. Clair Ervin and Isabelle (Eichelberger) F.; m. Judith Ann McClannan, June 15, 1963; children: Cynthia, Jennifer, Stephen. BA cum laude, Ohio State U., 1963; JD with distinction, U. Mich., 1965. Ohio 1966, U.S. Supreme Ct. 1970. Assoc. Porter, Wright, Morris & Arthur, Columbus, 1966-70, ptnr., 1971—. Past trustee Columbus Symphony Orch. and Ballet; past trustee, sec. United Cerebral Palsy of Columbus; past trustee, treas. Goodwill Industries; past trustee, pres. Cen. Community House; former advisor, bd. dirs. United Negro Coll. Fund; trustee Columbus Assn. for Performing Arts, Columbus Law Libr. Assn. Mem. Columbus Bar Assn., Phi Beta Kappa, Delta Upsilon (treas.). Banking, Contracts commercial, Real property. Home: 4630 Burbank Dr Columbus OH 43220-2806

FUNDERBURK, RAYMOND, judge; b. Phila., Mar. 2, 1944; s. Walter and Inez (Prince) F.; m. Alfreida Livingston. AA, Olive-Harvey Coll., 1972; BA, U. Ill., 1974; MPA, Roosevelt U., 1975; JD, U. Ill., 1978. Bar: Ill. 1979, U.S. Dist. Ct. (no. dist.) Ill. 1979, U.S. Ct. Appeals (7th and fed. cirs.) 1983, U.S. Supreme Ct. 1983. Staff atty. Cook County Legal Assistance, Harvey, Ill., 1978-80, mng. atty., 1980-82; assoc. O. Kenneth Thomas Ltd., 1982-83, Jones, Ware & Grenard, Chgo., 1983-88, Earl L. Neal and Assocs., Chgo., 1988-93; judge Cir. Ct. of Cook County, 1993—. Bd. dirs. Cook County Legal Assistance Found., Oak Park, Ill., chmn. 1985-87; active legal adv. bd. Thornton Community Coll., South Holland, Ill., 1982—, Aunt Martha's Service, Park Forest, Ill., 1981-83. Chmn. Zoning Bd. of Appeals, Park Forest, 1988-99, Housing Bd. of Appeals, Park Forest, 1988-99, Equal Employment Opportunity Bd., Park Forest, 1988-99, Housing Rev. Bd., Park Forest, 1988-99; bd. dirs. Park Forest Pub. Library, 1982. Served with U.S. Army, 1965-67. Recipient Cert. of Appreciation Aunt Martha's Youth Svc., 1980, Thornton C.C., 1985, Wendell Phillips H.S., 1985, South Suburban YMCA, 1986, 1987, City Ptnr. award U. Ill. Chgo., 1995; named Disting. Grad., U. Ill. Coll. of Law, 1998-99, Olive-Harvey Jr. Coll., 2001. Mem. ABA, Chgo. Bar Assn., Cook County Bar Assn., Ill. Jud. Coun., Ill. Judges Assn., Phi Alpha Delta, Alpha Phi Alpha. Democrat. Avocations: running, chess, tennis. Office: Cir Ct of Cook County Ill Rm 2600 Richard J Daley Ctr Dearborn & Randolph Sts Chicago IL 60602

FUNK, DAVID ALBERT, retired law educator; b. Wooster, Ohio, Apr. 22, 1927; s. Daniel Coyle and Elizabeth Mary (Reese) F.; children— Beverly Joan, Susan Elizabeth, John Ross, Carolyn Louise; m. Sandra Nadine Henselmeier, Oct. 2, 1976 Student, U. Mo., 1945-46, Harvard Coll., 1946; BA in Econs., Coll. of Wooster, 1949; MA, Ohio State U., 1968; JD, Case Western Res. U., 1951, LLM, 1972, Columbia U., 1973. Bar: Ohio 1951, U.S. Dist. Ct. (no. dist.) Ohio 1962, U.S. Tax Ct. 1963, U.S. Ct. Appeals (6th cir.) 1970, U.S. Supreme Ct. 1971. Ptnr. Funk, Funk & Eberhart, Wooster, Ohio, 1951-72; assoc. prof. law Ind. U. Sch. Law, Indpls., 1973-76, prof., 1976-97, prof. emeritus, 1997—. Vis. lectr. Coll. of Wooster, 1962-63; dir. Juridical Sci. Inst., Indpls., 1982—. Author: Oriental Jurisprudence, 1974, Group Dynamic Law, 1982; (with others) Rechtsgeschichte und Rechtssoziologie, 1985, Group Dynamic Law: Exposition and Practice, 1988; contbr. articles to profl. jours. Chmn. bd. trustees Wayne County Law Library Assn., 1956-71; mem. Permanent Jud. Commn., Synod of Ohio, United Presbyn. Ch. in the U.S., 1968. Served to seaman 1st class USNR, 1945-46 Harlan Fiske Stone fellow Columbia U., 1973; recipient Am. Jurisprudence award in Comparative Law, Case Western Res. U., 1970 Mem. Assn. Am. Law Schs. (sec. comparative law sect. 1977-79, chmn. law and religion sect. 1977-81, sec.-treas. law and social sci. sect. 1983-86), Am. Soc. for Legal History, Pi Sigma Alpha. Republican Home: 6208 N Delaware St Indianapolis IN 46220-1824

FUNK, WILLIAM F. lawyer, educator; b. Boston, Nov. 29, 1945; s. Ward L. and Mary Roberts (Fergusson) F.; m. Renate Dieckmann, June 5, 1971; children: Andrew Christopher, Jonas Peter, Rebecca Matthea. BA, Harvard U., 1967; JD, Columbia U., 1973. Bar: N.Y. 1974, D.C. 1979, U.S. Supreme Ct. 1983. Law clk. to Hon. James Oakes U.S. Ct. Appeals 2d Cir., Brattleboro, Vt., 1973-74; atty. advisor Office Legal Counsel Dept. Justice, Washington, 1974-77; prin. staff Intelligence Com. U.S. Ho. of Reps., 1977-78; asst. gen. counsel U.S. Dept. Energy, 1978-83; assoc. prof. Lewis and Clark Coll. Law Sch., Portland, Oreg., 1983-86, prof., 1986—. Cons. U.S. Dept. Energy, Washington, 1983-84, U.S. Adminstr. Conf., Washington, 1985-86. 1st lt. U.S. Army, 1967-70. Mem. ABA (coun. mem.). Home: 22 Grouse Terr Lake Oswego OR 97035 Office: Lewis and Clark Law Sch 10015 SW Terwilliger Blvd Portland OR 97219-7768 E-mail: funk@lclark.edu

FUOCO, PHILIP STEPHEN, lawyer; b. Riverside, N.J., Oct. 28, 1946; s. Francis and Mary Helen Fuoco; m. Carol Freeman, June 7, 1969; 1 child. BA in Philosophy, U. Notre Dame, 1968; JD, Villanova (Pa.) U., 1971. Bar: N.J. 1972, U.S. Dist. Ct. N.J. 1972, Pa. 1973, U.S. Dist. Ct. (ea. dist.) Pa. 1975, U.S. Ct. Appeals (3d cir.) 1977, U.S. Supreme Ct. 1980; cert. criminal trial atty. N.J. Supreme Ct. Trial atty. civil rights div. U.S. Dept. Justice, Washington, 1971-75; asst. U.S. atty. U.S. Dist. Ct. (ea. dist.) Pa., Phila., 1975; pvt. practice N.J., 1975—. Adj. prof. law Rutgers U., Camden, 1997-2000. Contbr. articles to profl. jours. and law revs. Bd. dirs. Steininger Ctr., 1990-92, Haddonfield Zoning Bd., 1984-88; mem. Haddonfield Environ. Commn., 1991-93; apptd. mem. com. on model jury charges-criminal N.J. Supreme Ct., 1996—, apptd. mem. dist. IV ethics com., 1997-2001; mem. steering com. First Night Haddonfield, 1999. Fellow NEH, 1978. Mem. ABA, ACLU, Nat. Assn. Dist. Attys., Nat. Assn. Criminal Def. Lawyers, Camden County Bar Assn. (trustee 1986-89), N.J. Bar Assn., Camden County Inns of Ct., Lions (Haddonfield pres. 1986-87). Civil rights, Federal civil litigation, Criminal. Office: 24 Wilkins Ave Haddonfield NJ 08033-2406

FUREY, JOHN J. lawyer; b. Coaldale, Pa., Nov. 3, 1949; s. James J. and Georgene C. (Young) F.; m. Jill A. Luscombe, Nov. 23, 1975; children: Matthew J., Andrew S. BS, Villanova U., 1971, JD, 1975, LLM, 1984. Bar: Pa. 1975, Fla. 1994; CPA, Pa. VISTA vol. Vols. in Service to Am., Rose Hill, N.C., 1971-72; staff atty. Legal Services N.E. Pa., Wilkes-Barre, 1975-77; atty. Legal Services Corp., Phila., 1977-80, dep. regional dir., 1980-81; assoc. corp. counsel Mrs. Paul's Kitchen's, 1981-82; asst. counsel, asst. sec. Campbell Soup Co., Camden, N.J., 1982-85, assoc. counsel, asst. sec., 1985-89, assoc. counsel, dep. corp. sec., 1989-90; corp. counsel, dep. corp. sec., 1990-92; corp. sec., corp. counsel Campbell Soup Co., Camden, N.J., 1992-97, corp. sec., 1997—. General corporate, Pension, profit-sharing, and employee benefits, Securities. Home: 1508 Spring Mill Ln Villanova PA 19085-2016 Office: Campbell Soup Co Campbell Pl Camden NJ 08103

FURMAN, HOWARD, mediator, arbitrator, lawyer; b. Newark, Nov. 30, 1938; s. Emanuel and Lilyan (Feldman) F.; m. Elaine Sheitleman, June 12, 1960 (div. 1982); children: Deborah Toby, Naomi N'chama, David Seth; m. 2d Janice Wheeler, Jan. 14, 1984. BA in Econs., Rutgers U., 1966; JD cum laude, Birmingham Sch. Law, 1985. Bar: Ala. 1985, U.S. Dist. Ct. (no. dist.) Ala. 1986, U.S. Dist. Ct. (so. dist.) Ala. 1996. Designer/draftsman ITT, Nutley, N.J., 1957-61; pers. mgr. Computer Products Inc., Belmar, 1962-64, Arde Engring. Co., Newark, 1964-66; econs. instr. Rutgers U., New Brunswick, N.J., 1966-74; dir. indsl. rels. Harvard Ind. Frequency Engring. Labs. Divsn., Farmingdale, 1966-74; commr. Fed. Mediation and Conciliation Svc., Birmingham, 1974-96; pvt. practice, 1985—. Instr. bus. law Jefferson State C.C., 1989-95; instr. human resources mgmt. Nova U., 1993; prof. personal property, adminstrv. law, sales and alternative dispute resolution Birmingham Sch. Law, 1993—. Pres. Ocean Twp. Police Res. (N.J.), 1968. Recipient ofcl. commendation Fed. Mediation and Conciliation Svc., 1979, 81-82, 88. Mem. ABA, Ala. Bar Assn., Birmingham Bar Assn., Soc. Profls. in Dispute Resolution, Fed. Soc. Labor Rels. Profls., Indsl. Rels. Rsch. Assn., Sigma Delta Kappa. Jewish. Home: 900 Kathryne Cir Birmingham AL 35235-1722 E-mail: hfesq@bellsouth.net

FURMAN, MARC, lawyer; b. Phila., Apr. 7, 1953; s. Mitchell Sydney and Eleanor (Rothstein) F.; m. Robin P. Fine, June 13, 1993; children: Andrea Lynn, Robert Elliot, Loren Elisha. BA cum laude, Temple U., 1974, JD, 1977, LLM in Labor Law, 1980. Bar: Pa. 1977, U.S. Dist. Ct. (ea. dist.) Pa. 1977, U.S. Ct. Appeals (3d cir.) 1985, U.S. Supreme Ct. 1987. Assoc. Rothenberg & Silverman, Elkins Park, Pa., 1979-97; ptnr. Rothenberg Silverman & Furman PC, 1997—; of counsel Cohen, Seglias, Pallas & Greenhall, P.C., 1999—. Adj. lectr. in labor practice Dickinson Sch. Law, Pa. State U., 1997—. Trustee, assoc. sec. Reform Congregation Keneseth Israel, 2000—. Mem. ABA (labor law sect.), Am. Arbitration Assn., Phila Bar Assn. (labor law com.), Montgomery Bar Assn. (labor law com.), Pa. Bar Assn. (labor law sect.), Pi Sigma Alpha. Labor. Home: 93 Kent Rd Huntingdon Valley PA 19006-6623 Office: Rothenberg Silverman & Furman PC 333 Township Line Rd Elkins Park PA 19027-2260 E-mail: laborlaw@home.com

FURNESS, PETER JOHN, lawyer; b. Providence, Jan. 30, 1956; s. Robert I. and Elsie R. (Mooradian) F.; children: Lindsey Elizabeth, Jonathan Peter. BA, U. R.I., 1979; JD, U. Pitts., 1982. Bar: Pa. 1982, U.S. Dist. Ct. (we. dist.) Pa. 1982, R.I. 1987, Mass. 1989, U.S. Dist. Ct. Mass. 1989. Atty. Mazzotta & Winters, Pitts., 1984-86, Hinckley, Allen, Snyder & Comen, Providence, 1986-91; ptnr. Nixon Peabody LLP, Boston/Providence, 1991—. Lectr. Nat. Bus. Inst., Inc., 1986—. Author: (seminar books) NBI Foreclosure in Rhode Island, 1986, NBI Basic Bankruptcy in Rhode Island, 1988, NBI Protection of Secured Interests in Bankruptcy, 1989. Bd. dirs. R.I. Chpt. for Prevention of Child Abuse. Mem. ABA, Am. Bankruptcy Inst., Fed. Bar Assn., Pa. Bar Assn., R.I. Bar Assn., Mass. Bar Assn., Comml. Law League, Phi Beta Kappa, Phi Kappa Phi. Avocations: photography, golf, vol. work with nonprofit orgns. Banking, Bankruptcy, Contracts commercial. Office: Nixon Peabody LLP 1 Citizens Plz Providence RI 02903-1344 E-mail: pfurness@nixonpeabody.com

FURNISH, DALE BECK, lawyer, educator; b. Iowa City, Iowa, Feb. 11, 1940; s. William Madison and Eula Bernice (Beck) F.; m. Roberta Rae Mahnke, Aug. 23, 1963 (div. Oct. 1975); 1 child, Katherine Elizabeth; m. Hannah Rose Arterian, May 27, 1978 (div. May 1994); children— William, Susannah, Diana, Cordelia; m. Diane Larkey, June 11, 1994. B.A., Grinnell Coll., 1962; J.D., U. Iowa, 1965; LL.M., U. Mich., 1970. Bar: Iowa, 1965; U.S. Ct. Appeals (8th cir.) 1966, Ariz. 1973, U.S. Ct. Appeals (9th cir.), Ariz. 1992; U.S. Dist. Ct. Ariz. 1976. Law clk. U.S. Ct. Appeals (8th cir.), Sioux City, Iowa, 1965-66; asst. prof. law U. Iowa, Iowa City, 1966-68; vis. prof. law Ford Found. Internat. Legal Ctr., Santiago, Chile, 1969-70; prof. law Ariz. State U., Tempe, 1970— ; ptnr. Molloy, Jones & Donahue, P.C., 1988-92; vis. prof. law U. Nacional Autonoma de Mexico, Mexico City, 1974-75; Fulbright prof. Pontificia U. Católica del Peru, 1984, 88, prof. law U. of Sonora, Mexico, 1994—; lectr. USIA, Latin Am., 1972—; chmn. Ariz. Supreme Ct. Project on Judicial Cooperation with Sonora, Mex., 1993—, Nat. Law Ctr. Inter-Am. Free Trade, 1991—. Author: Usury and the Monetary Control Act of 1980, 1981, Legal Aspects of the North American Free Trade Agreement, 1992. Bd. editors Am. Jour. Comparative Law, 1972-89, 96—, Revista Peruana del Derecho Internat., 1979— . Mem. Fgn. Relations Com., Phoenix, 1979— , mem. exec. bd. 1986-91; mem. Gov.'s Ariz.-Mex. Commn., 1981— , chmn. legal adv. com., 1988-93. Mem. Am. Assn. Law Schs. (chmn. creditor debtor sect. 1978, chmn. comparative law sect. 1979), ABA, Ariz. Bar Assn., Iowa Bar Assn., Interam. Bar Assn., Am. Bankruptcy Inst. (bd. dirs. 1984-91), Order of Coif. Republican. Office: Ariz State U Coll Law Tempe AZ 85287-7906

FUSCO, ANDREW G. lawyer; b. Punxsutawney, Pa., Jan. 11, 1948; s. Albert G. and Virginia N. (Whitesell) F.; m. Deborah K. Lucas; children: Matthew, Geoffrey, David. BS in Bus. Adminstrn. and Fin., W.Va. U., 1970, JD, 1973. Bar: W.Va. 1973, U.S. Ct. Appeals (4th cir.) 1974, U.S. Supreme Ct. 1977, U.S. Ct. Appeals (fed. cir.) 1985, U.S. Tax Ct. 1995. Pvt. practice, Morgantown, W.Va., 1973-85; prin. Fusco & Newbraugh, L.C., 1985-98, The Fusco Legal Group, L.C., Morgantown, 1998-2001; pros. atty. Monongalia County, W.Va., 1977-81; mem. Eckert Seamans Cherin & Mellott, LLC, 2001—. Instr. Coll. Bus. and Econs., Law Ctr., W.Va. U., 1975-76, mem. vis. com., 2000—; instr. W.Va. U. Sch. Journalism, 1997—; dir. Pitts. Environ. Systems Inc., 1983-86. Author: Antitrust Law (West Virginia Practice Handbook), 1991; editor, contbg. author: Twenty Feet From Glory (John R. Goodwin), 1970, Business Law (John R. Goodwin), 1972, Beyond Baker Street (Michael Harrison), 1976. Bd. dirs. W.Va. Career Colls., 1971-76; mem. profl. adv. bd. Childbirth and Parent Edn. Assn., 1975-82, Rape and Domestic Violence Info. Ctr., 1977-81; mem. W.Va. Sec. State's Tribunal on Election Reform, 1977-81; chmn. Monongalia County Drug Edn. Task Force, 1978-80; mem. bd. advisors Nat. Smokers Alliance, 1998-99; mem. vis. com. W.Va. U. Coll. Law, 2000—. Recipient Am. Jurisprudence award Bancroft-Whitney Publ. Co., 1971; named Outstanding Young Man of Morgantown, 1979. Mem. ABA (Civil RICO com., antitrust law sect.), ATLA, Monongalia County Bar Assn., Am. Judicature Soc., W.Va. Bar Assn., Baker St. Irregulars of N.Y., Sherlock Holmes Soc. London, Bootmakers of Toronto, Nat. Dist. Attys. Assn., Sons of Italy, W.Va. Law Sch. Assn., Monongalia Arts Ctr. (pres., treas., trustee). Democrat. Roman Catholic. Antitrust, General civil litigation, General corporate. Home: 332 Horseshoe Rd Morgantown WV 26508-5308 Office: Eckert Seamans Cherin & Mellott 2400 Cranberry Sq Morgantown WV 26508-9209 Fax: 304-594-1181. E-mail: agf@escm.com, agr@wvlaw.com

FUSCO, JOHN ANTHONY, lawyer; b. N.Y.C., Sept. 7, 1937; s. Michael and Rose (Marinelli) F.; m. Carol Ann Odessa, July 21, 1967; children— Michael John, Michelle Lynn. B.S., St. Peters Coll., 1959; J.D., New Eng. Sch. Law, Boston, 1963. Bar: Mass. 1963, N.Y. 1967, U.S. Supreme Ct. 1972, U.S. Dist. Ct. (ea. and so. dists.) N.Y. 1975, U.S. Ct. Appeals (2d cir.) 1975. Claims adjuster Allstate Ins. Co., N.Y.C., 1965-68; law sec. N.Y. State Supreme Ct., N.Y.C., 1969-71; ptnr. Russo, Fusco, Scano, Scamardella & Fredreck, S.I., N.Y., 1972— ; civil ct. arbitrator, 1982— . Law chmn. Richmond County Republican Com., 1971, vice chmn. 1973; mem. S.I. Heart Assn. Mem. ABA, Richmond County Bar Assn. (past dir.), N.Y. State Bar Assn. Republican. Roman Catholic. Clubs: Italian (S.I.); Holy Name Soc. Lodge: Lions. Family and matrimonial, Probate, Real property. Home: 2314 Richmond Rd Staten Island NY 10306-2562 Office: Russo Fusco Scano et al 1010 Forest Ave Staten Island NY 10310-2415

FUSCO, MARTA ANGELA, lawyer; b. Milan, Apr. 5, 1967; '. Giovanni and Elsa (Pelaia) F. Assoc. Simmons & Simmons, Rome, 1990-98, ptnr., 1998—. Intellectual property, Private international, Patent. Office: Simmons & Simmons Grippo via Barnaba Oriani 85 Rome Italy Office Fax: 06 809551. E-mail: marta.fusco@simmons_simmons.com

FUSELIER, LOUIS ALFRED, lawyer; b. New Orleans, Mar. 26, 1932; s. Robert Howe and Monica (Hanemann) F.; m. Eveline Gasquet Fenner, Dec. 27, 1956; children: Louis Alfred, Henri de la Claire, Elizabeth Fenner. B.S., La. State U., 1953; LL.B., Tulane U., 1959. Bar: La. 1959, Miss. 1964, U.S. Supreme Ct. 1965. Trial atty. NLRB, New Orleans, 1959-62; pres., ptnr. Fuselier, Hector, Robertson & Ott and successor firms, 1969-94; v.p., ptnr. Young, Williams, Henderson & Fuselier, P.A., Jackson, Miss., 1994—. Capt. USAF, 1953-56. Fellow Am. Acad. Hosp. Attys., Am. Coll. Labor and Employment Lawyers, The Am. Employment Law Coun., Am.

Law Inst.; mem. ABA (practice and procedure com. of labor law sect.), La. Bar Assn. (past chmn. labor law sect.), Miss. Bar Assn., Hinds County Bar Assn., Miss. Bar Found., Miss. Def. Lawyers, Miss. Wildlife Fedn. (pres. 1975-76), Newcomen Soc., Soc. Human Resource Mgmt. (accredited pers. diplomate), Miss. Econ. Coun. (dir. 1996-97), Miss. Mfrs. Assn., Boston Club (New Orleans), Country Club of Jackson, Univ. Club (Jackson), Rotary (Paul Harris fellow). Administrative and regulatory, Civil rights, Labor. Home: 3804 Old Canton Rd Jackson MS 39216-3521 E-mail: lfuselier@ywhf.com, lfuse1@aol.com

FUSTÉ, JOSÉ ANTONIO, federal judge; b. San Juan, Puerto Rico, Nov. 3, 1943; BBA, U. P.R., San Juan, 1965, LLB, 1968. Ptnr. Jimenez & Fuste, Hato Rey, P.R., 1968-85; judge U.S. Dist. Ct. P.R., San Juan, 1985—. Prof. U. P.R., 1972-85, 96—. Roman Catholic. Office: US Courthouse CH-133 150 Ave Carlos Chardon San Juan PR 00918-1758

FUSTER, JAIME B. supreme court justice; b. Guayama, P.R., Jan. 12, 1941; s. Jaime L. and Maria Luisa (Berlingeri) F.; m. Mary Jo Fuster, Dec. 19, 1966; children: Maria Luisa, Jaime. BA, Notre Dame U., 1962; JD, U. P.R., 1965; LLM, Columbia U., 1966; SJD, Harvard U., 1974; LLD (hon.), Temple U., 1985. Bar: P.R. Prof. law U. P.R., 1966-73, 78-80, project dir. Study on Legal Profession of P.R., Ctr. Social Research, 1970-73, dean Law Sch., 1974-78; ednl. cons. Office of Cts. Adminstrn. Govt. of P.R., 1978-80; dep. asst. atty. gen. U.S. Dept. Justice, Washington, 1980-81; pres. Cath. U. P.R., 1981-84; mem. Congress from P.R., Washington, 1984-92; resident commr. Commonwealth of P.R., 1984-92; assoc. justice P.R. Supreme Ct., 1992—. Cons., lectr. in field Author: Political and Civil Rights in Puerto Rico, 1968, The Duties of Citizens, 1973, The Lawyers of Puerto Rico: A Sociological Study, 1974, Law and Problems of Elderly People, 1978; editor-in-chief U. P.R. Law Rev., 1964-65; contbr. chpts. to books, articles to profl. jours. Named One of Outstanding Young Men of Am., U.S. Jr. C. of C., 1978. Mem. Assn. Am. Colls. (adv. bd. 1980-84), Interam. Bar Found. (bd. dirs. 1975-79). Democrat. Roman Catholic. Avocation: tennis. Office: PO Box 2392 San Juan PR 00902-2392 E-mail: jaimefb@tribunales.prstar.net

FUTRELL, JOHN MAURICE, lawyer; b. Bryan, Tex., Jan. 12, 1956; s. Maurice Chilton and Mary Dean (Feltner) F.; m. Ingrid Elizabeth Jones, May 9, 1981; children: Richard Landy Jones, Cathryn Grace. BS, Miss. State U., 1978; JD, U. Miss., 1981; LLM, Tulane U., 1982. Bar: Miss. 1981, La. 1981, U.S. Dist. Ct. (ea. dist.) La. 1982, U.S. Ct. Appeals (5th cir.) 1983, U.S. Ct. Appeals (11th cir.) 1990, U.S. Dist. Ct. (we. dist.) La. 1991, Tex. 1994. Assoc. Faris, Ellis, Cutrone & Gilmore, New Orleans, 1982-91, ptnr., 1991-93, Lee, Futrell & Perles, L.L.P., New Orleans, 1993—. Lectr. U. New Orleans Paralegal Inst., 1983, Hattiesburg (Miss.) Legal Secs. Assn. Continuing Legal Edn. Seminar, 1993; judge Tulane Moot Ct. Bd., 1983—. Editor: Miss. Law Jour., 1980. Co-founder Maurice Futrell Social Svcs. Ctr. and Michael Futrell Orphanage, Banglor, India, Global Outreach, Tupelo, Miss., 1979, 1991; vestry mem., lay eucharistic min. St. Andrew's Episcopal Ch.; v.p. state Palmer and Calhoun Neighborhood Assn., 1995-97; den leader Pack 108 New Orleans Coun. Boy Scouts Am. Mem. ABA (regional reporter Excess, Reinsurance and Surplus Lines Com. Tort and Insurance Practice Sect.), U.S. Maritime Law Assn., 5th Fed. Cir. Bar Assn., Lambda Chi Alpha, Omicron Delta Kappa. Episcopalian. Avocation: running. Admiralty, Appellate, Insurance. Office: Lee Futrell & Perles LLP 201 Saint Charles Ave Ste 2409 New Orleans LA 70170-2409

FUTTER, VICTOR, lawyer; b. N.Y.C., Jan. 22, 1919; s. Leon Nathan and Merle Caroline (Allison) F.; m. Joan Babette Feinberg, Jan. 26, 1943; children: Jeffrey Leesam, Ellen Victoria Futter Shutkin, Deborah Gail Futter Cohan. AB in Govt. and English with honors, Columbia U., 1939, JD, 1942. Bar: N.Y. 1942, U.S. Supreme Ct. 1948. Assoc. Sullivan & Cromwell, 1946-52; with Allied Corp. (now Honeywell Internat.), Morristown, N.J., 1952-84, assoc. gen. counsel, 1976-78, v.p., sec., 1978-84; dir. Allied Chem. Nuclear Products, 1977-84; gen. counsel, sec. to bd. trustees Fairleigh Dickinson U., 1984-85. Spl. prof. law Hofstra Law Sch., 1976-78, 88-89, 94—, spl. cons. to the dean, 1997—; lectr., seminar on corp. in modern soc. Columbia U. Law Sch., 1986-98. Editor: Columbia Law Rev; gen. editor Nonprofit Governance: An Executive's Guide, 1997; contbr. articles to profl. jours. Trustee, dep. mayor Village of Flower Hill, N.Y., 1974-76; mem. senate Columbia U., 1969-75; chmn. bd. Columbia Coll. Fund, 1970-72; pres. parents and friends com. Mt. Holyoke Coll., 1978-80; pres. Flower Hill Assn., 1968-70; bd. dirs. N.Y. Young Dems., 1948-52, Nat. Exec. Svc. Corps, 1997—, Soc. Columbia Grads., 1998—; co-chmn. fund drive Port Washington Cmty. Chest, 1965-66, bd. dirs., 1965-75; mem. coun. overseers C.W. Post, 1984-85; bd. dirs. Acad. Polit. Sci., 1986-94; bd. dirs. Greenwich House, 1985—, dep. chair, 1999-2000, sr. vice chair, 2000—; bd. dirs. Nat. Assn. Local Arts Agys.-Arts for Am., 1989-91, Am. Soc. Corp. Secs., 1987-90, pres. N.Y. chpt., 1983-84; chmn. Com. on Nonprofits, 1992-97; bd. dirs. Justice Resource Ctr., 1992-97; chair ad hoc Lunch Group for Nonprofits, 1993—. Maj. AUS. Recipient Alumni medal Columbia U., 1970, Disting. Svc. award Am. Soc. Corp. Secs., 1994; James Kent scholar. Fellow Am. Bar Found.; mem. ABA (coun. sr. lawyers divsn. 1989-97, chair 1995-96, chair Editl. Bd. Experience, 1989-95, liaison to ABA CEELI program 1990-99, sec. on bus. law, corp. laws com., com. on non-profit corps., com. on corp. govs., sect. on internat. law and practice 1990—, bd. govs., program and planning com. 1999—), Assn. of Bar of City of N.Y. (com. on internat. human rights 1993-96, com. on 2d century 1985-89, sr. lawyers com. 1989—, chair 1992-95, nonprofit com. 1995-96, Disting. Svc. award Individual Mentor Program 1995), Am. Law Inst. (consultative group for restatement of law governing lawyers 1987-98), Nat. Assn. Corp. Dirs. (pres. N.Y. chpt. 1988-89), Nat. Assn. Coll. Univ. Attys. (sec. on personal rels., tenure and retirement programs 1984-86), Am. Judicature Soc., N.Y. Lawyers Alliance for World Security, Columbia Coll. Alumni Assn. (pres. 1972-74, Pres.'s Cup award 1999), The Supreme Ct. Hist. Soc., Playwrights First, U.S. Lawn Tennis Assn., Am. Philatelic Soc., Univ. Club (coun. 1996-99, chair spl. events com. 1993-2000, chair club activities com. 1996-99), Manhasset Bay Yacht Club, Cold Spring Harbor Beach Club, Village Club of Sands Point (golf com. 1999-2000), Phi Beta Kappa. E-mail: vandjfut@optonline.net

FUTTERMAN, RONALD L. lawyer; b. Chgo., Mar. 5, 1943; s. Sol and Edythe (Greenberg) F.; m. Pamela Ann Hayes, June 5, 1966; children; Elizabeth, Samantha. BBA, U. Wis., Madison, 1964; JD, Northwestern U., 1967. Bar: Ill. 1967, U.S. Dist. Ct. (no. dist.) Ill. 1967, U.S. Ct. Appeals (7th cir.) 1975, U.S. Ct. Appeals (D.C. cir.) 1977, U.S. Supreme Ct. 1984. Atty. anti-trust divsn. U.S. Dept. Justice, Chgo., 1967-73; assoc. Pressman & Hartunian, 1973-78, ptnr., 1978-82, Hartunian, Futterman & Howard, Chartered, Chgo., 1982-91, Futterman & Howard, Chartered, Chgo., 1991—. Instr. law and psychology Adler Sch. Profl. Psychology, Chgo., 1999—. Active Ill. Sch. Dist. 113 Polit. Caucus, Deerfield, 1976-78, chmn. publicity, 1977-78; pres. South Park Elem. Sch. PTO, Deerfield, 1980-81. Mem. ABA, Chgo. Bar Assn., Chgo. Coun. Lawyers (v.p. 1983-84, 88—, bd. govs. 1984-88). Civil rights, Federal civil litigation, Securities. Office: Futterman & Howard Chartered 122 S Michigan Ave Ste 1850 Chicago IL 60603-6199 E-mail: fhlawi@aol.com

GAAL, JOHN, lawyer; b. Flushing, N.Y., Oct. 10, 1952; s. Stephen Alfred and Marjorie (Lappin) G.; m. Barbara Jeanne Zacher, Aug. 5, 1973; children: Bryan A., Adam C., Benjamin Z. BA cum laude, U. Notre Dame, 1974, JD magna cum laude, 1977. Bar: N.Y. 1978, U.S. Ct. Appeals (D.C. cir.) 1978, U.S. Dist. Ct. (no. dist.) N.Y. 1979, U.S. Supreme Ct. 1986. Law clk. to judge U.S. Ct. Appeals (D.C. cir.), Washington, 1977-78; assoc. Bond, Schoeneck & King, Syracuse, N.Y., 1978-85, ptnr., 1986—. Bd. dirs. Legal Svcs. of Ctrl. N.Y., Syracuse, 1981-87, 94-2000, pres. 1999-2000—; adj. prof. Sch. of Mgmt., Syracuse U., 1989-92, Coll. of Law, 2001. Editor: Senior Citizens Handbook, 1988; contbg. author: Public Sector Labor and Employment Law, 1988; co-chair editl. bd. Jour. Coll. and Univ. Law, 2000—; columnist The Bus. Jour., 1998-2000; mem. bd. advs. N.Y. Employment Law Practice Newsletter, 2001-; contbr. articles to profl. publs. Bd. dirs. Transitional Living Svcs., 2001—. Fellow Am. Bar Found.; mem. ABA (labor and employment law sect.), N.Y. State Bar Assn. (exec. com. labor and employment law sect., chair young lawyer sect. 1989-90, spl. com. on AIDS and the law 1988, spl. com. on mandatory pro bono svc. 1989, ho. of dels. 1987-89, 90-91, co-chair adhoc com. ethics 1999—). Democrat. Roman Catholic. Labor. Home: 6732 Serah Ln Jamesville NY 13078-9690 Office: Bond Schoeneck & King 1 Lincoln Ctr Fl 18 Syracuse NY 13202-1324 E-mail: jgaal@bsk.com

GAAR, NORMAN EDWARD, lawyer, former state senator; b. Kansas City, Mo., Sept. 29, 1929; s. William Edward and Lola Eugene (McKain) G.; children: Anne, James, William John; m. Marilyn A. Wiegraffe, Apr. 12, 1986. Student, Baker U., 1947-49; AB, U. Mich., 1955, JD, 1956. Bar: Mo. 1957, Kans. 1962, U.S. Supreme Ct. 1969. Assoc. Stinson, Mag, Thomson, McEvers & Fizzell, Kansas City, 1956-59; ptnr. Stinson, Mag & Fizzell, 1959-79; mng. ptnr. Gaar & Bell, Kansas City, St. Louis, Overland Park, Wichita, Kans., 1979-87; ptnr. Burke, Williams, Sorensen & Gaar, Overland Park, L.A., Camarillo, Fresno, Costa Mesa, Calif., 1987-96; shareholder McDowell, Rice, Smith & Gaar, Overland Park, 1996—. Mem. Kans. Senate, 1965-84, majority leader, 1976-80; faculty N.Y. Practising Law Inst., 1969-74; adv. dir. Panel Pubs., Inc., N.Y.C. Mcpl. judge City of Westwood, Kans., 1959-63, mayor, 1963-65. With USN, 1949-53. Decorated Air medal (2); named State of Kans. Disting. Citizen, 1962. Fellow Am. coll. Bd. Coun.; mem. ABA, Am. Radio Relay League, Nat. Assn. Bond Lawyers, Calif. Assn. Bond Lawyers (charter), Flying Midshipmen Assn., Assn. Naval Aviators, Tailhook Assn., Antique Airplane Assn., Exptl. Aircraft Assn., People to People. Republican. Episcopalian. Municipal (including bonds), Securities. Office: Ste 200 40 Executive Hills Shawnee Mission KS 66210-1891 E-mail: lgaar@unicom.net, ng@mrsg.com

GABAY, DONALD DAVID, lawyer; b. Bklyn., Apr. 25, 1935; s. Harry I. and Rachel Gabay. BBA, CCNY, 1956; LLB, Bklyn. Law Sch., 1961. Bar: N.Y. 1962. Pvt. practice law, N.Y.C., 1962-75; chief counsel N.Y. State Assembly Com. on Ins., Albany, 1975-78; 1st dep. supt. N.Y. State Ins. Dept., N.Y.C., 1978-84; ptnr. Stroock & Stroock & Lavan, LLP, 1984—. Pres. Ins. Fedn. N.Y., 1994-98, 99—, chmn. Served with U.S. Army, 1956-58. Named Ins. Man of Yr., Ind. Ins. Brokers Assn., 1973; recipient Pub. Service award Bklyn. Ins. Brokers Assn., 1977, ann. achievement award Council Ins. Brokers, 1981, Outstanding Achievement award CCNY Alumni Assn., 1981, Pub. Service award Ind. Ins. Agts. Assn., 1984, Torch of Liberty award ins. div. Anti-Defamation League, 1984. Insurance. Office: Stroock Stroock & Lavan LLP 180 Maiden Ln New York NY 10038-4925 E-mail: dgabay@stroock.com

GABBARD, DOUGLAS, II (JAMES GABBARD), judge; b. Lindsay, Okla., Mar. 27, 1952; s. James Douglas and Mona Dean (Dodd) G.; m. Connie Sue Mace, Dec. 30, 1977 (div. Feb. 1979); m. Robyn Marie Kohlhaas, June 18, 1981; children: Resa Marie, David Ryan, James Douglas III, Michael Drew. BS, Okla. U., 1974, JD, 1977; grad., Nat. Jud. Coll., 1987, U. Kans. Law Orgnl. Econs., 1997. Bar: Okla. 1978. Ptnr. Stubblefeild & Gabbard, Atoka, Okla., 1978; sole practice, 1979; asst. dist. atty. State of Okla., 1979-82, 1st asst. dist. atty. Atoka, Durant and Coalgate, 1982-85; dist. judge 25th Jud. Dist. State of Okla., Atoka and Coalgate, 1985—; presiding judge South East Adminstrn. Dist., Okla., 1992—, State Ct. Tax Review, 1992—. Presiding judge of emergency panel of State Ct. Criminal Appeals, State Ct. on Judiciary (Trial divsn.), 1997—; dir. Okla. Trial Judges Assn., 1996—; mcpl. judge City of Atoka, 1978-79 Mem. Bryan County/Durant Arbitration Com., 1984; negotiator Bryan Meml. Hosp. Bd., Durant, 1984-85. Mem. Okla. Bar Assn. (legal ethics com. 1988-90, jud. adminstrv. com. 1988-90, resolutions com., 1998—, long range planning com. 1999—, bench and bar com. 1999—), Okla. Jud. Conf., Am. Judges Assn., Masons. Democrat. Methodist. Avocations: painting, carpentry, reading, jogging. Home: 1401 S Walker Dr Atoka OK 74525-3611 Office: County Ct House Atoka OK 74525

GABEL, GEORGE DESAUSSURE, JR. lawyer; b. Jacksonville, Fla., Feb. 14, 1940; s. George DeSaussure and Juanita (Brittain) G.; m. Judith Kay Adams, July 21, 1962; children: Laura Gabel Hartman, Meredith Gabel Harris. AB, Davidson Coll., 1961; JD, U. Fla., 1964. Bar: Fla. 1964, D.C. 1972. With Toole, Taylor, Moseley, Gabel & Hair, Jacksonville, 1966-74, Gabel & Hair (formerly Wahl & Gabel), Jacksonville, 1974-98, Holland & Knight, Jacksonville, 1998—. Mem. Fla. Jud. Nominating Commn., 4th cir., 1982-86. Pres. Willing Hands, Inc., 1971-72; chmn. N.E. Fla. March of Dimes, 1974-75; mem. budget com. United Way, 1972-74, chmn. rev. com., 1976; bd. dirs. Ctrl. and So. brs. YMCA, 1973-79, Camp Immokalee, 1982-86; elder Riverside Presbyn. Ch., 1970-77, 80-86, 90-92, 97—, clk. session, 1975-76, 85-86, trustee, 1988-91; pres. Riverside Presbyn. Day Sch., 1977-79; chmn. Nat. Eagle Scout Assn., 1974-75; pres. Boy Scouts Am., North fla. Coun. 1993-96, silver Beaver award, 1978; trustee Davidson Coll., 1984-95; Norwegian Consul, 1989—; pres. Jacksonville Consular Corps, 1992-93, 96—. Capt. U.S. Army, 1964-66. Fellow Am. Coll. Trial Lawyers, Am. Bar Found.; mem. ABA (chmn. admiralty and maritime law com., 1980-81. chmn. media law and defamation torts com. 1988-89. tort and ins. practice sect.), Am. Counsel Assn. (bd. dirs. 1980-82, pres. 1992-93), Assn. Trial Lawyers Am., Maritime Law Assn. U.S. (bd. dirs. 1994-97), Assn. Average Adjusters (overseas subscriber), Fla. Bar (chmn. grievance com. 1973-75, chmn. admiralty law com. 1978-89, chmn. media and comms. law com. 1990-91), Southeastern Admiralty law Inst. (bd. govs. 1973-75), Duval County Legal Aid Assn. (bd. dirs. 1971-74, 81-84), Am. Inn of Ct. (master of bench, sec.-treas. 1990-95), Rotary of Jacksonville (bd. mem. 1982-84, 88-89, pres. 87-88), World Affair Coun. of Jacksonville (exec. com. 2001—). Democrat. Admiralty, Federal civil litigation, State civil litigation. Home: 1850 Shadowlawn St Jacksonville FL 32205-9430 Office: Holland & Knight 50 N Laura St Ste 3900 Jacksonville FL 32202-3622

GABELL, MARGARET M. lawyer; b. Phila., Jan. 26, 1968; d. Thomas J. and Marie D. Cunningham; m. Michael V. Gabell, Dec. 28, 1991. BS, Drexel U., 1990; JD, Widener U., 1997. Bar: N.C. 1997, U.S. Dist. Ct. (mid. dist.) N.C. 1997; CPCU; cert. assoc. in claims Ins. Inst. of Am. Claims rep. Aetna Ins. Co., Phila., 1990-94, Nationwide Ins. Co., Westchester, Pa., 1994-96, Kemper Ins. Co., Raleigh, N.C., 1997; assoc. Tuffle Duggins & Meschan, Greensboro, 1997—. Mem. ABA, Greensboro Bar Assn., N.C. Bar Assn. Avocation: golf. Family and matrimonial, Insurance. Home: 4019 Quartergate Dr High Point NC 27265 Office: Tuggle Duggins & Meschan 228 W Market St PO Box 2888 Greensboro NC 27402

GABERINO, JOHN ANTHONY, JR. lawyer; b. Tulsa, Aug. 6, 1941; s. John A Sr and Elizabeth (McCafferty) Gaberino; m. Marjory Ann Diamond, Aug. 21, 1965; children: Christina M, Megan E, Courntey L, John A III, Kathleen A. AB cum laude, Georgetown U., 1963, JD, 1966. Bar: Okla 1966, US Dist Ct (no & we dists) Okla, US Ct Appeals (10th cir) 1968, US Tax Ct 1968, US Supreme Ct 1994. Assoc. Huffman, Arrington & Kihle, Tulsa, 1968-75; ptnr. Arrington, Kihle, Gaberino & Dunn, 1975-87, also bd. dirs., 1987-97; sr. v.p., gen. counsel ONEOK, Inc., 1998—. Counsel, bd dirs St Francis Health Sys, Inc, Tulsa, Okla., 1989—97. Chmn Georgetown Univ Law Ctr Alumni Bd, 1990—92; bd govs Georgetown Univ , 1990—, chair, 2000—, bd dirs, 2000—; pres Georgetown Univ Club Okla; chmn Georgetown Univ AAP Okla; past chmn Christ the King Bd Educ; past pres bd trustees Monte Cassino Sch; chmn bd trustees Monte Cassino Sch Endowment Fund; bd dirs W K Warren Found, Tulsa Area United Way; chmn bd dirs Operation Aware Inc, 1991. Capt U.S. Army, 1966—68. Recipient John Carroll Medal, Georgetown Univ, 1993. Fellow: Am Bar Found (chair 2000—01); mem.: NCCJ (bd dirs Tulsa chpt, pres 1993—95), Okla Bar Asn (mem bd govs 1990—92, mem bd govs 1995, mem bd govs 1997—99, vpres 1995, pres 1998), Tulsa Bar Asn (chmn construction and bylaws comt, bd dirs 1989, chmn construction and bylaws comt, bd dirs 1991—94, secy 1988, pres 1993), Tulsa County Bar Found (bd dirs 1993—99, pres 1994), Metropolitan Tulsa CofC (bd dirs 1996—, chair 2001), Southern Hills Country Club (mem bd govs 1990—95, 1st vpres 1991—93, pres 1994), Knights Holy Sepulchre (hon soc Cath ch), Phi Beta Kappa. Republican. Roman Catholic. Avocations: golf, tennis. General corporate, Health, Public utilities. Office: ONEOK Inc 100 W 5th St Tulsa OK 74103-4240

GABOVITCH, STEVEN ALAN, lawyer, accountant; b. Newton, Mass., Feb. 7, 1953; s. William and Annette (Richman) G.; m. Rhonda Merle Kitover, Aug. 6, 1978; childre: Daniel J., Lindsey D. BS in Acctg., Boston Coll., 1975, JD, 1978; LLM in Taxation, Boston U., 1982. Bar: Mass. 1978, R.I. 1979, U.S. Dist. Ct. R.I. 1979, U.S. Tax Ct. 1980, U.S. Ct. Appeals (1st cir.) 1980, U.S. Dist. Ct. Mass. 1981, U.S. Ct. Appeals (fed. cir.) 1982, U.S. Supreme Ct. 1983; CPA, Mass. Tax specialist Peat, Marwick, Mitchell & Co., Providence, 1978-80; prin. William Gabovitch & Co., Boston, 1980-97; pvt. practice Stoughton, Mass., 1998—. Lectr. on bankruptcy taxation. Contbr. articles to profl. jours. Mem. Am. Bankruptcy Inst., Nat. Soc. Tax Profls., R.I. Bar Assn., Mass. Bar Assn., Boston Bar Assn., Beta Gamma Sigma. Bankruptcy, Estate taxation, Personal income taxation. Office: 378 Page St 3 Deerfield Corp Ctr Stoughton MA 02072 E-mail: steve@gabovitch.com

GABOVITCH, WILLIAM, lawyer, accountant; b. Boston, June 18, 1922; s. Ezra and Lena Ruth (Elkins) G.; m. Annette Richman, Sept. 19, 1925; children: Steven A., Ellis. BSBA, Boston U., 1943; JD, Boston Coll., 1949; LLM in Taxation NYU, 1950. Bar: Mass. 1949, U.S. Dist. Ct. Mass., U.S. Dist. Ct. R.I., U.S. Ct. Appeals (1st cir.), U.S. Tax Ct., U.S. Ct. Claims, U.S. Ct. Appeals (fed. cir.), U.S. Supreme Ct.; C.P.A., Mass. Sr. ptnr. William Gabovitch & Co., C.P.A.s, Boston, 1962—; lectr. in legal acctg. and taxation Boston Coll. Law Sch., 1959-70; examiner and trustee in bankruptcy, state ct. receiver. Campaign treas. Congressman Robert F. Drinan, 1970-84. Lt. (s.g.) USNR, 1943-46. Mem. ABA, Am. Inst. CPA's, Mass. Soc. CPA's, Mass. Bar Assn., Boston Bar Assn., Mensa, Masons. Home: 33 Old Nugent Farm Rd Gloucester MA 01930-3169 Office: 148 State St Boston MA 02109-2506

GABRIEL, EBERHARD JOHN, lawyer; b. Bucharest, Romania, Mar. 22, 1942; brought to U.S., 1952, naturalized, 1955; s. William and Margaret (Eberhart) Krzyzewski; m. Janice Josephine Jedrzejewski, Aug. 21, 1965; children: John, Stephanie, Christopher. BA in English, St. Joseph's Coll. of Ind., 1963; JD, Georgetown U., 1966. Bar: Md. 1966, Minn. 1993, U.S. Supreme Ct. 1972. Staff atty. Fgn. Claims Settlement Commn., Washington, 1966-68; corp. atty. GEICO and Govt. Employees Fin. Corp., Denver, 1968-87; pres., CEO MNC Am. Corp./Am. Indsl. Banks, 1987-89; v.p., asst. gen. counsel and compliance officer ITT Consumer Fin. Corp., Mpls., 1989-94; pvt. practice, 1994-95; coun. Comml. Credit Co., Balt., 1995-99; sr. v.p., gen. counsel Citibank USA, Wilmington, Del., 1995—. Fellow St. Joseph's Coll.; pres. Indsl. Bankers Assn. Colo., 1985-86, 87-89; bd. dirs., sec., treas. Indsl. Bank Savs. Guaranty Corp. Colo., 1973-83, pres., 1983-87; lectr. Am. Fin. Svcs. Assn., Advanced Mgmt. Program, 1974-81, 85, 87; mem. AFSA law com., 1978-89, bd. dirs., 1988-89. Bd. dirs. Jeffco/Lakewood (Colo.) C. of C., 1974-80, 82-86, chmn., 1984-85; mem. Jefferson County DA Adult Diversion Coun., 1985-89; mem. Jefferson Found., 1985-87; mem. adv. coun. Colo. Office Regulatory Reform, Colo. Dept. Regulatory Agys., 1984-89; trustee Lakewood Polit. Action Com., 1978-89, chmn., 1986-87, Lakewood on Parade, 1980, chmn. bd. govs., 1982; vice chmn. fin. divsn. United Way Metro Denver, 1982. Mem. ABA, Am. Corp. Counsel Assn., Md. Bar Assn., Phi Alpha Delta. Roman Catholic. Banking, Consumer commercial, General corporate. Home: 6178 Mississippi Ln New Market MD 21774-6247 E-mail: gabelex@aol.com, gabrielg@citibankusa.com

GACK, KENNETH DAVID, lawyer; b. Bucyrus, Ohio, July 28, 1951; s. William E. and Vera Ann (Welsh) G.; children: Vanessa Theodora (dec.), Colin David. BA in Anthropology, Calif. State U., Dominguez Hills, 1973; JD, Pepperdine U., 1976. Bar: Calif. 1976, U.S. Dist. Ct. (cen. dist.) Calif. 1977, U.S. Dist. Ct. (ea. dist.) Calif. 1982, U.S. Dist. Ct. (no. dist.) Calif. 1983, U.S. Ct. Appeals (9th cir.) 1977. Assoc. Law Office Robert L. Charbonneau Inc., Newport Beach, Calif., 1976-78; pvt. practice Sebastopol, 1978-80; assoc. Spridgen, Barrett et al, Santa Rosa, 1980-82; ptnr. James, Gack, Bernheim & Hicks, 1982-94; pvt. practice, 1994-96, 96—. Planning commr. City of Sebastopol, 1979-80. Mem. Am. Trial Lawyers Assn., Calif. Trial Lawyers Assn. Democrat. General civil litigation, Insurance, Personal injury. Office: JAMS/Endispute 418 B St Ste 200 Santa Rosa CA 95401-8500

GADON, STEVEN FRANKLIN, lawyer; b. Roxbury, Mass., Oct. 27, 1931; s. Sydney A. and Sarah G. (Feinstein) G.; m. Barbara Kaminsky, Sept. 5, 1954; children: Richard, Susan, Amy, Beth. BS, U. Pa., 1954; LLB, Temple U., 1959; LLM, NYU, 1964. Bar: Pa. 1963; CPA, Pa. Acct. Main, Lafrentz & Co., Phila., 1956-62; ptnr. MacCoy, Evans & Lewis, 1962-66, Meltzer & Schiffrin, Phila., 1966-76, Spector, Gadon & Rosen, Phila., 1976—. Sec., bd. dirs. Simkins Industries, Inc., New Haven. Mem. Am. Assn. Attys.-CPA's, AICPA, Pa. Inst. CPA's. Jewish. Avocations: running, opera. General corporate, Pension, profit-sharing, and employee benefits, Corporate taxation. Home: Grays Lane House 500 100 Grays Ln Haverford PA 19041-1727 Office: Spector Gadon & Rosen 1635 Market St Fl 7 Philadelphia PA 19103-2217

GADSDEN, CHRISTOPHER HENRY, lawyer, educator; b. Bryn Mawr, Pa., Aug. 7, 1946; s. Henry White and Patricia (Parker) G.; m. Eleanore R.B. Hoeffel, July 27, 1968; children: William C., Eleanore P., Patricia C. BS, Yale U., 1968, JD, 1973. Bar: Pa. 1973, U.S. Dist. Ct. (ea. dist.) Pa. 1973. Assoc. Drinker Biddle & Reath, Phila., 1973-80, ptnr., 1980-98, mng. ptnr., 1998-2001; founding ptnr. Gadsden Schneider & Woodward LLP, King of Prussia, Pa. Lectr. law U. Pa. Law Sch., Phila., 1986-89, 93. Author: Pennsylvania Estate Planning, 1996; contbg. author: Local Public Finance and the Fiscal Squeeze, 1977; co-editor: Administration of Estates, 1983. Mem. vestry St. Thomas Ch., Whitemarsh, Ft. Washington, Pa., 1980-82; trustee Abington (Pa.) Meml. Hosp., 1980—, chair bd. trustees, 1994-98; pres. bd. trustees Germantown Acad., Ft. Washington, 1987-90. With U.S. Army, 1968-70. Fellow Am. Coll. Trust and Estate Counsel; mem. Phila. Bar Assn. (probate and trust law sect., chair 1994), Phila. Cricket Club. Democrat. Avocations: squash, tennis, gardening. Estate planning, Non-profit and tax-exempt organizations, Probate. Home: 140 W Chestnut Hill Ave Philadelphia PA 19118-3702 Office: Gadsden Schneider & Woodward LLP 700 S Henderson Rd Ste 345 King Of Prussia PA 19406 E-mail: cgadsden@gsw-llp.com

GAERTNER, GARY M., SR. judge; b. St. Louis; m. Maureen Gaertner: children: Gary M., Lisa, Mark. Student, JD, St. Louis U.; grad., Nat. Jud. Coll., U. Nev., Mo. Trial Jedges Coll., Am. Acad. Jud. Edn., U. N.H., Sch. Law U. Va., Stanford U. Laaw Sch., Harvard U. Sch. Law. Bar: Mo., Ill., U.S. Dist. Ct., U.S. Ct. Appeals, U.S. Supreme Ct. After pvt. practice; served as asst. city counselor City of St. Louis, until 1964, assoc. city counsel, 1964-97, city counselor, 1967-69; judge 22d Jud. Cir. Mo.,

1969-85, including presiding judge criminal divs., juvenile judge, asst. presiding judge, and presiding judge and chief adminstrv. officer; chief judge Ct. Appeals, Ea. Dist. Mo., 1985. Past pres. Mo. Council Juvenille Ct. Judges; former chmn. juvenile subcom. Mo. Council Criminal Justice, region 5; former mem. St. Louis Commn. on Crime and Law Enforcement. Bd. dirs. Boys Town Mo.; v.p. Khoury Internat. Leagues, Policeman and Fireman's Fund of St. Louis, Shared Resource Enterprises Inc.; former dist. chmn., now dist. vice-chmn. Tomahawk dist Boy Scouts Am.; past mem. exec. bd. St. Louis Area council Boy Scouts Am. Served with USCG. Recipient awards, including Judiciary award St. Louis Grand Jury Assn., Man of Yr. award George Khoury Internat. Assn., Spl. Act. award U.S. Assn. Fed. Investigators; named an Outstanding Young St. Lousiaian, St. Louis Jaycees; diploma Jud. Ksills Am. Acad. Jud. Edn. Mem. ABA, Mo. Bar Assn., Mo. Assn. Trial Attys., Bar Assn. Met. St. Louis, Lawyers Assn. Met. St Louis. Am. Judicature Soc., Phi Delta Phi. Office: 111 N 7th St Saint Louis MO 63101-2100

GAFFNEY, MARK WILLIAM, lawyer; b. Spokane, Wash., July 3, 1951; s. William Joseph and Anne Veronica (McGovern) G.; m. Jean Elizabeth O'Leary, Oct. 8, 1988. BA, U. Notre Dame, 1973; JD, George Washington U., 1976. Bar: Wash. 1976, N.Y. 1982, D.C. 1984, Conn. 1984. Law clk. antitrust divsn. U.S. Dept. Justice, Washington, 1974-76; trial atty. N.Y.C., 1976-81; assoc. Solin & Breindel, P.C., 1982-83; ptnr. Chapman, Moran & Gaffney, Stamford, Conn., 1984-85; of counsel Kaplan & Kilsheimer, N.Y.C., 1985-93; corp. counsel Sta. WLNY-TV, Inc., Melville, N.Y., 1993-95. Recipient Spl. Achievement award U.S. Dept. Justice, 1978, 79. Mem. ABA, Assn. of Bar of City of N.Y., Conn. Bar Assn., N.Y. Athletic Club. Republican. Roman Catholic. Antitrust, Federal civil litigation, State civil litigation. Home: 1395 Roosevelt Ave Pelham NY 10803-3605 Office: 1328 Boston Post Rd Larchmont NY 10538 E-mail: mgaffney@concentric.net

GAFFNEY, RICHARD COOK, lawyer; b. Sewickley, Pa., July 14, 1931; s. John Edward and Florence Loretta (Cook) G.; m. Virginia Brady, May 15, 1954; children: Richar dCook, Charles, Kathleen, Robert, Virginia, Eileen. BS in Chem. Engring., Carnegie-Mellon U., 1953; JD, Duquesne U., 1959; exec. MBA, U. Pitts., 1982. Bar: Pa. 1960, U.S. Dist. Ct. (we. dist.) Pa. 1960. Mng. patent atty. Chevron Corp., Moraga, Calif. Mem. Patent Law Assn. Pitts. (asst. program chmn. 1981, program chmn. 1982). Computer, Patent. Mailing: 2915 Crystal Falls Dr Humble TX 77345-1303 E-mail: txgaffney@aol.com

GAGAN, JAMES EPHRIAM, lawyer; b. Pawtucket, R.I., Dec. 24, 1916; s. Walter Joseph and Eva (Audette) G.; m. Claire R. Mazerolle, 1939 (div. 1947); 1 child, Barbara Ann; m. Gertrude Durgin, July 18, 1950; children—Jamie, Brian, Patricia. J.D., U. Maine, 1952. Bar: Maine 1952, U.S. Dist. Ct. Maine 1953, U.S. Tax Ct. 1953. City solicitor, corp. counsel City of Westbrook, Maine, 1960-86; ptnr. Gagan & Desmond, Westbrook, 1976-86; of counsel Desmond & Rand, Westbrook, 1986—. Mem. Maine Gov.'s Exec. Council, 1965-66. Served with USN, 1943-45, ATO. Mem. Maine Bar Assn., Cumberland Bar Assn. (pres. 1980). Democrat. Roman Catholic. Lodge: Kiwanis (pres. Westbrook 1972). General practice, Probate. Home: 6600 Sunset Way Apt 204 Saint Petersburg Beach FL 33706-2171 Office: Desmond & Rand Westbrook ME 04092

GAGLIARDO, JOSEPH M(ICHAEL), lawyer; b. Chgo., Nov. 21, 1952; s. Joseph Anthony and Marie Vivian (Aiello) G.; m. Jennifer Ann Vozella, June 7, 1980; children: Joseph Michael Jr., Michael Anthony, John Richard. BS in Commerce, DePaul U., 1974; JD, John Marshall Law Sch., 1977. Bar: Ill. 1977, U.S. Dist. Ct. (no. dist.) Ill. 1977. Asst. corp. counsel law dept. City of Chgo., 1978-82, sr. atty. supr., 1982-83, chief asst. corp. counsel, 1983-85, dep. corp. counsel, 1985-86, first dep. corp. counsel, 1986—; ptnr. Laner, Muchin, Dombrow, Becker, Levin & Tominberg, 1988—. Editor: (annual report) Personnel and Labor Relations 1984-1985, 1985. Mem. ABA, Ill. State Bar Assn., Chgo. Bar Assn., Justinian Soc. Lawyers, Assembly Ill. State Bar Assn., Delta Mu Delta, Delta Epsilon Sigma. Office: Laner Muchin Dombrow Becker Levin Tominberg Ltd 515 N State St Ste 2800 Chicago IL 60610-4321 Fax: 312-467-9479. E-mail: jgagliardo@lmdblt.com

GAILLOT, LAURENT D, lawyer; b. Paris, France, Mar. 29, 1950; m. Katheryn Stoiano, April, 1981; 1 child: Arthur. Licence en droit, Paris Law Sch., France, 1972, D.E.S. Business and Tax Law, 1973, D.E.S. Criminal Law, 1974; LL.M., Harvard Law Sch., France, 1978. Ptnr. Gaillot, Bouchony, & Assocs., Paris, France. Treas. Harvard Law Sch. Assn. of Europe, 1986-1989. Co-author: Vers une Europe de l'Industrie, 1981, International Loan Workouts and Bankruptcies, 1989; contributor: Current Issues in Cross-Borde Insolvency and Reorganizations, 1994, Practioner's Guide to Cross-Border Insolvencies, 2000; contbr. articles to International Financial Law Review, 1986, contbr. articles to profl. jours. Alliance Francaise fellow, 1977, French Ministry of Foreign Affairs fellow, 1977. Mem. Paris Bar Assn., New York Bar, International Bar Assn. (sec. on Business Law), Harvard Law Sch. Assn. of Europe, Internat. Insolvency Inst. Contracts commercial, Private international, Mergers and acquisitions. Office: Gaillot Bouchony & Associes 4 Rue Bayard 25008 Paris France Fax: 0142895160. E-mail: gba@bayard-advocats.com

GAINER, RONALD LEE, lawyer; b. Lansing, Mich., Aug. 7, 1934; s. Asher Leroy and Gladys Irene (Harvey) G.; m. Alice Louise Sherwood, June 15, 1957; children— Gregory Sherwood, Geoffrey Scott. B.A., Mich. State U., 1956; J.D., U. Mich., 1959. Bar: N.Y. 1960, D.C. 1963, U.S. Supreme Ct. 1963. Atty. appellate sect., criminal div. Dept. Justice, Washington, 1963-69, dep. chief legis. and spl. projects, 1969-73, chief legis. and spl. projects, 1973-75, dir. Office of Policy and Planning, 1975-77; dep. asst. atty. gen. Office for Improvements in Adminstrn. of Justice, 1977-81, Office of Legal Policy, 1981-83, dep. assoc. atty. gen., 1984-85, assoc. dep. atty. gen., 1985-86, dep. assoc. atty. gen., 1986-89; ptnr. Gainer, Rient and Hotis (and successor Gainer and Rient), Washington, 1990—. U.S. expert mem. UN Com. on Crime Prevention and Control, 1979-92; designated mem. U.S. Sentencing Commn., 1985-88; bd. dirs., mem. adv. com. Internat. Centre Criminal Law Reform and Criminal Justice Policy, 1992—. Editorial bd.: Criminal Law Forum, 1989—. Served to capt. U.S. Ar, 1960-63. Recipient Disting. Service award U.S. Atty. Gen., 1973. Mem. Am. Law Inst., Am. Soc. Internat. Law, Internat. Soc. for Reform of Criminal Law (bd. dirs., mem. mgmt. com., 1989—), Internat. Assn. Penal Law, D.C. Bar Assn. Criminal, Public international. Home: 3000 N Monroe St Arlington VA 22207-5371 Office: Gainer and Rient 818 Eighteenth ST NW Ste 410 Washington DC 20006 E-mail: gr@us.net

GAINES, CHERIE ADELAIDE, lawyer; b. Queens, N.Y., May 17, 1935; d. Charles Oscar and Billie (Robinson) Gaines; m. Eugene Merwyn Swann, Apr. 15, 1960 (div. Oct. 1978); children— Liana Jane, Eugene Michael, Elliott Mark. B.A., Barnard Coll., 1956; J.D., U. Pa., 1960. Bar: Calif. 1963, N.Y. 1981. Assoc. prof. law Golden Gate U., San Francisco, 1970-71; city atty. Berkeley, Calif., 1971; asst. prof. law U. San Francisco Law Sch., 1971-73; asst. regional atty. EEOC, San Francisco, 1973-79, regional atty., N.Y.C., 1979-81; dep. gen. counsel N.Y.C. Housing Authority, 1981— ; asst. to asst. regional adminstr. HUD, San Francisco, 1970; practice law, San Francisco, 1963-65; chief atty. Alameda County Legal Aid Soc., Oakland, Calif., 1965-70. Founder, Phoenix Elem. Sch., Berkeley, 1969. Bd. dirs., treas., chmn. mgmt. com. Consumers Coop., Berkeley, 1972-76; bd. dirs. ACLU Berkeley-Albany chpt., Berkeley, 1968, San Francisco Regional Council, Berkeley, 1978. Recipient Commendation plaque Alameda Affirmative Action Com., 1971, Alameda County Human Relations Commn., 1973, Assn. Real Property Brokers, 1975. Mem. Calif. State Bar (commn. of profl. competence 1973-76, med. malpractice commn. 1972), N.Y. State Bar, Charles Houston Law Club (v.p. 1979). Episcopalian.

GAINES, HOWARD CLARKE, retired lawyer; b. Washington, Sept. 6, 1909; s. Howard Wright and Ruth Adeline-Clarke Thomas Gaines; m. Audrey Allen, July 18, 1936; children: Clarke Allen, Margaret Anne. J.D., Cath. U. Am., 1936. Bar: D.C. bar 1936, U.S. Supreme Ct. bar 1946, U.S. Ct. Claims bar 1947, Calif. bar 1948. Individual practice law, Washington, 1938-43, 46-47, Santa Barbara, Calif., 1948-51; asso. firm Price, Postel & Parma, 1951-54, partner, 1954-88; of counsel, 1989-94; ret., 1994. Chmn. Santa Barbara Bench and Bar Com., 1972-74 Chmn. Santa Barbara Police and Fire Commn., 1948-52; mem. adv. bd. Santa Barbara Com. on Alcoholism, 1956-67; bd. dirs. Santa Barbara Humane Soc., 1958-69, 85-92; bd. trustees Santa Barbara Botanic Garden, 1960— , v.p., 1967-69; bd. trustees Cancer Found. Santa Barbara, 1960-77; dir. Santa Barbara Mental Health Assn., 1957-59, v.p., 1959; pres. Santa Barbara Found., 1976-79, trustee, 1979— . Fellow Am. Bar Found.; mem. ABA, Bar Assn. D.C., State Bar Calif. (gov. 1969-72, v.p. 1971-72, tres. 1971-72), Santa Barbara County Bar Assn. (pres. 1957-58), Am. Judicature Soc., Santa Barbara Club. Republican. Episcopalian. Home: 1306 Las Alturas Rd Santa Barbara CA 93103-1600

GAINES, IRVING DAVID, lawyer; b. Milw., Oct. 14, 1923; s. Harry and Anna (Finkelman) Ginsburg; m. Ruth Rudolph, May 22, 1947 (dec. Apr. 5, 1979); children: Jeffrey S., Howard R., Mindy S. Gaines Pearce; m. Lois Shier, Nov. 25, 1979. BA, U. Wis., Madison, 1943; JD, 1947; postgrad., U. Pa., 1943-44. Bar: Wis. 1947, Fla. 1971, U.S. Dist. Ct. (ea. dist.) Wis. 1947, U.S. Dist. Ct. (we. dist.) Wis. 1970, U.S. Dist. Ct. (so. dist.) Fla. 1972, U.S. Dist. Ct. (mid. dist.) Fla. 1976, U.S. Ct. Appeals (7th cir.) 1954, U.S. Ct. Appeals (11th cir.) 1981, U.S. Supreme Ct. 1954. Sole practice, Milw., 1947-72; ptnr. Gaines & Saichek, S.C. (and predecessor firm), 1972-78; sr. ptnr. Gaines Law Offices, S.C., 1979—. Arbitrator N.Y. Stock Exchange, Nat. Assn. Securities Dealers, Am. Stock Exchange, Am. Arbitration Assn. 1988—. Mem. bd. visitor U. Wis. Law Sch., 1987-96, Cir. Ct. Commn., 1997—. Served with AUS, 1943-46. Mem. ABA (various coms.), Fla. Bar Assn. (past mem. exec. com., cts. com., econs. law com., past chn. unauthorized practice of law com., past chmn. negligence sect., lectr. programs, seminars), State Bar Assn. Wis. (bd. govs. 1982-85, comms. com. 1981-85, 88-91), 7th Fed. Cir. Bar Assn., Wis. Acad. Trial Lawyers (pres. 1958-59, 70-71). State civil litigation, Insurance, Real property. Home: 7821 N Mohawk Rd Milwaukee WI 53217-3123 Office: 312 E Wisconsin Ave Ste 208 Milwaukee WI 53202-4305

GAINES, WEAVER HENDERSON, lawyer; b. Ft. Meade, S.D., Aug. 31, 1943; s. Weaver Henderson and Bertha Louise (Harris) G. AB in Philosophy, Dartmouth Coll., 1965; LLB, U. Va., 1968. Bar: N.Y. 1969, Pa. 1979, U.S. Dist. Ct. (so. dist.) N.Y. 1973, U.S. Dist. Ct. (ea. dist.) N.Y. 1975, U.S. Ct. Appeals (2d cir.) 1975. Assoc. Dewey, Ballantine, Bushby, Palmer & Wood, N.Y.C., 1970-79; sr. staff counsel INA Corp., Phila., 1979; asst. gen. counsel, sec. Thyssen-Bornemisza Inc., N.Y.C., 1979-82, v.p. strategic projects, 1982-85; v.p., dep. gen. counsel Mut. of N.Y., 1985-86, sr. v.p., gen. counsel, 1986-90, exec. v.p., gen. counsel, 1990-92; pres. Unified Mgmt. Corp., 1989-90; chmn., CEO Ixion Biotechnology, Inc., Alachua, Fla., 1993—. Bd. dirs. First ING Life Ins. Co. of N.Y., Unified Fin. Svcs., Inc., Voyetra Turtle Beach, Inc., Ixion Biotechnology, Inc., BIO Fla. Inc., Enterprise North Fla., Inc., Dance Alive!. Bd. dirs. N.Y. Lawyers for Nixon, 1972; sr. advisor Bush/Quayle '92. Capt. U.S. Army, 1968-70, Vietnam. Decorated Bronze Star. Mem. ABA, Assn. of Bar of City of N.Y., Am. Corp. Counsel Assn., N.Y. Athletic Club, Haile Plantation Golf and Country Club. Republican. Episcopalian. Antitrust, General corporate, Insurance. Office: Ixion Biotechnology Inc 13709 Progress Blvd Ste 207 Alachua FL 32615-9495 E-mail: wgaines@ixion.biotech.com

GAITHER, JOHN FRANCIS, JR. lawyer; b. Evansville, Ind., Mar. 31, 1949; s. John F. and Marjilee G.; m. Christine Luby, Nov. 26, 1971; children: John F. III, Maria Theresa. BA in Acctg., U. Notre Dame, 1971, JD, 1974. Bar: Ind. 1974, Ill. 1975, U.S. Ct. Appeals (7th cir.) 1975, U.S. Ct. Mil. Appeals 1977. CPA, Ind. Law clk. to Hon. Wilbur F. Pell, Jr. Ct. of Appeals 7th Cir., Chgo., 1974-76; assoc. atty. Bell, Boyd & Lloyd, 1979-82; sr. atty. Baxter Healthcare Corp., Deerfield, Ill., 1982-83, asst. sec., sr. atty., 1983-84, asst. sec., asst. gen. counsel, 1984-85; sec., assoc. gen. counsel Baxter Internat. Inc., 1985-87, sec., dep. gen. counsel, 1987-91; v.p. law/devel. Baxter Diagnostics Inc., 1991-92; v.p. law, strategic planning Baxter Global Businesses, 1992-93; dep. gen. counsel, v.p. strategic planning Baxter Internat. Inc., 1993-94, corp. v.p., corp. devel., 1994-2001; v.p., sec., gen. counsel Global Healthcare Exch., LLC, Westminster, Colo., 2001—. Editor-in-chief Notre Dame Lawyer, 1973-74; contbr. articles to profl. jours. Lt. comdr. USNR, 1976-79. Mem. ABA, Ill. Bar Assn., Ind. Bar Assn., Chgo. Bar Assn., Ind. Assn. CPAs. Avocations: sailing, skiing. General corporate, Mergers and acquisitions, Securities. Office: Global Healthcare Exch LLC 1425 Lake Cook Rd Deerfield IL 60015 also: 10385 Westmoor Dr Westminster CO 80021 E-mail: jgaither@ghx.com

GAJARSA, ARTHUR J. circuit court judge; b. Norcia, Italy, Mar. 1, 1941; came to U.S., 1949; m. Melanie E. BSEE, Rensselaer Polytech Inst, 1962; JD, Georgetown U., 1967; MA in Econs., Cath. U., 1968. Bar: U.S. Patent Office 1963, D.C. 1968, U.S. Dist. Ct. D.C. 1968, U.S. Ct. Appeals (D.C. cir.) 1968, Conn. 1969, U.S. Supreme Ct. 1971, U.S. Superior Ct. 1972, U.S. Ct. Appeals (D.C. cir.) 1972, U.S. Ct. Appeals (9th cir.) 1974, U.S. Dist. Ct. (no. dist.) N.Y. 1980. Patent examiner U.S. Patent Office, Dept. Commerce, 1962-63; patent adviser USAF, Dept. Def., 1963-64, Cushman, Darby & Cushman, 1964-67; law clk. to Judge Joseph C. McGarraghy U.S. Dist. Ct. (D.C.), Washington, 1967-68; atty. office gen. counsel Aetna Life and Casualty Co., 1968-69; spl. counsel, asst. to commr. Indian affairs Bur. Indian Affairs, Dept. Interior, 1969-71; assoc. Duncan and Brown, 1971-72; ptnr. Gajarsa, Liss & Sterenbuch, 1972-78, Gajarsa, Liss & Conroy, 1978-80, Wender, Murase & White, 1980-86; ptnr., officer Joseph, Gajarsa, McDermott & Reiner, P.C., 1987-97; judge U.S. Ct. Appeals Fed. Cir., Washington, 1997—. Bd. dirs. Eyring Corp., 1992-96. Contbr. articles to profl. jours. Trustee Rensselaer Neuman Found., 1973—, Found. Improving Understanding of Arts, 1982-96, Outward Bound, 1987-96, Rensselaer Polytech Inst., 1994—; gov. John Carroll Soc., 1992-99; regent Georgetown U., 1995-2000, bd. dirs., 2000—. Recipient Sun and Balance medal Rensselaer Polytech Inst., 1990, Rensselaer Key Alumni award, 1992, Albert Demers Fox award, 1999, Gigi Pieri award Camp Hale Assn., 1992, 125th Anniversary medal Georgetown U. Law Ctr., 1995, Order of Commendatore, Republic Italy, 1995, Alumni Fellows award Rensselaer Alumni Assn., 1996, Paul Dean award Georgetown U., 1999. Mem. Fed. Cir. Bar Assn., Nat. Italian Am. Found. (bd. dirs. 1976-99, gen. counsel 1976-89, pres. 1989-92, vice-chair 1993-96), D.C. Bar Assn., Am. Judicature Assn. Office: US Ct Appeals Fed Cir 717 Madison Pl NW Washington DC 20439-0002

GALANIS, JOHN WILLIAM, lawyer; b. Milw., May 9, 1937; s. William and Angeline (Koroniou) G.; m. Patricia Caro, Nov. 29, 1969; children: Lia Galanis Economou, William, Charles, John. BBA cum laude, U. Wis., 1959; JD, U. Mich., 1963; postgrad. (Ford Found. grantee), London Sch. Econs., 1964. Bar: Wis. 1965; CPA, Wis. Assoc. firm Whyte & Hirschboeck S.C., Milw., 1964-68; sr. v.p., gen. counsel, sec. MGIC Investment Corp. and Mortgage Guaranty Ins. Corp., 1968-88; ptnr. Galanis, Pollack & Jacobs, S.C., 1988—. Assoc. editor: Mich. Law Rev, 1962-63. Bd. visitors Law Sch. U. Mich., Sch. Bus. U. Wis.; past chmn. Milw. Found.; bd. dirs., past pres. Milw. Boys' and Girls' Club; bd. dirs. Milw. Heart Found.; pres. Family Svc. Milw.; trustee Milw. Pub. Mus. Friends. Recipient Disting. Svc. award Internat. Inst., Hope Chest award Nat. MS Soc., Disting. Alumni award Milw. Boys' Club, Disting. Svc. award Milw. Civic Alliance Club, 1989. Mem. ABA, Wis. Bar Assn., Milw. Bar Assn., Am. Hellenic Ednl. Progessive Assn., Order of Coif, Milw. Athletic Club, Blue Mound Golf and Country Club. Greek Orthodox. General corporate, Finance, Insurance. Home: 1200 Woodlawn Cir Elm Grove WI 53122-1639 Office: MGIC Pl Milwaukee WI 53201

GALATZ, HENRY FRANCIS, lawyer; b. N.Y.C., Feb. 5, 1947; s. Julius D. and Dorothy (Kirschen) G.; m. Colleen Prager, Aug. 19, 1973; children: Benjamin Chase, Brandon Kyle. BA, U. Ariz., 1970, MEd, MA with honors, 1973; JD, U. the Pacific, 1979. Bar: Ill. 1981, U.S. Ct. Appeals (7th cir.) 1981, U.S. Dist. Ct. (no. dist.) Ill. 1982, U.S. Dist. Ct. (ea. dist.) Mich. 1982, U.S. Ct. Appeals (6th cir.) 1982, U.S. Dist. Ct. (ea. dist.) Mo. 1985, U.S. Supreme Ct. 1985, U.S. Dist. Ct. Mont. 1986, U.S. Dist. Ct. (we. dist.) Tex. 1987, U.S. Dist. Ct. (no. dist.) Calif. 1992, U.S. Dist. Ct. Nebr. 1993, U.S. Dist. Ct. (no. dist.) Ohio 1997, U.S. Ct. Appeals (11th cir.) 2000; cert. coach and referee U.S. Soccer Fedn. Cons. labor rels. Phoenix Closures, Chgo., 1974-75, Galatz Elec. Corp., Las Vegas, Nev., 1975-80; labor counsel W.W. Grainger, Inc., Skokie, Ill., 1980—; pvt. practice Olympia Fields, 1981—. Hearing officer Ill. State Bd. Edn., Chgo., 1982—: atty. Chgo. Legal Svcs. Found., 1983—, Ill. Inst. for Dispute Resolution, 1992—; mem. com. Employment Law Inst., Northwestern U., Evanston, Ill.; adv. coun. H-F Bus. Ptnr., 2000; mem. pres. counsel McGeorge Sch. Law, 2001-. Pres., coach Homewood-Flossmoor (Ill.) Soccer Club, 1985—, Intercollegiate Varsity Athletics (soccer and lacrosse); co-chair soccer Ill. Prairie State Games, 1992; pres. P.O.P.S. Homewood-Flossmoor H.S., 1996—; mem. bd. edn., pers. chairperson Homewood-Flossmoor H.S., 1998—, mem. improvement coun., 2001-. Recipient Judge Mason Rothwell Award, 1979, Cert. of Merit Chgo. Legal Svcs. Found., 1983. Mem. ABA, ATLA, Am. Corp. Counsel Assn. (labor and employment sect.), Ill. Bar Assn., Chgo. Bar Assn., Am. Arbitrators Assn. (arbitrator), Am. Judicature Soc., Ill. Trial Lawyers Assn., North Shore (Ill.) Labor Counsel Assn., Phi Delta Phi, Alpha Epsilon Pi. Democrat. Jewish. Avocations: soccer, lacrosse. Federal civil litigation, Education and schools, Labor. Home: PO Box 374 Flossmoor IL 60422-0374 Office: W W Grainger Inc 100 Grainger Pkwy Lake Forest IL 60045-5201

GALBRAITH, ALLAN LEE, lawyer; b. Feb. 16, 1955; s. Graeme C. and Joanne (Brack) Galbraith; m. Lorena Gail Boyd, May 28, 1982. BS in Bus., U. Idaho, 1977, JD, 1980. CPA Wash.; bar: Wash. 1980. Staff acct. Boyd Olofson & Co., C.P.A.s, Yakima, Wash., 1980—82; ptnr. Carlson Drewelow Galbraith Card & McMahon P.S., Wenatchee, 1982—92, Card & Galbraith PS, Wenatchee, 1992—97, Davis, Arneil Law Firm, LLP, Wenatchee, 1997—. Instr. bus. law Wenatchee Valley C.C.; dir., pres. Chelan-Douglas County Cmty. Action Coun., Wenatchee. Mem.: ABA, Wash. Bar Assn. (com. of bar examiners 1986—94, spl. dist. counsel profl. conduct sect. 1995—), Wash. Soc. C.P.A.s, Wenatchee Area C. of C., Ctrl. Wash. Hosp. Found., Rotary (Wenatchee). Contracts commercial, Probate, Real property.

GALBRAITH, COLIN ROBERT, lawyer; b. Melbourne, Victoria, Australia, Mar. 23, 1948; s. Colin Alfred and Dorothy Elizabeth Galbraith; m. Rhonda May Russell; children: Emma, Jamie, Robert, Stephen. LLB with honors, U. Melbourne, Australia, 1971, LLM, 1976. Bar: Victoria, New South Wales, Queensland, High Court Australia. Ptnr. Arthur Robinson & Hedderwicks, Melbourne, 1978—. Bd. dires. Commonwealth Bank Australia, Onesteel Ltd.; sec. Coun. Legal Edn., 1984—. Chmn. BHP Cmty. Trust, Melbourne, 1988—. General corporate, Mergers and acquisitions. Office: Arthur Robinson & Heddewics 530 Collins St Melbourne 3000 VIC Australia

GALBRAITH, ROBERT LYELL, JR. lawyer; b. Rochester, N.Y., May 18, 1960; s. Robert Lyell and Barbara Williams Galbraith; m. Debra Lee Dastyck, June 25, 1985; children: Taylor, Mary. BA, Hamilton Coll., 1982; JD, U. Buffalo, 1986. Bar: N.Y. 1987, U.S. Dist. Ct. (we. dist.) N.Y. 1987. Assoc. Osborn, Reed, VandeVate & Burke, Rochester, N.Y., 1986-88, Saperston & Day, P.C., Rochester, 1989-92, ptnr., 1992-98, chmn. R.E. practice group, 1994-98; ptnr. Davidson, Fink, Cook, Kelly & Galbraith LLP., 1998-2001, mng. ptnr., 2001—. Adv. bd. mem. Ticor/Chgo. Title Ins. Co., Rochester, 1991—; assoc. mem. N.Y. State Econ. Devel. Coun., Rochester, 1991-2000; adv. bd. dirs. Rochester Binding and Finishing, Rochester, 1993-96. Bd. mem., pres. Mental Health Assn., Rochester, 1991-2000; coach Brighton (N.Y.) Town Soccer, 1996—. Named Vol. of the Yr., Mental Health Assn., Rochester, 1995, one of 40 under 40 Rochester Bus. Jour., 1996. Mem. N.Y. State Bar Assn. (exec. com. for young lawyers sect., liason to real property exec. 1992-97), Monroe County Bar Assn. (real estate sect., pres. 1992-2000). Avocations: skiing, reading, soccer, football. Banking, Contracts commercial, Real property. Office: Davidson Fink Cook Kelly & Galbraith LLP 28 E Main St Ste 900 Rochester NY 14614-1916 E-mail: rgalbraith@dfckg.com

GALBUT, MARTIN RICHARD, lawyer; b. Miami Beach, Fla., June 27, 1946; s. Paul A. and Ethel (Kolnick) G.; m. Cynthia Ann Slaughter, June 4, 1972; children: Keith Richard, Lindsay Anne. BS in Speech, Northwestern U., 1968, JD cum laude, 1971. Bar: Ariz. 1972, U.S. Dist. Ct. Ariz. 1972, U.S. Ct. Appeals (9th cir.) 1972. Assoc. Brown, Vlassis & Bain PA, Phoenix, 1971-75; founder, ptnr. McLoone, Theobald & Galbut PC, 1975-86; of counsel Furth, Fahrner, Bluemle & Mason, 1986-89; pres., founder Galbut, Hunter & Conant, PC, Phoenix, 1989—. Presenter guest Law Talk cable TV; former judge pro tem Maricopa County Superior Ct.; lectr. comml. real estate litigation, arbitration, mediation and intellectual property law Lorman Bus. Seminars. Contbr. articles to profl. jours. Chmn., law rev. Ariz. State Air Pollution Control Hearing Bd., 1984-89; mem. Govs. Task Force on Urban Air Quality, 1986, City Phoenix Environ. Quality Commn., 1987-88; bd. dirs. Men's Art Council Phoenix Art Mus.; bd. dirs., founder Ariz. Asthma Found. Clarion de Witt Hardy scholar, Kosmerl scholar; Russel Sage grantee. Mem. ABA, Ariz. State Bar Assn. (lectr., securities law and litigation com. and sect.), Am. Arbitration Assn. (arbitrator), Nat. Assn. Securities Dealers (arbitrator, trainer and lectr.). Democrat. Jewish. Avocations: painting, collecting antiques and fine art, international travel, golf. Antitrust, General civil litigation, Securities. Office: Galbut Hunter & Conant PC 2425 E Camelback Rd Ste 1020 Phoenix AZ 85016-4216

GALE, FOURNIER JOSEPH, III, lawyer; b. Mobile, Ala., Aug. 3, 1944; s. Fournier J. Jr. and Clara (Beckham) G.; m. Louise Smith, Aug. 7, 1965; children: Carolyn, Jeanette. BA, U. Ala., 1966, JD, 1969; postgrad., Oxford U., summer 1968. Bar: Ala. 1969. From assoc. to ptnr. Cabaniss, Johnston, Gardner, Dumas & O'Neal, Birmingham, Ala., 1969-84; ptnr. Maynard, Cooper & Gale, PC, 1984—. Bd. dirs. McWane, Inc., Birmingham; gen. counsel, bd. dirs. Bus. Coun. Ala., Birmingham, 1977—; mem. Ala. Permanent Study Commn. on Judiciary, 1977-83; mem. Jefferson County Jud. Nominating Commn., 1993—; chmn. Ala. Commn. on Higher Edn., 1998—; spl. counsel to Gov. Don Siegelman, 1999—. Mem. Leadership Birmingham, 1986-87; pres. U. Ala. Law Sch. Found., 1987—. Mem. ABA (standing com. on environ. law, standing com. on fed. judiciary), Birmingham Bar Assn. (pres. 1989), Ala. Young Lawyers Assn. (pres. 1976-77), Am. Judicature Soc. (bd. dirs. 1980-85), Jud. Conf. Ala., Am. Bar Found., Kiwanis. Roman Catholic. Administrative and regulatory, General civil litigation, Environmental. Home: 2937 Southwood Rd Birmingham AL 35223-1232 Office: Maynard Cooper & Gale PC 2400 Amsouth Harbert Plz Birmingham AL 35203-2600

GALE, JOHN QUENTIN, lawyer; b. Hartford, Conn., June 16, 1951; s. John J. and Doris A. (Boissoneault) G.; m. Tracy Thompson, Sept. 23, 1978; children: Adrienne Hope, Calabria T., Aurelia D., Nathaniel J. BSEE, U. Pa., 1973; JD, U. Conn., 1977. Bar: Conn. 1977, U.S. Dist. Ct. 1978. Engr. GE, Valley Force, Pa., 1972-74; staff atty., corp. counsel City of Hartford, 1977; ptnr. Calvocoressi & Gale, Hartford, 1977—2000, Gale & Kowalyshyn, LLC, 2000—. Bd. dirs. New Horizons, Inc., pres., 1998-2000; bd. dirs. Farmington, Conn. Vision Svcs., Inc., Hartford, Immanuel House, Inc. Founder, editor Professional Discipline Digest, 1991. Trustee Bloomfield (Conn.) United Meth. Ch., 1991—; treas. Hartford Dem. Town Com., 1994—. Recipient Salutation for Improving City award Hartford Courant Columnist-Tom Condon, 1993. Mem. Conn. Bar Assn. (mem. profl. discipline com. 1987—, chmn. profl. discipline com. 1994—), Greater Hartford C. of C. (govt. affairs com. 1988-93), Lions Club (dir. 1980—), Phi Delta Phi (hon.). Avocations: recreational sports, bluegrass mandolin, 1941 Oldsmobile, golf, 1897 house. General practice, Personal injury, Probate. Office: Gale & Kowalyshyn LLC 363 Main St Fl 4 Hartford CT 06106-1845

GALKIN, LEE D. lawyer; b. Providence, Nov. 28, 1972; s. James Paul and Gail Marcia G.; m. Erika B. Silverman, Oct. 24, 1998. BA, Emory U., 1994; JD cum laude, Suffolk U., 1997. Bar: N.Y., Mass. Atty. SFX Sports Group, Inc., N.Y.C., 1997—. Mem. N.Y.C. Bar Assn. (com. mem.). Sports. Office: SFX 220 W 42nd St 12th Fl New York NY 10036

GALL, JOHN R. lawyer; b. San Francisco, 1945; BA, Miami U., 1967; JD, Ohio State U., 1970. Bar: Ohio 1971. Ptnr. Squire, Sanders & Dempsey, Columbus, Ohio. Construction, Patent, Trademark and copyright. Office: Squire Sanders & Dempsey 1300 Huntington Ctr 41 S High St Columbus OH 43215-6101 E-mail: jgall@ssd.com

GALLAGHER, BRIAN JOHN, lawyer; b. Bklyn., Oct. 24, 1939; s. John Joseph and Margaret R. Gallagher; m. Mary Loughney, Sept. 10, 1966; children: Amanda, Ian. BS, Fairfield U., 1961; JD, Fordham U., 1964; postgrad., NYU Law Sch., 1969-70. Bar: N.Y. 1965, U.S. Dist. Ct. (so. dist.) N.Y. 1967, U.S. Ct. Appeals (2d cir.) 1971, U.S. Dist. Ct. (ea. dist.) N.Y. 1974, U.S. Ct. Appeals (11th cir.) 1982, U.S. Ct. Appeals (D.C. cir.) 1986. Asst. U.S. Atty. So. Dist. N.Y., 1967-71; ptnr. Kronish, Lieb, Weiner & Hellman, LLP, N.Y.C., 1976—. Mayor Village of Pelham Manor, N.Y., 1995-97, trustee, 1989-95. Mem. ABA, N.Y. State Bar Assn., Assn. Bar City N.Y., Fed. Bar Coun., Larchmont (N.Y.) Yacht Club, Williams Club, N.Y. Athletic Club. Antitrust, Federal civil litigation, Private international. Office: 1114 Avenue Of The Americas New York NY 10036-7703 E-mail: bgallagher@klwhHp.com

GALLAGHER, BYRON PATRICK, JR. lawyer; b. Bay City, Mich., Feb. 29, 1964; s. Byron Patrick and Ethel Jean (Gebowski) G.; m. Michelle Francis Burdick, May 21, 1994; children: Byron Patrick III, Grace Katherine. AB, Kenyon Coll., Gambier, Ohio, 1986; JD, Washington U., St. Louis, 1989. Bar: Mich. 1989, U.S. Dist. Ct. (we. dist.) Mich. 1990, U.S. Dist. Ct. (ea. dist.) Mich. 1995. Ptnr. Gallagher Duby, PLC, Lansing, 1998—. Bd. dirs. Ingham County Social Svc. Bd., Mason, Mich., 1991-92, Ingham County Commn., Mason, 1993-97, Mich. Underground Storage Tank Fin. Assurance Authority, 1996—; Rep. cand. Mich. State Senate, 1998. Mem. Ingham County Bar Assn. (bd. dirs. 1996-99, bench bar com. 2000—), County Club of Lansing, Mich. Athletic Club. Republican. Avocations: flying, golf. General corporate, Probate, Real property. Home: 951 Walbridge Dr East Lansing MI 48823 Office: Gallagher Duby PLC 2510 Kerry St Ste 210 Lansing MI 48912-3671

GALLAGHER, EDWARD JOHN, II, lawyer; b. Detroit, Jan. 22, 1949; s. Edward John and Audrey (Robinson) G.; m. Diane Mary Powers, Sept. 18, 1976; children— Patrick Brian, Kerry Edward. Student St. Joseph's Coll., Rensellaer, Ind., 1966-68; BA, Western Mich. U., 1970; JD, Wayne State U., 1973. Bar: Mich. 1973, U.S. Dist. Ct. (ea. dist.) Mich. 1977. Assoc. Perica, Breithart & Carmody P.C., Warren, Mich., 1973-80; chief referee Macomb County Juvenile Ct., Mt. Clemens, Mich., 1980; assoc. B.M. Freid & Assocs., P.C., Saginaw, Mich., 1980-89, ptnr., 1989—; ptnr. Freid, Gallagher, Taylor & Assocs., P.C., Saginaw, 1989—. Mem. Assn. Trial Lawyers Am., Macomb Bar Assn., Saginaw Bar Assn., Inc. Soc. Irish-Am. Lawyers, Am Arbitration Assn. (panel arbitrators), Bay County Bar Assn., Mich. Trial Lawyers Assn. Democrat. Roman Catholic. State civil litigation, Insurance, Workers' compensation. Home: 28 Center Ct Bay City MI 48708-6901 Office: Freid Gallagher Taylor & Assocs PC 604 S Jefferson St Saginaw MI 48604-1416

GALLAGHER, GEORGE R. judge; Sr. judge D.C. Ct. Appeals. Office: 500 Indiana Ave NW Ste 6000 Washington DC 20001-2131

GALLAGHER, JEROME FRANCIS, JR. lawyer; b. Passaic, N.J., Sept. 16, 1958; s. Jerome F. and Iris (Torres) G.; m. Deirdre O. Stewart, Sept. 27, 1992; children: Nicholas, Colin, Caroline. BS in Man and Tech. with distinction, N.J. Inst. Tech., Newark, 1980; JD, Rutgers U., Newark, 1983. Bar: N.J. 1983, U.S. Dist. Ct. N.J. 1983, U.S. Ct. Appeals (3d cir.) 1994. Assoc. Shanley & Fisher, P.C., Morristown, N.J., 1983-84, Dunn, Pashman, Sponzilli, Swick & Finnerty, Esq., Hackensack, 1984-90; ptnr. Baron, Gallagher & Perzley, Esq., Parsippany, 1990-99, Greiner Gallagher & Cavanaugh LLC, Parsippany, 1999—. Mem. adv. coun. civil and environ. engring. dept. N.J. Inst. Tech., 1999—. Mem. adv. bd. dept. civil and environ. engring. N.J. Inst. Tech.; panelist Lorman N.J. Collections Practice Seminar, 2000; pres. St. Mary's H.S. Assn., Wharton, NJ, 1993—95, 2000—01. Mem. N.J. State Bar Assn., Bergen County Bar Assn., Comml. Law League Am. Bankruptcy, State civil litigation, Consumer commercial. Office: Greiner Gallagher & Cavanaugh LLC 2001 Route 46 Ste 202 Parsippany NJ 07054-1315 E-mail: jerrygal@greinergallagherlaw.com

GALLEGOS, LARRY DUAYNE, lawyer; b. Cheverly, Md., Mar. 23, 1951; s. Belarmino R. and Helen (Schlotthauer) G.; m. Claudia M. King, Oct. 1, 1994; 1 child, Will Adam. BS summa cum laude, U. Puget Sound, 1978; JD, Harvard U., 1981. Bar: Colo. 1981, U.S. Dist. Ct. Colo. 1981, U.S. Tax Ct. 1989. Assoc. Pendleton & Sabian, Denver, 1981-83, O'Connor & Hannan, Denver, 1983-86, ptnr., 1986-89, Rossi & Judd, P.C., Denver, 1989-92, Berliner Zisser Walter & Gallegos, P.C., Denver, 1992—. Served with U.S. Army (ARCOM), 1972-74. Mem. ABA (real property, probate and trust law sect.), Colo. Bar Assn., Colo. Trial Lawyers Assn., Denver Bar Assn., U.S. Golf Assn. Avocations: tennis, golf. General civil litigation, Contracts commercial, Finance. Office: Berliner Zisser Walter & Gallegos PC 1700 Lincoln St Ste 4700 Denver CO 80203-4547

GALLERANO, ANDREW JOHN, lawyer; b. Houston, Dec. 2, 1941; s. Andrew H. and Victoria J. (LaNasa) G.; m. Evelyn Cornelius, June 6, 1964; children: Kelly Lynn, Wendy Michelle. BA, U. Tex., Austin, 1964; JD, South Tex. Coll. Law, 1968. Bar: Tex. 1968, U.S. Supreme Ct. 1973. Asst. atty. gen., State of Tex., 1968-71; regional atty. Montgomery Ward & Co., 1971-72; v.p. Foley's, div. Federated Dept. Stores Inc., 1972-79; v.p., gen. counsel, sec. Nat. Convenience Stores Inc., Houston, 1979-89; sr. v.p., gen. counsel, sec. Nat. Convience Stores Inc., 1989-96; ptnr. Baker, Boldt & Gallerano, Dripping Springs, Tex., 1996-2000; v.p., gen. counsel K.C. Engring., Inc., Austin, 2000—. Adj. prof. South Tex. Coll. Law, 1973-75; mem. adv. coun. U. Tex. Coll. Bus., 1993-98. Pres. S. Tex. Hosp. Fin. Agy., 1979—; mem. devel. bd. U. Tex. Health Sci. Ctr., Houston, 1978-93; bd. dirs. YMCA, 1973-86, 90-92, Assn. Cmty. TV, 1974-80; chmn. bd. trustees Star of Hope Mission, 1990-96. Mem. Tex. Bar Assn. (grievance com. 1986-89), U. Tex. Ex-Students Assn., Houston Retail Mchts. Assn. (bd. dirs. 1973—, pres. 1976-78), Tax Rsch. Assn. (bd. dirs. 1975-92). General corporate. Home: 3167 Yeager Creek Rd Johnson City TX 78636-9712 Office: KC Engring Inc 1801 S Mopac Ste 150 Austin TX 78746

GALLIAN, RUSSELL JOSEPH, lawyer; b. San Mateo, Calif., Apr. 24, 1948; m. Pauline R. Davis, Sept. 29, 2000; children: Lisa, Cherie, Joseph, Russell, Yvette, Jason, Ryan, Jennifer. BS, U. San Francisco, 1969, JD with honors, 1974. Bar: Calif. 1974, Utah 1975, U.S. Ct. Appeals (10th cir.) 1975, U.S. Supreme Ct. 1990; CPA, Calif. Staff acct. Arthur Andersen & Co., CPAs, San Francisco, 1969-71; treas., contr. N.Am. Reassurance Life Svc. Co., Palo Alto, Calif., 1972-74; assoc. VanCott Bagley Cornwell & McCarthy, Salt Lake City, 1975-77; sr. ptnr. Gallian & Westfall, Wilcox & Welker, St. George, Utah, 1977—. Chmn. bd. dirs. Dixie Title Co., St. George. Chmn. Tooele (Utah) City Planning Commn., 1978; atty. City of Tooele, 1978-80, Town of Ivins, Utah, 1982-2000, Town of Springdale, Utah, 1987-90, Town of Rockville, Utah, 1987—, Town of Virgin, 1995-2000, City of Santa Clara, 2001—; commr. Washington County, 1993-96; chmn . Washington County Econ. Devel. Coun., 1993-96; bd. dirs. Dixie Ctr., 1993-96; mem. Habitat Conservation Plan Steering Com., 1993-99. Mem. ABA, Utah State Bar Assn., Tooele County Bar Assn. (pres. 1978-79), So. Utah Bar Assn. (pres. 1986-87). Republican. Mormon. Banking, Real property. Office: Gallian & Westfall Wilcox & Welker LC 59 S 100 E Saint George UT 84770-3422 E-mail: gwww@infowest.com

GALLIGAN, THOMAS C., JR. dean, law educator; AB, Stanford U., 1977; JD, U. Puget Sound (now U.Seattle), 1981; LLM, Columbia U., 1986. With Lane Powell Moss & Miller, Seattle; prof. law Paul Hebert Law Ctr. La. State U., Dale E. Bennett prof. law, 1997, exec. dir. La. Jud. Coll., 1996-98; dean, prof. law U. Tenn., Knoxville, 1998—. Spkr. on legal topics to various groups, 1987—. Co-author: Legislation and Jurisprudence on Maritime Personal Injury Law, 1997, 98, 99, 2000, Louisiana Tort Law, 1996, supplemented 1997, 2000, Personal Injury in Admiralty, 2000, Admiralty in a Nutshell, 4th edit., 2000; contbr. articles to law revs. and acad. jours. Recipient John Minor Wisdom award for acad. excellence in legal scholarship Tulane Law Rev., 1996-97. Office: 1505 W Cumberland Ave Ste 278 Knoxville TN 37996-0001 Fax: 423-974-6595. E-mail: galligan@libra.law.uth.edu

GALLIHER, KEITH EDWIN, JR. lawyer; b. Fond du Lac, Wis., July 29, 1947; s. Keith Edwin and Dolores Mae (Hazen) G.; m. Linda Lee Dessauer, May 18, 1985; children: Patrick, Christy Lyn. B.S, U. Nev. at Las Vegas, 1970; J.D., Ariz. State U., 1974. Bar: Nev. 1974, U.S. Dist. Ct. Nev. 1974, U.S. Ct. Appeals (9th cir.) 1976. Assoc. Lionel, Sawyer & Collins., Las Vegas, 1974-75; atty. Clark County Pub. Defender, Las Vegas, 1975-76; sr. ptnr. Mills, Galliher, Lukens, Gibson, Schwartzer & Shinehouse, Las Vegas, 1976-80, Galliher & Tratos, Las Vegas, 1980-83; pres., sr. ptnr. Keith E. Galliher, Jr., Chartered, Las Vegas, 1983— ; instr. hotel law U. Nev.-Las Vegas, 1980; alt. mcpl. judge City Las Vegas, 1983— . Author: Supplement to Comparison Analysis of ABA Criminal Justice Standards to Nevada Law, 1976. State del. Democratic Party, 1976; bd. govs. March of Dimes, Las Vegas, 1978. Mem. Nat. Assn. Trial Lawyers, Nev. Trial Lawyers Assn., ABA, Nev. Bar Assn., Clark County Bar Assn., State Bar Nev. (mem. fee dispute com. 1983), Comml. Law League Am., Real Estate Securities and Syndication Inst., Nat. Coll. Criminal Def. Lawyers and Pub. Defenders. Lutheran. State civil litigation, Criminal, Personal injury. Home: 8609 Titleist Cir Las Vegas NV 89117-5844 Office: 1850 E Sahara Ave Ste 100 Las Vegas NV 89104-3744

GALLO, JON JOSEPH, lawyer; b. Santa Monica, Calif., Apr. 19, 1942; s. Philip S. and Josephine (Sarazan) G.; m. Jo Ann Broome, June 13, 1964 (div. 1984); children: Valerie Ann, Donald Philip; m. Eileen Florence, July 4, 1985; 1 child, Kevin Jon. BA, Occidental Coll., 1964; JD, UCLA, 1967. Bar: Calif. 1968, U.S. Ct. Appeals (9th cir.) 1968, U.S. Tax Ct. 1969. Assoc. Greenberg, Glusker, Fields, Claman & Machtinger, L.A., 1967-75, ptnr., 1975—. Bd. dirs. USC Probate and Trust Conf., L.A., 1980—, UCLA Estate Planning Inst., chmn. 1992—. Contbr. articles to profl. jours. Fellow Am. Coll. Trust and Estate Counsel; mem. ABA (chair Generation Skipping Taxation com. 1992-95, co-chair life ins. com. 1995—), Internat. Acad. Estate and Trust Law, Assn. for Advanced Life Underwriting (assoc. mem.). Avocation: photography. Estate planning, Probate, Estate taxation. Office: Greenberg Glusker Fields Claman & Machtinger LLP Ste 2100 1900 Avenue Of The Stars Los Angeles CA 90067-4502

GALTON, SIDNEY ALAN, judge; b. Portland, Oreg., Jan. 9, 1947; s. Herbert B. and Ida Mae G.; m. Cynthia Weintraub Weber, Aug. 6, 1970 (div. Dec. 1980); children: Amy Louise, Allen Weintraub. AB in Polit Sci. with honors, Stanford U., 1969; JD, U. Calif., Berkeley, 1972. Assoc. Galton, Popick & Scott, Portland, 1972-81; adminstrv. law judge Oreg. Workers Compensation Bd., 1982-98; judge U.S. Cir. Ct., 1998—. Attys.' fee arbitrator Oreg. State Bar, 1977-78, 81, 84; chmn. disciplinary trial bd. Oreg. State Bar, 1984; judge Northwestern Regional Moot Ct. Competition, 1977. Contbr. articles to profl. jours. Chmn. adv. com. Bridlemile Elem. Local Sch., Portland, 1978-80; pres., gen. mgr. Rose City Performing Arts, 1984-86; treas. GALA Choruses, 1985-86, pres., 1986-88. Florence-Virginia K. Wilson scholar, 1969-70. Mem. Oreg. State Bar Assn., Multnomah Bar Assn., Oreg. Workers Compensation Attys. Assn. (pres. 1976-78), Order of Coif, Phi Beta Kappa. Democrat. Jewish. Office: Multnomah County Courthouse 1021 SW 4th Ave Portland OR 97201-1123 E-mail: sidney.a.galton@ojd.state.or.us

GALVIN, CHARLES O'NEILL, law educator; b. Wilmington, N.C., Sept. 29, 1919; s. George Patrick and Marie (O'Neill) G.; m. Margaret Edna Gillespie, June 29, 1946; children: Katherine Marie, George Patrick, Paul Edward, Charles O'Neill, Elizabeth Genevieve. BSc, So. Meth. U., 1940; MBA, Northwestern U., 1941, JD, 1947; SJD, Harvard U., 1961; LLD, Capital, 1990. Bar: Ill. 1947, Tex. 1948, U.S. Dist. Ct. (no. dist.) Tex. 1948, U.S. Tax Ct. 1949; CPA, Tex. Pvt. practice, Dallas, 1947-52; from asst. to assoc. prof. So. Meth. U., 1952-55, prof., 1955-82, dean Sch. Law, 1963-78; Centennial prof. law Vanderbilt U., Nashville, 1983-90, Centennial prof. emeritus, 1990—, exec. in residence, 1990-93; of counsel Haynes and Boone, LLP, Dallas, 1994—. Thayer tchg. fellow Harvard U., 1956-57; vis. prof. U. Mich., 1957, Duke U., 1979, Pepperdine U., 1980; Raymond Rice Disting. vis. prof. U. Kans., 1990; adj. prof. law U. Tex., 1995-97, So. Meth. U., 1996—; bd. dirs. State Farm Ins., Bloomington, Ill., 1980-95; trustee Am. Tax Policy Inst., 1992-97. Author: Estate Planning Manual, 1987; tax editor Oil and Gas Reporter; co-editor: Texas Will Manual, 1972—. Chmn. Dallas County Community Action, Dallas 1970-72; pres. Cath. Found., Dallas, 1963-67. Served to lt. comdr. USNR, 1942-46. Recipient Disting. Alumnus award So. Meth. U., 1984, Disting. Alumnus award Northwestern U., Chgo., 1993, John Rogers award Southwestern Legal Found., Dallas, 1997, McGill award Cath. Found., 1997. Fellow Am. Bar. Found., Tex. Bar Found.; mem. AICPA, ABA, Tex. Bar Assn., Dallas Bar Assn., Am. Law Inst. (life), Am. Judicature Soc., Tex. Soc. CPA's, Order of Coif, Am. Tax Policy Inst., U.S. Supreme Ct. Soc. (trustee), Phi Delta Theta, Beta Gamma Sigma. Roman Catholic. Home: 4240 Twin Post Rd Dallas TX 75244-6741 Office: Haynes and Boone LLP 3200 Nations Bank Plz 901 Main St Dallas TX 75202-3789 E-mail: cogalvin@swbell.net

GALVIN, ROBERT J. lawyer; b. New Haven, Dec. 10, 1938; s. Herman I. and Freda (Helfand) G.; m. Susan I. Goldstein, Oct. 15, 1960 (div.); children: David B., Peter J. AB, Union Coll., Schenectady, N.Y., 1961; JD, Suffolk U., Boston, 1967. Bar: Mass. 1967, U.S. Dist. Ct. Mass. 1967, U.S. Supreme Ct. 1988. Pvt. practice law, Boston, 1967-78; ptnr. Lippman & Galvin, 1978-84; of counsel Gage, Tucker & Vom Baur, 1984-86; ptnr. Davis, Malm & D'Agostine, 1986—. Lectr. Boston Ctr. Adult Edn., 1972-89, Northeastern U., Boston, 1977-78. Real estate columnist Boston Ledger, 1981; co-author, editor Massachusetts Condominium Law, 1988, 91, 93, 96, 97, 98; contbg. author: Crocker's Notes on Common Forms, 1995-96, 99, 2000; contbr. numerous articles to profl. jours. Bd. dirs., v.p. Rental Housing Assn. divsn. Greater Boston Real Estate Bd., 1974, Boston Ctr. Adult Edn., 1979—, chmn. fin. com. 1985-86, pres. 1987-91; bd. dirs. Thoreau Soc., Inc., 1993—, chmn. fin. com., chmn. exec. com., 1999-2000, v.p., 2001—, Walter Harding Disting. Svc. award 2001; bd. dirs. Beech Hill Found., Inc., 1989—, pres. 1989—. Fellow Mass. Bar Found. (life mem. Greater Boston 3 grantmaking adv. com. 1997, 98, 99, Mass. Hist. Soc.; housing employment small bus. assistance grantmaking adv. com. 2001); mem. Mass. Bar Assn. (coun. mem. property law sect. 1977-80, chmn. condominium com. 1979-91), Mass. Continuing Legal Edn. (real estate curriculum adv. com. 1983-87), Am. Arbitration Assn. (comml. arbitration panel), Abstract Club, Mass. Conveyancer's Assn., Cmty. Assns. Inst. (atty.'s com. New Eng. chpt.), Soc. for Censure, Reproof and Arraignment of Pub. Error. Real property. Home: 344 Pond St Jamaica Plain MA 02130-2447 Office: Davis Malm & D'Agostine PC One Boston Pl Ste # 3700 Boston MA 02108 E-mail: rgalvin@davismalm.com

GALYON, LUTHER ANDERSON, III, lawyer; b. Knoxville, Tenn., Apr. 24, 1946; s. Luther Anderson and Betty (Paxton) G.; m. Victoria Charline Hardison, Sept. 12, 1971; children: Luther Anderson, William Davis. BS, U. N.C., 1968; JD, U. Tenn., 1971. Bar: Tenn. 1972, U.S. Dist. Ct. (ea. dist.) Tenn. 1972, U.S. Ct. Appeals (6th cir.) 1972. Assoc. firm Kennerly, Montgomery, Howard & Finley, Knoxville, 1971-76; ptnr. firm Kennerly, Montgomery & Finley, Knoxville, 1976-84, Kennerly, Montgomery & Finley, P.C., 1985—, pres., 1991—. Recipient Alumni Leadership award U. Tenn. Coll. Law, 1985. Mem. Tenn. Def. Lawyers Assn. (v.p. 1982-84, sec.-treas. 1986-87, pres. elect 1987-88, pres. 1988-89), ABA (co-chmn. subcom. on role of design profls. in construction 1986-87), Internat. Assn. Def. Coun. (faculty mem. Def. Counsel Trial Acad. 1993), Knoxville Bar Assn., Tenn. Bar Assn., Def. Research Inst., Am. Arbitration Assn. (panel of arbitrators), Order of Coif. Republican. Presbyterian. General civil litigation, Contracts commercial, Construction. Office: Kennerly Montgomery & Finley PC PO Box 442 Knoxville TN 37901-0442

GAMBARO, ERNEST UMBERTO, lawyer, consultant, engineer; b. Niagara Falls, N.Y., July 6, 1938; s. Ralph and Teresa (Nigro) G.; m. Winifred Sonya Porter, June 3, 1961 (div.); m. Monica Cuellar, Sept. 30, 1994. BA in Aeronautical Engring., Purdue U., 1960, MS with honors, 1961; JD with honors, Loyola U., L.A., 1975. Bar: Calif. 1975, U.S. Tax Ct. 1976, U.S. Supreme Ct. 1979, U.S. Ct. Appeals (9th cir.). With Aerospace Corp., El Segundo, Calif., 1962-80, counsel, 1975-80; asst. gen. counsel, asst. sec. Computer Scis. Corp., 1980-88; sr. v.p., gen. counsel, sec. INFONET Svcs. Corp., 1988-2000. Cons. bus. fin. and mgmt., 1968— ; bd. dirs. STM Wireless, Govt. Systems, Inc., Networks Telephony Corp. Newspaper columnist Europe Alfresco; contbr. articles to profl. publs. Fulbright scholar Rome U., 1961-62; recipient USAF commendation for contributions to U.S. manned space program, 1969. Mem. ABA (internat., taxation sects.), L.A. Bar Assn. (exec. com. 1976—, founder chmn. sect. law and technology 1976-78, chmn. bar reorgn. com. 1981-82), Am. Arbitration Assn. L.A. Ctr. Internat. Comml. Arbitrations (found., bd. dirs.), Internat. Law Inst. (faculty), St. Thomas More Law Soc., Phi Alpha Delta, Omicron Delta Kappa (past pres.), Tau Beta Pi, Sigma Gamma Tau (past pres.), Phi Eta Sigma. Republican. E-mail: ernest. General corporate, General practice, Private international. Home: PO Box 3033 Palos Verdes Peninsula CA 90274-9033 Office: 2160 E Grand Ave El Segundo CA 90245-5024 E-mail: gambaro@infonet.com

GAMBLE, DONALD GEOFFREY BIDMEAD, lawyer; b. Apr. 11, 1945; s. Donald Edward and Gamble Elizabeth (Binheimer); m. Dorcas Hall, Feb. 14, 1976; children: Thomas, Elizabeth, Mary, Ann, Katherine, Victoria, Margaret. BA, Haverford Coll., 1967; JD, Cath. U., Washington, 1975. Bar: D.C. 1975, Del. 1976, U.S. Tax Ct. 1975. Law clk. Hon. D.S. Smith, Washington, 1973—75; assoc. Killoran & Van Brunt, Wilmington, Del., 1975—76; atty. Du Pont Co., 1976—78, sr. internat. Counsel, 1984—85, mng. counsel legal dept., 1985—94, assoc. gen counsel, 1994—96, chief internat. counsel, 1996—. Regional legal counsel Du Pont Asia Pacific, Hong Kong, 1978—82; dir. Du Pont Taiwan Ltd., Taipei, 1980—84, Du Pont Taiwan Chems. Ltd., Taipei, 1980—84, Nat. Fgn. Trade Counsel, 1990—; chmn. U.S. Industry Sector adv. com. for chems. and allied products, 1996—. Pres. Kennett Consol. Sch. Bd., 1997—; bd. dir. Cath. Ministry to the Elderly, Inc., 1985—, New Castle Civic Assn., Del., 1984. Capt. USMC, 1967—70, Vietnam. Named Knight of the Sovereign, Military Order of Malta; recipient Presdl. Commendation, Rep. of Vietnam. Mem.: Del. State Bar Assn., Internat. Bar Assn., Army-Navy Club (Washington). Republican. Roman Catholic. General corporate, Private international, Public affairs. Home: 560 Chandlers Mill Rd Avondale PA 19311-9626 Office: Du Pont Co Legal Dept D # 7052 Wilmington DE 19898-0001

GAMBOL, ROBERT ALAN, lawyer; b. Cleve., July 26, 1947; s. Frank Clarence and Anna Delores (Janitor) G.; m. Suzanne Louise McCollum, Nov. 22, 1975; children: Melissa, Katrina, Frank, Anthony. AB, Boston Coll., 1969; JD, Duke U., 1973. Bar: Ohio 1973, U.S. Dist. Ct. (no. dist.) Ohio 1974, U.S. Supreme Ct. 1975. Counsel CIC Lake County, Madison, Ohio, 1974—, Lake County 503 Corp., Madison, 1983—; magistrate Painesville (Ohio) Mcpl. Ct., 1989—. Instr. Am. Inst. Paralegal Studies, 1982-85, Lakeland C.C., 1989—, Kent State U., 1989—. Trustee Birthright Lake County, Ohio, 1979; evaluator Mentor High Sch., 1985; mem. Lake County Bd. Revision, 1999—. Mem. Ohio State Bar Assn., Lake County Bar Assn. Democrat. Roman Catholic. Home: 1813 Sandgate Rd Madison OH 44057-1846 Office: 9853 Johnnycake Ridge Rd Mentor OH 44060-6700 Fax: (440) 639-9010

GAMBONI, CIRO ANTHONY, lawyer; b. Bklyn., Aug. 16, 1940; m. Gail Pollack, Aug. 1, 1965; children: Dina, Lee. BBA cum laude, CCNY, 1963; LLB cum laude, NYU, 1965; LLM in Taxation, Georgetown U., 1969. Bar: N.Y., U.S. Dist. Ct. (so. dist.) N.Y., U.S. Tax Ct. Ptnr. Cahill, Gordon & Reindel, N.Y.C. Mem. patron com. Lincoln Ctr. Theatre, N.Y.C. Served to capt. JAGC, U.S. Amry, 1966-69. Mem. N.Y. State Bar Assn. (tax. sect.), NYU Law Review, Order of Coif, Beta Gamma Sigma, Beta Alpha Psi. Clubs: Downtown Assn., Lotos (N.Y.C.). Avocation: non-profit theater. Corporate taxation. Office: Cahill Gordon & Reindel 80 Pine St Fl 17 New York NY 10005-1790

GAMBRO, MICHAEL S. lawyer; b. N.Y.C., July 15, 1954; s. A. John and Rose A. (Grandinetti) G.; m. Joan L. Thurneyssen, Aug. 9, 1980; children: Dana E., Merrill R., Christopher J. BS summa cum laude, Tufts U., 1976; JD, Columbia U., 1980. Bar: N.Y. 1981, U.S. Dist. Ct. (so. dist.) N.Y. 1981, U.S. Dist. Ct. N.J. 1981, N.J. 1983, Calif. 1988. Assoc. Cadwalader, Wickersham & Taft, N.Y.C., 1980-86, ptnr., 1987-88, L.A., 1988-94, N.Y.C., 1994—. Harlan Fiske Stone scholar, 1978-79, 1979-80. Mem. ABA, Phi Beta Kappa, Psi Chi. General corporate, Securities. Office: Cadwalader Wickersham & Taft 100 Maiden Ln New York NY 10038-4818

GANDY, H. CONWAY, retired judge, state official; b. Washington, Nov. 3, 1934; s. Hoke and Anne B. (Conway) G.; m. Carol Anderson, Aug. 29, 1965; children: Jennifer, Constance, Margaret. BA, Colo. State U., 1962; JD, U. Denver, 1968. Bar: Colo. 1969, U.S. Dist. Ct. Colo. 1969. Pvt. practice, Ft. Collins, Colo., 1969-81; adminstrv. law judge divsn. adminstrv. hearings State of Colo., Denver, 1981-99. Bd. dirs. Foothills-Gateway Rehab. Ctr., 1970-80, Colo. State Bd. Dental Examiners, 1976-81; Dem.

candidate for Colo. Senate, 1974, dist. atty., 1976; trustee Internat. Bluegrass Music Assn. Trust Fund, 1990—; pres. Colo. chpt. Nat. Assn. Adminstrv. Law Judges, 1985-86. With USN, 1954-58. Mem. Sertoma (Centurion award 1973, Tribune award 1975, Senator award 1977, 79, sec. Honor club 1977-78, pres. Ft. Collins club 1978-79, pres. Front Range club 1988-89). Home: 724 Winchester Dr Fort Collins CO 80526-2636 E-mail: gandy@verinet.com

GANGLE, SANDRA SMITH, arbitrator, mediator; b. Brockton, Mass., Jan. 11, 1943; d. Milton and Irene M. (Powers) Smith; m. Eugene M. Gangle, Dec. 21, 1968; children: Melanie Jean, Jonathan Rocco. BA, Coll. New Rochelle, 1964; MA, U. Oreg.; JD, Willamette U., 1980. Bar: Oreg. 1980. Instr. French Oreg. State U., Corvallis, 1968-71, Willamette U., Salem, Oreg., 1971-74; instr. ESL Chemeketa C.C., 1975-79; labor arbitrator, 1980—; pvt. practice, 1980-86, 96—; ptnr. Depenbrock, Gangle & Greer, 1986-96. Mem. Oreg., Idaho, Wash., Mont., Calif. and Alaska Arbitration Panels; mem. NASD securities arbitration and mediation panel, mediator employment bus. and disabilities disputes; clin. prof. Portland State U., 1981-84; cons. State Oreg., 1981; mem. mediation panel for disabilities issues Key Bridge Found.; mem. USPS Redress mediation panel. Contbr. articles to profl. jours. Land-use chmn. Faye Wright Neighborhood Assn., Salem, 1983-84; mem. Civil Svc. Commn., Marion County Fire Dist., Salem, 1983-89; mem. U.S. Postal Svc. Expedited Arbitration Panel, 1984-91; mem. Salem Neighbor-to-Neighbor Mediation Panel, 1986-91; mem. labor arbitrator panel Fed. Mediation & Conciliation Svc., 1986—; mem. panel Prudential APCOM reviewers, 1999-2000; ct. apptd. arbitrator, mediator Marion, Polk & Yamhill Counties, 1996—; mem. Marion County Cir. Ct. Dispute Resolution Commn., 1993-95; trustee Salem Peace Plaza, 1985-97; convenor Salem Peace Roundtable, 1995; bd. dirs. Salem YWCA, 1997—; bd. dirs. Salem City Club, 1999—, pres., 2001; chair planning com. joint conf. between Oreg. Women Lawyers and Assn. Women Solicitors, 1998. NDEA fellow, 1967. Fellow Chartered Inst. Arbitrators (London); mem. Am. Arbitration Assn. (arbitrator/mediator), Assn. for Conflict Resolution (chpt. co-pres. 1993-94), Oreg. State Bar Assn. Alternative dispute resolution. Office: Sandra Smith Gangle PC PO Box 904 Salem OR 97308 E-mail: gangle@open.org

GANGSTAD, JOHN ERIK, lawyer; b. New Brunswick, N.J., May 16, 1948; s. Edward Otis and Ruth Margaret (Fletcher) G.; m. Cynthia Diane Coffman, July 5, 1974; children: Allison, Erik, Amy. BA, U. Tex., 1970, JD, 1974. Bar: Tex. 1974, U.S. Dist. Ct. (no. dist.) Tex. 1974. Assoc. Turner, Hitchins, McInnery, Webb & Hartnett, Dallas, 1974-76, ptnr., 1977-81, Brown McCarroll & Oaks Hartline, L.L.P., Austin, Tex., 1982-2000, Bickerstaff, Heath et al., Austin, 2000—. Partnership com. State Bar Tex., 1981-98. Bd. dirs. Found. for the Homeless, Austin, 1988—. With USNG. Mem. ABA, Tex. Bar Assn., Order of Coif. Presbyterian. Avocations: golf, reading. General corporate, Mergers and acquisitions, Securities. Home: 3106 Eaneswood Dr Austin TX 78746-6717 Office: Bickerstaff Heath et al 1700 FrostBank Plz 816 Congress Ave Ste 1700 Austin TX 78701-2443 E-mail: jgangstad@bickerstaff.com

GANN, PAMELA BROOKS, academic administrator; b. 1948; BA, U. N.C., 1970; JD, Duke U., 1973. Bar: Ga. 1973, N.C. 1974. Assoc. King & Spalding, Atlanta, 1973, Robinson, Bradshaw & Hinson, P.A., Charlotte, N.C., 1974-75; asst. prof. Duke U. Sch. Law, Durham, 1975-78, assoc. prof., 1978-80, prof., 1980-99, dean, 1988-99; pres. Claremont McKenna Coll., Claremont, Calif., 1999—. Vis. asst. prof. U. Mich. Law Sch., 1977; vis. assoc. prof. U. Va., 1980 Author: (with D. Kahn) Corporate Taxation and Taxation of Partnerships and Partners, 1979, 83, 89; article editor Duke Law Jour. Mem. Am. Law Inst., Coun. Fgn. Rels., Order of Coif, Phi Beta Kappa Office: Claremont McKenna Coll Office Pres 500 E 9th St Claremont CA 91711-5903

GANNAM, MICHAEL JOSEPH, lawyer; b. Savannah, Ga., Nov. 10, 1922; s. Karam George and Annie (Abraham) G.; m. Marion Collins DeFrank, June 11, 1949; children: James, Ann, Elizabeth, Joseph. JD, U. Ga., 1948; MA, U. N.C., 1950. Bar: Ga. 1948, U.S. Dist. Ct. (so. dist.) Ga. 1950, U.S. Supreme Ct. 1971, U.S. Ct. Appeals (11th cir.) 1971. Assoc. Bouhan, Lawrence, Williams & Levy, Savannah, Ga., 1950-59; ptnr. Findley, Shea, Friedman, Gannam, Head & Buchsbaum, 1959-70, atty. pvt. practice, 1970-81; sr. ptnr. Gannam and Gnann, 1981—. Instr. bus. law polit. sci. and history Armstrong State coll., 1951-62. Bd. dirs. Historic Savannah Found.; bd. dirs., legal counsel Telfair Acad. Arts & Scis.; past pres. Legal Aid Soc. Savannah; mem. Savannah-Chatham Bd. Zoning Appeals, 1961-63, Savannah Arts Com., 1982-85; chmn. Gilmer Lectr. Series Fund, 1980—; bd. dirs. Savannah Coun. World Affairs, 1983-87; pres. Savannah Bar Assn.; bd. govs. State Bar Ga., 1968-99. With USAAF, PTO, 1943-46. General civil litigation, General practice, Probate. Home: 235 E Gordon St Savannah GA 31401-5003 Office: Gannam & Gnann 130 W Bay St Savannah GA 31401-1109 E-mail: gamgan@bellsouth.net

GANNON, JOHN SEXTON, lawyer, management consultant, arbitrator/mediator; b. East Orange, N.J., Apr. 7, 1927; s. John Joseph and Agnes (Sexton) G.; m. Diane Ditchy, Aug. 11, 1951; children: Mary Catherine, John, Lanie Elizabeth, James. BA, U. Mich., 1951; JD, Wayne State U., Detroit, 1961. Bar: Mich. 1962, Tenn. 1971, U.S. Ct. Appeals (6th cir.) 1977, U.S. Dist. Ct. (mid. dist.) 1989; Rule 31 approved mediator Tenn. Supreme Ct. Labor negotiator, mgr. employee rels. Chrysler Corp., Highland Park, Mich., 1951-61; labor counsel, mgr. employee rels. Ex-Cell-O Corp., 1961-65; assoc. Constangy & Powell, Atlanta, 1966; v.p. employee rels., labor counsel Werthan Industries, Nashville, 1967-80; ptnr. Dearborn & Ewing, 1980-90; pvt. practice, 1991—. Mem. adj. faculty Owens Sch., Vanderbilt U., Nashville, 1975-85; instr. Soc. Human Resource Mgmt. Profl. cert. program Mid. Tenn. State U., 1993-2000; pres. Employee Rels. Svcs., Inc., Nashville, 1987—. Contbr. articles to profl. jours. Mem. Birmingham (Mich.) Bd. Zoning Appeals, 1963-66; mem. Human Rels. Commn., Nashville, 1979-89; chmn. Tenn. Citizens for Ct. Modernization, Nashville, 1979-80; mem. Pvt. Industry Coun., Nashville, 1986-95. With USN, 1945-47. Mem. ABA, FBA (chmn. sr. lawyers divsn. mediatin and arbitration com.), Tenn. Bar Assn., Mich. Bar Assn., Nashville Bar Assn., Soc. Human Resource Mgmt., Am. Arbitration Assn. (panel employment mediators and arbitrators), Univ. Club, Hillwood Country Club, Kiwanis. Alternative dispute resolution, Labor, Pension, profit-sharing, and employee benefits. Home: 216 Jackson Blvd Nashville TN 37205-3300 E-mail: jg216@msn.com

GANS, WALTER GIDEON, lawyer; b. Trutnov, Czechoslovakia, Jan. 11, 1936; came to U.S., 1949, naturalized, 1957; s. Frederick and Erna (Mueller) G.; m. Harriet Arlene Goldhagen, Oct. 6, 1938 (dec.); children: David Ian, Erik Anthony; m. Katherine Elizabeth Halligan, Feb. 10, 1947. BA, Bowdoin Coll., 1957; JD, NYU, 1961, LLM in Comparative Law, 1967. Bar: N.Y. 1961. Assoc. Fried, Frank, harris, Shriver & Jacobson, N.Y.C., 1961-63; internat. atty. Latex Corp., 1963-67; assoc. counsel Olin Corp., New Haven and Stamford, Conn., 1967-71, counsel, 1972-75, sr. counsel internat., 1975-79; v.p., gen. counsel and sec. Siemens Corp., N.Y.C., 1979-99; spl. counsel Kaye Scholer, 2001. Active CPR Inst. for Dispute Resolution, mem. exec. com. 1995—; active European Am. Gen. Counsel Group; dir. Food and Drug Law Inst.; mem. Conf. Bd. Coun. of Chief Legal Officers; mem. lawyers com. Human Rights' Internat. Rule Coun. Mem. ABA (mem. antitrust, bus. law, dispute resolution, litigation, internat. law and practice sects.), Am. Arbitration Assn. (internat. panel arbitrators, corp. counsel com.), Am. Fgn. Law Assn., Am. Corp. Counsel Assn. (N.Y.C. chpt. bd. dirs.), N.Y. State Bar Assn., Assn. Bar City of N.Y. (fgn. and comparative law com. 1973-75, 82-85, com. corp. law depts. 1986-89, fed. cts. com. 1992-95, adv. com. corp. lawyers 1992-95, 125th anniversary campaign com.), Internat. Bar Assn., The Corp. Bar. Alternative dispute resolution, General corporate, Private international. Office: Kaye Scholer 425 Park Ave New York NY 10022

GANZ, DAVID L. lawyer; b. N.Y.C., July 28, 1951; s. Daniel M. and Beverlee (Kaufman) G.; m. Barbara Bondanza, Nov. 3, 1974 (div. 1978); m. Sharon Ruth Lamnin, Oct. 30, 1981 (div. 1996); children: Scott Harry, Elyse Toby, Pamela Rebecca; m. Kathleen Ann Gotsch, Dec. 28, 1996. BS in Fgn. Svc., Georgetown U., 1973; JD, St. John's U., 1976. Bar: N.Y. 1977, D.C. 1980, N.J. 1985; cert. mediator U.S. Dist. Ct. (N.J.). Assoc. Regan, Dorsey & De Riso, Flushing, N.Y., 1977-79; ptnr. Durst & Ganz, N.Y.C., 1979-80; mng. ptnr. Ganz, Hollinger & Towe, 1981-98, Ganz & Hollinger, N.Y.C., 1999—. Exec. com. Industry Coun. Tangible Assets, Washington, 1983—, bd. dirs.; cons. in field. Author: A Critical Guide to the Anthologies of African Literature, 1973, A Legal and Legislative History of 31 USC Sec 342d-324i, 1976, The World of Coin Collecting, 1980, 3d edit., 1998, The 90 Second Lawyer, 1996, The 90 Second Lawyer's Guide to Selling Real Estate, 1997, How to Get an Instant Mortgage, 1997, Planning Your Rare Coin Retirement, 1998, Guide Commemorative Coin Values, 1999, Official Guide to America's State Quarters, 2000; corr. Numis. News Weekly, 1969-73, 96—, asst. editor, 1973-74, spl. corr., 1974-75, columnist, 1969-76, 96—; contbg. editor, columnist COINage Mag., 1974—; columnist Coin World, 1974-96, COINS Mag., 1973-83; contbr. articles to profl. jours. Mem. U.S. Assay Commn., 1974; bd. dirs. Georgetown Libr. Assocs., Washington, 1982—; mem. N.Y. County Draft Bd., 1984, Bergen County, N.J., 1985—, vice chair, 1996—; mem. LLoyd Bentsen Citizens Commemorative Coin Adv. Com. U.S. Treas., 1993-96; sec., mem. Zoning and Adjustment Bd., Fair Lawn, N.J., 1988-92, chmn., 1993-97; elected mem. Dem. County Com. Bergen County, 1988-96, borough coun. Borough of Fair Lawn, 1998—, mayor, 1999—; bd. dirs., Bialystoker Home & Infirmary for the Aged, N.Y.C., 2001—. Decorated Order of St. Agatha (Republic of San Marino). Fellow Am. Numis. Soc. (life); mem. Am. Numis. Assn. (life, legis. coun. 1978-81, 83-95, elected bd. govs. 1985-95, v.p. 1991-93, pres. 1993-95), Assn. of Bar of City of N.Y. (com. on state legis. 1987-90), N.Y. State Bar Assn. (mem. civil practice com., chmn. subcom. 1978-84), Profl. Numis. Guild Inc. affiliated mem. 1989—, gen. coun. 1981-92), Am. Soc. Internat. Law, Nat. Assn. Coin and Precious Metals Dealers (asoc. mem., gen. coun. 1981-85), Flushing Lawyers Club (pres. 1982-83). Democrat. Jewish. Avocation: numismatics. Contracts commercial, Private international, Legislative. Office: Ganz & Hollinger LLD 1394 3rd Ave New York NY 10021-0404 E-mail: DavidLGanz@aol.com

GANZ, HOWARD LAURENCE, lawyer; b. N.Y.C., Apr. 3, 1942; s. Myron and Beatrice (W.) G.; children: Beth, David. BA, Colgate U., 1963; LLB, Columbia U., 1966. Bar: N.Y. 1966, U.S. Dist. Ct. (so. dist.) N.Y. 1968, U.S. Dist. Ct. (ea. dist.) N.Y. 1969, U.S. Dist. Ct. (no. dist.) Calif. 1984, U.S. Ct. Appeals (3rd cir.) 1974, U.S. Ct. Appeals (4th cir.) 1985, U.S. Dist. Ct. (9th cir.) 1984, U.S. Dist. Ct. (D.C. cir.) 1986, U.S. Supreme Ct. 1986. Law clk. to Hon. Marvin E. Frankel U.S. Dist. Ct., N.Y.C., 1966-68; assoc., ptnr., co-chair sports law group, mem. exec. com. Proskauer Rose LLP, 1968—. Named One of 100 Best Lawyers in N.Y., N.Y. Mag., 1995, One of Best Lawyers in America, 1997. Mem. Fed. Bar Coun., N.Y. State Bar Assn., N.Y. County Lawyers Assn., Assn. of Bar of City of N.Y. General civil litigation, Labor, Sports. Office: Proskauer Rose LLP 1585 Broadway New York NY 10036-8299 Fax: 212-969-2999. E-mail: hganz@proskauer.com

GANZ, MARC DAVID, lawyer; b. N.Y.C., Oct. 10, 1969; s. Melvin and Bette Carol G.; m. Jodi Berlin, June 15, 1996. BA in History and Polit. Sci., U. Wis., 1991; JD, Washington U., St. Louis, 1994; LLM in Taxation, NYU, 1995. Bar: N.Y. 1995, U.S. Tax Ct. 1995, U.S. Dist. Ct. (so. dist.) N.Y. 1995. Law clk. U.S. Tax Ct., Washington, 1995-96; internat. tax cons. Price Waterhouse Cooper, LLP, N.Y.C., 1996-98; tax assoc. Kelley, Drye & Warren, 1998—. Contbr. articles to profl. jours. Mem. N.Y. Cares, 1998—, Children's Hearing Inst., N.Y.C., 1997—, Cure For Lymphona, N.Y.C., 1996—. With U.S. Army, 1987-89. Mem. ABA, N.Y. State Bar Assn., NYU Tax Soc. Public international, Corporate taxation, Taxation, general. Office: Kelley Drye & Warren LLP 101 Park Ave New York NY 10178-0002

GANZ, MARY KEOHAN, lawyer; b. Weymouth, Mass., Nov. 17, 1954; d. Francis and Margaret (Quinn) Keohan; m. Alan H. Ganz, Sept. 7, 1980. BA magna cum laude, Emmanuel Coll., 1976; JD, Suffolk U., 1979. Bar: Mass. 1979, U.S. Dist. Ct. Mass. 1979, N.H. 1981, U.S. Dist. Ct. N.H. 1981. Pvt. practice, Seabrook, N.H., 1981—. Bd. dirs. My Greatest Dream Inc., Seabrook, 1985—. Mem. ABA, N.H. Bar Assn., Rockingham County Bar Assn., Seabrook Bus. and Profl. Assn. (pres. 1986-87), Seacoast Vis. Nurses Assn. (bd. dirs. 1994-2001, sec. 1997-98, v.p. 1998-99, pres. 1999-2001), Phi Delta Phi, Kappa Gamma Pi. Roman Catholic. General practice. Office: 779 Lafayette Rd Seabrook NH 03874-4215

GANZI, VICTOR FREDERICK, lawyer; b. N.Y.C., Feb. 14, 1947; s. Walter John and Gertrude (Meyer) G.; m. Patricia Frances Martin, July 10, 1971; children: Danielle Martin, Victoria Louise. BS, Fordham U., 1968; JD, Harvard U., 1971; LLM in Taxation, NYU, 1981. Bar: N.Y. 1973, U.S. Dist. Ct. (so. and ea. dists.) N.Y. 1975, U.S. Ct. Appeals (2d cir.) 1975, U.S. Tax Ct. 1975; CPA, Colo. Tax acct. Touche Ross & Co., Denver, 1971-73; assoc. Rogers & Wells, N.Y.C., 1973-78, ptnr., 1978-86, mng. ptnr., 1986-90; v.p., sec., gen. counsel Hearst Corp., N.Y.C., 1990-92, CFO, chief legal officer, sr. v.p., 1992-94, also bd. dirs.; exec. v.p., pres. Hearst Books/Bus. Pub. Group, 1997-98; exec. v.p., COO The Heart Corp, 1998—. Speaker various insts.; bd. dirs. Palm Mgmt. Corp., N.Y.C., PGA Tour, Inc., ESPN, N.Y.C., IMI Sys. Inc., N.Y.C., N.Y.C. Econ. Devel. Corp., Olsten Corp.; mem. Coun. future of Law Sch., NYU Sch. Law. Mem. ABA, AICPA, Colo. Soc. CPAs, Sky Club, Cherry Valley Club (Garden City, N.Y.). Municipal (including bonds), Real property, Corporate taxation. Home: 303 Captains Way Bay Shore NY 11706-8106 Office: The Hearst Corp 959 8th Ave New York NY 10019-3795

GARABEDIAN, DANIEL, lawyer, educator; b. Brussels, Belgium, Dec. 20, 1959; LLB, Free U. Brussels, 1982, Spl. Degree in Tax Law, 1983; LLM, U. Mich., 1985. Lawyer Liedekerke Wolters Waelbroeck Kirkpatrick & Cerfontaine, Brussels, 1982—, Free U. Brussels, 1996—. Dir. spl. degree in tax law Free U. Brussels, 1998—. Contbr. articles to legal jours. Mem.: Internat. Fiscal Assn. (v.p. Belgian sect.). Office: Liedekerke Wolters et al Blvd de l'Empereur 3 B-1000 Brussels Belgium E-mail: d.garabedian@liedekerke-law.be

GARANCE, DOMINICK (D. G. GARAN), lawyer, author; b. Varaklani, Latvia, Oct. 14, 1912; came to U.S., 1950, naturalized, 1955; s. John and Virginia (Cakuls) Garans. LL.M., U. Riga, Latvia, 1935; J.U.D., U. Freiburg, Germany, 1945; LL.D., U. Paris, France, 1947; Ph.D., U. London, Eng., 1949. Bar: N.Y. 1958. Atty.-at-law, legal counsel Ministry of Welfare, Riga, 1936-42; law sec. French Mil. Govt. in Germany, Freiburg, 1945-46; documentary officer Harvard Law Sch. Internat. Program of Taxation, 1952-57; pvt. practice law N.Y.C., 1958—. Author: The Paradox of Pleasure and Relativity, 1963, Relativity for Psychology, A Causal Law for the Modern Alchemy, 1968, The Key to the Sciences of Man, 1975, Against Ourselves: Disorders from Improvements under the Organic Limitedness of Man, 1979, Our Sciences Ruled by Human Prejudice, 1987. Mem. ABA, N.Y. State Bar Assn., N.Y. State Trial Lawyers Assn., N.Y. Acad. Sci., Philosophy of Sci. Assn., Am. Assn. Advancement Sci., Lacuania. Address: 2926 E 196th St Bronx NY 10461-3804

GARBARINI, CHAS. J. lawyer, trade association consultant; b. N.Y.C., July 5, 1911; s. Victor Emanuele and Maria (Balzarini) G.; m. Lillian Michelina Penna, Jan. 23, 1937; children— Charles J., Rita Garbarini Nugent, Stephen A. B.A., Fordham Coll., 1933; J.D., St. John U., N.Y.C., 1936; trade assn. mgmt. cert. Eastern U. at Yale U., 1952. Bar: N.Y. 1941, U.S. Dist. Ct. (so. dist.) N.Y. 1947, U.S. Tax Ct. 1966, U.S. Ct. Internat. Trade 1966, U.S. Dist. Ct. (ea. dist.) N.Y. 1951, U.S. Supreme Ct. 1956. Ptnr. Garbarini & Kroll, N.Y.C., 1944-60, Garbarini, Scher & De Cicco, N.Y.C., 1961— ; cons. trade assns. Penn Affiliates, Inc., New Rochelle, N.Y., 1960-80; cons.-constrn. Garco Constrn. Corp., N.Y.C., 1940-54. Mem. ABA, Assn. Bar City N.Y., N.Y. County Lawyers Assn., Columbian Lawyers Assn. (pres. 1967). Roman Catholic. Lodge: K.C. (grand knight 1974). Insurance, Personal injury. Home: 956 Edgewood Ave Pelham NY 10803-2902 Office: Garbarini & Scher PC Rm 3500 1114 Avenue Of The Americas New York NY 10036-7790

GARBARINO, ROBERT PAUL, retired administrative dean, lawyer; b. Wanaque, N.J., Oct. 6, 1929; s. Attillio and Theresa (Napello) G.; m. Joyce A. Sullivan, June 29, 1957; children: Lynn, Lisa, Mark, Steven. BBA cum laude, St. Bonaventure U., 1951; JD with highest class honors, Villanova U., 1956. Bar: Pa. 1956, U.S. Dist. Ct. (ea. dist.) Pa. 1956, U.S. Ct. Appeals (3d cir.) 1962, U.S. Supreme Ct. 1962, U.S. Tax Ct. 1966, U.S. Ct. Internat. Trade 1966. Law clk. U.S. Dist. Ct. (ea. dist.) Pa., Phila., 1956-57; asst. counsel Phila. Electric Co., 1957-60, asst. gen. counsel, 1960-62; ptnr. Kania & Garbarino & predecessor firm, Phila. and Bala Cynwyd, Pa., 1962-81; assoc. dean adminstrn. Sch. Law Villanova (Pa.) U., 1981-96. Right-of-way cons. Edison Electric Inst., N.Y.C., 1960-62; trustee reorgn. Tele-Tronics Co., Phila., 1962-64; mem. bd. consultors Law Sch. Villanova U., 1967-81, chmn., vice chmn. bd. consultors, 1971-96, chmn. Profl. Sports Career Counseling Panel Villanova U.; mem pres.'s adv. coun. St. Bonaventure U., N.Y., 1975-86, chmn., 1976-78. Contbr. articles to profl. jours. Mem. community leadership seminar Fels Inst. Local and State Govt., 1961. Staff sgt. USMC, 1951-53. Mem. ABA, Phila. Bar Assn., Order of Coif. Home: 120 Ladderback Ln Devon PA 19333-1815

GARBER, BRUCE SAMUEL, lawyer; b. Detroit, Aug. 6, 1949; s. Jack and Freida (Fox) G.; m. Gloria Jeanne Elfond, Nov. 3, 1974; children— Jodi Gwen, Dustin Alan. B.A., U. Mich., 1971; J.D., Wayne State U., 1974. Bar: N.Mex. 1974, U.S. Dist. Ct. N.Mex. 1974, Calif. 1975, U.S. Ct. Appeals (D.C. cir.) 1975, U.S. Ct. Appeals (10th cir.) 1978, U.S. Supreme Ct., 1997. Staff atty. N.Mex. Environ. Improvement Div., Santa Fe, 1975-78, chief counsel, 1978-83; sole practice, Santa Fe, 1983-86; ptnr. Garber & Hallmark, P.C., Santa Fe, 1986—. Contbr. articles to profl. publs. Mem. N.Mex. Bar Assn., N.Mex. Supreme Ct. Specialization Bd. (chair), Calif. Bar Assn. General civil litigation, Environmental, Real property. Office: Garber & Hallmark PC 200 W Marcy St Ste 203 Santa Fe NM 87501-2036

GARBER, PHILIP CHARLES, lawyer; b. Boston, Nov. 16, 1934; s. Rubin E. and Sarah Rose (Schick) G. BA cum laude, Harvard U., 1956, JD, 1961. Bar: Mass. 1961, U.S. Ct. Appeals (1st cir.) 1977. Ptnr. Garber & Garber, Boston, 1961—. Title examiner Land Ct., Mass., 1966. Translator: The Political Constitution of Chile, 1980. Pres. West End House Boys Club Alumni Assn., Allston, Mass., 1982-83, Spellman Mus. Stamps & Postal History, 1993—; hon. consul, Chile, 1982. Named Comendador, Order of Bernardo O'Higgins, Republic of Chile. Mem. Harvard Club (Boston), Caleuche Club (Valparaiso). Consumer commercial, Contracts commercial. Office: Garber & Garber Esquires PC 19 Lanark Rd Boston MA 02135-7840

GARBER, ROBERT EDWARD, lawyer, insurance company executive; b. N.Y.C., Jan. 4, 1949; s. Edward Robert and Estelle (Rosenberg) G.; m. Mary Ellen Roche, Jan. 17, 1981; 1 child, Edward Thomas A.B., Princeton U., 1970; J.D., Columbia U., 1973. Bar: N.Y. 1974. Law clk. U.S. Dist. Ct. (so. dist.), N.Y.C., 1973-75; assoc. Debevoise, Plimpton, Lyons & Gates, 1976-79; assoc. counsel, v.p. Irving Trust, 1979-82, sr. v.p., 1982-87; gen. counsel Irving Bank Corp. and Irving Trust Co., 1987-89; sr. v.p., dep. gen. counsel Equitable Life Assurance Soc. U.S., 1989-93; sr. v.p., gen. counsel Equitable Cos., Inc. and Equitable Life Assurance Soc. U.S., 1993-94, exec. v.p., gen. counsel, 1994-99; exec. v.p., chief legal officer Equitable Life Assurance Soc. U.S., 1999—2001; exec. v.p., gen. counsel AXA Fin., Inc., 1999—2001. Dir. Am. Arbitration Assn. Served to capt. USAR, 1970-78 Mem. Assn. of Bar of City of N.Y. Banking, General corporate, Insurance. Home: 45 Sturgis Rd Bronxville NY 10708-5012

GARBER, SAMUEL B. lawyer, business/turnaround management consultant; b. Chgo., Aug. 16, 1934; s. Morris and Yetta G.; m. Marietta C. Bratta; children: Debra Lee, Diane Lori. JD, U. Ill., 1958; MBA, U. Chgo., 1968. Bar: Ill. 1958. Ptnr. Brown, Dashow and Langluttig, Chgo., 1960-62; corp. counsel Walgreen Co., 1962-69; v.p., gen. counsel, exec. asst. to the pres. Carlyle & Co., 1969-73; dir. legal affairs Stop & Shop Co., Inc., 1973-74; gen. counsel Goldblatt Bros., Inc., 1974-76; v.p., sec., gen. counsel, dir. Evans, Inc., 1976-99, pres., CEO, 1999-2000; prof. mgmt. DePaul U., 1975—; prin. The Garber Group, Bus. Cons. and Turnaround Management Firm, Chgo., 2000—. Adj. prof. bus. law grad. sch. bus. U. Chgo., 1993; arbitrator N.Y. Stock Exch., 1996, Chgo. Merc. Exch., 1996, Am. Stock Exch., 1997, Nat. Futures Assn., 1997; columnist Garber's Gurus Tribune Media Svcs., 1999—. With U.S. Army, 1958-60. Mem. ABA, NYSE (arbitrator 1996—), Am. Arbitration Assn. (arbitrator 1993—), Nat. Retail Fedn., Ill. Retail Mchts. Assn. General corporate, Landlord-tenant, Securities. Home: 2626 N Lakeview Ave Chicago IL 60614-1809 Office: DePaul U 1 E Jackson Blvd Ste 7010 Chicago IL 60604-2287

GARBIS, MARVIN JOSEPH, judge; b. Balt., June 14, 1936; s. Samuel and Adele E. (Warshaw) G.; m. Phyllis Lorraine Zaroff, Aug. 27, 1961; children: Kendall Rose, Jason Anders, Kerri Jill. BES., Johns Hopkins U., 1958; JD, Harvard U., 1961; LLM, Georgetown U., 1962. Bar: D.C. 1961, Md. 1962. Trial atty. Tax Div., Dept. Justice, Washington, 1962-67; sole practice Balt., 1967-71; ptnr. Garbis, Marvel & Junghans, 1971-86, Melnicove, Kaufman, Weiner, Smouse & Garbis, Balt., 1986-88, Johnson & Gibbs, Washington, 1988-89; judge U.S. Dist. Ct. Md., 1989—. Lectr. U. Md. Law Sch., 1970-85, NYU Fed. Tax Inst., 1970, 74, 79, 87-88; adj. prof. Georgetown U. Law Sch., 1978-80, U. Balt. Law Sch., 1982—; adviser on tax procedure study, jud. com. U.S. Senate, 1969-70; mem. adv. commr. to commr. IRS, 1982; mem. adv. coun. U.S. Claims Ct., 1982—; mem. Md. Inst. for Continuing Profl. Edn. for Lawyers, 1978-80, pres., 1980-82. Author: (with Frome) Procedures in Federal Tax Controversy, 1968, (with Schwait) Tax Refund Litigation, 1971, Tax Court Practice, 1974, (with Struntz) Cases and Materials on Federal Tax Procedure, Civil and Criminal, 1981, (with Junghans and Struntz) Federal Tax Litigation, 1985, (with Struntz and Rubin) Cases and Materials on Tax Procedure and Tax Fraud, 2d edit., 1987, (with Rubin and Morgan) Cases and Material on Tax Procedure and Tax Fraud, 3d edit., 1991; contbr. articles to profl. jours. Recipient Jules Ritholz Meml. Merit award, 1996; E. Barrett Prettyman fellow Georgetown Law Sch., 1961-62; named hon. justice Fed. Ct. Australia, 1998. Mem. Fed. Bar Assn. (pres. Balt. chpt. 1972-73, nat. vice chmn. tax com. 1974-76), Md. Bar Assn. (chmn. tax sect. 1970-71, chmn. continuing legal edn. 1973-80), ABA (chmn. ct. procedure com., tax sect. 1975-77), Balt. Bar Assn. (bd. govs. 1974-79), Fed. Cir. Bar Assn. (bd. dirs. 1985—). Am. Law Inst., Md. Inst. Continuing Profl. Education Lawyers (pres. 1981-82) judge. Office: US Dist Ct 101 W Lombard St Ste 530 Baltimore MD 21201-2605 E-mail: garbis@mdd.uscourts.gov

GARCIA, BONIFACIO BONNY, lawyer; b. Fresno, Calif., Oct. 27, 1956; s. Bonifacio Mata and Corrine (Miranda) G. B.A. magna cum laude, Loyola Marymount U., Los Angeles, 1978; J.D., Harvard U., 1981. Bar: Calif. 1981. Assoc. Fulop & Hardee, Beverly Hills, Calif., 1981-82; assoc. law firm Leff & Stephenson, Beverly Hills, Calif., 1983-84; assoc. Allen Matkins, Leck, Gamble & Mallory, Los Angeles, 1984-85; assoc. Lillick McHose & Charles, Los Angeles, 1985-88; ptnr. Tobin & Tobin, 1988—; adj. prof. history Loyola Marymount U., 1984. Author: (with others) Law and Justice, 1987. Recipient Loyola Marymount U. Pres.'s citation, 1978. Mem. Los Angeles County Bar Assn., Alpha Sigma Nu; Phi Alpha Theta. Democrat. Roman Catholic. Home: 901 E Domingo Dr San Gabriel CA 91775-2112

GARCIA, LUIS CESAREO, lawyer; b. Hato Rey, P.R., Apr. 19, 1949; came to U.S., 1965; s. Cesareo and Evelina Maura Garcia; foster s. John B. and Elena Amos.; m. Kathy Jo Mims, Dec. 4, 1970; children: Joseph Amos, Evelyn Kathleen, Jeremy Adam. Student Columbus Coll., 1967-70; JD, John Marshall Law U., Atlanta, 1973; postgrad. Harvard U., 1978, 84. Bar: Ga. 1974, U.S. Dist. Ct. (mid. dist.) Ga. 1974, U.S. Ct. Appeals (11th cir.) 1983, U.S. Supreme Ct. 1977, Vt. 1991, Vt. Supreme Ct. 1991. Assoc. Keil, Riley & Fort, Columbus, Ga., 1974-75; pvt. practice, Columbus, 1975-76, 89—; sr. ptnr. Garcia & Hirsch, P.C., Columbus, 1976-79; regional mgr. Am. Family Life Assurance Co., Columbus, 1979-82, exec. v.p., chief counsel, 1982-87; sr. v.p. counsel internat. ops., 1986-88; legal counsel LMI, Inc., 1979-82; mem. legis. com. Am. Prepaid Legal Inst., Chgo., 1983-86. Bd. dirs. Better Bus. Bur. of W. Ga.-E. Ala., 1984-87; mem. bd. adv. council CETA, 1979-83; adv. bd. Ga. Pub. TV, 1979-82; chmn., bd. dirs. March of Dimes, Columbus, 1989-91. Mem. ABA, Assn. Trial Lawyers Am., Vt. Bar Assn., Ga. Bar Assn., Franklin-Grand Isle Bar Assn., Columbus Lawyers Club, Younger Lawyers Club, Sigma Delta Kappa. Episcopalian. Bankruptcy, General civil litigation, Criminal. Office: PO Box 75 340 Malletts Bay Ave Colchester VT 05446-1462

GARCIA, PATRICIA A. lawyer; b. New Orleans, Feb. 18, 1956; d. Martin F. and Shirley (Polders) G. BA in History, U. New Orleans, 1976; JD, Loyola U., New Orleans, 1980. Bar: La. 1980, U.S. Tax Ct. 1982, U.S. Dist. Ct. (ea. dist.) La. 1984, U.S. Dist. Ct. (mid. dist.) La. 1986. Staff atty. office of chief counsel IRS, Washington, 1980-82; law clk. U.S. Ea. Dist. Ct. of La., New Orleans, 1983-86; assoc. Law Office of Eric A. Holden, 1986-89; ptnr. Holden & Garcia, 1990—2001; private practice, 2001—. Bd. dirs. La. Ctr. for Law and Civic Edn., 1992-96, pres., 1994-95, New Orleans Legal Assistance Corp., 1995-2000. Co-chair No/AIDS Task Force, 1997-01, sec./treas., 1994-97. Mem. ABA (comm. chair, exec. com. young lawyers divsn. 1990-91, gen. practice sect. gen. practice link conf. team 1994-99, vice chair sole practitioners and small firms com. 1990-92, vice chair law students com. 1991-96, vice chair law sch. curriculum com. 1991-94, La. dist. gov. 1979-80, project dir. model project for effective delivery of law-related edn. to low income families 1985-87, project dir. com. on substance abuse, chmn. delivery of legal svcs. com. young lawyers divsn. 1987, chmn. law student outreach com. 1988-91, asst. editor Affiliate mag. 1988-90, liaison to law student divsn. 1987-91, recipient Gold Key award 1980, regional coord. state and local bar liaison com. 1992-98, standing com. on Gavel awards 1994-97, project dir. com. on substance abuse 1994-97, ann. mtg. 1994 host com., ho. dels. 1994, 97-2000), La. Bar Assn. (chmn. law week 1986, mem. young lawyers sect. 1986-92, Achievement award 1985, 86, 87, mem. local and splty. bars com. 1992-98), New Orleans Bar Assn. (1st v.p. 1990-91, pres.-elect 1991-92, pres. 1992-93, chmn. TV com. 1992-98, com. on drugs and violence 1992-96, vice chmn. young lawyers sect. 1984-86, chmn. 1987-88, chmn. membership com. 1988-91, exec. com. 1988-94, vice chmn. increasing membership com. 1986-87, pub. rels. com. 1984-92, project grantee 1985-87), La. Ctr. for Law and Civic Edn. (pres. 1994-95, v.p. 1993-94, bd. dirs. 1992-96). Democrat. Roman Catholic. Federal civil litigation, State civil litigation, Contracts commercial. Home: 35 Dove St New Orleans LA 70124 Office: PO Box 24098 New Orleans LA 70184-4098 E-mail: pagarcia@bellsouth.net

GARCIA, RUDOLPH, lawyer; b. Phila., June 22, 1951; s. Rudolph Sr. and Assunta Rita (Marrara) G.; m. Randi Ellen Pastor, Aug. 3, 1980; 1 child, Jonathan P. BA magna cum laude, Temple U., 1974, JD cum laude, 1977. Bar: Pa. 1977, U.S. Dist. Ct. (ea. dist.) Pa. 1977, U.S. Ct. Appeals (3d cir.) 1982, U.S. Supreme Ct. 1982. Assoc. Wright, Thistle & Gibbons, Phila., 1977-78, Saul Ewing LLP, Phila., 1978-84, ptnr., 1984—. Judge pro tem Phila. Ct. Common Pleas. Fellow Acad. of Adv.; mem. ABA, Pa. Bar Assn., Phila. Bar Assn. (chmn. local rules subcom. 1988-92, chmn. state civil com. 1999, bd. govs. 2000—), Phila. Assn. Def. Counsel, Justinian Soc. (bd. govs. 1999—), Phi Beta Kappa. Avocations: computers, photography, golf. Federal civil litigation, State civil litigation, Insurance. Home: 235 Lloyd Ln Wynnewood PA 19096-3323 Office: Saul Ewing Remick & Saul 3800 Centre Sq W Philadelphia PA 19102-2174

GARCIA-BARRON, GERARD LIONEL, lawyer; b. L.A., Nov. 29, 1965; s. Jose Sergio and Maria (de Jesus) Barron; m. Irene Silva Garcia, May 16, 1992; children: Nicolas, Tomas. BA, U. So. Calif., 1987, JD, 1990. Bar: Calif. 1992, U.S. Dist. Ct. (ctrl. dist.) Calif. 1992. Assoc. Seals & Tenenbaum, Anaheim, Calif., 1990-92, Mazura & Arguelles, Newport Beach, 1992-95, Parker Stanbury, LLP, L.A., 1995—. Mem. L.A. Trial Lawyers Assn., Mex.-Am. Bar Assn. Democrat. Roman Catholic. Avocations: running, golf. General civil litigation, Criminal, Personal injury. Office: Parker Stanbury LLP 611 W 6th St Fl 33 Los Angeles CA 90017-3101

GARCIA BARRON, RAMIRO, lawyer; b. H. Matamoros, Mexico, Aug. 18, 1966; s. Ramiro Garcia Jimenez and Lourdes Barron Schoellkopf; m. Cecilia Garcia Moreno, Mar. 5, 1994; 1 child, Ramiro A. Garcia. BBA, U. Monterrey, Mexico, 1989; MBA, U. Dallas, 1992; JD, So. Meth. U., 1993; grad. program of instrn. for lawyers, Harvard Law Sch., 2000. Bar: U.S. Dist. Ct. (no. dist.) Tex. 1995, U.S. Ct. Internat. Trade 1997, U.S. Ct. Appeals (5th cir.) 1997, U.S. Supreme Ct. 1998. Accts. aide investigational divsn. edn. dept. U. Monterrey, 1988-89; rsch. asst. Banco Nacional de Comercio Exterior, Dallas, 1993, Trade Commn. Mexico, Dallas, 1993; assoc. Roberts Cunninham, 1993-99; pvt. practice Law Offices of Ramiro Garcia, P.C., Dallas, 1999—. Cons. in field; spkr. in field. Mem. ABA, Am. Soc. Internat. Law, Coll. State Bar Tex., Dallas Bar Assn. Avocations: swimming, cycling, hunting, fishing, triathlons. General civil litigation, General corporate, Private international. E-mail: rgblegis@aol.com

GARCIA-MONTOYA, LUIS ALBERTO, lawyer; b. Caracas, Miranda, Venezuela, Nov. 6, 1951; s. Alejandro Garcia Acebes and Maria Del Carmen Montoya; m. Beatriz Armas, Dec. 19, 1974; children: Valentina Garcia, Andreina, Luis Alberto. Bachelor, Colegio La Sallas La Colina, Caracas, 1969; Law Degree, U. Catolica Andres Bello, Caracas, 1974; LLM, Harvard U., 1977. Exec. v.p. Banco Indsl. de Venezuela, Caracas, 1980-83; pres. Citimerca Mercado de Capitales, 1983-85; v.p. Citibank NA, 1983-85; sr. ptnr. Garcia Montoya & Assocs., 1985-89; gen. dir. for investment promotion Ministry Devel., 1989-91; pres. Commn. Nat. de Valores (SEC), 1992-94; sr. ptnr. Viso, Rodriguez, Cottin & Garcia, 1994—. Prof. comml. banking and capital markets law Cath. U., Caracas, 1977—; prof. fin. law and fin. negotiations IESA, Caracas, 1979—; bd. dirs. Century 21 (Venezuela), Caracas, Fondo de Valores Inmobilia Rios, Caracas, Seguros Suramerica Zurich Group, Caracas, Banco Union and Affiliates, Caracas. Contbr. articles to profl. jours. Avocations: reading, horse racing, baseball, soccer. Banking, Mergers and acquisitions, Securities. Home: Calle AC3 Qta Las Munecas Caurimare Caracas Miranda Venezuela Office: Viso Rodriguez Cottin et al Piso 13 Av Francisco 1050 Solano Caracas Venezuela Office Fax: 582 7624562. E-mail: montoya@cantv.net, esaitorio@visonodriguezcottin.com

GARC$_8$A-PERROTE, IGNACIO, lawyer, law educator; b. Madrid, Oct. 19, 1956; s. José María García-Perrote and María Angeles Escartin; m. Paloma Rodulfo, Apr. 14, 1982; children: Guillermo, Pablo. Lic. in Law, U. Autonoma, Madrid, 1979; PhD in Law, 1986. Prof. labor law U. Autonoma, Madrid, 1987-92; chaired prof. of labor law U. Cantabria, Santander, Spain, 1992-98, U. Castilla La Mancha, Cuenca, Spain, 1998—; ct. atty. Constitutional Ct., Madrid, 1989-92; ptnr. Uría & Menéndez Abogados, 1999—. Arbitrator Interconferal Svc. Mediation and Arbitration, 1999—. Author: Ley y Autonomía Colectiva, 1987 (PhD award 1987), Instituciones y Derecho del Trabajo, 2nd edit., 1991, La Prueba en el Proceso de Trabajo, 1994, Derecho de Seguridad Social, 2nd rev. edit., 1999; chief editor: Labour Law Jour., 1999—. With Red Cross, Madrid, 1980—. Mem. Spanish assn. Labour and Social Security Law, Assn. Ct. Attys. of Constitutional Ct., DAR Assn. Avocations: travel, reading, sports, music. , Pension, profit-sharing, and employee benefits, Workers' compensation. Office: Uría Menéndez Abogados Jorge Juan 6 28001 Madrid Spain Fax: +34 915 860 330. E-mail: igp@uria.com

GARCIA RUIZ-HUIDOBRO, MAGALI, lawyer; b. Lima, Peru, June 6, 1974; d. Luis Alfredo Garcia Mseinas and Maria Isabel Ruiz-Huidobro. Degree in law, U. Lima, 1997. Bar: Lima 1998; registered mediator. Legal asst. Nat. Inst. Def. Comp. & Intellectual Property Protection, Lima, 1992-94, Estudio Osterling, Arias Schreiber, Vega, Orbegos & Assocs., Lima, 1994-96; assoc. Fernandini Abogados Asociados, 1996—. Asst. prof. San Ignacio Loyola U., Lima, 1999-2000; mediator Cepscon, Lima, 1999—. Contbr. articles to profl. jours. Mem. Lima Bar Assn., Am. C. of C. Roman Catholic. Avocations: travel, poetry, music. Office fax; 511-460-5458. Consumer commercial, General corporate, Intellectual property. Office: Fernandini Abogados Asocs Av. San Felipe 539 Lima 11 Peru E-mail: mgarcia@fernandini.com.pe

GARDE, JOHN CHARLES, lawyer; b. Lyndhurst, N.J., Aug. 17, 1961; s. John Charles and Jean (Sheperd) G.; m. L. Allison Ghenn, Aug. 9, 1986. BA, Drew U., 1983; JD, William and Mary, 1986. Bar: N.J. 1986, U.S. Ct. N.J. 1986, U.S. Ct. Appeals (2nd, 3rd and 7th cirs.) 1990. Law sec. to presiding judge Superior Ct Appellate div., Hackensack, N.J., 1986-87; assoc. McCarter & English, Newark, 1987-94, ptnr., 1995—. Contbr. William and Mary Law Rev. Warden St. Thomas Epis. Ch., 1987—; trustee St. Phillip's Acad., 1996-2000; trustee Diocese of Newark Episcopal Properties and Fin., 1996-2001, judge ecclesiastical ct. Mem. ABA, N.J. State Bar Assn., Essex County Bar Assn., Order of the Coif, Phi Beta Kappa. Republican. Episcopalian. General civil litigation, Insurance, Product liability. Office: McCarter & English 100 Mulberry St Newark NJ 07102-4004

GARDINER, LESTER RAYMOND, JR. lawyer; b. Salt Lake City, Aug. 20, 1931; s. Lester Raymond and Sarah Lucille (Kener) G.; m. Janet Ruth Thatcher, Apr. 11, 1955; children: Allison Gardiner Bigelow, John Alfred, Annette Gardiner Weed, Leslie Gardiner Crandall, Robert Thatcher, Lisa Gardiner West, James Raymond, Elizabeth Gardiner Smith, David William, Sarah Janet Boyden. BS with honors, U. Utah, 1954; JD, U. Mich., 1959. Bar: Utah 1959, U.S. Dist. Ct. Utah 1959, U.S. Ct. Appeals (10th cir.) 1960. Law clk. U.S. Dist. Ct., 1959; assoc. then ptnr. Van Cott, Bagley, Cornwall & McCarthy, Salt Lake City, 1960-67; ptnr. Gardiner & Johnson, 1967-72, Christensen, Gardiner, Jensen & Evans, 1972-78, Fox, Edwards, Gardiner & Brown, Salt Lake City, 1978-87, Chapman & Cutler, 1987-89, Gardiner & Hintze, 1990-92; CEO and pres. Snowbird Ski and Summer Resort, Snowbird Corp., 1993-97; prin., mgmt. cons. Ray Gardiner Assocs., 1998—. Reporter, mem. Utah Sup. Ct. Com. on Adoption of Uniform Rules of Evidence, 1970-73, mem. com. on revision of criminal code, 1975-78; master of the bench Am. Inn of Ct. I, 1980-90; mem. com. bar examiners Utah State Bar, 1973; instr. bus. law U. Utah, 1965-66; adj. prof. law Brigham Young U., 1984-85. Mem. Republican State Central Com. Utah, 1967-72, mem. exec. com. Utah Rep. Party, 1975-78, chmn. state convs., 1980, 81; mem. Salt Lake City Bd. Edn., 1971-72; bd. dirs. Salt Lake City Pub. Library, 1974-75; trustee Utah Sports Found., 1987-91; bd. dirs. and exec. com. Salt Lake City Visitors and Conv. Bur., 1988-91, 93-98. Served to 1st lt. USAF, 1954-56. Mem. Utah State Bar Assn., Sons of Utah Pioneers, Rotary. Mormon. Office: Ray Gardiner Assocs 93 Laurel St Salt Lake City UT 84103-4349

GARDNER, BRIAN E. lawyer; b. Des Moines, July 13, 1952; s. Lawrence E. and Sarah I. (Hill) G.; m. Rondi L. Veland, Aug. 7, 1976; children: Meredith Anne, Stephanie Lynn, John Clinton. BS, Iowa State U., 1974; JD, U. Iowa, 1978. Bar: Iowa 1978, Mo. 1978, Kans. 1979, U.S. Ct. Appeals (10th cir.) 1980, U.S. Dist. Ct. Kans. 1979, U.S. Dist. Ct. (we. dist.) Mo. 1978. Assoc. Morrison, Hecker, Curtis, Kuder & Parrish, Kansas City, Mo., 1978-80, Parker & Handsaker, Nevada, Iowa, 1980-81, Morrison, Hecker, Curtis, Kuder & Parrish, Overland Park, Kans., 1981-83; ptnr. Morrison & Hecker, Kansas City, Mo., 1983—, mng. ptnr., 1990-93, 96—; city atty. Mission Hills, Kans., 1992—. Bd. dirs. Overland Park Conv. and Visitors Bur., 1985-97, chmn., 1988-90; dir., mem. exec. com. Johnson County C.C. Found., Overland Park, 1990—, pres., 1997-98; bd. dirs. KCPT, 1993-99, 2000—, chmn., 1997-98; active Kansas City Area Devel. Coun., 1992—, Civic Coun. Greater Kansas City, 1998—. Mem. Kans. Bar Assn., Kans. Assn. Def. Counsel, Kansas City Met. Bar Assn., Mo. Bar Assn., Johnson County Bar Assn., Blue Hills Country Club, Cardinal Key, Phi Beta Kappa. Lutheran. Avocation: golf. Environmental, Land use and zoning (including planning). Office: Morrison & Hecker LLP 2600 Grand Blvd Kansas City MO 64108-4606

GARDNER, BRUCE ELWYN, lawyer; b. N.Y.C., Jan. 28, 1953; s. Parker and Mary P. (Pinkston) G. BA, UCLA, 1975; JD, Syracuse U., 1978; LLM in Taxation, Georgetown U., 1987. Bar: Ill. 1981, U.S. Dist. Ct. (no. dist.) Ill. 1981, U.S. Ct. Appeals (5th cir.) 1981, U.S. Dist. Ct. (so. dist.) Tex. 1982, U.S. Ct. Appeals (7th cir.) 1982, U.S. Ct. Appeals (9th cir.) 1983, U.S. Claims Ct. 1983, U.S. Ct. Mil. Appeals 1983, U.S. Supreme Ct. 1985, Tex. 1988, D.C. 1990. Estate tax atty. IRS, Chgo., 1979-80; appeals officer Ill. Dept. Revenue, 1980-81, hearing officer, 1981-82; agt. IRS, Houston, 1982-84, tax law specialist Washington, 1984-86, appeals officer Houston, 1986-87, atty. Washington, 1987-91, sr. trial atty. Sacramento, 1991-94; atty., dept. fin. and revenue D.C. Ct., 1995-96; asst. gen. counsel Office of Chief Fin. Officer, D.C. Govt., 1995-96; atty. The Gardner Kane Firm, P.C., 1994—; asst. gen. counsel United Negro Coll. Fund, 1999—. Named one of Outstanding Young Men Am., U.S. Jaycees, 1983, 84, 85, 86, 90; recipient Spl. Achievement award IRS, 1986, 90. Mem. ABA. Avocations: tennis, racquetball, music, travel. Office: IRS 1111 Constitution Ave NW Washington DC 20224-0001 also: PO Box 6183 Washington DC 20044-6183

GARDNER, DALE RAY, lawyer; b. Broken Arrow, Okla., May 8, 1946; s. Edward Dale and Dahlia Faye (McKeen) G.; m. Phyllis Ann Weinschrott, Dec. 27, 1969. BA in History, So. Ill. U., 1968; MA in History, St. Mary's U., San Antonio, 1975; JD, Tulsa U., 1979. Bar: Okla. 1979, Colo. 1986, Tex. 1991, U.S. Ct. Mil. Appeals 1988, U.S. Ct. Claims 1989, U.S. Dist. Ct. (no. dist.) Okla. 1981, U.S. Dist. Ct. Colo. 1986, U.S. Dist. Ct. (so. dist.) Tex. 1992, U.S. Ct. Appeals (10th cir.) 1986. Pvt. practice, Sapulpa, Okla., 1979-80, 94—; asst. dist. atty. child support enforcement unit 24th Dist. Oklahoma, 1980-86, 94-95; pvt. practice Aurora, Colo., 1986-91, Houston, 1991-94; mng. atty. Hyatt Legal Svcs., Aurora, 1988-89; city atty. City of Sapulpa, Okla., 1996-99. Author: Immigration Act of 1965: The Preliminary Results, 1974, Teapot Dome: Civil Legal Cases that Closed the Scandal, 1989. Mem. Child Support Enforcement, Sapulpa, 1980-86, 94-96; trustee United Way, Sapulpa, 1985, 95; Domestic Violence Counsel, Sapulpa, 1985; chmn. bd. trustees 1st Presbyn. Ch., Sapulpa, 1985. Capt. U.S. Army, 1969-75, Vietnam., lt. col Res., judge adv., ret. Mem. Okla. Bar Assn., Tex. Bar Assn., Creek County Bar, Tulsa County Bar, Gold Coat Club (pres.), Sertoma (pres. Sapulpa 1985, pres. Collumbine 1988, 90, Sertoman of Yr. 1985), Rotary Internat. Democrat. Avocations: fishing, post card collecting. Home: 1533 Terrill Cir Sapulpa OK 74066-2567 Office: 7 S Park St Sapulpa OK 74066-4219 E-mail: ltcja@swbell.net

GARDNER, ERIC RAYMOND, lawyer; b. Derry, N.H., Nov. 13, 1946; s. William Rudolph and Lois Brooks (Wilson) G.; m. Kathleen Linda Chertok, June 14, 1969 (div. Mar. 1985); children: Matthew Eric, Thomas Martin; m. Melissa Rae Hastings, Oct. 21, 1988. BA in Polit. Sci., U. N.H., 1969; JD, Boston U., 1972. Bar: N.H. 1972, Mass. 1972, U.S. Dist. Ct. Vt., 1987, U.S. Supreme Ct. 1979. Law clk. N.H. Supreme Ct., Concord, 1972-73; assoc. Goodnow, Arwe, Ayer & Prigge, Keene, N.H., 1973-76; ptnr. Goodnow, Arwe, Ayer, Prigge & Gardner, 1977-81; pvt. practice, 1981—. Appointee N.H. Supreme Ct. Profl. Conduct Com., Concord, 1984-93; sr. counsel Am. Coll. Barristers. Editor Boston U. Law Rev., 1971-72. Clk., dir. Monodnock United Way, Keene, 1975-80; dir. Keene Family YMCA, 1974-82; chair Cheshire County Crimestoppers, Inc., 1997-98. Fellow N.H. Bar Found.; mem. ABA, ATLA, Am. Bd. Trial Advocates, Nat. Bd. Trial Advocacy, N.H. Trial Lawyers Assn., Million Dollar Advocates Forum, Greater Keene C. of C. (clk., dir. 1975-80). Avocations: flying, golf, tennis, skiing, travel. Personal injury, Product liability, Professional liability. Office: PO Box C 372 West St Keene NH 03431-2455

GARDNER, J. STEPHEN, lawyer; b. Dayton, Ohio, May 10, 1944; s. David L. and Mary (Webb) Gardner; m. Sandra Ellen Ott, Dec. 23, 1967; children: Stephen, Truett, P.J. BA in Math., U. Fla., 1966, JD, 1969. Bar: Fla. 1969, U.S. Dist Ct. (mid. dist.) Fla. 1971. Co-founder, ptnr. Ott & Gardner, Tampa, Fla., 1971-72, Bucklew, Ramsey, Ott & Gardner, Tampa, 1972-75; ptnr. Trinkle & Redman, Brandon, 1976-81; co-founder, shareholder Bush, Ross, Gardner, Warren & Rudy, P.A., Tampa, 1981—. Mem. adv. bd. SouthTrust Bank, 1986, South Hillsborough Cmty. Bank, 1988-92. Past chmn. Tampa Downtown Partnership; past pres. Davis Islands Civic Assn.; bd. dirs. Young Life Tampa, 1972, 88; bd. dirs. F.L.O.A.T., Inc., 1986-87, v.p. 1987; mem. Leadership Tampa Class of 1980; mem. bd. counelors U. Tampa, 1976-84; chmn. pastor-parish com. Hyde Park United Meth. Ch., 1982, chmn. ch. and society com., 1975, chmn. budget raisning com., 1984, lay leader, 1985, Sunday sch. supt., 1986-87, Sunday sch. tchr., 1973-86, mem. adminstrv. bd., 1974-87, chmn., 1976, co-chmn. capital campaign com., 1997, chmn. bd. trustees, 2000. 1st lt. U.S. Army, 1969-71, Vietnam; capt. USAR, 1972-75. Decorated Bronze star with oak leaf cluster. Mem. AMA, Fla. Bar Assn. (probate rules com. 1985-87), Hillsborough County Bar Assn., Tampa Tennis Assn. (past pres.), Ye Mystic Krewe Gasparilla, Tampa Yacht and Country Club (past commodore), Exch. Club (past pres. Tampa), Univ. Club Tampa (past pres.). Methodist. Banking, Probate, Real property. Office: Bush Ross Gardner Warren & Rudy PA PO Box 3913 Tampa FL 33601

GARDNER, KATHLEEN D. gas company executive, lawyer; b. Fayetteville, Ark., July 14, 1947; d. Harold Andrew and Bess (Gunn) Dulan; m. Robert Gardner, June 7, 1969 (dec. Sept. 1974); m. Cecil Alexander, Feb. 4, 1995; 1 child, Christina Ann. BS, U. Ark., 1969, JD, 1978; MA, U. Ala., 1972. Atty., corp. officer SW Energy Co., Fayetteville, 1978-85; asst. gen. counsel, asst. v.p. Reliant Energy Akrla a divsn. of Reliant Energy Resources, Little Rock, 1985-86, gen. counsel, v.p., 1986-2000, sr. v.p., 2000—. Chmn. Regional Tng. Program, Birmingham, Ala., 1972-75. Bd. dirs. the New Sch. Fayetteville, 1978-79, Robert K. Gardner Meml. Fund, Fayetteville; past bd. dirs. Keep Ark. Beautiful Commn., Ballet Ark., Ark. Mus. Sci. and History, Vis. Nurse Corp. Named Outstanding Young woman Fayetteville Jaycettes, Ark. Jaycettes, recipient Woman of Achievement in Energy award, 1990; named to Top 100 Women in Ark., Ark. Bus. Newspaper, 1995, 96, 97, 98, 99, 2000. Mem. ABA, Ark. Bar Assn. (sec. natural resources sect. 1981), Pulaski County Bar Assn., Am. Gas Assn., DAR, Ark. Assn. Def. Counsel, Am. Arbitration Assn. (Ark. adv. coun.), Alpha Delta Pi. Episcopal. Office: Reliant Energy Arkla Reliant Energy Resources Co 401 E Capitol Ave Ste 102 Little Rock AR 72202-2459

GARDNER, MARTIN RALPH, law educator; b. Salt Lake City, Nov. 3, 1944; s. Ralph John and Elaine (Ward) G.; children: Joshua, Erin, Bryn, Linsey, Jacob. BS, U. Utah, 1969, JD, 1972. Bar: Utah 1972, Nebr. 1979. Instr. law U. Ind., Bloomington, 1972-73; asst. prof. law U. Ala., Tuscaloosa, 1973-77, U. Nebr., Lincoln, 1977-78, assoc. prof. law, 1978-80, prof. law, 1980—. Contbr. articles to profl. pubis. Served with USNG, 1962—. Home: 7100 Old Post Rd Unit 8 Lincoln NE 68506-2940 Office: Coll Law U Nebr 40th and Holdredge Streets Lincoln NE 68583

GARDNER, PETER JAGLOM, lawyer, publisher; b. N.Y.C., 1958; s. Ralph David and Natalie (Jaglom) G.; m. Victoire Taittinger, 1984; children: Evan, Emma, Nadya, Parker. BA, Middlebury (Vt.) Coll., 1980; JD, M in Environ. Law magna cum laude, Vt. Law Sch., 1999. Pres. Transatlantic Comml. Svcs. Corp., 1985-90; pub. Northern Centinel, Kinderhook, N.Y., 1991—; pres., CEO Centinel Co., 1991—. Contbr. articles. Trustee Ford Sayre Meml. Ski Coun., 2000—. Mem.: ABA, N.H. Bar Assn., N.Y. Bar Assn., Frank Rowe Kenison Inn of Ct. (treas. 1999—2001), Am. Intellectual Property Law Assn., Licensing Execs. Soc. (USA and Can. chpts.), Vt. Bar Assn., Overseas Press Club. General corporate, Intellectual property, Trademark and copyright. Office: 41 S Park St Hanover NH 03755-2109

GARDNER, RUSSELL MENESE, lawyer; b. High Point, N.C., July 14, 1920; s. Joseph Hayes and Clara Emma-Lee (Flynn) G.; m. Joyce Thresher, Mar. 7, 1946; children: Winthrop G., Page Stansbury, June Thresher. AB, Duke U., 1942, JD, 1948. Bar: Fla. 1948, U.S. Ct. Appeals (5th cir.) 1949, U.S. Tax Ct. 1949, U.S. Supreme Ct. 1985. Ptnr. McCune, Hiaasen, Crum, Gardner & Duke and predecessor firms, Ft. Lauderdale, Fla., 1948-90, Gunster, Yoakley, & Stewart, 1990—. Bd. govs. Shepard Broad Law Ctr. Nova S.E. U. Trustee Mus. of Art, Inc., Ft. Lauderdale, pres., 1964-67; bd. dirs. Stranahan House, Inc., 1981—, pres., 1983-85; bd. dirs. Ft. Lauderdale Hist. Soc., 1962—, pres. 1975-85, pres. emeritus, 1985—; mem. estate planning council Duke U. Sch. Law; bd. dirs., vice chmn. Broward Performing Arts Found., Inc., 1985—. Served to lt. USNR, 1943-49. Fellow Am. Coll. Trust and Estate Counsel; mem. ABA (real property, probate, trust sect.), Am. Judicature Soc., Fla. Bar Assn. (probate, guardianship rules com.), Broward County Bar Assn. (estate planning council), Coral Ridge Country Club, Lauderdale Yacht Club, Tower Club. Republican. Presbyterian. Probate, Real property, Estate taxation. Office: PO Box 14636 Fort Lauderdale FL 33302-4636 E-mail: rgardner@gunster.com

GARDNER, TRUDI YORK, lawyer, insurance company executive; b. Portland, Oreg., Mar. 19, 1947; d. Harry and Martha (Gevurtz) York; m. Alan Joel Gardner, Dec. 19, 1971; children: Jordan Casey, Andrew Ryan. BA, UCLA, 1969; MS, Portland State U., 1971; postgrad. N.Y. Law Sch., 1975-76; JD Lewis and Clark Law Sch., 1977. Bar: Washington 1978, U.S. Dist. Ct. (we. dist.) Wash. 1979; cert. tchr. Calif., Oreg. Law clk. U.S. Atty.'s Office (so. dist.) N.Y.C., 1976, to law firm, Portland, Oreg., 1977; fin. relations specialist Puget Sound Power & Light Co., Bellevue, Wash., 1978-79; asst. atty. gen. Dept. Labor and Industries, State of Wash., Seattle, 1979-80; sole practice, Bellevue, 1980-81; regional atty. for Mont., Idaho, Wash., Oreg, Utah and Wyo., Ins. Corp. of Am., Houston, 1981-84,

regional v.p., 1984-87; sr. legis. counsel Indsl. Indemnity Corp., San Francisco, 1990—; curriculum cons. Portland (Oreg.) Pub. Schs., 1972. Assoc. editor: Multnomah Lawyer, Multnomah County Bar Assn., Portland, 1973. Contbr. articles, cover stories to Sunday supplement of The Oregonian, radio scripts for Am. Heritage Assn. to Sta. KWJJ; contbr. short stories to mags. Mem. King County United Way Conf. Panel for Developmentally Disabled, Seattle, 1978-79. Mem. Wash. State Bar Assn. (pub. relations com. 1978-81), Seattle-King County Bar Assn., Portland City Club, Seattle Mcpl. League, Pi Sigma Alpha, Pi Lambda Theta. Clubs: Women's Univ.; Bellevue Athletic. Home and Office: 215 Tiburon Ct Walnut Creek CA 94596-3437

GARFIELD, MARTIN RICHARD, lawyer; b. N.Y.C., Feb. 19, 1935; s. Harry and Sarah (Spielman) G.; m. Susan Scher, July 20, 1978 (div. Oct. 1990); 1 child, Robin. BA, Hunter Coll., 1957; JD, Bklyn. Law Sch., 1964. Bar: N.Y. 1965, U.S. Dist. Ct. (ea. and so. dists.) N.Y. 1979, U.S. Supreme Ct. 1996. Assoc. Figueroa & Madow, N.Y.C., 1965-68, Schneider Kleinick & Weitz, N.Y.C., 1968-70; ptnr. Breadbar Garfield & Solomon, 1970-86; sr. ptnr. Breadbar Garfield & Schmelkin, 1986—. Arbitrator Civil Ct. N.Y. County, 1986—; mgr. N.Y. State Athletic Commn., 1996—. Mem. Am. Trial Lawyers Assn., N.Y. State Bar Assn. (torts, ins. sect.), N.Y. Trials Lawyers Assn. Avocations: tennis, basketball, boxing analysis, body building. State civil litigation, Personal injury, Product liability. Office: Breadbar Garfield & Schmelkin 11 Park Pl Fl 10 New York NY 10007-2895

GARFINKEL, BARRY HERBERT, lawyer; b. Bklyn., June 19, 1928; s. Abraham and Shirley (Siegel) G.; m. Gloria Lorenz, Feb. 16, 1969; children— David, James, Paul. BSS, CCNY, 1950; LLB, Yale U., 1955. Bar: N.Y. State 1955, U.S. Supreme Ct. 1959. Law clk. to Hon. Edward Weinfeld U.S. Dist. Ct., N.Y.C., 1955-56; assoc. Skadden, Arps, Slate, Meagher & Flom, 1956-61, ptnr., 1961-2000, of counsel, 2000—. Trustee, chmn. Practising Law Inst., Law Ctr. Found. of N.Y. U. Sch. Law Aperture Found., program com. 2d. Cir. Jud. Conf. Mng. editor: Yale Law Jour. Bd. dirs., former dir. Jewish Mus., Legal Aid Soc.; former trustee N.Y. Community Trust; pres. coun. Mus. City of N.Y.; chmn. lawyers' div., spl. gifts campaign United Jewish Appeal/Fedn. Jewish Philanthropies, 1979-81; mem. print com. Whitney Mus., Com. on Rsch. Libraries N.Y. Pub. Lib. Recipient Torch of Learning award Am. Friends of Hebrew U., 1983, Brandeis Distingish. Community Svc. award Brandeis U., 1985. Fellow Am. Coll. Trial Lawyers, Am. Bar Found.; mem. ABA, Am. Arbitration Assn., Assn. of Bar of City of N.Y. (exec. com., judiciary com., past chmn. fed. cts. com.), N.Y. State Bar Assn., Am. Law Inst. Club: Yale (N.Y.C.). Federal civil litigation, State civil litigation, Private international. Home: 211 Central Park W New York NY 10024-6020 Office: Skadden Arps Slate Meagher & Flom 4 Times Sq Fl 24 New York NY 10036-6595

GARFINKEL, NEIL B. lawyer; b. New Hyde Park, N.Y., Jan. 29, 1964; s. Elliot Z. and Diana (Fein) G.; m. Shari Chaitin, Aug. 14, 1988; children: Alyssa Hope, Joshua Phillip. BA summa cum laude, SUNY, Albany, 1986; JD, Cornell U., 1989. Bar: N.Y. 1990. Assoc. Proskauer, Rose, Goetz & Mendelsohn, N.Y.C., 1989-91, Bank & Bank, Garden City, N.Y., 1992-94; pntr. Abrams, Garfinkel & Rosen, LLP, N.Y.C., 1994—. Mem. N.Y. State Bar Assn., Phi Beta Kappa. Banking, Real property. Office: Abrams Garfinkel & Rosen LLP 237 W 35th St 4th Fl New York NY 10001 also: 12301 Wilshire Blvd Ste 402 Los Angeles CA 90025-1000 E-mail: ngarfinkel@agrlaw.com

GARGIULO, ANDREA W. lawyer; b. Hartford, Conn., Apr. 26, 1946; d. Charles M. and Irma S. (Rubin) Weiner; m. Richard A. Gargiulo, Nov. 26, 1975; 1 child, John K. BA, Smith Coll., 1968; JD cum laude, Suffolk U., 1972. Bar: Mass. 1972, U.S. Dist. Ct. Mass. 1975, U.S. Ct. Appeals (11th cir.) 1981, U.S. Supreme Ct. 1983. Asst. dist. atty. Middlesex County, Mass., 1972-75; chmn. Boston Fin. Commn., 1975-77; counsel Gargiulo, Rudnick, & Gargiulo, Boston, 1976—. Chmn. Boston Licensing Bd., 1977-89; lectr. Northeastern U. Coll. Criminal Justice, Boston, 1978, 80; bd. dirs. Arbella Mut. Ins. Co.; host (TV show) Women Today, 1994-96. Mem. Mass. Ethics Commn., 1985-88; mem. bd. overseers Children's Hosp., Boston, 1983-99; chmn. Mass. Bd. Overseers, 1996. Mem. Bay Club, Beacon Hill Garden Club, Harvard Mus. Assn., Wianno Yacht Club, Univ. Club. Democrat. Avocation: sailing, acting. Administrative and regulatory, General civil litigation, General practice. Home: 13 W Cedar St Boston MA 02108-1211 Office: Gargiulo Rudnick & Gargiulo 66 Long Wharf Boston MA 02110-3605

GARIBALDI, MARIE LOUISE, former state supreme court justice; b. Jersey City, Nov. 26, 1934; d. Louis J. and Marie (Serventi) G. BA, Conn. Coll., 1956; LLB, Columbia U., 1959; LLM in Tax. Law, NYU, 1963. Atty. Office of Regional Counsel, IRS, N.Y.C., 1960-66; assoc. McCarter & English, Newark, 1966-69; ptnr. Riker, Danzig, Scherer, Hyland & Pernutti, 1969-82; assoc. justice N.J. Supreme Court, 1982-2000. Contbr. articles to profl. jours. Trustee St. Peter's Coll.; co-chmn. Thomas Kean's campaign for Gov. of N.J., 1981, mem. transition team, 1981; mem. Gov. Byrne's Commn. on Dept. of Commerce, 1981. Recipient Disting. Alumni award NYU Law Alumni of N.J., 1982; recipient Disting. Alumni award Columbia U., 1982 Fellow Am. Bar Found.; mem. N.J. Bar Assn. (pres. 1982), Columbia U. Sch. Law Alumni Assn. (bd. dirs.) Roman Catholic.

GARLAND, MERRICK BRIAN, federal judge; b. Chgo., Nov. 13, 1952; s. Cyril and Shirley Garland. AB summa cum laude, Harvard U., 1974, JD magna cum laude, 1977. Bar: D.C. 1979, U.S. Dist. Ct. D.C. 1980, U.S. Ct. Appeals (D.C. and 9th cirs.) 1980, U.S. Ct. Appeals (4th cir.) 1983, U.S. Supreme Ct. 1983. Law clk. to judge U.S. Ct. Appeals (2d cir.), N.Y.C., 1977-78; law clk. to justice U.S. Supreme Ct., Washington, 1978-79; spl. asst. to U.S. atty. gen. Dept. Justice, 1979-81; from assoc. to ptnr. Arnold & Porter, 1981-89; asst. U.S. atty. Dept. Justice, 1989-92; ptnr. Arnold & Porter, 1992-93; dep. asst. atty. gen., criminal divsn. Dept. Justice, 1993-94, prin. assoc. dep. atty. gen., 1994-97; circuit judge U.S. Ct. Appeals, 1997—. Lectr. on law Harvard U. Law Sch., 1985-86. Author: Antitrust and State Action Yale Law Jour., 1983, Deregulation and Jud. Rev., Harvard Law Rev., 1985. Mem. Phi Beta Kappa. Office: US Courthouse 333 Constitution Ave NW Washington DC 20001-2802

GARLAND, RICHARD ROGER, lawyer; b. Princeton, Ill., Aug. 20, 1958; s. Louis Roger and Irene Marie (Tonozzi) G. BA in Polit. Sci. summa cum laude, U. S. Fla., 1979; JD with honors, U. Fla., 1982. Bar: Fla. 1982, U.S. Dist. Ct. (mid. dist.) Fla. 1983, U.S. Ct. Appeals (11th cir.) 1987, U.S. Supreme Ct. 1988, U.S. Ct. Appeals (fed. cir.) 1995; Fla. Bar cert. in appellate practice, 1995. Instr., supr. appellate advocacy U. Fla., Gainesville, 1981-82; assoc. Dickinson, O'Riorden, Gibbons, Quale, Shields & Carlton, Venice, Fla., 1983-85, Sarasota, 1986-90; ptnr., sr. atty. Dickinson & Gibbons, 1991—. Pres. parish coun. San Pedro Cath. Ch., North Port, Fla., 1986-92; mem. Sarasota County Libr. Adv. Bd., 1999-2001. Mem. ABA, Fla. Bar Assn., Sarasota County Bar Assn. (editor newsletter 1991-93, bd. dirs. 1994-96, treas. 1996-97, sec. 1997-98, v.p. 1998-99, pres.-elect 1999-2000, pres. 2000-01), Judge John M. Scheb Am. Inn of Ct. (treas. 1998-99, counselor 1999-2000, pres.-elect 2000-01, pres. 2001—, master), U. South Fla. Alumni Assn., Phi Kappa Phi, Pi Sigma Alpha. Democrat. Roman Catholic. Appellate, General civil litigation, Health. Office: Dickinson & Gibbons PA 1750 Ringling Blvd Sarasota FL 34236-6836 E-mail: rgarland@dglawyers.com

GARLAND, SYLVIA DILLOF, lawyer; b. N.Y.C., June 4, 1919; d. Morris and Frieda (Gassner) Dillof; m. Albert Garland, May 4, 1942; children: Margaret Garland, Paul B. BA, Bklyn. Coll., 1939; JD cum laude, N.Y. Law Sch., 1960. Bar: N.Y. 1960, U.S. Ct. Appeals (2d cir.) 1965, U.S. Ct. Claims 1965, U.S. Supreme Ct. 1967, U.S. Customs Ct. 1972, U.S. Ct. Appeals (5th cir.), 1979. Assoc. Borden, Skidell, Fleck and Steindler, Jamaica, N.Y., 1960-61, Fields, Zimmerman, Skodnick & Segall, Jamaica, 1961-65, Marshall, Brater, Greene, Allison & Tucker, N.Y.C., 1965-68; law sec. to N.Y. Supreme Ct. justice Suffolk County, 1968-70; ptnr. Hofheimer, Gartlir & Gross, N.Y.C., 1970—. Asst. adj. prof. N.Y. Law Sch., 1974-79; mem. com. on character and fitness N.Y. State Supreme Ct., 1st Jud. Dept., 1985—, vice chmn., 1991—. Author: Workman's Compensation, 1957, Labor Law, 1959, Wills, 1962; contbg. author: Guardians and Custodians, 1970; editor-in-chief Law Rev. Jour., N.Y. Law Forum, 1959-60 (svc. award 1960); contbr. articles to mag. Trustee N.Y. Law Sch., 1979-90, trustee emeritus, 1991—; pres. Oakland chpt. B'nai Brith, Bayside, N.Y., 1955-57. Recipient Disting. Alumnus award N.Y. Law Sch., 1978, Judge Charles W. Froessel award N.Y. Law Sch., 1997. Mem. ABA (litigation sect., family law sect.), N.Y. State Bar Assn. (family law sect.), Queen's County Bar Assn. (sec. civil practice 1960-79), N.Y. Law Sch. Alumni Assn. (pres. 1976-77), N.Y. Law Forum Alumni Assn. (pres. 1963-65). Jewish. General civil litigation, State civil litigation, Family and matrimonial. Home: 425 E 58th St New York NY 10022-2300

GARLICK, MICHAEL, lawyer, franchise consultant; b. N.Y.C., Oct. 20, 1944; s. Nathan S. and Gertrude (Finkel) G.; m. Judith Ann Schaufeld, May 12, 1977; children: Nathan S., Max Aaron. B.A., Lehigh U., 1966; J.D., NYU, 1969. Bar: N.Y. 1970, Fla. 1971, Calif. 1973, D.C. 1974, U.S. Dist. Ct. (so. dist.) Fla. Gen. counsel Internat. House of Pancakes Fla., Miami, 1970-74, cons., 1983— ; sr. ptnr. Garlick, Cohn, Darrow & Hollander, Miami, 1974-79; gen. counsel Internat. Adv. Group, Inc., Miami, 1980—; dir. Tao Inst., Inc.; chmn. bd. Attys. Profl. Assn., Inc., Miami, 1981-83. Author: The Karate Decision, 1984. Editor Lawletter, 1981-83. Mem. Floridians United for Safe Energy, Miami. Served with U.S. Army, 1969. Mem. Forum Com. on Franchising, ABA, Dade County Bar Assn. North Miami Beach Karate (pres. 1970-80), Tai Chi Chaun Assn. (pres. 1983—), Phi Beta Kappa, Beta Alpha Psi. Office: 1515 N Federal Hwy Boca Raton FL 33432-1911

GARMAN, RITA B. judge; b. Aurora, Ill., Nov. 19, 1943; m. Gill Garman; children: Sara Ellen, Andrew Gill. BS in econs. suma cum laude, U. Ill. , 1965; JD with distinction, U. Iowa, 1968. Asst. state atty. Vermilion County, 1969—73; pvt. practice Sebat, Swanson, Banks, Lessen & Garman, 1973; assoc. cir. judge, 1974—86; cir. judge Fifth Jud. Cir., 1986—95, presiding cir. judge, 1987—95; judge Fourth Dist. Appellate Ct., 1996—2001; Supreme Ct. justice Ill. State Supreme Ct., 2001—. Mem.: Ill. State Bar Assn., Iowa Bar Assn., Vermilion County Bar Assn., Ill. Judge's Assn. Office: 2832 N Vermilion St Rm 4 Danville IL 61832*

GARNER, BRYAN ANDREW, law educator, consultant, writer; b. Lubbock, Tex., Nov. 17, 1958; s. Gary Thomas and Mariellen (Griffin) G.; m. Pan Anurugsa, May 26, 1984; children: Caroline Beatrix, Alexandra Bess. BA, U. Tex., 1980, JD, 1984; LLD (hon.), Thomas M. Cooley Law Sch., 2000. Bar: Tex. 1984, U.S. Ct. Appeals (5th cir.) 1985, U.S. Dist. Ct. (no. dist.) Tex. 1986. Law clk. to judge U.S. Ct. Appeals (5th cir.), Austin, Tex., 1984-85; assoc. Carrington, Coleman, Sloman & Blumenthal, Dallas, 1985-88; dir. Tex./Oxford Ctr. for Legal Lexicography U. Tex. Sch. Law, Austin, 1988-90; adj. prof. law So. Meth. U., Dallas, 1990—. Vis. assoc. prof. law U. Tex., 1988-90; pres. LawProse, Inc., 1990—; vis. scholar U. Salzburg, 1995, U. Glasgow, 1996, U. Cambridge, Eng., 1997; chmn. plain-lang. com. State Bar Tex., 1989-95; lectr., cons. in field. Author: A Dictionary of Modern Legal Usage, 1987, 2d edit., 1995, The Elements of Legal Style, 1991, Guidelines for Drafting and Editing Court Rules, 1996, A Dictionary of Modern American Usage, 1998, Securities Disclosure in Plain English, 1999, The Winning Bried, 1999, Legal Writing in Plain English, 2001; editor Scribes Jour. Legal Writing, 1989-2000; editor: Texas, Our Texas, 1984, Black's Law Dictionary, 1996, 7th edit., 1999, A Handbook of Basic Law Terms, 1999, A Handbook of Business Law Terms, 1999, A Handbook of Family Law Terms, 2001; mem. editl. bd. Tex. Law Rev., 1983-84; contbr. articles to profl. jours. Recipient Henry C. Lind award Assn. Reporters Judicial Decisions, 1994, Clairty award State Bar Mich., 1997; named one of Outstanding Young Tex. Ex award, 1998. Fellow Tex. Bar Found.; mem. ABA, Am. Law Inst. (commn. on bylaws and coun. rules 1993-94), Tex. Bar Assn. (chmn. plain lang. com. 1990—), Dallas Bar Assn., 5th Cir. Bar Assn., Am. Judicature Soc., Am. Dialect Soc., Dictionary Soc. N.Am., Philos. Soc. Tex., Bent Tree Country Club, Scribes (exec. bd. 1990-2001, pres. 1997-98), Friars (abbot 1983-84), Phi Beta Kappa. Republican. Avocation: golf. Home: 6478 Lakehurst Ave Dallas TX 75230-5131

GARNER, ROBERT EDWARD LEE, lawyer; b. Bowling Green, Ky., Sept. 26, 1946; s. Alto Luther and Katie Mae (Sanders) G.; m. Suzanne Marie Searles, Aug. 22, 1981; children: Jessica Marie, Abigail Lee. BA, U. Ala., Tuscaloosa, 1968; JD, Harvard U., 1971. Bar: Ga. 1971, U.S. Dist. Ct. (no. dist.) Ga. 1974, U.S. Ct. Appeals (5th cir.) 1974, U.S. Ct. Appeals (11th cir.) 1981, Ala. 1982, U.S. Ct. Appeals (4th cir.) 1991, S.C. 1992. Assoc. Gambrell, Russell & Forbes, Atlanta, 1972-76, ptnr., 1976-80, Haskell, Slaughter & Young and predecessors, Birmingham, Ala., 1981-88, mng. ptnr., 1986-87, of counsel, 1988-90; gen. counsel, sec. Builders Transport, Inc., 1988-90; ptnr. Nelson, Mullins, Riley & Scarborough, Atlanta and Columbia, S.C., 1991-96; mem. Haskell Slaughter & Young, L.L.C., Birmingham, 1996-2000, mng. ptnr., 2000—. 1st lt. JAGC, USAF, 1971-72. Mem. ABA (com. on fed. regulation of securities, subcom. on disclosure matters and continuous reporting, ad hoc com. on pub. co. info. practices), State Bar Ga., Ala. State Bar, Birmingham Bar, S.C. Bar, U. Ala. Alumni Assn., Harvard U. Alumni Assn., Am. Soc. Corp. Secs. (mem. tech. com.), Phi Alpha Theta, Pi Sigma Alpha. Republican. General corporate, Finance, Securities. Home: 284 Kings Crest Ln Pelham AL 35124-2846 Office: Haskell Slaughter Young & Rediker LLC 1200 Am South/Harbert Plaza 1901 6th Ave N Birmingham AL 35203-2618 E-mail: relg@hsy.com

GARNER, WILLIAM MICHAEL, lawyer; b. Huntington, W.Va., Sept. 28, 1949; s. William Max Garner and Celeste (Eichling) Neuffer; m. Christine Ann McElligott, Aug. 18, 1997. AB, Columbia U., 1971; JD, NYU, 1975. Bar: N.Y. 1976, N.J. 1994, Minn. 1997, U.S. Dist. Ct. (so. dist.) N.Y. 1977, U.S. Dist. Ct. (ea. dist.) N.Y. 1980, U.S. Dist. Ct. N.J. 1994, U.S. Dist. Ct. Minn. 1998, U.S. Ct. Appeals (2d cir.) 1980, U.S. Ct. Appeals (11th cir.) 1985, U.S. Ct. Appeals (7th cir.) 1993. Assoc. Hughes Hubbard & Reed, N.Y.C., 1976-80, Rivkin, Sherman & Levy, N.Y.C., 1980-84; ptnr. Schnader, Harrison, Segal & Lewis, 1985-97, Dady & Garner, P.A., Mpls., 1997—. Author: Franchise and Distribution Law and Practice, 1990; editor Franchise Law Jour., 1988-93; contbr. articles to publs. Fellow Am. Bar Found.; mem. ABA, Assn. of Bar of City of N.Y. Home: 1815 Summit Ave Saint Paul MN 55105-1835 Office: Dady & Garner PA 4000 IDS Ctr 80 S 8th St Minneapolis MN 55402-2100 E-mail: wmgarner@dadygarner.com

GARNETT, STANLEY IREDALE, II, lawyer, utility company executive; b. Petersburg, Va., Aug. 11, 1943; s. Stanley Arthur and Edith (Keirstead) G.; children: Matthew S.A., Andrew F.W. BA, Colby Coll., 1965; MBA, U. Pa., 1967; JD, NYU, 1973. Bar: N.Y. 1974. Sr. fin. analyst Standard Oil Co. of N.J., N.Y.C., 1967-70; assoc. Milbank, Tweed, Hadley & McCloy, 1973-81; v.p.-legal and regulatory Allegheny Power Sys., Inc., 1981-90, v.p. fin., 1990-94, sr. v.p. fin., 1994-95; sr. advisor Putnam, Hayes & Bartlett, 1996-97, 98-00; exec. v.p. Fla. Progress Corp., St. Petersburg, 1997-98; ptnr. PA Consulting Group, 2000—. Bd. dirs. Bay Corp Holdings, Inc. Vice chmn. Episcopal Ch. Bldg. Fund; trustee, sec. ICB Internat. Ctr. for Disabled. Joseph P. Wharton scholar, 1965-67. Mem. ABA, N.Y. State Bar Assn. Republican. Episcopalian. Real property. Home: 1000 Monterey Blvd NE Saint Petersburg FL 33704-2310 E-mail: stan.garnett@paconsulting.com

GARODIA, ANIRUDDH, lawyer; b. Calcutta, India, Oct. 20, 1971; s. Bijoy Kumar and Bimala Devi Garodia; m. Anuranjita Kedia, Dec. 1, 1995. LLB, Calcutta U., 1998. Bar: India 1999. Law asst. L.P. Agarwalla & Co., Calcutta, 1992-95, Choudhury & Co., Calcutta, 1995-98; legal exec. S. Jalan & Co., 1998-99; proprietor Garodia Assocs. Advocates, 1999—. Cons. Bhubhandar Tea Co., 1995—, Internat. Bus. Orgn., 1998—, Titagarh Industries Ltd., 1999—. Mem. Incorporated Law Soc., Indian Coun. Arbitration, Adv. Club Calcutta. Mem. Manau Vikash Party. Avocations: sports, reading. Patent, Real property, Transportation. Home: GD 203 Sector III Salt Lake City 700091 Calcutta India Office: Garodia Assocs Bookmann 6 Kiran Shankar Roy Rd 700001 Calcutta India E-mail: aniruddhgarodia@hotmail.com

GARRELS, SHERRY ANN, lawyer; b. Chgo., Feb. 5, 1956; d. William Henry and Jacqueline Ann G.; m. Timothy Anthony Marion, Aug. 1, 1987 (div. June 1988); 1 child, William Garrels-Marion; 1 child, Georgianna Garrels-Rogers. BA, Barat Coll., 1980; certificate, Trinity Coll., 1989; JD, Western State U., 1990. Bar: Calif. 1992, U.S. Dist. Ct. (ctrl. dist.) Calif. 1992, U.S. Dist. Ct. (no. dist.) Calif. 1993, U.S. Dist. Ct. (so. dist.) Calif. 1996, U.S. Ct. Appeals (9th cir.) 1994, U.S. Tax Ct. 1996. Pvt. practice, Huntington Beach, Calif., 1992—. Arbitrator Nat. Panel Consumer Arbitrators, Huntington Beach, 1996, State Panel Consumer Arbitrators, Huntington Beach, 1996, Better Bus. Bureau, 1996—, U.S. C. of C., 1996, Huntington Beach C. of C., 1996. Editor The Dictum, 1989. Active 4th of July Exec. Bd., Huntington Beach, 1996—. Mem. Assn. Trial Lawyers, L.A. Trial Assn., Orange County Bar Assn., St. Bonny Golf Classic (dir. 1991-97), Delta Theta Phi. Republican. Presbyterian. Avocations: swimming, golf, scuba diving. State civil litigation, Criminal, Real property. Office: 5942 Edinger Ave Ste 113-702 Huntington Beach CA 92649-1763 Fax: 714-374-0104

GARRETT, RICHARD G. lawyer; b. N.Y.C., Oct. 16, 1948; BA magna cum laude, Emory U., 1970, JD, 1973. Bar: Ga. 1973, Fla 1979; U.S. Dist. Ct. (no. dist.) Ga. 1973, (so. dist.) Fla. 1979, U.S. Dist. Ct. (so. dist. trial bar) Fla. 1979; U.S. Ct. Appeals (5th cir.) 1974; U.S. Ct. Appeals (9th. cir., 11 cir.) 1981; U.S. Supreme Ct. 1981. Program dir., instr. rsch., writing and advocacy Emory U. Sch. Law, 1972-73; gen. counsel Greenberg, Traurig, Miami, Fla. Past chmn. litigation dept., exec. com. bd. dirs. Greenberg, Traurig, Miami. Editor Emory Law Journal, 1972-73. Recipient 1st place and Best Brief award Region V Nat. Moot Ct. Competition, 1972. Mem. ABA, The Fla. Bar Assn., State Bar Ga., Omicron Delta Kappa, Order of the Barristers. Banking, Real property, Securities. Office: Greenberg Traurig 1221 Brickell Ave Miami FL 33131-3224

GARRIDO DE LAS HERAS, MIGUEL, lawyer; b. Madrid, Spain, Sept. 6, 1973; s. Jose Garrido and Maria Luisa de las Heras. Law Degree, U. Carlos III, Madrid, 1995; LLM, Instituto de Empresa, Madrid, 1996. Lawyer J & A Garrigues, N.Y.C., 1995, Melchor de las Heras, Albinana & Suarez de Lezo, Madrid, 1997—. Invited prof. ICADE, Madrid, 2000, U. Carlos III, Madrid, 1998; asst. prof. Instituto de Empresa, Madrid, 1997-99. Mem. Medrid Bar Assn. General corporate, Mergers and acquisitions, Securities. Office: Melchor de las Heras et al c Jose Abascal 58 Madrid 28003 Spain

GARRIGLE, WILLIAM ALOYSIUS, lawyer; b. Camden, N.J., Aug. 6, 1941; s. John Michael and Catherine Agnes (Ebeling) G.; m. Jeannette R. Regan, Aug. 15, 1965 (div.); children: Maeve Regan, Emily Way; m. Rosalind Chadwick, Feb. 17, 1984; 1 child, Susan Chadwick. BS, LaSalle U., 1963; LLB, Boston Coll., 1966. Bar: N.J. 1966, U.S. Dist. Ct. N.J., U.S. Ct. Appeals (3rd cir.) 1973, U.S. Supreme Ct., 1973; cert. civil trial atty., N.J.; cert. civil trial adv., Nat. Bd. Trial Advocacy; diplomate Am. Bd. Profl. Liability Attys. Assoc. Taylor, Bischoff, Neutze & Williams, Camden, 1966-67, Moss & Powell, Camden, 1967-70; ptnr. Garrigle and Palm, Cherry Hill, N.J., 1970—. Pres. South Jersey chpt. Am. Bd. Trial Advocates, 2001. With USAR, 1959-67. Mem. ABA, N.J. State Bar Assn., Burlington County Bar Assn., Camden County Bar Assn., Internat. Assn. Def. Counsel, Def. Rsch. Inst., N.J. Def. Assn., Am. Bd. Trial Advs. (diplomate), Fedn. of Ins. and Corp. Counsel, Trial Attys. N.J., Camden County Inn of Ct. (master of the bench, chmn. 1989-96, treas. 1996—), Tavistock Country Club. Federal civil litigation, State civil litigation, Insurance. Home: 223 E Main St Moorestown NJ 08057-2905 Office: Garrigle and Palm 1415 Route 70 E Ste 204 Cherry Hill NJ 08034-2237 E-mail: garrigle@aol.com

GARRISON, PITSER HARDEMAN, lawyer, mayor emeritus; b. Lufkin, Tex., Mar. 7, 1912; s. Homer and Mattie (Milam) G.; m. Berneice Jones, Dec. 3, 1936 (dec. Apr. 1992); m. Reba Brent, Sept. 29, 1993. Student, Lon Morris Jr. Coll., 1929-30, Stephen F. Austin State U., 1930-32; LLB, U. Tex., 1935. Bar: Tex. 1935, U.S. Dist. Ct. (ea. dist.) Tex. 1936, U.S. Dist. Ct. (so. dist.) Tex. 1938, U.S. Ct. Appeals (5th cir.) 1939. Ptnr. Garrison, Renfrow, Zeleskey, Cornelius & Rogers, Lufkin, 1935-52, sr. ptnr., 1952-68; chmn., gen. counsel Lufkin Nat. Bank, 1968-81; sole practice Lufkin, 1981-99; ptnr. Garrison & Williams PLLC, 1999—. Mayor City of Lufkin, 1970-88, mayor emeritus, 1988—; past bd. dirs., past pres. Angelina and Neches River Authority, Lufkin; past pres. Deep East Tex. Coun. of Govts., Jasper; past bd. dirs., past chmn. Angelina County Tax Appraisal Dist., Lufkin; bd. dirs. Meml. Hosp., Lufkin, 1975-91. Maj. U.S. Army, 1942-46. Recipient Disting. Alumnus award Lon Morris Jr. Coll., 1974, Disting. Alumnus award Stephen F. Austin State U., 1976; named East Texan of the Month, East Tex. C. of C., 1981, East Texan of Yr., Deep East Tex. Coun. of Govts., 1980. Fellow Am. Coll. Trial Lawyers, Tex. Bar Found. (charter); mem. ABA, Tex. Bar Assn., Angelina County Bar Assn. (past pres.), Rotary (past pres.), Masons, Shriners, Phi Delta Phi. Democrat. Methodist. State civil litigation, General practice, Probate. Home: 1302 Tom Temple Dr Apt 302 Lufkin TX 75904-5592 Office: 609 E Lufkin Ave Lufkin TX 75901

GARRY, JOHN THOMAS, II, lawyer; b. Albany, N.Y., Dec. 12, 1923; s. Joseph A. II and Jean Theresa (Cramond) G.; m. Mary Regina Hoffman (dec.); children: John, Michael, Regina, Maureen, Suzanne, Patricia; m. Claire Baynes, 1989. Student, Cornell U., 1942-43; BA, St. Bernadine of Siena Coll., 1949; LLB, JD, Union U., 1952. Bar: N.Y. 1952, U.S. Supreme Ct. 1952. Asst. corp. counsel City of Albany, 1953-55, asst. dist. atty., 1955-58; dist. atty. Albany County, 1958-68; sr. ptnr. Garry & Cahill, Albany, 1968—. Exec. chmn. Dem. Cen. Com., Albany, Albany Big Bros./Big Sisters Am., 1971; trustee Siena Coll., Loudonville, N.Y., 1987-97; mem. Empire State Art Commn., 1990-95, N.Y. State Plz. Art Commn. Served with USAAF, 1943. Decorated Air medal. Mem. ABA, N.Y. State Bar Assn. (character com. admission), Albany County Bar Assn., Am. Judicature Soc., Internat. Narcotic Enforcement Officers Assn., N.Y. State Dist. Attys. Assn. (v.p. 1967), St. Bernadine of Siena Coll. Alumni Assn. (pres. 1964, trustee 1989-97), Am. Legion, VFW, KC (Grand Knight 1956). Club: Wolfert's Roost Country. Lodges: K.C., Elks. Criminal, Estate planning, General practice.

GARSON, JACK A. lawyer; b. San Juan, P.R., Dec. 19, 1960; BA cum laude with deptl. honors, U. Md., 1982; JD cum laude, George Washington U., 1985. Bar: Md. 1985, D.C. 1987. Mem. Garson & Assocs., Bethesda, Md. Mem. ABA, Md. State Bar Assn., Montgomery County Bar Assn., Phi Alpha Delta General corporate, Real property, Technology law. Office: Garson & Assocs Ste 600 6905 Rockledge Dr Bethesda MD 20813

GARTEN, DAVID BURTON, lawyer; b. Iowa City, Mar. 23, 1952; s. William B. and Linda (Laird) G.; m. Anita Wallner, Mar. 12, 1983. BA summa cum laude, honors in Econs., Yale U., 1974, JD, 1977. Law clk. to Hon. Anthony M. Kennedy U.S. Ct. Appeals (9th cir.), Sacramento, 1977-78; assoc. Kirkland & Ellis, Chgo., 1979-84, ptnr., 1984-90; v.p., gen. counsel NL Industries Inc., Houston, 1990—. Mem. Phi Beta Kappa. Avocations: skiing, golf. Antitrust, General civil litigation, Securities. Office: NL Industries Inc 16825 Northchase Dr Ste 1200 Houston TX 77060-6012

GARTH, BRYANT GEOFFREY, law educator, foundation executive; b. San Diego, Dec. 9, 1949; s. William and Patricia (Feild) G.; children: Heather, Andrew, Daniela. BA magna cum laude, Yale U., 1972; JD, Stanford U., 1975; PhD, European U. Inst., Florence, Italy, 1979. Bar: Calif. 1975, Ind. 1988. Law clk. to judge U.S. Dist. Ct. (no. dist.) Calif., San Francisco, 1978-79; asst. prof. Ind. U., Bloomington, 1979-82, assoc. prof., 1982-85, prof., 1985-92, dean Law Sch., 1986-90; dir. Am. Bar Found., Chgo., 1990—. Cons. Ont. Law Reform Commn., 1984-85, 94, World Bank Argentina Project, 1993-94, World Bank Peru Project, 1996; vis. assoc. prof. U. Mich., Ann Arbor, 1983-84; bd. dirs. Internat. Human Rights Law Inst.; mem. bd. visitors Stanford U. Law Sch., 1993-2000. Author: Neighborhood Law Firms for the Poor, 1980; co-editor: Access to Justice: A World Survey, 1978, Access to Justice: Emerging Issues and Perspectives, 1979, Dealing in Virtue, 1996; contbr. articles to profl. jours. V.p. H.G. & K.F. Montgomery Found. Rsch. grantee NSF, 1982, 91, 92, 95, 99, 2001, Nat. Inst. Dispute Resolution, 1985, Ind. Supreme Ct., 1989, Italian Coun. Rsch., 1989, Keck, 1995, MacArthur, 1997. Mem. Am. Law Inst., Law and Soc. Assn., Internat. Assn. Procedural Law. Democrat. Office: Am Bar Found 750 N Lake Shore Dr Chicago IL 60611-4403 E-mail: bggarth@abfn.org

GARTH, LEONARD I. federal judge; b. Bklyn., Apr. 7, 1921; s. Frank A. and Anne F. (Jacobs) Goldstein; m. Sarah Miriam Kaufman, Sept. 6, 1942; 1 child, Tobie Gail Garth Meisel. BA, Columbia U., 1942; postgrad., Nat. Inst. Pub. Affairs, 1942-43; LLB, Harvard U., 1952. Bar: N.J. 1952. Mem. firm Cole, Berman & Garth (and predecessors), Paterson, N.J., 1952-70; judge U.S. Dist. Ct. for Dist. N.J., Newark, 1970-73; U.S. cir. judge Ct. Appeals for 3d Cir., 1973—; lectr. Inst. Continuing Legal Edn.; lectr., coadj. mem. faculty Rutgers U. Law Sch., 1978-98, Seton Hall Law Sch., 1980-95. Mem. N.J. Bd. Bar Examiners, 1964-68; mem. com. on revision gen. and admiralty rules Fed. Dist. Ct. N.J.; former mem. com. on fin. disclosure Jud. Conf. U.S.; adv. bd. Fed. Cts. Study Com. Pres., trustee Harvard Law Sch. Assn. N.J., 1958-63; adv. bd. Law and Soc. Major of Ramapo Coll.; Served as 1st lt. AUS, 1943-46. Mem. ABA (N.J. fellows, appellate judges conf.), Fed. Bar Assn., Passaic County (N.J.) Bar Assn. (pres. 1967-68), Am. Law Inst. Office: Ct Appeals ML King Jr Fed Bldg 50 Walnut St Rm 5040 Newark NJ 07102-3506 also: 20613 US Courthouse Philadelphia PA 19106 E-mail: chambers_of_judge_leonard_garth@ca3.uscourts.gov

GARTNER, HAROLD HENRY, III, lawyer; b. L.A., June 23, 1948; s. Harold Henry Jr. and Frances Mildred (Evans) G.; m. Denise Helene Young, June 7, 1975; children: Patrick Christopher, Matthew Alexander. Student, Pasadena City Coll., 1966-67, George Williams Coll., 1967-68, Calif. State U., Los Angeles, 1969; JD cum laude, Loyola U., Los Angeles, 1972. Bar: Calif. 1972, U.S. Dist. Ct. (cen. dist.) Calif. 1973, U.S. Ct. Appeals (9th cir.) 1973. Assoc. Hitt, Murray & Caffray, Long Beach, Calif., 1972; dep. city atty. City of L.A., 1972-73; assoc. Patterson, Ritner & Lockwood, L.A., 1973-79; mng. ptnr. all offices Patterson, Ritner, Lockwood, Gartner & Jurich, L.A., Ventura, Bakersfield, and San Bernardino, Calif., 1991—. Instr. law Ventura Coll., 1981. Recipient Am. Jurisprudence award Trusts and Equity, 1971. Mem. ABA, Am. Bd. Trial Advocates, Calif. Bar Assn., Ventura County Bar Assn., Nat. Assn. Def. Counsel, Assn. Am. Bd. Trial Advocates, So. Calif. Def. Counsel, Ventura County Trial Lawyers Assn. Republican. Club: Pacific Corinthian Yacht. Avocations: sailing, scuba diving, flying. State civil litigation, Insurance, Personal injury. Home: 6900 Via Alba Camarillo CA 93012-8279 Office: Patterson Ritner Lockwood Gartner & Jurich 260 Maple Ct Ste 231 Ventura CA 93003-3570 E-mail: hgartner@dock.net

GARVEY, JOHN HUGH, dean, law educator; b. Sharon, Pa., Sept. 28, 1948; s. Cyril T. and Claudia C. (Evans) G.; m. Jeanne Barnes Walter, Aug. 30, 1975; children: Kevin, Elizabeth, Katherine, Michael, Clare. AB, U. Notre Dame, 1970; JD, Harvard U., 1974. Bar: Ky. 1976, U.S. Supreme Ct. 1982. Law clk. to chief judge U.S. Ct. Appeals (2d cir.), N.Y.C., 1974-75; assoc. Morrison & Foerster, San Francisco, 1975-76; asst. prof. Coll. Law U. Ky., Lexington, 1976-79, assoc. prof. Coll. Law, 1979-80, prof. Coll. Law, 1981-94; Univ. Rsch. prof. Coll. Law, 1989-90, Ashland prof., 1990-94; prof. Notre Dame Law Sch., South Bend, Ind., 1994-99; dean Boston Coll. Law Sch., Chestnut Hill, 1999—. Asst. to Solicitor Gen., U.S. Dept. Justice, Washington, 1981-84; vis. prof. law sch. U. Mich., Ann Arbor, 1985-86; chmn. constl. law sect. Assn. Am. Law Schs., Washington, 1991-93, chmn. law and religion sect., 1998-99. Author: Modern Constitutional Theory, 1989, 4th edit., 1999, The First Amendment, 1992, 2d edit., 1995, What Are Freedoms For?, 1996. Fellow Danforth Found., 1970. Mem. Am. Law Inst. Office: Boston Coll Law Sch Chestnut Hill MA 02167

GARVEY, RICHARD ANTHONY, lawyer; b. N.Y.C., Jan. 10, 1950; s. James Joseph Garvey and Janet Mary (Mooney) Rowse. AB, Boston Coll., 1972; JD, Harvard U., 1975. Bar: N.Y. 1976. Assoc. Simpson Thacher & Bartlett, N.Y.C., 1975-82, ptnr., 1982-93, 97—. Mem. ABA, N.Y. State Bar Assn., Assn. Bar City N.Y., Phi Beta Kappa. E-mail: r. General corporate, Mergers and acquisitions, Securities. Home: Flat 2A 1-3 Pollock's Path The Peak Hong Kong Hong Kong Office: Simpson Thacher & Bartlett 3 Garden Rd Hong Kong Hong Kong E-mail: garvey@stblaw.com

GARWOOD, WILLIAM LOCKHART, federal judge; b. Houston, Oct. 29, 1931; s. Wilmer St. John and Ellen Burdine (Clayton) G.; m. Merle Castlyn Haffler, Aug. 12, 1955; children: William Lockhart, Mary Elliott. BA, Princeton U., 1952; LLB with honors, U. Tex., 1955. Bar: Tex. 1955, U.S. Supreme Ct. 1959. Law clk. to judge U.S. Ct. Appeals (5th cir.), 1955-56; mem. Graves, Dougherty, Hearon, Moody & Garwood (and predecessor firms), Austin, Tex., 1959-79, 81; justice Supreme Ct. Tex., 1979-80; judge U.S. Ct. Appeals (5th cir.), 1981-97, sr. judge, 1997—; dir. Anderson, Clayton & Co., 1976-79, 81, exec. com., 1977-79, 81. Mem. adv. com. on appellate rules U.S. Ct.s, 1994—2001, chair, 1997—2001. Pres. Child and Family Service of Austin, 1970-71, St. Andrew's Episcopal Sch., Austin, 1972; bd. dirs. Community Council Austin and Travis County, 1968-72, Human Opportunities Corp. Austin and Travis County, 1966-70, Mental Health and Mental Retardation Ctr. Austin and Travis County, 1966-69, United Fund Austin and Travis County, 1971-73; mem. adv. bd. Salvation Army, Austin, 1972— . Served with U.S. Army, 1956-59. Fellow Tex. Bar Found. (life); mem. Tex. Law Rev. Assn. (pres. 1990-91, dir. 1986-96), Am. Law Inst. (life), Am. Judicature Soc., Order of Coif, Chancellors, Phi Delta Phi. Episcopalian. Office: US Ct Appeals Homer Thornberry Jud Bldg 903 San Jacinto Blvd Austin TX 78701-2451

GARY, MARC, lawyer; b. Englewood, N.J., July 14, 1952; BA with highest distinction, Northwestern U., 1974; JD, Georgetown U., 1977. Bar: Va. 1977, D.C. 1978, U.S. Ct. Appeals (D.C. cir. and 4th cir.) 1978, U.S. Dist. Ct. D.C. 1978, U.S. Supreme Ct. 1982, U.S. Ct. Appeals (6th cir.) 1983, U.S. Dist. Ct. Md. 1985, U.S. Ct. Appeals (9th cir.) 1989. Ptnr. Mayer, Brown & Platt, Washington; v.p., assoc. gen. counsel Bell South Corp. Mem. regulatory agy. task force Pres'. pvt. sector survey cost control, 1982-83. Contbr. articles to profl. jours. Bd. dirs., coun. trustees Am. Friends of Hebrew U., 1995-2000; nat. bd. dirs. United Synagogue of Conservative Judaism, 1994—; bd. dirs. D.C. Jewish Cmty. Ctr., 1990-2000. Mem. ABA, D.C. Bar (pub. dvc. activities com., steering com., antitrust, trade rresolution and consumer affairs sect.), Va. State Bar, Washington Coun. Lawyers (bd. dirs. 1982-2000), Phi Eta Sigma. Office: Bell South Corp ste 1700 1155 peachtree St NE Atlanta GA 30309

GARY, RICHARD DAVID, lawyer; b. Richmond, Va., Apr. 25, 1949; s. Morton Nathan and Blanche (Rudy) G.; m. Linda Levene, Aug. 6, 1972; children: Brent Ryan, Lauren Renee. AB in Econs., U. N.C., 1971; JD, U. Va., 1974. Bar: Va. 1974. From assoc. to ptnr. Hunton & Williams, Richmond, 1974—. Guest lectr. law Coll. William and Mary, Williamsburg, 1983-90. Pres. Beth Sholom Home Cen. Va., Richmond, 1989-91; chmn. Beth Sholom Home Va., 1991-92. Recipient Disting. Svc. award Beth Sholom Home Cen. Va., 1984. Mem. ABA (pub. utilities sect. council mem.), Va. State Bar (chmn. adminstrn. law sect. 1982-83), Va. Bar Assn., Richmond Bar Assn., Fed. Energy Bar Assn. Avocation: sports. Administrative and regulatory, FERC practice, Public utilities. Home: 1518 Helmsdale Dr Richmond VA 23233-4722 Office: Hunton & Williams Riverfront Plz East Twr PO Box 1535 Richmond VA 23218-1535 E-mail: rgary@hunton.com

GARZA, EMILIO M(ILLER), federal judge; b. San Antonio, Aug. 1, 1947; s. Antonio Peña and Dionisia (Miller) G. BA, U. Notre Dame, 1969, MA, 1970; JD, U. Tex., 1976. Assoc. Clemens, Spencer, Welmaker & Finck, San Antonio, 1976-82, ptnr., 1982-87; dist. judge 225th Dist. Ct., Bexar County, 1987-88; U.S. dist. judge U.S. Dist. Ct. (we. dist.) Tex., 1988-91; U.S. cir. judge U.S. Ct. Appeals (5th cir.), 1991—. Bd. dirs. Symphony Soc. San Antonio, 1987-89; mem. Century Club San Antonio, 1987-88; adv. coun. U. Tex. San Antonio Coll. Fine Arts and Humanities, 1992-98; adv. bd. Phoenix Inst., 1992—; bd. advisors Hispanic Law Jour. U. Tex. at Austin Sch. Law, 1992-96; adv. com. Notre Dame Law Sch., 1998—. Capt. USMCR, 1970-79, active duty, 1970-73. Mem. State Bar Tex., San Antonio Bar Assn. Office: 8200 I-10 W Ste 501 San Antonio TX 78230*

GARZA, REYNALDO G. federal judge; b. Brownsville, Tex., July 7, 1915; s. Ygnacio and Zoila (Guerra) G.; m. Bertha Champion, June 9, 1943; children: Reynaldo G., David C., Ygnacio Daniel, Bertha Victoria, Monica Bernadette. BA, LLB, U. Tex.; LLD (hon.), U. St. Edwards, Austin, Tex., 1965. Bar: Tex. 1939. Sole practice, 1939-42, 46-50; ptnr. Sharpe, Cunningham & Garza, 1950-60, Cunningham, Garza & Yznaga, 1960-61; judge U.S. Dist. Ct. Tex., Brownsville, from 1961, chief judge, 1974-79; senior judge U.S. Ct. Appeals (5th cir.), 1979—. Treas. Cameron County Child Welfare Bd., 1950-52; mem. Tex. Good Neighbor Commn., 1957-61; commr. City of Brownsville, 1947-49; trustee Brownsville Ind. Sch. Dist., 1941-42. Served with USAAF, 1942-45. Recipient Pro Ecclesia et Pontifice medal Pope Pius XII, 1952; decorated knight Order St. Gregory the Great, Pius XII, 1954 Mem. Cameron County Bar Assn., State Bar Tex. Office: US Ct Appeals 600 E Harrison St Brownsville TX 78520*

GASAWAY, LAURA NELL, law librarian, legal educator; b. Searcy, Ark., Feb. 24, 1945; d. Merel Roger and Carnell (Miller) G. BA, Tex. Woman's U., 1967, MLS, 1968; JD, U. Houston, 1973. Bar: Tex. 1974. Catalog libr. U. Houston, 1968-70, catalog-circulation libr., 1970-72, asst. law libr., 1972-73, law libr., asst. prof. law, 1973-75; dir. law libr., prof. law U. Okla., Norman, 1975-85; dir. law libr., prof. law U. N.C., 1985—; copyright cons. Recipient Calvert prize U. Okla., 1978, 81, Compton award Ark. Librs. Assn., 1986. Fellow Spl. Librs. Assn. (H.W. Wilson award 1983, John Cotton Dana award 1987, Fannie Simon award, 1992); mem. ABA, State Bar Tex., N.C. Bar Assn., Am. Assn. Law Librs. (pres. 1986-87). Democrat. Author: Growing Pains: Adapting Copyright for Libraries, Education and Society, 1997; co-author: (with Maureen Murphy) Legal Protection for Computer Programs, 1980, (with James Hoover and Dorothy Warden) American Indian Legal Materials, A Union List, 1981, (with Bruce S. Johnson and James M. Murray) Law Library Management during Fiscal Austerity, 1992, (with Sarah K. Wiant) Libraries and Copyright: A Guide to Copyright in the 1990s, 1994, (with Michael D. Chiorazzi) Law Librarianship: Historical Perspectives, 1996, Growling Pains: Adapting Copyright for Libraries, Education and Society, 1997. Office: U NC Law Libr Clb # 3385 Chapel Hill NC 27599-0001

GASIORKIEWICZ, EUGENE ANTHONY, lawyer; b. Milw., Jan. 7, 1950; s. Eugene Constantine and Loretta Ann (Kasprzak) G.; m. Jana Jamieson, Jan. 12, 1980; children: Suzanne A., Alexei E. AB, Regis Coll., 1971; JD, U. Miss., 1974. Bar: Wis. 1974, U.S. Supreme Ct. 1986. Law clk. to presiding justice Miss. Supreme Ct., Jackson, 1974-75; assoc. Schoone, McManus & Hanson SC, Racine, Wis., 1975-79; ptnr. Hanson & Gasiorkiewicz SC, 1979-90; pres., shareholder Hanson, Gasiorkiewicz & Weber, SC, 1990-96, Hanson & Gasiorkiewicz, SC, Racine, 1997—. Lectr. labor law U. Wis., Racine, 1975-76, worker's comp., State Bar Wis., 1984-86, med. malpractice, Wis. Acad. Trial Lawyers, 1986. Mcpl. judge Village of Wind Point, Wis., 1983-85; moot ct. instr., The Prairie Sch., Racine, 1986-87. Mem. State Bar Wis. (spl. ethics com. regarding trust accts. 1988-89), Assn. Trial Lawyers Am., Am. Arbitration Assn., Wis. Acad. Trial Lawyers (bd. dirs. 1999—), Nat. Bd. Trial Advocacy (cert. civil trial advocate), Racine County Bar Assn. (liaison local physicians and attys. 1990—). Roman Catholic. Avocation: tennis. Federal civil litigation, Personal injury. Home: 3929 S Brook Rd Franksville WI 53126-9303 Office: Hanson & Gasiorkiewicz SC 2932 Northwestern Ave Racine WI 53404-2249

GASS, RAYMOND WILLIAM, lawyer, consumer products company executive; b. Chgo., Apr. 6, 1937; s. William Frederick and Clara Gertrude (Grotman) G.; m. Patricia Ann Thomas, Apr. 20, 1968; children: Elizabeth Ann, Katharine Patricia, Christina Susanne. BS, Purdue U., 1959; LLB, U. Ill., 1962. Bar: Ill. Patent examiner U.S. Patent Office, Washington, 1962-63; atty. Armour and Co., Chgo., 1963-70; sr. atty. Greyhound Corp., 1970-71; sr. v.p., gen. counsel, sec. John Morrell & Co., 1971-89; v.p., gen. counsel Alberto-Culver Co., Melrose Park, Ill., 1989-98. Bd. dirs. Am. Chemet Corp., Columbia Paint and Coating Co. Mem. ABA, Chgo. Bar Assn. (chmn. corp. law depts. 1975-77) Antitrust, General corporate, Labor.

GASTFREUND, IRVING, lawyer; b. Landsberg, Ger., Nov. 27, 1947; s. Morris and Sally G.; m. Diane Lynn Cohen, June 14, 1970; children—Sarah Heather, Michael. B.A., Brown U., 1969; J.D., Boston U., 1973. Bar: D.C. 1973, U.S. Dist. Ct. D.C. 1974, U.S. Ct. Appeals (D.C. cir.) 1974, U.S. Supreme Ct. 1977. Atty., adviser FCC, Washington, 1973-76; assoc. Fly, Shuebruk, Gaguine, Boros, Schulkind & Braun, Washington, 1976-81, ptnr. 1981-85; of counsel Finley, Kumble, Wagner, Heine, Underberg, Manley, Myerson and Casey, 1985-87; counsel Kaye, Scholer, Fierman, Hays & Handler, Washington, 1987—. Served with USAR, 1969-75. Recipient William Gaston prize for excellence in oratory Brown U., 1969. Mem. ABA (broadcast and spectrum use com. communications law div., vice chmn. 1982-83, chmn. 1983—), Fed. Bar Assn., Fed. Communications Bar Assn. Jewish. Administrative and regulatory, Communications, Trademark and copyright. Office: Kaye Scholer Fierman Hays & Handler 901 15th St NW Washington DC 20005-2327

GASZNER, DAVID GEORGE, lawyer; b. Adelaide, Australia, Dec. 14, 1957; LLB with honors, Adelaide U., South Australia, 1979. Bar: barrister, solicitor South Australia, New South Wales, Victoria, We. Australia; High Ct. Roll. Assoc. Mollison Litchfield, South Australia, 1979-85; ptnr., 1985-89, Corrs Chambers Westgarth, Australia, 1989-92, Thomson Playford, South Australia, 1992—. Fellow Australian Inst. Mgmt. (pres. 1995-97), Australian Inst. Co. Dirs.; mem. Law Coun. Australia (chmn. fed. ct. practice com. 1996—, chmn. fed. litigation sect. 1998—), Law Soc. South Australia. Avocations: gardening, reading, history, model making. Alternative dispute resolution, Intellectual property. Office: Thomson Playford 101 Pirie St SA 5066 Adelaide Australia Fax: 61 8 82321961. E-mail: dgaszner@thomson-playford.com.au

GATES, STEPHEN FRYE, lawyer, business executive; b. Clearwater, Fla., May 20, 1946; s. Orris Allison and Olga Betty (Frye) G.; m. Laura Daignault, June 10, 1972. BA in Econs., Yale U., 1968; JD, MBA, Harvard U., 1972. Bar: Fla. 1972, Mass. 1973, Ill. 1977, Colo. 1986. Assoc. Choate Hall & Stewart, Boston, 1973-77; atty. Amoco Corp., Chgo., 1977-82, gen. atty., 1982-86; regional atty. Amoco Prodn. Co., Denver, 1987-88; asst. treas. Amoco Corp., Chgo., 1988-91, assoc. gen. counsel, corp. sec., 1991-92; v.p. Amoco Chem. Co., 1993-95; v.p., gen. counsel Amoco Corp., Chgo., 1995-98; exec. v.p., group chief of staff BP Amoco p.l.c., London, 1999-2000; sr. v.p., gen. counsel, sec. FMC Corp., Chgo., 2000—. Bd. dirs. Nat. Legal Ctr. Pub. Interest, Wash., 1999—. Trustee Newberry Libr., Chgo., 1998—; bd. dirs. Chgo. Sister Cities Internat. Program, Inc., Friends of Prentice Hosp., 1994-98; mem. adv. coun. Chgo. Schweitzer Urban Fellows Program, 1996—; mem. adv. bd. Chgo. Vol. Legal Svcs. Found., 1996-98; mem. Chgo. Crime Commn., 2000—, bd.dirs. 2000—. Knox fellow, 1972-73. Fellow Royal Soc. Arts (London); mem. ABA, Univ. Club, Mid-Am. Club, Chgo. Club, Yale Club. General corporate, Securities. Office: FMC Corp 200 E Randolph Dr Chicago IL 60601 E-mail: steve_gates@fmc.com

GATEWOOD, TELA LYNNE, lawyer; b. Cedar Rapids, Iowa, 23 Mar. d. Chester Russell and Cecilia Mae (McFarland) Weber. BA with distinction, Cornell Coll., Mt. Vernon, Iowa, 1970; JD with distinction, U. Iowa, 1972. Bar: Iowa 1973, Calif. 1974, U.S. Supreme Ct. 1984. Instr. LaVerne Coll., Pt. Mugu, Calif., 1973; asst. city atty. City of Des Moines, 1973-78; sr. trial atty. and supervisory atty. EEOC, Dallas, Phila., 1978-91, acting regional atty. Dallas Dist., 1987-89, adminstrv. judge Dallas, 1991-94; adminstrv. law judge Social Security Adminstrn., Oklahoma City, 1994—. Bd. dirs. Day Care Inc., Des Moines, 1975-78, sec., 1977, pres., 1978. Mem. ABA (labor law, litigation, govt. svc., judiciary sects.), NAFE, Nat. Assn. Female Judges, Fed. Bar Assn., U.S. Supreme Ct. Bar Assn., Calif. Bar Assn. Office: Social Security Adminstrn Office of Hearings and Appeals 420 W Main St Ste 400 Oklahoma City OK 73102-4435

GATHRIGHT, HOWARD T. lawyer; b. Phila., May 3, 1935; s. Howard W. and Rose (McGurk) G.; m. Natalie Acquaviva, June 22, 1963 (div. May 1991); children: Donna Marie, Gary Thomas. BA, U. Pa., 1957; JD, Temple U., 1963. Bar: Pa. 1964, Alaska, 2001, U.S. Dist. Ct. Pa. 1964, U.S. Supreme Ct. 1968. Ptnr. Pratt, Gathright & Brett, P.C., Doylestown, Pa., 1964-78; with Gathright & Leonard, 1990—. Asst. dist. atty. of Bucks County, Pa., 1966-69; solicitor Doylestown Twp., Pa., 1970-75, New Hope Sewage Project of Bucks County Water and Sewer Authority, 1971-76; bd. dirs. Bean, Mason & Eyer, Doylestown. Bd. dirs. Am. Lung Assn., 1970—; pres. Bucks County Estate Planning Coun., 1972; active Bucks County Emergency Health Coun., Inc., 1977-79; apptd. by gov. to Bucks County Spl. Trial Ct. Nominating Commn., 1987. Served in U.S. Army, 1957, USAR, 1958-63. Mem. ABA, Phila. Bar Assn., Pa. Bar Assn., Bucks County Bar Assn. (pres. 1986-87), Assn. Trial Lawyers Am., Pa. Trial Lawyers Assn., Cen. Bucks C. of C. (pres. 1975, chmn. bd. dirs. 1976, Man of Yr. 1975). Democrat. Roman Catholic. Avocations: sports, tennis. State civil litigation, Estate planning, Real property. Address: PO Box 248 Bethel AK 99559 Fax: 907-543-5537. E-mail: gathrightg@aol.com

GAUNT, JANET LOIS, arbitrator, mediator; b. Lawrence, Mass., Aug. 23, 1947; d. Donald Walter and Lois (Neuhart) Bacon; m. Frank Peyton Gaunt, Dec. 21, 1969; children: Cory C., Andrew D. BA, Oberlin Coll., 1969; JD, Wash. U., St. Louis, 1974. Bar: Wash. 1974, U.S. Dist. Ct. (we. dist.) Wash. 1974, U.S. Ct. Appeals (9th cir.) 1978. Assoc. Davis, Wright, Todd, Riese & Jones, Seattle, 1974-80; arbitrator/mediator, 1981—. Dir. Seattle King County Labor Law Sect., 1976-77; mem. Pacific Coast Labor Law Planning Com., 1977-83; com. vice chmn. Wash. State Task Force on Gender and Justice on the Cts., 1987-89; chmn. Wash. Pub. Employment Rels. Commn., Olympia, 1989-96. Author, editor: Alternative Dispute Resolution, 1989; author: Public Sector Labor Mediation and Arbitration, Arbitration and Mediation in Washington, 2d edit., 1995. Pres. State Bd. of Wash. Women Lawyers, 1986. Mem. Nat. Acad. Arbitrators (dir. rsch. and edn. found. 1991-96, bd. govs. 1998-2001), Am. Arbitration Assn., Wash. State Bar Assn. E-mail: jlgaunt@aol.com

GAVER, FRANCES ROUSE, lawyer; b. Lexington, Ky., Mar. 13, 1929; d. Colvin P. Rouse and Elizabeth Turner Sympson; m. Donald Paul Gaver, Jan. 24, 1953; children: Elizabeth, Donald, William. BA, Wellesley Coll., 1950; MA, U. Pitts., 1968; JD, Monterey (Calif.) Coll. of Law, 1986. Bar: Calif. 1986, U.S. Dist. Ct. (no. dist.) Calif. 1986; cert. specialist in probate, estate planing and trust law, Calif. Assoc. Hoge, Fenton, Jones & Appel, Monterey, 1986-93, Fenton & Keller, Monterey, 1993-97; ptnr. Johnson, Gaver & Leach, 1997-99, of counsel, 2000—. Bd. dirs. Carmel (Calif.) Unified Sch. Dist., 1973-81, Monterey Coll. of Law, 1991-97, Legal Svcs. for Srs., Pacific Grove, Calif., 1994—; bd. dirs. Monterey Peninsula Coll. Found. Mem. Monterey County Bar Assn. Avocations: playing recorder, swimming. Estate planning, Probate, Estate taxation. Office: Johnson Gaver & Leach LLP 2801 Monterey Salinas Hwy Monterey CA 93940-6401 E-mail: fgaver@jglllp.com

GAVIN, JOHN NEAL, lawyer; b. Chgo., Aug. 31, 1946; s. John Anthony and Mary Anne (O'Donnell) G.; m. Louise A. Sunderland, June 16, 1979; children: Anne, Matthew. AB, Coll. of Holy Cross, Worcester, Mass., 1968; JD, Harvard U., 1975. Bar: Ill. 1975. Law clk. to Hon. Charles M. Merrill U.S. Ct. Appeals (9th cir.), San Francisco, 1975-76; atty. office of legal counsel U.S. Dept. Justice, Washington, 1976-79; ptnr. Hopkins & Sutter, Chgo., 1981-2001. Served to lt. USNR, 1968-71. Mem. ABA, Chgo. Bar Assn. Administrative and regulatory, General corporate, Insurance. Office: Foley & Lardner 3 First National Plz Chicago IL 60602 Business E-Mail: jgavin@foleycaw.com

GAY, CARL LLOYD, lawyer; b. Seattle, Nov. 11, 1950; s. James and Elizabeth Anne (Rogers) G.; m. Robin Ann Winston, Aug. 23, 1975; children: Patrick, Joel, Alexander, Samuel, Nora. Student, U. of Puget Sound, 1969-70; BS in Forestry cum laude, Wash. State U., 1974; JD, Willamette U., 1979. Bar: Wash. 1979, U.S. Dist. Ct. (we. dist.) Wash. 1979. With Taylor & Taylor, 1979-82, Taylor, Taylor & Gay, 1982-85; prin. Greenaway & Gay, Port Angeles, Wash., 1985-91, Greenaway, Gay & Tassie, Port Angeles, 1991-96, Greenaway, Gay & Angier, Port Angeles, 1996—. Judge pro tem Clallam County, Port Angeles, 1981-85; commr. superior Ct., 1985-91; judge Juvenile Ct., 1985-87; instr. Guardian Ad Litem Program, Port Angeles, 1985—, Peoples Law Sch., 1989—. Bd. dirs.

Cmty. Concert Assn., Port Angeles, 1982-85, 94—, pres., 1984-85, 88-89, 99-2000; bd. dirs. Am. Heart Assn., 1987—, Clallam County YMCA, 1988—, exec. com., 1995—; adv. bd. Salvation Army, Port Angeles, 1982—; subdivsn. chmn., bd. dirs. United Way Clallam County, 1987—; bd. dirs., pres. Friends of Libr., Port Angeles, 1983-91; trustee Fisher Cove, 1988—; advisor youth in govt. program YMCA, 1986—; advisor United Meth. Youth Coun., 1987—, trustee, 1989—; chmn. long-range planning com. Port Angeles Sch. Dist.; bd. govs. Peninsula Coll. Found., 2000—; pres. Holy Trinity Luth. Ch., 2001—. Mem. ABA (real property, probate and trust and gen. practice sects.), ATLA, Wash. Bar Assn. (real property, probate, elder law and trust sects.), Clallam County Bar Assn. (pres. 1995), Nat. Coun. Juvenile and Family Ct. Judges, Superior Ct. Judges Assn. (com.), Wash. State Trial Lawyers Assn., Kiwanis (local bd. dirs. 1982-84, pres. 1986-87, Kiwanian of Yr. 1983-84), Elks. Lutheran. Avocations: backpacking, cross country skiing, raquetball, sailing. Contracts commercial, Probate, Real property. Home: 3220 Mcdougal St Port Angeles WA 98362-6738 Office: Greenaway Gay & Angier 829 E 8th St Ste A Port Angeles WA 98362-6452 E-mail: clgay@tenforward.com

GAY, E(MIL) LAURENCE, lawyer; b. Bridgeport, Conn., Aug. 10, 1923; s. Emil D. and Helen L. (Mihalich) G.; m. Harriet A. Ripley, Aug. 2, 1952; children: Noel L., Peter C., Marguerite S., Georgette A. BS, Yale U., 1947; JD magna cum laude, Harvard U., 1949. Bar: N.Y. 1950, Conn. 1960, Calif. 1981, Hawaii 1988. Assoc. Root, Ballantine, Harlan, Bushby & Palmer, N.Y.C., 1949-51; mem. legal staff U.S. High Commr. for Germany, Bad Godesberg, 1951-52; law sec., presiding justice appellate div. 1st dept. N.Y. Supreme Ct., N.Y.C., 1953-54; assoc. Debevoise, Plimpton & McLean, 1954-58; v.p., sec.-treas., gen. counsel Hewitt-Robins, Inc., Stamford, Conn., 1958-65; pres. Litton Gt. Lakes Corp., N.Y.C., 1965-67; sr. v.p. finance AMFAC, Inc., Honolulu, 1967-73, vice chmn., 1974-78; fin. cons. Burlingame, Calif., 1979-82; of counsel Pettit & Martin, San Francisco, 1982-88, Goodsill, Anderson, Quinn & Stifel, Honolulu, 1988—. Editor Harvard Law Rev., 1948-49. Pres. Honolulu Symphony Soc., 1974-78; trustee Loyola Marymount U., 1977-80, San Francisco Chamber Soloists, 1981-86, Honolulu Chamber Music Series, 1988—; officer, dir. numerous arts and ednl. orgns. 2d lt. AUS, 1943-46. Mem. ABA, State Bar of Hawaii, Pacific Club (Honolulu), Nat. Assn. of Securities Dealers, Am. Arbitration Assn. (mem. arbitration panels), Phi Beta Kappa. Republican. Roman Catholic. Avocations: music, arts. Home: 1159 Maunawili Rd Kailua HI 96734-4641 Office: Goodsill Anderson Quinn & Stifel PO Box 3196 Honolulu HI 96801-3196

GAYER, ELLIOTT, lawyer; b. Bklyn., June 29, 1951; s. Frank Wolf and Amelia Charlotte (Luftig) G.; m. Belle Linda Tuchinsky, June 30, 1972; 1 child, Sheridan J. B.S. in Laws, J.D., Western State U., San Diego. Bar: Ga. 1980, Calif. 1980, U.S. Dist. Ct. (so. dist.) Calif. 1980, U.S. Dist. Ct. (cen. dist.) Calif. 1982, U.S. Cir. Ct. Appeals 1982. Atty. Am. Tax & Law Ctr., San Diego, 1980-82; ptnr. Repici & Gayer, Newport Beach, Calif., 1982—; atty. Fine Artists Guild, Newport Beach, 1983—. Mem. Calif. Trial Lawyers Assn., Calif. Attys. Criminal Justice. Democrat. Jewish. Home: General Delivery New York NY 10001-9999

GEAN, THOMAS C. prosecutor; BA, U. Ark.; JD, Vanderbilt U. Atty. Alston and Bird, Atlanta, 1988—92, Gean, Gean and Gean, Ft. Smith, Ark., 1992—96; prosecuting atty. Sebastian County Dist. Atty.'s Office, 1997—2001; U.S. atty. We. Dist. Ark. U.S. Dept. Justice, 2001—. Office: PO Box 1524 Fort Smith AR 72902*

GEAREN, JOHN JOSEPH, lawyer; b. Wareham, Mass., Sept. 1, 1943; BA, U. Notre Dame, 1965; MA (Rhodes Scholar), Oxford U., 1967; JD, Yale U., 1970. Bar: Ill. 1972. Ptnr. Mayer, Brown & Platt, Chgo., 1970—. Democrat. Roman Catholic. Home: 179 Linden Ave Unit 2 Oak Park IL 60302-1661 Office: Mayer Brown & Platt 190 S La Salle St Ste 3100 Chicago IL 60603-3441 E-mail: jgearen@mayerbrown.com

GEARHISER, CHARLES JOSEF, lawyer; b. Dyersburg, Tenn., Aug. 14, 1938; s. Charles Josef Gearhiser and Mary Josephine (Plant) Wickham; m. Joy Edwards; children: Charles J. III, Laura, Christy. BS, Austin Peay State U., 1960; LLB, U. Tenn., 1961. Bar: Tenn. Assoc. Strang, Fletcher, Carriger & Walker, Chattanooga, 1961-63; law clk. to presiding justice U.S. Dist. Ct. (ea. dist.) Tenn., 1963-64; asst. U.S. atty. Dept. Justice, 1964-66; ptnr. Stophel, Caldwell & Heggie, 1966-74, Gearhiser, Peters, Lockaby & Tallant and predecessor firms, Chattanooga, 1974—. U.S. commnr., 1966-73; U.S. magistrate U.S. Dist. Ct. (ea. dist.) Tenn., 1973-78, Chattanooga. Chmn. bd. dirs. S.E. Tenn. Legal Services, Chattanooga, 1978-81. Fellow Am. Coll. Trial Lawyers, Tenn. Bar Found.; mem. ABA, Tenn. Bar Assn. (bd. govs. 1992-93, 94-, pres. 2001-, Chattanooga Bar Assn. (sec., treas 1972-73, pres. 1973-74), Assn. Trial Lawyers Am., Tenn. Trial Lawyers Assn., Chattanooga Trial Lawyers Assn., Nat. Inst. Trial Advocacy (civil trial adv. 1981), Am. Bd. Trial Advs. (charter mem. Tenn. chpt.), Order of Coif. Democrat. Methodist. Federal civil litigation, General civil litigation, Personal injury. Home: 12 N Crest Rd Chattanooga TN 37404-1827 Office: Gearhiser Peters Lockaby & Tallant 320 McCallie Ave Chattanooga TN 37402-2018*

GEARY, MICHAEL PHILIP, lawyer; b. Harvey, Ill., Dec. 19, 1954; s. John Thomas and Patricia Ann (Carpenter) G. BA, Georgetown U., 1977; JD, St. Mary's U., San Antonio, 1980. Bar: Tex. 1980, D.C. 1986, Ohio 1989. Asst. legis. counsel Office of Legis. Counsel, U.S. Senate, Washington, 1980-90; pvt. practice Westlake, Ohio, 1990-94; exec. dir. Ashtabula County Legal Aid Corp., Jefferson, 1994-2000, McNair & Bobulsky Co., LPA, Jefferson, 2000—. Trustee Contact-Ashtabula County, 1995-96, Ashtabula County Cmty. Housing Devel. Orgn., Inc., 1998-2000; mem. Leadership Ashtabula County, Jefferson, 1994—. Mem. Ohio State Bar Assn., Ashtabula County Bar Assn. Republican. Roman Catholic. State civil litigation, Family and matrimonial, General practice. Office: McNair & Bobulsky Co LPA 35 W Jefferson St Jefferson OH 44047-1027

GEDDIE, ROWLAND HILL, III, lawyer; b. Tuscaloosa, Ala., Jan. 7, 1954; s. Rowland Hill Jr. and Mary Martha (McGaughy) G.; m. Peggy O'Neal Emmons, Aug. 13, 1977; children: Mary Catherine, Virginia Jane. BA, U. Miss., 1976, JD, 1978. Bar: Miss. 1978, U.S. Dist. Ct. (no. dist.) Miss. 1978, Tex. 1979, Mo. 1995. Assoc. Baker & Botts, Houston, 1978-87; assoc. gen. counsel Lower Colo. River Authority, Austin, Tex., 1987-88; sr. counsel Houston Industries Inc./Houston Lighting & Power Co., 1988-92; contract atty. Tandy Corp./TE Electronics Inc., Ft. Worth, 1993; v.p., gen. counsel, sec. O'Sullivan Industries Holdings Inc., Lamar, Mo., 1993—. Treas. Southgate Civic Club, Houston, 1991-92. Presdl. scholar U.S. Govt., Washington, 1972. Mem. ABA, Am. Corp. Counsel Assn. (co-chair EDGAR issues practice group of corp. and securities law com. 1997-98, chair ann. meeting shareholders and proxy statement issues practice group corp. and securities, 1999, co-chair litigation 2000, chair 2001), Lamar Swim Team Assn., Inc. (pres. 2000-2002), Rotary Club (v.p. 2001-02). Methodist. Avocations: personal computers, cycling, scuba diving, swimming. General corporate, Securities. Home: 1503 Gulf St Lamar MO 64759-1830 Office: O'Sullivan Industries Inc 1900 Gulf St Lamar MO 64759-1899 E-mail: rowland.geddie@osullivan.com

GEE, ROBERT NEIL, law librarian; b. Miami, Okla., June 22, 1956; s. Robert Sanford and Nancy Ann (Neil) G. AA, Tulsa Jr. Coll., 1976; BA, U. Okla., 1978, JD, 1981; LLM, George Washington U., 1984. Bar: Okla. 1981, U.S. Suprem Ct. 1986, D.C. 1989. Legal reference specialist Library of Congress, Washington, 1984-94; chief law libr. pub. svcs. Law Libr. of Congress, 1994—. Mem. ABA (recipient Silver Key cert. 1981), Fed. Bar Assn., Okla. Bar Assn., Am. Judicature Soc., D.C. Bar Assn., Phi Delta Phi. Avocations: reading, bowling, travel, current events.

GEESEMAN, ROBERT GEORGE, lawyer; b. Shreveport, La., Oct. 23, 1944; s. George Robert and Cora (Hamilton) Glasgow; m. Rosemary Monahan, Aug. 19, 1967; 1 child, Regan Glasgow. BA, Yale U., 1966; JD, U. Mich., 1969. Bar: Pa. 1969, U.S. Dist. Ct. (we. dist.) Pa. 1969, U.S. Tax Ct. 1979, U.S. Supreme Ct. 1973. Assoc. Blaxter, O'Neill, Houston & Nash, Pitts., 1969-75; ptnr. Lynch, Lynch, Carr & Kabala, 1975-81, Lynch, Kabala & Geeseman, Pitts., 1981, Kabala & Geeseman, Pitts., 1981—. Lectr. on tax law and employee benefits; legal adv. bd. Small Bus. Coun. Am. Mem. ABA (mem. profl. svc. corps. com. sect. on taxation, chmn. prof. corp. com. sect. on econs., bd. editors Withdrawal Retirement and Disputes, What You and Your Firm Should Know), Pa. Bar Assn., Allegheny County Bar Assn., Pitts. Inst. Legal Medicine, Phi Delta Phi. Clubs: Rosslyn Farms Country, Rivers, Chartiers Country, Mory's (New Haven, Conn.), John's Island Country (Vero Beach, Fla.). Health, Pension, profit-sharing, and employee benefits, Taxation, general. Address: Kabala & Geeseman 625 Liberty Ave Fl 29 Pittsburgh PA 15222-3110

GEHAN, MARK WILLIAM, lawyer; b. St. Paul, Dec. 19, 1946; s. Mark William and Jean Elizabeth (McGee) G.; m. Lucy Lyman Harrison, Aug. 25, 1971; children: Hark Harrison, Alice McGee. BA, U. Notre Dame, 1968; JD, U. Minn., 1971. Bar: Minn. Asst. county atty. Ramsey County Atty.'s Office, St. Paul, 1972-76; prosecutor, Met. Area Dist. Urban County Attys. Bd., 1976-77; ptnr. Collins Buckley Sauntry & Haugh, 1978—. Bd. dirs. Minn. State Bd. Pub. Def., St. Paul, 1982-90. Pres. St. Paul Charter Commn., 1986-94. Mem. Minn. Bar Assn. (pres. 1998-99), Ramsey County Bar Assn. (pres. 1990-91). Avocations: scuba diving, tennis, guitar. State civil litigation. Office: Collins Buckley Sauntry & Haugh First Nat Bank Bldg 332 Minnesota St Ste W1100 Saint Paul MN 55101-1379 E-mail: mgehan@cbsh.net

GEHRES, JAMES, lawyer; b. Akron, Ohio, July 19, 1932; s. Edwin Jacob and Cleora Mary (Yoakam) G.; m. Eleanor Agnew Mount, July 23, 1960. BS in Acctg., U. Utah, 1954; MBA, U. Calif.-Berkeley, 1959; JD, U. Denver, 1970, LLM in Taxation, 1977. Bar: Colo. 1970, U.S. Dist. Ct. Colo. 1970, U.S. Tax Ct. 1970, U.S. Supreme Ct. 1973, U.S. Ct. Appeals (10th cir.) 1978, U.S. Ct. Claims 1992. Atty. IRS, Denver, 1965-80, atty. chief counsel;s office, 1980—. Contbr. articles to profl. jours. Treas., dir. Colo. Fourteeners Initiative. With USAF, 1955-58, capt. Res. ret. Mem. ABA, Colo. Bar Assn., AICPA, Colo. Soc. CPAs, Am. Assn. Atty.-CPAs, Am. Judicature Soc., Order of St. Ives, The Explorers Club, Am. Alpine Club, Colo. Mountain Club (bd. dirs.), Colo. Mountain Club Found. (bd. dirs., pres.), Beta Gamma Sigma, Beta Alpha Psi. Democrat. Office: 935 Pennsylvania St Denver CO 80203-3145

GEHRIG, MICHAEL FORD, lawyer; b. Cin., Jan. 25, 1947; s. John Richard and Mary Bonita (Ford) G.; m. Barbara Jane Rigg, June 16, 1973; children: Michael Ford, Caroline Cristina, Angela Victoria. BA, Ohio State U., 1970; JD, Chase Coll. Law, Cin., 1974. Bar: Ohio 1974, U.S. Dist. Ct. (so. dist.) Ohio 1974, U.S. Dist. Ct. (ea. dist.) Ky. 1983, U.S. Supreme Ct., 1985. Assoc. Beall, Hermanies & Bortz, Cin., 1974-76; mem. firm Gehrig & Gehrig, Cin., 1976-79, Gehrig, Parker & Baldwin, Cin., 1979-88, Fingerman, Guckenberger & Gehrig, 1988-96, Gehrig, Gelwicks & Eynon, 1996—; lectr. various legal seminars. Contbr. articles to jours., chpts. to books. Recipient book awards Chase Coll. Law, 1971, 73, 74. Mem. ABA, Ohio State Bar Assn., Cin. Bar Assn., Assn. Trial Lawyers Am. (sustaining), Am. Bd. Trial Advocates, Ohio Acad. Trial Lawyers (sustaining), Cin. Hist. Soc., English Speaking Union, Cin. Athletic Club, Univ. Club, Hyde Park Golf & Country Club, Phi Gamma Delta. Episcopalian. Personal injury. Office: Gehrig Gelwicks & Eynon 1140 Bartlett Bldg 36 E 4th St Ste 1140 Cincinnati OH 45202-3809

GEHRING, RONALD KENT, lawyer; b. Ft. Wayne, Ind., Feb. 5, 1941; s. Ronald G. and Beverly M. (Failor) G.; m. Teresa L. Eyer, June 18, 1966; children: Gregory D., Douglas K., Suzanne C. AB, Ind. U., 1963, JD, 1967. Bar: Ind. 1967, U.S. Dist. Ct. (no. and so. dists.) Ind. 1967, U.S. Ct. Appeals (7th cir.) 1975. Assoc. Peters, McHie, Enslen & Hand, Hammond, Ind., 1967-70; ptnr. Tourkow, Danehy, Crell, Hood & Gehring, Ft. Wayne, 1971-79, Grossman, Boeglin & Gehring and predecessor, Ft. Wayne, 1980-84; pvt. practice, 1984—. Panelist Ind. Collection Law Seminar, 1982-83; atty. Ind. Dist. Luth. Ch. Bd. dirs. Concordia Cemetery Assn., 1982-83, Luth. Assn. Broadcasting, Inc. Mem. ABA, Ind. Trial Lawyers, Comml. Law League, Ind. Bar Assn., Allen County Bar Assn., Phi Delta Phi. Consumer commercial, Probate, Real property. Office: 202 W Berry St Ste 321 Fort Wayne IN 46802-2242

GEIGER, ALEXANDER, lawyer; b. Kosice, Czechoslovakia, May 21, 1950; came to U.S., 1965; s. Emil and Alice (Brickmann) G.; m. Helene R. Mortar, May 28, 1972; children: Theodore, Aviva. AB, Princeton U., 1972; JD, Cornell U., 1975. Bar: N.Y. 1976, U.S. Dist. Ct. (we. dist.) N.Y. 1976, U.S. Supreme Ct. 1980, U.S. Ct. Appeals (2d cir.) 1985, U.S. Tax Ct. 1986. Assoc. Nixon, Hargrave, Devans & Doyle, Rochester, N.Y., 1975-82; sr. ptnr. Geiger & Rothenberg, 1982—. Adj. asst. prof. St. John Fisher Coll., Rochester, 1977-78. Mem. N.Y. State Bar Assn., Monroe County Bar Assn., Assn. Trial Lawyers Am., Rochester Inns of Ct. (master). Jewish. Federal civil litigation, State civil litigation, Personal injury. Home: 227 Brittany Ln Pittsford NY 14534 also: 30 Newport Pkwy # 3009 Jersey City NJ 07310 Office: Geiger & Rothenberg 45 Exchange Blvd Ste 800 Rochester NY 14614-2093 also: Geiger and Rothenberg 83 Maiden Ln 13th Fl New York NY 10038

GEIGER, JAMES NORMAN, lawyer; b. Mansfield, Ohio, Apr. 5, 1932; s. Ernest R. and Margaret L. (Bauman) G.; m. Paula Hunt, May 11, 1957; children: Nancy G., John W. Student Wabash Coll., Crawfordsville, Ind., 1950-51; BA, Ohio Wesleyan U., 1954; JD, Emory U., 1962, LLD, 1970. Bar: Ga. 1961, U.. Dist. Ct. (mid. dist.) Ga. 1966, U.S. Ct. Appeals (5th and 11th cirs.) 1980, U.S. Dist. Ct. (so. dist.) Ga. 1983. Ptnr. Henderson, Kaley, Geiger and Thurmond, Marietta, Ga., 1962-64, Nunn, Geiger and Hunt, Perry, Ga., 1964-72, Geiger & Geiger, P.C. and predecessors, 1972—. Trustee Westfield (Ga.) Schs., 1970-74; mem. civilian adv. bd. Warner Robins AFB, 1976; chmn. coun. ministries Perry United Meth. Ch., 1970-71, mem. adminstrv. bd., 1968—. Capt. USAF, 1954-57. Mem. ABA, Ga. Bar Assn., Houston County Bar Assn., South Ga. C. of C. (bd. dirs.) Perry C. of C. (pres. 1976, 90), Perry Kiwanis (pres. 1968, Man of Yr. 1968), Perry Club Coun. (pres. 1967), Phi Delta Phi, Pi Sigma Alpha. Methodist. Contracts commercial, General practice, Real property. Home: 1910 Northside Rd Perry GA 31069-2223 Office: Geiger & Geiger 1007 Jernigan St Perry GA 31069-3325

GEIGER, RICHARD STUART, lawyer; b. Dallas, Feb. 21, 1936; s. Gilbert A. and Letitia (Wells) G.; m. Phyllis Scott McGee, June 4, 1954; children— R. Scott, Angela G., Margaret L., P. Claire, Amy S. LL.B., So. Meth. U., 1962. Bar: Tex. 1962, U.S. Ct. Appeals (5th cir.) 1969, U.S. Supreme Ct. 1968. Sole practice, Dallas, 1962-75; ptnr. Thompson, Coe, Cousins & Irons, Dallas, 1975—. Editor in chief Tex. Ins. Law Reporter. Mem. Tex. Ho. of Reps., 1972-76. Democrat. Episcopalian. Clubs: Austin, Crescent (Dallas). E-mail: rgeiger@thompsoncoe.com. Administrative and regulatory, Insurance, Legislative. Office: Thompson Coe Cousins & Irons 200 Crescent Ct # 11th Dallas TX 75201-1853

GEIMAN, J. ROBERT, lawyer; b. Evanston, Ill., Mar. 5, 1931; s. Louis H. and Nancy O'Connell-Crowe G.; m. Ann L. Fitzgerald, July 29, 1972; children: J. Robert, William Patrick, Timothy Michael. BS, Northwestern U., 1953; JD, Notre Dame U., 1956. Bar: Ill. 1956, U.S. Ct. Appeals (7th cir.) 1956, U.S. Supreme Ct. 1969. Assoc. Eckert, Peterson & Lowry, Chgo., 1956-64; ptnr. Peterson, Lowry, Rall, Barber & Ross, 1964-70, Peterson & Ross, Chgo., 1970-96, of counsel, 1996—. Mem. com. on civil jury instructions Ill. Supreme Ct., 1979-81. Case editor Notre Dame Law Rev., 1956. Bd. advisors Cath. Charities of Archdiocese of Chgo., 1973-96. Fellow Internat. Acad. Trial Lawyers, Am. Coll. Trial Lawyers, Ill. Bar Found.; mem. ABA (aviation com., tort and ins. practice sect. 1980-90), Ill. Bar Assn. (sec. 1969-70, sec. bd. govs. 1969-71), Chgo. Bar Assn. (aviation law com. 1970-73), Bar Assn. of 7th Fed. Ct. (meetings com. 1968-70, vice chmn. membership com. 1973-75), Soc. Trial Lawyers, Cath. Lawyers Guild of Chgo. (bd. advisors 1973-96), Law Club Chgo., Chgo. Athletic Assn. (pres. 1973). Republican. Aviation, Federal civil litigation, Health. Home: 900 SW Bay Point Cir Palm City FL 34990-1758 Office: Peterson & Ross 200 E Randolph St Ste 7300 Chicago IL 60601-7012

GEIS, JEROME ARTHUR, lawyer, legal educator; b. Shakopee, Minn., May 28, 1946; s. Arthur Adam and Emma Mary (Boegemann) G.; m. Beth Marie Bruger, Aug. 11, 1979; children: Jennifer, Jason, Joan, Janice. BA in History, Govt. magna cum laude, St. John's U., Collegeville, Minn., 1968; JD cum laude, U. Notre Dame, 1973; LLM in Taxation, NYU, 1975. Bar: Minn. 1973, U.S. Dist. Ct. Minn. 1973, U.S. Tax Ct. 1973, U.S. Ct. Appeals (8th cir.) 1973. Law clk. to presiding justice Minn. Supreme Ct., St. Paul, 1973-74; assoc. Dudley & Smith, 1975-76, Briggs & Morgan P.A., St. Paul, 1976-79, chief tax dept., 1983-95. Prof. tax law William Mitchell Coll. of Law, St. Paul, 1976—. Columnist Minn. Law Jour., 1986-89, Bench & Bar, 1990—; editl. cons.: Sales and Use Tax Alert; former reviewer Summary Reporter: Finance and Commerce, Minnesota State Bar Assn.; corr. State Tax Notes. Bd. dirs. Western Townhouse Assn., West St. Paul, 1979, St. Matthews Cath. Ch., West St. Paul, 1981; adv. bd. Minn. Inst. of Legal Edn., 1984—. Served to specialist 4th class U.S. Army, 1969-71. Fellow Am. Coll. Tax Counsel; mem. ABA, Am. Law Inst., Tax Inst. Am. (chmn. sales and use tax commn. 1988-90), Nat. Tax Assn., Am. Judicature Soc., Minn. Bar Assn. (bd. dirs. tax coun. sect. 1984-93, 94-97, 99—, chmn. 1990-91), Ramsey County Bar Assn., Minn. Taxpayers Assn. (bd. dirs. 1988—), Inst. Property Taxation, Supreme Ct. Hist. Soc., Nat. Assn. State Bar Tax Sects. (exec. com. 1993—), Citizens League, Minn. Club (bd. dirs. 1997-2000—), KC, Kiwanis (bd. dirs. 1997-2000). Corporate taxation, Personal income taxation, State and local taxation. Home: 1116 Dodd Rd Saint Paul MN 55118-1821 Office: Briggs & Morgan PA 2200 1st St N Saint Paul MN 55109-3210 E-mail: Geiger@Briggs.com

GEISLER, THOMAS MILTON, JR. lawyer; b. Orange, N.J., Jan. 16, 1943; s. Thomas M. and Helen K. (Thomas) G.; m. Sarah Ann Farrell Geisler, Aug. 6, 1977; children: Sarah C., Ann C. AB in Math. (cum laude), Harvard Coll., Cambridge, Mass., 1965; JD, Harvard Law Sch., Cambridge, Mass., 1968. Bar: N.J., N.Y., Conn., U.S. Dist. Cts. (2nd cir.), U.S. Supreme Ct. Asst., base legal officer U.S. Naval Submarine Base, New London, Conn., 1969-71; appellate def. counsel Naval Appellate Review Activity, Washington, 1971-72; assoc. Shearman & Sterling, N.Y.C., 1973-80, ptnr., 1980-91; pvt. practice, 1991-96, New Haven, 1994—. Dir., bd. dirs. Friends of Harvard Law Record, Cambridge, Mass., 1997—. Author: Am. Jur. Proof of Facts 3d, 1995, 96, 98, 99; editor: Trial Practice Newsletter, 1986—. Lt., USNR, 1969-72. Recipient Litigation Star ABA Litigation Sect., 1997, Navy Achievement award USN, Washington, 1971. Mem. ABA (trial practice com.), Conn. Bar Assn., Harvard Club of So. Conn., Harvard Club of N.Y.C., Quinnipiack Club, Madison Beach Club. Presbyterian. Avocations: tennis. squash, theater, concerts. Appellate, Federal civil litigation, State civil litigation. Office: 205 Church St Ste 508 New Haven CT 06510-1805 E-mail: T1827@aol.com

GEISSLER, BERNHARD HEILO, lawyer; b. Berlin, Germany, Mar. 16, 1939; m. Ingrid; children: Katrin, Florian, Barbara. Dr.jur., Tech. U. Munich, Germany, 1971, diploma in physics, 1963; M of Comparative Law, George Washington U., 1980. Rsch. physicist Tech. U. Munich, Germany, 1963-65; patent atty. clk. German Fed. Patant Ct., Munich, 1964-68; patent atty. Kalle AG, 1971-73; asst. gen. patent counsel Phillips Petroleum Co., 1973-85; ptnr. Munich, 1985—. Sec. LES, Germany. Author: Licence Agreements, Semiconductor Protection Act. Legal rsch. fellow Max Planck Inst., Munich, 1968-71. Mem. AIPPI, GRUR, FILPI. Avocations: mathematical games, golf, skiing. Intellectual property, Patent, Product liability. Office: Patent-U Rechtsanwalte Galileiplatz 1 81679 Munich Germany

GELB, GEORGE EDWARD, lawyer; b. Miami, Fla., June 23, 1946; s. Monroe and Violet (Abelson) G.; m. Kathryn Mary Peterson, Dec. 21, 1973; children— Christine Mary, Joseph Edward. B.A., U. Miami, 1968; J.D., U. Del., 1975; LL.M., NYU, 1978. Bar: Fla. 1977, N.J. 1977, Pa. 1977, U.S. Dist. Ct. (so. dist.) Fla. 1977, U.S. Ct. Appeals (5th cir.) 1977, U.S. Ct. Appeals (11th cir.) 1981, U.S. Supreme Ct. 1983. Asst. atty. gen. Del. Atty. Gen.'s Office, Wilmington, 1975-76; pres., atty. George E. Gelb, P.A., Miami, Fla., 1978— . Chmn., Wilmington Young Republicans, atty. City of Wilmington Rep. Com., asst. counsel Del. Rep. State Com., 1975-76. Roman Catholic. Club: Coral Gables Country. Family and matrimonial. Office: George E Gelb P A 19 W Flagler St Ste 1116 Miami FL 33130-4410

GELB, JOSEPH DONALD, lawyer; b. Wilkes-Barre, Pa., Dec. 13, 1923; s. Edward and Esther (Fierman) G. m. Anne Mirman, July 3, 1955; children: Adam, Roger. Student, Pa. State Coll., 1943; BS, U. Scranton, 1950; LLB, George Washington U., 1952. Bar: D.C. 1954, Md. 1963, U.S. Supreme Ct. 1972. Adjudicator War Claims Commn., 1952-54; pvt. practice Washington and Md., 1954-69; ptnr. Gelb & Pitsenberger, Washington, 1969-74; prin. Joseph D. Gelb Chartered, 1974-80, Gelb, Abelson & Siegel, P.C., Washington, 1980-82, Gelb & Siegel, P.C., Washington, 1982-85, Joseph D. Gelb, Chartered, Washington, 1985-93, Gelb & Gelb, P.C., Washington, 1994—. Served with USAAF, 1943-46 Mem. Md. Bar Assn., D.C. Bar Assn., Bethesda Country Club, B'nai B'rith, Masons. General civil litigation, Personal injury, Product liability. Home: 9620 Annlee Ter Bethesda MD 20817-1410 also: 525 N Ocean Blvd Pompano Beach FL 33062-4640 Office: Gelb & Gelb PC 1120 Connecticut Ave NW Washington DC 20036-3902 E-mail: lawyers@gelbandgelb.com

GELB, JUDITH ANNE, lawyer; b. N.Y.C., Apr. 5, 1935; d. Joseph and Sarah (Stein) G.; m. Howard S. Vogel, June 30, 1962; 1 child, Michael S. BA, Bklyn. Coll., 1955; JD, Columbia U., 1958. BAr: N.Y. 1959, U.S. Dist. Ct. (so. and ea. dists.) N.Y. 1960, U.S. Ct. Appeals (2d cir.) 1960, U.S. Ct. Mil. Appeals 1962. Asst. to editor N.Y. Law Jour., N.Y.C., 1958-59; confidential asst. to U.S. atty. ea dist. N.Y., Bklyn., 1959-61; assoc. Whitman & Ransom, N.Y.C., 1961-70, ptnr., 1971-93, Whitman Breed Abbott & Morgan LLP, N.Y.C., 1993-2000, Winston & Strawn, N.Y.C., 2000—. Mem. ABA (individual rights sect., real property and trust law sect.), Fed. Bar Counsel, N.Y. State Bar Assn. (trusts and estates com.),

N.Y. State Dist. Attys. Assn., Assn. Bar City N.Y., Columbia Law Sch. Alumni Assn., (bd. dirs.), Girls, Inc. (resources com.), Princeton Club. Estate planning, Probate, Estate taxation. Home: 169 E 69th St New York NY 10021-5163 Office: Winston & Strawn 200 Park Ave New York NY 10166-0005 E-mail: jgelb@winston.com

GELBER, DON JEFFREY, lawyer; b. L.A., Mar. 10, 1940; s. Oscar and Betty Sheila (Chernitsky) G.; m. Jessica Jeasun Song, May 15, 1967; children: Victoria, Jonathan, Rebecca, Robert. Student UCLA, 1957-58, Reed Coll., 1958-59; AB, Stanford U., 1961, JD, 1963. Bar: Calif. 1964, Hawaii 1964, U.S. Dist. Ct. (cen. and no. dists. Calif.) 1964, U.S. Dist. Ct. Hawaii 1964, U.S. Ct. Appeals (9th cir.) 1964, U.S. Supreme Ct. 1991. Assoc. Greenstein, Yamane & Cowan, Honolulu, 1964-67; reporter Penal Law Revision Project, Hawaii Jud. Council, Honolulu, 1967-69; assoc. H. William Burgess, Honolulu, 1969-72; ptnr. Burgess & Gelber, Honolulu, 1972-73; prin. Law Offices of Don Jeffrey Gelber, Honolulu, 1974-77; pres. Gelber & Wagner, Honolulu, 1978-83, Gelber & Gelber, Honolulu, 1984-89, Gelber, Gelber, Ingersoll, Klevansky & Faris, Honolulu, 1990—; legal counsel Hawaii State Senate Judiciary Com., 1965; adminstrv. asst. to majority floor leader Hawaii State Senate, 1966, legal counsel Edn. Com., 1967, 68; majority counsel Hawaii Ho. of Reps., 1974; spl. counsel Hawaii State Senate, 1983. Contbr. articles to legal publs. Mem. State Bar Calif., ABA (sect. bus. law), Am. Bankruptcy Inst., Hawaii State Bar Assn. (sect. bankruptcy law, bd. dirs. 1991-93, pres. 1993). Clubs: Pacific, Plaza (Honolulu). Bankruptcy, Federal civil litigation, Real property. Office: Gelber Gelber Ingersoll Klevansky & Faris 745 Fort Street Mall Ste 1400 Honolulu HI 96813-3877

GELBER, LINDA CECILE, lawyer, banker; b. Hackensack, N.J., Oct. 30, 1950; d. Melvin W. and Beverly E. (Gilman) Gelber. B.A., Ind. U., 1972, M.B.A., 1974, J.D., 1978; cert. fin. svcs. counselor, Am. Bankers Assn. Nat. Grad. Trust Sch. , 1983. Bar: Ind. 1978, U.S. Dist. Ct. (so. dist.) Ind. 1978, U.S. Supreme Ct. 1983, N.J. 1988, U.S. Dist. Ct. N.J. 1988. Program analyst Ind. Legis. Svcs. Agy., Indpls., 1978-80; v.p., trust officer First Nat. Bank, Kokomo, Ind., 1980-85, asst. v.p. Mchts. Nat. Bank, Indpls., 1985-87, Midlantic Nat. Bank, Edison and Englewood, N.J., 1987-90; pvt. con. N.J., N.Y., 1990—; part-time instr. Indiana U., Kokomo, 1981-82, Ball State U., Muncie, Ind., 1979-80. Bd. dirs. United Way, Kokomo, 1983-85, div. chmn. fund raising campaign, 1983; mem. Estate Planning Coun. Indpls. Mem. ABA, Am. Inst. Banking (v.p. 1983-85), Howard County (Ind.) Bar Assn. (sec.-treas. 1981), Indiana State Bar Assn., N.J. State Bar Assn., Bergen County Bar Assn. Club: Altrusa (Kokomo). Probate. Office: Midlantic Nat Bank 1 Engle St Englewood NJ 07631-2910

GELBER, LOUISE C(ARP), lawyer; m. Milton Gelber (dec.); children: Jack, Bruce, Julie McCoy. BA, JD, U. Calif., 1944. Bar: Calif. 1945, U.S. Dist. Ct. (so. dist.) Calif. 1945, U.S. Supreme Ct. 1965. Pvt. practice; commr. Calif. Bd. Examiners for Nursing Home Adminstrs.; adminstr. Calif. Dept. Consumer Affairs. Speaker local drug rehab. hosp.; mem. Vis. Nurses Bd.; commr. Calif. Adv. Cost Control to State Govt.; mem. temporary judge panel L.A. County; settlement officer dispute resolution svc. Pasadena Superior Ct. Mem. editorial staff U. Calif. Law Rev. Calif. nominee for State Assembly, 1992; judge pro tem Rio Hondo Mcpl. Ct.; pro bono Bd. Legal Aid; v.p. local PTA; mem., invocator Arcadia Coord. Coun.; bd. dirs. Foothill Apt. Assn., People-For People; active ARC, Community Chest, United Way, Boy Scouts Am., Girl Scouts U.S. Mem. ABA, Calif. Bar Assn., Foothill Bar Assn., L.A. County Bar ASsn., Pomona Valley Bar Assn., Citrus Bar Assn., Arcadia C. of C. (legis. com.), So. Calif. Women Lawyers (treas.), Pasadena C. of C., Bus. and Profl. Women Lawyers (past state legis. chmn., state legis. adv.), Order of Eastern Star, LWV, Sierra. General corporate, Estate planning, Probate. Home and Office: 1225 Rancho Rd Arcadia CA 91006-2241 E-mail: french.court@verizon.net

GELDON, FRED WOLMAN, lawyer; b. N.Y.C., July 18, 1946; s. Earl R. and Ruth Judith (Abrahams) G.; m. Anne Wolman, June 2, 1974; children: Todd Wolman, Elise Wolman. AB magna cum laude, Princeton U., 1968; MA in Physics, U. Calif., Berkeley, 1970; JD magna cum laude, Harvard U., 1973. Bar: Calif. 1973, D.C. 1974, U.S. Dist. Ct. D.C. 1974, U.S. Ct. Appeals (D.C. cir.) 1974, U.S. Supreme Ct. 1978, U.S. Ct. Claims 1981, Md. 1984, U.S. Ct. Appeals (4th cir.) 1984. Law clk. to hon. William Bryant U.S. Dist. Ct. (D.C. dist.), Washington, 1973-74; from assoc. to ptnr. Leva, Hawes, Symington, Martin & Oppenheimer, 1974-83; asst. dir. torts br. civil div. U.S. Dept. Justice, 1983-85; ptnr. Janis, Schuelke & Wechsler, 1985-87; dep. gen. counsel Electronic Data Sys. Corp., Herndon, Va., 1987-89, gen. counsel govt. sys. group, 1989—, dir. govt. strategic bus. unit support, 1994—; gen. counsel EDS Fed., 1999—. Contbr. articles to profl. jours. Pres. Potomac Springs Civic Assn., Rockville Md., 1983-84, 1988-89. Mem. ABA, Fed. cir. Bar Assn. (vice chmn. govt. contracts appeals com. 1986), Sigma Xi, Phi Beta Kappa. Democrat. Jewish. Avocations: tennis, softball, music, computer programming, stamp collecting. Administrative and regulatory, Federal civil litigation, Government contracts and claims. Office: Electronic Data Systems 13600 Eds Dr Herndon VA 20171-3225

GELHAUS, ROBERT JOSEPH, lawyer, publisher; b. Missoula, Mont., Oct. 17, 1941; s. Francis Joseph and Bonnie Una (Mundhenk) G. AB magna cum laude, Harvard Coll., 1963; LlB, Stanford U., 1968. Bar: Calif. 1970, U.S. Dist. Ct., U.S. Ct. Appeals 1970. Assoc. firm Howard, Prim, Rice, Nemerovski, Canady & Pollak, San Francisco, 1970-74; sole practice, 1974—. Editor in chief Harcourt Brace Jovanovich Legal & Profl. Publs., Inc., 1974-78; pres. Robert J. Gelhaus, A Profl. Corp., 1978—; instr. econs. U. Wash., 1964-65; instr. law Stanford Law Sch., 1968-69; cons. FCC, 1968-69; asst. Calif. Law Revision Commn., 1967-68. Author: (with James C. Oldham) Summary of Labor Law, 11th edit., 1972. Mem. Calif. Bar Assn., Harvard Club San Francisco, Order Coif, Omicron Delta Epsilon. Antitrust, Federal civil litigation, Labor. Home: 1756 Broadway San Francisco CA 94109-2458

GELLER, KENNETH STEVEN, lawyer; b. N.Y.C., Sept. 22, 1947; s. Edward and Sylvia R. (Tannenbaum) G.; m. Judith B. Ratner, Sept. 9, 1990; children: Eric Jonathan, Lisa Beth. BA magna cum laude, CCNY, 1968; JD magna cum laude, Harvard U., 1971. Bar: N.Y. 1972, U.S. Dist. Ct. (so. and ea. dists.) N.Y. 1972, U.S. Ct. Appeals (2d cir.) 1972, U.S. Ct. Appeals (D.C. cir.) 1974, U.S. Supreme Ct. 1975, U.S. Ct. Appeals (10th cir.) 1976, D.C. 1986, U.S. Ct. Appeals (6th cir.) 1987, U.S. Ct. Appeals (4th cir.) 1987, U.S. Ct. Appeals (9th cir.) 1988, U.S. Ct. Appeals (5th and 11th cirs.) 1990, U.S. Dist. Ct. D.C. 1991, U.S. Ct. Appeals (3rd and 7th cirs.) 1991, U.S. Ct. Appeals (Armed Forces) 1995, U.S. Ct. Appeals (8th cir.) 1996, U.S. Ct. Appeals (fed. cir.) 1999. Law clk. U.S. Ct. Appeals (2d cir.), 1971-72; assoc. Nickerson, Kramer, Lowenstein, Nessen & Kamin, N.Y.C., 1972-73; asst. spl. prosecutor Watergate Spl. Prosecution Force, Washington, 1973-75; asst. to solicitor gen. Dept. Justice, 1975-79, dep. solicitor gen., 1979-86; ptnr. Mayer, Brown & Platt, 1986—, mng. ptnr., 1995—. Mem. adv. bd. State and Local Legal Ctrs., 1986-92; mem. adv. com. on rules U.S. Ct. Appeals for Armed Forces, 1994—; mem. adv. com. on procedures Ct. Appeals D.C. Cir., 2000—. Co-author: (Stern, Gressman, Shapiro & Geller) Supreme Court Practice, 7th edit., 1993; contbg. author: Business and Commercial Litigation in Federal Courts, 1998; contbr. articles to profl. jours. Mem. vis. com. Harvard U. Law Sch.; trustee, chmn. publs. com. Supreme Ct. Hist. Soc. Recipient Younger Fed. Lawyer award FBA, 1981, Presdl. Disting. Exec. award. Office: Mayer Brown & Platt 1909 K St NW Washington DC 20006-1152 E-mail: kgeller@mayerbrown.com

GELLER, WILLIAM ALAN, criminal justice researcher, police and public safety consultant; b. Bklyn., June 4, 1950; s. Maurice and Shirley F.E. (Scherker) G.; m. Julia Marie Arment, Oct. 1, 1978. BA, SUNY, Buffalo, 1972; JD, U. Chgo., 1975. Bar: Ill. 1975, U.S. Dist. Ct. (no. dist.) Ill. 1975. Law clk. to Hon. Walter V. Schaefer Ill. Supreme Ct., Chgo., 1975-76; exec. dir. Chgo. Law Enforcement Study Group, 1976-81; project dir. Am. Bar Found., Chgo., 1981-86; spl. counsel Chgo. Park Dist., 1986-88; assoc. dir. Police Exec. Rsch. Forum, 1987-97; dir. Geller & Assocs. Consulting, Wilmette, Ill., 1997—. Mem. Pres. Clinton's Transition Team (U.S. Dept. Justice search team mem.), 1992-93; mem. staff Office Presdl. Pers., Washington, 1993; commr. Wilmette Fire and Police Commn., 1985-88; cons. Local Initiatives Support Corp., 1995—, Nat. Inst. Justice, U.S. Dept. Justice, Washington, 1980—, Office of Cmty. Oriented Policing Svcs., U.S. Dept. Justice, 1994-, fellow, 1999-2001, N.Y.C. Police Dept., 1985-88, 93, FBI, Washington, 1986—, Police Found., 1986-92, N.Y.C. Met. Transp. Authority, 1991, Fed. Signal Corp., 1990, Chgo. Police Bd., 1991-95, St. Louis Police Dept., 1991—, Office of the Mayor, Washington, 1992-93, St. Louis, 1997-2001, Boulware & Assocs., 1992—, Burkhalter & Assocs., 1992-95; mem. rsch. com. Chgo. Police Dept., 1983-86; mem. Cook County Sheriff's adv. com. on internal affairs, 1986; mem. exec. com. Chgo. Ethics Project. Author: Split-Second Decisions: Shootings Of and By Chicago Police, 1981, Deadly Force: A Practitioner's Desk Reference on Police-Involved Shootings in the United States, 1991, Police Violence: Understanding the Controlling Police Abuse of Force, 1996, And Justice For All, 1995, Managing Police Innovation, 1995; also many articles to profl. jours., mags., and newspapers; editor: Police Leadership in America: Crisis and Opportunity, 1985, Local Government Police Management, 1991; script cons. (TV show) L.A. Law, 1991—. Co-chmn. Citizens for Safety Vests, Chgo., 1982-83; mem. adv. bd. March of Dimes Met. Chgo., 1983; bd. dirs. John Howard Assn., Chgo., 1978—, Bus. and Profl. People for Pub. Interest, 1988—, Travel Light Theatre, Chgo., 1980-82; mem. adv. bd. Yale U. Nat. Ctr. Children Exposed to Violence, 2000—; mem. priority grants com. United Way Met. Chgo., 1990-92; mem. task force on criminal justice studies, Clark-Atlanta U., 1991—; mgr. Harvard Exec. Session on Drugs and Cmty. Policing, Cambridge, Mass., 1990-92. Recipient Richard J. Daley Police medal of honor, City of Chgo., 1983, commendation N.Y.C. Police Commr., 1986, commendation St. Louis Police Chief, 1997; grantee Nat. Inst. Justice, 1980, 84, 88, 90, 91, Chgo. Bar Found., 1980, Chgo. Cmty. Trust, 1976-80, 84, 85, Charles Stewart Mott Found., 1990. Mem. ABA (com. on stds. for criminal justice 1983-86, prison and jail problems com. 185-86), Internat. Assn. Chiefs Police, Police Exec. Rsch. Forum, NOBLE, am. Soc. Criminology, Acad. Criminal Justice Scis. Home and Office: 2116 Thornwood Ave Wilmette IL 60091-1452 E-mail: wageller@aol.com

GELLERMANN, MARIAN DEBELLE, retired lawyer; b. Winslow, Ill., Nov. 9, 1905; d. Vernon LeRoy and Mae (Fetterhoff) DeBelle; m. Josef Egmond Gellermann, Dec. 31, 1955 (dec. Aug. 16, 1956). Diploma in Bus. Edn., Strayer Coll., Washington, 1932; LLB, George Washington U., 1937, AB, 1939, SJD, 1940. Bar: D.C. 1940, U.S. Supreme Ct. 1944. Corp. sec. Fed. Svcs. Fin. Corp., Washington, 1932-66; asst. to multiple agts. State Mutual Life Assurance, 1966; house atty. Doctor's Hosp., 1967; sec. to gen. agt. Penn Mutual Life Ins. Co., 1980-85; pvt. practice law, 1983-96; ret. Active in helping to build World War II Meml., Washington. Mem. Pres.'s Club of ABA (2 awards, including 5 Year award), D.C. Bar Assn., Women's Bar Assn. of D.C., Nat. Genealogical Assn., O.E.S., The Codrington Club (Oxford). Home: 2122 Massachusetts Ave NW Washington DC 20008-2833

GELLHORN, ERNEST ALBERT EUGENE, lawyer; b. Oak Park, Ill., Mar. 30, 1935; s. Ernst and Hilde Betty (Obermeier) G.; m. Jaquelin Ann Silker, Feb. 1, 1958; children: Thomas Ernest, Ann Lois. BA cum laude, U. Minn., 1956, LLB magna cum laude, 1962. Bar: Ohio 1962, Va. 1975, Ariz. 1976, D.C. 1986, Calif. 1990. Assoc. Jones, Day, Reavis & Pogue, Cleve., Washington, L.A., 1962-66; prof. law Duke U. Law Sch., 1966-70, U. Va. Law Sch., 1970-75; dean Coll. Law, Ariz. State U., Tempe, 1975-78, U. Wash. Law Sch., Seattle, 1978-79; T. Munford Boyd prof. U. Va. Law Sch., Charlottesville, 1979-82; dean, Galen J. Roush prof. Case Western Res. U. Sch. Law, Cleve., 1982-86; prtnr. Jones, Day, Reavis & Pogue, L.A., Washington, 1986-94; George Mason U. Found. prof. law, 1995—. Sr. counsel Commn. CIA Activities Within U.S., 1975. Co-author: Antitrust Law and Economics, 4th edit., 1994, Administrative Law and Process, 4th edit., 1997, The Administrative Process, 4th edit., 1993. Lt. USNR, 1956-59. Mem. ABA, Ariz. Bar Assn., Va. Bar Assn., Ohio Bar Assn., D.C. Bar Assn., Calif. Bar Assn., Phi Beta Kappa, Order of Coif. Administrative and regulatory, Antitrust, Appellate. Home: 2907 Normanstone Ln NW Washington DC 20008-2725 E-mail: gellhorn@pipeline.com

GELMAN, ANDREW RICHARD, lawyer; b. Chgo. s. Sidney S. and Beverly Gelman; m. Amy H., 1985; children: Stephen S., Adam P., Elizabeth F. BA, U. Pa., 1967; JD, U. Va., 1970. Bar: Va. 1970, Ill. 1971. Assoc. Roan & Grossman Law Firm, Chgo., 1971-74, McBride, Baker & Coles Law Firm, Chgo., 1974-77, ptnr., 1978—. Mem. com. on character and fitness of Ill. Supreme Ct., Chgo., 1979-95. Bd. dirs. Scholarship and Guidance Assn., Chgo., 1979—, Inst. for Edn. and Rsch. of Children's Meml. Hosp., Chgo., 1991—, vice-chair, 1998—; chmn. Med. Rsch. Inst. Coun., 1983-86, 91-92; trustee Michael Reese Hosp. and Med. Ctr., Chgo., 1987-91. Recipient Weigle award Chgo. Bar Found., 1980. Mem. ABA (standing com. jud. selection, tenure and compensation 1982-87, pub. understanding about the law com. 1987-91, chair probate and estate planning com. gen. practice sect. 1994-97, commn. on mental and phys. disability law 1995-97), Chgo. Bar Assn. (past chmn. divsn. probate practice com., bd. mgrs. 1978-80, chmn. young lawyers sect. 1976-77), Chgo. Estate Planning Coun. Estate planning, Probate, Estate taxation. Office: McBride Baker & Coles 500 W Madison St Fl 40 Chicago IL 60661-2511 E-mail: gelman@mbc.com

GELMAN, SANDOR M. lawyer; b. Pitts., Aug. 26, 1938; s. Harold Milton and Elsie (Markus) G.; m. Judith Ilene Meyers, Feb. 16, 1969; children: Jascha David, Gabriel Elliot. BBA, U. Mich., 1960, JD, 1963. Bar: Mich. 1964, U.S. Dist. Ct. (ea. dist.) Mich. 1964. Assoc., Bellinson & Doctoroff, Detroit, 1963-64, Goldman & Grabow, Detroit, 1964-65; legal advisor, prosecutor Oakland County, Pontiac, Mich., 1965-68; ptnr. Gelman & Baumkel, Troy, Mich., 1968— . Pres. Oakland Family Services, Pontiac, Mich., 1980-82. Mem. ABA, Am. Trial Lawyers Assn., State Bar Mich. (mem. family law council 1981-87, chmn. advt., certification and specialization com. 1980-86), Oakland County Bar Assn. (pres. 1984-85, bd. dirs. 1975-85), Detroit Bar Assn. Democrat. Jewish. Lodges: Kiwanis, B'nai B'rith. State civil litigation, Family and matrimonial, Personal injury. Home: 6745 Woodside Trl West Bloomfield MI 48322-3914

GELOSO-BARONE, ROSALIA A. lawyer; b. Rye, N.Y., Apr. 21, 1962; d. Vincent M. and Patricia (Checca) G. BA in Journalism with honors, Boston Coll., 1984; JD cum laude, Pace U., 1988. Bar: N.Y. 1988, Conn. 1988, U.S. Dist. Ct. (so. and ea. dists.) N.Y. 1988. Project asst. Fin. Acctg. Standards Bd., Stamford, Conn., 1984-85; legal asst. Merrill Lynch Realty, Inc., 1985-86, U.S. Attorney's Office, N.Y.C., 1987-88; legal asst./staff atty. Westchester County Attorney's Office, White Plains, N.Y., 1988-92; sr. staff atty. U.S. Dist. Ct. (so. dist.) N.Y., 1995-98; law lectr. bus. dept and legal assistant program Norwalk (Conn.) C.C., 1998—. Adj. prof. bus. law Norwalk C.C., Berkeley Coll., Katherine Gibbs Sch., U. Conn., 1992-95. Alumni admissions counselor Boston Coll., Fairfield County, Conn., 1984—. Recipient Merit Scholarship Pace Law Sch., 1986-88. Mem. ABA, N.Y. State Bar Assn., Conn. Bar Assn.

GELTMAN, EDWARD ALAN, lawyer; b. Newark, Apr. 14, 1946; s. Donald and Muriel G.; m. Elizabeth Ann Glass, Jan. 2, 1989; children: Andrew, Jeffrey, Rachel. BA with honors, Franklin & Marshall Coll., 1968; JD with honors, George Washington U., 1971. Bar: D.C. 1971, U.S. Ct. Appeals (D.C. cir.) 1971, U.S. Supreme Ct. 1980. Trial atty. FTC, Washington, 1971-73; assoc., then ptnr. Nicholson & Carter, 1973-79; ptnr. Squire, Sanders & Dempsey, 1979—. Contbr. articles to profl. jours. Mem. ABA (antitrust sect.), Order of Coif. Office: Squire Sanders & Dempsey 1201 Pennsylvania Ave NW Washington DC 20004-2491

GENBERG, IRA, lawyer; b. Newark, July 27, 1947; s. Jack and Ann (Lerman) G.; m. Rosemary Lawlor, Jan. 15, 1981; children: Jack Michael, Anne Rebecca. AB magna cum laude, Rutgers U., 1969; JD, U. Pa., 1972. Bar: Ga. 1972, D.C. 1978. Assoc. Haas, Holland, Levison & Gibert, Atlanta, 1972-75; ptnr. Stokes, Shapiro, Fussell & Genberg, 1975-87; ptnr., head litigation sect. Smith, Gambrell & Russell LLP, 1987—. Spkr. Seminar on Constrn. Litigation, Atlanta, 1985, Seminar on Constrn. Law, Atlanta, 1986; co-chmn. Seminar on Trying A Complex Constrn. Case, 1994. Contbr. articles to Constrn. Bus. Review Mag. Mem. ABA, Ga. Bar Assn., Atlanta Bar Assn., D.C. Bar Assn. Antitrust, General civil litigation, Construction. Office: Smith Gambrell & Russell LLP 1230 Peachtree St NE Atlanta GA 30309-3592

GENEGO, WILLIAM JOSEPH, lawyer; b. Albany, Mar. 27, 1950; s. William Joseph and Olga Alice (Sultan) G. BS in Bus. and Pub. Adminstrn. magna cum laude, NYU, 1972; JD, Yale U., 1975; LLM, Georgetown U., 1977. Bar: D.C. 1975, Calif. 1982, U.S. Supreme Ct. 1984, other dist. and appellate cts. Spl. asst. state's atty. Cir. and Dist. Cts. Montgomery County, Md., 1975-77; staff atty. legal intern program Georgetown U. Law Ctr., Washington, 1975-77, adj. prof., dep. dir. legal intern program, 1977-79; cons., vis. supervising atty. Yale Legal Svcs. Orgn., Law Sch. Yale U., New Haven, 1977; with Baker & Fine, Cambridge, Mass., 1980-81; asst. clin. prof. Law Ctr. U. So. Calif., L.A., 1981-83, assoc. clin. prof., 1983-86, clin. prof., 1986-89, adj. prof., 1990-92; vis. prof. law Boston U., 1990, UCLA, 1991-92; pvt. practice Law Offices of William J. Genego, Santa Monica, Calif., 1990-2000; ptnr. Nasatir, Hirsch, Podberesky & Genego, 2000—. Mem. practitioners' adv. group U.S. Sentencing Commn., 1989—; presenter in field. Mem. adv. bd. Criminal Practice Manual, Bur. Nat. Affairs, 1987-2000; editor Yale Law Jour., 1974-75; contbr. articles to legal publs. Bd. dirs. Nat. Network for Right to Counsel, 1986-88. Recipient Ann. Humanitarian award inmate rep. com. Fed. Correctional Instn., Danbury, Conn., 1974. Mem. NACDL (chairperson com. on rules of practice and procedure 1991—, Pres.'s award 1988), ABA (mem. ad hoc com. on U.S. Sentencing Commn. 1986—, chairperson competency com. sect. criminal justice 1983-85), Nat. Legal Aid and Defender Assn. (chairperson def. counsel competency com. 1984-87), Calif. Pub. Defenders Assn., Calif. Attys. for Criminal Justice. Appellate, Criminal. Office: Main St Law Bldg 2115 Main St Santa Monica CA 90405-2215

GENIA, JAMES MICHAEL, lawyer; b. Chgo., Sept. 16, 1964; s. Anthony Leo and Anne Louise (Hawley) G. BA, Augsburg Coll., 1987; JD, William Mitchell Coll. Law, 1990. Bar: Minn. 1990, U.S. Dist. Ct. Minn. 1992, U.S. Ct. Appeals (8th cir.) 1994, U.S. Supreme Ct. 1999. Judicial law clk. State Minn., Duluth, 1990-92; dep. solicitor gen. Mille Lacs Band of Ojibwe Indians, Onamia, Minn., 1992-93, solicitor gen., 1993-99; atty. Lockridge Grindal Nauen, Mpls., 1999—. Bd. dirs. Woodlands Nat. Bank, Onamia, 1996—, chmn., 1997—; vice-chmn. bd. dirs. Anishinabe O.I.C., Onamia, 1992-99; bd. dirs. Johnson Inst. Found., 1998—; bd. dirs. Minn. Am. Indian C. of C., 2001—; lectr. Am. Indian sovereignty and treaty rights various univs., cntinuing edn. seminars, civic groups, 1992—; adj. prof. St. Cloud State U., 1999—. Actor Mille Lacs Cmty. Theater, Onamia, 1996—. Bd. dirs. Johnson Inst. Found., 1998—. Named Atty. of Yr., Minn. Lawyer Newspaper, 1999, named One of Top 100 All-Time Grads., William Mitchell Coll. Law, 2000. Mem. ATLA, Fed. Bar Assn., Minn. Am. Indian Bar Assn., Minn. State Bar Assn., William Mitchell Coll. Law Alumni Assn. (bd. dirs. 1996-99). Avocations: softball, golf, jogging, reading, acting. Office: Lockridge Grindal Nauen 100 Washington Ave S Ste 2200 Minneapolis MN 55401-2179 E-mail: jmgenia@locklaw.com

GENIESSE, ROBERT JOHN, lawyer; b. Appleton, Wis., Sept. 16, 1929; s. Arthur John and Rhoda (Miller) G.; m. Jane Elizabeth Fletcher, June 10, 1961; children: Julia Forrest, Thomas Guy. BA magna cum laude, Williams Coll., 1951; LLB cum laude, Harvard U., 1957. Bar: N.Y. 1958, D.C. 1982. Assoc. Debevoise and Plimpton, N.Y.C., 1957-61, 64-66, ptnr., 1966-94; asst. U.S. atty. So. Dist. N.Y., 1962-63, chief appellate atty., 1963-64. Editor Harvard Law Rev., 1955-57. Bd. dirs. Legal Action Ctr., N.Y., 1973-78, Environ. Def. Fund, 1974-82; trustee Williams Coll., 1974-87; trustee World Monuments Fund, 1993—, sec., gen. counsel, 1995—; trustee Nat. Bldg. Mus., 1994-2000, Ringling Mus. Art, Sarasota, Fla., 2001—; trustee Sterling and Francine Clark Art Inst., Williamstown, Mass., 1974—, pres., 1987-98; trustee Ringling Mus. Art, Sarasota, Fla., 2001—. 1st lt. Inf. U.S. Army, 1952-54. Mem. N.Y. State Bar Assn., D.C. Bar ASsn., Soc. Alumni of Williams Coll. (pres. 1973-74), Phi Beta Kappa. Federal civil litigation, Criminal, Private international. Home: PO Box 516 Boca Grande FL 33921-0516 also: 2101 Connecticut Ave NW Apt 61 Washington DC 20008-1757 Office: Devevoise & Plimpton 555 13th St NW Ste 1100E Washington DC 20004-1163

GENKIN, BARRY HOWARD, lawyer; b. Phila., Aug. 8, 1949; s. Paul and Pearl (Rosenfeld) G.; m. Marian Block, Aug. 15, 1975; children: Matthew Todd, Kimberly Beth. BS cum laude, Pa. State U., 1971; JD cum laude, U. Balt., 1974; LLM in Taxation, Georgetown U., 1977. Bar: Pa. 1975, Wash. 1977, N.Y. 1995. Spl. counsel divsn. corp. fin. SEC, Washington, 1975-78; ptnr. Blank Rome Comisky & McCauly LLP, Phila., 1979-93, co-chmn. corp. dept., dist. com., mgmt. com., chmn. budget com. Bd. dirs. Smeal Bus. Sch., Pa. State U.; lectr. various orgns. Contbr. U. Balt. Law Rev., 1991—; lectr. various orgns. Mem. ABA, Pa. Bar Assn., Savs. Insts., Pa. Savs. League, N.J. Savs. League, Meadowlands Country Club, Heuisler Honor Soc., Omicron Delta Kappa. Banking, Mergers and acquisitions, Securities. Home: 544 Howe Rd Merion Station PA 19066-1129 Office: Blank Rome Comisky & McCauley LLP One Logan Sq Philadelphia PA 19103

GENOVA, DIANE MELISANO, lawyer; b. Aug. 8, 1948; d. Joseph Louis and Ines (Fiumana) Melisano; m. Joseph Steven Genova, Jan. 15, 1983; children: Anthony Robert, Matthew Edward. AB, Barnard Coll., 1970; postgrad., Harvard U., 1970-71; JD, Columbia U., 1975. Assoc. Milbank, Tweed, Hadley & McCloy, N.Y.C., 1975-80; v.p., asst. resident counsel Morgan Guaranty Trust Co. N.Y., 1981-90, mng. dir., assoc. gen. counsel, 1990-2000, J.P. Morgan Chase & Co., N.Y.C., 2000—. Harlan Fiske Stone scholar, 1972-75. Mem. Assn. of Bar of City of N.Y., N.Y. State Bar Assn., Internat. Swaps and Derivatives Assn. (bd. dirs. 1999—). Roman Catholic. Banking, Finance. Office: J P Morgan Chase & Co 60 Wall St New York NY 10260-0001 E-mail: genova_diane@jpmorgan.com

GENOVA, JOSEPH STEVEN, lawyer; b. Red Bank, N.J., Nov. 12, 1952; s. M. Leonard and Margaret (Coons) G.; m. Janet Scott, May 18, 1974 (div. Dec. 1980) ; m. Diane Melisano Genova, Jan. 15, 1983; children: Anthony Robert, Matthew Edward. BA, Dartmouth Coll., 1974; JD, Yale U., 1977. Bar: N.Y. 1978, U.S. Dist. Ct. (no., so. and ea. dists.) N.Y., Calif. 1993. Assoc. Milbank, Tweed, Hadley & McCloy, N.Y.C., 1977-85, ptnr., 1986—. Ct. appointed arbitrator U.S. Dist. Ct. (ea. dist.) N.Y., 1986—; mediator U.S. Dist. Ct. (so. dist.) N.Y., 1992—. Bd. dirs. Legal Aid Soc., N.Y.C., 1995-2000; N.Y. Lawyers Pub. Interest, 1997—, Legal Svcs. N.Y.C., 2001—; apptd. N.Y. Chief Judge Pro Bono Review Com. (1990-94), Legal Svcs. Project., 1997-2000 Fellow Am. Bar Found., N.Y. Bar

Found.; mem. ABA (Pro Bono Pub. award 1992, William Reece Smith award 1996, ABA Commn. on Iolta 1996-99), Assn. Bar City N.Y. (com. on housing and urban devel. 1982-85, com. on judiciary 1988-91, vice chmn. 1990-91, frequent interim mem., com. pro bono legal svcs., 1993-99, project on homelessness 2001—), N.Y. State Bar Assn. (com. on legal aid 1980—), chmn. 1986-91, pres.'s com. on access to justice 1990—, co-chmn. 1990-99, mem. task force on law guardian sys. 1989-99, mem. special com. future profession, 1998-2000), Fed. Bar Coun. (com. on 2d cir. cts. 1988-98, com. pub. svc. responsibility 1991—, chmn. 1994-2000, trustee 1998—). Roman Catholic. Avocations: fishing, skiing. General civil litigation, Government contracts and claims, Trademark and copyright. Office: Milbank Tweed Hadley & McCloy 1 Chase Manhattan Plz Fl 47 New York NY 10005-1413 E-mail: jgenova@milbank.com

GENTRY, MACK A. lawyer; b. Knoxville, Tenn., July 18, 1944; s. Edgar C. and Elizabeth (Cates) G.; m. Cheryl T. Gentry; children: Tucker J., Carter L., Cates E. BSBA, U. Tenn., 1966, JD, 1968; LLM in Taxation, NYU, 1976. Bar: Tenn. 1969, U.S. Dist. Ct. (ea. dist.) Tenn. 1983, U.S. Tax Ct. 1972, U.S. Claims Ct. 1983, U.S. Ct. Appeals (6th cir.) 1985, U.S. Ctl. Appeals (fed. cir.) 1986, Colo. 2001. Assoc. Kramer, Johnson, Rayson, Greenwood & McVeigh, Knoxville, 1972-75; pres. Gentry, Tipton, Kizer & McLemore, P.C., 1976—. Bd. dirs. First & Farmers Bank, Somerset, Ky. Trustee Tenn. Fed. Tax Inst.; bd. dirs. Met. YMCA, Knoxville Zoo, U. Tenn. Coll. Law Alumni Adv. Coun. Mem. Tenn. Bar Assn., Knoxville Bar Assn. (chmn. tax sect. 1978-79), Beta Alpha Psi, Phi Delta Phi (v.p. 1966). Estate planning, Taxation, general. Office: Gentry Tipton Kizer & McLemore PC 800 S Gay St Ste 2610 Knoxville TN 37929-2610

GEORGE, ALEXANDER ANDREW, lawyer; b. Missoula, Mont., Apr. 26, 1938; s. Andrew Miltiadin and Eleni (Efstathiou) G.; m. Penelope Mitchell, Sept. 29, 1968; children: Andrew A., Stephen A. BBA honors, U. Mont., 1960, JD, 1962; postgrad., John Marshall U., 1964-66. Bar: Mont. 1962, U.s. Ct. Mil. Appeals 1964, U.S. Tax Ct. 1970. Sole practice, Missoula, 1966—. Mem. adv. com. U. Mont. Tax Inst., 1973-76; adj. lectr. U. Montana Law Sch. Corp. Taxation. Pres. Missoula Civic Symphony, 1973; nat. dir. Assn. Urban and Cmty. Symphony Orch., 1974, Mont. Eye Endowment Found.; pres. Greek Orthodox Ch., 1978, 91. Served to capt. JAG U.S. Army, 1962-66. Recipient Jaycee Disting. Svc. award, 1973. Mem. State Bar Mont. (pres. 1981), Western Mont. Bar Assn. (pres. 1971, lifetime achievement award 1998), Mont. Law Found. (treas. 1986-92), Mont. Soc. CPA, Phi Delta Phi, Alpha Kappa Psi, Sigma Nu (alumni trustee 1966-71), Rotary (pres. 1972, state chmn. found. 1977, membership com. chmn. 1978), Ahepa (pres. 1967, state gov. 1968). General corporate, Probate, Corporate taxation. Home: 4 Greenbrier Ct Missoula MT 59802-3342 Office: 210 N Higgins Ave Ste 234 Missoula MT 59802-4497

GEORGE, ANNA-BRITT KRISTIN, solicitor; b. London, May 27, 1973; d. Christopher Walter and Grethe George. BA in Politics with honors, Exeter (Eng.) U., 1994; grad., Coll. of Law, London, 1997. Solicitor Beaumont and Son Solicitors, London, 1997—. Mem. Law Soc. Aviation, General civil litigation, Insurance. Office: Beaumont and Son Solicitors 1 Portsoken St London E1 8AW England Fax: 0207 481 3353. E-mail: ageorge@beaumont.co.uk

GEORGE, JOHN MARTIN, JR. lawyer; b. Normal, Ill., Dec. 17, 1947; s. John and Ada George; m. Judy Ann Watts; children: Sarah, Michael. AB with high honors, U. Ill., 1970, AM, 1971; PhD, Columbia U., 1976; JD cum laude, Harvard U., 1982. Bar: Mass. 1982, U.S. Dist. Ct. Mass. 1983, Ill. 1984, U.S. Dist. Ct. (no. dist.) Ill. 1984, U.S. Ct. Appeals (11th cir.) 1987, U.S. Ct. Appeals (9th cir.) 1988, U.S. Ct. Appeals (7th cir.) 1992, U.S. Ct. Appeals (3d cir.) 2000. Assoc. Hill & Barlow, Boston, 1982-84, Sidley & Austin (now Sidley, Austin, Brown & Wood), Chgo., 1984-89, ptnr., 1989—. Editor Harvard U. Law Rev., 1980-82. Sr. warden Trinity Ch., 1998-2000. Mem. ABA, Chgo. Bar Assn., Mid-Day Club, Phi Beta Kappa. Democrat. Episcopalian. Federal civil litigation, Professional liability, Securities. Office: Sidley Austin Brown & Wood Bank One Plz Chicago IL 60603-2003 E-mail: jgeorge@sidley.com

GEORGE, JOYCE JACKSON, lawyer, judge emeritus; b. Akron, Ohio, May 4, 1936; d. Ray and Verna (Popadich) Jackson; children: Michael Eliot, Michelle René. BA, U. Akron, 1962, JD, 1966; postgrad., Nat. Jud. Coll., Reno, 1976, NYU, 1983. Bar: Ohio 1966, U.S. Dist. Ct. (no. dist.) Ohio 1966, U.S. Ct. Appeals (6th cir.) 1968, U.S. Supreme Ct. 1968. Tchr. Akron Bd. Edn., 1962-66; asst. dir. law City of Akron, 1966-69, pub. utilities advisor, 1969-70, asst. dir. law, 1970-73; pvt. practice Akron, 1973-76; referee Akron Mcpl. Ct., 1975, judge, 1976-83, 9th dist. Ct. Appeals, Akron, 1983-89, Peninsula, Ohio, 1989; U.S. atty. No. Dist., 1989-93; v.p. adminstrn. Telxon Corp., Akron, 1993-96; pres. Ind. Bus. Info. Svcs., Inc., 1996—. Tchr., lectr. Ohio Jud. Coll., Nat. Jud. Coll.; cons. in field. Author: Judicial Opinion Writing Handbook, 1981, 3d edit., 1993, Referee's Report Writing Handbook, 1992; contbr. articles to profl. publs. Recipient Outstanding Woman of Yr. award Akron Bus. and Profl. Women's Club, 1982; Alumni Honor award U. Akron, 1983, Alumni award U. Akron Sch. Law, 1991; Dept. Treasury award, 1992; named Woman of Yr. in politics and govt. Summit County, Ohio, 1983. Mem. ATLA, ABA, Ohio Bar Assn., Ohio Trial Lawyers Assn., Akron Bar Assn. Fax: 330-668-2910

GEORGE, NICHOLAS, lawyer, entrepreneur; b. Seattle, July 11, 1952; s. Harry and Mary (Couroúnes) G.; children: Harry Nicholas, James Michael. BA in Polit. Sci. cum laude, Whitman Coll., 1974; MBA in Mktg. and Corp. Planning, U. Chgo., 1979; JD, U. Puget Sound, 1989. Bar: Wash. 1991, U.S. Dist. Ct. (we. dist.) Wash. 1991, U.S. Ct. Appeals (9th cir.) 1991, U.S. Tax Ct. 1992, U.S. Dist. Ct. (ea. dist.) Wash. 1994, U.S. Supreme Ct. 1994. Fin. cons. Pacific Western Investment Co., Lynnwood, Wash., 1975-77; planning dir. Clinton Capital Ventures, Seattle, 1979-81; corp. planning mgr. Tacoma Boatbldg., 1981-83; pres. MegaProf Investors, Bellevue, Wash., 1983-89; practice trial-settlement law bus., Seattle, 1989—. Free-lance coll. counselor, Seattle, 1980—. Author: Legitimacy in Government: Ideal, Goal, or Myth? 1974. Bd. auditor St. Demetrios Greek Orthodox Ch., Seattle, 1982-83; bd. dirs. Hellenic Golfers Assn., Seattle, 1981-83. Mem. ABA, Assn. Trial Lawyers Am., Wash. State Bar Assn., Wash. Assn. Criminal Def. Lawyers, Wash. State Trial Lawyers Assn., Fed. Bar Assn., Nat. Assn. Criminal Def. Lawyers, Tacoma-Pierce County Bar Assn., Seattle-King County Bar Assn., Wash. Defender Assn., Wash. State Hist. Soc., Am. Inst. Archeol., Phi Alpha Delta. Greek Orthodox. Avocations: weightlifting, travel, family history, football coaching, writing. Home: 5007 80th St SW Lakewood WA 98499-4077 Office: Ste 102 2412 N 30th Tacoma WA 98407-4322

GEORGE, RICHARD NEILL, retired lawyer; b. Watertown, N.Y., Apr. 6, 1933; s. Wendell Dow and Frances Laura (Small) G.; m. Patricia Harman Jackson, June 21, 1958; children: Frances Harman, Richard Neill, Mary Elizabeth AB, Yale U., 1955; JD, Cornell U., 1962. Bar: N.Y. 1962. Assoc. Nixon Peabody, LLP (formerly Nixon, Hargave, Devans & Doyle), Rochester, N.Y., 1962-70, ptnr., 1970-2000, ret., 2000. Committeeman, Brighton Town Republican Com., Rochester, 1966-78; ruling elder Twelve Corners Presbyn. Ch., Rochester, 1977-79, 84-87; mem. permanent jud. commn. Presbytery of Genesee Valley, 1988-94, moderator. Capt. USAF, 1956-59. Mem. ABA, N.Y. State Bar Assn., Monroe County Bar Assn., Fed. Energy Bar Assn., Exeter Alumni Assn. of Rochester (pres. 1970—), Country Club of Rochester, Yale Club (N.Y.C.), Amelia Island Club. Republican. Avocations: golf, reading. Administrative and regulatory, FERC practice, Public utilities. Home: 14 Oakfield Way Pittsford NY 14534-1888

GEORGE, RONALD M. state supreme court chief justice; b. L.A., Mar. 11, 1940; AB, Princeton U., 1961; JD, Stanford U., 1964. Bar: Calif. 1965. Dep. atty. gen. Calif. Dept. Justice, 1965-72; judge L.A. Mcpl. Ct., L.A. County, 1972-77, Superior Ct. Calif., L.A. County, 1977-87, supervising judge criminal divsn., 1983-84; assoc. justice 2d dist., divsn. 4 Calif. Ct. Appeal, L.A., 1987-91; assoc. justice Calif. Supreme Ct., San Francisco, 1991-96, chief justice, 1996—. Mem. Calif. Judges Assn. (pres. 1982-83). Avocations: hiking, skiing, running. Office: Calif Supreme Court 350 Mcallister St Fl 5 San Francisco CA 94102-4713

GEORGES, MARA STACY, lawyer; b. Sept. 2, 1963; JD, Loyola U., 1988; BA, U. Notre Dame, 1985. Ptnr. Rock, Fusco, Reynolds, Crowe & Garvey, 1995-97; 1st asst. corporation counsel City of Chgo., 1997-99, corporation cousel, 1999—.

GEORGES, PETER JOHN, lawyer; b. Wilmington, Del., Sept. 8, 1940; s. John Peter and Olga Demetrius (Kazitoris) G. BS in Chemistry, U. Del., 1962; JD, John Marshall Law Sch., 1970; LLM in Patent and Trade Regulations, George Washington U., 1973. Bar: Ill. 1970, U.S. Ct. Appeals (fed. cir.) 1972, D.C. 1973, U.S. Supreme Ct. 1973, Del. 1977. Chemist engrng. labs Bell & Howell Co., Chgo., 1966; patent coordinator Armour & Co., 1967; patent agt., atty. UOP Inc., 1968-71, Washington counsel Arlington, Va., 1972-77; ptnr. Kile, Gholz, Bernstein & Georges, 1977-78; assoc., then ptnr. Law Office Sidney W. Russell, 1978-83; mng. officer Breneman & Georges (and predecessor law firms), Alexandria, 1983—; founding ptnr. Lenastri Properties and Joanastri Properties, Va. Served to 1st lt. USMC, 1963-65, Vietnam. Mem. ABA, Ill. Bar Assn., D.C. Bar Assn., Del. Bar Assn., Fed. Cir. Bar Assn., Assn. Trial Lawyers Am., Am. Intellectual Property Law Assn., Am. Hellenic Lawyers Soc. Federal civil litigation, Patent, Trademark and copyright. Home: 1637 13th St NW Washington DC 20009-4302 Office: Breneman & Georges 3150 Commonwealth Ave Alexandria VA 22305-2712

GERARD, STEPHEN STANLEY, lawyer; b. N.Y.C., June 2, 1936; m. Nancy Mercer Keith, Apr. 25, 1969; children: Robert, Lillian, Stephen. BS, NYU, 1958, JD, 1963; cert. in employee relations law, Inst. for Applied Mgmt. and Law, Newport Beach, Calif., 1983. Bar: N.Y. 1964, U.S. Dist. Ct. (so. and ea. dists.) N.Y. 1967, U.S. Ct. Appeals (2d cir.) 1968. Commd. 2d lt. U.S. Army, 1954, advanced through grades to capt. M.I. Corps, 1966, ret., 1974; assoc. Haight, Gardner, Poor & Havens, N.Y.C., 1965-72; counsel Am. Hoechst Corp., Somerville, N.J., 1972-77, asst. sec., sr. counsel, 1977-87; assoc. gen. counsel Hoechst Celanese Corp., 1987-99, Celanese Ams. Corp., Summit, N.J., 1999-2000, cons., 2000-01; freelance cons., 2001—. Patron Colonial Symphony, 1988—; mem. Am. Mus. Natural History. Mem. ABA, Am. Corp. Counsel Assn., Am. Immigration Lawyers Assn., Navy League, Bonaventure Hist. Soc., Smithsonian Inst. Nat. Assocs. Immigration, naturalization, and customs, Labor, Pension, profit-sharing, and employee benefits. Office: 71 Hutchins Ln Savannah GA 31410-3826

GERBER, DAVID JOSEPH, legal educator, lawyer; b. St. Louis, Aug. 14, 1945; s. Joseph Harding and Elvera Louise (Duesenberg) G.; m. Ulla-britt Junemark, Aug. 16, 1981; children: Eric David, Marcus David. BA, Trinity Coll., 1967; MA, Yale U., 1969; JD, U. Chgo., 1972. Bar: N.Y. 1973. Assoc. Casey, Lane & Mittendorf, N.Y.C., 1972-75; asst. to dirs. Inst. Fgn. Law, U. Freiburg, W.Ger., 1975-76; legal adv. Peltzer and Riesenkampff, Frankfurt, W.Ger., 1977-78; vis. prof. U. Stockholm, 1979; assoc. prof. law Chgo.-Kent Coll. Law, Ill. Inst. Tech., 1982-88, prof., 1988—, disting. prof., 1996—. Vis. prof. U. Freiburg. Author: The German Law on Standard Business Conditions, 1977; mem. bd. editors Am. Jour. Comparative Law. Norman and Ena Freehling scholar, 1989-92. Mem. ABA, Am. Fgn. Law Assn. Office: Ill Inst Tech Kent Coll Law 565 W Adams St Chicago IL 60661-3613 E-mail: dgerber@kentlaw.edu

GERBER, EDWARD F. lawyer, educator; b. Houston, Oct. 10, 1932; s. Edward F. and Lucille (Beaver) G.; m. Eileen Healy, Sept. 1, 1956; children: Gretchen, Eric, Nils. BS, Syracuse U., 1957, LLB, 1960, JD, 1968. Bar: N.Y. 1960, U.S. Dist. Ct. (no. dist.) N.Y. 1960. Pvt. practice law, Syracuse, N.Y., 1960-64; first asst. dist. atty. Onandaga County, 1964-67, spl. prosecutor, 1976; pvt. practice law, 1977—. Lectr. Coll. of Law Syracuse U., 1968—; counsel Onondaga County Sheriff, 1978-94, N.Y. State Police Benevolent Assn., 1983—, N.Y. State Police Investigators Assn.; faculty Criminal Law Services Syracuse U. Trial Practice Sessions. Bd. dirs. Onandaga County Young Rep. Club, 1964-66. With USN, 1951-54. Named one of Best Lawyers in Am., 1989. Fellow Am. Coll. Trial Lawyers; mem. Upstate Trial Lawyers Assn. (pres. 1978-79), Onandaga County Bar Assn. (dir. 1969-71), Onandaga Bar Found. (pres. 1983). Federal civil litigation, State civil litigation, Criminal. Home: 21 Drumlins Ter Syracuse NY 13224-2217 Office: 224 Harrison St Ste 500 Syracuse NY 13202-3060 Fax: (315) 472-8299. E-mail: efgesq@yahoo.com

GERBER, JOEL, federal judge; b. Chgo., July 16, 1940; s. Peter H. and Marcia L. (Weber) G.; m. Judith R. Smilgoff, Aug. 18, 1963; children—Jay Lawrence, Jeffrey Mark, Jon Victor B.S.B.A., Roosevelt U., Chgo., 1962; J.D., DePaul U., Chgo., 1965; LL.M., Boston U., 1968. Bar: Ill. 1965, Ga. 1974, Tenn. 1978. Trial atty. IRS, Boston, 1965-72, staff asst. to regional counsel Atlanta, 1972-76, dist. counsel Nashville, 1976-80, dep. chief counsel Washington, 1980-83, acting chief counsel, 1983-84; judge U.S. Tax Ct., 1984—; gen. counsel ATF Credit Union, Boston, 1968-70; lectr. Vanderbilt U. Sch. Law, Nashville, 1976-80. Lectr. U. Miami Grad. Law Sch., 1986-90. Recipient awards U.S. Treasury Dept., 1979, 81, 82; Presdl. Meritorious Exec. Rank award, 1983. Mem. ABA (chmn. spl. com. for lawyers in govt. 1986-90). Office: US Tax Ct 400 2nd St NW Rm 432 Washington DC 20217-0002

GERBER, ROBERT EVAN, judge; b. N.Y.C., Feb. 12, 1947; s. Milton M. and Miriam (Simon) G.; m. Jane Flanagan, Nov. 10, 1996; 1 child, Ruslan Michael. BS with high honors, Rutgers U., 1967; JD magna cum laude, Columbia U., 1970. Bar: N.Y. 1971, U.S. Dist. Ct. (so. and ea. dists.) N.Y. 1972, U.S. Ct. Appeals (2d cir.) 1973, U.S. Ct. Appeals (9th cir.) 1974, U.S. Ct. Appeals (10th cir.) 1975, U.S. Ct. Appeals (11th cir.) 1983, U.S. Supreme Ct. 1983, U.S. Ct. Appeals (5th cir.) 1987, U.S. Ct. Appeals (6th cir.) 1989, U.S. Ct. Appeals (3d cir.) 1997. Assoc. Fried, Frank, Harris, Shriver & Jacobson, N.Y.C., 1970-71, 72-78, ptnr., 1978-2000; judge U.S. Bankruptcy Ct. (so. dist.) N.Y., 2000—. Served to 1st lt. USAF, 1971-72. James Kent scholar, 1970, Harlan Fiske Stone scholar, 1969. Mem. ABA, Assn. Bar City N.Y. (sec. spl. com. on energy 1974-79), Fed. Bar Coun., Am. Bankruptcy Inst., Tau Beta Pi. Office: US Bankruptcy Ct US Custom House One Bowling Green New York NY 10004

GERBERDING, MILES CARSTON, lawyer; b. Decatur, Ind., Oct. 25, 1930; s. Arnold H. and Luella E. (Lapp) G.; m. Ruth H. Hostrup, Aug. 20, 1955 (dec. Mar. 1992); children: Karla M. Smith, Greta E. Cowart, Kent E., Brian K.; m. Joan W. Fackler, Jan. 2, 1993; stepchildren: Stephen W. Fackler, Deborah E. Holbrook. BS, Ind. U., 1954, JD, 1956. Bar: Ind. 1956, U.S. Dist. Ct. (so. and no. dists.) Ind. 1956, Mich. 1984. Ptnr. Nieter & Smith, Ft. Wayne, Ind., 1956-58, Barrett, Barrett & McNagny, Ft. Wayne, 1958-85, Barnes & Thornburg, Ft. Wayne, 1985-97; retired Running, Wise, Ford & Phillips, Traverse City, Mich., 1998; pvt. practice Frankfort, 1998-2001; mem. Gerlending & Wolf, PLC, 2001—. Lectr., writer Ind. Continuing Legal Ednl. Forum. Contbr. articles to profl. jours. Pres. Luth. Assn. Elem. Edn., 1968-69; vice chmn., mem. Ind. Supreme Ct. Commn. on Continuing Legal Edn., sec.; bd. dirs. Big Bros., Ft. Wayne, Jr. Achievement, Ft. Wayne, United Way Allen County; pres. Concordia Ednl. Found., Greater Ft. Wayne C. of C. Found.; chmn. bd. visitors Ind. U. Sch. Law, Bloomington, 1984-85, mem. 1979-94; vice chmn. United Way of Allen County Campaign, 1990-92, chmn., 1992-93, dir., 1992-98; trustee Boys and Girls Club Ft. Wayne; sec. Willoughby Rotary Found., 1999. With USMC, 1950-52. Decorated UN medal, Korean Svc. medal with star; recipient Christus Magister award Luth. Edn. Assn., 1971, Disting Svc. award Ind. U. Sch. Law, 1999; named Grad. of Yr., Concordia Alumni Assn., 1993. Fellow Am. Bar Found., Am. Coll. Trust and Estate Counsel, Am. Coll. Tax Counsel, Ind. Bar Found.; mem. ABA (rep. Nat. Conf. Lawyers and CPAs 1980-86), nominating com., ho. dels. credentials com., chmn. Ind. del. 1985-94, ho. dels. mem. com., standing com. on bar svc., coordinating com. on outreach, med. profl. liability com., com. on pub. understanding about law, vice-chmn. com. on state and local bars-sr. lawyers divsn., marital deduction com. taxation sect.), Ind. Bar Assn. (pres. 1979-80, del. ABA 1979-94), State Bar Mich. (treas. Sr. Lawyers 1999-2000, chmn.-elect 2000-01, chmn. 2001—, com. on mandatory CLE com. on quality profl. life), Benzie County Bar Assn. (pres. 1999-2000), Allen County Bar Assn. (dir.), Lawyer-Pilot Bar Assn., Allen County Bar Found. (former bd. dirs., sec.), TerraLex (former co-vice chmn. N.Am., dir. 1993-96), Am. Judicature Soc., Ind. Continuing Legal Edn. Forum (pres. 1978-79), Ind. Bar Found. (dir.), Nat. Conf. Bar Pres. (exec. coun. 1983-86), Mich. State Bar Found., Arcadia Lions Club (bd. dirs.), Benzie Area Hist. Soc. (dir.), Frankfort Rotary Club, Am. Legion, Korean War Vets. Assn., VFW. Republican. Lutheran. Home: 17726 N Ridgewood PO Box 6 Arcadia MI 49613-0006 Office: PO Box 272 Frankfort MI 49635-0272 E-mail: mcgerb@northlink.net, jupnorth@northlink.net

GERBERDING COWART, GRETA ELAINE, lawyer; b. Ft. Wayne, Ind., Aug. 17, 1960; d. Miles Carston G. and Ruth (Hostrup) G., stepmother Joanie Wyatt Gerberding; m. T. David Cowart, Aug. 12, 1995. BS with high distinction, Ind. U., 1982; JD cum laude, 1985. Bar: Ind. 1985, U.S. Dist. Ct. (so. dist.) Ind., CPA, Ind., CEBS. Sr. tax cons. Ernst & Whinney, Indpls., 1985-87; assoc. Klineman, Rose, Wolf and Wallack P.C., 1987-89, Hall Render Killian Heath & Lyman P.C., Indpls., 1989-95; ptnr. Haynes and Boone, L.L.P., Dallas, 1996—. Presenter at seminars. Author: (with G.P. Gooch) Trust and Estate Income Tax Reporting and Planning, 1985; contbr. chpts. to books, articles to profl. jours. including Jour. Deferred Compensation, 403(b) Answer Book, Benefits Law Jour. Chmn. hospitality area Virginia Slims Tennis Tournament, Indpls., 1987-89; vol. Jello Tennis Classic Tennis Tournament, Indpls., 1990-91; coord. Hospitality and Ball Kids, 1990, Jr. Jamboree GTE Tennis Tournament, Indpls., 1990; vol. Ctr. for Exploration The Children's Mus., Indpls., 1991-94; com. on funding Vision 2002 Luth. Camp Assn., Inc., 1993-94, bd. dirs., 1997—; com. mem. Arcadia Found.; women's retreat com. King of Glory Lutheran Ch., 1997—, fin. com., 2000—; bd. dirs. Brianwood Retreat Ctr., 1998-2001. Glen Peters fellow Ind. U., 1984. Fellow Ind. Bar Found.; mem. ABA (com. marital deduction legis. real property and probate sect. 1986-87, tax section, gen. income tax com. 1987-89, employee benefits com. 1988—, subcom. health plan design and state regulation 1993—, health care task force 1994—, chmn. COBRA subcom. 1997—), Ind. Bar Assn. (acct.-lawyers com. 1986-89, co-chmn. com. on legis. 1988-92, coun. tax sect. 1988-96, sec.-treas. 1991-92, vice-chmn. tax sect. 1992-93, chair elect 1993-94, chair 1994-95), Indpls. Bar Assn., Indpls. Jaycees (treas. 4th Festival 1987 monthly dinner meetings 1988), West Indy Racquet Club (USTA Volvo Tennis Team 1986-87, RCA tounament credentials com. 1993-94), Indpls. Racquet Club (USTA Volvo tennis team 1988-91, 96). Avocations: tennis, sailing, golf, skiing, swimming, artwork. Health, Pension, profit-sharing, and employee benefits, Taxation, general. Office: Haynes and Boone LLP 901 Main St Ste 3100 Dallas TX 75202-3789

GERDE, CARLYLE NOYES (CY GERDE), lawyer; b. Long Beach, Calif., Oct. 22, 1946; m. Priscilla A. Murphy, July 4, 1976. BA in Am. Studies, Purdue U., 1967; JD, Ind. U., 1970. Bar: Ind. 1971, U.S. Supreme Ct. 1976, U.S. Tax Ct. 1980. Ptnr. Hanna & Gerde, Lafayette, Ind., 1972-86; registered lobbyist Ind. Twp. Assn., 1975-86; spl. counsel Nat. Assn. Towns and Twps., Washington, 1976-86. Adj. prof. indsl. engrng. Purdue U., 1972-96; participant White House Conf. Rural Policy, 1978, White House Conf. on Block Grants, 1981, White House Conf. on Liability Ins., 1986; mem. Ind. Gen. Assembly Study Commn. Bd. of govs. Tippecanoe County Hist. Assn., Lafayette, 1976-00, Ams. for Nuclear Energy, Washington (co-founder, v.p. 1977-00); pres. Battle Ground (Ind.) Hist. Corp., 1986; del. State of Ind. GOP Conventions. Mem. Ind. State Bar Assn., Tippecanoe County Bar Assn., Assn. Trial Lawyers Am., Nat. Assn. Town and Twp. Attys. (co-founder, v.p. 1985-88), Am. Agrl. Lawyers Assn., Lafayette Country Club, Skyline Club, Columbia Club. Office: Hanna & Gerde PO Box 1098 Lafayette IN 47902-1098 E-mail: gerde@hannagerde.com

GERDES, DAVID ALAN, lawyer; b. Aberdeen, S.D., Aug. 10, 1942; s. Cyril Fredrick and Lorraine Mary (Boyle) G.; m. Karen Ann Hassinger, Aug. 3, 1968; children: Amy Renee, James David. BS, No. State Coll., Aberdeen, 1965; JD cum laude, U. S.D., 1968. Bar: S.D. 1968, U.S. Dist. Ct. S.D., 1968, U.S. Ct. Appeals (8th cir.) 1973, U.S. Supreme Ct. 1973. Assoc. Martens, Goldsmith, May, Porter & Adam, Pierre, S.D., 1968-73; ptnr. successor firm May, Adam, Gerdes & Thompson, 1973—. Chmn. disciplinary bd. S.D. Bar, 1980-81, mem. fed. practice com. U.S. Dist. Ct., S.D., 1986-91, 94—; mem. fed. adv. com. U.S. Ct. Appeals (8th cir.), 1989-93; bd. dirs. U.S.D. Law Sch. Found., 1973-84, pres., 1979-84. Mng. editor U. S.D. Law Rev., 1967-68. Chmn. Hughes County Rep. Ctrl. Com., 1979-81; del. Rep. State Conv., co-chair platform com., 1988, 90; state ctrl. committeeman, 1985-91. Served to lt. Signal Corps, AUS, 1965-68. Mem. ABA, Nat. Coun. Bar Pres., Internat. Assn. Def. Counsel, Assn. Def. Trial Attys., Am. Judicature Soc., Am. Bd. Trial Advocates, State Bar S.D. (chmn. professionalism com. 1989-90, pres. 1992-93), Pierre Area C. of C. (pres. 1980-81), S.D. C. of C. (bd. dirs. 1998—), Lawyer-Pilots Bar Assn., Def. Rsch. Inst., Am. Soc. Med. Assn. Counsel, Kiwanis, Elks. Republican. Methodist. Author: Physician's Guide to South Dakota Law, 1982. Federal civil litigation, Health, Insurance. Office: May Adam Gerdes & Thompson PO Box 160 503 S Pierre St Pierre SD 57501-4522

GERDY, HARRY, lawyer; b. Chgo., Nov. 19., 1935; s. Abraham and Frances (Koerner) G.; m. Marianne B. Burke, 1970. B.S. in Commerce, Roosevelt U., 1957; J.D., DePaul U., 1966. Bar: Ill. 1966, U.S. Dist. Ct. (no. dist.) Ill. 1967. Spl. agt. Criminal Investigation div. IRS, Chgo., 1961-67; atty. Law Offices of Merwin Auslander, Chgo., 1967-69; chief counsel Ill. Dept. Gen. Services, Chgo., 1969-73; pvt. practice law, Chgo., 1973-75; regional counsel U.S. Gen. Services Adminstrn., Chgo., 1975—. Mem. bus. adv. council Jones Comml. High Sch., Chgo., 1976-79; adv. council Nat. Assn. State Purchasing Ofcls., Washington, 1974. Mem. ABA, Ill. Bar Assn., Fed. Bar Assn. (dir. 1976-79). Home: 2318 N Lakewood Ave Chicago IL 60614-3149 Office: GSA Regional Counsel 230 S Dearborn St Ste 3820 Chicago IL 60604-1562

GEREN, GERALD S. lawyer; b. Chgo., Nov. 10, 1939; s. Ben and Sara (Block) G.; m. Phyllis Freeman, Feb. 11, 1962; children: Suzanne, Gregory, Bradley. BSMetE, Ill. Inst. Tech., 1961; JD, DePaul U., 1966. Bar: Ill. Supreme Ct. 1966, U.S. Ct. Customs and Patent Appeals 1967, U.S. Patent and Trademark Office 1967, U.S. Dist Ct. (no. dist.) Ill. 1969, U.S. Supreme Ct. 1972, U.S. Ct. Appeals (7th cir.) 1972, U.S. Ct. Appeals (fed. cir.) 1982. Engr. Internat. Harvester, Chgo., 1961-64; atty. Corning Glass Works, Corning, N.Y., 1966-69; assoc. Silverman & Cass, Chgo., 1969-70, Siegal & Geren, Chgo., 1970-71; ptnr. Epton, Mullin & Druth, 1971-84, Hill, Steadman & Simpson, Chgo., 1984-94, Gerald S. Geren Ltd., Chgo., 1994-96, Lee, Mann, Smith, McWilliams, Sweeney & Ohlson, 1997—. Contbr. articles to Indsl. Rsch. and Devel., Design News mags. Pres. Chgo. High Tech. Assn., 1981-86, v.p., 1986-87; mem. strategic planning com. Econ. Devel. Commn., Chgo., 1986-91; mem. Ill. Ctr. for Indsl. Tech.,

1984-90, Ill. Mfg. Tech. Network, Chgo., 1986-91; mem. pres.' coun., rsch. coun., alumni bd. Ill. Inst. Tech., 1991—, The Leukemia Soc. Am. (Ill. chpt. bd. mem. 1988-90). Mem. ABA, Ill. Bar Assn., Chgo. Bar Assn., Patent Law Assn. Chgo., Am. Intellectual Property Law Assn., Execs. Club, Chgo. Econ. Club, Comml. Club Chgo. (small bus. com. 1985—), Met. Club Chgo. Federal civil litigation, Patent, Trademark and copyright. Office: Lee Mann Smith McWilliams Sweeney & Ohlson 209 S La Salle St Ste 410 Chicago IL 60604-1203

GERHART, STEVEN GEORGE, lawyer; b. Osage, Iowa, July 9, 1948; s. Grant George and Marjory Justine (Heckel) G.; m. Victoria Rae Cobb, Nov. 24, 1973; children: Sarah Jean, Melissa Rae, Nathaniel Scott, Abigail J. BA, U. Iowa, 1970, JD, 1973; postgrad. N.Am. Bapt. Sem., Sioux Falls, S.D., 1992—. Bar: Iowa 1973, Ill. 1975, N.D. 1982; postgrad. N.Am. Bapt. Sem., 1992—. Atty., FPC, Washington, 1973-75, People's Gas Co., Chgo., 1975-76; asst. gen. atty. Iowa Electric Light & Power Co., Cedar Rapids, Iowa, 1976-82; gen. counsel, sec. Montana-Dakota Utilities Co. (now MDU Resources Group Inc), Bismarck, N.D., 1982-87; legal com. Midwest Gas Assn., Mpls., 1977-87, Edison Electric Inst., Washington, 1983-87, Am. Gas Assn., Arlington, Va., 1983-87; legal counsel Profl. Christian Counseling Ctr., Inc., Bismarck, N.D., 1987-91, resigned; bd. dirs. Steer, Inc., Liberty House, Inc. Mem. elder-deacon bd. Century Baptist Ch., Bismarck, 1984-90. Mem. ABA, N.D. Bar Assn. Administrative and regulatory, General corporate, FERC practice. Home: 3826 Cheyenne Blvd Sioux City IA 51104-4332 Office: Profl Christian Resource Ctr 1501 N 12th St Bismarck ND 58501-2713

GERLING, JOSEPH ANTHONY, lawyer; b. Dayton, Ohio, Feb. 25, 1952; s. Clarence Anthony and Betty Jane (Blue) G.; m. Janet Mary Cox, July 6, 1974; children: Anthony, Andrew, Christopher. BCE, U. Notre Dame, 1974; JD, Ohio State U., 1977. Bar: Ohiho 1977. Rsch. scientist Battelle Meml. Inst., Columbus, Ohio, 1974-77; assoc. Lurie Gifford & Davis, 1977-78, Lane Alton & Horst, Columbus, 1978—. Mem. Columbus Def. Assn. (pres. 1987-88), Athletic Club Columbus. Avocations: sports, basketball, softball, photography. Personal injury, Product liability, Professional liability. Home: 2278 Viburnum Ln Columbus OH 43235-4266 Office: Lane Alton & Horst 173 S 3rd St Columbus OH 43215-5152 E-mail: jgerling@lah4law.com

GERMAN, G. MICHAEL, lawyer; b. Gary, Ind., June 15, 1952; s. George N. and Mary Ann (Lucas) G. Student, Wabash Coll., Crawfordsville, Ind., 1970-72; BA, U. Ill., 1976; JD, U. San Francisco, 1981. Bar: Calif. 1982, U.S. Ct. Appeals (9th cir.) 1983, U.S. Supreme Ct. 1988, U.S. Ct. Appeals (D.C. cir.) 1990, U.S. Dist. Ct. (no., so., ea. and cen. dists.) Calif. 1982, U.S. Dist. Ct. (no. dist.) Ind. 1983. Assoc. Acret & Perrochet, San Francisco, 1979-84; ptnr. German & Siggins, 1984-86; pvt. practice law, 1987-2000; with Calif. Dept Justice, 2000—. Pres. bd. Dolores Plaza Condo Assn., San Francisco, 1984-86; v.p., treas., then pres. Log Cabin Club of San Francisco, gen. counsel Log Cabin of Calif., 1995—; mem., gen. counsel San Francisco County Rep. Ctrl. Com., 1996— . With USN, 1972-75. Mem. League Am. Bicyclists (legal advisor 1989—), Assn. Trial Lawyers Am., Maritime Law Assn. U.S. (proctor in admiralty 1984—), Olympic Club, Sigma Chi. Roman Catholic. Avocations: swimming, cycling. Admiralty, Civil rights, Personal injury. Office: State Calif Dept Justice 455 Golden Gate Ave Ste 1100 San Francisco CA 94102-3660

GERMAN, JUNE RESNICK, lawyer; b. N.Y.C., Feb. 24, 1946; d. Irving and Stella (Weintraub) Resnick; m. Harold Jacob German, May 31, 1974; children: Beth Melissa, Heather Alice, Bret. BA, U. Pa., 1965; JD, NYU, 1968. Bar: N.Y. 1968, U.S. Dist. Ct. (ea. and so. dists.) N.Y. 1974, U.S. Ct. Appeals (2d cir.) 1973, U.S. Supreme Ct. 1973. Atty., sr. atty., supervising atty. Mental Health Info. Svc., N.Y.C., 1968-77; atty., advisor Course in Human Behavior Mems. of N.Y. State Judiciary, Nassau and Suffolk County, 1980; pvt. practice Huntington, N.Y., 1985—. Contbg. author: Bioethics and Human Rights, 1978, Mental Illness, Due Process and the Acquitted Defendant, 1979; contbr. chpts. to books, articles to profl. jours. Chmn. Citizen's Ad Hoc Com. Constrn. of the Dix Hills Water Adminstrn. Bldg., Huntington, N.Y., 1985-90; mem. Citizens Adv. Com. for Dix Hills Water Dist., Huntington, 1992—; dir. House Beautiful Assn. at Dix Hills, 1986—, Citizens for a Livable Environment and Recycling, Huntington, 1989-93; active Suffolk County (N.Y.) Dem. Com., 1986—, Deer Park Avenue Task Force, Town of Huntington, 1997-98, Dix Hills Revitalization Com., 1999-2000. Mem. Suffolk County Bar Assn. Jewish. Avocations: tennis, hiking, travel. Civil rights, Federal civil litigation, General practice. Office: 150 Main St Huntington NY 11743-6908

GERMUS, GÁBOR, lawyer; b. Miskolc, Hungary, May 23, 1970; s. Bertalan G. and Lenke Remenyik; m. Éva Szabó; 1 child: András. LLD, U. Eötvös, Budapest, Hungary. Trainee SBGK Law Offices, Budapest, 1994-97, atty., 1997-99, ptnr., 1999—. Mem. supr. bd. MATAV, Budapest, 2000—. Office: SBGK Law Office Andrassy 113 1062 Budapest Hungary Fax: 36 1 342 4323

GERRARD, JOHN M. state supreme court justice; b. Schuyler, Nebr., Nov. 2, 1953; BS, Nebr. Wesleyan U., 1976; MPA, U. Ariz., 1977; JD, U. of Pacific, 1981. Pvt. practice, Norfolk, 1981-95; city atty. City of Battle Creek, Nebr., 1982-95; justice Nebr. Supreme Ct., Lincoln, 1995—. Office: Nebr Supreme Ct 2219 State Capitol Lincoln NE 68509-8000 also: PO Box 98910 Lincoln NE 68509*

GERRARD, KEITH, lawyer; b. Malden, Mass., Feb. 8, 1935; s. William Francis and Mary Ethel (Compton) G.; Linda Jane Fay, Apr. 16, 1974; children by previous marriage: Jessica, Elizabeth; stepchildren: Elizabeth Perera, Jonathan Perera. AB, Harvard U., 1956, LLB, 1963. Bar: Wash. 1963. Assoc., Perkins Coie, Seattle, 1963-70, ptrn., 1970—. Served to 1st lt. USAF, 1956-59. Fellow Am. Coll. Trial Lawyers; mem. ABA, Wash. State Bar Assn., Seattle-King County Bar Assn., Rainier Club (Seattle). Aviation, General civil litigation. Office: Perkins Coie 1201 3rd Ave Fl 40 Seattle WA 98101-3029

GERSON, JEROME HOWARD, lawyer; b. Chgo., Sept. 9, 1928; s. Bernard Jay and Minnie (Cooper) G.; m. Marjorie Korshak, Nov. 22, 1985; children: Daniel, Bradley, Mitchell. Student U. Ill., 1946-48; JD, Chgo. Kent Coll. Law, 1951. Bar: Ill. 1951, U.S. Dist. Ct. (no. dist.) Ill. 1952. Assoc. Teller, Levit & Silvertrust, Chgo., 1952-56, Joseph W. Bernstein, 1957-60, Philip Goodman, 1961-63; ptnr. Yacker & Gerson, Chgo., 1963-76; sr. ptnr. Rudnick & Wolfe, Chgo., 1976-88; chmn. real estate dept. Winston & Strawn, Chgo., 1988-95, of counsel, 1995—. Contbr. articles to profl. publs. Fellow Honor Council, Chgo. Kent Coll. Law. Mem. ABA, Chgo. Bar Assn., Ill. State Bar Assn., Lake Shore Country Club, Standard Club. Real property. Office: Winston & Strawn 35 W Wacker Dr Ste 4200 Chicago IL 60601-1695

GERSON, MERVYN STUART, lawyer; b. Cleve., Nov. 1, 1936; s. Philip Gerson and Rena (Friedman) Davis; m. Linda Hanff, Feb. 14, 1965; children: Laurie Jean Powazek, Philip Stuart, Michael Craig. AB, U. Mich., 1957; JD, 1960. Atty. advisor U.S. Tax Ct., Washington, 1960-62; atty. Gerson, Grekin & Wynhoff, Honolulu, 1981—. Fellow Am. Coll. Trust and Estate Counsel (regent 1995—), Am. Coll. Tax Counsel. Estate planning, Probate, Estate taxation. Office: Gerson Grekin & Wynhoff 1001 Bishop St Ste 780 Honolulu HI 96813-3410

GERSON, STUART MICHAEL, lawyer; b. N.Y.C., Jan. 16, 1944; s. James and Ethel (Cherney) G.; m. Pamela Somers, July 28, 1979; children: James Barker, Somers Elizabeth, Lindsey Dakota. BA in Polit. Sci., Pa. State U., 1964; JD, Georgetown U., 1967. Bar: D.C. 1968, N.Y. 1999, U.S. Supreme Ct. 1974, U.S. Ct. Appeals (DC cir.) 1972, U.S. Ct. Appeals (5th cir.) 1972, 81, U.S. Ct. Appeals (9th cir.) 1978, U.S. Ct. Appeals (2d cir.) 1979, U.S. Ct. Appeals (11th cir.) 1981, U.S. Ct. Appeals (6th cir.) 1982, U.S. Ct. Appeals (4th cir.) 1984, U.S. Ct. Appeals (3d cir.) 1985, U.S. Ct. Appeals (8th cir.) 1986, U.S. Ct. Appeals (1st, 7th, 10th, fed. cirs.) 1989. Asst. U.S. atty. City of Washington, 1972-75; assoc., then ptnr. Reed Smith Shaw & McClay, Washington, 1975-80; pvt. practice; ptnr. in charge litigation Epstein, Becker & Green, Washington, N.Y.C., 1980-89; adj. prof. of law Georgetown U., 1991; asst. atty. gen. in charge civil div. U.S. Dept. Justice, Washington, 1989-93; acting Atty. Gen. U.S., 1993; atty. and head of litigation Epstein, Becker & Green, P.C., Washington and N.Y.C. Bd. dirs. CHANGE-All Souls Housing Corp., Washington, Counsel for Ct. Excellence. Contbr. articles to profl. jours. Gen. counsel Nat. Rep. Senatorial Com., Washington, 1985-86; sr. advisor presdl. campaign George Bush, 1988; leader transition team Office Pres. Elect, 1988; advisor Transition Office Pres. Elect, 2000. Capt. USAF, 1967-72. Decorated Meritorious Svc. Medal. Fellow Am. Bar Found.; mem. ABA, D.C. Bar Assn. (steering com. litigation 1985-93), The Barristers (pres.), Am. Health Lawyers Assn., Am. Inns of Ct., Metro. Club, Lawyers Club. Episcopalian. Avocations: competitive running, national track and field official, sailing, reading history. Office: Epstein Becker & Green PC 1227 25th St NW Ste 700 Washington DC 20037-1175 also: 250 Park Ave New York NY 10177-0001

GERSTEIN, MARK DOUGLAS, lawyer; b. Chgo., Nov. 16, 1959; s. Robert Henry and Helene Roberta Gerstein; m. Julia Sara Wolf, Apr. 13, 1986; children: Allison Ruth, Evan Benjamin. BA, U. Mich., 1981; JD, U. Chgo., 1984. Bar: Ill., U.S. Dist. Ct. (no. dist.) Ill. Ptnr., assoc. Katten Muchin & Zavis, Chgo., 1984-96; equity ptnr. Latham & Watkins, 1996—, equity ptnr., global co-chair mergers and acquisitions group, 1999—. Global co-chair mergers and acquisitions group Latham & Watkins. Dir. Assocs. Ravinia Festival, Chgo., 1996—, Youth Guidance, Chgo., 1995—. Mem. Chgo. Bar Assn. (chmn. com. on corp. control 1998-99), Standard Club. Avocations: sailing, cycling. General corporate, Mergers and acquisitions, Securities. Office: Latham & Watkins 233 S Wacker Dr Ste 5800 Chicago IL 60606-6362 E-mail: mark.gerstein@lw.com

GERTLER, MEYER H. lawyer; b. New Orleans, Oct. 28, 1945; s. David and Sadie (Redman) G.; m. Marcia Raye Goldstein, Aug. 23, 1967; children— Louis, Danielle, Joshua. B.A., Tulane U., 1967, J.D. 1969. Bar: La. 1970, U.S. Dist. Ct. (ea. and mid. dists.) 1970, U.S. Ct. Apppeals (5th cir.) 1970, U.S. Supreme Ct. 1970. Ptnr. Uddo & Gertler, New Orleans, 1970-76, Gertler & Gertler, New Orleans, 1977-86, Gertler, Gertler & Vincent, New Orleans, 1986—; mem. Asbestos Litigation Group. Mem. La. Trial Lawyers Assn., Am. Trial Lawyers Assn., ABA, Sup. Ct. Hist. Soc., Am. Judicature Soc. Democrat. Jewish. Clubs: B'nai B'rith, Masons. Federal civil litigation, State civil litigation, Product liability. Home: 5462 Bellaire Dr New Orleans LA 70124-1035 Office: Gertler Gertler & Vincent 127129 Carondelet New Orleans LA 70130

GERTZ, THEODORE GERSON, lawyer; b. Chgo., Sept. 8, 1936; s. Elmer and Ceretta (Samuels) G.; m. Suzanne C., June 19, 1960; children: Craig M., Candace C., Scott W. BA, U. Chgo., 1958; JD, Northwestern U., 1962. Bar: Ill. 1962, U.S. Dist. Ct. (no. dist.) Ill. 1962. Assoc. Marks, Marks & Kaplan, Chgo., 1962-64, Lowitz, Vihons & Stone, Chgo., 1964-66, ptnr., 1966-71, Pretzel & Stouffer, Chgo., 1971-94, Shefsky, Froelich, Chgo., 1995—. Gen. counsel Hull House Assn., Chgo., 1977—, Blind Svc. Assn., Chgo., 1987—, Citizens Against Suburban Sprawl, Mettawa, Ill., 1995—, Am. Student Dental Assn., Chgo., 1977—. Author: A Guide to Estate Planning, Illinois Advance Estate Planning. Dir., treas. Mettawa Open Lands, 1987—; former trustee Village of Mettawa, 1994—, Pub. Interest Law Initiative, Chgo. With U.S. Army, 1962-64. Fellow Ill. Bar Found., Ill. Bar Assn., Chgo. Bar Assn., Law Club. Democrat. Jewish. Avocations: reading, nature, working out, dancing, traveling. Estate planning. Home: 950 Benson Ln Libertyville IL 60048-2406 Office: Shefsky and Froelich 444 N Michigan Ave Ste 2600B Chicago IL 60611-3998

GERWIN, LESLIE ELLEN, lawyer, public affairs and community relations executive; b. L.A., May 18, 1950; d. Nathan and Beverly Adele (Wilson) G.; m. Bruce Robert Leslie, July 3, 1978; 1 child, Jonathan Gerwin Leslie. BA, Prescott Coll., 1972; JD, Antioch Sch. Law, 1975; MPH, Tulane U., 1988. Bar: D.C. 1975, N.Y. 1981, U.S. Dist. Ct. D.C. 1977, U.S. Dist. Ct. (so. dist.) N.Y. 1980. Staff asst. U.S. Congress, Washington, 1970-72; cons. Congl. Subcom., 1972-73; instr. U. Miami Law Sch., Coral Gables, Fla., 1975-76; assoc. prof. law Yeshiva U., N.Y.C., 1976-86; vis. assoc. prof. law Tulane Law Sch., New Orleans, 1983-84; pub. policy cons., 1987—; pres. Ariadne Cons., 1994—; dir. devel. and community rels. Planned Parenthood La., Inc., 1989-90; legal advisor La. Coalition for Reproductive Freedom, 1990-92; exec. v.p. Met. Area Com., New Orleans, 1992-94; exec. dir. Met. Area Com. Edn. Fund, 1992-94. Bd. dirs. Inst. for Phys. Fitness Rsch., N.Y.C., 1982-86, Challenge/Discovery, Crested Butte, Colo., 1977-80; cons. FDA, Washington, 1977-78, U. Judaism, L.A., 1974-75; mem. Met. Area Com. Leadership Forum, New Orleans, 1988; adj. asst. prof. La. State U. Sch. Medicine, 1996—, La. State U. Med. Sch., Dept. of Public Health and Preventive Medicine. Contbr. articles to profl. jours. Mem. Ind. Dem. Jud. Screening Panel, N.Y.C., 1980; bd. dirs. New Orleans Food Bank for Emergencies, 1987-89; profl. adv. com. MAZON-A Jewish Response to Hunger, L.A., 1986-89; bd. dirs. Second Harvesters Food Bank Greater New Orleans, 1989-94, La. State LWV, 1990-91, Anti-Defamation League, New Orleans, 1989-95, Jewish Endowment Found., 1987-93; trustee Jewish Fedn. Greater New Orleans, 1989-95, 97-99, mem. exec. com., 1997-99; trustee Emergency Food and Shelter Program, S.E. La., 1988—; v.p. Tulane U. B'nai B'rith Hillel Found., 1987-90; steering com. Citizens for Pers. Freedom, 1989-91; steering com. Metro 2000, 1989-90; sec. New Orleans sect. Nat. Coun. Jewish Women, 1990-91, state pub. affairs chmn., 1992-96; bd. Contemporary Arts Ctr., 1993-97; chair, bd. advocates Planned Parenthood La., 1995—; v.p. Edn. Tikvat Shalom Conservative Congregation, 1995-97, chair New Orleans Israel Bonds, 1996-98; mem. Cmty. Rels. Com., 1986-99, vice chair, 1995-97, chair 1997-99; adminstr. Area Tng. Ctr., USTA, New Orleans, 1996-2001. Fellow Inst. of Politics, 1990-91; scholar Xerox Found., 1972-75; Decorated Order of Barristers; named One of Ten Outstanding Young Women of Am., 1987; recipient Herbert J. Garon Young Leadership award Jewish Fedn. Greater New Orleans, 1990; named YWCA Role Model, 1992. Mem. ABA, N.Y. Bar Assn., N.Y. Acad. Scis., Am. Pub. Health Assn., D.C. Bar Assn., Nat. Moot Ct. Honor Soc., Pub. Health Honor Soc., Calif. State Dem. Club (Key Svc. award 1988), Delta Omega.

GESHELL, RICHARD STEVEN, lawyer; b. Colorado Springs, Colo., Aug. 6, 1943; s. Peter Steven and Ann Elizabeth (Irwin) G.; m. Carol Ann Reed, Sept. 6, 1965; 1 child, Carmen Marie. BA in Chemistry, Ariz. State U., 1965; JD, U. Nebr., 1968. Bar: Nebr. 1968, U.S. Dist. Ct. Nebr. 1968, Hawaii 1983, U.S. Dist. Ct. Hawaii 1983, U.S. Ct. Appeals (9th cir.) 1984, U.S. Supreme Ct. 1986. With Robak and Geshell, Columbus, Nebr., 1968-83; ptnr. R. Steven Geshell, Honolulu, 1983—. Lawyer; b. Colorado Springs, Colo., Aug. 6, 1943; s. Peter Steven and Ann Elizabeth (Irwin) G.; m. Carol Ann Reed, Sept. 6, 1965; 1 child, Carmen Marie. BA in Chemistry, Ariz. State U., 1965; JD, U. Nebr., 1968. Bar: Nebr. 1968, U.S. Dist. Ct. Nebr. 1968, Hawaii 1983, U.S. Dist. Ct. Hawaii 1983, U.S. Ct. Appeals (9th cir.) 1984, U.S. Supreme Ct. 1986. Mem. Robak and Geshell, Columbus, Nebr., 1968-83; ptnr. R. Steven Geshell, Honolulu, 1983—. Served to capt. USAR, 1974-83. Mem. Hawaii Bar Assn., Blue Key (pres. 1964-65), Elks (chief forum 1984, trustee), Phi Sigma Kappa. Republican. Capt. USAR, 1974-83. Mem. Hawaii Bar Assn., Blue Key (pres. 1964-65), Elks (chief forum 1984, trustee), Phi Sigma Kappa. Republican. General civil litigation, Personal injury, Professional liability. Home: 1155 Kaluanui Rd Honolulu HI 96825-1357 Office: Ste #116 6600 Kalanianaole Hwy Honolulu HI 96825 E-mail: geshell@lava.net

GESKE, ALVIN JAY, lawyer; b. Whitefish, Mont., Apr. 17, 1942; s. Alvin Emil and Ada Jay (Best) G.; m. Cheryl S. Glaze, Aug. 10, 1968; children: David, Daniel. BA in Econs. with high honors, So. Meth. U., 1964; JD with honors, U. Chgo., 1967; LLM in Taxation with high honors, George Washington U., 1974. Bar: Tex. 1967, D.C. 1972, U.S. Ct. Appeals (4th cir.) 1984, U.S. Tax Ct. 1982, U.S. Ct. Claims 1992. Atty. Jackson, Walker, Winstead, Cantwell & Miller, Dallas, 1967-68; from atty. to asst. br. chief legis. and regulation divsn. Office Chief Counsel IRS, Washington, 1970-74; atty. Childs, Fortenbach, Beck & Guyton, Houston, 1974-75; legis. atty. Joint Com. on Taxation U.S. Congress, Washington, 1975-78, asst. legis. counsel, 1978-81; atty. Davis & McLeod, 1981-83, Richard P. Sills PC, Washington, 1983-85, Stein, Sills & Brodsky PC, Washington, 1985-87, Wickham & Geske, Washington, 1987, Sills & Brodsky PC, Washington, 1988-93, Holland & Knight, Washington, 1993—. Contbr. articles to profl. jours. With U.S. Army, 1968-70. Mem. ABA (past chmn. com. on agr. sect. taxation), Order of Coif, Phi Beta Kappa, Phi Delta Phi. Estate taxation, Taxation, general. Office: Holland & Knight 2099 Pennsylvania Ave NW Washington DC 20006 E-mail: ageske@hklaw.com

GESKE, JANINE PATRICIA, law educator, former state supreme court justice; b. Port Washington, Wis., May 12, 1949; d. Richard Braem and Georgette (Paulissen) Geske; m. Michael Julian Hogan, Jan. 2, 1982; children: Mia Geske Berman, Sarah Geske Hogan, Kevin Geske Hogan. Student, U. Grenoble, U. Rennes; BA, MA in Tchg., Beloit Coll., 1971; JD, Marquette U., 1975, LLD, 1998, LLD (hon.), 1994; DHL (hon.), Mt. Mary Coll., 1999. Bar: Wis. 1975, U.S. Dist. Ct. (ea. & we. dists.) Wis. 1975, U.S. Supreme Ct. 1978. Tchr. elem. sch., Lake Zurich, Ill., 1970-72; staff atty., chief staff atty. Legal Aid Soc., Milw., 1975-78; asst. prof. law, clin. dir. Law Sch. Marquette U., 1978-81; hearing examiner Milw. County CETA, 1980-81; judge Milw. County Circuit Ct., 1981-93; justice Supreme Ct. Wis., 1993-98; disting. prof. law Marquette U. Law Sch., Milw., 1998—. Dean Wis. Jud. Coll.; mem. faculty Nat. Jud. Coll.; instr. various jud. tng. programs, continuing legal edn. Fellow ABA, mem. Am. Law Inst., Am. Arbitration Assn., Soc. Profls. in Dispute Resolution, Wis. Bar Assn., Wis. Assn. Mediators, Milw. Bar Assn., Nat. Women Judges Assn., 7th Cir. Bar Assn., Alpha Sigma Nu. Roman Catholic. Office: Marquette U Law Sch PO Box 1881 Milwaukee WI 53201-1881

GESLER, ALAN EDWARD, lawyer; b. Milw., Aug. 25, 1945; s. Paul and Caroline Gesler; m. Judith A. Joy, May 6, 1967; children: Amy, Molly, Joshua. BS cum laude, U. Wis., Milw., 1967; JD, U. Wis., Madison, 1970. Bar: Wis. 1970, U.S. Dist. Ct. (ea. dist.) Wis. 1971, U.S. Supreme Ct. 1974. Mem. Warshafsky, Rotter, Tarnoff, Gesler, Reinhardt & Bloch, S.C., Milw., 1970-94; of counsel Slattery & Hausman, Ltd., Waukesha, Wis., 1994—. Assoc. editor Litigation News, 1978-80. Vice chmn. County Task Force on Mental Retardation, Milw., 1974; active health adv. subcom. Milw. County Suprs., 1975. Fellow Internat. Acad. Trial Lawyers; mem. ABA, Wis. Bar Assn., Assn. Trial Lawyers Am. (bd. govs. 1985-88), Wis. Acad. Trial Lawyers (bd. govs. 1979—, pres. 1983), Am. Bd. Trial Advs. (pres. Wis. chpt. 1991, nat. bd. rep. 1992-95). E-mail: alan. Office: Slattery & Hausman Ltd W240n1221 Pewaukee Rd Waukesha WI 53188-1659 E-mail: gesler@yahoo.com

GETCHELL, CHARLES WILLARD, JR. lawyer, publisher; b. L.A., May 29, 1929; s. Charles Willard and Katharine (Fitch) G.; m. Angela Winthrop, Sept. 16, 1961; children: Katharine Chisholm, Emily Erskine, Sarah Fields. AB, Stanford U., 1951, JD, 1954. Bar: Calif. 1955, Mass. 1979, U.S. Dist. Ct. (no. dist.) Calif. 1960, Mass. 1983, U.S. Ct. Appeals, 9th cir. 1960, U.S. Supreme Ct. 1985. Atty. Air Materiel Force, Chateauroux, France, 1958-59; asst. U.S. atty. No. Dist. Calif., San Francisco, 1960-61; asst. mgr. Citibank, N.Y.C., Brussels, 1961-68; v.p. Wood Struthers & Winthrop, 1969-77; ptnr. Gray, Wendell, Chalmers & Dahlen, Boston, 1981-87; pub. The Ipswich (Mass.) Press, 1980—. Pres., dir. Yorkham Timber Co., Inc., 1986—; bd. dirs. Sabre Trust (UK); chmn. Sabre Europe (Belgium); sec. Sabre Found., 1995—; sr. fellow Salzburg Seminar, 1997—. Trans.: European Monetary Unity: For Whose Benefit? (Pascal Salin), 1980; contbr. occasional essays, verse, to N.Y. Times, Boston Globe, Beverly (Mass.) Times. Mem. steering com. Bilderberg Meetings, The Hague, 1980-85; bd. dirs. Salzburg Seminar, 1985-89, trustee Shore Country Dah Sch., 1978-84. Served to lt. (j.g.), USNR, 1955-58. Mem. Belgian Am. Ednl. Found., Mass. Hist. Soc., Tavern Club. Republican. General corporate, Private international. Office: Ipswich Press PO Box 291 Ipswich MA 01938-0291

GETCHES, DAVID HARDING, law educator, state environmental executive, lawyer; b. Abington, Pa., Aug. 17, 1942; s. George Winslow Getches and Ruth Erskine (Harding) Fossette; m. Ann Marks, June 26, 1964; children: Matthew, Catherine, Elizabeth. AB, Occidental Coll., 1964; JD, U. So. Calif., 1967. Bar: Calif. 1968, U.S. Supreme Ct. 1971, D.C. 1972, Colo. 1973. Assoc. Luce, Forward, Hamilton & Scripps, San Diego, 1967-69; directing atty. Calif. Indian Legal Services, Escondido, 1969-70; founding dir. Native Am. Rights Fund, Boulder, Colo., 1970-76; ptnr. Getches & Greene, 1976-78; prof. U. Colo. Sch. Law, 1978—; exec. dir. Colo. Dept. Natural Resources, Denver, 1983-87. Ptnr. MB Land Co., Centro Bldg. Devel. Co. Author: Water Law in a Nutshell, 1997; co-author: Cases and Materials on Federal Indian Law, 1998, Water Resources Management, 1993; contbr. articles to profl. jours. Chmn. bd. dirs. Land and Water Fund of Rockies; chmn. bd. trustees Grand Canyon Trust. Mem. Colo. Bar Assn., D.C. Bar, Calif. Bar, Wilderness Soc. (governing bd.), Defenders of Wildlife (bd. dirs.). Democrat. Home: 627 Pine St Boulder CO 80302-4739 Office: U Colo Sch Law Boulder CO 80309-0401 E-mail: getches@colorado.edu

GETTEN, THOMAS FRANK, lawyer; b. Akron, Ohio, Oct. 11, 1947; s. Frederick Bush and Edna (Vandever) G.; m. Nancy Hobson, Aug. 16, 1972; children: Elisabeth, Douglas, Ted. B.S. in Petroleum Engring., La. State U., 1970, J.D., 1974. Bar: La. 1974. Petroleum engr. Standard Oil of Calif., L.A. and New Orleans, 1970-71; shareholder Liskow & Lewis, New Orleans, 1974—. Mem. ABA, La. Bar Assn., La. Bankers Assn. (bank counsel com.), New Orleans Bar Assn., Order of Coif, Tau Beta Pi. Republican. Episcopalian. Banking, Contracts commercial, Real property. Home: 170 E Oakridge Park Metairie LA 70005-4019 Office: Liskow & Lewis One Shell Square 50th Fl New Orleans LA 71039

GETTNER, ALAN FREDERICK, lawyer; b. N.Y.C., Dec. 25, 1941; s. Victor Salomon and Henriette Seldner (Herrmann) G.; m. Monah Lawrence, Jan. 19, 1969. BA, Yale U., 1963; MA, U. Chgo., 1964; PhD, Columbia U., 1971, JD, 1979. Bar: N.Y. 1980. Assoc. Debevoise & Plimpton, N.Y.C. and Paris, 1979-84, Holtzmann, Wise & Shepard, N.Y.C., 1984-85, ptnr., 1986-95, mem. exec. com., 1992-94; ptnr. Patterson, Belknap, Webb & Tyler, LLP, 1995—, chmn. bus. devel. co., 2000—. Mem. ABA (sect. on bus. law, com. on opinions), Assn. Bar City N.Y., Internat. Bar Assn., Internat. Law Assn., The Lotos Club. General corporate, Private international, Mergers and acquisitions. Office: Patterson Belknap Webb & Tyler LLP 1133 Ave Americas New York NY 10036-6710 E-mail: agettner@pbwt.com

GETZOFF, WILLIAM MOREY, lawyer; b. Chgo., Mar. 2, 1947; s. Byron M. and Mabel A. (Chapman) G.; m. JoAnne D. Goclan, Oct. 27, 1974; children— David, Claire. B.A., Oberlin Coll. (Ohio), 1968; J.D., U. Ill., 1972. Bar: Ill. 1972, U.S. Dist. Ct. (no. dist.) Ill. 1972, U.S. Ct. Appeals (7th cir.) 1972, U.S. Tax Ct. 1973. Ptnr. Getzoff & Getzoff, Chgo., 1972—. Mem. Chgo. Bar Assn., Ill. State Bar Assn. Federal civil litigation, State civil litigation, General practice. Home: 1515 Colfax St Evanston IL 60201-2320 Office: Getzoff & Getzoff 150 S Wacker Dr Ste 650 Chicago IL 60606-4197

GEWIRTZ, PAUL D. lawyer, legal educator; b. May 12, 1947. s. Herman and Matilda (Miller) G.; m. Zoë Baird, June 8, 1986, children: Julian, Alec. AB summa cum laude, Columbia U., 1967; JD, Yale U., 1970. Bar: D.C. 1973, U.S. Supreme Ct. 1976. Law clk. to Hon. Marvin E. Frankel U.S. Dist. Ct. So. Dist. N.Y., 1970-71, to Justice Thurgood Marshall, U.S. Supreme Ct., Washington, 1971-72; assoc. Wilmer, Cutler & Pickering, Washington, 1972-73; atty. Ctr. Law and Social Policy, Washington, 1973-76; assoc. prof., then prof. Yale Law Sch., New Haven, 1976—; Potter Stewart prof. of law, 1992—; director The China Law Ctr., Yale Law Sch., 1999—, Special Rep. the Presidential Rule of Law Initiative, US Dept. of State, 1997-98; U.S. rep. European Commn. on Democracy through Law, 1996-2000. Author: Law's Stories, 1996; The Case Law System in America, 1989; contbr. numerous articles to profl. jours. Office: Yale U Law Sch PO Box 208215 New Haven CT 06520-8215

GEYSER, LYNNE M. lawyer, writer; b. Queens, N.Y., Mar. 28, 1938; d. Henry and Shirley Dannenberg; m. Lewis P. Geyser, 1956 (div. 1974); 1 child, Russell B. Geyser. BA, Queens Coll., 1960; JD, UCLA, 1968. Bar: Calif. 1969. Atty. Zagon, Schiff, Hirsch & Levine, Beverly Hills, Calif., 1969-70; atty., registered legis. advocate Beverly Hills, Malibu, 1973-75; atty. Freshman, Marantz, Comsky & Deutsch, 1971-74; prof. law Glendale (Calif.) U. Law, 1974-76, U. Iowa Sch. Law, Iowa City, 1976-77, Pepperdine U., Malibu, 1977-78; pvt. practice Newport Beach, Calif., 1978-81, San Clemente, 1978—. Part-time prof. law Western State Law Sch., Fullerton, Calif., 1978; cons. atty. The Irvine Co., Newport Beach, 1981-86, Std. Mgmt. Co., L.A., 1987-88; instr. Saddleback Coll., Mission Viejo, Calif., early 1990's; lectr., instr. Calif. Assn. Realtors Grad. Realty Inst., 1972-78, U. So. Calif. brokers tng. courses, L.A., 1978-80, UCLA real estate and corp. courses for paralegals, 1973-76; creator and lectr. course on disclosure for licensees, L.A., San Diego and Orange Counties, Calif., 1978-81; faculty advisor, rev. advisor Glendale U. Coll. Law, 1975-76. Chief articles editor UCLA Law Rev., 1967; adv. bd. The Rsch. Jour., 1976; contbr. poetry and short stories to jours. Mem. exec. bd. L.A. County Art Mus. Contemporary Art Coun., L.A., 1971-73; bd. trustees Westwood (L.A.) Art Assn., 1974; bd. govs. La Costa Beach Homeowners Assn., Malibu, 1975; pres. Dana Point (Calif.) Coastal Arts Coun., 1989-90; teaching participant Jr. Achievement, Newport Beach, 1985. Recipient 6 Am. Jurisprudence awards, 1966-68, 2 West Hornbook awards, 1967; nom. Douglas Law Clk. UCLA Law Sch., 1967. Fellow The Legal Inst.; mem. AALS (chair-elect environ. law sect. 1977), San Clemente Sunrise Rotary, Order of Coif. Avocations: world travel, fine arts, writing, computers, performing arts, graphics. Contracts commercial, General corporate, Real property. Office: PO Box 4715 San Clemente CA 92674-4715

GHANTOUS, KARYNE THERESE, lawyer; b. Hollywood, Calif., Apr. 30, 1972; d. Joseph Elias and Mary Yacoub Ghantous; m. Kyle MacLeod, June 15, 1996. BA in Psychology, UCLA, 1994; JD, U. Calif., San Francisco, 1997. Bar: Calif. 1997. Assoc. Hardin, Cook, Loper, Engel & Bergez, LLP, Oakland, Calif., 1998—. Democrat. Office: Hardin Cook Loper Engel & Bergez 1999 Harrison St Fl 18 Oakland CA 94612-3520

GHERLEIN, GERALD LEE, lawyer, former diversified manufacturing company executive; b. Warren, Ohio, Feb. 16, 1938; s. Jacob A. and Ruth (Matthews) G.; m. Joycelyn Hardin, June 18, 1960; children: David, Christy. Student, Ohio Wesleyan U., 1956-58; B.S. in Bus. Adminstrn, Ohio State U., 1960; J.D., U. Mich., 1963. Bar: Ohio 1963. Assoc. Taft Stettinius & Hollister, Cin., 1963-66; corp. atty. Eaton Corp., Cleve., 1966-68, European legal counsel Zug, Switzerland, 1968-71, asst. sec., assoc. counsel Cleve., 1971-76, v.p., gen. counsel, 1976-91, exec. v.p., gen. counsel, 1991-2000, ret., 2000. Pres. Citizens League Greater Cleve., 1979-81; trustee Cleve. Ballet, 1983-88, vice chmn. 1985-87; trustee WVIZ Pub. Television, 1990-99, Armada Funds, 1997—. Mem. ABA, Greater Cleve. Bar Assn. (pres. 1989, trustee), Ohio Bar Assn., Am. Soc. Corp. Secs. (pres. Ohio regional group 1977), Pepper Pike Country Club, Union Club, Mayfield Country Club. Clubs: Union, Tavern, Mayfield Country. General corporate. Home: 3679 Greenwood Dr Cleveland OH 44124-5502 Office: Eaton Corp 1111 Superior Ave E Cleveland OH 44114-2507

GIAIMO, JOSEPH OCTAVIUS, lawyer; b. July 12, 1934; married; children: James, Cynthia, Jennifer. BBA, St. John's U., 1959, LLB, 1961; Hon, 1986. Assoc. Havens, Wandless, Stitt and Tighe, N.Y.C., 1961-64; asst. legis. rep. Office of Mayor, 1964-66; ptnr. Adams & Giaimo, 1966-70, Giaimo & Kaufman, N.Y.C., 1970-71, Manton & Giaimo, N.Y.C., 1972-76; sole practice, 1976-82; ptnr. Giaimo & Vreeburg, 1982—. Asst. counsel to various N.Y. state assemblymen, 1966-77; legis. asst. Ins. com., 1978-80; counsel to com. on govtl. employees, 1981-84. Contbg. editor St. John's U. Law Rev., 1959-60, research editor, 1961. Mem. N.Y. State Mental Health Services Council, 1984-89. Served with USN. Mem. St. John's U. Sch. Law Alumni Assn. (bd. dirs., pres.), St. John's Alumni Fedn. (bd. dirs.). Home: 113 Warwick Ave Flushing NY 11363-1037 E-mail: jogktg@aol.com

GIALLANZA, CHARLES PHILIP, lawyer; b. Hornell, N.Y., Nov. 18, 1950; s. Charles Joseph Jr. and Rena Eugena (Foster) G.; children: Charles Edward, Juleah Marie. AS in Aerospace Sci., U. Albuquerque, 1977; BA in Polit. Sci. and English, U. South Fla., 1979; JD, John Marshall Law Sch., 1982. Bar: Ga. 1983, U.S. Dist. Ct. (no. dist.) Ga. 1983; cert. air traffic contr. FAA. With USAF, 1971-79; air traffic contr. USAF Res., Tampa, 1977-79, Dobbins AFB, 1980-81, USN Res., Dobbins AFB; assoc. James B. Pilcher, P.C., Atlanta, 1982-83; pvt. practice Snellville, Ga., 1983—. Advocate assisting Cubans detained in Atlanta prison, 1985, 86; capt. Ga. Def. Force, 1985-86. Recipient photography awards USAF, 1975. Mem. Ga. Bar Assn., Atlanta Bar Assn., Gwinnet Bar Assn. (law day com. 1987-88, Pro Bono Project award for outstanding svc. to citizens of Gwinnett County and the legal cmty. 2000). Avocations: cross-training, running, weightlifting. State civil litigation, Family and matrimonial, Personal injury. Office: 3881 Stone Mountain Hwy Ste 5 Snellville GA 30039-3978 Fax: 770-978-4450. E-mail: Charles@GiallanzaLaw.com

GIAMPIETRO, WAYNE BRUCE, lawyer; b. Chgo., Jan. 20, 1942; s. Joseph Anthony and Jeannette Marie (Zeller) G.; m. Mary E. Fordeck, June 15, 1963; children: Joseph, Anthony, Marcus. BA, Purdue U., 1963; JD, Northwestern U., 1966. Bar: Ill. 1966, U.S. Dist. Ct. (no. dist.) Ill. 1966, U.S. Ct. Appeals (7th cir.) 1967, U.S. Tax Ct. 1977, U.S. Supreme Ct. 1971. Assoc. Elmer Gertz, Chgo., 1966-73; mem. firm Gertz & Giampietro, 1974-75; sole practice, 1975-76; ptnr. Poltrock & Giampietro, 1976-87, Witwer, Burlage, Poltrock & Giampietro, 1987-94, Witwer, Poltrock & Giampietro, 1995—. Former cons. atty. Looking Glass divsn. Traveler's Aid Soc. Contbr. articles to profl. jours. Pres. Chgo. 47th Ward Young Republicans, 1968; bd. dirs. Ravenswood Conservation Commn. Lutheran. Avocation: stamp collecting. General civil litigation, Constitutional, Labor. Home: 23 Windsor Dr Lincolnshire IL 60069-3410 Office: Witwer Poltrock & Giampietro 125 S Wacker Dr Ste 2700 Chicago IL 60606-4401 E-mail: wgiampietro@wpglawyers.com

GIANNINI, MATTHEW CARLO, lawyer, educator; b. Youngstown, Ohio, July 12, 1950; s. Matthew and Graziella (Nistri) G. BS, Youngstown State U., 1973, postgrad., 1973-75; JD, U. Dayton, 1978. Bar: Ohio 1978, U.S. Dist. Ct. (no. dist.) Ohio 1978, U.S. Supreme Ct. 1982. Assoc. D'Apolito, Infante, Huberman and Gentile, Youngstown, 1978-84; ptnr. D'Apoloito, Infante and Giannini, 1984—; asst. prof. forensic psychiatry Northeastern Ohio U. Coll. Medicine, 1981-84, assoc. prof. forensic psychiatry, 1984—. Agt. Safeco Title Ins. Co., 1978—; sr. cons. forensic medicine Fair Oaks Psychiatry Hosp., Summit, N.J., 1979—; instr. Paralegal Inst. Ohio, 1980—; instr. comml. law Youngstown State U., 1980—. Author: (with A.J. Giannini and A.E. Slaby) Physicians Guide to Overdose and Detoxification, 1984; contbr. numerous articles to profl. jours., chpts. to books. Mem. ABA, Am. Inst. Biol. Scis., Ohio Bar Assn. Republican. Roman Catholic. Avocations: tennis, golf. General corporate, Family and matrimonial, Personal injury. Home: 7284 Yellow Creek Dr Poland OH 44514-2647 Office: 1040 S Commons Pl Ste 200 Youngstown OH 44514

GIANOULAKIS, JOHN LOUIS, lawyer; b. St. Louis, Nov. 22, 1938; s. Louis John and Marie (Pappas) G.; m. Louise Marotta, Jan. 1961 (dec. 1970); children: Christopher Louis, Kia Louise, Candlin Hamilton Dobbs; m. Dora Rodliff Deady, Sept. 2, 1972. AB, Wash. U., 1960; JD, Harvard U., 1963. Bar: Mo. 1963, U.S. Dist. Ct. (ea. dist.) Mo. 1963, U.S. Ct. Appeals (8th cir.) 1974, U.S. Supreme Ct. 1975, U.S. Ct. Appeals (7th cir.) 1982, U.S. Ct. Appeals (6th cir.) 1987. From assoc. to ptnr. Thompson, Walther & Shewmaker, St. Louis, 1963-70; ptnr. Kohn, Shands & Gianoulakis, 1971-73, Kohn, Shands, Elbert, Gianoulakis & Giljum, LLP, St. Louis, 1973—. Mem., pres. bd. dirs. Legal Svcs. of Ea. Mo., Inc., St. Louis, 1972-81; mem. bar com. 22d Jud. Cir., St. Louis, 1977-85. Mem., v.p., pres. University City (Mo.) Sch. Bd., 1970-76; vice-chair Washington U. Alumni Bd. Govs., 2000-2001, exec. vice-chair, 2001—; bd. trustees Washington U., 2001—. Recipient Arts and Scis. Disting. Alumnus award Washington U., 2000. Fellow Am. Coll. Trial Lawyers; mem. ABA, Mo. Bar Assn., Bar Assn. Met. St. Louis, Norwood Hills Country Club, Noon Day Club, Mo. Bluffs Assn. (pres. 1999—), Spanish Lake Cmty. Assn. (dir. 1999—). Democrat. Federal civil litigation, Education and schools, Labor. Home: 44 Clearview Park Saint Louis MO 63138-3302 Office: Kohn Shands Elbert Gianoulakis & Giljum LLP One Mercantile Ctr 24th Fl Saint Louis MO 63101 E-mail: jgianoulakis@ksegg.com

GIBB, ROBERTA LOUISE, lawyer, artist; b. Cambridge, Mass., Nov. 2, 1942; d. Thomas Robinson Pieri and Jean Knox Gibb. BS, U. Calif., La Jolla, 1969; JD, New Eng. Sch. Law, 1982. Bar: Mass. 1978. Legal aide Mass. State Legis., 1973; practice law Mass., 1980—. Author: To Boston With Love, 1980, The Art of Inflation, 1981, The Art of Economics, 1982; contbr. articles to profl. jours.; executed sculptures of Albert Einstein, Pres. Carter, Pres. Johnson, Pres. Reagan, Mother Theresa, Eleanor Roosevelt, The Marathon, Fire Dancers, Birth, Olympia, The Family, The Left Handed Squash Player, Basketball, Germain Gliddin, numerous others; exhibited in group shows at Geraci Galleries, 1996—, Rockport, Mass., Rockport Art Assn. Gallery, 1996—; permanent collection Nat. Art Mus. Art, Indpls.; executed 5 murals; prodr. Where the Spirit Leads (TV documentary), 2000; producer Where the Spirit Leads, TV documentary, 1980—. Mem. Essex County Environ. and Conservation, Rockport, 1980-88. Women winner Boston Marathon, 1966, 67, 68, 1st woman to run Boston Marathon, 1966; inducted into Road Runners of Am. Hall of Fame, 1982 Mem. Mass. Bar, Nat. Sculpture Soc., Rockport Art Assn., Inst. Study of Natural Sys. (founder, pres. 1976—), Boston Athletic Assn., U.S. Assn. for Art Clubs (sec. bd. dirs. 1999—). E-mail: bobbigibb@aol.com

GIBBES, WILLIAM HOLMAN, lawyer; b. Hartsville, S.C., Feb. 25, 1930; s. Ernest Lawrence and Nancy (Watson) G.; m. Frances Hagood, May 1, 1954; children: Richard H., William H. Jr., Lynn. BS, U. S.C., 1952, LLB, 1953. Bar: S.C. 1953, U.S. Ct. Mil. Appeals 1954, U.S. Dist. Ct. S.C. 1956, U.S. Supreme Ct. 1959, U.S. Ct. Appeals (4th cir.) 1965. Asst. atty. gen., Columbia, S.C., 1957-62; ptnr. Berry & Gibbes, 1962-68, Berry, Lightsey, Gibbes, Columbia, 1968-72; mem. Gibbes Law Firm, P.A., 1972—; house of dels. S.C. Bar, 1994-96. Chief judge U.S. Army Legal Svcs. Agy., 1980-83. Author: Control of Highway Access - Its Prospects and Problems, Legal Dimensions of Community Health Planning, 1969, Manual for Fee Appraisors, 1960; contbr. articles to S.C. Law Review, Law Rev. Digest, 1960. Chmn. bd. dirs. U. S.C. YMCA, 1956-60. Brig. gen. JAGC, USAR 1980-83. Recipient Legion of Merit, U.S. Army, 1983. Mem. ABA (mil. laws com. 1984-90, meml. com.), S.C. Bar Assn. (exec. com. 1961-62), Am. Bd. Trial Advocates (sec.-treas. 1994-95, pres.-elect 1995-96, pres. 1996-97), Judge Advs. Assn. (pres. 1982-83), Richland County Bar Assn., S.C. Credit Ins. Assn. (gen. counsel 1963-94), Tarantella Club, Caprician Club, Summit Club, Forest Lake Country Club, Kiawah Island Club, Kappa Sigma Kappa, Omicron Delta Kappa. Episcopalian. E-mila. General civil litigation, Estate planning, Probate. Home: 4925 Forest Lake Pl Columbia SC 29206-4965 E-mail: BillGibbes@aol.com

GIBBONS, JULIA SMITH, federal judge; b. Pulaski, Tenn., Dec. 23, 1950; d. John Floyd and Julia Jackson (Abernathy) Smith; m. William Lockhart Gibbons, Aug. 11, 1973; children: Rebecca Carey, William Lockhart Jr. BA, Vanderbilt U., 1972; JD, U. Va., 1975. Bar: Tenn. 1975. Law clk. to judge U.S. Ct. Appeals, 1975-76; assoc. Farris, Hancock, Gilman, Branan, Lanier & Hellen, Memphis, 1976-79; legal advisor Gov. Lamar Alexander, Nashville, 1979-81; judge 15th Jud. Cir., Memphis, 1981-83, U.S. Dist. Ct. (we. dist.) Tenn., Memphis, 1983—, chief judge, 1994-2000. Fellow: Am. Bar Found., Tenn. Bar Found., Memphis and Shelby County Bar Found.; mem.: Memphis Bar Assn., Order of Coif, Phi Beta Kappa. Presbyterian. Office: US Dist Ct 1157 Federal Bldg 167 N Main St Memphis TN 38103-1816

GIBBONS, WILLIAM JOHN, lawyer; b. Chgo., Jan. 22, 1947; s. Edward and Lottie (Gasiorek) G.; children: Maximilian Clay, Bartholomew David, Ariel Katherine. BA, Northwestern U., 1968, JD, 1972. Bar: Ill. 1972, U.S. Dist. Ct. (no. dist.) Ill. 1972, U.S. Ct. Appeals (9th cir.) 1980, U.S. Supreme Ct. 1982, U.S. Ct. Appeals (7th cir.) 1984. Assoc. Kirkland and Ellis, Chgo., 1972-76; ptnr. Hedlund, Hunter and Lynch, 1976-82, Latham and Watkins, Chgo., 1982—, mng. ptnr. Chgo. office, 1995-2000. Bd. dirs. Pegasus Players, Chgo. Served with USAR, 1968-74. Mem. ABA, Chgo. Bar Assn. (chairperson class action com. 1994-95), Chgo. Coun. Lawyers, Seventh Cir. Bar Assn. Met. Club, Riverpark Club (Chgo.). Antitrust, Federal civil litigation, State civil litigation. Home: 4900 S Kimbark Ave Chicago IL 60615-2922 Office: Latham & Watkins Sears Tower Ste 5800 Chicago IL 60606-6306

GIBBS, FREDERICK WINFIELD, lawyer, communications company executive; b. Buffalo, Mar. 22, 1932; s. Walter L. M. and Elizabeth Mari (Georgi) G.; m. Josephine Janice Jarvis, Dec. 20, 1954; children: Michael, Mathew, Robyn. BA cum laude, Alfred U., 1954; JD with Tax honors, Rutgers U., 1989. Bar: Pa. 1989, N.J. 1989, U.S. Dist. Ct. N.J. 1989. With N.Y. Tel. Co., 1954-65, ITT, 1965-86; mng. dir. ITT Standard Electrica, S.A., 1971-75; chief exec. officer ITT Standard Electrica, Brazil, 1975-77; exec. dir. ops. ITT Communications Ops. Group ITT Communications Ops. Group, 1977; corp. v.p. ITT, 1977-80; pres. U.S. Tel. and Tel. Corp., 1977-79, exec. dir., sr. group exec., 1980-86; dir. System 12, ITT, 1979-80; exec. v.p. ITT, 1980-86, ITT Telecommunications Corp., 1983-86; pvt. practice law Pemberton, N.J., 1989-95; founding ptnr. Gibbs & Gregory Attys. at Law, 1995—. Cons. ITT, 1986-89, The World Bank/IFC, 1989—; pres. Mulberry Hill Enterprises, 1989—; bd. dirs. CMC Ind., ACT Mfg. Trustee Alfred U., 1981—; trustee Whitesbog Found., 1996—, pres. bd. trustees, 2000—; mem. planning bd. Barnegat Light, N.J., elected Borough Coun., Barnegat Light, 1992, re-elected, 1995, 98; bd. dirs. Burlington County Red Cross, 1999—. Named Hon. Citizen of Rio de Janeiro, 1973; inducted to Alfred Univ. Athletic Hall of Fame, 1993. Mem. ABA, N.J. Bar Assn., Pa. Bar Assn., Burlington County Bar Assn., Barnegat Light Taxpayers Assn. (v.p. 1989-90, pres. 1990-92), Rotary Internat. (bd. dirs. Pemberton club 1996-97, v.p. 1997-98, pres. 1999-00, Pemberton Rotarian of Yr. 1996-97). Home: 12 E 17th Street Rd Barnegat Light NJ 08006

GIBBS, L(IPPMAN) MARTIN, lawyer; b. N.Y.C., Feb. 27, 1938; s. Harold and Shirley (Marks) G.; m. Dona Lynn Fagg, May 2, 1968; 1 child, Bradford M. BA, Brown U., 1959; JD, Columbia U., 1962. Bar: N.Y. 1963. Atty. various orgns., 1963-69; assoc., then ptnr. Finley, Kumble, Wagner, Heine & Underberg, N.Y.C., 1969-87; ptnr. Clifford Chance Rogers & Wells, LLP, 1987—. Bd. dirs. First Republic Bank, San Francisco. Regional dir. United Fund Drive of Rye, N.Y., 1979; trustee South St. Seaport Mus., 1995—. With USAR, 1962-68. Mem. ABA, NY. State Bar Assn., Assn. Bar City N.Y. Avocations: sailing, golf. Contracts commercial, General corporate. Office: Clifford Chance Rogers & Wells LLP 200 Park Ave New York NY 10166-0005 E-mail: martin.gibbs@cliffordchance.com

GIBSON, ERNEST WILLARD, III, retired state supreme court justice; b. Brattleboro, Vt., Sept. 23, 1927; s. Ernest William and Dorothy Pearl (Switzer) G.; m. Charlotte Elaine Hungerford, Sept. 10, 1960; children: Margaret, Mary, John. BA, Yale U., 1951; LLB, Harvard U., 1956. Bar: Vt. State's atty. Windham County, Vt., 1957-61; mem. Vt. Ho. of Reps., 1961-63, chmn. judiciary com., 1963; chmn. Vt. Pub. Svc. Bd., 1963-72; judge Vt. Superior Ct., 1972-83; assoc. justice Vt. Supreme Ct., 1983-97, ret., 1997. Chancellor Episcopal Diocese Vt., 1977-98, trustee, 1972-99, pres. bd. trustees, 1991-99, dep. to gen. conv., 1976-94. Served in U.S. Army, 1945-46, 51-53, Major Army Nat. Guard, 1956-71. Mem. Vt. Bar Assn. Avocations: bridge, tennis. Home: 11 Baldwin St Montpelier VT 05602-2110

GIBSON, FLOYD ROBERT, federal judge; b. Prescott, Ariz., Mar. 3, 1910; s. Van Robert and Katheryn Ida G.; m. Gertrude Lee Walker, Apr. 23, 1935; children: Charles R., John M., Catherine L. A.B., U. Mo., 1931, LL.B., 1933. Bar: Mo. 1932. Practiced law, Independence, 1933-37, Kansas City, 1937-61; mem. firm Johnson, Lucas, Bush & Gibson (and predecessor), 1954-61; county counselor Jackson County, 1943-44; judge U.S. Dist. Ct. (we. dist.) Mo., 1961-65, chief judge, until 1965; judge U.S. Ct. Appeals (8th cir.), Kansas City, Mo., 1965-79, sr. judge, 1979—, chief judge, 1974-80. Former chmn. bd. Mfrs. & Mechanics Bank, Kansas City, Mo., Blue Valley Fed. Savs. & Loan Assn.; mem. Nat. Conf. Commrs. Uniform State Laws, 1957—, Jud. Conf. U.S., 1974-80; chmn. Chief Judges Conf., 1977-78; bd. mgrs. Coun. State Govts., 1960-61; pres. Nat. Legis. Conf., 1960-61 Mem. Mo. Gen. Assembly from 7th Dist., 1940-46; mem. Mo. Senate, 1946-61, majority floor leader, 1952-56, pres. pro tem, 1956-60; del. Nat. Democratic Conv., 1956, 60; Mem. Mo. N.G. Named 2d most valuable mem. Mo. Legislature Globe Democrat, 1958, most valuable, 1960; recipient Faculty-Alumni award U. Mo., 1968; citation of merit Mo. Law Sch. Alumni, 1975; Spurgeon Smithson award Mo. Bar Found., 1978 Fellow ABA (adv. bd. editors Jour., chmn. jud. adminstrn. div. 1979-80, chmn. conf. sect. 1980-81, chmn. appellate judges conf. 1973-74, mem. ho. of dels.); mem. Fed. Bar Assn., Mo. Bar, Kansas City Bar Assn. (Ann. Achievement award 1980), Lawyers Assn. Kansas City (past v.p., Charles Evans Whittaker award 1985), Mo. Law Sch. Found. (life), Mo. Acad. Squires, Order of Coif, Phi Delta Phi, Phi Kappa Psi (Man of Yr. 1974). Democrat. Roman Catholic. Clubs: University, Carriage, Mercury.

GIBSON, JOHN ROBERT, federal judge; b. Springfield, Mo., Dec. 20, 1925; s. Harry B. and Edna (Kerr) G.; m. Mary Elizabeth Vaughn, Sept. 20, 1952 (dec. Aug. 1985); children: Jeanne, John Robert; m. Diane Allen Larrison, Oct. 1, 1986; stepchildren: Holly, Catherine. AB, U. Mo., 1949, JD, 1952. Bar: Mo. 1952. Assoc. Morrison, Hecker, Curtis, Kuder & Parrish, Kansas City, Mo., 1952-58, ptnr., 1958-81; judge U.S. Dist. Ct. (we. dist.) Mo., 1981-82, U.S. Ct. Appeals (8th cir.), Kansas City, 1982-94, sr. judge, 1994—. Mem. Mo. Press-Bar Commn., 1979-81; mem. com. on adminstrn. of magistrate sys. Jud. Conf. U.S., 1987-91, mem. security and facilities com., 1995—. Vice chmn. Jackson County Charter Transition Com., 1971-72; mem. Jackson County Charter Commn., 1970; v.p. Police Commrs. Bd., Kansas City, 1973-77. Served with AUS, 1944-46. Recipient Citation of Merit award U. Mo. at Columbia Sch. of Law, 1994. Fellow Am. Bar Found.; mem. ABA, Mo. State Bar (gov. 1972-79, pres. 1977-78; Pres.' award 1974, Smithson award 1984), Kansas City Bar Assn. (pres. 1970-71), Lawyers Assn. Kansas City (Charles Evan Whittaker award 1980), Fed. Judges Assn. (bd. dirs. 1991-97), Phi Beta Kappa, Omicron Delta Kappa. Presbyterian. Office: US Ct Appeals 8th Cir 400 E 9th St Ste 1040 Kansas City MO 64106-2695*

GIBSON, JOSEPH LEE, lawyer, lecturer; b. Lufkin, Tex., Mar. 12, 1940; s. Mitchell Osler and W. Christine (Bennett) Gibson; m. Bethanna Bunn, May 27, 1983; 1 child, Mark Corbett. BA, Baylor U., 1962; LLB, Harvard U., 1965. Bar: Tex. 1965, D.C. 1967. Legis. counsel Maritime Adminstrn., Washington, 1965-66; counsel govt. activities subcom. U.S. Ho. of Reps., Washington, 1966-68; assoc. Kirkland & Ellis, and predecessor, Washington, 1968-69; ptnr. Gibson, Branham & Farmer, Washington, 1969-73; counsel Montgomery Ward & Co., Washington, 1974-78; gen. counsel Credit Union Nat. Assn., Washington, 1978-79; counsel Diplomat Nat. Bank, Washington, 1979-80, also dir.; asst. solicitor Econ. Regulatory Adminstrn., Dept. Energy, Washington, 1980—; lectr. on equal employment in broadcasting, 1971-77, on consumer credit, privacy, electronic fund transfers, 1975—; atty. for mem. Nat. Commn. on Electronic Fund Transfers, Washington, 1976-78. Mem. various campaign and conv. staffs Democratic Party, Young Democrats, Tex. and Washington, 1965-80. Recipient Disting. Service award Maritime Adminstrn., 1966, Disting. Service award Dept. Energy, 1983. Methodist. Address: 966 Towlston Rd Mc Lean VA 22102-1026 Office: Dept Energy Econ Regulatory Adminstrn 1000 Independence Ave SW Washington DC 20585-0001

GIBSON, KEITH RUSSELL, lawyer, educator; b. Fulton, N.Y., Feb. 24, 1954; s. Keith Melvin and Retha (Thatcher) G.; m. Victoria Jean Carroll, Mar. 22, 1986; children: Emily Michelle, Robin Bethany, Kyle Russell. BA, Lycoming Coll., 1976; paralegal cert., Adelphi U., 1977; JD, Oklahoma City U., 1984. Bar: Okla. 1984, U.S. Dist. Ct. (no., we., ea. dists.) Okla. 1984. Paralegal Thatcher & Miller, Lewistown, Pa., 1978-81; law clk. Chief Justice Don Barnes Okla. Supreme Ct., Oklahoma City, 1983-84; assoc. Pate & Payne, 1984-91; sr. atty. Williams, Box, Forshee & Bullard, P.C., 1991—. Instr. Oklahoma City U. Legal Asst. Program, 1990-98, officer Sch. of Law Alumni Assn., 1994-96; lectr. Okla. Foreclosure and Repossession Nat. Bus. Inst.; paralegal issues instr. Inst. for Paralegal Edn.; legal advisor Okla. Just Compensation Act. Originator and participant Met. Ch. Legal Clearinghouse, Oklahoma City, 1995. Mem. Oklahoma City U. Law Alumni Assn. (officer 1994-96, participant fundraising 1996), North Oklahoma City Rotary (bd. dirs. 1994-95, sec. 1995-96, Newcomer of Yr. 1991, Pres.'s award 1993-94, Benefactor award Rotary Found. 1993), Citizen's League of Oklahoma City, Friends of the Oklahoma City Libr. Assn., Federalist Soc. (Okla. chpt.), Conf. Consumer Fin. Law. Republican. Bankruptcy, General civil litigation, Consumer commercial. Home: 2713 NW 158th St Edmond OK 73013-8819 Office: Williams Box Forshee & Bullard PC 522 Colcord Dr Oklahoma City OK 73102-2202

GIBSON, REGINALD WALKER, federal judge; b. Lynchburg, Va., July 31, 1927; s. McCoy and Julia Ann (Butler) G.; 1 child, Reginald S. B.S., Va. Union U., 1952; postgrad., Wharton Grad. Sch. Bus. Adminstrn., U. Pa., 1952-53; LL.B., Howard U., 1956. Bar: D.C. 1957, Ill. 1972. Agt. IRS, Washington, 1957-61; trial atty. tax div. U.S. Dept. Justice, 1961-71; sr. tax atty. Internat. Harvester Co., Chgo., 1971-76, gen. tax atty., 1976-82; judge

U.S. Ct. of Fed. Claims, Washington, 1982-95; sr. judge U.S. Ct. Fed. Claims, 1995—. Mem. bus. adbv. council Chgo. Urban League, 1974-82. Served with AUS, 1946-47. Recipient cert. award U.S. Dept. Justice Atty. Gen., 1969, recipient spl. commendation U.S. Dept. Justice Atty. Gen., 1970, Wall St. Jour. award, 1952, Am. Jurisprudence award, 1956; named Alumni of Yr. Howard U. Sch. Law, 1984. Mem. D.C. Bar Assn., Chgo. Bar Assn., Fed. Bar Assn., Nat. Bar Assn., Claims Ct. Bar Assn., J. Edgar Murdock Am. Inn of Ct. (taxation com.). Baptist. Club: Nat. Lawyers (Washington). Home: 6305 Chaucer View Cir Alexandria VA 22304-3548 Office: US Ct Fed Claims 717 Madison Pl NW Washington DC 20005

GIBSON, VIRGINIA LEE, lawyer; b. Independence, Mo., Mar. 5, 1946; BA, U. Calif., Berkeley, 1972; JD, U. Calif., San Francisco, 1977. Bar: Calif. 1981. Assoc. Pillsbury, Madison & Sutro, San Francisco, 1980-83; ptnr. Chickering & Gregory, 1983-85, Baker & McKenzie, San Francisco, 1985—. Mem. ABA (tax sect.), Nat. Assn. Stock Plan Profls., Nat. Ctr. for Employee Ownership, Calif. Bar Assn. (exec. com. tax sect. 1985-88), San Francisco Bar Assn. (internat. taxation sect.), Western Pension and Benefits Conf. (pres. San Francisco chpt. 1989-91, program com. 1984-88). Pension, profit-sharing, and employee benefits, Environmental. Office: Baker & McKenzie 2 Embarcadero Ctr Ste 2400 San Francisco CA 94111-3909

GIERBOLINI-ORTIZ, GILBERTO, federal judge; b. 1926; B.A., U. P.R., 1951, LL.B., 1961. Asst. U.S. atty. Commonwealth P.R., 1961-66; judge Superior Ct. Bayamon, P.R., 1966-67, Superior Ct. Caguas, 1967-69; solicitor P.R., 1969-72, asst. atty. gen. for antitrust, 1970-72; pvt. practice Jose H. Pico, 1973-74, Arias Cestero, Gierbolini & Garcia Soto, 1974-75, Nido, Berrios, Menendez & Gierbolini, 1975-77, Dubon, Gonzalez & Berrios, 1977-80; judge U.S. Dist. Ct. P.R., San Juan, 1980—, chief judge, 1991-93; sr. judge, 1993—. Prof. U. P.R., Cath. U. Law Sch. Chmn. State Elections Bd., P.R., 1972. Capt. U.S. Army, 1951-57. E-mail: Gilberto. Office: US Courthouse and PO Bldg 3d Fl Ste 342 300 Recinto Sur St Hato Rey San Juan PR 00901-1907 E-mail: Gierbolini@prd.uscourts.gov

GIFFORD, WILLIAM C. lawyer, educator; b. Aurora, Ill., Sept. 18, 1941; AB, Dartmouth Coll., 1963; LLB, Harvard U., 1966. Bar: Ill. 1966, D.C. 1968, N.Y. 1976. Assoc. ptnr. Ivins, Phillips & Barker, Washington, 1967-74; assoc. prof. Cornell Law Sch., 1974-78; counsel, ptnr. Wilmer, Cutler & Pickering, 1978-83; ptnr. Davis, Polk & Wardell, N.Y.C., 1983-98, sr. counsel, 1998—; prof. law Cornell U. Law Sch., 2001—. Author: International Tax Planning, 1974, 2d edit., 1979; (with E.A. Owens) International Aspects of U.S. Taxation, 1982. General practice, Corporate taxation, Taxation, general. Office: Davis Polk & Wardwell 450 Lexington Ave New York NY 10017-3911 E-mail: gifford@dpw.com

GIL, GUILLERMO, prosecutor; U.S. atty. Dept. Justice, Hato Rey, P.R., 1993—. Office: US Attys Office Fed Bldg Rm 452 Carlos E Chardon Ave Hato Rey San Juan PR 00918*

GILBERG, KENNETH ROY, lawyer; b. Phila., Feb. 2, 1951; s. Leonard David and Roslyn (Tennis) G.; m. Nanci Jane Schwartz, Sept. 7, 1974. BA, Lebanon Valley Coll., 1973; JD, Widener U., 1976. Bar: Pa. 1976. Assoc. Pechner, Dorfman et. al., Phila., 1976-84, ptnr., 1984-87, Myerson & Kuhn, Phila., 1988-89; prin. Kenneth R. Gilberg and Assocs., Bala Cynwyd, 1989—99; ptnr. Mesirov Gelman Jaffe Cramer & Jamieson, LLP, Phila., 1990—, Schnader Harrison Segal & Lewis, LLP, Phila., 2000—. Contbr. articles to profl. jours. Past pres. Golden Slipper Camp; pres. Golden Slipper Club and Charities. Recipient Meritorious Achievement award Pa. Sports Hall of Fame, 1974; named Most Valuable Player Mid-Atlantic Conf., 1973. Mem. Phi Alpha Delta (charter). Republican. Avocations: lacrosse, racquetball, photography, golf, tennis. Labor, Pension, profit-sharing, and employee benefits. Office: Schnader Harrison Segal & Lewis LLP 1600 Market St Ste 3600 Philadelphia PA 19103-7286 E-mail: kgilberg@schnader.com

GILBERT, ALAN JAY, lawyer; b. Newark, Oct. 11, 1951; s. Stanley David and June Helene (Gordon) G. Sc.B. magna cum laude, Brown U., 1973; J.D. magna cum laude, U. Mich., 1977. Bar: Colo. 1977, U.S. Dist. Ct. Colo. 1977, U.S. Ct. Appeals (10th cir.) 1977, U.S. Ct. Appeals (9th cir.) 1978, U.S. Ct. Appeals (D.C. cir.) 1979. Environ. engr. U.S. EPA, State of Rhode Island, Providence, 1973-74; mem. firm Sherman & Howard, Denver, 1977—; adj. prof. Sch. Bus. Adminstrn., lectr. Law Sch., U. Denver, 1984-92. Mem. editl. adv. bd. Environ. Law Reporter, 1994—. Trustee at large, Rocky Mt. Mineral Law Found., 1991-93, 95. Mem. ABA (vice chair natural resources sect.). Administrative and regulatory, Environmental. Home: 1965 S Adams St Denver CO 80210-3614 Office: Sherman & Howard 633 17th St Ste 3000 Denver CO 80202-3665

GILBERT, BLAINE LOUIS, lawyer; b. Phila., Aug. 26, 1940; s. Arthur I. and Marcia R. (Kaufman) G.; m. Sondra Gilbert; children: Beth M., Kimberly J. AA, Balt. Jr. Coll., 1961; postgrad., Am. U., 1962; JD, U. Balt., 1965. Bar: Md. 1966, U.S. Dist. Ct. Md. 1968, U.S. Supreme Ct. 1974. Exec. asst. ins. commr. State of Md., Balt., 1965-66; assoc. Polovoy & Polovoy, 1966-72; ptnr. Angeletti & Gilbert, 1972-79, Gilbert & Levin, Balt., 1979-92, Blaine L. Gilbert and Assocs. P.A., Balt., 1993—. Mem. ABA, Balt. Bar Assn., Am. Immigration Lawyers Assn., Am. Judicature Soc., Md. Trial Lawyers Assn. Avocations: music, screenwriting. State civil litigation, Entertainment, Immigration, naturalization, and customs. Home: 2B Dorsett Hills Ct Owings Mills MD 21117-1131 Office: Blaine L Gilbert & Assocs PA Lower Level 200 E Lexington St Baltimore MD 21202-3530 Fax: 410-539-6440. E-mail: blglaw@aol.com

GILBERT, HOWARD N(ORMAN), lawyer, director; b. Chgo., Aug. 19, 1928; s. Norman Aaron and Fannie (Cohn) G.; m. Jacqueline Glasser, Feb. 16, 1957; children: Norman Abraham, Harlan Wayne, Joel Kenneth, Sharon. PhB, U. Chgo., 1947; JD, Yale U., 1951. Bar: Ill 1951, U.S. Dist. Ct. (no. dist.) Ill. 1955, U.S. Ct. Appeals (7th cir.) 1956. Ptnr. Rusnak, Deutsch & Gilbert, Chgo., 1962-79, Aaron, Schimberg, Hess & Gilbert, Chgo., 1980-84; sr. ptnr. Holleb & Coff, 1984-2000, Wildman, Harrold, Chgo., 2000—. Bd. dirs. Jewish Fedn. Met. Chgo., 1977-83; chmn. bd. dirs., pres. Mt. Sinai Hosp. Med. Ctr., Chgo., 1968-69; trustee Chgo. Hosp. Coun., 1979-84; mem. Bd. Jewish Edn., 1972-77; mem. vis. com. Coll. of U. Chgo., 1997—. Mem. ABA, Chgo. Bar Assn., Chgo. Coun. Lawyers, Ill. Soc. Health Lawyers, Standard Club, Bryn Mawr Country Club. Democrat. Jewish. Health, Real property. Office: Wildman Harrold Allen & Dixon 225 W Wacker Dr Ste 3000 Chicago IL 60606-1224 E-mail: gilbert@wildmanharrold.com

GILBERT, HOWARD WILLIAM, JR. lawyer; b. Washington, Dec. 10, 1931; s. Howard William and Mirian Keener (King) G.; m. Lillian Janine Poitte, Oct. 3, 1953 (div. Jan. 1983); children: Elizabeth, Linda, Wayne, Scott; m. Lois Histand, Apr. 23, 1983. AB, U. Md., 1953; JD, Georgetown U., 1961. Bar: Md. 1962, U.S. Dist. Ct. Md. 1965. Asst. mgr. underwriting GEICO, Washington, 1955-65; mem. Gilbert, Marks & DiGirolamo and predecessor firms, Hagerstown, Md., 1965—. Served to capt. USAF, 1953-55, 59-60. Mem. Washington County Bar Assn. (pres. 1981, 82), Md. State Bar Assn. Democrat. Presbyterian. Personal injury, Real property, Workers' compensation. Office: Gilbert Marks & DiGirolamo 35 E Washington St Hagerstown MD 21740-5605

GILBERT, JAMES H. judge; b. Mpls., Mar. 11, 1947; s. Kenneth H. and Virginia E. (Ekstrand) G.; m. Mary M. Makepeace, Sept. 17, 1971; children: Alisson K., Erica M., Kristina L. BA, U. Minn., 1969, JD, 1972. Bar: Minn. 1972, Wis. 1984, U.S. Dist. Ct. Minn. 1974, U.S. Tax Ct. 1978, U.S. Ct. Appeals (8th cir.) 1989, U.S. Supreme Ct. 1988. Lawyer, v.p., mng. ptnr. Meshbesher, Singer & Spence Ltd., Mpls., 1971—; assoc. justice Minn. State Supreme Ct., 1998—. Park Commr. City of Orono, Minn., 1988—; bd. dirs. Minn. Drug Abuse Resistance Edn. Inc. Mem. Minn. Bar Assn., Minn. Trial Lawyers Assn., Lafayette Club. Avocations: skiing, hunting, golf, tennis, snowmobiling. Office: Minn Judicial Ctr 25 Constitution Ave Rm 422 Saint Paul MN 55155*

GILBERT, KEITH THOMAS, lawyer, consultant; b. Harlingen, Tex., Jan. 29, 1959; BBA, Baylor U., 1982; JD, South Tex. Coll. Law, Tex. A & M U., 1989. Bar: Tex. 1990, U.S. Dist. Ct. (so. dist.) Tex. 1992. Ptnr. Gilbert & Mestemaker, Houston, 1991-96; pvt. practice, 1996-2000, Gilbert & Maxwell, 2000—. Legal rep., cons. North Channel Tribune Newspaper, Galena Park, Tex., Sandy Ridge Vineyards, Safeco, Colonial Gen., Provider Law. Editor: World Trade Policy, 1979. Avocations: chess, muscle cars, stamp collecting, wine. Appellate, State civil litigation, Election. Office: PO Box 1984 Houston TX 77251-1984

GILBERT, PENNY XENIA, lawyer; b. West Bromwich, U.K., Jan. 7, 1960; d. R. L. and M.K. Gilbert; m. John Whittaker, Aug. 3, 1991; children: Max, Emilia. BA, U. Oxford, U.K., 1982, DPhil, 1987. Tech. asst. Bristows, London, 1986-87, trainee solicitor, 1989-91, solicitor, 1991-98, ptnr., 1998—. Intellectual property, Patent. Office: Bristows 3 Lincoln's Inn Fields London WC2A 3AA England Fax: 011-44-207-400-8050. E-mail: penny.gilbert@bristows.com

GILBERT, RICHARD ALLEN, lawyer; b. Pitts., Dec. 13, 1948; s. Donald T., Sr. and Sara Margaret (Fife) G.; m. Patricia Ann Ramsdale, Jan. 21, 1972; 1 child, Stephanie Ann. B.A., Miami U., Oxford, Ohio, 1970; J.D., U. Cin., 1973. Bar: Ohio 1973, Fla. 1974, U.S. Dist. Ct. (mid. dist.) Fla. 1975, U.S. Ct. Appeals (5th and 11th cirs.) 1975, U.S. Supreme Ct. 1985; cert. trial lawyer. Assoc. Fowler, White, Gillen, Boggs, Villareal & Banker, PA, Tampa, Fla., 1974-78; ptnr. de la Parte & Gilbert PA, Tampa, 1979— . Editorial bd. U. Cin. Law Rev., 1972. Co-chmn. United Way Tampa, 1984; mem. State Fla. Ethics Commn. Mem. Acad. Fla. Trial Lawyers, Assn. Trial Lawyers Am., Fla. Bar Assn., Ohio Bar Assn., ABA, Hillsborough County Bar Assn. Republican. Presbyterian. Federal civil litigation, State civil litigation, General practice. Home: 4141 Bayshore Blvd Tampa FL 33611-1800

GILBERT, RONALD RHEA, lawyer; b. Sandusky, Ohio, Dec. 29, 1942; s. Corvin and Mildred (Millikin) G.; children: Elizabeth, Lynne, Lisa. BA, Wittenberg U., 1964; JD, U. Mich., 1967, postgrad., 1967-68, Wayne State U., 1973-74. Bar: Mich. 1968, U.S. Dist. Ct. (ea. and we. dists.) Mich. 1968, U.S. Ct. Appeals (6th cir.) 1968, U.S. Ct. Appeals (9th cir.) 1977, U.S. Ct. Appeals (7th cir.) 1984, U.S. Ct. Appeals (3d cir.) 1988, U.S. Ct. Appeals (4th cir.) 1989, U.S. Ct. Appeals (8th cir.) 1990, U.S. Ct. Appeals (10th cir.) 1991, U.S. Ct. Appeals (11th cir.) 1992, U.S. Ct. Appeals (2nd cir.), 1992. Assoc. prosecutor Wayne County, Mich., 1969; assoc. Rouse, Selby, Dickinson, Shaw & Pike, Detroit, 1969-72; ptnr. Charfoos, Christensen, Gilbert & Archer, P.C., 1972-84; sole practice, 1984—. Instr. Madonna Coll., Detroit, 1977-81; mem. faculty Inst. Continuing Legal Edn., 1977—; speaker symposium on social security law Detroit Coll. Law, 1984; state bar grievance investigator; vol. chmn. Aquatic Injury Safety Found; mgr. web sites Found. for Spinal Cord Injury Prevention, Care and Cure (fscip.org), Found. for Aquatic Injury Prevention (aquaticisf.org). Co-author: Social Security Disability Claims, 1983; contbr. articles to legal jours. Founder, chmn. Aquatic Injury Safety Group, 1982, chmn., 1982-89; founder, chmn. Found. for Aquatic Injury Prevention, 1988, Found. for Spinal Cord Injury Prevention, 1988, founder websites; chmn. aquatic safety com. Nat. Safety Coun., 1987; mem. data collection subcom. of Nat. Swimming Safety Com. for Consumer Products Safety Commn.; bd. dirs. Nat. Coordinating Coun. on Spinal Cord Injuries; patron Detroit Art Inst., Detroit Zool. Soc.; mem. Pres.' Club U. Mich.; mem. Detroit Council on World Affairs, 1968-73, Council for Nat. Coop. in Aquatics; mem. combined fed. campaign Nat. Health Agy. Mich.; founder Spinal Cord Injury Traumatic Brain Injury Adv. Com. Mich. Pub. Health Chronic Adv. Com.; co-founder Safe Kids Coalition Southeastern Mich.; mem. Nat. Safe Kids Coalition. Mem. Assn. Trial Lawyers Am., Mich. Trial Lawyers Assn., System Safety Soc., ABA, Mich Bar Assn., Detroit Bar Assn., Am. Arbitration Assn., Am. Judicature Soc., Nat. Spinal Cord Injury Assn. (sec. 1988, bd. dirs., exec. com., chmn. prevention com.), Nat. Head Injury Assn., Mich. Head Injury Assn., Am. Standards and Testing Materials (com. F-24 on water parks and playgrounds, mem. com. F-8), World Water Parks Assn., Nat. Environ. Health Assn., Nat. Pub. Health Assn., Nat. Eagle Scout Assn. (alumni), Blue Key, Pi Kappa Alpha, Pi Sigma Alpha, Pi Delta Epsilon, U. Mich. Club. State civil litigation, Insurance, Personal injury. Office: 19223 Roscommon Harper Woods MI 48225 Office Fax: 313-245-0812. E-mail: ron@fscip.org, ron@aquaticisf.org, rrgpc@aol.com

GILBERT, STEPHEN ALAN, lawyer, organization executive; b. N.Y.C., Feb. 20, 1939; s. Ben Gilbert and Elsie (Alweiss) G. AB, Cornell U., 1960, JD, 1962. Bar: N.J. 1963, Fla. 1964, N.Y. 1984. From clk. to assoc. Carpenter, Bennett & Morrissey, Newark, 1961-63; assoc. Milton M. and Adrian M. Unger, 1963-67; pres. Preserver Goup, Inc. (formerly Motor Club Am.), Paramus, 1967—. Pres. MCA Ins. Co., 1988-92, Property-Casualty Co. MCA, 1988-93, Motor Club Am. Ins. Co., 1989—, Preserver Ins. Co., 1992—, Am. Colonial Ins. Co., 1999—, Mountain Valley Ind. Co., 2000—; chmn. bd. N.E. Ins. Co., 1999—. Asst. editor Plain Language Law Dictionary, 1979, assoc. editor, 1995. Active Boys and Girls Clubs, Newark, 1970—, pres., 1977-80, 96-97, chmn. bd., 1980-81, 97—; active Newark Mus. Coun., 1975-87, chmn., 1981; active Natural Sci. Solar Ctr., Milford, Pa., 1981-87, v.p., 1982-84; trustee Natural Sci. for Youth Found., 1984-87. Recipient Man and Boy award Boys Clubs, Newark, 1980. Mem. Nat. Assn. Ind. Insurers (bd. govs.). Jewish. General corporate, Insurance. Home: 8909 Francis Pl North Bergen NJ 07047-6001 Office: Preserver Group Inc 95 Rte 17 S Paramus NJ 07653-0931 E-mail: sgilbert@preserver.com

GILBERTSON, DAVID, state supreme court justice; Former judge S.D. Cir. Ct. (5th jud. cir.), Pierre; assoc. justice S.D. Supreme Ct., 1995—. Office: 500 E Capitol Ave Pierre SD 57501-5070

GILBERTSON, JOEL WARREN, lawyer; b. Valley City, N.D., Nov. 9, 1949; s. Roy W. and Gwen D. (Haugen) G.; m. Jan Erikson, June 11, 1972; children: David, Lisa. BA, Concordia Coll., Moorhead, Minn., 1972; JD, U. N.D., 1975. Bar: N.D. 1976, U.S. Dist. Ct. N.D. 1976. Ptnr. Binek & Gilbertson, Bowman, N.D., 1976; atty. N.D. Supreme Ct., Bismarck, 1976-78; exec. dir. N.D. Bar Assn., 1978-81; ptnr. Pearce & Durick, 1981-97; exec. v.p., gen. counsel Ind. Cmty. Banks of N.D., 1997—. Served with U.S. Army N.G., 1972-78. Mem. N.D. Bar Assn. (bd. govs. 1989-95, pres. 1992-93), N.D. Bar Found. (vice chmn. 1982-84, chmn. bd. dirs. 1986-89), South Cen. Dist. Bar Assn. (pres. 1987-89). Republican. Lutheran. Avocations: piano, softball. Federal civil litigation, Insurance, Personal injury. Home: 1025 Crescent Ln Bismarck ND 58501-2463 Office: Ind Comty Banks ND PO Box 6128 Bismarck ND 58506-6128

GILDAN, PHILLIP CLARKE, lawyer; b. West Palm Beach, Fla., July 17, 1959; s. Herbert Leonard and Kathleen (Yeager) G.; m. Laurie Beth Leinwand, Aug. 25,1985; children: Tyler Ross, Jacob Lee. AB magna cum laude, Dartmouth Coll., 1981; JD cum laude, Harvard U., 1984. Bar: Fla. 1984, U.S. Ct. Appeals (11th cir.) 1986, U.S. Supreme Ct. 1989. Assoc. Nason, Gildan, Yeager, Gerson & White, P.A., West Palm Beach, 1984-89, shareholder, 1989-96, Greenberg Traurig PA, West Palm Beach, 1997—. Lectr. Reinventing Govt. Symposium, Hollywood, Fla., 1994, Risk Mgmt. State Conf., Deerfield Beach, Fla., 1995. Contbr. articles to profl. jours. Dir. Com. for Good Govt., Palm Beach, Fla., 1990-94. Mem. Fla. Bar Assn., Palm Beach County Bar Assn., Am. Inns of Ct. LIV (exec. com. 1991-94), Phi Beta Kappa. General civil litigation, General corporate, Public utilities. Office: Greenberg Traurig Hoffman Lipoff Rosen & Quentel PA 777 S Flagler Dr Ste 300 West Palm Beach FL 33401-6161

GILDEA, BRIAN MICHAEL, lawyer; b. New Haven, Nov. 1, 1939; s. Thomas Michael and Lillian Frances (Reilly) G.; m. Lisa Gildea; children: Larysa Albina, Stefan Bohdan. AS, New Haven U., 1964; BA, Providence Coll., 1967; JD, Suffolk U., 1970. Bar: Conn. 1970, U.S. Dist. Ct. Conn. 1971, U.S. Ct. Appeals (2d cir.) 1975, U.S. Ct. Appeals (3d cir.) 1979, U.S. Ct. Appeals (5th cir.) 1984, U.S. Supreme Ct. 1975. Legal adviser City of Boston, 1969-70; assoc. Celentano, Ivey & Gery, New Haven, 1970-73; ptnr. Celentano & Gildea, 1973-74; pvt. practice, 1974—. Bd. dirs. St. Mary's High Sch., New Haven, 1975-77; mem. Bethany (Conn.) Town Charter Commn., 1976; del. U.S./Japan Bilateral Session, 1988, U.S./China Joint Session on Trade and Econ. Law, 1987. With USAF, 1958-62. Recipient Svc. award Providence Coll., New Haven, 1979, Friar award St. Mary's Alumni Assn., 1980. Mem. ABA, Def. Rsch. Inst., Conn. Bar Assn., New Haven County Bar Assn., Am. Lawyers Assn. Democrat. Roman Catholic. Avocations: bicycling, tennis, skiing, photography. Federal civil litigation, Immigration, naturalization, and customs, Insurance. Office: 512 Blake St New Haven CT 06515-1287

GILDEN, RICHARD HENRY, lawyer; b. Waterbury, Conn., May 28, 1946; s. Samuel and Adele (Lipshez) G.; m. Lorraine Ellen Bitner, Aug. 23, 1970; children: Sarah, Andrew. AB, Lafayette Coll., 1968; JD, Cornell U., 1971. Bar: N.Y. 1972, U.S. Dist. Ct. (no. dist.) N.Y. 1972. Assoc. Rosenman & Colin, N.Y.C., 1971-80, ptnr., 1980-86, Gelberg & Abrams, N.Y.C., 1986-87, Fulbright & Jaworski, N.Y.C., 1987-2000, Brobeck, Phleger & Harrison, 2000—. Bd. dirs. Cotswold Assn., 1983-89, Edgemont Community Coun. Inc., 1991-96. Mem. ABA, Assn. of Bar of City of N.Y., N.Y. State Bar Assn. General corporate, Private international, Securities. E-mail: rgilden@brobeck.com

GILES, JACK MICHAEL, lawyer; b. Vancouver, B.C., Can., Feb. 6, 1936; s. Henry George and Alice Maude (Frewen) G.; m. Virginia Cumming Grant; children: J. Graham, David M., E. Peter. B of Commerce, U. B.C., 1956, LLB, 1959. Bar: B.C. 1960, created Queen's Counsel, 1982. Assoc. Farris, Vaughan, Wills & Murphy, Vancouver, 1959-67, ptnr., 1967-73, sr. ptnr., 1973—. Fellow Am. Coll. Trial Lawyers; mem. Can. Bar Assn. (past mem. provincial and nat. councils), Vancouver Bar (past bd. dirs.), Justice Inst. B.C. (past bd. dirs.), Lawyers Inn B.C. (pres. 1981-82). Home: 2665 Point Grey Rd Vancouver BC Canada V6K 1A4 Office: Farris Vaughan Wills & Murphy 2600-700 W Georgia St Vancouver BC Canada V7Y 1B3

GILES, WILLIAM JEFFERSON, III, lawyer; b. Manila, The Philippines, Apr. 10, 1936; came to U.S., 1938; s. William Jefferson and Gardner (Anderson) G.; m. Nancy Gifford Seff, May 9, 1957; children: William Jefferson IV, Gregory Gifford. BS, U. Calif., Berkeley, 1957; postgrad., Golden Gate Coll., 1958-59, Stanford U., 1960; JD, U. S.D., 1961. Bar: Iowa 1961, U.S. Dist. Ct. Iowa 1961, U.S. Ct. Appeals (8th cir.) 1971, U.S. Supreme Ct. 1971, Nebr. 1982, U.S. Ct. Appeals (9th cir.) 1988. Pvt. practice, Sioux City, Iowa, 1961—. Of counsel Whicher & Whicher, Sioux City, 1966-75, Whicher & Hart, Sioux City, 1975-77; lectr. in field. Contbr. articles to profl. jours. Bd. dirs. Sioux City Mus. and Hist. Soc., 1976-79, Sioux City Cmty. Theatre, 1974-76. Capt. USAR, 1957-68. Recipient Gold Seal award Phi Beta Kappa, 1953. Fellow Am. Acad. Matrimonial Lawyers (chmn. bankruptcy com. 1992-99), Internat. Acad. Matrimonial Lawyers; mem. ABA, ATLA, Iowa Bar Assn., Iowa Assn. Trial Lawyers, Comml. Law League Am., Sioux City Country Club, Phi Delta Phi, Phi Phi. Republican. Bankruptcy, Family and matrimonial, Personal injury. Home: 3827 Country Club Blvd Sioux City IA 51104-1327 Office: 322 Frances Bldg 505 5th St Sioux City IA 51101 also: 3940 Hideaway Acres Crofton NE 68730-0088 also: 3 Sloane Gardens London SW1 W8EA England

GILFORD, STEVEN ROSS, lawyer; b. Chgo., Dec. 2, 1952; s. Ronald M. and Adele (Miller) G.; m. Anne Christine Johnson, Jan. 2, 1974; children: Sarah Julia, Zachary Michael, Eliza Rebecca. BA, Dartmouth Coll., 1974; JD, M of Pub. Policy Scis., Duke U., 1978. Bar: Ill. 1978, U.S. Dist. Ct. (no. dist.) Ill. 1978, U.S. Ct. Appeals (7th cir.) 1981, U.S. Ct. Appeals (D.C. cir.) 1984, U.S. Ct. Appeals (5th cir.) 1988, U.S. Dist. Ct. (ea. dist.) Mich. 1995. Assoc. Isham, Lincoln & Beale, Chgo., 1978-85, ptnr., 1985-87, Mayer Brown & Platt, Chgo., 1987—. Adminstrv. law editor Duke Law Jour., 1976-77. Bd. dirs. Evanston (Ill.) YMCA, 1982-92, sec., 1985, vice chmn., 1986-92; participating atty. ACLU, 1983—, bd. dirs. Ill., 1991-96, v.p. devel., 1993-96; bd. dirs. Roger Bawldwin Found., 1993-96; elected mem. bd. edn. dist. 202 Evanston Twp. H.S., 1993—, v.p., 1995-96, pres., 1996-98, mem. joint task force on safety, 1995-96; mem. Met. Family Svcs., Evanston Skokie Valley Cmty. Adv. Bd., 1997; mem., bd. dirs. Met. Family Svcs., 1998—, Legal Aid Soc., 2001—. Mem. ABA, Ill. Bar Assn., Chgo. Bar Assn. General civil litigation, Insurance, Libel. Home: 2728 Harrison St Evanston IL 60201-1216 Office: Mayer Brown & Platt 190 S La Salle St Ste 3100 Chicago IL 60603-3441

GILHOUSEN, BRENT JAMES, lawyer; b. Anacortes, Wash., Sept. 24, 1946; s. Darrell J. and Jean Sarah (Sabatine) G.; m. Sandra M. King, Aug. 13, 1983; 2 children: Lindsay Elizabeth, Shane Shroeder. BA, Wash. State U., 1968; JD, U. Oreg., 1973. Bar: Wash. 1973, U.S. Dist. Ct. (we. dist.) Wash. 1973, U.S. Ct. Appeals (9th cir.) 1973, U.S. Supreme Ct. 1980, Mo. 1981, U.S. Ct. Appeals (4th cir.) 1986. From atty.-advisor to sr. atty. U.S. EPA, Seattle, 1973-80; from environ. atty. to asst. gen. counsel-environ. Monsanto Co., St. Louis, 1980-97; asst. gen. counsel-environ. Solutia Inc., 1997—. Mem. Superfund Settlements Project, Washington, 1988-95, 2001—; legal com. Chem. Industry Inst. Toxicology, Rsch. Triangle Park, N.C., 1986-99; mem. environ. law adv. com. Nat. Chamber Litigation Ctr., Washington, 1992-97. Mem. editl. bd. Hazardous Waste Strategies Update, 1994—. With USAR, 1968-74. Mem. ABA (sect. environ., energy and resources, chair corp. counsel com. 1994-96, vice-chair hazardous waste com. 1991-99), Am. Chem. Coun. (mem. enforcement subgroup 1995—), Def. Rsch. Inst., Forest Hills Country Club, Indian Wells Country Club, Am. Legion. Republican. Avocations: skiing, golf, boating. Administrative and regulatory, Federal civil litigation, Environmental. Home: 1 Peakmont Ln Chesterfield MO 63005-6806 Office: Solutia Inc 575 Maryville Centre Dr Saint Louis MO 63141-5813 E-mail: bjgilh@solutia.com

GILL, E. ANN, lawyer; b. Elyria, Ohio, Aug. 31, 1951; d. Richard Henry and Laura (Beeler) G.; m. Robert William Hempel, Aug. 4, 1973; children: Richard, Peter, Mary. AB, Barnard Coll., 1972; JD, Columbia U., 1976. Bar: N.Y. 1977, U.S. Supreme Ct. 1982. Assoc. Mudge, Rose, Guthrie & Alexander, N.Y.C., 1976-77, Dewey Ballantine L.L.P., N.Y.C., 1977-84, ptnr., 1985—. Mem. ABA, Nat. Assn. Bond Lawyers. General corporate, Finance, Municipal (including bonds). Home: 255 W 90th St New York NY 10024-1109 Office: Dewey Ballantine 1301 Ave Of The Americas New York NY 10019-6022 E-mail: agill@deweyballantine.com

GILL, RICHARD LAWRENCE, lawyer; b. Chgo., Jan. 8, 1946; s. Joseph Richard and Dolores Ann (Powers) G.; m. Mary Helen Walker, July 14, 1990; children: Kyla Marie, Matthew Joseph. BA, Coll. of St. Thomas, St. Paul, 1968; JD, U. Minn., 1971. Bar: Minn. 1971, U.S. Dist. Ct. Minn. 1971, U.S. Supreme Ct. 1979, U.S. Ct. Appeals (8th cir.) 1983, U.S. Ct. Appeals (4th cir.) 1990, Ill. 1992. Spl. asst. atty. gen. State of Minn., St. Paul, 1971-73; assoc. Maun, Hazel, Green, Hayes, Simon & Aretz, 1974-77; ptnr. Gill & Brinkman, 1978-84, Robins, Kaplan, Miller & Ciresi, Mpls., 1984—. Vol. Courage Ctr., Golden Valley, Minn., 1981—; youth football coach Maplewood (Minn.) Athletic Assn., 1978-80; youth basketball coach Orono (Minn.) Athletic Assn., 1999—. Mem. ABA, Minn. Bar Assn., Hennepin County Bar Assn., Ramsey County Bar Assn., Assn. Trial Lawyers Am., Minn. Trial Lawyers Assn., Town and Country Club. Avocations: skiing, tennis, golf. General civil litigation, Patent, Product liability. Office: Robins Kaplan Miller & Ciresi 800 Lasalle Ave Ste 2800 Minneapolis MN 55402-2015 E-mail: rlgill@rkmc.com

GILLECE, JAMES PATRICK, JR. lawyer; b. Annapolis, Md., May 26, 1944; s. James Patrick and Erna Virginia (Barling) G.; m. Jane C. Szczepaniak, Apr. 24, 1971 (div. 1998); children: Jessica K., Jocelyn J., Jillian N., James P. III, Juliette A., John M. Szczepaniak -Gillece; m. Rosa Beza, Feb. 12, 1999. BA, LaSalle U., 1966; JD, U. Notre Dame, 1969. Bar: Md. 1969, U.S. Dist. Ct. Md. 1969, U.S. Ct. Appeals (4th cir.) 1972, U.S. Supreme Ct. 1974, U.S. Ct. Appeals (7th cir.) 1992, U.S. Ct. Appeals (8th and 11th cir.) 1995, U.S. Ct. Appeals (D.C. cir.) 2000. Assoc. Piper & Marbury, Balt., 1969-77, ptnr., 1977-92, dir. poverty law program, 1971-72; ptnr. Miles & Stockbridge, 1992-93; prin. Miles and Stockbridge, 1994-98; ptnr. McGuire, Woods, Battle & Boothe, 1998—. Cons. Mercy Hosp. Dietitians Program, Balt., 1986-95. Bd. dirs. Balt. City Fair, 1984-88, Legal Aid Soc. Balt., 1984, Family Cirsis Ctr. Baltimore County, Inc., 1992-97, Everyman Theatre, 1995—; mem. law adv. coun. U. Notre Dame, 1983-95; mem. Com. to Keep Supreme Bench Judges, Com. for Mayor Kurt Schmoke, 1987, Lawyers Com. for Jerry Brown, 1976; trustee Everyman Theatre, 1996—; mem. fin. com. Mayor Martin O'Malley, 2001—. Mem. ABA, FBA, Am. Judicature Soc. (bd. dirs. 1988-90), Md. State Bar Assn. (Disting. Svc. award), Balt. Bar Assn., Notre Dame Law Assn. (pres. 1983-99, bd. dirs. 1977—, exec. coun., life mem.), U. Notre Dame Law Assocs., Internat. Childbirth Edn. Assn. (cons. 1987-97). Democrat. Roman Catholic. General civil litigation, Criminal, Labor. Home: 3809 Greenway Baltimore MD 21218-1826 Office: McGuire Woods Battle & Boothe 7 Saint Paul St Ste 1000 Baltimore MD 21202-1671 Fax: 410-659-4484. E-mail: jpgillec@mwbb.com

GILLEN, JAMES ROBERT, lawyer, insurance company executive; b. N.Y.C., Nov. 14, 1937; s. James Matthew and Katharine Isabel (Fritz) G.; m. Rita Marie Wahleithner, June 15, 1963 (div. 1992); children: Jennifer Elaine, Nancy Louise, Paula Anne; m. Edda Lya Pacheco, Dec. 10, 1994. AB magna cum laude, Harvard U., 1959, LLB cum laude, 1965. Bar: N.Y. 1966, N.J. 1975. Assoc. firm White & Case, N.Y.C., 1965-72; v.p., assoc. gen. counsel Prudential Ins. Co. Am., Newark, 1972-77, sr. v.p., assoc. gen. counsel, 1977-80, sr. v.p. pub. affairs, 1980-84, sr. v.p., gen. counsel, 1984-98. Mem. bd. trustees Columbia Inst. Investor Project, 1991-97; legal adv. com. New York Stock Exch., 1986-89; mem. adv. bd. Ascertain Solutions Inc., 2001—. Trustee United Way Essex and West Hudson Counties, 1981-90, pres., 1986-88; mem. Mendham Twp. (N.J.) Bd. Edn., 1981-82; trustee N.J. Shakespeare Festival, 1991-99, Mendham Twp. Libr., 1979-82; dir., chmn. Neurol. Inst. N.J., 1998—. Lt. (j.g.) USN, 1959-62. Mem. ABA, N.J. Bar Assn., Assn. Life Ins. Counsel, Harvard Club (N.Y.C.), Morris Country Golf Club. General corporate, Finance, Insurance. Home: 72 Washington Valley Rd Morristown NJ 07960-3332

GILLESPIE, GEORGE JOSEPH, III, lawyer; b. N.Y.C., May 18, 1930; s. George Joseph Jr. and Dorothy Elizabeth (McKenna) G.; m. Eileen Tracy Dealy, July 27, 1955; children: Gail Gillespie Garcia, John D., Myles D., Eileen G. Fahey. A.B. magna cum laude, Georgetown U., 1952; LL.B. magna cum laude, Harvard U., 1955. Bar: N.Y. 1957. Assoc. Cravath, Swaine & Moore, N.Y.C., 1956-62, ptnr., 1963—. Bd. dirs. Washington Post Co., White Mountains Holdings Inc. Trustee, pres., John M. Olin Found.; pres., trustee Pinkerton Found., Arthur Ross Found., William S. Paley Found., Edmond J. Safra Philanthropic Found.; bd. dirs., sec. Mus. TV and Radio; trustee NYU Med. Ctr., chmn. exec. com. Madison Square Boys and Girls Club; bd. dirs., chmn. emeritus Nat. Multiple Sclerosis Soc.; mem. Corp. Jackson Lab.; trustee Convent of The Sacred Heart, Greenwich, Conn., 2001—. Frederick Sheldon traveling fellow Harvard U., 1955-56. Mem. Century Assn., Winged Foot Golf Club, Prouts Neck Country Club, Falmouth Country Club, Double Eagle Club, Am. Yacht Club, Portland Country Club. Republican. Roman Catholic. Office: Cravath Swaine & Moore Worldwide Pla 825 8th Ave Fl 38 New York NY 10019-7475

GILLESPIE, JANE, lawyer; b. Cin., Aug. 18, 1935; d. William Pembroke and Elizabeth (Biermann) G. Student, Vassar Coll., 1953-55; cert. Polit. Sci. U. Strasbourg, France, 1956; BA, Northwestern U., 1958; LLB, Yale U., 1962. Bar: N.Y. 1964, U.S. Dist. Ct. (so. and ea. dists.) N.Y. 1972. with McLanahan, Merritt, Ingraham, N.Y.C., 1964-69, Olwine, Connelly, Chase, O'Donnell & Weyher, N.Y.C., 1969-78; atty. Interpublic Group of Cos., Inc., N.Y.C., 1978— , sec. various advt. agys. including McCann-Erickson, U.S.A., Inc., Muir, Cornelius & Moore, Inc., McCann Direct Inc., The Phillips-Ramsey Co., LUL Software Systems, Inc. Mem. Darien Rep. Town Meeting, Conn., 1980-84, Five Mile River Commn., 1981— . Mem. ABA (subcom. on fed. regulation securities 1969—), Assn. of Bar of City of N.Y., Yale Club (N.Y.C.). Private international, Mergers and acquisitions, Securities. Office: Interpublic Group Cos Inc Ste 383 1271 Avenue Of The Americas Fl 44 New York NY 10020-1459

GILLESSEN, FREDERICK, lawyer; b. Bonn, Germany, Nov. 12, 1967; Degree in law, U. Bonn, 1993, JD, 1999, PhD, 1999. Bar: Regional Ct. Düsseldorf. Rsch. asst. U. Bonn., 1990-97; assoc. Bruckhaus Westrick Heller Löber, Düsseldorf, 1998-2000, Freshfields Brickha+388s Deringer, Düsseldorf, 2000—. Author: European Transnational Mergers and Company Migration in the U.K. and Ireland, 2000. With German Army, 1986-88. Banking, General corporate, Mergers and acquisitions. Office: Freshfields Bruckhaus Deriugo Freiligrathstrasse 1 Düsseldorf D-40479 Germany Office Fax: 49 211 4979103

GILLETTE, W. MICHAEL, state supreme court justice; b. Seattle, Dec. 29, 1941; s. Elton George and Hazel Irene (Hand) G.; m. Susan Dandy Marmaduke, 1989; children: Kevin, Saima, Ali, Quinton. AB cum laude in German, Polit. Sci., Whitman Coll., 1963; LLB, Harvard U., 1966. Bar: Oreg. 1966, U.S. Dist. Ct. Oreg. 1966, U.S. Ct. Appeals (9th cir.) 1966, Samoa 1969, U.S. Supreme Ct. 1970, U.S. Dist. Ct. Vt. 1973. Assoc. Rives & Rogers, Portland, Oreg., 1966-67; dep. dist. atty. Multnomah County, 1967-69; asst. atty. gen. Govt. of Am. Samoa, 1969-71, State of Oreg., Salem, 1971-77; judge Oreg. Ct. Appeals, 1977-86; justice Oreg. Supreme Ct., 1986—. Avocation: officiating basketball.*

GILLIAM, EARL B. federal judge; b. Clovis, N.Mex., Aug. 17, 1931; s. James Earl and Lula Mae G.; m. Rebecca L. Prater; children: Earl Kenneth, Derrick James. B.A., Calif. State U., San Diego, 1953; J.D., Hastings Coll. Law, 1957. Bar: Calif. 1957. Dep. dist. atty. San Diego, 1957-62; judge San Diego Mcpl. Ct., 1963-74, Superior Ct. Calif., San Diego County, 1975-80, U.S. Dist. Ct. (so. dist.) Calif., San Diego, 1980-93, sr. judge, 1993-2001. Head Trial Practice Dept. Western State U. Law Sch., San Diego, 1969—. Recipient Trial Judge of Yr. award San Diego County Trial Lawyers Assn., 1981. Office: US Dist Ct Ste 5195 US Ct House 940 Front St San Diego CA 92101-8994

GILLIAM, JOHN A. lawyer; b. Goldthwaite, Tex., Nov. 3, 1935; s. Ed Burr and Emily Corine (Anderson) G.; m. Sara Ann Swindell, Dec. 26, 1963; children— Joanna, John, Jason. B.A., Baylor U., 1958; LL.B., U. Tex., 1961. Bar: Tex. 1961, U.S. Dist. Ct. (no. dist.) Tex. 1961, U.S. Dist. Ct. (ea. and we. dists.) Tex., U.S. Ct. Appeals (5th, 10th and 11th cirs.) Assoc. then ptnr. Thompson & Knight, Dallas, 1961-74; sr. ptnr. Jenkens & Gilchrist, Dallas, 1975— . Assoc. editor Tex. Law Rev., 1959. Fellow Tex. Bar Found., Am. Coll. Trial Lawyers; mem. Tex. Assn. Def. Counsel (dir.), Dallas Bar Assn. (dir. 1981-85), Order of Coif, Alpha Chi, Phi Delta Phi, Phi Gamma Delta. Baptist. Federal civil litigation, State civil litigation. Home: 4617 Meadowood Rd Dallas TX 75220-2014 Office: Jenkens & Gilchrist 1445 Ross Ave Ste 3200 Dallas TX 75202-2785

GILLIGAN, MARY ANN, law librarian; b. Elizabeth, N.J., June 20, 1956; d. John Francis and Margaret Mary (Boyle) G. BA, Park Coll., 1977; MLS, Rutgers U., 1980. Asst. Time Inc., N.Y.C., 1981-83; law libr. Chubb & Son, Inc., Warren, N.J., 1985, Pennie & Edmonds LLP, N.Y.C., 1985—. Exec. committeewoman Monmouth County Dem. Party, 2000. Mem. ABA, Am. Assn. Law Librs., Spl. Librs. Assn., Law Libr. Assn. Greater N.Y. (bd. dirs. 1998—), Preservation Red Bank, Red Bank Women's Club. Democrat. Roman Catholic. Avocations: crafts, singing. Office: Pennie & Edmonds LLP Ste 1120 1155 Avenue Of The Americas Fl 17 New York NY 10036-2720

GILLILAND, JOHN CAMPBELL, II, lawyer; b. Bellefonte, Pa., June 4, 1945; s. John Campbell and Miriam Ruth (Forsythe) G.; m. Karen Gardner, Nov. 2, 1997; children: Jennifer, John, David. BA, Pa. State U., 1967; JD, Georgetown U., 1971. Bar: Pa. 1971, Ind. 1979, Ky. 1991, Ohio 1992. Ptnr. McQuaide, Blasko & Brown, Inc., State College, Pa., 1974-79, DeFur, Voran, Hanley, Radcliff & Reed, Muncie, Ind., 1979-90; prin. Gilliland & Assocs., Covington, Ky., 1991-2000; sr. counsel Locke Reynolds LLP, Indpls., 2000—01; prin. Gilliland Law Office, 2001—. Lectr. econs. dept. Ball State U., Muncie. Bd. dirs. United Way Delaware County, v.p., 1983-85; bd. dirs. Vis. Nurses Assn.; v.p. Muncie chpt. ARC, 1983-85; bd. govs. Friends of Bracken Libr. Served to capt. U.S. Army, 1971-72. Fellow Rotary Found., Queens Coll., Belfast, Ireland, 1968-69. Mem. ABA, Ind. Bar Assn., Ky. Bar Assn., Ohio Bar Assn., Am. Health Lawyers Assn., Ind. Soc. Hosp. Attys. (chmn. 1989), Pa. Soc. Hosp. Attys. (pres. 1978-79), East Central Ind. Pers. Assn. (bd. dirs.). Republican. Presbyterian. General corporate, Health, Labor. Home: 38 Kathryn Ave Florence KY 41042-1536 Office: 6650 Telecom Dr Ste 100 Indianapolis IN 46278 E-mail: jcg@gilliland.com

GILLILAND, SCOTT ALAN, lawyer; b. Winfield, Ala., Dec. 1, 1970; s. Charles Oman and Sharron Ann G. BS, U. North Ala., 1993; JD, Birmingham (Ala.) U., 1997. Bar: Ala. 1997, U.S. Dist. Ct. (mid. dist.) Ala. 1997, U.S. Dist. Ct. (no. dist.) Ala. 1998, U.S. Ct. of Appeals (11th cir.) 1998. Assoc. Gordon Silberman Wiggins & Childs, Birmingham, 1997—. Mem. ABA, Birmingham Bar Assn., Ala. Trial Lawyers Assn. Democrat. Baptist. Civil rights, Labor. Home: 12201 Kenley Way Birmingham AL 35242 Office: Gordon Silberman Wiggins & Childs 1400 South Trust Tower Birmingham AL 35203

GILLINGHAM, STEPHEN THOMAS, financial planner; b. St. Paul, May 30, 1944; s. Thomas Elmwood and Barbara Alice (Sickles) G.; m. Carolyn Jean Alvey, June 5, 1976; children: Kenneth, Brett. BA, Juniata Coll., 1966; JD, The George Washington U., 1969. Bar: Va. 1971; CFP. Tax specialist Price Waterhouse, Washington, 1969-71; tax law specialist IRS, 1971-77; sr. tax lawyer Internat. Paper Co., N.Y.C., 1977-83; dir. tax rsch. and planning The Singer Co., Stanford, Conn., 1983-88; tax counsel Am. Cyanamid Co., Wayne, N.J., 1988-95; fin. planner The Thompson Group, Inc., White Plains, N.Y., 1995—. Lectr. World Trade Inst., 1980-90. Contbg. editor Tax Lawyer, 1984-88. Trustees coun. Juniata Coll. With U.S. Army, 1970-75. Named one of Outstanding Young Men in Am., Jaycees, 1979. Mem. Va. Bar Assn., N.J. Tax Group (chmn. 1991-95), Tax Execs. Inst., Inst. Cert. Fin. Planners. Avocations: golf, swimming, hiking. Home: 4 Northway Hartsdale NY 10530-2109 Office: The Thompson Group Inc 244 Westchester Ave White Plains NY 10604-2907 E-mail: stgill@cyburban.com

GILLIS, JOAN, legal administrative assistant; b. Dallas, Mar. 10, 1944; d. John Malcolm and Nancy (Pollock) G.; m. Roger H. Sevigny, July 10, 1965 (div. Sept. 1982); children: R. Erik, Lisa M.; m. Allen R. Burrell, June 5, 1993. BA, Mt. St. Mary Coll., 1976; MBA, Rivier Coll., 1984. Admissions officer Mt. St. Mary Coll., N.H., 1976-77; adminstrv. asst. Weight Watchers of N.H., Nashua, 1977-79; sales assoc. Thelma Katz Real Estate, Manchester, N.H., 1979-80; program dir. N.H. Dental Soc., Concord, 1980-81; officer mgr. New Eng. Life, Bedford, N.H., 1981-87; adminstrn. mgr. Wiggin & Nourie, P.A., Manchester, 1987—. Mem. allocations com. United Way, Manchester, 1984-86, 98-99; bd. dirs. YWCA, Manchester, 1983-90, mem. membership com., 1996-97. Mem. Assn. Legal Adminstrs. (pres. 1999, sec. 1997-98). Avocations: bicycling, sewing. Office: Wiggin & Nourie PA 20 Market St Manchester NY 03101

GILLIS, JOHN LAMB, JR. lawyer; b. St. Louis, June 13, 1939; 5. John L. and Carol (Randolph) G.; m. Nichola Mitchell, Aug. 1965; children: John Mitchell, Suzanne Lamb. Student, Brown U.; AB, Washington U., 1965; LLB, Stanford U., 1968. Bar: Mo. 1968. Ptnr., chmn. securities dept. Armstrong Teasdale LLP, St. Louis. Finance, Mergers and acquisitions, Securities. Address: Armstrong Teasdale LLP 1 Metropolitan Sq Saint Louis MO 63102-2733 E-mail: jgillis@armstrongteasdale.com

GILLMORE, KATHLEEN CORY, lawyer; b. Louisville, July 10, 1947; d. Elmer Louis and Frances (Cory) Hoehn; m. David Newton Gillmore, Dec. 14, 1974. Student, U. Mich., 1965-66; B.A., Purdue U., 1969; J.D., Ind. U., 1972. Bar: Ind. 1972, D.C. 1973, Ky. 1979, Tex. 1986. Ptnr., firm E.L. Hoehn, Washington, 1972-78; staff atty. Ashland Oil, Inc., Ky., 1978-82, sr. atty., 1982-85; staff atty., Shell Oil Co., Houston, Tex., 1985-87, sr. environ. atty., 1987-96, sr. environ. counsel, 1996—. Mem. ABA, D.C. Bar Assn., Ind. Bar Assn., Ky. Bar Assn., Tex. Bar Assn., Houston Bar Assn. (bd. dirs. environ. section), Am. Petroleum Inst. (vice chmn. subcomm. on environ. and health law 1995-95, chmn. 1996—). Administrative and regulatory, General corporate, Environmental. Office: Shell Oil Co PO Box 2463 1 Shell Plz Houston TX 77252-2463

GILMAN, RONALD LEE, judge; b. Memphis, Oct. 16, 1942; s. Seymour and Rosalind (Kuzin) G.; m. Betsy Dunn, June 11, 1966; children: Laura M., Sherry I. BS, MIT, 1964; JD cum laude, Harvard U., 1967. Bar: Tenn. 1967, U.S. Supreme Ct. 1971. Mem. Farris, Mathews, Gilman, Branan & Hellen, Memphis, 1967-97; judge U.S. Ct. Appeals (6th cir.), 1997—. Judge Tenn. Ct. of Judiciary, 1979-87; lectr. trial advocacy U. Memphis Law Sch., 1980-97. Contbr. articles to profl. jours. Regional chmn. edn. coun. MIT, 1968-88; bd. dirs. Memphis Jewish Home, 1984-87, Chickasaw coun. Boy Scouts Am., 1993-2000; mem. Leadership Memphis. Recipient Sam A. Myar Jr. Meml. award for outstanding svc. to legal profession and cmty., 1981 Mem. ABA (ho. of dels. 1990-97), Am. Law Inst., Am. Judicature Soc., Am. Coll. Trust and Estate Counsel, Memphis Bar Assn. (pres. 1987), Tenn. Bar Assn. (spkr. ho. of dels. 1985-87, pres. 1990-91), 6th Cir. Jud. Conf. (life), Am. Arbitration Assn. (mem. large, complex case panel 1993-97). Democrat. Jewish. Office: Fed Bldg 167 N Main St Ste 1176 Memphis TN 38103-1824

GILMAN, SHELDON GLENN, lawyer; b. Cleve., July 20, 1943; BBA, Ohio U., 1965; JD, Case Western Res. U., 1967. Bar: Ohio 1967, Ky. 1971, Ind. 1982, Fla. 1984, D.C. 1985, Tenn. 1985, U.S. Supreme Ct. 1987. Assoc./ptnr. Louisville law firms, 1972—; ptnr. Lynch, Cox, Gilman & Mahan, P.S.C., Louisville, 1987—. Gen. counsel Louisville Assn. Life Underwriters, 1977, 78, 90; adj. prof. law U. of Louisville Sch. of Law. Bd. dirs., chmn. Louisville Minority Bus. Resource Ctr., 1975-80; pres. Congregation Adath Jeshurun, 1986-88; bd. dirs., v.p., sec. Louisville Orch., 1982-85; bd. dirs. City of Devondale, Ky., 1976, United Synagogue of Cons. Judaism, N.Y., 1989-98, also pres. Ohio Valley region. With JAGC, AUS, 1968-71. Fellow Am. Coll. Trust and Estate Counsel, Am. Bar Found.; mem. ACLU (bd. dirs. 1998—), Ky. Bar Assn. (ethics com. 1982—, ethics hotline com. 1990), Louisville Employee Benefit Council (pres. 1980). Pension, profit-sharing, and employee benefits, Probate, Corporate taxation. Office: Lynch Cox Gilman & Mahan 400 W Market St Ste 2200 Louisville KY 40202-3354 E-mail: SGilman@lcgandm.com

GILMORE, CARL W. lawyer; b. Phoenixville, Pa., July 23, 1965; BS, U. Ill., 1987; JD, U. Wis., 1994. With Mohr Mangianele Bruce & Gilmore, McHenry, Ill. Author: (book) Deconstructing Leases. Method and Critique of Lease Valuation in Divorce Proceedings, 1997; contbr. articles to law jours. Bd. dirs. Am. Cancer Soc., McHenry County, Ill., 1998. Mem. ABA (editl. bd. Family Advocate Mag. family law sect. 1997—), McHenry County Bar Assn. (sec. 1998-99), Woodstock Morning Rotary Club. Family and matrimonial. Office: Mohr Mangianele Bruce & Gilmore 3402 W Elm St Mchenry IL 60050

GILMORE, JAMES STUART, III, governor; b. Richmond, Va., Oct. 6, 1949; s. James Stuart, Jr. and Margaret Kandle G.; m. Roxane Gilmore; children: Jay, Ashton BA, U. Va., 1971, JD, 1977. Atty. Harris, Tuck, Freasier & Johnson, 1977-80, Benedetti, Gilmore, Warthen & Dalton, 1984-87; commonwealth's atty. Henrico County, Va., 1987-93; atty. gen. Commonwealth of Va., 1993-97; pntr. LeClair Ryan, Richmond, Va., 1997; gov. Commonwealth of Va., 1998—. Alt. del. Rep. Nat. Conv., 1976; chmn. Henrico County Rep. Com., 1982-85. With U.S. Army, 1971-74. Mem. Nat. Dist. Atty. Assn., Va. Bar Assn., Va. Trial Lawyers Assn., Va. Commonwealt Attys. Assn. Methodist. Office: Office of Gov State Capitol Bldg Richmond VA 23219*

GILMORE, VANESSA D. federal judge; b. St. Albans, N.Y., Oct. 26, 1956; BS, Hampton U., 1977; JD, U. Houston, 1981. Bar: Tex. 1982, U.S. Ct. Appeals (5th cir.), U.S. Dist. Ct. (so. dist.) Tex. Fashion buyer Foley's Dept. Store, 1977-79; ptnr. Vickery, Kilbride, Gilmore & Vickery, Houston, 1981-85, 86-94; atty. Sue Schecter & Assocs., 1985-86; judge U.S. Dist. Ct. (So. dist.) Tex., 1994—. Spkr. ATLA, San Diego, 1990, ABA, Atlanta, 1991, N.Y.C., 1993, Leadership Tex., Austin, 1992, Hampton U. Alumni Assn., Dallas, 1992, Laredo Bus. and Profl. Women's Assn., 1993, XI Ann. Border Gov.'s Conf., Monterrey, Mex., 1993, Gov.'s Bus. Devel. Coun., Ausitn, 1993, Tex. A&M U., 1993, State Bar of Tex., Austin, 1993, Houston Bus. Coun., 1993, Minority Enterprise Devel. Week, Houston, 1993, Holman St. Bapt. Ch., 1994, Greater Houston Women's Found., 1994, The Kinkaid Sch., 1995, So. Meth. U., Dallas, 1996, South Tex. Coll. of Law, 1996, among others. Contbr. articles to profl. jours. Bd. dirs. Houston Ballet, Tex. So. Univ. Found., Neighborhood Recovery Community Redevel. Corp., 1992-95; chair African Am. Art Adv. Assn., Mus. Fine Arts; mem. scv. acad. nominations bd. Rep. Jack Fields, Tex., 1993, 94; active Texans for NAFTA; mem. Tex. Dept. Commerce, 1991-94, chairperson, 1992-94; mem. adv. bd. St. Joseph's Hosp.; mem. Leadership Tex. Named One of Houston's Black Achievers, Human Enrichment of Life Program, 1989; recipient Citizen of the Month award Houston Defender, 1990, YWCA award, 1991, Austin Met. Resource Bus. Ctr. award, 1991, Houston Bus. and Profl. Men's Club award, 1992, Disting. Svc. award Nat. Black MBA Assn., 1994, Cmty. Svc. award Holman St. Bapt. Ch., 1994. Mem. ABA, NAACP (chair chs. and orgns. com. Freedom Fund banquets 1989-93), ATLA, Am. Leadership Forum, Tex. Trial Lawyers Assn., Tex. Lyceum Assn., Houston Bar Assn., Houston Lawyers Assn., U. Houston Law Alumni (bd. dirs. 1993—), W.J. Durham Legal Soc., Links, Inc. (Mo. chpt., chair LEAD substance abuse and teen pregnancy prevention program 1990-91). Office: US Courthouse 515 Rusk Ave Rm 9513 Houston TX 77002-2605

GILMORE, WEBB REILLY, lawyer; b. Lake Forest, Ill., Dec. 9, 1944; s. Durward Wilson and Dorothy Angeline (DeField) G.; m. Denise Regina Dever, May 9, 1970; children— Kara Anne, Kimberly Erin, Katharine Reilly. B.S., U.S. Naval Acad., 1966; J.D., U. Mo.-Columbia, 1973. Bar: Mo. 1973. Assoc. firm Stinson Mag & Fizzell, Kansas City, Mo., 1973-77, ptnr., 1977-79; ptnr. firm Gaar & Bell, Kansas City, Mo., 1979-87, Gilmore & Bell (formerly Garr & Bell), Kansas City, Mo., 1987— ; dir. Glasgow Savs. Bank, Mo., 1970— ; dir. Oran State Bank, 1984—. Mem. Mo. Lottery Commn., 1985—. Served with USN, 1966-70. Mem. ABA, Mo. Bar Assn., Nat. Assn. Bond Lawyers. Democrat. Roman Catholic. Municipal (including bonds), Securities. Home: 833 Westover Rd Kansas City MO 64113-1121 Office: Gilmore & Bell 1200 Main St 40th Floor One Kansas City Pl Kansas City MO 64105

GILROY, TRACY ANNE HUNSAKER, lawyer; b. St. Louis, Aug. 13, 1959; d. Raymond Thomas Hunsaker and Dorothy Jayne (Hickman) Hunsaker Reilly. BA, U. Dayton, 1981; JD, St. Louis U., 1984. Bar: Mo. 1984, Ill. 1985. Atty. Mo. State Hwy. and Transp. Dept., St. Louis, 1984-89; of counsel Draheim & Pranschke, 1989-94; pvt. practice The Gilroy Law Firm, 1994—. Mem. ABA (strategic comms. bar svcs. standing com., reporter The Affiliate, bd. dirs. LPM solo divsn.), Mo. Bar Assn. (chair eminent domain com., legis. com., bd. govs. 1998—), St. Louis Bar Found. (pres. 1998-99), St. Louis Met. Bar Assn. (pres. 1997-98, chair young lawyers sect. 1993, chair legis. com. 1985-87, chair, vice-chair, chair trial sect., chair social com., chair auction com., media com.), Woman Lawyers Assn. (mem.-at-large, chair legis. com. 1984-87, sec. 1987), Lawyers Assn., Assn. Trial Lawyers Am. Avocations: golf, skiing, running, writing, painting. Office: Gilroy Law Firm 1610 Des Peres Rd # 300 Saint Louis MO 63131-1813

GILSTER, PETER STUART, lawyer; b. Carbondale, Ill., Dec. 10, 1939; s. John Sprigg and Ruth Gilster; m. Carol Clevenger, June 30, 1968; children: John F., Thomas B. BS, U. Ill., 1962, JD, 1965. Bar: Ill. 1965, Mo. 1968, U.S. Dist. Ct. (ea. dist.) Mo. 1969, U.S. Patent Office 1970, U.S. Ct. Appeals (8th cir.) 1978, U.S. Supreme Ct. 1978, U.S. Ct. Customs and Patent Appeals 1980, U.S. Ct. Appeals (fed. cir.) 1983. Assoc. Koenig, Senniger, Powers & Leavitt, St. Louis, 1967-71, ptnr., 1971-72; patent atty. Monsanto Co., 1972-77; ptnr. Kalish & Gilster, 1977-96, Peper, Martin, Jensen, Michael and Hetlage, St. Louis, 1997-98, Blackwell, Sanders, Peper Martin, LLP, St. Louis, 1998-99; head patent sect. Kalish & Gilster Intellectual Property Group; officer, shareholder Greensfelder, Hemker & Gale, P.C. Intellectual Property Grp., 1999—; sr. patent counsel; chmn. internat. pratice Peper Martin, 1998. Seminar lectr. U. Mo.-St. Louis, 1976-83. Contbr. articles to legal publs. Capt. USAR, 1966-67. Decorated Army Commendation medal. Mem. ABA, IEEE, AAAS, Ill. Bar Assn., Mo. Bar Assn. (patent, trademark, and copyright com.), Lawyer Pilots Bar Assn., Fed. Cir. Bar Assn., Bar Assn. Met. St. Louis (chmn. patent sect. 1975-76), Assoc. Pilots St. Louis (v.p. 1977-83, bd. dirs. 1975-87), World Affairs Coun. St. Louis (bd. dirs. 2000—), Soc. Hispano-Am. St. Louis (bd. dirs. 1993-96, treas. 1994-96), Media Club St. Louis, Phi Delta Phi. Federal civil litigation, Patent, Trademark and copyright. Office: Equitable Bldg Ste 2000 10 S Broadway Saint Louis MO 63102 E-mail: psg@greensfelder.com

GINDIN, WILLIAM HOWARD, judge; b. Perth Amboy, N.J., Sept. 1, 1931; s. Jac Paul and Belle Ruth (Steinberg) G.; m. Jane Hersh, June 24, 1954; children: Thomas L., Suzanne Hinsdale; m. Emily Shimkin, Dec. 25, 1965; children: Geoffrey A. Drucker, Janine Drucker Gordon. AB, Brown U., 1953; JD, Yale U., 1956. Bar: N.J. 1956, U.S. Supreme Ct. 1965, U.S. Ct. Appeals (3d cir.) 1980. Assoc. Gindin & Gindin, Plainfield, N.J., 1956-62, ptnr. Plainfield & Bridgwater, 1962-82; adminstrv. law judge Newark, 1982-85; U.S. bankruptcy judge Trenton, 1985-90, 99—; chief, 1990-98. Adj. prof. Rutgers Camden Law Sch., 1988-93; lectr. Inst. Continuing Legal Edn., Profl. Edn. Systems, Inc.; bd. govs. Nat. Conf. Bankruptcy Judges (3d cir.), 1989-92. Mem. editl. bd. N.J. Bar Assn. Jour., 1962-72. Mem. Plainfield Human Relations Commn., 1965-72, chmn., 1968-72; pres. Temple Sholom, Plainfield, 1979-81; regional v.p. Union Am. Hebrew Congregations, 1983-86; trustee Princeton Jewish Ctr., Jewish Cmty. Found. of Mercer-Bucks; mem. Opera Festival of N.J. Fellow Am. Bar Found., Assn. Fed. Bar (adv. bd.), Bankruptcy Inn of Ct. N.J. (pres. 1995-99); mem. ABA, Plainfield Bar Assn., Union County Bar Assn., Mercer County Bar Assn., N.J. Bar Assn., Am. Judicature Soc., Plainfield Rotary (pres. 1974-75, Paul Harris fellow). Home: 30 James Ct Princeton NJ 08540-2633 Office: US Bankruptcy Ct 402 E State St Trenton NJ 08608-1507

GINGOLD, HARLAN BRUCE, lawyer; b. Syracuse, N.Y., Jan. 3, 1946; s. Eli and Sarle (Greenhouse) G.; m. Diane Port, Dec. 20, 1970; children: Alan R., Brian M., Eric R. BA, Syracuse U., 1967, JD, 1970. Bar: N.Y. 1971, U.S. Dist. Ct. (no. dist.) N.Y. 1971, U.S. Supreme Ct. 1977. Assoc. Primo & Marino, Syracuse, 1971-72, Driscoll, Mathews, Gingold and Cass, Syracuse, 1972-73; ptnr. Gingold & Gingold, 1973-85; ptnr., v.p., sec. Macht, Brenizer & Gingold, P.C., 1985—. Pub. adv. coun. N.Y.S. Ethics Com., 1998—. Bd. visitors Syracuse U. Coll. Law, 1982-84; bd. dirs. Temple Adath Yeshurun, Syracuse, 1984-90, Am. Diabetes Assn., Syracuse, 1989-96, Hiscock Legal Aid Soc., 1998—. Mem. ABA, ATLA, N.Y. State Bar Assn. (ho. dels. 1994-96, 98—, com. on profl. discipline 1999—), N.Y. State Bar Leaders (exec. counsel 1994-2000), Onondaga County Bar Assn. (bd. dirs. 1990-97, past pres., officer 1990-97), N.Y. State Supreme Ct. (appellate div. 4th dept., 5th dist. grievance com. 1995-2001). Avocation: golf. Consumer commercial, Family and matrimonial. Office: Macht Brenizer & Gingold PC State Tower Bldg Ste 510 Syracuse NY 13202-1798

GINGOLD, NEIL MARSHALL, lawyer; b. Syracuse, N.Y., Jan. 3, 1946; s. Eli and Sarle (Greenhouse) G.; m. Susan Lite, Aug. 15, 1970; children—Scott, Jason, Samantha. AB in Polit. Sci., Syracuse U., 1967, JD, 1970. Bar: N.Y. 1971, U.S. Dist. Ct. (no. dist.) N.Y. 1971, U.S. Supreme Ct. 1977, U.S. Dist. Ct. (we. dist.) N.Y. 1988, U.S. Dist. Ct. (ea. dist.) Mich. 1989. Assoc. Michaels & Michaels, Syracuse, 1970-71; asst. atty. gen. N.Y. State Dept. Law, Syracuse, 1971-73; regional atty. N.Y. State Dept. Environ. Conservation, Syracuse, 1973-79; counsel N.Y. State Assembly, Albany, 1980; ptnr. Gingold & Gingold, Syracuse, 1980-82; asst. dist. counsel U.S. SBA, Syracuse, 1982-85; gen. counsel Envirosure Mgmt. Corp., Buffalo, 1985-88; assoc. Pinsky & Skandalis, Syracuse, 1988-92; sr. assoc. Hancock & Estabrook, LLP, Syracuse, 1992—. Co-chmn. fund raising CNY Charities Open, Inc., Syracuse, 1980-85; successively treas., v.p., pres. Jewish Family Service Bur., Inc., Syracuse, 1975-82; bd. dirs. Temple Adath Yeshurun, Syracuse, 1972-76, Syracuse Jewish Fedn., 1975-78, Upstate N.Y. chpt. Am. Diabetes Assn. Syracuse, 1981-85, U.S. Com. for Israel Environment, N.Y.C., 1981-85, Finger Lakes Land Trust, Ithaca, 1997—. Office: Hancock & Estabrook LLP PO Box 4976 Syracuse NY 13221-4976

GINSBERG, ERNEST, lawyer, banker; b. Syracuse, N.Y., Feb. 14, 1931; s. Morris Henry and Mildred Florence (Slive) G.; m. Harriet Gay Scharf, Dec. 20, 1959; children: Alan Justin, Robert Daniel. BA, Syracuse U., 1953, JD, 1955; LLM, Georgetown U., 1963. Bar: N.Y. 1955, U.S. Supreme Ct. 1964. Pvt. practice law, Syracuse, 1957-61; mem. staff, office chief counsel IRS, Washington, 1961-63; tax counsel Comptr. of Currency, 1964-65, assoc. chief counsel, 1965-68; v.p. legal affairs, sec. Republic Nat. Bank N.Y., N.Y.C., 1968-74; sr. v.p. legal affairs, sec. Republic Nat. Bank, 1975-86, exec. v.p., gen. counsel, sec., 1984-86, vice chmn. bd., gen. counsel, 1986-94, vice chmn. bd., 1990-99. Sr. v.p., sec. legal affairs Republic N.Y. Corp., N.Y.C., 1974-84, exec. v.p., gen. counsel, sec., 1984-86, vice chmn. bd., gen. counsel, sec., 1986-94, vice chmn. bd., 1986-99, also bd. dirs.; bd. visitors Syracuse U. Coll. Law. Chmn. emeritus Roundabout Theatre Co., N.Y.C. With U.S. Army, 1955-57. Mem. Am. Bankers Assn. (bd. dirs. 1995-97), Am. Bankers Coun. (co-chmn. 1992-94), N.Y. State Bankers Assn. (pres. 1993-94), Bankers Roundtable (bd. dirs. 1995-97), Phi Sigma Delta, Phi Delta Phi. Administrative and regulatory, Banking, General corporate.

GINSBERG, EUGENE STANLEY, lawyer, arbitrator, mediator; b. Bklyn., Dec. 11, 1929; m. Barbara A. Proskauer, May 31, 1953 (dec.); children: Debra, Mara; m. Estelle Strauss, June 29, 1980; stepchildren: William, Robert, Steven. BBA, CCNY, 1951; JD, NYU, 1954. Bar: N.Y. 1955, U.S. Dist. Ct. (ea. and so. dists.) N.Y. 1957, U.S. Ct. Appeals (2d cir.) 1966, U. S. Supreme Ct. 1966. Ptnr. Krainin & Ginsberg, N.Y.C., 1958-62; sole practice Bklyn. and Mineola, N.Y., 1962-70; ptnr. Jaspan, Ginsberg, Schlesinger, Silverman & Hoffman, Garden City, 1970-96; pvt. practice, 1996—. Arbitrator Nassau County Dist. Ct., 1980— ; mem. nat. panel arbitrators Am. Arbitration Assn., 1966—, nat. labor panel, 1991—; arbitrator BBB, 1982-86, among others. With U.S. Army, 1953-55. Fellow N.Y. Bar Found., Coll. of Labor and Employment Lawyers; mem. ABA (co-chmn. subcom. on profl. responsibility in labor arbitration 1977-83, subcom. on publ. of labor arbitration awards 1984-86, historian 1994—, ADR in labor and employment law com., formerly labor arbitration and law of collective bargaining agreements com., 1975—), N.Y. State Bar Assn. (ADR com. co-chmn. 2001-, exec. com. 1996-, labor and employment law sect.), Nassau County Bar Assn. (dir. 1997-2000, chmn. 1993-95, labor and employment law com. 1973—, ADR com. 1973—, chmn. 1985-87, grievance com. 1983-88). Alternative dispute resolution, Labor. Home: 67 Hilton Ave Apt D26 Garden City NY 11530-2811 Office: 300 Garden City Plz Garden City NY 11530-3302 E-mail: esginsberg@aol.com

GINSBERG, MARC DAVID, lawyer; b. Chgo., Aug. 14, 1951; s. Marshall Leonard and Gloria Barbara (Goldfus) G.; m. Janice Diane Gordon, Jan. 23, 1977; 1 child, Brian. B.A. with honors, U. Ill., 1972; M.A., Ind. U., 1975; J.D. with highest distinction, John Marshall Law Sch., 1977. Bar: Ill. 1977, U.S. Dist. Ct. (no. dist.) Ill. 1977, U.S. Ct. Appeals (7th cir.) 1977, U.S. Supreme Ct. 1981. Law clk. to presiding justice Ill. Appellate Ct., Chgo., 1977-79; assoc. Tenney & Bentley, Chgo., 1979-83, Rooks, Pitts & Poust, Chgo., 1984— . Lead articles editor John Marshall Jour., 1976-77. Contbr. articles to profl. jours., chpts. to book. Recipient Hornbook award, West Pub. Co., 1977. Mem. ABA, Ill. State Bar Assn., Chgo. Bar Assn., Appellate Lawyers Assn. Ill., Am. Judicature Soc. Federal civil litigation, State civil litigation.

GINSBERG, PHILLIP H(ENRY), lawyer; b. N.Y.C., May 1, 1939; s. Benedict and Adele Harriett (Wall) G.; children: Elizabeth Clare Ginsberg-Lytle, Raphael Trapido Ginsberg-Lytle. AB, Princeton U., 1961; LLB, Harvard U., 1964. Bar: Ill. 1964, U.S. Dist. Ct. (no. dist.) Ill. 1964, Wash. 1970, U.S. Dist. Ct. (we. dist.) Wash. 1970, U.S. Dist. Ct. (ea. dist.) Wash. 1972, U.S. Ct. Appeals (7th cir.) 1967, U.S. Ct. Appeals (9th cir.) 1971. Assoc. Ross, Hardies & O'Keefe, Chgo., 1964-68; asst. prof. law U. Chgo., 1968-70; chief atty. Seattle King County Defender Assn., Seattle, 1970-74, dir., 1974-76; prin. Skellenger Ginsberg & Bender, Seattle, 1976-86; ptnr. Ginsberg & Stanich, Seattle, 1986—. Author books and articles in field. Mem. com. on appellate reorgn. Wash. Supreme Ct., 1976, com. on pattern jury instrns., 1974-78; mem. King County Adv. Com. for Indigent Def., 1984. Democrat. Jewish. Federal civil litigation, State civil litigation, Contracts commercial. Home: 6034 Lake Shore Dr S Seattle WA 98118-3038

GINSBURG, CHARLES DAVID, lawyer; b. N.Y.C., Apr. 20, 1912; s. Nathan and Rae (Lewis) G.; m. Marianne Laïs; children by previous marriage: Jonathan, Susan, Mark. AB, W.Va. U., 1932; LLB, Harvard U., 1935. Bar: W. Va. 1935, U.S. Supreme Ct. 1940, D.C. 1946, U.S. Ct. Appeals (2d, 3rd, 4th, 7th, and Fed. cirs.) 1946, U.S. Claims Ct. 1960, U.S. Tax Ct. 1961. Atty. for public utilities div. and office of gen. counsel SEC, 1935-39; law sec. to Justice William O. Douglas, 1939; asst. to commr. SEC, 1939-40; legal adviser Price Stblzn. Div., Nat. Def. Adv. Com., 1940-41; gen. counsel Office Price Adminstrn. and Civilian Supply, 1941-42, OPA, 1942-43; pvt. practice law Ginsburg, Feldman and Bress, Washington, 1946-98; founding ptnr. Ginsburg, Feldman & Bress, 1946-98; sr. counsel, firm Powell, Goldstein, Frazer & Murphy, LLP, 1998; adminstrv. asst. to Senator M.M. Neely, W.Va., 1950; adj. prof. internat. law Georgetown U. (Grad. Sch. Law), 1959-67. Dep. commr. U.S. del. Austrian Treaty Commn., Vienna, 1947; adviser U.S. del. Council Fgn. Ministers, London, 1947; Mem. Presdl. Emergency Bd. 166 (Airlines), 1966; mem. Pres.'s Commn. on Postal Orgn., 1967; chmn. Presdl. Emergency Bd. 169 (Railroads), 1969; exec. dir. Nat. Adv. Commn. Civil Disorders, 1967 Author: The Future of German Reparations; Contbr. to legal jours. Bd. mem., chmn. exec. com. Nat. Symphony Orch. Assn., 1960-69; bd. govs. Weizmann Inst., 1965 (hon. fellow 1972); mem. vis. com. Harvard-Mass. Inst. Tech. Joint Ctr. on Urban Studies, 1969; trustee St. John's Coll., 1969-76, chmn. bd., 1974-76; overseers com. Kennedy Sch. Govt. Harvard, 1971—; mem. coun. Nat. Harvard Law Sch. Assn., 1972—, gen. counsel Dem. Nat. Com., 1968-70. Served from pvt. to capt. AUS, 1942-46; dep. dir. econs. div. Office Mil. Govt., 1945-46, Germany. Decorated Bronze Star, Legion of Merit; recipient Presdl. Cert. of Merit. Mem. ABA, Fed. Bar Assn, Am. Law Inst., Coun. on Fgn. Rels., Met. Club, Army and Navy Club, Phi Beta Kappa. Democrat. Administrative and regulatory, Federal civil litigation, General corporate. Home: 619 S Lee St Alexandria VA 22314-3819 Office: 1001 Pennsylvania Ave NW Washington DC 20004-2505 E-mail: DGinsbur@PGMF.com

GINSBURG, DOUGLAS HOWARD, federal judge, educator; b. Chgo., May 25, 1946; s. Maurice and Katherine (Goodmont) G.; m. Claudia De Secundy, May 31, 1968 (div. Sept. 1980); 1 child, Jessica DeSecundy; m. Hallee Perkins Morgan, May 9, 1981; children: Hallee Katherine Morgan, Hannah Maurice Morgan. Diploma, Latin Sch. Chgo., 1963; BS, Cornell U., 1970; JD, U. Chgo., 1973. Bar: Ill. 1973, Mass. 1982, U.S. Supreme Ct. 1984, U.S. Ct. Appeals (9th cir.) 1986. Assoc. Covington & Burling, Washington, 1972; law clk. U.S. Ct. Appeals, 1973-74, U.S. Supreme Ct., Washington, 1974-75; prof. Harvard U., 1975-83; dep. asst. atty. gen. for regulatory affairs antitrust divsn U.S. Dept. Justice, Washington, 1983-84, asst. atty. gen. antitrust divsn., 1985-86; adminstr. for info. and regulatory affairs Exec. Office Pres., Office Mgmt. and Budget, 1984-85; judge U.S. Ct. Appeals (D.C. cir.), 1986—, chief judge. Vis. prof. law Columbia U., N.Y.C., 1987-88; lectr. law Harvard U., Cambridge, Mass., 1987-91; disting. prof. law George Mason U., Arlington, Va., 1988—; Charles J. Merriam vis. scholar, sr. lectr. U. Chgo., 1990—. Author: Regulation of Broadcasting: Law and Policy Towards Radio, Television and Cable Communications, 1979, Antitrust, Uncertainty, and Technological Innovation, 1980; co-author: Regulation of the Electronic Mass Media, 1991; editor: (with W. Abernathy) Government, Technology and the Future of the Automobile, 1980; contbr. articles to profl. jours. Mecham scholar U. Chgo. Law Sch., 1970-73; recipient Casper Platt award U. Chgo. Law Sch., 1972 Mem. ABA (jud. rep. sect. coun. 2000-2003), Am. Econ. Assn., Am. Law and Econs. Assn., Mont Pelerin Soc., Order of Coif, Phi Kappa Phi. Avocations: historic preservation, antiques, fox hunting. Office: US Ct Appeals 333 Constitution Ave NW Washington DC 20001-2866*

GINSBURG, MARTIN DAVID, lawyer, educator; b. N.Y.C., June 10, 1932; s. Morris and Evelyn (Bayer) G.; m. Ruth Bader, June 23, 1954; children: Jane, James. AB, Cornell U., 1953; JD, Harvard U., 1958; LLD (hon.), Lewis and Clark Coll., 1992, Wheaton Coll., 1997. Bar: N.Y. 1959, D.C. 1980. Practiced in N.Y.C., 1959-79; mem. firm Weil, Gotshal & Manges, N.Y.C., 1963-79; of counsel firm Fried, Frank, Harris, Shriver and Jacobson, Washington, 1980—; Charles Keller Beekman prof. law Columbia U. Law Sch., N.Y.C., 1979-80; prof. law Georgetown U. Law Center, Washington, 1980—; lectr. U. Leiden, The Netherlands, 1982; lectr. Salzburg Seminar Austria, 1984; mem. tax div. adv. group Dept. Justice, 1980-81; mem. adv. group to Commr. Internal Revenue, 1978-80; mem. adv. bd. U. Calif. Securities Regulation Inst., 1973-91. Adj. prof. law NYU, 1967-79; vis. prof. law Stanford (Calif.) U., 1978, Harvard U., Cambridge, Mass., 1986, U. Chgo., 1990, NYU, 1993; cons. joint com. on taxation U.S. Congress, 1979-80, acad. advisor, 2000-01; chmn. tax adv. bd. Commerce Clearing House, 1982-94; mem. bd. advisors NYU/IRS Continuing Profl. Edn. Program, 1983-88, co-chmn., 1986-88; sub coun. on capital allocation, co-chmn. taxation expert group Competitiveness Policy Coun., 1993-95; chmn. tax adv. bd. Little, Brown, 1994-96; bd. dirs. Millennium Chems., Inc., Chgo. Classical Rec. Found.; lectr. various tax insts. Co-author, editor: Tax Consequences of Investments, 1969; co-author: Mergers, Acquisitions, Buyouts, 2001; contbr. articles to legal jours. Mem. vis. com. Harvard Law Sch., 1994-98. 1st lt., arty. U.S. Army, 1954-56. Chair in taxation named in his honor, Georgetown U. Law Ctr., 1986; recipient Marshall-Wythe Medallion, Coll. of William and Mary Sch. Law, 1996, Outstanding achievemnt award Tax Soc. of NYU, 1993, Viccenial medal Georgetown U., 2000. Fellow Am. Coll. Tax Counsel, Am. Bar Found. (bd. dirs.); mem. Am. Law Inst. (cons. Fed. Income Tax Project 1974-93), N.Y. State Bar Assn. (mem. tax sect. exec. com. 1969—, chmn. tax sect. 1975, ho. of dels. 1976-77), Assn. Bar City N.Y. (chmn. com. taxation 1977-79, mem. audit com. 1980-81), ABA (mem. com. corp. taxation, tax sect. 1973—, chmn. com. simplification 1979-81, mem. tax sect. coun. 1984-87), Am. Bar Found. (bd. dirs.). Office: 600 New Jersey Ave NW Washington DC 20001-2022 E-mail: martin_ginsburg@ffhsj.com

GINSBURG, RUTH BADER, United States supreme court justice; b. Bklyn., Mar. 15, 1933; d. Nathan and Celia (Amster) Bader; m. Martin David Ginsburg, June 23, 1954; children: Jane Carol, James Steven. AB, Cornell U., 1954; postgrad., Harvard Law Sch., 1956-58; LLB Kent scholar, Columbia Law Sch., 1959; LLD (hon.), Lund (Sweden) U., 1969, Am. U., 1981, Vt. Law Sch., 1984, Georgetown U., 1985, DePaul U., 1985, Bklyn. Law Sch., 1987, Amherst Coll., 1991, Rutgers U., 1991, Lewis and Clark Coll., 1992, Radcliffe Coll., 1994, NYU, 1994, Columbia U., 1994, Smith Coll., 1994, L.I. U., 1994, U. Ill., 1995, Brandeis U., 1996, Wheaton Coll., 1997, Jewish Theol. Sem. of Am., 1997, George Washington U. Law Sch., 1997; DHL (hon.), Hebrew Union Coll., 1988. Bar: N.Y. 1959, D.C. 1975, U.S. Supreme Ct. 1967. Law sec. to judge U.S. Dist. Ct. (so. dist.) N.Y., 1959-61; rsch. assoc. Columbia Law Sch., N.Y.C., 1961-62, assoc. dir. project internat. procedure, 1962-63; asst. prof. Rutgers U. Sch. Law, Newark, 1963-66, assoc. prof., 1966-69, prof., 1969-72, Columbia U. Sch. Law, N.Y.C., 1972-80; U.S. Cir. judge U.S. Ct. Appeals, D.C. Cir., Washington, 1980-93; assoc. justice U.S. Supreme Ct., 1993—. Phi Beta Kappa vis. scholar, 1973-74; fellow Ctr. for Advanced Study in Behavioral Scis., Stanford, Calif., 1977-78; lectr. Aspen (Colo.) Inst., 1990, Salzburg Seminar, Austria, 1984; gen. counsel ACLU, 1973-80, bd. dirs., 1974-80. Author: (with Anders Bruzelius) Civil Procedure in Sweden, 1965; Swedish Code ofJudicial Procedure, 1968; (with others) Sex-Based Discrimination, 1974, supplement, 1978; contbr. numerous articles to books and jours. Fellow Am. Bar Found.; mem. AAAS, Am. Law Inst. (coun. mem. 1978-93), Coun. Fgn. Rels. Office: US Supreme Ct One First St NE Washington DC 20543*

GIOFFRE, BRUNO JOSEPH, lawyer; b. June 27, 1934; s. Anthony B. and Louise (Giorno) G.; m. Kathleen M. Bartlik, Nov. 14, 1959; children: Kathleen, Lisa, Michael, Christopher, B. Scott, David, Kerry. BA, Cornell U., 1956, JD, 1958. Bar: N.Y. 1958, U.S. Dist. Ct. (so. dist.) N.Y. 1973. Prin., sr. mem. Gioffre & Gioffre, P.C., Purchase, N.Y., 1958-99, counsel, 2000—. Justice Town of Rye (N.Y.), 1965-99. Chmn. bd. dirs. Sound Fed. Savs. & Loan Assn.; trustee United Hosp.; counsel Port Chester Pub. Library. Mem. ABA, N.Y. Bar Assn., N.Y. Magistrate's Assn., Westchester County Magistrate's Assn., Westchester Bar Assn., Port Chester-Rye Bar Assn., Elks, KC. Probate, Real property. Home and Office: 2900 Westchester Ave Purchase NY 10577-2552

GIOFFRE BAIRD, LISA ANN, lawyer; b. Port Chester, N.Y., Oct. 19, 1961; d. Bruno Joseph and Kathleen (Bartlik) Gioffre; m. Wayne Robert Baird, Oct. 15, 1989. BA, Villanova U., 1983; JD, Pace U., 1987. Bar: Conn. 1987, N.Y. 1988. Assoc. Gioffre & Gioffre P.C., Port Chester, 1987—. Advisor Port Chester Youth Ct., 1989—. Mem. ABA, N.Y. State Bar Assn., Port Chester Bar Assn. (sec. 1990—), Westchester County Bar Assn., Columbian Lawyers Assn., Conn. State Bar Assn. Republican. Roman Catholic. Avocations: reading, sports, travel. General practice, Probate, Real property. Home: 19 W Bank Ln Stamford CT 06902-1309 Office: Gioffre & Gioffre PC 220 Westchester Ave Port Chester NY 10573-4557

GIOIELLA, RUSSELL MICHAEL, lawyer; b. Camden, N.J., Mar. 10, 1954; s. Michael S. and Mildred (Leonardo) G.; m. Nerissa M. Radell, June 28, 1980; 1 child, Natalya. BA summa cum laude, Cath. U., 1976; JD, NYU, 1979, MA, 1980. Bar: N.Y. 1980, U.S. Dist. Ct. (so. and ea. dists.) N.Y. 1980, U.S. Ct. Appeals (2nd and 3rd cirs.) 1980, U.S. Dist. Ct. (no. dist.) N.Y. 1982, U.S. Supreme Ct. 1984. Assoc. Litman, Kaufman and Asche, N.Y.C., 1979-84; ptnr. Litman, Kaufman, Asche and Lupkin, 1985, Litman, Asche, Lupkin & Gioiella, N.Y.C., 1986-93, Litman, Asche, Lupkin, Gioiella & Bassin, N.Y.C., 1994-96, Litman, Asche & Gioiella LLP, N.Y.C., 1996—. Mem. First Jud. Dept. Assigned Counsel Screening Panel, 1998—. Mem. steering com. N.Y. State Coalition to Abolish the Death Penalty, 1992. Mem. ABA, NACDL, Assn. of Bar of City of N.Y. (mem. com. on product liability 1988-91, mem. criminal cts. com. 1992-94), N.Y. Criminal Bar Assn. (pres. 1997-98), N.Y. State Assn. Criminal Def. Lawyers (pres. 2001), Phi Beta Kappa. Democrat. Avocations: fatherhood, music, biking, wine, Russian literature. General civil litigation, Criminal, Personal injury. Office: Litman Asche & Gioiella 45 Broadway New York NY 10006-3007

GIORDANO, LAWRENCE FRANCIS, lawyer; b. Buffalo, Feb. 17, 1953; s. Anthony Jerome and Martha Ann (Taylor) G.; m. Elaine Kristie Thomas, May 29, 1976; children: Bradley Thomas, Evan Taylor. BS with highest honors in Psychology, Denison U., 1975; JD, Georgetown U., 1978. Bar: Tenn. 1978, U.S. Dist. Ct. (ea. dist.) Tenn. 1979, U.S. Ct. Appeals (6th cir.) 1980, U.S. Supreme Ct. 1983. Assoc. Stone & Hinds, P.C., Knoxville, Tenn., 1978-81, ptnr., 1981-88, Thomforde & Giordano, P.C., Knoxville, 1988-90, McCampbell & Young, P.C., Knoxville, 1990-91, London, Amburn & Giordano, Knoxville, 1991-92, Susano, Sheppeard & Giordano, Knoxville, 1993-94; spl. counsel Lewis, King, Krieg, Waldrop & Catron, P.C., 1994-97, shareholder, 1997—. Spl. judge Knox County Gen. Sessions Ct., 1988—; adminstrv. law judge State of Tenn. Dept. Edn., 1994-96; adj. prof. U. Tenn. Coll. Law, 1993—; instr. Knoxville Police Acad., 1989. Mem. exec. bd. Knoxville Metro Soccer League, 1980-85; mem. community network Knox County Youth Alcohol Hwy. Safety Project, Knoxville, 1987-90. Nat. Merit scholar, 1971-75, Kenneth I. Brown scholar, 1974. Mem. ABA, Tenn. Bar Assn. (Law Through Liberty award, 2000), Knoxville Bar Assn. (bd. govs. 1986-92, treas. 1986-90, sec. 1991-92), Def. Rsch. Inst., Am. Inns of Ct. (master of the bench 1991—, pres. 1994-95), Sertoma (v.p. chpt. 1987-89, pres. 1989-90), Phi Beta Kappa, Omicron Delta Kappa. Democrat. Roman Catholic. Avocations: soccer, gardening, reading, theater. General civil litigation, Criminal, General practice. Home: 1822 Nantasket Rd Knoxville TN 37922-5769 Office: Lewis King Krieg Waldrop & Catron PC 620 Market St Fl 5 Knoxville TN 37902-2231

GIPPIN, ROBERT MALCOLM, lawyer; b. Cleve., Feb. 3, 1948; s. Morris and Helena (Weil) G.; children: Sarah, Joshua, Rebecca, Alanna; m. Susan Smith. AB, Dartmouth Coll., 1969; JD, Harvard U., 1973. Bar: Ohio 1973. Asst. to dir. Ohio Dept. Commerce, Columbus, 1973; exec. sec. Ohio Real Estate Commn., 1974-75; pros. Mcpl. Ct., Cuyahoga Falls, Ohio, 1975; ptnr. Thompson, Hine, Cleve. Active exec. com. Summit County Dem. Party, Akron, 1975, Planned Parenthood; pres. Summit County Coun., 1982-84, Project Learn, 1997—. Mem. Akron Bar Assn., Ohio Bar Assn., Phi Beta Kappa. Jewish. Avocations: reading, tennis, cooking. Administrative and regulatory, General civil litigation, Environmental. Home: 929 Eaton Ave Akron OH 44303-1311 Office: Thompson Hine 3900 Key Ctr Cleveland OH 44114 E-mail: robert.gippin@thompsonhine.com

GIPSON, ROBERT EDGAR, lawyer; b. Boise, Idaho, Aug. 31, 1946; s. Tracy Greer and Marjorie (Lynch) G.; m. Penelope Helen Brandt, Aug. 20, 1966; children— Christopher, Jonathan, Elliot. A.B., Harvard U., 1967; J.D., Yale U., 1973. Bar: Calif. 1973. Assoc., Irell & Manella, Los Angeles, 1973-75, Armstrong Hendler & Hirsch, Los Angeles, 1975-82; ptnr. Gipson Hoffman & Pancione, Los Angeles, 1982— ; trustee Sundance Film Inst., Salt Lake City, 1981-84. Mng. editor Yale Law Jour., 1972-73. Served to 1st lt. U.S. Army, 1968-71, Thailand. Mem. ABA. Democrat. Methodist. Club: Century City. Lodge: Rotary. General corporate, Corporate taxation, Personal income taxation. Home: 656 Westholme Ave Los Angeles CA 90024-3248 Office: Gipson Hoffman & Pancione Bldg 1100 1901 Avenue of the Stars Los Angeles CA 90067-6002

GIPSTEIN, MILTON FIVENSON, lawyer, psychiatrist; b. Schenectady, N.Y., Aug. 31, 1951; s. Milton and Evelyn G.; m. Carol Grace Gipstein, July 21, 1974; children: Steven Mark, Richard Seth. BA, Columbia U., 1972; MD, SUNY, Syracuse, 1976; JD, U. N.C., 1981. Bar: Mass., 1982; diplomate Am. Bd. Psychiatry and Neurology. Resident psychiat. U. N.C., Chapel Hill, 1976-79; practice medicine specializing in psychiat. Dept. Corrections N.C., Raleigh, 1979-81; med. dir. Brockton (Mass.) Dist. Ct. Clinic, 1981-86, Bridgewater (Mass.) St. Hosp., 1986-87, Charter Hosp. of Aurora, Colo., 1988-97; med. dir. of forensic svcs. Columbine Psychiatric Hosp., Littleton, 1991-98; med. dir. forensic psychiatry divsn. Marvin Foote Youth Detention Facility, Englewood, 1997-2000; med. dir. forensic svcs. Ctrl. Region N.C. Dept. Correction, 2000—. Cons. med.-legal N.C. Legal Aid Soc., Raleigh, 1976-81, forensic Mass. Treatment Ctr. Sexually Dangerous, Bridgewater, 1981-88, psychiat. La. Gov.'s Task Force Mental Health, Baton Rouge, 1982, Jefferson Ctr. Mental Health, 1996-2000; med.-legal cons. Med. Evaluators, Inc., Denver, 1991-2000, SAFE HOUSE adolescent residential treatment ctr., Denver, 1997-2000; legal counsel indigent clients mental health Com. Pub. Counsel Svcs., Boston, 1982-88; lectr. mental health legal advisors com. Law and Mental Health for Mass. Supreme Ct., Boston, 1982-88. Cons. Pub. Health Adv. Com. Town of

Sharon, Mass., 1983-88, Mental Health Legal Advisors Com. Mass. Supreme Ct., Boston, 1985-88; v.p. cmty. affairs Heights Elem. Sch. PTA, Sharon, 1983-88; adv. com. gifted and talented Cherry Creek H.S., 1992-97, Campus Middle Sch., 1993-96. Mem. ABA, Mass. Bar Assn., Am. Profl. Practice Assn. Avocation: boating, antique documents, swimming.

GIRARD, NETTABELL, lawyer; b. Pocatello, Idaho, Feb. 24, 1938; d. George and Arranetta (Bell) Girard Student, Idaho State U., 1957-58; BS, U. Wyo., 1959, JD, 1961. Bar: Wyo. 1961, D.C. 1969, U.S. Supreme Ct. 1969. Practiced in, Riverton, 1963-69; atty.-adviser on gen. counsel's staff HUD; assigned Office Interstate Land Sales Registration, Washington, 1969-70; sect. chief interstate land sales Office Gen. Counsel, 1970-73; ptnr. Larson & Larson, Riverton, 1973-85; pvt. practice, 1985—. Guest lectr. at high schs.; condr. seminar on law for layman Riverton br. A.A.U.W., 1965; condr. course on women and law; lectr. equal rights, job discrimination, land use planning. Editor Wyoming Clubwoman, 1966-68; bd. editors Wyo. Law Jour., 1959-61; writer Obiter Dictum column Women Lawyers Jour., Dear Legal Advisor column Solutions for Seniors, 1988-94; featured in Riverton Ranger, 1994; also articles in legal jours. Chmn. fund dr. Wind River chpt. ARC, 1965; chmn. Citizens Com. for Better Hosp. Improvement, 1965; chmn. subcom. on polit. legal rights and responsibilities Gov.'s Commn. on Status Women, 1965-69, mem. adv. com., 1973-93; rep. Nat. Conf. G ovs. Commn., Washington, 1966; local chmn. Law Day, 1966, 67, county chmn. Law Day, 1994, 95, 96, 97; mem. state bd. Wyo. Girl Scouts USA, sec. 1974-89, mem. nat. bd., 1978-81; state vol. adv. Nat. Found., March of Dimes, 1967-69; legal counsel Wyo. Women's Conf., 1977; gov. apptd. State Wyo. Indsl. Siting Coun., 1995—. Recipient Spl. Achievement award HUD, 1972, Disting. Leadership award Girl Scouts U.S.A., 1973, Franklin D. Roosevelt award Wyo. chpt. March of Dimes, 1985, Thanks Badge award Girl Scout Coun., 1987, Women Helping Women award in recognition of effective advancement status of women Riverton Club of Soroptimist Internat., 1990, Spl. award plaque in appreciation and recognition of 27 yrs. of svc. to State of Wyo., Wyo. Commn. for Women, 1964-92, Appreciation award Wyo. Sr. Citizens and Solutions for Srs., 1994, Arts in Action Pierrot award for outstanding musician, 1998. Mem. AAUW (br. pres.), Wyo. Bar Assn., Fremont County Bar Assn. (Spl. Recognition cert. 1997), D.C. Bar Assn., Women's Bar Assn. D.C., Internat. Fedn. Women Lawyers, Am. Judicature Soc., Assn. Trial Lawyers Am., Wyo. Trial Lawyers Assn., Nat. Assn. Women Lawyers (del. Wyo., nat. sec. 1969-70, v.p. 1970-71, pres. 1972-73), Wyo. Fedn. Women's Clubs (state editor, pres.-elect 1968-69, treas. 1974-76), Prog. Women's Club (pres.-elect. 1994-95), Riverton Chautauqua Club (pres. 1965-67, 2000-01), Riverton Civic League (pres. 1987-89), Kappa Delta, Delta Kappa Gamma (state chpt. hon.). Bankruptcy, Contracts commercial, General practice. Home: PO Box 687 Riverton WY 82501-0687 Office: 513 E Main St Riverton WY 82501-4440

GIRARD, ROBERT DAVID, lawyer; b. Pitts., Aug. 2, 1946; s. Oscar L. and Ruth (Alpern) G. AB, UCLA, 1967; LLB, Yale U., 1970. Bar: Calif. 1971, U.S. Dist. Ct. (cen. dist.) Calif. 1971. Ptnr. Musick, Peeler & Garrett, L.A., 1970-85, Girard, Ellingsen, Christensen & West, L.A., 1985-88, Jones, Day, Reavis & Pogue, L.A., 1988-92, Musick Peeler & Garrett, L.A., 1992-98; with Sonnenschein Nath & Rosenthal, 1998—. Bd. dirs. Calif. Pediatric Ctr., L.A., 1980—, chmn., 1998—. Mem. ABA, L.A. County Bar Assn., Am. Acad. Hosp. Attys., Nat. Health Lawyers Assn., Calif. Health Care Lawyers Assn. (bd. dirs. 1982-85), Jonathan, Phi Beta Kappa. Administrative and regulatory, General corporate, Health. Office: Sonnenschein Nath & Rosenthal 601 S Figueroa St Ste 1500 Los Angeles CA 90017-5720

GIRARD-DICARLO, DAVID FRANKLIN, lawyer; b. Bryn Mawr, Pa., Jan. 20, 1943; s. John J. Girard-DiCarlo and Elizabeth (Patton) Ward; m. Constance Jean Bricker, Apr. 5, 1973. BS, St. Joseph's U., 1970; JD, Villanova U., 1973. Bar: U.S. Dist. Ct. (ea. dist.) Pa. 1973, Pa. 1973, U.S. Ct. Appeals (3d cir.) 1973, U.S. Supreme Ct. 1978. Assoc., Wolf, Block, Schorr & Solis-Cohen, Phila., 1973-74; assoc. Dilworth, Paxson, Kalish, Levy & Kauffman, Phila., 1974-78, ptnr., 1979; ptnr. Fell, Spalding, Goff & Rubin, Phila., 1979-82; ptnr. Blank, Rome, Comisky & McCauley, Phila., 1982— , chmn. labor and employment law sect., 1982-86, adminstrv. ptnr., 1986-87, mng. ptnr., 1987—; mem. hearing com. Disciplinary Bd. of Supreme Ct. of Pa., Phila., 1981-84, chmn. hearing com., 1984-87; faculty mem. Workshop on Urban Mass Transp., Practicing Law Inst., San Francisco and Washington, 1978; bd. dirs. Midlantic Corp.; trustee Phila. Belt Line R.R. Co., 1992—; lectr. in field. Editor-in-chief Villanova Law Rev., 1972, Transit Law Rev., 1977-81; contbr. articles to legal jours. Mem. Phila. Cmty. Leadership Seminar Program, 1978-79; chmn. bd. Southeastern Pa. Transp. Authority, 1979-82; mem. transp. taxation task force Tax Commn. of Commonwealth of Pa., 1981-82; chmn. N.E. Corridor Commuter Rail Authorities Com., 1981-83; mem. Pa. Rep. State Fin. Com., 1982— ; bd. dirs. Greater Phila. Partnership, 1981-83, Urban Affairs Partnership, 1983-85, Hermitage Homeowners Assn., 1982-86; mem. World Affairs Coun., Phila., bd. dirs., 1993—; trustee Walnut St. Theatre, 1986-93, Harcum Jr. Coll., 1987-92, Drexel U., 1988-92, Phila. Acad. Music and Phila. Orch., 1988-95, mem. exec. com., 1988-95, vice chmn., 1991-94; mem. sch. of law bd. of consultors Villanova U., 1992—; chmn. transition team Pa. Gov. Elect Tom Ridge, 1994; bd. mgrs. The Phila. Found., 1994—; trustee St. Joseph's U., 1994—. Fellow Am. Bar Found.; mem. ABA, Pa. Bar Assn., Phila. Bar Assn., Am. Pub. Transit Assn. (bd. dirs. 1979-82, chmn. bd. dirs. 1982, chmn. legis. com. 1980-81, mem. exec. com. 1980-82, v.p. govt. affairs 1981-82, mem. various coms.), Greater Phila. C. of C. (bd. dirs., sec., mem. exec. com. 1990—). Episcopalian. Clubs: Union League of Phila., Vesper (Phila.), Waynesborough Country (Paoli, Pa.), Pyramid Club (Phila., bd. dirs. 1992—), Stonewall Golf Club, The Boulders (Carefree, Ariz.). General corporate, General practice, Labor. Office: Blank Rome Comisky & McCauley 4 Penn Ctr Fl 10-13 Philadelphia PA 19103-2808

GIRARDS, JAMES EDWARD, lawyer; b. Manhasset, N.Y., Aug. 16, 1963; s. H.V. and Barbara (Davis) G.; m. Julie Ann Calame, June 27, 1987; children: Jessica Lauren, James Edward. BS, Baylor U., 1986; JD, St. Mary's Law Sch., 1989. Bar: Tex. 1989, U.S. Dist. Ct. (no., so. and ea. dists.) Tex. 1991, U.S. Ct. Appeals (5th cir.) 2000. Assoc. Law Offices Windle Turley, P.C., Dallas, 1989-94; prin. Tracy & Girards, 1994-97, The Girards Law Firm, Dallas, 1997—. Contbr. articles to profl. jours. Recipient Am. Jurisprudence Contracts award AmJur Pub. Co., 1986. Mem. ABA, ATLA (pres.'s club 1999), Tex. Trial Lawyers Assn. (dir. 1999—), Dallas Trial Lawyers Assn. (dir. 1998—), Dallas Bar Assn., Dallas Assn. Young Lawyers, State Bar Tex., Coll. of State Bar of Tex., Am. Mensa, Ltd., Million Dollar Advocates Forum. Personal injury. Office: La Sierra Bldg 5445 La Sierra Dr Ste 250 Dallas TX 75231-4153

GIRBAU, MIGUEL ANGEL, lawyer; b. Lima, Peru, Jan. 21, 1956; s. Miguel Girbau and Delia Flores. Grad., U. Nat. Mayor San Marcos, Lima, Peru, 1979. Atty. Min. Trabajo Promocion Social, Lima, Peru, 1980-84, Petroleos del Peru, Lima, 1984-94, Estudio Barreda Mollr, Lima, 1996—. Atty. Mut. Peru, Lima, 1995-96. Mem. Indsl. Property Assn., Peruvian Labor Law Assn., Lawyer's Orgn. Lima. General practice, Intellectual property, Personal injury. Office: Estudio Barreda Moller Av Angamos Oeste 1200 Lima 18 Peru Fax: 511-441-1916. E-mail: mail@barreda.com.pe

GIRDWOOD, GRAHAM WILLIAM, lawyer; b. London; s. Robert William and Caroline G. BA in Law, U. Stellenbosch, South Africa, 1991, LLB, 1993; LLM cum laude, U. Cape Town, South Africa, 1994; H.Dip.Arbitration Assn. Arbitration South Africa. Dir. Cliffe Dekker Fuller Moore, Inc., Johannesburg, South Africa, 1999—. Contbr. articles to profl. jours. Fellow Assn. Arbitrators. Bankruptcy, General civil litigation, Product liability. Home: Unit 41 Athol Village 115 Dennis Rd Johannesburg 2196 South Africa Office: Cliffe Dekkar Fuller Moore Private Bag X7 Johannesburg 2010 South Africa Fax: 27 11 290 7300. E-mail: girdwood@cdfm.co.za

GIRVIN, JAMES EDWARD, lawyer; b. Albany, N.Y., Dec. 7, 1955; s. James Joseph and Joan (Haggerty) G.; m. Theresa Kelly, Dec. 12, 1981; children: James P., Kevin P., Kelly M. BA in Polit. Sci. cum laude, Siena Coll., Loudonville, N.Y., 1978; JD, Albany Law Sch., 1981. Bar: N.Y., Mass., U.S. Dist. Ct. (no. dist.) N.Y., U.S. Ct. Appeals (2d cir.), U.S. Supreme Ct., U.S. Ct. Mil. Appeals. From assoc. to profl. O'Connell and Aronowitz, PC, Albany, 1986-91; ptnr. Ruberti, Girvin & Ferlazzo, PC, 1991—. Instr. bus. law McKendrie Coll., Radcliffe, Ky., 1993. Author: Interview/Selection Procedures for Shared Decision Making Teams and Advisory Committees, 1995. Counsel, Albany Sports Found., 1995—; bd. dirs. St. Catherine's Home for Children, Albany, 1996—. Capt. U.S. Army, 1982-85. Recipient VIP award Capital Dist. Ctr. for the Disabled, 1994. Mem. N.Y. State Bar Assn., Albany County Bar Assn., KC, Siena Coll. Alumni Assn. (trustee scholarship com. 1996—). Education and schools, Labor, Municipal (including bonds). Home: 2723 Doellner Cir Castleton On Hudson NY 12033-9752 Office: Ruberti Girvin & Ferlazzo 120 State St Albany NY 12207-1606

GITLITZ, STUART HAL, lawyer; b. Bklyn., Sept. 22, 1951; s. Jerome I. and Ruth (Moskowitz) G.; m. Marilyn June Mittentag, Apr. 28, 1979; children: Gina Ilyse, Keith Vance. BA, SUNY-Binghamton, 1972; JD, U. Miami, 1975. Bar: Fla. 1976, D.C. 1975, U.S. Dist. Ct. (D.C.) 1976, N.Y. 1977, U.S. Supreme Ct. 1979, U.S. Dist. Ct. (so. dist.) Fla. 1979, U.S. Ct. Appeals (5th cir.) 1979, U.S. Ct. Appeals (D.C.) 1976, U.S. Ct. Appeals (11th cir.) 1983, U.S. Ct. Mil. Appeals 1984, U.S. Dist. Ct. (mid dist.) Fla. 1984. Asst. pub. defender Office Pub. Defender for 11th Jud. Cir., Miami, Fla., 1977-80; ptnr. Gitlitz & Keegan, Miami, 1980-81, Gitlitz, Keegan & Dittmar, P.A., Miami, 1981-87, Sheppard Faber, P.A., Coral Gables, Fla., 1987-89, Faber & Gitlitz, P.A., Coral Gables, 1989—. Prettyman fellow Georgetown U. Law Ctr., Washington, 1975-77. Mem. Mortgage Bankers Assn. Am., Mortgage Bankers Assn. Fla., Mortgage Bnkers Assn. Greater Miami, Atty.'s Title Ins. Fund Inc. Democrat. Jewish. Bankruptcy, Consumer commercial, Real property. Office: Faber & Gitlitz PA 1570 Madruga Ave Ste 300 Miami FL 33146-3013

GITTER, MAX, lawyer; b. Samarkand, Uzbekistan, Nov. 17, 1943; came to U.S., 1950; s. Wolf and Paula (Nissenbaum) G.; m. Elisabeth Karla Gesmer, June 22, 1969; children: Emily F., Michael A. AB, Harvard U., 1965; LLB, Yale U., 1968. Bar: N.Y., D.C., U.S. Dist. Ct. (so. and ea. dists.) N.Y., U.S. Ct. Appeals (2d, D.C., 4th and 9th cirs.), U.S. Supreme Ct. Instr. U. Chgo. Law Sch., 1968-69; assoc. Paul, Weiss, Rifkind, Wharton & Garrison, N.Y.C., 1969-76, ptnr., 1976-99, Cleary, Gottlieb, Steen & Hamilton, N.Y.C., 1999—. Vis. lectr. law Yale U., 1986-88; mem. Internat. Steering Com. on Free Trade with Israel; vice-chmn., Yivo Inst. for Jewish Rsch. Spl. counsel Mayor of N.Y.C. to Investigate Office of Chief Medical Examiner, 1985. Mem. Fed. Bar Coun., Assn. Bar City of N.Y. (vice chmn. com. on profl. and jud. ethics 1985-86), Am. Law Inst. (spkr., panelist 1985-89), Practicing Law Inst. (spkr., panelist 1983-92), N.Y. State Bar Assn. (exec. com. sect. on comml. and fed. litigation 1994—). Federal civil litigation, State civil litigation. Office: Cleary Gottlieb Steen & Hamilton Rm 200 One Liberty Plz Ste 4300 New York NY 10006-1470 E-mail: mgitter@cgsh.com

GIUFFRÉ, JOHN JOSEPH, lawyer; b. Bklyn., Nov. 30, 1963; s. John B. and Marilyn N. G.; m. Lauren P. Dippel, Sept. 1, 1990; children: John Paul, Danielle Emily. BA, Columbia Coll., 1984; JD cum laude, U. Pa., 1987. Bar: N.J. 1987, N.Y. 1988, Conn. 1988, Pa. 1988, U.S. Dist. Ct. (so. and ea. dists.) N.Y. 1989. Assoc. labor and employment law sect. Morgan, Lewis & Bockius, N.Y.C., 1987-88; assoc. McLaughlin & McLaughlin, Bklyn., 1988-93; founding ptnr. Giuffré & Kaplan, PC, Hicksville, N.Y., 1994—. Editor: U. Pa. Jour. Comparative Bus. and Capital Market Law, 1985-86; sr. editor: U. Pa. Jour. Internat. Bus. Law, 1986-87. Vol. lawyer Bklyn. Bar Assn. Vol. Lawyer Project, 1992-93; trustee 1st Presbyn. Ch., Flushing, N.Y., 1991-92, pres. bd. trustees, 1993, elder, 1996—; bd. dirs. Flushing Christian Sch., 1994—. Mem. Nassau County Bar Assn., Phi Beta Kappa. Avocations: reading, studying history, teaching Sunday school. General civil litigation, Personal injury, Probate. Office: Giuffré & Kaplan PC 28 E Old Country Rd Hicksville NY 11801-4207

GIUSTI, WILLIAM ROGER, lawyer; b. N.Y.C., Oct. 27, 1947; s. John Eletto and Rita Marie (Lucarini) G.; m. Ingrid Gerke, Dec. 12, 1980. AB, Columbia Coll., 1969; postgrad., Oxford U., 1969-71; JD, Yale U., 1974. Bar: N.Y. 1975. Law clk. to judge U.S. Ct. Appeals (2d cir.), N.Y.C., 1974-75; assoc. Cravath, Swaine & Moore, 1975-80, Shearman & Sterling, N.Y.C., 1980-82, ptnr., 1983—. Roman Catholic. Club: Yale (N.Y.C.). Contracts commercial, Finance, Oil, gas, and mineral. E-mail: wgiusti@shearman.com

GIVAN, RICHARD MARTIN, retired state supreme court justice; b. Indpls., June 7, 1921; s. Clinton Hodel and Glee (Bowen) G.; m. Pauline Marie Haggart, Feb. 28, 1945; children: Madalyn Givan Hesson, Sandra Givan Chenoweth, Patricia Givan Smith, Elizabeth Givan Whipple. LL.B., Ind. U., 1951. Bar: Ind. 1952. Ptnr. with Clinton H. Givan, 1952-59, Bowen, Myers, Northam & Givan, 1960-69; justice Ind. Supreme Ct., 1969-74, chief justice, 1974-87, assoc. justice, 1987-95; ret.; dep. pub. defender Ind., 1952-53; dep. atty. gen., 1953-54; dep. pros. atty. Marion County, 1965-66; ret., 1995. Mem. Ind. Ho. Reps., 1967-68 Served to 2d lt. USAAF, 1942-45. Mem. Ind. Bar Assn., Indpls. Bar Assn., Ind. Soc. Chgo., Newcomen Soc. N.Am., Internat. Arabian Horse Assn. (past dir., chmn. ethical practices rev. bd.), Ind. Arabian Horse Club (pres. 1971-72), Indpls. 500 Oldtimers Club, Lions, Sigma Delta Kappa. Mem. Soc. of Friends. Home: 6690 S County Road 1025 E Indianapolis IN 46231-2495

GIVHAN, ROBERT MARCUS, lawyer; b. Mineral Wells, Tex., May 10, 1959; s. Walter Houston Givhan and Marion Blackwell Callen Stothart; m. Janet Lee Dothard, May 6, 1989; children: Vivian Lee, Charlotte Ann, Virginia Mae. BA, U. Ala., Tuscaloosa, 1981; JD, Cumberland Sch. Law, Birmingham, Ala., 1986. Bar: Ala. 1987, D.C. 1989, U.S. Supreme Ct. 1989, U.S. Ct. Appeals (D.C. and 11th cirs.), U.S. Dist. Ct. (so., mid. and no. dists.) Ala. 1987. Assoc. Perry and Russell, Montgomery, Ala., 1987-88; dep. dist. atty. 15th Jud. Cir. of Ala., 1988-91; dep. atty. gen. Office of Atty. Gen. of Ala., 1991-95; ptnr. Johnston Barton Proctor & Powell LLP, Birmingham, 1995—. Fellow Am. Coll. Pros. Attys.; mem. ABA (vice chmn. antitrust competition and trade regulation com. of adminstrv. law sect. 1994-00), Ala. State Bar Assn., Birmingham Bar Assn. (co-chmn. econs. of law practice com. 1998, 99), Am. Health Lawyers Assn. Episcopalian. Avocations: whitewater rafting, hiking, music collecting, book collecting. Antitrust, General civil litigation, Health. Home: 427 Cliff Pl Birmingham AL 35209-5201 Office: 2900 AmSouth/Harbert Plz 1901 6th Ave N Birmingham AL 35203-2618 E-mail: rmg@jbpp.com

GIZA, DAVID ALAN, lawyer; b. Chgo., May 16, 1958; s. Bruno Frank and Marianne Theresa (Mozdren) G.; m. Karen Ann Van Maldegiam, Nov. 5, 1988. BS, DePaul U., 1981; JD, John Marshall U., 1984. Bar: Ill. 1985, U.S. Dist. Ct. (no. dist.) Ill. 1985. Atty. pvt. practice, Chgo., 1985-86; assoc. Larry Karchmar, Ltd., 1986-87, Kovitz, Shifrin & Waitzman, Chgo., 1987; atty. W.W. Grainger, Inc., Skokie, Ill., 1987-91, Lincolnshire, 1991—, divsn. atty., 1993-96, sr. atty., 1996-98, asst. gen. counsel, 1998—. Trustee Village of Libertyville, Ill., 1995—; chmn. Camp Lake (Wis.)/Ctr. Lake Rehab. Dist., 1990—. Mem. Am. Trial Lawyers Assn., Am. Corp. Counsel Assn., Ill. State Bar Assn., Chgo. Bar Assn., Lake County Bar Assn. Republican. Roman Catholic. Avocations: politics, water sports, reading, travel, cooking. General civil litigation, Contracts commercial, General corporate. Office: W W Grainger Inc 100 Grainger Pkwy Lake Forest IL 60045-5201 Fax: 847-535-9243. E-mail: giza.d@grainger.com

GJERTSEN, O. GERARD, lawyer; b. Bklyn., June 24, 1932; s. Ole Gerhard and Hilma (Jorgensen) G.; m. Carol Ann Jurkops, June 2, 1962; children: Gerard, Gary, Krista, Karen. BA, Columbia Coll., 1954; JD, NYU, 1958. Bar: N.Y. 1958, U.S. Dist. Ct. (so. dist.) N.Y. 1960. Ptnr. Thacher Proffitt & Wood, N.Y.C., 1964—. Vice chmn. Tuckahoe (N.Y.) Urban Renewal Agy. With U.S. Army, 1954-55. Mem. ABA, N.Y. State Bar Assn., Assn. of Bar of City of N.Y., Westchester County Bar Assn., White Plains Bar Assn., Scarsdale Golf Club. Avocations: music, sports. Estate planning, Real property. Home: 262 Dante Ave Tuckahoe NY 10707-3015 Office: Thacher Proffitt & Wood 50 Main St White Plains NY 10606-1934

GLADDEN, JAMES WALTER, JR. lawyer; b. Pitts., Feb. 23, 1940; s. James Walter and Cynthia Unice (Hales) G.; m. Patricia T. Kuehn, Aug. 21, 1993; children: James, Thomas, Robert. AB, DePauw U., 1961; JD, Harvard U., 1964. Bar: Ill. 1964, U.S. Sup. Ct. 1978. Ptnr. Mayer, Brown & Platt, Chgo., 1964—. Mem. ABA. Federal civil litigation, Environmental, Labor. Home: 2212 Lincoln St Evanston IL 60201-2202 Office: Mayer Brown & Platt 190 S La Salle St Ste 3900 Chicago IL 60603-3441 E-mail: jgladden@mayerbrown.com

GLADDEN, JOSEPH RHEA, JR. lawyer; b. Atlanta, Oct. 5, 1942; s. Joseph Rhea Sr. and Frances (Baker) G.; m. Sarah Elizabeth Bynum, Aug. 21, 1965; children: Joseph III, Elizabeth. AB, Emory U., 1964; LLB, U. Va., 1967. Bar: Ga. 1968, U.S. Dist. Ct. (no. dist.) Ga. 1968, U.S. Ct. Appeals (5th cir.) 1968, U.S. Ct. Appeals (11th cir.) 1985. Assoc. King & Spalding, Atlanta, 1967-73, ptnr., 1973-85; v.p., sr. staff counsel The Coca-Cola Co., 1985-87, v.p. dep. gen. counsel, 1987-90, v.p., gen. counsel, 1990-91, sr. v.p., gen. counsel, 1991—. Bd. dirs. Coca-Cola Enterprises, Emory Healthcarere; chmn. bd. dirs. Wesley Woods Ctr. of Emory U., Inc., Coca-Cola Amatil. Chmn. bd. trustees Agnes Scott Coll..; bd. dirs. Atlanta Ballet; trustee Lovett Sch., Acad. Search Cons. Svc. Mem. ABA (com. corp. law gen. counsel), Am Corp. Counsel Assn., Ga. Bar Assn., State Bar Ga., Assn. Gen. Counsel, Atlanta Bar Assn., Commerce Club, Piedmont Driving Club. Antitrust, Federal civil litigation, General corporate. Office: The Coca-Cola Co PO Box 1734 Atlanta GA 30301-1734 E-mail: sjgladden@mindspring.com

GLANSTEIN, JOEL CHARLES, lawyer; b. Jersey City, May 16, 1940; s. Harry I. and Katherine G.; m. Eleanor Elovich, July 2, 1966; children: David Michael, Stacey Alison. BA with honors, Lehigh U., 1962; LLB, NYU, 1965, LLM in Labor Law, 1969. Bar: N.Y. 1967, D.C. 1975, U. S. Ct. Appeals (2d cir.) 1970, U.S. Supreme Ct. 1971, U.S. Ct. Appeals (1st cir.) 1972, U.S. Ct. Appeals (3d cir.) 1978, U.S. Ct. Appeals (11th and 9th cirs.) 1981, U.S. Ct. Appeals (5th cir.) 1982, U.S. Ct. Appeals (6th cir.) 1984, U.S. Ct. Appeals (7th cir.) 1999. Assoc. Pressman & Scribner, N.Y.C., 1968-69; ptnr. Scribner, Glanstein & Klein, 1970-72, Markowitz & Glanstein, N.Y.C., 1972-79, O'Donnell & Schwartz, N.Y.C., 1980-90, O'Donnell, Schwartz, Glanstein & Rosen, N.Y.C., 1991-99, O'Donnell, Schwartz, Glanstein, Rosen et al, LLP, N.Y.C., 1999-2001, O'Donnell, Schwartz & Glanstein, N.Y.C., 2001—. Adj. assoc. prof. N.Y. Law Sch., N.Y.C., 1980-95. Fellow Coll. of Labor and Employment Lawyers, Inc.; mem. ABA (labor and employment law sect., com. on internat. labor law 1976, com. on law of alternative dispute resolution 1976), N.Y. State Bar Assn. (labor and employment law sect., chmn. 1987-88), N.Y. County Lawyers Assn., D.C. Bar Assn., Maritime Law Assn. U.S., Downtown Athletic Club. Admiralty, Labor, Pension, profit-sharing, and employee benefits. Office: O'Donnell Schwartz & Glanstein 305 Madison Ave Rm 1022 New York NY 10165-0100

GLANTZ, WENDY NEWMAN, lawyer; b. L.I., N.Y., Dec. 16, 1956; d. Sidney and Sarah (Rudnitsky) Newman; m. Ronald Paul Glantz, Dec. 29, 1983. BS, SUNY, Stonybrook, 1978; JD, Nova Law Ctr., 1982. Bar: Fla., 1983. Assoc. Glazer & Glazer, Hallandale, Fla., 1983-85; ptnr. Pasin & Glantz, Lauderhill, 1985-86, Glantz & Glantz, Plantation and Miami, 1986—. Seminar leader Marital Strategies, Ft. Lauderdale, 1985—. Editor Pipeline, 1985-86; contbr. articles to profl. mags. Co-chairperson, editor Parents Anonymous, 1986—, mem. adv. bd.; chairperson Bus. Profl. Group of Sunrise Jewish Ctr., 1988—; sponsor Jewish Community Ctr., mem. fund raising com.; mem. South Fla. Symphony, Women of Fine Arts. Mem. ABA (family law sect.), NAFE (pres. S.E. chpt. 1985—), Fla. Bar Assn. (family law sect.), Assn. Trial Lawyers Am., Broward County Bar Assn. (program coord. continuing legal edn. family law sect.), West Broward Bar Assn. (pres. 1989-90), Fla. Assn. Women Lawyers (bd. dirs.), Broward County Women Lawyers Assn. (pres. 1988-90), Nat. Assn. Women Bus. Owners (Broward chpt.), Plantation C. of C. Family and matrimonial. Office: Glantz & Glantz 7951 SW 6th St Ste 200 Fort Lauderdale FL 33324-3223

GLASER, ARTHUR HENRY, lawyer; b. Jersey City, May 1, 1947; s. Ned C. and Lorraine I. (Neil) G.; m. Waynelia Potter, Mar. 19, 1994; children: Kimberly N., Kevin M., Daniel J. BS, Hampden-Sydney Coll., 1968; JD, U. Va., 1973. Bar: Ga. 1973, U.S. Dist. Ct. (no. and mid. dists.) Ga., U.S. Ct. Appeals (11th cir.). Assoc. Swift, Currie, McGhee & Hiers, Atlanta, 1973-78, ptnr., 1978-83, Drew, Eckl & Farnham, Atlanta, 1983-98, Self, Glaser & Davis, LLP, Atlanta, 1999—. Mem. ABA, Ga. Bar Assn., Atlanta Bar Assn. Presbyterian. Insurance, Libel, Personal injury. Home: 1540 Burnt Hickory Rd NW Marietta GA 30064-1308 Office: Self Glaser & Davis LLP Ste 1650 400 Interstate North Pkwy SE Atlanta GA 30339-5029 E-mail: ahg@sgdlaw.com

GLASER, STEVEN JAY, lawyer; b. Tacoma, Dec. 5, 1957; s. Ernest Stanley and Janice Fern (Stone) G.; 1 child, Jacob Andrew. Student, Oxford (Eng.) U., 1979; BSBA, Georgetown U., 1980; JD, John Marshall Law Sch., 1983. ABar: Ill. 1983, Ariz. 1984, U.S. Dist. Ct. Ariz. 1984, U.S. Ct. Appeals (9th and D.C. cirs.) 1984. Law clk. to judge Maricopa County Superior Ct., Phoenix, 1983-84; asst. atty. gen. State of Ariz., 1984-85; staff atty. Ariz. Corp. Commn., 1985-90; sr. atty. regulatory affairs Tucson Electric Power Co., 1990-92, mgr. legal dept., 1992-94, mgr. contracts and wholesale mktg., 1994, v.p. wholesale/retail pricing and system planning, 1994—; v.p. Energy Svcs., 1996-00, sr. v.p., COO, 2000—. Mem. Tucson C. of C. Mem. ABA, Ariz. Bar Assn., Ill. Bar Assn., Pima County Bar Assn., So. Ariz. Water Resources Assn. (bd. dirs. 1991-93), Tucson Parks Found., Georgetown U. Alumni Assn., Phi Delta Phi. Republican. Jewish. Avocations: golf, tennis. Administrative and regulatory, General corporate, Public utilities. Office: Tucson Electric Power Co PO Box 711 1 South Church Tucson AZ 85701-1093

GLASGOW, NORMAN MILTON, lawyer; b. Washington, Aug. 14, 1922; children: Norman M., Heather Glasgow Harris, Glenn. BS, U. Md., 1943; LLB, JD, BA, George Washington U., 1949. Bar: D.C. 1949, U. Supreme Ct. 1956, Md. 1960. Assoc. Wilkes, McGarraghy & Artis, Washington, 1949-55; ptnr. Wilkes & Artis, 1955-82; pres. Wilkes, Artis, Hedrick & Lane, 1982-86, sr. prin., 1988-2000; ptnr. Holland & Knight, LLP, 2001—. Bd. dirs., gen. counsel Greater Washington Bd. Trade, 1966, 87, 88; mem., chmn. Md. PAC, 1981-93; bd. govs. Washington Bldg. Congress; mem. Citizens Tech. Adv. Com. for Drafting Bldg. Code and Zoning Regulations, Washington, Commrs. Citizens Adv. Com. on Zoning, Washington, Balt. conv. Ctr. Authority Transp. Revenue Com., Gov.'s Salary Commn., Gov.'s Spl. Com. Vehicle Emissions Inspection Program, Gov.'s Adv. Redistricting Com.; chmn. Gov.'s Task Force Statewide Bldg. Performance Stds., Md. Stadium Authority, 1993-97, Md. Econ. Growth, Resource Protection and Planning Commn., co-chair subcom. for updating state planning and zoning laws, 1993-97; chmn. Md. Econ. Growth Task Force; mem. Gov.'s Western Md. Econ. Devel. Strategies Task Force, 1998—, co-chair Updating Md. Zoning and Planning Regulations (Article 66B). 1st lt. U.S. Army, 1942-46, ETO. Recipient Outstanding Alumni award George Washington U., 1985, Outstanding Svc. award D.C. Real Estate, Greater Washington Bd. Trade, 1978, named Convenor Class of 1949 50th Reunion. Mem. Supreme Ct. Bar Assn., D.C. Bar Assn., Md. Bar Assn., Urban Land Inst., Am. Soc. Planning Ofcls., Washington Bldg. Congress, Nat. Assn. Bus. Economists, Nat. Conf. States in Bldg. Codes and Stds., Lambda Alpha. Avocation: gardening. Land use and zoning (including planning), Real property. Home: 9012 Brickyard Rd Potomac MD 20854-1634 Office: Holland & Knight 2099 Penn Ave NW Washington DC 20006-2803

GLASGOW, ROBERT EFROM, lawyer; b. Portland, Oreg., Nov. 13, 1944; s. Joseph and Lee (Friedman) G.; m. Lesley G. Veltman, June 16, 1968; children: Jordan Robert, Emily Samantha. BA, George Washington U., 1966, JD, 1969. Bar: Oreg. 1969. Assoc. Dusenbery, Martin, Beatty, Bischoff & Templeton, Portland, 1969-72; ptnr. Martin, Bischoff, Templeton & Biggs, 1973-76, Glasgow & Kelly, Portland, 1977-79, Glasgow & Kelly, PC, 1980-85, pres., 1982-85, Glasgow & Wight, PC, 1985-92; of counsel Black Helterline LLP, Portland, 1992—. Trustee Multnomah County Legal Aid Svc., 1974-76, chmn., 1976; trustee Jewish Family and Child Svc., 1972-77, treas., 1976; trustee Jewish Cmty. Ctr., 1975-76, 86—, v.p., 1987—; trustee Mittlemann Jewish Cmty. Ctr., 1975-76, 86-97, pres., 1991-93; trustee Oreg. Legal Svcs. Corp., 1980-82, Am. Jewish Com., Oreg., 1996—, treas., 1998-99, v.p., 1999-2000, pres., 2000—; activities coun. Oreg. Art Inst., 1984-87; Dem. precinctman, 1986-87. Mem. ABA, Oreg. Bar Assn., Multnomah Bar Assn., West Hills Racquet Club (Portland). Contracts commercial, General corporate, Family and matrimonial. Office: 506 SW 6th Ave Ste 1111 Portland OR 97204-1530

GLASS, DOUGLAS B. lawyer; b. Houston, Aug. 19, 1949; BA, U. Tex., 1971, JD, 1974. Bar: Tex. 1974. Mem. Vinson & Elkins L.L.P., Houston. Private international. Office: Vinson & Elkins 2500 First City Tower 1001 Fannin St Ste 3300 Houston TX 77002-6706

GLASS, FRED STEPHEN, lawyer; b. Asheboro, N.C., Oct. 17, 1940; s. Emmett Frederick and Colene F. (Foust) G.; m. Gloria A. Grant, June 12, 1964; 1 child, Elizabeth Foust; m. Martha G. Daughtry, June 9, 1982. BA, Wake Forest U., 1963, JD, 1966. Bar: N.C. 1966, U.S. Dist. Ct. (ea. dist.) N.C. 1966, (mid. dist.) N.C., (we. dist.) N.C.; U.S. Ct. Appeals (4th cir.), U.S. Supreme Ct. Rsch. asst. presiding justice N.C. Supreme Ct., 1966-67; ptnr. Miller, Beck, O'Briant and Glass, Asheboro, N.C., 1971-77; exec. dir. and legal counsel N.C. Democratic Party, 1977-78; dep. commr. N.C. Indsl. Commn., 1978; spl. Congl. asst. 4th Congl. Dist., N.C., 1979; ptnr. Harris, Cheshire, Leager and Southern, Raleigh, 1979-86, Poyner and Spruill, Raleigh, 1987-94, Brooks, Stevens & Pope, P.A., Cary, 1994-98; mng. ptnr. Glass & Vining, LLC, 1998-2000, Johnson, hearn, Vinegar & Gee PLLC, 2001—. Prof. law and govt. Asheboro Jr. Coll. Bus., 1973-76; bd. dirs. Capital Bank. Author: The Legal Handboook for North Carolina Businesses, 2000, Your Estate Planning Handbook, Business Considerations for North Carolina Healthcare Providers; contbg. editor: N.C. Will Drafting and Probate Practice Handbook, 1983; contbr. articles to profl. jours. Pub. chmn., United Appeal; bd. dirs., Randolph County Emergency Med. Technician Bd., Capital Bank; chmn.-elect Cary C. of C., bd. dirs., vice-chair govt. relations com.; mem. adv. bd. Naval War Coll. ops. law; active Dem. campaigns, Boy Scouts Am., council commr. for Roundtables, 1980-89, asst. dist. commr. 1979-84, asst. scoutmaster; mem. nat. com. Boy Scouts of Am., council ex. bd., council commr., chancellor, council commrs. coll., 1980-83, Boy Scouts Am. Nat. Com., 1987-90, coun. pres. 1994-96; force judge adv. COMRNCF, 1985-89; v.p. Healthcare Bus. Mgmt., LLC. Rear adm. JAGC, USNR. Disting. Svc. Medal award, 1996. Meritorious Svc. medal with gold star, Meritorious Unit Commendation, Nat. Meritorious Svc. award USNR, 1995, Navy Commendation medal with Gold Star, Nat. Defense Svc. medal with Bronze Star, Seabee Combat Warfare Specialist Cert.; recipient numerous Scouters Tng. award Boy Scouts Am., Disting. Eagle Scout award, 1991, Young Man of Yr. award City Asheboro. Mem. ABA (standing com. on armed forces law), Randolph County Bar Assn. (pres. 1971-74), 19th Jud. Dist. Bar Assn. (pres. 1974-75), N.C. Bar Assn. (chmn. young lawyer sect. Randolph County), N.C. Def. Lawyers Assn. (computer in litigation support 1989), N.C. Bar Assn. (computers in law office 1995), N.C. Coun. Entrepreneurial Devel., N.C. Bar Found., Cary C. of C. (bd. dirs., chmn. elect), Rotaray, Sovereign Mil. Order Temple Jerusalem, Naval Order U.S. Democrat. Methodist. General civil litigation, Nuclear power, Health. Home: 113 Whispering Pines Ct Cary NC 27511-4059 Office: PO Box 1776 Raleigh NC 27602 Fax: 919-743-2201. E-mail: sglass@jhvglaw.com

GLASS, JOEL, lawyer; b. N.Y.C., Nov. 17, 1942; s. Sam and Ruth (Neselrod) G.; m. Sheila Zolenge, Apr. 30, 1983. BA, U. Buffalo, 1965; JD, Bklyn. Law Sch., 1968. Bar: N.Y. 1968. Assoc. Ackerman, Salwen & Linzer, N.Y.C., 1968-74; ptnr. Ackerman, Salwen & Glass, 1974-97, Saretsky, Katx, Dranoff & Glass, N.Y.C., 1997—. Lectr. Mt. Sinai Sch. Medicine, Emergency Care Inst., Sch. for Continuing Edn. Montefiore Hosp. and Med. Center, N.J. Hosp. Assn., Acad. Medicine, Hosp. Edn. and Research Fund, United Hosp. Fund.; cons. N.Y. State Assembly Ins. Com.; vol. hosp. rep. McGill Commn. on Malpractice and other med. hearings; mem. med. malpractice task force Am. Hosp. Assn. Author: (with Gallet, Glass & Minkowitz) Rent Stabilization and Control Laws of New York, 1972. Served with USNG, 1970. N.Y. State Regents scholar, 1961, Nat. Merit scholar, 1961. Mem. ABA (med. legal com., health com.), N.Y. State Bar Assn., Assn. of Bar of City of N.Y. (liability ins. com., medicine and law com., med. malpractice com.), Greater N.Y. Hosp. Assn. (legal com. study of arbitration and mapractice), Non-Profit Coordinating Com. N.Y. (liability ins. com.). Health, Insurance, Personal injury. Office: Saretsky Katz Dranoff & Glass 331 Madison Ave New York NY 10017 E-mail: Joelg@skdglaw.com

GLASSER, IRA SAUL, civil liberties organization executive; b. Bklyn., Apr. 18, 1938; s. Sidney and Anne (Goldstein) G.; m. Trude Maria Robinson, June 28, 1959; children: David, Andrew, Peter, Sally BS in Math., Queens Coll., 1959; MA in Math., Ohio State U., 1960. Instr. math. Queens Coll., N.Y.C., 1960-63; lectr. math. Sarah Lawrence Coll., Bronxville, N.Y., 1962-65; assoc. editor Current Mag., N.Y.C., 1962-64, editor, 1964-67; assoc. dir. N.Y. Civil Liberties Union, 1967-70, exec. dir., 1970-78, ACLU, 1978-2001. Cons. U. Ill.-Champaign-Urbana, 1964-65; dir. Asian Am. Legal Def. and Edn. Fund., N.Y.C., 1974—; pres., pres., bd. dirs. Lindesmith Ctr./Drug Policy Found., Washington, 1991—. Author: Visions of Liberty: The Bill of Rights for All Americans, 1991; co-author: Doing Good: The Limits of Benevolence, 1978; contbr. articles to profl. jours. Chmn. St. Vincents Hosp, N.Y.C., Cmty. Adv. Bd., N.Y.C., 1970-72. Recipient Martin Luther King, Jr. award N.Y. Assn. Black Sch. Suprs., 1971, Gavel award ABA, 1972, Allard K. Lowenstein award Park River Ind. Dem., 1981, Malcolm, Martin, Mandela award Greater Bapt. Trinity Ch., 1993. Avocation: sports.

GLASSER, ISRAEL LEO, federal judge; b. N.Y.C., Apr. 6, 1924; s. David and Sadie (Krupp) G.; m. Grace Gribetz, Aug. 24, 1952; children—Dorothy, David, James, Marjorie. LL.B., Bklyn. Law Sch., 1948; B.A., CUNY, 1976. Bar: N.Y. 1948. Fellow Bklyn. Law Sch., 1948-49, instr., 1950-52, asst. prof. law, 1952-53, asso. prof., 1953-55, prof., 1955-69, adj. prof., 1969-77, dean, 1977-81; judge U.S. Dist. Ct. N.Y., 1981—99, sr. judge, 1993—. Judge N.Y. State Family Ct., N.Y.C., 1969-77 Mem. ABA, Assn. of Bar of City of N.Y. Office: US Dist Ct 225 Cadman Plz E Brooklyn NY 11201-1818 E-mail: leo_glasser@nyed.uscourts.gov

GLASSER, MICHAEL A. lawyer; b. Norfolk, Va., Nov. 17, 1953; BA with distinction, U. Va., 1975; JD, U. Richmond, 1978. Bar: (Va.) 1978, U.S. Dist. Ct. Va. (ea. dist.) 1978, U.S. Ct. Appeals (4th cir.) 1978, U.S. Supreme Ct. 1997. Ptnr. Glasser & Glasser, Norfolk. Mem.: Va. State Bar (pres. 2001—). Office: Glasser & Glasser Crown Ctr Bldg 580 E Main St Ste 600 Norfolk VA 23510*

GLASSMAN, CAROLINE DUBY, state supreme court justice; b. Baker, Oreg., Sept. 13, 1922; d. Charles Ferdinand and Caroline Marie (Colton) Duby; m. Harry Paul Glassman, May 21, 1953; 1 son, Max Avon. LLB summa cum laude, Williamette U., 1944. Bar: Oreg. 1944, Calif. 1952, Maine 1969. Atty. Title Ins. & Trust Co., Salem, Oreg., 1944-46; assoc. Belli, Ashe, Pinney & Melvin Belli, San Francisco, 1952-58; ptnr. Glassman & Potter, Portland, Maine, 1973-78, Glassman, Beagle & Ridge, Portland, 1978-83; justice Maine Supreme Judicial Ct., 1983-97. Lectr. Sch. Law, U. Maine, 1967-68, 80 Author: Legal Status of Homemakers in State of Maine, 1977. Mem. Am. Law Inst., Oreg. Bar Assn., Calif. Bar Assn., Maine Bar Assn., Maine Trial Law Assn. Roman Catholic. Home: 56 Thomas St Portland ME 04102-3639

GLASSMAN, RICHARD, lawyer; b. Memphis, Nov. 11, 1946; s. Julius and Julia (Baker) G.; m. Susan Lawless, Nov. 23, 1980; children: Samantha, Lauran, Kathryn, Zoë. BS, Memphis State U., 1969, LLB, 1972. Bar: Tenn. 1972, U.S. Dist. Ct. (we. dist.) Tenn. 1972, U.S. Dist. Ct. (no. and mid. dists.) Miss., U.S. Ct. Appeals (6th cir.) 1973, U.S. Dist. Ct. (ea. dist.) Ark, 1980, U.S. Supreme Ct. 1982. Salesman Hertz Corp., Memphis, 1965-69; sr. ptnr. Glassman, Edwards, Wade & Wyatt PC, 1974—. Mem. ABA (litigation sect. 1982—), Am. Bd. Trial Advocates, Memphis Bar Assn., Shelby County Bar Assn. (fee dispute com. 1980-84). Admiralty, Banking, Insurance. Home: 7787 Dogwood Rd Germantown TN 38138-4912 Office: Glassman Edwards Wade & Wyatt PC 26 N 2nd St Memphis TN 38103-2600

GLASSMOYER, THOMAS PARVIN, lawyer; b. Reading, Pa., Sept. 4, 1915; s. James Arthur and Margaretha (Parvin) G.; m. Frances Helen Thierolf, May 9, 1942; children— Deborah Jane Beck, Nancy Parvin Brittingham, Wendy Jean Parsons. AB, Ursinus Coll., 1936, LLB (hon.), 1972; LLB, U. Pa., 1939. Bar: Pa. 1940. Law clk. Common Pleas Ct. 6, Phila., 1939-40; assoc. Murdoch, Paxson, Kalish & Green, 1940-42; atty. Dept. Justice and Office Price Adminstrn., 1942-43; assoc. Schnader, Harrison, Segal & Lewis, Phila., 1946-50, ptnr., 1950-87, retired ptnr., 1988—, chmn. pension com., 1969-84, chmn. tax dept., 1972-84, chmn. investment com., 1984-86, chmn. bd. trustees of Retirement Trust, 1986-89. Sec. The Lawrewnce McFadden Co., Phila., 1992, dir., 1994—; lectr. NYU Inst. Fed. Taxation; adv. bd. U. Pa. Tax Conf., 1968-88. Author: (with Sherwin T. McDowell) Legal Problems in Tax Returns, 1949; editor-in-chief U. Pa. Law Rev., 1938-39 Past pres. Upper Dublin Twp. PTA Council; mem. Zoning Bd. Adjustment Upper Dublin Twp., Montgomery County, Pa., 1957-59, bd. commrs., 1959-71, pres., 1968-69; mem. Upper Dublin Environ. Control Bd., 1972-82; bd. dirs. Ursinus Coll., Collegeville, Pa., 1956—, 1st v.p., 1978-81, pres., 1981-90, chmn. exec. com., 1981-97; bd. dirs. Wissahickon Valley Watershed Assn., 1974-76; trustee Bernard G. Segal Found., Phila., 1969-98, Charlotte W. Newcombe Found., Princeton, N.J., 1982—. Served to 1st lt. JAG Dept., AUS, 1943-46. Recipient Eagle Scout award, Boy Scouts Am. Fellow Pa. Bar Found. (life, sec. 1993—); mem. ABA, FBA, Pa. Bar Assn. (ho. of dels. 1982-88, membership com., by-laws com.), Phila. Bar Assn., Judge Advs. Assn., Pa. Folklife Soc. (bd. dirs., sec.), Nat. Assn. Coll. and Univ. Attys., Lawyers Club Phila., Manorlu Club, Mfrs. Golf and Country Club, Union League of Phila., Order of Coif, Order of Arrow. Republican. Lutheran. Avocation: golf, philately. Home: 1648 N Hills Ave Willow Grove PA 19090-4231 Office: Schnader Harrison Segal & Lewis 1600 Market St Ste 3600 Philadelphia PA 19103-7287

GLAUBERMAN, MELVIN L. lawyer; b. Bklyn., Nov. 3, 1927; s. Sam and Beatrice (Jacobs) G.; m. Maxine Dvorsetz, Dec. 25, 1955 (div.); children: David J., Nancy J., Jane C.; m. Naomi Alexander, Jan. 6, 1980. B.A., Bklyn. Coll., 1948; J.D., Harvard U., 1951. Bar: N.Y. 1951, U.S. Dist. Ct. (so. dist.) N.Y. 1953, U.S. Dist. Ct. (ea. dist.) N.Y. 1954, U.S. Supreme Ct. 1972. Sole practice, N.Y.C., 1951-56, 73-74, 88—; ptnr. Berman & Glauberman, N.Y.C., 1957-60, Berman, Glauberman & Raives, N.Y.C., 1960-72; sr. ptnr. Berman, Glauberman & Bernstein, N.Y.C., 1975-87; mediator under N.Y. State Alternative Dispute Resolution Procedures; N.Y. State no-fault ins. arbitrator. Contbr. to book Manual for Theatre Owners, 1955; contbr. NYU Tax Law Rev. Vice-pres. League in Aid of Crippled Children, Inc., N.Y.C., 1969; mem. Ins. Industry Ednl. Adv. Com. Mem. N.Y. State Trial Lawyers Assn. (lectr. 1984), Am. Arbitration Assn. (master arbitrator, 1978-88, lectr. 1982—, N.Y. state permanent profl. no-fault arbitrator 1988—). General practice, Probate. Home: 32 Sheffield Ct Ardsley NY 10502-1524 Office: 32 Sheffield Ct Ardsley NY 10502-1524

GLAVIN, A. RITA CHANDELLIER (MRS. JAMES HENRY GLAVIN III), lawyer; b. Schenectady, N.Y., May 11, 1937; d. Pierre Charles and Helen C. (Fox) Chandellier; m. James H. Glavin, III, June 1, 1963; children: Helene, James, Rita, Henry. AB cum laude, Middlebury Coll., 1958; JD, Union U., 1961. Bar: N.Y. 1961, U.S. Dist. Ct. (no. dist.) N.Y. 1961, U.S. Tax Ct. 1965, U.S. Supreme Ct. 1978. Assoc. Eugene Steiner, Albany, N.Y., 1961-64, Helen Fox Chandellier, Schenectady, 1965-76; mem. Glavin and Glavin, Waterford, Schenectady, 1965-86, 87—, Albany, 1965-86, 87—. Del. 4th Jud. Dist. Nominating Conv., 1966-67; confidential law clk. presiding justices N.Y. State Ct. Claims, 1968-71; surrogate judge Saratoga County, 1986; dir. assn. coun. mems. and coll. trustees SUNY, 1991—, sec., 1996—, Mem. editl. bd. Albany Law Rev., 1960-61. Bd. dirs., chmn. fin. com. Schenectady YWCA, 1979-81; mem. Univ. Coun. SUNY, Albany, 1985—; tech. advisor HSA of Northeastern N.Y. Maternity and Pediat. Com., 1976; bd. dirs. Schenectady Jr. League, 1974, 76; del. N.Y. State Jr. League Pub. Affairs Com., 1976; sec. Bellevue Maternity Hosp., Inc., 1966—, bd. dirs. 1966-83, bd. advisors, 1984—; trustee Middlebury Coll., 1978-88, chmn. law com., 1982-88, vice chmn. bd. dirs., 1986-87; trustee Waterford Hist. Mus. and Cultural Ctr., Inc., 2000—. Mem. N.Y. State Bar Assn. (mem. ho. of dels. 1987-88, nominating com. 1988-90), Saratoga County Bar Assn. (exec. com. 1981—, v.p. 1985, pres. 1986), Schenectady County Bar Assn., Phi Beta Kappa, Kappa Kappa Gamma. General practice. Office: Glavin & Glavin PO Box 40 69 2nd St Waterford NY 12188-2422

GLAVIN, KEVIN CHARLES, lawyer, educator; b. Providence, Aug. 1, 1949; s. Charles Francis and Lola Glavin; m. Donna Bettencourt, Aug. 23, 1980. AB, Providence Coll., 1971; JD, Suffolk Law Sch., 1974. Bar: R.I. 1975, Mass. 1984, U.S. Dist. Ct. R.I. 1975, U.S. Supreme Ct. 1979. Spl. asst. atty. gen. R.I. Dept. Atty. Gen., Providence, 1975-79; mng. atty. Kemper Ins. Co., 1979-94; arbitrator R.I. Superior Ct., 1989—; ptnr. Murray, Cutcliffe & Glavin, 1994-2001, Cutcliffe, Glavin & Archetto, Providence, 2001—. Adj. faculty Roger Williams U., Bristol, R.I., 1986—. V.P. Kent Heights PTA, East Providence, 1989; treas. Colt Andrews PTA, Bristol, 1993; judge Acad. Decathlon R.I., 1999-00. Recipient Order of the Gavel, Newport Ski Club, 1982. Mem. R.I. Superior Ct. (bench bar com. 1992—), Pawtucket Bar Assn. (exec. com. 2001). Avocations: tennis, skiing, sailing. General civil litigation, Personal injury, Product liability. Office: Cutcliffe Glavin & Archetto 155 S Main St Providence RI 02903-2963

GLAZE, THOMAS A. state supreme court justice; b. Jan. 14, 1938; s. Phyllis Laser; children: Steve, Mike, Julie, Amy, Ashley. BSBA, U. Ark., 1960, JD, 1964. Exec. dir. Election Research Council Inc., 1964-65; legal advisor Winthrop Rockefeller, 1965-66; staff atty. Pulaski County Legal Aid, 1966-67, asst. then dep. atty. gen., 1967-70; pvt. practice law, 1970-79; chancellor Ark. Chancery Ct., 6th Jud. Cir., 1979-80; judge Ark. Ct. Appeals, 1981-86; assoc. justice Ark. Supreme Ct., 1987—. Co-author Ark. Election Act, 1969, Ark. Consumer Act; lectr. U. Ark.; adj. faculty U. Ark., Little Rock. Past bd. dirs. Vis. Nurses Corp., Youth Home Inc. Office: Ark Supreme Ct Justice Building 625 Marshall St Little Rock AR 72201-1054

GLAZER, DONALD WAYNE, lawyer, business executive, educator; b. Cleve., July 26, 1944; s. Julius and Ethel (Goldstein) G.; children: Elizabeth M., Mollie S. AB summa cum laude, Dartmouth Coll., 1966; JD magna cum laude, Harvard U., 1969; LLM, U. Pa., 1970. Bar: Mass. 1970. Assoc. Ropes & Gray, Boston, 1970-78, ptnr., 1978-92, counsel, 1992-96; ptnr. Am. Bus. Ptnrs. LLC, 1996-98; pres. Mugar/Glazer Holdings, Inc., 1992-95; vice chmn. fin. New Eng. TV Corp. and WHDH-TV, Inc., 1992-93; adv. counsel Goodwin Procter LLC, 1997—; co-founder, corp. sec. Provant, Inc., 1998—. Instr. corp. fin. Boston U. Law Sch., 1975; lectr. law Harvard U., Cambridge, Mass., 1978-91; trustee GMO Trust, Boston, 2000—; past dir. Teleco Oilfield Svcs., Inc., Kronos, Inc. Co-author: Massachusetts Corporation Law and Practice, 1991, Fitzgibbon and Glazer on Legal Opinions, 1992; co-editor First Ann. Inst. on Securities Regulation, 1970; contbr. articles to legal jours. Past chmn., trustee Cowen Slavin Found.; past trustee Santa Fe Neuroscis. Inst.; past dir. Newton Girls Soccer League, past co-chmn. intramural com.; past trustee, past treas. Hillel Founds. of Greater Boston Inc.; past trustee Program for Young Negotiators. Fellow Salzburg Seminar in Am. Studies, 1975 Mem. ABA (chmn. legal opinions com., co-reporter Legal Opinion Prins., past chmn. subcom. on employee benefits and exec. compensation, fed. securities law com., past co-chmn. task force on sec. 16 devels.), Boston Bar Assn. (past chmn., corp. sec., past chmn. securities law com., past co-chmn. legal opinions com.), Am. Law Inst., Tri-Bar Legal Opinions Com. (co-reporter Third-party Closing Opinions). Jewish General corporate, Finance, Securities. Home: 225 Kenrick St Newton MA 02458-2731

GLAZER, JACK HENRY, lawyer; b. Paterson, N.J., Jan. 14, 1928; s. Samiel and Martha (Merkin) G.; m. Zelda d'Angleterre, 1979. BA, Duke U., 1950; JD, Georgetown U., 1956; postgrad., U. Frankfurt, Germany, 1956-57, U. Calif., Berkeley, 1977. Bar: D.C. 1957, Calif. 1968. Atty. GAO and NASA, 1958-60; mem. maritime divsn. UN Internat. Labour Office, Geneva, Switzerland, 1960, spl. legal adv. Switzerland, 1960-62; atty. NASA, Washington, 1963-66; chief counsel NASA-Ames Rsch. Ctr., Moffett Field, Calif., 1966-88; gov. Calif. Maritime Acad., 1975-78; asst. prof. Hastings Coll. Law, 1985-87; prof., assoc. dean bus. sch. San Francisco State U., 1988-92; dir. San Francisco Palace Fine Arts, 1995. Contbr. articles to profl. jours. Comdr. Calif. Naval Militia, ret. Capt. JAGC, USNR, ret. Mem. Calif. Bar Assn., D.C. Bar Assn., White's Inn (reader). Office: White's Inn 37 White St San Francisco CA 94109-2609 E-mail: whitesinn@aol.com

GLAZIER, JONATHAN HEMENWAY, lawyer; b. Hartford, Conn., May 14, 1949; s. Orman Hemenway and Susan (Micka) G.; m. Susan Gayle Davis, Dec. 12, 1983; children: Martin Hemenway, Gregory Stephen. Student, Australian Nat. U., Canberra, 1969; BA, Rice U., 1972; JD, George Washington U., 1980. Bar: Tex. 1980, U.S. Dist. Ct. (so. dist.) Tex. 1981, U.S. Ct. Appeals (5th cir.) 1981, U.S. Ct. Internat. Trade 1984, U.S. Ct. Appeals (D.C. and Fed. cirs.) 1984, D.C. 1986, U.S. Dist. Ct. D.C. 1989, U.S. Tax Ct. 1989, U.S. Supreme Ct. 1991. Assoc. Chamberlain, Hrdlicka, White, Johnson and Williams, Houston, 1980-84, Busby, Rehm and Leonard, Washington, 1984-88, Dorsey & Whitney, Washington, 1988-91; assn. counsel Nat. Rural Elec. Coop. Assn., 1992—. Thomas J. Watson fellow, 1972-73. Mem. ABA (chmn. sub. com. on internat. tax and trade, 1988-90), Fed. Cir. Bar Assn. Avocations: sailing, bicycling. General practice, Private international, Taxation, general. Office: Nat Rural Elec Coop Assn 4301 Wilson Blvd Arlington VA 22203-1867 E-mail: jonathan.glazier@nreca.org

GLEESON, PAUL FRANCIS, retired lawyer; b. Bronx, June 20, 1941; s. William Francis and Julia Anne (Dargis) G.; children: Kevin F., Sean W., Brendan J., Colleen J. AB in History, Fordham U., 1963; JD, U. Chgo., 1966. Bar: Ill. 1966, Fed. Trial Bar Ill. 1969, U.S. Ct. Appeals (6th cir.) 1972, U.S. Ct. Appeals (7th cir.) 1973, U.S. Ct. Appeals (8th cir.) 1997. Assoc. Vedder, Price, Kaufman & Kammholz, Chgo., 1966-73, ptnr., 1973-2000; ret., 2000. Adj. prof. DePaul U. Sch. of Law, 1991. Co-author (with Day, Green & Cleveland) The Equal Employment Opportunity Compliance Manual, 1978; columnist: (with B. Alper) Gleeson and Alper on Employment Law, Merrill's Illinois Legal Times, 1988-90. Capt. U.S. Army, 1966-68, Vietnam. Decorated Bronze Star; Floyd Russell Mechem scholar, 1963-66. Mem. Order of Coif, Phi Beta Kappa. Roman Catholic. Labor.

GLEIN, RICHARD JERIEL, lawyer; b. L.A., Aug. 20, 1929; s. Henry Carl Glein and Elsie B. (Drummond) Schurman; m. Rosalind Bell; children: Valerie, Kimberly, Richard Jr., Stacy. Student, U. Wash., 1953-58. Bar: Wash. 1963, U.S. Dist. Ct. (ea. and we. dists.) Wash. 1963, U.S. Ct. Appeals (9th cir.) 1963. Police officer, Seattle, 1952-63; dep. pros. atty. King County, 1963-65; from assoc. to ptnr. Clinton, Fleck & Glein, Seattle, 1965-92; pvt. practice, 1992—; pro-tem judge, arbitrator Dist and Superior Ct.; owner Legal Alternatives, LLC, Ancortes, Wash. Sgt. 1st class USAF, 1946-49, U.S. Army, 1950-51. Mem. FBA, Wash. State Bar Assn., Snohomish County Bar Assn., Internat. Footprint Assn. (pres. Seatle chpt. 1969-70, grand pres. 1982-83), Masons (master 1973). Republican. Alternative dispute resolution, State civil litigation, General practice. Home and Office: 5301 Sterling Dr Anacortes WA 98221-3037 Fax: 360-293-0404. E-mail: rnrlegalt@aol.com

GLEISS, HENRY WESTON, lawyer; b. Detroit, Nov. 22, 1928; s.George Herman and Mary Elizabeth (Weston) G.; m. Joan Bette Christopher, July 23, 1955; children: Kent G., Keith W. BA, Denison U., 1951; JD, U. Mich., 1954. Bar: Mich. 1955, U.S. Dist. Ct. (ea. dist.) Mich. 1955, U.S. Dist. Ct. (we. dist.) Mich. 1960, U.S. Ct. Appeals (6th cir.) 1964, U.S. Supreme Ct. 1967. Sole practice, Benton Harbor, Mich., 1957-61; ptnr. Globensky, Gleiss, Bittner & Hyrns, P.C., St. Joseph, 1961—. Spl. asst. atty. gen. Mich., 1960—. Bd. dirs. United Fund. Served with U.S. Army, 1955-57.

Mem. ABA, Mich. Bar Assn., Berrien County Bar Assn. (pres 1974), Twin Cities C. of C. (v.p. 1975), Kiwanis, Moose, Jaycees (officer), Economic of S.W. Mich., Elks. Congregational. State civil litigation, Condemnation, Personal injury. Home: 2409 Langley Ave Saint Joseph MI 49085-2150 Office: 610 Ship St Saint Joseph MI 49085-1120 E-mail: hgleiss@bhlr.com

GLEKEL, JEFFREY IVES, lawyer; b. N.Y.C., Apr. 8, 1947; s. Newton and Gertrude (Burr) G.; m. Cynthia R. Leder, June 18, 1988; 1 child, David L. AB, Columbia U., 1969; JD, Yale U., 1972. Bar: N.Y. 1973, U.S. Supreme Ct. 1981, U.S. Ct. Appeals (2d cir.) 1974, U.S. Dist. Ct. (so. dist.) N.Y. 1974. Law clk. to judge U.S. Dist. Ct. (so. dist.) N.Y., 1972-73; asst. U.S. atty. So. Dist. N.Y., 1973-77; law clk. to justice Byron R. White U.S. Supreme Ct., Washington, 1977-78; ptnr. Skadden, Arps, Slate, Meagher and Flom, N.Y.C., 1980—. Editor, contbr.: Civil Litigation Practice, 1990; Business Crimes, 1982; note and comment editor Yale Law Jour., 1971-72; contbr. articles to law jours. Mem. Assn. Bar City of N.Y. (chmn. com. fed. legislation 1984-87), ABA. Federal civil litigation, Constitutional, Criminal. Office: Skadden Arps Slate Meagher & Flom 4 Times Sq New York NY 10036-6522

GLENDENNING, DON MARK, lawyer; b. Dallas, Dec. 24, 1953; s. Don Thomas and Nancy (Malloy) G.; m. Carol Peterson, Dec. 30, 1979. BA, Rice U., 1976; JD, Stanford U., 1979. Bar: Tex. 1979. Assoc. Rain Harrell Emery Young & Doke, Dallas, 1979-85; ptnr. Rain, Harrell, Emery, Young & Doke, 1985-87; shareholder Locke Liddell & Sapp (formerly Locke Purnell Rain Harrell, P.C.), 1987-98; ptnr. Locke Liddell & Sapp LLP, 1999—. Bd. dirs. Nat. Tree Trust, Dallas Trees and Park Found., Thanks-Giving Found., Scenic Dallas, Scenic Tex., Scenic Dallas, Dallas Zool. Soc.; pres. Human Rights Initiative North Tex. Republican. Presbyterian. General corporate, Securities. Office: Locke Liddell & Sapp LLP 2200 Ross Ave Ste 2200 Dallas TX 75201-6776

GLENDON, MARY ANN, law educator; b. 1938; BA, U. Chgo., 1959, JD, 1961, M Comparative Law, 1963. Bar: Ill. 1964, Mass. 1980. Legal intern. EEC, Brussels, Belgium, 1963; assoc. Mayer, Brown & Platt, Chgo., 1963-68; prof. Boston Coll., 1968-86; vis. prof. Harvard U., 1974-75, prof., 1986—. Vis. prof. U. Chgo., 1983, 84, 86. Author: Rights Talk, 1991, A Nation Under Lawyers, 1994, A World Made New: Eleanor Roosevelt and the Universal Declaration of Human Rights, 2001. Foreign Law fellow U. Libre de Bruxelles, 1962-63, Ford Found. fellow, 1975-76. Mem. Am. Acad. Arts & Scis. Office: Harvard U Law Sch Cambridge MA 02138

GLESSNER, JOHN JACOB, III, lawyer; b. Boston, Oct. 28, 1931; s. John Jacob and Martha Greenfield (Sluder) G.; A.B., Harvard U., 1953; LL.B., Columbia U., 1962; m. Susan LeBourgeois Crockett, June 17, 1972; children— John Jacob, Ian Macbeth, Elizabeth Charless. Dept. supr. Dewey & Almy Chem. Co., Acton, Mass., 1956-59; admitted to Mass. bar, 1962; assoc. Ropes & Gray, Boston, 1962-72; v.p., sec. Eastern Gas and Fuel Assos., Boston, 1972— . Bd. dirs. Animal Rescue League Boston; trustee White Mountain Sch. Served with U.S. Army, 1954-56. Mem. Am. Bar Assn., Mass. Bar Assn. Clubs: Cruising of Am.; Union (Boston). Office: Eastern Gas & Fuel Assoc One Beacon St Boston MA 02107

GLICK, PAUL MITCHELL, lawyer, educator; b. N.Y.C., Dec. 7, 1948; s. Gene H. and Ethel (Scott) G.; m. Roberta Wallenstein, Aug. 8, 1970; children: Geoffrey, Peter. Student Columbia U., 1969; BA with distinction, U. Wis., 1970. JD cum laude, DePaul U., 1973. Bar: Ill. 1973, U.S. Dist. Ct. (no. dist.) Ill. 1973, U.S. Ct. Claims 1976, U.S. Tax Ct. 1976, U.S. Supreme Ct 1976. Ptnr. Friedman & Koven, Chgo., 1973-86, Neal, Gerber & Eisenberg, Chgo., 1986; ptnr., pres. Paul M. Glick, Chartered, Chgo., 1986—; adj. prof. DePaul U. Grad. Sch. Law, Chgo., 1977-83; Author: When Should Rabbi Trusts Be Used To Secure Non-Qualified Deferred Compensation Arrangements, Estate Planning, 1988; pub. mem. Ill. Pub. Employees Pension Laws Comm., 1983-84; mem. Ill. Task Force on Funding of State Retirement System, 1985. NSF grantee, 1969. Mem. ABA, Chgo. Bar Assn., Am. Judicature Soc., Ill. Bar Assn., Midwest Pension Conf., Profit Sharing Council Am. Pension, profit-sharing, and employee benefits. Home: 2505 Stonebridge Ln Northbrook IL 60062-8107 Office: 3500 Three First Nat Plz Chicago IL 60602

GLICKMAN, STEPHEN, state supreme court justice; Ptnr. Zuckerman, Spaeder, Goldstein, Taylor & Kolker, 1980-99; judge D.C. Ct. Appeals, 1999—. Office: DC Ct Appeals 6th Pl 500 Indiana Ave NW Ste 2 Washington DC 20001-2131*

GLICKSMAN, ELLIOT BORIS, educator, lawyer; b. Detroit, Jan. 25, 1942; s. B.H. and Sylvia (Bier) G.; m. Thea Schwartz, Dec. 27, 1970. B.A., Eastern Mich. U., 1964; M.A., Wayne State U., 1966; J.D., U. Detroit, 1969. Bar: Mich. 1969. Practice, Detroit, 1969-70; asst. pros. atty. Wayne County (Mich.), 1970-72; staff atty. Burroughs Corp. UNYSIS, Detroit, 1972-75; assoc. prof. law Thomas H. Cooley Law Sch., Lansing, Mich., 1975-80, prof. law, 1980—; lectr. Nat. Jud. Coll., U. Nev. Reno, Mich. Jud. Inst., Lansing;ad hoc hearing referee Mich. Dept. Civil Rights, 1975— ; vis. reseach fellow, faculty of law U. Birmingham (Eng.), 1984-85. Recipient Faculty award Mich. Jud. Inst., 1981-88, Disting. Men of Achievement award Cambridge U., 1986. Mem. Mich. Bar Assn., Ingham County Bar Assn. (10 yr. award, Disting. alumnus award 1997), ABA (select com. on rules on criminal procedure and evidence, Assn. Trial Lawyers Am., Scribes, Thomas M. Cooley Law Sch. Faculty Writers Assn. (charter). Contbr. chpts. to books, articles to profl. jours. Office: Thomas M Cooley Law Sch 300 S Capitol Ave PO Box 13038 Lansing MI 48901-3038

GLICKSMAN, EUGENE JAY, lawyer; b. N.Y.C., Aug. 10, 1954; s. David and Elsie (Lerner) G.; m. Patricia Cardoso, Sept. 23, 1984; 1 child, Elizabeth Ann. BA in Polit. Sci., CUNY, 1975, JD, 1978. Bar: N.Y. 1980, U.S. Dist. Ct. (so. and ea. dists.) N.Y. 1980, U.S. Supreme Ct. 1992. Immigration inspector U.S. Dept. Justice, Immigration and Naturalization Svc., N.Y.C., 1976-80; assoc. Antonio C. Martinez, 1980-81, Harry Spar, N.Y.C., 1981-83; pvt. practice pvt. practice, 1983-93; ptnr. Glicksman & Cardoso, 1993—. Arbitrator N.Y.C. Civil Cts., 1982-91; adminstrv. law judge N.Y.C. Taxi & Limousine Commn., 1991-98, N.Y.C. Environ. Control Bd., 1999-2000; aux. police officer N.Y.C. Police Dept., 1972-75. Mem. Am. Immigration Lawyers Assn. (N.Y. chpt. treas. 1993-94), N.Y. State Bar Assn., N.Y. County Lawyers Assn. (chair com. immigration and nationality law 1994-97). Immigration, naturalization, and customs. Office: Glicksman & Cardoso 150 Broadway Rm 1115 New York NY 10038-4302

GLICKSTEIN, HOWARD ALAN, law educator; b. N.Y.C., Sept. 14, 1929; s. Samuel and Fannie (Greenblat) G. BA magna cum laude, Dartmouth Coll., 1951; LLB, Yale U., 1954; LLM, Georgetown U., 1962. Bar: N.Y. 1954, U.S. Supreme Ct. 1962, D.C. 1980. Assoc. proskauer, Rose, Goetz & Mendelsohn, N.Y.C., 1956-60; staff atty. Civil Rights divsn. Dept. of Justice, 1960-65; gen. counsel U.S. Commn. on Civil Rights, Washington, 1965-68, staff dir., 1968-71. Cons. in law, 1971-73; adj. prof., dir. Ctr. for Civil Rights U. Notre Dame, 1973-75; prof., dir. equal employment litigation clinic Howard U. Sch. Law, Washington, 1976-80; dir. Task Force on Civil Rights Reorgn., Exec. Office of Pres., Washington, 1977-78; dean, prof. U. Bridgeport Sch. Law, Conn., 1980-85, Touro Coll. Law, 1986—. Contbr. articles to profl. jours. Bd. dirs. Fund for Modern Cts.; commr. Suffolk County Human Rights Commn.; chair Town Huntington Bd. Ethics and Fin. Disclosure, 1999—. With U.S. Army, 1954-56. Mem. ABA (former chmn. affirmative action com., sect. legal edn. and admissions to bar), Soc. Am. Law Tchrs. (bd. dirs., former pres.), N.Y. State Commn. on Fiduciary Appointments, N.Y. State Bar Assn. (mem. spl. com. pub. trust and confidence in the legal sys.). Office: Touro Coll Sch Law Coll Law 300 Nassau Rd Huntington NY 11743-4346

GLICKSTEIN, STEVEN, lawyer; b. Bklyn., Jan. 3, 1952; s. Alexander and Esther (Camhi) G. BA, Lehigh U., 1973; JD, Columbia U., 1976. Assoc. Kaye, Scholer, Fierman, Hays & Handler, N.Y.C., 1976-84, ptnr., 1985—. Mem. ABA, D.C. Bar Assn., Fla. Bar Assn., N.Y. State Bar Assn. Antitrust, Federal civil litigation. Home: 1619 3rd Ave Apt 9ae New York NY 10128-3459 Office: Kaye Scholer Fierman 425 Park Ave New York NY 10022-3506

GLIEGE, JOHN GERHARDT, lawyer; b. Chgo., Aug. 3, 1948; s. Gerhardt John Gliege and Jane Heidke; children: Gerhardt, Stephanie, Kristine. BA, Ariz. State U., 1969, MPA, 1970, JD, 1974. Bar: Ariz. 1974. Pvt. practice, Scottsdale, Ariz., 1974-81, Flagstaff, 1981-94, 98—, Sedona, 1994-97, Williams, 1997-98. Prof. paralegal studies No. Ariz. U., Flagstaff, 1981-83, prof. urban planning and cmty. devel., 1984—; prof. paralegal studies Yavapai Cmty. Coll., Prescott, Ariz., 1995-97. Administrative and regulatory, Environmental, Municipal (including bonds). Address: PO Box 1388 Flagstaff AZ 86002-1388 E-mail: jgliege@uswest.net

GLINN, FRANKLYN BARRY, lawyer; b. Newark, Oct. 22, 1943; s. Dave and Gertrude (Weinstein) G.; m. Sandra Lee Scales, Nov. 3, 1943; children: MacAdam Jordan, Dara Elisabeth, Daniel Garrett. BAE, U. Fla., 1965, JD, 1968. Bar: Fla. 1969, U.S. Ct. Appeals (5th cir.) 1969, U.S. Dist. Ct. (so. dist.) Fla. 1970. Assoc. Ser, Greenspahn & Keyfetz, Miami, Fla., 1969-70, Ser & Keyfetz, 1970-72, Rabin, Sassoon & Ratiner, Miami, 1972-74; ptnr. Ratiner & Glinn, 1974—2000. Mem. ABA, Am. Judicature Soc., Am. Trial Lawyers Assn., Acad. Fla. Trial Lawyers, Am. Arbitration Assn. Democrat. Jewish. State civil litigation, Personal injury, Workers' compensation. Office: Glinn & Somera PA Ste 680 2801 Ponce De Leon Blvd Coral Gables FL 33134-6920

GLINSEK, GERALD JOHN, lawyer; b. Akron, Ohio, Jan. 16, 1939; s. Rudolph Paul and Angela Louise (Stanger) G.; m. Karen Rosemary Mehen, Oct. 17, 1968 (div. Aug. 1990); children: Kelli, Daniel; m. Maureen Louise Nuosce, May 7, 1994 (dec. Aug. 1998); 1 child from previous marriage, Rebecca Ann. BA, U. Akron, 1963, JD, 1967. Bar: Ohio 1967, U.S. Dist. Ct. (no. dist.) Ohio 1969, U.S. Ct. Appeals (6th cir. 1986), U.S. Supreme Ct. 1986. Asst. pros. atty. Summit County Prosecutors Office, Akron, 1967-71; pvt. practice, 1971—. With U.S. Army, 1957. Mem. ABA, Ohio Bar Assn., Akron Bar Assn. (treas. 1981), Summit County Legal Aid Soc. (pres. 1978-82), Phi Kappa Tau (advisor 1982—). Democrat. Roman Catholic. Avocations: travel, skiing. Criminal, Family and matrimonial, Personal injury. Home: 1861 Wiltshire Rd Akron OH 44313-6101 Office: 88 S Portage Path Akron OH 44303-1023

GLOBER, GEORGE EDWARD, JR. lawyer; b. Edwards AFB, Calif., Aug. 10, 1944; s George Edward and Catharine (Crain) G.; m. Deirdre Denman, May 22, 1971; children: Denman, Nancy King. AB, Cornell U., 1966; JD, Harvard U., 1969. Bar: Tex. 1969, U.S. Supreme Ct. 1976. Tchg. fellow natural scis. Harvard U., 1967-69; assoc. Vinson & Elkins, Houston, 1969-77; dir. Houston Dept. Pub. Svc., 1977-78; mem. law dept. Exxon Mobil Corp. and Affiliates, Irving, Tex., 1978—; sr. counsel Exxon Mobil Corp., 1995—. Asst. gen. counsel Exxon Chem. Co., 1991-94; chief atty. refining, environ. and health Exxon Co. USA, 1988-91; gen. counsel Exxon Prodn. Rsch. Co., 1982-88. With Air N.G., 1969-75. Fellow Houston Bar Assn.; mem. ABA, Internat. Law Assn., Tex. Bar Assn., Dallas Bar Assn., Assn. Corp. Patent Counsel. General corporate, Environmental, Patent. Office: Exxon Mobil Corp 5959 Las Colinas Blvd Irving TX 75039-2298

GLOSBAND, DANIEL MARTIN, lawyer; b. Salem, Mass., July 3, 1944; s. Leon Glosband and Ruth Pauline (Wentworth) Glosband School; m. Merrily Cotton, Dec. 23, 1967; children: Alexander, Gabriel, Oliver. BA, U. Mass., 1966; JD, Cornell, U., 1969. Bar: Mass. 1969, U.S. Dist. Ct. Mass. 1970, U.S. Ct. Appeals (1st cir.) 1971, U.S. Dist. Ct. Conn. 1971, U.S. Dist. Ct. Vt. 1974, U.S. Supreme Ct. 1982. Assoc., then ptnr. firm Widett & Widett, Boston, 1969-75; ptnr. Goldstein & Manello, 1976-87, Goodwin, Procter LLP, Boston, 1988—. Advisor Am. Law Inst. Transnat. Insolvency Project, 1994—2000. Contbr. numerous articles on bankruptcy to profl. jours. Fellow: Am. Coll. Bankruptcy (dir. 1999—), Am. Bar Found., Mass. Bar Found.; mem.: ABA (sect. on corps., chmn. internat. bankruptcy com. 1990—95), Internat. Bar Assn. (sect. bus. law, vice chmn. insolvency and creditors rights com. 1997—2000, del. UN Commn. Internat. Trade Law), Mass. Bar Assn. (chmn. bankruptcy com. 1980—83), Boston Bar Assn. (chmn. bankruptcy com. 1977—80). Democrat. Jewish. Bankruptcy. Home: 34 Atlantic Ave Swampscott MA 01907-2404 Office: Goodwin Procter LLP Exchange Pl Boston MA 02109-2803 E-mail: dglosband@goodwinprocter.com

GLOSSER, WILLIAM LOUIS, lawyer; b. Johnstown, Pa., Aug. 30, 1929; s. Saul I. and Eva (Hurwitz) G.; m. Patricia Freeman, Feb. 5, 1932; children: Alix Paul, Jill P., Jonathan. BS, Temple U., 1951; LLB, U. Pa., 1954. Bar: Pa. 1954, Fla. 1956, U.S. Dist. Ct. (we. dist.) Pa. 1956, U.S. Dist. Ct. (so. dist.) Fla. 1957. Assoc. Broad and Cassel, Miami Beach, Fla., 1956-57; sole practice Coral Gables, 1957-61, Johnstown, 1962—. Magistrate judge U.S. Dist. Ct. (we. dist.) Pa., 1972-93; corp. sec., dir. Glosser Bros., Inc., Johnstown, 1969-85; of counsel Smorto, Persio, Webb & McGill, Johnstown, 1988—. Bd. dirs. Lee Hosp., Johnstown, Greater Johnstown (Pa.) Cmty. Found., ret.; mem. Johnstown adv. coun. Pa. Human Rels. Commn.; pres. United Jewish Fedn. Johnstown, 1970-75, 2000—; chmn. fund drive United Way, 1985, pres., 1987-88; bd. dirs. Mt. Aloysius Coll., 1980-84, Cmty. Found. Greater Johnstown, Pa., 1990—. With U.S. Army, 1954-56. Mem. Pa. Bar Assn., Fla. Bar Assn., Cambria County Bar Assn., Greater Johnstown C. of C. (pres. 1985), Rotary (pres. 1990), B'nai B'rith (pres. lodge 1965-67, 83-84). Jewish. General corporate, Criminal, Estate planning. Home: 521 Luzerne St Johnstown PA 15905-2324 Office: Smorto Persio Webb & McGill 430 Main St Johnstown PA 15901-1823

GLOTTA, RONALD DELON, lawyer; b. Lajunta, Colo., Mar. 18, 1941; s. John Wallace and Marian (Kisner) G.; m. Sharon S. Glotta, Aug. 27, 1961 (div. Mar. 1986); children: Holly Ann, Jeffrey Delon; m. Marietta Lynn Baba, June 23, 1990 (div. Oct. 1998). BA with honors, U. Kans., 1963; JD, U. Mich., 1966. Bar: Mich. 1966. Atty. Marcus, McCroskey, Libner, Reamon, Williams & Dilley, Muskegon, Mich., 1966-68; ptnr. Philo, Maki, Moore, Pitts, Ravitz, Glotta, Cockrel & Robb, Detroit, 1968-70; prin. Glotta & Adelman, 1970-85, Glotta, Rawlings & Skutt, Detroit, 1985-96, Glotta, Skutt & Assts, Detroit, 1996—. Mem. Phi Beta Kappa. Labor, Personal injury, Workers' compensation. Home: 2065 Hyde Park Rd Detroit MI 48207-3885 E-mail: rglotta@winstarmail.com

GLOVSKY, SUSAN G. L. lawyer; b. Boston, Apr. 16, 1955; d. Leonard B. and Marilyn S. (Shapiro) Loitherstein; m. Steven M. Glovsky, May 25, 1980; 1 child, Lowell Eliott. BS in Chemistry, U. Vt., 1977; JD, Boston U., 1980. Bar: Mass. 1980, Mich. 1980, U.S. Dist. Ct. (ea. dist.) Mich. 1980, U.S. Patent Office 1981, N.Y. 1982, U.S. Dist. Ct. Mass. 1982, U.S. Ct. Appeals (1st cir.) 1982, U.S. Ct. Appeals (fed. cir.) 1991, U.S. Supreme Ct. 1995. Assoc. Levin, Levin, Garvett & Dill, Southfield, Mich., 1980-81, Ladas & Parry, N.Y.C., 1981-82, Dahlen & Gatewood, Boston, 1982-83; ptnr. Dahlen & Glovsky, 1983-85; pvt. practice Boston and Salem, Mass., 1985-93; of counsel Hamilton, Brook, Smith & Reynolds, Lexington, 1993-97, prin., 1998—. Adj. prof. Suffolk U. Law Sch. Mem. ABA, Mass. Bar Assn., Boston Bar Assn., Boston Patent Law Assn. (past pres., chmn. litigation com. 1989—), Am. Arbitration Assn. (panel arbitrators 1985—, co-chmn. intellectual property adv. com. 1999—). Jewish. Avocations: swimming, skiing. Federal civil litigation, Patent, Trademark and copyright. Home: 36 Shaw Dr Wayland MA 01778-3214 Office: Hamilton Brook Smith & Reynolds 2 Militia Dr Lexington MA 02421-4799 E-mail: susan.glovsky@hbsr.com

GLUSBAND, STEVEN JOSEPH, lawyer; b. Berlin, Jan. 15, 1947; came to U.S., 1949; s. Morris and Docia (Waitman) G.; m. Roberta Gail Jacobs, Nov. 22, 1981; children: Ilana, Jonathan. BBA, CCNY, 1969; JD, Fordham U., 1973; LLM, NYU, 1978. Bar: N.Y. 1974, U.S. Dist. Ct. (so. dist.) N.Y. 1974, U.S. Ct. Appeals (2nd cir.) 1974. Trial atty. SEC, N.Y.C., 1974-75, spl. trial counsel, 1976-77; assoc. Sage Gray Todd & Sims, 1977-80, ptnr., 1981-87; mem. exec. com. Carter, Ledyard & Milburn, 1987—. Dir. MER Telemanagement Solutions Ltd. Mem. ABA (com. fed. regulation of securities, securities litigation), Assn. of Bar of N.Y.C. (com. on futures regulation 1986-88). General corporate, Securities, Commodities. Home: 343 E 30th St New York NY 10016-6417 Office: Carter Ledyard & Milburn 2 Wall St Fl 13 New York NY 10005-2072

GLUSHIEN, MORRIS P. lawyer, arbitrator; b. Bklyn., Oct. 15, 1909; s. Isaac and Minnie (Hoffman) G.; m. Anne Williams, Nov. 18, 1945; children: Minna Taylor, Ruth Wedgwood. A.B. with honors, Cornell U., 1929, J.D. with honors, 1931. Bar: N.Y. 1932, U.S. Supreme Ct. 1940. Pvt. practice, Bklyn., 1932-38; mem. faculty Cornell Law Sch., 1938-39, New Sch. for Social Rsch., 1977-78; chief U.S. Supreme Ct. sect., assoc. gen. counsel NLRB, 1939-47; gen. counsel Internat. Ladies Garment Workers Union, AFL-CIO, 1947-72; arbitrator, 1972—; spl. master fed. ct., 1976-78. Mem. Nat. Acad. Arbitrators; mem. arbitration panels Am. Arbitration Assn., Fed. Mediation and Conciliation Service, various state and city agys. Editorial bd.: Cornell Law Quar, 1930-31; Contbr. legal periodicals. Bd. dirs. Nat. Legal Aid and Defender Assn., 1954-72. Served with AUS, as cryptanalyst, 1942-45. Mem. ABA (past chmn. labor law sect.), N.Y. State Bar Assn. (labor rels. com.), Assn. of Bar of City of N.Y. (past chmn. com. labor and social security legis.), Indsl. Rels. Rsch. Assn., Practicing Law Inst., Am. Jewish Congress (com. law and social action), Am. Judicature Soc., AFL-CIO (past mem. nat. legis. coun.), Civil Svc. Reform Assn. (exec. com.), N.Y. Com. for Modern Cts. (past v.p., bd. dirs.), Nat. and N.Y. State Against Discrimination in Housing Coms., ACLU (com. free speech and assn.), Ams. for Dem. Action, NYU Conf. on Labor, Curia, Phi Beta Kappa, Phi Kappa Phi. Home: 2228 Westwood Blvd Los Angeles CA 90064-2018

GLYNN, ROBERT, lawyer, foundation chairman; b. N.J., Oct. 30, 1929; 1 child, Katherine F.J. Glynn. BA, Harvard U., 1951, LLB, 1956. Staff atty. Internat. Fin. Corp., Washington, 1961-65; ptnr. Fox, Glynn & Melamed, N.Y., 1968-87, Becker, Glynn, Melamed & Muffly LLP, N.Y., 1987—; chmn. bd. dirs. and dir. gen. Lampadia Found., 1993—. Office: Becker Glynn Melamed & Muffly LLP 299 Park Ave Fl 16 New York NY 10171-0002

GNICHTEL, WILLIAM VAN ORDEN, lawyer; b. Summit, N.J., Jan. 11, 1934; s. William Stone and Edith Parrot (Van Orden) G.; m. Emily Hopkins Martenet, July 11, 1959 (dec.); children: William Van Orden Jr., Edwin Martenet; m. Mary B. Gayley, June 7, 1996. BA, Trinity Coll., 1956; LLB, Columbia U., 1959. Bar: N.Y. 1961, Mass. 1997. Ptnr. Whitman & Ransom, N.Y.C., 1968-88, resident ptnr. Saudi Arabia, 1980-85; ptnr. Chadbourne & Parke, N.Y.C., 1988-92; spl. counsel Law Firm of Salah Al-Hejailan, Riyadh, Saudi Arabia, Saudi Arabia, 1986-95. Lectr. in field. Contbr. articles to profl. jours. Mem. ABA, Assn. of Bar of City of N.Y., Union Club, Knickerbocker Club (N.Y.C.), Somerset Club (Boston), Onteora Club (Tannersville, N.Y.; exec. vp. 1974-75, pres. 1976-77, bd. dirs. 1970-77), Masons, Phi Delta Phi. Episcopalian. Banking, Finance, Private international. Address: PO Box 431 Lincoln MA 01773-0431 E-mail: WVOGLAW@mindspring.com

GOANS, JUDY WINEGAR, lawyer; b. Knoxville, Tenn., Sept. 27, 1949; d. Robert Henry and Lula Mae (Myers) Winegar; m. Ronald Earl Goans, June 18, 1971; children: Robert Henson, Ronald Earl Jr. Student, Sam Houston State U., 1967-68; BS in Engring. Physics, U. Tenn., 1971, postgrad., 1971-74, JD, 1978. Bar: Tenn. 1978, U.S. Dist. Ct. (ea. dist.) Tenn. 1979, U.S. Patent Office 1980, U.S. Ct. Appeals (Fed. cir.) 1980, U.S. Supreme Ct. 1983. Instr. legal rights Knoxville Women's Ctr., 1977-78; patent analyst nuclear div. Union Carbide Corp., Oak Ridge, Tenn., 1978-79; patent atty. U.S. Dept. Energy, Washington, 1979-82; legis. and internat. intellectual property specialist Patent and Trademark Office, 1982-89; pvt. practice law Clinton, Tenn., 1990-96; cons. internat. intellectual property law Clinton and Washington, 1993—. Judge Rich Moot Ct. competition, Washington, 1984, Knoxville, 1991; head U.S. Del. 13th session World Intellectual Property Orgn. Permanent Com. for Devel. Cooperation Related to Intellectual Property, 1989; mem. hearing com. Bd. Responsibility of the Supreme Ct. Tenn., 1992—; dir. and chief of party SIPRE Project, Cairo, Nathan Assocs., Inc. Del. Nat. Women's Conf., Houston, 1977; bd. dirs. Nat. Orgn. for Women, Washington, 1977-79, Good Shepherd Kingergarten, 1987, Knoxville Women Ctr. 1992-93; legal adv. bd. Knoxville Rape Crisis Ctr., 1979. Mem. ABA, Tenn. Bar Assn., Am. Intellectual Property Law Assn., Govt. Patent Lawyers Assn. (sec. 1981-83), Patent and Trademark Office Soc. (bd. dir. 1986-88), East Tenn. Laywers Assn. for Women (pres. elect 1990-91, pres. 1992, bd. dirs.), Knoxville Assn. Women Execs. (bd. dirs.), Greater Knoxville Lions Club, Tau Beta Pi (bd. dirs. Greater Smoky Mountain Alumni Chpt. 1991—), Sigma Pi Sigma, (sec. U. Tenn. chpt. 1970-71). Episcopalian. Home: 1422 Eagle Bend Dr Clinton TN 37716-4029 Office: 2021 Wilson Blvd Ste 1200 Arlington VA 22201-3006

GOBBEL, LUTHER RUSSELL, lawyer, business executive; b. Durham, N.C., May 17, 1930; s. Luther and Marcia R. (Russell) G.; m. Jean M. Mollison, Apr. 4, 1959; children— Robert R., Katharine S. A.B., Duke U., 1952; J.D., Harvard U., 1955. Bar: Tenn. 1955, Md. 1972. Asst. counsel Bur. Ordnance, Navy Dept., Washington, 1955-59, asst. counsel Bur. Naval Weapons, San Diego, 1959-65; sr. atty. elec. div. Gen. Dynamics Corp., Rochester, N.Y., 1965-70; counsel Amecom div. Litton Systems, Inc., College Park, Md., 1970— ; adv. bd. Bur. Nat. Affairs Fed. Procurements Report, Washington, 1968-79. Mem. Harper's Choice Village Bd., Columbia, Md., 1972-75; chmn. Columbia Combined Bds., 1973; Mem. Howard County Criminal Justice Task Force, Md., 1975-76; mem. Howard County Police Tng. Adv. Bd., 1976; mem. Howard County Charter Rev. Com., 1979, Md. Gen. Assembly Compensation Commn., 1984— , Prince Georges County Econ. Devel. Adv. Commn. Mem. ABA, Md. Bar Assn., Fed. Bar Assn. (nat. council 1962-71, nat. v.p. for 9th dist. 1963-64, pres. San Diego chpt. 1962-63), Am. Arbitration Assn. (panel of arbitrators 1969—). Democrat. Methodist. General corporate, Government contracts and claims. Home: 10701 Symphony Way Columbia MD 21044-4922 Office: Litton Systems Inc 5115 Calvert Rd College Park MD 20740-3808

GODBEY, RONALD LEE, lawyer, meteorologist; b. Milford, Tex., July 11, 1934; s. Paschal Lee and Catherine Esta (Williams) G.; m. Martha Jane Worsham, May 14, 1954; children— Gary Lee, Julie Ann. B.S., North Tex. State U., 1960; postgrad. Tex. A&M U., 1960-61; J.D., So. Meth. U., 1971. Bar: Tex. 1971, U.S Dist. Ct. (no. dist.) Tex. 1971, Ill. 1982. Quality control mgr. Gen. Dynamics Corp., Ft. Worth, 1955-57; meteorologist WBAP TV and Radio, Ft. Worth, 1964-78; mem. firm Godbey, Simpson, Lynch & Wiley, Ft. Worth, 1971-81; lawyer Dept. Def., Belleville, Ill., 1982— ; cons. meteorologist, Ft. Worth, 1972-81; mcpl. ct. judge City of Keller, Tex., 1974-78. Co-author: Texas Weather, 1976. Bd. dirs. Grapevine Meml.

Hosp., Tex. 1973-77. Served with USAF, 1960-64, Korea. Mem. Tex. Trial Lawyers Assn., Ill. Bar Assn. (environ. council 1983—), Ill. Trial Lawyers Assn., Am. Meteorol. Soc. (cert. cons. meteorologist, TV seal of approval), Nat. Guard Assn. U.S., DAV, VFW, Chi Epsilon Pi Democrat. Methodist. Club: Ft. Worth Lions.

GODBOLD, GENE HAMILTON, lawyer; b. Mullins, S.C., June 14, 1936; s. John Dalton and Mildred (Stalvey) G.; m. Janice Louise McKay, June 24, 1960; children: Lori McKay, Scott Hamilton, Stephanie Louise. BA, Furman U., Greenville, S.C., 1958; LLB, Tulane U., 1963. Bar: Fla. 1963, U.S. Dist. Ct. (mid. dist.) Fla. 1964, U.S. Ct. Appeals (5th cir.) 1964. Assoc. Maguire, Voorhis & Wells, Winter Park, Fla., 1963-68, ptnr., 1968-84, pres., 1978-84, Godbold, Allen, Brown and Builder, P.A., Winter Park, 1984-88, Goldbold & Downing, P.A., 1988-94, Godbold, Downing, Sheahan & Bill, P.A., 1994—. Served to 1st lt. U.S. Army, 1958-60. Mem. Fla. Bar, Orange County Bar Assn (mem. exec. com. 1968-72, pres. 1971-72), Winter Parl Racquet Club, Interlachen Country Club. State civil litigation, Real property. Address: 222 W Comstock Ave Ste 101 Winter Park FL 32789-4272 E-mail: ggodbold@gdslaw.com

GODBOLD, JOHN COOPER, federal judge; b. Coy, Ala., Mar. 24, 1920; s. Edwin Condie and Elsie (Williamson) G.; m. Elizabeth Showalter, July 18, 1942; children: Susan, Richard, John C., Cornelia. BS, Auburn U., 1940; JD, Harvard U., 1948; LLD (hon.), Samford U., 1981, Auburn U., 1988, Stetson U., 1994. Bar: Ala. 1948. With firm Richard T. Rives, Montgomery, 1948-49; ptnr. Rives & Goldbold, 1949-51, Godbold & Hobbs and successor firms, 1951-66; cir. judge U.S. Ct. Appeals (5th cir.), 1966-81, chief judge, 1981, U.S. Ct. Appeals (11th cir.), 1981-86, sr. judge, 1987—; dir. Fed. Jud. Ctr., Washington, 1987-90. Mem. Fed. Jud. Ctr. Bd., 1976-81. With field arty. AUS, 1941-46. Mem. ABA, Fed. Bar Assn., Ala. Bar Assn., Montgomery County Bar Assn., Alpha Tau Omega, Omicron Delta Kappa, Phi Kappa Phi. Episcopalian. Office: US Ct Appeals 11th Circuit 15 Lee Street Rm 438 Montgomery AL 36104

GODBOUT, ARTHUR RICHARD, JR. lawyer; b. Hartford, Conn., Oct. 7, 1957; s. Arthur Richard and Elizabeth Anne (Desmond) G. BSBA, Georgetown U., 1979, JD, 1986. Bar: Conn. 1987. Pres. A.R. Godbout & Co., Avon, Conn., 1987—. Real property. Home: 8 Cheltenham Way Avon CT 06001-2444 Office: PO Box 1175 Avon CT 06001-1175

GODDARD, CLAUDE PHILIP, JR. lawyer; b. Long Beach, Calif., Oct. 31, 1952; s. Claude Philip and Doris Marian (Dow) G.; m. Ellen Kohn, May 23, 1981; children: Marian Laura, Nora Margaret. BS with distinction, U.S. Naval Acad., 1974; JD cum laude, U. Pa., 1979. Bar: N.H. 1979, D.C. 1985, Va. 1999, U.S. Dist. Ct. D.C. 1989, U.S. Ct. Appeals (9th cir.) 1985, U.S. Ct. Appeals (fed. cir.) 1991. Ensign U.S. Navy, 1974, advanced through grades to lt. comdr., 1987, atty., 1979-87, resigned, 1987; assoc. Keck, Mahin & Cate, Washington, 1987-89, ptnr., 1990, Jenner & Block, Washington, 1990-95; shareholder Kilcullen, Wilson and Kilcullen, Chartered, 1995-99, Wickwire Gavin, P.C., Vienna, 1999—. Federal civil litigation, General civil litigation, Government contracts and claims. E-mail: cgoddard@wickwire.com

GODDARD, JO ANNA, lawyer; b. Iowa City, May 1, 1951; d. William B. and Yvonne (Franzke) G.; m. J. Greg Faith, Mar. 18, 1977; children: Maxwell G., Jessica A. BA, U. Colo., 1972; JD, U. Denver, 1980. Bar: Colo. 1980. Atty. Holme, Roberts & Owen, Denver, 1980-82; contracts mgr. Midcon Exploration, 1982-87; atty. Goddard & Goddard, P.C., 1987—. Mem. adv. bd. U. Denver Law Rev., 1997-99. Co-leader PTO, Boulder Sch., 1992-94, Girl Scouts, Boulder, 1991-94; mem. Leadership Denver, 1996-97. Mem. ABA (trust and estates), CLE (speaker, writer), Colo. Bar Assn. (trusts and estates), Colo. Womens Bar Assn. (v.p. 1980-97), Rotary (bd., program chair 1995-97). Estate planning, Probate, Estate taxation. Home: 6788 Harvest Rd Boulder CO 80301-3649 Office: Goddard & Gaddard PC 1900 Wazee St Ste 203 Denver CO 80202-1258

GODDARD, TERRY, lawyer; BA, Harvard U., 1969; JD, Ariz. State U., 1976. Mayor City of Phoenix, 1983-90; of counsel Bryan Cave, Phoenix, 1990-94. Bd. dirs. Ariz. Theater Co., Ariz. Family and Child Devel. Ctr., Homeward Bound, Neighborhood Coalition of Phoenix; former pres. Nat. League of Cities, 1989; former chmn. Ariz. Mcpl. Water Users Assn., Maricopa Assn. Govts., govt. and non-profit group Valley of the Sun United Way, Regional Pub. Transp. Authority, Rebuild Am. Coalition; adv. bd. State and Local Legal Ctr. Comdr. USNR, 1970—. Mem. ABA, State Bar Ariz., Maricopa County Bar Assn. Office: 502 W Roosevelt St Bldg 2 Phoenix AZ 85003-1331

GODFREY, CULLEN MICHAEL, lawyer; b. Ft. Worth, Apr. 8, 1945; s. Cullen Aubrey and Agnes (Eiland) G.; m. Melinda McDonald, Aug. 29, 1970. BA, U. Tex., 1968, JD, 1970. Bar: Tex. 1969, U.S. Dist. Ct. (we. dist.) Tex. 1971, U.S. Ct. appeals (5th cir.) 1979, U.S. Ct. Appeals (11th cir.) 1981. Ptnr. Sloan, Muller & Godfrey, Austin, Tex., 1969-72; staff atty. Hunt Oil Co., Dallas, 1972-74, Tesoro Petroleum Corp., San Antonio, 1974-75, sr. atty., 1975-78, asst. gen. counsel, 1978-82, FINA, Inc., Dallas, 1982-88; gen. counsel Am. Petrofina, Inc (now FINA, Inc.), 1988-90, v.p., sec., gen. counsel, 1990-95, sr. v.p., sec., gen. counsel, 1995-2000; vice chancellor, gen. counsel U. Tex. Sys., Austin, 2000—. Bd. dirs. Normandy Life Ins. Co., Fina Oil & Chem. Co., Trust pipe Line Co., River Pipeline Co. Author: Legal Aspects of the Purchase and Sale of Oil and Gas Properties, 1992; contbr. articles to profl. jours. Bd. trustees Dallas Mus. Art, 1993-95, 98-2000, chmn. corp. com., 1993-95; bd. dirs. United Way Met. Dallas, Inc., 1999-2000, gen. campaign chmn., 1999; bd. dirs. Dallas County Heritage Soc., 1998-2000; mem. exec. bd. dirs. Cir. 10, Boy Scouts Am., 1999-2000. Recipient Anti-Defamation League Jurispirdence award, 1999. Fellow: Tex. Bar Found., Dallas Bar Found.; mem.: ABA (chmn-.subcom. on fgn. investment reporting, internat. law sect. 1984—87), State Bar Tex. (coun. oil, gas and mineral law sect. 1992—95, coun. bus. law sect. 1998—, v.p. bus. law sect. 2001—, coll. mem. 1989—, com. on continuing legal edn. 1997—2000, com.legal aspect arts 1998—, Cert. Merit 1999), Tex. Bd. Legal Specialization (bd. cert. oil, gas and mineral law), Tex. Bus. Law Found. (bd. dirs. 1990—, chmn. bd. dirs. 1995—98), Greater Dallas Crime Commn. (bd. dirs. 1991—2000, chmn. bd. dirs. 1995—98), Southwestern Legal Found. (rsch. fellow, adv.bd. internat. oil, gas edn.ctr., co-chmn. 44th-45th inst. on oil and gas law and taxation). General corporate, Oil, gas, and mineral, Private international. Office: U Tex Sys Office Gen Counsel 201 W 7th St Austin TX 78701

GODINER, DONALD LEONARD, lawyer; b. Bronx, N.Y., Feb. 21, 1933; s. Israel and Edith (Rubenstein) G.; m. Caryl Mignon Nussbaum, Sept. 7, 1958; children: Clifford, Kenneth. AB, NYU, 1953; JD, Columbia U., 1956. Bar: N.Y. 1956, Mo. 1972. Gen. counsel Stromberg-Carlson, Rochester, N.Y., 1965-71; assoc. gen. counsel Gen. Dynamics Corp., St. Louis, 1971-73; v.p., gen. counsel Permaneer Corp., 1973-75; ptnr. Gallop, Johnson, Godiner, Morganstern & Crebs, 1975-80; sr. v.p., gen. counsel, sec. Laclede Gas Co., 1980-98; of counsel Stone, Leyton and Gershman, P.C., 1999—. Editor Columbia U. Law Rev., 1955-56. Served with U.S. Army, 1956-58. Mem. ABA, N.Y. State Bar Assn., Met. St. Louis Bar Assn., Assn. of Bar of City of N.Y. Contracts commercial, General corporate, Public utilities. Home: 157 Trails West Dr Chesterfield MO 63017-2553 Office: Stone Leyton & Gershman PC 7133 Forsyth Blvd Ste 500 Saint Louis MO 63105-2122

GODONE-MARESCA, LILLIAN, lawyer; b. Buenos Aires, June 9, 1958; came to the U.S., 1991; d. Armand C.E. Godone-Signanini and E. Nydia Soracco-Godone; m. Paul Alexander Maresca-Lowell (dec.); children: Catherine Victoria, Gerard Frank, Warren Paul. BA, Cath. U. Buenos Aires, 1975, MA, 1977, JD summa cum laude, 1979, advanced tchg. degree in jud. sci., 1981. Bar: Dist. Ct. Buenos Aires 1980, Calif. 1995, U.S. Dist. Ct. (ea. dist.) Calif. 1995, U.S. Dist. Ct. (so. dist.) Calif. 1998; lic. real estate broker, Calif. Advisor Sub-Sec. of State for Fgn. Trade, Buenos Aires, 1982; pvt. practice law, 1982-86; therapist Ocean Pkwy. Developmental Ctr., N.Y., 1992; pvt. practice law Sacramento, 1995-96, San Diego, 1997—. Asst. instr. Cath. U., Buenos Aires, 1983-86; adj. instr. U.S. Internat. U., San Diego, spring 1998. Contbr. articles to profl. jours.; author of poetry. Vol. San Diego Vol. Lawyer Program, 1993-94, Legal Svcs. No. Calif., Sacramento, 1995-96; catechist St. Ignatius, Sacramento, 1995-96, St. Michael's, Poway, Calif., 1997-98. Mem. Internat. Soc. Poets (disting.), State Bar Calif., Mothers Twins Club. Republican. Roman Catholic. Avocations: spending time with her children, the right to life, writing. Bankruptcy, Family and matrimonial, Personal injury. Home: 11551 Avenida Sivrita San Diego CA 92128-4519

GODWIN, KIMBERLY ANN, federal agency administrator, lawyer; b. Fargo, N.D., July 18, 1960; d. Robert Chandler and Kathryn Marie (Haney) G. BA in Polit. Sci., U. N.H., 1980; MS in Mass Comm., JD, Boston U., 1984. Bar: D.C. 1984, U.S. Supreme Ct. 1990. Legal intern Army Corps of Engrs., Waltham, Mass., 1983-84; assoc. Booz, Allen & Hamilton, Inc., Bethesda, Md., 1986-88; cons. Dept. State, Washington, 1984-86, asst. dir. comm. interag. affairs, 1988-92, chief of policy diplomatic telecom. svc., 1992-96, dir. external affairs, 1997—. Cons. Elton Assocs., Inc., Arlington, Va., 1984—. Mem. ABA (vice chmn. internat. comm. com. 1989—), Phi Beta Kappa, Pi Sigma Alpha. Avocations: flying, tennis, skiing. E-mial. Home: 6215 Walhonding Rd Bethesda MD 20816-2138 Office: Dept State IRM/EA Rm 4428 2201 C St NW Washington DC 20520-0001

GOEBEL, WILLIAM HORN, lawyer; b. N.Y.C., Dec. 7, 1941; s. Harry H. and Maxine (Hamburger) G.; m. Barbara Golden, July 30, 1966; children: Jason, Pamela. AB, Columbia U., 1963; JD, NYU, 1966. Bar: N.Y. 1966. Assoc. Bernard Trencher, N.Y.C., 1966-69; real estate atty. J.C. Penney Co., Inc., 1969-71; assoc. gen. counsel N.K. Winston Corp., 1971-72, Teachers Ins. and Annuity Assn. Am./Coll. Retirement Equities Fund, N.Y.C., 1972-2000; bus. devel. and legal cons. Stewart Title Ins. Co., 2000—. Lectr. NYU Sch. Continuing Edn., 1985—; sr. coun. Team Leader, 1991-2000; mem. adv. bd. Commonwealth Land Title/Transamerica Title Ins. Co., 1992-2000; v.p. M.O.A. Enterprises, Inc./M.O.A Holdings, Inc., 1992-2000. Mem. Assn. of Bar of City of N.Y., N.Y. State Bar Assn. (fin. subcom. of real estate sect. 1998—, subcom. on zoning and land use planning). Contracts commercial, Real property. Office: Stewart Title Ins Co 4th Fl 300 E 42nd St New York NY 10017 E-mail: bgoebel@optonline.net, bgoebel@stewart.com

GOELZER, DANIEL LEE, lawyer; b. Milw., Feb. 14, 1947; s. Gerald Howard and Roberta (Hart) G.; m. Angela C. Carcone, Jan. 9, 1988; children: Christina H., Mary E.; 1 child by previous marriage, Michael W. BBA, U. Wis., 1969, JD, 1973; LLM, George Washington U., 1979. Bar: Wis. 1973, D.C. 1979, U.S. Dist. Ct. (we. dist.) Wis. 1973, U.S. Ct. Appeals (7th cir.) 1974, U.S. Ct. Appeals (2d, 9th and D.C. cirs.) 1975, U.S. Supreme Ct. 1976. Auditor Touche, Ross & Co., Milw., 1969-70; law clk. to Hon. U.S. Ct. Appeals, Chgo., 1973-74; atty. SEC, Washington, 1974-78, exec. asst. to chmn., 1978-83, gen. counsel, 1983-90; ptnr. Baker and McKenzie, 1990—. Adj. prof. Georgtown U. Law Ctr., Washington, 1986-92. Contbr. articles to profl. jours. With USAR, 1969-75. Mem. ABA, AICPA, Fed. Bar Assn. Republican. Congregationalist. Avocation: amateur radio. Administrative and regulatory, General corporate, Securities. Home: 5941 Searl Ter Bethesda MD 20816-2022 Office: Baker & Mckenzie 815 Connecticut Ave NW Washington DC 20006-4004 E-mail: daniel.l.goelzer@bakernet.com

GOETSCH, CHARLES CARNAHAN, lawyer, legal historian; b. New Haven, Nov. 9, 1950; s. John Black and Miriam Goetsch; m. Cecilia Cartwright Moffitt, Mar. 31, 1980; children: Benjamin John, Megan Elizabeth. AB magna cum laude, Brown U., 1973; JD, U. Conn., 1976; LLM, Harvard U., 1977; postgrad., Yale Law Sch., 1978-79. Bar: Conn. 1978, N.Y. 1984, U.S. Dist. Ct. Conn. 1978, U.S. Dist. Ct. (so. dist.) N.Y. 1982, U.S. Ct. Appeals (2d cir.) 1982, U.S. Supreme Ct. 1984. Law clk. to judge U.S. Dist. Ct. Conn., 1978-79, U.S. Ct. Appeals 2d cir., 1979-80; assoc. Tyler, Cooper & Alcorn, New Haven, 1980-81; ptnr. Cahill & Goetsch, P.C., 1982—. Chmn. civil justice adv. group U.S. Dist. Ct. Conn., 1990-95. Author: Essays on Simeon E. Baldwin, 1981, The Autobiography of Tomas L. Chadbourne, 1985; contbr. articles to legal jours.; editor Conn. Law Rev., 1974-76, Conn. Bar Jour., 1983-95. Am. Bar Found. fellow, 1978, NEH fellow, 1979. Fellow Am. Bar Found.; mem. ABA, Am. Trial Lawyers Assn., Conn. Bar Assn. (fed. practice com., chmn. legal history com.), Am. Soc. Legal History, Harvard Club, Brown Club (N.Y.C.), Phi Beta Kappa. Federal civil litigation, Personal injury. Home: 39 Round Hill Rd Woodbridge CT 06525-1228 Office: 43 Trumbull St New Haven CT 06510-1003

GOETTEL, GERARD LOUIS, federal judge; b. N.Y.C., Aug. 5, 1928; s. Louis and Agnes Beatrice (White) G.; m. Elinor Praeger, June 4, 1951; children: Sheryl, Glenn, James. Student, The Citadel, 1946-48; B.A., Duke U., 1950; J.D. (Harlan Fiske Stone scholar), Columbia U., 1955. Bar: N.Y. 1955. Asst. U.S. atty. So. Dist. N.Y., N.Y.C., 1955-58; dep. chief atty. gen.'s spl. group on organized crime Dept. Justice, 1958-59; asso. firm Lowenstein, Pitcher, Hotchkiss, Amann & Parr, 1959-62; counsel N.Y. Life Ins. Co., 1962-68; with Natanson & Reich, 1968-69; asso. gen. counsel Overmyer Co., 1969-71; asst. counsel N.Y. Ct. on the Judiciary, 1971; U.S. magistrate U.S. Dist. Ct., So. Dist. N.Y., 1971-76, U.S. dist. judge, 1976—; now sr. judge. Adj. prof. law Fordham U. Law Sch., 1978-87, Pace U. Law Sch., 1988-91; mem. com. on criminal justice act Jud. Conf. U.S., 1981-87, mem. cir. com. on pretrial phase of civil litigation, chmn. dist. coms. on discovery and criminal justice act 1982-85. Mem. council Fresh Air Fund, N.Y.C., 1961-64; bd. dirs. Community Action Program, Yonkers, N.Y., 1964-66. Served to lt. (j.g.) USCG, 1951-53. Mem.: Greenwood Country Club (Winsted, Conn.), Boyne South Golf Club (Naples, Fla.). Club: Greenwoods Country (Winsted, Conn.). Office: 14 Cottage Pl Waterbury CT 06702-1904

GOETZ, CLARENCE EDWARD, retired judge, retired chief magistrate judge; b. Balt., Feb. 4, 1932; AA, U. Balt., 1961, LLB, 1964. Bar: Md. 1964. Assoc. Hackney & Yourtee, Anne Arundel County, Md., 1965-66; asst. U.S. atty. for Md., 1966-70; U.S. magistrate judge for Md. Balt., 1970-97. Asst. prof. U. Balt., 1975, Towson State Coll., 1976; cons., arbitrator, mediator. Mem. Fed. Magistrate Judges Assn. E-mail: CKGoetz@home.com

GOFF, BETSY KAGEN, lawyer, international management group executive; b. York, Pa., July 3, 1948; d. Kenneth Stanford Kagen and Charlotte (Senn) Isen; m. William Miller Goff, Mar. 8, 1973; 1 child, Kenneth Steven. B.S. in Econs., U. Pa., 1970; J.D., Temple U., 1974. Bar: N.Y. 1975. Asst. exec. dir. Writers Guild of Am., N.Y.C., 1974-75; contract atty. ABC Sports, N.Y.C., 1975-78, asst. gen. atty. ABC News, N.Y.C., 1978-81; N.Y. v.p. Internat. Mgmt. Group Trans World Internat., N.Y.C., 1981— ; atty.-on-call Vol. Lawyers for the Arts, N.Y.C., 1974— , NOW, N.Y.C., 1975-79; dir. Living Arts, Inc., N.Y.C. Mem. Voters for Choice, Women in Sports. General corporate, Entertainment, Sports. Office: Internat Mgmt Group 22 E 71st St New York NY 10021-4975

GOGLIA, CHARLES A., JR. lawyer; b. Phila., Aug. 26, 1931; s. Charles and Marie A. (Beckman) G.; m. Patricia A. Morrissey, July 26, 1958; children: Philip L., Catherine A. BS, St. Joseph's U., Phila., 1953; LLB, Boston Coll., 1958. Bar: Mass. 1958, U.S. Dist. Ct. Mass. 1959, U.S. Ct. Appeals (1st cir.) 1964, U.S. Tax Ct. 1977, U.S. Supreme Ct. 1993. Atty. Sheff & Gens, Boston, 1958-61, Foley, Hoag & Eliot, Boston, 1961-68, ptnr., 1968-74; pvt. practice Wellesley, Mass., 1974—. Corporator, trustee, mem. bd. investment, exec. com. Bank Five for Savings, Burlington, Mass., 1974-92; mem. hearing com. Bd. Bar Overseers, Boston, 1984-86. Counsel Town of Nantucket, Mass., 1970-82, spl. counsel, 1982-85, Town of Weston, Mass., 1974-85, town counsel, 1986-92, spl. counsel, 1992—, mem. zoning bd. appeals, 1964-66, 74-85, mem. planning bd., 1973-74; spl. counsel Mass. Cable TV Commn., Boston, 1973-74. With USNAR, 1951-59. Mem. Wellesley Country Club (past pres.). Avocations: golf, travel. State civil litigation, General corporate, Real property. Home: 1 Hopewell Farm Rd Natick MA 01760-5570 Office: Wellesley Office Pk 65 William St Wellesley MA 02481-3802

GOGO, GREGORY, lawyer; b. Varos, Lemnos, Greece, Oct. 6, 1943; s. Soterio and Christina (Choleva) G.; m. Paraskevi Vivi Batzaka, July 15, 1989; 1 child, Chloe. BA, U. Chgo., 1966; MA, Rutgers U., 1972; JD, Seton Hall U., 1980. Bar: N.J. 1980, U.S. Dist. Ct. N.J. 1980. Reporter The Trentonian, Trenton, N.J., 1968-69; asst. project dir. Trenton Health Ctr., 1969-71; dir. planning UPI, Trenton, 1973-77; instr. sociology Trenton State Coll., 1973-77; assoc. Merlino, Rottkamp, Trenton, 1980-83; pvt. practice, 1983—. Corp. counsel Coronis Bldg. Sys. Mem. parish coun. St. George Orthodox Ch., Hamilton Twp., NJ, 1984—88, atty. for St. George, 1995; exec. bd. dirs. ARC, Trenton, 1972—77; spl. advisor to Pres. NAACP, 1973—74; mem. mass disaster response team NJSBA, 1996—. Recipient Archon Politis award Am. Hellenic Ednl. Prog. Assn., 1981, Cert. Merit, ARC, Trenton, 1977. Mem. N.J. Bar Assn., Mercer County Bar Assn., N.J. Assn. Trial Lawyers, Hellenic Vision (founding mem. 1992, pres. 1999—). Democrat. State civil litigation, Personal injury, Workers' compensation. Home: 14 Carla Way Lawrenceville NJ 08648-1500 Office: 1542 Kuser Rd Ste 1B Trenton NJ 08619-3829 E-mail: gogolaw@juno.com

GOHLKE, DAVID ERNEST, lawyer; b. Misawa AB, Japan, Apr. 20, 1963; s. Ernest E. and D. Annette Gohlke; m. Nancy Ann Brounstein, Jan. 16, 1988; 1 child, Christopher Aaron. AB in Polit. Sci., Washington U., St. Louis, 1985; MS in Criminal Justice Adminstrn., Cen. Mo. State U., 1988; MBA, JD magna cum laude, U. Houston, 1996. Bar: Tex. 1997. Commd. 2d lt. USAF, advanced through grades to capt., security police officer, 1985-92; assoc. Andrews & Kurth LLP, Dallas, 1997—. General corporate, Mergers and acquisitions, Securities. Office: Andrews & Kurth LLP Ste 1717 1717 Main St Dallas TX 75201

GOLD, ALAN STEPHEN, federal judge; b. N.Y.C. s. Frank and Geraldine (Guenzberg) G.; m. Susan Fine, May 28, 1965; children: Carol, Natalie. BA with high honors, U. Fla., 1966; JD, Duke U., 1969; M in Taxation, U. Miami, Fla., 1974. Bar: Fla., 1969, Dade County, Fla. (11th judicial cir.), 1992. Law clk. to Hon. Charles Carrol Fla. 3d Dist Ct. Appeal, Miami, 1969-71; asst. atty. Met. Dade County Atty's Office, 1971-75; ptnr. Greenberg, Traurig, Hoffman, Lipoff, Rosen & Quentel, P.A., 1975-92; apptd. judge 11th Circuit Ct., Dade County, Fla., 1992-97; appt. judge U.S. Dist. Ct. (so. dist.) Fla., Miami, 1997—. Contbr. articles to profl. jours. Co-gen. counsel Fla. High Speed Rail Transp. Commn., 1985—; city atty. Village of Bal Harbour, Fla., 1976-82; spl. counsel Broward County, Fla., 1984-88; trustee Palmer Sch., Miami, 1987-88; bd. dirs. Actor's Playhouse, Miami, 1989—, South Dade Jewish Community Ctr., Miami, 1985-85; apptd. Fla. Environ. Land Mgmt. Com., 1987. Disting. scholar Fla. State U., 1990; recipient award for outstanding contbn. in field of legis. affairs South Fla. Bldrs. Assn., 1989. Mem. ABA, Fla. Bar Assn. (com. on environment and land use law 1983-84, Disting. Svc. award 1984), Urban Land Inst. (nat. policy coun. 1988—), Greater Miami C. of C. (chmn. land use com. 1989-90), Am. Coll. Real Estate Attys. Democrat. Jewish. Avocations: trekking, vacationing, raising horses, sail fishing, reading. Office: US Dist Ct Fla 301 N Miami Ave Fl 10 Miami FL 33128-7702

GOLD, EDWARD DAVID, lawyer; b. Detroit, Jan. 17, 1941; s. Morris and Hilda (Robinson) G.; m. Francine Sheila Kamin, Jan. 8, 1967; children: Lorne Brian, Karen Beth. Student, Wayne State U., 1958-61; JD, Detroit Coll. Law, 1964. Bar: Mich. 1965, U.S. Dist. Ct. (ea. dist.) Mich. 1965, U.S. Ct. Appeals (6th cir.) 1965, D.C. 1966. Atty. gen. counsel FCC, Washington, 1965-66; ptnr. Conn, Conn & Gold, Detroit, 1966-67, May, Conn, Conn & Gold, Livonia, Mich., 1967-69, Hyman, Gurwin, Nachman, Gold & Alterman, Southfield, 1971-88, Butzel Long, Bloomfield Hills, 1988—. Chmn. Friend of Ct. Adv. Com., Lansing, Mich., 1982-88; mem. Oakland County Criminal Justice Coordinating Coun., 1976-77; contbr. lectr. Inst. Continuing Legal Edn., Ann Arbor, Mich., 1981—, Mich. Trial Lawyers Assn.; adj. prof. U. Detroit Mercy Sch. Law, 2001—. Author: Michigan Family Law, 1988; contbr. articles to legal jours. Mem. Southfield Transp. Commn., 1975-77; chmn. attys.' divsn. Jewish Welfare Fedn., Detroit, chairperson atty. disp. bd. Tri-County Hearing Panel 71, 1994-2001; mem. nat. young leadership cabinet United Jewish Appeal, N.Y.C., 1978-80; bd. dirs. Oakland County Legal Aid Soc., 1979-84; pres. Jewish Family Svc., Detroit, 1988-90. Tau Epsilon Rho scholar, 1963. Fellow Am. Coll. Family Trial Lawyers, Am. Acad. Matrimonial Lawyers (bd. dirs. 1986-93, pres. Mich. chpt. 1992-93, nat. bd. govs. 1998—); mem. Mich. Bar Assn. (coun. real property law sect. 1973-81, coun. family law sect. 1974-75, 77-82, chmn. family law sect. 1981-82, rep. assembly 1978-82, lifetime achievement award), Oakland County Bar Assn. (bd. dirs. 1984-93, pres. 1992-93), Southfield Bar Assn. (pres. 1975-76), Bar Assn. D.C., Am. Arbitration Assn., Alpha Epsilon Pi (nat. pres. 1976-77, Order of Lion award 1986). Avocation: golf. General corporate, Family and matrimonial, Real property. Office: Butzel Long Ste 200 100 Bloomfield Hills Pkwy Bloomfield Hills MI 48304 E-mail: Gold@Butzel.com

GOLD, GEORGE MYRON, lawyer, editor, writer, consultant; b. Bklyn., June 28, 1935; s. Harry and Rose Miriam (Meyerson) G.; m. Bunny Winters, Dec. 24, 1960; 1 child, Seth Harris A.B., U. Rochester, 1956; J.D., NYU, 1959. Bar: N.Y. 1960. Practice, N.Y.C., 1960-64, 67-78; legal editor Prentice-Hall, Inc., Englewood Cliffs, N.J., 1960-62; assoc. Speiser, Shumate, Geoghan & Law, N.Y.C., 1962-64; assoc. editor Rsch. and Rev. Svc. Am., Inc., Indpls., 1964-67; dir. publs., mng. editor Estate Planners Quar., Farnsworth Pub. Co., Inc., Rockville Centre, N.Y., 1967-69; editor-in-chief Trusts & Estates, N.Y.C., 1969-76; mng. editor Trust News, 1976-78; dir. news publs. and info. ABA, Chgo., 1978-83; sr. assoc. editor and dir. book divsn. ABA Jour., 1984-87; dir. publs. and editor Trial Mag. Assn. Trial Lawyers Am., 1988-89; cons. North Potomac, Md., 1989-90; exec. sr. law editor Mead Data Cen., Dayton, 1990-93; exec. editor Stevens Pub., Washington, 1993-94, corp. editl. dir., 1994-95, v.p. editorial, 1995. Cons., Ashburn, Va., 1995—. Author: The Propriety, Procedure and Evidentiary Effect of a Jury View, 1959, Investments by Trustees, Executors and Administrators, 1961, What You Should Know About Intestacy, 1962, What You Should Know About the Common Disaster, 1962, The Powers of Your Trustee, 1962, What You Should Know About the Antenuptial Agreement, 1963, Who May Be the Beneficiary of Your Will, 1963, What You Should Know About The Spendthrift Trust, 1963, Comprehensive Estate Analysis, 1966, You're Worth More Than You Think, 1966, Medicare Handbook, 1966, The ABCs of Administering Your Estate, 1966, The Will: An Instrument for Service and Sales, 1966, A Tax-Sheltered Pension Plan for the Close-Corporation Stockholder, 1968, Social Security Law in Nutshell, 1968, What You Should Know About Custodial Gifts to Minors, 1968, The Short-Term Trust and Estate

Planning, 1976, The Importance of a Will, 1976, The Need for an Experienced Executor, 1976, Tax Tips-99 Ways to Reduce the Bite, 1976, Investment Management: No Job for the Amateur, 1971, Who Manages Your Securities, 1972, A Woman's Need for Financial Planning, 1972, The Lawyer's Role in the Search for Peace, 1982, True Counselors: Helping Clients Deal with Loss, 1983, Evaluating and Settling Personal Injury Claims, 1991, Cite Checking: A Guide to Validating Legal Research, 1992, The Compliance Pak for HR Managers-Book I (Hiring, Evaluation & Separation), Book II (Severance), 1993, Selling Life Insurance: Overcoming Objections, 1996; editor: Fundamentals of Federal Income Estate and Gift Taxes, 1965-67, The R & R Tax Handbook, 1965-67, Tax-Free Reorganizations, 1968, Guide to Pension and Profit Sharing Plans, 1968, A Life Underwriter's Guide to Equity Investments, 1968, The Tired Tirade, 1968, A Handbook of Personal Insurance Terminology, 1968, The 15th Anniversary Edition of Estate Planners Quar., 1968, You, Your Heirs and Your Estate, 1968, The Farnsworth Letter for Estate Planners, 1968-69, How to Use Life Insurance in Business and Estate Planning, 1969, Human Drama in Death and Taxes, 1970, Don't Bank on It, 1970, The Feldman Method, 1970, Directory of Trust Instns. (ann.), LawTalk, 1986-87, The Supreme Court and Its Justices, 1987, Aaron J. Broder on Trial: Reflections of a Famous Litigator, 1994, Examining the Science Behind Nutraceuticals, 2001. Mem. Soc. Law Writers (dir. 1972-75), ABA, Am. Law Inst., N.Y. State Bar Assn., Assn. Bar City N.Y., Estate Planning Council N.Y.C., Nat. Press Club, Soc. Bus. Press Editors, Soc. Scholarly Publ., Soc. Human Resources Mgmt., Am. Soc. Assn. Execs., Newsletter and Electronic Publishers Assn., Washington Independent Writers, Loudoun County Cable TV Adv. Commn., Kappa Nu, Pi Alpha Lambda. Club: KP Estate planning, Personal injury, Probate. Office: 43325 Dovetail Pl Ashburn VA 20147-5312 E-mail: gmgold@erols.com

GOLD, HAROLD ARTHUR, lawyer; b. Pitts., Jan. 13, 1929; m. Anita Hubert, Aug. 18, 1937; children: Howard, Bradley. BBA, U. Pitts., 1952; JD, Georgetown U., 1956. Bar: Pa. 1956, D.C. 1956. Sole practice law, Pitts., 1956-64; atty. City of Pitts., 1960-69; ptnr. Baskin and Sears, Pitts., 1965-84, Reed, Smith, Shaw & McClay, Pitts., 1985-93; pres., chief exec. officer Coventry Care, Inc., Monongahela, Pa., 1970-86, chmn. bd., chief exec. officer, 1986-87. Adj. prof. law Duquesne U. Pres. Young Dem. Club of Pitts., 1960-66; presdl. elector Pa., 1960; chmn. bd. Mayview State Hosp., Pitts., 1971-75. Served to lt. U.S. Army, 1948-49, 52-53. Mem. ABA, Pa. Bar Assn., Allegheny County Bar Assn. (real property council 1983-86). Banking, Finance, Real property. Office: The Pitt Bldg 213 Smithfield St Pittsburgh PA 15222-2224

GOLD, I. RANDALL, lawyer; b. Chgo., Nov. 2, 1951; Albert Samuel and Lois (Rodrick) G.; m. Marcey Dale Miller, Nov. 18, 1978; children: Eric Matthew, Brian David. BS with high honors, U. Ill., 1973, JD, 1976. Bar: Ill. 1976, U.S. Dist. Ct. (no. dist.) Ill. 1976, Fla. 1979, U.S. Dist. Ct. (so. dist.) Fla. 1979, U.S. Ct. Appeals (5th and 7th cirs.) 1979, U.S. Tax Ct. 1979, U.S. Ct. Appeals (11th cir.) 1981, U.S. Supreme Ct. 1982, U.S. Dist. Ct. (mid. dist.) Fla. 1987; CPA, Ill., Fla. Tax staff Ernst & Ernst, Chgo., 1976-77; asst. state atty. Cook County, Ill., 1977-78, Dade County, Miami, Fla., 1978-82; spl. atty. Miami Strike Force U.S. Dept. Justice, 1982-87; pvt. practice Miami, 1987-92; asst. U.S. atty. U.S. Dist. Ct. (mid. dist.) Fla., 1992—. Lectr. Roosevelt U., Chgo., 1976-77; vice chmn. fed. practice com. on criminal sect. Fla. Bar, 1986-88, profl. ethics com., 1992-2001; instr. Rollins Coll. paralegal program, 1992-97; adj. prof. criminal justice program U. Ctrl. Fla., 1994—; adj. prof. law U. Orlando, 1998-99. Co-chmn. Greater Oviedo Cmty. Devel. Program, 1992-93; adviser Jr. Achievement, Chgo., 1976-78, Miami, 1982-84; coach, judge Nat. Trial Competition, U. Miami Law Sch., 1983-86, 88, 90; mentor Seminole County Sch., 1994—; coach mock trial program legal project Dade County Pub. Schs., 1985-89, 91-92, ptnr. program, 1989-92. Mem. ABA (govt. litigation counsel com., complex crimes com. litigation sect.), FBA, AICPA, ATLA, Fla. Bar, Ill. Bar Assn., Ill. Soc. CPAs, Fla. Inst. CPAs (com. on rels. with Fla. Bar 1985-86, bd. dirs. South Dade chpt. 1987-92), Ctrl. Fla. Bankruptcy Lawyers Assn., Orange County Bar Assn. (professionalism com., bankruptcy com.), Seminole County Bar Assn., Am. Assn. Atty. CPAs, Am. Inns of Ct. (master), U. Ill. Alumni Club (v.p.), Delta Sigma Pi. Jewish. Office: 80 N Hughey Ave Ste 201 Orlando FL 32801-2224

GOLD, PETER FREDERICK, lawyer; b. N.Y.C., Nov. 10, 1945; s. John and Dolores (Soyer) G.; m. Dee Crafferty, June 6, 1982; children: Joshua, Katharine. BA, Cornell U., 1967; MSc, London Sch. Econs., 1968; JD, NYU, 1971. Bar: D.C. 1988, N.Y. 1972, U.S. Dist. Ct. (so. dist.) N.Y. 1972, U.S. Dist. Ct. (ea. dist.) N.Y. 1972. Assoc. atty. Paul, Weiss, Rifkind, Wharton & Garrison, N.Y.C., 1971-75; legis. dir. Senator Gary Hart, Washington, 1975-81; ptnr. Wellford, Wegman, Krulwich, Gold & Hoff, 1981-84, Winthrop, Stimson, Putnam & Roberts, Washington, 1984-94; pres. The Gold Group, Chartered, 1994—, C.G. Sloan & Co., Inc., 1995-97. Editor in chief Review of Law and Social Change, 1970. Nat. policy dir. Hart for Pres. Campaign, Washington, 1984; chmn., founder First Book, Washington, 1992—; dir. Share Our Strength, Washington, 1990—; mem. Clinton-Gore Transition Team, Washington, 1992. Recipient Disting. Visitor Program European Econ. Community, Brussels, Belgium, 1982. Mem. D.C. Bar Assn., Fed. Bar Assn., N.Y.C. Bar Assn., Kenwood Golf & Country Club, Four Streams Golf Club. Democrat. Jewish. Avocation: tennis, golf. Antitrust, Private international, Legislative. Home: 13640 Glenhurst Rd North Potomac MD 20878-3921 Office: The Gold Group Chartered 1319 F St NW Ste 1000 Washington DC 20004-1106

GOLD, SIMEON, lawyer; b. Hartford, Conn., Jan. 3, 1949; s. Charles and Claire (Goldschein) G.; m. Heide Aline Turkel, Aug. 30, 1970; children: Jana, Craig. BS, Cornell U., 1970; JD, Harvard U., 1973. Bar: N.Y., U.S. Dist. Ct. (so. dist.) N.Y., U.S. Ct. Appeals (2d cir.). Assoc. Weil, Gotshal & Manges LLP, N.Y.C., 1973-81, ptnr., 1981—. Bd. dirs. Lawyers Alliance for N.Y. Contbr. articles to profl. jours. Mem. Coun. of Bus. Exec. Assn. for Help of Retarded Children, N.Y.C., Legal Aid Soc., N.Y.C.; bd. trustees Dalton Sch., 1997-2000. Mem. ABA, N.Y. State Bar Assn. (chair bus. law sect. 2000-01, former chair corp. law com. 1993-97), Assn. of Bar of City of N.Y., N.Y. County Lawyers Assn., Harmonie Club, Old Oaks Country Club. Avocations: skiing, tennis, golf, travel. General corporate, Securities, Restructuring. Office: Weil Gotshal & Manges LLP 767 5th Ave Fl Concl New York NY 10153-0119 E-mail: simen.gold@weil.com

GOLD, STEPHEN ALLEN, lawyer; b. Bklyn., May 24, 1942; s. George and Rose (Kaplan) G.; m. Winifred Atlas, June 5, 1966; children— Aliza, Shoshana. A.B., Columbia U., 1964; J.D., St. Johns U., 1967. Bar: N.Y. 1968, D.C. 70, U.S. Ct. Appeals (D.C. cir.) 1971, U.S. Supreme Ct. 1972. Atty., adviser FCC, Washington, 1967-68; assoc. law offices Samuel Miller, Washington, 1968-72; asst. gen. counsel Nat. Cable TV Assn., Washington, 1972-74; trial atty. U.S. Postal Rate Commn., Washington, 1974-75, dep. gen. counsel, 1975-82, consumer advocate, 1982— . Contbr. articles to legal jours. Pres. Lawyers North Civic Assn., Vienna, Va., 1981-83. Mem. Fed. Bar Assn. (chmn. postal law com. 1980-82), Am. Contract Bridge League (No. Va.). Jewish. Administrative and regulatory. Home: 2202 Loch Lomond Dr Vienna VA 22181-3231 Office: US Postal Rate Commn 1333 H St NW Washington DC 20005-4707

GOLD, STEVEN MICHAEL, lawyer; b. Bklyn., Sept. 19, 1953; s. Joseph and Gladys (Guss) G.; m. Susan Schwartz, Jan. 9, 1977; children: Rachel, David, Hannah. BA, Hobart Coll., 1975; JD, Cornell U., 1978. Bar: Conn. 1979, N.Y. 1979, U.S. Dist. Ct. Conn. 1979, U.S. Dist. Ct. (no. dist.) N.Y. 1979. Confidential law asst. 3d dept. appellate div. N.Y. Supreme Ct., Albany, 1978-79; assoc. Schatz & Schatz, Ribicoff & Kotkin, Hartford & Stamford, Conn., 1979-86, ptnr. Stamford, 1987-96, Shipman & Goodwin, LLP, Stamford, 1996—. Treas. Cmty. Coun. Westport/Weston, Conn., 1985, 1st v.p., 1987, bd. dirs., 1985-87; bd. dirs., counsel Urban League Greater Bridgeport, 1987-92; bd. dirs., v.p. Stamford Symphony Soc., 1990-95, counsel, 1994-95; bd. dirs. Nursing & Home Care, 1996-97; mem. adv. bd. Women's Bus. Develop. Ctr., 2001-. Mem. ABA, N.Y. State Bar Assn., Conn. Bar Assn., Stamford/Norwalk Regional Bar Assn., Assn. Comml. Fin. Attys., Assn. Corporate Growth, Nat. Assn. Transp. Practitioners (treas. Conn. chpt. 1983-85), Entrepreneurship Inst. (adv. bd. 1989-91), Phi Delta Phi, Pi Gamma Mu. Democrat. Jewish. Avocation: squash. Contracts commercial, Computer, General corporate. Office: Shipman & Goodwin LLP One Landmark Sq Stamford CT 06901 E-mail: sgold@goodwin.com

GOLD, STUART WALTER, lawyer; b. N.Y.C., Mar. 3, 1949; s. Morris I. and Barbara (Walters) G.; m. Michele M. Cardella, June 26, 1983. BA in Polit. Sci., Bklyn. Coll., 1969; JD, NYU, 1972. Bar: N.Y. 1973, U.S. Supreme Ct. 1983, U.S. Ct. Appeals (2d, 8th, 9th and D.C. cirs.). Law clk. to judge U.S. Dist. Ct. (so. dist.) N.Y., 1972-73; assoc. Cravath, Swaine & Moore, N.Y.C., 1973-80, ptnr., 1980—. Bd. dirs. N.Y. Lawyers for Pub. Interest, N.Y.C., 1982—. Mem. ABA, N.Y. State Bar Assn., Assn. of Bar City of N.Y. Democrat. Avocations: tennis, travel. Antitrust, Federal civil litigation, Libel. Office: Cravath Swaine & Moore 825 8th Ave Fl 39 New York NY 10019-7475

GOLDBERG, CHARLES NED, lawyer; b. San Antonio, Dec. 6, 1941; s. Harry and Mamie G.; children— Donald Harris, Allison Beth, William Korash. B.B.A., U. Tex., 1963, J.D., 1966. Bar: Tex. 1966, U.S. Dist. Ct. (so. dist.) Tex. 1969, U.S. Ct. Appeals (5th cir.) 1972. Mng. ptnr. Goldberg Brown, Houston, 1980— ; sec., dir. Affiliated Capital Corp., Houston, 1968-80. Mem. Southwest regional bd. Anti Defamation League, Houston, 1978—, mem. nat. commn., N.Y.C., 1982—; bd. govs. Houston Grand Opera, 1983-85. Served to capt. U.S. Army, 1966-68. Banking, Bankruptcy, Real property. Home: 1310 Chardonnay Dr Houston TX 77077-3102 Office: Goldberg Brown 5918 San Felipe St Apt 12 Houston TX 77057-1950

GOLDBERG, DAVID, lawyer, law educator; b. N.Y.C., Dec. 31, 1934; s. Philip and Esther (Dobbs) G.; m. Emily Ruth Messing, Aug. 17, 1958; children: Sara, Ari. BA, CUNY, 1956; LLB, Yale U., 1959. Bar: N.Y. 1960. Law clerk to judge U.S. Dist. Ct., N.Y.C., 1960-62; assoc. Kaye, Scholer, Fierman, Hays and Handler, 1962-68, ptnr., 1969-83, Cowan, Liebowitz and Latman, N.Y.C., 1983—. Adj. prof. law NYU, 1976-96. Contbr. articles on copyright and trademark law to N.Y. Law Jour., other profl. jours. Pres. Hillcrest Jewish Ctr., Jamaica Estates, N.Y., 1987-89. Served as sgt. U.S. Army, 1959-60. Mem. ABA (fin. officer sect. intellectual property law 1986-89, spkr. on copyright devels. 1984, 85, 87, 90, 2000), Copright Soc. USA (pres. 1978-80, hon. trustee 1980—, spkr. on copyright devels. annually 1984—), U.S. Trademark Assn. (spkr. on trademarks and copyright overlap 1987). Democrat. Avocation: fishing. Entertainment, Trademark and copyright. Office: Cowan Liebowitz and Latman 1133 Avenue Of The Americas New York NY 10036-6710 E-mail: dxg@cll.com

GOLDBERG, JOLANDE ELISABETH, law librarian, lawyer; b. Pforzheim, Germany, Aug. 11, 1931; came to U.S., 1967; d. Eugen and Luise Rosa (Thorwarth) Haas; m. Lawrence Spencer Goldberg, Sept. 7, 1969; children: Daniel Scott, Elisa Miriam, Clarissa Anna. Referendar, U. Heidelberg, 1957, PhD, 1963; postdoctoral, U. London, 1976-77. Bar: Germany 1961. Mem. rsch. staff Acad. Scis. and Humanities, Heidelberg, 1961-67; rsch. assoc. U. Heidelberg, 1964-67; cataloger, law specialist Libr. of Congress, Washington, 1967-72, asst. law classification specialist, 1972-80, law classification specialist, 1980—, sr. cataloging policy specialist, 1997—. Sculptor, potter Torpedo Factory Art Ctr., Alexandria, Va., 1974—; lectr. Smithsonian Inst., Washington, 1988—. Author: Probschlag & Meistersignatur, 1963; contbr. articles to profl. jours. Exec. bd. dirs. Friends Torpedo Factory Art Ctr., Alexandria, 1987—. Volkswagenwerk Found. rsch. fellow, Fed. Republic of Germany, 1964-65, German Rsch. Assn. fellow, 1966, German Libr. Inst. grantee, 1981, Robbins Collection sr. rsch. fellow U. Calif. Berkeley, 1995. Mem. ABA, ALA (Marta Lange award for disting. librarianship in law and polit. sci. 1999, Assn. Coll. and Rsch. Librs. divsn. Marta Lange Congl. Quarterly award 1999), Internat. Soc. for Knowledge Orgn., Am. Assn. Law Librs. (Tech. Svcs. Spl. Interest sect. exec. bd. dirs. 1987-91, citation for exceptional contbn. 1992, Reneé Chapman Meml. award 1999), Torpedo Factory Artist Assn., The Art League, Nat. Wildlife Fedn., Corcoran Gallery of Art. Democrat. Jewish. Office: Libr Of Congress Washington DC 20540-4305 Fax: (202) 707-6629. E-mail: jgol@loc.gov

GOLDBERG, JOSEPH, lawyer; b. Washington, Aug. 21, 1950; s. Morris and Rose (Levin) G.; m. Christine Marie Riggott, Mar. 29, 1980; children: Benjamin R., Louis E. BS, Ohio U., 1972; JD, U. Pa., 1975. Bar: Pa. 1975, N.J. 1981, D.C. 1980, U.S. Ct. Appeals (3d cir.) 1980, U.S. Dist.Ct. (mid. dist.) Pa. 1987, U.S. Supreme Ct. 1989. Assoc. Margolis, Edelstein & Scherlis, Phila., 1975-81; ptnr. Margolis Edelstein, 1982—. Author: State and Local Government Immunity to Tort Claims, 1992, 2d edit., 1997. Mem. ABA, Pa. Def. Rsch. Inst., Pa. Jud. Rules Com., Phila. Assn. Def. Counsel, Phila. Bar Assn. Avocation: scuba diving. Civil rights, General civil litigation, Personal injury. Office: Margolis Edelstein The Curtis Ctr 4th Fl Independence Sq West Philadelphia PA 19106

GOLDBERG, MARK JOEL, lawyer; b. Pitts., June 2, 1941; s. Charles J. and Eleanore (Letwin) G.; m. Wendy Witt, Dec. 23, 1988; children: Michael, Wendy, Josh, Jamie. BA, Washington and Jefferson Coll., 1963; JD, Case Western Res. U., 1966. Bar: Pa. 1966, Ohio 1966, U.S. Tax Ct. 1969, U.S. Supreme Ct. 1972. Assoc. Jerome Silver, Cleve., 1966-67; pvt. practice, Pitts., 1967-69; ptnr. Goldberg & Wender, 1969-80; ptnr., shareholder Gillotti Goldberg & Capristo, 1981-91, Goldberg Gentile & Voelker, Pitts., 1991-92, Goldberg, Gruener, Gentile, Horoho & Avalli, P.C., Pitts., 1992—. Mem. drafting com. Pa. Divorce Code, 1978-80, 88; frequent lectr. Pa. Bar Inst., Pa. Trial Lawyers Assn., Am. Acad. Matrimonial Lawyers. Contbr. articles to profl. jours. Committeeman Dem. Party, Pitts., 1970's; pres. bd. dirs. Parent and Child Guidance Ctr., Pitts., 1984-86. Fellow Am. Acad. Matrimonial Lawyers (pres. Pa. chpt. 1988-90, nat. bd. govs. 1991-95); mem. Am. Coll. Family Trial Lawyers (diplomate, officer), Allegheny County Bar Assn. (coun. mem. family law sect. 1972—, chmn. 1982-84), Pa. Bar Assn. (family law sect. chmn. 1986-88), Westmoreland Country Club, Rivers Club. Jewish. Avocations: golf, travel. Family and matrimonial. Home: 14 Carmel Ct Pittsburgh PA 15221-3618 Office: Goldberg Gruener Et Al 230 Grant Bldg Pittsburgh PA 15219-2200

GOLDBERG, MARVIN ALLEN, lawyer, business consultant; b. Phila., Jan. 9, 1943; s. Daniel and Elizabeth (Katz) G.; m. Kathryn Elizabeth Balotsky, Apr. 27, 1974; children: Robert Andrew, MaryBeth Anne. BS, Temple U., 1964, JD, 1967. Bar: Pa. 1968, U.S. Dist. Ct. (ea. dist.) Pa. 1980, U.S. Supreme Ct. 1976, U.S. Tax Ct. Estate tax atty. IRS, U.S. Tax Ct., Phila., 1967-68; staff atty. Legal Aid Soc. Northampton County, Easton, Pa., 1969-70, Northampton County Pub. Defender, Easton, 1969-70; pvt. practice law Phila., 1970-76; tchr. Inst. for Paralegal Tng., 1973; staff atty. Legal Aid Soc. Phila., 1974-76; CEO Goldberg & Assocs., P.C., Phila., 1976—. Cons. Butcher Trade Exchange, Ft. Washington, Pa., 1982-92. Mem. Chestnut St. Assn., Phila; dir. Sr. Citizen Judicare Project, Phila., 1977. With USAF, 1967-73. Fellow Roscoe Pound Inst.; mem. ABA, Phila. Bar Assn., Phila. Trial Lawyers Assn., Assn. Trial Lawyers Am., Pa. Trial Lawyers Assn., Attys. Across Am. (founding mem.), Jewish War Vets, Beta Gamma Sigma, Phi Alpha Delta. Avocations: running, flying, sailing, chess, Algebra, 19th century physics. Aviation, Insurance, Personal injury. Office: Goldberg & Assocs PC 1334 Walnut St Fl 5 Philadelphia PA 19107-5311

GOLDBERG, MAUREEN MCKENNA, state supreme court justice; b. Pawtucket, R.I., Feb. 11, 1951; m. Robert D. Goldberg. Grad., St. Mary's Acad., 1969; AB cum laude, Providence Coll., 1973; JD cum laude, Suffolk U., 1978. Bar: R.I. 1978, Mass. 1978, U.S. Ct. of Appeals (1st cir.) 1979. Asst. atty. gen. Adminstr. of the Criminal Divsn., 1978-84; town solicitor South Kingstown, 1985-87, Town of Westerly, 1987-90, acting town mgr., 1990; spl. legal counsel R.I. State Police; apptd. assoc. justice Superior Ct., 1990-96; assoc. justice R.I. Supreme Ct., 1997—. Mem. ABA, R.I. Bar Assn., R.I. Trial Judges Assn., Pawtucket Bar Assn. Office: Rhode Island Supreme Ct 250 Benefit St 7th Fl Providence RI 02903-2719

GOLDBERG, NEIL A. lawyer; b. N.Y.C., Dec. 24, 1947; s. Bernard G.; children: Jane Hana, Robert Saul. BA cum laude, SUNY, Stony Brook, 1969; JD cum laude, SUNY, Buffalo, 1973. Bar: N.Y. 1974, U.S. Dist. Ct. (we. dist.) N.Y. 1974. Sr. ptnr. Saperston & Day P.C., Buffalo, 1974—, also bd. dirs. Editor Products Liaility in New York, 1997; co-editor in chief Preparing for and Trying the Civil Lawsuit. Mem. ABA, Internat. Assn. Def. Counsel, Def. Rsch. Inst. (pres.), Am. Arbitration Assn. (bd. dirs. 1985—, product liability adv. coun.), N.Y. State Bar Assn. (chmn. product liability com. torts, ins. and compensation law sect. 1986—), Erie County Bar Assn. State civil litigation, Insurance, Personal injury. Office: Goldberg Segalla LLP Ste 500 120 Delaware Ave Buffalo NY 14202 Office Fax: 716-566-5401. Business E-Mail: ngoldberg@goldbergsegalla.com

GOLDBERG, RICHARD ROBERT, lawyer; b. New York, Apr. 27, 1941; s. Joseph and Anne (Blumfield) G.; m. Rita Ann Zieve, June 30, 1963; 1 child, Andrew Louis. BA, Pa. State U., 1961; LLB, U. Md., 1964. Bar: Md. 1964, U.S. Ct. Appeals (4th cir.) 1970, U.S. Supreme Ct. 1974, U.S. Ct. Appeals (5th cir.) 1978, U.S. Ct. Appeals (D.C. cir.) 1992, Pa. 1994, N.J. 1994. Asst. city solicitor to Mayor and City Coun. City of Balt., 1965-70; atty. The Rouse Co., Columbia, Md., 1970-78, v.p., assoc. gen. counsel, 1978-94; ptnr. Ballard, Spahr, Andrews & Ingersoll, Phila., 1994—. Author: Real Estate Development of Downtown Projects, 1981; author and editor: (handbooks) Commercial Real Estate Leasing, Commercial Real Estate Financing; contbr. numerous articles to profl. publs. Chmn. Jewish Coun. of Howard County, Md., 1975-77, chmn. ann. campaign, 1978, 80, 87; pres. Temple Isaiah, Columbia, 1978-79; bd. trustees Jewish Fedn. Howard County, 1993-94. Mem. ABA (sec. real property, probate and trust law, chmn. prohibited transactions com. 1983-85, chmn. mgmt. property com. 1985-87, chmn. nat. insts. and satellite programs 1987-89, advisor UCC drafting com. article 1, article 3, article 9), Md. State Bar Assn., Pa. Bar Assn., Phila. Bar Assn., Am. Law Inst. (advisor restatement of the law of mortgages), Anglo-Am. Real Property Inst. (sec. 1990-92, chair-elect 1994, chair 1995), Am. Coll. Real Estate Lawyers (v.p. 1989-90, pres.-elect 1990-91, pres. 1991-92), Urban Land Inst., Am. Coll. of Mortgage Attys. Real property. Home: 325 S 2nd St Philadelphia PA 19106-4317 Office: Ballard Spahr Andrews & Ingersoll 1735 Market St Ste 5100 Philadelphia PA 19103-7599 E-mail: goldbergr@ballardspahr.com

GOLDBERG, STANLEY JOSHUA, federal judge; b. Balt., Feb. 16, 1939; s. Isidore and Lillian Frances (Kravatz) G.; m. Susan Jane Coplin, July 1, 1962; Rachel Hilary, David Mark. BS, U. Md., 1960, LLB, 1964; postgrad., NYU, 1966-69. Bar: Md. 1964, U.S. Dist. Ct. Md. 1964, N.J. 1967, U.S. Dist. Ct. N.J. 1967, U.S. Tax Ct. 1968. Tax trial atty. office of chief counsel IRS, N.Y.C., 1965-69, 1971-76, spl. trial atty., 1976-84, asst. dist. counsel, 1984-85; assoc. Buckmaster, White, Mindel & Clarke, Balt., 1970; spl. trial judge U.S. Tax Ct., Washington, 1985—. Mem.: Am. Coll. Tax Counsel (hon.), D.C. Bar Assn. (hon.)). Office: US Tax Ct 400 2nd St NW Washington DC 20217-0002

GOLDBERG, VICTOR PAUL, law educator; b. 1941; BA, Oberlin (Ohio) Coll., 1963, MA, 1964; PhD, Yale U., 1970. From asst. to full prof. U. Calif., Davis, 1967-83; prof. Northwestern U., Evanston, Ill., 1983-88; prof., co-dir. Ctr. Law and Econ. Studies Columbia U., N.Y.C., 1988—. Assoc. prof. U. Calif., Berkeley, 1977; prof. U. Va., Charlottesville, 1981; mem. Inst. for Advanced Study, Princeton, N.J., 1978-79. Fellow Ctr. for Study of Pub. Choice, Blacksburg, Va., 1975-76. Office: Columbia U Sch Law 435 W 116th St New York NY 10027-7297 E-mail: vpgol@yahoo.com

GOLDBERGER, ALLEN SANFORD, lawyer; b. N.Y.C., Apr. 18, 1933; s. William S. and Elsa (Goldman) G.; m. Gail Davidman, Jan. 15, 1966; children— Michael, Lynn. B.A., NYU, 1954; J.D., Boston U. 1959. Bar: N.J. 1960, N.Y. 1982, U.S. Dist. Ct. N.J., U.S. Supreme Ct. Ptnr. Goldberger Seligsohn & Shinrod and predecessor firms, West Orange, N.J., 1981—. Served with U.S. Army, 1954-56. Mem. N.J. State Bar Assn. (chmn. workers compensation sect. 1983-85, exec. com.), Assn. Trial Lawyers Am., Essex County Bar Assn. (chmn. workers compensation sect.), N.J. State Bar Assn., N.Y. Workers Compensation Bar Assn. Jewish. Pension, profit-sharing, and employee benefits, Workers' compensation.

GOLDBERGER, ROBERT R. lawyer; b. N.Y.C., May 16, 1908; s. Charles Kalman and Ann (Green) G. BA, Yale U., 1930, LLB, 1933. Bar: Conn. 1933, U.S. Dist. Ct. Conn. 1935. Factfinder, arbitrator Superior Ct. Fairfield County, Bridgeport, Conn., 1983, atty., trial referee, 1984—. Arbitrator Am. Arbitration Assn., Conn., 1976-82. Served with AUS, 1942-45. Mem. Greater Bridgeport Bar Assn. (pres. 1975-77), Conn. Bar Assn. (50 Yr. Pin 1983, ho. of dels. 1977-78, bd. govs. 1978-80), Am. Legion, Grasso-Seavey Club (comdr. 1947-49), Yale Club of Ea. Fairfield County (bd. dirs. 1972-75), 25 Sportsmen Club Bridgeport (pres. 1959—). Republican. Jewish. State civil litigation, General practice, Probate. Home: 195 Jackman Ave Fairfield CT 06432-1727 Office: 955 Main St Bridgeport CT 06604-4300

GOLD-BIKIN, LYNNE Z. lawyer; b. N.Y.C., Apr. 23, 1938; d. Herbert Benjamin Zapoleon and Muriel Claire (Wimpfheimer) Sarnoff; m. Roy E. Gold, Aug. 20, 1956 (div. July 1976); children: Russell, Sheryl, Lisa, Michael; m. Martin H. Feldman, June 28, 1987. BA summa cum laude, Albright Coll., 1973; JD, Villanova Law Sch., 1976; hon., 1996. Bar: Pa. 1976, U.S. Dist. Ct. (ea. dist.) Pa. 1976, U.S. Supreme Ct. 1979. Assoc. Pechner, Dorfman, Wolffe, Rounick & Cabot, Norristown, Pa., 1976-81; ptnr. Olin, Neil, Frock & Gold-Bikin, 1981-82; pres. Gold-Bikin, Welsh & Assocs., 1982-96, Wolf, Block, Schorr & Solis-Cohen, Norristown, 1996—. Course planner for 12 manuals on continuing legal edn., 1978—; pres. coun. Albright Coll., Reading, Pa., 1982-87. Author: Pennsylvania Marital Agreements, 1984, Divorce Practice Handbook, 1994; contbg. editor, Fairshare Mag., 1987—. Named to Pa. Honor Roll of Women, 1996. Fellow Am. Acad. Matrimonial Lawyers, Internat. Acad. Matrimonial Lawyers, Am. Bar Found., Am. Law Inst., Pa. Bar Found.; mem. ABA (family law sect. chair 1994-95, ho. of dels. 1995, bd. govs. 1998-2001), Pa. Bar Assn. (family law sect. coun. mem. 1980-89), Montgomery County Bar Assn. (chmn. family law com. 1984-86), Pa. Trial Lawyers Assn. (chmn. family law sect. 1988-90). Family and matrimonial. Office: Wolf Block Schorr & Solis-Cohen PO Box 869 Norristown PA 19404-0869

GOLDBLATT, STEVEN HARRIS, law educator; b. Bklyn., Apr. 30, 1947; s. J. Irving and Ethel (Epstein) G.; m. Irene P. Burns, June 12, 1981; children: Sarah P., Elizabeth G.B. BA, Franklin & Marshall Coll., 1967; JD, Georgetown U., 1970. Bar: Pa. 1970, D.C. 1981. With Phila. Dist. Atty.'s Office, 1970-81; dir. Appellate Litigation Program Georgetown U. Law Ctr., Washington, 1981-83, prof. law, dir. Appellate Litigation Progam, 1983—. Chair rules adv. com. U.S. Ct. Appeals for Armed Forces, 2001—. Co-author: Analysis and Commentary to the Pennsylvania Crime Code, 1973, Three Prosecutors Look at the Crimes Code, 1974, Ineffective Assistance of Counsel: Attempts to Establish Minimum Standards for Criminal Cases, 1983; reporter Criminal Justice in Crisis, 1988, Achieving Justice in a Diverse America, 1992, An Agenda for Justice: ABA Perspectives on Criminal and Civil Justice Issues, 1996. Mem. ABA (criminal justice sect. chmn. amicus curiae briefs com. 1981-99, crisis in criminal justice com. 1990-91, criminal justice standards com.). Office: Georgetown U Law Ctr 600 New Jersey Ave NW Washington DC 20001-2075 E-mail: goldblat@law.georgetown.edu

GOLDBLUM, A. PAUL, lawyer; b. N.Y.C., July 26, 1925; s. Meyer and Rebecca (Glassman) G.; m. Chantal Mona Laurent, Sept. 2, 1951. B.S. cum laude, Harvard U., 1947, LL.B., 1950. Bar: N.Y. 1951, U.S. Dist. Ct. (ea. and so. dists.) 1952, U.S. Ct. Appeals (2d cir.) 1973. Trial atty. Liberty Mutual Ins. Co., N.Y.C., 1950-55, sr. trial atty., 1962-76, N.Y. div. gen. atty., appellate counsel, 1977— ; ptnr. Dent, Goldblum & Witschieben, N.Y.C., 1956-62; asst. counsel Ambulance Chasing Investigation, Bklyn., 1958-59. Contbr. articles to law jours. Chmn. law com. N.Y. Com. for Dem. Voters, 1956-60, 2d and 11th Jud. Dists. grievance com., 1974-82; bd. dirs. Greater Jamaica Devel. Corp., 1981— ; vice chmn. adv. bd. Paralegal Inst. Queens Coll., 1980—; mem. exec. com. Flushing Meadows-Corona Park Corp., 1987—. Served to lt. (j.g.) USN, 1943-46, PTO. Fellow N.Y. Bar Found.; mem. Queens County Bar Assn. (pres. 1979-80, chmn. com. profl. ethics 1984-88), N.Y. State Bar Assn. (del. 1981-87, v.p. 11th Jud. Dist. 1987—, chmn. Com. on Profl. Discipline 1978-81, vice chmn. Com. to Improve Ct. Facilities 1983—), Assn. of Bar of City of N.Y. Club: Harvard (N.Y.C.); Huguenot Yacht (New Rochelle, N.Y.). State civil litigation, Personal injury. Home: 34-21 80th St Jackson Heights NY 11372

GOLDEN, DONALD ALAN, lawyer; b. Olean, N.Y., Aug. 31, 1953; s. Clayton Alexander and Dorothea Ann (Pfeil) G.; m. Carol Anne Metz, Jan. 1, 1982; children: Allyson Michelle, Christina Ann. BS, SUNY, Brockport, 1975; JD, U. Miami, 1978. Bar: Fla. 1979. Asst. counsel Am. Title Ins. Co., Miami, Fla., 1980; assoc. corp. counsel Burger King Corp., 1980-82; ho. counsel Senior Corp., Miami Beach, Fla., 1982-86; assoc. Blackwell, Walker, Fascell & Hoehl, Miami, 1986-87, ptnr., 1988; prin. Moretz Walker & Golden P.A., 1988-91, Donald A. Golden, P.A., Miami, 1991-93, 97—, Wampler, Buchanan & Green, P.A., Miami, 1993-97. Mem. Fla. Bar Assn. Avocation: golf. Contracts commercial, General corporate, Real property. Home: 11755 SW 62nd Ave Miami FL 33156-4909 Office: Donald A Golden PA 11755 SW 62nd Ave Miami FL 33156-4909 Fax: (305) 740-0513. E-mail: goldmiami@mindspring.com

GOLDEN, E(DWARD) SCOTT, lawyer; b. Miami, Fla., Sept. 25, 1955; s. Alvan Leonard and Fay Betty (Gray) G.; m. Jane Eileen DeKlavon, June 9, 1979; children: Daniel Bryan, Kimberly Michelle. Student, So. Fla. Christian Coll., 1975-76; BS, MIT, 1978; JD, Harvard U., 1981. Bar: Fla. 1981, U.S. Dist. Ct. (so. dist.) Fla. 1982, U.S. Tax Ct. 1982, U.S. Supreme Ct. 1991, U.S. Dist. Ct. (mid. dist.) Fla. 1993. Assoc. Roberts and Holland, Miami, 1981-82, Valdes-Fauli, Richardson, Cobb & Petrey, P.A., Miami, 1982-83; v.p. Buck and Golden, P.A., Ft. Lauderdale, Fla., 1983-88; sole practice, 1988—. Judge negotiations competition Nova Southeastern U. Editor-in-chief Harvard Jour. of Law and Pub. Policy, 1980-81; contbr. articles to profl. jours. Mem. West Lauderdale Bapt. Ch., Broward County, Fla., 1982-98, chmn. deacons, 1984-86, 87-88, elder, 1994-98; mem. MIT Ednl. Coun., 1995—; del. Fla. Rep. Conv., 1987, 90; mem. Rep. Exec. Com., Broward County, 1984-94. Named one of Outstanding Young Men of Am., 1986; nominee Order of Silver Knight; Western Electric grantee, 1972-74. Mem. Christian Legal Soc., Broward County Christian Legal Soc. (pres. 1985-86, 94-95, 2000), Zeta Beta Tau. Lodge: Optimists (treas. Dade County Carol City High Sch., 1971-72). Avocations: sports, politics, Bible study. General corporate, Estate planning, Real property. Home: 5410 Buchanan St Hollywood FL 33021-5708 Office: 644 SE 4th Ave Fort Lauderdale FL 33301-3102 E-mail: esglaw@bellsouth.net

GOLDEN, ELLIOTT, judge; b. Bklyn., June 28, 1926; s. Barnet David and Rose (Fistel) G.; m. Ana Valbuena, July 8, 1990; children: Jeffrey Stephen, Marjorie Ruth, Peter Michael (dec.); stepchildren: Robert, Elizabeth, William, John. Student, Maritime Acad., 1944-46, NYU, 1947-48; LLB, Bklyn. Law Sch., 1951. Bar: N.Y. 1952, U.S. Dist. Ct. (ea. dist.) N.Y. 1953, U.S. Tax Ct., U.S. Dist. Ct. (so. dist.) N.Y. 1953, U.S. Supreme Ct. 1961. Assoc. Golden & Golden, 1952-64; asst. dist. atty. Kings County, N.Y., 1956-64, chief asst. dist. atty., 1964-76, acting dist. atty. N.Y., 1968; judge Civil Ct. of City of N.Y., 1977-78; justice Supreme Ct. State of N.Y., 1979-98, jud. hearing officer, 1998-2000. Adj. assoc. prof. N.Y.C. Tech. Coll., 1987-93; arbitrator, mediator Nat. Arbitration & Mediation, 1998—; cons. in field. Contbr. articles to profl. jours. Bd. trustees Greater N.Y. coun. Boy Scouts Am.; hon. vice chmn. March of Dimes; bd. dirs. Bklyn. Philharmonia; mem. adv. bd. Bklyn. PAL; chmn. Bklyn. Lawyers div. Fedn. Jewish Philanthropies; co-chmn. Bklyn. Lawyers div. State of Israel Bonds; assoc. trustee Temple Beth Emeth of Flatbush; mem. exec. com. Lawyers div. United Jewish Appeal; past pres. counsel Hosp. Relief Assn ; bd. dirs. Kings Bay YM-YMHA of Bklyn.; bd. dirs. Bklyn. ARC, Archway Sch. for Spl. Children, Bklyn. Sch. for Spl. Children. Recipient Cert. of Merit, Hosp. Relief Assn., numerous plaques, awards and certs. of appreciation various civic orgns. Mem. Nat. Dist. Attys. Assn. (dir. 1976-77, Disting. Svc. award), Combined Coun. Law Enforcement Ofcls. State N.Y., N.Y. State Dist. Attys. Assn. (sec. 1965-77), K.P. (supreme coun.). Avocations: golf, fishing, computers. E-mail: GoldenE@att.net

GOLDEN, GREGG HANNAN STEWART, lawyer; b. N.Y.C., Nov. 24, 1953; s. Edmond Jerome and Alvia Grace (Weinberger) G.; m. Laura Jean George, Apr. 26, 1992. Grad., Phillips Exeter Acad., 1971; AB with honors, Grinnell Coll., 1975; JD cum laude, Georgetown U., 1980. Bar: Pa. 1980, U.S. Dist. Ct. (mid. dist.) Pa. 1980, U.S. Ct. Appeals (3d and D.C. cirs.) 1981, Calif. 1982, N.J. 1983, D.C. 1984, U.S. Supreme Ct. 1984. Dep. atty. gen. State of Pa., Harrisburg, 1980-83; assoc. Hogan & Hartson, Washington, 1983-86; atty. Office of Enforcement Fed. Home Loan Bank Bd., 1986-88, assoc. dep. dir., 1988-89; assoc. dep. dir. enforcement Office Thrift Supervision U.S. Dept. Treasury, 1989-91, dist. counsel 12th Dist., 1990-91; counsel Resolution Trust Corp., 1991-94, sr. counsel, 1994-95; sr. counsel corp. affairs FDIC, 1996-99, counsel receivership ops. and litigation, 1999—. Trustee, sec. InterFuture, N.Y.C., 1979-89, chairing officer bd. of trustees, 1989—. Rsch. editor: American Criminal Law Review, 1979-80. Lectr. YWCA Rape Crisis Svcs. div., Harrisburg; spl. counsel Pa. State Ethics Commn., Harrisburg, 1981-82; competition judge moot ct. bd. Cath. U. of Am., Washington, 1988-89. Fellow Johnson Found., 1972, Thomas J. Watson Found., 1975. Mem. ABA, D.C. Bar (com. on ct. rules 1985—, co-chmn. com. 1987-90, com. on representation for needy civil litigants 1985-88), Fed. Bar Assn., Pa. Bar Assn. Democrat. Jewish. Administrative and regulatory, Federal civil litigation, Contracts commercial. Office: FDIC 550 17th St NW Washington DC 20429-0001

GOLDEN, JOHN DENNIS, lawyer; b. Providence, May 18, 1954; s. Edward J. and Ann V. (Cahill) G.; m. Olga Iglesias, Aug. 2, 1980; children: Jennifer, Jackelyn, John. BA, Providence Coll., 1976; JD, Thomas M. Cooley, 1980. Bar: Mich. 1980, Fla. 1981. Assoc. Harvey Kruse & Weston, Detroit, 1980-82, Blackwell & Walker, Miami, Fla., 1982-83; ptnr. Rumburger Kirk et al, 1983-89; mng. ptnr. Roth, Edwards & Smith, 1989-91; shareholder, dir. Popham, Haik, Schnobrich & Kaufman, Ltd., 1991-95; shareholder Carlton, Fields, Ward, Emmanuel, Smith & Cutler, 1996—. Sustaining mem. Product Liability Adv. Coun. Mem. ABA (sustaining, mem. products liability adv. coun.), Mich. Bar Assn., Fla. Bar Assn., Dade County Bar Assn. Republican. Roman Catholic. Avocations: golf, snow skiing. Insurance, Product liability. Office: Carlton Fields Ward Emmanuel Smith & Cutler PO Box 01901 4000 International Pl Miami FL 33131-9101

GOLDEN, MARC ALAN, investment banker; b. Phila., Dec. 26, 1953; s. Mano Robert and Sue E. (Aronsohn) G. B.A., Yale Coll., 1975; M.B.A., J.D., Harvard U., 1980. Bar: N.Y. 1981, U.S. Dist. Ct. (so. and ea. dists.) N.Y. 1984, U.S. Supreme Ct. 1985. Legis. asst. U.S. Senator Richard Stone (Fla.), Washington, 1975; legis. aide, issues analyst U.S. Rep. William Green (Pa.), Washington, 1975-76; legis. counsel U.S. Senate Com. on Vets. Affairs, Washington, 1976; asst. to dep. dir. Fed. Jud. Ctr., Washington, 1978; assoc. Cravath, Swaine & Moore, N.Y.C., 1981-86; v.p. Goldman, Sachs & Co., N.Y.C., 1986-88, mng. dir., head takeover def. and recapitalization group Prudential-Bache Capital Fundings, N.Y.C., 1988—. Active N.Y. chpt. Lawyers' Alliance for Nuclear Arms Control, 1983— . Mem. ABA, N.Y. State Bar Assn., Assn. Bar City N.Y. Office: Prudential Bache Capital Funding 199 Water St Fl 24 New York NY 10038-3592

GOLDEN, T. MICHAEL, state supreme court justice; b. 1942; BA in History, U. Wyo., 1964, JD, 1967; LLM, U. Va., 1992. Bar: Wyo. 1967, U.S. Dist. Ct. 1967, U.S. Ct. Appeals (10th cir.) 1967, U.S. Supreme Ct. 1970. Mem. firm Brimmer, MacPherson & Golden, Rawlins, Wyo., 1971-83, Williams, Porter, Day & Neville, Casper, 1983-88; justice Wyo. Supreme Ct., Cheyenne, 1988—, chief justice, 1994—. Mem. Wyo. State Bd. Law Examiners, 1977-82, 86-88. Capt. U.S. Army 1967-71. Office: Wyo Supreme Ct Bldg PO Box 1737 2301 Capitol Ave Cheyenne WY 82002*

GOLDEN, WILSON, lawyer; b. Holly Springs, Miss., Feb. 15, 1948; s. Woodrow Wilson and Constance Annette (Harris) G.; m. Krista Nix, July 10, 1999; children from previous marriage: Wilson Harris, Lewis Hamilton, Pamela Camille. BPA, U. Miss., 1970, JD, 1977. Bar: Miss. 1977, U.S. Dist. Ct. (no. and so. dists.) Miss. 1977, U.S. Ct. Appeals (5th cir.) 1977. Pub. affairs journalist PBS/Miss. Authority for Ednl. TV, Jackson, 1970-72; asst. sec. Miss. State Senate, 1972-76; ptnr. Lane & Henderson, Greenville, Miss., 1977-80, Watkins Ludlam & Stennis, Jackson, 1980-89; pvt. practice Jackson, Washington, 1990-96; v.p. govt. rels. ICF Kaiser Internat., Inc., Fairfax, Va., 1996—99; sr. congl. liaison U.S. Dept. Transp., Washington, 1999-2001; v.p. Jefferson Govt. Rels., 2001—. Mem. Dem. State Exec. Com., 1976-84, 88-96; mem. Miss. Gov.'s Constl. Study Commn., 1988; mem. Dem. Nat. Com., 1990-92; charter mem. Dem. Leadership Coun. NETWORK, 1988; USDOT rep. Miss. Spl. Task Force for Econ. Devel. Planning, 2000—. Major USAR, 1970-90. Recipient Disting. Reporting award Am. Polit. Sci. Assn. 1971, U.S. Law Week award Bur. Nat. Affairs, Inc., Washington, 1978. Mem. ABA, Miss. Bar Assn. Democrat. Presbyterian. Legislative. Home: 7037 E Haycock Rd Falls Church VA 22043-2319 E-mail: Wilsongolden@aol.com

GOLDFARB, BERNARD SANFORD, lawyer; b. Cleve., Apr. 15, 1917; s. Harry and Esther (Lenson) G.; m. Barbara Brofman, Jan. 4, 1966; children: Meredith Stacey, Lauren Beth. A.B., Case Western Res. U., 1938, J.D., 1940. Bar: Ohio bar 1940. Since practiced in, Cleve.; sr. ptnr. firm Goldfarb & Reznick, 1967-95; pvt. practice Cleve., 1997—. Spl. counsel to atty. gen. Ohio, 1950, 1971—74; mem. Ohio Commn. Uniform Traffic Rules, 1973—80. Contbr. legal jours. Served with USAAF, 1942-45. Mem. Am., Ohio, Greater Cleve. bar assns. Federal civil litigation, General practice, Labor. Home: 39 Pepper Creek Dr Pepper Pike OH 44124-5279 Office: 55 Public Sq Ste 1500 Cleveland OH 44113-1998

GOLDFARB, RONALD CARL, lawyer, educator; b. Bklyn., Apr. 20, 1947; s. Abe and Minnie G.; Marianne Kelleher, Apr. 10, 1983; 1 child, Rachel. BA, Richmond Coll., 1971; JD, New York Law Sch., 1975. Bar: N.Y. 1976, U.S. Dist. Cts. (so. and ea. dists) N.Y. 1976, U.S. Ct. Appeals (2d cir.) 1976, N.J. 1977, U.S. Supreme Ct. 1979. Pvt. practice, N.Y.C., N.J., 1976-94; assoc. prof, chmn. acctg. and legal studies Middlesex County Coll., Edison, NJ, 1995—2001, dean divsn. bus., computer sci and engring. techs., 2001—. Adj. instr. Middlesex County Coll., 1988-94; adj. asst. prof. Fordham U. Grad. Sch. Bus., 1991-93. Contbr. articles to profl. jours. Arbitrator N.Y. Civil Ct., 1978-88. Mem. Am. Assn. Paralegal Edn. (bd. dirs.), North East Acad. Legal Studies in Bus. (past pres.), Phi Delta Phi. Jewish. General corporate, General practice, Real property. Office: Middlesex County Coll 2600 Woodbridge Ave Edison NJ 08837-3604 E-mail: ronald_goldfarb@middlesex.cc.nj.us

GOLDFEIN, SHEPARD, lawyer; b. Englewood, N.J., 1948; AB, Rutgers U., 1970, JD, 1975; MA, U. Chgo., 1977. Bar: N.Y. 1976, N.J. 1977. Ptnr. Skadden, Arps, Slate, Meagher & Flom LLP, N.Y.C. Editor: Rutgers Law Rev., 1974-75. Mem. Phi Beta Kappa, Pi Sigma Alpha. E-mail. Office: Skadden Arps Slate Meagher & Flom LLP 4 Times Sq Fl 24 New York NY 10036-6595 E-mail: sgoldfei@skadden.com

GOLDIE, RAY ROBERT, lawyer; b. Dayton, Ohio, Apr. 1, 1920; s. Albert S. and Lillian (Hayman) G.; m. Dorothy Roberta Zatman, Dec. 2, 1941; children: Marilyn, Deanne, Dayle, Ron R. Student, U. So. Calif., 1943-44, JD magna cum laude, 1957; student, San Bernardino Valley Coll., 1950-51. Bar: Calif. 1957; cert. specialist estate planning, trusts and probate law, Calif. Bd. Legal Specialization. Elec. appliance dealer, various locations, 1944-54; dep. atty. gen. State Bar of Calif., L.A., 1957-58, 1957-58; pvt. practice San Bernardino, Calif., 1958-87, Rancho Mirage, 1987—. Pres. Trinity Acceptance Corp., 1948-53. Mem. World Peace Through Law Ctr., 1962—; regional dir. Legion Lex U. So. Calif. Sch. Law 1959-75; chmn. San Bernardino United Jewish Appeal, 1963; v.p. United Jewish Welfare Fund, San Bernardino, 1964-66; Santa Anita Hosp., Lake Arrowhead, 1966-69; bd. dirs. San Bernardino Med. Arts Corp.; trustee McCallum Theater, Bob Hope Cultural Ctr., 1996-99, Friends of Cultural Ctr. Found.; bd. dirs. Palm Canyon Theater, 1998—; legal counsel Lake Arrowhead Skating Found., 1998. Fellow Internat. Acad. Law and Sci.; mem. ABA, Assn. Naval Aviation Desert Storm Sqdn. (adminstrv. officer, sec.), San Bernardino County Bar Assn., Riverside County Bar Assn., State Bar Calif. (cert. specialist estate planning, probate and trust law), Am. Judicature Soc., Am. Soc. Hosp. Attys., Calif. Trial Lawyers Assn. (v.p. chpt. 1965-67, pres. 1967-68), Am. Arbitration Assn. (nat. panel arbitrators), Coachella Valley Desert Bar Assn. (chmn. taxation and estate planning, trusts, wills and probate com. 1992-94), Order of the Coif, Lake Arrowhead Country Club (pres. 1972-73, 80-81), Lake Arrowhead Yacht Club, Club at Morningside (CFO 1992-93, sec. 1993-94), Nu Beta Epsilon (pres. 1956-57). E-mail: ray r. General corporate, Non-profit and tax-exempt organizations, Real property. Home and Office: 1 Hampton Ct Rancho Mirage CA 92270-2585 E-mail: goldie@earthlink.net

GOLDMAN, ERIC SCOT, lawyer; b. Quincy, Mass., Mar. 5, 1957; s. Terry and Harriet (Goldstein) G.; m. Lora Anderson, June 18, 1983; children: William, Daniel, Leigh. BA, Boston Coll., 1979; MSc in Criminal Justice, Northeastern U., 1980; JD, Suffolk U., 1987. Bar: Mass. 1987, U.S. Dist. Ct. Mass. 1987, U.S. Mil. Ct. Appeals. Adminstr. McLean Hosp., Belmont, Mass.; caseworker Norfolk County Dist. Atty.'s Office, Dedham; atty. McDermott & Padis, Milton, 1983-93; assoc. Lynch & Lynch, South Easton, 1993-98, Lang & Morgera, Boston, 1998-99; ptnr. Finneran, Byrne & Drechsler, LLP, 1999—. Mediator Norfolk-Plymouth County; bd. dirs. Criminal Justice Scis. Inst., Washington. Recipient Cert. of Recognition, Norfolk County Dist. Atty., Commonwealth of Mass. Dist. Ct. Mem. Mass Acad. Trial Attys., Norfolk, Plymouth and Bristol County Bar Assn., Braintree Rifle and Pistol Club (pres. 1988—). Avocations: scuba diving, karate, music, firearms training. General civil litigation, Criminal, Insurance. Home: 36 Forge Way Duxbury MA 02332-4743 Office: Finneran Byrne & Drechsler Eastern Harbor Office Pk 50 Redfield St Boston MA 02122-3630

GOLDMAN, GARY CRAIG, lawyer; b. Dec. 28, 1951; s. Ronald Walter and Connie Sylvia (Stein) G.; m. Diane Rose Lane, Oct. 1, 1977; children: Justin Edward, Gregory David. BA magna cum laude, Temple U., 1973; JD, Villanova U., 1976. Bar: Pa. 1976, U.S. Dist. Ct. (ea. dist.) Pa. 1981. Jud. law clk. Common Pleas Ct., Northampton County, Pa., 1976-77; asst. atty. gen. office of legal counsel Pa. Dept. Pub. Welfare, Phila., 1977-81, asst. counsel, 1981-84; staff counsel CDI Corp., 1984-86, v.p., assoc. gen. counsel, 1986—. Mem. faculty, planning chmn. Nationwide Comml. Real Estate Leasing Programs. Author: Drafting a Fair Office Lease, 1989, 2d edit., 2000; contbg. author: The Commercial Real Estate Tenant's Handbook, 1987, The Practical Real Estate Lawyer's Manual, 1987, Commercial Tenants' Leasing Transactions Guide, 1991, Office Planning and Design Desk Reference, 1992, Negotiating and Drafting Office Leases, 1995; assoc. editor: Villanova Law Rev., 1974-76; contbr. articles to legal jours. Mem. ABA, Am. Corp. Counsel Assn., Phila. Bar Assn. Republican. Jewish. Avocation: golf. General corporate, Labor, Landlord-tenant. Home: 210 Fox Hollow Dr Langhorne PA 19053-2477 Office: CDI Corp 1717 Arch St Fl 35 Philadelphia PA 19103-2713

GOLDMAN, JANIS MERESMAN, lawyer, law firm executive; b. N.Y.C., Oct. 13, 1944; d. Harry and Helen (Chafets) Meresman; m. Michael David Goldman, Dec. 26, 1965; children— Melissa Lee, Lori Michelle. B.A. with honors in Psychology, U. Pa., 1965; J.D., Georgetown U. Law Center, Washington, 1969. Bar: D.C., Md. Sole practice, Washington, 1971-77; assoc. David Epstein, Esq., Washington, 1977-80; cons. Margolius, Davis & Finkelstein, Washington, 1980-82; pres. Lawyer's Lawyer, Inc., Washington, Chevy Chase, Md., 1983— , also chmn. bd. Co-author article in field. Chmn. U. Pa. Secondary Schs. Admissions Committee, Md., 1980— ; trustee D.C. Bd. Library Trustees, 1972-74; bd. dirs. Washington Urban League, 1972-74. New York State Regents scholar, 1961. Mem. D.C. Bar Assn., Montgomery County Bar Assn., Supreme Court Bar. Home: 3 Pinehurst Cir Bethesda MD 20815-3233 Office: Lawyer's Lawyer Inc 1725 K St NW Suite 907 Washington DC 20006

GOLDMAN, JERRY STEPHEN, lawyer; b. Bklyn., Sept. 7, 1951; s. Bernard I. and Charlotte (Emerling) G.; children by previous marriage: Rachel Dawn, Samantha. BA with honors, NYU, 1973; JD, Boston U., 1976; LLM in Taxation, Temple U., 1983. Bar: Mass. 1977, N.Y. 1977, U.S. Dist. Ct. (ea. and so. dists.) N.Y. 1980, U.S. Supreme Ct. 1981, Pa. 1982, U.S. Tax Ct. 1983, U.S. Dist. Ct. (ea. dist.) Pa. 1983, U.S. Ct. Appeals (3d cir.) 1983, U.S. Dist. Ct. Mass. 1997, U.S. Ct. Appeals (1st cir.) 1997. Sr. asst. dist. atty. Kings County Dist. Atty.'s Office, Bklyn., 1976-82; pvt. practice N.Y.C., Phila., 1982—. Dir., pres. Huntingdon Brook Cmty. Assn., Bucks Co, Pa., 1985-89. Mem. bd., counsel Citizen's Crime Commn., Phila., 1983-95; atty. Phila. Vol. Lawyers for the Arts, 1983—; chmn. Upper Southampton Planning Commn., 1984-90; bd. dirs. NYU Alumni Assn.; v.p. Coll. Arts and Scis. Mem. ABA, N.Y. State Bar Assn., Mass. Bar Assn., Pa. Bar Assn., Phila. Bar Assn., Fed. Bar Assn., N.Y. New Media Assn. Avocations: cross-country skiing, music. General corporate, Estate planning, Taxation, general. Office: 1601 Market St Philadelphia PA 19103 also: 13th Fl 111 Broadway New York NY 10006

GOLDMAN, JOEL J. retired lawyer; b. N.Y.C., Sept. 7, 1940; s. Myron and Pearl (Jacobs) G.; m. Jane I. Stalker, July 23, 1973; children: Elizabeth Ann, Rebecca Lynn. BS, U. Va., 1962; JD, Syracuse U., 1965. Bar: N.Y. 1966, U.S. Dist. Ct. (we. dist.) N.Y. 1966. Law clk. Myron Goldman, N.Y.C., 1965; staff atty., chief trial counsel Legal Aid Soc., Rochester, N.Y., 1966-73; ptnr. Kaman, Berlove, Marafioti, Jacobstein & Goldman, 1973-97; ret., 1997. Lectr. family law; spl. investigator N.Y. State Spl. Commn. on Attica, 1972; mem. panel arbitrators Am. Arbitration Assn..; mem. faculty Nat. Bus. Inst., 1985-97. Author continuing edn. materials; contbg. editor Bender's Forms for Civil Practice, 1986, Medina's Bostwick, 1986. Referee Ea. Assn. Inter-Collegiate Football Ofcsls., 1974-95, v.p. Empire chpt., 1988, pres., 1989, Observer, Ea. Coll. Athletic Conf., 1996—. Inductee Jewish Athletes Sports Hall of Fame, 1996. Fellow Am. Acad. Matrimonial Lawyers (ret.); mem. ABA, N.Y. State Bar Assn. (exec. com. family law sect. 1982, mem. exec. com. 1981-97), Monroe County Bar Assn. (chmn. family law sect. 1982, exec. com. 1981-86), Assn. Trial Lawyers Am. Jewish. Family and matrimonial. Home: 67 Mountain Rd Rochester NY 14625-1816 also: 21 Bluebill Ave Apt 1005B Naples FL 34108-1765 E-mail: jjgesq@gateway.net

GOLDMAN, LAWRENCE SAUL, lawyer; b. Phila., Mar. 25, 1942; s. Ephraim Lederer and Belle Joan (Finkelstein) G.; m. Kathi Sue Schleifer, June 20, 1965; children: Carolyn, Jonathan. BA, Brandeis U., 1963; JD, Harvard U., 1966. Bar: N.Y. 1966. Asst. dist. atty. New York County, N.Y.C., 1966-71; asst. gen. counsel N.Y. State Commn. To Investigate N.Y.C., 1971-72; pvt. practice N.Y.C., 1972-2001; principal Law Offices of Lawrence S. Goldman, 2001—. Cons. N.Y.C. Commn. on Police Corruption, 1972. Contbg. author: Criminal Trial Advocacy, 1980-99. Trustee Congregation Rodeph Sholom, N.Y.C., 1983-92; bd. dirs. William F. Ryan Comty. Health Ctr., N.Y.C., 1986-88, Bronx Defenders, 1997—; mem. N.Y. State Commn. on Jud. Conduct, 1990—, mem. adv. com. on the criminal law, 1992—. Recipient Man of Yr. award Hogan Assocs., 1984. Mem. NACDL (chmn. ethics adv. com. 1988-92, white collar com. 1992-97, Robert C. Heeney award 1998, pres.-elect 2001—), N.Y. State Assn. Criminal Def. Lawyers (pres. 1987-89, Thurgood Marshall award 1999), N.Y. Criminal Bar Assn. (pres. 1982-85, Outstanding Practitioner award 1994), N.Y. State Bar Assn. (Outstanding Practitioner award criminal justice sect. 1996), Harvard Club. Democrat. Criminal. Office: 500 Fifth Ave New York NY 10110-0002 E-mail: lsgoldman2@hotmail.com, lsg@lsgoldmanlaw.com

GOLDMAN, LOUIS BUDWIG, lawyer; b. Chgo., Apr. 11, 1948; s. Jack Sydney and Lorraine (Budwig) G.; m. Barbara Marcia Berg, Oct. 2, 1983; children: Jacqueline Ilyse, Annie Dara, Michael Louis. BA magna cum laude, U. Calif., Berkeley, 1970; JD cum laude, U. Chgo., 1974. Bar: Calif. 1975, U.S. Dist. Ct. (no. dist.) Calif. 1975, U.S. Ct. Appeals (9th cir.) 1975, N.Y. 1976, U.S. Dist. Ct. (so. and ea. dists.) N.Y. 1976, U.S. Ct. Appeals (2nd cir.) 1976, Ill. 1991, Czech Republic, 1997; registered fgn. lawyer, Eng. 1999, Wales 1999. Law clk. U.S. Dist. Ct., San Francisco, 1974-75; assoc. Cleary, Gottlieb, Steen & Hamilton, N.Y.C. and Paris, 1975-81, Edwards & Angell, N.Y.C., 1981-83, ptnr., 1986-88, Wald, Harkrader & Ross, N.Y.C., 1983-86, Altheimer & Gray, Chgo., 1989—, co-chmn., 1999—. Mng. dir. Abacus & Assocs. Inc., N.Y.C.; supervisory bd. Pudliszki S.A. Mem. U. Chgo. Law Rev.; contbr. articles to profl. jours. Mem. Chgo.-Prague Sister Cities Com., Chgo.-China Sister Cities Com.; bd. dirs. Lyric Opera Ctr. for Am. Artists, New Trier Swim Club; sec. class of 1970, U. Calif., Berkeley; bd. trustees The Ravinia Festival. Mem. ABA (com. on privatization), Calif. Bar Assn., N.Y. State Bar Assn. (com. on internat. banking, securities and fin. transactions), Assn. of the Bar of City of N.Y., N.Y. County Lawyers Assn., Chgo. Bar Assn., Ill. State Bar Assn., Internat. Bar Assn., Order of Coif, Northwestern Assocs., Chgo. China Sister Cities Comm., Old Willow Club, The Law Club, Phi Beta Kappa. Private international, Mergers and acquisitions, Securities. Home: 465 Grove St Glencoe IL 60022-1844 Office: Altheimer & Gray 10 S Wacker Dr Ste 4000 Chicago IL 60606-7407 E-mail: killian@nortexinfo.net

GOLDMAN, MICHAEL P. lawyer; b. Chgo., June 10, 1960; s. William J. and Judith Ann (Holleb) G.; m. Karla Sue Berman, June 26, 1983; children: Joshua, Adam, David. BS in Accountancy, U. Ill., 1982; JD cum laude, Loyola U. Chgo., 1985. Bar: Ill. 1985, U.S. Dist. Ct. (no. dist.) Ill. 1985; CPA, Ill. Acct. L. Karp & Sons Inc., Elk Grove Vill., Ill., 1979-81; tax analyst Beatrice Foods Corp., Chgo., 1981-84; ptnr. Katten Muchin & Zavis, 1984-2000, Sidley & Austin, Chgo., 2000—. Lectr. in field. Contbr. articles to profl. jours. Bd. dirs. K.I.D.S.S. for Kids (auxiliary of Children's Meml. Hosp., Chgo.), 1993—. Mem. ABA (tort and ins. and bus. law sects.), Chgo. Bar Assn.(ins. and corp. lawcoms.), Ill. CPA Soc. (chmn ins. co. com.), Soc. Fin. Ins. Examiners. Republican. Jewish. Avocations: skiing, handball. General corporate, Insurance, Securities. Office: Sidley & Austin Bank One Plz 10 S Dearborn Chicago IL 60603 Fax: 312-853-7036. E-mail: mgoldman@sidley.com

GOLDMAN, NATHAN CARLINER, lawyer, educator; b. Charleston, S.C., Mar. 19, 1950; s. Reuben and Hilda Alta (Carliner) G.; m. Judith Tova Feigon, Oct. 28, 1984; children: Michael Reuben, Miriam Esther. BA, U. S.C., 1972; JD, Duke U., 1975; MA, Johns Hopkins U., 1978, PhD, 1980. Bar: N.C. 1975, Tex. 1985, U.S. Dist. Ct. (mid. dist.) N.C. 1975. Paralegal City Atty.'s Office, Durham, N.C., 1975-76; asst. prof. govt. dept. U. Tex., Austin, Tex., 1980-85; pvt. practice Houston, 1985-86; assoc. Liddell, Sapp, Zivley, Hill & LaBoon, 1986-88; pvt. practice, 1988-2000; atty. Amour Law Office, 2000—. Adj. prof. space law U. Houston, 1985-88; rsch. assoc. Rice U. Inst. Policy Analysis, 1986—; lectr. bus. law, 1988-95; mem. coordinating bd. Space Architecture, U. Houston, 1985—; v.p. Internat. Design in Extreme Environments Assn., U. Houston, 1991—; vis. asst. prof. U. Houston-Clear Lake, 1989-91, 99—; adj. prof. South Tex. Coll. Law, 1994-95; gen. counsel Internat. Space Enterprises, 1993—, Globus Ltd. Co., 1994—; info. officer Israel Consulate, 1996-97, atty. Judith G. Cooper, P.C. Author: Space Commerce, 1985, American Space Law, 1988, 2d edit., 1996, Space Policy: A Primer, 1992; editor: Space and Society, 1984; assoc. editor Jour. Space Commerce, 1990-91; exec. editor Space Governance, 1996-99; also articles. Mem. com. on governance of space U.S. Bicentennial Commn., 1986-88, Clear Lake (Tex.) Area Econ. Devel. Found., 1987, Space Collegium, Houston Area Rsch. Ctr., 1987; pres. Windermere Civic Assn., 1990-92; bd. dirs. Hebrew Acad., 1994-96, Men's Club United Orthodox Synagogues, 1994—, pres., 1999—. U.S. Dept. Justice grantee, 1979-80, U. Tex. Inst. for Constructive Capitalism U. grantee, 1983; E.D. Walker Centennial fellow, 1984; NASA Summer fellow U. Calif., 1984. Fellow Internat. Inst. Space Law; mem. ABA, Tex. Bar Assn., Nat. Space Soc. (v.p. 1989-91), Inst. for Social Sci. Study Space (mem. adv. bd. 1990, editor Space Humanization Jour. 1993-2000), Am. Astronautical Soc., Inst. for Design in Extreme Environment Assn. (v.p. 1991-96), Space Bus. Roundtable. Avocations: reading, hiking, baseball, softball. General corporate, Immigration, naturalization, and customs, Private international. Home: 4419 Meyerwood Dr Houston TX 77096-3523 Office: 6161 Savvy Dr 450 Houston TX 77036

GOLDMAN, RICHARD HARRIS, lawyer; b. Boston, June 17, 1936; s. Charles M. and Irene M. (Marks) G.; m. Patricia Grollman, June 21, 1959; children: Elaine, Stephen. BA, Wesleyan U., 1958; LLB, NYU, 1961. Bar: Mass. 1961, U.S. Dist. Ct. Mass. 1961. Mem. Slater & Goldman, Boston, 1961-76, Widett, Slater & Goldman, PC, Boston, 1976-93; Sullivan & Worcester LLP, 1993—; past trustee, chmn. audit com. Grove Bank. Co-author: The Ritual Dance Between Lessee and Lender; contbr. articles to profl. jours. Trustee, v.p. Temple Israel; former chmn. Newton (Mass.) Human Rights Commn. Mem. ABA, Mass. Bar Assn., Boston Bar Assn. (chmn. leasing com. 1996-97, lectr., chmn. seminar comml. real estate fin. 1997, real estate steering com. 1997—, co-chair real estate sect. 1999—), Mass. Conveyancers Assn., Belmont Country Club (past v.p., sec.). General corporate, Probate, Real property. Home: 47 Vaughn Ave Newton MA 02461-1038 Office: Sullivan & Worcester LLP 1 Post Office Sq Ste 2300 Boston MA 02109-2129

GOLDMAN, STANLEY IRWIN, lawyer; b. Richmond, Va., Sept. 19, 1939; s. Robert and Alice Dorothy (Feldman) G.; m. Patricia Mae Samuel, Apr. 8, 1962 (div. 1967); 1 child, Linda S.; m Carol G. Malamud, Aug. 4, 1991. BA, U. Va., 1962, LLB, 1965. Bar: Va. 1965, U.S. Dist. Ct. D.C. 1972, U.S. Ct. Appeals (D.C. cir.) 1972, U.S. Ct. Appeals (2d cir.) 1975, U.S. Ct. Appeals (8th cir.) 1981, U.S. Ct. Appeals (7th cir.) 1982, U.S. Supreme Ct. 1980. Atty. ICC, Washington, 1965-67; ptnr. Denning & Wohlstetter, 1967—. Mem. Va. State Bar Assn., D.C. Bar Assn., Transp. Lawyers Assn., Assn. Transp. Practitioners. Republican. Jewish. Administrative and regulatory, Transportation. Home: 10009 Colebrook Ave Potomac MD 20854-1808 Office: Denning & Wohlstetter 1700 K St NW Washington DC 20006-3817

GOLDMAN, STEVEN JASON, lawyer, accountant; b. Boston, Nov. 11, 1947; s. Philip Charles and Selma Laura (Goldblatt) G. BSBA, Northeastern U., Boston, 1970, MBA, 1974; JD, New Eng. Sch. Law, 1987. Bar: R.I., 1987, U.S. Dist. Ct. R.I. 1988, U.S. Tax Ct. 1987; CPA, R.I. Staff auditor CPA firms, Boston and Providence, 1970-72; sr. accountant Peat, Marwick, Mitchell & Co., Providence, 1972-73; contr. Warwick Fed. Savs. & Loan Assn. (R.I.), 1974, v.p., 1975-79, exec. v.p., 1980-82; pres. Fin. Adv. Svcs., Unltd., 1982-87; pvt. practice, Warwick, 1987—. Fellow AICPA; mem. ABA (taxation div.), Nat. Soc. Tax Profls., R.I. Soc. CPAs, R.I. Bar Assn. (taxation com.), Turk's Head Club, Aircraft Owners and Pilots Assn., Edgewood Yacht Club. Jewish. Avocations: flying, sailing, tennis. Estate planning, Probate, Taxation, general. Office: 1009 Post Rd Warwick RI 02888-3362

GOLDSAMT, BONNIE BLUME, lawyer; b. N.Y.C., July 31, 1946; d. Frank and Evelyn (Tobias) Blume; m. Jay S. Goldsamt, June 25, 1967; children: Seth, Kathryn, Deborah. BA, Sarah Lawrence Coll., 1967; MA, NYU, 1971; JD, Rutgers U., 1979. Bar: N.J. 1979, N.Y. 1990, U.S. Dist. Ct. N.J. 1979, U.S. Supreme Ct. 1987. Law sec. to judge Superior Ct. N.J. Chancery Family Part, Newark, 1979-80; assoc. Cole, Schotz, Bernstein, Meisel and Forman, Rochelle Park, N.J., 1980-82; asst. county counsel govtl. affairs Essex County, Newark, 1982-84; assoc. Rose & DeFuccio, Hackensack, N.J., 1984-87; sr. assoc. Steven Morey Greenberg, 1987-89; pvt. practice, 1989—, Verona, 1992—. Speaker Women Bankers Assn., Hackensack, 1982, Seton Hall Law Sch., Newark, 1983; appointed mem. family practice com. N.J. Supreme Ct., 1990-92, ct. apptd. contract arbitrator, Essex County, 1996—, Task Force on Alternative Work Arrangements, State Bar Assn. Dispute Resolution Com.; asst. clin. prof. law Seton Hall Law Sch.; mem. complementary dispute resolution com. N.J. Supreme Ct. Bd. dirs. Downtown Bklyn. Planning Bd., 1974-75; committeeperson Essex County Com., 1987-96; ward co-chair Dem. County Com., Montclair, 1988-91, ward chair, 1993-96; fundraiser, speaker, chair women's issues No. N.J. Clinton Campaign; fin. com. Clinton/Gore campaign; chair women's issues Women's Coalition for Clinton/Gore; surrogate speaker Clinton for Pres. campaign; active Dem. Nat. Conv., Women's Leadership Forum. Named one of Bklyns. Women of the Yr., Bklyn. NOW, 1974. Mem. ABA, Am. Arbitration Assn. (arbitrator 1990—), Essex and Bergen County Comml. Bar Assns. (trustee Bergen County 1988-97, com. mem.), N.J. State Bar Assn. (chair dispute resolution sect. 1999—, family law exec. com., chair child abuse protocol com., elder law com., state bar family law exec. com., exec. com., judicial adminstrn. programming, pro bono com., sec. gen. coun. 1996-97, dispute resolution sect. 1999-2001), N.J. Assn. of Profl. Mediators (2nd vice-chair, chmn. dispute resolution sect. 1999-2001), Women Lawyers in Bergen County (pres. 1985-87, trustee Jean Robertson Found. 1987-88, dir. at large 1987-88, Merit award 1987), N.J. Assn. Profl. Mediators (sec. bd. dirs. 1997-98), Bergen County Bar Found. (trustee 1990-95), Nat. Acad. Elder Law Attys., Acad. of Family Mediators (practitioner mem.), N.J. Supreme Ct. Complementary Dispute Resolution Com., Hadassah. Democrat. Jewish. Avocations: reading, travel. Alternative dispute resolution, Family and matrimonial, General practice. Office: 1 University Plaza Dr Ste 14 Hackensack NJ 07601-6229 also: 25 Pompton Ave Verona NJ 07044-2934

GOLDSCHMID, HARVEY JEROME, law educator; b. N.Y.C., May 6, 1940; s. Bernard and Rose (Braiker) G.; m. Mary Tait Seibert, Dec. 22, 1973; children: Charles Maxwell, Paul MacNeil, Joseph Tait. AB, Columbia U., 1962, JD, 1965. Bar: N.Y. 1965, U.S. Supreme Ct. 1970. Law clk. to judge 2d Circuit Ct. Appeals, N.Y.C., 1965-66; assoc. firm Debevoise & Plimpton, 1966-70; asst. prof. law Columbia U., 1970-71, assoc. prof., 1971-73, prof., 1973-84, Dwight prof. law, 1984—, founding dir. Ctr. for Law and Econ. Studies, 1975-78; gen. counsel SEC, 1998-99, adv. to chmn., 2000; of counsel Weil, Gotshal & Manges, N.Y.C., 2000—. Cons. in field to pub. and pvt. orgns.; mem. planning and program com. 2d Cir. Jud. Conf., 1982-85; reporter 2d Cir. Jud. Conf. Evaluation Com., 1980-82, 88-89; mem. legal adv. com. N.Y.S.E., 1997-98, chmn. subcom. on corp. governance. Author(with others) Cases and Materials on Trade Regulation, 1975, 4th edit., 1997; editor: (with others) Industrial Concentration: The New Learning, 1974, Business Disclosure: Government's Need to Know, 1979, The Impact of the Modern Corporation, 1984. Chmn. bd. advisors program on philanthropy and the law NYU Sch. Law, 1992-94; bd. dirs. Nat. Ctr. on Philanthropy and the Law, 1996—; nat. coun. Washington U. Sch. of Law, 1999—; bd. dirs. Greenwall Found., 1996—, vice chair, 1999—. Fellow Am. Bar Found.; mem. ABA (task force on lawyers polit. contbrns. 1997-98), Am. Law Inst. (reporter part IV, duty of care and the bus. judgment rule, corp. governance project 1980-93), N.Y. State Bar Assn., Assn. Bar City N.Y. (v.p. 1985-86, chmn. exec. com. 1984-85, chmn. com. on antitrust and trade regulation 1971-74, com. on the 2d century, chmn. com. on securities regulation 1992-95, chmn. audit com. 1988-96, chmn. com. on corp. takeover legislation 1985-86, 88-92, treas., mem. exec. com. 1996-98, chmn. nominating com. 2000-01), Assn. Am. Law Schs. (chmn. sect. antitrust and econ. regulation 1976-78), Am. Assn. Internat. Commn. Jurists (sec.-treas., bd. dirs.), Century Assn., Riverdale Yacht Club (bd. dirs. 1987-90), Phi Beta Kappa. Office: Columbia Univ Sch of Law 435 West 116th St New York NY 10027 E-mail: goldschm@law.columbia.edu

GOLDSMITH, WILLIS JAY, lawyer; b. Paris, Feb. 21, 1947; came to U.S., 1949; s. Irving and Alice (Rosenfeld) G.; m. Marilynn Jacobson, Aug. 12, 1973; children: Andrew Edward, Helene Sara. AB, Brown U., 1969; JD, NYU, 1972. Bar: N.Y. 1973, U.S. Ct. Appeals (2d cir.) 1975, D.C. 1978, U.S. Ct. Appeals (4th cir.) 1979, U.S. Ct. Appeals (D.C. cir.) 1979, U.S. Supreme Ct. 1980, U.S. Ct. Appeals (6th cir.) 1985, U.S. Ct. Appeals (7th cir.) 1989, U.S. Ct. Appeals (3d cir.) 1991, U.S. Ct. Appeals (5th cir.) 1998. Atty. Dept. Labor, Washington, 1972-74; assoc. Guggenheimer & Untermyer, N.Y.C., 1974-77, Seyfarth, Shaw, Fairweather & Geraldson, Washington, 1977-79, ptnr., 1979-83, Jones, Day, Reavis & Pogue, Washington, 1983—, chmn. labor and employment law practice, 1991—. Adj. prof. law Georgetown U., 1988-91; fellow Coll. Labor and Employment Law, 1997—. Contbg. editor Employee Rels. Law Jour., 1983-91; assoc. editor Occupl. Safety and Health Law; mem. editl. adv. bd. Benefits Law Jour., 1991—. Mem. ABA (sect. labor and employment law com. on employee benefits, com. on occupl. safety and health), NYU Ctr. for Labor and Employment Law (bd dirs. 1997—), D.C. Bar Assn., Met. Club (Washington), Kenwood Golf and Country Club (Bethesda, Md.). Democrat. Jewish. Labor, Pension, profit-sharing, and employee benefits. Home: 6409 Elmwood Rd Chevy Chase MD 20815-6621 Office: Jones Day Reavis & Pogue 51 Louisiana Ave NW Washington DC 20001-2113 E-mail: wgoldsmith@jonesday.com

GOLDSON, AMY ROBERTSON, lawyer; b. Boston, Jan. 16, 1953; d. Irving Edgar and E. Emily (Lippman) Robertson; m. Alfred Lloyd Goldson, June 29, 1974. BA magna cum laude, Smith Coll., 1973; JD, Cath. U., 1976. Bar: D.C. 1976, U.S. Dist. Ct. D.C. 1976, U.S. Ct. Appeals (D.C. and 4th cirs.) 1976. Atty. office of chief counsel, tax ct. litigation div. IRS, Washington, 1976-77; assoc. Smothers, Douple, Gayton & Long, 1977-82; sole practice, 1982—. Gen counsel Congl. Black Caucus Found., Inc., Washington, 1977—. Mem. ABA, Nat. Bar Assn., Washington Bar Assn., D.C. Bar Assn., Phi Beta Kappa. Democrat. Roman Catholic. Club: Links (Washington). Avocations: swimming, skiing, tennis. General corporate, Entertainment, General practice. Home and Office: 4015 28th Pl NW Washington DC 20008-3801

GOLDSTEIN, ABRAHAM SAMUEL, lawyer, educator; b. N.Y.C., July 27, 1925; s. Isidore and Yetta (Crystal) G.; m. Ruth Tessler, Aug. 31, 1947 (dec. Feb. 1989); children: William Ira, Marianne Susan; m. Sarah Feidelson, May 7, 1995. B.B.A., CCNY, 1946; LL.B., Yale U., 1949, M.A. (hon.), 1961, Cambridge (Eng.) U., 1964; LL.D. (hon.), N.Y. Law Sch., 1979, DePaul U., 1987. Bar: D.C. bar 1949. Law clk. to judge U.S. Ct. Appeals, 1949-51; partner firm Donohue & Kaufmann, Washington, 1951-56; mem. faculty Yale Law Sch., 1956—, prof. law, 1961—, dean, 1970-75, Sterling prof. law, 1975—. Vis. prof. law Stanford Law Sch., summer 1963; vis. fellow Inst. Criminology, fellow Christ's Coll. Cambridge U., 1964-65; faculty Salzburg Seminar in Am. Studies, 1969, Inst. on Social Sci. Methods on Legal Edn., U. Denver, 1970-72; vis. prof. Hebrew U., Jerusalem, 1976, UN Asia and Far East Inst. for Prevention Crime, Tokyo, 1983, Tel Aviv U., 1986; cons. Pres.'s Com. Law Enforcement, 1967; mem. Conn. Bd. of Parole, 1967-69, Conn. Commn. Revise Criminal Code, 1966-70; mem. of the Conn. Planning Com. on Criminal Adminstrn., 1967-71; sr. v.p. Am. Jewish Congress, 1977-84, mem. exec. com., 1977-89, gov. coun., 1989-94. Author: The Insanity Defense, 1967, The Passive Judiciary, 1981, (with L. Orland) Criminal Procedure, 1974, (with J. Goldstein) Crime, Law and Society, 1971; contbr. numerous articles and revs to profl. jours. Served with AUS, 1943- 46. Guggenheim fellow, 1964-65, 75-76, Am. Acad. Arts & Scis., 1975—. Office: Yale Law Sch PO Box 208215 New Haven CT 06520-8215

GOLDSTEIN, BENJAMIN, lawyer, law educator; b. Phila., Dec. 2, 1949; s. Harry and Bella (Hochman) G. BS in Education, Temple U., 1971; JD, John Marshall U., Chgo., 1975. Bar: Ill. 1975, N.J. 1976, U.S. Ct. Appeals (7th cir.) 1975, (3rd cir.) 1978; U.S. Supreme Ct. 1978. Law clerk Cir. Ct. Cook County, Chgo., 1973-75; pvt. practice, 1975-76, Voorhees, N.J., 1976-80; atty., shareholder Maressa, Goldstein, Birsner, Patterson, Drinkwater & Oddo, Berlin, 1980—; solicitor Zoning Bd., Waterford, 1987-90, Township Com., Winslow, 1987-90; solicitor for mayor and coun. City of Lavallette (N.J.), 1995—. Adj. prof. law Camden County Coll., Blackwood, N.J., 1984—; arbitrator Superior Ct. N.J., Camden, 1990—; cons. Camden County Dem. Com., Runnemede, N.J., 1988-89; solicitor Kennedy Hosp. Sys., Stratford, N.J., 1994—. Author: (chpt.) Opening Statements, 1995; speaker in field. Mem. ATLA, N.J. Trial Lawyers Assn., ABA, N.J. State Bar Assn. (mock trial judge 1994—). Avocations: flying, scuba diving, boating, horseback riding, piano. Health, Personal injury, Professional liability. Office: Maressa Goldstein Birsner Patterson Drinkwater & Oddo 191 W White Horse Pike Berlin NJ 08009-2021 E-mail: Maressalaw@snip.net

GOLDSTEIN, CHARLES ARTHUR, lawyer; b. N.Y.C., Nov. 20, 1936; s. Murray and Evelyn V. Goldstein; m. Judith Stein, Sept. 29, 1962 (div. 1982); 1 child, Deborah Ruth; m. Carol Sager, Nov. 10, 1990 (div. 1995). AB, Columbia U., 1958; JD cum laude, Harvard U., 1961. Bar: N.Y. 1962. Law clk. U.S. Ct. Appeals (2d cir.), 1961-62; assoc. Fried, Frank, Harris, Shriver & Jacobson, N.Y.C., 1962-69; ptnr. Schulte Roth & Zabel, 1969-79, Weil, Gotshal & Manges, N.Y.C., 1979-83, counsel, 1983-85; ptnr. Shea & Gould, 1985-94, Sutherland, Asbill & Brennan, N.Y.C., 1994-95; counsel Squire, Sanders & Dempsey, 1996-01; counsel to amb. Ronald S. Lauder, 2001—. Lectr. Columbia U. Law Sch. Gen. counsel to Citizens Budget Commn., 1980-87; mem. Temp. Commn. on City Fins., 1975-77; mem. Gov.'s Task Force on World Trade Ctr. Mem. Am. Coll. Real Estate Lawyers. Republican. Real property. Home: 220 E 65th St New York NY 10021-6620 Office: 767 Fifth Ave Ste 4200 New York NY 10153 E-mail: cgoldstein@rslmgmt.com

GOLDSTEIN, DEBRA HOLLY, judge; b. Newark, Mar. 11, 1953; d. Aaron and Erica (Schreier) Green; m. Joel Ray Goldstein, Aug. 14, 1983; children: Stephen Michael, Jennifer Ann. BA, U. Mich., 1973; JD, Emory U., 1977. Bar: Ga. 1977, Mich. 1978, D.C. 1978, Ala. 1984. Tax analyst atty. Gen. Motors Corp., Detroit, 1977-78; trial atty. U.S. Dept. Labor, Birmingham, Ala., 1978-90; U.S. adminstrv. law judge office hearing and appeals Social Security Adminstrn., 1990—. New judge faculty U.S. adminstrv. law judges Social Security Adminstrn., 1991, 93—; co-chair Girl Scout Pluralism Think Tank, 1999. Mem. editl. bd. The Ala. Lawyer, 1994-99, The Addendum, 1995-99. Active United Way, Birmingham, 1983, 87, 90, 98, mem. vis. allocation team, 1998—, planning com., 2001—; bd. dirs. Temple Beth-El, 1993-94, co-chair workshop initiative group, 1993-94; adminstrv. v.p. Sisterhood, 1989-92; mem. steering com. Birmingham Bus. and Profl. Women Fedn., 1987-88, 95-2000; leader Brownie Troop, 1992—, bd. dirs. Cahaba Girl Scout Coun., 1996—; bd. dirs. Temple Emanu-El, 2000—; mem. Leadership for Diversity Initiative, 1995-96, Leadership Birmingham, 1997-98, Women's Network, 1997—. Mem. ABA, Ga. Bar Assn., D.C. Bar Assn., Mich. Bar Assn., Birmingham Bar Assn. (lay day com., scholarship com. 1994-99, 2001—, memls. com. 2000-01, women's liaison and project coms. 1998-99, bd. dirs. women's sect. 1999—, chmn. long range planning com. 1998-2000), Ala. Bar Assn., Zonta (v.p. 1983-84, bd. dirs. 1988-89, 90-92, intercity chmn. 1995, co-pres. 1996-98), B'nai B'rith Women (chair S.E. region 1984-86, Women's Humanitarian award 1981), Hadassah (local bd. dirs. 1979-83, adminstrv. v.p. 1989-90, 90-92, social action v.p. 2000-01). Jewish. Office: Social Security Adminstrn 1910 3rd Ave N Birmingham AL 35203-3585

GOLDSTEIN, E. ERNEST, lawyer, consultant; b. Pitts., Oct. 9, 1918; s. Nathan E. and Annie (Ginsberg) G.; m. Peggy Janet Rosenfeld, June 22, 1941; children: Susan M. Goldstein Lipsitch, Daniel F. A.B. cum laude, Amherst Coll., 1939; student, U. Chgo. Law Sch., 1940-42; LL.B., Georgetown U., 1947; S.J.D., U. Wis., 1956. Bar: D.C. 1947, Tex. 1958, U.S. Supreme Ct. 1967, conseil juridique, France 1973-79. Pvt. practice, Washington, 1947; with Dept. Justice, also War Claims Commn., 1947-50; assoc. counsel crime com. U.S. Senate, 1950-51; gen. counsel antitrust subcom. jud. Ho. of Reps., 1951-52; restrictive trade practices specialist Office U.S. Spl. Rep., Paris; also U.S. rep. productivity and applied research com. OEEC, 1952-54; prof. law U. Tex., 1955-65; spl. asst. to Pres. U.S. Lyndon B. Johnson, 1967-69; counsel Coudert Freres, Paris, 1966-67, ptnr., 1969-79; cons. CBS, Inc., 1980-85; advisor Ransom Humanities Rsch. Ctr. U. Tex., 1995—. Cons. on antitrust European coal and steel cmty., Luxembourg, 1956, on trade regulation Justice Sec., P.R., 1962; internat. law cons. Naval War Coll., 1962, 64; lectr. Inst. Advanced European Studies, U. Nice, France, 1967, Free U. Brussels, 1967, Europa Inst., Amsterdam, 1970; vis. prof. U. P.R. Law Sch., 1962; prof. Am. sem., Salzburg, Austria, 1963, 79; adj. prof. law U. Tex., 1993-95; chmn. Internat. Lawyers Ann. Conf. Mgmt. Ctr., Europe, 1971-79. Author: Patent, Trademark and Copyright Law, 1959, American Enterprise and Scandinavian Antitrust Law, 1962; contbr. author: LBJ: To Know Him Better, 1995, procs. of The Conference on Global Responsibility of Law Librarians, 1990; founder Tex. Internat. Law Jour., 1963, mem. adv. bd., 1983—. Membership chair Am. Vets. Com., Washington, 1946-47; chmn. S.W. regional adv. bd. Anti-Defamation League, 1964-65; bd. dirs. Am. C. of C. in France, 1970-79, Ctr. Internat. Formation Europèene, 1971—; trustee Leadership Enrichment Arts Program, 1996—; dir. Bus. Alliance for Vietnamese Edn., 1996—, chmn. adv. bd., 1994, co-chmn. adv. bd., 1995—; bd. govs. Am. Hosp. Paris, 1972-79, sec., 1974-79; chmn. fund raising Dem. Party Com. in France, 1973-77; mem. nat. com. Lyndon B. Johnson Meml. Grove, 1972-74; mem. nat. fin. coun. Dem. Nat. Com., 1975-77. With AUS, 1942-46. Decorated Legion of Merit; chevalier Légion d'Honneur, 1971; chevalier Ordre des Arts et des Lettres, 1981; recipient Carl Fulda Internat. Law award U. Tex., 1978; Medal of Honor, Am. C. of C., Paris, 1984; Carnegie Found. fellow, 1954-55, Ford. Found. Internat. Studies fellow, 1959, 60. Mem. Am. Club Paris (pres. 1976-78), Philos Soc. of Tex., Tex. Internat. Law Soc. (founder), Headliners Club, Austin Town and Gown Club, Order of Coif, Phi Delta Phi. Home: Cambridge Tower 1801 Lavaca St Apt 15F Austin TX 78701-1333 Office: U Tex Harry Ransom Humanities Rsch Ctr PO Box 7219 Austin TX 78713-7219

GOLDSTEIN, EUGENE E. lawyer; b. Bklyn., Jan. 5, 1946; s. Lester R. and Hannah (Strauss) G.; m. Anita Lorraine Wolis, June 10, 1975; children— Michael Jonathan, Lawrence Evan. B.A., CCNY, 1967; J.D., Washington U., 1970. Bar: N.Y. 1971, U.S. Dist. Ct. (ea. dist.) N.Y. 1973, U.S. Dist. Ct. (so. dist.) N.Y. 1974, U.S. Ct. Appeals (2d cir.) 1975, U.S. Supreme Ct. 1982. Law clk. VISTA, Portland, Oreg., 1970-71; assoc. firm Forscher, Glassman & Elias, N.Y.C., 1971-76; sole practice, N.Y.C., 1976-78; mem. firm Newman, Aronson & Neumann, P.C., N.Y.C., 1978-88. Mem. Am. Immigration Lawyers Assn., ABA, N.Y. State Bar Assn., N.Y. County Lawyers Assn., FBA, Assn. Internat. Educators, Jewish, B'nai B'rith, Anti-Defamation League (exec. com. N.Y. regional bd.). General corporate, Immigration, naturalization, and customs, Real property. Office: 150 Broadway Rm 1115 New York NY 10038-4302

GOLDSTEIN, HOWARD SHELDON, lawyer; b. Apr. 22, 1952; s. Jerome Harold and Goldie G.; m. Amy Ruth, 1980. BA, CUNY, 1974; JD, Bklyn. Law Sch., 1977. Bar: N.Y. 1978, U.S. Dist. Ct. (so. and ea. dists.) N.Y. 1978. Assoc. Loew & Cohen, Esquires, N.Y.C., 1976-82, ptnr., 1982-87, Cohen & Goldstein, N.Y.C., 1988—. Contbr. articles to profl. jours. Mem. N.Y. State Bar Assn. (family law com., legis. com.), N.Y. County Lawyers Assn., Nassau County Bar Assn., N.Y.C. Bar Assn. (legal referral svcs.). Republican. Jewish. General civil litigation, General corporate, Family and matrimonial. Office: Cohen & Goldstein Esqs LLP 32 Broadway Rm 1700 New York NY 10004-1670 E-mail: cohengolds@aol.com

GOLDSTEIN, KENNETH B. lawyer; b. Bklyn., Sept. 16, 1949; s. Nathan and Isabella (Solow) G. BA, Tulane U., 1973, JD, 1974; postdoctoral, Fordham U., 1979. Bar: N.Y. 1977, U.S. Dist. Ct. (so. and ea. dist.) N.Y. 1980, U.S. Ct. Appeals (D.C. cir.) 1981. Gen. mgr., v.p. Middletown (N.Y.) Window Cleaning Co., Inc., 1974; tchr. various schs., Middletown and Chester, N.Y., 1975-77; asst. sr. v.p., dir. mktg. Saks Fifth Ave, N.Y.C., 1977-79; sr. asst. dist. atty. Orange County, Goshen, N.Y., 1979-81; assoc. Zola & Zola, N.Y.C., 1981-83, Freedman, Weisbein & Samuelson P.C., Garden City, N.Y., 1983-85, Jaffe & Asher, N.Y.C., 1985-91, Raoul Lionel Felder P.C., N.Y.C., 1991—. Bd. dirs. Middletown Window Cleaning Co., Inc. Bd. dirs. New Orleans Jazz and Heritage Found., 1972-74, Jewish Family Svcs. Orange County, 2000—. Named one of Outstanding Young Men in Am., 1980. Mem. ABA, N.Y. State Bar Assn., Middletown Bar Assn., Orange County Bar Assn., Order of DeMolay. Republican. Jewish. Avocations: swimming, art, dance, opera. State civil litigation, Family and matrimonial, Landlord-tenant. Home: 145 E 35th St Apt 2ne New York NY 10016-4121 also: PO Box 3 Middletown NY Office: Raoul Lionel Felder PC 437 Madison Ave New York NY 10022-7001

GOLDSTEIN, M. ROBERT, lawyer, judge; b. N.Y.C., Nov. 18, 1927; s. Samuel and Dorothy (Kliban) G.; m. Susan Wallach, Nov. 17, 1932; children— Ellen Iris Goldstein Wasserson, Ivan. A.B., Pa. State U. 1947; J.D., NYU, 1949. Bar: N.Y. 1949, U.S. Dist. Ct. (so. and ea. dists.) N.Y. 1956, U.S. Supreme Ct. 1959, U.S. Ct. Appeals (2d cir.) 1969. Ptnr. Samuel Goldstein & Sons, N.Y.C., 1949—; judge Village Ct., Great Neck, N.Y., 1977-88. Columnist, Condemnation, Certiorari in N.Y. Law Jour., 1972—. Chmn. Great Neck Planning Bd., 1966-69, Great Neck Bd. Zoning and Appeals, 1969-73; trustee, dep. mayor Village of Great Neck, 1973-77; past pres. Couple's Club, Temple Beth El, Great Neck, United Community Fund, Great Neck; past bd. dirs. Men's Club, Temple Beth El. Mem. Assn. of Bar of City of N.Y., Nassau County Bar Assn., N.Y. County Lawyers' Assn. (chmn. real property com. 1979-84, sec. and bd. dirs. 1982—), Pi Lambda Phi (pres. nat. coun. 1970s, pres. endowment fund 1972—), Glen Head Country Club (N.Y., v.p. 1983-85), Boca West Club. Democrat. Jewish. Condemnation, State and local taxation. Home: 13 Locust Cove Ln Great Neck NY 11024-1117 Office: Samuel Goldstein & Sons 30 Vesey St New York NY 10007-2914

GOLDSTEIN, MARVIN MARK, lawyer; b. Bklyn., Jan. 24, 1944; s. Abraham and Regina (Winkler) G.; m. Linda Ann Sinkoff, Aug. 4, 1969; 1 child, Randal Ian. BS, Cornell U., 1966; JD, Boston U., 1969. Bar: N.Y. 1969, N.J. 1972. Corp. labor counsel Gen. Cable Corp., N.Y.C., 1970-72; assoc. Grotta, Oberwager & Glassman, Newark, 1972-76; ptnr. Grotta, Glassman & Hoffman P.A., Roseland, 1976-99; resident, ptnr. Proskauer Rose LLP, Newark, 1999—. Asst. sec. Hackensack (N.J.) Univ. Med. Ctr., 1987-93, mem. exec. com., 1987-96; bd. trustees United Jewish Community Bergen County, N.J., 1984-90; bd. visitors Sch. Law Boston U., 1998—. Mem. ABA (chmn. subcom. fair labor standards act labor law sect.), N.J. Bar Assn. (chmn. adminstrv. law sect. 1987-89, co-chair NLRB subcom. 1999—). Labor. Office: Proskauer Rose LLP 1 Newark Ctr Fl 18 Newark NJ 07102-5211

GOLDSTEIN, MICHAEL B. lawyer; b. N.Y.C., Sept. 29, 1943; s. Isaac and Betty (Friedman) G.; m. Jinny M. Loewenthal, Dec. 18, 1966; 1 child, Eric Loren. BA in Govt., Cornell U., 1964; JD, NYU, 1967. Bar: N.Y. 1967, Ill. 1974, D.C 1978. Spl. asst., dep. mayor Office of Mayor, N.Y.C., 1965-66, asst. city adminstr., dir. univ. rels., 1969-72; dir. N.Y.C. Urban Corps, 1966-69; assoc. vice chancellor for urban and govtl. affairs, assoc. prof. urban scis. U. Ill., Chgo., 1972-78; mem. Dow, Lohnes & Albertson PLLC, Washington, 1978—. Practice leader Ednl. Inst. Rels.; chmn. task force on pub. policy Commn.on Higher Edn. and Adult Learner Am. Coun. on Edn.; mem. bd. advisors Stanford Forum for Coll. Financing. Contbr. articles to profl. texts and jours. Pres. Nat. Ctr. for Pub. Svc. Internship Programs, 1975-77; bd. dirs., officer Washington Ctr. Internships and Acad. Seminars, 1977—; bd. dirs. and gen. counsel Washington Ballet, 1978—; bd. dirs. Greater Washington Rsch. Ctr., 1982-96, Chgo. Urban Corps, 1972-75, Am. Assoc. Higher Edn., 1998—; trustee Fielding Inst., 1989-94, 98—; trustee, chmn. fin. com. Mt. Vernon Coll., 1991-96; dir. Am.-Russian Cultural Cooperation Found., 1995—; bd. visitors Mt. Vernon Coll., 1996-98; bd. dirs. Sta. WETA, 1997-99, Am. Assn. Higher Edn., 1998—. Wall St. Jour. Newspaper Fund fellow, 1963, Loeb fellow Harvard U., 1972. Mem. ABA (chmn. edn. law com. 1991-92), D.C. Bar Assn. (vice chair edn. task force 1999—), FBA (co-chmn. edn. grants com. 1985-86, 91-92), Nat. Assn. Coll. and Univ. Attys. (mem. ctrl. office com. 1986-88, vice chmn. pvt. bar com. 1989-90, chair continuing legal edn. com. 2001—), Nat. Soc. Internships and Exptl. Edn. (pres. 1972), Am. Assn. Higher Edn. (dir. 1997—), Am. Assn. Univ. Adminstrs. (dir. 1998—). Democrat. Jewish. Administrative and regulatory, Education and schools, Legislative. Office: Dow Lohnes & Albertson 1200 New Hampshire Ave NW Washington DC 20036-6802

GOLDSTEIN, MICHAEL GERALD, lawyer, director; b. St. Louis, Sept. 21, 1946; s. Joseph and Sara G. (Finkelstein) G.; m. Ilene Marcia Ballin, July 19, 1970; children: Stephen Eric, Rebecca Leigh. BA, Tulane U., 1968; JD, U. Mo., 1971; LLM in Taxation, Washington U., 1972. Bar: Mo. 1971, U.S. Dist. Ct. (ea. dist.) Mo. 1972, U.S. Tax Ct. 1972, U.S. Ct. Appeals (8th cir.) 1974, U.S. Supreme Ct. 1976. Atty. Morris A. Shenker, St. Louis, 1972-78; ptnr. Lashly, Caruthers, Baer & Hamel and predecessor, 1979-84, Suelthaus & Kaplan, P.C. and predecessors, St. Louis, 1974-91; ptnr., chmn. dept. tax & estate planning Husch & Eppenberger, 1991-99; pres., CEO 1st Fin. Resources, 1999—; sr. v.p. EPS Fin. Solutions Corp., 1999-2000. Adj. prof. tax law Washington U. Sch. Law, 1986-97; planning com. Mid-Am. Tax Confs., chmn. ALI/ABA Tax Seminar; lectr., author taxation field. Author: BNA Tax Mgmt. Portfolios, ABA The Insurance Counselor Books; contbr. articles to profl. jours. Bd. dirs. Jewish Family and Children's Svc. St. Louis, 1980—, pres., 1986-88; bd. dirs. Jewish Fedn. of St. Louis; trustee United Hebrew Temple, 1986-88; grad. Jwish Fedn. St. Louis Leadership Devel. Coun.; co-chmn. lawyers divsn. Jewish Fedn. St. Louis Campaign, 1981-82, Leadership St. Louis, 1988-89. Capt. USAR, 1970-78. Fellow Am. Coll. Tax Counsel, Am. Coll. Trust and Estate Counsel; mem. ABA (chmn. tax seminar, group editor newsletter for taxation sect.), Am. Law Inst., Mo. Bar Assn., Bar Assn. Met. St. Louis, St. Louis County Bar Assn. Corporate taxation, Estate taxation, State and local taxation. Home: 2011 Yacht Mischief Newport Beach CA 92660-6713 Office: 18101 Von Karman Ste 540 Irvine CA 92612

GOLDSTEIN, MORT, lawyer, industrial engineer; b. N.Y.C., Apr. 13, 1942; s. Morris and Sarah (Elbaum) G.; children: Scott, Janice, Annette. BS in Indsl. Engring., Mont. State U., 1964; JD, U. Mont., 1969. Bar: Mont. 1970, Calif. 1970, U.S. Dist. Ct. (no. dist.) Calif. 1970, U.S. Supreme Ct. 1973, U.S. Dist. Ct. (cen. dist.) Calif. 1974, U.S. Dist. Ct. Mont. 1975, U.S. Dist. Ct. (ea. dist.) Calif. 1981. Assoc., Mintz, Giller, Himmelman & Minz, Oakland, Calif., 1969-75; ptnr. Hauge, Ober, Thompson & Goldstein, Havre, Mont., 1975-80; pres. Goldstein Law Firm, P.C., Havre, 1980— . Recipient award Am. Soc. Composers, Authors and Pubs., 1969. Mem. ABA, Calif. Bar Assn., Mont. Trial Lawyers Assn., Assn. Trial Lawyers Am. (inst. judge candidate 1989). Lutheran. Personal injury, Probate. Office: Goldstein Law Firm PC PO Box 706 Havre MT 59501-0706

GOLDSTEIN, ROBIN, lawyer; b. Bklyn., Sept. 23, 1957; s. Jerome and Edna (Cohen) G. SB, MIT, 1979, M of City Planning, 1980; JD, Union U., 1983. Bar: N.Y. 1984, U.S. Patent Office 1984, U.S. Dist. Ct. (ea. and so. dists.) N.Y. 1985, Mass. 1992, U.S. Supreme Ct. 1992, Ct. of Appeals for Fed. Cir. 1992. Patent clk. Internat. Paper Co., N.Y.C., 1982; assoc. Blum, Kaplan, Friedman, Silberman & Beran, 1983; patent atty. Digital Equipment Corp, Maynard, Mass., 1984-86; patent counsel SONY Corp Am., Park Ridge, N.J., 1986-91; of counsel Schiller & Kusmer, Boston, 1991-93; pvt. practice Palo Alto, Calif., 1993-95, 97—; sr. counsel Apple Computer, Inc., Cupertino, 1995-97, 98—; gen. counsel Newton, Inc., 1997. Talk show host Stas. KSCO-KOMY, 1998—; with the Schnauzer Logic Radio Co., 1999-2001. Mem. ABA, Am. Intellectual Property Law Assn. (mem. group 220 oversight com.), N.Y. Patent Law Assn., Sigma Phi Epsilon. Computer, Patent, Trademark and copyright. Home and Office: 4842 National Ave San Jose CA 95124-4919 E-mail: robin@schnauzerlogic.com, robin@weblegal.com

GOLDSTOCK, BARRY PHILIP, lawyer; b. Chgo., Sept. 10, 1941; s. George Arthur and Beatrice (Shapiro) G.; m. Eve-Ellen Schneider; children— Brian Steven, Michelle. B.A., UCLA, 1964, J.D., 1967. Bar: Calif. 1968, U.S. Dist. Ct. (ctrl. dist.) Calif. 1968, U.S. Supreme Ct. 1971; cert. family law specialist. Law clk. U.S. Dist. Ct. (ctrl. dist.) Calif., 1967-68; assoc. firm Epport & Delevie, L.A., 1968-69; ptnr. Stern & Goldstock, Newport Beach, Calif., 1969-88, Goldstock & Morris, Newport Beach, 1988-89; sole practice, 1989—. Pres. Lakewood Coordinating Council, 1972-74; chmn. bd. Helpline Youth Counseling, 1979-81. Named Man of Yr., Bellflower Jaycees, 1972; recipient commendation Los Angeles County Bd. Suprs., 1974. Mem. Los Angeles County Bar Assn., Orange County Bar Assn., Lions Internat. (dep. gov. dist. 1982-83, regional chair 1995-96). Democrat. Jewish. E=mail: bgoldstock@col.com. Consumer commercial, Family and matrimonial, Landlord-tenant. Office: 2 Park Plz Ste 300 Irvine CA 92614-8513

GOLDWEITZ, JULIE, lawyer; Assoc. counsel Reed Publishing USA. Office: 275 Washington St Newton MA 02458-1646*

GOLEMON, RONALD KINNAN, lawyer; b. Atlanta, Nov. 22, 1938; s. William Layton and Avis (Bogle) G.; m. Jacqueline Alice Burst, Sept. 2, 1966; children: Donald Brent, Jennifer Alice. BS in Indsl. Mgmt. Engring., U. Okla., 1961; LLB, U. Tex., 1967. Bar: Tex. 1967, U.S. Ct. Appeals (5th cir.) 1970, U.S. Dist. Ct. (so. dist.) Tex. 1968, U.S. Dist. Ct. (we. dist.) Tex. 1981, U.S. Dist. Ct. (no. dist.) 1986. Engr. asst. Tex. Water Pollution Control Bd., Austin, 1964-67; assoc. Keys, Russell, Watson & Seaman, Corpus Christi, Tex., 1967-71, ptnr., 1971-73, Brown McCarroll, LLP (formerly Brown McCarroll & Oaks Hartline), Austin, 1973—; mng. ptnr. Brown McCarroll & Oaks Hartline, 1989-94. Contbg. author The Southwestern Legal Foundation, 40th Annual Institute on Oil and Gas Law and Taxation, 1989, The Southwestern Legal Foundation, 43rd Annual Institute on Oil and Gas Law and Taxation, 1992; contbr articles to profl. jours. Alt. mem. RCRA permit adv. com. U.S. EPA, 1983; mem. Gov.'s Hazardous Waste Task Force, 1984-85; v.p. St. Stephen's Sch. PTA, 1985-86, pres., 1986-87; mem. cmty. adv. bd. Ronald McDonald House, Austin, 1990—. Mem. ABA (chmn. standing com. constnl. and by-laws 2001—, ho. dels. 2000—, mem. standing com. membership & liaison 1997-2000, mem. market rsch. task force 1995-96, chmn. sect. natural resources, energy and environ. law 1994-95, chmn.-elect 1993-94, vice-chmn. 1992-93, mem. coun. liaison environ. group 1989-91, chmn. air quality com. 1986-89, vice chmn. 1982-86), State Bar Tex. (chmn. environ. law sect. 1971-72), Tex. Mining and Reclamation Assn. (dir. 1988-2000), Travis County Bar Assn., U. Tex. Law Alumni Assn. (pres. 1984-85, mem. exec. bd. 1984-86). Avocations: hunting, skiing, golf. Administrative and regulatory, Environmental. Office: Brown McCarroll LLP 111 Congress Ave Ste 1400 Austin TX 78701-4043 E-mail: kgolemon@mailbmc.com

GOLIS, PAUL ROBERT, lawyer; b. San Francisco, Sept. 25, 1954; BA with high distinction, Calif. State U., Long Beach, 1977; JD, Syracuse U., 1981. Bar: Fla. 1984, U.S. Dist. Ct. (so. dist.) Fla. 1985, U.S. Ct. Appeals (11th cir.) 2000. Assoc. Russell L. Forkey, P.A., Ft. Lauderdale, Fla., 1984-85, Josias & Goren, P.A., Ft. Lauderdale, 1985-88; sr. trial atty. State of Fla. Dept. Transp., 1988-90; asst. county atty. Palm Beach County, West Palm Beach, Fla., 1990-91; assoc. Scott, Royce, Harris, Bryan & Hyland, Palm Beach Gardens, 1991-93, Watterson, Hyland & Klett, Palm Beach Gardens, 1993-98; pvt. practice, Boca Raton, Fla., 1998—. Featured spkr. on eminent domain issues Palm Beach County Bar Assn., West Palm Beach, 1993, 96, 99, 2001, on legal ethics Nat. Bus. Inst., West Palm Beach, 1999, 2000, on land use, 2000, 2001. Bd. dirs. Aid to Victims of Domestic Abuse, Inc., 1990-99, v.p., 1993-97, pres. 1997-99, mem. adv. bd., 1999-2001; bd. dirs. Boca Raton Soc. for Disabled, Inc., 1999—, treas. 2001-. Mem. ABA, Fla. Bar Assn. (eminent domain com. 1989—), Palm Beach County Bar Assn. (vice chmn. environ., land use and eminent domain CLE com. 1993-95, chmn. 1995-99, mem. 2000—, jud. rels. com. 1996-99, professionalism com. 2001-). State civil litigation, Condemnation. Office: 2000 Glades Rd Ste 208 Boca Raton FL 33432-1420 E-mail: Parogo@worldnet.att.net

GOLOMB, DAVID BELA, lawyer; b. Bklyn., Apr. 19, 1949; s. Maurice and Rita (Pick) G.; m. Lisa Ann Cutler, June 17, 1984. BA, Cornell U., 1970; JD, St. John's U., 1974. Bar: N.Y. 1975, U.S. Dist. Ct. (so. dist.) N.Y. 1977, U.S. Dist. Ct. (ea. dist.) N.Y. 1978, U.S. Ct. Appeals (2d cir.) 1979, U.S. Supreme Ct. 1979. Trial atty. N.Y.C. Legal Aid Soc., 1974-77; adminstr. N.Y.C. Office of Dep. Mayor, 1977-78; spl. asst. atty. gen. N.Y. State Office of Medicaid Fraud Control, 1978-80; trial atty. Fuchsberg and Fuchsberg, N.Y.C., 1980-83, Paul D. Rheingold, PC, N.Y.C., 1983-84; ptnr. Rheingold & Golomb PC, 1984-87; pvt. practice, 1987—. Lectr. ABA Nat. Inst. on Med. Malpractice, 1985, Ross Labs. Ann. Roundtable on Pediats., 1986. Mem. ABA, ATLA (N.Y. state del. 1992-94, gov. 1994—, exec. com. 2000—), Am. Bd. Trial Advs., Am. Inn of Ct., N.Y. State Bar Assn., Assn. of Bar of City of N.Y. (tort litigation com.), N.Y. State Trial Lawyers Assn. (bd. dirs. 1990-92, parliamentarian 1992-93, treas. 1993-95, sec. 1995-96, 2d v.p. 1996-97, 1st v.p. 1997-98, pres.-elect 1998-99, pres. 1999—, immediate past pres. 2000—, chmn. jud. screening com., chmn. med. malpractice com., mem. com. on state legis., co-chmn. seminars on malpractice), N.Y. County Lawyers Assn. Federal civil litigation, State civil litigation, Personal injury. Home: 40 Hampton Rd Scarsdale NY 10583-3025 Office: 230 Park Ave New York NY 10169-0005 E-mail: golomblaw@aol.com

GOLUBOCK, RHONA, lawyer; b. Suffern, N.Y., May 22, 1969; d. Harvey Lewis and Barbara (Polevoy) Golubock; m. Andrew Jay Rotter, Mar. 13, 1999. BA, Emory U., 1991; JD, Benjamin N. Cardozo Sch. Law, N.Y.C., 1994. Bar: N.Y. 1995, N.J. 1994. Atty. Instinct Records, N.Y.C., 1995-98; corp. cousnel Am. Softworks Corp., Darien, Conn., 1998—. Vol., Dem. Party, N.Y.C., 1995-96, Jewish Home and Hosp. for the Aged, N.Y.C., 1996-98. Mem. ABA, N.Y. State Bar Assn., B'nai B'rith. Avocations: reading, sports.

GOMEZ, DAVID FREDERICK, lawyer; b. Los Angeles, Nov. 19, 1940; s. Fred and Jennie (Fujier) G.; m. Kathleen Holt, Oct. 18, 1977. BA in Philosophy, St. Paul's Coll., Washington, 1965, MA in Theology, 1968; JD, U. So. Calif., 1974. Bar: Calif. 1975, U.S. Dist. Ct. (cen. dist.) Calif. 1975, U.S. Dist. Ct. (ea. dist.) Calif. 1977, Ariz. 1981, US. Dist. Ct. Ariz. 1981, U.S. Ct. Claims 1981, U.S. Ct. Appeals (9th cir.) 1981, U.S. Supreme Ct. 1981; ordained priest Roman Cath. Ch., 1969. Staff atty. Nat. Labor Relations Bd., Los Angeles, 1974-75; ptnr. Gomez, Paz, Rodriguez & Sanora, 1975-77, Garrett, Bourdette & Williams, San Francisco, 1977-80, Van O'Steen & Ptnrs., Phoenix, 1981-85; pres. Gomez & Petitti, PC, 1985—. Faculty Practicing Law Inst., 1989; instr. contracts law Peoples Coll. Law., L.A., 1975-76, Nat. Lawyers Guild; mem. Missionary Soc. St. Paul the Apostle (Paulist Fathers), 1963-75. Author: Somos Chicanos: Strangers in Our Own Land, 1973; co-author: Advanced Strategies in Employment Law, 1988, Arizona Employment Law Handbook, Vol. 2, 1995. Named to, Best Lawyers in Am., 1997—98, 1999—2000, 2001—. Fellow: Ariz. Bar Found.; mem.: ABA, Maricopa County Bar Assn., Los Abogados Hispanic Bar Assn., Nat. Employment Lawyer's Assn., Calif. State Bar Assn., Ariz. Employment Lawyers Assn. (bd. dirs. 1996—), Ariz. State Bar Assn. (com. on rules of profl. conduct 1991—97, civil jury instrns. com. 1992—94, peer rev. com. 1992—2000, task force on future of the legal profession 1998—). Democrat. Federal civil litigation, State civil litigation, Labor. Office: 2525 E Camelback Rd Ste 860 Phoenix AZ 85016-4279 E-mail: dfg@gomezlaw.net

GOMEZ, JOSE, lawyer; b. San Jose, Costa Rica, Jan. 8, 1948; s. Fabio and Claudia (Cortés) G.; m. Ana G. Tristán, July 20, 1972; children: Adriana, Antonio, María. JD, U. Costa Rica, 1972. Ptnr. Lara, López, Matamoros, Rodríguez & Tinoco, San Jose, 1969—; exec. dir. Union de Cámaras, Costa Rica, 1974-83; legal counsel Codesa, Costa Rica, 1986-90, Banco de Costa Rica, 1987—, Grupo Taca, El Salvador, 1987—, Stone Container and Ston Forestal, Costa Rica, 1989-99. Prof. U. Costa Rica, 1977-80, Escuela Libre de Derecho, Costa Rica, 1985-88. Avocations: diving, fishing, outdoor sports. General corporate, Real property. Office: Lara Lopez Matamoros et al calle 3 avenidas 6 y 8 652 San Jose 14741000 Costa Rica

GOMEZ, LYNNE MARIE, lawyer; b. Highland Park, Ill., May 9, 1952; d. John Ferdinand and Lucille Elizabeth (Devereaux) G.; m. William Joseph Coffey, Dec. 17, 1977; 1 child William Joseph Coffey III.. B.A., U. Tex.-Austin, 1972, M.A., 1974, J.D., 1977. Bar: Tex. 1977, U.S. Dist. Ct. (so. dist.) Tex. 1978, U.S. Ct. Appeals (5th Cir.) 1981, U.S. Dist. Ct. (we. dist.) Tex. 1984, U.S. Supreme Ct. 1983. Sole practice, Houston, 1978; staff atty. U.S. Dist. Ct., Houston, 1979-81; judicial clk. U.S. Dist. Judge, Houston, 1981-83; assoc. Blackburn, Gamble, & Henderson, Houston, 1983— ; adj. prof. law U. Houston, 1984— . Vol. March of Dimes, Houston, 1979-80, Am. Heart Assn., Houston, 1980-81, mem. com. to celebrate the Bicentennial of the Constn., dir. The Women's Advocacy Group, The Sheltering Arms, Houston, 1981— ; mem. The Met. Orgn., Houston, 1982— . Mem. ABA, State Bar Tex., Houston Young Lawyers' Assn. (chmn. courthouse visitation com. 1980-82), Am. Bus. Women's Assn. (sec. 1982-83, treas. 1983-84). Democrat. Roman Catholic. Federal civil litigation, State civil litigation, Consumer commercial. Office: Blackburn Gamble & Henderson 1900 West Loop S Ste 800 Houston TX 77027-3214

GONG, GLORIA M. lawyer, pharmacist; b. Yreka, Calif., Oct. 12, 1953; d. Kenneth Wayne and Patricia Ann (Farley) McCain; m. Peter-Poon Ming Gong, Apr. 3, 1976; children: George-Wayne, Cynthia-May, Miranda-Lin. Pharmacist Degree, U. of the Pacific, Stockton, Calif., 1976; JD, Calif. Pacific Law Sch., Bakersfield, 1992. BAr: Calif. 1992, U.S. Dist. Ct. (ea., ctr. and so. dists.) Calif. 1992. Pharmacist Gong's Pharmacy, Tehachapi, Calif., 1978-93; atty. Gong & Hirsch, Bakersfield, 1994-97; pvt. practice, 1997—. Mem. L.A. County Bar Assn., Kern County Bar Assn., Lambda Kappa Sigma. Alternative dispute resolution, Estate planning, Immigration, naturalization, and customs. Office: 818 "H" St Bakersfield CA 93304 Office Fax: 661-327-3792. E-mail: ggong@legalemail.com

GONSON, S. DONALD, lawyer; b. Buffalo, June 13, 1936; s. Samuel and Laura Rose (Greenspan) G.; m. Dorothy Rose, Aug. 28, 1960; children: Julia, Claudia A.B., Columbia U., 1958; J.D., Harvard U., 1961; postgrad., U. Bombay, India, 1961-62. Bar: Mass. 1962, N.Y. 1983. With Hale and Dorr, Boston, 1962—, sr. ptnr., 1972-2000, of counsel, 2000—. Co-chmn. Speech-Tech., N.Y.C., 1987; instr. in law Boston U., 1963-65, bd. trustees Boston Five Cents Savs. Bank, 1978-83, bd. advisors, 1983-88; adj. prof. internat. law Tufts U. Fletcher Sch. Law and Diplomacy, 1999—; lectr. Fin. Times (U.K.), Instnl. Investors, New Eng. Law Inst., Mass. Soc. CPA's. Chmn. Mass. Comty. Devel. Fin. Corp., 1976-82; pres. Cambridge Ctr. for Adult Edn., 1985-88; bd. dirs. Boston Psychoanalytic Soc. and Inst., 1994—. Fulbright scholar, 1961-62. Fellow Am. Bar Found.; mem. ABA, Internat. Bar Assn., Mass. Bar Assn., Boston Bar Assn. (chmn. internat. law sect. 1998-2001), Harvard Club. Private international, Mergers and acquisitions, Education and schools. Home: 32 Hubbard Park Rd Cambridge MA 02138-4731 Office: Hale & Dorr LLP 60 State St Boston MA 02109-1816 E-mail: donald.gonson@haledorr.com

GONYNOR, FRANCIS JAMES, lawyer; b. Cambridge, Mass., Nov. 6, 1959; s. James Francis and Beverly Joan (Lintz) G.; m. Deborah Lynn Snyder, July 25, 1981; children: Brian Christopher, Caroline Jane, Madeline Marie. AA, U. Fla., 1978, BA, 1980; JD, U. Houston, 1983. Bar: Tex. 1983, U.S. Dist. Ct. (so. dist.) Tex. 1983, U.S. Ct. Appeals (5th cir.) 1983. Assoc. Eastham Watson Dale & Forney, Houston, 1983-88, ptnr., 1988—. Mediator Am. Arbitration Assn., 1992. Contbr. articles to profl. jours. Mem. Maritime Law Assn., Houston Bar Assn., Coll. of the State Bar of Tex., Galveston Bay Found. Admiralty, Federal civil litigation, Environmental. Home: 3327 Spring Trail Dr Sugar Land TX 77479-3050 Office: Eastham Watson Dale Forney 808 Travis St Fl 20 Houston TX 77002-5706 E-mail: gonynor@eastham/aw.com

GONZALES, ALBERTO R. state supreme court justice, former secretary of state; b. San Antonio, Aug. 4, 1955; Student, U.S. Air Force Acad., 1975-77; BA, Rice U., 1979; JD, Harvard U., 1982. Bar: Tex. Ptnr. Vinson & Elkins, LLP, Houston, 1982-95; gen. counsel Gov. George W. Bush, 1995-97; sec. of state State of Tex., 1997-98; justice Supreme Ct of Texas, Austin, TX, 1999—. Trustee Tex. Bar Found., 1996—; mem. Tex. Jud. Dists. Bd., 1996-97; bd. dirs. United Way of Tex. Gulf Coast, 1993-94; pres. Leadership Houston, 1993-94; chair Commn. for Dist. Decentralization of Houston Ind. Sch. Dist., 1994; mem. com. on undergrad. admissions Rice U., 1994; chair Rep. Nat. Hispanic Assembly of Houston, 1992-94; pres. Houston Hispanic Forum, 1990-92; chair adv. com. Tex. Real Estae Ctr., 1989-90; bd. dirs. Big Bros. and sisters, Houston, 1985-91, Cath. Charities, Houston, 1989-93, others. Recipient Commitment to Leadership award United Way, 1993, Hispanic Salute award Houston Metro Ford Dealers, 1989, others; named one of Five Outstanding Young Texans, Tex. Jaycess, 1994, Outstanding Young Lawyer of Tex., Tex. Young Lawyers Assn., 1992. Mem. Houston Bar Assn., State Bar Tex. (bd. dirs. 1992-94). Republican. Office: Supreme Court of Texas PO Box 12248 Austin TX 78711-2248*

GONZALES, DANIEL S. lawyer; b. San Antonio, Nov. 10, 1959; s. Sam and Mary Louise (Stewart) G.; m. Mary David McCauley, May 16, 1980 (div. 1983); m. Devon Elaine Cattell, Jan. 1, 1988 (div. 2001). BA, U. Notre Dame, 1981; JD, Stanford U., 1984. Bar: Calif. 1986, U.S. Dist. Ct. (no. dist.) Calif. 1986, U.S. Tax Ct. 1987, U.S. Ct. Appeals (9th cir.) 1988, U.S. Dist. Ct. (ea. dist.) Calif. 1990. Trivia game writer Axlon Games, Sunnyvale, Calif., 1984; legal writer Matthew Bender & Co., San Francisco, 1984-86, assoc. Carey & Carey, Palo Alto, Calif., 1986-96, Ferrari, Olsen, Ottoboni & Bebb, San Jose, 1996-97, Bryant, Clohan, Eller, Maines & Baruh, San Jose, 1997—. Mng. editor Stanford Jour. Internat. Law, 1983-84. Candidate Menlo Park (Calif.) City Coun., 1988; bd. dirs. Page Mill YMCA, Palo Alto, 1993-99, YMCA of the Midpeninsula, 1999—, Project Match, San Jose, 1997—, pres., 1998-99; pres. Menlo Park Dispute Resolution Svc., 1994-95. U. Notre Dame scholar, 1977, Nat. Merit scholar, 1977, scholar Nat. Hispanic Scholarship Bd., 1980. Mem. ABA, San Mateo County La Raza Lawyers (pres. 1994), Santa Clara County Bar Assn. (chmn. minority access com. 1994, chmn. judiciary com. 1995), San Mateo County Bar Assn., Palo Alto Area Bar Assn. Democrat. Avocations: guitar, college football. General corporate, Land use and zoning (including planning), Real property. Office: Bryant Clohan Eller Et Al 303 Almaden Blvd 5th Fl San Jose CA 95110-2721 E-mail: dgonzales@bcemb.com

GONZALES, EDWARD JOSEPH, III, lawyer; b. Baton Rouge, Aug. 15, 1950; s. Edward Joseph Jr. and Ruth (Attaway) G.; m. Marear Ann Hathorn, Aug. 20, 1977; 1 child, Edward J. IV. BA, Southeastern La. U., 1975; JD, La. State U., 1982. Bar: La. 1982, U.S. Dist. Ct. (mid. dist.) La. 1985, U.S. Ct. Appeals (5th cir.) 1985, U.S. Ct. Appeals (11th cir.) 1997. Law clk. La. 19th Jud. Dist., Baton Rouge, 1982-83; pvt. practice, 1983-84; asst. U.S. att. Dept. Justice, 1985-95; spl. master La. Ins. Receiverships Office, 1995-96; assoc. Shows, Cali & Berthelot, 1997—. Recipient commendations FBI, 1989, 94, U.S. Atty. Gen., 1994, Spl. Achievement awards U.S. Dept. Justice, 1988, 89, 90. Administrative and regulatory, General civil litigation, Criminal. Office: Shows Cali & Berthelot PO Box 4425 Baton Rouge LA 70821-4425

GONZÁLEZ, CARLOS A. lawyer; b. Havana, Cuba, July 24, 1960; s. Jorge A. and Ondina (Santos) G.; m. Marilyn Marvin, Aug. 22, 1988; children: Matthew M., Jordan R. BS, Fla. State U., 1983; MA in Religion, Yale U., 1986; JD, Vanderbilt U., 1989. Bar: Ga. 1989, U.S. Dist. Ct. (no. dist.) Ga. 1991, U.S. Ct. Appeals (11th cir.) 1992, U.S. Dist. Ct. (mid. dist.) Ga. 1993. Law clk. to Judge Harold L. Murphy U.S. Dist. Ct. (no. dist.) Ga., Rome, 1989-91; fed. ct. appointed mediator Geier U. Tenn., U.S. Dist. Ct. (mid. dist.), Tenn., 1999-2000, fed. ct. appointed monitor, 2001—; fed. ct. monitor, spl. master Knight v. Alabama, U.S. Dist. Ct. (no. dist.) Ala.,

Birmingham, Ala., 1993—; assoc. Rogers & Hardin, Atlanta, 1992-93; pvt. practice, 1993—; ptnr. Evans & Gonzalez, 1997-99; assoc. editor Vanderbilt Law Rev., 1988-89. Cons. in higher edn., 1994—, civil rights, 1996. Fellow Inst. for Ministry, Law and Ethics, Salt Lake City. Mem. ABA, Am. Judicature Soc., Atlanta Bar Assn., Fed. Bar Assn., Hispanic Bar Assn., Phi Delta Phi. Methodist. Civil rights, Federal civil litigation, Education and schools. Home: 3087 Belingham Dr NE Atlanta GA 30345-1574 Office: PO Box 450888 Atlanta GA 31145-0888

GONZALEZ, JOSE ALEJANDRO, JR. federal judge; b. Tampa, Fla., Nov. 26, 1931; s. Jose A. and Luisa Secundina (Collia) G.; m. Frances Frierson, Aug. 22, 1956 (dec. Aug. 1981); children— Margaret Ann, Mary Frances; m. Mary Sue Copeland, Sept. 24, 1983 B.A., U. Fla., 1952, J.D., 1957; LLD, Nova Southeastern U., 1998. Bar: Fla. 1958, U.S. Dist. Ct. (so. dist.) Fla. 1959, U.S. Ct. Appeals 1959, U.S. Supreme Ct. 1963. Practice in, Ft. Lauderdale, 1958-64; claim rep. State Farm Mut., Lakeland, Fla., 1957-58; assoc. firm Watson, Hubert and Sousley, 1958-61, ptnr., 1961-64; asst. state atty. 15th Cir. Fla., 1961-64; cir. judge 17th Cir. Ft. Lauderdale, 1964-78, chief judge, 1969-70; assoc. judge 4th Dist. Ct. Appeals, West Palm Beach; U.S. dist. judge So. Dist. Fla., 1978—, sr. judge, 1996—. Bd. dirs. Arthritis Found., 1962-72; bd. dirs. Henderson Clinic Broward County, 1964-68, v.p., 1967-68. Served to 1st lt. AUS, 1952-54. Recipient Kupferman award Laymen's Nat. Bible Assn., 1991; named Broward County Outstanding Young Man, 1967, one of Fla.'s Five Outstanding Young Men, Fla. Jaycees, 1967, Broward Legal Exec. of Yr., 1978. Mem. ABA, Am. Judicature Soc., Fed. Bar Assn., Fla. Bar Assn., Broward County Bar, Ft. Lauderdale Jaycees (dir. 1960-61), Fla. Blue Key, Sigma Chi (Significant Sig), Phi Alpha Delta. Democrat. Clubs: Kiwanian (pres. 1971-72), Lauderdale Yacht, Greenock Country, Country Club Pittsfield. Home: 631 Intracoastal Dr Fort Lauderdale FL 33304-3618 Office: US Dist Ct 205 US Courthouse 299 E Broward Blvd Fort Lauderdale FL 33301-1944

GONZALEZ, MARIANO PABLO, lawyer; b. Buenos Aires, May 24, 1969; s. Abel and Nelly Gonzalez; m. Erica Silvana Pedruzzi, July 29, 1995; 1 child, Olivia. LLB, U. Belgrano, Argentina, 1993; LLM, Columbia U., N.Y.C., 1996. Assoc. Nat. Securities Commn., Argentina, 1993-94; fgn. assoc. Milbank Tweed, U.S., 1994-95, Linklaters, U.S., 1996-97; sr. assoc. Marval O'Farrell, Argentina, 1997-98, Estudio Beccar Varela, Buenos Aires, 1998—. Cons. in law Argentine Indsl. Union, 1997-98. Mem. Buenos Aires Bar. Avocations: golf, fishing, literature. Contracts commercial, General corporate, Finance. Home: Vueta de Obligado 1159 8o 1426 Buenos Aires Argentina Office: Beccar Varela Cerrito 740 1309 Buenos Aires Argentina

GONZALEZ, RAUL A. retired state supreme court justice, lawyer; b. Weslaco, Tex., Mar. 22, 1940; s. Raul G. and Paula (Hernandez) G.; m. Dora Blanca Champion, Dec. 22, 1963; children— Celeste, Jaime, Marco, Sonia BA in Govt., U. Tex., Austin, 1963; JD, U. Houston, 1966; LLM, U. Va., 1986. Bar: Tex. 1966. Asst. U.S. atty. U.S. Dist. Ct. (so. dist.) Tex., Brownsville, 1969-73; ptnr. Joe Walsh & Assocs., 1973, Gonzalez & Hamilton, Brownsville, 1974-78; judge 103d Dist. Ct. Tex., 1978-81, Ct. Appeals (13th cir.), Corpus Christi, Tex., 1981-84; justice Tex. Supreme Ct., Austin, 1984-98; ret., 1998; of counsel Locke Liddell & Sapp LLP, Austin, 1998—. Bd. dirs. Brownsville Boy's Club, Brownsville Community Devel. Corp., So. Tex. Rehab. Ind. Sch. Dist.; U.S. Recipient Outstanding Performance Rating award Dept. Justice, 1972, Toll fellow, 1987. Mem. Christian Legal Soc., Christian Conciliation Service, ABA, Tex. Bar Found. Avocations: jogging; racquetball. Home: 10511 River Plantation Dr Austin TX 78747-1125 Office: Locke Liddell & Sapp LLP 100 Congress Ave Ste 300 Austin TX 78701-2748 E-mail: rgonzalez@lockeliddell.com

GOOCH, ANTHONY CUSHING, lawyer; b. Amarillo, Tex., Dec. 3, 1937; s. Cornelius Skinner and Sidney Seale (Crawford) G.; m. Elizabeth Melissa Ivanoff, May 27, 1963 (div. Nov. 1983); children: Katherine C., Jennifer C. Gooch Avery, Melissa G., Andrew E.; m. Linda B. Klein, Nov. 7, 1987. BA, U. of South, 1959; diploma, Coll. of Europe, 1960; JD, NYU, 1963, M in Comparative Law, 1964. Bar: N.Y. 1963. Assoc. Cleary, Gottlieb, Steen & Hamilton, N.Y.C., Paris, Brussels, 1963-72, ptnr. Rio de Janeiro, 1973-78, N.Y.C., 1978-99, of counsel, 2000—; gen. counsel Internat. Inst. Rural Reconstruction, 2000—. Co-author: Loan Agreement Documentation, 1982, 2d edit., 1991, Swap Apreement Documentation, 1987, 2d edit., 1988, Documentation for Derivatives, 1993, Credit Support Supplement, 1995, Cross-Product Risk Mgmt. Supplement, 2000, Documentation for Loans, Assignments and Participations, 1996; articles editor NYU Law Rev., 1962-63. Mem. ABA, N.Y. State Bar Assn., Assn. Bar City N.Y., New York County Lawyers Assn. Episcopalian. Home: 7 Mine Hill Rd Redding CT 06896-2701 E-mail: agooch@cgsh.com, tonygooch@aol.com

GOOD, DOUGLAS JAY, lawyer; b. Bklyn., Mar. 29, 1947; s. Sidney B. and Sophie (Mohel) G.; m. Lynda Edes, Feb. 25, 1979; 1 child, Sara. BA, Columbia U., 1967; JD, NYU, 1971. Bar: N.Y. 1972, U.S. Dist. Ct. (so. and ea. dists.) N.Y. 1973, U.S. Ct. Appeals (2d cir.) 1975, U.S. Supreme Ct. 1976, U.S. Ct. Appeals (11th cir.) 1989. Staff atty. Legal Aid Soc. Rockland County, Inc., New City, N.Y., 1972-73, dir. N.J., 1973-81; assoc. Ruskin, Moscou, Evans & Faltishchek, P.C., Mineola, N.Y., 1981-85, ptnr., 1985—; mng. ptnr. Ruskin, Moscou, Evans & Faltischek, P.C., 1990-98. Adj. lectr. NYU Inst. for Paralegal Studies, N.Y.C., 1982-85; adj. asst. prof.; bd. dirs. Nassau/Suffolk Law Svcs. Com., Inc., 1986—, chairperson, 1987—; bd. dirs. Nassau Bar Tech. Ctr., Inc., 1995-2000, sec., 1995, vice chmn., 1996, pres. 1998. Mem.: ABA, N.Y. State Bar Assn., Nassau County Bar Assn. (bd. dirs. 1996—99, adv. bd. We Care Fund 2000—, sec. 2001—). Jewish. General civil litigation, Contracts commercial. Office: Ruskin Moscou Evans & Faltischek PC 170 Old Country Rd Mineola NY 11501-4307

GOODALL, CAROLINE MARY HELEN, lawyer; b. Eng. d. Peter and Sonja Jeanne Goodall; m. Vesey John Munnings Hill. BA, Cambridge U., Eng., 1977, MA, 1980. Bar: Supreme Ct. Judicature. Articled clk., asst. solicitor Slaughter & May, London, 1978-84; asst. solicitor Herbert Smith, 1984-87, ptnr., 1987—, joint head corp. fin., 1994-2000, head corp. divsn., 2000—. Assoc. Newnham Coll., Cambridge, 1998—. Rebecca Squire scholar Cambridge U., 1975; scholar Newnham Coll., 1975. Fellow Royal Soc. Arts; mem. Law Soc., City of London's Solicitor Co. Avocations: theatre, ballet, tennis, sailing, walking, reading. General corporate, Mergers and acquisitions, Securities. Office: Herbert Smith Exchange House Primrose St London EC2A 2HS England

GOODART, NAN L. lawyer, educator; b. San Francisco, Apr. 4, 1938; BA, San Jose State U., 1959, MA, 1965; JD, U. of the Pacific, 1980. Bar: Calif. 1980, U.S. Dist. Ct. (ea. dist.) Calif. 1981. Tchr. Eastside Union High Sch., San Jose, Calif., 1960-65; counselor San Jose City Coll., 1965-75; atty. Sacramento, 1981—. Speaker numerous seminars throughout no. Calif. and other western states, 1988—. Author: Who Will It Hurt When I Die? A Primer on the Living Trust, 1992 (Nat. Mature Media award 1993), The Truth About Living Trusts, 1995 (Nat. Mature Media award 1996). Judge pro tem Sacramento County Small Claims Ct., 1988-96; instr. continuing edn. of bar Am.'s Legal Ctr., Sacramento, 1992—. Mem. Nat. Acad. Elder Law Attys., Calif. State Bar Assn., Sacramento County Bar Assn. Estate planning, Probate, Estate taxation. Office: 7230 S Land Park Dr Ste 121 Sacramento CA 95831-3658

GOODE, BARRY PAUL, lawyer; b. N.Y.C., Apr. 11, 1948; s. Hy and Charlotte (Langer) G.; m. Erica Tucker, Sept. 1, 1974; children: Adam, Aaron. AB magna cum laude, Kenyon Coll., 1969; JD cum laude, Harvard U., 1972. Bar: Mass. 1972, Calif. 1975, Hawaii 1995, U.S. Dist. Ct. Mass. 1972, U.S. Dist. Ct. (no. dist.) Calif. 1975, U.S. Dist. Ct. (ctrl. dist.) Calif. 1983, U.S. Dist. Ct. Hawaii 1995, U.S. Ct. Appeals (9th cir.) 1976, U.S. Ct. Appeals (6th cir.) 1999, U.S. Supreme Ct. 1986. Spl. asst. Sen Adlai E. Stevenson III, Washington, 1972-74; assoc. McCutchen, Doyle, Brown & Enersen, San Francisco, 1974-80, ptnr., 1980-2001; legal affairs sec. Gov. Gray Davis, 2001—. Co-author: Federal Litigation Guide, 1985. Advisor Gov.'s Com. to Review Water Law, San Francisco, 1979; bd. dirs. Stanford Pub. Interest Law Found., 1979-82; bd. dirs. Coro No. Calif., 1997—. Mem. San Francisco Bar Assn. (exec. com. environ. law sect. 1989-91), Am. Law Inst. Federal civil litigation, State civil litigation, Environmental. Office: Gov Gray Davis State Capitol Sacramento CA 95814

GOODHARTZ, GERALD, law librarian; b. N.Y.C., Oct. 23, 1938; s. Jack and Anna (Sperling) G.; m. Carol Scialli, Aug. 18, 1969; children: Joanna, Allison. BSCE, CCNY, 1961; MLS, U. So. Calif., 1970. Night reference asst. Assn. Bar of City of N.Y., 1956-61; libr. asst. Cravath, Swaine & Moore, N.Y.C., 1961-65; head libr. Rosenman, Colin, Freund, Lewis & Cohen, 1965-69, Keatinge & Sterling, L.A., 1969-70, Kaye, Scholer, Fierman, Hays & Handler, N.Y.C., 1970-98; mgr. info. svcs. Broad and Cassel, Orlando, 1998-99; dir. libr. svcs. Brown Raysman Millstein Felder & Steiner LLP, N.Y.C., 1999—. Libr. planning cons. Olympic Towers, N.Y.C., 1975; lectr. in field. Mem. ABA, ALA, Am. Assn. Law Librs. (cert.), Law Libr. Assn. Greater N.Y., Assn. Law Librs. of Upstate N.Y., Spl. Librs. Assn., Am. Soc. Info. Scientists, Am. Mgmt. Assn., Assn. Info. Mgrs., Nat. Micrographics Assn. Office: Brown Raysman Millstein Felder & Steiner LLP 900 3d Ave New York NY 10022 E-mail: ggoodhartz@brownraysman.com

GOODING, DAVID MICHAEL, lawyer, mediator; b. Jacksonville, Fla., June 10, 1952; s. Marion William and Eunice (Drawdy) G.; m. Cathy Rhoden, Aug. 3, 1974; chidlren: Sara Lynn, John Thomas Gooding. BA, U. Fla., 1974; JD, U. Miami, 1988. Bar: U.S. Dist. Ct. (mid. dist.) Fla. 1988. Asst. state atty. Office of State Atty., Jacksonville, Fla., 1988-89; assoc. Penland & Penland, P.A., 1989-92; shareholder Kent, Ridge & Crawford, 1992-97, Kent, Crawford & Gooding, Jacksonville, 1997—. Bd. dirs. Anastasia Advertising Art, Inc., St. Augustine, Fla., 1990-97, Samaritan Counseling Ctr., Jacksonville, 1990-94. Bd. dirs. Girls, Inc., Jacksonville, 1997—, pres., 1999-2000, endowment trustee, 2000—; bd. dirs. Southside United Meth. Preschool, Jacksonville, 1995-97; adult tchr. Christ Ch., 1994-96—, nursery vol., 1991-94; elder South Jacksonville Presbyn. Ch., 1991-94. Mem. ABA, ATLA, Fla. Bar, Fla. Trial Lawyers Assn., Jacksonville Trail Lawyers Assn., Masons, Scottish Rite, Royal Order of Jesters, Shriners (1998 imperial conv. com. counsel 1995—), Christian Legal Soc. (trustee 1997-2000). Democrat. Presbyterian. Avocations: running. Contracts commercial, Family and matrimonial, Personal injury. Office: Kent Crawford & Gooding 225 Water St Ste 900 Jacksonville FL 32202-5142

GOODMAN, ALFRED NELSON, lawyer; b. Jan. 21, 1945; s. Bernard R. and Mildred (Schlanger) Goodman. BS in Mech. and Aerospace Scis., U. Rochester, 1966; JD, Georgetown U., 1969. Bar: N.Y. 1970, D.C. 1971, U.S. Supreme Ct. 1974. Patent examiner U.S. Patent Office, Washington, 1969—71; assoc. Roylance, Abrams, Berdo & Goodman, 1971—74, ptnr., 1975—. Mem.: ABA, Am. Patent Law Assn., Bar Assn. D.C. (chmn. patent, trademark and copyright law sect. 1984—85, bd. dir. 1985—86). Antitrust, Patent, Trademark and copyright. Home: 4948 Sentinel Dr Bethesda MD 20816-3556 Office: Roylance Abrams Berdo & Goodman 1300 19th St NW Ste 600 Washington DC 20036-1649

GOODMAN, BARRY JOEL, lawyer; b. N.Y.C., May 28, 1953; s. Walter Louis and Shirley (Lenzer) G.; m. Nicole Goodman; children: Aaron, Rebecca, Noah. BA, Bradley U., 1974; JD with honors, Stetson U., 1977. Bar: Fla. 1977, U.S. Ct. Appeals 1978, Mich. 1979, U.S. Dist. Ct. (we. dist.) Fla., U.S. Dist. Ct. (ea. dist.) Mich. With Diecidue, Ferlita & Prieto, Tampa, Fla., 1977-78; assoc. Provizer, Eisenberg et al, Southfield, Mich., 1979-82, Thurswell, Chayet & Weiner, Southfield, 1982-87, ptnr., 1987-93; owner Gordon, Goodman & Acker, 1993-98, Goodman Acker, Southfield, 1998—. Lectr. Inst. Continuing Legal Edn., Ann Arbor, Mich., Mich. Trial Lawyer's Assn., State Bar of Mich. Pres., bd. dirs. West Bloomfield (Mich.) Woods Homeowners Assn., 1980-83; bd. dirs., v.p. Anti-Defamation League, Mich., 1983—; bd. dirs. B'nai B'rith Youth Orgn., Mich., 1995-97. Mem. ATLA, Mich. Trial Lawyers Assn. (bd. dirs. 1985—, treas. 1995, sec. 1996, v.p. 1997, pres.-elect 1998, pres. 1999-2000), Oakland County Bar Assn., Oakland County Trial Lawyers Assn. Democrat. Jewish. Avocations: tennis, golf, reading, theater. Personal injury. Office: Goodman Acker PC 17000 W 10 Mile Rd Ste 150 Southfield MI 48075-2945 E-mail: bjgnic@aol.com

GOODMAN, BARRY S. lawyer; b. Jersey City, June 7, 1951; s. Milton and Margaret Goodman; m. Emily J. Reynolds, Dec. 5, 1982. BA cum laude, Rutgers Coll., 1973; JD, Rutgers U., Newark, 1977. Bar: N.J., U.S. Dist. Ct. N.J., U.S. Ct. Appeals (3rd cir.), U.S. Supreme Ct. Jud. law clk. hon. Eugene L. Lora Superior Ct. N.J. Appellate Divsn., Hackensack, 1977-78; atty. Essex-Newark Legal Svcs., Orange, N.J., 1978-79, Crummy, Del Deo, Dolan & Purcell, Newark, 1979-84, Greenbaum, Rowe, Smith, Ravin, Davis & Himmel LLP, Woodbridge, N.J., 1984—. Author: (manual) New Jersey Students' Rights, 1977; mem. editl. bd. Rutgers Law Rev., 1976-77; contbr. articles to profl. jours. Vol. atty. Essex-Newark Legal Svcs., 1979-81; mem. Kinoy Fellowship Adv. Com., Newark, 1991-96; mem. 20th reunion conf. com. Rutgers Constnl. Litigation Clinic, Newark, 1991; co-chairperson Hunterdon County Dems. for Clinton Com., Flemington, N.J., 1992; mem. Hunterdon County Dem. Com., Flemington, 1994—, mem. exec. com., 1996-2001; mem. funds allocation com. United Way Hunterdon County, Clinton, 1995—, agy. admissions com., 1996, trustee, 1997—, treas. 1998-99, exec. com., 1998—, spl. gifts com., 1998—, cmty. rels. com., 1998—, v.p., 1999-2001, pres., 2001—; mem. Hunterdon County Health and Human Svcs. Adv. Coun., Flemington, 1998-2000. Mem. ABA (litigation sect., antitrust sect.), Fed. Bar Assn. N.J., N.J. State Bar Assn. (civil trial sect., antitrust sect., real property and probate sect.), Trial Attys. N.J. (trustee 1996—), Middlesex County Bar Assn., Hunterdon County Bar Assn., Rutgers-Newark Sch. Law Alumni Assn. (annual reunion dinner com. 1992, co-chair 1999, annual spring dinner com. 1995-98, treas. 1999-2000, sec. 2000-01, v.p. 2001—), Phi Beta Kappa, Phi Kappa Phi. Antitrust, General civil litigation, Professional liability. Office: Greenbaum Rowe Smith Ravin Davis & Himmel LLP 99 Wood Ave S Iselin NJ 08830-2715

GOODMAN, ELLIOTT I(RVIN), retired lawyer; b. Mar. 28, 1934; s. Sidney W. and Jean (Strauss) G.; m. Sybil J. Shapiro, Dec. 25, 1957; children: Jessica, Paul, Jonathan. BS, Northwestern U., 1955, JD, 1958. Bar: Ill. 1958, U.S. Dist. Ct. (no. dist.) Ill. 1959; CPA, Ill. With Gottlieb & Schwartz, Chgo., 1959-90, ptnr., 1966-90, mng. ptnr., 1981-88; ptnr. D'Ancona and Pflaum, 1990-95; exec. v.p. ATI Carriage House, Inc., Lombard, Ill., 1995-99. Permanent arbitrator Amalgamated Social Benefit Ins. Plan. Sec., bd. dirs. Ind. Basketball Players Assn., 1971-74, Abe Saperstein Found., Athletes for Better Edn. Found., 1975-79 Mem. Highland Park Housing Commn. (Ill.), 1980-87. Mem. ABA (labor law com. 1977-97, environ. law com. 1988-97), Chgo. Bar Assn. (past chmn. Am. citizenship com. 1967-69, mem. labor law com. 1971—, environ. law com. 1988-97), Human Resource Mgmt. Assn. Chgo., Lake Geneva Yacht Club. Environmental, Labor. Home: 211 Rivershire Ln Apt 201 Lincolnshire IL 60069-3817 Office: ATI Carriage House Inc 1111 N Ridge Ave Lombard IL 60148-1212

GOODMAN, GARY A. lawyer; b. N.Y.C., Mar. 8, 1948; s. Nathaniel and Edith (Rosen) G.; m. Susan Schachter, Aug. 13, 1972; children: Max, Jonah, William, Zachary, Holden. AB in History summa cum laude, Economics with honors, U. Rochester, 1970; JD, NYU, 1973. Bar: N.Y. 1974, U.S. Dist. Ct. (so. dist. and ea. dist.) N.Y. 1974, U.S. Dist. Ct. Guam, 1975, U.S. Ct. Appeals (2d cir.) 1975, Calif. 1996, Tex. 1996. Ptnr. Akin, Gump, Strauss, Hauer & Feld, L.L.P., N.Y.C., 1996—, co-head N.Y.O. real estate practice group. Contbr. numerous articles to profl. jours.. Mem. bd. edn. Locust Valley (N.Y.) Ctrl. Sch. Dist., 1995-96, v.p., 1996-97, pres., 1997-98. Mem. ABA (vice chmn. internat. investment in real estate com. 1983-90, chmn. Pacific Rim trans. subcom. real estate financing com. 1987-88), N.Y. State Bar Assn. (chmn. fgn. investment in U.S. real estate com. 1987-88), Assn. of Bar of City of N.Y. (uniform state laws com. 1978-80, real property law com. 1991-94, 97-2000, land use com. 1994-97), Internat. Coun. Shopping Ctrs. (task force environ. issues 1987-90, law com. 1991-94), Real Estate Bd. N.Y. Office: Akin Gump Strauss Hauer & Feld LLP 590 Madison Ave New York NY 10022-2524 E-mail: ggoodman@akingump.com

GOODMAN, JOHN M. lawyer; b. N.Y.C., Oct. 31, 1947; s. Melvin D. and Margaret H. (Barnett) G.; children: Andrew, Nicholas. AB, Princeton U., 1969; JD, Harvard U., 1973. Bar: N.Y. 1974, U.S. Dist. Ct. (so. and ea. dists.) NY 1974, U.S. Ct. Appeals (2d cir.) 1975, D.C. 1984, U.S. Ct. Appeals (D.C. cir.) 1984. Assoc. Dewey, Ballantine, Bushby, Palmer & Wood, N.Y.C., 1973-83; gen. atty. Bell Atlantic, Washington, 1983— . Antitrust, General civil litigation, Communications. Office: Bell Atlantic 1300 I St NW Washington DC 20005-3314

GOODMAN, LEWIS ELTON, JR. lawyer; b. Lynchburg, Va., Jan. 27, 1936; s. Lewis Elton and Mary (Oliver) G.; m. Elizabeth Shumaker, July 10, 1960; children: William L., Lee E. JD, U. Richmond, 1973. Bar: Va. 1973, U.S. Dist. Ct. (we. dist.) Va. 1973, U.S. Ct. Appeals (4th cir.) 1979, U.S. Supreme Ct. 1986. Pvt. practice, Danville, Va., 1973—. Bankruptcy, Probate, Real property. Office: 520 Piney Forest Rd Danville VA 24540-3352

GOODMAN, MARK N. lawyer; b. Phoenix, Jan. 16, 1952; s. Daniel H. and Joanne Goodman; m. Gwendolyn A. Langfeldt, Oct. 24, 1982; children: Zachary A., Alexander D. BA, Prescott Coll., 1973; JD summa cum laude, Calif. Western Sch. Law, 1977; LLM, U. Calif., Berkeley, 1978. Bar: Ariz. 1977, U.S. Dist. Ct. Ariz. 1978, U.S. Ct. Appeals (9th cir.) 1978, U.S. Supreme Ct. 1981. Practice Law Offices Mark N. Goodman, Prescott, Ariz., 1978-79, 81-82, Mark N. Goodman, Ltd., Prescott, 1983-86; ptnr. Alward and Goodman, Ltd., 1979-81, Perry, Goodman, Drutz & Musgrove, Prescott, 1986-87, Goodman, Drutz & Musgrove, Prescott, 1987-88, Sears & Goodman, P.C., Prescott, 1988-92, Goodman Law Firm, P.C., Prescott, 1992—. Author: The Ninth Amendment, 1981; contbr. articles to profl. jours.; notes and comments editor Calif. Western Law Rev., 1976. Bd. dirs. Yavapai Symphony Assn., Prescott, 1981-84, N. Ariz. chpt. Alzheimer's Assn., 1995-97. Mem. ABA, Def. Rsch. Inst., State Bar Ariz. (fee arbitration com. vice chmn. 1988—), Yavapai County Bar Assn. (v.p. 1981-82). State civil litigation, Consumer commercial, Real property. Office: Goodman Law Firm PC PO Box 2489 Prescott AZ 86302-2489 E-mail: info@goodmanlaw.com

GOODMAN, SAMUEL J. lawyer; b. East Chicago, Ind., Nov. 6, 1942; s. Max M. Goodman and Rosetta (Weinberg) Goodman Small; m. Nancy Marx, Oct. 5, 1968; children— Greer, Max. B.A., Purdue U., 1964; J.D., U. Mich., 1967. Bar: Ind. 1967, U.S. Dist. Ct. (no. and so. dists.) Ind. 1967. Assoc., then ptnr. firm Given, Dawson & Cappas, East Chicago, 1967-77; founding ptnr. firm Goldsmith, Goodman, Ball & Van Bokkelen, Highland, Ind., 1977— . Sec. Lake County Jud. Nominating Com., 1973— . Mem. Ind. Bar Assn. (chmn. family law sect. 1983—), Lake County Ind. Bar Assn. (bd. dirs. 1981—). Democrat. Jewish. Family and matrimonial. Home: 6534 Forest Ave Hammond IN 46324-1016 Office: Goodman Ball et al 9013 Indianapolis Blvd Highland IN 46322-2502

GOODMAN, STEPHEN MURRY, lawyer; b. Phila., Oct. 8, 1940; s. Edward and Jean (Landau) G.; m. Janis Freeman, Jan. 8, 1983; children: Carl, Rachel. BS cum laude, U. Pa., 1962, LLB magna cum laude, 1965. Bar: D.C. 1967, Pa. 1969. Law clerk to Hon. David Bazelon U.S. Ct. Appeals (D.C. cir.), Washington, 1965-66; law clk. to Hon. William J. Brennan Jr. U.S. Supreme Ct., 1966-67; ptnr. Goodman & Ewing, Phila., 1970-83, Wolf, Block, Schorr & Solis-Cohen, Phila., 1983-94, Morgan, Lewis & Bockius LLP. Mem. Order of Coif. Democrat. Jewish. Avocation: profl. jazz pianist. Office: Morgan Lewis & Bockius LLP 1701 Market St Philadelphia PA 19103-2903

GOODMAN, WILLIAM FLOURNOY, III, lawyer; b. Aberdeen Miss., June 8, 1952; s. William Flournoy, Jr. and Edwina (McDuffie) G.; m. Tommie E. Goodman, July 19, 1992; children: William F. IV, Nancy Elizabeth. BA cum laude, Millsaps Coll., 1974; JD, U. Miss., 1977. Bar: Miss. 1977, U.S. Dist Ct. (so. and no. dists.) Miss. 1977, U.S. Ct. Appeals (5th cir.) 1977, U.S. Ct. Appeals (11th cir.) 1981. Assoc. Watkins & Eager PLLC, Jackson, Miss., 1977-81; ptnr., 1982—. Mem. ABA, Hinds County Bar Assn., Miss. Bar Assn., Miss. Def. Lawyers Assn., Def. Rsch. Inst., Internat. Assn. Def. Counsel, Omicron Delta Kappa. Methodist. Federal civil litigation, State civil litigation. Home: 1256 Belvoir Pl Jackson MS 39202-1205 Office: Watkins & Eager PO Box 650 Jackson MS 39205-0650

GOODPASTURE, PHILIP HENRY, lawyer; b. Lisbon, Portugal, Sept. 16, 1960; s. Henry McKennie and Ellen Ingabor (Moller) G.; m. Paige Everett Hargroves, June 25, 1994. BA with high distinction, U. Va., 1982, JD, 1985. Bar: Va. 1985, U.S. Dist. Ct. (ea. dist.) Va. 1985. Assoc. Christian & Barton and predecessor firm, Richmond, Va., 1985-92, ptnr., 1993—, vice-chmn. corp. team, 1994-97, mem. exec. com., 1998. Dir. Downtown Presents Inc., Richmond, 1993—, Va. League for Planned Parenthood, Richmond, 1989-95, Vol. Emergency Families for Children, Richmond, 1998-2000; dir. Parliament City of Richmond, 1997-98; mem. Leadership Metro Richmond, 1994; mem. leadership devel. coun. ARC, 1995. Mem. Va. Bar Assn., Richmond Bar Assn. General corporate, Entertainment, Mergers and acquisitions. Office: Christian & Barton 909 E Main St Ste 1200 Richmond VA 23219-3013 E-mail: pgoodpasture@cblaw.com

GOODRICH, THOMAS MICHAEL, engineering and construction executive, lawyer; b. Milan, Apr. 28, 1945; s. Henry Calvin and Billie Grace (Walker) G.; m. Gillian Comer White, Dec. 28, 1968; children: Michael, Braxton, Charles, Grace. BSCE, Tulane U., 1968; JD, U. Ala., 1971. Bar: Ala. 1971. Adminstrv. asst. Supreme Ct. Ala., Montgomery, 1971-72; various mgmt. positions BE & K, Inc., Birmingham, Ala., 1989-95, pres., CEO, 1995—, also bd. dirs. Bd. dirs. First Comml. Bank, Birmingham, Energen Corp. Bd. dirs. Birmingham Civil Rights Inst., Constrn. Industry Inst., Birmingham Area coun. Boy Scouts Am., U. Ala. Health System; trustee Nat. Bldg. Mus., Elsenhowen Exchg. Fellow. Capt. U.S Army, 1970-72. Mem. TAPPI, ABA, Ala. State Bar Assn., Assn. Builders and Contractors (pres. 1990), Constrn. Industry Roundtable. Presbyterian. Avocations: hunting, jogging. Office: B E & K Inc 2000 Internat Park Dr Birmingham AL 35243

GOODSON, HARLAN WAYNE, state regulator, educator; b. Newhall, Calif., Mar. 9, 1947; s. Robert Thurman Goodson and Margeret Loraine Underwood; m. Darla Kay Hinderks, (div. Feb. 1987); children: Kimberly, Marc. BA, Golden Gate U., 1976; JD, John F. Kennedy U., 1995; MPA, Golden Gate U., 1999. Sgt. of police Oakland (Calif.) Police Dept., 1971-92; cons. to pres. pro tempore Calif. State Senate, Sacramento,

1994-99; dir. Divsn. of Gambling Control Office of the Atty. Gen. Adj. prof. law John F. Kennedy U. Sch. Law, Orinda, Calif., 1996—; mem. gov.'s adv. panel Calif. Earthquake Authority, Sacramento, 1996, 97, mem. governing bd., 1996, 97. Del. Dem. Conv., Sacramento, 1997, L.A., 1998. With USN, 1967-71. Mem. ABA, Calif. State Bar, Oakland Police Activities League (founder, exec. dir. 1982-85, Wish Upon a Star Spl. Recognition 1988), Sigma Chi (charter Zeta Omicron chpt.). Democrat. Avocations: reading, golfing. Home: 1208 Grand River Dr Sacramento CA 95831-4420 Office: Office of the Atty Gen 1435 River Park Dr Fl 2D Sacramento CA 95815-4509 E-mail: hgoodson@hdcdojnet.state.ca.us

GOODWILLIE, EUGENE WILLIAM, JR. lawyer; b. Montclair, N.J., May 14, 1941; s. Eugene W. G. and Janet (Williams) G.; children: David Todd, Douglas Linn. BA, Williams Coll., 1963; LLB, JD, Columbia U., 1966. Bar: N.Y. 1966. Assoc. White & Case, N.Y.C., 1966-75, ptnr., 1975—. Bd. dirs. MAT Internat. Group, London. Stone scholar Columbia U., 1964-66; grantee Noble Found., 1963-65. Mem. ABA, Montclair Golf Club (pres. 1985-86), Phi Beta Kappa. General corporate, Finance, Private international. Office: White & Case Bldg Ll 1155 Avenue Of The Americas New York NY 10036-2787

GOODWIN, ALFRED THEODORE, federal judge; b. Bellingham, Wash., June 29, 1923; s. Alonzo Theodore and Miriam Hazel (Williams) G.; m. Marjorie Elizabeth Major, Dec. 23, 1943 (div. 1948); 1 son, Michael Theodore; m. Mary Ellin Handelin, Dec. 23, 1949; children: Karl Alfred, Margaret Ellen, Sara Jane, James Paul. B.A., U. Oreg., 1947; J.D., 1951. Bar: Oreg. 1951. Newspaper reporter Eugene (Oreg.) Register-Guard, 1947-50; practiced in Eugene until, 1955; circuit judge Oreg. 2d. Jud. Dist., 1955-60; assoc. justice Oreg. Supreme Ct., 1960-69; judge U.S. Dist. Ct. Oreg., 1969-71, U.S. Ct. Appeals for (9th cir.), Pasadena, Calif., 1971-88, chief judge, 1988-91, sr. judge, 1991—. Editor Oreg. Law Rev., 1950-51. Bd. dirs. Central Lane YMCA, Eugene, 1956-60, Salem (Oreg.) Art Assn., 1960-69; adv. bd. Eugene Salvation Army, 1956-60, chmn., 1959. Served to capt., inf. AUS, 1942-46, ETO. Mem. Am. Judicature Soc., Am. Law Inst., ABA (ho. of dels. 1986-87), Order of Coif, Phi Delta Phi, Sigma Delta Chi, Alpha Tau Omega. Republican. E-mila. Office: US Ct Appeals 9th Cir PO Box 91510 125 S Grand Ave Pasadena CA 91105-1621

GOODWIN, JAMES JEFFRIES, lawyer; b. San Juan, P.R., Aug. 24, 1949; s. David Badger and Elizabeth Ann (Ryan) G.; m. Mary Ann Schweikert, Nov. 29, 1981; 1 child, David Charles. B.A., U. Ky., 1971; M.P.A., Golden Gate U., 1977; J.D., U. Pacific, Sacramento, 1981. Bar: Calif. 1981, U.S. Dist. Ct. (ea. dist.) Calif. 1981, U.S. Ct. Appeals (9th cir.) 1983, U.S. Supreme Ct. 1984. Atty. Sacramento Pub. Defender's Office, 1980-82; sole practice, Sacramento, 1982— ; legis. advocate Aircraft Owners and Pilots Assn., Washington, 1982— ; legal counsel Emergency Med. Services, Sacramento, 1984. Served to capt. U.S. Army, 1971-77. Mem. Assn. Trial Lawyers Am., Calif. Trial Lawyers Assn. Episcopalian. Federal civil litigation, State civil litigation, Personal injury. Office: 175 Stonington Way Folsom CA 95630-6811

GOODWIN, JOHN ROBERT, lawyer, law educator, author; b. Morgantown, W.Va., Nov. 3, 1929; s. John Emory and Ruth Iona Goodwin; m. Betty Lou Wilson, June 2, 1952; children: John R., Elizabeth Ann Paugh, Mark Edward, Luke Jackson, Matthew Emory. BS, W.Va. U., 1952, LLD, 1964, JD, 1970. Bar: W.Va., U.S. Supreme Ct. Formerly city atty., county commr., spl. pros. atty.; then mayor City of Morgantown; prof. bus. law W.Va. U., Morgantown; prof. hotel and casino law U. Nev., Las Vegas; pvt. practice, Morgantown. Author: Legal Primer for Artists, Craftspersons, 1987, Hotel Law, Principles and Cases, 1987, Twenty Feet from Glory, Bus. Law, 3d edit., High Points of Legal History, Travel and Lodging Law, Desert Adventure, Gaming Control Law; editor Hotel and Casino Letter; past editor Bus. Law Rev., Bus. Law Letter. Ith U.S. Army, Korea. Named Outstanding West Virginian, State of W.Va. Democrat. Consumer commercial, Entertainment, Real property. Home: Casa Linda 48 5250 E Lake Mead Blvd Las Vegas NV 89156-6751 also: Goodwin Bldg 2d Fl Morgantown WV 26505

GOODWIN, JOSEPH R. judge; b. 1942; BS, W.Va. U., 1965, JD, 1970. Ptnr. Goodwin & Goodwin, 1970-95; judge U.S. Dist. Ct. (so. dist.) W.Va., Charleston, 1995—. Editor W.Va. Law Rev. Mem. W.Va. U. Bd. Advisors, 1981-86; bd. visitors W.Va. U. Coll. Law, 1995-98, chmn., 1998. With USAR, 1965-67. Mem. ABA, W.Va. State Bar Assn., Jackson County Bar Assn., 4th Cir. Jud. Conf. Office: US Dist Ct So Dist WVa PO Box 2546 Charleston WV 25329-2546

GOODWIN, ROBERT CRONIN, lawyer; b. Cleve., Mar. 17, 1941; s. Robert Clifford and Marion (Schmadel) G.; m. Judith Mary Baxter, June 7, 1968; children: Anne, Helen, Sharon, Katherine. AB, Fordham U., 1963; JD, Georgetown U., 1969. Bar: D.C. 1970, Md. 1990. Vol. Peace Corps, Thailand, 1964-65; asst. cmty. devel. advisor AID, Thailand, 1965-66; atty. advisor Office Gen. Coun., Dept. Commerce, 1969-74; dep. asst. gen. coun. internat. & resouce devel. programs Fed. Energy Adminstrn., Washington, 1974-77, asst. gen. coun. internat. conservation & resource devel., 1977; asst. gen. coun. internat. trade & emergency preparedness Dept. Energy, 1977-79; ptnr. Thompson, Hine & Flory, 1979-82; v.p., gen. coun. China Energy Ventures, Washington, 1982-86; ptnr. Goodwin & Soble, 1986-90; pvt. practice, 1990-92; exec. v.p., gen. coun., dir. U.S.-China Indsl. Exch., Inc., 1992—; dir. Med. Adv. Sys., Inc., 1999—. Guest lectr. internat. petroleum contracts East China Petroleum Inst. Beijing, 1985; frequent lectr. on internat. contracts and Chineses legal and bus. issues; adj. assoc. prof. internat. mgmt. progam, U. Md., 1990—. Editor-in-chief Law and Policy in International Business, 1968-69; co-editor Legal Environ. for Fgn. Direct Investment in U.S., 1994; contbr. articles to profl. jours. Mem. bd. sch. bd., 1980-83. Recipient cert. of Merit Fed. Energy Adminstrn., 1974, cert. Spl. Acheivement, 1974, 76. Mem. ABA, D.C. Bar Assn., Thai-Am. Assn. (chmn. bus. com. 1991, pres. 1995), Nat. Coun. U.S. China Trade (chmn. legal com. 1987), Am. Corp. Counsel Assn., Md.-China Bus. Coun. (bd. dirs., v.p. 1999—). Administrative and regulatory, Contracts commercial, Private international. Home: 3710 Bradley Ln Chevy Chase MD 20815-4257 Office: 7201 Wisconsin Ave Ste 703 Bethesda MD 20814-4850

GOOGASIAN, GEORGE ARA, lawyer; b. Pontiac, Mich., Feb. 22, 1936; s. Peter and Lucy (Chobanian) G.; m. Phyllis Elaine Law, June 27, 1959; children— Karen Ann, Steven George, Dean Michael B.A., U. Mich., 1958; J.D., Northwestern U., 1961. Bar: Mich. 1961. Assoc. Marentay, Rouse, Selby, Fischer & Webber, Detroit, 1961-62; asst. U.S. Atty. U.S. Dept. Justice, 1962-64; assoc. Howlett, Hartman & Beier, Pontiac and Bloomfield Hills, Mich., 1964-81; ptnr. Googasian Hopkins Hohauser & Forhan, Bloomfield Hills, 1981-96, The Googasian Firm, Bloomfield Hills, 1996—. Bd. law examiners State of Mich., 1997—. Author: Trial Advocacy Manual, 1984, West Groups Michigan Practice Torts, vols. 14, 15, 1998. Pres. Oakland Parks Found., Pontiac, 1984-89; chmn. Oakland County Dem. party, Pontiac, 1964-70; state campaign chmn. U.S. Senator Philip A. Hart, Detroit, 1970; bd. dirs. Big Bros. Oakland County. 1968-73 Fellow Am. Bar Found., Am. Coll. Trial Lawyers, Internat. Acad. Trial Lawyers; mem. ABA (del. 1992-93, exec. coun. nat. conf. bar pres. 1993-96), ATLA, Am. Bd. Trial Advocates, State Bar Mich. (pres. elect 1991-92, pres. 1992—), Oakland County Bar Assn. (pres. 1985-86), Oakland Bar Found. (pres. 1990-92). Presbyterian. Club: U. Mich. Club Greater Detroit Federal civil litigation, State civil litigation, Personal injury. Home: 3750 Orion Rd Oakland MI 48363-3029 Office: 6895 Telegraph Rd Bloomfield Hills MI 48301-3138

GOOGINS, ROBERT REVILLE, lawyer, insurance company executive; b. Cambridge, Mass., June 2, 1937; s. Robert Wendell and Patricia M. (Reville) G.; B.S., U. Conn., 1958, J.D., 1961; M.B.A., U. Hartford, 1970; m. Sonya Ann Forbes, June 21, 1958; children— Shawn W., Glen R. Bar: Conn. 1961. Atty. Conn. Mut. Life Ins. Co., Hartford, 1961-62, asst. counsel, 1964-67, assoc. counsel, 1967-70, counsel, 1970-72, counsel, sec., 1972-74, v.p., counsel, sec., 1974-75, v.p., gen. counsel, sec., 1975-77, sr. v.p., gen. counsel, 1977-80, exec. v.p., gen. counsel, 1980—, exec. v.p., 1982-89; ptnr. Hoberman & Pollock, P.C., 1989-90; dir. Ins. Law Ctr., adj. prof. law U. Conn. Sch. Law, 1990-91; ins. commr. State of Conn., 1991-94; bd. dirs. Thermodynectics; dep. mayor Town of Glastonbury, Conn., 1976; majority leader Glastonbury Town Council, 1977. Served to capt. U.S. Army, 1962-64. Mem. ABA, Conn. Bar Assn., Assn. Life Ins. Counsel, Nat. Assn. Securities Dealers (gov.-at large 1976-79). Republican. Roman Catholic. General corporate. Office: Ins Commr PO Box 816 Hartford CT 06142-0816

GOOLRICK, ROBERT MASON, lawyer; b. Fredericksburg, Va., Mar. 25, 1934; s. John T. and Olive E. (JOnes) G.; m. Audrey J. Dippo (div.); children: Stephanie M., Meade A. BA with distinction, U. Va., 1956, JD, 1959. BAr: Va. 1959, D.C. 1959, U.S. Dist. Ct. D.C. 1961, U.S. Ct. Appeals (D.C. cir.) 1961. Assoc. Steptoe & Johnson, Washington, 1959-65, ptnr., 1965-79; sole practice Alexandria, Va., 1979-83; cons. bus., oil and gas fin. Instr. U. Va. Law Sch. Author: Public Policy Toward Corporate Growth, 1978, Corporate Mergers and Acquisitions under Federal Securities Laws, 1978. Mem. ABA (corps. sect.), Jefferson Soc., Raven Soc., Order of Coif, Phi Beta Kappa. Contracts commercial, General corporate. Home: 3320 Woodburn Vill Dr No 22 Annandale VA 22003-6860 Office: PO Box 1233 Mc Lean VA 22101-1233 E-mail: rmgoolrick@starpower.net

GOOTEE, JANE MARIE, lawyer; b. Jasper, Ind., July 5, 1953; d. Thomas H. and Anne M. (Dreifke) G. BA, Ind. U., 1974; JD cum laude, St. Louis U., 1977. Bar: Ind. 1977, Mo. 1978, Mich. 1980, Ohio 1983, U.S. Dist. Ct. (so. dist.) Ind. 1977, U.S. Dist. Ct. (ea. dist.) Mich. 1980, U.S. Ct. Appeals (7th cir.) 1978, U.S. Supreme Ct. 1980, U.S. Ct. Appeals (6th cir.) 1982, U.S. Ct. Appeals (4th cir.) 1986. Dep. atty. gen. Ind., Indpls., 1977-79; corp. atty. Dow Chem. Co., Midland, Mich., 1979-81, ea. div. counsel, 1981-84, sr. atty., 1984-86, Mich. div. counsel, 1986-90, Dow Europe sr. staff counsel, 1990—; mem. issue mgmt. team Dow Chem. Groundwater, 1986-87; adv. com. Nat. Chamber Litigation Ctr. Environ. Law, 1985-90; mem. Great Lakes Community Coll. Adv. Bd., 1987-89; chair Dow Epidemiology Instl. Rev. Bd., 1984-90; pro-bono def. Midland Cir. Ct., 1980-81; adj. prof. Saginaw Valley State Coll., University Center, Mich., 1979-80. Bd. dirs. Big Sisters Midland, 1979-81, 84-86, Big Bros./Big Sisters Midland, 1986-90, also pres., 1988-89; exec. bd. Boy Scouts Am. Lake Huron Area Council, 1988-90, N.Y.C. YWCA Acad. of Women Achievers, 1988. Contbr. to profl. publs. Fellow Mich. State Bar Found; mem. ABA, Mo. Bar, Mich. Bar Assn. Contbr. articles to profl. jours. Federal civil litigation, General corporate, Environmental. Home: 1303 Foxwood Dr Midland MI 48642 Office: Dow Legal Dept 2030 Dow Ctr Midland MI 48674

GORDAN, CYNTHIA LEE, lawyer, textile company executive; b. Decatur, Ill., Apr. 4, 1947; d. Delbert R. and Jacqueline (McKinney) Smith; children: Rebecca, Elisabeth. A.B., Oberlin Coll., 1969; J.D., Boston U., 1975, LL.M. in Taxation, 1976. Bar: Mass. 1975, Ill. 1987. Assoc. counsel New Eng. Mut. Boston, 1976-80; assoc. counsel, asst. sec. Puritan Life Ins. Co., Providence, 1980-81, v.p., gen. counsel, sec., 1981-85, bd. dir.; mgr. ops. planning GE Capital, Stmaford, Conn., 1985-86; sr. assoc. Katten Muchin, Chgo., 1986-87; v.p., gen. counsel Quaker Fabric Corp., Fall River, Mass., 1988—. Mem. Am. Soc. CLU. Administrative and regulatory, General corporate, Corporate taxation. Home: 15 Sherman St Quincy MA 02170-1113 Office: Quaker Fabric Corp 931 Grinnell St Fall River MA 02721-5215

GORDESKY, MORTON, lawyer; b. Egg Harbor, N.J., Apr. 11, 1929; s. Benjamin and Rose (Suskin) G.; m. Marcelline D. Fallick, June 8, 1952 (div. 1982); children: Benjamin Todd, Nancy Hope Hafuta. BS, Temple U., 1950; JD, Rutgers U., 1954. Bar: Pa. 1955, U.S. Dist. Ct. (ea. dist.) Pa. 1958, U.S. Dist. Ct. Md. 1991, U.S. Ct. Appeals (3d cir.) 1983, U.S. Ct. Appeals (4th cir.) 1990, U.S. Supreme Ct. 1983. Sole practice, Phila., 1954—. Active Dem. Nat. Com., B'nai Brith. Served with U.S. Army, 1954-56. Mem. Phila. Bar Assn., Amvets (judge adv. 1961-64), Am. Legion. Bankruptcy, Federal civil litigation, State civil litigation. Office: Carlton Bus Ctr 1819 John F Kennedy Blvd Philadelphia PA 19103-1733

GORDON, ARNOLD MARK, lawyer; b. Norwich, Conn., Oct. 2, 1937; s. Barney and Rose (Bilsky) G.; m. Carolyn. BSBA, Wayne State U., Detroit, 1959, JD, 1962. Bar: Mich. 1962. With Gordon & Gordon P.C. and predecessor firms, Southfield, Mich.; arbitrator Am. Arbitration Assn., 1969—. Lectr. in field. Mem. Am. Coll. Trial Lawyers, State Bar Mich. (chmn. med.-legal com. 1976—, negligence sect. 1977-78, pub. negligence sect. bull.), Detroit Bar Assn. (co-chmn. trial advocacy program continguing legal edn. 1972—), Assn. Trial Lawyers Am. (exec. bd. Mich. 1967—), Mich., Detroit trial lawyers assns., Tau Epsilon Rho. Club: Masons. Office: Gordon & Gordon PC 18411 W 12 Mile Rd Ste 101 Southfield MI 48076-2663 E-mail: agordon101@aol.com

GORDON, COREY LEE, lawyer; b. Mpls., Aug. 22, 1956; s. Jack I. and LaVerne (Shedlov) G.; m. Ciel Schaeffer, Aug. 29, 1982; children: Jared Isaac, Lian Miriam. BA, Macalester Coll., 1976; JD cum laude, U. Minn., 1980. Bar: Minn. 1980, U.S. Dist. Ct. Minn. 1981, U.S. Ct. Appeals (8th cir.) 1983, U.S. Supreme Ct. 1983, Wis. 1987, U.S. Dist. Ct. (ea. and we. dists.) Wis. 1987, N.Y. 1991, U.S. Dist. Ct. (so. dist.) N.Y. 1991, U.S. Ct. Appeals (3d cir.) 1992, Ill. 1993, U.S. Dist. Ct. (no. dist.) Ill. 1995, Fla. 1995, U.S. Dist. Ct. (we., ea., and no. dists.) N.Y. 1999, U.S. Ct. Appeals (11th cir.) 1999, U.S. Ct. Appeals (7th cir.) 1999, U.S. Dist. Ct. (so. and ctrl. dists.) Ill. 1999, U.S. Ct. Appeals (2d cir.) 1999, U.S. Dist. Ct. (so. and no. dists.) Fla. 2000. Assoc. Fried, Frank, Harris, Shriver & Jacobson, N.Y.C., 1980-81; ptnr. Shapiro, Lavintman & Gordon P.A., Mpls., 1982-85; assoc. Robins, Zelle, Larson & Kaplan, St. Paul, 1986-88; ptnr. Robins, Kaplan, Miller & Ciresi, Mpls., 1989—. Bd. dirs. Jewish Family and Children's Svc. of Mpls., 1992-96, Mpls. Fedn. for Jewish Svc., 1994-99. Treas. The H.H.H. Fund, Minn., 1984-89; bd. dirs., sec.-treas. Minn. Humane Soc., 1985-86; active Dem. Farm Labor Party; trustee Bet Shalom Synagogue, 1992-93, v.p., 1993-97, pres., 1997-99. Mem. ABA, ATLA (co-chair inadequate security litigation group 1992-95). Jewish. Avocations: folk music, scuba diving, photography. Personal injury. Home: 2640 Glenhurst Pl Saint Louis Park MN 55416-3957 Office: Robins Kaplan Miller & Ciresi 2800 LaSalle Pla 800 Lasalle Ave Ste 2800 Minneapolis MN 55402-2015

GORDON, DAVID ELIOT, lawyer; b. Santa Monica, Calif., Mar. 8, 1949; s. Sam and Dee G.; m. Mary Debora Lane, Mar. 5, 1978. BA, Harvard U., 1969, JD, 1972. Bar: Calif. 1972. Ptnr. O'Melveny & Myers, L.A., 1980—. Adj. prof. Loyola Law Sch., 2000—. Founder, editor ERISA Litigation Reporter; contbr. articles on tax and employee benefits to profl. jours. Trustee Ctr. for Early Edn., 1997—. Fellow Los Angeles County Bar Found. (life, pres. 1984-85, bd. dirs. 1980-86); mem. ABA (employee benefits com. 1986—), Am. Coll. Tax Counsel, Los Angeles County Bar Assn. (tax sect., pres. 1990-91). Republican. Avocations: tennis, squash, racquetball. Pension, profit-sharing, and employee benefits, Corporate taxation, Personal income taxation. Office: O'Melveny & Myers 400 S Hope St Los Angeles CA 90071-2899

GORDON, DAVID ZEVI, retired lawyer; b. Bklyn., Mar. 2, 1943; s. Isidore and Yaffa S. (Stern) G.; m. Karen Baranker, Apr. 25, 1971; children: Ilana, Naomi. BA magna cum laude, Yeshiva U., 1964; JD cum laude, MBA, Columbia U., 1969. Bar: N.Y. 1970, U.S. Dist. Ct. (so. dist.) N.Y. 1973, U.S. Ct. Appeals (2d cir.) 1973. Assoc. Spear and Hill, N.Y.C., 1969-71; sr. assoc. LeBoeuf Lamb Lieby & McRae, 1971-77; ptnr. Finley Kumble Heine & Underburg, 1977-78, David Z. Gordon and Assocs., N.Y.C., 1978-81; mng. ptnr. Moroze Sherman Gordon & Gordon, P.C., 1981-96. Trustee, exec. com. Stern Coll. for Women, 1990-96; co-chmn. United Jewish Appeal, Operation Exodus, 1991-96, Project Renewal, 1987-96, exec. com. Israel econ. devel.; chmn. Israel Bonds, Bronx, 1988-96. Recipient Heritage award Yeshiva U., 1988. Mem. ABA, N.Y. State Bar Assn., N.Y.C. Bar Assn. (mem. com. condemnation and tax certiorari), Real Estate Tax Bar Assn. Democrat. General corporate, Real property, Securities. E-mail: FLASHGORDON@peoplepc.com

GORDON, EDGAR GEORGE, lawyer; b. Detroit, Feb. 27, 1924; s. Edgar George and Verna Florence (Hay) G.; m. Alice Irwin, Feb. 4, 1967; children: David A., J. Scott. AB, Princeton U., 1947; JD, Harvard U., 1950. Bar: Mich. 1951, U.S. Supreme Ct. 1953. Assoc. Poole, Warren & Littell, Detroit, 1950-54; ptnr. Poole, Warren, Littell & Gordon, 1953-63; gen. counsel Hygrade Food Products Corp., 1963-69, sec., 1966-69, v.p., 1968-69; v.p., sec. counsel City Nat. Bank of Detroit, 1969-81; v.p., sec., gen. counsel No. States Bancorp, 1970-81; v.p., sec., counsel First of Am. Bank Corp., Kalamazoo, 1981-84; also ptnr. Howard & Howard, 1981-2000. Dir. First Citizens Bank, Troy, Mich., 1973-81, First Nat. Bank, Plymouth, Mich., 1974-81; pres., chmn. bd. First of Am. Mortgage Co., Kalamazoo, 1978-84. Commr. City of Kalamazoo, 1995—. Lt. (j.g.) USN, 1943-46. Mem. ABA, Mich. Bar Assn., Kalamazoo Bar Assn., Country Club of Detroit (Grosse Pointe, Mich.). Republican. Presbyterian. Banking, General corporate, Probate. Home: 4339 Lakeside Dr Kalamazoo MI 49008-2802 Office: 241 W South St Kalamazoo MI 49007

GORDON, HARRISON J. lawyer; b. Newark, Aug. 21, 1950; s. Carl and Rose (Katz) G.; children by previous marriage: Caryn Rachel, Robert Jonathan. BS, U. Bridgeport, 1972; JD, U. Miami, 1975. Bar: N.J. 1976, D.C. 1995, N.Y., 1997, U.S. Dist. Ct. N.J. 1976, U.S. Supreme Ct. 1980. Sole practice, West Orange, N.J., 1976-78, Montclair, 1978-83; ptnr. Gordon & Gordon, West Orange, 1983-87, Gordon, Gordon & Haley, West Orange, 1987-90, Gordon & Gordon, PC, West Orange, 1990—. Adj. prof. Montclair State Coll., Upper Montclair, N.J., 1979. Recipient West Orange Cmty. Svc. award, 2001. Mem. N.J. State Bar Assn. (exec. com. young lawyers div. 1981-83), Assn. Trial Lawyers Am. (chmn. automobile and premises liability sect.), N.J. Trial Lawyers Assn. (bd. govs. 1987-90, sec. 1990-91, treas. 1991-92, 3d v.p. 1992-93, 2d v.p. 1993-94, 1st v.p. 1994-95, pres.-elect 1995—, assoc. editor mag. 1987—, pres. 1996-97), Am. Arbitration Assn. (arbitrator), Soc. Bar and Gavel, Optimists Club (pres. 1981-82), Psi Chi, Phi Alpha Theta. Democrat. Federal civil litigation, State civil litigation, Personal injury. Office: Gordon & Gordon PC 80 Main St West Orange NJ 07052-5460

GORDON, JAMES S. lawyer, director; b. N.Y.C., Feb. 15, 1941; s. George S. and Sylvia A. (Wolfson) G.; m. Marcia G. Gordon, Dec. 22, 1968 (dec.); children: Daniel, Sarah; m. Debbie S. Pase, June 15, 1996. BA with high honors, U. Fla., 1962; LLB, Yale U., 1965. Bar: Ill. 1965, Fla. 1966, U.S. Supreme Ct. 1974. Asst. prof. Ind. U. Sch. Law, Bloomington, 1967-68, assoc. prof., 1969; ptnr. Feiwell, Galper & Gordon, Chgo., 1970-72; sole practice, 1972-80; pres. James S. Gordon, Ltd., 1981-93; chmn. Gordon, Glickman, Flesch & Woody, 1994—. Editor Yale Law Jour., 1963-65; contbr. articles to profl. jours. Mem. Winnetka Caucus, 1981-82. Ford Found. grantee, 1965-66. Mem. Yale U. Law Alumni Assn. (exec. com. 1987-94), Lawyers Club of Chgo., Birchwood Club (Highland Park, Ill.), Order of Coif, Phi Beta Kappa, Phi Alpha Delta. Antitrust, Bankruptcy, Federal civil litigation. Office: 140 S Dearborn St Ste 404 Chicago IL 60603-5202 E-mail: gordfinance/@ameritech.net

GORDON, JEFFREY (JACK GORDON), lawyer; b. Boston, Sept. 6, 1964; BA, Tulane U., 1986, JD, 1989. Bar: Fla. 1990, U.S. Dist. Ct. (mid. dist.) Fla. 1995. Law clk. intern 1st dist. Ct. Appeal Fla., Tallahassee, 1989; spl. asst. pub. defender Dade County, Miami, Fla., 1990-92; cert. cir. ct. arbitrator Palm Beach County, West Palm Beach, 1990-92; ptnr. Maney & Gordon, P.A., Tampa, 1992—. Fellow Roscoe Pound Inst. Teen ct. judge pro bono Hillsborough County, Tampa, 1992-98. Fellow Roscoe Pound Inst. Mem. ATLA, Acad. Fla. Trial Attys., Animal Legal Def. Fund, Hillsborough County Bar Trial Lawyers (lawyers sect.). General civil litigation, Personal injury. Office: Maney & Gordon PA 101 E Kennedy Blvd Ste 3170 Tampa FL 33602-5151 E-mail: J.Gordon@ManeyGordon.com

GORDON, JEFFREY SHEPPARD, lawyer; b. Bklyn., Oct. 30, 1942; s. David and Fay G.; m. Diana Gordon, Apr. 19, 1988; 1 child, Joshua. B.A., Golden Gate U., 1974; J.D., U. Calif.-Davis, 1977. Bar: Calif. 1978, U.S. Dist. Ct. (cen. dist.) Calif., U.S. Ct. Appeals (9th cir.) U.S. Ct. Claims. Clk., to judge U.S. Dist. Ct. (cen. dist.) Calif., 1977-78; mem. firm Miller, Carlson & Beardsley, L.A., 1978-82, O'Donnell & Gordon, L.A., 1982-88, Kaye, Scholer, Fierman, Hays & Handler L.L.P., L.A., 1988—; Mem. Ind. Citizens' com. to Keep Politics Out of the Courts (treas., mem. steering com.). General civil litigation. Office: Kaye Scholer Fierman Hays & Handler LLP Ste 1600 1999 Avenue Of The Stars Los Angeles CA 90067-4612

GORDON, JOHN BENNETT, lawyer; b. Des Moines, Nov. 21, 1947; s. Bennett and Mary (Adelman) G.; m. Joanne Dunbar Westgate, Jan. 17, 1976; children: Anne Dunbar, Bennett Westgate, Susan Julia. AB, Princeton U., 1969; JD, Harvard U., 1973. Bar: Minn. 1974, U.S. Dist. Ct. Minn. 1974, U.S. Ct. Appeals (8th cir.) 1974, U.S. Supreme Ct. 1985. Clerk U.S. Ct. Appeals (5th cir.), Newnan, Ga., 1973-74; assoc. law firm Faegre & Benson, Mpls., 1974-80, ptnr., 1981—. Mem. Minn. State Bar Assn., Hennepin County Bar Assn. (pres. 1985-86). Federal civil litigation, State civil litigation, Environmental. Office: Faegre & Benson 90 S 7th St Ste 2200 Minneapolis MN 55402-3901 E-mail: jgordon@faegre.com

GORDON, KEVIN DELL, lawyer; b. Oklahoma City, June 23, 1958; s. James Dell and Mary Lurana (Tracewell) G.; m. Janice Linn Mathews, Aug. 4, 1979; children: Tracewell, Elise. BA cum laude, Westminster Coll., 1981; JD, Washington U., 1984. Bar: Okla. 1984, U.S. Dist. Ct. (we., no. and ea. dists.) Okla. 1984, U.S. Ct. Appeals (10th cir.) 1985, U.S. Supreme Ct. Shareholder, dir. Crowe & Dunlevy, Oklahoma City, 1984—. Adj. prof. health law U. Okla. Law Sch., 1997—. Editor Washington U. Law Quarterly, 1982-84. Trustee, past pres. Youth Svcs. Oklahoma County, 1986—; chair adv. com. Okla. Assn. Youth Svcs., 1994-98. Mem. ABA (ins. coverage com. 1990—), Okla. Bar Assn. (uniform laws com. 1994-97, coord./moderator ann. ins. law update 1999—, mentorship com. 1999—, Outstanding CLE award 1999), Am. Health Lawyers Assn. (HMO and ins. coms. 1998—), Oklahoma County Bar Assn. (professional com. 2000—, legal aid com. 1990-98, cmty. svc. com. 1997-99), Ruth Bader Ginsberg Am. Inn of Ct. (chair mentoring com. 1996-99, chair membership com. 1999-2000, pres.-elect 2000—, Master of Yr. 1998), Order of Coif. Avocations: sports, gardening, guitar, reading. General civil litigation, Health, Insurance. Home: 8309 Glenwood Ave Oklahoma City OK 73114-1111 Office: Crowe & Dunlevy 20 N Broadway Ave Ste 1800 Oklahoma City OK 73102-8273

GORDON, L(ELAND) JAMES, lawyer; b. Phila., Mar. 17, 1927; s. Leland James and Doris Mellor (Gilbert) G.; m. Jane Busby, June 10, 1950; children: James Douglas, Leslie Anne, John Scott. BA, Denison U., 1950; JD, Yale U., 1953. Bar: Ohio 1953, U.S. Dist. Ct. (so. dist.) Ohio 1957, U.S. Tax Ct. 1979, U.S. Supreme Ct. 1978, U.S. Ct. Appeals (6th dist.) 1992. Assoc. E. Clark Morrow, Newark, 1953-60; ptnr. Morrow & Gordon, 1960-67; sr. ptnr. Morrow, Gordon & Byrd, 1967-98, of counsel, 1998—. Counsel Weakley Apts, Inc. Co., Newark. Pres. bd. end., Granville Exempted Village, Ohio, 1969-79; pres. United Way of Licking County, Newark, 1972-74; pres. Granville Found., 1991-92. Served with USAF, 1945-47. Fellow Am. Coll. Trial Lawyers, Am. Bar Found., Ohio Bar Found., Am. Bd. Trial Advs. (adv.); mem. Ohio State Bar Assn. (chmn. negligence law com. 1986), Licking County Bar Assn. (pres. 1968), Mental Health Assn. Licking County (pres. 1986), Newark Area C. of C. (treas. 1983-84), Symposiarchs Club (pres. 1981-82), Masons, Kiwanis (pres. 1965), Rotary (pres. 1992-93). Democrat. Baptist. General civil litigation, General practice, Probate. Home: 732 Mount Parnassus Dr Granville OH 43023-1444 Office: Morrow Gordon & Byrd 33 W Main St PO Box 4190 Newark OH 43058-4190 E-mail: Gorden@nextech.net

GORDON, LOUIS, lawyer; b. Detroit, May 10, 1933; s. Isador and Esther (Kraizman) G.; m. Patricia Janis, Nov. 25, 1973 (div. Mar. 1986); children: Aaron, Marla; m. Johanna C. Gordon, Aug. 15, 1987 (dec.); children: Susan, Laurie. BSBA, Wayne State U ., 1955, JD, 1958. Sole practitioner, Detroit, 1959-75; owner Louis Gordon, P.C., Southfield, Mich., 1976—; spl. asst. atty. gen. State of Mich., Lansing, 1975—. Mem. ABA, Mich. Trial Lawyers Assn., Oakland Bar Assn. Avocations: tennis, golf, sailing, skiing, power boating. Insurance, Personal injury, Product liability. Office: Gordon & Pont PC 21700 Northwestern Hwy Ste 1100 Southfield MI 48075-4923 Fax: 248 395 4101. E-mail: Lawmich@aol.com

GORDON, MICHAEL MACKIN, lawyer; b. Boston, Apr. 15, 1950; s. Lawrence H. and Gladys (Mackin) G.; m. Linda Lowry, June 8, 1991; children: Alexandra, Harrison. AB, Vassar Coll., 1972; JD, Columbia U., 1976. Bar: N.Y. 1977, U.S. Dist. Ct. (so. and ea. dists. N.Y. 1977), D.C. 1980, U.S. Ct. Appeals (2d cir.) 1985, U.S. Supreme Ct. 1985, U.S. Claims Ct. 1991, U.S. Ct. Appeals (3d cir.) 1992, U.S. Dist. Ct. (no. dist.), Tex. 1993, U.S. Ct. Appeals (5th cir.) 1995, U.S. Dist. Ct. (ea. dist.) Tex. 1996, U.S. Dist. Ct. (no. dist. N.Y.) 1999. Assoc. Seward & Kissel, N.Y.C., 1977-79, Cadwalader, Wickersham & Taft, N.Y.C., 1979-85, ptnr., 1985—. Mem. ABA, N.Y. State Bar Assn., N.Y. County Lawyers Assn. Club: Vassar (N.Y.C.). General civil litigation, Environmental, Labor. Home: 12 W 72nd St New York NY 10023-4163 Office: Cadwalader Wickersham & Taft 100 Maiden Ln New York NY 10038-4818 E-mail: mgordon@cwt.com

GORDON, MICHAEL ROBERT, lawyer, state legislator; b. Montgomery County, Md., July 5, 1947; s. Frank and Frances (Fox) G. BA, Towson State U., 1969; JD, Georgetown U., 1972. BAr: D.C. 1973, Md. 1973, U.S. Supreme Ct. 1980. Student tech. asst. Sec. of State, Annapolis, Md., 1969-70; adminstrv. and legis. aide State Senator U. Crawford, 1971—72; mem. Md. Ho. of Dels., 1983—, vice chair econs. com., 1995—, chair fiscal affairs and govt. ops. subcom., 1996—98, exec. com. alt., 1998—; ptnr. Ehrlich & Gordon, Rockville, 1984—. Arbitrator Am. Arbitration Assn., 1975-79, Md. Med. Malpractice Commn., Balt., 1979—; gen. counsel Rockville Little Theater, 1974—. Pres. Rockville Civil Fedn., 1980-81, West End Citizens Assn., Rockville, 1979-80; mem. Rockville Alternative Cmty. Svc., 1981-83; mem. Rockville and Gaithersburg C. of C. Named Outstanding Young Dem. of Yr., Montgomery County Young Dems., 1973, Outstanding State-Eleced Ofcl., Md. Young Dems., 1986, Most Outstanding Legislator, 1985; recipient Disting. Svc. award, Md. Mcpl. League, 1983, 1984, 1988, 1991, 1998, award of achievement, 1985, 1986, 1989, 1992, 1993, 1995, 1999, 2000, 2001. Mem. ABA, Md. Bar Assn., Montgomery County Bar Assn. State civil litigation, Criminal, Family and matrimonial. Office: Ehrlich & Gordon 416 Hungerford Dr Ste 330 Rockville MD 20850-4127 Address: Md Ho of Dels Lowe House Ofc Bldg Rm 151 84 College Ave Annapolis MD 21401-1991 E-mail: delgordon1@aol.com

GORDON, MICHAEL WALLACE, law educator; b. Middletown, Conn., May 4, 1935; s. Seery Clarence and Anne Catharine (Gregory) G.; m. Elsbeth Leimomi Kunzig, Mar. 15, 1958; children: Huntly Milne, Elsbeth Wallace. BS U. Conn., 1957, JD, 1963; MA, Trinity Coll., 1967; Dipl. de Droit Compare, U. Strasbourg, France, 1973; Maestro en Derecho, U. Mex., 1982; student, L'Academie de Droit de la Haye, 1973, 82. Bar: Conn. 1963. Assoc., Shipman & Goodwin, Hartford, Conn., 1963-66, asst. dean U. Conn. Sch. of Law, Hartford, 1966-68; prof. law U. Fla., Gainesville, 1968-94, Chesterfield Smith prof. law, 1994—; vis. prof. Nat. U. Costa Rica, 1970, Duke U., 1984; Lyle T. Alverson vis. prof. George Washington U., 1986—, U. Konstanz, 1995; Fulbright prof. U. Mex., U. Guatemala, U. Frankfurt; Centennial prof. London Sch. Econs., 1992; John Stone prof. U. Ala., 1998; vis. lectr. U. Bombay, U. Brasilia, U. Nairobi, Zagreb U., U. Nicaragua, U. Regensburg, U. peking, Hong Kong U., U. Tamaulipas; external examiner U. Khartoum; of counsel Ogarrio y Díaz, Mexico City, 1976—; cons. govt. agys. in Nigeria, Brazil, Paraguay, Panama, Oman, Sudan. Contbg. editor Lawyer of the Americas; mem. adv. bd. Syracuse Jour. Internat. Law and Commerce; mem. editl. bd. Fla. Jour. Internat. Trade Law; mem. adv. bd. UCLA Pacific Basin Jour.; lectr. Coun. Fgn. Rels., Brit. Inst. Internat. and Comparative Law. Served to lt. j.g. USNR, 1957-60. Presdl. scholar, U. Fla., 1977. Mem. Am. Soc. Internat. Law, Am. Fgn. Law Assn., Brit. Inst. Internat. and Comparative Law, Am. Assn. for Comparative Study of Law (dir.). Republican. Episcopalian. Author: Florida Corporation Law Manual, 5 vols., 1975; The Cuban Nationalizations—The Demise of Foreign Private Property, 1976; Multinational Corporations Law-Mexico, Central America, Panama and the CACM (2 vols.) 1978; The Civil Code of Mexico, 1978; (with Glendon & Osakwe) Comparative Legal Traditions, 1982, 2nd edit., 1994; Commercial, Business and Trade Laws of Mexico, 1983; Foreign State Immunity in Commercial Transactions, 1990; (with Folsom & Spanogle) International Business Transactions, 1985, 3d edit., 1995, 4th edit., 2000; (with Foloom and Spangle) Handbook on NAFTA Dispute Settlement, 1999; (with Foloom and Lopez) Law on NAFTA, 2000. Office: Coll Law U Fla Gainesville FL 32611

GORDON, PHILLIP, lawyer; b. S. Africa, July 7, 1943; m. Norma. BA, U. Witwaterstrand, S. Africa, 1964, BA (hon.), 1965; BA, Oxford U., 1967, MA, 1973; JD, U. Chgo., 1969. Bar: Ill. 1969, N.Y. 1973. Acted as interim gen. counsel Strategic Hotel Capital, Chgo., 1997-98. Tchg. assoc. Northwestern U. Sch. Law, Chgo., 1967-68. Author: Ill. Practice Consultant, Midwest Transactional Guide, 1981. Dir. Lyric Opera Chgo.; trustee Spertus Inst. Jewish Studies, Chgo.; advising fellow Oxford U. Ctr. Socio-Legal Studies, London. Mem. ABA, Chgo. Bar Assn., Hotel Devel. Coun., Urban land Inst. Mergers and acquisitions, Securities, International Real E. Office: Altheimer & Gray 10 South Wacker Dr # 3800 Chicago IL 60606

GORDON, ROBERT, utility company executive, lawyer; b. Price, Utah, Aug. 15, 1927; s. Harry N. and Sarah (Bontsik) G.; m. Rosanne Cline, Nov. 29, 1952; children— Steven, Cindy, Gary. LL.B., U. Utah, 1952. Bar: Utah 1953. Sole practice, Salt Lake City, 1953-66; atty. Utah Power & Light Co., Salt Lake City, 1966-80, asst. corp. sec., 1973-76, corp. sec., 1976-80, v.p., corp. sec., 1980— . Pres. United Cerebral Palsy of Utah, Salt Lake City, 1965; trustee Ballet West, Salt Lake City, 1982-86 . Served with USAF, 1945-46. Mem. Utah Taxpayers Assn. (dir. 1981—), Utah State Bar Assn. (chmn. Law Day com. Salt Lake City 1983, 84). Republican. Jewish. Club: Salt Lake Tennis (pres. 1979-81). Administrative and regulatory, General corporate, Public utilities. Office: Utah Power & Light Co 1407 W North Temple Salt Lake City UT 84140-0002

GORDON, WILLIAM STOUT, lawyer; b. Liberty Center, Ind., Apr. 12, 1913; s. James Orin and Pearl Elizabeth (Stout) G.; m. Laura Kenner, Sept. 17, 1935; children: James Kenner, William Sumner. BS in Bus., Ind. U., 1934; JD with distinction, U. Mich., 1937. BAr: Ind. 1937, U.S. Dist. Ct. (no. dist.) Ind. 1937. Assoc. Slaymaker, Merrell, Locke, Indpls., 1937-42; spl. agt. FBI, 1942-45; ptnr. Gordon, Glenn, Miller, Bendall & Branham, Huntington, Ind., 1945—. Dir. Garrett Industries, Inc., Weaver Popcorn Co., Inc., Shuttleworth, Inc. Bd. dirs. Huntington YMCA Found., Huntington Coll. Found.; trustee Huntington Coll., 1971-80. Fellow Am. Coll. Trial Lawyers, Am. Bar Found., Ind. Bar Found.; mem. ABA, Ind. Satte Bar Assn. (pres. 1973-74), Am. Judicature Soc., Ft. Wayne Country Club, Oak Arbor Club (Vero Beach, Fla.), Masons Republican. Presbyterian. Banking, General corporate, Probate. Home: 1510 Oak Harbor Blvd Apt 301 Vero Beach FL 32967-7360 Office: 533 Warren St PO Box 269 Huntington IN 46750

GORES, CHRISTOPHER MERREL, lawyer; b. N.Y.C., Aug. 27, 1943; s. Guido James and Mary (Callaway) G.; children: Ellen, Eugenia, James. AB, Princeton U., 1965; LLB, Columbia U., 1968. Bar: N.Y. 1968, Tex. 1973, U.S. Dist. Ct (no. dist.) Tex. 1977. Assoc. Akin, Gump, Strauss, Hauer & Feld, LLP, Dallas, 1973-78, ptnr., 1979—. Bd. dirs. Shakespeare Festival of Dallas, 1982-88. Lt. USNR, 1969-72. Contracts commercial, General corporate, Mergers and acquisitions. Office: Akin Gump Strauss Hauer & Feld LLP 1700 Pacific Ave Ste 4100 Dallas TX 75201-4675 E-mail: cgores@akingump.com

GORES, THOMAS C. lawyer; b. Milw., Sept. 24, 1948; s. Kenneth W. and Carolyn (Camblin) G.; m. Ann P. Pacelli, June 13, 1970; children: Lauren, Jake, Kathryn. BA, U. Notre Dame, 1970, JD, 1973; LLM, U. Miami, 1977. Bar: Wash. 1973, U.S. Tax Ct. 1973. Assoc., then ptnr. Bogle & Gates, Seattle, 1973-78, ptnr., 1978-93, Gores & Blais, Seattle, 1993-2001, Perkins Coie LLP, 2001—. Fellow Am. Coll. Trust and Estate Counsel; mem. Wash. State Bar Assn., Seattle Estate Planning Coun. (pres.). Estate planning, Probate, Estate taxation. Office: Gores & Blais 1420 5th Ave Ste 2600 Seattle WA 98101-1357 E-mail: tgores@goresblais.com

GORINSON, STANLEY M. lawyer; b. Bklyn., May 30, 1945; s. Rubin and Lena (Shulman) G.; m. Barbara Jorgenson, Jan. 28, 1983; children: Ross Evan, Hunter Lloyd. BA cum laude, Bklyn. Coll., 1967; JD with honors, Rutgers U., 1973. Bar: N.Y. 1974, U.S. Dist. Ct. (so. dist.) N.Y. 1976, U.S. Ct. Appeals (2nd cir.) 1976, Md. 1984, D.C. 1984, U.S. Dist. Ct. D.C. 1984, U.S. Ct. Appeals (D.C. cir.) 1985, U.S. Dist. Ct. (ea. dist.) Mich. 1986, U.S. Ct. Appeals (6th cir.) 1988, U.S. Supreme Ct. 1979. Atty. judgments sect. U.S. Dept. Justice, Washington, 1973-76, asst. chief transp. sect., 1977-80, chief spl. regulated industries, 1980-84; assoc. Wachtell, Lipton, Rosen & Katz, N.Y.C., 1976-77; chief counsel Pres. Com. on Three Mile Island, Washington, 1979; ptnr. Pillsbury, Madison & Sutro, 1984-91, Winthrop, Stimson, Putnam & Roberts, Washington, 1991-93, Preston Gates Ellis & Rouvelas Meeds, Washington, 1993-2001, Kilpatrick Stockton LLP, Washington, 2001—. Contbg. author: Report on Regulatory Reform, 1985; also articles. Cons. NSF, Washington, 1982-83. Mem. ABA (bd. editors Antitrust Law Devels. 1984-87, chmn. comms. subcom. antitrust sect. 1985-88, chmn. criminal practice subcom. litigation sect. 1985-89, adminstrv. law sect., chmn. industry regulation com. antitrust sect. 1988-92, mem. edn. com. dispute resolution sect. 1994—), Fed. Comm. Bar Assn., N.Y. State Bar Assn. Administrative and regulatory, Antitrust, Federal civil litigation. Office: Kilpatrick Stockton LLP 607 14th St NW Ste 900 Washington DC 20005 E-mail: sgorinson@kilpatrickstockton.com

GORMAN, CHRIS, lawyer; b. Frankfort, Ky., Jan. 22, 1943; m. Vicki Lynn Beekman; two sons. Grad., U. Ky. Bar: Ky., 1967. Former ptnr. Conliffe, Sandman, Gorman, and Sullivan, Louisville; former dir. civil divsn. Jefferson County Attys. Office; atty. gen. Ky., 1992-95; gen. counsel Taylor Bldg. Corp. Am., Louisville, 1996—; ptnr. Sheffer, Hutchinson, Kinney, 1999—. Address: Nat City Tower 101 S 5th St Ste 1600 Louisville KY 40202-3107 E-mail: CGorman@kylaw.com

GORMAN, GERALD PATRICK, lawyer; b. Buffalo, Oct. 6, 1948; s. Gerald Joseph and Ellen Patricia (Lynch) G.; m. Julia Lucille Pericek, Aug. 21, 1971; children— Jonathan G., Jillian L., Jared P. BA in English, Canisius Coll., Buffalo, 1970; JD, SUNY-Buffalo, 1973. Bar: N.Y. 1974, U.S. Supreme Ct. 1978, U.S. Dist. Ct. (we. dist.) N.Y. 1980, U.S. Ct. Apls. (2d cir.). Asst. dist. atty. Erie County, Buffalo, 1974-77; ptnr. Manz & Gorman Buffalo, 1977-83, Lankes, Semple, Waible & Gorman, Buffalo, 1983— . Mem. ABA, N.Y. State Bar Assn., Am. Trial Lawyers Assn., Erie County Bar Assn. (Trial Lawyers award 1973). Democrat. Roman Catholic. Club: Young Am. Soccer (v.p. 1984—), Southtowns Exc. Federal civil litigation, State civil litigation, Criminal. Office: Lankes Semple Waible & Gorman 350 Elmwood Ave Buffalo NY 14222-2204

GORMAN, GERALD WARNER, lawyer; b. North Kansas City, Mo., May 30, 1933; s. William Shelton and Bessie (Warner) G.; m. Anita Belle McPike, June 26, 1954; children: Guinevere Eve, Victoria Rose AB cum laude, Harvard U., 1954, LLB magna cum laude, 1956. Bar: Mo. 1956. Assoc. firm Dietrich, Tyler, Davis, Burrell & Dicus, Kansas City, 1956-62; ptnr. Dietrich, Davis, Dicus, Rowlands, Schmitt & Gorman, 1963-90; dir. Slagle, Bernard & Gorman, P.C., 1990—. Bd.dirs. Musser-Davis Land Co., Curry Investment Co. Bd. govs. Citizens Assn. Kansas City, 1962—; trustee Harvard/Radcliffe Club Kansas City Endowment Fund, chmn. bd. trustees, 1977-83; trustee Kansas City Mus., 1967-82; chmn. bd. trustees Avondale Meth. Ch., 1969-92; mem. Citizens Bond Com. of Kansas City, 1973-2000, chmn. 7th jud. cir. citizens com., 1982-84; chmn. Downtown Coun. Allis Plaza Reconstrn., 1983-85; bd. dirs. Spofford Home for Children, 1972-77, Clay County Econ. Devel. Commn., 1989-94, mem. exec. com., 1991-93, bd. dirs. Jackson County Hist. Soc. 2001—. With U.S. Army, 1956-58; capt. USAR, 1958-64. Mem. Lawyers Assn. Kansas City (exec. com. 1968-71), ABA, Mo. Bar Assn., Kansas City Bar Assn., Clay County Bar Assn., Harvard Law Sch. Assn. Mo. (pres. 1973), Harvard Club (pres. 1966), Univ. Club (bd. dirs. 1983-86, 88-93, pres. 1990-91), Kansas City Club (bd. dirs. 1993-97), 611 Club (bd. dirs. 1987-91, pres. 1990), Kansas City Country Club, Old Pike Country Club, River Club., Nat. Golf Club of Kansas City. Republican. General corporate, Probate, Taxation, general. Home: 917 NE Vivion Rd Kansas City MO 64118-5317 Office: 4600 Madison Ave Ste 600 Kansas City MO 64112-3012 E-mail: ggorman@sbg-law.com

GORNISH, GERALD, lawyer; b. Phila., July 14, 1937; s. Edward H. and Sylvia (Elkan) G.; m. Rochelle Schildkraut, Mar. 5, 1961; children: Karen, Edward H. BA with honors, U. Pa., 1958; LLB, Harvard U., 1961. Bar: Pa. 1962. Pvt. practice, Phila., 1962-66; asst. city solicitor City of Phila., 1964-66; with Goodis, Greenfield, Henry, Shaiman & Levin, Phila., 1966-71; from dep. atty. gen. to atty. gen. Pa. Dept. Justice, 1971-78; with Wolf, Block, Schorr and Solis-Cohen, Phila., 1979—. Atty. gen. State of Pa., 1978; dir. Office Civil Law, Pa. Dept. Justice, 1975-78; mem. Supreme Ct. Adv. Com. on Appellate Ct. Rules, 1974-85. Mem. ABA, Pa. Bar Assn. (coun. pub. utility law sect. 1984-86, vice-chmn. 1988, chmn. 1989), Phila. Bar Assn. (chmn. appellate cts. com. 1987, treas. campaign for qualified judges 1986—). Administrative and regulatory, Health, Public utilities. Home: 511 Anthwyn Rd Merion Station PA 19066-1328 Office: Wolf Block Schorr & Solis-Cohen 12th Floor Packard Bldg SE Corner 15 & Chestnut Sts Philadelphia PA 19102 E-mail: ggornish@wolfblock.com

GORRIN, EUGENE, lawyer; b. Irvington, N.J., Apr. 22, 1956; s. Harry and Ruth (Goldberg) G. BA, Rutgers U., 1978; JD, George Washington U., 1981; LLM in Taxation, NYU, 1982. Bar: N.J. 1981, U.S. Dist. Ct. N.J. 1981, U.S. Tax Ct. 1982, U.S. Supreme Ct. 1985. Assoc. Ozzard, Rizzolo, Klein, Mauro & Savo, Somerville, N.J., 1982-83; Assoc. Levine, Furman & Davis, East Brunswick, 1984-88; ptnr. Cole, Schotz, Meisel, Forman & Leonard, P.A., Hackensack, 1988-98; v.p., corp. adv. specialist Family Office Group Merrill Lynch Trust Co., Princeton, 1999-2000, chief spl. assets officer spl. assets group NJ, 2001—. Contbr. articles to profl. pubs. Mem. ABA (taxation sect.), N.J. Bar Assn. (taxation sect.), Phi Alpha Delta. E-mail: eugene. Estate planning, Corporate taxation, Personal income taxation. Home: 2607 Frederick Ter Union NJ 07083-5603 Office: Merrill Lynch Trust Co Spl Assets Group 7 Roszel Rd 1st Fl Princeton NJ 08540-5735 E-mail: gorrin@ml.com

GORSKE, ROBERT H. retired lawyer; b. Milw., June 8, 1932; s. Herman Albert and Lorraine (McDermott) G.; m. Antonette Dujick, Aug. 28, 1954; 1 child, Judith Mary (Mrs. Charles H. McMullen). Student, U. Wis., Milw., 1949-50; BA cum laude, Marquette U., 1953, JD magna cum laude, 1955, MS in Clin. Psychology, 1996; LLM (W.W. Cook fellow), U. Mich., 1959; student, Hague Acad. Internat. Law, The Netherlands, 1981. Bar: Wis. bar 1955, D.C. bar 1975, U.S. Supreme Ct. bar 1970. Assoc. firm Quarles, Spence & Quarles, Milw., 1955-56; atty. Allis-Chalmers Mfg. Co., West Allis, Wis., 1956-62; instr. law U. Mich. Law Sch., Ann Arbor, 1958-59; lectr. law Marquette U. Law Sch., Milw., 1963; assoc. firm Quarles, Herriott & Clemons, 1962-64; atty. Wis. Electric Power Co., 1964-67, gen. counsel, 1967-94, v.p., 1970-72, 76-94, dir., 1991-94; mem. firm Quarles & Brady, 1972-76; gen. counsel Wis. Energy Corp., 1981-94. Tutor in psychiatry Med. Coll. Wis., 1995. Contbr. articles to profl. jours.; Editor-in-chief: Marquette Law Rev, 1954-55. Bd. dirs. Guadalupe Children's Med. Dental Clinic, Inc., Milw., 1976-86; bd. dirs. Milw. Urban League, 1991-94, treas., 1993-94; trustee Ronald McDonald House, Wauwatosa, Wis., 1987-94. Mem. State Bar Wis., Edison Electric Inst. (vice chmn. legal com. 1975-77, chmn. 1977-79), Am. Arbitration Assn. (panelist comml. arbitrators 1985—), Ctr. for Pub. Resources (com. on alt. dispute resolution 1985-94, exec. com. 1991-94, panel disting. neutrals 1991-94). Alternative dispute resolution, General corporate, Public utilities.

GORSKI, WALTER JOSEPH, lawyer, insurance company executive; b. New Britain, Conn., Jan. 11, 1943; s. Walter J. and Jayne D. (Kancewicz) G.; m. Joan Pernal, Aug. 20, 1967; 1 child, Walter. BS, U. Conn., 1964; JD, U. Conn.-West Hartford, 1967. Bar: Conn. 1967, U.S. Ct. Appeals (2d cir.). With Phoenix Mut. Life Ins. Co., Hartford, Conn., then assoc. firm Januszewski, Mc Quillan & Denigris, New Britain, 1969-72; sr. v.p., gen. counsel Conn. Mut. Life Ins. Co., Hartford, Conn., 1972—. Author: Insurable Interest, 1990; co-author: Connecticut Law of Zoning, 1967. Mem. Am. Coun. Life Ins. (sec. legal sect.), Assn. Life Ins. Counsel, Conn. Bar Assn. Democrat. Roman Catholic. General corporate, Insurance. Office: Conn Mut Life Ins Co 140 Garden St Hartford CT 06154-0001

GORTON, NATHANIEL M. federal judge; b. 1938; m. Jodi Linnell; 3 children. AB, Dartmouth Coll., 1960; LLB, Columbia U., 1966. Bar: Mass. 1966, U.S. Dist. Ct. Mass. 1967, U.S. Ct. Appeals (5th cir.) 1975, U.S. Ct. Appeals (9th cir.) 1977, U.S. Ct. Appeals (1st cir.) 1979, U.S. Ct. Appeals (11th cir.) 1990. Assoc. Nutter, McClennen & Fish, Boston, 1966-69, Powers & Hall, P.C., Boston, 1970-74, ptnr., dir., 1975-92; judge U.S. Dist. Ct., Mass., 1992—. Trustee Buckingham Browne & Nichols Sch., Cambridge, Mass., 1984-93, chmn., 1989-93; mem. corp. New Eng. Home for Little Wanderers; mem. Wellesley Town Meeting, 1971-86; sr. warden All Saints Episcopal Ch., Brookline, Mass., 1975-80; apptd. Mass. Citizens Commn. on Gen. Ct., 1976; mem. com. Modern Legis., 1967-69; coach Wellesley Little League and Youth Hockey, 1983-87; bd. dirs. Rep. Club Mass., 1991-92; mem. fin. com. Citizens for Joe Malone, 1989-90; mem. Weld/Cellucci Com., 1989-90; program chmn. Boston chpt. Ripon Soc., 1967-68. (Lt. (j.g.) USNR, 1960-62. Mem. Boston Bar Assn. (law day classroom program, 1987-93, litigation, adminstrn. justice sect.). Avocations: hockey, tennis, skiing, sailing, mem. Boston Atoms Hockey N.Am.-(nat. finalist 1988, 91). Office: US Dist Ct 595 Main St Worcester MA 01608-2093

GORUP, GEARY N. lawyer, judge; b. 06 Feb. s. Ted J. and Thelma (Ihle) G.; m. Sylvia Gorup, Aug. 3, 1974; children: Geoffrey K., Genee Bree. ABA, Kansas City (Kans.) Comm. Col., 1969; BA in Polit. Sci., Kans. State U., 1971; JD, U. Kans., 1974. Prosecutor City of Wichita, Kans., 1974-75; dep. county atty. Butler County Atty.'s Office, El Dorado, 1975-76, county atty., 1976-80; trial divsn. atty. Sedgwick County Dist. Atty.'s Office, Wichita, 1980-82, chief appellate divsn., 1982-87, asst. dist. atty., 1980-87; of counsel Moore & Rapp, P.A., 1987-88, Law Office of Leslie F. Hulnick, Wichita, 1988-91; pvt. practice, 1987-93, 97-99; mcpl. ct. judge City of Wichita, 1993-97; of counsel Render, Kamas, L.C., Wichita, 1997—; mcpl. ct. judge City of Bel Aire, 1998—, City of Cheney, 1999—. Contbr. articles to profl. jours.; author/editor: The Defense Never Rests, 1989-92; author/lectr. seminars/books and materials. Pres. Am. Youth Soccer Orgn., Hawthorne, Calif., 1998-2000, nat. sec., 1997-98, nat. bd. dirs., 1997-2000, sect. 4 dir., 1992-96, area dir., Kans.-Okla., 1991-92, regional commr., 1988-90. Mem. Kans. Assn. Criminal Def. Lawyers (bd. dirs., newsletter editor), Kans. County and Dist. Atty. Assn. (bd. dirs. 1978-80, Prosecutor of the Yr. 1980), Kans. Bar Assn. (chmn. criminal law sect. 1991-92), Wichita Bar Assn. (continuing legal edn. 1988-92, criminal law com. 1986-92), Kans. Trial Lawyers Assn. (chmn. criminal law com. 1990-92), Kans. Assn. Criminal Def. Lawyers. Mem. NACDL, Kans. Assn. Criminal Def. Lawyers (bd. dirs., newsletter editor), Kans. County and Dist. Attys. Assn. (bd. dirs. 1978-80, Prosecutor of Yr. award 1980), Kans. Bar Assn. (chmn. criminal law sect. 1991-92), Kans. Trial Lawyers Assn. (chmn. criminal law com. 1990-92), Wichita Bar Assn. (CLE com. 1988-92, criminal law com. 1986-92), Kans. Mcpl. Judges Assn. (manual com. 1995—). Appellate, General civil litigation, Criminal. Office: 11108 W 14th St N Wichita KS 67212-1137

GOSE, RICHARD VERNIE, lawyer; b. Hot Springs, S.D., Aug. 3, 1927. MS in Engring., Northwestern U., 1955; LLB, George Washington U., 1967; JD, George Washington U., 1968. Bar: N.Mex. 1967, U.S. Supreme Ct. 1976, Wyo. 1979; registered prof. engr., Wyo.; children: Beverly Marie, Donald Paul, Celeste Marlene. Exec. asst. to U.S. Senator Hickey, Washington, 1960-62; mgr. E.G. & G., Inc., Washington, 1964-66; asst. atty. gen. State of N.Mex., Santa Fe, 1967-70; pvt. practice law, Santa Fe, 1967—, Santa Fe/Prescott, 1989—; assoc. prof. engring. U. Wyo., 1957-60; owner, mgr. Gose & Assocs., Santa Fe, 1967-78; pvt. practice law, Casper, Wyo., 1978-83; pres. Argosy Internat., Inc., 1994—; ranch mgr., foreman, 1945-49; mem. Phoenix com. on fgn. rels., 1980—; co-chmn. Henry Jackson for Pres., M.Mex., 1976, Wyo. Johnson for Pres., 1960. With U.S. Army, 1950-52. Mem. N.Mex. Bar Assn., Wyo. Bar Assn., Yavapai County Bar Assn., Masons, High Country Hounds, Phoenix Com. Foreign Rels., High Country Hounds, Phi Delta Theta, Pi Tau Sigma, Sigma Tau. Methodist. General civil litigation, Oil, gas, and mineral, Real property. Home and Office: PO Box 3998 Prescott AZ 86302-3998

GOSS, JAMES WILLIAM, lawyer; b. London, Can., Mar. 10, 1941; s. Joseph Allen and Virginia Ruth (Farrah) G.; m. Rita Meyer, Aug. 2, 1969; children: Anne Candace, Jennette Courtney. BBA, West Mich. U., 1966; MS, U. Ill., 1972; JD, Georgetown U., 1974. Bar: Mich. 1974, U.S. Dist. Ct. (ea. dist.) Mich. 1974, U.S. Ct. Appeals (6th cir.) 1974. Sr. acct. Price Waterhouse & Co., Washington, 1969-71; assoc. Miller, Canfield, Paddock & Stone, Detroit, 1974-82, James W. Goss P.C., Southfield, Mich., 1982-88; ptnr. Dean & Fulkerson, Troy, 1988-95, James W. Goss P.C., Grosse Pointe Farms, 1995—. Adj. lectr. U. Mich. Law, Ann Arbor, 1978-82. Bd. dirs. Old Newsboys Goodfellow Fund of Detroit, 1990-96, Adrian Coll., 1991-96; bd. dirs., v.p. Svc. to Older Citizens Soc., Grosse Pointe, Mich., 1997-2001; bd. govs. William L. Clements Libr., U. Mich., 1998—. Named Outstanding Goodfellow, Old Newsboys Goodfellows of Detroit, 1991; recipient Disting. Alumni award Western Mich. U., 1995. Mem. Georgetown U. Law Alumni Assn., Grosse Pointe Yacht Club, Georgetown Club of Mich., Commanderie de Bordeaux, Hundred Club, Rotary (Grosse Pointe Rotarian of Yr. 2000-01), Masons. Presbyterian. Avocations: philately, wine collecting, cartographic collecting. General civil litigation, Estate planning, Taxation, general. Home: 398 Rivard Blvd Grosse Pointe MI 48230-1629 Office: 230 Punch and Judy Bldg 21 Kercheval Ave Grosse Pointe MI 48236-3698 E-mail: jameswgoss@earthlink.net

GOSSAGE, ROZA, lawyer, educator; b. Landreis Celle Lohheide, Germany, Mar. 21, 1947; came to U.S., 1949; d. Abram and Lola (Strubel) Berlinski; m. David Jordan Gossage, Feb. 21, 1970; children: Brenda, Sara, Leah. BA, U. Ill., 1968; JD, DePaul Sch. Law, 1971. Bar: Ill. 1971, Fla. 1972, Mo. 1981, U.S. Dist. Ct. (no. dist.) Ill. 1971, U.S. Dist. Ct. (so. dist.) Ill. 1978, U.S. Ct. Appeals (7th cir.) 1972. Law clk. U.S. Dist. Ct. (no. dist.) Ill., Chgo., 1971-72; atty. State's Atty.'s Office of Cook County, Ill., 1972-74, State's Atty.'s Office of St. Clair County, Belleville, 1974-78; ptnr. Hutnick & Gossage, 1978—. Atty. Commn. to Revise and Rewrite Pub. Aid Code of Ill., Springfield, 1978-80; atty. Village of Summerfield, Ill., 1983— ; arbitrator Better Bus. Bur., St. Louis, 1982—. Bd. dirs. YWCA, St. Clair County, Ill., 1981; co-chair continuing legal edn. Women's Lawyers of Greater St. Louis, 2001—. Mem. St. Clair County Bar Assn., Met. Women's Bar Assn. (bd. dirs. 1981—), Ill. Bar Assn. (family law sect. 1998—), Mo. Bar Assn., Fla. Bar Assn., So. Ill. Network of Women. Consumer commercial, Family and matrimonial, Personal injury. Office: 525 W Main St Ste 130 Belleville IL 62220-1535

GOSSELS, CLAUS PETER ROLF, lawyer; b. Berlin, Aug. 11, 1930; came to U.S., 1941; s. Max and Charlotte (Lewy) G.; m. Nancy Lee Tuber, June 29, 1958; children: Lisa Rae, Amy Devra, Daniel Joshua. AB, Harvard U., 1951, LLB, 1954. Bar: Mass. 1955, U.S. Dist. Ct. Mass. 1957, U.S. Ct. Appeals (1st cir.) 1957, U.S. Supreme Ct. 1965. Assoc. Sullivan & Worcester, Boston, 1956-65; mem. Zelman, Gossels & Alexander, 1965-72, Weston, Patrick, Willard & Redding, Boston, 1972—. Master Superior Ct., Mass., 1984—. Co-author, editor: Vetaher Libenu, 1980, Chadesh Yameynu, 1997. Moderator Town of Wayland, Mass., 1982—. With U.S. Army, 1954-56. Mem. Mass. Bar Assn., Boston Bar Assn., Mass. Moderators Assn., Mass. Acad. Trial Lawyers. Jewish. Avocations: reading, tennis, travel, gardening, theatre. General civil litigation, Education and schools, Family and matrimonial. Home: 32 Hampshire Rd Wayland MA 01778-1021 Office: Weston Patrick Willard & Redding 84 State St Boston MA 02109-2299

GOSTIN, LAWRENCE O. lawyer, educator; b. Oct. 19, 1949; s. Joseph and Sylvia (Berkman) G.; m. Jean Catherine Allison, July 30, 1977; children: Bryn Gareth, Kieran Gavin. BA summa cum laude, SUNY, Brockport, 1971; LLD (hon.), SUNY; JD, Duke U., 1974. Bar: N.Y. 1981, Coun. Europe. Legal dir. Nat. Assn. Mental Health, London, 1975-82; vis. fellow U. Oxford Ctr. for Criminol. Rsch., 1982-83; gen. sec. Nat. Coun. Civil Liberties, London, 1983-85; sr. fellow in health law Harvard U. Sch. Pub. Health, 1985—. Vis. prof. social policy McMaster U., Hamilton, Ont., Can., 1978-79; exec. dir. Am. Soc. Law, Medicine, and Ethics, Boston, 1987-94; adj. assoc. prof. Sch. Pub. Health, Harvard U., 1988—, adj. prof., 1990—, lectr. Law Sch., 1990—; vis. prof. Georgetown U. Law Ctr., 1993-94, assoc. prof., 1994-95, prof., 1996—; prof. Johns Hopkins Sch. Hygiene and Pub. Health, 1994—; co-dir. Georgetown/Johns Hopkins Program on Law and Pub. Health; dir. CDC Collaborating Ctr. on Law and the Pub.'s Health; legis. coun. U.S. Senate Labor and Human Resources Com., Washington, 1987, 88; bd. dirs., nat. exec. com. Am. Civil Liberties Union, 1987—; assoc. dir. Harvard U. WHO Internat. Collaborating Ctr. on Health Legis., 1989— Western European editor Internat. Jour. Law and Psychiatry, London, 1978-81; editor in chief: Law Medicine & Health Care; exec. editor: Am. Jour. Law and Medicine; sect. editor Jour. AMA; editor: Secure Provision, 1985, AIDS and the Health Care System, 1990, Surrogate Motherhood: Politics and Privacy, 1990, Implementing the Americans with Disabilities Act, 1993; co-editor: Law, Science and Medicine, 2d edit., 1996; author: Human Rights and Public Health in the AIDS Pandemic, 1997, The Rights of Persons with HIV Disease, 1996, Mental Health Services: Law and Practice, 1986, Institutions Observed, 1986, Mental Health: Tribunal Procedure, 1984, 2d edit., 1992, A Human Condition, 1975, 2d vol., 1977, Civil Liberties in Conflict, 1988, Public Health Law: Power, Duty, Restraint, 2000. Legal affairs com. Internat. League Socs. for Mentally Handicapped, Brussels, 1980—; trustee Cobden Trust, London, 1983-85; chmn. Advocacy Alliance, London, 1981-84; sec. All Party Parliamentary Civil Liberties Group, London, 1984-85; bd. dirs. ACLU, 1986—, exec. com., 1988—; mem. com. experts drafting conventions on human experientation UN, Siracusa, Italy, 1980-82. Recipient Rosemary Deldridge Meml. award Nat. Consumer Coun. U.K., 1983; fellow Kennedy Inst. Ethics, 1994—, Fulbright fellow U. Oxford, 1974-75. Avocations: climbing, vegetable growing. Home: 10413 Masters Ter Potomac MD 20854-3862 Office: Georgetown U Law Ctr 600 New Jersey Ave NW Washington DC 20001-2075 E-mail: gostin@law.georgetown.edu

GOTKIN, MICHAEL STANLEY, lawyer, director; b. Washington, Aug. 15, 1942; s. Charles and Florence (Rosenberg) G. m. Diana Rubin, Aug. 22, 1964; children: Lisa, Steven. AA, Montgomery C.C., 1962; BS, Columbia U., 1964; JD, Vanderbilt U., 1967. Bar: D.C. 1968, Tenn. 1973, Ill. 1997. Trial atty. Bur. Restraint of Trade FTC, Washington, 1967-70; atty. H.J. Heinz Co., Pitts., 1970-73; ptnr. Moseley & Gotkin, Nashville, 1973; atty. K.F.C. Corp., Louisville, 1974-75; sr. v.p., gen. counsel Farley Candy Co., Chgo., 1975-98; ptnr. Pullman and Gotkin, Northbrook, Ill., 1998—; also. bd. dirs. Mem. ABA, Am. Corp. Counsel Assn. (past v.p., pres., bd. dirs. Chgo. chpt., pres. 1990-91), D.C. Bar Assn., Tenn. Bar Assn., Montgomery C.C. Assn. (past pres.), Skokie C. of C. (past pres., dir.), Columbia U. Alumni Assn., Candy Prodn. Club, Vanderbilt U. Alumni Assn., Sprotsmans Country Club (Northbrook), B'nai Brith. General corporate, Intellectual property, Trademark and copyright. Office: 4820 Searle Pkwy Skokie IL 60077-2918

GOTLIEB, LAWRENCE BARRY, lawyer; b. L.A., July 24, 1948; s. Samuel and Sally (Friedman) G.; m. Virginia L. Moorman, Oct. 4, 1975; children: Shana E., Kenneth H., Rebecca J. AB, Dartmouth Coll., 1970; JD, Harvard U., 1973. Bar: Calif. 1973, D.C. 1984, N.Y. 1984, U.S. Supreme Ct. 1981. Asst. U.S. atty. Dept. Justice, L.A., 1978-82; asst. gen. counsel Distilled Spirits Coun., Washington, 1982-86; sr. counsel, v.p., asst. sec. First Interstate BanCorp, L.A., 1987-96; v.p. govt. and pub. affairs, assoc. corp. counsel Kaufman & Broad Home Corp., 1996—. Dep. gen. counsel ind. commn. on Christopher Commn., 1991; instr. Atty. Gen.'s Advocacy Inst., Washington, 1981-86; pro tem judge L.A. Mcpl. Ct., 1991. Mem. Housing Mediation Bd., Pasadena, Calif., 1981-82; bd. dirs. Juvenile Gang Prevention, L.A., 9174-77, pasadena Redistricting Commn., 1981-82; chmn. Calif. Workforce Investment Bd., 1999—; trustee Orthopaedic Hosp. Found., 1998—, Hugh O'Brian Youth Found., 1998-2000. Mem. ABA, State Bar Calif., D.C. Bar Assn., N.Y. State Bar Assn., Los Angeles County Bar Assn. (chmn. com. on professionalism, trustee 1995-97), Phi Beta Kappa. Jewish. Antitrust, Banking, General civil litigation. E-mail: lgotlieb@kbhome.com

GOTTLIEB, DANIEL SETH, lawyer; b. Los Angeles, Sept. 19, 1954; s. Seymour and Blanche Joyce (Kaufman) G.; m. Marilynn Jeanne Payne, July 21, 1985; children: Gwendolyn Z., Rebecca Lucinda. BA summa cum laude, Columbia U., 1976; JD, Harvard U., 1980. Bar: Wash. 1980, U.S. Dist. Ct. (we. dist.) Wash. 1980. Assoc. Riddell, Williams, Bullitt & Walkinshaw, Seattle, 1980-86, ptnr., 1986-95; prin. Graham & James LLP/Riddell Williams P.S., 1996-97; mem. Gottlieb, Fisher & Andrews, PLLC, 1997—. Coord. S.E. Legal Clinic, Seattle, 1984-86. Mem. Seattle Fremont Adv. Com. Recipient Achievement award Seattle-King County Econ. Devel. Coun., 1990. Mem. ABA, Nat. Assn. Bond Lawyers, Wash. State Bar Assn., King County Bar Assn. (treas. 1993-95, 2d v.p. 1995-96, 1st v.p. 1996-97, pres. 1997-98, bd. dirs. young lawyers divsn. 1987-90, treas. 1987-88, vice-chmn. 1988-89, chmn. 1989-90, chmn. legal info. and referral clinics com. 1986-87, Helen Geisuess award 2001), Wash. State Assn. Mcpl. Attys., Wash. Coun. Sch. Attys., Wash. State Soc. Hosp. Attys., Bainbridge Island-North Kitsap Jewish Chavurah (v.p. and sec. 1993-95). Jewish. Avocations: tuba, hiking, bicycling. Municipal (including bonds). Home: 4880 NE North Tolo Rd Bainbridge Island WA 98110-3461 Office: Gottlieb Fisher & Andrews PLLC 1325 Fourth Ave Ste 1200 Seattle WA 98101-2531 E-mail: dan@goandfish.com

GOTTLIEB, JAMES RUBEL, federal agency administrator, lawyer; b. N.Y.C., July 2, 1947; s. Robert J. Gottlieb and Mildred C. Blaufox; m. Roberta James, 1974; children: Zoe, Zachary. BA, Mich. State U., 1969; MA, NYU, 1970; JD, N.Y. Law Sch., 1974. Bar: N.Y. 1974, D.C. 1983. Trial asst. Fuchsberg & Fuchsberg, 1971-74, assoc., 1974-77; adminstrv. asst., legis. dir., counsel for rep. Ted Weiss U.S. House of Reps., 1977-83, staff dir., chief counsel Human Resources & Intergovt. Rels. Subcom., 1983-93; chief counsel, staff dir. Senate Com. on Vets. Affairs, Washington, 1993-94; minority chief counsel, staff dir. Senate Com. Vets. Affairs, 1995—; chief of staff Senator John D. Rockefeller IV, 2000—. Office: Senate Com on Vets Affairs 202 Hart Senate Ofc Washington DC 20510-0001

GOTTLIEB, JONATHAN W. lawyer; b. Washington, June 24, 1959; s. Julius Judah and Charlotte (Papernick) G.; m. Deborah Jo Levine, June 28, 1987; children: Maya Lane, Seth Joseph. BA with honors, DePaul U., 1982; student, Am. U., 1984-85; JD, N.Y. Law Sch., 1985. Bar: Pa. 1986, D.C. 1989, U.S. Ct. Appeals (D.C. cir.) 1990. Trial atty. Fed. Energy Regulatory Commn., Washington, 1987-88; assoc. Wickwire, Gavin & Gibbs, 1988-89, Ballard Spahr Andrews & Ingersoll, Washington, 1990-92, Reid & Priest, Washington, 1992-94, ptnr., 1995-98, Thelen Reid & Priest, Washington, 1998-99, Baker & McKenzie, Washington, 1999—. Chmn. legal affairs task force Nat. Hydropower Assn., 1992-95; counsel Mid-Atlantic Ind. Power Producers; gen. counsel Power Markets Devel. Co. (PPL Global), 1995-96; adv. bd. Bradley Energy Internat., 1997—; acting gen. counsel Packard Bell NEC, Inc., 1998. Contbg. editor Project Fin. Monthly; editor Competitive Utility, 1993—. Donor mem. Corning Mus. Glass. Mem. Fed. Energy Bar Assn., Pa. Bar Assn., D.C. Bar Assn., Southeastern Energy Soc. Republican. Avocations: glass collecting, stained glass making, gardening. Finance, Public utilities. Home: 9317 W Parkhill Dr Bethesda MD 20814-3966 E-mail: jonathan.w.gottlieb@bakernet.com

GOTTLIEB, PAUL MITCHEL, lawyer; b. N.Y.C., Mar. 30, 1954; s. Henry Gottlieb and Thelma Ethel (Friedman) Miller; m. Helene Manya Roiter, Apr. 3, 1982; children: Jordan Seth, Zachary Michael. BA, Hobart Coll., 1976; JD, MBA, Washington U., St. Louis, 1980. Bar: Ill. 1980, U.S. Dist. Ct. (no. dist.) Ill. 1980, N.Y. 1988. Assoc. Rudnick & Wolfe, Chgo., 1980-81; ind. trader Chgo. Bd. of Trade, 1981-83; staff atty. Chgo. Merc. Exch., 1983-84; v.p. market regulation Chgo. Merc. Exchange, 1984-87; commodity counsel Morgan Stanley and Co. Inc., N.Y.C., 1987-89; spl. counsel commodities, futures and derivative products Skadden, Arps, Slate, Meagher & Flom, 1989-92; ptnr., chair derivative products practice group Seward & Kissel, 1992-96; dir., sr. counsel structured products & commodities Union Bank of Switzerland, 1996-98; sr. v.p., dep. gen. counsel PaineWebber Inc., 1988-2000; exec. dir. UBS Warburg LLC, 2000-01; mng. dir., COO RBC Dominion Securities Corp., 2001—. Eisenhower fellow to New Zealand, 1992; adj. prof. Ctr. for Tech. & Fin. Svcs. Polytechnic U. Contbr. chpts. to books, articles to profl. jours. Mem. Futures Industry Assn. (law and compliance divsn.), Securities Industry Assn. (law and compliance divsn.), Bond Market Assn. Jewish. Avocations: coaching youth hockey and lacrosse, golf, skiing. Administrative and regulatory, Finance, Securities. Home: 11 Highpoint Pl West Windsor NJ 08550-5238 Office: RBC Dominion Securities Corp 1 Liberty Pla 165 Broadway New York NY 10006-1404

GOTTS, ILENE KNABLE, lawyer; b. Phila., Nov. 25, 1959; d. Harry Lee and Ethel Beatrice (Teitelman) Knable; m. Michael D. Gotts, May 25, 1986; children: Isaac, Samuel. BA magna cum laude with hon., U. Md., 1980; JD cum laude, Georgetown U., 1984. Bar: D.C. 1984, N.Y., 1997, U.S. Dist. Ct. D.C. 1986, U.S. Ct. Appeals (D.C. cir.) 1985, U.S. Dist. Ct. Md. 1987, U.S. Ct. Appeals (fed. cir.) 1989, U.S. Supreme Ct. 1988. Staff atty. FTC, 1984-86; assoc. Foley & Lardner, Washington, 1986-92, ptnr., head legis./adminstrv. group, antitrust practice group, 1992-96; ptnr. Wachtell, Lipton, Rosen & Katz, N.Y.C., 1996—. Adj. prof. George Washington U. Law Ctr., 1995-96. Mem. editorial bd. The Practical Lawyer, 1994—; mem. editorial adv. bd. The Antitrust Counselor, 1995—; contbr. articles to profl. jours. Recipient Sklar award U. Md., 1980; Mary Elizabeth Robey scholar. Mem. ABA (health care com. antitrust sect. 1988—, vice chair intellectual property com. 1994-97, consumer protection com. 1994-96, vice chair Clayton Act com. 1997-98, chmn. 1998-2001, coun. 2001—), FBA (chair health care com. of antitrust sect. 1991-95, chair antitrust and trade regulation sect. 1995-97), D.C. Bar (steering com., antitrust and trade regulation com. 1994-95), N.Y. Bar Assn. (task force of women and the law), Am. Law Inst., Washington Coun. Lawyers (exec. com. and bd. dirs. 1988-97, pres. 1994-95), N.Y. State Bar Assn. (exec. com. antitrust law sect. 2000—), N.Y. Women's Bar Assn., Internat. Bar Assn., Mortar Board, Phi Beta Kappa, Phi Kappa Phi, Pi Sigma Alpha, Phi Alpha Theta. Democrat. Jewish. Administrative and regulatory, Antitrust. Office: Wachtell Lipton Rosen & Katz 51 W 52d St New York NY 10019 E-mail: ikgotts@wlrk.com

GOUGELMAN, PAUL REINA, lawyer; b. Chgo., Mar. 16, 1951; s. Paul Reina Gougelman and Jayne Bohus. BA, Fla. Internat. U., Miami, 1975; JD, Nova Law Sch., Ft. Lauderdale, 1980. Bar: Fla. 1981, U.S. Ct. Appeals (11th cir.) 1981, US. Dist. Ct. (mid. dist.) Fla. 1983. Atty. 1st Dist. Ct. Appeals, Tallahassee, 1980-83; ptnr. Holland & Knight LLP, Melbourne, Fla., 1996-99; city atty. Indialantic, 1989—, Melbourne Beach, 1990—, Melbourne, 1996—, Cocoa Beach, 1998-99. Spl. counsel for land use and growth mgmt. City of Maitland, 1984-88; spl. counsel for code enforcement bd. City of Longwood, Fla., 1985-87; cons. growth mgmt. City of Lake Mary, Fla., 1985-87; gov.'s appointee East Ctrl. Fla. Regional Planning Coun., 1986-98; mem. Seminole County Charter Adv. Com., 1987-88; gen. counsel City of Cocoa Redevel. Agy., 1990-99, Brevard Met. Planning Orgn., 1993—, Space Coast League of Cities, 1991—; gen. coun., adv. coun. Fla. Met. Planning Orgn., 1994—. With Orange County Bar Task Force, 1985, Brevard County Planning and Zoning Bd., 1989-92, chmn., 1991-92; chmn. Brevard County Charter Com., 1993-94; chmn. bd. dirs. Harbor City Vol. Ambulance Squad, 1994-97. Mem. ABA, Fla. Bar (local govt. law sect., elected exec. coun. environ. and land use law sect.). Republican. Presbyterian. Office: City of Melbourne 900 E Strawbridge Ave Melbourne FL 32901-4739

GOUGH, JOHN FRANCIS, lawyer; b. Phila., Nov. 28, 1934; s. John Joseph and Honora Veronica (Garrity) G.; m. Natalie Smith, Mar. 8, 1984; children: David, Robert, J. Joseph II, Richard, Jonathan, Kristin. AB cum laude, St. Joseph's U., 1957; JD, Yale Law Sch., 1960. Bar: Pa. 1961, N.J. 1994, U.S. Dist. Ct. (ea. dist.) Pa. 1961, U.S. Ct. Appeals (3d cir.) 1966, U.S. Supreme Ct. 1967. Assoc. Erskine, Barbieri & Sheer, Phila., 1960-65, White and Williams, Phila., 1965-68, ptnr., 1968-80, Toll, Ebby & Gough, Phila., 1980-87; ptnr., chmn. corp. dept. Abrahams & Loewenstein, 1987-88; ptnr. Hoyle, Morris & Kerr, 1988-92, Montgomery, Mccracken, Walker & Rhoads, LLP, Phila., 1992-98, co-chair bus. bankruptcy sect., 1998; ptnr. Hoyle, Morris & Kerr LLP, 1998-2000; of counsel Montgomery, McCracken, Walker & Rhoads, LLP, 2000—. Exec. com. Ea. Dist Bankruptcy Conf., 1989—; faculty co-chmn. and lectr. Temple Grad. Sch. Law C.L.E. Program, 1989-92; lectr. U. Pa. Grad. Sch., Temple Law Sch., 1990—. Author course materials for profl. and edn. orgns. Pres. Highfield Sch. PTA, Plymouth, Pa., 1966-68, Greene Towne Montessori Sch., Phila., 1979-80; chmn. bd., exec. com. Schuylkill River Devel. Coun., 2000—; chmn. Tidal Schuylkill River Master Plan Task Force; treas. Rittenhouse Savoy Owners Assn. Mem. ABA, Am. Law Inst., Phila. Bar Assn. (pres. Jr. Bar Assn. 1964-65), Hosp. Attys. S.E. Pa. (pres. 1977-79), Am. Bankruptcy Inst. (bd. cert. in bus. bankruptcy), Yale Club Phila. Avocations: tennis, gardening, fitness. Bankruptcy, General corporate, Mergers and acquisitions. Office: Montgomery, McCracken, Walker & Rhoads, LLP 123 South Broad Street Philadelphia PA 19109 Fax: 215-772-7620. E-mail: jgough@mmwr.com

GOULD, ALAN I. lawyer; b. Phila., Jan. 4, 1940; s. Louis and Yvette (Balasny) G.; m. Joyce P. Feinstein, Sept. 19, 1965; 1 child, Traci Eve. BBA, U. Miami, Fla., 1961, JD, 1964. Bar: Fla. 1964, N.J. 1966, U.S. Dist. Ct. N.J. 1966, U.S. Supreme Ct. 1983, U.S. Ct. Appeals (3rd cir.) 1985. Assoc. George M. James Esq., Wildwood, N.J., 1966-70; pvt. practice, 1970-75; ptnr. Gould & Neidig, 1975-80, Alan I. Gould, Wildwood, 1980-82, Valore, McAllister, Westmoreland, Gould, Vesper & Schwartz, Wildwood and Northfield, 1982-87, Mairone, Biel, Gould, Zlotnick, Feinberg & Griffith, Wildwood and Atlantic City, 1988, Cooper, Perskie, April, Niedelman, Wagenheim & Levenson, Wildwood, Northfield and Atlantic City, 1989-95; prin. Alan I. Gould, P.C., Wildwood, 1996—. Chmn. N.J. Lawyers Fund for Clients Protection, 1987-91, chmn. 1991; mem. N.J. Commn. on Professionalism in Law; lectr. in field. Mem. editl. bd. N.J. Lawyer, Weekly Newspaper. Solicitor Lower Twp. Pub. Schs., 1980-85, Wildwood Crest Pub. Schs., 1985-95, Cape May County Drug Abuse Coun., Parking Authority, City of Wildwood, 1973-87, Cape May County br. Am. Cancer Soc., Cape Ednl. Fund Inc.; trustee in bankruptcy U.S. Trustee of N.J.; mem. Supreme Ct. N.J. Task Force on Spl. Civil Part, 1986-88; Supreme Ct. apptd. trustee Interest on Lawyers Trust Accts. (IOLTA) Fund, 1993-97, chair, 1997; chmn. bd. govs. Burdette Tomlin Meml. Hosp., 1985-89, mem., 1976-79, pres., 1979-84. Recipient Profl. Lawyer of Yr. award N.J. Commn. on Professionalism in the Law and Cape May County Bar Assn., 1997, N.J. State Bar Found. medal of honor, 1998. Fellow Am. Bar Found.; mem. ABA, Cape May County Bar Assn. (pres. 1982), N.J. Bar Assn. (trustee 1982-89, chair jud. and prosecutor appts. com., mem. jud adminstrn. com.), N.J. Bar Found. (trustee), Fla. Bar Assn., Fed. Bar Assn., Assn. Trial Lawyers Am., Am. Judicature Soc., Assn. Criminal Def. Lawyers, Navy League of U.S., Lions (pres. 1974), N.J. Lawyer (editl. bd. weekly newspaper). Avocations: running, golf, tennis, basketball. Bankruptcy, State civil litigation, Contracts commercial. Office: 3000 Pacific Ave Wildwood NJ 08260-4945 Fax: 609-729-2111. E-mail: Aigould@jerseycape.com

GOULD, RONALD MURRAY, judge; b. St. Louis, Oct. 17, 1946; s. Harry H. and Sylvia C. (Sadofsky) G.; m. Suzanne H. Goldblatt, Dec. 1, 1968; children: Daniel, Rebecca. BS in Econs., U. Pa., 1968; JD, U. Mich., 1973. Bar: Wash. 1975, U.S. Dist. Ct. (we. dist.) Wash. 1976, U.S. Ct. Appeals (9th cir.) 1980, U.S. Supreme Ct. 1981, U.S. Dist. Ct. (ea. dist.) Wash. 1982, U.S. Ct. Appeals (fed. cir.) 1986. Law clk. to hon. Wade H. McCree Jr. U.S. Ct. Appeals (6th cir.), Detroit, 1973-74; law clk. to hon. justice Potter Stewart U.S. Supreme Ct., Washington, 1974-75; assoc. Perkins Coie, Seattle, 1975-80, ptnr., 1981-99; judge U.S. Ct. Appeals (9th cir.), 2000—. Editor-in-chief Mich. Law Rev., 1972-73; editor: Washington Civil Procedure Deskbook, 1981, author with others, 1986, 92. Exec. bd. chief Seattle coun. Boy Scouts Am., Seattle, 1984—; mem. cmty. rels. coun. Jewish Fedn. of Greater Seattle, 1985-88; bd. dirs. econ. devel. coun. Seattle and King County, 1991-94; citizens cabinet mem. Gov. Mike Lowry, Seattle, 1993-96; bd. trustees Bellevue Cmty. Coll., 1993-99, chair bd. 1995-96. Fellow ABA (antitrust sect., litigation sect.); mem. Wash. State Bar Assn. (bd. govs. 1988-91, pres. 1994-95), King County Bar Assn. (Award for Disting. Svc. 1987), Supreme Ct. Hist. Soc., 9th Jud. Cir. Hist. Soc. (bd. dirs. 1994—). Jewish. Avocations: reading, chess. Office: US Courthouse 1200 6th Ave Fl 21 Seattle WA 98101-3123

GOULDING, NICK, lawyer, solicitor; b. Sheffield, Eng., May 22, 1973; s. James and Susan Mary Goulding; m. Claire Williams, May 8, 1999; 1 child, Grace. LLB, U. Liverpool, 1994. Trainee solicitor Tofield Swann & Smythe, Sheffield, Eng., 1995-97; solicitor Pinsent Curtis, Leeds, Eng., 1997-98, Irwin Mitchell Solicitors, Sheffield, 1998—. Mem. Law Soc. of Eng. and Wales. Avocations: soccer, squash, sports, reading. General corporate, Mergers and acquisitions. Office: Irwin Mitchell Solicotors St Peters House Hartshead Sheffield S1 2EL England Office Fax: 44-0-114-275-3306. E-mail: GouldingN@irwinmitchell.co.uk

GOUNLEY, DENNIS JOSEPH, lawyer; b. Jan. 29, 1950; s. George Gerard and Elizabeth Mary (Maggioncalda) G.; m. Martha Ann Zatezalo, Sept. 25, 1976. BA, St. Joseph's Coll., Phila., 1971; JD, Dickinson Sch. Law, 1974. Bar: Pa. 1974, U.S. Dist. Ct. (we. dist.) Pa. 1995, U.S. Ct. Appeals (3d cir.) 1976, U.S. Supreme Ct. 1977. Pvt. practice, Greensburg, Pa., 1974-83, 90—; ptnr. Gounley & O'Halloran, 1984-90. Westmoreland County mental health rev. officer, 1991—. Coun. mem. Franklin Towne Condominium Assn., Murrysville, Pa., 1976-79. Mem. Pa. Bar Assn., Westmoreland Bar Assn., Murrysville-Export Rotary Club (pres. 1999-00). Republican. Roman Catholic. General civil litigation, Probate, Real property. Home: 3590 N Hills Rd Murrysville PA 15668-1438 Office: 15 E Otterman St Greensburg PA 15601-2543

GOURVITZ, ELLIOT HOWARD, lawyer; b. Lewiston, Pa., Sept. 21, 1945; s. Louis and Irene (Brass) Gourvitz; m. Bonnie S. Hirsch; children: Evan, Amy, Ross, Ari. BA, Rutgers U., 1966, JD, 1969. Bar: N.J. 1969, N.Y. 1985, U.S. Dist. Ct. N.J. 1969, U.S. Dist. Ct. (ea. dist.) Wis. 1985, U.S. Ct. Appeals 93d cir.) 1972, U.S. Ct. Appeals (2d, 4th, 5th, 7th, 8th, 9th, 10th, and fed. cirs.) 1982, U.S. Tax Ct. 1970, U.S. Ct. Claims 1970, U.S. Ct. Internat. Trade 1985, U.S. Supreme Ct. 1973, cert.: N.J. (matrimonial atty.). Pvt. practice, Springfield. Chmn., Early Settlement Panel of Union County, NJ; panelist Essex and Middlesex Counties. Contbr. articles to profl. jours. Named Man of Yr., United Cerebral Palsy League Union County, 1980. Fellow: Am. Acad. Matrimonial Attys. (pres. N.J.), Internat. Acad. Matrimonial Lawyers; mem.: Am. Coll. Trial Lawyers (diplomate), N.J. Bar Assn., N.Y. State Bar Assn. Family and matrimonial.

GOUTTIERE, JOHN P. lawyer; b. Toledo, Mar. 18, 1949; BA in American Studies, Bowling Green State U., 1971; JD, Ohio No. U., 1974. Bar: Ohio 1974, U.S. Dist. Ct. (no. dist.) Ohio 1975, U.S. Supreme Ct. 1997. Ptnr. Ferstle & Gouttiere, Toledo, 1975-85; pres. John P Gouttiere Co. LPA, 1985—. Adj. prof. U. Toledo Coll. Law. Pres. Corp. for Legal Svcs. and Assistance to the Poor, 1996-99, Toledo Legal Aid Soc., bd. trustees, 1987-96, pres., 1994-96. Mem. Am. Bankruptcy Inst., Ohio State Bar Assn., Lucas County Bar Assn. (pres. 1986), Toledo Bar Assn. Contracts commercial, Probate, Real property. Office: John P Gouttiere Co LPA 310 Bell Bldg 709 Madison Ave Toledo OH 43624-1637

GOVER, ALAN SHORE, lawyer; b. Lyons, N.Y., Sept. 5, 1948; s. Norman Marvin and Beatrice L. (Shore) G.; m. Ellen Rae Ross, Dec. 4, 1976; children: Maxwell Ross, Mary Trace. AB, Tufts U., 1970; JD, Georgetown U., 1973. Bar: Tex. 1973, D.C. 1980, U.S. Dist. Ct. (so. dist.) Tex. 1974, U.S. Dist. Ct. (we. dist.) Tex. 1976, U.S Dist. Ct. (no. dist.) Tex. 1988, U.S. Dist. Ct. (ea. dist.) Tex. 1990, U.S. Ct. Appeals (5th cir.) 1974, U.S. Ct. Appeals (D.C. cir.) 1977, U.S. Dist. Ct. (we. dist.) 1979, U.S. Ct. Appeals (2d cir.) 1979, D.C. 1980, U.S. Ct. Appeals (9th and 11th cirs.) 1981, U.S. Ct. Appeals (8th cir.) 1981, U.S. Supreme Ct. 1976. Assoc. Baker & Botts, Houston, 1973-80, ptnr., 1981-85, Weil, Gotshal & Manges, Houston, 1985—. Co-author: The Texas Nonjudicial Foreclosure Process, 1990; editor, chmn. editorial bd. P.L.I. Oil and Gas and Bankruptcy Laws, 1985. Trustee Congregation Beth Israel, Houston, 1980-86, v.p., 1996-2001, pres., 2001—; trustee Houston Ballet, 1986—, v.p., 1993-96; chmn. ann. fund St. John's Sch., Houston, 1993-95, trustee 1996—; trustee Retina Rsch. Found., Houston, St. John's Sch., Houston, 1996—; chmn. East Downtown Mgmt. Dist., Houston, 2000—. Fellow Tex. Bar Found.; mem. ABA, Coronado Club, N.Y. Athletic Club, The Argyle (San Antonio). Jewish. Finance, Mergers and acquisitions, Public utilities. Office: Weil Gotshal & Manges 700 Louisiana St Ste 1600 Houston TX 77002-2784

GOWEN, THOMAS LEO, JR. lawyer; b. Phila., June 22, 1949; s. Thomas L. and Jacqueline Gowen; m. Michele F. Charrier, Sept. 25, 1971; children: Christopher, Jonathan. BA, Haverford Coll., 1971; JD, Villanova U., 1977. Bar: Pa. 1977, U.S. Dist. Ct. (ea. dist.) Pa. 1977. Securities analyst Continental Bank, Phila., 1971-74; ptnr. Caiola, Caiola & Gowen, Norristown, Pa., 1977—. V.p., counsel Phila. Tennis Patrons, 1977—; bd. dirs. WHRC Radio Corp., Haverford, Pa., Phila. Internat. Tennis Corp.; chmn. Comcast U.S. Indoor Tennis Tournament, Phila., 1991-96; mem. faculty Nat. Coll. Advocacy, 1987—, lectr. Developments in Traumatic Brain Injury Litifation, Assn. Trial Lawyers Am., NJ, 2001. Contbr. articles to profl. jours. Fellow Nat. Coll. Advocates; mem. Montgomery County Bar Assn. (continuing legal edn. com.), Assn. Trial Lawyers Am. (exchange com. 1985-86), Pa. Trial Lawyers Assn. (chmn. headtrauma seminar 1986, bd. govs. 2000—), Nat. Jr. Tennis League of Phila. (pres. 1980-83, 87—, vice-chmn. bd. dirs. 1983-87), Phila. Tennis Assn. (Seymour Coren award 1976), Phila. Sports Congress (World Cup Soccer com. 1991—), Pa. Supreme Ct. Bd. (chmn. special hearing com. 1994-2000). Federal civil litigation, State civil litigation, Personal injury. Home: 36 Glenbrook Rd Ardmore PA 19003-1025 Office: Murphy Oliver Caiola and Gowen 43 E Marshall St Norristown PA 19401-4828

GRABEN, ERIC KNOX, lawyer; b. Knoxville, Tenn., June 10, 1965; s. H. Willingham and Ann Mason Graben; m. Helen Shock, Aug. 20, 1988; 1 child, Harrison Willingham. BS in Physics, Clemson U., 1986; MA in Polit. Sci., U. Va., 1988, PhD in Polit. Sci., 1991, JD, 1997. Assoc. Wyche, Burgess, Freeman & Parham, PA, Greenville, S.C., 1997—. Mem. ABA. Contracts commercial, General corporate, Securities. Office: Wyche Burgess Freeman & Parham PO Box 728 44 E Camperdown Way Greenville SC 29602-0728

GRABER, SUSAN P. federal judge; b. Oklahoma City, July 5, 1949; d. Julius A. and Bertha (Fenyves) G.; m. William June, May 3, 1981; 1 child, Rachel June-Graber. BA, Wellesley Coll., 1969; JD, Yale U., 1972. Bar: N.Mex. 1972, Ohio 1977, Oreg. 1978. Asst. atty. gen. Bur. of Revenue, Santa Fe, 1972-74; assoc. Jones Gallegos Snead & Wertheim, 1974-75, Taft Stettinius & Hollister, Cin., 1975-78; assoc., then ptnr. Stoel Rives Boley Jones & Grey, Portland, Oreg., 1978-88; judge, then presiding judge Oreg. Ct. Appeals, Salem, 1988-90; assoc. justice Oreg. Supreme Ct., 1990-98; judge U.S. Ct. Appeals (9th cir.), Portland, 1998—. Mem. Gov.'s Adv. Coun. on Legal Svcs., 1979-88; bd. dirs. U.S. Dist. Ct. of Oreg. Hist. Soc., 1985—, Oreg. Law Found., 1990-91; mem. bd. visitors Sch. Law, U. Oreg., 1986-93. Mem. Oreg. State Bar (jud. adminstrn. com. 1985-87, pro bono com. 1988-90), Ninth Cir. Jud. Conf. (chair exec. com. 1987-88), Oreg. Jud. Conf. (edn. com. 1988-91, program chair 1990), Oreg. Appellate Judges Assn. (sec.-treas. 1990-91, vice chair 1991-92, chair 1992-93), Am. Inns of Ct. (master), Phi Beta Kappa. Office: US Ct Appeals 9th Cir Pioneer Courthouse 555 SW Yamhill St Portland OR 97204-1336*

GRABOW, RAYMOND JOHN, mayor, lawyer; b. Cleve., Jan. 27, 1932; s. Joseph Stanley and Frances (Kalata) G.; m. Margaret Jean Knoll, Nov. 27, 1969; children: Rachel Jean, Ryan Joseph. BSBA, Kent State U., 1953; JD, Western Res. U., 1958. Bar: Ohio 1958. Counsel No. Ohio Petroleum Retailers Assn., Cleve., 1965-78; counsel, trustee Alliance of Poles Fed. Credit Union, 1972; also gen. counsel Alliance of Poles of Am., Parma Polish Am. League; councilman City of Warrensville Heights (Ohio), 1962-68, mayor, 1968-98. Sec. Space Comfort Co., S.S.K., Inc.; fed. panelist U.S. Dist. Ct.; active Dem. Exec. Com., Cuyahoga County, 1966-98, precinct com., 1966-80; trustee Brentwood Hosp., Nat. League Cities, Brentwood Found.; bd. govs. Meridia Southpoint Hosp., 1996-99; pres. West Harbor Lagoons Assn. Mem. Ohio Jud. Conf. (life), Ohio State Bar Assn., Cuyahoga County Bar Assn., Cleve. Bar Assn., U.S. Conf. of Mayors, Am. Legion, PLAV Vets, Cleve. Soc., Warrensville Heights C. of C. (trustee 1989-98), Ohio Assn. Pub. Safety Dirs., Ohio Mcpl. League, Mcpl. Treas. Assn., Order of Alhambra, Fraternal Order of Eagles, West Harbor Lagoons Assn. (pres.). Home: 20114 Gladstone Rd Cleveland OH 44122-6644 Office: 5005 Rockside Rd Cleveland OH 44131-2194

GRACE, BRIAN GUILES, lawyer; b. Lawrence, Kans., Dec. 26, 1942; s. Bernard and Theola Avida (Guiles) G.; children: Kevin A., Jeff S., Brady A. BBA, U. Kans., 1964, JD, 1967. Bar: Kans. 1967, U.S. Dist. Ct. Kans. 1967, U.S. Ct. Appeals (10th cir.) 1974, U.S. Supreme Ct. 1991. Assoc., ptnr. Curfman, Harris, Stallings, Grace & Snow and predecessor firm, Wichita, Kans., 1967-84; ptnr. Grace Unruh & Pratt and predecessor firms, 1984—. Mem. Fed. Bench and Bar Comm., 1992-96. Bd. dirs. Leukemia Soc. Kans. Inc., Wichita, 1974-77; chmn. bd. edn. Desegretion Com., 1990-95. Mem. ABA (vice chmn. constn. litigation com. 1974-76), Assn. of Trial Lawyers of Am., Kans. Bar Assn. (bench and bar com. 1991—, chmn. 1993-96), Kans. Trial Lawyers Assn. (editor jour. 1989-91). Avocations: golf, tennis, bridge. General civil litigation, Personal injury, Product liability. Home: 7027 Woodbury Ct Wichita KS 67226-2513 Office: 501 N Market St Wichita KS 67214-3513 E-mail: bggpace@guplaw.com

GRACE, (WALTER) CHARLES, prosecutor; b. Elmira, N.Y., Mar. 4, 1947; s. Claude Henry and Grace Anne (Richardson) G.; m. Barbbara Lynn Eaglen, Oct. 3, 1981; children: Katherine Anne, Charles Brigham. BA History, Duke U., 1969; JD, U. Tenn., 1972. Bar: Ill., 1972; U.S. Dist. Ct. (ea. and so. dists.) Ill., 1972. Asst. state's atty. Jackson County, Murphysboro, Ill., 1972-73; assoc. Donald R. Mitchell Law Office, Carbondale, 1973-74; atty. Jackson County Pub. Defender, Murphysboro, 1974-77; ptnr. Lockwood & Grace, Carbondale, 1977-78, pvt. practice, 1978-79; ptnr. Hendricks, Watt & Grace, Murphysboro, 1979-82; assoc. Feirich, Schone, Mager, Green & Assocs., Carbondale, 1982-83, Feirch, Schoen, Mager, Green & Assocs., Carbondale, 1983-88; state's atty. Jackson County State's Atty., Murphysboro, 1988-93; U.S. Atty. U.S. Atty.'s Office, Fairview Heights, Ill., 1993—. Chmn. Jackson County Child Advocacy Adv. Bd., 1988-93; adv. bd. Ill. State Violent Crime Victim's Adv. Bd., 1988-90; com. mem. Jackson County Juv. Justice Task Force, 1988-93; exec. com. Ill. State's Atty.'s Assn., 1991-93; legis. com. Ill. Sate's Atty.'s Assn., 1992-93; co-chmn. Jackson County SAFE Policy/Gang Policy Interagy. Steering Com. Adv. Bd., 1991-93; master So. Ill. Am. Inn. of Ct., 1992—; others. Active NAACP, Carbondale; mem. Jackson County Heart Fund Campaign, 1976-77; bd. dirs. Carbondale United Way, 1978-80, capt. campaign drive, profl. div., 1980; mem. planning com. John A. Logan Coll.-Jackson County Bar Assn. Continuing Edn. Programs; mem. adv. com. to Corrections and Law Enforcment Programs, So. Ill. U. Sch. of Tech. Careers, 1978-89; mem. Hill House Board, Inc., 1979-84; pres. 1980-82; lector St. Francis Xavier Ch., Carbondale. Mem. Jackson County Bar Assn. (sec. 1978-79, pres. 1980-81), Ill. State Bar Assn. (mem. criminal law sect., family law sect., tort law sect.), ABA (family law and criminal law sects.), Assn. Trial Lawyers of Am., Nat. Legal Aid and Defender Assn., Ill. Pub. Defenders Assn., So. Ill. Am. Inns of Ct. (barrister 1993-95). Democrat. Roman Catholic. Avocations: golf, swimming, cooking, enology. Home: 431 Phillips Rd Carbondale IL 62901-7459 Office: US Attys Office 9 Executive Dr Ste 300 Fairview Heights IL 62208-1344*

GRACE, JAMES MARTIN, JR. lawyer; b. Columbus, Ohio, Sept. 6, 1967; s. James Martin and Letitia Jean (Stively) G.; m. Michèle Lee Sirna, June 22, 1991. BA, U. Notre Dame, 1989; JD cum laude, U. Houston, 1992. Bar: Tex. Law clk. to Hon. Samuel B. Kent U.S. Dist. Ct. (so. dist.) Tex., Galveston, 1992-93; assoc. Baker Botts, LLP, Houston, 1993-2000; sr. counsel Enron N.Am. Corp., 2000-2001; mgr. Enron Wholesale Svcs., 2001—. Author tchr.'s guide: Copyright Law, 1992. Adv. coun. Local Initiatives Support Corp.; pres. R Club PAC, 1998-99; mem. Tex. Accts. and Lawyers for the Arts, 1998—; co-chair Young Profls. for Aspiring Youth, 2000—. Mem. State Bar Tex., Houston Bar Assn., Houston Jaycees (dir. edn. 1993-94, legal counsel 1994, Outstanding Leadership award 1993, Silver Key award 1994), U. Notre Dame Alumni Assn. (treas. Class of '89), Notre Dame Club of Houston (bd. dirs.), Houston Law Rev. Alumni Assn. (dir.), Order of the Barons, Phi Delta Phi. Republican. Roman Catholic. Avocations: soccer, football, reading. Mergers and acquisitions, Securities. Office: Enron NAm Corp 1400 Smith St Houston TX 77002 E-mail: james.grace@enron.com

GRAD, FRANK PAUL, law educator, lawyer; b. Vienna, May 2, 1924; came to U.S., 1939, naturalized, 1943; s. Morris and Clara Sophie (Scher) G.; m. Lisa Szilagyi, Dec. 6, 1946; children: David Anthony, Catharine Ann. BA magna cum laude, Bklyn. Coll., 1947; LLB, Columbia U., 1949. Bar: N.Y. 1949. Assoc. in law Columbia U. Law Sch., N.Y.C., 1949-50, asst. dir. Legis. Drafting Research Fund, 1953-55, assoc. dir., 1956-68, dir., 1969-95, faculty, 1954-69, prof., 1969—, Joseph P. Chamberlain prof. legis., 1982-95, Joseph P. Chamberlain prof. emeritus legis. and spl. lectr., 1995—; legal adv. com. U.S. Council Environ. Quality, 1970-73; mem. N.Y. Deptl. Com. Ct. Adminstrn., Appellate Div., 1st Dept., 1970-74; counsel N.Y. State Spl. Adv. Panel Med. Malpractice, 1975; legal counsel Nat. Mcpl. League, 1967-88. Cons. in field; reporter U.S. Superfund Study group, 1981-82; dir. rsch. N.Y.C. Charter Revision Commn., 1982-83, N.Y. State-City Commn. on Integrity in Govt., 1986. Author: Public Health Law Manual, 1st edit., 1965, 2d rev. edit., 1990, The Drafting of State Constitutions, 1963, Environmental law: Sources and Problems, 3d edit., 1985, 4th edit. (with Joel Mintz), 2000, Treatise on Environemntal Law, 8 vols., 1973—; co-author other legal reports; contbr. articles to profl. jours.; draftsman mcpl. codes and state legislation. With AUS, 1943-46. 10th Horace E. Read Meml. lectr. Dalhousie Law Sch., 1984. Mem. ABA, APHA, Assn. of Bar of City of N.Y., N.Y. Bar Assn., Am. Law Inst., Am. Soc. Law and Medicine, World Conservation Union (commn. on environ. law 1991—), Human Genome Orgn., Internat. Coun. Environ. Law, N.Y. Soc. Med. Jurisprudence. Office: Columbia U Sch Law 435 W 116th St New York NY 10027-7297 E-mail: fgrad@law.columbia.edu

GRADY, GREGORY, lawyer, banker; b. Takoma Park, Md., Oct. 10, 1945; s. Francis Joseph Grady and Deane (McGehee) Black; m. Carol Love Harrison, Feb. 25, 1978; children: Olivia Love, Blake McGregor, Harrison Edwards. BA in Econs., U. Va., 1969; JD, Tulane U., 1972. Bar: D.C. 1973, U.S. Ct. Appeals (D.C. cir.) 1973, U.S. Ct. Appeals (4th cir.) 1975, U.S. Supreme Ct. 1976, U.S. Ct. Appeals (5th cir.) 1977, U.S. Ct. Appeals (10th cir.) 1979, U.S. Ct. Appeals (11th cir.) 1981, U.S. Ct. Appeals (6th cir.) 1982, U.S. Dist. Ct. 1988. Staff atty., supervisory atty. FPC, Washington, 1972-74; assoc. Littman, Richter, Wright & Talisman, P.C., 1974-79; mem. Wright & Talisman, P.C., 1979—, pres., chmn. bd. dirs., chmn. exec. com., 1997-98, mng. mem., 1999—. Bd. dirs. Bank of Franklin, Miss., D.R. McGehee Ins. Agy., Inc., Miss. Mem. Energy Bar Assn., D.C. Bar Assn., The Federalist Soc., Congl. Country Club. Republican. Episcopalian. Administrative and regulatory, Federal civil litigation, FERC practice. Home: 666 Live Oak Dr Mc Lean VA 22101-1569 Office: Wright & Talisman PC 1200 G St NW Ste 600 Washington DC 20005-3838

GRADY, JOHN F. federal judge; b. Chgo., May 23, 1929; s. John F. and Lucille F. (Shroder) G.; m. Patsy Grady, Aug. 10, 1968; 1 child, John F. BS, Northwestern U., 1952, JD, 1954. Bar: Ill. 1955. Assoc. Sonnenschein, Berkson, Lautmann, Levinson & Morse, Chgo., 1954-56; asst. U.S. atty. No. Dist. Ill., 1956-61, chief criminal divsn., 1960-61; assoc. Snyder, Clarke, Dalziel, Holmquist & Johnson, Waukegan, Ill., 1961-63; practice law, 1963-76; judge U.S. Dist. Ct. (no. dist.) Ill., Chgo., 1976-86, chief judge, 1986-90, sr. judge, 1994—. Mem. com. criminal law U.S. Jud. Conf., 1982-87, adv. com. civil rules, 1984-90, chair, 1987-90; mem. bench book com. Fed. Jud. Ctr., 1988-93; mem. Nat. State-Fed. Jud. Coun., 1990-92, Jud. Panel on Multidist. Litigation, 1992-2000. Assoc. editor: Northwestern U. Law Rev. Mem. Phi Beta Kappa Office: US Dist Ct Rm 2286 219 S Dearborn St Ste 2286 Chicago IL 60604-1802

GRADY, KEVIN E. lawyer; b. Charlotte, N.C., Jan. 19, 1948; s. Thomas F. and Rosemary (Loughran) G.; m. Mary Beth O'Brien, Dec. 27, 1975; children: Martin E., Donald F. BA, Vanderbilt U., 1969; JD, Harvard U., 1974. Bar: Ga. 1974, U.S. Dist. Ct. (no. dist.) Ga. 1975, U.S. Ct. Appeals (11th cir.) 1981, U.S. Supreme Ct. 1990. Assoc. Jones, Bird & Howell, Atlanta, 1974-76; trial atty. Antitrust divsn. U.S. Dept. Justice, 1976-77; ptnr. Alston & Bird, 1977—. Editor: Georgia Hospital Law Manual, 1997. Mem. bd. trust Vanderbilt U., 1995-97; hon. consul gen. of Sri Lanka to Georgia, 2000—. Recipient Top Hat award St. Vincent de Paul Soc., 1995. Mem. ABA (mem. coun. antitrust sect. 1995-98, publs. officer 1998-2000, fin. officer 2000-2001, vice chair 2001—), Ga. Acad. Healthcare Attys. (pres. 1997-98), Am. Health Lawyers Assn. (vice chair antitrust program 1992-99, chair 1999—), Am. Counsel Assn. (dir. 1991-2000, pres. 1995), State Bar Ga. (vice chair health law sect. 1998-99, chair 1999-2000). Democrat. Roman Catholic. Avocations: running, reading. Antitrust, Federal civil litigation, Health. Office: Alston & Bird 1201 W Peachtree St NW Ste 4200 Atlanta GA 30309-3449

GRADY, MARK F. dean, law educator; b. 1948; AB, UCLA, 1970, JD, 1973. Bar: Pa. 1975. Dir. office of policy planning & evaluation FTC, Washington, 1975-77; project mgr. Am. Mgmt. Systems, Inc., Arlington, Va., 1978-79; prof. Northwestern U., Chgo., 1985—92; John M. Olin vis. prof. law and econs. Duke U., 1992—93; prof. law UCLA; dean and prof. law George Mason U., Arlington, Va. Minority Counsel Senate Jud. Com., Washington, 1979; mem. Cons. Dept of Energy, Washington, 1978. Fellow U. Chgo. 1977, Civil Liability Yale, 1982. Mem. Phi Beta Kappa. Office: George Mason U Sch Law 3301 N Fairfax Dr Arlington VA 22201-4498*

GRADY, MAUREEN FRANCES, lawyer; b. N.Y.C., Oct. 6, 1960; d. Frank J. and Pauline (Laberge) G. BA, Manhattan Coll., 1982; JD, Georgetown U., 1985. Bar: N.Y. 1986, U.S. Dist. Ct. (so. and ea. dists.) N.Y. 1987, U.S. Ct. Appeals (2d cir.) 1990. Assoc. Griffin, Scully & Savona, N.Y.C., 1985-87, Morris & Duffy, N.Y.C., 1987-88, Summit, Rovins & Feldesman, N.Y.C., 1988-89; asst. gen. counsel N.Y.C. Transit Authority, 1989-92; trial atty. Fireman's Fund Ins. Co., N.Y.C., 1992-97; sr. assoc. DeCicco Gibbons & McNamara, P.C., 1998-99; assoc. Kral Clerkin Redmond Ryan Perry & Girvan, 1999-2000, Schwartzapfel Novick Truhowsky & Marcus, P.C., 2000-2001. Asst. vice pres. Am. Arbitration Assn., 2001—. Recipient Bur. Nat. Affairs award. Mem. Assn. Bar City N.Y. (young lawyers com. 1987-90, constrn. law com. 1991-92, spl. com. on alcoholism and substance abuse 1994-97, sec. spl. com. on alcoholism and substance abuse 1995-97, product liability com. 1995-98), Phi Beta Kappa, Epsilon Sigma Pi, Phi Alpha Theta. Insurance, Personal injury, Product liability. Office: Am Arbitration Assn 335 Madison Ave New York NY 10017 Fax: 212-716-5907. E-mail: GradyM@adr.org

GRADY, THOMAS MICHAEL, lawyer; b. Boston, Nov. 10, 1952; s. John C. and Jean M. (Harvey) G.; m. Jacquelyn Roberts, May 15, 1982; children: David R., Caroline M. AB, Harvard U., 1975; JD, Suffolk U., 1981. Bar: Ill. 1981, Pa. 1987. Atty. Container Corp. Am., Chgo., 1981-84, regional atty. Carol Stream, Ill., 1984-86, sr. regional atty. Valley Forge, Pa., 1986; sr. counsel Rohm & Haas Co., Phila., 1986—. Mem. Am. Corp. Counsel Assn., Nat. Agrl. Chems. Assn. (law com. 1990-93). Antitrust, General corporate, Mergers and acquisitions. Home: 537 Beaumont Cir West Chester PA 19380-6437 Office: Rohm and Haas Co Independence Mall Philadelphia PA 19105

GRAEFE, FREDERICK H. lawyer; b. Des Moines, Apr. 16, 1944; s. Harry B. and Harriet (Sargent) G.; m. Mary Pat Kelley, May 12, 1970; children: Erin, Caroline, Maureen, Mary Kate. AB, Loyola U., New Orleans, 1966; MA, Georgetown U., 1971, JD, 1973. Bar: Iowa 1973, D.C. 1974, U.S. Supreme Ct. 1976. Law clk. to Hon. Howard F. Corcoran U.S. Dist. Ct. Washington, 1973-75; assoc. Howrey & Simon, Washington, 1975-79; ptnr. Finley, Kumble, Wagner, Heine, Underberg, Manley, Myerson & Casey (formerly Perito, Duerk & Pinco, P.C.), 1980-87, Baker & Hostetler, Washington, 1988—. Meets sr. health care policymakers in Cong., White House, NIH, others; counsel health care trade assns., coalitions hosps., physicians, mfrs., others. Capt. USMC, 1967-70, Vietnam. Mem. Fed. Bar Assn. (chmn. health law com. 1984-85), Kenwood Country Club (Bethesda, Md.), Columbia Country Club. Democrat. Roman Catholic. Office: Baker & Hostetler 1050 Connecticut Ave NW Washington DC 20036-5304 E-mail: fgraefe@bakerlaw.com

GRAFFEO, VICTORIA A. judge; b. Rockville Centre, NY, Apr. 13, 1952; m. Edward E. Winders; 2 children. BA, SUNY, Oneonta, 1974; JD Albany Law Sch., Union U., 1977. Pvt. practice, 1978—82; asst. counsel N.Y. State Div. Alcoholism and Alcohol Abuse, 1982—84; counsel to minority leader pro tempore Kemp Hannon N.Y. State Assembly, 1984—89, chief counsel to minority leader Clarence D. Rappleyea Jr., 1989—94; solicitor gen. State of NY, 1995—96; judge NY State Supreme Ct. (3d jud. dist.), 1996—98; assoc. justice Appellate div., 3d dept., 1998—2000; assoc. judge N.Y. Ct. Appeals, 2000—. Office: Albany County Courthouse Albany NY 12207*

GRAFSTEIN, JOEL M. lawyer; b. N.Y.C., May 27, 1948; s. Max G. and Elaine (Weisner) G.; m. Andree M. Clement, Aug. 4, 1974; 1 son, Michael Louis. BS, U. Bridgeport, 1970; JD, N.Y. Law Sch., 1973; LLM, NYU, 1974. Bar: N.Y. 1973, Conn. 1973, U.S. Dist. Ct. Conn. 1973, U.S. Tax Ct. 1973. Assoc. Rome & Case, Bloomfield, Conn., 1974-82, Albrecht, Zelman, Hartford, Conn., 1982-83; ptnr. Lublin, Wolfe, Kantor & Silver, East Hartford, Conn., 1984—. Author: Connecticut Collection Law 1982, 83; Connecticut Foreclosure Law, 1984, 87; Bankruptcy: A Primer, 1984, 2d edit., 1987; The Connecticut Unfair Trade Practices Act, 1986, Problem Loans in Connecticut, 1988. Chmn. Republican Town Com., Barkhamstead, Conn., 1980-82; region chmn. Disaster Relief Com., Hartford, 1978-83. Mem. ABA, Conn. Bar Assn. (exec. com. 1978-83), Hartford County Bar Assn. Club: Lions (treas. 1976-80) (Bloomfield, Conn.). Bankruptcy, General corporate. Home: 20 Pond Rd Canton CT 06019-2623 Office: Bahrenburg & Grafstein 24 E Main St Avon CT 06001-3801

GRAHAM, DAVID, lawyer; b. Newcastle Upon Tyne, Eng., Sept. 14, 1958; s. Arthur and Audrey Graham; m. Janette Tuerese Flynn, July 4, 1990; children: Emma Jane, Samantha Frances. BA, Oxford U., 1981. Bar: Eng. and Wales 1984, Hong Kong 1998. Trainee solicitor Freshfields, London, 1982-84, solicitor, 1984-87, N.Y.C., 1987-90, ptnr. London, 1992-98, Hong Kong, 1998—; acting gen. counsel Asia Pacific Morgan Stanley Dean Witter, 1999—. Joint sec. Panel on Takeovers adn Mergers, London, 1990-92. Author: (book) Practitioners Guide to U.K. Takeovers and Mergers, 3d. edit., 1997. Mem. City of London Solicitors Co., Law Soc. Eng. and Wales, Law Soc. Hong Kong. Avocations: golf, tennis. General corporate, Mergers and acquisitions. Home: House 41 Strawberry Hill 8 Plunketti Rd The Peak Hong Kong Hong Kong Office: Freshfields Bruckhauss Exchange Sq II 11F Ctrl Hong Kong Hong Kong

GRAHAM, HAROLD STEVEN, lawyer; b. Kansas City, Mo., Feb. 1, 1950; s. Martie Sydney and Elsie Helen (Bradford) G.; m. Deborah Ruth Glick, Apr. 8, 1973; children: Elizabeth, Jonathan, Joshua, Lauren. BS with distinction, U. Wis., 1972; JD, U. Chgo., 1976. Bar: Mo. 1976. Assoc. Lathrop, Koontz & Norquist, Kansas City, 1976-81; mem. Lathrop & Norquist, L.C., 1982-95, Lathrop & Gage L.C., Kansas City, 1996—. Active Kansas City Tomorrow Alumni Assn. Year X; bd. dirs. Hyman Brand Hebrew Acad., Kansas City, 1985-99, Beth Shalom Synagogue, Kansas City, 1983-88, Jewish CCommunity Campus, 1992-98. Mem. ABA (sect. on real property and trust law, sect. on bus. law), Mo. Bar Assn. (property law com.), Kansas City Met. Bar Assn. Avocations: tennis, running. Banking, General corporate, Finance. Office: Lathrop & Gage LC 2345 Grand Blvd Ste 2600 Kansas City MO 64108-2617

GRAHAM, JAMES LOWELL, federal judge; b. 1939; BA, JD summa cum laude, Ohio State U., 1962. Pvt. practice Crabbe, Brown, Jones, Potts & Schmidt, Columbus, Ohio, 1962-69, Graham, Dutro, Nemeth, and predecessors, Columbus, 1969-86; judge U.S. Dist. Ct. (so. dist.) Ohio, 1986—. Faculty Ohio Jud. Coll., Ohio Legal Inst. Chmn. Ohio Bar Examiners, 1974, Devel. Commn. City of Columbus, 1976-77; mem. legal svcs. Salvation Army of Columbus, 1967-77, legal sect. United Way Campaign, 1976-80. Fellow Am. Coll. Trial Lawyers; mem. Capital U. Coll. of Law Assn. (dean's coun.), Ohio State U. Alumni Assn. Office: US Dist Ct 169 US Courthouse 85 Marconi Blvd Columbus OH 43215-2823

GRAHAM, JOHN STUART, III, lawyer; b. N.Y.C., Dec. 21, 1944; s. John Stuart and Alma Agnes (Tofty) G.; m. Cynthia Jean Haslam, Aug. 20, 1988; children from previous marriage: Elizabeth Love, Nicola Stuart. BA, Washington and Lee U., 1967; BPhil, U. St. Andrews (Scotland), 1969; JD, Yale U., 1974. Bar: Va. 1974, D.C. 1975, Md. 1992, U.S. Dist. Ct. (ea. dist.) Va. 1975, U.S. Dist. Ct. (Md.) 1996, U.S. Ct. Appeals (4th cir.) 1976, U.S. Supreme Ct. 1993, U.S. Tax Ct. 1994. Mem. Alston, Miller & Gaines, Washington, 1974-75, Browder, Russell, Morris & Butcher, Richmond, Va., 1975-90, McGuire Woods Battle & Boothe, Richmond and Balt., 1990-98, Akin, Gump, Strauss, Hauer & Feld L.L.P., Washington, 1998-99, Ober Kaler Grimes & Shriver, Washington and Balt., 1999—. Sec., bd. dirs. World Trade Ctr. Inst., Balt. Trustee, mem. exec. com. Living Classrooms Found., Balt., 1992—; trustee B&O Railroad Mus., 1995—. Mem. ABA, Va. Bar Assn., Fed. Bar Assn., Md. Bar Assn., D.C. Bar Assn.,

Internat. Bar Assn., Am. Arbitration Assn. (nat. energy panel 1997—), Inter-Am. Bar Assn. Democrat. Clubs: Commonwealth (Richmond); Md. Club (Balt.), Chartwell (Annapolis). General corporate, Oil, gas, and mineral, Municipal (including bonds). Home: 216 Springdale Ave Severna Park MD 21146-4428 Office: Ober Kaler Grimes & Shriver 1401 H St NW Ste 500 Washington DC 20005-2175 Fax: 202-408-0640. E-mail: jsgraham@ober.com

GRAHAM, JUL ELIOT, lawyer, educator; b. Bklyn., June 14, 1953; s. Arnold Harold and Roselle (Lesser) G.; m. Sherry Robin Goldberg, Nov. 2, 1980. BA in Polit. Sci. cum laude, NYU, 1975; JD magna cum laude, N.Y. Law Sch., 1978. Bar: N.Y. 1979, U.S. Supreme Ct. 1984. Cons. Consumer Law Tng. Ctr., N.Y. Law Sch., 1976, mem. adj. faculty, 1980—; prin. appellate law rsch. asst. appellate div. 1st Dept., Supreme Ct. of State of N.Y., N.Y.C., 1978-79, staff atty., 1979-82, assoc. atty., 1982-83, law asst. to the justices, 1983-88, exec. sec. deptl. adv. com. to family ct., 1979-82, editor criminal trial advocacy handbook, 1980—, prin. appellate ct. atty. to the justices, 1988—, 1st Dept., 1990—; Assoc. editor N.Y. Law Sch. Law Rev., 1976-78, contbg. author, 1975. Guest lectr. Joe Franklin Show, WOR-TV, 1982—. Mem. N.Y. County Lawyers Assn. (com. on communications and entertainment law 1980—, com. on penal and correctional reform 1980— , spl. com. on practical legal edn. 1979—), Am. Arbitration Assn. (arbitrator 1985—), Internat. Radio and TV Soc., Am. Film Inst., Phi Delta Phi, Phi Sigma Alpha. Home: 249 Adelaide Ave Staten Island NY 10306-3949 Office: NY State Supreme Ct Appellate Div 1st Jud Dept 27 Madison Ave New York NY 10010-2201

GRAHAM, KENNETH ALBERT, lawyer, educator; b. Bridgeport, Conn., Aug. 15, 1948; s. Albert Charles and Rosemary (Farrell) G. BA, U. Bridgeport, 1971; MA, Northeastern U., 1974; JD, Suffolk U., 1977. Bar: Conn. 1977, U.S. Dist. Ct. Conn. 1979, U.S. Ct. Appeals (2d cir.) 1980, U.S. Supreme Ct. 1981. Sole practice, Stratford, Conn., 1977-78; asst. clk. Conn. Superior Ct., Norwich, 1978; staff atty. Conn. Dept. Consumer Protection, Hartford, 1978-81; asst. atty. gen. Conn. Atty. Gen.'s Office, Hartford, 1981— ; assoc. prof. history Sacred Heart U., 1979— . Pres., Stratford Tennis Assn., 1983—. Served with U.S. Army, 1970-73. Mem. ABA, Bridgeport Bar Assn., Conn. Bar Assn. (exec. com. adminstrv. law sect. 1983-92, exec. com. consumer law sect. 1978-84), Stratford Hist. Soc., New Eng. Hist. Assn., Am. Hist. Assn., Delta Theta Phi (vice dean 1976-77, Scholarship Key 1976), Phi Alpha Theta. Home: 155 Butternut Ln Stratford CT 06614-2457 Office: Conn Atty Gens Office 1115 Main St Ste 604 Bridgeport CT 06604-4406

GRAHAM, MICHAEL PAUL, lawyer; b. Leavenworth, Kans., May 15, 1948; s. K.L. and Norma D. (Whiteside) G.; m. Pamela Jeanne Haymes, Feb. 21, 1976; children— Sarah Kathryn, Patrick Edward. A.B., Dartmouth Coll., 1970; J.D., Harvard, 1973. Bar: Tex. 1973. Assoc., Baker & Botts, Houston, Tex., 1973-80, ptnr., 1981—; bd. govs. Texans for Lawsuit Reform. Mem. Houston Bar Assn., Houston Bar Found. Federal civil litigation, State civil litigation. Office: Baker & Botts 910 Louisiana St Ste 3000 Houston TX 77002-4991

GRAHAM, ROBERT CLARE, III, lawyer; b. Albuquerque, Mar. 24, 1955; s. Robert C. Jr. and Helen (Hoagland) G.; children: Jennifer, Jessica, Kourtney, Kate. BA, DePauw U., 1977; JD magna cum laude, Pepperdine U., 1980. Bar: Mo. 1980, Ill. 1981, U.S. Dist. Ct. (ea. dist.) Mo. 1981. Assoc. Shephard, Sandberg & Phoenix, St. Louis, 1980-82, Suelthaus & Kaplan, PC and predecessors, St. Louis, 1982-91, Armstrong Teasdale, LLP, St. Louis, 1991—. Chmn. Kirkwood (Mo.) Greentree Festival, 1985. Named one of Outstanding Young Men in Am. Jaycees, 1981; recipient Outstanding Service to the Community of Kirkwood award. Mem. ABA, Ill. Bar Assn., Mo. Bar Assn., Bar Assn. Met. St. Louis, St. Louis County Bar Assn. Republican. Presbyterian. Banking, General corporate, Real property. Office: Armstrong Teasdale LLP 1 Metropolitan Sq Ste 2600 Saint Louis MO 63102-2740 E-mail: rgraham@armstrongteasdale.com

GRAHAM, SIMON, lawyer; b. Stockport, Cheshire, Eng., Apr. 13, 1962; s. John Redfern and Violet Edna (Taylor) G. LLB with honors, Birmingham (Eng.) U., 1983; MBA, Cranfield Sch. Mgmt., Eng., 1997. Bar: Calif. 2000. Ptnr. Wragge & Co., Solicitors, Birmingham, 1986—. Mem. Law Soc. Eng. General corporate, Mergers and acquisitions. Office: Wragge & Co 55 Colmore Row Birmingham B3 2AS England

GRAHAM, STEPHEN MICHAEL, lawyer; b. Houston, May 1, 1951; s. Frederick Mitchell and Lillian Louise (Miller) G.; m. Joanne Marie Sealock, Aug. 24, 1974; children: Aimee Elizabeth, Joseph Sealock, Jessica Anne. BS, Iowa State U., 1973; JD, Yale U., 1976. Bar: Wash. 1977. Assoc. Perkins Coie, Seattle, 1976-83, ptnr., 1983-2000, Orrick, Herrington & Sutcliffe LLP, Seattle, 2000—. Bd. dirs. Wash. Spl. Olympics, Seattle, 1979-83, pres., 1983; mem. Seattle Bd. Ethics, 1982-88, chmn., 1983-88; mem. Seattle Fair Campaign Practices Commn., 1982-88; trustee Cornish Coll. Arts, 1986-91, mem. exec. com., 1989-91; trustee Arboretum Found., 1994-96; mem. exec. com. Sch. Law, Yale U., 1988-92, 93-97; bd. dirs. Perkins Coie Cmty. Svc. Found., 1988-91; trustee Seattle Repertory Theatre, 1993-95; trustee Seattle Children's Theatre, 1996-98, mem. exec. com., 1997-98; bd. dirs. Wash. Biotech. and Biomed. Assn., 1996—, mem. exec. com., 1997—; trustee Fred Hutchinson Cancer Rsch. Ctr., 1999-2001, Sr. Citizens Ctr. Mem. ABA, Wash. State Bar Assn., Seattle-King County Bar Assn., Wash. Athletic Club, Rainier Club. Episcopalian. Contracts commercial, General corporate, Securities. Office: Orrick Herrington & Sutcliffe Ste 900 719 Second Ave Seattle WA 98104-7063

GRAHAM, WILLIAM EDGAR, JR. lawyer, retired utility company executive; b. Jackson Springs, N.C., Dec. 31, 1929; s. William Edgar and Minnie Blanch (Autry) G.; m. Jean Dixon McLaurin, Nov. 24, 1962; children: William McLaurin, John McMillan, Sally Faircloth. AB, U. N.C., 1952, JD with honors, 1956. Bar: N.C. bar. Law clk. U.S. Ct. Appeals 4th Circuit, 1956-57; individual practice law Charlotte, N.C., 1957-69; judge N.C. Ct. Appeals, 1969-73; sr. v.p., gen. counsel Carolina Power & Light Co., Raleigh, N.C., 1973-81, exec. v.p., 1981-85, vice chmn., 1985-93; counsel Hunton & Williams, 1994—. Served with USAF, 1952-54. Mem. ABA, N.C. Bar Assn., Wake County Bar Assn. Presbyterian. Home: 510-508 Glenwood Ave Raleigh NC 27603 Office: Hunton & Williams PO Box 109 Raleigh NC 27602-0109 E-mail: dgraham@hunton.com

GRAMMIG, ROBERT JAMES, lawyer; b. Oceanside, Calif., June 15, 1956; s. Richard Adolf and Mary Elizabeth (Spisak) G.; m. Laurel Jean Lenfestey, Aug. 10, 1996. BA, MA, U. Pa., 1978; JD, Harvard U., 1981. Bar: Fla. 1982, D.C. 1986, U.S. Dist. Ct. (mid. dist.) Fla. 1982, U.S. Ct. Appeals (11th and 5th cirs.) 1982, U.S. Supreme Ct. 1985. Law clk. to Hon. Thomas A. Clark U.S. Ct. Appeals (5th and 11th cirs.), Atlanta, 1981-82; assoc. Holland & Knight, Tampa, Fla., 1982-88, ptnr., 1989—. Bd. dirs. Child Abuse Coun., Tampa, 1993-97; mem. Leadership Tampa, 1994-95; Sec. Tampa Bay Internat. Trade Coun., 1994, vice chmn., 1995. Mem. Tampa Bay Coun. on Fgn. Rels., German Am. C. of C., U.S.-Austrian C. of C., Phi Beta Kappa. Republican. Roman Catholic. General corporate, Private international, Securities. Home: 21 Bahama Cir Tampa FL 33606-3317 Office: Holland & Knight 400 N Ashley Dr Ste 2300 Tampa FL 33602-4322

GRANADE, FRED KING, lawyer; b. Mobile, Ala., Mar. 3, 1950; s. Joe C. and Lucille (Williams) G.; m. Callie Virginia Smith, Oct. 9, 1976; children: Taylor Rives, Milton Smith, Joseph Kee. BA, Auburn U., 1972; JD, Washington and Lee U., 1975. Bar: Ala. 1975, Fla. 1976, U.S. Dist. Ct. (so. and mid. dists.) Ala., 1977, U.S. Supreme Ct. 1979, U.S. Ct. Appeals (5th and 11th cirs.) 1981. Law clk. to presiding justice Ala. Ct. of Criminal Appeals, Montgomery, 1975-76; ptnr. Stone, Granade & Crosby P.C., Bay Minette, Daphne, Ala., 1986—. Bd. dirs. First Community Bank, Chatom, Ala., S.W. Bancshares, Mt. Vernon, Ala. Bd. dirs. Historic Blakeley Authority, Ala., 1983-85, North Baldwin Hosp.; chmn. profl. div. North Baldwin United Fund, Bay Minette, 1987. Mem. Ala. Bar Assn., Fla. Bar Assn., Baldwin County Bar Assn., Omicron Delta Kappa. Presbyterian. General civil litigation, General practice, Probate. Office: Stone Granade & Crosby 34 N Pine St Bay Minette AL 36507-3202 E-mail: FKG@SGClaw.com

GRANADE, GINNY S. prosecutor; US atty. Ala. So. Dist. , 2001—. Office: Riverview Plz 63 S Royal St Mobile AL 36602 Office Fax: 334-441-5277*

GRANAT, RICHARD STUART, lawyer, educator; b. N.Y.C., Nov. 11, 1940; s. George and Judith G.; m. Nancy Ruth Wruble, Dec. 23, 1962; children: Lisa, Hilary, Peter, David. BA, Lehigh U., 1962; JD (Harlan Fiske Stone scholar), Columbia U., 1965. Bar: Md. 1966, D.C. 1977. Asst. counsel U.S. OEO, Washington, 1965-67, dir. housing programs, 1967-78; asst. dir. Model Cities Agy. Office of Mayor, Balt., 1968-69; dir. Cmty. Planning and Evaluation Inst., 1970-71; pres. Univ. Rsch. Corp. Mgmt. Svcs. Corp., 1970-77; pvt. practice Washington and Md., 1969—. Pres. Automated Legal Systems, Inc., Phila., 1984-89; dir. M.A. in Legal Studies Program, Antioch Sch. Law, 1979-83; pres., chmn. bd. Ctr. for Legal Studies, Washington, 1979-89; chmn. bd. dirs. Ctr. Sch., Rockville, Md.; pres. Inst. Paralegal Tng., Inc., Phila., 1982-89, The Phila. Inst. 1987-89; pres. Nat. Ctr. for Edn. Testing Inc., 1986-89, Inst. for Employee Benefits Tng., 1986-89; pres. The Inst. for Law and Tech., Phila., 1990-92; pres. Interactive Legal Media, Inc., 1992-96; instr. Rutgers Sch. Law, Camden, N.J., 1992-94, Sch. Lang., U. Balt., 1995-96; adj. prof. Sch. Law U. Md., 1994-96, dir. Ctr. for Law Practice Tech., 1994—, Peoples Law Libr. of Md., 1996—, dir. Ctr. for On-Line Mediation, Inc., 1996-99; pres. mylawyer.com, Inc., 1998—. Mem. ABA, Md. Bar Assn., D.C. Bar Assn. Civil rights. Home: 320 Morgause Pl N Baltimore MD 21208-1430 Office: 207 G Redwood St Baltimore MD 21202 E-mail: richard@granat.com

GRANATA, LINDA M. lawyer; b. Montreal, June 9, 1951; d. Albert Joseph and Marylka (Aksamit) G. BS in Broadcasting, U. Fla., 1974; JD, Nova U., 1988. Bar: Fla. 1988, U.S. Dist. Ct. (so. dist.) Fla. 1989, U.S. Ct. Appeals (11th cir.) 1990, U.S. Tax Ct. 1990. Pres. Mkt. Makers, Inc., Miami, Fla., 1978-88, Ethylene Eaters, Inc., North Miami, 1981-88, 92—; law clk. to Hon. Paul M. Marko III 17th Cir. Ct., Ft. Lauderdale, 1986-87; corp. counsel Quantum Assocs., Inc., Miami Beach, 1988-89; assoc. Richard C. Fox, P.A., Boca Raton, Fla., 1989-90; pvt. practice North Miami, 1990-93; corp. counsel World Trade Consortium, Inc., Miami, 1993-99; pvt. practice, 2000—. Arbitrator Nat. Assn. Securities Dealers, Ft. Lauderdale, 1990—, Nat. Futures Assn., Ft. Lauderdale, 1990-95; guardian ad litum 17th Cir. Ct. Broward County, 1996-99. Mem. Am. Arbitration Assn., Nat. Panel Consumer Arbitrators. Contracts commercial, General corporate, Securities. Office: 19085 NE 3rd Ct Miami FL 33179-3829 E-mail: legal-1@law.com

GRAND, RICHARD D. lawyer; b. Danzig, Feb. 20, 1930; came to U.S., 1939, naturalized, 1944; s. Morris and Rena Grand; m. Marcia Kosta, Jan. 27, 1952. BA, NYU, 1951; JD, U. Ariz., 1958. Bar: Ariz. 1958, Calif. 1973, U.S. Supreme Ct. 1973; cert. specialist in injury litigation Ariz. Bd. Legal Specialization. Dep. atty., Pima County, Ariz., 1958-59; pvt. practice trial law Tucson, 1959—; founder, 1st pres. Inner Circle Advocates, 1972-75; founder Richard Grand Found., 1966, now chmn.; hon. pres. Richard Grand Soc., 1997—. Contbr. articles to legal publs. Mem. bd. visitors law sch. Ariz. State U. Recipient citation of honor Lawyers Coop. Pub. Co., 1964 Fellow Am. Acad. Forensic Scis., Internat. Soc. Barristers; assoc. mem. Internat. Med. Soc. Paraplegia, Am. Coll. Legal Medicine; mem. ABA (vice-chmn. com. govtl. liability law, sect. of tort and ins. practice 1986-87), Pima County Bar Assn., N.Y. State Trial Lawyers Assn., Calif. Trial Lawyers Assn., Am. Bd. Trial Advs. (cert. in civil trial advocacy), Brit. Acad. Forensic Scis., President's Club of U. Ariz., Richard Grand Soc. (hon. pres.), Bohemian Club. Personal injury. Address: 127 W Franklin St Tucson AZ 85701-1020 E-mail: richard_d_grand@msn.com

GRANGE, GEORGE ROBERT, II, lawyer; b. Alexandria, Va., Apr. 14, 1947; s. George Robert and Lucille (Bell) G.; m. Kathy McPeek, Aug. 21, 1971; children: Steven, John, George Robert III, Sarah Ruth, Peter Mark. BA with honors, U. Va., 1969; postgrad., Yale U., 1970-71; JD, Harvard U., 1974. Bar: Mass. 1975, D.C. 1975, U.S. Supreme Ct. 1980, U.S. Dist. Ct. D.C. 1984, U.S. Ct. Appeals (D.C. cir.) 1984, U.S. Ct. Appeals (fed. cir.) 1988, U.S. Claims Ct. 1989. Assoc. Zuggert, Scott & Rasenberger, Washington, 1975-77; prin. Gammon & Grange, 1977—. CEO Dialogs, 1990—. Bd. dirs. Evang. Coun. for Fin. Accountability, Washington, 1980-88, Christian Mgmt. Assn., 1988-91. Mem. Christian Legal Soc. (nat. bd. dirs. 1983-91), D.C. Bar Assn., Va. Bar Assn., Nat. Bar Assn., Phi Beta Kappa. Republican. Administrative and regulatory, Non-profit and tax-exempt organizations, Corporate taxation. E-mail: GRG@GandGLaw.com

GRANHOLM, JENNIFER MULHERN, state attorney general; b. Vancouver, B.C., Can., Feb. 5, 1959; came to U.S., 1962; d. Victor Ivar and Shirley Alfreda (Dowden) G.; m. Daniel Granholm Mulhern, May 23, 1986; children: Kathryn, Cecelia, Jack. BA, U. Calif., Berkeley, 1984; JD, Harvard U., 1987. Bar: Mich. 1987, U.S. Dist. Ct. (ea. dist.) Mich. 1987, U.S. Ct. Appeals (6th cir.) 1987. Jud. law clk. 6th Cir Ct. Appeals, Detroit, 1987-88; exec. asst. Wayne County Exec., 1988-89; asst. U.S. atty. Dept. Justice, 1990-94; corp. counsel Wayne County, 1994—; elected atty. gen., 1999. Gen. counsel Detroit/Wayne County Stadium Authority, 1996—. Contbr. articles to profl. jours. V.p., bd.dirs. YWCA, Inkster, Mich., 1995—; del. Dem. Nat. Conv., Chgo., 1996; chair sel. com. U.S. Sen., Detroit, 1997; mem. Leadership Detroit, 1990—. Mem. Detroit Bar Assn., Women's Law Assn., Inc. Soc. Irish Lawyers. Roman Catholic. Avocations: running, family, laughing. Office: Atty Gen PO Box 30212 Lansing MI 48909-7712*

GRANO, JOSEPH DANTE, law educator; b. Olympia, Wash., Nov. 11, 1943; s. Dante J. and Sara R. (Giuffrida) G.; m. Maura D. Corrigan, July 11, 1976; children: Megan, Daniel. AB, Temple U., 1965, JD, 1968; LLM, U. Ill., 1970. Bar: Pa. 1970, Mich. 1977. Asst. dist. atty. Phila. Dist. Attys. Office, 1970-71; asst. prof. U. Detroit, 1971-74, assoc. prof., 1974-75; prof. law Wayne State U., Detroit, 1975—. Dep. asst. atty. gen. U.S. Dept. Justice, 1988; vis. prof. law Cornell U., 1978-79, U. Calif., Berkeley, 1981-82; reporter Mich. Criminal Procedure Rules Com., 1982—; lectr. Mich. Jud. Inst., 1978—, Am. Jud. Coll., 1986. Author: Problems in Criminal Procedure, 2d edit., 1981; (with James Haddad and Yale Kamisar) Sum and Substance of Criminal Procedure, 1977; contbr. articles to profl. jours. Mem. ABA, Am. Law Inst. Home: 880 Bishop Rd Grosse Pointe MI 48230-1924

GRANOFF, GAIL PATRICIA, lawyer; b. Phila., July 25, 1952; d. Jerome Claymont and Jean (Kessler) G.; m. Stanley B. Edelstein; children: Jessica, Jonathan. A.B., Temple U., 1973; J.D., U. Pa., 1976. Bar: Pa. 1976, U.S. Dist. Ct. (ea. dist.) Pa. 1977, U.S. Ct. Appeals (3d cir.) 1977, U.S. Supreme Ct. 1981. Law clk. to Judge Kalodner U.S. Ct. Appeals (3d cir.), Phila., 1976-77; assoc. Pepper Hamilton & Scheetz, 1977-84; counsel Rohm and Haas Co., 1984-86, sr. counsel, 1987-90, corp. sec., sr. counsel, 1990-93, asst. gen. counsel and corp. sec., 1993—. Mem. ABA (chair Reporting Cos. Under the '34 Act, Fed. Securities Com., Bus. Law sect. 1995—), Phila. Bar Assn. (exec. young lawyers sect. 1983-86, sec. 1984-86, commn. on jud. selection and retention investigative divsn. 1985-95, exec. com. bus. law sect. 1998—), Am. Corp. Counsel Assn. Antitrust, General corporate, Securities. Office: Rohm & Haas Co 100 Independence Mall W Philadelphia PA 19106-2399

GRANOFF, GARY CHARLES, lawyer, investment company executive; b. N.Y.C., Feb. 2, 1948; s. N. Henry and Jeannette (Trum) G.; m. Leslie Barbara Resnick, Dec. 21, 1969; children: Stephen, Robert, Joshua. BBA in Acctg., George Washington U., 1970, JD with honors, 1973. Bar: N.Y. 1974, Fla. 1974, U.S. Dist. Ct. (so. dist.) N.Y. 1976. Assoc. Dreyer & Traub, N.Y.C., 1973-75; ptnr. Ezon, Langberg & Granoff, 1975-78, Granoff & Walker, N.Y.C., 1982-92, Granoff, Walker & Forlenza PC, N.Y.C., 1993—; pvt. practice, 1978-81; pres., also bd. dirs. Elk Assocs. Funding Corp., 1979—, GCG Assocs., Inc., N.Y.C., 1982—; pres., dir. Gemini Capital Corp., 1996—; pres., chmn. Ameritrans Capital Corp., 1999—. Atty. del. to U.S.-China Joint Session on Trade, Investment and Econ. Law, Beijing, 1987; dean's adv. bd. George Washington U. Law Sch., 1993—. Campaign vol. Mondale for Pres., N.Y.C., 1984; fundraiser Robert Garcia for Congress, N.Y.C., Dem. Senatorial Campaign Com., N.Y.C., 1987-88; active N.Y. Lawyers for Dukakis Com., 1988; chmn. N.Y.C. chpt. George Washington U. Nat. Law Ctr. Leadership Gifts Com.; trustee George Washington U., 1998—, Parker Jewish Inst. for Health Care and Rehab., 2001—. Recipient Jacob Burns award George Washngton U. Law Sch., 1998. Mem. ABA, N.Y. State Bar Assn., Fla. Bar Assn., Assn. Bar City N.Y., People to People Internat., Nat. Assn. Investment Cos. (legis com.), George Washington U. Alumni Assn. (chmn. N.Y.C. chpt., bd. dirs. law sch. alumni assn., alumni com. 21 century, trustee), North Shore Country Club (chmn. legal com., bd. govs. 1994-96, 98-2001, chmn. admissions com. 1999-2001). Avocations: golf, tennis, skiing. Contracts commercial, Finance, Real property. Office: Granoff Walker & Forlenza 747 3rd Ave Fl 4 New York NY 10017-2803

GRANT, ARTHUR GORDON, JR. lawyer, educator; b. New Orleans, May 16, 1945; s. Arthur Gordon and Martha (McCutchon) G.; children: Arthur Gordon III, Kathryn S., Douglas M. BA, U. N.C., 1967; JD, Tulane U., 1970. Bar: La. 1970, U.S. Ct. Appeals (5th cir.) 1970, U.S. Dist. Ct. (ea. and mid. dists.) La. 1970, U.S. Dist. Ct. (we. dist.) La. 1970, U.S. Ct. Appeals (11th cir.) 1981, U.S. Supreme Ct. 1990, U.S. Dist. Ct. (so. dist.) Tex. 1998. Assoc. Montgomery, Barnett, Brown, Read, Hammond & Mintz, New Orleans, 1970-73, ptnr., 1973—. Admiralty and maritime law instr. U. New Orleans Sch. Naval Architecture, 1990—; bd. dirs. Am. Boat and Yacht Coun., Millersville, Md., 1990-98. Author: Recreational Craft, Jurisdiction, Claims and Coverage, 1989; contbg. author: Recreational Boating Law, 1992, Benedict on Admiralty, Vol. 8, 7th edit., 1995. Bd. govs. Propellor Club Port of New Orleans, 1989-90, 92-94. Fellow La. Bar Found.; mem. Fed. Bar Assn., Navy League of U.S., La. Bar Assn., Soc. Naval Architects and Marine Engrs., Maritime Law Assn. U.S. (vice chmn. recreational boating com. 1990-94), Bar Assn. 5th Fed. Cir., Southeastern Admiralty Law Inst., So. Yacht Club, Thomas More Inn of Ct. Episcopalian. Avocations: hunting, fishing, boating, Civil War history. Admiralty, Federal civil litigation, Product liability. Office: Montgomery Barnett Brown Read Hammond & Mintz 3200 Energy Ctr New Orleans LA 70163 E-mail: ggrant@monbar.com

GRANT, ISABELLA HORTON, retired judge; b. L.A., Sept. 24, 1924; d. John Daniel and Hannabelle (Horton) Grant. BA, Swarthmore Coll., 1944; MA, UCLA, 1946; JD, Columbia U., 1950; LLD (hon.), Molloy Coll., 1976. Jr. profl. asst. OSS, Washington, 1944-45; economist Inst. Indsl. Rels., UCLA, 1946-47, Office Price Stblzn., L.A., 1951-52; ptnr. Livingston, Grant, Stone & Kay, San Francisco, 1953-79; judge Mcpl. Ct., 1979-82, Superior Ct., San Francisco, 1982-97; ret., 1997. Bd. dirs. Kid's Turn, Pocket Opera. Fellow ABA; mem. Am. Arbitration Assn., San Francisco Ethics Commn. (chair 1999), San Francisco Bar Assn. (bd. dirs. 1978-79), Acad. Matrimonial Lawyers (pres. No. Calif. chpt. 1976), Assn. Family and Conciliation Cts. (pres. Calif. chpt. 1987-89), Nat. Coll. Probate Judges (William W. Treat award 2000), Queen's Bench (pres. 1964), Calif. Tennis Club, Phi Beta Kappa.

GRANT, JOHN HALLORAN, lawyer; b. Mpls., Aug. 15, 1950; s. Clarence John and Virginia Louise (Dwinnell) G.; m. Mary Elizabeth Davy; children— Elizabeth Ann, Virginia Marie. B.A., U. Mont., 1972; J.D., Gonzaga U., 1977. Bar: Mont. 1977, U.S. Dist. Ct. Mont. 1977, U.S. Supreme Ct. 1982. Shareholder, Jackson Murdo and Grant P.C., Helena, Mont., 1977— . Contracts commercial, General practice, Personal injury. Office: Jackson Murdo and Grant 203 N Ewing St Helena MT 59601-4202

GRANT, MERWIN DARWIN, lawyer; b. Safford, Ariz., May 7, 1944; s. Darwin Dewey and Erma (Whiting) G.; m. Charlotte Richey, June 27, 1969; children: Brandon, Taggart, Christian, Brittany. BA in Econs., Brigham Young U., 1968; JD, Duke U., 1971. Bar: Ariz. 1971, U.S. Dist. Ct. Ariz., U.S. Dist. Ct. (we. dist.) Tex., U.S. Ct. Appeals (5th, 7th, 8th, 9th and 10th cirs.), U.S. Tax Ct., U.S. Supreme Ct. Pres. Merwin D. Grant, P.C., Phoenix, 1977—; ptnr. Beus, Gilbert & Morrill, 1984-93; pres. Grant, Williams & Dangerfield P.C., 1994—. Guest condr. Phoenix Symphony Orch., 1989. Bd. dirs. Grand Canyon coun. Boy Scouts Am., Phoenix, 1974-76, Maricopa Hosp., Health Sys. Bd., 1997—, Ariz. Motorsports Charitable Found.; pres., bd. dirs. Golden Gate Settlement, Phoenix, 1975-80, 84-88, Phoenix Internat. Raceway Charities, Ariz. Acad. Decathalon Assn., exec. com., 1999—; charter mem. Rep. Presl. Task Force, Washington, 1984—. Fellow Ariz. Bar Found.; mem. ABA (litigation sect.), Assn. Trial Lawyers Am., Kiwanis (bd. dirs. Phoenix chpt. 1972-79). Federal civil litigation, State civil litigation, Private international. Office: Grant Williams & Dangerfield 302 N 1st Ave Phoenix AZ 85003-1500 E-mail: grant@phxlaw.com

GRANT, PATRICK ALEXANDER, lawyer, association administrator; b. Denver, Nov. 14, 1945; s. Edwin Hendrie and Mary Belle (McIntyre) G.; m. Carla Clyde Yancey, Aug. 16, 1975; children: Mary Cameron, Sara Mansur, Alexis Hendrie. BA with honors, Colgate U., 1967; MBA, Denver U., 1973; JD, Drake U., 1976. Bar: Colo. 1977. Law clk. to Judge Donald P. Smith, Jr. Colo. Ct. Appeals, Denver, 1976-77; assoc. Grant, McHendrie, Haines & Crouse, PC, 1977-83, ptnr., v.p., 1984-91, also bd. dirs.; state rep. Colo. Gen. Assembly, 1984-92, vice-chmn. fin. com., 1987-88, chmn. audit com., 1989-90, chmn. judiciary com., 1988-92, chmn. legal svcs. com., 1988-89. Mem. Colo. Coun. Elected Ofcls. for Soviet Jewry, Denver, 1985-92, Colo. Spl. Task Force Tort Liability and Ins., Denver, 1985; bd. dirs. Colo. Sports Hall of Fame, 1992-98, Colo. State U. Livestock Leader Coun. Kent Denver Leadership Fund, 1996-97, upper sch. chmn. parents divsn.; mem. Denver Cmty. Mental Health Commn., 1985-86; mem. exec. coun., planning com. St. Joseph Hosp., Denver, 1985-88; mem. Denver Bd. for Developmentally Disabled, 1987-88; vestryman, jr. warden St. Barnabas Parish, Denver, 1979-84; mem. adv. com. Nat. Ctr. Preventive Law, 1987-90; bd. dirs. Colo. Jud. Inst., 1990-96; mem. exec. bd. Parents Assn., Gettysburg (Pa.) Coll., 1997-2001, chmn. parents fund, 2000-01, mem. Gettysburg Coll. nat. campaign steering com., 2000-01, Colgate U. (N.Y.) Soc. of Families steering com.; exec. bd. Denver coun. Boy Scouts Am., scout show chmn., 1997—; mem. Roundup Riders of Rockies, 1989—; mem. Colo. State Bd. Agr., 2001—, Gates Found. fellow John F. Kennedy Sch. Govt. Harvard U., 1985, Toll Fellow Coun. of State Govts., 1987; recipient Outstanding Alumni award Kent Denver Country Day Sch., 1986, Colo. Wildlife Fedn. Appreciation award, 1987, Disting. Svc. to Higher Edn. award U. Denver, 1988, Bus. Legis. of Yr., award Colo. Pub. Affairs Coun., 1989, Outstanding Achievement award EPA, 1989, award of honor Hist. Denver, 1989, Stephen H. Hart award Colo. Hist. Soc., 1990, Spl. Recognition award AIA; named one of Outstanding Young Men in Am.,

U.S. Jaycees, 1980, Legislator of Yr. Associated Builders and Contractors, 1991, Gen. Heritage award for Former Legislator, 1997. Mem. Colo. Med. Soc. Found. (bd. dirs., pres. 1997-99, pres. emeritus 1999—), Western Stock Show Assn. (exec. com., bd. dirs. 1984—, exec. v.p. and CEO 1990-91, pres. and CEO 1991—), Metro Denver C. of C. (chmn. econ. devel. coun. 1995-96, co-chmn. pub. affairs coun. 1999-2000). Republican. Episcopalian. Avocation: wood chopping, horseback riding. Environmental, Real property, Transportation. Home: 3777 S Dahlia St Englewood CO 80110-4215 Office: 4655 Humboldt St Denver CO 80216-2818

GRANT, RUSSELL PORTER, JR. lawyer, petroleum land man; b. Ft. Sill, Okla., Nov. 5, 1943; s. Russell Porter and Jimmie (Bell) G.; m. Janice Rae Lockley, Nov. 19, 1966; 1 child, Russell Porter III. BS, U.S. Mil. Acad., 1966; JD, U. Miss., 1974. Bar: Miss. 1974, U.S. Dist. Ct. (no. dist.) Miss. 1974, U.S. Ct. Appeals (5th cir.) 1980, U.S. Dist. Ct. (so. dist.) Miss. 1992. Ptnr. Patterson & Patterson, Aberdeen, Miss., 1974-80; petroleum landman, 1980-81; ops. landman Hughes & Hughes Oil and Gas, Jackson, Miss., 1981-84; mgr. gas contracts Hughes Ea. Petroleum, Ltd., 1984-88; corp. counsel Hughes Ea. Petroleum, Inc., 1988-89; pvt. practice, 1989-90, 91; assoc. Overstreet & Kuykendall, 1990-91; ptnr. McKibben, Grant & Assocs., 1991-95; pvt. practice, 1995-2000; petroleum landman, 2000—. Mem. legal com. Interstate Oil and Gas Compact Commn., Oklahoma City, 1992—; speaker Oil and Gas Inst., U. Ala., 1990, natural gas seminar Miss. Natural Gas Assn., 1986. Co-chair exec. com. Monroe County Rep. Party, Aberdeen, 1980; pres. Aberdeen Exch. Club, 1978-79; mem. Monroe County (Miss.) Port Authority, 1979-80. Capt. U.S. Army, 1966-72. Named Outstanding Com. Chair, Aberdeen C. of C., 1979. Mem. Miss. Oil and Gas Lawyers (pres. 1986-87), Miss. Assn. Petroleum Landmen (v.p. 1987-88, pres. 1994-95), Miss. Bar (chmn. natural resources sect. 1988-89), Am. Assn. Profl. Landmen (cert. profl. landman), The Federalist Soc., Nat. Lawyers Assn. Episcopalian. Avocations: art, architecture, gardening, music, history. Contracts commercial, Oil, gas, and mineral, Real property. Home and Office: 1818 Aztec Dr Jackson MS 39211-6503 E-mail: grantjr@unidial.com

GRANT, STEPHEN ALLEN, lawyer; b. N.Y.C., Nov. 4, 1938; s. Benton H. and Irene A. Grant; m. Anne. K. Bagley, Feb. 11, 1961 (div. Nov. 1975); children: Stephen, Katharine, Michael; m. Anne-Marie Laignel, Dec. 8, 1975; children: Natalie, Elizabeth, Alexandra. AB, Yale U., 1960; LLB, Columbia U., 1965. Bar: N.Y. 1965, U.S. Supreme Ct. 1969. Law clk. to judge U.S. Ct. Appeals (2d cir.), N.Y.C., 1965-66; assoc. Sullivan & Cromwell, 1966-73, ptnr., 1973—. Mem. Japan-U.S. Friendship Commn., U.S.-Japan Conf. on Cultural and Ednl. Interchange, 1989-92. Lt. (j.g.) USNR, 1960-62. Mem. ABA, N.Y. State Bar Assn., Assn. of Bar of City of N.Y., Coun. Fgn. Rels. Clubs: Down Town, Links. General corporate, Private international, Securities. Home: 200 E 66th St Apt C2103 New York NY 10021-9187 Office: Sullivan & Cromwell 125 Broad St Fl 28 New York NY 10004-2489

GRANT, WALTER MATTHEWS, lawyer, corporate executive; b. Winchester, Ky., Mar. 30, 1945; s. Raymond Russell and Mary Mitchell (Rees) G.; m. Ann Carol Straus, Aug. 5, 1967; children— Walter Matthews II, Jean Ann, Raymond Russell II ABJ, U. Ky., Lexington, 1967; JD, Vanderbilt U., 1971. Bar: Ga. 1971, Tenn. 1992. Assoc. Alston & Bird, Atlanta, 1971-76, ptnr., 1976-83; v.p., gen. counsel, sec. Contel Corp., 1983-91; sr. v.p., gen. counsel Smith & Nephew N.Am., Memphis, 1991-93; sr. v.p., gen. counsel, sec. The Actava Group Inc., Atlanta, 1993-96, Bruno's Supermarkets, Inc., Birmingham, Ala., 1996—. Editor in chief Vanderbilt Law Rev., 1970-71, Ga. State Bar Jour., 1979-82 Baptist. General corporate, Mergers and acquisitions. Home: 23 Rose Gate Dr NE Atlanta GA 30342-4161 Office: Bruno's Supermarkets Inc PO Box 2486 Birmingham AL 35201-2486

GRASSI, JOSEPH F. lawyer; b. N.Y.C., Dec. 6, 1949; BA, Queens Coll., 1970; JD, NYU, 1974. Bar: N.Y. 1974, U.S. Dist. Ct. (so. and ea. dists.) N.Y., U.S. Ct. Appeals (2d cir.), U.S. Claims Ct. Law asst. appellate divsn., 2d judicial dept. Supreme Ct. State of N.Y., 1975-76; assoc. Milbank, Tweed, Hadley & McCloy, N.Y.C., 1976-79; asst. corp. counsel Corp. Counsel of N.Y.C., 1979-83; pvt. practice N.Y.C., 1983—. Mem. ABA, N.Y. County Lawyers' Assn., N.Y. Bldg. Congress. General civil litigation, Construction, Government contracts and claims. Office: 275 Madison Ave Rm 900 New York NY 10016-0601

GRASSIA, THOMAS CHARLES, lawyer, writer; b. Westfield, Mass., Aug. 26, 1946; s. Thomas C. and Assunta (Abatiell) G.; m. Judith Chace Cranshaw, Aug. 15, 1970; children: Susan C., Joseph C. BA, Boston U., 1968; JD, Suffolk U., 1974. Bar: Mass. 1974, U.S. Dist. Ct. Mass. 1976, U.S. Supreme Ct. 1980. Asst. v.p. Plymouth Rubber Co., Canton, Mass., 1969-71; ptnr. P.T.S. Computer Svcs., Waltham, 1971-81, D'Angio & Grassia, Waltham, 1974-85, Grassia & Assocs., P.A., Natick, Mass., 1985-98, Grassia, Murphy & Whitney, P.A., Natick, 1998—. Agt. Lawyers Title Ins. Co., Richmond, Va., First Am. Title Ins. Co., Fidelity Nat. Title Ins. Co.; bd. dirs. many regional corps; pres., treas., bd. dirs. Lender's Title & Abstract Co., Ltd., Natick. Author: Campfires, 2000; contbr. articles to profl. publs., lectr. on law, pub. interest subjects. Mem. Bd. Health, Sherborn, Mass., 1976-81, Bd. Selectmen, Sherborn, 1981-85; trustee Leonard Morse Hosp., Natick, 1981-84; mem. Met. Boston Hosp. Coun., Burlington, Mass., 1983-84; mem., team leader Sherborn Fire and Rescue Dept., 1974—; former mem. Sherborn Sch. Bd. Long Planning com., sherborn Police Chief Selection com., Sherborn Emergency Med. Com. Mem. ABA, Mass. Bar Assn., Mass. Conveyances Assn., Am. Arbitration Assn. (comml. arbitration bd.), New Eng. Helicopter Pilots Assn. (past pres., chmn. bd. dirs.). General corporate, Real property, Sports. Home: PO Box 178 Sherborn MA 01770-0178 Office: Grassia Murphy & Whitney PA 5 Commonwealth Rd Natick MA 01760-1526 E-mail: tgrassia@gmwclientcare.com

GRATKE, FRED EDWARD, lawyer; b. Chgo., Apr. 27, 1938; s. Paul Frederick and Conice May (Devol) G. B.S., U. Wis.-Milw., 1960; LL.B., U. Wis.-Madison, 1962. Bar: Wis. 1962, N.J. 1972. Investigator Office of Insp. Gen., Dept. Agrl., Chgo., 1962-65; atty. IRS, Phila., 1965— . Served with USNG, 1956-62. Recipient High Performance award IRS, 1975. Mem. ABA, Wis. Bar Assn., N.J. Bar Assn. Democrat. Unitarian. Clubs: Toastmasters (Independence Sq. 1983—) (treas. 1983-86, pres. 1986—) (asst. gov. Dist. 38 1984-85, gov. 1985-86, lt. gov. Div. C 1986—), IRS Golf League (treas. 1977, 86—, pres. 1978, 84-85). Home: 10102 Delaire Landing Rd Philadelphia PA 19114-5124 Office: IRS 600 Arch St Ste 1507A Philadelphia PA 19106-1612

GRAUBARD, JOHN J(OSEPH), lawyer; b. N.Y.C., Aug. 19, 1944; s. David J. and Florence (Pearl) G.; m. Myra L. Lubitz, June 10, 1967; children: Naomi, Michael. AB, N.Y. U., 1965; JD, Yale U., 1968. Bar: N.Y. 1968, U.S. Dist. Ct. (so. and ea. dists.) N.Y. 1970, U.S. Ct. Appeals (2d cir.) 1970, Conn. 1972, U.S. Supreme Ct. 1972, U.S. Dist. Ct. Conn. 1973, U.S. Dist. Ct. N.D. N.Y., 1995, U.S. Dist. Ct. W.D. N.Y. 1998, U.S. Tax Ct. 1982, U.S. Ct. Appeals (1st cir.) 1990, U.S. Ct. Appeals (3d cir.) 1997. Atty. opinions and appeal div. Port Authority N.Y. and N.J., 1968-72; assoc. firm Wofsey, Rosen, Kweskin & Kusiansky, Stamford, Conn., 1972-78; ptnr. firm Graubard and Graubard, Stamford, 1978-86; regional atty. Fed. Deposit Ins. Corp., 1987-89, litigation counsel, 1990-97; atty. Securities & Exch. Commn., N.Y.C., 1997—. Mem. Personnel Bd. of Appeals, City of Stamford, 1982-87. Mem. ABA. E-mail: graubard@scc.gov.

GRAVES, BRUCE, lawyer, director; b. Oct. 5, 1939; s. Forrest J and Lillian (Kurtz) Graves; m. Jeanne M. Rooney; children: Gwendolyn Sue, Daniel Curtis, Brian Patrick. BS, U. Omaha, 1961; JD cum laude, U. Nebr.-Lincoln, 1964. Bar: Iowa 1964, Nebr. 1964, U.S. dist. Ct. (so. dist.) Iowa 1964, U.S. Dist. Ct. Nebr. 1964, U.S. Ct. Claims 1964, U.S. Ct. Appeals (8th cir.) 1968, U.S. Ct. Appeals (fed. cir.) 1991, U.S. Tax Ct. 1968, U.S. Supreme Ct. 1972. Bd. dir., West Des Moines Devel. Corp. Contbr. articles to law revs., mags. Dir. West Des Moines Sch. Bd., 1967—76, Polk-Des Moines Taxpayers Assn., 1982—84. Named Citizen of Yr., West Des Moines, 1983. Mem.: ABA (subcom. on litigation, com. on ins. cos. 1982—), Iowa Bar Assn. (bd. govs. 1994—98, pres. 2000—01), Nebr. Bar Assn., Polk County Bar Assn., Des Moines C. of C., Des Moines Club (past pres., dir.), Order of Coif, Omicron Delta Kappa, Sigma Phi Epsilon. Republican. Federal civil litigation, General corporate, Corporate taxation. Office: 601 Locust St Suite 1100 Two Ruan Ctr Des Moines IA 50309

GRAVES, JOHN WILLIAM, state supreme court justice; b. Paducah, Ky., Oct. 17, 1935; m. Mary Ann Breivo; children: James Anthony, Kevin Andrew. BS, U. Notre Dame, 1957; postgrad., U. Louisville, 1957-58; JD, U. Ky., 1963. Bar: Ky. 1963. Dist. judge, 1984-88; circuit ct. judge McCracken Cir., 1989-95; justice Ky. Supreme Ct., 1995—. Col. U.S. Army Res. Decorated Army Commendation medal, Army Meritorious Svc. medal. Office: State Capitol 700 Capitol AveRm 230 Frankfort KY 40601-3410*

GRAVES, PATRICK LEE, lawyer; b. Pasadena, Calif., Sept. 16, 1945; s. James Edward and Virginia (Dudley) G.; children: Carrie Kathleen, Michael Patrick. AS, Citrus Jr. Coll., Glendora, Calif., 1969; BS, Calif. State Polytechnic U., 1973; BS in Law, Western State U., 1973, JD, 1975. Bar: Calif. 1975, U.S. Dist. Ct. (cen. dist.) Calif. 1976, U.S. Ct. Appeals (9th cir.) 1978, U.S. Supreme Ct. 1980. Assoc. Lynberg & Watkins, Los Angeles, 1975-80, ptnr., 1981-93, Graves & King, Irvine, Calif., 1993—. Settlement officer Los Angeles Superior Ct., 1988—, arbitrator, 1981—; arbitrator San Bernardino Superior Ct., 1990—; mediator L.A. Superior Ct., 1993—, Riverside Superior Ct., 1996—, AAA-Inland Empire, 1996—. Judge pro tem L.A. Superior Ct., 1992—. Sustaining mem. Rep. Nat. Com., Washington, 1979—; mem. Nat. Rep. Congl. Com., 1980—. Mem. ABA, San Bernardino County Bar Assn., Assn. So. Calif. Def. Counsel (chmn. 1988, bd. dirs. 1996—), Def. Rsch. Inst., Upland (Calif.) C. of C. Avocations: flyfishing, golf. Government contracts and claims, Personal injury, Real property. Home: 424B Monterey Ln San Clemente CA 92672-5329 Office: Graves & King 6 Venture Ste 395 Irvine CA 92618-7315

GRAVES, RAY REYNOLDS, retired judge; b. Tuscumbia, Ala., Jan. 10, 1946; s. Isaac and Olga Ernestine (Wilder) G.; children: Claire Elise, Reynolds Douglass. BA, Trinity Coll., Hartford, Conn., 1967; JD, Wayne State U., 1970. Bar: Mich. 1971, U.S. Dist. Ct. (ea. dist.) Mich. 1971, U.S. Ct. Appeals (6th cir.) 1972, U.S. Supreme Ct. 1976, D.C. 1977. Defender Legal Aid and Defender Assn., Detroit, 1970-71; assoc. Liberson, Fink, Feiler, Crystal & Burdick, 1971-72, Patmon, Young & Kirk, 1972-73; ptnr. Lewis, White, Clay & Graves, 1974-81; mem. legal dept. Detroit Edison Co., 1981; judge U.S. Bankruptcy Ct., Ea. Dist. Mich., Detroit, 1982-2002; chief judge U.S. Bankruptcy Ct., 1991-95. Mem. U.S. Ct. Com., State Bar Mich. Bd. dirs. Mich. Cancer Found.; trustee Mich. Opera Theatre, 1986-88; vestry Christ Ch. Episcopal, Grosse Pointe, Mich., 1994-97; del. Diocesan Conv. of the Episcopal Ch., Mich., 1997. Fellow Am. Coll. Bankruptcy; mem. Nat. Conf. Bankruptcy Judges (bd. govs. 1984-88), World Assn. Judges, World Peace Through Law Conf., Assn. Black Judges Mich., Wolverine Bar Assn., Detroit Bar Assn., D.C. Bar Assn., Delta Kappa Epsilon, Sigma Pi Phi, Iota Boulè (sire archon 1999-2001). Episcopalian. Office: 600 Church St Rm 104 Flint MI 48502

GRAVES, ROBERT, lawyer; b. Portland, Maine, May 26, 1940; s. William W. and Lillian Graves. BS, Boston U., 1963; JD, Suffolk U., Boston, 1969. Bar: Mass. 1969, U.S. Dist. Ct. 1969, U.S. Ct. Appeals 1969, U.S. Mil. Appeals 1974, U.S. Supreme Ct. 1974, U.S. Tax Ct. 1978. Judge advocate gen. USAR, 1968-69; propr. Robert Graves & Assocs., Burlington, Mass. Mem. Corp. Winchester (Mass.) Hosp., 1986—; alumni bd. dirs. Boston U., 1994—. Mem. Mass. Bar Assn., Boston Bar Assn., Masons, Shriners. General civil litigation, State civil litigation, Family and matrimonial. Home: 5 Coolidge Rd Winchester MA 01890-2222 Office: Robert Graves & Assocs 44 Mall Rd Ste 202 Burlington MA 01803-4530

GRAVES, TODD PETERSON, prosecutor; BA, U. Mo., 1988; JD, U. Va. Assoc. Skadden Arps, N.Y.C.; with Bryan Cave, 1992—94; prosecutor Platte County, Mo.; U.S. atty. Mo. western dist. U.S. Dept. Justice, 2001—. Republican. Office: 400 E 9th St 5th Fl Kansas City MO 64106*

GRAVING, RICHARD JOHN, law educator; b. Duluth, Minn., Aug. 24, 1929; s. Lawrence Richard and Laura Magdalene (Loucks) G.; m. Florence Sara Semel; children: Daniel, Sarah. BA, U. Minn., 1950; JD, Harvard U., 1953; postgrad., Nat. U. Mex., 1964-66. Bar: Minn. 1953, N.Y. 1956, U.S. Dist. Ct. (so. dist.) N.Y. 1956, Pa. 1968, U.S. Dist. Ct. (we. dist.) Pa. 1968, Tex. 1982, U.S. Dist. Ct. (so. dist.) Tex. 1982. Assoc. Reid & Priest, N.Y.C., 1955-61, Mexico City, 1961-66; v.p. Am. & Fgn. Power Co., Inc., 1966-68; atty. Gulf Oil Corp., Pitts., 1968-69, Madrid, 1969-73, London, 1973-80, Houston, 1980-82; pvt. practice London, 1982-84; prof. law South Tex. Coll., Houston, 1983—. With U.S. Army, 1953-55. Mem. Am. Soc. Internat. Law. Home: 8515 Ariel St Houston TX 77074-2806 Office: Inst Transnat Arbitration 1303 San Jacinto St Houston TX 77002-7000

GRAY, ARCHIBALD DUNCAN, JR. lawyer; b. Houston, July 12, 1938; s. Archibald Duncan and Lucie (Hill) G.; m. Suzanne Curtis, July 27, 1963 (div. Nov. 1978); 1 child, Archibald Duncan III; m. Nina Carol Wheeley, June 9, 1984; children: Matthew Hill, Joseph Sharp, Michael Branch. AB with distinction, Dartmouth Coll., 1960; JD, U. Mich., 1963; LLM in Taxation, NYU, 1964. Bar: Tex. 1963, U.S. Dist. Ct. (so. dist.) Tex. 1968, U.S. Ct. Appeals (5th cir.) 1976, Colo. 1982. Assoc. Baker & Botts, Houston, 1964-72; gen. atty. Pennzoil Co., 1972-74, v.p., 1977-79, Pennzoil Producing Co., Houston, 1974-79; of counsel Ireland, Stapleton, Pryor & Pascoe, Denver, 1981; ptnr. Mayer, Brown & Platt, 1981-82, ptnr. in charge Houston, 1982-96, ptnr., 1982-97; also sr. mgmt. com., 1992-96; co-founder, ptnr. Baker & McKenzie, Houston, 1997-2000; ptnr. King & Spalding, 2000—. Mem. ABA, Colo. Bar Assn., Tex. Bar Assn., Houston Bar Assn. Republican. Methodist. Clubs: Houston Country, Houston, Cherry Hills Country (Denver), Hills Country Club (Austin). Avocations: golf, hunting, skiing. Private international, Natural resources, General corporate. Home: 6046 Riverview Way Houston TX 77057-1450 Office: King & Spalding 1100 Louisiana St Ste 4000 Houston TX 77002-5219 E-mail: duncangray@kslaw.com

GRAY, BRIAN MARK, lawyer, researcher; b. Detroit, Dec. 21, 1939; s. Joseph Clay and Mary Jane (Bond) G.; m. Patricia Kay Gillett, Aug. 19, 1967; children: Diana Lisa, Amy Noel. BA, U. Mich., 1961, JD, 1964; postgrad., U. London, 1965, U. Brussels, 1966. Bar: Mich. 1967, U.S. Dist. Ct. Mich. 1967, U.S. Ct. Customs and Patent Appeals 1981, U.S. Ct. Appeals (fed. cir.) 1985, U.S. Supreme Ct. 1974. Assoc. Butzel, Eamon, Long, Gust & Kennedy, Detroit, 1964; sr. rsch. clk., chief judge Mich. Ct. Appeals, Grand Rapids, 1967-68; ptnr. Krueger, Gray & Lesica, Muskegon, Mich., 1967-74; pvt. practice Anchorage, 1975—. Of counsel in patent matters; cons. in field. Author: Your Estate Plan, 1980, European Community Corporate Mergers. Del. U.S.-Japan Bilateral Session Legal and Econ. Rels., 1988; del. designate Moscow Conf. Law and Econ. Rels., 1990. Rsch. grantee U. London, 1965. Mem. ABA, Mat-Su Borough Bar Assn., Mich. Bar Assn., Alaska Bar Assn., Soc. Gray's Inn (life), Phi Alpha Delta, Phi Beta Kappa. Lutheran. Avocations: breeding and training Arabian horses, building and flying experimental aircraft. Estate planning, Patent, Trademark and copyright.

GRAY, CHARLES ROBERT, lawyer; b. Kirksville, Mo., Aug. 22, 1952; s. George Devon and Bettie Louise (McCormick) G.; m. Dana Elizabeth Kehr, June 1, 1974; children: Jennifer, Jessica, Marcus, Gregory, Victoria. BS, N.E. Mo. State U., 1974; JD, U. Mo., Kansas City, 1978. Bar: Mo. 1978, Va. 1993, U.S. Dist. Ct. (we. dist.) Mo. 1978, U.S. Ct. Appeals (fed. cir.) 1992, U.S. Ct. Appeals (4th cir.) 1995, U.S. Supreme Ct. 1981; cert. mediator; cert. hearing officer Va. Supereme Ct., 1997. Pvt. practice, Parkville, Mo., 1978-81; asst. pub. defender 5th Judicial Cir. Ct. Mo., St. Joseph, 1978-79; pub. defender 6th Judicial Cir. Ct. Mo., Platte City, 1981; asst. dist. counsel Army Corps of Engrs., Kansas City, 1981-82, Vicksburg, Miss., 1982-83; chief counsel space shuttle, MX missile U.S. Army, Vandenberg AFB, Calif., 1983-85, chief counsel troop support agy. Ft. Lee, Va., 1985-87; fraud counsel Def. Gen. Supply Ctr. Dept. of Def., Richmond, 1987-93; pvt. practice, Chester, 1993-99; owner Pvt. Jud. Svcs., Inc., 1993—; asst. atty. gen. Atty. Gen.'s Office State of Va., 1999—. Adj. prof. St. Leo Coll., Ft. Lee, 1986-91, John Tyler Coll., Chester, Va., 1994—. Mem. Selective Svc. Draft Bd., Brookfield, Mo., 1972-74; pres. Old Towne Parkville Assn., 1979-81, Chester (Va.) Youth Sports Boosters, 1989-91; den leader Boy Scouts Am., Chester, 1991—. Victor Wilson honor scholar, 1977; recipient Am. Jurisprudence award Coop-Bancroft-Whitney, 1989. Mem. ATLA, Am. Arbitration Assn. (mem. nat. panel arbitrators 1994—, mem. govt. disputes panel 1995—, mem. constrn. panel 1995—, mem. comml. panel 1995—), Def. Rsch. Inst. (approved mem. panel on mediation and arbitration), Mo. Bar Assn., Va. Bar Assn., Va. Trial Lawyers Assn. Methodist. Avocations: coaching youth sports, cub scouts, softball, tennis, basketball. Construction, General practice, Personal injury. Home: 3813 Terjo Ln Chester VA 23831-1839 Office: Pres Presiding Ofcl PO Drawer B Chester VA 23831 E-mail: cgray@oag.state.va.us

GRAY, ELIZABETH CHRETIEN, criminal justice educator, real estate salesperson; b. Lafayette, La., June 9, 1932; d. John Hiram and Caroline Ophelia (Ivey) Chretien; m. Noel Gray, Feb. 3, 1953 (div. Nov. 1962); 1 child, Mark Thaddeus. B.S., So. U. and A&M Coll., Baton Rouge, 1957; M.Ed. in Spl. Edn., Coppin State Coll., 1975; M.A. in Guidance-Psychology, Cath. U. Am., 1968; student Georgetown U., 1979, George Washington U., 1980, U. Md., 1982, Temple U., 1983— , SUNY, 1978. Tchr., adminstr. Lafayette Parish Pub. Schs., 1951-52; sec. So. U., Baton Rouge, 1953-56; sci. tchr. New Orleans Pub. Schs., 1956-58; reading-spl. edn. tchr. Montgomery County Pub. Schs., Rockville, Md., 1958-64; asst. prin. Washington Pub. Schs., 1964-72; assoc. prof. dept. criminal justice Coppin State Coll., Balt., 1972— ; pres. Confidential Counseling Components, Balt., 1979-82; cons. delinquency prevention KOBAR Mgmt. Cons. Assocs., Washington, 1980; speaker Md. Commn. on Women's Speakers Bur. Democratic candidate for Congress from Md. 7th dist., 1982, 84. Mem. Md. Assn. Tchr. Educators, Am. Assn. Counseling and Devel., Md. Mental Health Counselors Assn., NAACP (life), Urban League, Alpha Kappa Alpha. Work study grantee So. U., 1951. Presbyterian. Office: Coppin State Coll 2500 W North Ave Baltimore MD 21216-3633

GRAY, ELIZABETH VAN DOREN, lawyer; b. Columbia, S.C., Jan. 3, 1949; d. Robert Lawson and Elizabeth Dacus (Gaines) Van Doren; m. James Cranston Gray, Jr., Apr. 30, 1982; children: James Cranston III, Elizabeth Gaines. BA in Internat. Studies, U. S.C., 1970, JD cum laude, 1976; student, St. Mary's Coll., Raleigh, N.C., 1966-67. Bar: S.C. 1977, U.S. Dist. Ct. S.C. 1977, U.S. Ct. Appeals (4th cir.) 1980, U.S. Ct. Appeals (6th cir.) 1989. Assoc. McNair Law Firm, PA, Columbia, 1977-82, shareholder, 1982-87; ptnr. Glenn Irvin Murphy Gray & Stepp, 1987—; now ptnr. Sowell Gray Stepp & Lafitte. Contbr. articles to profl. jours. Mem. ABA, John Belton O'Neill Inn of Ct., S.C. Bar (pres. 2001-), S.C. Women Lawyers Assn. (bd. dirs. 1995-99, sec. 1997-98), Richland County Bar Assn. Episcopalian. General civil litigation, Criminal. Home: 1412 Westminister Dr Columbia SC 29204-2358 Office: Sowell Gray Stepp & Lafitte PO Box 11449 Columbia SC 29211*

GRAY, J. CHARLES, lawyer, cattle rancher; b. Leesburg, Fla., Mar. 26, 1932; s. G. Wayne and Mary Evelyn (Albright) G.; m. Saundra Hagood, Aug. 18, 1955; children: Terese Ren. John Charles Jr., Lee Jerome. BA, U. Fla., 1955, JD, 1968. Bar: Fla. 1958. County atty. Orange County, Fla., 1978-85; chmn. Gray, Harris & Robinson, P.A. Chmn. Fla. Turnpike Authority, 1965-67; city solicitor City of Orlando (Fla.), 1960-61; pres. Santa Gertrudis Breeders Internat., 1981-83. Chmn. pres.'s coun. advisors U. Ctrl. Fla., 1978-84; pres. U. Ctrl. Fla. Found., 1990-91; pres. Orange County U. Fla. Alumni Assn., Pi Kappa Alpha Alumni Assn.; past dist. v.p. U. Fla. Alumni Assn.; mem. U. Fla. Pres.'s Coun.; mem. Com. of 100; founding bd. dirs. Fla. Epilepsy Found.; chmn. Econ. Devel. Commn. Mid. Fla., 1987-89; mem. Fla. Econ. Devel. Adv. Coun. Recipient J. Thomas Guerney Lifetime Svc. award, James B. Green award for Econ. Devel.; inducted into U. Fla. Hall of Fame. Mem. ABA, Fla. Bar Assn., Orange County Bar Assn., Citrus Club of Orlando (past dir.), Univ. Club of Orlando (past dir.). Republican. Episcopalian. Real property. Home: PO Box 3068 Orlando FL 32802-3068 Office: Ste 1400 301 E Pine St Orlando FL 32801-2725 E-mail: cgray@ghrlaw.com

GRAY, KARLA MARIE, state supreme court chief justice; BA, MA in African History, Western Mich. U.; JD, Hastings Coll. of Law, San Francisco, 1976. Bar: Mont. 1976, Calif. 1977. Law clk. to Hon. W. D. Murray U.S. Dist. Ct., 1976-77; staff atty. Atlantic Richfield Co., 1977-81; pvt. practice law Butte, Mont., 1981-84; staff atty., legis. lobbyist Mont. Power Co., 1984-91; justice Supreme Ct. Mont., Helena, 1991-2000, chief justice, 2000—. Mem. Mont. Supreme Ct. Gender Fairness Task Force. Fellow Am. Bar Found., Am. Judicature Soc., Internat. Women's Forum; mem. State Bar Mont., Silver Bow County Bar Assn. (past pres.), Nat. Assn. Women Judges. Avocations: travel, reading, piano, family genealogy, cross-country skiing. Office: Supreme Ct Mont PO Box 203001 Helena MT 59620-3001

GRAY, KATHLEEN ANN, lawyer; b. Reading, Pa., May 16, 1947; d. Sebastian and Helen Mary)Zajac) Vespico; m. George A. Gray, Oct. 22, 1966 (dec. 1968). BSBA, Drexel U., 1971, MBA, 1978; JD, Wake Forest U., 1977. Bar: Pa. 1977. Computer programmer Ednl. Testing Svc., Princeton, N.J., 1971-73, dir. EDP tng., 1973-74; assoc. Barley, Snyder, Cooper & Barber, Lancaster, Pa., 1977-83; ptnr. Barley, Snyder, Senft & Cohen, 1983—. Mem. Wake Forest Law Rev., 1975-77. Bd. dirs. Hist. Preservation Trust of Lancaster County, 1978-88, v.p., 1984; sec. bd. dirs. Lancaster Integrated Specialized Transp. Sys., 1981-85; bd. dirs. Am. Lung Assn. of Lancaster and Berks Counties, 1982-99, v.p., 1987-90, pres., 1994-96; bd. dirs. Leadership Lancaster, 1983-92, Lancaster Pub. Libr., 1987-90, Am. Lung Assn. Pa., 1993-98; sec. bd. dirs. Found. Lancaster Chamber, 1985-96, v.p., 1997-98, pres., 1999-2000; chmn. Lancaster County Parks and Open Space Funding Task Force, 1989-90. Mem. ABA, Nat. Assn. Bond Lawyers, Pa. Bar Assn., Pa. Assn. Bond Lawyers (bd. dirs., sec. 1988-94), Lancaster County Bar Assn., Jr. League of Lancaster (sustaining). Republican. Computer, General corporate, Municipal (including bonds). Office: Barley Snyder Senft & Cohen 126 E King St Lancaster PA 17602-2832

GRAY, MARVIN LEE, JR. lawyer; b. Pitts., May 9, 1945; s. Marvin L. and Frances (Stringfellow) G.; m. Jill Miller, Aug. 14, 1971; children: Elizabeth Ann, Carolyn Jill. AB, Princeton U., 1966; JD magna cum laude, Harvard U., 1969. Bar: Wash. 1973, U.S. Supreme Ct. 1977, Alaska 1984. Law clk. to judge U.S. Ct. Appeals, N.Y.C., 1969-70; law clk. to justice U.S. Supreme Ct., Washington, 1970-71; asst. U.S. atty. U.S. Dept. Justice, Seattle, 1973-76; ptnr. Davis Wright Tremaine, 1976—, mng. ptnr., 1985-88. Staff counsel Rockefeller Commn. on CIA Activities in U.S., Washington, 1974; lectr. trial practice U. Wash. Law Sch., Seattle, 1979-80. Lay reader Episcopal Ch. of Ascension, Seattle, 1982-94. Capt. USAF, 1971-73. Fellow Am. Coll. Trial Lawyers; mem. ABA, Am. Law Inst. Antitrust, Federal civil litigation. Office: Davis Wright Tremaine 1501 4th Ave Ste 2600 Seattle WA 98101-1688

GRAY, PAUL BRYAN, lawyer, historian, arbitrator; b. L.A., Apr. 10, 1938; s. Sylvester Bryan and Alice Esther (Flick) G.; m. Dorothy Jo Knorpp, Aug. 13, 1963 (div. May 1977); children: Christopher, Mark; m. Felipa Rios, July 31, 1987. JD, Hastings Coll. Law, U. Calif., San Francisco, 1968. Assoc. Unthoff, Gomez Vega and Unthoff, Mexico City, 1968-70; pvt. practice, South El Monte, Calif., 1970-93, Claremont, 1993—. Judge pro tem Mcpl. Ct. L.A., 1975—; arbitrator Superior Ct. L.A., 1990—. Author: Forster v. Pico: The Struggle for the Rancho Santa Margarita, 1997. Reader The Huntington Libr., San Marino, Calif., 1985—. General civil litigation. Office: 250 W 1st St Ste 318 Claremont CA 91711-4740

GRAY, RANDALL JOSHUA, information services administrator; b. Santa Monica, Calif., Sept. 30, 1949; s. Joshua and Eunice M. (Serr) G.; BA in English, San Fernando Valley State Coll., 1972; MLS, UCLA, 1974, cert. law librarianship, 1974; m. Roberta Christine Johnson, June 15, 1973. Intern, L.A. County Law Libr., 1973-74; asst. libr. O'Melveny & Myers, L.A., 1974-76; law libr. Adams, Duque & Hazeltine, L.A., 1976-82, dir. info. svcs., 1982-84; sales rep. Callaghan & Co. Law and Tax Publs., 1984-85; mgr. info. svcs. Haight, Brown & Bonesteel, Santa Monica, Calif., 1986—; instr. Inst. Pvt. Law Librs., Biltmore Hotel, L.A., 1980, UCLA Extension, 1980, Practising Law Inst., 1981; participant Calif. State Colls. Internat. Studies Program, Uppsala, Sweden, 1971; chmn. 10th Ann. Inst. on Calif. Law, 1982. Cert. law libr., 1980— . Mem. Am. Assn. Law Libr., Def. Rsch. Inst., So. Calif. Assn. Law Librs. (chmn. cons. com. 1980, v.p. 1981-82, pres. 1982-83), Spl. Librs. Assn., UCLA Grad. Sch. Libr. and Info. Sci. Students Assn. (pres. 1973-74). Author: Effective Administration: Better Decisions through Information, 1981. Home: 521 Ramona Ave Sierra Madre CA 91024-2230 Office: Haight Brown & Bonesteel 201 Santa Monica Blvd PO Box 680 Santa Monica CA 90406-0680

GRAY, WHITMORE, law educator, lawyer; b. 1932. A.B., Principia Coll., 1954; J.D., U. Mich., 1957; postgrad. U. Paris, 1957-58, U. Munich (W.Ger.), 1962, LLD, Adrian Coll., 1982. Bar: Mich. 1958. Assoc. Casey, Lane & Mittendorf, N.Y.C., 1958-60; asst. prof. U. Mich., 1960-63, assoc. prof., 1963-66, prof., 1966—; assoc. Cleary, Gottlieb, N.Y.C., 1981; of counsel LeBoeuf, Lamb, greene & MacRae, N.Y.C., 1994—; mem. adv. bd. Bulletin on Rsch. in Soviet Law and Govt. and Soviet Statues and Decisions. Japan Found. fellow U. Tokyo, 1977-78; lectr. contract law Chinese Acad. Social Scis., 1982; summer faculty Jilin U., People's Republic of China, 1985; mem. panel arbitrators, Hongkong Arbitration Ctr., adviser, 1993—, Cambodia, 1994, Indonesia, 1995-96. Mem. Am. Assn. Law Schs. (past chmn. comparative law sect.), Am. Fgn. Law Assn. (dir.), Internat. Acad. Comparative Law, Japanese-Am. Soc. Legal Studies (bd. dirs.), Assn. Asian Studies. Contbr. articles on comml. arbitration and alternative dispute resolution to profl. jours. Translator Russian Republic Civil Code, General Principles of Civil Law of People's Republic of China. Past editor-in-chief Mich. Law Rev.; bd. editors Am. Jour. Comparative Law. Home: S 4th Ave Ann Arbor MI 48104 Office: U Mich Law Sch 625 S State St Ann Arbor MI 48109-1215 also: 125 W 55th St New York NY 10019-5369

GRAY, WILLIAM OXLEY, retired lawyer; b. Iowa Falls, Iowa, Nov. 23, 1914; s. Clarence O. and Hazel (Oxley) G.; m. Mary Florence Comstock, Oct. 19, 1940; children: William Scott, John Steven, Mary Ellen Gray Hart, James C. B.A., Coe Coll., 1936; J.D., U. Iowa, 1938. Bar: Iowa 1938, U.S. Dist. Ct. (no. and so. dists.) Iowa 1938. Ptnr. Silliman & Gray, Cedar Rapids, Iowa, 1938-42; spl. agt. FBI, 1942-46, ptnr. Silliman, Gray & Stapleton, Cedar Rapids, 1946-85, Gray, Stefani & Mitvalsky, 1986-91; dir. Brenton Bank & Trust Co., Cedar Rapids. Chmn. Iowa Hwy. Commn., 1969-73; chmn. bd. trustees Coe Coll., Cedar Rapids, 1964-84. Mem. ABA, Iowa State Bar Assn., Linn County Bar Assn., Ex-Agts. FBI (pres. 1970-71), Cedar Rapids C. of C. (bd. dirs. 1968). Republican. Congregationalist. Club: Union League (Chgo.). Lodge: Masons. Office: Gray Stefani & Mitvalsky 200 American Bldg Cedar Rapids IA 52401

GRAY, WILLIAM R. lawyer; b. Peoria, Ill., Aug. 25, 1941; s. John J. and Alverna K. (Kennedy) G.; m. Tiana M. Yeager, June 12, 1982; children: Ann Katherine, Thomas William. BA, U. Colo., 1963, JD, 1966. Bar: Colo. 1966; U.S. Dist. Ct. Colo. 1966; U.S. Ct. Appeals (10th cir.) 1976. Dep. dist. atty. Dist. Atty.'s Office/10th Jud. Dist., Pueblo, Colo., 1967-69, Dist. Atty.'s Office/20th Jud. Dist., Boulder, 1969-70; dep. state pub. defender Colo. State Pub. Defender, 1970-72; ptnr. Miller & Gray, 1973-85, Purvis, Gray & Gordon, LLP, Boulder, 1985—. Mem./vice chair, chmn., Colo. Supreme Ct. grievance com., 1983-88, mem. criminal rules com., 1982-84; adj. prof. law U. Colo. Sch. of Law, Boulder, 1984. Bd. dirs. Mental Health Ctr. of Boulder County, 1972-78. Fellow Am. Coll. Trial Lawyers (Courageous Advocacy award 1985), Internat. Soc. Barristers, Internat. Acad. Trial Lawyers, Am. Bar Found., Colo. Bar Foun., Colo. Bar Assn. (Professionalism award 1995), Am. Bd. Trial Advocates. Democrat. Environmental, Personal injury, Product liability. Office: Purvis Gray & Gordon LLP 1050 Walnut St Ste 501 Boulder CO 80302-5144 E-mail: wgray@pgglaw.com

GRAYSHAW, JAMES RAYMOND, judge; b. Cleve., Apr. 3, 1948; s. Thomas J. and Bettie Lee (Griffith) G.; m. Susan Hancher, Oct. 15, 1980; 1 child, John H. BA, L.I. U., Bklyn., 1970; JD, Bklyn. Law Sch., 1975. Legal asst. Cadwalader, Wickersham & Taft, N.Y.C., 1975-77; law asst. Civil Ct., City N.Y., 1977-80; sr. law asst. Supreme Ct., State N.Y., 1980-82; judge housing part Civil Ct., City N.Y., 1983—. Judge advocate Cmty. Advocacy Ctr., N.Y.C., 1996. Sgt. U.S. Army, 1970-72. Mem. Queens Bar Assn., Protestant Lawyers N.Y.C. (dir. 1980—), Vietnam Vets. Am., 16th Inf. Reg. Assn., Masons. Democrat. Episcopalian. Home: 21107 28th Ave Bayside NY 11360-2508 Office: Civil Ct City NY 89-17 Sutphin Blvd Jamaica NY 11435 E-mail: jgrayshaw@aol.com, jgraysha@courts.state.ny.us

GRAYSON, BETTE RITA, lawyer; b. Newark, July 10, 1947; d. Sidney and Joan (Rosenman) G.; m. Stanley Noah Kruzweil, Aug. 17, 1975; children: Jeremy, Cynthia. BA, NYU, 1969; JD, Bklyn. Law Sch., 1977. Bar: N.J. 1977. Pvt. practice, Union and Springfield, N.J., 1977—. Former real estate counsel City of Plainfield, N.J.; former spl. real estate counsel City of Orange; former rev. atty. for State Bank South Orange, N.J.; chairperson Fee Arbitration Com. Union County, N.J.; mem. adv. bd. Crown Bank, 1998—. V.p. Millburn (N.J.) Hadassah, 1985-87, mem. steering com. for planned gifts, 1996-99; trustee Internat. Youth Orgn., 1997—; treas. Millburn Hoopsters, 1997-99. Recipient Trust Bklyn. Law Sch., 1974, Woman of Excellence award Union County, 1998. Mem. Women Lawyers Union County (pres. 1990-92, v.p. 1988-90, sec. 1983-84, treas. 1986-88). Democrat. Family and matrimonial, Land use and zoning (including planning), Real property. Office: 140 Mountain Ave Springfield NJ 07081-1725

GRAYSON, EDWARD DAVIS, lawyer, manufacturing company executive; b. Davenport, Iowa, June 20, 1938; s. Charles E. and Isabelle (Davis) G.; m. Alice Ann McLaughlin; children: Alice Anne, Maureen Isabelle, Edward Davis Jr. B.A., U. Iowa, 1960, LLB, 1964. Bar: Iowa 1964, Mass. 1967. Atty. Goodwin, Procter & Hoar, Boston, 1967-74; sr. v.p., gen. counsel Wang Labs., Inc., Lowell, Mass., 1974-92; v.p., gen. counsel Honeywell, Inc., Mpls., 1992—. Trustee U. Lowell, Mas., 1981-87, chmn. bd. trustees, 1982-85, 87; dir. Bus. Econs. Edn. Found., 1992—. Capt. USAF, 1964-67. Mem. ABA (com. corp. law depts.), Mass. Bar Assn. (bd. dels. 1977-80), Greater Mpls. C. of C. (dir. 1992—). General corporate. Office: Honeywell Inc Honeywell Plz PO Box 524 Minneapolis MN 55440-0524

GRAZIANO, CRAIG FRANK, lawyer; b. Des Moines, Dec. 7, 1950; s. Charles Dominic and Corrine Rose (Comito) G. BA summa cum laude, Macalester Coll., 1973; JD with honors, Drake U., 1975. Bar: Iowa 1976, U.S. Dist. Ct. (no. and so. dists.) Iowa 1978, U.S. Ct. Appeals (8th cir.) 1977, U.S. Supreme Ct. 1988. Law clk. to Hon. M. D. Van Oosterhout U.S. Ct. Appeals (8th cir.), Sioux City, Iowa, 1976-78; pvt. practice Dickinson, Mackaman, Tyler & Hagen, PC, Des Moines, 1978-98; with Office of Consumer Advocate, Iowa Dept. Justice, 1999—. Mem. Gov.'s Task Force on Quality and Efficiency in Government, 1999—. Mem. Iowa Bar Assn. (chair specialization com. 1993-96, chair adminstrv. law sect. 1996-99), Order of Coif, Phi Beta Kappa. Administrative and regulatory, Appellate, Public utilities. Home: 500 44th St Des Moines IA 50312-2408 Office: 310 Maple St Des Moines IA 50319-0063 E-mail: craig.graziano@home.com, cgraziano@mail.oca.state.ia.us

GRAZIANO, RONALD ANTHONY, lawyer; b. N.Y.C., Aug. 13, 1948; s. Charles and Anna (DiPasquale) G.; m. Helen Ann McFadden, Aug. 4, 1973. B.A. in Polit. Sci., Fordham U., 1970; J.D., Rutgers-Camden Sch. Law, 1973. Bar: N.Y. 1974, N.J. 1974, U.S. Dist. Ct. N.J. 1974, U.S. Ct. Appeals (2d and 3d cirs.) 1975, U.S. Ct. Appeals (D.C. cir.) 1978, U.S. Supreme Ct. 1979; cert. civil trial atty Supreme Ct. of N.J. Law clk. to presiding judge U.S. Dist. Ct., N.J., 1973-74; assoc. Tomar, Parks, Seliger, Simonoff & Adourian, Haddonfield, N.J., 1974-79, ptnr., 1979— . Assoc. editor Rutgers-Camden Law Jour., 1972-73. Bd. dirs. Camden Regional Legal Services, 1977-80; mem. Planning Bd., Mount Laurel, N.J., 1981, 83, 84; councilman Mount Laurel Twp., 1981-83, mayor, 1984. Mem. Rutgers-Camden Law Sch. Alumni Assn. (chancellor 1976-77), Am. Arbitration Assn. (nat. panel 1979—), Camden County Bar Assn., N.J. State Bar Assn., ABA, Assn. Trial Lawyers Am. (exec. com. N.J. chpt. 1975). Democrat. Roman Catholic. Civil rights, Family and matrimonial, Personal injury. Office: Tomar Parks Seliger Simonoff Adourian& O'Brien 41 S Haddon Ave Haddonfield NJ 08033-1800

GREAGAN, WILLIAM JOSEPH, lawyer; b. Albany, N.Y., Feb. 11, 1963; s. William Joseph Greagan and Dolores Sandra Stiles. BA in Polit. Sci., Siena Coll., 1985; JD, Union U., Albany, 1988. Bar: N.Y. 1989, U.S. Dist. Ct. (no. dist.) N.Y. 1989, U.S. Dist. Ct. (we. dist.) N.Y. 1997. From assoc. to ptnr. Carter, Conboy, Case, Blackmore, Napierski & Maloney, P.C., Albany, 1989—. Mem. Def. Rsch. Inst., N.Y. State Bar Assn. General civil litigation, Environmental, Product liability. Home: 165 S Manning Blvd Albany NY 12208-1811 Office: Carter Conboy Case Blackmore Napierski & Maloney PC 20 Corporate Woods Blvd Ste 8 Albany NY 12211-2362

GREANEY, JOHN M. state supreme court justice; b. Westfield, Mass., Apr. 8, 1939; s. Patrick Joseph and Margaret Irene (Fitzgerald) G.; m. Susan H. Greaney, Nov. 23, 1967. 1 child, Jessica S. BA summa cum laude, Holly Cross Coll., 1960; JD, NYU, 1963; LLD (hon.), Westfield State Coll., 1967, Western New England Coll., 1969; LLD, New England Law Sch., 1991. Bar: Mass., Supreme Judicial Ct., U.S. Dist. Ct., U.S. Supreme Ct. Ptnr. Ely & King, Springfield, Mass., 1963-73; presiding judge Hampden County Housing Ct., 1973-75; assoc. judge Mass. Superior Ct., Boston, 1975-76; assoc. justice Mass. Appeals Ct., 1976-84, 1976-84, chief justice, 1984-89; assoc. justice Mass. Supreme Judicial Ct., 1989—. Former faculty mem. Western New England Law Sch., Westfield State Coll.; co-chair. Supreme Judicial Ct's Gender Bias Study Commn; mem. bd. Tribunes WGBY-Channel #57. Former assoc. editor Mass. Law Review. Trustee, dir. Westfield Atheneum, participant Child and Family Svcs. Program. Fellow Am. Bar Found.; mem. ABA (litigation, judicial adminstrn. section), Hampden County Bar Assn.(former mem. exec. com., grievance com., treas.), Mass. Bar Assn.(former chmn. Young Lawyers section, bd. delegates, exec. com., grievance com., legal svc. to the poor com.,(current) civil litigation, criminal law sections), Am. Law Inst. Avocations: competitive running, reading. Office: Mass Supreme Jud Court Pemberton Sq 1300 New Courthouse Boston MA 02108-1701*

GREAVES, JOHN ALLEN, lawyer; b. Kansas City, Mo., Feb. 18, 1948; s. John Allen Greaves and Nancy Lee (Farmer) Greaves-Meltzer; m. Sharon Louise Peace Ventura, Dec. 23, 1967 (div. Mar. 1971); 1 child, Karen Christine Greaves Calogne; m. Jerri Lynn Crawford, Sept. 5, 1981. BA in Polit. Sci., U. Mo., 1976; MPA, JD with honors, Drake U., 1992. Bar: Iowa 1992, U.S. Dist. Ct. (so. dist.) Iowa 1992, Calif. 1994, U.S. Dist. Ct. (no. and cen. dists.) Calif. 1994, U.S. Dist. Ct. (so. and ea. dists.) Calif. 1995, U.S. Dist. Ct. N.Mex. 1995, U.S. Ct. Appeals (9th cir.) 1995, U.S. Dist. Ct. (no. dist.) N.Y. 1996, U.S. Dist. Ct. S.C. 1995, U.S. Ct. Appeals (4th and 10th cirs.) 1996, U.S. Dist. Ct. (no. dist.) Ill. 2000; lic. airline transport pilot. Pres., CEO VIPilot Svcs., Inc., Kansas City, 1980-83; pilot Air Illinois, Carbondale, Ill., 1983-84, Wright Airlines, Cleve., 1983-84, ComAir Airlines, Cin., 1984-88; jud. law clk. to Hon. Arthur E. Gamble Iowa Dist. Ct., Des Moines, 1990-91; pvt. practice, 1992-94; assoc. Baum, Hedlund, Aristei, Guilford & Downey, L.A., 1994—. Mem. plaintiffs' steering com. Atlantic S.E. Airlines crash, Carrollton, Ga., 1995. Mem. ABA (mem. forum on air and space com.), ATLA, Air Line Pilots Assn. (coun. 37, chmn. contract adminstrn. com. 1985-87, Disting. Svc. award), Lawyer/Pilot Bar Assn., State Bar Calif., State Bar Iowa, Iowa Trial Lawyers Assn., Inn Ct., Delta Theta Phi. Avocations: aviation, snow and water skiing, boating and sailing, tennis, golf. Aviation, Personal injury, Product liability. Home: 3664 May St Los Angeles CA 90066-3606 Office: Baum Hedlund Aristei Guilford & Downey 12100 Wilshire Blvd Ste 950 Los Angeles CA 90025-7107 E-mail: jgreaves@baumhedlundlaw.com

GREBEL, LAWRENCE BOVARD, lawyer; b. St. Louis, Jan. 7, 1951; s. Clement Bovard and Jean Estelle (Schrieber) G.; children: David, Mark, Benjamin. BA, St. Louis U., 1973, JD, 1977. Bar: Mo. 1977, Ill. 1978, U.S. Dist. Ct. (ea. dist.) Mo. 1977. Mem. Moser, Marsalek, Carpenter, Cleary, Jaeckel, Keaney & Brown, St. Louis, 1977-80, Brown & James PC, St. Louis, 1980—. Mem. Internat. Assn. Def. Counsel, Assn. Def. Trial Attys., Mo. Bar Assn. (treas. 1981, sec. 1982, chmn. 1984), St. Louis Met. Bar Assn., Def. Rsch. Inst., Lawyers Assn. St. Louis. Roman Catholic. Federal civil litigation, State civil litigation, Personal injury. Home: 8822 Ryegate Saint Louis MO 63127 Office: Brown & James PC 705 Olive St Ste 1100 Saint Louis MO 63101-2270 E-mail: lgrebel@bjpc.com

GREEN, CAROL H. lawyer, educator, journalist; b. Seattle, Feb. 18, 1944; BA in History/Journalism summa cum laude, La. Tech. U., 1965; MSL, Yale U., 1977; JD, U. Denver, 1979. Reporter Shreveport (La.) Times, 1965-66, Guam Daily News, 1966-67; city editor Pacific Jour., Agana, Guam, 1967-68, reporter, editl. writer Guam, 1968-76, legal affairs reporter Guam, 1977-79; asst. editor editl. page Denver Post, 1979-81, house counsel, 1980-83, labor rels. mgr., 1981-83; assoc. Holme Roberts & Owen, 1983-85; v.p. human resources and legal affairs Denver Post, 1985-87, mgr. circulation, 1988-90; gen. mgr. Distbn. Systems Am., Inc., 1990-92; dir. labor rels. Newsday, 1992-95, dir. comm. & labor rels., 1996-97; v.p. Weber Mgmt. Cons., 1997-98; v.p. human resources Denver Post, 1998-2000, Denver Newspaper Agy., 2000—. 1985 speaker for USIA, India, Egypt; mem. Mailers Tech. Adv. Com. to Postmaster Gen., 1991-92. Recipient McWilliams award for juvenile justice, Denver, 1971, award for interpretive reporting Denver Newspaper Guild, 1979. Mem. ABA (forum on comm. law), Colo. Bar Assn. (bd. govs. 1985-87, chair BAR-press com. 1980), Newspaper Assn. Am. (mem. human resources and labor rels. com.), Denver Bar Assn. (co-chiar jud. sel. and benefits com. 1982-85, 2st v.p. 1986), Colo. and Internat. Women's Dorum, Leadership Denver, Human Resources Planning Soc., Soc. Human Resources Mgmt., Indsl. Rels. Rsch. Assn., Colo. Assn. Human Resources Assn., Huntington Camera Club. Episcopalian.

GREEN, CLIFFORD SCOTT, federal judge; b. Phila., Apr. 2, 1923; s. Robert Lewis and Alice (Robinson) G.; m. Carol Greene. B.S., Temple U., 1948, J.D., 1951. Bar: Pa. 1952. Pvt. practice law, Phila., 1952-64; dep. atty. gen. State of Pa., 1954; judge County Ct., Phila., 1964-68, Ct. Common Pleas, 1968-71, U.S. Dist. Ct. for Eastern Dist. Pa., Phila., 1971-88, sr. judge, 1988—. Former lectr. in law Temple U. Former bd. dirs. Children's Aid Soc. of Pa.; former bd. mgrs. Children's Hosp., Phila.; trustee Temple U. Served with USAAF, 1943-46. Recipient Judge William Hastie award NAACP Legal Def. Fund, 1985, awards for community service Women's Christian Alliance, awards for community service Health and Welfare Council, awards for community service Opportunities Industrialization Center, J. Austin Norris Barrister's award, 1988, Temple Law Alumni Assn. award 1994, Justice Thurgood Marshall Meml. award Nat. Bar Assn., 1994, gen. alumni award Temple U., 1999. Mem. Sigma Pi Phi. Presbyterian. Office: US Courthouse Independence Mall W #15613 601 Market St Philadelphia PA 19106-1713

GREEN, CUMER L. lawyer; b. Moscow, Oct. 6, 1941; s. Leon Grant and Gwen Pratt G.; m. JoAnne Ames; children: Scott, Cliff, Holly, Stephen, Chris. BS in Bus., U. Idaho, 1963, MA in Acctg., JD, U. Idaho, 1969. Bar: Idaho 1969; U.S. Dist. Ct. Idaho, 1969, U.S. Ct. Appeals (9th cir.) 1971, U.S. Tax Ct. 1971, U.S. Dist. Ct. (cen. dist.) Calif. 1987; CPA, Idaho. Assoc. Eberle & Berlin, Boise, 1969-71; pvt. practice, 1971-72; ptnr. Green & Bithell, 1972-75, Green & Frost, Boise, 1973-75, Green & Cantrill, Boise, 1975-80, Green & Sullivan, Boise, 1980-81; owner Green Law Offices, 1981-88, 91-01; ptnr. Green & Nyman, 1988-90. Treas. Ford for Pres., Boise; chmn. Gov's Task Force on Local Govt. Revenue Problems, 1970; prin. sponser Law Inst., Boise, 1992—. With USMC, 1959-60. Mem. ABA, Nat. Bd. Sch. Attys., Idaho State Bar Assn. (commr. 1995-98, pres. 1998), Idaho State Code Commn. (commr. 1998—), Phi Alpha Delta. Republican. Avocation: jogging, skiing. General civil litigation, Education and schools, Taxation, general. Office: PO Box 2597 Boise ID 83701-2597 E-mail: clgreen@micron.com

GREEN, ERIC HOWARD, lawyer; b. N.Y.C., Jan. 5, 1950; s. Bernard and Edith Green; m. Mona M. Green, July 10, 1982; children: Zachary Samuel, Shawn Alexander. BA, SUNY, Buffalo, 1972, JD, 1976. Bar: N.Y. 1977, U.S. Dist. Ct. (so. and ea. dists.) N.Y. 1979, U.S. Supreme Ct. 1985. Assoc. Pops & Estrin, N.Y.C., 1976-77, Karp & Silver, Queens, N.Y., 1977-81, Edward Leshaw, Esq., N.Y.C., 1981-82; mng. ptnr. Eric H. Green, Esq., 1982—. Instr. Nat. Inst. of Trial Advocacy, Cardoza Law Sch., N.Y.C., 1987—, U. Buffalo, coll. of Urban Studies, 1974-76; lectr. NYU, Sch. Continuing Edn., N.Y.C., 1986-90; arbitrator Am. Arbitration Assn., 1987—. Mem. N.Y. Dem. Judicial Screening Panel, N.Y.C., 1989; advisor, vol. N.Y.C. Open Doors Edn. Program, 1985-89. Mem. ATLA, N.Y. County Lawyers Assn., N.Y. State Bar Assn., N.Y. State Trial Lawyers Assn. (bd. dirs., speaker cmty. speakers bur. 1988—), N.Y. County Lawyers Assn. (fee dispute com., Supreme Ct. com.), Assn. Bar City N.Y. (tort litigation com., chmn. mediation subcom.). Avocations: sports, theatre, antiques. General civil litigation, General practice, Personal injury. Office: 295 Madison Ave New York NY 10017-6304 E-mail: greenlegal@msn.com

GREEN, JEFFREY C. lawyer; b. Newark, July 6, 1941; s. Albert and Mildred (Rosenberg) G.; m. Iris Landow, Aug. 23, 1964; children: Michelle, Marlene. BA, Rutgers U., 1963, JD, 1966; postgrad., Nat. Coll. State Judiciary, Reno, 1974-75. Bar: N.J. 1966, U.S. Dist. Ct. N.J. 1966. Law clk. to judge N.J. Superior Ct., Middlesex County Ct., New Brunswick, 1966-67; assoc. Toolan, Romond & Burgess, Perth Amboy, N.J., 1967-68; ptnr. Green & Green and predecessors, Somerset, 1968—. Prosecutor Franklin Twp. Mcpl. Ct., Somerset, 1969-70, mcpl. judge, 1970-76, 97—; judge Millstone (N.J.) Mcpl. Ct., 1970-76, Manville (N.J.) Mcpl. Ct., 1972-73; atty. Cranbury (N.J.) Bd. Adjustment, 1978—. Legal counsel Temple Beth El, Somerset, 1974—; bd. dirs. Middlesex County Legal Svcs. Corp., New Brunswick, 1983—. Named Man of Yr., Temple Beth El, 1984; recipient Pro Bono Achievement award Middlesex County Legal Svcs. Corp., 1985, 87. Mem. N.J. State Bar Assn. (trustee 1997—, Gen. Practitioner of Yr. award 1997), Middlesex County Bar Assn. (pres. 1985-86), Middlesex County Bar Found. (trustee 1990—, pres. 1994-95), Franklin Twp. Jaycees (pres. 1970-71), Lions Club. Democrat. Contracts commercial, General corporate, General practice. Home: 3 Denise Ct Somerset NJ 08873-2834 Office: Green & Green PO Box 5321 Somerset NJ 08875-5321

GREEN, JEFFREY STEVEN, lawyer; b. N.Y.C., July 7, 1943; s. Morris and Fannie (Mandel) G.; m. Sydell Joan Loewenthal, Nov. 1, 1964; children: Robin Janet, Philip Peter. BA in Polit. Sci., CCNY, 1965; JD, NYU, 1969; grad. advanced mgmt. program, Harvard U., 1982. Bar: N.Y. 1969, U.S. Dist. Ct. (so. and ea. dists.) N.Y. 1983, U.S. Supreme Ct. 1989. Atty. Port Authority N.Y. and N.J., N.Y.C., 1969-77, asst. chief fin divsn. law dept., 1977-78, dep. chief fin. divsn. law dept., 1978-79, chief fin. divsn. law dept., 1979-85, asst. gen. counsel, 1985-90, dep. gen. counsel, 1990-91, gen. counsel, 1991—. Mem. Anthony Commn. on Pub. Fin. Mem. editl. bd. Mcpl. Fin. Jour.; contbr. articles to profl. jours. Trustee Pearl River Pub. Libr., 1985-96, pres., 1989-96; bd. dirs. Rockland County YM-YWHA, 1989—, v.p., 2000—; trustee Pearl River Sch. Bd., 1975-84, pres., 1977-80; mem. exec. com. Rockland County Sch. Bds. Assn., 1976-84, pres., 1980-82. Fellow Am. Bar Found.; mem. Nat. Assn. Bond Lawyers, N.Y. State Bar Assn., Assn. Bar City N.Y., Govt. Fin. Officers Assn. (chmn. com. govtl. debt and fiscal policy 1984-91, disclosure task force 1989-95, bd. dirs. 1991-94), Mcpl. Forum N.Y., N.Y. State Govt. Fin. Officers Assn.

GREEN, JERSEY MICHAEL-LEE, lawyer; b. Washington, Feb. 29, 1952; m. Jonelle Sue Burke, May 12, 1988. BA in criminology, U. Md., 1976; JD, Syracuse U., 1983. Bar: Colo. 1983, U.S. Dist. Ct. Colo. 1983, U.S. Ct. Appeals (10th cir.) 1983, U.S. Tax Ct. 1983, U.S. Ct. Appeals (9th cir.) 1987, U.S. Supreme Ct. 1988, U.S. Ct. Appeals (2d cir.) 1990, U.S. Dist. Ct. Ariz. 1994. Atty. Wagner & Waller, P.C., Denver, 1983-86, Waller, Mark & Allen, P.C., Denver, 1986-89, Orten & Hindman P.C., Denver, 1989-90, Elrod, Katz, Preeo, Look, Moison & Silverman, P.C., Denver, 1990-97, Preeo, Silverman & Green, P.C., Denver, 1998-99, Preeo, Silverman, Green & Egle, P.C., Denver, 1999—. Mem. exec. com. staff Lawyers for Romer, Denver, 1986; precinct committeeman, 1989-92. Recipient Syracuse (N.Y.) Def. Group scholarship, 1982. Mem. Assn. Trial Lawyers Am., Colo. Trial Lawyers Assn., Arapahoe County Bar Assn., Syracuse U. Alumni Assn. (pres. Colo. 1987-89). Democrat. Avocations: mountaineering, skiing, running. General civil litigation. Office: Preeo Silverman Green & Eagle PC 1401 17th St Ste 800 Denver CO 80202-1246 E-mail: Jersey@preeosilv.com

GREEN, JOSEPH LIBORY, lawyer; b. St. Louis, Mar. 20, 1960; s. Joseph Richard and Kathleen Ann Green; m. Sherry Michelle Fedder, Oct. 7, 1989; children: Bryan Smith, Samantha Joe Green, Jacob Fedder Green, Jacqueline Michelle Green. BSBA, Truman State U., 1982; JD, St. Louis U., 1987. Bar: Mo. 1988, U.S. Dist. Ct. (ea. dist.) Mo. 1993, U.S. Dist. Ct. (we. dist.) Mo. 1996, U.S. Ct. Appeals (8th cir.) 1998, U.S. Supreme Ct. 1998. Asst. pub. def. St. Joseph (Mo.) Pub. Def.'s Office, 1988; chief trial atty. St. Louis County Pub. Def.'s Office, Clayton, Mo., 1989-90; capital litigation atty. Mo. State Pub. Def.'s Office, St. Louis, 1990-93; assoc. Wittner, Poger, Rosenblum & Spewak, P.C., Clayton, 1993-96; sole practitioner St. Charles, Mo., 1996; ptnr. Baerveldt, Bagsby, Lee & Green, L.L.C., 1996—. Dem. candidate for county prosecutor, St. Charles, 1994, 98. Mem. Nat. Assn. Criminal Def. Lawyers, Mo. Assn. Criminal Def. Lawyers. Civil rights, Criminal, Personal injury. Office: Baerveldt Bagsby Lee & Green LLP 566 1st Capitol Dr Saint Charles MO 63301-2726

GREEN, JOYCE HENS, federal judge; b. N.Y.C., Nov. 13, 1928; d. James S. and Hedy (Bucher) Hens; m. Samuel Green, Sept. 25, 1965 (dec.); children: Michael Timothy, June Heather, James Harry. BA, U. Md., 1949; JD, George Washington U., 1951, LLD, 1994. Practice law, Washington, 1951-68, Arlington, Va., 1956-68; ptnr. Green & Green, 1966-68; assoc. judge Superior Ct., D.C., 1968-79; judge U.S. Dist. Ct. for D.C., 1979—; judge presiding U.S. Fgn. Intelligence Surveillance Ct., 1988-95. Bd. advisors George Washington U. Law Sch.; jud. br. com. Jud. Conf. U.S. Co-author: Dissolution of Marriage, 1986, supplements, 1987-89; contbr. supplements Marriage and Family Law Agreements, 1985-89. Chair Task Force on Gender, Race and Ethnic Bias for the D.C. Cir. Recipient Alumni Achievement award George Washington U., 1975, Profl. Achievement award, 1978, Outstanding Contbn. to Equal Rights award Women's Legal Def. Fund, 1976, hon. doctor of Laws George Washington U., 1994, U.S. Dept. Justice Edmund J. Randolph award, 1995. Fellow Am. Bar Found.; ABA (jud. adminstrn. divsn., chair nat. conf. fed. trial judges), Fed. Judges Assn., Nat. Assn. Women Judges, Va. Bar Assn., Bar Assn. D.C. (jud. honoree of Yr. 1994), D.C. Bar, D.C. Women's Bar Assn., (pres. 1960-62, woman lawyer of yr. 1979), Exec. Women in Govt. (chmn. 1977), Woman's Forum of Washington D.C. Office: US Dist Ct E Barrett Prettyman US Courthouse 333 Constitution Ave NW Washington DC 20001-2802

GREEN, MARSHALL MUNRO, lawyer; b. Staten Island, N.Y., Feb. 23, 1938; s. Thomas Marshall and Mary (Tibbitts) G.; m. Lucy Featherstone Abbott, June 15, 1959; children: Eleanor Thurston, John Marshall, Lucy Gatewood. AB, Harvard U., 1959, LLB cum laude, 1965. Bar: N.Y. 1965, Conn. 1976, Fla. 1976, U.S. Dist. Ct. Conn. 1984. Assoc. Breed, Abbott & Morgan, N.Y.C., 1965-72; ptnr. Williamson & Green, 1972-76, Bisset, Atkins & Green, N.Y.C., 1976-82, LeBoeuf, Lamb, Leiby & MacRae, N.Y.C., 1982-90; v.p. Carter-Wallace, Inc., 1990—. Adj. prof. N.Y. Law Sch., N.Y.C., 1993—. Trustee Childrens Aid Soc., N.Y.C., 1972—, Fedn. Protestant Welfare Agys., N.Y.C., 1980—, United Charities Inc., N.Y.C., 1983—; mem. bd. mgrs. Episcopal Social Svcs., N.Y.C., 1995—; mem. Nat. Choral Council, 1976—. Fellow Am. Coll. Trusts and Estates Counsel; mem. The Century Assn. (N.Y.C.), Univ. Club (N.Y.C.), Harvard Club (N.Y.C.), City Island Yacht Club. Democrat. Episcopalian. Probate, Estate taxation. E-mail: greenm@earthlink.net

GREEN, RICHARD, lawyer, psychiatrist, educator; b. Bklyn., June 6, 1936; s. Leo Harry and Rose (Ingber) G.; m. Melissa Hines; 1 child, Adam Hines-Green. AB, Syracuse U., 1957; MD, Johns Hopkins U., 1961; JD, Yale U., 1987. Diplomate Am. Bd. Psychiatry and Neurology; bar: Calif. 1987, D.C. 1989. Intern Kings County Hosp., Bklyn., 1962-64; resident in psychiatry UCLA Neuropsychiat. Inst., 1962-64, NIMH, Bethesda, Md., 1965-66; from asst. prof. to prof. dept. psychiatry UCLA, 1968-74; prof. psychiatry and psychology SUNY, Stony Brook, 1974-85; prof. psychiatry UCLA, 1986-94, prof. law, 1988-90, prof. emeritus psychiatry, 1994—; affiliated lectr., faculty of law Cambridge U., 1994-2001. Faculty mem. law sch. UCLA, 1991-92; head dir. of rsch., cons. psychiatrist Gender Identity Clinic Charing Cross Hosp., London; vis. fellow, sr. rsch. fellow Inst. Criminology, Cambridge U., 1994-2001. Author: Sexual Identity Conflict in Children and Adults, 1974, The Sissy Boy Syndrome and the Development of Homosexuality, 1987, Sexual Science and the Law, 1992; co-editor: Impotence, 1981, Transsexualism and Sex Reassignment, 1969, Sociolegal Control of Homosexuality: A Multination Comparison, 1997; editor: Human Sexuality: A Health Practitioner's Text, 1975, 2d edit., 1979; editor Jour. Archives of Sexual Behavior, 1971-2000. Vol. atty., ACLU, LA. Vis. scholar U. Cambridge, Eng., 1980-81, Fulbright scholar King's Coll., London, and Univ. Cambridge, 1992; fellow Ctr. Advanced Study in Behavioral Scis., Stanford, Calif., 1982-83. Fellow Royal Coll. Psychiatrists, Soc. Sci. Study of Sex (pres. 1974-77), Internat. Acad. Sex Rsch. (founding pres. 1973, elected pres. 1998—); mem. Calif. Bar Assn., D.C. Bar Assn., Harry Benjamin Internat. Gender Dysphoria Assn. (pres. 1998-99). Avocations: photography, traveling, antiques. Office: Charing Cross Hosp Gender Identity Clinic Dept Psychiatry London W6 8RF England E-mail: richard.green@ic.ac.uk

GREEN, SAUL A. lawyer; B.A., U. Mich. , 1969; J.D., U. Mich. Law , 1972. Asst. U.S. Atty., eastern dist. Mich U.S. Dept Justice, Mich., 1973—76; chief counsel U.S. Dept. of Housing and Urban Devel., Detroit, 1976—89; corp. counsel Wayne County, 1989—93; U.S. atty. Ea. Dist. Mich., Detroit, 1994—2001; sr. counsel Miller, Canfield, Paddock and Stone, PLC , 2001—, dir., Minority Bus Practice Group, 2001—. Office: Miller, Canfield, Paddock and Stone, PLC 150 West Jefferson, Suite 2500 Detroit MI 48226 Office Fax: 313-496-8453. E-mail: greens@millercanfield.com*

GREEN, WILLIAM PORTER, lawyer; b. Jacksonville, Ill., Mar. 19, 1920; s. Hugh Parker and Clara Belle (Hopper) G.; m. Rose Marie Hall, Oct. 1, 1944; children: Hugh Michael, Robert Alan, Richard William. BA, Ill. Coll., 1941; JD, Northwestern U., Evanston, Ill., 1947. Bar: Ill. 1947, Calif. 1948, U.S. Dist. Ct. (so. dist.) Tex. 1986, U.S. Ct. Customs and Patent Appeals, U.S. Patent and Trademark Office 1948, U.S. Ct. Appeals (fed. cir.) 1982, U.S. Ct. Appeals (5th and 9th cir.), U.S. Supreme Ct. 1948, U.S. Dist. Ct. (cen. dist.) Calif. 1949, (so. dist.) Tex.1986. Pvt. practice, L.A., 1947—; mem. Wills, Green & Mueth, 1974-83; of counsel Nilsson, Robbins, Dalgarn, Berliner, Carson & Wurst, 1984-91; of counsel Nilsson, Wurst & Green, 1992—. Del. Calif. State Bar Conv., 1982—, chmn., 1986. Bd. editors Ill. Law Rev., 1946; patentee in field. Mem. L.A. world Affairs Coun., 1975—; deacon local Presbyn. Ch., 1961-63. Mem. ABA, Calif. State Bar, Am. Intellectual Property Law Assn., L.A. Patent Law Assn. (past. sec.-treas., mem. bd. govs.), Lawyers Club L.A. (past treas., past sec., mem. bd. govs., pres. 1985-86), Los Angeles County Bar Assn. (trustee 1986-87), Am. Legion (past post comdr.), Northwestern U. Alumni Club So. Calif., Big Ten Club So. Calif., Town Hall Calif. Club, PGA West Golf Club (La Quinta, Calif.), Phi Beta Kappa, Phi Delta Phi, Phi Alpha. Republican. Patent, Trademark and copyright. Home: 3570 Lombardy Rd Pasadena CA 91107-5627 Office: 707 Wilshire Blvd Ste 3200 Los Angeles CA 90017-3514 E-mail: wpgreen@aol.com

GREENAWALT, ROBERT KENT, lawyer, law educator; b. Bklyn., June 25, 1936; s. Kenneth William and Martha (Sloan) G.; m. Sanja Milic, July 14, 1968 (dec. Nov. 1988); children: Robert Milic, Alexander Kent Anton, Andrei Milenko Kenneth; m. Elaine Pagels, June 1995; children: Sarah Pagels, David. A.B. with honors, Swarthmore Coll., 1958; Ph.B.; Keasbey fellow, Oxford (Eng.) U., 1960; LL.B.; Kent scholar, Columbia U., 1963. Bar: N.Y. 1963. Law clk. to Justice Harlan, U.S. Supreme Ct., 1963-64; spl. asst. AID, Washington, 1964-65; mem. faculty Columbia U. Law Sch., 1965—, prof. law, 1969—, Cardozo prof., 1979—, Univ. prof., 1990—. Dep. solicitor gen. U.S., 1971-72; assoc. dir. N.Y. Inst. Legal Edn., 1969; vis. prof. Stanford U. Law Sch., 1970, Northwestern U. Law Sch., 1983, Marshall-Wythe Sch. Law, 1985, N.Y.U. Law Sch., 1989-90; atty. Lawyers Com. Civil Rights, 1965, trustee, 1992; mem. staff Task Force Law Enforcement N.Y.C., 1965; vis. fellow All Souls Coll. Oxford (Eng.) U., 1979 Co-author: The Sectarian College and The Public Purse, 1970; author: Legal Protections of Privacy, 1976, Discrimination and Reverse Discrimination, 1983, Conflicts of Law and Morality, 1987, Religious Convictions and Political Choice, 1988, Speech, Crime and the Uses of Language, 1989, Law and Objectivity, 1992, Private Consciences and Public Reasons, 1995, Fighting Words, 1995, Statutory Interpretation: Twenty Questions, 1999; editor in chief Columbia U. Law Rev., 1962-63; contbr. articles to legal jours. Recipient Ivy award Swarthmore Coll., 1958; fellow Am. Council Learned Soc., 1972-73. Fellow Am. Acad. Arts and Scis.; mem. Am. Philos. Soc., Am. Law Inst., Am. Soc. Polit. and Legal Philosophy (pres. 1992-93). Office: Columbia U Law Sch 435 W 116th St New York NY 10027-7201

GREENAWALT, WILLIAM SLOAN, lawyer; b. Bklyn., Mar. 4, 1934; s. Kenneth William and Martha Frances (Sloan) G.; m. Jane DeLano Plunkett, Aug. 17, 1957 (div. May 1986); m. Peggy Ellen Freed Tomarkin, Oct. 31, 1987; children: John DeLano, David Sloan, Katherine Downs. AB, Cornell U., 1956; LLB, Yale U., 1961. Bar: N.Y. 1962, U.S. Dist. Ct. (so. and ea. dists.) N.Y. 1962, U.S. Ct. Apls. (2d cir.) 1962, U.S. Supreme Ct. 1966. Assoc. Sullivan & Cromwell, N.Y.C., 1961-65; N.E. regional legal svcs. dir. U.S. Office Econ. Opportunity, 1965-68; assoc. Rogers & Wells, 1968-69, ptnr., 1969-77, sr. ptnr., 1977-81, Halperin, Shivitz, Eisenberg, Schneider & Greenawalt, N.Y.C., 1981-86, Eisenberg Honig Fogler Greenawalt & Davis, N.Y.C., 1986-91, Bangser Klein Rocca & Blum, N.Y.C., 1991-93, Loselle Greenawalt Kaplan Blair & Adler, N.Y.C., 1993-97, Loselle Greenawalt Kaplan & Blair, N.Y.C., 1997-99, Meyer Greenawalt Taub & Wild, LLP, N.Y.C., 1999-2001; pvt. practice, 2001—. Lectr. in field. Bd. editors: Yale Law Jour., 1959-61; contbr. articles in field to profl. jours. Chmn. bd. dirs. Applied Resources, Inc., N.Y.C., 1968-70; chmn. Cmty. Aid Employment of Ex-Offenders, Westchester, N.Y., 1971; pres. Westchester Legal Svcs., 1971-74, bd. dirs., 1975-91; mem. N.Y. State Gov.'s Task Force on Elem. and Secondary Edn., 1974-75; mem. Pres. Carter's Task Force on Criminal Justice, 1976; mem. adv. coun. N.Y. State Senate Dems., 1978—; asst. and acting treas. N.Y. State Dem. Party, 1990-96, vice chair, 1996-2000, mem. state com., 1974—; chair Greenburgh Dem. Party, 1997—; mem. Greenburgh Recreation Commn., 1976-83, Dem. Statewide Spl. Commn. on Polit. Ethics, 1986-87, Statewide Spl. Commn. on Election Law and Campaign Spending Reform, 1989-95; pres. Westchester Crime Victims Assistance Agy., 1981-82; commr. Taconic State Pks., Recreation and Hist. Preservation Commn., 1984-96, chmn., 1989-96; vice chmn. N.Y. State Coun. on Pks., Recreation and Hist. Preservation, 1989-94; moderator Scarsdale Congl. Ch., 1988-90; mem. Westchester County Parks, Recreation and Conservation Bd., 1998—, vice chmn., 1999—; mem. Westchester County Execs. Transition Team on Planning, 1997. Lt. comdr. USN, 1956-58, with Res., 1961-68. Fellow N.Y. Bar Found.; mem. ABA, Am. Arbitration Assn. (mem. panel comml. arbitrators 1977—), N.Y. State Bar Assn. (chmn. com. on availability of legal svcs. 1968-70, chmn. action unit 3 1979-81, chmn. spl. commn. on alternatives to jud. resolution of disputes 1981-85), Assn. of Bar of City of N.Y., Nat. Legal Aid and Defenders Assn., Sphinx Head, Aleph Samach, County Tennis Club Westchester (Scarsdale, N.Y., pres. 1979-80), Yale Club (Yale Law jour. 1959-61), Phi Alpha Delta, Chi Psi. Democrat. Congregationalist. Federal civil litigation, State civil litigation, Securities. Home: 24 Lewis Ave Hartsdale NY 10530 Office: Law Offices William S Greenawalt 230 Park Ave Rm 2525 New York NY 10169-0199

GREENBAUM, KENNETH, lawyer; b. N.Y.C., July 24, 1944; s. Nathan and Beatrice (Lieboff) G.; BA, Hobart Coll., 1966; JD, Suffolk U., 1969; LLM, N.Y. U., 1970; m. Ellyn Greenstein, June 30, 1968; children: Debra Renee, Jeffrey Scott. Admitted to N.Y. bar, 1969; assoc. Del Rosso & Weinstein, Hempstead, N.Y., 1970-72; sr. atty. Kane Miller Corp., Tarrytown, N.Y., 1972-75; with Condec Corp., Old Greenwich, Conn., 1975-85, gen. counsel, 1982-85; with Farley Industries, 1985—, v.p., gen. counsel, 1985—, sec. 1988—. Mem. ABA, Counsel Assn. Banking, General corporate, Securities. Office: Farley Industries 233 S Wacker Dr Chicago IL 60606-6306

GREENBAUM, SHELDON MARC, lawyer; b. Bklyn., July 1, 1950; s. Emil and Edith (Greenbaum) G.; m. Susan M. Weisberg, May 27, 1971; children— Diana, Elizabeth. B.S. magna cum laude, NYU, 1971, J.D., 1974. Bar: N.Y. 1975, U.S. Dist. Ct. (so. and ea. dists.) N.Y. 1975, U.S. Ct. Appeals (2d cir.) 1975, U.S.Ct. Appeals (fed. cir.) 1987, U.S. Ct. Internat. Trade 1986, U.S. Supreme Ct. 1978. Law clk. Parker, Chapin, Flattau & Klimpl, N.Y.C., 1968-70; litigation atty., 1974-77; acct. Berkowitz & Brody, N.Y.C., 1971-72; asst. controller WaSko Gold Products Corp., N.Y.C., 1972-73; litigation atty. Hess, Segall, Guterman, Pelz & Steiner, N.Y.C., 1978-81; ptnr. Goldman and Greenbaum, P.C., N.Y.C., 1981-84, Goldman , Greenbaum & Milner, P.C., N.Y.C., 1984-86, Goldman & Greenbaum, P.C., N.Y.C., 1986—; adj. asst. prof. law Grad. Sch. Bus. Adminstrn. and Coll. Bus. and Pub. Adminstrn., NYU, 1978-83. Mem. bd. appeals Village of Port Washington North, N.Y., 1980-88, chmn., 1989—. Served with USAR, 1970-76. Mem. ABA, N.Y. State Bar Assn., Assn. Bar City NY. Federal civil litigation, State civil litigation, Family and matrimonial. Home: 89 Radcliff Ave Port Washington NY 11050-1616 Office: Goldman & Greenbaum PC 60 E 42nd St New York NY 10165-0006

GREENBERG, GARY HOWARD, lawyer; b. N.Y.C., Mar. 2, 1948; s. Leo and Elizabeth P. (Weissman) G.; m. Sherri Snyder, June 21, 1987; children: Benjamin, Laura, Nicholas. BA, Johns Hopkins U., 1970; JD, N.Y.U., 1974. Bar: N.Y. 1975, U.S. Dist. Ct. (so. dist.) N.Y. 1975, U.S. Dist. Ct. (ea. dist.) N.Y. 1975, U.S. Ct. Appeals (2d cir.) 1984. Assoc. Orans, Elsen & Lupert, N.Y.C., 1975-83, ptnr., 1983—. Instr. trial acad. direct and cross exam. skills N.Y. County Lawyers' Assn.-Nat. Inst. of Trial Advocacy, 1995. Mem. ABA, Assn. of Bar of City of N.Y. (mem. com. on fed. legis. 1983-86), N.Y. State Bar Assn., N.Y. County Lawyers' Assn. (chair appellate cts. com. 1996-99). Federal civil litigation, General civil litigation, Criminal. Office: Orans Elsen & Lupert 1 Rockefeller Plz New York NY 10020-2102

GREENBERG, HAROLD, legal educator; b. Phila., Jan. 19, 1938; s. George and Sarah (Elkins) G. Teaching cert. Gratz. Coll., Phila., 1957; A.B. summa cum laude, Temple U., 1959; J.D. magna cum laude U. Pa., 1962. Bar: Pa. 1963, U.S. Ct. Appeals (3d cir.) 1964, Ind. 1979. Law clk. Supreme Ct. of Pa., Phila. and Erie, 1963-64. Assoc., then ptnr. firm Cohen, Shapiro, Polisher, Shiekman & Cohen, Phila., 1964-77; assoc. prof. law Ind. U., Indpls., 1977-88, prof., 1988—. Author: Rights and Remedies Under U.C.C. Article 2, 1987. Mem. ABA, Ind. Bar Assn., Indpls. Bar Assn. Democrat. Jewish. Office: Sch Law Ind U 735 W New York St Indianapolis IN 46202-5222

GREENBERG, IRA GEORGE, lawyer; b. N.Y.C., May 8, 1946; s. Julius M. and Florence Greenberg; m. Linda Sharon Padell, Apr. 29, 1979; children: Amanda, Glenn. AB, Harvard U., 1968, JD, 1971. Bar: N.Y. 1972, D.C. 1980. Asst. to gen. counsel Office of Sec. of Army, Washington, 1971-74; assoc. Dewey Ballantine, N.Y.C., 1974-81, Summit Solomon & Feldesman and predecessor firms, N.Y.C., 1981-83, ptnr., 1983-92, Edwards & Angell LLP, N.Y.C., 1992—. Capt. U.S. Army, 1971-74. Mem. ABA, Assn. Bar City N.Y. Democrat. Federal civil litigation, State civil litigation. Office: Edwards & Angell LLP 750 Lexington Ave Fl 12 New York NY 10022-1253 E-mail: igreenberg@ealaw.com

GREENBERG, JACK, lawyer, law educator; b. N.Y.C., Dec. 22, 1924; s. Max and Bertha (Rosenberg) G.; m. Sema Ann Tanzer, 1950 (div. 1970); children: Josiah, David, Sarah, Ezra; m. Deborah M. Cole, 1970; children: Suzanne, William Cole. AB, Columbia U., 1945, LLB, 1948, LLD, 1984, Morgan State Coll., Central State Coll., 1965, Lincoln U., 1977, John Jay Coll. Criminal Justice, 1983, De Paul U., 1994. Bar: N.Y. 1949. Rsch. asst. N.Y. State Law Revision Commn., 1949; asst. counsel NAACP Legal Def. and Ednl. Fund, 1949-61, dir.-counsel, 1961-84; argued in sch. segregation, sit-in, employment discrimination, poverty, capital punishment, other cases before U.S. Supreme Ct.; adj. prof. Columbia U. Law Sch., 1970-84, prof., vice-dean, 1984-89; dean Columbia Coll., 1989-93; prof. Columbia U. Law Sch., 1993—. Cons. Ctr. Applied Legal Studies, U. Witwatersrand, 1978; vis. lectr. Yale U. Law Sch., 1971; vis. prof. CCNY, 1977, Tokyo U., 1993-94, 99, St. Louis U. Law Sch., 1994, Lewis and Clark Law Sch., 1994-98, Princeton U., 1995, U. Munich, 1998; lectr. Harvard U. Law Sch., 1983, Shikes fellow, 1981; disting. lectr. humanities Columbia Coll. Physicians and Surgeons, 1998, U. Nurenberg-Erlangen, 1999. Author: (with H. Hill) Citizens Guide to Desegregation, 1955, Race Relations and American Law, 1959, Judicial Process and Social Change, 1976, (with James Vorenberg) Dean Cuisine or the Liberated Man's Guide to Fine Cooking, 1990, Crusaders in the Courts, 1994; contbg. author: Race, Sex and Religious Discrimination in International Law, 1981; contbr. articles to profl. jours. Bd. dirs. N.Y.C. Legal Aid Soc., Internat. League for Human Rights, Mex.-Am. Legal Def. Fund, 1968-75, Asian Am. Legal Def. Fund, 1980—, Human Rights Watch, 1978-98, NAACP Legal Def. and Ednl. Fund. Co-recipient Grenville Clark prize, 1978; hon. fellow U. Pa. Law Sch., 1975. Fellow AAAS, Am. Coll. Trial Lawyers; mem. ABA (commn. to study FTC, adv. com. to spl. com. on crime prevention, sect. on individual rights and responsibilities, Silver Gavel award, Thurgood Marshall prize, Presdl. Citizens medal 2001), N.Y. State Bar Assn. (exec. dir. spl. com. study state antitrust laws 1956), Am. Law Inst., Bar Assn. City N.Y. (Cardozo lectr. 1973) Adminstrv. Conf. U.S. Home: 118 Riverside Dr New York NY 10024-3708 Office: Columbia Law Sch 435 W 116th St New York NY 10027-7297

GREENBERG, MICHAEL J. lawyer; b. Bklyn., July 25, 1972; s. Arnold K. and Barbara W. Greenberg; m. Erica M. Golden, Mar. 28, 1998. BA, Washington U., St. Louis, 1994, JD, 1997. Bar: N.Y. 1998. Assoc. Curto, Burton & Alesi, P.C., Melville, N.Y., 1998—. Mem. ABA, N.Y. State Bar Assn. Contracts commercial, General corporate, Real property. Office: Curto Burton & Alesi PC Ste 1N5 1 Huntington Quadrangle Melville NY 11747

GREENBERG, MORTON IRA, federal judge; b. Philadelphia, Pa., Mar. 20, 1933; s. Harry Arnold and Pauline (Hofkin) G.; m. Barbara-Ann Kissel, May 29, 1987; children from first marriage: Elizabeth, Suzanne, Lawrence. AB, U. Pa., 1954; LLB, Yale U., 1957. Bar: N.J. 1958, U.S. Dist. Ct. N.J. 1958, U.S. Ct. Appeals (3d cir.) 1972, U.S. Supreme Ct. 1973. Law clk.office of atty. gen. State of N.J., Trenton, 1957-58, dep. atty. gen., 1958-60, asst. atty. gen., 1971-73; pvt. practice, Cape May, N.J., 1960-71; judge law div. Superior Ct. N.J., New Brunswick, 1973-76, judge chancery and gen. equity divs. Trenton, 1976-80, judge appellate div., 1980-87; judge U.S. Ct. Appeals (3d cir.), Trenton and Phila., 1987—. Office: US Ct Appeals US Courthouse 402 E State St Ste 7050 Trenton NJ 08608-1507

GREENBERG, MORTON PAUL, lawyer, consultant, life settlement broker; b. Fall River, Mass., June 2, 1946; s. Harry and Sylvia Shirley (Davis) G.; m. Louise Beryl Schindler, Jan. 24, 1970; 1 child, Alexis Lynn. BSBA, NYU, 1968; JD, Bklyn. Law Sch., 1971. Bar: N.Y. 1972; CLU Am. Coll., 1975. Atty. Hanner, Fitzmaurice & Onorato, N.Y.C., 1971-72; dir., counsel, cons. on advanced underwriting The Mfrs. Life Ins. Co., Toronto, 1972-98; mng. gen. agt. for life settlements Viaticus, Inc., Chgo., 1999—; mng. gen. agt. Coventry Fin., Ft. Washington, Pa., 1999—. Mem. sales ideas com. Million Dollar Roundtable, Chgo., 1982-83; 4th ann. George M. Graves meml. lectr., 1991; mem. adv. bd. Keeping Current, 1999—; speaker on law, tax, life settlements, and advanced underwriting to various profl. groups, U.S., Can. Author: (tech. jour.) ManuBriefs. Mem. ABA, N.Y. State Bar Assn., Assn. for Advanced Life Underwriting (mem. bus. ins. and estate planning steering com. 1989-93), Internat. Platform Assn., Nat. Assn. Life Underwriters, Soc. of Fin. Svcs. Profls., NYU Alumni Assn., Stern Sch. Bus. Alumni Assn. Estate planning, Corporate taxation, Personal income taxation. Office: PO Box 183 7617 E Sunrise Trail Parker CO 80134-6915

GREENBERG, MYRON SILVER, lawyer; b. L.A., Oct. 17, 1945; s. Earl W. and Geri (Silver) G.; m. Shlomit Gross; children: David, Amy, Sophie, Benjamin. BSBA, UCLA, 1967; JD, 1970. Bar: Calif., 1971, U.S. Dist. Ct. (middle dist.) Calif. 1971, U.S. Tax Ct. 1977; cert. splst. in taxation law bd. legal specialization State Bar Calif.; CPA, Calif. Staff acct. Touche Ross & Co., L.A., 1970-71; assoc. Kaplan, Livingston, Goodwin, Berkowitz, & Selvin, Beverly Hills, Calif., 1971-74; ptnr. Myron S. Greenberg, a Profl. Corp., Larkspur, 1982—. Professorial lectr. tax. Golden Gate U.; instr. U. Calif., Berkeley, 1989—; mem. taxation law adv. commn. Calif. Bd. Legal Specialization, 1998—, chair, 2001. Author: California Attorney's Guide to Professional Corporations, 1977, 79; bd. editors UCLA Law Rev., 1969-70. Mem. San Anselmo Planning Commn., 1976-77; mem. adv. bd. cert. program personal fin. planning U. Calif., Berkeley, 1991—. Mem. AHA (bd. dirs. Marin county chpt. 1984-90, pres. 1988-89), ABA, AICPAs, L.A. County Bar Assn., Marin County (Calif.) Bar Assn. (bd. dirs. 1994-2001, pres. 1999), Real Estate Tax Inst. Calif. Cont. Edn. Bar (planning com.), Larkspur C. of C. (bd. dirs. 1985-87), Calif. Bd. Legal Specialization, 2001. Democrat. Jewish. Corporate taxation, Estate taxation, Personal income taxation. Office: # 205 700 Larkspur Landing Cir Larkspur CA 94939-1711 E-mail: msg@eplaw.com

GREENBERG, PHILIP ALAN, lawyer; b. Bklyn., Aug. 2, 1948; s. Harry and Jeannette (Nataf) G. BA cum laude, Bklyn. Coll., 1970; JD, N.Y.U., 1973. Bar: N.Y. 1974, U.S. Dist. Ct. (ea. and so. dists.) N.Y. 1975, U.S. Ct. Appeals (2d cir.) 1975, U.S. Supreme Ct. 1977 N.J. 1988. Assoc. Kamerman & Kamerman, N.Y.C., 1973-78, ptnr., 1978-82, Segal, Liling, Erlitz & Greenberg, N.Y.C., 1982, Segal, Liling & Greenberg, N.Y.C., 1982-84, Segal & Greenberg, N.Y.C., 1984; mng. ptnr. Segal, Post, DeMott & Crow, 1985, Segal, Greenberg, McDonald & Maher, N.Y.C., 1985-86, Segal, Greenberg & McDonald, N.Y.C., 1986-87, Segal & Greenberg, N.Y.C., 1987-93, Bizar & Martin, N.Y.C., 1993-95; ptnr. Wallman Greenberg Gasman & McKnight, 1995-2000, Law Offices of Philip A. Greenberg, N.Y.C., 2000—. Mem. faculty para legal Sobelsohn Sch. Trustee Congregation Emunath Israel, 1984—, chmn. law and ins. com., 1987—. Mem. ABA (com. mem., lit. mem.), N.Y. Bar Assn., Assn. of Bar of City of N.Y., Mason (Maimonides-Marshall #739, master), Masters & Wardens Assn. (past pres. 6th Manhattan 1990-91, sec. 2000—), Internat. Assoc. Tribune, Phi Alpha Delta. Democrat. Jewish. General civil litigation, General corporate, Family and matrimonial. Home: 7 Francisco Ave Little Falls NJ 07424-2316 Office: Law Offices of Philip A Greenberg 350 5th Ave Ste 7720 New York NY 10118 E-mail: lawman802@aol.com

GREENBERG, ROBERT JAY, law educator; b. N.Y.C., Nov. 22, 1959; s. Murray Louis and Jeanette (Adams) G.; m. Dafna Rena Fuerst, June 29, 1993; children: Ashira Esther, Aliza Gila, Leora Adina. BA, Yeshiva U., 1981, JD, 1984, LLM, 2000. Bar: N.Y. 1986, N.J. 2000, D.C. 2001, U.S. Dist. Ct. N.Y. (ea. and so. dists.) 1986, (no. and we. dists.) 2000, U.S. Dist. Ct. N.J., 2000, U.S. Ct. Appeals (2nd. cir.) 1998, U.S. Supreme Ct., 1989; lic. real estate broker, N.Y.; notary public, N.Y. Asst. to judge N.Y. Civil Ct., Bklyn., 1982; assoc. Simon, Meyrowitz, Meyrowitz and Schlussel, N.Y.C., 1983-86; instr. Bruriah High Sch. for Girls, Elizabeth, N.J., 1985-87; lectr. Nat. Acad. for Paralegal Studies, Mahwah, 1987-88; sr.

legal editor Matthew Bender and Co., Inc., N.Y.C., 1987-94. Adj. asst. prof. bus. law Yeshiva U., N.Y.C., 1994-98, asst. prof., 1998—; lectr. NYU Inst. Paralegal Studies, N.Y.C., 1994-2000, adj. assoc. prof., 2001—; instr. dept. paralegal studies Queens College CUNY, 1994—. Asst. to author: Judaism and Vegetarianism, Judaism and Global Survival. Lectr. in Jewish law, Young Israel of Staten Island, 1976-93, Congregation Beth Yehuda, Staten Island, 1980-93, Young Israel of Forest Hills, Queens, 1993—. Recipient Disting. Svc. award Congregation Beth Yehuda, 1988, Outstanding Svc. award, 1991. Mem. ABA, N.Y. State Bar Assn., N.Y. County Lawyers Assn. Democrat. Office: 6939 Yellowstone Blvd Apt 508 Forest Hills NY 11375-3734

GREENBERG, RONALD DAVID, lawyer, law educator; b. San Antonio, Sept. 9, 1939; s. Benjamin and Sylvia (Ghetlzer) G. BS, U. Tex., 1957; MBA, Harvard U., 1961, JD, 1964. Bar: N.Y., 1966, U.S. Dist. Ct. (ea. and so. dists.) N.Y. 1970, U.S. Ct. Appeals (2d cir.) 1975, U.S. Supreme Ct. 1975. Engring. lab. instr. U. Tex., 1957; engr. Redstone Arsenal, Army Ballistic Missile Agy., 1957; engr., bus. analyst Exxon Corp., N.Y.C., 1957-64; rsch. asst. Harvard Bus. Sch.; with Smithsonian Astrophys. Observatory and Ednl. Testing Svc., N.J., 1961-62; atty., engr. Allied Corp., N.Y.C., 1964-67; assoc. Arthur, Dry, Kalish, Taylor & Wood, 1967-69, Valicenti, Leighton, Reid & Pine, N.Y.C., 1969-70; instr. faculty Columbia U., 1972-81, adj. prof. bus. law and taxation, 1970-71, 82-98; of counsel Delson & Gordon, 1973-87; sole practitioner Harrison, N.Y., 1988—. Lectr., cons. AICPA, Inst. Internal Auditors, New Haven C. of C., Citibank, Mfrs. Hanover Trust Co., Harcourt, Brace, Jovanovich, Inc., Prudential-Bache, Drexel, Burnham & Lambert, E.F. Hutton; vol. instr. vol. income tax program, Columbia U., N.Y.C., 1991-92; vis. prof. Stanford U., Palo Alto, Calif., 1978, Harvard U., Boston, 1981. Author: Business Income Tax Materials, 1994; (with others) Business Organizations: Corporations, General Practice in New York, 1998, Business/Corporate Law and Practice, 2000; editor: The Compleat Lawyer, 1985-88, Tax Lawyer, 1982-95; editor in chief N.Y. Internat. Law Rev., 1988-91, chair adv. bd., 1992—; editor in chief Internat. Law Practicum, 1987-91; contbr. chpts. to books, articles to profl. jours. Cons. coun. City of N.Y., 1971-72, Manhattan C.C., 1974-76. Lt. USNR, 1957-59. Recipient Outstanding Prof. award Columbia U. Grad. Sch. Bus., 1973, MIT Fellowship Mech. Engring. Dept., 1959, Harvard U., Teagle Found., 1959-61; grantee Ford Found., 1977, Columbia U. Ctr. Internat. Studies, Sch. Internat. Pub. Affairs, 1992, Columbia Bus. Sch., 1976, 92, 93, 94. Mem. ABA (chmn. com. on taxation gen. practice sect. 1978-83, chmn. com. on corp. banking and bus. law. gen. practice sect. 1985-87, moderator, chair profl. edn. programs 1986, 87), ASME, NSPE, N.Y. State Bar Assn. (gen. practice sect., chmn. tax law com. 1983-92, chmn. bus. law com. 1985-88, internat. law & practice sect., chmn. pubs. com. 1988-91, coord. study com. on med. malpractice legislation, 1980-82), Assn. of Bar of City of N.Y., N.Y. Acad. Scis., Mensa, Rye Golf Club, Tau Beta Pi, Pi Tau Sigma, Phi Eta Sigma. General corporate, Private international, Corporate taxation. E-mail: rdgreenberg@hotmail.com

GREENBERG, STEVEN MOREY, lawyer; b. Jersey City, Apr. 9, 1949; s. Joseph and Rhoda (Weisenfeld) G. AB cum laude, Syracuse U., 1971; JD, U. Pa., 1974. Bar: N.J. 1974, U.S. Dist. Ct. N.J. 1974, N.Y. 1980, U.S. Dist. Ct. (so. dist.) N.Y. 1986, U.S. Dist. Ct. (ea. dist.) N.Y. 1986, U.S. Ct. Appeals (3d cir.) 1987, U.S. Ct. Fed. Claims 1989. Assoc. Carpenter, Bennett & Morrissey, Newark, 1974-77, Cole, Berman & Belsky, Rochelle Park, 1977-79; pvt. practice Hackensack, 1979-94; atty. Bergenfield (N.J.) Rent Leveling Bd., 1985-89, 92-93, 99, Bergenfield Planning Bd., 1993-96; ptnr. Greenberg & Marmorstein, Hackensack, N.J., 1994-97, Greenberg & Lanz, Hackensack, 1997—. Trustee, past chmn. youth activities com. Jewish Ctr. of Teaneck, NJ, 1978—, mem. exec. com., 1992—97, v.p., 1992—94, pres., 1994—97, Jewish Inst. Bioethics NY, 1998—; trustee United Jewish Appeal Fedn. Bergen County and N. Hudson, 1997—, exec. com., 2000—, chmn. planning and allocations com., 2000—, chmn. sub-com. Jewish educ., 1997—, chmn. com. campus youth servs., 1998—2000, v.p., 2001—; mem. N.J. Leadership Think Tank The Allen and Joan Bildner Ctr. Study of Jewish Life Rutgers Univ., 2001—; mem. adv. bd. dirs. jewish Home and Rehab. Ctr. Jersey City and River Vale, NJ, 1982—90; chmn. pers. com. Jewish Home and Rehab. Ctr. Jersey City and River Vale, 1986—, mem. various coms., 1986—; mem. gov. body, exec. com., chmn. pers. com. Jewish Home at Rockleigh , NJ, 1999—; trustee numerous orgs.; dir. Union for Traditional Judaism, United Jewish Appeal Fedn. Bergen County, others. Recipient Second Century award Jewish Theol. Sem. Am., 1988. Mem. ABA, N.J. Bar Assn., Bergen County Bar Assn., N.Y. State Bar Assn., Assn. Transp. Practitioners, Phi Kappa Phi, Pi Sigma Alpha. State civil litigation, Contracts commercial, General corporate. Home: 96 Westminster Ave Bergenfield NJ 07621-3916 Office: 2 University Plaza Hackensack NJ 07601-6202 E-mail: smg@greenberglanz.com

GREENBERG, STEWART GARY, lawyer; b. Flushing, N.Y., Feb. 2, 1955; s. Herman Leo and Constance Ann G.; m. Wendy L., Dec. 25, 1976; childre: Melissa, Jonathan, Jennifer, Michael. BA, NYU, 1976; JD, U. Miami, 1979. Bar: Fla. 1979, N.Y. 1986. Assoc. Rizzo & Koltun, Miami, Fla., 1976-83; ptnr. Koltun & Greenberg, 1983-93; atty. pvt. practice, 1993—. CEO, dir. Upscale Techs., Inc., Miami, 1996-97. Pres. Bet Shira Congregation, Miami, 1990-91, v.p., 1984-90; bd. dirs. Jewish Adoption & Foster Care Options, Sunrise, Fla., 1998—. Mem. Assn. Trial Lawyers Am., Acad. Fla. Trial Lawyers, Dade County Trial Lawyers Assn. Avocations: golf, sailing, fishing. Insurance, Personal injury, Product liability. Office: 11440 N Kendall Dr Ste 400 Miami FL 33176-1025

GREENBERGER, HOWARD LEROY, lawyer, educator; b. Pitts., July 16, 1929; s. Abraham Harry and Alice (Levine) G.; m. Bette Jo Bergad, June 15, 1959. BS magna cum laude, U. Pitts., 1951; JD cum laude, NYU, 1954; diploma in law (Fulbright scholar), Oxford (Eng.) U., 1955. Bar: Pa. 1955, D.C. 1954, N.Y. 1969, U.S. Supreme Ct. 1964. Law clk. U.S. Ct. Appeals (3d cir.), 1958-60; assoc. Kaufman & Kaufman, Pitts., 1960-61; assoc. prof. law NYU, 1961-65, prof., 1965—; assoc. dean NYU Sch. Law, 1968-72; dean and dir. Practising Law Inst., 1972-75; senator NYU, 1994—. Cons. in field.; v.p. Nat. Ctr. Para-Legal Tng.; pres. Early Am. Industries Assn., 1979-82; chmn. Commn. on Fgn. Grad. Study, AALS. Author: (with G. Cole) The Meriden Experiment, 1973; Study of the Quality of Continuing Legal Education in the U.S, 1980; contbr. articles to legal publs.; chmn. editorial bd. Jour. Legal Edn, 1974-77. Pres. N.Y.C. chpt. Am. Jewish Com., 1977-79, nat. bd. govs., 1979-85; vice chmn., gen. counsel Coalition to Free Soviet Jews, 1977—; trustee Law Ctr. Found., 1973-91, Am. Friends of Hebrew U. Jerusalem, 1986—; chair New Amsterdam dist. Boy Scouts Am., 1990—, Ctr. on Social Welfare Policy and Law, 1991—, Blaustein Inst. on Human Rights, 1992—. Capt. JAGC, U.S. Army, 1955-58. Recipient Alumni Meritorious Svc. award NYU, 1977, Stanley Isaacs award Am. Jewish Com., 1982, Gt. Tchr. award NYU, 1993, Friendship award Govt. of Germany, 1988, Robert B. McKay Disting. Svc. award N.Y.U. Sch. of Law, 1997, Great Tchr. award 1999; Root-Tilden grantee NYU, 1954. Fellow Am. Bar Found.; mem. ABA, Assn. of Bar of City of N.Y., N.Y. County Lawyers Assn. (bd. dirs. 1990—), Am. Law Inst., Assn. Am. Law Schs., NYU Club (pres. 1981-83, Masons, Sojourners, Order of Coif, Phi Epsilon Pi. Democrat. Jewish. Home: 4 Washington Square Vlg Apt 16 New York NY 10012-1936 Office: NYU Sch Law Vand Hall 40 Washington Sq S New York NY 10012-1005

GREENBERGER, I. MICHAEL, lawyer; b. Scranton, Pa., Oct. 30, 1945; s. David and Betty (Kabatchnick) G.; m. Marcia Devins, July 19, 1969; children: Sarah Devins, Anne Devins AB, Lafayette Coll., 1967; JD, U. Pa., 1970. Bar: D.C. 1971, U.S. Dist. Ct. D.C. 1971, U.S. Ct. Appeals (D.C. cir.) 1971, U.S. Supreme Ct. 1975. Law clk. to Judge Carl McGowan U.S. Ct. Appeals for D.C. Circuit, Washington, 1970-71; legis. asst. to U.S. Congresswoman Elizabeth Holtzman, 1972-73; atty., advisor Office of Criminal Justice, Office U.S. Atty. Gen., 1973; assoc. Shea & Gardner, Washington, 1973-77, ptnr., 1977-97; dir. divsn. of trading and markets U.S. Commodity Futures Trading Commn., 1997-99; counselor to U.S. Atty. Gen., 1999, prin. dep. assoc., atty. gen., 1999-2001. Vis. prof. U. Md. Law Sch., 2001—; bd. govs. D.C. Bar 1995-98, com. on legal ethics, 1993-95; mem. D.C. Cir. Adv. Com. on Procedures, 1983-89; mem. steering com. D.C. Pro Bono Partnership, 1994-97, Lafayette Coll. Leadership Coun., 1994-99; mediator office of cir. exec. U.S. Cts. for D.C., 1989—; mem. D.C. Cir. Jud. Conf., 1983—; legal cons. Software Engring. Inst., Carnegie-Mellon U., 1986-87; mem. steering com. Pres.'s Working Group on Fin. Mkts., 1997-99; mem. hedge fund task force Internat. Orgn. of Secs. Commrs., 1999. Editor-in-chief U. Pa. Law Rev., 1969-70; contbr. articles to profl. jours. Bd. dirs. Washington Legal Clinic for the Homeless, 1993-98, Am. Rivers, 1993-98, sec., 1995-98; bd. dirs. MIT Enterprise Forum Washington, 1984-87, Advanced Tech. Assn. Md., 1985-87, D.C. Prisoners' Legal Svc. Project, 1997-98. Mem. Am. Law Inst., Phi Beta Kappa. Contracts commercial, Intellectual property, Securities. Address: 2757 Brandywine St NW Washington DC 20008-1041 E-mail: greenbergerm@aol.com

GREENBLATT, MORTON HAROLD, retired assistant attorney general; b. Waterbury, Conn., Oct. 31, 1916; s. Samuel F. and Dorothy K. (Katz) G.; m. Evelyn Lipman, Oct. 26, 1947; children: Sarah Beth, Ruth, David. BA, Yale U., 1937; LLB, Harvard U., 1940. Bar: Conn. 1941, U.S. Dist. Ct. Conn. 1947, U.S. Supreme Ct. 1961, U.S. Ct. Appeals (7th cir.) 1971. Pvt. practice, Waterbury, Conn., 1941, 46-47; v.p., of counsel Ellmore Silver Co., Meriden, 1946-61; pvt. practice, 1961-67; asst. pros. atty. 7th Cir. Ct., 1962-66; asst. corp. counsel City of Meriden, 1966-81; asst. atty. gen. State of Conn., Hartford, 1982-86; of counsel Pomeranz, Orayton and Stabnich, 1986-96; ret., 1996. Sec. Meriden Planning Commn., 1953-55; pres. Meriden Bd. Edn., 1959-61; active Temple B'nai Abraham, 1946-85, pres., 1977-79; chmn. Solid Waste Mgmt. Commn. Branford, 1986-92, rep. policy bd. South Cen. Conn. Regional Water Dist., 1988-92; bd. assessment appeals Branford, 1987-91, 97—. Maj. USAAF, 1942-46. Mem. Meriden-Wallingford Bar Assn., Conn. Bar Assn., Am. Arbitration Assn., Conn. Assn. Mcpl. Attys. (treas.), New Haven County Bar Assn. Jewish. Home: 50 Turtle Bay Dr Branford CT 06405-4974

GREENE, ADDISON KENT, lawyer, accountant; b. Cardston, Alta., Can., Dec. 23, 1941; s. Addison Allen and Amy (Shipley) G.; m. Janice Hanks, Aug. 30, 1967; children: Lisa, Tiffany, Tyler, Darin. BS in Acctg., Brigham Young U., 1968; JD, U. Utah, 1973. Bar: Utah 1973, Nev. 1974, U.S. Tax Ct. 1979. Staff acct. Seidman and Seidman, Las Vegas, Nev., 1968-69, Peat Marwick Mitchell, Los Angeles, 1969-70; atty. Clark Greene & Assocs., Ltd., Las Vegas, 1973—. Instr. Nev. Bar Rev., Las Vegas, 1975-78; bd. dirs. Cumorah Credit Union. Mem. Citizen's for Responsible Gov't, Las Vegas, 1979—; asst. dist. com. mem. Boy Scouts Am., Las Vegas, 1985—. Mem. ABA, Utah Bar Assn., Nev. Bar Assn., Nev. Soc. CPA's (assoc.), Am. Assn., Pension Actuaries (assoc.). Republican. Mormon. Avocations: golf, snow skiing. Estate planning, Pension, profit-sharing, and employee benefits, Probate. Office: Clark Greene & Assocs Ltd 3770 Howard Hughes Pkwy Ste 195 Las Vegas NV 89109-0976

GREENE, IRA S. lawyer; b. N.Y.C., Nov. 21, 1946; s. Melvin and Syd (Semmelman) G.; m. Robin Colin, Dec. 29, 1973; children: Jessica, Alexander. BA, Syracuse U., 1968; postgrad., U. Buffalo, 1968-69; JD, N.Y. U., 1971. Bar: N.Y. 1972, U.S. Dist. Ct. (ea. dist.) N.Y. 1972, U.S. Ct. Appeals (2d cir.) 1974. Counsel Gainsburg, Gottlieb, Levitan & Cole, N.Y.C., 1982-84; ptnr. Gainsburg, Gottlieb, Levitan, Greene & Cole, 1984-86, Gainsburg, Greene & Hirsch, Purchase, N.Y., 1986-91, Squadron, Ellenoff, Plesent & Sheinfeld, N.Y.C., 1991—. Lectr. in field. Mem. Assn. Comml. Fin. Attys., Bank Lawyers Conf., Bankruptcy Lawyers Bar Assn., Assn. of Bar of City of N.Y. Banking, Bankruptcy, Contracts commercial. Office: Squadron Ellenoff Plesent & Sheinfeld 551 5th Ave Fl 22 New York NY 10176-0049

GREENE, JOHN JOSEPH, lawyer; b. Marshall, Tex., Mar. 19, 1946; s. William Henry and Camille Anne Greene. BA, U. Houston, 1969, MA, 1974; JD, South Tex. Coll., 1978. Bar: Tex. 1978, U.S. Supreme Ct. 1982. Asst. atty. City of Amarillo, Tex., 1978-79, Harris County, 1979-83; pvt. practice, 1983—; city atty. City of Conroe (Tex.), 1983-89; sr. asst. city atty. City of Austin (Tex.), 1990—. Capt. USAR, 1969-76. Decorated Bronze Star, Air Medal. Roman Catholic. Office: 114 W 7th St Ste 400 Austin TX 78701-3008

GREENE, JOHN THOMAS, judge; b. Salt Lake City, Nov. 28, 1929; s. John Thomas and Mary Agnes (Hindley) G.; m. Dorothy Kay Buchanan, Mar. 31, 1955; children: Thomas Buchanan Greene, John Buchanan Greene, Mary Kay Greene Platt. BA in Polit. Sci., U. Utah, 1952, JD, 1955. Bar: Utah 1955, U.S. Dist. Ct. (10th cir.) 1955, U.S. Supreme Ct. 1966. Pvt. practice, Salt Lake City, 1955-57; asst. U.S. atty., 1957-59; ptnr. Marr, Wilkins & Cannon (and successor firms), 1959-75; ptnr., pres., chmn. bd. dirs. Greene, Callister & Nebeker, 1975-85; judge U.S. Dist. Ct., 1985—. Author: (manual) American Mining Law, 1960; contbr. articles to profl. jours. Chmn. Salt Lake City Cmty. Coun., 1970-75, Utah State Bldg. Authority, Salt Lake City, 1980-85; Regent Utah State Bd. Higher Edn., Salt Lake City, 1982-86. Recipient Order of Coif U. Utah, 1955, Merit of Honor award, 1994, Utah Fed. Bar Disting. Svc. award, 1997. Fellow ABA Found. (life); ABA ho. of dels. 1972-92, bd. govs. 1987-91; mem. Dist. Judges Assn. (pres. 10th cir. 1998-2000), Utah Bar Assn. (pres. 1971-72, Judge of Yr. award 1995), Am. Law Inst. (life, panelist and lectr. 1980-85, advisor 1986-98); Phi Beta Kappa. Mormon. Avocations: travel, reading, tennis. Office: US Dist Ct 350 S Main St Ste 447 Salt Lake City UT 84101-2180 E-mail: JTGJR@hotmail.com

GREENE, NORMAN L. lawyer; b. Mt. Vernon, N.Y., Aug. 31, 1948; s. Martin M. and Vera R. Greene. AB, Columbia U., 1970; JD, NYU, 1974. Bar: N.Y. 1975, U.S. Supreme Ct., U.S. Ct. Appeals (2d, 3d and 5th cirs.), U.S. Dist. Cts. (so., ea. and no.) N.Y. Assoc. Paskus Gordon & Hyman, N.Y.C., 1974-76, Guggenheimer and Untermyer, N.Y.C., 1976-83, ptnr., 1983-85, Rosenman & Colin, N.Y.C.; now ptnr. Schoeman, Marsh & Updike. Mem. N.Y. State Uniform Law Commn. Contbr. articles to profl. jours. Mem. Assn. Bar City N.Y. (chmn. com. on lectures and continuing edn., former chmn. com. uniform state laws, former mem. product liability com.), Nat. Conf. Commrs. on Uniform State Laws (mem. standby com. on proposed tort reform, drafting com. model punitive damages act). Contracts commercial, Land use and zoning (including planning), Product liability. Office: Schoeman Marsh & Updike 60 E 42nd St Fl 39 New York NY 10165-0048

GREENE, ROBERT MICHAEL, lawyer; b. Buffalo, Jan. 14, 1945; s. Gerald Henry and Dorothy Louise (Doll) G.; m. Catherine Ellen Ostanski, Sept. 28, 1974; children: Amy, Megan, Timothy, Daniel. BA, Canisius Coll., 1966; JD, U. Notre Dame, 1969; LLM, NYU, 1971. Bar: N.Y. 1970, U.S. Dist. Ct. (we. dist.) N.Y. 1970, U.S. Ct. Appeals (2d cir.) 1970. Atty. VISTA, N.Y.C., 1969-71; assoc. Phillips, Lytle, Hitchcock, Blaine & Huber, Buffalo, 1971-75, ptnr., 1976-81, mng. ptnr., 1982-95, CEO, 1995—. Del. White House Conf. on Small Bus., 1986; bd. dirs. Fed. Home Loan Bank of N.Y., Cello Pack Corp., Gioia Mgmt., Inc. Author: Managing Partner 101: A Primer on Law Firm Leadership, 1990, Making Partner, A Guide for Law Firm Associates, 1992; co-author: Summary of Land Use Regulation in the State of New York and State Land Use Programs, 1974; editor: The Quality Pursuit: Assuring Standards in the Practice of Law, 1989; bd. editors Law Practice Mgmt. mag., 1989-93, articles editor, 1992-93. Trustee Canisius Coll., 1971-77, 92-2000, chmn. 1993-97; chmn. Shea's Ctr. for Performing Arts, Buffalo, 1981-85; pres. Zool. Soc. of Buffalo, 1987-92; chmn. Buffalo Philharm. Orch., 1997-99; pres. bd. Cath. Edn. Diocese of Buffalo, 1987-97; trustee Western N.Y. Pub. Broadcasting Assn., 1984—, chmn. 1993-96; Greater Buffalo Devel. Found., 1992-93; bd. dirs. Greater Buffalo Partnership, 1993-2000, sec. 1996-2000. Recipient LaSalle award Canisius Coll., 1980, Bd. Regents Dist. Citizens Achievement award, 1987, Disting. Alumni award 1991, Signum Fidei award St. Joseph's Collegiate Inst., 1990, Golden Marquee award Shea's Buffalo Theatre, 1984, Theodore Roosevelt Exemplary Citizen award, 1993, Person of Yr. award Notre Dame Club of Buffalo, 1994. Mem. N.Y. State Bar Assn., Erie County Bar Assn., U. Notre Dame Law Assn. (bd. dirs. 1988—), Buffalo Club (bd. dirs. 1997-2000), Country Club Buffalo. Democrat. Roman Catholic. General corporate, Health. Office: Phillips Lytle Hitchcock Blaine & Huber 3400 HSBC Ctr Buffalo NY 14203-2887 Fax: 716-852-6100. E-mail: rgreene@phillipslytle.com

GREENE, STEPHEN CRAIG, lawyer; b. Watertown, N.Y., Apr. 27, 1946; s. Harold Adelbert and Mildred Esther (Baker) G.; m. Nancy Jean Adams, Mar. 28, 1965; children: Kathryn, Stephen, Hilary. AB, Syracuse U., 1967, JD, 1970. Bar: N.Y. 1971, U.S. Tax Ct., 1977. Asst. to pres. SUNY, Oswego, 1970-73; assoc. firm Leyden E. Brown, 1973-75; ptnr. Brown and Greene, 1976-81; pvt. practice law, 1981—. Bd. dirs. Found. Corp. Legal Studies, Inc., 1968-70, United Way of Oswego County, Inc., 1985-88, Campbell's Point Assn., 1994-96, Oswego Hosp., 1981-2000, mem. exec. com., 1985-2000, pres., 1996-98; pres. Oswego Health, Inc., 1997—; town atty. Oswego, 1972—; counsel Oswego County Bd. Realtors, 1978—; mem. Oswego County Rep. com., 1974-85, counsel, 1980-83; gen. counsel Express Abstract Co., 1992-95. Recipient Inst. Counsel, 1970. Mem. ABA, N.Y. Bar Assn., Oswego County Bar Assn., Greater Oswego C. of C. (bd. dir. 1980-87), Oswego Country Club (counsel 1977-81), Masons, Shriners, Phi Delta Phi. General corporate, Probate, Real property. Home: 611 W 1st St Oswego NY 13126-4137 Office: 85 W Bridge St Oswego NY 13126-2011

GREENE, TIMOTHY GEDDES, lawyer; b. Lewiston, Idaho, May 12, 1939; s. George and Norma (Geddes) G.; m. Patricia Apcar, Sept. 13, 1969; children: Andrew Apcar, Jonathan Apcar. BA cum laude, U. Idaho, 1961; LLB, George Washington U., 1965. Bar: D.C., 1966, Tex., 1990. Exec v.p., gen. counsel Sallie Mae SEC, Washington, 1965-69, exec. asst. to the chmn., 1969-71; spl. asst. to gen. counsel U.S. Treasury Dept., 1971-73; sec. U.S. Emergency Loan Guarantee Bd., 1971-73; exec. v.p., gen. counsel Student Loan Mktg. Assn. Sallie Mae, 1973-79; prin. Eggers & Greene, Dallas, 1979-90, Stuart Mill Capital, Inc., Arlington, Va., 1997—. Bd. dirs. Wolf Trap Found. for the Performing Arts, Vienna, Va., 1991-97, NCCJ, 1993-98. Ford Found. fellow Brown U. Grad. Sch. Econs., 1961-62. Republican. Mem. LDS Ch. Avocations: sports, golf, tennis. General corporate, Legislative. Home: 1006 Bellview Rd Mc Lean VA 22102-1102

GREENEBAUM, LEONARD CHARLES, lawyer; b. Langgoens, Germany, Feb. 6, 1934; came to U.S. 1937, naturalized, 1952; s. Norbert and Henny Lisa (Greenbaum) G.; m. Barbara Rosendorf, Feb. 10, 1957; children: Beth Lynn, Cathy Sue, Steven I. BS cum laude in Commerce, Washington and Lee U., 1956, JD cum laude, 1959. Bar: D.C. 1959, Va. 1959., Md. 1965. Atty. Sachs, Greenebaum & Tayler and predecessor firms, Washington, 1959-64, ptnr., 1964-75, mng. ptnr., 1975-90; ptnr., D.C. coord. litigation Baker & Hostetler, 1990-95, firmwide litigation group chair, 1996-2000. Arbitrator Am. Arbitration Assn., Washington, 1975-2000; mem. Washington and Lee U. Law Coun. Chmn. bd. Davis Meml. Goodwill Industries, Washington, 1979-82; bd. dirs. Coun. for Ct. Excellence. Capt. U.S. Army, 1957. Recipient Svc. to Handicapped People award Davis Meml. Goodwill Industries, 1982. Fellow Am. Bar Found. (life); mem. D.C. Bar Assn., Md. Bar Assn., Bethesda (Md.) Country Club, Wild Dunes Club (Isle of Palms S.C.), Dunes West Club (Charleston, S.C.), Order of Coif, Phi Delta Phi. Jewish. Federal civil litigation, Criminal, General practice. Office: Baker & Hostetler 1050 Connecticut Ave NW Washington DC 20036-5304

GREENER, RALPH BERTRAM, lawyer; b. Rahway, N.J., Sept. 23, 1940; s. Ralph Bertram and Mary Ellen (Esch) G.; m. Jean Elizabeth Wilson, Mar. 21, 1964; children: Eric Wilson, Erin Hope, Nicholas Christian. BA, Wheaton Coll., 1962; JD, Duke U., 1968. Bar: Minn. 1969, U.S. Dist. Ct. 1969, U.S. Tax Ct. 1988. With Fredrikson & Byron P.A., Mpls., 1969—. Chmn. Minn. Lawyers Mutual Ins. Co., Mpls. 1981—; pres. Nat. Assn. of Bar-Related Ins. Cos., 1989-90. 1st Lt. USMCR, 1962-65. Recipient award of profl. excellence Minn. State Bar Assn., 1993. Mem. Rotary Club. General corporate, Insurance, Non-profit and tax-exempt organizations. Home: 1018 W Minnehaha Pky Minneapolis MN 55419-1161 Office: Fredrikson & Byron PA 1100 International Ctr 900 2nd Ave S Minneapolis MN 55402-3314 E-mail: rgreener@fredlaw.com

GREENFELD, ALEXANDER, lawyer; b. Wilmington, Del., Jan. 19, 1929; s. Abraham and Annie (Colton) G. BA, U. Del., 1949; LLB, U. Pa., 1953. Bar: D.C. 1953, Del. 1953, U.S. Ct. Appeals (D.C. cir.) 1953, U.S. Ct. Appeals (3d cir.). Assoc. Albert Simon, Wilmington, 1956; dep. atty. gen. Office Atty. Gen., 1957-58; pvt. practice, 1959-60, Washington, 1990-95; atty. FCC, 1960-61; U.S. atty. for Del., U.S. Dept. Justice, Wilmington, 1961-69; corp. counsel N.Y. Times Co., N.Y.C., 1972-79; prof. media law U. Calif., Berkeley, 1979-84, U. Md., College Park, 1984-89; legal rschr., Washington, 1992—. Sr. counsel Reports Commn. for Freedom of Press, Washington, 1984—; corp. counsel U.S. News & World Report, Washington, 1985-88; atty. U.S. Senate, Washington, 1992. Contbr. articles to legal jours. Pres. Del. Ednl. TV Assn., 1956, Del. chpt. Am. Assn. for UN, 1956; counsel to state chmn. Dem. Com. Del., 1970. Mem. Del. Bar Assn., D.C. Bar Assn. General civil litigation, Criminal, Libel. Home and Office: 4201 Butterworth Pl NW Apt 314 Washington DC 20016-4552

GREENFIELD, ESTER FRANCES, lawyer; b. Chgo., July 4, 1951; d. Aaron Arthur and Lea (Brody) Greenfield. BA, U. Chgo., 1973; JD, U. Ill., 1976. Bar: Ill. 1976, Wash. 1978, U.S. Dist. Ct. (no. dist.) Ill. 1976, U.S. Dist. Ct. (we. dist.) Wash. 1978. Law clk. U.S. Dist. Ct. Ill., Chgo., 1976-78; assoc. MacDonald, Hoague & Bayless, Seattle, 1978-83, dir., 1983—, mng. dir., 1993. Cooperating atty. ACLU, Seattle, 1982-86, Northwest Women's Law Ctr., Seattle, 1982-90; adj. prof. U. Puget Sound Law Sch., 1986-88. Sr. editor Am. Immigration Lawyers Assn., Immigration and Nationality Law Handbook. Pres. New Beginnings Shelter for Battered Women, Seattle, 1982-83; mem. Seattle Human Rights Commn., 1986-90. Recipient Gov.;s Disting. Vol. award Wash., 1983. Mem. Am. Immigration Lawyers Assn. (chmn. Wash. state chpt. 1986-87), Wash. State Bar Assn., Seattle-King County Bar Assn. Democrat. Immigration, naturalization, and customs. Home: 5955 49th Ave SW Seattle WA 98136-1326 Office: MacDonald Hoague & Bayless 705 2nd Ave Ste 1500 Seattle WA 98104-1796 E-mail: esterg@mhb.com

GREENFIELD, JAMES ROBERT, lawyer; b. Phila., Mar. 31, 1926; s. Milton and Katherine E. (Rosenberg) G.; m. Phyllis Chaplowe, Aug. 17, 1947 (dec. May 1978); m. Joyce MacDonald Koehler, Mar. 22, 1980. B.S., Bates Coll., 1947; J.D., Yale U., 1950. Bar: Conn. 1950, U.S. Dist. Ct. Conn. 1951, U.S. Ct. Appeals (2d cir.) 1966, U.S. Supreme Ct. 1959. Atty. Chaplowe & Greenfield, 1950-54, Markle & Greenfield, New Haven, 1954-58; sr. ptnr. Lander, Greenfield & Krick, 1958-80, Greenfield, Krick & Jacobs, New Haven, 1980-90, Greenfield & Murphy, New Haven, 1990-98; of counsel Tyler Cooper & Alcorn, 1998—. Lectr. U. Conn., 1966-67, 71-72, 75-76 Mem. editorial bd. Conn. Bar Jour, 1963-77. Pres. New Haven Symphony, 1976-78, Conn. Bar Found., 1976-77; bd. dirs. Nat. Jud. Coll., 1978-84. With USNR, 1944-46. Fellow Am. Bar Found.

(state chmn. 1985-90); mem. ABA (state del. 1975-78, bd. govs. 1978-81, ho. of dels. 1972-83, spl. com. on governance 1983-84, chmn. various coms.), Conn. Bar Assn. (pres. 1973-74, Disting. Profl. Svc. award 1989), Judicature Soc. (bd. dirs. 1983-87), Am. Law Inst., Am. Acad. Matrimonial Lawyers (pres. Conn. chpt. 1993-94), Internat. Acad. Matrimonial Lawyers, New Haven County Bar Assn. (pres. 1969-70, Lifetime Achievment award 1993), Yale Law Sch. Assn. (sec. 1977-80), Quinnipiack Club. Family and matrimonial. Office: Tyler Cooper & Alcorn 205 Church St New Haven CT 06510-1805 E-mail: greenfield@tylercooper.com

GREENFIELD, MICHAEL C. lawyer; b. Chgo., May 4, 1934; BA, U. Ill., 1955; JD, Northwestern U., 1957. Bar: Ill. 1957, Ind. 1982, U.S. Suprmee Ct. 1974. Asst. states atty. Cook County, Ill., 1957-58; ptnr. Asher, Gittler & Greenfield, Ltd., Chgo., 1959—, Asher, Gittler, Greenfield & D'Alba, Ltd., Chgo. Mem. inquiry bd. Ill. Supreme Ct. Disciplinary Commn., 1973-77, mem. hearing bd., 1978-94, 97—, vice chmn., 1984, chmn., 1985, mem. oversight comm., 1995-96. Mem. ABA, Ill. Bar Assn., Chgo. Bar Assn., Internat. Found. Employee Benefit Plans (bd. dirs. 1977-80, 85-88, 92-94). Labor, Pension, profit-sharing, and employee benefits. Office: Asher Gittler Greenfield & D'Alba Ltd 125 S Wacker Dr Ste 1100 Chicago IL 60606-4397 E-mail: mcg@ulaw.com

GREENLEAF, WALTER FRANKLIN, lawyer; b. Griffin, Ga., Sept. 21, 1946; BA, Mich. State U., 1968; MA, U. N.C., 1970; JD, U. Ala., 1973. Law clk. U.S. Dist. Ct., Birmingham, Ala., 1973-74; assoc. Sirote, Permutt, et al., 1975-76; assoc., then ptnr. Welbaum Guernsey, Hingston, Greenleaf & Gregory, LLP, Miami, Fla., 1976—. Construction, Insurance, Probate. Home: 417 Madeira Ave Miami FL 33134-4234 Office: Welbaum Guernsey Hingston Greenleaf & Gregory LLP 901 Ponce De Leon Blvd Miami FL 33134-3073

GREENLEE, JIM MING, prosecutor; BA, JD, U. Miss. Atty. Taylor and Whitehall, 1981—85; ptnr. Taylor, Jones, Alexander, Greenlee, Seale and Ryan, 1985—87; asst. U.S. atty. No. Dist. Miss. U.S. Dept. Justice, 1987—2001, U.S. atty., 2001—. Office: 800 Jefferson Ave Oxford MS 38655*

GREENSPAN, JEFFREY DOV, lawyer; b. Chgo., July 19, 1954; s. Philip and Sylvia (Haberman) G.; m. Eleanor Helen Goldman, Aug. 28, 1983. BS in Econs., U. Ill., Urbana, 1976; JD, Ill. Inst. Tech., 1979. Bar: Ill. 1979, U.S. Dist. Ct. (no. dist.) Ill. 1979, U.S. Ct. Appeals (7th cir.) 1979. Atty. Govs. Office Consumer Services, Chgo., 1978-80; asst. pub. defender Cook County Pub. Defenders Office, 1980-81; asst. corp. counsel Village of Skokie, Ill., 1981-91; of counsel Fioretti & Des Jardins, 1990-91; with Ancel, Glink, Diamond, Cope & Bush, P.C., 1991-99, Fioretti & Des Jardins, 1999-2001; gen. counsel, dir. land acquisition CorLands, 2001—. Sec., treas. Polit. Cons., Inc., Skokie, 1984—. Author polit. computer software Master Campaigner, 1984. Mem. Niles (Ill.) Twp. Dem. Orgn., 1976—; chmn. Niles Twp. Com. on Youth, 1982-85, TRY-Citizens for Drug Awareness, Niles, 1983-84; mem. Centereast Bd. Authority, 1998—; bd. dirs. Niles Twp. H.S., 1999—. Mem. Chgo. Bar Assn. (chmn. devel. of law com. 1990-91, chmn. local govt. law com. 1992-93). Environmental, Land use and zoning (including planning), Real property. Home: 9445 Keeler Ave Skokie IL 60076-1442 Office: 25 E Washington Ste 1650 Chicago IL 60603 E-mail: jgreenspan@corlands.org

GREENSPAN, LEON JOSEPH, lawyer; b. Phila., Feb. 10, 1932; s. Joseph and Minerva (Podolsky) G.; m. Irene Gordon, Nov. 2, 1958; children: Marjorie, David, Michael, Lisa. AB, Temple U., 1955, JD, 1958. Bar: N.Y. 1959, U.S. Supreme Ct. 1969, N.J. 1985, Fla. 1985, Pa. 1986, Conn. 1991. Pvt. practice law, White Plains, N.Y., 1959-64; ptnr. Greenspan and Aurnou, 1964-77, Greenspan, Jaffe & Rosenblatt, White Plains, 1987-91, Greenspan & Greenspan, White Plains, 1992—. Counsel Brown, Boston; lectr. Fla. Bar CLER Program, 1991, 92, 99; atty. Tarrytown (N.Y.) Housing Authority. Pres. Hebrew Inst., White Plains; vice chmn. ann. dinner NCCJ. Recipient Pres.'s award Union Orthodox Synagogues, 1982, Owl Club award Temple Univ., 2001; honoree Hebrew Inst., White Plains, 1983. Mem. ABA, Westchester County Bar Assn., White Plains Bar Assn., N.Y. State Trial Lawyers Assn., Criminal Cts. Bar Assn. Westchester County, N.J. Bar Assn. General civil litigation, Criminal, Taxation, general. Home: 14 Pinebrook Dr White Plains NY 10605-4713 Office: Greenspan & Greenspan 34 S Broadway 6th Fl White Plains NY 10601-4400

GREENSPAN, MICHAEL EVAN, lawyer; b. White Plains, N.Y., Jan. 18, 1967; s. Leon Joseph and Irene (Gordon) G.; m. Diane Gloria Blum, July 2, 1989; children: Daniel, Marc, Julia. BA magna cum laude, Temple U., 1988, JD, 1991. Bar: N.Y. 1992, U.S. Dist. Ct. (so. and ea. dists.) N.Y. 1992, U.S. Dist. Ct. Conn. 1992, U.S. Ct. Appeals (2d cir.) 1993, U.S. Ct. Appeals (11th cir.) 1996. Assoc. Greenspan, Jaffe & Rosenblatt, White Plains, 1991-92; ptnr. Greenspan & Greenspan, 1992—. Mem. com. civil practice laws and rules State Bar N.Y.; Temple U. del. Symposium on the Presidency, Washington, 1987. Mem. exec. com. Loucks Track & Field Games, White Plains, 1991—. Recipient Lewis F. Powell Jr. medallion Am. Coll. Trial Lawyers Assn., 1991, James J. Manderino award Phila. Trial Lawyers Assn., 1991. Mem. ATLA, N.Y. Trial Lawyers Assn., Barristers Soc., N.Y. State Bar Assn., Westchester County Bar Assn., White Plains Bar Assn., Westchester Track and Field and Cross-Country Ofcls. Orgn., Golden Key, Order of Omega, Phi Beta Kappa, Pi Sigma Alpha, Phi Alpha Theta, Delta Tau Delta. Republican. Jewish. Avocations: officiating high school track and field, race walking, basketball. General civil litigation, Criminal, Personal injury. Office: Greenspan & Greenspan 34 S Broadway Ste 605 White Plains NY 10601-4428 E-mail: GandGEsqs@aol.com

GREENSPON, BURTON EDWARD, lawyer; b. Hartford, Conn., Dec. 9, 1946; s. Bernard and Anne (Mitnick) G.; m. Donna Carol Wallins, June 4, 1971; children— Amy Susan, Marc Jeffrey. B.A. with honors, U. Conn., 1969; J.D., U. Va., 1972. Bar: Conn. 1972, U.S. Dist. Ct. Conn. 1974, N.Y. 1980. Sole practice, Hartford, 1973-74; asst. house counsel Sanitas Service Corp., Bethany, Conn., 1974-75; counsel Delaware North Cos., Inc., Buffalo, 1976-82, asst. gen. counsel, 1982-86; v.p., gen. counsel Synder Corp., 1986—; guest lectr. dept. communications SUNY-Buffalo, summer 1981. Mem. communal services commn. Jewish Fedn. Buffalo, 1983-85, mem. planning and allocation com. and young men's cabinet, 1985-86. Served to capt. USAR, 1972-79. Mem. Niagara Frontier Corp. Counsel Assn., Alpha Epsilon Pi, Phi Alpha Delta. Contracts commercial, General corporate, Real property. Home: 419 Wood Acres Dr East Amherst NY 14051-1669 Office: Snyder Corp 6 Fountain Plz # Plazalv Buffalo NY 14202-2211

GREENSPON, ROBERT ALAN, lawyer; b. Hartford, Conn., Apr. 17, 1947; s. George Arthur and Shirley Jean (Shelton) G.; m. Claire Alice Stone, Aug. 21, 1971; children: Colin Haynes, Alison Shelton. AB, Franklin and Marshall, 1969; JD, Columbia U., 1972. Bar: Conn. 1973, N.Y. 1998, U.S. Dist. Conn. 1973, U.S. Ct. Appeals (2d cir.) 1983. Assoc. Robinson & Cole, Hartford, Conn., 1972-78, ptnr., 1978-81, Stamford, Conn., 1981-86; sr. v.p., gen. counsel Guinness Peat Aviation Corp., Stamford, N.Y.C., N.Y.C., Shannon, Ireland, 1985-92; ptnr. Latham & Watkins, N.Y.C., 1992—. Contbr. articles to profl. jours. Mem. ABA (comml. fin. services, aircraft fin.), Conn. Bar Assn., N.Y. State Bar Assn., Internat. Bar Assn., Southwestern Legal Found. (bd. advisors internat. and comparative law ctr.). Federal civil litigation, Contracts commercial, Private international. Home: 49 Old Farm Rd Darien CT 06820-6119 Office: Latham & Watkins 885 3rd Ave Fl 10 New York NY 10022-4834

GREENSTEIN, RICHARD HENRY, lawyer; b. Newark, June 29, 1946; s. Jacob Harold and Florence G.; m. Irene Beth Polishuk, July 4, 1973; children: Suzanne Beth, Jonathan Henry. AB, Rutgers Coll., 1968; JD, Boston U., 1971. Bar: N.J. 1971, U.S. Dist. Ct. N.J. 1971, U.S. Supreme Ct. 1985. Law clk. Superior Ct. N.J., Elizabeth, 1971-72; asst. county prosecutor Union County Prosecutor, 1972-74; assoc. atty. Mandel, Wysoker, Sherman, et al, Perth Amboy, N.J., 1974-77, Fox and Fox, Newark, 1977-83; ptnr. Kein, Pollatschek & Greenstein, Union, N.J., 1983—. Atty. Young Astronauts N.J. Inc., 1989—; mem. ethics com. Supreme Ct. Dist. N.J., 1991-95. Lighting dir. Wash. Sch. PTA Show, Westfield, N.J., 1985-94. Mem. Exchange Club Union (pres.-elect, dir. 1983—). Jewish. Avocations: skiing, hiking, reading. Banking, General corporate, Land use and zoning (including planning). Home: 743 Saint Marks Ave Westfield NJ 07090-2035 Office: Kein Pollatschek & Greenstein 2042 Morris Ave Union NJ 07083-6028

GREENWALD, ANDREW ERIC, lawyer; b. N.Y.C., May 31, 1942; s. Harold and Lillian G.; m. Paula S., Aug. 20, 1967; children: Brooke Ellen, Karen Michelle. BS, U. Wis., 1964; JD, Georgetown U., 1967. Bar: D.C. 1968, Md. 1969, U.S. Ct. Appeals Md. 1969. Lawyer Nat. Labor Rels. Bd., Washington, 1967-68; asst. corp. counsel D.C. Govt., 1968-69; shareholder Joseph, Greenwald & Laake PA, Greenbelt, Md., 1969—. Past mem. dept. family and cmty. devel. U. Md. Contbr. articles to profl. jours. Active adv. com. Georgetown U. Continuing Legal Edn., 1991, Georgetown U. Law Ctr. Alumni Bd., 1995. Mem. ATLA (chmn. tort sect. 1985), ABA, Nat. Inst. Trial Advocacy, Am. Bd. Profl. Liability Attys., Am. Bd. Trial Advocates, William B. Bryant Inn, Am. Inns of Ct. General civil litigation, Personal injury, Product liability. Office: Joseph Greenwald & Laake PA 6404 Ivy Ln Ste 400 Greenbelt MD 20770-1407

GREENWOOD, DANN E. lawyer; b. Dickinson, N.D., Sept. 21, 1952; s. Lawrence E. and Joyce E. (Henley) G.; m. Debra K. Ableidinger, June 15, 1975; children: Jay, Lindsey, Paige. BSBA magna cum laude, U. N.D., 1974, JD, 1977. Bar: N.D. 1977, U.S. Dist. Ct. N.D. 1980. Ptnr. Greenwood, Greenwood & Greenwood and predecessor firms, Dickinson, 1977-98, Greenwood & Ramsey PLLP, 1998—. Mem. N.D. Supreme Ct. Disciplinary Bd., 1984—, Northern Lights Boy Scouts Council, Dickinson, 1985—; bd. dirs. Legal Assistance N.D., Bismarck, 1980-86. Mem. N.D. Bar Assn. (pres. 1998-99), Stark-Dunn County Bar Assn., N.D. Trial Lawyers Assn. (sec. 1983-84, treas. 1984-85, v.p. 1985-86, pres. 1987-88). Lutheran. Lodges: Kiwanis, Masons, Shriners, Elks. General civil litigation, Family and matrimonial, Personal injury. Home: PO Box 688 Dickinson ND 58602-0688 E-mail: shadyln@pop.ctctel.com, grlawdg@ndsupernet.com

GREER, CHARLES EUGENE, company executive, lawyer; b. Columbus, Ohio, Mar. 28, 1945; s. Earl E. Greer and Margaret I. Cavanass; 1 child, Erin Elizabeth. BS, Ind. U., 1972, JD, 1976. Bar: Ind. 1976. Pres. Willoughby Industries, Inc., Indpls., 1976-91, pres., CEO, 1991-93; ptnr. Ice Miller Donadio & Ryan, 1976-91; pres. ECM Corp., Indpls., 1993—, Loggins, Inc., Indpls., 1995—, bus. turnaround specialist, 1995—. Served to sgt. USAF, 1965-68, Vietnam. Mem. Ind. Bar Assn., Order of Coif, Phi Eta Sigma, Beta Gamma Sigma. Office: 5581 Sunset Ln Indianapolis IN 46228-1468

GREER, GORDON BRUCE, lawyer; b. Butler, Pa., Feb. 17, 1932; s. Samuel Walker and Winifred (Fletcher) G.; m. Nancy Linda Hannaford, June 14, 1959; children: Gordon Bruce, Alison Clark. BA, Harvard U., 1953, JD cum laude, 1959. Bar: Wis. 1959, Mass. 1961. Assoc. Foley, Sammond & Lardner, Milw., 1959-61; assoc. Bingham Dana LLP, Boston, 1961-67, ptnr., 1967-97, of counsel, 1997—. Lectr. Boston U. Sch. Law. Editor Harvard Law Rev. Vos. 71, 72. Maj. USAFR. Mem. Mass. Bar Assn., Boston Bar Assn., Brae Burn Country Club, Harvard Club (Boston). Republican. General corporate, Private international. Home: 45 Fieldmont Rd Belmont MA 02478-2606 Office: Bingham Dana LLP 150 Federal St Boston MA 02110-1713

GREER, RAYMOND WHITE, lawyer; b. Port Arthur, Tex., July 20, 1954; s. Mervyn Hardy Greer and Eva Nadine (White) Swain; m. Pamela V. Brown; children: Emily Ann, Sarah Kelly, Jonathan Collin. BA magna cum laude, Sam Houston State, 1977; JD, U. Houston, 1981. Assoc. Hoover, Cox & Shearer, Houston, 1980-83, Hinton & Morris, Houston, 1983-85; pvt. practice, 1985-86; prin. Morris & Greer, P.C., 1986-90, Raymond W. Greer & Assocs., P.C., Houston, 1990-98, Rigg & Greer, Houston, 1998—. Lectr. in field; mem. dist. 4 grievance com. State Bar Tex. Mem. adv. com. Enterprising Girls Scouts Beyond Bars, San Jacinto coun., 1996-98. Recipient Outstanding Alumnus award, Dept. English, Sam Houston U., 1986, Disting. Alumni Alpha Chi., 1996. Mem. ABA, State Bar Tex., Houston Bar Assn., Fort Bend County Bar Assn., Rotary (Houston chmn. fresh start com. 1997-98, dir. 1998-2001), Sam Houston State U. Alumni Assn. (2d v.p., chmn. membership com., combined charter and membership com. 1995-96, 1st v.p. 1996-97, pres. 1997-98). Avocations: golf, reading. General civil litigation, Consumer commercial, Family and matrimonial. Office: Rigg & Greer 13333 Southwest Fwy Ste 100 Sugar Land TX 77478-3545

GREEVEN, RAINER, lawyer; b. Berlin, Dec. 6, 1936; s. Wolf and Marianne Kolck G.; m. Regina Jouvin, June 13, 1964; children— Andrea, Cristina. B.A., Cornell U., 1959; LL.B., Columbia U., 1962. Bar: N.Y. 1964, U.S. Dist. Ct. (so. dist.) N.Y. 1964. Assoc., Lord, Day & Lord, N.Y.C., 1963-67; assoc. Burke & Burke, N.Y.C., 1967-70, ptnr., 1971-77; ptnr. Morris & McVeigh, N.Y.C., 1977-87, Greeven & Ercklentz, N.Y.C., 1987—; dir. Continental Can Co., N.Y.C., Smith Barney World Funds, Smith Barney Travelers Funds; pres. Stuart (Fla.) Land Co., 1985-89. Founder, bd. dirs. South Fork Land Found., 1974. Mem. ABA, N.Y. State Bar Assn., Assn. Bar of City of N.Y., Internat. Bar Assn. Clubs: Knickerbocker (N.Y.C.); Meadow (Southampton, N.Y.). General corporate, Oil, gas, and mineral, Private international. Home: 200 E 71st St New York NY 10021-5137 Office: Greeven & Ercklentz 630 5th Ave Ste 1905 New York NY 10111-0100

GREGG, JOHN PENNYPACKER, lawyer; b. Phila., May 25, 1947; s. William Pemberton and Sarah E. (High) G. AB, Trinity Coll., 1969; JD, Villanova U., 1974. Bar: Pa. 1974, U.S. Dist. Ct. (ea. dist.) Pa. 1974. Tchr., dir. student activities The Pennington (N.J.) Sch., 1969-71; atty. Pub. Defenders Office, Norristown, Pa., 1974—, High, Swartz, Roberts & Seidel, Norristown, 1975—. Bd. dirs. Rittenhouse Book Distbr. Inc., King of Prussia, Pa. Bd. dirs. Phila. Toboggan Co., Lansdale, 1987-91, Lower Merion Shared Housing Corp., Ardmore, Pa., 1991-95, Lower Merion Affordable Housing Corp., Narberth, Pa., 1995—, The Episcopal Acad., Merion, Pa., 1986-89; ann. giving com. Inglis House, Phila., 1991-92. Recipient Legion of Honor Chapel of the Four Chaplains, Phila., 1980, Harry L. Green Svc. award, 1990, Disting. Svc. award Episcopal Acad., 1990. Mem. Pa. Bar Assn., Montgomery Bar Assn. (com. chmn. 1991-94). Criminal, Family and matrimonial. Home: 635 Walnut Ln Haverford PA 19041-1225 Office: High Swartz Roberts & Seidel 40 E Airy St Norristown PA 19401-4803

GREGG, RICHARD, lawyer; b. Cananea, Mex., May 24, 1946; came to U.S., 1949; s. Enrique Francisco and Carolina (Rivas) G.; m. Jean Ann Pharris, June 2, 1973; 1 child, Jessica Raquel. BA, Calif. State U., 1972; JD, U. Calif., Davis, 1977. Bar: Calif. 1977, U.S. Dist. Ct. (ea. dist.) Calif. 1977, U.S. Dist. Ct. (no. dist.) Calif. 1984. Adminstrv. analyst City of Redondo Beach, Calif., 1972-74; ct. interpreter Yolo County Cts., 1975-79; legal asst. Calif. Dept. Motor Vehicles, Sacramento, 1976-77; ct. probate investigator Yolo County, 1978-83, ct. commr., 1983; ptnr. Lauricella & Gregg, Woodland, Calif., 1978-83; assoc. Boccado Law Firm, San Jose, 1983-89, Schneider & Wallerstein, San Jose, 1989-90, The Alexander Law Firm, San Jose, 1990-93, Zazueta & Gregg, San Jose, 1993-95, The Boccardo Law Firm, San Jose, 1995—. Editor Yolo County Bar Newsletter, 1981-83, Santa Clara County La Raza Lawyers Newsletter, 1984. Chmn. Safe Harbor Crisis House, Davis, Calif., 1982. 1st lt. U.S. Army, 1966-69, Vietnam. Decorated Air medal. Mem. Calif. State Bar Assn., Calif. Trial Lawyers Assn., Santa Clara County Bar Assn., Santa Clara County La Raza Lawyers Assn. (pres. 1986), Yolo County Bar Assn. (pres. 1983), La Raza Lawyers Assn. (pres. Santa Clara County chpt. 1986, TV moderator 1982), Toastmasters (pres. Sacramento 1982, pres. Woodland 1981, Dist. Toastmaster of Yr. 1982). Democrat. Federal civil litigation, State civil litigation, Personal injury. Office: Boccardo Law Firm 111 W Saint John St Fl 11 San Jose CA 95113-1113 E-mail: rgreggesq@msn.com

GREGOIRE, CHRISTINE O. state attorney general; b. Auburn, Wash. m. Michael Gregoire; 2 children. BA, U. Wash.; JD cum laude, Gonzaga U., 1977. Clerk, typist Wash. State Adult Probation/ Parole Office, Seattle, 1969; caseworker Wash. Dept. Social and Health Scis., Everett, 1974; asst. atty. gen. State of Wash., Spokane, 1977-81, sr. asst. atty. gen., 1981-82, dep. atty. gen. Olympia, 1982-88; dir. Wash. State Dept. Ecology, 1988-92; atty. gen. State of Wash., 1992—. Dir. Wash. State Dept. Ecology, 1988-92. Chair Puget Sound Water Quality Authority, 1990-92, Nat. Com. State Environ. Dirs., 1991-92, States/B.C. Oil Spill Task Force, 1989-92. Recipient Conservationist of Yr. award Trout Unlimited/N.w. Steelhead & Salmon Coun., 1994, Gov.'s Child Abuse Prevention award, 1996, 5th Annual Myra Bradwell award, 1997, Wyman award, 1997-98, Bd. of Gov.'s award for professionalism WSBA, 1997, Kick Butt award The Tobacco Free Coalition of Pierce County, 1997, award Wash. State Hosp. Assn., 1997, Citizen Activist award Gleitsman Found., 1998, Woman of Achievement award Assn. for Women in Comm. Matrix Table, 1999, WSTLA Pub. Justice award, 1999, Excellence in Pub. Health award Wash. State Assn. Local Pub. Health Ofcls., 1999, Women in Govt. award Good Housekeeping, 1999, Woman of Yr. award Am. Legion Aux., 1999, Spl. Recognition award Wash. State Nurses Assn., 2000; named one of 25 Most Influential Working Mothers, Working Mother mag., 2000. Mem. Nat. Assn. Attys. Gen. (consumer protection and environment com., energy com., children and the law subcom.). Office: Attorney Generals Office PO Box 40100 Olympia WA 98504*

GREGORY, GEORGE G. retired lawyer; b. Whittier, Calif., Dec. 21, 1932; BA, Harvard U., 1954, LLB, 1957. Bar: Calif. 1957, U.S. Supreme Ct. 1962. Assoc. Gibson, Dunn & Crutcher, L.A., 1957-65, ptnr., 1966-69; v.p., sec. Cordura Corp. (formerly Computing & Software), 1969-74; ptnr. Collins, Gregory & Rutter, 1974-77, Hughes, Hubbard & Reed, L.A., 1977-83; exec. v.p. H.F. Ahmanson & Co., 1983-97; ret., 1997. Mem. State Bar Calif., Phi Beta Kappa. Banking, General corporate, Real property.

GREGORY, LEWIS DEAN, trust company executive; b. Wichita, Kans., May 13, 1953; s. Harry Samuel III and Virginia Dorothy (Womer) G.; m. Laura Lorraine Davis, March 4, 1978; children: Paul Lewis, Erin Elizabeth. BA in Communications, U. Kans., Lawrence, 1975; MS in Journalism, U. Kans., 1976; JD, Washburn U., 1983. Bar: Kans. 1984, U.S. Dist. Ct. Kans. 1984. Cons. Delta Upsilon Frat., Inc., Indpls., 1975-76; mktg. rep. IBM, Kansas City, Mo., 1976-80; assoc. Hershberger, Patterson, Jones & Roth, Wichita, 1983-84; trust mktg. mgr. Bank IV Wichita, 1984-86; v.p., trust officer, sales mgr. BancOklahoma Trust Co., Tulsa, 1986-88, Boatmen's Trust Co., Kansas City, 1988-97; sr. v.p., dist. trust mgr. Merrill Lynch Trust Co., 1997—. Dir. Am. Heart Assn., Wichita, Kans., 1985-86; pres. YMCA Men's Club, Tulsa, 1987-88; del. Rep. Party, Tulsa, 1988; trustee Leukemia Soc., 1992-96. Mem. ABA, Kans. Bar Assn., Johnson County Bar Assn., Kansas City Met. Bar Assn., Estate Planning Soc. (bd. dirs. 1996-98), Kiwanis, Kans. Univ. Alumni Assn. (pres. Greater Kansas City chpt. 1994-96, nat. bd. dirs. 1997—), Delta Upsilon (Indpls. dir. 1987-90, dir. Kans. chpt. 1977-90). Republican. Methodist. Avocation: running. E-mail: lewis. Home: 12205 Aberdeen Rd Leawood KS 66209-1208 E-mail: gregory@ml.com

GREGORY, ROGER LEE, judge; b. Phila., July 17, 1953; s. George Lee and Fannie Mae (Washington) G.; m. Carla Eugenia Lewis, Sept. 6, 1980; children: Adriene Leigh, Rachel Leigh. BA, Va. State U., 1975; JD, U. Mich., 1978. Bar: Mich. 1978, Va. 1980, U.S. Ct. Appeals (6th cir.) 1978, U.S. Ct. Appeals (4th cir.) 1980. Assoc. atty. Butzel, Long, Gust, Klein & Van Zile, Detroit, 1978-80, Hunton & Williams, Richmond, Va., 1980-82; ptnr. Wilder & Gregory, 1982—2001; judge U.S. Ct. Appeals (4th cir.). Bd. visitors Va. Commonwealth U., Richmond, 1985—. Bd. dirs. Indsl. Devel. Authority, Richmond, 1984—, Richmond chpt. YMCA, 1989—. Me. Cen. Va. Legal Aid Soc. (exec. com.), Old Dominion Bar Assn. (pres.), Richmond Bar Assn. (bd. dirs.), Metro C. of C. (bd. dirs. 1989—), Alpha Kappa Mu, Alpha Mu Gamma. Baptist. Office: US Ct Appeals 4th cir 1100 E Main St Rm 212 Richmond VA 23219*

GREGORY, WILLIAM STANLEY, lawyer; b. Greenwood, Miss., Mar. 12, 1949; s. Carlyle and Charlotte Ruby (Richardson) G.; m. Vicki Sue Lovelady, Aug. 15, 1970. BS in Commerce and Bus. Adminstrn., U. Ala., 1971, MBA, 1973, JD, 1974. Bar: Ala. 1974, U.S. Dist. Ct. (mid. dist.) Ala. 1979, U.S. Ct. Appeals (5th cir.) 1979, U.S. Ct. Appeals (11th cir.) 1980, U.S. Tax Ct. 1979, U.S. Dist. Ct. (no. dist.) Ala. 1991. Assoc. Johnson, Thorington, North, Haskell & Slaughter, Montgomery, Ala., 1974-78; jr. ptnr. Johnson & Thorington, 1979-90; sr. ptnr. Thorington & Gregory, 1990-2000; ptnr. Bradley, Arant, Rose & White LLP, 2000—. Spl. asst. atty. gen. State of Ala., Montgomery, 1978-82; mem. taxpayer bill of rights drafting com. tax sect. Ala. State Bar, Montgomery, 1990-91. Pres. Montgomery Symphony Assn., 1980, 92, Highland Ave. Adult & Sr. Citizens Ctr., Montgomery, 1986-99; mem. Montgomery Estate Planning Coun. Capt. USAR, 1971-75. Mem. SAR, Kiwanis (v.p. 1989-90). Presbyterian. Avocation: music. General corporate, Municipal (including bonds), State and local taxation. Home: 8218 Wynlakes Blvd Montgomery AL 36117-5101 Office: 504 S Perry St Montgomery AL 36104-4616 E-mail: sgregory@barw.com

GREIF, JOSEPH, lawyer; b. N.Y.C., June 25, 1943; s. Jacob J. and Dorothy (Harrison) G.; m. Aline Bohm, Jan. 1, 1966; children: Jeffrey, Julie. BBA, U. Pitts., 1964; JD, NYU, 1967. Bar: N.Y. 1967, D.C. 1968, U.S. Tax Ct. 1986; CPA, Md., D.C. Instr. No. Va. C.C., Annandale, 1967-68; mgmt. cons. Computer Sci. Corp., Silver Spring, Md., 1967-70; tax mgr. Arthur Andersen & Co., Washington, 1970-75; sr. assoc. Ginsberg, Feldman & Bress, 1975-77; ptnr. Touche Ross & Co., 1977-84, McGuffie, Greif, Whitney & Handal, Washington, 1984-90; of counsel McNeily, Rosenfeld & Rubenstein, 1991-98, Neimark & Nadel, Ft. Lauderdale, Fla., 1998—, Washington, 1998—. Lectr. George Washington U. Grad. Sch. Bus., Washington, 1993-95. Co-author, editor: Managing Membership Societies, 1979; contbr. articles on taxation, comml. leasing, computer systems contracting, exec. compensation, exec. contracts to profl. jours. Bd. dirs. Nat. Assn. for Mental Health, Washington, 1973-75, Combined Health Appeal, Washington, 1980-81, Assn. Devel. Coun., Washington, 1987-89; task force mem. White House Task Force on Charitable Giving, Washington, 1979-80. Mem. AICPA (chmn. fed. tax divsn. task force on exempt orgns. 1983-86), ABA, D.C. Bar Assn., Am. Soc. Assn. Execs. (mem. govt. affairs and long range planning coms., Outstanding Svc. award, tech. sect. coun. 1996—), D.C. Inst. CPAs, Greater Washington Soc. Assn. Execs. (tech. task force 1994—), Computer Law Assn. Avocations: boating, squash. Home: 4701 Willard Ave Apt 207 Chevy Chase MD 20815-4607 Office: Neimark & Nadel 1730 K St NW Ste 304 Washington DC 20006 Fax: 202-204-2235

GREIG, BRIAN STROTHER, lawyer; b. Austin, Tex., Apr. 10, 1950; s. Ben Wayne Greig and Virginia Ann (Strother) Higgins; m. Jane Ann Sentilles, June 17, 1972; children: Travis Darden, Grace Hanna. BA, Washington and Lee U., 1972; JD, U. Tex., 1975. Bar: Tex. 1975, U.S. Dist. Ct. (ea. dist.) Tex. 1976, U.S. Ct. Appeals (5th cir.) 1976, U.S. Dist. Ct. (so. dist.) Tex. 1977, U.S. Dist. Ct. (we. dist.) Tex. 1980, U.S. Supreme Ct. 1980, U.S. Dist. Ct. (no. dist.) Tex. 1984, U.S. Ct. Appeals (11th cir.) 1984. Law clk. to chief judge U.S. Dist. Ct., Beaumont, Tex., 1975-76; sr. ptnr. Fulbright & Jaworski L.L.P., Austin, 1976—. Mem. Austin Tomorrow On-Going Goals Assembly Com., 1981; pres. Austin Mgmt. Lawyers Forum, 1987, 93. Editor-in-chief Tex. Assn. Bus. and C. of C. Employment Law Handbook; mem. editl. bd. Tex. Labor Letter, 1994-2001. Pres. Austin Lawyers and Accts. for Arts, 1981; trustee Laguna Gloria Art Mus., Austin, 1983-91, pres., 1989-90, chmn., 1990-91; bd. dirs. Zachary Scott Theater Ctr., Austin, 1981; mem. devel. bd. Inst. Texan Cultures, 1991-98; trustee Westminster Manor Health Facilities Corp. of Travis County, Tex., 1991-96, sec., 1995-96; trustee St. Stephen's Episcopal Sch., 1995-2001; pres. Austin Mus. Art, 1991-92, trustee, 1991-93. Fellow Tex. Bar Found. (life), Am. Coll. Labor and Employment Lawyers; mem. ABA, FBA, Am. Arbitration Assn. (employment adv. coun. 1995—), Tex. Bar Assn., Travis County Bar Assn., Tex. Commn. on Human Rights (chmn.'s task force), Tarry House Club, Headliners Club (trustee 1998—), Austin Assembly. Methodist. Avocations: hunting, fishing. General civil litigation, Construction, Labor. Office: Fulbright & Jaworski LLP 600 Congress Ave Ste 2400 Austin TX 78701-3271 E-mail: bgreig@fulbright.com

GREIGG, RONALD EDWIN, lawyer; b. Washington, June 29, 1946; s. Edwin E. and Helen Marie (Marcy) G.; m. Patricia Anne Crowe, June 5, 1968; children: Elizabeth, Rebecca. BBA, Am. U., 1969, MBA in Fin., 1971; JD, Stetson U., 1976. Registered patent atty.; bar: Fla. 1976, D.C. 1978, Va. 1985, U.S. Dist. Ct. (mid. dist.) Fla. 1976, U.S. Dist. Ct. (ea. dist.) Va. 1988, U.S. Ct. Appeals (D.C. cir.) 1979, U.S. Ct. Appeals (fed. cir.) 1982, U.S. Supreme Ct. 1980. Assoc. David E. De Serio, St. Petersburg, Fla., 1977-78, Edwin E. Greigg, Washington, 1979-82, Harris, Barrett & Dew, St. Petersburg, Fla., 1982-84; ptnr. Greigg & Greigg, Arlington, Va., 1984-99; mng. dir. Greigg & Greigg PLLC, Alexandria, 1999—. Author: A Guide to the FTC Franchise Disclosure Rule, 1979, Patent Infringement Damages, 1988. Mem. D.C. Bar Assn., Fla. Bar Assn., Va. Bar Assn., Inst. of Trademark Attys. (London), Internat. Trademark Assn., Phi Alpha Delta. Republican. Episcopalian. Avocations: sailing, classic cars. Computer, Patent, Trademark and copyright. Office: Greigg & Greigg PLLC #1 1423 Powhatan St Ste 1 Alexandria VA 22314-1389 Fax: 703-838-5554. E-mail: rgreigg@greigg.com

GREINER, STEPHEN W. lawyer; b. N.Y.C., Dec. 14, 1944; BA, Syracuse U., 1965; JD, NYU, 1968. Bar: N.Y. 1969. Mem. Willkie Farr & Gallagher, N.Y.C. Mem. Assn. Bar City N.Y. (sec. com. legal edn. and admissions 1977-80, mem. fed. legislation com. 1981-84), Order of Coif. Office: Willkie Farr & Gallagher 787 7th Ave New York NY 10019-6018 E-mail: sgreiner@willkie.com

GRENIER, EDWARD JOSEPH, JR. lawyer; b. N.Y.C., Nov. 26, 1933; s. Edward Joseph and Jane Veronica (Farrell) G.; m. Patricia J. Cederle, June 22, 1957; children: Victoria-Anne, Edward Joseph III, Peter C. BA summa cum laude, Manhattan Coll., N.Y.C., 1954; LLB magna cum laude, Harvard U., 1959. Bar: D.C. 1959, N.Y. 1983, U.S. Ct. Appeals (D.C. cir.) 1959, U.S. Ct. Mil. Appeals 1960, U.S. Ct. Appeals (3d cir.) 1966, U.S. Supreme Ct. 1966, U.S. Ct. Appeals (9th cir.) 1973, U.S. Ct. Appeals (10th cir.) 1977, U.S. Ct. Appeals (5th cir., 11th cir.) 1982. Law clk. U.S. Ct. Appeals (D.C. cir.), 1959-60; assoc. Covington & Burling, Wahsington, 1960-68; ptnr. Sutherland, Asbill & Brennan, 1968—. Speaker in field of energy related issues to profl. orgns. Contbr. articles in field to legal jours. Chmn. bd. trustees, mem. exec. com. Connelly Sch. Holy Child, Potomac, Md., 1976-85, trustee, 1976-88; bd. dirs. D.C. Recording for the Blind, Washington, 1977-89. 1st lt. USAF, 1954-56. Fellow Am. Bar Found.; mem. ABA (chmn. sec. adminstrv. law 1986-87, sec., del. Ho. of Dels. 1991-97), FBA, D.C. Bar Assn., Energy Bar Assn. (bd. dirs. 1986-89, 95-2001, v.p. 1995-96, pres.-elect 1996-97, pres. 1997-98, del. Ho. of Dels. 1999-2001), Am. Inns of Ct. (master of bench Prettyman-Leventhal Inn of Ct. 1988—, pres. 1991-92, counselor 1997-98), Met. Club. Congl. Country Club. FERC practice. Office: Sutherland Asbill & Brennan LLP 1275 Pennsylvania Ave NW Washington DC 20004-2415 E-mail: egrenier@sablaw.com

GRESHAM, ZANE OLIVER, lawyer; b. Mobile, Ala., Dec. 16, 1948; S. Charles Brandon and Lillian Ann (Oliver) G.; m. Marian Gan, Mar. 3, 1988. BA cum laude, Johns Hopkins U., 1970; JD magna cum laude, Northwestern U., 1973. Bar: Calif. 1973. Assoc. Morrison & Foerster, San Francisco, 1973-79, ptnr., 1980—, co-chair land use and environ. law group, 1987-97, co-chair airports and aviation law group, 1996—; chair Latin Am. Group, 1998—. Dir., v.p. (Latin Am.) Internat. Private Water Assn., 1999—; dir. Fromm Inst., 2000—. Cons. editor: Environ. Compliance and Litigation Strategy. Pres. San Francisco Forward, 1980-85; bd. dirs. Regional Inst. Bay Area, Richmond, Calif., 1989-95, Regional Parks Found., Oakland, Calif., 1992—, pres., 1995; spl. counsel Grace Cathedral, San Francisco, 1991—; dir., exec. v.p. Pan Am. Soc. Calif., 1995-97, pres. 1998—; vice chmn. Nat. Youth Sci. Found., 1997—. Mem. State Bar Calif., Urban Land Inst., Lambda Alpha. Avocations: opera, sketching. Private international, Land use and zoning (including planning). Office: Morrison & Foerster 425 Market St Ste 3100 San Francisco CA 94105-2482 E-mail: zgresham@mofo.com

GRETICK, ANTHONY LOUIS, lawyer, judge; b. Chgo., June 26, 1936; s. Anthony L. and Martha M. (Leinar) G.; m. Caroline Hogue, Dec. 30, 1955; children: Kirsten, David. AB, Northwestern U., 1958, JD, 1964. Bar: Ill. 1964, Ohio 1965, U.S. Supreme Ct. 1971. Assoc. Gebhard, Hogue, Dwyer & Wilson, 1964-67, ptnr., 1967-71; exec. asst. Atty. Gen. Ohio, 1971-72, also chief trial divsn. of spl. litigation sect., 1971-72; ptnr. Hogue, Dwyer, Gretick, Bish & Lowe, Bryan, Ohio, 1972-82, Gretick, Bish, Lowe & Roth, Bryan, 1982—. Pros. atty., Williams County, Ohio, 1977—94; judge gen. divsn. Ct. Common Pleas, Williams County, 1995—. Mem. Gov.'s Commn. on Prison Crowding, 1984—. Servd with USNR, 1958-75. Fellow Ohio Bar Found.; mem. Ohio Pros. Attys. Assn. (dir. 1978-94, pres. 1982). Home: 115 Deerfield Cir Bryan OH 43506-9368 Office: 1 Courthouse Sq Bryan OH 43506-1751

GREW, ROBERT RALPH, lawyer; b. Metamora, Ohio, Mar. 25, 1931; m. Anne Gano Bailey, Aug. 2, 1958. AB in Letters and Law, U. Mich., 1953, JD, 1955. Bar: Mich. 1955, N.Y. 1958. Assoc. Carter, Ledyard & Milburn, N.Y.C., 1957-68, ptnr., 1968-98, of counsel, 1999—. Lectr. legal problems in banking and in venture capital investments Practising Law Inst. Mem. Pilgrims of U.S., English Speaking Union (nat. v.p. 1989-93), Union Club, Lansdowne Club (London). Republican. Banking, General corporate, Real property. Office: Carter Ledyard & Milburn 2 Wall St New York NY 10005-2001 also: 1401 Eye I St NW Washington DC 20005 E-mail: grew@clm.com

GRIER, JEAN HEILMAN, lawyer; b. Rapid City, S.D., Jan. 27, 1947; d. Henry and Edna (Baum) Heilman; m. David Alan Grier, Mar. 20, 1986. BA in Polit. Sci., S.D. State U., 1969; JD, U. Minn., 1972; LLM, U. Wash., 1987. Bar: D.C., Minn. Asst. atty. gen. Minn. State Gov., St. Paul, 1972-83; sr. counsel trade agreements Dept. Commerce, Washington, 1987—. Adj. asst. prof. George Washington U., Washington, 1994-98. Mem. editl. bd. Pub. Procurement Law Rev.; contbr. articles to profl. jours. Fellow Fulbright Assn, 1985-86. Mem. ABA, Asia Soc., Washington Fgn. Law Soc., Japan-Am. Soc. Office: Dept Commerce 14th and Constitution Washington DC 20016 E-mail: jgrier@doc.gov

GRIER, PHILLIP MICHAEL, lawyer, former association executive; b. Quitman, Ga., Aug. 31, 1941; s. Phillip Moore and Helen Dale Parrish (Cottingham) G. BA, Furman U., 1963; JD, U. S.C., 1969. Bar: S.C. 1969, U.S. Dist. Ct. S.C. 1969, U.S. Ct. Appeals (4th cir.) 1972, U.S. Supreme Ct. 1978, U.S. Ct. Appeals (fed. cir.) 1985. Assoc. Haynsworth, Perry, Bryant, Marion & Johnstone, Greenville, S.C., 1969-70; asst. to pres. U. S.C., Columbia, 1969, staff counsel, 1970-74, gen. counsel, 1974-79; exec. dir., CEO Nat. Assn. Coll. and Univ. Attys., Washington, 1979-96; cons. Fulbright & Jaworski, 1996-2000. Bd. dirs. Am. Coun. Edn., 1992-94; mem. adv. bd. Ctr. for Constl. Studies, U. Notre Dame and Mercer U., 1981-92; mem. secretariat of nat. higher edn. orgns. Nat. Ctr. for Higher Edn., Washington, 1979-96. Author: (with Joseph P. O'Neill) Financing in a Period of Retrenchment: A Primer for Small Private Colleges, 1984. Editor: The Corporate Counsellors Deskbook (Non-Profit Organizations Supplement), 1983; editor, contbg. author: Legal Deskbook for Administrators of Independent Colleges and Universities, 1982, 83, 84; editor Coll. Law Digest, 1980-96; mem. editorial adv. com. West Pub. Co., St. Paul, 1980-96; editorial bd. Jour. Coll. and Univ. Law, U. Notre Dame, Ind., 1979-96. With U.S. Army, 1963-66, USAR, 1966-74. Mem. Order of St. John, Soc. Colonial Wars, St. Nicholas Soc. of N.Y., Mil. Order Fgn. Wars, Ancient and Honorable Artillery Co., City Tavern Club (bd. govs. 1992-2000, sec. 1994, v.p. 1996-99), Cosmos Club (legal affairs com. 1986-90, com. reciprocity 1988-90, house com. 1990-95, chmn. 1992-95). Administrative and regulatory, Federal civil litigation, General corporate.

GRIESA, THOMAS POOLE, federal judge; b. Kansas City, Mo., Oct. 11, 1930; s. Charles Henry and Stella Lusk (Bedell) G.; m. Christine Pollard Meyer, Jan. 5, 1963. A.B. cum laude, Harvard U., 1952; LL.B., Stanford U., 1958. Bar: Wash. 1958, N.Y. 1961. Atty. Justice Dept., 1958-60; with firm Symmers, Fish & Warner, N.Y.C., 1960-61, Davis Polk & Wardwell, N.Y.C., 1961-72, partner, 1970-72; judge U.S. Dist. Ct. So. Dist. N.Y., 1972—, chief judge, 1993-2000. Mem.: Stanford Law Rev., 1956-58. Bd. visitors Stanford Law Sch., 1982-84; bd. dir. Greater N.Y. Coun. Boy Scouts of Am. Served to lt. (j.g.) USCGR, 1952-54. Mem. Bar Assn. City N.Y., Union Club N.Y.C. Christian Scientist. Office: US Dist Ct US Courthouse 500 Pearl St New York NY 10007-1316

GRIEVE, GORDON THOMAS, lawyer; b. Brisbane, Queensland, Australia, July 13, 1956; s. Robert Blyth and Marjorie Ellis (Mitchell) G.; m. Suzanne Gloria Vera Jarosik, Mar. 17, 1990; children: Annabella, Imogene. BA, U. Queensland, 1978, LLB, 1979. Bar: Australia, Queensland, South Australia, NSW. Commr. corp. affairs Commn. Corp. Affairs South Australia, 1980-91; cons. Piper Alderman Lawyers, Adelaide, Australia, 1991-92, ptnr. Australia, 1992—. Mem. com. bus. law sect. Law Coun. Australia, 1994—. Editorial bd. Internat. Co. and Comml. Law Review, 2000. Bd. dirs. Australian Fin. Inst. Commn., 1992-99, dep. chmn., 1996-99. Administrative and regulatory, Contracts commercial, Mergers and acquisitions. Home: 3 Clifton St Sydney 2088 NSW Australia Office: Piper Alderman Level 23 Gov Macquarie Tower 1 Farrer Pl Sydney NSW 2000 Australia Office Fax: 612 92539900. E-mail: gandsgrieve@one.net.au, ggrieve@piper-alderman.com.au

GRIFF, HARRY, lawyer; b. Worcester, Mass., May 27, 1952; s. Joseph J. and Dorothy J. (Goldsmith) G.; m. Joan G. Garovoy, May 27, 1973; children: Joshua, Jordana. BA with high distinction, U. Mich., 1973, JD with distinction, 1977. Bar: Mich. 1977, Colo. 1982. Legal counsel Social Security Adminstrn., HHS, Balt., 1978-79; trial atty. U.S. Dept. Justice, Washington, 1979-81; assoc. Dufford, Waldeck, Ruland, Wise & Milburn, Grand Junction, Colo., 1981-83; atty. Harmon & Griff, P.C., Grand Junction, 1983-86; ptnr. Foster, Larson, Laiche & Griff, 1986-99, Griff, Larson, Laiche & Volkmann, 1999—; legal counsel Grand Junction br. NAACP, 1983-84, Walker Field, Colo. Pub. Airport Authority, Grand Junction, 1984-97. Mem. organizing com. pro bono program for Western Colo., Grand Junction, 1982-84; bd. dirs. Paradise Hills Homeowners Assn., Grand Junction, 1984-87, Grand Junction Jewish Cmty. Ctr., 1984-89, Colo. Lawyers Trust Acct. Found., 1986-92, Ptnrs., Inc., 1988-94, KPRN Pub. Radio Sta., 1989-91; active Mus. Western Colo., 1997—, Vol. Ctrl., 1996-99, Grand Valley Pub. Radio, 1995—. Mem. Assn. Trial Lawyers Am., ABA, Colo. Bar Assn., Mesa County Bar Assn. (bd. dirs. legal aid program 1984-89). Democrat. General civil litigation, Family and matrimonial, Personal injury. Home: 2636 Chestnut Dr Grand Junction CO 81506-8390 Office: Griff Larson Laiche & Volkmann 422 White Ave Fl 3 Grand Junction CO 81501-2555

GRIFFIN, CAMPBELL ARTHUR, JR. lawyer; b. Joplin, Mo., July 17, 1929; s. Campbell Arthur and Clara M. (Smith) G.; m. Margaret Ann Adams, Oct. 19, 1958; children: Campbell A., Laura Ann. BA, U. Mo., 1951, MA in Acctg., 1952; JD, U. Tex., 1957. Bar: Tex. 1957. Assoc. Vinson & Elkins, LLP, Houston, 1957-67, ptnr., 1968-92, mgmt. com., 1981-90, mng. ptnr., 1986-89. Adj. prof. adminstrv. sci. Jones Grad. Sch. Adminstrn., Rice U., 1992-94. Mem. ofcl. bd. Bethany Christian Ch., Houston, 1962-69, chmn. bd. elders, 1968; bd. dirs. Houston Pops Orch., 1982-87; councilman City of Hunters Creek Village, Tex., 1993-95; pres. Windcliff Property Owners Assn., Estes Park, Colo., 1995-96; active St. Martin's Episcopal Ch., Houston. Mem. Houston Bar Assn., State Bar Tex. (bus. law sect. chmn. 1974-75), Tex. Bus Law Found. (chmn. 1988-89, dir. 1988-2001), Houston Racquet Club (dir. 1992-94). General corporate, Securities.

GRIFFIN, DEBORAH S. lawyer; b. N.Y., Oct. 31, 1953; d. William Daniel and Cora Shelton; m. James Robert Griffin, Mar. 1, 1982 (div. Mar. 1985); children: Jamal C. Wright, Jonathan James Griffin. BA, U. Pa., 1976; JD, U. Mo., 1988. Atty. Supreme Ct. Pa., 1988—. Recipeint Shirley Chisholm award for leadership, Nat. Political Congress Black Women, Phila. chapt., 1999. Mem. Nat. Assn. Criminal Defense Attys., Phila. Bar Assn. Avocations: tennis, singing, gourmet cooking. Offce: 1315 Walnut St Ste 1105 Philadelphia PA 19107-4711 E-mail: eyedefendu@aol.com

GRIFFIN, MALVERN ULYSSES, lawyer; b. Huntsville, Ala., May 27, 1924; s. Malvern Ulysses and Harriett Bass Griffin; m. Linda Anne Condra, Dec. 10, 1963; children: Malvern U., Tracy Barton, Christopher Edward. BS in Law, U. Ala., 1950, LLB, 1951. Bar: Ala. 1951. Assoc. Griffin, Ford, Calwell & Ford, Huntsville, Ala., 1951-58; ptnr. Griffin & Griffin, 1958-90; pvt. practice, 1990—. Author: (anthology) Son of Dark and Stormy Night, 1980. Pres. Huntsville Lit. Assn., Burritt Mus. Bd., Huntsville; pres. bd. Boys and Girls Club of Am., Huntsville, 1960—. With USN, 1943-46. Recipient Appreciation award Huntsville Boys and Girls Club, 1990, 37 Yr. Svc. award, 1995, Svc. to Youth award, 1993, Man and Boy award, 1986, 89. Mem. Huntsville-Madison County Bar Assn. Presbyterian. Avocations: reading, hunting, fishing. Personal injury, Probate. Home: 308 Shadybrook Dr Huntsville AL 35801 Office: 200 Randolph Ave Huntsville AL 35801

GRIFFIN, PATRICK EDWARD, lawyer; b. Palos Verdes Estates, Calif., Nov. 14, 1969; BBA in Mktg., U. Houston, 1992; JD, Creighton U., 1997. Bar: Nebr., U.S. Dist. Ct. Nebr. 1997. Lectr. Inst. Paralegal Edn. Author: (manual) Effective Legal Writing for Paralegals, 1998. Mem. Assn. of Trial Lawyers of Am. (pres. Creighton chpt. 1996-97). Avocations: mountain biking, traveling, reading, running. General corporate, Landlord-tenant, Mergers and acquisitions. Office: 872 West Dodge #400 Omaha NE 68114

GRIFFIN, ROBERT PAUL, former United States senator, state supreme court justice; b. Detroit, Nov. 6, 1923; s. J.A. and Beulah M. G.; m. Marjorie J. Anderson, 1947; children— Paul Robert, Richard Allen, James Anderson, Martha Jill. AB, BS, Central Mich. U., 1947, LLD, 1963; JD, U. Mich., 1950, LLD, 1973; LL.D., Eastern Mich. U., 1969, Albion Coll., 1970, Western Mich. U., 1971, Grand Valley State Coll., 1971, Detroit Coll. Bus., 1972, Detroit Coll. Law, 1973; L.H.D., Hillsdale (Mich.) Coll., 1970; J.C.D., Rollins Coll., 1970; Ed.D., No. Mich. U., 1970; D. Pub. Service, Detroit Inst. Tech., 1971. Bar: Mich. 1950. Pvt. practice, Traverse City, Mich., 1950-56; mem. 85th-89th congresses from 9th Dist. Mich., Washington, 1957-66; mem. U.S. Senate from Mich., 1966-79; counsel Miller, Canfield, Paddock & Stone, Traverse City, 1979-86; assoc. justice Mich. Supreme Ct., Lansing, 1987-95. Trustee Gerald R. Ford Found. Served with inf. AUS, World War II, ETO. Named 1 of 10 Outstanding Young Men of Nation U.S. Jaycees, 1959 Mem. ABA, Mich. Bar Assn., D.C. Bar Assn., Kiwanis. E-mail: npgriffin@aol.com

GRIFFIN, RONALD CHARLES, law educator; b. Washington, Aug. 17, 1943; s. Roy John and Gwendolyn (Points) G.; m. Vicky Tredway, Nov. 26, 1967; children: David Ronald, Jason Roy, Meg Carrington. BS, Hampton Inst., 1965; JD, Howard U., 1968; LLM, U. Va., 1974. Bar: D.C. 1970, U.S. Supreme Ct. 1973. Asst. corp. counsel Govt. of D.C., 1970; asst. prof. law U. Oreg., 1974-78; assoc. prof. law Washburn U., Topeka, 1978-81, prof. law, 1981—. Vis. prof. U. Notre Dame, 1981-82; vis. scholar Faculty of Law Queen's U., Kingston, Ont., Can., 1988; dir. Council on Legal Ednl. Opportunity, Summer Inst., Great Plains Region, 1983; grievance examiner Midwest region EEOC, 1984-85; arbitrator consumer protection complaints Northeast Kans. Better Bus. Bur., 1989—; commr. Continuing Legal Edn. Commn. for Kans., 1989-95. Contbr. articles to legal jours. Capt. JAGC, U.S. Army, 1970-74. Named William O. Douglas Outstanding Prof. of Yr., 1985-86, 94-95; Rockefeller Found. grantee Howard U., 1965-68; fellow Parker Sch. Fgn. and Comparative Law, Columbia U., summer 1981; Kline sabbatical rsch. and study, Japan, 1985. Mem. ABA, Ctrl. States Law Sch. Assn. (pres.-elect 1987—), Phi Kappa Phi, Phi Beta Delta. Home: 3448 SW Birchwood Dr Topeka KS 66614-3214 Office: Washburn U Sch Law Topeka KS 66621

GRIFFIN, WILLIAM MELL, III, lawyer; b. Tallahassee, Feb. 1, 1957; s. William Mell Jr and June Winona (Cooper) G.; m. Kathryn Elizabeth Lawson, Dec. 11, 1993; children: William Mell IV, George Lawson. BA, U. Va., 1979; JD, So. Meth. U., 1982. Bar: Ark. 1982, U.S. Dist. Ct. (ea. and we. dists.) Ark. 1982, U.S. Ct. Appeals (8th cir.) 1983. Assoc. Friday, Eldredge & Clark, Little Rock, 1982-87, ptnr., 1987—. Mem. ABA (torts and ins. practice sect.), Am. Bd. Trial Advocates (advocate), Ark. Bar Assn., Pulaski County Bar Assn., William R. Overton Inn of Ct., Ark. Def. Counsel, Def. Rsch. Inst., Fedn. Ins. and Corp. Counsel, Leadership Greater Little Rock, Phi Delta Phi. Democrat. Avocations: running, hunting. Federal civil litigation, State civil litigation, Insurance. Home: 420 Midland St Little Rock AR 72205-4177 Office: Friday Eldredge & Clark 2000 1st Commercial Bldg Little Rock AR 72201

GRIFFITH, DONALD KENDALL, lawyer; b. Aurora, Ill., Feb. 4, 1933; s. Walter George and Mary Elizabeth G.; m. Susan Smykal, Aug. 4, 1962; children: Kay, Kendall. Grad. in history with honors, Culver Mil. Acad., 1951; BA, U. Ill., 1955, JD, 1958. Bar: Ill. 1958, U.S. Supreme Ct. 1973. Assoc. Hinshaw & Culbertson, Chgo., 1959-65, ptnr., 1965-98, of counsel, 1999—. Spl. asst. atty. gen. Ill., 1970-72; lectr. Ill. Inst. Continuing Legal Edn., 1970-90. Mem. editl. bd. Ill. Civil Practice After Trial, 1970; co-editor The Brief, 1975-83; contbg. author Civil Practice After Trial, 1984, 89; contbr. articles to legal jour. Trustee Lawrence Hall Youth Svcs., 1967—, v.p. for program, 1969-74; bd. dirs. Child Care Assn. Ill., 1970-73; mem. Lake Forest H.S. Bd. Edn., 1983-84. 2d lt. USAF, 1956. Fellow Am. Acad. Appellate Lawyers; mem. ABA (chmn. appellate advocacy com., tort and ins. practice sect. 1983-84), Ill. Bar Assn., Chgo. Bar Assn., Appellate Lawyers Assn. Ill. (pres. 1973-74), Def. Rsch. Inst., Ill. Def. Counsel, Chgo. Trial Lawyers Club, Univ. Club Chgo., Knollwood Club, Alpha Chi Rho (chpt. pres.), Phi Delta Phi. Federal civil litigation, State civil litigation, Insurance. Office: Hinshaw & Culbertson 222 N LaSalle St Ste 300 Chicago IL 60601-1081 E-mail: kgriffit@hinshawlaw.com

GRIFFITH, EDWARD, II, lawyer; b. Wilkes-Barre, Pa., Feb. 9, 1948; s. Edward Meredith Griffith and Jane (Randall) Griffith Jones; m. Linda Christine Scribner, Aug. 9, 1969 (div. July 1982); children: Trevor Scribner, Stewart Randall; m. Katherine Greybill, Oct. 24, 1987. BA, Lehigh U., 1970; JD, Dickinson Sch. Law, 1973. Bar: Pa. 1973, U.S. Dist. Ct. (ea. dist.) Pa. 1973, U.S. Ct. Appeal (3rd cir.) 1973, U.S. Supreme Ct. 1978. Ptnr. Duane, Morris & Heckscher LLP, Phila., 1973—. Cons. Pa. State Bd. Law Examiners, Phila, 1974-77. Master John E. Stively Inn of Ct.; mem. ABA, Pa. Bar Assn., Chester County Bar Assn., Def. Rsch. Inst., Pa. Def. Inst. Republican. Presbyterian. Avocations: hunting, fishing, gardening. General civil litigation, Insurance, Personal injury. Office: Duane Morris & Heckscher LLP Ste 100 200 Chesterfield Pkwy Malvern PA 19355-8704 E-mail: griffith@duanemorris.com

GRIFFITH, ELWIN JABEZ, lawyer, university administrator; b. Barbados, W.I., Mar. 2, 1938; came to U.S., 1956, naturalized, 1963; s. Vincent and Ermie G.; m. Norma Joyce Rollins, June 9, 1962; 1 child, Traci. BA, L.I. U., 1960; JD, Bklyn. Law Sch., 1963; LLM, NYU, 1964. Bar: N.Y. 1963. Asst. counsel Chase Manhattan Bank, N.Y.C., 1964-68, 68-71; asst. prof. law Cleveland Marshall Law Sch., Cleve. State U., 1968; asst. counsel Tchrs. Ins. and Annuity Assn., N.Y.C., 1971-72; asst. dean Drake U. Law Sch., 1972-73; assoc. prof. U. Cin., 1973-76, prof., 1976-78, assoc. dean, 1974-78; dean DePaul U. Law Sch., 1978-85; prof. Fla. State U. Coll. Law, Tallahassee, 1986—. Legal counsel Bedford-Stuyvesant Jaycees, 1968-71; vis. prof. colls.; vis. prof. Black Exch. program Nat. Urban League, 1970-75 Contbr. articles to law revs. Mem. ABA, N.Y. State Bar Assn. Office: Fla State U Coll Law Tallahassee FL 32306

GRIFFITH, RICHARD LATTIMORE, lawyer; b. Abilene, Tex., Feb. 8, 1939; s. Richard Allan and Lorayne (Lattimore) G.; m. Sarah Brewster, Feb. 16, 1963 (dec. 1979); 1 child, Grey; m. Betsy Brooks, Apr. 19, 1980. BA, U. Okla., 1961; LLB, U. Tex., 1963. Bar: Tex. 1965, U.S. Dist. Ct. (no. dist.) Tex. 1966, U.S. Ct. Appeals (5th cir.) 1981, U.S. Dist. Ct. (ea. dist.) Okla. 1976, U.S. Dist. Ct. (we. dist.) Okla. 1967. Ptnr., chmn. health law sect. Cantey & Hanger, Ft. Worth, 1965—. Chmn. Health Law Sect. State Bar of Tex., 1988. Co-author: Texas Hospital Law, 1988, 3d edit., 1998; contbr. articles to profl. jours. 1st lt. U.S. Army, 1963-65. Fellow Am. Coll. Trial Lawyers, Tex. Bar Found. (life); mem. Am. Bd. Trial Advocates (chpt. pres. 1985, state chmn. 1995), Def. Counsel Trial Acad. (faculty 1988), Coll. of State Bar of Tex., Tex. Assn. Def. Counsel (v.p. 1984-85, regional v.p. 1986-88, 92-93), Tarrant County Bar Assn., Tex. Bar Assn. Eldon Mahon Inn of Ct. (emeritus), Def. Rsch. Inst. (dir. 1993-2000). Avocations: gardening, fishing, hunting, cooking. General civil litigation, Health, Personal injury. Home: 6332 Curzon Ave Fort Worth TX 76116-4604 Office: Cantey & Hanger 2100 Burnett Plaza 801 Cherry St Ste 2100 Fort Worth TX 76102-6821

GRIFFITH, STEVEN FRANKLIN, SR. lawyer, real estate title insurance agent and investor; b. New Orleans, July 14, 1948; s. Hugh Franklin and Rose Marie (Teutone) G.; m. Mary Elizabeth McMillan Frank, Dec. 9, 1972; children: Steven Franklin Jr., Jason Franklin. BBA, Loyola U., New Orleans, 1970, JD, 1972. Bar: La. 1972, U.S. Dist. Ct. (ea. dist.) La. 1975, U.S. Ct. Appeals (5th cir.) 1975, U.S. Supreme Ct. 1976. With Law Offices

of Senator George T. Oubre, Norco, La., 1971-75; sole practice Destrehan, 1975—. Pres. 29th Jud. Dist. Bar Assn., 1999—. Fellow La. State Bar Found.; mem. ABA, ATLA, La. State Bar Assn. (ho. of dels. 1987—), La. Trial Lawyers Assn., New Orleans Trial Lawyers Assn., Fed. Bar Assn., St. Charles Parish Bar Assn. (pres. 1999—), Lions. Democrat. Insurance, Personal injury, Real property.

GRILLER, GORDON MOORE, legal administrator; b. Sioux City, Iowa, Feb. 3, 1944; s.Joseph Edwards and Arlene (Searles) G. m. Helen Mary Friederichs, aug. 20, 1966; children: Heather, Chad. BA in Political Sci., U. Minn., 1966, MA in Pub. Affairs, 1969. Mgnt. analyst Hennepin County Adminstr., Mpls., 1968-72; asst. court adminstr. Hennepin County Municipal Ct., 1972-77, ct. adminstr., 1977-78; judicial dist. adminstr. 2nd Dist. Ct. Minn., St. Paul, 1978-87; ct. adminstr. Superior Ct. Ariz., Phoenix, 1987—. Bd. dirs. Nat. Ctr. State Cts., 1997—, Nat. Conf. Metro Cts., 1999—. Vice-chmn. Bloomington Sch. Bd., Minn., 1981-87. Sgt. USAAF, 1968-74 Res. Recipient Warren E. Burger award Inst. Ct. Mgnt.,1988, Leadership Fellows award Bush Leadership Program, 1974. Mem. Nat. Assn. Trial Ct. Adminstrs.(pres. 1983-84), Ariz. Ct. Assn., Nat. Assn Ct. Mgmt., Am. Judicature Soc., (bd. dirs. 1997—). Lutheran. Avocations: running, kyaking, racquetball, scuba diving. Home: 8507 E San Jacinto Dr Scottsdale AZ 85258-2576 Office: Superior Ct Ariz 201 W Jefferson St Fl 4 Phoenix AZ 85003-2243

GRIMES, STEPHEN HENRY, retired state supreme court justice; b. Peoria, Ill., Nov. 17, 1927; s. Henry Holbrook and June (Kellar) G.; m. Mary Fay Fulghum, Dec. 29, 1951; children: Gay Diane, Mary June, Sue Anne, Sheri Lynn. Student, Fla. So. Coll., 1946-47; BS in Bus. Adminstrn. with honors, U. Fla., 1951, LLB with honors, 1954; LLD (hon.), Stetson U., 1980. Bar: Fla. 1954, U.S. Dist. Ct. (no. and so. dists.) 1954, U.S. Ct. Appeals (5th cir.) 1965, U.S. Supreme Ct. 1972. Since practiced in, Bartow, Fla.; ptnr. Holland and Knight and predecessor firm, Tallahassee, 1954-73, 98—; judge Ct. Appeal 2d Dist. Fla., Lakeland, Fla., 1973-87, chief judge, 1978-80; chmn. Conf. Fla. Dist. Cts. Appeal, 1978-80; justice Fla. Supreme Ct., Tallahassee, 1987-97, chief justice, 1994-96; chair Article V Task Force, 1994-96, Supreme Ct. Workload Study Commn., 2000-2001. Mem. Fla. Jud. Qualification Commn., 1982-86, vice chmn., 1985-86; chmn. Fla. Jud. Coun., 1989-94. Contbr. articles U. Fla. Law Rev., 1951, 54. Bd. dirs. Bartow Meml. Hosp., 1958-61, Bartow Library, 1968-78; trustee Polk Community Coll., Winter Haven, Fla., 1967-70, chmn., 1969-70; bd. govs. Polk Pub. Mus., 1976-97; bd. dirs. Fla. History Found. Lt. (j.g.) USN, 1951-53. Fellow Am. Coll. Trial Lawyers; mem. ABA, Fla. Bar Assn. (bd. govs. jr. bar 1956-58, bd. dirs. trial lawyers sect. 1967-69, sec. 1969, vice chmn. appellate rules com. 1976-77, vice chmn. tort litigation rev. commn. 1985-86), 10th Cir. Bar Assn. (pres. 1966), Am. Judicature Soc., Bartow C. of C. (pres. 1964), Rotary (dist. gov. 1960-61). Episcopalian (sr. warden 1964-65, 77). Office: Holland & Knight LLP 315 S Calhoun St Tallahassee FL 32301-1856

GRIMSHAW, LYNN ALAN, lawyer; b. Portsmouth, Ohio, Sept. 14, 1949; s. Vaughn Edwin and Margaret (Jordan) G.; m. Beverly Gay Moore, Oct. 21, 1978; children: Jordan, Stuart. BS in Indsl. Mgmt., Purdue U., 1971; JD, U. Cin., 1975. Bar: Ohio 1978. Atty. Gerlach & Grimshaw, Portsmouth, 1975-76; pros. atty. Scioto County, 1977—. Mem. Gov.'s Organized Crime Cons. Com., Ohio, 1984. Chmn. Scioto County Dem. Party, 1980-81. Mem. Ohio Pros. Atty. Assn. (pres. 1985), Nat. Dist. Atty.'s Assn. (bd. dirs. 1987), Scioto County Bar Assn. (pres. 1997), Kiwanis. Democrat. Methodist. Office: Scioto County Courthouse 6th and Courts Sts Portsmouth OH 45662

GRINNELL, JOSEPH FOX, financial company executive; b. July 4, 1923; s. Robert L. and Mary King G.; m. Marjorie Volwiler, Aug. 24, 1946; children: Stephen F., Christine K. Burcham, James W. BA, Yale U., 1945; JD, Northwestern U., 1949. Bar: Ill. 1949, U.S. Dist. Ct. (no. dist.) Ill. 1949, Minn. 1954. Assoc. Winston-Strawn, Chgo., 1949-54; sr. v.p. law Investors Diversified Svcs., Mpls., 1954-83; of counsel Pepin Dayton Herman Graham & Getts, 1983-87. Bd. dirs. Guthrie Theater, Mpls., 1970-71, Minn. Orch. Assn., Mpls., 1976-78; bd. dirs., chmn. Minn. Pollution Control Agy., Mpls., 1973-81. Served to lt. (j.g.) USN, 1942-46, PTO. Democrat. Presbyterian. Home: 6101 Idylwood Dr Minneapolis MN 55436-1232

GRISCHKE, ALAN EDWARD, lawyer; b. Milw., Mar. 2, 1945; s. Rupert Edward and Velma Pearl (Springer) G.; m. Christine A. Bremer, July 4, 1981. BS, U. Wis., Stevens Point, 1968; postgrad., U. Miami, Fla., 1969; JD, Loyola U., Chgo., 1971. Bar: Ill. 1971, Wis. 1982, U.S. Dist. Ct. (no. dist.) Ill. 1971, U.S. Dist. Ct. (we. and ea. dist.) Wis. 1982, U.S. Ct. Appeals (7th cir.) 1979, U.S. Supreme Ct. 1979; cert. civil trial specialist. Asst. atty. gen. Ill. Atty. Gens. Office, Chgo., 1971-73; regional counsel Ill. Dept. Mental Health, 1973-75, gen. counsel, 1975-80; ptnr. Grischke & Assocs., Ltd., 1980-82; assoc. Trembath, Hess, Miller & Seidl, Wausau, Wis., 1982; ptnr. Mallery Law Offices SC, 1983-85; pvt. practice, 1985-89; pres. Grischhke & Bremer LLSC, 1989—. Adj. prof. John Marshall Law Sch., Chgo., 1975-81; faculty U. Ill., Abraham Lincoln Sch. Medicine, Chgo., 1976-80, Loyola U., Stritch Sch. Medicine, Chgo., 1980-82; chmn. Midwest Consortium Mental Health Attys., 1975-76, Nat. Assn. State Mental Health Attys., 1976-80. Mem. ABA (sustaining), Am. Trial Lawyers Assn., Wis. State Bar Assn. (bd. profl. responsibility dist. 16 1990-98), Marathon County Bar Assn., Wis. Acad. Trial Lawyers (sustaining, bd. dirs. 1986-88). State civil litigation, Personal injury, Product liability. Home: 608 Excel Dr Wausau WI 54401-2165 Office: PO Box 847 1400 Merrill Ave Wausau WI 54402-0847 E-mail: aeg@grischkeandbremer.com

GRISHAM, RICHARD BOND, lawyer, retired oilfield service company executive; b. Dallas, Feb. 18, 1945; s. Nellson Norman and Patricia Jean (Ritchie) G.; children: Jeffrey Claassen, Rebeccah Claassen, Blair. BA in Math., Centenary Coll., 1967; JD, So. Meth. U., 1972. Bar: Tex. 1972. V.p. legal Halliburton Energy Svcs., Houston, 1993-2000; ret., 2000. Mem. State Bar Tex. Nuclear power, Private international. E-mail: meowbark@houston.rr.com

GRIZANTI, ANTHONY J. lawyer; b. Cin., Jan. 27, 1949; s. Anthony Joseph and Mary Emma (Schroeder) G.; m. Judith L. Grizanti, July 26, 1969; children: Virginia A. Madonna, Christina E., Anthony J. III, Michael F. BA, Canisius Coll., 1971; MBA, SUNY, Buffalo, 1980; JD, Syracuse U., 1984. Bar: N.Y. 1985, Pa. 1990, U.S. Dist. Ct. (no. dist.) N.Y. 1986, U.S. Ct. Claims 1985, U.S. Supreme Ct. 1991. V.p. Grizanti Music Co., Inc., Niagara Falls, N.Y., 1972—; atty. advisor U.S. Tax Ct., Washington, 1984-85; ptnr. Scolaro, Shulman, Cohen, Lawler & Burstein, P.C., Syracuse, N.Y., 1985—. Dir. Syracuse Symphony Orch., 1993-98. Mem. Estate Planning Coun. Ctrl. N.Y. (pres. 1996-97), Performing Arts Medicine Assn. (pres. 1994-97). Estate planning, Probate, Estate taxation. Office: Scolaro Shulman Cohen Lawler & Burstein PC 90 Presidential Plz Ste 500 Syracuse NY 13202-2200

GRODD, LESLIE ERIC, lawyer; b. N.Y.C., Feb. 18, 1946; s. Abe and Celia G.; m. Judith Cota, June 18, 1967; children: Elissa, Katharine, Matthew. BA, U. Vt., 1966; JD, St. John's U., 1969; MBA, NYU, 1971. Bar: N.Y. 1969, Conn. 1974, D.C. 1982, U.S. Dist. Ct. Conn. 1975, U.S. Tax Ct. 1980, U.S. Supreme Ct. 1975. With tax dept. Coopers & Lybrand, N.Y.C., 1969-74; prin. Blazzard, Grodd & Hasenauer, PC, Westport, Conn., 1974—. Mem. ABA (chair closely held bus. com., tax sect. 1998-99, vice chair 2000-2001, chair 2001—), AICPA, Conn. Soc. CPAs (chmn. fed. tax com. 1988-89), Conn. Bar Assn. (chmn. tax sect. 1991-94), N.Y. Bar Assn., D.C. Bar Assn. Jewish. Corporate taxation, Estate taxation, Personal income taxation. Office: Blazzard Grodd & Hasenauer PC 943 Post Rd E PO Box 5108 Westport CT 06880-5399 E-mail: lgrodd@aol.com, leslie.grodd@bghpc.com

GRODNER, GEOFFREY MITCHELL, lawyer; b. Houston, Aug. 22, 1950; s. Murray and Leah (Cohen) G.; m. Lorelei Meeker, Dec. 22, 1974; 1 child, Andrew Meeker. B.A., Ind. U., 1972, J.D. cum laude, 1975. Bar: Ind. 1975, U.S. Dist. Ct. (so. dist.) Ind. 1975, U.S. Ct. Appeals (7th cir.) 1978. Assoc., Rogers Wilder & McDonald, Bloomington, Ind., 1975; counsel Subcom. on Constl. Amendments, U.S. Senate, Washington, 1975-76; ptnr. Rogers McDonald & Grodner, Bloomington, 1977-81, Grodner & Fore, Bloomington, 1981-85; sole practice, Bloomington, 1985— ; pres., dir. Westside Mgmt., Inc., Bloomington, 1983— ; ptnr. gen. Devel. Group, Bloomington, 1983— ; dir. Bloomington Datsun, Inc., Chmn., bd. dirs. Bloomington Pub. Transp. Corp., 1982— ; mem. Bloomington Ind. Bd. Pub. Works, 1972-75; pres., bd. dirs. Girl's Club, Bloomington, 1978-82. Mem. Monroe County Bar Assn., Ind. Bar Assn. Democrat. State civil litigation, General corporate, Personal injury. Home: 705 S Meadowbrook Dr Bloomington IN 47401-4230

GROETZINGER, JON, JR. lawyer, consumer products executive; b. N.Y.C., Feb. 12, 1949; s. Jon M. and Elinor Groetzinger; m. Carol Marie O'Connor, Jan. 24, 1981; 3 children. AB magna cum laude, Middlebury Coll., 1971; JD in Internat. Legal Affairs, Cornell U., 1974. Bar: N.H. 1974, N.Y. 1980, Mass. 1980, Fla. 1982, Md. 1985, Ohio 1991, U.S. Supreme Ct. 1980. Assoc. McLane, Graf, Greene, Raulerson and Middleton, P.A., Manchester, N.H., 1974-76; atty. John A. Gray Law Offices, Boston, 1978-81; pvt. practice N.H., Boston, 1977-81; chief internat. counsel Martin Marietta Corp., Bethesda, Md., 1981-88; pres., exec. v.p. Martin Marietta Overseas Corp., 1984-88; sr. v.p., gen. counsel, corp. sec. Am. Greetings Corp., Cleve., 1988—. Chmn. internat. adv. bd. Case Western Res. U. Law Sch., 1995—, disting. adj. prof., 1998—. Trustee Middlebury (Vt.) Coll., 1974-76, mem. bd. overseers, 1977—; bd. dirs. Cleve. Coun. on World Affairs, 1991-98, 99—, chmn. strategic planning com., 2000—, mem. exec. com., 2000—; bd. dirs. Can.-U.S. Law Inst.; mem. exec. com. The Conf. Bds. Coun. Chief Legal Officers, 1996—, membership chmn., 1997-98, program chair, 1999-2000, coun. chmn., 2000—; chmn. Greater Cleve. Gen. Counsels, 2000—. Mem. ABA, N.H. Bar Assn., Fla. Bar Assn., Ohio Bar Assn., Cleve. Bar Assn., Md. Bar Assn., N.Y. Bar Assn., Mass. Bar Assn., Supreme Ct. Bar Assn., Am. Soc. Corp. Secs. (sec. Ohio chpt. 1995—, v.p. 1996-97, pres. 1997-98), Soc. of Benchers, Phi Beta Kappa. Contracts commercial, General corporate, Private international. Office: Am Greetings Corp 1 American Rd Cleveland OH 44144-2301 E-mail: jgroetzi@yahoo.com

GROGAN, LYNN LANGLEY, lawyer; b. Rockingham, N.C., Jan. 16, 1957; d. John Wesley and Hilda Maske Langley; m. Lee Roy Grogan Jr., Oct. 29, 1983; children: Erin Margaret, Hannah Elizabeth, Mary-Stamper. AB, Davidson Coll., 1979; JD, Mercer U., 1983. Counselor Jack Eckerd Found., Tampa, Fla., 1979-80; assoc. Hirsch, Beil & Partin, P.C., Columbus, Ga., 1983-86, ptnr., 1986-89, Hirsch, Partin, Grogan & Grogan, P.C., Columbus, 1989—. Chmn. Child Fatality/Abuse Protocol, Columbus, 1990-93; lectr. CLE, Atlanta. Bd. dirs. Muscogee Edn. Excellence Found., Columbus, 1994-97; founding bd. dirs. Easter Seal Soc. West Ga., Columbus, 1986; bd. dirs. March of Dimes, Columbus, 1984-86; chmn. State Public Affairs Com., Atlanta, 1991-92. Recipient Leadership award Leadership Columbus, 1995, Woman of Achievement award Concharty Order of Girl Scouts U.S., 1998. Fellow Am. Acad. Matrimonial Lawyers; mem. Ga. State Bar Assn., Columbus Bar Assn., Jr. League of Columbus (pres. 1996-97). Avocations: biking, reading, stitchery. Family and matrimonial. Home: 2715 Lynda Ln Columbus GA 31906-1248 Office: Hirsch Partin Grogan & Grogan PC 1021 3d Ave Columbus GA 31901

GROGAN, ROBERT HARRIS, lawyer; b. Feb. 25, 1933; s. Robert Michael and Nora Howarth (Johnson) G.; m. Delia Ann Grossi, Dec. 23, 1967 (div. 1982); m. Lynn D. Habian, June 20, 1987. AB, Harvard U., 1955; LLB, U. Va., 1961. Bar: Va. 1961, N.Y. 1962, Ill. 1977, Fla. 1986; cert. cir. ct. mediator, Fla. Assoc. Milbank, Tweed, Hadley & McCloy, N.Y.C., 1961-66; counsel Anaconda Co., 1966-68; assoc. Shearman & Sterling, 1968-75; v.p., gen. counsel staff Citibank, 1975-76; ptnr. Mayer, Brown & Platt, Chgo., 1976-81; of counsel Olwine, Connelly, Chase, O'Donnell & Weyher, N.Y.C., 1981-87; sr. v.p., dep. sr. counsel S.E. Bank, N.A., Miami, Fla., 1987-91; sr. v.p., gen. counsel Republic Nat. Bank of Miami, 1992-96; ind. bank, bus. and legal cons., 1996-2001; program adminstr. Broward County (Fla.) Legal Aid Svc., 2001—. Vice chmn. exec. adv. coun. Andreas Bus. Sch. Barry U., Miami Shores, Fla., 1995-97; lectr. in field. Contbg. author: The Local Economic Development Corporation, 1970. Sec., bd. dirs. 3d Equity Owners Corp., coop. housing corp., 1975-77, pres., bd. dirs., 1982-86. With U.S. Army, 1956-58. Mem. ABA, Fla. Bar, N.Y. Bar, Va. State Bar Assn., Ill. State Bar Assn., Am. Arbitration Assn. (comml. panel neutral arbitrators 1997-2001), Phi Delta Phi, Harvard Club (N.Y.C.), Harvard Faculty Club (Cambridge, Mass.). Address: PO Box 666 Palm Beach FL 33480-0666 Fax: 561-848-5922. E-mail: rgrogan@legalaid.org

GROH, JENNIFER CALFA, law librarian; b. Patchogue, N.Y., Mar. 28, 1970; d. Anthony Bernard and Mary (Fogerty) C.; m. William Matthew Groh, May 10, 1997. BA in Social Sci., St. Joseph's Coll., 1992; MA in Internat. Edn., NYU, 1993; MSLS, Pratt Inst., Bklyn., 1996. Reference page Patchogue (N.Y.)-Medford Libr., 1986-93; from libr. asst. to sr. libr. Morgan & Finnegan, N.Y.C., 1994—. NYU grad. scholar, 1992, Law Libr. Assn. scholar, N.Y. 1995, Am. Assn. Law Librs. scholar, 1996. Mem. ALA, Spl. Librs. Assn., Law Libr. Assn. Greater N.Y. Home: 21 Mohawk Dr North Babylon NY 11703-3303 Office: Morgan & Finnegan 345 Park Ave New York NY 10154-0053

GRONER, BEVERLY ANNE, retired lawyer; b. Des Moines; d. Benjamin L. and Annabelle (Miller) Zavat; m. Jack Davis; children: Morrilou Davis Morell, Lewis A. Davis, Andrew G. Davis; m. Samuel Brian Groner, Dec. 17, 1962. Student, Drake U., 1939-40, Cath. U., 1954-56; JD, Am. U., 1959. Bar: Md. 1959, U.S. Supreme Ct. 1963, D.C. 1965. Pvt. practice, Bethesda Md., Washington, 1959-99; ret., 1999. Chmn. Md. Gov.'s Commn. on Domestic Relations Laws 1977-87; exec. com. trustee Montgomery-Prince George's Continuing Legal Edn. Inst., 1983-99, pres., 1992-98; lectr. to lay, profl. groups; speaker to Bar Assns. and numerous seminars; participant continuing legal edn. programs, local and nat.; participant, faculty mem. trial demonstration films Am. Law Inst.-ABA Legal Consortium; participant numerous TV, radio programs; seminar leader, expert-in-residence Harvard Law Sch., 1987, Family Law, Georgetown U. Law Ctr., 1988, 89; mem. gov.'s com. ERA, 1978-80; faculty mem. Montgomery County Bar Assn. Law Sch. for the Pub., 1991, Inst. on Professionalism, 1992. Cons. editor Family Law Reporter, 1986-90, MD Family Law Monthly, 1993-99; mem. bd. editors Fairshare 1992-97; contbr. numerous articles to profl. jours. Pres. Am. Acad. Matrimonial Lawyers Found., 1994-98. Named One of Leading Matrimonial Practitioners in U.S., Nat. Law Jour., 1979, 87, Best Divorce Lawyer in Md., Washingtonian Mag., 1981, One of Best Matrimonial Lawyers in U.S., Town and Country mag., 1985, Best Lawyers in Am., 1987—; recipient Disting. Svc. award Va. State Bar Assn., 1982, Okla. Bar Assn., 1987, Md. Gubernatorial citation, 1987. Fellow Am. Acad. Matrimonial Lawyers (pres. Md. chpt. 1992-98, pres.-elect found. 1993-94); mem. Bar Assn. Montgomery County (exec. com. chmn. family law sect. 1976, chmn. fee arbitration panel 1974-77, legal ethics com.), Md. State Bar Assn. bd. of govs., (gov., chmn. family law sect. 1975-77, vice chmn. com. continuing legal edn., ethics com. 1991-99, mem. inquiry panel and grievance com., 1991-99, faculty mem. on Professionalism 1992), ABA (chmn. family law sect. 1986-87, rep. to White House conf. on Yr. of Child 1984, sec. family law sect. 1983-84, vice chmn. 1984-85, chmn. sect. marital property com., assn. adv. to nat. conf. commrs. on uniform marital property act, mem. faculty family law advocacy inst. 1988, 90), Am. Acad. of Matrimonial Lawyers, Md. State Bar Assn. (mem. inquiry panel and grievance com. 1991—), Phi Alpha Delta. Family and matrimonial. Home: 5600 Wisconsin Ave Apt 1602 Chevy Chase MD 20815-4413

GRONER, ISAAC NATHAN, lawyer; b. Buffalo, Oct. 22, 1919; s. Louis and Lena (Blinkoff) G.; m. Estelle Kaye, Sept. 14, 1941; children— Phyllis Gross, Robert, Lois. B.A. in econs. and gen. studies with distinction, Cornell U., 1939; M.A., NYU, 1942; LL.B. cum laude, Yale U., 1948. Bar: N.Y. 1948, U.S. Supreme Ct. 1953, D.C. 1954, U.S. Ct. Appeals (D.C. cir.) 1954, Md. 1955. Law clk. Chief Justice Fred M. Vinson, U.S. Supreme Ct., Washington, 1948-50; atty. Dept. Justice, Washington, 1950-51; chief counsel Wage Stabilization Bd., Washington, 1951-53; pvt. practice, Washington, 1953-64, 90—; ptnr. Cole and Groner, P.C., Washington, 1964-90. Contbr. articles to law jours. Tech. sgt. U.S. Army, 1943-46. Mem. ABA (co-chmn. com. on law govt. employee relations sect. labor relations law 1962-64), Order of Coif, Phi Beta Kappa, Phi Kappa Phi. Federal civil litigation, Labor. Home: 3304 Wake Dr Kensington MD 20895-3217 Office: 1015 18th St NW Washington DC 20036-5203

GRONER, SAMUEL BRIAN, retired lawyer; b. Buffalo, Dec. 27, 1916; s. Louis and Lena (Blinkoff) G.; m. Beverly Anne Groner; children: Jonathan B. (dec. 1962), Morri Lou Morell, Lewis A. Davis, Laurence M., Andrew G. Davis. AB, Cornell U., 1937, JD, 1939; MA in Econs., Am. U., 1950. Bar: N.Y. 1939, D.C. 1952, Md. 1953, U.S. Supreme Ct. 1944. Pvt. practice law, Buffalo, 1939-40; atty. U.S. Dept. War and Office Price Adminstrn., 1940-43; atty.-adviser U.S. Dept. Justice, Washington, 1946-53; pvt. practice law Md. and Washington, 1953-63; ptnr. Groner, Stone & Greiger, Washington, 1955-57, Groner & Groner, Silver Spring and Bethesda, Md., 1962-98; ret. U.S. Govt., 1995. Asst. counsel Naval Ship Systems Command, Washington, 1963-73; trial atty. Office Gen. Counsel, Dept. Navy, Washington, 1973-74, assoc. chief trial atty., 1974-79; adminstrv. law judge and mem. Bd. Contract Appeals U.S. Dept. Labor, Washington, 1979—, acting chmn., 1987, mem. Bd. Alien Labor Certification Appeals, 1990—, acting adminstrv. appeals judge Benefits Rev. Bd., 1988-89; instr. Terrell Law Sch., Washington, 1948; mem. faculty USDA Grad. Sch., 1972—; reporter Md. Gov.'s Commn. on Domestic Rels. Laws, 1977-87; participant in continuing legal and jud. edn. Author: Modern Business Law, 1983, (with others) The Improvement of the Administration of Justice, 6th edit., 1981; assoc. editor Fed. Bar Jour., 1948-55; contbr. articles to profl. jours. Active PTA, civic assns., Jewish Community Coun., Community Chest; mem. Montgomery County Commn. on Handicapped Individuals, 1977-85, vice chmn., 1980-81. 1st lt. inf. and M.I.S., U.S. Army, 1943-46, ETO. Recipient Navy Superior Civilian Service award, 1979. Mem. ABA (liaison commn. on professionalism 1985—, advisor to standing com. on lawyer competence 1986—, family law sect., jud. adminstrn. div., vice chmn. pub. contract law sect., com. on adminstrv. claims and remedies 1976-79, chmn. 1979-80), Fed. Bar Assn., Montgomery County Bar Assn. and Bar Found., Bar Assn. of D.C., Bar Assn. Met. St. Louis, Cornell Law Assn. (pres. D.C. chpt. 1947-54), Am. Law Inst., Inst. for Jud. Adminstrn., Am. Judicature Soc.,. Supreme Ct. Hist. Soc., Govt. Adminstrv. Trial Lawyers Assn., Nat. Lawyers Club, Cosmos Club, Cornell Club N.Y.C., Officers and Faculty Club (U.S. Naval Acad., Annapolis), Phi Beta Kappa. Government contracts and claims, Workers' compensation. Home: 5600 Wisconsin Ave Apt 1602 Chevy Chase MD 20815-4413

GRONOW, GEOFFREY REES, lawyer, consultant; b. Melbourne, Victoria, Australia, July 21, 1937; s. William Rees and Brier G.; m. Geraldine Joan Craw, Feb. 23, 1963; children: Michael, Claire, Jeremy. BS, Melbourne, 1961; Cert. Acctg., RMIT, Melbourne, 1963; LLB, Melbourne U., 1965; postgrad., Monash U., Melbourne, 1974, Cambridge U., 1989. Bar: barrister, solicitor Supreme Ct. Victoria, 1967, Supreme Ct. Capital Ter. 1976; High Ct. Australia 1967. Commd. Royal Australian Inf., 1957; advanced through grades to lt. col.; legal officer Atty. Gen.'s Dept., Melbourne, 1959-68; solicitor AXA (NALA), 1968-69; dir. News Ltd., 1974-80; ptnr. Middletons Moore & Bevins, 1980-2000; cons., 2000—. Chair editl. com. Law Inst. Victoria, 1988, sr. counsellor, 1998—; vis. lectr. Law Sch. Melbourne U. Chmn. Sea Care Authority Australia, 1999—; chmn. Vol. Marine Rescue, Victoria, 1995—; comdr. Royal Vol. Coastal Patrol, 1978—; dep. chair We. Port Safety Coun., 1995—. Recipient Efficiency Decoration Govt. of Australia, 1974. Fellow Australian Inst. Mgmt., Taxation Inst. Australia. Avocations: reading, sailing, music, classic cars. Alternative dispute resolution, Communications, Libel. Home: 21 Huntingfield Rd Brighton VIC 3186 Australia Office: Level 29 200 Queen St Melbourne VIC 3000 Australia Fax: (03) 9205 20 55

GROPPER, ALLAN LOUIS, bankruptcy judge; b. N.Y.C. ; m. Jane Evangelist, Aug. 10, 1968 (dec. Feb. 1999). BA, Yale U., 1965; JD, Harvard U., 1969. Bar: N.Y. 1969, U.S. Dist. Ct. (so. and ea. dists.) N.Y. 1971, U.S. Ct. Appeals (2d cir.) 1971, U.S. Supreme Ct. 1974. Atty. Civil Appeals Bur., Legal Aid Soc., N.Y.C., 1969-71; assoc. White & Case, 1972-77, ptnr., 1978-2000; bankruptcy judge U.S. Bankruptcy Ct., 2000—. Bd. dirs. Browning Sch., 1990—, pres., 1997-2000; bd. dirs. Legal Aid Soc., 1990-2000, v.p., 1996-2000; bd. dirs. N.Y. Lawyers for Pub. Interest, 1990-2000. Mem. ABA, Assn. of Bar of City of N.Y. (v.p. 1995-96, mem. exec. com. 1991-96, chmn. 1994-95), N.Y. State Bar Assn. Office: US Bankruptcy Ct Alexander Hamilton Custom House 1 Bowling Green New York NY 10004

GROSECLOSE, LYNN HUNTER, lawyer; b. Marion, Va., Apr. 22, 1943; s. Byron Glen and Wilma Comer G.; m. Sharon L. Pair; children: Seth, Zachery, Meredith. BA, Emory & Henry Coll., 1964; postgrad., Emory U., 1964-65; JD, U. Va., 1970. Bar: Fla. 1971, U.S. Dist. Ct. (mid. dist.) Fla. 1972, U.S. Ct. Appeals (5th cir.) 1980, U.S. Ct. Appeals (11th cir.) 1981, Colo. 1993. Prof. Orlando Jr. Coll., Fla., 1965-67; atty. Langston & Massey, Attys., Lakeland, 1971-75; ptnr. Sprott & Groseclose, Attys., 1975-80, Jacobs, Valentine, Groseclose, Lakeland, 1980-84, Lane, Trohn, Bradenton, Fla., 1984-96, Brown, Clark, Sarasota, 1996-99, Thompson, Goodis, Thompson, Groseclose & Richardson, Sarasota, 1999—. Sr., jr. warden St. Davids Episcopal Ch.; pres., bd. dirs. Vols. in Svc. to Elderly, Gulfcoast Legal Svcs., Sarasota Manatee Legal Aid. Mem. Sarasota County Bar Assn., Manatee County Bar Assn., Colo. Bar Assn., Fla. Def. Lawyers Assn., Fedn. Ins. and Corp. Counsel, Fla. Bar Found. (legal assistance to poor com. 1997—). Democrat. Avocations: history, remodeling, golf. Insurance, Personal injury, Professional liability. Home: 7512 Preserves Ct Sarasota FL 34243-3700 Office: Thompson Goodis Thompson Groseclose & Richardson PO Box 730 Bradenton FL 34206

GROSENHEIDER, DELNO JOHN, lawyer; b. Litchfield, Ill., Feb. 10, 1935; s. Junas Louis Henry and Esther O'Neil (Knabel) G.; m. Margaret Noel Adams, Aug. 30, 1959; children— John Stephen, Michael Del. Student So. Ill. U., 1953-54; B.A., U. Tex., 1961, LL.B., 1964. Bar: Tex. 1963, U.S. Dist. Ct. (we. dist.) Tex., 1966, U.S. Ct. Appeals (5th cir.) 1985, U.S. Supreme Ct., 1986. Atty. Tex. Securities Bd., Austin, 1964-66, House, Mercer, House & Brock, Austin, 1966-77; ptnr. Wilson, Grosenheider & Burns, Austin, 1977—. Judge, City of Rollingwood, Tex., 1968; city atty. City of Rollingwood, 1969; mem. Bd. of Adjustment, City of Rollingwood,

1975-84. Mem. State Bar of Tex., Travis County Bar Assn., Tex. Assn. Def. Counsel, Def. Rsch. Inst., Internat. Assn. Ins. Counselors, Met. Club. Republican. Episcopalian. Federal civil litigation, State civil litigation, Insurance. Home: 3005 Stratford Dr Austin TX 78746-4650 Office: Wilson Grosenheider & Burns 400 W 15th St Suite 1100 Austin TX 78767

GROSMAN, ALAN M. lawyer; b. Mar. 13, 1935; s. Charles M. and Grace (Fishman) G.; m. Bette Bloomenthal, Dec. 27, 1967; children, Ellen, Carol. BA, Wesleyan U., 1956; MA, Yale U., 1957; JD, N.Y. Law Sch., 1965. Bar: N.J. 1965, U.S. Dist. Ct. N.J. 1965, U.S. Supreme Ct. 1969. Ptnr. Grosman & Grosman and predecessors, Millburn, N.J., 1965—; asst. prosecutor Essex County, 1968-69; prosecutor Millburn, 1981—. Mem. family part practice com. N.J. Supreme Ct., 1984-88, mem. dispute resolution task force, 1987-88, com. on women in the cts., 1991-93; chmn. N.J. World Trade Coun., 1975-77, dir., 1978—; lectr. in field. Reporter New Haven Jour., 1959-60, Newark Evening News, 1961-62; author: New Jersey Family Law, 1999; contbr. articles to profl. jours. Mem. ABA (chmn. alimony, maintenance and support com. family law sect. 1983-87, editor ABA Family Law Quar. 1993—), N.J. State Bar Assn. (exec. editor N.J. Family Lawyer 1980-91, mem. exec. com. family law sect. 1980—, chmn. sect. 1987-88, appellate practice com. 1995—), Am. Acad. Matrimonial Lawyers (pres. N.J. chpt. 1983-85, nat. bd. govs. 1984-88, editor Jour. AAML 1980-90), Essex County Bar Assn. (chmn. family law com. 1970-72), N.Y. Law Sch. Alumni Assn. (bd. dirs. 1988-98), Millburn-Short Hills Rep. Club, Inc. (counsel 1988—), Phi Beta Kappa. Family and matrimonial. Address: 75 Main St Ste 205 Millburn NJ 07041-1322

GROSS, ALLEN JEFFREY, lawyer; b. Wheeling, W.Va., May 2, 1948; s. Arthur and Bertyl (Kahn) G.; m. Carolyn McGuire, May 2, 1982; children: Alexander, Lindsay. BS, Ohio State U., 1970; JD, Georgetown U., 1974. Bar: Pa. 1974, U.S. Dist. Ct. (ctrl. and we. dists.) Pa., Calif. 1989, U.S. Dist. Ct. (no., so. and ctrl. dists.) Calif. 1989, U.S. Ct. Appeals (3d and 6th cirs.). Ptnr. Morgan, Lewis & Bockius, Phila., 1974-89, Orrick, Harrington & Sutcliffe, L.A., 1989-93; now with Mitchell, Silberberg & Knupp. Mem. Corp. Counsel Inst. adv. bd. Georgetown U. Law Ctr. Author: Survey of Wrongful Discharge Cases in the United States, 1979, Employee Dismissal Laws, Forms, Procedures, 1986, 2d edit. 1992. Fellow Coll. Labor and Employment Lawyers Inc.; mem. ABA (chair trial advocacy supcom. 1989-93, employee rights and responsibilities com. 1991—, co-chair Nat. Advocacy Inst. 1992), Calif. Bar Assn., Pa. Bar Assn. (mgmt. chair Employee Rights Responsibilities com., Sect. Insts. Spl. Programs sub-com.), L.A. County Bar Assn. Labor. Office: Mitchell Silberberg & Knupp 11377 W Olympic Blvd Los Angeles CA 90064-1625

GROSS, CAROL ANN, lawyer; b. St. Louis, May 25, 1951; m. William H. Gross. B in journalism, U. Mo., 1973; JD cum laude, Seton Hall U. Sch. Law, 1985. Bar N.J., 1985, Pa., 1985, N.Y., 1995, U.S. Dist. Ct., 1985. Law clerk N.J. office atty. gen., Trenton, 1983-85; assoc. Lowenstein, Sandler, Kohl, Fischer & Boylan, Roseland, N.J., 1985-90, Jones, Day, Reavis & Pogue, N.Y., 1990-96; ptnr. pvt. practice, Somerville, N.J., 1996—. Co-Author: (book) N.J. Environmental Law Handbook, 1989; contbr. Environmental Reporter's Handbook, 1988; co-editor (newsletter) Enviro-Notes, 1989-90; contbr. author: Legal Guide to Working with Environmental Consultants. Recipient Responsible Journalism award, N.J. Press Assn., 1982, Interpretive Writing award, N.J. Press Assn., 1980, Journalistic Excellence Under Deadline Pressure award, Soc. Profl. Journalists, 1979, Good Citizen award, Gannett Co., Inc., 1979, Merit award, Union Co. Civil Defense/Disaster Control, 1978. Mem. ABA, N.J. Bar Assn., Pa. Bar Assn. Avocations: gardening, guitar, cooking. Office: 79 Davenport St Somerville NJ 08876-1921

GROSS, LESLIE JAY, lawyer; b. Coral Gables, Fla., July 24, 1944; s. Bernard Charles and Lillian (Adler) G.; m. Frances L. Londow, June 16, 1968; children: Jonathan Eric, Jason Marc. BA magna cum laude, Harvard U., 1965, JD, 1968. Bar: Fla. 1971, U.S. Dist. Ct. (so. dist.) Fla. 1971, U.S. Ct. Appeals (5th cir.) 1971, U.S. Tax Ct. 1971, U.S. Supreme Ct. 1971; registered real estate broker, registered mortgage broker, registered securities broker. Rsch. aide Fla. 3d Dist. Ct. Appeal, Miami, Fla., 1968-69; prof. social sci. Miami-Dade Community Coll., 1969-70; assoc. Greenberg, Traurig, et al., Miami, 1969-70, Patton, Kanner, et al., Miami, 1970-71, Fromberg, Fromberg, Roth, Miami, 1971-72; ptnr. Fromberg, Fromberg, Gross, et al., 1973-88; assoc. Thornton, David, Murray, et al., 1988-94. Atty. agt. Atty.'s Title Ins. Fund, First Am. Title, Miami, 1971-94; adj. prof. U. Miami Sch. Law, 1984; lectr. seminar Nat. Aircraft Fin. Assn., 1990. Contbr. articles to profl. jours. Mem. transp. com. Greater Miami C. of C., 1984-85; v.p., pres., bd. dirs. Kendale Homeowners Assn., Miami, 1970-81; vol. Dem. candidates in state and nat. elections, Miami, 1968, 70, 72, 87, 88; mem. Vision Coun. Land Use Task Force, Miami, 1988-89; judge Silver Knight awards Miami Herald, 1987, 92, 93, 94, 95, judge spelling bee, 1987; bd. dirs. Internat. Assn. Fin. Planning, 1983-84; founding mem., bd. dirs. The Actors Playhouse, 1987—, sec., 1990—. Mem. Harvard Law Sch. Assn., Harvard Club of Miami (v.p. 1985-90, pres. 1990-94, dir. 1985-99). Democrat. Jewish. Avocations: gardening, humorous creative writing, photography, aerobics, travel. General corporate, Finance, Real property. Home: 10471 SW 126th St Miami FL 33176-4749

GROSS, MALCOLM JOSEPH, lawyer; b. Allentown, Pa., Oct. 2, 1940; s. John Tilghman and Agnes Amelia (Lieberman) G.; m. Lona Mae Farr, Aug. 24, 1963 (div. Apr. 1976); m. Sally Lorensen Oeler, Apr. 9, 1976 (div. Nov. 1990); m. Janet Abramson, Nov. 21, 1992; children: Andrea, Stacey, John, Peter. AB cum laude, Muhlenberg Coll., 1962; JD, Villanova U., 1965. Bar: Pa. 1965, U.S. Dist. Ct. (ea. and mid. dists.) Pa. 1965, U.S. Ct. Appeals (3rd cir.), U.S. Supreme Ct. Law clk. to chief justice Pa. Supreme Ct., 1966; ptnr. Brennen & Gross, Allentown, 1966-72, Gross & Brown, Allentown, 1972-76; sr. ptnr. Gross, McGinley & McGinley, 1976-83, Gross, McGinley, LaBarre & Eaton, Allentown, 1983—. Asst. pub. defender Lehigh County, 1969-72; disciplinary com. Pa. Sup. Ct., 1975-79; solicitor Lehigh Valley Child Care, Inc., 1971-83, Lehigh County Office Children and Youth Svcs., 1972-87, Head Start Lehigh Valley, 1980—, Kidspeace, 1981—; v.p., pres. Allentown Symphony Assn., 1990-2000; sec. Lehigh Valley Conf. Health Care, 1994—; pres. Grandview Cemetery Assn., Allentown, 1966-95; law lectr. Muhlenberg Coll., 1972-87, Lehigh U., 1988; chmn., sec., treas. Sta. WLVT-TV 39, 1969-94; lectr. in field. Bd. editors Villanova Law Rev., 1964-65; contbr. articles to legal and social work hist. publs. Mem. collections com. Muhlenberg Coll.; mem. exec. com., bd. assocs. Allentown Art Mus., Cedar Crest Coll.; bd. dirs. Lehigh Valley Conservancy, 1969-72; mem. Gov.'s Coun. on Alcohol and Drug Abuse, 1969-75; bd. dirs. YMCA, 1971-76; pres., dir. Lehigh Valley Child Care, 1971-79; chmn. parish coun. Cathedral of St. Catherine of Siana, 1968-70; mem. exec. fin. com. Pa. State Dem. Party, 1981-86; bd. dirs., exec. com. Lehigh Valley United Way, 2000—; trustee Trexler Trust, 2000—, Sacred Heart Hosp., 2001-. Rrecipient Disting. Svc. award YMCA, Allentown, 1976; Dubach scholar, 1961. Mem. ABA, Pa. Bar Assn. (constl. law and child abuse coms.), Lehigh County Bar Assn. (orphan ct. rules and juvenile ct. media rels. coms.), Pa. Trial Lawyers Assn. (bd. govs.), Am. Inns of Ct., Sigma Phi Epsilon. General civil litigation, Family and matrimonial, Libel. Home: 4648 Pleasant View Dr Coopersburg PA 18036-9354 Office: 33 S 7th St PO Box 4060 Allentown PA 18105-4060 E-mail: mgross@gmle.com

GROSS, RICHARD BENJAMIN, lawyer; b. Santa Monica, Calif., Sept. 26, 1947; s. Edward L. and Adele P. Gross; m. Pamela McGovern, June 1, 1985; 1 child, Hannah McGovern. Student, UCLA, 1965-68; BA, U. Calif., Berkeley, 1970; JD, Harvard U., 1973; postgrad., Cambridge (Eng.) U., 1973-74. Bar: N.Y. 1975, U.S. Dist. Ct. (so. dist.) N.Y. 1975, U.S. Ct. Appeals (2d cir.) 1975, Ill. 1987. Assoc. White & Case, N.Y.C., 1974-77; assoc. counsel Am. Express Co., 1977-82; sr. v.p., gen. counsel and sec. Citicorp Diners Club, Inc., Chgo., 1982-90; sr. v.p., gen. counsel Citicorp Ins. Group, Inc., N.Y.C., 1990-91; sr. v.p., gen. counsel, sec. Ambac Fin. Group, Inc., 1991-98; mng. dir., gen. counsel U.S. Trust Corp., 1998—. Bd. dirs. Randall's Island Sports Found., 1999—, sec., treas., 2000—. Mem. ABA (com. of corp. gen. counsel, com. on fed. regulation of securities, com. on banking), N.Y. Bankers Assn. (mem. lawyers adv. com., mem. govt. rels. com.), N.Y. State Bar Assn., Assn. of the Bar of the City of N.Y., Am. Soc. Internat. Law, Am. Soc. Corp. Secs., Am. Corp. Counsel Assn., Am. Bankers Coun., Fin. Svcs. Roundtable (mem. lawyers coun., govt. affairs coun.). Banking, General corporate, Securities. Office: US Trust Corp 114 W 47th St New York NY 10036-1510 Fax: (212) 852-1310. E-mail: rgross@ustrust.com

GROSS, STEVEN ROSS, lawyer; b. N.Y.C., June 15, 1946; s. Alexander and Lola (Mandelbaum) G.; m. Georgette Francine Kleinhaus, Dec. 14, 1968; children: Amy, Jillian. BA, Columbia U., 1968, MA, 1969; LLB, Cambridge U., 1971; JD, Yale U., 1973. Bar: U.S. Dist. Ct. (ea. and so. dists.) N.Y. 1974. Assoc. Debevoise & Plimpton, N.Y.C., 1973-80, ptnr., 1981—. Co-author: Collier Business Workout Guide; contbr. articles to profl. jours. Mem. ABA, Assn. of Bar of City of N.Y. Jewish. Bankruptcy. Home: 145 E 74th St New York NY 10021-3225 Office: Debevoise & Plimpton 919 3rd Ave Fl 23 New York NY 10022-3094 E-mail: srgross@debevaise.com

GROSSBERG, MARC ELIAS, lawyer; b. Houston, Dec. 26, 1940; s. Sylvester and Leah (Hochman) G.; m. Eva M. Wolski, Jan. 3, 1981; 1 child, Nicole; children from previous marriage: Lee Ann Krishnan, Toni Oreck. BS in Polit. Sci., U. Houston, 1961; JD with honors, U. Tex., 1965. Bar: Tex. 1965, Calif. 1966, Fla. 1980, U.S. Supreme Ct. 1980; bd. cert. fed. income taxation, Tex. Acct. Brochstein Toomim & Co CPAs (now Deloitte Touche), Houston, 1961-62; law clk. hon. Walter Ely U.S. Ct. Appeals (9th cir.), L.A., 1965-66; assoc. Fulbright & Jaworski, Houston, 1966-71; ptnr. Schlanger Mills Mayer & Grossberg, LLP, 1974-99, Thompson & Knight LLP, Houston, 1999—. Pres. Imprint, Inc., 2000—. Advanceman, speech writer 1968 Hubert Humphry Presdl. Campaign; pres. Tex. Bill of Rights Found., Houston, 1971-72, Jewish Family Svc., Houston, 1986-87, U. Tex. Law Rev. Assn.; commr. Housing Authority City of Houston, 1974-78. Mem. ABA (tax sect. and litig. sects.). Democrat. Jewish. Avocations: computers, racquetball. General civil litigation, Taxation, general, Personal income taxation. Office: Thompson & Knight LLP 1200 Smith St Ste 3600 Houston TX 77002-4595 E-mail: grossbergm@tklaw.com

GROSSMAN, DEBRA A. lawyer, real estate manager, radio talk show host; b. Cleve., July 29, 1951; d. Morris M. and Idelle R. (Bialosky) G. BA, Syracuse U., 1973; JD, Suffolk U., 1976. Bar: Mass. 1977, U.S. Dist. Ct. Mass. 1977. Sole practice, Lexington, Mass., 1977-79; ptnr. Kurland & Grossman, P.C., Lowell, 1979-94; property mgr. KD Mgmt. Co., 1983—, Chelmsford, Mass., 1994-98; talk show host "Legal Briefs" WCCM Radio, Lawrence, 1989-97. Bd. dirs. Downtown Lowell Bus. Assn., 1987; lectr. Greater Lowell Alzheimers Assn., 1987; vice chair Lowell Hist. Bd., 1995-97, chair, 1997—; mem. corp. adv. bd. Suitability, Inc., 2001—. Mem. Mass. Assn. Women Lawyers (asst. treas. 1981-82, bd. dirs. 1979-81), Mass. Bar Assn. (mem. family law sect.), Mass. Acad. Trial Lawyers, Greater Lowel Bar Assn. (bd. dirs. 1993-96, Lawyer for the Day program dir. 1990-92), Syracuse U. Alumni Club, Greater Boston Club, Assn. Trial Lawyers Am., Mass. Family and Probate Am. Inn Ct. General civil litigation, Family and matrimonial, Personal injury. Office: Kurland & Grossman PC 139 Billerica Rd Chelmsford MA 01824-3619 E-mail: dgrossman@nrmail.com

GROSSMAN, JEROME KENT, lawyer, accountant; b. St. Louis, Apr. 15, 1953; s. Marvin and Myra Lee (Barnholtz) G.; m. Debbie Ada Kogan, Aug. 7, 1977; children: Hannah Felicia, Marni Celeste. AB cum laude, Georgetown U., 1974, JD, 1977. Bar: Mo. 1977, D.C. 1978, U.S. Ct. Claims 1979, U.S. Tax Ct. 1979, Del. 1980, U.S. Dist. Ct. Del. 1982; CPA, Mo. Acct., controller U.S. Dept. State, Washington, 1974-77; acct. Arthur Andersen & Co., St. Louis, 1977-79; mem. firm Bayard, Handelman and Murdoch, P.A., Wilmington, Del., 1979-88; ptnr. Young Conaway Stargatt & Taylor LLP, 1988—. Co-author: ALI-ABA Course of Study on the Reform Act of 1984, 86. V.p. Jewish Cmty. Ctr., Wilmington, 1986—88, 1989—90, treas., 1989—90; trustee Milton & Hattie Kutz Found., 2001—; mem. Congregation Beth Shalom, Wilmington, 1988—90, pres., 1990—92; treas. Jewish Fedn. Del., 1989—90; pres. Del. Gratz Hebrew H.S., 1997—2000, trustee, 1995—, Jewish. Com. of Del. Endowment Fund., 1988—95; co-chmn. Del. State Com. State of Israel Bonds, 1992—95, chmn., 1995—2000; bd. dirs., trustee Del. Symphony Assn., 1998—, vice chmn., 1999—2001. Fellow Am. Coll. Tax Counsel; mem. ABA (tax sect., chmn. inventories subcom. 1982-86, vice chmn. 1986-88, chmn. 1988-90, com. on tax acctg.), AICPA (mem. coun. 2000—), Del. Bar Assn. (chair sect. of taxation 1996-97), Del. Tax Inst. (planning com. 1985-86, 94—), Del. Soc. CPAs (chmn. tax com. 1980-85, coun. 1985-87, 93—, ethics com. 1989-92, pres. 2000-01), Alpha Sigma Nu. Democrat. Avocations: choir, opera, bridge. Estate planning, Corporate taxation, Taxation, general. Home: 803 Westover Rd Wilmington DE 19807-2978 Office: Young Conaway Stargatt & Taylor LLP PO Box 391 Wilmington DE 19899-0391 E-mail: jgrossman@ycst.com

GROSSMAN, ROBERT LOUIS, lawyer; b. Cleve., Dec. 20, 1954; s. Sidney and Lillian Belle (Davis) G.; m. Rochelle Carol Shear, Nov. 7, 1987; children: Zachary, Jonathan, David, Andrew. BA with honors, Ohio State U., 1975, JD with Honors, 1978, MA with honors, 1979. Bar: Ohio 1978, U.S. Ct. Appeals (5th cir.) 1979, Fla. 1982. Law clk. U.S. Dist. Ct. (so. dist.) Ohio, Columbus, 1977-78; sr. atty. U.S. Govt. EEOC, Houston, 1979-82; shareholder Greenberg, Traurig, Hoffman, Lipoff, Rosen & Quentel, P.A., Miami, 1982—. Editor: Florida Corporate Practice, 2d edit., 1991. Chmn. South Dade Jewish Leadership Coun., 1997-99; bd. dirs. Greater Miami Jewish Fedn. South Dade, Miami, 1987—, campaign chmn., 1995-97; bd. dirs. Greater Miami Jewish Fedn., 1995—, exec. com., 1997-99, Alper Jewish Comm. Ctr., 1997-2000, exec. com., 1998-2000; bd. dirs. Children's Bereavement Ctr., 2000—, Beacon coun., 2000—. Donald Becker Meml. scholar Ohio State U., 1975, 76, fellow, 1978; Robert Russehl fellow Greater Miami Jewish Fedn., 1998; recipient Stanley C. Myers Young Leadership award Greater Miami Jewish Fedn., 1999. Mem. ABA (corp. securities sect.), Fla. Bar Assn., Dade County Bar Assn., Order of Coif. Avocations: sports, reading, travel. General corporate, Mergers and acquisitions, Securities. Office: Greenberg Traurig 1221 Brickell Ave Miami FL 33131-3224

GROSSMANN, RONALD STANYER, lawyer; b. Chgo., Nov. 9, 1944; s. Andrew Eugene and Gladys M. Grossmann; m. Jo Ellen Hanson, May 11, 1968; children: Kenneth Frederick, Emilie Beth. BA, Northwestern U., 1966; JD, U. Mich., 1969. Bar: Oreg., 1969. Law clk. Oreg. Supreme Ct., Salem, 1969-70; assoc. Stoel Rives LLP, Portland, Oreg., 1970-76; ptnr. Stoel Rives Boley Jones & Grey, 1976—. Mem.: ABA, Oreg. Bar Assn., Am. Coll. Employee Benefits Counsel. General corporate, Pension, profit-sharing, and employee benefits, Personal income taxation. Office: Stoel Rives LLP 900 SW 5th Ave Ste 2600 Portland OR 97204-1268 E-mail: rsgrossmann@stoel.com

GROTON, JAMES PURNELL, lawyer; b. Newport News, Va., Oct. 29, 1927; s. Lafayette Watson and Mary (Skidmore) G.; m. Lora Frances Webster, June 13, 1953; children: James Purnell, Hunter W., Molly Groton Urban, Lora Groton Rust. AB cum laude, Princeton U., 1949; LLB, U. Va., 1954. Bar: D.C. 1954, Ga. 1955, U.S. Supreme Ct. 1964. Assoc. Sutherland, Asbill & Brennan, Atlanta, 1954-61, ptnr., 1961—; lectr. to profl. socs. on alternative dispute resolution and constrn. Editor articles Va. Law Rev., 1953-54; contbr. to profl. jours. Bd. dirs. Atlanta Council for Internat. Visitors, 1968-75; bd. dirs., treas. N.W. Ga. council Girl Scouts U.S., 1973-79; trustee South Kent Sch., Conn., 1973-77, Nat. Assn. Women in Constrn. Edn. Found., 1993—; chmn. Constrn. Industry Dispute Avoidance and Resolution Task Force. Capt. USMC, 1946-48, 50-52. Recipient medal Excellence, Engineering News-Record, 1993. Fellow Am. Coll. Constrn. Lawyers; mem. State Bar Ga., Atlanta Bar Assn. (chmn. construction sect., 1992—), AIA (hon., Bronze medal 1984), Am. Arbitration Assn. (nat. panel constrn. arbitrators 1970—, bd. dirs. 1990—, nat. constrn. dispute resolution com., 1992—, Whitney North Seymour medal 1983), Nat. Sch. Bds. Assn. Council of Sch. Attys., Nat. Assn. Coll. and Univ. Attys., Ga. Council Sch. Bd. Attys. (exec. com. 1971-78), Ctr. for Pub. Resources (Arbitration award 1988), Princeton Alumni Assn. Ga. (v.p. 1964-77), Phi Delta Phi. Democrat. Episcopalian. Clubs: Peachtree, Piedmont Driving, Commerce, Old War Horse Lawyers. Construction, Education and schools. Home: 37 Lakeview Ave NE Atlanta GA 30305-3722 Office: Sutherland Asbill & Brennan 999 Peachtree St NE Ste 2300 Atlanta GA 30309-3996

GRUBBS, DONALD SHAW, JR. retired actuary; b. Bellvue, Pa., Dec. 15, 1929; s. Donald Shaw and Zora Fay (Craven) G.; m. Margaret Helen Crooke, Dec. 27, 1969; children: David, Deborah, Daniel, Dawson, Dwight, Douglas. AB, Tex. A&M U., 1951; postgrad., L.A. State Coll., 1953-54, Fresno State Coll., 1954-55, Boston U., 1955-57, Princeton Theol. Sem., 1959-60, Westminster Theol. Sem., 1960-61; JD, Georgetown U., 1979. Bar: D.C. 1979. Actuarial asst. New Eng. Mut. Life Ins. Co., Boston, 1955-58, Warner Watson, Inc., Boston, 1958-59; cons. actuary John B. St. John, Penllyn, Pa., 1959-65, Grubbs & Co., Phila., 1965-72; v.p. actuary Nat. Health and Welfare Retirement Assn., N.Y.C., 1972-74; dir. actuarial div. IRS, Washington, 1974-76; cons. actuary Buck Cons., Inc., 1976-86; pres. Grubbs and Co., Inc., Silver Spring, Md., 1986-95, retired, 1995—. Chmn. Joint Bd. for Enrollment Actuaries, Washington, 1975-76. Author: (with G.E. Johnson) The Variable Annuity, 1967; (with D.M. McGill) Fundamentals of Private Pensions, 6th edit., 1989. V.p. NAACP, Ambler, Pa., 1961-62; chmn. Warminster (Pa.) Child Day Care Assn., 1962-64. 1st lt. U.S. Army, 1951-53, Korea. Decorated Bronze Star with V U.S. Army, 1953; recipient Employee Benefits Outstanding Achievement award Pension World, 1986. Fellow Soc. of Actuaries (sec. 1983-84), Conf. Consulting Actuaries; mem. ABA, Middle Atlantic Actuarial Club (pres. 1981-82), UN Assn. (v.p. nat. capital area divsn. 1996-98, 2000—). Democrat. Unitarian. Home: 10216 Royal Rd Silver Spring MD 20903-1613 E-mail: dongrubbs@aol.com

GRUBE, KARL BERTRAM, judge; b. Elmhurst, Ill., Jan. 13, 1946; s. Karl Ludwig and Gerturde (Bertram) G.; m. Mary B. Harr, May 4, 1974 (div. Aug. 1991); m. Julia Ross, Dec. 28, 1998. BSBA, Elmhurst Coll., 1967; JD, Stetson U., 1970; M in Judicial Studies, U. Nev., 1992. Asst. pub. defender State of Fla., Clearwater, 1970-73, county ct. judge St. Petersburg, 1977—; pvt. practice Seminole, Fla., 1973-76; city atty. City of Redington Beach, 1975-76. Asst. dean Fla. Jud. Coll., Tallahassee, 1984-85; faculty mem., course coord., mem. faculty coun. Nat. Jud. Coll., chair faculty coun., 2000—; mem. Nat. Hwy. Traffic Safety Jud. Tng. Implementation Bd. Contbr. articles to profl. jours. Dir. Pinellas Comprehensive Addiction Svcs., Clearwater, 1982-88. Jud. fellow U.S. Dept. Transp., 1998, Nat. Hwy. Traffic Safety Adminstrn., 1999. Mem. ABA (conf. chmn. divsn. jud. adminstrn. 1992, del. to jud. divsn. coun. 1997—, Dedicated Svc. award 1991), Fla. Bar Assn. (civil rule com.), Colo. Bar Assn., Fla. Conf. County Ct. Judges (pers. com. 1984-85), Rolls Royce Owner's Club (editor 1982-84). Lutheran. Avocations: collecting fountain pens, collecting antique watches, auto restoration. Office: Pinellas County Ct 501 1st Ave N Ste A212 Saint Petersburg FL 33701-3732

GRUENDER, RAYMOND W. prosecutor; BA, MBA, JD, Washington U. Assoc. Lewis, Rice and Fingersh, 1987—90; asst. US atty. Eastern Dist. , Mo., 1990—94, Eastern Dist., 2000; ptnr. Thompson Coburn, 1994—2000; US Atty. Eastern Dist., Mo. Office: Thomas F Eagelton US Courthouse 111 S St Rm 20 Saint Louis MO 63102 Office Fax: 314-539-2309*

GRUETTNER, DONALD W. retired lawyer; b. Milw., Oct. 13, 1930; BS, Marquette U., 1952; JD, U. Mich., 1955. Bar: Ohio 1956. Ptnr. Baker & Hostetler, Cleve., et al., 1996. Mem. Delta Theta Phi. Office: 3200 National City Ctr 1900 E 9th St Ste 3200 Cleveland OH 44114-3475

GRUNEWALD, MARK HOWARD, law educator; BA, Emory U., 1969; JD with highest honors, George Washington U., 1972. Bar: D.C. 1973, Va. 1979. Assoc. Arent, Fox, Kintner, Plotkin & Kahn, Washington, 1972-73; atty. advisor Office of Legal Counsel U.S. Dept. Justice, 1973-76; from asst. prof. to assoc. prof. law Washington and Lee U., Lexington, Va., 1976-86, prof. law, 1986—, assoc. dean, 1992-96, interim dean, 1999-2000. Editor-in-chief George Washington Law Rev. Mem. Order of Coif. Office: Washington and Lee U Sch Law Lexington VA 24450-0303

GRUSH, JULIUS SIDNEY, lawyer; b. Los Angeles, Dec. 4, 1937; children: Robin, Randi, Ronna, Rodney. BS, UCLA, 1960; postgrad., U. Calif., San Francisco, 1960-62; LLB, Southwestern U., 1964. Bar: Calif. 1965. Dep. city atty. City of Los Angeles, 1965-67; sole practice Los Angeles, 1967—. Prof. Bar-Bri Harcourt Brace Pubs. Bar Course, Los Angeles, 1986—. Pres. Lockhurst Booster Club; mem. City of Hope (past pres.). Mem. ABA, Los Angeles Bar Assn., Beverly Hills Bar Assn., Century City Bar Assn., Phi Alpha Delta. Republican. State civil litigation, General corporate, Real property. Office: 1900 Avenue Of The Stars Fl 25 Los Angeles CA 90067-4301

GRUSHKO, PAVEL GREGORY, lawyer; b. Kyiv, Ukraine; B in Internat. Rels. with honors, Kyiv Nat. U., 1998, LLM, 1999. Counsellor at law Supreme Coun. Ukraine, Kyiv, 1993-95; lawyer Vasil Kisil & Ptnrs. Antitrust, General corporate, Taxation, general. Office: Vasil Kisil & Ptnrs 5/60 Zhylyanska St Ste 1-2 01033 Kyiv Ukraine Office Fax: 380 44 220 4877. E-mail: pavel.grushko@vkp.kiev.ua

GRUSON, MICHAEL, lawyer; b. Berlin, Sept. 17, 1936; came to U.S., 1962; s. Rudolf and Barbara Gruson; m. Hiroko Tsubota, July 11, 1964; children: Rudolf, Andreas, Sebastian, Matthias, Florian, Konrad. LLB, U. Mainz, Fed. Republic of Germany, 1962; M in Comparative Law, Columbia U., 1963, LLB, 1965; Dr. iur, Freie Univ., Berlin, 1966. Bar: N.Y. 1969, U.S. Ct. Appeals (2d cir.) 1969, U.S. Dist. Ct. (so. dist.) N.Y. 1971, U.S. Supreme Ct. 1977. Assoc. Shearman & Sterling, N.Y.C., 1966-73, ptnr., 1973—. Bd. dirs. Fuji Bank and Trust Co. Author: Die Bedurfniskompetenz, 1967; co-author: Sovereing Lending: Managing Legal Risk, 1984, Legal Opinions in International Transactions, 3d edit., 1997, Regulation of Foreign Banks, 2 vols., 3d edit., 2000, Acquisition of Shares in a Foreign Country, 1993; contbr. articles to profl. jours. Mem. Internat. Bar Assn. (past vice chmn. com. banking law, past chmn. subcom. on legal opinions, hon. treas. Am. br.), N.Y. State Bar Assn. (com. internat. banking, securities and fin. transaction, internat. law and practice sect.), Internat. Law Assn. (com. on internat. monetary law, hon. treas. Am. br.). Banking, Mergers and acquisitions. Home: 850 Park Ave New York NY 10021-1845 Office: Shearman & Sterling 599 Lexington Ave Fl C2 New York NY 10022-6069

GRZECA, MICHAEL G(ERARD), lawyer, mediator; b. Milw., Aug. 5, 1949; s. Leonard George and Katherine Anne Grzeca; m. Linda Gail Schultz, Aug. 15, 1970; children: Amy Marie, Laura Elizabeth. BA, Marquette U., 1971, JD, 1974. Bar: Wis. 1974, U.S. Dist. Ct. (ea. and we. dists.) Wis. 1974, U.S. Supreme Ct. 1977. Assoc. Everson, Whitney, Everson & Brehm, S.C., Green Bay, Wis., 1974-80, shareholder, 1980-86;

prin. Grzeca & Stanton, S.C., 1986-95; pvt. practice, Green Bay, 1995-99; cir. ct. judge, 1999-2000; mediator, 2000—. Spl. counsel Wis. Bd. Attys. Profl. Responsibility, 1983-97; cir. ct. commr., 1991-99, 2000—. Editor Wis. Ins. Issues, 1984-99. Bd. dirs. Big Bros.-Big Sisters of Northeastern Wis., Green Bay, 1977-86, pres., 1979-81, 85, legal counsel, 1985-99. Served as officer USAR, 1974-80. Mem. ABA, Order of Barristers, Robert J. Parins Inn of Ct., Wis. Assn. Mediators. Alternative dispute resolution, State civil litigation, Personal injury. Office: 712 Bordeaux Rue Green Bay WI 54301-1430

GUBLER, JOHN GRAY, lawyer; b. Las Vegas, June 16, 1942; s. V. Gray and Loreta N. (Newton) G.; m. Mollie Boyle, Jan. 10, 1987; 1 child, J. Gray; children from previous marriage: Laura, Matthew. BA, U. Calif.-Berkeley, 1964; JD, U. Utah, 1971; LLM in Taxation, NYU, 1973. Bar: Nev. 1971, U.S. Dist. Ct. Nev. 1973, U.S. Tax Ct. 1974, U.S. Ct. Appeals (9th cir.) 1978. Dep. pub. defender Clark County, Nev., 1973-74; ptnr. Gubler & Gubler, Las Vegas, 1974-88, ptnr. Gubler and Peters, Las Vegas, 1989—; instr. continuing edn. community coll. Served with U.S. Army, 1966-68. Mem. Clark County Bar Assn., ABA, State Bar of Nev. (disciplinary com. 1979-88), Las Vegas-Paradise Rotary (pres. 1981-82), Knife & Fork Club (pres. 1978-80). Ch of Jesus Christ of Latter Day Saints. Estate planning, Probate. Office: Gubler & Peters 302 E Carson Ave Ste 601 Las Vegas NV 89101-5989

GUENTER, RAYMOND ALBERT, lawyer, banker; b. Buffalo, May 31, 1932; s. Albert and Anna Matilda (Pfeiffer) G.; B.A., Syracuse U., 1954; LL.B, Harvard U., 1957; m. Doris Ruth Honig, Feb. 8, 1963; 1 child, Joshua Samuel. Bar: N.Y. With Chase Manhattan Bank, N.Y.C., 1958-76, v.p., asst. sec., 1971-76; sr. v.p., gen. counsel Conn. Nat. Bank, Hartford, 1976-79; exec. v.p., sec., gen. counsel Shawmut Nat. Corp., Hartford, 1979—; lectr. in law U. Conn. Law Sch.; mem. banking adv. com. Conn. Law Revision Commn., 1992—; dir. New England Legal Found., Greater Hartford Archtl. Conservancy. Mem. exec. com. N.Y. County Dem. Com., 1965-73; mem. N.Y. State Dem. Com., 1962-66; mem. West Hartford Archtl. Heritage Com., 1985—, chmn., 1985-86. Served with AUS, 1958-59, 61-62. Mem. Assn. Bank Holding Cos. (chmn. lawyers com. 1986-87), Conn. Bar Assn., Boston Bar Assn. (co-chmn. banking law commn.). General corporate. Home: 52 Woodpond Rd West Hartford CT 06107-3526

GUESS, JAMES DAVID, lawyer; b. Lampasas, Tex., Jan. 21, 1941; s. David Ira and Lila Blanch (Reagan) G.; m. Susan Lawyer, Dec. 19, 1981; children: Corey, Stephanie, Casey, Chris. BS in Edn., Southwestern U., 1963; JD, St. Mary's U., 1968. Bar: Tex. 1968, U.S. Dist. Ct. (we. dist.) Tex. 1974, U.S. Ct. Appeals (5th cir.) 1974, U.S. Dist. Ct. (so. dist.) Tex. 1978, U.S. Dist. Ct. (no. dist.) Tex. 1982. Assoc. Groce Locke & Hebdon, San Antonio, 1968-74, ptnr., 1975-86; shareholder Groce Locke & Hebdon P.C., 1986-96, Jenkens & Gilchrist, San Antonio, 1996-99, Law Offices of James D. Guess, San Antonio, 1999—. Sustaining mem. Products Liability Adv. Coun.; mem. Am. Bd. Trial Advs. With USN, 1961-67, Vietnam. Mem. Tex. Assn. Def. Coun. (past pres.), Def. Rsch. Inst. (bd. dirs. 1998—), Internat. Assn. Def. Counsel. Avocations: sports, golf, hunting. Aviation, Product liability. Home: 13318 Southwalk St San Antonio TX 78232-4843 Office: Law Offices James D Guess 615 NW Loop 410 Ste 200 San Antonio TX 78216-5504 E-mail: jguess@lgtlaw.com

GUEST, BRIAN MILTON, lawyer; b. Vineland, N.J., Mar. 18, 1948; s. Edmund James Jr. and Vivian D. Guest. AB in Polit. Sci. with distinction, Rutgers U., 1970; JD, Boston U., 1973. Bar: N.J. 1973, U.S. Dist. Ct. N.J. 1973, U.S. Supreme Ct. 1978, U.S. Ct. Appeals (3d cir.) 1981; diplomate N.J. Mcpl. Govt. Law, 1994. Assoc. Hartman & Schlesinger, Mt. Holly, N.J., 1973-78, ptnr., 1978-82, Bookbinder & Guest, Burlington, N.J., 1982-83, Bookbinder, Guest & Domzalski, Burlington, 1983-90, Guest, Domzalski, Kurts & Langraf, Burlington, 1990-91, Guest, Domzalski, Kurts, Landgraf & McNeill, Burlington & Cherry Hill, N.J., 1991-94, Kearns, Vassallo, Guest & Kearns, Willingboro, 1994—. Pres. Raritan Sigma Phi Epsilon Corp., New Brunswick, N.J., 1983-89, trustee, 1982-92. Bd. dirs. Drenk Mental Health Svcs., Inc., pres. bd. trustees, 2000—; trustee 1st United Meth. Ch., Moorestown, N.J., 1995-97, Meml. Health Alliance, 1999-00, Virtua Health Sys. Ambulatory Svcs., 2000—, sec. bd., 2000—. Mem. ABA, Trial Attys. N.J., N.J. Bar Assn. (gen. counsel del. 1983-86), Burlington County Bar Assn. (trustee 1982-84), Burlington County C. of C. (bd. dirs. 1987—, treas. 1989, v.p. 1990, pres. 1991), Masons (worshipful master Mt. Holly club 1982), Rotary, Sigma Phi Epsilon (trustee 1982-91). Land use and zoning (including planning), Probate, Real property. Office: Kearns Vassallo Guest & Kearns 630 Beverly Rancocas Rd Willingboro NJ 08046-3736

GUETHLEIN, WILLIAM O. lawyer; b. Cin., May 4, 1927; s. William O. and Catherine (Sandmann) G.; m. Bette Mivelaz, Aug. 4, 1961 (dec. 1974). LLD, U. Louisville, 1950. Bar: Ky. 1950, U.S. Dist. Ct. Ky. 1954, U.S. Ct. Appeals (6th cir.) 1954. Assoc. Boehl Stopher and Graves, Louisville, 1950-60, sr. ptnr., 1960—. Lt. USAR, 1952-60. Fellow Am. Acad. Trial Lawyers; mem. ABA, Jefferson County Bar Assn., Ky. Bar Assn., Am. Assn. Hosp. Attys. Avocation: tennis. Federal civil litigation, State civil litigation, Environmental. Office: Phillips Parker Orberson and Moore PLC 716 W Main St Ste 300 Louisville KY 40202-2634

GUGGENHEIM, MARTIN FRANKLIN, law educator, lawyer; b. N.Y.C., May 29, 1946; s. Werner and Fanny (Monatt) G.; m. Denise Silverman, May 29, 1969; children: Jamie, Courtney, Lesley. BA, SUNY, Buffalo, 1968; JD, NYU, 1971. Bar: N.Y. 1972, U.S. Dist. Ct. (so. dist. and ea. dist.) N.Y. 1973, U.S. Ct. Appeals (2d cir.) 1974, U.S. Ct. Appeals (3d cir.) 1979, U.S. Ct. Appeals (6th cir.) 1977, U.S. Supreme Ct. 1976. Staff atty. Legal Aid Soc., N.Y.C., 1971-72, dir. spl. litig. unit, juvenile rights divsn., 1972-73; clin. instr. NYU Sch. Law, 1973-75; staff atty. juvnile rights project ACLU, 1975-79, acting dir., 1976-77; asst. prof. clin. law NYU, 1975-77, assoc. prof. clin. law, 1977-79, prof. clin. law, 1980—. Exec. dir. Washington Sq. Legal Svcs., Inc., N.Y.C., 1986-2000; pres. Nat. Coalition for Child Protection Reform, 2000—; pres., founding dir. Family Def. Law Project, Inc., N.Y.C., 1992-2000; advisor program for children Edna McConnell Clark Found., 1993—; dir. clin. and advocacy programs NYU, 1989—; cons. juvenile justice stds. project ABA/Inst. Jud. Adminstrn., 1979-81; acting dir. Clin. Advocacy Programs, Sch. of Law NYU, 1988-89. Author: (with Alan Sussman) The Rights of Parents, 1980, Abuse and Neglect Volume, 1982, The Rights of Young People, 2d edit., 1985, (with Anthony G. Amsterdam and Randy Hertz) Trial Manual for Defense Attorneys in Juvenile Court, 1991, (with Alexandra Lowe and Diane Curtis) The Rights of Families, 1996. Dir. William J. Brennan Ctr., NYU, 1995-2000; mem. adv. bd. N.Y.C. Adminstrn. Children, 1997—; pres. Nat. Coalition for Child Protection Reform, 2000—. Arthur Garfield Hays Civil Liberties fellow, 1970-71, Criminal Law Edn. and Rsch. fellow, 1969-70; Kathryn A. McDonald award Assn. of the Bar of the City of N.Y., 2000. Mem. ABA, Am. Assn. Law Schs. Office: NYU Sch Law 161 Ave of the Americas New York NY 10013 E-mail: guggenh@juris.law.nyu.edu

GUGGENHIME, RICHARD JOHNSON, lawyer; b. San Francisco, Mar. 6, 1940; s. Richard E. and Charlotte G.; m. Emlen Hall, June 5, 1965 (div.); children: Andrew, Lisa, Molly; m. Judith Perry Swift, Oct. 3, 1992. AB in Polit. Sci. with distinction, Stanford U., 1961; JD, Harvard U., 1964. Bar: Calif. 1965, U.S. Dist. Ct. (no. dist.) Calif. 1965, U.S. Ct. Appeals (9th cir.) 1965. Assoc. Heller, Ehrman, White & McAuliffe, 1965-71, ptnr., 1972—. Spl. asst. to U.S. Senator Hugh Scott, 1964; bd. dirs. Comml. Bank of San Francisco, 1980-81, Global Savs. Bank, San Francisco, 1984-86, North Am. Trust Co., 1996-99. Mem. San Francisco Bd. Permit Appeals, 1978-86; bd. dirs. Marine World Africa USA, 1980-86; mem. San Francisco Fire Commn., 1986-88, Recreation and Parks Commn., 1988-92; chmn. bd. trustees San Francisco Univ. H.S., 1987-90; trustee St. Ignatius Prep. Sch., San Francisco, 1987-96; dir. Olympic Club, 2000—. Mem. Am. Coll. Probate Counsel, San Francisco Opera Assn. (bd. dirs.), Bohemian Club, Wine and Food Soc. Club, Olympic Club (dir. 1999—), Chevaliers du Tastevin Club (San Francisco), Thunderbird Country Club (Rancho Mirage, Calif.). Estate planning, Probate, Estate taxation. Home: 2621 Larkin St San Francisco CA 94109-1512 Office: Heller Ehrman White & McAuliffe 333 Bush St San Francisco CA 94104-2806

GUIDA, TONI M. lawyer; b. Bklyn., Nov. 10, 1961; d. Peter and Susan G.; m. Jeffrey P. Rogan, Apr 1, 1989; children: Madeline Elsie, Peter Dylan Jeffrey. BA with honors, Binghamton U., 1984; JD with honors, Syracuse U., 1987. Bar: N.Y. 1987, U.S. Dist. Ct. (ea. and so. dists.) N.Y. 1989. Jud. clk. appellate divsn. 3rd dept. N.Y. Supreme Ct., Albany, 1987-88; litig. atty. Kelley, Drye & Warren, N.Y.C., 1988-93; sr. spl. counsel divsn. enforcement N.Y. Stock Exch., 1993-94; founding ptnr. Rogan, Guida & Orenstein, White Plains, N.Y., 1996—. Alumni admissions rep. Binghamton U., 1996—. Notes and Comments editor Syracuse Jour. Internat. Law & Commerce, 1985-86. Vol. White Plains Sch. Dist., 1997—; mem. The Women's Guild, White Plains, 1997—. Mem. N.Y. Met. Club. Harper Coll./Binghamton U., Syracuse Met. Alumni Assn. Avocations: writing instructional books and articles, reading. General civil litigation, Personal injury, Real property. Office: Rogan Guida & Orenstein 235 Mamaroneck Ave White Plains NY 10605-1315

GUILD, CLARK JOSEPH, JR. lawyer; b. Yerington, Nev., May 14, 1921; s. Clark Joseph and Virginia Ellen (Carroll) G.; m. Elizabeth Ann Ashley, July 20, 1945 (div. 1977); children: Clark J. III, Jeffrey S., Daniel E. (dec.), Jann Cademartori. BA, U. Nev., 1943; JD, Georgetown U., 1948. Bar: Nev. 1948, D.C. 1948, U.S. Dist. Ct. (no. dist.) Nev. 1948, U.S. Ct. Appeals (D.C. cir.) 1948, U.S. Supreme Ct. 1959, U.S. Ct. Appeals (9th cir.) 1984. Ptnr. Guild, Hagen & Clark, Ltd., Reno, Nev., 1953-88, Guild, Russell, Gallgher & Fuller Ltd., Reno (formerly Guild, Hagen & Clark Ltd.), 1988—. Pres. YMCA, Reno, 1954, 64; regent U. Nev. System, 1972. Capt. inf. U.S. Army, 1942-46. Recipient Disting. Nevadan award U. Nev., 1989. Fellow Am. Coll. Trial Lawyers; mem. ABA, State Bar Nev., Clark County Bar Assn., Washoe County Bar Assn. (pres. 1959-60), Masons, Elks. Democrat. Episcopalian. Federal civil litigation, State civil litigation, General practice. Office: Guild Russell Gallagher & Fuller Ltd 100 W Liberty St Reno NV 89501-1962

GUILFORD, ROBERT E. lawyer; b. Cleve., Apr. 14, 1933; s. Isadore H. and Malvene G.; m. Edel Singer, 1960 (div. 1963); 1 child, Steven; m. Judith Cagen, May 5, 1990. BA in Philosophy with honors, U. Va., 1955; JD, Harvard U., 1958. Bar: Calif. 1959, U.S. Dist. Ct. (cen. dist.) Calif. 1959, U.S. Dist. Ct. (no. dist.) Calif. 1964, U.S. Dist. Ct. (no. dist.) N.Y. 1996, U.S. Ct. Appeals (9th cir.) 1959. Asst. U.S. atty. Dept. Justice, L.A., 1958-59; legal staff MCA Universal, Universal City, Calif., 1959-65; gen. counsel World Horizons Inst., Newport Beach, 1965-70; ptnr. Bryant, Maxwell, Guilford & Sheahan, 1970-75; outside counsel Home Savings & Loan Assn., Beverly Hills, Calif., 1975-80; pvt. practice Santa Monica, 1980-85; gen. counsel Mus. of Flying, 1985-90; assoc. counsel Am. Golf Corp., 1987-90; shareholder Baum, Hedlund, Aristei, Guilford & Downey, 1993—. V.p., chief pilot, trustee Mus. Flying, Santa Monica; v.p. Supermarine Aviation Ltd., Liberty Aero Corp., NATO Aviation. Mem. State Bar Calif., Lawyer-Pilot's Bar Assn., Aircraft Owners and Pilots Assn., Exptl. Aircraft Assn., Classic Jet Aircraft Assn. (chmn. bd. dirs.), Warbirds Am. (co-founder), Hunter Flight Test Ltd. (v.p.), Mustang Pilots Club (founder, pres.), Phi Eta Sigma. Avocation: pilot. Office: Baum Hedlund Aristei Guilford and Downey 12100 Wilshire Blvd Ste 950 Los Angeles CA 90025-7107 E-mail: bguilford@bhagd.com

GUILFOYLE, ROBERT THOMAS, lawyer; b. Chgo., Mar. 23, 1936; s. Joseph Leo and Nellie (Powers) G.; m. Jacqueline Gardner, May 21, 1964; B.S., U. San Francisco, 1958; J.D., DePaul U., 1964. Bar: Ill. 1964. Atty. Allstate Ins. Co., Chgo., 1964-95. With USN, 1958-60. Mem. ABA, Chgo. Bar Assn., Ill. Bar Assn., Ill. Def. Assn., Trial Lawyers Club. Roman Catholic. State civil litigation, Insurance, Personal injury. Home: 524 N 5th Ave Des Plaines IL 60016-1125 Office: 200 N La Salle St Chicago IL 60601-1014

GUILLOT, PATRICK CARL, lawyer, judge; b. Dallas, Apr. 12, 1945; s. L.E. and Helen Ruth (Gallagher) G.; m. Rebecca Nichols, Jan 20, 1945; children— Christian, Claire, Drouard. B.A., U. Tex., 1967, J.D., 1969. Bar: Tex. 1969, U.S. Dist. Ct. (no. dist.) Tex. 1969, U.S. Ct. Appeals (5th cir.) 1973. Assoc. Bailey & Williams, Dallas, 1969-73; mem. Collie, McSpedden & Roberts, Dallas, 1969-79; judge 254th Dist. Ct., Dallas, 1979-81; judge Ct. Appeals, Dallas, 1981-86; mem. Godwin & Carlton 1986-93; mem. True, Rohde & Sewell, 1993—. mem. Nat. Conf. Commrs. on Uniform State Laws, 1982— . Fellow Tex. Bar Found. Republican. Roman Catholic. Office: US Ct Appeals 8080 N Central Expy Ste 9 Dallas TX 75206-1838

GUIN, DON LESTER, insurance company executive; b. Shreveport, La., Nov. 5, 1940; s. Lester and Ethelyn (Dumas) G.; m. Mary Ann Guin, Feb. 3, 1979. BBA in Ins., U. Ga., 1962; BS in Law, Kensington U., Glendale, Calif., 1987, JD, 1989. Bar: Calif. 1990, U.S. Ct. Appeals (5th and 9th cirs.) 1990, U.S. Dist. Ct. (no. dist.) Calif. 1990, U.S. Ct. Appeals (fed. cir.) 1991, U.S. Dist. Ct. (ea. dist.) Tex. 1991, U.S. Ct. Internat. Trade 1991, U.S. Ct. Fed. Claims 1992, U.S. Supreme Ct. 1994. Adjuster, supr. Lindsey & Newsom, Beaumont, Tex., 1963-71, mgr. Port Arthur, 1968-71, asst. to pres. Tyler, 1971-74, v.p. ops., 1977-84, sr. v.p., 1984—; sr. v.p. adminstrn. and legal Lindsey Morden, 1990—; sr. v.p., corp. sec. Lindsey Morden Claims Svc. Inc., Lindsey Morden Claims Mgmt., 1992-93, sr. v.p., treas. U.S. Ops., 1993—, sr. v.p., corp. treas., chief legal officer, 1995—; sr. v.p., corp. treas. and sec. Vale Nat. Training Ctrs, Inc., 1993—; exec. v.p., corp. treas, corp. sec., chief legal officer, 1995—; exec. v.p Cunningham Lindsey U.S., Inc., 2000—, Vale Nat. Tng. Ctr., 2001—. Bd. dirs. Lindsey Morden Claims Svc., Inc., Lindsey Morden Claims Mgmt., Inc., exec. com., mgmt. com., compensation com., incentive com., Vale Nat. Tng. Ctrs., Lindsey & Newsom Inc.; trustee Lindsey and Newsom Benefit Trusts, 1990-91, plan adminstr. Lindsey Morden Profit Sharing Retirement Trust, 1994, Lindsey & Newsom Retirement Funds, 1990—; sr. v.p., corp. sec., CLO Lindsey Morden Group, Inc., 1996—; mem. adv. bd. Kemper Ins. Group; sr. v.p., corp. sec. Lindsey & Newsom, Vale Nat; bd. dirs. Tyler Mus. Art, chmn. pers. policy com., chair fin. com., 1999; exec. v.p. Cunningham Lindsey, U.S., Inc., 2000. Author: Analysis of Garage Liability, 1972, Dishonesty Claims Handling, 1973, Casualty Reporting Manual, 1975, Sexual Harassment in the Workplace, 1986, (audio cassette) Beating the Bears of Bad Faith, 1991, (video cassette) Bad Faith and Preventing Errors and Omissions Claims, 1987. Trustee Lindsey Morden Benefit Trusts, Lindsey Morden Retirement Trusts, 1992—; dir. assoc. U. Tex Health Ctr., 1995; budget allocation panelist United Way Tyler/Smith County, Tex., 1995; bd. dirs. Tyler Mus. of Art, 1996. Mem. ABA (internat. law sect., corp. law sect.), Can. Bar Assn., Nat. Assn. Def. Counsel, Nat. Assn. Ind. Ins. Adjusters (data processing com. 1976, legis. com. 1990), Bar Assn. D.C., Bar Assn. U.S. Fed. Cir., Defense Inst. Trial Lawyers Assn. (ins. law com.), State Bar Calif. (internat. law sect., tort sect., litigation sect., labor and employment law sect.), Nat. Employee Benefit Found., Def. Rsch. Inst., Alameda County Bar Assn., Inter-Pacific Bar Assn., Italian-Am. Bar Assn., Bar Assn. 5th Fed. Cir., Optimist Club, Kiwanis Club, Sabre Club, Lawyers Club San Francisco, Ins. Soc. U. Ga. (charter mem.), Circle K-Kiwanis. Home: 17389 Hidden Valley Ln Flint TX 75762-9611 Office: Lindsey Morden Claims Svcs Inc 211 Brookside Dr Tyler TX 75711

GUIN, JUNIUS FOY, JR. federal judge; b. Russellville, Ala., Feb. 2, 1924; s. Junius Foy and Ruby (Pace) G.; m. Dorace Jean Caldwell, July 18, 1945; children: Janet Elizabeth Smith, Judith Ann Mullican, Junius Foy III, David Jonathan. Student, Ga. Inst. Tech., 1940-41; AB magna cum laude, U. Ala., JD with honors, 1947; LLD, Magic Valley Christian Coll., 1963. Bar: Ala. 1948. Pvt. practice law, Russellville; sr. ptnr. Guin, Guin, Bouldin & Porch, 1948-73; fed. dist. judge U.S. Dist. Ct. (no. dist.) Ala., Birmingham, from 1973, now sr. judge; commr. Ala. Bar, 1965-73, 2d v.p., 1969-70. Pres. Abstract Trust Co., Inc., 1958-73; sec. Iuka TV Cable Co., Inc., Haleyville TV Cable Co., Inc., 1963-73; former dir., gen. counsel First Nat. Bank of Russellville, Franklin Fed. Savs. & Loan Assn. of Russellville.; Lectr. Cumberland-Samford Sch. Law, 1974— , U. Ala. Sch. Law, 1977— Chmn. Russellville City Planning Com., 1954-57; 1st chmn. Jud. Commn. Ala., 1972-73; mem. Ala. Supreme Ct. Adv. Com. (rules civil procedure), 1971-73; mem. adv. com. on standards of conduct U.S. Jud. Conf., 1980-87, mem. com. on Fed.-State Jurisdiction, 1982-88, mem. ad hoc com. on cameras in the courtroom, 1982-83; Rep. county chmn., 1954-58, 71-72, Rep. state fin. chmn., 1972-73; candidate for U.S. Senator from, Ala., 1954; Ala. Lawyers' Finance chmn. Com. to Re-elect Pres., 1972; former trustee Ala. Christian Coll., Faulkner U., Magic Valley Christian Coll., Childhaven Children's Home; elder Ch. of Christ. Served to 1st lt., inf. AUS, 1943-46. Named Russellville Citizen of Year, 1973; recipient Dean's award U. Ala. Law Sch., 1977 Mem. ABA (mem. spl. com. on resdl. real estate transactions 917-73), Am. Radio Relay League, Ala. Bar Assn. (com. chmn. 1965-73, Award of Merit 1973), Jefferson County Bar Assn., Fed. Bar Assn., Am. Law Inst., Ala. Law Inst. (dir. 1969-73, 76—), Am. Judicature Soc., Farrah Law Soc., Farrah Order Jurisprudence (now Order of Coif), Phi Beta Kappa, Omicron Delta Kappa, Delta Chi. Office: US Dist Ct 619 US Courthouse 1729 5th Ave N Birmingham AL 35203-2000

GUINN, STANLEY WILLIS, lawyer; b. Detroit, June 9, 1953; s. Willis Hampton and Virginia Mae (Pierson) G.; m. Patricia Shirley Newgord, June 13, 1981; children: Terri Lanae, Scott Stanley. BBA with high distinction, U. Mich., 1979, MBA with distinction, 1981; MS in Taxation with distinction, Walsh Coll., 1987; JD cum laude, U. Mich., 1992. CPA, Mich.; cert. mgmt. acct., Mich. Tax mgr. Coopers & Lybrand, Detroit, 1981-87; tax cons. Upjohn Co., Kalamazoo, 1987-89; litigation atty. Brobeck, Phleger & Harrison, 1992-94, Coughlan, Semmer & Lipman, San Diego, 1994-95; consumer fin. atty. Bank Am. NT & SA, San Francisco, 1995-98, GreenPoint Credit, LLC, San Diego, 1998—. Served with USN, 1974-77. Mem. AICPA, ABA, Calif. State Bar Assn., Inst. Cert. Mgmt. Acctg., Phi Kappa Phi, Beta Gamma Sigma, Beta Alpha Psi, Delta Mu Delta. Republican. Mem. Christian Ch. Avocations: tennis, racquetball, running. General civil litigation, Consumer commercial, Taxation, general. Home: 3125 Crystal Ct Escondido CA 92025-7763 Office: GreenPoint Credit 10089 Willow Creek Rd San Diego CA 92131-1603 E-mail: stan.guinn@greenpoint.com

GUINTO, BOB LIM, lawyer; b. Quezon City, Philippines, Dec. 18, 1967; s. Mariano Oliveros and Eufemia Lim G.; m. Valerie Prado Tiempo, Nov. 2, 1969. BA, U. Philippines, 1989, LLB, 1994; MLS, Cambridge U., U.K., 1998. Bar: Philippines. Assoc. lawyer PECABAR Law Offices, Makati City, Manila, Philippines, 1994-96, sr. assoc. lawyers Philippines, 1998—; lawyer, dir. Office of the Pres. of the Philippines, Philippines, 1996-97. Assoc. corp. sec. Air Liquide and subsidiaries, Philippines, 2000—. Contbr. articles to profl. jours. British Chevening scholarship British Govt., 199798. Mem. Integrated Bar of the Philippines, U. of the Philippines Collegian Editors Alumni Assn., Philippines Oxford and Cambridge Soc. Avocation: travel. Consumer commercial, General corporate, Finance. Office: PECABAR Law Offices Vernida IV Bldg Leviste St Makati City 1227 The Philippines Fax: (632) 818-7355; 8187391. E-mail: bobguinto@pecabar.com

GULLAND, EUGENE D. lawyer; b. Endicott, N.Y., Aug. 27, 1947; s. George Raymond and Virginia (Fisher) G.; m. Kristin Spearing, Aug. 29, 1970; children: Michael Spearing, Molly Spearing, Samuel Spearing. AB, Princeton U., 1969; JD, Yale U., 1972. Bar: D.C., Va., U.S. Supreme Ct., U.S. Ct. Appeals (1st, 2d, 3d, 4th, 6th, 7th, 9th, D.C., Fed. cirs.), U.S. Dist. Ct. D.C., (ea. dist.) Va., Md., Ariz., Ind. Assoc. Covington & Burling, Washington, 1973-80, ptnr., 1980—. Practitioner before London Ct. Internat. Arbitration, Internat. C. of C., Am. Arbitration Assn., also other arbitral tribunals; mem. faculty Nat. Inst. for Trial Advocacy, Am. Judicature Soc. Trustee Loudoun Day Sch., Leesburg, Va., 1986-98; vestryman, treas. Our Redeemer Ch., 1987-97; mem. alumni schs. com. Princeton U. Capt. U.S. Army, 1972-73. Woodrow Wilson scholar Princeton U., Princeton U. scholar. Mem. Nat. Assn. Coll. and Univ. Attys., Phi Beta Kappa. Administrative and regulatory, Federal civil litigation, Private international. Home: Little River Farm Aldie VA 20105 Office: Covington & Burling PO Box 7566 1201 Pennsylvania Ave NW Washington DC 20004-2401 E-mail: egulland@cov.com

GULOTTA, FRANK ANDREW, JR. lawyer; b. N.Y.C., Nov. 2, 1939; s. Frank A. and Josephine M. (Giardina) G.; m. Joanne C. DeLessio, Jan. 29, 1966; children: Lisa, Frank A. BA, Trinity Coll., 1961; JD, Columbia U., 1964. Bar: N.Y. 1965, U.S. Dist. Ct. (ea. dist.) N.Y. 1972, U.S. Supreme Ct. 1970. Asst. dist. atty. Nassau County (N.Y.), 1965-69; prin. Gulotta & Stein, Mineola, N.Y., 1969-95. Dir. Am. Com. Italian Migration; dir. Syosset Little League, 1981-83, Edn. Assistance Corp., 1991-95; mem. Nassau County Police Boys Club; counsel for Sen. Ralph Marino, Com. on Crime, 1979-82. Mem. ABA, Nat. Assn. Criminal Def. Attys., N.Y. State Sheriffs Assn. (grievance com. 10th jud. dist. 1986-95, chmn. 1993-95), N.Y. State Bar Assn., Nassau County Bar Assn. (chmn. grievance com. 1983-85, bd. dirs. 1984—, pres. 1996-97) Criminal Courts Bar Assn., Former Asst. Dist. Attys. Assn. (dir., past pres.), N.Y. State Dist. Atty. Assn., N.Y. State Assn. Criminal Def. Attys., Am. Acad. Profl. Law Enforcement, Nat. Dist. Attys. Assn., Am. Judicature Soc., Columbian Lawyers Assn. (dir.), Am. Diabetes Assn., South Woodbury Civic Assn., Order Sons Itay, Elks, KC. Recipient Frank A. Gullata Criminal Justice award Former Dist. Attys. Assn., Man of Yr. award Middle Earth Crisis Ctr. Roman Catholic. Criminal, Family and matrimonial, General practice. Office: 262 Old Country Rd Mineola NY 11501-4255

GUMM, MARGARET R. lawyer; b. East Orange, N.J., June 25, 1940; d. John R. Gumm and Margaret M. (Clay) Wahl. B.A., William Smith Coll., 1962; J.D., NYU, 1969. Bar: NY 1970. Asst. to pub. relations officer Exec. Council Episc. Ch., N.Y.C., 1963-70; assoc. Ponzan & Goldblum, Queens, N.Y., 1970-73, Norman S. Reich, 1973-78; atty. Human Resources Adminstrn. Office of Legal Affairs, City of N.Y., 1978-83, assoc. atty., 1983— ; counsel Episc. Women's Caucus, 1971-73, mem. Exec. Council, Episc. Diocese of N.Y., 1972-75. Mem. Canons Com., Episc. Diocese of N.Y., 1971-76; sr. warden St. Clement's Episc. Ch., N.Y.C., 1982— , mem. vestry, 1973— . Mem. Hobart and William Smith Club. of N.Y. (bd. govs. 1978-84), Phi Beta Kappa, Phi Sigma Iota. Office: Human Resources Adminstrn Office of Legal Affairs 220 Church St Fl 6 New York NY 10013-2904

GUNDERSON, BRENT MERRILL, lawyer; b. Vernal, Utah, Apr. 16, 1960; s. Merrill Ray and Betty Velate (Norton) G.; m. Julie Phillips, Oct. 28, 1983; children: Adam Brent, Jeremy Phillip, Matthew Norton, Hannah, Rachel, Mariah, Kayla, Jacob Elden. BA, Brigham Young U., 1984; JD, Columbia U., 1987. Bar: Ariz. 1987, U.S. Dist. Ct. Ariz. 1987, U.S. Tax Ct. 1994. Ptnr. Brown & Bain, Phoenix, 1987-96; pvt. practice Mesa, Ariz., 1996—. Pres. Ariz. Mgmt. Soc., Phoenix, 1996-97. Asst. dist. commr. Boy Scouts Am., Mesa, Ariz., 1994-97, scoutmaster troop 611, Mesa, 1991-94, troop 761, Mesa, 1999—, chair varsity scout com., 1997-98; precinct capt.

Mesa Rep. Precincts 47 & 17, 1988-94; cubmaster pack 761, Boy Scouts Am., 1998-99; mem. Ariz. Cmty. Found. Breakfast eries com., 2001—; mem. profl. advisors. com. Leave a Legacy, Ariz. Recipient Mesa Dist. award of Merit, 1997, Scoutmaster award of Merit Boy Scouts Am., 1992, named to Scout Leader Hall of Fame, 1993, Scouting Family Hall of Fame, 1999. Mem. Am. Immigration Lawyers Assn. (v.p. Ariz. chpt. 1992-93, Maricopa County Bar Found. (bd. dirs. 1991-95), East Valley Estate Planning Coun. (bd. dirs. 1997-2001, pres. 1999-2000), Am. Immigration Lawyers Assn., Ariz. Mgmt. Soc. (bd. dirs. 1997—). Mem. LDS Ch. Avocations: backpacking, fishing, China. Estate planning, Immigration, naturalization, and customs, Probate. Office: Gunderson & Denton PC 123 N Centennial Way Ste 150 Mesa AZ 85201-6747

GUNDERSON, MICHAEL ARTHUR, lawyer; b. Flint, Mich., Nov. 3, 1952; s. Robert Edward and Phyllis Elaine (Cronin) G.; m. Patricia Beatrice Holstein, Jan. 4, 1980; children: Eric Brendan, Ryan Dane. BA, U. Mich., 1974; postgrad. Gonzaga U. Law Sch., 1974; JD, Detroit Coll. Law, 1978. Bar: Mich. 1978, U.S. Dist. Ct. (ea. dist.) Mich. 1978, U.S. Dist. Ct. (we. dist.) Mich. 1980. Mem. firm Harvey, Kruse & Westen, P.C., Detroit, 1978-79, Fitgerald, Hodgman, Kazul, Rutledge, Cawthrone & King, P.C., Detroit, 1979-85; ptnr. Rutledge, Manion, Rabaut, Terry & Thomas, P.C., Detroit, 1986—; rep. assembly State Bar Mich., 1987—. Notes and comment editor Detroit Coll. Law Rev., 1976-77. Mem. ABA, Catholic Lawyers Soc. Detroit (pres. 1984-86, bd. dirs. 1981—), Mich. Bar Assn. , Detroit Bar Assn., Oakland County Bar Assn., Def. Research Inst., Am. Arbitration Assn. (arbitrator), Mich. Def. Trial Counsel, Incorp. Soc. Irish Am. Lawyers (bd. dirs. 1987—), Assn. Def. Trial Counsel, Wayne County Mediator Tribunal (mediator), Delta Theta Phi. Republican. Roman Catholic. State civil litigation, Insurance, Personal injury. Home: 659 Rivard Blvd Grosse Pointe MI 48230-1253 Office: Rutledge Manion Rabaut Terry & Thomas PC 2300 Buhl Bldg Detroit MI 48226

GUNDERSON, ROBERT VERNON, JR. lawyer; b. Memphis, Dec. 4, 1951; s. Robert V. and Suzanne (McCarthy) G.; m. Anne Durkheimer, May 15, 1982; children: Katherine Paige, Robert Graham. BA with distinction, U. Kans., 1973; MBA, U. Pa., 1974; MA, Stanford U., 1976; JD, U. Chgo., 1979. Bar: Calif. 1979, U.S. Dist. Ct. (no. dist.) Calif. 1979. Assoc. Cooley, Godward, Castro, Huddleson & Tatum, San Francisco and Palo Alto, Calif., 1979-84, ptnr., 1984-88, Brobeck, Phleger & Harrison, Palo Alto, 1988-95, mem. exec. com., 1991-95, chmn. bus. and tech. practice, 1992-95; founder, ptnr. Gunderson Dettmer Stough Villeneuve Franklin & Hachigian, Menlo Park, Calif., 1995—. Panelist Venture Capital and Pub. Offering Negotiation, San Francisco and N.Y.C., 1981, 83, 85, 92, Practicing Law Inst., N.Y.C. and San Francisco, 1986; moderator, panelist Third Ann. Securities Law Inst., 1985; dir. Heartport, Inc., Redwood City, Calif.; sec. Dionex Corp., Sunnyvale, Calif., 1983-88, Southwall Techs., Inc., Palo Alto, 1985-88, Conductus, Inc., Sunnyvale, 1992-2001, Remedy Corp., Mountain View, Calif., 1995-97; vis. lectr. U. Santa Clara Law Sch., 1985, 89. Exec. editor U. Chgo. Law Rev., 1978-79; contbr. articles to profl. jours. Mem. ABA (bus. law sect., various coms.), State Bar Calif. (panelist continuing legal edn. 1984), San Francisco Bar Assn., Am. Fin. Assn., Wharton Club (San Francisco Bay area). Avocations: contemporary art, music, travel. General corporate, Securities. Home: 243 Polhemus Ave Menlo Park CA 94027-5442 Office: Gunderson Dettmer Franklin & Hachigian 155 Constitution Dr Menlo Park CA 94025-1106

GUNGER, RICHARD WILLIAM, lawyer; b. Auburn, N.Y., Aug. 7, 1963; s. William Bruce and Lita Patricia G.; m. Barbara Jean Taber, Nov. 24, 1984; children: William Robinson, James Taber. BA magna cum laude, Alfred U., 1985; JD cum laude, Syracuse U., 1988. Bar: N.Y. 1989, U.S. Dist. Ct. (no. dist.) N.Y. 1991, U.S. Dist. Ct. (we. dist.) N.Y. 1993, U.S. Supreme Ct. 1993. Assoc. Albert D. DiGiacomo, Syracuse, N.Y., 1988-89, Cuddy, Durgala & Timian, Auburn, 1989-90; atty. pvt. practice, 1990—. Bd. dirs. Cayuga Counseling, Auburn. Alan L. Ponyman scholar, 1985. Mem. ABA, N.Y. State Bar Assn. Cayuga County Bar Assn., KC. Bankruptcy, Family and matrimonial, General practice. Office: 5 Court St Auburn NY 13021-3713

GUNN, ALAN, law educator; b. Syracuse, N.Y., Apr. 8, 1940; s. Albert Dale and Helen Sherwood (Whitnall) G.; m. Bertha Ann Buchwald, 1975; 1 child, William BS, Rensselaer Poly. Inst., 1961; JD, Cornell U., 1970. Bar: D.C. 1970. Assoc. Hogan & Hartson, Washington, 1970-72; asst. prof. law Washington U., St. Louis, 1972-75, assoc. prof., 1975-76; assoc. prof. law Cornell U., Ithaca, N.Y., 1977-79, prof., 1979-84, J. duPratt White prof., 1984-89; prof. law U. Notre Dame, Ind., 1989-96, John N. Matthews prof., 1996—. Author: Partnership Income Taxation, 1991, 3d edit., 1999; (with Larry D. Ward) Cases, Text and Problems on Federal Income Taxation, 4th edit., 1998; (with Vincent R. Johnson) Studies in American Tort Law, 1994, 2d edit., 1999. Methodist. Office: U Notre Dame Law Sch Notre Dame IN 46556

GUNN, MICHAEL PETER, lawyer; b. St. Louis, Oct. 18, 1944; s. Donald and Loretto Agnes (Hennelly) G.; m. Carolyn Ormsby Ritter, Nov. 27, 1969; children: Mark Thomas, Christopher Michael, John Ritter, Elizabeth Jane. JD, St. Louis U., 1968. Bar: Mo. 1968, U.S. Dist. Ct. (ea and we. dists.) Mo. 1968, U.S. Tax Ct. 1972. Assoc. Gunn & Gunn, St. Louis, 1968-81; ptnr. Gunn & Lane, 1981-86; pvt. practice Ballwin, Mo., 1986—. Rep. ea. dist. Mo. Ct. Appeals. Sgt. U.S. Army, 1969-75. Mem. ABA (del. Ho. of Dels. 1988—), St. Louis Bar Assn., The Mo. Bar (bd. govs. 1990—, exec. com. 1993-94, pres.-elect 1998-99, pres. 1999-2000), Lawyers Assn. St. Louis (pres. 1981-82), St. Louis Bar Found. (pres. 1988-89), Bar Assn. Met. St. Louis (pres. 1987-88), Nat. Conf. Bar Founds. (trustee 1990—, pres. elect 1993-94). Roman Catholic. State civil litigation, Estate planning, Probate. Home: 2232 Centeroyal Dr Saint Louis MO 63131-1910 Office: Gunn & Rossetes PC Ste 240 1714 Deer Tracks Trail Saint Louis MO 63131

GUNNING, FRANCIS PATRICK, lawyer, insurance association executive; b. Scranton, Pa., Dec. 10, 1923; s. Frank Peter and Mary Loretta (Kelly) G.; m. Nancy C. Hill, Aug. 10, 1951; 1 son, Brian F. Student, City Coll. N.Y., 1941-43; LLB, St. John's U., 1950. Bar: N.Y. 1950. Legal editor Prentice Hall Pub. Co., N.Y.C., 1950-51; legal specialist Tchrs. Ins. & Annuity Assn. Am., Coll. Retirement Equities Fund, 1951-53, asst. counsel, 1953-57, assoc. counsel, 1957-60, counsel, 1960-65, asst. gen. counsel, 1965-67, assoc. gen. counsel, 1967, v.p., assoc. gen. counsel, 1967-73, sr. v.p., gen. counsel, 1973-74, exec. v.p., gen. counsel, 1974-88, ret., 1988. Trustee, mem. exec. and audit coms. Mortgage Growth Investors (now MGI Properties). Contbr. articles on mortgage financing to profl. jours. With USAAF, 1943-46. Mem. ABA, N.Y. State Bar Assn., Am. Land Title Assn., Am. Law Inst., Assn. of Bar of City of N.Y., Assn. Life Ins. Counsel, Nat. Assn. Coll. Univ. Attys., Am. Coll. Real Estate Lawyers. Republican. Roman Catholic. Home and Office: 32 Kewanee Rd New Rochelle NY 10804-1324

GUNTER, MICHAEL DONWELL, lawyer; b. Gastonia, N.C., Mar. 26, 1947; s. Daniel Cornelius and DeNorma Joyce (Smith) G.; m. Barbara Jo Benson, June 19, 1970; children: Kimberly Elizabeth, Daniel Cornelius III. BA in History with honors, Wake Forest U., 1969; JD with honors, U. N.C., 1972; MBA with honors, U. Pa., 1973. Bar: N.C. 1972, U.S. Dist. Ct. (mid. dist.) N.C. 1974, U.S. Tax Ct. 1975, U.S. Supreme Ct. 1979, U.S. Claims Ct. 1982, U.S. Ct. Appeals (D.C. cir.) 1985, U.S. Ct. Appeals (4th cir.) 1992. Ptnr. Womble Carlyle Sandridge & Rice PLLC, Winston-Salem, N.C., 1974—; chmn. employee benefits practice group. Bd. dirs. G & J Enterprises Inc., Gastonia, Indsl. Belting Inc., Gastonia. Contbr. articles to profl. jours. Coach youth basketball Winston-Salem YMCA, 1981-90; advisor Winston-Salem United Way Christmas Cheer Toy Shop, 1975; fundraiser Deacon Club Wake Forest U., also mem. exec. com., strategic planning com., athletic coun., 1987—, v.p., pres., 1990-92; bd. dirs. Goodwill Industries, Winston-Salem, 1987—, past chmn. bd., sec., chmn. fin. com., chmn. elect; bd. dirs. Centenary Meth. Ch., 1980, vice chmn. bd. dirs.; mem. community problem solving com. United Way, 1988—; mem. Leadership Winston-Salem, Alumni Coun. Wake Forest U., Cert. Com. NCAA, long range planning com. athletic dept. William E. Newcombe scholar U. Pa., 1972-73; selected One of Best Employee Benefits and Corp. Lawyers in Am., Nat. Law Jour. Fellow Am. Coll. Employee Benefits Counsel (charter); mem. ABA, So. Pension Conf., N.C. Bar Assn. (former chmn. tax sect., mem. continuing legal edn. com., sports and entertainment law com.), Forsyth County Bar Assn., Forsyth County Employee Benefit Coun., Winston-Salem Estate Planning Coun. (past bd. dirs.), Profit Sharing Coun. Am., ESOP Assn., Profit Sharing Coun., Assn. of Pvt. Pension and Welfare, Forsyth Country Club (former pres., bd. dirs.) Piedmont Club, Order of Coif, Rotary (former bd. dirs. Reynolda club). Democrat. Avocations: golf, fishing. Mergers and acquisitions, Pension, profit-sharing, and employee benefits, Corporate taxation. Home: 128 Ballyhoo Dr Lewisville NC 27023-9633 Office: Womble Carlyle Sandridge & Rice PLLC PO Drawer 84 1600 BB&T Financial Ctr Winston Salem NC 27102

GUNTER, RUSSELL ALLEN, lawyer; b. Amarillo, Tex., Feb. 21, 1950; s. J.B. and Shirley Ann (Russell) G.; children: Kim, Sarah, Laura, Rachel, Lindsay. BS in Polit. Sci., So. Ark U., 1972; JD, Tex. Tech U., 1975. Bar: Ark., 1975, Tex, 1975, U.S. Dist. Ct. (ea. and we dists.) Ark. 1975, U.S. Supreme Ct. (8th cir.) 1975, U.S. Dist. Ct. (no. dist.) Tex. 1976, U.S. Ct. Appeals (5th cir.), 1980, U.S. Supreme Ct. 1986. Assoc. Gaines N. Houston, Little Rock, 1975-79, Wallace, Dover & Dixon, P.A., Little Rock, 1979-90, McGlinchey Stafford Lang P.L.L.C., Little Rock, 1990-97; Cross, Gunter, Witherspoon & Galchus P.C., 1997—. Mem. ABA (com. on practice and procedure before NLRB labor sect.), Soc. for Human Resource Mgmt. (cert. sr. profl. in human resources), Ark. Bar Assn., Tex. Bar Assn. Labor. Office: 500 E Markham St Ste 200 Little Rock AR 72201-1747

GURFEIN, RICHARD ALAN, lawyer; b. N.Y.C., Nov. 4, 1946; s. Jack and Ruth (Kronowitz) G.; m. Erica P. Temchin, Oct. 20, 1978; children: Jared L., Amanda, Jessica M., Sarah R. BE, NYU, 1967; JD, Bklyn. Law Sch., 1971. Bar: N.Y. 1972, U.S. Dist. Ct. (so. and ea. dists.) N.Y. 1973, U.S. Supreme Ct. 1976, U.S. Ct. Appeals (2d cir.) 1990. Assoc. Mark B. Wiesen, PC, N.Y.C., 1972-78; ptnr. Wiesen & Gurfein, 1978-82, Wiesen, Gurfein & Jenkins, N.Y.C., 1982-2001; pres. Trial1.com, Inc., 1997—; founder Richard A. Gurfein & Assocs., PLLC, 2001—. Moderator, lectr. Nassau Acad. Law, 1984—, N.Y. State Trial Lawyers Inst., 1985—, treas., 1989-91, pres. 1995-96. Recipient Crown of Good Name award Inst. Jewish Humanities, 1996. Mem. Assn. Trial Lawyers Am., N.Y. State Trial Lawyers Assn. (lectr. continuing legal edn. 1985—, bd. dirs. 1986—, chmn. com. on coms. 1987-88, exec. com. 1987—, dep. treas. 1988-89, treas. 1989-91, sec. 1991-92, v.p. 1992-94, pres. elect 1994-95, pres. 1995-96, past pres. 1996—), N.Y. County Lawyers Assn., Nassau County Bar Assn. (chmn. com. on med. jurisprudence 1983-86), Million Dollar Advocates Forum. Avocations: astronomy, amateur radio, photography, golf, computing. State civil litigation, Personal injury, Product liability. Office: Richard A Gurfein & Assocs PLLC 11 Park Pl Rm 1100 New York NY 10007-2889 E-mail: rgurfein@trial1.com

GURION, HENRY BARUCH, lawyer; b. Duluth, Minn., Mar. 30, 1950; s. Maximilian and Gina (Spinner) G.; m. Joanne Francesca Bohman, Aug. 21, 1971; children: Lisa, David, Daniel, Charles. BA, U. Ill., 1972; JD, Loyola U., Chgo., 1975. Bar: Ill. 1975, U.S. Dist. Ct. (no. dist.) Ill. 1976. Assoc., Law Offices of Thomas J. Keevers, Chgo., 1975-79, Garretson & Santora, Chgo., 1979-81, Purcell & Wardrope Chartered, Chgo., 1981-85, Henry B. Gurion and Assocs., 1985-88; mng. atty. midwest region AIG Inc., 1988-91; v.p., gen. counsel MJML, 1991—. Mem. Ill. Bar Assn. Federal civil litigation, State civil litigation, Personal injury. Office: MJMC 3111 167th St Hazel Crest IL 60429-1025

GÜRLICH, RICHARD, lawyer; b. Prague, Czech Republic, Sept. 13, 1972; married. Law Degree, Charles U., Prague, 1996. Jr. asst. Law Firm Kocian Solc Balastik, Prague, 1996-98; jr. asst. firm Fiala Profous Maisner, 1998-2000, atty. firm, 2000—. Mem. Common Law Soc. Prague. Home: Katovicka 312 Prague 181 00 Czech Republic Office: Fiala Profous Maisner Vodickova 30 Prague 110 00 Czech Republic Fax: 420224215823. E-mail: gurlich@fpm.cz

GURSTEL, NORMAN KEITH, lawyer; b. Mpls., Mar. 24, 1939; s. Jules and Etta (Abramowitz) G.; m. Jane Evelyn Golden, Nov. 24, 1984; children: Todd, Dana, Marc. BA, U. Minn., 1960, JD, 1962. Bar: Minn. 1962, U.S. Dist. Ct. Minn. 1963, U.S. Supreme Ct. 1980. Assoc. Robins, Davis & Lyons, Mpls., 1962-67; prin. Gurstel & Gurstel, 1967-97. Arbitrator Hennepin County Dist. Ct., 1988-91; parttime referee family ct. Hennepin County Dist.; lectr. U. Minn. Family Law Seminar. Mem. ABA (corp. banking and bus. law and family law sects.), Minn. Bar Assn. (co-chmn. family ct. com. bankruptcy law sect. 1966-67, family law and bankruptcy law), Hennepin County Bar Assn. (chmn. family law com. 1964-65, vice chmn. 1981-91, fee arbitration bd., creditors remedy com.), Fed. Bar Assn., Assn. Trial Lawyers Am., Minn. Trial Lawyers Assn., Am. Acad. Matrimonial Lawyers, Nat. Council Juvenile and Family Ct. Judges, Comml. Law League Am. (recording sec. 1980-81, bd. govs. 1983-89, pres. 1987-88), Comml. Law League Fund for Pub. Edn. (sec. 1981-83, pres. 1989-92, bd. dirs. 1989-94), Phi Delta Phi. Jewish. Club: Oak Ridge Country (Mpls.). Lodges: Shriners, Masons. Bankruptcy, Contracts commercial, Family and matrimonial. Office: Marc Shawn Inc 3330 Galleria Edina MN 55435 E-mail: marcshawmen@att.com

GUSEWELLE, ANNE ELIZABETH, lawyer; b. Kansas City, Jan. 7, 1969; d. Charles Wesley and Katie Jane Gusewelle. BA, Vassar Coll., 1991; JD, U. Kans., 1996. Bar: Mo. 1996, Kans. 1997. Atty., law clk. hon. Joseph E. Stevens, Jr. U.S. Dist. Ct. (we. dist.) Mo., Kansas City, 1996-98; assoc. Shughart Thomson & Kilroy, 1998—. Mem. ABA, Kans. Bar Assn., Kansas City Met. Bar Assn. Democrat. Avocations: travel, skiing, painting, wine tasting, fishing. Office: Shughart Thomson & Kilroy 120 W 12th St Ste 1500 Kansas City MO 64105-1929 E-mail: agusewelle@kc.stklaw.com

GUSMAN, ROBERT CARL, lawyer; b. N.Y.C., Nov. 17, 1931; s. Samuel and Esther (Zuckerman) G.; m. Harriet Wish, Aug. 21, 1955; children: Amy, Jennifer, Julie. BA, NYU, 1953; JD, Cornell U., 1956. Bar: N.Y. 1957, D.C. 1960, Calif. 1962. Asst. counsel Office Gen. Counsel, Dept. of Navy, Washington, 1956-58; spl. legal advisor fleet ballistic missile program USN, 1958-60; asst. gen. counsel Aerojet-Gen. Corp., El Monte, Calif., 1960-70, Lockheed Corp., Calabasas, 1970-87, asst. sec., 1987-95, v.p., asst. gen. counsel, 1992-95. Editl. cons. fed. contract reports Bur. Nat. Affairs, Washington, 1970-84, adv. bd., 1984-95; spl. legal advisor Commn. on Govt. Procurement, Washington, 1970; instr. law Loyola U., L.A., 1971-72; chmn. indemnification project group Aerospace Industries Assn., Washington, 1984-86, chmn. legal com., 1986-88. Contbr. articles to profl. jours. Mem. ABA (chmn. pub. contract law subcoms.), Fed. Bar Assn. (conf. chmn. 1985-88), Am. Arbitration Assn. (arbitrator 1964—).

GUST, JOHN DEVENS, lawyer; b. Phoenix, Aug. 31, 1918; s. John Lewis and Ada Lee (Rebstock) G.; m. Mary Elizabeth Montgomery, Sept. 1, 1942; children— John Devens, Morgan M. A.B., Stanford U., 1940, J.D., 1942. Bar: Ariz. 1943. Ptnr., Gust, Rosenfeld, Divelbess & Henderson, Phoenix, 1946-86, sr. ptnr., 1968-86; sr. counsel, 1986—; dir. Valley Nat. Bank Ariz. Served to lt. j.g. USNR, 1941-46. Mem. ABA, State Bar Ariz. (past pres., dir.), Maricopa County Bar Assn. (past pres., dir.). Republican. Club: Ariz. Banking, Agricultural. Office: 3300 Valley Bank Ctr Phoenix AZ 85073

GUSTAFSON, ANNE-LISE DIRKS, lawyer, foreign consul; b. Vejle, Denmark, Aug. 14, 1934; came to U.S., 1955; d. Hans and Edith Margerita Dirks; m. William L. Gustafson, June 23, 1958. BA cum laude, U. Miami, 1963, JD, 1971, LLM, 1973. Vice consul Nation of Denmark, Miami, Fla., 1973-76; consul, 1976—; assoc. atty. Aronovitz & Weksler, 1976-83; pvt. practice, 1983—. Knighted by Queen of Denmark, 1976, 96. Mem. Fla. Bar Assn., Consular Corps Miami, Alpha Lambda Delta, Delta Phi Alpha, Kappa Delta Pi. Republican. Lutheran. General civil litigation, General practice, Probate. Home and Office: 2655 S Le Jeune Rd Ph 1D Coral Gables FL 33134-5827 Fax: 305-448-4151, 305-448-9707

GUSTE, ROY FRANCIS, lawyer, banker, planter, restaurateur; b. New Orleans, Nov. 28, 1923; s. William Joseph and Marie Louise (Alciatore) G.; BA, Loyola U. at New Orleans, 1943, LLB, 1948; m. Beverly Taylor, July 1, 1948; children: Roy Francis, Taylor, Colette, Robert, Beatrice, Michael. Admitted to La. bar, 1948, since practiced in New Orleans; ptnr. firm, Guste & Guste; owner, dir. Antoine's Restaurant, New Orleans, 1972—, Guste Island Plantation, Madisonville, La.; v.p., dir. Continental Savs. & Loan Assn., New Orleans, 1966-83. Pres. Young Men's Bus. Club, New Orleans, 1955-56, Pres's. Coun. Loyola U., 1973-77. Mem. adv. bd. Delgado Trade Sch., New Orleans, 1955-56; bd. dirs. Internat. House, New Orleans, 1955-56, Nat. Cath. Conf. for Interracial Justice, 1974-76; trustee Loyola U., 1980-88. Served with USNR, 1943-46. Mem. New Orleans, La. State, Am. bar assns., St. Thomas More Law Club, Alpha Delta Gamma, Delta Theta Phi. Republican. Roman Catholic (pres. archdiocese human rels. com., 1971-73). K.C. (4 deg.), Knight Grand Cross, Order of Holy Sepulchre of Jerusalem. Order of St. Louis. Home: 500 Guste Island Rd Madisonville LA 70447-9626

GUSTMAN, DAVID CHARLES, lawyer; b. Yokuska, Japan, Mar. 16, 1954; came to U.S., 1955; s. David C. and Marilyn N. Gustman; m. Lisa S. Seyferth, Mar. 7, 1987; children: Hunter, David, Corrie. BA in Econs., U. Mich., 1975; JD, George Washington U., 1979. Bar: Ill. 1979, U.S. Dist. Ct. (no. dist.) Ill. 1979, U.S. Dist. Ct. (ea. dist.) Wis. 1988, U.S. Dist. Ct. (ctrl. dist.) Ill. 1990, U.S. Dist. Ct. (so. dist.) Ill. 1991, U.S. Ct. Appeals (fed. cir.) 1988, U.S. Ct. Appeals (7th cir.) 1990, U.S. Supreme Ct. 1994, U.S. Ct. Appeals (8th cir.) 1997, U.S. Dist. Ct. (ea. dist.) Mich. 1997. Clk. Arter & Hadden, Washington, 1977-78; assoc. Rooks, Pitts & Poust, Chgo., 1979-84, Freeborn & Peters, Chgo., 1984-86, ptnr., 1986—, chmn., mng. ptnr., 1996-2000, chmn., 2000—. Operating com. Freeborn & Peters, 1992-2000. Articles editor: Jour. Internat. Law & Econs., 1978-79. Bd. dirs. Constitutional Rights Found., Chgo., 1982-88. Mem. ABA, Ill. State Bar Assn., Mich. Shores Club, Met. Club, Sheridan Shores Yacht Club. Avocations: skiing, sailing, running. Antitrust, General civil litigation. Office: Freeborn & Peters 311 S Wacker Dr Ste 3000 Chicago IL 60606-6679 Fax: 312-360-6571. E-mail: dgustman@freebornpeters.com

GUTHEINZ, JOSEPH RICHARD, JR. lawyer, politician, expert witness, investigative consultant; b. Camp Lejune, N.C., Aug. 13, 1955; s. Joseph R. Sr. and Rita A. (O'Leary) G.; m. Lori Ann Bentley, Jan. 16, 1976; children: Joseph, Christopher, Michael, Jim, Bill, Dave. AS, AA, Monterey Peninsula Coll., Calif., 1975; BA, Calif. State U., Sacramento, 1978, MA, 1979; postgrad., U. Calif., Davis, 1979-80; grad., U.S. Army Tactical Intelligence Schs., 1980, U.S. Army Flight Sch., 1984; MS in Sys. Mgmt., U. So. Calif., 1985; JD, S. Tex. Coll. Law, 1996; grad. (hon.), Fed. Law Enforcement Tng. Ctrs., 1988; grad. (disting.), Fed. Law Enforcement Tng. Ctrs. Office Inspector Gen., 1989. Bar: Tex. 1997, U.S. Dist. Ct. (so. dist.) Tex. 1997, U.S. Vets. Ct. Appeals 1998, U.S. Armed Forces Ct. Appeals 1998, U.S. Ct. Appeals (5th, 10th, 11th and fed. cirs.) 1998, U.S. Tax Ct. 1998, (U.S. Supreme Ct.). Officer U.S. Army, Kitzigen, Fed. Rep. Germany, 1980-82, capt., mil. intelligence officer Stuttgart, Fed. Rep. Germany, 1982-84, capt., aviator Ft. Polk, La., 1984-86; spl. agt. civil aviation security FAA, Oklahoma City, 1986-87; spl. agt. U.S. Dept. Transp., Denver, 1987-90; sr. spl. agt., acting sr. resident agent in charge Office Insp. Gen. NASA, Houston, 1990-2000; pvt. practice atty., 1996—. Pres. Citizen's for Fair Tax Funding, Calif., 1976—79; instr. Ctrl. Tex. Coll., Nelligan, Germany, 1983; guest spkr. Internat. Bus. Forum, 1995, Assn. Govt. Accts., 1996, NASA OIG Auditor Conf., 2000; task force leader Nine Agy. Fed. Omniplan, 1992—96; chief NASA OIG investigator Russian Mir Space Stas. fire and collision, 1997; chief investigator and arresting agt. Jerry Whittridge the astronaut and CIA assassin impersonator, 1998, Op. Lunar Eclipse, 1998—2000; task force leader Bid and Proposal Investigation Rockwell Space and Ops. Co., 1996—2000; task force leader Fed. Agy. Investigation Rockwell Internat./Boeing N.Am. and U.S. Alliance, 2000, others; mem. bd. dirs. Sea Isle Tex., 2001; spkr. in field. Pres. Citizens for Fair Tax Funding, 1977—79, Calif. State U. United Students for Life, 1976—79; proponent Calif. Pro-Life Initiative, 1977, 1978; organizer, active Morton Downey Dem. Presdl. campaign, 1979; Briefed Pres. Yeltsin's econ. advisors, 1995. Recipient U.S. Army Meritorious Svc. medal, 1986, Commendation medal, 1984, Commendation FBI dir. Louis Freeh, 1995, Tex. Spl. Commendation U.S. Atty. Office So. Dist., 1996, NASA Exceptional Svc. medal, 2000, Pres.'s Coun. for Integrity and Efficiency Career Achievement award, 2000; named Hon. Lt. Gov. Okla., 1987; Merit scholar S. Tex. Coll. Law; guest spkr. Cert. Fraud Examiners Conv., 2001. Mem. ATLA, Assn. Certified Fraud Examiners, Tex. Bar Assn. Republican. Roman Catholic. Avocations: reading, pistol shooting, volleyball, chess, weight lifting. General practice. Office: 205 Woodcombe Houston TX 77062 E-mail: jguteinz@cs.com

GUTHERY, JOHN M. lawyer; b. Broken Bow, Nebr., Nov. 22, 1946; s. John M. and Kay G.; m. Diane Messineo, May 26, 1972; 1 child, Lisa. BS, U. Nebr., 1969, JD, 1972. Bar: Nebr. 1972. Pres. Perry, Guthery, Haase & Gessford, P.C., L.L.O., Lincoln, Nebr., 1972—. Mem. ATLA, ABA (mem. litigation section), Nebr. Bank Attys. Assn. (past pres., 1985-86), Nebr. Assn. Trial Attys., Nebr. State Bar Assn. (pres. 1998-99, mem. Nebr.State Bar Found. mem. ho. dels. 1979-83, 87-95, exec. coun. 1988-94 pres. elect. 1997-98, chair Nebr. bankruptcy sect.), Lincoln Bar Assn. (bd. trustees, 1985-88, pres. 1990-91). Banking, General civil litigation, Personal injury. Office: Perry Guthery Haase & Gessford PC LLO 233 S 13th St Ste 1400 Lincoln NE 68508-2003 E-mail: jguthery@perrylawfirm.com

GUTHRIE, JUDITH K. federal judge; b. Chgo., July 13, 1948; d. David Curtis and Kathleen McAfee G.; m. John H. Hannah, Jr., May 9, 1992. Student, Ariz. State U., 1966-68; BA, St. Mary's U., 1971; JD cum laude, U. Houston, 1980; postgrad., Harvard U., 1990. Bar: Tex. 1981, U.S. Dist. Ct. (ea. dist.) Tex. 1982, U.S. Ct. Appeals (5th cir.) 1982, U.S. Dist. Ct. (no. dist.) Tex. 1983, U.S. Dist. Ct. (we. dist.) Tex. 1984. Editor Am. Coun. Edn., Washington, 1972-73; exec. asst. Tex. Ho. Reps., Austin, 1973-75; lobbyist Bracewell & Patterson, 1975-80, assoc. Houston, 1980-81; briefing atty. Tex. Ct. Appeals, Tyler, 1981-82; ptnr. Hannah & Guthrie, Tex., 1982-86; magistrate judge U.S. Dist. Ct. (ea. dist.) Tex., 1986—. Instr. legal asst. program, Tyler Jr. Coll., 1986-87; apptd. Tex. Judicial Coun., 1991-97, gender bias task force, 1991-92; lectr. in field. Contbr. articles to profl. jours. Bd dirs. Found. Women's Resources, Leadership Am., Leadership Tex.; adv. bd. Main St. Project; former Dem. chmn. Smith County; legal asst. adv. bd. Tyler Jr. Coll., 1986—, chmn. of adv. bd. 1996—; mem.

Citizens Commn. Tex. Judicial System, 1992-93. Mem. ABA (fed. trial judges legis. com. 1991-93), Am. Judges Assn., Fed. Magistrate Judges Assn., 5th Cir. Bar Assn., State Bar Tex. (dist. 2A grievance com. 1990-96, chmn. 1995-96, coun. mem. women and law sect. 1981-84, bd. dirs. lawyers' credit union 1983-84, citizens and law focused edn. com. 1984-85), Smith County Bar Assn. (chmn. law libr. com. 1985-2001). Office: US District Court 300 Federal Bldg & US Ct House 211 W Ferguson St Tyler TX 75702-7212

GUTMAN, HARRY LARGMAN, lawyer, educator; b. Phila., Feb. 23, 1942; s. I. Cyrus and Mildred B. (Largman) G.; m. Anne G. Aronsky, Aug. 28, 1971; children: Jonathan, Elizabeth. AB cum laude, Princeton U., 1963; BA, U. Coll., Oxford, Eng., 1965; LLB cum laude, Harvard U., 1965; MA (hon.), U. Pa., 1984. Bar: Mass. 1968, Pa. 1989, D.C. 1996, U.S. Tax Ct. 1969. Assoc. Hill & Barlow, Boston, 1968-75; ptnr., 1975-77; clin. assoc. Law Sch. Harvard U., Cambridge, Mass., 1971-77; instr. Boston Coll., 1974-77; atty.-advisor Office of Tax Legis. Counsel U.S. Dept. Treasury, 1977-78; dep. tax law legis. counsel, 1978-80; assoc. prof. law U. Va., Charlottesville, 1980-84; prof. Law Sch. U. Pa., 1984-89; ptnr. Drinker Biddle & Reath, Phila., 1989-91; chief of staff joint com. on taxation U.S. Congress, 1991-93; ptnr. King & Spalding, Washington, 1994-99, KPMG LLP, Washington, 1999—. Cons. Office Tax Policy U.S. Dept. Treasury, 1980; cons. Am. La Inst., 1980-84, reporter Generation-Skipping Tax project, Arden House III Conf.; vis. prof. Law Sch. U. Va., 1985-89, Ill. Inst. Tech., 1986. Author: Transactions Between Partners and Partnerships, 1973, Minimizing Estate Taxes: The Effects of Inter Vivos Giving, 1975, (with F. Sander) Tax Aspects of Divorce and Separation, 1985, (with D. Lubick) Treasury's New Views on Carryover Basis, 1979, Effective Federal Tax Rates on Transfers of Wealth, 1979, (with others) Federal Wealth Transfer Taxes after ERTA, 1983, Reforming Federal Wealth Transfer Taxes After ERTA, 1983, A Comment on the ABA Tax Section Task Force Report on Transfer Tax Restructuring, 1988, Where Does Congress Go From Here? Base Timing and Measurement Issues in the Transfer Tax, 1989. Fellow Am. Coll. Tax Counsel (trustee); mem. Am. Tax Policy Inst. (trustee). Office: KPMG LLP 2001 M St NW Washington DC 20036-3310 E-mail: hgutman@kpmg.com

GUTMAN, RICHARD EDWARD, lawyer; b. New Haven, Apr. 9, 1944; s. Samuel and Marjorie (Leo) G.; m. Jill Leslie Senft, June 8, 1969 (dec.); 1 child, Paul Senft; m. Rosann Seasonwein, Dec. 10, 1987. AB, Harvard U., 1965; JD, Columbia U., 1968. Bar: N.Y. 1969, U.S. Ct. Appeals (2d cir.) 1969, U.S. Dist. Ct. (so. and ea. dists.) N.Y. 1975, U.S. Supreme Ct. 1982, Tex. 1991. Counsel Exxon Corp., N.Y.C., 1978-90, Dallas, 1990-91, asst. gen. counsel, 1992-99, Exxon Mobil Corp., Dallas, 1999—. Pres. 570 Park Ave Apts., Inc., N.Y.C., 1984-89, past bd. dirs. Fellow Am. Bar Found. (life); mem. ABA (fed. regulation securities com., vice-chmn. 1995-98), Am. Law Inst., N.Y. State Bar Assn. (exec. com. 1983-86, 93—, securities regulation com. 1980—, chmn. 1993-97, chmn. bus. law sect. 2001), Assn. of Bar of City of N.Y. (securities regulation com. 1980-81, 83-86), Dallas Bar Assn., Coll. of the State Bar of Tex., N.A.M. (corp. fin. and mgmt. com.), Harvard Club (N.Y.C., admissions com. 1983-86, chmn. 1985-86, nominating com. 1986-87, bd. dirs. 1988-91, v.p. 1990-91), Harvard Club (Dallas bd. dirs. 1998—). General corporate, Finance, Securities.

GUTSTEIN, SOLOMON, lawyer; b. Newport, R.I., June 18, 1934; s. Morris Aaron and Goldie Leah (Nussbaum) G.; m. Carol Feinhandler, Sept. 3, 1961; children: Jon Eric, David Ethan, Daniel Ari, Joshua Aaron. AB with honors, U. Chgo., 1953, JD, 1956. Bar: Ill. 1956, U.S. Dist. Ct. (no. dist.) Ill. 1957, U.S. Ct. Appeals (7th cir.) 1958, U.S. Ct. Appeals (5th cir.) 1971, U.S. Supreme Ct. 1980; rabbi, 1955. Assoc. Schradzke, Gould & Ratner, Chgo., 1956-60; ptnr. firm Schwartz & Gutstein, 1961-65, Gutstein & Cope, Chgo., 1968-72, Gutstein & Schwartz, Chgo., 1980-83, Gutstein & Sherwin, Chgo., 1983-85; ptnr. Arvey, Hodes, Costello & Burman, 1991-92, Tenney & Bentley LLc, Chgo., 2000—. Spl. asst. atty. gen. State of Ill., 1968-69; adj. prof. law John Marshall Law Sch., 1993-96; lectr. bus. law U. Chgo. Grad. Sch. Bus., 1973-82; cons. Ill. Real Property Svc., Bancroft Whitney Co., 1988-89; lectr. in field; real estate broker. Author: Illinois Real Estate, 2 vols., 1983, rev. ann. updates, 1984—95; co-author: Construction Law in Illinois, annually, 1980—84, Judaism in Art (The Windows of Shaare Tivkah), 1995, Illinois Real Estate Practice Guide, 2 vols., 1996, rev. ann. edit., 1997—2001;contbr. chpt. to Commercial Real Estate Transactions, 1962-76; assoc. editor U. Chgo. Law Rev., 1954—56, editl. advisor Basic Real Estate I, also Advanced Real Estate II, 1960—70; author: Analysis of the Book of Psalms, 1962;contbr. articles to profl. publs. Mem. Cook County Citizens Fee Rev. Com., 1965; alderman from 40th ward Chgo. City Coun., 1975-79; mem. govt. affairs adv. com. Jewish Fedn., 1984-94. Fuerstenberg scholar U. Chgo., 1950-56; Kosmerl fellow U. Chgo., 1953-56. Mem. Ill. State Bar Assn. (real estate law sect. coun. 2001), Chgo. Bar Assn., Decalogue Soc. Lawyers, B'nai B'rith. Health, Probate, Real property. Office: Tenney & Bentley 111 W Washington St Ste 1900 Chicago IL 60602-2769 E-mail: tenben@interaccess.com, sol.gut@prodigy.com

GUTTMAN, EGON, law educator; b. Neuruppin, Germany, Jan. 27, 1927; came to U.S., 1958, naturalized, 1968; s. Isaac and Blima (Liss) G.; m. Inge Weinberg, June 12, 1966; children: Geoffrey David, Leonard Jay. Student, Cambridge U., 1945-48; LLB, U. London, 1950, LLM, 1952; postgrad., Northwestern U. Sch. Law, 1958-59. Barrister: Eng. 1952. Sole practice, Eng., 1952-53; faculty Univ. Coll. and U. Khartoum Sudan, 1953-58; legal advisor to chief justice Sudan, 1953-58; founder, editor Sudan Law Jour. & Reports, 1956-57; researcher, lectr. Rutgers U. Sch. Law, Newark, 1959-60; asst. prof. U. Alta., Edmonton, Can., 1960-62; prof. Howard U. Law Sch., Washington, 1962-68, vis. adj. prof., 1968-96; adj. prof. law Washington Coll. Law, Am. U., 1964-68, Levitt Meml. Trust scholar-prof., 1968—, dir. JD-MBA joint degree program, 1990-2000; lectr. Practicing Law Inst., 1964—. Adj. prof. law Georgetown U. Law Ctr., 1972-74, Johns Hopkins U., Balt., 1973-81; vis. prof. Faculty of Law, U. Cambridge, Wolfson Coll., Eng., 1984, U. Haifa, Israel, 2000; atty.-fellow SEC, 1976-79; cons. to various U.S. agys. and spl. commns.; U.S. rep. to UNCITRAL working groups; mem. various ALI-ABA working groups on the revision of the uniform comml. code; mem. Sec. of State's Adv. Com. on Pvt. Internat. Lawl arbitrator N.Y. Stock Exch. and NASD, 1997—. Author: Crime, Cause and Treatment, 1956, (with A. Smith) Cases and Materials on Domestic Relations, 1962, Modern Securities Transfers, 1967, 3d edit. 1987, cumulative supplement, 2000, (with R.G. Vaughn) Cases and Materials on Policy and the Legal Environment, 1973, rev. 1978, 3d edit. 1980, (with R.B. Lubic) Secured Transactions- A Simplified Guide, 1996; (with L.F. Del Duca and A.M. Squilante) Problems and Materials on Secured Transactions Under the Uniform Commercial Code, Commercial Transactions, vol. 1, 1992, (with F. Miller) supplement, 1996-98, Problems and Materials on Sales Under the Uniform Commercial Code and the Convention on International Sale of Goods, Commercial Transactions, vol. 2, 1990, supplement, 1997-98, Problem and Materials on Negotiable Instruments under the Uniform Commerical Code and the U.N. Convention on International Bills of Exchange and International Promissory Notes, Commercial Transactions vol. 3, 1993, supplement, 1997-98, Securities Laws in the United States - A Primer for Foreign Lawyers, 1996-99; contbr. numerous articles, revs., briefs to profl. lit. Howard U. rep. Fund for Edn. in World Order, 1966-68; trustee Silver Spring Jewish Ctr., Md., 1976-79; mem. exec. com. Sha'are Tzedek Hosp., Washington, 1971-72, 97—. Leverhulme scholar, 1948-51; U. London studentship, 1951-52; Ford Found. grad. fellow, 1958-59, NYU summer workshop fellow, 1960, 61, 64; Levitt Meml. Trust scholar-professor 1982; recipient Outstanding Svc. award Student Bar Assn., Am. U., 1970, Law Rev. Outstanding Svc. award, 1981, Washington Coll. of Law Outstanding Contbn. to Acad. Program Devel. award, 1981. Mem. Am. Law Inst., ABA, Fed. Bar Assn. Assn. Trial Lawyers Am., Brit. Inst. Internat. and Comparative Law, Soc. Pub. Tchrs. Law (Eng.), Hon. Soc. Middle Temple, Hardwick Soc. of Inns of Ct., Sudan Philos. Soc., Assn. Can. Law Tchrs., Am. Soc. Internat. Law, Can. Assn. Comparative Law, B'nai Brith Club, Argo Lodge, Phi Alpha Delta (John Sherman Myers award 1972). Home: 14801 Pennfield Cir Silver Spring MD 20906-1580 Office: Am U Washington Coll Law 4801 Massachusetts Ave NW Washington DC 20016-8196 Fax: (202) 274-4130. E-mail: guttman@wcl.american.edu

GUY, JAMES MATHEUS, lawyer, realtor; b. Wichita, Kans., Aug. 26, 1945; s. Jesse Milton and Roberta Aldine (Housholder) G.; m. Cindy K. Sundell, Dec. 31, 1978. BA, U. Kans., 1967; JD, Washburn Coll., 1970. Bar: Kans. 1970, U.S. Dist. Ct. Kans. 1970. Assoc., Coombs & Brick, Wichita, Kans., 1970-71; atty. Fed. Land. Bank, Wichita, 1971-76, sr. atty., 1976-78, prin. atty., 1978-84, asst. gen. counsel litigation, 1985-86; realtor, gen. counsel and owner Century 21 Consol. Realty, Inc., Wichita, 1986—. Founding mem. Kans. Preservation Alliance, Topeka, 1979—; pres. Midtown Citizens Assn., Wichita, 1984-85, mem MCA Exec. Bd., 1984-87; bd. dirs., exec. com. Hist. Wichita-Sedgwick County, Inc., 1974—; mem. Wichita Hist. Landmarks Preservation Com., 1981—; bd. dirs., pres. Victorian Soc. in Am., Kans. chpt., Wichita, 1974-84, Skinner Lee Victorian House Mus., Wichita, 1976-84; mem., chmn. Wichita Hist. Landmarks Preservation Council, 1981—. Washburn U. law scholar, 1967, law research fellow, 1968-70. Mem. Wichita Area Corp. Counsels (sec. 1982-83), Washburn Law Sch. Assn., Kans. U. Alumni Assn. Lodges: Mason, Shriners. Banking, Bankruptcy, Real property. Home: 1043 Jefferson St Wichita KS 67203-3575 Office: Century 21 Consolidated Realty Inc 1999 Amidon St Ste 105 Wichita KS 67203-2122

GUY, JOHN MARTIN, lawyer; b. Detroit, July 16, 1929; s. Alvin W. and Ann G. (Martin) G.; B.S., Butler U., 1958; J.D., Ind. U., 1961; children—Janice Lynn, Robert John. Bar: Ind. 1962. Practice law, Monticello, 1962—; atty. firm Guy, Christopher, Loy, 1962— ; mem. Ind. Ho. of Reps., 1971-74, house majority leader, 1973-74; mem. Ind. Senate, 1977-84, majority leader, 1979-80; Pros. atty. 39th Jud. Circuit, 1963-67. Pres. White County Mental Health Assn., 1965-68. Trustee Monticello-Union Twp. Library Bd., pres., 1970-71. Served with USAF, 1951-55. Named Outstanding Republican Freshman Ind. Ho. of Reps., 1971, Ind. Senate, 1977. Mem. Ind., Monticello Bar Assns., Am. Judicature Soc., Am. Trial Lawyers Assn., Monticello C. of C. (pres. 1975-76), Am. Legion, Masons, Shriners, Moose. Banking, Federal civil litigation, Probate. Office: 115 W Broadway PO Box 925 Monticello IN 47960-0925

GUY, RICHARD P. retired state supreme court justice; b. Coeur d'Alene, Idaho, Oct. 24, 1932; s. Richard H. and Charlotte M. Guy; m. Marilyn K. Guy, Nov. 16, 1963; children: Victoria, Heidi, Emily. JD, Gonzaga U., 1959. Bar: Wash. 1959, Hawaii 1988. Former judge Wash. Superior Ct., Spokane, from 1977; chief justice Wash. Supreme Ct., Olympia, 1998—. Capt. USAS. Mem. Wash. State Bar, Spokane County Bar Assn. Roman Catholic. Office: Wash Supreme Ct Temple Justice PO Box 40929 Olympia WA 98504-0929

GYEMANT, ROBERT ERNEST, lawyer, merchant banker; b. Managua, Nicaragua, Jan. 17, 1944; s. Emery and Magda (Von Rechnitz) G.; came to U.S., 1949, naturalized, 1954; A.B. magna cum laude, U. Calif. Los Angeles, 1965; J.D., U. Calif. Berkeley, 1968; children from previous marriage: Robert Ernest Jr., Anne Elizabeth; m. Sally Bartch Libhart, Oct. 17, 1992; children: Emily Bartch, Amanda Nancy, Katherine Libhart. Tax accountant Ernst & Ernst, CPAs, Oakland, Calif., 1966-68; CPA, Calif., 1967; admitted to Calif. bar, 1969, N.Y., 1981; asso. atty. Orrick, Herrington, Rowley & Sutcliffe, San Francisco, 1968-69; partner law firm Skornia, Rosenblum & Gyemant, San Francisco, 1969-74; law offices Robert Ernest Gyemant profl. corp., San Francisco, 1975; exec. v.p. finance Topps & Trowsers, San Francisco, 1977-79; cons., pvt. investor, 1979; with ComDial Corp, San Francisco; co-founder Com Vu Corp., N.Y.C., 1979-83; ptnr. Rosen, McCarthy, Gyemant & Babbits, P.C., San Francisco, 1993-97; prin. Knapp, Petersen & Clarke, P.C., Glendale, Calif., 1997-99, Hill, Farrer & Burrill, LLP, L.A., 1999-2000; mng. dir. Copp Wheelock Ptnr., LLC; instr. U. Calif. at Berkeley, 1968. Mem., ptnr. Calif. Council Criminal Justice Jud. Process Task Force, 1971-73. Mem. Calif. State Rep. Ctrl. Com.; trustee French-Am. Bilingual Sch., San Francisco, 1978-82; hon. vice consul Republic of Costa Rica, 1981—. Mem. ABA, San Francisco Bar Assn. (co-chmn. sect. on juvenile justice 1971) State Bar Calif. (cert. specialist criminal law 1988-93, com. on unauthorized practice law 1974-76, spl. com. on juvenile justice 1974, commr. San Francisco County juvenile justice comm. 1976—), AICPA, Calif. CPA Soc. (mem. accounting prins. com. 1969), Assn. Def. Counsel, Calif. Trial Lawyers Assn., San Francisco Downtown Assn., San Francisco World Trade Club, N.Y. Athletic Club, Racquet and Tennis Club (N.Y.C.). Author publs. in field; editor: Calif. Law Rev., 1967-68. Email: rgyemant@hfbllp.com.

HAAR, CHARLES MONROE, lawyer, educator; b. Dec. 3, 1920; came to U.S., 1921; s. Benjamin and Dora (Eisner) H.; children: Jeremy, Susan Eve, Jonathan. AB, N.Y.U., 1940; LLB, Harvard, 1948; MA, U. Wis., 1941; LLD, Lake Erie U., 1968, Hebrew Coll., 1988. Bar: N.Y. 1949, U.S Dist. Ct. (so. dist.) N.Y. 1950, U.S. Supreme Ct. 1968, Mass. 1978. Practice law, N.Y.C., 1949-52; asst. prof. law Harvard, 1952-54; prof., 1954-66, 69—, Louis D. Brandeis prof. law, 1972—; disting. prof. U. Miami Law Sch., 1998—. Chmn. Joint Ctr. for Urban Studies, Mass. Inst. Tech. and Harvard, 1969—, chmn. land policy roundtable Lincoln Inst. Land Policy; dir. Charles River Assocs.l asst. sec. met. devel. Dept. Housing and Urban Devel., Washington, 1966-69. Author: Land Planning Law in a Free Society, Feeral Credit and Private Housing, 1960, Law and Land, 1964, Golden Age of American Law, 1966, The End of Innocence, 1972, Housing the Poor in Suburbia, 1973, Suburban Problems, 1973, Property and Law, 1977, 2d edit., 1985, Of Judges, Politics and Flounders: Perspectives on the Cleaning Up of Boston Harbor, 1985; (with others) The Wrong Side of the Tracks, 1986, Fairness and Justice, 1987, Land-Use Planning: A Casebook in the Use, Misuse and Re-use of Urban Land, 4th edit., 1989, Landmark Justice, 1989, Zoning and the American Dream, 1989; editor: Beacon Classics of the Law, Suburbs Under Siege, 1992; contbr. articles to profl. jours. Chief reporter Am. Land Inst. project model code land devel. 1964-66; mem. Cambridge Redevel. Authority, Met. Area Planning Coun., Mass. Gov.'s Com. on Resource Mgmt., 1974, Fin. Adv. Bd., 1978—, Uniform Commn. State Laws, 1979—, Jerusalem Com., 1970—; chmn. Pres.'s Task Force Preservation Natural Beauty, Task Force on Model Cities, on Suburban Problems; chmn. com. on met. governance RFF, 1970-72; cons. WHite House AID, HHFA, U.S. Senate state and city agys.; mem. U.S. del. to UN Conf. on Habitat, 1976; pres. Regional and Urban Planning Implementation, Onc., bd. dirs. Zelda Zinn Found.; trustee Mass. Gen. Hosp., 1979—. Lt. (j.g.) USNR, 1942-46. Fellow Urban Land Inst.; mem. Am. Acad. Arts and Scis., Am. Inst. Planners, Brit. Town Planning Inst., Am. Bar Assn., Am. Law Inst., Phi Beta Kappa. Office: Harvard Law Sch Griswold 300 Cambridge MA 02138

HAARMANN, WILHELM, lawyer, tax advisor; b. Hagen, Westfalia, Germany, May 24, 1950; s. Wilhelm and Hilde (Rüsseler) H.; m. Elisabeth Strabl; 1 child, Elisabeth. JD, U. Münster, 1979. Bar: Germany; cert. tax advisor, pub. auditor. Intern Arthur Young & Co., Frankfurt, Germany, 1977-79; ptnr. Peat Marwick Mitchell, Munich, 1979-87; founding ptnr. Haarmann Hemmelrath & Ptnrs., Frankfurt, 1987—. Bd. dirs. R. Oldenberg, IBG, Genres, IXOS, chmn., Haussler AG, chmn.; supr. bd. SAP, AG, Walldorf, Germany, 1988, Mannesmann AG, Dusseldorf, Germany, 1999. Contbr. articles to profl. jours. With German army, 1968-69. Mem. Bar Germany, German Inst. Chartered Accountants (chmn. tax com. 1998—), German Internat. Fiscal Assn. (bd. dirs. 1999—). Contracts commercial, Mergers and acquisitions, Taxation, general. Office: Haarmann Hemmelrath & Ptnrs Neue Mainrer Str 75 60311 Frankfurt Germany E-mail: wilhelm.haarmann@hhpde

HAAS, JOSEPH ALAN, court administrator, lawyer; b. Riverside, Calif., June 30, 1950; s. Garland August and Pauline (Anderson) H.; m. Barbara Roberts, May 27, 1978; children: Natalie C., Christina R. BA in Econs., U. Wash., 1972, MA in Econs., 1974; JD, U. Puget Sound, 1983. Bar: Wash. 1984, U.S. Dist. Ct. (we. dist.) Wash. 1984, Md. 1986, U.S. Ct. Appeals (4th cir.) 1986. Regional coord. Adminstrv. Office U.S. Cts., Washington, 1975-80; chief dep. clk. U.S. Dist. Ct. for Western Wash., Seattle, 1981-84; clk. U.S. Dist. Ct. Md., Balt., 1984-96, U.S. Dist. Ct. for S.D., Sioux Falls, 1996—. Mem. Nat. Assn. for Ct. Mgmt., Fed. Ct. Clks. Assn. (pres. 1987-88, pres. elect 2000-01, pres. 2001—), Fed. Bar Assn. (bd. govs. 1989-96, treas. 1991-95), Wash. State Bar Assn. Office: US Dist Ct 400 S Phillips Ave Rm 128 Sioux Falls SD 57104-6851

HABECK, JAMES ROY, lawyer; b. Berlin, Aug. 11, 1954; s. Roy J. and Phyllis J. (Hazelwood) H.; m. Penny Ann Gillman. BS, U. Wis., Stevens Point, 1976; JD, Marquette U., 1979. Bar Wis. 1979, U.S. Dist. Ct. (ea. and we. dists.) Wis. 1979, U.S. Supreme Ct. 1990. Atty. Rutgers Law Office, Sheboygan Falls, Wis., 1979-80; pvt. practice Shawano, 1980—. Family ct. commr. Shawano, Menominee County, 1983—; corp. counsel Shawano County, 1984-87, 90, 93; legal counsel Wis. Towns Assn., Shawano, 1987—. Contbr. newsletter articles Wis. Towns Assn., 1987—. Pres. Big Brothers/Big Sisters, Shawano, 1984-88; v.p. Rep. Ctrl. Com., Shawano County, 1993-99, chmn. 1999—; atty. St. James Lutheran Ch., Shawano, 1983—. Named Friend of 4-H Shawano County 4-H, 1990. Mem. Shawano County Bar Assn. (sec.-treas., pres. 1987-93), Wis. Family Ct. Commrs. Assn. (sec.-treas., pres. 1992-96, dir. 1998—), Shawano County Agrl. Soc., Rotary, Shawano Area C. of C. (bd. dirs. 2000—), White Tails Unltd., Wild Turkey Fedn. Republican. Lutheran. Avocations: scoring high sch. basketball games. Family and matrimonial, Municipal (including bonds), Probate. Office: Habeck Law Office 141 N Main St Shawano WI 54166-2355

HABER, STEPHEN K. lawyer; b. Phila., Jan. 3, 1945; s. Benjamin F. and Dorothy L. (Kurtz) H.; A.B. cum laude, U. Pa., 1964; J.D., Yale U., 1968; m. Dorine Myriam Caddous, Nov. 4, 1982. Admitted to Pa. bar, 1968; with Sheriff Securities Corp., N.Y.C., 1968— , pres., dir., 1979— . Pres., Am. Friends of Haifa Maritime Mus., Inc. Mem. Pa. Bar Assn., N.Y. Bar Assn., N.Y. Stock Exchange. Jewish. Clubs: Explorers, Yale (N.Y.C.). Home: 5 E 22d St Penthouse C New York NY 10010 Office: 630 5th Ave Ste 2415 New York NY 10111-0100

HABERMANN, TED RICHARD, lawyer; b. Waupaca, Wis., Nov. 1, 1957; s. Richard Dale and Laura Aleen (Defrates) H. BS, U. Wis., 1980; JD, Valparaiso U., 1983. Bar: Ind. 1983, Tenn. 1989, U.S. Dist. Ct. (no and so. dists.) Ind. 1983, U.S. Dist. Ct. (mid. dist.) Tenn. 1990, U.S. Tax Ct. 1984, U.S. Supreme Ct., 1989. Mng. atty. Davisson & Davisson, P.C., Anderson, Ind., 1984-89; corp. counsel Spectra Distbn./Sound Stage Cos., Nashville, 1989-91; gen. counsel, sec. Servpro Industries, Inc., Gallatin, 1991-98; asst. gen. counsel, asst. sec. Shoney's Inc., Nashville, 1998-2000; gen. counsel, sec. Servpro Industries, Inc., Gallatin, Tenn., 2000—. Contbr. Valparaiso U. Law Rev. Mem. ABA, Ind. Bar Assn. (mem. forum on franchising), Tenn. Bar Assn., Jaycees (v.p. 1987), Exchange Club (dir. 1987), Sigma Phi Epsilon, Delta Theta Phi. Republican. Methodist. Franchising. Home: 4724 Aaron Dr Antioch TN 37013-4218 Office: Servpro Industries Inc 575 Airport Blvd Gallatin TN 37066 E-mail: tedhabermann@msn.com, thabermann@servpronet.com

HABUSH, ROBERT LEE, lawyer; b. Milw., Mar. 22, 1936; s. Jesse James and Beatrice (Liebenberg) H.; m. Miriam Lee Friedman, Aug. 25, 1957; children: Sherri Ellen, William Scott, Jodi Lynn. BBA, U. Wis., 1959, JD, 1961. Bar: Wis. 1961, U.S. Dist. Ct. (ea. and we. dists.) Wis. 1961, U.S. Ct. Appeals (7th cir.) 1965, U.S. Supreme Ct. 1986. Pres. Habush, Habush & Rottier, S.C., Milw., 1961—. Lectr. U. Wis. Law Sch., Marquette U. Law Sch., State Bar Wis., other legal orgns. Author: Cross Examination of Non Medical Experts, 1981; contbr. articles to legal jours. Capt. U.S. Army, 1959-75. Recipient Evan P. Helfaer Donor award Nat. Assn. Fundraising Execs., 200; named in his honor The Wis. Acad. of Trial Lawyers Robert L. Habush Trial Lawyer of Yr. Award, 2000. Mem. ATLA (bd. govs. 1983-86, pres. 1986-87, Harry Philo award 1999), ABA, Internat. Acad. Trial Lawyers (bd. dirs. 1983-87, 91-92), Internat. Soc. Barristers, Nat. Coll. Advocacy, Nat. Bd. Trial Advs., Am. Bd. Trial Advs., Am. Soc. Writers on Legal Subjects, Wis. Bar Assn., Wis. Acad. Trial Lawyers (pres. 1968-69), Inner Circle Advs., Trial Lawyers for Pub. Justice, Roscoe Pound Found. Federal civil litigation, State civil litigation, Personal injury. Office: Habush Habush & Rottier 777 E Wisconsin Ave Ste 2300 Milwaukee WI 53202-5381

HACKER, GARY LEE, lawyer; b. Denver, Nov. 28, 1939; s. Andrew Aris and Lena May (Brandt) H.; m. Aleta Szemcsak, Nov. 14, 1975; 1 child, Andrew John. BA, U. Colo., 1963; MA, U. Denver, 1971; JD, Baylor U., 1976. Bar: Tex. 1977, Fla. 1978. Commd. 2d lt. U.S. Army, 1963, advanced through grades to maj.; asst. city atty., Abilene, Tex., 1977; asst. dist. atty. Taylor County, Abilene, 1978; shareholder Whitten & Young, Abilene, 1978—; dir. Steamboat Mountain Water Corp., Tuscola, Tex., 1984—. Mem. ABA, ATLA, Tex. Bar Found., Abilene Bar Assn. Democrat. Lutheran. Avocation: golf. Bankruptcy, Contracts commercial, Oil, gas, and mineral. Office: Whitten & Young PC PO Box 208 Abilene TX 79604-0208

HACKETT, BARBARA (KLOKA), federal judge; b. 1928; B of Philosophy, U. Detroit, 1948, JD, 1950. Bar: Mich. 1951, U.S. Dist. Ct. (ea. dist.) Mich. 1951, U.S. Ct. Appeals (6th cir.) 1951, U.S. Supreme Ct. 1957. Law clk. U.S. Dist. Ct. (ea. dist.) Mich., 1951-52; chief law clk. Mich. Ct. Appeals, 1965-66; asst. pros. atty. Wayne County, Mich., 1967-72; pvt. practice Detroit, 1952-53, 72-73; assoc. Frasco, Hackett & Mills, 1984-86; U.S. magistrate U.S. Dist. Ct. (ea. dist.) Mich., Detroit, 1973-84, judge, 1986-2001. Mem. Interstate Commerce Commn., 1964. Trustee U. Detroit, 1983-89, Mercy High Sch., Farmington Hills, Mich. 1984-86, Detroit Symphony Orch., Orch. Hall Assocs., Detroit Sci. Ctr., United Community Svcs. Recipient Pres.'s Cabinet award U. Detroit Mercy, 1991. Mem. ABA (spl. ct. judge discovery abuse com. 1978-79, com. on cts. in cmty. 1979-84), Am. Judicature Soc., Fed. Bar Assn. (sec. 1981-82), Fed. Judges Assn., Nat. Assn. Women Judges, Nat. Dist. Attys. Assn., Nat. Assn. R.R. Trial Counsel, State Bar Mich., Women Lawyers Assn. Mich. Pros. Attys. Assn. Mich. (Disting. Svc. award 1971), Oakland County Bar Assn., U. Detroit Law Alumni Assn. (officer 1970-75, pres. 1975-77, Alumni Tower award 1976), Washtenaw County Bar Assn., Women's Econ. Club (bd. dirs. 1975-80, pres. 1980-81, named Detroit's Dynamic Women 1992), Econ. Club Detroit (bd. dirs. 1979-85, 88—), Phi Gamma Nu. Home: PMB 182 4195 S Tamiami Trl Venice FL 34193

HACKETT, KEVIN R. lawyer; b. Atlantic City, Apr. 16, 1949; BA summa cum laude, Boston Coll., 1971; JD, Harvard U., 1974. Bar: N.Y. 1975. Ptnr. Shearman & Sterling, N.Y.C. Fellow Am. Coll. Real Estate Lawyers; mem. ABA, N.Y. State Bar Assn., Assn. Bar City of N.Y., Phi Beta Kappa. Contracts commercial, Landlord-tenant, Real property. Office: 599 Lexington Ave Fl 1448 New York NY 10022-6030

HACKETT, ROBERT JOHN, lawyer; b. N.Y.C., Feb. 6, 1943; s. John P. and Marie S. (Starace) H.; m. Anita Carlile, Apr. 19, 1969; children: Robert J. Jr., John Peter, Kathryn Marie. AB, Rutgers U., 1964; JD, Duke U., 1967. Bar: N.Y. 1967, Ariz. 1972. Assoc. Milbank, Tweed, Hadley, McCloy, N.Y.C., 1967-71; ptnr. Evans, Kitchel & Jenckes, Phoenix, 1971-89; dir. Fennemore Craig, 1989—, course dir. seminar on mergers and acquisitions, 1996, 99. Mem. editl. bd. Duke Law Jour. Bd. dirs. Xavier Coll. Prep. Mem. ABA (com. on fed. securities regulation), State Bar Ariz. (past chmn. securities regulation sect.), Maricopa County Bar Assn., Assn. Corp. Growth (past bd. dirs., past pres. Ariz. chpt.), Phoenix Duke U. Law Alumni Club (past pres.), Pi Sigma Alpha. Republican. Roman Catholic. Banking, General corporate, Securities. E-mail: rhackett@fclaw.com

HACKETT, WESLEY PHELPS, JR. lawyer; b. Detroit, Jan. 3, 1939; s. Wesley P. and Helen (Decker) H.; children: Kelly D. Hackett Pell, Robin C. BA, Mich. State U., 1960; JD, Wayne State U., 1968. Bar: Mich. 1968, U.S. Dist. Ct. (we. dist.) Mich. 1971, U.S. Ct. Appeals (6th cir.) 1972, U.S. Dist. Ct. (ea. dist.) Mich. 1972, U.S. Supreme Ct. 1972, U.S. Ct. Mil. Appeals 1991. Law clk. Mich. Supreme Ct., Lansing, 1968-70; ptnr. Brown & Hackett, 1971-73; pvt. practice, 1973-84; ptnr. Starr, Bissell & Hackett, 1984-87; pvt. practice East Lansing, Mich., 1987-98, Saranac, 1998—. Adj. prof. Thomas M. Cooley Law Sch., Lansing, 1973—; instr. Lansing C.C., 1981-99. Author: Evidence: A Trial Manual for Michigan Lawyers, 1981, Hackett's Evidence: Michigan and Federal, 2d edit., 1995; co-author: Hiring Legal Staff, 1990. Mem. City of East Lansing Planning Commn., 1969-72; mem. Village of Saranac Planning Commn., 2000—; bd. dirs. St. Vincent Home for Children, Lansing, 1974-82. 1st lt. USAF, 1961-65. Fellow Coll. Law Practice Mgmt.; mem. ABA (sec. gen. practice sect. 1990-91, vice-chair 1991-92, chair 1993-94, standing com. on lawyer referral and info. svcs. 1997—, sole practitioner of yr. 1994, founders award 1997), State Bar Mich. (chair legal econs. sect. 1990-91). General corporate, Estate planning, Real property.

HACKLEY, DAVID KENNETH, lawyer; b. Chgo., Mar. 31, 1940; s. Kenneth Lewis and Helen (Sievers) H.; m. Janey D., June 2, 1962 (div. 1970); children: Gretchen Ann, David Edward; m. Sara E. Hayward, Mar. 5, 1985 (div. 1990). BA, Miami U., Oxford, Ohio, 1960; MA, U. Wyo., 1961; postgrad., U. Minn., 1961-62, JD, 1965. Bar: Minn. 1965. Law clk. Hennepin County Dist. Ct., Mpls., 1965-66; pvt. practice, 1966-83, 85—. Author: New Panama Canal Company and American Isthmian Diplomacy: 1894-1904, 1961. Chmn. Mpls. Bd. Housing Appeals, 1968-83. Mem. Minn. State Bar Assn., Hennepin County Bar Assn. (ethics com. 1982-87, fee arbitration com. 1977-88, chmn. 1986-87), Toastmasters. Contracts commercial, General corporate, Labor. Office: 3400 W 66th St # 325407 Minneapolis MN 55435-2111

HACKMAN, MARVIN LAWRENCE, lawyer; b. Jasper, Ind., Jan. 29, 1934; s. Theodore Peter and Sarah Rose (Bellner) H.; m. Jane Marie Sermersheim, Aug. 23, 1958; children: Stephen J., Anne M., Michael A., Daniel T. AB summa cum laude, St. Joseph Coll., 1956; JD magna cum laude, Ind. U., 1959. Bar: Ind. 1959, U.S. Dist. Ct. (so. dist.) Ind. 1959, U.S. Ct. Appeals (7th cir.) 1960. Law clk. to chief judge U.S. Dist. Ct., Indpls., 1959-61; mem. Hackman Hulett & Cracraft LLP, 1961—. Mem. ABA, Ind. State Bar Assn., Indpls. Bar Assn., Phi Delta Phi, Order of Coif. General corporate, Finance, Real property. Home: 4021 Royal Pine Blvd Indianapolis IN 46250-2272

HACKNEY, HUGH EDWARD, lawyer; b. McGregor, Tex., July 17, 1944; BA, So. Meth. U., 1966, JD, 1969. Bar: Tex. 1970. Mem. Fulbright & Jaworski, LLP, Dallas, 1970-97; lawyer Locke Purnell Rain Harrell, 1998-99, Locke Liddell & Sapp LLP, Dallas, 1999—. Fellow: Coll. of Labor and Employment Lawyers; mem. ABA, State Bar Tex., Dallas Bar Assn., Houston Bar Assn., Phi Alpha Delta, Soc. Internat. Bus. Fellows, Internat. Bar Assn. General civil litigation, Private international, Labor. Office: Locke Liddell and Sapp LLP 2200 Ross Ave Dallas TX 75201-6776

HACKNEY, VIRGINIA HOWITZ, lawyer; b. Phila., Jan. 11, 1945; d. Charles Rawlings and Edith Wrenn (Pope) Howitz; m. Barry Albert Hackney, Feb. 15, 1969; children: Ashby Rawlings, Roby Howison, Trevor Pope. BA in Econs., Hollins Coll., 1967; JD, U. Richmond, 1970. Bar: Va. 1970. Assoc. Hunton & Williams, Richmond, Va., 1970-77, ptnr., 1977—. Pres. Am. Acad. Hosp. Attys. Chgo., 1992-93. Mem. agy. evaluation com. United Way of Greater Richmond, 1981-86; sustainer Jr. League of Richmond; mem. Am. Health Lawyers Assn. (pres. 1992-93, bd. dirs. 1988-94). Named Outstanding Woman in field of law, YWCA, Richmond, 1981. Mem. ABA (bus. law sect. 1984—, forum com. on health law 1982—), Va. State Bar (long range planning com. 1985-90, chmn. standing com. lawyer discipline 1986-90, exec. com. 1988-90, Bar Coun. mem. 1984-90). Avocations: tennis, skiing, reading, boating, walking. Administrative and regulatory, Health, Legislative. Office: Hunton & Williams Riverfront Plz East Tower 951 E Byrd St Richmond VA 23219-4074

HADDAD, ERNEST MUDARRI, lawyer; b. Boston, Oct. 30, 1938; s. Abraham and Elaine (Mudarri) H.; m. Kathleen L. Tracy; 1 child, Barton Edward; children from previous marriage: Scott Cochrane, Mark Mudarri. BA, Trinity Coll., Hartford, Conn., 1960; LLB, Boston U., 1964. Bar: Mass. 1964, U.S. Dist. Ct. Mass. 1966, U.S. Supreme Ct., 1981. Asst. dean and mem. faculty sch. law Boston U., 1966-71; asst. sec., gen. counsel Commonwealth of Mass. Exec. Office Human Svcs., Boston, 1971-76; gen. counsel Blue Cross and Blue Shield Mass. Inc., 1976-80; sec., gen. counsel The Mass. Gen. Hosp., 1981—, Ptnrs. HealthCare Sys., Inc., Boston, 1995—. Program chmn., mem. exec. com. Boston Study Group, 1979—; bd. commrs. Black Achievers Br. Greater Boston YMCA, 1995—. Bd. dirs. New Eng. Legal Found., 2001—. Recipient Trinity Coll. Alumni medal for Excellence, 1990. Mem. ABA, Am. Corp. Counsel Assn., Am. Health Lawyers Assn., Boston Bar Assn. (mem. coun. 1998—, exec. com. 1999—, fin. com. 1999—, treas. 2001—), Boston Bar Found. (trustee, 1998—), Boston U. Law Sch. Alumni Assn. (pres. 1998-99). General corporate, Health, Non-profit and tax-exempt organizations. Home: 144 Mount Vernon St Boston MA 02108-1128 Office: 800 Boylston St Ste 1150 Boston MA 02199-8001 E-mail: ehaddad@partners.org

HADEN, CHARLES HAROLD, II, federal judge; b. Morgantown, W.Va., Apr. 16, 1937; s. Charles H. and Beatrice L. (Costolo) H.; m. Priscilla Ann Miller, June 2, 1956; children: Charles H., Timothy M., Amy Sue. BS, W.Va. U., 1958, JD, 1961. Ptnr. Haden & Haden, Morgantown, W.Va., 1961-69; state tax commr. W.Va., 1969-72; justice Supreme Ct. Appeals W.Va., 1972-75, chief justice, 1975; judge U.S. Dist. Ct. No. and So. Dists. W.Va., Parkersburg, 1975-82; chief judge U.S. Dist. Ct. (so. dist.) W.Va., 1982—. Mem. W.Va. Ho. of Dels., 1963-64; asst. prof. Coll. Law, W.Va. U., 1967-68; mem. com. adminstrn. probation system Jud. Conf., 1979-86; mem. 4th Cir. Jud. Coun., 1986-91, 96-2000, U.S. Jud. Conf., 1997—, chair exec. com., 2000—. Mem. Bd. Edn., Monongalia County, W.Va., 1967-68; bd. dirs. W.Va. U. Found., 1986—; past. mem. vis. coms. W.Va. U. Coll. Law & Sch. Medicine. Recipient Outstanding Alumnus award W.Va. U., 1986; named Outstanding Appellate Judge in W.Va., W.Va. Trial Lawyers Assn., 1975, Outstanding Trial Judge in W.Va., 1982. Fellow Am. Bar Found., W.Va. State Bar Found.; mem. ABA, W.Va. Bar Assn., W.Va. State Bar Assn., Am. Judicature Soc., 4th Cir. Dist. Judges Assn. (pres. 1993-95), W.Va. U. Alumni Assn. (pres. 1982-83), W.Va. U. Order of Vandalia. Office: US Dist Ct PO Box 351 Charleston WV 25322-0351 E-mail: judge_haden@wvsd.uscourts.gov

HADLEY, RALPH VINCENT, III, lawyer; b. Jacksonville, Fla., Aug. 20, 1942; s. Ralph V. and Clare (Cason) H.; m. Carol Fox Hadley, Sept. 18, 1993; children: Graham Kimball, Christopher Bedell, Blair Vincent. BS, U. Fla., 1965, JD, 1968. Bar: Fla. 1968, Calif. 1972. Assoc. Kurz, Toole, Taylor & Moseley, Jacksonville, 1968-69; asst. atty. gen. State of Fla., Orlando, 1972-73; ptnr. Davids, Henson & Hadley, Winter Garden, Fla., 1973-80; sr. ptnr. Hadley & Asma, 1980-89, Parker, Johnson, Owen, McGuire, Michaud, & Hadley, Orlando, 1989-91, Owen & Hadley, Orlando, 1991-94, Hadley, Gardner & Ornstein, P.A., Winter Park, Fla., 1994-95; Swann, Hadley & Alvarez, P.A., 1995-2000; with Swann & Hadley, 2000—. Vice chmn. bd. dirs. Tucker State Bank, Winter Garden, 1981-88; vice chmn. bd. dirs., sec. Tucker Holding Co., Jacksonville, 1984-88; bd. dirs. BankFIRST, All Sign Products. Bd. dirs. Orange County Dem. Exec. Com., Orlando, 1974-81, Spouse Abuse, Inc., Orlando, 1975-81. Lt. comdr. USN, 1969-72, Vietnam. Recipient award of merit Orange County Legal Aid Soc., 1989, Disting. Svc. award Judge J.C. Jake Stone Legal Aid Soc., 1989, Pres. Pro Bono Svc. award Fla. Bar, 1992. Mem. ABA, Fla. Bar Assn., Calif. Bar Assn., Orange County Bar Assn. (legis. chmn. 1979, 82), Am. Inn of Ct. (master), Winter Park C. of C. (bd. dirs. 1979-80), West Orange C. of C. (bd. dirs. 1979-82), Rotary. Presbyterian. Banking, Contracts commercial, Real property. Office: 1031 W Morse Blvd Winter Park FL 32789-3715

HAEMIG, MARY JANE, religious studies educator; b. Mpls., Aug. 21, 1954; d. Ernest Albert and Jean Louise (Hafermann) Haemig. AB, U. Minn., 1977; MTheol. Studies, Harvard Div. Sch., 1981; JD, Harvard U., 1981, ThD, 1996. Bar: Ill. 1981. Atty., law dept. Continental Ill. Bank & Trust Co. of Chgo., 1982-89; asst. prof. religion Pacific Luth. U., 1994-99; assoc. prof. ch. history Luther Sem., 1999—. German Acad. Exch. fellow, 1981-82. Mem. ABA. Lutheran. Office: Luther Sem 2481 Como Ave Saint Paul MN 55108 E-mail: mhaemig@luthersem.edu

HAFER, JOSEPH PAGE, lawyer; b. Harrisburg, Pa., June 28, 1941; s. George Horace and Betty (Page) H.; children: Bradford G., Susan P., David E. AB, Lafayette Coll., 1963; JD with distinction, U. Mich., 1966. Bar: Pa. 1966, U.S. Dist. Ct. (mid. dist.) Pa. 1966, U.S. Supreme Ct. 1969, U.S. Ct. Appeals (3d cir.) 1976. Assoc. Metzger, Hafer, Keefer, Thomas & Wood, Harrisburg, 1966-77; mng. ptnr. Thomas, Thomas & Hafer, 1977—. Adj. prof. law Dickinson Law Sch., Carlisle, Pa. Pres. Cumberland Valley Sch. Bd., Mechanicsburg, Pa., 1976-85; pres. Hampden Twp. Rep. Assn., Camp Hill, Pa. Fellow Am. Coll. Trial Lawyers; mem. ABA, Pa. Bar Assn., Assn. Trial Lawyers Am., Pa. Trial Lawyers Assn., Dauphin County Bar Assn. (ct. rels. com.). Methodist. Insurance, Personal injury, Workers' compensation. Home: 1530 Waterford Camp Hill PA 17011-9000 Office: Thomas Thomas & Hafer PO Box 999 Harrisburg PA 17108-0999 E-mail: jph@tthlaw.com

HAFETS, RICHARD JAY, lawyer; b. N.Y.C., Apr. 23, 1951; s. Meyer Hafets and Marilyn (Glanzrock) Bell; m. Claire Margolis, June 18, 1972; children: Brooke, Amy. BS in Bus. summa cum laude, Am. U., Washington, 1973, JD magna cum laude, 1976. Bar: Md. 1976, U. S. Dist. Ct. Md. 1976, U.S. Ct. Appeals (4th cir.) 1976, U.S. Supreme Ct. 1981, D.C. 1997, U.S. Dist. Ct. (D.C.) 1997. Assoc. Piper & Marbury, Balt., 1976-84, ptnr., 1984—, chmn. labor and employment practice, 1990—, chmn. hiring and assoc. coms., 1988-91. Labor atty. Balt. Symphony Orch., 1986-93; bd. dirs., gen. counsel Am. Cancer Soc., Balt., 1983-89; bd. dirs. Md. Ballet, Balt., 1978-80. Mem. ABA, Md. Bar Assn., Balt. City Bar Assn., Order of Coif. Avocations: horses, skiing. General civil litigation, Labor. Home: 7346 Narrow Wind Way Columbia MD 21046-1262 Office: Piper Marbury Rudnick & Wolfe 6225 Smith Ave Baltimore MD 21209-3600 E-mail: richard.hafets@piperrudnick.com

HAFLING, MARILYN E. lawyer; b. Apr. 26, 1950; BA in Psychology, BS in Comm. Disorders, U. Minn., 1972; MS in Counseling Psychology, Nova U., 1984; JD, Stetson U., 1992. Bar: Fla. 1992. Clk. typist, tchr. asst., presch. dir., rsch. asst., 1966-73; speech pathologist Faribault (Minn.) State Hosp., 1973-75; program dir. REM Inc., Mpls., 1975-78; human svcs. counselor, supr. devel. svcs. State of Fla. Human Resource Svcs., 1979-89; atty. in pvt. practice Largo, Fla., 1992—. Mem. legal panel Pinellas ACLU, 1992—, bd. dirs., 1996-97; pres. bd. dirs. Resource Ctr. for Women, 1998—; mem. Women On the Way. Mem. NOW, ABA, Fla. Bar Assn., Clearwater Bar Assn., Assn. Women Lawyers (pres. 1992). Office: 11740 Currie Ln Largo FL 33774-3843

HAFNER, THOMAS MARK, lawyer; b. Evansville, Ind., Aug. 8, 1943; s. Theodore Paul and Josephine Margaret (Herpolsheimer) H.; m. Joy Ruth Roller, June 10, 1967; children: Mark, Sharon, Matthew, Michael, Martin. BA with distinction, Valparaiso U., 1965, JD, 1968. Bar: Ind. 1968, Tenn. 1980. Assoc. Nieter, Smith, Blume, Wyneken & Dixon, Ft. Wayne, Ind., 1968-70; atty. Magnavox Co., 1970-73, group counsel, 1973-77; sr. counsel N.Am. Philips Corp., 1977-80, Knoxville, Tenn., 1980-87, divsn. gen. counsel, 1988-89; v.p., gen. counsel Philips Consumer Electronics Co., 1989-97, Atlanta, 1997-2000, Philips Consumer Electronics N.Am., Atlanta, 2000—. Dir. Cherokee Health Sys., Inc., 1995-97. Mem. Electronic Industries Assn. (chmn. govt. and consumer affairs coun. 1981-86, vice chmn. law com. 1986, chmn. 1987-88, bd. dirs. consumer electronics group 1991-94), Am. Corp. Counsel Assn. (bd. dirs. at large Tenn. chpt. 1986-88, 90-97). Antitrust, Contracts commercial, Private international.

HAGAN, PETER ANTHONY, lawyer; b. Staten Island, N.Y., Nov. 30, 1947; s. Peter Anthony and Frances Theresa (Golumb) H.; m. Barbara Ann Sibulski, Apr. 29, 1973; children: Marygrace, Patrick, Michael, Elizabeth. AB, Fordham U., 1969; JD, St. John's U., 1972; MLS, Pratt Inst., 1978; LLM, NYU, 1983. Bar: N.Y. 1973, U.S. Dist. Ct. (ea. and so. dists.) N.Y., U.S. Ct. Appeals (2nd cir.) 1977, Pa. 1989. Sr. atty. Consol. Edison, N.Y.C., 1973—. Atty. Pax Christi, N.Y.C., 1983—. Author: Scout Leaders Legal Guidebook. Lt. JAGC USMC, 1969-73. Recipient Eagle Scout award Boy Scouts Am. Mem. Emerald Soc., Right to Life Party, Phi Beta Kappa. Roman Catholic. Avocations: running, weightlifting, scouting. Home: 134 Greeley Ave Staten Island NY 10306-3213 Office: Consol Edison 4 Irving Pl New York NY 10003-3502

HAGBERG, CHRIS ERIC, lawyer; b. Steubenville, Ohio, Dec. 19, 1949; s. Rudolf Eric and Sara (Smith) H.; m. Viola Louise Wilgus, Feb. 19, 1978. BS, Duke U., 1975; JD, U. Tulsa, 1978; postgrad., Nat. Law Ctr., George Washington U. Bar: Okla. 1978, Va. 1979, U.S. Ct. Appeals (4th cir.) Calif. 1986. Law clk. to presiding justice U.S. Dist. Ct. (no. dist.) Okla.; asst. counsel ADP Selection Office Dept. Navy, Navy Regional Contracting Ctr., Washington; counsel Naval Supply Ctr., Pearl Harbor, Hawaii; Pacific area counsel Naval Supply Sys. Command, Dept. Navy, Makakilo; assoc. counsel Navy Supply Sys. Command, Washington; atty. Pettit & Martin, L.A., 1985-87, Seyfarth, Shaw, Fairweather and Geraldson, Washington, 1988-91, U.S. Coast Guard HQ, Washington, 1992-93, USN, 1993-95, Dept. Navy OGC/NSWC Carderock, West Bethesda, Md., 1995—. Contbr. articles to legal jours. Lt. USN, 1970-74. Recipient David I. Milsten award, 1978, 7 Am. Jurisprudence awards, 1976-78, First prize Dept. Navy Legal Writing Contest, 1981. Mem. ABA, FBA, Nat. Contract Mgmt. Assn., Order of Coif. Democrat. Presbyterian. Administrative and regulatory, Government contracts and claims, Labor. Home: 9810 Meadow Valley Dr Vienna VA 22181-3215

HAGBERG, VIOLA WILGUS, lawyer; b. Salisbury, Md., July 3, 1952; d. William E. and Jean Shelton (Barlow) Wilgus; m. Chris Eric Hagberg, Feb. 19, 1978. BA, Furman U., Greenville, S.C., 1974; JD, U. S.C., 1978, U. Tulsa, 1978; DOD Army Logistics Sch. honor grad. basic mgmt. def. acquisition, def. small purchase, advanced fed. acquisition regulation, Fort Lee, Va., 1981-82. Bar: Okla. 1978, Va. 1979, U.S. Ct. Appeals (4th cir.) 1979. With Lawyers Com. for Civil Rights, Washington, 1979; pub. utility specialist Fed. Energy Regulatory Commn., Washington, 1979-80; contract specialist U.S. Army, C.E., Ft. Shafter, Hawaii, 1980-81; contract officer/supervisory contract specialist Tripler Army Med. Ctr., Hawaii 1981-83; supervisory procurement analyst and chief policy Procurement Div. USCG, Washington, 1983; contracts officer and chief Avionics Engring Contracting Br., 1984; procurement analyst office of sec. Dept. Transp., 1984-85; contracting officer Naval Regional Contracting Ctr., Long Beach, Calif., 1985-87; chief acquisition rev. and policy, Hdqrs. Def. Mapping Agy., Washington, 1987-92, dir. acquisitions, Fairfax, Va., 1992-93, dir. acquisition policy, 1994-96; dir. acquisition polity, tech., and legis. programs Nat. Mapping and Imagery Agy., 1996-97, Office of Gen. Counsel. Mem. ABA (law student div. liaison 1977-78), Nat. Contract Mgmt. Assn., Va. State Bar Assn., Okla. Bar Assn., Phi Alpha Delta, Kappa Delta Epsilon. General corporate, Environmental, Government contracts and claims. Home: 9810 Meadow Valley Dr Vienna VA 22181-3215 Office: Nat Imagery and Mapping Agy Office Gen Counsel 4600 Sangamore (MS-D-10) Bethesda MD 20816

HAGEN, DAVID WARNER, judge; b. 1931; BBA, U. Wis., 1956; LLB, U. San Francisco, 1959. Bar: Washoe County 1981, Nev. 1992. With Berkley, Randall & Harvey, Berkeley, Calif., 1960-62; pvt. practice Loyalton, 1962-63; with Guild, Busey & Guild (later Guild, Hagen and Clark Ltd. and Guild & Hagen Ltd.), Reno, 1963-93; judge U.S. Dist. Ct. Nev., 1993—, chmn. 9th Cir. Art. III, judge edn. com., 1998-2000. Lectr U. Nev., 1968-72; acting dean Nev. Sch. of Law, 1981-83, adj. prof., 1981-87; mem. Nev. Bd. Bar Examiners, 1972-91, chmn., 1989-91; chmn. Nev. Continuing Legal Edn. Com., 1967-75; mem. Nev. Uniform Comml. Code Com. S/sgt. USAF, 1949-52. Fellow Am. Coll. Trial Lawyers (state chmn. 1983-85); mem. VFW, Nev. Bar Assn., Calif. Bar Assn., Washoe County Bar Assn., Am. Bd. Trial Advocates (advocate), Nat. Maritime Hist. Soc., U.S. Sailing Assn. Office: US Dist Ct Fed Bldg & US Courthouse 400 S Virginia St Reno NV 89501-2193

HAGEN, GLENN W(ILLIAM), lawyer; b. Detroit, July 8, 1948; s. William A. and Lilian (Abrolat) H.; m. Cynthia Winn, July 21, 1984. BS in Chemistry, U. Ala., 1970; JD, Valparaiso U., 1973. Bar: Mich. 1973, U.S. Dist. Ct. (we. dist.) Mich. 1974, Colo. 1981, U.S. Dist. Ct. Colo. 1982. Ptnr. Peters, Seyburn & Hagen, Kalamazoo, 1973-76; dep. city atty. City of Battle Creek, Mich., 1976-79; staff and regulatory counsel CF&I Steel Corp., Pueblo, Colo., 1979-81; gen. counsel Commonwealth Investment Properties Corp., Littleton, 1981-82; assoc. Berkowitz & Brady, Denver, 1982-83, Zarlengo, Mott, Zarlengo & Winbourn, Denver, 1983-87; pvt. practice Glenn W. Hagen, P.C., 1987—. Lectr. law office mgmt., personnel matters, small and mid-size bus. issues, corp. entity and formation issues Colo. Bar Assn. and Nat. Bus. Inst. Del. Colo. Rep. Com., 1986, 90, 92, 94, 96, 98, 2000; referee property tax appeals Douglas and Jefferson Counties; chmn. 18th Jud. Dist., 1999—; small bus. cons. South Met. Denver C. of C., 1994-2000. Mem.: ABA (young lawyers exec. coun. 1978—81, chmn. small bus. enterprises 1986, regional dir. constabars 1992—94, nat. editors conf. 1995, mem. constrn. forum 1996—), Mich. Bar Assn. (young lawyers exec. coun. 1978—80), Colo. Bar Assn. (chmn. long range planning com. 1983—86, gen. practice exec. coun. 1985, chmn.small firm section 1991—96, law office mgmt. com. 1995—, constrn. law sect. 1996—, chmn. 2001—, mem. exec. bd. chmn. budget com. 1987—89, mem. svcs. com. 1987—89, bus. law sect. 1986—91, alt. dispute resolutions com. 1990—94), Denver Bar Assn, Douglas-Elbert County Bar Assn., Am. Arbitration Assn., Colo. Lawyers for Arts, Highlands Ranch C. of C. (founder, bd. dirs., chmn. elect). Lutheran. Avocations: travel, photography, golf. General civil litigation, Construction, General corporate. Home: 2303 E Lansdowne Pl Highlands Ranch CO 80126-4936 Office: Highlands Ranch Bus Pk Ste 108 8925 S Ridgeline Blvd Highlands Ranch CO 80129-2354 Fax: 303-683-3521. E-mail: hagenlaw4biz@earthlink.net

HAGENDORF, STANLEY, lawyer, writer; b. Bklyn., Mar. 1, 1930; s. David and Fanny (Hammer) H.; m. Tilbeth Greene, Nov. 18, 1962; children: Lauren, Wayne, Richard. BS in Econs., U. Pa., 1953; JD cum laude, Harvard U., 1956; LLM in Taxation, NYU, 1961. Bar: N.Y. 1956, Fla. 1975. Assoc. Hellerstein, Rosier & Brudney, N.Y.C., 1957-59; pvt. practice, 1960-70; ptnr. Karow & Hagendorf, 1970-75, Hagendorf & Schlesinger, N.Y.C., Coral Gables, Fla., 1975-84, Hagendorf, Deason & Frank, 1984-85; pvt. practice N.Y.C., 1985-2000, Hagendorf Law Firm, Las Vegas, Nev., 2000—. Assoc. prof. U. Miami Law Sch., Coral Gables, 1975-80; dir.-lectr. Hagendorf Tax Workshop, N.Y.C. Author: Tax Manual for Corporate Liquidations, Redemptions and Estate Planning Recapitalizations, 1978, Liquidations, Redemptions and Recapitalizations: Taxation and Planning, 1986, Tax Guide for Buying and Selling a Business; editor: Tax Hotline, 2001; contbr. articles to profl. jours. Emeritus fin. and estate planning adv. bd. Commerce Clearing House. With U.S. Army, 1948-51. Recipient Disting. Lectr. award Nat. Soc. Pub. Accts. Scholarship Found., 1980, Cert. Appreciation, N.Y. County Lawyers Assn., 1982. Mem. ABA, N.Y. State Bar Assn., Fla. Bar Assn. (cert. tax lawyer). Corporate taxation, Estate taxation, Personal income taxation. Office: Hagendorf Law Firm 2000 S Jones Blvd Ste 240 Las Vegas NV 89146 E-mail: stanleyhagendorf@hagendorflaw.com

HAGERMAN, JOHN DAVID, lawyer; b. Houston, Aug. 1, 1941; s. David Angle and Noima L. (Clay) H.; m. Linda J. Lambright, June 25, 1975; children: Clayton Robert, Holly Elizabeth. BBA, So. Meth. U., 1963; JD, U. Tex., Austin, 1966. Bar: Tex. 1966, U.S. Ct. Appeals (5th cir.) 1967, U.S. Supreme Ct. 1969; cert. civil trial law, 1980-95; real estate broker Tex. Pres., owner Hagerman & Sereau, Inc., The Woodlands, Tex., 1966—. Condr. bank creditor rights seminars; mem. adv. bd. Klein Bank. Contbr. articles to profl. jours. Res. dep. sheriff Montgomery County, Tex.; former bd. dirs. Montgomery County Fair Assn., 1978—, Montgomery County Hosp. Dist. Found., Seven Coves Homeowners Assn. Mem. ABA, Tex. Bar Assn., Houston Bar Assn., Houston Outdoor Advtsg. Assn., Tex. Assn. Civil Trial Splsts., Tex. Assn. Bank Counsel, Comml. Real Estate Assn. Montgomery County, Houston Philosoph. Soc., Petroleum Club (Houston), Woodlands Country Club, Beta Theta Pi. Republican. Avocations: swimming, tennis, jogging, shooting. Banking, State civil litigation, Contracts commercial. Office: Hagerman & Seureau Inc 24800 Interstate 45 Ste 100 The Woodlands TX 77386-1987

HAGERMAN, MICHAEL CHARLES, lawyer, arbitrator, mediator; b. Webster City, Iowa, Aug. 20, 1951; s. Charles Arnold and Jill Hamilton (Son de Regger) H.; m. Birgit A. Hagerman; children: Kelly, Douglas, Alexander, Christine, Jacqueline. BA with honors, U. Iowa, 1973; MBA, U. Utah, 1978; JD, Drake U., 1981; Grad., U.S. Army Command/Gen. Staff, Coll., Ft. Leavenworth, Kans., 1988. Bar: Iowa 1981, Mass. 1995. Clk. Iowa Resources, Legal Aid of Polk County, and State of Iowa, Des Moines, 1978-81; contract atty. Fisher Controls Internat., Inc., Marshalltown, Iowa, 1981-84; contracts mgr. Emerson & Cuming, Inc., Canton, Mass., 1984-85; contract atty. GTE Govt. Sys., Taunton, 1986-90; v.p., gen. counsel, sec. ISI Sys., Inc., Andover, 1990-94; legal counsel Swan Tech. Inc., Marlboro, 1994-95; pvt. practice Franklin, 1995—; sr. contracts mgr.

Fleet Boston Fin., 1998—. Contbr. articles to profl. jours. Capt. U.S. Army, 1973-78, Germany; lt. col. U.S. Army Res. ret. Mem. Mass. Bar Assn., Sigma Chi (chpt. Balfour award 1973), Phi Alpha Delta (chpt. pres. 1980-81). Avocations: sailing, writing, travel. Contracts commercial, Computer, Labor. E-mail: mchagermanesq@msn.com

HAGGARD, WILLIAM ANDREW, lawyer; b. Miami, Feb. 20, 1942; s. Curtis Andrew and Marjorie (Tumlin) H.; m. Carole Ann Erali; children: Michael Andrew, Rebecca M. BA, Fla. State U., 1964; JD, Mercer U., 1967. Bar: Fla. 1967, U.S. Dist. Ct. (5th cir.) 1972, U.S. Supreme Ct. 1972, U.S. Ct. Appeals 1981. Clk. Fla. State Atty.'s Office, 1967; asst. state atty. Eleventh Jud. Cir., 1967-68; chief prosecutor, mil. judge, trial counsel USAF, 1968-71; assoc. Frates, Floyd, Pearson & Stewart, 1971-72; ptnr. Rentz, McClellan & Haggard, 1972-79, Rentz & Haggard, 1979-82; sr. ptnr. Haggard & Kirkland, 1982-89, Wm. Andrew Haggard & Assoc., 1989-93, Haggard & Stone, Coral Gables, Fla., 1993-95, Haggard Parks & Stone, P.A., 1995—, Haggard & Parks, P.A., 1999—. Instr. Fla. bar continuing legal edn., 1977-82; vis. lectr. U. Fla. Law Sch., 1977-82 Commr. Fla. Commn. on Ethics, 1990-91; mem. Mercer U. Alumni Bd.; bd. dirs. Fla. State U. Found.; chmn. Fla. State U. Coll. of Arts and Scis. Leadership Counsel. Fellow Internat. Acad. Trial Lawyers (state chair); mem. ATLA, ABA, Am. Bd. Trial Advocates, Dade County Bar Assn., Acad. Fla. Trial Lawyers (bd. dirs. 1995-96), Internat. Soc. Barristers, Million Dollars Advocates Club, Phi Delta Phi, Sigma Chi. Office: 330 Alhambra Cir Coral Gables FL 33134-5004 E-mail: mail@haggardparks.com

HAGGERTY, ROBERT HENRY, lawyer; b. N.Y.C., Feb. 25, 1919; s. Daniel A. and Helen Marie (Henry) H.; m. Mary Rita O'Neil, Aug. 28, 1945 (dec. 1990); children: Robert Jr., Daniel J., Nancy D., Thomas H; m. Nadia Ismail, 1991. BBA, Manhattan Coll., 1940; LLB, Harvard U., 1953. Bar: N.Y. 1954, Fla. 1977. Assoc. Root, Ballantine, Harlan, Bushby & Palmer (now Dewey, Ballantine), N.Y.C., 1965-95, 96—, ptnr., 1965—; atty. Gen. Electric Co., N.Y.C. and Schenectady, N.Y., 1956-62. Bd. dirs. Ticor Title Guarantee Co., N.Y.C. Editor: PLI Real Estate Construction Current Problems, 1973; editor (vols. 8, 29, 58) PLI Real Estate Construction, 1969-72. Bd. dirs. Plandome (N.Y.) Property Assocs., 1965-76, pres., 1970-76; pres. Plandome Mills Property Owners, 1980-82; village justice of Plandome Manor, 1983-89, mayor, 1989-93. Served to maj. USMC, 1941-45, PTO. Decorated Silver Star, Purple Heart. Mem. Plandome Country Club, Grand Harbor Golf and Country Club. Roman Catholic. Home: 146 I U Willets Rd Albertson NY 11507-2023 also: 1870 Paseo Del Lago Ln Vero Beach FL 32967-7260 Address: Dewey Ballantine 1301 Avenue Of The Americas New York NY 10019-6022

HAGGERTY, WILLIAM FRANCIS, lawyer; b. Orange, N.J., June 4, 1943; s. Francis Anthony and Grace Agnes (Cullen) H.; m. Emily Catherine Giacobazzi, Sept. 3, 1965; 1 child, Erin Catherine. AB, U. Detroit, 1965, JD, 1979; MA, Eastern Mich. U., 1970. Bar: Mich. 1980, U.S. Dist. Ct. (ea. dist.) Mich. 1980, U.S. Supreme Ct. 1992. Assoc. Greenbaum & Greenbaum, Southfield, Mich., 1979-80; legal editor Mich. Supreme Ct., Lansing, 1980-81, sr. legal editor, 1981-82, asst. reporter of decisions, 1982-84, acting reporter of decisions, 1984-85, reporter of decisions, 1985—. Adj. prof. Thomas M. Cooley Law Sch., Lansing, 1983-90; bd. trustees Libr. of Mich., 1990-93. Mem. Assn. Reporters of Jud. Decisions (sec. 1989-90, v.p. 1990-91, pres. 1991-92), Mich. Bar Assn. (adv. bd. Mich. Bar Jour.), Legal Authors Soc., Clarity, Irish Am. Cultural Inst. Office: Mich Supreme Ct PO Box 30048 Lansing MI 48909-7548 E-mail: haggertyb@jud.state.mi.us

HAGGLUND, CLARANCE EDWARD, lawyer, publishing company owner; b. Omaha, Feb. 17, 1927; s. Clarance Andrew and Esther May (Kelle) H.; m. Dorothy Souser, Mar. 27, 1953 (div. Aug. 1972); children: Laura, Bret, Katherine; m. Merle Patricia Hagglund, Oct. 28, 1972. BA, U. S.D., 1949; JD, William Mitchell Coll. Law, 1953. Bar: Minn. 1955, U.S. Ct. Appeals (8th cir.) 1974, U.S. Supreme Ct. 1963; diplomate Am. Bd. Profl. Liability Attys. Ptnr. Hagglund & Johnson and predecessor firms, Mpls., 1973—; mem. Hagglund, Weimer and Speidel, PA; publ., pres. Common Law Publishing Inc., Golden Valley, Minn., 1991—. Pres. Internat. Control Sys., Inc., Mpls., 1979—, Hill River Corp., Mpls., 1976—; gen. counsel Minn. Assn. Profl. Ins. Agts., Inc., Mpls., 1965-86; CFO, Pro-Trac, software for profl. liability ins. industry. Contbr. articles to profl. jours. Served to lt. comdr. USNR, 1945-46, 50-69. Fellow Internat. Soc. Barristers; mem. Lawyers Pilots Bar Assn., U.S. Maritime Law Assn. (proctor), Acad. Cert. Trial Lawyers Minn. (dean 1983-85), Nat. Bd. Trial Advocacy (cert. in civil trial law, bd. dirs.), Douglas Amdahl Inns of Ct. (pres.), Ill. Athletic Club (Chgo.), Edina Country Club (Minn.), Calhoun Beach Club (Mpls.). Roman Catholic. Avocation: flying. Federal civil litigation, State civil litigation, Insurance. Home: 3168 Dean Ct Minneapolis MN 55416-4386 Office: Common Law Publishing Inc 5101 Olson Memorial Hwy Golden Valley MN 55422-5149 E-mail: hagglund@prons.net

HAGIN, T. RICHARD, lawyer; b. Thomasville, Ga., Sept. 13, 1941; s. Wesley R. and Elizabeth (Skinner) H.; m. Deborah Hayes, June 19, 1981; children: Jennifer Bridges, Lori Mikula; children from previous marriage: John Wesley Hagin, Grace Elizabeth Hagin. AA, North Fla. C.C., Madison, 1961; student, Fla. State U., 1961-62; JD, Stetson U., 1964. Fla. 1964, Oreg. 1992, U.S. Dist. Ct. (mid. dist.) Fla. 1965, U.S. Ct. Appeals (5th cir.) 1965, U.S. Ct. Appeals (11th cir.) 1981, U.S. Ct. Mil. Appeals 1991, U.S. Supreme Ct. 1971. Atty. Law Offices of David A. Davis, Bushnell, Fla., 1964; ptnr. Davis and Hagin, 1965; atty. in pvt. practice, 1966-67; ptnr. Hagin, Hughes, Rardon & Rodriguez, 1989-1996, Getzen and Hagin, Bushnell, 1967-71; pres. Getzen & Hagin, P.A., 1971—. Local counsel CSX R.R., Bushnell, 1967-87, gen. counsel Tax Collector of Sumter County, Bushnell, 1976-95; forfeiture atty. Sumter County Sheriff Dept., Bushnell, 1983-89; county atty. Sumter County, Fla., 1969-76; city atty. City of Webster, Fla., 1966-87, City of Coleman, Fla., 1969-73; gen. counsel Sumter County Indsl. Authority, Bushnell, 1979-89, Sumter County Hosp. Authority, Bushnell, 1969-85. Mem. City Coun., Bushnell, 1967-69; pros. atty. Sumter County, 1969-73; chmn. Withlacochee Regional Planning Coun., Ocala, Fla., 1973-75; chmn. 5th Jud. Cir. Grievance Com., 1973-76. Mem. ABA, Assn. Trial Lawyers Am., Fla. Bar, Oreg. Bar Assn., Acad. Fla. Trial Lawyers. Democrat. Personal injury, Product liability, Workers' compensation. Office: Getzen and Hagin P A PO Box 248 Bushnell FL 33513-0248

HAGOOD, LEWIS RUSSELL, lawyer; b. Persia, Tenn., July 13, 1930; s. Hobart Verlin and Stella Rose (Carter) H.; m. Mary Evelyn Morrisette, Mar. 15, 1952; children: Lewis Russell Jr., Mary Victoria, Paul Gregory. Student, Lincoln Meml. U., Harrogate, Tenn., 1947-49; BS, East Tenn. State U., 1952; JD, U. Tenn., 1963. Bar: Tenn. 1964, U.S. Dist. Ct. (ea. dist.) Tenn. 1964, U.S. Dist. Ct. (ea. dist.) Ky. 1975, U.S. Tax Ct. 1984, U.S. Ct. Appeals (6th cir.) 1968, U.S. Supreme Ct.; cert. fed. mediator for Ea. Dist. Tenn.; cert. mediator Tenn. Supreme Ct. Ptnr. McLellan, Wright, Hagood, Attys., Kingsport, Tenn., 1964-65; assoc. Arnett & Draper, Attys., Knoxville, 1965-67; ptnr. Arnett, Draper & Hagood, 1967—. Mem., v.p. Tenn. Bd. Law Examiners, 1994—; spkr., lectr. in field. Editor-in-chief: Tennessee Law Review, 1963-64; contbr. articles to profl. jours. Bd. dirs. Knoxville Symphony Soc., 1977—; mem. East Tenn. chpt. March of Dimes, 1981-84; bd. dirs. Knoxville Teen Ctr., Inc., 1975-97. With U.S. Army, 1954-56. Fellow Tenn. Bar Found.; mem. ABA, Tenn. Bar Assn. (past chmn. labor law sect.), Knoxville Bar Assn. Republican. Presbyterian. Avocations: golf, fishing, antique autos. Federal civil litigation, State civil litigation, Labor. Office: Arnett Draper & Hagood Plz Towers Ste 2300 Knoxville TN 37929

HAGOORT, THOMAS HENRY, lawyer; b. Paterson, N.J., May 30, 1932; s. Nicholas Hugh and Rae (Sytsma) H.; m. Lois Ann Bennett, Sept. 6, 1954; children: Nancy Lynn Hagoort Treuhold, Susan Audrey Hagoort Bick. A.B. cum laude, Harvard U., 1954, LL.B. magna cum laude, 1957. Bar: N.Y. 1959. Assoc. firm Cleary, Gottlieb, Steen & Hamilton, N.Y.C., 1957-67, ptnr., 1968-90, of counsel, 1991—; gen. counsel Albany Internat. Corp., 1991—. Note editor, Harvard Law Rev., 1956-57. Pres. Mountainside Hosp., Montclair, N.J., 1983-85, chmn. bd. trustees, 1985-88; pres. Internat. Baccalaureate of N.Am., N.Y.C., 1980-91, Montclair Bd. Edn. 1966-70; mem., Coun. of Found. Internat. Baccalaureate Orgn., Geneva, 1982-96, pres. and chair exec. com., 1990-96. Mem. ABA, N.Y. State Bar Assn., Harvard Club of N.J. (pres. 1977-78), Montclair Golf Club, S.C. Yacht Club. Democrat. General corporate, Finance, Mergers and acquisitions. Home: PO Box 3229 Hilton Head Island SC 29928-0229

HAGOPIAN, JACOB, federal judge; b. Providence; s. Bedros and Varvar (Leylegian) H.; m. Mary L. Pomoranski; children: Mark Jay, Dana Aquinas, Mary Lou, Jan Christian, Jon Gregory. AB, George Washington U., 1957; JD, Am. U., 1960; grad. in internat. law, Judge Advocate Gen.'s Sch., 1964; postgrad., Indsl. Coll. Armed Forces, 1967. Bar: Va. 1961, R.I. 1964, U.S. Supreme Ct. 1964, U.S. Dist. Ct. R.I., U.S. Dist. Ct. (ea. dist.) Va., U.S. Ct. Appeals (D.C. cir.), U.S. Ct. Customs and Patent Appeals, U.S. Ct. Claims, U.S. Tax Ct. Enlisted U.S. Army, 1944, advanced through grades to 1st sgt. 11th Airborne Divsn., 2d lt. to 1st lt. 82d Airborne Divsn., 1948-50; capt. U.S. Army Security Agency, Washington, 1950-53, 56-60, with 501st Recon group Korea, 1953, Tokyo, 1954-56; advanced through grades to col. U.S. Army, 1953-68; appellate judge U.S. Ct. Mil. Rev. U.S. Army Ct. Criminal Appeals, Washington, 1968-70; ret. U.S. Army, 1970; appellate judge U.S. Army Judiciary, Washington, 1968-70; dir. law ctr. Roger Williams Coll., Providence, 1970-71; U.S. magistrate judge U.S. Dist. Ct., 1971—. Legal adv. to intelligence cmty. Spl. Ops., Berlin, 1960-63; group supv. def. appellate divsn. USA Judiciary, Washington, 1964-66; dep. and chief criminal law divsn. OTJAG dept. of army The Pentagon, Washington, 1966-68 mem. U.S. Army and U.S. Air Foce Clemency and Parole Bd.: lectr. Fed. Judicial Ctr., Washington; adj. prof. Am. U., 1971—, Suffolk U. Law Sch.; vis. prof. Naval War Coll.; mem. hon. faculty fellow AV, 1997—, hon. program U. R.I. Contbr. articles to profl. jours. Decorated Legion of Merit (2) with first oak leaf cluster; recipient Army Commendation medal with oak leaf cluster. Mem. ABA (former cons. sect. criminal justice, vice chmn. com. on adequate def. and incentives in mil., former sec.-reporter com. mil. law, Houston Justice Assist award 1987, mem. code com. uniform code mil. justice 2000—), Fed. Bar Assn. (past pres. R.I. chpt., mem. nat. coun., mem. nat. chmn. com. criminal law, chmn. U.S. magistrate judge's com.), Am. Judges Assn., Inst. Jud. Adminstrn., U.S. Naval War Coll. Found., Nat. Def. U. Found. Office: US Dist Ct Two Exchange Ter Providence RI 02903 Fax: 401-752-7006

HAHN, ELLIOTT JULIUS, lawyer; b. San Francisco, Dec. 9, 1949; s. Leo Wolf and Sherry Marion (Portnoy) H.; m. Toby Rose Mallen; children: Kara Rebecca, Brittany Atira Mallen, Michael Mallen, Adam Mallen. BA cum laude, U. Pa., 1971, JD, 1974; LLM, Columbia U., 1980. Bar: N.J. 1974, Calif. 1976, D.C. 1978, U.S. Dist. Ct. N.J. 1974, U.S. Dist. Ct. (cen. dist.) Calif. 1976, U.S. Supreme Ct. 1980. Assoc. von Malitz, Derenberg, Kunin & Janssen, N.Y.C., 1974-75; law clk. L.A. County Superior Ct., 1975-76; atty. Atlantic Richfield Co., L.A., 1976-79; prof. Summer in Tokyo program Santa Clara Law Sch., 1981-83; assoc. prof. law Calif. Western Coll. Law, San Diego, 1980-85; atty. Morgan, Lewis & Bockius, L.A., 1985-87; assoc. Whitman & Ransom, 1987-88, ptnr., 1989-93, Sonnenschein Nath & Rosenthal, L.A., 1993-97, Hahn & Bolson LLP, 1997—. Vis. scholar Nihon U., Tokyo, 1982; vis. lectr. Internat. Christian U., Tokyo, 1982; adj. prof. law Southwestern U. Sch. Law, 1986-93, Pepperdine U. law Sch., 1986-93, U. So. Calif. Law Sch., 1997-98; lectr. U. Calif., Davis, Law Sch. Orientation in U.S.A. Law Program, 1994-97. Author: Japanese Business Law and the Legal System, 1984; contbr. chpt. on Japan to The World Legal Ency.; internat. law editor Calif. Bus. Law Reporter. Vice-chmn. San Diego Internat. Affairs Bd., 1981-85; bd. dirs. San Diego-Yokohama Sister City Soc., 1983-85, L.A.-Nagoya Sister City Soc., 1986-1996; mem. master planning com. City of Rancho Palos Verdes, Calif., 1989-91; advisor, exec. com. Calif. Internat. Law Sect., 1990-91, 95, appointee exec. com., 1991-94, vice-chmn., 1992-93, chair, 1993-94; appointee, trustee Palos Verdes Libr. Dist., 1993-94; bd. dirs. Internat. Student Ctr. UCLA, 1996—, pres., 2000-01. Mem. ABA, State Bar Calif., L.A. County Bar Assn. (bd. dirs. internat. sect., exec. com. Internat. Legal Sec. 1987—, sec. 1995-96, 2d v.p. 1996-97, 1st v.p. 1997-98, chmn. 1998-99, appointee Pacific rim com. 1990-98, chmn. 1991-92, 95-98, trustee 1997-98), Assn. Asian Studies, U. Pa. Alumni Club (pres. San Diego chpt. 1982, pres. coun. Phila. 1983), Anti Defamation League, Japanese-Am. Soc. (book rev. editor Seattle 1983-85). Jewish. General corporate, Private international, Labor. Office: Hahn & Bolson LLP 1000 Wilshire Blvd # 1600 Los Angeles CA 90017-2457 E-mail: ehahn@hahnbolsonllp.com

HAHN, JOHN STEPHEN, lawyer; b. Sikeston, Mo., July 30, 1952; s. James William and Mary Margaret (Heady) H.; m. Jane Louise Trantham, Aug. 3, 1974; children: Elisabeth Peyton, David Trantham. AB, Duke U., 1974; JD, Yale U., 1977. Bar: D.C. 1977. Assoc. ptnr. Kirkland & Ellis, Washington, 1977-87; ptnr. Sonnenschein Nath & Rosenthal, 1987—. Recipient Oak Leaf award The Nature Conservancy, 1991. Mem. ABA (mem. environ. sect.), Duke Club (Washington), Yale Club (Washington). Republican. Methodist. Environmental. Office: Sonnenschein Nath & Rosenthal East Tower 1301 K St NW Ste 600 Washington DC 20005-3317

HAHN, PAUL BERNARD, lawyer; b. Prague, Czechoslovakia, Aug. 13, 1947; came to U.S. 1949, naturalized, 1954; s. George and Edith (Blum) H.; m. Denise Szabo, Aug. 7, 1976; children: Aaron, Ross. BA, Queens Coll., 1969; MS, L.I.U., 1971; JD, Bklyn. Law Sch., 1976. Bar: N.Y. 1977, U.S. Dist. Ct. (ea., so. dists.) N.Y. 1977. Tchr. Bklyn. Pub. Schs., 1969-77; assoc. J.V. Salierno Law Firm, Middle Village, N.Y., 1977-78; dist. office counsel SBA, N.Y.C., 1978-82; sr. assoc. Goldman, Horowitz & Cherno, Mineola, N.Y., 1982-83; sr. atty. Heller Fin., Inc., N.Y.C., 1983—; spl. asst. U.S. Atty. U.S. Atty.'s Office, so. dist., N.Y.C., 1981-82. Contbr. articles to profl. jours. Mem. ABA, Assn. of Bar of City of N.Y., Assn. Comml. Fin. Attys. (sec., bd. dirs.). Bankruptcy, Contracts commercial. Office: Heller Financial Inc 101 Park Ave New York NY 10178-0002

HAHN, WILLIAM EDWARD, lawyer; b. Bklyn., Sept. 3, 1946; s. Ernest Edward and Alice Elizabeth (Moench) H.; m. Elizabeth Weiler Fowles, Mar. 14, 1970; children: Bethany Elyce, Tara Elizabeth, Jillian Lisa. BA, Marietta Coll., 1968; JD, U. Fla., 1972. Bar: Fla. 1972, U.S. Dist. Ct. (mid. dist.) Fla. 1972, U.S. Dist. Ct. (so. and no. dists.) Fla. 1975. Ptnr. MacFarlane, Ferguson, Allison & Kelly, Tampa, Fla., 1972-78; shareholder Newman & Hahn, P.A., 1978-79, Shear, Newman & Hahn, P.A., Tampa, 1979-85, Shear, Newman, Hahn & Rosenkranz, P.A., Tampa, 1985—. Com. mem. civil jury instructions Fla. Supreme Ct., 1994-2000. Bd. dirs. Hillsborough County Crisis Ctr., Inc., Tampa, 1975—, indep. day sch., 1985-90. Mem. ABA, Am. Bd. Trial Adv. (pres. Tampa Bay chpt. 1999), Fla. Bar Assn. (chmn. grievance com. 1992-94; exec. com. Trial Lawyers sect. 2000—), Fla. Supreme Ct. (civil jury instrns. com.), Fedn. Ins. and Corp. Counsel, Hillsborough County Trial Lawyers (com. mem. 1990-94). Democrat. Methodist. Avocations: scuba diving, biking, tennis, swimming. General civil litigation, Personal injury, Professional liability. Home: 11742 Lipsey Rd Tampa FL 33618-3620 Office: Hahn Morgan & Lamb PA 2701 N Rocky Point Dr Ste 410 Tampa FL 33607-5919 E-mail: whahn@hml-law.com

HAIG, ROBERT LEIGHTON, lawyer; b. Plainfield, N.J., July 30, 1947; s. Richard Randall and Edith (Remington) H. AB, Yale U., 1967; JD, Harvard U., 1970. Bar: N.Y. 1971, U.S. Dist. Ct. (so. and ea. dists.) N.Y., U.S. Ct. Appeals (2d cir.). Assoc. Kelley Drye & Warren, N.Y.C., 1970-79, ptnr., 1980—. Mem. bd. advisers Law Dept. Mgmt. Adviser, 1995—. Co-author: Preparing for and Trying the Civil Lawsuit, 1987, 91, 94, 97, 2000, Federal Civil Practice, 1989, 93, 97, 2000, Federal Litigation Guide, 1992, 93, 94, Corporate Counsel's Guide, 1996, 97, Products Liability in New York, 1997; also contbr. chpts. to books, articles to profl. jours.; mem. bd. editors Fed. Litigation Guide Reporter, 1989—, In-House Law Practice Management, 1997—; editor-in-chief Comml. Litigation in N.Y. State Cts., 1995, Bus. and Comml. Litigation in Fed. Cts., 1998, Successful Partnering Between Inside and Outside Counsel, 2000. Co-chair Comml. Cts. Task Force, 1995—; mem. legis. com. Com. for Modern Cts., N.Y.C., 1986—, bd. dirs., 1994—, exec. com., 2001—; mem. Am. Law Inst., 1998—; mem. N.Y. State Conf. Bar Leaders, exec. coun., 1988-90, dept. disciplinary com. appellate divsn., 1996—, hearing panel chair, 1999—; mem. N.Y. State Jud. Salary Commn., 1997—. Recipient award for excellence in continuing legal edn. Assn. Continuing Legal Edn. Adminstrs., 1991. Fellow Am. Bar Found. (life), N.Y. Bar Found. (life, bd. dirs. 2001—); mem. ABA (del. 1991—, standing com. on jud. selection, tenure and compensation 1995-96, com. on bus. cts. 1996—, chair subcom. on rels. between inside and outside counsel 1997—), Assn. of Bar of City of N.Y. (mem. jud. com. 1985-88, chmn., 1989-92, mem. coun. on jud. adminstrn. 1989-92, chmn. 1996-99), N.Y. County Lawyers Assn. (exec. com. 1986-95, v.p. 1986-92, pres. 1992-94, dir. 1985—, chmn. com. on supreme ct. 1984-86, chmn. fin. com. 1988-90, lectr. 1984—, pres. Found. 1992-94), N.Y. State Bar Assn. (chmn. com. on fed. cts. 1986-88, del. 1988—, chmn. comml. and fed. litig. sect. 1988-90, lectr. 1985—, exec. com. 1991-94, mem. steering com. on commerce and industry 1997—, chair com. on multi-disciplinary practice and the legal profn. 1998-99, 1st Ann. award for Disting. Pub. Svc. comml. and fed. litig. sect. 1995). Federal civil litigation, General civil litigation, State civil litigation. Office: Kelley Drye & Warren LLP 101 Park Ave Fl 30 New York NY 10178-0062 E-mail: rhaig@kelleydrye.com

HAIGHT, CHARLES SHERMAN, JR. federal judge; b. N.Y.C., Sept. 23, 1930; s. Charles Sherman and Margaret (Edwards) H.; m. Mary Jane Peightal, June 30, 1953; children: Nina E., Susan P. B.A., Yale U., 1952, LL.B., 1955. Bar: N.Y. State 1955. Trial atty., admiralty and shipping dept. Dept. Justice, Washington, 1955-57; assoc. firm Haight, Gardner, Poor & Havens, N.Y.C., 1957-68, ptnr., 1968-76; judge U.S. Dist. Ct. for So. Dist. N.Y., 1976—. Bd. dirs. Kennedy Child Study Ctr.; adv. trustee Am.-Scandinavian Found., chmn., 1970-76; bd. mgrs. Havens Fund. Mem. Maritime Law Assn., U.S., N.Y. State Bar Assn., Bar Assn. City N.Y., Fed. Bar Council. Episcopalian. Office: US Dist Ct US Courthouse 500 Pearl St New York NY 10007-1316

HAILE, LAWRENCE BARCLAY, lawyer; b. Atlanta, Feb. 19, 1938; children: Gretchen Vanderhoof, Eric McKenzie (dec.), Scott McAllister. BA in Econs, U. Tex., 1958, LLB, 1961. Bar: Tex. 1961, Calif. 1962. Law clk. to U.S. Judge Joseph M. Ingraham, Houston, 1961-62; pvt. practice San Francisco, 1962-67, L.A., 1967—. Instr. UCLA Civil Trial Clinics, 1974, 76; lectr. law Calif. Continuing Edn. of Bar, 1973-74, 80-89; nat. panel arbitrators Am. Arbitration Assn., 1965—. Mem. editl. bd. Tex. Law Rev, 1960-61; contbr. articles profl. jours. Mem. State Bar Calif., Tex., U.S. Supreme Ct. Bar Assn., Internat. Assn. Property Ins. Counsel (founding mem., pres. 1980), Vintage Motorsports Coun. (past pres.), Phi Delta Phi, Delta Sigma Rho. Federal civil litigation, State civil litigation, Insurance. Office: 425 E Ocean Blvd Unit 340 Long Beach CA 90802-4951 E-mail: lhaile1938@aol.com

HAINES, TERRY L. lawyer, consultant; b. Washington, Oct. 2, 1957; s. John A. and Ann C. Haines; m. Cathy MacFarlane. BA, Oberlin Coll., 1979; JD, Vt. U., 1982. Bar: Pa. 1983, U.S. Dist. Ct. (we. dist.) Pa. 1983. Legis. asst. com. on judiciary Pa. Assembly, Harrisburg, 1983; sr. staff atty. FCC, Washington, 1983-87; rep. counsel com. on energy and commerce U.S. Ho. of Reps., 1987-91; chief of staff FCC, 1991-93; divsn. gen. counsel TCI East, Inc., Bethesda, Md., 1993-94; chief oper. officer, gen. counsel Boland & Madigan, Inc., Washington, 1995-2001; chief counsel, staff dir. U.S. Ho. of Reps. Com. on Fin. Svcs., 2001—. Avocations: golf, history. Antitrust, Communications, Computer. Office: US Ho of Reps Com on Fin Svcs 2129 Rayburn House Ofc Bldg Washington DC 20515

HAINES, THOMAS W. W. lawyer; b. Balt., Oct. 10, 1941; s. John Summer and Clara Elizabeth (Ward) H.; m. Vivienne Wilson, Jan. 3, 1981; children: Robert S., Elizabeth E., John M. BA, Cornell U., 1963; LLB, U. Md., 1967. Bar: Md. 1967, U.S. Dist. Ct. Md. 1968, U.S. Ct. Appeals (4th cir.) 1972, U.S. Tax Ct. 1973, U.S. Supreme Ct. 1975. Assoc. Semmes, Bowen & Semmes, Balt., 1968-75, ptnr., 1975-95, Venable, Baetjer & Howard, LLP, Balt., 1995—. Fellow Am. Coll. Trust and Estate (counsel); mem. ABA, Md. Bar Assn., Bar Assn. Balt. City, Gibson Island Club, Maryland Club. Episcopalian. Banking, General corporate, Intellectual property. Office: Venable Baetjer & Howard LLP 1800 Mercantile Bank Trust 2 Hopkins Plz Ste 2100 Baltimore MD 21201-2982 E-mail: twhaines@venable.com

HAIRSTON, GEORGE W. lawyer; b. Ironton, Ohio, Aug. 1, 1942; BBA, So. Meth. U., 1965; JD cum laude, Ohio State U., 1968. Bar: Ohio 1968. Mng. ptnr. Baker & Hostetler, Columbus, Ohio. Office: Baker & Hostetler Capitol Sq 65 E State St Ste 2100 Columbus OH 43215-4260

HAJE, PETER ROBERT, lawyer; b. N.Y.C., July 31, 1934; s. Arnold John and Edna Marie (Bossert) H.; m. Helen Heineman, Aug. 13, 1943; children: Michael James, Katherine Joy, Lily Elizabeth. BA, Cornell U., 1955; LLB, Harvard U., 1960. Bar: N.Y. 1961, U.S. Dist. Ct. (so. dist.) N.Y. 1965, U.S. Ct. Appeals (2d cir.) 1965, D.C. 1970, U.S. Ct. Appeals (D.C. cir.) 1981. Assoc. Paul, Weiss, Rifkind, Wharton & Garrison, N.Y.C., 1960-68, ptnr., 1969-90; exec. v.p., gen. counsel Time Warner Inc., 1990-99, gen. counsel emeritus, 2000—; counselor AOL Time Warner, 2000—. General corporate, Mergers and acquisitions, Securities. Office: Time Warner Inc Fl 30 1285 Ave of Americas New York NY 10019

HAJEK, FRANCIS PAUL, lawyer; b. Hobart, Tasmania, Australia, Oct. 21, 1958; came to U.S., 1966; s. Frank Joseph and Kathleen Beatrice (Blake) H. BA, Yale U., 1980; JD, U. Richmond, 1984. Bar: Va. 1984, U.S. Dist. Ct. (ea. dist.) Va. 1984, U.S. Ct. Appeals (4th cir.) 1986. Law clk. to presiding magistrate U.S. Dist Ct., Norfolk, Va., 1984-85; assoc. Seawell, Dalton, Hughes & Timms, 1985-87, Weinberg & Stein, Norfolk, 1987-89, I'Anson-Hoffman Am. Inn of Ct., 1991-97; ptnr. Wilson, Hajek & Shapiro, P.C., Virginia Beach, Va., 1989—. Legal counsel United Transp. Union, 1999—. Mem. ABA, ATLA, Am. Rail Labor Acad., Va. Bar Assn., Norfolk-Portsmouth Bar Assn. (chmn. exec. com. young lawyer's sect. 1990-91). Roman Catholic. Avocations: squash, tennis. Federal civil litigation, State civil litigation, Personal injury. Home: 1001 Caton Dr Virginia Beach VA 23454 Office: Wilson Hajek & Shapiro PO Box 5369 Virginia Beach VA 23471-0369 E-mail: fhajek@whslaw.com

HALAGAO, AVELINO GARABILES, lawyer; b. Santa Lucia, Ilocos Sur, The Philippines, Nov. 4, 1938; came to U.S., 1972; s. Manuel Habon and Marciana Garabiles H.; m. Concepcion Lorenzana Jimeno, aug. 1, 1962; children: Jesus Michael, Arleen Bernadette, Avelino Jr., Anna Maria, Amanda Marie. LLB, San Beda Coll. Law, Manila, 1962; M in Comparative Law, George Washington U., 1986. Bar: Va. 1987, D.C. 1992, The Philippines 1963. Ptnr. Bello, Halagao & Pimentel, Manila, 1963-65; atty. Commn. on Elections, 1965-70; judge Republic of The Philippines,

1970-72; trust officer Nat. Bank Washington, 1973-87; assoc. Coates & Davenport, McLean, Va., 1987-88; mng. ptnr. Avelino G. Halagao & Assocs., Tysons Corner, 1989—. Pres., chmn. bd. dirs. Manuel H. Halagao & Sons Transp. Co., Manila, 1968-72; chmn. bd. dirs. QX, Inc., Washington, 1995-97. Mem. Philippine-Am. Bar Assn. (founder, treas. 1976-78, pres. 1984-85, Leadership and Disting. Membership award 1990), Ilocano Soc. Am. (co-founder, pres. 1983-84). Roman Catholic. Avocations: basketball, golfing, fishing, dancing, singing. General corporate, Immigration, naturalization, and customs, Personal injury. Home: 3311 Cullers Ct Woodbridge VA 22192-1086 Office: Avelino G Halagao & Assocs 7799 Leesburg Pike Ste 900N Falls Church VA 22043-2413

HALE, JAMES THOMAS, retail company executive, lawyer; b. Mpls., May 14, 1940; s. Thomas Taylor and Alice Louise (Mc Connon) H.; m. Sharon Sue Johnson, Aug. 27, 1960; children: David Scott, Eric James, Kristin Lynn. BA, Dartmouth Coll., 1962; LLB, U. Minn., 1965. Bar: Minn. Law clk. Chief Justice Earl Warren, U.S. Supreme Ct., 1965-66; asso. firm Faegre & Benson, Mpls., 1966-73, ptnr., 1973-79; v.p., dir. corp. growth Gen. Mills, Inc., 1979-80, v.p. fin. and control consumer non-foods, 1981; sr. v.p., gen. counsel, corp. sec. Dayton-Hudson Corp., Mpls., 1981-2000; exec. v.p., gen. counsel, corp. sec. Target Corp., 2000—. Adj. prof. U. Minn., 1967-73. Mem. exec. com. Fund Legal Aid Soc., others. Mem. Order of Coif, Phi Beta Kappa. Office: Target Corp 777 Nicollet Mall Minneapolis MN 55402-2004

HALE, ZAN, editor, publisher; Editor Legal Intelligencer Daily Legal Jour., Phila. Office: American Lawyer Media Ste 1750 1617 John F Kennedy Blvd Philadelphia PA 19103-1821

HALEY, GEORGE PATRICK, lawyer; b. Bad Axe, Mich., Sept. 23, 1948; s. Glen Kirk and Bernice (Cooper) H.; m. Theresa L. Thomas, Dec. 24, 1975. BS, U. Mich., 1970; MS, U. Calif., Berkeley, 1971; JD, Harvard U., 1974. Bar: Calif. 1974, U.S. Dist. Ct. (no. dist.) Calif. 1974, U.S. Dist. Ct. (ea. dist.) Calif. 1980. Assoc. Pillsbury Winthrop LLP, San Francisco, 1974-81, ptnr., 1982—. Prof. U. Shanghai, Shanghai-San Francisco Sister City Program, 1986—. Author numerous articles uniform commercial code, project fin. Dir. Calif. Shakespeare Festival, Berkeley, 1986-93; dir. Nat. Writing Project, 1996—. Mem. ABA (chmn. com. 1976-93), Am. Coll. Comml. Fin. Lawyers, State Bar Calif. (chmn. fin. instns. com. 1980, commercial code com. 1988). Republican. Methodist. Avocations: tai chi chuan, golf, cooking. Home: 1825 Marin Ave Berkeley CA 94707-2414 E-mail: ghaley@pillsburywinthrop.com

HALEY, JOHN HARVEY, lawyer; b. Hot Springs, Ark., May 29, 1931; s. Harvey H. and Anne (Tanner) H.; m. Cynthia Martin, Sept. 7, 1997. AB, Emory U., 1952; LLB, U. Ark., 1955. Bar: Ark. 1955, U.S. Dist. Ct. (we. dist.) Ark. 1955, U.S. Ct. Appeals (8th cir.) 1955, U.S. Supreme Ct. 1971. Clk. Ark. Supreme Ct., Little Rock, 1955-56; ptnr. Rose Law Firm, 1956-71, Haley, Young, Bogard & Gitchell, Little Rock, 1971-73, Laser, Sharp, Haley, Young & Boswell, Little Rock, 1973-82, Haley, Polk & Heister, Little Rock, 1982-86, Arnold, Grobmyer & Haley, Little Rock, 1986-96; owner Haley Law Firm, 1996—. Bd. dirs. North Ark. Telephone Co., Flippin, Ark.; Munro and Co., Hot Springs, Ark., Binnacle Industries, Rose Creek Industries, Kappa Realty, Little Rock, Plaza Partnership, Talweg, LLC, Memphis; lectr. U. Ark. Law Sch., Little Rock, 1956-60, CLU instr., 1961-65; spl. counsel liquidation and rehab. Ark. Ins. Dept., 1967-71; pres. Combustion Technologies LLC, Little Rock, 1996—. Editor Ark. Law Rev., 1954-55. Chmn. Ark. State Bd. Correction, 1967-72, Ark. State Bd. Law Examiners, 1960-63, Election Rsch. Coun., Little Rock, 1961-64; dir. Wildwood Ctr. Performing Arts, Little Rock, 1994-99, Florence Crittenden Home, Little Rock, 1994-99; scoutmaster Second Presbyn. Ch. Troop, Little Rock, 1962-65. Methodist. Avocations: piloting, sailing, bicycling, underwater photography, skiing. General corporate, Real property, Taxation, general. Home: 3614 Doral Dr Little Rock AR 72212-2920 Office: Haley Law Firm PO Box 3730 Little Rock AR 72203-3730 Fax: 501-664-7539. E-mail: enginery@aol.com

HALFORD, RAYMOND GAINES, lawyer; b. Columbia, S.C., Apr. 10, 1925; s. Richard Eugene and Henrietta (Levy) H.; m. Wilma Eleazer, Dec. 31, 1960; children— Anne Lindsey, Richard Gaines. B.S., U. S.C., 1949, LL.B. cum laude, 1950. Bar: S.C. 1950, U.S. Dist. Ct. S.C. 1971, U.S. Ct. Appeals (4th cir.) 1978. Atty./advisor U.S. C.E., Aiken, S.C., 1950-52; account exec. Harris Upham & Co., Columbia, 1952-54; mortgage banker, Columbia, 1954-65; asst. atty. gen. Office Atty. Gen., Columbia, 1966— ; dep. atty. gen., gen. counsel S.C. Dept. Social Service, Columbia, 1983-84, S.C. Health and Human Services Fin. Commn., Columbia, 1984— . Div. chmn. United Fund, Columbia, 1958-59; Mem. YMCA; trustee United Community Services, Columbia, 1966-68. Served with U.S. Army, 1943-46. Named Outstanding Mem., Jr. C. of C., 1958; Disting. Service award Region IV, Nat. Welfare Fraud Assn., 1978. Mem. Clariosophic Literary Soc., , Order of Wig and Robe (chief justice), Delta Sigma Pi., Omicron Delta Kappa. Episcopalian. Home: 1162 Eastminister Dr Columbia SC 29204-3309 Office: SC Health and Human Services Fin Comm Jefferson Sq PO Box 8206 Columbia SC 29202

HALICZER, JAMES SOLOMON, lawyer; b. Ft. Myers, Fla., Oct. 27, 1952; s. Julian and Margaret (Shepard) H.; m. Paula Fleming, Oct. 3, 1987. BA in English Lit., U. So. Fla., 1976, MA in Polit. Sci., 1978; JD, Stetson U., 1981. Bar: Fla. 1982. Assoc. Conrad, Scherer & James, Ft. Lauderdale, Fla., 1982-86, ptnr., 1988-92; assoc. Bernard & Mauro, 1985-86; shareholder Cooney, Haliczer, Mattson, Lane, Blackburn, Pettis & Richards, 1992-96, Haliczer, Pettis & White, P.A., Ft. Lauderdale, Fla., 1996—. Mem. ABA, Fla. Bar Assn., Broward County Bar Assn., Assn. Trial Lawyers Am., Def. Rsch. Inst., Am. Acad. Healthcare Attys., Phi Kappa Phi, Pi Sigma Alpha, Omicron Delta Kappa. Democrat. Methodist. Avocations: reading, jogging. State civil litigation, Personal injury. Office: Haliczer Pettis & White PA 101 NE 3rd Ave Fort Lauderdale FL 33301-1162

HALKET, THOMAS D(ANIEL), lawyer; b. N.Y.C., July 20, 1948; SB in Physics, SM in Physics, MIT, 1971; JD, Columbia U., 1974. Bar: Mass. 1974, N.Y. 1979. Ptnr. Bingham Dana LLP, N.Y.C. Mem. ABA (chmn. divsn. aerospace law 1979-83, ventures and entrepreneur divsn. 1986-89, sect. sci. and tech. coun. 1982-85, program chmn. 1981-86, sec. 1985-86, vice-chmn. 1986-87, chmn. 1988-89), AAAS, AIAA (sr.), Am. Arbitration Assn. (chmn. tech. com. 1998—, computer disputes adv. com. 1992-96), Am. Phys. Soc., Bar Assn. City N.Y. (law and sci. com. 1987-90, computer law com. 1993-96, 1997-2000, tech. in law practice com. 1993-96, chmn. subcom. on software and uniform comml. code 1993-96, 97-99), Computer Law Assn. Computer, General corporate, Private international. Office: Binghham Dana LLP 399 Park Ave New York NY 10004 E-mail: tdhalket@bingham.com

HALL, ADAM STUART, lawyer; b. Atlanta, June 19, 1971; s. Andrew Clifford Hall and Patricia Ann Bursten. BA with honors, U. Fla., 1993, JD with honors, 1996. Bar: Fla. 1997, U.S. Dist. Ct. (so. dist.) Fla. 1997, U.S. Dist. Ct. (mid. dist.) Fla. 1998. Intern Supreme Ct. Fla., Tallahassee, 1995; assoc. Andrew Hall & Assocs., P.A., Miami, Fla., 1997-98, Hall, David and Joseph, P.A., Miami, 1998—. Chmn. unsecured creditor's com. Inre Telephone Co. Ctrl. Fla., Inc., Orlando, 1998-99. Mem. U. Fla. Coll. Law Alumni Coun., Gainesville, 1997—; mem. young leadership coun. United Way of Dade County, Miami, 1997—. Mem. ABA, ATLA, Acad. Fla. Trial Lawyers, Dade County Bar Assn. Avocations: scuba diving, skiing, football. General civil litigation, Professional liability, Securities. Office: Hall David and Joseph PA 1428 Brickell Ave Penthouse Miami FL 33131

HALL, CLYDE MATTHEW, lawyer, advocate; b. Pocatello, Idaho, Apr. 8, 1951; s. William Mckinley and Charlotte Rose (Truchot) H. Student Idaho State U., 1968-75; Cert. in Broadcasting , Career Acad.-San Francisco, 1970; JD, Utah State U., 1980. Bar: Idaho 1981, Tribal 1981. Park ranger Grand Teton Nat. Park, Moose, Wyo., 1975-79; art instr. Sho-Ban High Sch., Ft. Hall, Idaho, 1979-80; chief judge Ft. Hall Tribal Ct., 1980-83; Indian art cons. Grant Teton Nat. Park, 1983— ; performer Am. Indian Art Exchange, Seattle, 1983— ; lawyer Ft. Hall Tribes, 1983— ; cons. D.T. Vernon Indian Arts Mus., Denver Mus. Natural History; others. Contbr. articles to profl. jours. Mem, New Alliance Party, Washington, Native Am. Ch.; chmn. bd. dirs. Alcohol Adv. Bd., Ft. Hall, 1981-88. Mem. Credit Assn. Idaho, Internat. Credit Assn., Shoshone Bannock Tribal Bar Assn., Am. Indian Broadcasters Assn., Imperial Gem. Ct. of Idaho (ambassador to native Ams.), G.A.I. Club. Democrat. Home: PO Box 135 West Agency Rd Fort Hall ID 83203 Office: Fort Hall Tribal Ct PO Box 306 Fort Hall ID 83203-0306

HALL, CYNTHIA HOLCOMB, federal judge; b. Los Angeles, Feb. 19, 1929; d. Harold Romeyn and Mildred Gould (Kuck) Holcomb; m. John Harris Hall, June 6, 1970 (dec. Oct. 1980) A.B., Stanford U., 1951, J.D., 1954; LL.M., NYU, 1960. Bar: Ariz. 1954, Calif. 1956. Law clk. to judge U.S. Ct. Appeals 9th Circuit, 1954-55; trial atty. tax div. Dept. Justice, 1960-64; atty.-adviser Office Tax Legis. Counsel, Treasury Dept., 1964-66; mem. firm Brawerman & Holcomb, Beverly Hills, Calif., 1966-72; judge U.S. Tax Ct., Washington, 1972-81, U.S. Dist. Ct. for central dist. Calif., Los Angeles, 1981-84; cir. judge U.S. Ct. Appeals (9th cir.), Pasadena, Calif., 1984—, sr. judge, 1997—. Served to lt. (j.g.) USNR, 1951-53. Office: US Ct Appeals 9th Cir 125 S Grand Ave Pasadena CA 91105-1621

HALL, DAVID, law educator, dean, law educator, department chairman; b. Savannah, May 26, 1950; s. Levi and Ethel H.; m. Marilyn Braithwaite-Hall; children: Sakile, Kiamsha, Rahsaan. BS in Polit. Sci., Kans. State U., 1972; MA in Human Rels., U. Okla., 1975, postgrad., 1975-78, JD, 1978; LLM, Harvard U., 1985, Doctor Juridical Scis., 1988. Bar: Ill. 1978, Mass. 1978, Okla. 1978. Profl. basketball player Spaidero Pallacanestro, Inc., Udine, Italy, 1972-74; grad. asst. human rels. dept. U. Okla., Norman, 1974-75; lawyer Chgo. regional office Fed. Trade Commn., 1978-80; assoc. prof. law Sch. Law U. Okla., Norman, 1983-85; asst. prof. law Sch. Law U. Miss., 1980-83; assoc. dean academic affairs Sch. Law Northeastern U., Boston, 1988-92, prof. law, 1985—, dean Sch. Law, 1993-99, provost, 1999—. Instr. ethnic studies dept. and law ctr. U. Okla., Norman, 1975-79; Robert D. Klien U. lectr. Northeastern U.; co-chair legal edn. forum Law Sch. Harvard U., Cambridge, Mass., 1984-85, co-coord. Nat. Symposium on the Constitution and Race, 1987; coord. law student outreach program Barron Assessment Ctr., Boston. Contbr. numerous articles to profl. jours. Mem. bd. Mass. Civil Liberties Union, 1987-88, Inst. Affirmative action, Boston, TransAfrica Forum Scholars Adv. Coun., Washington, commn. on equal justice Mass. Legal Assistance Corp., 1995—, Nat. Consumer Law Ctr., 1993—; pres. African Cultural Soc. St. Paul A.M.E. Ch., Cambridge, Mass.; bd. dirs. Gang Peace Inc., 1995—. Named Professor of the Year NAACP, to Savannah Athletic Hall of Fame; honoree African Am. Ist. Oratory Competition; recipient Black Rose award Sigma Gamma Rho., Humanitarian award Nat. Conf. Cmty. and Justice, Outstanding Dean of Yr., Nat. Assn. Pub. Interest Lawyers, 1997. Fellow Am. Sociol. Assn.; mem. ABA (standing ocm. lawyers' pub. svc. responsibility 1995—), Assn. Law Sch. (diversity in legal edn. 1995-96), Boston Bar Assn., Mass. Bar Assn. (mem. bd. minorities in the profession 1995-96), Okla. Bar Assn. (Outstanding Sr. award), Nat. Conf. Black Lawyers (pres. Mass. chpt. 1986—), Black Faculty and Staff Orgn., Nat. Black Wholistic Soc. (pres. 1993, mem. bd. 1984—), Order of the Coif. Office: Northeastern U Office of Provost 112 Hayden Hall 360 Huntington Ave Boston MA 02115-5005 E-mail: d.hall@nunet.neu.edu

HALL, FRANKLIN PERKINS, lawyer, banker, state official; b. Amelia, Va., Dec. 12, 1938; s. Perkins Lee and Lois E. Hall; m. Phoebe Ann Poulterer, July 26, 1969; children: Kimberly Ann, Franklin P. Jr. BS, Lynchburg Coll., 1961; MBA, Am. U., 1964, JD, 1966. Bar: Va. 1966. Aide to U.S. Senate, Washington, 1964; asst. sec. Dept. HUD, 1968-69; sr. ptnr. Hall & Hall, Richmond, 1969—. Chmn. bd. Cardinal Savs. and Loan Assn., Richmond, Va., 1979-84; chmn. bd. Commonwealth Bank, Richmond, 1984— ; spl. counsel Va. Gen. Assembly, Richmond, 1970-75. Del. Va. House of Dels.; active Va. Gen. Assemly, 1976—; chmn. bd. Cen. Richmond Assn., 1974-75; pres. Richmond Jaycees, 1972-73. Recipient Disting. Svc. award Richmond Jaycees, 1972, Award Va. Jaycees, 1974, Disting. Citizen award Nat. Mcpl. League, 1976; named Outstanding Young Man of Va. award, 1973. Mem. Va. Trial Lawyers Assn. (bd. govs. 1982-84), Richmond Bar Assn. (exec. com. 1973-76), Soc. Advancement Mgmt., Newcomen Soc. Democrat. Presbyterian. Administrative and regulatory, Federal civil litigation, General corporate. Office: Hall & Hall 1401 Huguenot Rd Ste 100 Midlothian VA 23113-2662

HALL, HOWARD HARRY, lawyer; b. Syracuse, N.Y., Jan. 9, 1933; s. Harold Gibner and Mildred E. (Way) H. AB, Syracuse U., 1953, JD, 1959. Bar: N.Y. 1960, U.S. Ct. Appeals (2d cir.) 1960, U.S. Dist. Ct. (we., no., so.dists.) N.Y. 1960, U.S. Supreme Ct. 1963, Calif. 1978, U.S. Ct. Appeals (9th cir.) 1978, U.S. Dist. Ct. (we. dist.) N.Y., U.S. Dist. Ct. (cen. and so. dist.) Calif., 1978. Assoc. Hiscock, Cowie, Bruce, Lee and Mawhinney, Syracuse, N.Y., 1959-61; pvt. practice, 1961-74, Long Beach, Calif., 1978-82, Paramount, 1982—. Commr. of edn. Syracuse, N.Y., 1968-72. Capt. USMC, 1953-56. Mem. State Bar of Calif., Calif. Trial Lawyers Assn. Criminal, Insurance, Personal injury. Office: 15559 Paramount Blvd Paramount CA 90723-4330

HALL, JOHN HERBERT, lawyer; b. Orange, N.J., Dec. 5, 1942; s. Embert Brown Hall and Elizabeth (Sullivan) Carnahan; m. Suzanne Steeger, Aug. 21, 1965 (div. Apr. 1988); children: Christopher Evan, Jeremy Randall; m. Lisa Gersh, June 19, 1988; children: Samantha Gersh, Madeleine Gersh. BA, Wesleyan U., 1965; MBA, NYU, 1966; JD, Columbia U., 1969. Bar: N.Y. 1970, U.S. Dist. Ct. (so. dist.) N.Y. 1972, (ea. dist.) N.Y. 1981, U.S. Ct. Appeals (2d cir.) 1974, (10th cir.) 1977, (5th cir.) 1980, (11th cir.) 1981, (4th cir.) 1989, (D.C. cir.) 1982, U.S. Supreme Ct. 1981. Assoc. Debevoise, Plimpton, Lyons & Gates, N.Y.C., 1969-72, 73-78; grad. bus. Community Law Offices, 1972-73; ptnr. Debevoise & Plimpton, 1979—, chair litigation dept., 1993—. Bd. dirs. Community Law Offices, Legal Aid Soc. N.Y. Co-author: Takeovers-Attack and Survival, 1987, 2d edit., 1993. Bd. dirs. Vols. Legal Svcs., 1990-96, Welfare Law Ctr. Mem. ABA (criminal, bus. law, litigation sects.), N.Y. Lawyers for Pub. Interest (bd. dirs. 1987-00), Assn. of Bar of City of N.Y. (fed. cts. com. 1981-84), Prep for Prep Inc. (dir. 1974), U.S. Cycling Fedn., Nat. Legal Aid/Defenders Assn. Avocations: bicycle racing, tennis. Federal civil litigation, State civil litigation, Mergers and acquisitions. Home: 300 Central Park W Apt 19C New York NY 10024-1513 Office: Debevoise & Plimpton 875 3rd Ave Fl 23 New York NY 10022-6225 E-mail: Jhhall@debevoise.com

HALL, JOHN HOPKINS, retired lawyer; b. Dallas, May 10, 1925; s. Albert Brown and Eleanor Pauline (Hopkins) H.; m. Marion Martin, Nov. 23, 1957; children: Ellen Martin, John Hopkins II. Student, U. Tex., 1942, U. of South, Sewanee, Tenn., 1942-43; LL.B., So. Meth. U., 1949. Bar: Tex. bar 1949. Ptnr. Strasburger & Price, Dallas, 1957-93, ret., 1993. Served with U.S. Army, 1943-45. Fellow Tex. Bar Found., Am. Bar Found., Internat. Acad. Trial Lawyers, Am. Coll. Trial Lawyers; mem. Tex. Bar Assn., Tex. Assn. Def. Counsel, Internat. Assn. Def. Counsel, Fin and Feather Club. Episcopalian. Federal civil litigation, General civil litigation, State civil litigation.

HALL, JOHN THOMAS, lawyer, educator; b. Phila., May 14, 1938; s. John Thomas and Florence Sara (Robinson) H.; m. Carolyn Park Currie, May 26, 1968; children: Daniel Currie, Kathleen Currie. AB, Dickinson Coll., 1960; MA, U. Md., 1963; JD, U. N.C., 1972. Bar: N.C. 1972. Chmn. dept. speech Mercersburg (Pa.) Acad., 1960-63, U. Balt., 1963-69; research asst. N.C. Ct. Appeals, Raleigh, 1972-73, dir. pre-hearing research staff, 1974-75, asst. clk., marshall, librarian, 1980-81; counsel Dorothea Dix Hosp., 1974; asst. dist. atty. State of N.C., 1975-80, 81-83; pvt. practice, 1973-74, 83—. Mem. faculty King's Bus. Coll., Raleigh, 1973-75, N.C. Bar Assn., 1987—; undercover inmate Cen. Prison Duke Ctr. on Law and Poverty, Durham, N.C., 1970; vis. lectr. dept. comm. N.C. State U., 2000—. Mem. Raleigh Little Theatre, Theatre in the Park, Raleigh; charter mem. Wake County Dem. Men's Club, 1977—. Named Best Actor, Raleigh Little Theatre, 1975, 77, 80, 82, 85, 86, 93, 98. Mem. ABA, N.C. Bar Assn., Wake County Bar Assn. (bd. dirs. 1986-89, vice chmn. exec. com. 1986-87), 10th Jud. Dist. Bar Assn. (bd. dirs. 1986-89, chmn. grievance com. 1987-90), Wake County Acad. Criminal Trial Lawyers (v.p. 1986-87), Scottish Clan Gunn Soc., Neuse River Valley Model R.R. (Raleigh). Roman Catholic. Avocations: model railroading, walking, reading. Appellate, Criminal. Office: PO Box 1207 Raleigh NC 27602-1207

HALL, LISA JELLISON, lawyer; b. Providence, Sept. 3, 1972; d. Gerald Earle Jr. and Mary Milkovich Jellison; m. Brian Keith Hall, Sept. 27, 1997. BA in English, U. Tenn., 1994, JD, 1997. Bar: Tenn. 1997, U.S. Dist. Ct. (ea. dist.) Tenn. 1998. Assoc. Hodges, Doughty & Carson, Knoxville, Tenn., 1997—. Mem. ABA, Tenn. Bar Assn., Knoxville Bar Assn., Defense Rsch. Inst., Am. Inns of Ct. Office: Hodges Doughty & Carson 617 Main Ave Knoxville TN 37902

HALL, PETER W. prosecutor; BA, MA, U. N.C.; JD, Cornell U. From asst. U.S. atty to 1st asst. U.S. Atty. Dist. Vt. U.S. Dept. Justice, 1978—86, U.S. atty., 2001—; ptnr. Reiber, Kenlan, Schwiebert, Hall and Facey, Rutland, Vt., 1986—2001. Office: 11 Elmwood Ave PO Box 570 Burlington VT 05402*

HALL, REED STANLEY, lawyer; b. Idaho Falls, Idaho, July 29, 1929; s. Reed LeRoy and Melba (Stevens) H.; m. Dorothy Stuart, Apr. 26, 1955; children— John, Christopher, Gary, Suzanne, Elizabeth, Andrew. B.S., Brigham Young U., 1951; M.A., U. Ill., 1953; J.D., Harvard U., 1958. Bar: Calif. 1959, U.S. Dist. Ct. (cen. dist.) Calif. 1959. Assoc. Price, Postel & Parma, Santa Barbara, Calif., 1960-68; atty. law dept. Sears, Roebuck and Co., Alhambra, Calif. and Chgo., 1968-91, ret., 1991—; sec., dir. Pacific Installers, Inc., Alhambra, 1976-85. Editor Yearbook Brigham Young U., 1951. Chmn. campaign for sch. tax rate election, Whittier, Calif., 1970. Republican. Mormon. Consumer commercial. Office: Sears Roebuck and Co Legal Dept Sears Tower Chicago IL 60606-6306

HALL, STEPHEN CHARLES, lawyer; b. Carmel, Calif., Sept. 14, 1948; s. Melvin Wiley and Dorothy Louise (Hoyt) H.; m. Kristi Lee Roberts, Feb. 23, 1983; children: Spencer Stephen Rodrigo, Rachel Genevieve Cristina, Trevor Charles. AB, Dickinson Coll., 1971; JD, Vt. Law Sch., 1977. Bar: Pa. 1978, Va. 1979, U.S. Dist. Ct. (ea. dist.) Va. 1982, U.S. Dist. Ct. (we. dist.) Va. 1990, U.S. Ct. Appeals (4th cir.) 1982. Title atty. Chgo. Title Inst. Co., Richmond, 1978-79; assoc. Edward E. Willey Jr., P.C., 1979-82; ptnr. Willey & Hall, P.C., 1983-88; assoc. Hazel & Thomas, P.C., 1988-90, ptnr., 1990-94, Keith & Hall, Richmond, 1994—. Contbr. articles to profl. jours. Past chmn. bd. trustees St. Michael's Episcopal Sch., mem. St. Michael's Sch. Found. Mem. Richmond Bar Assn. (past chmn. publs. com.), Chesterfield Bar Assn. (1st v.p. 2001-02), Bon Air Bus. and Profl. Assn. (past pres.). Episcopalian. Avocations: golf, photography. Federal civil litigation, General civil litigation, State civil litigation. Office: Keith & Hall 2727 Mcrae Rd Richmond VA 23235-3055

HALLANAN, ELIZABETH V. federal judge; b. Charleston, W.Va., Jan. 10, 1925; d. Walter Simms and Imogene (Burns) H. , U. Charleston, 1946; JD, W.Va. U., 1951; postgrad, U. Mich., 1964. Atty. Crichton & Hallanan, Charleston, 1952-59; mem. W.Va. State Bd. Edn., 1955-57, Ho. of Dels., W.Va. Legis., Charleston, 1957-58; asst. commr. pub. instns., 1958-59; mem., chmn. W.Va. Pub. Service Commn., 1969-75; atty. Lopinsky, Bland, Hallanan, Dodson, Deutsch & Hallanan, 1975-83; sr. judge U.S. Dist. Ct. for So. Dist. W.Va., 1983—. Recipient Hannah G. Solomon award Nat. Coun. Jewish Women, 1997, Justitia Officium award W.Va. U. Coll. Law, 1997; named Woman of Achievement, YWCA, 1997, West Virginian of Yr., Charleston Gazette, 1997. Mem. W.Va. Bar Assn. E-mail: judge. Office: US Dist Ct PO Box 2546 Charleston WV 25329-2546 E-mail: Hallanan@wvsd.uscourts.gov

HALL-BARRON, DEBORAH, lawyer; b. Oakland, Calif., Oct. 7, 1949; d. John Standish Hall and Mary (Swinson) H.; m. Eric Levin Meadow, Feb. 1973 (div. June 1982); 1 child, Jesse Standish Meadow Hall; m. Richie Barron, 1997. Paralegal cert., Sonoma State U., Rohnert Park, Calif., 1984; JD, John F. Kennedy U., Walnut Creek, Calif., 1990. Bar: Calif. 1991. Paralegal Law Offices Marc Libarle/Quentin Kopp, Cotati, Calif., 1983-84, MacGregor & Buckley, Larkspur, 1984-86, Law Offices Melvin Belli, San Francisco, 1987-88, Steinhart & Falconer, San Francisco, 1988; mgr. Computerized Litigation Assocs., 1986; law clk. Morton & Lacy, 1989-91, assoc., 1991-96; atty. Law Offices of Charlotte Venner, 1996-97, Plastiras & Terrizzi, San Francisco, San Rafael, Calif., 1998, Bishop, Barry, Howe, Haney & Ryder, San Francisco, 1998-99, McLemore, Collins and Toschi, Oakland, Calif., 1999-2000, Nevin Levy, LLP, Walnut Creek, 2000—. Atty. Vol. Legal Svcs., San Francisco, 1991-96; judge San Francisco Youth Ct., 1995-97; com. chmn. Point Richmond (Calif.) coun., 1994-96. Recipient Whiley Manuel Pro Bono award State Bar Calif., 1993. Mem. Nat. Assn. Ins. Women, Def. Rsch. Inst., Bar Assn. San Francisco (del. 4th world conf. on women 1995, chair product liability com.), Internat. Com. Lawyers for Tibet (litigation com. 1991-97, co-chair women's com.), Ins. Claims Assn. (chmn. membership com. 1994-96), Hon. Order of Blue Goose Internat., Queen's Bench (chmn. employment com. 1994-97, bd. dirs. 1996—, newsletter editor and webmaster 1999), BASF intellectual property/entertainment law). Democrat. Avocations: sailing, playing guitar and saxaphone, home brewing, mountain biking, human rights advocate. Construction, Personal injury, Real property. E-mail: lawbarron@mlode.com

HALLENBERG, ROBERT LEWIS, lawyer; b. Oct. 21, 1948; s. Daniel Ward and Anna Mae (Lewis) H.; m. Susan Annette Shaffer, Nov. 29, 1980; children: Shea F., Jonathan E.R., Robert Lewis Jr. BA, U. Ky., 1970, JD, 1973; LLM in Taxation, U. Miami, Fla., 1974. Bar: U. Ky. 1970, U.S. Dist. Ct. (we. dist.) Ky. 1975, U.S. Tax Ct. 1986. Ptnr. Woodward, Hobson & Fulton, Louisville, 1974—. Adj. prof. U. Louisville Sch. Law, 1974-80. Bd. dirs. Louisville Theatrical Assocs., 1980-90, v.p., sec., 1985-90; bd. dirs. Goodwill Industries Ky., 1987-93, sec., 1988-91; pres. Louisville Estate Planning Coun., 1979-80; bd. dirs. Louisville Estate Planning Forum, 1986-93, sec., 1992-93; mem. Estate Planning Coun. of Louisville, bd. dirs., 1989-95, pres., 1993-94. Fellow Am. Coll. Trust and Estate Counsel; mem. ABA (subchpt. com. 1974-77, real property, probate and trust com. 1985—), Ky. Bar Assn. (sec. tax com. 1984-85), Owl Creek Country Club (bd. dirs. 1988-91, pres. 1989-90, treas. 1990-91). Republican. Episcopalian. Estate planning, Pension, profit-sharing, and employee benefits, Probate. Office: Woodward Hobson & Fulton 2500 Nat City Tower Louisville KY 40202 E-mail: bhallenberg@WHF-law.com

HALLIDAY, JOSEPH WILLIAM, lawyer; b. N.Y.C., Aug. 9, 1938; s. Joseph John and Marie (Marro) H.; m. Vivian Ross Talbird, July 10, 1960; children: Katherine Ann Langan, Mary Allison Shaw. AB, Fordham U., 1960, LLB, 1963. Bar: N.Y. 1964, D.C. 1965. Assoc. White & Case, N.Y.C., 1965-72, ptnr., 1972-85, Skadden Arps Slate Meagher & Flom, LLP, N.Y.C., 1985—. Mem. tribar legal opinion com., lectr. Ctr. for Internat. Banking Studies, U. Va., Banking Law Inst., Inst. Internat. Rsch., Law and Bus., Euromoney, Practicing Law Inst. Editor-in-chief Fordham Law Rev., 1962-63. Served to 1st lt. U.S. Army, 1963-65. Mem. ABA, N.Y. State Bar Assn., Assn. of Bar of City of N.Y., N.Y. County Lawyers Assn., Larchmont Yacht Club (commodore 1985-86). Republican. Roman Catholic. Avocations: yachting, skiing, golf. Banking, Bankruptcy, Contracts commercial. Office: Skadden Arps Slate Meagher & Flom LLP 4 Times Sq Fl 24 New York NY 10036-6595

HALLIDAY, WILLIAM JAMES, JR. lawyer; b. Detroit, Nov. 16, 1921; s. William James and Katherine Elizabeth (Krantz) H.; A.B. (scholar), U. Mich., 1943, J.D., 1948; m. Lois Jeanne Streelman, Sept. 6, 1947; children: Carol Lynn Halliday Murphy, Richard Andrew, Marcia Katherine, James Anthony. Admitted to Mich. bar, 1948; assoc. Schmidt, Smith & Howlett and successors, Grand Rapids, Mich., 1952-56, ptnr., 1956-66, counsel Varnum, Riddering, Schmidt & Howlett, 1984—; sec. Amway Corp. Ada, Mich., 1964-84, gen. counsel, 1966-71, v.p., 1970-79, exec. v.p., 1979-84, also dir.; asst. pros. atty., Kent County, Mich., 1949-51; twp. atty., Wyoming Twp., Mich., 1955-57; city atty., Wyoming, Mich., 1961-66. Bd. dirs. Met. YMCA of Grand Rapids. Served with M.I., U.S. Army, 1943-46, with JAGC, 1951-52. Decorated Bronze Star; recipient William Jennings Bryan award U. Mich., 1943. Mem. ABA, Mich. Bar Assn. (chmn. client protection fund com.), Grand Rapids Bar Assn., Phi Beta Kappa, Phi Kappa Phi, Delta Sigma Rho, Phi Eta Sigma. Republican. Presbyterian. Club: Kiwanis. Home: 3020 Uplands Dr SE Grand Rapids MI 49506-1933 Office: Varnum Riddering Schmidt & Howlett PO Box 352 Grand Rapids MI 49501-0352

HALLIGAN, BRENDAN PATRICK, lawyer; b. Tipperary, Ireland, Nov. 19, 1958; came to U.S., 1959; s. Joseph and Christina Ann (O'Connell) H.; m. Bethann Reed, Sept. 17, 1988; children: Katherine, Kevin, Michael. BA, L.I. U., 1980; JD, New Eng. Sch. of Law, 1994. Bar: Mass. 1994, U.S. Dist. Ct. Mass. 1995, U.S. Ct. Appeals (1st cir.) 1996. Asst. money mgr. Securities Settlement Corp., N.Y.C., 1980-82; securities rsch. Chem. Bank, 1982-84; commodities trader Paine Webber, 1984-86; instnl. trader Carroll, McEntee & McGinley, 1986-89, Sanwa-BGK Securities, N.Y.C., 1989; legal asst. Cravath, Swaine & Moore, 1989-91; asst. counsel Liberty Mut. Ins. Co., Boston, 1994-97, counsel, 1997-2000; atty. Gadsby Hannah LLP, 2000—. Contbr. chpt. to book in field. Mem. Town of Plymouth (Mass.) Zoning Bd. Appeals, 1992-94; commr. Town of Duxbury (Mass.) Conservation Commn., 1998—; trustee, mem. Worcester Kiltie Pipe Band, 1998—. General corporate, Mergers and acquisitions, Securities. Office: Gadsby Hannah LLP 225 Franklin St Boston MA 02110-2804

HALLINGBY, JO DAVIS, lawyer, arbitrator; b. N.Y.C. d. Irwin and Ruth Davis; m. Paul Hallingby Jr., Nov. 17, 1994. BA, Boston U., 1966; JD cum laude, Bklyn. Law Sch., 1973. Bar: N.Y. 1974, U.S. Ct. Appeals (2nd cir.) 1974. Legal intern counsel to chmn. N.Y.C. Planning Commn., summer 1972; law clk. Hon. John R. Bartels U.S. Dist. Judge Ea. Dist. N.Y., 1973; law clk. Hon. William C. Conner U.S. Dist. Judge So. Dist. N.Y., 1974; staff atty. Criminal Appeals Bur., Legal Aid Soc., 1974-77; asst. U.S. atty. Ea. Dist. N.Y., 1978-83; assoc. Kass, Goodkind, Wechsler & Labaton, 1977-78; litigation counsel CBS, Inc., 1983-84; N.Y. counsel Kaye, Scholer, Fierman, Hays & Handler, 1984-93; arbitrator Nat. Assn. Securities Dealers, N.Y. Stock Exch., 1994—. Mem. U.S. Commn. on Civil Rights-N.Y. State Adv. Com., 1984-86; jud. com. Assn. of the Bar of the City of N.Y., 1984-90, fed. cts. com., 1990-94; dir. Riverside Park Fund, 1986-93; ct. adv. group com. on civil litigation U.S. Dist. Ct. Ea. Dist. N.Y., 1990-95; dir. Landmarks Preservation Found., 1995—; spkr. in field. Notes editor Bklyn. Law Rev., 1972-73. Office: Nat Assn Securities Dealers NY Stock Exch 1 Sutton Pl S New York NY 10022-2471

HALLMAN, LEROY, lawyer; b. Grandview, Tex., July 16, 1915; s. Ernest L. and Willa (Prestridge) H.; m. Martha Booker, Nov. 12, 1944; children— Martha B., Willa Anne, Samuel John. Diploma Hillsboro Jr. Coll., 1934; LL.B. with highest honors, U. Tex., 1939. Ptnr. Phinney Hallman & Coke, Dallas, 1946-84, Storey, Armstrong, Steger & Martin, 1984— ; dir. Frozen Food Express Industries, Inc., Dallas, Hub Hill, Inc., Dallas. Contbr. articles to profl. jours. Mem. City of University Park Planning and Zoning Commn., Tex., 1972-80. Served to maj. USAAF, 1940-46, PTO. Fellow Tex. Bar Found.; mem. ABA, Dallas Bar Assn., State Bar Tex., Motor Carrier Lawyer Assn. (pres. 1970-71), Delta Theta Phi, Democrat. Baptist. Clubs: Northwood, Petroleum. Administrative and regulatory, General corporate. Home: 3212 Southwestern Blvd Dallas TX 75225-7651 Office: 4600 1st Interstate Bank Tower 1445 Ross Ave Dallas TX 75202-2812

HALLORAN, MICHAEL JAMES, lawyer; b. Berkeley, Calif., May 20, 1941; s. James Joseph and Fern (Ogden) H.; m. Virginia Smedberg, Sept. 6, 1964; children: Pamela, Peter, Shelley. BS, U. Calif., Berkeley, 1962, LLB, 1965. Bar: Calif. 1966, D.C. 1979, Wyo. 1996. Assoc. Keatinge & Sterling, L.A., 1965-67, Pillsbury, Madison & Sutro, San Francisco, 1967-72, ptnr., 1973-90, 97—, mng. ptnr. Washington, 1979-82; exec. v.p., gen. counsel BankAm. Corp. and Bank of Am., San Francisco, 1990-96. Mem. legal adv. com. N.Y. Stock Exch., 1993-96; bd. overseers Inst. Civil Justice, 1994-98; chair sect. corp. securities banking and emerging cos. Pillsbury Madison & Sutro, 1997-2000. Editor: Venture Capital and Public Offering Negotiation, 1982—. Mem. corp. governance, shareholder rights and securities transactions com. Calif. Senate Commn., 1986-98; bd. dirs. Am. Conservatory Theater, 1994-2000. Mem. ABA (chmn. state regulation of securities com. 1981-84, mem. coun. of sect. of bus. law 1986-90, chmn. banking law com. 1992-96, mem. corp. laws com. 1997—), Bar Assn. San Francisco (bd. dirs. 1993-96). Avocations: skiing, golf, fishing, hiking. E-mail: halloran. Banking, General corporate, Securities. Office: Pillsbury Madison & Sutro LLP 50 Fremont St Fl 10 San Francisco CA 94105-2233 also: 2550 Hanover St Palo Alto CA 94304-1115 E-mail: mj@pillsgurylaw.com

HALLORAN, MICHAEL JOHN, lawyer; b. St. Louis, June 4, 1951; s. Edward Anthony Halloran and Helen M. (Kickham) Phillips; m. Gwen V. Carroll, July 25, 1983 (div. Oct. 1984). BS in Commerce, St. Louis U., 1972, JD, 1975. Bar: Ill. 1975, U.S. Dist. Ct. (no. dist.) Ill. 1975, U.S. Ct. Appeals (7th cir.) 1975. Assoc. Seyfarth, Shaw, Fairweather & Geraldson, Chgo., Washington, 1975-78; atty. Beinhauer & Rouhana, N.Y.C., 1978-79; assoc. William B. Hanley & Assocs., Chgo., 1979-81, Bell, Boyd & Lloyd, Chgo., 1981-83, ptnr., 1983-86; pvt. practice, 1987—. Federal civil litigation, General civil litigation, State civil litigation. Home: # 552 800 S Wells St Apt 552 Chicago IL 60607-4531 Office: 53 W Jackson Blvd Ste 319 Chicago IL 60604-3607 E-mail: mhalloran7@hotmail.com

HALLUIN, ALBERT PRICE, lawyer; b. Nov. 8, 1939; children: Russell, Marcus. BA, La. State U., 1964; JD, U. Balt., 1969. Bar: Md. 1970, N.Y. 1985, Calif. 1991. Assoc. Jones, Tullar & Cooper, Arlington, Va., 1969-71; sr. patent atty. CPC Internat. Inc., Englewood Cliffs, N.J., 1971-76; counsel Exxon Rsch. & Engring. Co., Florham Park, 1976-83; v.p., chief intellectual property counsel Cetus Corp., Emeryville, Calif., 1983-90; ptnr. Fleisler, Dubb, Meyer & Lovejoy, San Francisco, 1990-92, Limbach & Limbach, San Francisco, 1992-94, Pennie & Edmonds, Menlo Park, Calif., 1994-97, Howrey, Simon, Arnold & White, LLP, Menlo Park, 1997—; pres., CEO, chmn. Halzyme Tech., Inc., 1995—. Contbr. articles to legal jours. Pres. Belle Roche Homeowners Assn., Redwood City, Calif., 1995—. Named One of Top 20 Intellectual Property Lawyers, Calif. Lawyer's mag., 1993. Mem. ABA, Am. Intellectual Property Law Assn. (chmn. chem. practice com. 1981-83, sec. 1984-85, bd. dirs. 1984-89, founding chmn. biotech. com. 1990-92), Licensing Exec. Soc., Assn. Corp. Patent Counsel, Bar Assn. San Francisco, San Francisco Patent Assn. Republican. Episcopalian. Intellectual property. Office: Howrey, Simon, Arnold & White LLP 301 Ravenswood Ave Menlo Park CA 94025-3434 Fax: 650-463-8400. E-mail: HalluinA@Howrey.com, Halzym@Earthlink.net

HALPER, EMANUEL B(ARRY), real estate lawyer, developer, consultant, author; b. Bronx, N.Y., June 24, 1933; s. Nathan N. and Molly (Rabinowitz) H.; m. Ilona Rubinstein, Mar. 5, 1961; children: Eve Brook, Dan Reed. AB, CCNY, 1954; JD, Columbia U., 1957. Bar: N.Y. 1958, Minn. 1982; real estate broker, N.Y. House counsel Howard Stores Corp., Bklyn., 1960; ptnr. Zissu, Berman, Halper & Gumbinger, N.Y.C., 1965-87, of counsel, 1987-97; ptnr. Can. Pacific Realty Co., Fairfield, N.J., 1970—; v.p. devel. Chase Enterprises, Hartford, Conn., 1987-89; pres. Texam Horizon Ventures, 1989-93, Am. Devel. and Cons. Corp., Greenvale, N.Y., 1989—. Adj. prof. real estate NYU, 1973-83; spl. prof. law Hofstra U., 1998—. Author: Wonderful World of Real Estate, 1975 (republished as Conversations in Real Estate, 1990), Shopping Center and Store Leases, 1979, Ground Leases and Land Acqusition Contracts, 1988; columnist N.Y. Law Jour., 1982—; contbg. editor Real Estate Review, N.Y.C., 1973-99; chmn. editorial policy com. Internat. Property Investment Jour., Hempstead, N.Y., 1982-87. With USAR, 1957-63. Recipient Disting. Teaching award NYU, 1978, Dean's award Hofstra U. Law Sch., 1987. Mem. ABA (chmn. comml. leasing com. 1986-93, chmn. comml. and indsl. leasing group 1993-94, mem. supervisory coun. of real property, probate and trust law sect. 1994-2000, mem. standing com. on CLE, 1994-96, mem. standing com. pubs. 1997-98, Gavel award 1977, mem. standing com. on diversity 1999—), World Assn. Lawyers (chmn. internat. real estate com. 1982-90), Internat. Inst. for Real Estate Studies (chmn. bd. 1980-87), Am. Coll. Real Estate Lawyers. Jewish. Avocations: writing, painting, gardening, yoga, running. Construction, Real property. Office: PO Box 261 Greenvale NY 11548-0261 E-mail: e1h@aol.com

HALPERN, ALEXANDER, lawyer; b. Tokyo, Aug. 13, 1948; came to U.S., Dec. 1948; s. Abraham Meyer and Mary (Fujii) H.; m. Carol Dreiling, May 12, 1973; children: Solomon J., Eve M., Peter N. BA in Sociology, Brandeis U., 1970; JD, U. Denver, 1976. Bar: Colo. 1976, U.S. Dist. Ct. Colo. 1976, U.S. Ct. Appeals (10th cir.) 1981, U.S. Supreme Ct. 1983. Ptnr. Caplan and Earnest, Boulder, Colo., 1976—. Pres. Ashoka Credit Union, Boulder, 1978—; bd. dirs. Shamshala Internat., 1991—; trustee Narpoa U., Boulder, 1991—. Mem. ABA, Colo. Bar Assn., Asian Am. Bar Assn. Colo., Boulder County Bar Assn. Democrat. Buddhist. Federal civil litigation, Constitutional, Education and schools. Office: Caplan and Earnest 2595 Canyon Blvd Ste 400 Boulder CO 80302-6737 E-mail: ahalpern@celaw.com

HALPERN, PHILIP MORGAN, lawyer; b. Derby, Conn., Apr. 17, 1956; s. Edwin Vincent and Carol Veronica (Gallagher) H.; m. Carolyn G. McElwreath, Mar. 11, 1989. BS magna cum laude, Fordham U., 1977; JD, Pace U., 1980. Bar: N.Y. 1981, U.S. Dist. Ct. (so. and ea. dists.) N.Y. 1981, U.S. Ct. Appeals (2d cir.) 1982, U.S. Tax Ct. 1984, U.S. Supreme Ct. 1985, U.S. Dist. Ct. Conn. 1989, Conn. 1989, U.S. Ct. Appeals (3d cir.) 1991. Law clk. to sr. judge U.S. Dist. Ct. (so. dist.) N.Y., N.Y.C., 1980-82; assoc. litigation dept. Kimmelman, Sexter & Sobel, 1982-83; ptnr. Pirro, Collier, Cohen, & Halpern LLP, 1983—; mng. ptnr. Collier, Haplern, Newberg, Nolletti & Bock LLP, White Plains, N.Y., 1996—. Arbitrator Civil Ct. City N.Y. and Am. Arbitration Assn., 1987-96; adv. coun. Bd. of Judges, So. Dist. of N.Y., 1995—; mediator U.S. Dist. (so. dist.) N.Y., 1998—, mem. adv. com. on civil practice, 1999—. Author: Age Discrimination in Employment Act: Employers Can Enforce Releases Too!, 1992, Fair Value Proceedings: Fixing Fair Value in New York, 1996; editor: Civil Pretrial Proceedings in New York, 2 vols., 1999, updated annually. Chmn. Young Reps., Tuckahoe, N.Y., 1975-77; chmn. taxi commn. Village of Mamaroneck, N.Y., 1986-87, mem. planning bd., 1987-89. Fellow Am. Bar Found.; mem. N.Y. State Bar Assn. (com. on lawyer competency, com. on fed. judiciary), Assn. of Bar of City of N.Y., ATLA, N.Y. Trial Lawyers Assn., N.Y. County Lawyers Assn., Fed. Bar Coun., Profl. Golfers Assn. (adv. coun. metro. sect. 1992—), Westchester Country Club. Roman Catholic. Federal civil litigation, General civil litigation, State civil litigation. Office: Collier Haplpern Newberg Nolletti & Bock LLP One N Lexington Ave White Plains NY 10601 also: 99 Park Ave New York NY 10016-1601

HALPERN, RALPH LAWRENCE, lawyer; b. Buffalo, May 12, 1929; s. Julius and Mary C. (Kaminker) H.; m. Harriet Chasin, June 29, 1958; children: Eric B., Steven R., Julie B. LL.B. cum laude, U. Buffalo, 1953. Bar: N.Y. 1953. Teaching assoc. Northwestern U. Law Sch., 1953-54; assoc. firm Jaeckle, Fleischmann, Kelly, Swart & Augspurger, Buffalo, 1957-58; asso. firm Raichle, Banning, Weiss & Halpern (and predecessors), 1958-59, ptnr., 1959-86, Jaeckle Fleischmann & Mugel LLP, Buffalo, 1986—. Pres. Buffalo Coun. World Affairs, 1972-74, Temple Beth Zion, Buffalo, 1981-83, Bur. Jewish Edn., 2000—; chmn. Buffalo chpt. Am. Jewish Com., 1975-77; bd. govs. United Jewish Fedn., Buffalo, 1972-78, 91-97, 99—, v.p., 1992-95. Served to capt. JAGC U.S. Army, 1954-57. Mem. ABA (ho. dels. 1989-95, 97-99), N.Y. State Bar Assn. (chmn. com. profl. ethics 1971-76, chmn. com. jud. election monitoring 1983-86, chmn. spl. com. to consider adoption of ABA model rules of profl. conduct 1983-85, sec. internat. law and practice sect. 1992-93, vice chmn. 1993-95), Erie County Bar Assn., Am. Judicature Soc., Am. Law Inst. Antitrust, Federal civil litigation, General corporate. Home: 88 Middlesex Rd Buffalo NY 14216-3618 Office: Jaeckle Fleischmann & Mugel LLP 800 Fleet Bank Bldg Buffalo NY 14202-2292 E-mail: rlhalpern@compuserve.com, rhalpern@jaeckle.com

HALPRIN, HENRY STEINER, lawyer, educator; b. N.Y.C., May 5, 1924; s. Abraham J. and Julia (Steiner) H.; divorced; children: Karen K. Sims, Bruce S. LLD, U. Va., 1949, JD, 1970. Bar: N.Y. 1949, U.S. Dist. Ct. (ea. and so. dists.) N.Y. 1950, U.S. Supreme Ct. 1961, U.S. Dist. Ct. Conn. 1963, Conn. 1967. Asst. dir. spl. programs U.S. Housing and Homes Fin. Agy., N.Y.C., 1955-61; sr. assoc. Demov & Morris, 1961-62, ptnr., 1962-64; sole practice N.Y.C., 1965-68; ptnr. Halprin & Goler, 1968-92, 1968-92; pvt. practice, 1992—. Adj. asst. prof. real estate NYU, 1979—; lectr. Baruch Coll., 1981-99. Bd. trustees Westport (Conn.) Libr., 1987-91. Non-profit and tax-exempt organizations, Real property. Home: 24 Buena Vista Dr Westport CT 06880-6603 Office: 60 E 42nd St New York NY 10165-0006 Fax: 212-490-3888

HALSEY, DOUGLAS MARTIN, lawyer; b. Warwick, R.I., 1953; s. Donald Post Jr. and Marita H.; m. Amy Klinow, Sept. 5, 1976; children: Mark, Meredith. BA, Columbia U., 1976; JD cum laude, U. Miami, 1979. Bar: Fla. 1979, U.S. Ct. Appeals (11th cir.), U.S. Dist. Ct. (so. dist.) Fla. Assoc. Paul & Thomson, Miami, Fla., 1979-85; ptnr. Thomson, Bohrer, Werth & Razook, 1985-88, Douglas M. Halsey, P.A., Miami, 1989-97, Halsey & Burns, P.A., Miami, 1997-2000, White & Case LLP, Miami, 2000—. Rsch. editor U. Miami Law Review, 1978-79. Mem. Alexis de Tocqueville Soc., United Way of Miami-Dade County, 1995—; chmn.Children's Home Soc. Fla., 2000—; chmn. Foster Care Rev., Inc., Miami, Fla., 1998-2000. Mem. Fla. Bar (chmn. environ. and land use law sect. 1993-94, President's Pro Bono Svc. award 1991). Environmental. Office: First Union Fin Ctr 200 S Biscayne Blvd Ste 4900 Miami FL 33131-2352

HALSTRÖM, FREDERIC NORMAN, lawyer; b. Boston, Feb. 26, 1944; s. Reginald F. and Margaret M. (Graham) H.; divorced, 1989, m. Lena Strelnikova, 2001; children: Ingrid Alexandra, Reginald Frederic II, Mikhail Strelnikova. Student, Northeastern U., 1961-63, USAF Acad., 1963-65; AB, Georgetown U., 1967; JD, Boston Coll., 1970. Bar: Mass. 1970, U.S. Dist. Ct. Mass., 1971, U.S. Dist. Ct. R.I. 1981, U.S. Tax Ct., 1981, U.S. Ct. Appeals (1st cir.) 1971, U.S. Ct. Appeals (11th cir.) 1991. Assoc. Schneider and Reilly, P.C., Boston, 1970-73; ptnr. Parker, Coulter, Daley and White, 1973-78; prin. Halström Law Office, 1978—. Spl. prosecutor Dist. Atty., Norfolk County, 1969-70; spl. asst. city solicitor City of Quincy, 1980. Editor Mass. Law Quar., 1972; contbr. articles to profl. jours. Fellow Boston Coll. Law Sch., v.p. 1988-91, pres. 1991—, benefactor Frederic N. Halström Nat. Moot Ct. Team. Mem. ABA (chmn. products liability com. gen. practice sect. 1980-85, award of achievement young lawyers divsn. 1978, vice chmn. taxation on ins. cos. sect. 1986-88), Assn. Trial Lawyers Am. (gov. 1981-84, 87—), state del. 1976-78, 86-87, chair various coms.), Mass. Acad. Trial Attys. (co-chmn. tort law sect. 1980—, bd. of govs. 1976—, sec. 1987-88, pres.-elect 1995-96, pres. 1996-97), Mass. Bar Assn. (pres. young lawyers divsn. 1977-78, bd. dels. 1978-80), Middlesex County Bar Assn., Mass. Trial Lawyers Assn. (mem/Bd. of Govs., 2001—), Trial Lawyers Pub. Justice (sustaining founder, v.p. 1989—), Thomas F. Lambert Jr. Endowed Chair Trust), Algonquin Club, Univ. Club (Boston). State civil litigation, Insurance, Personal injury. Home: 483 River Rd Carlisle MA 01741-1873 Office: 132 Boylston St Boston MA 02116-4616 Fax: 617-426-4791. E-mail: FHalstrom@aol.com

HALTOM, B(ILLY) REID, lawyer; b. Artesia, N. Mex., Sept. 9, 1945; s. Felix Tucker and Shirley Mae (Lucado) H.; m. Elizabeth Ann Berger, Dec. 25, 1964; 1 child, Robb Reid. BA in Philosophy, U. N.Mex, 1969; JD, Tex. Tech U., 1972. Bar: N.Mex. 1973, U.S. Dist. Ct. N.Mex. 1977, U.S. Ct. Appeals (10th cir.) 1980, U.S. Ct. Claims 1980, U.S. Supreme Ct. 1992, U.S. Dist. Ct. Ariz. 1992. Ptnr. Nordhaus, Haltom, Taylor, Taradash & Frye, Albuquerque, 1980—. Fellow ABA, N.Mex. State BAr Assn., Albuquerque Bar Assn., Albuquerque Lawyers Club. Avocations: snow and water skiing, tennis, gourmet cooking. General corporate, Oil, gas, and mineral, Finance. Office: Nordhaus Haltom Taylor Taradash & Frye 500 Marquette Ave NW Ste 1050 Albuquerque NM 87102-5310

HALVERSON, LOWELL KLARK, lawyer, writer; b. Tacoma, May 4, 1942; s. Sidney Lawrence and Jeannette (Thompson) H.; m. Diane E. Vosburgh, June 13, 1964; children: Liana Kay, Ward Vosburgh. AB, Harvard U., 1964; JD, U. Wash., 1968. Bar: Wash. 1968, N.Y. 1981, U.S. Supreme Ct. 1979, Alaska 1989. Bd. dirs. Wash. Legal Found., 1984-87, pres. Wash. State Bar Assn., 1990-91. Author, editor: Washington Lawyer Practice Manual, 3 vols., 1972-78; author: (with others) Divorce in Washington-A Humane Approach, 1985, 2d edit., 1990, (with others) Divorce in New York, 1987. Fellow Am. Acad. Matrimonial Lawyers; mem. ABA, Wash. State Bar Assn. (gov. 7th congl. dist. 1977-80, merit award 1988, editor-in-chief Family Law Deskbook), Alaska State Bar Assn., N.Y. State Bar Assn., Seattle-King County Bar Assn. (trustee 1975-77, chmn. young lawyers sect. 1974-75, Disting. Service award 1986). Clubs: Harvard of Wash. (pres. 1974), Rainier. Civil rights, Family and matrimonial. Home: 13721 Tastad Rd Arlington WA 98223-9413 Office: 3035 Island Crest Way Mercer Island WA 98040-2919

HALVERSON, STEVEN THOMAS, lawyer, construction executive; b. Enid, Okla., Aug. 29, 1954; s. Robert James Halverson and Ramona Mae (Ludke) Selenski; m. Diane Mary Schueller, Aug. 21, 1976; children: John Thomas, Anne Kirsten. BA cum laude, St. John's U., 1976; JD, Am. U., 1979. Bar: Va. 1979. Asst. project dir. ABA, Washington, 1977-79; with Briggs & Morgan, St Paul., 1980-83; sr. v.p. M.A. Mortenson Cos., Denver, 1984-99; pres., CEO Haskell Co., Jacksonville, Fla., 1999—. Chmn. Lowell Whiteman Sch., Design Build Inst. Am., Regis U.; bd. dirs. U. North Fla. Co-author: Federal Grant Law, 1982, The Future of Construction, 1997; contbr. articles to profl. jours. Bd. dirs. Jacksonville Symphony. Mem. Fla. Coun. 100, Jacksonville C. of C. (bd. dirs.), Constrn. Industry Roundtable. Republican. Roman Catholic. Home: 825 Mapleton Ter Jacksonville FL 32207-5204 Office: Haskell Co Haskell Bldg 111 Riverside Ave Fl 1 Jacksonville FL 32202-4950 E-mail: sthalver@thehaskellco.com

HALVORSON, NEWMAN THORBUS, JR. lawyer; b. Detroit, Dec. 17, 1936; s. Newman Thorbus and Virginia Westbrook (Markle) H.; m. Sally Clark Stone, May 3, 1969; children: Christina English, Charles Burgess Westbrook. AB, Princeton U., 1958; LLB, Harvard U., 1961. Bar: Ohio 1962, D.C. 1963, U.S. Supreme Ct. 1965. Assoc. Covington & Burling, Washington, 1962-70; asst. U.S. atty. Office of U.S. Atty., 1983-85; assoc. ind. counsel (spl. prosecutor under Ethics in Govt. Act), 1987-90; ptnr. Covington & Burling, Washington, 1970-83, 85—. Editor, Harvard Law Rev., 1960-61; author: Intermediate Sanctions Regs: Many Questions Remain, Tax Notes, 1998. Sr. warden, Jr. warden, vestryman Christ Ch. Georgetown, Washington, 1983-86, 89-92, chmn. fin. com., 1992-96; bd. dirs. Lupus Found. D.C., 1974-85; mem., bd. dirs. Eugene and Agnes E. Meyer Found., Washington, 1976-91, chmn., 1989-90; bd. mgrs. Hist. Soc. Washington, 1995—, chmn. investment com., 1999—; bd. dirs. Coun. for Ct. Excellence, Washington, 1995—; trustee Potomac Sch., McLean, Va., 1980-86, chmn., 1981-83; mem. com. of 100 on Federal City, 1970—, trustee, treas., 1975-79; bd. trustees, mem. exec. com. Greater Washington Rsch. Ctr., 1997—; v.p., trustee Cleveland Park Hist. Soc., 1997—. With USMCR, 1961-67. Mem. ABA, D.C. Bar. Republican. Episcopalian. Clubs: Met. (Washington), Chevy Chase (Md.). General corporate, Corporate taxation, State and local taxation. Home: 3500 Lowell St NW Washington DC 20016-5025 Office: Covington & Burling 1201 Pennsylvania Ave NW PO Box 7566 Washington DC 20044-7566

HAMANN, DERYL FREDERICK, lawyer, bank executive; b. Lehigh, Iowa, Dec. 8, 1932; s. Frederick Carl Hamann and Ada Ellen (Hollingsworth) Hamann Geis; m. Carrie Svea Rosen, Aug. 23, 1954 (dec. 1985); children: Karl E., Daniel A., Esther Hamann Brabec, Julie Hamann Bunderson; m. Eleanor Ramona Nelson Curtis, June 20, 1987. AA, Ft. Dodge Jr. Coll., Iowa, 1953; BS in Law, U. Nebr., 1956, JD cum laude, 1958. Bar: Nebr. 1958, U.S. Dist. Ct. Nebr. 1958, U.S. Ct. Appeals (8th cir.) 1958. Law clk. U.S. Dist. Ct. for Nebr., Lincoln, 1958-59; ptnr. Baird, Holm, McEachen, Pedersen, Hamann & Strasheim, Omaha, 1959—. Chmn. adv. com. Supreme Ct. Nebr., Omaha, 1986-95; chmn. bd. Midwestern Cmty. Banks. Past pres. Omaha Estate Planning Coun. Mem. Nebr. Bar Found. (pres. 1981-86), Nebr. Assn. Bank Attys. (pres. 1985-86). Republican. Lutheran. Avocations: boating, reading. Banking, General corporate, Estate planning. Office: Baird Holm McEachen Pedersen Hamann & Strasheim 1500 Woodmen Tower Omaha NE 68102

HAMBLEN, LAPSLEY WALKER, JR. judge; b. Chattanooga, Dec. 25, 1926; s. Lapsley Walker Sr. and Libby (Shipley) H.; m. Claudia Royster Terrell, Mar. 20, 1971; children by previous marriage: Lapsley Walker III, Allen M., William Shipley. BA, U. Va., 1949, LLB, 1953. Bar: W.Va. 1954, Ohio 1955, Va. 1957. Trial atty. IRS, Atlanta, 1955; atty. advisor U.S. Tax Ct., 1956; ptnr. Caskie Frost Hobbs & Hamblen and predecessor firms, Lynchburg, Va., 1957-82; dep. asst. atty. gen. tax divsn. U.S. Dept. Justice, 1982; judge U.S. Tax Ct., Washington, 1982-92, chief judge, 1992-94, 94-96, sr. judge, 1996-2000, ret., 2000. Mem. adv. bd. Va. tax rev. U. Va. Law Sch., Charlottesville, 1990—; former trustee So. Fed. Tax Inst.; former co-dir. ann. conf. on fed. taxation U. Va. Served with USN, 1945-46. Fellow Am. Coll. Tax Counsel, Am. Coll. Trust and Estate Counsel, Raven Soc., Order of Coif, Omicron Delta Kappa, Phi Alpha Delta. Presbyterian.

HAMBLEN, NICHOLAS, barrister; b. London, Sept. 23, 1957; s. Derek and Pauline Hamblen; m. Kate Hayden, July 13, 1985; children: Eleanor, James. MA, Oxford U., 1979; LLM, Harvard U., 1980. Bar: Eng. and Wales 1981. Barrister, London, 1981—; apptd. Queen's Counsel, 1997; apptd. Recorder, 1999. Office: 20 Essex St London SW18 3RW England

HAMBLET, MICHAEL JON, lawyer, city official, former state official; b. Rapid City, S.D., Aug. 10, 1940; s. Herbert F. and Helen F. (Tice) H.; m. Maureen Anne Murphy, Nov. 26, 1966 (div. May 1986); children: Tracy Anne, Michael Jon; m. Mary K. Harvick, Aug. 12, 1995. B.A., U. Ill., 1962; m. Mary Katherine Harvick, Aug. 12, 1995; J.D., U. Mich., 1965. Bar: Ill. 1965. Assoc. Mayer, Brown, Chgo., 1965-69; ptnr. Herrick, NcNeill, McElroy & Peregrine, Chgo., 1969-78, 82-83, Greenberg, Keele, Lunn & Aronberg, Chgo., 1979-81; Hamblet, Casey, Oremus, & Vacin (formerly Mathewson, Hamblet & Casey), Chgo., 1983—; mem. Ill. State Bd. Elections, Chgo. and Springfield, 1978— , chmn., 1979-81, 83-85, vice chmn., 1981-83; commr. Chgo. Bd. Elections, 1987-90, chmn. 1990—; mem. Ill. Bldg. Authority, Chgo., 1973-78, chmn., 1977-78. Mem. Cook County Econ. Devel. Adv. Com., 1982-87. Federal civil litigation, State civil litigation, General corporate. Home: 1322 N Sutton Pl Chicago IL 60610-2008

HAMBURG, CHARLES BRUCE, lawyer; b. Bklyn., June 30, 1939; s. Albert Hamburg and Goldie (Blume) H.; m. Stephanie Barbara Steingesser, June 23, 1962; children: Jeanne M., Louise E. B.Chem. Engring., Poly. Inst. Bklyn., 1960; JD, Geroge Washington U., 1964. Bar: N.Y. 1964. Patent examiner U.S. Patent Office, 1960-63; patent atty. Celanese Corp. Am., N.Y.C., 1963-65, Burns, Lobato & Zelnick, N.Y.C., 1965-67, Nolte & Nolte, N.Y.C., 1967-75; prin. C. Bruce Hamburg, 1976-79; ptnr. Jordan & Hamburg, L.L.P., 1979—. U.S. corr. Patents and Licensing, Japan, 1986—. Author: Patent Fraud and Inequitable Conduct, 1972, 78, Patent Law Handbook, 1983-84, 84-85, 85-86, (in Japanese) Doctrine of Equivalents in U.S., 1995, 2nd edit. (in Korean), 1998; monthly columnist Patent and Trademark Rev., 1976-85; contbr. chpt. on U.S. patents: Patents Throughout the World, 1976—. Mem. ABA, Am. Intellectual Property Law Assn., N.Y. Patent Trademark Copyright Law Assn., Internat. Assn. Protection Intellectual Property, Queens Bar Assn., Bklyn. Bar Assn., Licensing Execs. Soc., Internat. Fedn. Intellectual Property Attys., Masons. Intellectual property, Patent, Trademark and copyright. Office: 122 E 42nd St New York NY 10168-0002 E-mail: jandh@ipattorneys.com

HAMEL, LEE, lawyer; b. N.Y.C., Oct. 1, 1940; s. Herman and Jessie Blanche (Mapes) H.; m. Carole Ann Holmes, Dec. 30, 1965; children: Todd Leland, Stuart Russell. BA, Duke U., 1962; JD, U. Tex., 1967; postgrad., U. Houston, 1997—. Bar: Tex. 1967, U.S. Ct. Appeals (5th and 11th cirs.) 1968, U.S. Ct. Mil. Appeals 1968, U.S. Dist. Ct. (so. dist.) Tex. 1968, U.S. Supreme Ct. 1971, U.S. Tax Ct. 1979, U.S. Dist. Ct. (we. dist.) Tex. 1984, U.S. Dist. Ct. (ea. dist.) Tex. 1994. Asst. U.S. atty. U.S. Dist. Ct. (so. dist.) Tex., Houston, 1968-71, chief Corpus Christi divsn., 1970-71; owner Lee Hamel & Assocs., 1971-74, 90-99; ptnr. Dickerson, Hamel, Early & Pennock, 1974-88, Hamel & Rouner, Houston, 1988-89, Hamel Bowers & Clark, LLP, Houston, 2000—. Instr. Nat. Inst. for Trial Advocacy, 1986—. Co-editor Nat. Law Jour. Health Care Fraud and Abuse Newsletter, 1998—. Former trustee St. Luke's Hosp., Houston, St. James Home for Aged, Baytown; former dir. exec. bd. Episcopal Diocese of Tex.; pres. St. Francis Endowment Fund, 1993-94; former councilman Hunters Creek Village, Tex. Comdr. USN, 1962-64, USNR, ret. 1993. Fellow Coll. of State Bar of Tex., Houston Bar Found., State Bar Tex.; mem. ABA (litig. sec., white collar crime com., bus. law sec., chair health care fraud subcomittee), FBA, Houston Bar Assn., Houston Vol. Lawyers Assn. (bd. dirs. 1998-99). Episcopalian. Avocations: backpacking. Federal civil litigation, State civil litigation, Criminal. Office: Hamel Bowers & Clark LLP 1200 Smith St Ste 2900 Houston TX 77002-4502

HAMEL, RODOLPHE, pharmaceutical company executive, retired lawyer; b. Lewiston, Maine, June 3, 1929; s. Rodolphe and Alvina Melanie (Bilodeau) H.; m. Marilyn Vivian Johnsen, June 10, 1957; children: Matthew Edward, Anne Melanie. BA, Yale U., 1950; LLB, Harvard U., 1953. Bar: Maine 1953, D.C. 1953, N.Y. 1957. Assoc. firm Shearman & Sterling, N.Y.C., 1956-66; v.p., corp. sec., gen. counsel Macmillan Inc., 1972-73; internat. counsel Bristol-Myers Squibb Co. (formerly Bristol-Myers Co.), 1966-72, 73, v.p., counsel internat. div., 1974-81, assoc. gen. counsel, 1978-89, v.p., 1983-92, gen. counsel, 1989-94, sr. v.p., 1992-94, cons., 1995—. 1st lt. AUS, 1953-56. Mem. ABA, N.Y. State Bar Assn., Assn. of Bar of City of N.Y., Yale Club. General corporate, Private international. Office: Bristol-Myers Squibb Co 345 Park Ave New York NY 10154-0004

HAMES, WILLIAM LESTER, lawyer; b. Pasco, Wash., June 21, 1947; s. Arlie Franklin and Nina Lee (Ryals) H.; m. Pamella Kay Rust, June 3, 1967; children: Robert Alan, Michael Jonathan. BS in Psychology, U. Wash., 1974; JD, Willamette U., 1981. Bar: Wash. 1981, U.S. Dist. Ct. (ea. dist.) Wash. 1982, U.S. Ct. Appeals (9th cir.) 1985, U.S. Dist. Ct. (we. dist.) Wash. 1985. Counselor Wash. Juvenile Ct., Walla Walla, Wash., 1974-76; reactor operator control rm. United Nuclear Inc., Richland, 1976-77; assoc. Sonderman, Egan & Hames, Kennewick, 1981-84, Timmons & Hames, Kennewick, 1984-86, Sonderman, Timmons & Hames, Kennewick, 1987-88; ptnr. Hames, Anderson & Whitlow, 1988—. Mem. Am. Trial Lawyers Assn., Wash. State Bar Assn., Wash. State Trial Lawyers Assn., Benton-Franklin County Bar Assn., Bankruptcy Bar Assn. (bd. dirs.), Fed. Bar Assn. (bd. dirs.). Democrat. Methodist. Bankruptcy, Consumer commercial, Personal injury. Home: 410 W 21st St Kennewick WA 99337 Office: Hames Anderson & Whitlow PO Box 5498 Kennewick WA 99336-0498 E-mail: Billh@hamlaw.com

HAMILTON, CLYDE HENRY, federal judge; b. Edgefield, S.C., Feb. 8, 1934; s. Clyde H. and Edwina (Odom) H.; children: John C., James W. BS, Wofford Coll., 1956; JD with honors, George Washington U., 1961. Bar: S.C. 1961. Assoc. J.R. Folk, Edgefield, 1961-63; assoc., gen. ptnr. Butler, Means, Evins & Browne, Spartanburg, S.C., 1963-81; judge U.S. Dist. Ct. S.C., Columbia, 1981-91, U.S. Ct. Appeals (4th cir.), Richmond, Va., 1991—. Reference asst. U.S. Senate Library, Washington, 1958-61; gen. counsel Synalloy Corp., Spartanburg, 1969-80 Mem. editorial staff Cumulative Index of Congl. Com. Hearings, 1935-58; bd. editors George Washington Law Rev., 1959-60 Pres., Spartanburg County Arts Council, 1971-73; pres. Spartanburg Day Sch., 1972-74, sustaining trustee, 1975-81; past mem. steering com. undergrad. merit fellowship program and estate planning council Converse Coll., Spartanburg; trustee Spartanburg Methodist Coll., 1979-84; mem. S.C. Supreme Ct. Bd. Commrs. on Grievances and Discipline, 1980-81; del. Spartanburg County, 4th Congl. Dist. and S.C. Republican Convs., 1976, 80; mem., past chmn. fin. com. and adminstrv. bd. Trinity United Meth. Ch., Spartanburg, trustee, 1980-83. Served to capt. USAR, 1956-62 Recipient Alumni Disting. Svc. award Wofford Coll., 1991. Mem. S.C. Bar Assn., John Belton O'Neall Am. Inn of Ct. (founding mem., past pres. 1987-88), Piedmont Club (bd. govs. 1979-81). Office: US Ct Appeals 4th Cir 1901 Main St Columbia SC 29201-2443

HAMILTON, DAGMAR STRANDBERG, lawyer, educator; b. Phila., Jan. 10, 1932; d. Eric Wilhelm and Anna Elizabeth (Sjöström) Strandberg; m. Robert W. Hamilton, June 26, 1953; children: Eric Clark, Robert Andrew Hale, Meredith Hope. A.B., Swarthmore Coll., 1953; J.D., U. Chgo. Law Sch., 1956, Am. U., 1961. Bar: Tex. 1972. Atty. civil rights divsn. U.S. Dept Justice, Washington, 1965-66; asst. instr. govt. U. Tex., Austin, 1966-71; lectr. Law Sch. U. Ariz., Tucson, 1971-72; editor, rschr. Assoc. William O. Douglas U.S. Supreme Ct., Washington, 1962-73, 75-76; editor, rschr. Douglas autobiography Random House Co., 1972-73; staff counsel Judiciary Com. U.S. Ho. of Reps., 1973-74; asst. prof. L.B. Johnson Sch. Pub. Affairs U. Tex., Austin, 1974-77, assoc. prof., 1977-83, prof., 1983—, assoc. dean., 1983-87. Interdisciplinary prof. U. Tex. Law Sch., 1983—; vis. prof. Washington U. Law Sch., St. Louis, 1982, U. Maine, Portland, 1992; vis. fellow Univ. London, QMW Sch. Law, 1987-88, Univ. Oxford Inst. European & Comparative Law, 1998. Contbr. to various publs. Mem. Tex. State Bar Assn., Am. Law Inst., Assn. Pub. Policy Analysis and Mgmt., Swarthmore Coll. Alumni Coun. (rep.), Kappa Beta Phi (hon.), Phi Kappa Phi (hon.). Democrat. Quaker. Civil rights, Constitutional. Home: 403 Allegro Ln Austin TX 78746-4301 Office: U Tex LBJ Sch Pub Affairs Austin TX 78713 E-mail: dagmar.hamilton@mail.utexas.edu

HAMILTON, DAVID F. judge; b. 1957; BA magna cum laude, Haverford Coll., 1979; JD, Yale U., 1983. Law clk. to Hon. Richard D. Cudahy U.S. Ct. Appeals (7th cir.), 1983-84; atty. Barnes & Thornburg, Indpls., 1984-88, 91-94; judge U.S. Dist. Ct. (so. dist.) Ind., 1994—. Counsel to Gov. of Ind., 1989-91; chair Ind. State Ethics Commn., 1991-94. V.p. for litigation, bd. dirs. Ind. Civil Liberties Union, 1987-88. Fulbright scholar, 1979-80; recipient Sagamore of the Wabash, Gov. Evan Bayh, 1991. Mem. Am. Inns of Ct. (Sagamore chpt., pres.-elect 1999-2001, criminal law com. jud. conf. 2000—). Office: US Dist Ct So Dist Ind 46 E Ohio St Rm 330 Indianapolis IN 46204-1921

HAMILTON, ELWIN LOMAX, lawyer; b. Lubbock, Tex. Mar. 18, 1934; s. Elwin Louis and Mildred (Hunt) H.; children: Lauren, Karen. A.S., Arlington State Coll., 1954; B.A., North Tex. State Coll., 1956; LL.B., U. Tex., Austin, 1959. Bar: Tex. 1959, U.S. Dist. Ct. (no. dist.) Tex. 1961, U.S. Dist. Ct. (we. dist.) Tex. 1972, U.S. Ct. Claims 1972, U.S. Ct. Appeals (5th cir.) 1961. Atty. Humble Oil Co., Corpus Christi, Tex., 1959-60; mem. firm Morton & Brownfield, Tex., 1960-66; mcpl. judge, Morton, Tex., 1960-61; county dist. atty., Terry County, 1963-66; asst. exec. dir. State Bar Tex., 1966-69; asst. atty. gen., State of Tex., 1969-73; atty. Tex. Securities Bd., Austin, 1973-74; asst. gen. counsel to Gov. of Tex., Austin, 1974-82; ptnr. Senterfitt & Childress, Hamilton & Shook, San Saba, Tex., 1982-86, law practice, R. Mayo Davidson, San Saba Legal Services, 1987—; instr. Legal Asst. Studies, Austin Community Coll. State civil litigation, Probate, Real property. Office: San Saba Legal Svcs PO Box 547 San Saba TX 76877-0547

HAMILTON, JACKSON DOUGLAS, lawyer; b. Cleve., Feb. 5, 1949; m. Margaret Lawrence Williams, Dec. 19, 1971; children: Jackson Douglas Jr., William Schuyler Lawrence. BA, Colgate U., 1971; JD, U. Pa., 1974. Bar: Calif. 1974, U.S. Dist. Ct. (cen. dist.) Calif. 1974, U.S. Tax Ct. 1978, U.S. Ct. Claims 1984, U.S. Ct. Appeals (6th and 11th cirs.) 1988, N.C. 1991, U.S. Supreme Ct. 1991. Ptnr. Kadison, Pfaelzer, Woodard, Quinn & Rossi, L.A., 1986-87, Spensley, Horn, Jubas & Lubitz, L.A., 1987-91, Roberts & Stevens, Asheville, N.C., 1991—. Adj. prof. law U. San Diego, 1981, Golden Gate U., San Francisco, 1981-85, U. N.C., Asheville, 1994; cons. Calif. Continuing Edn. Bar, 1983-84, select com. on sports Calif. Senate, 1983-85. Editor Entertainment Law Reporter, 1979—; contbr. articles to profl. jours. Mem. ABA (tax sect., internat. law sect.), N.C. Bar Assn. (tax. sect. coun.). Republican. Episcopalian. General corporate, Corporate taxation, Taxation, general. Office: Roberts & Stevens BB & T Bldg Asheville NC 28802

HAMILTON, JEAN CONSTANCE, judge; b. St. Louis, Nov. 12, 1945; AB, Wellesley Coll., 1968; JD, Washington U., St. Louis, 1971; LLM, Yale U., 1982. Atty. Dept. of Justice, Washington, 1971-73, asst. U.S. atty. St. Louis, 1973-78; judge 22d Jud. Circuit State of Mo., 1982-88; judge Mo. Ct. Appeals (ea. dist.), 1988-90, U.S. Dist. Ct. (ea. dist.) Mo., 1990—, chief judge, 1995—. Office: US Courthouse 111 S 10th St Saint Louis MO 63102

HAMILTON, JOHN THOMAS, JR. lawyer; b. Delhi, N.Y., Apr. 17, 1951; s. John Thomas and Theresa Anastasia (L'Ecuyer) H.; m. Julia Ann Whitlow, Sept. 3, 1977; children: John Thomas III, Sara Baer. BS, Hamilton Coll., 1973; JD cum laude, Union U., Albany, N.Y., 1976. Bar: N.Y. 1977, U.S. Dist. Ct. (no., so., ea. and we. dists.) N.Y., U.S. Ct. Appeals (2d cir.). Law clerk Lynn & Lynn, PC, Albany, 1974-75; law clk. Solomon & Solomon, P.C., 1975-77, assoc., 1977, George S. Evans, N.Y.C., 1977-78, Frank E. Maher, Bklyn., 1978-80; pvt. practice, Delhi, 1980—; atty., counsel Sen. Chas. D. Cook, Albany, 1981-98; counsel N.Y.C. Watershed Negotiations, 1990-97. Counsel local govt. com. N.Y. Senate, 1983-92, counsel agrl. com., 1981-82, asst. counsel to majority leader, 1999—, senate home rule counsel, 1999—. Mem. law guardian adv. com. Supreme Ct. Appellate Divsn. 3d Dept., 1992—; law guardian liaison Delaware County 6th Jud. Dist., 1992—; mem. jud. screening com. So. Tier Trial Lawyers Affiliate; mem. Assn. Retarded Children (life); v.p. Del. County Hist. Assoc., 1985-87, pres. 1988-96; chmn., treas. Cook for Senate, 1978-98; exec. bd. dirs. Otschodela coun. Boy Scouts Am., 1992—; Hamilton Coll. alumni coun., 1994—; adv. com. Allen Resdl./Sgt. Henry Johnson Youth Leadership Facility, 1990—. Mem. ATLA, N.Y. State Bar Assn., N.Y. County Lawyers Assn., N.Y. State Trial Lawyers Assn., Delaware County Bar Assn. Republican. General civil litigation, Personal injury, Real property. Home and Office: 145 Main St Delhi NY 13753-1282

HAMM, DAVID BERNARD, lawyer; b. Bklyn., Oct. 6, 1948; s. Isidore I. and Sarah (Lamm) H.; m. Margaret Weiss, June 20, 1971; children: Jennifer A. Maltz, Michael S. BA cum laude, CUNY, Bklyn., 1971; JD magna cum laude, N.Y. Law Sch., 1977. Bar: N.Y. 1978, U.S. Dist. Ct. (no. dist.) N.Y. 1978, U.S. Dist. Ct. (so. and ea. dists.) N.Y. 1979, U.S. Supreme Ct. 1981, U.S. Ct. Appeals (2d cir.) 1982, (3d cir.) 1988. Law clk. to presiding judges N.Y. State Ct. Appeals, Albany, 1977-79; assoc. Herzfeld & Rubin P.C., N.Y.C., 1979-85, mem., 1986—. Mem. Commn. Legis. and Civic Action Agudath Israel of Am., N.Y.C., 1979—. Recipient Community Service award Agudath Israel of Am., 1986. Mem. ABA, N.Y. State Bar Assn. (com. civil practice law and rules), N.Y. County Lawyers Assn. (torts law sect., appellate advocacy com.), Jewish Lawyers Guild, N.Y. Law Sch. Alumni Assn. (Prof. Vincent LoLordo award 1977). Democrat. Appellate, Insurance, Product liability. Home: 2015 E 22nd St Brooklyn NY 11229-3615 Office: Herzfeld & Rubin PC 40 Wall St 53d Fl New York NY 10005-2301 E-mail: dhamm@herzfeld-rubin.com

HAMMEL, JOHN WINGATE, lawyer; b. Indpls., Dec. 25, 1943; s. Walter Francis and Mary Vivian (Patterson) H.; m. Linda Ann Yarling, Dec. 22, 1972; children: William Wingate II, Kathryn Christine, Rebecca Ann. BS, Butler U., 1967; postgrad., So. Ill. U., 1967-68; JD, Ind. U., 1975. Bar: Ind. 1975, U.S. Dist. Ct. (so. dist.) Ind. 1975, U.S. Ct. Mil. Appeals 1978, U.S. Ct. Appeals (7th crct.) 1982. Assoc. Yarling, Winter, Tunnell & Robinson, Indpls., 1975-86; ptnr. Yarling & Robinson, 1986—. Lt. col. Ind. Army N.G. Mem. ABA, Ind. Bar Assn., Indpls. Bar Assn., 7th Cir. Bar Assn. Republican. Consumer commercial, Insurance, Personal injury. Home: 5242 Rucker Cir Indianapolis IN 46250-2329 Office: Yarling & Robinson 151 N Delaware St Ste 1535 Indianapolis IN 46204-2539 E-mail: jhammel@yarling.com

HAMMER, DAVID LINDLEY, lawyer, writer; b. Newton, Iowa, June 6, 1929; s. Neal paul and Agnes Marilyn (Reece) H.; m. Audrey Lowe, June 20, 1953; children: Julie, Lisa, David. BA, Grinnell Coll., 1951; JD, U. Iowa, 1956. Bar: Iowa 1956, U.S. Dist. Ct. (no. dist.) Iowa 1959, U.S. Dist. Ct. (so. dist.) Iowa 1969, U.S. Ct. Appeals (8th cir.) 1996, U.S. Supreme Ct. 1977. Ptnr. Hammer Simon & Jensen, Galena, Ill. and, Iowa; mem. grievance commn. Iowa Supreme Ct., 1973-85; mem. adv. rules com., 1986-92. Author: Poems from the Ledge, 1980, The Game is Afoot, 1983, For the Sake of the Game, 1986, The 22nd Man, 1989, To Play the Game, 1986, The Quest, 1993, My Dear Watson, 1994, The Before Breakfast Pipe, 1995, A Dangerous Game, 1997, The Vital Essence, 1999, A Talent for Murder, 2000, Yonder in the Gaslight, 2000, Straight Up with a Twist, 2001. Bd. dirs. Linwood Cemetery Assn., 1973—, pres., 1983-84; bd. dirs. Dubuque Mus. Art, 1998-2001, hon. dir.; bd. dirs., past pres. Finley Hosp., hon. dir.; bd. dirs. Finley Found., 1988-95; past campaign chmn., past pres. United Way; past bd. dirs. Carnegie Stout Pub. Libr. With U.S. Army, 1951-53. Fellow Am. Coll. Trial Lawyers; mem. ABA, Young Lawyers Iowa (past pres.), Iowa Def. Counsel Assn. (pres. 1991-92, del. to Def. Rsch. Inst. 1992-93), Assn. Def. Trial Attys. (exec. coun. 1983-86, past chmn. Iowa chpt.), Iowa State Bar Assn. (past chmn. continuing legal edn. com.), Iowa Acad. Trial Lawyers, Dubuque County Bar Assn. (past pres.), Baker St. Irregulars. Republican. Congregationalist. General civil litigation, Insurance. Office: 700 Locust St Ste 190 Dubuque IA 52001-6824

HAMMERSON, MARC CHARLES, solicitor; b. London, Nov. 12, 1970; s. David Graham and Palette Sandra Hammerson; m. Ruth Anne Stembridge, May 30, 1998. LLB with honors, U. Manchester, Eng., 1993; LLM, London Sch. Econs., 1994. Solicitor Denton Hall, London and Tokyo, 1995-99, Vinson & Elkins, London, 1999—. Counsel Tomen Corp., Tokyo, 1998-99. Contbr. articles to profl. jours. Mem. Law Soc. England and Wales. Avocation: chess. Contracts commercial, FERC practice, Oil, gas, and mineral. Home: 25 Carysfort Rd Crouch End London N8 8RA England Office: Vinson & Elkins 45 King William St London EC4R 9AN England Office Fax: 44 207 618 6001. E-mail: mhammerson@velaw.com

HAMMOND, FRANK JEFFERSON, III, lawyer; b. Moss Point, Miss., Sept. 18, 1953; s. Frank Jefferson Jr. and Jane (Laird) H.; m. Gale Ray, May 30, 1975; children: Katharine Blakeney, Benjamin Laird. BBA, U. Miss., 1974, JD, 1976; LLM, U. Fla., 1978. Bar: Miss. 1977, U.S. Dist. Ct. (no. dist.) Miss. 1977, U.S. Dist. Ct. (so. dist.) Miss. 1977, U.S. Ct. Appeals (5th cir.) 1977, U.S. Tax Ct. 1978, U.S. Ct. Appeals (11th cir.) 1980, U.S. Supreme Ct. 1989. Mem. Corlew, Krebs & Hammond, P.A., Pascagoula, Miss., 1978-84, Watkins & Eager, PLLC, Jackson, 1984—. Adj. prof. U. Ala. Sch. Law, Mobile, 1983; adj. faculty U. So. Miss., Gautier, 1983-84; bd. dirs. Merchants and Marine Bank, Pascagoula, Miss. Bd. trustees Dantzler Meml. Meth. Ch., Moss Point, 1981-84. U. Fla. Grad. Council fellow, 1977; Richard B. Stephens scholar, 1978. Mem. ABA, Miss. State Bar (chmn. sect. estates and trusts 1988-89), Phi Kappa Phi, Beta Alphs Psi, Beta Gamma Sigma, Omicron Delta Kappa. Banking, Real property, Taxation, general. Home: PO Box 650 Jackson MS 39205-0650 Office: Watkins & Eager PLLC 400 E Capitol St Ste 300 Jackson MS 39201-2610

HAMMOND, GLENN BARRY, SR. lawyer, electrical engineer; b. Roanoke, Va., Sept. 3, 1947; s. Howard Reichard and Billie (Cromer) H.; m. Vickie McComb, Dec. 29, 1973 (div.); 1 child, Glenn Barry II. BA, Va. Mil. Inst., 1969; MBA, So. Ill. U., 1974; JD, U. Richmond, 1978; BSEE, Nova Coll., 1995. Bar: Va. 1979, U.S. Dist. Ct. (we. dist.) Va. 1979, U.S. Ct. Appeals (4th cir.) 1981, U.S. Ct. Mil. Appeals 1989, Air Force Ct. Mil. Rev. 1989, U.S. Supreme Ct., 1992. Assoc. Wilson, Hawthorne & Vogel, Roanoke, 1978-79; pvt. practice, 1979-80, 86—; atty., advisor to chief adminstrv. law judge Social Security Adminstrn., HHS, 1980-86; ptnr. Wooten & Hart P.C., 1995-98; pres. R.F. Cons., Inc., Roanoke, Va., 1998—. Pres., bd. dirs. LCH Broadcasting Group, Inc. Roanoke. Editor: Psychiatry in Military Law, 1988. Sr. vice-comdr. Mil. Order World Wars, Roanoke, 1981. Col. JAGC, USAF, 1969-75, Res. 1975—. Mem. Air Commando Assn. (life), DAV (life), VFW (life), AFA (life), Nat. Mil. Intelligence Assn. (life), Armed Forces Comms. Electronics Assn., Nat. Orgn. Social Security Claimants Reps., Masons. Pension, profit-sharing, and employee benefits. E-mail: bluetig@earthlink.net

HAMMOND, HERBERT J. lawyer, mediator, arbitrator; b. Santa Fe, May 19, 1951; m. Myra Hammond; children: Ariel, Jay. BS magna cum laude, U. N.Mex., 1973; JD, NYU, 1976. Bar: Tex. 1977, U.S. Patent and Trademark Office 1977. Sr. ptnr. Thompson & Knight, Dallas, 1994—. Contbr. articles to profl. jours. Mem. State Bar Tex. (vice-chmn. com. on computerization of the profession 1989-92, chair computer sect. 1994-95, newsletter editor computer sect.), Am. Intellectual Property Law Assn., Dallas Bar Assn. (chmn. intellectual property sect. 1998), Phi Beta Kappa, Phi Kappa Phi, Kappa Mu Epsilon. Computer, Entertainment, Intellectual property. Office: Thompson & Knight 1700 Pacific Ave Ste 3300 Dallas TX 75201-4693 E-mail: hhammond@tklaw.com

HAMMOND, JANE LAURA, retired law librarian, lawyer; b. nr. Nashua, Iowa; d. Frank D. and Pauline Hammond. BA, U. Dubuque, 1950; MS, Columbia U., 1952; JD, Villanova U., 1965, LHD, 1993. Bar: Pa. 1965. Cataloguer Harvard Law Libr., 1952-54; asst. libr. Sch. Law Villanova (Pa.) U., 1954-62; libr. Sch. Law, Villanova (Pa.) U., 1962-76; prof. law Sch. Law Villanova (Pa.) U., 1965-76; law libr., prof. law Cornell U., Ithaca, N.Y., 1976-93. Adj. prof. Drexel U., 1971-74; mem. depository libr. coun. to pub. printer U.S. Govt. Printing Office, 1975-78; cons. Nat. Law Libr., Monrovia, Liberia, 1989. Fellow ALA; mem. ABA (coun. sect. legal edn. 1984-90, mem. com. on accreditation 1982-87, mem. com. on stds. rev. 1987-95), PEO, Coun. Nat. Libr. Assn. (sec.-treas. 1971-72, chmn. 1979-80), Am. Assn. Law Librs. (sec. 1965-70, pres. 1975-76). Episcopalian. Office: Cornell U Sch Law Myron Taylor Hall Ithaca NY 14853

HAMNER, LANCE DALTON, prosecutor; b. Fukuoka, Japan, Sept. 18, 1955; parents Am. citizens; s. Louie D. and Mary Louise (Sloan) H.; m. Karla Jean Cleverly, Sept. 22, 1980; children: Lance Dalton Jr., Nicholas James, Louie Alexander, Samuel Sean, Victoria Jean. BS summa cum laude, Weber State Coll., 1984; JD magna cum laude, Ind. U., 1987. Bar: Ind., U.S. Dist. Ct. (no., so. dist.) Ind. 1988. Atty. Barnes & Thornburg, Indpls., 1988-89; dep. prosecuting atty. Marion County Prosecutor's Office, 1989-90; pros. atty. Johnson County, Franklin, Ind., 1990—. Legal corr. WGGR Radio News, Indpls., 1995; adj. prof. law Sch. Law Ind. U., In dpls., 1995-96, Bloomington, 1996—; frequent spkr. on legal topics including search and seizure and interrogation law; lectr. Ind. Continuing Legal Edn. Forum, Indpls., 1992; faculty mem. Newly-Elected Pros. Sch., Ind. Pros. Attys. Coun., 1999, Indpls. Police Acad., 1999, Ind. Police Corps, 2000. Author: Indiana Search & Seizure Courtroom Handbook, 2001; editor: Ind. Law Jour., 1987. Asst. scoutmaster Boy Scouts Am., Franklin, Ind., 1995-99, scoutmaster, 1999—. Mem. Nat. Dist. Attys. Assn., Assn. Govt. Attys. in Capital Litigation, Ind. Prosecuting Atty.'s Coun., Nat. Eagle Scout Assn., Order of the Coif. Republican. Mem. LDS Ch. Avocations: family, fitness, writing. Office: Prosecutor's Office Courthouse Annex N 18 W Jefferson St Franklin IN 46131-2353

HAMNER, REGINALD TURNER, lawyer; b. Tuscaloosa, Ala., June 4, 1939; s. Raiford Samuel and Ellie Wells (Turner) H.; m. Anne Ellen Young, Nov. 8, 1969; children: Patrick Turner, William Christian. BS, U. Ala., 1961, JD, 1965. Bar: Ala. 1965, U.S. Dist. Ct. (mid. dist.) Ala. 1966, U.S. Ct. Appeals (5th cir.) 1966, U.S. Ct. Mil. Appeals 1968, U.S. Supreme Ct. 1968, U.S. Ct. Appeals (11th and 5th cirs.) 1981. Law clk. Supreme Ct. Ala., Montgomery, 1965; dir. legal-legis. affairs Med. Assn., State of Ala., 1968-69; sec., exec. dir. Ala. State Bar, Montgomery, 1969-94; ct. project coord. U.S. Dist. Ct. for Mid. Dist.) Ala., 1995—. Coord. ct. project, U.S. Dist. Ct. (mid. dist.) Ala., 1995—. Bd. dirs. SE br., YMCA, Montgomery, 1978-81; former legal counsel govtl. adv. panels investigating Ala. Prison System; vice chmn. State Child Welfare Com.; dir. Attys. Ins. Mut. of Ala., Inc.; sec., treas. Ala. Law Found., 1987-93; chmn. Ala. Rhodes Scholarship Com., 1989-94. With USAF, 1965-68, col. USAFR, ret. Fellow Am. Bar Found. (life, state chmn. 1994-95); mem. ABA (com. mem., mem. ho. of dels. 1972-76, 85-89, 93, 96—), Am. Judicature Soc., Nat. Assn. Bar Execs. (pres. 1978-79), Am. Soc. Assn. Execs. (commr. certification com.

1991-94), Ala. Coun. Assn. Execs. (pres. 1984), Ala. Law Inst. (council), Jud. Conf. U.S. Ct. Appeals (11th cir. 1981-95), Ala. Nat. Alumni Assn. (pres. 1989-90), Montgomery Country Club, Omicron Delta Kappa, Alpha Epsilon Delta, Phi Alpha Delta, Delta Tau Delta. Episcopalian. E-mail: reginald. Home: 7518 Wynford Cir Montgomery AL 36117-7498 Office: US Dist Ct 15 Lee St Ste 401 Montgomery AL 36104 E-mail: hamner@almd.uscourts.gov

HAMPTON, CLYDE ROBERT, lawyer; b. Worland, Wyo., May 10, 1926; s. Clyde E. and Mabel L. (Lasley) H.; m. Dorothy Laura Gaebelein, June 3, 1949; 1 dau.: Dorothy Norma. B.A., Columbia Coll., 1949; LL.B., U. Colo., 1952. Bar: Colo. 1952. Atty., then counsel, sr. counsel and now gen. atty. Conoco, Inc., Denver, 1952-85, ret., 1985—, sole practice, 1985—; lectr., educator in field. Republican committeeman; bd. dirs. Denver Theol. Sem.; ch. officer Presbyterian ch. Served to capt. USNR. Recipient numerous awards in energy-related fields. Mem. Am. Petroleum Inst. (past chmn. environ. law com.; Disting. Merit award 1982), ABA (past chmn. Natural Resources Law Sect.), Aurora Bar Assn., Colo. Bar Assn., Sigma Chi, Phi Alpha Delta. Clubs: Petroleum, Columbia U. Alumni (Denver). Author: Landman's Legal Handbook, 1970; contbr. numerous articles on environ. law, natural resources to profl. jours. General corporate, Oil, gas, and mineral, Environmental. Home and Office: 14830 E Jefferson Ave Aurora CO 80014-4070

HANBERY, DONNA EVA, lawyer; b. Framingham, Mass.; d. Donald Taylor and Jacqueline Joyce (LaVine) H. B.A. summa cum laude, Hamline U., 1974; J.D. magna cum laude, U. Minn., 1977. Bar: Minn. 1977, U.S. Dist. Ct. D.C. 1977. Ptnr., Curtin, Mahoney & Cairns, P.A., Mpls., 1976— ; chmn., lectr. Advanced Legal Edn. Seminar on Landlord Tenant Law, 1982, 83, 84. Columnist New Homes mag., 1979— , Multi Housing mag., 1978— . Co-author: Why Cucumbers Are Better Than Men, 1983. Fundraiser, performer Law Revue for Family Plus, Mpls., 1982-83, bd. dirs., sec., counsel Crime Stoppers Minn., 1979— . Mem. ABA, Minn. Bar Assn., Hennepin County Bar Assn., Loring Mall Bus. Assn. (chmn. 1980-84), Minn. Multi-Housing Assn. Republican. Lutheran. Contracts commercial, General corporate, Landlord-tenant. Office: Curtin Mahoney & Cairns PA 4150 Multifoods Tower Minneapolis MN 55402

HANCOCK, CHRISTOPHER PATRICK, barrister; b. London, June 7, 1960; s. Alan Hancock and Ann Turner; m. Diane Galloway, Aug. 3, 1985; children: Philip Robin, Oliver James. MA, Trinity Coll., Cambridge, Eng., 1982; LLM, Harvard U., 1984. Barrister, London, 1985—. Named Queen's Counsel Queen on Advice of Lord Chancellor, 2000. Office: 20 Essex St London WC2R 3AL England Fax: 0207-583-1341. E-mail: chancock@20essexst.com

HANCOCK, HELEN MATHIAS, lawyer; b. Ebbw VAle, Wales, June 25, 1964; d. Robert Frederik Corbett and Margaret Elizabeth H.; m. Robin Lindsay Chubb, June 30, 1990; 1 child, James. LLB with honors, U. Bristol (Eng.), 1985; Law Soc. Finals with 2nd class honors, Guildford (Eng.) Coll. Law, 1986. Bar: solicitor 1956. Articled clk. Simmons & Simmons, London, 1986-88; solicitor, 1988-94; ptnr., 1995—; head transaction mgmt. Natwest Markets, London, 1994-95. Fulbright fellow , 1991. Avocations: reading, theatre. Securities. Office: Simmons & Simmons 21 Wilson St EC2M 2TX London England

HANCOCK, JAMES HUGHES, federal judge; b. 1931; B.S., U. Ala., 1953, LL.B., 1957. Bar: Ala. Ptnr. firm Balch and Bingham, Birmingham, Ala., 1957-73; judge U.S. Dist. Ct. (no. dist.) Ala., 1973—; now sr. judge. Mem. Ala. Bar Assn. Office: US Dist Ct 681 US Courthouse 1729 5th Ave N Birmingham AL 35203-2000

HANCOCK, S. LEE, business executive; b. Knoxville, Tenn., Aug. 11, 1955; s. Melton Donald and Alma Helen (McDaniel) H.; m. Kathleen Ann Koll, July 26, 1986. BS summa cum laude, Southwest Mo. State U., 1975; JD cum laude, So. Meth. U., 1979. Bar: Mo. 1979, U.S. Dist. Ct. (we. dist.) Mo. 1979, U.S. Tax Ct. 1982, U.S. Ct. Claims Calif. 1983, Calif. 1988, U.S. Supreme Ct., 1992; CPA, Mo. Assoc. Blackwell, Sanders, Matheny, Weary & Lombardi, Kansas City, Mo., 1979-83, ptnr., 1984-88, Allen, Matkins, Leck, Gamble & Mallory, Newport Beach, Calif., 1988-98, of counsel, 1998-99; pres., CEO Go2 Systems, Inc., 1998—. Pres., CEO Go2 Systems, Inc. Bd. dirs. Calif./Orange County Venture Forum; bd. dirs. Orange County Cmty. Found., 1991—, sec. 1994-95, pres. 1995-97. Mem. ABA, Young Execs. Am. (bd. dirs. Orange County chpt. 1992-96, pres. 1994-95), Calif. Bar Assn., Mo. Bar Assn., Orange County Bar Assn., Lawyers Assn. Kansas City (pres. young lawyers sect. 1986-87, bd. dirs. 1986-87), Young Pres. Assn., Order of Coif. Republican. Avocations: flying, sailing, skiing, photography. Home: 4 Hampshire Ct Newport Beach CA 92660-4933 Office: G02 Systems Inc Ste 900 18400 Von Karman Ave Irvine CA 92612-1514

HANCOCK, STEWART F., JR. law educator, judge; b. Syracuse, N.Y., Feb. 2, 1923; s. Stewart F. and Marion (MCLennan) H. BS, U.S. Naval Acad., 1945; LLB, Cornell U., 1950; LLD (hon.), Syracuse U., 1993, Le Moyne Coll., 1999. Corp. counsel, chief legal officer City of Syracuse, 1961-63; justice 5th judicial dist. N.Y. Supreme Ct., 1971-77, assoc. justice appellate divsn. 4th judicial dept., 1977-86; assoc. judge N.Y. Ct. Appeals, Albany, 1986-93; disting. vis. prof. law, jurist in residence Syracuse U., 1994—; counsel Hancock & Estabrook, Syracuse, 1994—. Mem. N.Y. State Com. on Profession and the Cts., 1994—. Rep. chmn. Onondaga County, 1964-66; Rep. candidate for Congress, 1966; former mem. Onondaga County Met. Water Bd.; mem. Syracuse Bd. Edn., ARC, Dunbar Ctr., Pebble Hill Sch., Crouse-Irving Meml. Hosp., Syracuse Symphony; mem. First Presbyn. Ch., Cazenovia. Line officer USN, 1945-47, lt. (s.g.) USNR, 1950-51. Fellow Am. Bar Found., New York State Bar Found.; mem. ABA, N.Y. State Bar Assn. (com. on jud. selection, com. on jud. independence, steering com. on commerce and industry, Gold medal for disting. svc. in law 2000), Onondaga County Bar Assn, dir. Frank H. Hiscock Legal Aid Soc. Office: Hancock & Estabrook 1500 Mony Tower 1 PO Box 4976 # 1 Syracuse NY 13221-4976 E-mail: shancock@hancocklaw.com

HAND, BENNY CHARLES, JR. lawyer, judge; b. Valley, Ala., Sept. 12, 1964; s. Benny Charles Sr. and Nelda Lee (Knight) H.; m. Martha Lynne Reynolds, May 29, 1988; children, Hannah Elisabeth, Abigail Faith, Ester Aliyn. BS in Bus. Mgmt., Auburn U., 1987; JD, Cumberland Sch. Law, 1990. Bar: Ga. 1990, Ala. 1990, U.S. Dist. Ct. (mid. dist.) 1990. Account mgr. Shamrock Rentables, Opelika, Ala., 1984-85; owner, pres. Suburban Pro, 1985-87; pres. Premier Car Care, 1991-94; pvt. practice, 1990—; judge Wedowee (Ala.) Mcpl., 1995—; city atty. City of Uniontown, Ala., 1995—; bd. dirs. Sim-Ptnrs., East Ala. Sickle Cell. Vice chmn. bd. Beacon Coll., Columbus, Ga., 1995—. Bd. dirs. East Ala. Mental Health Human Rights, Opelika, 1994—; deacon Believers Bapt. Ch., Auburn, 1995—; Rep. nominee U.S. Ho. of Reps., 1994; mem. Lee County Rep. Club. Recipient Rutherford Inst. for Outstanding Svc., 1994. General corporate, Personal injury, Sports. Office: 114 Nth 8th Opelika AL 36801-6040

HANDEL, RICHARD CRAIG, lawyer; b. Hamilton, Ohio, Aug. 11, 1945; s. Alexander F. and Marguerite (Wilks) H.; m. Katharine Jean Carter, Jan. 10, 1970. AB, U. Mich., 1967; MA, Mich. State U., 1968; JD summa cum laude, Ohio State U., 1974; LLM in Taxation, NYU, 1978. Bar: Ohio 1974, S.C. 1983, U.S. Dist. Ct. (so. dist.) Ohio 1975, U.S. Dist. Ct. S.C. 1979, U.S. Tax Ct. 1977, U.S. Ct. Appeals (4th cir.) 1979, U.S. Supreme Ct. 1979; cert. tax specialist. Assoc. Smith & Schnacke, Dayton, Ohio, 1974-77; asst. prof. U. S.C. Sch. Law, Columbia, 1978-83; ptnr. Nexsen, Pruet, Jacobs & Pollard, 1983-87, Moore & Van Allen, Columbia, 1987-88, Nexsen Pruet Jacobs & Pollard, Columbia, 1988-89; chief tax policy and appeals S.C. Tax Commn., 1989-95; chief coun. Policy S.C. Dept. of Revenue, 1995—. Adj. prof. U. S.C. Sch. Law, 1990—. Contbr. articles to legal jours. Bd. dirs. Friends of Richland County Pub. Libr., 1993-99. With U.S. Army, 1969-70, Vietnam. Recipient Outstanding Law Prof. award, 1980-81; Gerald L. Wallace scholar, 1977-78. Mem. ABA (com. state and local taxes, chmn. membership com. 1997—, vice-chmn. com. tax procedures 1993-94, com. stds. tax practice), S.C. Bar Assn., Order of Coif. Office: SC Dept Revenue PO Box 125 301 Gervais St Columbia SC 29214-0702 E-mail: rickch@aol.com, handelr@sctax.org

HANDLER, ARTHUR M. lawyer; b. N.Y.C., Feb. 16, 1937; BS, Queens Coll., 1957; LLB, Columbia U., 1960. Bar: N.Y. 1960, U.S. Dist. Ct. (ea. dist.) N.Y. 1960, U.S. Dist. Ct. (so. dist.) N.Y. 1963, U.S. Tax Ct. 1971, U.S. Ct. Appeals (2d cir.) 1971, U.S. Supreme Ct. 1965. Staff counsel SEC, Washington, 1960-61; law clk. U.S. Dist. Ct. for So. Dist.N.Y., N.Y.C., 1961-62; asst. U.S. atty. So. Dist. N.Y., 1962-65; assoc. Proskauer, Rose, Goetz & Mendelsohn, 1965-67, Golenbock and Barell, N.Y.C., 1967-70, ptnr., 1970-89, Whitman & Ransom, N.Y.C., 1990-93, Burns Handler & Burns, N.Y.C., 1993-99, Handler & Goodman, N.Y.C., 1999—. Arbitrator Am. Stock Exchange, N.Y.C., 1986—. Vol. atty. Pres.'s Com. for Civil Rights under Law, Jackson, Miss., 1966. Mem. ABA, N.Y. State Bar Assn., Bar Assn. of City of N.Y., Fed. Bar Council, Am. Arbitration Assn. (arbitrator 1969—). Clubs: University (N.Y.C.); Lords Valley Country (Hawley, Pa.) (bd. govs. 1977-80). Avocations: golf, skiing, theatre, travel. Administrative and regulatory, General civil litigation. Office: Handler & Goodman LLP 805 3d Ave New York NY 10022

HANDLER, HAROLD ROBERT, lawyer; b. Jersey City, Aug. 24, 1935; s. Morris Sidney and Fan (Krieger) Handler; children from previous marriage: Maren, Jeremy, Jolyon. BS, Lehigh U., 1957; LLM, Columbia U., 1961. Bar: N.Y. 1961, U.S. Tax Ct. 1963, U.S. Ct. Appeals (2d cir.) 1980. Atty., advisor U.S. Tax Ct., Washington, 1961-63; assoc. Simpson Thacher & Bartlett, N.Y.C., 1963-69, ptnr., 1970-97, of counsel, 1998—. Adj. assoc. prof. law NYU, 1978-80. Chmn. fin. com., citizens adv. com. Met. Transp. Authority, N.Y.C., 1975—79; trustee Citizens Budget Commn.; chmn. bd. Jewish Cmty. Ctr. in Manhattan, N.Y.C.; trustee Jewish Cmty. Found. Fellow Am. Coll. Tax Counsel; mem. ABA, N.Y. State Bar Assn. (chmn. subcom. tax sect. 1979-83, mem. exec. com. tax sect. 1990—, officer 1996-2000, chair 1999-20000), Assn. of Bar of City of N.Y. (chmn. tax com. 1983-86, mem. tax coun. 1990-98), Am. Law Inst., Inst. Fed. Taxation (panelist), Inst. Securities Regulation (panelist corp. taxation, personal income taxation). Corporate taxation, Personal income taxation.

HANDZLIK, JAN LAWRENCE, lawyer; b. N.Y.C., Sept. 21, 1945; s. Felix Munso and Anna Jean Handzlik; children: Grant, Craig, Anna. BA, U. So. Calif., 1967; JD, UCLA, 1970. Bar: Calif. 1971, U.S. Dist. Ct. (cen. dist.) Calif. 1971, U.S. Ct. Appeals (9th cir.) 1971, U.S. Supreme Ct. 1975, U.S. Tax Ct. 1979, U.S. Dist. Ct. (no. dist.) Calif. 1979, U.S. Dist. Ct. (ea. dist.) Calif. 1981, U.S. Dist. Ct. (so. dist.) Calif. 1982, U.S. Ct. Appeals (2d cir.) 1984, U.S. Ct. Internat. Trade 1984. Law clk. to Hon. Francis C. Whelan, U.S. Dist. Ct. (cen. dist.) Calif., L.A., 1970-71; asst. U.S. atty. fraud and spl. prosecutions unit criminal div. U.S. Dept. Justice, 1971-76; assoc. Greenberg & Glusker, 1976-78; ptnr., prin. Stilz, Boyd, Levine & Handzlik, P.C., 1978-84; prin. Jan Lawrence Handzlik, P.C., 1984-91; ptnr. Kirkland & Ellis, 1991—. Del. U.S. Ct. Appeals for 9th cir. Jud. Conf., L.A., 1983-85; counsel to ind. Christopher Commn. Study of the L.A. Police Dept., 1991; dep. gen. counsel to Hon. William H. Webster, spl. advisor to L.A. Police Commn. for Investigation of Response to Urban Disorders, 1992; mem. adv. com. for Office of L.A. County Dist. Atty., 1994-96; mem. standing com. on discipline U.S. Dist. Ct. Ctrl. Dist. Calif., 1997—; deputy gen. counsel Rampart ind. rev. panel L.A. Police Commn., 2000. Mem. editl. adv. bd. DOJ Alert, 1994-95. Bd. dirs. Friends of Child Advs., L.A., 1987-91, Inner City Law Ctr., L.A., 1993—; mem. bd. judges Nat. and Calif. Moot Ct. Competition Teams, UCLA Moot Ct. honors program. Mem. ABA (sect. criminal justice nat. com. on white collar crime 1991—, vice-chair 1998-2000, chair 2000—, co-chair securities fraud subcom. 1994-98, west coast white collar crime com., exec. com. 1993-98, vice-chair 1994-96, chair 1996-98, mem. sect. litigation, criminal litigation com. 1989—), Fed. Bar Assn., State Bar Calif., L.A. County Bar Assn. (exec. com. criminal justice sect. 1997—, coms. on fed. cts. 1988—, chair criminal practice subcom. 1989-90, fed. appts. evaluation 1989-93, white collar crime com., exec. com. 1991-97, fed. cts. coord. com. 2001—). Federal civil litigation, State civil litigation, Criminal. Office: Kirkland & Ellis 777 S Figueroa St Ste 3700 Los Angeles CA 90017-5835 E-mail: jan_handzlik@la.kirkland.com

HANEY, THOMAS DWIGHT, lawyer, educator; b. St. Paul, May 17, 1948; s. Thomas Dwight and Helen Elizabeth (Johnson) H.; m. Barbara Jeanne Tozer, Aug. 23, 1969. Student Kans. State U., 1966-69; B.A., Washburn U., 1970, J.D., 1973. Bar: Kans. 1973, U.S. Dist. Ct. Kans. 1973, U.S. Ct. Appeals (10th cir.) 1973, U.S. Supreme Ct. 1980. Asst. dist. atty., chief consumer protection and career criminals Shawnee County Dist. Attys. Office, Topeka, 1973-78; chief counsel enforcement dir. Kans. Securities Commn., Topeka, 1978; chief criminal div. Kans. Atty. Gen.'s Office, Topeka, 1979-82; asst. U.S. atty., supr. U.S. Atty. Dist. Kans., Topeka, 1982-84; mem. firm Eidson, Lewis, Porter & Haynes, Topeka, 1984-89; ptnr. Porter, Fairchild & Haney, Topeka, 1989—; adj. instr. Washburn U. Law Sch.; lectr. in field. Author: Civil Liability for Police, 1982; A Guide for the Kansas Peace Officer, 1982. Mem. adv. bd. Indian Ctr., Topeka, 1982, Shawnee Court Jail Constrn. Com., Topeka, 1983— ; bd. dirs. Campfire; parliamentarian 2d Dist. Republican Com., Topeka, 1981-82. Named Alumnus of the Year Kans. State U. Delta Chi, 1995. Mem. ABA, Am. Judicature Soc., Kans. Bar Assn., Topeka Bar Assn., Kans. Assn. Def. Counsel. Federal civil litigation, Criminal. Office: Fairchild Haney & Buck NationsBank Towers # 1000 Topeka KS 66603

HANGLEY, WILLIAM THOMAS, lawyer; b. Long Beach, N.Y., Mar. 11, 1941; s. Charles Augustus and Faustine Charmillot H.; m. Mary Dupree Hangley, July 24, 1965; children: Michele Dupree, William Thomas, Katherine Charmillot. BS in Music, SUNY-Coll. at Fredonia, 1963; LLB cum laude, U. Pa., 1966. Bar: Pa. 1966, U.S. Ct. Appeals (3d cir.) 1966, U.S. Dist. Ct. (ea. dist.) Pa. 1966. Assoc. Schnader, Harrison, Segal & Lewis, Phila., 1966-69; mem., CEO, Hangley Connolly Epstein Chicco Foxman & Ewing, Phila, 1969-94, CEO Hangley Aronchick Segal & Pudlin, 1994—; judge protem Phila. Ct. of Common Pleas, 1991—; mem. adv. bd. Pub. Interest Law Ctr. Phila. Contbr. articles to profl. publs. Bd. dirs. Ams. for Dem. Action, 1972-81. Fellow Am. Coll. Trial Lawyers (chmn. Com. on Fed. Rules of Evidence, 2001-, mem. Pa. State Com.), Am. Bar Found.; mem. ABA (co-chmn. litigation sect. com. on fed. procedure 1990-95—, co-chair task force on merit selection of judges 1995-97, mem. task force on discovery 1997-98, task force on judiciary 1998—), Pa. Bar Assn. (corp. and litigation coms., securities and antitrust subcoms., ho. dels. 1989-92), ACLU, Am. Law Inst., Phila. Bar Assn., Legal Club, Jr. Legal Club, Order of Coif, U. Pa. Inns of Ct. (master of the bench). Roman Catholic. Federal civil litigation, Securities. Office: Hangley Aronchick Segal & Pudlin 1 Logan Sq Fl 27 Philadelphia PA 19103-6995

HANKET, MARK JOHN, lawyer; b. Jan. 28, 1943; s. Laddie W. and Florence J. (Kubat) H.; m. Carole A. Dalpiaz, Sept. 14, 1968; children: Gregory, Jennifer, Sarah. AB magna cum laude, John Carroll U., 1965; JD cum laude, Ohio State U., 1968; MBA, Xavier U., 1977. Bar: Ohio 1968, Mich. 1993. Atty. Chemed Corp., Cin., 1973-77, asst. sec., 1977-82, sec., 1982-84, v.p., sec., 1984-86; v.p., gen counsel DuBois Chems. Divsn., 1986-87; v.p., sec. gen. counsel DuBois Chems., Inc., 1987-91; sec. gen. counsel Diversey Corp., 1991-94, v.p., sec. gen. counsel, 1994-96; v.p. law and people excellence, sec. Americlean Sys., Inc., 1996-99; asst. gen. counsel Diversey Lever, Inc., 1999—. Capt. U.S. Army, 1968-73. Decorated Meritorious Svc. medal, Army Commendation medal with oak leaf cluster. Mem. ABA, Mich. Bar Assn., Am. Corp. Counsel Assn., Ohio Bar Assn. Contracts commercial, General corporate, Pension, profit-sharing, and employee benefits. Office: Diversey Lever 360 E Kemper Rd Sharonville OH 45241 E-mail: mark.hanket@diverseylever.com

HANKIN, MITCHELL ROBERT, lawyer; b. Phila., May 16, 1949; s. Samuel and Harriet (Cohen) H. BA, Trinity Coll., Hartford, Conn., 1971; JD, Columbia U., 1974. Bar: Pa. 1974, U.S. Dist. Ct. (ea. dist.) Pa. 1975, U.S. Ct. Appeals (3d cir.) 1975. Assoc. Blank, Romeklaus, Comisky, Phila., 1974-75; asst. U.S. atty. U.S. Atty.'s Office, 1975-76; ptnr. Hankin Enterprises, Willow Grove, Pa., 1976—. Bd. dirs. Bank of Old York, Bank of King of Prussia (Pa.), Royal Bank of Pa. Mem. ABA, Pa. Bar Assn., Montgomery County Bar Assn., Phila. Bar Assn., Phi Beta Kappa. State civil litigation, Contracts commercial, Real property. Home: 1115 Barberry Rd Bryn Mawr PA 19010-1907

HANKINSON, DEBORAH G. state supreme court justice; BS with distinction, Purdue U.; MS, U. Tex., Dallas; JD, So. Meth. U. Bar: Tex., U.S. Ct. Appeals (5th cir.) 1995; cert. civil appellate law Tex. Bd. Legal Specialization. Spl. edn. tchr. Plano (Tex.) Ind. Sch. Dist.; assoc. Thompson and Knight, Dallas, 1983-95; judge U.S. Ct. Appeals (5th cir.), 1996, Tex. Supreme Ct., Dallas, 1997—. Liaison Gender Bias Reform Implementation Com., family law sect. Dallas Bar. Editor-in-chief Southwestern Law Jour. Fellow Tex. Bar Found., Dallas Bar Found. Mem. ABA (litigation sect., com. appellate practice, judicial sect.), State Bar Tex. (judicial, litigation, appellate sects.), Dallas Bar Assn. (apellate law sect.), 5th Cir. Bar Assn., Coll. of State Bar Tex., Order of the Coif. Office: Supreme Court PO Box 12248 Austin TX 78711-2248*

HANKS, GEORGE CAROL, JR. state judge; b. Breaux Bridge, La., Sept. 25, 1964; s. George Carol and Quenola Reese Hanks; m. Stacey L. Hanks, Apr. 29, 1995. JD, Harvard U., 1989; BA summa cum laude, La. State U., 1986. Bar: Tex. 1989, U.S. Dist. Ct. (so. dist.) Tex. 1992, U.S. Ct. Appeals (5th cir.) 1993, U.S. Dist. Ct. Ariz. 1994. Judicial law clk., Houston, 1989-91; assoc. atty. Fulbright & Jaworski, 1991-96; shareholder Wickliff & Hall PC, 1996-2001; judge 157th Dist. Ct., State of Tex., 2001—. Panel chmn. grievance com., spl. disciplinary counsel State Bar Tex., Houston, 1993-99. Contbr. articles to profl. jours. Bd. dirs. Big Bros. and Big Sisters, Houston, 1995-97, Houston chpt. ARC, 2001—. Fellow Houston Bar Assn.; mem. Fed. Bar Assn., Nat. Bar Assn., Houston Bar Assn. (mem. editl. bd.), Coll. State Bar Tex. (panel chmn. grievance com. 1993-99, spl. disciplinary counsel 1993—). Avocations: aviation, ice hockey, scuba diving. Home: 12035 E Circle Dr Houston TX 77071 Office: 1310 Prairie St 11th Fl Houston TX 77002 E-mail: ghanks@prodigy.net, george_hanks@jusex.net

HANNA, HARRY MITCHELL, lawyer; b. Portland, Oreg., Jan. 13, 1936; s. Joseph John and Amelia Cecelia (Rask) H.; m. Patricia Ann Shelly, Feb. 4, 1967; 1 child, Harry M. Jr. BS, U. Oreg., 1958; JD, Lewis and Clark Coll., 1966. Bar: Oreg. 1966, U.S. Tax Ct. 1967, U.S. Dist. Ct. Oreg. 1970, U.S. Supreme Ct. 1971, U.S. Ct. Appeals (9th cir.) 1973, U.S. Ct. Claims 1973. Airport mgr. Port of Portland, 1964-66; mng. ptnr. Hanna & Purcella, Portland, 1966-80, Niehaus, Hanna, Murphy, Green, Holloway & Connolly, Portland, 1980-88; shareholder, v.p. Hanna, Kerns & Strader, P.C., 1988—. Judge pro-tempore U.S. Dist. Ct. Oreg., 1973-78; adj. prof. N.W. Sch. Law, Lewis and Clark Coll., Portland, 1976-77. Trustee Emanuel Med. Ctr. Found., 1989—; pres. Ctrl. Cath. H.S. Bd., 1992-95; vice chair Life Flight Devel. Bd., 1994-97, chair, 1997—. Mem. ABA, Fed. Bar Assn., Oreg. State Bar Assn., Multnomah Bar Assn., Rotary (pres. East Portland club 1989-90). Avocations: tennis, hunting, fishing, coaching youth athletics. General corporate, Real property, Taxation, general. Office: Hanna Kerns & Strader PC 1300 SW 6th Ave Ste 300 Portland OR 97201-3461

HANNA, TERRY ROSS, lawyer, small business owner; b. Wadsworth, Ohio, May 17, 1947; s. Harry Ross and Geraldine (Frensley) H.; m. Max Anna Hindes, Jan. 20, 1968; children: Travis, Taylor, Molly. BBA, U. Okla., 1968, JD, 1972; LLM, NYU, 1973; MA in Bibl Studies, Dallas Theol. Sem., 1988. Bar: Okla. 1972, U.S. Tax Ct. 1974, U.S. Ct. Appeals (10th cir.) 1979, U.S. Supreme Ct. 1989; CPA, Okla. Mem. McAfee & Taft, Oklahoma City, 1972-80; pres. P 356 Inc., 1980—; of counsel Crowe & Dunlevy, 1987—. Owner Mo Jo Video, 1995—; spl. lectr. Oklahoma City U. Sch. Law, 1974-75. Editor Okla. U. Law Rev., 1970-72. Mem. internat. com. Boy Scouts Am., 1988—; dir. U.S. Found. for Internat. Scouting, Irving, 1989—. Baden-Powell fellow World Scout Found., 1988—; recipient Silver Beaver award Boy Scouts Am., 1988. Mem. Okla. Bar Assn. (pres. taxation sect. 1978-79), Sports Lawyers Assn., Order of Arrow (lodge advisor 1989—), Kappa Sigma (chpt. advisor 1974-75), Phi Delta Phi (magister 1972). Republican. Mem. Christian Ch. Avocations: coach, patch collector, fishing, softball, computers. Home: 2600 W Coffee Creek Rd Edmond OK 73003-3326 Office: Crowe & Dunlevy 1800 Mid America Towers Oklahoma City OK 73102 E-mail: HANNAT@crowedunlevy.com, thanna@ionet.net

HANNAH, JIM, judge; b. Dec. 26, 1944; BSBA in Acctg., U. Ark., JD. Pvt. practice Lightle, Tedder, Hannah & Beebe; city atty. City of Searcy, Ark., 1969—78; juvenile judge White County, 1976—78; chancery,probate judge 17th Jud. Dist., 1979—99; justice Supreme Ct. Ark., 2000. Office: Justice Bldg Rm 230 625 Marshall St Little Rock AR 72201*

HANNAH, LAWRENCE BURLISON, lawyer; b. Urbana, Ill., Aug. 5, 1943; s. Lawrence Hugh and Margaret Alene (Burlison) H.; m. Kathleen O'Hara, Nov. 8, 1969; 1 child, Scott David. BA, Dartmouth Coll., 1965; JD cum laude, U. Pa., 1968. Bar: Wash. 1971, U.S. Dist. Ct. (we. dist.) Wash. 1971, Ct. of Appeals (9th cir.) 1971, U.S. Supreme Ct. 1990. Analyst U.S. Central Intelligence Agency, Langley, Va., 1969-71; ptnr. Perkins Coie, Bellevue, Wash., 1971—. Contbr. articles to profl. jours. Mem. King County Personnel Bd., Wash., 1984-90; mem. fin. com. Mcpl. Gov. Candidates, King County, 1972—. 1st lt. USAF, 1968-69. Mem. ABA, Wash. State Bar Assn., Seattle-King County Bar Assn. Methodist. Avocations: jogging, boating, tennis. Labor, Municipal (including bonds). Home: 1610 W Lake Sammamish Pky SE Bellevue WA 98008-5229 Office: Perkins Coie 411 108th Ave NE Ste 1800 Bellevue WA 98004-5584

HANNAN, MYLES, lawyer, banker; b. Rye, N.Y., Oct. 14, 1936; s. Joseph A. and Rosemary (Edwards) H.; children from previous marriages: Myles Jr., Paul F., Thomas J., Kerry E. BA, Holy Cross Coll., 1958; LLB, Harvard U., 1964. Bar: N.Y. 1964, Mass. 1970, Md. 1994, D.C. 1996, U.S. Dist. Ct. (so. and ea. dists.) N.Y. 1966, U.S. Dist. Ct. Md. 1995. Assoc. Cadwalader, Wickersham & Taft, N.Y.C., 1964-69; v.p., gen. counsel, sec. High Voltage Engrng. Corp., Burlington, Mass., 1969-73; v.p., sec. Stop & Shop Cos., Inc., Boston, 1973-79; group v.p. law and adminstrn. Del. North Cos., Inc., Buffalo, 1979-81; v.p., fin., gen. counsel, sec. Anacomp, Inc., Indpls., 1981-84; exec. v.p. Empire of Am. FSB, Buffalo, 1984-89; adminstrv. v.p. Berkeley Group Inc., 1990-91; ptnr. Linowes and Blocher LLP, Washing-

ton, 1992—. Trustee Studio Arena Theatre, Buffalo, 1986-89; bd. dirs. Buffalo Philharm. Orch., 1987-89. Lt. USNR, 1958-61. Finance, Landlord-tenant, Real property. Home: 2445 Lyttonsville Rd Apt 1209 Silver Spring MD 20910-1936 Office: Linowes and Blocher LLP 1010 Wayne Ave Ste 1000 Silver Spring MD 20910-5615 E-mail: mh@linowes-law.com

HANNAY, WILLIAM MOUAT, III, lawyer; b. Kansas City, Mo., Dec. 3, 1944; s. William Mouat and Gladys (Capron) H.; m. Donna Jean Harkins, Sept. 30, 1978; children: Capron Grace, Blaike Ann, William Mouat IV. BA, Yale U., 1966; JD, Georgetown U., 1973. Bar: Mo. 1973, D.C. 1974, N.Y. 1975, Ill. 1980. Law clk. to Judge Myron Bright, U.S. Ct. Appeals, 8th Cir., St. Louis, 1973-74; law clk. to Justice Tom Clark U.S. Supreme Ct., Washington, 1974-75; assoc. Weil Gotshal & Manges, N.Y.C., 1975-77; asst. dist. atty. New York County Dist. Atty.'s Office, 1977-79; ptnr. Schiff Hardin & Waite, Chgo., 1979—. Adj. prof. IIT/Chgo.-Kent Law Sch., 1983—. Author: International Trade: Avoiding Criminal Risks, Designing an Effective Antitrust Compliance Program, Tying Arrangements; contbr. articles to profl. jours. Chmn. bd. dirs. Gilber and Sullivan Soc. Chgo., 1984-87, Served with U.S. Army, 1967-68, Vietnam. Mem. ABA (chair sect. internat. law and practice 1998-99, chair Africa law initiative coun. 2000—), Chgo Bar Assn. (chmn. antitrust com. 1986-87), Yale Club (pres. 1987-89), Chgo. Yacht Club, Union League Club (Chgo.). Democrat. Episcopalian. Antitrust, Trademark and copyright, Unfair trade regulation. Home: 591 Plum Tree Rd Barrington Hills IL 60010-2329 Office: Schiff Hardin & Waite 7200 Sears Tower Chicago IL 60606

HANNON, TIMOTHY PATRICK, lawyer, educator; b. Culver City, Calif., Nov. 29, 1948; s. Justin Aloysius and Ann Elizabeth (Ford) H.; m. Patricia Ann Hanson, May 1, 1976; children: Sean Patrick, James Patrick. Student, U. Vienna, 1968-69, Naval War Coll., 1988; BA, U. Santa Clara, 1970, JD cum laude, 1974. Bar: Calif. 1974, U.S. Dist. Ct. (no. dist.) Calif. 1974, U.S. Dist. Ct. (so. and dists.) Calif. 1978, U.S. Ct. Appeals (9th cir.) 1978, Ct. Appeals Armed Forces 1979, D.C. 1981, U.S. Tax Ct. 1983, U.S. Ct. Claims 1983; cert. trial and def. lawyer Univorm Code Mil. Justice; cert. pilot with tailwheel endorsement, FAA. Assoc. N. Perry Moerdyke, Jr., Palo Alto, Calif., 1975-81; ptnr. Myerdyke & Hannon, 1982-84, Attwood, Hurst, Knox & Anderson, 1984-86; pvt. practice Campbell, Calif., 1986-97; U.S. Adminstrv. law judge Social Security Adminstrn., 1997—. Instr. San Jose State U., 1985-89; instr. De Anza Jr. Coll., Cupertino, Calif., 1987-97, instr. extension courses U. Calif., Santa Cruz, 1982-83; lectr. Lincoln Law Sch., San Jose, Calif., 1988-97, 2001—; arbitrator Santa Clara County Superior Ct., Santa Clara County Mcpl. Ct.; sr. mil. mem. expanded Internat. Mil. Edn. Tng., Uganda; judge pro temp Santa Clara County Mcpl. Ct. Chmn., Menlo Park Housing Commn., 1979-81; mem. allocations com. vol. United Way Clara County, 1987-90; mem. San Jose Vets. Meml. Com., 1993-99, treas., 1996-99. Admiral Tex. Navy, 1998. With Calif. Army NG, 1970-76, capt., USNR, 1979—, commdg. officer, 1999-2001. Mem. Santa Clara County Bar Assn. (exec. com.), Santa Clara U. Nat. Alumni, U. Santa Clara Law Alumni Assn. (bd. dirs. 1980-81, sec. 1981-83, v.p. 1983-85, pres. 1985-87), Kiwanis. Roman Catholic. Avocation: flying. State civil litigation, Consumer commercial, General practice. Home: 806 Buckwood Ct San Jose CA 95120-3306 Office: Social Security Adminstrn 280 S 1st St # 300 San Jose CA 95113-3002 E-mail: tpatrick.hannon@ssa.gov

HANRAHAN, MICHAEL G. lawyer, business consultant; b. Mount Vernon, N.Y., June 1, 1949; s. G. Michael and Florence M. (Quinn) H.; m. Barbara L. Fluhr, June 11, 1977; children: Thomas M., Elizabeth L. BA, Saint Bonaventure U., 1971; JD, Fordham U., 1974. Bar: N.Y., 1975; U.S. Dist. Ct. (ea. dist.) N.Y. 1975, U.S. Ct. Appeals (2nd cir.) 1975, Supreme Ct. 1997. Ptnr. Hanrahan & Hanrahan, Pelham, N.Y., 1975—, Hanrahan & Curley, Chappaqua, 1995—. Bd. dirs. John Langenbacher Co., Inc., Bronx, N.Y., U.S. Veneer Co., Inc., 1985—. Pres., dir. Pelham (N.Y.) Family Svc., Inc., 1976-80. Mem. Rotary Internat. (pres., dir. 1976—, Paul Harris fellow 1988). Estate planning, General practice, Probate. Office: Hanrahan & Hanrahan 438 5th Ave Pelham NY 10803-1257

HANSBURY, STEPHAN CHARLES, judge; b. Mt. Holly, N.J., Nov. 3, 1946; s. Charles Clark and Kathryn Irene (Meyer) H.; m. Sharon Buckley; children: Elizabeth Kathryn, Jillian Judith, Stephanie Clark. BA, Allegheny Coll., 1968; MBA, Fairleigh Dickinson U., 1973; JD, Seton Hall U., 1977; cert. civil trial atty., Supreme Ct. N.J., 1989. Bar: N.J. 1977, U.S. Dist. Ct. (no. dist.) N.J. 1977, U.S. Supreme Ct. 1982. Dir. spl. programs Bloomfield (N.J.) Coll., 1968-71; dir. fin. aid Monmouth Coll., West Long Branch, N.J., 1971-72; asst. adminstr. Morris View, Morris Plains, 1972-78; assoc. Hansbury, Martin & Knapp, 1978-87, pres., 1987-92; ptnr. Kummer Knox, Naughton & Hansbury, Parsippany, N.J., 1992-99, pres., 1996-97; ptnr. Cooper, Rose & English, LLP, 2000-2001; judge Superior Ct. of N.J., 2001—. Mem., gen. counsel Cheshire Home, Florham Park, N.J., 1978-2000, Ciba-Geigy Corp., Summit, N.J., 1980-92. Legis. aide Assemblyman Arthur Albohn, Morristown, N.J., 1980-83; mem. Morris County Bd. of Social Svcs., 1989-96, chmn. 1992-94; bd. dirs. Colonia Symhony. Mem. ABA, N.J. Bar Assn., Morris County Bar Assn. (trustee 1987-90), Rotary (pres. 1998-99), Morristown Club. Republican. Episcopalian. Avocations: tennis, golf, reading. Office: Courthouse PO Box 910 Morristown NJ 07963-0910 E-mail: shansbury@crelaw.com

HANSELL, DEAN, lawyer; b. Bridgeport, Conn., Mar. 24, 1952; BA, Denison U., 1974; JD, Northwestern U., 1977. Bar: Ill. 1977, U.S. Dist. Ct. (no. dist.) Ill. 1977, U.S. Ct. Appeals (7th cir.) 1978, U.S. Ct. Appeals (D.C. cir.) 1978, U.S. Ct. Appeals (9th cir.) 1979, U.S. Ct. Appeals (8th cir.) 2001, Calif. 1980, U.S. Dist. Ct. (cen. dist.) Calif. 1981, U.S. Dist. Ct. (so. dist.) Calif. 1989, U.S. Supreme Ct. 1998. Asst. atty. gen. for environ. control State of Ill., Chgo., 1977-80; atty. FTC, L.A., 1980-83; assoc. Lillick, McHose & Charles, 1983-84, Donovan Leisure Newton & Irvine, L.A., 1984-86; ptnr. LeBoeuf, Lamb, Greene & MacRae, 1986-01, mng. ptnr., 2001—. Adj. assoc. prof. Southwestern U. Sch. Law, L.A., 1982-86; mem. Ill. Solar Resources Adv. Panel, 1978-80; judge pro tem L.A. County Mcpl. Ct., 1987-97, L.A. County Superior Ct., 1989—; mem. adv. bd. Fayette Haywood Legal Svcs., Tenn., 1979-83, Nat. Inst. for Citizen Edn. in Law, 1989-94. Mem. editl. bd. L.A. Lawyer Mag., 1995—, Internat. Reins. Dispute Reporter, 1996—; contbr. articles to profl. jours. Bd. dirs. Jewish Fed. Coun. Met. L.A. Region, 1984-87, Project LEAP, Legal Elections in All Precincts, Chgo., 1976-80, Martin Luther King, Jr. Ctr. Nonviolence, L.A., 1991-95, L.A. Pub. Libr. Found., 1997—; commr. L.A. Bd. Police Commrs., 1997-2001, v.p., 2001; commr. L.A. Bd. Info. Tech. Comrs., 2001-. Mem. L.A. County Bar Assn. (mem. exec. com. antitrust sect. 1982-92, chair 1989-90), Calif. Bar Assn., Phi Beta Kappa, Omicron Delta Kappa. General civil litigation, Environmental, Insurance. Office: LeBoeuf Lamb Greene & MacRae 725 S Figueroa St Ste 3100 Los Angeles CA 90017-5404 E-mail: dhansell@llgm.com

HANSELMANN, FREDRICK CHARLES, lawyer; b. Phila., Sept. 1, 1955; s. Helmuth Fredrick and Maria Elizabeth (Dougherty) H.; m. Mary Nina Johnson, May 7, 1983; children: Elizabeth Ryan, Peter Cornelius, Kevin Andrew, Charlotte Mary. BA magna cum laude, La Salle Coll., 1977; JD, U. Notre Dame, 1980. Bar: Pa. 1980, U.S. Dist. Ct. (ea. dist.) Pa. 1981, U.S. Dist. Ct. (mid. dist.) Pa. 1987, U.S. Ct. Appeals (3d cir.) 1981. Assoc. German, Gallagher & Murtagh, P.C., Phila., 1981-85, Wilson, Elser, Moskowitz, Edelman & Dicker, Phila., 1985-90; ptnr. Mylotte David & Fitzpatrick, 1990-99; of counsel McBreen, McBreen and Kopko, 1999—. Mem. ABA, Pa. Bar Assn., Phila. Bar Assn., Def. Rsch. Inst., Profl. Liability Underwriting Soc., Lawyers Club Phila., Notre Dame Club Phila., Avalon Yacht Club, Glen Lake (Mich.) Assn. Republican. Roman Catholic. General civil litigation, Insurance, Personal injury. Home: 118 Azalea Way Flourtown PA 19031-2008 Office: McBreen McBreen & Kopko 1760 Market St Ste 900 Philadelphia PA 19103-4134 Fax: 215 864-2610. E-mail: fchlaw2@aol.com

HANSEN, CHRISTOPHER AGNEW, lawyer; b. Yakima, Wash., Dec. 10, 1934; s. Raymond Walter and Christine F.M. (Agnew) H.; m. Sandra Ridgely Pindell, Aug. 4, 1959; Anne Ridgely, Christopher Agnew Jr., Eric Bruce. BS, Cornell U., 1957; JD, U. Md., 1963. Bar: Md. 1963, U.S. Supreme Ct. 1973, U.S. Ct. Appeals (4th cir.) D.C. 1978. Law clk. Cir. Ct. for Balt. County, Towson, Md., 1960-63; assoc. Piper & Marbury, Balt., 1963-74; of counsel Casey, Scott, Canfield & Heggestad PC, Washington, 1982-93; ptnr. Constable, Alexander & Skeen, Towson, 1984-86, Parks, Hansen & Ditch, Towson, 1986-94; of counsel Heggestad & Weiss, PC, Washington, 1993—; pvt. practice Towson, 1974-83, 95—. With U.S. Army, 1957-60. Mem. ABA, D.C. Bar, Md. State Bar Assn., Bar Assn. Balt. County, Balt. City Bar Assn., Phi Alpha Delta. Episcopalian. Federal civil litigation, State civil litigation, Insurance. Home: 800 Hatherleigh Rd Baltimore MD 21212-1614

HANSEN, CURTIS LEROY, federal judge; b. 1933; BS, U. Iowa, 1956; JD, U. N.Mex., 1961. Bar: N.Mex. Law clk. to Hon. Irwin S. Moise N.Mex. Supreme Ct., 1961-62; ptnr. Snead & Hansen, Albuquerque, 1962-64, Richard C. Civerolo, Albuquerque, 1964-71, Civerolo, Hansen & Wolf, P.A., 1971-92; dist. judge U.S. Dist. Ct., N.Mex., 1992—. Mem. State Bar N.Mex., Albuquerque Bar Assn., Am. Coll. Trial Lawyers, Am. Bd. Trial Advocates, Albuquerque Country Club. Office: US Courthouse Chambers 660 333 Lomas Blvd NW Albuquerque NM 87102-2272

HANSEN, DAVID RASMUSSEN, federal judge; b. 1938; BA, N.W. Mo. State U., 1960; JD, George Washington U., 1963. Asst. clk. to minority House Appropriations Com. Ho. of Reps., 1960-61; adminstrv. aide 7th Dist. Iowa, 1962-63; pvt. practice law Jones, Cambridge & Carl, Atlantic, Iowa, 1963-64; capt., judge advocate General's Corps U.S. Army, 1964-68; pvt. practice law Barker, Hansen & McNeal, Iowa Falls, Iowa, 1968-76; ptnr. Win-Gin Farms, 1971—; judge Police Ct., Iowa, 1969-73, 2d Jud. Dist. Iowa Dist. Ct., 1976-86, U.S. Dist. Ct. (no. dist.) Iowa, Cedar Rapids, 1986-91, U.S. Ct. Appeals (8th cir.), Cedar Rapids, 1991—. Office: US Courthouse 101 1st St SE Cedar Rapids IA 52401-1202*

HANSEN, ERIC PETER, lawyer; b. Mpls., June 12, 1951; s. Donald Arthur and Florence (Paulsen) H.; m. Janet G. Bostrom, Mar. 21, 1981; children: Lindsey Elizabeth, Jessie Johanna. BA, St. Olaf Coll., 1973; JD, Duke U., 1976. Bar: Minn. 1976, .S. Dist. Ct. Minn. 1979, U.S. Ct. Appeals (8th cir.) 1979. Atty. 3M Co., St. Paul, 1976-80, divsn. atty., 1980-83, sr. atty., 1983—. Mem. Minn. Bar Assn. Republican. Antitrust, Contracts commercial, General corporate. Office: 3M Co PO Box 33428 3M Center Saint Paul MN 55144-1001 E-mail: ephansen@mmm.com

HANSEN, H. REESE, dean, educator; b. Logan, Utah, Apr. 8, 1942; s. Howard F. and Loila Gayle (Reese) H.; m. Kathryn Traveller, June 8, 1962; children: Brian T., Mark T., Dale T., Curtis T. BS, Utah State U., 1964; JD, U. Utah, 1972. Bar: Utah, 1974. Atty. Strong, Poelman & Fox, Salt Lake City, 1972-74; from asst. prof. to assoc. prof. Brigham Young U., Provo, Utah, 1974-79, prof., 1979—, from asst. dean to assoc. dean, 1974-89, dean, 1989—. Commr. ex officio Utah State Bar, Salt Lake City, 1989—; commr. Nat. Conf. Commrs. on Uniform State Laws, 1988-95. Co-author: Idaho Probate System, 1977, Utah Probate System, 1977, Cases and Text on Laws of Trusts, 6th edit., 1991; editor: Manual for Justices of Peace--Utah, 1978; contbr. articles to profl. jours. Mem. LDS Ch. Office: Brigham Young U 348A Jrcb Provo UT 84602-1029

HANSMANN, HENRY BAETHKE, law educator; b. Highland Park, Ill., Oct. 5, 1945; s. Elwood Hansmann and Louise Frances (Baethke) Moore; m. Marina Santilli, 1992; 1 child, Lisa Santilli. BA, Brown U., 1967; JD, Yale U., 1974, PhD, 1978. Asst. prof. law U. Pa. Law Sch., Phila., 1975-81, assoc. prof. law, econs. and pub. policy, 1981-83; prof. law Yale U., New Haven, 1983-88, Harris prof., 1988—. Author: The Ownership of Enterprise, 1996. John Simon Guggenheim Found. fellow, 1985-86. Mem. Am. Econs. Assn., Am. Law and Econ. Assn. Home: 240 Mercer St # 1603 New York NY 10012-1507 Office: Yale U Law Sch PO Box 208215 New Haven CT 06520-8215 E-mail: henry.hansmann@yale.edu

HANSON, ARNOLD PHILIP, JR. lawyer, publishing company executive; b. Boston, Nov. 24, 1949; s. Arnold Philip Sr. and Della Ann (Lavernoich) H.; m. Barbara Jean Davis, Oct. 19, 1974; children: Christopher Davis, Stephanie Ann, Jonathan Robert. AB, Dartmouth Coll., 1971; JD, Boston U., 1974; M in Mgmt., Yale U., 1982. Bar: N.H. 1974, U.S. Dist. Ct. N.H. 1974. Assoc. Bergeron & Hanson, Berlin, N.H., 1974-79, ptnr., 1979-80; mgmt. teaching asst. Yale U., New Haven, 1980-82; internal cons. Insilco Corp., Meriden, Conn., 1981, asst. to chmn. bd. dirs., 1982-83; dir. pub. Taylor Pub. Co. subs. Insilco Corp., Dallas, 1984-88, vp. publ., new product devel., 1988— ; cons. Hanson and Assocs., Plano, Tex., 1983—. Pres., drive chmn. United Way, Berlin, 1976-80; pres., v.p., bd. dirs. Androscoggin Valley C. of C., Berlin, 1977-80. Mem. ABA, N.H. Bar Assn. (bd. govs. 1979-80), Am. Mktg. Assn., Assn. MBA Execs. Republican. Clubs: Androsloggin Valley Country (Gorham, N.H.) (pres., bd. dirs. 1978-80); Canyon Creek Country (Richardson, Tex.). Avocations: golf, tennis. Home: PO Box 186 Berlin NH 03570-0186 Office: Taylor Pub Co PO Box 597 Dallas TX 75221-0597

HANSON, BRUCE EUGENE, lawyer; b. Lincoln, Nebr., Aug. 25, 1942; s. Lester E. and Gladys (Diessner) H.; m. Peggy Pardun, Dec. 25, 1972 (dec. Nov. 1989). BA, U. Minn., 1965, JD, 1966. Bar: Minn. 1966, U.S. Dist. Ct. Minn. 1966, U.S. Tax Ct. 1973, U.S. Ct. Appeals (8th cir.) 1973, U.S. Ct. Appeals (fed. cir.) 1983, U.S. Supreme Ct. 1970. Shareholder Doherty, Rumble & Butler, P.A., St. Paul, 1966-99; ptnr. Oppenheimer, Wolff & Donnelly, LLP, Mpls., 1999—. Dir., sec. Am. Saddlebred Horse Assn.; bd. trustees, chair United Hosp., 1996-98. Mem. ATLA, Hennepin County Bar Assn., Minn. State Bar Assn., Am. Health Lawyers Assn., Minn. Soc. Hosp. Attys., North Oaks Golf Club, Order of Coif, Phi Delta Phi. Federal civil litigation, State civil litigation, Health. Home: 23 Evergreen Rd Saint Paul MN 55127-2077 Office: Oppenheimer Wolff & Donnelly LLP 45 S 7th St Ste 3300 Minneapolis MN 55402-1614 E-mail: BHanson@Oppenheimer.com

HANSON, DAVID JAMES, lawyer; b. Neenah, Wis., July 20, 1943; s. Vernon James and Dorothy O. Hanson; m. Diana G. Severson, Aug. 25, 1965 (div. Sept. 1982); children: Matthew Vernon, Maja Kirsten, Brian Edward; m. Linda Hughes Bochert, May 28, 1983; children: Scott Charles, Sarah Katherine. BS, U. Wis., 1965, JD, 1968. Bar: Wis. 1968, U.S. Dist. Ct. (we. dist.) Wis. 1968, U.S. Dist. Ct. (ea. dist.) Wis. 1969, U.S. Ct. Appeals (7th cir.) 1970, U.S. Supreme Ct. 1971. Asst. atty. gen. State of Wis. Dept. of Justice, Madison, 1968-71, dep. atty. gen., 1976-81; asst. chancellor, chief legal counsel U. Wis., 1971-76; ptnr. Michael, Best & Friedrich LLP, 1981—. Lectr. Law Sch., U. Wis., Madison, 1972-75; chair govt. law sect. State Bar Wis., Madison, 1979-88. Contbr. articles to profl. jours. Bd. dirs. Sand County Found., Madison, 1988—, Wis. Ctr. for Academically Talented Youth, Madison, 1991-94, bd. trustees Edgewwod Coll., Madison, 1997—. Mem. ABA, Madison Club, Blackhawk Country Club. Democrat. Unitarian. Avocations: canoeing, skiing, golf, biking, hunting. General corporate, Health, Public utilities. Office: Michael Best & Friedrich PO Box 1806 Madison WI 53701-1806 E-mail: djhanson@mbflaw.com

HANSON, GARY A. lawyer, legal educator; b. Santa Fe, Sept. 30, 1954; s. Norman A. Hanson and Mary Gene (Moore) Garrison; m. Tracey J. Tannen, Mar. 11, 1982; children: Paul, Carly, Sean. BS magna cum laude, U. Utah, 1976; JD, Pepperdine U., 1980. Bar: Calif. 1980, U.S. Dist. Ct. (cen. dist.) Calif. 1980, U.S. Ct. Appeals (9th cir.) 1980. Pvt. practice, Westlake Village, Calif., 1980-82; assoc. gen. counsel Pepperdine U., Malibu, 1982-83, acting gen. counsel, 1983-84, univ. gen. counsel, 1984—. Adj. prof. law Pepperdine U., Malibu, 1982—, lectr. bus. law, 1986—; pro bono atty. San Fernando Valley Christian Sch., L.A., 1982-83; mem. Pro Bono Estate Adv. Svc., San Diego, 1983-86; cons. West Ednl. Pub. Co., 1988. Contbr. articles to profl. jours.; pres. Ind. Colls. and Univs. jour., 1989. Recipient Pres.'s award San Diego Christian Found., 1984. Mem. ABA, L.A. County Bar Assn., Nat. Assn. Coll. and Univ. Attys. Republican. General corporate, Education and schools. Office: Pepperdine U Gen Counsel Office TAC 421 24255 Pacific Coast Hwy Malibu CA 90263-0002

HANSON, JEAN ELIZABETH, lawyer; b. Alexandria, Minn., June 28, 1949; d. Carroll Melvin and Alice Clarissa (Frykman) H.; m. H. Barndt Hauptfuhrer, May 15, 1982; children: Catherine Jean, Benjamin Colman (twins). BA, Luther Coll., 1971; JD, U. Minn., 1976. Bar: N.Y. 1977, U.S. Dist. Ct. (so. dist.) 1977. Probation officer Hennepin County, Mpls., 1972-73; law clk. Minn. State Pub. Defender, 1975-76; assoc. Fried, Frank, Harris, Shriver & Jacobson, N.Y.C., 1976-83, ptnr., 1983-93, 94—. Gen. counsel U.S. Treasury, Washington, 1993-94; mem. bd. regents Luther Coll.; mem. bd. visitors Law Sch. U. Minn. Recipient Disting. Svc. award Luther Coll., 1991, Outstanding Achievement award U. Minn., 1999. Mem. ABA, N.Y. State Bar Assn., Assn. of Bar of City of N.Y. (securities regulation com. 1991-98, mem. task force women in the profession 1995-98), U. Minn. Law Alumni Assn. Democrat. Lutheran. Office: Fried Frank Harris Shriver & Jacobson One New York Plaza New York NY 10004 E-mail: jean.hanson@ffhsj.com

HANSON, JOHN J. lawyer; b. Aurora, Nebr., Oct. 22, 1922; s. Peter E. and Hazel Marion (Lounsbury) H.; m. Elizabeth Anne Moss, July 1, 1973; children from their previous marriages— Mark, Eric, Gregory. A.B., U. Denver, 1948; LL.B. cum laude, Harvard U., 1951. Bar: N.Y. bar 1952, Calif. bar 1955. Asso. firm Dewey, Ballantine, Bushby, Palmer & Wood, N.Y.C., 1951-54; ptnr. firm Gibson, Dunn & Crutcher, L.A, 1954—, mem. exec. com., 1978-87, adv. ptnr., 1991—. Contbr. articles to profl. jours. Trustee Palos Verdes (Calif.) Sch. Dist., 1969-73. Served with U.S. Navy, 1942-45. Fellow Am. Coll. Trial Lawyers; mem. Am. Bar Assn., Los Angeles County Bar Assn. (chmn. antitrust sect. 1979-80), Bel Air Country Club. Antitrust. Home: 953 Linda Flora Dr Los Angeles CA 90049-1630 Office: Gibson Dunn & Crutcher 333 S Grand Ave Ste 4400 Los Angeles CA 90071-3197

HANSON, KENT BRYAN, lawyer; b. Litchfield, Minn., Sept. 17, 1954; s. Calvin Bryan and Muriel (Wessman) H.; m. Barbara Jane Elenbaas, Aug. 24, 1974; children: Lindsay Michal, Taylor Jordan, Chase Philip. AA with high honors, Trinity Western Coll., 1974; BA, U. B.C., Vancouver, 1976; JD magna cum laude, U. Minn., 1979. Bar: Minn. 1979, U.S. Dist. Ct. Minn. 1980, U.S. Ct. Appeals (8th cir.) 1980, U.S. Dist. Ct. (we. dist.) Wis. 1983, Wis. 1985, U.S. Ct. Appeals (9th cir.) 1989, U.S. Dist. Ct. Ariz. 1992, Ohio 1993, Calif. 1994. Assoc. Grossman, Karlins, Siegel & Brill, Mpls., 1979-81, Gray, Plant, Mooty, Mooty & Bennett, Mpls., 1981-85; ptnr. Bowman & Brooke, 1986-95; CEO Hanson, Marek, Bolkcom & Greene, Ltd., 1996—. Bd. dirs. Inner City Boys Club, Ctrl. Free Ch., Mpls., 1979-81; 12th ward del. Mpls. Dem. Farmer Labor Com. Conv., 1982; mem. exec. bd. Ctrl. Free Ch., Mpls., 1986; chair exec. bd. Ctrl. Community Ch., 1993-96. Mem. ABA, State Bar Assn. Wis., Minn. Def. Lawyers Assn., Minn. State Bar Assn., Hennepin County Bar Assn., Calif. State Bar Assn., State Bar of Ohio, Def. Rsch. Inst. Avocations: classical music, golf, tennis, computers, motorcycles. Federal civil litigation, State civil litigation, Product liability. Office: Hanson Marek Bolkcom & Greene Ltd 2200 Rand Tower 527 Marquette Ave Minneapolis MN 55402-1302

HANSON, ROBERT DELOLLE, lawyer; b. Harrisburg, Pa., Dec. 13, 1916; s. Henry W. A. and Elizabeth (Painter) H.; m. Barbara Esmer, Apr. 22, 1949 (dec. Mar. 2000). BA, Gettysburg Coll., 1939; LLB, Dickinson Law Sch., 1942. Bar: Pa. 1942. Practice in Harrisburg, 1946-98; solicitor Dauphin County, 1958-76, Dauphin County Redevel. Authority, 1959-98. Pres. coun. of congregation Luth. Ch., 1953-55, 57-59; pres. Family and Children's Svc. of Harrisburg, 1956-57; mem. Harrisburg Sch. Bd., 1952-57, Dauphin County Housing Authority, 1960-98; gen. chmn. Tri-County United Fund, 1969, pres., 1971-72; trustee Gettysburg Coll., 1974—, sec., 1980, vice chmn., 1983-86; pres. Keystone area coun. Boy Scouts Am., 1980-82. Maj. inf. AUS, 1942-46, ETO. Decorated Bronze Star, Purple Heart; recipient Silver Beaver award Boy Scouts Am., 1980, Eagle award Boy Scouts Am., 1990, Alexis de Tocqueville award United Way of Am., 1991, Others award Salvation Army, 1992, Lavern Brenneman award Gettysburg Coll., 1996, Wisdom award of honor The Wisdom Soc. for the Advancement of Knowledge, Learning and Rsch. in Edn., 1999. Mem. ABA, Pa. Bar Assn. (sec., treas. taxation sect. 1948-59), Dauphin County Bar Assn. (dir. 1958-59), Gettysburg Coll. Alumni Assn. (treas. 1958-59, v.p. 1968-71, pres. 1971-72), Masons (33 deg., past master, pres. bd. trustees 1982-85), Execs. Club (pres. 1953), Harrisburg Rotary (pres. 1979). Lutheran. General corporate, Estate planning, General practice. Home: 2500 N 2nd St Harrisburg PA 17110-1106 Office: 111 Locust St Harrisburg PA 17101-1426

HANSON, RONALD WILLIAM, lawyer; b. Aug. 3, 1950; s. Orlin Eugene and Irene Agnes Hanson; m. Sandra Kay Cook, Aug. 21, 1971; children: Alec Evan, Corinn Michele. BA summa cum laude, St. Olaf Coll., 1972; JD cum laude, U. Chgo., 1975. Bar: Ill. 1975, U.S. Dist. Ct. (no. dist.) Ill. 1975, U.S. Ct. Appeals (7th cir.) 1978, U.S. Ct. Appeals (10th cir.) 1989. Assoc. Sidley & Austin, Chgo., 1975-83, ptnr., 1983-88, Latham & Watkins, Chgo., 1988—. Ofcl. advisor to Nat. Conf. of Commrs. on Uniform State Laws; lectr. Ill. Inst. Continuing Legal Edn., Springfield, 1979—, Am. Bankruptcy Inst., Washington, 1984—, Banking Law Inst., 1985, Practicing Law Inst., 1985—, Am. Law Inst., 1987. Contbr. articles to profl. jours. Mem. ABA, Ill. Bar Assn., Chgo. Bar Assn., Order of Coif, Met. Club, Phi Beta Kappa. Republican. Lutheran. Banking, Bankruptcy, Federal civil litigation. Home: 664 W 58th St Hinsdale IL 60521-5104 Office: Latham & Watkins Sears Tower Ste 5800 Chicago IL 60606-6306 E-mail: ronaldhanson@lw.com

HANTEL, PHILIP EDWARD, lawyer; b. Los Alamos, N.Mex., Aug. 4, 1972; s. Lawrence W. and Elizabeth G. Hantel. BA in Polit. Sci., U. Wash., 1994; JD, South Tex. Coll. Law, 1997. Bar: La. 1997, U.S. Dist. Ct. (we., mid. and ea. dists.) La. 1997, U.S. Ct. Appeals (5th cir.) 1997. Staff atty. La. Indigent Defender Bd., New Orleans, 1997, juvenile atty. Harvey, La., 1998; assoc. Beevers & Beevers LLP, Gretna, 1998-2000; pvt. practive Havey, 2000—. Mem. La. Criminal Def. Lawyers Assn., La. Pub. Defenders Assn., 5th Cir. Bar Assn., Fed. Bar Assn. Civil rights, Criminal, Human rights. Home: 2606 Royal St New Orleans LA 70117 Office: Philip Hantel Atty at Law PO Box 1900 Harvey LA 70059

HANZLIK, RAYBURN DEMARA, lawyer; b. L.A., June 7, 1938; s. Rayburn Otto and Ethel Winifred (Membery) H.; children: Kristina, Rayburn N., Alexander, Geoffrey. BS, Principia Coll., 1960; MA, Woodrow Wilson Sch. Fgn. Affairs, U. Va., 1968; JD, U. Va., 1974. Bar: Va. 1975, D.C. 1977. Staff asst. to Pres. U.S., Washington, 1971-73; assoc. dir. White House Domestic Council, 1975-77; of counsel Danzansky Dickey Tydings Quint & Gordon, Washington, 1977-78, Akin Gump Strauss Hauer & Feld, Washington, 1978-79; pvt. practice L.A., 1979-81; adminstr. Econ. Regulatory Adminstrn., Dept. Energy, Washington, 1981-85; ptnr. Heidrick and Struggles, Inc., 1985-91, McKenna & Hanzlik, Irvine, Calif., 1991-92; chmn. Lanxide Sports Internat., Inc., San Diego, 1992-95, Stealth Propulsion Internat., Ltd., San Diego, Calif. and, Melbourne, Australia, 1994-97; exec. v.p. Commodore Corp., N.Y.C. and McLean, Va., 1997-98; mng. dir. Brewer-Hanzlik Nuclear Ptnrs., LLC, 1998-99; atty. Trainum, Snowdon & Deane, Washington, 1999—; ptnr. Boyden Global Exec. Search, 2001—. Contbg. author: Global Politics and Nuclear Energy, 1971, Soviet Foreign Relations and World Communism, 1965. Alt. del. Republican Nat. Conv., 1980; dir. Calif. Rep. Victory Fund, 1980; candidate U.S. Senate, 1980. Served to lt. USN, 1963-68, Vietnam. Mem. ABA, Va. Bar Assn., D.C. Bar Assn. Republican. Christian Scientist. Administrative and regulatory, Legislative, Mergers and acquisitions. E-mail: rdhanzlik@aol.com

HARBAUGH, DANIEL PAUL, lawyer; b. Wendell, Idaho, May 18, 1948; s. Myron and Manuelita (Garcia) H. BA, Gonzaga U., 1970, JD, 1974. Bar: Washington 1974, U.S. Dist. Ct. (ea. dist.) Wash. 1977, U.S. Ct. Appeals (9th cir.) 1978. Asst. atty. gen. State of Wash., Spokane, 1974-77; ptnr. Richter, Wimberley & Ericson, 1977-83, Harbaugh & Bloom, P.S., Spokane, 1983—. Bd. dirs. Spokane Legal Svcs., 1982-86; bd. govs. LAWPAC, Seattle, 1980-92. Bd. dirs. Spokane Ballet, 1983-88; chpt. dir. Les Amis du Vin, Spokane, 1985-88; mem. Spokane County Civil Svc. Commn., 1991—, chmn., 1999—, Gonzaga U. Pres'. Coun., 1991-2000. Mem. ATLA, Wash. State Bar Assn. (spl. dist. counsel 1982-95, mem. com. rules for profl. conduct 1989-92, mem. legis. com. 1995-96), Spokane County Bar Assn. (chair med.-legal com. 1991), Wash. State Trial Lawyers Assn. (v.p. 1988-89, co-chair worker's compensation sect. 1992, 93, spl. select. com. on workers' corp. 1990—, forum 1994—, vice-chmn. 1994-97, mem. legis. com. 1995-98), Nat. Orgn. Social Security Claimants Reps., Internat. Wine and Food Soc. (pres. local chpt. 1989-91, cellar master 1994-96, cellar com. 2001—), Empire Club, Spokane Club, Spokane Country Club (adminstrv. com. 1995-98, chmn. 1991-98, trustee 1996-99, sec.-treas. 1997-98, pres. 1998-99, ex-officio 1999-2000, long range planning com. 1999—), Alpha Sigma Nu, Phi Alpha Delta. Roman Catholic. Alternative dispute resolution, Personal injury, Workers' compensation. Office: Harbaugh & Bloom PS PO Box 1461 Spokane WA 99210-1461 E-mail: harbl@msn.com

HARBECK, DOROTHY ANNE, lawyer; b. Elizabeth, N.J., Sept. 19, 1962; d. Jay Cleveland and Ella Anne (Phillips) H. BA, Wellesley Coll., 1984; JD, Seton Hall U., 1989. Bar: N.J. 1990, U.S. Dist. Ct. N.J. 1990, U.S. Ct. Appeals (3d cir.) 1992, U.S. Supreme Ct. 1995. Assoc. Drazin & Warshaw, Red Bank, N.J., 1990-94, Donington, Karcher, Salmond, Ronan & Raimone, Tinton Falls, 1994-95, Graham, Curtin & Sheridan, Trenton, 1995—. Editor: (jour.) Dictum, 1992; contbr. articles to profl. jours. Bd. dirs. Red Bank Environ. Commn., 1997—. Recipient Nathan Burkan Copyright Law prize ASCAP, 1988, prize Am. Acad. of Poets, 1983; Wellesley Coll. scholar, 1984. Fellow Am. Inns of Ct. Found.; mem. N.J. Bar Assn. General civil litigation, Personal injury, Election. Home: 65 E River Rd Apt 24 Rumson NJ 07760-1646 Office: Graham Curtin & Sheridan 50 W State St Ste 1008 Trenton NJ 08608-1220

HARBOUR, NANCY CAINE, lawyer; b. Cleve., July 30, 1949; d. William Anthony and Bernadette (Frohnapple) Caine; m. Randall Lee Harbour, Sept. 29, 1979. B.A. magna cum laude, U. Detroit, 1970; J.D., Cleve. State U., 1978. Bar: Mich. 1978. Writer Project Map, Inc., Washington, 1971-72; newspaper reporter Alexandria (Va.) Gazette, 1972-73, Times Herald Record, Goshen, N.Y., 1973-75; atty. Conklin, Benham, et al., Detroit, 1978-82, Martens, Ice & Geary, P.C., Detroit, 1982-90; ptnr. Martens, Ice, Geary, 1990—. Mem. Am. Trial Lawyers Assn., Mich. Trial Lawyers Assn., Mich. Bar Assn., State Bar Mich. (mem. compensation council 1983-85), Gamma Pi Epsilon. Democrat. Office: Martens Ice Geary 17117 W 9 Mile Rd Ste 1400 Southfield MI 48075-4520 E-mail: caineharbour@martensice.com

HARDGROVE, JAMES ALAN, lawyer; b. Chgo., Feb. 20, 1945; s. Albert John and Ruth (Noonen) H.; m. Kathleen M. Peterson, June 15, 1968; children: Jennifer Anne, Amy Kristine, Michael Sheridan. BA, U. Notre Dame, 1967; cert. English law, U. Coll. Law, 1969; JD, U. Notre Dame, 1970. Bar: Ill. 1970, U.S. Ct. Appeals (7th cir.) 1970, U.S. Dist. Ct. (no. dist.) Ill. 1970, U.S. Dist. Ct. (cen. dist.) Ill. 1978, U.S. Supreme Ct. 1980. Law clk. to presiding justice U.S. Ct. Appeals (7th cir.), Chgo., 1970-71; assoc. Sidley & Austin, 1971-76, ptnr., 1977—. Mem. ABA, Ill. Bar Assn., Chgo. Bar Assn., Legal Club. Antitrust, Federal civil litigation, State civil litigation. Home: 948 Ridge Ave Evanston IL 60202-1720 Office: Sidley Austin Brown & Word Bank One Plz 10 S Dearborn St Chicago IL 60603-2000 E-mail: jhardgro@sidley.com

HARDIE, JAMES HILLER, lawyer; b. Pitts., Dec. 1, 1929; s. James H. and Elizabeth Gillespie (Alcorn) H.; m. Frances P. Curtis, Dec. 5, 1953; children: J. Hiller, Janet Hardie Harvey, Andrew G., Michael C., Rachel Hardie Share. A.B., Princeton U., 1951; LL.B., Harvard U., 1954. Bar: Pa. 1955. Assoc. Reed Smith LLP, Pitts., 1954-62, ptnr., 1962-99, of counsel, 1999—. Mem. ABA, Am. Law Inst., Pa. Bar Assn. General corporate, Mergers and acquisitions, Securities. Office: Reed Smith LLP PO Box 2009 Pittsburgh PA 15230-2009 E-mail: jhardie@reedsmith.com

HARDIN, ADLAI STEVENSON, JR. judge; b. Norwalk, Conn., Sept. 20, 1937; s. Adlai S. and Carol (Moore) H. BA, Princeton U., 1959; LLB, Columbia U., 1962. Bar: N.Y. 1963, U.S. Dist. Ct. (so. and ea. dists.) N.Y. 1965, U.S. Supreme Ct. 1967, U.S. Ct. Appeals (2d cir.) 1965, U.S. Ct. Appeals (5th cir.) 1974, U.S. Ct. Appeals (3d cir.) 1977, U.S. Ct. Appeals (9th cir.) 1982, U.S. Ct. Appeals (4th and D.C. cirs.) 1985, U.S. Ct. Appeals (7th cir.) 1988. Assoc. Milbank, Tweed, Hadley & McCloy, N.Y.C., 1963, ptnr., 1971; judge U.S. Bankruptcy Ct., 1995—. Judge Bankruptcy Appellate Panel for 2d Circuit, 1996-2000. Trustee Spence Sch., 1981-87; former elder, trustee Madison Ave. Presbyn. Ch. With USAR, 1962-68. Mem. ABA (past chmn. N.Y. State membership com., antitrust sect., litigation sect.), Fed. Bar Coun. (trustee 1983-92, v.p. 1986-88, chmn. bd. dirs. 1990-92), Fed. Bar Found. (pres. 1992-94), N.Y. State Bar Assn. (mem. com. on profl. ethics, mem. jud. election monitoring com., mem. internat. litigation com.), Assn. of Bar of City of N.Y. (sec. 1979-82, chmn. com. on profl. and jud. ethics 1970-73, mem. spl. com. on lawyers role in securities transactions, mem. spl. com. to cooperate with ABA in revision of Canons of Ethics, mem. nominating com., mem. com. on membership, mem. com. on profl. discipline), Nat. Conf. Bankruptcy Judges, Am. Bankruptcy Inst., Westchester County Bar Assn. Office: US Bankruptcy Ct US Courthouse 300 Quarropas St White Plains NY 10601-4140

HARDIN, EDWARD LESTER, JR. lawyer; b. Wetumpka, Ala., Mar. 29, 1940; s. Edward Lester and Katherine (Williams) H.; m. Lila Manor, June 10, 1962; children: Leigh Hardin Hancock, Caroline Hardin Butler, Laura Elizabeth, Edward Lester III. BA, Birmingham So. Coll., 1962; JD, U. Ala., 1965. Bar: Ala. 1965, U.S. Dist. Ct. (no., mid. and so. dists.) Ala. 1965, U.S. Ct. Appeals (11th cir.), U.S. Supreme Ct. Assoc., then ptnr. Hare Wynn Newell and Newton, Birmingham, Ala., 1965-71; sr. ptnr. Hardin and Hawkins, 1971-98; exec. v.p., gen. counsel, bd. dirs. Caremark Rx, Inc., 1998—. Bd. dirs. Am. Sports Medicine Inst., Birmingham. Editorial bd. U. Ala. Law Rev., 1964-65; contbr. to profl. publs. Mem. ABA, Am. Bd. Trial Advocates, Assn. Trial Lawyers Am. (bd. govs. 1976), Ala. Bar Assn., Ala. Trial Lawyers Assn. (exec. com., pres. 1975-76), Omicron Delta Kappa, Phi Alpha Delta. Methodist. Avocations: Marlin fishing, golf, hunting. Antitrust, General civil litigation, Personal injury. Office: Caremark Rx Inc 3000 Galleria Towers Ste 1000 Birmingham AL 35244-2359

HARDIN, HAL D. lawyer, former United States attorney, former judge; b. Davidson County, Tenn. BA, Middle Tenn. State U., 1966; JD, Vanderbilt U., 1968; student, State Jud. Coll., Reno, 1976. Bar: Tenn. 1969, D.C. 1983, Tex. 1990, U.S. Ct. Claims 1983, U.S. Tax Ct. 1983, U.S. Ct. Mil. Appeals 1983, U.S. Supreme Ct. 1973. Fingerprint technician FBI, 1961; dir. St. Louis Job Corps Ctr., 1968; asst. dist. atty. Nashville, 1969-71; pvt. practice, 1971-75; presiding judge Nashville Trial Cts., 1976-77; spl. judge Ct. of Appeals, 1977; U.S. atty. Middle Dist. Tenn., 1977-81; practice law Nashville, 1981—. Adj. prof. Aquinas Coll., Tenn. State Coll., 1975—76; adj. instr. fed. sentencing, criminal practice and procedure Nashville Sch. Law, 1994—. Vol. Peace Corps, Columbia, 1963—65; bd. dirs. Nat. Assn. Former U.S. Attys., 1993—96, Nat. Assocs. Peace Corps Vols., 2001—, Leadership Nashville, 1983, Capital Case Resource Ctr., 1988—95. Named one of Best Lawyers in Am., 1993-2000. Fellow Tenn. Bar Found.; mem. Nashville Bar Assn. (bd. dirs. 1983-85, v.p. 1985), Ky. Bar Assn., Tenn. Bar Assn. (gen. counsel 1982-90), D.C. Bar, Tex. Bar Assn., Tenn. Criminal Def. Attys., Am. Bd. Trial Advs. (sec. Tenn. chpt. 1987, nat. bd. dirs. 1988-89, pres. Tenn. chpt. 1990), Inns of Ct. (master), 6th Cir. Jud. Coun. (life mem.). Federal civil litigation, State civil litigation, Criminal. Office: 218 3d Ave N Nashville TN 37201

HARDING, JOHN EDWARD, lawyer; b. San Francisco, Sept. 5, 1963; s. Merle Lewis and Trudy (Evertz) H.; m. Lisa Elliott; children: Jack Joseph, Ryan Elise. BA, St. Mary's Coll., Moraga, Calif., 1986; JD, Golden Gate U., 1989. Bar: Calif. 1989, U.S. Dist. Ct. (no. dist.) Calif. 1989, U.S. Ct. Appeals (9th cir.) 1989, D.C. 1991, Wyo. 1996, U.S. Dist. Ct. (ctrl. dist.) Calif. 1997. Assoc. Law Offices of Merle L. Harding, Pleasanton, Calif., 1989; ptnr. Harding & Harding, 1990-2000, Harding & Assocs., Pleasanton, 2000—. Bd. dirs. Tri-Valley br. Am. Heart Assn., Oakland, Calif., 1992-93, Valley Community Health Ctr., Pleasanton, 1992-96. Mem. ABA, ATLA, Consumer Atty. Calif., State Bar Calif., D.C. Bar Assn., Wyo. Bar Assn., Pleasanton C. of C. (bd. dirs. 1993-96, v.p. pub. affairs 1994). Avocations: golf, softball, backpacking, fishing, spectator sports, reading, travel. General civil litigation, General practice, Personal injury. Office: Harding & Assocs 78 Mission Dr Ste B Pleasanton CA 94566-7683 E-mail: jharding@hardinglaw.com

HARDING, MAJOR BEST, state supreme court chief justice; b. Charlotte, N.C., Oct. 13, 1935; m. Jane Lewis, Dec., 1958; children: Major B. Jr., David L., Alice Harding Sanderson. BS, Wake Forest U., 1957, also LLD; LLM in Jud. Process, U. Va., 1995; LLD, Stetson U., 1991, Fla. Coastal Sch. Law, 1999. Bar: N.C. 1959, Fla. 1960. Staff judge adv. hdqrs., Ft. Gordon, Ga., 1960-62; asst. county solicitor Criminal Ct. of Record, Duval County, Fla., 1962-63; pvt. practice law, 1964-68; judge Juvenile Ct., Duval County, 1968-70, 4th Jud. Cir. of Fla., 1970-74, chief judge, 1974-77; justice Supreme Ct. of Fla., Tallahassee, 1991—, chief justice, 1998-2000. Supervisory judge Family Mediation Unit, 1984-90; mem. Matrimonial Law Commn. and Gender Bias Study Commn.; chair Fla. Ct. Edn. Coun., past mem. Jud. Conf.; 1st dean New Judges Coll., 1975, faculty mem. in probate and juvenile areas, until 1979; dean Fla. Jud. Coll., 1984-92, faculty mem., 1984—, mem. bench-bar commn.; chmn. Supreme Ct. com. on law-related edn., 1997—. Bd. dirs. Legal Aid Assn., Family Consultation Svc., Daniel Meml. Home; mem. bd. visitors Wake Forest Sch. Law, Winston-Salem, N.C., Reformed Theol. Sem., Orlando, Fla.; past pres. Rotary Club of Riverside, Jacksonville, Fla., Rotary Club of Tallahasee; chmn. U.S. Constn. Bicentennial Commn., Jacksonville; past mem., deacon, elder St. John's Presbyn. Ch.; commr. Gen. Assembly Presbyn. Ch. U.S., 1971. Recipient Award for Outstanding Contbn. to Field of Matrimonial Law Am. Acad. Matrimonial Lawyers, 1986, Disting. Svc. award Nat. Ctr. State Cts., 2001, William A. Dugger Profl. Integrity award Capital Rotary Club. Mem. ABA (mem. bar admission com., Commn. Lawyer Assistance Programs Jud. Recognition award), Am. Bd. Trial Advocates (Jurist of Yr. Jacksonville chpt. 2000), The Fla. Bar, N.C. State Bar Assn., Chester Bedell Inn of Ct. (past pres., ex-officio bd. mem., master emeritus Chester Bedell), Dade County Trial Lawyers Assn. (Justice Harry Lee Anstead professionalism award 1998), Scabbard and Blade, Tallahassee Am. Inn of Ct. (ex officio trustee), Tallahassee Bar Assn., Sigma Chi (Significant Sig award 1997), Phi Delta Phi. Episcopalian. Office: Supreme Ct of Fla 500 S Duval St Tallahassee FL 32399-6556

HARDING, RAY MURRAY, JR. judge; b. Logan, Utah, Nov. 23, 1953; s. Ray M. Sr. and Martha (Rasmussen) H.; m. Anne Harding; children: Michelle, Nicole, Justin. BS, Brigham Young U., 1975; JD, J. Reuben Clark Law Sch., 1978. Bar: Utah 1978. Ptnr. Harding & Harding, American Fork and Pleasant Grove, Utah, 1978-85; owner Harding & Assoc., 1986-95; judge Utah County 4th Jud. Dist. Ct., 1995—. Atty. Lindon City and Pleasant Grove City, Utah, 1983-95, Alpine City, 1985-94, American Fork, Utah, 1985-95. Bd. trustees Utah Valley State Coll., 1986-95, chmn., 1991-93. Named Businessman of Yr., Future Bus. Leaders of Am., 1983. Mem. ABA, Utah State Bar Assn. Avocations: skiing, scuba diving, hiking, hunting, travel. Home: 11165 Yarrow Cir Highland UT 84003-9598 Office: Utah County 4th Judicial Dist Ct 125 N 100 W Provo UT 84601-2849

HARDMAN, JAMES CHARLES, lawyer, motor carrier executive; b. Chgo., Sept. 22, 1931; s. William Pryor and Mary Margaret (O'Donnell) H.; children: James Pryor, Katie Maura. BS in Bus., Quincy Coll., 1953; MBA, Northwestern U., 1958, JD, 1961. Bar: Ill. 1961, Minn. 1984, U.S. Dist. Ct. (no. dist.) Ill. 1962, U.S. Ct. Appeals (7th cir.) 1968, U.S. Dist. Ct. D.C. 1971, U.S. Supreme Ct. 1971, U.S. Ct. Appeals D.C. Cir. 1978. Gen. atty. Swift & Co., Chgo., 1961-62; sole practice, 1962-83; v.p. adminstrn., gen. counsel Dart Transit Co., St. Paul, 1984-94; atty. Law Offices James C. Harman, 1994—. Vis. prof. law U. Denver, 1978-79; lectr. small bus. mgmt. Northeastern Ill. U., Chgo., 1982; exec. com. Interstate Truckload Carriers Conf. of Am. Trucking Assns. Author: Fair Labor Standard Act and Motor Carrier Operations, 1974, Motor Carriage: The Interstate Commerce Commission, 1976, Welcome to the Wonderful World of Political Action, 1990; contbr. articles to profl. jours. V.p. Sauganash Cmty. Assn., Chgo., 1980-83; chmn. bd. govs. Transp. Law Jour., Denver, 1976-78. Served to lt. (j.g.) USN, 1953-55. Recipient Am. Jurisprudence Labor Law award, 1961, award of Merit Transp. Law Inst., 1968, 72. Mem. Transp. Lawyers Assn. (pres. 1980, chmn. 1982), Minn. Trucking Assn. (chmn.), Ill. State Bar Assn., Chgo. Bar Assn. (Legal Writing award 1970), Elks. Roman Catholic. Administrative and regulatory, General corporate, Legislative. Home: 753 Carla Ln Saint Paul MN 55109-1925 Office: Law Offices James C Hardman 753 Carla Ln Little Canada MN 55109-1925

HARDY, ASHTON RICHARD, lawyer; b. Gulfport, Miss., Aug. 31, 1935; s. Ashton Maurice and Alice (Baumbach) H.; m. Katherine Ketelsen, Sept. 4, 1959; children: Karin H. Wood, Katherine H. Foster. BBA, Tulane U., 1958, JD, 1962. Bar: La. 1962, FCC, 1976. Ptnr. Jones, Walker, Waechter, Poitevent, Carrere & Denegre, New Orleans, 1962-74, 76-82; gen. counsel FCC, Washington, 1974-76; ptnr. Fawer, Brian, Hardy, Zatzkis, New Orleans, 1982-86, Hardy & Popham, 1986-88, Walker, Bordelon, Hamlin, Theriot & Hardy, New Orleans, 1988-92, Hardy, Carey & Chautin, New Orleans, 1992—. Gen. counsel La. Assn. Broadcasters, 1976-86, Greater New Orleans Assn. Broadcasters, 1976—, La. Assn. Advt. Agys., 1982-86; lectr. in field; advance rep. to Pres. U.S., 1971-74. Bd. dirs. New Orleans Mission, 1989—, Met. Crime Commn. New Orleans, 1993—, vice-chmn., 1997—, United Christian Charities, 1993-99, Prison Fellowship/La., 1976—. Lt. USN, 1958-60. Mem. La. Bar Assn. (del. ho. of dels. 1987-92), FCC Bar Assn., Nat. Religious Broadcasters (bd. dirs. S.W. chpt. 1994—), Christian Legal Soc., Metairie Country Club (pres. 1986), Comm Club. Administrative and regulatory, Contracts commercial, Communications. Home: 306 Cedar Dr Metairie LA 70005-3902 Office: Hardy Carey & Chautin LLP Ste 300 110 Veterans Memorial Blvd Metairie LA 70005-4960 E-mail: arhardy@hardycarey.com

HARDY, HARVEY LOUCHARD, lawyer; b. Dallas, Dec. 2, 1914; s. Nat L. and Winifred H. (Fouraker) H.; m. Edna Vivian Bedell, Feb. 14, 1948; children: Victoria Elizabeth Hardy Pursch, Alice Anne Hardy Gannon. Bar: Tex. 1936, U.S. Dist. Ct. (so. and we. dists.) Tex. 1946, U.S. Ct. Appeals (5th cir.) 1946, U.S. Supreme Ct. 1949. First asst. dist. atty. Bexar County, San Antonio, 1947-50, acting dist. atty., 1950-51; city atty., 1952-53, Castle Hills, 1959-96, Helotes, 1984-96, Fair Oaks Ranch, 1973-96; legal adviser bd. trustees Fireman and Policemen's Pension Fund of San Antonio, 1956-96. Legal advisor Grey Forest Utilities, 1986-96. Author: A Lifetime at the Bar: A Lawyer's Memoir, 1999. 1st lt. inf. U.S. Army, 1941-45. Decorated Bronze Star with cluster. Fellow Tex. Bar Found.; mem. Tex. Bar Assn., San Antonio Bar Found., Tex. Assn. City Atts., San Antonio Bar Assn. Methodist. Home: 2008 NW Mil San Antonio TX 78213

HARDY, MICHAEL LYNN, lawyer; b. St. Louis, Aug. 28, 1947; s. William Frost and Ruth (Shea) H.; m. Martha Bond, Sept. 2, 1972; children: Brian M., Kevin S. AB, John Carroll U., 1969; JD, U. Mich., 1972. Bar: Ohio 1972. Assoc. Guren, Merritt, et al, Cleve., 1972-77, ptnr., 1977-84, Thompson Hine LLP and predecessor, Cleve., 1984—. Editor-in-chief Ohio Environ. Monthly, 1989-94, Ohio Environ. Law, 1992; bd. advisors Harvard Environ. Law Rev., 1976-78, The Environ. Counselor, 1988—. Trustee Nature Ctr. at Shaker Lakes. Capt. U.S. Army, 1969-74. Mem. ABA (nat. resources sect.), Ohio State Bar Assn. (sec. environ. law com. 1983-84, vice-chmn. 1984-86, chmn. 1987-91), Def. Rsch. Inst. (chmn. industrywide litig. com. 1989-91), Canterbury Golf Club. Administrative and regulatory, Federal civil litigation, Environmental. Home: 30649 Summit Ln Cleveland OH 44124-5836 Office: Thompson Hine LLP 3900 Key Ctr 127 Public Sq Cleveland OH 44114-1216 E-mail: mike.hardy@thompsonhine.com

HARDY, ROBERT PAUL, lawyer; b. San Francisco, Apr. 30, 1958; s. David John Hardy and Constance Catherine (Parrette) Morris; m. Mary Louise Stevens, Aug. 6, 1988; children: Nicholas Paul, Jackson Robert. BA, UCLA, 1981; JD, U. So. Calif., 1984. Bar: Calif. 1984, U.S. Dist. Ct. (ctrl. dist.) Calif. 1984, U.S. Ct. Appeals (9th cir.) 1984, N.Y. 1995. Assoc. Kindel & Anderson, L.A., 1984-86, Jones, Day, Reavis & Pogue, L.A., 1986-91, N.Y., 1991-93, ptnr., 1994-97, Brown & Wood, N.Y.C., 1997—. Recipient Am. Jurisprudence award The Lawyers Co-operative Pub. Co. and Bancroft-Whitney Co., 1982. Mem. ABA. Democrat. Episcopalian. Pension, profit-sharing, and employee benefits. E-mail: rhardy@brownwoodlaw.com

HARDYMON, DAVID WAYNE, lawyer; b. Columbus, Ohio, Aug. 22, 1949; s. Philip Barbour and Margaret Evelyn (Bowers) H.; m. Monica Ella Sleep, Mar. 13, 1982; children: Philip Garnet, Teresa Jeanette. BA in History, Bowling Green State U., 1971; JD, Capital U., Columbus, Ohio, 1976. Bar: Ohio 1976, U.S. Dist. Ct. (so. dist.) Ohio 1976, U.S. Supreme Ct. 1980, U.S. Ct. Appeals (6th cir.) 1982, Ky. 1999, U.S. Dist. Ct. (no. dist.) Ohio 1999, W.Va. 2000, U.S. Dist. Ct. (so. dist.) W.Va. 2000. Asst. prosecuting atty. Franklin County Prosecutor's Office, Columbus, Ohio, 1976-81; assoc. Vorys, Sater, Seymour & Pease, 1981-86, ptnr., 1987—. Mem. Chmn's. Club Franklin Country Rep. Orgn., 1983. Fellow Columbus Bar Found.; mem. Ohio State Bar Assn., Columbus Bar Assn. Avocations: sailing, archery. General civil litigation, Environmental, Product liability. Office: Vorys Sater Seymour & Pease PO Box 1008 52 E Gay St Columbus OH 43215-3161

HARFF, CHARLES HENRY, lawyer, retired diversified industrial company executive; b. Wesel, Germany, Sept. 27, 1929; s. Philip and Stephanie (Dreyfuss) H.; m. Marion Haines MacAfee, July 19, 1958; children—Pamela Haines, John Blair, Todd Philip B.A., Colgate U., 1951; LL.B., Harvard U., 1954; postgrad., U. Bonn, Fed. Republic Germany, 1955. Bar: N.Y. 1955. Assoc. Chadbourne & Parke, N.Y.C., 1955-64, ptnr., 1964-84; sr. v.p., gen. counsel, sec. Rockwell Internat. Corp., Pitts., 1984-94, sr. v.p., spl. counsel, 1994-96, ret., 1996. Cons., 1996—2001; bd. dirs. Arvin Meritor, Inc. Trustee Christian A. Johnson Endeavor Found., N.Y.C., 1984-2001; bd. dirs. Atlantic Legal Found., 1989-98, Fulbright Assn., 1995—, pres., 2001. Fulbright scholar U. Bonn, Germany, 1955. Mem. ABA, N.Y. State Bar Assn., The Assn. Gen. Counsel, Econ. Club N.Y., Harvard Club, Duquesne Club, Allegheny Country Club, Laurel Valley Golf Club, Farm Neck Golf Club (Martha's Vineyard, Mass.). General corporate, Securities.

HARGESHEIMER, ELBERT, III, lawyer; b. Cleve., Jan. 4, 1944; s. Elbert and Agnes Mary (Heckman) H.; children: Heather Leigh, Elbert IV, Jon-Erik, Piper Elizabeth, Kevin R. Cross, Mark R. Dziob. AB, Cornell U., 1966; JD, SUNY, Buffalo, 1969. Bar: N.Y. 1970, U.S. Dist. Ct. (we. dist.) N.Y. 1971. Assoc. Miller, Bouvier, O'Connor & Cegielski, Buffalo, 1970-73, ptnr., 1973-74, Godinho & Hargesheimer, Hamburg, N.Y., 1974-84; pvt. practice law, 1984—. Chief counsel Joint Legis. Commn. to Revise Bus. and Corp. Law, N.Y. State Assembly and Senate, 1974-75; prosecutor Village of Blasdell (N.Y.), 1978-80, 83-87, village atty. 1980-82; fund chmn. South Towns Hosp. Found., Inc., 1973-76, fin. chmn., bd. dirs., 1976-77, v.p., 1978-82; chmn. Hamburg Town Rep. Com., 1978-88; coord. Erie County Pretrial Svcs. Program, 1987-88; counsel Erie County Rep. Com., 1980-92; mem. Erie County Bd. Ethics, 1979-89, chmn. 1983.; charter mem., counsel S.W. Hamburg Taxpayers Assn. Named Mr. Rep., Town of Hamburg Rep. Club, 1982, Rep. of Yr., Hamburg Twon Rep. Com., 1988. Mem. Western N.Y. Trial Lawyer's Assn., Theta Chi. Methodist. General corporate, Family and matrimonial, General practice. Home and Office: 22 Buffalo St Hamburg NY 14075-5002

HARGIS, DAVID MICHAEL, lawyer, writer; b. Warren, Ark., Feb. 10, 1948; s. James Von Hargis and Noma Lee (Anderson) Watkins; m. Carolyn Jane Sangster (div. 1981); children— Michelle Leigh, Michael Bradley; m. Linda Jane Huckelbury, Jan. 8, 1981; 1 child, Christopher Key. B.S.B.A. with honors, U. Ark., 1970, J.D., 1973. Bar: Ark. 1973, U.S. Dist. Ct. (ea. and we. dists.) Ark. 1974. Assoc. Williamson Law Firm, Monticello, Ark., 1973-74; asst. U.S. atty. Eastern Dist. Ark., Little Rock, 1974-75; assoc. House, Holmes & Jewell, Little Rock, 1975-79; ptnr. House, Holmes & Jewell, P.A., Little Rock, 1979-85; founder Wilson, Wood & Hargis, 1985—; atty. Legal Services Corp., Little Rock, 1977; county atty. Pulaski County, Ark., 1980-82; atty. Pulaski County Quorum Ct., 1980-82; spl. circuit judge Pulaski County Circuit Ct., 1982; atty. Office of Spl. Prosecutor, Pulaski County Grand Jury, 1983-84; spl. counsel Ark.Ins. Dept., 1984. Editor-in-chief Ark. Law Rev., 1972-73; guest columnist Ark. Gazette, 1984. Contbr. articles to legal jours. Co-author: Quality Assurance in Health Test, American College of Pathologists, 1986. Recipient spl. commendation Legal Services Corp., 1977, Ark. Edn. Assn., 1984. Mem. ABA (legal edn. sect., corp. sect.), Ark. Bar Assn., Omicron Delta Kappa, Beta Gamma Sigma. Methodist. Federal civil litigation, State civil litigation, Contracts commercial. Home: 10 Durance Dr Little Rock AR 72223-9106 Office: 807 W 3rd St Little Rock AR 72201-2103

HARGIS, V. BURNS, lawyer; b. Victoria, Tex., Oct. 29, 1945; s. A.V. and Rosalie (Burns) H.; m. Ann Whiting, June 8, 1969; children: Matthew Burns, Kathryn Ann. BS, Okla. State U., 1967; JD, U. Okla., 1970. Bar: Okla. 1970. Pvt. practice law, Okla. City, 1970-75; ptnr. Reynolds, Ridings & Hargis, 1975-89; dir. Hartzog, Conger, Cason & Hargis, 1989-94; shareholder McAfee & Taft, Oklahoma City, 1994-97; vice chmn. Bank of Okla., 1997—. Pres., bd. dirs. Neighborhood Homes, Inc., 1973. Vice chmn. Okla. State Election Bd., 1975-80; legal counsel Okla. State Rep. Com., 1971-73; bd. dirs. Neighborhood Services Orgn.; pres., bd. dirs. Oklahoma City Community Food Bank, 1978-87; exec. com. Last Frontier Council, 1988—; chmn. Mayor's Econ. Devel. Com., Oklahoma City, 1986; chmn. Okla. Commn. Human Services, 1987; sr. warden All Souls Episcopal Ch., 1974-78. Served to capt. U.S. Army, 1970-76. Fellow Am. Bar Found., Okla. Bar Found. (trustee, pres. 1987); mem. ABA, Okla. Bar Assn. (outstanding cmty. svc. award 1986), Okla. County Bar Assn. (pres. 1982, leadership award 1986), Oklahoma City Golf and Country Club, Rotary (pres., bd. dirs. Oklahoma City 1986). Republican. Avocations: golf, tennis, squash. Bankruptcy, Consumer commercial, General corporate.

HARGRAVE, RUDOLPH, state supreme court justice; b. Shawnee, Okla., Feb. 15, 1925; s. John Hubert and Daisy (Holmes) H.; m. Madeline Hargrave, May 29, 1949; children: Cindy Lu, John Robert, Jana Sue. LLB, U. Okla., 1949. Bar: Okla. 1949. Pvt. practice, Wewoka, Okla., 1949; asst. county atty. Seminole County, 1951-55; judge Seminole County Ct., 1964-67, Seminole County Superior Ct., 1967-69; dist. judge Okla. Dist. Ct., Dist. 22, 1969-79; justice Okla. Supreme Ct., Oklahoma City, 1978—, former vice chief justice, currently chief justice. Mem. Seminole County Bar Assn., Okla. Bar Assn., ABA Democrat. Methodist. Lodges: Lions; Masons. Office: Okla Supreme Ct State Capitol Bldg Room 202 Oklahoma City OK 73105*

HARIRI, V. M. arbitrator, mediator, lawyer, educator; BS, Wayne State U.; JD, Detroit Coll. Law; LLM, London Sch. Econs. and Polit.Sci.; diploma arbitration, Reading (Eng.) U. Pvt. practice internat. and domestic bus. law, Detroit. Drafting com. Republic of Kazakhstan Code on Arbitration Procedure, Free Econ. Zone Legislation, Republic of Belarus; instr. internat. comml. arbitration Chartered Inst. Arbitrators, Am. Arbitration Assn. Fellow Chartered Inst. Arbitrators (exec. com. N.Am. br., founding com.); mem. ABA, Internat. Bar Assn., Am. Soc. Internat. Law, Am. Arbitration Assn., London Ct. Internat. Arbitration, World Jurist Assn., Mich. Trial Lawyers Assn. Office: 325 N Center St Ste E3 Northville MI 48167-1244

HARKEY, JOHN NORMAN, judge; b. Russellville, Ark., Feb. 25, 1933; s. Olga John and Margaret (Fleming) H.; m. Willa Moreau Charlton, May 24, 1959; children— John Adam, Sarah Leigh. AS, Marion (Ala.) Inst., 1952; LLB, BS, BSL, U. Ark., 1959, JD, 1969. Bar: Ark. 1959. Since practiced in, Batesville; pros. atty. 3d Jud. Dist. Ark., 1961-65; ins. commr. Ark., 1967-68; chmn. Ark. Commerce Commn., 1968-69; spl. justice Ark. Supreme Ct., 1988; judge juvenile divsn. Ark. 16th Dist., 1989-90; sr. ptnr. Harkey, Walmsley and related firms, Batesville, 1970-92; chancery and probate judge 16th Jud. Dist., Ark., 1993-98, circuit and chancery judge, 1999-2001, circuit judge, 2001—. 1st lt. USMCR, Korea. Mem. Ark. Bar Assn., Am. Bar Register, U.S. Marine Corps League. Home: 490 Harkey Rd Batesville AR 72501-9294 Office: PO Box 2656 Batesville AR 72503-2656

HARKEY, ROBERT SHELTON, lawyer; b. Charlotte, N.C., Dec. 22, 1940; s. Charles Nathan and Josephine Lenora (McKenzie) H.; m. Barbara Carole Payne, Apr. 2, 1983; 1 child, Elizabeth McKenzie. BA, Emory U., 1963, LLB, 1965. Bar: Ga. 1964, U.S. Dist. Ct. (no. dist.) Ga. 1964, U.S. Ct. Appeals (1st, 5th, 7th, 9th and 11th cirs.) 1964-86, U.S. Supreme Ct. Assoc. Swift, Currie, McGhee & Hiers, Atlanta, 1965-68; atty. Delta Air Lines, 1968-74, gen. atty., 1974-79, asst. v.p. law, 1979-85, assoc. gen. counsel, v.p., 1985-88; gen counsel, v.p., 1988-90; gen. counsel, sr. v.p. Delta Air Lines, Atlanta, 1990-94, gen. counsel, sr. v.p., sec., 1994—. Mem. coun. Emory U. Law Sch., 1997—. Unit chmn. United Way, Atlanta, 1985; trustee Woodruff Arts Ctr., 1995—; bd. visitors Emory U., 1996-99. Mem. ABA (com. gen. counsels), Air Transport Assn. (chmn. law coun. 1996-98), State Bar Ga. (chmn. corp. counsel sect. 1992-93), Atlanta Bar Assn., Corp. Counsel Assn. Greater Atlanta (bd. dirs. 1990), Commerce Club, Lawyers Club of Atlanta, Cherokee Town and Country Club. Presbyterian. Avocations: tennis, reading. Aviation, General corporate, Labor. Office: Delta Air Lines Hartsfield Atlanta Internat Airport Atlanta GA 30320

HARKINS, PATRICK NICHOLAS, III, lawyer; b. Jackson, Miss., Apr. 27, 1941; s. Patrick Nicholas and Mary Ruth (Gammon) H.; m. Mary Elizabeth Wilson, Apr. 12, 1969; children: Elizabeth Glenn, DeMatt Henderson. BBA, U. Notre Dame, 1963; JD, U. Miss., 1965. Bar: Miss. 1965, U.S. Dist. Ct. (no. and so. dists.) Miss. 1965, U.S. Ct. Appeals (5th cir.) 1965, U.S. Supreme Ct. 1968. Legis. asst. U.S. Congressman G.V. Montgomery, 1967-68; assoc. atty. Watkins, Pyle, Ludlam, Winter & Stennis, Jackson, 1969; atty. Watkins & Eagen PLLC, 1970—, ptnr., 1973—. Served to capt. U.S. Army, 1965-67. Fellow Am. Coll. Trial Lawyers, Miss. Bar Found.; mem. ABA, DRI (pres.-elect),

HARKLESS, ANGELA, lawyer, publishing executive; b. Jackson, Miss., Oct. 7, 1964; d. Wesley and Julia L. (Murrell) H. BA in Comm., Loyola U., Chgo., 1986; JD, Ind. U., 1995; postgrad., London Law Consortium, 1995. Bar: Ill. 1995. Rsch. asst. WFYR-FM, Chgo., 1983-86; editl. asst. Chgo. Tribune, 1987-88; adminstrv. exec. asst. CBS, Inc., N.Y.C., 1989-90; atty. Harkless Law Firm, Chgo., 1996—; editor, pub. Cachét Mag., 1999—. Notes editor Fed. Comm. Law Jour., 1993-95, Law News Ctr. Mem. amb. com. Chgo. Sister Cities Internat., 1990-92; bd. dirs. Young Adult Bd. DuSable Mus., Chgo., 1996—. Scholar RKO Broadcast, Inc. Black Media Coaliton, 1985, Journalism scholar McGraw-Hill, 1986; law fellow Coun. on Legal Edn., 1992-95. Mem. ABA, Ill. State Bar Assn., Chgo. Bar Assn., Fed. Comm. Bar Assn. (mem. planning com. Chgo. chpt.), Chgo. Assn. Black Journalists (pres. 1999—), Multicultural Journalism Consortium (pres. 1994—), Alpha Kappa Alpha Sorority Inc. Avocations: learning foreign languages, golf, tennis, collecting antiques. Communications, Entertainment, Intellectual property.

HARLAN, JANE ANN, lawyer; b. Newton, Iowa, Oct. 8, 1947; d. Ellis and Julia (Blount) H.; m. Adel Zahian Hanna, 1971 (div. 1981); children: Samuel, Laura, Magda. BA, Drake U., 1969; JD, DePaul U., 1974. Bar: Ill. 1975, Wis. 1978, Iowa 1984. Pvt. practice, Chgo., 1975-78, Greendale, Wis., 1978-84, Newton, Iowa, 1984-94; adminstrv. asst. Office of State Pub. Defender, Racine, Wis., 1994-95, Milw., 1995-99; atty. Appalachian Rsch. and Defense Fund, Somerset, Ky., 1999—. Cooperating atty. Wis. Civil Liberties Union, Milw., 1978-84; chairperson S.W. Suburban Dems., Milwaukee County, Wis., 1982-83. Recipient Outstanding Svc. plaque, Milw. Dems., 1983, citation for outstanding contbns. Wis. State Assembly, 1984. Mem. NOW, ACLU, Ky. Bar Assn., Wis. Bar Assn., Assn. for Retarded Citizens. Avocation: band music, pipe organ. Family and matrimonial, General practice. Office: Appalachian Rsch and Def Fund PO Box 1334 Somerset KY 42502-1334

HARLAN, NANCY MARGARET, lawyer; b. Santa Monica, Calif., Sept. 10, 1946; d. William Galland and Betty M. (Miles) Plett; m. John Hammack, Dec. 01, 1979; children: Laryssa Maria Rebello, Leea Elyce. BS magna cum laude, Calif. State U., Hayward, 1972; JD, U. Calif., Berkeley, 1975. Bar: Calif. 1975, Fed. Bar, U.S. Dist. Ct. (ctrl. dist. 9th cir.) 1976. Assoc. Poindexter & Doutr+248, L.A., 1975—80; residential counsel Coldwell Banker Residential Brokerage Co., Fountain Valley, Calif., 1980—81; sr. counsel for real estate subs. law dept. Pacific Lighting Corp., Santa Ana, 1981—87; sr. v.p., gen. counsel The Presley Cos., 1987—. Bd. dirs. La Casa; exec. v.p. student body U. Calif., Berkeley, 1974—75. Mem.: ABA, NAFE, State Bar Calif., L.A. County Bar Assn., Orange County Bar Assn. (dir. corp. counsel sect. 1982—), Bus. and Profl. Women, Calif. Women Lawyers Assn., Orange County Women Lawyers Assn., L.A. Women Lawyers Assn. General corporate, Real property. Office: William Lyon Homes Inc 4490 Von Karman Ave Newport Beach CA 92660-2008

HARLEY, COLIN EMILE, lawyer; b. Columbia, S.C., Mar. 27, 1940; s. William Hummel and Caroline (Monteith) H.; m. Emilia Saint Amand, June 5, 1965; children: Emile, Gray; m. Anita H. Laudone, May 20, 1978; children: Clayton, Victoria. AB, Dartmouth Coll., 1962; LLB, U. S.C., 1965; LLM, NYU, 1967. Bar: S.C. 1965, N.Y. 1968. Sole practice, Laurens, S.C., 1965; assoc. Davis Polk & Wardwell, N.Y.C., 1967-72, ptnr., 1973—; adj. asst. prof. taxation NYU Sch Law, 1970-75. Trustee Greenwich (Conn.) Country Day Sch., 1987-96, pres., 1994-96. With USMCR, 1961-67. Oil, gas, and mineral, Corporate taxation, Equipment leasing. Office: Davis Polk & Wardwell 450 Lexington Ave Fl 31 New York NY 10017-3982 E-mail: colin.harley@dpw.com

HARLEY, HALVOR LARSON, banker, lawyer; b. Atlantic City, Oct. 7, 1948; s. Robison Dooling and Loyde Hazel (Gauchnauer) H. BSc, U. S.C., 1971, MA, 1973; JD, Widener U., 1981. Bar: Pa. 1982, D.C. 1989, U.S. Ct. Appeals (3d cir.) 1987, U.S. Dist. Ct. (ea. dist.) Pa. 1987, U.S. Supreme Ct., 1988, U.S. Ct. Appeals D.C., 1989. Staff psychologist Columbia Area Mental Health Ctr., S.C., 1971-73; dir. Motivational Rsch. Cons., Columbia, 1973-79; psychologist Family Ct. Del., Wilmington, 1979; pvt. practice law Phila., 1982; v.p. investment banking Union Bank, L.A., 1982-88; v.p., mgr. Tokai Bank, Newport Beach., Calif., 1988-94; first v.p., regional mgr. Mellon Pvt. Asset Mgmt., Newport Beach, 1994-97, first v.p., 1994—; regional sales mgr. So. Calif. Pvt. Asset Mgmt., 1994—. Author: Help for Herpes, 1982; contbr. articles to profl. jours. Fundraiser Orange County Performing Art Ctr., 1983-84; trustee, exec. com. Orange County Mus. Arts; vol. Hosp. Ship HOPE, Sri Lanka, 1968-69; bd. dirs., v.p. exec. com. alzheimers Assn. Orange County; bd. dirs. Lido Sands Homeowners Assn., Newport Beach, 1984-85, So. Calif. Entrepreneurship Acad., 1995—, pres./bd. dirs.; bd. dirs. United Cerebral Palsy of Orange County, chmn. Bastile Day com. Mem. ATLA, Calif. Bankers Assn., Am. Judicature Soc., Indsl. League Orange County (membership com. 1983-84), Am. Bankers Assn., World Trade Ctr. Assocs. Orange County (directing com. 1983-85), Orange County Performing Arts Fraternity (trustee), Psi Chi (chpt. pres. 1971-73). Home: 5015 Lido Sands Dr Newport Beach CA 92663-2403 Office: Mellon Bank 4695 Macarthur Ct Ste 240 Newport Beach CA 92660-8851

HARLEY, ROBISON DOOLING, JR. lawyer, educator; b. Ancon, Panama, July 6, 1946; s. Robison Dooling and Loyde Hazel (Goehenauer) H.; m. Suzanne Purviance Bendel, Aug. 9, 1975; children: Arianne Erin, Lauren Loyde. BA, Brown U., 1968; JD, Temple U., 1971; LLM, U. San Diego, 1985. Bar: Pa. 1971, U.S. Ct. Mil. Appeals 1972, Calif. 1976, U.S. Dist. Ct. (cen. and so. dists) Calif. 1976, N.J. 1977, U.S. Dist. Ct. N.J. 1977, U.S. Supreme Ct. 1980, D.C. 1981, U.S. Ct. Appeals (9th cir.) 1982, U.S. Dist. Ct. (ea. dist.) Pa. 1987, U.S. Ct. Appeals (3rd cir.) 1986. Cert. criminal law specialist Calif. Bd. Legal Specialization, 1981, recertified 1986, 91, 96; cert. criminal trial adv. Nat. Bd. Trial Advocacy, 1982, recertified, 1987, 92, 97. Asst. agy. dir. Safeco Title Ins. Co., L.A., 1975-77; ptnr. Cohen, Stokke & Davis, Santa Ana, Calif., 1977-85; prin. Harley Law Offices, Santa Ana, Calif., 1985—; adj. prof. Orange County Coll. Trial Advocacy, adj. prof., paralegal program U. Calif., trial adv. programs U.S. Army, USN, USAF, USMC; judge pro-tem Orange County Cts. Author: Orange County Trial Lawyers Drunk Driving Syllabus; contbr. articles to profl. jours. and reports. Bd. dirs. Orange County Legal Aid Soc. Served to lt. col. JAGC, USMCR, 1975-94; trial counsel, def. counsel, mil. judge, asst. staff judge adv. USMC, 1971-75, regional def. counsel Western Region, 1986-90, instr., program coord. Army, Navy, Air Force, Marines, Coast Guard Trial Adv. Programs worldwide. Recipient Commendation medal U.S. Navy, Nat. Defense Svc. medal, Reserve medal, 23 Certs. of Commendation and/or Congratulations. Mem. ABA, ATLA, Orange County Bar Assn. (judiciary com., criminal law sect., adminstrn. of justice com.), Orange County Trial Lawyers Assn., Calif. Trial Lawyers Assn., Calif. Attys. for Criminal Justice, Calif. Pub. Defenders Assn., Nat. Assn. for Criminal Def. Attys., Assn. Specialized Criminal Def. Advs., Orange County Criminal Lawyers Assn. (found. com.), Res. Officers Assn., Marine Corps Reserve Officers Assn., Marine Corps Assn. Republican. Avocations: sports, physical fitness, reading. Criminal, Military. Home: 31211 Paseo Miraloma San Juan Capistrano CA 92675-5505 Office: Harley Law Offices 825 N Ross St Santa Ana CA 92701-3419

HARMAN, DONNA A. lawyer; b. Elkhart, Kans., Aug. 6, 1959; d. Donald E. and Pearl Duvall Akers; m. John R. Harman III, Aug. 20, 1988; children: Caitlin, Caroline. BA in Pub. Affairs and Econs., Anderson U., 1981; JD, Am. U., 1988. Bar: D.C. 1989. Fin. dir. Rep. Party La., Baton Rouge, 1981-83; legis. aide U.S. Rep. W. Henson Moore, Washington, 1983-85; mgr. govt. rels. The Dow Chem. Co., 1985-89; dir. govt. rels. Champion Internat., 1989-99, counsel govt. affairs, 1999—. Chairperson Alternative Minimum Tax Coalition, Washington, 1993—; bd. co-chair Tax Coalition, Washington, 1996. Bd. dirs. Nat. Presbyn. Ch., Washington, 1998—; leader Girls Scouts Am. Avocation: girls soccer. Office: Champion Internat Corp 1875 I St NW Ste 540 Washington DC 20006-5425

HARMAN, JOHN ROYDEN, retired lawyer; b. Elkhart, Ind., June 30, 1921; s. James Lewis and Bessie Bell (Mountjoy) H.; m. Elizabeth Rae Crosier, Dec. 12, 1943 (dec. May 1995); 1 child, James Richard. B.S., U. Ill., 1943; J.D., Ind. U., 1949. Bar: Ind. 1949. Assoc. Proctor & Proctor, Elkhart, 1949-51; pvt. practice, 1952-60; ptnr. Cawley & Harman, 1960-65, Thornburg, McGill, Deahl, Harman, Carey & Murray, 1965-82, Barnes & Thornburg, Elkhart, 1982-89; ret., 1989. Atty. City of Elkhart, 1952-60. State del. Ind. Republican Com., 1962-70; pres., bd. dirs. Crippled Childrens Soc.; bd. dirs. United Community Services Elkhart County. 1st lt., F.A.,AUS, 1943-46, PTO. Fellow Ind. Bar Found; mem. ABA, Ind. Bar Assn. , Elkhart County Bar Assn. (pres. 1977), Elkhart City Bar Assn. (pres. 1970), Elkhart C. of C. (pres. 1977, bd. dirs. 1972-75), Elcona Country Club (bd. dirs.), Phi Kappa Psi, Alpha Kappa Psi, Phi Delta Phi. Republican. Presbyterian. Avocation: golf. General corporate, Estate planning. Office: NBD Bank Bldg 121 W Franklin St Ste 200 Elkhart IN 46516-3200

HARMAN, TERRIE, lawyer; b. Williamsport, Pa., May 23, 1953; d. Lyle Eugene H. and Phyllis Ann Stuart; m. Thomas David McCarron, Oct. 5, 1989. AB, Wilson Coll., 1975; JD, Franklin Pierce Law Ctr., 1978. Bar: N.H. 1978, Maine 1978. Staff atty. Pine Tree Legal Assistance, Bangor, Maine, 1975-79; assoc. Myers & Laufer, Concord, N.H., 1979-82; atty. pvt. practice, Portsmouth, 1982—. Bd. dirs. Feminist Health Ctr., Portsmouth, 1997—. Mem. N.H. Bar Assn., Maine Bar Assn., Portsmouth Men's Chorus (founder, exec. dir. 2000—). Avocations: church organist, piano teacher, auctioneer. Bankruptcy, General civil litigation, Taxation, general. Home: PO Box 463 New Castle NH 03854-0463 Office: 59 Deer St Unit 1B Portsmouth NH 03801-3765

HARMAN, WALLACE PATRICK, lawyer; b. El Paso, Tex., Jan. 22, 1949; s. Wallace Irvin and Dorothy Louise (Pearson) H.; m. Gina Marie Ries, Dec. 31, 1988; children: Loren Patrick, Claire Marie. BA, Stanford U., 1972; JD, U. Calif., 1977. Bar: Calif. 1977, U.S. Ct. Appeals (9th cir.) 1977, N.Mex. 1978, U.S. Dist. Ct. N.Mex. 1978, U.S. Ct. Appeals (10th cir.) 1978. Zone adminstrn. mgr. Am. Motors Corp., Burlingame, Calif., 1972-74; atty., shareholder Sutin, Thayer & Browne, APC, Albuquerque, 1977-87, group leader comml. group, 1985-87; atty., shareholder, mng. ptnr., leader bus. group The Payne Law Firm, P.C., 1987-91; atty., ptnr. Hisey & Wainwright, P.A., 1991-92; atty., pres., chief exec. officer The Harman Law Firm, P.C., Littleton, CO, 1992—. Mem. N.Mex. Supreme Ct. Med.-Legal Panel, Albuquerque, 1978-80, 91—; mem. N.Mex. Supreme Ct. Lawyers Assistance Com., Albuquerque, 1991—; area rep. The Taft Sch., Watertown, Conn., 1992—; mem. mentorship program Hatings Coll. Law. Co-author: Recent Developments in Commerical Law, University of New Mexico Law Review, 1989. Bd. advisors Lovelace Med. Ctr., Albuquerque, 1980-89; mem. state bd. trustees The Nature Conservancy, N.Mex., 1984-88; adv. bd. Assistance League Albuquerque, 1982-89, Jr. League Albuquerque, 1984-87, Make-a-Wish Found. of N.Mex., Inc., 1996-97. Recipient AV Rating award Martindale-Hubbell, 1990. Mem. ABA, Albuquerque Bar Assn. Democrat. Avocations: photography, sports, computers, landscaping, writing. Banking, General civil litigation, Real property. E-mail: harman@sandia.net

HARMON, GAIL MCGREEVY, lawyer; b. Kansas City, Kans., Mar. 15, 1943; d. Milton and Barbara (James) McGreevy; m. John W. Harmon, June 11, 1966; children: James, Eve. BA cum laude, Radcliffe Coll., 1965; JD cum laude, Columbia U., 1969. Bar: Mass. 1970, D.C. 1976, U.S. Dist. Ct. D.C. Assoc. Gaston Snow & Ely Bartlett, Boston, 1970-75, Steptoe & Johnson, Washington, 1975-76, Roisman, Kessler & Cashdan, Washington, 1976-77; ptnr. Harmon, Curran & Tousley, 1977-90, Harmon, Curran, Spielberg & Eisenberg, Washington, 1990—. Pres. Women's Legal Def. Fund, 1982-84; steering com. Emily's List, 1985—; bd. dirs. Population Svcs. Internat., 1998—. Mem. Population Svcs. Internat. (bd. dirs.) Democrat. Episcopalian. General corporate, Taxation, general. E-mail: gharmon@harmoncurran.com

HARMS, DONALD C. lawyer; b. Detroit, May 27, 1941; s. Herbert R. and Elsa J. (McClelend) H.; m. Sue J. Kingsley, June 15, 1963; children: Kristin, Sharon, Melissa. BA, U. Mich., 1963; JD cum laude, Wayne State U., 1967. Bar: Mich. 1967, U.S. Dist. Ct. (ea. dist.) Mich. 1967. Ptnr. Larson & Harms, P.C., Farmington Hills, Mich., 1968—. Arbitrator Am. Arbitration Assn., Detroit, 1975—. Clk., Ward Evangel. Presbyn. Ch., Livonia, Mich., 1979-80, moderator Evang. Presbyn. Ch., 1984-85. Mem. State Bar of Mich. (pres. gen. practice sect. 1975-77), Farmington Hills C. of C. (pres. 1979), Kiwanis. General corporate, Estate planning, Real property. Office: Larson & Harms PC 37899 W 12 Mile Rd Ste 300 Farmington MI 48331-3026 E-mail: larsonharms@prodigy.net, donharms@prodigy.net

HARMS, STEVEN ALAN, lawyer; b. Detroit, Feb. 15, 1949; s. Herbert Rudolph and Elsa Jane (McClelland) H.; m. Nancy Gayle Banta, June 26, 1971; children: Jennifer Elizabeth, Heather Lynn, Robin Ann. BA, Hope Coll., 1970; JD, Detroit Coll. Law, 1975. Bar: Mich. 1975, U.S. Dist. Ct. (so. dist.) Mich. 1975, U.S. Ct. Appeals (6th cir.) 1982; bd. cert. creditors rights specialist. Ptnr. Muller, Muller, Richmond, Harms, Myers & Sgroi, P.C., Birmingham, Mich.; sec. gen. practice session State Bar Mich., 1982-83; mediator Oakland County Cir. Ct., 1990—. Lectr. in field; adj. prof. Bus. Law Walsh Coll., Troy, Mich., 1990—. Author: Successful Collection of a Judgement, 1981, Rights of Commercial Creditors, 1982, Post Judgement Collection, 1988, Handling the Collection Case in Michigan, 1989, rev. edit., 1999; co-author: Attorney Fee Agreements, 1995, contbg. editor Michigan Business Formbook, 1997, rev. edit., 2000, Michigan Civil Procedure, 1997; editor: General Practitioner, State Bar Mich., 1978-82. Bd. dirs. fin. com. YMCA, North Oakland County, Mich., 1987—, chmn. bd., 1990-91. Republican. Club: Pearson Yacht Owners Assn. (commodore 1988-90), Hunter Sailing Assn. (vice commodore 1985-86, commodore 1987-88). Consumer commercial, Contracts commercial. Office: Muller Muller Richmond Harms Myers & Sgroi PC 33233 Woodward Ave Birmingham MI 48009-0903 E-mail: steve@mullerfirm.com

HARMSEN, CHRISTIAN, lawyer; b. Hamburg, Germany, May 24, 1968; Abitur, Stormarnschule, Ahrensburg, 1987. Bar: 1997. Rechtsreferendar Higher Regional Ct., Hamburg, 1995-97; with WESSING, Dusseldorf, Germany, 1997-2001, Anderson Legal, Dusseldorf, 2001—. Mem. GRUR, AIPLA. Intellectual property, Patent, Trademark and copyright. Office: Andersen Legal Verdinger Str 88 40474 Dusseldorf Germany Fax: 49 211 4974-320

HARNACK, DON STEGER, retired lawyer; b. Milw., June 19, 1928; s. Benjamin John and Katherine (Steger) H.; m. Rose Marie Ball, Oct. 17, 1959; children: Christopher Wallen, Gretchen Marie, Pamela Ann. BS, U. Wis., 1950; LLB, Harvard U., 1953. Bar: Wis. 1953, U.S. Dist. Ct. (ea. dist.) Wis. 1955, U.S. Tax Ct. 1957, Ill. 1959, U.S. Dist. Ct. (no. dist.) Ill. 1962, U.S. Ct. Appeals (6th and 7th cirs.) 1963, U.S. Ct. Claims 1966, U.S. Ct. Appeals (8th cir.) 1971, U.S. Supreme Ct. 1972. Assoc. Quarles, Spence & Quarles, Milw., 1955-57; trial atty. regional counsel IRS, Chgo., 1957-61; assoc. Dixon, Todhunter, Knouf & Holmes, 1961-65; ptnr. McDermott, Will & Emery, 1965-96, of counsel, 1997-98; ret., 2001. Contbr. articles to profl. jours. Active Winnetka (Ill.) Zoning Bd., 1971-75; park bd. atty. Winnetka Park Dist., 1978-83; pres. N.E. Ill. coun. Boy Scouts Am., 1982-83; life trustee ULC Boys and Girls Club, Chgo.; trustee Village of Winnetka, 1984-88. Lt. USNR. Recipient Silver Beaver award Boy Scouts Am., 1984, named distinguished Eagle Scout, 1996. Mem. ABA, Ill. Bar Assn., Wis. Bar Assn., Union League Club (bd. dirs., officer, v.p. 1981-87, pres. 1987-88). Republican. Avocations: fishing, golf, reading, flying. Federal civil litigation, Corporate taxation, State and local taxation. E-mail: bigcoho2@aol.com

HARNDEN, EDWIN A. lawyer; BA Columbia U., 1969, JD Columbia U., 1972. Mng. ptnr. Barran Liebman LLP, Portland, Oreg.; pres.-elect Oreg. State Bar. Past pres. Profl. Liability Fund. Fellow: Am. Bar Found. (life). Office: ODS Tower 601 SW 2d Ave Ste 2300 Portland OR 97204-3159 Office Fax: 503-274-1212. E-mail: eharnden@barran.com*

HARNER, TIMOTHY R. lawyer; b. Clarkson, N.Y., Sept. 1, 1955; s. Roy Seymour and Helen Belle (Dowden) H.; m. Suzanne Lee Daggs, May 22, 1982; children: Sarah, Andrew. BA, Houghton Coll., 1977; JD cum laude, Harvard Law Sch., 1980. Bar: N.Y., 1981. Law clk. U.S. Ct. Appeals 2nd Cir., N.Y.C., 1980-81; assoc. Nixon, Hargrave, Devans & Doyle, Rochester, N.Y., 1981-85; gen. counsel Upstate Farms Coop., Inc., LeRoy, 1985—. Dir. Palmer Food Svcs., Rochester. Editor: Harvard Law Rev., 1978-79, devel. officer, 1979-80. Trustee, sec. Roberts Wesleyan Coll., Rochester, 1989. Mem. Am. Corp. Counsel Assn. (past pres. Ctrl. and Western N.Y. chpts. 1997). Republican. Methodist. Avocations: astronomy, golf, jogging. Administrative and regulatory, General corporate, Mergers and acquisitions. Office: Upstate Farms Coop Inc 25 Anderson Rd Buffalo NY 14225

HARON, DAVID LAWRENCE, lawyer; b. Detroit, Sept. 24, 1944; s. Percy Hyman and Bess (Holland) H.; m. Pamela Kay Colburn, May 25, 1969; children: Eric, Andrea. BA, U. Mich., 1966, JD, 1969. Bar: Mich. 1969, U.S. Dist. Ct. (ea. dist.) Mich., 1969, U.S. Supreme Ct. 1974, U.S. Ct. of Appeals (6th cir.) 1996. Law clk. to chief judge Mich. Ct. Appeals, Detroit, 1969-70; assoc. Barris, Sott, Denn & Driker, 1970-74; sr. ptnr. Josephson, Tennen, Haron and Bennett, Southfield, Mich., 1974-90; prin., shareholder, sr. v.p. Frank, Stefani, Haron and Hall, Troy, 1990—; arbitrator Mich. Prudential Securities, Inc. Expedited Arbitrations, 1994-

96. Cons. Universe Computer Software, 1985; pres., bd. dirs. S&H Licensing Corp., Southfield; panelist Ct. TV Law Ctr. Bar Assn. Mem. editorial bd. Prospectus Jour. Law Reform, 1969, (newsletter) Atty.'s Mktg. Report, 1986-88; contbr. articles to profl. jours. Mem. Farmington Hills Planning Commn., 1996—, vice-chair, 2000-01, chair, 2001—; vol. handicap parking enforcement officer Farmington Hills Police Dept., 1990-93; bd. dirs. Forest Elem. Sch. PTO, 1983, 87-88; v.p. North Farmington Baseball for Youth, 1984; mem. Sta. WTVS Auction, Detroit, 1985-88; trustee Caring Athletes Team for Children's and Henry Ford Hosps., 1996—, Temple Israel, West Bloomfield, Mich., 1987-93, tchr. Sunday Sch., 1986-88, chmn. Ritual com., 1988-93, advisor youth group, 1987-90; chmn. Farmington Hills Com. to Increase Voter Participation, 1987-89; bd. dirs. Met. Detroit chpt. Zionist Orgn. Am., 1987-90; pres. North Farmington H.S. Parent Club, 1989-95; mem. bd. advisors Farmington Hills Corps.-Salvation Army, 1997-2000; mem. site selection com. South Oakland County Habitat for Humanity; chair Cardozo Law Soc. of the Jewish Fedn. Met. Detroit, 1999—. Recipient Outstanding Alumnus award Mumford H.S., Detroit, 1985, Cert. recognition City of Farmington Hills, 1986. Fellow The Roscoe Pound Found., Mich. State Bar Found.; mem. ABA (mem. com. on comml. leasing 1987—, real property, probate and trust law sect., mem. bus. law sect. com. on fed. regulation of securities, mem. subcom. on alternative dispute resolution, SEC enforcement matters), ASTM (mem. com. on environ. assessment 1992—), ATLA, Nat. Arbitration Forum (arbitrator), Assn. Health Lawyers Am. (co-chmn. fraud & abuse SISLC false claims/qui tam working group), Mich. Trial Lawyers Assn., Am. Soc. Writers on Legal Subjects, Internat. Assn. Jewish Lawyers and Jurists, Million Dollar Advocates Forum, State Bar Mich. (mem. pro bono com. real property sect. 1996-98, mem. professionalism com. 1994—, chmn. professionalism com. 1996-98, chmn. unauthorized practice of law com. 1990-92, mem. unauthorized practice of law com. 1999—, chmn. Ct. Appeals com. 1977-78, mem. representative assembly 1999—), Nat. Assn. Securities Dealers (mediator 1996—, arbitrator 1997—), Am. Arbitration Assn. (arbitrator, mediator, spkr.), Comml. Law League Am., Detroit Bar Assn., Jewish Fedn., Cardozo Legal Soc. (chmn. 1999—), Oakland County Bar Assn. (participant Mich. law-related edn. project 1988-89, real estate com. 1990—, environ. law com. 1992-95, lawyer dispute conciliator, spkr. 1993, chmn. professionalism com. 1995-97; Cir. Ct. facilitator, master Inn of Ct. 1997—), Oakland Bar Found. (trustee), U. Mich. Alumni Assn., U. Mich. Victor's Club, Zionist Orgn. (bd. dirs. Detroit 1987-90), Tau Epsilon Rho, Tau Delta Phi. Jewish. General corporate, Real property. Home: 34685 Old Timber Rd Farmington Hills MI 48331-1436 Office: Frank Stefani Haron & Hall 5435 Corporate Dr Ste 225 Troy MI 48098-2624 Fax: 248-952-0890. E-mail: dharon@fsh-law.com

HARP, JOHN ANDERSON, lawyer; b. Helena, Ark., Nov. 30, 1950; s. Bert Seth and Mary Eleanor (Jolley) H.; m. Jane Van Cleave, Apr. 26, 1980; children: Anderson, Elizabeth, William, Hamilton. BA, Am. U., Washington, 1973; JD, Mercer U., Macon, Ga., 1980. Bar: Ga., Ala. Ptnr. Taylor, Harp & Callier, Columbus, Ga., 1985—. Co-author: Litigating Head Trauma Cases, 1991; bd. editors Neurolaw Letter, 1991—, IATROGENICS, 1992-93, Topics in Spinal Cord Injury Rehab., 1994—; contbr. articles to profl. jours. Reservist USMCR with Office of Asst. Sec. of Def., The Pentagon, 1996-2000. Col., USMCR, 1995-2000, Marine Forces Pacific G-3, 2000—. Mem. ABA, ATLA, Ga. Bar Assn., Ala. Bar Assn., Nat. Spinal Cord Assn. (bd. dirs. 1987-95), Marine Corps Res. Officers Assn. (bd. dirs. 1995-98, nat. pres. 1997-98, vice-chmn. bd. dirs. 1998-99, Non Sibi Sed Patriae award), Mercer U. Law Sch. Alumni Assn. (nat. v.p. 1997-98, nat. pres.-elect 1998-99, nat. pres. 1999—). Avocations: running, skiing. General civil litigation, Personal injury, Product liability. Office: Taylor Harp & Callier 233 12th St Ste 900 Columbus GA 31901-2449

HARPER, CONRAD KENNETH, lawyer, former government official; b. Detroit, Dec. 2, 1940; s. Archibald Leonard and Georgia Florence (Hall) H.; m. Marsha Louise Wilson, July 17, 1965; children: Warren Wilson, Adam Woodburn. BA, Howard U., 1962; LLB, Harvard U., 1965; LLD (hon.), CUNY, 1990, Vt. Law Sch., 1994. Bar: N.Y. 1966. Law clk. NAACP Legal Def. and Ednl. Fund, N.Y.C., 1965-66, staff lawyer, 1966-70; assoc. Simpson Thacher & Bartlett, 1971-74, ptnr., 1974-93, 96—; legal adviser U.S. Dept. of State, Washington, 1993-96. Lectr. law Rutgers U., 1969-70; vis. lectr. law Yale U., 1977-81; cons. HEW, 1977; chmn. admissions and grievances com. U.S. Ct. Appeals, 2d cir., 1987-93; co-chmn. Lawyers' Com. for Civil Rights Under Law, 1987-89; mem. Permanent Ct. of Arbitration, The Hague, 1993-96, 98—, Adminstrv. Conf. U.S., 1993-95, Harvard Corp., 2000—; bd. dirs. N.Y. Life Ins. Co., Pub. Svc. Enterprise Group. Trustee Inst. Internat. Edn., 1992-93, N.Y. Pub. Libr., chmn. exec. com., 1990-93, vice-chmn. bd. trustees, 1991-93; trustee William Nelson Cromwell Found., 1990—, Met. Mus. of Art, 1996—; bd. mgrs. Lewis Walpole Libr., 1989-93; bd. visitors Fordham Law Sch., 1990-93, CUNY, 1989-93; vestryman Ch. of St. Barnabas, Irvington, N.Y., 1982-85; bd. dirs. Phi Beta Kappa Assocs., 1992-93; chancellor The Episc. Diocese of N.Y., 1987-92; bd. legal advisors Martindale-Hubbell, 1990-93. Fellow Am. Bar Found., N.Y. Bar Found., Am. Coll. Trial Lawyers, Am. Acad. Arts and Scis.; mem. ABA (bd. editors jour. 1980-86), Internat. Bar Assn., Nat. Bar Assn., N.Y. State Bar Assn., Assn. of Bar of City of N.Y. (chmn. exec. com. 1979-80, pres. 1990-92), Am. Law Inst. (mem. coun. 1985—, 2nd v.p. 1998-2000, 1st v.p. 2000—), Am. Assn. for Internat. Commn. Jurists (bd. dirs. 1988-93), Am. Soc. Internat. Law (mem. exec. coun. 1997-2000, exec. com. 1998-2000, counselor 2000—), Met. Black Bar Assn., Internat. Law Assn., N.Y. Law Inst. (exec. com. 1997—), Am. Arbitration Assn. (bd. dirs. 1990-93, 97-2001, exec. com. 1998-2001), Acad. Polit. Sci. (bd. dirs. 1998—), Coun. Fgn. Rels., Acad. Am. Poets (bd. dirs. 1990-93), Grolier Club (coun. mem. 1993, 97—), Century Assn., Harvard Club (mem. bd. mgrs. 1993), Yale Club, Phi Beta Kappa. Democrat. Episcopalian. Office: 425 Lexington Ave New York NY 10017-3954

HARPER, STEVEN JAMES, lawyer; b. Mpls., Apr. 25, 1954; s. James Henry and Mary Margaret H.; m. Kathy Joseph Loeb, Aug. 21, 1976; children: Benjamin James, Peter William, Emma Suzanne. BA with distinction, MA in Econs., Northwestern U., 1976; JD magna cum laude, Harvard U., 1979. Bar: Ill. 1979, U.S. Dist. Ct. (no. dist.) Ill. 1979. Assoc. Kirkland & Ellis, Chgo., 1979-85, ptnr., 1985—. Mem. ABA. Club: University (Chgo.). Federal civil litigation, State civil litigation. Office: Kirkland & Ellis 200 E Randolph Dr Fl 54 Chicago IL 60601-6636

HARPER, VESTA TAMORA, lawyer, paralegal educator; b. Vicksburg, Miss., Sept. 25, 1971; d. Gregory Duwayne and Sara Susette (Jackson) H. BS, Alcorn State U., 1993; MBA, JD, Tex. Tech. U., 1996. Bar: Tex. 1997. Extern Criminal Dist. Ct. No. 2, Dallas, 1989; legal rsch. asst. West Tex. Legal Svcs., Lubbock, 1995, staff atty. Ft. Worth, 1998—; contract atty. Exec. Secretariat Sch., Dallas, 1997—. Pvt. practice law, Dallas, 1997-98; extern 5th Dist. Ct. Appeals, Dallas, 1997; contract atty. Southeastern Paralegal Inst., Dallas, 1998. Mem. ABA. Home: 9433 Timberleaf Dr Dallas TX 75243-6123 Office: West Tex Legal Svcs 600 E Weatherford St Fort Worth TX 76102-3264

HARPOOTLIAN, RICHARD ARA, lawyer, political party official; b. Bklyn., Jan. 23, 1949; s. Harold C. and Joan (Williams) H.; m. Pamela McCreery, Jan. 1, 1972. BS, Clemson U., 1971; JD, U. S.C., 1974. Bar: S.C. 1974. Asst. solicitor Solicitor's Office (5th cir.), Columbia, S.C., 1975-77, dep. solicitor, 1977-83; ptnr. Swerling & Harpootlian, 1983-90; solicitor Solicator's Office (5th cir.), Cola, S.C., 1991-95; pvt. practice, 1995—. Chmn. S.C. Dem. Party, 1998—. Methodist. Criminal, Family and matrimonial, Personal injury. Home: 1721 Enoree Ave Columbia SC 29205-2907 Office: 1410 Laurel St Columbia SC 29201-2516 E-mail: ratt@harpootlianlaw.com

HARR, LAWRENCE FRANCIS, lawyer; b. Broken Bow, Nebr., Sept. 1, 1938; s. Joseph and Dorothy (Gleason) H.; m. Susan Smithberger; children: Sharyl, Steve, Brian, Burke, BSBA, Creighton U., 1960, JD, 1962. Bar: Nebr. 1962, Ill. 1971. Dept. atty. Nebr. Ins. Dept., Lincoln, 1963-69; gen. counsel, chief adminstrv. officer Consumer Credit Ins. Assn., Chgo., 1969-75; exec. v.p., exec. counsel Mut. of Omaha Ins. Cos., 1975—; chmn. Nebr. Guarantee Assn.; chmn. Nat. Orgn. of Life & Health Ins. Guaranty Assn.; bd. dirs. Omaha Indemnity Co., Mutual of Omaha Investors Svcs., Inc., Omaha Property and Casualty. Mem. exec. com., former chmn. Nebr. Ins. Fedn., Lincoln. Capt. U.S. Army 1962-1963. Mem. ABA, Nebr. Bar Assn., Omaha Bar Assn., Omaha C. of C. (past chmn. ins. execs. com.). Roman Catholic. General corporate, Insurance. Home: 9834 Harney Pkwy N Omaha NE 68114-4945 Office: Mut of Omaha Ins Co Mutual Of Omaha Plz Omaha NE 68175-0001

HARRAL, JOHN MENTEITH, lawyer; b. Ancon, Panama Canal Zone, June 25, 1948; s. Brooks Jared and Sara (Mumma) H.; m. Marjorie Van Fosson, Aug. 15, 1970; children: Alyse, Jessica. BBA, U. Miss., 1971, JD, 1974. Bar: Miss. 1974, U.S. Dist. Ct. (so. dist.) Miss. 1974, U.S. Ct. Appeals (5th cir.) 1977. Law clk. to Judge J.P. Coleman, U.S. Ct. Appeals (5th cir.), New Orleans, 1978-79; ptnr. White & Morse, Gulfport, Miss., 1979-92, Eaton & Cottrell, P.A., Gulfport, 1993-97; sole practitioner, 1997—. Mem. Miss. Gov.'s Jud. Nominating Com., 1990-93; instr. bus. law William Carey Coll.; mem. adv. bd. dirs. Whitney Nat. Bank. Chmn. Episc. Svcs. for Aging, Mississippi Gulf Coast, 1981-85, also bd. dirs.; bd. dirs. Make-A-Wish Found. Miss.; founder, pres. Gulfport Excellence, 1991—; bd. dirs., exec. com. Christmas in April, Harrison County, 1994—, pres., 1995-96; bd. dirs. Lynn Meadows Discovery Ctr., 1996—, sec., exec. com., 1997-2000; lay eucharistic min. St. Mark's Episcopal Ch., Gulfport, 1980, vestryman, sr. and jr. warden, Sunday sch. tchr.; pres. Gulfport Downtown Assn., Inc., 1997-98, dir., 1998-2001; mentor Gulfport Schs., 1991—; Miss. commr. Nat. Conf. Commrs. on Uniform State Laws, 2000—. Lt. JAGC, USNR, 1974-78. Fellow Miss. Bar Found.; mem. ABA, Miss. Bar Assn. (bd. dirs. young lawyers divsn. 1982-84, commr. 1991-94), Harrison County Bar Assn. (pres. young lawyers sect. 1982, pres. 1987-88), Gulf Coast Law Inst. (bd. dirs. 1988-93), Gulfport C. of C. (bd. dirs. 1995-97, pres. 1997), Miss. Coast C. of C. (bd. dirs. 1994—), Rotary (bd. dirs. Gulfport chpt. 1997-99, pres. elect 2001—), Bayou Bluff Tennis Club, Gulfport Yacht Club, Gulfport Bus. Club (founder, v.p. 1999, pres. 2001). Republican. Banking, General civil litigation, Insurance. Home: 12 Old Oak Ln Gulfport MS 39503-6210 Office: 1418 20th Ave Gulfport MS 39501-2029 E-mail: navyjag@aol.com

HARRELL, GLENN T., JR. judge; b. Ashland, Ky., June 27, 1945; BA, U. Md., 1967, JD, 1970. Bar: Md. 1970. Assoc. O'Malley, Miles & Harrell, 1973-76, ptnr., 1977-91; assoc. county atty. Prince George's County, 1971-73; judge at large Ct. Spl. Appeals, 1991-99; judge Ct. Appeals (4th cir.), Prince George's County, Md., 1999—. Chair Commn. on Jud. Disabilities, 1996-98; mem. exec. com. Md. Jud. Conf., 1997-99; adj. prof. legal writing Sch. Law U. Balt., 1997-99; lectr. in field. Mem. Md. Bar Found., Prince George's County Bar Found. Mem. MD. Bar Assn., Prince George's County Bar Assn. Office: Ct Appeals PO Box 209 Upper Marlboro MD 20773-0209*

HARRELL, LIMMIE LEE, JR. lawyer; b. Jackson, Tenn., Aug. 15, 1941; s. Limmie Lee Sr. and Mary Benthal (Nowell) H.; m. Betsy D. Harrell; children: Limmie Lee III, Mary Kimberley. BS, Memphis State U., 1963, JD, 1966. Bar: Tenn. 1966, U.S. Dist. Ct. (we. dist.) Tenn. 1968, U.S. Supreme Ct. Ptnr. Harrell & Harrell, Attys., Trenton, Tenn., 1966—. Bd. dirs. Bank of Commerce, Trenton. Pres. Gibson County Young Dems., Trenton, Tenn., 1968. Named one of Outstanding Young Men in Am. Mem. ABA, Tenn. Bar Assn., Gibson County Bar Assn., Assn. Trial Lawyers Am., Tenn. Trial Lawyers Assn., Memphis State Alumni Assn. (pres. 1984-85). Baptist. Club: Pinecrest Country Club (Trenton, Tenn.) (pres. (3) terms). Lodges: Elks (exalted ruler 1971-72), Moose. Avocations: golf, fishing, hunting, water skiing. Criminal, General practice, Personal injury. Home: 300 Rosemont Dr Trenton TN 38382-3116 Office: Harrell & Harrell Attys Court Sq Trenton TN 38382-1862

HARRER, HERBERT, lawyer; b. Munich, Germany, Apr. 15, 1961; s. Florian and Elisabeth Harrer. First State Exam., U. Munich, 1987, Doctorate in Law, 1989, Second State Exam., 1991; LLM, Columbia U., 1992. Bar: Frankfurt, Germany 1992, N.Y. 1992, U.S. Dist. Ct. (so. dist.) N.Y. 1993. Lawyer Shearman & Sterling, N.Y.C. and Frankfurt, 1992-97; ptnr. Oppenhoff & Rädler, Frankfurt, 1998—. Recipient German Army Hon. medal Fed. Republic of Germany, 1981; Hanns-Seidel-Found. scholar, 1988, Fulbright scholar, 1990-91. Mem. N.Y. State Bar Assn., Internat. Bar Assn., German Am. Lawyers Assn. General corporate, Securities. Home: Bernusstrasse 25 60487 Frankfurt am Main Germany Office: Linklaters Oppenhoff Radler Mainzer Landstrasse 16 60325 Frankfurt am Main Germany E-mail: herbert.harrer@linklaters.com

HARRINGTON, BRUCE MICHAEL, lawyer, investor; b. Houston, Mar. 12, 1933; s. George Haymond Harrington and Doris (Gladden) Maginnis; m. Anne Griffith Lawhon, Feb. 15, 1958; children: Julia Griffith, Martha Gladden, Susan McIver B.A., U. Tex., 1960, J.D. with honors, 1961. Bar: Tex. 1961, U.S. Dist. Ct. (so. dist.) Tex. 1962, U.S. Ct. Appeals (5th cir.) 1962, U.S. Supreme Ct. 1973. Assoc. Andrews & Kurth and predecessor firm, Houston, 1961-73, ptnr., 1973-84. Dir. Offenhauser Co., Houston, Allied Metals, Inc., Houston Trustee St. John's Sch., Houston, 1981-92, chmn. bd., CEO, 1986-92; chmn. bd. Covenant House, Tex., 1991-95; trustee St. Luke's Episcopal Hosp., Tex. Med. Ctr., Houston, 1983-86; bd. dirs. YMCA Bd. Mgmt., Am. Cancer Soc., 1992-94, Ctr. for Hearing and Speech, 1993, chmn. bd., 1995-98; vice chmn. Gateway Found., 1993-95; mem. adv. com. Assn. Governing Bds. of Colls. and Univs. Mem. ABA, Nat. Assn. Ind. Schs. (chmn. trustee com.), Ind. Schs. Assn. S.W. (chmn. trustee com., bd. exec. com.), Tex. Bar Assn., Houston Bar Assn., The Mil. and Hosp. Order of St. Lazarus, The Venerable Order of St. John (U.K.), The Order of Saints Maurice and Lazarus (Savoy), Houston Country Club, Petroleum Club, Houston Club, Phi Delta Phi, Order of Coif. Republican. Episcopalian. General corporate. Home: 3608 Overbrook Ln Houston TX 77027-4128

HARRINGTON, CAROL A. lawyer; b. Geneva, Feb. 13, 1953; d. Eugene P. and M. Ruth (Bowersox) Kloubec; m. Warren J. Harrington, Aug. 19, 1972; children: Jennifer Ruth, Carrie Anne. BS summa cum laude, U. Ill., 1974, JD magna cum laude, 1977. Bar: Ill. 1977, U.S. Dist. Ct. (no. dist.) Ill. 1977, U.S. Tax Ct. 1979. Assoc. Winston & Strawn, Chgo., 1977-84, ptnr., 1984-88, McDermott, Will & Emery, 1988—. Speaker in field. Co-author, co-author: The New Generation Skipping Tax, 1986co-author: Generation-Skipping Transfer Tax, Warren, Gorham & Lamont, 2000. Fellow Am. Coll. Trusts and Estate Coun. (bd. regents 1999—); mem. ABA (chmn. B-1 generation skipping transfer com. 1987-92, coun. real property, probate and trust law sect. 1992-98), Ill. State Bar Assn., Chgo. Bar Assn. (trust law com. divsn. 1), Chgo. Estate Planning Coun. Estate planning, Probate, Estate taxation. Office: McDermott Will & Emery 227 W Monroe St Ste 3100 Chicago IL 60606-5096

HARRINGTON, JAMES TIMOTHY, lawyer; b. Chgo., Sept. 4, 1942; s. John Paul and Margaret Rita (Cunneen) H.; m. Roseanne Strupeck, Sept. 4, 1965; children: James Timothy, Roseanne, Maris Zajdela. BA, U. Notre Dame, 1964, JD, 1967. Bar: Ill. 1967, Ind. 1968, U.S. Dist. Ct. (no. dist.) Ill. 1967, U.S. Dist. Ct. (no. and so. dists.) Ind. 1968, U.S. Ct. Appeals (7th cir.) 1969, U.S. Ct. Appeals (4th cir.) 1977, U.S. Ct. Appeals (8th cir.) 1979, U.S. Ct. Appeals (3d cir.) 1981, U.S. Supreme Ct. 1979, U.S. Ct. Appeals (D.C. cir.) 1993. Law clk. U.S. Dist. Ct. (no. dist.) Ind., 1967-69; assoc. Rooks, Pitts & Poust, Chgo., 1969-75, ptnr., 1976-87, Ross & Hardies, Chgo., 1987—. Lectr. environ. law, fed. procedures, adminstrv. law, 1960—. Vice chmn. Mid Am. Legal Found.; vice-chmn., bd. dirs. Ill. Safety Coun. Fellow Am. Bar Found.; mem. Ill. Bar Assn., Ind. Bar Assn., Chgo. Bar Assn. (environ. law com., real estate com.), Indsl. Water Waste and Sewer Group (past chmn.), Air and Waste Mgmt. Assn. (bd. dirs. Lake Mich. sect.), Assn. Environ. Law Inst., Lawyers Club Chgo., Exec. Club Chgo., Union League Club Chgo. Roman Catholic. Federal civil litigation, State civil litigation, Environmental. Home: 746 Foxdale Ave Winnetka IL 60093-1908 Office: Ross & Hardies 150 N Michigan Ave Ste 2500 Chicago IL 60601-7567 E-mail: james.harrington@rosshardies.com

HARRINGTON, KEVIN PAUL, lawyer; b. Paterson, N.J., Jan. 1, 1951; s. James John and theresa Elizabeth (Giblin) H. BA, Niagara U., 1973; JD, N. E. Sch. Law, Boston, 1978. Bar: N.J. 1978, U.S. Dist. Ct. N.J. 1978, U.S. Supreme Ct. 1983. Judicial clerkship to hon. Thomas R. Rumana, Paterson, N.J., 1978-79; asst. prosecutor Passaic County Prosecutor's Office, 1979-80; assoc. DeYoe & Guiney, 1980-87; ptnr. Catania & Harrington, N. Haledon, 1987-99, Harrington and Lombardi, LLP, N. Haledon, 2000—. Pres., bd. trustees Clinic for Mental Health Svc., Paterson, N.J., 1990—. Recipient Civil Trial Atty. cert., Supreme Ct. N.J., 1986—. Master Am. Inns of Ct.; mem. ATLA, N.J. Def. Assn., N.J. Bar Assn., Passaic County Bar Assn. (trustee), Def. Rsch. Inst. Avocations: sports, golf, scuba diving. General civil litigation, Insurance, Personal injury. Office: Harrington and Lombardi LLP 909 Belmont Ave Ste 3 North Haledon NJ 07508-2568

HARRIS, ALVIN LOUIS, lawyer; b. Boston, Jan. 27, 1959; s. Morton Allen and Judye Rose Harris; m. Kathy Lynn Howerton, June 19, 1982; children: Jeffrey Louis, Natalie Rosemary. BA, Vanderbilt U., 1981, JD, 1985. Bar: U.S. Dist. Ct. (mid. dist.) Tenn. 1986, U.S. Ct. Appeals (11th cir.) 1986, U.S. Dist. Ct. (mid. dist.) Ga. 1990. Law clk. hon. R. Lanier Anderson 11th Cir. Ct. Appeals, Macon, Ga., 1985-86; atty. O'Hare, Sherrard & Roe, Nashville, 1986-89, Page, Scrantom, Harris & Chapman, Columbus, Ga., 1990-93, Greene & Greene, Nashville, 1993-97; ptnr. Weed, Hubbard, Berry & Doughty PLLC, 1997—. Adj. bus. law instr. Columbus (Ga.) Coll., 1990-91. Pres. Nashville Chess Ctr., 1996-2000. Mem. ABA, Tenn. Bar Assn., Cmty. Assn. Inst., Phi Beta Kappa, Order of the Coif. Avocations: chess, running. General civil litigation, Contracts commercial, Construction. Office: Weed Hubbard Berry & Doughty PLLC 201 4th Ave N Ste 1420 Nashville TN 37219-2089 E-mail: alvinharris@home.com, aharris@whbdlaw.com

HARRIS, BAYARD EASTER, lawyer; b. Washington, July 22, 1944; s. Edward Bledsoe and Grace (Childrey) H.; m. Rebecca Bond Jeffress, June 10, 1967; children: Nicholas Bayard, Nathan Bedford (dec. 1989), Ellen Coley. AB in History, U. N.C., 1966; JD cum laude, U. S.C., 1973. Bar: Va. 1974, U.S. Dist. Ct. (we. dist.) Va. 1974, U.S. Ct. Appeals (4th cir.) 1974, U.S. Supreme Ct. 1982. Assoc. Woods, Rogers, Muse, Walker & Thornton, Roanoke, Va., 1973-79, ptnr., 1979-85, Woods, Rogers & Hazlegrove, Roanoke, 1985-90; pres. Ctr. for Employment Law, 1991-98; of counsel Woods, Rogers and Hazlegrove, PLC, 1998—. Mem. Transp. Safety Bd., 1992-96. Comments and rsch. editor U. S.C. Law Rev., 1972-73. Chpt. chmn. ARC, Roanoke Valley, 1985-87, chmn. ea. ops. hdqrs., 1988-91. Lt. USNR, 1966-70. Recipient Clara Barton award ARC Roanoke Valley chpt., 1986. Mem. ABA (labor and employment sect. 1974—), Va. Bar Assn. (labor and employment com. and sect. 1974—), Rotary. Republican. Episcopalian. Avocations: golf, gardening. Civil rights, Federal civil litigation, Labor. Office: Woods Rogers & Hazlegrove 10 S Jefferson St Ste 1400 Roanoke VA 24011-1331 E-mail: bharris@woodsrogers.com

HARRIS, BENJAMIN HARTE, JR. lawyer; b. Sept. 12, 1937; s. Ben H. and Mary Cade (Aldridge) H.; m. Martha Elliott Lambeth, Aug. 26, 1961; children: Benjamin Harte, Wayt. AB, Davidson Coll., 1959; JD, U. Ala., 1962. Bar: Ala. 1964, U.S. Dist. Ct. (so. dist.) Ala. 1965, U.S. Ct. Appeals (5th cir.) 1981, U.S. Supreme Ct. 1971, U.S. Ct. Appeals (11th cir.) 1981. Assoc. Johnstone, Adams, Bailey, Gordon & Harris (formerly Johnstone, Adams, May, Howard & Hill, LLC), Mobile, Ala., 1964-70; mem. Johnstone, Adams, Bailey, Gordon & Harris, 1971. Chmn. Atty's Ins. Mut. Ala., bd. dirs. Past bd. dirs. Boys' Club, 1989-95; past chmn., past trustee UMS Prep Sch.; v.p., bd. dirs. Gordon Smith Ctr.; mem. stds. com. United Way. Fellow Am. Bar Found. (life), Ala. Law Found.; mem. ABA (past ho. of dels., past bd. govs.), Ala. Law Found. (past pres., past trustee), Mobile County Bar Assn. (exec. com. 1980-87), Ala. State Bar (bd. commrs. 1978-87, mem. exec. com., trustee bar found., past chmn. disciplinary commn., past pres.), Ala. Law Inst., Ala. Law Sch. Found. (past pres., trustee), Ala. Def. Lawyers Assn., Am. Judicature Soc., Am. Arbitration Assn., Ala. Jud. Commn., 11th Cir. Ct. Appeals Hist. Soc. (trustee, v.p.), Nat. Conf. Bar Pres. (past exec. coun.), Brock Inn of Ct. (pres. 1996-98), Mobile Rotary Club (Paul Harris fellow), Athelstan Club. Episcopalian. General civil litigation, Oil, gas, and mineral, Workers' compensation. Office: PO Box 1988 Mobile AL 36633-1988

HARRIS, BRIAN CRAIG, lawyer; b. Newark, Sept. 8, 1941; s. Louis W. and Lillian (Frankel) H.; m. Ellen M. Davis, Aug. 20, 1978; children; Andrea, Keith. BS, boston U., 1963; JD, Rutgers U., 1966. Bar: N.J. 1968, D.C. 1968, U.S. Ct. Appeals (3d cir.) 1968, N.Y. 1984, U.S. Ct. Appeals (2d cir.) 1985. Asst. corp. counsel, Newark, 1968-70; assoc. Braff, Litvak & Ertag, East Orange, N.J., 1970-72; ptnr. Braff, Litvak, Ertag, Wortmann & Harris, 1972-85, Braff, Ertag, wortmann, Harris & Sukoneck, Livingston, N.J., 1985-91, Braff, Harris & Sukoneck, 1991—. Adj. lectr. law and medicine Seton Hall U., South Orange, N.J., 1982-83, trial preparation Rutgers U. Law Sch., 1983, strategy of def. United Tech. Corp., Chgo., 1986. Sustaining mem. Product Liability Adv. Coun., Inc.; contbg. mem. Nat. Ileitis found., N.Y.C., 1983—. Named Master of Inns. of Ct., Arthur J. Vanderbilt Sect., 1988. Mem. ABA (employment law sect., tort and ins. sect.), Internat. Assn. Def. Counsel, Profl. Liability Underwriters Soc., N.Y. State Bar Assn., N.Y. Trial Lawyers Assn., Essex County Trial Lawyers Assn., Middlesex County Trial Lawyers Assn., Def. Rsch. Inst. (mem. com. employment law, mem. com. profl. liability, trustee Hamonie Group), N.J. Trial Lawyers Assn., N.J. Def. Assn., East Hampton Indoor Outdoor Tennis Club, Orange Lawn Tennis Club. Jewish. Avocations: running, basketball, theater, tennis, study of military strategy of land forces in World War II. Personal injury, Product liability, Transportation. Home: Llewellyn Pk West Orange NJ 07052-5402 Office: Braff Harris & Sukoneck 570 W Mount Pleasant Ave Ste 18 Livingston NJ 07039-1688 also: 305 Broadway Fl 7 New York NY 10007-1109

HARRIS, CHARLES MARCUS, lawyer; b. Orange, N.J., July 5, 1943; s. Roger Kennedy and Margaret Louise (Adams) H.; m. Jean Ellen Redding, July 6, 1968; children: Charles Redding, Anna Dean. AB, Duke U., 1965, JD, 1972; MA, U. Ariz., 1966. Bar: N.C. 1972, U.S. Dist. Ct. (we. dist.) N.C. 1972, U.S. Dist. Ct. (ea. dist.) N.C. 1976, U.S. Dist. Ct. (mid. dist.) N.C. 1977. Field examiner NLRB, Winston-Salem, N.C., 1966-69; ptnr. Smith Helms Mulliss & Moore, Charlotte, N.C., 1972-93; ptnr. Poyner & Spruill, Charlotte, 1993—. Mem. editorial bd. Duke Law Jour., 1971-72. Jr. warden Christ Episc. Ch., Charlotte, 1983-84, 89-90; pres. United Family Svcs., Charlotte, 1986; pres. Friendship Trays Bd., Charlotte, 1991-93. Mem. ABA, N.C. Bar Assn., Duke U. Alumni Assn. (pres. Mecklenburg chpt. 1979-81, gen. alumni bd. 1993—), Charlotte City Club, Charlotte Country Club. Republican. General corporate, Pension, profit-sharing, and employee benefits, Securities. Home: 4733 Cambridge Crescent Dr Charlotte NC 28226-3324 Office: Poyner & Spruill 100 N Tryon St Ste 4000 Charlotte NC 28202-4010

HARRIS, CHRISTOPHER KIRK, lawyer; b. Aluquerque, July 6, 1951; s. Paul and Margureite (Kirk) H. BA, Yale U., 1973; MSc, London Sch. Econs., 1974; JD, Boston Coll., 1977. Bar: Mass. 1977, D.C. 1980, Mont. 1986, U.S. Supreme Ct. 1981. Atty. GAO, Washington, 1977-78; chief counsel U.S. Senate Judiciary Subcom., 1979; atty. land and natural resources divsn. U.S. Dept. Justice, Washington, 1979-83; counsel Ho. of Reps. Energy and Commerce Com., 1983-84; ptnr. McCutchen Doyle Brown & Enersen, 1991-94, Harris, Tarlow & Stonecipher, Bozeman, Mont., 1994-2000; mem. Mont. Ho. of Reps., 2001—. Mem. Mont. Environ. Quality Coun.; gen. counsel Nat. Oil Recyclers Assn., 1985—. Author: Hazardous Waste: Confronting the Challenge, 1987, Report That Spill!, 1990, Environmental Crimes, 1992, Hazardous Chemicals and the Right to Know, 1993, Used Oil: Management Practices and Potential Liability, 1988, (with others) Environmental Litigation, 1999. Recipient Cert. of Merit energy and minerals divsn. GAO, 1978, Spl. Achievement award U.S. Atty. Gen., 1981. Environmental, Legislative. Office: 519 N Black Bozeman MT 59715

HARRIS, CHRISTY FRANKLIN, lawyer; b. Greensboro, N.C., Dec. 8, 1945; s. Luther Franklin and Rebecca Ann (Bluster) H.; children: Stacey Lynn, Aubrey Leigh. AA, Oxford Coll., Emory U.; BA, U. Fla., 1967, JD with honors, 1970. Bar: Fla. 1970, U.S. Dist. Ct. (mid. dist.) Fla. 1970, U.S. Ct. Mil. Appeals 1971, U.S. Ct. Appeals (11th cir.) 1984. Assoc. Holland & Knight, Lakeland, Fla., 1970, 1973-74; pres. Canan & Harris P.A., 1974-76; pres., sr. atty. Harris, Midyette & Clements P.A., 1976-89, Harris & Midyette, P.A., Lakeland, 1989-91, Harris, Midyette, Geary, Darby & Morrell, P.A., Lakeland, 1991-98, Harris, Midyette & Darby, P.A., Lakeland, 1998-2000; shareholder Peterson & Myers, P.A., 2000—. Mem. 10th cir. Grievance Com., Lakeland, 1976-79, 83-86, chmn. 1979, vice chmn., 1986; mem. Unauthorized Practice of Law Com., 1983-86; bd. dirs. Internat. Speedway Corp., 1984—. Bd. dirs. Program to Aid Drug Abusers, Lakeland, 1975-76, Campfire, 1979-85. Served to capt. USMCR, 1968-73, mil. judge, 1972-73. Named to Hon. Order of Ky. Cols., 1974. Mem. Lakeland Bar Assn., Attys. Title Ins. Fund, Grand Am. Rd. Racing Assn., LLC (founding mem.), Order of Coif, Phi Beta Kappa, Phi Kappa Phi. Republican. Avocations: motor sports, sport fishing. Contracts commercial, General corporate, Estate planning. Home: 1335 Longoak Dr N Lakeland FL 33811-2146 Office: Peterson & Myers PA PO Box 24628 Lakeland FL 33806-2451 E-mail: cfh@pmlawoffice.com

HARRIS, DALE RAY, lawyer; b. Crab Orchard, Ill., May 11, 1937; s. Ray B. and Aurelia M. (Davis) H.; m. Toni K. Shapkoff, June 26, 1960; children: Kristen Dee, Julie Diane. BA in Math., U. Colo., 1959; LLB, Harvard U., 1962. Bar: Colo. 1962, U.S. Dist. Ct. Colo. 1962, U.S. Ct. Appeals (10th cir.) 1962, U.S. Supreme Ct. 1981. Assoc. Davis, Graham & Stubbs, Denver, 1962-67, ptnr., 1967—, chmn. mgmt. com., 1982-85. Spkr., instr. various antitrust and comml. litig. seminars; bd. dirs. Lend-A-Lawyer, Inc., 1989-94. Mem. campaign cabinet Mile High United Way, 1986—87, chmn., atty. adv. com., 1988, sec., legal counsel, trustee, 1989—94, 1996—2001, mem. exec. com., 1989—2001, chmn. bd. trustees, 1996, 1997; trustee The Spaceship Earth Fund, 1986—89, Legal Aid Found. Colo., 1989—95, 2000—01; mem. devel. coun. U. Colo. Arts and Scis. dept., 1985—93; area chmn. law sch. fund Harvard U., 1978—81; bd. dirs. Colo. Jud. Inst., 1994—, vice chari, 1998; bd. dir. Colo. Lawyers Trust Account Found., 1996—2001; steering com. Youth-At-Work, 1994, School-To-Work, 1995; mem. jud. adv. coun. Colo. Supreme Ct., 2001—. With reserves USAR, 1962—68. Recipient Williams award, Rocky Mountain Arthritis Found., 1999. Fellow: Am. Bar Found. (Colo. state chmn. 1998—); mem.: ABA (antitrust and litigation sects.), Colo. Bar Found. (pres.-elect 1992—93), Colo. Bar Assn. (chmn. antitrust com. 1980—84, coun. corp. banking and bus. law sect. 1978—83, bd. govs. 1991—95, bd. govs. 1999—, chmn. family violence task force 1996—2000, pres.-elect 1999—2000, pres. 2000—01, co-chair multi-disciplinary practice task force 1999—2000, chmn. profl. reform initiative task force 2001—), Denver Bar Assn. (chmn. centennial com. 1990—91, pres. 1993—94, bd. trustees 1992—95, Merit award 1997), Colo. Assn. Corp. Counsel (pres. 1973—74), Denver Law Club (pres. 1976—77, Lifetime Achievement award 1997), Rotary (Denver), The Two Percent Club (exec. com. 1994—), Citizens Against Amendment 12 Com. (exec. com. 1994), Univ. Club, Colo. Forum, Phi Beta Kappa. Antitrust, General civil litigation. Home: 2032 Bellaire St Denver CO 80207-3722 Office: Davis Graham & Stubbs 1550 17th St Ste 500 Denver CO 80202-1202 E-mail: dale.harris@dgslaw.com

HARRIS, DARLENE, lawyer, county legislator; d. Robert and Novella Harris. BA, U. Pa., 1986; postgrad., U. London, 1988; JD, Hofstra U., 1989. Bar: N.Y. 1989. Staff atty. Juvenile Rights divsn. Legal Aid Soc., N.Y.C., 1989-90, Appeals Bur. Legal Aid Soc., Hempstead, N.Y., 1990; sr. ct. atty. Dist. Ct. of Nassau County, 1991-95; atty. Atty.'s Office Town of Hempstead, 1995-97, Law Offices of Elliot Bloom, Mineola, N.Y., 1996-97; pvt. practice Uniondale, 1997—. Mem. R.E.A.C.H. Project, Hempstead. Mem. NAACP (exec. bd.), Women in Cts. (Nassau county jud. com.), Nassau County Bar Assn., N.Y. State Bar Assn., Black and Hispanic Bar Assn., Kiwanis Club, 100 Black Women. Republican. Office: Office of the County Legislature One West St Mineola NY 11501

HARRIS, EDWARD MONROE, JR. former office equipment company executive; b. Phila., June 5, 1923; s. Edward Monroe and Grace Ida (Wilson) H.; m. Marion Hoyt Stevens, Sept. 16, 1950; children: Edward Monroe, Marion Olney, Peter Duncan. BA, Yale U., 1943; LLB, U. Pa., 1949. Bar: N.Y. 1949. Assoc. Sullivan & Cromwell, N.Y.C., 1949-57; assoc. counsel Kennecott Copper Corp., N.Y.C., 1957-62; corp. counsel, sec. MacMillan Inc., N.Y.C., 1963-67; sec., gen. counsel Pitney Bowes Inc., Stamford, Ct., 1967-88, v.p., 1969-88. Dir. Conn. Joint Council on Econ. Edn., 1974-88; trustee Conn. Pub. Expenditure Council, 1979-85, exec. com., 1983-85; dir. Stamford Mus. and Nature Ctr. Inc., 1980-90, treas., 1982-84, first v.p., 1984-86, pres., 1986-88; trustee Edward W. Hazen Found., 1981-91; mem. adv. com. Conn. Comprehensive Plan for Secondary, Vocat. Career and Adult Edn., 1985; mem. bd. edn., Darien, Conn., 1966-90, chmn., 1967-90. Served to 1st lt. USMCR, 1943-46. Mem. C. of C. U.S. (edn., employment tng. com. 1976-86, environ. com. 1987-88), Conn. Bus. and Industry Assn. (bd. dirs. 1974-77). Republican. Presbyterian. Club: Wee Burn Country (Darien). Avocations: tennis, skiing, golf, travel, gardening. General corporate.

HARRIS, GEORGE BRYAN, lawyer; b. Columbia, S.C., July 8, 1964; s. A. Bryan and Beverly Gaye (Bennett) H. BA, U. Ala., 1986; JD, U. Va., 1989. Bar: Ala. 1989, U.S. Dist. Ct. (no., mid., and so. dists.) Ala. 1990, U.S. Ct. Appeals (11th cir.) 1990, D.C. 1991, U.S. Ct. Appeals (5th cir.) 1992, U.S. Supreme Ct. 1993, London Ct. Internat. Arbitration 1995, U.S. Dist. Ct. (no. dist.) Tex. 1996, U.S. Ct. Appeals (4th cir.) 2000, U.S. Ct. Appeals (fed. cir.) 2000. Ptnr. Bradley Arant Rose & White LLP, Birmingham, Ala., 1996—. Spl. asst. atty. gen. for environment State of Ala., Montgomery, 1990-92. Mem. ABA (co-chairperson Y2K com. 2000—), Birmingham Bar Assn., U. Va. Law Alumni Assn., U. Ala. Alumni Assn., Bus. Coun. Ala. (charter mem., young exec. com.), Birmingham Mon. Morning Quarterback Club, Birmingham Kiwanis Club, Birmingham Area C. of C. (chair govt. action com.), Delta Tau Delta (v.p., bd. dirs. chpt. 1991-94). Methodist. General civil litigation, Legislative, Public utilities. Office: Bradley Arant Rose & White LLP 2001 Park Pl Ste 1400 Birmingham AL 35203-2736 E-mail: gbharris@barw.com

HARRIS, HARVEY ALAN, lawyer; b. St. Louis, Nov. 5, 1936; s. Irvin S. and Sylvia Zelda (Goodman) H.; m. Gloria Goldman, Aug. 14, 1960; children: Stephen J., David A., Linda A.; m. Linda Ruth Everett, Mar. 17, 1977; m. Judith A. Stackhouse, Dec. 19, 1992. AB magna cum laude, Harvard U., 1958, JD, 1961. Bar: Mo. 1961, U.S. Dist. Ct. (ea. dist.) Mo. 1963, U.S. Ct. Appeals (8th cir.) 1979, U.S. Supreme Ct. 1979. Ptnr. and chmn. The Stolar Partnership and predecessors, St. Louis, 1961—. Cons. Office Policy Devel. and Rsch., HUD; owner, ptnr. Fox Assocs., Inc., Metrotix. Author: Schumpeter's Theory of Innovation, 1958. Commr., treas., trustee St. Louis Sci. Ctr.; former chmn. St. Louis bi-state chpt. ARC; chmn. emeritus Sta. KETC-TV, St. Louis; commr., chmn. Bi-State Transit Authority Met. St. Louis; bd. dirs. Jewish Fedn. St. Louis, Barnes Jewish Hosp., St. Louis, St. Louis Symphony. Mem.: ABA, Mo. Bar Assn., St. Louis Bar Assn., Westwood (treas.), Harvard of St. Louis (v.p. 1983), St. Louis Racquet, Noonday, Phi Beta Kappa. Democrat. General corporate, Estate planning, Real property. Home: 31 Westmoreland Pl Saint Louis MO 63108-1227 Office: 911 Washington Ave 7th Floor Saint Louis MO 63101 E-mail: harveystl@aol.com, hah@stolarlaw.com

HARRIS, ISAAC RON, lawyer; b. Haifa, Israel, Oct. 1, 1954; came to U.S., 1955; s. Lee B. and Leah (Jacobson) H.; m. Shari E. Shapiro, Sept. 6, 1981; children: Jessica Sara, Emma Rachel. BA, Brown U., 1976; JD, Georgetown U., 1980. Bar: N.Y. 1981, U.S. Dist. Ct. (so. and ea. dists.) N.Y. 1981. Asst. dist. atty. Kings County, Bklyn., 1980-84; assoc. Hall, Dickler, Lawler, Kent & Friedman, N.Y.C., 1984-85; ptnr. Scheffler, King & Casper, Mt. Kisco, N.Y., 1990-2000; prin. I. Ron Harris, Esq., 2000—. Mem. N.Y. State Bar Assn., Westchester County Bar Assn., No. Westchester Bar Assn. Home: 44 North Way Chappaqua NY 10514-2214 Office: I Ron Harris Esq 100 S Bedford Rd Ste 200 Mount Kisco NY 10549

HARRIS, JAY STEPHEN, lawyer, producer; b. L.A., May 2, 1938; s. Nathan and Leah (Spector) H.; m. Fredda Lee Levin, June 20, 1981; m. Marie Masters, Apr. 15, 1967 (div. 1976); children: Jenny, Jesse. AB, Cornell U., 1961; LLB, NYU, 1965. Bar: N.Y. 1966, U.S. Dist. Ct. (so. dist.) N.Y. 1967. Asst. dist. atty. New York County, 1965-67; assoc. Phillips, Nizer, Benjamin, Krim & Ballon, N.Y.C., 1967-68, Weissberger & Frosch, N.Y.C., 1969-73; ptnr. Weissberger & Harris, 1973-81, Gottlieb Schiff Ticktin & Harris, N.Y.C., 1981-85; pvt. practice, 1985-89, 2000—; of counsel Hall, Dickler, Kent, Friedman & Wood, 1991-2000. Exec. producer NBC spls. Ann. TV Guide Spls., 1979-82. Author: TV Guide: The First 25 Years, 1978; prodr. Weissberger Theater Group. Bd. dirs. Am. Theatre Wing, N.Y.C., 1977—, Williamstown Theatre Festival, 1993—. Recipient Tony award for Best Play, 1999. Mem. N.Y. State Bar Assn. Entertainment. E-mail: jayharrisnyc@aol.com

HARRIS, JERALD DAVID, lawyer; b. July 14, 1947; s. Donald W. and Dorothy (Botwin) H.; m. Carol Sue Fohlen, Mar. 25, 1972; children: Alyse, Jeffrey, Danielle. BA, Miami U., Oxford, Ohio, 1969; JD, U. Cin., 1972. Bar: Ohio 1972, U.,S. Dist. Ct. (so. dist.) Ohio 1972, U.S Ct. Appeals (6th cir.) 1977, U.S. Dist. Ct. (ea. dist.) Ky. 1978, U.S. Supreme Ct. 1978. Assoc. Kondritzer, Gold & Frank, Cin., 1972-75; ptnr., 1975-79; sole practice Cin., 1979-81; sr. ptnr. Harris and Katz Co. LPA, 1982-88, Harris, Bella & Burgin A Legal Profl. Assn., 1988—. Lectr. U. Cin. Coll. of Law, 1986—. Author: Ohio Workers' Compensation Act. 1986; editor Workers' Compensation Jour. Ohio. Co-chmn. young profl. div. Jewish Welfare fund; bd. dirs. Hillel; vice chmn. Isaac M. Wise Temple Bldg. Fund campaign; mem. Young Leadership Coun. of Jewish Fedn. of Cin.; v.p., bd. dirs. Bonds for Israel; mem. Jewish Cmty. Rels. Coun.-WCET; active Jerry Springer for Gov. campaign; county chmn. Supreme Ct. campaign; bd. dirs. ARC, 1975-79; founding sponsor Civil Justice Found.; adv. Atty. General's Workers' Compensation Coun.; mem. Indsl. Commn. Ohio. Mem. Cin. bar Assn. (past chmn. workers compensation com. 1983-86, other coms.), Ohio Bar Assn. (workers compensation com.), Assn. Trial Lawyers Am., Ohio Acad. TrialLawyers (chmn. social security and adminstrv. law sect. 1981-85, chmn. workers compensation edn., com., 1985, vice chmn., regional coord. workers compensation com., chmn. workers compensation sect. 1992-93, legis. coord. com. 1993, Service to legal Profession award 1981, Cert. of Appreciation 1983, Disting. Svc. award, 1985, 87, Hall of Fame award, 1998, trustee), Nat. Orgn. Social Security Claimants Reps. (Ohio chmn. 1981-83), Am. Soc. Law and Medicine, Ohio State Bar Assn. Coll. Cuyahoga bar Assn.) worker's compensation com.), Phi Alpha Theta. Personal injury, Workers' compensation. Home: 10592 Cinderella Dr Cincinnati OH 45242-4909 Office: Harris & Burgin A Legal Profl Assn 9545 Kenwood Rd Ste 301 Cincinnati OH 45242-6100

HARRIS, JOEL B(RUCE), lawyer; b. N.Y.C., Oct. 15, 1941; s. Raymond S. and Laura (Greene) H.; m. Barbara J. Rous, June 13, 1965 (div.); l child, Clifford S.; m. Deborah Sherman, Apr. 1, 1986 (div.); children: Sydney Anne, Cassidy Raye. AB, Columbia U., 1963; LLB, Harvard U., 1966; LLM, U. London, 1967. Bar: N.Y. 1968, U.S. Dist. Ct. (so. dist.) N.Y. 1970, U.S. Ct. Appeals (2d cir.) 1970, U.S. Dist. Ct. (ea. dist.) N.Y. 1975, U.S. Supreme Ct. 1976, U.S. Ct. Appeals (3d cir.) 1980, U.S. Dist. Ct. (we. dist.) N.Y. 1981. Assoc. Simpson, Thacher & Bartlett, N.Y.C., 1967-70; asst. U.S. atty. So. Dist. N.Y., 1970-74, chief civil rights unit, 1973-74; assoc. Weil, Gotshal & Manges, N.Y.C., 1974-76, ptnr., 1976-86, Thacher, Proffitt & Wood, N.Y.C., 1986—; chmn. litigation dept., Latin Am. practice group. Speaker, panelist, moderator confs. Contbr. articles to profl. jours. Knox Meml. fellow, 1966-67. Fellow Am. Bar Found.; mem. ABA (chmn. com. internat. litigation 1981-84, chmn. com. personal rights litigation 1984-87), N.Y. State Bar Assn. (mem. internat. law and practice sect., sect. chair 1997-98, mem. exec. com. 1990—, chmn. internat. dispute resolution com. 1990-93, chmn. seasonal meeting 1993, 2001), Assn. Bar City N.Y., Inter-Am. Bar Assn., Fed. Bar Coun., Am. Soc. Internat. Law, Internat. Law Assn., Am. Judicature Soc. Federal civil litigation, State civil litigation, Private international. Home: 40 Prince St New York NY 10012-3426 Office: Thacher Proffitt & Wood 11 West 42nd St New York NY 10036 E-mail: jharris@thacherproffitt.com

HARRIS, K. DAVID, state supreme court justice; b. Jefferson, Iowa, July 29, 1927; s. Orville William and Jessie Heloise (Smart) H.; m. Madonna Theresa Coyne, Sept. 4, 1948; children: Jane, Julia, Frederick. BA, U. Iowa, 1949, JD, 1951. Bar: Iowa 1951, U.S. Dist. Ct (so. dist.) Iowa, 1958. Sole practice Harris & Harris, Jefferson, 1951-62; dist. judge 16th Judicial Dist., Iowa, 1962-72; justice Iowa Supreme Ct., Des Moines, 1972-99, sr. justice, 1999—. Served with U.S. Army, 1944-46, PTO. Mem. VFW, Am. Legion, Rotary. Roman Catholic. Avocation: writing poetry. Office: Iowa Supreme Ct State Capitol Bldg Des Moines IA 50319-0001

HARRIS, MICALYN SHAFER, lawyer, educator; b. Chgo., Oct. 31, 1941; d. Erwin and Dorothy (Sampson) Shafer. AB, Wellesley Coll., 1963; JD, U. Chgo., 1966. Bar: Ill. 1966, Mo. 1967, U.S. Dist. Ct. (ea. dist.) Mo. 1967, U.S. Supreme Ct. 1972, U.S. Ct. Appeals (8th cir.), 1974, N.Y. 1981, N.J. 1988, U.S. Dist. Ct. N.J., U.S. Ct. Appeals (3d cir.) 1993. Law clk. U.S. Dist. Ct., Mo., 1967-68; atty. The May Dept. Stores, St. Louis, 1968-70, Ralston-Purina Co., St. Louis, 1970-72; atty., asst. sec. Chromalloy Am. Corp., 1972-76; pvt. practice, 1976-78; atty. CPC Internat., Inc., 1978-80; divsn. counsel CPA N.Am., 1980-84, asst. sec., 1981-88; gen. counsel S.B. Thomas, Inc., 1983-87; corp. counsel CPC Internat., Englewood Cliffs, NJ, 1984-88; assoc. counsel Weil, Gotshal & Manges, N.Y.C., 1988-90; pvt. practice, 1991; v.p., sec., gen. counsel Winpro, Inc., 1991—. Arbitrator Am., Arbitration Assn., NYSE, NASD, The Aspen Ctr. Conflict Mgmt.; adj. prof. Lubin Sch. Bus. Pace U. Mem. consultative groups Restatement of Agy. and UCC Article 2. Mem.: ABA (Ctr. Profl. Responsibility com., bus. law sect., chair corp. comm. subcom., past chair subcom. counseling the mktg. function, mem. securities law com., tender offers and proxy statements subcom., legal bus. ethics com., chair task force on e-mail privacy, vice chair subcom. on computer software contracting, task force on electronic contracting, task force on conflicts of interest, ad hoc com. on tech. strategic planning com.), N.Y. State Bar Assn. (exec. com. bus. law sect., securities regulation com., chair technology and internet law com., past chair subcom. on licensing, task force on shrink-wrap licensing), N.J. Bar Assn. (computer law com.), Assn. Bar City N.Y., Bar Assn. Metro St. Louis (past chair TV com.), Mo. Bar Assn. (part chmn. internat. law com.), Am. Corp. Counsel Assn. N.Y. (mergers and acquisitions com., corp. law com.), N.J. Gen. Coun., Computer Law Assn., Am. Law Inst. (mem. consultative groups, restatement of agy., 3d, UCC article 2 and internat. judgements project). Computer, General corporate, Finance. Address: 625 N Monroe St Ridgewood NJ 07450-1206

HARRIS, MICHAEL DAVID, lawyer; b. Cleve., Mar. 16, 1946; s. Harold E. and Belle (Silver) H.; m. Amy L. Jacobson, July 3, 1971; children—Jeffrey Marshall, Andrew Jay. B.S. in Engring., Purdue U., 1969; J.D., Am. U., 1972. Bar: D.C. 1972, U.S. Patent Office 1972, Calif. 1973, U.S. Dist. Ct. (cen. dist.) Calif. 1973, U.S. Ct. Appeals (9th cir.) 1974, U.S. Ct. Customs and Patent Appeals 1981. Examiner U.S. Patent Office, Washington, 1969-72; assoc. then ptnr. Poms, Smith, Lande & Rose, Los Angeles, 1972-82, 87—; ptnr. Koppel & Harris, Westlake Village, Calif., 1982-87; judge pro tem Los Angeles Mcpl. Ct., 1976-84; instr. So. Calif. Inst. Law, Ventura, 1984. Editor Century City Bar Jour., 1977. Mem. Century City Bar Assn. (pres. 1983-84, bd. govs. 1976-86), Los Angeles County Bar Assn. (trustee 1984-85), Los Angeles Patent Law Assn., Ventura County Bar Assn. Libertarian. Jewish. Patent, Trademark and copyright. Home: 5025 Jacobs Ct Oak Park CA 91377-4716 Office: Best & Krieger PO Box 2710 Palm Springs CA 92263-2710

HARRIS, MICHAEL GENE, optometrist, educator, lawyer; b. San Francisco, Sept. 20, 1942; s. Morry and Gertrude Alice (Epstein) H.; m. Dawn Block; children: Matthew Benjamin, Daniel Evan, Ashley Beth, Lindsay Meredith. BS, U. Calif., 1964, M in Optometry, 1965, D in Optometry, 1966, MS, 1968; JD, John F. Kennedy U., 1985. Bar: Calif., U.S. Dist. Ct. (no. dist.) Calif. Assoc. practice optometry, Oakland, Calif., 1965-66, San Francisco, 1966-68; instr., coord. contact lens clinic Ohio State U., 1968-69; asst. clin. prof. optometry U. Calif., Berkeley, 1969-73, dir. contact lens extended care clinic, 1969-83, chief contact lens clinic, 1983—, assoc. clin. prof., 1973-76, asst. chief, then assoc. chief contact lens svc., 1970—, lectr., then sr. lectr., 1978—, vice chmn. faculty Sch. Optometry, 1983-85, 95—, prof. clin. optometry, 1984-86, clin. prof., 1986—, dir. residency program, 1993-95, asst. dean, 1994-95, assoc. dean, 1995—, acting dean, 2000; lectr. Peter's Meml. U. Calif. Sch. Optometry, 2000. Peter's Meml. lectr. U. Calif. Sch. Optometry, 2000; John de Carle vis. prof. City U., London, 1984; vis. rsch. fellow U. NSW, Sydney, Australia, 1989; sr. vis. rsch. scholar U. Melbourne, Victoria, Australia, 1989, 92; pvt. practice optometry, Oakland, 1973-76; mem. ophthalmic devices panel, med. device adv. com. FDA, 1990—, interim chair, 1994; lectr., cons. in field; mem. regulation rev. com. Calif. Bd. Optometry; cons. hypnosis Calif. Optometric Assn., Am. Optometric Assn.; cons. Nat. Bd. Examiners in Optometry, Soflens divsn. Bausch & Lomb, 1973—, Barnes-Hind Hydrocurve Soft Lenses, Inc., 1974-87, Pilkinton-Barnes Hind, 1987-94, Contact Lens Rsch. Lab., 1976-80, Wesley-Jessen Contact Lens Co., 1977-2001, Palo Alto VA, 1980, Primarius Corp., Cooper Vision Optics Alcon, 1980—, CIBA, 1976—, Vistakon, 1980-2000; co-founder Morton D. Sarver Rsch. Lab., 1986; Max Shapero meml. lectr., 1995. Editor current comments sect. Am. Jour. Optometry, 1974-77; editor Eye Contact, 1984-86; assoc. editor The Video Jour. Clin. Optometry, 1988-92; cons. editor Contact Lens Spectrum, 1988—; author: Contact Lenses: Treatment Options for Ocular Disease, Contact Lenses for Pre & Post-Surgery; editor: Problems in Optometry, Special Contact Lens Procedures; Contact Lenses in Ocular Disease, 1990; mem. editl. bd. Contact Lens and Anterior Eye Jour.; contbr. chpts. to books, articles to profl. jours. Planning commr. Town of Moraga, Calif., 1986, vice-chmn., 1987-88, chmn., 1988-90; mem. Town Coun., Moraga, 1992-96, vice-mayor, 1994-95, mem. Medi-Cal. adv. planning commn., 1993-95, chair, 1994-96, with Managed Care commn., 1995—, chair, 1996-98; city county rels. com. Contra Costa County, Calif.; planning commr. City of Pleasant Hill, Calif., 1999—; founding mem. Young Adults divsn. Jewish Welfare Fedn., 1965-69, chmn., 1967-68; commr. Sunday Football League, Contra Costa County, 1974-78; chmarer mem. Jewish Cmty. Ctr. Contra Costa County; founding mem. Jewish Cmty. Mus. San Francisco, 1984; Para-Rabbinic, Temple Isaiah, Lafayette, Calif., 1987, bd. dirs., 1990; life mem. Bay Area Coun. for Soviet Jews, 1976; bd. dirs. Jewish Cmty. Rels. Coun. Greater East Bay, 1979-83, Campolindo Homeowners Assn., 1981-85; grantor Michael G. Harris Family Endowment Fund, U. Calif., Dr. Michael G. Harris Tchg. award U. Calif. Named Alumnus of Yr., U. Calif. Sch. Optometry, 1999; U. Calif. fellow, 1971; Calif. Optometric Assn. scholar, 1965, George Schneider meml. scholar, 1964. Fellow British Contact Lens Assn., British Controller Assn., Am. Acad. Optometry (diplomate cornea and contact lens sect., chmn. contact lens papers, mem. contact lens com. 1974—, vice-chmn. contact lens sect. 1980-82, chmn. sect. 1982-84, immediate past chmn. 1984-86, chmn. jud. com. 1989-2001, chmn. bylaws com. 1989—, ethics taskforce 1999—), Assn. Schs. and Colls. Optometry (coun. on acad. affairs), AAAS, Prentice Soc. (pres.-elect 1994-96, pres. 1996-98); mem. ABA, Internat. Assn. Contact Lens Educators, Am. Optometric Assn. (proctor 1969-79, cons. on hypnosis, mem. contact lens sect., position papers com., mem. com. on ophthalmic stds., subcom. on testing and certification, cons. editor Jour.), Calif. Optometric Assn., Assn. Optometric Contact Lens Educators, Am. Optometric Found., Mexican Soc. Contactology (hon.), Nat. Coun. on Contact Lens Compliance, Internat. Soc. Contact Lens Rsch., Calif. State Bd. Optometry (regulation rev. com.), Calif. Acad. Scis., U. Calif. Optometry Alumni Assn. (life), Contrac Costa Bar Assn., Mus. Soc., JFK U. Sch. Law Alumni Assn., Benjamin Ide Wheeler Soc. U. Calif., Pleasant Hill C. of C., Mensa, Robert Gordon Sproul Assn. U. Calif. Democrat. Office: U Calif Sch Optometry Berkeley CA 94720-0001 E-mail: mharris@spectacle.berkeley.edu

HARRIS, PATRICIA SKALNY, lawyer; b. Detroit, Mar. 28, 1949; d. John Francis and Sophie Skalny. B.A., U. Mich., 1970, J.D., 1974. Bar: Mich. 1974, U.S. Dist. Ct. (ea. dist.) Mich. 1976. Atty. Gen. Motors Corp., Detroit, 1974— . Mem. ABA, Mich. Bar Assn., Women Lawyers Assn., Soc. Automotive Engrs. Federal civil litigation, State civil litigation, Personal injury. Office: Gen Motors Corp 3044 W Grand Blvd Detroit MI 48202-3037

HARRIS, RANDOLPH BURTON, lawyer; b. Highland Park, Ill., June 29, 1951; s. Robert Norman and Mildred (Burton) H.; m. Ruby Harris; children: Taryn, Kyra. AB, Stanford U., 1973; JD, Northwestern U., 1977; MS in Indsl. Rels., Cornell U., 1980. Bar: Oreg. 1978, Wis. 1980, U.S. Ct. Appeals (7th and 9th cirs.) 1978, U.S. Dist. Ct. Oreg. 1978, U.S. Dist. Ct. (ea. and we. dists.) Wis. 1980, U.S. Supreme Ct. 1984. Field rep. Oreg. Bur. Labor, Portland, 1975-77, conciliator, 1977-78; asst. atty. gen. Oreg. Dept. Justice, 1978-79; gen. counsel Pluswood Inc., Oshkosh, Wis., 1980-85; atty. Boglet Gate, Portland, 1986-87, SAIF Corp., Portland, 1987-93, Littler, Mendelson, Portland, 1993-96; area mgr. Pacific N.W. Majestic Ins. Co., Seattle, 1996—. Spkr. NWLAA, Gov.'s Safety Com., LCA. Mem. Am. Jewish Com. Mem. ABA (labor-spl. com. civil rights, litigation com.), Assn. Trial Lawyers Am. Labor, Workers' compensation. E-mail: randyh@maj.esystem.com

HARRIS, SCOTT BLAKE, lawyer; b. N.Y.C., June 18, 1951; s. Stanley Robert and Adele Jean (Ganger) H.; m. Barbara Straughn Harris, Aug. 5, 1978. AB magna cum laude, Brown U., 1973; JD magna cum laude, Harvard U., 1976. Bar: D.C. 1977, U.S. Ct. Appeals (D.C. cir.) 1978, U.S. Supreme Ct. 1983. Law clk. to presiding justice U.S. Dist. Ct., Washington, 1976-77; assoc. Williams & Connolly, 1977-84, ptnr., 1984-93; chief counsel Bur. Export Adminstrn., U.S. Dept. Commerce, 1993-94; chief internat. bur. FCC, 1994-96; ptnr. Gibson, Dunn & Crutcher, Washington, 1996-98; mng. ptnr. Harris, Wiltshire & Grannis LLP, 1998—. Mem. adv. bd. Ctr. for Wireless Tech., Va. Tech. U., 1996-2000, Satellite Comms. Mag., 1996-2000, Time Domain Sys., Inc., 1999—, Critical Infrastructure Fund LLP, 1999—, Telecom. Reports Internat., 2000—, Seriga Networks Inc., 2000—, Morphics Tech., Inc., 2000—. Trustee Fed. Comms. Bar Assn. Found., 1997-2000. Mem. ABA (co-chair telecoms. com., sect. internat. law 1999—), FCBA (co-chair online comms. com.), Phi Beta Kappa. Federal civil litigation, Communications, Private international. Home: 3409 Fulton St NW Washington DC 20007-1436 Office: Harris Wiltshire & Grannis LLP 1200 18th St NW Washington DC 20036-2506 E-mail: sharris@harriswiltshire.com

HARRIS, STANLEY S. judge; b. Washington, Oct. 19, 1927; s. Stanley Raymond and Elizabeth (Sutherland) H.; m. Rebecca Ashley, Aug. 1, 1964; children: Scott Sutherland, Todd Ashley, Mark Ashley. BS, U. Va., 1951, JD, 1953. Bar: D.C. 1953, U.S. Supreme Ct. 1964. Assoc., then ptnr. Hogan & Hartson, Washington, 1953-70; judge Superior Ct. D.C., 1971-72, D.C. Ct. Appeals, 1972-82; U.S. atty. for D.C. Dept. Justice, 1982-83; judge U.S. Dist. Ct. D.C., 1983—, sr. judge, 1996—. Mem. com. on criminal law Jud. Conf. U.S., 1988-94, chmn. com. intercircuit assignments, 1994-2000. Served with U.S. Army, 1945-47. Recipient Judiciary award Assn. Fed. Investigators, 1982. Mem. Bar Assn. D.C. (bd. dirs. 1970-72, Lawyer of Yr. award 1982, Disting. Career award 1996), Lawyers' Club of Washington (pres. 1998-99). Republican. Home: 4982 Sentinel Dr Apt 406 Bethesda MD 20816-3579 Office: US Dist Ct US Courthouse 333 Constitution Ave NW Washington DC 20001-2802

HARRIS, TERRELL LEE, prosecutor; BA, Rhodes Coll.; JD, U. Miss. Assoc. Kirkpatrick, Kirkpatrick and Efird, Memphis, 1986—87; asst. dist. atty. gen. Shelby County Dist. Atty.'s Office, 1987—2001; U.S. atty. We. Dist. Tenn. U.S. Dept. Justice, 2001—. Office: 800 Clifford Davis fed Office Bldg 167 N Main St Memphis TN 38103-1898*

HARRIS, THOMAS V. lawyer; b. N.Y.C., Apr. 6, 1948; s. Bernard V. and Miriam (Sullivan) H.; m. Marcia Elizabeth Vogler, Aug. 11, 1979; children: Stephen Charles, Laura Jane. A.B. cum laude, Harvard U., 1970; J.D., Cornell U., 1973. Bar: Wash. 1973, U.S. Dist. Ct. (we. dist.) Wash. 1973, U.S. Dist. Ct. (ea. dist.) Wash. 1980, U.S. Ct. Appeals (9th cir.) 1973. Shareholder, dir. Merrick, Hofstedt & Lindsey, P.S., Seattle, 1973— ; moot ct. judge U. Wash., 1981— . Contbr. articles to profl. jours. Mem. ABA, Internat. Assn. Ins. Counsel. Roman Catholic. Club: Wash. Athletic. Federal civil litigation, Insurance, Personal injury. Home: 8860 SE 74th Pl Mercer Island WA 98040-5700 Office: Merrick Hofstedt & Lindsey PS 710 9th Ave Seattle WA 98104-2017

HARRIS, WAYNE MANLEY, lawyer; b. Dec. 28, 1925; s. George H. and Constance M. Harris; m. Diane C. Quigley, Sept. 30, 1978; children: Wayne, Constance, Karen, Duncan, Claire. LLB, U. Rochester, 1951. Bar: N.Y. 1952, U.S. Supreme Ct. 1958. Ptnr. Harris, Chesworth & O'Brien (and predecessor firms), Rochester, N.Y., 1958—. Drafter 5 laws passed in N.Y. State. Pres. Delta Labs, Inc. (non-profit environ. lab.) Adopt-A-Stream program, 1971—, Friends of Bristol Valley Playhouse Found., 1984-87, Monroe County Conservation Coun. Inc., 1956-61, v.p., 1984-87; v.p. Powder Mills Pk. Hatchery Preservation Inc., 1993-95, pres., 1995—. With combat inf., Germany, 1944-46. Decorated Bronze Star; recipient Sportsman of Yr. award Genesee Conservation League, Inc., 1960, Conservationist of Yr. award Monroe County Conservation Coun., Inc., 1961, Kiwanian of Yr. award Kiwanis Club, 1965, Livingston County Fedn. of Sportsmen award, 1966, N.Y. State Conservation Coun. Nat. Wildlife Fedn. Water Conservation Conservationist of Yr. award, 1967, Rochester Acad. Sci. Hon. Fellowship award, 1970, Conservation award Nat. Am. Motor Corp., 1971, Meritorious Leadership in Civic Devel. award Rochester C. of C., 1972, Svc. award Rochester Against Intoxicated Drivers, 1989, Vol. Conservationist of Yr., N.Y. State Conservation Coun. Inc., 2000, N.Y. State Conspicuous Svc. Cross, 2000, NY Senate Resolution 241 award, 2001. Mem. ATLA, N.Y. State Trial Lawyers Assn., AIDA Reins. and Arbitration Soc., Indsl. Mgmt. Coun., Wild Turkey Fedn. State civil litigation, General corporate, Probate. Home: 60 Mendon Center Rd Honeoye Falls NY 14472-9363 Office: Harris Chesworth & O'Brien 1820 East Ave Rochester NY 14610-1829

HARRISON, BRYAN GUY, lawyer; b. Norman, Okla., Nov. 22, 1963; s. Danny Guy and Judith Kay (Dalke) H.; m. Kathleen Hazel Cody, May 8, 1993. BS, Lehigh U., 1986; JD, Emory U., 1989. Bar: Tex. 1989, Ga. 1991. Assoc. Shank, Irwin, Conant, Lipshy & Casterline, Dallas, 1989-90; trial atty. antitrust div. U.S. Dept. Justice, 1990-91; assoc. Morris, Manning & Martin, Atlanta, 1991-97, ptnr., 1998—. Antitrust, General civil litigation, Computer. Office: Morris Manning & Martin 3343 Peachtree Rd NE Ste 1600 Atlanta GA 30326-1044

HARRISON, DAVID GEORGE, lawyer; b. Albany, Oreg., Apr. 6, 1945; s. Russell Benjamin and Altha Edna (Green) H.; m. Katherine Scott Crockett, Jan. 2, 1971; children— Elizabeth, Scott. B.S., Oreg. State U., 1967; M.B.A., Am. U., 1973; J.D., U. Oreg., 1973. Bar: Oreg. 1973, D.C. 1974, Tenn. 1975, Va. 1978, U.S. Dist. Ct. (ea. dist.) Tenn. 1975, U.S. Dist. Ct. (we. dist.) Va. 1978, U.S. Dist. Ct. (ea. dist.) Va. 1982, U.S. Ct. Appeals (4th cir.) 1978. Legal counsel, sec. Tenn. Forging Steel Corp., Harriman, Tenn., 1974-77; atty. Martin, Hopkins & Lemon, Roanoke, Va., 1977-81, Wetherington & Melchionna, Roanoke, 1981— . Bd. dirs. Family Service of Roanoke Valley, 1982-84, mem. exec. com., 1983-84. Served with U.S. Army, 1968-71. Mem. ABA (mem. antitrust and labor relations com. of labor and employment law sect. 1978), Va. State Bar, Va. Bar Assn., Roanoke Bar Assn., D.C. Bar, Oreg. State Bar. Presbyterian. Club: Kiwanis. Contracts commercial, General corporate, Securities. Office: Weatherington & Melchionna 1100 United Va Bank Bldg Roanoke VA 24011

HARRISON, DONALD, lawyer; b. N.Y.C., Mar. 2, 1946; s. David and Arlene Beverly (Johnson) H. BA magna cum laude, Harvard U., 1967, JD magna cum laude, 1971. Bar: D.C. 1973, U.S. Ct. Internat. Trade 1975, U.S. Ct. Appeals (Fed. cir.) 1982, U.S. Supreme Ct. 1979. Law clk. to judge Francis L. Van Dusen U.S. Ct. Appeals 3d circuit, Phila., 1972-73; ptnr. Gibson, Dunn & Crutcher, 1988—. Editor Harvard Law Rev., 1969-71. Private international. Office: Gibson Dunn & Crutcher Washington Sq 1050 Connecticut Ave NW Ste 900 Washington DC 20036-5306

HARRISON, EARL DAVID, lawyer, real estate executive; b. Bryn Mawr, Pa., Aug. 25, 1932; divorced; 1 child, H. Jason. BA, Harvard U., 1954; JD, U. Pa., 1960. Bar: D.C. 1960. Pvt. practice, Washington; exec. v.p. Washington Real Estate Corp., 1986-94; pres. EDH Assocs., Inc., 1994—. Capt. U.S. Army, 1954-57. Decorated Order of Rio Branco (Brazil); Order of Merit (Italy). Mem.: ABA, Internat. Coun. Shopping Ctrs., D.C. Bar Assn., Washington Assn. Realtors, Greater Washington Comml. Assn. Realtors, Nat. Assn. Realtors, Nat. Restaurant Assn., Met. Washington Restaurant Assn., Coun. Internat. Restaurant Real Estate Brokers Ltd. (v.p., gen. coun.), Harvard Club, Nat. Press Club, U. Pa. Club. Contracts commercial, Private international, Real property. Office: 1077 30th St NW Ste 706 Washington DC 20007-3834 E-mail: david@edhassoc.com

HARRISON, FRANK J. lawyer; b. Streator, Ill., Dec. 5, 1919; s. Frank Joseph and Nell (Webb) H.; children: Ellen Harrison Greinacher, Paul, Janice Harrison Tienhaara, Mark. AB, U. Chgo., 1941, JD, 1947; LLM, Harvard U., 1947. Bar: Ill. 1942. Atty. Chgo. Title and Trust Co., 1948-51, Pub. Housing Adminstrn., Chgo., 1951-53; pvt. practice Streator, 1953—; city atty. City of Streator, 1965-71, 73-87; twp. atty., 1990-97. Sr. law clk. Ill. Appellate Ct. 3d Dist., Ottawa, 1971-76; atty. Streator Twp. High. Sch., 1975-83. Compiler, editor: Streator Mcpl. Code of 1968, 1968. Sgt. Signal Intelligence Svc. AUS, 1942-46, PTO, 1st lt. JAGC, 1949. Mem. Ill. Bar Assn., La Salle County Bar Assn., Streator Bar Assn. (pres. 1986-96). Presbyterian. Avocations: tennis, music. General practice, Probate, Real property. Home: 135 W 1st St Streator IL 61364-1241 Office: 114 N Bloomington St Streator IL 61364-2208

HARRISON, JOHN CONWAY, state supreme court justice; b. Grand Rapids, Minn., Apr. 28, 1913; s. Francis Randall and Ethlyn (Conway) H.; m. Ethel M. Strict; children: Nina Lyn, Robert Charles, Molly M., Frank R., Virginia Lee LLD, George Washington U., 1940. Bar: Mont. 1947, U.S. Dist. Ct. 1947. County atty. Lewis and Clark County, Helena, Mont., 1934-60; justice Mont. Supreme Ct., 1961-98, ret., 1998. Pres. Mont. TB Assn., Helena, 1951-54, Am. Lung Assn., N.Y.C., 1972-73, Mont. coun. Boy Scouts Am., Great Falls, Mont., 1976-78. Col. U.S. Army Mem. ABA, Mont. Bar Assn., Kiwanis (pres. 1953), Sigma Chi. Home: 215 S Cooke St Helena MT 59601-5143

HARRISON, KEITH MICHAELE, law educator; b. Washington, Nov. 6, 1956; s. Charles Thomas Harrison Sr. and June Earlene (Bell) Harrison-Russ; m. Karen Marie Anderson, Aug. 21, 1982; children: Michaele Marie, David Tyler. BA, St. John's Coll., Santa Fe, N.Mex., 1977; JD, U. Chgo., 1981. Bar: Ill. 1981, D.C. 1982, N.Y. 1985. Clin. teaching fellow Antioch Sch. Law, Washington, 1985-86; asst. prof. law No. Ill. U., DeKalb, 1986-89, U. Denver, 1989-94, assoc. prof. law, 1994-2001; pres.-elect faculty senate, 1995-96; pres. faculty senate, 1996-98; assoc. dean Coll. Law, 1998-2000; vice dean, prof. law Franklin Pierce Law Ctr., Concord, New Hampshire, 2001—. Vis. prof. Syracuse U. Coll. Law, 1993; vis. lectr. Escuela de Relaciones Internacionales, Universidad Nacional, Heredia, Costa Rica, 1993. V.p. Sam Cary (Colo.) Scholarship Endowment Fund, 1991. Served to lt. USCG, 1981-85. Mem. D.C. Bar Assn., Sam Cary Bar Assn. (treas. 1991), Multiplikatoren Group (Germany). Office: Franklin Pierce Law Ctr 2 White St Concord NH 03301

HARRISON, MARION EDWYN, lawyer; b. Phila., Sept. 17, 1931; s. Marion Edwyn and Jessye Beatrice (Cilles) H.; m. Carmelita Ruth Deimel, Sept. 6, 1952; children: Angelique Marie (Mrs. Kevin B. Bounds), Marion Edwyn III, Henry Deimel. BA, U. Va., 1951; LLB, George Washington U., 1954, LLM, 1959. Bar: Va. 1954, D.C. 1958, Supreme Ct. 1958. Spl. asst. to gen. counsel Post Office Dept., 1958-60, assoc. gen. counsel, 1960-61, mem. bd. contract appeals, 1958-61; ptnr. firm Harrison, Lucey & Sagle (and predecessors), Washington, 1961-78, Barnett & Alagia, 1978-84; ptnr. Scott, Harrison & McLeod, 1984-86, Law Offices Marion Edwyn Harrison, Washington, 1986—. Mem. coun. Adminstrv. Conf. U.S., 1971-78, sr. conf. fellow, 1984-88; mem. D.C. Law Revision Commn., 1975-92; lectr. Nat. Jud. Coll., Reno, 1979, La. State U. Law Sch., Aix-en-Provence, 1987, 89, Tulane U. Law Sch., Crete, 1997, Hofstra U. Law Sch., Nice, 1999, Pa. State U. Dickinson Law Sch., Vienna, 2000, Tulane U. Law Sch., Thessalonika, 2001; adv. dir. NationsBank, N.A., 1987-93. Contbr. articles to profl. pubs.; editor-in-chief Fed. Bar News, 1960-63; mem. editorial bd. Adminstrv. Law Rev., 1976-89. Trustee AEFC Pension Fund, Chgo., 1986-92; pres. Young Rep. Fedn. Va., 1954-55; mem. Va. Rep. Cen. Com., 1954-55; bd. visitors Judge Adv. Gen. Sch., Charlottesville, Va., 1976-78; chmn. Wolf Trap Assn., 1984-87; bd. dirs. Wolf Trap Found., 1984-88; pub. mem. USIA Insp. Mission, Argentina, 1971. Officer AUS, 1955-58. Decorated Commendation medal. Fellow Am. Bar Found. (life); mem. ABA (chmn. sect. adminstrv. law 1974-75, ho. of dels. 1978-88, bd. govs. 1982-86, chmn. com. on fgn. and internat. orgns. 1986-87, lawyers in govt. com. 1980-82), FBA (nat. coun. 1966-82), Inter-Am. Bar Assn., Bar Assn. D.C. (chmn. adminstrv. law sect. 1970-71, bd. dirs. 1971-72), George Washington U. Law Assn. (pres. 1974-77), Smithsonian Instn. (nat. bd. dirs. 1991-97), Federalist Soc., Soc. Mayflower Desc., Washington Golf and Country Club, Met. Club, Nat. Lawyers Club (Washington), Farmington Country Club (Charlottesville, Va.), Gainey Ranch Golf Club (Scottsdale, Ariz.), Knight of Malta. Republican. Roman Catholic. Administrative and regulatory, General practice, Private international. Home: 4111 N Ridgeview Rd Arlington VA 22207-4617 Address: 7222 E Gainey Ranch Rd Scottsdale AZ 85258-1529 Office: 1700 K St NW Ste 700 Washington DC 20006-3813 Address: 107 Park Washington Ct Falls Church VA 22046-4519 also: Dufourstrasse 32 8008 Zurich Switzerland

HARRISON, MARK ISAAC, lawyer; b. Pitts., Oct. 17, 1934; s. Coleman and Myrtle (Seidenman) H.; m. Ellen R. Gier, June 15, 1958; children: Lisa, Jill. AB, Antioch Coll., 1957; LLB, Harvard U., 1960. Bar: Ariz. 1961, Colo. 1991. Law clk. to justices Ariz. Supreme Ct., 1960-61; ptnr. Harrison, Harper, Christian & Dichter, Phoenix, 1966-93, Bryan Cave, LLP, Phoenix, 1993—. Adj. prof. U. Ariz. Coll. Law, 1995-97, Ariz. State Coll. Law, 2001—; nat. bd. visitors, 1996—. Co-author: Arizona Appellate Practice, 1966; editorial bd. ABA/BNA Lawyers Manual on Profl. Conduct, 1983-86; contbr. articles to profl. jours. Fellow Am. Bar Found., Am. Acad. Appellate Lawyers (pres. 1993-94); mem. ABA (chmn. commn. pub. understanding law 1984-87, standing com. profl. discipline 1976-84, chmn. 1982-84, chmn. coord. com. on professionalism 1987-89, com. on women in the profession, ethics com. 1999—, Michael Franck Profl. Responsibility award 1996), Assn. Profl. Responsibility Lawyers (pres. 1992-93), Maricopa County Bar Assn. (pres. 1970), Am. Bd. Trial Advocates, State Bar Ariz. (bd. govs. 1971-77, pres. 1975-76), Ariz. Bar Found. (pres. 1991), Am. Inns of Ct. (master, pres. Sandra Day O'Connor chpt. 1993-94), Nat. Conf. Bar Pres. (pres. 1977-78), Western States Bar Conf. (pres. 1978-79), Am. Judicature Soc. (exec. com. 1983-86, bd. dirs. 1983-87), Ariz. Civil Liberties Union, Ariz. Policy Forum (bd. dirs. 2000—), , Harvard Law Sch. Assn. (nat. exec. coun. 1980-84), Am. Law Inst. (nat. coun., lawyers com. for human rights), Law Coll. Assn. U. Ariz. (bd. dirs. 1999—). E-mila. General civil litigation, Professional liability. Office: Bryan Cave 2 N Central Ave Ste 2200 Phoenix AZ 85004-4406 E-mail: ellenmark@aol.com, miharrison@bryancave.com

HARRISON, MICHAEL GREGORY, judge; b. Lansing, Mich., Aug. 4, 1941; s. Gus and Jean D. (Fuller) H.; m. Deborah L. Dunn, June 17, 1972; children: Abigail Ann, Adam Christopher, Andrew Stephen. AB, Albion (Mich.) Coll., 1963; JD, U. Mich., 1966; postgrad., George Washington U. Bar: Mich. 1966, U.S. Dist. Ct. (ea. and we. dists.) Mich. 1967. Asst. pros. atty. County of Ingham, Lansing, 1968-70, corp. counsel, 1970-76; judge 30th Jud. Cir. State of Mich., 1976-2000; chief judge 30th Jud. Cir. State of Mich., 1980-91; judge Ct. of Claims, 1979-2000; of counsel Foster, Swift, Collins and Smith, Lansing, 2000—. Counsel Capital Region Airport Authority, Lansing, 1970-76, Ingham Med. Ctr., Lansing, 1970-76; chmn. Ingham County Bldg. Authority, Mason, Mich., 1971-76; adj. prof. Thomas M. Cooley Law Sch., Lansing, 1976—. Editor Litigation Control, 1996; contbr. chpt. to Michigan Municipal Law, Actions of Governing Bodies, 1980; contbr. articles to profl. jours. Mem. shared vision steering com. United Way-C. of C.; mem. adv. bd. Hospice of Lansing, 1989—; pres. Greater Lansing Urban League, 1974-76, Lansing Symphony Assn., 1974-76; chmn. Mid. Mich. chpt. ARC, Lansing, 1984-86; bd. dirs., sec. St. Lawrence Hosp., Lansing, 1980-88; bd. dirs. ARC Gt. Lakes Regional Blood Svcs., 1991-95, Lansing 2000, 1987—; mem. exec. bd. Chief Okemos coun. Boy Scouts Am.; mem. criminal justice adv. com. Olivet Coll.; hon. bd. dirs. Lansing Area Safety Coun.; mem. State Bar Bd. Commrs., 1993-96; mem. felony sentencing guidelines steering com., mem. caseflow mgmt. coordinating com., mem. juror use and mgmt. task force Mich. Supreme Ct. Recipient Disting. Citizens award Boy Scouts Am., Disting. Vol. award Ingham County Bar Assn., Disting. Alumni award Albion Coll. Fellow: Am. Bar Found., Mich. Bar Assn.; mem.: ABA (coun.mem.judicial divsn., coun. mem. tort and ins. practice session), Am. Judicature Soc. (bd. dirs. 1996—), Mich. State U. Am. Inn of Ct. (pres. 2001—, master), Mich. Judges Assn. (treas. 1991, sec. 1992, 2d v.p. 1993, 1st v.p. 1994, pres. 1995), Nat. Conf. State Trial Judges (exec. com. 1991—94, vice chmn. 1995—96, chmn. 1997—98), Country Club, Lansing, Rotary Club, Lansing. Republican. Congregationalist. Avocations: skiing, golf, tennis, travel, photography. Office: 313 S Washington Sq Lansing MI 48933-2193 E-mail: mharrison@fosterswift.com*

HARRISON, MOSES W., II, state supreme court chief justice; b. Collinsville, Ill., Mar. 30, 1932; m. Sharon Harrison; children: Luke, Clarence. BA, Colo. Coll.; LLB, Washington U., St. Louis. Bar: Ill. 1958, Mo. 1958. Pvt. practice, 1958-73; judge 3d Jud. Cir., Ill., 1973-79, 5th Dist. Appellate Ct., 1979-92; chief justice Ill. Supreme Ct., 1992—. Mem. ABA, Am. Judicature Soc., Ill. State Bar Assn. (former bd. govs.), Madison County Bar Assn. (former pres.), Tri-City Bar Assn., Met. St. Louis Bar Assn., Justinian Soc. Office: 333 Salem Pl Ste 170 Fairview Heights IL 62208-1363

HARRISON, PATRICK WOODS, lawyer; b. St. Louis, July 14, 1946; s. Charles William and Carolyn (Woods) H.; m. Rebecca Tout, Dec. 23, 1967; children: Heather Ann, Heath Aaron. BS, Ind. U., 1968, JD, 1972. Bar: Ind. 1973, U.S. Dist. Ct. (so. dist.) Ind. 1973, U.S. Dist. Ct. Nebr. 1982, U.S. Supreme Ct. 1977. Assoc. Goltra, Cline, King & Beck, Columbus, Ind., 1972-73; ptnr. Goltra & Harrison, 1973-78; pvt. practice, 1979-80; ptnr. Cline, King, Beck and Harrison, 1980-85, Beck, Harrison & Dalmbert, Columbus, 1985—. Ind. Jud. Nominating Commn. nominee Ind. Supreme Ct., 1984. With U.S. Army, 1968-70. Fellow Ind. Trial Lawyers Assn. (bd. dirs. 1984, emeritus dir. 1999, Co-Trial Lawyer of Yr. 1999); mem. Am. Trial Lawyers Assn. Republican. Baptist. Avocation: golf. State civil litigation, Personal injury. Home: 14250 W Mount Healthy Rd Columbus IN 47201-9309 Office: Beck Harrison & Dalmbert 320 Franklin St Columbus IN 47201-6732 E-mail: beckyt@iquest.net, harrison@hsonline.net

HARRISON, RICHARD WAYNE, lawyer; b. Marfa, Tex., June 23, 1944; Ptnr. Florence & Harrison, Hughes Springs, Tex., 1968-69; pvt. practice, 1969-73; asst. atty. gen. Atty. Gen.'s Office of Tex., Austin, 1973-74, chief tax divsn., 1974-76, spl. asst. atty. gen., 1976-78; ptnr. McGinnis, Lochridge & Kilgore, 1978-87, Jones, Day, Reavis & Pogue, Austin, 1987-94; mng. ptnr. Harrison & Rial, L.L.P., 1994-2000; owner Rick Harrison & Assocs., 2000—. Trustee, treas. St. Andrew's Episcopal Sch., Austin; precinct chmn. Cass County Dem. Com., 1969-73; pres. Hughes Springs Indsl. Found., 1970; Cass County chmn. Salvation Army, 1970-72; area coord. Lloyd Bentsen for Senate Com., 1970; chmn. Hughes Springs United Fund Drive, 1972; mem. Austin Convocation Cursillo Steering Com., 1983-86, chmn., 1985-86; sr. warden St. Luke's-on-the-Lake Episcopal Ch., 1984. Fellow Tex. Bar Found.; mem. State Bar of Tex. (fed. jud. com. 1980-83, bar jour. com. 1980-83), Travis County Bar Assn., Cass County Bar Assn. (past pres.), Schreiner Coll. Former Student Assn. (bd. dirs. 1984-88), Austin Club, Horseshoe Bay Country Club, Barton Creek Country Club, Masons. Democrat. Federal civil litigation, State civil litigation, State and local taxation. Home: 1730 Camp Craft Rd Austin TX 78746-7317 Office: Rick Harrison & Assocs 100 Congress Ave Ste 1550 Austin TX 78701-2744

HARRISON, SAMUEL HUGHEL, lawyer; b. Atlanta, Jan. 12, 1956; s. Gresham Hughel and Leslie (Powell) H.; m. Margaret Mary Carew, June 24, 1978; 1 child, Peter James. Student, Mercer U., 1974-75; BA magna cum laude, Washington & Lee U., 1978; JD cum laude, U. Ga., 1981. Bar: Ga. 1981, U.S. Dist. Ct. (no. dist.) Ga. 1981, U.S. Ct. Appeals (11th cir.) 1981, U.S. Dist. Ct. (mid. dist.) Ga. 1985. Ptnr. Harrison & Harrison, Lawrenceville, Ga., 1981-86, 87—; solicitor state ct. Gwinnett County, 1986. Vestryman St. Edward the Confessor Episcopal Ch., Lawrenceville, 1983-86; coun. del. Episcopal Diocese of Atlanta, 1986, 88; chancellor St. Matthew's Episcopal Ch., Snellville, Ga., 1998-99; mem. Gwinnett County Bd. Registrations and Elections, 1991-96; mem. exec. com. Gwinnett Dems., 1991-96; troop scoutmaster Boy Scouts Am. Mem. Ga. Bar Assn. (mock trial com. young lawyers sect. 1987-88), Ga. Assn. Criminal Def. Lawyers, Nat. Assn. Criminal Def. Lawyers. Avocations: photography, history (Revolutionary War reenactor), books. Criminal, Family and matrimonial. Office: Harrison & Harrison 151 W Pike St # 88 Lawrenceville GA 30045-4939

HARRISON, THOMAS FLATLEY, lawyer; b. N.Y.C., Jan. 11, 1942; s. John P. and Mary F. (Flatley) H.; m. Lorraine Brereton, Aug. 16, 1969; children: John J., Jane C., Ann B., Peter T. AB, Holy Cross Coll., 1963; JD, Fordham U., 1966. Bar: N.Y. 1967, Ill. 1979, Ohio 1981, D.C. 1988, Conn. 1989. Asst. counsel N.Y.C. Dept. Rent and Housing, 1966-69; asst. atty. gen. N.Y. State Dept. Law, 1969-74; chief enforcement N.Y. region U.S. EPA, 1974-76, regional counsel Chgo., 1976-80; sr. corp. counsel B.F. Goodrich Co., Akron, Ohio, 1980-87; ptnr. Manatt, Phelps, Rothenberg & Evans, Washington, 1987-88; ptnr., co-chmn. environ. and land use dept. Day, Berry & Howard LLP, Hartford, Conn., 1988—. Faculty Practising Law Inst. Contbr. articles to profl. jours. Mem. 49th Assembly Dist. Rep. Orgn., N.Y.C., 1963-73, bd. govs., 1969-73; active Silver Lake, Ohio, Rep. Orgn., 1981-87; mem. Rep. Town Com., Avon, Ct., 1991—, Inland Wetlands Commn., Avon, 1992-95, Bd. Fin. 1995—, Conn. Coun. on Environ. Quality, 1997—; mem. Conn. Small Bus. Compliance Adv. Panel, 1996—; bd. dirs. Conn. League of Conservation Voters, 2000—. Recipient Outstanding Performance award EPA, 1976. Mem. Conn. Bar Assn. (exec. com. environ. law sect. 1989—, sect. chair 1998-99). Roman Catholic. Administrative and regulatory, General corporate, Environmental. Home: 51 Briar Hill Rd Avon CT 06001-4007 Office: Day Berry & Howard LLP City Place Hartford CT 06103-3499 E-mail: tfharrison@dbh.com

HARROD, DANIEL MARK, lawyer; b. Peoria, Ill., Sept. 23, 1945; s. Samuel Glenn and Dorothe Grace (White) H.; m. Amy Lynn Moore, June 4, 1993; children: Maggie, Emily. BA, Eureka (Ill.) Coll., 1967; JD, John Marshall Law Sch., 1975. Bar: Ill., U.S. Dist. Ct. Ill., U.S. Supreme Ct. Pub. defender Woodford County, Eureka, 1980-90; prin. Harrod Law Firm. Chmn., bd. dirs. Peoria Area Civic Chorale, Peoria, 1990—. Lt. col. Ill. Air N.G., 1967-88. Mem. Rotary (sgt. at arms 1985—). Avocations: tennis, racquetball. Criminal, Family and matrimonial, Real property. Home: 206 Moody St Eureka IL 61530-1705 Office: Harrod Law Firm 107 E Eureka Ave Eureka IL 61530-1239

HARROLD, BERNARD, lawyer; b. Wells County, Ind., Feb. 5, 1925; s. James Delmer and Marie (Mounsey) H.; m. Kathleen Walker, Nov. 26, 1952; children— Bernard James, Camilla Ruth, Renata Jane. Student, Biarritz Am. U., 1945; AB, Ind. U., 1949, LLB, 1951. Bar: Ill. 1951. Since practiced in, Chgo.; assoc., then mem. firm Kirkland, Ellis, Hodson, Chaffetz & Masters, 1951-67; sr. ptnr. Wildman, Harrold, Allen & Dixon, 1967—. Note editor: Ind. Law Jour, 1950-51; contbr. articles to profl. jours. Served with AUS, 1944-46, ETO. Fellow Am. Coll. Trial Lawyers, Acad. Law Alumni Fellows Ind. U. Sch. Law; mem. ABA, Ill. Bar Assn. (chmn. evidence program 1970), Chgo. Bar Assn, Lawyers Club, Univ. Club, Order of Coif, Phi Beta Kappa, Phi Eta Sigma. Antitrust, General civil litigation, Environmental. Home: 809 Locust St Winnetka IL 60093-1821 Office: Wildman Harrold Allen & Dixon 225 W Wacker Dr Fl 28 Chicago IL 60606-1229

HARSHMAN, RAYMOND BRENT, lawyer; b. Athens, Ala., Feb. 16, 1948; s. L. Raymond and B. Katherine (Laubenthal) H.; m. Letha Lee, Nov. 30, 1974; 3 children. BSBA, U. Tenn., 1969; JD, So. Meth. U., 1973. Bar: Tex. 1973, U.S. Ct. Appeals (D.C. and 5th cirs.) 1986, U.S. Ct. Appeals (6th cir.) 1989, Colo. 1992, U.S. Ct. Appeals (11th cir.) 1992. Instr., atty. Abilene (Tex.) Christian U., 1973-74; tax acct./tax atty. Exxon Co., USA, Houston, 1974-76; gas contract rep. Tex. Gas Transmission Corp., 1976-78; atty. Diamond Shamrock Corp., Amarillo, Tex., 1978-81; sr. atty. Diamond Shamrock Exploration Co., f1981-86; assoc. counsel Maxus Energy Corp., Dallas, 1986-90, sr. counsel, 1991-99; ind. atty., 2000; sr. atty. Austin Energy, 2001—. Mem. State Bar Tex., Fed. Energy Bar Assn. Mem. Ch. of Christ. FERC practice, Oil, gas, and mineral.

HART, B. CLARENCE, lawyer; b. Promise City, Iowa, Mar. 19, 1923; s. Harry H. and Alfreda (DeBolt) H.; m. Jean E. Hart, July 7, 1933; children: Nannette, Kyle, Charles, Charlotte. AB, U. Iowa, 1947; JD, Harvard U., 1950. BAr: Minn. 1951, U.S. Ct. Mil. Appeals 1956, U.S. Supreme Ct. 1956. Ptnr. Briggs and Morgan, P.C., St. Paul, 1951-76, pres., 1976-83, Hart, Bruner, O'Brien & Thprnton and predecessors, Mpls., 1983—. V.p. Downtown St. Paul, 1956—59; bd. dirs. Lakewood Coll. Found., 1974—76; mem. Minn. Citizens Com. for Voyageurs Nat. Park, 1975—; co. chmn. United Fund, bd. dirs., 1958—61, 1981—; mem. midwest regional adv. com. Nat. Park Svc. Lt. col. USAR. Recipient Cornerstone award Forum Commn. on Constrn. Industry, others. Fellow: Am. Bar Found.; mem.: ATLA, ABA (chmn. tort and ins. practice sect. 1980—81, Martin J. Andrew Lifetime Achievement award, Tips Andrew Hecker Lifetime Achievement award), Minn. Bar Assn. (chmn.ct. rules com. 1973—77), Fed. Bar Assn., Ramsey County Bar Assn., Internat. Assn. Ins. Counsel, Am. Coll. Trial Lawyers, Am. Bd. Trial Advocates (state pres. 1973), Am. Coll. Constrn. Arbitrators, Am. Coll. Constr. Lawyers, Harvard Law Sch. Assn. (state pres. Minn., nat. v.p.), St. Paul Athletic Club, Minn. Club (bd. dirs. 1980—86), Phi Beta Kappa. Federal civil litigation, State civil litigation, Construction. Office: Fabyanske Westra & Hart 920 2d Ave S Ste 1100 Minneapolis MN 55402 E-mail: bchart@minnlaw.com

HART, BROOK, lawyer; b. N.Y.C., Aug. 24, 1941; s. Walter and Julie H.; divorced; children: Morgan M., Leilani L., Ashley I., Ariel J. BA, Johns Hopkins U., 1963; LL.B., Columbia U., 1966. Bar: N.Y. 1966, U.S. Ct. Appeals (9th cir.) 1967, Hawaii 1968, U.S. Supreme Ct. 1972, Calif. 1973. Law clk. to chief judge U.S. Dist. Ct. Hawaii, 1966-67; assoc. counsel Legal Aid Soc. Hawaii, 1968; assoc. Greenstein and Cowan, Honolulu, 1968-70; chief pub. defender State of Hawaii, 1970-72; co-founder, ptnr. Hart, Leavitt, Hall and Hunt, Honolulu, 1972-80, Hart and Wolff, Honolulu, 1980-96; sr. ptnr. Law Offices of Brook Hart, 1996—. Instr. course U. Hawaii, 1972-73, lectr. Sch. Law, 1974—; apptd. Nat. Commn. to Study Def. Svcs., 1974, Planning Group for U.S. Dist. Ct. Hawaii, 1975; spl. counsel City Coun. of City and County of Honolulu, 1976-77, spl. investigative counsel to trustee in bankruptcy THC Fin. Corp., 1977; mem. Jud. Coun. STate of Hawaii com. on revision state penal codes, 1984—; lectr. schs., profl., civic groups; mem. com. to select Fed. Pub. Defender Dist. of Hawaii, 1981, 95. Contbr. chpts. to books, articles to profl. publs. Recipient Reginald Heber Smith award Nat. Legal Aid and Defender Assn., 1971; named Bencher, Am. Inn of Ct., Hawaii, 1982—. Fellow Am. Bd. Criminal Lawyers; mem. ABA, Hawaii Bar Assn., State Bar Calif., Am. Judicature Soc., Nat. Legal Aid and Defender Assn., Nat. Assn. Criminal Def. Lawyers, Calif. Attys. for Criminal Justice. Federal civil litigation, General civil litigation, Criminal. Office: 333 Queen St Honolulu HI 96813-4726 E-mail: hartlaw@hawaii.rr.com

HART, CHRISTOPHER ALVIN, lawyer; b. Denver, June 18, 1947; s. Judson Duncan and M. Murlee (Shaw) H.; 1 child, Adam Christopher. B.S. in Aerospace Engring., Princeton U., 1969, M.S. in Aerospace Engring., 1971; J.D., Harvard U., 1973. Bar: D.C. 1973, U.S. Dist. Ct. D.C. 1973, U.S. Ct. Appeals (D.C. cir.) 1973, U.S. Ct. Appeals (8th cir.) 1981, U.S. Supreme Ct. 1985. Assoc. Peabody, Rivlin & Lambert, Washington, 1973-76, Dickstein, Shapiro & Marin, Washington, 1979-81; gen. atty. Air Transport Assn., Washington, 1976-77; dep. asst. gen. counsel U.S. Dept. Transp., Washington, 1977-79; charter, prin. firm Hart & Chavers, Washington, 1981-90; mem. Nat. Transp. Safety Bd., 1990-93; dep. adminstr. Nat. Highway Traffic Safety Adminstrn., 1993-94; assoc. adminstr. for system safety Fed. Aviation Adminstrn., 1994—. Bd. dirs. Howard U. Hosp. Cancer Ctr., Washington, 1983-88, WPFW (Pacific Found.)-FM, 1984-90, Nat. Sleep Found., 1997—. Recipient Superior Performance award U.S. Dept. Transp., 1979. Mem. D.C. Bar (com. ethics 1983-89, mem. bd. profl. responsibility 1989-94), ABA, Nat. Bar Assn., Washington Bar Assn., Fed. Bar Assn., Fed. Communications Bar Assn., Lawyer-Pilots Bar Assn., Black Princeton Alumni (dir. N.Y.C. 1981-87). Democrat. Episcopalian. Administrative and regulatory, Federal civil litigation, Securities. Home: 1612 Crittenden St NW Washington DC 20011-4218 Office: Fed Aviation Adminstrn 800 Independence Ave SW Washington DC 20591-0001

HART, CLIFFORD HARVEY, lawyer; b. Flint, Mich., Nov. 12, 1935; s. Max S. and Dorothy H. (Fineberg) H.; m. Alice Rosenberg, June 17, 1962; children: Michael F., David E., Steven A. AB, U. Mich., 1957, JD, 1960. Bar: Mich. 1960, U.S. Dist. Ct. (ea. and we. dists.) Mich. 1962; cert. civil trial advocate. Assoc. Stevens & Nelson, Flint, 1960-62; ptnr. White, Newblatt, Nelson & Hart, 1962-64; with Dean, Dean, Segar & Hart, P.C. and predecessor firms, 1965-97; pvt. practice Law Offices Clifford H. Hart, 1997—. Adj. assoc. prof. Flint Sch. Mgmt., U. Mich., 1972—; lectr. Inst. Continuing Legal Edn., Mich.; lectr.iMIch. Jud. Inst. Pres. Vis. Nurse Assn., Flint, 1967; pres. Temple Beth El, 1973-75; trustee United Way Genesee County, 1981—, chmn. bd., 1990-91, sec., 1988-89, chmn. bd. dirs. Genesee County and Lapeer County, 1990-91; chair corp. adv. bd. U. Mich., Flint, 1988-93; mem. faculty Inst. Continuing Legal Edn., Ann Arbor, Mich., 1984—. Fellow: Mich. Bar Found., Roscoe Pound Found.; mem.: ABA, ATLA (bd. govs. 1979—, lectr., home budget and office com 1987—89, chair 1989—91, chair 1998—, exec. com. 1984—85, exec. com. 1990—93, exec. com. 2001—, chmn. elections com. 1984—87, nat. parliamentarian 1990—91, nat. treas. 1991—92), Mich. State Bar Assn. (chmn. negligence law sect. 1981—82, rep. assembly 1975—81), Mich. Trial Lawyers Assn. (pres. 1977—78, lectr.), Genesee County Bar Assn. (pres. 1975—76), Am. Judicature Soc., Nat. Bd. Trial Advocacy (lectr., home budget and office com 1980—84, cert.), B'nai B'rith (past pres.). Democrat. Federal civil litigation, General civil litigation, State civil litigation. Office: 1410 Mott Found Bldg 503 S Saginaw St Flint MI 48502-1807 E-mail: clhart@umich.edu

HART, JOHN CLIFTON, lawyer; b. Chgo., Apr. 29, 1945; s. Clifton Edwin and Eleanor (Zielinski) H.; m. Dianne Lynn Wenzel, Jan. 18, 1969; children: David Clifton, Steven Philip, Kristin Dianne. BS, Loyola U., 1967; postgrad., Northwestern U., 1967-69; JD, U. N.D., 1972. Bar: Minn. 1973, U.S. Dist. Ct. Minn. 1973, Tex. 1979, U.S. Dist. Ct. (no. dist.) Tex. 1979, U.S. Dist. Ct. (we dist.) Tex. 1981, U.S. Dist. Ct. (ea. dist.) Okla. 1981, U.S. Dist. Ct. (ea. dist.) Tex. 1984, U.S. Dist. Ct. (no. dist.) Okla. 1999, U.S. Ct. Appeals (5th and 8th cirs.) 1980, U.S. Supreme Ct., 1997. Ptnr. Robins, Zelle, Larson & Kaplan, Mpls., 1973-81; v.p. Gollaher & Hart, Dallas, 1981-84; pres. Hart & Engen, 1984-87, Hart & Assocs., Dallas, 1987-88; mng. ptnr. S.W. regional office Robins, Kaplan, Miller & Ciresi, 1988-93; ptnr. Cantey & Hanger L.L.P., 1993-98, Brown, Herman, Dean, Wiseman, Liser & Hart, L.L.P., 1998—. Contbr. articles to profl. jours. Maj. USAF, 1969-73. Mem. ABA, State Bar Tex., Tarrant County Bar Assn., Fedn. Ins. and Corporate Counsel, Loss Exec. Assn. Republican. Lutheran. Federal civil litigation, State civil litigation, Insurance. Office: Brown Herman Dean Wiseman Liser & Hart LLP 306 W 7th St Ste 200 Fort Worth TX 76102-4905 E-mail: jhart@brownherman.com

HART, JOHN EDWARD, lawyer; b. Portland, Oreg., Nov. 21, 1946; s. Wilbur Elmore and Daisy Elizabeth (Bowen) H.; m. Bianca Mannheimer, Mar. 29, 1968 (div. 1985); children: Ashley Rebecca, Rachel Bianca, Eli Jacob; m. Serena Callahan, Nov. 9, 1991; 1 child, Katelyn Elizabeth. Student, Oreg. State U., 1965-66; BS, Portland State U., 1971; JD, Lewis and Clark Coll., 1974. Bar: Oreg. 1974, U.S. Dist. Ct. Oreg. 1974, U.S. Ct. Appeals (9th cir.) 1975. Ptnr. Schwabe, Williamson and Wyatt, Portland, 1973-92, Hoffman, Hart & Wagner, Portland, 1992—. Adj. faculty U. Oreg. Dental Sch., 1987—; legal cons. Oreg. Chpt. Obstetricians, Gynecologists, Portland, 1985—, Am. Cancer Soc. Mammography Project, 1987—. Contbr. articles to profl. jours. Co-chmn. Alameda Sch. Fair, Portland, 1983. With U.S. Army, 1967-68. Mem. ABA, Am. Coll. Trial Lawyers, Am. Bd. Trial Advocates (pres. 1995) Am., Inns of Ct., Oreg. State Bar Assn., Oreg. Assn. Def. Counsel (pres. 1989), Multnomah Athletic Club. Democrat. Presbyterian. Avocations: jogging, weight lifting, outdoor activities. General civil litigation, Health, Personal injury. Office: Hoffman Hart & Wagner 1000 SW Broadway Ste 2000 Portland OR 97205-3072

HART, LARRY CALVIN, lawyer; b. Lawton, Okla., Dec. 24, 1942; s. Clifford C. and Evelyn M. (Dupler) H.; m. Leslie K. Bolek, April 1986. A.B.A., Otero Coll., 1963; B.S., Colo. State U., 1967; J.D., Loyola U., Los Angeles, 1974. Bar: Calif. 1974, US. Dist. Ct. (cent. dist.) Calif. 1974, U.S. Ct. Appeals (9th cir.) 1979, U.S. Dist. Ct. (ea. and no. dists.) Calif. 1980. Assoc., Ned Good, Los Angeles, 1974-76, Hagenbaugh & Murphy, Los Angeles, 1976-77; ptnr. Hart & Michaelis, Los Angeles, 1977-84, Brill, Hunt & Hart, Los Angeles, 1984-86, Musick, Peeler & Garrett, Los Angeles, 1987—; instr. Inst. Safety and Systems Mgmt., Univ. So. Calif., Los Angeles, 1982—; hearing officer Los Angeles Superior Ct., 1982—. Mem. Assn. So. Calif. Def. Counsel (bd. dirs. 1980-83), Aviation Ins. Assn. Calif. (v.p. 1983-84, pres. 1986-87), Def. Research Inst., Calif. Bar Assn., Lawyer Pilots Bar Assn. Federal civil litigation, State civil litigation, Insurance. Office: Musick Peeler & Garrett 1 Wilshire Blvd Ste 2000 Los Angeles CA 90017-3876

HART, RUSSELL HOLIDAY, retired lawyer; b. Chgo., May 1, 1928; s. Russell Holiday and Allegra (Prince) H.; m. Mary Gehres, June 16, 1951; children: Holiday Hart McKiernan, Robert Russell, Andrew Richard. AB, DePauw U., 1950; JD, Ind. U., 1956. Bar: Ind. 1956, U.S. Dist. Ct. (no. and so. dists.) Ind. 1956, U.S. Ct. Appeals (7th cir.) 1965, U.S. Supreme Ct. 1973. Assoc. Stuart & Branigin, Lafayette, Ind., 1956-61, ptnr., 1961-99; ret., 1999. Lectr. Ind. Continuing Legal Edn. Forum; tchr. trial lawyers Nat. Inst. for Trial Advocacy. Served with U.S. Army, 1951-53. Fellow: Am. Coll. Trial Lawyers, Am. Bar Found., Internat. Soc. Barristers, Internat. Acad. Trial Lawyers, Ind. Bar Found. (sec., v.p. 1985), Acad. Law Alumni Ind. U. Sch. Law;; mem.: ABA (del.), Ind. Bar Assn. (pres.-elect 1986—87, pres. 1987—88, bd. mgrs., former treas., chmn. trial lawyers sect.), Tippecanoe County Bar Assn. (past pres.), Ind. Def. Trial Counsel (diplomate), Ind. Def. Lawyers Assn. (past pres.), Nat. Assn. Railroad Trial Counsel (past pres.). General civil litigation, Environmental, Insurance. Office: Stuart & Branigin PO Box 1010 Lafayette IN 47902-1010

HART, WILLIAM THOMAS, federal judge; b. Joliet, Ill., Feb. 4, 1929; s. William Michael and Geraldine (Archambeault) H.; m. Catherine Motta, Nov. 27, 1954; children: Catherine Hart Fornero, Susan Hart DaMario, Julie Hart Boesen, Sally Hart Collins, Nancy Hart McLaughlin. JD, Loyola U., Chgo., 1951. Bar: Ill. 1951, U.S. Dist. Ct. 1951, U.S. Ct. Appeals (7th cir.) 1954, U.S. Ct. Appeals (D.C. cir.) 1977. Asst. U.S. atty. U.S. Dist. Ct. (no. dist.) Ill., Chgo., 1954-56; assoc. Defrees & Fiske, 1956-59; spl. asst. atty. gen. State of Ill., 1957-58; assoc. then ptnr. Schiff, Hardin & Waite, 1959-82; spl. asst. state's atty. Cook County, Ill., 1960; judge U.S. Dist. Ct. Ill., 1982—; now sr. judge. Mem. exec. com. U.S. Dist. Ct. (no. dist.) Ill., 1988-92; mem. com. on adminstrn. fed. magistrates sys., Jud. Conf. U.S., 1987-92, 7th cir. Jud. Coun., 1990-92; mem. edn. com. Fed. Jud. Ctr., 1994-99; chair No. Dist. Ill. Ct. Hist. Assoc., 1998—. Pres. adv. bd. Mercy Med. Ctr., Aurora, Ill., 1980-81; v.p. Aurora Blood Bank, 1972-77; trustee Rosary H.S., 1981-82, 93-98; bd. dirs. Chgo. Legal Asst. Found., 1974-76. Served with U.S. Army, 1951-53. Decorated Bronze Starl named to Joliet/Will County Hall of Pride, 1992. Mem. 7th Cir. Bar Assn., Law Club, Legal Club, Soc. Trial Lawyers, Union League Club of Aurora, Ill. (hon.), Inn of Ct., Serra Club of Aurora (v.p. 2000—). Office: US Dist Ct No Dist Ill US Courthouse Rm 2246 219 S Dearborn St Chicago IL 60604-1702

HARTER, RALPH MILLARD PETER, lawyer, educator; b. Auburn, N.Y., Mar. 15, 1946; s. Donald Robert and Ruth (Ashdown) H.; m. Robin Ann Bampton, June 29, 1968 (div. Oct. 1994); m. Leslie J. Teague, Sept. 13, 1997; children: Robin Brooke, Donald Bampton. BA, Hobart Coll., 1968; JD, Cornell U., 1972; postgrad., Colgate Rochester Divinity Sch., 2001—. Bar: Pa. 1972, U.S. Dist. Ct. (ea. dist.) Pa. 1972, N.Y. 1981, U.S. Dist. Ct. (we. dist.) N.Y. 1981. Assoc. Duane, Morris & Heckscher, Phila., 1972-81, Harter, Secrest & Emery, Rochester, N.Y., 1981-83; ptnr. Goldstein, Goldman, Kessler & Underberg, 1983-91, Sutton, DeLeeuw, Clark & Darcy, Rochester, 1991-94; mng. ptnr. Burke, Albright, Harter & Reddy, LLP, 1994—. Educator elder law issues, right to die, ethics, trusts and estates issues. V.p., gen. counsel, bd. dirs. Otetiana council Inc., Boy Scouts Am., Rochester, 1982-2000; mem. various coms. Episcopal Diocesen and Ch., Phila. and Rochester, 1972—; chair bd. dirs. Episcopal Sr. Life Cmtys., 1997-99, bd. dirs., 1995—; trustee Colls. of Seneca (Hobart & William Smith Colls.), 1987-96; bd. dirs. Allendale Columbia Sch., 1991-96; trustee Sigma Phi Ednl. Found., N.Y.C., 1990—; pres., gen. coun., bd. dirs. Rochester chpt. Alzheimer's Assn., 1981—. Served with USAR, 1969-75. Mem. ABA, N.Y. State Bar Assn. (various sects., lectr.), Pa. Bar Assn., Phila. Bar Assn., Monroe County Bar Assn., Nat. Acad. Elder Law Attys., Rochester Area C. of C. (United Way coms. 1984-96), Alzheimer's Disease and Related Disorders Assn. Inc. (pres., gen. counsel, bd. dirs. 1981—), Assn. of Adirondack Scout Camps (bd. dirs. 1986-93), Cornell U. Law Sch. Assn., Hobart Coll. Alumni Assn. and Alumni Council (pres. 1984-86), Hobart Coll. Statesmen Athletic Assn. (gen. counsel, bd. dirs. 1983—), Hobart Coll. Club of Rochester (pres. 1984-86), The Genesse Valley Club (Rochester), Webhannet Golf Club (Kennebunkport, Maine), Delta chpt. Sigma Phi. Republican. Avocations: flyfishing, duck decoy carving, white water rafting, canoeing, golf. Estate planning, Probate, Estate taxation. Home: Tuckaway Farm 98 Canfield Rd Pittsford NY 14534-9709 Office: Burke Albright Harter & Reddy LLP 1800 Hudson Ave Rochester NY 14607-1912 E-mail: harter@rochesterlawyer.com

HARTLEY, CARL WILLIAM, JR. lawyer; b. Carthage, Mo., Aug. 12, 1946; s. Carl William and Doris Eillene (Wilcox) H.; m. Martha Anderson Gouch (div. 1991); children: Zach, Jordan. BS, U. Fla., 1968, JD with High Honors, 1976. Bar: Fla. 1976, U.S. Dist. Ct. (so. dist.) Fla. 1976, U.S. Dist. Ct. (mid. dist.) Fla. 1980. Sales rep. Scott Paper Co., Miami, Fla., 1971-73; assoc. Grenbherg, Traurig et al., 1976-80; ptnr. Thomas Thomas Hartley & Spraker, Orlando, Fla., 1980-83, Holland & Knight, Orlando, 1983-85, Hartley, Wall & Norman, Orlando, 1985—. Editor U. Fla. Law Rev., 1976. Democrat. Methodist. Avocations: fishing, hunting, camping. General civil litigation, Contracts commercial, Real property. Office: Hartley Wall & Norman PO Box 2168 Orlando FL 32802-2168 E-mail: cwhsec@hwnlaw.com

HARTLEY, JASON SCOTT, lawyer, educator; b. Calif., Oct. 1, 1971; s. Virgil Otis Jr. and Louise Ann H. BA, U. Calif., San Diego, 1993; JD cum laude, Tulane U., 1997. Bar: Calif. 1997, U.S. Dist. Ct. (so. and ctrl. dist.) Calif. Law clk. New Orleans City Atty., 1995-96, Montgomery, Barnett, Brown, Reed, New Orleans, 1996-97; lectr. law Thomas Jefferson Law Sch., San Diego, 1998; atty. Kay Rose & Ptnrs. LLP, 1997—. Advisor MCM Music, Würzburg, Germany, 1994—, Dirty Dogma Records, San Diego, 1997—. Editor Tulane Jour. Comp. and Internat. Law, 1995-97; contbr. articles to profl. jours. Recipient Nathan F. Burkan Meml. award ASCAP, 1997. Avocations: composing and recording music, sailing, swimming, cooking. Admiralty, Entertainment, Product liability. Office: Kaye Rose & Ptnrs 402 W Broadway Ste 2100 San Diego CA 92101

HARTMAN, MARSHALL J. lawyer; b. Chgo., Mar. 9, 1934; s. Paul and Anna Lily (Rose) H.; m. Patricia Gail Henig, July 30, 1961; children: Ann, Judy, Danny. A.B., U. Chgo., 1954; BHebrew Letters, Coll. Jewish Studies, Chgo., 1954; JD, U. Chgo., 1957. Bar: Ill. 1958, U.S. Dist. Ct. (no. Dist.) Ill., U.S. Ct. Appeals (7th cir), U.S. Supreme Ct. 1962. Youth dir. South Side Hebrew Congregation, Chgo., 1958-61; asst. pub. defender, Cook County, Chgo., 1963-70; probation officer Cook County Juvenile Ct., 1958-60, asst. to presiding judge, 1960-63; nat. dir. defender services Nat. Legal Aid and Defender Assn., 1970-76; vis. assoc. prof. U. Ill., Chgo., 1978— ; exec. dir. Criminal Def. Consortium of Cook County, Chgo., 1976-78; treas., gen. counsel Nat. Defender Inst., Chgo., 1978-89; with Lake County Pub. Defender, Waukegan, Ill. 1989—; chief pub. defender 19th jud. cir. Lake County, Ill. Author: Hartman's Handy Guide, 1968, Constitutional Criminal Procedure Handbook, 1986; contbr. articles to profl. jours. Mem. Am. Jewish Congress. 1st lt. USAR, 1961-62. Recipient Reginald Heber Smith award, Nat. Legal Aid and Defender Assn., 1978; Silver Circle award U. Ill., 1982, 85. Mem. Ill. Pub. Defender Assn. (pres.), Ill. Acad. Criminology (v.p., pres.), ABA (ho. of dels.), Chgo Bar Assn. Democrat. Home: 6554 S Spaulding Ave Chicago IL 60629-3445 Office: Lake County Pub Defender 18 N County St Waukegan IL 60085-4304

HARTMANN, CARL JOSEPH, lawyer, consultant; b. Rochester, N.Y., Apr. 21, 1954; s. Carl Joseph and Mary (Ercel) H.; m. Kimberly Lynn Japinga, Feb. 15, 1998. JD, Antioch Coll., 1979. Bar: N.Mex. 1980, V.I. 1993, U.S. Dist. Ct. N.Mex. 1981, U.S. Ct. Appeals (10th cir.) 1982, U.S. Ct. Appeals (3d cir.) 1988, D.C. 1994, U.S. Supreme Ct. 1985. Jud. intern U.S. Supreme Ct., Washington, 1979; jud. clk. N.Mex. Ct. Appeals, Santa Fe, 1980-81; asst. prof. law Antioch Coll. Sch. Law, Washington, 1982-85; ptnr. Law Offices of Carl Hartmann, Albuquerque, 1985-87; assoc. Campbell, Arellano & Rich, St. Thomas, V.I., 1988-89; special counsel Merrill Lynch Pvt. Capital, N.Y.C., 1989-91; ptnr. Law Offices of Carl Hartmann, 1991—. Gen. counsel Emerging Comms., Inc., St. Croix, V.I., 1997-98, Innovative Comms., Corp., St. Croix, 1998—; spl. counsel U.S. Park Svc., Santa Fe, 1987. Author: Legal Analysis for Clinical Students, 1981; co-author: Private Law: An Introduction to Torts, 1980, Clinical Perspectives on Fair Employment, 1979; co-editor-in-chief Antioch Sch. of Law--Law Rev., 1979. Adv. bd. Our Lady of Czestochowa Sch., Paulus Hook, N.J., 1998-2001. Mem. Assn. of the Bar of the City of N.Y., V.I. Bar Assn. Roman Catholic. Avocations: fencing, flying, scuba, skiing, golf. Federal civil litigation, General corporate, Labor. Home: 126 Sussex St Jersey City NJ 07302-6405 Office: 72-08 243rd St New York NY 11363 E-mail: hartmann@federal-litigation.com

HARTMANN, JAMES M. lawyer; b. N.Y.C., Mar. 8, 1946; s. Morton Woodrow and Miriam Rose H.; m. Nancy K. Deming, May 20, 1988. BA, St. Lawrence U., 1967; MA, U. Wis., 1968; JD, Bklyn. Law Sch., 1974. Bar: N.Y. 1975, U.S. Dist. Ct. (so. and ea. dists.) N.Y. 1975, U.S. Ct. Appeals (2d cir.) 1975, U.S. Dist. Ct. (no. and we. dists.) N.Y. 1989, U.S. Supreme Ct. 1991. Gen. atty. U.S. Dept. Justice, N.Y.C., 1975-76, trial atty., 1976-79; pvt. practice, 1979-86, Delhi, N.Y., 1989—; head dept. litig. Frenkel & Hershkowitz, N.Y.C., 1986-89. Spl. dist. atty. Del. County, Delhi; mem. libr. com. Supreme Ct., Delhi, 1992—. Mem. N.Y. State Bar Assn., N.Y. Trial Lawyers Assn., N.Y. State Criminal Def. Lawyers Assn., Del. County Bar Assn. (mem. grievance com. 1994—), Pi Sigma Alpha. General civil litigation, Criminal. Office: PO Box 206 Rte 10 Delhi NY 13753

HARTMANN, KENNETH, lawyer; b. Chgo., Apr. 2, 1950; s. Orvel Arthur and Anita (Everding) H.; m. Carol Beth Draeger, Aug. 5, 1978; children— Elizabeth Ann, Kristen Carol. B.A. with high honors, U. Ill., 1971; J.D., U. Chgo., 1977. Bar: Ill. 1977, U.S. Dist. Ct. (no. dist.) Ill. 1977. Assoc., Sonnenschein, Carlin, Nath & Rosenthal, Chgo., 1977-79, Coffield, Ungaretti, Harris & Slavin, Chgo., 1979-81; ptnr. Rudnick & Wolfe, Chgo., 1981-85; pres. Cen. Chgo. Distributing Co., 1985—. Mem. Phi Beta Kappa. Republican. Lutheran. Banking, General corporate, Real property.

HARTMANN, UWE, lawyer; b. Zell/Mosel, Germany, Aug. 25, 1963; m. Uta Friedlein; 1 child, Michael. JD, U. Wuerzburg, Germany, 1992, PhD, 1994. Cert. dist. ct. Frankfurt, Germany; advocat in Czech Republic. Assoc. BBLP Beiten Burkhardt Mittl & Wegener, Frankfurt, 1995-96, Prague, Czech Republic, 1997-98, ptnr. Duesseldorf, Germany, 1998-99, Frankfurt, 1999—2001; ptnr. Weil Gotshalz Nanges, 2001—. Bank clk. Deutsche Bank AG, Paris, 1990, Wuerzburg, Germany, 1988; spkr. Inst. for Internat. Rsch. Diverse, Germany, 1997, Gustav Stresemann Inst., Bonn, Germany, 1995-96. Contbr. articles to profl. jours. Lt. German Fed. Armed Forces, 1985-87. Scholarship Konrad-Adenauer-Stiftung, 1989-92. Mem. German-Am. Lawyers Assn., Assn. Internat. étudiants des anciens étudiants en droit comparé. General corporate, Finance, Mergers and acquisitions. Office: Weil Gotshal nanges Main Tower Nene Mainzer Landstr 52-58 60311 Frankfurt am Main Germany Home Fax: 49-6192-309765; Office Fax: 49-69-21659-699

HARTNETT, MARY, lawyer; b. St. Louis, Jan. 17, 1959; d. William Joseph and Kathleen (Hannefin) Hartnett; m. Richard Boyce Norland, Oct. 25, 1980; children: Daniel Richard Hartnett Norland, Kathleen Patricia Hartnett Norland. BA with honors, Grinnell Coll., 1980; postgrad., NYU, 1983; JD magna cum laude, Georgetown U., 1985. Bar: D.C. 1985, U.S. Ct. Appeals (D.C. cir.) 1985, U.S. Dist. Ct. D.C. 1986. Correspondent Middle East Exec. Reports, Bahrain, 1981-82; assoc. Vinson & Elkins, Washington, 1985-86, Coudert Bros. Internat. Law Firm, Washington and Moscow, 1989-96, of counsel Washington, 1996-98; adj. prof. law Georgetown U. Law Ctr., 1999—, exec. dir., bd. dirs. Women's Law and Pub.

Policy Fellowship, 1998—. Mem. civil pro bono panel U.S. Dist. Ct., Washington, 1991-95; mem. Edmund Muskie Fellowship Legal Selection Com., Washington and N.Y.C., 1994. Contbr. more than 30 articles to profl. jours. Vol. atty. D.C. Emergency Domestic Rels. Project, Women's Legal Def. Fund, Washington, 1994-95; patient vol. Hospice of No. Va., Arlington, 1994-95; local coord. Meals on Wheels, Arlington, 1994-95; Dem. candidate for State Rep. from 71st Dist. Iowa, 1980. Root-Tilden scholar, 1980. Mem. ABA, Women's Bar Assn., D.C. Bar Assn. Congregationalist. Avocations: tennis, hiking. Office: Georgetown U Law Ctr Women's Law/Pub Policy Fell 600 New Jersey Ave NW Fl 334 Washington DC 20001-2075

HARTNETT, MAURICE A., III, state supreme court justice; b. Dover, Del., Jan. 20, 1927; s. Maurice and Anna Louise (Morris) H.; m. Elizabeth Anne Hutchinson, Aug. 21, 1965; 1 child, Anne Elizabeth. Student, Washington Coll.-Chestertown, Md., 1946-47; BS, U. Del.-Newark, 1951; postgrad., Georgetown U., 1951; JD, George Washington U., 1954; EdM, U. Del., 1956. Bar: Del. 1954, U.S. Dist. Ct. Del. 1957, U.S. Supreme Ct. 1959. Pvt. practice law, Dover, Del., 1955-76; exec. dir. Del. Legis. Ref. bur., 1961-69; vice chancellor Del. Ct. Chancery, 1976-94; justice Del. Supreme Ct., 1994—. Code revisor Del. Rev. Code Commn., 1961-72; commr. Nat. Conf. Com. Uniform State Laws, Chgo., 1962— , sec., exec. com., 1977-83; chmn. State Tax Appeal Bd., Wilmington, Del., 1973-76. Served with U.S. Army, 1945-46. Mem. ABA, Del. Bar Assn., Kent County Bar Assn. (pres. 1974), Am. Law Inst. Democrat. Home: 144 Cooper Rd Dover DE 19901-4926 Office: Del Supreme Court 55 The Grn Dover DE 19901-3611

HARTNETT, WILL FORD, lawyer; b. Austin, Tex., June 3, 1956; s. James Joseph and Emily (High) H.; m. Tammy Lynn Cotton, Dec. 7, 1996; 1 child, Will. BA, Harvard U., 1978; JD, U. Tex., 1981. Bar: Tex. 1981, U.S. Ct. Appeals (5th cir.) 1985, U.S. Supreme Ct. 1985; cert. in Estate Planning and Probate Law Tex. Bd. Legal Specialization. Assoc. Turner & Hitchins, Dallas, 1981-82; ptnr. The Hartnett Law Firm, 1982—. Bd. dirs. Tex. Guaranteed Student Loan Corp., Austin, 1987-90. Co-author: Annual Survey of Wills and Trusts, 1986. Mem. Tex. Ho. of Reps., 1991—; vice-chmn. House Jud. Affairs Com., 1995—. Fellow Am. Coll. Trust and Estate Coun., Tex. Bar Found.; mem. SAR, Dallas Bar Assn., St. Nicholas Soc., Mensa, Harvard Club Dallas (bd. dirs., treas. 1983-95), Rotary. Republican. Roman Catholic. State civil litigation, Probate. Home: 4722 Walnut Hill Ln Dallas TX 75229-6354 Office: The Hartnett Law Firm 4900 Thanksgiving Tower Dallas TX 75201 E-mail: will@hartnettlawfirm.com

HARTRICK, JANICE KAY, lawyer; b. Baytown, Tex., Oct. 15, 1952; BA, Rice U., 1974; JD, U. Houston, 1976. Bar: Tex. 1977, La. 1980. With contracts sect. Texaco Corp., Houston, 1977-78; asst. gen. counsel Cities Exploration Co., Watson Oil Corp., 1978-79; sr. atty. Coastal Corp., 1979-87; chief counsel, v.p. Seagull Energy Corp., 1987-97; gen. counsel, sr. v.p. EEX Corp., 1997-2000; cons., 2000—. Mgmt. cons. Contbg. editor Regulation of the Natural Gas Industry, 1980-84. Vice chair adv. bd. Internat. Oil and Gas Ednl. Ctr., Southwestern Legal Found., co-chair 50th Inst. on Oil and Gas Law and Tax. Mem. ABA, Tex. Bar Assn., State Bar of Tex. (oil, gas and mineral law sect. chair 1999), La. Bar Assn. Avocation: track. General corporate, FERC practice, Public utilities. Office: 3836 Oberlin St Houston TX 77005-3634

HARTSHORN, ROLAND DEWITT, lawyer; b. Cordele, Ga., May 27, 1921; s. George DuBois and Nola Nancy (Redwine) H.; m. Mildred Stromick, Aug. 15, 1953; children— Marie Anne Hartshorn Kuhn, Elizabeth Lee, Roland David. J.D., Emory U., 1948. Bar: Va. 1956, D.C., 1956, Ga. 1948. Sole practice, Atlanta, 1948-50; sole practice, 1956-70; ptnr. Thomas, Thomas & Hartshorn, Springfield, Va., 1970-75; ptnr. Holst & Hartshorn, Arlington and Falls Church, Va., 1975— . Served to capt. U.S. Army, 1950-56. Mem. Fairfax County Bar Assn. Republican. Presbyterian. Lodges: Lions, Moose. General practice, Personal injury, Probate. Home: 3103 Sleepy Hollow Rd Falls Church VA 22042-3126 Office: Holst & Hartshorn 6400 Arlington Blvd Falls Church VA 22042-2336

HARTT, GROVER, III, lawyer; b. Dallas, Apr. 12, 1948; s. Grover Jr. and Dorothy June (Wilkins) H. BA with high honors, So. Meth. U., 1970, LLM in Tax, 1986; JD with high honors, Tex. Tech U., 1973. Bar: Tex. 1973, U.S. Dist. Ct. (no. dist.) Tex. 1974, U.S. Dist. Ct. (we. dist.) Tex. 1975, U.S. Ct. Appeals (5th cir.) 1975, U.S. Supreme Ct. 1976, U.S. Dist. Ct. (ea. dist.) Tex. 1999. Law clk. to presiding justice Ct. Criminal Appeals Tex., Austin, 1973-75; atty. Hartt and Hartt, Dallas, 1975-79; atty., advisor Office Spl. Counsel U.S. Dept. Energy, 1979-80, dep. chief counsel, 1981-83; trial atty. tax divsn. U.S. Dept. Justice, 1983-86, dep. atty.-in-charge tax divsn., 1986-95, asst. chief southwestern region civil trial sect. tax divsn., 1995—. Nat. spkr. on taxation, bankruptcy and litigation. Contbg. author: Collier on Bankruptcy; contbr. articles to profl. jours. Recipient Atty. Gen's award for disting. svc., 1996. Mem. ABA (mem. ct. procedure com. tax sect., chmn. bankruptcy litigation subcom. 1995—, mem. bus. bankruptcy com. bus. law sect., vice chmn. tax and fed. claims subcom. 1996-2000, chmn. 2000—), Tex. Bar Assn., Dallas Bar Assn., Am. Bankruptcy Inst., Coll. of State Bar of Tex., John C. Ford Am. Inn of Ct. (master of the bench 2000—). Office: US Dept Justice Tax Div 717 N Harwood St Ste 400 Dallas TX 75201-6506 E-mail: grover.hartt@usdoj.gov

HARTY, JAMES QUINN, lawyer; b. Phila., Dec. 10, 1925; s. William Lawrence and Marie Sarita (Quinn) H.; m. Ann Elizabeth McGeeney, July 23, 1955; children: Michael, Martha Harty Scheines, Christopher, Patrick, Mark, Paul. AB, LaSalle Coll., 1949; MBA, U. Pa., Phila., 1952, LLB, 1959. Bar: Pa. 1961. Personnel mgr. Corning (N.Y.) Glass Works, 1952-56; lectr. Wharton Sch. U. Pa., Phila., 1956-59; assoc. Reed, Smith, Shaw & McClay, Pitts., 1961-70, ptnr., 1971-95, Plummer DeWalt & Linn, Pitts., 1995—. Research editor: Office Management Handbook, 1958. Mem. Thornburg Zoning Rev. Bd., Thornburg Borough Coun., Pitts., 1968-76. With USN, 1943-46, PTO, CBI. Fulbright lectr. U. Kanazawa, Japan, 1959-60. Mem. ABA, Pa. Bar Assn. (chmn. labor sect. 1982), Allegheny Bar Assn., Pitts. Athletic Assn. Roman Catholic. Clubs: Pitts. (gov. 1986-87), Chartiers Country (Pitts.). Avocation: golf. Civil rights, Labor, Workers' compensation. Office: Plummer & Harty LLP Gulf Tower 28th Floor 707 Grant St Pittsburgh PA 15219-1912 E-mail: jharty@p2law.com

HARTZ, STEVEN EDWARD MARSHALL, lawyer, educator; b. Cambridge, Mass., July 11, 1948; s. Louis and Stella (Feinberg) H.; m. Janice Lindsay, June 12, 1976. AB magna cum laude, Harvard Coll., 1970; JD, U. Chgo., 1974. Bar: N.Y. 1975, U.S. Dist. Ct. (so. and ea. dists.) N.Y. 1975, U.S. Ct. Appeals (2d cir.) 1975, Fla. 1979, U.S. Dist. Ct. (so. dist.) Fla. 1979, U.S. Tax Ct. 1979, U.S. Ct. Appeals (5th cir.) 1979, U.S. Supreme Ct. 1979, U.S. Ct. Appeals (11th cir.) 1981, U.S. Dist. Ct. (mid. dist.) Fla. 1984. Assoc. Cleary, Gottlieb, Steen & Hamilton, N.Y.C., 1974-79; asst. U.S. atty. U.S. Dept. Justice, Miami, Fla., 1979-82, dep. chief criminal divsn., chief fraud and pub. corruption sect., 1981-82; sole practice Fla., 1982-90; of counsel Akerman, Senterfitt & Eidson, P.A., 1980, ptnr., shareholder, 1991—. Lectr. dept. English, U. English, U. Miami, 1984, adj. assoc. prof., 1985-86. Co-author: Housing, A Community Handbook, 1973. Vol. atty. Mobilization for Youth Legal Svcs., N.Y.C., 1978. Recipient Dirs.' award U.S. Dept. Justice, 1981; Fulbright Hays scholar, 1970. Mem. ABA, FBA, Fla. Bar Assn., N.Y. State Bar Assn., Dade County Bar Assn., Assn. Bar City N.Y., Phi Beta Kappa. General civil litigation, Consumer commercial, Criminal. Office: One Southeast 3rd Ave 28th Fl Miami FL 33131-4943

HARUTUNIAN, ALBERT T(HEODORE), III, judge; b. San Diego, May 15, 1955; s. Albert Theodore Jr. and Elsie Ruth H.; m. Rebecca Blair, Oct. 16, 1999. BA, Claremont McKenna Coll., 1977; JD, U. Calif., Berkeley, 1980. Bar: Calif. 1980, U.S. Dist. Ct. (so. dist.) Calif. 1980, U.S. Ct. Apppeals (9th cir.) 1982, U.S. Supreme Ct. 1984. Law clk. to Hon. Howard B. Turrentine U.S. Dist. Ct., San Diego, 1980-81; assoc. Luce, Forward, Hamilton & Scripps, 1982-87, ptnr., 1988-95; judge San Diego Mcpl. Ct., 1995-98, San Diego Superior Ct., 1998—. Spl. counsel standing com. on discipline U.S. Dist. Ct. Calif., San Diego, 1983-85; chmn. San Diego Bar Labor and Employment Sect., 1988-89; chmn. fed. cts. com. Calif. State Bar, 1989-90. Bd. dirs. ARC San Diego chpt., 1992—, Crime Victims Fund, 1995-97; bd. govs. Muscular Dystrophy Assn., San Diego, 1985; mem. LEAD Inc., San Diego, 1986—; planning com. San Diego United Way, 1986-92. Named one of Outstanding Young Men of Am., 1983; recipient Outstanding Service award 9th Cir. Jud. Conf., 1986. Mem. ABA, Calif. State Bar Ct. (referee 1985-88), Am. Arbitration Assn. (arbitrator 1986-95), Calif. Judges Assn. (mem. criminal law and procedure com. 1997-2000), Boalt Hall Alumni Assn. (bd. dirs. 1994-97), Claremont McKenna Coll. Alumni Assn. (founding dir. San Diego chpt. 1984-2000), Rotary (bd. dirs. San Diego club 1995—). Republican. Avocations: music, golf. Office: San Diego Superior Ct PO Box 122724 San Diego CA 92112-2724

HARVEY, ALBERT C. lawyer; m. Nancy Rutherford; children: Anne, Elizabeth. BS, U. Tenn., 1961, JD, 1967. Asst. pub. defender Tenn. Supreme Ct.; asst. to pub. defender Shelby County, 1969-71; ptnr. Thomason, Hendrix, Harvey, Johnson & Mitchell, Memphis. Instr. med. and dental jurisprudence U. Tenn., Memphis. Bd. editors Tennessee Law Review. Pres. Goodwill Boys Club, 1983-85; active YMCA, Arthritis Found., Citizens Assn. Memphis and Shelby County, Shelby County War Memls.; sr. warden of vestry Calvary Episcopal Ch. Maj. gen. USMCR, comdg. gen. 4th Marine divsn. Recipient Sam A. Myar, Jr. award Tenn. Bd. Law Examiners, 1978. Fellow: Am. Bar Found. (life), Tenn. Bar Found. (pres. 1993—94); mem.: ABA (bd. govs., ho. dels. charter mem. and coun. sect. litigation, young lawyers sect., fellow young lawyers divsn., com. on ethics and profl. responsibility, ethics 2000 spl. com.), Am. Judicature Soc. (nat. bd. dirs.), Am. Bd. Trial Advocates (adv.), Tenn. Bar Assn. (bd. govs., pres. young lawyers conf., v.p. 2000—, pres. elect 2001—), Memphis Area C. of C. (pres. mil. affairs coun.), Memphis Bar Assn. (v.p. 1989, pres. elect 1990, pres. 1991, pres. young lawyers divsn.), Am. Inns. of Ct., Ctrl. Garden Area Assn. (pres.), Phoenix Club (1st v.p.), Kiwanis, Univ. Club Memphis (pres.), U. Tenn. Nat. Alumni Assn. (pres. Memphis chpt., nat. bd. govs.), Navy League. Construction, Personal injury, Product liability. Office: 1 Commerce Sq 29th Fl Memphis TN 38103

HARVEY, ALEXANDER, II, federal judge; b. Balt., May 3, 1923; s. Fred B. and Rose (Hopkins) H.; m. Mary E. Williams, Feb. 24, 1951; children: Elizabeth H., Alexander IV. BA, Yale U., 1947; LLB, Columbia U., 1950. Bar: Md. 1950. Assoc. Ober, William, Grimes & Stinson, Balt., 1950-66, ptnr., 1953-66; asst. atty. gen. Md., 1957-58; judge U.S. Dist. Ct. Md., 1966-86, chief judge, 1986-91, sr. judge, 1991—. Mem. Gov.'s Com. To Study Blue Sky Law of Md., 1961; mem. character com. Ct. Appeals Md. for 8th Jud. Cir. Bd. dirs. Balt. Symphony Assn., 1966-68; pres., dir. Balt. Opera Guild, 1960; bd. dirs. Balt. Coun. Social Agys., 1957-63; trustee Ch. Home and Hosp., Balt., 1952-71. 1st lt. AUS, World War II, ETO. Mem. Am., Md., Balt. bar assns., Phi Beta Kappa. Episcopalian (vestry 1967-70). Home: 7300 Brightside Rd Baltimore MD 21212-1011 Office: US Dist Ct 101 W Lombard St Ste 404 Baltimore MD 21201-2605

HARVEY, ALICE ELEASE, lawyer; b. Haddonfield, N.J., Apr. 10, 1968; d. Lucious James and Doris Arleen Harvey; m. Joseph Edward Koren, Aug. 17, 1996. BS, Drexel U., 1986; JD, U. Pa., 1994. Bar: Pa. 1995. Law clk. U.S. SEC, Phila., summer 1992; assoc. Morgan, Lewis & Bockius, LLP, 1994-97, Hangley, Aronchick, Segal & Pudlin, Phila., 1997-99; corp. counsel The Franklin Mint, Franklin Center, Pa., 1999—. Tutor Future Investments Tutoring Program, Phila., 1995-98; vol. lawyer Phila. Vol. Lawyers for Arts, 1997—. Editor/mng. editor Housing Law Jour., 1991-94; editor Univ. Pa. Law Rev., 1992-94. Mem. Pa. Bar Assn., Phila. Bar Assn. Avocations: travel, writing, equestrian. General corporate, Entertainment, Mergers and acquisitions. Office: The Franklin Mint Media PA 19091-0001

HARVEY, CHARLES ALBERT, JR. lawyer; b. Beverly, Mass., Sept. 28, 1949; s. Charles A. and Phyllis B. (O'Rourke) H.; m. Whitney Ann Neville, Sept. 21, 1985; children: John Whitney, Charlotte Baird. AB, Assumption Coll., 1971; JD, U. Maine, 1974. Bar: Maine 1974, Mass. 1974, U.S. Supreme Ct. 1979. Assoc. Verrill & Dana, Portland, Maine, 1974-79, ptnr., 1979-95, Harvey & Frank, Portland, 1995—. Assoc. chief counsel President's Commn. on Accident at Three Mile Island, Washington, 1979; mem. adv. com. on civil rules Maine Supreme Jud. Ct., 1978-91, chmn. adv. com. on cameras in trial cts., 1991-93, cons. on civil rules, 1996—, chmn. adv. com. on civil rules, 1987-91; chmn. adv. com. on local rules U.S. Dist. Ct. Maine, 1985—, mem. civil justice adv. com., 1992-97; chmn. Maine Gov.'s Select Com. on Jud. Appointments, 1987-91; chmn. grievance commn. Maine Bd. Overseers of the Bar, 1996-97. Contbr. articles to profl. jours. Trustee Portland Sympnony Orch., 1980-89, pres., 1987-89, adv. trustee, 1989—; trustee Portland Stage Co., 1984-87, adv. trustee, 1987—; trustee Waynflete Sch., 1990-96; adv. trustee Maine Childrens Mus., 1992—, Maine Vol. Lawyers for the Arts, 1994—. Fellow Portland Mus. of Art, 1993—. Fellow Am. Coll. Trial Lawyers, Maine Bar Found.; mem. Am. Law Inst. Republican. Federal civil litigation, State civil litigation. Office: Harvey & Frank Two City Ctr Portland ME 04112

HARVEY, GREGORY MERRILL, lawyer; b. Morris Twp., N.J., Jan. 6, 1937; s. Merrill Piercy and Dorothy Ceola (Gregory) H.; m. Emily Mitchell Wallace, June 14, 1969. AB, Harvard U., 1959; JD, Harvard Law Sch., 1962. Bar: Pa. 1963. Assoc. Morgan, Lewis & Bockius, Phila., 1962-69, ptnr., 1969-99, Montgomery, McCracken, Walker & Rhoads, Phila., 1999—. Bd. dirs. Pub. Interest Law Ctr. of Phila., Inc., 1980—. Chmn. City of Phila. Bd. Ethics, 1984-91; trustee Fairmount Park Art Assn., Phila., 1981—; co-chmn. 8th Ward Dem. Exec. Com., Phila., 1984—; bd. dirs. Ams. for Dem. Action Southeastern Pa. chpt., 1966—. Recipient James Madison award Soc. Profl. Journalists, 1986, Judge Learned Hand Human Rels. award Am. Jewish Com., 1991. Fellow Am. Coll. Trial Lawyers; mem. ABA, Pa. Bar Assn., Phila. Bar Assn., Phi Beta Kappa. Clubs: Merion Cricket (Haverford, Pa.), Racquet (Phila.). Appellate, General civil litigation, Libel. Home: 1939 Panama St Philadelphia PA 19103-6609 Office: Montgomery McCracken et al 123 S Broad St Philadelphia PA 19109-1030 E-mail: gharvey@mmwr.com

HARVEY, JONATHAN MATTHEW, lawyer; b. Worcester, Mass., July 6, 1955; s. Irwin and Hannah H.; m. Lyssa Lynn Kligman, Dec. 17, 1977; children: Laurel Eden, Jordane Mills, Kyle Michael. BA cum laude, U. Ga., 1977; JD, U. S.C., 1981. Bar: S.C. 1981, U.S. Dist. Ct. S.C. 1982, U.S. Ct. Appeals (4th cir.) 1992. Asst. solicitor Fifth Judicial Circuit Solicitor's Office, Columbia, S.C., 1982-83; asst. atty. gen. Office of the Atty. Gen., 1983-86; lawyer pvt. practice, 1986—. Vice chair Richland Sch. Dist. 2 Ednl. Found., 2001—; Fin. dir. Richland County Dems. , Columbia, SC, 1987—88, mem. exec. com., 1987—90, 1998—2000; commr. East Richland County Pub. Svc. Dist., Richland County, SC, 1990—99, chmn., 1999—2000. Mem. ATLA, S.C. Bar Assn., S.C. Assn. Criminal Def. Lawyers (bd. dirs. 5th jud. cir. 1998—), S.C. Trial Lawyers Assn., Richland County Bar Assn. Democrat. Avocations: tennis, outdoor activities. Administrative and regulatory, Criminal, Personal injury. Office: 1804 Bull St Columbia SC 29201-2506

HARVEY, MORRIS LANE, lawyer; b. Madisonville, Ky., Apr. 22, 1950; s. Morris Lee and Margie Lou (Wallace) H.; m. Mary Topel; children: Morris Lane Jr., John French, Laura Kathleen. BS, Murray State U., 1972; JD, U. Ky., 1974. Bar: Ill. 1975, U.S. Dist. Ct. (so. dist.) 1979. Assoc. Hanagan & Dousman, Mt. Vernon, Ill., 1975-77; ptnr. Feiger, Quindry, Molt & Harvey and successor firms, Fairfield, 1977-85; sole practice, 1986-97, Mt. Vernon, 1997—. Instr. Frontier C.C., Fairfield, 1977-79; spl. asst. atty. gen. State of Ill., Fairfield, 1977-82; Ill. pres. Woodman of World Life Inst. Soc., 1985-87; mem. nat. fraternal com., 1987-89, nat. legis. com., 1989-93, nat. jud. com., 1993-97. Recipient Outstanding Young Man Am. U.S. Jaycees, 1978, 81, 89. Mem. ABA, Ill. Bar Assn., Assn. Trial Lawyers Am., Ill. Trial Lawyers Assn., Am. Judicature Soc. Civil litigation, Family and matrimonial, Personal injury. Home: 5 Webster Hill Est Mount Vernon IL 62864-2346 Office: 2029 Broadway St Mount Vernon IL 62864-2910

HARVIE, CRAWFORD THOMAS, lawyer; b. N.Y.C., Mar. 28, 1943; s. William Mead and Barbara Adele (Johnson) H.; m. Iris Ruth Alofsin, June 10, 1972; children: Katherine, Edward. AB, Stanford U., 1965; LLB, Yale U., 1968; cert. advanced mgmt. program, Harvard U., 1992. Bar: N.Y. 1969. Assoc. Debevoise & Plimpton, N.Y.C., 1971-75; counsel TRW, Inc., Cleve., 1976-77, sr. counsel, 1978-79, asst. gen. counsel, v.p., 1980-83; v.p. law TRW Automotive, 1983-90; v.p., assoc. gen. counsel TRW Inc., 1990-95; sr. v.p., gen. counsel, sec. Goodyear Tire and Rubber Co., Akron, Ohio, 1995—. Trustee Cleve. Inst. of Music, 1989—, Akron Art Mus.; bd. overseers Blossom Music Ctr. Mem. Am. Corp. Counsel Assn., Assn. of Gen. Counsel, Chief Legal Officer Roundtable-U.S. General corporate. Home: 6537 Thornbrook Cir Hudson OH 44236-3552 Office: Goodyear Tire and Rubber Co 1144 E Market St Akron OH 44316-0001

HARWELL, DAVID WALKER, retired state supreme court chief justice; b. Florence, S.C., Jan. 8, 1932; s. Baxter Hicks and Lacy (Rankin) H.; divorced; children: Robert Bryan, William Baxter. LL.B., J.D., U. S.C., 1958; HHD (hon.), Frances Marion U., 1987. Bar: S.C. 1958, U.S. Dist. Ct. S.C. 1958, U.S. Ct. Appeals 1964, U.S. Supreme Ct. 1961. Circuit judge 12th Jud. Ct. S.C., 1973-80; justice S.C. Supreme Ct., 1980-91, chief justice, 1991-94; ret., 1994; spl. counsel Nelson, Mullins, Riley and Scarborough. Mem. S.C. Ho. of Reps., 1962-73. Served with USNR, 1952-54. Mem. Am. Bar Assn., Am. Trial Lawyers Assn., S.C. Bar Assn., S.C. Trial Lawyers Assn. (Portrait and Scholarship award 1986). Presbyterian. Office: PO Box 2459 Myrtle Beach SC 29578-2459

HARWOOD, ROBERT BERNARD, JR. judge; b. Oct. 17, 1939; Student, U. of the South, 1958—59; BS in Commerce and Bus. Adminstrn., U. Ala., 1962, JD, 1963. Spl. asst. atty. gen. State of Ala., 1969—75; dep. city judge City of Tuscaloosa, Ala., 1975—80; cir. judge Tuscaloosa County, 1991—2001; assoc. justice Ala. Supreme Ct., 2001. Lectr. law and trial advocacy U. Ala., 1979—83, 1989—99. Mem. exec. bd. Black Warrior coun. Boy Scouts Am., 1976—, pres., 1993; mem. leadership assn. United Way Tuscaloosa County; mem. Carroll Creek Vol. Fire Dept.; bd. dirs. FOCUS on Sr. Citizens of Tuscaloosa County. Recipient Silver Beaver award, Black Warrior Coun. Boy Scouts Am., 1994. Mem.: ABA, Ala. Bar Assn., Tuscaloosa Inn of Ct. (pres. 1991—92), Am. Judges Assn., Tuscaloosa County Bar Assn. (pres. 1978—79), Ala. Cattlemen's Assn., Tuscaloosa County Cattlemen's Assn., Order of the Coif. Republican. Episcopalian. Office: Ala Supreme Ct 300 Dexter Ave Montgomery AL 36104-3741*

HASELTON, RICK THOMAS, lawyer; b. Albany, Oreg., Nov. 5, 1953; s. Shirley (Schantz) H. AB, Stanford U., 1976; JD, Yale U., 1979. Chair Oreg. State Bd. Bar Examiners, 1988-89, bd. dirs., 1986-88; mem. adv. com. on rules of practice 9th Cir. Ct., 1991-93. Law clk. U.S. Ct. Appeals (9th cir.) Oreg., Portland, 1979-80; from assoc. to ptnr. Lindsay, Hart, Neil & Weigler, 1979-93; sole practice, 1993-94; assoc. judge Oreg. Ct. Appeals, Salem, 1994—. Chair Multnomah County Legal Aid, Portland, 1985-86, bd. dirs., 1982-87. Mem. ABA, Oreg. Bar Assn., ACLU (cooperating atty. 1982-94), Phi Beta Kappa. Jewish. Federal civil litigation, State civil litigation. Office: 300 Justice Blvd Salem OR 97310-0001

HASKELL, DONALD MCMILLAN, lawyer; b. Toledo, July 2, 1932; s. Irwin Wales and Grace (Lee) H.; m. Carol Jean Ross, June 19, 1954; children: Deborah Lee, Catherine Jean, David Ross. BA, Coll. of Wooster, 1954; JD, U. Mich., 1957. Bar: Ill. 1957, U.S. Dist. Ct. (no. dist.) Ill. 1958, U.S. Ct. Appeals (7th cir.) 1960, U.S. Supreme Ct. 1963, U.S. Ct. Appeals (10th cir.) 1974, Oreg. 1990. Ptnr. McKenna, Storer, Rowe, White & Haskell and predecessors, Chgo., 1957-75; sr. ptnr. Haskell & Perrin, 1975-89, of counsel, 1989-2000. Commr. Clatsop County, Oreg., 1991-94; bd. dirs. N.W. Oreg. Econ. Alliance, 1993-98. Trustee Columbia River Maritime Mus., 1991—; chmn. Clatsop County Rep. Com., 1994-95; Mem. Astoria Planning Commn., 1999—, chmn., 2001—. Fellow Am. Bar Found., Ill. Bar Found.; mem. ABA (ho. of dels. 1982-92, bd. govs. 1987-90), Law Club Chgo., Legal Club Chgo., Astoria Country Club. Lutheran. Home: 600 W Lexington Ave Astoria OR 97103-5726 Office: Wecoma Ptnrs Ltd PO Box 777 100 16th St Astoria OR 97103-3634 E-mail: haskell@seasurf.net

HASKELL, WYATT RUSHTON, lawyer; b. Birmingham, Ala., May 15, 1940; s. Preston Hampton and Mary Wyatt (Rushton) H.; m. Susan Porter Nabers, June 1, 1968; children: John Howze, Henry Devereux, Samuel Drayton. AB, Amherst Coll., 1961; LLB, Yale U., 1965. Bar: Ala. 1965. Assoc. Bradley, Arant, Rose & White, Birmingham, 1966-71; staff atty. So. Natural Gas Co., 1971-73; ptnr. Haskell, Slaughter & Young, 1973—. Vis. rsch. asst. U. Muenster, Fed. Republic Germany, 1965-66; vis. prof. U. Ala. Law Sch., 1970-73; bd. dirs. Realty South, Bio Horizons Implant Systems, Inc. Contbr. articles to profl. jours. Bd. dirs. Alahause Shakespeare Fest., Montgomery, Ala., Folger Shakespeare Library, Washington. Thomas Pope fellow Trinity Coll., Oxford. Mem. ABA, Ala. Bar Assn., Birmingham Bar Assn., Mountain Brook Club. Presbyterian. Municipal (including bonds). Home: 2964 Cherokee Rd Birmingham AL 35223-2609 Office: Haskell Slaughter et al 800 First National Birmingham AL 35223 E-mail: wrh@hsy.com

HASKIN, J. MICHAEL, lawyer; b. Kansas City, Mo., Sept. 25, 1949; s. Harley V. and Geraldine E. (Porterfield) H.; m. Pamela J. Lutz, May 22, 1999. BA, Baker U., 1971; JD, U. Mo., 1976. Bar: Kans. 1976, Mo. 1987, U.S. Fed. Tax Ct., U.S. Supreme Ct. Ptnr., atty. Haskin, Hinkle, Slater & Snowbarger, Olathe, Kans., 1976-83, Dietrich, Davis, Dicus, Rowlands, Schmitt & Gorman, Kansas City, Mo., 1984-88; pres., atty. J. Michael Haskin, PA, Olathe, 1989—. Bd. dirs., exec. com., The Assn. K-10 Corridor Devel., Inc., Lawrence, 1993-95. City councilman-at-large City of Olathe, 1989-93, mayor, 1993-95; mem., vice chmn., chmn. Stormwater Mgmt. Adv. Coun., Johnson County, Kans., 1989-95; bd. dirs. Olathe Pub. Libr., 1989-90, 93-95; bd. dirs. Hidden Glen Arts Festival, vice chmn., chmn., 1990—); mem. Mid-Am. Regional Coun. Perimeter Transp. Com., 1995—. Recipient Boss of Yr. award Johnson County Legal Secs. Assn., 1991-92, Cmty. Leadership award Olathe Area C. of C., 1992. Mem. Kans. Bar Assn., Mo. Bar Assn., Olathe Rotary Club (bd. dirs., pres. 1981—, Paul Harris award 1992, Olathe Rotarian of Yr. 1995), Olathe Arts Alliance (pres. 1988), Kaw Valley Philological Soc. Republican. Methodist. Avocations: golfing, sailing. Estate planning, Probate, Real property. Office: PO Box 413 100 E Park St Ste 203 Olathe KS 66061-3463 E-mail: haskinlawoffice@aol.com

HASKINS, CHARLES GREGORY, JR. lawyer; b. Chgo., Jan. 27, 1951; s. Charles G. and Ellen Barbara (Essman) H.; m. Gail Beaubien Ferbend, June 14, 1987; 1 child, Charles Robert. BA, U. Ill., 1972; JD, John Marshall Law Sch., 1976. Bar: Ill. 1976, U.S. Dist. Ct. (no. dist.) Ill. 1976. Assoc. George J. Cullen, Ltd., Chgo., 1976-82; shareholder George J. Cullen & Assoc., Ltd., 1982-89, Cullen, Haskins, Nicholson & Menchetti, Chgo., 1989—. Mem. ATLA, Workers Compensation Lawyers Assn. (bd. dirs. 1986-96, pres. 1989), Ill. Bar Assn., Ill. Trial Lawyers Assn. (bd. mgrs. 1989—, treas. 1997, co-chmn. Workers Compensation com. 1991—, co-editor Case Notebook 1992—), Chgo. Bar Assn. (cham. indsl. commn. com. 1987-88), Workplace Injury Litigation Group (bd. dirs. 1997—). Democrat. Roman Catholic. Avocations: golf, water skiing, snow skiing. Workers' compensation. Office: Cullen Haskins Nicholson & Menchetti 35 E Wacker Dr Ste 1760 Chicago IL 60601-2271

HASSAN, ALLEN CLARENCE, lawyer, physician, surgeon, educator; b. Red Oak, Iowa, Mar. 29, 1936; s. Oman Diab Hassan and Dorothea Tuttle. DVM, Iowa State U., 1962; MD, U. Iowa, 1966; JD, Lincoln U., 1978. Bar: Calif. 1981, U.S. Dist. Ct. (ea. dist.) Calif. 1981, U.S. Supreme Ct. 1981; diplomate Am. Bd. Family Practice, Am. Bd. Sports Medicine. Intern Mt. Zion Hosp., San Francisco, 1966-67; residency Mendolino State Hosp. Psychiatry, Talmage, Calif., 1967-70; sole practice Sacramento, 1981—. Clin. instr. family practice, U. Calif., Davis, 1976-86. Author: Failure to Atone, 1969, Diagnosis and Treatment of Brain and Spinal Cord Trauma, 1992, True Story of a Jungle Surgeon in Vietnam. Served as sgt. USMC, 1954-57, comdr. USCG. Fellow Coll. of Legal Medicine; mem. AMA, Am. Acad. Family Physicians (program chmn. 1973-76, sec., treas. 1974, 75, pres. 1975-76), Calif. Bar Assn., Calif. Trial Lawyer Assn., Calif. Med. Assn. Avocations: reading, jogging, golf, flying, scuba diving. Personal injury, Professional liability, Workers' compensation. Home: 401 Bret Harte Rd Sacramento CA 95864-5602 Office: 2933 El Camino Ave Sacramento CA 95821-6012

HASSELL, LEROY ROUNTREE, SR. state supreme court justice; b. Aug. 17, 1955; BA in Govt. and Fgn. Affairs, U. Va., 1977; JD, Harvard U., 1980. Bar: Va. Former ptnr. McGuire, Woods, Battle and Boothe; now justice Supreme Ct. of Va. Former mem. Va. gen. assembly task force to study violence on sch. property. Former mem. adv. bd. Massey Cancer Ctr.; mem. policy com., former chmn. Richmond Sch. Bd., ; former bd. dirs. Richmond Renaissance, Inc., Richmond chpt. ARC, Garfield childs Fund, Carpenter Ctr. for Performing Arts, St. John's Hosp., Legal Aid Ctrl. Va.; vol. Richmond Pub. Schs., Hospice vol.; elected sch. bd. chmn. 4 terms. Recipient Liberty Bell award 1985, 86, Black Achievers award, 1985-86, Outstanding Young Citizen award Richmond Jaycees, 1987, Outstanding Young Virginian award Va. Jaycees, 1987; one of youngest persons to both serve on the Richmond Sch. Bd. and to serve as bd. chmn. Mem. Va. Trial Lawyers Assn., Assn. Trial Lawyers Am., Va. Assn. Def. Attys., Old Dominion Bar Assn., Va. Bar Assn. Office: Supreme Ct of Virginia PO Box 1315 Richmond VA 23218-1315

HASSETT, JOSEPH MARK, lawyer; b. Buffalo, May 1, 1943; m. Carol A. Melton, June 23, 1984; children: Matthew, Meredith. B.A. summa cum laude, Canisius Coll., 1964; LL.B. cum laude, Harvard U., 1967; M.A. with 1st class honors, Univ. Coll. Dublin, 1981, Ph.D., 1985. Bar: N.Y. 1967, D.C. 1970, U.S. Supreme Ct. 1976. Assoc. Hogan & Hartson, Washington, 1970-74, ptnr., 1974—. Bd. trustees Canisius Coll. Author: Yeats and the Poetics of Hate, 1986; contbr. articles to profl. publs. Mem. ABA, D.C. Bar Assn. Federal civil litigation, General civil litigation, State civil litigation. Home: 6035 Crimson Ct Mc Lean VA 22101-1818 Office: 555 13th St NW Washington DC 20004-1109

HASSON, JAMES KEITH, JR. lawyer, law educator; b. Knoxville, Tenn., Mar. 3, 1946; s. James Keith and Elaine (Biggers) H.; m. Jayne Young, July 27, 1968; 1 son, Keith Samuel. BA, Duke U., 1967, JD, 1970. Bar: Ga. 1971, D.C. 1971. Assoc. Sutherland, Asbill & Brennan, Atlanta, 1970-76, ptnr., 1976—; prof. law Emory U., Atlanta, 1976-94; dir. House-Hasson Hardware Co., Knoxville, 1971—. Editor Jour. Taxation; contbr. and editor articles to profl. jours. Chmn. Met. Atlanta Crime Commn., 1986-87, also trustee; trustee Reinhardt Coll., 1989—; mem. Atlanta Civilian Review Bd.; mem. Leadership Atlanta, 1981-82; mem. IRS Commr. exempt orgn. adv. group; chmn. bd. dirs. Foxfire Fund, 1988—. 1st lt. U.S. Army, 1970-71. Mem. ABA (com. chmn. 1983-85), Atlanta Bar Assn. (counsel 1977-80, Pres's. Disting. Svc. award 1980), Lawyers Club. Presbyterian. General corporate, Health, Corporate taxation. Home: 3185 Chatham Rd NW Atlanta GA 30305-1101 Office: Sutherland Asbill & Brennan 999 Peachtree St NE Ste 2300 Atlanta GA 30309-3996

HASSON, KIRKE MICHAEL, lawyer; b. East St. Louis, Ill., Oct. 25, 1949; s. David S. and Audrey (Leber) H.; B.A., Yale U., 1971; J.D., Harvard U., 1974. Bar: Calif. 1974, U.S. Dist. Ct. (no. dist.) Calif. 1974. Assoc., Pillsbury, Madison & Sutro, San Francisco, 1974-81, ptnr., 1982—; mem. Am. Arbitration Commn., Internat. Found. Employee Benefit Plans. Bd. dirs., chmn. Bread and Roses, Mill Valley, Calif., 1985-91. Federal civil litigation, State civil litigation, Pension, profit-sharing, and employee benefits. Office: Pillsbury Madison & Sutro 235 Montgomery St # 540 San Francisco CA 94104-2902

HASTINGS, DOUGLAS ALFRED, lawyer; b. Oak Park, Ill., July 28, 1949; s. Douglas A. and Elaine M. (Schramm) H.; m. Virginia Joslin, June 28, 1982; children: Corey, Douglas. BA, Duke U., 1971; MPA, Memphis State U., 1977; JD, U. Va., 1981. Bar: D.C. 1981. Assoc. dir. Inst. for Govt. Studies, Memphis State U., 1976-77; adminstrv. intern Fed. Exec. Inst., Charlottesville, Va., 1977-78; project coord. Assn. Acad. Health Ctrs., 1978-80; cons. Shenandoah PSRO, 1980-81; ptnr. Epstein Becker & Green, Washington, 1981—. Vis. lectr. dept. health adminstrn. Duke U., Durham, N.C., 1985-90. Contbr. articles to profl. jours. Mem. ABA, Washington Coun. Lawyers, Am. Health Lawyers Assn. (bd. dirs. 1991—), Order of Coif, Phi Beta Kappa. Democrat. Unitarian. Avocations: karate, tennis, basketball, coaching. Administrative and regulatory, General corporate, Health. Home: 5301 Burke Dr Alexandria VA 22309-3310 Office: Epstein Becker & Green 1227 25th St NW Fl 7 Washington DC 20037-1156

HASTINGS, EDWIN H(AMILTON), lawyer; b. Yonkers, N.Y., Jan. 2, 1917; s. Edwin H. Jr. and Emily (Clark) H.; m. Mabel Hurst, July 12, 1941 (div. June 1957); children: Judy H. Hastings Johnson, Jill S. Hastings Cane; m. Suzanne Saul, July 1, 1957; 1 child, Andrew C. AB, Amherst Coll., 1938; LLB, Columbia U., 1941. Bar: N.Y. 1941, R.I. 1946, U.S. Dist. Ct. R.I. 1947, U.S. Ct. Appeals (1st cir.) 1950, Mass. 1951. Assoc. Larkin, Rathbone & Perry, N.Y.C., 1941-42, Tillinghast, Collins & Tanner, Providence, 1946-53; ptnr. Tillinghast Collins & Graham, 1953-96, Tillinghast Licht Perkins Smith & Cohen, Providence, 1996—, cons. ptnr. estate planning and adminstrn. Bar examiner State of R.I., 1968-74, chmn. of bd., 1972-74; chmn. com. on future of criminal law R.I. Supreme Ct., 1973-75; bar examiner U.S. Dist. Ct. R.I., 1981-84. 1st lt. U.S. Army, 1942-46, 51-52, Korea. Mem. ABA, R.I. Bar Assn., Lawyers Alliance World Security. Baptist. Avocation: bird watching. Estate planning, Probate. Home: 210 Payton Ave Warwick RI 02889-5133 Office: Tillinghast Licht Perkins Smith & Cohen 10 Weybosset St Providence RI 02903-2818 E-mail: ehastings@tlslaw.com

HASTINGS, LAWRENCE VAETH, lawyer, physician, educator; b. Flushing, N.Y., Nov. 23, 1919; m. Doris Lorraine Erickson, Dec. 11, 1971. Student, Columbia U., 1939-40, student Law Sch., 1949-50; student, U. Mich. Engring. Sch., 1942-43, Washington U., 1943-44, U. Vt., 1943; MD, Johns Hopkins U., 1948; JD, U. Miami, 1953. Bar: Fla. 1954, U.S. Supreme Ct. 1960, D.C. 1976; cert. Am. Bd. Legal Medicine. Intern U.S. Marine Hosp., S.I., N.Y., 1948-49; asst. surgeon, sr. asst. surgeon USPHS, 1949-52; asst. resident surgery Bellevue Hosp. Med. Ctr., 1951; med. legal cons., trial atty. Miami, Fla., 1953—; ptnr. Lawrence V. Hastings, P.A.; asst. prof. medicine U. Miami, 1964-70, lectr. law, 1966; past adj. prof. St. Thomas U. Law Sch., Miami, Fla. Contbr. articles to profl. publs. Bd. dirs. Miami Heart Inst.; past trustee Barry U., Miami; trustee Fla. Internat. U., 1979-82. Served with AUS, 1943-46. Fellow Acad. Fla. Trial Lawyers, Am. Coll. Legal Medicine, Law-Sci. Acad. Found. Am.; mem. ABA, AMA, ATLA, Fla. Bar Assn., Dade County Bar Assn., Am. Acad. Forensic Scis., Fla. Med. Assn., Dade County Med. Assn., Fla. Bar (vice chmn. med. legal com. 1957, vice chmn. trial tactics com. 1963-65, chmn. steering com. trial tactics and basic anatomy seminars), Pitts. Inst. Legal Medicine, Johns Hopkins Med. and Surg. Assn., Pithotomy Club, Assn. Mil. Surgeons, U. Miami Law Alumni Assn. (pres. 1967), Acad. Psychosomatic Medicine, Fairbanks Ranch Country Club (Rancho Santa Fe, Calif.), Alpha Delta Phi, Phi Eta Sigma, Phi Alpha Delta. Roman Catholic. Clubs: Surf (bd. govs. 1976—, chmn. bd. 1980-82, pres. 1978-80), Com. 100, Indian Creek Country, Miami Beach, River of Jacksonville; N.Y. Athletic, Metropolitan, Princeton (N.Y.C.). Federal civil litigation, State civil litigation, Personal injury. Address: Palm Beach Towers 44 Coconut Row Palm Beach FL 33480

HASTINGS, WILLIAM CHARLES, retired state supreme court chief justice; b. Newman Grove, Nebr., Jan. 31, 1921; s. William C. and Margaret (Hansen) H.; m. Julie Ann Simonson, Dec. 29, 1946; children—Pamela, Charles, Steven. B.Sc., U. Nebr., 1942, J.D., 1948; LHD (hon.), Hastings Coll., 1991. Bar: Nebr. 1948. With FBI, 1942-43; mem. firm Chambers, Holland, Dudgeon & Hastings, Lincoln, 1948-65; judge 3d jud. dist. Nebr., 1965-79, Supreme Ct. Nebr., Lincoln, 1979-88, chief justice, 1988-95; ret., 1995. Bd. dirs. Nat. Conf. Chief Justices, 1989-91. Pres. Child Guidance Ctr., Lincoln, 1962, 63; v.p. Lincoln Community Coun., 1968, 69; vice chmn. Antelope Valley coun. Boy Scouts Am., 1968, 69; pres. 1st Presbyn. Ch. Found., 1968—; mem. Lincoln Parks and Recreation Adv. Bd., Govs. task force correctional dept. medical svcs., 2000; mem. Nebr. Pub. Employees Retirement Bd. Served with AUS, 1943-46. Named to Nebr. Jaycee Hall of Fame, 1998. Mem. ABA, Nebr. Bar Assn. (George H. Turner award 1991, Pioneer award 1992), Am. Jud. Soc., Lincoln Bar Assn., Nebr. Dist. Judges Assn. (past pres.), Nat. Conf. Chief Justices (past bd. dirs.), Am. Judicature Soc. (Herbert Harley award 1997), Phi Delta Phi. Republican. Presbyterian (deacon, elder, trustee). Club: East Hills Country (pres. 1959-60). Home: 1544 S 58th St Lincoln NE 68506-1407

HASTY, WILLIAM GRADY, JR. lawyer; b. Canton, Ga., July 7, 1947; s. William Grady and Hazel Bonnie (Wyatt) H.; m. Linda Lacey Nichols, Aug. 9, 1969; children: William Grady III, Lauren Elise, Jeffrey Nichols. AA, Reinhardt Coll., 1967; BS, U. Ga., 1969; JD, Mercer U., 1974. Bar: Ga. 1974, U.S. Dist. Ct. (no. dist.) Ga. 1975, U.S. Ct. Appeals (11th cir.) 1975. Bd. dirs. Bank of Canton, The Presdl. Roundtable. Chmn. Cherokee County Recreation Commn., 1975-85; charter mem. Leadership Cherokee County, 1987, steering com., 1988—; mem. Leadership Ga.; trustee Canton 1st United Meth. Ch., sec., exec. com.; bd. trustees Reinhardt Coll., Cherokee County Hosp. Authority, Northside Hosp., Cherokee; exec. bd. Cherokee Founder's Club; bd. dirs. Northside Hosp., Cherokee. Named Outstanding Citizen Cherokee County Commr., 1986, 87. Mem. VFW, ATLA, Ga. Bar Assn., Canton Bar Assn., Blue Ridge Bar Assn., Trial Lawyers Assn. Ga., Phoenix Soc. Atlanta, Canton Golf Club, Moose Club, Atlanta Track Club, Cherokee County C. of C., Commerce Club Atlanta. Avocations: tennis, running, fishing, hunting. Banking, General civil litigation, Personal injury. Home: 1746 Cumming Hwy Canton GA 30114-8043 Office: William G Hasty Jr PC PO Box 1818 211 E Main St Canton GA 30114-2710

HATCH, DENISON HURLBUT, JR. lawyer; b. Greenwich, Conn., Sept. 7, 1949; s. Denison Hurlbut and Louise (Bingham) H.; m. Wendy Ann Swanson, Sept. 4, 1971;children: Denison H. III, Erica Swanson. AB, Cornell U., 1971; JD, Northwestern U., 1980. Bar: Del. 1980, U.S. Dist. Ct. Del. 1980, U.S. Ct. Appeals (3rd cir.) 1983, U.S. Ct. Claims 1984, U.S. Tax Ct. 1984, U.S. Supreme Ct. 1983. Assoc. Morris, Nichols, Arsht & Tunnell, Wilmington, Del., 1980-88, ptnr., 1989—. Mem. ABA (taxation sect.), Del. Bar Assn. (asst. to pres. 1983-84), Richard Rodney Inn of Ct., Wilmington, 1985-87. Republican. Contracts commercial, Pension, profit-sharing, and employee benefits, Corporate taxation. Home: PO Box 1347 Wilmington DE 19899-1347 Office: Morris Nichols Arsht & Tunnell 1201 N Market St Ste 1347 Wilmington DE 19899-1347 E-mail: dhatch@mnat.com

HATCH, MIKE, state attorney general; m. Patti Hatch; 3 children BS in Polit. Sci. with honors, U. Minn., Duluth, 1970; JD, U. Minn., 1973. Commr. of commerce State of Minn., 1983-89; pvt. practice law; atty. gen. State of Minn., 1999—. Office: Minn Atty Gen's Office 1400 NCL Tower 445 Minnesota St Saint Paul MN 55101*

HATCHER, JAMES GREGORY, lawyer; b. Charleston, S.C., May 30, 1968; m. Quinton Larue and Wilma Pearl H.; m. Julia Kate Harris, Sept. 20, 1997. BA in History, Philosophy, Vanderbilt U., 1990; JD, Wake Forest U., 1993. Bar: N.C. 1993, S.C. 1995, U.S. Dist. Ct. (we. dist.) N.C. Atty. Russell & King, PA, Asheville, N.C., 1993-94, Erdman & Hockfield, LLP, Charlotte, 1995-98, The McIntosh Law Firm P.C., Charlotte, 1998—. Mem. N.C. Bar Assn., S.C. Bar Assn., N.C. Acad. Trial Lawyers, Mecklenburg County Bar Assn. (family law sect.). Family and matrimonial. Office: The McIntosh Law Firm PC 428 E 4th St Ste 201 Charlotte NC 28202-2496

HATFIELD, DEBORAH L. lawyer; b. Kenosha, WI, Apr. 28, 1970; d. James Oscar and Charlotte Ann (Hess) H. AA in Arts & Scis., Univ. Wisconsin-Marathon Ctr., Wansau, WI, 1990; BA Bus. Admin., Univ. Wisconsin-Whitewater, Whitewater, WI, 1992; JD, Univ. Wisconsin, Madison, WI, 1996. Bar, Wisconsin, 1996. Atty. Hatfield Law Office, Elcho, WI, 1996—, Langlade Co. Child Support Agency, Antigo, 1999—. Judge, mock trial, 1997—. 1st vice pres., Lions-Hyland Lakes, Deerbrook, WI, 1997—. Recipient Woman of the yr., AAUW, Wansau, WI, 1992. Mem. Wisconsin Bar Assn., Langlade County Bar Assn. Lutheran. Office: Hatfield Law Office N11226 Antigo St Elcho WI 54428-9613

HATFIELD, JACK KENTON, lawyer, accountant; b. Medford, Okla., Jan. 26, 1922; s. Loate L. and Cora (Walsh) H.; m. D. Ann Keltner, Dec. 5, 1943 (dec. Sept. 1988); children: Susan Kathryn Hatfield Bechtold, Sally Ann Hatfield Clark; m. K. Dean Walker, Aug. 7, 1997; m. Dores Hamaker, Aug. 9, 2000. BS in BA, Phillips U., Enid, Okla., 1947; BA, Phillips U., 1953; LLB, Oklahoma City U., 1954, JD, 1967. Bar: U.S. Dist. Ct. (we. dist.) Okla. 1954, U.S. Supreme Ct. 1961, U.S. Dist. Ct. (no. dist.) Okla. 1967, U.S. Ct. Appeals (10th cir.) 1968; CPA 1954. Pvt. practice, Enid, Okla., 1954-58; with Dept. Interior, Tulsa, 1958-77; pvt. practice, 1977—. Mem. ABA, Okla. Bar Assn., Tulsa Co. Bar Assn., Am. Inst. CPA's, Okla. Soc. CPA's. Club: Petroleum. Avocations: photography, tennis. Estate planning, Probate, Personal income taxation. Home: 4013 E 86th St Tulsa OK 74137-2609 Office: 7060 S Yale Ave Ste 601 Tulsa OK 74136-5739

HATHAWAY, GARY RAY, lawyer; b. Liberal, Kans., July 5, 1942; s. Addison E. And Helen M. (Nix) H.; m. Sonja J. Brewer, Aug. 6, 1977. BA, Southwestern Coll., Winfield, Kans., 1964; JD, Washburn U., 1969. Bar: Kans. 1969, U.S. Dist. Ct. Kans. 1969, U.S. Ct. Appeals (10th cir.) 1979, U.S. Supreme Ct. 1978. County atty. Grant County, Ulysses, Kans., 1971-72, 80-84; ptnr. Hathaway, Kimball and Campbell, 1972-2000; pvt. practice, 2000—. City atty. City of Ulysses, 1972-76. Mem. N.Am. Elk Breeders Assn., Am. Legion, Elks, Kiwanis, Phi Alpha Delta. Republican. Oil, gas, and mineral, General practice, Probate. Home: 218 N Wilson St Ulysses KS 67880-1950 Office: Hathaway Kimball & Campbell PO Box 27 Ulysses KS 67880-0527

HATHAWAY, STANLEY KNAPP, lawyer; b. Osceola, Nebr., July 19, 1924; s. Franklin E. and Velma Clara (Holbrook) H.; m. Roberta Louise Harley, Nov. 26, 1948; children: Susan Garrett, Sandra D'Amico. AB, U. Nebr., 1948, LLB, 1950; LLD, U. Wyo., 1975. Bar: Nebr. 1950, Wyo. 1950, U.S. Dist. Ct. Wyo., Nebr., Mont. 1950, U.S. Supreme Ct. 1964. Sole practice, Torrington, Wyo., 1950-66; gov. State of Wyo., 1967-75; sec. U.S. Dept. Interior, 1975; assoc. Hathaway, Speight & Kunz, Cheyenne, Wyo., 1975—. County atty. Goshen County (Wyo.), 1955-62. Decorated Air medals with 5 clusters. Mem. ABA, Wyo. State Bar Assn., Masons (Cheyenne), Shriners (Rawlins, Wyo.). Anglican. Administrative and regulatory, General corporate, General practice. Office: Hathaway Speight & Kunz 2515 Warren Ave Cheyenne WY 82001-3113

HAUBERG, ROBERT ENGELBRECHT, JR. lawyer; b. Jackson, Miss., Oct. 26, 1943; s. Robert Engelbrecht and Robbie Mae (Bowen) H.; m. Claudia Carithers; children: Greta, Patrick, Michael. BA, U. Miss., 1965; MA, Yale U., 1967, JD, 1970. Bar: N.Y. 1971, U.S. Dist. Ct. (so. dist.) N.Y. 1971, U.S. Ct. Appeals (2d cir.) 1971, D.C. 1974, U.S. Dist. Ct. D.C. 1974, U.S. Ct. Appeals (D.C. cir.) 1974, U.S. Supreme Ct. 1974, U.S. Ct. Appeals (5th cir.) 1988, U.S. Dist. Ct. (no. dist.) Tex. 1989, U.S. Dist. Ct. (so. dist.) Miss. 1989, Miss. 1991, U.S. Dist. Ct. (no. dist.) Miss. 1991. Assoc. Donovan, Leisure, Newton & Irvine, N.Y.C., 1970-73; asst. U.S. atty. U.S. Dept. Justice, Washington, 1973-76, trial atty., 1976-79, asst. chief, 1979-86, sr. trial atty., 1986-90, sr. litigation counsel Dallas Bank Fraud Task Force, 1990-91; ptnr. Watkins, Ludlam, Winter & Stennis, P.A., Jackson, Miss., 1991-98; shareholder Baker, Donelson, Bearman & Caldwell, Jackson/Washington, 1998—. Contbr. numerous articles to profl. jours. Mem. ABA (mem. anti-trust, criminal justice, litigation sects.), D.C. Bar Assn., Miss. Bar, Internat. Bar Assn., Yale Law Sch. Assn. (D.C. pres. 1986-87, exec. com. 1987-88, 93-97), Beta Theta Pi. Episcopalian. Avocations: sports, music. Antitrust, Federal civil litigation, Criminal. Home: 4656 Calnita Pl Jackson MS 39211-5801

HAUBOLD, SAMUEL ALLEN, lawyer; b. Watertown, S.D., July 29, 1938; s. Gustuv Herman and Leone Marjorie (York) H.; m. Caroline V. Thompson. Sept. 27, 1969; 1 child, Caroline A. BS in Engring., Northwestern U.; JD, Harvard U. Bar: Ill. 1966, N.Y. 1990, U.S. Dist. Ct. (no. dist.) Ill. 1966, U.S. Ct. Appeals (7th cir.) 1970, U.S. Ct. Appeals (9th cir.) 1979, U.S. Supreme Ct. 1974. Assoc. Kirkland & Ellis, Chgo., 1966, ptnr., 1972—; resident ptnr. Kirkland & Ellis Internat., London, 1994—. Served to lt. USN, 1960-63. Mem. ABA, Ill. Bar Assn., Internat. Bar Assn., Mid-Am. Club, Saddle and Cycle Club (Chgo.), The Hurlingham Club (London), City of London Club. Presbyterian. Antitrust, Federal civil litigation, Nuclear power. Home: 40 S Eaton Pl London SW1W 9JJ England Office: Kirkland & Ellis Internat Old Broad St London EC2N 1HQ England

HAUER, JAMES ALBERT, lawyer; b. Fond du Lac, Wis., Apr. 3, 1924; s. Albert A. and Hazel M. (Corcoran) H.; children: Stephen, John, Paul, Christopher, Patrick. BCE, Marquette U., 1948, LLB, 1949; bank mgmt. cert., Columbia U., 1957, U. Wis., 1959. Bar: Wis., U.S. Dist. Ct. (ea. dist.), U.S. Ct. Appeals (9th cir.), U.S. Dist. Ct. (fed. dist.) 1958. Patent counsel Ira Milton Jones, Milw., 1949; chief counsel Wauwatosa Realty, 1950-57; v.p. Wauwatosa (Wis.) State Bank, 1957-67; pres. Milw. We. Bank, 1967-69, Prem Constrn. Co., Milw., 1969-73; pvt. practice Elm Grove, Wis., 1973-86, Sun City, Ariz., 1986—. Pres., bd. dirs. Sunshine Svc., Sun City, Meals on Wheels, Sun City. With USMCR, 1942-45. Mem. Wis. Bar Assn., Ariz. Patent Law Assn. (charter). Roman Catholic. Land use and zoning (including planning), Patent, Real property. Office: 9915 W Royal Oak Rd # Gh1078 Sun City AZ 85351-3163

HAUGHT, WILLIAM DIXON, lawyer, writer; b. Kansas City, Kans., June 12, 1939; s. Walter Dixon and Florence Louise (Rhoads) H.; m. Julia Jane Headstream, July 22, 1967; 1 dau., Stephanie Jane. B.S., U. Kans., 1961; LL.B., U Kans., 1964; LL.M., Georgetown U., 1968. Bar: Kans. 1964, Ark. 1971. Assoc. Stanley, Schroeder, Weeks, Thomas & Lysaught, Kansas City, Kans., 1968-70; ptnr. Wright, Lindsey & Jennings, Little Rock, 1970-91; pvt. practice, 1991-95; ptnr. Haught & Wade, 1996—. Author: Arkansas Probate System, 1977, 5th ed. 1992, (with others) Probate and Estate Administration: The Law in Arkansas, 1983. Served to capt. USAR, 1964-68, Korea, Washington. Mem. ABA (coun. chmn. coms.), Am. Coll. Trust and Estate Counsel (regent, editor studies program, chmn. editl. bd., state chair), Internat. Acad. Estate and Trust Law, Am. Law Inst., Am. Counsel Assn., Ark. Bar Assn. (chmn. probate law sect., chmn. econs. of law practice com., chmn. agrl. law com., chmn. juris law reform com.), Ctrl. Ark. Estate Coun., Pulaski County Bar Assn., Ark. Bar Found., Country Club of Little Rock. Presbyterian. Estate planning, Probate, Estate taxation. Office: Haught & Wade 111 Center St Ste 1320 Little Rock AR 72201-4405 E-mail: wdh@haughtwade.com

HAUHART, ROBERT CHARLES, lawyer, educator; b. St. Louis, Dec. 17, 1950; s. Shields and Naomi (Allen) H. BS, So. Ill. U., 1972; MA, Washington U., St. Louis, 1973; JD, U. Balt., 1981; PhD, U. Va., 1982. Bar: Md. 1982, Pa. 1984, U.S. Dist. Ct. (mid. dist.) Pa. 1984, U.S. Ct. Appeals (3d cir.) 1984, U.S. Dist. Ct. (no. dist.) N.Y. 1987, U.S. Ct. Appeals (2d cir.) 1987, N.Y. 1988, D.C. 1989, U.S. Dist. Ct. D.C. 1989, U.S. Ct. Appeals (4th and D.C. cirs.) 1989. Sole practice, Balt., 1982-84; assoc. Rieders, Travis Law Firm, Williamsport, Pa., 1985-86; atty. Lewisburg (Pa.) Prison Project, 1984-86, Prisoners Legal Services N.Y., 1986-88, D.C. Pub. Defender Service, 1988—2001. Adj. prof. SUNY-Plattsburgh, 1987-88, George Washington U., Washington, 1992; vis. assoc. prof. Towson (Md.) State U., 1980-84. Author: Paralegal Manual for Prisoner Advocacy, 1985, Prisoners' Civil Actions in Federal Court, 1986, Due Process Administration Reviews, 1986, Rule 37 F.R.C.P. Motions to Compel, 1987. Mem. ABA, Am. Sociol. Assn., Balt. City Bar Assn. (dir. speaker's bur. 1982-83). Home and Office: 6112 Stuart Ave Baltimore MD 21209-4022 Business E-Mail: vze2dtmm@verizon.net

HAURY, JOHN CARROLL, lawyer; b. Louisville, Aug. 24, 1948; s. Harry Clay and Louise (Rose) H.; children: Amanda, Jonas Dylan, Samuel Compton; m. Sarah Belinda Polk. BA, Wesleyan U., 1970; JD, Ind. U., 1975. Bar: Ind. 1975, U.S. Dist. Ct. (so. dist.) Ind. 1975. Chief dep. Lawrence County Prosecutor's Office, Bedford, Ind., 1975-78; ptnr. Robbins & Haury, 1975-83, Haury & Nelson, Bedford, 1983-89; pvt. practice, 1990-92; ptnr. Haury & Hall, 1992-96, Haury & Woodward, Bedford, 1996—. Past bd. dirs., pres. Lawrence County United Way, 1980-84; past pres., bd. dirs. Lawrence county Park Bd., past Ind. Legal Services Orgn. Mem. Ind. State Bar Assn., Lawrence County Bar Assn. (past pres. and sec.), Assn. Trial Lawyers Am. Avocations: basketball, tennis (USTA umpire), running, golf. Criminal, Family and matrimonial, Personal injury. Home: 2201 Olcott Blvd Bloomington IN 47401-7106 Office: 1534 I St Bedford IN 47421-3836

HAUSELT, DENISE ANN, lawyer; b. Wellsville, N.Y., Oct. 12, 1956; BS, Cornell U., 1979, JD, 1983. Bar: N.Y. 1984, Ill. 1984, U.S. Dist. Ct. (we. dist.) N.Y. 1984, U.S. Bankruptcy Ct. 1984. Summer assoc. Wildman, Harrold, Allen & Dixon, Chgo., 1982; assoc. Nixon Peabody LLP, Rochester, N.Y., 1983-86; asst. counsel Corning (N.Y.) Inc., 1986-93, divsn. counsel, 1993-99, asst. gen. counsel, 1999-2000, asst. gen. counsel, asst. sec., 2000—01, corp. sec., 2001—. Bd. dirs. 171 Cedar Arts Ctr., The Rockwell Mus., The Corning Found., The Corning Mus. Glass. Adv. coun. Cornell Law Sch.; sec. Rockwell Mus. and Corning Inc. Found. Recipient Am. Jurisprudence Constl. Law prize, Cornell U., 1981. Mem. ABA, Am. Corp. Counsel Assn., Cornell Law Assn., Keuka Yacht Club. Republican. Avocations: sailing, skiing. Antitrust, Contracts commercial, General corporate. Office: Corning Inc Riverfront Plz Mp Hq E2 Corning NY 14831-0001

HAUSER, CHRISTOPHER GEORGE, lawyer; b. Syracuse, N.Y., May 15, 1954; s. W. Dieter and Nancy (Keating) H. BA, Washington & Jefferson Coll., 1976; JD, Dickinson Sch. Law, 1979. Bar: Pa. 1979, U.S. Dist. Ct. (we. dist.) Pa. 1981, N.Y. 1987, U.S. Supreme Ct. 1992. Legal asst. Pa. Dept. of Justice, Harrisburg, 1978-79; assoc. McDowell, McDowell, Wick & Daly, Bradford, 1979-83; ptnr. McDowell, Wick, Daly, Gallup, & Hauser, and predecessor firm McDowell, McDowell, Wick & Daly, 1983—; broker, owner Re/Max Alpine Sales, Ellicottville, N.Y., 1991-93. Pres./owner Alpine Sales and Rental Mgmt., Inc., Ellicottville, N.Y., 1987-94; chmn. adv. bd. Office Econ. Cmty. Devel., Bradford, 1988—. Chmn. campaign Bradford Area United Way, 1984, v.p., 1987-89, pres., 1990-92; chmn. Downtown Bradford Revitalization Corp., 1986—; Bradford Parking Authority, 1986-94, 99—; pres. Alleghany Highlands coun. Boy Scouts Am., Falconer, N.Y., 1986-88; dir. Bradford Econ. Devel. Corp., 1987—, Exch. Club, 1989-91; sec., treas. Bradford Redevel. Authority, 1992-96, chmn., 1996—; active Bradford Area Citizens Adv. Com., 1992; dir. Pa. Economy League, 1997—; dir., sec. Bradford Area Alliance, 1997-98; bd. dirs. Rte. 219 Assn., 1996-98; v.p. Continental One, 1998—, pres., 2000—; dist. justice McKean County, Pa., 2000—. Recipient Outstanding Svc. award Bradford Area United Way, 1985, Silver Beaver award Allehany Highlands coun. Boy Scouts Am., 1990, Founder's award Order Arrow Boy Scouts Am., 1991, Cmty. Svc. award City of Bradford Office Econ. and Cmty. Devel., 1995; named Bus. Person of Yr. Bradford C. of C., 1986, One of Outstanding Young Men Am. U.S. Jaycees, 1983. Mem. N.Y. Bar Assn., Pa. Bar Assn., McKean County Bar Assn. (v.p. 1992-93, pres. 1994-96), Bradford Area Jaycees (pres. 1983-85), Pennhills Club (sec. 1985-90, 99-2000, pres. 1990-92, 2000—), Bradford Club. Republican. Episcopalian. General corporate, Finance, Real property. Home: 110 Congress St Bradford PA 16701-2228 Office: McDowell Wick Daly Gallup & Hauser PO Box 361 78 Main St Bradford PA 16701-2026 E-mail: cghauser@penn.com, mwalaw@penn.com

HAUSER, HARRY RAYMOND, lawyer; b. N.Y.C., July 12, 1931; s. Milton I. and Lillian (Perlman) H.; m. Deborah Marlowe, Aug. 6, 1954; children: Mark Jeffrey, Joshua Brook, Bradford John, Matthew Milton. AB, Brown U., 1953; JD, Columbia U., 1959. Bar: N.Y. 1959, Mass. 1963, Wash. 1972. Practice in, N.Y.C., 1959-61, Boston, 1962—; atty. Sperry Rand Corp., 1959-61, Hotel Corp. Am., N.Y.C., 1961-62, v.p., sec., gen. counsel, 1962-70; mem. firm Gadsby & Hannah, 1971—. Life trustee Temple Israel, Boston; pres. emeritus, dir. N. Bennett St. Sch.; trustee, gen. counsel The Boston Harbor Assn., Inc. Mem. ABA, N.Y. State Bar Assn., Mass. Bar Assn., D.C. Bar Assn., Internat. Bar Assn., Brown U. Club. General corporate, Real property. Home: 1175 Chestnut St #2 Newton Upper Falls MA 02464-1336 Office: Gadsby & Hannah 225 Franklin St Boston MA 02110-2804 E-mail: hhauser@ghlaw.com

HAUSER, RITA ELEANORE ABRAMS, lawyer; b. N.Y.C., July 12, 1934; d. Nathan and Frieda (Litt) Abrams; m. Gustave M. Hauser, June 10, 1956; children: Glenvil Aubrey, Ana Patricia. AB magna cum laude, CUNY Hunter Coll., 1954; D in Polit. Economy with highest honors, U. Strasbourg, France, 1955; Licence en Droit, U. Paris, 1958; student, Harvard U., 1955-56; LLB with honors, NYU, 1959; LLD (hon.), Seton Hall U., 1969, Finch Coll., 1969, U. Miami, Fla., 1971, Colgate U., 1995. Bar: D.C. 1959, N.Y. 1961, U.S. Supreme Ct. 1967. Atty. U.S. Dept. Justice, 1959-61; pvt. practice N.Y.C., 1961-67; ptnr. Moldover, Hauser, Strauss & Volin, 1968-72; sr. ptnr. Stroock & Stroock & Lavan, N.Y.C., 1972-92, of counsel, 1992—; pres. The Hauser Found., 1990—. Handmaker lectr., Louis Brandeis Lecture Series, U. Ky. Law Sch.; lectr. internat. law Naval War Coll. and Army War Coll.; Mitchell lectr. in law SUNY, Buffalo; USIA lectr. constl. law Egypt, India, Australia, New Zealand; bd. dirs. The Eisenhower World Affairs Inst.; U.S. chmn. Internat. Ctr. for Peace in Middle East, 1984-92; bd. dirs. Internat. Peace Acad., chair 1993—; U.S. pub. del. to Vienna follow-up meeting of Conf. on Security and Cooperation in Europe, 1986-88; mem. adv. panel in internat. law U.S. Dept. State, 1986-92, Am. Soc. Internat. Law Award to honor Women in Internat. Law; mem. Pacific Coun. on Internat. Policy, 1998-2000; bd. dirs. The Rand Corp. Contbr. articles to profl. jours. U.S. rep. to UN commn. on Human Rights, 1969-72; mem. U.S. del. to Gen. Assembly UN, 1969; vice chmn. U.S. Adv. Com. on Internat. and Cultural Affairs, 1973-77; mem. N.Y.C. Bd. Higher Edn., 1974-76, Stanton Panel on internat. info., edn., cultural rels. to reorganize USIA and Voice of Am., 1974-75, Mid. East Study Gruop Brookings Inst., 1975, 87-88, U.S. del. World Conf. Internat. Women's Yr., Mexico City, 1975; co-chair Com. for Re-election Pres., 1972, Presdl. Debates project LVW, 1976, Coalition for Regan/Bush; adv. bd. Nat. News Coun., 1977-79; bd. dirs. Bd for Internat. Broadcasting, 1977-80, Catalyst, Internat. Peace Acad., The Aspen Inst., The RAND Corp., U.S. Coun. Germany; trustee, exec com. N.Y. Philharm. Soc.; trustee Lincoln Ctr. Performing Arts; adv. bd. Ctr. For Law and Nat. Security, U. Va. Law Sch., 1978-84; vis. com. Ctr. Internat. Affairs Harvard U., 1975-81, John F. Kennedy Sch. Govt., Harvard U., 1992—, chair adv. bd. Hauser Ctr. for Non-Profit Orgns. at Harvard U.; dean's bd. advisor's Harvard Law Sch., 1996—, vice-chair, nat. co-chair univ. fund-raising campaign, 1997-2000; bd. advisors Mid. East Inst., Harvard U.; bd of visitors Georgetown Sch. Fgn. Svc., 1989-94; chmn. adv. panel Internat. Parlimentary Group for Human Rights in Soviet Union, 1984-86; mem. Lawyers Com. for Human Rights, 1995—; mem. spl. refugee adv. panel Dept. State, 1981; bd. fellows Claremont U. Ctr. & Grad. Sch., 1990-94; former trustee Internat. Legal Ctr., Legal Aid Soc. N.Y., Freedom House; mem. Lawyer's Comm. Human Rights, 1996—. Fulbright grant U. Strasbourg, 1955; Intellectual Exch. fellow Japan Soc.; recipient Jane Addams Internat. Women's Leadership award, 1996, Women in Internat. Law award Am. Soc. Internat. Law, 1995, Fulbright award for Fulbright Alumni, 1997, Servant of Justice award, Legal Aid Soc. N.Y., 2000. Fellow ABA (life, mem. standing coms. on law and nat. security 1979-85, standing com. on world order under law 1969-78, standing com. on jud. selection, tenure, compensation 1977-79, coun. sect. on ind. rights and responsibilities 1970-73, advisor bd. jour. 1973-78); mem. Am. Soc. Internat. Law (v.p. 1988—, mem. exec. com. 1971-76), Am. Fgn. Law Assn. (bd. dirs.), Am. Arbitration Assn. (past bd. dirs.), Ams. Soc. (bd. dirs. 1988—), Coun. Fgn. Rels. (bd. dirs.), Internat. Inst. for Strategic Studies (London, bd. dirs. 1994—), Internat. Adv. Bd., Jaffee Ctr. for Strategic Studies, Tel Aviv Univ. (1999—), Am. Coun. on Germany, The Atlantic Coun. U.S., Friends of the Hauge Acad. Internat. Law (bd. dirs.), Assn. of Bar of City of N.Y., Catalyst (bd. dirs. 1989-96). Republican. Banking, Private international, Public international. Office: Stroock & Stroock & Lavan 180 Maiden Ln Fl 17 New York NY 10038-4937 also: The Hauser Found Office of Pres 712 5th Ave New York NY 10019-4108

HAUSMAN, C. MICHAEL, lawyer, judge; b. Chgo., Oct. 4, 1940; s. Charles Martin and Evelyn (Partridge) H.; children: Laura, Sarah, Craig, Karen, Richard, Ronald, Charles, Ashley, Courtney Megan. BS, Marquette U., 1962, JD, 1967. Bar: Wis. 1967, U.S. Dist. Ct. (ea. dist.) Wis. 1967, U.S. Supreme Ct. 1972. Ptnr. Frisch, Dudek & Slattery, Ltd., Milw., 1967-88; mcpl. judge City of Delafield, 1983—; ptnr. Slattery & Hausman, Ltd., Waukesha, 1988—2001, C. Michael Hausman and Assocs. Ltd., Delafield, 2001—. Lectr. State Bar of Wis. Family Law Seminars, Am. Acad. Matrimonial Lawyers; bd. dirs. Collaborative Family Law Coun. Wis., Inc., 2001—. Named Outstanding Young Man Brookfield (Wis.) Jaycees, 1975. Fellow: Internat. Acad. Matrimonial Lawyers, Am. Acad. Matrimonial Lawyers (pres. Wis. chpt. 1988—89); mem.: ATLA, Am. Arbitration Assn., Wis. Acad. Trial Lawyers, State Bar Wis., Milw. Jr. Bar Assn. (bd. dirs. 1969—71), Brookfield C.of C. (pres. 1977—78), Brookfield Rotary (pres. 1980—81). Avocations: fishing, hiking, stamp and coin collecting. Family and matrimonial, Personal injury, Workers' compensation. Home and Office: 329 GeneseeSt Delafield WI 53018

HAUSNER, JOHN HERMAN, judge; b. Detroit, Oct. 31, 1932; s. John E. and Anna (Mudrak) H.; m. Alice R. Kieltyka, Aug. 22, 1959. Ph.B. cum laude, U. Detroit, 1954, M.A., 1957, J.D. summa cum laude, 1966. Bar: Mich. 1967, U.S. Ct. Appeals (6th cir.) 1968, U.S. Supreme Ct. 1971, U.S. Tax Ct. 1976, U.S. Ct. Claims 1976, U.S. Ct. Mil. Appeals 1976. Tchr. Detroit Pub. Schs., 1954, 56-59; tchg. fellow U. Cin., 1959-61; instr. U. Detroit, 1961-74, sole practice, 1967-69; asst. U.S. atty., 1969-73; chief asst. U.S. atty. ea. dist. Mich., 1973-76; judge 3rd Jud. Cir. Mich., Wayne County, 1976-94; ret. 3d Jud. Cir. Mich., 1994, 1994. Lectr. Law Sch.; faculty adviser Nat. Jud. Coll., 1978-79. Author: Sebastian, The Essence of My Soul, 1982; contbr. articles to Detroit Advertiser. Active Civic Searchlight. Served with U.S. Army, 1954-56. Mem. Fed. Bar Assn. (mem. exec. bd. Detroit chpt. 1976-82), State Bar Mich., Mich. Retired Judges Assn., Blue Key, Alpha Sigma Mu. Republican. Home: 22433 Louise St Saint Clair Shores MI 48081-2034 also: 8420 E Desert Palm Tucson AZ 85730-4723

HAUTZINGER, JAMES EDWARD, lawyer; b. Apr. 15, 1936; s. Julius M. and Iva (Beach) H,; m. Susan Jean O'Brien, June 20, 1959; childrn: Peter Grattan, Sarah Jean, Andrew Beach; m. Leslie Ann Walker, Apr. 21, 1979; m. Anne Phillips, Oct. 28, 2000). BA, Grinnell Coll., 1958; JD, U. Chgo., 1961. Bar: Colo. 1961, U.S. Dist. Ct. Colo. 1961, U.S. Supreme Ct. 1973, U.S. Ct. Appeals (10th cir.) 1961, U.S. Ct. Appeals (5th cir.) 1981, U.S. Ct. Appeals (9th cir.) 1980. Assoc. Sherman & Howard, Denver, 1961-67; ptnr., 1967-98; counsel, 1999—. Mem. exec. com.; lectr. Coll. Labor and Employment Lawyers, Legal counsel People for Haskell campaign, 1972-78, Hart for Senate campaign, 1980; alt. del. Dem. Nat. Conv., 1968; mem. vis. com. U. Chgo. Law Sch., 1978-80. Mng. editor Chgo. Law Rev., 1960. Mem. ABA, Colo. Bar Assn. (labor law com.), denver Bar Assn., Indsl. Rels. Rsch. Assn., Phi Beta Kappa, Order of Coif. Clubs: Denver Athletic. Antitrust, Labor. Office: Sherman & Howard 633 17th St Ste 3000 Denver CO 80202-3665 E-mail: jhautzin@sah.com

HAVEL, RICHARD W. lawyer; b. Fairmont, Minn., Sept. 20, 1946; s. Thomas Earl and Elizabeth (Shiltz) H.; m. Arlene Havel, July 6, 1968; children: Stephanie, Derek. BA, Notre Dame U., 1968; JD, UCLA, 1971. Bar: Calif., U.S. Dist. Ct. (no., ea., cen. and so. dists.) Calif., U.S. Ct. Appeals (9th cir.). Atty. Shutan & Trost, L.A., 1971-80, Sidley & Austin, L.A., 1980—. Instr. law U. Loyola, 1975-80; bd. govs. Fin. Lawyers Conf., 1991-94, 95-98, officer, 1998-2001; spkr., panelist Bankruptcy Litigation Inst., 1989-95, ALI-ABA, 1989, 90, 91; chmn. L.A. City Indsl. Devel. Authority, 1993-98, bd. dirs., 1998-2000. Contbr. articles to profl. jours. Trustee Jonsson/UCLA Cancer Ctr., 1998—. Fellow Am. Coll. Bankruptcy, 1997; mem. ABA, Calif. Bar Assn., L.A. County Bar Assn. (comml. law & bankruptcy sect. bankruptcy subcom. 1986-89, exec. com. 1987-90, lawyer assistance com. 1985—), UCLA Law Alumni Assn. (trustee 1996—). Bankruptcy, Mergers and acquisitions. Office: Sidley & Austin 555 W 5th St 40th Fl Los Angeles CA 90013-1010 E-mail: RHavel@Sidley.com

HAVEN, MILTON M. lawyer; b. Paterson, N.J., July 12, 1909; s. Harry and Minnie (Brown) H.; m. Phyllis Grossman, Dec. 23, 1938; children: Miles J., Constance A. AB, Syracuse U., 1931, LLB, 1933, JD, 1968. Bar: N.Y. Assoc. Hon. John E. Mack, Poughkeepsie, N.Y., 1933-46; rent examiner OPA, 1946-50; acting sitting city judge, clk. of City Ct., 1950-54; assoc. Edward J. Mack, 1954-62, 66-70; judge City Ct., 1962-66, 70-72; counsel to firm McCabe & Mack, 1972-80, Corbally, Gartland & Rapplelyea, Poughkeepsie, 1980—; jud. hearing officer 9th Jud. Dist., 1978-81. Mem. N.Y. State Mental Hygiene Coun. Pres. Poughkeepsie Jewish Ctr., 1942-43; pres. Temple Beth-El, Poughkeepsie, 1959-60, hon. trustee, 1985—; mem. adv. com. police sci. and correction adminstrn. CC, 1966-71; pres. Dutchess County Mental Health Assn., 1970-71, hon. trustee, 1990—; mem. adv. com. Pub. Welfare, Poughkeepsie, 1966-71; chmn. City Trial Com., Poughkeepsie, 1972-75; budget chair Dutchess County Area Chest and Coun., Poughkeepsie, 1952-54; mem. adv. bd. Marist Coll., Poughkeepsie, 1970-75; chmn. Dem. Com. City of Poughkeepsie, 1954-57; mem. bd. visitors Hudson River Psychiat. Ctr., 1977-88. Served with U.S. Army, 1942-43. Recipient Cert. of Appreciation Dutchess C.C., 1965, Dutchess Interfaith Coun., Poughkeepsie, 1990, Disting. Svc. award Mental Health Assn., Poughkeepsie, 1992, Van Bramer award, 1992. Mem. N.Y. State Bar Assn., Dutchess County Bar Assn. (pres. 1977-78), Masons, Harding Club (pres. 1937-38). Avocation: choir singing. Estate planning, General practice, Estate taxation. Home: 3 Ivy Ter Poughkeepsie NY 12601-4804

HAVIGHURST, CLARK CANFIELD, law educator, educator, law educator; b. Evanston, Ill., May 25, 1933; s. Harold Canfield and Marion Clay (Perryman) H.; m. Karen Waldron, Aug. 28, 1965; children: Craig Perryman, Marjorie Clark. BA, Princeton U., 1955; JD, Northwestern U., 1958. Bar: Ill. 1958, N.Y. 1961. Assoc. Debevoise Plimpton Lyons & Gates, N.Y.C., 1958, 61-64; assoc. prof. law Duke U., Durham, N.C., 1964-68, prof., 1968-86, William Neal Reynolds prof., 1986—; interim dean Duke U. Sch. Law, 1999. Dir. Program on Legal Issues in Health Care Duke U., 1969-88; adj. scholar Am Enterprise Inst. Pub. Policy Rsch., 1976—; resident cons. FTC, Washington, 1978, Epstein, Becker & Green, Washington, 1989-90; scholar in residence Inst. Medicine of NAS, Washington, 1972-73, RAND Corp., Santa Monica, 1999. Author: Deferred Compensation for Key Employees, 1964, Regulating Health Facilities Construction, 1974, Deregulating the Health Care Industry, 1982, Health Care Law and Policy, 1988, 2d edit., 1998, Health Care Choices: Private Contracts as Instruments of Health Reform, 1995; editor Law and Contemporary Problems jour., 1965-70. With U.S. Army, 1958-60. Mem. Inst. Medicine of Nat. Acad. Sci., Order of Coif Office: Duke U Sch Law PO Box 90360 Durham NC 27708-0360 E-mail: hav@law.duke.edu

HAWKEY, G. MICHAEL, lawyer, real estate developer; b. Apr. 17, 1941; m. Frances Tripp, Feb. 27, 1971; children: Samuel, Eliza, MacKenzie. AB, Princeton U., 1963; postgrad., Columbia Bus. Sch., 1964; LLB, Cornell U., 1967. Bar: Mass. 1967. Ptnr. Sullivan & Worcester LLP, Boston. Lectr. Mass. Restaurant Assn. Author: The Union-Management Controversy Over Subcontracting and Plant Relocation, 1963. Bd. dirs. Pacific Internat. Inst., Lewiston, Idaho, 1992-97, St. Lukes Cancer Rsch. Found., Cork, Ireland, 1994-97, Village Condominiums, Sun Valley, Idaho, 2001—; mem. N.Am. bd. Michael Smurfit Grad. Sch. Bus., Univ. Coll., Dublin, Ireland, 1994-98; trustee Maruzen Hawthorne Coll., Antrim, N.H., 1991-92; gov. Wianno Club, 1982-98; founder Sun Valley Properties, Pocatello, Idaho, Mettowee Valley Properties, Pawlet, Vt. Mem. Internat. Coun. Shopping Ctrs., Real Estate Fin. Assn. (bd. dirs. 1989-92), Sr. Execs. Club of Mass. Real Estate Fin. Assn., Mass. Conveyancers Assn., The Country Club (Brookline, Mass.). Avocations: golf, tennis, skiing, real estate development. Land use and zoning (including planning), Landlord-tenant, Real property. Home: 26 Arlington Rd Wellesley MA 02481-6129 Office: Sullivan & Worcester 1 Post Office Sq Ste 2300 Boston MA 02109-2129

HAWKINS, CARMEN DOLORAS, lawyer; b. L.A., Sept. 17, 1955; d. Lenell Herman Hawkins and Doloras Mondy. BA, U. Calif., Santa Cruz, 1977; JD, Georgetown U., 1981. Bar: Washington 1981, Calif. 1982, U.S. Dist. Ct. (cen. dist. Calif.) 1982, U.S. Ct. Appeals (9th cir.) 1982. Assoc. Law Offices of Thomas G. Neusom, L.A., 1982-83; pvt. practice law, 1984-88; atty. L.A. Community Coll., 1984-85; gen. counsel L.A. Trade Tech. Coll. Found., 1986-88; of counsel Wilson, Becks & Pyfrom, L.A., 1986-88; dep. city atty., 1988—. Bd. dirs. Calif. Dems. for New Leadership, Los Angeles, 1985-88; mem. New Frontier Dem. Club, Los Angeles, 1984-88, New Dem. Channel, Los Angeles, 1984-88; commr. City of Los Angeles Commn. on Bicentennial of U.S. Constitution, 1976, 87-89. Recipient Community Service award Los Angeles City Council, 1985, Community Service award Calif. State Senator Diane Watson, 1985, Community Service award Black Women Lawyers, 1986, Community Service award Los Angeles Councilman David Cunningham, 1986. Mem. ABA, Calif. Bar Assn. (com. on ethnic minorities 1988-92), L.A. County Bar Assn., L.A. County Barristers Assn. (exec. com. 1986-91), NAACP, Black Women Lawyers of L. A. (parliamentarian 1985-86), John M. Langston Bar Assn., Jack & Jill of Am., Los Angeles Chapter. Democrat. African Methodist Episcopalian. Avocations: bicycling, tennis. State civil litigation, Insurance, Probate. E-mail: chawkin@atty.lacity.org

HAWKINS, EDWARD JACKSON, lawyer; b. Fall River, Mass., June 24, 1927; s. Edward Jackson and Harriet (Sherman) H.; m. Janet Schwerdt; children: Daniel, George, Robert, Harriet. Grad., Phillips Acad., Andover, Mass., 1945; AB summa cum laude, Princeton U., 1950; LLB magna cum laude, Harvard U., 1953. Bar: Ohio 1954, D.C. 1990. Assoc., ptnr. Squire, Sanders & Dempsey, Cleve., 1953-78, ptnr. Cleve. and Washington, 1982-96, counsel, 1997-99; ret., 2000. Chief tax counsel U.S. Senate Fin. Com., Washington, 1979-80, minority tax counsel, 1981; gen. chmn. Cleve. Tax Inst., 1969. Contbr. articles to profl. jours. With U.S. Army, 1945-46. Mem. ABA (vice chmn. govt. rels. tax sect. 1987-89), Ohio Bar Assn., D.C. Bar Assn., Phillips Acad. Alumni Assn. (alumni coun. 1967-70), Quadrangle Club. Democrat. Home: 7404 Park Terrace Dr Alexandria VA 22307-2039 E-mail: ejhawkins2@aol.com

HAWKINS, FALCON BLACK, JR. federal judge; b. Charleston, S.C., Mar. 16, 1927; s. Falcon Black Sr. and Mae Elizabeth (Infinger) H.; m. Jean Elizabeth Timmerman, May 28, 1949; children: Richard Keith, Daryl Gene, Mary Elizabeth Hawkins Eddy, Steely Odell II. BS, The Citadel, 1958; LLB, U. S.C., 1963, JD, 1970. Bar: S.C. bar 1963. Leadingman electronics Charleston (S.C.) Naval Shipyard, 1948-60; salesman ACH Brokers, Columbia, S.C., 1960-63; from assoc. to sr. ptnr. firm Hollings & Hawkins and successor firms, Charleston, 1963-79; U.S. dist. judge Dist. of S.C., 1979—, chief judge, 1990-93, sr. status, 1993—. Served with Mcht. Marines, 1944-45, with AUS, 1945-46. Mem. Jud. Conf. 4th Jud. Circuit, ABA, S.C. Bar Assn., Charleston County Bar Assn., Am. Trial Lawyers Assn., S.C. Trial Lawyers Assn., Carolina Yacht Club, Hibernian Soc. Charleston, Masons. Democrat. Presbyterian. Office: Hollings Jud Ctr PO Box 835 Charleston SC 29402-0835 Fax: 843-579-1499

HAWKINS, MICHAEL DALY, federal judge; b. Winslow, Ariz., Feb. 12, 1945; s. William Bert and Patricia Agnes (Daly) H.; m. Phyllis A. Lewis, June 4, 1966; children: Aaron, Adam. BA, Ariz. State U., 1967, JD cum laude, 1970; LLM, U. Va., 1998. Bar: Ariz. 1970, U.S. Ct. Mil. Appeals 1971, U.S. Supreme Ct. 1974. Pvt. practice law, 1973-77, 80-94; U.S. atty. Dept. Justice, Phoenix, 1977-80; judge U.S. Ct. Appeals (9th cir.), 1994—. Mem. Appellate Cts. Jud. Nominating Commn., 1985-89. Staff editor: Ariz. State U. Law Jour, 1968-70. Mem. Ariz. Lottery Commn., 1980-83, Commn. on Uniform State Laws, 1988-93. Capt. USMC, 1970-73. Recipient Alumni Achievement award Ariz. State U., 1995. Mem. ABA, Maricopa County Bar Assn. (bd. dirs. 1975-77, 81-89, pres. 1987-88), State Bar of Ariz., Ariz. Trial Lawyers Assn. (bd. dirs. 1976-77, state sec. 1976-77), Phoenix Trial Lawyers Assn., Adminstrv. Conf. U.S. (pub. mem. 1985-94), Nat. Assn. Former U.S. Attys. (pres. 1989-90).

HAWKINS, RICHARD MICHAEL, lawyer; b. Nevada City, Calif., July 23, 1949; s. Robert Augustus and Virginia June (Hawke) H.; m. Linda Lee Chapman, Sept. 27, 1975; child, Alexandra Michelle. BS in Math., U. Calif., Davis, 1971; JD, U. Calif., San Francisco, 1974; LLM in Taxation, U. Pacific, 1983. Bar: Calif. 1974, U.S. Dist. Ct. (ea. dist.) Calif. 1974, U.S. Dist. Ct. (no. dist.) Calif. 1982, U.S. Ct. Claims 1982, U.S. Tax Ct. 1982, U.S. Ct. Appeals (9th cir.) 1982, U.S. Supreme Ct. 1982. From assoc. to ptnr. Larue & Francis, Nevada City, 1974-76; ptnr. Larue, Roach & Hawkins, 1977-78; of counsel Berliner & Ellers; ptnr. Berliner, Spiller & Hawkins, 1981; sole practice Grass Valley, Calif., 1981—. Bd. dirs. 49er Fire Dist., Nevada City, 1977-81, 89-98, asst. fire chief, 1981-83, fire chief, 1983-89. Mem. ABA, Calif. State Bar (cert. specialist in estate planning, trust and probate law 1990), Nevada County Bar Assn. (v.p. 1976), Order of Coif, Phi Kappa Phi. Republican. Roman Catholic. Avocations: bicycling, running, showing Morgan horses. Estate planning, Probate, Estate taxation. Home: 14762 Banner Quaker Hill Rd Nevada City CA 95959-8813 Office: 10563 Brunswick Rd Ste 2 Grass Valley CA 95945-7801 Fax: (530) 272-7861. E-mail: rhawk53@aol.com

HAWKINS, SCOTT ALEXIS, lawyer; b. Des Moines, Nov. 24, 1954; s. Alexis Merrill and Rosemary Kathryn (Carney) H. BS, Drake U., 1977, JD, 1981. Bar: Iowa 1982, U.S. Dist. Ct. (no. dist.) Iowa, Tex. 1983, U.S. Dist. Ct. (no. and we. dists.) Tex., U.S. Ct. Appeals (5th cir.) Tex. 1988. In house counsel Internat. Housing Systems Inc., Dallas, 1982-84; assoc. Durant & Mankoff, 1984-85; ptnr. Hawkins & Hawkins, 1985—. Gen. counsel Wednesday's Child Benefit Corp., Dallas, 1987-88; pres., gen. counsel Hunger Solutions, Inc., a non-profit orgn., 1989. Mem. ABA, State Bar Tex. General civil litigation, Landlord-tenant, Personal injury. Office: Hawkins & Hawkins 5747 Ridgetown Cir Dallas TX 75230-2657

HAWLEY, ROBERT CROSS, lawyer; b. Douglas, Wyo., Aug. 7, 1920; s. Robert Daniel and Elsie Corienne (Cross) H.; m. Mary Elizabeth Hawley McClellan, Mar. 3, 1944; children— Robert Cross, Mary Virginia, Laurie McClellan. BA with honors, U. Colo., 1943; LLB, Harvard U., 1949, JD, 1989. Bar: Wyo. 1950, Colo. 1950, U.S. Dist. Ct. Colo. 1950, U.S. Dist. Ct. Wyo. 1954, U.S. Ct. Appeals (10th cir.) 1955, Tex. 1960, U.S. Ct. Appeals (5th cir.) 1960, U.S. Supreme Ct. 1960, U.S. Dist. Ct. (so. dist.) Tex. 1961, U.S. Ct. Appeals (D.C. cir.) 1961, U.S. Ct. Appeals (8th cir.) 1979, U.S. Ct. Appeals (11th cir.) 1981, U.S. Dist. Ct. (we. dist.) Tex. 1987. Assoc. Bannister Weller & Friedrich, Denver, 1949-50; sr. atty. Continental Oil Co., Denver, 1952-58, counsel, Houston, 1959-62; ptnr., v.p. Ireland, Stapleton & Pryor, Denver, 1962-81; ptnr. Dechert Price & Rhoads, Denver, 1981-83, Hawley & VanderWerf, Denver, 1983-94; sole practice, Denver, 1994—; pres. Highland Minerals, Denver; bd. dirs. Bank of Denver; speaker oil and gas insts. Contbr. articles to Oil & Gas Pubs. Bd. dirs. Am. Cancer Soc., Denver, 1967-87, treas., 1981-82; chmn. U. Colo. Devel. Found., 1960-61; bd. dirs. Rocky Mountain Arthritis Found., 1987—, sec., 1993-94, vice chmn. Colo., 1994—; mem. adv. bd. ARC, 1988—; chmn. 1st Annual Retarded Children Campaign, 1963; dir. East Seal Chpt., 1966-68; bd. dirs. Craig Hosp., 1964-68. Lt. col. U.S. Army, Korean War. Recipient Alumni Recognition award U. Colo., Boulder, 1958, Meritorious Service award Monticello Coll., Godfrey, Ill., 1967, Humanitarian award Arthritis Found., 1992, Honored Lawyer award Law Club,

1993; Sigma Alpha Epsilon scholar, 1941-43. Mem. Denver Assn. Oil and Gas Title Lawyers (pres. 1983-84), Denver Petroleum Club (pres. 1978-79), Harvard Law Sch. Assn. Colo. (pres. 1980-81), Associated Alumni U. Colo. (pres. and bd. dirs. 1956-57), Law Club, Denver (pres. 1958-59), ABA, Colo. Bar Assn., Denver Bar Assn., Tex. Bar Assn., Wyo. Bar Assn., Fed. Energy Bar Assn. (legal and lands com.), Interstate Oil and Gas Compact Comn., Harvard Alumni Assn., Rocky Mountain Oil and Gas Assn., Rocky Mountain Petroleum Pioneers (pres. 1991-92), Wyo. Pioneer Assn., Chevaliers du Tastevin, Denver Country Club, Petroleum Club, Gyro Club, Univ. Club Denver, Garden of the Gods Club (Colo. Springs), Colo. Arlberg Club, Mile High Club, U. Colo. Alumni Club (Living Legend award). Republican. Episcopalian. Author, co-author: Landman's Handbook, Law of Federal Oil and Gas Leases, Problems of Surface Damages, Federal Oil and Gas Leases--The Sole Party in Interest Debacle. FERC practice, Oil, gas, and mineral. Home: 4401 E 3rd Ave Denver CO 80220-5627 Address: Hawley & Hawley 4401 E 3rd Ave Denver CO 80220-5627

HAWS, ROBERT JOHN, lawyer; b. Highland Park, Ill., Aug. 1, 1947; s. Robert William and Ardyth E. (Meintzer) H.; m. Theresa M. Giaimo, Oct. 9, 1982; children: Benjamin Robert, Theodore Matthew. BA, Rutgers Coll., 1969; JD, Seton Hall U., 1976. Bar: N.J. 1976, U.S. Dist. Ct. N.J. 1976, U.S. Supreme Ct. 1986; cert. civil trial atty. Dep. atty. gen. State of N.J., Trenton, 1977-83; pvt. practice, East Brunswick, N.J. Mem. ABA, Assn. Trial Lawyers Am., N.J. Trial Lawyers Assn., N.J. State Bar Assn., Middlesex County Bar Assn. Democrat. Roman Catholic. Avocation: skiing, travel, mountain biking. State civil litigation, Personal injury, Professional liability. Home: 275 Edlys Ln North Brunswick NJ 08902-3057 Office: 4 Cornwall Dr Ste 201 East Brunswick NJ 08816-3332

HAY, DENNIS LEE, lawyer; b. L.A., Feb. 18, 1958; s. Frank Henry, Jr. and Kyoko (Sukuya) H.; m. Kerry Lynne Hatfield, Aug. 11, 1984; children: Michelle, Jason, Katheryne. BS in Fin., San Jose State U., 1984; JD, U. Honolulu, 1988. Bar: Calif. 1989. Law clk. Legal Aid Soc. of Alameda Co., Hayward, Calif., 1985-87, Cohn, Becker & Jacquint, Hayward, 1987, Souza, Coats, McInnis, Mehlhaff & Hay, Tracy, 1987-89, assoc. counsel atty., 1989-92; ptnr. Mehlhaff & Hay, 1992—; judge pro tem San Joaquin Superior Cts. Prof. law U. Honolulu Law Sch., Modesto, Calif. Mem. Calif. Bar Assn., San Joaquin County Bar Assn. (chairperson bus. litig. sect. com. 1997-98). Republican. Presbyterian. Avocations: drag racing, horse back riding, raquetball. General civil litigation, Consumer commercial, Contracts commercial. Office: Mehlhaff & Hay PO Box 1129 23950 S Chrisman Rd Tracy CA 95378-1129

HAY, JOHN LEONARD, lawyer; b. Lawrence, Mass., Oct. 6, 1940; s. Charles Cable and Henrietta Dudley (Wise) H.; m. Ruth Murphy, Mar. 16, 1997; 1 child, Ian. AB with distinction, Stanford U., 1961; JD, U. Colo., 1964. Bar: Colo. 1964, Ariz. 1965, D.C. 1971. Assoc. Lewis and Roca, Phoenix, 1964-69, ptnr., 1969-82, Fannin, Terry & Hay, Phoenix, 1982-87, Allen, Kimerer & LaVelle, Phoenix, 1987-94, Gust Rosenfeld, Phoenix, 1994—; judge pro tem Ariz. Ct. Appeals, 1999—. Bd. dirs. Ariz. Life and Disability Ins. Guaranty Fund, 1984-95, chmn., 1993-95. Co-author: Arizona Corporate Practice, 1996, Representing Franchisees, 1996. Mem. Dem. Precinct Com., 1966-78, Ariz. State Dem. Com., 1968-78; chmn. Dem. Legis. Dist., 1971-74; mem. Maricopa County Dem. Cen. Com., 1971-74; bd. dirs. ACLU, 1973-78; bd. dirs. Community Legal Svcs., 1983-89, pres., 1987-88; bd. dirs. Ariz. Club, 1994-96. Mem. ABA, Ariz. Bar Assn., Maricopa County Bar Assn. (bd. dirs. 1972-85), Assn. Life Ins. Counsel, Ariz. Licensors and Franchisors Assn. (bd. dirs. 1985—, pres. 1988-89), Ariz. Civil Liberties Union (bd. dirs. 1967-84, 95—, pres. 1973-77, 97-2000, Disting. Citizen award 1979), Phoenix C. of C. (chmn. arts and culture task force 1997-99). General corporate, Franchising, Insurance. Home: 201 E Hayward Ave Phoenix AZ 85020-4037 Office: Gust Rosenfeld 201 N Central Ave Ste 3300 Phoenix AZ 85073-3300 E-mail: jhay@gustlaw.com

HAY, PETER HEINRICH, law educator, dean; b. Berlin, Germany, Sept. 17, 1935; s. Edward and Margot (Tull) H.; 1 child, Cedric. BA, JD, U. Mich., 1958. Prof. law U. Ill., Champaign, 1963-91; dean Coll. Law U. Ill., 1979-89; L.Q.C. Lamar prof. law Emory U., Atlanta, 1991—, currently interim dean, chief exec. and acad. officer. Hon. prof. U. Freiburg, Germany, 1976—; prof. U. Dresden, Germany, 1994—. Author: An Introduction to U.S. Law; co-author: Conflict of Laws, 2d edit., 1992; author other books and more than 50 articles. Recipient Rsch. prize von Humboldt Found., Germany, 1990; Fulbright rsch. prof., 1992; Jean-Monnet prof., Bonn, Germany, 1994. Mem. Am. Law Inst., Am. Acad. Fgn. Law, Internat. Acad. Comparative Law. Office: Emory U Sch Law G501 Gambrell Hall 1301 Clifton Rd Atlanta GA 30322-0001*

HAYASE, PAUL HIROMI, lawyer; b. Warren, Ohio, Mar. 20, 1955; s. Charles Koji and Michiko (Watanabe) H.; m. Aug. 12, 1978. BA, Yale Univ., 1976; JD, Univ. Pa., 1980. Bar: Calif. 1980, U.S. Dist. Ct. (cen. dist.) Calif. 1980, U.S. Ct. Appeals (9th cir.) 1980. Assoc. MacDonald, Halsted & Laybourne, L.A., 1980-85; sr. v.p., gen. counsel Knapp Communications Corp., L.A., 1985—. V.p., bd. dirs. Japanese Evang. Missionary Soc., L.A., 1981-85. Internat. scholar Svc. Employees Internat., Washington, 1973-77; Centennial scholar Japanese C. of C., L.A., 1973. Mem. Japanese-Am. Bar Assn., L.A. County Bar Assn., L.A. Jr. C. of C. Democrat. Baptist. Office: Knapp Communications Corp 5900 Wilshire Blvd Los Angeles CA 90036-5013

HAYDEN, JOSEPH A., JR. lawyer; b. Newark, Apr. 2, 1944; s. Joseph A. and Mary (Giblin) H.; m. Donna Heinrich, Aug. 26, 1967; children: Kathryn Elizabeth, Patrick Joseph; m. Katharine Jackson Sweeney, July 19, 1987. Student, Boston Coll., 1966; JD magna cum laude, Rutgers U., 1969. Bar: N.J. 1969, U.S. Dist. Ct. N.J. 1969, N.Y. 1981. Law sec. to chief justice N.J. Supreme Ct., Trenton, 1969-70; dep. atty. gen. organized crime and spl. prosecution sect. Div. Criminal Justice, Atty. Gen.'s Office, 1970-73; pvt. practice DeCotis, Fitzpatrick, Glack, Hayden & Cole, Newark, Hoboken and Weehawken, N.J., 1973—. Mem. editl bd. N.J. Law Jour., 1998—. Counsel to Essex County Dems., 1976-80; mem. adv. com. U.S. Dist. Ct. N.J. Named Top Lawyer N.J. Monthly mag., 1997-2000. Fellow Am. Coll. Trial Lawyers, Am. Bar Found.; mem. FBA (trustee 1996-99), N.J. State Bar Assn. (prosecutorial and jud. appointment com. 1992-97, trustee 1998-99), Assn. Criminal Def. Lawyers N.J. (trustee 1985—, founder, 1st pres.), Ct. of Appeal Lawyers 3rd cir. (adv. com.), Fed. Bar Assn. (program chair 1998-99, treas. 2000-2001). Democrat. Avocations: running, recreational basketball, skiing. General civil litigation, Criminal, Environmental. Home: 811 Hudson St Hoboken NJ 07030-5003 Office: DeCotis Fitzpatrick Slack Hayden & Cole 500 Frank W Burr Blvd Teaneck NJ 07666-6802

HAYDEN, RAYMOND PAUL, lawyer; b. Rochester, N.Y., Jan. 15, 1939; s. John Joseph and Orpha (Lindsay) H.; m. Suzanne Saloy, Sept. 1, 1962; children: Thomas Gerard, Christopher Matthew. BS in Marine Transit, SUNY Maritime Coll., 1960; LLB, Syracuse U., 1963. Bar: N.Y. 1963, U.S. Ct. Appeals (2d cir.) 1963, U.S. Dist. Ct. (ea. and so. dists.) N.Y. 1964, U.S. Supreme Ct. 1967. Assoc. Haight Gardner Poor & Havens, N.Y.C., 1963-70; asst. gen. counsel Commonwealth Oil Co., 1970-71; ptnr. Hill Rivkins & Hayden LLP, 1971—. Mem. Coll. Coun., SUNY Maritime Coll., 1977-98, chmn., 1983-98; mem. adv. coun. Tulane U. Admiralty Law Inst. Served as lt. (j.g.) USNR, 1960-70. Mem. ABA (chmn. standing com. on admiralty and maritime law 1982-86), Maritime Law Assn. U.S. (chmn. com. on admissions 1974-82, exec. com. 1988-91, membership sec. 1996-98, 2nd v.p. 1998-2000, 1st v.p. 2000—), India House Club, Brookville Country Club (N.Y.). Email: HR NYC. Admiralty, Insurance, Private international. Office: Hill Rivkins & Hayden LLP 90 West St New York NY 10006-1039 E-mail: RPH@compuserve.com

HAYDEN, WILLIAM TAYLOR, lawyer; b. Cin., Feb. 14, 1954; s. Joseph Page Jr. and Lois Elaine (Taylor) H.; m. Debbie Jane Kraus, Nov. 27, 1976; children: Page Ann, William Taylor, Michael Joseph, Amy Weber. BA in Econs., Denison U., 1976; JD, U. Cin., 1979. Bar: Ohio 1979, U.S. Dist. Ct. (so. dist.) Ohio 1979. Assoc. Cohen, Todd, Kite & Stanford, Cin., 1979-85, ptnr., 1986-96, mng. ptnr., mem. mgmt. com., 1988-96. Sec. to bd. dirs. The Midland Co., 1988—, also bd. dirs.; trustee Fernald Litigation Settlement Fund, 1990—. Bd. dirs., mem. exec. com. Cin. Restoration, Inc., 1989-98, chair bd. dirs., 1995-96; dir. Clermont Bank, 1998-99, Ctr. Bank, 2000—; mem. audit com. Ctr. Bank, 2000—. Mem. ABA (corp. sect., tort and ins. law sect., tax sect., real estate and trust sect.), Ohio State Bar Assn., Queen City Club, Coldstream Country Club, Met. Club. Republican. Methodist. Bankruptcy, Contracts commercial, General corporate. Home: 7266 Nottinghill Ln Cincinnati OH 45255-3964 Office: PO Box 1104 Cincinnati OH 45201-1104

HAYEK, CAROLYN JEAN, retired judge; b. Portland, Oreg., Aug. 17, 1948; d. Robert A. and Marion L. (DeKoning) H.; m. Steven M. Rosen, July 21, 1974; children: Jonathan David, Laura Elizabeth. BA in Psychology, Carleton Coll., 1970; JD, U. Chgo., 1973; webmaster cert., Lake Washington Tech. Coll., 2000. Bar: Wash. 1973. Assoc. Jones, Grey & Bayley, Seattle, 1973-77; pvt. practice Federal Way, Wash., 1977-82; judge Federal Way Dist. Ct., 1982-95; ret., 1995. Task force Alternatives for Wash., 1973-75; mem. Wash. State Ecol. Commn., 1975-77; columnist Tacoma News Tribune Hometown Sect., 1995-96; bus. law instr. Lake Washington Tech. Coll., 2000-2001. Bd. dirs. 1st Unitarian Ch., Seattle, 1986-89, vice-chair 1987-88, pres. 1988-89; ch. adminstr. Northlake Unitarian Universalist Ch.; treas. Eastshore Unitarian Universalist Ch. Women's Perspective, 2001—; den leader Mt. Rainier coun. Boy Scouts Am., 1987-88, scouting coord., 1988-89; bd. dirs. Twin Lakes Elem. Sch. PTA; v.p. Friends of the Libr. Kirkland, 2000—. Recipient Women Helping Women award Federal Way Soroptimist, 1991, Martin Luther King Day Humanitarian award King County, 1993, Recognition cert. City of Federal Way Diversity Commn., 1995. Mem. AAUW (co-pres. Kirland-Redmond br. 1999-2000, co-v.p. Lake Washington br. 2001—, pres. Federal Way br. 1978-80, 90-92, chair state level conf. com. 1986-87, diversity com. 1991-98, state bd. mem. 1995-97, dir. ESL project), ABA, Wash. Women Lawyers, Wash. State Bar Assn., King County Dist. Ct. Judges Assn. (treas., exec. com. 1990-93, com. chair, chair and rules com. 1990-94), Elected Wash. Women (dir. 1983-87), Nat. Assn. Women Judges (nat. bd. dirs., dist. bd. dirs. 1984-86, chmn. rules com. 1988-89, chmn. bylaws com. 1990-91), Fed. Way Women's Network (bd. dirs. 1984-91, 95-97, pres. 1985, program co-chair 1989-91, co-editor newsletter), Greater Fed. Way C. of C. (dir. 1978-82, sec. 1980-81, v.p. 1981-82), Sunrise Rotary (com. svc. chair, bd. dirs., membership com., Federal Way chpt. 1991-96, youth exch. officer 1994-95), Washington Women United (bd. dirs. 1995-97), Unitarian Universalist Women's Assn. (chair bylaws com. 1996), Eliot Inst. (bd. dirs. 1996-2000, vice-chair 1998-99, bd. chair 1999-2000, webmaster 1999—), Plaza on State Owners Assn. (bd. dirs. 1997-2000, pres. 1997-99, sec. 1999-2000, webmaster 2000—). E-mail: cjh@kirklandplaza.com

HAYERS, PAUL HUGH, lawyer; b. Wichita Falls, Tex., Dec. 2, 1942; s. Carl Edward and Emogene (Wagoner) H.; m. Jannis Baker, Aug. 16, 1964; children: Stephanie Laura, Christopher Mark. BBA, So. Meth. U., 1964; JD, Georgetown U., 1967. Bar: Tex. 1967, U.S. Dist. Ct. (no. dist.) Tex. 1968, U.S. Ct. Appeals (5th cir.) 1975, U.S. Ct. Appeals (11th cir.) 1981. Ptnr. McKelvey & Hayers, Electra, Tex., 1967-84, mng. owner, 1984—. Commr. City of Electra, 1972-75, 80-86, mayor pro-tem, 1974, 75, 85, city atty., 1976-80, 86—; chmn. Wichita County Tax Appraisal Dist., Wichita Falls, Tex., 1980-87, bd. dirs. Tex. Assn. Appraisal Dists., 1985-86; chmn. Wichita County Child Welfare Bd., 1979-84. Mem. State Bar Tex., Wichita County Bar Assn., Electra C. of C., Rotary (pres. 1984), Lions (pres. 1971-72). Democrat. Methodist. Probate, Real property, Personal income taxation. Home: PO Box 391 Electra TX 76360-0391 Office: McKelvey & Hayers 109 N Main Electra TX 76360

HAYES, BURGAIN GARFIELD, lawyer; b. Ft. Ord, Calif., May 20, 1948; children: Christine, Katherine, Burgain IV, Mary Margaret. BA, Am. U. Sch. Internat. Studies, 1969; JD, U. Tex., 1975. Bar: Tex. 1975, U.S. Dist. Ct. (we. dist.) Tex. 1976, U.S. Ct. Appeals (5th cir.) 1981, U.S. Dist. Ct. (so. dist.) Tex. 1983, U.S. Dist. Ct. (ea. dist.) Tex. 1984, U.S. Dist. Ct. (no. dist.) Tex. 1985, U.S. Dist. Ct. (we. dist.) Okla. 1986, U.S. Dist. Ct. (no. dist.) Okla. 1986, U.S. Ct. Appeals (10th cir.) 1986, U.S. Supreme Ct. 1985. Trial prosecutor, chief civil sect. County Atty.'s Office, Austin, Tex., 1974-77; assoc. Clark, Thomas, Winters and Shapiro, 1977-82; ptnr. Clark, Thomas & Winters, 1982—. Editor: Tex. Internat. Law Jour., 1973-74. Served to 1st lt. U.S. Army, 1969-72. Mem. ABA (product liability adv. coun.), Fed. Bar Assn., Internat. Assn. Def. Counsel, Tex. State Bar Assn., Tex. Assn. Def. Counsel, Def. Rsch. Inst. Avocations: fishing, sports. General civil litigation, Construction, Product liability. Home: 2802 Deercreek Cir Austin TX 78703 Office: Clark Thomas & Winters 700 Lavaca St Austin TX 78701-3109 E-mail: bgh@ctw.com

HAYES, BYRON JACKSON, JR. retired lawyer; b. L.A., July 9, 1934; s. Byron Jackson and Caroline Violet (Scott) H.; m. DeAnne Saliba, June 30, 1962; children: Kenneth Byron, Patricia DeAnne. Student, Pomona Coll., 1952-56; BA magna cum laude, Harvard U., LLB cum laude, 1959. Bar: Calif. 1960, U.S. Supreme Ct. 1963. Assoc. McCutchen, Black, Verleger & Shea, L.A., 1960-68, ptnr., 1968-89, Baker & Hostetler, 1990-97; ret., 1998. Trustee L.A. Urban Found., 1996—, CFO, 1998-2000, v.p., CFO, 2000—; trustee L.A. Ch. Ext. Soc. United Meth. Ch., 1967-77, pres., 1974-77, chancellor ann. conf. Pacific and S.W., 1979-86, dir. 1010 devel. corp., 1993—, v.p., 1995—; dir., pres. Pacific and S.W. United Meth. Found., 1978-84; dir., v.p. Padua Hills, Inc., 1999—. Named Layperson of yr. Pacific and S.W. Ann. Conf., United Meth. Ch., 1981; recipient Bishop's award, 1992, 2000. Mem. ABA, Am. Coll. Mortgage Attys. (regent 1984-93, pres. 1993-94), Calif. Bar Assn., Los Angeles County Bar Assn. (chmn. real property sect. 1982-83), Toluca Lake Property Owners Assn. (sec. 1990-94), Toluca Lake C. of C. (dir. 2001—), Pomona Coll. Alumni Assn. (pres. 1984-85), Lakeside Golf Club.

HAYES, DAVID JOHN ARTHUR, JR. legal association executive; b. Chgo., July 30, 1929; s. David J.A. and Lucille (Johnson) H.; m. Anne Huston, Feb. 20, 1963; children— David J.A. III, Cary AB, Harvard U., 1952, JD, 1961. Bar: Ill. Trust officer, asst. sec. First Nat. Bank of Evanston, Ill., 1961-63; gen. counsel Ill. State Bar Assn., Chgo., 1963-66; asst. dir. ABA, 1966-68, div. dir., 1968-69, asst. exec. dir., 1969-87, v.p., 1987-88, assoc. exec. v.p., 1989-90, sr. assoc. exec. v.p., 1990, exec. dir., 1990-94, exec. dir. emeritus, 1994—; exec. dir. Naval Res. Lawyers Assn., 1971-75; asst. sec. gen. Internat. Bar Assn., 1978-80, 90—, Inter-ABA, 1984—. Contbr. articles to profl. jours. Capt. JAGC, USNR Fellow Am. Bar Found. (life); mem. Ill. State Bar Assn. (ho. of dels. 1972-76), Nat. Orgn. Bar Counsel (pres. 1967), Chgo. Bar Assn., Michigan Shores Club. Home: 908 Pontiac Rd Wilmette IL 60091-1349 Office: ABA 750 N Lake Shore Dr Chicago IL 60611-4403 E-mail: djahayes@aol.com

HAYES, DAVID MICHAEL, lawyer; b. Syracuse, N.Y., Dec. 2, 1943; s. James P. and Lillie Anna (Wood) H.; m. Elizabeth S. Tracy, Aug. 26, 1972; children: Timothy T., AnnElizabeth S. AB, Syracuse U., 1965; LLB, U. Va., 1968. Bar: Va. 1968, N.Y. 1969. Assoc. Hiscock & Barclay, Syracuse, 1968-72; asst. gen. counsel Agway Inc., 1972-81, gen. counsel, sec., 1981-87, v.p., gen. counsel, sec., 1987-92, sr. v.p., gen. counsel, sec., 1992-2001; of counsel Bond, Schoeneck & King, 2001—. Adj. prof. law Syracuse U. Coll. Law, 1995—; former chmn. Nat. Coun. of Farmer Coops. Legal Tax and Acctg. Com. Bd. dirs., former pres. Boys and Girls Club of Syracuse. With Army N.G., 1968-74. Fellow N.Y. Bar Found.; mem. ABA, Onondaga County Bar Assn. (pres. 1998), N.Y. State Bar Assn. (ho. of dels., 1995-99), Va. State Bar, Century Club, Skaneateles Country Club. Democrat. Office: Agway Inc PO Box 4933 Syracuse NY 13221-4933 E-mail: dhayes@bsk.com

HAYES, GEORGE NICHOLAS, lawyer; b. Alliance, Ohio, Sept. 30, 1928; s. Nicholas John and Mary Irene (Fanady) H. BA, U. Akron, 1950; MA, Western Res. U., 1953, LLB, 1955. Bar: Ohio 1955, U.S. Dist. Ct. Alaska 1957, U.S. Ct. Appeals (9th cir.) 1958, Alaska 1959, U.S. Supreme Ct. 1964, Wash. 1972. Mcpl. ct. prosecutor, asst. county prosecutor Portage County, Ravenna, Ohio, 1955-57; asst. U.S. atty. Fairbanks and Anchorage, Alaska, 1957-59; dep. atty gen. State of Alaska, Anchorage, 1959-62; dist. atty. 3d Jud. Dist., 1960-62; atty gen. Juneau, Alaska, 1962-64; spl. counsel to Gov. on earthquake recovery program State of Alaska, Washington, 1964; stockholder Delaney, Wiles, Hayes, Gerety & Ellis, Inc. and predecessor, Anchorage, 1964-92, of counsel, 1992. Mem. ABA, Alaska Bar Assn, Anchorage Bar Assn. Democrat. Office: Delaney Wiles Hayes 1007 W 3rd Ave Anchorage AK 99501-1936

HAYES, GERALD JOSEPH, lawyer; b. Bronx, N.Y., July 24, 1950; s. James Joseph and Gladys (Guest) H.; m. Diane Elizabeth Willoughby, July 21, 1984; children: Erin Jane, Thomas Joseph, Cara Elizabeth. BA, U. Mass., 1972; JD, U. Miami, 1978. Bar: N.Y. 1979, U.S. Dist. Ct. (so. dist.) N.Y. 1979. Assoc. Baker & McKenzie, N.Y.C., 1978-85, ptnr., 1985—, mng. ptnr., 1995, 97, 99—, mem. policy com., 1997—. Mem. Bus. Coun. for UN, 1990-95. Nat. alumni adv. bd. U. Miami Sch. Law, 1992—. Mem. ABA (atomic energy com. publ utility law sect. 1983, vice chair internat. tort & ins. law com., tort & ins. practice sect. 1997—), Assn. Bar City N.Y. (com. on nuclear tech. and law 1979-82, 85-88, com. on ins. law 1983-84), Nat. Assn. Ins. Commrs. (adv. com. on internat. law 1989-90), Nat. Risk Retention Assn. (govt. affairs com.). Nuclear power, Insurance, Private international. Office: Baker & McKenzie 805 3rd Ave New York NY 10022-7513

HAYES, J. MICHAEL, lawyer; b. St. Louis, Dec. 10, 1946; s. Frank J. and Louise J. (Lough) H.; m. Vicky J. Verbocy, May 27, 1972; children: Thomas K., James M. BS summa cum laude, SUNY, Brockport, 1973; JD, SUNY, Buffalo, 1976. Bar: N.Y. 1977, U.S. Dist. Ct. (we. dist.) N.Y. 1977. Assoc. Smith, Murphy & Schoepperle, Buffalo, 1977-79, Tenney, Smith & Scott, Buffalo, 1979-82, Terry D. Smith, Buffalo, 1982-86; ptnr. Smith, Keller, Hayes & Miner, 1986-94; pvt. practice, 1994—. General civil litigation, Personal injury, Product liability. Office: 69 Delaware Ave Rm 1111 Buffalo NY 14202-3805 E-mail: jmh@jmichaelhayes.com

HAYES, LARRY B. lawyer; b. Atlanta, Oct. 4, 1939; s. Luther F. and Ruby (Thomas) H.; m. Rebecca Thomason, Feb. 12, 1959; children: Laura Alison, Lawrence Bruce. BS in Pharmacy, U. Fla., 1962; JD, St. Mary's U., 1977. Bar: Tex. 1978, U.S. Dist. Ct. (no. dist.) Tex. 1979, U.S. Ct. Appeals (5th cir.) 1979; cert. personal injury trial law, Tex. Trial counsel Windle Turley PC, Dallas, 1978-82; ptnr. Ware & Hayes, 1982-83; sr. trial atty. Green, Hayes & Ryan, 1983-86; ptnr. Cantey & Hanger, Ft. Worth, 1986—. Mem. Tex. Bar Assn., Tex. Assn. Def. Counsel, Def. Rsch. Inst., Tarrant County Bar Assn., Tarrant County Civil Trial Lawyers Assn., Ridglea Country Club, Phi Delta Phi. Health, Personal injury, Product liability. Home: 910 Houston St Apt 802 Fort Worth TX 76102-6228 Office: Cantey & Hanger Burnett Plaza 801 Cherry St Ste 2100 Fort Worth TX 76102-6898

HAYES, MARGARET MARY, lawyer; b. Southington, Conn., Oct. 26, 1957; d. Michael Francis and Ann Theresa (Draper) H. BA magna cum laude, Tufts U., 1979; JD, U. Conn., 1982. Bar: Conn. 1982, U.S. Dist. Ct. Conn. 1982. Assoc. Anderson & Alden, Bristol, Conn., 1982-86, ptnr., 1986-87, Anderson, Alden & Hayes, Bristol, 1987—. 1st v.p. Bristol Girls' Club Family Ctr., 1986-88, pres., 1988-90; co-chair Bristol United Way Campaign, 1993, bd. dirs., 1993-94; v.p. Am. Heart Assn. (local), 1993-94; housing commr. City of Bristol, 1999—; bd. dirs. Bristol Boys & Girls Club, 1998—, Bristol Hosp. and Health Care, 2000—. Mem. ABA, Conn. Bar Assn., Hartford County Bar Assn., Bristol Bar Assn. (treas. 1986-88, v.p. 1988-89, pres. 1989-90), Assn. Trial Lawyers Am., Conn. Trial Lawyers Assn., Bristol C. of C., Rotary. Democrat. Roman Catholic. State civil litigation, Family and matrimonial, Personal injury. Office: Anderson Alden Hayes Ziogas PO Box 1197 Bristol CT 06011-1197 E-mail: mhayes@aahzs.com

HAYES, NORMAN ROBERT, JR. lawyer; b. Schenectady, N.Y., Apr. 12, 1948; s. Norman Robert Sr. and Ethel May (Blair) H.; m. Alice S. Margitan, Oct. 14, 1972; children: Robert, Charles. BS, Clarkson U., 1970; JD, Union U., 1973. Bar: N.Y. 1974, U.S. Dist. Ct. (no. dist.) N.Y. 1974, U.S. Supreme Ct. 1978. Ptnr. Wemple, Daly, Casey, Hayes, Watkins & Harter, Schenectady, 1973-86; pvt. practice Clifton Park, N.Y., 1986-96; ptnr. Gordon, Siegel, Mastro, Mullaney, Gordon & Galvin, 1996—. Pres. Hayes Indsl. Inc., 1998—; chmn. Saratoga Econ. Devel. Corp., Saratoga Springs, NY; bd. dirs. Provantage Funding Corp., Ebeling Assocs.; adv. bd. dirs. Chase Manhattan Bank. Pres. County Knolls South Civic Assn., Clifton Park, 1975-76. Served to capt. U.S. Army, 1973-74. Mem. ABA, N.Y. State Bar Assn., Schenectady County Bar Assn. Republican. E-mila. Banking, Contracts commercial, General corporate. Home: 3380 State Route 9L Lake George NY 12845-5511 Office: 3380 State Route 9L Lake George NY 12845-5511 E-mail: bob6@capital.net

HAYES, PHILIP HAROLD, lawyer; b. Battle Creek, Mich., Sept. 1, 1940; s. Robert Harold and Maurine (Page) H.; m. Robin Hayes, May 20, 1995; 1 child, Rian; children from previous marriage: Elizabeth, Courtney. AB, Ind. U., 1963, JD, 1967. Bar: Ind. 1967, U.S. Dist. Ct. (so. dist.) Ind. 1967, D.C. 1977, U.S. Ct. Appeals (7th cir.) 1992. Dep. prosecutor Vanderburgh County, Evansville, Ind., 1967-68; ptnr. Cox & Hayes, 1969-72; senator State of Ind., 1971-74; pvt. practice, 1973-74, 77-79, 1980—; U.S. congressman U.S. Ho. of Reps., Washington, 1975-77; ptnr. Hayes & Young, Evansville, 1980-90, Hayes & Tornatta, Evansville, 1990-92. Legal counsel Airport Authority Dist., Evansville, 1980-84, Redevel. Commn., Evansville, 1984-88, Health and Hosp. Corp., Evansville, 1984-88, Vanderburgh County Atty., 2001—. Editor, moderator pub. affairs TV program, 1977-78. Mem. Evansville Bar Assn., D.C. Bar Assn., Ind. Bar Assn. Democrat. Administrative and regulatory, General civil litigation, Real property. Home: 218 Glenview Dr Evansville IN 47710-3737 Office: 400 Court St Evansville IN 47708 E-mail: phaylaw@aol.com

HAYES, TIMOTHY GEORGE, lawyer, consultant; b. New London, Conn., June 27, 1954; s. George Melen and Lauretta C. (Bresnahan) H.; m. Barbara Joan White, Jan. 27, 1983; children: Laura Katherine, Kevin Michael. BS, Fla. State U., 1976, MS, 1977; JD, Stetson Coll. Law, 1982. Bar: Fla. 1982, U.S. Dist. Ct. (mid. dist.) Fla. 1983. Legis. aide Fla. State Rep. George H. Sheldon, Tallahassee, 1978-79; assoc. Alice K. Nelson, P.A., Tampa, Fla., 1982-83; ptnr. Cotterill, Gonzalez & Hayes, Lutz, 1983-84, Cotterill, Gonzalez, Hayes & Grantham, Lutz, 1984-88; sr. ptnr. Hayes & McClelland, 1988-90, Hayes, Winick & Albrechta, Lutz, 1990-91, Hayes & Albrechta, P.A., Lutz, 1991-93, Hayes & Assocs., Lutz, 1993—. V.p. Hillsborough County Young Dems., Tampa, 1978, pres., 1979; bd. dirs. Tampa Bay Commuter Rail Authority, Tampa, 1990-97,

Pasco County Econ. Devel. Coun., New Port Richey, Fla., 1990-92, Pasco Food Bank, 1996—, Sunshine Youth Soccer Assn., 1997-99; bd. dirs., coach Ctrl. Pasco United Soccer Assn., 1995—, pres., 1996-98; mem. Tampa-Orlando High-Speed Transp. Study Task Force, 1992-94; mem. adv. bd. Pasco-Hernando C.C., 1994-95; bd. dirs., v.p. Heritage Park Found., 1997—; citizens adv. com. Pasco County Pks. and Recreation, 1999—, Pasco County Natural Gas Pipeline, 2000; pres. United Soccer Assn., 2000—. Named Outstanding Young Man in Am. by Jaycees, 1980; recipient Sam Walton Bus. Leader award, 1998. Mem. ABA (real property, probate and trust law sect.), Fla. Bar Assn. (environ. and land use law sect., real property, probate and trust law sect.), Hillsborough County Bar Assn. (environ. and land use law sect.), Land O' Lakes C. of C. (v.p. 1988-89, pres. 1991-92, chmn. bd. 1992-93, bd. dirs. 1995—). Roman Catholic. Avocations: soccer, bicycling, camping, gardening. Land use and zoning (including planning), Probate, Real property. Office: Hayes & Assocs 21859 State Road 54 Ste 200 Lutz FL 33549-6986

HAYNER, HERMAN HENRY, lawyer; b. Fairfield, Wash., Sept. 25, 1916; s. Charles H. and Lillie (Reifenberger) H.; m. Jeannette Hafner, Oct. 24, 1942; children: Stephen, James K., Judith A. BA, Wash. State U., 1938; JD with honors, U. Oreg., 1946. Bar: Wash. 1946, Oreg. 1946, U.S. Dist. Ct. Wash. 1947, U.S. Ct. Appeals (9th cir.) 1947. Asst. U.S. atty. U.S. Dept. Justice, Portland, Oreg., 1946-47; atty. City of Walla Walla, Wash., 1949-53; ptnr. Minnick-Hayner, Walla Walla, 1949—. Mem. Wash. State exec. bd. U.S. West, Seattle, 1988-95. Regent Wash. State U., Pullman, 1965-78; dir. YMCA, Walla Walla, 1956-67. Lt. col. Infantry, 1942-46. Decorated Bronze Star medal and four Battle Stars; recipient Disting. Svc. award Jr. C. of C., 1951, Wash. State U. Alumni award, 1988. Fellow ABA, Am. Coll. Trust & Estate Counsel; mem. Wash. State Bar Assn., Walla Walla County Bar Assn. (pres. 1954-55), Walla Walla C. of C. (merit award 1977, dir. 1973-88), Rotary (pres. 1956-57), Walla Walla Country Club (pres. 1956-57). Republican. Lutheran. Avocations: golf, photography. General corporate, Probate. Home: PO Box 454 Walla Walla WA 99362 Office: Minnick-Hayner PO Box 1757 Walla Walla WA 99362 E-mail: hhhayner@aol.com

HAYNES, GEORGE CLEVE, lawyer, author; b. St. Louis, Jan. 15, 1946; s. George Cave and Helen Marie (Cleve) H. B.A., So. Ill. U., Edwardsville, 1969; J.D., Ill. Inst. Tech., 1974. Bar: Wash. 1977, U.S. Dist. Ct. (we. dist.) Wash. 1977, U.S. Ct. Appeals (9th cir.) 1978, U.S. Supreme Ct. 1982. judge pro tem Seattle Mcpl. Ct., 1977-84, King County Superior Ct., 1980; instr. Edmonds Community Coll., Wash., 1983-84; gen. counsel Alternative Intervention Resources King County, Seattle, 1984—; literary agt., Harold Matson Co., N.Y. Mem. Wash. State Bar Assn., Sherlock Holmes Soc. of London, La Soc. Dante Alighieri. Club: Diogenes. Criminal, General practice. Office: Harold Matson Co 276 5th Ave New York NY 10001-4509

HAYNES, JEAN REED, lawyer; b. Miami, Fla., Apr. 6, 1949; d. Oswald Birnam and Arleen (Wiedman) Dow. AB with honors, Pembroke Coll., 1971; MA, Brown U., 1971; JD, U. Chgo., 1981. Bar: Ill. 1981, U.S. Ct. Appeals (7th cir.) 1982, U.S. Dist. Ct. (no. dist.) Ill. 1983, U.S. Dist. Ct. (cen. dist.) Ill., 1988, N.Y. 1991, U.S. Dist. Ct. (so. dist.) N.Y. 1991, U.S. Dist. Ct. (no. and ea. dists.) N.Y. 1992, U.S. Ct. Appeals (10th cir.) 1993, U.S. Ct. Appeals (11th cir.) 1995. Tchr. grades 1-4 Abbie Tuller Sch., Providence, 1971-72; tchr., facilitator St. Mary's Acad., Riverside, R.I., 1972-74; tchr., head lower sch. St. Francis Sch., Goshen, Ky., 1974-78; law clk. U.S. Ct. Appeals (7th cir.), Chgo., 1981-83; assoc. Kirkland & Ellis, 1983-87, ptnr., 1987-2001; pres. J.R. Haynes, Inc., 2001—. Assoc. editor Litigation Mag., 1997-99. Assoc. editor: Litigation Mag., 1997-99. Governing mem. Art Inst. Chgo., 1982-90, mem. aux. bd., 1986-90, membership com. aux. bd., 1987-90, v.p. for devel., 1988-90; vis. com. U. Chgo. Law Sch., 1990-92; pres. com. All Stars Project, Inc., 1997—; adv. com. Youth Devel. Ct, 1997—, bd. dirs. 1999—. Mem. ABA (com. on affordable justice litigation sect. 1988—), Ill. Bar Assn. (life), Assn. Bar City N.Y., Internat. Bar Assn., Am. Judicature Soc. (life, chmn. membership com. 1991-97, treas. 1997-99, chmn. fin. com. 1997-99, v.p. 1994-97, exec. com. 1992—, pres. 1999—, bd. dirs. 1991—, chair adminstrv. com. 1997—), Three Lincoln Ctr. Condominium Assn. (pres. 1995-99, v.p. 1999-2001), Law Club Chgo. Bankruptcy, Federal civil litigation, State civil litigation. Office: JR Haynes Inc JR Haynes Co 160 W 66th Ste 54B New York NY 10023-6569 E-mail: jeanrhaynes@earthlink.net

HAYNES, WILLIAM J(AMES), II, lawyer; b. Waco, Tex., Mar. 30, 1958; s. William James and Caroline H.; m. Margaret Frances Campbell, Aug. 21, 1982; children: William, Sarah, Taylor. BA, Davidson Coll., 1980; JD, Harvard U., 1983; LLD (hon.), Stetson U., 1999. Bar: N.C. 1983, Ga. 1989, D.C. 1990. Law clk. to Hon. James B. McMillan U.S. Dist. Ct. N.C., Charlotte, 1983-84; assoc. Sutherland, Asbill & Brennan, Washington, 1989; spl. asst. to gen. counsel Dept. Def., 1989-90; gen. counsel Dept. Army, 1990-93; ptnr. Jenner & Block, 1993-96; v.p., assoc. gen. counsel Gen. Dynamics Corp., Falls Church, Va., 1996-98; gen. counsel Gen. Dynamics Marine Group, 1997-98; ptnr. Jenner & Block, Washington, 1999-2001; gen. counsel Dept. of Defense, 2001—. Capt. U.S. Army, 1984-88. Mem. ABA, N.C. Bar Assn., D.C. Bar Assn., Ga. Bar Assn., Army-Navy Club. Presbyterian. Avocation: tennis. Federal civil litigation, Environmental, Government contracts and claims. Office: General Counsel Dept of Defense 1600 Defense Pentagon Washington DC 20301 E-mail: hayneswj@osdgc.osd.mil

HAYNIE, TONY WAYNE, lawyer; b. Houston, Sept. 26, 1955; m. Mary E. Steward, Sept. 1, 1978. BA, U. Okla., 1978; postgrad., Boston U., Heidelberg Br., Fed. Republic Germany, 1980-81; JD, U. Tulsa, 1984; MBA, Okla. State U., 1993. Bar: Okla. 1985, U.S. Dist. Okla. 1985, U.S. Ct. Appeals (10th cir.) 1987, U.S. Ct. Appeals (5th cir.) 1992, U.S. Ct. Appeals (7th and D.C. cirs.) 1998, U.S. Supreme Ct. 1990. Assoc. Conner & Winters, Tulsa, 1984-90, ptnr., 1991-92, shareholder, 1992—; pres., CEO The Colonneh Co., 1991—. Arbitrator N.Y. Stock Exch., 1991-93; trustee Transvoc, Inc., 1995-2000, pres. bd. trustees, 1998-99. Adv. bd. mem. Tulsa Area United Way, 1998-99. 1st lt. U.S. Army, 1978-82. Mem. ABA (sect. bus. law and litig., chair subcom. on expert witness on trial evidence com. of litig. sect. 1991-94), Am. Inns of Ct. (barrister Hudson-Hall-Wheaton chpt. 1996—), Okla. Bar Assn., Okla. Bar Found., Tulsa County Bar Assn., Tulsa County Bar Found., Phi Delta Phi. Democrat. Methodist. Bankruptcy, Federal civil litigation, General civil litigation. Office: Conner & Winters 3700 1st Place Tower 15 E 5th St Tulsa OK 74103-4391 E-mail: thaynie@cwlaw.com

HAYS, STEELE, retired state supreme court judge; b. Little Rock, Mar. 25, 1925; s. L. Brooks and Marion (Prather) H.; m. Peggy Wall, July 12, 1980; children from previous marriage: Andrew Steele, Melissa Louise, Sarah Anne. B.A., U. Ark., 1948; J.D., George Washington U., 1951. Bar: Ark. 1951. Adminstrv. asst. to Congressman Brooks Hays, 1951-53; practice in Little Rock, 1953-79; mem. firm Spitzberg, Mitchell & Hays, 1953-79; circuit judge 6th Jud. Circuit Ark., Little Rock, 1969-70; judge Ark. Ct. Appeals, 1979-81; assoc. justice Ark. Supreme Ct., 1981-95; ret., 1995. Chmn. Bd. Law Examiners, 1968-70 Mem. Ark. com. U.S. Civil Rights Commn.; del. Presbyn. Ch. Consultation on Ch. Union, 1968-70; trustee Presbyn. Found.; chancellor Episcopal Diocese of Ark. Mem. Ark. Bar Assn. (past sec.-treas.), Sigma Chi, Delta Theta Phi. Home: 12 Deerwood Dr Conway AR 72032-6113

HAYS, THOMAS CLYDE, lawyer; b. Franklin, Ind., Mar. 3, 1951; s. Clyde Gilbert and Anna Marie (Hill) H.; m. Mary Linda Lux, June 19, 1976; children: Thomas Clyde Jr., Lindsay Marie. AB, Ind. U., 1973; JD, Woodrow Wilson Coll. of Law, 1977. Bar: Ga. 1977, U.S. Dist. Ct. (no. dist.) Ga. 1977, Ind., 1979, U.S. Dist. Ct. (so. dist.) Ind. 1979. Assoc. Spence, Garrett & Spence, Alpharetta, Ga., 1977-78, Reeves and Collier, Atlanta, 1978-79, Kitley and Schreckengast, Beech Grove, Ind., 1979-82; ptnr. Schreckengast and Hays, Indpls., 1982-85, Lewis, Bowman, St. Clair & Wagner (now Lewis & Wagner), Indpls., 1985—. Pres. Briar Ln. Homeowners Assn., 1984. Mem. ABA, Ind. State Bar Assn., Ga. State Bar Assn., Indpls. Bar Assn. (litigation sect.), Def. Trial Counsel of Ind., Nat. Inst. for Trial Advocacy (diplomate, advanced sem. 1987), Def. Rsch. Inst., Am. Bd. Trial Advocates, Carmel Dad's Club, Optimist Club (pres. Southdside club 1984-85). Republican. Roman Catholic. Avocations: golf, bicycling. State civil litigation, Insurance, Personal injury. Home: 11214 Westminster Ct Carmel IN 46033-3702 Office: Lewis & Wagner 500 Place 501 Indiana Ave Ste 200 Indianapolis IN 46202-6146 E-mail: thays@lewiswagner.com

HAYTHE, WINSTON MCDONALD, lawyer, educator, consultant, real estate investor; b. Reidsville, N.C., Oct. 10, 1940; s. McDonald Swann and Henrietta Elizabeth (East) H.; m. Glenann Leigh Rogers, Aug. 17, 1963 (div. 1977); children: Sheila Elaine, Kevin McDonald, Rhonda Leigh. BS, S.W. Mo. State U., 1963; JD, Coll. William and Mary, 1967; postgrad., U. Va., 1968-69; grad., Command and Gen. Staff Sch., Ft. Leavenworth, Kans., 1982, U.S. Def. U., 1984; LLM, U.S. Army JAG Sch., 1976. Bar: Va. 1967, D.C. 1969. Assoc. Rhyne & Rhyne, Washington, 1969-72; sr. trial atty. AEC, 1972-73; asst. gen counsel, sr. atty. Consumer Produce Safety Commn., 1973-82; staff dir. legal office EPA, 1982-83, sr. atty. for enforcement policy, 1985-91, sr. atty. Nat. Enforcement Tng. Inst., 1991-94, asst. dir., 1994-96, sr. legal counsel, 1996-2001; sr. counsel Office of Criminal Enforcement Forensics, 2001—. Legis. fellow U.S. Senate, Washington, 1983-85; mem. adv. com. paralegal studies U. Md., 1980-95, chmn., 1992-95; adj. prof. law, 1978-94; mem. law faculty U.S. Army Judge Adv. Gen.'s Sch., Charlottesville, Va., 1969-94, Nat. Advocacy Ctr. U.S. Dept. Justice, Columbia, S.C., 1999—; cons. Barrister Ent., Washington, 1978—; elected mem. undergrad. programs adv. coun. U. Md., 1993-95; guest lectr. George Washington U. Sch. Law, 1999—. Trustee Georgetown Presbyn. Ch., 1995-98, v.p. trustees, 1996, pres. trustees, 1997-98, elder, mem. session, 2000-03. Col. JAGC, USAR, 1967-94, ret. Mem. Va. State Bar Assn., D.C. Bar Assn., Fed. Bar Assn. (chmn. nat. com. 1981—), Coll. William and Mary Law Sch. Assn. (bd. dirs. 1988-95), The Social List of Washington, Cosmos Club, Kappa Mu Epsilon. Presbyterian. Avocations: playing organ, piano, theater, concerts, reading. Home: 2141 P St NW Apt 402 Washington DC 20037-1031 Office: EPA (MC-2235A) 1200 Pennsylvania Ave NW Washington DC 20460-0001 E-mail: whaythe@hotmail.com

HAYWARD, ELIZABETH, lawyer, artist; b. Quincy, Mass., Aug. 27, 1964; d. William and Patricia Hayward. BS, Salem (Mass.) State Coll., 1986; JD, New Eng. Sch. Law, Boston, 1993. Bar: Mass. 1994. Legis. aide Mass. Ho. of Reps., Boston, 1987-88, rsch. asst., 1988-89; staff counsel Mass. Office Inspector Gen., 1993-96, asst. gen. counsel, 1996-97, dep. gen. counsel, 1997—. Vol. Youth Enrichment Svcs., Boston, 1999—. Recipient Am. Jurisprudence award in consti. law Lawyer's Coop. Pub., Boston, 1992. Mem. ABA, Assn. Inspectors Gen. (bd. dirs. 1996—), S-Kimos Ski Club. Democrat. Roman Catholic. Avocations: oil and acrylic painting, snowboarding, golf. Office: Office Inspector Gen 1 Ashburton Pl Boston MA 02108-1518

HAYWARD, THOMAS ZANDER, JR. lawyer; b. Oct. 21, 1940; s. Thomas Z. and Wilhelmina (White) H.; m. Sally Madden, June 20, 1964; children: Thomas Z., Wallace M., Robert M. BA, Northwestern U., 1962, JD, 1965; MBA, U. Chgo., 1970. Bar: Ill. 1966, Ohio 1966, U.S. Dist. Ct. (no. dist.) Ill. 1966, U.S. Supreme Ct. 1970. Assoc. Defrees & Fiske, Chgo., 1965-69, ptnr., 1969-81, Boodell, Sears, Giambalvo & Crowley, Chgo., 1981-87, Bell, Boyd, Lloyd, Chgo., 1987—. Mem. mgmt. and exec. coms. Bell, Boyd, Lloyd. Trustee, vice chmn. Northwestern U., 1980-84, 97—, vice-chmn., 2000—; bd. dirs. Ill. Continuing Legal Edn., 1987-92, Chgo. area Found. for Legal Svcs., 1983—. Recipient Northwestern U. Alumni Svc. award, 1973. Mem. ABA (ho. of dels. 1984—, fed. jud. com. 1993-97, bd. govs., exec. com. 1998-2001, chmn. fin. com.), Ill. State Bar Assn., Chgo. Bar Assn. (pres. 1983-84), Chgo. Club, Casino Club, Barrington Hills Country Club (pres. 1985-87). Republican. Presbyterian. General corporate, Real property. Home: 8 W County Line Rd Barrington IL 60010-2613 Office: Bell Boyd & Lloyd 3 1st Nat Plz 70 W Madison St Ste 3300 Chicago IL 60602-4284

HAZARD, GEOFFREY CORNELL, JR. law educator; b. Cleve., Sept. 18, 1929; s. Geoffrey Cornell and Virginia (Perry) H.; m. Elizabeth O'Hara; children: James G., Katherine W., Robin P., Geoffrey Cornell III. BA, Swarthmore Coll., 1953, LLD (hon.), 1988; LLB, Columbia U., 1954; LLD (hon.), Gonzaga U., 1985, U. San Diego, 1985, Ill. Inst. Tech., 1990, Republica Italiana, 1998. Bar: Oreg. 1954, Calif. 1960, Conn. 1982, Pa. 1994. Assoc. Hart, Spencer, McCulloch, Rockwood & Davies, Portland, Oreg., 1954-57; exec. sec. Oreg. Legis. Interim Com. Jud. Adminstrn., 1957-58; assoc. prof. law, then prof. U. Calif., Berkeley, 1958-64; prof. law U. Chgo., 1964-71, Yale U., 1971-94, prof. mgmt., 1979-83, acting dean Sch. Orgn. and Mgmt., 1980-81, Sterling prof. law, 1986-94; trustee prof. U. Pa., Phila., 1994—. Mem. Adminstrv. Conf. U.S., 1971-78; jud. conf. U.S. com. on rules practice and procedure, 1994-2000. Author: (Law text) Research in Civil Procedure, 1963, Ethics in the Practice of Law, 1978; author: (with D.W. Louisell, C. Tait, W. Fletcher) Pleading and Procedure, 1972; author: 8th rev. edit., 1999; author: (with M. Taruffo) (Law text) American Civil Procedure, 1994; author: (with S. Koniak and R. Cramton) Law and Ethics of Lawyering 3d edit., 1999; author: (with W.W. Hodes) Law of Lawyering 3d edit., 2000; author: (with F. James and J. Leubsdorf) Civil Procedure 5th rev.edit., 2001; editor: Law in a Changing America, 1968; editor: (with D. Rhode) Legal Profession: Responsibility and Regulation , 1985, ;contbr. . Served with USAF, 1948-49. Fellow Am. Bar Found. (exec. dir. 1964-70, rsch. award 1986), Am. Acad. Arts and Scis.; mem. ABA (cons. code jud. conduct 1970-72, reporter stds. jud. adminstrn. 1971-77, reporter model rules of profl. conduct 1978-83), Am. Law Inst. (reporter restatement of judgments 1973-81, dir. 1984-99), Nat. Legal Aid and Defender Assn., Inst. Jud. Adminstrn., Am. Judicature Soc., Selden Soc., Pa. Bar Assn., Calif. State Bar, Assn. Bar City N.Y., Phi Beta Kappa. Episcopalian. Avocations: tennis, history, golf. E-mail: ghazard@law.upenn.edu

HAZARD, NICOLE FLEUR, lawyer, social worker; b. Mpls., June 30, 1971; d. Thomas Nathan and Ann Elizabeth Hazard. AB, Dartmouth Coll., 1993; JD, MSW, U. Conn., 1997. Bar: N.Y. 1998. Grant writer Village for Families and Children, Hartford, Conn., 1996-97; stds. assoc. Coun. on Accreditation, N.Y.C., 1997—. Mem. task force on adoption Office N.Y.C. Comptr., N.Y.C., 1998—; mem. task forces on kinship care and cultural competency Child Welfare League Am ., Washington, 1998—. Pub. Interest Law grantee U. Conn., 1995. Mem. ABA, Bar Assn. City N.Y. (children and law com. 1998—). Democrat. Jewish. Avocations: sports, children's issues, film, public interest law. Home: 865 1st Ave Apt 11-C New York NY 10017

HAZELTON, PENNY ANN, law librarian, educator; b. Yakima, Wash., Sept. 24, 1947; d. Fred Robert and Margaret (McLeod) Pease; m. Norris J. Hazelton, Sept. 12, 1971; 1 child, Victoria MacLeod. BA cum laude, Linfield Coll., 1969; JD, Lewis and Clark Law Sch., 1975; M in Law Librarianship, U. Wash., 1976. Bar: Wash. 1976, U.S. Supreme Ct. 1982. Assoc. law libr., asst. prof. U. Maine, 1976-78, law libr., assoc. prof., 1978-81; asst. libr. for rsch. svcs. U.S. Supreme Ct., Washington, 1981-85, law libr., 1985, U. Wash., Seattle, 1985—, prof. law. Tchr. legal rsch., law librarianship, Indian law; cons. Maine Adv. Com. on County Law Librs., Nat. U. Sch. Law, San Diego, 1985-88, Lawyers Cooperative Pub., 1993-94. Author: Computer Assisted Legal Research: The Basics, 1993; contbr. articles to legal jours. Recipient Disting. Alumni award U. Wash., 1992. Mem. ABA (sect. legal edn. and admissions to bar, chair com. on librs. 1993-94, vice chair 1992-93, 94-95, com. on law sch. facilities 1998—), Am. Assn. Law Schs. (com. law librs. 1991-94), Law Librs. New Eng. (sec. 1977-79, pres. 1979-81), Am. Assn. Law Librs. (program chmn. ann. meeting 1984, exec. bd. 1984-87, v.p. 1989-90, pres. 1990-91, program co-chair Insts. 1983, 95), Law Librs. Soc. Washington (exec. bd. 1983-84, v.p., pres. elect 1984-85), Law Librs. Puget Sound, Wash. State Bar Assn. (chair editl. adv. bd.), Wash. Adv. Coun. on Librs., Westpac. Office: U Wash Marian Gould Gallagher Law Libr 1100 NE Campus Pkwy Seattle WA 98105-6605

HAZELWOOD, KIMBALL ELLEN, lawyer; b. Alberta, Canada; d. John Ernest Gilmer, Aug. 22, 1998. BA, Trinity Western U., Langley, B.C., Can., 1992; JD, Stanford (Calif.) U., 1996. Bar: Va. 1998, U.S. Ct. Appeals (4th cir.) 1998. Jud. clk. Chief Judge J. Harvie Wilkinson U.S. Ct. Appeals, Charlottesville, Va., 1996-97; regional coord. The Rutherford Inst., 1997—. Recipient Govs. Gen.'s Silver medal Gov. Gen. of Can., 1992. Mem. ABA, Christian Legal Soc., Am. Immigration Lawyers Assn. Avocations: running, assisting internat. students. Civil rights, Constitutional, Immigration, naturalization, and customs. Office: The Rutherford Inst 1445 East Rio Rd Charlottesville VA 22901

HEAD, ALLAN BRUCE, bar association executive; b. Norwood, Mass., May 15, 1944; s. E. Putnam and Tillie (Mentz) H.; m. Patricia Ann Reed, June 10, 1968; children— David, Darryl, Jayme. B.A., Wake Forest U., 1966, J.D., 1969. Bar: N.C. 1969. Mem. legal staff Hanes Corp., 1969; exec. sec. N.C. Bar Assn., Raleigh, 1974-80, exec. dir., 1981— . Office: NC Bar Assn PO Box 3688 8000 Weston Pkwy Cary NC 27519

HEAD, BEN THOMAS, lawyer; b. Oklahoma City, Nov. 1, 1920; s. Ben Thomas Head and Virginia (Broados) Pine; m. Mary C. Johnston, June 17, 1949 (div. June 1983); children: Marcy, Paul, Eric; m. June Leftwich, Mar. 22, 1986. BBA, U. Okla., 1942, LLB, 1948, JD, 1970. Bar: Okla., Tex. Pres., chmn., chief exec. officer RepublicBank, Austin, Tex., 1978-84; sr. lectr. banking U. Tex., 1984-88; U.S. trustee U.S. Dist. Ct. (so. and we. dists.) Tex., Houston, 1988-93. Pres., CEO United Va. Bank (now Sun-Trust), Newport News, Va., 1975-78; chmn. City Savs., San Angelo, Tex., 1986-87. V.p. Oklahoma City C. of C., 1973, chmn. Austin C. of C., 1983; pres. progress com. Newport News., Va., 1978; bd. dirs., chmn. fin. com. Austin Presbyn. Sem., 1982-90; bd. dirs. fin. com. Tex. Presbyn. Found., 1988—; trustee, vice chmn. bd., Hampton U., 1980—. Col. U.S. Army, 1942-46, India. Named Exec. of Yr. Austin C. of C., 1983. Mem. Rotary. Avocations: golf, walking. Home: 3234 Tarryhollow Dr Austin TX 78703-1639 Office: 816 Congress Ave Ste 1200 Austin TX 78701-2442

HEAD, HAYDEN WILSON, JR. judge; Student, Washington and Lee U., 1962-64; BA, U. Tex., 1967, LLB, 1968. Bar: Tex. Assoc. Head & Kendrick, Corpus Christi, Tex., 1968-69, 1972-76, ptnr., 1976-81; judge U.S. Dist. Ct. (so. dist.) Tex., 1981—. Lt. JAGC, USNR, 1969-72 Fellow Tex. Bar Found.; mem. State Bar Tex., Jud. Conf. of U.S. Office: US Dist Ct 1133 N Shoreline Blvd Corpus Christi TX 78401

HEAD, PATRICK JAMES, lawyer; b. Randolph, Nebr., July 13, 1932; s. Clarence Martin and Ellen Cecelia (Magirl) H.; m. Eleanor Hickey, Nov. 24, 1960; children: Adrienne, Ellen, Damian, Maria, Brendan, Martin, Sarah, Daniel, Brian. A.B. summa cum laude, Georgetown U., 1953, LL.B., 1956, LL.M. in Internat. Law, 1957. Bar: D.C. 1956, Ill. 1966. Assoc. John L. Ingolsby (and predecessor firm), Washington, 1956-64; gen. counsel internat. ops. Sears, Roebuck & Co., Oakbrook, Ill., 1964-70, counsel midwest ter. Skokie, 1970-72; v.p. Montgomery Ward & Co., Inc., Washington, 1972-76, v.p., gen. counsel, sec. Chgo., 1976-81; v.p., gen. counsel FMC Corp., 1981-96; ptnr. Altheimer E. Gray, 1997—. Bd. visitors Northwestern Law, 1988-91. Mem. Chgo. Crime Commn.; bd. regents Georgetown U., Washington, 1981-87; bd. visitors Georgetown Law Sch., 1992—. Mem. ABA, D.C. Bar Assn., Chgo. Bar Assn., Am. Law Inst. Democrat. Roman Catholic. Clubs: Met. (Washington); Chgo, Internat. Administrative and regulatory, Federal civil litigation, General corporate. Office: Altheimer & Gray 10 S Wacker Dr Fl 36 Chicago IL 60606-7407

HEAD, WILLIAM CARL, lawyer, author; b. Columbus, Ga., Mar. 4, 1951; s. Louis Bernice and Betty June (Vickery) H.; m. Sandra Earle, Sept. 3, 1972 (div. 1979); m. Kathleen Crenshaw, Aug. 8, 1981 (div. 1988); 1 stepchild, Stephanie A. Hansen; m. Kris L. Foreman, Feb. 14, 1990; children: Lauren Ansley, Shelby Jordan. BA cum laude, U. Ga., 1973, JD, 1976. Bar: Ga. 1976, U.S. Dist. Ct. (mid. dist.) Ga. 1976, U.S. Ct. Appeals (5th and 11th cirs.) 1979, S.C. 1990. Ptnr. Galis, Timmons, Andrews & Head, Athens, Ga., 1977-79, Andrews & Head P.C., Athens, 1979-82; pvt. practice, 1982-85; ptnr. McDonald, Head, Carney & Haggard, 1985-88; real estate developer, 1979-88; ptnr. Head, Thomas, Webb & Willis, LLC, Atlanta, 1995—. Regent, co-founder Nat. Coll. DUI Def., Inc. Author: The Georgia DUI Trial Practice Manual, 1998, Handling License Revocations and Suspensions in Georgia, 1993, Georgia DUI Trial Practice, 1998; co-author: 101 Ways to Avoid A Drunk Driving Conviction, 1991. Pres. Joseph Henry Lumpkin Found., Inc., Athens, 1979; chmn. Bridge the Gap seminar, Atlanta, 1980. Awardee Athens-Clarke Heritage Found. Inc., Athens, 1983. Mem. ABA, Ga. Bar Assn., S.C. Bar Assn., Assn. Trial Lawyers Am., Ga. Trial Lawyers Assn., Def. Drinking Drivers Network (founder), Order of Barristers, U. Ga. Pres.'s Club. Democrat. Presbyterian. Criminal, Personal injury, Product liability. Home: 6115 Spalding Bluff Ct Norcross GA 30092-4540 Office: 750 Hammond Dr NE Bldg 5 Atlanta GA 30328-5532 E-mail: wchead@mindspring.com

HEADY, EUGENE JOSEPH, lawyer; b. Poughkeepsie, N.Y., Jan. 25, 1958; s. William and Margaret Patricia Heady; m. Susan Leigh Snead, July 31, 1987; children: Anthony Ray, Emily Rene, Katie Shanell. BS in Engring., U. Hartford, 1981; JD cum laude, Tex. Tech. U., 1996. Bar: Tex. 1996, Ga. 1997, Colo. 1997, Fla. 1998, Supreme Ct. Ga. 1997, U.S. Dist. Ct. (no. dist.) Ga. 1997, Ct. Appeals Ga. 1997. V.p. Heady Electric Co., Inc., Poughkeepsie, N.Y., 1980-83; project mgr. ANECO, Inc., West Palm Beach, Fla., 1987-93; assoc. Smith, Currie & Hancock LLP, Atlanta, 1996—. Editor-in-chief: Tex. Tech Law Rev. vol. 27, 1995-96; student editor: Tex. County Ct. Bench Manual, 1996, Bench Book for the Tex. Jud., 1996; editor: Tex. Tech Legal Rsch. Bd., 1995-96; co-author: Ga. Suppl. to Fifty State Construction Lien and Bond Law, 1996, 97, 98, Ga. chpt. Fifty State Construction Lien and Bond Law, 2000; author: chpts. in Alternative Clauses to Standard Construction Contracts, 1998, 99, 2000; contbr. numerous articles to profl. jours. Mem. ABA (forum on the constrn. industry, vice-chmn. region IV sect. of pub. contract law), Scribes-The Am. Soc. Writers on Legal Subjects. Avocations: writing, reading. Construction, Government contracts and claims. Home: 2412 Waterscape Trl Snellville GA 30078-7740 Office: Smith Currie & Hancock LLP 2600 Harris Tower 233 Peachtree St NE Ste 2600 Atlanta GA 30303-1530 Fax: 404-688-0671. E-mail: gjheady@smithcurrie.com

HEALY, GEORGE WILLIAM, III, lawyer, mediator; b. New Orleans, Mar. 8, 1930; s. George William and Margaret Alford H.; m. Sharon Saunders, Oct. 26, 1974; children: George W. IV, John Carmichael, Floyd Alford, Hyde Dunbar, Mary Margaret. BA, Tulane U., 1950, JD, 1955. Bar: La. 1955, U.S. Supreme Ct. 1969. Assoc. Phelps, Dunbar, Marks, Claverie & Sims, New Orleans, 1955-58; ptnr. Phelps Dunbar LLP, 1958-95; of counsel Phelps Dunbar, 1996—. Mem. U.S. del. Comité Maritime Internat., Tokyo, 1969, Lisbon, 1985, Paris, 1990, Sydney, 1994, titulary mem. Mem. planning com. Tulane U. Admiralty Law Inst., dir. World Trade Ctr.,

1993—; dir. New Orleans Pro Bono Project, 1995-97, La. Orgn. for Jud. Excellence, 1997—. Fellow Am. Bar Found., Am. Coll. Trial Lawyers, Maritime Law Assn. U.S. (mem. exec. com. 1984-87, 2d v.p. 1988-90, 1st v.p. 1990-92, pres. 1992-94), La. Bar Found.; mem. ABA (ho. dels. 1993-95, 97-2000), New Orleans Bar Assn. (pres. 1992), Def. Rsch. Inst., La. Assn. Def. Counsel, New Orleans Assn. Def. Counsel, Com. Maritime Internat. Am. Found. (dir. 1990—), New Orleans Bar Assn. Inn of Ct. (master), Boston Club., La. Club, Stratford Club, Plimsoll Club, Recess Club (pres. 1978), Pinfeathers Hunting Club, New Orleans Lawn Tennis Club, Propeller Club, Mariners Club. Republican. Episcopalian. Admiralty. Home: 6020 Camp St New Orleans LA 70118-5902 Office: Canal Place 365 Canal St Ste 2000 New Orleans LA 70130-6534 Fax: 504-568-9130. E-mail: healyg@phelps.com

HEALY, JAMES CASEY, lawyer; b. Washington, Feb. 19, 1956; s. Joseph Francis Jr. and Patricia Ann (Casey) H.; m. Kelly Anne Quinn, Nov. 4, 1995; 1 child, Caitlin Quinn. BS, Spring Hill Coll., 1978; JD, Emory U., 1982. Bar: Ga. 1983, Conn. 1983, U.S. Dist. Ct. Conn. 1984, U.S. Tax Ct. 1984, U.S. Supreme Ct. 1987. Assoc. Gregory and Adams PC, Wilton, Conn., 1982-87, ptnr., 1988-89, mng. ptnr., 1990-94, v.p., 1995—. Spl. counsel Wilton Police Commn., 1986-98; mem. Parks and Recreation Commn., 1991—, sec., 1991-93, chmn., 1997—; corporator Ridgefield Bank, 1997—. Bd. dirs. Mark Lavin Meml. Offshore Med. and Safety Found., Empire, Mich., 1987—97; bd. dirs. Village Market, Inc. , 1988—90; chmn. leadership giving program United Way, 1991; bd. mgrs. Wilton Children's Ctr., 1996—98; mem athletic fields subcom.of building com. Wilton H.S., 1998—99; mem. steering com. Wilton Family Recreation and Activity Ctr., 2000; mem. bd. trustees Wilton Hist. Soc., 2001—; adv. com. Wilton Teen Ctr., 2001—. Mem. ABA, State Bar Ga., State Bar Conn. (exec. com., planning and zoning sect. 1992-94, 98—), Am. Planning Assn., Stamford/Norwalk Regional Bar Assn. (law office mgmt. com. 1994-96, co-chmn. land use com. 1996—, real estate broker's contract com. 1997-98), Wilton C. of C. (bd. dirs. 1994-96), Real Estate Fin. Assn., Silver Spring Country Club, Real Estate Fin. Assn. Republican. Roman Catholic. Land use and zoning (including planning), Real property. Office: Gregory and Adams 190 Old Ridgefield Rd Wilton CT 06897-4023 E-mail: jhealy@gregoryandadams.com

HEALY, JOSEPH FRANCIS, JR. lawyer, arbitrator, retired airline executive; b. N.Y.C., Aug. 11, 1930; s. Joseph Francis and Agnes (Kett) H.; m. Patricia A. Casey, Apr. 23, 1955; children: James C., Timothy, Kevin, Cathleen M., Mary, Terence. BS, Fordham U., 1952; JD, Georgetown U., 1959. Bar: D.C. 1959. With gen. traffic dept. Eastman-Kodak Co., Rochester, N.Y., 1954-55; air transp. examiner CAB, Washington, 1955-59; practiced in, 1959-70, 80-81; asst. gen. counsel Air Transport Assn. Am., 1966-70; v.p. legal Eastern Air Lines, Inc., N.Y.C. and Miami, Fla., 1970-80; ptnr. Ford, Farquhar, Kornblut & O'Neill, Washington, 1980-81; v.p. legal affairs Piedmont Aviation, Inc., Winston Salem, N.C., 1981-84, sr. v.p., gen counsel, 1984-89, ret., 1989; sr. v.p., gen. counsel Trans World Airlines Inc., Mt. Kisco, N.Y., 1993-94. Mem. bd. visitors Sch. Law Wake Forest U., 1988-96. 1st lt. USAF, 1952-54. Mem. FBA, Am. Arbitration Assn. (mem. nat. panel arbitrators 1989—), Nat. Aero. Assn., Internat. Aviation Club (Washington), Univ. Club (Washington), Beta Gamma Sigma, Phi Delta Phi. Home: 104 Overlink Ct Lynchburg VA 24503-3200

HEALY, JOSEPH ROBERT, lawyer; b. Troy, N.Y., Apr. 15, 1939; s. Thomas Francis and Isabel Kathryn (Eagle) H.; m. Sylvia Anne Tuccillo, May 14, 1976; 1 child, Daniel Joseph. BA in Sociology, Siena Coll., 1961; JD, Albany Law Sch., 1965. Bar: N.Y. 1973, U.S. Dist. Ct. (no. dist.) N.Y. 1973. Claims examiner Social Security Adminstrn., Glens Falls, N.Y., 1961-62; personnel examiner N.Y. State Dept. Civil Svc., Albany, 1962-69, sr. legal examiner, 1969-71, atty., 1971-75, sr. atty., 1975-82; assoc. atty., 1982-87; dir. civil svc. security ops., 1987-88; adminstrv. counsel internal controls, 1988-92; dir. investigations, 1992—. Author newsletter N.Y. State Orgn. Mgmt. Condifential Employees News Network. Active Woodland Hills Homeowners Assn., Clifton Park, N.Y. Republican. Roman Catholic. Home: 5 George Dr Clifton Park NY 12065-1811 E-mail: JHealy71@Hotmail.com

HEALY, NICHOLAS JOSEPH, lawyer, educator; b. N.Y.C., Jan. 4, 1910; s. Nicholas Joseph and Frances Cecilia (McCarthy) H.; m. Margaret Marie Ferry, Mar. 29, 1937; children: Nicholas, Margaret Healy Parker, Rosemary Healy Bell, Mary Louise Healy White, Donall, Kathleen Healy Hamon. AB, Holy Cross Coll., 1931; JD, Harvard U., 1934. Bar: N.Y. 1935, U.S. Supreme Ct. 1949. Pvt. practice, N.Y.C., 1935-42, 48—, 1935-42, 48—; mem. Healy & Baillie (and predecessor firms), 1948—. Spl. asst. to atty. gen. U.S., 1945-48; tchr. admiralty law NYU Sch. Law, 1947-86, adj. prof., 1960—; Niels F. Johnsen vis. prof. maritime law Tulane Maritime Law Ctr., 1986; vis. prof. maritime law Shanghai Maritime Inst. (now Shanghai Maritime U.), 1981, 86, 88. Contbr. chpts. to Ann. Survey Am. Law, 1948-87; author: (with Sprague) Cases on Admiralty, 1950; (with Currie) Cases and Materials on Admiralty, 1965; (with Sharpe) Cases and Materials on Admiralty, 1974, 3rd edit., 1998; (with Sweeney) The Law of Marine Collision, 1998; editor: Jour. Maritime Law and Commerce, 1980-90, mem. editl. bd., 1969-79, 91—; assoc. editor: American Maritime Cases; mem. scientific bd. Il Dirittimo Marittimo; contbr. to Ency. Brit. Chmn. USCG Adv. Panel on Rules of the Road, 1966-72; mem. permanent adv. bd. Tulane Admiralty Law Inst. Lt. (s.g.) USNR, 1942-45. Fellow Am. Coll. Trial Lawyers; mem. ABA (ho. of dels. 1964-66), N.Y. State Bar Assn., Assn. of Bar of City of N.Y., N.Y. County Lawyers Assn., Maritime Law Assn. U.S. (pres. 1964-66), Assn. Average Adjusters U.S. (chmn. 1959-60), Com. Maritime Internat. (exec. coun. 1972-79, v.p. 1985-91, hon. v.p. 1991—), Ibero-Am. Inst. Maritime Law (hon.). Admiralty. Home: 132 Tullamore Rd Garden City NY 11530-1139 Office: Healy & Baillie 29 Broadway Fl 27 New York NY 10006-3201 Fax: 212-425-0131. E-mail: nhealy@healy.com

HEARD, DAVID JAMES, lawyer, solicitor; b. Kaikoura, Canterbury, New Zealand, June 27, 1958; s. Richard Kemp and Margaret Elizabeth H.; m. Rebecca Clare Gibbons, Oct. 1, 1994; children: Hugo, Rory. Diplome Française, Toulouse (France) U., 1980; LLB with honors, Victoria U., Wellington, New Zealand, 1984. Bar: barrister, solicitor High Ct. New Zealand; solicitor Supreme Ct. Eng. and Wales. Trainee, barrister, solicitor Izard Weston, Wellington, 1984-86; solicitor, ptnr. Warner Cranston, London, 1986—. Mem. French C. of C., Australia-New Zealand C. of C. Avocations: cricket, golf, skiing, fishing, shooting. Contracts commercial, General corporate, Mergers and acquisitions. Office: Warner Cranston Pickfords Wharf Clink St SE1 9DG London England E-mail: david-heard@warner-cranston.com

HEARN, SHARON SKLAMBA, lawyer; b. New Orleans, Aug. 15, 1956; d. Carl John and Marjorie C. (Wimberly) Sklamba; m. Curtis R. Hearn. BA magna cum laude, Loyola U., New Orleans, 1977; JD cum laude, Tulane U., 1980. Bar: La. 1980, Tex. 1982; cert. tax specialist. Law clk. to presiding judge U.S. Ct. Appeals Fed. Cir., Washington, 1980-81; assoc. Johnson & Swanson, Dallas, 1981-84, The Kullman Firm, New Orleans, 1984—. Recipient Am. Legion award, 1970. Mem. ABA, La. State Bar Assn., Tex. State Bar Assn., Dallas Women Lawyers Assn. Democrat. Roman Catholic. Labor, Pension, profit-sharing, and employee benefits, Taxation, general. Home: 106 Bordeaux St Metairie LA 70005-4231 Office: The Kullman Firm 1600 Energy Ctr 1100 Poydras St New Orleans LA 70163-1101

HEARNE, MARY, retired legal secretary, artist; b. Dallas County, Ark., Aug. 2, 1934; d. Henry Evans Hearne and Olive Glover Abbott. Student, U. Ark., Little Rock, 1975-80. Dance instr. Arthur Murray Dance Studio, Orlando, Fla., 1958-61; sec., ct. reporter Little Rock AFB, 1967-81; legal sec. Friday, Eldridge & Clark, Little Rock, 1982-92; ret., 1992. Represented by The Collector Art Gallery, Design Ctr., Washington. One-woman shows at Ark. State Capitol Bldg., Little Rock, 1980, Ark. Arts Coun., Little Rock, 1980, Ark. Terr. Restoration, Little Rock, 1982, Ozark Folk Ctr., Mountain View, Ark., 1985, Gov.'s Conf. Rm., 1986, Plantation Agr. Mus., Scott, Ark., 1994; exhibited at group shows at Ark. Arts Ctr., Little Rock, 1979, Gallery 4, St. George, Utah, 1984, Gallery 2, Charlottesville, Va., 1984, The Collector Art Gallery, Hot Springs, Ark., 1994, The Collector Art Gallery, Washington, 1996, Statehouse Conf. Ctr., 1999, H. Lee Moffitt Cancer Ctr. and Rsch. Inst., Tampa, Fla., 1999; represented in permanent collection of Naval Nuclear Guided Missile Cruiser; 4 paintings selected for Ark. Sesquicentennial commemorative mugs, 1986; 3 paintings selected for 1-year display at office of Senator David Pryor, Washington, 1994-95, included in White House collection. Recipient Ambassador of Goodwill cert., 1980. Mem. N.Y. Artists Equity Assn., Nat. Mus. Women in the Arts (registered). Avocations: horseback riding, gardening, hiking. Home: 424 Burnside Dr Little Rock AR 72205-2235

HEATH, CHARLES DICKINSON, lawyer, telephone company executive; b. Waterloo, Iowa, June 28, 1941; s. George Clinton and Dorothy (Dickinson) H.; m. Carilyn Frances Cain, June 3, 1972. BBA, U. Iowa, 1962, JD, 1966; MBA, U. Ariz., 1963. Bar: Iowa 1966, Pa. 1969, Ind. 1970, U.S. Supreme Ct. 1971, Wis. 1973, Ariz. 1975, Mich. 1979, Fla. 1979, Calif. 1989. Asst. gen. counsel Kohler Co., Wis., 1973-79; securities and tax counsel Kellogg Co., Battle Creek, Mich., 1979-81; assoc. gen. counsel Universal Telephone Inc., Milw., 1981-89, also corp. sec., 1987-89; atty. CenturyTel, Inc., LaCrosse, Wis., 1989—. Public utilities, Securities, Corporate taxation.

HEATH, JOSEPH JOHN, lawyer; b. Watertown, N.Y., Mar. 19, 1946; s. Robert Edward and Lucille Frances (Ferringer) H.; 1 child, Travis Jackson. B.A., Syracuse U., 1968; J.D., SUNY-Buffalo, 1974. Bar: N.Y. 1975, U.S. Dist. Ct. (no. dist.) N.Y. 1976. Trial atty. Attica Bros. Legal Def., Buffalo, 1975-76; ptnr. Heath, Rosenthal & Weissman, Syracuse, 1976—; adj. prof. SUNY-Oswego, 1982-83; clin. prof. Syracuse U., 1982; sec. bd. dirs. G.C. Hanford Co., Syracuse, 1986, Allflex Mfg. Co., Syracuse, 1986. Mem. Onondaga County Child Abuse Citizen's Adv. Coun., Onondaga County Dist. Atty.'s Adv. Coun; bd. dirs. Hiscock Legal Aid Soc., 1984. Served with USN, 1968-70. Mem. Nat. Lawyers Guild, Onondaga County Bar Assn., N.Y. State Bar assn., N.Y. State Defenders Assn. Democrat. Roman Catholic. Civil rights, Criminal, Family and matrimonial. Office: 716 E Washington St Ste 104 Syracuse NY 13210-1550

HEATH, THOMAS CLARK, lawyer; b. Sarasota, Fla., Feb. 6, 1948; s. Roy Fulmer and Ruby (Clark) H.; m. Marsha Robert Hubbard, June 26, 1971 (div. Dec. 1977)); m. Anne Frances Wilson, Sept. 6, 1980; 1 child, Benjamin. BSBA, U. Fla., 1970, JD, 1973. Bar: Fla. 1973, U.S. Dist. Ct. (so. dist.) Fla. 1976, U.S. Ct. Appeals (11th cir.) 1976. Assoc. Howell, Kirby, Montgomery et al, Ft. Lauderdale, Fla., 1973-75, Carey, Dwyer, Cole, Selwood & Bernard, Ft. Lauderdale, 1975-81; ptnr. Hainline, Billing, Cochran & Heath, 1981-85, Billing, Cochran, Heath, Lyles & Mauro, Ft. Lauderdale, 1985—, West Palm Beach, 1985—. Fellow Am. Bd. Trial Advocacy (charter); mem. Am. Assn. Hosp. Attys., Assn. Trial Lawyers Am., Trial Attys. Am., Fla. Defense Lawyers Assn. Avocations: fishing, hunting. General civil litigation, Personal injury, Product liability. Office: Billing Cochran Heath Lyles & Mauro 888 SE 3rd Ave Ste 301 Fort Lauderdale FL 33316-1159

HEAVICAN, MICHAEL G. prosecutor; BA, JD, U. Nebr. From dep. county atty. yo chief dep. county atty. Lancaster County, Nebr., 1975—81, county atty., 1981—91; chief of criminal div. U.S. Atty.'s Office Nebr., 1991—2001; U.S. atty. Dist. Nebr. U.S. Dept. Justice, 2001—. Office: 1620 Dodge St Ste 1400 Omaha NE 68102-1506*

HECHT, FRANK THOMAS, lawyer; b. Ann Arbor, Mich., June 18, 1944; s. Hans H. and Ilse (Wagner) H. AB, Stanford U., 1966; postgrad., Johns Hopkins U., 1966-68, U. Chgo., 1968, JD, 1975. Bar: Ill. 1975, U.S. Dist. Ct. (no. dist.) 1975, U.S. Ct. Appeals (7th cir.) 1975, U.S. Supreme Ct. 1981, Colo. 1991. Lawyer Migrant Farmworker Litigation Project, Chgo., 1978-81, dir., 1981-82; assoc. Levy & Erens, 1982-85, ptnr., 1985-86, Hopkins & Sutter, Chgo., 1986-2001; vice chair trial sect., pro bono coord., ptnr. Ungaretti & Harris, 2001—. Cooperating atty. ACLU, Ill., 1983—, bd. dirs. 1985—; bd. dirs. Cook County Legal Assistance Found., 1984-85, Nat. Inst. for Trial Advocacy, 1978. Contbr. Civil Rights Law Reporter. Exec. dir. New Univ. Conf., 1970-72, Indochina Peace Campaign, 1973-75; exec. com. ACLU, 1986-87. Reginald Heber Smith fellow, 1975-78. Mem. ATLA, Assn. Trial Lawyers Am., Def. Rsch. Inst. Civil rights, Federal civil litigation, State civil litigation. Home: 240 Maplewood Rd Riverside IL 60546-1846 Office: Ungaretti & Harris 3 First National Plz Chicago IL 60602

HECHT, NATHAN LINCOLN, state supreme court justice; b. Clovis, N.Mex., Aug. 15, 1949; s. Harold Lee and Mary Loretta (Byerly) H. BA, Yale U., 1971; JD cum laude, So. Meth. U., 1974. Bar: Tex. 1974, D.C. 1975, U.S. Dist. Ct. D.C. 1975, U.S. Dist. Ct. (no. and we. dists.) Tex. 1976, U.S. Ct. Appeals (D.C. cir.) 1975, U.S. Ct. Appeals (5th cir.) 1976, U.S. Supreme Ct. 1979. Law clk. to judge U.S. Ct. Appeals (D.C. cir.), 1974-75; assoc. Locke, Purnell, Boren, Laney & Neely, Dallas, 1976-80, ptnr., 1981; dist. judge 95th Dist. Ct., 1981-86; justice Tex. 5th Dist. Ct. Appeals, 1986-89, Texas Supreme Ct., Austin, 1989—. Contbr. articles to profl. jours. Bd. visitors So. Meth. U., Dallas, 1984-87; trustee Children's Med. Found., Dallas, 1983-89; bd. dirs. Children's Med. Ctr. North, Dallas, 1985-89; elder Valley View Christian Ch., Dallas, 1981—. Lt. USNR, 1971-79. Named Outstanding Young Lawyer of Dallas, Dallas Assn. of Young Lawyers, 1984. Fellow Tex. Bar Found., Am. Bar Found.; mem. ABA, Dallas Bar Assn., D.C. Bar Assn., Am. Law Inst. Republican. Avocations: piano, organ, jogging, bicycling. Office: Tex Supreme Ct PO Box 12248 201 West 14th Room 104 Austin TX 78711*

HECHT, ROBERT D. lawyer; b. Seneca, Kans., Oct. 17, 1934; s. Jesse J. and Flossie Isabel (Ridgeway) H.; children— Lisa Fay, Julia Paige. B.B.A., Washburn U., 1956, J.D., 1958. Bar: Kans. 1958, U.S. Dist. Ct. Kans. 1958, U.S. Ct. Appeals (10th cir.) 1969, U.S. Supreme Ct. 1969. Asst. county atty. Shawnee County, Kans., 1961-65, county atty., 1965-69, county counselor, 1969-75; ptnr. Gray, Freidberg & Davis, Topeka, 1965-69, Scott, Quinlan & Hecht, Topeka, 1969— ; past adj. prof. Washburn U. Sch. Law, Topeka; dir. Benchmark Securities, Topeka; sch. atty. Unified Sch. Dist. 345, Topeka, 1979— ; Contbr. articles to Kans. Trial Lawyers Jour. Co-chmn. Shawnee County March of Dimes, 1963; candidate for atty. gen. State of Kans., 1968. Served as capt. JAGC, USAF, 1958-61. Mem. ABA, Kans. Bar Assn., Assn. Trial Lawyers Am., Kans. Trial Lawyers Assn. (bd. govs. 1974— , v.p. 1981-82), Am. Judicature Soc. Republican. Administrative and regulatory, Federal civil litigation, Criminal. Office: Scott Quinlan & Hecht 3301 SW Van Buren St Topeka KS 66611-2225

HECKENKAMP, ROBERT GLENN, lawyer; b. Quincy, Ill., June 29, 1923; s. Joseph Edward and Ethel E. (Requet) H.; m. Jean E. Duker, June 22, 1946 (dec. 1983); children: Gae Kelly, Joy Heckenkamp-Roate; m. Wilma E. Dobbs, Nov. 15, 1985. BS, Quincy Coll., 1947; JD, DePaul U., 1949. Bar: Ill. 1949, U.S. Dist. Ct. (cen. and so. dists.) Ill. 1949, U.S. Ct. Appeals (7th cir.) 1952, U.S. Supreme Ct. 1965. Sr. ptnr. Heckenkamp, Simhauser, Ward & Zerkle, Springfield, Ill. Fellow Am. Coll. Trial Lawyers (com. chmn. 1983-86), Internat. Acad. Trial Lawyers; mem. ATLA, ABA, Ill. State Bar Assn. (pres. 1980-81), Sangamon County Bar Assn., Ill. Trial Lawyers Assn. (pres. 1977-78). Soc. Trial Lawyers. Avocations: hunting, fishing. General civil litigation, Insurance, Personal injury. Home: 2201 W Washington Unit 1 Springfield IL 62704 Office: Heckenkamp Simhauser Ward & Zerkle 1610 S Sixth St Springfield IL 62703

HECKLER, GERARD VINCENT, lawyer; b. Utica, N.Y., Feb. 18, 1941; s. Gerard Vincent and Mary Jane (Finocan) H. BA, Union Coll., Schenectady, 1962; JD, Syracuse U., 1970; MA in Clin. Psychology, Antioch U., 1994; postgrad., The Fielding Inst., 1995—. Bar: Ill. 1971, Calif. 1980, Mass. 1986, N.Y. 1986, U.S. Supreme Ct. 1985. Assoc. Martin, Craig, Chester & Sonnenschein, Chgo., 1970-73, Goldstein, Goldberg & Fishman, Chgo., 1973-76; ptnr. Heckler & Enstrom, 1976-80; pvt. practice law L.A., Irvine, 1980-85; sr. trial atty. Law Office of Harden Bennion, L.A., 1985-87, Rafferty & Polich, Cambridge, Mass., 1987-8; trial atty. Acret, Gropman & Turner, L.A., 1989-92. Instr. trial skills and evidence Calif. State Bar, 1987—; judge pro tem L.A. Mcpl. Ct., 1991—. Lt. USCG, 1964-67, Vietnam. Mem. Calif. State Bar (Bd. Govs. commendation 1986), L.A. County Bar Assn., Acad. Family Mediators, Ill. Bar Assn., Mass. Bar Assn., N.Y. Bar Assn. Avocations: sports, theater, public speaking. Bankruptcy, General civil litigation, Construction. Office: 400 N Tustin Ave Ste 120 Santa Ana CA 92705-3879

HECKMAN, JEROME HAROLD, lawyer; b. Washington, June 7, 1927; s. Morris and Pauline (German) H.; m. Margot Resh, June 16, 1948 (div. Oct. 1977); children: Eric Stephen, Carey Eugene; m. Ilona Ely Grenadier, Jan. 2, 1986. BSS, Georgetown U., 1948, LLB, 1953, JD, 1967. Bar: D.C. 1953, U.S. Supreme Ct. 1965. Assoc. Dow, Lohnes & Albertson, Washington, 1954-59, ptnr., 1959-62; sr. ptnr. Keller and Heckman, 1962—. Gen. counsel Soc. of Plastics Industry Inc., N.Y.C., Washington, 1954—, Broadcasting Publs. Inc. Mag., Washington (co. sold to L.A. Times), 1968-87, Disposables Assn. Inc. (now named Internat. Nonwovens and Disposables Assn.), 1958-67. Contbr. articles to profl. jours. Chmn. regional Rep. com., Md., 1966-72; pres. Plastics Acad., 1995-97. Named to Hall of Fame of Plastics Industry, 1987; recipient Spes Hominum award, Nat. Sanitation Found., 1987, William Bradbury award, Soc. Plastics, 2000, Paul R. Dean Disting. Alumni award Georgetown U. Law Ctr., 2001; Dirs. Citation, Ctr. Food Safety and Applied Nutrition, 2000. Mem. ABA, Bar Assn. D.C., George Town Club, Woodmont Country Club, Phi Delta Phi. Avocations: golf, tennis. Administrative and regulatory, Antitrust, Communications. Office: Keller & Heckman 1001 G St NW Ste 500 Washington DC 20001-4545

HEDGES, RICHARD HOUSTON, lawyer, epidemiologist; b. Louisville, July 16, 1952; s. Houston and Frances Ruth (Zemo) H.; m. Donna Jean Hough. BA, U. Ky., 1974; MA, Ea. Ky. U., 1975, MPA, 1983; PhD, U. Ky., 1986; JD, Capital U. Law, 1994. Bar: Ohio 1995. Rehab. specialist Commonwealth of Ky., Somerset, 1976-81, chief health planner Frankfort, 1981-82; asst. prof. U. Ky., Lexington, 1985-87; rsch. assoc. dept. med. behavioral sci. U. Ky. Coll. Medicine, 1982-85; program adminstr. Rollman Psychiat. Inst., Cin., 1987-88; asst. prof. Ohio U., 1988-92, assoc. prof., 1992—; assoc. Garry Hunter, LPA, Athens, Ohio, 1997-98; ptnr. Thomas & Hedges LLC, 1998-99; pvt. practice, Athens, 1999—. Asst. city atty. City of Nelsonville, Ohio, 1997—2001, city pros., 1997—2001; dir. divsn. on aging Ohio U. Health Promotion and Rsch., 1990—92, MHA grad. program coord., 1995—96; bd. dirs. Washington County Mental Health and Addiction Recovery Svcs., 1998—99; exec. dir. pro tem Health Recovery Svcs., 1998; solicitor Village of Chauncey, 2000. Author: Bioethics, Healthcare and the Law, 1999; contbr. articles to profl. jours. Mem. Athens County Domestic Violence Task Force, Athens County Victim's Assistance Adv.; treas. Athens County Heart Assn.. 1998. Fellow NIMH, 1984-86. Mem.: ABA, ATLA, Ohio Acad. Trial Lawyerrs, Soc. Ohio Healthcare Attys., Healthcare Fin. Mgmt. Assn., Nat. Health Lawyers Assn., Ohio Bar Assn., Washington County Bar Assn. (trustee at large 2000—), Athens County Bar Assn., Pi Sigma Alpha, Phi Delta Phi. Democrat. Episcopalian. Avocations: backpacking, volleyball, bicycling, sailing. Family and matrimonial, Health, Labor. Home: RR 2 Box 14 Belpre OH 45714-9702 Office: 8 N Court St Ste 506 Athens OH 45701-2450 also: Ohio U Sch Health Sci 413 Tower Athens OH 45701 Fax: 740-592-3724

HEDIEN, COLETTE JOHNSTON, lawyer; b. Chgo., 1939; d. George A. and Catherine (Bugan) Johnston; m. Wayne E. Hedien; 3 children. BS with honors, U. Wis., 1960; JD, DePaul U., 1981. Bar: Ill. 1981. Tchr. Sch. Dist. 39, Wilmette, Ill., 1960-63, Tustin (Calif.) Pub. Schs., 1964-66; extern law clk. to judge Chgo., 1980, U.S. Atty.'s Office, 1980; pvt. practice Northbrook, Ill., 1981—. Atty. Chgo. Vol. Legal Svcs.; mem. Chgo. Appellate Law Com., 1982-83, chmn., 1987-88; chmn. Northbrook Planning Commn., 1984-89; founder Am. Women of Surrey (Eng.), 1975-77; founding dir. U. Irvine Friends of Libr., 1965-66; guidance vol. Glenbrook High Sch., 1984-89; trustee Village of Northbrook, 1989—; mem. Women's Bd. Field Mus. Bd. dirs. Ill. Project for Spl. Needs Children, 1998—. NSF scholar, 1962. Mem. ABA (com. on real property), Ill. Bar Assn., Chgo. Bar Assn., North Shore Panhellenic Assn. (rep. 1989—), Phi Kappa Phi, Kappa Alpha Theta (bd. dirs.).

HEDLUND, KAREN JEAN, lawyer; b. Chgo., Oct. 27, 1948; d. Reuben E. and Jane C. (Scarborough) H.; m. Barry M. Schneider; children— Erik, Alexander. A.B., Harvard U., 1970; J.D., Georgetown U., 1974. Bar: Ill. 1974, U.S. Dist. Ct. (no. dist.) Ill. 1974, Calif. 1989. Assoc. Mayer, Brown & Platt, Chgo., 1974-80, ptnr., 1980-84; ptnr. Skadden, Arps, Slate, Meagher & Flom, Chgo., L.A., 1984-93, Sun America Inc., 1993-94. Advisor debt com. Govt. Fin. Officer's Assn. Mem. ABA (mem. Tax sect. tax exempt fin. com. 1983—), Nat. Assn. Bond Lawyers, Assn. for Govtl. Leasing and Fin., Univ. Club, Banking Club. Banking, Municipal (including bonds), Securities. Office: SunAmerica Inc 1 Sun America Ctr Los Angeles CA 90067-6121

HEDLUND, PAUL JAMES, lawyer; b. Abington, Pa., June 26, 1946; s. Frank Xavier and Eva Ruth (Hoffman) H.; m. Marta Louise Brewer, Dec. 7, 1985; children: Annemarie Kirsten, Brooke Ashley, Tess Kara. BSME, U. Mich., 1968; JD, UCLA, 1973. Bar: Calif. 1973, D.C. 1994, U.S. Dist. Ct. (ctrl. dist.) Calif. 1977, U.S. Dist. Ct. (ea. dist.) Calif. 1991, U.S. Dist. Ct. (no. dist.) N.Y. 1994, U.S. Patent and Trademark Office 1978, U.S. Ct. Appeals (9th cir.) 1994, U.S. Supreme Ct. 1997. Staff engr. So. Calif. Edison, L.A., 1968-70; ptnr. Hedlund & Samuels, 1974-88, Kananack, Murgatroyd Baum & Hedlund (and predecessor firms), L.A., 1988-92; shareholder Baum, Hedlund, Aristei, Guilford & Downey (and predecessor firms), 1993—. Mem. discovery and trial teams MDL 817 aircrash at Sioux City Iowa United Airlines, Chgo., 1989; lectr. in field. Mem. State Bar Calif., D.C. Bar Assn., Consumer Attys. of L.A. and L.A. County Bar Assn. Aviation, Personal injury, Product liability. Office: Baum Hedlund Aristei Guilford & Downey 12100 Wilshire Blvd Ste 950 Los Angeles CA 90025-7107 E-mail: paul@bhagd.com

HEFFELFINGER, THOMAS BACKER, lawyer; b. Mpls., Feb. 13, 1948; BA in History, Stanford U., 1970; JD, U. Minn., 1975. Bar: Minn. 1976, U.S. Dist. Ct. Minn. 1977, U.S. Ct. Appeals (8th cir.) 1983. Law clk. Office of the Hennepin County Atty. , 1974-76; asst. atty. juvenile divsn. Office of the Hennepin County Atty., 1976, asst. atty. criminal divsn. trial sect., 1977-82, asst. atty. major offender unit, 1978-81, supr. burglary unit, 1981-82; asst. U.S. atty. criminal divsn. Dist. Minn., U.S. Dept. Justice, 1982-88, atty. white collar crime sect., 1982-85, supr. narcotics and firemans sect., 1985-86; ptnr. Opperman Heins & Paquin, 1988-91; U.S.

atty. Dist. Minn., U.S. Dept. Justice, 1991-93, 2001—; ptnr. Bowman and Brooke, 1993—2000, Best & Flanagan, 2000—01. Contbr. articles to profl. jours. Candidate Hennepin County Atty., 1986; bd. dirs. Mpls. Chpt. ARC, 1987—; mem. Hennepin County Task Force on Youth and Drugs, 1987-88, Minn. Ho. of Reps. Rep. Caucus Drug Task Force, 1989-90, Minn. Commn. on Violent Crime, 1991; chmn. Minn. Commn. on Jud. Selection, 1990-91; lectr. in field. Mem. Fed. Bar Assn., Minn. Bar Assn., Hennepin County Bar Assn. General civil litigation, Criminal, Native American. Office: 600 US Courthouse 300 S 4th St Minneapolis MN 55415*

HEFFERNAN, JAMES VINCENT, lawyer; b. Washington, Oct. 6, 1926; s. Vincent Jerome and Hazel Belle (Wiltfong) H.; m. Virginia May Adams, June 26, 1954; children: David V., Douglas J., Alan P., Margaret L., Thomas A. AB, Cornell U., 1949, JD with distinction, 1952. Bar: D.C., 1953, Md., 1959, U.S. Ct. Claims, 1955, U.S. Tax Ct., 1953, U.S. Supreme Ct., 1958. Assoc. Sutherland, Asbill & Brennan, Washington, 1952-59, ptnr., 1959—. Adj. prof. Georgetown U., Washington, 1978-79. Contbr. articles to profl. jours. With USN, 1945-46. Mem. ABA, Fed. Bar Assn., Bar Assn. of D.C., Order of Coif, KC, Phi Alpha Delta. Democrat. Roman Catholic. Clubs: Metropolitan (Washington); Kenwood Golf and Country (Bethesda, Md.). Corporate taxation, Estate taxation, Personal income taxation. Home: 5216 Falmouth Rd Bethesda MD 20816-2913 Office: Sutherland Asbill & Brennan LLP 1275 Pennsylvania Ave NW Washington DC 20004-2428 E-mail: jheffernan@sablaw.com, jvheff@gateway.net

HEFFERNAN, NATHAN STEWART, retired state supreme court chief justice; b. Frederic, Wis., Aug. 6, 1920; s. Jesse Eugene and Pearl Eva (Kaump) H.; m. Dorothy Hillemann, Apr. 27, 1946; children: Katie (Mrs. Howard Thomas), Michael, Thomas. BA, U. Wis., 1942, LLB, 1948; postgrad. in bus., Harvard U. Sch. Bus. Adminstrn., 1943-44; LLD (hon.), Lakeland Coll., 1995; LLD, U. Wis., 1999. Bar: Wis. 1948, U.S. Dist. Ct. (we. dist.) Wis. 1948, U.S. Dist. Ct. (ea. dist.) Wis. 1950, U.S. Ct. Appeals (7th cir.) 1960, U.S. Supreme Ct. 1960. Assoc. firm Schubring, Ryan, Peterson & Sutherland, Madison, Wis., 1948-49; practice in Sheboygan, 1949-59; partner firm Buchen & Heffernan, 1951-59; counsel Wis. League Municipalities, 1949; research asst. to gov. Wis., 1949; asst. dist. atty. Sheboygan County, 1951-53; city atty. City of Sheboygan, 1953-59; dep. atty. gen. State of Wis., 1959-62; U.S. atty. Western Dist. Wis., 1962-64; justice Wis. Supreme Ct., 1964—, chief justice, 1983-95. Lectr. mcpl. corps., 1961-64, appellate procedure and practice U. Wis. Law Sch., 1971-83; faculty Appellate Judges Seminar, Inst. Jud. Adminstrn., NYU, 1972-87; former mem. Nat. Council State Ct. Reps., chmn., 1976-77; ex-officio dir. Nat. Ctr. State Cts., 1976-77, mem. adv. bd. appellate justice project; former mem. Wis. Jud. Planning Com.; chmn. Wis. Appellate Practice and Procedure Com., 1975-76; mem. exec. com. Wis. Jud. Conf., 1978—, chmn., 1983; pres. City Attys. Assn., 1958-59; chair Citizens Panel on Election Reform; co-chair Equal Justice Coalition. Wis. chmn. NCCJ, 1966-67; past exec. bd. Four Lakes Coun., Boy Scouts Am.; gen. chmn. Wis. Dem. Conv., 1960, 61; mem. Wis. Found.; bd. dirs. Inst. Jud. Adminstrn.; visitors U. Wis. Law Sch., 1970-83, chmn., 1973-76; past mem. corp. bd. Meth. Hosp.; former curator Wis. Hist. Soc., curator emeritus, 1990; trustee Wis. Meml. Union, Wis. State Libr., William Freeman Vilas Trust Estate; v.p. U. Wis. Meml. Union Bldg. Assn.; former deacon Conglist. Ch. Lt. (s.g.) USNR, 1942-46, ETO, PTO. Recipient Disting. Svc. award NCCJ, 1968, Ann. Disting. Svc. award Wis. Mediation Assn., 1995, Lifetime Achievement award Milw. Bar Assn., 1995, Disting. Svc. award Dem. Party Sheboygan County, 1995; Disting. Jud. fellow Marquette U. Law Sch., 1996. Fellow Am. Bar Found. (life), Inst. for Jud. Adminstrn. (hon., bd. dirs., mem. faculty seminar), Wis. Bar Assn. (chmn. Wis. bar com. study on legal edn. 1995-96, hon. chmn. Equal Justice Coalition 1997—, Goldberg award for disting. svc.), Wis. Bar Found.; mem. ABA (past mem. spl. com. on adminstrn. criminal justice, mem. com. fed.-state delineation of jurisdiction, jud. adminstrn. com. on appellate ct., com. appellate time standards), Am. Law Inst. (life, adv. com. on complex litigation), Dane County Bar Assn., Sheboygan County Bar Assn., Am. Judicature Soc. (dir. 1977-80, chmn. program com. 1979-81), Wis. Law Alumni Assn. (bd. dirs., Disting. Alumni Svc. award 1989), Nat. Conf. Chief Justices (bd. dirs.), Nat. Assn. Ct. Mgmt., Wis. Rivers Alliance (bd. dirs.), Order of Coif, Iron Cross, U. Club (Madison, Wis.), Phi Kappa Phi, Phi Delta Phi. Clubs: Madison Lit. (pres. 1979-80); Harvard (Milw.); Harvard Bus. Sch. (Wis.). Home: 17 Thorstein Veblen Pl Madison WI 53705

HEFFINGTON, JACK GRISHAM, lawyer, banker, insurance company executive, horse breeder; b. Lawrenceburg, Tenn., Mar. 8, 1944; s. Charles Alexander and Kathlyn (Grisham) H.; m. Nancy Caroline Heffington, Sept. 29, 1979; children: Jacquelyn Elliott, Caroline Sutherland. B.S., Memphis State U., 1967; J.D., U. Ark., 1971. Bar: Tenn. 1971, Ala., 1972. Ptnr., Heffington & Thomas, Murfreesboro, Tenn., 1972— ; pres., chmn. Middle Tenn. Mortgage Co., Murfreesboro, 1973— ; pres., chmn. Keg Life Ins. Co. of S.C., Columbia, 1977— ; pres. South Tex. Bankers Life Ins. Co., Birmingham, Ala., 1993—; vice chmn. World Svc. Life Ins. Co. of Am., Winchester, Tenn., 1993—; owner Tan Oak Farms, Murfreesboro; dir. 1st Nat. Bank of Rutherford County, Murfreesboro. Mem. ABA, Ala. Bar Assn., Tenn. Bar Assn., Sigma Delta Chi. Mem. Ch. of Christ. General corporate. Home: PO Box 64 Christiana TN 37037-0064 Office: Heffington & Thomas 520 S Church St Murfreesboro TN 37130-4922

HEFTER, LAURENCE ROY, lawyer; b. N.Y.C., Oct. 13, 1935; s. Charles S. and Rose (Postal) H.; m. Jacqulyn Maureen Miller, June 13, 1957; children: Jeffrey Scott, Sue-Anne. B.M.E., Rensselaer Poly. Inst., 1957, M.S. in Mech. Engring., 1960; J.D. with honors, George Washington U., 1964. Bar: Va. 1964, N.Y. 1967, D.C. 1973. Instr. Rensselaer Poly. Inst., Troy, N.Y., 1957-59; patent engr. Gen. Electric Co., Washington, 1959-63; sr. patent atty. Atlantic Research Corp., Alexandria, Va., 1963-66; assoc. firm Davis, Hoxie, Faithfull & Hapgood, N.Y.C., 1966-69; mem. firm Ryder, McAulay & Hefter, 1970-73, Finnegan, Henderson, Farabow, Garrett & Dunner, LLP, Washington, 1973—. Professorial lectr. trademark law George Washington U., 1981-90; mem. adv. com. U.S. Patent and Trademark Office, 1988-92, Trademark Rev. Commn., 1986-89. Bd. govs. Brand Names Ednl. Found., 2001—. Named in Best Lawyers in Am., Best Lawyers in Washington. Mem. ABA (chmn. patent office affairs com. patent, trademark and copyright sect. 1976-80, unfair competition com. 1980-81, governing com. franchise forum 1994-97), N.Y. State Bar Assn., D.C. Bar Assn., Va. Bar Assn. (dir. patent, trademark and copyright sect. 1976-78), Internat. Bar Assn. (chmn. trademark com. 1986-90), Am. Patent Law Assn. (chmn. trademark com. 1979-81, dir. 1981-84), U.S. Trademark Assn. (dir. 1982-84, elected Guide to World's Leading Experts in Trademark Law, Guide to World's Leading Experts in Patent Law), Brand Names Ednl. Found. (dir. 2001—), Order of Coif, Alpha Epsilon Pi. Federal civil litigation, Patent, Trademark and copyright. Home: 6904 Loch Lomond Dr Bethesda MD 20817-4756 Office: 1300 I St NW Washington DC 20005-3314

HEFTLER, THOMAS E. lawyer; b. Jersey City, 1943; AB, Princeton U., 1965; JD cum laude, NYU, 1968. Bar: N.Y. 1968. Mem. Stroock & Stroock & Lavan LLP, N.Y.C. General corporate, Securities, Commodities. Office: Stroock & Stroock & Lavan LLP 180 Maiden Ln New York NY 10038-4925

HEGARTY, MARY FRANCES, lawyer; b. Chgo., Dec. 19, 1950; d. James E. and Frances M. (King) H. BA, DePaul U., 1972, JD, 1975. Bar: Ill. 1975, U.S. Dist. Ct. (no. dist.) Ill. 1976, U.S. Supreme Ct. 1980. Ptnr. Lannon & Hegarty, Park Ridge, Ill., 1975-80; pvt. practice, 1980—. Dir. Legal Assistance Found. Chgo., 1983—. Mem. revenue study com. Chgo. City Coun. Fin. Com., 1983; mem. Sole Source Rev. Panel, City of Chgo., 1984; pres. Hist. Pullman Found., Inc., 1984-85; apptd. Park Ridge Zoning Bd., 1993-94. Mem. Ill. State Bar Assn. (real estate coun. 1980-84), Chgo. Bar Assn., Women's Bar Assn. Ill. (pres. 1983-84), NW Suburban Bar Assn., Park Ridge Women Entrepreneurs, Chgo. Athletic Assn. (pres. 1992-93). Democrat. Roman Catholic. General corporate, Probate, Real property. Office: 301 W Touhy Ave Park Ridge IL 60068-4204

HEIDER, JON VINTON, retired lawyer, corporate executive; b. Moline, Ill., Mar. 1, 1934; s. Raymond and Doris (Hinch) H.; m. Barbara L. Bond, Dec. 27, 1960 (div.); children: Loren P., John C., Lindsay L.; m. Mary R. Murray, Jan. 27, 1984. AB, U. Wis., 1956; JD, Harvard U., 1961; grad., Advanced Mgmt. Program, 1974. Bar: Pa. 1962, U.S. Dist. Ct. (ea. dist.) Pa. 1962, U.S. Ct. Appeals (3d cir.) 1962, U.S. Supreme Ct. 1991. Assoc. Morgan Lewis & Bockius, Phila., 1961-66; counsel Catalytic, Inc., 1966-68, Houdry Process & Chem. Co., Phila., 1968-70; counsel chems. group Air Products & Chems., Inc., Valley Forge, Pa., 1970-75, asst. gen. counsel, 1975-76, assoc. gen. counsel, 1976-78, gen. counsel Allentown, 1978-80; v.p. corp. affairs, sr. adminstrv. officer-Europe, Air Products Europe, Inc., London, 1980-83; v.p. corp. devel. Air Products & Chems., Inc., 1983-84; v.p., gen. counsel BF Goodrich Co., Akron, Ohio, 1984-88, sr. v.p., gen. counsel, 1988-94, exec. v.p., gen. counsel, 1994-98; ret., 1998. Trustee U. Akron, Bluecoats, Inc.; mem. distbn. com. Charles E. and Mabel M. Ritchie Meml. Found. Lt. USNR, 1956-58. Mem. ABA, Am. Law Inst., Assn. Gen. Counsel, Blossom Music Ctr. Bd. Overseers, Sisler McFawn Found. (chmn. distbn. com.), U. Wis. Found., Portage Country Club, Rolling Rock Club, Key Biscayne Yacht Club. General corporate. E-mail: JHeider@msn.com

HEIDRICH, ROBERT WESLEY, lawyer; b. Chgo., Aug. 1, 1927; s. Carl G. and Harriet B. (Butzlaff) H.; m. Lennice L. Hubenbecker, June 19, 1948; children: John G., Robert G., Kimberly L. Student, U. Wis., 1944-45, 47-48; JD, DePaul U., 1951. Bar: Ill. 1951, Calif. 1974, Tenn. 1980. Atty. Brunswick Corp., Chgo., 1953-60, 65-69; v.p. Brunswick AG (Switzerland), 1960-61; dir. Brunswick Internat. Fin. AG (Switzerland), 1962-65; sec., corp. counsel Nat. Can Corp., Chgo., 1969-73; v.p., sec., gen. counsel, dir. Rohr Industries, Inc., Chula Vista, Calif., 1973-79; corp. v.p., gen. counsel Holiday Hotels, 1979-85; counsel Kaiser Steel Corp., 1985-87, LaJolla (Calif.) Devel., 1987—. Chmn. Riverside-Brookfield CMty. Caucus, 1972; bd. dirs., Am. Internat. Sch. Zurich, 1964-65; chmn. Jr. Achievement, Chgo., 1970-75. Served with U.S. Army, 1945-47. Mem. Frederick Law Olmstead Soc. (founding pres. 1967-69). General corporate, Real property. Home: 5157 Long Branch Ave Apt 4 San Diego CA 92107-2032 Office: La Jolla Devel PO Box 7001 San Diego CA 92167-0001

HEILIGENSTEIN, CHRISTIAN E. lawyer; b. St. Louis, Dec. 7, 1929; s. Christian A. and Louisa M. (Dixon) H.; children: Christie; m. Liselotte Warbanoff, Feb. 6, 1981. BS in Law, U.Ill., 1953, JD, 1955. Bar: Ill. 1956, U.S. Dist. Ct. (so. dist.) Ill. 1956, U.S. Ct. Appeals (7th cir.) 1956, U.S. Dist. Ct. (cen. dist.) Ill. 1960, U.S. Supreme Ct. 1978. Assoc. Listeman & Bandy, East St. Louis, Ill., 1955-61; sole practice Belleville, 1962-84; ptnr., pres. Heiligenstein & Badgley, 1984-98; pres. C.E. Heiligenstein, P.C., 1998—. Bd. dirs. Union Planters Corp., Union Planters Bank NA, 1998-2000, audit com. 1999-2000, Magna Bank and Magna Group, Inc., 1984-98; chair audit com. Magna Group, Inc., 1994-98. Bd. visitors U. Ill. Coll. of Law, 2000. Recipient Alumni of Month award U. Ill. Law Sch., 1982; C.E. Heiligenstein Chair in Law named in his honor U. Ill., 1999. Mem. Ill. State Bar Assn., Internat. Acad. Trial Lawyers (bd. dirs. 1991-97), St. Clair County Bar Assn., St. Louis Bar Assn., Inner Circle Advs., Am. Bd. Trial Advs. (nat. bd. dirs. 1992, pres. St. Louis, So. Ill. region 1993), Am. Acad. Profl. Liabilities Attys. (Nat. bd. dirs., 1990-99), ATLA (bd. govs. 1985-87), Ill. Trial Lawyers Assn. (bd. mgrs. 1975-88, pres. 1989), Mo. Athletic Club, Beach Club (bd. dirs. 1996, v.p. 1998), Old Guard Soc. of Palm Beach. Democrat. Personal injury, Product liability, Workers' compensation. Home: 5200 Turner Hall Rd Belleville IL 62220-5628 also: 225 Eden Rd Palm Beach FL Office: CE Heiligenstein PC 5200 Turner Hall Rd Belleville IL 62220 E-mail: l.warbanoj@aol.com

HEILMAN, PAMELA DAVIS, lawyer; b. Buffalo, July 2, 1948; d. George Henry and Natalie (Maier) Davis; m. Robert D. Heilman, June 27, 1970. AB, Vassar Coll., 1970; JD, SUNY, Buffalo, 1975. Bar: N.Y. 1976, Fla. 1980. Assoc. Hodgson, Russ, Andrews, Woods & Goodyear, Buffalo, 1975-84, ptnr., 1984—. Bd. dirs. United Way Buffalo, 1985-97, vice chmn., 1989-92, chair, 1993-97, gen. campaign chair, 1992; bd. dirs. D'Youville Coll. Ctr. for Women in Mgmt., Buffalo, 1985-90. Mem. ABA, N.Y. State Bar Assn. (vice chmn., exec. com., sect. on internat. law and practice 1988-90), Fla. Bar Assn., Erie County Bar Assn. General corporate, Private international, Non-profit and tax-exempt organizations. Office: Hodgson Russ Andrews Woods & Goodyear LLP One M&T Plz Buffalo NY 14211-1638 E-mail: pheilman@hodgsonruss.com

HEINDL, PHARES MATTHEWS, lawyer; b. Meridian, Miss., Dec. 14, 1949; s. Paul A. and Leila (Matthews) H.; m. Linda Ann Williamson, Sept. 21, 1985; children: Lori Elizabeth, Jesse Phares, Jared Matthews. BSChemE, Miss. State U., 1972; JD, U. Fla., 1981. Bar: Fla. 1981, Calif. 1982, U.S. Dist. Ct. (cen. dist.) Calif. 1983, U.S. Dist. Ct. (mid. dist.) Fla. 1983; cert. civil trial lawyer Fla. Bar. Assoc. Lafollette, Johnson et al, L.A., 1982-83, Sam E. Murrell & Sons, Orlando, Fla., 1983-84; pvt. practice, 1984-93, Altamonte Springs, 1993—. Bd. cert. civil trial lawyer. Precinct coord. Freedom Coun., Orlando, 1986; pres. Friends of the Wekiva River, 1999-2001. Mem. Fla. Bar Assn., Calif. Bar Assn., Seminole County Bar Assn. (pres. civil trial sect. 1998), ATLA, Christian Legal Soc. (past pres. Ctrl. Fla.), Fla. Acad. Trial Lawyers, Workers Compensation Rules Com. Republican. Avocation: kayak racing. State civil litigation, Personal injury, Workers' compensation. Home: 2415 River Tree Cir Sanford FL 32771-8334 Office: 222 S Westmonte Dr Ste 208 Altamonte Springs FL 32714-4269

HEINEMAN, ANDREW DAVID, lawyer; b. N.Y.C., Nov. 5, 1928; s. Bernard and Lucy (Morgenthau) H. BA, Williams Coll., 1950; LLB, Yale U., 1953. Bar: N.Y. 1953. Assoc. Proskauer Rose Goetz & Mendelsohn, N.Y.C., 1953-63; ptnr. Proskauer Rose LLP, 1963—. Pres., chmn. bd. dirs. Ernest and Mary Hayward Weir Found., N.Y.C., 1969-87, trustee Mt. Sinai Hosp. Med. Sch. and Med. Ctr., 1976—, Williams Coll., 1980-95, Abelard Found., 1976-96; Asphalt Green, 1992-96; bd. dirs. Jewish Home and Hosp. for Aged, 1967—, vice chmn. bd. dirs., 1992, chmn. bd. dirs. 1993-97; exec. asst. Citizens for Kennedy and Johnson, N.Y.C., 1960; mem. N.Y. Gov.'s Commn. on Minorities in Med. Schs., 1982. Mem. Yale Law Sch. Assn. N.Y. (pres. 1970-73), Yale Law Sch. Alumni Assn. (v.p. 1973-76, exec. com.). Estate planning. Office: Proskauer Rose LLP 1585 Broadway Fl 27 New York NY 10036-8299

HEINKE, REX S. lawyer; b. Harrisburg, Ill., June 9, 1950; s. William Richard and Versa Lee Heinke; m. Margaret Ann Nagle, May 6, 1978; children: William Rex, Meghan Bradley. BA, U. Witwatersrand, Johannesburg, Republic of South Africa, 1971; JD, U. Columbia, 1975. Bar: Calif. 1975. Ptnr. Gibson, Dunn & Crutcher, L.A., 1983-99, Greines, Martin, Stein & Richland, Beverly Hills, Calif., 1999—. Appellate, Libel, Trademark and copyright. Office: 9601 Wilshire Blvd Ste 544 Beverly Hills CA 90210-5207 E-mail: rheinke@gmsr.com

HEINLE, RICHARD ALAN, lawyer; b. New Kensington, Pa., May 13, 1959; s. Robert Alan and Barbara Jane (Klimeck) H.; m. Sharon Eileen Farrell, Oct. 20, 1990; children: Kelly, Kyra, Casey. AB with highest honors, U. Chgo., 1981; JD cum laude, Georgetown U., 1984. Bar: Ill. 1984, Fla. 1994. Assoc. Arnstein & Lehr, Chgo., 1984-89, Foley & Lardner, Chgo., 1989-93, ptnr. Orlando, Fla., 1994—. Counsel Better Bus. Bur. Ctrl. Fla., Orlando, 1996—. Mem. Mfrs. Assn. Ctrl. Fla. (bd. dirs. 1995—), Fla. C. of C. (bd. dirs. 1999—), Phi Beta Kappa. Roman Catholic. Avocations: golf, running. Mergers and acquisitions, Securities. Home: 8100 Vineland Oaks Blvd Orlando FL 32835-8215 Office: Foley & Lardner 111 N Orange Ave Ste 1800 Orlando FL 32801-2386 E-mail: rheinle@foleylaw.com

HEINRICH, RANDALL WAYNE, lawyer; b. Houston, Nov. 29, 1958; s. Albert Joseph Sr. and Beverly June Earles; m. Linda Carol Cheek, June 6, 1993; children: Angela Leigh, Conrad Randall. BA, Baylor U., 1980, postgrad., 1981, Rice U., 1981-82; JD, U. Tex., 1985. Bar: Tex. 1985. Assoc. Baker & Botts, Houston, 1985-87, Chamberlain, Hrdlicka, White, Williams & Martin, Houston, 1987-91, Norton & Blair, Houston, 1991-92; of counsel Gillis & Slogar, 1992—; mng. dir. Baytree Investors, 1993-97. Mem. dirs.' circle Houston Grand Opera, 1991, The Arts Symposium, 1991, Center Stage, Alley Theater, Houston, 1992-93, Houston Entrepreneurs' Forum, 1990-91; bd. dirs. The Cadre, 1991-92; pres. Exchange Club of Bayou City, 1992-93. Mem. ABA (YLD securities law com. 1993-95, vice chmn. 1994-95), NASD Pool Securities Arbitrators, Am. Arbitration Assn. (mem. nat. panel neutrals), Houston Bar Assn., Forum Club Houston, Phi Delta Theta. Republican. Baptist. Home: 4318 Saint Michaels Ct Sugar Land TX 77479-2986 Office: Gillis & Slogar 1000 Louisiana St Ste 6905 Houston TX 77002-5014

HEINY, JAMES RAY, lawyer; b. Albert Lea, Minn., Oct. 7, 1928; s. Albin James and Lola Marguerite (Keig) H.; m. Wava Jeanine Isaacson, Sept. 2, 1951 (dec. 1980); children: Jon Carl, Jane Ellen Heiny Smith, Ann Elizabeth Heiny Hohenshell, Thomas James; m. Norma Lou West, July 24, 1982. BA, Grinnell Coll., 1950; JD, U. Iowa, 1953. Bar: Iowa 1953. Assoc. Westfall, Laird & Burington, Mason City, Iowa, 1955-58; ptnr. Laird, Heiny, McManigal, Winga, Duffy & Stambaugh, 1958—. Pres. Good Shepherd Geriatric Ctr., Inc., Mason City, 1960-72; bd. dirs. YMCA, Mason City, 1972-75; pres. Luth. Social Svcs. Iowa FODN, 1987—. With U.S. Army, 1953-55. Mem. ABA, Iowa State Bar Assn. (bd. govs. 1986-91), Cerro Gordo County Bar Assn. (pres. 1976). Republican. Avocations: amateur radio, bird watching, sports. Probate, Real property, Personal income taxation. Home: 2040 Hunters Ridge Dr Mason City IA 50401-7500 Office: Laird Heiny McManigal Winga Duffy & Stambaugh 300 Norwest Bank Bldg Mason City IA 50401 E-mail: jamesrh4@home.com, laird@netconx.net

HEINZ, WILLIAM DENBY, lawyer; b. Carlinville, Ill., Nov. 26, 1947; s. William Henry and Margaret (Denby) H.; children: Kimberly, Rebecca, Elizabeth; m. Catherine Lamb Heinz. BS, Millikin U., 1969; JD, U. Ill., 1973. Bar: Ill. 1973, U.S. Dist. Ct. (no. dist.) Ill. 1974, U.S. Ct. Appeals (3d cir.) 1982, U.S. Ct. Appeals (5th cir.) 1973, U.S. Ct. Appeals (7th cir.) 1976, U.S. Supreme Ct. 1979. Law clk. to judge U.S. Ct. Appeals (5th cir.), Tuscaloosa, Ala., 1973-74; assoc. Jenner & Block, Chgo., 1974-80, ptnr., 1980—; mem. faculty NITA, 1981—. Adj. prof. Northwestern U. Sch. Law, 1995—; bd. visitors U. Ill. Coll. Law, 1990-93, pres.'s coun. U. Ill.; bd. dirs., chair Legal Aid Bur., Chgo.; bd. dirs. exec. com. Met. Family Svcs. Chgo. Recipient Disting. Grad. award U. Ill. Coll. Law, 1995. Fellow Am. Coll. Trial Lawyers; mem. ABA, Ill. Bar Assn. (civil practice and procedure sect. coun., com. on liaison with Ill. ARDC, task force on multi-disciplinary practice), Chgo. Bar Assn. (jud. evaluation com. 1990-93), ARDC Ill. Profl. Responsibility Inst., Cribbett Soc., U. Ill. Coll. Law, Legal Club (bd. dirs. 1998-2000), Westmoreland Country Club. General civil litigation, General corporate, Professional liability. Home: 437 Sheridan Rd Kenilworth IL 60043-1220 Office: Jenner & Block 1 E Ibm Plz Fl 46 Chicago IL 60611-3586 E-mail: wheinz@jenner.com

HEINZEN, BERNARD GEORGE, lawyer; b. Hendricks, Minn., Sept. 18, 1930; s. Bernard Martin and Thelma Harrington (Bowers) H.; m. Maryann Mullen, Aug. 25, 1978; children from previous marraige: John Masters, Robert Kenneth (dec.), James Warren, William Martin. BA, Carleton Coll., 1953; LLB, NYU, 1956. Bar: Minn. 1956, U.S. Supreme Ct. 1969, Pa. 1978. Atty., legal adviser U.S. Dept. State, Washington, 1956-58; assoc. Dorsey & Whitney, Mpls., 1960-65, ptnr., 1966-76; spl. asst. atty. gen. State of Minn., St. Paul, 1967-70; gen. counsel Consol. Rail Corp., Phila., 1976-77; counsel Harvey, Pennington, Herting & Renneisen, Ltd., 1977-83; pres. Bernard G. Heinzen, Ltd., 1978—; ptnr. Stassen, Kostos & Mason, 1983-85; pres., bd. dirs. Rittenhouse Town Watch, Inc., 1993—; gen. counsel Logan Capital Mgmt., Inc., 1995—. Dir. Chamber Orch. of Phila., 1995—; adviser U.S. del. to Geneva Conf. on Law of Sea, 1958. Contbr. Stanford Law Rev., 1959; assoc. editor NYU Law Rev., 1955-56. Mem. Citizens Com. on Pub. Edn., Mpls., 1964-76; exec. com. state cen. com. Minn. Rep. Party, 1967-71; vestryman The Ch. of the Holy Trinity, Phila., 1998—. 1st lt. U.S. Army, 1957-60. Mem. ABA, Phila. Bar Assn., Minn. Bar Assn. (chmn. com. on ins. 1970-73), Am. Judicature Soc. (life), Racquet Club Phila., Union League Phila., Phi Beta Kappa. Republican. Episcopalian. Insurance, Public international. Home: 1901 Walnut St Philadelphia PA 19103-4640 Office: 1 Liberty Pl 1650 Market St Ste 5200 Philadelphia PA 19103-7305

HEIPLE, JAMES DEE, state supreme court justice; b. Peoria, Ill., Sept. 13, 1933; s. Rae Crane and Harriet (Birkett) H.; B.S., Bradley U., 1955; J.D., U. Louisville, 1957; Certificate in Internat. Law, City of London Coll., 1967; grad. Nat. Jud. Coll., 1971; LLM U. Va., 1988; m. Virginia Kerswill, July 28, 1956 (dec. Apr. 16, 1995); children: Jeremy Hans, Jonathan James, Rachel Duffield. Bar: Ill. 1957, Ky. 1958, U.S. Supreme Ct. 1962; partner Heiple and Heiple, Pekin, Ill., 1957-70; circuit judge Ill., 10th Circuit 1970-80; justice Ill. Appellate Ct., 1980-90; justice Ill. Supreme Ct., 1990—. V.p., dir. Washington State Bank (Ill.), 1959-66; dir. Gridley State Bank (Ill.), 1958-59; village atty., Tremont, Ill., 1961-66, Mackinaw, Ill., 1961-66; asst. pub. defender Tazewell County, 1967-70., jud. clerk Ill. Appellate Ct., 1968-70. Chmn. Tazewell County Heart Fund, 1960. Pub. Adminstr. Tazewell County, Ill., 1959-61; sec. Tazewell County Republican Central Com. 1966-70; mem. Pekin Sch. Bd., 1970; mem. Ill. Supreme Ct. Com. on Profl. Responsibility, 1978-86. Recipient certificate Freedoms Found., 1975, George Washington honor medal, 1976, Bradley Centurion award Bradley U., 1995; named Disting. Alumnus, U. Louisville, 1992. Fellow ABA (life), Ill. Bar Found. (life), Ky. Bar Found. (life); mem. Ky., Ill. (chmn. legal edn. com. 1972-74, chmn. jud. sect. 1976-77, chmn. Bench and Bar Council 1984-85), Tazewell County Bar Assn. (pres. 1967-68), Ill. Judges Assn. (pres. 1978-79), Ky., Ill., Pa. hist. socs., S.A.R., War of 1812, Sons of Union Vets., Delta Theta Phi, Sigma Nu, Pi Kappa Delta. Methodist. Clubs: Filson; Union League (Chgo.), Country (Peoria). Lodge: Masons (33 degree). Office: 207 Main St Ste 500 Peoria IL 61602-1362

HEISERMAN, ROBERT GIFFORD, lawyer; b. El Paso, July 5, 1946; s. Robert Gifford and Nancy Mildred (Wardlow) H.; m. Nancy Fay Price, Oct. 20, 1973; 1 child, Laura. BA, U. Oreg., 1968; JD, U. Denver, 1971. Bar: Ct. Colo. 1972, U.S. Dist. Ct. Colo. 1972, U.S. Dist. Ct. N.Mex. 1972, U.S. Dist. Ct. D.C. 1972, U.S. Dist. Ct. (so. dist.) Ala. 1974, U.S. Ct. Appeals (10th cir.) 1975, U.S. Supreme Ct. 1976. Legis. draftsman N.Mex. Legislature, Santa Fe, 1972-73; pvt. practice, 1973, Denver, 1974—. Adj. prof. immigration and nationality law and profl. responsibility courses U. Denver, 1981—. Mem. Emergency Med. Svcs. Coun., Denver, 1981-84. Mem. Am. Immigration Lawyers Assn. (nat. bd. govs., chmn. profl. ethics

and grievances com. 1982-89, 98-2000, founder Colo. chpt., treas. Colo. chpt. 1978-81), ABA, Colo. Bar Assn., Denver Bar Assn., D.C. Bar Assn., Internat. Bar Assn., InterAm. Bar Assn. Democrat. Methodist. Immigration, naturalization, and customs. Office: 1675 Broadway Ste 2280 Denver CO 80202-4675 E-mail: rheiserman@heiserman.com

HEISLER, STANLEY DEAN, lawyer; b. The Dalles, Oreg., Jan. 11, 1946; s. Donald Eugene and Roberta (Van Valkenburgh) H. BA, Willamette U., 1968, JD, 1972. Bar: Oreg. 1972, U.S. Ct. Claims 1972, U.S. Tax Ct. 1972, U.S. Ct. Appeals (9th cir.) 1972, D.C. 1973, U.S. Ct. Appeals (fed. cir.) 1973, U.S. Ct. Mil. Appeals 1973, N.Y. 1985, U.S. Supreme Ct. 1985. Assoc. Heisler & Van Valkenburgh, The Dalles, 1973-74; ptnr. Heisler, Van Valkenburgh & Coats, 1975-81, Heisler & Heisler, The Dalles, 1982-84, Cohen & Shalleck, N.Y.C., 1985-88, Phillips, Nizer, Benjamin, Krim & Ballon, N.Y.C., 1988-91, Squadron, Ellenoff, Plesent, Sheinfeld & Sorkin, N.Y.C., 1991-94; mng. ptnr. Shays & Kemper, LLP, 1994-98, Shays, Rothman, & Heisler, LLP, N.Y.C., 1999-2000, Shays, Heisler & Rosenthal, LLP, N.Y.C., 2000-01; pvt. practice Stanley D. Heisler, PC, 2001—. Speechwriter Sec. of State Tom McCall, Salem, 1965, Gov. Tom McCall, Salem, 1966-68; speechwriter, legis. asst. U.S. Senator Bob Packwood, Washington, 1969-73; vice chmn. Pres.'s Air Quality Adv. Bd., Washington, 1973-76. Mem. ABA, N.Y. State Bar Assn., Assn. of Bar of City of N.Y., Arlington Club, Univ. Club (N.Y.C. and Portland, Oreg.), Soc. Mayflower Descs. (bd. dirs. N.Y. State chpt. 2001—), Soc. of the Descs. Washington's Army at Valley Forge, Soc. for the Promotion of Hellenic Studies (London), Edmund Rice (1638) Assn. Republican. State civil litigation, Family and matrimonial. Home: 400 E 77th St Apt 8J New York NY 10021-2342 Office: Stanley D Heisler PC 276 5th Ave New York NY 10001-4509 E-mail: s.heisler@worldnet.att.net

HEISMAN, NORMAN M. lawyer; BS, Temple U., LLB, U. Pa., 1957. Bar: Pa. 1957. With U.S. Dept of Justice, until 1959; asst. legal counsel, Scott Paper Co., Phila., 1959-62, assoc. counsel, 1962-63, counsel, 1963-67, asst. gen. counsel, 1967-71, gen. counsel, sr. legal exec., 1971, v.p., 1972, sr. v.p. gen. counsel, 1975-91, counsel, bd. dirs., 1991—. General corporate. Office: Scott Paper Co Scott Plz Philadelphia PA 19113

HEISNER, JOHN RICHARD, lawyer, novelist; b. Dinuba, Calif., May 11, 1947; s. Robert Irving and Elinor May (Van Duyne) H.; m. Peggy Jean Opfer, July 20, 1968 (div. 1981); children— John Richard, Sara Lynn; m. Margo Elizabeth Sanchez, Apr. 17, 1982; stepchildren— John L. Cook, James P. Cook. B.S., U. Oreg., 1969; J.D., U. San Diego, 1972. Bar: Calif. 1973, U.S. Dist. Ct. (ea. dist.) Calif. 1980, U.S. Dist. Ct. (so. dist.) Calif. 1982, U.S. Dist. Ct. (cen. dist.) Calif. 1987. Dep. dist. atty. County of San Diego, San Diego, 1981-86; asst. dist. atty. County of Tulare, Visalia, Calif., 1979-80; sr. ptnr. Heisner, Yoshimoto and Cline, Visalia, 1980-81; spl. asst. U.S. atty. So. Dist. Calif., San Diego, 1982-86; civil litigator Morgan, Lewis & Bockius, San Diego, 1986-87; Mulvaney & Kahan, 1987-93; Lorenz Alhadeff Cannon & Rose, 1993—. Author: Like a Thief in the Night, 1983; Tentacles of Corruption, 1984; Seeds of Ambition, 1985. Campaign chmn. Robert Van Auken for Judge, Visalia, 1981; campaign organizer Charles R. Hayes for Judge, San Diego, 1982; examiner Eagle Scout rev. bd. San Diego council Boy Scouts Am., 1982—; adj. prof. U. San Diego Sch. of Law, 1993—; cons. J. Leslie Duchnick for Judge, San Diego, 1984, Leo McCarthy for Lt. Gov., 1986. Named Citizen of Week, Oceanside Blade Tribune, Calif., 1974. Mem. ABA, Calif. Bar Assn., Calif. Dist. Attys. Assn., Tulare County Bar Assn., San Diego County Bar Assn. Democrat. Lodges: Kiwanis, Masons, Shriners. Contracts commercial. Home: 1829 Lola Ln El Cajon CA 92019-3850

HEITNER, KENNETH HOWARD, lawyer; b. Jersey City, Apr. 1, 1948; s. Charles Fred and Molly (Vogelman) H.; m. Anne Barbara Siegel, June 14, 1970; children: Douglas, Andrew, Elizabeth. BA, Rutgers U., 1969; JD, NYU, 1973, LLM, 1977. Bar: N.Y. 1974, U.S. Dist. Ct. (so. and ea. dists.) N.Y. 1975, U.S. Tax Ct. 1976. Assoc. Weil, Gotshal & Manges, N.Y.C., 1973-81, ptnr., 1981—. With U.S. Army, 1969-75. Mem. ABA, N.Y. State Bar Assn. (exec. com. on bankruptcy , corps., net oper. losses, reorgns.), Tax Club, Assn. Bar City N.Y., Fairview Country Club (Greenwich, Conn., bd. govs. 1983-90). Corporate taxation, Personal income taxation. Office: Weil Gotshal & Manges LLP 767 5th Ave Fl Concl New York NY 10153-0119 E-mail: Kenneth.Heitner@Weil.com

HEJTMANEK, DANTON CHARLES, lawyer; b. Topeka, July 22, 1951; s. Robert Keith and Bernice Louise (Krause) H.; m. Julie Hejtmanek; 1 child, Brian J. BBA in Acctg., Washburn U., 1973, JD, 1975. Bar: Kans. 1976, U.S. Dist. Ct. Kans. 1976, U.S. Tax Ct. 1976. Ptnr. Schroer, Rice, Bryan & Lykins, P.A., Topeka, 1975-86, Bryan, Lykins & Hejtmanek, P.A., Topeka, 1986—. Mem. ABA (rep. young lawyers Kans. and Nebr.), ATLA, Kans. Bar Assn. (pres. young lawyers 1985), Kans. Trial Lawyers Assn., Sertoma (pres. 1983, internat. pres. 1998-99). Republican. Presbyterian. Avocations: snow skiing, travel. Family and matrimonial, Personal injury, Probate. Home: 2800 SW Burlingame Rd Topeka KS 66611-1316 Office: Bryan Lykins & Hejtmanek PA 222 SW 7th St Topeka KS 66603-3734

HELDMAN, JAMES GARDNER, lawyer; b. Cin., Mar. 7, 1949; s. James Norvin and Jane Marie (Gardner) H.; m. Wendy Maureen Saunders, Sept. 3, 1978; children: Dustin A., Courtney B. AB cum laude, Harvard U., 1971; JD with honors, George Washington U., 1974. Bar: D.C. 1975, U.S. Dist. Ct. (D.C. dist.) 1975, U.S. Ct. Appeals (D.C. cir.) 1975, U.S. Supreme Ct. 1980, Ohio 1981. Assoc. Perazich & Kolker, Washington, 1974-79, Wyman, Bautzer, Kuchel & Silbert, Washington, 1979-81, Strauss & Troy, Cin., 1981-83, ptnr., 1984—. Mem. ABA, Ohio State Bar Assn., Cin. Bar Assn. Avocations: tennis, platform tennis, biking. Finance, Real property, Securities. Office: Strauss & Troy The Fed Res Bldg 150 E Fourth St Cincinnati OH 45202-4018

HELFER, MICHAEL STEVENS, lawyer, business executive; b. N.Y.C., Aug. 2, 1945; s. Robert Stevens and Teresa (Kahan) H.; m. Ricki Rhodarmer Helfer; children: Lisa, David, Matthew. BA summa cum laude, Claremont Men's Coll., 1967; JD magna cum laude, Harvard U., 1970. Bar: D.C. 1971. Law clk. to chief judge U.S. Ct. Appeals D.C., 1970-71; asst. counsel subcom. on constl. amendments Senate Judiciary Com., 1971-73; assoc. Wilmer, Cutler & Pickering, Washington, 1973-78, ptnr., 1978-2000, mgmt. com., 1990-98, chmn., 1995-98; exec. v.p. for corp. strategy Nationwide Ins./Fin. Svcs., Columbus, Ohio, 2000—. Bd. dirs. 1st Cmty. Bankshares, Inc., Houston, 1997-2000. Trustee Legal Aid Soc. D.C., 1983-95, pres., 1990-92; bd. dirs. Lawyers for Children Am., Inc. Mem. Am. Law Inst. Democrat. Administrative and regulatory, Banking, Federal civil litigation. Home: 173 S Parkview Ave Columbus OH 43209 Office: Nationwide Ins/Fin Svcs Mail Code 1-37-09 Columbus OH 43215 E-mail: helferm@nationwide.com

HELLER, PHILIP, lawyer; b. N.Y.C., Aug. 12, 1952; s. Irving and Dolores (Soloff) Heller; 1 child Howard Philip. Attended, Harvard Coll.; BA summa cum laude, Boston U., 1976, JD, 1979. Bar: Mass 1979, NY 1980, US Ct Appeals (1st, 2d & 9th cirs) 1980, US Supreme Ct 1983, Calif 1984, US Dist Ct (all dists) Calif, US Dist Ct (ea & so dists) NY, US Dist Ct Mass. Law clk. to judge Cooper So. Dist. N.Y., N.Y.C., 1979; ptnr. Fagelbaum & Heller LLP, L.A. Mem.: ABA (litigation sect), Calif Bar Asn, Los Angeles County Bar Asn. Federal civil litigation, General civil litigation, State civil litigation. Office: Fagelbaum & Heller LLP 2049 Century Park E Ste 2050 Los Angeles CA 90067-3168 Fax: 310-286-7086. E-mail: fhllp@pacbell.net

HELLER, ROBERT MARTIN, lawyer; b. N.Y.C., Feb. 12, 1942; s. Philip B. and Mildred S. (Friedman) H.; m. Amy S. Wexler, July 11, 1965; children: David B., Pamela L. BA, Columbia U., 1963, LLB, 1966. Bar: N.Y. 1967, D.C. 1992, U.S. Dist. Ct. (so. and ea. dists.) N.Y. 1970, U.S. Ct. Appeals (2d cir.) 1967, U.S. Supreme Ct. 1976. Law clk. to judge U.S. Ct. Appeals (2d cir.), N.Y.C., 1966-67; atty. adviser to commr. FTC, Washington, 1967-69; asst. to mayor for housing, city planning, transp. and model cities, sec. to cabinet City of N.Y., 1971-73; ptnr. Kramer Levin Naftalis & Frankel LLP, N.Y.C., 1974—, mng. ptnr., 1991-94. Adj. prof. architecture Columbia U., 1975-77; bd. visitors Columbia Law Sch., 1992—. Bd. govs. Hebrew Union Coll./Jewish Inst. Religion, 1996—; pres. bd. dirs. 1056 Fifth Ave. Corp., 1994-96; vice chair Union Am. Hebrew Congregations, 1999—; trustee Rabbi Marc H. Tanenbaum Found. James Kent scholar; Harlan Fiske Stone scholar. Mem. ABA, N.Y. State Bar Assn., Assn. of Bar of City of N.Y. (com. on antitrust and trade regulation 1996—), Phi Beta Kappa. Avocations: aerobic walking, photography. Antitrust, Federal civil litigation, Mergers and acquisitions. Home: 1056 5th Ave New York NY 10028-0112 Office: Kramer Levin Naftalis & Frankel LLP 919 3rd Ave New York NY 10022-3902

HELLER, RONALD IAN, lawyer; b. Cleve., Sept. 4, 1956; s. Grant L. and Audrey P. (Lecth) H.; m. Shirley Ann Stringer, Mar. 23, 1986; 1 child, David Grant. AB with high honors, U. Mich., 1976, MBA, 1979, JD, 1980. Bar: Hawaii 1980, U.S. Ct. Claims 1982, U.S. Tax Ct. 1981, U.S. Ct. Appeals (9th cir.) 1981, U.S. Supreme Ct. 1992; Trust Ter. Pacific Islands 1982, Rep. Marshall Islands 1982; CPA, Hawaii. Assoc. Hoddick, Reinwald, O'Connor & Marrack, Honolulu, 1980-84; ptnr. Reinwald, O'Connor & Marrack, 1984-87; stockholder, bd. dirs. Torkildson, Katz, Fonseca, Jaffe & Moore, 1988—. Adj. prof. U. Hawaii Sch. Law, 1981; arbitrator ct.-annexed arbitration program First Cir. Ct., State of Hawaii; author, instr. Hawaii Taxes. Bd. dirs. Hawaii Women Lawyers Found., Honolulu, 1984-86, Hawaii Performing Arts Co., Honolulu, 1984-93; panel of arbitrators Am. Arbitration Assn., 1987-99; actor, stage mgr. Honolulu Cmty. Theatre, 1983-87, Hawaii Performing Arts Co., Honolulu, 1982-87. Named NFIB Hawaii outstanding sm. bus. vol. 1998. Fellow Am. Coll. Tax Counsel; mem. AICPAs (coun. 1994-96), ABA, Hawaii State Bar Assn. (chair tax sect. 1997-98, chair state and local tax com. 1994-95), Hawaii Soc. CPAs (chmn. tax com. 1985-86, legis. com. 1987-88, bd. dirs. 1988-98, pres. 1994-95), Hawaii Women Lawyers. General civil litigation, Taxation, general, State and local taxation. Office: Torkildson Katz Fonseca Jaffe & Moore 700 Bishop St Fl 1500 Honolulu HI 96813-4187 E-mail: rheller@torkidson.com

HELLERSTEIN, WALTER, lawyer; b. N.Y.C., June 21, 1946; s. Jerome Robert and Pauline Alice (Lefkowitz) H.; m. Nina Laurie Salant, Aug. 31, 1970; childre; Michael, Margaret. AB, Harvard U., 1967; JD, U. Chgo., 1970. Bar: D.C. 1970, Ill. 1976, N.Y. 1989. Law clk. U.S. Ct. Appeals (3d cir.), N.Y.C., 1967-71; atty. Air Force Gen. Counsel's Office, Washington, 1971-73; assoc. Covington & Burling, 1973-75; asst. prof. law U. Chgo., 1976-78; assoc. prof. laws U. Ga., Athens, 1978-84, prof. law, 1984-98, Francis Shackelford prof. taxation, 1999—; of counsel Morrison & Foerster, N.Y.C., 1986-96; ptnr. Sutherland, Asbill & Brennan, Atlanta, 1996-98; counsel KPMG, 1999—. Cons. Orgn. Econ. Coop. and Devel., 1999—, UN, 2000—; mem. sci. com. Centro Europeo di Studi Tributarie sall'Electroic Commerce, 1999—. Co-author: State and Local Taxation, 7th edit., 2001, State and Local Taxation of Natural Resources, 1986, State Taxation, vols. 1 & 2, 3d edit., 1998; editl. adv. bd. Nat. Tax Jour., 1983—, Multistate Tax Analyst, 1986—; chmn. editl. adv. bd. State Tax Notes, 1991—, Jour. Taxation, 1993—; contbr. articles to profl. jours. Recipient Multistate Tax Commn. 25th Ann. award for outstanding contbn. 1992. Fellow Am. Coll. Tax Counsel; mem. ABA, Nat. Tax Assn. (dir. 1981-83), Ill. State Bar Assn., D.C. Bar Assn., N.Y. State Bar Assn., Am. Law Inst., Order of Coif, Phi Beta Kappa. Home: 239 Westview Dr Athens GA 30606-4731 Office: U Ga Law Sch Athens GA 30602-6012 E-mail: wallyh@arches.uga.edu

HELLMUTH, THEODORE HENNING, lawyer; b. Detroit, Mar. 28, 1949; s. George F. and Mildred Hellmuth; m. Laurie Hellmuth, May 29, 1970; children: Elizabeth Ann, Theodore Henning, Sara Marie. BA, U. Pa., 1970; JD cum laude, U. Mo.-Columbia, 1974. Bar: Mo. 1974, U.S. Dist. Ct. (ea. dist.) Mo. 1974, U.S. Ct. Appeals (8th cir.) 1978. Assoc., then ptnr. Armstrong Teasdale LLP, St. Louis, 1974—. Author: Missouri Real Estate, 1985, 2d edit., 1998, Lease Audits: The Essential Guide, 1994; editor Distressed Real Estate Law Alert, 1987-88, Litigated Commercial Real Estate Document Reports, 1987-95. Mem. ABA (vice-chmn., chmn. litigation and dispute resolution com. real property and probate sect. 1991-95, editor, then mng. book editor real property and probate sect. 1996-2000), Am. Coll. Real Estate Lawyers (chmn. alternative dispute resolution com. 1993-96), Order of Coif. General civil litigation, Real property. Office: Armstrong Teasdale LLP 1 Metropolitan Sq Ste 2600 Saint Louis MO 63102-2740 E-mail: thelmut@armstorngteasdale.com

HELMAN, STEPHEN JODY, lawyer; b. Houston, Dec. 14, 1949; m. Gail Stevenson, 1974; children: Kimberley Brooke, Courtney Elizabeth, Caitlin Rebecca. BA in Spanish and Religion, So. Meth. U., 1971; postgrad., Perkins Sch. Theology, 1971-73; JD with honors, U. Tex., 1978. Bar: Tex., 1978; cert. estate planning and probate law, 1987. Assoc. Graves, Dougherty, Hearon & Moody, Austin, Tex., 1978-85, ptnr., shareholder, 1985-93; ptnr. Osborne, Lowe, Helman & Smith, L.L.P., 1993-2000, Osborne & Helman, L.L.P., Austin, 2001—. Exam commr. in estate planning and probate law, Tex. Bd. Legal Specialization, 1990-94. Contbr. articles to profl. jours. Fellow Am. Coll. Trust and Estate Counsel (mem. profl. standards com. 1990-93); mem. ABA (mem. real property, probate, and trust law sects.), Coll. of the State Bar of Tex., State Bar Tex. (mem. real property, probate and trust law sects.), Travis County Bar Assn. (mem. probate and estate planning sect., pres. 1991-92, dir. 1989-92, ex-officio dir. 1992-93), Order of Coif. Avocations: nature photography, hiking. Estate planning, Probate, Estate taxation. Office: Osborne & Helman LLP 301 Congress Ave Ste 1910 Austin TX 78701-4041 E-mail: sjhelman@osbornehelman.com

HELMER, DAVID ALAN, lawyer; b. Colorado Springs, May 19, 1946; s. Horton James and Alice Ruth (Cooley) H.; m. Jean Marie Lamping, May 23, 1987. BA, U. Colo., 1968, JD, 1973. Bar: Colo. 1973, U.S. Dist. Ct. Colo. 1973, U.S. Ct. Appeals (10th cir.) 1993, U.S. Ct. Claims 1990, U.S. Supreme Ct. 1991. Assoc. Neil C. King, Boulder, Colo., 1973-76; mgr. labor rels., mine regulations Climax Molybdenum Co., Inc. divsn. AMAX, Inc., Climax, 1976-83; prin. Law Offices David A. Helmer, Frisco, 1983—. Sec., bd. dirs. Z Comm. Corp., Frisco, 1983-90; cmty. bd. dirs. Wells Fargo Bank, N.A., Frisco, 1996—. Editor U. Colo. Law Rev., 1972-73; contbr. articles to legal jours. Bd. dirs. Summit County Coun. Arts and Humanities, Dillon, Colo., 1980-85; advisor Advocates for Victims of Assault, Frisco, 1984—; legal counsel Summit County United Way, 1983-95, v.p., bd. dirs., 1983-88; bd. dirs., legal counsel Summit county Alcohol and Drug Task Force, Inc., Summit Prevention Alliance, 1984—, Pumpkin Bowl Inc./Chldren's Hosp. Burn Ctr., 1989—; chmn. Summit County Reps., 1982-89; chmn. 5th Jud. Dist. (Colo.) Rep. Com., 1982-89; chmn. resolutions com. Colo. Rep. Conv., 1984, del. Rep. Nat. Com., 1984; chmn. reaccreditation com. Colo. Mountain Coll., Breckenridge, 1983, mem. steering com., 1997-99; founder, bd. dirs. Dillon Bus. Assn., 1983-87, Frisco Arts Coun., 1989—; atty. N.W. Colo. Legal Svcs. Project, Summit County, 1983—; mcpl. judge Town of Dillon, 1982—, Town of Silverthorne, Colo., 1982—; dir. Snake River Water Dist., 1998—. Sgt. USAR, 1968-74. Mem. ABA, Colo. Bar Assn., (bd. govs. 1991-93, mem. exec. com. 1995-97), Continental Divide Bar Assn. (prs. 1991-95, v.p. 1995-97), Summit County Bar Assn. (pres. 1990-99), Dillon Corinthian Yacht Club (commodore local club 1987-88, 95-97, vice commodore 1994, club champion 1989-91, 94, 95, 97, 98, winner Colo. Cup, Colo. State Sailing Championships 1991, Dist. Champion 2000), Phi Gamma Delta. Lutheran. State civil litigation, General practice, Real property. Home: PO Box 300 352 Snake River Dr Dillon CO 80435-0300 Office: PO Box 868 611 Main St Frisco CO 80443-0868 E-mail: dave@helmerlaw.com

HELMHOLZ, R(ICHARD) H(ENRY), law educator; b. Pasadena, Calif., July 1, 1940; s. Lindsay and Alice (Bean) H.; m. Marilyn P. Helmholz. AB, Princeton U., 1962; JD, Harvard U., 1965; PhD, U. Calif., Berkeley, 1970; LLD, Trinity Coll., Dublin, 1992. Bar: Mo. 1965. Prof. law and hist. Washington U., St. Louis, 1970-81; prof. law U. Chgo., 1981—. Maitland lectr. Cambridge U., 1987; Goodhart prof. Cambridge U., 2000-01. Author: Marriage Litigation, 1975, Select Cases on Defamation, 1985, Canon Law and the Law of England, 1987, Roman Canon Law in Reformation England, 1990, Spirit of Classical Canon Law, 1996, The IUS Commune in England: Four Studies, 2001. Guggenheim fellow, 1986; recipient Von Humboldt rsch. prize, 1992. Fellow Brit. Acad. (corr.), Am. Acad. Arts and Scis., Am. Law Inst., Medieval Acad. Am.; mem. ABA, Am. Soc. Legal History (pres. 1992-94), Selden Soc. (v.p. 1984-87), Univ. Club, Reform Club. E-mail: dick. Home: 5757 S Kimbark Ave Chicago IL 60637-1614 Office: U Chgo Law Sch 1111 E 60th St Chicago IL 60637-2776 E-mail: helmholz@law.uchicago.edu

HELMRICH, JOEL MARC, lawyer; b. Bklyn., Apr. 15, 1953; s. William and Edna (Steigman) H.; m. Barbara Ellen Richter, Sept. 2, 1984; children: Joshua David, Rachel Marysa. BS, Cornell U., 1975, MBA, 1976; JD, Syracuse U., 1979. Bar: Pa. 1979, U.S. Dist. Ct. (we. dist.) Pa. 1979, U.S. Ct. Appeals (3d cir.) 1997. Assoc. Tucker Arensberg, PC, Pitts., 1979-86; shareholder Tucker Arensberg, 1986-99; ptnr. Meyer, Unkovic & Scott, LLP, 1999—. Mem. Pa. Bar Assn., Allegheny County Bar Assn., Comml. Law League Am., Am. Bankruptcy Inst., Cornell Club. Avocations: golf, tennis. Bankruptcy, Consumer commercial, General corporate. Office: Meyer Unkovic & Scott LLP 1300 Oliver Bldg Pittsburgh PA 15222-2304 E-mail: jmh@muslaw.com

HELMS, DAVID ALONZO, lawyer, real estate broker; b. Evanston, Ill., July 5, 1934; s. Hugh Judson and Edna (Peterson-Holmes) H.; div.; children— Donald Anthony, Cybil Estelle. BBA, Northwestern U., 1956; JD, U. Calif.-Berkeley, 1969. Bar: N.Y. 1972, Calif. 1973, Ill., 1974; lic. real estate broker. With Matson Navigation Co., San Francisco, 1958-66, mgr. mktg. rsch., passenger ops., 1963-66; assoc. law firm Paul, Weiss, Rifkind, Wharton & Garrison, Esqs., N.Y.C., 1969-72; spl. asst. to mayor of Berkeley, Calif., 1972-73; dep. sec. state, spl. asst. to gov. Calif., 1973-75; exec. sec. Civil Rights Bar Assn., San Francisco, 1975-80; asst. dean, mem. faculty Chgo.-Kent Coll. Law, Ill. Inst. Tech., Chgo., 1979-81; atty., regional coun. FAA, Des Plaines, Ill., 1982-84; vol. atty. Howard Area and Cabrini-Green Law Clinics, Chgo. Vol. Legal Svcs. Found., 1981— ; sole practice law, David A. Helms & Assocs., Evanston and Chgo., 1981— ; legal advisor to nat. pres. op. Push, 1986. Author: Rehabilitation as a Housing Policy, 1980, The Quality of Life; editor: Civil Rights Law Jour., Vol. I & II, 1974-78. Recipient Image award NAACP, 1974, Disting. Svc. award Chgo. Vol. Legal Asst. Found., 1986, Community Svc. award Op. Push, Chgo., 1986-87. Bd. dirs. Pub. Advocates, San Francisco, 1977-79, Elizabeth B. Hill Meml. Scholarship Fund, Evanston, 1986—. Mem. ABA, Chgo. Coun. Lawyers, Cook County Bar Assn., Chgo. Bar Assn. Baptist (mem. legal com., law clinic 1984—), Civil Rights Bar Assn., Ill. State Bar Assn., Nat. Bar Assn. Democrat. Baptist. Avocations: bicycling, jogging, exercising, antiques, photography.

HELMS, ROGER D. lawyer; b. Orlando, June 11, 1953; s. V.S. and Eunice Helms. BS magna cum laude, U. Ctrl. Fla., 1980; JD, U. Fla. Sch. Law, 1982. Bar: Fla. From assoc. to ptnr. Troutman, Williams, Irvin & Green, Winter Park, Fla., 1983—. Mem. ABA, Acad. Fla. Trial Lawyers. Avocations: offshore fishing, boating. Home: 2840 Bear Island Pointe Winter Park FL 32792-9426 Office: Troutman Williams Irvin Green & Helms 311 W Fairbanks Ave Winter Park FL 32789-5094

HELTON, ARTHUR CLEVELAND, advocate, lawyer, scholar, writer; b. St. Louis, Jan. 24, 1949; s. Arthur Cleveland Sr. and Marjorie Jane (Russell) H.; m. Jacqueline Dean Gilbert, May 14, 1982. AB, Columbia Coll., 1971; JD, NYU, 1976. Bar: N.Y. 1977, U.S. Dist. Ct. (so. and ea. dists.) N.Y. 1977, U.S. Ct. Appeals (2d cir.) 1978, U.S. Ct. Appeals (1st cir.) 1980, U.S. Ct. Appeals (4th and 9th cir.) 1988, U.S. Ct. Appeals (5th, 7th and 11th cir.) 1989, U.S. Ct. Appeals (3d cir.) 1994, U.S. Supreme Ct. 1980. Assoc. appellate counsel Legal Aid Soc., N.Y.C., 1976-79; assoc. Mailman & Rutheizer, 1979-82; dir. refugee project Lawyers Com. Human Rights, 1982-94; dir. migration programs, forced migration projects Open Soc. Inst., 1994-99; vis. prof. internat. rels. Ctrl. European U., 1997-2000; course co-dir. Summer U. Ctrl. European U., 1999-2000; adj. prof. Columbia Law Sch., 2001—. Adj. prof. law NYU, 1986-99; sr. fellow Coun. Fgn. Rels., 1999—; program dir. Peace and Conflict, Coun. Fgn. Rels., 2001—; chair Internat. Social Svcs., USA br.; adj. faculty Columbia U. Sch. Law, 2001—. Author: (with others) Forced Displacement and Human Security in the Former Soviet Union: Law and Policy, 2000, The Rights of Aliens and Refugees: The Basic ACLU Guide to Alien and Refugees Rights, 1990; editor: Transnational Pubs., Inc.; series editor Free Movement, Forced Displacement and Human Security, Transnational Pubs., Inc.; contbr. articles to profl. jours. Recipient Pub. Svc. award Law Alumni Assn. NYU, 1987, Immigration and Refugee Policy award, Ctr. for Migration Studies, 2000; grantee The German Marshall Fund, The Ford Found. Fellow Am. Bar Found.; mem. Coun. Fgn. Rels., ABA (co-chmn. immigration and nationality law com. sect. internat. law and practice 1997—, coord. com. on immigration law 1997-2000, adv. com. immigration pro bono devel. and bar activation project 2000—), Internat. Bar Assn., Assn. Bar N.Y.C. (chmn. com. on immigration and nationality law 1982-85, legal assistance com. 1985-88, civil rights com. 1988-91, internat. human rights com. 1991-94, internat. law com. 1995-98, adminstrv. law com. 1999—), Pub. internat. imm., naturalization, and customs. Home: 245 7th Ave Apt 10B New York NY 10001-7301 Office: Coun Fgn Rels 58 E 68th St New York NY 10021-5953 E-mail: ArthurHelton@msn.com, ahelton@car.org

HEMINGWAY, RICHARD WILLIAM, law educator; b. Detroit, Nov. 24, 1927; s. William Oswald and Iva Catherine (Wildfang) H.; m. Vera Cecilia Eck, Sept. 12, 1947; children: Margaret Catherine, Carol Elizabeth, Richard Albert. B.S. in Bus, U. Colo., 1950; J.D. magna cum laude (J. Woodall Rogers Sr. Gold medal 1955), So. Meth. U., 1955; LL.M. (William S. Cook fellow 1968), U. Mich., 1969. Bar: Tex. 1955, Okla. 1981. Assoc. Fulbright, Crooker, Freeman, Bates & Jaworski, Houston, 1955-60; lectr. Bates Sch. Law, U. Houston, 1960; assoc. prof. law Baylor U. Law Sch., Waco, Tex., 1960-65; vis. assoc. prof. So. Meth. U. Law Sch., 1965-68; prof. law Tex. Tech U. Law Sch., Lubbock, 1968-71, Paul W. Horn prof., 1972-81, acting dean, 1974-75, dean ad interim, 1980-81; prof. law U. Okla., Norman, 1981-83, Eugene Kuntz prof. oil, gas and natural resources law, 1983-92, Eugne Kuntz prof. emeritus oil, gas & natural resources law, 1992—. Author: The Law of Oil and Gas, 1971, 2d edit., 1983, lawyer's edit., 1983, 3d edit., 1991, West's Texas Forms (Mines and Minerals), 1977, 2d edit., 1991, 85; contbg. editor various law reports, cases and materials. Served with USAAF, 1945-47. Mem. Tex. Bar Assn., Scribes, Order of Coif (faculty), Beta Gamma Sigma. Lutheran. Home: 5000 Old Shepard Pl Apt 516 Plano TX 75093-4402

HEMMENDINGER, NOEL, retired lawyer; b. Bernardsville, N.J., Dec. 25, 1913; s. Max and Jeannette (Harris) H.; m. Marjorie Knebelman, Aug. 28, 1948; children: Eric, Lucy, John. AB, Princeton U., 1934; JD, Harvard U., 1937. Bar: D.C. 1937, N.Y. 1938, U.S. Dist. Ct. (so. dist.) N.Y. 1938, U.S. Supreme Ct. 1956. Law clk. U.S. Ct. Appeals (2d cir.), N.Y.C., 1937-38; asst. U.S. atty. So. Dist., 1938-40; spl. asst. to U.S. atty. gen. U.S. Dept. Justice, 1940-42; staff official U.S. Dept. State, Washington, 1946-56; ptnr. Stitt & Hemmendinger and successor firms, 1957-77, Arter, Hadden & Hemmendinger, Washington, 1977-83, Wald, Harkrader & Ross, Washington, 1983-85; of counsel Willkie, Farr & Gallagher, 1985—; now ret. Dep. dir. U.S. Japan Trade Council, Washington, 1957-77, bd. dirs. Trustee, counsel Japan Am. Soc. Washington, 1957—. Served to capt. U.S. Army, 1942-46, ETO. Decorated Bronze Star, 1945; named to Japanese Order of the Sacred Treasure 2d class, 1981. Mem. ABA, D.C. Bar Assn. Democrat. Clubs: Cosmos. Avocation: tennis. Home: 2007 Marthas Rd Alexandria VA 22307-1954 Office: Willkie Farr & Gallagher 1155 21st St NW Fl 6 Washington DC 20036-3384

HEMNES, THOMAS MICHAEL SHERIDAN, lawyer; b. Chgo., Nov. 10, 1948; s. Paul Gene and Dorothy Marion (Carl) H.; m. Carole Elizabeth Powers Dec. 20, 1970; children: Anna Ryan, Abigail Powers, Jonathan James. AB, Harvard U., 1970, JD, 1974. Bar: Mass. 1976, U.S. Dist. Ct. Mass., 1976, U.S. Dist. Ct. (no. dist.) N.Y. 1985. Law clk. U.S. Ct. Appeals (3d cir.), Phila., 1974-75; assoc. Foley, Hoag & Eliot, Boston, 1975-81, ptnr., 1981—; lectr. Northeastern U. Co-compilor: The Legal Word Book, 1978, rev. edit., 1982; contbr. articles on copyright, trademark, law firm mgmt. and other topics; editor, officer Harvard Law Rev., 1973-74. Corporator Handel & Hayden Soc., Boston, 1980-85, The Trademark Reporter, 1985—. Mem. ABA, Mass. Bar Assn., Boston Bar Assn., Boston Patent Law Assn., U.S. Trademark Assn. (assoc.). Contracts commercial, Trademark and copyright. Home: 49 Hammond Rd Belmont MA 02478-2249 Office: Foley Hoag & Eliot One Post Office Sq Boston MA 02109

HEMPHILL, MEREDITH, JR. retired lawyer; b. Spring Lake, N.J., Oct. 12, 1931; s. Meredith and Katharine (Dilworth) Hemphill; m. Beverly Bell, Feb. 06, 1960; children: Mary, M. Scott, Geoffrey G., Mark A. BChemE, Rensselaer Poly. Inst., 1953; JD, U. Mich., 1959. Bar: N.Y. 1960, Pa. 1976. Assoc. Cravath, Swaine & Moore, N.Y.C., 1959-67; atty., gen. atty. Bethlehem (Pa.) Steel Corp., 1967-73, asst. gen. counsel, 1973-79, asst. v.p., asst. gen. counsel, asst. sec., 1979-85, asst. gen. counsel, asst. sec., 1985-87, dep. gen. counsel, asst. sec., 1987-96; ret., 1996. With USMCR, 1953-55. Mem. ABA, Pa. Bar Assn., Northampton County Bar Assn., Saucon Valley Country Club. Republican. Federal civil litigation, State civil litigation, General corporate. Home: 238 E Market St Bethlehem PA 18018-6232

HEMPSTEAD, GEORGE H., III, lawyer, diversified company executive; b. 1943; BBA, St. Johns U., 1965, LLB, 1967. Bar: N.Y. 1968, Del. 1979. Atty. antitrust div. U.S. Dept. Justice, Washington, 1967-70; with Simpson, Thacher & Bartlett, N.Y.C., 1970-74; gen. counsel Burmah Oil, Inc., 1974-76; asst. gen. counsel Hanson Industries Inc., Iselin, N.J., 1976-78; sr. coord. coun. ICI Am. Inc., Wilmington, Del., 1978-81; dir., v.p. sec., gen. counsel Hanson Industries, Iselin, 1982-96; sr. v.p. Millennium Chems., Red Bank, N.J., 1996—. Assoc. dir. Hanson PLC, London and NYSE, 1990-96; chmn. bd. trustees Christian Brother Acad., 1993-95, Lincroft, N.J.; sr. v.p. law, sec. Millennium Chemicals Inc., 1996—; bd. suprs. Suburban Propane LLP, 1996-99. Office: Millennium Chemicals Inc PO Box 7015 230 Half Mile Rd Red Bank NJ 07701-5683

HENDEL, CLIFFORD JAMES, lawyer; b. Boston, Nov. 11, 1957; s. Seymour L. and Patricia T. H.; m. Catherine Armand, Aug. 22, 1998; children: Paloma, Pedro. BA, Wesleyan U., Middletown, Conn., 1979; JD, U. Conn. Sch. Law, 1983. Solicitor Eng., Wales; bar: N.Y. 1984; adv. Paris; abogado, Madrid. Jud. law clk. to hon. Peter C. Dorsey U.S. Dist. Ct., Conn., 1983-85; assoc. White & Case, N.Y.C., 1985-92, of counsel Paris, 1992-96; ptnr. Araoz & Rueda, Madrid, 1997—. Contbr. articles to profl. jours.; subject of chpt. in ABA's Careers in Internat. Law, 2d edit. Arbitrator N.Y.C. Small Claims Ct., 1990-91. Mem. ABA, Union Internat. Avocates, Internat. Bar Assn., N.Y. Bar Assn. (co-chair Madrid chpt. sect. internat. law and practice). Alternative dispute resolution, Private international, Mergers and acquisitions. Office: Araoz & Rueda Castellana 15 28046 Madrid Spain E-mail: hendel@araozyruedaabogados.es

HENDEL, MAURICE WILLIAM, lawyer, consultant; b. Holyoke, Mass., Feb. 24, 1909; s. Richard and Helen (Katz) H.; m. Evelyn F. Berger, Dec. 30, 1934; children— Richard C., Eugene L. Ph.B., Brown U., 1930; J.D., Harvard U., 1933. Bar: R.I. 1933, U.S. Dist. Ct. R.I. 1935. Counsel to Sec. of State of R.I., Providence, 1949-79, editor Pub. Laws, 1949-79; cons. to constl. convs. State of R.I., 1954, 62, 68-69, 86; cons. home rule charters cities and towns, 1960— , mem., sec. Statute Consolidation Commn., 1953-56; parliamentarian R.I. Senate, 1949-79. Mem. editorial bd. R.I. Bar Jour. Mem. Dem. City Com., Providence, 1940-60, Dem. Town Com., Lincoln, R.I., 1961-86. Mem. R.I. Bar Assn., Pawtucket Bar Assn. Jewish. Clubs: Kirkbrae Country (Lincoln); Faculty of Brown U. (Providence). Lodge: Masons (past master, high priest). Office: McMahon Hendel McMahon 200 Main St Pawtucket RI 02860-4119 Address: 4 Morgan Ct Lincoln RI 02865-4647

HENDERSON, DONALD BERNARD, JR. lawyer; b. Birmingham, Ala., June 27, 1949; s. Donald B. and Pauline V. (Szulinski) H.; m. Ruth Ann Jeffers, Sept. 12, 1981. BS, U. Ala., 1971, JD, 1974; LLM in Taxation, NYU, 1976. Bar: Ala. 1974, N.Y. 1983. Ptnr. Sirote and Permutt, Birmingham, 1976-83; sr. assoc. Mound, Cotton and Wollan, N.Y.C., 1983-85; ptnr. Kroll & Tract, 1985-88, LeBoeuf, Lamb, Greene & MacRae, L.L.P., N.Y.C., 1988—. Lectr. Birmingham chpt. Am. Coll., Bryn Mawr, Pa., 1977-82; dir. Jackson Nat. Life Ins. Co. N.Y., SunLife Assurance Co. N.Y., Zurich Kemper Life Ins. Co. N.Y.; counsel to Bronxville Planning Bd., 1994-2001. Contbr. articles to profl. jours. Pres. Lenox Hill Dem. Club, N.Y.C., 1989-90; mem. Ala. State Dem. Com., 1978-83, N.Y.C. Cmty. Bd. Number 8, 1987-88, Republican Club of Bronxville, Bronxville Planning Bd. Mem. ABA, N.Y. Bar Assn., Ala. Bar Assn. (sec. tax sect. 1982-83). General corporate, Insurance, Corporate taxation. Home: 108 Midland Ave Bronxville NY 10708-3206 Office: LeBouf Lamb Greene & MacRae LLP 125 E 55th St New York NY 10022-3502 E-mail: Dhenders@llgm.com

HENDERSON, GEORGE ERVIN, lawyer; b. Pampa, Tex., June 7, 1947; s. Ervin L. and Elizabeth (Yoe) H.; m. Linda L. Dalrymple, Aug. 22, 1970; children: Andrew, Elizabeth. BA, Tex. Christian U., 1969; JD, Yale U., 1972. Bar: Tex. 1972, U.S. Dist. Ct. (so. dist.) Tex. 1974, U.S. Dist. Ct. (we. dist.) 1978. Assoc. Fulbright & Jaworski, Houston and Austin, 1972-79, ptnr. Austin, 1983—, Sneed & Vine, Austin, 1979-82. Adj. instr. law U. Tex., Austin, 1983-85. Contbr. articles to profl. jours. Mem. S. Tex. Youth Soccer Assn. Rules Com., 1993-2001, Greater Austin Soccer Coalition, 1995-98; elder Univ. Presbyn. Ch., Austin, Tex., 2001—. Capt. USAR, 1972-78. Mem. ABA, State Bar of Tex. (chmn. corp. banking and bus. law sect. 1983, mem. coun. corp. banking and bus. law sect. 1985-88), Tex. Assn. Bank Counsel (pres. 1985-86), Travis County Bar Assn. (bankruptcy law sect., chmn. 1988-89, vice-chmn. 1997-98), Tex. Law Found., San Antonio Bankruptcy Bar Assn., Uniform Comml. Code Com., Austin Yacht Club, Capital Soccer Club (pres. 1993-95). Banking, Bankruptcy. Office: Fulbright & Jaworski 600 Congress Ave Ste 2400 Austin TX 78701-3271

HENDERSON, HELENA NAUGHTON, legal association administrator; b. New Orleans, Mar. 19, 1956; d. John Francis and Helen Naughton; div.; children: William Henry Henderson, Kevin Richard Henderson. BS in Psychology, Harvard U., 1976, Newcomb Coll, 1978; postgrad., Tulane U., 1990—. Exec. dir. New Orleans Bar Assn. Mem. La. Commn. on Policy and Rsch., 1999-2001, chair Juvenile Law Conf. for La., 1999. Bd. dirs. La. Ctr. for Law-Related Edn., New Orleans, 1992—, New Orleans Police Found., 1996—, Voices for Children, 1997—. Mem. ABA (assoc.), Am. Soc. Assn. Execs., Nat. Assn. Bar Execs. (chair strategic planning com. 1996-98), Nat. Ctr. for Nonprofit Bds. Office: New Orleans Bar Assn 228 Saint Charles Ave Ste 1223 New Orleans LA 70130-2643

HENDERSON, JOHN ROBERT, lawyer; b. Ft. Worth, Apr. 21, 1950; s. Julius Adrian and Jane Marie (Fitts) H.; m. Cynthia Lynn Wendland, May 27, 1972; 1 child, Michael Robert. B.B.A., U. Tex., 1972; J.D. with honors, Tex. Tech. U., 1975. Bar: Tex. 1975, U.S. Dist. Ct. (no. dist.) Tex. 1976, U.S. Dist. Ct. (ea. dist.) Tex. 1981, U.S. Ct. Appeals (5th and 11th cirs.) 1981, U.S. Dist. Ct. (we. dist.) Tex. 1983, U.S. Dist. Ct. (so. dist.) Tex. 1988. Briefing atty. 12th Dist. Tex. Ct. Appeals, Tyler, 1975-76; assoc. Stalcup, Johnson, Meyers & Miller, Dallas, 1976-78, Meyers, Miller & Middleton, Dallas, 1978-80; assoc. Jones, Day, Reavis & Pogue, Dallas, 1981-83, ptnr., 1984— . Bd. dirs. The 500 Inc., Dallas, 1982-83, sponser, 1984, 85; bd. dirs. Dallas Opera, 1982-84, Dallas Repertory Theater, 1983-84, Dallas Civic Music Assn., 1987—. Fellow Tex. Bar Found.; mem. ABA (litigation sect., forum com. on constrn. industry), Tex. Bar Assn. (mem. litigation and constrn. sects.), Tex. Assn. Def. Counsel, Tex. Bd. Legal Specialization (cert.), Dallas Bar Assn. (council constrn. law sect. 1983-85), Order of Coif. Episcopalian. Club: Argyle. Federal civil litigation, State civil litigation, Construction.

HENDERSON, KAREN LECRAFT, federal judge; b. 1944; BA, Duke U., 1966; JD, U. N.C., 1969. Ptnr. Wright & Henderson, Chapel Hill, N.C., 1969-70, Sinkler, Gibbs & Simons, P.A., Columbia, S.C., 1983-86; asst. atty. gen., 1973-78; sr. asst. atty. gen., dir. of spl. litigation sect., 1978-82; deputy atty. gen., dir. of criminal div., 1982; judge U.S. Dist. Ct. S.C., Columbia, 1986-90, U.S. Ct. Appeals (D.C. cir.), Washington, 1990—. Apptd. Dist. Ct. Adv. Com. Mem. ABA (litigation sect. and urban, state and local government law sect.), N.C. Bar Assn., S.C. Bar (government law sect., trial and appellate practice sect., fed. judges assn.). Office: US Ct Appeals DC Cir US Courthouse 333 Constitution Ave NWRm 3118 Washington DC 20001-2802*

HENDERSON, THOMAS HENRY, JR. lawyer, legal association executive; b. Birmingham, Ala., Feb. 4, 1939; s. Thomas Henry and Edna (Green) H.; m. Elaine Dauphin (div. 1983); children: Ashley, Michelle; m. Paulette Maehara, June 1988. BSBA, Auburn U., 1961; JD, U. Ala., 1966; LLM, Nat. Law Ctr., George Washington U., 1987. Bar: D.C. 1970, Ala. 1966. Trial atty. organized crime and racketeering sect. U.S. Dept. Justice, Washington, 1966-70, dep. sect. chief mgmt. labor sect., 1970-73; dep. chief counsel, subcom. on adminstrn. practice and procedure U.S. Senate, 1973-74; dep. sect. chief mgmt. and labor sect. Dept. Justice, 1974-76, chief pub. integrity sect., 1976-80, sr. counsel criminal div., 1980-83; bar counsel D.C. Ct. Appeals, 1983-87; CEO, ATLA, 1988—. Columnist Bar Counsels Page, Washington Lawyer mag., bi-monthly, 1983-87. Pres. Christmas in April, Washington, 1986-87. Mem. Am. Soc. Assn. Execs. (bd. dirs. 1994-97, vice chair 1997-98), Omicron Delta Kappa. Avocations: golf, skiing, fitness, outdoor adventure. Home: 6698 Glenbrook Rd Chevy Chase MD 20815-6515 Office: ATLA 1050 31st St NW Washington DC 20007-4409

HENDREN, JIMM LARRY, federal judge; b. 1940; BA, U. Ark., 1964, LLB, 1965. With Little & Enfield, 1968-69; pvt. practice Bentonville, Ark., 1970-77, 79-92; chancellor, probate judge Ark. 16th Chancery Dist., 1977-78; U.S. dist. judge We. Dist. Ark., 1992-96, chief judge, 1997—. Served to lt. comdr. JAGC, USN, 1965-70, USNR, 1970-83. Mem. ABA, Ark. Bar Assn. Office: US Dist Ct PO Box 3487 Fayetteville AR 72702-3487

HENDRICK, BENARD CALVIN, VII, lawyer; b. Odessa, Tex., Oct. 7, 1964; s. Benard Calvin IV and Marita Hendrick; m. Amy Camille Weatherby, Nov. 17, 1990; children: Benard Calvin VIII, Kaitlin Camille. BBA summa cum laude, Angelo State U., San Angelo, Tex., 1987; JD, U. Tex., 1990. Bar: Tex. 1990, U.S. Dist. Ct. (ea., we. and no. dists.) Tex. 1991, U.S. Ct. Appeals (5th cir.) 1995. Assoc. Shafer, Davis, Ashley, O'Leary & Stoker, Odessa, 1990-92, ptnr., 1992—. Bd. dirs. Permian Basin Rehab. Ctr., Odessa, 1992-97, Crystal Ball Found., Odessa, 1993-96; elder First Christian Ch., Odessa, 1995-98, 2000—. Fellow Tex. Bar Found.; mem. Tex. Assn. Def. Counsel (bd. dirs. 1998-2000), State Bar Tex., Ector County Bar Assn. (pres. 1998-99), Ector County Young Lawyers Assn. (pres. 1995), Def. Rsch. Inst. Republican. Mem. Christian Ch. Avocations: hunting, fishing, karate. General civil litigation, Insurance, Personal injury. Home: 2301 La Due Ln Odessa TX 79762 Office: Shafer Davis Ashley O'Leary & Stoker 700 N Grant Ave Ste 201 Odessa TX 79761-4576

HENDRICKS, RANDAL ARLAN, lawyer; b. Nov. 18, 1945; s. Clinton H. and Edith T. (Anderson) H.; m. Suann Rose, June 1, 1965 (div. 1976); children: Kristin Lee, Daehne Lynn; m. Jill Edith Duke, Mar. 22, 1982; 1 child, Bret Larson-Hendricks. Student, U. Mo., Kansas City, 1963-65; BS with honors, U. Houston, 1968, JD with honors, 1970. Bar: Tex. 1970, U.S. Dist. Ct. (so. dist.) Tex. 1970, U.S. Tax Ct. 1985. Assoc. Baker & Botts, Houston, 1970-71; pvt. practice, 1971—; sr. v.p., mng. dir. Baseball, SFX Sports Group, Inc., 1999-2001, chmn., pres., CEO, 2001—, SFX Baseball Group Inc., 2001—. Ptnr. Hendricks Sports Mgmt., Houston, 1977-81; pres. Hendricks Mgmt. Co., Inc., Houston, 1981-99; expert witness U.S. Senate Subcom. on Antitrust and Monopoly, 1972; mem. pub. adv. com. Houston/Harris County Sports Facility, 1995-96. Author: Inside the Strike Zone, 1994. Dir. profl. div. Excellence Campaign, U. Houston, 1971; bd. dirs. Cypress Creek Christian Ch., Spring, Tex., 1979-85. Mem. Houston Bar Assn., Assn. Reps. Profl. Athletes (bd. dirs. 1978-88, mem. at large 1978-79, treas. 1979-80, v.p. 1980-81, pres. 1981-82, chmn. ethics com. 1978-80, chmn. baseball com. 1981-88), Sports Lawyers Assn. (bd. dirs. 1992-2000), Order of Barons (chancellor 1969-70), Phi Kappa Phi, Phi Delta Phi. Real property, Sports, Personal income taxation. Home: 20802 Highet Pl Tomball TX 77375-7042 Office: 400 Randal Way Ste 106 Spring TX 77388-8908 E-mail: randy.hendricks@SFX.com

HENDRY, ANDREW DELANEY, lawyer, consumer products company executive; b. N.Y.C., Aug. 9, 1947; s. Andrew Joseph and Virginia (Delaney) H.; 1 child, Robert. AB in Econs., Georgetown U., 1969; JD, NYU, 1972. Bar: N.Y. 1973. Va. 1981, Mich. 1984, Pa. 1987. Assoc. Battle and Fowler, N.Y.C., 1972-79; sr. corp. and fin. atty. Reynolds Metals Co., Richmond, Va., 1979-82; sr. staff counsel Burroughs Corp., Detroit, 1982-83, assoc. gen. coun., 1983-86, dep. gen. counsel, 1986-87; v.p. legal affairs Unisys Corp, Blue Bell, Pa., 1987-88, v.p., gen. counsel, 1988-91; sr. v.p., gen. counsel, sec. Colgate-Palmolive Co., N.Y.C., 1991—. Dir., chmn., corp. adv. bd. Nat. Legal Aid and Def., Washington, 1992-99—. With JAGC USAF, 1973. Mem. ABA (corp. gen. counsel, com. chmn. 1996-98, standing com. on substance abuse, com. on corp. laws), Am. Law Inst., Am. Corp. Counsel Assn. (pres. Mich. chpt. 1985, bd. dirs. emeritus N.Y. chpt., chmn. nat. pro bono com. 1985-88), N.Y. Athletic Club. General corporate, Mergers and acquisitions, Securities. Office: Colgate-Palmolive Co 300 Park Ave New York NY 10022-7499

HENDRY, JOHN, state supreme court justice; b. Omaha, Aug. 23, 1948; BS, U. Nebr., 1970, JD, 1974. Pvt. practice, Licoln, 1974-1995; county ct. judge 3d Jud. Dist., 1995-98; chief justice Nebr. Supreme Ct., 1998—. Office: Rm 2214 State Capitol Lincoln NE 68509*

HENDRY, NANCY H. lawyer; b. Beijing, China, Jan. 28, 1949; m. William Joseph Baer, 1979; two children. BA, Radcliffe Coll., Cambridge, MA, 1970; J.D., Stanford U Law Sch., CA, 1975. Vol. Peace Corps, Senegal, 1970-72; Assoc. Wald Harkrader and Ross, 1975-80; special asst. to the general counsel Dept. of Edn., 1980-81; VP, dep. general counsel and asst. corp. secy. Public Broadcasting Service, 1981-96; general counsel Peace Corps, 1996-2000; adjunct prof. Georgetown U Law Sch., Washington, 1989-90.

HENDRY, ROBERT RYON, lawyer; b. Jacksonville, Fla., Apr. 23, 1936; s. Warren Candler and Evalyn Marguerite (Ryon) H.; children by previous marriage: Lorraine Evalyn, Lynette Comstock, Krista Ryon; m. Janet LaCoste. BA in Polit. Sci., U. Fla., 1958, JD, 1963. Bar: Fla. 1963; bd. cert. in internat. law. Assoc. Harrell, Caro, Middlebrooks & Whiltshire, Pensacola, Fla., 1963-66, Hewlliwell, Melrose & DeWolf, Orlando, 1966-67, ptnr., 1967-69; ptnr., pres. Hoffman, Hendry, Parker & Smith and predecessor Hoffman, Hendry & Parker, 1969-77, Hoffman, Hendry & Stoner and predecessor, Orlando, 1977-82, Hendry, Stoner, Sims & Sawicki, Orlando, 1982-88, Hendry, Stoner, Townsend Sawicki & Brown, 1988-92, Hendry, Stoner, Sawicki & Brown, 1992—. Author: U.S. Real Estate and the Foreign Investor, 1983; contbr. articles to profl. jours. Mem. Dist. Export Coun., 1977-91, vice chmn., 1981, chair, 1995—, mem. nat. steering com., 1997—; bd. dirs. World Trade Ctr. and predecessor, Orlando, 1979-89, pres., 1980-82, 84; chmn. Fla. Gov.'s Conf. on World Trade, 1983; chmn. Fla. coun. on internat. edn., 1993-96; mem. internat. fin. and mktg. adv. bd. U. Miami Sch. Bus., Fla., 1979-90, Commn. on Internat. Edn., 1986-88; bd. dirs. Econ. Devel. Commn. of Mid-Fla., 2001—; mem. Metro Orlando Internat. Bus. Coun., 1994-96, Metro Orlando Internat. Affairs Commn., 1995—, Fla. Econ. Summit, 1996—; mem. internat. trade and econ. devel. bd. and audit com. Enterprise, Fla., 1997-2000; chmn. Fla. Trade Grant Review Panel, 1998—; mem. adv. com. Enterprise Fla. Internat. Bus. Devel., 2000—; mem. internat. programs adv. com. U. Fla. Levin Coll., 2000—. Lt. U.S. Army, 1958-60, capt. Army N.G., 1960-70. Mem. Fla. Coun. Internat. Devel. (bd. dirs. 1972-85, chmn. 1977-79, adv. bd. 1985-95, chmn. emeritus, 1991—, vice chair 1995-96, chair 1996-98), Fla. Bar (bd. cert. internat. lawyer 1999—, vice chmn. internat. law com. 1974-75, chmn. com. 1976-77, mem. exec. coun. internat. law sect. 1982—, original internat. law certification com. 1998—, chmn. 2001—), Fla. Assn. Voluntary Agys. for Caribbean Action (bd. dirs. 1987—, pres. 1989-91, past pres. 1991—), Orange County Bar Assn. (treas. 1971-74), Soc. Internat. Bus. Fellows, Brit.-Am. C. of C. (bd. dirs. 2000—, sec. 1984-85), Swiss Am. C. of C. (sec. Fla. chpt. 1996—), German Am. Bus. Chamber of Fla., Univ. Club. General corporate, Private international, Real property. Office: Hendry Stoner Sawicki Et Al 200 E Robinson St Ste 500 Orlando FL 32801-1956

HENEGAN, JOHN C(LARK), lawyer; b. Mobile, Ala., Oct. 14, 1950; s. Virgil Baker and Marie (Fife) Gunter; m. Morella Lloyd Kuykendall, Aug. 5, 1972; children: Clark, Jim. BA in English and Philosophy, U. Miss., 1972, JD with honors, 1976. Bar: Miss. 1976, U.S. Dist. Ct. (no. dist.) Miss. 1976, N.Y. 1978, U.S. Dist. Ct. (so. dist.) N.Y. 1979, U.S. Ct. Appeals (5th and 11th cirs.) 1982, U.S. Ct. Appeals (2nd cir.) 1984, U.S. Dist. Ct. (so. dist.) Miss. 1984, U.S. Ct. Appeals (fed. cir.) 1995, U.S. Supreme Ct. 1995. Law clk. to judge U.S. Ct. Appeals (5th cir.), N.Y.C., 1976-77; atty. Dewey, Ballantine, Bushby, Palmer & Wood, N.Y.C. and Washington, 1977-81; exec. asst., chief of staff to Gov. William Winter Jackson, Miss., 1981-84; atty. Butler, Snow, O'Mara, Stevens & Cannada, PLLC, 1984—. Lectr. U. Miss. Ctr. for Continuing Legal Edn., 1985, 87, Miss. Jud. Coll., Oxford, 1982; mem. lawyers adv. com. U.S. Ct. Appeals for 5th Cir. Jud. Conf., 1991-93. Editor-in-chief Miss. Law Jour., 1976; editor Miss. Lawyer, 1985; contbr. articles to legal jours. Bd. dirs. Mississippians for Ednl. Broadcasting, Jackson, 1983-90, North Jackson Youth Baseball, Inc., 1991-97, Ctrl. Miss. Legal Svcs., 1997—; co-pres. Chastain Mid. Sch. Parent Tchrs. Students Assn., 1995-96; mem. Miss. Ethics Commn., Jackson, 1984-87; del. Hinds County Dem. Conv., 1988; mem. Miss. Dem. Fin. Coun., 1988, Hinds County Dem. Exec. Com., 1989-92; Sunday sch. supt. Covenant Presbyn. Ch., 1989-90, elder, 1996—, deacon, 1991-96, moderator of diaconate, 1993-94. Recipient Cmty. Svc. award Hinds County Bar Assn., 1998. Mem. ABA, FBA, Miss. Bar Assn. (chmn. Law Day U.S.A. 1983), Miss. Def. Lawyers Assn., Miss. Law Jour. Alumni Assn. (bd. dirs. 1985—), 5th Cir. Bar Assn., Jackson C. of C., Am. Inns of Ct. (barrister Charles Clark chpt. 1991-93), Phi Kappa Phi, Phi Delta Phi, Omicron Delta Kappa. Avocations: reading, running. Antitrust, Federal civil litigation, Libel. Home: 2441 Eastover Dr Jackson MS 39211-6727 Office: 210 E Capitol St Fl 17 Jackson MS 39201-2306 E-mail: john.henegan@butlersnow.com

HENES, SAMUEL ERNST, lawyer; b. Oberlin, Ohio, Jan. 28, 1937; s. Ernst Louis and Martha Hannah (Artz) H. A.B. with honors, Cornell U., 1959; LL.B., Harvard U., 1962. Bar: Ohio, 1962. Assoc. Arter & Hadden, Cleve., 1962-70, ptnr., 1971-89. Trustee Musart Soc., Cleve., 1980— , pres. 1985-94; trustee Young Audiences Greater Cleve., Inc., 1982-85, George P. Bickford Found., 1981-90; hon. trustee So. Lorain County Hist. Soc., Wellington, Ohio, 1988—. Served to 1st lt. U.S. Army, 1963-65 Mem. ABA, Cleve. Bar Assn., Ohio State Bar Assn. Republican. Methodist. Club: Rowfant (Cleve.) (sec. 1985-89). Avocations: book collecting, amateur harpsichordist, swimming, travel. Home: 13605 Shaker Blvd Apt 2B Cleveland OH 44120-1503

HENG, DONALD JAMES, JR. lawyer; b. Mpls., July 12, 1944; s. Donald James and Catharine Amelia (Strom) H.; m. Kathleen Ann Bailey, Sept. 2, 1967; 1 child, Francesca Remy BA cum laude, Yale U., 1967; JD magna cum laude, Minn., 1971. Bar: Calif. 1971, U.S. Dist. Ct. (no. dist.) Calif. 1971, U.S. Ct. Appeals (9th cir.) 1971. Assoc. Brobeck, Phleger & Harrison, San Francisco, 1971-73, ptnr., 1978-90; atty.-adviser Office Internat. Tax Counsel, Dept. Treasury, Washington, 1973-75; pvt. practice law San Francisco, 1990—. Lectr., writer on tax-related subjects Note and comment editor Minn. Law Rev., 1970-71 Co-recipient award for outstanding performance Am. Lawyer Mag., 1981; Fulbright scholar, Italy, 1967-68 Mem. ABA, Calif. Bar Assn., Oakland Mus. Assn. (pres. 1985-87, bd. dirs. 1983-89), Mus. Soc. San Francisco, Fine Arts Mus. (bd. dirs. 1989-90), Order Coif. Republican. Congregationalist Private international, Personal income taxation. Office: 388 Market St Ste 500 San Francisco CA 94111-5313

HENG, GERALD C. W. lawyer; b. London, Mar. 6, 1941; came to U.S., 1964; s. Chong-Kwai and York-Choo (Eng); m. Eileen B-Y Tang; 1 child, Sharmaine. BS with honors, Harvard U., 1967; LLM in Taxation, Boston U., 1985; LLB, London U., 1973; JD, Suffolk U., 1983. Tchr. Malay and English langs. Ministry of Edn., Malaysia and Singapore, 1959-60; adminstr. hosp. and health Ministry of Health, Malaysia and Singapore, 1960-64; Fulbright fellow, scholar Inst. Internat. Edn., N.Y.C., 1964-69; atty. Heng Assocs., London, 1973-83, ptnr. Brookline, Mass., 1983—. Contbr. articles to newspapers including Boston Globe, Singapore Mirror, Boston Mag. and community newspapers. Com. mem. internship program Sch. Theology, Boston U., 1987; founding sponsor Civil Justice Found., 1987—; campaign vol., amb. Elliot L. Richardson for U.S. Senate, Boston, 1984. Mem. ABA, ATLA, Asian-Am. Lawyers Assn., Internat. Assn. Asian

Ams. (pres. Boston chpt. 1981—), Boston Bar Assn. (specialist on internat. trade and human rights 1987—, gen. law practice and coms.), Mass. Acad. Trial Attys. Avocations: travel, hiking, horseback riding, sailing, golf. Communications, General practice, Taxation, general. Home and Office: 19 Lillian Rd Framingham MA 01701-4820 E-mail: gcwebheng@gis.net

HENGSTLER, GARY ARDELL, publisher, editor, lawyer; b. Wapakoneta, Ohio, Mar. 23, 1947; s. Luther C. and N. Delphine (Sims) H.; m. Linda K. Spreen, Mar. 8, 1969 (div. Aug. 1986); children: Dylan A., Joel S.; m. Laura M. Williams, Dec. 15, 1986. BS, Ball State U., 1969; JD, Cleve. State U., 1983. Bar: Ohio 1984, U.S. Dist. Ct. (no. dist.) Ohio 1984. Assoc. Blaszak, Schilling, Coey & Bennett, Elyria, Ohio, 1984-85; editor The Tex. Lawyer, Austin, 1985-86; news editor ABA Jour., Chgo., 1986-89, editor, pub., 1989-2000; dir. Donald W. Reynolds Nat. Ctr. Cts. & Media, Reno, 2000—. Home: 5055 Carnoustie Dr Reno NV 89502-9724 Office: Donald W Reynolds Nat Ctr Cts & Media U Nev Jud Coll Bldg 358 Reno NV 89557-0001 Fax: 775 327 2160. E-mail: hengstler@judges.org

HENKE, DAN, law educator; b. San Antonio, Feb. 18, 1924; BS, Georgetown U., 1943, JD, 1951; LLM, U. Wash., 1956. Bar: Tex. 1951, D.C. 1951, Calif. 1962, U.S. Supreme Ct. 1959. Bus. economist, office bus. econs. Dept. Commerce, Washington, 1948-51; practice law San Antonio, 1951-55; asst. to law libr. U. Wash., Seattle, 1955-56; head N.J. Bur. Law and Legis. Reference, Trenton, 1956-59; lectr. law U. Calif., Berkeley, 1959-64, prof., 1965-70, law libr., 1959-70; prof. law, dir. legal info. ctr. Calif. Hastings Coll. Law, San Francisco, 1970-91, emeritus prof. law, 1991—. Cons. Am. Bar Found., 1965-66, Fed. Jud. Ctr., 1976. Author: (with Mortimer D. Schwartz) Anglo-American Law Collections, 1971, California Legal Research Handbook, 1971, California Law Guide, 1976, (with Betty W. Taylor) Law in the Digital Age: The Challenge of Research in Legal Information Centers, 1996; contbr. articles to legal jours. Mem. ABA, ALA, State Bar Calif. (chmn. com. on computers and the law 1975-76), Am. Judicature Soc., Am. Assn. Law Librs. (Disting. Svc. award 1996), Am. Soc. Info. Sci., Assn. Am. Law Schs., Order of Coif, Beta Phi Mu. E-mail: DFHenke!aol.com. Office: 200 Mcallister St Ste 407 San Francisco CA 94102-4707

HENKE, MICHAEL JOHN, lawyer, educator; b. Evansville, Ind., Aug. 3, 1940; s. Emerson Overbeck and Beatrice (Arney) H.; m. Leni Edith Anderson, Mar. 20, 1966; children: Blake, Paige, Britt. BA summa cum laude, Baylor U., 1962, LLB, 1965; LLM, NYU, 1966. Bar: Tex. 1965, D.C. 1967. Assoc. Covington & Burling, Washington, 1966-73, Vinson & Elkins, Washington, 1974-76, ptnr., 1976—. Adj. prof. U. Va. Law Sch., 1988-94, 96—; chmn. pro bono adv. com. Legal Aid Soc., D.C., 1990-96, trustee, 1992—, chmn. ways & means com., 1997-2000, v.p., 2000—; Washington adv. coun. Baylor Washington Program, 1989-92; sesquicentennial coun. of 150 Baylor U., 1993-95. Author: (with others) Petroleum Regulation Handbook, 1980, Natural Gas Yearbook, 1995; mem. editl. bd. Nat. Gas Mag., 1992-97, Best Lawyers in America, 1989—, Best Lawyers in Washington, 1997, Worlds Leading Competition and Antitrust Lawyers, 1997—, World's Leading Litigation Lawyers, 1997—; contbr. articles to profl. jours. Founder, chmn. Old Presbyn. Meeting House Day Care Ctr., Alexandria, Va., 1970-74; trustee Alexandria Country Day Sch., 2000—. Kenneson fellow. Mem. ABA (chmn. energy antitrust subcom. litigation sect. 1987-88, vice chmn. energy litigation com. 1988-89, chmn. 1989-92, chmn. ann. fall meeting 1993, divsn. dir. 1993-95, co-chmn. audiotaping & videotaping com. 1995-96, co-chmn. ins. coverage litigation com. 1996-98, coun. mem. 1998—), D.C. Bar Assn., Tex. Bar Assn., Coll. State Bar Tex., Baylor U. Alumni Assn. (bd. dirs. 1994-98), Am. Civil Trial Bar Roundtable, Met. Club, Belle Haven Country Club, Farmington Country Club (Charlottesville). Democrat. Avocations: skiing, flyfishing, tennis, backpacking. Administrative and regulatory, Antitrust, Federal civil litigation. Home: 310 Charles Alexander Ct Alexandria VA 22301-1500 Office: Vinson & Elkins 1455 Pennsylvania Ave NW Fl 7 Washington DC 20004-1013 E-mail: mhenke@velaw.com

HENKE, ROBERT JOHN, lawyer, mediator, consultant, engineer; b. Chgo., Oct. 13, 1934; s. Raymond Anthony and May Dorothy (Driscoll) H.; m. Mary Gabrielle Handrigan, June 18, 1960; children: Robert Joseph, Ann Marie. BSEE, U. Ill., 1956; MBA, U. Chgo., 1964; JD, No. Ill. U., 1979; postgrad., John Marshall Law Sch. Bar: Ill. 1980, Wis. 1980, U.S. Dist. Ct. (no. dist.) Ill. 1980, U.S. Dist. Ct. (we. and ea. dists.) Wis. 1980, U.S. Supreme Ct. 1984; registered profl. engr., Ill, Wis. Sr. elec. engr. Commonwealth Edison Co., Chgo., 1956-80; elec. engr. Peterson Builders, Sturgeon Bay, Wis., 1982-83; sr. elec., cost estimating engr. Sargent & Lundy Engrs., Chgo., 1985-94; instr. econs. and criminal law NE Wis. Tech. Inst., 1981-82; asst. dist. atty. Door County, Wis., 1981, ct. commr., 1981-82, sole practice, 1981-84, Lake County, Ill., 1984-94; pvt. practice cons., mediator Fish Creek, Wis., 1995-99; cons. Pittsboro, N.C., 1999—. Dir. Scand, Door County, 1981-82. Vice chmn. Door County Bd. Adjustment, 1983-84; atty. coach Wis. Bar Found. H.S. Moot Ct. Competition, Door County, 1984; vol. lawyers program, Lake County, Ill., 1985-95; sec., counsel, bd. dirs. Woodland Hills Condominium Assn., Gurnee, Ill., 1993-94. Served with USAR, 1958-63. Recipient award for pro bono work, 1994. Mem. ABA, IEEE, Wis. Bar Assn., Door Kewaunee Bar Assn. (pres. 1983-84), Chgo. Bar Assn., Am. Assn. Cost Engrs. Roman Catholic.

HENKEL, KATHRYN GUNDY, lawyer; b. West Columbia, Tex., Oct. 16, 1952; d. Louis Ory Jr. and Patricia Dolores (Fields) Gundy. BA cum laude, Rice U., 1973; JD cum laude, Harvard U., 1976. Bar: Tex. 1976, U.S. Dist. Ct. (no. dist.) Tex. 1982, U.S. Ct. Appeals (5th cir.) 1994, U.S. Tax Ct. 1981, U.S. Supreme Ct. 1983; bd. cert. estate planning and probate law, Tex. Bd. Legal Specialization. Ptnr. Hughes & Luce, L.L.P., Dallas, 1982—. Author: Estate Planning and Wealth Preservation: Strategies and Solutions, 1997; mem. editl. bd. Estate Planning mag. Mem. adv. coun. Cmtys. Found. Tex. Inc., 1982—; mem. planned giving com. Dallas Symphony Orch., 1987—; mem. planned giving adv. com. Children's Med. Ctr., Dallas; bd. dirs., chmn. bd. advisors to found. com. Dallas Opera. Fellow Am. Coll. Trust and Estate Counsel; mem. ABA (vice chair sect. real property, probate and trusts com. on generation-skipping transfers 1992-95, chair sect. of taxation com. on estate and gift taxes 1993-95, coun. dir. sect. taxation 1996-99, co-chair sect. real property, probate and trust law estate planning study com. on law reform), State Bar Tex. (chair sect. taxation 1992-93), Dallas Bar Assn. (past chair sect. taxation), Tex. Bar Found. Roman Catholic. Avocations: reading, travel. Estate planning, Probate, Taxation, general. Office: Hughes & Luce LLP 1717 Main St Ste 2800 Dallas TX 75201-4685 E-mail: henkelk@hughes.luce.com

HENKIN, LOUIS, lawyer, law educator; b. Russia, Nov. 11, 1917; came to U.S., 1923, naturalized, 1930; s. Yoseph Elia and Frieda Rebecca (Kreindel) H.; m. Alice Barbara Hartman, June 19, 1960; children: Joshua, David, Daniel. AB, Yeshiva Coll., 1937; DHL, Yeshiva U., 1963; LLB, Harvard U., 1940; LLD, Columbia U., 1995; JD (hon.), Bklyn. Law Sch., 1997. Bar: N.Y. 1941, U.S. Supreme Ct. 1947. Law clk. to Judge Learned Hand, 1940-41; law clk. to Justice Frankfurter, 1946-47; cons. legal dept. UN, 1947-48; with State Dept., 1945-46, 48-57; U.S. rep. UN Com. Refugees and Stateless Persons, 1950; adviser U.S. del. UN Econ. and Social Coun., 1950, UN Gen. Assembly, 1950-53, Geneva Conf. on Korea, 1954; assoc. dir. Legis. Drafting Rsch. Fund, lectr. law Columbia U., 1956-57; prof. law U. Pa., 1958-62; prof. internat. law and diplomacy, prof. law Columbia U., 1962, mem. Inst. War and Peace Studies, 1962—, Hamilton Fish prof. internat. law and diplomacy, 1963-78, Harlan Fiske Stone prof. constl. law, 1978-79, univ. prof., 1979-88, u. prof. emeritus and spl. svc. prof., 1988—; co-dir. Ctr. for Study of Human Rights, 1978-86, chmn. of directorate, 1986—. U.S. mem. Permanent Ct. Arbitration, 1963-69; adviser U.S. Del. UN Conf. on Law of the Sea, 1972-80; adv. panel on internat. law Dept. State, 1975-80, 93—; human rights com. U.S. Commn. for UNESCO, 1977-80, Internat. Covenant Civil and Polit. Rights, 1999—; Carnegie lectr. Hague Acad. Internat. Law, 1965; Frankel lectr. U. Houston, 1969; Gottesman lectr. Yeshiva U., 1975; Lockhart lectr. U. Minn. Law Sch., 1976; Francis Biddle lectr. Harvard Law Sch., 1978; lectr. Columbia U., 1979; Sherrill lectr. Yale U. Law Sch., 1981; Jefferson lectr. U. Pa. Law Sch., 1983; Irvine lectr. Cornell U., 1986; disting. lectr. Coll. Physicians and Surgeons, Columbia U., 1988; Solf lectr. Judge Adv. Gen.'s Sch., 1988; Cooley lectr. U. Mich. Law Sch., 1988; White lectr. La. State U., 1989; prin. lectr. The Hague Acad. Internat. Law, 1989; Blaine Sloane lectr. Pace U. Law Sch., 1991; Gerber lectr. U. Md. Law Sch., 1991; Nathanson lectr. law sch. U. San Diego, 1994; Sibley lectr. U. Ga. Law Sch., 1994; Brandeis lectr. Israel Acad. Scis. and Humanities, 1994; Phi Kappa Phi lectr., James Madison U., 1996, Doris and A. Leo Levin lectr. Bar Ilan U., Israel, 1996; cons. to govt., pres. U.S. Inst. Human Rights, 1970-93, Robert L. Levine lectr. Fordham Law Sch.; chief reporter Am. Law Inst., Restatement of the Law (3d), Fgn. Rels. Law of the U.S., 1979-87; bd. dirs. Lawyers Com. Human Rights, Immigration and Refugee Svcs. Am., v.p., 1994—; pres. Am. Soc. Internat. Law, 1992-94; vis. prof. U. Pa., 1957-58; mem. human rights com. UN, 2000—. Author: Arms Control and Inspection in American Law, 1958, The Berlin Crisis and the United Nations, 1959, Disarmament: The Lawyer's Interests, 1964, Law for the Sea's Mineral Resources, 1968, Foreign Affairs and the Constitution, 1972, 2nd edit., 1996, The Rights of Man Today, 1978, How Nations Behave: Law and Foreign Policy, 2nd edit., 1979; (with others) Human Rights in Contemporary China, 1986, Right v. Might: International Law and the Use of Force, 1989, 2nd edit., 1991, The Age of Rights, 1990, Constitutionalism, Democracy and Foreign Affairs, 1990, International Law: Politics and Values, 1995; editor: Arms Control: Issues for the Public, 1961, (with others) Transnational Law in a Changing Society, 1972, World Politics and the Jewish Condition, 1972, The International Bill of Rights: The International Covenant of Civil and Political Rights, 1981; (with others) International Law: Cases and Materials, 3d edit., 1993, 4th edit., 2001, Constitutionalism and Rights: The Influence of the United States Constitution Abroad, 1989, Foreign Affairs and the U.S. Constitution, 1990, Human Rights: Cases and Materials, 1999; bd. editors: Am. Jour. Internat. Law, 1967—, co-editor-in-chief, 1978-84; bd editors Ocean Devel. and Internat. Law Jour., 1973—, Jerusalem Jour. Internat. Relations, 1976—; contbr. articles to profl. jours. Served with AUS, 1941-45. Decorated Silver Star; recipient Law Alumni medal of excellence Columbia U. Sch. Law, 1982, Friedmann Meml. award Columbia Soc. Internat. law, 1986, Hudson medal Am. Soc. Internat. Law, 1995, Leadership in Human Rights award Columbia Human Rights Law Rev., 1995, Human Rights award Lawyers Com. for Human Rights, 1995, Outstanding Rsch. in Law and Govt. award Fellows of Am. Bar Found., 1997; Guggenheim fellow, 1979-80; Festschrift (Liber Amicorum): Politics, Values and Functions, Internat. Law in the 21st Century, Essays on Internat. Law in his honor, 1997, Louis Henkin Professorship in Human and Constitutional Rights established in his honor Columbia Law Sch., 1999. Fellow Am. Acad. Arts and Scis.; mem. Coun. Fgn. Rels., Am. Soc. Internat. Law (v.p. 1975-76, 88-90, pres. 1992-94, hon. v.p. 1994—), Internat. Law Assn. (v.p. Am. br., 1973—), Am. Soc. Polit. and Legal Philosophy (pres. 1985-87), Inst. de Droit Internat., Am. Polit. Sci. Assn., Internat. Assn. Constl. Law (v.p. 1982-95, hon. pres. 1995—), U.S. Assn. Constl. Law (hon. pres. 1997—), Am. Philos. Soc. (Henry M. Phillips prize in jurisprudence 2000). Home: 460 Riverside Dr New York NY 10027-6801 E-mail: lhenkin@law.columbia.edu

HENNEKE, EDWARD GEORGE, lawyer; b. Flint, Mich., Jan. 28, 1940; s. Edward G. and Anna I. (Kielhorn) H.; m. Donna M. Wardosky, Jan. 24, 1970; children: Dawn, Shelley, Charlene; stepchildren: Scott, Tracy, Kurt Fraim. AA, Flint Jr. Coll., 1960; BS, U. Mich., Flint, 1962; JD, U. Mich., Ann Arbor, 1965. Bar: Mich. 1965, U.S. Dist. Ct. (ea. dist.) Mich. 1967, U.S. Ct. Appeals (6th cir.) 1974, U.S. Supreme Ct. 1971. Asst. pros. atty. Genesee County Pros. Atty., Flint, 1965-67; assoc. Ransom, Fazenbaker & Ransom, 1967-74; prin. ptnr. Keil, Ransom & Henneke, 1975-88, Henneke, McKone Fraim & Dawes, P.C. (and predecessor firm), Flint, 1988—. Flushing city atty., 1999—. Mem. planning com. Flushing Twp., 1986-92; bd. appeals, 1993—. Named Outstanding Alumnus, Flint U. Mich., 1971. Mem. Genesee County Bar Assn. (dir. 1978-81, pres. 1981-83), ABA. Avocations: hunting, golf, skiing. General civil litigation, Insurance, Probate. Office: Henneke McKone Fraim & Dawes PC 2222 S Linden Rd Ste G Flint MI 48532-5413 E-mail: ehenneke@bignet.net

HENNELLY, EDMUND PAUL, lawyer, oil company executive; b. N.Y.C., Apr. 2, 1923; s. Edmund Patrick and Alice (Laccorn) H.; m. Josephine Kline; children: Patricia A. Anglin, Pamela J. Farley. BCE, Manhattan Coll., 1944; JD, Fordham U., 1950. Bar: N.Y. 1950. Instr. Manhattan Coll., 1947-50; litigation assoc. Cravath, Swaine & Moore, 1950-51, sr. litigation assoc., 1953-54; asst. gen. counsel CIA, Washington, 1951-52; assoc. counsel Time, Inc., N.Y.C., 1954-56; asst. legis. cons. Mobil Oil Corp., 1956-60, legis. cons., 1960-61, mgr. domestic govt. rels. dept., 1961-67, mgr. govt. rels. dept., 1967-73, gen. mgr. govt. rels. dept., 1974-78, gen. mgr. pub. affairs dept., 1978-86; pres., CEO C. Remainder Corp., 1986—. Bd. dirs. South Cay Trust. Contbr. articles on engring. and law to profl. jours. Trustee, vice chmn. Daytop Village Found.; mem. adv. com. N.Y. State Legis. Com. on Higher Edn., Nassau County (N.Y.) Energy Commn., L.I. Citizens' Com. for Mass Transit, N.Y. State Def. Coun.; mem. White House Conf. on Natural Beauty, 1963; bd. dirs. Nat. Coun. on Aging; exec. com. Pub. Affairs Rsch. Coun. of Conf. Bd.; mem. Nassau County Econ. Devel. Planning Coun.; commr. nat. com. Commn. for UNESCO, 1982-85, head U.S. del. with personal rank of amb. 22d Gen. Conf., 1983, mem. internat. adv. panel, 1989—; mem. Pres.' Intelligence Transition Team, 1980-81; cons. Pres.'s Intelligence Oversight Bd.; trustee Austen Riggs Ctr., Pub. Affairs Found. Lt., USNR, 1943-46, PTO, ETO. Decorated Knight of Malta, Knight of Holy Sepulchre. Mem. ABA, Fed. Bar Assn., Assn. Bar City of N.Y., Acad. Polit. and Social Scis., Am. Good Govt. Soc. (trustee), Tax Coun. (bd. dirs.), Pub. Affairs Coun. (bd. dirs.), Freedom House (trustee), Am. Mgmt. Assn., Pi Sigma Epsilon, Delta Theta Phi, Army-Navy Club, Meadows Country Club, Sarasota Yacht Club, Island Hills Country Club, Explorers Club, Knights of Malta, Knights Holy Sepulchre. Clubs: Army-Navy, Explorers. Lodges: K.M., Knights Holy Sepulcher. Oil, gas, and mineral. Home: 84 Sequams Ln E West Islip NY 11795-4508 also: 3941 Hamilton Club Cir Sarasota FL 34242-1109 Office: C Remainder Corp 21 Argyle Sq Babylon NY 11702-2712

HENNEN, THOMAS WALDO, lawyer; b. Tacoma, Nov. 28, 1945; s. Waldo Gerhart and Ruth Elzora (George) H. AA, Highline Coll., 1966; BS in Mech. Engring., Wash. State U., 1969; JD, U. Maine, 1973. Bar: Wash. 1973, U.S. Ct. Claims 1975, U.S. Patent Office 1975, U.S. Ct. Customs and Patent Appeals 1975. Design engr. Boeing Aircraft Co., Seattle, 1969-70; patent atty. Office Naval Rsch., Arlington, Va., 1975, Naval Sea Sys. Command, Washington, 1978-79; patent staff asst. for tech. and administrv. ops. Office Naval Rsch., Arlington, Va., 1979-82; patent atty. Naval Weapons Ctr., China Lake, Calif., 1975-78; dpe. patent counsel Ridgecrest, 1982-86; counsel info., space and def. sys. Boeing, Kent, Wash., 1986-97, counsel info. and comm. sys. Seattle, 1998; counsel Boeing Space and Comm Group, Seal Beach, Calif., 1999—. Instr. basic patent prosecution Naval Weapons Ctr. Coach Civitan Soccer Club, Arlington, Va., 1981-82. Mem. ASME, Wash. State Bar Assn., Wash. State Patent Law Assn., Govt. Patent Lawyers Assn., Nat. Rifle Assn. (life), Indian Wells Valley Bar Assn. (pres. 1977). Intellectual property, Patent, Trademark and copyright. Office: Boeing Space and Comm Group 2515 MC 110 SB50 Seal Beach CA 90740-1515 E-mail: thennen@socal.rr.com

HENNESSY, DEAN MCDONALD, lawyer, multinational corporation executive; b. McPherson, Kans., June 13, 1923; s. Ernest Weston and Beulah A. (Dunn) H.; m. Marguerite Sundheim, Sept. 6, 1946 (div. Sept. 1979); children: Joan Hennessy Wright, John D., Robert D. (dec.), Scott D. (dec.); m. Darlene MacLean, Apr. 4, 1981. AB cum laude, Harvard U., 1947, LLB, 1950; MBA, U. Chgo., 1959. Bar: Ill. 1951. Assoc. Carney, Crowell & Leibman, Chgo., 1950-53; atty. Borg-Warner Corp., 1953-62; with Emhart Corp., Farmington, Conn., 1962-88, asst. sec., 1964-67, sec., gen. counsel, 1967-74, v.p., sec., gen. counsel, 1974-76, v.p., gen. counsel, 1976-86, sr. v.p., gen. counsel, 1986-88, ret., 1988. Incorporator Ill. Citizens for Eisenhower, 1952; chmn. Citizens Activities, Ill. Citizens for Eisenhower, 1952, 56; Justice of the peace, mem. bd. suprs. Proviso Twp., Ill., 1952-56; vice chmn. Jr. Achievement Chgo., 1959; program chmn. trade and industries divsn. United Rep. Fund Ill., 1961; trustee West Hartford Bicentennial Trust, Inc., 1976-77, Friends and Trustees of Bushnell Meml., Hartford, 1978-84; bd. dirs. Royal Homestead Condominium Assn., Juno Beach, Fla., 1990-93. Served to lt. (j.g.) USNR, 1943-46. Sheldon fellow Harvard U., 1947. Mem. ABA, Mfrs. Alliance for Productivity and Innovation (vice chmn. law coun. 1984-87, chmn. 1987, 88), John Harvard Soc. Republican. Presbyterian. General corporate. E-mail: dmha1@aol.com, subastra@aol.com

HENNESSY, ELLEN ANNE, lawyer, benefits compensation analyst, educator; b. Auburn, N.Y., Mar. 3, 1949; d. Charles Francis and Mary Anne (Roan) H.; m. Frank Daspit, Aug. 27, 1974. BA, Mich. State U., 1971; JD, Cath. U., 1978; LLM in Taxation, Georgetown U., 1984. Bar: D.C. 1978, U.S. Ct. Appeals (D.C. cir.) 1978, U.S. Supreme Ct. 1984. Various positions NEH, Washington, 1971-74; atty. office chief counsel IRS, 1978-80; atty.-advisor Pension Benefit Guaranty Corp., 1980-82; assoc. Stroock & Stroock & Lavan, 1982-85, Willkie Farr & Gallager, Washington, 1985-86, ptnr., 1987-93; dep. exec. dir. and chief negotiator Pension Benefit Guaranty Corp., 1993-98; sr. v.p. Aon Cons. Inc., 1998—. Adj. prof. law Georgetown U., Washington, 1985—; mem. com. on continuing profl. edn. Am. Law Inst./ABA, 1994-97; pres. ASA Fiduciary Counselors, Inc., 1999—. Mem. ABA (supervising editor taxation sect. newsletter 1984-87, mem. standing com. on continuing edn. 1990-94, chairperson joint com. on employee benefits 1991-92), Worldwide Employee Benefits (pres. 1987-88), D.C. Bar Assn. (mem. steering com. tax sect. 1988-93, chairperson continuing legal edn. com. 1993-95), Am. Coll. Employee Benefits Counsel (bd. govs. 2000—). Democrat. Avocation: whitewater canoeing. Home: 1926 Lawrence St NE Washington DC 20018-2734 Office: South Bldg Ste 900 601 Pennsylvania Ave NW Washington DC 20004-2601 E-mail: nell_hennessy@aoncons.com

HENNIGER, DAVID THOMAS, lawyer; b. Cuyahoga Falls, Ohio, Dec. 12, 1936; s. Herman Harrison and Wilma (Weeks) H.; m. LaRayne Virginia Kerlin, Apr. 9, 1965; children: Mark, Jill, Matthew, Michael. AA, St. Petersburg Jr. Coll., 1957; BS summa cum laude, Fla. So. Coll., 1959; JD cum laude, Stetson U., 1965. Bar: Fla. 1965, U.S. Dist. Ct. (mid. dist.) Fla. 1965, U.S. Ct. Appeals (5th cir.) 1966, U.S. Supreme Ct. 1971, U.S. Ct. Appeals (11th cir.) 1981. Diplomate Nat. Bd. Trial Advocacy. Assoc. Masterson, Lloyd, Sundberg & Rogers, St. Petersburg, Fla., 1965-75; ptnr. Lloyd and Henniger, P.A., 1975-84; assoc. Greene and Mastry, P.A., 1984-91; coll. atty. St. Petersburg Jr. Coll. Instr. Stetson Coll. Law, Gulfport, Fla., 1972-73; St. Petersburg Jr. Coll., 1968-73; pres. St. Petersburg Legal Aid Soc., 1976. Pres. Christian Arbitration Ctr., St. Petersburg, 1987—; v.p. Christian Businessmen's Com., 1981-82; chmn. sch. adv. com. Dixie Hollins High Sch., Kenneth City, Fla., 1985-86, pres. Parent Tchrs. Student Assn., 1987-88. Mem. ABA, Fed. Bar Assn., Am. Judicare Soc., Assn. Trial Lawyers Am., Fla. Trial Lawyers Soc., Am. Arbitration Assn. (panel arbitrators 1977-88), Christian Legal Soc. (treas. St. Petersburg 1984—). Avocations: basketball, photography. General civil litigation. Home: 5862 32nd Ave N Saint Petersburg FL 33710-1837 Office: St Petersburg Jr Coll PO Box 13489 Saint Petersburg FL 33733-3489

HENNING, JOEL FRANK, lawyer, author, publisher, consultant; b. Chgo., Sept. 15, 1939; s. Alexander M. and Henrietta (Frank) H.; m. Grace Weiner, May 24, 1964 (div. July 1987); children: Justine, Sarah-Anne, Dara; m. Rosemary Nadolsky, June 21, 1992; 1 child, Alexandra. AB, Harvard U., 1961, JD, 1964. Bar: Ill. 1965. Assoc. Sonnenschein, Levinson, Carlin, Nath & Rosenthal, Chgo., 1965-70; fellow, dir. program Adlai Stevenson Inst. Internat. Affairs, 1970-73; nat. dir. Youth Edn. for Citizenship, 1972-75; dir. profl. edn. Am. Bar Assn., Chgo., 1975-78; asst. exec. dir. comm. and edn. ABA, 1978-80; ptnr. Joel Henning & Assocs., 1980-87; sr. v.p., gen. counsel, mem. exec. com. Hildebrandt, Internat., Inc., 1987—; pres., pub. LawLetters, Inc., 1980-89; pub. Lawyer Hiring and Tng. Report, 1980-89; Chgo. theater critic Wall St. Jour., 1989—; pub. Almanac of Fed. Judiciary, 1984-89; editor Bus. Lawyer Update, 1980-87. Mem. faculty Inst. on Law and Ethics, Council Philos. Studies; chmn. Fund for Justice, Chgo., 1979-85 Author: Law-Related Education in America: Guidelines for the Future, 1975, Holistic Running: Beyond the Threshhold of Fitness, 1978, Mandate for Change: The Impact of Law on Educational Innovaiton, 1979, Improving Lawyer Productivity: How to Train, Manage and Supervise Your Lawyers, 1985, Law Practice and Management Desk Book, 1987, Lawyers Guide to Managing and Training Lawyers, 1988, Maximizing Law Firm Profitability: Hiring, Training and Developing Productive Lawyers, 1991-98, also articles. Chmn. Gov.'s Commn. on Financing Arts in Ill., 1970-71; bd. dirs. Ill. Arts Council, 1971-81, Columbia Coll., Chgo.; bd. dirs., v.p., pub. edn. exec. com. ACLU of Ill.; trustee S.E. Chgo. Commn.; mem. Joseph Jefferson Theatrical Awards Com. Fellow Am. Bar Found. (life); mem. Am. Law Inst., ABA (ho. of dels.), Chgo. Bar Assn., Chgo. Council Lawyers (co-founder), Social Sci. Edn. Consortium. General corporate, General practice. Office: 150 N Michigan Ave Ste 3600 Chicago IL 60601-7572

HENRICK, MICHAEL FRANCIS, lawyer; b. Chgo., Feb. 29, 1948; s. John L. and A. Madeline (Hafner) H.; m. Cissi F. Henrick, Aug. 9, 1980; children: Michael Francis Jr., Derry Patricia. BA, Loyola U., 1971; JD with honors, John Marshall Law Sch., 1974. Bar: Ill. 1974, U.S. Dist. Ct. (no. dist.) Ill. 1974, U.S. Supreme Ct. 1979, Wis. 1985, U.S. Dist. Ct. (ea. dist.) Wis. 1985. Ptnr. Hinshaw & Culbertson, Chgo., Waukegan, Ill., 1974—. Recipient Corpus Juris Secundum award West Publ. Co., 1974. Mem. ABA, Def. Rsch. Inst., Ill. Bar Assn., Lake County Bar Assn., Ill. Hosp. Attys. Assn., Internat. Assn. of Def. Counsel, Ill. Def. Attys. Assn., Soc. Trial Lawyers Def. Rsch. Inst., Am. Inns of Ct. Personal injury. Office: Hinshaw & Culbertson 110 N West St Waukegan IL 60085-4330 E-mail: m.henrick@hinshawlaw.com

HENRY, BRIAN THOMAS, lawyer; b. Chgo., Dec. 25, 1954; s. Thomas Joseph and Shirley Grace (Pfaff) H.; m. Mary Elizabeth Collins, Sept. 17, 1983; children: Kyle Justin, Erin Maureen, Colin Thomas. BA Honors in History magna cum laude, Loyola U., Chgo., 1977; JD, U. Ill., 1980. Bar: Ill. 1980, U.S. Dist. Ct. (no. dist.) Ill. 1980. Ptnr. Pretzel & Stouffe Chtd., Chgo., 1980—. Faculty instr. Ill. Assn. of Def. Trial Counsel Trial Acads., 1990-2001; seminar speaker Chgo. Bar Assn. Comparative Negligence Seminar, 1990, '91; cons. health care com. Inst. of Medicine of Chgo.; frequent lectr. med. groups. Editor-in-chief Recent Decisions Sect. of Ill. Bar Jour., 1979-80 Mem. ASTL, ABA, Ill. Assn. Hosp. Attys., Ill. Assn. Defense Trial Counsel, Internat. Assn. Defense Counsel (faculty instr. trial acad. 2001), Chgo. Bar Assn., Ill. Bar Assn., Phi Alpha Theta, Phi Alpha Delta. General civil litigation, Personal injury, Professional liability. Office: Pretzel & Stouffer Chtd 1 S Wacker Dr Ste 2500 Chicago IL 60606-4614

HENRY, CARL NOLAN, lawyer; b. Washington, Sept. 30, 1965; s. Robert Benjamin Covington III and Inola Francis Henry. BA in Polit. Sci., U. Calif., Berkeley, 1987, JD, 1993. Bar: Calif. 1993, U.S. Supreme Ct. 1997, U.S. Ct. Appeal (9th cir.) 1993, U.S. Dist. Ct. (no., ctrl. dists.) Calif. 1993. Dep. atty. gen. Calif. Dept. Justice, L.A., 1994-99, 99—; staff atty. to Hon. Janice Rogers Brown Calif. Supreme Ct., San Francisco, 1999. Career Awareness Acad. scholar Home Savings Am., 1983; Liberal Arts award Bank Am., 1983. Mem. L.A. Angel City Links Assn. (O. J. Simpson Acad. scholar 1983), L.A. Ephebian Honor Soc. Democrat. Methodist. Avocations: sports, politics, music, history, education. Office: Calif Dept Justice 300 S Spring St Ste 5000 Los Angeles CA 90013-1230

HENRY, DAVID PATRICK, lawyer; b. Terre Haute, Ind., June 2, 1960; s. Joseph C. and Sara F. Henry; children: Hannah Lane, Blake Ryan. BS, U. Mo., 1982; JD, Oklahoma City U., 1985. Bar: Okla., U.S. Dist. Ct. (we., no. and ea. dists.) Okla., U.S. Ct. Appeals (10th cir.). Assoc. Hughes & Nelson, Oklahoma City, 1985-88; ptnr. Coyle & Henry, P.C., 1988-91, Henry Law Office, Oklahoma City, 1991—. Mem. ATLA, Okla. Criminal Def. Bar Assn., Okla. County Bar Assn. Democrat. Baptist. Avocations: golf, poker. Criminal, Family and matrimonial, Personal injury. Office: Henry Davidson & Hill 3315 NW 63rd St Oklahoma City OK 73116-3787

HENRY, DELYSLE LEON, lawyer; b. Cumberland, Apr. 17, 1935; s. Clarence Philip and Lillian Pauline (Hartley) H.; m. Kaye Claire Grulke, June 23, 1960; children: Reginald DeLysle, Lisa Kay. BA, Ea. Nazarene Coll., 1956; MA, U. Pa., 1958; JD, U. Balt., 1966; postgrad., Mich. State U. Bar: Mich. 1971, U.S. Dist. Ct. (ea. dist.) Mich. 1978, U.S. Ct. Appeals (6th cir.) 1979. Instr. law and govt. Alpena (Mich.) Community Coll., 1959-61, 66-89; pvt. practice Alpena, 1971—. Commr. County of Alpena, 1974-76. Mem. ABA, Nat. Orgn. Social Security Claimants' Reps., State Bar Mich., Am. Judicature Soc., Am. Bus. Law Assn., Fed. Bar Assn. (Detroit chpt.). Presbyterian. Avocations: hiking, swimming. Federal civil litigation, Pension, profit-sharing, and employee benefits.

HENRY, EDWIN MAURICE, JR. lawyer, electrical engineer, consultant; b. Cambridge, Md., June 26, 1930; s. Edwin Maurice Henry Sr. and Emma Lee (Wilson) Clayton; m. Barbara Ann Brittingham, Feb. 2, 1952; children: Barbara Jo, Kim M. Student, U.S. Naval Acad., 1949-51; BSEE, John Hopkins U., 1957; JD, U. Balt., 1972. Bar: Md. 1974, U.S. Dist. Ct. Md. 1974; registered profl. engr., Md. Assoc. Pairo & Pairo, Balt., 1973-76; ptnr. Pairo & Henry, Ellicott City, Md., 1976-86; sole practice, 1986-95; pvt. practice LLC, 1996-00. Mem. Md. Atty. Grievance Rev. Bd., 1980-83. Author: Defense of Speeding Vascar, 1974. Served with USN, 1947-51. Mem. Am. Legion, Masons, Shriners, Jesters, Eastern Shore Soc., St. Andrew's Soc. Methodist. Avocations: travel. Estate planning, Family and matrimonial, General practice. Home: 9035 Overhill Dr Ellicott City MD 21042-5246 Office: PO Box 309 8433 Main St Ellicott City MD 21043-4607 E-mail: henryllc@erols.com

HENRY, FREDERICK EDWARD, lawyer; b. St. Louis, Aug. 28, 1947; s. Frederick E. and Dorothy Jean (McCulley) H.; m. Vallie Catherine Jones, June 7, 1969; children: Christine Roberta, Charles Frederick. AB, Duke U., 1969, JD with honors, 1972. Bar: Ill. 1972, U.S. Dist. Ct. (no. dist.) Ill. 1972, Calif. 1982. Assoc. Baker & McKenzie, Chgo., 1972-79, ptnr., 1979—. Bd. dirs. Lincoln Park Conservation Assn., Chgo., 1983-85, Old Town Triangle Assn., Chgo., 1980-83, pres., 1984; elder, session mem. Fourth Presbyn. Ch., Chgo., 2000—. Recipient Willis Smith award Duke U. Law Sch., 1972. Mem. ABA, Chgo. Bar Assn., Calif. State Bar, Order of Coif. Private international, Corporate taxation. Home: 164 W Eugenie St Chicago IL 60614-5809 Office: Baker & McKenzie 1 Prudential Pla 130 E Randolph St Ste 3700 Chicago IL 60601-6342 E-mail: frederick.e.henry@bakernet.com

HENRY, KAREN HAWLEY, lawyer; b. Whittier, Calif., Nov. 5, 1943; d. Ralph Hawley and Dorothy Ellen (Carr) Hawley; m. John Dunlap, 1968; m. Charles Gibbons Henry, Mar. 15, 1975; children: Scott, Alexander, Joshua; m. Don H. Phemister, June 21, 1991; children: Justin Phemister, Johnathan Phemister, Keith Phemister. BS in Social Scis., So. Oreg. Coll., 1965; MS in Labor Econs., Iowa State U., 1967; JD, U. Calif., Hastings, 1976. Instr. Medford (Oreg.) Sch. Dist., 1965-66; rsch. asst. dept. econs. Iowa State U., Ames, 1966-67; dir. rsch. program Calif. Nurses Assn., San Francisco, 1967-72; labor rels. coord. Affiliated Hosps. of San Francisco, 1972-79, labor counsel, 1979-88; ptnr. Littler, Mendelson, Fastiff & Tichy, San Francisco, 1979-86; mng. ptnr. labor and employment law Weissburg and Aronson, Inc., 1986-88; prin. Karen H. Henry, Inc., Auburn, Calif., 1991—. Author: Supervisors Guide to Labor Relations, 1981, Supervisor's Legal Guide, 1984, Nursing ADA: Ten Steps to Compliance, 1992, 6th edit., 2001; contbr. articles on employment issues to profl. jours. Mem. State Bar Calif., Thurston Soc., Order of Coif. General civil litigation, Labor. Office: Karen H Henry Inc 1141 High St Auburn CA 95603-5132

HENRY, PETER YORK, lawyer, mediator; b. Washington, Apr. 28, 1951; s. David Howe II and Margaret (Beard) H.; children: Ryan York, Zachary Price, Chance Hagdorn; m. Deidra B. Hagdorn, May 1995; 1 child, Chance Hagdorn Henry; stepchildren: Nathan Hebert, Christopher Hebert. B.B.A., Ohio U., 1973; J.D. St. Mary's U., San Antonio, 1976. Bar: Tex. 1976. Sole practice, San Antonio, 1976—. Mem. ATLA, Tex. Bar Assn., Tex Trial Lawyers Assn., San Antonio Trial Lawyers Assn. (bd. dirs. 1989-90), San Antonio Bar Assn., Phi Delta Phi. Insurance, Personal injury, Workers' compensation. Home: 7642 Bluesage Cove San Antonio TX 78249-2541

HENRY, ROBERT HARLAN, federal judge, former attorney general; b. Shawnee, Okla., Apr. 3, 1953; BA, U. Okla., 1974, JD, 1976. Bar: Okla. 1976. Atty. Henry, West, Still & Combs, Shawnee, Okla., 1977-83, Henry, Henry & Henry, Shawnee, 1983-87; mem. Okla. Ho. of Reps., 1976-86; atty. gen. State of Okla., Oklahoma City, 1987-91; dean, prof. law. Law Sch. Okla. City U., 1991-94; judge U.S. Ct. Appeals (10th cir.), Oklahoma City, 1994—. Mem. Nat. Conf. Commrs. on Uniform State Law. Fellow Am. Bar Found.; mem. Okla. Bar Assn., Am. Coun. Young Polit. Leaders, Nat. Assn. Attys. Gen. (chmn. state constl. law adv. com., vice-chmn. civil rights com.). Office: US Ct Appeals 10th Cir 200 NW 4th StRm 2021 Oklahoma City OK 73102-3026*

HENRY, ROBERT JOHN, lawyer; b. Chgo., Aug. 1, 1950; s. John P. and Margaret P. (Froelich) H.; children: Cherylyn, Deanna, Laurin. BA cum laude, Loyola U., Chgo., 1973, JD cum laude, 1975. Bar: Ill 1975, U.S. Dist. Ct. (no. dist.) Ill. 1975. Atty. Continental Ill. Nat. Bank, Chgo., 1975-77, Allied Van Lines, Inc., Chgo., 1977-81, assoc. gen. counsel, 1981-88, gen. counsel, 1988-90, v.p. adminstrn., gen. counsel, 1990-93, v.p. gen. counsel, 1993-99; v.p., assoc. gen. counsel Allied Worldwide, Inc., 1999—. Gen. counsel NFC N.Am., 1996-99. Alt. scholar Weymouth Kirkland Found., 1971. Mem. ABA, Chgo. Bar Assn., Am. Corp. Counsel Assn. Contracts commercial, General corporate, Securities. Office: Allied Van Lines Inc PO Box 4403 Chicago IL 60680-4403 E-mail: robert.henry@alliedvan.com

HENRY, RONALD GEORGE, lawyer, consultant; b. Beaver Falls, Pa., May 14, 1949; s. Ronald S. and Alice (Ross) H.; m. Linda Callahan, Aug. 28, 1976; 1 child, Elizabeth Walton. AB with honors, Georgetown U., 1971, JD, 1974. Bar: Pa. 1974, D.C. 1978, U.S. Supreme Ct. 1977. Asst. atty. gen. Pa. Dept. Commerce, Harrisburg, Pa., 1974-76; counsel to lt. gov. State of Pa., 1976-79; assoc. Ballard, Spahr, Andrews & Ingersoll, Phila., 1979-83; v.p. pub. fin. Prudential Bache, Inc., 1983-85, Smith Barney, Harris Upham & Co., Phila., 1985-90; chief counsel Phila. Regional Port Authority, 1990-91; exec. dir. Pa. Intergovtl. Coop. Authority, Phila., 1991-94, coord. spl. projects, 1994-95; pvt. practice Bryn Mawr, Pa., 1995-97; mng. dir. The Harriton Group, Inc., Broomall, 1997-99. Author: (with others) Financing Colleges and Universities, 1983. Mem. task force on econ. devel. fin. alternatives Pa. Dept. Commerce, 1987; mem. water supply adv. com. Pa. Dept. Environ. Resources, 1990; trustee Internat. Visitors Coun. Phila., 1991—, chmn., 1997—. Mem. ABA, Pa. Bar Assn., D.C. Bar Assn., Phila. Bar Assn. Health, Legislative, Municipal (including bonds). Office: 711 Pennstone Rd Bryn Mawr PA 19010-2939 E-mail: rhenry1949@aol.com

HENRY, THORNTON MONTAGU, lawyer; b. Bermuda, May 8, 1943; s. Otis R. and Barbara M. Henry; m. Ann Portlock, Aug. 28, 1971; children: Ruth Montagu, Thornton Bradshaw, John Gordon. BA, Washington and Lee U., 1966, LLB, 1969; LLM, Georgetown U. Bar: Fla. 1972, U.S. Dist. Ct. (so. dist.) Fla., U.S. Ct. Appeals (11th cir.), U.S. Tax Ct., U.S. Ct. Claims; cert. in taxation, Fla. Tax law specialist IRS, Washington, 1972-74; bd. dirs., chmn., pvt. client svcs. group Jones, Foster, Johnston & Stubbs, P.A., West Palm Beach, Fla., 1974—. Vice-chmn., bd. dirs., exec. com., counsel Cmty. Found. Palm Beach and Martin Counties; bd. dirs., 1st v.p., counsel Internat. Children's Mus. Pres., elder Meml. Presbyn. Ch.; trustee Sch. Found.; bd. dirs. The Benjamin Sch.; bd. dirs., past pres. Rehab. Ctr. Children and Adults, Inc., Palm Beach.; past pres. Planned Giving Coun., Palm Beach County. Served to capt. C.E., U.S. Army, 1970-72. Mem. ABA (tax com.), Fla. Bar Assn., Fla. Bar (exec. coun. tax sect.), East Coast Estate Planning Coun. (dir., past pres.), Palm Beach Tax Inst., Kiwanis (past pres.). Order St. John of Jerusalem (sec., knight). Republican. Avocations: jogging, furniture restoration, reading, photography, missionary work. Estate planning, Probate, Estate taxation. Office: Jones Foster Johnston & Stubbs 505 S Flagler Dr West Palm Beach FL 33401-5923

HENSCHEL, JOHN JAMES, lawyer; b. Mineola, NY, Aug. 11, 1954; s. John Jr. and Lilyan Marie (Dodge) H.; m. Yasmin Islami, May 26, 1980; children: John Christopher, Theodore Martin, Jessamyn Susanna. BA in Psychology, Fairfield U., 1976; JD, Seton Hall U., 1984. Bar: N.J. 1984, U.S. Dist. Ct. N.J. 1984, U.S. Dist. Ct. (so. and ea. dists.) N.Y. 1985, U.S. Ct. Appeals (3d cir.) 1996. Law sec. Hon. Marshall Selikoff, J.S.C., Freehold, N.J., 1984-85; assoc. McElroy, Deutsch & Mulvaney, Morristown, 1985-88, Bumgardner, Hardin & Ellis, Springfield, 1988-90; ptnr. Tompkins McGuire & Wachenfeld, Newark, 1990-97; trial counsel Caron McCormick Constants & Wilson, Rutherford, N.J., 1997—; mediator Superior Ct. N.J., 1999—. Trustee Abdol H. Islami M.D. Found. for Med. Edn. Mem. ABA, N.J. Bar Assn., N.J. Bar Found. (trustee 1995-99, treas. 1999-2001, second v.p. 2001—), Am. Inns of Ct. (Justice William Brennan Jr. chpt.; master Seton Hall Law Alumni chpt., Marie L. Garibaldi chpt.), Essex County Bar Assn. Avocations: reading, sports. Alternative dispute resolution, General civil litigation, Insurance. Home: 3 Birchmont Ln Warren NJ 07059-5437 Office: 201 Route 17 Rutherford NJ 07070-2574

HENSLEIGH, HOWARD EDGAR, lawyer; b. Blanchard, Iowa, Oct. 29, 1920; s. Albert Dales and Eula Fern (Bair) H.; m. Janice Lee Pedersen, Aug. 15, 1948; children: Susan Lee Hensleigh Harvey, Nancy Ann Hensleigh-Quinn, Jonathan Blair. BA, Iowa U., 1943, JD, 1947; postgrad., Columbia U., 1954-55. Bar: Iowa 1947, N.Y. 1955, Mass. 1968. Commd. U.S. Army, 1943, advanced through grades to col., 1965, ret., 1973; legal adviser U.S. Mission to NATO, Paris, 1958-60; dep. asst. gen. counsel office of Sec. Def. U.S. Govt., Washington, 1960-67, dep. asst. to sec. treas., 1967-68; asst. gen. counsel Raytheon Co., Bedford, Mass., 1968-91, ret., 1991; pvt. practice Carlisle, 1991—. Participated in U.S. Italy Internat. Ct. Justice, The Hague, 1989. Chmn. town com. Carlisle Reps., 1972-80, sch. com. Carlisle, 1973-75, bd. selectmen, 1977-80. Mem. ABA (chmn. region I), Fed. Bar Assn., Am. Soc. Internat. Law. Government contracts and claims, Private international, Public international. Home and Office: 50 School St Carlisle MA 01741-1709 E-mail: hhensleigh@earthlink.net

HENSON, HAROLD EUGENE, lawyer; b. Belleville, Kans., May 31, 1932; s. Charles Nelson and Alice Marie (Harbers) H.; m. Virginia Louise Hurtig, Aug. 4, 1958; children— Rebecca Ann, Christopher Eric. B.A., U. Kans., 1954, LL.B., 1959. Bar: Kans. 1959, Mo. 1965; C.L.U. Trust officer Commerce Trust Co., Kansas City, Mo., 1960-63; atty. BusinessMens Assurance Co., Kansas City, 1963-66, counsel, 1966-72, assoc. gen. counsel, 1972-80, v.p., gen. counsel, 1980-87, cons., 1987—. Served to 1st lt. USAF, 1954-56. Mem. ABA, Mo. Bar Assn., Kansas City Bar Assn., Am. Council Life Ins., Assn. Life Ins. Counsel, Lawyers Assn. Kansas City, Phi Delta Phi. Republican. Methodist. General corporate, Insurance. Home: 7905 Dearborn Dr Shawnee Mission KS 66208-4820 Office: Bus Mens Assurance Co PO Box 419458 Kansas City MO 64141-6458

HENTULA, ISMO TAPANI, lawyer; b. Turku, Finland, Oct. 22, 1960; s. Unto Aleksander and Katri (Tuulikki) H.; m. Irene Katariina Parssinen, Nov. 11, 1967; children: Eero, Lauri, Taneli. LLM, Helsinki U., 1985; eMBA, Helsinki U. Tech., Espoo, Finland, 1996. Assoc. Procopé & Hornborg Law Offices, Helsinki, 1992-97, ptnr., 1997—, mng. ptnr., 2000—. Mem. commn. on fin. svcs. and ins. ICC, 1997-2000. Finnish Cultural Found. scholar, 1985. Mem. Finnish Bar Assn., Internat. Bar Assn. General corporate, Mergers and acquisitions, Securities. Home: Ristiniementie 32 L 54 Espoo 02320 Finland Office: Procope & Hornborg Law Ofcs Mannerheimintie 20B Helsinki 00100 Finland Fax: 35896948651. E-mail: ismo.hentula@procope-hornborg.fi

HERALD, J. PATRICK, lawyer; b. Latrobe, Pa., Sept. 27, 1947; s. John P. and Doris Faye (Galvin) H.; m. Bridget Grace Tobin, Aug. 17, 1973; children: Brian Michael, Matthew Patrick, Molly Bridget, John Francis. AB in History, John Carroll U., 1969; JD, U. Notre Dame, 1972. Bar: Ill. 1972, U.S. Dist. Ct. (no. dist.) Ill. 1972, U.S. Ct. Appeals (7th cir.) 1975, U.S. Supreme Ct. 1978. Assoc. Baker & McKenzie, Chgo., 1972-79, ptnr., 1979—. Fellow Am. Coll. Trial Lawyers; mem. ABA, Ill. Bar Assn., Chgo. Bar Assn., 7th Cir. Bar Assn., Soc. Trial Lawyers (bd. dirs. 1987-89), Internat. Assn. Def. Counsel, Chgo. Trial Lawyers Club (pres. 1982-83). Roman Catholic. Federal civil litigation, General civil litigation, State civil litigation. Home: 1721 N Normandy Ave Chicago IL 60707-3925 Office: Baker & McKenzie 1 Prudential Plz 130 E Randolph St Fl 3500 Chicago IL 60601-6213 E-mail: j.patrick.herald@bakernet.com

HERAUF, WILLIAM ANTON, lawyer; b. Dickinson, N.D., Feb. 26, 1957; s. Herbert Henry and Nancy Dann (Rabe) H.; m. Joan Thompson, May 17, 1986. BSBA, U. N.D., 1979, JD, 1982. Bar: N.D. 1982, Minn. 1982, U.S. Dist. Ct. N.D. 1982. Assoc. Mackoff, Kellogg, Kirby & Kloster, Dickinson, 1982-84; corp. atty. Multi Nat. Diving Educators Assn., Marathon, Fla., 1984-89; asst. city atty. City of Dickinson, 1985-90; assoc. Ficek Law Office, Dickinson, 1985-90; state's atty. Slope County, N.D., 1985-87. Fireman Dickinson Vol. Fire Dept., 1985-88; bd. dirs. Dickinson Underwater Search and Recovery Team, 1985-88. Mem. ABA (Bronze Key 1982, bd. govs. cert. 1982), N.D. Trial Lawyers Assn. (bd. dirs. 1985—, treas. 1988-89, sec. 1989-90, pres. elect 1990-91, pres. 1991-92), Assn. Trial Lawyers Am., Stark County Bar Assn. Methodist. Lodge: Elks. Avocations: skiing, scuba diving, running, swimming, reading. State civil litigation, General practice, Personal injury. Home: 1055 5th Ave W Dickinson ND 58601-3836 Office: Reichert Herauf PC 34 1st St SE # K Dickinson ND 58601-5612

HERB, F(RANK) STEVEN, lawyer; b. Cin., Nov. 9, 1949; s. Frank X. and Jean M. (Zurcher) H.; m. Jean L. Jeffers, June 21, 1971; children: Tracy Lynn, Jacquelyn Anne. BS, Bowling Green U., 1971; JD, U. Cin., 1974. Bar: Ohio 1974, Fla. 1978, U.S. Dist. Ct. (no., mid., and so. dists.) Fla., U.S. Ct. Appeals (11th cir.); cert. county and cir. ct. mediator, Fla. Supreme Ct. Assoc. Connaughton Law Offices, Hamilton, Ohio, 1974; jud. advocate gen., chief of civil law USAF, Tyndall AFB, Fla., 1975-78; mng. ptnr. Nelson Hesse, Sarasota, 1979—. Author: (with others) Bennedicts on Admiralty, 1996, 97, 98; contbr. chpts. to books. Bd. dirs. Brock Wilson Found., Sarasota, 1983-92; pres. Riegels Landing Assn., Sarasota, 1986-90, 98-2000; dir., vice chmn. Siesta Key Utilities Assn., 1994—; mem. govt. rels. com. Nat. Marine Mfrs. Assn. Capt. JAGC USAF, 1975-78. Decorated USAF Meritorious Svc. medal. Mem. Ohio Bar Assn., Fla. Bar Assn. (chmn. 12th Jud. cir. unauthorized practice of law com. 1986-93, fee arbitration com. 12th jud. cir. 1996—), Sarasota Bar Assn., Def. Rsch. Inst., Maritime Law Assn., Am. Boat and Yacht Counsel, Nat. Marine Mfrs. Assn. (govt. rels. com.), The Field Club (dir. exec. com.). Republican. Roman Catholic. Avocations: boating, woodworking, skiing, tennis. Admiralty, General corporate, Product liability. Office: Nelson Hesse 2070 Ringling Blvd Sarasota FL 34237-7002

HERBERT, DAVID LEE, lawyer, author; b. Cleve., Oct. 1, 1948; s. William Clayton and Virginia Margaret (Battersby) H.; m. Lynda Jane Rosenkranz, Aug. 23, 1970; children: Laurance, Jason, Meredith. BBA, Kent State U., 1971; JD, U. Akron, 1974. Bar: Ohio 1974, U.S. Dist. Ct. (no. dist.) Ohio 1974, U.S. Ct. Appeals (6th cir.) 1984. Asst. prosecutor Stark County Prosecutors Office, Canton, Ohio, 1974-80; ptnr. Herbert & Benson, 1975—. Pres. Profl. Reports Corp., 1986—; assoc. prof. Kent State U., Ohio, 1980-87; sec., asst. chmn. Ohio Govs. Organized Crime Law Enforcement Cons. Com., Columbus, 1976-78; sec. Stark County Pub. Defender Com., Canton, 1982-87. Author: Attorneys' Master Guide to Psychology, 1980, Legal Aspects of Preventive and Rehabilitative Exercise Programs, 1984, Corporations of Corruption: The Systematic Study of Organized Crime, 1984, Legal Aspects of Sports Medicine, 1990, others; editor The Exercise Stds. and Malpractice Reporter, 1986—, The Sports Medicine Stds. and Malpractice Reporter; contbr. articles to profl. jours. Pres., trustee Lake Twp. Trustees, Hartville, Ohio, 1983-87; bd. dirs. Stark County Jr. Achievement, Canton, 1983; mentor pupil enrichment program Lake Local Sch. Bd., Hartville, 1981-85. Recipient Continuing Legal Edn. award ABA/Am. Law Inst., 1975 Mem. ABA (liaison to jud. adminstrn. divsn. 1972-73), Am. Arbitration Assn. (comml. arbitrator 1983—), Def. Rsch. Inst., Am. Coll. Sports Medicine, Stark County Trustees and Clks. Assn., Stark County Bar Assn. (exec. com. 1984, grievance com. 1979-82), Akron/Canton Def. Lawyers Assn., Ducks Unltd., North Canton Jaycees (com. chmn. 1975-76). State civil litigation, General corporate, Insurance. Home: 1055 Clearvale St NE Hartville OH 44632-9463 Office: Herbert & Benson 4571 Stephen Cir NW Canton OH 44718-3633 E-mail: herblegal@aol.com

HERBST, ABBE ILENE, lawyer; b. N.Y.C., June 19, 1955; d. Seymour and Charlotte (Wolper) H. BA summa cum laude, Fordham U., 1976, JD, 1979. Bar: N.Y. 1980, N.J. 1980, U.S. Supreme Ct. 1986. Law clk. Keenan, Powers & Andrews, N.Y.C., 1978-79, assoc., 1980-83, DeForest & Duer, N.Y.C., 1983-90, ptnr., 1991—. Editor: Fordham Urban Law Journal, 1978-79. Recipient Outstanding Presentation award Cmty. Svc. Soc., N.Y.C., 1986. Mem. ABA, N.Y. State Bar Assn., N.J. State Bar Assn., N.Y. County Lawyers Assn., Fin. Women's Assn. N.Y., Riverdale Mental Health Assn., Phi Beta Kappa. Avocations: travel, collecting miniature cat figurines. Estate planning, Probate, Estate taxation. Office: DeForest & Duer 90 Broad St Fl 18 New York NY 10004-2276

HERBST, TODD L. lawyer; b. N.Y.C., July 15, 1952; s. Seymour and Charlotte (Wolper) H.; m. Robyn Beth Kellman, June 3, 1979; children: Scott Marshall, Carly Nicole. BA, CUNY, 1974; JD, John Marshall Law Sch., 1977. Bar: N.Y. 1978. Assoc. Max E. Greenberg, Cantor & Reiss, N.Y.C., 1977-83, mng. ptnr., 1984-87; sr. ptnr. Max E. Greenberg, Trager, Toplitz & Herbst, 1988—. Bus. cons. Shimizu Corp., U.S., 1983—, NTT Internat. Corp., Japan and U.S., 1996—, Dillingham Constrn. Holdings, Inc., San Francisco, 1987—, Gottlieb Skanska, Inc., N.Y.C., 1980—, Jolly Hotels, Italy, 1993—, Legal Commentary UPN News, N.Y.; lectr. Nat. Assn. Corp. Real Estate Execs. Exec. editor John Marshall Law Rev. Mem. ABA (A/V rated), Am. Inst. Archs., N.Y. State Bar Assn., Am. Corp. Counsel Assn., N.Y. County Lawyers Assn. Avocations: writing poetry, automobiles. Contracts commercial, Construction, Real property. Home: 7 Brookwood Ln New City NY 10956-2203 Office: Max E Greenberg Trager Toplitz & Herbst 100 Church St New York NY 10007-2601 E-mail: tlh@megbuildlaw.com

HERCHENROETHER, PETER YOUNG, lawyer; b. Pitts., Apr. 14, 1954; s. Henry C. and Nell E. (Young) H.; m. Susan E. Suomi, Aug. 4, 1979; children: Gregory A., Emily A. BA, Westminster Coll., 1976; JD, Vanderbilt U., 1979. Bar: Pa. 1979, U.S. Dist. Ct. (we. dist.) Pa. 1979, U.S. Ct. Appeals (3d cir.) 1984, U.S. Supreme Ct. 1985. Mem. Alter, Wright & Barron, Pitts., 1979-90, Sherrard, German & Kelly, P.C., Pitts., 1990—. Mem. Pa. Bar Assn., Allegheny County Bar Assn. Republican. Presbyterian. General corporate, General practice, Probate. Office: Sherrard German & Kelly PC FreeMarkets Ctr 35th Fl Pittsburgh PA 15222-2600

HERDEG, JOHN ANDREW, lawyer; b. Buffalo, Sept. 15, 1937; s. Franklin Leland and Susannah Estelle (Clark) H.; m. Judith Coolidge Carpenter, June 24, 1961; children: Judith Leland Herdeg Wilson, Andrew Carpenter Herdeg, Fell Coolidge Herdeg. BA, Princeton U., 1959; LLB, U. Pa., 1962. Bar: Conn. 1963, Del. 1964. Atty. Wilmington (Del.) Trust Co., 1963-75, sr. v.p. in charge of trust dept., 1975-85, bd. dirs., chmn. trust com., corp. sec., 1977-85; pres. Herdeg & Assocs., Wilmington, 1986-98; ptnr. Herdeg, duPont & Dalle Pazze, LLP, 1999—. Co-founder, chmn. bd. dirs. Christiana Bank & Trust Co., Greenville, Del., 1992—. Bd. trustees Henry Francis duPont Winterthur (Del.) Mus., 1970—, chmn., 1977-86; trustee Med. Ctr. of Del., Stanton, 1965—; supr. Pennsbury Twp., Chester County, Pa., 1968-74; mem. Westminster Presbyn. Ch. Mem. Wilmington Club (bd. govs. 1997—, treas. 1999—), Vicmead Hunt Club (bd. govs. 1977-84), Walpole Soc., Confrerie des Chevalier du Tastevin, Mill Reef Club, West Chop Club, Mill Reef Club. Avocations: tennis, photography, decorative arts. Estate planning, Probate, Estate taxation. Home: PO Box 216 Mendenhall PA 19357-0216 Office: Herdeg DuPont & Dalle Pazze LLP 12th & Orange St Ste 500 Wilmington DE 19801-1140 E-mail: jherdeg@dellaw.com

HERGE, J. CURTIS, lawyer; b. Flushing, N.Y., June 14, 1938; s. Henry Curtis and Josephine E. (Breen) H.; m. Joyce Dorean Humbert, Aug. 20, 1960 (div. 1988); children: Cynthia Lynda, Christopher Curtis; m. Shirley Brooks Labonte, Dec. 22, 1989. Student, Cornell U., 1956-58; BA, Rutgers U., 1961, JD, 1963. Bar: N.Y. 1964, U.S. Supreme Ct. 1970, U.S. Ct. Claims 1974, D.C. 1974, Va. 1976. Assoc. Mudge Rose Guthrie & Alexander, N.Y.C., 1963-71; spl. asst. to atty. gen. U.S. Dept. Justice, Washington, 1973; assoc. solicitor conservation and wildlife U.S. Dept. Interior, 1973-74, asst. to sec. and chief staff, 1974-76; ptnr. Sedam & Herge, McLean, Va., 1976-85, Herge, Sparks & Christopher LLP, McLean, 1985—. Bd. dirs. Diversified Labs., Inc., Ann E.W. Stone & Assocs., Inc., Palmer Tech. Svcs., Inc., Eaton Design Group, Inc., George Washington Banking Corp., Eaton Purchase Mgmt., Inc., George Washington Nat. Bank, Congl. Inst. Inc., Citizens United for Am., Am. Def. Lobby, Coun. Nat. Def., Renascence Found., The Am. Lobby Econ. Recovery Taskforce, Nat. Bank No. Va., Am. Freedom Found., Creative Response Concepts Inc., Congl. Inst., Inc.; spkr. in field. Adv. bd. Washington Legal Found., Nat. Taxpayers Legal Fund; Va. Commonwealth escheator Loudoun

County and City of Fairfax, 1979-83; co-dir. spokesmen resources Com. for Re-election of Pres., 1971-72; mem. No. Va. Estate Planning Council; mem. natural resources coun. Rep. Nat. Com.; mem. Fairfax County Rep. Com., Conservative Rep. Com.; mem. Office Pres.-Elect Fed. Election Commn. Transition Team, 1980; co-chmn. N.Y. Honor Am. Day, 1970; expert witness, charitable fund-raising, U.S. Tax Ct. Sebastian Gaeta scholar Rutgers U., 1963. Mem. ABA, N.Y. State Bar Assn., Va. Bar Assn., D.C. Bar Assn., Capitol Hill Club, Phi Kappa Sigma. Club: Capitol Hill. Administrative and regulatory, Non-profit and tax-exempt organizations, Probate. Home: 35 Rutherford Cir Potomac Falls VA 20165-6221 Office: Herge Sparks & Christopher LLP 6862 Elm St Ste 360 Mc Lean VA 22101-3867

HERLONG, HENRY MICHAEL, JR. federal judge; b. Washington, June 1, 1944; s. Henry Michael Sr. and Josie Payne (Blocker) H.; m. Frances Elizabeth Thompson, Dec. 30, 1983; children: Faris Elizabeth, Henry Michael III. BA, Clemson U., 1967; JD, U. S.C., 1970. Bar: S.C. 1970, U.S. Ct. Appeals (4th cir.) 1972, U.S. Dist. Ct. S.C. 1972. Legis. asst. U.S. Senator Strom Thurmond, Washington, 1970-72; asst. U.S. atty. Dept. Justice, Greenville, S.C., 1972-76, Columbia, 1983-86; U.S. Magistrate judge U.S. Dist. Ct., 1986-91, U.S. Dist. judge Greenville, 1991—; prin. Coleman & Herlong, Edgefield, 1976-83. Dir. Edgefield (S.C.) Devel. Bd., 1978-83, S.C. Assn. of Counties, 1980-83; active S.C. Rural Devel. Bd., 1980-83, Edgefield County Coun., 1979-83. Capt. USAR, 1970-75. Mem. S.C. Bar, Edgefield County Bar, Lions Club, Sertoma Club. Republican. United Methodist. Avocations: hunting, fishing, gardening. Office: US Dist Courts PO Box 10469 300 E Washington St Greenville SC 29603-1000

HERMAN, CHARLES JACOB, lawyer, accounting firm executive; b. Balt., May 31, 1937; s. Jacob and Edna M. (Hackett) H.; m. Frances L. Leonard, Oct. 25, 1958; children— Alison, Charles J., Leonard. B.A., U. Balt., 1958, J.D., 1961. Bar: Md. 1961. Atty. Fidelity & Deposit, N.Y.C., 1958-69, Aetna Ins. Co., Hartford, Conn., 1969-71, INA, Phila., 1971-76; officer Home Ins. Co., N.Y.C., 1976-80; nat. ptnr., dir. litigation support services Laventhol & Horwath, Phila., 1980—; ptnr. Margolis Edelstein Scherles and Kraemer; founder, chief exec. officer Curtis Cons. Group Ltd. Co-author: (manual) Bonds on Public Works, 1986. Past pres. St. John's Lutheran Ch., Morrisville, Pa; bd. dirs. Luth. Home, Germantown, Germantown Home. Served to sgt. U.S. Army, 1961-66. Mem. ABA, Internat. Assn. Ins. Counsel, Am. Arbitration Assn., Md. Bar Assn. Republican. Lutheran. State civil litigation, Contracts commercial, Insurance. Home: 957 Randolph Dr Morrisville PA 19067-4207 Office: Curtis Cons Group Ltd The Curtis Ctr 4th Fl Independence Sq W Philadelphia PA 19106

HERMAN, FRED L. lawyer; b. New Orleans, Mar. 25, 1950; s. Harry and Reba (Hoffman) H.; m. Amanda Luria, Mar. 4, 1975. BA, Tulane U., 1972; JD, Loyola U.-New Orleans, 1975. Bar: La. 1975, U.S. Dist Ct. (ea. dist.) La. 1975, U.S. Ct. Appeals (5th cir.) 1978, U.S. Dist. Ct. (we. and mid. dists.) La. 1981, U.S. Ct. Appeals (11th cir.) 1981. Assoc. Herman & Herman, New Orleans, 1975-80; ptnr. Herman, Herman, Katz & Cotlar, 1980-87; sole practice, 1987—; of counsel Garner and Munoz, Attys. at Law, 1988—. Ltd. ptnr. New Orleans Saints, 1985, legis. counsel, chief negotiator for mng. ptnr., 1987; adj. faculty Tulane U.; lectr. Loyola Sch. Law, New Orleans, La. Trial Lawyers Assn. Commr. New Orleans Pub. Belt R.R. Commn., 1983-93; mem. Jefferson Parish Child Abuse Advocacy Program, 1980-81; spl. counsel litigation, State of La.; spl. counsel City of New Orleans; judge pro tem., First City Ct., New Orleans, 1998; mem. adv. coun. Adult Rehab. Ctr. Salvation Army, 1991—. Mem. ATLA, Am. Arbitration Assn. (mediator, arbitrator), Nat. Health Lawyer Assn. (panel of mediators and arbitrators), Fed. Bar Assn. (bank counsel sect.), La. Bankers' Assn., La. State Bar Assn. General civil litigation, General practice, Personal injury. Office: 1010 Common St Ste 3000 New Orleans LA 70112-2421

HERMAN, SIDNEY N. lawyer; b. Chgo., May 14, 1953; s. Leonard M. and Suzanne (Nierman) H.; m. Meg Dobies. BA, Haverford Coll., 1975; JD, Northwestern U., 1978. Bar: Ill. 1978, U.S. Dist. Ct. (no. dist.) Ill. 1978, U.S. Ct. Appeals (7th cir.) 1982, U.S. Supreme Ct. 1983. Assoc. Kirkland & Ellis, Chgo., 1978-84, equity ptnr., 1984-93; founding ptnr. Bartlit Beck Herman Palenchar & Scott, 1993—. Bd. dirs. Todd Shipyards Corp., Sigmatron, Inc., Chgo., Am. Steel Wool Mfg., Inc., Chgo. Articles editor Northwestern U. Law Rev. Trustee Francis W. Parker Sch. Mem. ABA, Ill. Bar Assn. Jewish. Federal civil litigation, General civil litigation, Libel. Office: Bartlit Beck Et Al Courthouse Pl 54 W Hubbard St Ste 300 Chicago IL 60610-4668

HERMAN, STEPHEN CHARLES, lawyer; b. Johnson City, N.Y., Apr. 28, 1951; s. William Herman and Myrtle Stella (Clark) Keithline; m. Jeanne Ellen Nelson, Sept. 9, 1972; children: Neelie Kristine, Stefanie Anne, Christopher William. Student, Cedarville Coll., 1969-72; BA, Wright State U., 1973; JD, Ohio No. U., 1976. Bar: Mo. 1977, Ill. 1977; U.S. Dist. Ct. (ea. dist.) Mo. 1978, U.S. Dist. Ct. (no. dist.) Ill. 1979, U.S. Dist. Ct. (ea. dist) Mich. 1988, U.S. Dist. Ct. (so. dist.) Tex. 1997; U.S. Ct. Appeals (D.C. cir.) 1979, U.S. Ct. Appeals (7th cir.) 1979, U.S. Ct. Appeals (5th cir.) 1980, U.S. Ct. Appeals (10th cir.) 1992; U.S. Supreme Ct. 1986, U.S. Ct. Internat. Trade, 1998. Atty. Mo. Pacific Railroad Co., St. Louis, 1977-78; assoc. Belnap, McCarthy, Spencer, Sweeney & Harkaway, Chgo., 1978-82; ptnr. Belnap, Spencer & McFarland, 1982-83, Belnap, Spencer, McFarland & Emrich, Chgo., 1983-84, Belnap, Spencer, McFarland, Emrich & Herman, Chgo., 1984-89, Belnap, Spencer, McFarland, Herman, 1990-96, McFarland & Herman, 1996-01; atty. Stephen C. Herman, P.C., Chgo., 2001—. Mem. ABA, Mo. Bar Assn., Met. Bar Assn. St. Louis, Ill. State Bar Assn., Chgo. bar Assn., Assn. Transp. Law, Logistics and Policy, Tower Club, Univ. Club (Chgo.). General civil litigation, Transportation, General practice. Home: 795 N Mckinley Rd Lake Forest IL 60045-1836 Office: 20 N Wacker Dr Ste 1828 Chicago IL 60606-2905 E-mail: schrmn@aol.com

HERMAN, WILLIAM CHARLES, lawyer; b. N.Y.C., Nov. 6, 1935; s. Milton and Hortense (Rosenthal) H.; m. Elizabeth Leitner; children: Howard, Sarah Jane (dec.). BA, CCNY, 1958; LLB, Columbia U., 1959. Bar: N.Y. 1960, U.S. Dist. Ct. (so. and ea. dists.) 1964, U.S. Ct. Appeals (2d cir.) 1964, U.S. Supreme Ct. 1964. Assoc. Howard H. Spellman, N.Y.C., 1960-61; pvt. practice law, 1962-65; assoc. Gilbert S. Rosenthal, 1965-70; ptnr. Rosenthal & Herman, 1970-82, Rosenthal, Herman & Mantel, P.C., N.Y.C., 1982-94, Rosenthal & Herman, P.C., N.Y.C., 1994—. Bd. dirs., Camphill Spl. Schs., Inc., Glenmoore, Pa., 1980—; bd. dirs. Camphill Found., Kimberton, Pa., 1987—; trustee Camphill Assn., N.Am., Copake, N.Y., 1982—. With U.S. Army, 1959-60. Fellow Am. Acad. Matrimonial Lawyers; mem. ABA, N.Y. State Bar Assn., N.Y. County Lawyers Assn. (bd. dirs. 1979-85, chmn. matrimonial law com. 1982-84), Am. Coll. Family Trial Lawyers (diplomate). Avocations: charitable activities, fishing, platform tennis. State civil litigation, Family and matrimonial. Home: 95 Lord Kitchner Rd New Rochelle NY 10804-2230 E-mail: rhpc8911@aol.com

HERMAN-GIDDENS, GREGORY, lawyer; b. Birmingham, Ala., Aug. 8, 1961; BA, U. N.C., 1984; JD, Tulane U., 1988; LLM in Estate Planning, U. Miami, 1993. Bar: N.C. 1988, U.S. Dist. Ct. (mid. dist.) N.C. 1988, Fla. 1992, U.S. Tax Ct. 2001, U.S. Supreme Ct. 1998, U.S. Tax Ct. 2001; cert. specialist in estate planning and probate law, N.C. State Bar Bd. Legal Specialization; grad. leadership triangle program 1996. Assoc. N. Joanne Foil, Atty. at Law, Durham, N.C., 1988-92, Catalano, Fisher, Gregory & Crown, Chartered, Naples, Fla., 1993, Northen, Blue, Rooks, Thibaut, Anderson & Woods, L.L.P., Chapel Hill, N.C., 1994-96; pvt. practice, 1996—. Profl. adv. com. Triangle Cmty. Found., 1999—. Mem. Chapel Hill Bd. Adjustment, 1989-92; bd. dirs. Friends of Chapel Hill Sr. Ctr., 1994-97; mem. Orange County Adv. Bd. on Aging, 1994-97, vice-chair, 1996-97; treas., bd. dirs. Orange County Literacy coun., Carrboro, N.C., 1994-98; mem. nat. com. on planned giving N.C. Planned Giving Coun. Mem.: ABA (coms. on stds. of tax practice and tax practice mgmt. of tax sect., coms. on lifetime and testamentary charitable gift planning, com. on planning for execs. and profls. of real property, probate and trust sect. 1996—), N.C. Bar Assn. (law and aging com. young lawyers divsn. 1994—98, elder law sect. coun. 1998—2001, career devel. com. young lawyers divsn. 1990—91, dir. young lawyers divsn. 1997—98, endowment com. 1997—), Nat. Acad. Elder Law Attys., Durham/Orange Estate Planning Coun., Phi Beta Kappa, Psi Chi. Estate planning, Probate, Estate taxation. Office: 1829 E Franklin St Ste 700D Chapel Hill NC 27514-5867 E-mail: ghigiddens@trust-specialist.com

HERMANN, DONALD HAROLD JAMES, lawyer, educator; b. Southgate, Ky., Apr. 6, 1943; s. Albert Joseph and Helen Marie (Snow) H. AB (George E. Gamble Honors scholar), Stanford U., 1965; JD, Columbia U., 1968; LLM, Harvard U., 1974; MA, Northwestern U., 1979, Ph.D., 1981; MA in Art History, Sch. Art Inst. Chgo., 1993; postgrad., U. Chgo., 1998—. Bar: Ariz. 1968, Wash. 1969, Ky. 1971, Ill. 1972, U.S. Supreme Ct. 1974. Mem. staff, directorate devel. plans U.S. Dept. Def., 1964-65; With Legis. Drafting Research Fund, Columbia U., 1966-68; asst. dean Columbia Coll., 1967-68; mem. faculty U. Wash., Seattle, 1968-71, U. Ky., Lexington, 1971-72, DePaul U., 1972—, prof. law and philosophy, 1978—, dir. acad. programs and interdisciplinary study, 1975-76, assoc. dean, 1975-78, dir. Health Law Inst., 1985—; lectr. dept. philosophy Northwestern U., 1979-81; counsel DeWolfe, Poynton & Stevens, 1984-89. Vis. prof. Washington U., St. Louis, 1974, U. Brazilia, 1976, U. P.R. Sch. Law, 1993; lectr. law Am. Soc. Found., 1975-78, Sch. Edn. Northwestern U., 1974-76, Christ Coll. Cambridge (Eng.) U., 1977, U. Athens, 1980; vis. scholar U. N.D., 1983; mem. NEH seminar on property and rights Stanford U., 1981; participant law and econs. program U. Rochester, 1974; mem. faculty summer seminar in law and humanities UCLA, 1978; Bicentennial Fellow of U.S. Constitution Claremont Coll., 1986; Law and Medicine fellow Cleve. Clinic., 1990; bd. dirs. Coun. Legal Edn. Opportunity, Ohio Valley Consortium, 1972, Ill. Bar Automated Rsch. Corp., 1975-81, Criminal Law Consortium Cook County, Ill., 1977-80; cons. Adminstrv. Office Ill. Cts., 1975-90; reporter cons. Ill. Jud. Conf., 1972-90; mem. Ctr. for Law Focused Edn., Chgo., 1977-81; faculty Instituto Superiore Internazionale Di Science Criminali, Siracusa, Italy, 1978-82; cons. Commerce Fedn., State of São Paulo, Brazil, 1975; residential scholar Christ Ch., Oxford, 1999. Editor: Jour. of Health and Hosp. Law, 1986-96, DePaul Jour. Healthcare Law, 1996—, AIDS Monograph Series, 1987—. Bd. dirs. Ctr. for Ch.-State Studies, 1982—, Horizons Cmty. Svcs., 1985-88, Chgo. Area AIDS Task Force, 1987-90, Howard Brown Health Ctr., 1994—; dir., v.p. Inst. for Genetics, Law and Ethics, Ill. Masonic Hosp., 1993—; trustee 860 N. Lakeshore Trust, Chgo., Ill., 1993-95; bd. visitors Oriental Inst., U. Chgo., 1995—, bd. dirs. Renaissance Soc., 1995—; mem. Cook County States Atty. Task Force on Drugs, 1985-90, Cook County States Atty. Task Force on Gay and Lesbian Issues, 1990—; mem. Ill. HIV Prevention Cmty. Planning Group, Ill. Dept. Pub. Health. John Noble fellow Columbia U., 1968, Internat. fellow, NEH fellow, Law and Humanities fellow U. Chgo, 1975-76, Law and Humanities fellow Harvard U., 1973-74, Northwestern U., 1978-82, Criticism and Theory fellow Stanford U. 1981, NEH fellow Cornell U., 1982, Judicial fellow U.S. Supreme Ct., 1983-84, U. Ill. fellow med. ethids rsch. group; Dean's scholar Columbia U., 1968, Univ. scholar Northwestern U., 1979. Mem. ABA, Ill. Bar Assn., Chgo. Bar Assn., Am. Acad. Polit. and Social Sci., Am. Law Inst., Am. Soc. Law, Medicine and Ethics, Am. Soc. Polit. and Legal Philosophy, Nat. Health Lawyers Assn., Am. Judicature Soc., Am. Philos. Assn., Soc. for Bus. Ethics, Soc. for Phenomenology and Existential Philosophy, Internat. Assn. Philosophy of Law and Soc., Soc. Writers on Legal Subjects, Internat. Penal Law Soc., Soc. Am. Law Tchrs., Am. Assn. Law Schs. (del., sect. chmn., chmn. sect. on jurisprudence), Am. Acad. Healthcare Attys., Ill. Assn. Hosp. Attys., Chgo. Coun. Fgn. Rels., Evanston Hist. Soc., Northwestern U. Alumni Assn., Signet Soc. of Harvard, Quadrangle Players, Hasty Pudding Club, University Club, Quadrangle Club, Tavern Club, Cliff Dwellers Club, Arts Club Chgo., Legal Club Chgo., Law Club Chgo. Episcopalian. Home: 1243 Forest Ave Evanston IL 60202-1451 Office: DePaul U Coll Law 25 E Jackson Blvd Chicago IL 60604-2287 also: 880 N Lake Shore Dr Chicago IL 60611-1761 also: 21 Nando-Machi Shinjukuko Tokyo 162 Japan

HERMANN, PHILIP J. lawyer; b. Cleve., Sept. 17, 1916; s. Isadore and Gazella (Gross) H.; m. Cecilia Alexander, Dec. 28, 1945; children: Gary, Ann. Student, Hiram Coll., 1935-37; B.A., Ohio State U., 1939; J.D., Western Res. U., 1942. Bar: Ohio 1942. With Hermann Cahn & Schneider and predecessors, Cleve., 1946-86. Founder, former chmn. bd. Jury Verdict Rsch., Cleve.; pres. Legal Info. Pubs. Author: 1956, Better Settlements Through Leverage, 1965, Do You Need a Lawyer?, 1980, Better, Earlier Settlements through Economic Leverage, 1989, Injured? How to Get All the Money You Deserve, 1990, The 96 Billion Dollar Game: You are Losing, 1993, How to Select Competent Cost-effective Legal Counsel, 1993, Profit With the Right Lawyer; contbr. articles to profl. jours. Served to lt. comdr. USNR, 1942-46, PTO. Mem. ABA (past vice chmn. casualty law com., past chmn. use of modern tech. com.), Ohio Bar Assn. (past chmn. ins. com., past chmn. fed. ct. com., past mem. ho. of dels.), Cleve. Bar Assn. (past chmn. membership com.), Am. Law Firm Assn. (past chmn. bd.), Fedn. Ins. Counsel. Club: Walden Golf and Tennis. Insurance, Personal injury, Product liability. Home: 615 Acadia St Aurora OH 44202

HERN, J. BROOKE, lawyer; b. Johnstown, Pa., May 19, 1964; s. Dennis Kay Hern and Sherrie Maureen Pesci; m. Stephanie Lynne Arnold, July 29, 1989; 1 child, Allyson Elizabeth. BA, Am. U., 1987; JD cum laude, So. Meth. U., 1998. Bar: N.J. 1998. Staff asst. U.S. Rep. Robert G. Torricelli, Hackensack, N.J., 1987; development rsch. specialist Drew U., Madison, 1987-89, coord. internal comms., 1989-91; dir. pub. affairs N.J. Dept. of Commerce, Trenton, 1991-94; chief of staff Office of N.J. Assemblyman Joseph F. Yuhas, 1994-95; assoc. Lowerstein Sandler P.C., Roseland, N.J., 1998—. Commr., designer Del. and Raritan Canal Transp. Safety Study Commn., Trenton, N.J., 1994-95; committeeman Mercer County Dem. Com., Mercer County, N.J., 1993-95; treas. Mercer County Young Dems., 1993-95. Mem. ABA, N.J. Bar Assn. Democrat. Methodist. Avocation: musician. General civil litigation, Construction, Intellectual property. Office: Lowentein Sandler PC 65 Livingston Ave Roseland NJ 07068

HERNANDEZ, DAVID N(ICHOLAS), lawyer; b. Albuquerque, Nov. 5, 1954; s. B.C. and Evangeline (C De Baca) H.; m. Alice A. McLish, June 7, 1975. BA, U. N.Mex., 1975, MBA, 1978, JD, 1979. Bar: N.Mex. 1979, U.S. Dist. Ct. N.Mex. 1979. Law clk. to presiding justice N.Mex. Supreme Ct., Santa Fe, 1979-80; assoc. Knight, Custer & Duncan, Albuquerque, 1980-82; sole practice, 1982—. Mem. com. rules appellate ct. procedure N.Mex. Supreme Ct., 1984—; bd. dirs. Delta Dental N.Mex., Albuquerque. Mem. Environ. Planning Commn., Albuquerque, 1984-86, PHS assocs. Presbyn. Healthcare Found., 1985—. Named one of Outstanding Young Men Am., 1980. Mem. ABA, N.Mex. Bar Assn. (pres. 2001-), Albuquerque Bar Assn., Am. Judicatur Soc., Greater Albuquerque C. of C. (bd. dirs. 1982-86, polit. action com. 1983-85). Avocations: tennis, golf, reading, fishing, politics. Contracts commercial, Probate, Real property.*

HERNÁNDEZ, FERNANDO VARGAS, lawyer; b. Irapuato, Mex., Sept. 8, 1939; came to U.S., 1942, naturalized, 1957; s. José Espinosa and Ana Maria (Vargas) H.; m. Bonnie Corrie, Jan. 8, 1966 (div. Feb. 1991); children: Michael David, Alexandra Rae, Marcel Paul. BS, U. Santa Clara, 1961; MBA, 1962; JD, U. Calif., Berkeley, 1966. Bar: Calif. 1967, U.S. Dist. Ct. (no. dist.) Calif. 1967. Sole practice law, San Jose, Calif., 1967—. Lectr. law Lincoln U.; lectr. bus. U. Santa Clara. Mem. San Jose Housing Bd., 1970-73; arbitrator Santa Clara County Superior Cts., 1979-99, judge pro tem, 1979—. Contbg. editor to legal pleadings books. Mem. San Jose Civic Light Opera, 1981-83. Served with AUS, 1962-63. Mem. Calif. State Bar Assn., Sant Clara County Bar Assn. (chmn. torts sect. 1977-78, features editor In Brief mag. 1990-93), Calif. Trial Lawyers Assn. (bd. govs. 1979-82), Santa Clara County Trial Lawyers Assn. (pres. elect 1981), U. Santa Clara Alumni Assn. (pres. San Jose chpt. 1977-78), La Raza Lawyers Assn., Democratic Century. Democrat. Roman Catholic. General civil litigation, Intellectual property, Personal injury. Office: 46 S 1st St San Jose CA 95113-2406 E-mail: fvhlaw@pacbell.net

HERNANDEZ, H(ERMES) MANUEL, lawyer; b. Bronx, N.Y., Mar. 16, 1955; s. Manuel and Aurora O'Neill H.; m. Hortensia Beatriz Carrasquillo, Aug. 28, 1980; children: Antonio, Victoria, Stephanie. BS in Criminal Justice magna cum laude, Met. State Coll. of Denver, 1976; JD, U. Denver, Denver, 1979. Bar: Colo. 1979, N.Y. 1986, D.C. 1986, Fla. 1988; cert. trial adv Nat. Bd. Trial Advocacy; cert. criminal trial specialist and criminal appellate specialist Fla. Bar 1993. Trial atty. criminal div. U.S. Dept. Justice, Washington, 1979-80; asst. U.S. atty. criminal and civil div. U.S. Dept. Justice (Colo., Puerto Rico, Fla. mid. dist.), 1980-89; pvt. practice Orlando, Fla., 1989—. Chmn. civilian rev. bd. Seminole County Sheriff's Office, Orlando, 1992-93. Mem. Nat. Criminal Def. Lawyers Assn., Fla. Fed. Bar Assn. (Orlando chpt., v.p. 1988-89, pres. 1989-90, 90-91, 99—, nat. del. 1991, 92, 93), Fla. Bar, Fla. Assn. Criminal Def. Lawyers, Hispanic Bar Assn. (charter mem. Orlando chpt.), Ctrl. Fla. Criminal Trial Lawyers Assn.. Republican. Roman Catholic. Avocations: music, history. Appellate, Federal civil litigation, Criminal. Office: 646 E Colonial Dr Orlando FL 32803-4603

HERNANDEZ, JUAN IGNACIO, lawyer; b. Torreon, Mex., May 13, 1954; s. Pascual Hernandez and Juana Guerra; m. Carolina Zambrano; children: Carolina, Ana Gabriela, Elizabeth. Mem. Assn. Nat. Abodagos de Emprza, Barra de Abogadis, Anade Seccion Comarca Lagunera (pres. 1996-98). Avocations: tennis, fishing. Banking, General civil litigation, General corporate. Office: Corp Juridico Ocampo 601 Oriente Coahuila CP 27000 Mexico Fax: (1) 7-17-75-44. E-mail: lic_hernandezguerra@hotmail.com

HERNANDEZ, JUAN LUIS, lawyer; b. Lima, Peru, Jan. 10, 1971; s. Luis and Aida (Gazzo) H.; m. Claudia Bernos, July 2, 1997. BA, Cath. U., Lima, 1994, JD, 1995; LLM, Harvard U., 1998. Lawyer-ptnr. Luis Hernandez Berenguel Law Firm, Lima, 1994—; legal asst. CONASEV, 1994; prof. comml. law Pacifico U., 1996; internat. assoc. Shearman & Sterling, N.Y.C., 1998-99; prof. corp. law Cath. U., Lima, 1996—. Contbr. articles to profl. jours. Fulbright scholar, 1997. Mem. Peruvian Inst. Corp. Law, Peruvian Inst. Tax Law, Ius et Veritas (exec. dir. 1994). Avocations: tennis, squash, soccer. General corporate, Mergers and acquisitions, Securities. Home: Manuel Tovar 647 Dpto 301 Miraflores Lima 18 Peru Office: Luis Hernandez Berenguel Av Javier Prado Oeste 795 Mag de Mar Lima 27 Peru Office Fax: 051-4615824. E-mail: jlhernandez@lhbabog.com.pe

HERNANDEZ, MACK RAY, lawyer; b. Austin, Tex., Sept. 8, 1944; s. Mack and Mary (Prado) Hernandez; 1 child John Christopher ; m. Jayne Webb Barrett, Aug. 02, 2001. BA, U. Tex., 1967, JD, 1970. Bar: Tex. 1970, U.S. Dist. Ct. (we. dist.) Tex. 1972. Staff atty. Travis County Legal Aid Soc, Austin, 1970-71; pvt. practice, 1971—. Bd. dirs. Austin C. of C., 1983-86, Meals on Wheels, Austin, 1972-76; trustee Austin C.C., 1988—; vice-chair, 1990-92, chair, 1992-94; chmn. bd. dirs. Am. Cancer Soc., Austin, 1988-95; trustee Austin Mus. Art, 2000—. Mem. Tex. Bar Assn., Travis County Bar Assn., Coll. of State Bar, Tex. Bar Found. Avocations: travel, jogging, hiking, backpacking. State civil litigation, Contracts commercial, Probate. Office: 524 N Lamar Blvd Ste 202 Austin TX 78703-5422 E-mail: mrhernandez@hernandezlaw.com

HERNANDEZ-DENTON, FEDERICO, supreme court justice; b. Santurce, P.R., Apr. 12, 1944; s. Federico and Teresa (Denton) Hernandez-Morales; m. Isabel Pico, 1966. BA, Harvard U., 1966, JD, 1969. Bar: P.R. 1971. Dir. Consumer Rsch. Ctr. and Bus. Adminstrn. Rsch. Ctr. U. P.R., 1970-72; dir. P.R. Consumer Svc. Adminstrn., 1973; sec. P.R. Dept. Consumer Affairs, 1973-76; asst. prof. Law Sch. Interam. U., P.R., 1977-84, dean, 1984-85; now justice Supreme Ct. P.R, San Juan. Chair Bd. Bar Examiners. Mem. ABA, Am. Law Inst., P.R. Bar Assn. Office: Supreme Ct of PR PO Box 9022392 San Juan PR 00902-2392

HEROLD, KARL GUENTER, lawyer; b. Munich, Feb. 3, 1947; came to U.S., 1963; s. Guenter K.B. and Eleonore E.E. H.; children: Deanna, Donna, Nicole, Jessica, Christine, Karl-Matthäus. BS, Bowling Green State U., 1969; JD, Case Western Res. U., 1972. Bar: Ohio 1972, N.Y. 1985; avocat, France, 1992; mem. Anwaltskamaret, Frankfurt, Germany. Ptnr.-in-charge, European bus. practice coord. Jones, Day, Reavis & Pogue, Frankfurt, Germany, 1972—, coord. bus. practice Europe and Ctrl. and Ea. Europe. Trustee Internat. and Comparative Law Ctr. Southwest Legal Found., Dallas, 1983; bd. dirs. Didier Taylor Refractories Corp., Cin., Redland Corp., San Antonio, v.p., Redland Credit Corp., San Antonio, v.p., Redland Fin. Inc., San Antonio, v.p., 1979-86, Zircoa Inc., Solon, Ohio, 1988-92. Contbr. numerous articles to legal jours. Trustee Cleve. Internat. Program, 1982-88; chmn. bd. dirs. Frankfurt Internat. Sch., 1991-93. Mem. ABA, Internat. Bar Assn., Order of Coif, Omicron Delta Kappa. General corporate, Private international. Office: Jones Day Reavis & Pogue 599 Lexington Ave Fl C1A New York NY 10022-6030 also: Jones Day Reavis & Pogue Hochhaus am Park Grueneburg Weg 60323 Frankfurt Germany E-mail: RGHerold@JonesDay.com

HERON, JULIAN BRISCOE, JR. lawyer; b. Washington, Dec. 17, 1939; s. Julian B. Sr. and Doris S. (Strange) H.; m. Kathleen Ann Sweeney, Aug. 13, 1983; children: Kimberle, Melissa, Julian III, Kevin, Kathleen. BS, U. Ky., 1962, LLB, 1965. Bar: Ky. 1965, D.C. 1966, U.S. Dist. Ct. D.C. 1966, Md. 1968, U.S. Ct. Appeals (D.C. cir.) 1968, U.S. Supreme Ct. 1968. Ptnr. Pope, Ballard & Loos, Washington, 1968-81, Heron, Burchette, Ruckert & Rothwell, Washington, 1981-90, Tuttle, Taylor & Heron, Washington, 1990—. Chmn. U.S. Agrl. Export Devel. Coun., 1983-85. Pres. Washington Internat. Horse Show, 1984, 85, Nat. Horse Show, 1994-96; mem. Dominican 3d Order Preachers. Capt. USAF, 1965-68. Fellow ABA (chmn. agr. com. of adminstrv. law sect.); mem. D.C. Bar Assn. (chmn. ethics com.), Ky. Bar Assn., Md. Bar Assn., Bar Assn. D.C., Barristers, Va. Angus Assn. (bd. dirs., treas. 2000—), Faquier Springs Country Club, KC, Knight of the Equestrian Order of the Holy Sepulchre of Jerusalem. Republican. Roman Catholic. Administrative and regulatory, Private international, Legislative. Office: Tuttle Taylor & Heron Ste 407 1025 Thomas Jefferson St NW Washington DC 20007-5201

HERPE, DAVID A. lawyer; b. Chgo., May 2, 1953; s. Richard S. and Beverly H.; m. Tina Demsetz, Aug. 21, 1977; children: Lauren E., Stacy P. BA in Econs., U. Ill., 1975; JD, U. Chgo., 1978. Bar: Ill. 1978, U.S. Dist. Ct. (no. dist.) Ill. 1979, U.S. Tax Ct. 1991. Assoc. then ptnr. Schiff, Hardin & Waite, Chgo., 1978-1996; ptnr. McDermott, Will & Emery, 1996—. Co-author: Illinois Estate Planning, Will Drafting and Estate Administration Forms-Practice, 2nd edit., 1994; contbr. articles to legal jours. Mem. and dir. Chgo. Estate Planning Coun. (pres. 2000-01). Fellow Am. Coll. of Trust and Estate Counsel; mem. ABA. Estate planning, Probate, Estate taxation. Office: McDermott Will & Emery 227 W Monroe St Ste 3100 Chicago IL 60606-5096

HERR, BRUCE, lawyer; b. Chgo., Aug. 12, 1943; s. Ross and Emilie (Robert) H.; m. Ellen Epstein, Feb. 22, 1968; children: Sarah, Rachel. BA cum laude, Harvard U., 1965, JD, 1968. Bar: N. Mex. 1969, Ill. 1970, U.S. Dist. Ct. N. Mex. 1969, U.S. Ct. Appeals (10th cir.) 1969, U.S. Supreme Ct. 1973. Staff atty. DNA Legal Svcs., Shiprock, N. Mex., 1969-70, Appellate Defender Project, Springfield, Ill., 1970-73; legal dir. Office of Ill. Appellate Defender, 1973; appellate defender N. Mex. Pub. Defender Dept., Santa Fe, 1973-76; assoc., shareholder Montgomery & Andrews, PA, 1976-99, of counsel, 1999-2000; with Office Lab. Counsel, Los Alamos Nat. Lab., 2000—. Mem. N. Mex. Supreme Ct. Com. on Civil Procedure Rules, 1983-98, chair, 1996-98, chair task force on electronic filing, 1994-96; mem. adv. opinions com. N. Mex. State Bar, 1985-88, 96—, chair employment and labor law sect., 1994-95. Pres. Friends of Santa Fe Pub. Libr., 1997-98; tutor Literacy Vols. Santa Fe, 1996—; bd. dirs. Santa Fe Bus. Incubator, Inc., 1995-96; v.p. Santa Fe Econ. Devel., Inc., 1999-2000. Lifetime hon. bd. mem. Santa Fe Bus. Incubator, Inc., 1996. Mem. ABA, First Jud. Dist. Bar Assn., Oliver Seth Am. Inn of Ct., Santa Fe County C. of C. (dir. 1992-96, chair 1995-96, Bd. Mem. of Yr. 1993-94). Avocations: running, hiking, reading, community activities. Civil rights, General civil litigation, Labor. Home: 148 Elena St # A Santa Fe NM 87501-6528 Office: Los Alamos Nat Lab PO Box 1663 MS A-187 Los Alamos NM 87545-0001 E-mail: herr@lanl.gov

HERR, STANLEY SHOLOM, law educator; b. Newark, Aug. 7, 1945; s. Louis J. and Ruth G. (Greenberg) H.; m. Raquel Schuster, June 17, 1979; children: David Louis, Deborah Ann, Ilana Ruth. BA cum laude, Yale U., 1967, JD, 1970; DPhil, Oxford U., 1979. Bar: D.C. 1971, U.S. Dist Ct. D.C. 1971, U.S. Ct. Appeals (5th cir.) 1972, Md. 1984, U.S. Supreme Ct. 1984. Staff atty. Stern Community Law Office, Washington, 1970-71; sr. staff atty. Nat. Law Office of Nat. Legal Aid Defender Assn., 1971-73; Joseph P. Kennedy Jr. fellow Balliol Coll. Oxford (Eng.) U., 1973-76; vis. scholar, instr. Law Sch. Harvard U., Cambridge, Mass., 1976-80; Rockefeller Found. fellow, vis. scholar Law Sch. Columbia U., N.Y.C., 1980-82; project dir. mental patients' rights guidebook NIMH, Northampton, Mass. and Bethesda, Md., 1982-83; vis. assoc. prof. law U. Md., Balt., 1983-84, assoc. prof. law, 1984-95, prof. law, 1995—. Sr. rsch. fellow Schell Ctr. for Internat. Human Rights, Yale Law Sch., 1995—; cons. U.S. Dist. Ct. Mass., Boston, 1979-81; co-founder, v.p. & bd. dir. Homeless Persons Representation Project, Balt., 1987—; vis. prof. Tel Aviv U., 1990-91; vis. scholar Law Sch., Hebrew U., Jerusalem, 1990-91, 1999-2000; Kennedy Pub. Policy fellow, The White House, 1993-95; cons. NAS; Switzer disting. rsch. fellow Nat. Inst. on Disability and Rehab. Rsch., 1999-2000; vis. Crossman prof. Haifa U., 1999-2000. Author: The New Clients: Legal Services for Mentally Retarded Persons, 1979, Rights and Advocacy for Retarded People, 1983, Legal Rights and Mental Health Care, 1983, A Guide to Consent, 1999, Aging, Rights and Quality of Life, 1999; contbr. articles to legal jours., chpts. to books. Bd. dirs. Am. Jewish Soc. for Svc., N.Y.C., 1972—, Am. Assn. Mental Retardation, Internat. Acad. Law & Mental Health; cons. U.S. Pres.'s Com. on Mental Retardation, 1978-80; mem. Md. Gov.'s Commn. to Revise Mental Retardation and Devel. Disability Laws, 1985-86; pres. Greater Balt. Shelter Network, 1987. Recipient Rosemary F. Dybwad Internat. award Nat. Assn. Retarded Citizens, 1973, Leadership award Region IX Am. Assn. Mental Deficiency, 1984, Thomas Ferciot Disting. Profl. Svc. award Balt. Assn. Retarded Citizens, 1987, Swartz medallion for Humanitarian Svc., Swartz found., 1990, Burton Blatt award Young Adult Inst., Rights of the Disadvantage award Md. Bar Found., 1999, Regent's faculty award for excellence in pub. svc., 1999; named Fulbright scholar 1990-91, fellow World Inst. on Disability, 1993, Paul Hearne Disability Rights award, 2001. Mem. Am. Assn. Mental Retardation (pres. legal process divsn. 1978-80, 82-84, bd. dirs. 1993-95, v.p. 1996, pres.-elect 1997, pres. 1998-99, Humanitarian award 1996, Sandra Jensen Humanitarian award Region II 1997), ABA (commn. on mental and phys. disability law 1997-2000, chair editl. adv. bd., mental and phys. disability law reporter, 1997-2000), Assn. Retarded Citizens U.S. (chmn. legal advocacy com. 1984-90). Avocations: foreign travel. Office: U Md Law Sch 515 W Lombard St Baltimore MD 21201-1602 E-mail: sherr@law.umaryland.edu

HERRELL, ROGER WAYNE, lawyer; b. Washington, July 29, 1938; s. Stanley D. and Lillian B. (Davis) H.; m. Eugenia Maupin, June 11, 1960; children: Sharon, Julie, Roger. BEE, U. Va., 1960, JD, 1963. Bar: Va. 1963, Pa. 1964, U.S. Patent Office 1964. Assoc. Howson & Howson, Phila., 1963-70, ptnr., 1970-73; pres. Dann, Dorfman, Herrell & Skillman and predecessors, 1973—. Corp. sec. Leo Pharm. Products, Inc., Leo Labs. Ltd. subs. Leo Pharm. Products, 1980—. Contbr. articles to profl. jours. Past mem. Franklin Inst., 1964-84; bd. dirs. Union League Phila., 1981-84, 86-89; mem. Greater Phila. Internat. Network, 1989-94; bd. vis. Eastern Coll., 2000-. Mem. ABA (chmn. econs. com. PTC sect. 1983-85), Pa. Bar Assn. (ho. of dels. 1979-97), Phila. Bar Assn. (chmn. econs. com. 1985), Va. State Bar, Am. Intellectual Property Law Assn., Phila. Intellectual Property Assn. (bd. govs. 1980-82, 94-96), Nat. Coun. Intellectual Property Law Assns. (coun. 1982-84), Am. Soc. Corp. Secs. (nat. conf. com. 1988-89), Merion Cricket Club (Haverford, Pa.), Phila. Country Club (Gladwyne, Pa.), Penn Club, Lawyers Club, Virginia Club. (Phila.) (past pres.), Unin League (Phila.) (bd. dirs. 1981-84, 86-89), Rotary. Republican. Presbyterian. Intellectual property, Patent, Trademark and copyright.

HERRICK, STEWART THURSTON, lawyer; b. Grenada, Miss., July 30, 1945; s. Samuel Thurston and Elizabeth Glenn (Stewart) H.; m. Gretchen Ann Schein, Sept. 9, 1967; children: Alisa, Craig, Ashlie. BA, Syracuse U., 1967; JD cum laude, Suffolk U., 1974. Bar: Mass. 1974, U.S. Dist. Ct. Mass. 1975, U.S. Ct. Claims 1975, U.S. Ct. Appeals (1st cir.) 1976, U.S. Supreme Ct. 1984. Assoc. atty. Law Offices of F. Lee Bailey, Boston, 1974-76; ptnr. Harrison & Maguire, Boston, 1976-85, Catanzaro, Effron & Herrick, Ashland, Mass., 1985-90, Stewart T., Herrick & Assocs.; pvt. practice law, Framingham, Mass., 1990—. Mem. Ashland (Mass.) Dem. Town Com., 1982-83; troop leader Patriots Trail council Girl Scouts Am., 1984; bd. dirs., coach Ashland Youth Soccer, 1986-92. Lt. (j.g.) USN, 1967-70. Mem. ATLA, ABA, Mass. Bar Assn., Boston Bar Assn., Mass. Trial Lawyers Assn., Mass. Assn. Bank Counsel, Internat. Platform Assn., Mass. Conveyancer's Assn., Lions (bd. dirs. Ashland chpt. 1993—). General civil litigation, General practice, Real property. Office: 1661 Worcester Rd Ste 303 Framingham MA 01701-5405

HERRING, CHARLES DAVID, lawyer, educator; b. Muncie, Ind., Mar. 18, 1943; s. Morris and Margaret Helen (Scherbaum) H.; children: David, Margaret, Christopher, Deneice. BA, Ind. U., 1965, JD cum laude, 1968. Bar: Ind. 1968, U.S. Dist. Ct. (so. dist.) Ind. 1971, Calif. 1971, U.S. Dist. Ct. (so. dist.) Calif. 1971. Rsch. assoc. Ind. U., 1965-68; intern Office of Pros. Atty., Monroe County, Ind., 1967-68; ptnr. Herring, Stubel & Lehr and predecessor Hering and Stabel, San Diego, 1972-88; pvt. practice, 1988—. Prof. law Western State U., 1972—. Author: (with Jim Wade) California Cases on Professional Responsibility, 1976. Vice chmn. Valle de Oro Planning Com., Spring Valley, Calif., 1972-75; chmn. Valle de Oro Citizens Exec. Com. for Community Planning, Spring Valley, 1975-78. Served with JAGC, U.S. Army, 1968-72. Mem. ABA (nat. best brief award 1968), Ind. Bar Assn., Calif. Bar Assn., San Diego County Bar Assn., Conf. Spl. Ct. Judges, Calif. Trial Lawyers Assn., Order of Coif, San Diego Lions Club (dir., bd. trustees 1991). Republican. Avocations: computers, gardening, swimming, golf. General civil litigation, Insurance, Real property. Home: 284 Sunnybrook Ln El Cajon CA 92021-7801 Office: Herring Spear & Loftus 755 Broadway Cir 2d Fl San Diego CA 92101-6160 E-mail: herringd@pacbell.net

HERRING, GROVER CLEVELAND, lawyer; b. Nocatee, Fla., Dec. 9, 1925; s. Joseph I. and Martha (Selph) H.; m. Dorothy L. Blinn, Apr. 17, 1947; children: Stanley T., Kenneth Lee. JD, U. Fla., 1950. Bar: Fla. 1950. Assoc. Haskins & Bryant, 1950-52; sole practice West Palm Beach, Fla., 1952-60, 64—; ptnr. Blakeslee, Herring & Bie and predecessor firm, 1953-60, Warwick, Paul & Herring, 1964-70, Herring & Evans now Arnstein & Lehr, 1970-95, Baldwin & Herring, West Palm Beach, Fla., 1995-96. Atty. City of Atlantis, Fla., City of West Palm Beach, 1960-63, Town of Ocean Ridge, Fla., 1953-61, 64-66, Village of Royal Palm Beach, Fla., 1964-72, Town of South Palm Beach, Fla., 1966-72; spl. master-in-chancery 15th Jud. Cir. Palm Beach County, 1953-54; judge ad litem Mcpl. Ct., West Palm Beach, 1954-55; bd. dirs. Lawyers Title Services Inc., West Palm Beach. Contbr. legal articles to profl. revs. Active PTA, Family Service Agy., Palm Beach County Mental Health Assn.; chmn. profl. sect. ARC, 1960; mem. Charter Revision Com. West Palm Beach, 1960-65, Palm Beach County Resources Devel. Bd., 1959-64, Dem. Exec. Com., 1965-70; apptd. mem. Govtl. Study Commn. by Fla. Legis.; bd. dirs. Community Chest. Served with USNR, 1944-46. Mem. ABA, Palm Beach County Bar Assn. (treas. 1960), John Marshall Bar Assn., Fla. Bar Assn., Am. Judicature Soc., Lawyers Title Guaranty Fund (field rep. 1955-60, 64-74), East Coast Estate Planning Council, Nat. Inst. Mcpl. Law Officers, Law-Sci. Acad., Assn. Trial Lawyers Am. (assoc. editor 1960-92), Lawyers Lit. Club, Nat. Mcpl. League, U. Fla. Law Ctr. Assn., World Peace Through Law Ctr., Fla. Sheriff's Assn. (hon.), U. Fla. Alumni Assn., VFW, Am. Legion, West Palm Beach C. of C., Civic Music Assn., Palm Beach County Hist. Soc. (pres. 1969-72), New Eng. Hist. Geneal. Soc. Boston. Clubs: West Palm Beach Country (hon.); Airways (N.Y.C.). Lodges: Eight Oaks River, Masons (32 deg.), Elks, Moose. Home: 509 56th St West Palm Beach FL 33407-4511

HERRING, JERONE CARSON, lawyer, bank executive; b. Kinston, N.C., Sept. 27, 1938; s. James and Isabel (Knight) H.; m. Patricia Ann Hardy, Aug. 6, 1961; children— Bradley Jerone, Ansley Carole. A.B., Davidson Coll., 1960; LL.B., Duke U., 1963. Bar: N.C. 1963. Assoc. McElwee & Hall, North Wilkesboro, N.C., 1965-69; ptnr. McElwee, Hall & Herring, 1969-71; exec. v.p., sec., gen. counsel Br. Banking & Trust Co., Winston-Salem, N.C., 1971—, BB&T Corp., Winston-Salem, 1995—. Served to capt. U.S. Army, 1963-65. Mem. ABA, N.C. Bar Assn., Am. Soc. Corp. Secs., Am. Corp. Counsel Assn. Presbyterian. Banking, General corporate. Office: 200 W 2d St Winston Salem NC 27101 E-mail: jherring@bbandt.com

HERRINGER, MARYELLEN CATTANI, lawyer; b. Bakersfield, Calif., Dec. 1, 1943; d. Arnold Theodore and Corinne Marilyn (Kovacevich) C.; m. Frank C. Herringer; children: Sarah, Julia. AB, Vassar Coll., Poughkeepsie, N.Y., 1965; JD, U. Calif. (Boalt Hall), 1968; student, Stanford Grad. Sch. Bus., 1994. Assoc. Davis Polk & Wardwell, N.Y.C., 1968-69, Orrick, Herrington & Sutcliffe, San Francisco, 1970-74, ptnr., 1975-81; v.p., gen. counsel Transamerica Corp., 1981-83, sr. v.p., gen. counsel, 1983-89; ptnr. Morrison & Foerster, 1989-91; sr. v.p. gen. counsel APL Ltd., Oakland, Calif., 1991-95, exec. v.p., gen. counsel, 1995-97; gen. counsel allied bus. Littler & Mendelson, San Francisco, 2000. Bd. dirs. Golden West Fin. Corp., World Savs. Bank, ABM Industries Inc. Author: Calif. Corp. Practice Guide, 1977, Corp. Counselors, 1982. Regent St. Mary's Coll., Moraga, Calif., 1986—, pres., 1990-92, trustee, 1990-99, chmn., 1993-95; trustee Vassar Coll., 1985-93, The Head-Royce Sch., 1993—, Mills Coll., 1999—, The Benilde Religious & Charitable Trust, 1999—, Alameda County Med. Ctr. Hosp. Authority, 1998—; bd. dirs. The Exploratorium, 1988-93. Mem. ABA, State Bar Calif. (chmn. bus. law sect. 1980-81), Bar Assn. San Francisco (co-chair com. on women 1989-91), Calif. Women Lawyers, San Francisco C. of C. (bd. dirs. 1987-91, gen. counsel 1990-91), Am. Corp. Counsel Assn. (bd. dirs. 1982-87), Women's Forum West (bd. dirs. 1984-87). Democrat. Roman Catholic. General corporate, Mergers and acquisitions, Securities. E-mail: mherringer@aol.com

HERSH, ROBERT MICHAEL, lawyer, insurance company executive; b. N.Y.C., Feb. 12, 1940; s. Isaac and Esther (Cohen) H.; m. Louise Sobin, Sept. 23, 1984; 1 child, Lauren. BA, Columbia U., 1960; JD, Harvard U. Bar: N.Y. 1964. Assoc. Malcolm A. Hoffmann, N.Y.C., 1964-66, Valicenti, Leighton, Reid & Pine, N.Y.C., 1966-68; atty. Kraftco Corp., 1968-74; assoc. counsel Equitable Life Assurance Soc. U.S., 1974-76, asst. gen. counsel, 1976-78, v.p., counsel, 1978-83, v.p., assoc. gen. counsel, 1983-88; v.p., gen. counsel Integrity Life Ins. Co., 1988-93; assoc. gen. counsel Met. Life ins. Co., 1994—. Dir. Ideal Mut. Ins. Co., 1972-74; chief announcer Madison Sq. Garden Track Meets, 1974—; chief Eng. lang. athletics announcer Olympic Games, 1984, 88, 92, 96 World Championships, 1991, 93, 95, 97, 99 World Indoor Championships, 1987, 99, World Jr. Championships, 1994, 98. Columnist: Track and Field News, 1973-84, sr. editor, 1974—; contbg. editor Runner Mag., 1980-87; contbr. articles to profl. jours. With USAR, 1963-69. Mem. Assn. Life Ins. Counsel, Assn. Bar City N.Y. (com. profl. and jud. ethics 1978-81, consumer affairs com. 1984-85, ins. com. 1985-88), USA Track & Field (dir. 1979—, chmn. records com. 1979-88, chmn. rules com. 1989—, gen. counsel 1989-98, chmn. grand prix 1982-96, Robert Giegengack award for outstanding svc. 1997), Internat. Amateur Athletic Fedn. (tech. com. 1984-99, coun. 1999—, competition commn. 1999—, mktg. commn. 1999—, juridical commn. 2000—), Assn. Track and Field Statisticians, Fedn. Am. Statisticians of Track. General corporate, Insurance, Securities. Home: 92 Club Dr Roslyn Heights NY 11577-2732 Office: MetLife 1 Madison Ave New York NY 10010-3603 E-mail: rhersh@metlife.com, bobhersh@compuserve.com

HERSHATTER, RICHARD LAWRENCE, lawyer, writer; b. New Haven, Sept. 20, 1923; s. Alexander Charles and Belle (Blenner) Hershatter; m. Mary Jane McNulty, Aug. 16, 1980; 1 stepchild Kimberly Ann Matlock Kleiman ;children from previous marriage: Gail Brook, Nancy Jill, Bruce Warren. BA, Yale U., 1948; JD, U. Mich., 1951. Bar: Conn 1951, Mich 1951, US Supreme Ct 1959. Pvt. practice, New Haven, 1951-85, Clinton, Conn., 1985—; state trial referee, 1984—. Author The Spy Who Hated Licorice novels, The Spy Who Hated Caramel, The Spy Who Hated Fudge, Hung Jury, The Spy Who Hated Taffy. Mem Branford Bd Educ, Conn., 1963—71; mem Clinton Rep Town Comt, 1982—2000, chmn, 1984—88. With Air Corps U.S. Army, 1942—44. Mem.: Conn Sch Attys Coun (pres 1977), Middlesex County Bar Asn, Mystery Writers Am, Banyan Bay Club (vpres, bd dirs 1988—), Masons. Alternative dispute resolution, Labor, Probate. Office: 41 West Rd Clinton CT 06413-2316 also: 166 Route 81 Killingworth CT 06419-1469 E-mail: hershatter@aol.com

HERSHCOPF, GERALD THEA, lawyer; b. Feb. 8, 1922; s. Paul Hershcopf and Rose (Thea) Hershcopt; m. Elaine Yeckes, June 10, 1950; 1 child Jane. AB, Cokumbia U., 1943; cert. in French Civilization, U. Paris, 1945; JD, Harvard U., 1949. Bar: N.Y. 1949, U.S. Dist. Ct. (so. dist.) N.Y. 1960, U.S. Supreme Ct. 1981. Assoc. Marshall, Bratter, Greene, Allison & Tucker, N.Y.C., NY, 1949—54; ptnr. Starr & Hershcopf, 1954—56, Herschcopf & Graham and successor firms, 1956—91, Eisen, Hershcopf & Schulman, 1991—. Gen. ptnr. Norfolk Realty Corp., N.Y.C., 1961—86; chmn. bd. N.Am. Planning Corp., N.Y.C., 1968—71; pres. Consortium Met. Law Schs., N.Y.C., 1983—. Served with U.S. Army, 1943—46, ETO. Mem.: Assn. Bar City N.Y., N.Y. State Bar Assn. (gen. practice sect.), Judge Advs. Assn., Real Estate Bd. N.Y., French-Am. C. of C., Doubles Club (N.Y.C.), N.Y. Athletic Club, Harvard Club, Columbia U. Tennis Club, Beta Sigma Rho. Bankruptcy, Real property, Securities. Home: 737 Park Ave New York NY 10021-4256 Office: 609 5th Ave Fl 6 New York NY 10017-1021

HERSHENSON, GERALD MARTIN, lawyer; b. Revere, Mass., May 14, 1941; s. Morris and Ida Rita (Engorn) H.; m. Sarah Shirley Knobel, June 15, 1969; children: David, Rachel. BSBA, Boston U., 1963, LLB, 1966. Bar: Mass. 1966, Pa. 1969, U.S. Dist. Ct. (ea. dist.) Pa. 1970, U.S. Supreme Ct. 1979. Law clk. Judge E. Hettrick, Boston, 1966-67; ptnr. Curtin & Heefner, Morrisville, Pa., 1969-88; pvt. practice, Morrisville, 1988—. Mem. Dem. Nat. Com., Washington, 1983, Mideast Trade Mission, 1983; officer Bucks County Dem. Com., Doylestown, Pa., 1984; mem. fin. com. Bob Edgar for Pa. Senate, 1986. Capt. U.S. Army, 1967-69. Decorated Army Commendation medal. Mem. Assn. Trial Lawyers Am., Pa. Bar Assn., Pa. State Dem. Fin. Com., Am. Arbitration Assn., Pa. Trial Lawyers Assn., Bucks Bar Assn. (treas. 1980-82), Syda Found., Comml. Law League Am., Jewish Fedn. Delaware Valley (Young Leadership award 1982, v.p. Bucks County chpt. 1980-86). State civil litigation, Consumer commercial, Workers' compensation. Home: 1637 Bluebird Dr # B Yardley PA 19067-6320 Office: 81 Big Oak Rd Morrisville PA 19067-7801

HERSHMAN, SCOTT EDWARD, lawyer; b. N.Y.C., Mar. 31, 1958; s. Harold Martin and Barbara (Goldberg) H. BA, Am. U., 1980; JD, Yeshiva U., 1983. Bar: N.Y. 1984, U.S. Dist. Ct. (so. and ea. dists.) N.Y. 1986, U.S. Supreme Ct. 1994. Asst. dist. atty. N.Y. County Dist. Atty.'s Office, N.Y.C., 1983-86; ptnr. Graubard, Mollen & Miller, 1986-2000, Hunton & Williams, N.Y.C., 2001—. Mem. ABA, N.Y. State Bar Assn., Assn. Bar City of N.Y. General civil litigation, Criminal, Securities. Office: Hunton & Williams 200 Park Ave New York NY 10166-0136 E-mail: shershman@hunton.com

HERSHNER, ROBERT FRANKLIN, JR. judge; b. Sumter, S.C., Jan. 21, 1944; s. Robert Franklin and Druie (Goodman) H.; m. Sally Sinclair, May 19, 1990; children: Bryan, Andrew. AB, Mercer U., 1966, JD, 1969. Bar: Ga. 1971, U.S. Dist. Ct. (mid. dist.) Ga. 1971, U.S. Dist. Ct. (so. dist.) Ga. 1979, U.S. Ct. Appeals (11th cir.) 1981, U.S. Supreme Ct. 1978. Atty. Ga. Legal Svcs. Corp., Macon, 1972; assoc. Adams, O'Neal, Hemingway & Kaplan, 1972-76; ptnr. Kaplan & Hershner, P.A., 1976-80; judge U.S. Bankruptcy Ct. for Mid. Dist. Ga., 1980—, chief bankruptcy judge, 1986—. Active Fed. Jud. Ctr. Com. on Bankruptcy Edn., 1990—99, chmn., 1994—99; elected mem. bd. Fed. Jud. Ctr., 2001—. Contbr. Georgia Lawyers Basic Practice Handbook, 2d edit., Post-Judgment Procedures, 1979; cons. Norton Bankruptcy Law and Practice. V.p. Macon Heritage Found., 1977-78. Capt. U.S. Army, 1970-75. Mem. Ga. Bar Assn., Macon Bar Assn., Nat. Conf. Bankruptcy Judges (gov., v.p. 1996-97, pres. 1997-98), Blue Key, Phi Eta Sigma. Methodist. Office: US Bankruptcy Ct PO Box 86 Macon GA 31202-0086

HERSKOVITZ, S(AM) MARC, lawyer; b. Munich, Jan. 1, 1949; came to U.S., 1949; s. Max and Bella Herskovitz; 1 child from previous marriage, David Michael; m. Barbara Hobbs, Nov. 28, 1990; 1 child, Daniel Max. BA, Pa. State U., 1970; MS in Edn. with high honors, So. Ill. U., 1974; JD with honors, Fla. State U., 1987. Bar: Fla. 1987, U.S. Dist. Ct. (mid. dist.) Fla. 1988, U.S. Ct. Appeals (11th cir) 1988. Agy. mgr. Sun Personnel Svcs., Inc., Sarasota, Fla., 1978-80; claims adjuster Allstate Inc. Co., Lake Worth, 1980-84; sr. litigation atty. Fla. Dept. Ins., Tallahassee, 1987—. Mem. ABA, Assn. Trial Lawyers Am., Phi Kappa Phi. Democrat. Jewish. Avocations: softball, reading. Home: 707 Lothian Dr Tallahassee FL 32312-2858 Office: Fla Dept Ins 612 Larson Bldg Tallahassee FL 32399-0333

HERTZ, DAWN LESLIE, lawyer; b. Michigan City, Ind., June 15, 1946; d. Wilbur Tracy and Norma (Elaine) Scrivnor; m. Ted Torpo Phillips, July 7, 1969 (div. Dec. 1988); 1 child, Kristin Ann; m. Roger Helmut Hertz, Aug. 5, 1989. BA, U. Mich., 1968, JD, 1971. Bar: Mich. 1971. Law clerk U.S. Dist. Ct., Detroit, 1971-73; assoc. Dickinson, Wright, 1973-78; ptnr. Keywell and Rosenfeld, Troy, Mich., 1978-90; pvt. practice Ann Arbor, 1990—. Gen. counsel Mich. Press Assn., Lansing Mich., 1980—. Author: Michigan Media Law, 1998. V.p. Mich. Edn. Trust, Lansing, 1991—; pres. Creative Arts Center, Pontiac, Mich., 1993—. Fellow Mich. Bar Found.; mem. ABA (co-chair com. 1997-99), Mich. Bar Assn., Women In Comm. Methodist. Avocations: golf, travel. Home: 7844 Fischers Way Dexter MI 48130-9405 Office: 301 E Liberty St Ste 250 Ann Arbor MI 48104-2266 E-mail: dlph@lawyers.com

HERZ, ANDREW LEE, lawyer; b. N.Y.C., Nov. 12, 1946; s. John W. and Elise J. H.; m. Jill K. Herz; children: Adam, Matthew, Daniel, Michael. BA, Columbia U., 1968, JD, 1971. Bar: N.Y. 1972. Assoc. Milbank, Tweed, Hadley & McCloy, N.Y.C., 1971-75, Nickerson, Kramer, Lowenstein, Nessen, Kamin & Soll, N.Y.C., 1975-76, Marshall, Bratter, Greene, Allison & Tucker, N.Y.C., 1977-80; gen. counsel N.Y. State Mortgage Loan Enforcement and Adminstrn. Corp., 1980-81; ptnr. Richards & O'Neil, LLP, 1981-2001, Bingham Dana, LLP, N.Y.C., 2001—. Lectr. Real Estate Inst., NYU, 1988-93; cons. N.Y. Real Property Svcs., 1987. Author: Office Lease Operating Expense Clauses-Definitional Problems, 1986, Renegotiating Commercial Leases, 1993, Liability Risks for Ducting Loan Commitments, 1995; co-author: Japanese Yen Financing of U.S. Real Estate, 1989, Real Estate Management Agreements, 1990; contbr. articles to profl. jours. Chmn. zoning bd. appeals Village of Ossining, N.Y., 1980-88; bd. dirs. Planned Parenthood N.Y.C., 1987-94, AIDS Resource Ctr., 1991-94. Harlan Fiske Stone Scholar, 1971. Mem. ABA (real property divsn., comml. office leasing com. 1999—, chair real estate mgmt. com. 1990-91, vice chmn. 1988-90, co-chair real estate asset mgmt. com. 1992-94, chair real estate asset mgmt. com. 1994-95, lending and financing subcom. 1997-99, co-chair comml. leasing com. 1999-2001), Am. Coll. Real Estate Lawyers (vice chair office leasing com. 1997-98, chair office leasing com. 1999-2001), N.Y. State Bar Assn. (co-chmn. comml. leasing com. 1991-96, exec. com. 1991-96, real property sect., editor N.Y. Real Property Jour. 1996-97), Assn. Bar City N.Y., Real Estate Bd. N.Y., Urban Land Inst., Columbia Law Sch. Alumni Assn. Democrat. Contracts commercial, Real property. Home: 31 Flint Ave Larchmont NY 10538-3807 Office: Bingham Dana LLP 399 Park Ave New York NY 10022-4689 E-mail: aherz@bingham.com

HERZ, CHARLES HENRY, lawyer; b. Newark, Oct. 28, 1939; s. Henry and Margaret (Boa) H.; m. Barbara Jane Knapp; children— Amy, Katherine. A.B., Princeton U., 1961; LL.B., Yale U., 1967. Bar: D.C. 1968. Assoc. Covington & Burling, Washington, 1967-76; gen. counsel NSF, Washington, 1976—. 1st lt. U.S. Army, 1962-64. Mem. Nat. Conf. Lawyers and Scientists (former chmn.), ABA, AAAS. Office: NSF 1800 G St NW Washington DC 20504-0002

HERZBERG, PETER JAY, lawyer; b. Newark, Feb. 3, 1950; s. Arno and Annelle (Baruch) H.; m. Lisa F. Chrystal, Mar. 13, 1982. BA, Haverford Coll., 1972; JD, U. Pa., 1975. Dep. atty. gen. N.J. Dept. Law and Pub. Safety, Trenton, 1975-78, 80, 82-83; staff atty. Sierra Club Legal Def. Fund, Washington, 1978-80; acting asst. counsel to gov. of N.J. Trenton, 1981; John F. Baker scholar, 1971; atty. Pitney Hardin Kipp & Szuch, Morristown, N.J. Mem. Phi Beta Kappa. Federal civil litigation, State civil litigation, Environmental. Office: Pitney Hardin Kipp & Szuch PO Box 1945 Morristown NJ 07962-1945 E-mail: pherzberg@phks.com

HERZECA, LOIS FRIEDMAN, lawyer; b. July 7, 1954; d. Martin and Elaine Shirley (Rapoport) Frideman; m. Christine S. Herzeca, Aug. 15, 1980; children: Jane Leslie, Nicholas Cameron. BA, SUNY-Binghamton, 1976; JD, Boston U., 1979. Bar: N.Y. 1980, U.S. Dist. Ct. (so. and ea. dist.) N.Y. 1980. Atty. antitrust div. U.S. Dept. Justice, Washington, 1979-80; assoc. Fried, Frank, Harris, Shriver & Jacobson, N.Y.C., 1980-86, ptnr., 1986—. Editor: Am. Jour. Law and Medicine, 1978-79. Mem. ABA, N.Y.C. Bar Assn. General corporate, Securities. Office: Fried Frank Harris Shriver Jacobson 1 New York Plz Fl 22 New York NY 10004-1980

HERZOG, BRIGITTE, lawyer; b. St. Sauveur, France, Jan. 11, 1943; came to the U.S., 1970, naturalized, 1976; d. Roger and Berthe (Niobey) Ecolivet; m. Peter E. Herzog, June 29, 1970; children: Paul Roger, Elizabeth Ann. Licence en Droit, Law Sch. Pantheon, Paris, 1967; diploma d'Etudes Superieures in internat. and criminal law, Law Sch. Pantheon, 1968; diploma, Acad. Internat. Law, The Hague, The Netherlands, 1969; JD, Syracuse Coll. Law, 1975. Bar: Paris 1968, N.Y. 1976. Assoc. Chardenon Law Firm, Paris, 1968-70, Cleary, Gottlieb et al, Paris, 1976-77; staff atty. Carrier Corp., Syracuse, N.Y., 1977-83, sr. atty., 1983-84, asst. gen. counsel, 1984-86, counsel European and Transcontinental Ops. Surrey, Eng., 1986-89, assoc. gen. counsel Syracuse, 1990; dir. legal affairs Otis, Paris, 1990-92; v.p. legal affairs European and Transcontinental Ops. Otis Internat., Inc., 1992-97; dep. gen. counsel Otis Elevator Co.-Europe; v.p. legal affairs Otis Elevator North European Area, 1998—. Contbr. to Harmonization of Laws in EEC Fifth Sokol Colloquium, 1983; contbr. articles on French and internat. law to profl. jours. Bd. dirs. Syracuse Stage Guild, 1974-77; chair legal com. European Elevator Assn. Mem. ABA, Am. Fgn. Law Assn. Roman Catholic. General corporate, Private international. Home: 112 Erregger Rd Syracuse NY 13224-2220 Office: Otis 4 Place Victor Hugo Courbevoie France

HERZOG, FRED F. law educator; b. Prague, Czech Republic, Sept. 21, 1907; s. David and Anna (Reich) H.; m. Betty Ruth Cohen, Mar. 27, 1947 (dec. Sept. 1984); children: Stephen E., David R. Dr. Juris, U. Graz (Austria), 1931; JD with high distinction U. Iowa, 1942; LL.D. (hon.), John Marshall Law Sch., 1983. Bar: Iowa 1942, Ill. 1946, U.S. Supreme Ct. 1965. Judge, Vienna, Austria, 1937-38; prof. and dean Chgo.-Kent Coll. Law, 1947-73; spl. atty. Met. San. Dist. Greater Chgo., 1962-70; 1st asst. atty. gen. Ill., 1973-76; dean John Marshall Law Sch., Chgo., 1976-83, prof., 1976—. Recipient Americanism award DAR, 1978; Golden Doctor diploma U. Graz, 1981; award of Excellence, John Marshall Law Sch. Alumni Assn., 1981; cert. of Appreciation, Ill. Dept. Registration and Edn., 1978; Ill. Atty. Gen.'s award for Outstanding Pub. Service, 1976; Torch of Learning award Am. Friends of the Hebrew U., 1986; named to Sr. Citizens Hall of Fame, City of Chgo., 1983. Mem. ABA, Ill. Bar Assn., Chgo. Bar Assn., Ill. Appellate Lawyers Assn., Decalogue Soc. Lawyers, Mid-Am. Club, Internat. Club (Chgo.), Union League Club (Chgo.). Contbr. articles to legal jours. Office: John Marshall Law Sch 315 S Plymouth Ct Chicago IL 60604-3969

HERZOG, LESTER BARRY, lawyer, educator; b. Presov, Czechoslovakia, July 3, 1953; came to U.S., 1965; s. Alexander and Flora (Braun) H.; m. Terry Lynn Hochhauser, Feb. 6, 1979; children: Simcha, Sarah, Chaim, Judah, Leah. BA, Rabbinical Sem. Belz, Bklyn., 1974; MBA with distinction, L.I. U., 1977; JD cum laude, Bklyn. Law Sch., 1983. Bar: N.Y. 1984, U.S. Dist. Ct. (ea. and so. dists.) N.Y. 1984; CPA, N.Y. Sr. auditor Seidman & Seidman, N.Y.C., 1977-83; sr. trial atty. Office Corp. Counsel N.Y.C. Law Dept., Bklyn., 1983-89; pvt. practice N.Y.C., 1989—. Adj. assoc. prof. law and acctg. L.I. U., Bklyn., 1985—. Contbr. articles to profl. jours. Mem. ABA, AICPA (exam grader 1981-83), N.Y. State Bar Assn. Democrat. Jewish. Avocations: chess, fishing, gardening. Home and Office: 1729 E 15th St Brooklyn NY 11229-2084

HESLIN, GARY PHILLIP, lawyer; b. Phila., Oct. 16, 1951; s. James Phillip and Margaret Mary (McConnell) H.; m. Maureen Ann Burnley, Feb. 13, 1982; 1 child, Lindsay. BA in Polit. Sci., La Salle U., Phila., 1973; JD, Loyola U., New Orleans, 1977. Bar: Pa., U.S. Dist. Ct. (ea. dist.) Pa. Law clk. Phila. Ct. Common Pleas, 1979-80; assoc. Woluv & Rosenberg, Phila., 1981-86; ptnr. Krain & Heslin, 1986-97. Mem. Pa. Bar Assn., Phila. Bar Assn., Pa. Trial Lawyers Assn., Phila. Trial Lawyers Assn. Personal injury, Workers' compensation. Office: Krain & Heslin The Bourse Bldg 21 S 5th St Ste 1002 Philadelphia PA 19106-2515

HESS, EMERSON GARFIELD, lawyer; b. Pitts., Nov. 13, 1914; AB, Bethany Coll., 1936; JD, U. Pitts., 1939. Bar: Pa. 1940. Sr. ptnr. Hess, Reich, Georgiades, Wile & Homyak and predecessor firm Emerson G. Hess & Assocs., Pitts., 1940-92; of counsel DeMarco & Assocs., 1992—. Solicitor Scott Twp. Sch. Bd., 1958-65; legal counsel Judiciary com. Pa. Ho. of Reps., 1967-69; solicitor Scott Twp., 1968-69, Crafton Borough, 1974-78, Authority for Improvements in Municipalities of Allegheny County, 1977-80. Bd. dirs. Golden Triangle YMCA, Pitts., 1945—, WQED Ednl. TV, Pitts., 1952-68; pres., dir. Civil Light Opera Assn., Pitts., 1967-68; mem. internat. com. YMCA World Svc., N.Y.C., 1968-78; trustee, chmn. Cen. Christian Ch., Pitts., 1962-63; pres. Anesthesia and Resuscitation Found., Pitts., 1964-88, Pa. Med. Rsch. Found., 1960-88. Mem. ABA, Pa. Bar Assn., Allegheny County Bar Assn. General corporate, Probate, Real property. Home: 43 Robin Hill Dr Mc Kees Rocks PA 15136-1238 Office: DeMarco & Assocs 946 Gulf Tower 707 Grant St Pittsburgh PA 15219-1908

HESS, GEORGE FRANKLIN, II, lawyer; b. Oak Park, Ill., May 13, 1939; s. Franklin Edward and Carol (Hackman) H.; m. Diane Ricci, Aug. 9, 1974; 1 child, Franklin Edward. BS in Bus., Colo. State U., 1962; JD, Suffolk U., 1970; LLM, Boston U., 1973. Bar: Pa. 1971, Fla. 1973, U.S. Tax Ct. 1974, U.S. Dist. Ct. (so. dist.) Fla. 1975. Assoc. Hart, Childs, Hepburn, Ross & Putnam, Phila., 1970-72; instr. Suffolk U. Law Sch., Boston, 1973-74; ptnr. Henry, Hess & Hoines, Ft. Lauderdale, Fla., 1974-79; with Mousaw, Vigdor, Reeves & Hess, 1979-94; pvt. practice, 1995—. Bd. dirs. Childrens Home Soc., Ft. Lauderdale, 1985-89, Nadeau Charitable Found., 1985-2000; trustee endowment fund All Sts. Ch., 1995—. Lt. USNR, 1963-66. Mem. ABA, SAR, Fla. Bar Assn., Broward County Bar Assn., Lauderdale Yacht Club, USN League, Phi Alpha Delta. Episcopalian. Estate planning, Probate. Home: 2524 Castilla Is Fort Lauderdale FL 33301-1505 Office: 333 N New River Dr E Fort Lauderdale FL 33301-2241

HESSE, CAROLYN SUE, lawyer; b. Belleville, Ill., Jan. 12, 1949; d. Ralph H. Hesse and Marilyn J. (Midgley) Hesse Dierkes; m. William H. Hallenbeck. BS, U. Ill., 1971; MS, U. Ill., Chgo., 1977; JD, DePaul U., 1983. Bar: Ill. 1983, U.S. Dist. Ct. (no. dist.) Ill. 1983. Rsch. assoc. U. Ill., Chgo., 1974-77; tech. adviser Ill. Pollution Control Bd., 1977-80; environ. scientist U.S. EPA, 1980-84; assoc. Pretzel & Stouffer, Chartered, 1984-87, Coffield Ungaretti Harris & Slavin, Chgo., 1987-88; ptnr. McDermott, Will & Emery, 1988-99; pvt. practice Chgo., 1999-2001; ptnr. Barnes & Thornburg, 2001—. Frequent spkr. seminars on environ. issues. Contbr. articles on environ. sci. to profl. jours. Mem. ABA. Environmental. Office: 2600 Chase Plaza 10 S LaSalle St Chicago IL 60603

HESTER, FRANCIS BARTOW, III (FRANK HESTER), lawyer; b. Interlachen, Fla., Oct. 13, 1920; s. Francis Bartow Jr. and Flora McRae H.; m. Joyce Slate, Dec. 21, 1946; children: Susan Hester Elmore, Blanche Hester Wolfson, F. Bartow Hester Jr. Student, Ga. Inst. Tech., 1938-42, U. Ga., 1946; LLB, Emory U., 1948. Bar: Ga. 1952, U.S. Dist. Ct. (no. dist.) Ga. 1952, U.S. Ct. Appeals (4th cir.) 1990, U.S. Ct. Appeals (5th cir.) 1955, U.S. Ct. Appeals (6th cir.) 1967, U.S. Ct. Appeals (7th cir.) 1994, U.S. Ct. Appeals (11th cir.) 1981, U.S. Bd. Immigration Appeals 1985, U.S. Supreme Ct. 1960. Spl. agt. FBI, Cleve., Phila., Atlanta, 1948-51; criminal case trial lawyer Hester & Hester, 1952-99. Spl. investigator of fraud in Ga. State Govt., 1958-59. With Air Corp., U.S. Army, 1942-45. Commendation Ga. Ho. of Reps., 1997. Mem. Ga. Bar Assn., Ga. Assn. Criminal Def. Lawyers, Former Spl. Agts. of FBI Assn., Inc., Atlanta Bar Assn., Mason (32d degree), 6th Bomb Group Assn. (Tinian 1945), Cherokee Town & Country Club, Shriner (Yaarab temple), Sigma Alpha Epsilon. Democrat. Avocation: boating. Criminal. Home and Office: 5350 Larch Ln Gainesville GA 30506-6282

HESTER, JULIA A. lawyer; b. L.A., Nov. 14, 1953; d. Robert William and Bertie Ella (Gilbert) H.; m. Fred M. Haddad, Aug. 2, 1980; children: Allison Hester-Haddad, Nancy Hester-Haddad. BA, Fla. Atlantic U., 1984; JD, Nova U., 1990. Bar: Fla. 1990, U.S. Dist. Ct. (mid. dist.) Fla. 1993. Asst. pub. defender Broward Pub. Defender, Ft. Lauderdale, Fla., 1990-93; atty., ptnr. Haddad & Hester, 1993-95, 97—. Bd. dirs. St. Anthony Found., Ft. Lauderdale, 1995—, Ft. Lauderdale Billfish Tournament, 1992-96, BACDL, St. Thomas Aquinas Found., 1999—; mem. Sunrise Intracoastal Bd., Ft. Lauderdale, 1995; bd. dirs., officer Kids Inn Distress Aux., Ft. Lauderdale, 1984-87; bd. dirs. St. Thomas Found., 1999—, mem. exec. bd., 1999. Avocations: skiing, fishing, swimming. Appellate, Criminal, Juvenile. Office: 1 Financial Plz Ste 2612 Fort Lauderdale FL 33394-0061

HESTER, PATRICK JOSEPH, lawyer; b. Worcester, Mass., Aug. 14, 1951; s. Joseph P. and Anne T. (O'Brien) H.; m. Ann E. Riley, July 11, 1987; children: Maureen M., Colleen A., Margaret R., Molly E. BS in Civil Engr., W.P.I., Worcester, Mass., 1973; MS in Civil Engr., Northeastern U., Boston, 1979; JD, Suffolk Law Sch., Boston, 1983. Bar: Mass. 1983, U.S. Dist. Ct. Mass. 1984, 1st Cir. Ct. Appeals, 1999, U.S. Supreme Ct. 2000. Civil engr. Stone & Webster, Boston, 1973; dist. engr. Algonquin Gas Transmission Co., 1973-75, engr., 1975-78, sr. engr., 1978-79, supr.,engr., 1979-82, project mgr., 1982-83, asst. mgr. gas supply, 1983-84, corp. atty., 1984-92, v.p., gen. counsel, 1992-97; asst. gen. counsel Duke Energy Corp., 1998—; gen. counsel M & N Mgmt. Co., 1998-99, sr. v.p., gen. counsel, 1999—. Profl. engr., Mass. Mem. Am. Bar Assn., Mass. Bar Assn., Fed. Energy Bar Assn., Boston Bar Assn., New England Corp. Counsel Assn., Guild Gas Mgrs., Chi Epsilon, Phi Delta Phi. Democrat. Roman Catholic. Avocation: sports. Contracts commercial, General corporate, FERC practice. Office: Duke Energy Corp 1284 Soldiers Field Rd Boston MA 02135-1003

HESTER, THOMAS PATRICK, lawyer, business executive; b. Tulsa, Okla., Nov. 20, 1937; s. E.P. and Mary J. (Layton) H; m. Nancy B. Scofield, Aug. 20, 1960; children: Thomas P. Jr., Ann S., John L. BA, Okla. U., 1961, LLB, 1963. Bar: Okla. 1963, Mo. 1967, N.Y. 1970, D.C. 1973, Ill. 1975. Atty. McAfee & Taft, Okla. City, 1963-66, Southwestern Bell Telephone Co., Okla. City, St. Louis, 1966-72, AT&T, N.Y.C., Washington, 1972-75; gen. atty. Ill. Bell Telephone Co., Springfield, 1975-77, gen. solicitor Chgo., 1977-83, v.p., gen. counsel, 1983-87; sr. v.p., gen. counsel Ameritech, 1987-91, exec. v.p., gen. counsel, 1991-97; ptnr. Mayer, Brown & Platt, 1997—; sr. v.p., gen. counsel, sec. Sears, Roebuck and Co., 1998-99, FMC Corp., 2000. Corp. counsel ctr. adv. bd. Northwestern U., 1987-97. Mem. Taxpayers Fedn. Ill., Springfield, 1987-97, chmn. bd. trustees 1987-88; mem. adv. bd. Ill. Dept. Natural Resources, 1991-2000—, chmn., 1993-98; trustee Art Inst. Chgo., 1995-2000. Fellow Am. Bar Found.; mem. Am. Law Inst. Administrative and regulatory, General corporate, Public utilities. Office: Mayer Brown & Platt 190 S LaSalle St Chicago IL 60603-3441 E-mail: thester@mayerbrown.com

HETHERWICK, GILBERT LEWIS, lawyer; b. Winnsboro, La., Oct. 30, 1920; s. Septimus and Addie Louise (Gilbert) H.; m. Joan Friend Gibbons, May 31, 1946 (dec. Aug. 1964); children: Janet Hetherwick Pumphrey, Ann Hetherwock Lyons Winegeart, Gilbert, Carol Hetherwick Sutton, Katherine Hetherwick Hummell; m. Mertis Elizabeth Cook, June 7, 1967. BA summa cum laude, Centenary Coll., 1942; JD, Tulane U., 1949. Bar: La. 1949. With legal dept. NorAm Energy Corp., Shreveport, La., 1949-53; dir. Blanchard, Walker, O'Quin and Roberts, PLC, 1953-99, of counsel, 2000—. Mem. Shreveport City Charter Revision Com., 1955; mem. Shreveport Mcpl. Fire and Police Civil Svc. Bd., 1956-92, vice chmn., 1957-78, chmn., 1978-88. Served with AUS, 1942-46. Recipient Tulane U. Law Faculty medal, 1949. Mem. ABA, La. Bar Assn., Shreveport Bar Assn. (pres. 1987), Energy Bar Assn., Order of Coif, Phi Delta Phi, Omicron Delta Kappa. Episcopalian. Home: 4604 Fairfield Ave Shreveport LA 71106-1432 Office: Bank One Tower Shreveport LA 71101

HETLAGE, ROBERT OWEN, lawyer; b. St. Louis, Jan. 9, 1931; s. George C. and Doris M. (Talbot) H.; m. Anne R. Willis, Sept. 24, 1960; children: Mary T., James C., Thomas K. AB, Washington U., St. Louis, 1952, LLB, 1954; LLM, George Washington U., 1957. Bar: Mo. 1954, U.S. Dist. Ct. (ea. dist.) Mo. 1954, U.S. Supreme Ct. 1957. Ptnr. Hetlage & Hetlage, 1958-65, Peper, Martin, Jensen, Maichel & Hetlage, St. Louis, 1966-97, chmn., 1994-97; of counsel Blackwell Sanders Peper Martin LLP, 1998—. 1st lt. U.S. Army, 1954-58. Fellow Am. Bar Found. (life, bd. trustees 1996—); mem. ABA (chmn. real property, probate and trust law sect. 1981-82), Bar Assn. Met. St. Louis (pres. 1967-68), Mo. Bar (pres. 1976-77), Am. Coll. Real Estate Lawyers (pres. 1985-86), Am. Judicature Soc., Anglo-Am. Real Property Inst. (chmn. 1991). Contracts commercial, Construction, Real property. Office: Blackwell Sanders Peper Martin LLP 720 Olive St Saint Louis MO 63101-2338 E-mail: rohelage@bspmlaw.com

HETLAND, JOHN ROBERT, lawyer, educator; b. Mpls., Mar. 12, 1930; s. James L. and Evelyn (Lundgren) H.; m. Mildred Woodruff, Dec. 1951 (div.); children: Lynda Lee Catlin, Robert John, Debra Ann Allen; m. Anne Kneeland, Dec. 1972; children: Robin T. Willcox, Elizabeth J. Pickett. B.S.L., U. Minn., 1952, J.D., 1956. Bar: Minn. 1956, Calif. 1962, U.S. Supreme Ct, 1981. Practice law, Mpls., 1956-59; prof. law U. Calif., Berkeley, 1959-91; prof. emeritus, 1991—; prin. Hetland & Kneeland, PC, Berkeley, 1959—. Vis. prof. law Stanford U., 1971, 80, U. Singapore, 1972, U. Cologne, Fed. Republic Germany, 1988. Author: California Real Property Secured Transactions, 1970, Commercial Real Estate Transactions, 1972, Secured Real Estate Transactions, 1974, 1977; co-author: California Cases on Security Transactions in Land, 2d edit., 1975, 3d edit., 1984, 4th edit., 1992; contbr. articles to legal, real estate and fin. jours. Served to lt. comdr. USNR, 1953-55. Fellow Am. Coll. Real Estate Lawyers, Am. Coll. Mortgage Attys., Am. Bar Found.; mem. ABA, State Bar Calif., State Bar Minn., Order of Coif, Phi Delta Phi. Home and Office: 20 Red Coach Ln Orinda CA 94563-1112 E-mail: hetlandj@law.berkeley.edu, jrhatk@home.com

HETTRICK, GEORGE HARRISON, lawyer; b. Piney River, Va., Aug. 15, 1940; s. Ames Bartlett and Frances Caryl (O'Brian) H.; children: Heather White Hettrick Brugh, Edward Lord. BA, Cornell U., 1962; JD, Harvard U., 1965. Bar: Va. 1965. Assoc. Hunton & Williams, Richmond, Va., 1965-73, ptnr., 1973—. Ptnr. in charge Church Hill Neighborhood Law Office Hunton & Williams, 1990—, chmn. Community Svc. com.; dir. Richmond Community Hosp., 1992—. Contbr. articles to profl. jours. Spl. counsel Gov. of Va., Richmond, 1971-72; vice chmn. bd. dirs. Va. Port Authority, Norfolk, 1970-75, former commr., vice chmn.; pres. bd. trustees Va. Episcopal Sch., Lynchburg, 1978-81; mem. Va. State adv. com. Neighborhood Assistance Program; past dir., chmn. Peter Paul Devel. Ctr., Inc.; bd. dirs. Richmond Better Housing Coalition, St. Mary's Hosp., Stuart Circle Hosp., Richmond Cmty. Hosp., 1995—, Regional Meml. Med. Ctr.; mem. Henrico County (Va.) Cmty. Svcs. Bd., 1997—. Capt. U.S. Army, 1966-68. Fellow Va. Law Found.; mem. ABA, Va. Bar Assn. (chmn. substance abuse com. 1995-96, Lawyers Helping Lawyers), Va. State Bar, Richmond Bar Assn. (chmn. pro bono com. 1998—). Republican. Episcopalian. Home: 6350 Memorial Dr Sandston VA 23150-6307 Office: Hunton & Williams PO Box 1535 Richmond VA 23218-1535 E-mail: ghettrick@hunton.com

HETZNER, MARC A. lawyer; b. Logansort, Ind., Apr. 24, 1953; s. John R. and Nelma L. (Byrt) H.; m. Rosalie M.; children: Collette N., Christopher R., Kimberly A. BA, Ind. U., 1975, MBA in Taxation, JD, Ind. U., 1983. Bar: Ind. 1983, U.S. Dist. Ct. (so. dist.) Ind. 1983, U.S. Tax Ct. 1983, U.S. Ct. Appeals (7th cir.) 1988. Ptnr. Krieg DeVault LLP, Indpls., 1989—. Contbr. articles to profl. jours. 1st lt. U.S. Army, 1975-79. Fellow Am. Coll. Trust & Estate Counsel, Ind. State Bar Found.; mem. Indpls. Estate Planning Coun. Estate planning, Estate taxation, Taxation, general. Office: Krieg DeVault LLP Ste 2800 1 Indiana Sq Indianapolis IN 46204-2079

HEUBEL, WILLIAM BERNARD, lawyer, international contract consultant; b. Sharon, Pa., Mar. 7, 1928; s. Herman J. and Margaret (Becker) H. Student, Gannon U., 1948-49; BS, Purdue U., 1952; JD, Ind. U., 1954. Bar: Ind. 1955, U.S. Dist. Ct. (so. dist.) Ind. 1955. Mem. profl. mgmt. staff AT&T Long Lines, 1955-61; contract adminstr. nuclear and def. Westinghouse Electric Corp., Pitts., 1961-68, mgr. mktg. adminstrn. nuclear, 1968-73, contract mgmt. cons. corp. mktg., 1973-81, contract cons. internat. sales contracts-law dept., 1981-87; pvt. practice, 1988—. Served with AUS, 1946-48. Mem. Internat. Bar Assn. Roman Catholic. Contracts commercial, Government contracts and claims, Private international. Office: 123 Franklin Dr Greensburg PA 15601-1304

HEUER, SAM TATE, lawyer; b. Batesville, Ark., July 11, 1952; s. Albert A. and Mary (Baker) H.; children: Noal Tate, Polly Anna, Charles Albert; m. Max Parker. BBA in Banking and Fin., U. Miss., 1974; JD, U. Ark., 1978. Bar: Ark. 1979, U.S. Dist. Ct. (ea. and we. dist.) Ark. 1979, U.S. Ct. Appeals (8th cir.) 1980. Dep. pros. atty. 4th Jud. Dist., Fayetteville, Ark., 1979-80; assoc. Davis Bracey & Heuer, Springdale, 1980-81; pvt. practice, Batesville, 1981-86; pros. atty. 16th Jud. Dist., 1983-86; assoc. salesman Crews & Assocs., Little Rock, 1987-88; assoc. John Wesley Hall P.C., 1988-93; ptnr. Heuer Law Firm, 2000—. Mem. ATLA, Ark. Prosecutor's Assn. (bd. dirs. 1984-86, v.p. 1985-86), Ark. Trial Lawyers Assn., Am. Trial Lawyers Assn., Pulaski County Attys. Assn. Democrat. Episcopalian. General civil litigation, Criminal, Family and matrimonial. Office: Heuer Law Firm 124 W Capitol Ave Ste 1650 Little Rock AR 72201-3758

HEUISLER, CHARLES WILLIAM, lawyer; b. Phila., May 24, 1941; s. Isaac Kilner and Mary Gertrude (Smith) H.; m. Judith Ann Hargadon, June 26, 1965; children: Karen L. Heuisler Murphy, Susan M. Heuisler McCabe, Charles W. Jr. BA in Modern Lang., Coll. of Holy Cross, 1963; JD, Villanova U., 1966. Bar: N.J. 1966, U.S. Dist. Ct. N.J. 1966, U.S. Ct. Appeals (3d cir.) 1970, U.S. Supreme Ct. 1972; cert. civil trial atty. Am. Bd. Trial Advs. Law clk. to Hon. John B. Wick, Superior Ct. of N.J., Chancery Divsn., Camden, 1966-67; shareholder Archer & Greiner, Haddonfield, N.J., 1972—. Counsel, mem. adv. bd. Haddonfield Symphony Soc., 1980—; chmn. South Jersey Performing Arts Ctr., 1992-98. Mem. FBA, N.J. Bar Assn. (trustee from Camden County 1989-93), Camden County Bar Assn. (pres. 1985-86, trustee, Peter J. Devine award 1991), Rotary (pres. Camden 1987-88). Avocations: tennis, sailing. General civil litigation, Intellectual property, Professional liability. Home: 1236 Folkestone Way Cherry Hill NJ 08034-3021 Office: Archer & Greiner PC One Centennial Sq Haddonfield NJ 08033 E-mail: cheuisler@archerlaw.com

HEUMAN, DONNA, lawyer; b. Seattle, May 27, 1949; d. Russell George and Edna Inez (Armstrong) H. BA in Psychology, UCLA, 1972; JD, U. Calif., San Francisco, 1985. Cert. shorthand reporter, Calif. Owner Heuman & Assocs., San Francisco, 1978-86; lic. real estate broker Calif., 1990—; co-founder, chair, CFO Atherton Park Foods, Inc., Menlo Park, 1996—. Mem. Hastings Internat. and Comparative Law Rev., 1984-85; bd. dirs. Saddleback, 1987-89. Jessup Internat. Moot Ct. Competition, 1985; mem. North Fair Oaks Adv. Coun., vice chair, sec. 1993-95. Mem. ABA, NAFE, ATLA, AOPA, Nat. Shorthand Reporters Assn., Women Entrepreneurs, Mensa, Calif. State Bar Assn., Nat. Mus. of Women in the Arts, Calif. Lawyers for the Arts, San Francisco Bar Assn., Commonwealth Club, World Affairs Coun., Zonta (bd. dirs.). Address: 750 18th Ave Menlo Park CA 94025-2018 E-mail: athpark@aol.com

HEWITT, JAMES WATT, lawyer; b. Hastings, Nebr., Dec. 25, 1932; s. Roscoe Stanley and Willa Manners (Watt) H.; m. Marjorie Ruth Barrett, Aug. 8, 1954; children: Mary Janet, William Edward, John Charles, Martha Ann. Student, Hastings Coll., 1950-52; BS, U. Nebr., 1954, JD, 1956, MA, 1994. Bar: Nebr. 1956. Practice, Hastings, 1956-57, Lincoln, Nebr., 1960—; v.p., gen. counsel Nebco, Inc., 1961—. Vis. lectr. U. Nebr. Coll. Law, 1970-71. Mem. state exec. com. Rep. Party, 1967-70, mem. state ctrl. com., 1967-70, legis chmn., 1968-70; bd. dirs. Lincoln Child Guidance Ctr., 1969-72, pres., 1972; bd. dirs. Lincoln Cmty. Playhouse, 1967-73, pres., 1972-73; trustee Bryan Meml. Hosp., Lincoln, 1968-74, 76-82, chmn., 1972-74; bd. dirs. Lincoln Libr., 1990-97; trustee U. Nebr. Found., 1979—; dir. Bryan Meml. Hosp. Found., Lincoln, 1994—; pres, dir. Nebr. State Hist. Soc. Found., Lincoln, 1994—; dir. Nebr. state chpt. The Nature Conservancy, 1993-97. Capt. USAF, 1957-60. Fellow Am. Bar Found. (Nebr. state chmn. 1988-92, 99—, chmn. 1994-95); mem. ABA (Nebr. state del. 1972-80, bd. govs. 1981-83), Nebr. State Bar (chmn. ins. com. 1972-76, chmn. pub. rels. com. 1982-84, pres. 1985-86), Fed. Bar Assn., Lincoln Bar Assn., Newcomen Soc. (Nebr. chair 1995—), Am. Rose Soc., Nebr. Rose Soc., Lincoln Rose Soc., Nebr. Club, Country of Lincoln Club, Round Table, Beta Theta Pi, Phi Delta Phi. Congregationalist. Administrative and regulatory, Construction, General corporate. Home: 2990 Sheridan Blvd Lincoln NE 68502-4241 Office: PO Box 80268 1815 Y St Lincoln NE 68508-1233

HEWITT, PAUL BUCK, lawyer; b. St. Louis, July 27, 1949; s. John York and Kathryn Louise (Buck) H.; m. Marla Ivy Zimmers, Feb. 17, 1985; children: Anna Ruth, Rachel Elizabeth. BA in Econs., Northwestern U., 1971; JD cum laude, U. Wis., 1974. Bar: D.C. 1979, Wis. 1974. Law clk. to chief justice Wis. Supreme Ct., Madison, 1974-75; atty. Bureau of Competition FTC, Washington, 1975-78; assoc. Akin Gump Strauss Hauer and Feld, 1978-82, ptnr., 1983—. Articles editor Wis. Law Rev., Madison, 1973-74. Mem. ABA, D.C. Bar, Wis. Bar Assn. Administrative and regulatory, Antitrust, Federal civil litigation. Office: Akin Gump Strauss Hauer and Feld Ste 400 1333 New Hampshire Ave NW Washington DC 20036-1564

HEYBURN, JOHN GILPIN, II, federal judge; b. 1948; m. Martha Keeney, 1976. BA, Harvard U., 1970; JD, U. Ky., 1976. Ptnr. Brown, Todd & Heyburn, Louisville, 1976-92; fed. judge U.S. Dist. Ct. (we. dist.), 1992—. Bd. dirs. Kentuckians for Jud. Improvement, 1975-76; mem. Budget Com. Jud. Conf.of U.S., 1994—, chmn. 1997—; chair Jefferson County Crime Commn.; mem. vis. com. U. Ky., 1980; active Leadership Louisville Found. With USAR, 1970-76. Mem. ABA, Ky. Bar Assn., Louisville Bar Assn., U. Ky. Coll. Law Alumni Assn., Louisville Com. Fgn. Rels. Office: US Dist Ct 601 W Broadway Ste 239 Louisville KY 40202-2227

HEYCK, THEODORE DALY, lawyer; b. Houston, Apr. 17, 1941; s. Theodore and Richard and Gertrude Paine (Daly) H. BA, Brown U., 1963; postgrad., Georgetown U., 1963-65, 71-72; JD, N.Y. Law Sch., 1979. Bar: N.Y. 1980, Calif. 1984, U.S. Ct. Appeals (2d cir.) 1984, U.S. Supreme Ct. 1984, U.S. Dist. Ct. (so. and ea. dists.) N.Y. 1980, U.S. Dist. Ct. (we. and no. dists.) N.Y. 1984, U.S. Dist. Ct. (cen. and so. dists.) Calif. 1984, U.S. Ct. Appeals (9th cir.) 1986. Paralegal dist. atty., Bklyn., 1975-79; asst. dist. atty. Bklyn. dist., Kings County, N.Y., 1979-85; dep. city atty. L.A., 1985—. Bd. dirs. Screen Actors Guild, N.Y.C., 1977-78. Mem. ABA, ATLA, AFTRA, NATAS, SAG, Bklyn. Bar Assn., N.Y. Trial Lawyers Assn., N.Y. State Bar Assn., Calif. Bar Assn., Fed. Bar Coun., L.A. Coun. Bar Assn., Actors Equity Assn. Home: 2106 E Live Oak Dr Los Angeles CA 90068-3639 Office: Office City Atty City Hall E 200 N Main St Los Angeles CA 90012-4110

HEYER, JOHN HENRY, II, lawyer; b. Rochester, N.Y., May 4, 1946; s. Joseph Lester and Margaret Mary (Darcy) H.; m. Charla Ann Prewitt (dec.); children: Thomas, William, John III, Richard, Mary. BA, U. Colo., 1969; JD, U. Denver, 1972. Bar: Colo. 1973, U.S. Dist. Ct. Colo. 1973, N.Y. 1976, Pa. 1979, U.S. Dist. Ct. (we. dist.) N.Y. 1980, U.S. Supreme Ct. 1982. Atty. Texaco, Inc., Denver, 1973-75; sole practice Olean, N.Y., 1975—. Pres. Northeastern Land Svcs., Inc., Olean, N.Y., 1982—; v.p. Vector Capital Corp., Rochester, N.Y., 1985-87; chpt. 7 trustee U.S. Bankruptcy Ct., we. dist. N.Y., 1986—. Editor: New York Oil and Gas Statutes, 1985. Asst. dist. atty. Cattaraugus County, Olean, 1978-81; bd. dirs. Olean YMCA, 1989—, v.p. 1993-94, pres., 1994-99, pres. bd. trustees, 1999—; bd. dirs. Buffalo Philharm. Symphony Cir., v.p., 1993, pres., 1994-95; bd. dirs. Friends of Good Music, pres. 1994-95. Mem. N.Y. State Bar Assn. (real property sect., real property devel. com.), Erie County Bar Assn., Cattaraugus County Bar Assn. (sec.-treas. 1997, v.p. 1998, pres. 1999), Eastern Mineral Law Found. (trustee 1984—, exec. com. 1994-95), Ind. Oil and Gas Assn. N.Y. (bd. dirs. 1986—, sec. 1986-87, v.p. 1988—), SAR, Selden Soc. Roman Catholic. Bankruptcy, Oil, gas, and mineral, Real property. Office: PO Box 588 201 N Union St Olean NY 14760-2738

HEYMANN, PHILIP BENJAMIN, law educator, academic director; b. Pitts., Oct. 30, 1932; B.A., Yale U., 1954; LL.B., Harvard U., 1960. Bar: D.C. 1960, Mass. 1969. Trial atty. gen. Dept. Justice, Washington, 1961-65, asst. atty. gen. criminal div., 1978-81, dep. atty. gen., 1993-94; dep. adminstr. Bur. Security and Consular Affairs, Dept. State, 1965, acting adminstr., to 1967; dep. asst. sec. of state for Bur. Internat. Orgns., 1967, exec. asst. to under sec. of state, 1967-69; with Legal Aid Agy. of D.C., 1969; faculty law Harvard U., 1969—, James Barr Ames prof. law, dir. Harvard Law Sch. Ctr. for Criminal Justice. Assoc. prosecutor and cons. to Watergate Spl. Prosecution Force, summers 1973-75 Served with USAF, 1955-57.

HEYWOOD, ROBERT GILMOUR, lawyer; b. Berkeley, Calif., May 18, 1949; m. Carolyn Cox, June 10, 1972. AB with distinction, Stanford U., 1971; MA, U. Calif., Berkeley, 1972; JD cum laude, Santa Clara U., 1975. Bar: Calif. 1975, U.S. Dist. Ct. (no. and ea. dists.) Calif. 1975, U.S. Ct. Appeals (9th cir.) 1976, U.S. Supreme Ct. 1979; cert. specialist workers' compensation law Calif. Bd. Legal Specialization, State Bar Calif. Of counsel Hanna, Brophy, MacLean, McAleer & Jensen, Oakland, Calif., 1976—. Instr. Santa Clara U., 1975-77, advocacy skills workshop Stanford U. Law Sch., 1994—; faculty ctr. for trial and appellate adv. Hasting Coll. of Law, San Francisco; mem. faculty Calif. Ctr. for Jud. Edn. and Rsch., 1998; mem. intensive advocacy program faculty U. San Francisco Sch. Law, 1995—; adj. prof. law U. Calif., Hastings, 1982-86; arbitrator Alameda County Superior Ct. Mem. bd. editl. cons. Calif. Compensation Cases. Bd. dirs. Alameda County Legal Aid Soc., Oakland, 1978-87, Cazadero Performing Arts Camp, 1994—; bd. govs. Oakland East Bay Symphony, pres., 1991-93. Mem. ABA, Calif. Bar Assn., Calif. Continuing Edn. of Bar (editor, lect., author), Alameda County Bar Assn., Calif. Compensaton Def. Attys. Assn. Insurance, Personal injury, Workers' compensation. Office: Hanna Brophy MacLean Et Al 155 Grand Ave Ste 600 Oakland CA 94612-3747

HIBBS, LOYAL ROBERT, lawyer; b. Des Moines, Dec. 24, 1925; s. Loyal B. and Catharine (McClymond) H.; children: Timothy, Theodore, Howard, Dean. BA, U. Iowa, 1950, LLB, JD, 1952. Bar: Iowa 1952, Nev. 1958, U.S. Supreme Ct. 1971. Ptnr. Hibbs Law Offices, Reno, 1972—. Moderator radio, TV Town Hall Coffee Breaks, 1970-72; mem. Nev. State Bicycle Adv. Bd., 1996-2000, Reno Bicycle Coun., 1995-99; chmn. Reno Park Recreation Commn., 2001—. Fellow Am. Bar Found. (Nev. chmn. 1989-94); mem. ABA (standing com. Lawyer Referral Svc. 1978-79, steering com. state dels. 1979-82, consortium on legal svcs. and the pub. 1979-82, Nev. State Bar del. to Ho. of Dels. 1978-82, 89-90, bd. govs. 1982-85, mem. legal tech. adv. coun. 1985-86, standing com. on nat. conf. groups 1985-91, chmn. sr. lawyers divsn. Nev. 1988—), Nat. Conf. Bar Pres.'s Iowa Bar Assn., Nev. Bar Assn. (bd. govs. 1968-78, pres. 1977-78), Washoe County Bar Assn. (pres. 1966-67), Nat. Jud. Coll. (bd. dirs. 1986-92, sec. 1988-92), Assn. Def. Counsel No. Calif., Assn. Def. Counsel Nev., Assn. Ski Def. Attys., Aircraft Owners and Pilots Assn. (legal svcs. plan 1991—), Washoe County Legal Aid Soc. (co-founder), Lawyer-Pilots Bar Assn. (chmn. Nev.), Greater Reno C. of C. (bd. dirs. 1968-72), Phi Alpha Delta. Aviation, General civil litigation, Probate. Home: 1489 Foster Dr Reno NV 89509-1209 Office: 290 S Arlington Ave Ste 100 Reno NV 89501-1793 E-mail: loyalhibbs@aol.com

HICKEN, JEFFREY PRICE, lawyer; b. Macomb, Ill., Oct. 25, 1947; s. Victor and Mary Patricia (O'Connell) H.; m. Mary Sarah Schmidt, Aug. 23, 1969; children: Andrew, Molly, Elizabeth. BA, Cornell Coll., 1969; JD, U. Ill., 1972. Bar: Minn. 1972, U.S. Dist. Ct. Minn. 1980, U.S. Ct. Appeals (8th cir.). Assoc. Weaver, Talle & Herrick, Anoka, Minn., 1972-77; sr. ptnr. Hicken, Scott & Howard, P.A., 1977-00, 1998—. Mem. Minn. Family Law Certification Commn., 1999. Bd. dirs. Anoka Lyric Arts; precinct chair Dem. Farmer-Labor Party, Anoka, 1976—. Capt. U.S. Army, 1969-77. Recipient J. Franklin Littel scholarship Cornell Coll., Mt. Vernon, Iowa, 1969 Fellow Am. Acad. Matrimonial Lawyers (cert. arbitrator, bd. mgrs.); mem. Minn. State Bar Assn., Anoka County Bar Assn. (pres. 1990-91), City of Anoka Charter Commn. (chmn. 1978—). Democrat. Avocations: running, violin. Family and matrimonial. Home: 1700 West Ln Anoka MN 55303-1923 Office: Hicken Scott & Howard PA 2150 3rd Ave Ste 300 Anoka MN 55303-2200

HICKEY, JOHN (JACK) HEYWARD, lawyer; b. Miami, Fla., Dec. 18, 1954; s. Weyman Park Hickey and Alice Joan (Heyward) Brown. BA magna cum laude, Fla. State U., 1976; JD, Duke U., 1980. Bars: Fla. 1980 (admiralty law com. 2000—), U.S. Dist. Ct. (so. dist) Fla. 1980, U.S. Dist. Ct. (mid. dist.) Fla. 1982, U.S. Ct. Appeals (5th cir.) 1982, U.S. Ct. Appeals (11th cir.) 1983, U.S. Supreme Ct. 1985. Trial lawyer Smathers & Thompson, Miami, 1980-85, Hornsby & Whisenand P.A., Miami, 1985—, ptnr., 1988, Hickey & Jones, Miami, 1988—. Lectr. securities litigation Internat. Assn. Fin. Planners, 1989, 90, Fla. Inst. CPAs, 1990, Flood Ins. Conf., Columbus, Ohio, 1991, Scottsdale, Ariz., 1992, Orlando, Fla., 1993; lectr. admiralty law, Fla. Bar, 1994. Contbg. author: Fla. Bar Jour., 1990, Trail mag., 2000, P&I Internat., 1998. Interviewer of prospective undergrads. Duke U. Alumni Adv. Com., 1984—; arbitrator Miami Marine Arbitration Coun. Mem. ABA (litigation mgmt./econs. com. 1986—, comml. transactions and banking com. 1986—), Fla. Bar (chmn. admiralty law com. 2000-01, chmn. grievance com. 1986-89, vice chmn. 1999—, lectr. Bridge the Gap seminars 1984-85, jud. evaluation com. 1985, chmn. 11th cir. fee arbitration com. 1991—, cert. civil trial lawyer 1990, lectr. admiralty law 1994, vice chair admiralty law com. 1997—, mem. admiralty law com. 2000—, chair 2000-2001), Dade County Bar Assn. (vice assessment 2001-2002, bd. dirs. 1998—, media rels. com. 1982-83, membership com. 1982-83, legal edn. com. 1983-84, cir. ct. com. 1983-84, dir. 1984-86, chmn. young lawyers sect. meetings and programs com. 1985-86, chmn. young lawyers sect. sports com. 1984-85, exec. com. 1985—, chmn. profl. arbitration subcom. 1986—, cert. of merit 1985, 88, 89, 91, 921, 93, bd. dirs. 1990-93, 97—, chmn. banking and corp. litigation com. 1990, 91, 92, chmn. civil litigation com. 1992-93, exec. com. 1992-93, treas. 1999—, sec. 2000—, pres. 2001—), Greater Miami C. of C., Coral Gables C. of C., Propellor Club of U.S. (Miami divsn.), Marine Coun. So. Fla. (bd. dirs.), Southeastern Admiralty Law Inst. (proctor), Maritime Law Assn., Miami Marine Arbitration Coun., Phi Beta Kappa. Admiralty, General civil litigation, Personal injury. Office: Hickey Law Firm PA 1401 Brickell Ave Ste 510 Miami FL 33131-3501

HICKEY, JOHN KING, lawyer, career officer; b. Mt. Sterling, Ky. s. John Andrew and Anna Christine H.; m. Elizabeth Jane Pattavina, Nov. 23, 1944; children: Roger Dennis, John King, Patricia Elizabeth Corsini. JD, U. Ky., 1948; M in Internat. Affairs, George Washington U., 1974. Bar: Ky. 1949, Colo. 1958, U.S. Ct. Military Appeals 1959, U.S. Supreme Ct. 1959. Commd. 2d. lt. U.S. Army Air Forces, 1942; advanced through grades to col. USAF, 1964, ret., 1970; dir. legal judicial adminstrn. Council State Govts., Lexington, Ky., 1971-73; dir. continuing legal edn. U. Ky. Coll. Law, 1973-86; pvt. practice, 1986—. Mem. Nat. Assn. Attorneys Gen. (outstanding contributions award 1973, sec.), U. Ky. Law Alumni Assn. (sec., treas. 1973-76, appreciation award 1976), Ctrl. Ky. Knife Club (plaque 1997). Democrat. Roman Catholic. Avocations: machairologist, reading, walking, swimming. General practice, Public international, Military. Office: 3340 Nantucket Dr Lexington KY 40502-3205

HICKEY, JOHN MILLER, lawyer; b. Cleve., June 4, 1955; s. Lawrence Thomas and Margaret (Miller) H.; m. Sharon Salazar, Aug. 4, 1984; children: Theodore James, John Salazar, Margaret Maureen. Student, U. Wales, U.K., 1975-76; BA, Tulane U., 1977; JD cum laude, Calif. We. Sch. Law, 1981; LLM in tax, NYU, 1982. Bar: Calif. 1981, N.Mex. 1983, U.S. Dist. Ct. N.Mex. 1983, U.S. Tax Ct. 1983, U.S. Ct. Appeals (10th cir.) 1983. Prodn. control mgr. Randall-Textron, Inc., Wilmington, Ohio, 1977-78; assoc. Montgomery & Andrews, Santa Fe, 1983-88; shareholder, dir. Compton, Coryell, Hickey & Ives, 1988-93, Hickey & Ives, Santa Fe, 1993-97, Hickey & Johnson PA, Santa Fe, 1998-99, White, Koch, Kelly & McCarthy, P.A., Santa Fe, 1999—. Bd. dirs. Los Alamos (N.Mex.) Econ. Devel., Hospice Ctr., Inc., Santa Fe; sec. Inst. Water Policy Studies, Santa Fe. Republican. Roman Catholic. Avocations: bicycling, squash, reading. Estate planning, Probate, Taxation, general. Home: 806 Camino Zozobra Santa Fe NM 87505-6101 Office: White Koch Kelly & McCarthy PA 433 Paseo De Peralta Santa Fe NM 87501-1958

HICKS, BETHANY GRIBBEN, judge, commissioner, lawyer; b. N.Y., Sept. 8, 1951; d. Robert and DeSales Gribben; m. William A. Hicks III, May 21, 1982; children: Alexandra Elizabeth, Samantha Katherine. AB, Vassar Coll., 1973; MEd, Boston U., 1975; JD, Ariz. State U., 1984. Bar: Ariz. 1984. Pvt. practice, Scottsdale and Paradise Valley, Ariz., 1984-91; law clk. to Hon. Kenneth L. Fields Maricopa County Superior Ct. S.E. dist., Mesa, 1991-93; commr., judge pro tem domestic rels. and juvenile depts. Maricopa County Superior Ct. Ctrl. and S.E. Dists., Phoenix and Mesa, Ariz., 1993-99; magistrate Town of Paradise Valley, 1993-94; judge ctrl. dist. domestic rels. dept. Maricopa County Superior Ct., Phoenix, 1999-2000, presiding judge family ct. dept., 2000—. Mem. Jr. League of Phoenix, 1984-91; bd. dirs. Phoenix Children's Theatre, 1988-90; parliamentarian Girls Club of Scottsdale, Ariz., 1985-87, 89-90, bd. dirs., 1988-91; exec. bd., sec. All Saints' Episcopal Day Sch. Parents Assn., 1991-92, pres., 1993-94; active Nat. Charity League, 1995-99, Valley Leadership Class XIX, 1997-98; vol., Teach for Am., 1997—. Mem. ABA, State Bar Ariz., Ariz. State Bar Assn., Maricopa County Bar Assn., Ariz. Women Lawyers' Assn. (steering com. 1998—), Assn. Family Ct. Conciliators (bd. dirs. 2001—). Republican. Episcopalian. Office: 201 W Jefferson St Phoenix AZ 85003-2205 E-mail: whicks@swlaw.com, bhicks@superiorcourt.maricopa.gov

HICKS, C. FLIPPO, lawyer; b. Fredericksburg, Va., Feb. 24, 1929; s. Robert A. and Nell (Jones) H.; m. Patricia DeHardit (dec. 1983); children: Robert, Patricia Shull, J. Flippo (dec. 1995), Paula Mooradian. BS in Commerce, U. Va., 1950, LLB, 1952. Bar: Va. 1952, U.S. Supreme Ct. 1955. Asst. atty. gen. Commonwealth of Va., Richmond, 1953-59; ptnr. Martin, Hicks, Ingles, Ltd., Gloucester, Va., 1959-91; gen. counsel Va. Assn. Counties, Richmond, 1991—. Bd. dirs., v.p. Williamsburg (Va.) Nat. Bank, 1965-75; bd. dirs. 1st Va. Bank, Hampton Roads. Presdl. elector 1968, 76, 80; pres. exec. coun. Episcopal Diocese of Va., 1970-71, mem. standing com., 1971-74. Fellow Am. Bar Found.; mem. ABA (Leader of Yr. award Gen. Practice Sect., Constbar Leader of Yr. 1992), Va. State Bar (pres. 1990-91), Nat. Assn. of Counties Civil Attys. (pres. 1999—, bd. dirs.), Defenders Commn. Va. Democrat. Episcopalian. Avocations: gardening, college sports. General civil litigation. E-mail: counsel@vaco.org

HICKS, C. THOMAS, III, lawyer; b. N.Y.C., Sept. 14, 1945; s. Charles Thomas and Jeane (Merritt) H.; m. Susan Massie, Dec. 30, 1967 (div. Dec. 1997); children: Melissa, Merritt. BSCE, Va. Tech. U., 1967; JD, U. Ga., 1970; LLM in Tax, Georgetown U., 1975. Bar: Ga. 1970, Va. 1972, D.C. 1981. Assoc. Boothe, Prichard & Dudley, Fairfax, Va., 1975-78; ptnr. Wickwire, Gavin & Gibbs, P.C., Vienna, 1978-83, Shaw, Pittman, Potts & Trowbridge, McLean, 1983-98; shareholder Greenberg Traurig, 1998-2001; ptnr. Wilmer, Cutler & Pickering, 2001—. Gen. counsel Wolf Trap Found. Performing Arts, 1998-2001. Judge advocate USMC, Washington, 1971-75; co-founder, dir. No. Va. Transp. Alliance, McLean, Va., 1987, gen. counsel, 1987—. Mem. Va. Bar Assn. (vice chair bus. law coun.), Va. State Bar (bus. law sec. bd. governors, chmn. 1997-99), Fairfax Bar Assn., Nat. Assn. Bond Lawyers, Va. Assn. Comml. Real Estate (co-founder, pres., dir.), Nat Assn. Indsl. and Office Properties (pres. 1989-92, dir. Va. chpt. 1985-91, pres. 1990), No. Va. Tech. Coun. (dir. 2000—, gen. counsel 1996-2000), Greater Washington Bd. Trade, Fairfax County C. of C. (dir. 1998—). Avocations: singing, sailing, tennis, golf. Home: 6443 Madison McLean Dr Mc Lean VA 22101 Office: Wilmer Cutler & Pickering 1650 Tysons Blvd Ste 950 Tysons Corner VA 22102-4856 E-mail: thicks@wilmer.com

HICKS, JAMES THOMAS, lawyer, physician; b. Brownsville, Pa. s. Thomas A. and Florence Julia (O'Donnell) H. AB, BS, MS, U. Pitts.; PhD, George Washington U.; MD, U. Ark.; JD, DePaul U.; LLM in Health Law, Loyola U., 1989. Bar: Ill. 1977, Pa. 1977, U.S. Supreme Ct. 1980, N.Y. 1988, D.C. 1988, U.S. Dist. Ct. D.C. 1988, U.S. Ct. Appeals (7th cir.) 1977, U.S. Ct. Appeals (D.C. and Ill. cirs.) 1988; lic. airline transport flight instr.; cert. sports trainer, nutrition, old age and strength devel. Tchr. DePaul U. Coll. Law, Chgo., 1990—; intern USPHS Hosp., Balt.; resident VA Hosp., Pitts.; pvt. practice River Forest, Ill., Oak Brook Terrace. Contbr. editor Hosp. Mgmt. mag. Asst. surgeon USPHS. Recipient Outstanding Alumnus award De Paul U., 1980. Fellow ACP, Am. Coll. Pathologists, Am. Acad. Forensic Scientists, Am. Soc. Clin. Pathologists; mem. ABA (com. on professionalism and ethics, vice-chmn. health law com. gen. practice sect.), Royal Coll Physicians (Eng.), Assn. Trial Lawyers Am., Pa. Bar Asns., Ill. Bar Assn., Chgo. Bar Assn. (health law com., ethics com.), Ill. Trial Lawyers Assn., D.C. Bar Assn., Pa. Trial Lawyers Assn., N.Y. Bar Assn., N.Y. Acad. Sci., Univ. Club, Carlton Club, Elks, Moose, Oak Park Country Club. Criminal. Office: Ste 218 17 W 706 Butterfield Rd Oakbrook Terrace IL 60181

HICKS, WILLIAM ALBERT, III, lawyer; b. Welland, Ont., Can., Apr. 6, 1942; s. William Albert and June Gwendolyn (Birrell) H.; m. Bethany G. Galvin, May 21, 1982; children: James Christopher, Scott Kelly, Alexandra Elizabeth, Samantha Katherine. AB, Princeton U., 1964; LLB, Cornell U., 1967. Bar: N.Y. 1967, Ariz. 1972, U.S. Dist. Ct. Ariz. 1972. Assoc. Seward & Kissel, N.Y.C., 1967-68, Snell & Wilmer LLP, Phoenix, 1972-75, ptnr., 1976—. Instr. Ariz. State U., 1974-75. Mem. U.S. Olympic Fencing Squad, 1964; mem. bd. advisors Casino USA, Inc., 1981-84; bd. dirs. Scottsdale Arts Ctr. Assn., 1984-88, v.p. devel,. 1985-87; bd. dirs. Valley Leadership, Inc., 1987-91, sec., 1988-89, sec.-treas., 1989-90; bd. dirs. Scottsdale Cultural Coun., 1988-97, vice chmn., 1992-95, chmn., 1995-96; active The Luke's Men, 1992—, bd. dirs., 1993-97, 99—, sec., 1993-94, v.p. 1995-96, pres., 1996-97; mem. adv. bd. Scottsdale Arts Ctr., 1988-91, chmn., 1988-90; bd. dirs., vice chmn. Ariz. Coun. on Econ. Edn., 1999-2000, chmn., 2000—. Capt. JAG Corps, USAF, 1968-72. Recipient DSM. Mem. ABA, N.Y. State Bar Assn., Nat. Assn. Bond Lawyers (vice chmn. on fin. health care facilities 1982-83, chmn. com. on fin. health care facilities 1983-86, securities law and disclosure com. 1994—), Assn. for Govtl. Leasing and Fin., Princeton U. Alumni Assn. Ariz. (pres. 1978-81, sec. 1981—), Paradise Valley (Ariz.) Country Club. General corporate, Municipal (including bonds), Securities. Office: Snell & Wilmer LLP One Arizona Ctr Phoenix AZ 85004-2202 E-mail: whicks@swlaw.com

HIDEN, ROBERT BATTAILE, JR. lawyer; b. Boston, May 8, 1933; s. Robert Battaile Sr. and Clotilda (Waddell) H.; m. Ann Eliza McCracken, Mar. 27, 1956; children: Robert B. III, Elizabeth Patterson, John Hughes. BA, Princeton U., 1955; LLB, U. Va., 1960. Bar: N.Y. 1961, U.S. Ct. Appeals (2d cir.) 1974, U.S. Dist. Ct. (so. dist.) N.Y. 1975. Assoc. Sullivan & Cromwell, N.Y.C., 1960-67, ptnr., 1968-98, of counsel, 1999-2000, sr. counsel, 2001—. Articles editor and contbr. U. Va. Law Rev., 1959-60; contbr., mem. bd. editors Futures Internat. Law Letter, 1987-92. Trustee Hampton (Va.) U. and Hampton Inst., 1984—; mem. Dillard scholarship com. U. Va. Law Sch., 1984-98, 2001—; commr. Larchmont Little League, N.Y., 1964-68; chmn. Larchmont Jr. Sailing Program, 1977-78; vestry, jr. warden St. John's Episc. Ch., Larchmont, 1982-86, 99—. Served to lt. (j.g.) USNR, 1955-57. Mem. ABA, N.Y. State Bar Assn., Assn. of Bar of City of N.Y., N.Y. County Bar Assn., Am. Judicature Soc., Larchmont U. Club (pres. 1976-77), Larchmont Yacht Club (trustee 1979-85, sec. 1990—), Yale Club (N.Y.C.), Coral Beach Club (Bermuda), Raven Soc., Order of Coif, Omicron Delta Kappa. Democrat. Avocations: skiing, golf, sailing, tennis. General corporate, Mergers and acquisitions, Securities. Home: 2 Walnut Ave Larchmont NY 10538-4232 Office: Sullivan & Cromwell 125 Broad St Fl 28 New York NY 10004-2489

HIEKEN, CHARLES, lawyer; b. Granite City, Ill., Aug. 15, 1928; s. Samuel and Margaret (Isaacs) H.; m. Donna Jane Clanin, Jan. 6, 1961; children: Tina Jane, Seth Paul. SBEE, SMEE, MIT, 1952; LLB, Harvard U., 1957. Bar: Ill. 1957, Mass. 1958, U.S. Supreme Ct. 1960, U.S. Ct. Customs and Patent Appeals 1961, U.S. Ct. Claims 1963, U.S. Ct. Appeals (fed. cir.) 1982. Patent asst. Lab. Electronics, Boston, 1954-56, Fish, Richardson & Neave, Boston, 1956-57; assoc. Hill, Sherman, Meroni & Simpson, Chgo., 1957, Joseph Weingarten, Boston, 1957-58, Wolf, Greenfield & Hieken, Boston, 1958-61, ptnr., 1961-70; prin. Charles Hieken Law Offices, Waltham, Mass., 1970-87; ptnr. Fish & Richardson, Boston, 1987-94, prin., 1995—. Mem. Pres. Carter's adv. com. on indsl. innovation, 1979. Mem. pres.'s adv. coun. Bentley Coll., 1993—; mem. coun. Harvard Law Sch. Assn., 1998—. Served with U.S. Merchant Marine, 1944-47, U.S. Army, 1952-54. Mem. Boston Bar Assn. (mem. civil procedure com. 1959—), Mass. Bar Assn. (chmn. intellectual property com. 1977-80), Ill. State Bar Assn., Boston Patent Law Assn. (chmn. pub. rels. com. 1965-66, chmn. antitrust law com. 1966-70, 78-80, treas. 1970-71, v.p. 1971-72, pres.-elect 1972-73, pres. 1973-74), IEEE (sr., life), Down Town Club (bd. govs., v.p. gen. counsel), Tau Beta Pi, Eta Kappa Nu. Federal civil litigation, Patent, Trademark and copyright. Home: 193 Wilshire Dr Sharon MA 02067-1561 Office: Fish & Richardson PC 225 Franklin St 31st Fl Boston MA 02110-2804 E-mail: hieken@fr.com

HIER, MARSHALL DAVID, lawyer; b. Bay City, Mich., Aug. 24, 1945; s. Marshall George and Helen May (Copeland) H.; m. Nancy Speed Brown, June 26, 1970; children: John, Susan, Ann. BA, Mich. State U., 1966; JD, U. Mich., 1969. Bar: Mo. 1969. Assoc. Peper, Martin, Jensen, Maichel and Hetlage, St. Louis, 1969-76, ptnr., 1976-95; prin. Bertram, Peper and Hier, P.C., 1996—. Bd. dirs. Gateway Ctr. Met. St. Louis, Mercantile Libr. Assn., St. Louis Soc. Blind and Visually Impaired. Contbr. articles to profl. jours. Mem. St. Louis Bar Assn. (editor jour. 1988—), St. Louis Civil Round Table (former pres.). Baptist. General corporate, Private international, Securities. Home: 17141 Chaise Ridge Rd Chesterfield MO 63005-4457

HIESTAND, SHEILA PATRICIA, lawyer; b. Levittown, Pa., July 10, 1969; d. John Douglas Lloyd and Eileen Ann Cassidy; m. David Michael Hiestand, July 25, 1992; 1 child, Michael David. BA in Spanish and English, Centre Coll., Danville, Ky., 1990; JD, U. Ky., 1993. Bar: Ky. 1993, U.S. Dist. Ct. (ea. and we. dists.) Ky. 1994, U.S. Ct. Appeals (6th cir.) 1997. Assoc. Landrum & Shouse, Lexington, Ky., 1993-98, ptnr., 1999—. Bd. dirs., officer Vol. Ctr. of the Bluegrass, 1995-98; girls basketball coach Christ the King Sch., 1993-98. Mem. Fayette County Bar Assn. (Outstanding Young Lawyer 1998, pres. young lawyers sect. 1996-98, bd. dirs. 1996-99), Ky. Bar Assn. (bd. dirs. young lawyers sect., convention CLE com. 1997-98). Roman Catholic. Civil rights, General civil litigation, Workers' compensation. Office: Landrum & Shouse 106 W Vine St Ste 800 Lexington KY 40507-1688

HIGGINBOTHAM, PATRICK ERROL, federal judge; b. Ala., Dec. 16, 1938; Student, U. Ala., 1956, Arlington State Coll., 1957, North Tex. State U., 1958, U. Tex., 1958; BA, U. Ala., 1960, LLB, 1961; LLD (hon.), So. Meth. U., 1989. Bar: Ala. 1961, Tex. 1962, U.S. Supreme Ct. 1962. Assoc. to ptnr. Coke & Coke, Dallas, 1964-75; judge U.S. Dist. Ct. (no. dist.) Tex., 1976-82, U.S. Ct. Appeals (5th cir.), Dallas, 1982—. Adj. prof. So. Meth. U. Law Sch., 1971—, adj. prof. constl. law, 1981—; adj. prof. constnl. law U. Tex. Sch. Law, fall 1998; M.D. Anderson pub. svc. prof. in residence Tex. Tech. U. Sch. Law, spring 1999; John Sparkman jurist-in-residence U. Ala. Sch. Law, fall 1995, 97, 99; conferee Am. Assembly, 1975, Pound Conf., 1976; bd. suprs. Inst. Civil Justice Rand. Contbr. articles to profl. jours. With USAF, 1961-64, JAG. Recipient Dan Meador award U. Ala., Samuel E. Gates Litigation award Am. Coll. Trial Lawyers, 1997; named Outstanding Alumnus U. Tex., Arlington, 1978, One of Nation's 100 Most Powerful Persons for the 80's Next Mag. Fellow Am. Bar Found.; mem. ABA (chmn. com. to compile fed. jury charges antitrust sect., mem. coun. antitrust sect., bd. editors Jour. chair appellate judges conf. 1989—), Dallas Bar Assn. (dir., chmn. cons. legal aid civic affairs), Dallas Bar Found. (bd. dirs.), Am. Law Inst., S.W. Legal Found. (chmn. bd. of trustees), Am. Judicature Soc. (bd. dirs., trustee), Nat. Jud. Coun. State and Fed. Cts., Dallas Inn of Ct. (pres. 1996—, chair adv. com. on civil rules jud. conf. U.S. 1993-96), Farrah Law Soc., Order of Coif (hon.), Bench and Bar, Am. Inns. of Ct. Found. (pres. 1996-2000), Omicron Delta Kappa. Office: US Ct Appeals 13E1 US Courthouse 1100 Commerce St Dallas TX 75242-1027

HIGGINS, JOHN PATRICK, lawyer, mediator, educator, lobbyist; b. Beloit, Wis., Feb. 13, 1952; s. John Eugene and Catherine Marie (Beaudry) H. BA cum laude, St. Norbert Coll., 1973; postgrad., DePaul U. Law Sch., 1974-76; JD, U. Wis., Madison, 1977; MBA, Keller Grad. Sch. Mgmt., Milw., 1986; postgrad., U. Wis., Milw. Bar: Wis. 1977, U.S. Dist. Ct. (ea. and we. dists) Wis., 1977, U.S. Ct. Appeals (7th cir.), 1977, U.S. Supreme Ct., 1983. Assessment technician Kenosha County Assessor, Wis., 1973-75; law clk. various firms, Madison, Wis., 1976-77; claims atty. Employers Ins. of Wausau (Wis.), 1977-80, trial counsel, 1980-99; counsel Guttorm-

sen, Hartley & Guttermsen, Kenosha, 2000—. Part time instr. North Ctrl. Tech. Inst., Wausau, 1980; adj. prof. Marian Coll., Fond du Lac, Wis., 1990-2000, Carthage Coll., Kenosha, Wis., 2000—; dir. , v.p. legal John E. Higgins Appraisal Co., Kenosha, 1977-97; lectr., spkr. various profl. and fraternal groups; mem. dist. 1 investigative com. Office of Lawyer Regulation Wis. Supreme Ct., 2001—. Author articles and monographs. Bd. dirs., arbitrator Roman Cath. Archdiocese of Milw., 1983-85; mem. human rels commn. City of Kenosha, 1997—, vice chair, 1999-2001; mem. City of Kenosha Zoning Appeals Bd., 2001—. Fellow Young Lawyers Assn.; mem. State Bar Wis. (bd. govs. 1990-91, bd. dirs. young lawyers divsn. 1978-87, sec. 1979-82, chmn. law reform com. 1984-87, chmn. planning conf. young lawyers divsn. 1986, chmn. gavel awards com. 1985-87, chmn. comm. com. 1984-87, interprofl. com. 1987-89, conv. & entertainment com. 1988-1992, 94-97, chmn., mem. various coms.), Thomas More Soc., State Bar Assn. Wis., Civil Trial Coun. Wis., Kenosha Bar Assn., St. Norbert Coll. Alumni Assn. (exec. bd. dirs. 1979-87, chpt. liaison, editor chpt. newsletter, class devel. agt. 1998-99), Nat. Assn. State Bar Journ. (bd. trustee 1986-89), Am. Corp. Coun. Assn. (bd. dirs. 1989-98, pres. Wis. chpt. 1997-98), Am. Acad. ADR Attorneys, Phi Alpha Delta. State civil litigation, General corporate, Private international, Insurance. Office: Guttormsen Hartley Guttormsen & Wilk Ste 200 600 52d St Kenosha WI 53140 E-mail: JPH@kenoshalawyers.com

HIGGINS, KENNETH DYKE, lawyer; b. Benton, Tenn., Aug. 21, 1916; s. Fredrick Dyke and Martha (Dunn) H.; m. Jane Blair Webb; children: Jane Webb, Kenneth Dyke. AA, Tenn. Wesleyan Coll., 1936, LLB (hon.), 1984; AB, Transylvania U., 1938; JD, Tulane U., 1942. Bar: Tenn. 1946. Ptnr. Higgins, Biddle, Chester & Trew, Athens, Tenn., 1946—. Trustee Tenn. Wesleyan Coll. Served to lt. USN, 1942-46, PTO. Named to Hall of Fame Transylvania U., 1998. Fellow Tenn. Bar Found.; mem. ABA, Tenn. Bar Assn. Lodge: Kiwanis (sec.). General practice. Home: 1200 Woodacre Dr Athens TN 37303-2743

HIGGINS, MARY CELESTE, lawyer, researcher; b. Chgo., Feb. 9, 1943; d. Maurice James and Helen Marie (Egan) H. AB, St. Mary-of-the-Woods Coll., Ind., 1965; JD, DePaul U., 1970; LLM, John Marshall Law Sch., Chgo., 1976; postgrad., Harvard U., 1981, 82, MPA, 1982; MPhil, U. Cambridge (Eng.), 1983. Bar: Ill., 1970, U.S. Dist. Ct. (no. dist.) Ill. 1970. Sole practice, Chgo., 1970-72, 79-80; atty. corp. counsel dept. Continental Bank, 1972-76; asst. sec., asst. counsel Marshall Field & Co., 1976-79; sr. atty. Mattel, Inc., Hawthorne, Calif., 1980-81; rch. in revitalization and adjustment of U.S. Industries in U.S. and world markets, 1981-83; legal cons., 1983-85; Midwest regional officer Legal Svcs. Corp., 1985-87, assoc. dir., 1986, acting dir. office of field svcs., 1986-87, dir., 1987-89, Meridian One Corp., Alexandria, Va., 1990—. Recipient Am. Jurisprudence awards for acad. excellence, 1966-70. Mem. Ill. Bar Assn. General corporate, Private international, Public international. Home: 203 Yoakum Pkwy Apt 508 Alexandria VA 22304-3711

HIGGS, CRAIG DEWITT, lawyer; b. Coronado, Calif., Mar. 19, 1944; s. DeWitt Alexander and Florence (Fuller) H.; children: Marisa DeWitt, Alexander Craig; m. Cynthia Aaron, May 19, 1993. B.S., U. Redlands, 1966; J.D., U. San Diego, 1969. Bar: Calif. 1971, U.S. Dist. Ct. (so. dist.) Calif. 1971. Dept. city atty. San Diego, 1970-71; assoc. Higgs, Fletcher & Mack, San Diego, 1971-76, ptnr., 1976—; del. 9th Cir. Jud. Conf., 1992-94; dir. San Diego Law Ctr., 1983-89. Bd. visitors U. San Diego Sch. Law, 1983—. Mem. San Diego Bar Found. (bd. dirs. 1983-89), Am. Bd. Trial Advocates (pres. 1995), San Diego Inn of Cts. (pres. 1993), State Bar Calif. (chmn. commn. on jud. nominees evaluation 1981), San Diego County Bar Assn. (pres. 1984). Democrat. Federal civil litigation, State civil litigation, Personal injury. Home: 12686 Crest Knolls Ct San Diego CA 92130-2411 Office: Higgs Fletcher & Mack 401 W A St Ste 2600 San Diego CA 92101-7913

HIGGS, JOHN H. lawyer; b. Balt., Mar. 10, 1934; s. E. Homer and Josephine (Doughty) H.; m. Helen Platt, Aug. 25, 1956; children: Sarah, Anne, Julia, Susan. AB, Dartmouth Coll., 1956; LLB, U. Pa., 1960. Bar: N.Y. 1961. Founder Higgs Pavements Co., Milford, Conn., 1953-56; assoc. Sullivan & Cromwell, N.Y.C., 1960-61, 62-68, Wickes, Riddell, Bloomer, Jacobi & McGuire, N.Y.C., 1968, ptnr., 1969-79, Morgan, Lewis & Bockius, LLP, N.Y.C., 1979-97, counsel, 1997—; ptnr. Skyport Indsl. Park, Newark; legal advisor NetCharge.com Inc., N.Y.C. Sec. Ea. States Bankcard Assn., Lake Success, N.Y., 1970-88; bd. dirs. Indsl. Bank Japan Trust Co., N.Y., 1974—, IBJ Found. Inc., N.Y., 1989—; mem. staff adv. com. on comml. bank supervision State N.Y., 1965-66. Contbr. articles to profl. jours. Mayor Village of Pelham Manor, N.Y., 1979-81. Banking, Finance, Private international. Home: John's Island 56 Wax Myrtle Way Vero Beach FL 32963-3721 Office: Morgan Lewis & Bockius 101 Park Ave Fl 44 New York NY 10178-0060

HIGH, DAVID ROYCE, lawyer; b. Oklahoma City, Aug. 28, 1950; s. Jack Eugene and Harriett Ann High; m. Charlotte Anne Bonsteel, Dec. 28, 1975; 1 child, Katie McKenzie. BA, U. Okla., 1973; JD, Oklahoma City U., 1978. Bar: Okla. 1978, U.S. Dist. Ct. (we. dist.) Okla. 1978, U.S. Ct. Appeals (10th cir.) 1990. Assoc. Tomerlin & High, Oklahoma City, 1978-80; ptnr. Tomerlin, High & High, 1980-92, pvt. practice law, 1992—. Legal counsel The Children's Ctr., Bethany, Okla., 1978—, Oklahoma City Beautiful Inc., 1982-89. Mem. ABA, Okla. Bar Assn. (gov. 1988-91), Oklahoma County Bar Assn. (bd. dirs. 1981-91, v.p. 1984-85, Outstanding Oklahoma County Young Lawyer award 1981). Avocation: tennis. State civil litigation, General corporate, Probate. Office: Tomerlin High & High 3601 N Classen Blvd Ste 203 Oklahoma City OK 73118-3269

HIGHSMITH, SHELBY, federal judge; b. Jacksonville, Fla., Jan. 31, 1929; s. Isaac Shelby and Edna Mae (Phillips) H.; m. Mary Jane Zimmerman, Nov. 25, 1972; children— Holly Law, Shelby. A.A., Ga. Mil. Coll., 1948; B.A., J.D., U. Kansas City, 1958. Bar: Fla. 1958. Trial atty., Kansas City, Mo., 1958-59, Miami, Fla., 1959-70; circuit judge Dade County, 1970-75; sr. ptnr. Highsmith, Strauss, Glatzer & Deutsch, P.A., Miami, 1975-91; judge U.S. Dist. Ct. (so. dist.) Fla., 1991—. Chief legal adviser Gov.'s War on Crime Program, 1967-68; spl. counsel Fla. Racing Commn., 1969-70; mem. Inter-Agy. Law Enforcement Planning Counsel of Fla., 1969-70. Served to capt. AUS, 1949-55. Decorated Bronze Star; recipient Outstanding Alumni Achievement Law award, U. Mo., 1998. Fellow Internat. Soc. Barristers; mem. ABA, Dade County Bar Assn., Bench and Robe, Torch and Scroll, Miami Nat. Golf Club, Wildcat Cliffs Country Club, (Highlands, N.C.), Omicron Delta, Phi Alpha Delta. Republican. Roman Catholic. Office: Fed Justice Bldg 99 NE 4th St Rm 1027 Miami FL 33132-2138

HIGHTOWER, JACK ENGLISH, former state supreme court justice, congressman; b. Memphis, Sept. 6, 1926; s. Walter Thomas and Floy Edna (English) H.; m. Colleen Ward, Aug. 26, 1950; children— Ann, Amy, Alison. B.A., Baylor U., 1949; JD, 1951; LLM, Univ. Va., 1992. Bar: Tex. 1951. Since practiced in, Vernon; mem. Tex. Ho. of Reps., 1953-54; dist. atty. 46th Jud. Dist. Tex., 1955-61; mem. Tex. Senate, 1965-75, pro tempore, 1971; mem. 94th-98th Congresses from 13th Tex. Dist., 1975-85; 1st asst. atty. gen. State of Tex., 1985-87; justice Texas Supreme Ct., Austin, 1988-95; ret., 1996. Mem. Tex. Law Enforcement Study Commn., 1957; del. White House Conf. Children and Youth, 1970; alt. del. Democratic Nat. Conv., 1968; bd. regents Midwestern U., Wichita Falls, Tex., 1962-65; trustee Baylor U., 1972-81, acting gov., 1971; trustee Wayland Bapt. Univ., Plainview, Tex., 1991—, Tex. Bapt. Children's Home, 1959-62, Tex. Scottish Rite Hosp. Children, 1991—, Human Welfare Commn.; bd. dirs. Bapt. Standard, 1959-68; mem. Nat. Commn. on Libra. and Info. Sci., 1999—. With USNR, 1944-46. Named Outstanding Dist. Atty, Tex., Tex. Law Enforcement Found., 1959, Disting. Alumnus, Baylor U., 1978; recipient Knapp-Porter award Tex. A&M Univ., 1980. Mem. Tex. Dist. and County Attys. Assn. (pres. 1958-59), Scottish Rite Ednl. Assn. Tex. (exec. com. 1990—), Tex. Supreme Ct. Historical Soc. (pres. 1991-98), Tex. Bar. Found. (fellow 1992), SAR, U.S. Supreme Ct. Historical Soc., Tex. State Historical Assn. (exec. coun. 1998—), Masons (grand master Tex. 1972), Lions (pres. Vernon 1961).

HIGINBOTHAM, JACQUELYN JOAN, lawyer; b. Dec. 15, 1951; d. Ivan Lyle and Ruth Harriet (La Point) H.; m. Robert Redditt; children: Altara Roxana, Rigel Rowena. AA, Northeastern Jr. Coll., Sterling, Colo., 1972; BA, U. No. Colo., 1974; JD, U. Colo., 1978. Bar: Colo. 1978, U.S. Dist. Ct. Colo. 1978, U.S. Ct. Appeals (10th cir.) 1983. Staff, mng. atty. Colo. Legal Svcs., Ft. Morgan, 1979—. Mem. adv. bd. Caring Ministries Morgan County, 1986-87. Mem. Colo. Bar Assn., Christian Legal Soc., Order of Colf. Democrat. Episcopalian. Avocations: astronomy, music, skating. Family and matrimonial, Health, Pension, profit-sharing, and employee benefits. Home: 702 Sherman St # 1123 Fort Morgan CO 80701-3540 Office: Colo Legal Svcs 209 State St Fort Morgan CO 80701-2115

HILBERT, OTTO KARL, II, lawyer; b. Colorado Springs, Colo., Feb. 9, 1962; s. Otto Karl and Mary Rachel (Shine) H.; m. Lucille Megan O'Shaughnessy, Apr. 21, 1995. BA, U. Notre Dame, 1984, postgrad., 1985; JD, U. Colo., 1988. Bar: Colo. 1989, Ariz. 1989, Wis. 1998, U.S. Dist. Ct. (no. dist.) Calif, U.S. Dist. Ct. (we. dist.) Mich. 2001, U.S. Ct. Appeals (9th cir.) 1991, U.S. Tax Ct. 1992, U.S. Ct. Appeals (10th cir.) 1993, U.S. Supreme Ct. 1995, U.S. Dist. Ct. (we. dist.) Mich. 2001. Assoc. Kelly, Stansfield & O'Donnell, Denver, 1988-89, 92-93, Russell Piccoli, Ltd., Phoenix, 1989-92, LeBoeuf, Lamb, Greene & MacRae LLP, Denver, 1993-96; shareholder Reinhart, Boerner, Van Deuren, Norris & Rieselbach PC, 1996-2000, Robinson Waters & O'Dorisio, PC, Denver, 2000—. Arbitrator Nat. Assn. Securities Dealers, Inc., 1993—, Nat. Futures Assn., 1993—, Nat. Arbitration and Mediator's Internat. div. bds. arbitration. Mem. law sch. adv. coun. U. Notre Dame, 1989-92; cons. Ariz. Spl. Olympics, Phoenix, 1989-92; mem. Edward Frederick Sorin Soc., Notre Dame, Ind., 1989—; bd. dirs. Denver Athletic Club, 2000—. Mem. ABA, Colo. Bar Assn., Denver Bar Assn., Ariz. Bar Assn., Wis. Bar Assn., Notre Dame Club of Phoenix (1st v.p. 1991-92, bd. dirs. 1989-92, Award of the Yr. 1992), Notre Dame Club of Denver (bd. dirs. 1995-97), Lakewood Country Club (bd. dirs. 1998—). Republican. Roman Catholic. Avocations: piano, guitar, golf. Federal civil litigation, Securities, Sports. Office: Robinson Waters & O'Dorisio PC 1099 18th St Ste 2600 Denver CO 80202 Address: Reinhart Boerner Van Deuren 1775 Sherman St Ste 2100 Denver CO 80203-4320 E-mail: ohilbert@twolaw.com

HILBOLDT, JAMES SONNEMANN, lawyer, investment advisor; b. Dallas, July 21, 1929; s. Grover C. and Grace E. (Sonnemann) H.; m. Martha M. Christian, Sept. 5, 1953; children: James, Katherine Hilboldt Farrell, Susanna Jean, Thomas. AB in Econs., Harvard U., 1952; postgrad., U. Chgo., 1952-53; JD, U. Mich., 1956. Registered investment advisor. With comml. and trust dept. No. Trust Co., Chgo., 1952-53; pvt. practice Kalamazoo, 1956—; pvt. practice as investment advisor, 1971—. Bd. dirs. Lafourche Realty Co., Inc., Kalamazoo, pres., 1971—. Bd. dirs. Kalamazoo Tennis Patrons, Inc., 1974-95, Downtown Devel. Authority, Kalamazoo, 1982-88, Downtown Tomorrow, Inc., Kalamazoo, 1985—, sec., treas., 1995, Downtown Kalamazoo Inc., 1988-91; treas., trustee The Power Found., 1967—, sec., 1967-94. Sgt. USMC, 1946-48. Mem. ABA, Mich. Bar Assn., Kalamazoo County Bar Assn., Harvard Club Western Mich. (pres. 1972-74), Kalamazoo Country Club, Park Club, Harvard Club N.Y.C. Avocations: tennis, swimming. Home: 4126 Lakeside Dr Kalamazoo MI 49008-2814 Office: 136 E Michigan Ave Ste 1201 Kalamazoo MI 49007-3918

HILDEBRAND, DANIEL WALTER, lawyer; b. Oshkosh, Wis., May 1, 1940; s. Dan M. and Rose Marie (Baranowski) H.; m. Dawn E. Erickson; children: Daniel G., Douglas P., Elizabeth A., Rachel E., Jacob E. BS, U. Wis., 1962, LLB, 1964. Bar: Wis. 1964, U.S. Dist. Ct. (we. dist.) Wis. 1964, N.Y. 1965, U.S. Dist. Ct. (so. and ea. dists.) N.Y. 1967, U.S. Ct. Appeals (2d cir.) 1968, U.S. Dist. Ct. (ea. dist.) Wis. 1970, U.S. Ct. Appeals (7th cir.) 1970, U.S. Supreme Ct. 1970, U.S. Tax Ct. 1986, U.S. Ct. Appeals (8th cir.) 1988, U.S. Ct. Appeals (D.C. cir.) 1991. Assoc. Willkie, Farr & Gallagher, N.Y.C., 1964-68; from assoc. to ptnr. DeWitt Ross & Stevens S.C., Madison, Wis., 1968—. Lectr. U. Wis. Law Sch., Madison, 1972—; mem. Joint Survey Com. on Tax Ememptions Wis. Editor: U. Wis. Law Rev., 1963-64. Pres. Wis. Law Foun., 1993-95, Wis. Jud. Commn., 1992-98, chairperson, 1997-98. Fellow Am. Bar Found. (life), Wis. Law Found. (life), Wis. Bar Found.; mem. ABA (com. pub. fin. judicial campaigns 2000—, mem. trial practice com. litigation sect., ho. of dels. 1992—, standing com. on ethics 1997—, Wis. state delegate 1995—), Wis. Bar Assn. (bd. govs. 1981-85, 86-93, mem. exec. com. 1987-93, chmn. 1988-89, pres. 1991-92), N.Y. State Bar Assn., Dane County Bar Assn. (pres. 1980-81), 7th Cir. Bar Assn., Am. Law Inst., Am. Acad. Appellate Lawyers, James E. Doyle Inn of Ct. Roman Catholic. Federal civil litigation, State civil litigation. Office: 2 E Mifflin St Ste 600 Madison WI 53703-2890 E-mail: dwh@dewittross.com

HILDEBRANDT, GEORGE FREDERICK, lawyer; b. Claverack, N.Y., Mar. 28, 1959; s. Harry K. and Sophie Evelyn (Reutenauer) H. BA, Syracuse U., 1981, JD, 1984. Bar: N.Y. 1985, U.S. Dist. Ct. (no. dist.) N.Y. 1986, U.S. Supreme Ct. 1997, U.S. Ct. Appeals (2d cir.) 1998. Atty. Frank H. Hiscock Legal Aid Soc., Syracuse, N.Y., 1985-88; pvt. practice, 1988—. Mem. Nat. Assn. Criminal Def. Lawyers, N.Y. State Trial Lawyers Assn., Onondaga County Bar Assn. Criminal, Personal injury. Office: 300 Crown Bldg 304 S Franklin St Syracuse NY 13202-1233

HILDEBRANDT, SHARRIE L. legal technology educator, paralegal; b. Berwyn, Ill., Sept. 1, 1940; m. Richard C. Hildebrandt, Dec. 10, 1960; children— Jeffrey, Laura, Douglas. A.A.S., William R. Harper Coll., 1973; B.A., DePaul U., 1975; M.Ed., U. Ill., 1982. Coordinator legal tech. program William R. Harper Coll., Palatine, Ill., 1974— ; owner Adminstrv. Paralegal Services, Arlington Heights, Ill., 1973— ; mem. adv. bd. Legal Asst. Today mag., 1984. Author: Legal Assistant Program Development Guide, 1978. Pres. Regional Bd. Sch. Trustees, Cook County, Ill., 1974-83. Mem. Am. Assn. Paralegal Edn. (bd. dirs. 1982-84), ABA (edn. com.), Am. Fedn. Tchrs., Nat. Fedn. Paralegals, Ill. Paralegal Assn. Club: N.W. Suburban Women's Republican (corr. sec. 1981-82, newsletter editor). Office: William R Harper Coll Algonquin And Roselle Rd Palatine IL 60067

HILDNER, PHILLIPS BROOKS, II, lawyer; b. Battle Creek, Mich., June 26, 1944; s. Phillips Brooks and Eva Marie (Burek) H.; divorced; 1 child, Phillips Brooks III. BS, Western Mich. U., 1967; JD, Detroit Coll. Law, 1971. Bar: Mich. 1971. Asst. prosecuting atty. Genesee County, Flint, Mich., 1971-73; ptnr. Conover, Hildner & Zielinski, Fenton, 1973-79; sole practice, 1980—. Sponsoring atty. Law Day, Fenton High Sch., 1973—. Mem. State Bar Mich., Genesee County Bar Assn., Fenton C. of C., 2d Century Club Detroit Coll. Law, Delta Theta Phi. Episcopalian. Avocations: fly fishing, hunting, running, exercise. General practice, Probate. Office: PO Box 87 111 W Shiawassee Ave Fenton MI 48430-2005

HILES, BRADLEY STEPHEN, lawyer; b. Granite City, Ill., Nov. 11, 1955; s. Joseph J. and Betty Lou (Goodman) H.; m. Toni Jonine Failoni, Aug. 12, 1977; children: Eric Stephen, Nina Catherine, Emily Christine. BA cum laude, Furman U., 1977; JD cum laude, St. Louis U., 1980. Bar: Mo. 1980, U.S. Dist. Ct. (ea. dist.) Mo., 1980, Ill. 1981. From assoc. to ptnr. Blackwell Sanders Peper Martin, St. Louis, 1980—. V.p., sec., gen. counsel Miss. Lime Co., 1992. Editor-in-chief St. Louis Univ. Law Jour., 1979-80; contbr. articles to profl. jours. Pres. Second Baptist Ch. of St. Louis, 1988. Mem. Bar Assn. of Met. St. Louis (chmn. environ. and conservation law com. 1993-94). Republican. Baptist. Avocations: gospel singing, cycling. Environmental, Labor. Home: 34 Meditation Way Ct Florissant MO 63031-6535 Office: Blackwell Sanders Peper Martin 720 Olive St Fl 24 Saint Louis MO 63101-2338

HILKER, WALTER ROBERT, JR. lawyer; b. L.A., Apr. 18, 1921; s. Walter Robert and Alice (Cox) H.; m. Ruth H. Hibbard, Sept. 7, 1943; children: Anne Katherine, Walter Robert III. BS, U. So. Calif., 1942, LLB, 1948. Bar: Calif. 1949. Sole practice, Los Angeles, 1949-55; ptnr. Parker, Milliken, Kohlmeier, Clark & O'Hara, 1955-75; of counsel Pacht, Ross, Warne, Bernhard & Sears, Newport Beach, Calif., 1980-84. Trustee Bella Mabury Trust; bd. dirs. Houchin Found. Served to lt. USNR, 1942-45. Decorated Bronze Star. Mem. ABA, Calif. Bar Assn., Orange County Bar Assn. Republican. Clubs: Spring Valley Lake Country (Apple Valley, Calif.); Balboa Bay (Newport Beach, Calif.). Home and Office: 143 Stonecliffe Aisle Irvine CA 92612-3778

HILL, ALFRED, lawyer, educator; b. N.Y.C., Nov. 7, 1917; m. Dorothy Turck, Aug. 12, 1960; 1 dau., Amelia. B.S., Coll. City N.Y., 1937; LL.B., Bklyn. Law Sch., 1941, LL.D., 1986; S.J. D., Harvard U., 1957. Bar: N.Y. State bar 1943, Ill 1958. With SEC, 1943-52; prof. law So. Meth. U., 1953-56, Northwestern U., 1956-62, Columbia U., 1962-75, Simon H. Rifkind prof. law, 1975-87, Simon H. Rifkind prof. law emeritus, 1988—. Contbr. articles on torts, conflict of laws, fed. cts. constl. law to legal jours. Mem. Am. Law Inst. Home: 79 Sherwood Rd Tenafly NJ 07670-2734 Office: Columbia Law Sch New York NY 10027

HILL, BRIAN DONOVAN, lawyer; b. Sanford, Fla., July 27, 1947; s. Herbert Charles and Catherine (Kenny) H.; m. Carol Ponton, Aug. 24, 1978; children: Erin, Chad, Michael, Matthew, Casey. BS, JD, U. Fla. Bar: Fla. 1975, U.S. Dist. Ct. (mid. dist.) Fla. Assoc. Maquire, Voorhis & Wells, Gainesville, Fla., 1974-80, Swann and Haddock, Orlando, 1980-82; ptnr. Taraska and Hill, 1983-86, Hill and Hill, Orlando, 1986-87, Hill & Ponton P.A., Orlando, 1987—. Served to lt. USN, 1969-74. Mem. Phi Beta Kappa, Phi Kappa Phi. Federal civil litigation, State civil litigation, Personal injury. Home: 103 Ocean Shore Blvd Ormond Beach FL 32176-5734 Office: Hill & Ponton PA PO Box 2673 Orlando FL 32802-2673

HILL, CHRISTOPHER T. lawyer; b. Washington, Oct. 10, 1971; s. Ralph J. and Penny G. H. BS in Psychology, Kansas State U., 1994; JD, Lewis and Clark Coll., 1997. Bar: Oreg. Assoc. Jeffrey Foote & Assocs., Portland, Oreg., 1997-98. Mem. ABA, Assn. of Trial Lawyers of Am. Avocations: guitar, shotokan karate of Am. Insurance, Personal injury, Product liability. Office: PO Box 1096 Portland OR 97205

HILL, EARL MCCOLL, lawyer; b. Bisbee, Ariz., June 12, 1926; s. Earl George and Jeanette (McColl) H.; m. Bea Dolan, Nov. 22, 1968 (dec. Aug. 1998); children: Arthur Charles, John Earl, Darlene Stern, Tamara Fegert. BA, U. Wash., 1960, JD, 1961. Bar: Nev. 1962, U.S. Ct. Claims 1978, U.S. Ct. Appeals (9th cir.) 1971, U.S. Supreme Ct. 1978. Law clk. Nev. Supreme Ct., Carson City, 1962; assoc. Gray, Horton & Hill, Reno, 1962-65, ptnr., 1965-73, Marshall Hill Cassas & de Lipkau (and predecessors), Reno, 1974—, Sherman & Howard, Denver, 1982-91. Judge pro tem Reno mcpl. ct., 1964-70; lectr. continuing legal edn.; mem. Nev. Commn. on Jud. Selection 1977-84; trustee Rocky Mountain Mineral Law Found. 1976-95, sec. 1987-88. Contbr. articles to profl. jours. Mem. ABA, ATLA, State Bar Nev. (chmn. com on jud. adminstrn. 1971-77), Washoe County Bar Assn., Am. Judicature Soc., Lawyer Pilots Bar Assn., Soc. Mining Law Antiquarians (sec.-treas. 1975—), Prospectors Club. General civil litigation, Environmental, Real property. Office: Holcomb Profl Ctr 333 Holcomb Ave Ste 300 Reno NV 89502-1665 E-mail: ehill1@mhcl-law.com

HILL, JAMES CLINKSCALES, federal judge; b. Darlington, S.C., Jan. 8, 1924; s. Albert Michael and Alberta (Clinkscales) H.; m. Mary Cornelia Black, June 7, 1946; children: James Clinkscales, Albert Michael. BS in Commerce, U. S.C., 1948; JD, Emory U., 1948. Bar: Ga. 1948, U.S. Supreme Ct. 1969. Assoc. Gambrell, Russell, Killorin & Forbes, Atlanta, 1948-55, ptnr., 1955-63, Hurt, Hill & Richardson, Atlanta, 1963-74; judge U.S. Dist. Ct. (no. dist.) Ga., 1974-76, U.S. Cir. Ct. (5th cir.), Atlanta, 1976-81, U.S. Cir. Ct. (11th cir.), Atlanta, 1981-89; sr. U.S. cir. judge U.S. Ct. Appeals, 1989—. Past chmn. com. on appellate ednl. programs Fed. Jud. Ctr.; former mem. com. on intercir. assignments Jud. Conf. U.S. With USAAF, 1943-45. Fellow ACTL, Am. Bar Found. (life); m. ABA, Am. Law Inst., World Assn. Judges, State Bar Ga., Atlanta Bar Assn., Am. Judicature Soc., Lawyers Club Atlanta (life), Old War Horse Lawyers. Republican. Baptist. Office: US Ct Appeals PO Box 52598 Jacksonville FL 32201-2598 E-mail: JCHretreat@aol.com

HILL, JOHN GLENWOOD, JR. university counsel, lawyer; b. Hartford, Conn., Aug. 2, 1929; John Glenwood and Marion E. (Cullen) H.; m. Barbara Oppel, Nov. 12, 1955; children— John G., Ellen E. B.A., LL.B., U. Conn., 1954, Ph.D., 1972; M.A., Trinity Coll., 1962. Bar: Conn. 1954, U.S. Dist. Ct. Conn. 1956, U.S. Supreme Ct. 1971; Mass. 1977, U.S. Dist. Ct. Mass. 1978, Wis. 1980. Asst. atty. gen., counsel pub. Utilities Commr., State of Conn., 1958-67; gen. counsel U. Conn., Storrs, 1967-76, Boston U., 1976-80, Marquette U., Milw., 1980— ; dir. Colloquium on Anglo Am. Law, London, 1984, 86. Co-author: The Student, The College, The Law, 1972; also articles. Served with USCG, 1954-56. Mem. Nat. Assn. Coll. and Univ. Attys. (exec. bd. 1980-83). Office: Marquette Univ 1212 W Wisconsin Ave Milwaukee WI 53233-2225

HILL, JOHN HOWARD, lawyer; b. Pitts., Aug. 12, 1940; s. David Garrett and Eleanor Campbell (Musser) H. B.A., Yale U., 1962, J.D., 1965. Bar: Pa. 1965, U.S. Dist. Ct. (we dist.) Pa. 1965, U.S. Ct. Appeals (3d cir.) 1965, U.S. Supreme Ct. 1982. Assoc. Reed, Smith, Shaw & McClay, Pitts., 1965-75, ptnr., 1975-90; of counsel Jackson, Lewis, Schnitzler & Krupman, 1991—. Bd. dirs. Travelers Aid Soc., Pitts., 1972-99, treas., 1982-87, pres., 1987-90; bd. dirs. Pitts. Opera, Pitts. Symphony Soc. Mem. ABA, Pa. Bar Assn., Allegheny County Bar Assn., Hosp. Assn. Pa., Pa. Soc., Duquesne Club, Fox Chapel Golf Club, Rolling Rock Club, Phi Gemma Delta. Republican. Presbyterian. Home: 4722 Bayard St Pittsburgh PA 15213-1708 Office: Jackson Lewis Schnitzler & Krupman One PPG Pl 28th Fl Pittsburgh PA 15222-5414 E-mail: hillj@jacksonlewis.com

HILL, LUTHER LYONS, JR. lawyer; b. Des Moines, Aug. 21, 1922; s. Luther Lyons and Mary (Hippee) H.; m. Sara S. Carpenter, Aug. 12, 1950; children— Luther Lyons III, Mark Lyons. BA, Williams Coll., 1947; LLB, Harvard U., 1950; LLD (hon.), Simpson Coll., 1979. Bar: Iowa 1951. Law clk. to Justice Hugo L. Black U.S. Supreme Ct., 1950-51; assoc., ptnr. Henry & Henry, Des Moines, 1951-69; mem. legal staff Equitable Life Ins. Co. of Iowa, 1952-87, exec. v.p., 1969-87, gen. counsel, 1970-87; of counsel Nyemaster, Goode, McLaughlin, Voigts, Wiest, Hansell O'Brien, Des Moines, 1992—. Counsel, adminstr. Iowa Life and Health Ins. Guaranty Assn. Bd. dirs., past pres. United Comty. Svcs. Greater Des Moines; past trustee, past chmn. Simpson Coll., Indianola, Iowa; bd. chmn. Iowa State Hist. Found., 1997-2001; trustee The Hoyt Sherman Pl. Found.

Capt. M.I., AUS, WWII, ETO. Mem. ABA, Iowa Bar Assn., Polk County Bar Assn., Assn. Life Ins. Counsel, Des Moines Club, Wakonda Club. Republican. Avocation: walking in the Swiss mountains. Insurance, Probate. Home: 2801 Park Ave Des Moines IA 50321-1515 Office: Ste 1600 700 Walnut St Des Moines IA 50309-3929

HILL, MILTON KING, JR. retired lawyer; b. Balt., Nov. 29, 1926; s. Milton King and Mary Fusselbaugh (Hall) H.; m. Agnes Ciotti, June 11, 1949; children: Thomas Michael, Milton King, III, Susan Hill. BS in Bus. and Pub. Adminstrn., U. Md., 1950, JD, 1952. Bar: Md. 1952, U.S. Dist. Ct. Md. 1952, U.S. Ct. Appeals (4th cir.) 1952. Assoc. Smith, Somerville & Case, Balt., 1952-55, ptnr., 1955-90; ret. Mem. faculty Md. Hosp. Ednl. Inst. Served with USAF, 1944-46. Fellow Am. Coll. Trial Lawyers, Internat. Soc. Barristers; mem. Md. State Bar Assn., Md. Bar Assn., Nat. Conf. Commrs. Uniform State Laws (pres. 1981-83, chmn. model punitive damages act drafting com.), Assn. Def. Trial Counsel (pres. 1964-65), Internat. Assn. Ins. Counsel, ABA (ho. of dels. 1981-83), Md. Bar Found., Am. Acad. Hosp. Attys. Clubs: Potapskut Sailing Assn., Wednesday Law. Federal civil litigation, State civil litigation, Insurance. Home: 8810 Walther Blvd Apt 2329 Parkville MD 21234-5762 E-mail: khill2329@aol.com

HILL, PHILIP, retired lawyer; b. East Saint Louis, Ill., Mar. 13, 1917; s. Nehemiah William and Lulu Myrtle (Johnson) H.; m. Betty Jean Stone, July 4, 1942; children: William Stone, Thomas Chapman, Nancy Layton, Mary Anne. AB in Chemistry, U. Ill., 1937; PhD in Chemistry, Ohio State U., 1941; JD, John Marshall Law Sch., Chgo., 1968. Bar: Ill. 1968, U.S. Patent Office 1969, U.S. Ct. Appeals (fed. cir.) 1982. With Standard Oil Co. Ind., 1941-78, patent atty., 1969-73, dir. petroleum and corp. patents and licensing, 1973-78; ptnr. Hill & Hill, Lansing, Ill., 1978-86; pvt. practice law Philip Hill, P.C., 1987-96; ret., 1996. Cons. Univ. Patents, Inc., Norwalk, Conn., 1980-89; treas. Am. Waste Reduction Corp., 1992-96. Contbr. articles to profl. jours.; patentee in field. Mem.: ABA, AAAS, Ill. State Bar Assn., Am. Intellectual Property Law Assn., Chgo. Patent Law Assn., Am. Chem. Soc., Kiwanis (Lansing, pres. 1959, 84), Phi Beta Kappa, Sigma Xi. Methodist. General corporate, Patent, Trademark and copyright. Home: 17946 Chicago Ave Lansing IL 60438-2261 Office: PO Box 187 Lansing IL 60438-0187

HILL, PHILIP BONNER, lawyer; b. Charleston, W.Va., May 1, 1931; AB, Princeton U., 1952; LLB, W.Va. U., 1957. Bar: W.Va. 1957, Iowa 1965. Assoc. Dayton, Campbell & Love, Charleston, W.Va., 1957-61; ptnr. Porter, Hill, Thomas, Williams & Hubbard, 1961-65; v.p. Thomas & Hill, 1961-65; assoc. counsel Equitable Life Ins. Co. of Iowa, Des Moines, 1965-68, counsel, 1968-75; ptnr. Reimenschneider, Hanes & Hill, 1975-79, Austin & Gaudineer, Des Moines, 1979-82, Snyder & Hassig, Des Moines, 1982-96, of counsel Sistersville & New Martinsville, W.Va., 1997-99, Bowles Rice McDavid Graff & Love, PLLC, Martinsburg, 2000—. Mem. staff W.Va. Law Rev., 1955-57; contbr. articles to profl. jours. Lt. USNR, 1952-54. Mem. ABA (exec. coun. young lawyers sect. 1966-67), W.Va. State Bar (chmn. jr. bar sect. 1961-62, bd. govs. 1989-92), W.Va. Bar Assn. (pres. 1998-99), Iowa State Bar Assn., Assn. Life Ins. Counsel, Am. Land Title Assn., Am. Judicature Soc., Phi Delta Phi. Office: Bowles Rice McDavid Graff & Love PLLC PO Drawer 1419 101 S Queen St Martinsburg WV 25402-1419

HILL, STEPHEN L., JR. lawyer, former prosecutor; m. Marianne Matteson; 2 children. BS in Polit. Sci., Southwest Mo. State U., 1981; JD, U. Mo., 1986; postgrad., London U. Staff U.S. Congressman Ike Skelton, 4th dist Mo., 1982; trial atty. Smith, Gill, Fisher & Butts, Kansas City, 1986-94; U.S. atty. Western Dist. Mo., 1993—2001; partner Blackwell Sanders Peper Martin, LLP, Mo., 2001—. Office: Blackwell Sanders Peper Martin, LLP Two Pershing Square 2300 Main St, Ste. 1000 Kansas City MO 64108 Office Fax: 816-983-8080. E-mail: shill@bspmlaw.com*

HILL, THOMAS ALLEN, lawyer; b. Salem, Ohio, Mar. 29, 1958; s. Charles Spencer and Dorothy Jane (Allen) H. BA magna cum laude, Hiram Coll., 1980; JD, George Washington U., 1984. Bar: Ohio 1984, Pa. 1987, D.C. 1988, U.S. Supreme Ct. 1989, Tex. 1990, Okla. 1991. Legis. intern Office of Hon. John Conyers, Jr., Washington, 1979; asst. to dean campus Life for Housing, conf. dir. Hiram (Ohio) Coll., 1980-81; corp. counsel Capital Oil & Gas Inc., Austintown, Ohio, 1984-93; gen. counsel, sec. North Coast Energy, Inc., Cleve., 1987-2001, Trinity Oil & Gas, Inc. subs. North Coast Energy Inc., Warren, Ohio, 1990-93; gen. counsel Eric Petroleum Corp., Canfield, 2001—. Mem. mini-task force on notices of violation Ohio Div. Oil and Gas, Columbus, 1988-90; part-time fin. analyst Primerica Fin. Svcs., Inc., 1997-2000; corp. sec. Peake Energy, Inc., Ravenswood, W.Va., 2000-01. Mem. ABA, Ohio Bar Assn., Mahoning County Bar Assn., Pa. Bar Assn., Okla. Bar Assn., D.C. Bar Assn., State Bar Tex., Trumbull County Bar Assn., Ohio Oil and Gas Assn., Christian Legal Soc., Energy Bar Assn., Ohio Land Title Assn., Ohio Geneal. Soc., Mahoning Valley Hist. Soc., Austintown Hist. Soc., Gen. Soc., War of 1812, SAR, Order of Arrow, Kappa Delta Pi, Pi Gamma Mu. Republican. Avocations: local history, study of Amaranth. General corporate, Oil, gas, and mineral, Real property. Home: 4841 Westchester Dr Apt 102 Youngstown OH 44515-2548 Office: Eric Petroleum Corp 4206 1/2 Boardman-Canfield Canfield OH 44406

HILL, THOMAS CLARK, lawyer; b. Prestonsburg, Ky., July 17, 1946; s. Lon Clay and Corinne (Allen) H.; m. J. Barbarie Friedly, June 13, 1968; children: Jason L., Duncan L. BA, Case Western Reserve U., 1968; JD, U. Chgo., 1973. Bar: Ohio 1973, U.S. Supreme Ct. 1976. Assoc. atty. Taft, Stettinius & Hollister LLP, Cin., 1973-81, ptnr., 1981—. Author: Monthly Meetings in North America: A Quaker Index, 4th edit., 1998. Trustee, treas. Wilmington (Ohio) Coll., 1982-94, 99—; treas. Ams. sect. Friends World Commn. for Consultation, 1990-95, presiding clk., 1995-99, interim com., presiding clk., London, 2000—; trustee Wilmington Yearly Meeting of Friends (Quakers), 1986-98, Friends United Meeting, 1999—. Mem. ABA, Ohio State Bar Assn., Cin. Bar Assn., Friends Hist. Assn. (bd. dirs. 1994-95). Republican. Mem. Soc. of Friends. Avocation: Quaker history. Antitrust, Environmental, Insurance. Office: 425 Walnut St Ste 1800 Cincinnati OH 45202-3923 E-mail: hill@taftlaw.com

HILL, THOMAS WILLIAM, JR. lawyer, educator; b. N.Y.C., Dec. 25, 1924; s. Thomas William Sr. and Marion (Bond) H.; m. Elizabeth Rowe, June 18, 1949; children: Gretchen P., Catharine B., Thomas William III. BS, U. Pa., 1948; MBA, NYU, 1950; JD, Columbia U., 1953. Bar: N.Y. 1953, D.C. 1954, U.S. Supreme Ct. 1958, Fla. 1989; CPA N.Y. Sr. tax acct. Hurdman & Cranstoun, 1949-50; asst. U.S. atty. So. Dist. N.Y., 1953-54; assoc. Cahill, Gordon, Reindel & Ohl, 1954-58; sr. ptnr. Spear & Hill, 1958-75; ptnr. Sidley & Austin, 1981-86; pres. Belco Petroleum Co., N.Y.C., 1962-63; legal adviser Sultanate of Oman, 1972-76. Adj. prof. law U. Miami, 1986-97. Contbr. articles to profl. jours. Vice chmn., pres., trustee Internat. Coll., Beirut, Lebanon, 1978-91. 1st lt. AUS, 1943-46. Decorated Bronze Star, Purple Heart, Medal of Oman (Sultanate of Oman), Order of Homayun (Iran). Mem. ABA, Assn. of Bar of City of N.Y., IBA, Racquet and Tennis Club (N.Y.C.), Mayacoo Golf Club, Taconic Golf Club, Phi Delta Phi, Kappa Sigma. Private international, Public international. Home: 2627 Muirfield Ct West Palm Beach FL 33414-7019 E-mail: twhilljr@aol.com

HILL, WILLIAM U. state supreme court justice; Atty. gen., Cheyenne, Wyo., 1995-98; justice Wyo. Supreme Ct., 1998—. Office: Wyoming Supreme Court 2301 Capitol Ave Cheyenne WY 82001-3656

HILLESTAD, CHARLES ANDREW, lawyer; b. McCurtain, Okla., Aug. 30, 1945; s. Carl Oliver and Aileen Hanna (Sweeney) H.; m. Ann Ramsey Robertson, Oct. 13, 1973. BS, U. Oreg., 1967; JD, U. Mich., 1972. Bar: Colo. 1972, U.S. Dist. Ct. Colo. 1972, U.S. Ct. Appeals (10th cir.) 1972, Oreg. 1993; lic. real estate broker, Colo. Law clk. to presiding justice Colo. Supreme Ct., Denver, 1972-73; ptnr. DeMuth & Kemp, 1973-83, Cornwell & Blakey, Denver, 1983-90, Scheid & Horlbeck, Denver, 1990-93, Gablehouse & Epel, Denver, 1993-94; pvt. practice Cannon Beach, Oreg., 1994—. Co-developer award winning Queen Anne Inn, Capitol Hill Mansion and Cheyenne Canyon Inn Hotels (4-diamond award AAA); mem. ad hoc com. Denver Real Estate Atty. Specialists. Author: Preventive Law for Innkeepers, co-author: Annual Surveys of Real Estate Law for Colorado Bar Association; contbr. articles to profl. jours.; assoc. editor Inn Times. Past coun. mem. Denver Art Mus.; past chmn. Rocky Mountain chpt. Sierra Club; past v.p., bd. dirs. Seaside C. of C.; past bd. dirs. Hist. Denver, Inc. Staff sgt. U.S. Army, 1968-70. Recipient Colo. Co. of Yr. award Colo. Bus. Mag., Award of Honor Denver Ptnrship., Newsmaker of Yr. and Outstanding Achievement awards Am. Assn. Hist. Inns, Tourism Person of Yr. award Denver Conv. and Visitor's Bur., Rocky Mountain Spectacular Inn award B&B Rocky Mountains Assn., Best Inns of Yr. awards County Inns Mag. and Adventure Rd. Mag., Best of Denver award Westward newspaper. Mem. ABA, Colo. Bar Assn., Oreg. Bar Assn., Denver Bar Assn., Colo. Lawyers for the Arts, POETS, Astoria C. of C., Seaside C. of C., Cannon Beach C. of C. Avocations: photography, art collecting, historic and environmental preservation, history and architecture reading, rafting. Contracts commercial, Landlord-tenant, Real property. Office: PO Box 1065 1347 S Hemlock Cannon Beach OR 97110

HILLIARD, DAVID CRAIG, lawyer, educator; b. Framingham, Mass., May 22, 1937; s. Walter David and Dorothy (Shortiss) H.; m. Celia Schmid, Feb. 16, 1974. BS, Tufts U., 1959; JD, U. Chgo., 1962. Bar: Ill. 1962, U.S. Supreme Ct. 1966. Mng. ptnr. Pattishall, McAuliffe, Newbury, Hilliard & Geraldson, Chgo., 1984—. Adj. prof. law Northwestern U., 1971—, chmn. Symposium Intellectual Property Law and the Corp. Client, 1987—; lectr. in advanced trademark law U. Chgo. Law Sch., 1999—. Author: Unfair Competition and Unfair Trade Practices, 1985, Trademarks, 1987, Trademarks and Unfair Competition, 1994, 4th edit., 2000, Trademarks and Unfair Competition Deskbook, 2001; editor-in-chief Chgo. Bar Record, 1978-81. Trustee Art Inst. Chgo., 1980—, vice-chmn., 1998-2000, exec. com., 1994-2000, chmn. sustaining fellows, 1981-85, chmn. adv. com. dept. architecture, 1981—, pres. aux. bd., 1977-79, chmn. exhbns. com., 1993—, chmn. bd. govs. of the sch., 1997-2000; trustee Newberry Libr., 1983—, exec. com., 1987—; pres. Lawyers Trust Fund Ill., 1985-88; vis. com. DePaul U. Law Sch., U. Chgo. Sch. of Law, chmn., 1987-88, Northwestern U. Assocs., 1985—; profl. adv. bd. Atty. Gen. Ill., 1982-84; mem. Ill. Commn. on Rights of Women, 1983-85; bd. dirs. Ill. Inst. Continuing Legal Edn., 1980-82; pres. Planned Parenthood Assn. Chgo., 1975-77. Lt. JAGC, USN, 1962-66. Recipient Maurice Weigle award, 1974, Chgo. Coun. Lawyers award for jud. reform, 1983. Fellow Am. Coll. Trial Lawyers (chmn. courageous adv. com. 1995-97); mem. ABA (chmn. trademark divsn. 1986-87, mem. coun. 1991-95, intellectual property law sect.), Ill. Bar Assn., Chgo. Bar Assn. (pres. 1982-83, founding chmn. young lawyers sect. 1971-72), Internat. Trademark Assn. (bd. dirs. 1989-91, ADR panel of neutrals 1994—), Arts Club, Chgo. Club, Econ. Club, Grolier Club, Lawyers Club, Legal Club (pres. 1989-90), Univ. Club, Casino, Wayfarers Club (pres. 1994-95). Federal civil litigation, Intellectual property, Trademark and copyright. Home: 1320 N State Pkwy Chicago IL 60610-2118 Office: Pattishall McAuliffe Newbury Hilliard & Geraldson 311 S Wacker Dr Ste 5000 Chicago IL 60606-6631 E-mail: dhilliard@pattishall.com

HILLJE, BARBARA BROWN, lawyer; b. Carlisle, Pa., Dec. 18, 1942; d. R. Morrison and Gladys M. (Lauver) Brown; m. John W. Hillje, Mar. 23, 1968. AB, Vassar Coll., 1964; BS in Edn., Ind. U. Pa., 1965; MA, Temple U., 1971, ABD, 1977; JD, Villanova U., 1984. Bar: Pa. 1984, U.S. Dist. Ct. (ea. dist.) Pa. 1984, N.J. 1985, U.S. Dist. Ct. N.J. 1985, U.S. Supreme Ct. 1990. English tchr. Council Rock Sr. High Sch., Newtown, Pa., 1965-68; assoc. Harry J. Agzigian and Assocs., Levittown, 1985-87; pvt. practice Langhorne, 1987—. Contbr. articles to profl. journals. Bd. dirs., pres. bd. Children of Aging Parents, Levittown, 1985-93; mem. facility ethics com. Statesman Health & Rehab. Ctr., Levittown, Pa., 1996—; bd. dirs. D'Youville Manor, 2001—. Recipient Women Helping Women award Soroptimists of Indian Rock, Inc., 1995; named Woman of Yr., Lower Bucks AAUW, 1985, Neshaminy BPW, 1987, Legal Humanitarian of Yr., Bucks County United Way, 1994, Consumer Connection award, 1996. Mem. AAUW (bd. dirs. 1978—, legis. cons. Pa. division 1990-92), Middletown-Newtown LWV (bd. dirs. 1983-89, citizen campaign watch adv. panel 1992, 94, 96), Pa. Bar Assn., Bucks County Bar Assn. (bd. dirs. 1991-93), Nat. Acad. Elder Law Attys., Older Women's League (legis. chair 1984-94, Women of Worth award 1993). Family and matrimonial, Probate, Elder. Office: 506 Corporate Dr W Langhorne PA 19047-8011

HILLMAN, DOUGLAS WOODRUFF, federal district judge; b. Grand Rapids, Mich., Feb. 15, 1922; s. Lemuel Serrell and Dorothy (Woodruff) H.; m. Sally Jones, Sept. 13, 1944; children: Drusilla W., Clayton D. (dec.). Student, Phillips Exeter Acad., 1941; A.B., U. Mich., 1946, LL.B., 1948. Bar: Mich. 1948, U.S. Supreme Ct. 1967. Assoc. Lilly, Luyendyk & Snyder, Grand Rapids, 1948-53; partner Luyendyk, Hainer, Hillman, Karr & Dutcher, 1953-65, Hillman, Baxter & Hammond, 1965-79; U.S. dist. judge Western Dist. Mich., Grand Rapids, 1979—, chief judge, 1986-91, sr. judge, 1991—. Instr. Nat. Inst. Trial Adv., Boulder, Colo; dir. Fed. Judges Assn.; mem. jud. conf. com. on Adminstrn. of Magistrate Judges Sys., 1993-99; chair 6th Circuit Standing Com. on Jud. Conf. Planning; mem. exec. com. ABA jud. adminstrn. divsn. Nat. Conf. Fed. Trial Judges, 1995-98. Co-author articles in legal publs. Chmn. Grand Rapids Human Relations Commn., 1963-66; chmn. bd. trustees Fountain St. Ch., 1970-72; pres. Family Service Assn., 1967. Served as pilot USAAF, 1943-45. Decorated DFC, Air medal; recipient Annual Civil Liberties award ACLU, 1970, Disting. Alumni award Ctrl. High Sch., 1986, Raymond Fox Advocacy award, 1989, Championship of Justice award State Bar Mich., 1990, Profl. & Cmty. Svc. award Young Lawyers Sect., 1996, Svc. to Profession award Fed. Bar Assn., 1991; named one of 25 Most Respected Judges Mich. Lawyers Weekly; Paul Harris fellow Rotary Internat. Fellow Am. Bar Found.; mem. ABA, Mich. Bar Assn. (chmn. client security fund), Grand Rapids Bar Assn. (pres. 1963), Am. Coll. Trial Lawyers (Mich. chmn. 1979, com. on teaching trial and appellate adv.), 6th Circuit Jud. Conf. (life), Internat. Acad. Trial Lawyers, Fedn. Ins. Counsel, Internat. Assn. Ins. Counsel, Internat. Soc. Barristers (pres 1977-78, chair annual Hillman Trial Adv. Seminar 1982—), M Club of U. Mich. (com. visitors U. Mich. Law Sch.), Univ. Club (Grand Rapids), Torch Club. Office: US Dist Ct 682 Fed Bldg 110 Michigan St NW Grand Rapids MI 49503-2363

HILLMAN, ROBERT ANDREW, law educator, former academic dean; b. N.Y.C., Dec. 23, 1946; s. Herman D. and Edith N. (Geilich) H.; m. Elizabeth Hall Kafka, Aug. 24, 1969; children: Jessica H., Heather D. BA, U. Rochester, 1969; JD, Cornell U., 1972. Bar: N.Y. 1973, Iowa 1976. Law clk. to judge U.S. Dist. Ct., N.Y.C., 1972-73; assoc. Debevoise & Plimpton, 1973-74; prof. law U. Iowa, Iowa City, 1975-82, Cornell U., Ithaca, N.Y., 1982—, acad. dean, 1990-97, Edwin Woodruff prof. law. Author: (with others) Common Law and Equity Under the UCC, 1985, Law: Its Nature, Functions, and Limits, 1986, Contract and Related Obligation: Theory, Doctrine, and Practice, 1987, 2d edit., 1992, 3d edit., 1997, The Richness of Contract Law, 1997, Modern American Contract Law, 2000; contbr. articles to profl. jours. Mem. Am. Law Inst. Avocations: tennis, bicycling. Office: Cornell U Law Sch Myron Taylor Hall Ithaca NY 14853 E-mail: rah16@cornell.edu

HILLS, CARLA ANDERSON, lawyer, former federal official; b. Los Angeles, Jan. 3, 1934; d. Carl H. and Edith (Hume) Anderson; m. Roderick Maltman Hills, Sept. 27, 1958; children: Laura Hume, Roderick Maltman, Megan Elizabeth, Alison Macbeth. AB cum laude, Stanford U., 1955; student, St. Hilda's Coll., Oxford (Eng.) U., 1954; LLB, Yale U., 1958; hon. degrees, Pepperdine U., 1975, Washington U., 1977, Mills Coll., 1977, Lake Forest Coll., 1978, Williams Coll., 1981, Notre Dame U., 1993, Wabash Coll., 1997. Bar: Calif. 1959, DC 1974, U.S. Supreme Ct. 1965. Asst. U.S. atty. civil divsn., L.A., 1958-61; ptnr. Munger, Tolles, Hills & Rickershauser, 1962-74; asst. atty. gen. civil divsn. Justice Dept., Washington, 1974-75; sec. HUD, 1975-77; ptnr. Latham, Watkins & Hills, Washington, 1978-86, Weil, Gotshal & Manges, Washington, 1986-88; U.S. trade rep. Exec. Office of the Pres., 1989-93; chmn., CEO Hills & Co. Internat. Cons., 1993—. Chair bd. dirs. Nat. Com. for U.S.-China Rels., vice chair bd. dirs. Inter-Am. Dialogue Coun. on Fgn. Rels.; bd. dirs. Am. Internat. Group, AOL-Time Warner, Lucent Techs., Inc., Bechtel Enterprises Holdings, Chevron Corp., TCW Group, Inc.; adj. prof. Sch. Law UCLA, 1972; mem. Trilateral Commn., 1977—82, 1993—, Am. Com. on East-West Accord, 1977—79, Internat. Found. for Cultural Cooperation and Devel., 1977—89, Fed. Acctg. Stds. Adv. Coun., 1978—80; mem. corrections task force L.A. County Sub-Regional; mem. adv. bd. Calif. Coun. on Criminal Justice, 1969—71; mem. standing com. discipline U.S. Dist. Ct. for Ctrl. Calif., 1970—73; mem. Adminstrv. Conf. U.S., 1972—74; mem. exec. com. law and free soc. State Bar Calif., 1973; bd. councillors U. So. Calif. Law Ctr., 1972—74; trustee Pomona Coll., 1974—79, Brookings Instn., 1985; mem. at large exec. com. Yale Law Sch., 1973—78; mem. com. on Law Sch. Yale U. Coun.; Gordon Grand fellow Yale U., 1978; mem. Sloan Commn. on Govt. and Higher Edn., 1977—79; mem. adv. com. Princeton U., Woodrow Wilson Sch. of Pub. and Internat. Affairs, 1977—80; trustee Am. Productivity and Quality Ctr., 1988; coun. mem. Calif. Gov. Coun. Econ. Policy Adv., 1993—98, Coun. on Fgn. Rels., 1993—. Co-author: Federal Civil Practice, 1961; co-author, editor: Antitrust Adviser, 1971, 3d edit., 1985; contbg. editor: Legal Times, 1978-88; mem. editorial bd. Nat. Law Jour., 1978-88. Trustee U. So. Calif., 1977-79, Norton Simon Mus. Art, Pasadena, Calif., 1976-80; trustee Urban Inst., 1978-89, chmn., 1983-89; co-chmn. Alliance to Save Energy, 1977-89; vice chmn. adv. coun. on legal policy Am. Enterprise Inst., 1977-84; bd. visitors, exec. com. Stanford U. Law Sch., 1978-81; bd. dirs. Am. Coun. for Capital Formation, 1978-82; mem. exec. com. Inst. for Internat. Econs., 1993—; mem. adv. com. MIT-Harvard U. Joint Ctr. for Urban Studies, 1978-82. Fellow Am. Bar Found.; mem. Am.'s Soc. (bd. dirs.), L.A. Women Lawyers Assn. (pres. 1964), ABA (chair publs. com. antitrust sect. 1972-74, council 1974, 77-84, chair 1982-83), Fed. Bar Assn. (pres. L.A. chpt. 1963), L.A. County Bar Assn. (fed. rules and practice com. 1963-72, chair issues and survey 1963-72, chair sub-com. revision local rules for fed. cts. 1966-72, jud. qualifications com. 1971-72), Am. Law Inst., Am.-China Soc. (bd. dirs. 1995—), Am. Soc. (bd. trustees), Asia Soc. (bd. trustees), Yale of So. Calif. Club (bd. dirs. 1972-74), Yale Club. Clubs: Yale of So. Calif. (dir. 1972-74); Yale (Washington). Antitrust. Office: Hills & Co 1200 19th St NW Ste 201 Washington DC 20036-2429

HILPERT, EDWARD THEODORE, JR. lawyer; b. Frazee, Minn., Apr. 29, 1928; s. Edward Theodore Sr. and Hulda Gertrude (Wilder) H.; m. Susan Hazelton, May 5, 1973. AB, U. Wash., 1954, JD, 1956. Bar: Wash. 1956, U.S. Dist. Ct. (we. dist.) Wash. 1956, U.S. Tax Ct. 1959, U.S. Ct. Appeals (9th cir.) 1959, U.S. Supreme Ct. 1970. Law clk. to Hon. George H. Boldt U.S. Dist. Ct. (we. dist.) Wash., Tacoma, 1956-58; assoc. Ferguson & Burdell, Seattle, 1958-63, ptnr., 1963-91; sr. ptnr. Schwabe, Williamson, Ferguson & Burdell, 1992—. Exec. com. 9th cir. Jud. Conf., San Francisco, 1987-90. Judge pro tem Seattle Mcpl. Ct., 1971-80. Capt. USAR, 1946-49, 50-52, Korea. Mem. ABA, Mensa, Rainer Club, Seattle Tennis Club, Broadmoor Golf Club, Sea Pines Country Club. Republican. Lutheran. General corporate, Estate planning, State and local taxation. Home: 1434 Broadmoor Dr E Seattle WA 98112-3744 Office: Schwabe Williamson Ferguson & Burdell US Bank Ctr 1420 5th Ave Ste 3500 Seattle WA 98101-1397 E-mail: sshathhi@aol.com, kanderson@schwabe.com

HILTON, STANLEY GOUMAS, lawyer, educator, writer; b. San Francisco, June 16, 1949; s. Loucas Stylianos and Effie (Glafkides) Goumas; m. Raquel Estrella Villalba, Feb. 25, 1996. BA with honors, U. Chgo., 1971; JD, Duke U., 1975; MBA, Harvard U., 1979. Bar: Calif. 1975, U.S. Dist. Ct. Calif. 1975, U.S. Ct. Appeals (9th cir.) 1983, U.S. Supreme Ct. 1985. Libr. asst. Duke U. Libr., Durham, N.C., 1972-75, Harvard U. Libr., Cambridge, Mass., 1977-79; minority counsel U.S. Senator Bob Dole, Washington, 1979-80; adminstrv. asst. Calif. State Senate, Sacramento, 1980-81; pvt. practice San Francisco, 1981—; CEO Froggg, Inc., 1999—, San Francisco Landlords Union, 1999—. Adj. assoc. prof. Golden Gate U., San Francisco, 1991—. Author: Bob Dole: American Political Phoenix, 1988, Senator for Sale, 1995, Glass Houses, 1998 (Best writer 1998). Pres. Com. to Stick With Candlestick Park, San Francisco, 1992-96, Value Added Tax Now, San Francisco, 1994—, Save the 4th Amendment, San Francisco, 1995—; pres., CEO Animalism, Inc., San Francisco Landlord's Union, 2001—; CEO Fountain of Youth. Mem. Calif. State Bar, Abolish the Fed. Res. Bank Assn. (pres. 1999—), Hellenic Law Soc., Bechtel Toastmasters Club (pres.), Rhinoceros Toastmasters Club. Democrat. Avocations: philately, photography, classical music, ancient Greek and Roman history. Constitutional, Labor. Office: 580 California St Ste 500 San Francisco CA 94104-1000

HILTS, EARL T. lawyer, government official, educator; b. Ilion, N.Y., Mar. 31, 1946; stepson Leon Thomas and Gertrude Annette (Daly) Butler; m. Mae Hwa Kim, Apr. 13, 1973; children: Troy Alan, Kimberly, Michelle. BS, St. Lawrence U., 1967; JD, Albany Law Sch., 1970. Bar: N.Y. 1972. Gen. atty.-advisor Dept. Army Watervliet Arsenal, N.Y., 1978-80, supervisory atty.-advisor, 1980-99; ret., 1999; pvt. practice, 1999—. Adj. prof. Schnectady C.C., 1985—, St. Rose Coll., 1999—. Catechism instr. St. Mary's Ch., 1990-97; pee wee football coach, wrestling coach Shenendehowa Sch., 1983-87; little league coach West Crescent Halfmoon Baseball League, 1980-90. Capt. JAGC, U.S. Army, 1972-76. Scholar St. Lawrence U., 1963-67, Albany Law Sch., 1967-70. Mem. N.Y. State Bar Assn., Am. Legion, Pi Mu Epsilon. Republican. Roman Catholic. Home and Office: 28 Oakwood Blvd Clifton Park NY 12065-7413

HIMELEIN, LARRY M. judge; b. Buffalo, June 27, 1949; s. Levant Maurice and Barbara McKenzie (Neilson) H.; m. Julie Ann Peglowski, Mar. 20, 1982; children: Ryan Charles, Brendan Levant, Meghan Lee. BA, Ithaca Coll., 1971; JD, Suffolk U., 1975. Bar: N.Y. 1976. Pvt. practice, Gowanda, N.Y., 1977-79; assoc. Levant Himelein, Jr., Gowanda, 1979-82; dist. atty. Cattaraugus County, Little Valley, N.Y., 1982-92; judge Cattaraugus County, Little Valley, 1993—; mem. Arson Task Force, Little Valley, 1982-92, Traffic Safety Bd., 1982-92, Cattaraugus County Police Chiefs, Little Valley, 1982-92. Bd. dirs. Tri-County Meml. Hosp., Gowanda, N.Y., 1987-96. Mem. N.Y. State Bar Assn., N.Y. State County Judges Assn., N.Y. State Family Judges Assn., N.Y. State Surrogate Ct. Assn., Cattaraugus County Bar Assn., Erie County Bar Assn., Am. Legion, Slovenian Club, Gowanda Country Club (bd. dirs. 1997—). Democrat. Episcopalian. Home: 40 W Hill St Gowanda NY 14070-1428 Office: 303 Court St Little Valley NY 14755-1028

HIMELFARB, STEPHEN ROY, lawyer; b. Washington, Feb. 19, 1954; s. Jordan Sheldon and Marion (Soloman) H.; m. Anne Patricia Spille, June 26, 1983; children: Kara Michelle, Bradley Richard. BSBA, Am. U., 1976; JD, George Mason U., 1980. Bar: D.C. 1982, Md. 1982, Va. 1988, U.S. Dist. Ct. D.C. 1982, U.S. Dist. Ct. Md. 1982, U.S. Ct. Appeals (D.C. and 4th cirs.) 1982, U.S. Dist. Ct. (ea. dist.) Va. 1988, U.S. Tax Ct. 1990, U.S.

Bankruptcy Ct. (ea. div.) Va. 1988, U.S. Supreme Ct. 1985. From v.p. to pres. ECA Bus. Comm. Network, Washington, 1982-85; ptnr. Himelfarb & Podryhula, 1984-93, Speights & Micheel, Washington, 1986-88, Sheeskin, Hillman & Lazar, PC, Rockville, Md., 1989-90, Ahmad & Himelfarb, PC, Rockville, 1993-95; pvt. practice Bethesda, 1995—. V.p. Video Shack Inc., Woodbridge, Va., 1984-95. Mem. ABA, Md. State Bar Assn., Va. Bar Assn., Assn. Trial Lawyers Am., Phi Delta Phi. Democrat. Jewish. Avocations: electronics, coin-op/americana collecting, model trains, radio control models. Contracts commercial, General corporate, Personal injury. Home: 1214 Winter Hunt Rd Mc Lean VA 22102-2434 Office: 4701 Sangamore Rd Ste S-225 Bethesda MD 20816-2508

HINCHEY, JOHN WILLIAM, lawyer; b. Knoxville, Tenn., June 18, 1941; s. Roy William and Ruth (Owenby) H.; m. Sherie Paulette Archer, May 12, 1968; children: Paul William, Meredith Marie, John Oliver. AB, Emory U., 1964, LLB, 1965; LLM, Harvard U., 1966; MLitt., Oxford U., 1980. Bar: Ga. 1965, U.S. Dist. Ct. (no., mid. and so. dists.) Ga. 1968, U.S. Ct. Appeals (11th cir.) 1968, U.S. Supreme Ct. 1969. Asst. atty. gen. State of Ga., Atlanta, 1968-72; ptnr. McConaughey & Hinchey, Decatur, Ga., 1972-76, Phillips & Mozley, Atlanta, 1976-84, Phillips, Hinchey & Reid, Atlanta, 1984-92, King and Spalding, Atlanta, 1992—. Contbr. to profl. jours. and treatises. Mem. ABA (chair Forum on Constrn. Industry), Am. Coll. Constitution Lawyers (bd. govs. 2001—), Am. Arbitration Assn., Ga. Bar Assn., Atlanta Bar Assn. (chair constrn. law sect. 1999-2000), London Ct. of Internat. Arbitration, Chartered Inst. Arbitrators, Druid Hills Golf Club. Republican. Methodist. Alternative dispute resolution, Contracts commercial, Construction. Office: King & Spalding 191 Peachtree St SW Atlanta GA 30303-1763 E-mail: jhinchey@kslaw.com

HINCKLEY, ROBERT CRAIG, lawyer; b. New Orleans, Sept. 5, 1947; s. Marsden Donald and Doris Camille (Engelhardt) H.; m. Marilyn J. Spence, Mar. 9, 1985. BS, U.S. Naval Acad., 1969; JD, Tulane U., 1976. Bar: La. 1976, Calif. 1977. Commd. Navigator, anti-submarine warfare officer USS Brinkley Bass, Long Beach, Calif., 1969-71; aide to dir. naval intelligence Pentagon, Washington, 1971-73; spl. asst. U.S. atty., legal officer Naval Air Sta., Alameda, Calif., 1976-79; with Lillick McHose & Charles, San Francisco, 1979-81, Jones, Walker, Waechter, Poitevent, Carrere & Denegre, New Orleans, 1981; v.p., gen. counsel, sec. NEC Electronics, Inc., Mountain View, Calif., 1981-87; sr. v.p., CFO Spectra Physics, San Jose, Calif., 1988-90; v.p. strategic programs, COO Xilinx, Inc., San Jose, 1991—. Bd. dirs. San Jose (Calif.) Symph., 1995. Mem. Assn. Publicly Traded Cos. (bd. dirs. 1995—). Computer, General corporate, Trademark and copyright. Home: 1974 Webster St Palo Alto CA 94301-4047

HINDMAN, LARRIE C. lawyer; b. Meservey, Iowa, Mar. 30, 1937; s. Marvin C. and Fredona E. (Lemke) H.; m. Jeannie Carol Richey, June 18, 1961; children: Bryant C., Derek Cory. BS, Iowa State U., 1959; JD, U. Iowa, 1962. Bar: Mo. 1963, Kans. 1975. Ptnr. Morrison & Hecker LLP, Kansas City, Mo., 1962-2000. Contbr. legal articles to profl. jours. Mem.: ABA, Am. Coll. Real Estate Lawyers, Am. Coll. Mortgage Attys., Am. Land Title Assn. (lender counsel), Club at Porto Cima. Finance, Real property, Native American. Home: 67 Grand Cove Dr Sunrise Beach MO 65079-9217 Office: Morrison & Hecker LLP 2600 Grand Blvd Ste 1200 Kansas City MO 64108-4606

HINER, LESLIE DAVIS, lawyer, political consultant; b. Canton, Ohio, Sept. 30, 1957; d. Wendell Hughes and Margaret Alvina (Klebaum) Davis; m. Ward Christopher Hiner, July 23, 1983; children: Elaine Margaret, Travis Davis. BA, Coll. of Wooster, Ohio, 1980; JD, U. Akron, Ohio, 1985. Bar: In. 1985. Intern Legis. Svcs. Agy., Indpls., 1984; assoc. Ecklund, Frutkin & Grant, 1985-87; co-owner, v.p., gen. counsel Hiner Van & Storage, Kokomo, Ind., 1987-91; assoc. Russell McIntrye Jessup Hilligoss & Raquet, 1991-91; Ind. senate majority atty., 1993-94; pvt. practice, 1994-95; gen. counsel, elections dep. Ind. Sec. of State, 1995-97; pvt. practice, session atty. Rep. caucus Ind. Ho. of Reps., Indpls., 1997-2000, policy dir., caucus atty. Rep. caucus, 2000—. Mem. adj. faculty U. Indpls., 1986-87, 1992—. Bd. dirs. United Way Howard County, 1990. exec. com. 1990, allocations coun. 1987-91, vice chmn. 1989, chmn. 1990, past chmn. 1991, campaign vol. 1988, 89; atty. Legal Aid, Kokomo, 1987-91; bd. dirs. Montessori Children's Home, 1989-90, community affairs com. chmn. 1990; mem. fin. com. Howard County Rep. Party, 1991; vol. Bona Vista Rehab. Ctr., Capital Campaign. Col. 1991; mem. Altrusa Cmty. Affairs Com., 1989-91; campaign chair Johnson for State Senate Re-election com., 1990; campaign mgr. Kenley for State Senate, 1992; mem. Indpls. Symphonic Choir. Named Howard County Women of Yr. in Bus. Industry, 1991. Mem. Ind. State Bar Assn., Federalist Soc. (bd. dirs. lawyers divsn. Indpls. chpt. 1994—), U. Akron Sch. Law Alumni Assn. (life), Grtr. Indpls. Rep. Women's club (life), Richard D. Lugar Excellence in Pub. Svc. Series Alumna, Brebeuf Jesuit Mother's Assn. Republican. Lutheran. Avocations: piano, reading, needlework, tennis, singing. Office: Ind Ho of Reps Statehouse 200 W Washington St Indianapolis IN 46204 E-mail: lhiner@iga.state.in.us

HINES, EDWARD FRANCIS, JR. lawyer; b. Norfolk, Va., Sept. 5, 1945; s. Edward Francis and Jeanne Miriam (Caulfield) H.; m. Elaine Geneva Carroll, Aug. 21, 1971; children: Jonathan Edward, Carolyn Adele. AB, Boston Coll., 1966; JD, Harvard U., 1969. Bar: Mass. 1969. Assoc. Choate Hall & Stewart, Boston, 1969-77, ptnr., 1977-2001, Hines & Corley LLP, Boston, 2001—. Bd. dirs. Univ. Hosp., Boston, 1990—96, v. chmn., 1994—96; bd. dir. Boston Med. Ctr., 1996—. With USAR, 1969-75. Recipient Boston Coll. High Sch. St. Ignatius award, 1998. Mem. Boston Bar Assn. (pres. 1988-89), Boston Bar Found. (pres. 1995-97), Mass. CLE (pres. 1985-87), Carroll Ctr. for Blind (bd. dirs. 1983-89, 90-96, chmn. 1994-96), Mass. Taxpayers Found. (bd. dirs. 1987—), Am. Heart Assn. (bd. dirs. Dallas 1984-86, 91-2000, chmn. 1998-99, award of merit 1983), Assoc. Industries Mass. (bd. dirs. 1990—, chmn. 1996-98), Am. Coll. Greece (Athens, bd. dirs., vice chmn. 1988-97), Fed. Tax Inst. New Eng. (treas. 1994-2001), Social Law Libr. (trustee 1993-98), Supreme Jud. Ct. Hist. Soc. (trustee 1989-96), Accion Internat. (bd. dirs. 1999—), North Andover Country Club, Boston Coll. Club, Bay Club. General corporate, Taxation, general, State and local taxation. Office: Hines & Corley LLP 225 Franklin St 26th Fl Boston MA 02109 E-mail: efh@hinesandcorley.com

HINES, N. WILLIAM, dean, law educator, administrator; b. 1936; AB, Baker U., 1958; LLB, U. Kans., 1961; LLD, Baker U., 1999. Bar: Kans. 1961, Iowa 1965. Law clk. U.S. Ct. Appeals 10th cir., 1961-62; tchg. fellow Harvard U., 1961-62; asst. prof. law U. Iowa, 1962-65, assoc. prof., 1965-67, prof., 1967-73, disting. prof., 1973—, dean, 1976—. Vis. prof. Stanford U., 1974-75. Notes and comments editor Kans. Law Rev. Grad. fellow Harvard U., 1961-62. Fellow ABA Found., Iowa State Bar Found.; mem. Environ. Law Inst. (assoc.), Jo. Co. Her. Trust (founder, pres.), Order of Coif. Office: U Iowa Coll Law Iowa City IA 52242-0001

HINES, PRESTON HARRIS, state supreme court justice; b. Atlanta, Sept. 6, 1943; AB in Polit. Sci., Emory U., 1965, JD, 1968. Bar: Ga. 1968, U.S. Dist. Ct. Ga. 1973. Law clk. Civil Ct. Fulton County, 1968-69; pvt. practice Marietta, Ga., 1969-74; judge State Ct. of Cobb County, 1974-82, Superior Ct. of Ga., 1982—. Chmn. attys. divsn. Cobb County United Appeal, 1972; participant Leadership Ga., 1975, Leadership Atlanta, 1978-79; pres. YMCA Cobb County, 1976; co-treas. Cobb Landmarks Soc., 1976-77; former bd. dirs. Cobb County Emergency Aid Assn., Cobb-Marietta Girls Club, Ga. chpt. Leukemia Soc. Am., Cobb County Children's Ctr., Met. Atlanta Red Cross, First Presbyn. Day Kindergarten; mem. cmty. adv. com. Marietta-Cobb County LWV; bd. dirs. Kennesaw Coll. Found.; trustee Cobb Cmty. Symphony. Named Outstanding Young Man of Yr., Ga. Jaycees, 1975, Boss of Yr., Cobb County Legal Secs. Assn., 1975-76, 83-84. Mem. ABA, State Bar Ga. (chmn. Law Day com. 1975, mem. exec. com. younger lawyers sec. 1974-76), Cobb Jud. Cir. (sec. 1972-73, chmn. Law Day com. 1972), Joseph Henry Lumpkin Inn of Ct. Ga., Atlanta Lawyers Club, Kiwanis (bd. dirs. Marietta chpt., chmn. Key Club com., past chmn. spiritual aims com., past pres.), Cobb County C. of C., Sigma Alpha Epsilon (Atlanta and Marietta chpts.). Office: Supreme Court 533 State Judicial Bldg Atlanta GA 30334

HINKLE, CHARLES FREDERICK, lawyer, clergyman, educator; b. Oregon City, Oreg., July 6, 1942; s. William Ralph and Ruth Barbara (Holcomb) H. BA, Stanford U., 1964; MDiv, Union Theol. Sem., N.Y.C., 1968; JD, Yale U., 1971. Bar: Oreg. 1971; ordained to ministry United Ch. of Christ, 1974. Instr. English, Morehouse Coll., Atlanta, 1966-67; assoc. Stoel Rives LLP (formerly Stoel, Rives, Boley, Jones & Grey), Portland, Oreg., 1971-77, ptnr., 1977—. Adj. prof. Lewis and Clark Law Sch., Portland, 1978—; bd. govs. Oreg. State Bar, 1992-95. Oreg. pres. ACLU, Portland, 1976-80, nat. bd. dirs., 1979-85; bd. dirs. Kendall Cmty. Ctr., 1987-93, Youth Progress Assn., 1994-98, Portland Baroque Orch., 1999-2000; mem. pub. affairs com. Am. Cancer Soc., 1994-99; mem. Oreg. Gov.'s Task Force on Youth Suicide, 1996. Recipient Elliott Human Rights award Oreg. Edn. Assn., 1984, E.B. MacNaughton award ACLU Oreg., 1987, Wayne Morse award Dem. Com. Oreg., 1994, Tom McCall Freedom of Info. award Women in Comm., 1996, Civil Rights award Met. Human Rights Commn., 1996, Pub. Svc. award Oreg. State Bar, 1997. Fellow Am. Bar Found.; mem. ABA (ho. of dels. 1998-2000), FBA, Multnomah County Bar Assn., City Club Portland (pres. 1987-88). Democrat. Communications, Constitutional, Libel. Home: 14079 SE Fairoaks Way Milwaukie OR 97267-1017 Office: Stoel Rives 900 SW 5th Ave Ste 2600 Portland OR 97204-1268 E-mail: cfhinkle@stoel.com

HINMAN, HARVEY DEFOREST, lawyer; b. Binghamton, N.Y., May 7, 1940; s. George Lyon and Barbara (Davidge) H.; m. Margaret Snyder, June 23, 1962; children: George, Sarah, Marguerite. BA, Brown U., 1962; JD, Cornell U., 1965. Bar: Calif. 1966. Assoc. Pillsbury, Madison & Sutro, San Francisco, 1965-72, ptnr., 1973-93, v.p., gen. counsel Chevron Corp., 1993—; bd. dirs. Legal Aid Soc., San Francisco. Bd. dirs., sec. Holbrook Palmer Park Found., 1977-86; bd. dirs. Phillips Brooks Sch., 1978-84, pres. 1983-84; trustee Castillija Sch., 1988-89; bd. govs. Filoli Ctr., 1988—, pres. 1994-95. Fellow Am. Bar Found.; mem. ABA, San Francisco Bar Assn. Contracts commercial, Oil, gas, and mineral, Private international. Office: Chevron Corporation 575 Market St San Francisco CA 94105-2856

HINOJOSA, FEDERICO GUSTAVO, JR. judge; b. Edinburg, Tex., Apr. 16, 1947; s. Federico Gustavo and Zulema (Trevino) H.; m. Yolanda Silva, 1970 (div. 1977); children: Cynthia, Zelda Cassandra; m. Magdalena Garza, Oct. 30, 1992. BA, Pan Am. U., 1969; JD, U. Houston, 1977. Bar: Tex. 1977, U.S. Dist. Ct. (so. dist.) Tex. 1977, U.S. Ct. Appeals (5th cir.) 1980, U.S. Supreme Ct. 1980. Assoc. Clark, Lowes & Carrithers, Houston, 1977-79; ptnr. Clark & Hinojosa, 1979-81; child support atty. Tex. Dept. Human Resources, McAllen, 1981-83; asst. dist. atty. Hidalgo County, Edinburg, 1983-84; assoc. Atlas & Hall, McAllen, 1984-87; ptnr. Lewis, Pettitt & Hinojosa, 1987-91; justice Tex. Ct. Appeals for 13th Dist., Corpus Christi, 1991—. Sgt. USAF, 1970-74. Mem. State Bar Tex., Mexican-Am. Bar Tex., Mexican-Am. Bar Assn. Coastal Bend (dir. 1993-94), Hidalgo County Bar Assn. (dir. 1986-90). Democrat. Office: 13th Ct Appeals 100 E Cano St Edinburg TX 78539-4548 E-mail: fghinojosa@courts.state.tx.us

HINSDALE, BETH A. lawyer; b. Montclair, N.J., June 25, 1965; d. Robert Joseph and Sandra Elvira Drew. BA, Pa. State U., 1987; JD, Villanova U., 1990. Bar: N.J. 1990, U.S. Dist. Ct. N.J. 1990, U.S. Ct. Appeals (3d cir.) 1996. Ptnr. Grotta, Glassman & Hoffman, Roseland, N.J., 1990—. Mem. ABA, N.J. Bar Assn. Labor. Office: Grotta Glassman & Hoffman 75 Livingston Ave Roseland NJ 07068-3701 E-mail: hinsdaleb@gghlaw.com

HINSHAW, CHESTER JOHN, lawyer; b. Sacramento, Mar. 10, 1941; s. Chester Edward and Gertrude Lorraine (Miller) H.; m. Karen Forbes Breakey, Feb. 19, 1977. AB, Stanford U., 1963; JD, U. Calif., Berkeley, 1966. Bar: Calif. 1966, U.S. Dist. Ct. (no. dist.) Calif. 1967, U.S. Ct. Appeals (9th cir.) 1967, N.Y. 1968, U.S. Dist. Ct. (so. dist.) N.Y. 1972, U.S. Dist. Ct. (ea. dist.) N.Y. 1974, U.S. Ct. Appeals (2d cir.) 1974, U.S. Dist. Ct. (no. dist.) N.Y. 1980, U.S. Dist. Ct. (ea. dist.) Mich. 1982, U.S. Dist. Ct. (no. dist.) Tex. 1983, Tex. 1984, U.S. Ct. Appeals (5th cir.) 1984, U.S Supreme Ct. 1991. Assoc. Chadbourne & Parke, N.Y.C., 1967-74, ptnr., 1974-83, Jones, Day, Reavis & Pogue, Dallas, 1983-99. Lectr. U. Calif. Berkeley, 1966. Mem. ABA, Tex. Bar Assn., Calif. Bar Assn. Antitrust, Federal civil litigation, Private international. Home: 5510 Park Ln Dallas TX 75220-2158

HINSHAW, DAVID LOVE, lawyer; b. Wichita, Kans., June 17, 1947; s. Wallace Bigham and Mary Elizabeth (Love) H.; m. Carol Lynn Green, Sept. 30, 1972; children— Cara Danielle, Derek Love. B.S. in Bus., U. Kans., 1969; J.D., U. Houston, 1972. Bar: Tex. 1972, U.S. Supreme Ct. 1979. Tax atty. Exxon Co., U.S.A., Houston, 1972-77, sr. tax atty., 1977-79, tax counsel, 1979-80; gen. tax counsel Reliance Electric Co., Cleve., 1980-82; asst. gen. tax counsel Esso Europe Inc., London, 1982-86, Exxon Co., Internat., Florham Park, N.J., 1986-87; tax mgr. Esso UK plc, London, 1987—. Mem. ABA (vice chmn. com. on state and local taxes, sect. taxation 1981-82, com. on taxation and fiscal policy), Internat. Fiscal Assn., Internat. C. of C. (com. on taxation), Am. C. of C. (chmn. corp. tax subcom.). Republican. Corporate taxation, Personal income taxation, International and English taxation. Office: Esso UK Expro House 21 Dartmouth St London SW1H 9BE England

HINTON, JAMES FORREST, JR. lawyer; b. Gadsden, Ala., Nov. 19, 1951; s. James Forrest Sr. and Juanita Grey (Weems) H.; m. Rosalind Flynn, Nov. 10, 1979. BA, Vanderbilt U., 1974; JD, U. Ala., 1977. Bar: Ala. 1977, D.C. 1979, U.S. Dist. Ct. (so. dist.) Ala. 1979, U.S. Ct. Appeals (5th cir.) 1980, U.S. Ct. Appeals (11th cir.) 1981, La. 1982, U.S. Dist. Ct. (ea. and mid. dists.) La. 1982, U.S. Dist. Ct. (no. dist.) Ala 1982, U.S. Supreme Ct. 1982, U.S. Dist. Ct. (we. dist.) La. 1983, U.S. Dist. Ct. (no. dist.) Ohio 1983, U.S. Ct. Appeals (D.C. cir.) 1984, U.S. Ct. Appeals (fed. cir.) 1985, U.S. Dist. Ct. (so. dist.) Tex. 1987, U.S. Dist. Ct. (no. dist.) Tex. 1991, Tex. 1992, Tenn. 1992, U.S. Dist. Ct. (ea. and we. dists.) Ark. 1992, U.S. Ct. Appeals (6th and 8th cirs.) 1992, U.S. Dist. Ct. (ea. and we. dists.) Tex. 1993, U.S. Dist. Ct. (mid. dist.) Ala. 1993, U.S. Dist. Ct. (ea. and mid. dist.) Tenn. 1994, U.S. Dist. Ct., Colo. 2000. Law clk. to chief judge U.S. Dist. Ct. (so. dist.) Ala., Mobile, 1977-79; ptnr. Darby, Myrick & Hinton, 1979-82; dir. McGlinchey Stafford Lang, New Orleans, 1982-93; ptnr. Adams & Reese, 1993-97; shareholder Berkowitz, Lefkovits, Isom & Kushner, Birmingham, 1997—. Contbr. articles to profl. jours. Mem. ABA (antitrust, intellectual property, litigation sects.), FBA, La. Assn. Def. Counsel, Order of Coif, Phi Beta Kappa. Antitrust, General civil litigation, Intellectual property. Office: Berkowitz Lefkovits Isom & Kushner 1600 South Trust Tower 420 20th St N Birmingham AL 35203-5200 E-mail: fhinton@blik.com

HINTON, PETER BRUCE, lawyer; b. Auckland, New Zealand, Aug. 24, 1954; m. Anne Elizabeth Gatfield; children: Andrew Bruce, Campbell Peter. LLB with honors, BCom, U. Auckland, 1977; LLM, Harvard U., 1979. Assoc. Simpson Grierson, Auckland, 1976—77, Covington & Burling, Washington, 1979—80, Russell McVeagh McKenzie Bartleet & Co., Auckland, 1980, Simpson Grierson, Auckland, 1981—82, ptnr., 1982—. Home: 11 Arney Cres Remuera Auckland New Zealand Office: Simpson Grierson 92-96 Albert St Auckland New Zealand Business E-Mail: peter.hinton@simpsongrierson.com

HINUEBER, MARK ARTHUR, lawyer; BA, Blackburn Coll., 1973; JD, John Marshall Law Sch., 1977. Bar: Ill. 1977, Calif. 1978, Ark. 1995, Nev. 2000. Assoc. Abrams, Mix & London, Chgo., 1977; counsel, asst. corp. sec. Scripps League Newspapers, Inc., San Mateo, Calif., 1978-94; dir. legal divsn. Donrey Media Group, Ft. Smith, Ark., 1994-98, gen. counsel, 1998—. Named one of Outstanding Young Men Am. Mem. ABA, Calif. Bar Assn., Ill. Bar Assn., Ark. Bar Assn., Nev. Bar Assn. Avocations: golf, reading. General corporate, Labor, Libel. Office: Donrey Media Group PO Box 70 Las Vegas NV 89125 E-mail: mhinueber@donrey.com

HIRSCH, BARRY, lawyer; b. N.Y.C., Mar. 19, 1933; s. Emanuel M. and Minnie (Levenson) H.; m. Myra Seiden, June 13, 1963; children: Victor Terry II, Neil Charles Seiden, Nancy Elizabeth. BSBA, U. Mo., 1954; J.D., U. Mich., 1959; LL.M., N.Y. U., 1964. Bar: N.Y. bar 1960. Assoc., then partner firm Seligson & Morris, N.Y.C., 1960-69; v.p., sec., gen. counsel dir. B.T.B. Corp., 1969-71; v.p., sec., gen. counsel Loews Corp. (and subsidiaries), 1971-86, sr. v.p., sec., gen. counsel, 1986—. Bds. dirs. Neuberger and Berman Funds. Served to 1st lt. AUS, 1954-56. Mem. ABA, Assn. of Bar of City of N.Y., N.Y. State Bar Assn., Zeta Beta Tau, Phi Delta Phi. General corporate, Finance, Securities. Home: 1010 5th Ave New York NY 10028-0130 Office: Loews Corp 667 Madison Ave Fl 8 New York NY 10021-8087 E-mail: bhirsch@loews.com

HIRSCH, DAVID L. lawyer, corporate executive; BA, Pomona Coll., 1959; JD, U. Calif., Berkeley, 1962. Bar: Calif. 1963. V.p. Metaldyne/NI Industries, Inc., Taylor, Mich., 1966—. V.p. mem. commn. on Govt. Procurement for U.S. Congress, 1971. Mem. editorial bd. Bur. Nat. Affairs' Fed. Contracts Report. Fellow Am. Bar Found.; mem. ABA (life fellow of fellows, chair emerging issues com. sect. pub. contract law, sec. pub. contract law sect. 1977-78, mem. council 1978-80, chmn. 1981-82), Calif. Bar (bd. advisors pub. law sect.), Los Angeles County Bar Assn., Fed. Bar Assn., Nat. Contract Mgmt. Assn. (nat. bd. advisors), Fin. Exec. Inst. (legal advisor com. on govt. bus.). Contracts commercial, Government contracts and claims. Office: Masco Tech Corp/NI Industries Inc 21001 Van Born Rd Taylor MI 48180-1340

HIRSCH, EDWIN PAUL, lawyer, mfg. co. exec.; b. Phila., Oct. 8, 1923; B.S. in Econs., U. Pa., 1947, M.B.A., 1948; LL.B., U. Va., 1951; postgrad. Parker Sch. Fgn. & Comparative Law, Columbia U. m. Dorothy L. Newhook, Aug. 2, 1979; 1 dau., Sharon L. Gonzalez. Admitted to D.C. bar, 1951, Va. bar, 1951, U.S. Supreme Ct. bar, 1951; with RCA Corp., Lancaster, Pa., 1952— , sr. counsel picture tube div., 1975-77, staff v.p., sr. counsel picture tube div., 1977-88 . Served with USAAF, 1943-46. Mem. Am. Bar Assn., Va. Bar Assn., D.C. Bar Assn., Phi Delta Phi. Asso. editor Va. Law Rev., 1951.

HIRSCH, JEROME S. lawyer; BA in Econs., SUNY, Binghamton, 1970; JD, Fordham U., 1974. Bar: N.Y. Assoc. Skadden, Arps, Slate, Meagher & Flom, N.Y.C., 1974-81, ptnr., 1982—. Mem. ABA, N.Y. State Bar Assn., Assn. of Bar of City of N.Y. Federal civil litigation, State civil litigation, Securities. Office: Skadden Arps Slate Meagher & Flom 4 Times Sq New York NY 10036-6595

HIRSCH, MILTON, lawyer; b. Chgo., Sept. 10, 1952; s. Charles Ira and Beverly Ruth (Kelner) H.; m. Ilene Lonnie Schreer, Feb. 16, 1986. BA, U. Calif., San Diego, 1974; MS, DePaul U., 1979; JD, Georgetown U., 1982. Bar: Fla. 1982, U.S. Dist. Ct. (so., mid. dists.) Fla. 1983, U.S. Dist. Ct. (no. dist.) Fla. 1985, U.S. Ct. Appeals (5th and 11th cirs.) 1983, U.S. Tax Ct. 1983, U.S. Ct. Claims 1983, U.S. Supreme Ct. 1988. Acct. Arthur Young & Co., CPAs, Chgo., 1977-79; asst. state atty. Office State Atty., Miami, Fla., 1982-84; assoc. Finley, Kumble, Wagner, Heine, Underberg, Manley et al, 1985-87; pvt. practice, 1987—. Adj. prof. Nova U. Law Sch., Ft. Lauderdale, Fla., 1988, 94, 95. Author: Florida Criminal Trial Procedure; contbg. editor Jour. Nat. Assn. Criminal Def. Attys., 1987—; contbr. articles to profl. jours. Mem. ABA (litigation sect.), Nat. Assn. Criminal Def. Lawyers, Fla. Bar Assn.), Fla. Criminal Def. Attys. Assn. (former pres., Presdl. award for Disting. Svc. 1987-88). Criminal, General practice. Office: 9130 S Dadeland Blvd Ste 1504 Miami FL 33156-7850

HIRSCH, RICHARD GARY, lawyer; b. L.A., June 15, 1940; s. Charles and Sylvia (Leopold) H.; m. Claire Renee Recsei, Mar. 25, 1967; 1 child, Nicole Denise. BA, UCLA, 1961; JD, U. Calif., Berkeley, 1965. Bar: Calif. 1967, U.S. Dist. Ct. (ctrl. dist.) Calif. 1967, U.S. Supreme Ct. 1972, U.S. Ct. Appeals (9th cir.) 1989, U.S. Dist. Ct. (ea. dist.) Calif. 1991. Dep. dist. atty. L.A. Dist. Atty.'s Office, 1967-71; ptnr. Nasatir, Hirsch & Podberesky, Santa Monica, Calif., 1971—. Commr. Calif. Coun. Criminal Justice, 1977-81; mem. Spl. Com. on Cts. in the Media/Judicial Coun. Calif., 1979. Co-author: California Criminal Law Proceedings/Practice, 1st edit., 2d edit., 3rd edit., 4th edit. Pres. bd. trustees Santa Monica Mus. Art, 1984-91; chmn. Greek Theatre Adv. Com., L.A., 1976-79; mem. L.A. Olympic Organizing Com., 1981-84; bd. dirs. Ocean Park Cmty. Ctr., 1995—, bd. chair, 1997-2001. Recipient Spl. Merit Resolution, L.A. City Coun., 1984, Criminal Def. Atty. of Yr. award Century City Bar Assn., 1996. Fellow Am. Bd. Criminal Lawyers (bd. dirs., v.p. 1998-2000, pres.-elect 2001); mem. Calif. Attys. Criminal Justice (pres. 1987, bd. trustees), Criminal Cts. Bar Assn. (pres. 1981, Spl. Merit award 1988), L.A. County Bar Assn. (Criminal Def. Atty. of Yr. 1999), Santa Monica C. of C. (bd. dirs. 1995-97). Avocations: cooking, reading, community service. Criminal. Office: Nasatir Hirsch Podberesky & Genego 2115 Main St Santa Monica CA 90405-2215

HIRSCH, ROBERT ALLEN, lawyer; b. Phila., July 1, 1946; s. Leon Sidney and Harriet Roselyn (Benson) H.; BS, Pa. State U., 1968; JD, U. Akron (Ohio), 1974; m. Victoria Ingold, Apr. 23, 1977; 1 child, Courtney Benson. Claims rep. State Farm Ins. Co., Springfield, Pa., 1968-69; claims mgr. Ins. Placement Facility Pa. and Del., Phila., 1970-71; Bar: D.C. 1974; atty. Bur. Enforcement, ICC, 1974-79; assoc. gen. counsel Am. Trucking Assns., Inc., Washington, 1979-87; gen. counsel, dir. govt. affairs Nat. Pvt. Trucking Assn., Washington, 1987-88; gen. counsel, dir. regulatory affairs Nat. Pvt. Truck Coun., Washington, 1988-91; sec., gen. counsel Pvt. Fleet Mgmt. Inst., 1990—; sr. assoc., office mgr. Krukowski & Costello, P.C., Washington, 1991—. Co-author: Drug Testing Handbook for the Trucking Industry. Mem. Hazardous Materials Adv. Coun. Served with USAR, 1969-76. Mem. ABA, Nat. Transp. Indsl. Rels. Assn., Assn. Transp. Practitioners, Va. Bar Assn., D.C. Bar Assn., Transp. Lawyers Assn. (chmn. fed. agy. practice com.), Phi Alpha Delta. Democrat. Administrative and regulatory, General corporate, Transportation. Home: 3323 Parkside Ter Fairfax VA 22031-2715 Office: 2011 Pennsylvania Ave NW Washington DC 20006-1813

HIRSCHFELD, MICHAEL, lawyer; b. Bronx, N.Y., July 4, 1950; s. Lawrence John and Ida (Miller) H.; m. Heidi P. Greenspan, June 17, 1973; children: Adam Lawrence, Philip Richard. BEE summa cum laude, CCNY, 1972; JD cum laude, U. Pa., 1975; LLM in Taxation, NYU, 1980. Bar: N.Y. 1976, U.S. Dist. Ct. (so. and ea. dists.) N.Y. 1976, U.S. Tax Ct. 1978.

Assoc. Shearman and Sterling, N.Y.C., 1975-80, Roberts and Holland, N.Y.C., 1980-83, Carro, Spanbock, Kaster and Cuiffo, N.Y.C., 1983-85, ptnr., 1985-88, Winstown & Strawn, N.Y.C., 1988-98, Dechert, N.Y.C., 1998—. Lectr. NYU, Assn. of Bar of City of New York, ABA, ALI-ABA, PLI, Syracuse U., U. Tex., Tulane U., Georgetown U.; chmn. NYU Inst. Real Estate Taxation; co-chmn. 49th, 50th, 52d, 53d and 54th ann. Fed. Income Taxation Confs.; 11th-23d ann. NYU Confs. on Fed. Taxation of Real Estate Taxations: mem. nat. edn. bd., Business Entities (RIA publ.) Real Estate Tax Digest, Jour. of Internat. Tax, Tax. Mgmt. Real Estate Jour.; mem. adv. bd. Tax Mgmt. Real Estate, Inst. Fed. Tax. Co-author: Real Estate Limited Partnerships, 3rd edit., 1991; bd. editors Real Estate Tax Digest, BNA Tax Mgmt.; editl. adv. bd. NYU Real Estate Adv. Bd. Mem. ABA (lectr. taxation sect., vice chmn. individual income taxpayers com. 2000—, coun. 1997-2000, coun. dir. tax sect. internat. com. 1997-2000, co-chmn. govt. subcom. 1992-94, chmn. govt. subcom. 1994-97, chmn. real estate tax problems com. 1989-91, chmn. syndications subcom. 1985-87, vice chmn. ACRS depreciation recapture subcom. 1983-85, task force pres.'s tax reform proposals minimum tax subcom. 1985-86, vice chmn. gov. submission com. 1992-95), Am. Law Inst. (lectr.), N.Y. State Bar Assn. (lectr., co-chmn. coms. on income from real property tax sect. 1988-91, co-chmn. com. on preferences and minimum tax 1991-92, co-chmn. com. in individuals 1992-93, co-chmn. com. U.S. activities of fgn. taxpayers 1993-96, co-chmn. com. on real property, 1996-98, co-chmn. tax accts. 1997-98, exec. com. 1987-97, com. on internat. members), Assn. of Bar of City of N.Y. (mem. com. on internat. transactions), Internat. Tax Assn., Am. Coll. Tax Counsel. Avocation: music (drum). Corporate taxation, Taxation, general, Personal income taxation. Office: Dechert 30 Rockefeller Plz Fl 22 New York NY 10112-2200 Fax: (212) 698-3599. E-mail: michael.hirschfeld@dechert.com

HIRSCHHORN, HERBERT HERMAN, lawyer; b. Bklyn., Apr. 13, 1909; s. Bernard and Rae (Greenberg) H.; m. Rose Berger, July 10, 1968. BA, NYU, 1930, JD, 1932, Dr. Jud. Sci., 1934, MA, 1937. Bar: N.Y. 1934, U.S. Supreme Ct. 1959, U.S. Dist. Ct. (so. and ea. dists.) N.Y. 1962, U.S. Dist. Ct. (we. dist.) N.Y. 1964, U.S. Ct. Appeals (2d cir.) 1966. Assoc. Gair Gair Conason Steigman & Mackauf and predecessor firms, N.Y.C., 1932—. Dir. emeritus NYU Alumni Fedn.; dir. Coll. Arts & Sci., Sch. Law & Grad. Sch. Arts 7 Sci. Alumni Assn., NYU. Recipient Alumni Meritorious Svc. award NYU, 1982, Disting. Svc. award NYU and Washington Sq. Coll., 1992, Judge Edward Weinfeld award NYU Law Ctr., 1993; inscribed on the Wall of Honor, NYU Sch. of Law 1996. Mem. ABA, N.Y. State Bar Assn., N.Y. County Lawyers Assn., Am. Judicature Soc., Assn. Trial Lawyers Am., Soc. Med. Jurisprudence, Met. Women's Bar Assn., N.Y. Women's Bar Assn., Internat. Assn. Jewish Lawyers and Jurists, N.Y. State Trial Lawyers Assn. (dir. 1954-80, dir. emeritus 1982—). Personal injury. Home: 40 Central Park S New York NY 10019-1633 Office: Gair Gair Conason Steigman & Mackauf 80 Pine St Fl 34 New York NY 10005-1768

HIRSCHKOP, PHILIP JAY, lawyer, educator; b. Bklyn., May 14, 1936; s. Abraham and Frances (Krumholz) H.; children: Jacqueline, Jon David, Adam Abraham. AB, Columbia Coll., 1960; BS in Engring., Columbia U., 1961; JD, Georgetown U., 1964. Bar: Va. 1964, D.C. 1964, U.S. Dist. Ct. (ea. and we. dists.) Va. 1964, U.S. Dist. Ct. D.C. 1964, U.S. Ct. Mil. Appeals 1964, U.S. Ct. Appeals (4th and D.C. cirs.) 1965, U.S. Supreme 1967, U.S. Ct. Claims 1969, U.S. Dist. Ct. (no. dist.) Tex. 1973, U.S. Ct. Appeals (5th cir.) 1973, U.S. Tax Ct. 1974, U.S Ct. Appeals (11th cir.), 1981, N.Y., 1982, U.S. Dist. Ct. (ea. dist.) N.C., U.S. Dist. Ct. D.C. Patent examiner U.S. Patent Office, Washington, 1961-63; legis. asst. congressman Richard Ichord, 1964; pvt. practice Alexandria, Va., 1964—. Adj. prof. law Georgetown U., Washington, 1969-75; profl. law lectr. George Washington U., 2001; chair steering com. Nat. Prison Project, Washington, 1975—; spkr. in field. Contbr. articles to profl. jours. Nat. bd. dirs. ACLU, N.Y.C., 1966-86. With Spl. Forces, U.S. Army, 1954-56. Recipient Disting. Svc. award, Va. Trial Lawyers Assn., 1999, War Horse award, So. Trial Lawyers Assn., 2000. Fellow Va. Law Found.; mem. ATLA (state committeman), PETA (gen. counsel), NCIA (dir., counsel), Va. Bar. Assn., Alexandria Bar Assn., Trial Lawyers for Pub. Justice (bd dirs., founder 1986—), Law Students Civil Rights Rsch. Coun. General civil litigation, Constitutional, Personal injury. Office: Hirschkop & Assocs PC 108 N Columbus St Alexandria VA 22314-3013

HIRSCHMAN, SHERMAN JOSEPH, lawyer, accountant, educator; b. Detroit, May 11, 1935; s. Samuel and Anna (Maxmen) H.; m. Audrey Hecker, 1959; children: Samuel, Shari. BS, Wayne State U., 1956, JD, 1959, LLM, 1968; D in Bus. Adminstrn., Nova Southeastern U., 1996. Bar: Mich. 1959, Fla. 1983; CPA, Mich., Fla.; cert. tax lawyer, Fla. Pvt. practice, Mich., 1959—; instr. comml. law Detroit Coll. Bus., 1971—. Adj. instr. Nova Southeastern U., 1997—, Ctrl. Mich. U., 1997—, Fla. Metro U., 2001—. With USAR, 1959-62. Mem. Mich. Bar Assn., Fla. Bar Assn., Am. Arbitration Assn., Am. Assn. CPA Attys. Pension, profit-sharing, and employee benefits, Corporate taxation, Personal income taxation. Office: 340 Woodlake Wynde Oldsmar FL 34677-2190 E-mail: rgwh2oa@aol.com

HIRSHFIELD, STUART, lawyer; b. N.Y.C., Dec. 31, 1941; s. William Louis and Anne (Frank) H.; m. Susanne Drucker, Jan. 22, 1967; children: Matthew S., Edward R. BA, Syracuse U., 1963, JD, 1966. Bar: N.Y. 1966, U.S. Dist. Ct. (so. and ea. dists.) N.Y. 1968, U.S. Ct. Appeals (2nd cir.) 1968. Assoc. Krauss & Krauss, N.Y.C., 1966-67; atty. N.Y. Cen. RR, 1967-69; assoc. Blum, Haimoff, Gersen, Lipson & Szabad, 1969; atty. CIT Fin., 1970-72; assoc. Shea & Gould, 1972-77, ptnr., 1977-88; ptnr., chmn. bankruptcy practice group Dewey Ballantine, 1988—. Bd. dirs. 565 Tenants Corp. Contbr. Asset Based Financing--A Transactional Guide, 1985. Assn. atty. Allenwood Civic Assn., Great Neck, N.Y., 1984; bd. visitors Syracuse U. Coll. Law, 1990—, exec. com., 1991-96. With USAR, 1966-72. Fellow Am. Coll. Bankruptcy (2d cir. admissions coun. 1994-2001, chair 1998-2001, bd. regents 1998-2001, bd. dirs. 2001—), Am. Bar Found.; mem. ABA (com. on bankruptcy 1983—), N.Y. Bar Assn., Assn. Bar City N.Y. (corp. reogn. com. 1975-78, 82-85), Assn. Comml. Fin. Attys. (dir. 1980-93), Rockefeller Ctr. Club. Bankruptcy, Contracts commercial. Office: Dewey Ballantine 1301 Avenue Of The Americas New York NY 10019-6022

HIRSHON, ROBERT EDWARD, lawyer; b. Portland, Maine, Apr. 2, 1948; s. Selvin and Gladys (Wein) H.; m. Roberta Lynn Miller, Aug. 16, 1969; children: Todd, Sara, Jason, Miriam. BA, U. Mich., 1970, JD, 1973. Bar: Maine 1973, U.S. Dist. Ct. Maine 1973, U.S. Ct. Appeals (1st cir.) 1977. Shareholder Drummond, Woodsum & MacMahon P.A., Portland, 1973—. Adj. prof. law U. Maine Law Sch. Contbr. articles to profl. jours. Chairperson Breakwater Sch Bd., Portland, 1978-85; mem. Zoning Bd. Appeals, Cape Elizabeth, Maine, 1983-90. Mem. ABA (mem. Ho. of Dels. 1992—, chair standing com. lawyers pub. svc. responsibility 1990-93, chair standing com. pro bono ctr. 1991-96, chair torts and ins. practice sect. 1996-97, chair standing com. on membership 1997-2000, pres.-elect 2000-01, pres. 2001—), Maine Bar Assn. (pres. 1986, chair continuing legal edn. com. 1975-83), Cumberland County Bar Assn., Maine Bar Found. (pres. 1990). Avocations: reading, tennis, skiing. Banking, General civil litigation, Insurance. Home: 3 Oakhurst Rd Cape Elizabeth ME 04107 Office: Drummond Woodsum & MacMahon PO Box 9781 Portland ME 04104-5081 E-mail: rhirshon@dwm.law.com

HIRSHON, SHELDON IRA, lawyer; b. Bklyn., Mar. 27, 1947; s. Jay and Jeanne (Benk) H.; m. Claudia Glenn Barasch; children: Ariel, Yaniv, Jessica. BS, NYU, 1968, JD, 1972, LLM, 1978. Bar: N.Y. 1972. Assoc. Graubard, Moskovitz, McGoldrick, Dannett & Horowitz, N.Y.C., 1972-76, Windels, Marx, Davies & Ives, N.Y.C., 1976-78, Krause, Hirsch & Gross, N.Y.C., 1978-80; assoc., ptnr. Stroock & Stroock & Lavan, 1980-87; ptnr. Proskauer, Rose, Goetz & Mendelsohn, 1987—. Mem. ABA, N.Y. Bar Assn., Assn. Bar City N.Y. Bankruptcy, General corporate. Office: Proskauer Rose LLP 1585 Broadway Fl 27 New York NY 10036-8299

HIRSHOWITZ, MELVIN STEPHEN, lawyer; b. N.Y.C., Dec. 11, 1938; s. Samuel Albert and Lillian Rose (Minkow) H.; m. Susan Bonnie Brezel, June 19, 1983; children: Lauren Allison, Emily Sara. BA with hons., Cornell U., 1960; LLB cum laude, Harvard U., 1963; MA in Biology, CUNY, 1977. Bar: N.Y. 1963, N.J. 1987, U.S. Dist. Ct. (so. dist.) N.Y. 1969, (ea. dist.) N.Y. 1977, N.J. 1993, U.S. Ct. Appeals (2d cir.) 1978, U.S. Supreme Ct. 1994. Assoc. atty. SEC, N.Y.C., 1963-65; sole practitioner Melvin Hirshowitz Law Office, 1968-76, 87--; of counsel Hyman Bravin Law Offices, 1976-87. Author: (manual) Proof of an Over the Counter Manipulation, 1964. Vice chmn. N.Y. Libertarian Party, 1970-72, candidate for surrogate ct. judge and ct. of appeals judge. Mem. N.Y. County Lawyers Assn. (com. on profl. ethics 1986-92, com. fed. legislation 1986-88), Assn. of Bar of City of N.Y. (com. on the civil ct. 1986-89), N.Y. State Bar Assn., Harvard Club of N.Y.C., Phi Beta Kappa, Pi Delta Epsilon. Republican. Jewish. Avocations: bird watching, art, tennis. General civil litigation, State civil litigation, Probate. Office: 630 3rd Ave New York NY 10017-6705 E-mail: mshlawoffices@aol.com

HITCHCOCK, BION EARL, lawyer; b. Muscatine, Iowa, Oct. 9, 1942; s. Stewart Edward and Arlene Ruth (Eichelberger) H. BSEE, Iowa State U., 1965; JD, U. Iowa, 1968. Bar: Iowa 1968, Okla. 1968, U.S. Ct. Customs and Patent Appeals 1973, U.S. Ct. Appeals (fed. cir.) 1982. Attyl Phillips Petroleum Co., Bartlesville, Okla., 1968-69, 73-76; mgr. licensing Phillips Petroleum Co. Europe-Africa, Brussels, 1977-80; sr. patent counsel Phillips Petroleum Co., Bartlesville, 1980-84, assoc. gen. patent counsel, 1984-2000; asst. gen. counsel intellectual property Chevron Phillips Chem. Co., LP, Houston, 2000—. Bd. dirs. Bartlesville Symphony Orch., 1973-77, 80-91, pres., 1975-77, 82-84; bd. dirs. Bartlesville Allied Arts and Humanities Coun., 1976-77, 80-86, 1st v.p., 1982-83; mem. Govt. and Fin. Goals for Bartlesville Com., 1974-75; bd. dirs. Bartlesville Cmty. Concert Assn., 1982-90, Okla. Assn. Symphony Orchs., 1983-88. Lt. JAGC, USN, 1969-73. Mem. ABA, Okla. Bar Assn. (dir. patent trademark and copyright sect. 1980-86, sec. 1982-83, vice chmn. 1983-84, chmn. 1984-85), Iowa Bar Assn., Washington County Bar Assn. (pres. 1981-82), Am. Intellectual Property Law Assn., Am. Judicature Soc., Am. Corp. Counsel Assn., Fed. Cir. Bar Assn., Licensing Execs. Soc., Eta Kappa Nu. Private international, Patent, Trademark and copyright. Home: 1227 Misty Lake Ct Sugar Land TX 77478-5613 Office: Chevron Phillips Chem Co LP 1301 McKinney Ste 3450 Houston TX 77010-3030

HITE, DAVID L. lawyer; b. Thornville, Ohio, Apr. 30, 1916; s. Frank C. Hite and Mary Pannabaker; m. Maxine Witherbee, July 15, 1943; 1 child, Diane. BS, Kent Sate U., 1938; JD, Capital U., 1946. Neuropsychiat. fellow Psychology Ct. Neuropsychiat. Inst., Hartford, Conn., 1939; pvt. practice Utica and Newark, Ohio, 1946—. Capt. OSS, 1942-46. Mem. ABA (pub. utilities sect., small trusts and estate com., adminstrn. and distbrn. of estates com.), Ohio Bar Ass., Cleve. Bar Assn., Licking Bar Assn. Probate, Public utilities. Office: Hite & Hite 964 N 21st St Ste D Newark OH 43055-7230 E-mail: hite@nextek.net

HITE, ROBERT GRIFFITH, lawyer; b. San Antonio, Nov. 24, 1932; s. Raymond Griffith and Violet (Peck) H.; m. Gay Ann Bickham, Aug. 25, 1971; m. Carol Jean Peterson, June 5, 1953 (div. Aug. 1971); children: R. David, Kevin L., Brent R. B.S., U. Utah, 1960, J.D., 1966. Bar: Hawaii 1966. Ptnr., Goodsill Anderson Quinn & Stifel, Honolulu, 1966— . Editor-in-chief Utah Law Rev., 1965-66. Fellow Am. Coll. Trust and Estates Counsel (Hawaii state chmn. 1983-88); mem. Hawaii State Bar Assn., Hawaii Estate Planning Council (exec. com. 1978-79, 81-82, pres. 1987). Estate planning, Probate, Estate taxation. Home: 92-1539 Aliinui Dr Apt F Kapolei HI 96707-2224 Office: Goodsill Anderson Quinn & Stifel 1099 Alakea St Ste 1800 Honolulu HI 96813-4512

HITT, LEO N. lawyer, educator; b. Pitts., Oct. 20, 1955; s. Joe Stephen and Laurene (Lally) H.; m. Mary Elizabeth Wolf, Jan. 26, 1985; children: Nancy Anne, Elizabeth Lea. BA summa cum laude, U. Pitts., 1977, JD cum laude, 1980; LLM in Taxation, N.Y.U., 1983. Bar: Pa. 1980, U.S. Dist. Ct. (we. dist.) Pa. 1983, U.S. Tax Ct. 1981, U.S. Ct. Fed. Claims, 1997. Atty., tax sr. Kenneth Leventhal & Co., N.Y.C., 1980-81; atty., tax counsel Touche Ross & Co., Pitts., 1981-83; assoc. Reed Smith LLP, 1983-88, ptnr., 1989—. Adj. prof. tax. grad. sch. Robert Morris Coll., Pitts., 1983—, tax grad. sch., law sch. Duquesne U., Pitts., 1987—, sch. law U. Pitts., 1988—; seminar speaker various profl. orgns., Pitts., 1983—. Comments editor: U. Pitts. Law Review, 1979-80. Mem. Allegheny County Bar Assn., Pitts. Internat. Tax Soc., Allegheny Tax Soc., Pitts. Tax Club. Democrat. Roman Catholic. Avocations: alpine skiing, opera, gourmet cooking. Corporate taxation, Taxation, general. Home: 4209 Summervale Dr Murrysville PA 15668-3515 Office: Reed Smith LLP 435 6th Ave Pittsburgh PA 15219-1886 E-mail: LHitt@ReedSmith.com

HITTER, JOSEPH IRA, lawyer; b. Bklyn., Nov. 1, 1944; s. Harry H. and Annette (Fidler) H.; m. Ann Lois Jaffe, May 28, 1966; children: Jonathan C., Evan R. BS in Acctg., L.I. U., 1966; JD, St. John's U., 1969; LLM in Taxation, NYU, 1973. Bar: N.Y. 1970, U.S. Tax Ct. 1971, U.S. Supreme Ct. 1974. Tax specialist Arthur Young & Co., N.Y.C., 1969-72; tax atty. Pfizer, Inc., 1972-73, supr. tax planning, 1973-74; sr. tax. specialist Mead Corp., Dayton, Ohio, 1974-76, mgr. fed. and internat. taxes, 1976-77, mgr. tax affairs, 1977-82, dir. taxation, 1982-98, v.p., 1999—. Bd. dirs. Dayton-Montgomery County Port Authority; chmn. tax policy com. Am. Paper Inst., 1987—. Advisor YWCA, Dayton, 1985-87; dir. Hillel Acad., Dayton, 1981-83. Mem. ABA Tax Execs. Inst. (chpt. pres. 1984-85), N.Y. State Bar Assn., Dayton Bar Assn. Republican. Clubs: Meadowbrook Country, Dayton Racquet. Avocations: golf, tennis. Corporate taxation, Taxation, general, State and local taxation. Office: The Mead Corp Courthouse Plz NE Dayton OH 45402

HITTNER, DAVID, federal judge; b. Schenectady, N.Y., July 10, 1939; s. George and Sophie (Moskowitz) H.; children: Miriam, Susan, George. BS, NYU, 1961, JD, 1964. Bar: N.Y. 1964, Tex. 1967. Pvt. practice, Houston, 1967-78; judge Tex. 133d Dist. Ct., 1978-86, U.S. Dist. Ct. (so. dist.) Tex., Houston, 1986—. Author 2 books; contbr. articles to profl. jours. Mem. Nat. coun. Boy Scouts Am. Capt. inf., paratrooper U.S. Army, 1965-66. Recipient Silver Beaver award Boy Scouts Am., 1974, Silver Antelope award Boy Scouts Am., 1988, Samuel E. Gates award Am. Coll. Trial Lawyers. Mem. ABA (Merit award), State Bar Tex. (Outstanding Lawyer in Tex. award), Houston Bar Assn. (Pres.'s and Dirs.' award), Am. Law Inst., Masons (33d degree), Order of Coif (hon.). Office: US Courthouse 515 Rusk St Ste 8509 Houston TX 77002-2603

HOAGLAND, KARL KING, JR. lawyer; b. St. Louis, Aug. 21, 1933; s. Karl King and Mary Edna (Parsons) H.; m. Sylvia Anne Naranick, July 13, 1957; children: Elizabeth Parsons, Sarah Stewart, Karl King III, Alison T. BS in Econs., U. Pa., 1955; LLB, U. Ill., 1958. Bar: Ill. 1958, U.S. Dist. Ct. (so. dist.) Ill. 1958. V.p., gen. counsel, sec. Jefferson Smurfit Corp., St. Louis, 1960-92, Container Corp. Am., St. Louis, 1986-92; of counsel Hoagland, Fitzgerald, Smith & Pranaitis, Alton, Ill., 1987—. Chmn. bd. dirs. Millers' Mut. Ins. Assn. Ill., 1989-92. Asst. editor: U. Ill. Law Forum, 1957-58. Trustee, treas. Monticello Coll. Found., 1965—. 1st lt. USAF, 1958-60. Mem. Ill. Bar Assn., Madison County Bar Assn., Alton-Wood River Bar Assn., Lockhaven Country Club, Mo. Athletic Club, Crystal Lake Club, Orcas Tennis Club, Order of the Coif, Beta Gamma Sigma. Episcopalian. Avocations: tennis, skiing, hunting, fishing, golf. General corporate. Home: PO Box 1454 Eastsound WA 98245

HOAGLAND, SAMUEL ALBERT, lawyer, pharmacist; b. Mt. Home, Idaho, Aug. 19, 1953; s. Charles Leroy and Glenna Lorraine (Gridley) H.; m. Karen Ann Mengel, Nov. 20, 1976; children: Hiliary Anne, Heidi Lynne, Holly Kaye. BS in Pharmacy, Idaho State U., 1976; JD, U. Idaho, 1982. Bar: Idaho 1982, U.S. Dist. Ct. Idaho 1982, U.S. CT. Appeals (9th cir.) 1984. Lectr. clin. pharmacy Idaho State U., Pocatello, 1976-78, lectr. pharmacy law, 1985-86, dean's adv. council Coll. Pharmacy, 1987-92; hosp. pharmacist Mercy Med. Ctr., Nampa, Idaho, 1978-79; retail pharmacist Thrifty Corp., Moscow, 1980-82; assoc. Dial, Looze & May, Pocatello, 1982-89, Prescott & Foster, Boise, Idaho, 1989-90; pvt. practice, 1990—; gen. counsel Design Innovations and Rsch. Corp., 1991-95. Chmn. malpractice panel Idaho Bd. Medicine, Boise, 1983-92, adminstrv. hearing officer, 1989-92. Contbr. to law publs. Bd. dirs. Cathedral Pines Camp, Ketchum, Idaho. Mem. Idaho State Bar Assn., Idaho Pharm. Assn., Idaho Trial Lawyers Assn., Boise Bar Assn., Capital Pharm. Assn., Am. Pharm. Assn., Idaho Soc. Hosp. Pharmacists (bd. dirs.), Am. Soc. Pharmacy Law, Flying Doctors Am. (Atlanta) (bd. dirs.). Administrative and regulatory, General civil litigation, General practice. Home: 11901 W Mesquite Dr Boise ID 83713-0813 Office: 1471 Shoreline Dr Ste 100 Boise ID 83702-9104

HOARD, HEIDI MARIE, lawyer; b. Mt. Clemons, Mich., Feb. 8, 1951; d. Duane Jay and Elizabeth Hoard; m. John B. Lunseth II, Jan. 11, 1980; children: John B. III, Steven J. BA, Macalester Coll., 1972; JD cum laude, U. Minn., 1976. Bar: Minn. 1976, U.S. Dist. Ct. Minn. 1976. Assoc. Faegre & Benson, Mpls., 1976-83, ptnr., 1984-93; sr. legal counsel Medtronic, Inc., 1993-95; v.p., gen. counsel, corp. sec. The Musicland Group, Minnetonka, 1995—. Mem. State Bd. Women in the Legal Profession Task Force, State Bd. Legal Cert., 1986-88, pres. Tel-Law, Bar Assn. Com., Mpls., 1978-80; bd. dirs. Fund for Legal Aid Soc. Mem. Minn. Region G, Law Enforcement Assistance Assn. Com., 1971-72; vol. aide U.S. Senate Nursing Home Investigation and Hearing, Mpls., 1971-72; student dir. Legal Aid Clinic, U. Minn., Mpls., 1975-76. Mem. Am. Soc. Corp. Secs. (bd. dirs. Minn. sect.), Am. Corp. Counsel Assn., Minn. Bar Assn., Phi Beta Kappa. Democrat. General corporate. Office: Musicland Group 10400 Yellow Circle Dr Hopkins MN 55343

HOBBS, CASWELL O., III, lawyer; b. Sherman, Tex., Aug. 25, 1941; s. Caswell Owen II and Marie Elizabeth (Bloomfield) H.; m. Anne Louise Simpson, June 7, 1968; children: Elizabeth Ellen, Emily Jane. BS, U. Kans., 1963; LLB, U. Pa., 1966. Bar: D.C. 1967, U.S. Ct. Appeals (4th cir.) 1975, U.S. Supreme Ct. 1972. Asst. to chmn., dir. Office of Policy Planning and Evaluation, FTC, Washington, 1970-73; assoc. Morgan Lewis & Bockius, Washington, 1973-76, ptnr., 1976—, chmn. Washington office mgmt. com., 1987-89, mem. governing bd., 1989-92, 95-99; lectr. Conf. Bd., ABA. Author: Antitrust Strategies for Mergers, Acquisitions, Joint Ventures and Strategic Alliances, 2000; contbr. articles to profl. jours. Trustee Legal Aid Soc. D.C., 1982-92, pres., 1989-91, pres. coun., 1991—. Served to capt. JAGC, USAR, 1966-72. Fellow ABA (chair antitrust sect. 1994-95, officer 1991-96, co-chair task force on competition policy 1993, mem. commn. to study the FTC, 1988); mem. Am. Law Inst. E-mail: cohobbs@morganlewis.com. Administrative and regulatory, Antitrust, General corporate. Office: Morgan Lewis & Bockius 1800 M St NW Lbby 6 Washington DC 20036-5828

HOBBS, GREGORY JAMES, JR. state supreme court justice; b. Gainesville, Fla., Dec. 15, 1944; s. Gregory J. Hobbs and Mary Ann (Rhodes) Frakes; m. Barbara Louise Hay, June 17, 1967; children: Daniel Gregory, Emily Mary Hobbs Wright. BA, U. Notre Dame, 1966; JD, U. Calif., Berkeley, 1971. Bar: Colo. 1971, Calif. 1972. Law clk. to Judge William E. Doyle 10th U.S. Cir. Ct. Appeals, Denver, 1971-72; assoc. Cooper, White & Cooper, San Francisco, 1972-73; enforcement atty. U.S. EPA, Denver, 1973-75; asst. atty. gen. State of Colo. Atty. Gen.'s Office, 1975-79; ptnr. Davis, Graham & Stubbs, 1979-92; shareholder Hobbs, Trout & Raley, P.C., 1992-96; justice Colo. Supreme Ct., 1996—. Counsel No. Colo. Water Conservancy, Loveland, Colo., 1979-96. Contbr. articles to profl. jours. Vol. Peace Corps-S.Am., Colombia, 1967-68; vice chair Colo. Air Quality Control Com., Denver, 1982-87; mem. ranch com. Philmont Scout Ranch, Boy Scouts Am., Cimarron, N.Mex., 1988-98; co-chair Eating Disorder Family Support Group, Denver, 1992—. Recipient award of merit Denver Area Coun. Boy Scouts, 1993, Pres. award Nat. Water Resources Assn., Washington, 1995. Fellow Am. Bar Found.; mem. ABA, Colo. Bar Assn., Denver Bar Assn. Avocations: backpacking, fishing, writing poetry. Office: Colo Supreme Ct 2 E 14th Ave Denver CO 80203-2115

HOBBS, J. TIMOTHY, SR. lawyer; b. Yakima, Wash., Sept. 23, 1941; s. Leonard M. and Virginia (Snider) H.; m. Barbara J. Hatfield, June 14, 1964; children: Amy Elizabeth, J. Timothy Jr. BA in Polit. Sci., U. Wash., 1964; JD, Am. U., 1968. Bar: D.C. 1969, U.S. Ct. Supreme Ct. 1973, U.S. Ct. Appeals Fed. Crct. 1982, U.S. Ct. Appeals (11th cir.) 1986, U.S. Ct. Appeals (5th cir.) 1989, U.S. Ct. Appeals (6th cir.) 1996. Assoc. Mason Fenwick & Lawrence, Washington, 1969-76, ptnr., 1977-82, sr. ptnr., 1982-91; ptnr., head intellectual property dept. Dykema Gossett, 1991-99; ptnr. Wiley, Rein & Fielding, Washington, 1999—. Author chpt. on copyright law, West's Federal Practice Manual, 1983. Pres. Arlington Outdoor Edn. Assn., 1990-92. Mem. D.C. Bar (chmn. trademark com. 1982-84), U.S. Trademark Assn. Forums (speaker 1988), Washington Golf and Country Club. Trademark and copyright. Home: 6135 Lee Hwy Arlington VA 22205-2134 Office: Wiley Rein & Fielding 1776 K St NW Washington DC 20006-2304

HOBELMAN, CARL DONALD, lawyer; b. Hackensack, N.J., Dec. 26, 1931; s. Alfred Charles and Marion (Gerrish) H.; m. Grace Palumbo, Apr. 25, 1964 BCE, Cornell U., 1954; JD, Harvard U., 1959. Bar: N.Y. 1960, U.S. Supreme Ct. 1975, D.C. 1980, Calif. 1993. Assoc. LeBoeuf, Lamb, Greene & MacRae, N.Y.C., 1959-64, ptnr. L.A., N.Y.C., Washington, 1965-94, of counsel Washington, 1995—. Contbr. articles on energy-related topics to profl. jours. Served to 1st lt. U.S. Army, 1954-56 Mem. Energy Bar Assn. (pres. 1980-81), D.C. Bar Assn., Met. Club (Washington), Univ. Club (N.Y.C.). Avocations: travel, philately. Office: LeBoeuf Lamb Greene & MacRae 1875 Connecticut Ave NW Washington DC 20009-5728

HOBERMAN, STUART A. lawyer; b. N.Y.C., Nov. 21, 1946; BBA, Baruch Coll., N.Y.C., 1969; JD, Bklyn. Law Sch., 1972; LLM, NYU, 1973. Bar: N.Y. 1973, N.J. 1977, Pa. 1979, U.S. Supreme Ct. 1976. Assoc. Windels & Marx, N.Y.C., 1973-77, Wilentz, Goldman & Spitzer, Woodbridge, N.J., 1977-80, ptnr., 1980—. Trustee, Emmanuel Cancer Found., Kenilworth, N.J., 1983-90. Mem. N.J. State Bar Assn. (trustee 1990-94, 97-2001, sec. 2001—, corp. and bus. law sect. chmn. 1988-90, bank law sect. chmn. 1986-87, chmn. exec. com. of gen. coun. 1990-92, trustee N.J. State Bar Found. 1992—, treas. 1995, 96, pres. 1999-2001). Banking, General corporate, Finance. Office: Wilentz Goldman & Spitzer PO Box 10 90 Woodbridge Ctr Dr Ste 900 Woodbridge NJ 07095-1142

HOCH, GARY W. lawyer; b. Duluth, Minn., Jan. 14, 1943; s. Roland J. and Virginia (Sandwick) H.; m. Marilyn Turnquist, June 13, 1970; children: Ryan M., Nicole S., Carrie L. BA in Polit. Sci., U. Minn., 1965, JD, 1968. Bar: Minn. 1968, U.S. Dist. Ct. Minn. 1968, U.S. Ct. Appeals (8th cir.). Assoc. Meagher & Geer PLLP, Mpls. Mem. ABA, Am. Coll. Trial Lawyers, Am. Bd. Trial Advs., Minn. Bar Assn., Internat. Soc. Barristers. General civil litigation, Insurance, Product liability. Office: Meagher & Geer 4200 Multifoods Tower 33 S 6th St Minneapolis MN 55402-3788 E-mail: ghoch@meagher.com

HOCHBERG, RONALD MARK, lawyer; b. Bklyn., Apr. 3, 1955; s. Fred S. and Adele (Gunsberg) H.; m. Sharon A. Berg, Aug. 11, 1985; children: Rachel, Sarah. BA, Rutgers U., 1977; JD, Bklyn. Law Sch., 1980; LLM, U. Miami, 1982. Assoc. Klatsky & Klatsky, Red Bank, N.J., 1980-81, Fuerst, Singer & Yusem, Somerville, 1982-83, Law Offices of Steven Schanker, Melville, N.Y., 1983-86; ptnr. Schanker & Hochberg, Attys., Huntington, 1986—. Frequent lectr. on estate planning; instr. Adelphi U., 1984-93. Columnist Financial World Mag., 1993-97; contbr. articles to profl. publs. Mem. ABA, N.Y. State Bar Assn., Estate and Tax Planning Coun. Avocations: skiing, sailing. Estate planning, Pension, profit-sharing, and employee benefits, Estate taxation. Office: Schanker & Hochberg 27 W Neck Rd PO Box 1905 Huntington NY 11743-2618 E-mail: mark@schankerhochberg.com

HOCHMAN, KENNETH GEORGE, lawyer; b. Mt. Vernon, N.Y., Nov. 12, 1947; s. Benjamin S. and Lillian (Gilbert) H.; m. Carol K. Hochman, Apr. 8, 1979; children: Brian Paul, Lisa Erin. BA, SUNY, Buffalo, 1969; JD, Columbia U., 1972. Bar: Ohio 1973, Fla. 1977, N.Y. 1979. Assoc. Jones, Day, Reavis & Pogue, Cleve., 1972-79, ptnr., 1980—. Trustee Katharine Kenyon Lippitt Found., Cleve., 1988, Kenridge Fund, Cleve., 1989, Bolton Found., Cleve., 1990, Elisha-Bolton Found., Cleve., 1993. Harlan Fiske Stone scholar Columbia U., 1971, 72. Fellow Am. Coll. Trusts and Estate Counsel; mem. Phi Beta Kappa, Oakwood Club (Cleve.) (trustee 1997, officer 2000). Estate planning, Probate, Estate taxation. Office: Jones Day Reavis & Pogue 901 Lakeside Ave E Cleveland OH 44114-1190

HOCK, FREDERICK WYETH, lawyer; b. Newark, July 10, 1924; s. Herbert Hummel and Carol (Wyeth) H.; m. Alfheld Catherine Larsen, Mar. 4, 1945; children: Carolyn, Sandra, Rhonda; m. Ellen Barbara Weidner, June 28, 1975. AA, Princeton U., 1944; BA, Rutgers U., 1948, LLB, 1950, JD, 1968. Bar: N.J. 1949. Assoc. Stevenson, Willette & McDermott, 1949-51; pvt. practice, 1951-65; ptnr. Hock & Sharkey, East Orange, N.J., 1965-79; sr. ptnr. Hock Silverlieb & Kramer, Livingston, 1979-93, Gulkin, Hock & Lehr, 1994-2000, Hock Graziano & Koprowski, 2000—. Acting judge East Orange Mcpl. Ct., 1954-57; mem. adv. bd. Maplewood Bank and Trust Co., Livingston, 1987-91, Summit Trust Co., 1991-98. Chmn. Juvenile Conf. Com., 1958-62; trustee Cmty. Day Nursery of the Oranges & Maplewood, 1962-75, pres. 1973-75; trustee Founders Endowment Fund, 1954-87, House of Good Shepherd, 1970-90, Nu Beta Found., 1970-91; bd. dirs. Essex County chpt. ARC, 1987-91; post adv. VFW post 5445, 1955-90. With USMC, 1942-46. Mem. ABA, N.J. Bar Assn., Northwestern N.J. Estate Planning Coun. (dir. 1988-90), No. N.J. Estate Planning Coun., Marina Bay Club (trustee 2000—). Estate planning, Probate. Office: 130 Pompton Turnpike Verona NJ 07044-0031

HOCKENBERRY, JOHN FEDDEN, counselor; b. Bronxville, N.Y., Sept. 2, 1945; m. Nina Gail Levitt; 1 child, Mark S. AB in Econ. summa cum laude, Princeton U., 1969; JD, Yale Law Sch., 1972. Bar: N.Y., D.C. Atty. Cravath, Swaine & Moore, N.Y.C., 1973-80; assoc. gen. counsel The Washington Post Co., 1980—. Office: The Washington Post Co 1150 15th St NW Washington DC 20071-0002

HOCKER, WESLEY HARDY, lawyer; b. Corpus Christi, Tex., Mar. 6, 1941; s. Thomas Tudor and Nola Vivian (Vandergriff) H.; m. Pamela Jean Zapp, Mar. 21, 1980; 1 son, Warner Vandergriff. B.J., U. Tex., 1963; J.D., South Tex. Coll. Law, 1970. Bar: Tex. 1971, U.S. Dist. Ct. (so. dist.) Tex., U.S. Ct. Appeals (5th and 11th cirs.), U.S. Supreme Ct. Gen. counsel Houston Inspection Services, Inc., 1980-84; of counsel White, Gilbreath & Squire; sr. ptnr. Hocker, Morrow & Mathews, Houston, 1984— ; bd. dirs. Coll. State Bar Tex., 1986-92. Editor South Tex. Law Jour., 1970. Former gen. counsel Harris County Democratic Party, Houston, dir. Houston LIvestock Show & Rodeo, 1986-. Served to capt. USMC, 1963-73. Fellow Tex. Bar Found.; mem. Harris County Criminal Lawyers Assn. (charter, dir. 1972-73, 79-80, Outstanding Lawyer award 1972, 73), Phi Alpha Delta. Democrat. Baptist. Lodge: Eagles. Criminal, Family and matrimonial. Home: 333 Woerner Rd Houston TX 77090-1054

HOCUM, MONICA CARROLL, lawyer; b. Waukesha, Wis., Sept. 16, 1966; d. Paul Eagan Carroll and Edith Carroll Oaks; m. Neal Eric Hocum, Sept. 22, 1990; 1 child, Matthew Eric. BS, U. Wis., 1989, MS, 1990; JD cum laude, Marquette U., 1997. Bar: U.S. Dist. Ct. (ea. and we. dists.) Wis., U.S. Supreme Ct. 1997. Vocat. rehab. counselor DS Assocs., Ventura, Calif., 1990-92; vocat. rehab. coord. Superior Nat. Ins., Calabasas, 1992-93, vocat. rehab. supr. San Francisco, 1993-94; atty. Bode, Carroll, McCoy & Hoefle S.C., Waukesha, 1997—. Mem. Wis. Women Entrepreneurs. Avocations: spending time with family, reading. General corporate, Estate planning, Health. Office: Bode Carroll McCoy & Hoefle SC # 250 20700 Swenson Dr Waukesha WI 53186

HODES, PAUL WILLIAM, lawyer, record company executive; b. N.Y.C., Mar. 21, 1951; s. Robert Bernard and Florence (Rosenberg) H.; m. Margaret Ann Horstmann; children: Maxwell, Ariana. BA, Dartmouth Coll., 1972; JD, Boston Coll., 1978. Bar: N.H. 1978, Mass. 1980. Asst. atty. gen. Office of N.H. Atty. Gen., Concord, 1978-82; pres. Big Round Records, Inc., N.H., 1986—. Co-owner Big Round Music, LLC, 1986—. Bd. dirs. Capital Ctr. for Arts, 1990-97, chair 1990-96; bd. dirs. Children's Entertainment Assn., 1995-99, Concord Cmty. Music Sch., 1997-99, N.H. Children's Alliance, 1997-2000, Tricinium Ltd., 2001—. Recipient hon. award Parents Choice Found., 1987, 96. Mem. Am. Bd. Trial Advocates, NARAS, ASCAP, ATLA, Nat. Assn. Criminal Def. Lawyers, N.H. Assn. Criminal Def. Lawyers, N.H. Trial Lawyers. Federal civil litigation, Criminal, Entertainment. Office: Shaheen & Gordon PA PO Box 2703 Concord NH 03302-2703 also: Big Round Records Inc PO Box 610 Concord NH 03302-0610 E-mail: gtrpaul@aol.com, phodes@shaheengondon.com

HODGES, RALPH B. state supreme court justice; b. Anadarko, Okla., Aug. 4, 1930; s. Dewey E. and Pearl R. (Hodges) H.; m. Janelle H.; children: Shari, Mark, Randy. B.A., Okla. Baptist U.; LL.B., U. Okla. Atty. Bryan County, Okla., 1956-58; judge Okla. Dist. Ct., 1959-65; justice Okla. Supreme Ct., Oklahoma City, 1965—. Office: Okla Supreme Ct State Capital Bldg Rm 200 Oklahoma City OK 73105*

HODOUS, ROBERT POWER, lawyer; b. Zanesville, Ohio, July 29, 1945; s. Robert Frank and Nancy Aurelia (Power) H.; m. Susan Cottrell Birkhead, Feb. 1, 1969; children: Robert Everett, Shannon Alycia. BA, Miami U., Oxford, Ohio, 1967; JD, U. Va., Charlottesville, 1970. Bar: Va. 1970. Assoc. firm McGuire, Woods & Battle, Charlottesville, 1970-71; asst. trust officer Nat. Bank & Trust Co., 1971-72, trust officer, 1972-75, sec., 1975-79, Jefferson Bankshares, Inc. (formerly NB Corp.), Charlottesville, 1979-91, v.p., sec., 1985-91, sr. v.p., sec., 1987-91; asst. to pres. Jefferson Nat. Bank, 1987-91; pvt. practice law, 1991-92; mem. firm Payne & Hodous, 1992—. Author: Let's Really Change Taxes, 1998. Chmn. profl. div. Thomas Jefferson Area United Way, 1973, vice-chmn., 1978-79, campaign chmn., 1979-80, v.p. planning, 1981, pres., 1983; bd. dirs. Central Va. chpt. ARC, 1972-78, treas., 1972-75, chmn., 1975-77; commr. Charlottesville Redevel. and Housing Authority, 1974-78; mem. Region X Community Mental Health and Retardation Services Bd., 1973-79, chmn., 1974-76, mem. exec. com., 1976-78; v.p. Soccer Orgn. of Charlottesville-Albemarle, 1985-86, pres., 1986-88; co-pres. Greenbier Sch. PTA, 1985-86; chmn. recreation precinct Charlottesville City Dem. Com., 1971, Rep. com., 1992—; chmn. City Rep. Com., 2000—; bd. dirs. Charlottesville-Albemarle Community Found., 1987-2000, chmn. devel. com., 1991-93, mem. exec. and fin. coms., 1991-2000, chmn. fin. com., 1997-2000. Mem. Va. Bar Assn., Charlottesville-Albemarle Bar Assn., Va. State Bar, Va. Bankers Assn. (com. drafted Va. Trust Subs. Act 1973, trust com. 1974-77, legal affairs com. 1986-91, large bank legis. coord. 1987-91), Computer Law Assn., Charlottesville C. of C. (legis. action com. 1996—), Fairview Club (Charlottesville, pres. 1974-75). Roman Catholic. Banking, General corporate, Pension, profit-sharing, and employee benefits. Home: 1309 Lester Dr Charlottesville VA 22901-3143 Office: 412 E Jefferson St Charlottesville VA 22902-5109

HODYL, RICHARD, JR. lawyer, educator; b. Chgo., May 25, 1964; s. Richard Sr. and Mildred Hodyl; m. Charlene E. Horvath, Mar. 24, 1990; children: Kyle, Kelley. BS, Western Ill. U., 1986; JD, DePaul U., 1989. Bar: Ill., U.S. Dist. Ct. (no. dist.) Ill., U.S. Ct. Appeals (7th cir.), U.S. Supreme Ct. Dir. comml. and environ. liability svcs. Liability Ins. Rsch. Bur., Schaumburg, Ill., 1990-92; atty. GRE Specialty Automobile, 1992-94, Nat. Assn. Ind. Insurers, Des Plaines, Ill., 1994-98; assoc. Williams Montgomery & John Ltd., Chgo., 1998—. Mem. St. Petronille Sch. Bd. Edn., Glen Ellyn, Ill., 1999-2000, Lake Park H.S. Bd. Edn., Roselle, Ill., 1995-99; bd. dirs. DuPage County Area Found., Addison, Ill., 1999-2000; trustee Glen Oaks Hosp. Found., Glendale Heights, Ill., 1995-6000; chmn. Village of Bloomingdale (Ill.) Old Town Plan Commn., 1988-90. Office: Williams Montgomery & John Ltd 20 N Wacker Dr Ste 2100 Chicago IL 60606 Fax: (312) 443-1323. E-mail: rh@willmont.com

HOELSCHER, MICHAEL RAY, lawyer; b. Rosebud, Tex., Dec. 15, 1947; s. Clarence Raymond and Helen (Buster) H.; m. Anita R. Clark, June 6, 1975; children: Jennie, Matt. BA, MBA, Baylor U., 1970, JD, 1972. Bar: Tex. 1972, U.S. Dist. Ct. (so. dist.) Tex. 1976. Assoc. Law Office of Phillip Goode, College Station, Tex., 1974-78; shareholder Hoelscher, Lipsey & Elmore, 1978—, 1995—. Lectr. Tex. A&M U., 1975-76; shareholder, officer Univ. Title Co., College Station, 1982—. Pres. Brazos Valley Rehab. Ctr., Bryan, Tex., 1980-82, Am. Heart Assn., 1992. Mem. Coll. State Bar Tex., Brazos County Bar Assn. (pres. 1988-89), The Dispute Resolution Ctr. (pres. 1997-99), Tex. Bar Found. (1999—), Lions (pres. College Station club 1982-83), Tiger Club (pres. 1995-96). State civil litigation, Family and matrimonial, Personal injury. Office: Hoelscher Lipsey Elmore PC 1021 University Dr E College Station TX 77840-2120

HOENICKE, EDWARD HENRY, lawyer, corporate executive; b. Chgo., Apr. 12, 1930; s. Edward Albert and Henrietta Christina (Hameister) H.; m. Janice Armande Gravel, Aug. 14, 1954; children— Jeanne E., Anne L. A.B., Cornell U., 1950; J.D., U. Mich., 1956. Bar: N.Y. 1956. Assoc. Cravath, Swaine & Moore, N.Y.C., 1956-59; div. counsel Olin Corp., N.Y.C., 1959-68; v.p., gen. counsel Beechnut, Inc., N.Y.C., 1968-69; pres. Beechnut Lifesavers Internat., N.Y.C., 1969-76; v.p., asst. gen. counsel Squibb Corp., N.Y.C., 1976-77; sr. v.p., gen. counsel, UAL, Inc. and United Airlines, Inc., Elk Grove Village, Ill., 1977—. Bd. dirs. Care, Inc., 1971—. With USAF, 1951-53. Mem. ABA, Exmoor Country Club (Highland Park, Ill.), Bronxville (N.Y.) Field Club. General corporate. Office: United Airlines Corp 1200 E Algonquin Rd Arlington Heights IL 60005-4786

HOERNER, ROBERT JACK, lawyer; b. Fairfield, Iowa, Oct. 12, 1931; s. John Andrew and Margaret Louise (Simmons) Hoerner; m. Judith Chandler, Apr. 21, 1954 (div. Feb. 1975); children: John Andrew II, Timothy Chandler, Blayne Marie Hoerner Murray, Michelle Margaret Hoerner Smith; m. Mary Paolano, June 03, 1989. BA, Cornell Coll., 1953; JD, U. Mich., 1958. Bar: Ohio 1960, US Supreme Ct 1964, US Ct Appeals (6th cir) 1972, US Ct Appeals (fed cir) 1990. Law clk. to hon. Chief Justice Earl Warren U.S. Supreme Ct., Washington, 1958-59; assoc. Jones, Day, Reavis & Pogue, Cleve., 1959-63, 65-66; chief evaluation sect. antitrust divsn. Dept. Justice, Washington, 1963-65; ptnr. Jones, Day, Reavis & Pogue, Cleve., 1967-93. Contbr. articles to profl jours; editor (editor-in-chief): (journal) Mich Law Rev. Trustee New Orgn Visual Arts, Cleveland, Ohio, 1976—80, 1987—90. With Counter Intelligence Corps U.S. Army, 1953—55. Mem.: ABA (antitrust sect, patent sect), Ohio Bar Asn, Greater Cleveland Bar Asn, Cleveland Intellectual Property Law Asn, Leland Country Club, Order of Coif. Democrat. Antitrust, Federal civil litigation, Patent. Home: 360 Darbys Run Bay Village OH 44140-2968 Office: Jones Day Reavis & Pogue 901 Lakeside Ave E Ste N-334 Cleveland OH 44114-1190 Business E-Mail: rjhoerner@jonesday.com

HOFF, JONATHAN M(ORIND), lawyer; b. Chgo., July 4, 1955; s. Irwin S. and Ida (Inditz) H. AB, U. Calif., Berkeley, 1978; JD, UCLA, 1981. Bar: Calif. 1981, U.S. Dist. Ct. (no. and cen. dists.) Calif. 1981, N.Y. 1982, U.S. Dist. Ct. (so. dist.) N.Y. 1982, U.S. Ct. Appeals (4th, 5th, 7th, 8th, 9th, 10th cirs.) 1982. Ptnr. Weil, Gotshal & Manges, N.Y.C., 1981-98, Cadwalader, Wickersham & Taft, N.Y.C., 1998—. Comment editor UCLA Law Rev., 1980-81; contbr. articles to law jours. Mem. ABA, Calif. Bar Assn. General civil litigation, Mergers and acquisitions, Securities. Office: Cadwalader Wickersham & Taft 100 Maiden Ln New York NY 10038-4818

HOFF, TIMOTHY, law educator, priest; b. Freeport, Ill., Feb. 27, 1941; s. Howard Vincent and Zillah (Morgan) H.; m. Virginia Nevill; children: Brian Charles, Morgan Witherspoon; stepchildren: Guy Baker, Katherine Baker. AB, Tulane U., 1963, JD, 1966; student, U. London, 1961-62; LLM, Harvard U., 1970. Bar: Fla. 1967, Ala. 1973, U.S. Dist. Ct. (mid. dist.) Fla. 1967; ordained priest Episcopal Ch. Assoc. Williams, Parker, Harrison, Dietz & Getzen, Sarasota, Fla., 1968-69; asst. legal editor The Fla. Bar, 1969; asst. prof. U. Ala., 1970-73, assoc. prof., 1973-75, prof. law, 1975-93, Gordon Rosen prof., 1993—. Cons. Ala. Law Inst.; reporter Ala. Adminstrv. Procedure Act, 1977—. Author: Alabama Limitations of Actions, 1984, 2d edit., 1992, Forms for Civil Trial Practice, 1991; contbr. articles to profl. jours. V.p., founding dir. Hospice of West Ala.; founding dir. Cmty. Soup Bowl, Inc.; Episc. priest assoc. Canterbury Chapel U. Ala.; rector St. Michael's Episc. Ch., Fayette, Ala., 1988-96. Recipient Hist. Preservation Svc. award, 1976. Mem. ACLU, AAUP, Maritime Law Assn. U.S., Coun. on Religion and Law, Episc. Soc. for Ministry in Higher Edn., Univ. Club, Phi Beta Kappa, Order of Coif, Omicron Delta Kappa, Eta Sigma Phi. Democrat. Home: 2601 Lakewood Cir Tuscaloosa AL 35405-2727 Office: U Ala Law Sch 101 Paul W Bryant Dr E PO Box 870382 Tuscaloosa AL 35487-0382 E-mail: thoff@law.ua.edu

HOFFHEIMER, DANIEL JOSEPH, lawyer; b. Cin., Dec. 28, 1950; s. Harry Max and Charlotte (O'Brien) H.; children: Rebecca, Rachel, Leah. Grad., Phillips Exeter Acad., 1969; AB cum laude, Harvard Coll., 1973; JD, U. Va., 1976. Bar: Ohio 1976, U.S. Dist. Ct. (so. dist.) Ohio 1976, U.S. Ct. Appeals (6th crct.) 1977, U.S. Ct. Appeals (D.C. and fed. crcts.) 1986, U.S. Ct. Internat. Trade 1986, U.S. Tax Ct. 1992, U.S. Supreme Ct. 1980, U.S. Tax Ct. 1992. Assoc. Taft, Stettinius & Hollister, Cin., 1976-84, ptnr., 1984—. Lectr. law Coll. Law, U. Cin., 1981-83; trustee Judges Hoadly & Porter Meml. Trust; mem. adv. bd. Ohio Dist. Ct. Rev. Editor-in-chief U. Va. Jour. Internat. Law, 1975-76; co-author: Practitioners' Handbook Ohio First District Court Appeals, 1984, 2d edit., 1991, Federal Practice Manual, U.S. 6th Circuit Court of Appeals, 1999, Manual on Labor Law, 1988; mem. editl. bd. Probate Law Jour. Ohio, 2000—; contbr. articles to profl. jours. Mem. Cin. Symphony Bus. Rels. Com., 1977-86, Cin. Composers Guild, 1988-93, Ohio Supreme Ct. Com. Racial Fairness, 1993-2000; trustee Underground R.R. Freedom Mus., 1995—; mem. adv. bd. for Consumer Protection, Cin., 1978-80, Hoxworth Blood Ctr. Univ. Cin. Hosp., 1994-99; mem. bd. Hebrew Union Coll. Jewish Inst. Religion, 1994—, WGUC-FM Pub. Radio, 1988—, vice chmn., 1993-96, chmn., 1996-98; trustee Cin. Chamber Orch., 1977-80, Seven Hills Sch., Cin., 1980-86, Internat. Visitors Ctr., Cin., 1980-84, Friends Coll. Conservatory of Music, Cin., 1985-86, Cin. Symphony Orch., 1988-94, 96—, sec., 1996-99, vice chair 1999-2000, chair, 2001—, Children's Psychiat. Ctr., Cin., 1986-89, treas., 1987-89; vice chmn. Jewish Hosp., Cin., 1989-92; Leadership Cin., 1989-90; sec., trustee Cin. Symphony Musicians Pension Fund, 1989-99, Jewish Cmty. Rels. Coun., 1990-98, v.p., 1996-98; sec. Nat. Conf. Commn. Justice, 1992-99, treas. 1999-2000, trustee emeritus, 2000—; counsel Cin. AIDS Commn., 1991—, Cin. Inst. Fine Arts Govt. Affairs Com., 1993-94, B'nai B'rith Nat. Coun. Legacy Devel., 1996-97; trustee Nat. Underground R.R. Freedom Ctr., 1995—. Named Outstanding Young Man, U.S. Jaycees, 1984, 98. Life fellow Am. Bar Found., Ohio Bar Found.; fellow Am. Coll. Trust and Estate Counsel; mem. ABA, Internat. Bar Assn., Internat. Trade Bar Assn., Internat. Arbitration Assn. (comml. arbitrator 1991-95), Fed. Bar Assn. (treas. 1984, sec. 1985, v.p. 1986-87, pres. 1987-88), Ohio State Bar Assn. (bd. govs. Est. Pl. Trust and Probate Law sect. 1996—), Cin. Bar Assn. (trustee 1988-93, v.p. 1990-91, pres. 1992-93, chair Cin. Acad. Leadership for Lawyers 1998-2000), Harvard Club of Cin. (bd. dirs. 1980-88, v.p. 1983-86, pres. 1986-87). Democrat. Avocations: music, tennis, Chinese and Japanese art. Estate planning, General practice, Probate. Home: 1 Forest Hill Dr Cincinnati OH 45208-1953 Office: 1800 Firstar Tower 425 Walnut St Cincinnati OH 45202-3923 E-mail: hoffheimer@taftlaw.com

HOFFLUND, PAUL, lawyer; b. San Diego, Mar. 27, 1928; s. John Leslie and Ethel Frances (Cline) H.; m. Anne Marie Thalman, Feb. 15, 1958; children: Mark, Sylvia. BA, Princeton (N.J.) U., 1950; JD, George Washington U., 1956. Bar: D.C. 1956, U.S. Dist. Ct. D.C. 1956, U.S. Ct. Appeals (D.C. cir.) 1956, Calif. 1957, U.S. Dist. Ct. (so. dist.) Calif. 1957, U.S. Ct. Mil. Appeals 1957, U.S. Ct. Claims 1958, U.S. Ct. Appeals (9th cir.) 1960, U.S. Supreme Ct. 1964, U.S. Tax Ct. 1989. Assoc. Wencke, Carlson & Kuykendall, San Diego, 1961-62; ptnr. Carlson, Kuykendall & Hofflund, 1963-65, Carlson & Hofflund, San Diego, 1965-72; Christian Sci. practitioner, 1972-84; arbitrator Mcpl. Cts. and Superior Ct. of Calif., 1984-99; pvt. practice, 1985—. Adj. prof. law Nat. U. Sch. Law, San Diego, 1985-94; judge pro tem Mcpl. Ct. South Bay Jud. Dist., 1990-99; disciplinary counsel to U.S. Tax Ct., 1989—; asst. U.S. atty. U.S. Dept. of Justice, L.A., 1959-60, asst. U.S. atty. in charge, San Diego, 1960-61, spl. hearing officer, San Diego, 1962-68; asst. corp. counsel Govt. of D.C., 1957-59. Author: (chpt. in book) Handbook on Criminal Procedure in the U.S. District Court, 1967; contbr. articles to profl. jours. Treas. Princeton Club of San Diego; v.p. Community Concert Assn., San Diego; pres. Sunland Home Found., San Diego, Trust for Christian Sci. Orgn., San Diego; chmn. bd. 8th Ch. of Christ, Scientist, San Diego. With USN, 1950-53, comdr. JAGC, USNR, 1953-72, ret. Mem. ABA, San Diego County Bar Assn., World Affairs Coun., Phi Delta Phi. Democrat. Avocations: theater, classical music, bridge, fine art, biblical study. Estate planning, General practice, Probate. Home and Office: 6146 Syracuse Ln San Diego CA 92122-3301

HOFFMAN, ALAN CRAIG, lawyer, consultant; b. Chgo., Oct. 1, 1944; s. Morris Joseph and Marie E. Hoffman; m. Pamela Hoffman. BA, Carthage Coll., 1968; JD, John Marshall Law Sch., 1973. Bar: Fla. 1973, Ill. 1973, U.S. Dist. Ct. (no. dist.) Ill. 1974, U.S. Dist. Ct. (mid. dist.) Fla. 1981, U.S. Ct. Appeals (7th cir.) 1975, U.S. Ct. Appeals (5th and 11th cirs.) 1981, U.S. Supreme Ct. 1977. Staff atty. Cook County Legal Assistance Found., Brookfield, Ill., 1973-74, Patient Legal Svcs., Chgo., 1974; pvt. practice law, 1973—, River Grove, Ill., 1973-86, Oak Brook, 1980-87, Hinsdale, 1987-93; with assocs., 1980—. Spl. asst. atty. gen. Ill. Criminal Justice Divsn., Chgo., 1977-79, Ill. Condemnation Divsn., Chgo., 1980-87; pres. Almar, Ltd., 1986-91; v.p. Marach, Ltd., 1986-89, Hoffman Realty, 1978—; pres., dir. North Shore Greenview Bldg. Corp., 1978—; asst. prof. Lewis U., 1974-79, vis. profl. Coll. Law Paraprofl. Ctr., 1974-76, adj. prof., 1979-80; assoc. prof. No. Ill. U., 1979-80; v.p. Adv. Svc., Inc.; cons. Med-legal cases, 1982—; adj. prof. law Health Law Inst., Loyola U. Coll. Law, Chgo., 2001—. Author: (with F. Lane and D. Birnbaum) Lane's Medical Litigation Guide, 1981; mem. editl. bd. Jour. Legal Medicine, 1980—, Med. Malpractice Prevention, 1986-96, Med. Malpractice Prevention Ob-Gyn, 1987-96; contbg. author: Legal Medicine: Legal Dynamics of Medical Encounters, 1988, 3d edit., 1995, supplements; contbr. articles to Med. Trial Technique Quar., others. Mem. Oak Park Twp. (Ill.) Mental Health Bd., 1975-80, v.p., 1975, chmn. program com., 1975-77, pres., 1978; mem. governing bd. Women In Need Growing Stronger, 1993-96; bd. govs. Jewish Fedn. Chgo., Coun. for Elderly, 1995-98; co-chair Rainbow House Bread and Roses Ann. Fundraiser, 1997-98. Mem. Am. Coll. Legal Medicine (assoc. in law 1975, profl. devel. com. 1990—, student awards com. 1992—, moot ct. competition com. 1992—, co-chair com. violence and abuse in the family 1993, textbook update com. 1988, program com. 1988—, legal com. 1988—, editl. bd. med. and legal textbook com. 1987—); mem. ABA (civil procedure and evidence com. 1993—, comml. tort com. 1993—), Ill. State Bar Assn. (vice chmn. standing com. on mentally disabled 1975-77, chmn. 1977-78), Chgo. Bar Assn., DuPage Bar Assn., West Suburban Bar Assn., Chgo. Acad. Law and Medicine, Am. Soc. Law and Medicine, Mensa, Ill. Trial Lawyers Assn. (profl. negligence com. 1982), Fla. Bar Assn., (health law com. 1983-84, out-of-state practitioner com. 1988-91), ATLA, Phi Alpha Delta. State civil litigation, Personal injury, Workers' compensation.

HOFFMAN, ALAN JAY, lawyer; b. Phila., Aug. 31, 1948; s. Heinz Julius and Sylvia (Wise) H.; children: Jennifer, Lauren, Allison. BBA, Temple U., 1970; JD, Villanova U., 1973. Bar: Pa. 1973, U.S. Dist. Ct. (ea. dist.) Pa. 1973, U.S. Dist. Ct. Del. 1973, U.S. Ct. Appeals (3rd cir.) 1973, Del. 1977, U.S. Supreme Ct. 1984, D.C. 1990. Asst. U.S. atty. U.S. Dept. Justice, Wilmington, Del., 1973-78; ptnr. Dilworth, Paxson, Kalish & Kauffman, Phila., 1979-92, mem. exec. mgmt. com., 1989-90, chmn. new bus. com., 1990-91; ptnr. Blank, Rome, Comisky and McCauley, 1992—, mem. exec. mgmt. com., 1998—, co-chmn. atty. recruiting com., adminstrv. ptnr. in charge Wilmington, Del., chmn. litigation and dispute resolution dept., 1996—. Lectr. Widener Del. Law Sch., Wilmington, 1974, Mealy's Conf. on Toxic Torts, 1999—, Mealy's Conf. on MTBE pollution, 2000. Contbg. co-editor Villanova Law Rev., 1972-73; contbr. articles to profl. jours. Bd. dirs. Men's Club Temple Adath Israel, Merion, Pa., 1993-94; pres. Villanova Law Sch. Inn of Ct., 1999—. Recipient Atty. Gen.'s Spl. Commendation U.S. Dept. Justice, Washington, 1977. Fellow Am. Bar Found.; mem. ATLA, ABA, Pa. Bar Assn., Fed. Bar Assn., Phila. Bar Assn.,

Del. Bar Assn., Del. Trial Lawyers Assn., Pa. Trial Lawyers Assn., White Manor Country Club (pres. 1993—, 1st v.p. 1990-93, bd. dirs. 1988-90, admissions chmn. 1989—), J. Willard O'Brien Villanova Law Sch. Inn of Ct. (pres. 1999—). Avocation: golf. General civil litigation, Criminal, General practice. Office: Blank Rome Comisky & McCauley One Logan Sq Philadelphia PA 19103-6998

HOFFMAN, BARRY PAUL, lawyer; b. Phila., May 29, 1941; s. Samuel and Hilda (Cohn) H.; m. Mary Ann Schrock, May 18, 1978; children: Elizabeth Barron, Hayley Rebecca. BA, Pa. State U., 1963; JD, George Washington U., 1968. Bar: Pa. 1972, Mich. 1983. Asst. U.S. Senator Wayne Morse, Oreg., Washington; spl. agt. FBI; asst. dist. atty. Phila. Dist. Atty.'s Office; exec. v.p., gen. counsel Valassis Communications, Inc., Livonia, Mich. 1st lt. U.S. Army, 1963-65, Korea. General corporate. Home: 49933 Standish Ct Plymouth MI 48170-2882 Office: Valassis Communications Inc 19975 Victor Pkwy Livonia MI 48152-7001 E-mail: hoffmanb@valassis.com

HOFFMAN, CARL H(ENRY), lawyer; b. St. Louis, May 28, 1936; s. Carl Henry and Anna Marie (Remlinger) H.; m. Pamela L. Polk, May 8, 1971 (div. Novl 1982); children: Kurt M., Jennifer K. BS, St. Louis U., 1958; postgrad., U. Mex., Mexico City, 1958, U. Nev., 1960-61, Tex. Technol. Coll., 1961-62; JD, Washington U., St. Louis, 1966. Bar: Mo. 1966, Fla. 1969, U.S. Supreme Ct. 1970; cert. civil trial adv. Nat. Bd. Trial Advocacy. Pilot Eastern. Airlines, Inc., Miami, Fla.; assoc. Spencer & Taylor, 1969-70; pvt. practice, 1970-80; ptnr. Hoffman & Hertzig, P.A., Coral Gables, Fla., 1980—. Capt. USAF, 1958-63. Mem. ABA, ATLA, Fla. Bar (cert. civil trial lawyer, cert. bus. litigation lawyer, chmn. aviation law com. 1997-98), Fla. Acad. Trial Lawyers, Am. Jurisprudence Am. Jurisprudence Soc., Greater Miami C. of C. (trustee). Aviation, General civil litigation, Personal injury. Office: Hoffman & Hertzig PA 241 Sevilla Ave Ste 900 Coral Gables FL 33134-6600 E-mail: hoffhertz@att.net

HOFFMAN, DANIEL STEVEN, lawyer, law educator; b. N.Y.C., May 4, 1931; s. Lawrence Hoffman and Juliette (Marbes) Ostrov; m. Beverly Mae Swenson, Dec. 4, 1954; children: Lisa Hoffman Ciancio, Tracy Hoffman Cockriel, Robin Hoffman Black. BA, U. Colo., 1951; LLB, U. Denver, 1958. Bar: Colo. 1958. Assoc., then ptnr. Fugate, Mitchem, Hoffman, Denver, 1951-55; mgr. of safety City and County of Denver, 1963-65; ptnr. Kripke, Hoffman, Carrigan, Denver, 1965-70, Hoffman, McDermott, Hoffman, Denver, 1970-78; of counsel Hoffman & McDermott, 1978-84; mem. Holme Roberts & Owen, LLC, 1984-94; dean Coll. Law, U. Denver, 1978-84, dean emeritus, prof. emeritus, 1984—; ptnr. McKenna & Cuneo LLP, Denver, 1994-2000, Hoffman Reilley Pozner & Williams LLP, 2000—. Chmn., mem. Merit Screening Com. for Bankruptcy Judges, Denver, 1979—84; chmn. subcom. Dist. Atty.'s Crime Adv. Commn., Denver, 1984—; chmn. Senator Wirth's jud. nomination rev. com., Cong. DeGette's jud. nomination rev. com. Contbr. chpts. to books Mem. Rocky Mountain region Anti-Defamation League, Denver, 1985; bd. dirs. Colo. chpt. Am. Jewish Com., 1985, Legal Ctr., Denver, 1985—; mem. adv. com. Samaritan Shelter, Denver, 1985; chmn. Rocky Flats Blue Ribbon Citizens Com., Denver, 1980-83; mem. bd. visitors J. Reuben Clark Law Sch. Brigham Young U., 1986-88. With USAF, 1951-55. Recipient Am. Jewish Com. Nat. Judge Learned Hand award, 1993, Humanitarian award Rocky Mountain chpt. Anti-Defamation League, 1984, Alumni of Yr. award U. Denver Coll. Law, 1997. Fellow: Am. Coll. Trial Lawyers (state chmn. 1975—76), Internat. Soc. Barristers, Colo. Bar. Found., Am. Bar Found.; mem.: Colo. Bar. Assn. (pres. 1976—77, Young Lawyer of Yr. award 1965), Colo. Trial Lawyers Assn. (pres. 1961—62, Lifetime Achievement award), Assn. Trial Lawyers Am. (nat. com. mem. 1962—63), Am. Judicature Soc. (bd. dirs. 1977—81), Order of Coif (hon.)). Democrat. Jewish Avocation: platform tennis. Federal civil litigation, State civil litigation, Personal injury. Office: Hoffman Reilly Pozner & Williamson LLP Kittredge Bldg 511 16th St Ste 700 Denver CO 80202-4248 E-mail: dhoffman@hrpwlaw.com

HOFFMAN, DARNAY ROBERT, management consultant; b. N.Y.C., Nov. 25, 1947; s. Bill and Toni (Darnay) H.; m. Jennifer Lea Sheppard, Aug. 20, 1984; children by previous marriage: Brandon, Brett; m. Sydney Biddle Barrows, May 14, 1994. BA, SUNY, 1977; MBA, CUNY, 1980; JD, Yeshiva U., 1982. Bar: N.Y. 1995, U.S. Dist. Ct. (so., ea., we. and no. dists.) N.Y. 1995, U.S. Ct. Appeals (fed. cir.) 1995, U.S. Tax Ct. 1995, U.S. Ct. Internat. Trade 1995, U.S. Dist. Ct. Colo. 2000, U.S. Dist. Ct. (no. dist.) Ga. 2000, U.S. Ct. Appeals (fed. cir.). Pres., mgmt. cons. Darnay Hoffman Assocs., Inc., 1969—; mgmt. cons. Hoffman Rsch. Group Inc., N.Y.C., 1977—; rsch. assoc. Baruch Coll., 1977-79. Bd. dirs. Hobton Realty Corp.; dir. Nat. Conf. Law Historians Am., 1987—. Author: Murder in the Wilderness, 1989, Allen Contact, 1989, (pamphlet) Products in Decline, 1980. Mem. ABA, ATLA, Am. Mgmt. Assn., Am. Mktg. Assn., Acad. Mgmt. Scis., Nat. Assn. Criminal Def. Attys., N.Y. State Bar Assn., N.Y. County Lawyers Assn., Assn. Bar of City of N.Y., N.Y. State Trial Lawyers Assn., Player's, Beta Gamma Sigma, Alpha Delta Sigma.

HOFFMAN, DAVID NATHANIEL, lawyer; b. N.Y.C., Aug. 10, 1960; s. Martin J. and Edith D. Hoffman; m. Joan Lynne Fiden, Feb. 18, 1990; children: Benjamin, Emily. JD, SUNY, Buffalo, 1986; cert. in bio-ethics, Columbia U., 1996. Bar: N.Y. 1997, U.S. Dist. Ct. (ea. dist.) N.Y. 1997, U.S. Dist. Ct. (so. dist.) N.Y. 1997. Litigation assoc. Martin, Clearwater & Bell, N.Y.C., 1986-88; assoc., then ptnr. Kanterman, Taub & Breitner, 1988-94; founding ptnr. Breitner & Hoffman, 1994-99, Hoffman & Arshack P.C., N.Y.C., 1999—. Guest lectr. Columbia U. Sch. Psychology, Wycoff Heights Med. Ctr., Flushing Hosp. Med. Ctr., N.Y. County Lawyers Assn. Mem. Am. Soc. Law Medicine and Ethics, Nature Conservancy, Amnesty Internat., Habitat for Humanity, Assn. of Bar of City of N.Y. (legis. liaison com. on med. malpractice 1988-96, chmn. 2000—, com. on bio-ethics). Avocations: sailing, SCUBA diving, woodworking, bicycling, philosophy. Alternative dispute resolution, Health, Professional liability. Office: 225 W 57th St New York NY 10019

HOFFMAN, DONALD ALFRED, lawyer; b. Milw., May 4, 1936; s. Harry Gustav and Emily Frances (Schwartz) H.; m. Louise Hardie Chapman, June 8, 1963; children: Donald Hardie, Richard Rainey. BBA, U. Wis., 1958, JD, 1968. Bar: La. 1969, U.S. Supreme Ct. 1972, U.S. Ct. Appeals (5th cir.) 1973, U.S. Dist. Ct. (ea., mid. and we. dists.) La. Assoc. Lemle & Kelleher, New Orleans, 1968-73; ptnr. Lemle, Kelleher, Kohlmeyer, Matthews & Schumacher, 1973-75, McGlinchey, Stafford, Mintz & Hoffman, New Orleans, 1975-78; city atty. City of New Orleans, 1978-79; dir. Carmouche, Gray & Hoffman, New Orleans, 1979-82, sr. dir., 1982-88, Hoffman, Siegel, Seydel, Bienvenu, Centola & Cordes, New Orleans, 1989—. Fellow Am. Bar Found., La. Bar Found.; mem. Am. Bd. Trial Advocates, French-Am. C. of C. (pres. La. chpt.). Presbyterian. General civil litigation, Personal injury. Home: 1524 4th St New Orleans LA 70130-5918 Office: Hoffman Siegel Seydel Bienvenu Centola & Cordes 650 Poydras St New Orleans LA 70130-6101

HOFFMAN, IRA ELIOT, lawyer; b. Highland Park, Mich., Jan. 3, 1952; s. Maxwell Mordecai and Leah (Silverman) H.; m. Ruth Felsen, Aug. 19, 1975 (div. 1981); 1 child, Daniel Gideon; m. Meredith Lippman, Dec. 17, 1988; 1 child, Lauren Samantha. BA, U. Mich., 1973; MSc in Econs., London Sch. Econs., 1975; JD cum laude, U. Miami, 1983. Bar: Fla. 1983, U.S. Ct. Appeals (D.C. cir.) 1984, D.C. 1985, Md. 1991, U.S. Ct. Appeals (10th cir., 4th cir) 1992, U.S. Dist. Ct. (D.C. dist.) 1992, U.S. Dist. Ct. Md., 1992, U.S. Ct. Appeals (fed. cir.) 1994, U.S. Ct. Fed. Claims, 1998, U.S. Ct. Appeals (11th cir.) 2001, U.S. Dist. Ct. (so. dist.) Fla. 2001. Tchr. London Sch. Econs., 1975-77; rsch. assoc. Shiloah Ctr. Mid. East Studies, Tel Aviv U., 1978-80; staff atty. FTC, Washington, 1983; law clk. U.S. Ct. Appeals (D.C. cir.), 1983-84; assoc. Fried, Frank, Harris, Shriver & Jacobson, 1984-86, 87-88; counsel Ministry of Def. Mission to the U.S., Govt. of Israel, N.Y.C., 1986-87; counsel to vice chmn. U.S. Internat. Trade Commn., Washington, 1988-89; assoc. Howrey & Simon, 1989-91; pres. Israel Housing Investors, Inc., Rockville, Md., 1990-92; v.p. H.P.F. Prefab Constrn., Ltd., Givatayim, Israel, 1991-92; of counsel Savage & Schwartzman, Balt., 1992-94, McAleese & Assocs., P.C., McLean, Va., 1995-98, Grayson & Kubli, P.C., McLean, 1998—; pres. Smart Planet, LLC, Rockville, Md., 1998—. Translator: The Emergence of Pan-Arabism in Egypt, 1980; contbr. articles to profl. jours. Spl. counsel Nat. Sudden Infant Death Syndrome Found., Landover, Md., 1984-86; hon. counsel to chmn. Nat. Holocaust Meml. Coun., Washington, 1985. Mem. ABA. Jewish. Avocations: travel, sports, history. Government contracts and claims, Private international, Public international. E-mail: hoffmani@cais.com

HOFFMAN, JAMES PAUL, lawyer, hypnotist; b. Waterloo, Iowa, Sept. 7, 1943; s. James A. and Luella M. (Prokosch) H.; 1 child, Tiffany K. B.A., U. No. Iowa, 1965, J.D. U. Iowa, 1967. Bar: Iowa 1967, U.S. Dist. Ct. (no. dist.) Iowa 1981, U.S. Dist. Ct. (so. dist.) Iowa 1968, U.S. Dist. Ct. (so. dist.) Ill, U.S. Tax Ct. 1971, U.S. Ct. Appeals (8th cir.) 1970, U.S. Supreme Ct. 1974. Sr. mem. James P. Hoffman, Law Offices, Keokuk, Iowa, 1967—; chmn. bd. Iowa Inst. Hypnosis. Fellow Am. Inst. Hypnosis; mem. ABA, Iowa Bar Assn., Lee County Bar Assn., Assn. Trial Lawyers Am., Ill. Trial Lawyers Assn., Iowa Trial Lawyers Assn. Democrat. Roman Catholic. Author: The Iowa Trial Lawyers and the Use of Hypnosis, 1980. State civil litigation, Personal injury, Workers' compensation. Home and Office: PO Box 1087 Middle Rd Keokuk IA 52632-1087

HOFFMAN, JOHN DOUGLAS, lawyer; b. Easton, Pa., Jan. 9, 1939; s. John Douglas and Margaret Shirley (Kummer) H.; m. Lynne Ellen Campbell, Feb. 4, 1967; children: Alison, Mark. BA magna cum laude, Yale U., 1960, LLB, 1964. Bar: N.Y. 1965, Calif. 1967, U.S. Ct. Appeals (2d cir.) 1966, U.S Ct. Appeals (9th cir.) 1967, U.S. Ct. Appeals (D.C. cir.) 1975, U.S. Ct. Appeals (fed. cir.) 1998, U.S. Dist. Ct. (so. and ea. dist.) N.Y. 1966, U.S. Dist. Ct. (no. dist.) Calif. 1967, U.S. Supreme Ct. 1972. Assoc. Cleary, Gottlieb, Steen & Hamilton, N.Y.C., 1964-67, Cooley, Godward, Castro, Huddleson & Tatum, San Francisco, 1967-71; exec. dir., atty. Sierra Club Legal Def. Fund, Inc., 1972-77, trustee, 1978—. Bd. dirs. Ellman, Burke, Hoffman & Johnson, San Francisco. Woodrow Wilson fellow, 1960; Fulbright scholar Free U. Berlin, 1960-61. Mem. ABA, San Francisco Bar Assn. Alternative dispute resolution, Appellate, Land use and zoning (including planning). Home: 14 Lincoln Ave Mill Valley CA 94941-1124 Office: One Ecker Bldg Ste 200 San Francisco CA 94105 E-mail: jhoffman@ellman-burke.com

HOFFMAN, JOHN FLETCHER, lawyer; b. N.Y.C., May 22, 1946; s. George Fletcher and Helen (Gilbert) H.; m. Coralie Tallman, June 29, 1969; children: Julie Gilbert, William Delano. BS, St. Lawrence U., 1969; JD, Washington and Lee U., 1975. Bar: N.Y. 1976, U.S. Dist. Ct. (so. dist.) N.Y. 1976, U.S. Dist. Ct. (ea. dist.) N.Y. 1978, U.S. Supreme Ct. 1980, U.S. Ct. Appeals (2d cir.) 1982, U.S. Dist. Ct. (no. dist.) Tex. 1988, U.S. Ct. Appeals (11th cir.) 1991, U.S. Ct. Appeals (fed. cir.) 1999. Assoc. Cadwalader, Wickersham & Taft, N.Y.C., 1975-83, ptnr., 1983-94; v.p., assoc. gen. counsel Schering-Plough Corp., Kenilworth, N.J., 1995—. Trustee First Unitarian Congl. Soc. Bklyn., 1980-83; trustee, treas. Bklyn. Children's Mus., 1985-95. Mem. ABA, Order of Coif, Omicron Delta Kappa. Antitrust, Federal civil litigation, State civil litigation. Office: Schering Plough Corp 2000 Galloping Hill Rd Kenilworth NJ 07033-1328

HOFFMAN, JOHN RAYMOND, lawyer; b. Rochester, N.Y., July 24, 1945; s. Raymond Edward and Ruth Emily (Karnes) H.; m. Linda Lee Moore, Aug. 22, 1970; 1 child, Heather Anne. BA, Washburn U., 1967; JD, U. Mo.-Kansas City, 1971. Bar: Mo. 1972, Tenn. 1976, Kans. 1980, U.S. Supreme Ct. 1975. Law clk. United Telecom, Kansas City, Mo., 1967-70, gen. atty., 1970-75; gen. counsel, sec. United Telephone Sys.-Southeast Group, Bristol, Tenn., 1975-80; v.p., gen. counsel United Telephone Sys. Inc., 1980-84; sr. v.p. legal, dir. US Telecom, Inc., 1984-86; sr. v.p. external affairs Sprint Corp., 1986-99; chmn. FCC N.Am. Numbering Coun., 1999—2000. Bd. dirs. United Telephone Co. of N.W., 1990-98. Author: The History of Sprint Corp.; That Was a Pin?, 2000. Bd. dirs. Ctr. Pub. Utilities, N.Mex. State U., 1989—90, Kansas City Area Econ. Devel. Coun., 1988—89, Trinity Luth. Hosp., Kansas City, 1984—89, Bishop Miege H.S. Found., 1990—92, 1999—2001, Health Initiatives, Inc., Kansas City, 1985—89, pres., 1986—89; bd. dirs. Kansas City Young Audiences, 1981—85, Johnson County Fire Dist., Prairie Village, Kans., 1982—86, Kansas City/Coro Found., 1983—84, Friends of the Zoo, Kansas City, 2000—01. Mem. ABA, Mo. Bar Assn., Tenn. Bar Assn., Kans. Bar Assn., Kansas City Bar Assn., Competative Telecommunications Assn. (chmn. 1986-88), Ind. Telephone Pioneers Assn., Phi Delta Phi. Club: Optimist. Administrative and regulatory, General corporate, Public utilities. Home: 17960 S Bond Ave Bucyrus KS 66013 E-mail: john_r_hoffman@yahoo.com

HOFFMAN, LARRY J. lawyer; b. N.Y.C., Aug. 20, 1930; s. Max and Pauline (Epstein) H.; m. Deborah E. Alexander, Oct. 2, 1954; children: Lisa, Ken, Heidi, Mark. AA, U. Fla.; JD, U. Miami. Bar: Fla. 1954. Chmn. Greenberg, Traurig, PA, Miami, 1968—; also bd. dirs. Greenberg, Traurig, Hoffman, Lipoff, Rosen & Quentel, PA. Mem. ABA, Fla. Bar Assn., Dade County Bar Assn. Avocations: music, art, tennis, computers, photography. Contracts commercial, General corporate, Securities. Office: Greenberg Traurig 1221 Brickell Ave Miami FL 33131-3224 E-mail: hoffmanl@gtlaw.com

HOFFMAN, MARK LESLIE, lawyer, film maker; b. Cleve., Jan. 12, 1952; s. Nathan Norman and Sally (Coleman) H. B.A. with spl. honors, George Washington U., 1973; J.D., Case Western Res. U., 1976, Ph.D., 1978. Bar: Ohio 1976, D.C. 1978, U.S. Dist. Ct. (no. dist.) Ohio 1976, U.S. Tax Ct. 1979, U.S. Ct. Appeals (6th cir.) 1981, U.S. Supreme Ct. 1981. Ptnr. Hoffman & Foote, Shaker Heights, Ohio, 1976— ; pres. Advocate Films, Inc. Shaker Heights, 1978— ; acting judge Cleveland Heights Mcpl. Ct., Ohio, 1983— . Mem. Assn. Trial Lawyers Am., Ohio State Bar Assn., Greater Cleve. Bar Assn., Ohio Acad. Trial Lawyers, Cleve. Acad. Trial Lawyers. General civil litigation, Personal injury, Real property. Office: Hoffman & Foote 20133 Farnsleigh Rd Cleveland OH 44122-3613

HOFFMAN, MICHAEL WILLIAM, lawyer, accountant; b. Bowling Green, Ohio, Feb. 5, 1955; s. Oscar William and Marie Louise (Carlson) H.; m. Lynne Ellen Steele, Aug. 31, 1975; children: Megan, Jessica, Kristine, Robert. BA in Acctg. summa cum laude, Bowling Green State U., 1976; JD, U. Toledo, 1981. Bar: Ohio 1981, Ga. 1983; CPA, Ga., Ohio. Acct. Ernst & Whinney, Toledo, 1976-81; acct., ptnr. Touche Ross & Co., Atlanta, 1981-86; v.p. Profl. Svcs. Network Inc., 1986; assoc. Chamberlain, Hrdlicka, White, Johnson & Williams, 1986-89; ptnr. Somers & Altenbach, 1989-91; atty. Hoffman & Assocs., 1991—. Organizing dir. Paces Bank & Trust Co., Atlanta; spkr. in field. Author: RIA's U.S.A. News for the Inbound Investor, 1983. Treas. Friendship Force Internat., 1984; mem. troop com. Boy Scouts Am. Recipient Leadership award Boy Scouts Am., 1986. Mem. ABA, AICPA, Am. Assn. Attys-Certified Public Accts., State Bar Ga. (v.p. mgmt. com., chmn. estate, gift and trust sect. 1997-2000, chmn. Atlanta chpt. estate, gift and trust sect., Disting. Com. Chair award 1998-99, Bowling Green State U.-Atlanta Alumni Assn. (pres. 1988-90, parents adv. coun., 1999-), Atlanta Country Club (bd. dirs. 1998-2001), State Bar Ohio, Ga. Soc. CPA's (bd. dir. 2000-2001). Republican. Roman Catholic. Avocations: golf, tennis, reading. Estate planning, Taxation, general, State and local taxation. Home: 535 Willow Knolls Dr Marietta GA 30067-4647 Office: 6075 Lake Forrest Dr NW Ste 200 Atlanta GA 30328-3845 E-mail: hoff_law@bellsouth.net

HOFFMAN, PATRICK ANDREW, lawyer; b. Florence, Ariz., Dec. 1, 1965; s. Ronald Ray Hoffman and June Harris; m. Angela Joyce Woodward, June 17, 1995. BA in English, Tex. Wesleyan U., 1993; JD, Washburn U., 1997; LLM in Taxation, So. Meth. U., 1998. Bar: Tex. 1997, N.Mex. 1998. Intern Judge Sam A. Crow, Topeka, 1995; assoc. Modrall, Sperling, Roehl, Harris & Sisk, Albuquerque, 1998—. With U.S. Army, 1984-88. Avocations: running, outdoor activities, music. General corporate, Taxation, general. Office: Modrall Sperling Roehl Harris & Sisk PA 500 4th St NE Ste 1000 Albuquerque NM 87103

HOFFMAN, PAUL SHAFER, lawyer; b. Harrisburg, Pa., Dec. 12, 1933; s. Paul and Lucy Rose (Shafer) H.; m. Patricia Ann Rudisill, 1958; children: Eric, Kathryn, Julia, Margot. AB in Physics, Gettysburg Coll., 1957; JD, Harvard U., 1962. Bar: N.Y. 1963, U.S. Patent Office 1963, U.S. Dist. Ct. (so. dist.) N.Y. 1977, U.S. Ct. Appeals (2d cir.) 1977, U.S. Supreme Ct. 1977. Assoc. Kenyon & Kenyon, N.Y.C., 1962-63; application analyst IBM-ASDD, Yorktown, N.Y., 1963-66; dir. tech. research Matthew Bender Co., N.Y.C., 1966-68; v.p. Bowne and Co., Inc., 1968-77; sole practice Croton-on-Hudson, N.Y., 1977—. Mem. Croton Sch. Bd., 1972-75, pres., 1974-75; trustee Village Croton-on-Hudson, 1977-81, acting village justice, 1991—; bd. dirs. Croton Caring Com., Inc., 1982—. Served to cpl. U.S. Army, 1952-54. Mem. N.Y. State Bar Assn. (assoc. editor-in-chief N.Y. State Bar jour. 1991-98), Westchester County Bar Assn., Computer Law Assn. (bd. dirs. 1984-94, 96-2001). Republican. Lutheran. Club: Harvard (N.Y.C.). Lodge: Masons. Contracts commercial, Computer, Trademark and copyright. Office: 139 Grand St Croton On Hudson NY 10520-2306

HOFFMAN, S. DAVID, lawyer, engineer, educator; b. N.Y.C., June 16, 1922; s. Joseph and Ida (Katz) H.; m. Naomi Barbara Brosterman, June 30, 1946; children: Mathew E., Robert Adam. BE in Elec. Engring., Yale U., 1945; JD, St. John's U., N.Y.C., 1955. Bar: N.Y. 1955, U.S. Supreme Ct. 1960, U.S. Ct. Mil. Appeals 1961, U.S. Patent Office 1964, Ill. 1981. Engr. Western Electric Co., N.Y.C., Newark, 1946-49; head elec. engring. Am. Nat. Stds. Inst., N.Y.C., 1949-66, resident legal counsel, 1955-66, dir. contracts and cert., 1955-66; v.p., gen. counsel Underwriters Labs. Inc., Northbrook, Ill., 1966-88, cons. counsel to the pres., 1988-90; arbitrator Lake and Cook County (Ill.) Cts., 1989—. Sec. U.S. nat. com. Internat. Electrotech. Commn., 1955-66; vol., cons. multimedia resource Highland Park (Ill.) H.S., 1990—; adj. prof. divsn. of indsl. and systems engring. dept. mech. engring. U. Ill., Chgo., 1974-92; vol. Internet tutor Highland Park Libr., 1996—; mgr. tech. activities Nat. Bur. Stds. for U.S. Consumer Products Safety Commn., 1970-71. Contbr. numerous articles to profl. jours. Mem. indsl. adv. bd. U. Ill., Chgo., 1974-95; commr. City of Highland Park (Ill.) Telecomms. Commn., 1998-2000; on-line instr. Sr. Net, 1998—. With USNR, 1942-46, 50-52, ret. comdr. JAG Corp. Recipient Achievement award U.S. Pres. Commn. on Exec. Interchange, 1973-74, Merit awards Am. Nat. Stds. Inst., Joint award ASTM-Stds. Engring. Soc., 1980, Margaret Dana award ASTM. Fellow IEEE (life), Stds. Engring. Soc. (Leo B. Moore medal 1980). Administrative and regulatory, General corporate, Personal injury. E-mail: dhoffman49@home.com

HOFFMAN, VALERIE JANE, lawyer; b. Lowville, N.Y., Oct. 27, 1953; d. Russell Francis and Jane Marie (Fowler) H.; m. Michael J. Grillo, Apr. 4, 1996. Student, U. Edinburgh, Scotland, 1973-74; BA summa cum laude, Union Coll., 1975; JD, Boston Coll., 1978. Bar: Ill. 1978, U.S. Dist. Ct. (no. dist.) Ill. 1978, U.S. Ct. Appeals (3rd cir.) 1981, U.S. Ct. Appeals (7th cir.) 1983. Assoc. Seyfarth Shaw, Chgo., 1978-87; ptnr. Seyfarth, Shaw, Fairweather & Geraldson, 1987—. Adj. prof. Columbia Coll., 1985. Contbr. articles to legal publs. Dir. Remains Theatre, Chgo., 1981-95, pres., 1991-93, v.p., 1991-95; dir. The Nat. Conf. for Cmty. and Justice, Chgo. Region, 1993—, nat. trustee, 1995—; trustee bd. advisors Union Coll., 1996-99, trustee, 1999—; dir. AIDS Found. of Chgo., 1997—, sec., 1999—; trustee Union Coll., 1999—. Mem. ABA, Chgo. Bar Assn., Law Club Chgo., Univ. Club Chgo. (bd. dirs. 1984-87), Phi Beta Kappa. Administrative and regulatory, Entertainment, Labor. Office: Seyfarth Shaw 55 E Monroe St Ste 4400 Chicago IL 60603-5713

HOFFMANN, CHRISTOPH LUDWIG, lawyer; b. Elsterwerda, Germany, Oct. 9, 1944; came to U.S., 1965; s. Gunther and Ruth (Hornschuh) H.; m. Susan Magnuson, June 18, 1983. Student, Freie U. Berlin, 1964-65; BA, U. Wis., 1966; JD, Harvard U., 1969. Bar: Mass. 1969, R.I. 1977. Assoc. Bingham, Dana & Gould, Boston, 1969-76; asst. gen. counsel Textron Inc., Providence, 1976-83; v.p., gen. counsel, sec. Pneumo Corp., Boston, 1983-85; sr. v.p., gen. counsel, sec. Pneumo Abex Corp., 1985-91; v.p., sec., gen. counsel Raytheon Co., Lexington, Mass., 1991-94, sr. v.p. law, human resources and corp. adminstrn., sec., 1994-95, exec. v.p. law and corp. adminstrn., sec., 1995-98; ltd. ptnr. Carlisle 1999, L.P., 1998—. Bd. dirs. Assoc. Industries Mass., 1994; vice-chmn., trustee Deaconess Glover Hosp., 1994—; mem. adv. bd. eLaw Forum Corp., 1999—. Mem. ABA, New Eng. Legal Found. (bd. dirs. 1991-98), Mass. Bar Assn., R.I. Bar Assn., Assn. Gen. Counsel.

HOFFMANN, MARIA ELISABETH, lawyer; b. Trier, Germany, Feb. 20, 1942; d. Klaus and Kathrina Hoffmann; m. Guy Brun d'Aubignosc, 1965 (div. 1978); children: Emmanuel, Karen; m. J. Lucien Lamoureux, 1983; 1 child, Isabelle. Lic es Lettres, U. Paris Sorbonne, 1967; Dr en Droit, Free U. Brussels, 1970. Bar: Brussels. Atty. Hoffman & Assocs., Brussels. Author: Elemente des Belgischen Handels-und Wirtschaftrecht, 1996; contbr. articles to profl. jours. Bd. dirs. Can. C. of C., Brussels, 1972—, German C. of C., Brussels, 1990—, Brussels C. of C. and Industry, 1991-96. Mem. Internat. Bar Orgn., Union Internationale des Avocats. Contracts commercial, General corporate, Intellectual property. Office: Hoffmann @ Assocs 385 Ave Louise B1050 Brussels Belgium E-mail: ehoffmann@hoffmann-partners.com

HOFFMANN, MARTIN RICHARD, lawyer; b. Stockbridge, Mass., Apr. 20, 1932; m. Margaret Ann McCabe; children: Heidi H. Slye, William, Bern. AB, Princeton U., 1954; LLB, U. Va., 1961. Bar: D.C. 1961. Law clk. U.S. Ct. Appeals (4th cir.), 1961-62; asst. U.S. atty. Washington, 1962-65; minority counsel com. on judiciary Ho. of Reps., 1965-67; legal counsel to Senator C. Percy, U.S. Senate, 1967-69; asst. gen. counsel Univ. Computing Co., Dallas, 1969-71; gen. counsel AEC, Washington, 1971-73; spl. asst. to sec. and dep. sec. def., 1973-74; gen. counsel Dept. Def., 1974-75; sec. Dept. Army, 1975-77; mng. ptnr. Gardner, Carton & Douglas, 1977-89; v.p., gen. counsel, sec. Digital Equipment Corp., Maynard, Mass., 1989-93; of counsel Skadden, Arps, Slate, Meagher & Flom, Washington, 1996-2000. Sr. vis. fellow Ctr. for Policy, Tech. and Indsl. Devel., MIT, Cambridge, 1993-95; bd. dirs. Castle Energy, Phila., Sea Change Corp., Maynard, Mass., Mitretek Systems, Inc., Beamhit LLC. Maj. USAR, 1954-73. Mem. Met. Club. Home: 1546 Hampton Hill Cir Mc Lean VA 22101

HOFFMEYER, WILLIAM FREDERICK, lawyer, educator; b. York, Pa., Dec. 20, 1936; s. Frederick W. and Mary B. (Stremmel) H.; m. Betty J. Hoffmeyer, Feb. 6, 1960 (div.); 1 child, Louise C.; m. Karen L. Semmelman, 1985. AB, Franklin and Marshall Coll., 1958; JD, Dickinson Sch. Law, 1961. Bar: Pa. 1962, U.S Dist Ct. (mid. dist.) Pa. 1981, U.S.

Supreme Ct. 1983. Pvt. practice law, 1962-81; sr. ptnr. Hoffmeyer & Semmelman, 1982—. Adj. prof. real estate law York Coll. Pa., 1980-92, real estate law, paral legal program Pa. State U., 1978—. Autor: Abstractor's Bible, 1981, Pennsylvania Real Estate Installment Sales Contrct Manual, 1981, Real Estate Settlement Procedures, 1982, Contracts of Sale, 1984, How to Plot a Deed Description, 1985; author, lectr., moderator and course planner numerous Pa. Bar Inst. CLE Programs. Recipient Disting. Svc. award Gen. Alumni Assn. Dickinson Sch. Law, 1993, Pa. Bar medal, 1997. Mem. ABA, Pa. Bar Assn. (co-chmn. unauthorized practice of law com.), York County Bar Assn. (chmn. continuing legal edn. com. 1992-96), Am. Coll. Real Estate Lawyers, Lions (past pres. East York club), York Area C. of C. (chair small bus. support network 1997-99), Masons, Shriners (past pres. York County). General practice, Probate, Real property. Address: 30 N George St York PA 17401-1214

HOGAN, ELWOOD, lawyer; b. Augusta, Ga., Mar. 4, 1929; s. William Elwood and Geneva Isabell H.; m. Myrtle Elizabeth McCall, June 15, 1957; children: Martha Elizabeth Ondrejca, Darrell William Hogan. BBA, U. Ga., 1954; JD, Stetson U., 1958. Bar: Fla. 1958, U.S. Ct. Appeals (6th cir.) Fla. 1958, U.S. Dist. Ct. Fla. 1959, U.S. Ct. Appeals (11th cir.) 1959, U.S. Tax Ct. 1965, U.S. Supreme Ct. 1973; cert. cir. ct. mediator. Assoc. Wolfe & Bonner Attys., Clearwater, Fla., 1958-63; ptnr. Wolfe, Bonner & Hogan, 1964-75; pres. Bonner & Hogan P.A., 1985-98, Hogan & Breakstone, P.A., Clearwater, 1998-99, McFarland, Gould, Lyons, Sullivan, Perenich & Hogan, P.A., Clearwater, 2000—. Prosecutor Mcpl. Ct., Clearwater, 1966-68, judge, 1968-74; bd. trustees Morton Plant Hosp., Clearwater, 1981-86, chmn., 1984-86; pres. Fla. Mcpl. Judges Assn., 1972; Fla. Cir. Ct. mediator. Mem. ABA, Fla. Acad. Profl. Mediators, Kiwanis Club (dist. gov. Fla. dist. 1979-80), Clearwater Bar Assn. (pres. 1972-73), Phi Alpha Delta (life). Avocations: swimming, tennis, fishing. Estate planning, Probate, Real property. Office: McFarland Gould Lyons Sullivan Perenich & Hogan 311 S Missouri Ave Clearwater FL 33756-5833 E-mail: ehogan@mglsplaw.com

HOGAN, KEMPF, lawyer; b. East Grand Rapids, Mich., May 11, 1939; s. Romain Grammel and Helen Maude (Kempf) H.; BBA, U. Mich., 1961; MBA with distinction, 1965; JD, 1966; postgrad. Harvard U., 1962. Security analyst Comerica Bank-Detroit, 1961-62; tax analyst Standard Oil Co. of N.J., N.Y.C., 1964; admitted to Mich. bar, 1967; assoc. firm Poole Littell & Sutherland, Detroit, 1967-71, partner, 1971-76; partner firm Butzel, Long, Gust, Klein & Van Zile, P.C., 1976-81, stockholder, 1982—; former mem. trust and trust investment com. Mich. Nat. Bank Detroit. Bd. dirs., founders jr. council Detroit Inst. Arts, 1971-78, mem. adv. bd., 1979—, patron and benefactor; active Friends of U. Mich. Mus. Art; friend Birmingham-Bloomfield Art Assn., Cranbrook Acad. Art Mus., Detroit Artists Market, Inc.; bd. dirs. Meadow Brook Art Gallery Oakland U.; bd. dirs., v.p. Friends of Modern Art Detroit Inst. Arts; past bd. dirs. The Children's Center, Planned Parenthood League, Inc., Readings for the Blind, Inc. Mem. State Bar Mich., Am., Detroit Bar Assn., Oakland County Bar, Am. Judicature Soc., Phi Kappa Phi, Beta Gamma Sigma, Beta Alpha Psi, Beta Theta Pi, Phi Delta Phi. Presbyterian. Clubs: Harvard (Detroit); Bloomfield Hills Country. Home: Piety Hill Place # 307 600 W Brown St Birmingham MI 48009 Office: 32270 Telegraph Rd Ste 200 Franklin MI 48025-2457

HOGAN, MICHAEL R(OBERT), judge; b. Oregon City, Oreg., Sept. 24, 1946; married; 3 children. AB, U. Oreg. Honors Coll., 1968; JD, Georgetown U., 1971. Bar: Oreg. 1971, U.S. Ct. Appeals (9th cir.) 1971. Law clk. to chief judge U.S. Dist. Ct. Oreg., Portland, 1971-72; assoc. Miller, Anderson, Nash, Yerke and Wiener, 1972-73; magistrate judge U.S. Dist. Ct. Oreg., Eugene, 1973-91, dist. judge, 1991—, chief judge, 1995—; bankduptcy judge U.S. Dist. Oreg., 1973-80. Mem. ABA, Oreg. State Bar Assn. Office: US Courthouse 211 E 7th Ave Eugene OR 97401-2773

HOGLUND, JOHN ANDREW, lawyer; b. Cleve., July 19, 1945; s. Paul Franklin and Louise (Anderson) H.; m. Patricia Olwell, May 27, 1972; children: Britt Hannah, Maeve Olwell, Marc Paul-Joseph. BA, Augustana Coll., 1967; JD, George Washington U., 1972. Bar: Wash. 1973, U.S. Dist. Ct. (we. dist.) Wash. 1973, U.S. Ct. Appeals (9th cir.) 1973. Law clk. Wash. State Supreme Ct., 1973-74; assoc. Mooney, Cullen & Holm, Olympia, 1973-75; ptnr. Cullen, Holm, Hoglund & Foster, 1975-81; pvt. practice, 1981—; pres. Hoglund Enterprises, 1987—. Adj. prof. law sch. U. Puget Sound, Tacoma, Wash., 1989-90, trustee, 1984-92. Co-author: SKYCYL Practicing Law Manual, 1986-95, WSBA Book Automobile Negligence Law, 1988. Vice chmn. Group Health Coop., Olympia, 1978, Thurston County Dem. Cen. Com., Olympia, 1980; chmn. bd. dirs. S.W. Wash. Health Sys. Agy., 1979; alumni bd. dirs. George Washington U. Nat. Law Ctr., 1994-97, emeritus mem., 1997—. With U.S. Army, 1967-69. Named Boss of Yr. Thurston County Legal Secs. Assn., 1985. Mem. ABA, Thurston County Bar Assn. (trustee 1988-90, Svc. awards 1987, 90), ATLA, Wash. State Trial Lawyers Assn. (pres. 1983-84, Brandeis award 1980), Wash. State Trial Lawyers Found. (pres. 1985-87), Wash. State Bar Assn. (chmn. UPL com. 1979, CPR com., pub. rels. com., chmn. Lawyer Protection Fund com. 1999), Nat. Law Ctr. George Washington U. (alumni bd. 1994—), Kiwanis (Disting. Pres. award 1980). Insurance, Personal injury. Address: Hoglund Counselors PO Box 11189 Olympia WA 98508-1189

HOGUE, TERRY GLYNN, lawyer; b. Merced, Calif., Sept. 23, 1944; s. Glynn Dale and Lillian LaVonne (Carter) H.; m. Joanne Laura Sharples, Oct. 3, 1969; children: Morgan Taylor, Whitney Shannon. BA, U. Calif., Fresno, 1966, postgrad., 1967; JD, U. Calif., San Francisco, 1972. Bar: Calif. 1972, Idaho 1975, U.S. Dist. Ct. (cen. dist.) Calif. 1973, U.S. Dist. Ct. Idaho 1975, U.S. Supreme Ct. 1976. Assoc. Reid, Babbage & Coil, Riverside, Calif., 1972-75; pvt. practice, Hailey, Idaho, 1975-77; ptnr. Campion & Hogue, 1977-80, Hogue & Speck, Hailey and Ketchum, Idaho, 1980-82, Hogue, Speck & Aanestad, Hailey and Ketchum, 1982-97, Hogue & Dunlap, L.L.P., Hailey and Ketchum, 1998—. Bd. dirs. Blaine County Med. Ctr., Hailey, 1975-91. Sgt. U.S. Army, 1969-71. Mem. ABA, Calif. Bar Assn., Idaho Bar Assn. (hearing panel of profl. conduct bd. 1991-97, chmn. profl. conduct bd. 1994-95), 5th Jud. Dist. Bar Assn. (magistrate com. 1991-93, ethics com. 1991-93), Idaho Trial Lawyers Assn. (bd. dirs. 1982-93, treas. 1985-86, sec. 1986-87, v.p. 1988-89, pres. 1989-90), Assn. Trial Lawyers Am. (sec. coun. of pres. 1989-90, Atla Weideman Wisocki award 1990), Am. Inns. of Ct. (charter Master Bench chpt.), Hailey C. of C. (bd. dirs. 1975-83), Rotary. General civil litigation, Family and matrimonial, General practice. Home: PO Box 1259 500 Onyx Dr Ketchum ID 83340-1259 Office: Hogue & Dunlap LLP PO Box 460 Hailey ID 83333-0460 also: PO Box 538 Ketchum ID 83340-0538

HOHMAN, A. J., JR. lawyer; b. San Antonio, Dec. 19, 1934; s. A.J. and Helen (Stehling) H.; m. Mary C. Leonard, Aug. 30, 1958; children: Kristin Marie, Jonathan David. BA in Econs., LLB, St Mary's U., 1959. Bar: Tex. 1961, U.S. Dist. Ct. (we. and so. dists.) Tex. 1970, U.S. Ct. Appeals (5th cir.) 1971; U.S. Supreme Ct. 1971. Asst. dist. atty. Bexar County, San Antonio, 1961-64; ptnr. Hohman, Georges & Gehring, 1964-93. Editor: Barrister News, 1958-59. Bd. dirs. St. Peter's and St. Joseph's Ch.'s Homes, San Antonio, 1974-87, 92-96, pres., 1980-81, 86-87; pres. Ursuline Acad., San Antonio, 1982-84, bd. dirs., 1984-87. 1st lt. U.S. Army, 1959-61. Fellow Am. Bd. Trial Advocates (pres. San Antonio chpt. 1983-84); mem. Tex. Trial Lawyers Assn. (assoc. dir. 1981-88), San Antonio Trial Lawyers Assn. (pres. 1980), Am. Trial Lawyers Assn. (1975-93). Democrat. Roman Catholic. Avocations: travel, all outdoor activities, reading. General civil litigation, State civil litigation, Personal injury. Office: Hohman Georges & Gehring 4940 Broadway Ste 101 San Antonio TX 78209 Fax: (210) 223-1496

HOHNHORST, JOHN CHARLES, lawyer; b. Jerome, Idaho, Dec. 25, 1952; m. Raelene Casper; children: Jennifer, Rachel, John. BS in Polit. Sci./Pub. Adminstrn., U. Idaho, 1975, JD cum laude, 1978. Bar: Idaho 1978, U.S. Dist. Ct. Idaho 1978, U.S. Ct. Appeals (9th cir.) 1980, U.S. Ct. Claims 1983, U.S. Supreme Ct. 1987. Adminstrv. asst. to Sen. John M. Barker Idaho State Senate, 1975; ptnr. Hepworth, Lezamiz & Hohnhorst, Twin Falls, Idaho, 1978—. Contbr. articles to profl. jours. Mem. planning & zoning commn. City of Twin Falls, 1987-90. Mem. ABA, ATLA, Idaho State Bar (commr. 1990-93, pres. 1993), Idaho Trial Lawyers Assn. (regional dir. 1985-86), 5th Dist. Bar Assn. (treas. 1987-88, v.p. 1988-89, pres. 1989-90), Am. Acad. Appellate Lawyers, Greater Twin Falls C. of C. (chmn. magic valley leadership program 1988-89, bd. dirs. 1989-92), Phi Kappa Tau (Beta Gamma chpt., Phi award 1988). Appellate, General civil litigation, Insurance. Office: Hepworth Lezamiz & Hohnhorst PO Box 389 133 Shoshone St N Twin Falls ID 83301-6150

HOINES, DAVID ALAN, lawyer; b. St. Paul, Oct. 18, 1946; s. Arnold H. and Patricia (Olson) H.; m. Bonnie K. Smith, June 4, 1983. BA, Calif. State U., San Jose, 1969; JD, Santa Clara U., 1972; LLM in Taxation, Boston U., 1973. Bar: Fla. 1975, Calif. 1975, N.Y. 1999, U.S. Dist. Ct. (so. dist.) Fla. 1975, U.S. Dist. Ct. (no. dist.) Calif. 1980, U.S. Dist. Ct. (mid. dist.) Fla. 1984, U.S. Dist. Ct. (ctrl. dist.) Calif. 1990, U.S. Ct. Claims 1980, U.S. Tax Ct. 1975, U.S. Ct. Appeals (fed. cir.) 1990, U.S. Ct. Appeals (4th cir.) 1985, U.S. Ct. Appeals (5th cir.) 1978, U.S. Ct. Appeals (9th cir.) 1980, U.S. Ct. Appeals (11th cir.) 1981, U.S. Supreme Ct. 1980; cert. civil trial lawyer. Pvt. practice, Ft. Lauderdale, Fla., 1975—. Adj. instr. Nova U. Ctr. for Study of Law, 1977. Author: Taxman and the Textbook, The Ripon Forum, 1972. Mem. ABA, ATLA., Broward County Bar Assn., Fla. Bar Assn., Calif. Bar Assn., State Bar of N.Y., Hundred Club of Broward County, Tau Delta Phi. Avocations: ocean diving (free and scuba), snowskiing, running, boating, reading. General civil litigation, Probate, Taxation, general. Office: 1290 E Oakland Park Blvd Fort Lauderdale FL 33334-4443 E-mail: dahfl@aol.com

HOKE, GEORGE PEABODY, lawyer; b. St. Paul, Mar. 18, 1913; s. George Edward and Carolyn Grahfs (Peabody) H.; m. Carolyn Elizabeth Glass, May 25, 1940 (div. 1963); children— Carolyn G., George G. Jared Peabody. A.B. cum laude, Dartmouth Coll., 1935; J.D., Yale U., 1938. Bar: Minn. 1939, U.S. Dist. Ct. Minn. 1940, U.S. Dist. Ct. (so. dist.) Iowa 1965, U.S. Tax Ct. 1945, U.S. Ct. Appeals (8th cir.) 1970. Ptnr., Snyder Gale Hoke, Richard & Janes, Minneapolis, 1943-57, Wheeler, Fredriksen, Hoke & Larson, Minneapolis, 1957-61; sr. ptnr. Hoke, Roehrdenz, Bigelow & Chamberlain, Mpls., 1975-86; central U.S. counsel Inter-provincial Pipe Line Co., Can., 1950-54; sec. and chmn. bd. Velie Ryan, Inc., Rochester, Minn., 1940-70; trustee Shattuck Sch., Faribault, Minn., 1940-70. Vestryman St. David's Episc. Ch., Hopkins, Minn., 1940-65, St. Paul's Episc. Ch., Mpls., 1985—; chmn. Henn County Civil Def., Mpls. and Wayzata, 1942-45; campaign sec. Republican State Central Com. Minn., St. Paul, 1944-48; campaign chmn., 1948; mem. Minn. Rep. Central Com., 1940-48. Served to lt. j.g., USN, 1942-1943. Mem. Am. Law Inst. (life mem., mem. joint com. A.B.A./Am. Law Inst. 1940-50), ABA (Minn. state dir. jr. bar conf. 1945-55), Hennepin County Bar Assn. (chmn. tax sect. and jr. bar sec. 1945-55), Minn. State Bar Assn., Am. Judicature Soc. (state dir. 1960), Phi Delta Phi (province pres. 1940-70), Beta Theta Pi. Republican. Episcopalian. Clubs: Minneapolis, Mory's Assn. (New Haven). General practice, Insurance, Probate. Home and Office: PO Box 102 Marine On Saint Croix MN 55047-0102

HOLBROOK, REID FRANKLIN, lawyer; b. Kansas City, Jan. 19, 1942; s. Henry Edmiston and Margaret Dorothy H.; m. Mary Lynn Rogers, Feb. 16, 1968; children: Ann Holbrook Johnson, Katherine Reid. AB in Econs., U. Kans., 1964, JD, 1966. Bar: Kans. 1967, U.S. Dist. Ct. Kans. 1967, U.S. Dist. Ct. D.C. 1970, U.S. Ct. Appeals (D.C. cir.) 1970, U.S. Mil. Ct. Appeals 1970, U.S. Supreme Ct. 1970, Mo. 1990, U.S. Dist. Ct. (we. dist.) Mo. 1981, U.S. Ct. Appeals (8th and 10th cirs.) 1977. Judge 29th Jud. Dist. Kans., Kansas City, 1967-71, spl. counsel to dist. atty., 1971-75; spl. asst. atty. gen. State of Kans., 1971-74; ptnr. Holbrook, Heaven & Osborn, 1975—. Co-author: Child Abuse and Neglect: A Medical Reference, 1982. Maj. U.S. Army, 1966-80. Fellow Am. Acad. Hosp. Attys.; mem. Kans. Assn. Hosp. Attys., Kansas City Soc. Hosp. Attys. Avocations: flying, golf, travel. General civil litigation, Health, Personal injury. Home: 11101 W 119th Ter Overland Park KS 66213-2051 Office: Holbrook Heaven & Osborn 757 Armstrong Ave Kansas City KS 66101-2701

HOLCOMB, LYLE DONALD, JR. retired lawyer; b. Miami, Fla., Feb. 3, 1929; s. Lyle Donald and Hazel Irene (Watson) H.; m. Barbara Jean Roth, July 12, 1952; children: Susan Holcomb Davis, Douglas J., Mark E. BA, U. Mich., 1951; JD, U. Fla., 1954. Bar: U.S. Ct. Appeals (5th and 11th cirs.) 1981, U.S. Supreme Ct. 1966. Ptnr. Holcomb & Holcomb, Miami, 1955-72; assoc. Copeland, Therrel, Baisden & Peterson, Miami Beach, Fla., 1972-75; ptnr. Therrel, Baisden, Stanton, Wood & Setlin, 1976-85, Therrel, Baisden & Meyer Weiss, Miami Beach, 1985-93; pvt. practice Tallahassee, 1993-95. Organizing pres. So. Fla. Migrant Legal Svcs. Program (now Fla. Rural Legal Svcs.), 1966-68. Mem. exec. coun. So. Fla. coun. Boy Scouts Am., 1958-93; past pres., past counselor Miami chpt. Huguenot Soc. Fla. Served with USNR, 1947-53. Recipient Silver Beaver award So. Fla. coun. Boy Scouts Am., 1966. Fellow Am. Coll. Trust and Estate Counsel, 1980-94, Acad. Fla. Probate and Trust Litigation Attys., 1980-95; mem. Dade County Bar Assn. (dir. 1960-71, sec. 1963-71), Miami Beach Bar Assn. (pres. 1980), Estate Planning Coun. Greater Miami, Soc. Mayflower Descs. (past pres. Miami club, past counselor soc.), SAR (past pres. Miami chpt.), Univ. Yacht Club. Republican. Mem. United Ch. of Christ. Home: 3538 Killarney Plaza Dr Tallahassee FL 32309-3491 E-mail: lholcomb23@aol.com

HOLDAWAY, RONALD M. federal judge; b. Afton, Wyo. m. Judy Janowski, Dec. 1958; children: Denise, Georgia. BA, U. Wyo., 1957, JD, 1959. Bar: Wyo. 1959, U.S. Dist. Ct. (Wyo.), U.S. Ct. Mil. Appeals, 1960, U.S. Army Ct. Mil. Rev., U.S. Supreme Ct., 1967. Commd. 2nd lt. U.S. Army, 1960, advanced through grades to brig. gen., 1989; legal staff officer U.S. Army, Ft. Lewis, Washington, 1960-63, legal staff instr. Hawaii, 1963-66, instr. criminal law, Judge Advocate Gen.'s Sch. Va., 1966-69, staff judge advocate 1st cav. divsn. Vietnam, 1969-70, chief govt. appellate divsn., 1971-75, chief of pers., 1975-77, staff judge advocate Stuttgart, Germany, 1978-80, exec. to judge advocate gen. Washington, 1980-81, asst. judge advocate gen., 1981-83; judge advocate U.S. Army Europe, Heidelberg, Germany, 1983-87; chief judge Ct. Mil. Review U.S. Army, Washington, 1987-89; judge U.S. Ct. of Vets. Appeals, Washington DC, 1990—. Decorated Bronze Star, Legion of Merit, Disting. Svc. medal with Oak Leaf Cluster, Meritorious Svc. medal with Oak Leaf Cluster, Air medal, Nat. Def. Svc. medal, Vietnam Campaign medal with 4 campaign stars, Vietnam Svc. medal, Overseas medal (3). Mem. Wyo. State Bar Assn., Assn. U.S. Army, Ft. Myer Officers Club, Army Navy Club. Office: US Ct of Appeals for Vets Claims 625 Indiana Ave NW Ste 900 Washington DC 20004-2917

HOLDEN, FREDERICK DOUGLASS, JR. lawyer; b. Stockton, Calif., Nov. 21, 1949; s. Frederick Douglass and Sarah Frances (Young) H.; m. Patricia Brierton, June 25, 1988; children: Elizabeth, Andrew. BA, U. Calif., Santa Barbara, 1971; JD, U. Calif., Davis, 1974. Bar: Calif. 1974, U.S. Dist. Ct. (no., cen., ea. and so. dists.) Calif. 1974, U.S. Ct. Appeals (9th cir.) 1974, D.C. 1996, U.S. Dist. Ct. D.C. 1996, U.S. Supreme Ct. 2001. Assoc. Brobeck, Phleger & Harrison LLP, San Francisco, 1974-81; ptnr. Brobeck, Phleger & Harrison, 1981—. Mem. faculty Practising Law Inst., 1990; speaker Nat. Conf. Bankruptcy Judges, 1987, 91, Banking Law Inst., 1986, Calif. Continuing Legal Edn. of Bar, Calif., 1983-85, Calif. State Bar, 1993. Mng. editor U. Calif. Davis Law Rev., 1974. Fellow Am. Coll. Bankruptcy; mem. ABA (bus. bankruptcy com., spkr. 1991, 95), Calif. Bar Assn. (commendation 1983), San Francisco Bar Assn. (cert. appreciation 1985, 88, 90, 95), Turnaround Mgmt. Assn. (dir., sec. 1994-96), Am. Bankruptcy Inst., San Francisco Yacht Club, Sigma Pi (pres. 1970). Democrat. Avocations: triathlons, skiing, sailing. Bankruptcy, Contracts commercial, Mergers and acquisitions. Home: 140 Bella Vista Ave Belvedere CA 94920-2466 Office: Brobeck Phleger & Harrison Spear St Tower 1 Market Plz Ste 341 San Francisco CA 94105-1420 E-mail: fholden@brobeck.com

HOLDEN, JULIA, lawyer; b. Liverpool, Eng. BA with Honors in Law and German, U. Sussex, Brighton, Eng., 1986. Bar: Eng. 1990, Wales 1990. Trainee solicitor Pritchard, Englefield & Tobin, London, 1988-90; asst. solicitor Slaughter & May, 1990-91; with Trevisan & Cuonzo Avvocati, Milan. Intellectual property, Private international, Trademark and copyright. Office: Trevisan & Cuonzo Avvocati Via Brera 6 Milan 20121 Italy E-mail: jholden@trevisan.inet.it

HOLDER, HOLLY IRENE, lawyer; b. Albuquerque, May 16, 1952; d. Howard George and Dorothy Evelyn (Doll) Holzum; m. William B. Holder Jr., June 4, 1974; 1 child, Eric James. BA with honors, U. Colo., 1974; JD with honors, U. Denver, 1980. Bar: Colo. 1980, U.S. Ct. Appeals (10th cir.) 1980. Chemist Indsl. Labs., Denver, 1974-76; law clk. to presiding justice Colo. Supreme Ct., 1979; assoc. Calkins, Kramer, Grimshaw and Harring, 1980-82, 84-88, McKenna, Conner & Cuneo, Denver, 1988-90, Saunders, Snyder, Ross & Dickson, Denver, 1990-93; pvt. practice, 1993—. Mem. adv. com. Regional Coun. Govts. Water Resources Mgmt., 1984—; chmn. Chatfield Basin Assn., Denver, 1987, Chatfield Basin Master Plan Task Force, Denver, 1986—. Recipient Disting. Svc. award Denver Regional Coun. Govts., 1987. Mem. Colo. Bar Assn., Denver Bar Assn., Mensa, Denver Rotary. Republican. Avocations: golf, reading, book-collecting. Environmental, Real property. Office: 17th St Ste 1500 Denver CO 80202-1202

HOLDER, JANICE MARIE, state supreme court justice; b. Canonsburg, Pa., Aug. 29, 1949; d. Louis V. and Sylvia (Abraham) H.; m. George W. Loveland II, June 5, 1976 (div. Mar. 1987). Student, Allegheny Coll., 1967-68, Sorbonne, 1970; BS summa cum laude, U. Pitts., 1971; JD, Duquesne U., 1975. Bar: Pa. 1975, Tenn. 1979, D.C. 1988. Sr. law clk. to chief judge U.S. Dist. Ct. for Western Dist. Pa., Pitts., 1975-77; assoc. Catalano & Catalano, P.C., 1977-79, Holt, Batchelor, Spicer & Ryan, Memphis, 1980-82; pvt. practice, 1983-87; assoc. James S. Cox & Assocs., 1987-89; pvt. practice law, 1989-90; judge 30th Jud. Dist., 1990-96; justice Tenn. Supreme Ct., 1996—. Solicitor Borough of McDonald (Pa.), 1978-79. Bd. dirs. Alliance for Blind and Visually Impaired, Memphis, 1985-94, Midtown Mental Health Ctr., 1995-97; trustee Memphis Botanical Garden Found., 1996—. Fellow Tenn. Bar Found. (trustee 1995-99); mem. ABA, Am. Bar Found., Tenn. Bar Assn., Memphis Bar Assn. (bd. dirs. 1986-87, 93-94, editor Memphis Bar Forum 1987-91, 93-94, sec. 1993, treas. 1994, Sam A. Myar award 1990, Judge of Yr. divorce and family law sect. 1992, Chancellor Charles A. Rond award Outstanding Jurist 1992), Assn. for Women Attys. (treas. 1989, v.p. 1991), Tenn. Jud. Conf., Am. Inns Ct., Memphis Trial Lawyers Assn. (bd. dirs. 1988-90), Tenn. Task Force Against Domestic Violence (mem. state coordinating coun. 1994-96), Tenn. Lawyers' Assn. for Women, Tenn. Trial Judges Assn. (exec. com. 1994-96), Tenn. Judicial Conf. (treas. 1993-94, exec. com. 1993-96). Office: Tenn Supreme Ct 119 S Main St Ste 310 Memphis TN 38103-3678

HOLLAND, LYMAN FAITH, JR. lawyer; b. Mobile, Ala., June 17, 1931; s. Lyman Faith and Louise (Wisdom) H.; m. Leannah Louise Platt, Mar. 6, 1954; children: Lyman Faith III, Laura. BS in Bus. Adminstrn, U. Ala., 1953, LLB, 1957. Bar: Ala. 1957, U.S. Supreme Ct. 1992. Assoc. Hand, Arendall & Bedsole, Mobile, 1957-62; ptnr. Hand, Arendall, Bedsole, Greaves & Johnston, 1963-94, mem., 1995, Hand Arendall LLC, 1996—. Mem. Mobile Hist. Devel. Com., 1965-69, v.p., 1967-68; bd. dirs. Mobile Azalea Trail, Inc., 1963-68, chmn. bd., 1963-65; bd. dirs. Mobile Mental Health Ctr., 1969-76, v.p., 1972, pres., chmn. bd., 1973; bd. dirs. Mobile chpt. ARC, 1969-89, 91-97, vice chmn., 1975-77, exec. vice chmn., 1978-80, chmn., 1980-82, life bd. dirs. emeritus, 1997—; bd. dirs. Deep South coun. Girl Scouts U.S., 1965-71, Gordan Smith Ctr. Inc., 1973, Bay Area Coun. on Alcoholism, 1973-76, Comty. Chest Coun. of Mobile County, Inc., 1976-81; bd. dirs. Greater Mobile Mental Health-Mental Retardation, 1975-81, pres., 1975-77; mem. exec. com. Mobile Estate Planning Coun., 1988-97, pres., 1994-95. 1st lt. USAF, 1953-55; lt. col. USAF ret. Mem. ABA, Mobile County Bar Assn., Ala. State Bar (chmn. sect. corp., banking and bus. law 1978-80), Am. Counsel Assn., Am. Coll. Trust and Estate Counsel, Am. Coll. Trust and Estate Counsel Found. (bd. dirs. 1990-96), Ala. Law Inst. (coun. 1978—), Athleston Club (Mobile), Country Club of Mobile, Bienville Club, Lions, Pi Kappa Alpha, Phi Delta Phi. Baptist (deacon, ch. trustee 1968-73, chmn. trustees 1971-73). Estate planning, Probate, Real property. Home: 3606 Provident Ct Mobile AL 36608-1534 Office: Hand Arendall LLC PO Box 123 Mobile AL 36601-0123 E-mail: lymanh@handarendall.com

HOLLAND, MARVIN ARTHUR, lawyer; b. Bklyn., Oct. 5, 1930; s. Leo and Rose (Auslander) H.; m. Barbara Lee Birnstein, Dec. 16, 1971 (div. 1979). B.A., Lafayette Coll., 1951; J.D., Cornell Law Sch., 1954. Bar: N.Y. 1955, U.S. Dist. Ct. (ea. and so. dists.) N.Y. 1960. Assoc., then ptnr. Holland & Radoyevich, Smithtown, N.Y., 1956-67, sole practice, Smithtown, 1967-69, 75-79; ptnr. Holland, Greshin & Sloan, Smithtown, 1969-75, Holland & Zinker, Smithtown, 1978— ; lectr. Practising Law Inst., N.Y.C., 1981, Suffolk Acad. Law, Ronkonkoma, N.Y., 1978— , Am. Acad. Matrimonial Attys., Chgo., 1981-83, Nassau County Acad. Law, Mineola, N.Y., 1982-83. Contbr. bankruptcy entry to Money Ency., 1984; also articles. Mem. B'nai B'rith Anti-defamation League, N.Y.C., 1974— , Nat. Law Com. Served with U.S. Army, 1954-56. Mem. Suffolk County Bar Assn. (bd. dirs. 1974-77), N.Y. State Bar Assn., Bankruptcy Bar Assn. , Nassau County Bar Assn. Jewish. Bankruptcy. Home: 10 Woodhollow Rd Smithtown NY 11787-3710 Office: Holland & Zinker 12 Bank Ave Smithtown NY 11787-2704 also: US District Court 75 Clinton St Brooklyn NY 11201-4201

HOLLAND, RANDY JAMES, state supreme court justice; b. Elizabeth, N.J., Jan. 27, 1947; s. James Charles and Virginia (Wilson) H.; m. Ilona E. Holland, June 24, 1972 BA in Econs., Swarthmore Coll., 1969; JD cum laude, U. Pa., 1972; LLM, U. Va., 1998. Bar: Del. 1972. Ptnr. Dunlap, Holland & Rich and predecessors, Georgetown, Del., 1972-80, Morris, Nichols, Arsht & Tunnell, Georgetown, 1980-86; justice Supreme Ct. Del., 1986—. Mem. Del. Bar Examiners, 1978-86; mem. Gov.'s Jud. Nominating Commn., 1978-86, sec., 1982-85, chmn., 1985-86; mem. Del. Supreme Ct. Consol. Com., 1985-86; pres. Terry-Carey Inn of Ct., 1991-94; v.p. Am. Inns of Ct., 1996-2000, pres., 2000—; co-chair Racial and Ethnic Task Force, 1995—; adj. prof. Widener U. Sch. Law, 1991—, U. Pa. Sch. Law, 1993-94; co-chair Del. Cts. Planning Com., 1996; chair nat. jud. adv. com. fed. Office of Child Support Enforcement; Jud. Ethics Adv. Commn., 1994—; del. Code Jud. Conduct Rev. Commn., 1991-94; del. Bar Bench Media Conf., 1990—. Mem. editL. bd. Del. Lawyer Mag., 1981-85; contbr. chpt. Del. Appellate Handbook, 1985—. Pres. adminstrv. bd. Ave. United Meth. Ch., Milford, Del. Bar Found.; hon. chmn. History of the Del. Bar in 20th Century, 1992—. Recipient Henry C. Loughlin prize for legal ethics U. Pa. 1972, St. Thomas More award, 1999; named Judge of the Yr. Nat. Child Support Enforcement Assn., 1992. Mem. ABA (standing com. on

lawyer competence, nat. jud. coll. adv. commn. model rules jud. disclosure enforcement 1996), Am. Judicature Soc. (nat. trustee 1992—), Am. Inns of Ct. Found. (trustee 1992—, nat. trustee 1996—, v.p. 1996-2000, nat. pres. 2000—), Am. Law Inst., Del. Bar Found., Am. Law Inst. Republican. Office: Del Supreme Ct Family Court Bldg 22 The Cir Georgetown DE 19947-1500

HOLLAND, ROBERT DALE, retired magistrate, consultant; b. Sayre, Okla., June 10, 1928; s. Claude Henry and Alva Mae (Joyce) H.; children: Arlene, Burton Dale, Rhonda Jo. Student, Tex. A&M, 1946, Internat. Corr. Schs., 1963, 65, 67-68; PhD of Sociology (hon.), Scholars U., 1975. Safety, security, loss prevention officer Copper Queen Br. Phelps Dodge Corp., Bisbee, Ariz., 1946-85; probation officer State of Ariz., 1986-87; safety dir., loss prevention dir. Spray Sys. Environ., Phoenix, 1987-93; city magistrate City of Bisbee, 1989-93; pres., owner Copper City Cons., Bisbee, 1989—. Referee & hearing officer Cochise County Juvenile Ct., 1969-78; juvenile ct. judge pro tem, 1990-93; justice ct. judge pro tem, 1991-93; bd. dirs. Southern Ariz. Safety Coun., Tucson, 1986-91. Councilman City of Bisbee, 1973-82; chmn. relief com. Salvation Army, 1980—; chmn., vice chmn. bd. dirs. Copper Queen Hosp. Corp., Bisbee, Ariz. With USMC, 1947-52. Mem. ADHS (water quality com. 1974), Am. Mining Congress (ad-hoc com. 1980), Perfect Ashlar Lodge F&AM (master 1964), Scottish Yorkrite Bodies Ariz. Democrat. Avocations: gun collecting, reading, church work. Home and Office: PO Box 5427 206 Black Knob View Bisbee AZ 85603-5427

HOLLANDER, BRUCE LEE, lawyer, business executive; b. Queens, N.Y., Aug. 16, 1943; s. I. Gerard and Argate (Polmer) H.; m. Beverly Ann Olund, Apr. 28, 1967; children— Aaron Gerard, Adam Robert. Student Cornell U., 1961-62; B.S. in Psychology, U. Miami, 1970; J.D. cum laude, 1973. Bar: Fla. 1973, U.S. Dist. Ct. (mid. and so. dists.) Fla. 1973, U.S. Ct. Appeals (5th cir.) 1973. Assoc. Snyder, Young, Stern & Tannenbaum, Miami, Fla., 1973-76; ptnr. Garlick, Cohn, Darrow & Hollander, Hollywood, Fla., 1976-82, Hollander & Assocs., P.A., Hollywood, 1982— ; lectr. in field; mem. adv. bd. Broward Bank, 1982, mem. elect, 1983; pres. Automated Title Services, Hollywood, Automated Credit Svcs., Hollywood. Contbr. articles to Mortgage Notes, Fla. Bar Jour. Bd. dirs. Broward County chpt. ARC, Fla., 1979-81. Mem. ABA, Broward County Bar Assn., Fla. Bar (rep. 17th jud. cir. for real property, probate and trust law sect. 1978— , exec. council real property, probate and trust law sect. 1979-83, chmn. 2d mortgage law subcom. 1979-83, also corp., banking and bus. law sect. and econs. and mgmt. law practice sect.), Nat. Second Mortgage Assn., Nat. Consumer Fin. Assn. (home equity sect.), Nat. Assn. Mortgage Brokers, Fla. Assn. Mortgage Brokers (bd. dirs. Gold Coast chpt.), Soc. Wig and Robe, Soc. Bar and Gavel (justice, honor council), Sports Car Club Am. (S.E. divisional champion 1968, 76-77, 86), Delta Theta Phi, Phi Kappa Phi. Jewish. Contracts commercial, General corporate, Real property. Office: Hollander & Assocs PA 1940 Harrison St Hollywood FL 33020-5082

HOLLENBAUGH, H(ENRY) RITCHEY, lawyer; b. Shelby, Ohio, Nov. 12, 1947; m. Diane Robinson Nov. 21, 1973 (div. 1989); children: Chad Ritchey, Katie Paige; m. Rebecca U., Aug. 8, 1995. BA, Kent State U., 1969; JD, Capital U., 1973. Bar: Ohio 1973, U.S. Dist. Ct. (so. dist.) Ohio 1974, U.S. Ct. Appeals (6th cir.) 1976, U.S. Supreme Ct. 1978. Investigator Ohio Civil Rights Com., Columbus, Ohio, 1969-72; legal intern City Atty.'s Office, 1972-73, asst. city prosecutor, 1973-75, sr. asst. city atty., 1975-76; ptnr. Hunter, Hollenbaugh & Theodotou, 1976-85, Delligatti, Hollenbaugh, Briscoe & Milless, Columbus, 1985-91, Climaco Seminatore Delligatti & Hollenbaugh, Columbus, 1991-93, Delligatti, Hollenbaugh & Briscoe, Columbus, 1993-95, Draper, Hollenbaugh, Briscoe, Yashko & Carmany, 1996-99, Carlile Patchen & Murphy, Columbus, 1999—. Mem. Ohio Pub. Defender Commn., 1988-94; chmn. Franklin County Pub. Defender Commn., 1986-92. Treas. The Gov's. Com., 1987-96, Friends With Celeste, Friends of Gov's. Residence, 1987-92, Participation 2000, 1987-91. Fellow ABA Found. (chair commn. on advt. 1993-97, ho. of dels. 1993—); mem. Ohio State Bar Assn. (bd. govs. 1989-94, pres. 1992-93), Columbus Bar Assn. (pres. 1987-88), Nat. Conf. Bar Pres., Nat. Assn. Criminal Def. Lawyers, Capital Club. Democrat. Methodist. Avocations: golf, politics. Federal civil litigation, State civil litigation, Criminal. Home: 8549 Glenalmond Ct Dublin OH 43017-9737 Office: Carlile Patchen & Murphy 336 E Broad St Columbus OH 43215-3202 E-mail: HRN@CPMCAW.com

HOLLEY, STEVEN LYON, lawyer; b. Ft. Wayne, Ind., Apr. 5, 1958; s. Wesley Lewis and Cornelia Alice (Reeder) H. BA in History/Polit. Sci., Ind. U., 1980; JD, NYU, 1983. Bar: N.Y. 1984, U.S. Dist. Ct. (so. and ea. dist.) N.Y. 1985, U.S. Dist. Ct. (no. dist.) N.Y. 1988. Law clk. Hon. Jose' A. Cabranes, Hartford, Conn., 1983-84; assoc. Sullivan & Cromwell, N.Y.C., 1984-90, ptnr., 1991—. Mem. Assn. Bar City of N.Y. (sec. com. on profl. and jud. ethics 1988-90). Democrat. Antitrust, Mergers and acquisitions, Securities. Home: 832 Broadway New York NY 10003-4813 Office: Sullivan & Cromwell 125 Broad St Fl 34 New York NY 10004-2498 E-mail: holleys@sullcrom.com

HOLLIN, SHELBY W. lawyer; b. Varilla, Ky., July 29, 1925; s. Herbert and Maggie Hollin; m. Martha Jane Fisch, Nov. 27, 1948; children— Sheila K, Henry T., Richard G., Roberta E., Nathan W., Jacob C. B.B.A., St. Mary's U., 1965, J.D., 1970. Bar: Tex. 1969, U.S. Supreme Ct. 1974, U.S. Claims, 1978, U.S. Ct. Appeals 1981, Ky. 1990. Sole practice, San Antonio, 1969— ; mem. nat. bd. advisors Am. Biog. Inst. Served with USAF, World War II. Decorated Air medal, Air Force Commendation medal with oak leaf cluster; recipient award for fighting discrimination Govt. Employed Mejures, 1981, others. Mem. Tex. State Bar, San Antonio Bar Assn., Res. Officers Assn. (life), Air Force Assn. (life), VFW (life), DAV (life), Am. Legion, Mil. Order World Wars. Baptist. Administrative and regulatory, General practice, Labor. Home and Office: 7710 Stagecoach Dr San Antonio TX 78227-3430

HOLLINSHEAD, EARL DARNELL, JR. lawyer; b. Pitts., Aug. 1, 1927; s. Earl Darnell and Gertrude (Cahill) H.; m. Sylvia Antion, June 29, 1957; children: Barbara, Kim, Earl III, Susan. AB, Ohio U., 1948; LLB, U. Pitts., 1951. Bar: Pa. 1952, U.S. Ct. Mil. Appeals 1954, U.S. Dist. Ct. (we. dist.) Pa. 1955, U.S. Supreme Ct. 1956, U.S. Ct. Appeals (3d cir.) 1959, U.S. Dist. Ct. (ea. dist.) Ohio 1978. Sole practice, Pitts., 1955-70; ptnr. Hollinshead and Mendelson, 1970-89, Hollinshead, Mendelson, Bresnahan & Nixon, P.C., Pitts., 1990-97; sole practitioner, 1997—. Mem. Pitts. Estate Planning Council. Contbr. articles to profl. jours. Served to lt. USNR, 1951-55. Fellow Pa. Bar Found. (life); mem. Pa. Bar Assn. (chmn. real property divsn. 1983-85, real property, probate and trust sects. 1985-86), Allegheny County Bar Assn. (chmn. real property sect. 1975-76), Pa. Bar Inst. (lectr., planner, bd. dirs. 1988-94), Am. Coll. Real Estate Lawyers. Bankruptcy, Probate, Real property. Home: 2535 Windgate Rd Bethel Park PA 15102-2730 Office: 630 Grant Bldg Pittsburgh PA 15219-2105

HOLLIS, DARYL JOSEPH, judge; b. Pitts., Oct. 22, 1946; s. Joseph and Margaret Clara (Meszar) H.; m. Linda Eardley, July 18, 1970. BS in Edn., Pa. State U., 1968, MEd in Remedial Reading, 1971; JD, Cath. U. Am., 1984. Bar: Pa. 1987, D.C. 1989, U.S. Supreme Ct. Law clk. D.C. Office of Employee Appeals, Washington, 1984-85, adminstrv. law judge, 1985-97, sr. adminstrv. law judge, 1997—. Lectr. D.C. Bar Assn. Pro Bono Svcs., Washington, 1985—; mem. Transplant Recipients Internat. Orgn., Nat. Capital Area Chpt., 1993—. Mem. Columbia Pines Citizens Assn., 1993—. Mem. Transplant Recipients Internat. Orgn. Democrat. Roman Catholic. Avocations: woodworking, hiking, Civil War, baseball history, sports. Home: 4002 Rose Ln Annandale VA 22003-1943

HOLLIS, SHEILA SLOCUM, lawyer; b. Denver, July 15, 1948; d. Theodore Doremus and Emily M. (Caplis) Slocum (dec.); m. John Hollis; 1 child, Windsong Emily Lanford. BS in Journalism with honors, BS in Gen. Studies cum laude, U. Colo., 1971; JD, U. Denver, 1973. Bar: Colo. 1974, D.C. 1975, U.S. Supreme Ct. 1980. Trial atty. Fed. Power Commn., Washington, 1974-75; assoc. firm Wilner & Scheiner, 1975-77; dir. office enforcement Fed. Energy Regulatory Commn., 1977-80; pvt. practice, 1980-87; ptnr. Vinson & Elkins, Washington, 1987-92; sr. ptnr. Metzger, Hollis, Gordon & Alprin, 1992-97; mng. ptnr. D.C., mem. ptnrs. bd., chair energy and environ. practice Duane, Morris & Heckscher, LLP, 1997—. Professorial lectr. in energy law George Washington U., 1980—. Co-author: Energy Decision Making, 1983, Energy Law and Policy, 1989; mem. editl. bd. Oil and Gas Reporter, Pub. Utility Fortnightly; contbr. articles to profl. publs. Established and developed enforcement program Fed. Energy Regulatory Commn.; mem. adv. bd. Pub. Utility Ctr., N.Mex. State U., 1986-94, Gas Industry Stds. Bd., 1998—; pres. Women's Coun. Energy and Environ., 1997—; mem. bd. dirs. Nat. Assn. Vets. Health Care, Wyo. State Soc. U. Denver scholar, 1972-73. Fellow: ABA (mem. ho. dels. 1992—2001, chair sect. environ., energy and resources, chair coord. group energy law 1989—92, chair coord. group energy law 1995—97, chair standing com. environ. law 1997—2000, mem. bd. editors ABA jour., Gavel Awards selection com.); mem.: Internat. Bar Assn., Am. Law Inst., Fed. Energy Bar Assn. (pres. 1991—92), Oil and Gas Ednl. Inst., Southwestern Legal Found. (trustee), Colo. Bar Assn., D.C. Bar Assn., Comml. Bar of England and Wales (hon.)), Women's Bar Assn. D.C., John Carroll Soc., Nat. Press Club, Cosmos Club, George Washington U. Club. Roman Catholic. Administrative and regulatory, FERC practice, Environmental. Office: Duane Morris & Heckscher LLP 1667 K St NW Ste 700 Washington DC 20006-1608 E-mail: sshollis@duanemorris.com

HOLLOWAY, DONALD PHILLIP, lawyer; b. Akron, Ohio, Feb. 18, 1928; s. Harold Shane and Dorothy Gayle (Ryder) H. BS in Commerce, Ohio U., Athens, 1950; JD, U. Akron, 1955; MA, Kent State U., 1962. Bar: Ohio 1955. Title examiner Bankers Guarantee Title & Trust Co., Akron, 1950-54; acct. Robinson Clay Product Co., 1955-60; libr. Akron-Summit Pub. Libr., 1962-69, head fine arts and music divsn., 1969-71, sr. libr., 1972-82; pvt. practice Akron, 1982—. Payroll treas. Akron Symphony Orch., 1957-61; treas. Friends Libr. Akron and Summit County, 1970-72. Mem. ABA, ALA, Ohio Bar Assn., Akron Bar Assn., Ohio Libr. Assn., Nat. Trust Hist. Preservation, Music Libr. Assn., Soc. Archtl. Historians, Coll. Art Assn., Art Librs. N.Am., Akron City Club, North Coast Soc. Republican. Episcopalian. Avocations: art and architecture, music, travel. Probate. Home: 601 Nome Ave Akron OH 44320-1682 Address: 293 Delaware Pl Akron OH 44303-1275

HOLLOWAY, GORDON ARTHUR, lawyer; b. Wichita, Kans., July 27, 1938; s. George Arthur and Margurite (Bondurant) H.; m. Carol H. Criss, Sept. 1, 1960; children: Gregory Arthur, Suzanne Criss, Garrett Austin. BBA, U. Tex., 1960, JD, 1963. Bar: Tex. 1963, Colo. 1993. Assoc. McGregor, Sewell, Junell & Riggs, Houston, 1963-71; ptnr. Sewell and Riggs, 1971-93, Holloway & Rowley, 1994—. Staff sgt. Air N.G., 1964-71. Mem. Am. Bd. Trial Advocates (diplomate), Nat. Assn. Railroad Trial Counsel, Internat. Assn. Defense Counsel, Tex. Bd. Legal Specialization (cert. personal injury, civil trial law, qualified atty.-mediator), Houston Club, Intertel. General civil litigation, Personal injury, Product liability. Office: Holloway & Rowley P C 1415 Louisiana St Ste 2550 Houston TX 77002-7378 E-mail: gordon_holloway@hotmail.com

HOLLOWAY, WILLIAM JUDSON, JR. federal judge; b. 1923; AB, U. Okla., 1947; LLB, Harvard U., 1950; LLD (hon.), Oklahoma City U., 1991. Ptnr. Holloway & Holloway, Oklahoma City, 1950-51; atty. Dept. Justice, Washington, 1951-52; assoc., ptnr. Crowe and Dunlevy, Oklahoma City, 1952-68; judge U.S. Ct. Appeals (10th cir.), 1968-84, chief judge, 1984-91, sr. judge, 1992—. Mem. ABA, Fed. Bar Assn., Okla. Bar Assn., Oklahoma County Bar Assn. Office: US Ct Appeals 10th Cir PO Box 1767 Oklahoma City OK 73101-1767

HOLLRAH, DAVID, lawyer; b. Norman, Okla., June 8, 1948; s. Victor and Dorothy E. (Friedland) H.; children: Kendall, Lauren. Student U. Heidelberg, Ger., 1969; B.A., U. Tex., 1970; postgrad. U. Tuebingen, Fed. Republic Germany, 1970-71; J.D., Harvard U., 1974. Bar: N.Y. 1975, Tex. 1977. Assoc. firm Briger & Assocs., N.Y.C., 1974-76, firm Butler & Binion, Houston, 1976-81; mng. ptnr. firm Hollrah, Lange & Thoma, Houston, 1981-92; dir. Morris, Lendais, Hollrah & Brown, Houston, 1992—. Editor-in-chief Harvard Internat. Law Jour., 1974. Mem. State Bar Tex., ABA. Lutheran. Contracts commercial, General corporate, Private international. Home: 4417 Acacia St Bellaire TX 77401-4301

HOLLYER, A(RTHUR) RENE, lawyer; b. Wycoff, N.J., July 28, 1938; s. Richard W. and Florence (Vervaet) H.; m. Lauraine Dennis, Apr. 8, 1978; children: James Richard, Jennifer Ashley. BA, Williams Coll., 1961; MPA, Woodrow Wilson Sch., Princeton, 1963; LLB, Columbia U., 1966. Bar: N.J. 1966, U.S. Dist. Ct. N.J. 1966, N.Y. 1968, U.S. Dist. Ct. (so. and ea. dists.) N.Y. 1969, U.S. Ct. Appeals (3rd cir.) 1970, U.S. Ct. Appeals (2d cir.) 1971, D.C. 1972, U.S. Supreme Ct. 1974. Law sec. to judge chancery divsn. N.J. Superior Ct., Newark, 1966-67; assoc. Olwine, Connelly, Chase, O'Donnell & Weyher, N.Y.C., 1968-70, 72-74; asst. U.S. atty. Dist. N.J., 1970-71; ptnr. Hollyer, Brady, Smith & Hines, L.L.P. and predecessor firms, N.Y.C., 1974—. Mem.: N.Y. State Bar Assn. (chair spl. com. on procedures for judicial discipline 2001—), Assn. of Bar of City of N.Y. (profl. discipline com. 1990—92, profl. discipline com. 1995—98, profl. discipline com. 2001—, chmn. complaint mediation panel 1991—92, ethics com. 1992—95, profl. responsibility com. 1998—2001). Federal civil litigation, State civil litigation, General practice. Home: 50 Hamilton Rd Glen Ridge NJ 07028-1109 Office: Hollyer Brady Smith & Hines LLP 551 5th Ave New York NY 10176-0001 E-mail: arh-esq@worldnet.att.net

HOLLYFIELD, JOHN SCOGGINS, lawyer; b. Harlingen, Tex., Aug. 20, 1939; m. Penny Pounds, Dec. 27, 1962; children: Jon Scott, Courtney. Bar: Tex. 1968. Assoc. Fulbright & Jaworski, Houston, 1968-75, ptnr., 1975—. Lt. USNR, 1961-65. Recipient Pres.'s award Houston Bar Assn., 1986. Mem. ABA (coun. real property sect. 1986-93, sec. 1993-94, vice chair real property divsn. 1994-96, chair elect 1996-97, chair 1997-98, ho. of dels. 1999—), Am. Coll. Real Estate Lawyers (pres. 1990-91), Anglo-Am. Real Property Inst. (chair 2001). Contracts commercial, Landlord-tenant, Real property. Office: Fulbright & Jaworski LLP 1301 Mckinney St Houston TX 77010-3031 E-mail: jhollyfield@fulbright.com

HOLMAN, BUD GEORGE, lawyer; b. N.Y.C., June 30, 1929; s. Harry and Fannie Abrams (Bass) H.; m. Kathleen Barbara McLean, Sept. 1, 1961; children: Jennifer Jean, Wayne George. BBA, CCNY, 1950; LLB, Yale U., 1956. Bar: N.Y. 1956, Conn. 1979, D.C. 1982. Law sec. to judge N.Y. Ct. Appeals, 1956-58; practice in N.Y.C., 1958—; ptnr. Kelley Drye & Warren (and predecessor firms), 1965—. Pres., chmn. bd. dirs. Sixty Sutton Corp., 1969-97; lectr. Practising Law Inst., Wage Price Inst., Young Pres. Orgn. Editor: The Bar, 1949-50, Yale Law Jour., 1955-56. Trustee U.S. Naval Acad. Found., 1978-85; bd. dirs. USO Met. N.Y. Mem. Naval Res. Assn. (pres. 3d naval dist. chpts. 1973-75, mem. nat. adv. coun. 1975-94), Am. Arbitration Assn. (bd. dirs., mem. exec. com.), Navy League (bd. dirs. coun. N.Y. chpt. 1979-99), Yale U. Law Sch. Assn. (mem. exec. com. 1987-90, 93-96, bd. dirs.), Yale Law Sch. Assn. N.Y.C. (bd. dirs.), Met. Club, Yale Club, Beta Gamma Sigma. Democrat. Presbyterian. Antitrust, General civil litigation, Product liability. Home: 350 Park Ave Box 978 Mattituck NY 11952 Office: Kelley Drye & Warren LLP 101 Park Ave New York NY 10178-0002 E-mail: bholman@kelleydrye.com, holmanbg@aol.com

HOLMAN, JOHN CLARKE, lawyer; b. Milw., Apr. 19, 1938; s. John Abner and Myrtle Vivian (Salter) H.; m. Jeanne Riba, Sept. 2, 1960 (div.1971); children: Lee Anne, Melaney Anne; m. Anne Elizabeth Wooster, Apr. 28, 1973; 1 child, Elizabeth Anne. BS, U. Wis., 1961; JD, Am. U., 1965; postgrad., Holborn Coll. Law, London, 1965-67. Bar: U.S. Dist. Ct. D.C. 1966, U.S. Ct. Appeals (D.C. and fed. cirs.) 1968, U.S. Supreme Ct. 1972. Examiner U.S. Patent Office, Washington, 1961-65; expert intellectual property Marks & Clerk, London, England, 1965-67; ptnr. Holman & Stern, Washington, 1967-77; pres. Holman & Stern, Chartered, 1977-89; ptnr. Fleit Jacobson Cohn Price Holman & Stern, 1989-92, Jacobson Holman PLLC, Washington, 1992—. Author: U.S. Patent Law, 1971. Mem. ABA, Licensing Execs. Soc., Assn. Internat. Patent Law Attys., Am. Inst. Mining Engrs., Internat. Fed. Indsl. Property Attys., Interam. Assn. Indsl. Property, Am. Intellectual Patent Law Assn., Internat. Assn. Protection Indsl. Property, U.S. Trademark Assn., Am. Soc. for Metals. Republican. Episcopalian. Patent, Trademark and copyright. Office: 400 7th St NW Ste 600 Washington DC 20004-2232 Fax: 202-393-5350. E-mail: JHOLMAN@JHIP.com

HOLMAN, KRISTINA SUE, lawyer; b. Seattle, Mar. 3, 1958; d. Carl Viking and Vernelda Clairefern (Leeb) Holman; m. Mark T. Hoepfner, Oct. 8, 1983; children: Matthew, Alicia. BS in Biology, Seattle U., 1980, JD, 1984. Bar: Minn. 1985, U.S. Dist. Ct. Minn. 1986, Nev. 1989, U.S. Dist. Ct. Nev. 1990, U.S. Ct. Appeals (9th cir.) 1998. Assoc. Gartner Shulman & Erwin, Rochester, Minn., 1985-88, Alverson Taylor Mortensen & Nelson, Las Vegas, Nev., 1989-90, Combs & England, Las Vegas, 1990-94; pvt. practice, 1994—. Appt. alt. panelist Nev. State Bar Disciplinary Panel, 1997. Contbr. articles to profl. jours. Bd. dirs. Nev. Disability Advocacy and Law Ctr. Mem. ABA, AAUW, ATLA, NAFE, Nat. Employment Lawyers Assn., Nev. Trial Lawyers Am., Nev. Bar Assn., So. Nev. Assn. Women Attys., Clark County Bar Assn., Alpha Sigma Nu. Roman Catholic. Avocations: gardening, reading. Civil rights, General civil litigation, Labor. Office: Kummer Kaempfer Bonner & Renshaw 3800 Howard Hughes Pkwy 7th Fl Las Vegas NV 89109

HOLME, JOHN CHARLES, JR. lawyer; b. N.Y.C., Aug. 3, 1940; s. John Charles and Anne Robinson (Mackey) H.; m. Diane Louise Stover, July 24, 1965; children: Christopher Scott, Jennifer Anne. Student Washington Coll., 1958-60; BA, U. Vt., 1962; LLB, Cornell U., 1965. Bar: N.Y. 1966, U.S. Dist. Ct. (we. dist.) N.Y. 1966, Ohio 1974, U.S. Dist. Ct. (no. dist.) Ohio 1974, U.S. Ct. Appeals 1979, Vt. 1982, U.S. Dist. Ct. Vt. 1983. Assoc. Dutcher, Witt, Sidoti & Considine, Rochester, 1966-69; assoc. Antell Harris, Githler & Calleri, Rochester, 1968-69; trust adminstr. Marine Midland Bank, Rochester, 1969-70, asst. trust officer, 1970-73, trust officer, 1973-74; staff atty. Advocates for Basic Legal Equality, Toledo, 1974-82; assoc. William E. Dakin, Jr., Chester, Vt., 1982-83; v.p., sec. Dakin & Holme, P.C., Chester, 1984-90; atty. pvt. practice, Chester, Vt., 1990-97, Springfield, Vt., 1997—. Mem. ABA, Am. Inn of Ct. (sec.-treas. 1994—), Vt. Bar Assn., Vt. Bar Found. (bd. dirs. 1995—, pres. 1996-97), Vt. Trial Lawyers Assn. (bd. govs. 1987—, treas. 1995—), Assn. Trial Lawyers Am., Rotary (Chester pres. 1997—). Democrat. Mem. United Ch. of Christ. State civil litigation, General practice, Real property. Home: PO Box 474 Chester VT 05143-0474

HOLMES, DALLAS SCOTT, lawyer, educator; b. L.A., Dec. 2, 1940; s. Donald Cherry and Hazel (Scott) H.; m. Patricia McMichael, Aug. 21, 1965; children: Mark Scott, Tobin John. AB cum laude, Pomona Coll., 1962; MS, London Sch. Econs., 1964; JD, U. Calif., Berkeley, 1967. Bar: Calif. 1968. Assoc. Best, Best & Krieger, Riverside, Calif., 1968-74, ptnr., 1974-96; mem. Calif. Jud. Coun., 1995-96; adj. prof. Hastings Coll. Law U. Calif., San Francisco, 1990; exec. asst. to Assembly majority fl. leader, Calif. State Legislature, Sacramento, 1969-70; asst. adj. prof. Grad. Sch. Mgmt., U. Calif.-Riverside, 1977-88; lectr. UCLA Extension, 1987—; Superior Ct. judge, 1996—; chair Riverside Superior Ct. Jury Com., 1997—; chair Calif. jud. coun. task force jury sys. improvements, 1998—; city atty. City of Corona, Calif., 1976-96; lectr. local govt. and univ. extension groups. Pres., Pomona Coll. Alumni Coun., 1973-74, Century Club, Riverside, 1974-76, Citizens Univ. Com., 1983-85, Downtown Riverside Assn., 1987-88; chmn. legal affairs com. Assn. Calif. Water Agys., 1985-91. Mem. bd. govs. State Bar Calif., 1990-93, v.p. 1992-93. Named Man of Yr., Riverside Press-Enterprise, 1962, Young Man of Yr., Riverside Jr. C. of C., 1972. Mem. Riverside County Bar Assn. (pres. 1982), Calif. State Bar Assn. (exec. com. pub. law sect. 1983-86), Am. Judicature Soc. Republican. Presbyterian. Contbr. articles on mass transit, assessment of farmland in Calif., exclusionary zoning and environ. law to profl. jours.; author proposed tort reform initiative for Calif. physicians. E-mail: dhomes1@co.riverside.ca.us. Office: Ct Ho 4050 Main St Riverside CA 92501-3702

HOLMES, JAMES HILL, III, lawyer; b. Birmingham, Ala., Sept. 10, 1935; s. Houston Eccleston and Celia Lindsey (Wearn) H.; m. Julia (Judy) Ryman, Aug. 17, 1963; children: James H. IV, Randell Ryman, Tucker Malone. BBA, So. Meth. U., 1957, LLB, 1959. Bar: Tex. 1959, U.S. Dist. Ct. (no. dist.) Tex. 1963, U.S. Dist. Ct. (ea. dist.) Tex. 1966, U.S. Dist. Ct. (we. dist.) Tex. 1979, U.S. Ct. Appeals (5th and 11th cirs.) 1981, U.S. Ct. Mil. Appeals 1960, U.S. Supreme Ct. 1974. Ptnr. Burford & Ryburn, Dallas, 1962—. Spkr. State Bar Tex. Profl. Devel. Program, 1987-93; mock trial participant Tex. Nurses Assn., 1978-86; co-chair Supreme Ct. Adv. Com. on Professionalism for Supreme Ct. Tex., 1989-90. Contbr. articles to profl. jours. Past mem. University Park (Tex.) Bd. Adjustment; chmn. University Park Planning and Zoning Commn., 1988-94; city councilman City of University Park, 1994-2000, mayor pro tem, 1998-2000; past. dir. Child Guidance Clinic; past dir., pres. All Sports Assn., Dallas, 1977; pres. University Park Cmty. League, 1987-88; past bd. dirs. Park Cities Town North YMCA; numerous other offices in civic orgns.; trustee, bd. trustees Tex. Ctr. Legal Ethics & Professionalism, 2001—; vice chmn. Adminstrv. Tex. Ctr. Legal Ethics & Professionalism, 2001—. With USAF, 1959-62. Recipient Presdl. Citation, State Bar of Tex., 1995, Judge Sam Williams Local Bar Leadership award, Professionalism award, Coll. of the State Bar Tex., 1999, Morris Harrell Professionalism award, Dallas Bar Assn. and Tex. Ctr. for Ethics and Professionalism, 2000. Fellow: Am. Coll. Trial Lawyers, Tex. Bar Found. (judge Sam Williams Local Bar Leadership Award 2001); mem.: ABA, Dallas Assn. Def. Counsel (chmn. 1975), Tex. Assn. Def. Counsel (pres. 1992—93, Founder's award 1997), Assn. Def. Trial Attys., Internat. Assn. Def. Counsel, Def. Rsch. Inst., Dallas Bar Assn. (numerous offices and coms.), Tex. Bar Assn., Am. Bd. Trial Advocates (sec.ptreas, pres.-elect Dallas chpt. 1999, pres. Dalls chpt. 2000), Patrick E. Higginbotham Am. Inn of Ct. (master 1989—95), Blue Key, Phi Alpha Delta, Phi Delta Theta. Episcopalian. Avocations: jogging, spectator sports, outdoors. General civil litigation, Personal injury, Product liability. Home: 3804 Lovers Ln Dallas TX 75225-7101 Office: Burford & Ryburn LLP 3100 Lincoln Pla 500 N Akard St Ste 3100 Dallas TX 75201-6697

HOLMES, JENANNE NELSON, lawyer; b. Evanston, Ill.; d. Oscar William and Anne L. (Moll) Nelson. B.S. magna cum laude, U. So. Calif., 1967, J.D., 1976. Admitted to D.C. bar, 1977, Calif. bar, 1983; sec., corp. officer Sta. KUPD-AM-FM, Phoenix, 1959-61; media dir. West, Weir & Bartel, Los Angeles, 1962-65; asso. media dir. Eisaman, Johns & Laws, Los Angeles, 1966-68; media supr. Ogilvy & Mathers, N.Y.C., 1968-69; v.p. media and mktg. services Smith-Gent Advt. Co., N.Y.C., 1969-71; media supr. The Media Dept., N.Y.C., 1971-72; v.p. media Perkal Advt. Co., Los Angeles, 1972-74; research asst. U. So. Calif. Law Center, 1975-76; atty. advisor FCC, Washington, 1977-80; gen. atty. U.S. Dept. Energy, 1980-88; supervisory hearing officer USDA Farmers Home Adminstrn., Memphis, 1988—; pro bono atty. Friends of Animals, N.Y.C.

Mem. ABA, Calif. Bar Assn., D.C. Bar Assn., Fed. Bar Assn., Los Angeles Advt. Women, U. So. Calif. Alumni, Presbyterian. Mensa, Cactus and Succulent Soc., Sierra Club, North Shore Animal League, Phi Beta Kappa, Beta Gamma Sigma. Office: Farmers Home Adminstrn Nat Appeals Staff 7777 Walnut Grove Rd Memphis TN 38120-2130

HOLMES, MICHAEL GENE, lawyer; b. Longview, Wash., Jan. 14, 1937; s. Robert A. and Esther S. Holmes; children: Helen, Peyton Robert. AB in Econs., Stanford U., 1958, JD, 1960. Bar: Oreg. 1961, U.S. Dist. Ct. Oreg. 1961, U.S. Ct. Appeals (9th cir.) 1961, Temp. Emergency Ct. Appeals 1976, U.S. Supreme Ct. 1976. Assoc. Spears, Lubersky, Bledsoe, Anderson, Young & Hilliard, Portland, 1961-67, ptnr., 1967-90, Lane Powell Spears Lubersky, Portland, 1990-95, of counsel, 1995. Mem. Oreg. Joint Com. of Bar, Press & Broadcasters, 1982-85, sec., 1983-84, chmn. 1985. Author Survey of Oregon Defamation and Privacy Law, ann., 1982-95. Trustee Med. Rsch. Found. Oreg., Portland, 1985-94, exec. com., 1986-94; hon. trustee Oreg. Health Scis. Found., 1995—; trustee Portland Civic Theatre, 1962-66. Mem. Oreg. Bar Assn., Phi Beta Kappa. Administrative and regulatory, General civil litigation, Labor.

HOLMES, ROBERT ALLEN, lawyer, educator, consultant, lecturer; b. Sewickley, Pa., Dec. 12, 1947; s. Lee Roy John and Nellie Ann (Kupits) H.; div.; children: Wesley Paige, Ashley Reagan. BA in Bus. Adminstrn., Coll. William and Mary, 1969, JD, 1972. Bar: Md. 1972, U.S. Dist. Ct. Md. 1972, Va. 1973, U.S. Dist. Ct. (ea. dist.) Va. 1973, U.S. Dist. Ct. (no. dist.) Ohio 1988, U.S. Ct. Appeals (6th cir.) 1988. Assoc. Ober, Grimes & Shriver, Balt., 1972-73, Kellam, Pickrell & Lawler, Norfolk, Va., 1973-75; ptnr. Holliday, Holmes & Inman, 1975-77; asst. prof. law Bowling Green State U., Ohio, 1977-82, assoc. prof., 1982-2001. Dir. Purchasing Law Inst., 1979—, EEO-Affirmative Action Rsch. Group, 1978—; lectr. in field. Author: (with others) Computers, Data Processing and the Law, 1984; numerous manuals on discrimination and affirmative action law, corp. purchasing law and internat. bus. law; contbg. editor, monthly columnist Midwest Purchasing, 1983-84. Recipient Outstanding Young Man award William and Mary Soc. Alumni, 1973. Mem. Md. Bar Assn., Va. Bar Assn., Am. Bus. Law Assn., Am. Soc. Pers. Adminstrs., Nat. Assn. Purchasing Mgmt., Mensa. Republican. Home: 1030 Conneaut Ave Bowling Green OH 43402-2118

HOLMSTEAD, JEFFREY RALPH, lawyer; b. American Fork, Utah, June 20, 1960; s. R. Kay and Mary L. (Gillison) H.; m. Elizabeth Tisdel, Aug. 17, 1985; children: Emily Kay, Eric Noble, Elizabeth Anne, Eli Jeffrey. BA, Brigham Young U., 1984; JD, Yale U., 1987. Bar: Pa. 1988, D.C. 1998. Jud. clk. to Hon. Douglas H. Ginsburg D.C. Cir. Ct. Appeals, Washington, 1987-88; assoc. Davis Polk & Wardwell, 1988-89; asst. counsel to Pres. of U.S. The White House, 1989-90, assoc. counsel, 1990-93; assoc. Latham & Watkins, 1993-95, ptnr., 1996—. Republican. Mem. LDS Ch. Administrative and regulatory, Environmental. Office: Latham & Watkins 4De 1300 555 11th St NW Ste 1000 Washington DC 20004-1304

HOLSCHUH, JOHN DAVID, JR. lawyer; b. Columbus, Ohio, Dec. 21, 1955; s. John D. and Carol Elouise (Stouder) H.; m. Wendy G. Ellis, Sept. 22, 1984; children: Heather Elyse, John David III, Jacob Alexander. BS, Miami U., Oxford, Ohio, 1977; JD, U. Cin., 1980. Bar: Ohio 1980, U.S. Dist. Ct. (so. dist.) Ohio 1980, U.S. Ct. Appeals (6th cir.) 1986, U.S. Supreme Ct. 1986, U.S. Dist. Ct. (ea. dist.) Ky. 1987, Ky. 1991. Assoc. Santen, Shaffer & Hughes, Cin., 1980-87, ptnr., 1987-89, Santen & Hughes, Cin., 1989—. Pros. atty. City of Loveland, Ohio, 1987-92, magistrate, 1992—; magistrate Village of Fairfax, Ohio, 1999—; mem. faculty Nat. Inst. Trial Advocacy, 1990, 91, 96; participant Pretrial Civil Litigation Skills Workshop, 1991. Author: Medical Malpractice, 1986, Tort Reform Pleading, 1987, Civil Procedure, 1986, rev. edit., 1989, Damages for Plaintiff and Defense Attorneys in Ohio, 1990, 2d edit., 1991, Tort Reform Update, 1990. Recipient merit award Ohio Legal Ctr. Inst., 1986. Mem.: ATLA, Am. Bd. Trial Advs., Ohio Acad. Trial Lawyers (trustee 1991—95, trustee 1998—2000), Ohio State Bar Assn., Hamilton County Trial Lawyers (pres. 1990—92), Cin. Bar Assn. (chmn. common pleas ct. 1991—93, trustee 1995—, sec. 1999—2000, v.p. 2000—, pres.-elect 2001—, co-chmn. bench-bar conf. 1997—98), Cin. Bar Found. (trustee 2001—), 6th Cir. Jud. Conf. (life; del. 1983—88), Potter Stewart Inns of Ct. (emeritus mem.), Order of Barristers. Avocations: sports, travel. Federal civil litigation, General civil litigation, Personal injury. Office: Santen & Hughes 312 Walnut St Ste 3100 Cincinnati OH 45202-4044

HOLSCHUH, JOHN DAVID, federal judge; b. Ironton, Ohio, Oct. 12, 1926; s. Edward A. and Helen (Ebert) H.; m. Carol Eloise Stouder, May 25, 1952; 1 child, John David Jr. BA, Miami U., 1948; JD, U. Cin., 1951. Bar: Ohio 1951, U.S. Dist. Ct. (so. dist.) Ohio 1952, U.S. Ct. Appeals (6th cir.) 1953, U.S. Supreme Ct. 1956. Atty. McNamara & McNamara, Columbus, Ohio, 1951-52, 54; law clk. to Hon. Mell. G. Underwood U.S. Dist. Ct., 1952-54; ptnr. Alexander, Ebinger, Holschuh, Fisher & McAlister, Ohio, 1954-80; judge U.S. Dist. Ct. (so. dist.) Ohio, 1980—, chief judge, 1990-96. Adj. prof. law Ohio State U. Coll. Law, 1970; mem. com. on codes of conduct Jud. Conf. U.S., 1985-90. Pres. bd. dirs. Neighborhood House, Columbus, 1969-70; active United Way of Franklin County, Columbus. Fellow Am. Coll. Trial Lawyers; mem. Order of Coif, Phi Beta Kappa, Omicron Delta Kappa. Office: US Courthouse 85 Marconi Blvd Columbus OH 43215 also: US Dist Ct 109 US Courthouse 85 Marconi Blvd Rm 109 Columbus OH 43215-2823

HOLSINGER, CANDICE DOREEN, lawyer; b. Pitts., June 9, 1955; d. Edward P. and Myrtle-Jane (Atwood) H.; m. Barry Alan McClune, Nov. 23, 1984. BA, Westminster Coll., 1977; JD, Duquesue U., 1981. Bar: Pa., U.S. Dist. Ct. (we. dist.) Pa., U.S. Supreme Ct. Law clk. Child Advocacy Assn., Pitts., 1981; assoc. Tarasi & Tyle, 1982-84, Metz, Cook, Hanna, Welsh Bluestone & Beamer, Pitts., 1984-87, Hyatt Legal Svcs., Pitts., 1987-94, Karlowitz & Cromer, 1994; pvt. practice Wilmerding, 1994—97; assoc. Kramer Thompson & Assoc, Pitts., 1997—. With H&R Block, 1997. Mem.: Allegheny County Bar Assn. State civil litigation, General practice. Home: 225 Welsh Ave Wilmerding PA 15148-1216 Office: Kramer Thompson & Assoc Acacia Bldg 875 Greentree Rd Ste 204 Pittsburgh PA 15220

HOLSTEIN, JOHN CHARLES, state supreme court judge; b. Springfield, Mo., Jan. 10, 1945; s. Clyde E. Jr. and Wanda R. (Polson) H.; m. Mary Frances Brummell, Mar. 26, 1967; children: Robin Diane Camacho, Mary Katherine Link, Erin Elizabeth Lary. BA, S.W. Mo. State Coll., 1967; JD, U. Mo., 1970; LLM, U. Va., 1995. Bar: Mo. 1970. Atty. Moore & Brill, West Plains, Mo., 1970-75; probate judge Howell County, 1975-78, assoc. cir. judge, 1978-82; cir. judge 37th Jud. Cir., 1982-87; judge so. dist. Mo. Ct. Appeals, Springfield, 1987-88, chief judge so. dist., 1988-89; judge Supreme Ct. Mo., Jefferson City, 1989—, chief justice, 1995-97. Instr. bus. law S.W. Mo. State Coll., 1976-77, pub. sch. law S.W. Bapt. U., 1999-2000. Lt. col. USAR, 1969-87. Office: Supreme Ct Mo PO Box 150 Jefferson City MO 65102-0150

HOLT, MARJORIE SEWELL, lawyer, retired congresswoman; b. Birmingham, Ala., Sept. 17, 1920; d. Edward Rol and Juanita (Felts) Sewell; m. Duncan McKay Holt, Dec. 26, 1946; children: Rachel Holt Tschantre, Edward Sewell, Victoria. Grad., Jacksonville Jr. Coll., 1945; JD, U. Fla., 1949. Bar: Fla. 1949, Md. 1962. Pvt. practice, Annapolis, Md., 1962; clk. Anne Arundel County Circuit Ct., 1966-72; mem. 93d-99th Congresses from 4th Dist. of Md., 1973-86; armed services com., vice chair Office Tech. Assessment, 1977; chair Republican Study com., 1975-76; of counsel Smith, Somerville & Case, Balt., 1986-90. Supr. elections Anne Arundel County, 1963-65; del. Rep. Nat. Conv., 1968, 76, 80, 84, 88; mem. Pres.'s Commn. on Arms Control and Disarmament; mem. ind. commn. USAR; bd. dirs. Annapolis Fed. Savs. Bank; adv. bd. Crestar; co-chair George W. Bush Presdl. campaign, Md., 2000. Co-author: Case Against The Reckless Congress, 1976, Can You Afford This House, 1978. Bd. dirs. Md. Sch. for the Blind, Hist. Annapolis Found. Recipient Disting. Alumna award U. Fla., 1975, Trustees award U. Fla. Coll. Law, 1984, Alumnae Outstanding Achievement award, 1997. Mem. ABA, Md. Bar Assn., Anne Arundel Bar Assn., Phi Kappa Phi, Phi Delta Delta. Presbyterian (elder 1959).

HOLT, MICHAEL BARTHOLOMEW, lawyer; b. Jersey City, July 10, 1956; s. William A. and Grace (Donohue) H.; m. Mary Patricia Butler, Aug. 14, 1982; children: Melissa Aislynn, Scott Michael, Eric Michael. BA magna cum laude, Providence Coll., 1978; JD, Seton Hall U., 1982. Bar: N.J. 1982, U.S. Dist. Ct. N.J. 1982, U.S. Dist. Ct. (ea. and so. dists.) N.Y. 1985, U.S. Ct. Appeals (3d cir.) 1985, U.S. Supreme Ct. 1986, N.Y. 1990. Assoc. Keane, Brady & Hanlon, Jersey City, 1982-84, Waters, McPherson, McNeill P.A., Secaucus, N.J., 1984-87; ptnr. O'Halloran, Holt and Assocs., Bayonne, 1987-89, Carroll & Holt, Secaucus, 1989-91; pvt. practice, 1991-95; corp. counsel NYK Lines (N.Am.) Inc., 1995—. Mem. N.Y. State Bar Assn. (corp. counsel com.). General corporate, General practice, Transportation. Home: 26 Oak Crest Pl Nutley NJ 07110-1516 Office: NYK Line Inc 300 Lighting Way Secaucus NJ 07094-3679 E-mail: mholt81176@aol.com

HOLT, PHILETUS HAVENS, IV, lawyer, consultant; b. Akron, Ohio, Aug. 12, 1936; s. Philetus Havens and Ottilia Dolina (Nichols) H.; B.A., Yale U., 1958, LL.B., 1961; m. Kathy Ann Kuryla, Dec. 2, 1978; children— Elizabeth Hopkins, Stephen. Admitted to Conn. bar, 1962; asso. Durey & Pierson, Stamford, Conn., 1962-64; dep. counsel, dir. downtown projects New Haven Redevel. Agy., 1964-69; partner Cogen Holt & Assos., cons., New Haven, 1969-76; spl. asst. to pres. Yale-New Haven Med. Center, 1976— ; acting pres., 1978-79; partner Holt Wexler & Crawford, New Haven, 1976— ; trustee Conn. Savs. Bank, New Haven, 1971— ; asso. fellow Jonathan Edwards Coll., Yale U., 1968. Bd. dirs. Shubert Performing Arts Ctr., New Haven Preservation Trust. Clubs: New Haven Yacht, New Haven Lawn, Mory's Assn. Home: 39 Wooster Pl New Haven CT 06511-6932 Office: 900 Chapel St New Haven CT 06510-2802

HOLTKAMP, JAMES ARNOLD, lawyer, educator; b. Albuquerque, Apr. 4, 1949; s. Clarence Jules and Karyl Irene (Roberts) H.; m. Marianne Coltrin, Dec. 28, 1973; children: Ariane, Brent William, Rachel, Allison, David Roberts. BA, Brigham Young U., 1972; JD, George Washington U., 1975. Bar: Utah 1976, U.S. Dist. Ct. Utah 1977, U.S. Ct. Appeals (10th cir.) 1979, Colo. 1995. Mem. staff U.S. Senate Watergate Com., Washington, 1974; atty.-advisor Dept. Transp., 1975; atty. Dept. Interior, 1975-77; assoc. Van Cott, Bagley, Cornwall & McCarthy, Salt Lake City, 1977-81, ptnr., 1981-89, Davis, Graham & Stubbs, Salt Lake City, 1989-92, Stoel Rives, Salt Lake City, 1992-97, LeBoeuf, Lamb, Greene & MacRae, Salt Lake City, 1997—. Adj. prof. Law Sch., Brigham Young U., Provo, Utah, 1979—, Coll. Law U. Utah, 1995—. Co-author: Utah Environmental and Land Use Permits and Approvals Manual, 1981; contbr. articles to legal jours. Missionary LDS Ch., 1968-70; active Gt. Salt Lake coun. Boy Scouts Am., 1977—; trustee Coalition for Utah's Future, 1996—. Mem. ABA (vice-chmn. air quality commn. 1985-89), Utah State Bar (chmn. energy and natural resources sect. 1984-85, chmn. pub. utilities law com. 1990-93, Lawyer of Yr. award 1981), Utah Mining Assn. (bd. dirs. 1999—), Rocky Mtn. Mineral Law Found. (trustee 1999—), Utah Petroleum Assn., George Washington Law Assn. (nat. bd. dirs. 1999—). Environmental, Legislative, Public utilities. Home: 7990 Deer Creek Rd Salt Lake City UT 84121-5752 Office: LeBoeuf Lamb Greene & MacRae 136 S Main St Ste 1000 Salt Lake City UT 84101-1685

HOLTON, WALTER CLINTON, JR. lawyer; b. Winston-Salem, N.C. s. Walter Clinton and Mabel (Hartsfield) H.; m. Lynne Rowley. BA in Polit. Sci., U. N.C., 1977; JD, Wake Forest U., 1984. Bar: N.C. 1984, U.S. Dist. Ct. (mid. dist.) N.C. 1986, U.S. Ct. Appeals (4th cir.) 1990, U.S. Supreme Ct., 1996. Asst. dist. atty. Office 21st Jud. Dist. Atty., Winston-Salem, 1985-87; assoc. White & Crumpler, 1987-88; pvt. practice, 1989; ptnr. Holton & Menefee, 1989-92, Tisdale, Holton & Menefee, PA, Winston-Salem, 1992-94; U.S. atty. Office U.S. Atty. Mid. Dist. N.C., Greensboro, N.C., 1994-2001; pvt. practice Grace Holton Tisdale & Clifton PA, Winston-Salem, 2001—. Democrat. Office: Grace Holton Tisdale & Clifton 301 N Main St Ste 100 Winston Salem NC 27101 Fax: (336) 721-1176. E-mail: wbolton@gbtclaw.com

HOLTZ, EDGAR WOLFE, lawyer; b. Clarksburg, W.Va., Jan. 18, 1922; s. Dennis Drummond and Oleta (Wolfe) H.; m. Alberta Lee Brinkley, May 6, 1944; children: Diana Hilary, Heidi Johanna. BA, Denison U., 1943; JD, U. Cin., 1949. Bar: Ohio 1949, U.S. Supreme Ct. 1957, D.C. 1961. Assoc. firm Matthews & Matthews, Cin., 1949-53; asst. dean Chase Law Sch., 1952-55; asst. solicitor City of Cin., 1950-55; asst. chief office of opinions and rev. FCC, Washington, 1955-56, dep. gen. counsel, 1956-60; mem. firm Hogan & Hartson, Washington, 1960—. Trustee Denison U., Granville, Ohio, 1974—: chmn. bd. Ctr. for the Arts, Vero Beach, Fla., 1995-97; bd. dirs. Cultural Coun. Indian River County, 1998—, chmn. 2000-01; bd. dirs. McKee Bot. Garden, 2001. Served to 1st lt. USAAF, 1943-45. Decorated D.F.C., Air medal with 2 clusters, 8 Battle Stars; recipient Alumni citation Denison U., 1993. Fellow Am. Bar Found.; mem. ABA (standing com. on gavel awards), Ohio Bar Assn., D.C. Bar Assn., Fed. Comms. Bar (pres. 1977-78), Am. Juicature Soc., Newcomen Soc. N.Am., Moorings Club (Vero Beach, Fla.), Met. Club (Washington, George Town Club (Washington). Republican. Methodist. Administrative and regulatory, Communications, General corporate. Office: Hogan & Hartson 555 13th St NW Ste 800E Washington DC 20004-1161

HOLTZMANN, HOWARD MARSHALL, lawyer, judge; b. N.Y.C., Dec. 10, 1921; s. Jacob L. And Lillian (Plotz) H.; m. Anne Fisher, Jan. 14, 1945 (dec. Aug. 1967); children: Susan Holtzmann Richardson, Betsey; m. Carol Ebenstein Van Berg, Dec. 23, 1972 AB, Yale Coll., 1942, JD, 1947; LittD (hon.), St. Bonaventure U., 1952; LLD (hon.), Jewish Theol. Sem., N.Y.C., 1990. Bar: N.Y. 1947. Atty. Colorado Fuel & Iron Corp., Buffalo, 1947-49; ptnr. Holtzmann, Wise & Shepard, N.Y.C., 1949-95; judge Iran-U.S. Claims Tribunal, The Hague, Netherlands, 1981-94; arbitrator and dispute resolution cons., 1994—; arbitrator Claims Resolution Tribunal for Dormant Accounts, Zurich, Switzerland, 1998—. U.S. del. UN Commn. on Internat. Trade Law, 1975—, Hague Conf. on Pvt. Internat. Law, 1985; advisor U.S.A. Arbitration agreements with USSR, Russian Fedn., China, Hungary, Bulgaria, Czechoslovakia, Poland and German Dem. Republic. Author, editor: A New Look at Legal Aspects of Doing Business with China, 1979; co-author: A Guide to the Unicitral Model Law on International Commercial Arbitration—Legislative History and Commentary, 1988 (cert. of merit Am. Soc. Internat. Law 1991); contbr. chpts. to books and articles to law jours. Mem. governing coun. Downstate Med. Sch. SUNY, Bklyn., 1961-78; trustee St. Bonaventure U., Olean, N.Y., 1968-90, trustee emeritus, 1990—; chmn. bd. Jewish Theol. Sem., N.Y.C., 1983-85, hon. chmn., 1985—; trustee Inst. Internat. Law, Pace U. Sch. Law, 1992—. Mem. ABA (chmn. com. code ethics comml. arbitrators 1973-77), Internat. Council for Comml. Arbitration (hon. vice chmn., chmn.), Am. Arbitration Assn. (hon. chmn., adv. bd. Stockholm arbitration Inst., Gotshal Internat. Arbitration award 1980), Internat. C. of C. (vice chmn. arbitration commn. 1979—), Am. Bar Found., N.Y. County Lawyers Assn., Internat. Law Assn., Am. Fgn. Law Assn. (v.p. 1995—), Internat. Bar Assn., N.Y. State Bar Assn., Assn. of Bar of City of N.Y., Am. Soc. Internat. Law (cert. merit 1991), Soc. Profls. in Dispute Resolution, Indsl. Rels. Rsch. Assn., N.Y. Law Inst., Am. Judicature Soc., Am. Assn. for Internat. Commn. of Jurists. General corporate, Private international.

HOLTZSCHUE, KARL BRESSEM, lawyer, author, educator; b. Wichita, Kans., Mar. 3, 1938; s. Bressem C. and Josephine E. (Landsittel) H.; m. Linda J. Gross, Oct. 24, 1959; children: Alison, Adam, Sara. AB, Dartmouth Coll., 1959; LLB, Columbia U., 1966. Bar: N.Y. 1967, U.S. Dist. Ct. (so. and ea. dists.) N.Y. 1968. Assoc. Webster & Sheffield, N.Y.C., 1966-73, ptnr., 1974-88; ptnr., head real estate dept. O'Melveny and Myers, 1988-90; pvt. practice, 1990—. Adj. prof. Fordham U. Law Sch., 1990—; adj. prof. Bus. Sch., Columbia U., 1990-96, Law Sch., 1991. Author: Holtzschue on Real Estate Contracts, 1999, New York Practice Guide: Real Estate, Vol. 1 on Purchase and Sale, 1999, Real Estate Transactions: Purchase and Sale of Real Property, 1999; editor: NYSBA's Res. R.E. Forms on Hot Docs. Trustee Soc. of St. Johnland, 1980-86, Ensemble Studio Theatre, 1986-88; bd. dirs. The Bridge, 1990—, pres., 1992-95; mem. alumni bd. Dartmouth Ptnrs. in Cmty. Svc., 1994—, chmn., 1994-99. Lt. (j.g.) USN, 1959-62. Mem. ABA (com. on internat. investment in real estate 1987-97, com. on legal opinions in real estate trans. 1990—), N.Y. State Bar Assn. (exec. com. real property sect. 1998—, com. on attys. opinions 1992—, com. on title and transfer 1998—, co-chmn. 1998—), Assn. Bar City N.Y. (com. on real property law 1977-80, chmn. 1987-90, 95-98, com. ctrl. and East Europe 1998-99), Am. Coll. Real Estate Lawyers (opinions com. 1989—, vice chmn. 1992-95), Tri Bar (opinions com. 1990-99). Episcopalian. E-mail: karl. Real property. E-mail: holt@msn.com

HOLZ, HARRY GEORGE, lawyer; b. Milw., Sept. 13, 1934; s. Harry Carl and Emma Louise (Hinz) H.; m. Nancy L. Heiser, May 12, 1962; children: Pamela Gretchen, Bradley Eric, Erika Lynn. BS, Marquette U., 1956, LLB, 1958; LLM, Northwestern U., 1960. Bar: Wis. 1958, Ill. 1960. Tchg. fellow Northwestern U. Sch. Law, 1958-59; assoc. Sidley & Austin, Chgo., 1960; ptnr. Quarles & Brady, Milw., 1968—. Lectr. law securities regulation U. Wis. Law Sch., 1971-74; adj. prof., Marquette U. Sch. Law, 1976—; faculty program on antitrust law Wis. State Bar Seminars, 1975-82, 89, 93; lectr., spkr. in field. Bd. visitors Marquette U. Sch. Law, 1990, 93. Capt. C.E. U.S. Army, 1960-67. Mem. ABA (Robinson-Patman com., corp. counsel com., antitrust litigation com.), Wis. Bar Assn. (chmn. dir. bus. law sect. 1978-79, bd. dirs. 1978-83, standing com. bus. law), Milw. Bar Assn., Marquette U. Sch. Law Woolsack Soc. (bd. dirs., pres.), Marquette U. Law Alumni Assn. (bd. dirs.), Western Racquet Club, Beta Gamma Sigma, Phi Delta Phi. Antitrust, General corporate, Mergers and acquisitions. Office: Quarles & Brady 411 E Wisconsin Ave Ste 2550 Milwaukee WI 53202-4497

HOMBURGER, THOMAS CHARLES, lawyer; b. Buffalo, Sept. 16, 1941; s. Adolf and Charolotte E. (Stern) H.; m. Louise Paula Shemin, June 6, 1965; children: Jennifer Anne, Richard Ephraim, Kathryn Lee. BA, Columbia U., 1963, JD, 1966. Bar: Ill. 1966, U.S. Dist. Ct. (no. dist.) Ill. 1966. Assoc., ptnr. Sonnenschein, Carlin, Nath & Rosenthal, Chgo., 1966-86; ptnr., chmn. real estate dept. Bell, Boyd & Lloyd, 1986-2001. Adj. prof. John Marshall Law Sch., Chgo., 1989—. Contbr. articles to profl. jours. Chmn. Chgo. regional bd. Anti-Defamation League, B'nai Brith, 1986-88; chmn. nat. exec. com. Anti-Defamation League, 2000—, Glencoe (Ill.) Bd. Edn., 1984-89; bd. dirs., exec. com. Ill. Ambs. Mem. ABA (real property divsn., probate & trust law sect., fin. subcom.), Ill. Bar Assn. (real property sect.), Chgo. Bar Assn. (chmn. real property law com. 1984-85), Am. Coll. Real Estate Lawyers (bd. govs. 2000—), Law Club Chgo., Chgo. Mortgage Attys. Assn. (pres. 1975-77), Lambda Alpha Internat., Std. Club, Met. Club. General corporate, Landlord-tenant, Real property. Home: 20 East Cedar St Apt 2F Chicago IL 60611-1149 Office: Bell Boyd & Lloyd 70 W Madison St Ste 3300 Chicago IL 60602-4284 E-mail: tc@homburger.cnchost.com, thomburger@bellboyd.com

HOMEIER, MICHAEL GEORGE, lawyer, educator; b. Santa Monica, Calif., Dec. 31, 1958; s. George Vincent Homeier and Nancy Van Noorden Field. BA cum laude, UCLA, 1979; JD, U. So. Calif., 1983. Bar: Calif. 1984, U.S. Dist. Ct. (ctrl. dist.) Calif. 1984. Corp. assoc. Zobrist, Vienna & McCullough, L.A., 1982-84, Ball Hunt Hart Brown and Baerwitz, L.A., 1984-86; staff counsel Hebalife Internat., Inc., 1986-87; assoc. prof. bus. law Calif. State U., Northridge, 1989-92; atty. Law Offices of Lewis W. Boies, Jr., Santa Monica, Calif., 1992-98; pvt. practice, 1999—. Adj. lectr. in bus. law Calif. State U., L.A., 1995, Northridge, 1997—. Dir. Young Adults Conquering Cancer Aux. to the Children's Cancer, L.A., 1992-95; peer counselor Teen Impact Program L.A. Children's Hosp., 1990-95; co-dir. The Vagabond Players Theatre Co., 1997—. Legion lex scholar U. So. Calif., 1982-84. Republican. Avocations: acting, theatre producing, art, writing. Contracts commercial, General corporate, Entertainment. Office: PO Box 3514 Santa Monica CA 90408-3514 E-mail: mhomeier@linkonline.net

HOMER, BARRY WAYNE, lawyer; b. Junction City, Kans., Jan. 13, 1950; BA, U. Kans., 1972; JD, U. Chgo., 1975. Bar: Calif. 1975, U.S. Dist. Ct. (no. dist.) Calif. 1975, U.S. Tax Ct. 1980. Assoc. Brobeck, Phleger & Harrison, San Francisco, 1975-82, ptnr., 1982—. Co-author: Attorney's Guide to Pension and Profitsharing Plans, 1985, Compensating the Executive with Stock: Some Planning Possibilities and the Effect of the Parachute Provisions, 1986; contbr. articles to profl. jours. Mem. ABA (employee benefits com. tax sect. 1978—), Western Pension & Benefits Conf. Pension, profit-sharing, and employee benefits, Corporate taxation. Office: Brobeck Phleger & Harrison Spear St Tower 1 Market Plz Ste 341 San Francisco CA 94105-1420

HONAKER, JIMMIE JOE, lawyer, ecologist; b. Oklahoma City, Jan. 21, 1939; s. Joe Jack and Ruby Lee (Bowen) H.; children: Jay Jimmie, Kerri Ruth. BA, Colo. Coll., 1963; MA, U. No. Colo., 1991; JD, U. Wyo., 1966, MS, 1995; postgrad., Utah State U., 1995—. Bar: Colo. 1966, U.S. Dist. Ct. Colo., U.S. Ct. Appeals (10th cir.), Ute Indian Tribal Ct. Utah. Pvt. practice, Longmont, Colo., 1966-91. Incorporator Longmont Boys Baseball, 1969; chmn. Longmont City Charter Commn., 1973; chmn. ch. bd. 1st Christian Ch., Longmont, 1975, 76; chmn. North Boulder County unit Am. Cancer Soc., 1978, 79. Recipient Disting. Svc. award Longmont Centennial Yr., 1971; named Outstanding Young Man, Longmont Jaycees, 1973. Mem. ABA, Colo. Bar Assn. (interprofl. com. 1972-91, environ. law sect. 1999—), Denver Bar Assn., Christian Legal Soc., Internat. Assn. Approved Basketball Ofcls. (cert.), Nat. Eagle Scout Assn., Ecol. Soc. Am., US-IALE, Colo. Mountain Club, Uintah Mtn. Club, Phi Alpha Delta, Alpha Kappa Psi, Xi Sigma Pi, Alpha Tau Omega. Avocations: private pilot, mountain climbing. Contracts commercial, Environmental, Real property. Address: Utah State U PO Box 1320 Logan UT 84322-0199

HONAN, WILLIAM JOSEPH, III, lawyer; b. Cleve., Jan. 8, 1945; s. William Joseph and Vernice Louise (Bryan) H. B.A., U. N.C., 1966, J.D., 1969. Bar: N.Y. 1970, U.S. Dist. Ct. (so. dist.) N.Y., U.S. Ct. Appeals (2d cir.). Assoc., Haight, Gardner, Poor & Havens, N.Y.C., 1969-76, ptnr., 1976— ; mem. documentary com. Intertanko, Oslo, Norway, 1981— ; dir. Bergen Lind, Inc., N.Y.C., 1984— . Mem. Maritime Law Assn., Assn. Bar City N.Y. Roman Catholic. Club: India House (N.Y.C.). Admiralty. Home: 235 E 22nd St New York NY 10010-4616 Office: Haight Gardner Poor & Havens 195 Broadway Rm 2400 New York NY 10007-3189

HONEY, WILLIAM CHIPMAN, lawyer, educator; b. Ferguson, Mo., Apr. 7, 1932; s. Albert Erroll and Helen Elizabeth (Chipman) H.; m. Roberta Alice Mare, July 19, 1955 (div. 1967); children: Craig (dec.), Sarah, Martha, Alice; m. Barbara Ann Blackwell, Apr. 17, 1968 (div. 1985); 1 son, Christopher. Student U. of South, Sewanee, Tenn., 1949-51; JD, Washington U., St. Louis, 1955; postgrad. U. South Fla., 1974, U. Ark., 1975-76. Bar: Mo. 1955, Ark. 1975, Ariz. 1979, Va. 1982, Fla. 1988, Ala. 1989. Sole practice, St. Louis, 1957-70; asst. prof. English, U. P.R., Mayaguez, 1970-74; exec. v.p. Delray Corp., 1974; sole practice, Rogers, Ark., 1975-79, Scottsdale, Ariz., 1979-81; asst. prof. dept. fin. Sch. Bus. Adminstr., Old Dominion U., Norfolk, Va., 1981-85; assoc. prof. Auburn U. Sch. Bus., Montgomery, Ala., 1985—; pvt. practice, St. Petersburg, Fla., 1988, Phoenix, 1989—; of counsel McPhillips, Shinbaum, Gill & Stoner, Attys., 1995—; mem. firms Kerth Thies & Schreiber, Clayton, Mo., Honey and Kehr, Clayton; pres. Video Learning Systems, Inc., 1985—, Soulard Assocs. Inc.; adj. prof., clin. law dir. U. Ark. Law Sch., Fayetteville, 1976-77; adj. prof. English composition Ariz. State U., Tempe, 1979-81; co-developer Spirit of St. Louis Airport and St. Louis Air Park, Chesterfield, Mo., 1960-67; developer Soulard Area Rehab., St. Louis, 1967-70; city atty. City of Rogers, 1975-79; cons. Human Relations Commn. East St. Louis, Ill., Mid-City Community Congress, St. Louis, OHSA Dept. Labor, others; lectr. various orgns. Author: Guide to Law and Business, 1986; pres., pub., editor-in-chief Montgomery Living Mag., 1996—; contbr. articles to profl. jours, stories, poetry to mags. Trustee U. of South, Sewanee, 1957-70; gen. counsel Mansion House Ctr., St. Louis; mem. vestry, ch. sch. supt. Episcopal Ch. Served with U.S. Army, 1955-57. Mem. Va. Bar Assn., Fla. Bar Assn., Ariz. Bar Assn., Ark. Bar Assn., Mo. Bar Assn., Ala. Bar Assn., Beta Theta Pi (pres. U. of South chpt. 1950). Home: 2094 Myrtlewood Dr Montgomery AL 36111-1000

HONEYCHURCH, DENIS ARTHUR, lawyer; b. Berkeley, Calif., Sept. 17, 1946; s. Winston and Mary Martha (Chandler) H.; m. Judith Ann Poliquin, Oct. 5, 1969; children: Sean, James, Thomas. BA, UCLA, 1968; JD, U. Calif., San Francisco, 1972. Bar: Calif. 1972, U.S. Dist. Ct. (no. dist.) Calif. 1972, U.S. Ct. Appeals (9th cir.) 1972. Dep. pub. defender Sacramento County Calif., Sacramento, 1973-75; supervising asst. pub. defender Solano County, Fairfield, Calif., 1975-78; ptnr. Honeychurch & Finkas and predecessor firm, 1978—. Bd. dirs. Fairfield-Suisun Unified Sch. Dist., Fairfield, 1979-83, Solano Coll., Fairfield, 1985—; chmn. bd. dirs. Downtown Improvement Dist., Fairfield, 1980-82; mem. Dem. Ctr. Com. Solano County, 1994-98. Mem. ABA, Nat. Assn. Criminal Def. Lawyers, Calif. Attys. Criminal Justice, Calif. Pub. Defenders Assn., Solano County Bar Assn. (pres. 1991), Calif. Bd. Legal Specialization (cert.), Nat. Bd. Trial Advocacy (cert.). Democrat. Criminal. Office: Honeychurch & Finkas 823 Jefferson St Fairfield CA 94533-5591

HOOD, MARY DULLEA, law librarian; b. Fargo, N.D., Jan. 3, 1947; d. Maurice Eugene and Rosemary (Melican) Dullea; m. Michael L. Hood, May 26, 1974; children: David Patrick, Michelle Marie. BA, U. Santa Clara, 1970, JD, 1975; MLS, San Jose State U., 1979. Bar: Calif. 1976. Libr. asst. Law Libr., U. Santa Clara, Calif., 1970-75, reference libr., 1975-78; instr. legal rsch. Paralegal Inst., 1976-84; head pub. svcs. U. Santa Clara, Calif., 1978-87, assoc. dir., 1987—, mem. univ. automation task force, 1986-91, mem. adj. faculty advanced legal rsch. Law Sch., 1998-99, 2001. Mem. Santa Clara CSC, 1976-78. Mem. Am. Assn. Law Librs. (placement com. 1999—), No. Calif. Assn. Law Librs. (pres. 1982-83), U. Santa Clara Law Sch. Alumni Assn. (treas. 1983-85). Avocatins: needlepoint, reading, stained glass. Office: Santa Clara U Law Libr Santa Clara CA 95053-0001

HOOD, ROBERT HOLMES, lawyer; b. Charleston, S.C., Oct. 5, 1944; s. James Albert and Ruth (Henderson) H.; m. Mary Agnes Burnham, Aug. 5, 1967; children: Mary Agnes, Elizabeth, Robert Holmes Jr., James Bernard. BA, U. of the South, 1966; JD, U. S.C., 1969. Bar: U.S. Supreme Ct. 1969, S.C. 1969, U.S. Dist. Ct. S.C. 1969, U.S. Ct. Appeals (4th cir.) 1969. Asst. atty. gen. State of S.C., Columbia, 1969-70; ptnr. Sinkler, Gibbs & Simons, Charleston, 1970-85; prin. Hood Law Firm, LLC, 1985--. Mem. Assn. Def. Trial Attys. (pres. 1985-86), Am. Bd. Trial Advs. (diplomate, pres. Charleston chpt. 1997), Internat. Assn. Def. Counsel, Def. Rsch. and Trial Inst. (bd. dirs. 1987-90), Fedn. Ins. and Corp. Counsel, S.C. Def. Trial Attys. Assn. (pres. 1980-81), Network of Trial Law Firms. Episcopalian. General civil litigation, Consumer commercial, Personal injury. Office: 172 Meeting St Charleston SC 29401-3126 E-mail: bobby-hood@hoodlaw.com

HOOGLAND, ROBERT FREDERICS, lawyer; b. Paterson, N.J., Apr. 3, 1955; s. Robert J. and Lucretia H.; m. Diane Wood, Sept. 21, 1983 (div. Mar. 1985). BA, U. Fla., 1976; MBA, Rollins Coll., 1977; JD, U. Fla., 1982. Bar: Fla. 1983, U.S. Dist. Ct. (mid. dist.) Fla. 1989; cert. real estate law. Assoc. Giles, Hedrick & Robinson, Orlando, Fla., 1983-89; ptnr. Hoogland & Durket, P.A., Longwood, 1989-92, Robert F. Hoogland, P.A., Altamonte Springs, 1992—. Mem. ABA, Fla. Bar Assn., Orange County Bar Assn., Winter Park C. of C., Phi Delta Phi. Republican. Roman Catholic. Avocations: tennis, golf, fishing. , State civil litigation, Personal injury. Home: 139 Olive Tree Cir Altamonte Springs FL 32714-3240 Office: PO Box 160021 Altamonte Springs FL 32716-0021

HOOKER, WADE STUART, JR. lawyer; b. Brockton, Mass., Sept. 23, 1941; s. Wade S. and Eleanor M. (Tolan) H.; m. Susan M. Levine, May 20, 1984; children: Thomas A., Richard P. BA, Harvard Coll., 1963; LLB, U. Va., 1966. Bar: N.Y. 1969. Assoc. Casey, Lane & Mittendorf, N.Y.C., 1968-77; ptnr. Burlingham Underwood LLP, 1979—. Spkr. in field. Contbr. articles to profl. jours. Maxwell fellow Syracuse U., Resident scholar Indian Law Inst., New Delhi, 1966-67. Mem. ABA, Assn. Bar City of N.Y. (chair aeronautics com.), Computer Law Assn., Inc., Internat. Bar Assn., Maritime Law Assn. U.S. (chair com. maritime regulation and promotion 1990-94), Mensa. Admiralty, Computer, Finance. Office: Burlingham Underwood LLP One Battery Pk Plaza New York NY 10004 E-mail: wadehooker@post.harvard.com

HOOVER, DAVID CARLSON, lawyer; b. Waterville, Maine, Apr. 22, 1950; s. Jack Cauldwell and Mary Elizabeth (Donavan) H.; m. Kathleen Delia Powell, June 28, 1981; children: Maegan Elizabeth, Peter Daniel, Christian Shaw. BA, U. N.H., 1972; JD cum laude, Suffolk U., 1976. Bar: Mass. 1977, U.S. Dist. Ct. Mass. 1982, U.S. Supreme Ct. 1982, U.S. Ct. Appeals (1st cir.) 1983. Atty. advisor NOAA, Washington, 1976-79; gen. counsel Mass. Div. Marine Fisheries, Boston, 1979-83; spl. asst. atty. gen. Mass. Dept. Atty. Gen., 1980—; gen. counsel Mass. Dept. of Fisheries, Wildlife and Environ. Law Enforcement, 1983—. Adminstrv. law judge Commonwealth of Mass., 1979; lectr. Franklin Pierce Law Ctr., Concord, N.H., 1984. Mem. editl. bd. Territorial Sea Jour., U. of Maine Sch. of Law; contbr. articles to profl. jours. Ch. lector; tchr. Youth Orgn.; vol. New Eng. Boys Shelter for Homeless Vets.; exec. dir. Mass. Wildcats AAU Basketball Club; asst. coach boy varsity basketball Trinity H.S., Newton. Recipient Am. Jurisprudence award Lawyers Cooperative Pub. Co. Mem. Mass. Bar Assn., Com. on Chemical Dependency, Atty. advisor to Mock-Trial Tournament, Law Related Edn. Com., Lawyers Concerned for Lawyers, Internat. Assn. of Approved Basketball Offcls. Avocations: miniaturist, woodworking, civil war history, coaching and officiating high school basketball. Home: 808 Watertown St Newton MA 02465-2116 Office: Dept Fisheries Wildlife and Environ Law Enforcement 100 Cambridge St Rm 1901 Boston MA 02202-0044

HOPE, HENRY WELCKER, lawyer; b. Chattanooga, Sept. 11, 1940; s. William Boyd and Eleanor Kate Roberson Hope; m. Sara Elizabeth Bailey, Aug. 6, 1961; children: Eleanor Hope Rooke, Julia Cathleen Falick. BS, U. Tenn., 1962; JD, George Washington U., 1966. Bar: Va. 1966, Tex. 1966, U.S. Patent Office 1966. Assoc. Fulbright & Jaworski, LLP, Houston, 1966-75, ptnr., 1975—. Bd. dirs. Royal Ten Cate, Inc., Atlanta, BCM Tech., Inc., Houston. Mem., bd. trustees Houston Ballet Found., 1997—, mem. adv. trustee, 2000-01; mem., corp. ptnrs. com. Mus. Fine Arts, Houston, 1997—; mem., adv. bd. dirs. Houston Jr. Forum, 1988-91; mem., adminstrv. bd. Meml. Dr. United Meth., Houston. Mem. ABA (com. mem. 1966—), Tex. Bar Assn. (com. mem. 1966—), Va. Bar Assn., Licensing Exec. Soc. (various chairs 1975—), MIT Enterprise Forum of Tex. (bd. dirs. 1989-94), Lakeside Country Club (bd. dirs. 1996-2000, pres. 1998-99). Methodist. Avocations: golf, reading, travel. Office: Fulbright & Jaworski LLP 1301 Mckinney St Ste 5100 Houston TX 77010-3031 E-mail: hhope@fulbright.com

HOPE, KARIN, lawyer, legislative staff member; b. Breckenridge, Minn., Mar. 14, 1967; d. George Huntington and Barbara Jesten H. BA in political sci., Bethel Coll., 1989; JD, Georgetown U. Law Ctr., 1994. Bar: Minn., 1994, U.S. Supreme Ct., 1998. Asst. legis. dir. U.S. Senator Dave Durenberger, Washington, 1987-88, 89-91, legis. asst., 1991-94; legis. counsel U.S. Rep. Jim Ramstad, 1995, legis. dir./counsel, 1996—. Legal and govt. affaris com., Christian Coll. Coalition, Washington, 1992-94. Tutor/Mentor Neighborhood Learning Ctr., Washington, 1994—, alumni bd. dirs., Bethel Coll., St. Paul, 1995-97, 2000—. Citizenship award, Iowa Bar Assn., Osage, Iowa, 1985. Mem. Tax Coalition. Republican. Baptist. Avocations: vocal and instrumental music, theatre. Office: US Rep Jim Ramstad 103 Cannon House Off Bldg Washington DC 20515-0001 E-mail: karin.hope@mail.house.gov

HOPE, RONALD ARTHUR, lawyer; b. Mineral Wells, Tex., Jan. 8, 1956; s. Arthur Virgil and Barbara Louise (Wester) H.; m. Mary Katharyn Howell, Oct. 3, 1987; children: Katharyn Rachel, Laura Anderson, John Arthur. BSBA in Acctg., U. Ark., 1978, JD, 1981. Bar: Ark. 1981, U.S.Dist. Ct. (ea. and we. dists.) Ark. 1982, U.S. Ct. Appeals (8th cir.) 1991, U.S. Supreme Ct. 1987. Atty. Howell, Price & Trice, PA, Little Rock, 1981-85; ptnr. Howell, Price, Trice, Basham & Hope, PA, 1985-93; shareholder Howell, Trice & Hope, PA, 1993-2001, Howell, Trice, Hope & Files PA, Little Rock, 2001—. City atty. City of Wrightsville, Ark., 1988—; atty. Ark. Property and Casualty Guaranty Fund. Legal com. NCIGF, 1996—. Century mem. Boy Scouts Am. Mem. ATLA, Ark. Bar Assn., Ark. Trial Lawyers Assn., Pulaski County Bar Assn., Rotary, Masons, Shriners, Phi Alpha Delta, Sigma Chi. Methodist. Avocations: duck hunting, deer hunting, golf. General civil litigation, Family and matrimonial, Insurance. Office: Howell Trice Hope & Files PA 211 S Spring St Little Rock AR 72201-2405 E-mail: ron@hthfirm.com

HOPKINS, ALBEN NORRIS, lawyer; b. Ripley, Miss., Feb. 14, 1941; s. Lloyd Carter and Reba Genova (Norris) H.; m. Ruth Boyd, May 31, 1963; children: Ashley Anne, A. Norris. BA, Delta State Coll., 1963; JD, U. Miss., 1965; BA, William Carey Coll., 1985; student, Blue Mountain Coll. Bar: U.S. Dist. Ct. (so. dist.) Miss. 1966, U.S. Dist. Ct. (no. dist.) Miss. 1970, U.S. Ct. Appeals (5th cir.) 1972, U.S. Supreme Ct. 1972, U.S. Ct. Appeals (11th cir.) 1981, U.S. Ct. Mil. Appeals 1986. Assoc. Daniel, Coker & Horton, Jackson also Gulfport, Miss., 1965-67, 1967-69, resident ptnr., 1969-77; sr. ptnr., mng. ptnr. Hopkins, Crawley, Bagwell & Upshaw, Gulfport, 1977—. Bd. dirs. Delta State U. Found., 1991-94, pres., 1994; bd. dirs. USO, 1974-75, 83—, Gulf Pines Coun. Girl Scouts U.S.A., 1974-82, 85—, United Way Harrison Coutny; bd. dirs., chmn. planned giving com., dist. dir. Am. Heart Assn.; asst. chmn. State Heart Fund, 1983, chmn., 1985; asst. adjutant gen. State of Miss., 1991-95, chief judge Mil. Ct. Appeals, 1996—. Served to maj. gen. U.S. Army N.G., 1965-95, ret. Fellow Miss. Bar Found.; mem. Internat. Assn. Def. Counsel, Fedn. Ins. Counsel, Maritime Law Assn. U.S., Southeastern Admiralty Assn., Hinds County Bar Assn., Harrison County Bar Assn. (v.p. 1976-77), Miss. Bar Assn. (mem. jud. selection com. 1978-79), ABA, Lamar Order, Fed. Bar Assn. (bd. dirs. 1979-82), Kappa Alpha, Pi Kappa Delta, Phi Alpha Delta, Omicron Delta Kappa, Windance Country Club, Gulfport Yacht Club, Univ. Club, Masons, Shriners, YorkRite, others. Republican. Baptist. Federal civil litigation, State civil litigation. Office: PO Box 1510 Gulfport MS 39502-1510 E-mail: AHopkins@MsLawyer.com

HOPKINS, CHARLES PETER, II, lawyer; b. Elizabeth, N.J., June 16, 1953; s. Charles Peter Sr. and Josephine Ann (Battaglia) H.; m. Elizabeth Anna Altinger, Jan. 21, 1984; children: Courtney Alexandra, Ashley Elizabeth, Brooke Anne, Brittany Emilia. AB summa cum laude, Boston Coll., 1975, JD, 1979; MBA, Rutgers U., 1987. Bar: N.J. 1979, U.S. Dist. Ct. N.J. 1979, U.S. Ct. Appeals (3d cir.) 1982, U.S. Supreme Ct. 1985, U.S. Tax Ct. 1988. Assoc. Gagliano, Tucci & Kennedy, West Long Branch, N.J., 1980; pvt. practice, 1980-81; assoc. Richard J. Sauerwein (formerly Sparks & Sauerwein), Shrewsbury, N.J., 1981-83, trial atty., 1983-87, sr. trial atty., 1987-90; mng. trial atty. Law Offices Charles Peter Hopkins II, 1990—. Arbitrator U.S. Dist. Ct. N.J., 1985—, N.J. Civil arbitrator program, 1987—, Am. Arbitration Assn., 1991—. Active West Long Br. Sch. Bd., 1980-82. Mem. Def. Rsch. Inst. (state rep. 1996-2000, chmn. tech. com. 1997-2000, annual meeting steering com. 1999-2000, membership steering com. 1999—, bd. dirs. 2000—), Monmouth Bar Assn., N.J. Def. Assn. (regional v.p. ctrl. region 1994-95, chmn. leadership com. 1994-98, chmn. pub. rel. com. 1994-98, chmn. tech. com. dir. 1995-98, 2000—, sec.-treas. 1996-97, pres.-elect 1997-98, pres. 1998-99, bd. dirs. 1995—, chmn. bd. dirs. 1999-2000). Republican. Roman Catholic. Avocations: fitness, politics, military history. General civil litigation, Insurance, Personal injury. Office: Shrewsbury Sq Office Ctr 655 Shrewsbury Ave Shrewsbury NJ 07702-4151

HOPKINS, GROVER PREVATTE, lawyer; b. Jacksonville, Fla., Sept. 2, 1933; s. John Taylor and Capitola (Prevatte) H.; m. Ann Hutchinson, Oct. 16, 1965 (dec.); children: John, George, James, Corbin; m. Connie Jefferys, June 7, 1973. AB, Fla. State U., 1958; JD, U. N.C., 1971. Bar: N.C. 1971, Fla. 1972, D.C. 1981, U.S. Dist. Ct. (ea. dist.) N.C. 1971, U.S. Ct. Appeals (4th cir.) 1974, U.S. Supreme Ct. 1974; cert. mediator N.C. Cts., 1997. Announcer Sta. WTAL, Tallahassee, 1951-54; pub. rels. dir. Inter-Am. U., San German, P.R., 1958-60; pers. mgr. Northridge Knitting Mills, 1960-62; cons. bus and pers. Mayaguez, P.R., Miami, Fla., 1963-69; mem. Weeks & Muse, Tarboro, N.C., 1971-73, Hopkins & Assocs., Tarboro, 1973—. Served with U.S. Army, 1954-57. Mem. ABA, N.C. Bar Assn., D.C. Bar Assn., Inter-Am. Bar Assn. (sec. gen. 1989-91). Republican. Computer, Family and matrimonial, Personal injury. Office: Hopkins & Assocs 212 N Main St Tarboro NC 27886-5008 E-mail: lawyergph@aol.com

HOPKINS, JOHN DAVID, lawyer; b. Memphis, Feb. 8, 1938; s. John and Helen (Sweeney) H.; m. Evelyn Harry, June 8, 1963 (div. Feb. 1985); children: John David III, Katharine Jane, Matthew Joseph; m. Laurie Eileen House, June 3, 1987. BA, Vanderbilt U., 1959; LLB, U. Va., 1965. Bar: Ga. 1966, D.C. 1979. From assoc. to ptnr. King & Spalding, Atlanta, 1965-93; exec. v.p., gen. counsel Jefferson-Pilot Corp., Greensboro, N.C., 1993—. Bd. dirs., mem. exec. com. Rock-Tenn Co., Atlanta, 1989—; mem. Guilford Coll. Bd. of Visitors, 1994-2000; bd. dirs. Univ. N.C. at Greensboro Excellence Found., 1995—. Bd. dirs. Atlanta Ballet, 1991-93, Greensboro United Arts Coun., 1994-97, Ea. Music Festival, 1998—; mem. alumni coun. U. Va. Law Sch. Alumni Assn., 2000—; trustee Children's Sch., Inc., Atlanta, 1971-79, 88-89, Nat. Assn. Children's Hosps. and Related Instns., Alexandria, Va., 1973-79. Lt. USN, 1959-62. Mem. Ga. Bar Assn. (chmn. corp. code revision com., corp. and banking sect. 1970-79), D.C. Bar Assn., Greensboro Country Club, Cherokee Town and Country Club (Atlanta), Order of Coif, Omicron Delta Kappa. Episcopalian. General corporate, Finance, Mergers and acquisitions. Office: 100 N Greene St Greensboro NC 27401-2507 E-mail: john.hopkins@jpfinancial.com

HOPP, DANIEL FREDERICK, manufacturing company executive, lawyer; b. Ann Arbor, Mich., Apr. 14, 1947; s. Clayton A. and Monica E. (Williams) H.; m. Maria G. Lopez, Dec. 20, 1968; children: Emily, Daniel, Melissa. BA in English, U. Mich., 1969; JD, Wayne State U., 1973. Bar: Ill. 1974, Mich. 1980. Atty. Mayer, Brown and Platt, Chgo., 1973-79, Whirlpool Corp., Benton Harbor, Mich., 1979-84, asst. sec., 1984-85, sec., asst. gen. counsel, 1985-89, v.p., gen. counsel, sec., 1989-98, sr. v.p., corp. affairs and gen. counsel, 1998—. Past co-chmn. Conf. Bd. Legal Quality Coun. Mem. City of St. Joseph (Mich.) Planning Comm.; bd. dirs. Lakeland Regional Health Sys., Joseph, Mich. With U.S. Army, 1969-71. Mem. Am. Soc. Corp. Secs. (past pres., bd. dirs. Chgo. chpt.), Mich. Bar Assn. (mem. Open Justice Commn.), Ill. Bar Assn., Berrien County Bar Assn. Republican. Mem. Ch. of Christ. Avocation: golf. Office: Whirlpool Corp Adminstrv Ctr 2000 N M 63 Benton Harbor MI 49022-2692

HOPPEL, ROBERT GERALD, JR. lawyer; b. Scranton, Pa., Dec. 26, 1921; s. Robert Gerald and Ellen Amelia (Casey) H. BS, U. Scranton, 1950; JD, Georgetown U., 1954. Bar: D.C. 1955, U.S. Ct. Appeals (D.C. cir.) 1955, U.S. Supreme Ct. 1974. Supervising auditor GAO, Washington, 1950-57; ptnr. Coles & Goertener, 1957-82, Hoppel, Mayer & Coleman, Washington, 1982-84; sole practice, 1984—. Served to cpl. USAAF, 1943-45. Mem. ABA, Maritime Admistrv. Bar Assn., D.C. Bar, Bar Assn. D.C., Internat. Platform Assn., Am. Legion, Nat. Lawyers Club, Propellor Club (Washington). Republican. Roman Catholic. Administrative and regulatory, Admiralty, Government contracts and claims. Office: 3600 Massachusetts Ave NW Washington DC 20007-1449

HOPPS, RAYMOND, JR. lawyer, film producer; b. Balt., July 26, 1949; s. Raymond Hopps Sr. and Ella Louise Dixon. BA cum laude, Howard U., 1971; JD, Loyola U., Chgo., 1974. Bar: Ill. 1975. CEO, art atty. Cmty. Legal Counsel, Chgo., 1972; staff and adminstr. Chgo. Vol. Legal Svcs., 1972-74; assoc. Archie B. Weston Sr. Ltd., Chgo., 1975-77; pvt. practice, 1977-78; film prodr., 1978; prodr. N.Y. Film Colony, 1979; with svc. work Internat. Econs.; owner, prodr., artist Am. Oriental Internat. Ltd., Balt., 1980—. Staff rschr. Task Force for Cmty. Broadcasting, Chgo., 1973-78; atty. cons. Assn. of AudioVisual Prodrs., Chgo., 1978; coord. N.Y. Film Colony, 1979; staff atty. Ebony Talent Assocs., Chgo. Composer: Concerto Impossible, 1987, For Your Eyes Only, 1981, Victory for the Free Planet, 1991; author: (prose) Master E, 1986; composer, author: Free Planet, 1991; writer, film prodr. for screen. Staff artist Eubie Blake Cultural Ctr., Balt., 1990—; assoc. Nat. Football League and Balt. Ravens 2001 Super Bowl Champions. With USAF, 1968-91, brig. gen. Res. Mem. NAACP, Internat. Mid. East Assn., Am. Mgmt. Assn., Equal Opportunity Found., Jim Straw Heritage Exch., WFI Corp. Democrat. Avocations: music, dancing, films, walking. Entertainment, Intellectual property, Trademark and copyright. Address: Garrison Bldg 2806 Ste 1 South Baltimore MD 21216 Office: AMI Ltd Motion Pictures PO Box 67585 Baltimore MD 21215-0016 also: 3704 Ferndale Ave Baltimore MD 21207-7163

HOPSON, EDWIN SHARP, lawyer; b. Louisville, Apr. 23, 1945; s. Henry Dockins and Martha (Linton) H.; m. Jane Mayo Fitzpatrick, July 20, 1968; children: Edwin Hopson Jr., Martha. BSL, U. Louisville, 1967, JD, 1969; LLM, George Washington U., 1971. Bar: Ky. 1969, Fla. 1969, U.S. Supreme Ct. 1972, U.S. Dist. Ct. (we. dist.) Ky. 1974, U.S. Ct. Appeals (6th cir.) 1977. Atty. Solicitor's Office, U.S. Dept. Labor, Washington, 1969-72; field atty. NLRB, Balt., 1972-74; assoc. Tarrant, Combs, Blackwell & Bullitt, Louisville, 1974-77; ptnr. Tarrant, Combs & Bullitt, 1977-80, Wyatt, Tarrant & Combs, L.L.P., Louisville, 1980—. Editor: (jour.) Ky. Bench & Bar, 1989—91, (chpt.) How Arbitration Works, 1989, 2nd edit., 2001—;contbr. articles. Bd. dirs. Bellewood Presbyn. Children's Home, Louisville, 1988-96, pres., 1991-93; bd. dirs. Louisville Ballet, 1991—, v.p., 1992-93, pres., 1993-94; bd. dirs. Bellewood Children's Found., 1995—, pres., 1995-96. Fellow Coll. Labor & Employment Lawyers, Inc.; mem. ABA (co-chmn. pub. of arbitration awards subcom. 2000—, adr. com. of labor and employment sect. 1999—), FBA (chpt. pres. 1991-92), Louisville Bar Assn. (co-chmn. labor and employment law sect. 1982-83), Ky. Bar Assn. (co-chmn. labor and employment law sect. 1987-89, mem. ho. of dels. 1996—, chair comms. com. 2001—). Republican. Presbyterian. Avocations: flying, various sports, reading. Labor. Home: 3003 Lightheart Rd Louisville KY 40222-6138 Office: Wyatt Tarrant & Combs LLP PNC Plz Louisville KY 40202-2823 E-mail: ehopson@wyattfirm.com

HOPSON, EVERETT GEORGE, retired lawyer; b. Stillwell, Ill., Sept. 4, 1922; s. Carman Roy and Adella (George) H.; m. Doris May Hutchins, Aug. 15, 1953 (dec.); children: Christine E., Eugene G. AA, Springfield Jr. Coll., 1942; BS, U. Ill., 1947, JD, 1949; MS in Internat. Affairs, George Washington U., 1967. Bar: Ill. 1949, U.S. Ct. Mil. Appeals 1957, U.S. Supreme Ct. 1957. Dep. collector U.S. Treasury, IRS, Carlinville, Ill., 1949-51; commd. officer USAF, 1951, advanced to col., judge advocate, 1951-71; spl. asst. to asst. sec. def. Dept. Def., Washington, 1971; sr. atty. U.S. Postal Svc., 1972-73; dep. chief gen. law divsn. USAF, 1973-75, chief gen. law divsn., 1975-94, ret., 1994. Trustee USAF JAG Sch. Found. Served with U.S. Army, 1943-46. Decorated Legion of Merit; recipient Presdl. Rank of Meritorious Exec., USAF, 1981, 87, 92, Freedoms Found. award, 1961, 62, 66. Mem. ABA, Ill. Bar Assn. (sr. counsellor 1999), Fed. Bar Assn., Judge Advocates Assn., Am. Inns of Ct., Phi Alpha Delta. Democrat. Methodist. Avocations: coin collecting, gardening. Home: 9719 Limoges Dr Fairfax VA 22032-1115 E-mail: eghdmh@aol.com

HORAN, JOHN DONOHOE, lawyer; b. N.Y.C., Mar. 4, 1948; s. Michael Joseph, Jr. and Anna Patricia (Donohoe) H.; m. Judith R. Levinson, Aug. 8, 1976; children— Michael L., Emily L. B.A., Fordham Coll., 1970; J.D., Rutgers U., 1974. Bar: N.J. 1974, U.S. Dist. Ct. N.J. 1974, U.S. Ct. Appeals (3d cir.) 1980, U.S. Supreme Ct. 1981. Ptnr., Goodman, Stoldt, Breslin & Horan, Hackensack, N.J., 1974-84, Stoldt, Horan & Cino, 1984— . Bd. dirs. Research Fund for Cystic Fibrosis, Inc., 1985— . Mem. Bergen County Bar Assn. (com. on employment discrimination 1979— , founder, chmn. com. environ. law 1983— , chmn. subcom. on hazardous waste litigation 1983—), Trial Attys. N.J., ABA (litigation), N.J. State Bar Assn. (com. on environ. law). Federal civil litigation, State civil litigation, Environmental. Office: Stoldt Horan & Kowal 401 Hackensack Ave Hackensack NJ 07601-6411

HORKOVICH, ROBERT MICHAEL, lawyer; b. Kew Gardens, N.Y., June 11, 1954; s. Andrew Horkovich and Amelia (Rauba) Patti. BA in Econs. and Govt., Fordham U., 1976, JD, 1979. Bar: N.Y. 1980, Md. 1987, U.S. Dist. Ct. (so. and ea. dists.) N.Y. 1980, U.S. Ct. Appeals (2d cir.) 1980, U.S. Ct. Mil. Appeals 1980, U.S. Dist. Ct. Md. 1987, U.S. Ct. Appeals (10th cir.) 1997. Clk. U.S. Senator James L. Buckley, N.Y., 1975-77; dir. ops. N.Y. State Polit. Action Com., 1977-79; assoc. Skadden, Arps, Slate, Meagher & Flom, N.Y.C., 1979-80, Cadwalader, Wickersham & Taft, N.Y.C., 1984-89; ptnr. Anderson Kill & Olick P.C., 1989—. Articles editor Fordham Urban Law Jour., 1978-79, bd. dirs. 1984—; contbr. articles to profl. jours. Served to capt. USAF, 1980-84. Named Co. Grade Officer of Yr. 1100 Air Base Wing, 1982, Eagle Scout Boy Scouts Am., 1972. Mem. Pi Sigma Alpha. Roman Catholic. Avocations: impressionist art, scuba diving. General civil litigation, Insurance. Office: Anderson Kill & Olick PC 1251 Avenue Of The Americas New York NY 10020-1104

HORLICK, GARY NORMAN, lawyer, legal educator; b. Washington, Mar. 12, 1947; s. Reuben S. and Gertrude V. (Cooper) H.; m. Kathryn L. Mann, June 1, 1986. AB, Dartmouth Coll., 1968; BA, MA, Diploma in Internat. Law, Cambridge (Eng.) U., 1970; JD, Yale U., 1973. Bar: Conn. 1974, U.S. Ct. Appeals (D.C. cir.) 1975), D.C. 1977, U.S. Supreme Ct. 1977, U.S. Ct. Internat. Trade 1979, U.S. Ct. Customs and Patent Appeals 1980. Asst. to rep. Ford Found., Santiago, Chile, 1973-74, asst. rep.

Bogota, Colombia, 1974-76; assoc. Steptoe & Johnson, Washington, 1976-80; internat. trade counsel U.S. Senate Fin. Com., 1981; dep. asst. sec. U.S. Dept. Commerce, 1981-83; ptnr. O'Melveny & Myers, 1983—. Lectr. law Yale U., New Haven, 1983-86, 2001—; adj. prof. Georgetown U. Law Ctr., Washington, 1986—; lectr. various orgns.; adv. com. U.S. Ct. Internat. Trade, 1993-97; mem. permanent group of experts World Trade Orgn., 1996-2001, chmn., 1996-97. Mem. ABA (chmn. standing com. on customs law 1993), Coun. Fgn. Rels., Internat. Law Assn. (mem. exec. coun. Am. br. 1983—), Internat. Bar Assn. (vice chmn. antitrust and trade law 1987-89), D.C. Bar Assn. (chmn. internat. divsn. 1984-85), Am. Soc. of Internat. Law (exec. coun. 1998-99). Private international, Public international. Office: O'Melveny & Myers 555 13th St NW Ste 500W Washington DC 20004-1159

HORN, ANDREW WARREN, lawyer; b. Apr. 19, 1946; s. George H. and Belle (Collin) H.; m. Melinda Fink; children: Lee Shawn, Ruth Belle. BBA in Acctg., U. Miami, 1968, JD, 1971. Bar: Fla. 1971, Colo. 1990, U.S. Dist. Ct. (so. dist.) Fla. 1972, U.S. Tax Ct. 1974. Ptnr. Gillman & Horn P.A., Miami, Fla., 1973-74; pvt. practice, 1974—. Active civic coun. Children's Hosp., Miami, Dade County, Fla., 1994—, Blue Ribbon Aviation Panel-Miami-Dade County, Fla., 2000. Recipient Am. Jurisprudence award Lawyers Coop. Pub. Co., 1970. Mem. ABA, ATLA, Fla. Bar, Acad. Fla. Trial Lawyers. State civil litigation, Consumer commercial, Personal injury. E-mail: lawofficehorn@msn.com

HORN, BRENDA SUE, lawyer; b. Beech Grove, Ind., Apr. 22, 1949; d. Donald Eugene Horn and Barbara Joyce (Waggoner) Christie. AB with distinction, Ind. U., 1971; MS, Purdue U., 1975; JD summa cum laude, Ind. U., 1981. Bar: Ind. 1981, U.S. Dist. Ct. (so. dist.) Ind. 1981. Assoc. Ice Miller, Indpls., 1981-87, ptnr., 1988—. Assoc. editor Ind. Law Rev., 1980-81. Bd. dirs. Ballet Internationale, 1995—, treas., 1996—; pres. Greenleaf Cmty. Ctr., 1992-93, 96-99, v.p., 1991, sec., 1990; bd. dirs., v.p. Cmty. Alliance for the Far East Side, 1997-98, hon. dir. 1998—; bd. dirs. Big Sisters of Ctrl. Ind., 1995-98, hon. dir., 1998—; bd. dirs. Indiana Edn. Svcs. Authority, 1996—, Cmty. Orgns. Legal Assistance Project, 2000—, treas., 2001—. Named among Influential Women in Indpls., Ind. Lawyer and Indpls. Bus. Jour., 1998; Disting. fellow Indpls. Bar Fond. Mem. ABA (com. on tax exempt fin.), Am. Coll. Bond Counsel (bd. dirs., v.p. 1995-98, pres. 1998—), Ind. Bar Assn., Indpls. Bar Assn. (bd. mgrs. 1992), Ind. Mcpl. Lawyers Assn., Nat. Assn. Bond Lawyers, Skyline Club (bd. dirs.), Phi Beta Kappa. Health, Municipal (including bonds). Office: Ice Miller One American Sq Box 82001 Indianapolis IN 46282 E-mail: horn@icemiller.com

HORN, CHARLES M. lawyer; b. Boston, Sept. 28, 1951; s. Garfield Henry and Alexandra (Matz) H.; m. Jane Charlotte Luxton, May 29, 1976; children: Andrew L., Caroline C. AB magna cum laude, Harvard Coll., 1973; JD, Cornell Law Sch., 1976. Bar: D.C. 1976, U.S. Dist. Ct. D.C. 1977, U.S. Ct. Appeals (D.C. cir.) 1977, U.S. Supreme Ct. 1980. Atty. U.S. Securities and Exchange Commn., Washington, 1976-82, br. chief divsn. enforcement, 1982-83; asst. dir. securities and corp. practices Office Comptroller of Currency, 1983-86, dir. securities and corp. practices, 1986-89; ptnr. Stroock & Stroock & Lavan, 1989-92, Mayer, Brown & Platt, Washington, 1992—. Mem. faculty Am. Bankers Assn. Nat. Grad. Compliance Sch., 1991-92, 94, Fed. Fin. Instns. Exam. Coun. (programs off-balance-sheet risk, Trust Exams. Sch.); lectr. in field. Edit. adv. bd. Bank Acctg. and Fin., 1993—; contbr. articles to profl. jours. Mem. ABA (banking law com., subcom. securities, com. fed. regulation securities), D.C. Bar Assn., Harvard Club Washington, Washington Golf and Country Club. Administrative and regulatory, Banking, Securities. Home: 1918 Massachusetts Ave Mc Lean VA 22101-4907 Office: Mayer Brown & Platt 1909 K St NW Washington DC 20006 E-mail: chorn@mayerbrown.com

HORN, EVERETT BYRON, JR. retired lawyer; b. Newton, Mass., Aug. 18, 1927; s. Everett Byron and Ella Frances (Doody) H.; m. Patricia Ann Reusch, Sept. 10, 1949; children: Everett B. III, John M., Daniel J., Cynthia A. Whetten. AB, Harvard U., 1949; JD, Boston Coll., 1954. Bar: Mass. 1954, U.S. Dist. Ct. Mass. 1955, U.S. Supreme Ct. 1965. Asst. counsel Liberty Mut. Ins. Co., Boston, 1954-63; sr. v.p. and gen. counsel Mass. Indemnity and Life Ins. Co., Hyannis, 1964-75; counsel New Eng. Mut. Life Ins. Co., Boston, 1976-77; ret. v.p. and gen. counsel Boston Mut. Life Ins. Co., Canton, Mass., 1977—. Vice chmn. bd. dirs. Vt. Life and Health Ins. Guaranty Assn.; bd. dirs. Maine Life and Health Ins. Guaranty Assn., R.I. Life and Health Ins. Guaranty Assn., Mass. Life and Health Ins. Guaranty Assn., Boston Mut. Mgmt. Corp., Life Ins. Co. of Boston and N.Y, Life Ins. Assn. Mass. (exec. com.). Pres. Seaside Park Taxpayers Assn., West Hyannis Port, Mass. 1961-64. Served as cpl. USAAF, 1945-46. Mem. ABA (vice chmn. life ins. law com. ins. law sect. 1985-89), Mass. Bar Assn., Barnstable County Bar Assn., Norfolk County Bar Assn., Assn. Life Ins. Counsel, Soc. Corp. Ins. Litigators, Hyannis Yacht Club, Harvard Club. Republican. Roman Catholic. Avocation: sailing. General corporate, Insurance. Home: 500 Ocean St Apt 120 Hyannis MA 02601-4759

HORN, JOHN HAROLD, lawyer; b. Eugene, Oreg., Mar. 4, 1927; s. Harold William and Mildred A. (Truesdale) H.; m. Deloris Eileen Davis, Aug. 22, 1948; children: Lorraine, Deborah, Lisa, Darren. BS, U. Oreg., 1949, JD, 1951. Bar: Oreg. 1951, U.S. Dist. Ct. Oreg. 1957. Ptnr. Horn & Slocum, Roseburg, Oreg., 1951-65, Riddlesbarger, Pederson, Young & Horn, Eugene, 1970-74, Young, Horn, Cass & Scott, Eugene, 1974-82; pvt. practice Roseburg, 1965-70, Eugene, 1982—. Chmn. fund raising Douglas County unit ARC, 1966, county chmn., 1968; exec. bd., legal advisor Eugene Mission, 1979—; pres. bd. dirs. Jubilee Ministries, Eugene, 1980—; v.p., bd. dirs. His Word Broadcasting, 1989-91, pres. bd. dirs., 1991—. Recipient Outstanding Svc. award ARC, 1968. Mem. ABA, Oreg. Bar Assn., Douglas County Bar Assn. (pres. 1960, chmn. grievance com. 1961-62), Lane County Bar Assn., Lions (dir. Eugene chpt. 2000—). Republican. Avocations: aviation, golf, skiing. General civil litigation, Probate, Real property. Home: 640 Elwood Ct Eugene OR 97401-2235 Office: 875 Country Club Rd Eugene OR 97401-2255 E-mail: jhhorn@hotmail.com

HORN, STEPHEN, lawyer; b. N.Y.C., Sept. 12, 1946; s. Leonard and Gladys H.; m. Kerry Corcoran, Oct. 9, 1977. B.S. in Indsl. Engring., Rutgers, 1968; J.D. cum laude, Seton Hall Sch., 1973. Bar: D.C. 1974, U.S. Dist. Ct. D.C. 1979, U.S. Ct. Appeals (D.C. cir.) 1979, Md. 1982. Trial atty. Dept. Justice, Washington, 1973-78; ptnr. Horn & Conroy, 1979-83, Schmeltzer, Aptaker & Sheppard, P.C., 1983— . Editor-in-chief Jour. Seton Hall Law Rev., 1972-73. Contbr. articles to profl. publs. Served to 1st lt. inf., U.S. Army, 1968-70, Vietnam. Recipient Spl. Achievement award U.S. Dept. Justice, 1976. Mem. ABA (chmn. com. 1981-85). Republican. Jewish. Federal civil litigation, Criminal, Franchising. Office: Schmeltzer Aptaker & Sheppard PC 2600 Virginia Ave NW Ste 1000 Washington DC 20037-1922

HORNBLASS, JEROME, lawyer, mediator, arbitrator, former judge; b. N.Y.C., June 20, 1941; s. Maurice and Betty (Krieger) H.; m. Ann Herman; children: Jonathan, Elliott, Jessica. BA, Yeshiva U., 1962; JD, Bklyn. Law Sch., 1965. Bar: N.Y. 1965. Commr. N.Y.C. Addiction Svcs. Agy., 1974-77; judge N.Y.C. Criminal Ct., 1977-81; justice N.Y. State Supreme Ct., 1982-97; atty., mediator, arbitrator U.S. Post Office, Bankruptcy Ct. & Family Disputes/Discrimination Matters, N.Y.C., 1997—. Assoc. prof. law and sociology CCNY; lectr. New Sch. U., throughout U.S. Past pres. Civic Ctr. synagogue, N.Y.C., 1979; pres. Yeshiva Etz Chaim Found., Bklyn., 1980—. Mem. ABA, Internat. Assn. Jewish Lawyers and Jurists (v.p. 1982-86, pres. Am. sect. 1986—). Office: 370 E 76th St New York NY 10021-2547

HORNBY, DAVID BROCK, federal judge; b. Brandon, Manitoba, Can., Apr. 21, 1944; s. William Ralph Hornby and Retha Patricia (Fox) Sword; m. Helaine Cora Mandel, Oct. 9, 1946; children: Kirstin, Zachary. BA, U. Western Ont., 1965; JD, Harvard U., 1969. Bar: Va. 1973, Maine 1974, U.S. Supreme Ct. 1980. Law clk. U.S. Ct. Appeals, New Orleans, 1969-70; assoc. prof. U. Va. Sch. Law, Charlottesville, 1970-74; ptnr. Perkins, Thompson, Hinckley & Keddy, Portland, Maine, 1974-82; U.S. magistrate Dist. Maine, 1982-88; assoc. justice Maine Supreme Jud. Ct., 1988-90; judge U.S. Dist. Ct. Maine, 1990—; chief judge, 1996—. Mem. Fed. Jud. Ctr.'s Com. on Dist. Judge Edn., 1994-98, chair 1995-98; com. on ct. adminstrn. and case mgmt. Jud. Conf. of the U.S., 1990-2000, chair 1997-2000.; judge rep. 1st cir. Jud. Conf. Dist., 2000—. Contbr. articles to profl. jours.; editor, officer Harvard Law Rev., 1967-69. Fellow Am. Bar Found.; mem. ABA, Am. Law Inst., Maine State Bar Assn., Maine Bar Found. (bd. trustees 1990-94), Cumberland County Bar Assn. Office: US Dist Ct Edward T Gignoux Courthouse 156 Federal St Portland ME 04101-4152

HORNE, MICHAEL STEWART, lawyer; b. Mpls., May 10, 1938; s. Owen Edward and Adeline (DiGeorgio) H.; m. Martha Brean, Sept. 11, 1965; children: Jennifer, Katherine, Sarah, Owen. BA, U. Minn., 1959; LLB, Harvard U., 1962. Bar: D.C. 1963, U.S. Ct. Appeals (D.C. cir.) 1964, U.S. Supreme Ct. 1968, U.S. Ct. Appeals (6th cir.) 1966, U.S. Ct. Appeals (9th cir.) 1978, U.S. Ct. Appeals (4th cir.) 1979, U.S. Ct. Appeals (5th cir.) 1979, U.S. Ct. Appeals (2d cir.) 1980, U.S. Ct. Appeals (11th cir.) 1983, U.S. Ct. Appeals (8th cir.) 1984, U.S. Ct. Appeals (10th cir.) 1997. Assoc. Covington & Burling, Washington, 1964-71, ptnr., 1971—. Lawyer; b. Mpls., May 10, 1938; s. Owen Edward and Adeline (DiGeorgio) H.; m. Martha Brean, Sept. 11, 1965; children: Jennifer, Katherine, Sarah, Owen. BA, U. Minn., 1959; LLB, Harvard U., 1962. Bar: D.C. 1963, U.S. Ct. Appeals (D.C. cir.) 1964, U.S. Supreme Ct. 1968, U.S. Ct. Appeals (6th cir.), 1966, U.S. Ct. Appeals (9th cir.) 1978, U.S. Ct. Appeals (4th cir.) 1979, U.S. Ct. Appeals (5th cir.), 1979, U.S. Ct. Appeals (2d cir.) 1980, U.S. Ct. Appeals (11th cir.) 1983, U.S. Ct. Appeals (8th cir.) 1984, U.S. Ct. Appeals (10th cir.), 1997. Assoc. Covington & Burling, Washington, 1964-71, ptnr., 1971—. Mem. D.C. Bar Assn., ABA, FCC Bar Assn., Am. Judicature Soc. Democrat. Co-author (with T.S. Williamson and A. Herman): The Contingent Workforce, Business and Legal Strategies, 2000. Mem. ABA, D.C. Bar Assn., FCC Bar Assn., Am. Judicature Soc. Democrat. Administrative and regulatory, Labor, Libel. Home: 9008 Levelle Dr Bethesda MD 20815-5608 Office: Covington & Burling 1201 Pennsylvania Ave NW PO Box 7566 Washington DC 20044-7566 E-mail: hornems@erols.com, mhorne@cov.com

HORN EPSTEIN, PHYLLIS LYNN, lawyer; b. Phila., Sept. 10, 1955; d. Harold and Bernice H. BA, Temple U., 1977, JD, 1980, LLM, 1984. Bar: Pa. 1980, U.S. Dist. Ct. (ea. dist.) Pa., U.S. Ct. Appeals (3rd cir.). Assoc. Blumstein, Block & Vanore, Phila., 1980-81, Epstein, Beller & Shapiro, Phila., 1982-85, ptnr., 1985-86, Epstein, Shapiro & Epstein, Phila., 1986—. Instr. LaSalle Coll., Phila., 1980-82; vice-chmn. Fee Dispute Com., Phila. 1985, chmn., 1986. Co-author: Procedure and Administration: Bender's Federal Tax Service, 1989. Bd. dirs. Phila. chpt. Friends of Bezalel, 1987—. Mem. ABA (tax sect., group editor newsletter 1982-85, editor Tax Commentary newsletter 1985-88, court procedure com. 1984—), Pa. Bar Assn., Phila. Bar Assn., Pa. Trial Lawyers Assn., Hadassah (life). E-mial. General corporate, Corporate taxation, Taxation, general. Office: Epstein Shapiro & Epstein 1515 Market St 15th Fl Three Penn Ctr Philadelphia PA 19102 E-mail: jeepsu@aol.com

HORNER, RUSSELL GRANT, JR. real estate investor, retired energy and chemical company executive, inv; BA, U. Okla., 1961, LLB, 1963. Bar: Okla. 1963. Ptnr. Kerr-Davis, 1963-69; internat. counsel Kerr-McGee Corp., Oklahoma City, 1969-75, sr. v.p., gen. counsel, corp. sec., 1997-99; v.p. land Transworld Drilling Co., 1975-82, exec. v.p., 1982-86, v.p. gen counsel, 1986-87. Office: 3635 Brownwood Dr Paris TX 75462-8101

HOROWITZ, DONALD LEONARD, lawyer, educator, researcher, political scientist, arbitrator; b. N.Y.C., June 27, 1939; s. Morris and Yetta (Hibscher) H.; m. Judith Anne Present, Sept. 4, 1960; children: Marshall, Karen, Bruce. AB, Syracuse U., 1959, LLB, 1961; LLM, Harvard U., 1962, AM, 1965, PhD, 1967. Bar: N.Y. 1962, D.C. 1979, U.S. Ct. Appeals (D.C., 6th, 7th and 10th cirs.) 1970, U.S. Supreme Ct. 1969. Law clk. U.S. Dist. Ct. (ea. dist.), Pa., 1965-66; rsch. assoc. Harvard U. Ctr. Internat. Affairs, 1967-69; atty. Dept. Justice, Washington, 1969-71; fellow Coun. on Fgn. Rels./Woodrow Wilson Internat. Ctr. Scholars, 1971-72; rsch. assoc. Brookings Instn., 1972-75; sr. fellow Rsch. Inst. on Immigration and Ethnic Studies/Smithsonian, 1975-81; prof. law and polit. sci. Duke U., Durham, N.C., 1980—, Charles S. Murphy Prof., 1988-93, James B. Duke prof., 1994—. Vis. prof. Charles J. Merriam scholar U. Chgo. Law Sch., 1988; vis. fellow Cambridge U., Eng., 1988; Sticerd Disting. visitor London Sch. Econs., 1998-2000, Centennial prof., 2001; vis. scholar Universiti Kebangsaan Malaysia Law Faculty, 1991; cons. Ford Found., 1977-82; mem. internat. adv. com. Office of the High Rep., Bosnia, 1998-99; McDonald-Currie Meml. lectr. McGill U., Montreal, 1980; mem. Coun. on Role of Cts., 1978-83; Opsahl lectr. Queen's U., Belfast, 2000. Author: The Courts and Social Policy (Nat. Acad. Public Adminstrn. Louis Brownlow prize for best book in pub. adminstrn. 1977), 1977; The Jurocracy: Government Lawyers, Agency Programs and Judicial Decisions, 1977; Coup Theories and Officers' Motives, 1980, Ethnic Groups in Conflict, 1985, A Democratic South Africa? Constitutional Engineering in a Divided Soc., 1991 (Am. Polit. Sci. Assn. Ralph J. Bunche award for best book in ethnic and cultural pluralism, 1992), The Deadly Ethnic Riot, 2001; mem. editl. bd. Ethnicity, 1974-82, Law and Soc. Rev., 1979-82, Law and Contemporary Problems, 1983-84, 89-2000, Jour. Democracy, 1993—. Guggenheim fellow, 1980-81; Nat. Humanities Ctr. fellow, 1984. Fellow Am. Acad. Arts and Scis. Office: Duke University School Law Durham NC 27706

HOROWITZ, ROBERT M. lawyer; b. N.Y.C., Feb. 14, 1963; s. Harold M. and Charlotte R. (Rosenblatt) H. BA, Coll. of William and Mary, 1985; JD, U. Colo., 1988. Bar: Colo. 1988, U.S. Dist. Ct. Colo. 1988, U.S. Ct. Appeals (10th cir.). Instr. People's Law Sch., 1991-93, Nat. Inst. Trial Advocacy, 1993; shareholder Pearson, Milligan & Horowitz, P.C., Denver, 1991—. Mem. faculty 3rd Ann. Rocky Mountain Child Advocacy Tng. Inst., Million Dollar Advs. Forum. Mem. ABA (litigation sect.), Denver Bar Assn., Colo. Bar Assn. (litigation sect.), Colo. Trial Lawyers Assn. Avocations: backpacking, rock climbing, music. Contracts commercial, Entertainment, Insurance. Office: Pearson Milligan & Horowitz PC 1999 Broadway Ste 2300 Denver CO 80202-5750 E-mail: rhorowitz@pmh-law.com

HOROWITZ, STEPHEN PAUL, lawyer; b. L.A., May 23, 1943; s. Julius J. and Maxine (Rubenstein) H.; m. Nancy J. Shapiro, Apr. 4, 1971; children: Lindsey Nicole, Keri Lyn, Deborah Arielle. B.S., UCLA, 1966; J.D., 1970; M. Acctg., U. So. Calif., 1967. Bar: Calif. 1971, U.S. Dist. Ct. 1971, U.S. Ct. Appeals 1972. CPA, Calif. Bookkeeper, various law and acctg. firms, 1963-70; staff acct. Touche, Ross & Co., C.P.A.s, L.A., 1968, 69. Pvt. practice law, L.A., 1971-77; partner firm Horowitz & Horowitz, L.A., 1978-79, prin. firm, 1979—; judge pro tem L.A. Mcpl. Ct.; classroom speaker L.A. County Bar Assn.; arbitrator Better Bus. Bur., L.A. County Bar Assn., Am. Arbitration Assn., L.A. Superior Ct.; ombudsman VA, 1970. Bd. dirs. Vols. Am. Detoxification and Rehab. Center, L.A., 1975-81, treas., 1979, vice chmn., 1980-81; legal adv. chmn., parliamentarian Temple Ramat Zion, Northridge, Calif., 1983-88, v.p., 1988. Served with U.S. Army, 1961-62. Mem. Calif. State Bar, L.A. Trial Lawyers. Jewish. Lodge: Masons. Editorial bd. UCLA-Alaska Law Rev., 1968-70, co-editor-in-chief, 1969-70. State civil litigation, Personal injury, Probate. Office: 8383 Wilshire Blvd Ste 528 Beverly Hills CA 90211-2404

HORSLEY, JACK EVERETT, lawyer, writer; b. Sioux City, Iowa, Dec. 12, 1915; s. Charles E. and Edith V. (Timms) H.; m. Sallie Kelley, June 12, 1939 (dec.); children: Pamela, Charles Edward; m. Bertha J. Newland, Feb. 24, 1950 (dec.); m. Mary Jane Moran, Jan. 20, 1973; 1 child, Sharon. AB, U. Ill., 1937, JD, 1939. Bar: Ill. 1939. Ptnr. Craig & Craig, Mattoon, Ill., 1939-93, sr. atty.-of counsel, 1983-99. Instr. Sch. of the Solder, U. Ill. ROTC, 1934—36; temp. prof. law NYU, N.Y.C., 1974, N.Y.C., 90, N.Y.C., 99, N.Y.C., 2000; mem. Harlan Moore Heart Rsch. Found., 1968—, asst. treas., 1996—; mem. lawyers adv. coun. U. Ill. Law Forum, 1960—63; lectr. Practicing Law Inst., N.Y.C., 1967—73, U. Ill., Champaign, 1974, Ct. Practice Inst., Chgo., 1974—, Coll. Law Inst. Continuing Legal Edn., U. Mich., 1967, Bankers' Seminar, 1999, 2000; vis. lectr. Orange County (Fla.) Med. Soc., 1985, San Diego Med. Soc., 1970, U. S.C., 1976, Duquesne Coll., 1970, U. Ill. Law Forum, 1972, alumni adv. com., 1991—; vis. lectr. trial practice NYU Coll. Law, 1972; faculty banker seminar Wis. Med. Assn., Lake Geneva, 1997; lectr. med./legal seminars on tour Chgo., Cleve., Pa., Orlando, 1995; chmn. rev. bd. Ill. Supreme Ct. Disciplinary Commn., 1973—76, adv. cons., 1976—; lectr. Cleve. Hosp., Shelby, NC, 1976; adv. dir. Ctrl. Nat. Bank of Mattoon, 1980—99; vis. prof. trial practice Fordham Law Sch., N.Y.C., 1969; vis. prof. U. Berkeley Coll. Law, 1999; legal advisor 1st Nat. Bank Mattoon, 1999—; vis. lectr. John Marshall Sch. Law, Chgo., 1999—2001; vis. lectr. trial practice U. Nebr. Law Sch., 1999, Columbia U., N.Y.C., 1999; vis. lectr. Trial Practice Columbia U., NY, 1999; Trial Laureate Ill. Trial Lawyers Acad., 1996, Laureata-emeritus, 2000. Narrator Poetry Interludes, Sta. WLBH-FM, 1977—91; author: Trial Lawyer's Manual, 1967, Voir Dire Examinations and Opening Statements, 1968, Current Development in Products Liability Law, 1969, Illinois Civil Practice and Procedure, 1970, The Medical Expert Witness, 1973; author, author, author(supplement 4th edit.): Testifying in Court, 1973, author: The Doctor and the Law, 1975, The Doctor and Family Law, 1975, The Doctor and Business Law, 1976, The Doctor and Medical Law, 1977; author, author(3d edit.): Anatomy of a Medical Malpractice Case, 1984, author: Trilogy: The Frivolous Law Suit, 2000, (municipals) G.O. of Revenue, 1992, World War II, D-Day, 1994, author: Life's Challenges Preparation, 1999, World War II Air Mus, Duxford, Eng., 1999, Trial Techniques, 1995, Legal Liability Exposure of Trust Co., 1996, author: On Trust Dept. Guide-lines and Risks, 1996; author, author, author: On Federal Evidence and Examination, 1995; author, author: Memories of World War II in the European Theater, 1997, suppl. on post World War II Reserve officer duties, 2000 (awarded Purple Heart, 1943), author: History of the Bar in East Central Illinois, 1997, Remembrances: An Autobiography, 1998, Memories of World War II in the European Theater, 1997, suppl. on post World War II Reserve officer duties, 2000 (awarded Purple Heart, 1943), author: Views of Christianity: Origin of Man, 1999, (pamphlet) A Doctor's Duty: Presciption Care, 1999, Thoughts to Ponder, 2001; co-author: RN Legally Speaking, 1998, Matthew Bender Forensic Sciences, 1988, (2d edit.) , 2000; editor: Med. Econs., 1969—, Fifty Eight Years as Attorney, 1997; legal cons. Mast-Head, 1972—;contbr. , , , ; cons., reviewer Civil Practice State and Fed. Cts., 1998—2001, Thoughts to Ponder, 2001, contbr., cons. editor Eagle Forum;contbr. ; author, reviewer Current Developments in Medical Malpractice Law;contbr. , 2d edit., supplement, ; editor, editor, editor: Fifty Eight Years as Attorney, 1998; author, author: Memories of World War II in the European Theater, 1997, suppl. on post World War II Reserve officer duties, 2000 (awarded Purple Heart, 1943). Alt. del. to Rep. Platform Com., 2000; active Senatorial Reelection Com., 1993; mem. exec. com. Ill. Rep. Election Campaign, 1997; founding mem. U.S. Air Mus., Am. Air Mus., U.S. Supreme Ct. Hist. Soc.; pres. bd. edn. sch. dist. 100, 1946-48; bd. dirs. Harlan Moore Heart Rsch. Found., 1968-91, hon. dir., 1991—; vol. reader in rec. texts Am. Assn. for Blind, 1970-72; chmn. exec. com. U. Ill. Law Forum, 1990-91; founding mem. Home for Law Alumni Found., Chgo., 1999; pres. Res. Officers Assn. East Cen. Ill., 1988-89, 99-2000, chair, bd. dirs., 2000—; founder Bertha Newland Horsley award St. John's Coll. Nursing, Springfield, Mary Jane Horsley award trophy Mattoon (Ill.) H.S.; mem. exec. com. Ill. Rep. Election Campaign, 1997. Full col. hon. res., 1997. Recipient Disting. Svc. award U. Ill., 1995. Fellow Am. Coll. Trial Lawyers (co-chair membership commn. 1998, acting regent 2000-01); mem. ABA, Ill. Bar Assn. (exec. coun. ins. law 1961-63, com. chmn. banking law 1972, lectr. law course for attys. 1962, 64-65, sr. counsellor 1989—, Disting. Svc. award 1982-83), Assn. of Bar of City of N.Y. (non-resident), Coles-Cumberland Bar Assn. (v.p. 1968-2000, pres. 1969-70, chmn. com. jud. inquiry 1976-80, chair meml. com. 1989-2000, mem. exec. com. 1998, sr. counsellor 1989, co-author Forensic Scis. Jour. 1991, 2d edit. 1999, Life-time Achievement award 1999), Am. Arbitration Assn. (nat. panel arbitrators, counsel advisor hearing officers in Ill. 1996-97), U. Ill. Law Alumni Assn. (life mem., pres. 1966-67, Alumni of Month Sept. 1974, exec. com. 1990-91, Sr. Alumni of Month 2001), Ill. Appellate Lawyers Assn., Soc. Legal Scribes (chair emeritus 1995—), Ill. Def. Counsel Assn. (pres. 1967-88), Soc. Trial Lawyers (chmn. profl. activities 1960-61, bd. dirs. 1966-67), Fed. Ct. Hist. Soc. (co-chmn.), Adelphic Debating Soc., Assn. Ins. Attys., Internat. Assn. Ins. Counsel, Am. Judicature Soc., Res. Officers Assn. (pres. 1997-98, chair exec. com., pres. emeritus 1999), U. Ill. Alumni Assn. (exec. com. 1990-91), Soc. Legal Scribes, Masons (lectr. ceremonial 32 degree Scottish Rite 2000, Sr. Master award 1992), Scabbard and Blade Soc. U. Ill. (pres. 1936), Delta Phi (exec. com. alumni assn. 1960-61, 67-68), Sigma Delta Kappa. Lutheran. State civil litigation, Health, Personal injury. Home: 913 N 31st St Mattoon IL 61938-2271

HORSLEY, WALLER HOLLADAY, lawyer; b. Richmond, Va., July 2, 1931; s. John Shelton Jr. and Lilian (Holladay) H.; m. Margaret Stuart Cooke, Dec. 3, 1955; children: Margaret Terrell, Stuart W., John Garrett. BA with distinction, U. Va., 1953, LLB, 1959. Bar: Va. 1959, U.S. Dist. Ct. (ea. dist.) Va. 1959, U.S. Tax Ct. 1959, U.S. Ct. Appeals (4th cir.) 1959, U.S. Supreme Ct. 1969. Ptnr. Hunton & Williams, Richmond, 1965-92, Horsley & Horsley, Richmond, 1992—. Lectr. taxation U. Va. Law Sch., 1961-65, 69. Mem. editorial bd. Taxation for Lawyers, 1975-86, Probate Lawyer, 1976-87, Probate Notes, 1976-87, editor, 1986-87; bd. advisors Va. Tax Rev., 1981—; contbr. articles to legal jours. Mem. adv. coun. Sch. Bus., Va. Commonwealth U., 1983-91; sr. warden St. Stephen's Episcopal Ch., 1977-79; gen. conv. dep. Diocese of Va., 1979, 85; pres. Richmond Tennis Patrons Assn., 1969, Va. Silver Star Found., 1985-86; mem. bd. visitors U. Va., 1988-92. With USN, 1953-56; to lt. comdr. USNR, 1956-62. Recipient Algernon Sydney Sullivan award, 1953; named Outstanding Young Man of Yr., Richmond Jr. C. of C., 1965. Fellow Am. Bar Found., Va. Bar Found.; mem. ABA, Va. State Bar (pres. 1982-83), Va. Bar Assn., Am. Coll. Trust and Estate Counsel (pres. 1990), Country Club of Va., Westwood Club, Omicron Delta Kappa, Phi Beta Kappa, Order of Coif. Democrat. Episcopalian. Estate planning, Probate, Estate taxation. Office: Horsley & Horsley 5020 Monument Ave Fl 2 Richmond VA 23230-3620 E-mail: shors45683@aol.com

HORTTOR, DONALD J. lawyer; b. May 3, 1932; s. Elmer J. and Cleda C. (Cox) Horttor; m. Jane Ann Ausherman, Mar. 22, 1959; children: Daun Ann, Bretton J. AB in Econs., U. Kans., 1953, JD, 1959; LLM in Taxation, NYU, 1961. Bar: Kans. 1959, U.S. Dist. Ct. Kans. 1959, U.S. Ct. Appeals (10th cir.) 1963, U.S. Supreme Ct. 1965, U.S. Tax Ct. 1965. Adj. prof. Washburn U. Law Sch., Topeka, 1965—76; assoc. Cosgrove, Webb and

Oman, 1959—63, ptnr., 1963—. Author: (pamphlet) Estate Planning, Why A Will, Kans. Estate Adminstrn. Fellow: Am. Coll. Trust and Estate Coun.; mem.: ABA, Topeka Bar Assn., Kans. Bar Assn., Topeka Country Club, Masons, Elks, Moose. Republican. Congregationalist. Probate, Estate taxation, State and local taxation. Office: Bank IV Tower 1100 Nations Bank Terr Topeka KS 66603-3477

HORVITZ, MICHAEL JOHN, lawyer; b. Cleve., Feb. 15, 1950; s. Harry Richard and Lois Joy (Unger) H.; m. Jane Rosenthal, Aug. 25, 1979; children: Katherine R., Elizabeth R. BS in Econs., U. Pa., 1972; JD, U. Va., 1975; LLM in Taxation, NYU, 1980. Bar: Ohio 1975, Fla. 1976. Assoc. Hahn, Loeser, Freedheim, Dean & Wellman, Cleve., 1975-78; counsel Hollywood, Inc., Fla., 1978-79; assoc. Jones, Day, Reavis & Pogue, Cleve., 1980-85, ptnr., 1985-2000, of counsel, 2001—. Mem. adv. bd. Kirtland Capital Ptnrs., L.P., 1992—; chmn. Parkland Mgmt. Co., 1992—; vice chmn. Horvitz Newspapers, Inc., 1994—; pres. H.R.H. Family Found., 1992—; chmn. H.R.H. Family Trust, 1992—; bd. dirs. Zephyr Mgmt., Inc.; corp. advisor Internat. Mgmt. Group, 1999—. Trustee Jewish Cmty. Fedn. Cleve., 1993—, Case Western Res. U., Musical Arts Assn., 1992—, Cleve. Ctr. Econ. Edn., 1992-95, Am. Cancer Soc., Cuyahoga County unit, 1989-95, Hathaway Brown Sch., Mt. Sinai Med. Ctr., Cleve. chpt. Am. Jewish Com., 1984-95, Montefiore Home for the Elderly, 1982-90, Health Hill Hosp. for Children, 1982-95, bd. pres., 1987-89; bd. dirs. Cleve. Mus. Art, 1991—, pres. bd., 1996—. General corporate, Estate planning, Taxation, general. Office: Jones Day Reavis & Pogue 901 Lakeside Ave E Cleveland OH 44114-1190 also: Parkland Mgmt Co 1001 Lakeside Ave E Ste 900 Cleveland OH 44114-1172

HORWIN, LEONARD, lawyer; b. Chgo., Jan. 2, 1913; s. Joseph and Jennie (Fuhrmann) H.; m. Ursula Helene Donig, Oct. 15, 1939; children: Noel Samuel, Leonora Marie. LLD cum laude, Yale U., 1936. Bar: Calif. 1936, U.S. Dist. Ct. (cen. dist.) Calif. 1937, U.S. Ct. Appeals (9th cir.) 1939, U.S. Supreme Ct. 1940. Assoc. Lawler, Felix & Hall, 1936-39; counsel Bd. Econ. Warfare, Washington, 1942-43; attache, legal advisor U.S. Embassy, Madrid, Spain, 1943-47; sole practice Beverly Hills, Calif., 1948—. Dir., lectr. Witkin-Horwin Rev. Course on Calif. Law, 1939-42; judge pro tempore Los Angeles Superior Ct., 1940-42; instr. labor law U. So. Calif., 1939-42. Author: Insight and Foresight, 1990, Plain Talk, 1931—; contbr. articles to profl. jours. U.S. rep. Allied Control Council for Ger., 1945-47; councilman City of Beverly Hills, 1962-66, mayor, 1964-65; chmn. transp. Los Angeles Goals Council, 1968; bd. dirs. So. Calif. Rapid Transit Dist., 1964-66; chmn. Rent Stabilization Com., Beverly Hills, 1980. Fellow Am. Acad. Matrimonial Lawyers; mem. ABA, State Bar Calif., Order of Coif, Balboa Bay Club, Aspen Inst., La Costa Country Club. Family and matrimonial, General practice, Real property. Office: 121 S Beverly Dr Beverly Hills CA 90212-3002 E-mail: lhorwin@mindspring.com

HORWITZ, ETHAN, lawyer; b. Binghamton, N.Y., May 9, 1952; s. Lester and Barbara (Goldstein) H.; m. Freddi Sue Firegood; children: Jessica Sara, Matthew Eli, Emily Cristal. BS, Poly. Inst. Bklyn., 1972; MS, NYU, 1974; JD, St. Johns U., 1976. Bar: N.Y. 1977. Assoc. Cooper, Dunham, Clark, Griffin & Moran, N.Y.C., 1976-77, Ladas & Parry, N.Y.C., 1977-80, Darby & Darby, N.Y.C., 1980-86, ptnr., 1986—. Author: (treatise) World Trademark Law and Practice, 1982; co-author: (treatise) Patent Litigation: Procedure and Tactics; co-editor: Intellectual Property Counseling and Litigation; mem. editl. bd. Trademark Reporter, 1980-82. Bd. dirs. Project Dorot, N.Y.C., 1977—, pres., 1984-89. Mem. N.Y. Patent Law Assn., U.S. Trademark Assn. (chmn. Western Europe com.), Inst. Trademark Agts. (overseas mem.), Internat. Assn. Protection Indsl. Property, Internat. Bar Assn. Fedn. Internat. de Conseils en Propriete Industrielle. Jewish. Federal civil litigation, Patent, Trademark and copyright. Office: Darby & Darby PC 805 3rd Ave Fl 27 New York NY 10022-7513

HORWITZ, KENNETH MERRILL, lawyer, accountant; b. Atlanta, Oct. 11, 1943; s. Sidney A. and Lillian Ann (Rappaport) H.; m. Barbara Lynn Smith, June 23, 1968; children: Seth A., Lisa E. BS in Psychology, Ga. Inst. Tech., 1965; JD, Emory U., 1968; LLM, George Washington U., 1972. Bar: Ga. 1968, D.C. 1969, Tex. 1974. Sr. tax specialist IRS, Washington, 1969-74; assoc. McDonald, Sanders et al, Ft. Worth, 1974-76; ptnr. Laventhol & Horwath, Dallas, 1978-83, Coopers & Lybrand, Dallas, 1989, Washington, 1983-89; ptnr. gen. bus. & taxation Vial, Hamilton, Koch & Knox, Dallas, 1989—. Contbr. articles to profl. jours. Mem. ABA, AICPA, Tex. Bar Assn., Tex. Soc. CPAs (bd. dirs., bd. govs. CPE Found.), , Dallas Bar Assn. (past chair internat. law sect.), Internat. Trade Assn. Dallas Ft. Worth (former treas.), Dallas Coun. World Affairs (bd. dirs.), Internat. Tax Assn. (chmn. Dallas chpt.). Corporate taxation, Estate taxation, Taxation, general. Office: Vial Hamilton Koch & Knox LLP 1717 Main St Ste 4400 Dallas TX 75201-7388

HOSEMAN, DANIEL, lawyer; b. Chgo., Aug. 18, 1935; s. Irving and Anne (Pruzansky) H.; m. Susan H. Myles, Aug. 7, 1960; children: Lawrence N., Joan E., Jonathan W. BS, U. Ill., 1956, JD, 1959. Bar: Ill. 1959, U.S. Dist. Ct. (no. dist.) Ill. 1960, U.S. Ct. of Appeals (7th cir.) 1969, U.S. Supreme Ct. 1976. Atty. pvt. practice, Chgo., 1959—. Mem. panel pvt. atty. trustees U.S. Bankruptcy Ct. No. Dist. Ill., 1979—; arbitrator Cir. Ct. Cook County. Trustee Ill. Legal Svcs. Fund, 1978—; v.p. Allied Jewish Sch. Bd. Met. Chgo., 1977—; v.p. United Synagogue Am., 1978—. With USAFR, 1959-65. Mem. Am. Bankruptcy Inst., Advs. Soc., Decalogue Soc. Lawyers (pres. 1981-82, award of merit 1979-80), Ill. Bar Assn. (gen. assembly, long-range planning com.), Lake County Bar Assn. (com. on bankruptcy 1980—), Chgo. Coun. Lawyers, Comml. Law League Am., Am. Bankruptcy Inst., Nat. Assn. Bankruptcy Trustees. Bankruptcy, Consumer commercial, Contracts commercial. Home: 2151 Tanglewood Ct Highland Park IL 60035-4231 Office: 77 W Washington St Ste 1220 Chicago IL 60602-2901

HOSSLER, DAVID JOSEPH, lawyer, law educator; b. Mesa, Ariz., Oct. 18, 1940; s. Carl Joseph and Elizabeth Ruth (Bills) H.; m. Gretchen Anne, Mar. 2, 1945; 1 child, Devon Annagret. BA, U. Ariz., 1969, JD, 1972. Bar: Ariz. 1972, U.S. Dist. Ct. Ariz. 1972, U.S. Supreme Ct. 1977. Legal intern to chmn. FCC, summer 1971; law clk. to chief justice Ariz. Supreme Ct., 1972-73; chief dep. county atty. Yuma County (Ariz.), 1973-74; ptnr. Hunt, Kenworthy and Hossler, Yuma, Ariz., 1974—. Instr. in law and banking, law and real estate Ariz. Western Coll.; instr. in bus. law, mktg., ethics Webster U.; instr. agrl. law U. Ariz.; co-chmn. fee arbitration com. Ariz. State Bar, 1990—; instr. employee/employer law U. Phoenix. Editor-in-chief Ariz. Adv., 1971-72. Mem. precinct com. Yuma County Rep. Ctrl. Com., 1974-2000, vice chmn., 1982; chmn. region II Acad. Decathalon competition, 1989; bd. dirs. Yuma County Ednl. Found. (Hall of Fame 2000), Yuma County Assn. Behavior Health Svcs., also pres., 1981; coach Yuma H.S. mock ct. team, 1987-94; bd. dirs. friends of U. Med. Ctr. With USN. Recipient Man and Boy award Boys Clubs Am., 1979, Freedoms Found. award Yuma chpt., 1988, Demolay Legion of Honor, 1991, Francis Woodward award Ariz. Pub. Svc., 2000; named Vol. of Yr., Yuma County, 1981-82, Heart of Yuma award, 2000. Mem. ATLA, Am. Judicature Soc., Yuma County Bar Assn. (pres. 1975-76), Navy League, VFW, Am. Legion, U. Ariz. Alumni Assn. (nat. bd. dirs., past pres., hon. bobcat 1996, Disting. Citizen award 1997), Rotary (pres. Yuma club 1987-88, dist. gov. rep. 1989, dist. gov. 1992-93, findings com. 1996, dist. found. chair 1996-2000, co-chmn. membership retention 2000-01, John Van Houton Look Beyond Yourself award 1995, Roy Slayton Share Rotary Share People award 1996, Al Face You Are the Key award 1997, Ted Day Let Svc. Light the Way award 1998, Rotary Found. citation for meritorious svc., Internat. Svc. Above Self award, Cliff Doctorman Real Happiness is Helping Others award). Episcopalian (vestry 1978-82). State civil litigation, Family and matrimonial, Personal injury. Home: 2802 S Fern Dr Yuma AZ 85364-2919 Office: Hunt and Hossler 330 W 24th St Yuma AZ 85364-6455 also: PO Box 2919 Yuma AZ 85366-2919 E-mail: dhossler@mindspring.com

HOSTNIK, CHARLES RIVOIRE, lawyer; b. Glen Ridge, N.J., Apr. 8, 1954; s. William John and Susan (Rivoire) H. AB, Dartmouth Coll., 1976; JD, U. Puget Sound, 1979. Bar: Wash. 1980, U.S. Dist. Ct. (we. dist.) Wash. 1980, U.S. Dist. Ct. (ea. dist.) Wash. 1982, U.S. Ct. Appeals (9th cir.) 1983, Hoh Tribal Ct. 1984, Nisqually Tribal Ct. 1984, Puyallup Tribal Ct. 1984, Shoalwater Bay Tribal Ct. 1984, Skokomish Tribal Ct. 1984. Asst. atty. gen. Atty. Gen.'s Office State of Wash., Olympia, 1980-84; assoc. Kane, Vandeberg, Hartinger & Walker, Tacoma, 1984-87; ptnr. Anderson, Burns & Hostnik, 1988—. Trial and appellate judge N.W. Intertribal Ct. Sys., Edmonds, Wash., 1986-00. Author: (chpt.) Washington Practice, 1989. General practice, Native American, Personal injury. Office: Anderson Burns & Hostnik 6915 Lakewood Dr W Ste A1 Tacoma WA 98467-3299

HOTH, STEVEN SERGEY, lawyer, educator; b. Jan. 30, 1941; s. Donald Leroy and Ina Dorothy (Barr) H.; m. JoEllen Maly, July 29, 1967; children: Andrew Steven, Peter Lindsey. AB, Grinnell Coll., 1962; JD, U. Iowa, 1966; postgrad., U. Pa., 1968, Oxford (Eng.) U., 1973. Bar: U.S. Ct. Appeals (8th cir.) 1966, U.S. Tax Ct. 1967, U.S. Ct. Claims 1967, U.S. Dist. Ct. Iowa 1968, U.S. Dist. Ct. N.D. 1968, U.S. Dist. Ct. S.D. 1968, U.S. Supreme Ct. 1973, U.S. Ct. Appeals (7th cir.) 1982. Law clk. to chief justice U.S. Ct. Appeals (8th cir.), Fargo, N.D., 1967-68; assoc. Hirsch, Adams, Hoth & Krekel, Burlington, Iowa, 1968-72, ptnr., 1972-91; pvt. practice, 1992—. Asst. atty. Des Moines County, Burlington, 1968-72, atty., 1972-83; alt. mcpl. judge, Burlington, 1968-69; lectr. criminal law Southeastern C.C., West Burlington, 1972-82; assoc. prof. polit. sci. Iowa Wesleyan Coll., Mt. Pleasant, 1981-82, Iowa Truck Rail; pres. Burlington Truck Rail, Burlington Short Line RR. Inc., Iowa Internat. Investments, Burlington Storage and Transfer; sec. Burlington Loading Co. Contbr. numerous articles to profl. jours. Chmn. Des Moines County Civil Svc. Commn.; trustee Charles H. Rand Lecture Trust; mem. Des Moines County Conf. Com., Des Moines County Conf. Bd.; dir. Burlington Med. Ctr. Staff Found.; moderator 1st Congl. Ch., Burlington; bd. dirs. UN Assn.; clk. Burlington North Bottoms Levy and Drainage Dist.; bd. mem., pres. Burlington Cmty. Sch. Dist. Bd. Edn., chmn. commn. on ministry, mem. exec. com. Nat. Assn. Congl. Christian Chs., moderator; treas. 1st dist. Dem. Com.; bd. dirs. Legal Aid Soc. Planned Parenthood Des Moines County. Recipient Chmn.'s award ARC, 1980; Reginald Heber Smith fellow in legal aid Cheyenne River Indian Reservation, Eagle Butte, S.D., 1967-68. Mem. Missionary Soc.-Nat. Assn. Congl. Christian Chs., ABA (internat. sect., tax sect.), Iowa State Bar Assn. (Med. Soc. liaison), Des Moines County Bar Assn., Am. Judicature Soc., Agrl. Law Com., Iowa Def. Coun., Iowa Archaeol. Soc., Soc. for German Am. Studies, Manorial Soc. Gt. Britain, Grinnell Coll. Alumni Assn. (bd. dirs.), Malawi Soc., Burlington-West Burlington C. of C. (bd. dirs.), Nat. Assn. Congrl. Christian Chs., Burlington Golf Club, New Crystal Lake Club (pres.), Elks, Eagles, Masons, Rotary. General corporate, General practice, Private international. Office: PO Box 982 Hoth Bldg 200 Jefferson St Burlington IA 52601 E-mail: attorney@interl.net

HOUCHINS, LARRY, legal association administrator; m. Pamela Palmer; children: Palmer, Peyton. BBA in Mgmt., U. Miss., 1975. Exec. dir. Miss. Trial Lawyers Assn., 1975-80, Miss. Bar, Jackson, 1980—. Mem. Nat. Assn. Bar Execs., Am. Soc. Assn. Execs., Miss. Soc. Assn. Execs. Presbyn. Office: PO Box 2168 Jackson MS 39225-2168 E-mail: houchins@msbar.org

HOUGH, THOMAS HENRY MICHAEL, lawyer, educator; b. Midland, Pa., Aug. 4, 1933; s. Bert Patrick and Marguerite (Mullen) H.; m. Jocelyn Peltz, Aug. 20, 1956; children: Jocelyn, Thomas Henry Michael. AB, Dickinson Coll., 1955; JD, Dickinson Sch. Law, 1958. Bar: Pa. 1959, U.S. Ct. Appeals (3d cir.) 1975, U.S. Supreme Ct. 1970. Field atty. NLRB, Pitts., 1959-60; atty. United Steelworkers Am., 1960-68; ptnr. Lucchino, Gaitens & Hough, Pitts., 1968-79, Hough & Gleason, P.C., Pitts., 1980-94, Barry Fasulo & Hough, P.C., Pitts., 1994—. Adj. assoc. prof. pub. sector arbitration and pub. sector collective bargaining Grad. Sch. Pub. and Internat. Affairs, U. Pitts., 1970-97. Health, Labor. Office: Barry Fasulo & Hough 3700 Gulf Tower 707 Grant St Pittsburgh PA 15219-1908

HOULE, JEFFREY ROBERT, lawyer; b. Biddeford, Maine, July 27, 1965; s. Marcel Paul and Lois Marie (Jackson) H.; m. Lorren Johnston Houle, Oct. 11, 1997; children: Grace Morgan, Hunter Jackson. AB, Boston Coll., Chestnut Hill, Mass., 1987; JD, Western New Eng. Coll., Springfield, Mass., 1991; LLM in Taxation, Cert. in Employee Benefits Law, Georgetown U., Washington, 1992, LLM in Securities Regulation, 1995. Bar: D.C., N.Y., Conn., Mass., Maine. Pres. A.F.I. Investments, Springfield, Mass., 1988-91, Washington Capital Ventures, LP, Washington, 1995-98; law clk. Stones Solicitors, Exeter, Devon, Eng., 1989; jud. intern to the Hon. Joan Glazer Margolis U.S. Magistrate Judge, New Haven, 1990; legal intern Office of Atty. Gen. Robert Abrams, N.Y.C., 1990; analyst The Bur. of Nat. Affairs, Inc., Washington, 1992; assoc. Andros, Floyd & Miller PC, Hartford, Conn., 1992-94, Elias, Matz, Tiernan & Herrick LLP, Washington, 1994-98; founding ptnr. Greenberg Traurig LLP, McLean, Va., 1998—. Contbr. articles to profl. jours. With U.S. Army, 1984-86. Mem. ABA, The Army and Navy Club, The Federalist Soc.,The Tower Club, Phi Alpha Delta. Republican. Roman Catholic. Avocations: hiking, swimming, horseback riding, international travel. General corporate, Securities, Taxation, general.

HOULIHAN, DAVID PAUL, lawyer; b. Youngstown, Ohio, May 14, 1937; s. Paul V. and Delcie (Norman) H.; m. Marlene K. Betras, Aug. 13, 1960; children: Kevin, Rex, Laura, Brian. BS, Youngstown State U., 1959; postgrad., Purdue U., 1960; LLB, Georgetown U., 1964. Bar: D.C. 1965, U.S. Ct. Appeals (D.C. cir.) 1965, U.S. Supreme Ct. 1968, U.S. Ct. Internat. Trade 1976, U.S. Ct. Customs and Patent Appeals 1976, U.S. Ct. Appeals (Fed. cir.) 1982. Analyst U.S. Internat. Trade Commn., Washington, 1960-64; counsel U.S.-Japan trade council Stitt & Hemmendinger, 1964-68; ptnr. Daniels, Houlihan & Palmeter P.C., 1968-84, Mudge, Rose, Guthrie, Alexander & Ferdon, Washington, 1984-95, White & Case, Washington, 1995—. Lectr. Oxford U., Eng., 1972; chmn. Keidanren Seminar: Dumping, Customs and Tax Aspects of Transfer Pricing. Contbr. articles to profl. jours. Mem. ABA, D.C. Bar Assn., British-Am. C. of C. Democrat. Roman Catholic. Avocations: sailing, music. Administrative and regulatory, Private international. Address: White & Case 601 13th St NW Washington DC 20005-3807 E-mail: dhowlihan@whitecase.com

HOULIHAN, GERALD JOHN, lawyer; b. Cortland, N.Y., Aug. 26, 1943; s. Robert Emmett and Helen (Corsi) H.; m. Claudia C. Kitchens; children: Andrea, Gerald Jr., Maureen, Katherine, Colleen. BS, U. Notre Dame, 1965; JD, Syracuse U., 1968. Bar: N.Y. 1968, U.S. Dist. Ct. (we. dist.) N.Y. 1968, U.S. Ct. Appeals (2nd cir.) 1972, U.S. Supreme Ct. 1980, U.S. Ct. Appeals (5th cir.) 1981, U.S. Ct. Appeals (11th cir.) 1981, Fla. 1985, U.S. Dist. Ct. (so. dist.) Fla. 1985, U.S. Dist. Ct. (so. dist.) N.Y. 1986, U.S. Dist. Ct. (no. dist.) Fla. 1986, U.S. Ct. Appeals (4th and D.C. cirs.) 1987, U.S. Dist. Ct. (middle dist.) Fla., 1987. Assoc. Harris, Beach, Keating et al., Rochester, N.Y., 1968-72; asst. U.S. atty. U.S. Atty.'s Office, 1972-81; sr. litigation counsel U.S. Dept. Justice, 1981-82; chief asst. U.S. atty. U.S. Atty.'s Office, Miami, Fla., 1982-85; ptnr. Steel Hector & Davis, 1985-91; mem. Greenberg, Traurig, Hoffman, Lipoff, Rosen & Quentel, P.A., 1991-95; ptnr. Houlihan & Ptnrs., P.A., 1995—. Advocate Am. Bd. Trial Advocates. Belle L. Landry scholar Syracuse Soc. Mem. Fed. Bar Assn. (pres. 1993-94, bd. dirs. Miami chpt. 1988—), Order of Coif. Democrat. Antitrust, Federal civil litigation, Criminal. Home: 5191 SW 76th St Miami FL 33143-6015 Office: Houlihan & Ptnrs PA 2600 S Douglas Rd Ste 600 Miami FL 33134-6100 E-mail: gjhoulihan@aol.com

HOUPT, JAMES EDWARD, lawyer; b. Calif., 1951; m. Leslie Ann Jones Houpt. BA with distinction, Calif. State U., Chico, 1976; JD cum laude, Harvard U., 1992. Bar: Va. 1992, D.C. 1992, U.S. Ct. Appeals (4th cir.) 1992, Md. 1993, Calif. 1997, U.S. Ct. Appeals (9th cir.) 1997. News dir. Sta. KNVR-FM, Paradise, Calif., 1978-80; anchor, reporter Sta. KHSL-AM-TV, Chico, 1980-85; sr. reporter Sta. KOLO-TV, Reno, 1985-89; assoc. Baker & Hostetler, Washington, 1992-97, Orrick, Herrington & Sutcliffe LLP, Sacramento, 1997—. Lectr. journalism Calif. State U., 1981, 85; adj. prof. law sch. U. Calif., Davis, vis. prof., 1999, 2000. Author: (booklet) Access to Electronic Records, 1990, The Libel Curtain: A Comparison of Canadian & American Libel Law, 1994, Going On-Line: Is the World Wide Web a Web for the Unwary?, 1996, Boarding a Moving Bus: Developing an Internet Risk Management Strategy, 1997, The Courts and the Internet: A Match Made in Hell?, 2000; contbr. articles to legal and gen. interest publs. With USN, 1970-74. Recipient Cert. of Merit, Calif.-Nev. AP TV-Radio Assn., 1983, 84, 86. Mem. ABA, Va. State Bar Assn., D.C. Bar, Calif. Bar Assn., VFW, Am. Legion. Avocations: photography, hiking, canoeing. General civil litigation, Libel, Trademark and copyright. Office: Orrick, Herrington & Sutcliffe LLP 400 Capitol Mall Ste 3000 Sacramento CA 95814-4497

HOUSEMAN, ALAN WILLIAM, lawyer; b. Colorado Springs, Colo., Apr. 23, 1943; s. Murl Clarence and Opal Juanita (Snyder) H.; m. Susan Hays Margolis, June 17, 1967; children: Alana Judith, Nora Suzanne. BA, Oberlin Coll., 1965; JD, NYU, 1968. Bar: Mich. 1968, U.S. Dist. Ct. (ea. dist.) Mich. 1969, U.S. Dist. Ct. (we. dist.) Mich. 1970, U.S. Ct. Appeals (6th cir.) 1973, U.S. Supreme Ct. 1976, D.C. 1979, U.S. Ct. Appeals (D.C. cir.) 1982, U.S. Ct. Appeals (3d cir.). Reginald Heber Smith fellow Wayne County Legal Services, Detroit, 1968-69; dir. Mich. Legal Services, 1969-76; dir. research inst. Legal Services Corp., Washington, 1976-81; dir. Ctr. for Law and Social Policy, 1981—. Author: (with others) Legal Services History, 1984; contbr. articles to profl. jours. Chmn. Orgn. of Legal Svcs. Back-Up Ctrs., N.Y.C., 1973-75; vice chmn. Project Adv. Group, Washington, 1974-76. Recipient Recognition award Mich. Welfare Rights Orgn., 1975, Achievement award Project Adv. Group, 1979, 88, Nat. Equal Justice award, 1994. Mem. ABA, Nat. Legal Aid and Defender Assn. (chmn. civil com. 1975-77, recipient spl. award 1973, 88, 2000), Law and Soc. Assn., Soc. Am. Law Tchrs. Democrat. Mem. United Ch. Christ. Avocations: hiking, tennis, music. Home: 1715 Crestwood Dr NW Washington DC 20011-5333 Office: Ctr for Law and Social Policy 1616 P St NW Washington DC 20036-1434 E-mail: ahouse@clasp.org

HOUSER, JOHN EDWARD, lawyer; b. Richmond, Va., Dec. 24, 1928; s. Aubrey Alphin and Winnifred (Savage) H.; m. Elizabeth Rives Pollard, Apr. 1, 1967; children— Allen Rives Cabell Lybrook, Andrew Murray Lybrook. B.S., U. Va., 1959, LL.B., 1959. Bar: Fla. 1959, U.S. dist. ct. (so. and mid. dists.) Fla. 1959, U.S. Ct. Appeals (5th cir.) 1963, U.S. Supreme Ct. 1970, U.S. Ct. Appeals (11th cir.) 1981. Assoc., Jennings, Watts, Clarke & Hamilton, Jacksonville, Fla., 1959-61, Howell, Kirby, Montgomery & Sands, Jacksonville, 1961-63; ptnr. Howell & Houser, Jacksonville, 1963-65; sole practice, Jacksonville, 1965—; lectr. on Long shore and Harbor works Comp. Act Loyola U., 1979, 88; dir. William P. Polythress & Co., Richmond, Neal F. Tyler & Sons, Jacksonville. Author: England's Legacy to America, 1996. Active Jacksonville U. Council, Jacksonville Symphony Assn., Fla. Hist. Soc., Jacksonville Hist. Soc., Cummer Gallery of Art, Jacksonville Art Mus.; mem. English-Speaking Union, dir., 1970-79, pres., 1974-78, nat. regional chmn., 1973-76, nat. dir., 1976-81; hon. sec. Live Oak Hounds; subscriber Exmoor Foxhounds; active Thomasville Landmarks, dir., 1991—, Thomasville Arts Guild, Thomasville Cultural Ctr., Thomas County Hist. Soc. Served with AUS, 1953-57. Mem. Internat. Assn. Indsl. Accident Bds. and Commns., Maritime Law Assn., Southeastern Admiralty Law Inst., Jacksonville Claimsmen Assn., Atlanta Claimsmen Assn., ABA, Jacksonville Bar Assn., Fla. Bar, Fla. Def. Scl. Assn., Am. Judicature Soc., Am. Arbitration Assn., Ga. Trust for His. Preservation, Nat. Trust Hist. Preservation, Fla. Inst. Pub. Affairs, Navy League, Jacksonville Assn. Def. Counsel, Def. Research Inst., Theta Delta Chi, Sigma Nu Phi. Clubs: Rotary Internat., River, Fla. Yacht, University (Jacksonville), Deerwood, Ponte Vedra River, Exchange, German, Ye Mystic Revellers, Univ., Princeton of N.Y., Glen Arven, Commonwealth (Richmond, Va.); 2300. Admiralty, Federal civil litigation, Workers' compensation. Office: PO Box 873 Jacksonville FL 32201-0873

HOUSER, RONALD EDWARD, lawyer, mediator; b. Fairbury, Nebr., Aug. 11, 1949; s. Edward Erle and Lois Charlotte (Dux) H.; m. Linda Marie Webber, June 13, 1971 (div. 1985); children: Angela Marie, Brian Edward, Darren James; m. Beatrice Virginia McMullen Bupp, July 24, 1993. DVM, U. Mo., 1974; MS, Ohio State U., 1979; JD, U. Ga., 1990. Bar: Ga. 1990, U.S. Dist. Ct. (mid., no. and so. dist.) Ga. 1990, U.S. Ct. Appeals (11th cir.) 1990, U.S. Ct. Mil. Appeals 1993, U.S. Supreme Ct. 1993. Asst. instr. Univ. Nebr., Lincoln, 1979-83; owner, mgr. Lincoln Animal Health Clinic, 1983-85; atty. Cook, Noell, Tolley, Bates & Michael, Athens, Ga., 1990—. Contbr. articles to profl. jours. Mem. Nebr. State Bd. Health, 1980-84. Mem. Nat. Lawyers Assn., Nebr. Vet. Med. Assn. (dist. pres. 1979-81), Christian Legal Soc., Res. Officers Assn., Am. Legion, Phi Alpha Delta, Sigma Xi. Avocations: sports, reading, gardening. Alternative dispute resolution, Appellate, Criminal. Home: PO Box 502 Athens GA 30603-0502 Office: Cook Noell Tolley Bates & Michael LLP 304 E Washington St Athens GA 30601-2751

HOUSTON, JAMES GORMAN, JR. state supreme court justice; b. Eufaula, Ala., Mar. 11, 1933; s. James Gorman and Mildred (Vance) H.; m. Martha Martin, Dec. 3, 1955; children: Mildred Vance, J. Gorman III. BS, Auburn U., 1955; LLB, U. Ala., 1956, JD, 1969. Bar: Ala. 1956. Law clk. to chief justice Ala. Supreme Ct., Montgomery, 1956-57; ptnr. Houston & Martin, P.C., Eufaula, 1960-85; assoc. justice Ala. Supreme Ct., Montgomery, 1985—. County atty. Barbour County, Clayton, Ala., 1961-79. Contbr. numerous opinions to So. Reporter; contbr. articles to profl. jours. Mayor pro tem, alderman City of Eufaula, 1964-70; pres. Heritage Assn., Eufaula, Ala., 1979-82; mem. Ala. Commn. on Uniform State Laws. 1st lt. JAGC, USAF, 1957-60. Named Citizen of Yr., City of Eufaula, 1979; recipient Alumni Achievement in Humanities award Auburn Univ., 1993. Fellow Am. Bar Found.; mem. ABA, Ala. Bar Assn., Ala. State Bar (examiner 1979-82, disciplinary commn. 1984-85, state bar commr. 1982-85), Barbour County Bar Assn. (pres. 1975), Eufaula C. of C. (pres. 1974). Republican. Methodist. Office: Ala Supreme Ct 300 Dexter Ave Montgomery AL 36104-3741

HOVDA, THEODORE JAMES, lawyer; b. Forest City, Iowa, Oct. 15, 1951; s. Ernest J. and Doris (Goodnight) H.; m. Susan J. Miller, Feb. 24, 1973; children: Theodore James III, Lee Joseph, Margaux Ann. BS, Iowa State U., 1973; JD, U. Iowa, 1977. Asst. county atty. Hancock County, Garner, Iowa, 1977-78, county atty., 1979-98; mem. Riehm & Hovda, 1977-98, Hovda Law Office, 1998—. County chmn. Hancock County Rep. Ctrl. Com., 1979-98. Mem. Iowa Bar Assn., Hancock County Bar Assn., Dist. 2A Bar Assn., Rotary, Masons. Republican. Methodist. Estate planning, Probate, Personal income taxation. Home: 785 11th Street Pl Garner IA 50438-1848 Office: Hovda Law Office PO Box 9 395 State St Garner IA 50438-1236 Fax: 641-923-3108. E-mail: tshovda@kalnet.com

HOVDE, F. BOYD, lawyer; b. Mpls., Aug. 7, 1934; s. Frederick L. and Priscilla L. (Boyd) H.; m. Alice Austell, Feb. 22, 1981; children by previous marriage: Frederick R., Debra L., Kristine L., Sarah L. AB, Princeton U., 1956; JD, U. Mich., 1959. Bar: Ind. 1959, U.S. Dist. Ct. (no. and so. dists.) Ind. 1959, U.S. Ct. Appeals (7th cir.) 1960, U.S. Supreme Ct. 1977. Assoc. Ice, Miller, Donadio & Ryan, Indpls., 1959-67, ptnr., 1967-69, Townsend, Hovde & Townsend, Indpls., 1969-77; mem. Townsend, Hovde, Townsend & Montross, P.C., 1977-84, Townsend, Hovde & Montross, P.C., 1984-97, F. Boyd Hovde, P.C., 1985—, Hovde Law Firm, 1997—. Mem. com. on character and fitness Ind. Supreme Ct., 1976-2000, rules of practice and procedure, 1980-92. Mem. Indpls. Bar Assn. (treas. 1969, v.p. 1974, pres. 1979), ABA (del. 1980-83), Ind. Trial Lawyers Assn. (bd. dirs. 1970—, pres. 1976-77), Assn. Trial Lawyers Am., Am. Coll. Trial Laywers, Internat. Acad. Trial Lawyers, Ind. Coll. Trial Lawyers, Indpls. Jaycees (pres. 1963-64), Ind. Golf Assn. (pres. 1974-75), Western Golf Assn. (dir. 1969-81, v.p. 1972-81), Crooked Stick Golf Club (Carmel, Ind.), Pine Valley Golf Club (Celmenton, N.J.), Old Marsh Golf Club (Palm Beach Gardens, Fla.). Personal injury, Product liability, Professional liability. Office: Hovde Law Firm Ste 345 10585 N Meridian St Indianapolis IN 46290-1068 E-mail: f.b.hovde@hovdelaw.com

HOVDE, FREDERICK RUSSELL, lawyer; b. Lafayette, Ind., Oct. 1, 1955; s. F. Boyd and Karen (Sorenson) H. BBA, So. Meth. U., 1977; JD, Ind. U., 1980. Bar: Ind. 1980, U.S. Dist. Ct. (no. and so. dists.) Ind. 1980, U.S. Ct. Appeals (7th cir.) 1980. Ptnr. Hovde Law Firm, Indpls., 1980—. Bd. visitors Ind. U. Sch. of Law, Indpls., 1993—. Bd. dirs. Ind. Golf Found., 1998—. Fellow Am. Coll. Trial Lawyers, Ind. Coll. Trial Lawyers, Indpls. Bar Found.; mem. ABA, Ind. Bar Assn. (bd. dirs. young lawyers sect. 1983-86), Indpls. Bar Assn. (bd. dirs. young lawyers sect. 1986-89), Assn. Trial Lawyers Am. (sustaining), Ind. Trial Lawyers Assn. (bd. dirs. 1990—, exec. com. 1995—, pres.-elect 2001), Am. Bd. Trial Advs., Tex. Trial Lawyers Assn., Ind. Golf Assn. (pres. 1995-97), Sagamore Inn of Ct., Crooked Stick Golf Club (pres. 1992-93). Personal injury, Product liability. Office: Hovde Law Firm 10585 N Meridian St Indianapolis IN 46290-1069 E-mail: rhovde@hovdelaw.com

HOWALD, JOHN WILLIAM, lawyer; b. St. Louis, Dec. 21, 1935; s. Herbert John and Irene Dorothy (Weber) H.; m. Nina M. Zierenderg, June 15, 1957 (div. 1970); children: Deborah A., Catherine A., Laura A., John William; m. Betty L. Curtis, Feb. 14, 1971 (div. 1999); 1 stepchild, Tracy L. BS, U. Mo., 1957; JD, St. Louis U., 1962. Bar: Mo. 1962, U.S. Dist. Ct. (ea. dist.) Mo. 1962, U.S. Ct. Appeals (8th cir.) 1965, U.S. Supreme Ct. 1985. V.p. sales Eureka Svc. and Equip. Co., Eureka, Mo., 1959-62; ptnr. Sheehan, Furtaw & Howald, Hillsboro, 1963-64, Thurman, Nixon, Smith & Howald, Hillsboro, 1964-70, Thurman, Nixon, Smith, Howald, Weber & Bowles, Hillsboro, 1970-80, Thurman, Smith, Howald, Weber & Bowles, Hillsboro, 1989-91, Thurman, Howald, Weber, Bowles & Senkel, Hillsboro, 1991-95, Thurman, Howald, Weber, Senkel & Norrick, L.L.C., Hillsboro, 1995—. Bd. dirs. LaBarque Ent. of Jefferson County, Hillsboro, 1965—, Rustic Hills Resort Ltd., Hillsboro, 1968—. Mem. Mo. Ethics Commn., 1994-98, vice-chmn., 1995-96, chmn., 1996-98. Lt. (j.g.) USN, 1957-59. Recipient Spl. award, Meramec Basin Assn., 1967, 69. Fellow Am. Bar Found., Am. Coll. Trust and Estate Counsel (Mo. chmn. 1987-92); mem. ABA, Estate Planning Coun. St. Louis (pres. 1990-91), Mo. Bar Assn. (bd. govs. 1975-87, Pres. Spl. award 1979), Jefferson County Bar Assn. (pres. 1963-64). Avocations: travel, golf. General corporate, Estate planning, Real property. Home: 9662 W Vista Dr Hillsboro MO 63050-3112 Office: Thurman Howald Weber Senkel & Norrick LLC PO Box 800 One Thurman Ct Hillsboro MO 63050

HOWARD, ALEX T., JR. federal judge; b. 1924; Student, U. Ala., 1942, student, 1946, Auburn U., 1942-44; JD, Vanderbilt U., 1950. U.S. probation officer, Mobile, Ala., 1950-51; ptnr. Johnstone, Adams, Howard, Bailey & Gordon, 1951-86; U.S. commr. U.S. Dist. Ct. (so. dist.) Ala., 1956-70, judge, 1986—, chief judge, 1989-94. Assoc. editor Am. Maritime Cases for Port of Mobile. Served to 2d lt. U.S. Army, 1943-46. Mem. ABA, Internat. Soc. Barristers, Internat. Assn. of Ins. Counsel, Maritime Law Assn. of U.S., Southeastern Admiralty Law Inst. (dir. 1978-80), Ala. Bar Assn., Ala. Def. Lawyers Assn. (dir. late 1950's), Mobile Bar Assn. (pres. 1973). Office: US Courthouse 113 Saint Joseph St Mobile AL 36602-3606

HOWARD, ANDREW BAKER, lawyer; b. Watertown, N.Y., July 26, 1969; s. Courtland Rogers and Maryanne H.; m. Elizabeth Edge, June 8, 1996; children: Christopher Baker, Paul Andrew. BA cum laude, St. Lawrence U., 1991; JD cum laude, Union U., 1994. Bar: N.Y. 1995. Atty. Connor, Curran & Schram, Hudson, N.Y., 1994—; asst. dist. atty. Columbia County Dist. Atty., 1995. Instr. Am. Inst. Banking, Albany, 1997—. Mem. N.Y. State Bar Assn., Columbia County Bar Assn., Justinian Soc., Columbia County C. of C. (bd. dirs.). Republican. Roman Catholic. Avocations: mountain biking, skiing, shooting. Banking, General civil litigation, Personal injury. Home: 216 Long Pond Rd Hewitt NJ 07421-3118 Office: Connor Curran & Schram PC 441 E Allen St Hudson NY 12534-2422 E-mail: abhccspc@capital.net

HOWARD, ARTHUR ELLSWORTH DICK, law educator; b. Richmond, Va., July 5, 1933; s. Thomas Landon and Marie Antoinette (Dick) H. BA, U. Richmond, 1954; LLB, U. Va., 1961; BA with honors, Oxford U., 1960, MA, 1965; LLD (hon.), James Madison U., 1983, U. Richmond, 1984, Campbell U., 1986, Coll. William and Mary, 1991, Wake Forest U., 2000. Bar: Va., D.C. 1961. Asso. Covington & Burling, Washington, 1961-62; law clk. to Supreme Ct. Justice Hugo L. Black, 1962-64; assoc. prof. law U. Va., Charlottesville, 1964-67, prof., 1967-76, White Burkett Miller prof. law and public affairs, 1976—, assoc. dean, 1967-69, dir. Ctr. for Pub. Svc., 1988-89, Roy L. and Rosamond Woodruff Morgan rsch. prof., 2001—. Counsel sessions Gen. Assembly Va., 1969, 70. Author: Commentaries on the Constitution of Virginia, 2 vols., 1974 (Phi Beta Kappa prize), The Road from Runnymede: Magna Carta and Constitutionalism in America, 1968, (with Baker and Derr) Church, State and Politics, 1982, Democracy's Dawn, 1991, Constitution-Making in Eastern Europe, 1993, Magna Carta: Text and Commentary, 1998; bd. editors The American Oxonian, 1968—, The Wilson Quar., 1977—. Chmn., exec. dir. Va. Commn. on Constl. Revision, 1968-69; chmn. Va. Commn. on Bicentennial of U.S. Constn., 1985-92; mem. Va. Ind. Bicentennial Commn., 1966-83; vice chmn. Magna Carta Commn. Va., 1965-66; Va. sec. Rhodes Scholarship Trust, 1970—; counselor to Gov. of Va., 1982-86; bd. dirs. James Madison Meml. Found. With U.S. Army, 1954-56. Recipient Disting. Prof. award U. Va., 1981, Randa medal Czech Republic, 1996; fellow Woodrow Wilson Internat. Center for Scholars, Smithsonian Instn., Washington, 1974-75, 76-77; fellow Ctr. Advanced Studies U. Va., 1970-71, 76-77, 82-83; Rhodes scholar Oxford U., 1958-60 Mem. Va. Bar Assn. (v.p. 1970-71), Va. Acad. Laureates (chmn. 1981-92), Cosmos Club (Washington), Oxford and Cambridge Club (London). Episcopalian. Home: 627 Park St Charlottesville VA 22902-4654 Office: U Va Sch Law 580 Massie Rd Charlottesville VA 22903-1738

HOWARD, BLAIR DUNCAN, lawyer; b. Alexandria, Va. s. T. Brooke and Elizabeth Duncan H.; m. Catherine Cremins; children: Thomas Brooke II, Caitlin Margaret. BA, U. Va., 1960; LLB, American U., 1963. Ptnr. Howard, Leino & Howard, Alexandria, Va., 1966—. Capt. USA, 1963-65. Named in Superstar Ohio Assn. Criminal Defense Lawyers, Columbus, 1994, One of Top Lawyers in Met. Washington, Washingtonian Mag. article, 1997. Fellow Am. Coll. Trial Lawyers; mem. ABA, ATLA, Alexandria Bar Assn., Va. State Bar Assn. (faculty professionalism course 1990-93). Criminal, Federal civil litigation, General civil litigation. Office: Howard Morrison & Howard 1 Wall Street Warrenton VA 20186-3319

HOWARD, CYNTHIA, lawyer, county official; b. Northampton, Mass., July 14, 1951; d. Robert TenBroeck and Margaret Eleanor (McCleary) H.; m. Thomas A. Lubeck, Oct. 27, 1990; children: Alice, Jacob. BA, Oberlin Coll., 1973; JD, U. Minn., 1978. Bar: Minn. 1978, S.D. 1979, Washington 1991. Staff mng. atty. Dakota Plains Legal Svcs., Eagle Butte, S.D., 1978-81; pvt. practice Deadwood, 1981-86; dir. No. Hills Pub. Defender, 1986-89; asst. pub. defender Minnehaha County Public Defender, Sioux Falls, S.D., 1991-98; dir. Minnehaha County Office of Pub. Adv., 1999—. Bd. dirs. Black Hills Legal Svcs., Rapid City, S.D., 1981-87. Bd. dirs. YWCA, Sioux Falls, 1992-2001; mem. Sioux Falls Historic Preservatin Commn., 1992-96, Mem. S.D. State Bar Assn. (criminal pattern jury instrn. com. 1991-97, mem. ethics com. 1999—). Democrat. Presbyterian. Avocation: weaving. Office: Pub Adv 415 N Dakota Ave Sioux Falls SD 57104-2412

HOWARD, GEORGE, JR. federal judge; b. Pine Bluff, Ark., May 13, 1924; Student, Lincoln U., 1951; B.S., U. Ark., J.D., 1954; LL.D., 1976. Bar: Ark. bar 1953, U.S. Supreme Ct. bar 1959. Pvt. practice law, Pine Bluff, 1953-77; spl. assoc. justice Ark. Supreme Ct., 1976, assoc. justice, 1977; justice U.S. Ct. Appeals, Ark., 1979-80; U.S. dist. judge, Eastern dist. Little Rock, 1980—. Mem. Ark. Claims Commn., 1969-77; chmn. Ark. adv. com. Civil Rights Commn.. Recipient citation in recognition of faithful and disting. svc. as mem. Supreme Ct. Com. of Profl. Conduct, 1980, disting. jurist award Jud. Coun. Nat. Bar Assn., 1980, Wiley A. Branton Issues Symposium award, 1990; voted outstanding trial judge 1984-85 Ark. Trial Lawyers Assn.; inducted Ark.'s Black Hall of Fame, 1994; recipient keepers of the spirit award Univ. Ark., Pine Bluff, 1995, quality svc. award Ark. Dem. Black Caucus, 1995. Mem. ABA, Ark. Bar Assn., Jefferson County Bar Assn. (pres.) Baptist.

HOWARD, GREGORY CHARLES, lawyer; b. Jan. 20, 1947; s. Robert L. and Nonamae (Lawlor) H.; m. Kathy Arlene Steinbacher, Oct. 1, 1983. Student, Clarkson Coll., 1965-67; BS, Boston U., 1969; JD, New Eng. Sch. Law, 1975. Bar: Mass. 1975, U.S. Dist. Ct. Mass. 1975, U.S. Supreme Ct. 1979. Assoc. Carmen L. Durso, Boston, 1975-77, Norris Kozodoy & Krasnoo, Boston, 1977-79; pvt. practice, 1979-80; ptnr. Hoff Ernstoff & Howard, 1980-86; pres. Gregory C. Howard, PC, 1986—. State civil litigation, Personal injury, Real property. Home: 5 Eliot Ave Chestnut Hill MA 02467-1455 Office: 28 State St Ste 1100 Boston MA 02109-1775 E-mail: greghoward@earthlink.net

HOWARD, JEFFREY HJALMAR, lawyer; b. N.Y.C., Aug. 23, 1944; s. Virgil Edward and Margaretta E. H.; m. Brenda H. Howard, June 19, 1966; children: Taggart Harrison, Brooke Kennedy. BA in Philosophy, Randolph-Macon Coll., 1966; postgrad. (English Speaking Union scholar) U. Edinburgh (Scotland), 1965; LLB, U. Va., 1969. Bar: D.C. 1970, U.S. Sup. Ct. 1978, Va. 1987. Law clk. Circuit Ct., Montgomery County, Md., 1969-70; assoc. Covington & Burling, Washington, 1970-74; assoc. gen. counsel for toxics, pesticides and solid waste U.S. EPA, Washington, 1974-76; ptnr. Crowell & Moring, 1989—; lectr. antitrust and environ. law U. Va. 1976-89; lectr. environ. law Peking U., Peoples Republic of China, 1986. Mem. ABA, D.C. Bar Assn., Va. Soc. Fellows, Order Coif, Alpha Psi Omega, Alpha Epsilon Pi, Delta Sigma Rho-Tau Kappa Alpha, Omicron Delta Kappa. Editorial bd. Va. Law Rev., 1967-69; contbr. chpts. to books and articles to profl. jours. Administrative and regulatory, Antitrust, Environmental. Home: 1021 Duchess St Mc Lean VA 22102-2007 Office: 1001 Pennsylvania Ave NW Washington DC 20004-2505

HOWARD, JOHN WAYNE, lawyer; b. Dec. 17, 1948; s. Joseph Leon and Irene Elizabeth (Silver) H.; m. Kathleen Amanda Busby, Oct. 7, 1978. BA, U. Calif., San Diego, 1971; JD, Calif. Western Sch. Law, 1976; postgrad., San Diego Inn of Ct., 1979, Hastings Coll. Advocacy, 1981; grad. Program of Instrns. for Lawyers, Harvard Law Sch., 1992. Bar: Calif. 1978, U.S. Dist. Ct. (so. dist.) Calif. 1978, U.S. Supreme Ct. 1989, Colo. 1989, U.S. Dist. Ct. (no. dist.) Calif., U.S. Dist. Ct. (ea. dist.) Calif., U.S. Ct. Appeals (9th cir.) 1995, U.S. Ct. Appeals (D.C. cir.) 1996, U.S. Ct. of Claims 1996. Assoc. Robert T. Dierdorff, San Diego, 1978-79; pvt. practice, 1979-82; ptnr. Howard & Neeb, 1982-84; prin. John W. Howard and Assocs., 1984-86; gen. counsel Ace Parking, Inc., 1986-89, CCCA Inc., 1989-93; pres. Individual Rights Found. Inc., 1993-95, Inst. for Constitutional Rights, Inc., 1995—, John W. Howard and Assoc., 1995—. Jud. arbitrator Superior Ct. Calif., 1983—. Chmn. San Diego County Indigent Def. Adv. Bd., 1981-84, mem. subcom. on def. monitoring and budget for Office Defender Svcs. of San Diego County; mem. select com. on small bus. Calif. State Assembly, 1983-90; chmn. San Diego Pub. Arts Adv. Bd.; mem. San Diego County Coun. of Com. Chairs; chmn. precinct orgn. Roger Hedgecock for Supt. Campaign Com., 1976, mem. steering com., 1976; chmn. steering com. Hedgecock for Mayor, 1982, Cleator for Mayor, 1986; chmn. Muscular Dystrophy Telethon, San Diego, 1983; vice chmn. San Diego Festival of Arts, 1983-84; pres. Bowery Theatre, San Diego, 1984-89; pres., bd. dirs. La Jolla Stage Co.; founder, bd. dirs. San Diego Theatre League; 1st v.p., bd. dirs. Muscular Dystrophy Assn.; bd. dirs. Patrick Henry Meml. Found., Brookneal, Va., The Poe Mus., Richmond, Va., San Diego Med. Oncology Rsch. Found., Ilan-Lael Found., Multiple Sclerosis Soc., Am. Ballet Found., Wellness Cmty., Teatro Macara Magica; bd. dirs., chmn. legal affairs subcom. Calif. Motion Picture Coun.; mem. adv. bd. dirs. San Diego Motion Picture Bur.; mem. pub. edn. com. Am. Cancer Soc.; founder, bd. dirs. San Diego Theatre Found., 1984—; mem. 44th Congl. Dist. Adv. Com.; mem. Com. to Re-Elect Congressman Bill Lowery; mem. San Diego County 4th Dist. Adv. Com. Mem. ABA, ATLA, Calif. State Bar Assn., Am. Corp. Counsel Assn., U. Calif.-San Diego Alumni Assn. (past v.p., bd. dirs.), Calif. Western Sch. Law Alumni Assn., Friendly Sons of St. Patrick, Delta Kappa Epsilon, Phi Alpha Delta, Kiwanis, Enright Inn of Ct., Am. Inns of Ct. Republican. Federal civil litigation, State civil litigation, Constitutional.

HOWARD, LEWIS SPILMAN, lawyer; b. Knoxville, Tenn., Oct. 10, 1930; s. Frank Catlett and Lillian (Spilman) H.; m. Anne Robinson, Dec. 26, 1953 (div. 1976); children: Catherine C., Martha S., Lewis S. Jr., Laura A. BSBA, JD, U. Tenn., 1953. Bar: Tenn. 1953, U.S. Ct. Mil. Appeals 1954, U.S. Dist. Ct. Ga. 1954, U.S. Dist. Ct. Tenn. 1956, U.S. Ct. Appeals (6th cir.) 1959. Ptnr. Kennerly, Montgomery, Howard & Finley, Knoxville, 1957-84, Howard & Ridge, Knoxville, 1984-99, Howard & Howard, Knoxville, 2000—. Gen. counsel Coal Creek Mining and Mfg. Co., Knoxville, 1969—, pres., 1971—. Vice chmn. Knoxville Bd. Edn., 1968-71. Capt. JAGC, USAR, 1953-56. Mem. ABA, Tenn. Bar Assn., Knoxville Bar Assn., Cherokee Country Club, Club LeConte. Republican. Presbyterian. Avocation: boating. General corporate, Mergers and acquisitions, Natural resources. Home: 1604 Kenesaw Ave Knoxville TN 37919-7863 Office: Howard & Howard 4800 Old Kingston Pike Knoxville TN 37919-6478

HOWARD, WILLIAM HERBERT, lawyer; b. June 27, 1953; s. Victor Jack and Dolores (Reiter) H.; m. Sara Conners Thomas, July 24, 1982; children: Claire Fontaine, Victoria Hill. BA, Case Western Res. U., 1975; JD, 1978. Bar: Ohio 1978, Pa. 1986, U.S. Dist. Ct. (so. dist.) Ohio 1978, U.S. Ct. Appeals (6th cir.) 1979, U.S. Dist. Ct. (ea. dist.) Pa. 1986, U.S. Ct. Appeals (3d cir.) 1987. Law clk. U.S. Dist. Ct. (so. dist.), Cin., 1978-80; assoc. Estabrook, Finn & McKee, Dayton, 1980-83, Porter, Wright, Morris & Arthur, Dayton, 1983-85, Cozen and O'Connor, Phila., 1985-87; ptnr., 1987-91; sr. ptnr., 1991—. Mem. ABA (ins. coverage litigation com., Natural Resources Environmental and En ergy Law, Tort and Ins. Law), Ohio Bar Assn., Pa. Bar Assn., (civil litigation sect., mem. environ. law, sports, entertainment and art law com.), Phila. Bar Assn. (mem. environ. law com.). Republican. Roman Catholic. Avocations: running, fitness, home repairs/gardening, movies, music. General civil litigation, Construction, Insurance. Office: Cozen and O'Connor 1900 Market St Philadelphia PA 19103-3527 Fax: 215-665-2013. E-mail: whoward@cozen.com

HOWE, DRAYTON FORD, JR. lawyer; b. Seattle, Nov. 17, 1931; s. Drayton Ford and Virginia (Wester) H.; m. Joyce Arnold, June 21, 1952; 1 son, James Drayton. AB, U. Calif., Berkeley, 1953; LLB, U. Calif., San Francisco, 1957. Bar: Calif. 1958. CPA Calif. Atty. IRS, 1958-61; tax dept. supr. Ernst & Ernst, San Francisco, 1962-67; ptnr. Bishop, Barry, Howe, Haney & Ryder, 1968—. Lectr. on tax matters U. Calif. extension, 1966-76. Mem. Calif. Bar Assn., San Francisco Bar Assn. (chmn. client relations com. 1977), Calif. Soc. CPA's. State civil litigation, Estate planning, Corporate taxation. Office: Bishop Barry Howe Haney & Ryder 2000 Powell St Ste 1425 Emeryville CA 94608-1861 E-mail: dhowe@bbhhr.com

HOWE, JAY EDWIN, lawyer; b. Omaha, Apr. 13, 1940; m. Catherine B. Olesen; children: Joseph E., Olivia G. BA, U. Iowa, 1963, JD, 1966. Bar: Iowa 1966, U.S. Dist. Ct. (so. dist.) Iowa 1966. County atty. Adair County, Iowa, 1973-79; ptnr. Howe & Olesen, Greenfield, 1979—. Served with U.S. Army, 1966-68. Mem. Iowa Bar Assn. Methodist. Club: Chamber (Greenfield) (pres.). General practice. Office: Howe & Olesen PO Box 86 Greenfield IA 50849-0086

HOWE, JONATHAN THOMAS, lawyer; b. Evanston, Ill., Dec. 16, 1940; s. Frederick King and Rosalie Charlotte (Volz) H.; m. Lois Helene Braun, July 12, 1963; children: Heather C., Jonathan Thomas Jr., Sara E. BA with honors, Northwestern U., 1963; JD with distinction, Duke U., 1966. Bar: Ill. 1966, U.S. Dist. Ct. (no. dist.) Ill. 1966, U.S. Ct. Appeals (7th cir.) 1967, U.S. Tax Ct. 1968, U.S. Supreme Ct. 1970, U.S. Ct. Appeals (D.C. cir.) 1976, U.S. Ct. Appeals (9th cir.) 1980, U.S. Ct. Appeals (4th, 5th, 11th dirs.) 1983, U.S. Claims Ct. 1990. Ptnr. Jenner & Block, Chgo., 1966-85, sr. ptnr. in charge assn. and adminstrv. law dept., 1978-85; founding and sr. ptnr., pres. Howe & Hutton, Chgo., Washington & St. Louis, 1985—. Exec. and adv. coms. to Ill. Sec. of State to revise the Ill. Not for Profit Act, 1983-86; dir. Pacific Mut. Realty Investors, Inc., 1985-86; dir. cable TV options for public Chgo. Access Corp., 1995-97, Bostrom Corp., 2001—. Contbg. editor Ill. Inst. for Continuing Legal Edn., 1973—, Sporting Goods Bus., 1977-91, Meeting News, 1978-88, Meetings Mgr., 1988—, Meetings and Convs., 1991—; contbr. articles to profl. jours.; legal editor Meetings and Convs., 1990—. Mem. Dist. 27 Bd. Edn., Northbrook, Ill., 1969-89, sec., 1969-72, pres., 1973-84; chmn. bd. trustees Sch. Employee Benefit Trust, 1979-85; founding bd. dirs., pres. Sch. Mgmt. Found. Ill., 1976-84; mem. exec. com. Northfield Twp. Rep. Orgn., 1967-71; bd. deacons Village Presbyn. Ch. Northbrook, 1975-78, trustee, 1981-83; mem. Arts and Music Forum, 4th Presbyn. Ch., Chgo., 1990-93; spl. advisor Pres.'s Coun. Phys. Fitness and Sports, 1983-87, Duke Univ. Sch. of Law Bd. of Visitors (life mem.). Named Industry Leader of Yr., Meeting Industry, 1987, Sch. Bd. Mem. Yr. (twice) , Ill. State Bd. Edn.; recipient Internat. Found. PaceSetters award Hospitality Sales Mktg. Assn., 1996. Fellow Internat. Forum of Travel and Tourism Advs., Am. Soc. Assn. Execs. (vice-chmn. legal com. 1983-86); mem. Internat. Assn. Conv. and Hosp. Indsl. Attys. (founder), ABA (antitrust sect. Nat. Inst. com., trade assn. law com. corp. banking and bus. law sect., sect. on litigation, adminstrv. law sect.; mem. internat. law com., continuing edn. com., tort and ins. practice, vice-chmn. com. sports law 1986—, standing com. meetings and travel 1988-93, spl. advisor 1993—), Task Force on Membership Benefits for Disabled Lawyers, Ill. Bar Assn. (antitrust sect., civil practice sect., sch. law sect., adminstrv. law sect.; co-editor Antitrust Newsletter 1968-70), Chgo. Bar Assn. (def. of prisoners com. 1966-83, antitrust law com. 1971—, continuing edn. com. 1977—, chmn. assn. and non-profit soc. law com. 1984-86), Am. Soc. Assn. Execs. (vice-chmn. legal com., founding mem. legal sect.), N.Y. Soc. Assn. Execs., Acad. Hospitality Industry Attys. (founder, bd. dirs. 1994—), Nat. Sch. Bds. Assn. (nat. bd. dirs. 1979-89, exec. com. 1981-89, sec.-treas. 1983-85, 2d v.p. 1985-86, chmn. devel. com. 1982-87, pres. 1987-88), D.C. Bar Assn., Am. Judicature Soc., Ill. Assn. Sch. Bds. (pres. 1977-79, bd. dirs. 1971-88), Chi Bar Found. (life), Assn. Forum Chicagoland (assoc., formerly Chgo. Soc. Assn. Execs.), Nat. Sch. Bds. Found. (pres./trustee 1995—), U.S. C. of C. (legal coun. 1998—), Greater Washington Soc. Assn. Execs., Legal Club, Law Club, Mid-Am. Club, Tower Club, Univ. Club Chgo., Psi Upsilon. General civil litigation, General practice, Non-profit and tax-exempt organizations. Home: 126 W Delaware Pl Chicago IL 60610-3252 Office: 20 N Wacker Dr Ste 4200 Chicago IL 60606-3191 E-mail: jth@howehutton.com

HOWE, KAREN LOUISE, lawyer; b. Corning, N.Y., Jan. 2, 1964; d. George R. Cleveland and Alberta B. Rhoda; m. William Earl Howe, May 1, 1993. BS, Keuka Coll., 1986; JD, Syracuse Coll., 1989. Bar: N.Y. 1990. Pub. defender Cortland (N.Y.) County Pub. Defender's Office, 1990-99; with Cortland (N.Y.) County Dist. Atty.'s Office, 2000—. Mem. N.Y. State Bar Assn., Cortland County Bar Assn. Office: Howe Law Office PO Box 5462 55 Main St Cortland NY 13045-2609

HOWE, RICHARD CUDDY, state supreme court chief justice; b. South Cottonwood, Utah, Jan. 20, 1924; s. Edward E. and Mildred (Cuddy) H.; m. Juanita Lyon, Aug. 30, 1949; children: Christine Howe Schultz, Andrea Howe Reynolds, Bryant, Valerie Howe Winegar, Jeffrey, Craig. BS, U. Utah, 1945, JD, 1948. Bar: Utah. Law clk. to Justice James H. Wolfe, Utah Supreme Ct., 1949-50; judge city ct. Murray, Utah, 1951; individual practice law, 1952-80; justice Utah Supreme Ct., Salt Lake City, 1980—. Mem. Utah Constnl. Revision Commn., 1976-85. Chmn., original mem. Salt Lake County Merit Coun.; mem. Utah Ho. of Reps., 1951-58, 69-72, Utah Senate, 1973-78. Named Outstanding Legislator Citizens' Conf. State Legislatures, 1972 Mem. ABA, Utah Bar Assn., Sons of Utah Pioneers. Mem. LDS Ch. Office: Utah Supreme Ct 450 S State St PO Box 140210 Salt Lake City UT 84114-0210*

HOWE, RICHARD RIVES, lawyer; b. Portland, Oreg., Dec. 21, 1942; s. Hubert Shattuck Jr. and Anna Gertrude (Moody) H.; m. Elizabeth Anne Crowell, Aug. 29, 1964; 1 child, Richard Rives Jr. BA, Yale U., 1964; JD, Harvard U., 1967. Bar: N.Y. 1968, U.S. Ct. Appeals (2d cir.) 1973, U.S. Dist. Ct. (so. and ea. dists.) N.Y. 1973, U.S. Supreme Ct. 1973. Assoc. Sullivan & Cromwell, N.Y.C., 1967-74, ptnr., 1974—. Mem. exec. com. Nat. Com. Am. Fgn. Policy, Inc., 2000—. Bd. dirs. Peoples' Symphony Concerts, N.Y.C., 1983—, Bar Assurance and Reinsurance Ltd., Bermuda, 1994—, Nat. Com. Am. Fgn. Policy, Inc., 1999—. Mem. ABA (mem. com. on corp. practice, bus. law sect.), N.Y. State Bar Assn. (mem. exec. com. 1982-99, chmn. 1992-93, bus. law sect., chmn. securities regulation com. 1982-86), Assn. Bar City of N.Y., Phi Beta Kappa, Pi Sigma Alpha. Democrat. General corporate, Mergers and acquisitions, Securities. Home: 86 Woodfield Dr Short Hills NJ 07078-1654 Office: Sullivan & Cromwell Fl 32 125 Broad St Fl 32 New York NY 10004-2498 E-mail: hower@sullcrom.com

HOWELL, ALLY WINDSOR, lawyer, editor; b. Montgomery, Ala., Mar. 10, 1949; s. Elvin and Bennie Merle (Windsor) H.; m. Donna K. Graffander, Sept. 2, 1989; children: Christopher Darby, Joshua Darby, Jeremiah Graffander. BA, Huntington Coll., 1971; JD, Jones Sch. Law, 1974. Bar: Ala. 1974, U.S. Supreme Ct. 1977, U.S. Ct. Appeals (fed. cir.) 1983, U.S. Ct. Appeals (11th cir.) 1981, U.S. Tax Ct. 1979, U.S. Claims Ct. 1982, U.S. Dist. Ct. (mid. dist.) Ala. 1975, U. Dist. Ct. (so. dist.) Ala. 1978. Archivist Hist. Rsch. Ctr. Air U., Maxwell AFB, Ala., 1972-75; pvt. practice Montgomery, 1975-82, 83-01; atty.-editor West Group, Rochester,

N.Y., 2001—. Adj. prof. Faulkner U., Montgomery, 1975—, law sch. 1983-85; asst. atty. gen., chief legal sect. Ala. Medicaid Agy., Montgomery, 1982-83. Author: Alabama Civic Practice Forms, 1986, 3d edit., 1992, Alabama Torts Case Finder, 1988, Alabama Personal Injury and Torts, 1996, Trial Handbook for Alabama Lawyers, 2d edit., 1998. Hon. lt. col., aide de camp Gov. Ala., 1974. Mem. ABA (contbr. editor profl. liability newsletter, litigation sect. 1990-92), Assn. Trial Lawyers Am., Montgomery County Bar Assn. (newsletter editorial com. 1984-85), Nat. Bd. Trial Adv. (cert. civil litigation 1981, 86, 91, examiner ethics, evidence and civil procedure), Nat. Lesbian and Gay Law Assn. (bd. dirs. 1999—, vice co-chair 2001—, editor newsletter 2000—). Mem. Ch. of Christ. Insurance, Personal injury, Probate.

HOWELL, ARTHUR, lawyer; b. Atlanta, Aug. 24, 1918; s. Arthur and Katharine (Mitchell) H.; m. Caroline Sherman, June 14, 1941; children: Arthur, Caroline, Eleanor, Richard, Peter, James; m. Janet Kerr Franchot, Dec. 16, 1972. AB, Princeton U., 1939; JD, Harvard U., 1942; LLD (hon.), Oglethorpe U., 1972. Bar: Ga. 1942. Assoc. F.M., 1942-45; ptnr. Alston & Bird (and predecessor firms), 1945-89, of counsel, 1989—. Bd. dirs., gen. counsel Atlantic Steel Co., 1960-93; chmn., bd. dirs. Summit Industries, Inc.; bd. dirs. Enterprise Funds; chmn. emeritus bd. dirs. Crescent Banking Co.; past pres. Atlanta Legal Aid Soc.; emeritus mem. bd. dirs. Crescent Bank and Trust Co., Crescent Banking Co. Pres. Met. Atlanta Cmty. Svcs., 1956, dir., 1953— ; pres. Cmty. Planning Coun., 1961-63; gen. chmn. United Appeal, 1955; spl. atty. gen. State Ga., 1948-55; spl. counsel Univ. Sys. Ga., State Sch. Bldg. Authorities, 1951-70; adv. com. Ga. Corp. Code, 1967— ; chmn. Atlanta Adv. Com. Pks.; trustee, past chmn. Oglethorpe U.; trustee Princeton, 1964-68, Atlanta Speech Sch., Westminister Schs., Atlanta, Episcopal H.S., Alexandria, Va.; emeritus trustee Morehouse Coll., past trustee Inst. Internat. Edn., mem. exec. com. 1969-72; elder, trustee, chmn. bd. trustees Presbyn. Ch., 1985-89. Named hon. alumnus Ga. Inst. Tech. Mem. ABA, Ga. Bar Assn., Atlanta Bar Assn., Am. Law Inst. (life), Lawyers Club of Atlanta (past pres.), Am. Judicature Soc., Soc. Colonial Wars, Capital City Club, Piedmont Driving Club, Commerce Club, Homosassa Fishing Club, Nassau Club, Princeton Club, Phi Beta Kappa. Home: 200 Larkspur Ln Highlands NC 28741-8388 Office: Alston & Bird One Atlantic Ctr 1 Atlantic Ctr Atlanta GA 30309-3400

HOWELL, DONALD LEE, lawyer; b. Waco, Tex., Jan. 31, 1935; s. Hilton Emory and Louise Howell; m. Gwendolyn Avera, June 13, 1957; children: Daniel Liege, Alison Avera, Anne Turner. BA cum laude, Baylor U., 1956; JD with honors, U. Tex., 1963. Bar: Tex. 1963. Assoc. Vinson & Elkins, Houston, 1963-70, ptnr., 1970—, mem. mgmt. com., 1980-99. Capt. USAFR, 1956-59. Fellow Am. Bar Found., Tex. Bar Found., Houston Bar Found., Am. Law Inst.; mem. ABA, Am. Coll. Bond Counsel, Houston Bar Assn., Nat. Assn. Bond Lawyers (pres. 1981-82, bd. dirs. 1979-83), Attys. Liability Assurance Soc. (Bermuda bd. dirs. 1992—, chmn. 2000—, U.S. bd. dirs. 1992—, chmn. 2000—), Houston Club, Houston Ctr. Club, Order of Coif, Phi Delta Phi. Democrat. Episcopalian. Finance, Municipal (including bonds), Public utilities.

HOWELL, GEORGE COOK, III, lawyer; b. New Orleans, June 27, 1956; s. George C. Jr. and Billie Grace (Webb) H.; children: Margaret Sloan, George C. IV. AB magna cum laude, Princeton U., 1978; JD, U.Va., 1981. Bar: Va. 1981, U.S. Dist. Ct. (ea. dist.) Va. 1982, U.S. Ct. Appeals (4th cir.) 1982. Law clk. U.S. Dist. Ct. (ea. dist.) Va., Alexandria, 1981-82; assoc. Hunton & Williams, Richmond, Va., 1982-89, ptnr., 1989—, team head tax & employee benefits, 1999—. Contbr. Va. Law Rev., 1980; editor-in-chief Va. Tax Rev., 1980-81; articles editor The Tax Lawyer, 1983-86, mng. editor, 1987-89. Mem. usher's guild 1st Presbyn. Ch., Richmond, 1986-90; participant Leadership Metro Richmond, 1987-88. Mem. ABA (taxation sect. chmn. remic task force 1987-88, chmn. mini-program on mortgage-backed securities 1988, chmn. subcom. on asset securitization 1988-90, corp. tax shelters tax force 2000-2001, vice chmn. com. on fin. trans. 1990-92, chmn. com. on fin. trans. 1992-94, sec. taxation 1995-97, sect. taxation coun., 1997-2000, vice chmn. comm. 2001—), Princeton Assn. Va. (treas. 1987-89, pres. 1989-91), Order of Coif, Phi Beta Kappa. Republican. Avocations: golf, tennis, basketball, running, the stock market. Corporate taxation. Office: Hunton & Williams 951 E Byrd St Ste 200 Richmond VA 23219-4074

HOWELL, HARLEY THOMAS, lawyer; b. Chgo., June 5, 1937; s. Harley W. and Geneva (Engelmann) H.; m. Aliceann A. McLaughlin, Apr. 23, 1983; children by previous marriage: Shelley A. Young, Rebecca L., Emily S. AB, Princeton U., 1959; JD, Yale U., 1962. Bar: Md. 1962, U.S. Supreme Ct. 1966, D.C. 1972. Law clk. to chief judge U.S. Ct. Appeals (4th cir.), 1962-63; assoc. Semmes, Bowen & Semmes, Balt., 1966-72, ptnr., 1972-92, Howell, Gately, Whitney & Carter LLP, Towson, Md., 1992-98, counsel, 1998-99; ptnr. Howell & Gately, Balt., 1998—. Mem. Gov.'s Commn. to Revise Annotated Code Md., 1975-85; mem. standing com. on rules of practice and procedure Ct. Appeals of Md., 1985-2000. Bd. dirs. Balt. Symphony Orch., 1975—, sec., 1986—; trustee Sheppard & Enoch Pratt Hosp., Towson, 1991-2001. Capt. JAG Corps, U.S. Army, 1963-66. Decorated Army Commendation medal. Fellow Am. Coll. Trial Lawyers, Am. Acad. Appellate Lawyers, Md. Bar Found.; mem. ABA, Md. State Bar Assn., Bar Assn. Balt. City, Balt. County Bar Assn., D.C. Bar Assn., Fed. Bar Assn., Wine and Food Soc., Wranglers Law Club (Balt.). Appellate, Federal civil litigation, State civil litigation. Home: 1012 Chestnut Ridge Dr Lutherville Timonium MD 21093-1716 Office: Howell & Gately One Charles Ctr 19th Fl 100 N Charles St Baltimore MD 21201 E-mail: hthomas37@home.com

HOWELL, JOEL WALTER, III, lawyer; b. Jackson, Miss., Dec. 25, 1949; s. Joel W. and Elizabeth (Harris) H.; m. Wilhelmina C. Pontus, June 25, 1983. BA, Millsaps Coll., 1971; JD, Columbia U., 1974. Bar: Tex. 1974, U.S. Ct. Appeals (5th cir.) 1974, Miss. 1975, U.S. Dist. Ct. (no. and so. dists.) Miss. 1975. Ptnr. Daniel, Coker, Horton, Bell & Dukes, Jackson, 1975-80; pvt. practice, 1981—. Adj. faculty law sch. Miss. Coll., Jackson, 1988. Contbg. editor, case notes and comments editor Columbia Jour. Transnat. Law, 1973-74. Mem. ABA, ATLA, Tex. Bar Assn., Miss. Bar, Hinds County Bar Assn. (small firm practice com. 1993-94, chair 1995, computer columnist newsletter 1996—, webmaster 1997—), Miss. Trial Lawyers Assn., Miss. Def. Lawyers Assn., Def. Rsch. Inst., Miss. Bankruptcy Conf. Federal civil litigation, State civil litigation, Personal injury. Home: 50 St Andrews Dr Jackson MS 39211-2466 Office: PO Box 16772 5446 Executive Pl Jackson MS 39206-4103 E-mail: jwh3@mindspring.com

HOWELL, R(OBERT) THOMAS, JR. lawyer, former food company executive; b. Racine, Wis., July 18, 1942; s. Robert T. and Margaret Paris (Billings) H.; m. Karen Wallace Corbett, May 11, 1968; children: Clarinda, Margaret, Robert. AB, Williams Coll., 1964; JD, U. Wis., 1967; postgrad., Harvard U., 1981. Bar: Wis. 1968, Ill. 1968, U.S. Dist. Ct. (no. dist.) Ill. 1968, U.S. Tax Ct. Assoc. Hopkins & Sutter, Chgo., 1967-71; atty. The Quaker Oats Co., 1971-77, counsel, 1977-80, v.p., assoc. gen. corp. counsel, 1980-84, v.p., gen. corp. counsel, 1984-96, corp. sec., 1994-96; of counsel Seyfarth Shaw, 1997—. Bd. dirs. Ill. Inst. of Continuing Legal Edn., Lawyers for Creative Arts. Editor (mags.) Barrister, 1975-77, Compleat Lawyer, 1983-87. Bd. dirs. Metro. Family Svcs.; bd. dirs. Chgo. Bar Found., 1987—, pres., 1991-93; trustee 4th Presbyn. Ch., Chgo., 1989-92, pres., 1994-96; bd. dirs. Chgo. Equity Fund, 1992-96. Capt. USAR, 1966-72. Mem. ABA, Ill. Bar Assn., Wis. Bar Assn., Chgo. Bar Assn. (bd. mgrs. 1977-79, chmn. young lawyers sect. 1974-75), LawClub Chgo., Econ. Club Chgo., Univ. Club Chgo. (bd. dirs. 1982-85, 87-88, v.p.). Presbyterian. Antitrust, General corporate, Mergers and acquisitions. Home: 853 W Chalmers Pl Chicago IL 60614-3233 Office: Seyfarth Shaw 55 E Monroe St Ste 4200 Chicago IL 60603-5863 E-mail: thowell@seyfarth.com

HOWELL, WELDON ULRIC, JR. lawyer; b. Dallas, July 16, 1947; s. Weldon U. and Betty (Temple) H.; m. Barbara Molina, July 14, 1973; children: Benjamin, Sarah. B.A., U. Ariz., 1969; postgrad. City London Poly. Sch., 1971; J.D., U. Tex., 1973. Bar: Tex. 1973, Calif. 1974, U.S. Dist. Ct. (cen., no., so. and ea. dists.) Calif., U.S. Ct. Appeals (9th cir.) 1984, U.S. Tax Ct. 1981, U.S. Ct. Claims 1981. Briefing atty to assoc. justice Supreme Ct. Tex., Austin, 1973-74; assoc. Schramm & Raddue, Santa Barbara, Calif., 1974-77, sr. ptnr., chmn. bus. and tax dept., 1977—; sr. ptnr. Howell Moore & Gough LLP, Santa Barbara. Mem. Santa Barbara County Bar Assn. (chmn. tax sect. 1984, bd. dirs. 1986-88, pres. 1994), Barristers Club Santa Barbara (pres. 1977-78), Pi Kappa Alpha. Democrat. Clubs: Tennis of Santa Barbara (chmn., 1980). General corporate, Securities, Personal income taxation. Home: 2525 Anacapa St Santa Barbara CA 93105-3511 Office: Howell Moore & Gough LLP Schramm & Raddue 812 Presidio Ave Santa Barbara CA 93101-2210

HOWELL, WILLIAM ASHLEY, III, lawyer; b. Raleigh, N.C., Jan. 2, 1949; s. William Ashley II and Caroline Erskine Greenleaf; m. Esther Holland, Dec. 22, 1973. BS, Troy State U., 1972; postgrad., U. Ala., Birmingham, 1974-75; JD, Birmingham Sch. Law, 1977. Bar: Ala. 1977, U.S. Dist. Ct. (no. dist.) Ala. 1977, U.S. Ct. Appeals (5th cir.) 1977, U.S. Supreme Ct. 1982, U.S. Ct. Appeals (11th cir.) 1983, U.S. Dist. Ct. (mid. dist.) Ala. 1987. Atty. pub. defender divsn. Legal Aid Soc. of Birmingham, 1977-78, civil divsn. Legal Aid Soc. of Birmingham, 1978-81; dist. office atty. SBA, Birmingham, 1980-82, supervising atty. Ala. Dist., 1982—; spl. asst. U.S. Atty. (Mid. Dist.), Ala., 1988—. Part-time instr. legal and social environ. and human resources mgmt. Jefferson State C.C., Birmingham, 1993. Contbr. articles to profl. jours. Bd. dirs. Hoover Homeowners Assn., 1977-81, Southside Ministries, Inc., 1990-91, v.p. bd. dirs., 1990-91; bd. dirs. SafeHouse of Shelby County, Inc., 1990-93, vice chmn., 1991-93; mem. outreach commn., Episc. Ch. of St. Francis of Assisi, Pelham, Ala., 1992, 95, 97; del. State Conv., alternate del., 1993, 94; vol. reader Radio Reading Svc. Network for Blind, 1991-93; mem. Shelby County Econ. Devel. Coun., 1993-94; dir. Hispanic Outreach Commn., 2000-2001. Recipient Am. Jurisprudence Criminal Procedure Book award. Mem. ABA (sect. corporation, banking and bus. law), Nat. Parks and Conservation Soc. (life), Fed. Bar Assn. (sec. Birmingham chpt. 1980-81, del. nat. conv. 1993, 94, del. mid yr. meeting, 1994-95), Ala. Bar Assn. (com. on future of the profession 1978-81, 83-84, com. on quality of life 1992-93, sect. bankruptcy and corp. law, sect. bankruptcy and comml. law, sect. corp. counsel, sect. banking and bus. law), Nature Conservancy (life), Birmingham Bar Assn., Birmingham Venture Club, Sierra Club (life), Sigma Delta Kappa (v.p., Outstanding Sr. award 1977). Episcopalian. Office: US Small Bus Adminstrn 801 Tom Martin Dr Ste 201 Birmingham AL 35211-4436 Fax: 205-290-7443. E-mail: william.howell@sba.gov

HOWES, BRIAN THOMAS, lawyer; b. Sioux Falls, S.D., July 23, 1957; s. Thomas A. and Joyce L. (McFarland) H.; m. Robin Kay Schoonover, June 2, 1979; children: Phillip, Adam, Jason. BSBA in Acctg., BA in Polit. Sci., Kans. State U., 1979; JD, U. Kans., 1982. Bar: Mo. 1982, U.S. Dist. Ct. (we. dist.) Mo. 1982, U.S. Supreme Ct. 1989. Assoc. Shughart, Thomson & Kilroy, Kansas City, Mo., 1982-85; exec. v.p., COO, gen. counsel Tenenbaum & Assocs., Inc., 1985-95; ptnr., nat. dir. property tax svcs. Ernst & Young LLP, 1995-99; of counsel Shughart Thomson & Kilroy, P.C., 2000—. Pres. Nat. Coun. Property Taxation, 1999-2000. Contr. articles to profl. jours; writer, speaker in field. Contbg. mem. Dem. Nat. Com.; bd. dirs. Kansas City Wheelchair Athletic Commn., 1987-89, Vol. Atty. Project, 1984—, Nat. Youth Sports Coaches Assn., 1994—. Mem. ABA, Kansas City Met. Bar Assn., Lawyers Assn. Kansas City, Am. Corp. Counsel Assn., Inst. for Profls. in Taxation, Internat. Assn. of Assessing Officers, Urban Land Inst. Episcopalian. General corporate, Real property, State and local taxation. Home: 4901 W 130th St Shawnee Mission KS 66209-1864 Office: Shughart Thomson & Kilroy PC Ste 1800 120 W 12th St Kansas City MO 64105-1929 E-mail: bhowes@kc.stklaw.com

HOWETT, JOHN CHARLES, JR. lawyer; b. Tampa, Fla., Feb. 11, 1946; s. John Charles and Martha Carlton (Durrance) H.; m. Mary K. Sheehan, Oct. 12, 1974; children: Timothy S., Julia K. BA, U. Pa., 1968; JD, Dickinson Sch. of Law, 1974. Bar: Pa. 1974, U.S. Supreme Ct. 1979. Law clk. Hon. Roy Wilkinson Commonwealth Ct. Pa., Harrisburg, 1974-75; sr. ptnr. Howett, Kissinger & Conley, P.C., 1975—. Contbr. articles to profl. jours. 1st lt. U.S. Army, 1968-71, Vietnam. Mem. Pa. Bar Assn. (chmn. family law sect. 1995-96, bd. govs. 1978-81, 88-91, pres. young lawyers divsn. 1979-80), Am. Acad. Matrimonial Lawyers (pres. Pa. chpt. 1999-2000), Dauphin County Bar Assn. (pres. 1994-95, chmn. family law sect. 1990-91), Internat. Acad. Matrimonial Lawyers. Family and matrimonial. Office: Howett Kissinger & Conley PC PO Box 810 130 Walnut St Harrisburg PA 17101-1612

HOWIE, JOHN ROBERT, lawyer; b. June 29, 1946; s. Robert H. and Sarah Francis (Caldwell) H.; children: John Robert, Ashley Elizabeth, Lindsey Leigh. BBA, North Tex. State U., 1968; JD, So. Meth. U., 1976. Bar: Tex. 1976, U.S. Dist. Ct. (no. dist.) Tex. 1977, U.S. Ct. Appeals (5th, 9th, 10th and 11th cirs.), U.S. Supreme Ct. 1985, U.S. Dist. Ct. (so., ea. and we. dists.) Tex. 1987; cert. in personal injury trial law Tex. Bd. Legal Specialization, 1982. With Law Offices of Windle Turley, Dallas, 1976-88, Misko & Howie, 1988-95; ptnr. Howie & Sweeney, LLP, 1995—. Adj. prof. trial advocacy So. Meth. U. Sch. Law, 1988-89, 92—, So. Meth. Sch. Law exec. bd. Lt. comdr. USN, 1968-73. Recipient Disting. Alumnus U. of North Tex., Disting. Alumnus Pvt. Practice, So. Meth. Sch. Law, 2001. Fellow So. Trial Lawyers Assn., Roscoe Pound Found. Civil Trial Adv.-Nat. Bd. Trial Adv. (cert. civil trial law), Internat. Acad. Trial Lawyers, Tex. Bar Found., Internat. Soc. Air Safety Investigators (contbr. Million Dollar Argument series 1989); mem. ABA (vice chmn. aviation law sect. 1986-91, chair 1992), Tex. Trial Lawyers Assn. (bd. dirs. 1983—), Dallas Trial Lawyers Assn. (sec.-treas. 1984, v.p. 1985, pres. 1986), Assn. Trial Lawyers Am. (vice chmn. aviation sect. 1984-85, chmn. 1986), Am. Bd. Trial Advocates (sec. Dallas chpt. 1988, pres. 1989), State Bar Tex. (aviation law sect. coun. 1994—, personal injury trial specialist), Lawyer/Pilots Bar Assn., Flight Safety Found., Trial Lawyers for Pub. Justice Found., Ark. Trial Lawyers Assn., Ga. Trial Lawyers Assn., N.Mex. Trial Lawyers Assn., Ind. Trial Lawyers Assn., So. Meth. U. Jour. Air Law and Commerce (bd. advs.), Pres.'s Coun. U. North Tex., Internat. Soc. of Barristers. Aviation, Personal injury, Product liability. Home: 6508 Turtle Creek Blvd Dallas TX 75205-1244 Office: Howie & Sweeney LLP 2911 Turtle Creek Blvd Ste 1400 Dallas TX 75219-6258 E-mail: jh@howie-sweeney.com

HOWLAND, JOAN SIDNEY, law librarian, law educator; b. Eureka, Calif., Apr. 9, 1951; d. Robert Sidney and Ruth Mary Howland. BA, U. Calif., Davis, 1971; MA, U. Tex., 1973; MLS, Calif. State U., San Jose, 1975; JD, Santa Clara (Calif.) U., 1983; MBA, U. Minn., 1997. Assoc. librarian for pub. svcs. Stanford (Calif.) U Law Library, 1975-83, Harvard U. Law Library, Cambridge, Mass., 1983-86; dep. dir. U. Calif. Law Library, Berkeley, 1986-92; dir. law libr., Roger F. Noreen prof. law U. Minn. Sch. of Law, 1992—, assoc. dean info. tech., 2001—. Questions and answers column editor Law Libr. Jour., 1986-91; memt. column editor Trends in Law Libr. Mgmt. & Tech., 1987-94. Mem. ALA, ABA (com. on accreditation 2001—), Am. Assn. Law Librs., Am. Assn. Law Schs., Am. Indian Libr. Assn. (treas. 1992—), Am. Law Inst. Office: U Minn Law Sch 229 19th Ave S Minneapolis MN 55455-0400

HOWLAND, RICHARD MOULTON, retired lawyer; b. Glen Cove, L.I., N.Y., Jan. 2, 1940; s. Richard Moulton and Natalie (Fuller) H.; m. Julie Rose Keschl, Sept. 28, 1974 (div.); children: Kimberly Merrill, Gillian Fuller. BA, Amherst Coll., 1961; JD, Columbia U., 1968. Bar: Mass. 1968. Assoc. firm Nutter, McLennen & Fish, Boston, 1968-69, DiMento & Sullivan, Boston, 1969-70; atty. for students U. Mass., Amherst, 1970-74; practice law, 1974-2000; Legal Infirmary Amherst, 1997-98; ret., 2001. Adj. prof. U. Mass., 1972-76, Western New Eng. Coll. Sch. Law, 1993-94; vis. lectr. Amherst Coll., 1983, mock trial team coach, 1989-98; mock trial team coach Tufts Coll., 1998, Deerfield Acad., 1999-2000, Southwick H.S., 1999-2000; constnl. law tchr. Springfield H.S. Sci. and Tech., 2001—. Co-editor Mass. Lawyers Weekly, 1979-94, emeritus, 1994; statistician New England Blizzard, 1996-98, Connecticut Pride, 1999-2000, Springfield Sirens Pro Soccer, 1999—. Asst. moderator Town of Leverett, 1988-93, moderator, 1993-96; mem. Leverett Sch. Bldg. Com., 1988-89; trustee Art Inst. Boston, 1990-92, Greenfield C. C. Found., 1991-97, Amherst Regional High Sch. Coun., 1993-95; trustee Amherst Hist. Soc., 1990-95; pres. Leverett PTO, 1981-85; mem. devel. com. Pioneer Valley High Sch. of the Performing Arts, 1996-97; pres. Interfaith Housing Corp., Amherst, 1984-93; bd. dirs. Leverett Craftsmen and Artists, Inc., 1986—, treas., 1988-89, v.p., 1988-89, pres., 1989—; bd. dirs. Community Multisvc. Inc., Northampton, Mass., 1987-93; trustee Wildwood Cemetery Assn., 1987—; bd. dirs., sec. Responsible Hospitality Inst., 1990-95; mem. host com. Russia-Amherst Exchange City of Petrozavadsk, 1988—; del. rep. Town of Amherst to Sister City, Kanegasaki, Japan, 1992-95; chair Amherst-Kanegasaki Sister Com., 1994-95; mem. bd. career com., Hampshire-Franklin Sch., 1995-98; cert. nat. ofcl. U.S. Assn. Track and Field, 1996—; Western Mass. track and field ofcl., 1995—; We. Mass. football ofcl., 1995—; referee FIFA Soccer, 1997—; collegiate water polo ofcl., 1997—; asst. coach varsity girls soccer Amherst Regional H.S., 1995-99. Lt. (j.g.) USNR, 1961-65. Mem. ABA (chmn. profl. liability com. Gen. Practice Sect. 1987-90, chmn. certification and specialization com. Gen. Practice Sect. 1992-95, chmn. family law com. 1995-96, chmn. certification, specialization and law sch. curriculum com. 1996-98, mem. coun. 1997-2001), Mass. Bar Assn. (chmn. com. on chem. dependency, Mass. Community Svc. award 1984), Franklin Bar Assn., Hampshire Bar Assn. (del. to Mass. Bar Assn., sec., v.p. 1986), Mass. Acad. Trial Lawyers, Amherst C. of C. (pres. 1985-93, Dakin medallion 1995), Nat. High Sch. Slavic Honor Soc. (hon.), Amherst Alumni Athletic Assn. (bd. dirs. 1995—), Skating Club (past v.p., treas. 1987-96, Amherst). Democrat. General civil litigation, Family and matrimonial, General practice. Home: 326 N Pleasant St Amherst MA 01002-1706 E-mail: howland@mediaone.net

HOWLETT, MICHAEL JOSEPH, JR. lawyer; b. Chgo., July 10, 1948; s. Michael Joseph and Helen (Geary) H.; m. Kathleen Fitzgerald, Oct. 2, 1970; children— Elizabeth, Melissa, Catherine. B.A., St. John's U., Collegeville, Minn., 1970; J.D., U. Notre Dame, 1973. Bar: Ill. 1973, U.S. Dist. Ct. (no. dist.) Ill. 1975, U.S. Ct. Appeals (7th cir.) 1975, Ind. 1980, U.S. Supreme Ct. 1980. Law clk. U.S. Dist. Ct., U.S. Ct. Appeals, Chgo., 1973-75; asst. U.S. atty. no. dist. Ill., Chgo., 1975; ptnr. firm Moriarty, Hultquist & Howlett, Chgo. and South Bend, Ind., 1980-83; assoc. judge Cir. Ct. Cook County (Ill.), Chgo., 1983-86; counsel, Hayes & Power, 1986-87; ptnr. Pope & John, Ltd., Chgo., 1987—; spl. outside counsel ethics com. U.S. House of Rep., 1988, dep. spl. outside counsel com. on offl. conduct (ethics), 1988-89; pub. dir. Mid-Am. Commodity Exchange, Chgo., 1981-83; spl. dep. prosecutor St. Joseph County (Ind.), South Bend, 1981-83; pres. Lawyers Assistance Program, Chgo., 1989-90, dir., intervenor, 1984—; panel atty. Fed. Defender Program, Inc., U.S. Dist. Ct. (no. dist.) Ill., 1977-83; adj. prof. trial practice and civil procedure John Marshall Law Sch., Chgo., 1977-79, 83-84; mem. fed. criminal jury instrns. com. 7th Cir. Ct. Appeals, Chgo., 1981— ; lectr. profl. responsibility Loyola U. Law Sch., Chgo., 1984— ; lectr. trial practice U. Chgo. Law Sch., 1985—; vice chmn. Ill. Task Force on Gender Bias in the Cts., 1987—. Candidate Ill. lt. gov. Adlai Stevenson Solidarity Party, 1986; dir. Great Books Found., 1987— . Mem. Chgo. Bar Assn., Ill. Bar Assn., ABA, Ill. Judges Assn. (bd. dirs. 1984-86), Ill. Trial Lawyers Assn. Democrat. Roman Catholic. State civil litigation. Office: Pope & John Ltd 444 N Michigan Ave Ste 2500 Chicago IL 60611-3997

HOWLEY, JAMES MCANDREW, lawyer; b. Dunmore, Pa., Oct. 3, 1928; s. Joseph Austin and Mary Helene (Ruddy) H.; m. Mary McDade; 1 child, Maura. BS, U. Scranton, 1952; LLB, U. Pa., 1955. Bar: Pa. 1956, U.S. Dist. Ct. (mid. dist.) Pa. 1956, U.S. Ct. Appeals (3d cir.) 1960. Pvt. practice, Scranton, Northeastern Pa., 1956—. Panel mem. and speaker at various legal symposiums; chmn. and commr. Pa. State Ethics Commn.; chmn. Gov.'s Spl. Trial Ct. nomination commn., Lackawanna County, Pa., 1987; disciplinary bd. Supreme Ct. Pa. hearing com., 1987; lawyer's adv. com. U.S. Ct. Appeals (3d cir.), 1983-86, U.S. Dist. Ct. (mid. dist.) Pa., 1981-86. Chmn. and trustee Marywood Coll., trustee St. Mary's Villa. Fellow Am. Coll. Trial Lawyers; mem. ABA, Pa. Bar Assn., Pa. Def. Inst., Am. Bd. Trial Advs. (cert.), Lackawanna County Bar Assn., Scranton C. of C. (bd. dirs.), Country Club of Scranton (pres. 1974-79), Friendly Sons of St. Patrick (pres. 1986). Roman Catholic. Avocation: golf. Federal civil litigation, General civil litigation, State civil litigation. Home: 115 Maple Ave Clarks Summit PA 18411-2513 Office: 1000 Bank Towers 321 Spruce St Scranton PA 18503-1400 E-mail: jmhowley@aol.com

HOWORTH, DAVID BISHOP, lawyer; b. Temple, Tex., Feb. 6, 1947; s. Marion Beckett and Mary Hartwell (Bishop) H.; m. Martha Ellen Peacock, Aug. 29, 1970; children: Katherine Somerville, Emily Hartwell. BA, Yale U., 1971; JD, U. Miss., 1975. ar: N.Y. 1976, Oreg. 1990, Wash. 1996, Miss. 2000, U.S. Dist. Ct. (so. and ea. dists.) N.Y. 1977, U.S. Ct. Appeals (2d cir.) 1984, U.S. Dist. Ct. Oreg. 1990, U.S. Ct. Appeals (9th cir.) 1991. Assoc. Dewey Ballantine, N.Y.C., 1975-77, 78-83, ptnr., 1984-90; asst. prof. law U. Miss., University, 1977-78; ptnr. Foster, Pepper & Shefelman, Portland, Oreg., 1990-2000; interim dir. Nat. Remote Sensing and Space Law Ctr. of Excellence, University, Miss., 2000—. Mem. ABA, N.Y. State Bar Assn., Assn. Bar City of N.Y. General civil litigation. Home: 1420 S 10th St Oxford MS 38655 Office: Sch Law U Miss University MS 38677 E-mail: dhoworth@olemiss.edu

HOWSER, RICHARD GLEN, lawyer; b. Tulsa, Apr. 5, 1951; s. Richard Glen and Mary Ann Howser; m. Judith Anne Howser, Sept. 1, 1986; children: Crystal, Benton, Elizabeth, Richard. BA, U. Ill., 1973; JD, Loyola U., 1977. Assoc. Clausen Miller P.C., Chgo., 1977-83, ptnr., 1983—, dir., 1992—, corp. sec., 1996—. Treas. Wilmette (Ill.) Luth. Ch., 1991-95, pres., 1995-96; area chmn. New Trier Republican Orgn., Kenilworth, Ill., 1992—. Mem. ABA, Soc. Trial Lawyers, Ill. State Bar Assn., Chgo. Bar Assn. Avocations: soccer coach, Sunday school teacher, gardener, history buff, politics. General civil litigation, Personal injury, Product liability. Office: Clausen Miller PC 10 S Lasalle St Ste 1600 Chicago IL 60603-1098

HOYNES, LOUIS LENOIR, JR. lawyer; b. Indpls., Sept. 23, 1935; s. Louis L. and Catharine (Parker) H.; m. Judith E. Kass, Oct. 12, 1958 (div. 1979); children: Thomas M., William D., Ellen B.; m. Virginia Devin, Dec. 9, 1979. AB, Columbia U., 1957; JD cum laude, Harvard U., 1962. Bar: N.Y. 1963, U.S. Supreme Ct. 1967, U.S. Dist. Ct. (so. dist.) N.Y., U.S. Ct. Appeals (2d, 7th and 9th cirs.). Assoc. Willkie, Farr & Gallagher, N.Y.C., 1962-68, ptnr., 1969-90; counsel Nat. League Profl. Baseball Clubs,

1970-90; sr. v.p., gen. counsel Am. Home Products Corp., 1990-2000, exec. v.p. gen. counsel, 2000—. Lectr. law Columbia U., N.Y.C., 1982-91; bd. dirs. Cytec Industries Inc.; trustee Food and Drug Law Inst. Served to lt. USNR, 1957-59, PTO. Mem. ABA, N.Y. State Bar Assn., Assn. of City of Bar of N.Y., The Assn. Gen. Counsel. Federal civil litigation, General corporate, Labor. Home: 47 Cornwells Beach Rd Sands Point NY 11050-1305

HRANITZKY, RACHEL ROBYN, lawyer; b. Irving, Tex., Mar. 16, 1968; d. Dennis Rogers and Jeanne Beverly (Crooks) H. BA, Tex. Christian U., 1987, U. Tex., 1988; JD, So. Meth. U., 1995. Bar: Tex. 1995, U.S. Dist. Ct. (no. dist.) Tex. 1997, U.S. Dist. Ct. (ea. dist.) Tex. 1999, U.S. Dist. Ct. (so. and we. dists.) Tex. 2000. Tchr. Grapevine (Tex.) H.S., 1988-92; clk. to Hon. Candace Tyson, 44th Dist. Ct., Dallas, 1993; assoc. coun. Mesa, Inc., 1995; assoc. Hiersche, Hayward, Drakeley & Urbach, 1996—. Rsch. asst. William V. Dorsaneo, III, 1993-95; clinic atty. So. Meth. U. Legal Clinics, Dallas, 1995. Mem. ABA, ATLA, Dallas Bar Assn., Dallas Assn. Young Lawyers, Delta Theta Phi. Avocations: art, music, sports, cooking, dancing. General civil litigation, Contracts commercial, Trademark and copyright. Home: 11251 Newberry Dr Frisco TX 75035-8614 Office: 15303 Dallas Pkwy Ste 700 Addison TX 75001-4610 E-mail: rhranitzky@hhdulaw.com

HRITZ, GEORGE F. lawyer; b. Hyde Park, N.Y., Aug. 28, 1948; s. George F. and Margaret M. (Callahan) H.; m. Mary Elizabeth Noonan; 1 child, Amelia C. Hritz. AB, Princeton U., 1969; JD, Columbia U., 1973. Bar: N.Y. 1974, D.C. 1978, U.S. Supreme Ct. 1979. Law clk. U.S. Dist. Ct. (ea. dist.) N.Y., N.Y.C., 1973; assoc. Cravath, Swaine & Moore, 1974-77; counsel U.S. Senate Select Com. Ethics Korean Inquiry, Washington, 1977-78; ptnr. Moore & Foster, 1978-80, Davis, Weber & Edwards, N.Y.C., 1980-2000; assoc. ind. counsel Washington, 1986-89; ptnr. Hogan & Hartson, LLP, N.Y.C., 2000—. Mem. adv. com. U.S. Dist. Ct. (ea. dist.) N.Y., 1990—. Trustee Fed. Bar Found., 1998—; bd. dirs. gen. counsel exec. com. Internat. Rescue Com., 1982—; chmn. planning bd. Village of Sleepy Hollow, N.Y., 1993-97; bd. dirs. exec. com. Princeton in Africa, 2000—. Mem. Fed. Bar Coun., D.C. Bar Assn. Federal civil litigation, State civil litigation, Private international. Home: 505 Cognewaugh Rd Greenwich CT 06807-1110 Office: Hogan & Hartson LLP 100 Park Ave Rm 3200 New York NY 10017-5516 E-mail: gfhritz@hhlaw.com

HRONES, STEPHEN BAYLIS, lawyer, educator; b. Boston, Jan. 20, 1942; s. John Anthony and Margaret (Baylis) H.; m. Anneliese Zion, Sept. 11, 1970; children: Christopher, Katja. BA cum laude, Harvard U., 1964; postgrad., U. Sorbonne, Paris, 1964-65; JD, U. Mich., 1968. Bar: Iowa 1969, Mass. 1972, U.S. Dist. Ct. Mass. 1973, U.S. Ct. Appeals (1st cir.) 1979, U.S. Tax Ct. 1985, U.S. Supreme Ct. 1991. Pvt. practice, Heidelberg, Germany, 1970-72; pvt. practice Boston, 1973-86; ptnr. Hrones and Harwood, 1986-90, Hrones and Garrity, Boston, 1990—. Clin. assoc. Suffolk U. Law Sch., Boston, 1979-82; faculty advisor Harvard Law Sch., 1988—; instr. Northeastern Law Sch., 1998; Mass. Continuing Legal Edn. Programs, 1988—. Author: How To Try a Criminal Case, 1982, Criminal Practice Handbook, 1995, 2d edit., 1999, Massachusetts Jury (Criminal) Instructions, 2d edit., 1999; contbr. articles to profl. jours. Trustee Orgn. for Assabet River, 1990-99; mem. schs. and scholarship com. Harvard U.; fundraiser Harvard Coll. Fund, 1985—. Recipient Edward J. Duggan Pvt. Counsel award for zealous advocacy and outstanding legal svcs. to the poor Com. for Pub. Counsel Svcs., 2000; Fulbright scholar, 1968-69. Mem. ACLU, Nat. Assn. Criminal Def. Lawyers, Mass. Assn. Criminal Def. Lawyers, Mass. Bar Assn., Boston Bar Assn., Nat. Lawyers Guild. Democrat. Avocations: squash, skiing, wind-surfing, vegetable gardening, reading. Civil rights, Criminal, Personal injury. Home: 39 Winslow St Concord MA 01742-3817 Office: Hrones and Garrity Lewis Wharf Bay 232 Boston MA 02110 Fax: (617) 227-3908. E-mail: azhro@aol.com

HSU, PAUL SHIU-PO, lawyer, educator; b. Hong Kong, Mar. 25, 1939; s. Pei Yuan and Hang Poo (Loh) H.; 1 child, Duncan Yuan Chung. LLB, Nat. Taiwan U., 1962; MA, Fletcher Sch. Law & Diplomacy, 1965; LLM, NYU, 1969. Lectr. Nat. Taiwan U. Law Sch., 1969-73, Soochow U. Law Sch., 1969-73; assoc. Lee & Li, Taipei, 1969-73, ptnr., 1973-90, sr. ptnr., 1990—. Assoc. prof. law Nat. Taiwan U., 1973-86, prof., 1986—; bd. dirs. China Airlines. Author: A Practical Legal Guide for Conducting Business in the Republic of China, Capital Market Development in the Republic of China, Future Legislative Trends Pertaining to Future Economic and Social Development of the R.O.C., Technology Transfer and Licensing; co-author: (Column) The Law and You, Econ. News Weekly, 1975-78, (monograph) Joint Ventures in the R.O.C.: A Study in Internat. Bus. Corp.; nat. corr. Investment Laws of the World; contbr. articles to profl. jours. Exec. dir. Republic of China-U.S.A./U.S.A.-Republic of China Econ. Coun.; exec. dir. Epoch Found.; chmn. Asia Found. Taiwan; chmn. Republic of China-New Zealand Bus. Coun.; dir. Bd. of the Euro-Asia Trade Orgn.; cons. Taiwan's Exec. Yuan; mem. nat. competitiveness enforcement task force, cons. com. for privatization; mem. Industry Tech. Planning and Assessment Com.; rsch. sect. Hong Kong/Macao Affairs of Mainland Affairs Coun. Recipient grant Asia Found. Mem. ABA, Internat. Bar Assn., Am. Mgmt. Assn., Internat. Liccensing Execs. Soc., Asia Soc. (corp. coun., internat. coun.), Young Pres.'s Orgn. (chmn. Taipei chpt. 1985-87, area v.p. 1987-88, internat. bd. dirs.), Chief Execs. Orgn., Internat. C. of C. Home: # 21-C Sect 2 60 Tun Hua South Rd Taipei Taiwan Office: Floor 7 #201 Tun Hua N Rd Taipei Taiwan

HUANG, THOMAS WEISHING, lawyer; b. Taipei, Taipan, Feb. 1, 1941; came to U.S., 1967; s. Lienden and Helen (Yen) H. BA, Taiwan U., 1964; JD magna cum laude, Ind. U., Indpls., 1970; LLM, Harvard U., 1971, SJD, 1975. Bar: D.C. 1975, Mass. 1976, U.S. Dist. Ct. Mass. 1976, U.S. Ct. Appeals (1st cir.) 1978, N.Y. 1980. Judge adv. Chinese Army, Taiwan, 1964-65; legal officer treaty and legal dept. Ministry Fgn. Affairs, Taiwan, 1966-67; assoc. Chemung County Legal Svcs., Elmira, N.Y., 1975-76, Taylor Johnson & Wieschhoff, Marblehead, Mass., 1980; prin. Reiser & Rosenberg, Boston, 1982-86, Huang & Assocs., Boston, 1987-88, Hale, Sanderson, Byrnes & Morton, Boston, 1988-96; of counsel Chin, Wright & Branson P.C., 1996-97; shareholder Sherburne, Powers & Needham, P.C., 1997-98; ptnr. Holland & Knight, LLP, 1998—. Exec. v.p. Excel Tech. Internat. Co., Brunswick, N.J., 1982-88; bd. dirs. Asian Am. Bank & Trust Co., Boston, exec. com., clk., 1993—; legal counsel Nat. Assn. Chinese Ams., Washington, 1979-80. Mem. editl. staff Ind. Law Rev., 1969-70; contbr. articles to legal jours. Bd. dirs. Chinese Econ. Devel. Coun., Boston, 1978-80; mem. Gov.'s Adv. Coun. on Guangdong, 1984-87; mem. minority bus task force Senator Kerry's Office, 1988—. Mem. Boston Bar Assn. (steering com. internat. law sect. 1979-90, ad hoc com. on code profl. conduct), Nat. Assn. Chines Ams. (v.p. Boston chpt. 1984-86, pres. 1986-88, 1st v.p. nat. assn. 1994-97), Taiwan C of C. in New Eng. (clk., bd. dirs. 1996-2000), N.E. Chinese Internet & Network Assn. (bd. dirs. 2000—). Democrat. Contracts commercial, Immigration, naturalization, and customs, Private international. Home: 30 Farrwood Dr Andover MA 01810-5233 Office: Holland & Knight LLP 10 St James Ave Boston MA 02116 E-mail: Thuang@hklaw.com

HUANG, VIVIAN WENHUEY CHEN, lawyer; b. Taipei, Taiwan, Aug. 10, 1942; came to U.S., 1968; d. Yi Song and Ling Yu (Lin) Chen; 1 child, Charlotte. BA in Law, Nat. Taiwan U., 1966; JD, Ind. U., 1971. Bar: Mass. 1975. Assoc. Mau Chun Chen's Law Office, Taipei, 1966-67; staff lawyer Urban and Econ. Devel. Com., Taipei, 1967-68; assoc. Ropes & Gray, Boston, 1973-89; of counsel Cuddy, Lynch & Bixby, 1990-92, Bloom & Witkin, 1992—; adv. coun. Gov. Mass., Boston, 1983—; bd. dirs., pres. Asian Am. Bank & Trust Co., Boston. Trustees Harry H. Dow Meml. Legal Assistance Fund, 1985—; advisory trustee Peabody & Essex Mus. of Salem, Mass., 1988-93, overseer, 1993-95. Mem. ABA, Mass. Bar Assn. (critical issue com. 1988—), Asian-Am. Lawyers Assn. Mass. (bd. dirs. 1983-88), Boston Bar Assn. (steering com. internat. law sect. 1983, chmn. Asian Pacific Rim com. 1988-90), Nat. Assn. Chinese Ams. (bd. dirs., sec. Boston chpt. 1983-94, v.p. 1990-92), Orgn. Chinese Ams. (bd. dirs. 1982-88). Democrat. Avocations: painting, skiing, tennis, hiking, music. Private international, Probate, Business. Home: 30 Farrwood Dr Andover MA 01810-5233 Office: Asian Am Bank & Trust Co 17 Kneeland St Boston MA 02111-1513

HUBBARD, FRED LEONHARDT, lawyer; b. Carlinville, Ill., Apr. 14, 1940; s. David Fred and Frances Pauline (Leonhardt) H.; m. Sharon L. Woodyard, Nov. 13, 1964; 1 child, Glenn Edward. BS in Commerce, U. Ill., 1961, JD, 1963. Bar: Ill. 1963. Ptnr. Lowenstein and Hubbard, Danville, Ill., 1965-73, Lowenstein, Hubbard & Smith, Danville, 1973-88, Hubbard, Smith & Kagawa, Danville, 1990-92, Gunn & Hickman, P.C., Danville, 1992-97, Fred L. Hubbard Law Office, Danville, 1997—. Chmn. Vermilion County Am. Cancer Soc., 1982-83; pres. Plankeshaw coun. Boy Scouts Am., 1984-85. Served to sgt., U.S. Army, 1963-69. Recipient Silver Beaver award Boy Scouts Am., 1980, also Dist. award of Merit. Mem. Vermilion County Bar Assn. (pres. 1991-92), Ill. State Bar Assn., Vermilion County Hist. Soc., Masons (33d degree). Republican. Methodist. Avocations: music, woodworking, photography, model railroading, antiques. Municipal (including bonds), Probate, Real property. Home: PO Box 434 Catlin IL 61817-0434 Office: 415 N Gilbert St PO Box 12 Danville IL 61834-0012

HUBBARD, MICHAEL JAMES, lawyer; b. N.Y.C., Dec. 8, 1950; s. William Neil and Elizabeth (Terleski) H. AB, U. Mich., 1976; JD, Marquette U., 1979. Bar: Wis. 1980, Mich. 1980. Assoc. Kidston, Peterson P.C., Kalamazoo, 1980, Barbier, Goulet & Petersmarck, Mt. Clemens, Mich., 1981; pvt. practice Detroit, 1982-86, Belleville, Mich., 1990-98; assoc. Lawrence J. Stockler, P.C., Southfield, 1987; staff atty. Hyatt Legal Svcs., Southgate, 1988; assoc. Dunchock, Linden & Wells, Coruna, 1989. Mem. Mich. Trial Lawyers Assn., State Bar Mich. Republican. Avocations: reading, racquetball. General practice, Other.

HUBBARD, PETER LAWRENCE, lawyer; b. Syracuse, N.Y., Apr. 4, 1946; s. Bardwell B. and Barbara (Bowen) H.; m. Hannah R., June 21, 1967; 1 child, Brian C. BA, Syracuse U., 1968, JD, 1971; postgrad., Judge Advocate Gen.'s Sch., Charlottesville, Va., 1976. Bar: N.Y. 1972, U.S. Dist. Ct. (no. and we. dists.) N.Y. 1972, U.S. Ct. Appeals (2d cir.) 1983. Assoc. Smith & Sovik, Syracuse, N.Y., 1971-72; asst. dist. counsel U.S. SBA, 1972-80; mng. ptnr. Menter, Rudin & Trivelpiece, 1980—. Lectr. in field. Contbr. articles to profl. jours. Pres. Reachout Inc., County Drug Rehab. Agy., Syracuse, 1979; mem. bd. trustees Loretto Mgmt. Corp., Syracuse, 2001. Banking, Bankruptcy, Contracts commercial. Office: Menter Rudin & Trivelpiece 500 S Salina St Ste 500 Syracuse NY 13202-3300 E-mail: phubbard@menterlaw.com

HUBBARD, THOMAS EDWIN (TIM HUBBARD), lawyer; b. Roseboro, N.C., July 10, 1944; s. Charles Spence and Mary Mercer (Reeves) H.; children: Marvin Gannon, Caitlin Kable York. BS in Biomed. Engring., Duke U., 1970, postgrad., 1970-71; JD, U. N.C., 1973. Bar: N.C. 1973. Regulation writer, med. devices FDA, Washington, 1974-75; asst. dir. clin. affairs Zimmer USA, Warsaw, 1975, dir. regulatory affairs, 1975-76; house counsel Gen. Med. Cor., Richmond, Va., 1976-79; pvt. practice Pittsboro, N.C., 1979—. Pres. Chathamborough Rsch. Group, Inc., Pittsboro, 1979—, Chathamborough Farms Inc., 1982—; sec.-treas. Hubbard-Corry, Inc., Pittsboro, 1981—; chmn. Hubbard Bros., Inc., Chapel Hill, N.C., 1982-87; bd. dirs. No. State Legal Svc., Hillsborough, N.C., 1980—, pres., 1986-89, MDR Svcs., Inc., 1991—; adj. instr. U. N.C. Law Sch., 1983. V.p. N.C. Young Dems. 4th Congl. Dist., 1970-71; mem. State Dem. Exec. Com., 1972-73; mem. paralegal adv. com. Ctrl. Carolina C.C., Sanford, N.C., 1987-93, legal svcs. N.C. Long Range Planning Com., 1987-93; bd. dirs. Chatham Soccer League, 1993—, sec.-treas., coach coord., 1994-98, v.p., 1998-99, pres., 1999-2001; mem. Chatham Coalition to Improve Quality of Life, 1992-93, chmn. single parent com.; pres. Pittsboro Elem. PTA, 1996-98; soccer coach Horton Mid. Sch., 2000—. Sgt. USMC, 1963-68. Named Top N.C. Young Dem., 1971. Mem. ABA (vice chmn. health law com. gen. practice sect. 1991-93), N.C. Bar Assn. (legal svcs. planning com. 1988-94), Chatham County Bar Assn., Assn. for Advancement Med. Instrumentation (govt. affairs com. 1976). Democrat. Methodist. Administrative and regulatory, Personal injury, Product liability. Office: PO Box 939 Pittsboro NC 27312-0939 also: Chathamborough Rsch Group Inc 105 West St Pittsboro NC 27312-9470

HUBBELL, BILLY JAMES, lawyer; b. Pine Bluff, Ark., May 21, 1949; s. Arley E. and Mary M. (Duke) H.; m. Judy C. Webb, Feb. 21, 1981; children: Jennifer Leigh, William Griffin. BE, U. Cen. Ark., 1971; JD, U. Ark, Little Rock, 1978. Bar: Ark. 1978, U.S. Dist. Ct. (ea. dist.) Ark. 1978, U.S. Ct. Appeals (8th cir.) 1987. Tchr. Grady (Ark.) High Sch., 1971-78; assoc. Smith and Smith, McGehee, Ark., 1978-79; ptnr. Smith, Hubbell and Drake, 1979-86, Griffin, Rainwater & Draper, P.A., Crossett, Ark., 1987-90; dep. prosecuting atty. Ashley County, Ark., 1989-90; mcpl. judge Crossett, 1991—; pvt. practice, 1991—. Candidate Ark. Ho. of Reps., Lincoln County, 1984, 10th Jud. Dist. Cir./Chancery Judge, 1998. Sgt. USAR, 1970-76. Mem. Ark. Bar Assn., S.E. Ark. Legal Inst. (chmn. 1984-85, Ashley County Bar Assn. (past pres.), Ark. Trial Lawyers Assn. Democrat. Seventh Day Adventist. Avocations: jogging, computers. General civil litigation, Contracts commercial, Personal injury. Office: PO Box 574 Crossett AR 71635-0574 E-mail: bjhubbell@starband.net

HUBBELL, ERNEST, lawyer; b. Trenton, Mo., Aug. 28, 1914; s. Platt and Maud Irene (Ray) H.; m. Nevah Smith, Apr. 25, 1943; 1 child, Platt Thorpe. AA, North Cen. Mo. Coll. (formerly Trenton Jr. Coll.), 1934; JD, Georgetown U., 1938. Bar: D.C. 1937, Mo. 1938, U.S. Supreme Ct. 1946. Practiced in, Trenton, 1938-39, Jefferson City, Mo., 1939-42; pvt. practice, Kansas City, 1947-52; ptnr. Hubbell, Sawyer, Peak, O'Neal & Napier (formerly Hubbell, Lane & Sawyer), 1952—. Asst. atty. gen. Mo., 1939-42; first chmn. bench, bar com. 16th Jud. Cir. Ct., Kansas City, 1964-69, mem 16th Cir. Jud. Nominating Commn., 1970-75; mem. U.S. Cir. Judge Nominating Commn., 1977-80. Trustee Legal Aid and Defender Soc. Greater Kansas City, 1964-73; mem. Law Found. U. Mo. Kansas City, 1966-71; chmn. Nat. Council on Crime and Delinquency, 1966-76; pres. Hubbell Family Hist. Soc., 1981-85; mem. Soc. Fellows Nelson Art Gallery. With USAAF, 1942-44, capt. JAGC, 1944-46. Mem. ABA, Kansas City Met. Bar Assn. (pres. 1963-64, ann. Achievement award 1974, 1st ann. Litigator Emeritus award), Mo. Bar Assn., Assn. Trial Lawyers Am. (assoc. editor R.R. law sect. of jour. 1951—), Mo. Assn. Trial Attys. (pres. 1954, editor bull. 1955), Lawyers Assn. Kansas City, Lawyers Assn. St. Louis, Archeol. Inst. Am., Sierra Club (life). Episcopalian. Democrat. Club: Kansas City. Federal civil litigation, State civil litigation, Personal injury. Home: 1210 W 63d St Kansas City MO 64113-1513 Office: Hubbell Sawyer Peak O'Neal & Napier Power and Light Bldg 106 W 14th St Fl 12 Kansas City MO 64105-1914

HUBEN, BRIAN DAVID, lawyer; b. Inglewood, Calif., May 14, 1962; s. Michael Gerald and Dorothy (Withers) H.; m. Kathy Henson Johnson, Apr. 6, 1991; children: Kaitlin Johnson, Mariana Johnson. BA, Loyola Marymount U., 1984; JD, Loyola Law Sch., 1987. Bar: Calif. 1988, U.S. Dist. Ct. (no., ce., ea. and so. dists.) Calif. 1988, Ariz., 1994, U.S. Ct. Appeals (9th cir.) 1988, D.C. 1989, U.S. Supreme Ct. 1996. Assoc. Steinberg, Nutter & Brent, Santa Monica, Calif., 1988-89, Smith & Hilbig, Torrance, 1989-95, Robie & Matthai, L.A., 1995-99; spl. master State Bar of Calif., 1995-99; counsel Katten Muchin Zavis, L.A., 1999—. Del. L.A. County Bar Assn. State Conv., 1990-99. Mem. instl. rev. bd. Torrance Meml. Med. Ctr., 1990-95. Mem. Calif. Bar Assn., D.C. Bar Assn., L.A. County Bar Assn., Loyola Marymount Univ. Alumni Assn. (dir., bd. dirs. 1995—). Democrat. Roman Catholic. Avocations: travel, sports, current events. Bankruptcy, General civil litigation, Contracts commercial. Office: Katten Muchin Zavis 14th Fl 1999 Avenue Of The Stars Fl 14 Los Angeles CA 90067-6022 E-mail: brian.huben@kmz.com

HUBER, RICHARD GREGORY, lawyer, educator; b. Indpls., June 29, 1919; s. Hugh Joseph and Laura Marie (Becker) H.; m. Katherine Elizabeth McDonald, June 21, 1950 (dec.); children: Katherine, Richard, Mary, Elizabeth, Stephen, Mark. BS, U.S. Naval Acad, 1942; JD, U. Iowa, 1950; LLM, Harvard U., 1951; LLD (hon.), New England Sch. Law, 1985, Northeastern U., 1987, Roger Williams U., 1996. Instr. law U. Iowa, 1950; assoc. prof. law U. S.C., 1952-54; assoc. prof. Tulane U., 1954-57, Boston Coll., 1957-59, prof., 1959-90, dean, 1970-85; disting. prof. Roger Williams U., Bristol, R.I., 1993-95; prof. New England Sch. Law, Newton, Mass., 1995-99. Adj. faculty Boston Coll., 1999—. Contbr. articles and book revs. to profl. jours. Past chairperson pers. and fin. coms. Mass. chpt. Multiple Sclerosis Soc.; past pres. bd. trustees Beaver Country Day Sch. With USN, 1941-47, 51-52. Mem. ABA (del., mem. coun. legal edn. 1981-85, trustee law sch. admissions coun 1983-85), Soc. Am. Law Tchrs., Assn. Am. Law Schs. (pres. 1988-89), Coun. Legal Edn. Opportunity (pres. 1975-79), Am. Judicature Soc., Mass. Bar Assn., Mass. Bar Found. Democrat. Roman Catholic. Home: 406 Woodward St Waban MA 02468-1523 Office: 885 Centre St Newton MA 02459-1148 E-mail: richard.huber1@worldnet.att.net, huber@monet.bc.edu

HUBER, THOMAS P. lawyer; b. Watertown, Wis., Oct. 26, 1936; s. Frederick O. and Isabel Mary (Coogan) H.; m. Gloria A. Parrella, Dec. 30, 1961; children— Patrick, Christopher, Mary. B.S., Marquette U., 1959; LL.B., George Washington U., 1967. Bar: Hawaii 1968. Assoc. Cades Schutte Fleming & Wright, Honolulu, 1967-73, ptnr., 1973— . Pres. Protection and Advocacy Agy. of Hawaii, Honolulu, 1978-81, 83-84. Chmn. Task Force on Guardianship, Civil Commitment and Protective Services in Hawaii, Honolulu, 1980-83; bd. dirs. Cath. Charities, Honolulu, 1985—. Served to 1st lt. USMC, 1959-62. Mem. ABA, Hawaii Bar Assn. Roman Catholic. Club: Pacific (Honolulu). Banking, Contracts commercial, General corporate. Home: 46-291 Auna St Kaneohe HI 96744-4110

HUBER, WILLIAM EVAN, lawyer; b. Celina, Ohio, Mar. 10, 1943; s. W. Evan and Genevieve Rose Huber; m. E. Marie Schwaberow, June 24, 1966 (div. Aug. 1994); m. Betty Jo Bowers, Aug. 23, 1999; children: Michael D., Mark William. BSEd, Ohio No. U., 1965, JD, 1968. Bar: Ohio 1968, U.S. Dist. Ct. (no. dist.) Ohio 1972, U.S. Supreme Ct. 1972, U.S. Ct. Appeals (6th cir.) 1990, U.S. Tax Ct. Ohio, U.S. Dist. Ct. (no. dist.) Ohio. Asst. pros. atty. Auglaize County, Ohio, 1969-76; pvt. practice St. Marys, 1969—. Asst. law dir. City of St. Marys, Ohio, 1972-79. Past pres., past state dir. St. Marys Jaycees; past state v.p. Ohio Jaycees, 1969; mem. Jr. Chamber Internat. Senate; past trustee Auglaize County Mental Health Assn.; past gen. chmn. St. Mary's Area United Way; past chmn. St. Marys City Recreational Adv. Bd.; past pres. St. Marys Nat. Little League; past chmn. St. Marys Medic-Search Com.; mem., past trustee St. Marys Cmty. Improvement Corp.; past mem. Mayor's Downtown Re-vitalization Com.; past mem., chmn. St. Marys Civil Svc. Commn., 1993-97; mem. Auglaize County Bd. Elections, 1994-97; past mem. Auglaize County Dem. Exec. Com., chmn., 1992-97. Named Outstanding Jaycee, St. Marys Jaycees, 1971; recipient Ohio Jaycees Presdl. award of Honor, 1972, Disting. Svc. award Ohio Dem. Party, 1997. Mem. Ohio State Bar Assn., Auglaize County Bar Assn. (past pres.), St. Marys C. of C. (past trustee, past pres.). General civil litigation, Family and matrimonial, General practice. Office: 137 E Spring St PO Box 298 Saint Marys OH 45885-0298

HUBERMAN, RICHARD LEE, lawyer; b. Lynn, Mass., Dec. 6, 1953; s. Irving Morris and Selma Edythe (Wolk) H. AB, Harvard U., 1975, JD, 1978. Bar: Mass. 1979, D.C. 1979. Atty. Office of Rail Pub. Counsel, Washington, 1978-80; counsel subcom. on commerce, consumer protection and competitiveness (formerly commerce, transp. and tourism) U.S. Ho. of Reps., 1980-95, mem. prof. staff Com. on Edn. and Workforce, 1995—97; pvt. practitioner, 1997-98; counsel to commr. and chmn. Occupl. Safety and Health Rev. Commn., 1998—. Mem. ABA, Mass. Bar Assn., Harvard Law Sch. Assn. Democrat. Club: Harvard (Washington). E-mail. Home: 2141 P St NW Apt 302 Washington DC 20037-1031 Office: Occupl Safety and Health Rev Commn Office of the Chmn 1120 20th St NW Washington DC 20036 E-mail: rhuberman@oshrc.gov

HUBERT, DONALD, lawyer; b. Chgo., Apr. 12, 1948; s. Issac Wade and Louise (Billingsly) H. BBA, Loyola U., Chgo., 1970; JD, U. Mich., 1973. Bar: Ill. 1974, U.S. Dist. Ct. (no. dist.) Ill. 1983, U.S. Ct. Appeals (7th cir.) 1976. Atty. gen. Lawyers for State, Chgo., 1974-77; assoc. Howard, Mann and Slaughter, 1977-80, Adam Bourgois & Assocs., Chgo., 1980; ptnr Hubert & Assocs., 1980—. Spl. asst. corp. counsel City of Chgo., 1983— ; mem. Ill. Criminal Justice Info. Authority, Chgo., 1980—; com. vistors U. Mich. Law Sch., 1993—; bd. overseers Chgo.-Kent Coll. Law, Ill. Inst. Tech., 1993—; mem. Ill. Supreme Ct. com. on profl. responsibility, 1993—, chmn., 2001. Co-chair county bd. pres. Cook County com. on Cts. for 21st Century, 1997—; mem. Gov's. commn. on capital punishment, 2000—, Chgo. Libr. Bd., 1999-2001, Ill. Criminal Justice Info. Council/Authority, 1977-91; chmn., bd. trustees. Hales Franciscan Catholic H.S. Inc, 1988-95. Named Chgo. Lawyer Person of Yr., 1992; recipient Abraham Lincoln award Chgo. Sun Times, 1992. Fellow Internat. Acad. Trial Lawyers, Am. Coll. Trial Lawyers; mem. ABA (Gambrell award 1992), Fed. Bar Assn. (Chgo. chpt., Just Beginning Found. Recognition award 1994), Chgo. Bar Assn. (pres. 1996-97), Cook County Bar Assn. (Westbrook award 1992). Democrat. Roman Catholic. Federal civil litigation, Criminal. Home: 1112 E 48th St Chicago IL 60615-1904 Office: Hubert & Assocs 188 W Randolph St 188 W Randolph St Chicago IL 60601 E-mail: Don@DonaldHubert.com

HUBSCHMAN, HENRY A. lawyer; b. Newark, Aug. 12, 1947; s. Morris and Esther (Weissman) H.; m. Joanne L. Goode; children: Lilly, Josie, Ellis, Nathan. BA summa cum laude, Rutgers U., 1969; JD magna cum laude, M Pub. Policy, Harvard U., 1973. Bar: Mass. 1973, N.J. 1974, D.C. 1974, Ohio 1994. Law clk. U.S. Dist. Ct. Mass., Boston, 1973-74; assoc. Fried, Frank, Harris, Shriver & Jacobson, Washington, 1974-77, 79-80, ptnr., 1980-92; v.p., gen. counsel, bus. devel. GE Aircraft Engines, Cin., 1992-97; pres., CEO GE Capital Aviation Svcs., Stamford, Conn., 1997—. Exec. asst. to Sec. HUD, Washington, 1977-79; bd. dir. Fed. Nat. Mortgage Assn., 1979-81. Jewish. Federal civil litigation, Insurance, Securities. Home: 37 Hillside Rd Greenwich CT 06830-4834 Office: GE Capital Aviation Svcs 201 High Ridge Rd Stamford CT 06905-3417

HUCHTEMAN, RALPH DOUGLAS, lawyer; b. Garland, Tex., Oct. 8, 1946; s. Ray Edwin and Hazel Laverne (Clark) H.; m. Sherry Lynn Horner, Mar. 12, 1994; children: Lara Victoria, Brett Norman, Bryan Randolff. AA, Okla. Mil. Acad., 1966; BA in Polit. Sci., Okla. State U., 1969; JD, Okla. U., 1972. Bar: Okla. 1972, U.S. Dist. Ct. (we. dist.) Okla. 1972. Ptnr. Doak & Huchteman, Oklahoma City, 1972-73, Wolf & Wolf P.C. (formerly Wolf, Wolf, Huchteman & Graven), Norman, Okla., 1982-88; prin. Huchteman Law Offices, 1989-98; staff atty. Legal Svcs. of Eastern Okla., Inc., Bartlesville, 1998-99, mng. atty., 1999—. Assoc. mcpl. judge, Noble, Okla., 1990-98, Blanchard, Okla., 1992-98; vis. asst. prof. Coll. Bus., Okla. U., 1972-73; temporary justice Okla. Ct. Appeals, Oklahoma City, 1982-83. State exec. sec. Student Lobby for Higher Edn., Stillwater, Okla., 1968-69. 1st lt. U.s. Army, 1973. T.A. Shadid scholar Okla. U., 1969; recipient A.C. Hunt Practice award Okla. U., 1972. Mem. ATLA, Okla. Bar

Assn., Okla. Trial Lawyers Assn. Democrat. State civil litigation, Family and matrimonial, Pension, profit-sharing, and employee benefits. Office: Legal Svcs Eastern Okla 217 S Choctaw Ave Bartlesville OK 74003-2837 E-mail: rhuchteman@aol.com, rhuchteman@lseo.org

HUCKABEE, HARLOW MAXWELL, lawyer, writer; b. Wichita Falls, Tex., Jan. 22, 1918; s. Edwin Cleveland and Gladys Idella (Bonney) H.; m. Gloria Charlotte Comstock, Jan. 10, 1942; children: Bonney M., David C., Stephen M. BA, Harvard U., 1948; JD, Georgetown U., 1951. Bar: U.S. Dist. Ct. D.C. 1952, U.S. Ct. Appeals (D.C. cir.) 1952. Cashier br. office Columbian Nat. Life Ins. Co., Boston, 1935-40; lawyer Fed. Housing Adminstrn., Washington, 1955-56; trial lawyer, criminal sect., tax divsn. U.S. Justice Dept., 1956-63; lawyer IRS, 1963-67; trial lawyer organized crime and racketeering sect. U.S. Justice Dept., 1967-68, trial lawyer criminal sect., tax divsn., 1968-80. Author: Lawyers, Psychiatrists and Criminal Law, 1980, Mental Disability Issues in the Criminal Justice System: What They Are, Who Evaluates Them, How and When, 2000; contbr. articles to profl. jours. and legal publs. including Diminished Capacity Dilemma in the Federal System, 1991. Maj. U.S. Army, 1940-45, 48-55, ETO, Korea; lt. col. USAR, 1961. Methodist. Home: 5100 Fillmore Ave Apt 913 Alexandria VA 22311-5048

HUCKIN, WILLIAM PRICE, JR. prosecutor; b. Okmulgee, Okla., Aug. 20, 1920; s. William Price and Mary Louise H.; m. Freda Croom, Nov. 15, 1947; children: William Price III, David, Elizabeth, Barbara. BA, U. Okla., 1942, LLB, 1947. Bar: Okla. 1947; U.S. Dist. Ct. (no. dist.) 1953, U.S. Dist. Ct. (we. dist.) 1950, U.S. Ct. Appeals, 1994. Asst. county atty., Tulsa, Okla., 1951-52; prosecutor, 1954-55; pvt. practice, 1956—. Apttd. city prosecutor, Tulsa. Active First Presbyn. Ch., clk. of session, permanent jud. commn. 1st lt., pilot, U.S. Army Air Corps, 1943-45. Decorated EAME (Rome Arno and Air Offensive Europe) Theatre ribbon with 2 bronze stars, air medal, 1944, 2nd oak leaf cluster, 1944, unit citation, 1944. Mem. ATLA, Okla. Bar Assn., Tulsa County Bar Assn. (Disting. Svc. award 1986), Beta Theta Pi (pres. Gamma Phi chpt. 1947). Republican. Avocations: genealogy, chess. Home: 6706 S Florence Ave Tulsa OK 74136-4556 Office: 1206 Philtower Bldg 427 S Boston Ave Tulsa OK 74103-4141

HUDDLESTON, JOSEPH RUSSELL, judge; b. Glasgow, Ky., Feb. 5, 1937; s. Paul Russell and Laura Frances (Martin) H.; m. Heidi Wood, Sept. 12, 1959; children: Johanna, Lisa, Kristina. AB, Princeton U., 1959; JD, U. Va., 1962, LLM, 1997. Bar: Ky. 1962, U.S. Ct. Appeals (6th cir.) 1963, U.S. Supreme Ct. 1970. Ptnr. Huddleston Bros., Bowling Green, Ky., 1962-87; judge Warren Cir. Ct. Divsn. I, 1987-91, Ky. Ct. appeals, Bowling Green, 1991—. Mem. Adv. Com. for Criminal Law Revision, 1969-71; exec. com. Ky. Crime Commn., 1972-77. Named Ky. Outstanding Trial Judge, 1990. Fellow Am. Bar Found.; mem. ABA, Ky. Bar Assn. (ho. of dels. 1971-80), Assn. Trial Lawyers Am. (state del. 1981-82), Ky. Acad. Trial Attys. (bd. govs. 1975-87, pres. 1978), Bowling Green Bar Assn. (pres. 1972), So. Ky. Estate Planning Coun. (pres. 1983), Bowling Green-Warren County C. of C. (bd. dirs. 1987-91), Port Oliver Yacht Club (commodore). Democrat. Episcopalian. Home: 644 Minnie Way Bowling Green KY 42101-9210 Office: 1945 Scottsville Rd Ste 101 Bowling Green KY 42104-5824

HUDIAK, DAVID MICHAEL, academic administrator, lawyer; b. Darby, Pa., June 27, 1953; s. Michael Paul and Sophie Marie (Glowaski) H.; m. Veronica Ann Barbone, Aug. 28, 1982; children: David Michael, Christopher Andrew, Jonathan Joseph. BA, Haverford Coll., 1975; JD, U. Pa., 1978. Bar: Pa. 1979, U.S. Dist. Ct. (ea. dist.) Pa. 1979, N.J. 1981, U.S. Dist. Ct. N.J. 1981. Assoc. Jerome H. Ellis, Phila., 1978-79, Berson, Fineman & Bernstein, Phila., 1979-80; pvt. practice Aldan, Pa., 1980-81; dir. tng. paralegal program PJA Sch., Upper Darby, 1982—, acting dir., 1983-89, dir., 1989—; v.p. The PJA Sch., Inc., 1989—, bd. dirs.; v.p., sec.-treas., bd. dirs. 7900 West Chester Pike Corp., 1994—. Mem. staff Nat. Ctr. Ednl. Testing, Phila., 1982-87; instr. Villanova (Pa.) U., 1985. Mem. Havertown Choristers; active U. Pa. Light Opera Co., 1977-84. Mem. ABA, Pa. Bar Assn., Founders Club Haverford Coll. Office: PJA Sch 7900 W Chester Pike Upper Darby PA 19082-1917 E-mail: dhudiak909@home.com

HUDKINS, JOHN W. lawyer; b. Inglewood, Calif., Jan. 12, 1946; s. Ralph Emerson and Genevieve Delores H.; m. Diana Byler, Feb. 16, 1969. BA, Calif. State U., Hayward, 1968; MBA, U. Nev., Las Vegas, 1971; JD, U. of Pacific, 1976; LLM, George Washington U., 1983. Bar: Iowa 1976, Calif. 1977, U.S. Ct. Mil. Appeals 1976, Fla. 1995. Commd. 2d lt. USAF, 1968, advanced through grades to lt. col., 1983, ret., 1988; sr. counsel Aerojet-Gen. Corp., Sacramento, 1988-94; dir. bus. mgmt. Olin Ordnance, Downey, Calif., 1994-95, sr. counsel St. Petersburg, Fla., 1995-96, v.p., chief counsel, 1996-97; v.p., dep. gen. counsel Primex Tech., Inc., 1997-2001; dep. gen. counsel Gen. Dynamics Ordnance and Tactical Sys., 2001—. Bd. dirs. Vandenberg Fed. Credit Union, Lompoc, Calif., 1983-85, Prince William (Va.) County Soccer Assn., 1985-88. Mem. ABA (pub. contract law sect.), Nat. Security Indsl. Assn. (chair legal com.). Administrative and regulatory, General corporate, Government contracts and claims. Home: 1339 Forestedge Blvd Oldsmar FL 34677-5119 Office: Gen Dynamics Ordnance and Tactical Sys 10101 9th St N Saint Petersburg FL 33716 E-mail: jwhudkins@stp.gd-ots.com

HUDSON, DENNIS LEE, lawyer, retired government official, arbitrator, educator; b. St. Louis, Jan. 5, 1936; s. Lewis Jefferson and Helen Mabel (Buchanan) H.; children: Karen Marie, Karla Sue, Mary Ashley. BA, U. Ill., 1958; JD, John Marshall Law Sch., 1972. Bar: Ill. 1972, U.S. Dist. Ct. (so. and no. dists.) Ill. 1972. Ins. IRS, Chgo., 1962-72; spl. agt. GSA, 1972-78, spl. agt.-in-charge, 1978-83, regional insp. gen., 1983-87; supervisory spl. agt. Dept. Justice-GSA Task Force, Washington, 1978; arbitrator Circuit Ct. Cook County, Ill., 1987-93; prof. criminal justice Coll. of DuPage, Glen Ellyn, 1996—. Bd. govs. Theatre Western Springs, Ill., 1978-81, 91-92; deacon Grace Luth. Ch., LaGrange, Ill., 1977-81; lay eucharistic min. All Sts. Episcopal Ch., Western Springs, Ill., 1999—. With U.S. Army, 1959-61. John N. Jewett scholar, 1972. Mem. ABA, Ill. Bar Assn. Home: 109 51st Pl Western Springs IL 60558-2002 Office: Coll Dupage Bus & Svcs Div 22D St Lambert Rd Glen Ellyn IL 60137 E-mail: hudsond@cdnet.cod.edu

HUDSON, FRANK N. real estate developer, lawyer; b. N.Y.C., Nov. 28, 1949; s. Alec N. Hudson. B.B.A., Sam Houston State U., 1971; J.D., St. Mary's U., 1974. Bar: Tex. 1975, U.S. Dist. Ct. (so. dist.) Tex. 1979, U.S. Supreme Ct., U.S. Ct. of Appeals, Atlanta, New Orleans and San Francisco, Mem. Nat. Assn. Home Builders, Nat. Multi Family Council, State Bar Assn. Tex. Office: PO Box 460029 Houston TX 77056-8029

HUDSON, ROBERT FRANKLIN, JR. lawyer; b. Miami, Fla., Sept. 20, 1946; s. Robert Franklin and Jane Ann (Reed) H.; m. Edith Mueller, June 19, 1971; children: Daniel Warren, Patrick Alexander. BSBA in Econs., U. Fla., 1968, JD, 1971; summer cert., U. London, 1970; LLM in Taxation, NYU, 1972. Bar: Fla. 1971, N.Y. 1975. Law clk. to judge Don N. Laramore U.S. Ct. Claims, Washington, 1972-73; assoc. Wender, Murase & White, N.Y.C., 1973-77; ptnr. Arky, Freed, Stearns et al, Miami, 1977-86, Baker & McKenzie, Miami, 1986—, mem. policy com., 1990-93, mem. client credit com., 1992-99, mng. ptnr. Miami office, 1996-98; N. Am. Tax Practice Group Mgmt. com., 2000—. Mem. adv. bd. Tax Mgmt., Inc., Washington, 1986—, Fgn. Investment N.Am., London, 1990-96; legal counsel to her majesty's Britanic Counsel, Miami. Author: Federal Taxation of Foreign Investment in U.S. Real Estate, 1986; contbr. articles to legal publs. Bd. dirs. Fla. Philharmonic, 1996-97, Performing Arts Ctr. Found., 1994—, vice chmn. 2000—; bd. dirs. Concert Assn. Fla., 1992—, exec. com., 1993-98, vice chmn., 1994-98. Mem. ABA, Fla. Bar Assn. (chmn. tax sect. 1989-90, Outstanding Spkr. 1995), Internat. Fiscal Assn. (v.p. S.E. region U.S. br. 1985-92, exec. coun. 1987—), Inter-Am. Bar Assn., Internat. Bar Assn., Internat. Tax Planning Assn., Coll. Tax Lawyers, World Trade Ctr. (bd. dirs. 1992-94), S.E./U.S. Japan Assn., Japan Soc. South Fla. (chmn. pub. affairs com. 1991-93, bd. dirs. 1993-2000, treas. 1995-96, pres. 1996-99 Democrat. Methodist. Avocations: skiing, boating, photography, travel, hiking. Private international, Corporate taxation. Office: Baker & McKenzie 1200 Brickell Ave Ste 1900 Miami FL 33131-3257 E-mail: bob.hudson@bakernet.com

HUDSPETH, HARRY LEE, federal judge; b. Dallas, Dec. 28, 1935; s. Harry Ellis and Hattilee (Dudney) H.; m. Vicki Kathryn Round, Nov. 27, 1971; children: Melinda, Mary Kathryn. BA, U. Tex., Austin, 1955, JD, 1958. Bar: Tex. 1958. Trial atty. Dept. Justice, Washington, 1959-62; asst. U.S. atty. Western Dist. Tex., El Paso, 1962-69; assoc. Peticolas, Luscombe & Stephens, 1969-77; U.S. magistrate, 1977-79; judge U.S. Dist. Ct. (we. dist.) Tex., 1979—; chief judge U.S. Dist. Ct. (we. dist) Tex., 1992-1999. Bd. dirs. Sun Carnival Assn., 1976, Met. YMCA El Paso, 1980-88. Mem. ABA, El Paso Bar Assn., U. Tex. Ex-students Assn. (exec. coun. 1980-86), Chancellors, Order of Coif, Phi Beta Kappa. Democrat. Mem. Christian Ch. (Disciples of Christ). Office: US Dist Ct We Dist Tex 903 San Jacinto Ste 350 Austin TX 78701

HUEBNER, EMILY ZUG, judicial administrator; b. Bryn Mawr, Pa., Apr. 17, 1942; d. Harry Coover and Anne (Mayer) Zug; m. John Stephen Huebner, June 16, 1962; children: Christopher, Jeffrey. BA, Goucher Coll., 1964, MEd, 1965. Alumni specialist Am. U., Washington, 1978-80, conf. coord., 1980-83, program specialist, 1983-87, assoc. dir. contract programs, 1987-90; tng. adminstr. Fed. Jud. Ctr., 1990-91, asst. dir. ct. edn., 1991-95, dir. ct. edn., 1995—. Cons. adult learning Coll. Bd., N.Y.C., 1985-88; cons. Coun. for Adult and Experienced Learning, Chgo., 1988-90. Contbr. articles to profl. jours. Mem. exec. bd. United Way/United Black Fund, Washington, 1988-91. Recipient Vol. Svc. award United Way/United Black Fund, 1990. Mem. Higher Edn. Group (pres. 1993-94), Am. Soc. Tng. and Devel. (Continuous Svc. award 1990), Assn. for Continuing Higher Edn. (chair human resources 1988-89), Women Adminstrs. in Higher Edn. Home: 6102 Cromwell Dr Bethesda MD 20816-3410 Office: Fed Jud Ctr 1 Columbus Cir NE Washington DC 20002-8000

HUEGEL, RUSSELL J. lawyer; b. N.Y.C., May 19, 1970; BA, Richard Stockton Coll. of N.J., 1992; JD, Pace U., 1996. Bar: N.J. Assoc. Paul B. Brickfield, P.C., River Edge, N.J., 1998—. Criminal, Personal injury. Office: Paul B Brickfield PC 70 Grand Ave River Edge NJ 07661

HUETTNER, RICHARD ALFRED, lawyer; b. N.Y.C., Mar. 25, 1927; s. Alfred F. and Mary (Reilly) H.; children: Jennifer Mary, Barbara Bryan; m. 2d, Eunice Bizzell Dowd, Aug. 22, 1971. Marine Engrs. License, N.Y. State Maritime Acad., 1947; B.S., Yale U. Sch. Engring., 1949; J.D., U. Pa., 1952. Bar: D.C. 1952, N.Y. 1954, U.S. Ct. Mil. Appeals 1953, U.S. Ct. Claims 1961, U.S. Supreme Ct. 1969, U.S. Ct. Appeals (fed. cir.) 1982, also other fed. cts, registered to practice U.S. Patent and Trademark Office 1957, Canadian Patent Office 1968. Engr. Jones & Laughlin Steel Corp., 1954-55; assoc. atty. firm Kenyon & Kenyon, N.Y.C, 1955-61, mem. firm, 1961-96, of counsel, 1996-98; specialist patent, trademark and copyright law. Trustee N.J. Shakespeare Festival, 1972-79, sec., 1977-79; trustee Overlook Hosp., Summit, N.J., 1978-84, 86-89, vice chmn. bd. trustees, 1980-82, chmn. bd. trustees, 1982-84; trustee Overlook Found., 1981-89 , chmn. bd. trustees, 1986-89, emeritus trustee, 1991; trustee Colonial Symphony Orch., Madison, N.J., 1972-82, v.p. bd. trustees 1974-76. pres. 1976-79; chmn. bd. overseers N.J. Consortium for Performing Arts, 1972-74; mem. Yale U. Council, 1978-81; bd. dirs. Yale Communications Bd., 1978-80; chmn. bd. trustees Center for Addictive Illnesses, Morristown, N.J., 1979-82; rep. Assn. Yale Alumni, 1975-80, chmn. com. undergrad. admissions, 1976-78, bd. govs., 1976-80, chmn. bd. govs., 1978-80; chmn. Yale Alumni Schs. Com. N.Y., 1972-78; assoc. fellow Silliman Coll., Yale U., 1976—; bd. dirs., exec. com. Yale U. Alumni Fund, 1978-81; mem. Yale Class of 1949 Council, 1980—; bd. dirs. Overlook Health Systems, 1984—. Served from midshipman to lt. USNR, 1945-47, 1952-54; cert. JAGC 1953; Res. ret. Recipient Yale medal, 1983, Disting. Svc. to Yale Class of 1949 award, 1989, Yale Sci. and Engring. Meritorious Svc. award, 1992. Fellow N.Y. Bar Found.; mem. ABA (life), N.Y. State Bar Assn., Assn. Bar City N.Y., N.Y. Intellectual Property Law Assn. (chmn. com. mtgs. 1961-64, chmn. com. econ. matters 1966-69, 72-74) (life), AAAS, N.Y. Acad. Scis., N.Y. County Lawyers Assn., Am. Intellectual Property Law Assn. (life), Internat. Patent and Trademark Assn., Am. Judicature Soc., Yale Sci. and Engring. Assn. (v.p. 1973-75, pres. 1975-78, exec. bd. 1972-79), Fed. Bar Coun. Clubs: Yale (N.Y.C.); Yale of Central N.J. (Summit) (trustee 1973-88, pres. 1975-77), Morris County Golf (Convent, N.J.); The Graduates (New Haven). Federal civil litigation, Patent, Trademark and copyright. Home: 150 Green Ave Madison NJ 07940-2513 Fax: (973) 377-2811. E-mail: huettnerrichard@aol.com

HUFFMAN, JAMES LLOYD, law educator; b. Fort Benton, Mont., Mar. 25, 1945; s. Roy E. and Menga (Herzog) H.; m. Leslie M. Spencer, Sept. 11, 1956; children: Kurt Andrew, Erica Leigh, James Spencer, Claire Menga, Margaret Murray. Student, Stanford U., 1963-64; BS, Mont. State U., 1967; MALD, Fletcher Sch. Law and Diplomacy, 1967-68; JD, U. Chgo., 1972. Bar: Mont., U.S. Ct. Appeals (Fed. cir.), U.S. Supreme Ct. Asst. prof., then assoc. prof. Lewis and Clark Law Sch., Portland, Oreg., 1973-78, prof. law, 1978—, assoc. dean, 1978-80, dir. natural resources law inst., dean, 1993—. Vis. prof. Auckland U. (N.Z.), 1980-81, U. Oreg. Law Sch., 1988, U. Athens, 1988-89; mem. com. socioecon. effects of earthquake prediction Nat. Acad. Scis., 1977-80. Author: The Allocation of Water to Instream Flows: A Comparative Study of Policy Making and Technical Information in the States of Colorado, Idaho, Montana and Washington, 1980, Government Liability and Disaster Mitigation: A Comparative Study, 1986; contbr. articles to profl. jours. Bd. mem. Bishop Street Funds. NSF grantee, 1976-77, 81-84; Office of Water Rsch. Dept. Interior grantee, 1978-80; Raymond fellow, 1973. Mem. Am. Soc. Legal History, Rocky Mountain Mineral Law Found. Home: 5340 SW Hewett Blvd Portland OR 97221-2254 Office: Lewis & Clark Sch Law Portland OR 97219

HUFFMAN, ROBERT ALLEN, JR. lawyer; b. Tucson, Dec. 30, 1950; s. Robert Allen and Ruth Jane (Hicks) H.; m. Marjorie Kavanagh Rooney, Dec. 30, 1976; children: Katharine Kavanagh, Elizabeth Rooney, Robert Allen III, Simeon Ross. BBA, U. Okla., 1973, JD, 1976. Bar: Okla. 1977, U.S. Dist. Ct. (no. dist.) Okla. 1977, U.S. Ct. Appeals (10th cir.) 1978, U.S. Supreme Ct. 1982. Assoc. Huffman, Arrington, Kihle, Gaberino & Dunn, Tulsa, 1977-81, ptnr. 1981-97, ptnr. Edwards & Huffmann LLP, 1997—. Mem. ABA, Tulsa County Bar Assn., Fed. Energy Bar Assn. Republican. Roman Catholic. Clubs: Southern Hills Country (Tulsa). General corporate, Public utilities, Real property. Home: 5937 S Columbia Ave Tulsa OK 74105-7319 Office: Edwards & Huffman LLP South Yale Ste 1470 Two Warren Pl 6120 Tulsa OK 74136

HUFFSTETLER, PALMER EUGENE, lawyer; b. Shelby, N.C., Dec. 21, 1937; s. Daniel S. and Ethel (Turner) H.; m. Mary Ann Beam, Aug. 9, 1958; children: Palmer Eugene, Ben Beam, Brian Tad. BA, Wake Forest U., 1959, JD, 1961. Bar: N.C. 1961. Practiced in, Kings Mountain, N.C., 1961-62, Raleigh, 1962-64; with State Farm Ins. Co., Orlando, Fla., 1962; gen. legal counsel Carolina Freight Corp., Cherryville, N.C., 1964-93, sec., 1969-90, sr. v.p., 1969-89, exec. v.p., 1985-93, pres., 1993-95; ret., 1995; pres., CEO Blue Chip Inc., 1997-99. Author, composer: Senior Man on Carolina Line, Fifty Years Ago. Chmn. Cherryville Zoning Bd. Adjustment, 1967-70; active N.C. Gasoline and Oil Insp. Bd., 1974-76; class chmn. Wake Forest Coll. Fund, 1971-79, decade chmn., 1981-82; governing body, chmn. adminstrv. com. So. Piedmont Health Systems Agy., 1975-77; mem. Cherryville Econ. Devel. Commn., 1982-87, Cherryville Econ. Devel. Com., 1995-97; pres. Cherryville Devel. Corp., 1986—; bd. dirs. C. Grier Beam Truck Mus., 1982—, pres. 1982-96; bd. dirs. Schiele Mus., Gastonia, N.C., 1985-88, Gaston Meml. Hosp., 1990-93, vice-chmn. bd.; active N.C. Gov.'s Hwy. Safety Commn., 1985-88, Gov.'s Bus. Com., N.C., 1993-95; v.p. Ctrl. and So. Rate Bur., 1984-89; trustee Brevard Coll., 1987-93. Mem. N.C. State Bar, N.C. Bar Assn. Methodist (mem. adminstrv. bd. 1965-69, 71-72, chmn. adminstrv. bd., trustee 1970-73, fin. com. 1994—). General corporate, Labor, Transportation. Home: 2141 Fairways Dr Cherryville NC 28021-2115

HUFSTEDLER, SHIRLEY MOUNT (MRS. SETH M. HUFSTEDLER), lawyer, former federal judge; b. Denver, Aug. 24, 1925; d. Earl Stanley and Eva (Von Behren) Mount; m. Seth Martin Hufstedler, Aug. 16, 1949; 1 son, Steven Mark. BBA, U. N.Mex., 1945, LLD (hon.), 1972; LLB, Stanford U., 1949; LLD (hon.), U. Wyo., 1970, Gonzaga U., 1970, Occidental Coll., 1971, Tufts U., 1974, U. So. Calif., 1976, Georgetown U., 1976, U. Pa., 1976, Columbia U., 1977, U. Mich., 1979, Yale U., 1981, Rutgers U., 1981, Claremont U. Ctr., 1981, Smith Coll., 1982, Syracuse U., 1983, Mt. Holyoke Coll., 1985; PHH (hon.), Hood Coll., 1981, Hebrew Union Coll., 1986, Tulane U., 1988. Bar: Calif. 1950. Mem. firm Beardsley, Hufstedler & Kemble, L.A., 1951-61; practiced in, 1961; judge Superior Ct., County L.A., 1961-66; justice Ct. Appeals 2d dist., 1966-68; circuit judge U.S. Ct. Appeals 9th cir., 1968-79; sec. U.S. Dept. Edn., 1979-81; ptnr. Hufstedler & Kaus, L.A., 1981-95; sr. of counsel Morrison & Foerster LLP, 1995—. Emeritus dir. Hewlett Packard Co., US West, Inc.; bd. dirs. Harman Internat. Industries. Mem. staff Stanford Law Rev, 1947-49; articles and book rev. editor, 1948-49. Trustee Calif. Inst. Tech., Occidental Coll., 1972-89, Aspen Inst., Colonial Williamsburg Found., 1976-93, Constl. Rights Found., 1978-80, Nat. Resources Def. Coun., 1983-85, Carnegie Endowment for Internat. Peace, 1983-94; bd. dirs. John T. and Catherine MacArthur Found., 1983—; chair U.S. Commn. on Immigration Reform, 1996-97. Named Woman of Yr. Ladies Home Jour., 1976; recipient UCLA medal, 1981. Fellow Am. Acad. Arts and Scis.; mem. ABA (medal 1995), L.A. Bar Assn., Town Hall, Am. Law Inst. (coun. 1974-84), Am. Bar Found., Women Lawyers Assn. (pres. 1957-58), Am. Judicature Soc., Assn. of the Bar of City of N.Y., Coun. on Fgn. Rels. (emeritus), Order of Coif. Antitrust, Federal civil litigation, State civil litigation. Office: Morrison & Foerster LLP 555 W 5th St Ste 3500 Los Angeles CA 90013-1024

HUG, PROCTER RALPH, JR. federal judge; b. Reno, Mar. 11, 1931; s. Procter Ralph and Margaret (Beverly) H.; m. Barbara Van Meter, Apr. 4, 1954; children: Cheryl Ann English, Procter James, Elyse Marie Pasha. BS, U. Nev., 1953; LLB, JD, Stanford U., 1958. Bar: Nev. 1958. Mem. Springer, McKissick & Hug, 1958-63, Woodburn, Wedge, Blakey, Folsom & Hug, Reno, 1963-77; U.S. judge 9th Circuit Ct. Appeals, 1977—, U.S. chief judge, 1996-2000. Dep. atty. gen. State of Nev.; v.p. dir. Nev. Tel. & Tel. Co., 1958-77. Mem. bd. regents U. Nev., 1962-71, chmn., 1969-71; bd. visitors Stanford Law Sch.; mem. Nev. Humanities Commn., 1988-94; vol. civilian aid sect. U.S. Army, 1977. Lt. USNR, 1953-55. Recipient Outstanding Alumnus award U. Nev., 1967, Disting. Nevadan citation, 1982; named Alumnus of Yr. U. Nev., 1988. Mem. ABA (bd. govs. 1976-78), Am. Judicature Soc. (bd. dirs. 1975-77), Nat. Judicial Coll. (bd. dirs. 1977-78, 2001—), Nat. Assn. Coll. and Univ. Attys. (past mem. exec. bd.), U. Nev. Alumni Assn. (past pres.), Stanford Law Soc. Nev. (pres.) Office: US Ct Appeals 9th Cir US Courthouse Fed Bldg 400 S Virginia St Ste 708 Reno NV 89501-2181

HUGHES, BYRON WILLIAM, lawyer, oil exploration company executive; b. Clarksdale, Miss., Nov. 8, 1945; s. Byron B. and Francis C. (Turner) H.; m. Sarah Eileen Goodwin, June 23, 1973 (div.); children: Jennife Eileen, Stephanie Ann. BA, U. Miss., 1968; JD, Jackson Sch. Law (now Miss. Coll. Law), 1971. Bar: Miss. 1971, U.S. Supreme Ct. 1975; cert. real estate appraiser. Atty., abstractor Miss. Hwy. Dept., 1971-76; atty., ind. landman Byron Hughes Oil Exploration Co., Jackson, Miss., 1976-92; prosecutor, child support enforcement atty. Miss. Dept. Human Svcs., 1992—. Tchr. high sch.; real estate broker. Mem. ABA, Miss. Bar Assn., Hinds County Bar Assn., Bolivar County Bar Assn., Am. Judicature Soc., Nat. Assn. Real Estate Appraisers, Miss. Child Support Assn., Miss. Assn. Petroleum Landmen, Ala. Landmen Assn., Black Warrior Basin Petroleum Landmen Assn., Am. Assn. Petroleum Landmen (cert. profl. landman 1991), Ole Miss. Alumni Assn., Miss. Coll. Alumni Assn., Miss. Art Assn., Cleve. Exch. Club, Sigma Delta Kappa. Methodist. Oil, gas, and mineral, Family and matrimonial, Real property. Home and Office: PO Box 1485 Jackson MS 39215-1485

HUGHES, JUDY ANNE, law library administrator, researcher, educator; b. South Pittsburg, Tenn., May 9, 1950; d. Leon Johnson and Fannie Mae (Hall) H. BS, David Lipscomb U., 1972; M of Libr. and Info. Sci., Vanderbilt U., 1982, EDd, 1995. Tchr. 3d grade Bridgeport (Ala.) Elem. Sch., 1972-75; asst. mgr. Bridgeport Home Furnishings, 1975-80; tchr., libr. Bridgeport Elem. Sch., 1980-85; cons. career ladder divsn. Tenn. Dept. Edn., Nashville, 1985-86; libr. Bridgeport Elem. Sch., 1986-88; dir. Jones Sch. of Law Libr., asst. prof. Faulkner U., Montgomery, Ala., 1988—. Mng. editor Thomas Goode Jones Sch. of Law-Law Review, 2001. Vol. Reach to Recovery, Am. Cancer Soc., Montgomery, 1989—. Mem. Am. Assn. Law Librs., Law Libr. Assn. Ala. (pres. 1997-98), South Ea. Assn. Law Librs., Sigma Delta Kappa (treas. 1989-91), Beta Phi Mu. Avocations: reading, swimming, water skiing, walking, tending to roses. Office: Faulkner U Jones Sch of Law 5345 Atlanta Hwy Montgomery AL 36109-3390

HUGHES, KEVIN JOHN, lawyer; b. St. Cloud, Minn., July 27, 1936; s. Fred James and Valeria Mary (Spaniol) H.; m. Joanne Margaret Robertson, July 27, 1936; children: Anne, Thomas, Jennifer, James, Emily. BA in Philosophy and Polit. Sci., St. John's U., Collegeville, Minn., 1958; JD, U. Minn., 1962. Bar: Minn. 1962, U.S. Dist. Ct. Minn. 1963, U.S. Ct. Appeals (8th cir.) 1973, U.S. Supreme Ct. 1973. Law clerk Minn. Supreme Ct., 1962-63; assoc. Fred J. Hughes Atty., St. Cloud, 1963; ptnr. Hughes Thoreen & Sullivan, Hughes Thoreen Mathews & Knapp, 1964-94, Hughes Mathews PA, St. Cloud, 1994—. Bd. dirs. Ctrl. Minn. Cmty. Found., United Way, YMCA. 1st lt. U.S. Army, 1959. Mem. Minn. State Bar, Am. Health Lawyers Assn., St. Cloud C. of C. General civil litigation, Contracts commercial, Labor. Home: 295 Waite Ave S Saint Cloud MN 56301-7335 Office: Hughes Mathews PO Box 548 Saint Cloud MN 56302-0548 E-mail: khughes@hughesmathews.com

HUGHES, KEVIN PETER, lawyer; b. N.Y.C., Sept. 8, 1943; s. George and Mae (Kilduff) H.; m. Margaret Ellen Comiskey, Nov. 18, 1967; children: Erin, Cara, Deirdre. BA, Manhattan Coll., 1965; JD, St. John's U., 1968. Bar: N.Y. 1968, U.S. Dist. Ct. (so. dist., ea. dist.) N.Y. 1971, U.S. Ct. Appeals (2d cir.) 1975, U.S. Supreme Ct. 1980. Law clerk to justice N.Y. Ct. Appeals, Albany, 1968-70; assoc. Weil, Gotshal & Manges, N.Y.C., 1970-77, ptnr., 1977—. Arbitrator Am. Arbitration Assn., N.Y.C., 1984—. Mem. ABA (litigation sect.), N.Y. State Bar Assn., Plandome Country Club (Manhasset, N.Y.), Eagle Creek Golf and Country Club (Naples, Fla.) Republican. Roman Catholic. Avocations: skiing, golf. Bankruptcy, Federal civil litigation, State civil litigation. Home: 27 Chapel Rd Manhasset NY 11030-3601 Office: Weil Gotshal & Manges 767 5th Ave Fl Concl New York NY 10153-0119 E-mail: kevin.hughes@weil.com

HUGHES, KIERAN PATRICK, lawyer; b. Orange, N.J., Dec. 19, 1959; s. Edward Patrick and Mary (Bland) H.; m. Jeannine Joy DeCheser, Jan. 1, 1989; children: Lauren Noelle, Aidan Thomas. BA, Rutgers U., Newark, 1981; JD, Seton Hall U., 1984. Bar: N.J. 1985, U.S. Dist. Ct. N.J. 1985; cert. civil trial atty. Law clk. to Hon. Edward F. Neagle, Jr. law divsn. Superior Ct. of N.J., Newark, 1984-85; assoc. Connel Foley & Geiser, Roseland, N.J., 1985-87, Lane & Mittendorf, N.Y.C., 1987-88, Bumgardner, Hardin & Ellis, Springfield, N.J., 1988-96; pvt. practice Kieran P. Hughes, Atty.-at-Law, Westfield, 1996—. Mem. Spkrs. Bur., N.J. State Bar Found., N.J. State Bar Mentor Program; active Juvenile Conf. Com., Westfield, N.J., 1989— (chair 1996—); trustee, v.p. Essex County Legal Aid, 1989—; coach Westfield Soccer Assn. Mem. N.J. Bar Assn. (health & law sect.), Essex County Bar Assn., Union County Bar Assn. Roman Catholic. Avocations: golf, reading. General civil litigation, Contracts commercial, General corporate. Home: 226 Edgewood Ave Westfield NJ 07090-3918 Office: Kieran P. Hughes Atty-at-Law 232 Saint Paul St Westfield NJ 07090

HUGHES, LYNN NETTLETON, federal judge; b. Houston, Sept. 9, 1941; m. Olive Allen. BA, U. Ala., 1963; JD, U. Tex., 1968; LLM, U. Va., 1992. Bar: Tex., 1966. Pvt. practice, Houston, 1966-79; judge Dist. Ct. Tex., 1979-85; U.S. dist. judge So. Dist. Tex., 1985—. Adj. prof. South Tex. Coll. Law, 1973—, U. Tex., 1990-91, 2000-01; Tex. del. Nat. Conf. State Trial Judges, 1983-85; cons. Tex. Jud. Budget Bd., 1984; lectr. Tex. Coll. Judiciary, 1983; mem. task force on revision rules of civil procedure Supreme Ct. Tex., 1993-94; cons. on constn. Moldova, 1993, European Community, 1989, Ukraine, 1995, Romania, 1996, Albania, 1997; mem. jud. adv. bd. Law and Econs. Ctr., George Mason U., 1999—. Mem. adv. bd. Houston Jour. Internat. Law, 1981—, chmn., 1989-99; mem. adv. dirs. Internat. Law Inst., U. Houston, 1995—. Trustee Rift Valley Rsch. Mission, 1978—; mem. St. Martin's Episcopal Ch.; dir. Houston World Affairs Coun., 1997—, co-chair 1999-00. Mem. ABA, FBA (bd. dirs. Houston chpt. 1986-89), Am. Law Inst., Maritime Law Assn., Houston Bar Assn., Tex. Bar Assn. (nominations com. jud. sect. 1983, court cost, delay and efficiency com. 1981-90, vice chmn. 1984-86, selection, compensation and tenure state judges com. 1981-85, vice chmn. 1982-83, liaison with law schs. com. 1987-92, plain lang. com. 1989-96), Am. Judicature Soc., Am. Soc. Legal History, Am. Anthrop Assn., Houston Philos. Soc. (mem. exec. com. 2000—), Coun. on Fgn. Rels., Am. Inns of Ct. XV (pres. 1986-92), Phi Delta Phi. Office: US Court House 11122 515 Rusk St Houston TX 77002-2605

HUGHES, MARCIA MARIE, lawyer, consultant, motivational speaker; b. Montrose, Colo., Oct. 12, 1949; d. John Atkinson and Catherine Marie (Buskirk) H.; m. James Terrell, Dec. 26, 1990; 1 child, Julia. BA, U. Colo., 1972; JD with honors, George Washington U., 1976; MA in Psychology, U. Colo. Bar: Colo. 1976, U.S. Dist. Ct. Colo. 1976, U.S. Ct. Appeals (10th cir.) 1976. Adminstrv. aide Bur. Accounts Treasury Dept., Washington, 1972-73; legis. aide to Congresswoman Patricia Schroeder, 1973-74; legal intern Consumer Product Info. Ctr., 1974-75, Media Access Project, Washington, 1975-76; law clk. to Hon. William E. Doyle U.S. Ct. Appeals (10th cir.), Denver, 1976-77; asst. atty. gen. Colo. Atty. Gen.'s Office, 1977-79; spl. asst. to dir. Colo. Dept. Health, 1979-81; assoc. Rothgerber, Appel, Powers & Johnson, 1982-85; ptnr. Cockrel, Quinn & Creighton, 1985-87; pres. Hughes, Duncan & Dingess, 1987-90, Marcia M. Hughes, P.C., Denver, 1990-99, Collaborative Growth, L.L.C., 1993—; exec. dir. Pntrs. Mentoring Assn., 1998-2000. Pub. spkr. on orgnl. growth, interpersonal dynamics, negotiation strategies, spirit in the workplace. Bd. dirs. Jefferson County chpt. ARC, 1999-2000, Influence Denver X, Capitol Hill United Neighborhoods, 1977-86; v.p. Nat. Assn. Neighborhoods, 1980-81; bd. dirs. Ecumenical Housing Corp., 1982-85; participant Leadership Denver, 1984-85; active Big Sisters Colo., Denver, 1987-93; vice chmn. Kempe Children's Found., bd. dirs., 1991-95, chair pub. affairs com.; bd. dirs. Colo. Found. Children and Families, 1993-96, pres., 1995-96; apptd. mem. family issues task force Colo. Legislature. Named one of Outstanding Young Women in Colo., 1980, Big Sister of Yr., 1991. Mem. Colo. Profl. Soc. on Abuse of Children (bd. dirs.), Colo. Bar Assn. (chmn. environ. sect., officer 1982-86), Colo. Hazardous Waste Com. (chmn. 1982-85). Avocations: writing, hiking, gardening, reading. Alternative dispute resolution, Environmental, Family and matrimonial. Home: PO Box 10758 Golden CO 80401-0610

HUGHES, MARGO GIBSON, legal assistant; b. Brookline, Mass., Mar. 21, 1964; m. Herbert Vincent Hughes, Apr. 30, 1997. AA, Villa Julie Coll., 1984; BA, U. Balt., 1988. Legal asst. Gallagher, Evelius & Jones, LLP, Balt., 1998—. Support group facilitator Parents Anonymous, The Family Tree, Balt., 1996—. Mem. Sigma Tau Delta. Office: Gallagher Evelius & Jones LLP Park Charles 218 N Charles St Baltimore MD 21201 Fax: (410) 837-3085

HUGHES, STEVEN JAY, lawyer; b. Fayetteville, Ark., Nov. 7, 1948; s. Howard and Jimmie Louise (Williams) H.; m. Leora Donna Halfhill, July 22, 1972; children: Christopher Blake, Clayton Brent. BS in Edn., U. Ark., Fayetteville, 1970; JD, U. Ark., Little Rock, 1978; LLM, DePaul U., 1993. Bar: Ark. 1978, U.S. Dist. Ct. (ea. dist.) Ark. 1978, U.S. Ct. Appeals (8th cir.) 1978, U.S. Supreme Ct. 1981, Mo. 1993. Sole practice, Jacksonville, Ark., 1978-92; owner Hughes Legal Rsch., 1994-96; assoc. Mickel Law Firm, PA, Little Rock, 1998—. Bd. dirs. Tiara Condominium Property Owners Assn., chmn., 1994-96. Alderman Jacksonville City Coun., 1979-81; commr. Jacksonville Planning Commn., 1982-85; mem. U. Ark. Razorback Letterman's Club, Little Rock, 1985, Ark. Sports Hall of Fame, 1985; bd. dirs. Jacksonville Boys Club, 1979-92, pres., 1982-83. Mem. Assn. Trial Lawyers Am., Ark. Bar Assn., Delta Theta Phi (life, dist. chancellor 1983-93). Baptist. Lodge: Kiwanis (pres. Jacksonville club 1983-84, Kiwanian of Yr. award 1979-80, Disting. Club Pres. award 1984). Avocation: sport. Bankruptcy, General practice, Real property. Home: 7502 W Markham St Little Rock AR 72205-2608 Office: 1501 N University Ave Ste 966 Little Rock AR 72207-5238

HUGHES, THOMAS MORGAN, III, lawyer; b. Racine, Wis., June 14, 1949; s. Thomas Morgan and Rosemary (Navratil) H.; m. Teresa Lee Cloud, Aug. 10, 1974; 1 child, Gwyneth Leigh. B.B.A., U. Wis.-Madison, 1971; J.D., St. Louis U., 1974. Bar: Ark. 1974, U.S. Dist. Ct. (ea. dist.) Ark. 1974. Sole practice, Beebe, Ark., 1974-78; ptnr., Hughes & Hughes, Searcy, Ark., 1978— ; instr. Ark. State U., Beebe, 1975. City atty. City of Beebe, 1975-76; treas. Beebe Indsl. Devel. Corp., Beebe, 1983— ; judge City Ct., Beebe, 1985-87, Beebe Mcpl. Ct., 1987—. Mem. Ark. Trial Lawyers Assn., White County Bar Assn. Prs. 1996), Beebe C. of C. (pres. 1984—). Democrat. Lodge: Kiwanis (pres. 1981-82, bd. dirs. 1979—). Family and matrimonial, Probate, Personal injury. Home: 807 W Louisiana St Beebe AR 72012-2623 Office: Hughes & Hughes PO Box 91 Searcy AR 72145-0091

HUGHES, VESTER THOMAS, JR. lawyer; b. San Angelo, Tex., May 24, 1928; s. Vester Thomas and Mary Ellen (Tisdale) H. Student, Baylor U., 1945-46; B.A. with distinction, Rice U., 1949; LLB cum laude, Harvard U., 1952. Bar: Tex. 1952. Law clk. U.S. Supreme Ct., 1952; assoc. Robertson, Jackson, Payne, Lancaster & Walker, Dallas, 1955-58; ptnr. Jackson, Walker, Winstead, Cantwell & Miller, 1958-76, Hughes, Luce, Hennessy, Smith & Castle, Dallas, 1976—, Hughes & Hill, Dallas, 1979-85, Hughes & Luce, Dallas, 1985—. Bd. dirs. Exell Cattle Co., Amarillo, Tex., LX Cattle Co., Amarillo Austin Industries, Dallas; adv. dir. First Nat. Bank Mertzon; tax counsel Communities Found. of Tex., Inc.; mem. adv. com. Tex. Supreme Ct., 1985-93. Contbr. articles on fed. taxation to profl. jours. Bd. dirs. Juvenile Diabetes Found. Inc., Dallas, 1982—; trustee Dallas Bapt. Coll., 1967-77; v.p., trustee, exec. com. Tex. Scottish Rite Hosp. for Children, 1967—; bd. overseers vis. com. Harvard Law Sch., 1969-75. 1st lt. JAGC U.S. Army, 1952-55. Mem. ABA (coun. sect. taxation 1969-73), Tex. Bar Assn., Dallas Bar Assn., Am. Law Inst. (coun. 1958—), Am. Coll. Tax Counsel, Southwestern Legal Found., Am. Coll. of Trust and Estate Counsel, Met. Club (Washington), Harvard Club (N.Y.C.), Masons, Order Ea. Star, Phi Beta Kappa, Sigma Xi. Democrat. Baptist. Avocations: traveling, community and church activities, reading. Corporate taxation, Estate taxation, Personal income taxation. Office: Hughes & Luce 1717 Main St Ste 2800 Dallas TX 75201-4685

HUGHES, WILLIAM EARLE, lawyer; b. Ft. Worth, June 14, 1944; s. Robert Earle and June Alice (Eldridge) H.; m. Cheryl Christine Dempsey, Oct. 4, 1965; children— Christine, Robert, Alexander. B.A., The Citadel, 1965, J.D., Harvard U., 1968. Bar: Mass. 1969, Okla. 1978, Okla. 1979. Assoc. Herrick and Smith, Boston, 1970-73, asst. U.S. atty. U.S. Dept. Justice, Boston, 1973-78; assoc. Doerner, Stuart, S.D. and A., Tulsa, 1978-82, ptnr. 1982—89; atty. Tulsa, 1989-2000; Fulbright Scholar and vis. prof. U. Tunis, Rep. of Tunisia, 2000-01. Served to capt. U.S. Army, 1968-70, Vietnam. Decorated Bronze Star. Mem. Okla. Bar. Assn. Republican. Roman Catholic. Federal civil litigation, State civil litigation, Public utilities. Home: 1020 E 18th St Tulsa OK 74120-7407 E-mail: blvegilltwo@earthlink.net

HUGHES, WILLIAM JEFFREY, lawyer; b. San Gabriel, Calif., Dec. 6, 1951; s. William Drennan and Rosetta Jane (Duff) H. B.A., Stanford U., 1973; J.D., Hastings Coll., 1977; M.L., London Sch. Econ., 1979. Bar: Calif., 1977, U.S. Dist. Ct. (no. dist.) Calif. 1977, U.S. Ct. Appeals (9th cir.) 1980, U.S. Supreme Ct. 1982. Assoc. Alexander Anolik, P.C., San Francisco, 1978-80; mem. Brooks & Hughes, San Leandro, Calif., 1980-83; inheritance tax referee State of Calif., Alameda County, 1981-83; gen. counsel Bicara, Ltd., Carson, Calif., 1983—; dir. Food Wholesalers Am., Carson, 1984— . Contbr. articles to profl. jours. Mem. Thomas Scotto Scholarship Fund Com., San Francisco, 1981-82. Mem. Los Angeles County Bar Assn. Democrat. Contracts commercial, General corporate, Private international. Home: 501 Lincoln Blvd Santa Monica CA 90402-2811 Office: Bicara Ltd PO Box 58834 Los Angeles CA 90058-0834

HUGHEY, RICHARD KOHLMAN, author, lawyer; b. Chgo., July 6, 1934; BA cum laude, Santa Clara U., 1958, JD cum laude, 1963. Bar: Calif. 1964, U.S. Ct. Appeals (9th cir.) 1964, U.S. Supreme Ct. 1972. Atty. Pacific Gas & Elec. Co., San Francisco, 1963-69, Berry, Davis & McInerny, Oakland, Calif., 1969-71; ptnr. Caputo, Liccardo, Rossi & Kohlman, San Jose, 1971-75; lectr. law, dir. CLE Santa Clara (Calif.) U., 1975-80; mng. editor Bancroft-Whitney Co., San Francisco, 1980-91, Lawyers Coop. Pub. Co., Rochester, N.Y., 1992-94; history and lit. biography writer, 1995—; columnist Mountain Democrat, Placerville, Calif., 1997—. Bd. editors Calif. State Bar Jour., 1972-75; editor-in-chief Santa Clara Law Rev., 1961-63; author: Jeffers Country Revisited: Beauty Without Price, 1996, Computer Technology in Civil Litigation, 1990, Trial Lawyers Manual, 1978; co-author: Petroglyphs: Poetry and Fiction, 1994, Hey Lew: Homage to Lew Welch, 1997; editor: Am Jur Trials, 1980-90, Proof of Facts, 1982-90. Mem. citizen's adv. commn. U.S. Postal Svc., San Francisco, 1989-92; mem. adv. bd. Commn. on Future of the Cts., Jud. Coun. of Calif., 1992; dir. Cmty. Legal Svcs., San Jose, 1973-78. Recipient Merit award Calif. Psychol. Assn., 1985, Santa Clara County Bar Assn., 1973-75. Mem. ABA, Am. Acad. Forensic Scis., Assn. Trial Lawyers Am., Practicing Law Inst., Def. Rsch. Inst., Internat. Platform Assn., Writers and Books Club, Acad. Am. Poets, Modern Poetry Assn., San Jose Ctr. for Poetry and Lit. Avocations: creative writing, photography.

HUGHSTON, THOMAS LESLIE, JR. judge; b. Spartanburg, S.C., July 25, 1943; s. Thomas Leslie and Eunice (Poole) H.; m. Mary Anne McLean, May 30, 1993; children: Karen, Greer, Mary. B.A., The Citadel, 1965; J.D., U. S.C., 1968. Bar: S.C. 1968, U.S. Dist. Ct. S.C. 1968. Assoc. Nicholson & Nicholson, Greenwood, S.C., 1968-72; ptnr. Bishop & Hughston, Greenwood, 1972-82, Bishop, Hughston & Daniel, 1983-85; resident cir. judge, 8th Jud. Cir., 1985—; mcpl. judge Greenwood, 1973-75; pub. defender Greenwood and Abbeville Counties (S.C.), 1973-75; mem. S.C. Ho. of Reps., 1977-85. Chmn. City of Greenwood Democratic Party, 1969-74; pres. Senators Club of Lander Coll., Greenwood, 1971-72; bd. dirs. Connie Maxwell Children's Home, Greenwood, 1983— . Recipient Disting. Service award S.C. Mcpl. Assn., 1981. Mem. Greenwood County Bar Assn. (pres. 1980), S.C. Bar Assn., Kiwanis. Baptist. General practice. Home: 286 Meeting St Apt A Charleston SC 29401-1564 Office: Greenwood County Courthouse PO Box 683 Greenwood SC 29648-0683

HUICI, HECTOR MARIA, lawyer; b. Buenos Aires, July 20, 1964; s. Saturnino Héctor Huici and Gladys Ana Miravalles; m. Maria Gabriela Rodgriguez, July 25, 1967; children: Francisco, Clara. Degree in law, U. Buenos Aires, 1989; M in Adminstrv. Law, Austral U. Bar: Buenos Aires 1990. Paralegal Huici & Arancet, Buenos Aires, 1986-89, assoc., 1990-92; dir. legal dept. CNC, 1992-93, mgr., 1993-94; ptnr. Sanchez Elia, Pinedo, 1994-99, Sanchez Elia, Pinedo, Diaz Bobillo & Richard, Buenos Aires, 2000—. Advisor City Coun., Buenos Aires, 1990-92, Sec. of Energy, Buenos Aires, 1993-99; ITU expert Sec. of Comm., Buenos Aires, 1997; tchg. staff U. Austral, Buenos Aires, 1996—, Cath. U., Buenos Aires, 1997—. Contbr. articles to profl. jours. Dir. Bar City Buenos Aires, 1997-2000; dir. bd. Law Sch., U. Buenos Aires, 1987-91, 99—; pres. conservative students UPAU, Buenos Aires, 1986-89; pres. Dem. Youth, Buenos Aires, 1985-87. Scholar Found. U. del Rio de la Plata, 1987. Mem. Assn. Argentina del Derecho de las Telecomm., U. Club Buenos Aires, Found. Univ. del Rio de la Plata, Pub. Bar Buenos Aires. Roman Catholic. Avocations: traveling, surfing, snowboarding. Office: Sanchez Elia Pinedo Diaz Bobillo et al 884 Fl 5 1001 Buenos Aires Argentina Fax: ++54 11 5554 4400. E-mail: hhuici@spdr.com.ar

HULIN, FRANCES C. prosecutor; AB, Northwestern U., 1957; JD, U. Ill., Urbana, 1971. Bar: Ill. 1973. Asst. states atty. Champaign County, Ill., 1973-76, Macon County, Ill., 1977-78; prosecutor U.S. Attys. Office, Ctrl. Dist. Ill., 1978-93; U.S. atty. Dept. Justice, Springfield, Ill., 1993—. Office: US Attys Office 600 E Monroe St Ste 312 Springfield IL 62701-1675*

HULL, DAVID JULIAN, lawyer; b. Birmingham, West Midlands, Eng., Oct. 18, 1961; s. Derek and Anne H.; m. Anne Louise Morgan, June 29, 1985; children: Gabriella, Olivia. LLB with honors, Sheffield U., 1983. Trainee Dibb Lupton & Broomheads, 1984-86; solicitor Hammond Suddards, 1986-87, Edge Ellison, 1987-88; assoc., 1998-90; ptnr., 1990-2000, Hammond Suddards Edge, Birmingham, 2000—, head corp. fin., chmn., 2001—. Spkr. in field. Dir. Birmingham Repertory Theatre, Midlands Art Ctr. Named Leading Expert in Corp. Law Legal 500, Chambers Guide to the Legal Profession, Top 30 Lawyer in the Regions Legal Bus., 1999. Mem. Brit./North Am. Group in the Midlands (founing dir.). General corporate, Entertainment, Mergers and acquisitions. Office: Hammond Suddards Edge Rutland House 148 Edmund St Birmingham B3 2JR England Fax: 44 (0) 121 222 3001. E-mail: david.hull@hammondsuddardsedge.com

HULL, FRANK MAYS, federal judge; b. Augusta, Ga., Dec. 9, 1948; d. James M. Hull Jr. and Frank (Mays) Pride; m. Antonin Aeck, Apr. 16, 1977; children: Richard Hull Aeck, Molly Hull Aeck. AB, Randolph-Macon Women's Coll., 1970; JD cum laude, Emory U., 1973. Bar: Ga. 1973, U.S. Ct. Appeals (5th cir.) 1973, U.S. Dist. Ct. (no. dist.) Ga. 1974, U.S. Ct. Appeals (11th cir.) 1982. Law clk. to Hon. Elbert P. Tuttle U.S. Ct. Appeals (5th cir.), Atlanta, 1973-74; assoc. Powell, Goldstein, Frazer & Murphy, 1974-80, ptnr., 1980-84; judge State Ct. Fulton County, 1984-90, Superior Ct. Fulton County, Atlanta, 1990-94, U.S. Dist. Ct. (no. dist.) Ga., 1994-97, U.S. Ct. Appeals (11th cir.), 1997—. Mem. commn. on family violence State of Ga., 1992-94, commn. on gender bias in jud. sys., 1988-90. Bd. dirs. Met. Atlanta Mediation Ctr., Inc., 1976-79, Atlanta Vol. Lawyers Assn., 1988-91; mem. Leadership Atlanta, 1986—, program co-chair criminal justice com., 1988-89; Sunday sch. tchr. Cathedral St. Philip, Atlanta, 1983-88, childrens com., 1981-82, outreach com., 1989-91. Fellow AAUW, 1973—. Mem. ABA (fin. sec. long range planning com. tort and ins. practice sect. 1979-82, chmn. contract documents divsn., forum com. on constrn. industry 1983-85, editl. staff jour. 1981-85, vice chmn. fidelity and surety law com. 1978-85), Ga. Bar Assn., Am. Judicature Soc. (bd. dirs. 1990-96), Atlanta Bar Assn., Ga. Assn. Women Lawyers, Nat. Assn. Women Judges, Order of Coif. Office: US Ct of Appeals 56 Forsyth St NWRm 300 Atlanta GA 30303-2289*

HULL, J(AMES) RICHARD, retired lawyer, business executive; b. Keokuk, Iowa, Dec. 5, 1933; s. James Robert and Alberta Margaret (Bouseman) H.; m. Patricia M. Kiesner, June 14, 1958; children— Elizabeth Ann Hull Whims, James Robert, David Glen. B.A., Ill. Wesleyan U., 1955; J.D., Northwestern U., 1958. Bar: Ill. 1958, Fla. 1978. V.p., sec., gen. counsel Honeggers & Co., Inc., Fairbury, Ill., 1959-65, also bd. dirs.; staff atty. Am. Hosp. Supply Corp., Evanston, 1965-68, chief atty., asst. sec., 1968-70, corp. sec., 1970-71, corp. sec., corp. gen. counsel, 1971-79, gen. counsel, 1979-84; sr. v.p., sec., gen. counsel Household Internat. Inc., Northbrook, 1984-93, sr. v.p., of counsel, 1993-94; ret. Mem. planning com. Northwestern U. Corp. Counsel Inst., 1992-93, chmn. Northwestern Corp. Counsel Ctr., 1993. Bd. trustees, bd. visitors Ill. Wesleyan U.; pres. Prestancia Cmty. Assn. Fellow Am. Bar Found., Am. Law Inst.; mem. ABA, Ill. Bar Assn., Fla. Bar Assn., Chgo. Bar Assn. (chmn. corp. law dept.), North Shore Gen. Counsels, Northwestern U. Sch. Law Alumni Assn. (pres.), Sigma Chi, Legal Club (Chgo.), Law Club (Chgo.), Skokie Country Club (Glencoe, Ill.), Gator Creek Golf Club (Sarasota, Fla.), T.P.C. Club (Prestancia, Fla.), Prestancia Cmty. Assn. (pres. 1995-96), Champion Hills Golf Club (Hendersonville, N.C.). Home (Winter): 4634 Mirada Way #24 Sarasota FL 34238 Home (Summer): 21 LaCoste Dr Hendersonville NC 28739

HULL, JOHN DANIEL, IV, lawyer; b. Washington, Feb. 27, 1953; s. John Daniel III and Arlene (Reemer) H. BA cum laude, Duke U., 1975; JD, U. Cin., 1978. Bar: D.C. 1980, U.S. Dist. Ct. D.C. 1983, U.S. Ct. Appeals (D.C. cir.) 1984, U.S. Ct. Appeals (10th cir.) 1986, Md. 1989, Pa. 1989, U.S. Dist. Ct. (we. dist.) Pa. 1989, U.S. Ct. Appeals (3d cir.) 1989, U.S. Supreme Ct. 1989. Legis. asst. 93d & 96th U.S. Congresses, Washington, 1974, 78-81; assoc. Rose, Schmidt & Dixon, 1981-87, ptnr., 1988-92; with Hull McGuire PC, Pitts., Washington, and San Diego, 1992—. Mem. U. Cin. Law Rev., 1976-77, editor student articles, 1977-78. Mem. ABA (sect. natural resources, energy and environ. law, litigation and intellectual property), Bar Assn. D.C., Md. Bar Assn., Pa. Bar Assn., Duke Club, Tara Club. Federal civil litigation, Environmental, Legislative. Office: Hull McGuire PC 32d Fl USX Tower 600 Grant St Pittsburgh PA 15219-2702 also: Hull McGuire PC 1155 Connecticut Ave NW Ste 300 Washington DC 20036-4306 also: Hull McGuire PC 15644 Via Calanova San Diego CA 92128-4462 E-mail: jdhull@hullmcguire.com

HULL, PHILIP GLASGOW, lawyer; b. St. Albans, Vt., Feb. 17, 1925; s. Charles Herman and Gladys Gertrude (Glasgow) H.; m. Gretchen Elizabeth Gaebelein, Oct. 24, 1952; children: Jeffrey R., Sanford D., Meredyth Hull Smith. AB, Middlebury Coll., 1949; LLB, Columbia U., 1952. Bar: N.Y. 1952, Fla. 1977. Staff mem. subcom. on adminstrn. internal revenue laws, com. on ways and means U.S. Ho. of Reps., Washington, 1951; assoc. Winthrop, Stimson, Putnam & Roberts, N.Y.C., 1952-63, ptnr., 1964-97, sr. counsel, 1998-2000, Pillsbury Winthrop, N.Y.C., 2001—. Mem. Sch. Revenue Com., Cold Spring Harbor, N.Y., 1963-65; bd. dirs. Eagle Dock Found., Cold Spring Harbor, 1971-74, People's Symphony Concerts, N.Y.C., 1977—, L.I. Philharm., 1979-81; trustee L.Am. Mission, Miami, Fla., 1969-79; elder Ctrl. Presbyn. Ch., Huntington, N.Y., 1956-78; mem. nat. mssions bd. United Presbyn. Ch., U.S.A., 1967-73; trustee Madison Avenue Presbyn. Ch., N.Y.C., 1989-94, pres., 1993-94; mem. Lloyd Harbor Conservation Adv. Coun., 1973-77. With U.S. Army, 1943-46. Ellis fellow, Kent scholar, Stone scholar Columbia U. Mem. Am. Coll. Trust and Estate Counel, N.Y. State Bar Assn., Fla. Bar Assn., Christian Legal Soc. (bd. dirs. 1984-97), Fellowship Christians in Univs. and Schs. (trustee 1983-90), Univ. Club N.Y.C. (bd. dirs. 1986-90), Cold Spring Harbor Beach Club, Blue Key, Phi Beta Kappa. Office: Pillsbury Winthrop One Battery Park Plz New York NY 10004-1490

HULL, ROBERT JOE, lawyer; b. Ft. Monmouth, N.J., Dec. 16, 1944; s. Thurman Beuford and Helen Louise (Bracey) H.; m. Susan Diane Hull, Mar. 12, 1966; 1 child, Robert Steven. BA, U. Tex., 1966, JD, 1969. Bar: Tex. 1969, Calif. 1970, U.S. Dist. Ct. (ctrl. dist.) Calif. 1970, U.S. Ct. Appeals (9th cir.) 1970, U.S. Tax. Ct. 1971, U.S. Supreme Ct. 1992. Assoc. Sheppard, Mullin, Richter & Hampton, L.A., 1969-76, ptnr., 1976-98, Bracewell & Patterson LLP, Houston, 1998—. Co-author: Representing Start-Up Companies, 1992, (annual) ABA Sales & Use Tax Handbook; mem. editorial bd., contbr. Jour. Multistate Taxation, 1991—. Mem. Tex. Bar Found., Brae Burn Country Club, Annandale Golf Club, PGA West Golf Club. Avocation: golf. Taxation, general, State and local taxation. Home: 2607 Sutton Ct Houston TX 77027-5246 Office: Bracewell & Patterson LLP S Twr Penzoil Pl 711 Louisiana St Ste 2900 Houston TX 77002-2781 E-mail: rjhull@bracepatt.com

HULL, THOMAS GRAY, federal judge; b. 1926; m. Joan Brandon; children: Leslie, Brandon, Amy. Student, Tusculum Coll.; JD, U. Tenn., 1951. Atty. Easterly and Hull, Greeneville, Tenn., 1951-63; mem. Tenn. Ho. of Reps., 1955-65; atty., prin. Thomas G. Hull, 1951-72; chief clk. Tenn. Ho. of Reps., 1969-70; judge 20th Jud. Cir., Greeneville, Morristown and Rogersville, Tenn., 1972-79; legal counsel to Tenn. Gov. Lamar Alexander, 1979-81; judge U.S. Dist. Ct. (ea. dist.) Tenn., 1983—. Served as cpl. U.S. Army, 1944-46. Mem. Tenn. Bar Assn. (chmn. East dist. com. 1969), Greenville Bar Assn. (pres. 1969-71), Tenn. Jud. Conf. (del. 1972-79, vice chmn. 1974-75, com. to draft uniform charges for trial judges). Republican. Office: Office of US Dist Judge 211 US Courthouse 101 W Summer St Greeneville TN 37743-4944

HUMES, JAMES CALHOUN, lawyer, communications consultant, writer, educator; b. Williamsport, Pa., Oct. 31, 1934; s. Samuel Hamilton and Elenor Kathryn (Graham) H.; m. Dianne Stuart, July 25, 1957; children: Mary Stuart Quillen, Rachel Bailey. Student, Hill Sch., Stowe Sch., Eng., Williams Coll., 1953-55; A.B., George Washington U., 1959, J.D., 1962. Bar: Pa. 1963. Mem. Pa. Ho. of Reps., Harrisburg, 1962-65; exec. dir. Phila. Bar Assn., 1967-69; presdl. asst. policy planning sect. White House, Washington, 1969-70; dir. Office Policy and Plans, U.S. Dept. State, 1970-72; presdl. asst. White House Staff; White House cons. to Pres. Ford, 1976-77; Woodrow Wilson fellow Smithsonian Instn., 1982-83; adj. prof. Williams Coll., 1986-87; Ryals Chair Leadership and Lang. U. So. Colo., Pueblo, 1997—. Mem. U.S. Commn. for UNESCO; adj. prof. U. Pa., 1985-99; editl. advisor Pres. Ford's memoirs A Time To Heal. Author: Sweet Dream, 1966, Instant Eloquence, 1973, Podium Humor, 1975, Roles Speakers Play, 1976, How to Get Invited to the White House, 1977, Winston Churchill: Speaker of the Century, 1980, Talk Your Way to the Top, 1980, Standing Ovation, 1988, Sir Winston Method, 1991, The Benjamin Franklin Factor, 1992, My Fellow Americans, 1992, Citizen Shakespeare, 1993, Wit and Wisdom of Churchill, 1994, Wit and Wisdom of Benjamin Franklin, 1995, Wit and Wisdom of Abraham Lincoln, 1996, Confessions of a White House Ghost Writer, 1997, Nixon's Ten Commandments of Statecraft, 1998, Churchill and Eisenhower: The Partnership that

Saved the World, 2001. Decorated Order of Brit. Empire. Fellow Royal Soc. of Art; mem. S.R., St. Nicholas Soc. N.Y., Soc. Pilgrims, St. Andrew's Soc. Phila., Soc. of Cin., Order of Magna Charta, Athenaeum Club, Union League Club, Phila. Cricket Club, Brook Club (N.Y.). Republican. Presbyterian. Home: 4404 Turnberry Cres Pueblo CO 81001-1162

HUMICK, THOMAS CHARLES CAMPBELL, lawyer; b. N.Y.C., Aug. 7, 1947; s. Anthony and Elizabeth Campbell (Meredith) H.; m. Nancy June Young, June 7, 1969; 1 child, Nicole Elizabeth Campbell. BA, Rutgers U., 1969; JD, Suffolk U., 1972; postgrad., London Sch. Econs.-Polit. Sci., 1977-78. Bar: N.J. 1972, U.S. Ct. Appeals (3d cir.) 1976, U.S. Supreme Ct. 1977, N.Y. 1981. Law clk. Superior Ct. N.J., 1972-73; assoc. Riker, Danzig, Scherer & Debevoise, Newark and Morristown, N.J., 1973-77; ptnr. Francis & Berry, Morristown, 1978-84, Dillon, Bitar & Luther, Morristown, 1985-92, Schenck, Price, Smith & King, Morristown, 1992—. Arbitrator U.S. Dist. Ct. N.J., 1985—; del. to Jud. Conf. for 3d Jud. Cir. U.S., 1975-79; mem. dist. X ethics com. N.J. Supreme Ct., 1983-87; mem. jud, selection com. Morris County, 1995-99. Contbg. author: Valuation for Eminent Domain, 1973; mem. editl. bd. Suffolk U. Law Rev., 1970-71, N.J. Lawyer, 1993-94. Trustee Peck Sch., 1993-98; trustee Richmond Fellowship N.J., 1982-89, pres., 1984. Mem. ABA, FBA, N.J. Bar Assn., Morris County Bar Assn. (trustee 1995-2000), Bay Head Yacht Club. Republican. Presbyterian. Federal civil litigation, State civil litigation, General corporate. Home: PO Box 191 Oldwick NJ 08858-0191 Office: Schenck Price Smith & King 10 Washington St Morristown NJ 07960-7117 E-mail: tcch@spsk.com

HUMMEL, GREGORY WILLIAM, lawyer; b. Sterling, Ill., Feb. 25, 1949; s. Osborne William and Vivian LaVera (Guess) H.; m. Teresa Lynn Beveroth, June 20, 1970; children: Andrea Lynn, Brandon Gregory. BA, MacMurray Coll., 1971; JD, Northwestern U., 1974. Bar: Ill. 1974, U.S. Dist. Ct. (no. dist.) Ill. 1974. Assoc. Rusnak, Deutsch & Gilbert, Chgo., 1974-78; ptnr. Rudnick & Wolfe, 1978-97; mem. Bell, Boyd & Lloyd LLC, 1997—. Editor Jour. Criminal Law & Criminology Northwestern U., 1973-74; co-author: Illinois Real Estate Forms, 1989; contbr. articles to law jours. Mem. gov. coun. Luth. Gen. Hosp. Advocate Health Care Sys.; trustee Mac Murray Coll., Jacksonville, Ill., 1986-2001; trustee, sec.-treas. Homes for Children Found; bd. dirs. Chgo. area coun. Boy Scouts Am., ChildServ. Mem. Nat. Inst. Constrn. Law and Practice, Internat. Bar Assn. (past co-chmn. com. internat. constrn. projects), Am. Coll. Constrn. Lawyers (past pres.), Urban Land Inst. (trustee), Chgo. Dist. Coun. (past chmn.), Lambda Alpha Internat. (Ely chpt. past pres.). Construction, Municipal (including bonds), Real property. Office: Bell Boyd & Lloyd LLC 3 1st Nat Plaza 70 W Madison St Ste 3300 Chicago IL 60602-4207 E-mail: ghummel@bellboyd.com

HUMPHREVILLE, JOHN DAVID, lawyer; b. Harrisburg, Pa., Feb. 4, 1953; s. Robert E. and Winifred (MacNulty) H.; m. Laurie Wettstone, Mar. 6, 1976; children: Caroline Elizabeth, John Ervin. BS, Pa. State U., 1977; MA in Govt. Adminstrn., U. Pa., 1984; JD, Cath. U. Am., 1986. Bar: Fla. 1986, U.S. Dist. Ct. (mid. dist.) Fla. 1987, D.C. 1988. Dir. bur. real estate Pa. Dept. Gen. Svcs., Harrisburg, 1979-80; dep. adminstrv. asst. to gov. State of Pa., 1980-83; assoc. Shackleford, Farrior, Stallings & Evans, P.A., Tampa, Fla., 1986-90; ptnr. Icard, Merrill, Cullis, Timm, Furren & Ginsburg, P.A., 1990; asst. to atty. gen. U.S. Dept. Justice, Washington, 1990-91, spl. counsel Asst. Atty. Gen. environ. divsn., 1991; ptnr. Quarles & Brady, Naples, Fla., 1991—. Mem. Fed. Jud. Adv. Commn., 1989-91. Avocations: surfing, swimming, triathlons. Environmental, Land use and zoning (including planning), Real property. Office: Quarles & Brady 4501 Tamiami Trl N Ste 300 Naples FL 34103-3023 E-mail: JDH@quarles.com

HUMPHRIES, EDWARD FRANCIS, lawyer; b. S.I., N.Y., May 25, 1957; s. Robert Edward and Joan D. (Mauter) H.; m. Colleen Kennedy, July 21, 1990; 1 child, Stephen Edward. BBA, Bernard M. Baruch Coll., 1981; JD, Fordham U., 1984. Bar: N.J. 1984, U.S. Dist. Ct. N.J. 1984, N.Y. 1985, U.S. Dist. Ct. (ea. and so. dists.) N.Y. 1985, U.S. Dist. Ct. (we. dist.) N.Y. 1987, Pa. 1990, Hawaii 1990, U.S. Supreme Ct. 1990, U.S. Dist. Ct. Hawaii 1991. Assoc. Amabile & Erman, Bklyn., 1984-86, 87-92, ptnr., 1993—; assoc. Pegalis & Wachsman, Great Neck, N.Y., 1986-87. Trustee Soc. Hill East Condominium Assn., East Brunswick, N.J., 1987-90, pres., 1988-90; co-chmn. Homeowners Assn. Coun. East Brunswick, 1988-90; vice chmn. East Brunswick Planning Bd., 1989-90; pres. East Brunswick Rep. Club, 1989-91. Recipient Morton Wollman medal in Mgmt. Bernard Baruch Coll., 1981. Mem. N.Y. State Bar Assn., N.J. State Bar Assn., Hawaii Bar Assn., Beta Gamma Sigma, Sigma Iota Epsilon. Republican. Roman Catholic. Personal injury, Real property. Home: 451 Manor Rd Staten Island NY 10314-2963 Office: Amabile & Erman 1000 South Ave Staten Island NY 10314-3430

HUND, EDWARD JOSEPH, lawyer; b. May 3, 1945; s. Edward J. and Josephine A. (Hoover) Hund; m. Marty M. Anderson, June 29, 1970; children: Corie Elizabeth, Cyrus Anthony, Hanna Christine. Student, Creighton U., 1963—64; AB in Polit. Sci., Hays Coll., 1967; JD, Washburn U., 1970. Asst. county atty. Sedgwick County, Wichita, Kans., 1971—72; assoc. Smith, Shay, Farmer, Wetta, 1972—75, ptnr., 1975—84, Focht, Hughey & Hund, Wichita, 1984—. 1st lt. NG USAR, 1968—74. Mem.: ABA, Am. Trial Lawyers Assn. (bd. govs. 1994—95), Am. Bd. Trial Advocates (pres. Kans. chpt. 1995), Kans. Trial Lawyers Assn. (pres. 1991), Kans. Bar Assn. (sec.-treas. 1981), Wichita Bar Assn. (pres. young lawyers 1978), East Y Mens Club (Wichita chpt.) (pres. 1980), Lions (v.p. 1979). Democrat. Congregationalist. Federal civil litigation, State civil litigation, Personal injury. Home: 325 Brookfield St Wichita KS 67206-1901 Office: Bradshaw Johnson & Hund 200 W Douglas Ave Ste 100 Wichita KS 67202-3001

HUNEYCUTT, ALICE RUTH, lawyer; b. New Haven, Jan. 10, 1951; d. C. Jerome and Alberta (Piner) H.; m. Howard Mark Bernstein, Nov. 28, 1981; children: Ashley Laughton, Laura Whitney. BA in History, Duke U., 1972; JD, U. Miami (Fla.), 1979. Bar: Fla. 1980, U.S. Dist. Ct. (so. dist.) Fla. 1980, U.S. Ct. Appeals (5th cir.) 1980, U.S. Dist. Ct. (mid. dist.) Fla. 1982, U.S. Ct. Appeals (11th cir.) 1982. Corp. counsel Burger King Corp., Miami, 1980-82; assoc. Stearns Weaver Miller Weissler Alhadeff & Sitterson, P.A., Tampa, Fla., 1982-84, ptnr., 1984—. Bd. dirs. Am. Heart Assn., Tampa, 1986-91, chmn. elect, 1988-89, chmn. 1990-91. Mem. ABA (subcom. franchising, small bus. com., corp., banking and bus law sect.), Fla. Bar Assn. (pres.'s Pro Bono Svc. award 1987), Fla. Assn. Women Lawyers. Democrat. Methodist. General civil litigation. Home: 1400 72nd Ave NE Saint Petersburg FL 33702-4610 Office: 401 E Jackson St Ste 2200 Tampa FL 33602-5251 E-mail: ahyneycutt@swmwas.com

HUNKINS, RAYMOND BREEDLOVE, lawyer, rancher; b. Culver City, Calif., Mar. 19, 1939; s. Charles F. and Louise (Breedlove) H.; m. Mary Deborah McBride, Dec. 12, 1967; children: Amanda, Blake, Ashley. BA, U. Wyo., 1966, JD, 1968. Ptnr. Jones, Jones, Vines & Hunkins, Wheatland, Wyo., 1968—. Local rules com. U.S. Dist. Ct., 1990—; spl. counsel U. Wyo., Laramie, State of Wyo., Cheyenne; mem. faculty Western Trial Adv. Inst., 1993-95, Wyo. Supreme Ct. Commn. Jud. Salary and Benefits, 1996-98; mem. Assn. Govt. Bds. of Univs. and Colls.; owner Thunderhead Ranches, Albany and Platte Counties, Wyo.; gen. ptnr. Split Rock Land & Cattle Co.; spl. asst. atty. gen., Wyo. Chmn. Platte County Reps., Wheatland, 1972-74, chmn. adv. coun. Coll. of Commerce and Industry, U. Wyo., 1978-79; bd. dirs. U. Wyo. Found., 1996—; mem. bd. advisors Am. Heritage Ctr., 1995-99; mem. Gov.'s Crime Commn., 1970-78; pres. Wyo. U. Alumni Assn., 1973-74, commr. Wyo. Aeronautics Commn., 1987-98; moderator United Ch. Christ, 1997-98. With USMCR, 1956-60. Recipient Big Horn Mountain Roundup Pax Irvine award, 1989, Outstanding Advisor award Phi Delta Theta, 1968. Fellow Am. Coll. Trial Lawyers (Wyo. state chmn. 1998-2000, nat. ethics com. 2000—), Internat. Soc. Barristers, Am. Bd. Trial Advs.; mem. ABA (aviation com. 1980-86, forum com. on constrn. industry litigation sect.), Wyo. Bar Assn. (chmn. grievance com. 1980-86, mem. com. on civil pattern jury instrns.), Wyo. Trial Lawyers Assn. (past pres.), Lions, Elks. Federal civil litigation, Construction, Personal injury. Office: Jones Jones Vines & Hunkins PO Drawer 189 9th and Maple Wheatland WY 82201

HUNSAKER, RICHARD KENDALL, lawyer; b. L.A., June 2, 1960; s. Richard Allan and Patricia Kendall (Cook) H.; m. Laura Constance Haile, Oct. 8, 1988; children, Charles Nicholas, Laura Caroline. BA, U. Ill., 1982, MA, 1983; JD, Washington U., St. Louis, 1986. Bar: Ill. 1986, U.S. Dist. Ct. (cen. and no. dists.) Ill. 1987, U.S. Ct. Appeals (7th cir.) 1990, Wis. 1992. Speech coach Champaign (Ill.) Central High Sch., 1979-81; instr. speech communications, asst. debate coach U. Ill., Urbana, 1982-83; assoc. Heyl, Royster, Voelker & Allen, Springfield, Ill., 1986-87, Rockford, 1987-93, ptnr., 1994—. Author: Advanced Real Estate Law in Illinois - Environmental Liabilities, 1992, (with others) Advanced Real Estate Law in Illinois: Environmental Liability, 1992. Mem. ABA (tort and ins. practice, litigation and natural resources, energy and environ. law sects.), Ill. Bar Assn. (assoc., ins. law sect. 1990-92, civil practice and procedure, workers compensation, tort law and environ. control law sects.), Ill. Assn. Def. Trial Counsel, Winnebago County Bar Assn. (editl. bd. lawyer, legal-med., trial practice and continuing legal edn. coms.), Seventh Cir. Bar Assn., Def. Rsch. Inst. Methodist. Avocations: golf, biking, backpacking. General civil litigation, Insurance, Workers' compensation. Home: 1418 National Ave Rockford Il 61103-7144 Office: Heyl Royster Voelker & Allen 321 W State St Rockford IL 61101-1137 E-mail: rhunsaker@hrva.com

HUNSAKER, RODERICK CASON, lawyer, insurance company executive; b. Newark, July 23, 1930; s. Herbert C. and Marion (Thompson) H. m. Gwynn Doyle, Nov. 1, 1959; children— Roderick, Bradford. B.B.A., Case Western Res. U., 1953, J.D., 1958. Bar: Ohio 1959, Mass. 1967. Atty. NLRB, Cin., also Cleve., 1958-62; sole practice law, Cleve., 1962-65; asst. counsel John Hancock Mut. Life Ins. Co., Boston, 1965-68, assoc. counsel, 1968-75, counsel, 1975— , v.p., 1985— . Bd. dirs. Equal Employment Adv. Council, Washington, 1983— . Served with U.S. Army, 1954-56. Mem. ABA. Club: University of Boston (v.p. 1983-84, gov. 1984—). Office: John Hancock Mut Life Ins Co PO Box 111 Boston MA 02117-0111

HUNSTEIN, CAROL, state supreme court justice; b. Miami, Fla., Aug. 16, 1944; AA, Miami-Dade Jr. Coll., 1970; BS, Fla. Atlantic U., 1972; JD, Stetson U., 1976, LLD (hon.), 1993. Bar: Ga. 1976; U.S. Dist. Ct. 1978; U.S. Ct. Appeals 1978; U.S. Supreme Ct. 1989. Legal practice, Atlanta, 1976-84; judge Superior Ct. of Ga. (Stone Mt. cir.), 1984-92; justice Supreme Ct. of Ga., Atlanta, 1992—. Chair Ga. Commn. on Gender Bias in the Judicial System 1989—; pres. Coun. of Superior Ct. Judges of Ga., 1990-91; adj. prof. Sch. Law Emory U., 1991—. Bd. dirs. Ga. Campaign Adolescent Pregnancy Prevention, 1992—; chair Ga. Child Support Commn., 1993, 98, Supreme Ct. Equality Commn. Recipient Clint Green Trial Advocacy award 1976, Women Who Made A Difference award Dekalb Women's Network 1986, Outstanding Svc. commendation Ga. Legislature, 1993, Cmty. Svc. award Emory U. Legal Assn. for Women Students., 1993, Gender Justice award Ga. Commn. Family Violence, 1999, Margaret Burns award ABA, 1999; inducted to Fla. Atlantic U. Hall of Fame, 1993. Mem. Ga. Assn. of Women Lawyers, Nat. Assn. of Women Judges (dir. 1988-90), Bleckley Inn of Ct., State Bar Ga. Office: Supreme Ct Ga 523 State Judicial Bldg Atlanta GA 30334-9007 E-mail: hunsteic@supreme.courts.state.ga.us

HUNT, DAVID EVANS, lawyer; b. Wilkes-Barre, Pa., May 10, 1953; s. James Dixon and Twyla (Burkert) H.; m. Denise M. Barbera, Aug. 21, 1976 (div. 1984); 1 child Christopher Evans; m. Elizabeth S. Pearce, Sept. 5, 1987; children: Alexandra Stacy, Thomas Dixon. AB, Dartmouth Coll., 1975; JD, U. Chgo., 1978. Bar: N.Y. 1979, U.S. Dist. Ct. (so. and ea. dists.) N.Y. 1979, Maine 1982, U.S. Dist. Ct. Maine 1982, U.S. Tax Ct. 1982, Fla. 1999. Assoc. Debevoise & Plimpton, N.Y.C., 1978-81; ptnr. Pierce, Atwood, Scribner, Allen, Smith & Lancaster, Portland, Maine, 1981-92, McCandless & Hunt, Portland, 1992-97; sole practitioner, 1997—. Adjunt prof. Univ. Maine Law Sch. Portland, Maine, 1991-92, 2000. Co-author: Maine Will and Trust Forms, 1994, Maine Estate Administration, 1996. Officer, dir. Maine Estate Planning Coun., Portland, 1986-94. Fellow Am. Coll. Trust and Estate Counsel (state chair 1997-2001); mem. ABA, Fla. Bar, Maine State Bar Assn., N.Y. State Bar Assn., Cumberland County Bar Assn., Woodlands Club. Episcopalian. Avocations: classical Latin, skiing. Estate planning, Probate, Taxation, general. Home: 6 Highland St Portland ME 04103-3005 Office: 511 Congress St Portland ME 04101-3411 E-mail: dhunt@mainewills.com

HUNT, DAVID WALLINGFORD, lawyer; b. Washington, Sept. 27, 1952; s. Donald Harvey and Dorothy Walter (Johnson) H.; m. Sylvia Fortney, Aug. 10, 1974; 1 child, David Wallingford Jr. BA with high distinction, U. Va., 1974, JD, 1977. Bar: Ga. 1977, D.C. 1982, U.S. Ct. Appeals (5th cir.) 1981, U.S. Ct. Appeals (11th cir.) 1982. Law asst. Ga. Supreme Ct., Atlanta, 1977-78; atty. Troutman, Sanders, Lockerman & Ashmore, Atlanta, 1978-80; counsel Turner Broadcasting System, Inc., Atlanta, 1980-81; atty. O'Neill & Haase, P.C., Washington, 1981-84, ptnr., 1985-86; prin. Taubman, Hunt, Hodin & Costelloe, P.C., Washington, 1986-87; mem. Swidler & Berlin chartered, Washington, 1987—; gen. counsel Congl. Award Bd., Washington, 1986—. Mem. editorial bd. Va. Law Review, 1975-77. Pres. Windgate of Arlington, Va., 1982-84. Dillard fellow U. Va., Charlottesville, 1976-77. Mem. ABA, Ga. Bar Assn., D.C. Bar Assn., Order of the Coif, Phi Beta Kappa. Episcopalian. Banking, General corporate, Securities. Home: 5850 Aspen Wood Ct Mc Lean VA 22101-2501 Office: Swidler & Berlin 3000 K St NW Fl 3 Washington DC 20007-5109

HUNT, GERALD WALLACE, lawyer; b. Portland, Oreg., Oct. 31, 1939; BSBA in Econs., U. Denver, 1961, JD, 1964; LLM in Taxation, Washington U., 1981. Bar: Colo. 1964, Ariz. 1968, Tex. 1996, Alaska, 1999; cert. tax splst. Ariz. Bd. Legal Specialization. Asst. trust officer The Ariz. Bank, Phoenix, 1967-69; atty. Westover, Keddie, et al, Yuma, Ariz., 1969-73; pvt. practice law, 1973-74; atty. Hunt & Clark, 1974-75, Hunt, Stanley & Hossler, Yuma, 1975-96, Hunt, Tallan & Hossler, Yuma, 1996-97, Hunt, Kenworthy and Hossler, Yuma, 1998—. Treas. Excel Group, Yuma, 1998-99, chair, 2000; vice chair Greater Yuma Port Authority, 2000. Fellow Am. Coll. Trust and Estate Counsel; mem. ABA, Internat. Mcpl. Lawyers Assn., Ariz. State Bar, Colo. State Bar. Estate planning, Probate, Taxation, general. Office: Hunt Kenworthy & Hossler 330 W 24th St Yuma AZ 85364-6455

HUNT, LAWRENCE HALLEY, JR. lawyer; b. July 15, 1943; s. Lawrence Halley Sr. and Mary Hamilton (Johnson) H.; m. Katherine Collins; children: Caroline Smith, Laura Hamilton, Darwin Halley. AB, Dartmouth Coll., 1965; cert., l'Inst. d'Etudes Politiques, Paris, 1966; JD, U. Chgo., 1969. Bar: N.Y. 1970, Ill. 1971, U.S. Ct. Appeals (9th cir.) 1980, U.S. Ct. Appeals (2d cir.) 1981, U.S. Supreme Ct. 1981. Assoc. Davis Polk & Wardwell, N.Y.C., 1969-70, Sidley & Austin, Chgo., 1970-75; ptnr. Sidley Austin Brown & Wood, 1975—, mem. exec. com., 1985—. Advisor securities adv. com. Ill. Sec. of State, Springfield, 1977-87; prof. grad. program fin. svcs. law Ill. Inst. Tech.-Chgo.-Kent Coll. Law, 1987—. Mng. editor U. Chgo. Law Review, 1968-69. James B. Reynolds scholar Dartmouth Coll., 1965-66. Mem. ABA (com. on commodity regulation, past chmn. subcom. on futures commn. merchants, mem. exec. coun.), Internat. Bar Assn. (past chmn. bus. law com. sub-com futures and options), Mid-Day Club, Chgo. Club, Indian Hill Club. Administrative and regulatory, Private international. Office: Sidley Austin Brown & Wood Bank One Plz Chicago IL 60603 E-mail: lhunt@sidley.com

HUNT, RONALD FORREST, lawyer, director; b. Shelby, N.C., Apr. 18, 1943; s. Forrest Elmer and Bruna Magnolia (Brackett) H.; m. Judy Elaine Shultz, May 19, 1965; 1 child, Mary A.B., U. N.C., 1966, J.D., 1968. Bar: N.C. 1968, D.C. 1973. Mem. staff SEC, Washington, 1968-69, legal asst. to chmn., 1970-71, sec. of commn., 1972-73; dep. gen. counsel, sec. Student Loan Mktg. Assn., 1973-78, sr. v.p., gen. counsel, sec., 1979-83, exec. v.p., gen. counsel, 1983-90; pvt. practice New Bern, N.C., 1991—. Vice chmn. First Capital Corp., Southern Pines, N.C., 1984-90; bd. dirs. Student Loan Mktg. Assn., Washington., SLM Holding Corp., Reston, Va., e-Numerate Solutions, Inc., McLean, Va.; chmn. bd. dirs. Nat. Student Loan Clearinghouse, Reston, 1993-95, 97—. Mem. Montgomery County Commn. Landlord and Tenant Affairs, Md., 1976-81, chmn., 1979-81; bd. dirs. D.C. chpt. ARC, 1976-83; trustee Arena Stage, Washington, 1984-89, Washington Theatre Awards Soc., 1988-90. Republican. Presbyterian Avocations: sailing; gardening. General corporate, Securities.

HUNT, WILLIAM E., SR. state supreme court justice; b. 1923; BA, LLB, U. Mont., JD, 1955. Bar: 1955. Judge State Workers' Compensation Ct., 1975-81; justice Mont. Supreme Ct., Helena, 1984—2001, retired justice Mo., 2001—. Office: Mont Supreme Ct Justice Bldg Rm 434 215 N Sanders St Helena MT 59601-4522

HUNTER, DONALD FORREST, lawyer; b. Mpls., Jan. 30, 1934; s. Earl Harvey and Ruby Cecilia (Lagerson) H.; m. Marlys Ann Zilge; Jeffrey, Cheri, Kathryn. BA, U. Minn., 1961, JD, 1963. Bar: Minn. 1963, U.S. Dist. Ct. Minn. 1965, U.S. Ct. Appeals (8th cir.) 1965, Ill. 1977, U.S. Dist. Ct. (no. dist.) Ill. 1991, U.S. Supreme Ct. 1986. Assoc., then ptnr. Gislason, Dosland, Hunter & Malecki, New Ulm, Minn., 1963-76; exec. v.p., sec., gen. counsel Wirtz Prodn. Ltd. Ice Follies/Holiday on Ice, Chgo., 1976-79; ptnr. Gislason, Dosland, Hunter & Malecki, Mpls., 1979-99; of counsel Gislason & Hunter, 1999—. Chmn. bd. dirs. Chgo. Milw. Corp., 1977-81; pres. Chgo. Milw. R.R., 1977-81; bd. dirs. First Security Bank, Chgo.; bd. dirs., officer First Security Bancorp, Inc., Chgo., 1993—; bd. dirs., sec. Wirtz Corp., Chgo. Blackhawk Hockey Team and related cos. Fellow Am. Coll. Trial Lawyers; mem. ABA, Am. Judicature Soc., Minn. Bar Assn. (bd. of govs. 1973-76), 5th Dist. Bar Assn. (pres. 1971-72), Hennepin County Bar Assn., Minn. Def. Lawyers Assn. (bd. dirs. 1976), Internat. Assn. Ins. Counsel, U.S. Supreme Ct. Hist. Assn. General civil litigation, Contracts commercial, General corporate. Office: Gislason & Hunter PO Box 5297 9900 Bren Rd E Ste 215E Hopkins MN 55343-9666

HUNTER, ELMO BOLTON, federal judge; b. St. Louis, Oct. 23, 1915; s. David Riley and Della (Bolton) H.; m. Shirley Arnold, Apr. 5, 1952; 1 child, Nancy Ann (Mrs. Ray Lee Hunt). AB, U. Mo., 1936, LLB, 1938; Cook Grad. fellow, U. Mich., 1941; PhD (hon.), Coll. of Ozarks, 1988. Bar: Mo. 1938. Pvt. practice, Kansas City, 1938-45; sr. asst. city counselor, 1939-40; ptnr. Sebree, Shook, Hardy and Hunter, 1945-51; state circuit judge Mo., 1951-57; Mo. appellate judge, 1957-65; judge U.S. Dist. Ct., Kansas City, Mo., 1965—, now sr. judge. Instr. law U. Mo., 1952-62; mem. jud. selection Elmo B. Hunter Citizens Ctr., Am. Judicature Soc. Contbr. articles to profl. jours. Mem. Bd. Police Commrs., 1949-51; Trustee Kansas City U., Coll. of Ozarks; fellow William Rockhill Nelson Gallery Art. 1st lt. M.I., AUS, 1943-46. Recipient 1st Ann. Law Day award U. Mo., 1964, Charles E. Whittaker award, 1994, SAR Law Enforcement Commendation medal, 1994, citation of Merit Mo. Law Sch., 1996. Fellow ABA; mem. Fed., Mo. bar assns., Jud. Conf. U.S. (mem. long range planning com., chmn. ct. adminstrn. com.), Am. Judicature Soc. (bd. govs., mem. exec. com., pres., chmn. bd., Devitt Disting. Svc. to Justice award 1987), Acad. Mo. Squires, Order of Coif, Phi Beta Kappa, Phi Delta Phi. Presbyterian (elder). Office: US Dist Ct 659 US Courthouse 811 Grand Blvd Ste 201 Kansas City MO 64106-1904

HUNTER, HOWARD OWEN, academic administrator, law educator; b. Brunswick, Ga., Oct. 14, 1946; m. Susan Frankel, Nov. 27, 1971; 1 child, Emily Atwood Plotkin. BA in Russian Studies, Yale U., 1968, JD, 1971. Bar: Ga. 1971. Assoc. atty. Hogan & Hartson, Washington, 1971-72, Hansell, Post, Brandon & Dorsey, Atlanta, 1972-76; asst. prof. Emory U. Sch. Law, 1976-79, assoc. prof., 1979-82, assoc. dean, 1979-80, prof., 1982—, prof. law, dean, 1989-2001. Dir. Ga. Vol. Lawyers for the Arts, Inc., 1975-89, sec., 1975-77, treas., 1978-80, v.p., 1980-82, pres., 1984-87; vis. prof. law U. Va. Sch. Law, Charlottesville, 1982-83; hon. prof. law U. Hong Kong, 1986; vis. Mills E. Godwin prof. law Coll. William & Mary, Williamsburg, Va., 1989; mem. Chief Justice Commn. on Professionalism, 1990—, Supreme Ct. Commn. on Indigent Def., 2000—; bd. trustees Fed. Def. Program, 1991-97; lectr. in field. Author: Freedom of Information Handbook: Georgia, 1979, Modern Law of Contracts: Breach and Remedies, 1986, supplements, 1987, 88, 89, 90, 91, 92, 93, Modern Law of Contracts: Formation, Performance, Relationships, 1987, supplements, 1988, 89, 90, 91, 92, 93, Modern Law of Contracts, revised edit., 1993, supplements, 1994, 95, 96, 97, 98, 2d rev. edit., 1999, supplements, 2000, 01, (with Mogens Pedersen) Recent Reforms in Swedish Higher Education, 1980; contbr. articles to profl. jours.; mem. editl. bd. Jour. of Contract Law, 1988—. Fulbright Sr. scholar U. Sydney, 1988. Mem. ABA, Assn. Am. Law Schs., Am. Law Inst. (mem. consultative com. on revisions to article 2 of UCC), State Bar Ga. (mem. editl. bd. Ga. State Bar Jour. 1977-82), Decatur-DeKalb Bar Assn., Atlanta Bar Assn. (vol. lawyer project on illegal Cuban immigrants 1985-87, vol. lawyer in representation of Cuban inmates at fed. prison in Talladega, Ala. 1988, bd. dirs. internat. transaction sect. 1995—), Inst. Continuing Legal Edn. (vice-chmn. bd. trustees 1993-97), Inst. Continuing Judicial Edn. (bd. trustees 1989-2001). Avocations: cycling, jogging, fishing, travel. Office: Emory U Sch Law Gambrell Hall 1301 Clifton Rd NE Atlanta GA 30322-1013 E-mail: hunter@emory.edu

HUNTER, IAN DALZELL, lawyer; b. Bangor, Northern Ireland, July 20, 1961; s. William Dalzell and Marian H. BA with honors, Bristol U., Eng., 1983. Bar: solicitor Supreme Ct. 1989. Articled clk. Drules & Atlee, London, 1987-89; solicitor, 1989-90, Fox Williams, London, 1990-96, Bird & Bird, London, 1996-98; ptnr., 1998—. Author: Employment Law for the Layman Which? Guide to Employement, 1999; co-author: Britain's Invisible Earnings, 1989; contbr. articles to Fin. Times, The Times. Mem. Law Soc., Employement Lawyers Assn. Avocations: writing, current affairs, reading. Labor. Office: Bird & Bird 90 Fetter Ln EC4A 1JP London England Fax: 0207-615-6111. E-mail: ian.hunter@twobirds.com

HUNTER, JACK DUVAL, lawyer; b. Elkhart, Ind., Jan. 14, 1937; s. William Stanley and Marjorie Irene (Upson) H.; m. Marsha Ann Goodsell, Nov. 14, 1958 (dec.); children: Jack, Jon, Justin. BBA, U. Mich., 1959, LLB, 1961. Bar: Mich. 1961, Ind. 1962. Atty. Lincoln Nat. Life Ins. Co., Ft. Wayne, Ind., 1961-64, asst. counsel, 1964-68, v.p., gen. counsel 1975-79, sr. v.p., gen. counsel, 1979-86, exec. v.p., gen. counsel, 1986-99. Asst. gen. counsel, asst. sec. Lincoln Nat. Corp., Ft. Wayne and Phila., 1968-71, gen. counsel, 1971—, v.p., 1972-79, sr. v.p., 1979-86, exec. v.p., 1986—, Life trustee Ind. Nature Conservancy, chmn. bd. trustees, 1993-95. Recipient Oak Leaf award Nature Conservancy, 1997. Mem. ABA, Ind. State Bar Assn., Allen County Bar Assn., Assn. Life Ins. Counsel (pres. 1995-96), Am. Coun. Life Ins. (chmn. legal sect. 1991). General corporate. Office: Lincoln Nat Corp 1500 Market St Ste 3900 Philadelphia PA 19102-2100 E-mail: jdhunter@lnc.com

HUNTER, JAMES AUSTEN, JR. lawyer; b. Phoenix, June 19, 1941; s. James Austen and Elizabeth Aileen (Holt) H.; m. Donna Gabriele, Aug. 24, 1973; 1 child, James A. A.B., Cath. U. Am., 1963, LL.B., 1966. Bar: N.Y. 1967, Pa. 1975, U.S. Supreme Ct. 1974. Assoc. firm Sullivan & Cromwell, N.Y.C., 1967-74; assoc. firm Morgan, Lewis & Bockius, Phila., 1974-77, ptnr., 1977—. Banking, General corporate, Real property. Home: 1001 Red Rose Ln Villanova PA 19085-2118 Office: Morgan Lewis & Bockius 1701 Market St Philadelphia PA 19103-2903 E-mail: jhunter@morganlewis.com

HUNTER, JAMES GALBRAITH, JR. lawyer; b. Phila., Jan. 6, 1942; s. James Galbraith and Emma Margaret (Jehl) H.; m. Pamela Ann Trott, July 18, 1969 (div.); children: James Nicholas, Catherine Selene; m. Nancy Grace Scheurwater, June 21, 1992. B.S. in Engring. Sci., Case Inst. Tech., 1965; J.D., U. Chgo., 1967. Bar: Ill. 1967, U.S. Dist. Ct. (no. dist.) Ill. 1967, U.S. Ct. Appeals (7th cir.) 1967, U.S. Ct. Claims, 1976, U.S. Ct. Appeals (4th and 9th cirs.) 1978, U.S. Supreme Ct. 1979, U.S. Dist. Ct. (cen. dist.) Ill. 1980, Calif. 1980, U.S. Dist. Ct. (cen. and so. dists.) Calif. 1980, U.S. Ct. Appeals (5th cir.) 1982, U.S. Ct. Appeals (fed. cir.) 1982. Assoc. Kirkland & Ellis, Chgo., 1967-68, 70-73, ptnr., 1973-76; ptnr. Hedlund, Hunter & Lynch, Chgo., 1976-82, Los Angeles, 1979-82; ptnr. Latham & Watkins, Hedlund, Hunter & Lynch, Chgo. and Los Angeles, 1982— . Served to lt. JAGC, USN, 1968-70. Mem. ABA, State Bar Calif., Los Angeles County Bar Assn., Chgo. Bar Assn. Clubs: Metropolitan (Chgo.), Chgo. Athletic Assn., Los Angeles Athletic. Exec. editor U. Chgo. Law Rev., 1966-67. Antitrust, Federal civil litigation, State civil litigation. Office: Latham & Watkins Sears Tower Ste 5800 Chicago IL 60606-6306 also: 633 W 5th St Los Angeles CA 90071-2005

HUNTER, LARRY DEAN, lawyer; b. Leon, Iowa, Apr. 10, 1950; s. Doyle J. and Dorothy B. (Grey) H.; m. Rita K. Barker, Jan. 24, 1971; children: Nathan (dec.), Allison. BS with high distinction, U. Iowa, 1971; AM, JD magna cum laude, U. Mich., 1974, CPhil in Econs., 1975. Bar: Va. 1975, Mich. 1978, Calif. 1992. Assoc. McGuire Woods & Battle, Richmond, Va., 1975-77; asst. counsel, internat. counsel Clark Equipment Co., Buchanan, Mich., 1977-80; ptnr. Honigman, Miller, Schwartz and Cohn, Detroit, 1980-93; asst. gen. counsel Hughes Electronics Corp., L.A., 1993-98, corp. v.p., 1998—; sr. v.p., gen. counsel DIRECTV, Inc., El Segundo, Calif., 1996-98; chmn. pres. DIRECTV Japan Mgmt., Inc., Tokyo, 1998-2000. Mem. faculty Wayne State U. Law Sch., Detroit, 1987-89. Mem. Order of Coif. Contracts commercial, General corporate, Securities. Home: 1101-B S Catalina Ave Redondo Beach CA 90277 Office: Hughes Electronics Corp 200 N Sepulveda El Segundo CA 90245 E-mail: larry.hunter@hughes.com

HUNTER, M(ILTON) REED, JR. lawyer; b. Salt Lake City, Oct. 5, 1932; s. Milton Reed and Ferne (Gardner) H.; m. Mary Anne Shumway, Dec. 19, 1968; children: Edward Lund, Anne Leslie, Maria Lynne, Jefferson Reed. BA with honors, Brigham Young U., 1953; JD, U. Utah, 1961. Bar: Utah 1961, Calif. 1969, U.S. Dist. Ct. Utah 1961, U.S. Ct. Appeals (9th cir.) 1969, U.S. Supreme Ct. 1978. Asst. atty. gen. Utah State Atty. Gen.'s Office, Salt Lake City, 1961-68; staff atty. Continuing Edn. of the Bar, U. Calif., Berkeley, 1968-71; assoc., ptnr. Goldstein, Barceloux & Goldstein, San Francisco, 1971-84; v.p., atty. Fadem, Berger & Norton, Santa Monica, Calif., 1984-89; sole practitioner Encino, 1989-90; ptnr. Crosby, Heafey, Roach & May, L.A., 1990-2000; sole practitioner, 2000—. Contbr. articles to profl. jours. Sgt. U.S. Army, 1953-55, Germany. Mem. Calif. State Bar, Calif. Acad. Appellate Lawyers (pres. 1979-80; chair state bar com. on appellate cts. 1985), Los Angeles County Bar Assn. (condemnation com.), Mensa, Phi Kappa Phi, Phi Alpha Theta. Republican. Mormon. Avocations: music, film, tennis, travel. Appellate, Land use and zoning (including planning). Home and Office: 17165 Avenida De Santa Ynez Pacific Palisades CA 90272-2134 E-mail: cumquat45@hotmail.com

HUNTER, RICHARD SAMFORD, JR. lawyer; b. Montgomery, Ala., May 8, 1954; s. Richard Samford and Anne (Arendell) H.; m. Jane Messer, June 28, 1981; children: Richard Samford III, Benjamin Arendell. Student, Berklee Coll. of Music, 1974-75; BA, U. N.C., 1977; JD, Cumberland Sch Law of Samford U., 1980. Bar: N.C. 1980, U.S. Dist. Ct. (ea. and mid. dists.) N.C. 1981; cert. Am. Bd. Trial Advs. Assoc. Green & Mann, Raleigh, N.C., 1980-82, Smith, Debnam, Hibbert & Pahl, Raleigh, 1982-85; ptnr. Futrell, Hunter & Bingham, 1985-97. Pres., North Carolina Acad. of Trial Lawyers, 1993-94; pres. elect, 1992-93; exec. comm., 1987-94; bd., 1984-87; chair, Auto Torts Sect., 1998—, program chmn. media law U. N.C., Chapel Hill, 1983-84; mem. faculty NCATL Nat. Inst. Trial Advocacy, 1987; lectr. in field. Author: How to Try a Civil Case, 1986, Traumatic Medicine, 1988, Insurance Law for the General Practitioner, 1992, North Carolina Bar Assn. Desk Book, 1992, Traumatic Medicine, 1988, Inadequate Offer? Try that P.I. Case, 1995; composer, performer (TV musical) The Tomorrow Show, 1975; contbr. articles to profl. jours. and mags. including Trial Briefs Mag., Fourth Quarter. Corp. fund raiser United Way, Wake County, N.C., 1984-85; mem. clergy's sermon evaluation com. Christ Episc. Ch., Raleigh; bd. dirs. Raleigh Chamber Music Guild, 1986-88; bd. dirs. Food Bank of N.C., 1990—. Fellow Roscoe Pound Found. Fellow So. Trial Lawyers Assn., Roscoe Pound Found.; mem. ABA (litig. sect.), ATLA, Am. Bd. Trial Advocates (cert.), N.C. Bar Assn. (litig. sect.), Wake County Bar Assn. (bd. dirs. 1987, 88, chmn. 1988), Assn. Trial Lawyers Am. (Stalwart fellow Roscoe Pound Found.), N.C. State Bar, N.C. Acad. Trial Lawyers (speaker various seminars, chmn. speakers bur. 1984-85, bd. govs. 1986—, v.p. pub. svc. and info. com. 1988-90, v.p. membership 1990-91, v.p. legis. 1991—, pres. 1993-94, exec. com. 1987-94, chmn. auto torts sect. 1998—, mem. edn. com. 1985-88, pres.-elect 1992-93, bd. dirs. 1984-87, co-chair auto torts sect. 1998-99, U. N.C. journalism press law seminar, 1983, 84), Kiwanis, Sphinx, Phi Alpha Delta. Democrat. Avocations: sports, music, hunting, fishing. Alternative dispute resolution, General civil litigation, Personal injury. Home: 813 Graham St Raleigh NC 27605-1124 Office: Law Offices of Richard S Hunter Jr Ste 300 133 Fayetteville St Mall Raleigh NC 27602-0470 Fax: 919-831-8734. E-mail: hunteratty@aol.com

HUNTLEY, DONALD WAYNE, lawyer; b. Chgo., Sept. 22, 1942; s. Joseph Edward and Emily Rose (Beran) H.; m. Margaret Helen Kopacek, Aug. 27, 1966 (div. 1994); children: Richard A. II, Scott J., Mark B., C. Frederick M. BS, U. Ill., 1963, JD, 1966. Bar: D.C. 1967, Del. 1981, U.S. Supreme Ct. 1973. Patent counsel E. I. du Pont de Nemours & Co., Wilmington, Del., 1966-92, Remington Arms Co., 1985-89; founder present firm, 1993; asst. pub. defender State of Del., Wilmington, 1972-78; ptnr. Huntley & Assocs. Bd. dirs. Del. Symphony Assn., 1972-86, 98—, pres., 1976-79, chmn. music com., 1979-86, trustee, 1988-98, chmn. past pres. coun., 1990—; bd. dirs. Kalmar Kyckel Commemorative Com., 1983-91, chmn. cultural com., 1983-86, mem. exec. com., 350th anniversary com., 1986-88; counsel Ctr. for Creative Arts, Yorklyn, Del., 1983-84. Mem. Rotary Club Wilmington, ABA, Del. Bar Assn., Phila. Intellectual Property Law Assn., Phi Delta Phi. Republican. Episcopalian. Intellectual property, Patent, Trademark and copyright. Home: 838 Summerset Dr Hockessin DE 19707-9338 Office: Huntley & Assocs PO Box 948 1105 N Market St Wilmington DE 19899-0948 E-mail: huntley@monopolize.com

HUPP, HARRY L. federal judge; b. L.A., Apr. 5, 1929; s. Earl L. and Dorothy (Goodspeed) H.; m. Patricia Hupp, Sept. 13, 1953; children: Virginia, Karen, Keith, Brian. AB, Stanford U., 1953, LLB, 1955. Bar: Calif. 1956, U.S. Dist. Ct. (cen. dist.) Calif. 1956, U.S. Supreme Ct. Pvt. practice law Beardsley, Hufstedler and Kemble, L.A., 1955-72; judge Superior Ct. of Los Angeles, 1972-84; appointed fed. dist. judge U.S. Dist. Ct. (cen. dist.) Calif., L.A., 1984-97, sr. judge, 1997—. Served with U.S. Army, 1950-52. Mem. Calif. Bar Assn., Los Angeles County Bar Assn. (Trial Judge of Yr. 1983), Order of Coif, Phi Alpha Delta. Office: US Dist Ct 312 N Spring St Ste 218P Los Angeles CA 90012-4704

HURABIELL, JOHN PHILIP, SR. lawyer; b. San Francisco, June 2, 1947; s. Emile John and Anna Beatrice (Blumenauer) H.; m. Judith Marie Hurabiell, June 7, 1969; children: Marie Louise, Michele, Heather, John Philip Jr. JD, San Francisco U., 1976. Bar: Calif. 1977. Atty. pvt. practice, San Francisco, 1977-86; ptnr. Huppert & Hurabiell, 1985—. Pres. San Francisco S.A.F.E., Inc., 1983-88, pres. emeritus, 1988—. Editor, primary author: C.A.L.U. Business Practices Guidelines, rev. edit., 1980. Treas. Rep. election coms.; 1st v.p. Bling Babies Found., 1989-91, bd. dirs., sec., 1995-97, 98-2000; bd. dirs. Calif. State Mining and Mineral Mus., 1990-93. With USN, Vietnam. Decorated Navy Commendation medal. Mem. Calif. Bar Assn., Assn. Trial Lawyers Am., San Francisco Trial Lawyers Assn., Lawyers Club San Francisco, St. Thomas More Soc., St. Francis Hook & Ladder Soc. (trustee), The Family Club, Ferrari Club Am. (pres., chmn. Pacific region 1997-98, regional dir. 1998—, nat. legal chmn. 2000—), Golden Gate Breakfast Club, KC, Alhambra Lodge (organizing regional dir. 1983-85). Roman Catholic. Avocation: racing vintage automobiles. Pension, profit-sharing, and employee benefits, Probate, Real property. Office: Huppert & Hurabiell 3101 Clement St San Francisco CA 94121-1615

HURFORD, CAROL, retired lawyer; b. Friedensburg, Pa., Sept. 30, 1940; d. Harvey Sydney and Ada Aldine (Lengle) Zerbe; m. John Boyce Hurford, Sept. 16, 1961 (div. 1975); m. Thomas W. McEnerney, Dec. 28, 1984. BA, UCLA, 1963; JD, Rutgers U., 1975. Bar: N.Y. 1976. Assoc. Breed, Abbott & Morgan, N.Y.C., 1975-78, Reavis & McGrath, N.Y.C., 1978-84; ptnr. Munves, Tannenhaus & Storch, 1984-90. Editor Rutgers U. Law Rev. Pres. West Brooklyn Ind. Dems., 1970; bd. dirs. Ballet Tech. Found., Inc., N.Y.C., 1994—. Mem. LWV (chair voter svc. New Castle chpt. 1993-96, v.p. 1994-96, pres. 1996-98, bd. dirs. 1999—, bd. dirs. Chappaqua summer scholarship program 1991—). Democrat. Avocations: travel, reading, skiing, cycling. Home: 49 Marcourt Dr Chappaqua NY 10514-2506

HURLEY, GEOFFREY KEVIN, lawyer; b. N.Y.C., Apr. 12, 1948; s. John J. and Evelyn M. (Hoffman) H.; m. C. Austin Fitts, May 19, 1979. B.A., Haverford Coll., 1970; J.D., Vanderbilt U., 1973. Bar: N.Y. 1974. Assoc., Brown, Wood, Ivey, Mitchell & Petty, N.Y.C., 1973-80; ptnr., 1981-84; ptnr. Skadden, Arps, Slate, Meagher & Flom, N.Y.C., 1984— . Articles editor Vanderbilt Law Rev., 1972-73. Mem. Assn. Bar City of N.Y., ABA, N.Y. State Bar Assn. Republican. Episcopalian. Securities. Home: 103 W 75th St New York NY 10023-1813 Office: Milbank Tweed, Hadley & McCoy 1 Chase Manhattan Plz Fl 47 New York NY 10005-1413

HURLEY, GRADY SCHELL, lawyer; b. New Orleans, Nov. 29, 1954; s. Daniel Patrick and Jocelyn Mary (Schell) H.; children: Joshua, Benjamin, Mary Elizabeth, William, John. BA, Tulane U., 1976, JD, 1979, LLM, 1981. Bar: La. 1979, U.S. Dist. Ct. (ea., mid. and we. dists.) La. 1979, U.S. Ct. Appeals (5th and 11th cirs.) 1980, U.S. Supreme Ct. 1986. Assoc. Jones, Walker, Waechter, Poitevent, Carrere and Denegre, New Orleans, 1979-84, ptnr., 1984—; mem. profl. employment com. Jones Walker Waecheter Poitevent Carrère & Denègre and predecessor firms, 1985—, mem. adminstrv. com., 1993—. Editor: Damages Recoverable in Maritime Matters, 1984, Briefly Speaking, 1993. Mem. ABA (chmn. subcom. on wrongful death and workers compensation 1990-94), Fed. Bar Assn., La. Bar Assn. (dist. rep. young lawyers sect. 1986, La. Bar examiner 1989—), New Orleans Bar Assn. (chmn. maritime law com. 1990-92, exec. bd. 1994—, pres.-elect 2001), Maritime Law Assn. (maritime pers. com., young lawyers com.), S.E. Admiralty Law Inst., Tulane U. Alumni Assn. (bd. dirs. 1986—, pres. 1995, chmn. 35th ann. ednl. conf.), Mariner Club (pres. 1982). Republican. Roman Catholic. Avocations: sports, reading, painting, movies. Admiralty, General civil litigation, Insurance. Office: Jones Walker Waechter Poitevent Carrère & Denègre 201 St Charles Ave Ste 5000 New Orleans LA 70170-5100 E-mail: ghurley@jwlaw.com

HURLEY, LAWRENCE JOSEPH, lawyer; b. Plainfield, N.J., Nov. 17, 1946; s. Luke Michael and Gertrude Marie (Bremer) H.; m. Allyson J. Kingsley, May 28, 1977; children: Michael William, Kathryn Elizabeth. BS, U. Dayton, 1969; JD, Cath. U. Am., 1974. Bar: N.J. 1974, U.S. Dist. Ct. N.J., 1974, D.C. 1976, N.Y. 1980, U.S. Ct. Appeals (3rd cir.) 1980, U.S. Dist. Ct. (ea. and so. dists.) N.Y. 1981, U.S. Ct. Appeals (2nd cir.) 1981, U.S. Ct. Appeals (D.C. cir.) 1982. Law clk. Superior Ct. N.J., New Brunswick, 1974-75; assoc. Lynch, Mannion, Lutz & Lewandowski, 1975-76, Stryker, Tams & Dill, Newark, 1976-79; atty. AT&T Comm., Basking Ridge, N.J., 1979-85; asst chief prosecutor econ. crimes and ofcl. corruption Morris County Prosecutor's Office, Morristown, 1985-89; ptnr. Voorhees & Acciavatti, 1989-91; sr. atty. AT&T, 1991-96; mng. corp. labor and employment counsel Lucent Techs., 1996—. With U.S. Army, 1969-71. Decorated Bronze Star. Mem. ABA (litig. sect. 1976-86, labor law sect. 1981-86, criminal law sect. 1985-91, labor law sect. 1991—), N.J. State Bar Assn. (labor law sect. 1981—). Labor. Office: Lucent Techs Rm D001 535 Mountan Ave New Providence NJ 07974 E-mail: ljhurley@lucent.com

HURLOCK, JAMES BICKFORD, retired lawyer; b. Chgo., Aug. 7, 1933; s. James Bickford and Elizabeth (Charls) H.; m. Margaret Lyn Holding, July 1, 1961; children: James Bickford III, Burton Charls, Matthew Hunter. AB, Princeton U., 1955; BA, Oxford U., 1957, MA, 1960; JD, Harvard U., 1959. Bar: N.Y. 1960, U.S. Supreme Ct. 1967. Assoc. White & Case, N.Y.C., 1959-66, ptnr., 1967-2000; ret., 2000. Dir. Orient Express Hotels, Ltd. Trustee N.Y. Presbyn. Hosp., Parker Sch. Fgn. and Comparative Law, Internat. Devel. Law Inst., Woods Hole Oceanog. Inst. Rhodes scholar, 1955. Mem. ABA, N.Y. State Bar Assn., Am. Law Inst., Am. Assn. Internat. Law, River Club, N.Y. Yacht Club. Republican. Episcopalian. Antitrust, General corporate, Private international. Home: 46 Byram Dr Greenwich CT 06830-7008 Office: White & Case Bldg Ll 1155 Avenue Of The Americas New York NY 10036-2787 E-mail: jhurlock46byram@aol.com

HURNYAK, CHRISTINA KAISER, lawyer; b. Noblesville, Ind., Dec. 22, 1949; d. Albert Michael and Lois Angie (Gatton) Kaiser; m. Cyril Hurnyak, June 24, 1972. BA cum laude, Wittenberg U., 1972; JD, SUNY-Buffalo, 1979. Bar: N.Y. 1980, Pa. 1996, U.S. Dist. Ct. (we. dist.) Pa. 1998. Mem. support staff McKinsey & Co., Inc., mgmt. cons., Chgo., 1972-75; law clk. Justice Norman J. Wolf, N.Y. Supreme Ct., Buffalo, 1980-81; assoc. Dempsey & Dempsey, 1979-80, 81-90, Grossman, Levine & Civiletto, Niagara Falls, N.Y., 1990-95, Tarasi, Tarasi & Fishman, P.C. (formerly Tarasi Law Firm), Pitts., 1998—. Mem. ABA, ATLA, Pa. State Bar Assn., Pa. Trial Lawyers Assn.. Allegheny County Bar Assn. Democrat. Lutheran. Federal civil litigation, State civil litigation, Personal injury. Office: Tarasi Tarasi & Fishman PC 510 3rd Ave Pittsburgh PA 15219-2107

HURST, CHARLES WILSON, lawyer; b. Salt Lake City, July 4, 1957; s. John Vann and Myra (Kasik) Piscane; m. Karen Buck, Jan. 5, 1985; children: Jeanette Q., Daniel C., Brian K., Matthew C., Robert W. Student, U. Chgo., 1975-77; BA cum laude, Wesleyan U., Conn., 1979; JD, Duke U., 1983. Bar: Pa. 1983, U.S. Dist. Ct. (ea. dist.) Pa. 1985, Calif. 1986, U.S. Dist. Ct. (cen. dist.) Calif. 1990. Assoc. Saul, Ewing, Remick & Saul, Phila., 1983-85, Wyman Bautzer Kuchel & Silbert, Orange County, Calif., 1985-89, ptnr., 1990, Snell & Wilmer LLP, Orange County, 1990—. Dir. Pacific Art Found., 1994-2000; trustee Pegasus Sch., 1996—. Mem. ABA (comml. leasing com. of real property, probate and trust law sect.), Orange County Bar Assn. Contracts commercial, Land use and zoning (including planning), Real property. Office: Snell & Wilmer 1920 Main St Ste 1200 Irvine CA 92614-7230 E-mail: churst@swlaw.com

HURT, MICHAEL CARTER, lawyer; b. Kokomo, Ind., Sept. 7, 1943; s. Eldon Carter and Jane Ann (McCool) H.; m. Susan Clay Lines, Jan. 18, 1964; children— Michael Carter II, Justin Patrick. J.D., U. Pacific, 1973. Bar: Wis. 1973, U.S. Dist. Ct. (ea. dist.) Wis. 1973, U.S. Ct. Appeals (7th cir.). Legal intern Sacramento County Pub. Defender, Sacramento, 1971-73; assoc. Laubenheimer, Patrick & Maegli, Menomonee Falls, Wis., 1973-74; ptnr. Patrick & Hurt, Menomonee Falls, 1974-86; pvt. practice, 1986—; chmn. SE Wis. Corrections Adv. Com., Waukesha, 1978— ; cir. ct. commr. Waukesha County Cir. Ct., 1983— ; acting family ct. commr. Waukesha County Family Ct., 1983— . Bd. mgrs. Tri-County YMCA, Menomonee Falls, 1975-87; panel mem. United Way of Waukesha County, 1981— ; vol. XIII Winter Olympic Games, Lake Placid, N.Y., 1980. Served to sgt. USAF, 1966-70. Mem. Wis. State Bar, Waukesha County Bar, Menomonee Falls C. of C. (bd. dirs. 1976-82), Phi Alpha Delta (chpt. justice 1971-73, outstanding mem. 1973). Republican. Methodist. Lodge: Kiwanis. Contracts commercial, Family and matrimonial, General practice. Home: N87w15611 Kenwood Blvd Menomonee Falls WI 53051-2911 Office: N84w15959 Appleton Ave Menomonee Falls WI 53051-3044

HURWICH, ROBERT ALLAN, lawyer, multimedia, manufacturing and services company executive; b. South Bend, Ind., Nov. 1, 1941; s. Abe and Carolyne C. (Neisner) H.; m. Judith A. Jones, May 31, 1969; children: Katherine A., David A. AB, Harvard U., 1963, LLB, 1966. Bar: N.Y. 1967; U.S. Dist. Ct. (ea. dist.) N.Y. 1968, U.S. Dist. Ct. (so. dist.) N.Y. 1968, Conn. 1990. Law clk. U.S. Dist. Ct. (ea. dist.) N.Y., 1966-68; assoc. Cravath, Swaine & Moore, N.Y.C., 1968-75; gen. counsel, sec. Moore McCormack Resources, Inc., Stamford, Conn., 1975-89, v.p., 1979-89; pvt. practice, 1990-93; v.p. adminstrn., gen. counsel, sec. Lynch Corp., Greenwich, Conn., 1994—. Communications, General corporate, Securities. Office: Lynch Corp 8 Sound Shore Dr Ste 290 Greenwich CT 06830-7272

HUSBAND, BERTRAM PAUL, lawyer; b. L.A., Aug. 15, 1950; s. Bertram Perry and Ruth (Eatough) H.; m. Beverly Ruth Hyams, May 1, 1987; children: Joseph Bertram, Daniel James, David Paul. BA, Occidental Coll., 1972; JD, UCLA, 1977. Bar: Calif. 1977, U.S. Dist. Ct. (cen. dist.) Calif. 1978, U.S. Ct. Appeals (9th cir.) 1979, U.S. Dist. Ct. (so. dist.) Calif. 1980, U.S. Dist. Ct. (no. dist.) Calif. 1988, U.S. Tax Ct. 1987. Assoc. Coskey, Coskey & Boxer, L.A., 1978-79, Cooper, Epstein & Hurewitz, Beverly Hills, Calif., 1979-81; pvt. practice L.A., 1981-84; ptnr. Husband & Morris, 1984-89, Husband & Roberts, L.A. and Encino, Calif., 1989-91; pvt. practice Encino, 1991-94, Valencia, Calif., 1994-97, Burbank, 1997—. Adj. prof. law Pepperdine U., Malibu, Calif.,1978-79. Author equine law column Jour. Agrl. Taxation and Law, 1987-93; writer, producer (ednl. video) Fighting Back: Successfully Representing Your Horse Business to the IRS, 1991; editl. adv. bd. Am. House Coun. Tax Bulletin, 1994—. Registered judge Am. Horse Shows Assn., 1975-94; recommended judge Equestrian Trials Inc., 1988-94; dir., gen. counsel Burbank Internat. Children's Film Festival, 2000—. Mem. ABA (tax sect., agrl. com., forum com. entertainment and sports industry, L.A. County Bar Assn. (chmn. pro bono oversight com. tax sect. 1987-88, officer entertainment tax com. of tax sect. 1993-96, chair 1995-96), Beverly Hills Bar Assn. (exec. com. entertainment sect. 1992-96), San Fernando Valley Bar Assn. (chair tax sect. 1993-94), Calif. State Bar (tax sect., lectr. 1988 seminar), Internat. Arabian Horse Assn. (vice chair fed. tax study com. 1979-92), Association Internationale du Film d'Animation (Hollywood chpt., dir. 1997, gen. counsel 1997—), Media Dist. Intellectual Property Assn., World Arabian Horse Orgn. Mem. Ch. of Christ. Avocation: speculative fiction. Entertainment, Taxation, general, Equine law. Office: 245 E Olive Ave Ste 400 Burbank CA 91502-1214 E-mail: bphusband@aol.com

HUSBAND, JOHN MICHAEL, lawyer; b. Elyria, Ohio, Apr. 7, 1952; s. Clint F. and Emma H.; m. Jan Lee Umbenhour, Sept. 15, 1975; children: Heather, John. BS, Ohio State U., 1974; JD, U. Toledo, 1977. Law clk. U.S. Ct. Appeals (10th cir.), Denver, 1977-78; ptnr. Holland & Hart, Denver, 1978—, chair labor and employment law dept., 1991—; counsel Western Gov.'s Office, Denver, 1984, Vols. of Am., Denver, 1984. Editor, The Colorado Lawyer, Employment and Labor Rev., 1984—; co-editor Colo. Employment Law Letter; contbr. articles to profl. jours. Bd. dirs. Colo. Safety Assn., 1984—, Denver Four Mile House, Town of Bow Mar, 1987-90, 1984; mem. Denver Leadership Assn.; sec., treas. Colo. Safety Assn., 1988—; bd. govs. U. Toledo Coll. Law. Inductee Elyria Sports Hall of Fame, 1997. Mem. ABA (labor law sect., individual rights and responsibilities com., co-chair pub. subcom. individual rights and responsibilities com.), Assn. Trial Lawyers Am., Nat. Inst. Trial Advocate, Ohio Bar Assn., Colo. Bar Assn. (labor sect.), Denver Bar Assn., Colo. Safety Assn. (exec. com. sec. treas. 1987—). Republican. Lutheran. Federal civil litigation, State civil litigation, Labor. Home: 5280 Ridge Trl Littleton CO 80123-1410 Office: Holland & Hart LLP PO Box 8749 555 17th St Ste 2900 Denver CO 80202-3979

HUSICK, LAWRENCE ALAN, lawyer; b. Bklyn., Feb. 15, 1958; s. Charles Bernard and Babette Ann (Kraus) H.; m. Margaret Levy, Aug. 23, 1987; children: Andrew Jacob, Carly Elizabeth. BSc cum laude, Muhlenberg Coll., 1980; JD, Washington Coll. of Law, 1983. Bar: Pa. 1983, U.S. Dist. Ct. (ea. dist.) Pa. 1983, U.S. Ct. Appeals (3d cir.) 1989, U.S. Ct. Appeals (fed. cir.) 1990. Chemist Air Products and Chem. Inc., Allentown, Pa., 1979-80; cons. Hilton-Alan Assoc., Chevy Chase, Md., 1980-83; assoc. Ratner & Prestia, Valley Forge, Pa., 1983-88; head intellectual property dept. Dilworth, Paxson, Kalish & Kauffman, Phila., 1988-91; sole practitioner Southeastern, Pa., 1991-95; ptnr. Lipton, Weinberger & Husick, Malvern, 1995—; co-founder, prin. Informatics, Inc., Wayne, 1992—. Mem. adv. com. for patents, Washington, 1987-91. Pres. Helen Beebe Speech and Hearning Ctr., Easton, Pa., 1989-92. Recipient Advocacy award Assn. Trial Lawyers Am., 1983. Avocations: computing, sailing. Federal civil litigation, Patent, Trademark and copyright. Office: PO Box 587 Southeastern PA 19399-0587 E-mail: Lawrence@LawHusick.com

HUSKEY, DOW THOBERN, lawyer; b. Sept. 23, 1946; s. Dow Thobern Huskey and Helen (Weathersbee) Morris; m. Julie Beth Coursin, May 17, 1975; children: Dow, III, Whitney. BS, Samford U., 1970; JD, Cumberland Sch. Law, 1976. Bar: Ala. 1977, U.S. Dist. Ct. (mid. dist.) Ala. 1977, U.S. Ct. Appeals (5th cir.) 1977, U.S. Ct. Appeals (11th cir.) 1981, U.S. Supreme Ct. 1981. Ptnr. Huskey & Etheredge, Dothan, 1977—82, Johnson Huskey Hornsby & Etheredge, Dothan, 1982—87; pvt. practice, 1987—. Author: (non-fiction) Landlord and Tenant, The Law in Alabama, 1980, Damages, The Law in Alabama, 1985. Pres. Houston County chpt. Am. Cancer Soc., Dothan, Ala., 1979—81, Houston County chpt. Ala. Soc. Crippled Children and Adults, Dothan, 1982—83. Mem.: Ala. Trial Lawyers Assn. (bd. govs. 1980—85), Nat. Assn. Coll. and Univ. Attys., Assn. Trial Lawyers Am., Am. Judicature Soc., Soc. Ala. Def. Lawyers Assn., Rotary (pres. 1989—). Republican. Episcopalian. Federal civil litigation, General corporate, Real property. Home: 27 Hampton Way Dothan AL 36305-6319 Office: 112 W Adams St Dothan AL 36303-4528

HUSNEY, ELLIOTT RONALD, lawyer, financier; b. Mpls., July 24, 1940; s. Edward and Betty (Malca) H.; m. Gloria Lynne Rudd, Dec. 15, 1962; children: Ronald Edward, Kenneth Logan, Evan James. AA, U. Minn., 1960; BSBA, U. Denver, 1962, JD, 1965. Bar: Colo. 1966. Staff examiner Nat. Assn. Security Dealers Inc., 1965-66; trial atty. U.S. SEC, 1966-68; house counsel Denver Corp., 1968-69, Colo. Corp., 1969-70; v.p.

Petro Search Inc., Denver, 1970-71; pres. Denver Venture Capital, Inc., 1972-75; ptnr. Husney & Pansing, Denver, 1975-77; of counsel Pansing & Pansing; chmn. Elliott Enterprise Group, Denver, 1977-86; pres. Walden Banking Ptnrs. Ltd., 1987—. Pres. Am. Heliothermal Corp., 1977-79; chmn, U.S. Israel Investments, 1977-83; chmn. Vital Sci. Corp. divsn. Vital Sci., Ltd., 1985-88, also dir.; dir. Pro Care Industries; pres. Elliott R. Husney PC, 1990—; ptnr. Dean McClure, Eggleston & Husney, 1990-94; of counsel McClure & Eggleston, 1995-96; spl. ltd. ptnr. Wolf Ventures, 1996-98, ptnr., 1998-2000. Bd. dirs. Am. Jewish Com., 1982—85, 1995—, Am.-Israel Friendship League, 1983—84, pres., 2001—. Recipient Young Leadership award Allied Jewish Fedn. of Denver; named Man of Yr. Denver Jaycees, 1978. Mem. ABA, Denver Bar Assn., Colo. Bar Assn. Office: 7802 E Iowa Ave Denver CO 80231-2690

HUSS, ALLAN MICHAEL, lawyer; b. Chgo., Sept. 29, 1949; s. Henry A. and Emily (Rosenheim) H.; m. Sandra Joyce Cohn, Aug. 16, 1970 (dec. Mar. 1992); children: Leah E., Samantha J.; m. Susan Irene Stanley Stallard, July 17, 1993; stepchildren: Michelle E. Stallard, Adam J. Stallard. BS, Mich. State U., 1970; JD, U. Cin., 1973. Bar: Ohio 1973, Mich. 1982. Staff atty. U. S. FTC, Cleve., 1973-81; sr. staff counsel Daimler Chrysler Corp. (formerly Chrysler Corp.), Detroit, 1982—. Mem. fed. adv. com. FTC, 1985-87; chmn. joint com. on admission to bar, Cuyahoga County, Ohio, 1980-81. Mem. ABA, State Bar Mich. (chmn. antitrust sect. 1995-96), Greater Cleve. Bar Assn. Avocation: computers. Antitrust, Franchising, Warranty, consumer lemon law. Home: 4934 Peggy St West Bloomfield MI 48322-4420 Office: DaimlerChrysler Corp 485-13-65 1000 Chrysler Dr Auburn Hills MI 48326-2766

HUST, BRUCE KEVIN, lawyer; b. Cin., Aug. 16, 1957; s. George Julius and Shirley Mae (Glaser) H. BA, U. Cin., 1979; JD, No. Ky. U., 1985. Bar: Ohio 1986, U.S. Dist. Ct. (so. dist.) Ohio 1987, U.S. Ct. Appeals (6th cir.) 2000. Pvt. practice, Cin., 1986-99; trial counsel Hamilton County Pub. Defender's Office, 1988-2000; assoc. Wm. Eric Minamyer Esq. Co., LPA, 1999-2000, ptnr., 2000—. Vol. Lawyers for Poor, Cin., 1986-87, 90—; precinct exec. mem. Hamilton County Rep. Ctrl. Com., 1988—. With Ohio Naval Militia, 1988-94; journalist USNR, 1994—. Mem. Ohio State Bar Assn., Cin. Bar Assn., Ohio Assn. Criminal Def. Lawyers, Masons, Odd Fellows. Mem. United Ch. of Christ. Avocations: reading, current events, politics, writing and performing comedy. Appellate, Criminal, General practice. Home: 4247 Delridge Dr Cincinnati OH 45205-2025 Office: 8280 Montgomery Rd Ste 202 Cincinnati OH 45236-6101

HUSTON, BARRY SCOTT, lawyer; b. Bronx, N.Y., July 17, 1946; s. Irving and Estelle Huston; m. Audrey Jill Kimmel, Mar. 29, 1970; children: Jared, Brett. BA, CUNY, 1969; JD, Bklyn. Law Sch., 1972. Bar: N.Y. 1973, U.S. Dist. Ct. ea. and so. dists.) N.Y. 1975, U.S. Ct. Appeals (2d cir.) 1975, U.S. Tax Ct. 1978, U.S. Supreme Ct. 1978. Assoc. Dreyer & Traub, N.Y.C., 1972-75, Reich & Reich, N.Y.C., 1975-77; pvt. practice, 1977-80, Gt. Neck, N.Y., 1985-87; sr. ptnr. Arenstein & Huston, PC, N.Y.C., 1980-85; ptnr. Edelman & Edelman, PC, 1987-94, Baron & Kesel, PC, Kew Gardens, N.Y., 1994; sr. trial atty. Schneider Kleinick Weitz Damashek & Shoot, N.Y.C., 1994-97; sr. ptnr. Huston & Schuller, PC, 1997—. Pres. Roslyn (N.Y.) Pines Civic Assn., 1983-85; bd. dirs. Sid Jacobson Jewish Cmty. Ctr., East Hills, N.Y., 1989—. Mem. Penn Club N.Y.C. Avocations: golf, travel, reading. Entertainment, Health, Personal injury. Home: 20 Melby Ln Roslyn NY 11576-2519 Office: Huston & Schuller PC 470 Park Ave S New York NY 10016-6819

HUSTON, STEVEN CRAIG, lawyer; b. Morris, Ill., June 3, 1954; s. Raymond P. and Evelyn M. (Bass) H. BA, Ill. Coll., 1977; JD, John Marshall Law Sch., 1980; MBA, Northwestern U., 1989. Bar: Ill. 1980, U.S. Dist. Ct. (no. dist.) Ill. 1980, U.S. Ct. Appeals (7th cir.) 1980. Assoc. Siegel, Denberg et al, Chgo., 1980-83; staff atty. Wm. Wrigley Jr. Co., 1983-84; asst. sec. legal William Wrigley Jr. Co., 1984-94, asst. v.p. legal, 1994-96, counsel North Am., 1996-2000; v.p., gen. counsel Brach's Confections, Inc., 2001—. Mem. ABA, Chgo. Bar Assn. General corporate, Securities, Trademark and copyright.

HUSZAGH, FREDRICK WICKETT, lawyer, educator, information management company executive; b. Evanston, Ill., July 20, 1937; s. Rudolph LeRoy and Dorothea (Wickett) H.; m. Sandra McRae, Apr. 4, 1959; children: Floyd McRae, Fredrick Wickett II, Theodore Wickett II. BA, Northwestern U., 1958; JD, U. Chgo., 1962, LLM, 1963, JSD, 1964. Bar: Ill. 1962, U.S. Dist. Ct. D.C. 1965, U.S. Supreme Ct. 1966. Market rschr. Leo Burnett Co., Chgo., 1958-59; internat. atty. COMSAT, Washington, 1964-67; assoc. Debevoise & Liberman, 1967-68; asst. prof. law Am. U., 1968-71; program dir. NSF, 1971-73; assoc. prof. U. Mont., Missoula, 1973-76, U. Wis., Madison, 1976-77; exec. dir. Dean Rusk Ctr., U. Ga., Athens, 1977-82; prof. U. Ga., 1982—. Chmn. TWH Corp., Athens, 1982—; chmn. Profession Mgmt. Techs., Inc., Athens, 1993-96; cons. TWH Scv. Corp.; cons. Pres. Johnson's Telcommunications Task Force, Washington, 1967-68; co-chmn. Nat. Gov.'s Internat. Trade Staff Commn., Washington, 1979- 81. Author: International Decision-Making Process, 1964, Comparative Facts on Canada, Mexico and U.S., 1979; editor Rusk Ctr. Briefings, 1981-82; contbr. articles to publs. Mem. Econ. Policy Coun., N.Y.C., 1981-89. NSF grantee, 1974-78. Republican. Presbyterian. Home: 151 E Clayton St Athens GA 30601-2702 Office: U Ga Law Sch Athens GA 30602 E-mail: huszagh@uga.edu

HUSZAR, ARLENE CELIA, lawyer, mediator; b. N.Y.C., May 1, 1952; d. Charles and Dora (Toffoli) H.; m. Victor M. Yellen, May 6, 1978; 1 child: Mariette Huszar Yellen. BA, Fla. Atlantic U., 1973; JD, U. Fla., 1976. Bar: Fla. 1977, U.S. Dist. Ct. (mid. and no. dists.) Fla. 1978, U.S. Ct. Appeals (5th and 11th cirs.) 1978, D.C. 1979, U.S. Supreme Ct. 1982; cert. fed. and cir. ct. mediator, arbitrator. Pvt. practice, Gainesville, Fla., 1977-80; exec. dir. Fla. Instl. Legal Svcs., 1980—2001; deputy ct. adminstrv. 8th Judicial Circuit , Fla., 2001—. Author: (with others) Adoption, 1992, Termination of Parental Rights, 1997. Mem. City of Gainesville Citizens Adv. Com. for Cmty. Devel., 1976-79, Fla. Bar Com. on the Legal Needs of Children, 1984-85; mem. steering com. juvenile law sect. Nat. Legal Aid and Defender Assn., 1986-87; vice chmn. Alachua County Citizens Adv. Com., Dept. Criminal Justice Svcs., 1986-95; precinct committeewoman Alachua County Dem. Exec. Com., 1986-96; Queen of Peach parish coun. (sec. 1995-97, pres. 1998). Named one of Outstanding Young Women of Am., 1975. Mem. ATLA, Fla. Acad. Profl. Mediators, North Ctrl. Fla. Mediation Coun. (sec. 1999-2000, pres. 2000-01). Roman Catholic. Office: Fla Instl Legal Svcs 1010-B NW 8th Ave Gainesville FL 32601-4969

HUTCHENS, MICHAEL D. lawyer; b. Chgo., Jan. 13, 1960; s. Duane Eugene and Deborah Ann (Hoffman) H.; m. Christie Lynn Simons, July 2, 1983; children: Camille Gwendolyn Maxwell. BA, Coll. St. Thomas, St. Paul, 1982; JD, Hamline Law Sch., 1985. Bar: Minn. 1985, U.S. Dist. Ct. (4th cir.) 1986. Ptnr. Meagher & Geer, Mpls., 1986—. Arbitrator Am. Arbitration Assn., Mpls., 1990—. Mem. Minn. Def. Lawyers Assn. General civil litigation, Personal injury, Product liability. Office: Meagher & Geer 33 S 6th St Ste 4200 Minneapolis MN 55402-3788

HUTCHEON, PETER DAVID, lawyer; b. S.I., N.Y., Sept. 11, 1943; s. Peter and Helen Christine (Buckley) H.; m. Elizabeth Ann Demy, June 8, 1969 (div. Jan. 1986); children: Rececca Leigh, Douglas Ian; m. Barbara Mary Silver, Feb. 14, 1986; 1 child, Peter Silver. BA, Williams Coll., 1965; postgrad., Ludwig-Maximilian Universität, Munich, 1965-66; JD, Harvard U., 1969. Bar: N.Y. 1970, N.J. 1975. Assoc. White & Case, N.Y., 1968-75, Norris, McLaughlin & Marcus, P.A., Somerville, N.J., 1975-76, mem., 1976—. Chmn. N.J. Corp. and Bus. Law Study Commn., 1989—; mem., sec. adv. com. N.J. Bur. Securities, 1993—, chmn., 1994—. Contbr. articles to profl. jours. Chmn. bd. mgrs. St. Andrews Soc. of N.Y., 1986—87; deacon United Reformed Ch., Somerville, 1977—80; elder Bound Brook Presbyn. Ch., 1996—99. Dankstipendium scholar govt. of the Fed. Republic of Gemany, 1965. Mem. ABA (chmn. sect. of sci. and tech. 1986-87), N.J. State Bar Assn. (chmn. banking law sect. 1982-83, chmn. corp. and bus. sect. 1990-92), N.Y. State Bar Assn., German-Am. Lawyers Assn., Nat. Conf. of Lawyers and Scientists (del. 1988-91), Princeton Area Alumni Assn. of Williams Coll. (pres. 1981-89), Clan Donald (N.Y.). Avocations: wine tasting, singing. Banking, General corporate, Securities. Office: Norris McLaughlin & Marcus PA PO Box 1018 721 Rt 202/206 Somerville NJ 08876

HUTCHESON, MARK ANDREW, lawyer; b. Phila., Mar. 29, 1942; s. John R. and Mary Helen (Willis) H.; m. Julie A. Olander, June 13, 1964; children: Kirsten Elizabeth, Mark Andrew II, Megan Ann. BA, U. Puget Sound, 1964; LLB, U. Wash., 1967. Bar: Wash. 1967, U.S. Dist. Ct. (we. and ea. dists.) Wash., U.S. Ct. Appeals (9th cir.), U.S. Supreme Ct. Staff counsel Com. on Commerce U.S. Senate, Washington, 1967-68; assoc. Davis Wright Tremaine, Seattle, 1968-72; ptnr. Davis, Wright Tremaine, 1973—; mng. ptnr., chief exec. officer Davis Wright Tremaine, 1989-94; chmn. Davis, Wright Tremaine, 1994—. Mem., co-founder labor law com. Nat. Banking Industry, 1984—. Co-author: Employer's Guide to Strike Planning and Prevention, 1986; contbr. articles to profl. jours. Chmn., trustee Virginia Mason Hosp., Seattle, 1980—, Overlake Sch., Redmond, Wash., 1984-89, Epiphany Sch., Seattle, 1982-84, Legal Aid for Wash. Fund, 1991—; bd. dirs. Vis. Nurse Svcs., Seattle-King County, 1985-88; trustee Pacific N.W. Ballet, 1991-99, Pacific N.W. Assn. Ind. Schs., 1996-98. Nelson T. Hartson scholar U. Wash., 1966; Deerfield fellow Heritage Found., Deerfield, Mass., 1963. Mem. ABA (health care forum, employment law sect.), Seattle-King County Bar Assn. (employment law sect.), Am. Acad. Hosp. Attys., Am. Hosp. Assn. (labor rels. adv. com. 1978—), Coll. Labor and Employment Lawyers, Greater Seattle C. of C. (bd. dirs. 1991-94), Rainier Club, Seattle Tennis Club, Univ. Club, Order of Coif. Episcopalian. Avocations: sailing, tennis, skiing, reading, travel. Health, Labor. Office: Davis Wright Tremaine 2600 Century Sq 1501 4th Ave Seattle WA 98101-1688 E-mail: markhutcheson@dwt.com

HUTCHINS, BRIAN R. attorney general; b. Oklahoma City, Aug. 18, 1954; BA in Polit. Sci., Calif. State U., Fullerton, 1976; JD cum laude, Calif. Western Sch. Law, San Diego, 1979. Law clk. to Assoc. Justice Noel E. Manoukian Nev. Supreme Ct., Carson City, 1979-80; dep. atty. gen. State Nev., 1980-86, chief dep. atty. gen. criminal justice divsn., 1987-89, chief dep. atty. gen. transp. and pub. safety divsn., 1990—. Home: 1696 Rankin Dr Carson City NV 89701-6857 Office: Office Atty Gen 1263 S Stewart St Carson City NV 89712-0001

HUTCHINS, PETER EDWARD, lawyer; b. Nashua, N.H., Jan. 20, 1958; s. Edward Peter and Joyce Martha Hutchins; m. Kathy Hutchins; 1 child, Jamie. BA cum laude, Dartmouth Coll., 1980; JD magna cum laude, Boston Coll., 1983. Bar: N.H. 1983, U.S. Dist. Ct. N.H. 1983. Ptnr. Wiggin & Nourie, P.A., Manchester, N.H., 1983-98, Hall & Hess, PA, Manchester, 1998—. Basketball referee, cert. Internat. Assn. Approved Basketball Officials, N.H., 1992—; girls softball umpire, cert. N.H. Softball Umpires Assn., 1994—. Mem. N.H. Bar Assn. (v.p., pres. 2001-). Avocation: officiating high school sports. Insurance, Personal injury, Product liability. Office: Hall & Hess PA 80 Memmick St Manchester NH 03101*

HUTCHINSON, DENNIS JAMES, law educator; b. Boulder, Colo., Dec. 28, 1946; s. Dudley Isom and Jane Wilcox (Sampson) H.; children: Kathryn Wood, David Office: U Chgo Law Sch 1111 E 60th St Chicago IL 60637-2776

HUTCHINSON, MICHAEL CLARK, lawyer; b. Quincy, Mass., Feb. 25, 1953; s. William Thomas and Marguerite J. (Gunning) H. BA cum laude, Bowdoin Coll., 1975; JD cum laude, Suffolk U., 1979. Bar: Minn. 1980, U.s. Dist. Ct. Minn. 1980. Law clk. 7th Jud. Dist. Ct., Moorhead, Minn., 1979-81; asst. county atty. Clay County Atty.'s Office, 1981-83; assoc. Clinton & O'Gorman P.A., Cottage Grove, 1983-90; asst. county atty. Washington County Atty.'s Office, Stillwater, 1990—. Mem. Washington County Bar Assn., Lions Club (pres. local club 1989-90). Roman Catholic. Criminal. Office: Washington County Atty Office PO Box 6 Stillwater MN 55082-0006 also: 14969 62d St N Stillwater MN E-mail: Michael.Hutchinson@co.washington.mn.us

HUTCHISON, STANLEY PHILIP, lawyer, retired; b. Joliet, Ill., Nov. 22, 1923; s. Stuart Philip and Verna (Kinzer) H.; m. Helen Jane Rush, July 25, 1945; children: Norman, Elizabeth. BS, Northwestern U., 1947; LLB, Ill. Inst. Tech., 1951. Bar: Ill. 1951. Legal asst. Washington Nat. Ins. Co., Evanston, 1947-51, asst. counsel, 1951-55, asst. gen. counsel, 1955-58, assoc. gen. counsel, 1958-60, gen. counsel, 1960-63, v.p., gen. counsel, dir., 1963-66, exec. v.p., gen. counsel, dir., 1966-67, exec. v.p., gen. counsel, sec., dir., 1967-70, chmn. exec. com., 1970-73, vice-chmn. bd., 1974-75, chmn. bd., CEO, 1976-88; pres. Wash. Nat. Corp., 1970-83, CEO, 1978-88, chmn. bd., 1983-88; ret., 1988-98. Bd. dirs. Washington Nat. Corp. Pres.'s coun. Nat. Coll. Edn., 1977-88, adv. coun. Kellogg Grad. Sch. Mgmt. Northwestern U., 1981-88; bd. dirs. Evanston Hosp. Corp., 1983-88. Lt. (j.g.) USNR, 1942-46. Mem. Assn. Life Ins. Counsel, Am. Coun. Life Ins. (bd. dir. 1977-81, 84-88), Ill. Life Ins. Coun. (bd. dir. 1978-86, pres. 1983-85), Inc. Econs. Soc. Am. (bd. dir. 1977-85, chmn. 1981-82), Health Ins. Assn. Am. (bd. dirs. 1982-88, chmn. 1987-88). Insurance. Home: PO Box 2339 Carefree AZ 85377-2339 E-mail: carefreesh@aol.com

HUTH, WILLIAM EDWARD, lawyer; b. South Bend, Ind., July 26, 1931; s. Edward Andrew and Margaret Mary (Emonds) H.; m. Mary Pamela Hall, Aug. 11, 1962; children: Katharine Louise, Stephen Edward (dec.), Alan Edward. BS, U. Dayton, 1952; JD, Yale, 1957. Bar: N.Y. 1958, U.S. Dist. Ct. (so. dist.) N.Y. 1959, Mich. 1962, U.S. Dist. Ct. (ea. dist.) Mich. 1962, U.S. Supreme Ct. 1969, Pa. 1975, Conn. 1978. Assoc. Kelley, Drye, Newhall & Maginnes, N.Y.C., 1958-61; group counsel Chrysler Corp., Detroit, 1962-72; ptnr. Ziegler, Dykhouse, Wise & Huth, 1973-74; assoc. gen. counsel Westinghouse Electric Corp., Pitts., 1974-76; asst. sec., asst. gen. counsel Combustion Engring., Inc., Stamford, Conn., 1976-90; ptnr. Huth, Grinnell & Flaherty, 1991-2000. Adj. prof. law Wayne State U., Detroit, 1969-74, adj. prof. law Pace U. Sch. of Law, 1999—. Contbr. articles to profl. publs. 1st lt. AUS, 1952-54. Mem. ABA (antitrust sect., internat. law sect., bus. law sect.), Am. Soc. Internat. Law, Am. Arbitration Assn. (Blue Ribbon Panel Arbitrators and Mediators, mem. copr. coun. com.), Inter-Am. Bar Assn., Inter-Pacific Bar Assn., Internat. Bar Assn., Conn. Bar Assn. (chmn. corp. coun. sec. 1991-94), Assn. of Bar of City of N.Y., Westchester-Fairfield Corp. Counsel Assn. (pres. 1987, bd. dirs. 1984-88), U.S. C. of C. (mem. antitrust adv. coun.), Yale Club N.Y.C., The Army and Navy Club (Washington), Indian Harbor Yacht Club (Greenwich), Order of Coif. Roman Catholic. Antitrust, Contracts commercial, Private international. Home: 39 Balmaha Ct Fairfield CT 06432-1173 Office: PO Box 320298 357 Commerce Dr Fairfield CT 06432 E-mail: huthwe@ix.netcom.com

HUTSON, JEFFREY WOODWARD, lawyer; b. New London, Conn., July 19, 1941; s. John Jenkins and Kathryn Barbara (Himberg) Hutson; m. Susan Office, Nov. 25, 1967; children: Elizabeth Kathryn, Anne Louise. AB, U. Mich., 1963, LLB, 1966. Bar: Ohio 1966, Hawaii 1990. Assoc. Lane, Alton & Horst, Columbus, Ohio, 1966-74, ptnr., 1974—. Arbitrator commercial construction panel Am Arbitration Asn, 1976—. Trustee, vice-chair 6 Pence Sch, 1983—88; mem comt creeds and professionalism Ohio Supreme Ct, 1989—90; chair, bd dirs NW Counseling Servs, 1990—92; regional vpres Def Research Inst, 1991—93. Lt comdr USNR, 1967—71. Fellow: Am Col Trials Lawyers, Am Arbit Asn, Am Bar Found, Ohio State Bar Found, Columbus Bar Found; mem.: Ohio Bar Asn, Ohio Asn Civil Trial Attys, Columbus Bar Asn, Int Asn Def Counsel, Faculty Def Coun Trail Acad, Scioto Country Club, Athletic Club. Avocations: cycling, reading, music. Alternative dispute resolution, State civil litigation, Construction. Office: Lane Alton & Horst 175 S 3rd St Ste 700 Columbus OH 43215-5100

HUTSON, MELVIN ROBERT, lawyer; b. Decatur, Ala., Dec. 7, 1947; s. John Robert and Katie Louise (Waddell) H.; m. Margaret Ann Shaddix; children: Melvin, Rachael, Katie, Jamie. BS, U. Ala., 1968, JD, 1971. Bar: Ala. 1971, Ga. 1972, S.C. 1975, D.C. 1978. Atty. NLRB, Atlanta, 1971-73; ptnr. Thompson Mann & Hutson, Greenville, S.C., 1974-98, Melvin Hutson, PA, Greenville, 1998—. Bd. dirs. Primesco, Inc. Chmn. bd. dirs. World Cancer Rsch. Fund, London, 1994—; chmn. AGC Labor Lawyers Coun., 1989-90. Mem. ABA (mem. com. on devel. of law under nat. labor relations act 1977—, chmn. subcom. on labor mgmt. litigation). Labor. Home: 1307 N Main St Greenville SC 29609-4716 Office: 306 E North St Ste 230 Greenville SC 29602 E-mail: mel.hutson@scbar.org

HUTTER, ROBERT GRANT, lawyer, educator; b. Cleve., May 7, 1948; s. Russell G. and Tresa V. (Ireland) H. B.S.Ch.E., Va. Poly. Inst., 1969; J.D., U. Md., 1973; M.B.A., St. Bonaventure U., 1978. Bar: N.Y. 1980, U.S. Dist. Ct. N.Y. Chem. engr. Westinghouse, Balt., 1969-73; prof. law Alfred U., N.Y., 1974— ; ptnr. Sootheran & Hutter, Andover, N.Y., 1981— . Contbr. numerous articles and book revs. to profl. publs. Mem. N.Y. State Bar Assn., Allegany County Bar Assn. (chmn. real estate law com. 1983—). Probate, Real property. Home: RR 1 Box 81H Wellsville NY 14895-9801 Office: 15 Main St Andover NY 14806

HWANG, ROLAND, lawyer; b. Detroit, May 17, 1949; s. David Nien-Tzu and Rose (Hsi) H.; m. Christina Grace Sieh, Aug. 19, 1983. BSME, U. Mich., 1971, MBA, 1976; JD, Wayne State U., 1980, LLM, 1984. Bar: Mich. 1981, U.S. Dist. Ct. (we. dist.) Mich. 1981. Substitute tchr. Livonia (Mich.) Pub. Schs., 1971-72; customer service rep. Manpower, Inc., Detroit, 1971; product engr. Ford Motor Co., Dearborn, Mich., 1972-81, staff atty., 1981-88; asst. atty. gen. State of Mich., Lansing, 1988—. Mem. adv. com. Madonna Coll. Legal Assistance Tng. Program, Livonia, 1982-88. Contbr. articles, reports to profl. jours. Chmn. Gov.'s Adv. Commn. on Asian Am. Affairs, Lansing, Mich., 1986-90; mem. state adv. bd. U.S. Commn. on Civil Rights, 1988—, chair 1997-98. Fellow State Bar Mich. Found.; mem. State Bar Mich. (civil liberties com. 1986-91, a community orgn. recognizing diversity 1991—), Am. Mgmt. Assn., Am. Citizens for Justice (treas. 1983, sec. 1985-86, pres. 1992), Soc. Automotive Engrs., Assn. Chinese Ams. Detroit (pres. 1982), Asian Am. Bar Assn. Mich. (co-founder 1986, pres. 1986-87), Internat. Inst. of Metro Detroit Inc. (bd. dirs. 1990-97, 2000—, pres. 1995-96, 2000-2001), Econ. Club (Detroit), Phi Alpha Delta. Methodist. Avocations: rafting, travel, aerobics, squash, reading. Oil, gas, and mineral, Environmental, Real property. E-mail: hwagnr@ag.state.mi.us

HYAMS, HAROLD, lawyer; b. Bklyn., May 19, 1943; s. Frank Charles and Celia (Silverstein) H.; m. Simone Elkeharrat, Nov. 18, 1973; children: Gabriel, Galite, Emilie, Jonathan. BA, U. Vt., 1965; MA in Latin Am. Studies, Georgetown U., 1966; JD, Syracuse U., 1970. Bar: N.Y. 1971, Ariz. 1974, U.S. Dist. Ct. Ariz. 1974, U.S. Ct. Appeals (9th cir.) 1974. Asst. to the gen. counsel Am. Express Co., N.Y.C., 1970-72; atty. Legal Aid Soc., Bklyn., 1973; ptnr. Harold Hyams and Assocs., Tucson, 1974—. Mem. panel of arbitrators Am. Arbitration Assn., N.Y.C., 1971-73. Mem. Commn. on Ariz. Environ., 1988. Mem. Am. Bd. Trial Advs., Ariz. Trial Lawyers Assn., Pima County Bar Assn., Assn. Trial Lawyers Am. (adv. bd. trial advocates 1990, cert. specialist in personal injury and wrongful death 1991). Avocation: travel. Federal civil litigation, Personal injury. Home: 3175 N Elena Maria Tucson AZ 85750-2915 Office: 680 S Craycroft Rd Tucson AZ 85711-7197

HYBL, WILLIAM JOSEPH, lawyer, foundation executive; b. Des Moines, July 16, 1942; s. Joseph A. and Geraldine (Evans) H.; m. Kathleen Horrigan, June 6, 1967; children: William J. Jr., Kyle Horrigan. BA, Colo. Coll., 1964; JD, U. Colo., 1967. Bar: Colo. 1967. Asst. dist. atty. 4th Jud. Dist. El Paso and Teller Counties, 1970-72; pres., dir. Garden City Co., 1973—; dir. Broadmoor Hotel, Inc., 1973—, also vice-chmn., 1987—; chmn., CEO, trustee El Pomar Found., Colorado Springs, Colo., 1973—; pres. U.S. Olympic Com., 1991-92,96-2000. Vice chair USAA, San Antonio; dir. Kinder Morgan Inc., Houston, FirstBank Holding Co. of Colo., Lakewood; mem. Colo. Ho. Reps., 1972-73; spl. counsel The White House, Washington, 1981. Pres. Air Force Acad. Found.; sec., dir. Nat. Jr. Achievement; vice chmn. bd. U.S. Adv. Commn. on Pub. Diplomacy, 1990-97; civilian aide to sec. of army, 1986—. Capt. U.S. Army, 1967-69. Republican. Real property.

HYDE, HOWARD LAURENCE, lawyer; b. Boston, Sept. 4, 1957; s. Morris Morton and Evelyn Lee (Weinstein) H.; m. Nancy J. Paulu, May 18, 1985; children: Emma Catherine, Benjamin Tuttle. AB, Dartmouth Coll., 1979; JD, Harvard U., 1982. Bar: Mass. 1983, D.C. 1987, U.S. Dist. Ct. Mass. 1984, U.S. Ct. Appeals (1st cir.) 1984. Jud. clk. Minn. Supreme Ct., St. Paul, 1982-83; assoc. Gaston Snow & Ely Bartlett, Boston, 1983-86, Arnold & Porter, Washington, 1986-91, spl. counsel, 1992—. Mem. ABA (Bus. law sect.). Avocations: fly fishing, canoeing. Banking, General corporate, Securities. Office: Arnold & Porter 555 12th St NW Washington DC 20004-1206 E-mail: Howard_Hyde@aporter.com

HYMAN, MICHAEL BRUCE, lawyer; b. Elgin, Ill., July 26, 1952; s. Robert I. and Ruth (Cohen) H.; m. Leslie Bland, Aug. 14, 1977; children: Rachel Joy, David Adam. BSJ with honors, Northwestern U., 1974, JD, 1977. Bar: Ill. 1977, U.S. Supreme Ct. 1989. Asst. atty. gen. Antitrust div. State of Ill., Chgo., 1977-79; trial atty. Much Shelist Freed Denenberg Ament & Rubenstein, 1979-85, ptnr., 1985—. Chmn. panelist various continuing legal edn. seminars. Columnist Editor's Briefcase, CBA Record, 1988-90, 93—, The Red Pencil, 1986-89; contbr. chpt. to book, articles to profl. jours.; host (cable TV program) You and the Law, 1995—. Trustee North Shore Congregation Israel, Glencoe, 1980-89, 95-2001, v.p., 1987-89. Mem. ABA (mem. sect. litigation, chmn. antitrust litigation com. 1987-90, editor-in-chief Litigation News 1990-92, mng. editor 1989-90, assoc. editor 1985-89, chmn. monographs and unpub. papers com. 1992-95, task force on civil justice reform 1991-93, editor-in-chief Litigation Docket, 1995-2001, Tips From the Trenches 2001-, mem. jud. divsn., lawyers conf., membership com. chair 1999—), Chgo. Bar Assn. (editor-in-chief CBA Record 1988-90, 93—, CBA News 1994-98, bd. mgrs. 1992-94, vice chair class action com. 1999-2000, chair 2000-01), Ill. Bar Assn. (rep. on assembly 1986-92, 94-99, 2001—, antitrust coun. 1981-87, chmn. coun. 1985-86, vice chair, sec., co-editor newsletter 1982-85, chmn. bench and bar sect. coun. 1990-91, bench and bar sect. coun. 1998—, professionalism com. 1992-95, chair 1993-94, vice chair ARDC com. 1995-96, chair ARDC com. 1996-97, mem. cable tv com. 1995—, chair 1997-99), Am. Soc. Writers on Legal Subjects (mem., chair book award com. 1997—), Decalogue Soc. Lawyers (trustee 2001—). Jewish. Avocations: writing, Abraham Lincoln. Antitrust, General civil litigation, Consumer commercial. Office: Much Shelist Freed Denenberg Ament & Rubenstein 200 N La Salle St Ste 2100 Chicago IL 60601-1026 E-mail: mbhyman@muchlaw.com

HYMAN, MONTAGUE ALLAN, lawyer, educator; b. N.Y.C., Apr. 19, 1941; s. Allan Richard and Lilyan P. (Pollock) H.; m. susann Podell, Jan. 25, 1965; children: Jeffrie-Anne, Erik. BA, Syracuse U., 1962; JD, St. Johns U., 1965. Bar: N.Y. 1965, U.S. Dist. Ct. (so. and ea. dists.) N.Y. 1967, U.S. Ct. Appeals (2d cir.) 1982, U.S. Supreme Ct. 1973. Assoc. Warburton, Hyman, Deeley & Connelly, Mineola, N.Y., 1965-67; ptnr. Hyman & Deeley, 1967-69, Koeppel, Hyman, Sommer, Lesnick & Ross, Mineola, 1969-72, Hyman & Hyman, P.C., Garden City, 1972-80, Costigan, Hyman, Hyman & Herman, P.C., Mineola, 1980-87, Certilman, Haft, Balin, Buckley, Adler & Hyman, Mineola, 1988—, Certilman Balin Adler & Hyman, 1988—. Lectr. Hofstra U., Adelphi U., Columbia Appraisal Soc., Practicing Law Inst. Contbr. articles to profl. jours. Bd. trustees North Shore L.I. Jewish Health System. Mem. Nassau County Bar Assn., N.Y. State Bar Assn., Inst. Property Taxation. Federal civil litigation, Real property, State and local taxation. Office: Certilman Balin Adler & Hyman LLP 90 Merrick Ave East Meadow NY 11554-1571 E-mail: ahymaw@cbah.com

HYMAN, ROGER DAVID, lawyer; b. Oak Ridge, Tenn., Apr. 23, 1957; s. Marshall Leonard and Vera Lorraine (McKinney) H.; m. Elsa Laurencio; children: Cristina Alicia, James Marshall. BA, Vanderbilt U., 1979; JD, U. Tenn., 1984. Clk. Oak Ridge Nat. Lab., 1977-78, 81; air personality, news reporter Stas. WKDA, WKDF, Nashville, 1979; program dir. Sta. WBIR-FM, Knoxville, Tenn., 1979-80; assoc. atty. Hindman & Holt, Attys., 1984-85; asst. atty. gen. State of Tenn., 1986-95; with Law Offices of Roger D. Hyman Powell, Tenn., 1995-97; ptnr. Hyman & Carter, Attys., 1997—. Bd. dirs. Knoxville Christian Sch., 1991-93. Democrat. Mem. Ch. of Christ. Home: 2713 Windemere Ln Powell TN 37849-3782 Office: Hyman & Carter PO Box 1304 Powell TN 37849-1304 E-mail: RDHymanLAW@aol.com

HYMEL, L(EZIN) J(OSEPH), lawyer, former prosecutor; b. Baton Rouge, July 2, 1944; s. Lezin Joseph Sr. and Alma K. Hymel; m. Linda N., Oct. 6, 1973; children: Traci Lyn, Shea Roach Bonaventure, Kimberly Kaye. BS in Geology, La. State U., 1966, JD, 1969. Bar: La., U.S. Dist. Ct. (ea. dist.) La., U.S. Dist. Ct. (mid. dist.) La., U.S. Dist. Ct. (we. dist.) La., U.S. Ct. Appeals (5th cir.). Pvt. practice, Baton Rouge, 1969-70; staff atty. Office State Atty. Gen., 1970-71, asst. atty. gen., 1972-78, dir. criminal divsn., 1992-93; asst. dist. atty. Office 19 Jud. Dist. Atty., 1978-79; city judge Baton Rouge City Ct., 1980-83; state dist. ct. judge criminal divsn. 19th Jud. Dist. Ct, Baton Rouge, 1983-90, state dist. ct. judge civil divsn., 1991-92; U.S. atty. Office U.S. Atty., Dept. Justice, 1994-2001; ptnr. Sharp Henry Cerniglia Calvin Weaver & Hymel, 2001—. Office: Sharp Henry Cerniglia et al Ste C 15171 So Harrells Ferry Rd Baton Rouge LA 70816 Fax: (225) 755-1065. E-mail: ljhymel@sharphenry.com

HYNES, PATRICIA MARY, lawyer; b. N.Y.C., Jan. 26, 1942; BA, CUNY, 1963; LLB, Fordham U., 1966. Bar: N.Y. 1966, U.S. Dist. Ct. (so. and ea. dists.) N.Y. 1969, U.S. Ct. Appeals (2d cir.) 1982. Law clk. Hon. Joseph C. Zavatt U.S. Dist. Ct. (ea. dist.) N.Y., 1966-67; asst. U.S. atty. U.S. Dist. Ct. (so. dist.) N.Y., 1967-82, exec. asst. U.S. atty., 1980-82, chief ofcl. corruption and spl. pros. unit, 1978-80, chief consumer fraud unit, 1971-78, mem. civil divsn., 1967-71; ptnr. Milberg Weiss Bershad Hynes & Lerach LLP, N.Y.C., 1983-99, of counsel, 2000—. Adj. prof. law Fordham U., 1978—83; lectr. trial advocacy Harvard U. Law Sch., 1983; lectr. Practising Law Inst.; mem. criminal justice act peer rev. panel U.S. Dist. Ct. (so. dist.) N.Y., 1982—83, mem. discovery com., 1982—84, mem. civil litig. com., 1983—84, mem. merit selection panel for N.Y. magistrate judges, 1994—. Mem. Fordham Law Rev., 1964-66; mem. editl. bd. N.Y. Law Jour., 1994—. Mem. Gov.'s Exec. Adv. Com. on Adminstrn. Criminal Justice, 1981-82, N.Y. Gov.'s Commn. on Govt. Integrity, 1987-90; mem. Mayor's Adv. Com. on Jud., 1994—; chairperson N.Y. Regional Consumer Protection Coun., 1971-72. Named one of 50 Top Women Lawyers Nat. Law Jour., 1998. Fellow Am. Coll. Trial Lawyers; mem. ABA (standing com. on fed. jud. 1995-2000, chair, 2000-2001, coun. litig. sect. 1989-92, chair pre-trial practice and discovery com. 1992-94, chair govt. litig. com. litig. sect. 1984-87, chair securities litig. com. 1987-89, criminal justice sect.), Am. Law Inst. (spl. adviser 1995—), Fordham Law Alumni Assn., Assn. of the Bar of the City of N.Y. (del. to ABA, ho. dels. 1990-94, chair fed. cts. com. 1992-95, sec. 1982-84, exec. com. 1984-88, second century com. 1988-92, criminal law com. 1980-84, police law and policy com. 1981-83, consumer affairs com. 1971-78), N.Y. State Bar Assn. (del., ho. dels. 1983-84), Fed. Bar Coun. (v.p. 1990, 96—, treas. 1987-90, trustee 1983-91), N.Y. Coun. Def. Lawyers. Federal civil litigation, General civil litigation, Securities. Office: Milberg Weiss Bershad Hynes & Lerach LLP One Penn Plz New York NY 10119

HYSLOP, RICHARD STEWART, law educator; b. Kitchener, Ont., Can., May 23, 1944; s. Stewart Lees and Joyce Elaine (Slater) H. B.A., Calif. State U., Fullerton, 1966; M.A., U. Calif. Irvine, 1967; J.D., UCLA,1970. Bar: Calif. 1971, U.S. Dist. Ct. (cen. dist.) Calif. 1971, U.S. Supreme Ct. 1982, U.S. Ct Appeals (9th cir.) 1982, U.S. Tax Ct. 1982. Mem. faculty Calif. State Poly. U. Pomona, 1970—, assoc. prof. govt. and Am. studies, 1975-79, prof., 1979—, assoc. v.p. acad. affairs, 1978-79, coordinator Am. Studies, 1975—; assoc. Friedemann & Menke Orange, Calif., 1973-78, 81-84; cons. Nat. Multilingual Multicultural Materials Devel. Ctr., Pomona, 1977-80, law sch. admissions test Am. Testing Service, Princeton, 1981-83. arbitrator Am. Arbitration Assn., Los Angeles, 1976—. Author: (with Crane Miller) California: Geography of Diversity, 1983: (with others). Essays in American History and Culture, 1983. Recipient Disting. Tchr. award Calif. State Poly. U., 1974. Mem. Am. Culture Assn., Western Social Scis. Assn., Can. Studies in U.S., Western Can. Studies Group, Pi Gamma Mu. Home: 1147 Picaacho Dr La Habra CA 90631-8031 : is 3801 W Temple Ave Pomona CA 91768

HYUN, JUNG-WEN, lawyer; b. Seoul; Student, Seoul Nat. U., 1989-90; BA, Columbia U., 1993, JD, 1997. Bar: N.Y. 1998. Assoc. Morison & Foerster LLP, N.Y.C., 1998—. General corporate, Mergers and acquisitions, Securities. Office: Morrison & Foerster LLP 1290 Ave of Americas New York NY 10104

IAMELE, RICHARD THOMAS, law librarian; b. Newark, Jan. 29, 1942; s. Armando Anthony and Evelyn Iamele; m. Marilyn Ann Berutto, Aug. 21, 1965; children: Thomas, Ann Marie. BA, Loyola U., L.A., 1963; MSLS, U. So. Calif., 1967; JD, Southwestern U., L.A., 1976. Bar: Calif. 1977. Cataloger U. So. Calif., L.A., 1967-71; asst. cataloger L.A. County Law Libr., 1971-77, asst. ref. libr., 1977-78, asst. libr., 1978-80, libr. dir., 1980—. Law librarian; b. Newark, Jan. 29, 1942; s. Armando Anthony and Evelyn Iamele; m. Marilyn Ann Berutto, Aug. 21, 1965; children: Thomas, Ann Marie. BA, Loyola U., L.A., 1963; MSLS, U. So. Calif., 1967; JD, Southwestern U., L.A., 1976. Bar: Calif. 1977. Cataloger U. So. Calif., L.A., 1967-71; asst. cataloger L.A. County Law Libr., 1971-77, asst. ref. libr., 1977-78, asst. libr., 1978-80, libr. dir., 1980—. Mem. ABA, Am. Assn. Law Librs., Calif. Libr. Assn., So. Calif. Assn. Law Librs., Coun. Calif. County Law Librs. (pres. 1981-82, 88-90). Office: LA County Law Libr 301 W 1st St Los Angeles CA 90012-3140 E-mail: richard@lalaw.lib.ca.us

IANNUZZI, JOHN NICHOLAS, lawyer, author, educator; b. N.Y.C., May 31, 1935; s. Nicholas Peter and Grace Margaret (Russo) I.; m. Carmen Marina Barrios, Aug. 1979; children: Dana Alejandra, Christina Maria, Nicholas Peter II, Alessandro Luca; children from previous marriage: Andrea Marguerite, Maria Teresa. BS, Fordham U., 1956; JD, N.Y. Law Sch., 1962. Bar: N.Y., U.S. Dist. Ct. (so. and ea. dists.) N.Y. 1964, U.S. Dist. Ct. (no. and we. dists.) N.Y. 1965, U.S. Ct. Appeals (2d cir.) 1965, U.S. Supreme Ct. 1971, U.S. Dist. Ct. Conn. 1978, U.S. Tax Ct. 1978, U.S. Ct. Appeals (5th and 11th cirs.) 1982, U.S. Ct. Appeals (4th cir.) 1988, Wyo. 1994. Assoc. Law Offices of H.H. Lipsig, N.Y.C., 1962, Law Offices of Aaron J. Broder, N.Y.C., 1963; ptnr. Iannuzzi & Iannuzzi, 1963—. Adj. prof. trial advocacy Fordham U. Law Sch. Author: (fiction) What's Happening, 1963, Part 35, 1970, Sicilian Defense, 1974, Courthouse, 1977, J.T., 1984, (non-fiction) Cross-Examination: The Mosaic Art, 1984, Trial Strategy and Psychology, 1992, Handbook of Cross-Examination, 1999, Handbook of Trial Strategy, 2000. Mem. ABA, N.Y. County Bar Assn., N.Y. Criminal Bar Assn., Columbian Lawyers Assn., Lipizzan Internat. Fedn. (v.p.). Roman Catholic. Federal civil litigation, State civil litigation, Civil rights. Home: 118 Via Settembre 9 Rome Italy Office: Iannuzzi & Iannuzzi 74 Trinity Place New York NY 10006 also: 775 Park Ave Huntington NY 11743-3976 also: 345 Franklin St San Francisco CA 94102-4427 also: 1592 Pine Ave W Montreal PQ Canada also: 120 Adelaide St W Toronto ON Canada H3B 3G3 E-mail: jni@iannuzzi.net

IATESTA, JOHN MICHAEL, lawyer; b. Orange, N.J., Dec. 29, 1944; s. Thomas Anthony and Marie Monica I.; m. Paulina Clare Pascuzzi, July 11, 1971. BS magna cum laude, Seton Hall U., 1967, JD cum laude, 1976; MS, Fordham U., 1968; LLM in Corp. Law, NYU, 1986. Bar: N.J. 1976, U.S. Dist. Ct. N.J. 1976, U.S. Ct. Appeals (3d cir.) 1981, N.Y. 1982, U.S. Supreme Ct. 1985. Law sec. to presiding judge appellate div. Superior Ct. N.J., Trenton, 1976-77; assoc. Wilentz, Goldman & Spitzer, Woodbridge, N.J., 1977-81, D'Alessandro, Sussman & Jacovino, Florham Park, 1981-83; corp. counsel, 1983—, Rhodia Inc., Cranbury, N.J. Recipient Book prize Tchrs. Coll. Columbia U., 1967. Mem. ABA, N.J. Bar Assn., Am. Corp. Counsel Assn., Order of the Cross & Crescent, Delta Epsilon Sigma, Kappa Delta Pi. General corporate, Finance, Real property. Office: Rhodia Inc 259 Prospect Plains Rd Cranbury NJ 08512 E-mail: john.iatesta@us.rhodia.com

IDEMAN, JAMES M. federal judge; b. Rockford, Ill., Apr. 2, 1931; s. Joseph and Natalie Ideman; m. Gertraud Erika Ideman, June 1, 1971. BA, The Citadel, 1953; JD, U. So. Calif., 1963. Bar: Calif. 1964, U.S. Dist. Ct. (cen. dist.) Calif. 1964, U.S. Ct. Mil. Appeals 1967, U.S. Supreme Ct. 1967. Dep. dist. atty. Los Angeles County, 1964-79; judge Los Angeles County Superior Ct., 1979-84; appointed judge U.S. Dist. Ct. (cen. dist.) Calif., L.A., 1984-98, sr. judge, 1998. Served to 1st lt. U.S. Army, 1953-56, col. AUS Ret. Republican.*

IDING, ALLAN EARL, lawyer; b. Milw., Apr. 29, 1939; s. Earl Herman and Erna Adeline (Albrecht) I.; m. Anne Louise Chaconas, July 9, 1961; children: Kent Earl, Krista Anne Templeman, Bradford A., Andrea Beth Brozynski. BS, Marquette U., 1961, LLB, 1963; DHL (hon.), Nashotah (Wis.) House, 1990. Bar: Wis. 1963, U.S. Dist. Ct. (ea. dist.) Wis. 1963, U.S. Ct. Appeals (7th cir.) 1963. Law clk. U.S. Ct. Appeals (7th cir.), Chgo., 1963-64; assoc. Whyte Hirschboeck Dudek, S.C., Milw., 1964-71, mem., 1971—. Bd. dirs. Elicar Corp. Trustee Nashotah House, 1976—; pres., bd. dirs. Wis. DeMolay Found., Milw., 1985—, Wis. Health and Ednl. Facilities Authority, 1978-85, Wis. Masonic Home, Inc.; v.-p., sec., bd. dirs. Wis. Masonic Home, Inc.; mem. Wauwatosa (Wis.) Police and Fire Commn., 1978-83. Mem. Blue Mound Golf and Country Club (sec., bd. dirs.), Milw. Athletic Club, Masons (grand master Wis. 1981-82). Republican. Episcopalian. Avocation: golf. General corporate, Estate planning, Probate. Home: 9212 Wilson Blvd Milwaukee WI 53226-1729 Office: Whyte & Hirschboeck Dudek SC Ste 2100 111 W Wisconsin Ave Milwaukee WI 53203-2501 E-mail: aiding@whdlaw.com

IEYOUB, RICHARD PHILLIP, state attorney general; b. Lake Charles, La., Aug. 11, 1944; s. Phillip Assad and Virginia Khoury I.; m. Caprice Brown, Feb. 3, 1995; children: Amy Claire, Nicole Anne, Brennan Jude, Richard Phillip Jr., Khoury Myhand, Christian Brown. BA in history, McNeese State U., 1968; JD, La. State U., 1972. Bar: La. 1972, U.S. Supreme Ct. Spl. prosecutor to atty. gen. State of La., Baton Rouge, 1972-74; assoc. Camp, Carmouche, Lake Charles, 1974-76; mem. Stockwell, Sievert, 1976-78, Baggett, McCall, Singleton, Ranier, Ieyoub, Lake Charles, from 1978; sole practice; dist. atty. Calcasieu Parish, 1985-92; atty. gen. State of La., 1992—. Instr. criminal law McNeese State U.; chmn. La. Drug Policy Bd., New Orleans Met. Crime Task Force; mem. La. Commn. on Law Enforcement, President's Commn. on Model State Drug Laws, 1992—; mem. bd. dirs. La. State U. Alumni Assn. Bd. dirs. S.W. La. Health Counseling Svcs., Crime Stoppers of Lake Charles, St. Jude Children's Rsch. Hosp., 1998-99; mem. Parish coun. Immaculate Conception Cathedral Parish, Lake Charles; vice chmn. La. coord. coun. on the prevention of drug abuse and treatment of drug use; mem. La. commn. on law enforcement; apptd. by gov. to adv. bd. La. D.A.R.E.; chmn. New Orleans Metropolitan Crime Task Force, Gov's. Military Adv. Commn. Named Outstanding Pub. Ofcl. for Diocese Lake Charles, 1990; recipient Disting. Alumnus award McNeese State U., 1994, Legis. Leadership award, Nat. Coun. Against Drinking and Driving, 1996, Ochsner Humanitarian award, 1998. Mem. ABA (vice chmn. prosecution function com.), Assn. Trial Lawyers Am., Nat. Assn. Criminal Def. Lawyers, La. Bar Assn. (lectr. criminal law), Nat. Dist. Attys. Assn. (pres., bd. dirs. 1990-91), Nat. Assn. Attys. Gen. (exec. working group on prosecutorial rels.), La. Dist. Attys. Assn. (pres., bd. dirs. 1989-90), Nat. Coll. Dist. Attys. (bd. regents 1991), S.W. La. Bar Assn. (exec. com. 1979), So. Attys. Gen. Assn. (elected chmn.), Sierra Club. Democrat. Roman Catholic. Office: Justice Dept PO Box 94005 Baton Rouge LA 70804-9005*

IGLESIAS, DAVID C. prosecutor; Graduate Wheaton Coll., JD U. NMex Sch. Law. Asst. atty. gen. N.Mex Atty. Gen. Office; asst. city atty. City of Albuquerque, 1991—94; Special Asst. to Sec. of Transp. White House Fellowship, 1995; Chief Counsel N.Mex Risk Mgmt. Legal Office, 1995—98; Gen. Counsel N.Mex Taxation and Revenue Dept., 1998—2001; Comdr. US Navel Reserve JAG Corps.; assoc. Walz and Assoc., Albuquerque; US Atty. Dist. of N.Mex, 2001—. Office: US Attorney PO Box 607 Albuquerque NM 87103 Fax: 505-346-7296*

IGO, LOUIS DANIEL, lawyer, educator; b. Boston, Sept. 21, 1939; s. L. Louis and Martha W. Igo; 1 child, John Daniel. B.S. in Econs. and Acctg., Mo. Valley Coll., 1963; postgrad. tax law U. Mo.-Kansas City, 1964-66; J.D., U. Tulsa, 1967; postgrad. Okla. Sch. Accountancy, 1967-68, U. So. Calif., 1979. Bar: Okla. 1968, U.S. Dist. Ct. (no. and so. dists.) Okla. 1968, U.S. Tax Ct. 1973, Calif. 1973, U.S. Dist. Ct. (cen. dist.) Calif. 1973, U.S. Ct. Mil. Appeals 1982, U.S. Ct. Appeals (9th cir.) 1982, U.S. Supreme Ct. 1973. pvt. practice, L.A., 1973—; prof. law and acctg. Los Angeles Community Coll. Dist., 1973—; farmer, 1991—; moderator, lectr. Instructional TV Show: Law for the Seventies, 1980; Mil. Magistrate, 1980-84; USNR Legal Assistance officer, 1976-92. With U.S. Army, 1964-68; comdr. JAGC USNR 1968-92. Cert. Scuba diver Nat. Assn. Underwater Instrs. Mem. ATLA, L.A. Consumer Lawyers Assn., Am. Arbitration Assn. (arbitrator), Calif. Trial Lawyers Assn., Naval Res. Assn., Res. Officers Assn., Alpha Phi Omega, Sigma Alpha Epsilon, Phi Alpha Delta. Episcopalian. Clubs: Skelton Congressional, Elks, Masons, Shriner, Navy Flying. Author scripts and syllabus for Law for the Seventies (Instructional TV award, 1976); revised The Time-Life Family Legal Guide, 1976; cons. editor Bus. Law West, 1984. State civil litigation, Estate planning, Family and matrimonial. Office: Los Angeles City Coll 855 N Vermont Ave Los Angeles CA 90029-3516

IKEDA, CNYTHIA YUKO, lawyer; b. San Francisco, Sept. 8, 1967; d. George and Miyako Ikeda. BA magna cum laude, UCLA, 1989; LLM, Keio U., Tokyo, 1993; JD, Yale U., 1996. Bar: N.Y. 1997. Assoc. Chadbourne & Parke LLP, N.Y.C., 1997-98, Morrison & Foerster LLP, N.Y.C., 1998—. Bd. dirs. N.Y. chpt. Japanese Am. Citizens League, 1997-98. Mem. ABA, N.Y. State Bar Assn., Assn. Am. Bar Assn., Assn. Am. Legal Def. and Edn. Fund, Assn. Bar City N.Y., Phi Beta Kappa. Avocations: piano, singing, Japanese classical dance. Contracts commercial, Intellectual property, Mergers and acquisitions.

IMBER, ANNABELLE CLINTON, state supreme court justice; b. Heber Springs, Ark., July 15, 1950; m. Ariel Barak Imber; 1 child, William Pierce Clinton. BA magna cum laude, Smith Coll., 1971; postgrad., Inst. for Paralegal Tng., 1971, U. Houston, 1973-75; JD, U. Ark., 1977. Atty. Wright, Lindsey & Jennings Law Firm, Little Rock, 1977-88; apptd. cir. judge (5th divsn.) Pulaski and Perry Counties, 1984, elected chancery and probate judge (6th divsn.), 1989-96; elected assoc. justice Ark. Supreme Ct., 1997—. Bd. dirs. Ark. Advs. for Children and Families, 1985-90, pres. 1986-88; bd. dirs Pulaski County Hist. Soc., 1992-95, Congregation B'Nai Israel, 1988-92, 2001-, Kiwanis Club 1995-98, YMCA of Greater Little Rock and Pulaski County, Our House-A Shelter for Homeless, 1992—, St. Vincent Devel. Found., 1989-93, UAMS Med. Ctr. Dept. Pastoral Care and Edn., 1996—. Mem. ABA, AAUW, Nat. Assn. Women Judges, Ark. Bar Assn., Ark. Women Exec., Assn. of Ark. Women Lawyers (pres. 1980-81, Judge of the Year award 1994), Pulaski County Bar Assn. (bd. dirs. 1982-84). Office: Ark Supreme Ct Justice Bldg 625 Marshall St Little Rock AR 72201-1054

IMMKE, KEITH HENRY, lawyer; b. Peoria, Ill., Jan. 18, 1953; s. Francis William and Pearl Lenora (Kime) I. BA, U. Ill., 1975; JD, So. Ill. U., 1978. Bar: Ill. 1978, U.S. Dist. Ct. (so. and ea. dist.) Ill. 1979. Assoc. Lawrence E. Johnson & Assocs., P.C., Champaign, Ill., 1979-87; staff atty. Dept. Ins. State Ill., Springfield, 1987-88; legal counsel Underground Storage Tank program (now Divsn. Petroleum and Chem. Safety), 1988-98; asst. legal counsel Office Fire Marshal State Ill., 1988—. Legal counsel Underground Storage Tank Program (now Div. Petroleum and Chem. Safety 1988-98), asst. legal counsel; Office Fire Marshal State Ill., 1998—. Mem. ABA, Ill. State Bar Assn., U. Ill. Alumni Assn., Phi Kappa Phi, Pi Sigma Alpha, Phi Alpha Delta. Environmental. Office: State Ill Office Fire Marshal Div Petroleum and Chem Safety 1035 Stevenson Dr Springfield IL 62703-4259

IMPERATO, JOSEPH JOHN, lawyer, composer; b. Jersey City, Mar. 14, 1956; s. Joseph Francis Imperato and Edith Roslyn (Dubin) Schwimmer. Student, Oberlin Coll., 1974-76; BA, Fla. State U., 1978, JD, 1981. Bar: Fla. 1983. Trial atty., tng. instr. Office of Pub. Defender, Miami, Fla., 1982—. Lectr., mock trial coach Dade County sec. schs. and univs., Miami, 1993—. Composer musical scores Fox TV Network, 1992-94; composer comml. jingles, 1975— (Addy award 1976), original songs, 1974— (Billboard Mag. Songwriting award 1995); composer, producer original childrens' musicals, 1997—. Mem. ASCAP, Audio Engring. Soc. Office: Office of Pub Defender 1320 NW 14th St Miami FL 33125-1609 E-mail: imperato@sprynet.com

IMRE, CHRISTINA JOANNE, lawyer; b. Gary, Ind., Oct. 25, 1950; d. Joseph and Ruth Leone I.; m. Richard Long, Dec. 31, 1991. BA, Mt. St. Mary's Coll., L.A., 1972; MA, U. Notre Dame, 1974; JD, Loyola Law Sch., L.A., 1980. Bar: Calif. 1980, U.S. Ct. Appeals (ninth cir.) 1982, U.S. Dist. Ct. (ctrl. dist.) Calif. 1983, U.S. Dist. Ct. (no. dist.) Calif. 1988,U.S. Dist. Ct. (so. dist.) Calif. 1995. Assoc. Lascher & Lascher, Ventura, Calif., 1980-83, Law Office of Errol Berk, Ventura, 1983-84, Pachter, Gold & Schaffer, L.A., 1984-87; sr. atty. Kornblum & McBride, 1987-89; atty. Horvitz & Levy LLP, Encino, Calif., 1989—. Bd. govs. Calif. Continuing Edn. of Bar, Berkeley, Calif., 1996—; chair Calif. Continuing Edn. of Bar Joint Adv. Com., Berkeley, 1995; editorial bd. L.A. Lawyer Mag., L.A., 1996-99; cons. Handling Civil Appeals, Berkeley, 1996, Calif. Trial Practice, Berkeley, 1995; lectr. in field. Editor-in-chief: Loyola of Los Angeles International & Comparative Law Journal, 1979-80; monthly columnist CEB Civil Litigation Reporter; contbr. articles to profl. jours. and chpts. to books. Named one of 50 Most Powerful Women in L.A. Law, L.A. Business Journal, 1998; Loyola Law Sch. fellow, 1979-80, U. Notre Dame fellow, 1972-74. Mem. L.A. County Bar Assn., Defense Rsch. Inst., So. Calif. Defense Counsel Assn. Avocations: music, Shakespeare, history, philosophy. Appellate, State civil litigation, Insurance. Office: Crosby Heafey Roach & May 700 S Flower St 22nd Fl Los Angeles CA 90017 E-mail: CImre@chrm.com

INDURSKY, ARTHUR, lawyer; b. Bklyn., Jan. 1, 1943; s. David and Anne (Levine) I.; m. Deanne Fiedler, Mar. 26, 1967; 1 child, Blake. BBA, CCNY, 1964; JD, Bklyn. Law Sch., 1967. Bar: N.Y., 1968. Entertainment counsel Columbia Pictures, N.Y.C., 1969-72; mng. ptnr. Grubman Indursky & Schindler P.C., 1973—. Bd. dirs. Alliance Artists and Rec. Cos.; guest spkr. Can. Rec. Industry Seminar, 1986, Entertainment Law Soc., Bklyn. Law Sch., 1987, 92, Copyright Soc., 1988, Disting. Alumni Lecture Series Bklyn. Law Sch., 1989, Hofstra Law Sch., 1995. Bd. dirs. T.J. Martell Found. for Leukemia, Cancer and AIDS Rsch., 1993—. Recipient 1st Ann. Alumni Achievement award Bklyn. Law Sch., 1992, Outstanding Leadership award Meml. Sloan Kettering Cancer Ctr., 1994, City of Hope award, 1995, Jule Styne Humanitarian award Childrens Hearing Inst., 1998. Entertainment. Office: Grubman Indursky & Schindler PC 152 W 57th St New York NY 10019-3310

INGERSOLL, RICHARD KING, lawyer; b. Algoma, Wis., Aug. 13, 1944; s. Robert Clive and Bernice Eleanore (Koehn) I.; m. Caroline Soi-Keu Yee, Aug. 31, 1968; children: Kristin Paula Juk-Yee, Karin Eleanor Juk-Ling. BBA, U. Mich., 1966; JD, U. Calif.-Berkeley, Berkeley, 1969. Bar: Ill. 1969, Hawaii 1973. Asst. prof. U. Ill.-Champaign, Champaign, 1969-70; assoc. Sidley & Austin, Chgo., 1970-73; ptnr. Rush, Moore, Craven, Kim & Stricklin, Honolulu, 1973-88, Gelber, Gelber, Ingersoll Klevansky & Faris, Honolulu, 1989—. Speaker tax law seminars. Author various law materials. Mem. ABA (taxation, bus. and internat. law coms.), Waialae Country Club (sec.). General corporate, Private international, Corporate taxation. Home: 944 Waiholo St Honolulu HI 96821-1226 E-mail: ringersoll@ggikf.com

INGRAM, DENNY OUZTS, JR. lawyer, educator; b. Kirbyville, Tex., Mar. 23, 1929; s. Denny Ouzts and Grace Bertha (Smith) I.; m. Ann Elizabeth Rees, July 11, 1952; children: Scott Rees, Stuart Tillman. B.A., U. Tex., 1955, J.D. with honors, 1957. Bar: Tex. 1956, N.Mex. 1967, Utah 1968. Editor Kirbyville Banner, 1949-50; mem. Tex. Ho. of Reps., 1951-52; assoc. Graves, Dougherty, Gee and Hearon (and predecessors), Austin, Tex., 1957, 59-60, partner, 1961-66; asst. prof. law U. Tex., 1957-59, U. N.Mex., 1966-67; prof. U. Utah, 1968-77; ptnr. McGinnis, Lochridge, and Kilgore, Austin, 1977-90, of counsel, 1991—; prof. law Tex. Wesleyan U. Sch. Law, 1991—. Vis. prof. U. Calif., Davis, 1973-74, U. Tex., summers 1968, 75, U. San Diego, 1993; research fellow Southwestern Legal Found., lectr. in field Contbr. numerous articles to law revs., chpts. to books; assoc. note editor: Tex. Law Rev., 1956-57. Research dir. Utah Constn. Revision Com., 1969-71, 73-74. Served with U.S. Army, 1951-54. Fellow Am. Coll. Trust and Estate Counsel, Am. Coll. Tax Counsel, Tex. Bar Found.; mem. ABA, Am. Law Inst. (life), Tex. Bar Assn., Utah Bar Assn., N.Mex. Bar Assn., Chancellors, Order of Coif, Phi Delta Phi. Democrat. Episcopalian. Home: 4055 Hildring Dr E Fort Worth TX 76109-4712 Office: Tex Wesleyan U Sch Law 1515 Commerce St Fort Worth TX 76102-6572

INGRAM, GEORGE CONLEY, lawyer, judge; b. Dublin, Sept. 27, 1930; s. George Conley and Nancy Averett (Whitehurst) I.; m. Sylvia Williams, July 26, 1952; children: Sylvia Lark, Nancy Randolph, George Conley. A.B., Emory U., 1949, LL.B., 1951. Bar: Ga. 1952. City atty. City of Smyrna, Ga., 1958-64, City of Kennesaw, 1964; judge Cobb County Juvenile Ct., 1960-64, Superior Ct., Cobb Jud. Cir., 1964-68; justice Supreme Ct. Ga., 1973-77; spl. asst. atty. gen. State of Ga., 1979-86; ptnr. Alston & Bird, Atlanta, 1977-98; sr. judge State of Ga., 1998—. Staff, faculty Judge Advocate Gen. Sch. U.S. Army U. Va., 1952-54. Former trustee Scott Coll., Kennesaw Coll. Found., Emory U., Agnes U.; trustee Cobb Cmty. Found., The Eleventh Cirs. Hist. Soc. Inc., Tommy Nobbis Ctr. Found., Inc.; emeritus mem. Emory Law Sch. Coun.; past pres. Cobb County YMCA, Cobb Landmarks Soc.; former chmn. ofcl. bd. 1st Meth. Ch. of Marietta, trustee. 1st lt. JAGC, USAR, 1952-54. Recipient Emory U. medal and Disting. Svc. award Kennesaw Mountain Jaycees, 1961, Ga. Jaycees, 1961, Emory Law Sch. Alumni Assn., 1985; Disting. Citizen award City of Marietta, Ga., 1973; Len Gilbert Leadership award Cobb County C. of C., 1985; Cobb County Citizen of Yr. award, 1990; hon. life mem. Ga. PTA. Fellow Am. Bar Assn. Found., Am. Coll. Trial Lawyers, Internat. Soc. Barristers, Am. Acad. Appellate Lawyers, Marietta-Cobb Mus. Art; mem. ABA, Am. Law Inst., State Bar Ga. (Tradition of Excellence award 1987), Cobb and Atlanta Bar Assn., Lawyers Club of Atlanta, Old War Horse Lawyers Club, Cobb County C. of C. (Pub. Svc. award, 1970) Georgian Club (bd. mem., founding chmn.), Rotary (award for vocat. excellence 1999), Order of Coif (hon.), Phi Delta Phi, Omicron Delta Kappa. Methodist. Federal civil litigation, State civil litigation, General practice. Home: 540 Hickory Dr Marietta GA 30064-3602

INGRAM, KENNETH FRANK, retired state supreme court justice; b. Ashland, Ala., July 7, 1929; s. Earnest Frank and Alta Mary (Allen) I.; m. Judith Louise Brown, Sept. 3, 1954; children: Jennifer Lynn Ingram Malone, Kenneth Frank Jr. BS, Auburn U., 1951; LLB, Jones Law Sch., 1963. Bar: Ala. 1963, U.S. Dist. Ct. (no. dist.) Ala. 1965, U.S. Dist. Ct. (mid. dist.) Ala. 1966. City councilman City of Ashland, Ala., 1956-58; mem. Ho. of Reps., 1958-66; presiding judge 18th Jud. Cir. Ct., 1968-87; judge Ala. Ct. Civil Appeals, Montgomery, 1987-89, presiding judge, 1989-91; assoc. justice Ala. Supreme Ct., 1991-97. Mem., chmn. Ala. Jud. Inquiry Commn., 1979-87. Contbr. articles on jud. ethics to profl. pubs. With USMC, 1952-54. Mem. Ala. Bar Assn., Masons. Democrat. Methodist. Avocations: woodworking, metalcrafting, tennis, swimming. Home: 264 1st St N PO Box 729 Ashland AL 36251-0729

INGRAM, SAMUEL WILLIAM, JR. lawyer; b. Utica, N.Y., Mar. 20, 1933; s. Samuel William and Mary Elizabeth (Rosen) I.; m. Jane Austin Stokes, Sept. 30, 1961; children: Victoria, William BS, Vanderbilt U., 1954; LLB, Columbia U., 1960. Bar: N.Y. 1960. Assoc. Sullivan & Cromwell, N.Y.C., 1960-67; assoc. Shea Gallop Climenko & Gould, 1967-68; ptnr. Shea & Gould and predecessors, 1968-89, Ingram, Yuzek, Gainen, Carroll & Bertolotti LLP, N.Y.C., 1989—. Bd. dirs. Legal Aid Soc., N.Y.C., 1974-86, sec., 1978-86; trustee Green Mountain Valley Sch., Waitsfield, Vt., 1984-87. Served to 1st lt. USMC, 1954-57 Mem. ABA, N.Y. State Bar Assn., Assn. of Bar of City of N.Y. Avocations: athletic and outdoor activities. Real property. Home: 332 Long Ridge Rd Pound Ridge NY 10576-2005 Office: Ingram Yuzek Gainen Carroll & Bertolotti LLP 250 Park Ave Ste 600 New York NY 10177-0699 E-mail: singram@ingramllp.com

INGRAM, WILLIAM AUSTIN, federal judge; b. Jeffersonville, Ind., July 6, 1924; s. William Austin and Marion (Lane) I.; m. Barbara Brown Lender, Sept. 18, 1947; children: Mary Ingram Mac Calla, Claudia, Betsy Ingram Friebel. Student, Stanford U., 1947; LL.B., U. Louisville, 1950; LLD honoris causas, Santa Clara U., 1994. Assoc., Littler, Coakley, Lauritzen & Ferdon, San Francisco, 1951-55; dep. dist. atty. Santa Clara (Calif.) County, 1955-57; mem. firm Rankin, O'Neal, Luckhardt & Center, San Jose, Calif., 1957-69; judge Mcpl. Ct., Palo Alto-Mountain View, 1969-71, Calif. Superior Ct., 1971-76, U.S. Dist. Ct. (no. dist.) Calif., San Jose, 1976-88, chief judge, 1988-90; sr. judge, 1990—. Served with USMCR, 1943-46. Fellow Am. Coll. Trial Lawyers. Republican. Episcopalian. Office: US Dist Ct 280 S 1st St Rm 5198 San Jose CA 95113-3002

INKLEY, JOHN JAMES, JR. lawyer; b. St. Louis, Nov. 7, 1945; s. John James Sr. and Morjorie Jane (Kenna) I.; m. Catherine Ann Mattingly, Apr. 13, 1971; children: Caroline Marie, John James III. BSIE, St. Louis U., 1967, JD, 1970; LLM in Taxation, Washington U., St. Louis, 1976. Bar: Mo. 1970, U.S. Dist. Ct. (we. dist.) Mo. 1970, U.S. Dist. Ct. (ea. dist.) Mo. 1975, U.S. Tax Ct. 1975, U.S. Supreme Ct. 1975. Assoc. Padberg, Raack, McSweeney & Slater, St. Louis, 1970-73; ptnr. Summer, Hanlon, Summer, MacDonald & Nouss, 1973-81; city atty. City of Town and Country, Mo., 1979-84, spl. counsel, 1984-88; ptnr. Hanlon, Nouss, Inkley & Coughlin, St. Louis, 1981-83; ptnr., chmn. banking and real estate dept. Suelthaus & Kaplan, 1983-91; ptnr. Armstrong Teasdale LLP (and predecessor firm), 1991—; co-chmn. bus. svcs. group, 1993-2000; exec. com. St. Louis, 1994—. Mem. ABA, Mo. Bar Assn., Bar Assn. Met. St. Louis. Roman Catholic. Banking, General corporate, Real property. Home: 35 Muirfield Ln Saint Louis MO 63141-7382 Office: Armstrong Teasdale LLP 1 Metropolitan Sq Ste 2600 Saint Louis MO 63102-2740

INNES, KENNETH FREDERICK, III, lawyer; b. San Francisco, May 15, 1950; s. Kenneth F. Jr. and Jean I.; m. Patricia Ann Graboyes, May 12, 1973; children: Kenneth F. IV, Julia Christine. BA, San Francisco State U., 1972, JD, 1984. Bar: Calif. 1984, U.S. Dist. Ct. (no. dist.) Calif. 1987, U.S. Dist. Ct. (ea. dist.) Calif. 1988. Tchr. secondary schs., Red Bluff, Calif., 1973-74; postal clk. U.S. Postal Svc., Vallejo, 1977-84, postal insp. Denver, 1984-87; regional atty. U.S. Postal Inspection Svc., Memphis, 1987-90, fin. auditor, 1990-92, regional atty. San Francisco, 1992—. Capt. USMCR, 1974-77. Mem. ABA, Calif. Bar Assn., Mensa, Elks. Democrat. Roman Catholic. Home: 157 Heartwood Ct Vallejo CA 94591-5638 Office: US Postal Insp Svc PO Box 882528 San Francisco CA 94188-2528

INSEL, MICHAEL S. lawyer; b. N.Y.C., Apr. 19, 1947; s. Ralph David and Lillian Ruth (Solomon) I.; married; 1 child, Louis Leo. BA, Duke U., 1969; JD, NYU, 1973. Bar: N.Y. 1974, Fla. 1984. Assoc. Kelley Drye & Warren, N.Y.C., 1973-82, ptnr., 1982—; pres. French Am. Vintners LLC. Bd. dirs. Kobrand Corp., N.Y.C., Maison Louis Jadot, S.A., Beaune, France, L & L, S.A., Boe, France, Western Wine Svcs., Inc., North Bergen, N.J., Kobrand Found., N.Y.C., The Kopf Family Found., Inc., St. Francis Vineyards, Sonoma, Calif., Domaine Carneros, Napa, Calif., Goodwill Industries, Astoria, N.Y.; trustee Elsie del Fierro Charitable Trust, N.Y.C., 1985—, Barbara Bell Cumming Found., N.Y.C., 1991—. Mem. ABA, N.Y. State Bar Assn., Fla. Bar, Assn. Bar of City of N.Y. Avocations: sailing, golf, opera. Office: Kelley Drye & Warren 101 Park Ave Fl 30 New York NY 10178-0062

INTRILIGATOR, MARC STEVEN, lawyer; b. Oceanside, N.Y., July 14, 1952; s. Alan and Sally (Jacobs) I.; m. Roxann Kathleen Hoff, Aug. 28, 1977; children: Seth Adam, Joshua Ross, Daniel Benjamin. BA, SUNY, Binghamton, 1974; JD, Boston U., 1977. Bar: N.Y. 1978. Assoc. Dreyer and Traub, N.Y.C., 1977-83, assoc. ptnr., 1984-85, sr. ptnr., 1985-96; of counsel Fischbein Badillo Wagner Harding, 1996—. Projects editor: Boston U. law rev., 1976-77. Past pres. Croton Jewish Ctr., Highlands Country Club. Mem. ABA, Assn. Bar City N.Y., The Country Club at Lake MacGregor, Tau Epsilon Phi. Landlord-tenant, Real property. Office: Fischbein Badillo Wagner Harding 909 3rd Ave New York NY 10022-4731 E-mail: mintrili@fbwhlaw.com

INZETTA, MARK STEPHEN, lawyer; b. N.Y.C., Apr. 14, 1956; s. James William and Rose Delores (Cirnigliaro) I.; children: Michelle, Margot, Mallory. BBA summa cum laude, U. Cin., 1977; JD, U. Akron, 1980. Bar: Ohio 1980, U.S. Dist. Ct. (no. dist.) Ohio 1980. Legal intern City of Canton, Ohio, 1979-80; assoc. W.J. Ross Co., LPA, Canton, 1980-84; asst. gen. counsel Wendy's Internat. Inc., Columbus, Ohio, 1984—. Instr. real estate law Stark Tech. Coll., Canton, 1983. Case and comment editor: Akron Law Rev., 1979-80. Instr. religious edn. St. Peter's Cath. Ch.; bd. dirs. Brookside Village Civic Assn., 1985-87, treas., 1986-87; chmn. campaign Earle Wise Appellate Judge, North Canton, Ohio, 1982; legis. dir. Children's and Parents' Rights assn., 1996-97, chmn., 1997—, State of Ohio Child Support Guidelines Commn., 1995-97, 99-2001; State of Ohio Task Force on Family Law and Children, 1998-2001, treas. Recipient Am. Jurisprudence award Lawyers Coop. Pub. Co., 1978, Dir. of Yr. award North Canton Jaycees, 1982, Presdl. award of honor, 1984, Dist. Dir. award of honor Ohio Jaycees, 1984, Vol. of Yr. award Children's Rights Coun., 2001. Mem. ABA, Ohio Bar Assn., North Canton Jaycees (bd. dirs. 1981-82, v.p. 1982-83, pres. 1983-84), North Canton C. of C. (bd. dirs. 1983-84). Democrat. Roman Catholic. E-mail: mark. General corporate, Private international, Real property. Home: 295 Weatherburn Ct Powell OH 43065 Office: Wendy's Internat Inc 4288 W Dublin Granville Rd Dublin OH 43017-1442 E-mail: inzetta@wendys.com

IOPPOLO, FRANK S., JR. lawyer; b. Rockville Centre, N.Y., Nov. 13, 1966; s. Frank S. and Carmella L. (Marrone) I. BA, Wake Forest U., 1988; JD, Fordham U., 1991. Bar: Fla. 1991, U.S. Dist. Ct. (mid. dist.) Fla. 1991, D.C. 1992, N.Y. 1992, U.S. Dist. Ct. (so. dist.) Fla. 1992, U.S. Supreme Ct. 1995. Assoc. Baker & Hostetler, Orlando, Fla., 1991-96; shareholder Greenberg Traurig, 1996—. Bd. regents Leadership Fla., 1995-96, 97-98; chmn. bd. Orlando Marine Insts., Inc., 1995-97; bd. dirs. Assoc. Marine Insts., Inc., 1995-97; pres., chmn. bd. Bay Point of Bay Hill Property Owners Assn., Inc., Orlando, 1994-96; bd. dirs. Communities in Schs., Orange County, Fla., 1997-99. Mem. ABA, Fla. Bar Assn., Orange County Bar Assn., N.Y. State Bar Assn., D.C. Bar Assn., Wake Forest U. Alumni Assn. Ctrl. Fla. (pres. 1995-98), Seminole County, CofC (gen. counsel, 2001-). Avocations: sailing, snow and water skiing, reading, fishing, target shooting. General corporate, Private international, Securities. Office: Greenberg Traurig 111 N Orange Ave Fl 20 Orlando FL 32801-2316

IRBY, HOLT, lawyer; b. Dodge City, Kans., July 4, 1937; s. Jerry M. and Virgie (Lorean) I.; m. LaVerne Smith, May 27, 1956; children: Joseph, Kathy, Kay, Karon, James. BA, Tex. Tech. U., 1959; JD, U. Tex., 1962. Bar: Tex. 1962, U.S. Dist. Ct. (no. dist.) Tex. 1963. Asst. city atty. City of Lubbock, Tex., 1962-63; assoc. Hugh Anderson, Lubbock, 1963-66; gen. counsel, sec. Merc. Fin. Corp., Dallas, 1966-69; gen. counsel, v.p. Ward Food Restaurants, inc., 1969-71; pvt. practice, Garland, Tex., 1971—. Mem. lawyer referal com. State Bar Tex., 1977, 78. Mem. bd. deacons First Bapt. Ch., Garland, 1979-90, chmn., 1976-77; bd. dirs. Garland Assistance Program, 1980, Habitat for Humanity of Greater Garland, Inc., 1997—, Dallas Life Found., 1980-90, Toler Children's Cmty., 1983-85; bd. dirs. Garland Civic Theatre, 1986—, pres., 1990-91, 92-93, v.p., 1991-92; mem. Garland Drug Task Force, 1990; deacon South Garland Bapt. Ch., 1992—, chmn., 1993-94, 98-99. Mem. Tex. Trial Lawyers Assn., Tex. Assn. Bank Counsel, Tex. Bar Assn., Garland Bar Assn. (bd. dirs. 1986-96, sec. 1992-93, v.p. 1993-94, pres. 1995-96), Dallas Bar Assn., Praetor Legal Frat. (named outstanding mem. 1962), Lubbock Jaycees (dir. 1963-65), Kiwanis (dir. 1973-74). State civil litigation, Contracts commercial, General practice. Office: Bank of Am Tower 705 W Avenue B Ste 404 Garland TX 75040-6241

IRELAND, FAITH, state supreme court justice; b. Seattle, 1942; d. Carl and Janice Enyeart; m. Chuck Norem. BA, U. Wash.; JD, Willamette U., 1969; M in Taxation with honors, Golden Gate U. Past assoc. McCune, Godfrey and Emerick, Seattle; pvt. practice Pioneer Square, 1974; judge King County Superior Ct., 1984-98; justice Wash. Supreme Ct., 1998—. Past dean Washington Jud. Coll., past mem. Bd. Ct. Edn. Served on numerous civic and charitable bds.; past pro-bono atty. Georgetown Dental Clin.; past bd. dirs. Puget Sound Big Sisters, Inc.; founding mem. Wing Luke Asian Mus., 1967—, past pres., past bd. dirs.; bd. dirs. Youth and Fitness Found., 1998. Recipient Disting. Svc. award Nat. Leadership Inst. Jud. Edn., 1998; named Judge of Yr. Washington State Trial Lawyer's Assn., Man of Yr. for efforts in founding Wing Luke Asian Mus. Mem. Washington Women Lawyer's (founding mem., Pres.'s award, Vanguard award), Wash. State Trial Lawyer's Assn. (past chair bd. dirs), Superior Ct. Judges Assn. (past bd. dirs., pres. 1996-97, vice chair bd. dirs. jud. adminstrn. 1996-98), Rainer Valley Hist. Soc. (founding mem., life), Rotary (bd. dirs. Seattle No. 4 1998). Office: Washington Supreme Ct Temple Justice PO Box 40929 Olympia WA 98504-1174*

IRELAND, RODERICK L. state supreme court justice; m. Alice Alexander. Bachelor's degree, Lincoln U., 1966; Master's degree, Harvard U.; JD, Columbia U., 1969; PhD, Northeastern U., 1998. Assoc. justice Mass. Supreme Jud. Ct., 1997—. Judge Boston Juvenile Ct., 1977, 90, Mass. Appeals Ct., 1990-97. Mem. Eliot Congregational Ch. Office: Mass Supreme Jud Ct Pemberton Square 1300 New Courthouse Boston MA 02108-1701

IRENAS, JOSEPH ERON, judge, director; b. Newark, July 13, 1940; s. Zachary and Bessie (Shain) I.; m. Nancy Harriet Jacknow, 1962; children: Amy Ruth, Edward Eron. AB, Princeton U., 1962; JD cum laude, Harvard U., 1965; postgrad., NYU Sch. Law, 1967-70. Bar: N.J. 1965, N.Y. 1982. Law sec. to justice N.J. Supreme Ct., 1965-66; assoc. McCarter & English, Newark, 1966-71, ptnr., 1972-92; judge U.S. Dist. Ct. N.J., 1992—. Trustee Hamilton Investment Trust, Elizabeth, N.J., 1980-83; mem. N.J. Supreme Ct. Dist. Ethics Com., 1984-86, vice chmn., 1986; adj. prof. law Rutgers Sch. Law, Camden, 1985-86, 88-97, 99—, N.J. Bd. Bar Examiners, 1986-88. Contbr. articles to legal jours. Chmn. bd. trustees United Hosps. of Newark, 1982-83; trustee United Hosps. Found., 1985-92, United Way Essex County, 1988-92, treas., 1990-92. Fellow Royal Chartered Inst. Arbitrators (London), Am. Bar Found.; mem. ABA, Am. Law Inst., N.J. Bar Assn., Camden County Bar Assn., Nassau Club, Harbor League Club, Union League Club. Republican. Jewish. Office: Mitchell H Cohen US Courthouse One John F Gerry Plaza PO Box 2097 Camden NJ 08101-2097

IRISH, LEON EUGENE, lawyer, educator, non-profit executive; b. Superior, Wis., June 19, 1938; s. Edward Eugene and Phyllis Ione (Johnson) I.; m. Karla W. Simon; children: Stephen T., Jessica L., Thomas A., Emily A. B.A. in History, Stanford U., 1960; J.D., U. Mich., 1964; D.Phil in Law, Oxford (Eng.) U., 1973. Law clk. to Assoc. Justice U.S. Supreme Ct. Byron R. White, 1967; cons. Office Fgn. Direct Investments, Dept. Commerce, 1967-68; spl. rep. sec. def. 7th session 3d UN Conf. Law of Sea; mem. Caplin & Drysdale, chartered, Washington, 1968-85; prof. law U. Mich. Law Sch., Ann Arbor, 1985-88; ptnr. Jones, Day, Reavis & Pogue, Washington, 1988-93; v.p., sr. counsel Aetna Life and Casualty Co., Hartford, Conn., 1993-95; pres., chmn. Internat. Ctr. Not-for-Profit Law, Washington, 1992—; pres., CEO United Way Internat., Alexandria, Va., 1996; sr. legal cons. World Bank NGO Law, 1997—. Adj. prof. Georgetown U. Law Ctr., 1975-85; regent Am. Coll. Tax Counsel, 1986-89; mem. IRS Commr.'s Adv. Group, 1987; bd. dirs. Vols. Tech. Assistance, Found. for Devel. of Polish Agr.; vis. fellow World Bank, 1995-96. Contbr. articles to legal jours. Bd. dirs., sec. Ctr. Comm., Health and Environ. Mem. ABA, D.C. Bar Assn., Am. Law Inst., Am. Coll. Tax Counsel, Coun. on Fgn. Rels. Democrat. Episcopalian. Labor, Public international, Non-profit and tax-exempt organizations. Home: 304 Kyle Rd Crownsville MD 21032 E-mail: lirish@icnl.org

IRTZ, FREDERICK G., II, lawyer; b. Ft. Knox, Ky., Aug. 23, 1944; married; children: Kimberly, Fred III, Andrew. BS in Commerce, Eastern Ky. U., 1968; JD, U. Louisville, 1973. Bar: Ky. 1973, U.S. Dist. Ct. (we. dist.) Ky. 1974, U.S. Ct. Appeals (6th cir.) 1974, U.S. Tax Ct. 1975, U.S. Supreme Ct. 1977, U.S. Dist. Ct. (ea. dist.) Ky. 1979, Calif. 1981, U.S. Ct. Claims 1998. Atty IRS, Louisville, 1974-78; sole practice Lexington, Ky., 1978—. Speaker U. Ky. Estate Planning Seminar, Ky. Bar Assn., U. Ky. Agrl. Law Seminar, No. Ky. Soc. CPAs, Louisville Estate Planning Coun., Lexington Soc. MBAs, Fayette County Bar Assn. Chmn. Dist. Internat. Youth Exch., 1985, legal staff Oleika Temple, atty., chmn. budget com.; pres. Oleika Brass Band, 1982; bd. dirs. Ctrl. Ky. Youth Orchs. Lt. Col. U.S. Army Reserve ret. 1994. Decorated Bronze Star; named one of Outstanding Young Men Am., 1977; recipient service award 4-H, 1987. Mem. Bluegrass Estate Planning Council (pres. 1978, speaker 1978, 83), ABA taxation, real property, and probate sect.), Ky. Bar Assn. (taxation sect., chair 1995-96), Fayette County Bar Assn. Lodge: Lions (pres. Bluegrass Breakfast club 1981-82, Lion of Yr. 1984). Home and Office: PO Box 22777 Lexington KY 40522-2777 Fax: 859-252-3692

IRVIN, CHARLES LESLIE, lawyer; b. Corpus Christi, Tex., Mar. 2, 1935; s. Joseph and Louise (Frelon) I.; m. Shirley Jean Smith, Feb. 8, 1964; children— Kimberley Antoinette, Jonathan Charles. B.A., Tex. So. U., 1961, LL.B., 1964. Bar: Tex. 1964, U.S. Dist. Ct. (so. dist.) Tex. 1973, U.S. Dist. Ct. (ea. dist.) Tex. 1973, U.S. Supreme Ct. 1971, U.S. Ct. Appeals (9th cir.) 1982. Atty. U.S. Dept. Labor, Kansas City, Mo., 1964-67, Chgo., 1964-73; atty. Texaco, Inc., Chgo., 1973-74, Houston, 1974-79, Harrison, N.Y., 1979-81, sr. atty., Houston, 1981-88; divsn. atty., Midland, Tex., 1988, Denver, 1989-93, regional atty., mng. atty. adminstrn., Harrison, 1993-94, pvt. practice, Conroe, Tex., 1994—. Sgt. U.S. Army, 1955-58. Mem. Tex. Bar Assn., Tex. Bar Found., Houston Lawyers Assn. Congregationalist. Oil, gas, and mineral, Family and matrimonial, Labor. Home: 314 Cochran St Conroe TX 77301-2559

IRVIN, ROBERT JULIAN, lawyer; b. Balt., Oct. 1, 1948; s. Julian Rowe and Gloria Virginia (Johnson) I.; m. Norma Ann Walsh, May 9, 1981; children— Catharine Leigh. B.A., U. Fla., 1970; J.D., U. Va., 1974. Bar: Fla. 1974. Assoc. Mahoney Hadlow & Adams, Miami and Jacksonville, Fla., 1974-76; assoc. Steel Hector & Davis, Miami, 1976-80, ptnr., 1980-87, chief exec. officer Collier Fin. Holding Co., Miami and Naples, 1987—. Bd. dirs. Internat. Ctr. Fla., Miami, 1984-86, chmn. investment in Fla. com., 1983-86; mem. Fla. Atty. Gen.'s Study Commn. on Money Laundering, Miami, 1983-84. Mem. Am. Land Title Assn. (mem. lenders' counsel group 1984—), Fla. Bar (mem. exec. council real property, probate and trust law sect. 1980-87, chmn. fgn. investment in real estate 1980-84, chmn. real estate investments by pension trusts 1984-87, real property sect. liaison to fgn. tax adv. com. tax sect. 1984). Republican. Episcopalian. Club: Coral Gables Country (Fla.). Home: 2843 S Bayshore Dr Apt P4D Miami FL 33133-6024 Office: Collier Fin Holding Co 3003 Tamiami Trl N Naples FL 34103-2714

IRVINE, JOHN ALEXANDER, lawyer; b. Sault Ste. Marie, Ont., Can., Mar. 10, 1947; s. Alexander and Ruth Catherine (Woolrich) I.; children from previous marriage: John Alexander, Allison Brooks; m. Lynda Kaye Myska Jenkins, May 24, 1981; children: James Woolrich, William Myska. BS, Auburn U., 1969; JD, Memphis State U., 1972. Bar: Tenn. 1972, Ohio 1982, Tex. 1985. Law clk. U.S. Dist. Ct. (we. dist.) Tenn., 1972-73; asst. dist. atty. gen. 15th Jud. Cir. Tenn., 1973-78; assoc. Glankler, Brown, Gilliland, Chase, Robinson and Raines, Memphis, 1978-81; asst. gen. counsel Mead Corp., Dayton, Ohio, 1981-84; ptnr. Porter & Clements, Houston, 1984-87; prin. Boyer, Norton & Blair, 1987-89; ptnr. Thelen, Marrin, Johnson & Bridges, 1989-94, mng. ptnr. Houston office, mem. mgmt. com., 1991-94; ptnr. Porter & Hodges, L.L.P., 1995—, mem. mgmt. com., 2000—. Bd. dirs. Make-A-Wish Found. Tex. Gulf Coast, 1985-86, mem. mgmt. com., 2000—. Fellow Tex. Bar Found. (chair Region 4 nominating com. 2000), Houston Bar Found.; mem. ABA (vice chmn. com. corp. counsel, litig. sect. 1989-91, co-chmn. intellectual properties litig. com. 1996-99, co-chmn. trial practice com. 2000—), Internat. Assn. Def. Counsel, Am. Arbitration Assn. (bd. arbitrators), Nat. Assn. Securities Dealers (bd. arbitrators), Tex. Bar Assn., Tenn. Bar Assn., Fed. Bar Assn. (treas. 1997-98, v.p. 1998-99, pres.-elect 1999-2000, pres. 2000—), Memphis Bar Assn. (YLS, bd. dirs. 1976, treas. 1977), Ohio Bar Assn., Houston Bar Assn., Coll. State Bar Tex., Memphis State U. Law Sch. Alumnae Assn. (pres. 1975-76, 77-78), 5th Cir. Ct. Appeals Bar Assn., U.S. C. of C. (coun. on antitrust policy 1983—), Phoenix Club of Memphis (bd. dirs. 1977-79), Def. Rsch. Inst., Champions Golf Club, Houston Met. Racquet Club, Briar Club. Republican. Presbyterian. Avocations: sports, travel, reading. Antitrust, General civil litigation, Securities.

IRWIN, R. ROBERT, lawyer; b. Denver, July 27, 1933; s. Royal Robert and Mildred Mary (Wilson) I.; m. Sue Ann Scott, Dec. 16, 1956; children: Lori, Stacy, Kristi, Amy. Student, U. Colo., 1951-54; BS in Law, U. Denver, 1955, LLB, 1957. Bar: Colo. 1957, Wyo. 1967. Asst. atty. gen. State of Colo., 1958-66; asst. divsn. atty. Mobil Oil Corp., Casper, Wyo., 1966-70; prin. atty. No. Natural Gas Co., Omaha, 1970-72; sr. atty., asst. sec. Coastal Oil & Gas Corp., Denver, 1972-83; ptnr. Baker & Hostetler, 1983-87; pvt. practice, 1987—. Mem. Colo. Bar Assn., Arapahoe County Bar Assn., Rocky Mountain Oil and Gas Assn., Los Verdes Golf Club, Petroleum Club, Denver Law Club. Republican. General corporate, Oil, gas, and mineral, Real property. Office: 650 S Alton Way Apt 4D Denver CO 80231-1669

ISAACS, MICHAEL BURTON, lawyer; b. Mar. 22, 1947; s. Richard and Bailey (Levine) I.; m. Mindy Isaacs, June 27, 1993; 1 stepchild, Tara Sousa. AB, U. Rochester, 1969; JD, Boston Coll., 1974. Bar: Mass. 1974, U.S. Dist. Ct. Mass. 1975, U.S. Ct. Appeals (D.C. cir.) 1975, D.C. 1979, U.S Ct. Appeals (9th cir.) 1979, R.I. 1988. Staff atty. Mass. Cable TV Commn., Boston, 1974-75; gen. counsel, 1975-78; asst. gen. counsel Nat. Cable TV Assn., Washington, 1978-80; dir. planning and govt. affairs Colony Communications Inc., Providence, 1980-82; sole practice L.A., 1982-84; dir. corp. devel. Providence Jour. Co., 1984-87, also. dir. devel., regulatory and legal affairs, 1987-92; dir. govt. affairs and pub. policy, 1992-94; v.p. govt. affairs and pub. policy, 1994-97; v.p. govt. & corp. rels., 1997; v.p. devel. Bresnan Comm., White Plains, N.Y., 1998-2000. Mem external com. on telecomm. and higher edn. R.I. Bd. Govs. for Higher Edn., 1995; panelist at numerous profl. convs. Bd. dirs. Jewish Srs. Agy., 2000—, Jewish Fedn. R.I., 2001—; mem. fin. bd. Town of East Greenwich, R.I., chair, 2001—; mem. R.I. Pub. Telecomms. Authority, 2001—. Mem. ABA, R.I. Bar Assn., Nat. Cable TV Assn. (utility rels. 1980-81, state-local coms. 1990, 94—), D.C. Bar Assn., Found for Cmty. Svc. Cable TV (bd. dirs. 1985-87), Fed. Comm. Bar Assn., New Eng. Cable TV Assn. (bd. dirs. 1981), Calif. Cable TV Assn. (bd. dirs. 1985-87), So. Calif. Cable TV Assn. (bd. dirs., v.p. 1986), City of L.A. Cable Operators Assn. (pres. 1986-87), Cellular Telecomm. Industry Assn. (legis. com. 1988-90), Cable Telecom. Assn. (bd. dirs.). Democrat. Jewish. Administrative and regulatory, Communications.

ISAACS, ROBERT CHARLES, retired lawyer; b. July 16, 1919; s. David and Elsie (Weiss) I.; m. Doris Frances Shapiro, Nov. 20, 1943 (dec. 1982); 1 child, Leigh Richard; m. Mary Lou Anderson, Dec. 12, 1986. BA cum laude, NYU, 1941, JD, 1943. Bar: N.Y. 1943. Dep. asst. atty. gen. N.Y. State Dept. Law, Albany, 1943, spl. asst. atty. gen., 1946; ptnr. Nordlinger Riegelman Benetar, N.Y.C., 1946-71, Aranow Brodsky Bohlinger Benetar & Einhorn, N.Y.C., 1972-79, Benetar Isaacs Bernstein & Schair, N.Y.C., 1979-88. Mem. Lebanon (N.H.) Zoning Bd. Adjustment, 1988—; adj. prof.

law St. John's U. Sch. Law, N.Y.C., 1961-72; mem. panel mediators and fact finders N.Y. State Pub. Employment Rels. Bd., 1968-88. Contbr. articles to profl. publs. Capt. U.S. Army, 1943-45, 51. Mem. ABA, ASCAP, Am. Arbitration Assn. (mem. panel arbitrators 1988), N.Y.C. Bar Assn., NYU Law Review Alumni Assn. Home: 5 Village Grn West Lebanon NH 03784-1506

ISAAK, GOTTHILF EUGENE, lawyer; b. Bismarck, N.D., Nov. 23, 1937; s. G. C. and Caroline (Jassman) I.; m. Elizabeth Baquet, Aug. 3, 1968; children: Jason E., Melissa E. BS, BA, U. N.D., 1959, JD, 1961; LLM in Taxation, NYU, 1962. Bar: N.D. 1961, Ariz. 1963, U.S. Dist. Ct. Ariz. 1963, U.S. Ct. Appeals (9th cir.) 1965, U.S. Supreme Ct. 1965; CPA, Ariz. Assoc. Dunseath, Stubbs & Burch, Tucson, 1962-73, Haralson, Miller, Pitt & McAnally, P.C., Tucson, 1973—. Chmn. U. Ariz. Sch. Law Probate workshop, 1982. Asst. nat. legal officer CAP, 1976—; pres., bd. dirs. Pima County Parklands Found., 1994—. Fellow Am. Coll. Trust and Estate Counsel; mem. ABA, Ariz. Bar Assn. (probate and trust sect. com. 1985-90, 96-2000), Pima County Bar Assn., Am. Brittany Club (nat. bd. dirs. 1982-87, legal counsel 1988—). Republican. Lutheran. Estate planning, Real property, Estate taxation. Office: Haralson, Miller Pitt & McAnally PC One S Church Ave Ste 900 Tucson AZ 85701-1620

ISABELLA, MARY MARGARET, lawyer; b. Pitts., Oct. 16, 1947; d. Sebastian C. and Joanna C. (dec.) (Ferris) I. BS in Biology, Duquesne U., 1969; cert. med. technologist, Mercy Hosp., Pitts., 1970; JD, Duquesne U., 1975. Bar: Pa. 1976, U.S. Dist Ct. (we. dist.) Pa. 1976, U.S. Supreme Ct., 1982. Sole practice, Pitts., 1977—. Instr. Wheeling (W.Va.) Coll., 1978-80. Mem. coun. Brentwood Whitehall Assn., Pitts., 1984-90; bd. dirs. Dukes Ct., Duquesne U.; bd. govs. Law Alumni Assn., treas., 1993, sec., 1994-95; sec., treas. Brentwood Bus. Owners' Assn., 2001—. Mem. ABA (vice chair sole practice sect., 1994—), Pa. Bar Assn., Allegheny County Bar Assn., Delta Theta Phi (past asst. dist. chancellor). Republican. Roman Catholic. Lodge: Italian Sons and Daughters of Am. (trustee local chpt.). Family and matrimonial, Probate. Office: 4101 Brownsville Rd Bldg 200 Pittsburgh PA 15227-3336 E-mail: mmiesq@juno.com

ISACOFF, RICHARD IRWIN, banker, lawyer; b. New Haven, Sept. 7, 1950; s. Paul and Doris (Tashman) I.; m. Bette Ann Francesconi, May 2, 1970; 1 child, Kira Lyn. Student Clark U., 1968-70; B.A., Western New Eng. Coll., 1972, J.D., 1977. Bar: Mass. 1977, U.S. Dist. Ct. Mass. 1978. Trust officer 3d Nat. Bank, Springfield, Mass., 1973-77, v.p. human resources, 1977-80; dir. human resources, corporate sec. Aspen Systems, Corp., Rockville, Md., 1980-82; sr. v.p., dir. corporate staff, corporate sec. Provident Bank Md., Balt., 1982— ; instr. U. Mass., Amherst, part time 1976; sole practice, Springfield, part time 1977-80. Mem. allocations com. United Way Pioneer Valley, 1977-80; mem. fin. com. PBS-WGBY TV, Springfield. Mem. ABA. Banking, Labor, Pension, profit-sharing, and employee benefits. Office: Provident Bank Md 114 E Lexington St Baltimore MD 21202-1746

ISAF, FRED THOMAS, lawyer; b. Jacksonville, N.C., Nov. 18, 1950; s. Thomas Fred and Rowanda (Maloof) I.; m. June J. Jeffcoat, Aug. 18, 1973; children: Julie, Thomas, Christa. BA, Duke U., 1972; JD, Emory U., 1975, LLM in Taxation, 1978. Bar: Ga. 1975. Ptnr. Peterson, Young, Self & Asselin, Atlanta, 1980-86; shareholder Roberts and Isaf, PC, 1986-94, Roberts, Isaf & Summers, PC, Atlanta, 1994-99; ptnr. McGuire Woods Battle & Boothe, 1999—. Contbr. article to profl. jour. Dir. Pinecrest Acad., 1995—. Mem. State Bar Ga., Cherokee Town and Country Club (dir. 1994-96, 99, sec. 1993, v.p. 1997, pres. 1998), Order of the Coif, Order of Barristers. General corporate, Real property, Securities. Office: McGuire Woods Ste 2100 1170 Peachtree St Atlanta GA 30309 E-mail: fisaf@mcguirewoods.com

ISBELL, DAVID BRADFORD, lawyer, legal educator; b. New Haven, Feb. 18, 1929; s. Percy Ernest and Dorothy Mae (Crabb) I.; m. Florence Bachrach, July 21, 1971; children: Christopher Pascal, Virginia Anne, Nicholas Bradford. BA, Yale U., 1949, LLB, 1956. Bar: Conn., 1956, D.C. 1957. Assoc. Covington & Burling, Washington, 1957-59, 61-65, ptnr., 1965-98, sr. counsel, 1998—; asst. staff dir. U.S. Commn. on Civil Rights, 1959-61. Lectr. Sch. Law U. Va., 1962—, Georgetown U. Law Ctr., 1996—. Bd. dirs. ACLU, 1965-92. 2nd lt. U.S. Army, 1951-53. Mem. ABA (mem. ho. dels. 1986-96, chairperson com. on ethics and profl. responsibility 1991-94), D.C. Bar (gov. 1978-82, pres. 1983-84), Cosmos Club. Federal civil litigation, General corporate, Libel. Home: 3709 Bradley Ln Bethesda MD 20815-4256 Office: Covington & Burling 1201 Pennsylvania Ave NW Washington DC 20004 E-mail: disbell@cov.com

ISELE, WILLIAM PAUL, lawyer; b. Sept. 8, 1949; s. Francis Joseph and Anna Mae (Hauser) I.; m. Linda Hean Bender, May 1, 1976; children: William Nicholas, Christopher Paul, David Francis. BA in Philosophy, Cath. U. Am., 1971; MA in Philosophy, 1972; JD, Georgetown U., 1975. Bar: Va. 1975, Ill. 1976, U.S. Dist. Ct. (no. dist.) Ill. 1976, U.S Dist. Ct. N.J. 1976; N.J. 1977, U.S. Supreme Ct. 1986, N.Y. 1989. Asst. dir. health law div. AMA, Chgo., 1976-81; assoc. Gross & Novak, East Brunswick, N.J., 1981-84; ptnr., 1985-88; of counsel Carella, Byrne, Bain & Gilfillan, Roseland, N.J., 1989; prin. Kern, Augustine, Conroy & Isele, P.C., Bridgewater, 1989-92; pvt. practice law, 1992-98; gen. counsel Office of Ombudsman for the Institutionalized Elderly, 1998-2000, N.J. Ombudsman for the Institutionalized Elderly, 2000—. Instr. So. Ill. U. Regional Health Edn. Programs, Springfield, 1980-81; adj. prof. Seton Hall U. Law Sch., 1987-91. Cubmaster Pack 33, Boy Scouts Am., 1987—. Author: Confidentiality of Medical Records in N.J., 1983, The Hospital Medical Staff, 1984, Medical Society of New Jersey Model Medical Staff Bylaws, 1990, Under Oath: Tips for Testifying, 1994; contbr. articles to profl. jours. Mem. ABA, N.J. State Bar Assn. (chmn. health and hosp. law sect. 1989-91), Nat. Health Lawyers Assn., Am. Acad. Hosp. Attys., N.J. Soc. Hosp. Attys., Middlesex County Bar Assn., Cath. Lawyers Guild (trustee Metuchen diocese 1989-91), Nat. Assn. Pastoral Musicians (treas. Metuchen chpt. N.J. 1981-87). Administrative and regulatory, Contracts commercial, Health. Home: 313 Brook Dr Milltown NJ 08850-1405 Office: PO Box 807 Trenton NJ 08625 E-mail: wisele@doh.state.nj.us

ISELY, HENRY PHILIP, association executive, integrative engineer, writer, educator; b. Montezuma, Kans., Oct. 16, 1915; s. James Walter and Jessie M. (Owen) I; m. Margaret Ann Sheesley, June 12, 1948; children: Zephyr, LaRock, Lark, Robin, Kemper, Heather Capri. Student, South Oreg. Jr. Coll., Ashland, 1934-35, Antioch Coll., Yellow Springs, Ohio, 1935-37. Organizer Action for World Fedn., 1946-50, N.Am. Coun. for People's World Conv., 1954-58, World Com. for World Constl. Conv., 1958, sec. gen., 1959-66, World Constn. and Parliment Assn., Lakewood, Colo., 1966—; organizer worldwide prep. confs. World Constnl. Convention, 1963, 66, 67, 1st session People's World Parliament and World Constl. Conv., Switzerland, 1968; editor assn, jour. Across Frontiers, 1959—; co-organizer Emergency Coun. World Trustees, 1971, World Constituent Assembly, Innsbruck, Austria, 1977, Colombo, Sri Lanka, 1978-79, Troia, Portugal, 1991; organizer Provisional World Parliament 1st session, Brighton, Eng., 1982, 2nd Session, New Delhi, India, 1985, 3d Session, Miami Beach, Fla., 1987; mem. parliament, 1982—. Sec. Working Commn. to Draft World Constn., 1971-77, pres. World Svc. Trust, 1972-78; co-founder Builder Found., Vitamin Cottages, 1955—, (chmn. bd. dir s., 1985—), pres. Earth Rescue Corps., 1984-90, sec.-treas. Grad. Sch. World Problems, 1984-99, pres., 1999—, cabinet mem. Provisional World Govt. , 1987—, pres. World Govt. Funding Corp., 1986—, Emergency Earth Rescue Adminstrn., 1995—, co-organizer Global Ratification and Elections Network, 1991— (sec. 1992—), prin. organizer 4th session Provisional World Parliament, Barcelona, Spain, 1996, 5th session, Malta, 2000, organizer first More Oxygen for the World conf., San Antonio, 1998; prof. world problems Grad. Sch. World Problems, 1990—; organizer Com. Five Global Expositions, 2001—; founding pres., CEO Only One Earth Enterprises, 2001—. Author: The People Must Write the Peace, 1950, A Call to All Peoples and All National Governments of the Earth, 1961, Outline for the Debate and Drafting of a World Constitution, 1967, Strategy for Reclaiming Earth for Humanity, 1969, Call to a World Constituent Assembly, 1974, Proposal for Immediate Action by an Emergency Council of World Trustees, 1971, Call to A Provisional World Parliament, 1981, People Who Want Peace Must Take Charge of World Affairs, 1982, Plan for Emergency Earth Rescue Administration, 1985, Plan for Earth Finance Credit Corporation, 1987, Climate Crisis, 1989, Technological Breakthroughs for A Global Energy Network, 1991, Bill of Particulars: Why the U.N. Must Be Replaced, 1994, Manifesto for the Inauguration of World Government, 1994, Call to the Fourth Session of the Provisional World Parliament, 1995, Fifth Session, 1997, Critique of the Report of the Commission on Global Governance, 1995, Using Crtedit Careds and Electronic Accountin to Initiate New Global Accounting, Credit and Finance System, 1996, Double Jeopardy and the Phytoplankton Project, 1997, The Fallacy of Treating Labor as a Commodity, 2000, The Immediate Economic Benefits of World Government, 2000; co-author, editor: A Constitution for the Federation of Earth, 1974, rev. edit., 1991, also author several other world legis. measures adopted at Provisional World Parliament, 1968-96; co-author: Plan for Collaboration in World Constituent Assembly, 1991, Creator treatment for screen drama History Hangs by a Thread, 1993; designer: prefab modular panel sys. constrn., master plan Guacamaya project, Costa Rica; planner five world fairs, five sessions World Parliament, 2000. Candidate for U.S. Congress, 1958. Recipient hon. rsch. doctorate in edn., 1989, Honor award Internat Assn. Educators for World Peace, 1975, Ghandi medal, 1977, Honor award Internat Soc. Universalism, 1993. Mem. ACLU, Am. Acad. Polit. Sci., Fellowship of Reconciliation, World Union, World Federalist Assn., World Future Soc., Earth Island Inst., Populatin Reference Bur., Earth Action, People's Congress, Life Ext. Found., Interfaith Alliance, Internat. Assn. for Hydrogen Energy, Friends of Earth, Wilderness Soc., Solar Energy Soc., Sierra Club, Amnesty Internat., World Resources Inst., Human Rights Watch, Nat. Nutritional Foods Assn., Environ. Def. Fund, Greenpeace, Ctr. for Study of Democratic Instns., War Resistors League, Audubon Soc., Worldwatch Inst., Internat. Assn. Constl. Law, Earth Regeneration Soc., Zero Population Growth, Cancr Control Soc., Mt. Vernon Country Club. Socialist. Home: Lookout Mountain 241 Zephyr Ave Golden CO 80401-9589 Office: 8800 W 14th Ave Lakewood CO 80215-4817 Fax: 303-237-7685, 303-526-7933. E-mail: wcparliament@uswest.net

ISHIZUKA, NOBUHISA, lawyer; b. N.Y.C., Dec. 29, 1960; s. Haruhisa and Ayako (Osawa) I.; m. Marcia Tsao-Ming Teng, Apr. 7, 1989; children: Megumi, Midori. BA in East Asian Studies, Columbia U., 1982, JD, 1986; cert. of study, U. Tokyo, 1988. Bar: N.Y., D.C. Fgn. legal cons. Kashiwagi Sogo Law Office, Tokyo, 1986-87; atty. White & Case, 1987-88, N.Y.C., 1988-94, Morgan, Lewis & Bockius LLP, N.Y.C., 1994-96, ptnr., 1996-2000, Tokyo, 1999—; registered fgn. legal cons. Gaikokuho Jimu Bengoshi, 1999-2000; ptnr. Skadden, Arps, Slate, Meagher & Flom LLP, Tokyo, 2000—. Legal counsel Ea. U.S. Kendo Fedn., N.Y.C., 1988-94; sec. JSR Am., Inc., N.Y.C., 1988—, NGK U.S.A., Inc., N.Y.C., 1992—, Teletechno, Inc., 1993-98. Sr. editor Columbia Law Rev., 1984-86. Mem. Phillips Acad. (Andover) Alumni Coun., 1998—. Japan Found. scholar, 1982; mem. U.S. Nat. Team-Kendo, 1982. Mem. ABA, N.Y.C. Bar Assn. (mem. standing com. on corp. law), N.Y. Athletic Club, Japanese Am. Assn. (mem. planning com. 1994-95, dir. 1995—, chmn. music scholarship com. 1995-99), Brit. Olympic Assn.-U.S. (N.Y. com. 1994-96), Sky Club, Dai-Ichi Tokyo Bar Assn. Avocation: rowing. General corporate, Finance, Mergers and acquisitions. Home: care Skadden Arps Et Al 4 Times Sq New York NY 10036-6522 Office: ATT Main Bldg 2-17-22 Akasaka Minato-ku Tokyo 107-0052 Japan E-mail: nishizuk@skadden.com

ISLA, EXU REIDEMER Q. corrections professional, lawyer; b. Villasis, Pangasinan, The Philippines, May 30, 1941; camd to U.S., 1990; s. Francisco Lopez and Rosenda (Quero) I.; m. Carmen Rosales Isla, June 7, 1970; children: Mary, Christian, John, Imelda, Theresa, Francis. AA, U. Pangasinan, 1960, edn. degree, 1965, postgrad., 1970-72, 80-81, JD, 1985; BA, U. of East, Manila, 1963; bus. adminstrn. degree, Arellano U., The Philippines, 1969; legal asst. diploma, Internat. Corr. Schs., 1969. Instr. social studies U. Pangasinan, 1964-68, 69-72; cmty. devel. worker Presdl. Arms Cmty. Devel., The Philippines, 1968-69; tchr. social studies Manila Pub. Schs., 1968-69; tng. officer Capital Planning Corp., The Philippines, 1971-74; regional tng. officer Bur. Lands, The Philippines, 1974-79; manpower devel. officer Nat. Manpower, The Philippines, 1979-87; election registrar Commn. on Elections, The Philippines, 1987-89; legal asst. Nat. Bur. Investigation, The Philippines, 1989-90; probation officer Gary (Ind.) City Ct., 1991—. Rural devel. cons. Presdl. Office for Devel., The Philippines, 1978-81; youth devel. cons. Youth Movement in Barrios, The Philippines, 1978-86. Columnist North Tribune and Ilocos Times, The Philippines, 1974-87, Weekly Express, The Philippines, 1987-89. Presdl. asst. for Province of Abra, Presdl. Regional Office for Devel. Regional Mgmt. Staff, 1978-81; regional sec. Rural Adv. Bd., The Philippines, 1978-81. Recipient provincial award Pangasinan-Dagupan City YMCA, nat. award Nat. YMCA, The Philippines, 1965, Found. for Youth Devel. in The Philippines, award of recognition Ministry Pub. Info., Ilocos Region, 1980, Pangasinan State U., 1981, Provincial Agr. Office Pangasinan, 1984, Mcpl. Coun. Urdaneta, Pangasinan, 1989, Outstanding Adminstr. award KC, The Philippines, 1982, Outstanding Parent award U. Pangasinan H.S., Dagupan City, 1989, Lew Wallace H.S., Gary, 1994. Mem. Am. Correctional Assn., Ind. Correctional Assn., Philippine Profl. Assn. (officer 1991—), Internat. Inst. N.W. Ind. (officer 1991—). Home: 5066 Pennsylvania St Gary IN 46409-2738 Office: Gary City Ct 1301 Broadway Gary IN 46407-1326

ISQUITH, FRED TAYLOR, lawyer; b. N.Y.C., June 6, 1947; s. Stanley and Rita (Hoskwith) I.; m. Susan Nora Goldberg, May 23, 1976: children: Fred, Rebecca. BA, CUNY, 1968; JD, Columbia U., 1971. Bar: N.Y. 1972, D.C. 1976, U.S. Dist. Ct. (so. and ea. dists.) N.Y. 1975, U.S. Dist. Ct. (no. dist.) N.Y. 1988, U.S. Dist. Ct. (we. dist.) Mich. 1992, U.S. Dist. Ct. Ariz. 1994, U.S. Dist. Ct. (ctrl. dist.) Ill. 1996, U.S. Ct. Appeals (2d cir.) 1975, U.S. Ct. Appeals (8th cir.) 1985, U.S. Ct. Appeals (3d cir.) 1986, U.S. Ct. Appeals (4th cir.) 1990, U.S. Supreme Ct. 1983, U.S. Dist. Ct. Colo. 1999, U.S. Dist. Ct. Nebr. 2000, U.S. Ct. Appeals (1st cir.) 2000. Assoc. Fulbright & Jaworski, N.Y.C., 1971-75, Kaye Scholer et al, N.Y.C., 1975-80; ptnr. Wolf Haldenstein Adler Freeman & Herz, 1980—. 'd. trustees St. Chad's Coll. Found.; bd. dirs. 103 East 84th St. Corp., N.Y.C., Sheinkopf Comm., Ltd.; lectr. Am. Conf. Inst., N.Y. State Bar Assn.; mediator Supreme Ct. State N.Y. County N.Y. Comml. Divsn.; arbitrator Am. Arbitration Assn.; lectr. in field. Author: An Introduction to Securities Arbitration, 1994, Real Estate Exit Strategies, 1994, Fundamental Strategies in Securities Litigation, 2000, Federal Civil Practice, 2000; editor, weekly columnist The Class Act. Mem. ABA (mem. internet com. anti-trust law sect.), N.Y. State Bar Assn. (coms. on securities and legis., arbitrator securities industry disputes sect.), N.Y. County Lawyers Assn. (chmn. bus. torts), D.C. Bar Assn., Assn. of Bar of City of N.Y. (Fed. Cts. com.), Bklyn. Bar Assn. (civil practice law and rules com., legis. com. and fed. cts. com.), Columbia Club. Federal civil litigation, State civil litigation, Securities. Office: Wolf Haldenstein Adler Freeman & Herz 270 Madison Ave New York NY 10016-0601

ISRAEL, BARRY JOHN, lawyer; b. Rockford, Ill., Mar. 14, 1946; s. Robert John and Bettie Jane (Erickson) I.; childn: Alison, Ashley, Brenna. BA, U. So. Calif., L.A., 1968; JD, George Washington U., 1974. Bar: Calif. 1975, D.C. 1976, U.S. Supreme Ct. 1978, U.S. Dist. Ct. Mariana Islands 1985. Assoc. Clifford & Warnke, Washington, 1975-83; ptnr. Stovall, Spradlin, Armstrong & Israel, 1983-86, Dorsey & Whitney, Washington, 1988-92, Stroock, Stroock & Lavan, Washington, 1992-95. Spl. counsel, pres. Federated States of Micronesia, 1982-84; spl. asst. atty. gen. Territory Guam, 1990-95; chmn. bd. Danao Internt. Holdings Co., Ltd.; bd. dirs. Bank of the Federated States of Micronesia, Bank of Saipan. Author: (guides) Investment Guides to the Federated States of Micronesia and the Republic of the Marshall Islands, 1989. 1st lt. U.S. Army, 1969-72. Democrat. Avocations: travel, tennis. Administrative and regulatory, Private international, Public international. Home: 1101 Luneta Plaza Santa Barbara CA 93109 E-mail: barryjon@aol.com

ISRAEL, SCOTT MICHAEL, lawyer; b. Milw., Oct. 22, 1955; s. Phillip David and Bella Dawn (Rubin) I. BBA, U. Wis., 1977; JD, Marquette U., 1980. Bar: Wis. 1980, U.S. Dist. Ct. (ea. and we. dist.) Wis. 1980. Atty. Rausch, Sturm, Israel & Hornik, S.C., Milw., 1980—. Bd. dirs. Yeshiva Elem. Sch., Milw., Inc.; v.p. Milw. Kollel, Inc., Beth Hamedrosh Hagodel Cemetery Assn. Mem. Comml. Law League Am., State Bar Wis., Phi Eta Sigma. Jewish. Bankruptcy, State civil litigation, Consumer commercial. Office: Rausch Sturm Israel Hornik SC 1233 N Mayfair Rd Ste 125 Milwaukee WI 53226-3255 E-mail: Sisrael@wiscollect.com

ISRAELS, MICHAEL JOZEF, lawyer; b. N.Y.C., Sept. 27, 1949; s. Carlos Lindner and Ruth Lucille (Goldstein) I.; m. Maija-Sarmite Jansons, Aug. 31, 1980; children: Aleksandrs Lehman, Peter Carlos. AB magna cum laude, Amherst Coll., 1972; JD, Harvard U., 1975. Bar: N.Y. 1976, U.S. Dist. Ct. (so. and ea. dists.) N.Y. 1976, D.C. 1977, N.J. 1980, U.S. Dist. Ct. N.J. 1980. Assoc. Shearman & Sterling, N.Y.C., 1975-79; sole practice, 1979-81; ptnr. Courter, Kobert, Laufer & Pease, P.A., Hackettstown, N.J., 1981-83, Fitzpatrick & Israels, Bayonne and Secaucus, 1983-87, 89-94; sr. ptnr. Waters, McPherson, McNeill, Fitzpatrick, PA., Secaucus, 1987-89; ptnr. Broscious, Israels, Glynn & Gentile, Washington, 1994-96; counsel Fitzpatrick & Waterman, 1996—. Gen. counsel Kearny (N.J.) Mcpl. Port Authority, 1985-90, Jersey City Mcpl. Port Authority, 1986-96; Kearny Mcpl. Utilities Authority, 1988-95; mem. N.J. Debt. Mgmt. Adv. Com., 1986—; cons. U.S./USSR Trade Council, N.Y.C., 1979, Council on Religion and Internat. Affairs, N.Y.C., 1980. Author: (with Moore, Thomson and Linsky) Report of the New England Conference on Conflicts Between Media and Law, 1977; contbr. articles to profl. jours. Bd. dirs. Cmty. Tax Aid, Inc., N.Y.C., 1976-82, Am. Jewish Com., N.Y.C., 1980-88, Anti-Defamation League N.J., Livingston, 1981—, U.S. Assn. Internat. Migration, 1988-94; mem. religious sch. com. Temple Emanu-El, N.Y.C., 1972-84. Mem. ABA (gov. law student divsn. 1974-75), Assn. Bar City N.Y., N.J. Bar Assn., Met. Opera Club, Harvard Club (N.Y.C.). General corporate, Municipal (including bonds), Estate taxation. Home: 160 W 66th St Apt 51E New York NY 10023-6567 Office: Fitzpatrick & Waterman 400 Plaza Dr Secaucus NJ 07094-3605

ISSLER, HARRY, lawyer; b. Cologne, Germany, Nov. 14, 1935; came to U.S., 1937; s. Max and Fanny (Grunbaum) I.; m. Doris Helen Lukow, June 1, 1958; children: Adriane P. Schorr, M. Valerie Priestley, Stephanie L. Beck. BS, U. Wis., 1955; JD, Cornell U., 1958. Bar: N.Y. 1958, U.S. Supreme Ct. 1962, U.S. Ct. Mil. Appeals 1967, U.S. Dist. Ct. (so. and ea. dists.) N.Y. 1960, U.S. Customs Ct. 1964, U.S. Tax Ct. 1964; cert. specialist in civil trial advocacy Nat. Bo. Trial Advocacy. Assoc. Wing & Wing, N.Y.C., 1958-60; assoc. Fuchsberg & Fuchsberg, 1960-62; ptnr. Issler & Fein, 1963-68, Shaw, Issler & Rosenberg, N.Y.C., 1968-70; pvt. practice, 1970-79; ptnr. Issler & Scrage, P.C., 1980-99; sr. ptnr. The Law Firm of Harry Issler PLLC, 1999—. Arbitrator Civil Ct., N.Y. County, 1979-91; hearing officer N.Y. State Tax Appeals, 1975-77, Supreme Ct. of N.Y., N.Y. County Med. Malpractice Panel, 1980-91; judge advocate N.Y. State; mem. neutral evaluator mediation panel Supreme Ct., N.Y. County, 1997—. Trustee N.Y. State Mil. Ednl. Found., 1997-2000; v.p. Sutton Area Cmty., Inc., 2000—; v.p., treas. 50 Sutton Pl. South Owners, Inc., 2000—. With U.S. Army, 1958-59, N.Y. Army N.G., 1963-88, ret. brig. gen., 1988. Ford Found. scholar, 1951-55. Mem. ABA, N.Y. State Bar Assn., Assn. of Bar of City of N.Y., Am. Trial Lawyers Assn., N.Y. State Trial Lawyers Assn., 42d Infantry Divsn. Officers Club (N.Y.C.pres. 1979-80), Officers Club (U.S. Mcht. Marine Acad.), 42d Infantry Rainbow Disn. Assn. (pres. 1989), Phi Alpha Delta, Pi Lambda Phi (Omega chpt. pres. 1953-54). thelawfirm.com. Family and matrimonial, Military, Personal injury. Home: 50 Sutton Pl S New York NY 10022-4167 Office: The Law Firm of Harry Issler PLC 32d Fl 1370 Ave of Americas New York NY 10019 E-mail: harryissler@lawyer.com

IVERACH, ROBERT JOHN, lawyer; b. Edmonton, Alta., Can., Dec. 13, 1947; s. David W. and Margaret L. (Ranton) I.; m. Susan Anne Long, May 6, 1977; children: Robert J., Michelle A. BA, U. Calgary, 1969; LLB, U. Alta., 1970; LLM, London Sch. Econs., 1971. Bar: Alta. 1972. Student, atty., Ballem, McDill & MacInnes, Calgary, Alta., 1971-74; ptnr. Fenerty & Co., Calgary, 1974-78; founding ptnr. Bell, Felesky & Iverach, Calgary, 1978— ; bd. dirs. Maxx Petroleum Ltd. Co-author: Canadian Income Tax Tips and Traps, 1979. Bd. dirs. Alta. Law Found., 1976-78. Viscount Bennett scholar, 1970. Mem. Law Soc. Alta., Can. Bar Assn. Progressive Conservative. Mem. United Ch. Can. Clubs: Ranchmen's, Petroleum, Glencoe (Calgary). Office: 350 7th Ave SW Suite 3400 Calgary AB Canada T2P 3N9

IVERS, DONALD LOUIS, judge; b. San Diego, May 6, 1941; s. Grant Perrin and Margaret (Ware) I. BA, U. N.Mex., 1963; JD, Am. U., 1971. Bar: U.S. Dist. Ct. (D.C. 1972), U.S. Ct. Appeals (D.C. cir.) 1972, U.S. Ct. Mil. Appeals 1972, U.S. Supreme Ct. 1975. Assoc. Brault, Graham, Scott, Brault, Washington, 1972-78; chief counsel Republican Nat. Com., 1978-81; gen. counsel 1980 Rep. Nat. Conv. Site Selection Com., 1979-80; chief counsel Fed. Hwy. Adminstrn., U.S. Dept. Transp., 1981-85; counselor to sec., chmn. sec.'s safety rev. task force U.s. Dept. Transp., 1984-85; gen. counsel VA, 1985-89; acting gen. counsel U.S. Dept. Vet. Affairs, 1989-90, asst. to the sec., 1990; assoc. judge U.S. Ct. Appeals Vet. Claims, 1990—. Capt. U.S. Army, 1963-68, Vietnam, lt. col. Res., ret. Mem. Delta Theta Phi. Office: US Ct Appeals Vet Claims 625 Indiana Ave NW Washington DC 20004-2923

IWAI, WILFRED KIYOSHI, lawyer; b. Honolulu, Aug. 21, 1941; s. Charles Kazuo and Michiko (Sakimoto) I.; m. Judy Tomiko Yoshimoto, Mar. 1, 1963; children: Kyle K., Tiffany Seiko. BS in Bus., U. Colo., 1963, JD, 1966. Bar: Hawaii 1966, Colo. 1966, U.S. Dist. Ct. Hawaii 1966, U.S. Ct. Appeals (9th cir.) 1966. Dep. corp. counsel State of Hawaii, Honolulu, 1966-71; assoc. Kashiwa & Kanazawa, 1971-75; ptnr. Kashiwa, Iwai, Motooka & Goto, 1975-82, also bd. dirs.; ptnr. Iwai & Morris, 1982—, also bd. dirs. Mem. ABA, Hawaii Bar Assn., Assn. Trial Lawyers Am., Bldg. Industry Assn., Bldg. Owners & Mgrs. Assn. Hawaii. Club: Draftsmen's (Honolulu) (pres.). State civil litigation, Construction, General practice. Office: Iwai & Morris 820 Mililani St Ste 502 Honolulu HI 96813-2935

JABLONSKI, JAMES ARTHUR, lawyer; b. Sheboygan, Wis., Nov. 12, 1942; s. John Alfred and Dena (Kaat) J. BBA, U. Wis., 1965, JD, 1968. Bar: Wis. 1968, Calif. 1969, U.S. Ct. Appeals (7th cir) 1969, U.S. Supreme Ct. 1974, Colo. 1976, U.S. Ct. Appeals (8th and 10th cirs.) 1976. Assoc. Pillsbury, Madison & Sutro, San Francisco, 1969-72; asst. prof. law

Washington U., St. Louis, 1972-76; ptnr. Gorsuch Kirgis L.L.C., Denver, 1976—. Mem. Colo. Bar Assn., Wis. Bar Assn. (bd. govs. 1990-92), Denver Bar Assn. Democrat. Club: Pinehurst Country (Denver). Federal civil litigation, Construction, Labor. Office: Gorsuch Kirgis Tower 1 1515 Arapahoe St Ste 1000 Denver CO 80202-2120

JACK, JANIS GRAHAM, judge; b. 1946; RN, St. Thomas Sch. Nursing, 1969; BA, U. Balt., 1974; JD summa cum laude, South Tex. Coll., 1981. Pvt. practice, Corpus Christi, Tex., 1981-94; judge U.S. Dist. Ct. (so. dist.) Tex., 1994—. Jud. mem. The Maritime Law Assn. U.S. Mem. ABA, Fed. Judges Assn., Fifth Cir. Dist. Judges Assn., Nat. Assn. Women Judges, Tex. Bar Found., State Bar Tex., The Philos. Soc. Tex., Order of Lytae, Phi Alpha Delta. Office: US Dist Ct 1133 N Shoreline Blvd Corpus Christi TX 78401

JACKOWIAK, PATRICIA, lawyer; b. Chgo., Feb. 3, 1959; d. Leonard John and Margaret Mary (Iozzi) J. BA, Loyola U., Chgo., 1981; JD, John Marshall Law Sch., 1984. Bar: Ill. 1985. Asst. state's atty. Cook County, Chgo., 1987-89, supr. trial atty. bur. child support enforcement, legal advisor law student's spl. and perjury projects, chmn. employee rels. com., 1988-89, com. mem. domestic rels. div. Pro-se task force, 1989; dep. commr. Consumer Protection div. Dept. Consumer Svcs. City of Chgo., 1989-96; dep. chief adminstrv. law judge Dept. Adminstrv. Hearings City of Chgo., 1996—. Summer atty. Ct. Claims and Antitrust divsn. Office of Ill. Atty. Gen., 1985, 86; com. mem. domestic rels. divsn. Cook County The Pro-Se Task Force Com.; mem. Chgo. divsn. Ford Consumer Appeals Bd., 1989-92, chair, 1991-92. Pres. Santa Lucia Sch. Bd., Chgo., 1987—; chairperson employee rels. com. Child Support divsn., 1988—89; mem. freshman recruiting and fundraising coms. Parents Assocs. Loyola U., Chgo., 1987—90; mem. elder care task force Dept. Health, Aging and Disability, Dept. Consumer Svcs. City of Chgo., 1989—96; chairperson Santa Lucia Parish Carnival Com., 1987—; dir. religious edn. Santa Lucia Parish, 1985—; commencement speaker St. Barbara High Sch., Chgo., 1993, 1997, adv. bd., 1994—2001, co-chair, 1998—99, chair, 1999—2001. Recipient Local Parish award Cath. Youth Orgn./Archdiocese of Chgo., 1991; disting. elem. grad. award Nat. Cath. Ednl. Assn., Santa Lucia Sch., 1994, Superior Pub. Svc. award, 1998. Mem. ABA, Nat. Assn. Adminstrv. Law Judges, Nat. Indsl. Scale Assn., Nat. Conf. Weights and Measures, Blue Key, Pi Sigma Alpha. Democrat. Roman Catholic. Office: Dept Adminstrv Hearings 740 N Sedgwick St Fl 6 Chicago IL 60610-3478 E-mail: pjackowiak@ci.chi.il.us

JACKSON, DARNELL, judge; b. Saginaw, Mich., Feb. 2, 1955; s. Roosevelt and Annie Lois (Pratt) J.; m. Yvonne Kay Givens, July 29, 1978; children: Brandon Darnell, Elliott Stephen. BA, Wayne State U., 1977, JD, 1981; AA, Kalamazoo C.C., 1993. Office mgr., shift supr. Wayne State U., Detroit, 1979-81; mng. ptnr. Allan & Jackson, P.C., Saginaw, 1983-85; asst. city atty. Saginaw City Atty.'s Office, 1985-86; asst. prosecuting atty. Saginaw County Prosecutor's, Saginaw, 1986-89; assoc. Braun, Kendrick, Finkbeiner et al, 1989-90; instr. Paralegal Inst. Delta Coll., University Center, Mich., 1986, instr. Northeastern Basic Police Acad., 1991-96; dep. chief asst. prosecuting atty. Saginaw County Prosecutor's Office, 1990-93; adminstrv. dep. chief of police Saginaw Police Dept., 1993-96; dir. Office of Drug Control Policy State of Mich., Lansing, 1996-2001; dist. ct. judge 70th Jud. Dist. Ct., Saginaw, Mich., 2001—. Mem. Drug Edn. Adv. Com., Lansing, Mich., 1996-2001, DARE Policy Adv. Bd., Lansing, 1996-2001, Mich. Dispute Resolution, Saginaw, 1989-92, Sen. Cisky Adv. Com., Saginaw, 1992-94; co-chair Partnership for Drug Free Mich., 1997-2001; speaker in field. Bd. dirs. United Way of Saginaw County, 1996, Westchester Village/Essex Manor, 1994-96, Saginaw County Child Abuse and Neglect Coun., 1994-96, Mr. Rogers Say No to Drugs Program, 1991-95; mem. Saginaw Valley Sate U. Multicultural Adv. Com., 1991-96; adv. bd. Saginaw St. Mary's Hosp., 1991-94, State Sen. Jon Cisky Minority Affairs Adv. Com., 1992-94. Recipient award for Profl. Excellence, FBI/Saginaw County Gang Crime Task Force, 1995, Frederick Douglass award for Community Svc., Mich. State Legis., 1991, award for Effort in War on Drugs, Saginaw Police Dept. Spl. Ops. Unit, 1989, Spl. Tribute for Community Svc., Mich. State Legis., 1985, Comm. Svc. awards Wayne State Univ. Free Legal Aid Clin, 1980-81. Mem. Mich. Bar Assn., Saginaw County Bar Assn., Fraternal Order of Police, Internat. Assn. of Chiefs of Police, Mich. Assn. of Chiefs of Police, Nat. Orgn. of Black Law Enforcement Execs. Office: State of Mich Saginaw County Ct Ho Saginaw MI 48602

JACKSON, JOHN HOLLIS, JR. lawyer; b. Mongomery, Ala., Aug. 21, 1941; s. John Hollis and Erma (Edgeworth) J.; m. Rebecca Mullins, May 27, 1967; 1 child, John Hollis III. AB, U. Ala., 1963, JD, 1966. Bar: Ala. 1966, U.S. Dist. Ct. (no. dist.) Ala. 1969, U.S. Ct. Appeals (11th cir.) 1993. Pvt. practice, Clanton, Ala., 1967—. County atty. Chilton County Commn., Clanton, 1969— ; mcpl. judge Clanton, 1971-99, city atty., 1999—; dir. First Nat. Bank, Clanton, 1974-83; mem. adv. bd. Colonial Bank, Clanton, 1983—; mcpl. judge, Jemison, Ala., 1984—. Bd. dirs. Chilton-Shelby Mental Health Bd., Calera, Ala., 1974-83, pres., 1974-79; mem. State Dem. Exec. Com., Birmingham, Ala., 1974-98, County Dem. Exec. Com., Chilton County, 1982-94; del. Dem. Nat. Conv., N.Y.C., 1976. 1st lt. U.S. Army, 1966-67. Mem. Ala. Young Lawyers Sect. (exec. com. 1969-70), Chilton County Bar Assn. (pres. 1969, 74), Ala. State Bar Assn. (bd. bar commrs. 1984-87, 93-99, chmn. adv. com. to bd. bar examiners 1986-87, 19th cir. indigent def. commn. 1983—, chmn. disciplinary panel II 1997-99), Kiwanis, Phi Alpha Delta. Democrat. Methodist. General practice. Home: Samaria Rd Clanton AL 35045 Office: PO Box 1818 500 2nd Ave S Clanton AL 35046-1818

JACKSON, MILLARD IRVING, JR. lawyer, banker; b. Phila., June 19, 1939; s. Millard Irving and Marion (Bennett) J.; A.B., Duke U., 1961; LL.B., U. N.C., 1964; m. Marilynn Louise White, June 15, 1963; children— Michael Howard, David Alan. Admitted to N.C. bar, 1964; mem. trust dept. 1st Citizens Bank & Trust Co., Raleigh, N.C., 1964-66; asst. v.p. Provident Nat. Bank, Phila., 1966-76; v.p., dir. tax and estate planning Janney Montgomery Scott, Inc., Phila., 1976— . Mem. N.C. Bar Assn., S.E. Conn. Estate and Tax Planning Council, Internat. Assn. Fin. Planners. Republican. Presbyterian. Home: 850 Lewis Ln Bryn Mawr PA 19010-1206 Office: 18th Floor Five Penn Center Plaza Philadelphia PA 19103

JACKSON, PATRICK RICHMOND, lawyer; b. Shreveport, La., Apr. 12, 1971; s. Henry Richmond and Michele Joan (McClure) J.; m. Tonya Rawls, Dec. 30, 1994; children: Lee Richmond, Luke Marshall. BA magna cum laude, La. Tech. U, 1994; JD, Baylor U., 1997. Bar: Tex. 1997, La. 1998, U.S. Dist. Ct. (no. dist.) Tex. 1998. Assoc. Harris, Finley & Bogle P.C., Ft. Worth, 1997-99; shareholder Patrick R. Jackson, PLC, Bossier City, La., 1999—. Campaign mgr. Henry Brown for La. Supreme Ct., Bossier City, La., 1995. Capt. U.S. Army N.G., 1988—. Mem. ABA, Tex. Bar Assn., La. Bar Assn., Shreveport Bar Assn., Bossier Parish Bar Assn. Republican. Roman Catholic. Avocations: basketball, running, reading, politics, antiquing. General civil litigation, Personal injury. Office: 1000 Benton Rd Bossier City LA 71111

JACKSON, RAYMOND A. federal judge; b. 1949; BA, Norfolk State U., 1970; JD, U. Va., 1973. Capt. U.S. Army JAGC, 1973-77; asst. U.S. atty. Ea. Dist. Va., Norfolk, 1977-93; judge U.S. Dist. Ct. (ea. dist.) Va., 1993—. Mem. judicial conf. U.S. Ct. Appeals (4th cir.); adj. faculty Marshall Wythe Sch. of Law, Coll. of William and Mary, 1993—. Active Day Care and Child Devel. Ctr., Tidewater, 1980—86; bd. dirs. Peninsula Legal Aid Ctr., 1977. Col. Res. USAR, ret. 1998. Fellow: Va. Bar Found.; mem.: U.S. Dist. Judges Assn., Old Dominion Bar Assn. (pres. 1984—86), Norfolk-Portsmouth Bar Assn., South Hampton Rds. Bar Assn., Am. Inn Ct. (Hoffman-l'Anson chpt. pres. 2000—01), Va. Law Found., U.S. Judicial Conf. Com. Adminstrn. Magistrate Judge Sys. Office: 600 Granby St Norfolk VA 23510-1915

JACKSON, RAYMOND SIDNEY, JR. lawyer; b. Bklyn., Sept. 17, 1938; s. Raymond Sidney and Mary Frost (McInerney) Van Vranken. BA, William Coll., 1960; JD, Harvard U., 1966. Bar: N.Y. 1967, U.S. Dist. Ct. (so. and ea. dists.) N.Y. 1969, U.S. Ct. Appeals (2d cir.) 1969. Assoc. Thacher, Proffitt & Wood, N.Y.C., 1966-76, ptnr., 1976-94, of counsel, 1994—. Mem. South St. Seaport Mus., N.Y.C., 1974—, Gramercy Neighborhood Assocs., N.Y.C., 1974—, Nat. Assn. Coll. and Univ. Attys., 1972. Mem. ABA (vice chmn. admiralty and maritime law com. sect. of tort and ins. practice 1990-92), N.Y. State Bar Assn. (admiralty and maritime com. internat. law and practice sect. 1989-94), Assn. Bar City N.Y. (admiralty com. 1984-85, 88-91), Maritime Law Assn. U.S. (com. on practice and procedure 1976-91). Admiralty, General civil litigation. E-mail: rsjacksonj@aol.com

JACKSON, RENEE LEONE, lawyer; b. Winter Park, Fla., Sept. 26, 1966; d. Richard Lee and Jean Karen (Bergmann) Wiechmann; m. J. David Jackson, Dec. 10, 1994; stepchildren: Ian, Kelsey. AA, Bethany Lutheran Coll., 1986; BS with high honors, U. Fla., 1988; JD magna cum laude, U. Minn. Law Sch., 1991. Lawyer Dorsey & Whitney, Mpls., 1991-93, Larkin, Hoffman, Daly & Lindgren, Bloomington, Minn., 1993—. Bd. dirs. Bloomington Cmty. Found., 1996—. Recipient Order of the Coif. Mem. ABA. Lutheran. General civil litigation, Intellectual property. Office: Larkin et al 7900 Xerxes Ave S Bloomington MN 55431-1106

JACKSON, ROBBI JO, agricultural products company executive, lawyer; b. Nampa, Idaho, Apr. 12, 1959; d. William R. Jackson and Marilyn K. Samp Jackson Nunez. BS in Fin., U. Colo., Boulder and Denver, 1981; JD, U. Denver, 1987, LLM in Taxation, 1990. Bar: Colo. Asst. office mgr. Jerome Karsh & Co., Denver, 1982; office mgr. Almirall & Assocs., Englewood, Colo., 1983-84; assoc. Moye, Giles, O'Keefe, Vermeire & Gorrell, Denver, 1989-90, Holme Roberts & Owen, Denver, 1990-92; in-house gen. counsel Cmty. Corrections Svcs., 1992-96; CEO Enviro Cons. Svc., LLC, Evergreen and Lakewood, Colo., 1996—. Mem. staff Adminstrv. Law Rev., Denver, 1985, editor, 1985, mng. editor, 1986-87; co-author course of study materials; presenter in field. Mem. fin. com. Mile-High chpt. ARC, Denver, 1990-92; food delivery person Vols. of Am., Meals-on-Wheels, Denver, 1990-92. Recipient scholarships. Mem. ABA, Colo. Bar Assn. (ethics com.). Republican. Avocations: running marathons and other races, biking, hiking, swimming, piano and organ playing.

JACKSON, THOMAS GENE, lawyer; b. N.Y.C., Mar. 9, 1949; s. Alan Clark and Clare Seena (Werther) J.; m. Beatrice Lafrance Korab, June 11, 1972; children: Sarah Ann, Alan Edward. AB magna cum laude in English, Dartmouth Coll., 1971; JD, U. Va., 1974. Bar: N.Y. 1975, U.S. Dist. Ct. (so. and ea. dists.) N.Y. 1975, U.S. Ct. Appeals (2d cir.) 1975, U.S. Ct. Appeals (5th cir.) 1978, U.S. Supreme Ct. 1978, U.S. Ct. Appeals (D.C. cir.) 1986. Editor The Rsch. Group, Charlottesville, Va., 1973-74; assoc. Phillips Nizer Benjamin Krim & Ballon LLP, N.Y.C., 1974-82, ptnr., 1982—. Mem. fed. bar coun. com. 2d Cir. Cts., 1997-2000, chmn. subcom. on tech. in the cts., 1997-2000. Mem. Village of Irvington Cable TV Adv. Com., N.Y., 1979-91, 95—, chmn. franchise renewal com., 1991-95; sec. Village of Irvington Environ. Conservation Bd., 1983-87, chmn., 1987—; mem. Dartmouth Coll. Alumni Coun., 1986-89. Mem.: ABA (sect. antitrust law, Clayton Act com., premerger notification subcom. 1982—), Am. Arbitration Assn. (panel of arbitrators, comml. tribunal 1986—), Assn. Bar City N.Y. (antitrust and trade regulation com. 1988—92, mergers acquisitions and joint ventures subcom. 1991—92), Dartmouth Coll. Club Officers Assn. (exec. com. 1988—91), Dartmouth Club Westchester (sec. 1984—87, pres. 1987—90), Dartmouth Coll. Class Secs. Assn. (v.p. 1984—85, pres. 1985—86). Antitrust, Federal civil litigation. Home: 32 Hamilton Rd Irvington NY 10533-2311 Office: Phillips Nizer Benjamin Krim & Ballon LLP 666 5th Ave New York NY 10103-0001

JACKSON, THOMAS PENFIELD, federal judge; b. Washington, Jan. 10, 1937; s. Thomas Searing and May Elizabeth (Jacobs) J. AB in Govt., Dartmouth Coll., 1958; LLB, Harvard U., 1964. Bar: D.C., Md., U.S. Supreme Ct. 1970. Assoc., ptnr. Jackson & Campbell, P.C., Washington, 1964-82; U.S. dist. judge U.S. Dist. Ct. D.C., 1982—. Vestryman All Saints' Episcopal Ch., Washington, 1969-75; trustee Gallaudet U., Washington, 1985-99, St. Marys Coll., Md., 2001—. Lt. (j.g.) USN, 1958-61. Fellow Am. Coll. Trial Lawyers; mem. ABA, Bar Assn. D.C. (pres. 1982-83), Rotary. Republican. Clubs: Chevy Chase, Metropolitan, Lawyers', Barristers. Office: US Dist Ct US Courthouse 3rd & Constitution Ave NW Washington DC 20001

JACOB, BRUCE ROBERT, law educator; b. Chgo., Mar. 26, 1935; s. Edward Carl and Elsie Berthe (Hartmann) J.; m. Ann Wear, Sept. 8, 1962; children: Bruce Ledley, Lee Ann, Brian Edward BA, Fla. State U., 1957; JD, Stetson U., 1959; LLM, Northwestern U., 1965; SJD, Harvard U., 1980; LLM in Taxation, U. Fla., 1995. Bar: Fla. 1959, Ill. 1965, Mass. 1970, Ohio 1972. Asst. atty. gen. State of Fla., 1960-62; assoc. Holland, Bevis & Smith, Bartow, Fla., 1962-64; asst. to assoc. prof. Emory U. Sch. Law, 1965-69; rsch. assoc. Ctr. for Criminal Justice, Harvard Law Sch., 1969-70; staff atty. Cmty. Legal Assistance Office, Cambridge, Mass., 1970-71; assoc. prof. Coll. Law, Ohio State U., 1971-73, prof., dir. clin. programs, 1973-78; dean, prof. Mercer U. Law Sch., Macon, Ga., 1978-81; v.p., dean, prof. Stetson U. Coll. Law, St. Petersburg, Fla., 1981-94, dean emeritus and prof., 1994—. Contbr. articles to profl. jours. Mem. Fla. Bar, Sigma Chi. Democrat. Home: 1946 Coffee Pot Blvd NE Saint Petersburg FL 33704-4632 Office: Stetson U Coll Law 1401 61st St S Saint Petersburg FL 33707-3246 E-mail: jacob@law.stetson.edu

JACOB, MARVIN EUGENE, lawyer; b. N.Y.C., Feb. 4, 1935; s. Sam Jacob and Ann (Garfinkel) Law; m. Atara Binnun, Mar. 27, 1960; children: Shalom J., Aviva, Asher. BA, Bklyn. Coll., 1961; JD cum laude, N.Y. Law Sch., 1964. Bar: N.Y. 1964, U.S. Supreme Ct. 1967. Assoc. regional adminstr. SEC, N.Y.C., 1964-79; ptnr. Weil, Gotshal & Manges, 1979—. Adj. prof. law N.Y. Law Sch., 1975—. Editor: Restructurings, 1993, Reorganizing Failing Businesses, 1999. Mem. ABA, N.Y. State Bar Assn. Bankruptcy, Federal civil litigation, Securities. Office: Weil Gotshal & Manges 767 5th Ave Fl 29 New York NY 10153-0023

JACOBI, JOHN ALBERT, lawyer, engineer; b. Columbus, Ohio, June 28, 1947; s. James Henry and Annabelle Marie (Koenig) J.; m. Jane Alice Rohrer, Aug. 26, 1967; children: Jill Ann, James Andrew. BSME with honors, Rose-Hulman Inst. Tech., 1969; MS in Indsl. Engring., Tex. A&M U., 1970; JD, U. Mo., Kansas City, 1975. Bar: Mo. 1976, Tex. 1979, Fla. 1980, U.S. Patent and Trademark Office 1982, U.S. Supreme Ct. 1985; registered profl. engr., Mo., Tex., Fla. Civilian gen. engr. Red River Army Depot, Texarkana, Tex., 1969-71; indsl. engr. U.S. Army Aviation Sys. Command, St. Louis, 1971-72; chief engr. Lake City Army Ammunition Plant, Independence, 1973-78; from mgr. environ. affairs to atty. Tenneco, Inc., Houston, 1978-84, mgr. remediation, 1989-91; gen. atty. Tenn. Gas Transmission, 1985-88; mgr. tech. svcs. Tenneco Gas Transp., 1988-89; prin. Ecology and Environment, Inc., 1991-92; v.p., sr. cons. Woodward-Clyde Cons., 1992, v.p., 1993-97; pvt. practice, 1995-96; chief bur. health Tex. Dept. Health, 1996-2000; gen. mgr. legal affairs Intercontinental Terminals Co., Houston, 2000—01. Phys. scientist Office Dir. Army Rsch., Pentagon, fall 1977; tech. dir. Harding Lawson Assocs., Houston, 1994-95; presdl. exch. exec. Tenneco Inc. Fed. Credit Union, 1978-79. Rsch. grantee Olin, 1968. Mem. ABA, NRA (life) Tex. Bar Assn., Fla. Bar Assn., Exptl. Aircraft Assn., Blue Springs Jaycees (bd. dirs. 1975-77, 1st v.p. 1977), Aircraft Owners and Pilots Assn., Blue Key, Tauy Beta Pi, Pi Tau Sigma, Alpha Pi Mu, Alpha Tau Omega. General corporate, FERC practice, Environmental. E-mail: jjacobi@iterm.com

JACOBOWITZ, HAROLD SAUL, lawyer; b. N.Y.C., Aug. 26, 1950; s. William and Miriam (Spector) J.; m. Estrella B. Rivera, Oct. 26, 1972. BA, CUNY, 1972; JD, Rutgers U., 1977. Bar: N.Y. 1977, U.S. Dist. Ct. (so. dist.) N.Y. 1978, U.S. Dist. Ct. (ea. dist.) N.Y. 1978. Assoc. Goldman & Heffernan, N.Y.C., 1977-78; assoc. Zola & Zola, 1978-79, Goldberg & Lysaght, N.Y.C., 1979-82; atty. of record Am. Internat. Group (Jacobowitz, Spessard, Garfinkel & Lesman), 1982-88, regional mng. atty., 1988-89, chief counsel, 1989-90, v.p., 1990—, chief tech. officer property/casualty claims, 1998—. Arbitration panel U.S. Dist. Ct. (ea. dist.) N.Y. Mem. ABA, N.Y. State Bar Assn., Assn. Bar City N.Y., N.Y. County Lawyers Assn., Assn. Trial Lawyers N.Y.C. (bd. dirs.). State civil litigation, Insurance, Personal injury. Office: Am Internat Group 70 Pine St New York NY 10270-0002 E-mail: harold.jacobowitz@aig.com

JACOBS, ANN ELIZABETH, lawyer; b. Lima, Ohio, July 28, 1950; d. Warren Charles and Virginia Elizabeth (Lewis) J.; m. Mark S. Bush, Nov. 26, 1988; 1 child, Whitney Elizabeth. BA, George Washington U., 1972; JD, Cath. U., 1976. Bar: Ohio 1977, Calif. 1977, U.S. Ct. Appeals (D.C. cir.) 1980, U.S. Dist. Ct. (no. dist.) Ohio 1982, S.C. 2000. Asst. atty. gen. State of Ohio, Columbus, 1977-78; trial atty. EEOC of Ohio, Miami, Fla., 1978-80; sole practice Lima, 1980—. Bd. dirs. Allen County Blackhoof Area Legal Svcs. Assn., Marimor Industries, Inc., Lima. Fundraiser Lima Symphony Orch., 1985; trustee Lima Art Assn., YWCA; bd. dirs. Sr. Citizens; mem. bd. elders Market St. Presbyn. Ch., chairperson mission com., 2001. Recipient Recognition award US Naval Air Sta., Jacksonville, Fla., 1979. Mem. LWV, Ohio Bar Assn., Calif. Bar Assn., D.C. Bar Assn., Allen County Bar Assn. (chmn. juvenile ct. com. 1993). Avocations: sailing, golf, reading. General civil litigation, General practice, Personal injury. Home: 1529 Shawnee Rd Lima OH 45805-3801 Office: Jacobs & Von der Embse 558 W Spring St Lima OH 45801-4728

JACOBS, CHARLES P. lawyer; b. Buffalo, Apr. 2, 1950; s. Phillip Roblin and Joyce Marilyn (Schwab) J.; m. Jill Lang, June 10, 1973; children—Eliza, Lauren. B.A. in History, U. Pa., 1972; J.D., SUNY-Buffalo, 1975. Bar: N.Y. 1976, U.S. Dist. Ct. (we. dist.) N.Y. 1976. Assoc. firm Moot & Sprague, Buffalo, 1975-80; v.p., gen. counsel Envirogas, Inc., Hamburg, N.Y., 1980-84; former assoc. Saperston, Day Lustig, Gallick, Kirschner & Gaglione, P.C., Buffalo; now with Nixon, Hargrave, Devans & Doyle, Buffalo. Mem. ABA, N.Y. State Bar Assn., Erie County Bar Assn. Club: Buffalo Tennis and Squash. General corporate, Oil, gas, and mineral, Securities. Office: Nixon Hargrave Devans & Doyle 1600 Empire Tower Buffalo NY 14202-3716

JACOBS, DENNIS, federal judge; b. N.Y.C., Feb. 28, 1944; s. Harry N. and Rose J.; m. Judith Weissman. BA, Queens Coll., 1964; MA, NYU, 1965, JD, 1973. Atty. Simpson Thacher & Bartlett, N.Y.C., 1973-92; judge U.S. Ct. Appeals (2d cir.), 1992—. Office: US Ct Appeals US Courthouse 40 Foley SqRm 1904 New York NY 10007-1502*

JACOBS, HARA KAY, lawyer; b. Phila., Dec. 22, 1969; d. Ellis R. Jacobs and Sandy K. Sacks; m. Clifford I. Ward, Oct. 10, 1998. BA, U. Mich., 1991; JD, Duke U., 1994. Bar: Pa. 1994, U.S. Dist. Ct. (ea. dist.) Pa. 1995, N.J. 1995, U.S. Dist. Ct. N.J. 1995, U.S. Dist. Ct. (ea. and so. dists.) N.Y. 1997, N.Y. 1998. Assoc. Ballard Spahr Andrews & Ingersoll, Phila., 1994-97, Hall Dickler, N.Y.C., 1997-98, Pryor Cashman Sherman & Flynn, N.Y.C., 1998—. Mem. ABA (intellectual property sect.), Internat. Trademark Assn. (project editl. bd.), N.Y. Bar Assn., Phi Beta Kappa. Avocations: basketball, skiing, running. General civil litigation, Trademark and copyright. Office: Pryor Cashman Sherman & Flynn 410 Park Ave Fl 10 New York NY 10022-4407

JACOBS, JACK BERNARD, judge; b. July 23, 1942; s. Louis K. and Phoebe J.; m. Marion Antiles, Apr. 2, 1967; 1 child, Andrew Seth. AB, U. Chgo., 1964; LLB, Harvard U., 1967. Bar: Del. 1968, U.S. Dist. Ct. Del. 1968, U.S. Ct. Appeals (3d cir.) 1968, U.S. Supreme Ct. 1975. Law clk. Del. Chancery and Superior Cts., 1967-68; assoc. Young, Conaway, Stargatt & Taylor, Wilmington, Del., 1968-71, ptnr., 1971-85; vice chancellor Ct. of Chancery State of Del., 1985—. Adj. prof. Widener U. Sch. Law, 1986—; chmn. Bar-Bench-Media Conf. Del., 1992-93; mem. various faculty continuing legal edn. programs. Contbr. articles to profl. jours. Vice chmn. Nat. Jewish Cmty. Rels. Adv. Coun., 1985-89; bd. dirs. Jewish Fedn. Del., 1981-87, Del. Symphony Assn., 1991-95, Del. Cmty. Found., 1994-2000, chair grants com., 1998-2000; pres. Milton & Hattie Kutz Home, 1990-92. Mem.: ABA (litigation sect., bus. law sect., mem. com. corp. laws 1999—), Am. Law Inst. (advisor Restatement (3d) Restitution), Am. Judicature Soc. (bd. dirs. 1999—), Del. Bar Assn., Harvard Law Sch. Del. (pres. 1986—87), Phi Beta Kappa. Democrat. Jewish. Home: 28 Beethoven Dr Wilmington DE 19807-1923 Office: Ct of Chancery 1000 N King St Wilmington DE 19801-3303 E-mail: JJacobs@state.De.us

JACOBS, JEFFREY LEE, lawyer, education network company executive; b. Boston, Jan. 20, 1951; s. Philip and Millicent T. (Katz) J.; m. Deborah R. Rath, June 7, 1981; children: Alison, Hannah. BA, U. Pa., 1973; MPA, U. So. Calif., 1979; JD, Pace U., 1985. Bar: Conn. 1985, N.Y. 1988. Asst. to comptroller gen. U.S. Gen. Acctg. Office, Washington, 1976-80; sr. rsch. assoc. Nat. Acad. Pub. Adminstrn., 1980-83; dir. of seminars Prentice Hall, Clifton, N.J., 1985-87; pres. Profl. Edn. Network, Inc., Westport, Conn., 1987—. Lectr. Ga. Tax Inst., Ohio Fed. Tax Inst.; adj. prof. Quinnipiac Coll., Univ. New Haven; cons. SmartPros Ltd. Co-author: GAO: Government Accountability, 1979; producer, writer TV series The CPA Report, 1988-91; producer, writer radio series Legal Practice Alert, 1990—. Trustee Westport Pub. Libr. Mem. ABA (taxation sect.), Acad. Legal Studies in Bus. Home: 16 Janson Dr Westport CT 06880-2568 Office: SmartPros Ltd 12 Skyline Dr Hawthorne NY 10532-2133 E-mail: jeffjacobs@keepsmart.com

JACOBS, JOHN PATRICK, lawyer; b. Chgo., Oct. 27, 1945; s. Anthony N. and Bessie (Montgomery) J.; m. Linda I. Grams, Oct. 6, 1973; 1 child, Christine Margaret. BA cum laude, U. Detroit, 1967, JD magna cum laude, 1970. Bar: Mich. 1979, U.S. Dist. Ct. Mich (ea. dist.) 1970, U.S. Ct. Appeals (6th cir.) 1974, U.S. Ct. Appeals (D.C. cir.) 1988, U.S. Supreme Ct. 1978, U.S. Ct. Appeals (4th cir.) 2001. Law clk. to chief judge Mich. Ct. Appeals, Detroit, 1970-71; assoc., then ptnr. Plunkett & Cooney P.C., 1972-92, also bd. dirs.; founding ptnr., prin. mem. O'Leary, O'Leary, Jacobs, Mattson, Perry & Mason P.C., Southfield, Mich., 1992-99; prin., owner John P. Jacobs, P.C., 1999—. Investigator Atty. Grievance Com., Detroit, 1975-84; mem. hearing panel Atty. Discipline Bd., Detroit, 1984-87, 94—; adj. prof. law Sch. Law, U. Detroit, 1983-84, faculty advisor, 1984-89, Pres.'s Cabinet, 1982—; elected rep. State Bar Rep. Assembly, Lansing, Mich., 1980-82, 91-92, 93-96; fellow Mich. State Bar Found., 1990-98; treas., mem. steering com. Mich. Bench-Bar Appellate Conf. Com., 1994—; apptd. mem. Mich. Supreme Ct. Com. on Appellate Fees, 1990; spl. mediator appellate negotiation program Mich. Ct. Appeals, 1995—; mem. exec. com. Mich. Appellate Bench-Bar Conf. Found., 1996—; appellate counsel to State Bar of Mich., mem. profl. ethics com., 1998, mem. multi-disciplinary practice com., 1999. Bd. editors Mich. Lawyers Weekly. Bd. dirs. Boysville of Mich., Clinton, 1988-95, 99—,

chmn. pub. policy com., 1993-95, pub. policy liaison, 1999—; apptd. mem. State Bar Mich. Blue Ribbon Com. Improving Def. Counsel-Insurer Rels., 1998-99. Recipient Robert E. Dice Med. Malpractice Def. Atty. award Mich. Physicians, 1986; Reginald Heber Smith fellow, 1971-72. Fellow Am. Acad. Appellate Lawyers, Mich. Std. Jury Instn. (subcom. employment law 1984-87); mem. ABA (litigation sect., appellate subcom., torts and ins. practice), Internat. Assn. Def. Counsel (v.p., amicus curiae com., med. and legal malpractice coms., product liability com.), Fedn. Ins. and Corp. Counsel, Mich. Def. Trial Counsel (chmn. amicus curiae com. 1986-88, chmn. future planning com., bd. dirs. 1989—, treas. 1993-94, sec. 1994-95, v.p. 1995-96, program chair 1990, 94, 95, pres., 1996-97), Def. Rsch. Inst. (state rep. 1997-98, Outstanding Performance Citation 1997, nat. appellate com. steering com. 1997—), Cath. Lawyers Soc. (bd. dirs. 1988-98, emeritus dir. 1998—, pres. 1994-95), Democrat. Roman Catholic. Avocations: collecting antique law books, film. Appellate, Federal civil litigation, State civil litigation. Office: 1 Towne Sq Ste 1400 Southfield MI 48076-3705

JACOBS, JOSEPH JAMES, lawyer, communications company executive; b. Toronto, Ont., Can., Mar. 18, 1925; came to U.S., 1925; s. Sidney and Hildred Veronica (Greenberg) J.; m. Carole Evelyn Bent, Jan. 22, 1946 (div. 1972); children— Carole Lynn Urgenson, Joseph James III; m. Edna Mae Meincke, Jan. 5, 1973. J.D., Tulane U., 1950. Bar: La. 1950, N.Y. 1951, U.S. Dist. Ct. (so. dist.) N.Y. 1953, U.S. Ct. Mil. Appeals 1953, U.S. Ct. Appeals (2d cir.) 1977, U.S. Ct. Appeals (D.C. cir.) 1980. Assoc. Proskauer, Rose, Goetz & Mendelsohn, N.Y.C., 1950-53; asst. gen. counsel, asst. to pres. Am. Broadcasting Co., N.Y.C., 1954-60; gen. atty. Metromedia, Inc., N.Y.C., 1960-61; dir. program and talent negotiations United Artists TV, Inc., 1961-66; atty. United Artists Corp., N.Y.C., 1966-69; v.p., counsel United Artists Broadcasting, Inc., N.Y.C., 1969-71; gen. atty. ITT World Communications Inc., N.Y.C., 1972-74; v.p., legal dir. ITT Communications Ops. and Info. Services Group (formerly U.S. Telephone & Telegraph Corp.), N.Y.C. and Secaucus, N.J., 1974-83, ITT Communications and Info. Services, Inc., Secaucus, 1983-87; v.p., gen. counsel U.S. Transmission Systems, Inc., Secaucus, 1984-87, ITT World Communications Inc., Secaucus, 1984-87; of counsel Seyfarth, Shaw, Fairweathr & Geraldson, N.Y.C., 1988-89; v.p., gen. counsel Graphic Scanning Corp., Englewood, N.J., 1989-91; v.p., gen. counsel Ram/BSE, L.P., Woodbridge, N.J., 1992; pvt. practice, Wainscott, N.Y., 1992-95. Bd. editors Tulane Law Rev., 1949, asst. editor-in-chief, 1950; cons. 1996—. Served with parachute inf. U.S. Army, 1943-46, ETO, PTO, to maj. USAFR ret. Mem. Assn. Bar City of N.Y., Fed. Bar Assn., Order of Coif. Republican. Jewish. Administrative and regulatory, General corporate, Entertainment. Office: 6380 Sweet Maple Ln Boca Raton FL 33433-1933

JACOBS, JULIAN I. federal judge; b. Balt., Aug. 13, 1937; s. Sidney and Bernice (Kellman) J.; m. Donna Buffenstein; children: Richard S., Jennifer K. B.A., U. Md., 1958, J.D., 1960; LL.M., Georgetown U., 1965. Bar: Md., 1960. Atty. chief counsel's office IRS, Washington, 1961-65, trial atty. regional counsel's office Buffalo, 1965-67; assoc. Weinberg & Green, Balt., 1967-69, Hoffberger & Hollander, Balt., 1969-72, Gordon Feinblatt Rothman Hoffberger & Hollander, Balt., 1972-74, ptnr., 1974-84; judge U.S. Tax Ct., Washington, 1984—. Chmn. study commn. Md. Tax Ct., 1978-79, mem. rules com., 1980; mem. spl. study group Md. Gen. Assembly, 1980; adj. prof. grad. tax program U. Balt., 1991-93; adj. prof. law, U. San Diego, 2001—; adj. prof. grad. tax program, U. Denver, 2001—, U. Wis., 2001—. Mem. U. Md. Law Rev. Bd. dirs. Md. Med. Research Inst., Inc. Mem. Md. State Bar Assn. (past chmn. taxation sect.), Balt. City Bar Assn. (past chmn. tax legis. subcom.). Office: US Tax Ct 400 2nd St NW Washington DC 20217-0002

JACOBS, MARY LEE, lawyer; b. Pitts., June 29, 1950; d. George and Mary Jane (Swinderman) Jacobs. BA in History, Wellesley Coll., 1972; JD, Boston U., 1974. BAr: Mass. 1975, U.S. Dist. Ct. Mass. 1976, U.S. Ct. Appeals (1st cir.) 1978, U.S. Supreme Ct. 1981. Gen. counsel Tufts U., Medford, Mass., 1984—. Mem. ABA, Boston Bar Assn., Nat. Assn. Coll. and Univ. Attys. Education and schools. Office: Tufts Univ Ballou Hall 3d Fl Medford MA 02155

JACOBS, PAUL, lawyer; b. N.Y.C., Sept. 29, 1946; s. William R. and Sylvia (Wanshel) J.; m. Lisette Simon, Oct. 10, 1979; children: Alexia, Caroline. BA, Colgate U., 1967; JD, Columbia U., 1971. Bar: N.Y. 1971, U.S. Dist. Ct. (so. dist.) N.Y. 1971. Assoc. Reavis & McGrath, N.Y.C., 1971-78, ptnr., 1978-89, Fulbright & Jaworski, N.Y.C., 1989-96, sr. ptnr., 1996—. Mem. adv. com. Grace Ventures Corp., Cupertino, Calif., 1988-98, Euro-Am.-I C.V., San Bruno, Calif., 1988-98; sec. Zygo Corp., Middlefield, Conn., 1992—. Mem. N.Y. Bar Assn., N.Y.C. Bar Assn., Phi Beta Kappa, The University Club. General corporate, Private international. Office: Fulbright & Jaworski 666 5th Ave Fl 31 New York NY 10103-0001 E-mail: p.jacobs@fulbright.com

JACOBS, PAUL ELLIOT, lawyer; b. Sioux City, Iowa, Feb. 11, 1946; s. Leonard D. and Ruth (Jelenk) J.; m. Renee M. Glennon, Mar. 4, 1972; children: Sarah, Andrew, Ian. BA, Northwestern U., 1968; JD, Santa Clara U., 1971. Bar: Calif. 1972. Dept. dist. atty. Santa Clara County Dist. Atty., San Jose, Calif., 1972-76; ptnr. Beauzay, Hammer, Ezgar, Bledsoe & Sprenkle, 1976-85, Hammer & Jacobs, San Jose, 1985—. Lectr. CEB, ABA, San Diego County Bar Assn., Santa Clara County Bar Assn., Calif. Family Law Reports. Contbr. articles on family law to profl. jours. Planning commr., City of Saratoga, Calif., 1992-94, mem. city coun., 1994-98, mayor, City of Saratoga, 1995-96; chmn. Santa Clara County Hist. Heritage Commn., 1977-80, San Jose Hist. Mus. Assn., 1977-80. Fellow Am. Acad. Matrimonial Lawyers (treas. No. Calif. chpt. 1983-85); mem. Santa Clara County Bar Assn. (chmn. family law com. 1981, 82), State Bar Calif. (lectr. family law sect., family law adv. commn. 1981-86, chmn. 1985-86). Family and matrimonial. E-mail: PaulJ@hammerandjacobs.com

JACOBS, RANDALL SCOTT DAVID, lawyer; b. Sept. 6, 1944; s. Irving and Lea Sylvia (Kerner) Jacobs; m. Jill Barbara Weiss, June 20, 1981; children: Evan, Todd. BSBA, NYU, 1967, LLM in Corp. Law, 1971; JD, Temple U., 1970. Bar: N.Y. 1977, U.S. Dist. Ct. (ea. dist.) N.Y. 1979, U.S. Dist. Ct. (so. dist.) N.Y. 1979, U.S. Ct. Appeals (2d cir.) 1980, U.S. Supreme Ct. 1980. Assoc. Coudert Brothers, N.Y.C., NY, 1968; with Comml. Coverage Corp., 1971—78; assoc. Levy, Tandet, Sohn and Loft, 1978—82; of counsel Harvis and Zeichner, 1982—84; ptnr. Rich, Krinsly, Dorman & Jacobs, P.C., 1984—91, Mintz and Fraade, PC, N.Y.C., 1991—94, Branin Investments, Inc., N.Y.C., 1995—96, Recap. Ptnrs., LLC, N.Y.C., 1996—2000, FMG Acquisitions Fund, LLC, N.Y.C., 2000—. Mem. staff Temple Law Quarterly Law Rev., 1969—70. Mem.: ABA, N.Y. State Bar Assn., Assn. of Bar of City of N.Y. Federal civil litigation, State civil litigation, Consumer commercial. Office: 67 Wall St Ste 1901 New York NY 10005

JACOBS, ROGER BRUCE, lawyer, educator; b. Newark, Apr. 9, 1951; s. Seymour B. and Pearle (Flaschen) J.; m. Robin Hodes, July 2, 1978; children: Joshua Seymour, Rachel Pearle. BS, Cornell U., 1973; JD, NYU, 1976, LLM in Labor Law, 1979. Bar: N.J. 1977, D.C. 1978, N.Y. 1980. Asst. prosecutor Hudson County Prosecutor's Office, Jersey City, 1977-79; assoc. Guggenheimer & Untermyer, N.Y.C., 1979-82, Rosen, Gelman & Weiss, Newark, 1982-83; ptnr. Jacobs and Assocs., N.Y.C. and Newark, 1983—. Adj. prof. N.Y. Law Sch., 1979-83, Rutgers U. Inst. Mgmt. and Labor Rels., Am. Mgmt. Assn., Law Sch. Fordham U., 1989—; mem. faculty ann. conf. labor NYU, 1987. Author: Labor and Employment in New Jersey, 1992, 2d edit., 2000, Legal Compliance Guide to Personnel Management, 1993, The Employee Handbook Kit, 1993, 2d edit., 1998, Defense of Claims under the Americans with Disabilities Act, 1994; contbr. articles to profl. jours. Counsel N.J. Zool. Soc.; trustee, mem. exec. com. Garden State Polit. Action Com., N.J., 1981-96; bd. dirs. Hamilton-Madison House, 1985-89; asst. sec. N.J YM-YWHA Camps, 1989-93; chmn. Cub pack 118 com. Essex coun. Boy Scouts Am., 1990-95, v.p. Essex coun., 1998-99; chmn. Essex coun. Friends of Scouting, 1997; trustee N.J. Jewish News of Metrowest, v.p., 1998—; chmn. cmty. rels. Jewish Fedn. of Metrowest. Lieberman fellow in labor law, 1978-79; recipient Jeffords prize for disting. writing N.Y. Law Sch., 1984, Shofar award, 2000, Silver Beaver award, 2000, Kuttner Pro Bono award, Essex Co. Bar Assn., 2000. Mem. ABA (labor and employment law sects., com. on equal opportunity law), N.J. State Bar Assn. (labor law, editl. bd. N.J. Lawyer newspaper 1993-95, mag. 1983-96), N.Y. County Lawyers Assn. (chmn. com. on labor 1987-90, chmn. com. sports law 1993-96), N.Y. State Bar Assn. (labor law com.), Cornell Club No. N.J., Cornell Club N.Y.C. Democrat. Labor. Home: 31 Undercliff Ter West Orange NJ 07052-3929 Office: 460 Park Ave New York NY 10022-1906 also: One Gateway Ctr Newark NJ 07102 E-mail: rjacobslaw@cs.com

JACOBS, ROLLY WARREN, judge; b. Nashville, Aug. 26, 1946; s. William Clinton Jr. and Eleanor Olive (Warren) J.; m. Karen Lee Ponist, Sept. 16, 1972; children: Collin Wayne, Tyler Warren. BA in Econs., Washington & Lee U., 1968; JD, U. S.C., 1974. Bar: S.C. 1975, U.S. Dist. Ct. for S.C. 1975. Assoc. Carl R. Reasonover, Camden, S.C., 1975-77; ptnr. Reasonover & Jacobs, 1977-80; pvt. practice law, 1980-99; judge family ct. 5th Jud. Cir., 1999—. Asst. city judge Mcpl. Ct., Camden, 1976-77; master in equity S.C. Jud. Sys., Camden, 1978-99; mem. Jud. Coun. for S.C., Columbia, 1989-2000; mem. fee dispute panel S.C. Bar Assn., 1986-93. Bd. dirs. ARC, Camden, 1976-78, Am. Cancer Soc., Camden, 1976-78, United Way, Camden, 1978-82; active Boy Scouts Am., Camden, 1984-96. Capt. U.S. Army, 1968-72. Recipient Dist. Award of Merit Indian Waters Coun. Boy Scouts Am., 1991; named Scouting Family of Yr., 1990. Mem. ABA, VFW, S.C. Bar Assn., Am. Legion, Res. Officers Assn., Elks. Methodist. Home: 418 Lafayette Way Camden SC 29020-1642 Office: Kershaw County Courthouse PO Box 664 Camden SC 29020-0664

JACOBS, WENDELL EARLY, JR. lawyer; b. Detroit, Nov. 15, 1945; s. Wendell E. and Mildred P. (Horton) J.; m. Elaine M. Lott (div.); children: Wendell Early III, Damon R. BFA, Denison U., 1969; JD, Wayne State U., 1972. Bar: Mich. 1972, U.S. Dist. Ct. (ea. dist.) Mich. 1973, Fla. 1974. Asst. prosecutor Jackson County, Mich., 1973-76; ptnr. Jacobs & Engle, Jackson, 1977—. Mem. Mich. Coun. on Crime and Delinquency. Mem. Nat. Assn. Criminal Def. Lawyers, Criminal Def. Attys. Mich., Jackson County Bar Assn., Eagles Club, Grotto Club, Elks. Avocations: paddleball, motorcycling. Criminal, Family and matrimonial, General practice. Home: 9281 Greenwood Rd Grass Lake MI 49240-9590 Office: Jacobs & Engle 1104 W Michigan Ave Jackson MI 49202-4123

JACOBS, WILLIAM RUSSELL, II, lawyer; b. Chgo., Oct. 26, 1927; s. William Russell and Doris B. (Desmond) J.; m. Shirley M. Spiegler, Mar. 21, 1950; children: William R. III, Richard W., Bruce Allen. BS, Northwestern U., 1950, JD, 1953. Bar: Ill. 1953, U.S. Dist. Ct. (no. dist.) Ill. 1958, U.S. Ct. Appeals (7th cir.) 1958, U.S. Supreme Ct., 1962. Atty. Continental Casualty Co., Chgo., 1955-58; assoc. Horwitz and Anesi, 1958-62; prin. William R. Jacobs and Assocs., 1962—. Adj. prof. Lewis Coll. Law, Glen Ellyn, Ill., 1975-76; dir., tchr. Ct. Practice Inst., Chgo., 1974—; lectr. Ill. Inst. Continuing Legal Edn., Chgo., 1967—. Elected alderman Des Plaines (Ill.) City Coun., 1953-54; mem. Ill. Bar Assembly, 1973—. 1st lt. inf. U.S. Army, 1946-48. Mem. Ill. State Bar Assn., Am. Acad. Matrimonial Lawyers. Congregationalist. General civil litigation, Family and matrimonial, Personal injury. Office: William R Jacobs & Assocs 601 Lee St Des Plaines IL 60016-4631 E-mail: spregler@home.com

JACOBSEN, RAYMOND ALFRED, JR. lawyer; b. Wilmington, Del., Dec. 14, 1949; s. Raymond Alfred and Margaret (Walters) J.; m. Marilyn Perry, Aug. 4, 1973; 1 child, Hunter Perry. BA, U. Del., 1971; JD, Georgetown U., 1975. Bar: D.C. 1975, U.S. Supreme Ct. 1982. From assoc. to ptnr. Howrey & Simon, Washington, 1975-97; dir. Antitrust/Trade Reg. Grp. McDermott, Will & Emery, 1997-, ptnr., 1997—. Adj. prof. internat. anti-trust law Am. U. Law Sch. Spl. projects editor Law & Policy in International Business, 1974-75. Served to capt. U.S. Army, 1975. Mem. ABA (antitrust law sect., adminstrv. law sect., corp. banking and bus. law sect., litigation sect., internat. law sect., pub. contract law sect.), D.C. Bar Assn., U.S. Supreme Ct. Bar Assn. Republican. Club: Army & Navy, City (Washington). Antitrust, Federal civil litigation, Mergers and acquisitions. Home: 4205 Maple Tree Ct Alexandria VA 22304-1035 Office: McDermott Will & Emery 600 13th St NW Fl 12 Washington DC 20005-3096 E-mail: rayjacobsen@mwe.com

JACOBSON, BARRY STEPHEN, lawyer, judge; b. Bklyn., Mar. 30, 1955; s. Morris and Sally (Ballaban) J.; m. Andrea Jacobson; children: Faith Blair, Matthew Aaron Jacobson. Cert. in drama, Sch. of Performing Arts, N.Y.C., 1973; BA, CUNY, 1977, MA, 1980; JD, Bklyn. Sch. Law, 1980. Bar: N.Y., 1981, U.S. Dist. Ct. (ea. and so. dists.) N.Y. 1981, U.S. Dist. Ct. (we. and no. dists.) N.Y., 1988, U.S. Dist. Ct. D.C., 1988, U.S. Ct. Appeals (2d cir.) 1981, U.S. Ct. Appeals (fed. and D.C. cirs.) 1988, U.S. Supreme Ct. 1984, U.S. Ct. Claims, 1985, U.S. Tax Ct. 1988 and others. Sole practice, Bklyn., 1981; asst. corp. counsel N.Y.C. Law Dept., 1981-84; asst. dist. atty. Borough of Queens, Kew Gardens, N.Y., 1984-85; judge adminstrv. law N.Y. Dept. Motor Vehicles, Bklyn., 1985-86, 87-92; assoc. counsel N.Y. State Dept. Health, N.Y.C., 1986; arbitrator N.Y.C. Small Claims Ct., 1986-91; pvt. practice Bklyn., 1992—. Gen. counsel Amersfort Flatlands Devel. Corp., Bklyn., 1981-82; arbitrator N.Y.C. Civil Ct. 1987-92; adminstrv. law judge N.Y.C. Parking Violators Bur., 1987-93; mem. Indigent Defenders Appeal Panel, 1988-96; sr. adminstrv. law judge N.Y.C. Parking Violation Bur., 1989-93; leader Nat. Jud. Coll., N.Y. Mem. Roosevelt Dem. Party, Bklyn., 1984-95, mem. adv. bd., 1989-92, treas., 1990-92; active Kings Hwy. Dem. Party, Bklyn., 1982-95, Dem. com. 1986-95; active King's County Young Dems., 1985-86; gen. counsel Bklyn. Coll. Hillel, Bklyn. Coll. Student Govts., 1980-90, also advisor; treas. local div. dept. mtr. vehicles pub. employees fedn. AFL-CIO; coun. ldr. div. #255 Pub. Employee's Fedn., 1989-92, conv. del. 1989, 90, 91; chmn. Bklyn. Traffic Employee Assistance Prog., 1989-92. Named one of Outstanding Young Men Am., 1983, 85, 86, 87, 88. Mem. ABA (judicial sect., spl. const. judges traffic cts. com.), Am. Judges Assn. (hwy. safety com.), Bklyn. Bar Found. (trustee, bd. dirs.), Am. Arbitration Assn. (forums 1988—), Am. Judicature Soc., Assn. Adminstrv. Law Judges (pres.), N.Y. State Dept. Motor Vehicles (v.p.), N.Y. State Adminstrv. Law Judges Assn. (pres. bd. dirs. parking violation com., v.p.), N.Y. State Bar Assn. (pres. for DMV, spl. com. juvenile justice, adminstrv. law jud. coms., jud. adminstrn. com.), Bklyn. Bar Assn. (family ct. com., chmn. young lawyers sect., trustee 1991, chmn. adminstrn. law com.), N.Y. County Lawyers Assn. (family Ct. Com.), Bklyn. Coll. Alumni Assn. (gen. counsel student govt. affiliate 1983-92, bd. dirs. 1985-92), Jaycees, B'nai B'rith, Hillel (bd. dirs. 1983-91, gen. counsel 1987-91), many others. Jewish. Avocations: motorcycling, drama, theatre, target shooting, flying. Administrative and regulatory, Criminal, Family and matrimonial. Home: 342 Coleridge Ln Jericho NY 11753-2605 Office: 26 Court St Ste 810 Brooklyn NY 11242-1108 E-mail: ticklan@aol.com

JACOBSON, DAVID EDWARD, lawyer; b. Port Chester, N.Y., May 17, 1949; s. Robert Herzel and Ruth Doris (Rosenzweig) J.; m. Debra Ann Denkensohn, Aug. 10, 1975; 1 child, Andrew. BA in Econs., U. Rochester, 1971; JD, SUNY, Buffalo, 1974; LLM in Taxation, Georgetown U., 1977. Bar: N.Y. 1975, D.C. 1976, U.S. Tax Ct. 1982, U.S. Ct. Appeals (fed. cir.) 1983. Atty.-advisor Office of Chief Counsel, IRS, Washington, 1974-79; tax counsel com. on fin. U.S. Senate, 1979-81; assoc. firm Thelen Reid & Priest LLP, 1981-86, ptnr., 1986—. Mem. Partnership Coun., 2001—. Vol. Income Tax Assistance, Arlington, Va., 1977-81; treas. Overlook Townhouse Homeowners Assn., Arlington. Mem. ABA (mem. tax sect. 1982—, vice chmn. regulated utilities com. 1988-90, chmn. 1990-92), N.Y. State Bar Assn. Avocations. Public utilities, Corporate taxation, Personal income taxation. Office: Thelen Reid & Priest LLP 701 Pennsylvania Ave NW Ste 800 Washington DC 20004-2608 E-mail: djacobson@thelenreid.com

JACOBSON, GARY STEVEN, lawyer; b. Holyoke, Mass., Sept. 4, 1951; s. Rudolph Milton and Frederika Helena (Vanderryn) J.; m. Sharon W. Turkish, June 16, 1974; children: Lowell Daniel, Lee Stuart. BA cum laude, Wesleyan U., Middletown, Conn., 1973; JD, Northwestern U., 1976. Bar: Conn. 1976, N.Y. 1977, N.J. 1977, U.S. Ct. Appeals (3d cir.) 1981, U.S. Ct. Appeals (2d cir.) 1996. Investigative atty. N.Y. State Commn. on Jud. Conduct, N.Y.C., 1976-77; spl. asst. atty. gen. Office Spl. State Prosecutor, 1977-79; assoc. Hofheimer, Gartlir, Gottlieb & Gross, 1979-80, Kleinberg, Moroney, Masterson & Schachter, Millburn, N.J., 1980-85, ptnr., 1986-90; of counsel Kelley Drye & Warren, N.Y.C., 1990-91, ptnr., 1992-96, Farer Siegal Fersko, Westfield, N.J., 1996-98; mem. Jacobson & Brecher LLC, Mountainside, 1998—. Co-author: Commercial Litigation in New York State Courts, 1995; editor: Judicial Discipline Reporter, 1976. Republican. Jewish. Bankruptcy, Federal civil litigation, Contracts commercial. Home: 99 Susan Dr Chatham NJ 07928-1055 Office: Jacobson & Brecher LLC PO Box 1220 608 Sherwood Pkwy Mountainside NJ 07092-2512

JACOBSON, JEFFREY E. lawyer, consultant; b. N.Y.C., Aug. 19, 1956; s. Murray and Adele (Ebert) J.; m. Linda Moel, Aug. 11, 1984; children: Justin Myles, Sari Amanda. BA, Fordham U., 1976; JD, N.Y. Law Sch., 1980. Bar: N.Y. 1982, D.C. 1982, U.S. Tax Ct. 1982, U.S. Ct. Internat. Trade 1982, U.S. Dist. Ct. (so. and ea. dists.) N.Y. 1982, U.S. Ct. Appeals (2nd cir.) 1988, U.S. Supreme Ct. 1988. Assoc. SESAC, Inc., N.Y.C., 1980-82; sole practice N.Y.C. and D.C., 1982-85; sr. ptnr. Jacobson & Colfin, P.C., N.Y.C., Washington, L.I., 1985-90, mng. mem., 1991—; exec. v.p., sec. Fifth Ave. Media, Ltd., N.Y.C., 1995—; assoc. prof. Five Towns Coll., N.Y., 1999—. Asst. mgr. Embassy Theatre, N.Y.C., 1975, Victoria Theatre, N.Y.C., 1975; asst. Theatre Confections, Inc., N.Y.C., 1975; mgr. Criterion Theatre, N.Y.C., 1976; mgr., sec. Squirrels Prodns. Ltd., N.Y.C., 1976-88; pres. Aldous Demian Prodns., Ltd., N.Y.C., 1980-82; counsel Box Office Media, N.Y.C., 1982-88, Eggink, N.Y.C., 1982-89, Performance Records, 1988-97, J&J Mus. Enterprises, Ltd., 1982-95,, Anamaze Records, 1982-95, Cynthia Entertainment Group, Ltd., 1989-91, Roir Records, Inc., 1992—, Super Bubble Music Corp., 1992-99, Sergei Artemiev Benefit, 1993, New Riders of the Purple Sage, 1985—, Mick Taylor Music, 1985—, Best Film and Video Corp., 1988-91, Marty Balin, 1988—, Andrew Tosh, 1990—; spkr. CMJ Music Marathon & Musicfest, 1995, Phila. Music Confs., 1993, 94, 95, 96, 97. Mem. editl. bd. Mealey's Intellectual Property Litigation Law Report, 1992-93; contbr. articles to profl. jours.; music and internat. promotion mgmt., 1984-85; columnist IMPS Jour., 1990-95; featured columnist Replication News Medialine, 1998—. Mem. Rep. candidate assembly; v.p. Pelham Pkwy., 1983-88; speaker Songwriter's Guild, N.Y.C., 1983-88, NARAS, 1991; entertainment arbitrator Am. Arbitration Assn., N.Y.C., 1984-95; guest speaker Ctr. for Media Arts, N.Y.C., 1985, Fordham U., N.Y.C., 1986, N.Y. Law Sch., 1987, Detroit Sch. Law, 1991, 93; counsel Pelham Pkwy. Block Assn., Inc., 1991; panelist Mid-Am. Music Conf., Detroit, 1993, Black Radio Exclusive, Econs. of Music, 1993; league lawyer Hewlett-Woodmere Little League, 1994-2000. Recipient Eagle Scout with Silver Palm award Boy Scouts Am., 1972, Cert. of Merit Bronx House, 1973, Nathan Burkan award ASCAP, 1980, Plaque of Appreciation, Am. Arbitration Assn., 1985; named Most Admired Men and Women of Yr., 1993, Two Thousand Notable Am. Men, 1993, Man of Yr., 1996. Mem. ABA (chmn. subcom. on satellites, chmn. subcom. on copyright compliance, chmn. subcom. on copyright renewal, mem. patent trademark, copyright law sect., forum com. on entertainment and sports law sects., mem. spl. com. on corp. practice 1992-97, mem. spl. com. on atty. opinions 1994—, mem. spl. com. on internet 1997—, sub. com. on broadcasting & music industry), forum com. on comm. law, young lawyer's divsn., vice chmn. 1992-94, patent, trademark, intellectual property sect. exec. com., 1992-93, media law com., young lawyers divsn., founder Urban Intellectual Property Law seminars 1993-95, dir., 1993-95, mem. com. on atty./client opinions, mem. spl. com. Internet usage), Assn. of Bar of City of N.Y. (entertainment law com. 1992-95, trademark law com. 1997-2000), Copyright Soc. USA (com. on Bicentennial of copyright, mem. editl. bd. Jour. of Copyright Soc. 1991-93, 97—, trustee 2001-04), Nat. Acad. Rec. Arts and Scis. (edn. com., columnist N.Y. chpt. newsletter 1997-2000), Rock and Roll Hall of Fame and Museum (founding mem.), Internat. Assn. Entertainment Lawyers, B'nai B'rith (v.p. 1988-91), Order of the Arrow Brotherhood, Sephardic Jewish Brotherhood Am., Masons (officer 1997-2000, planning bd. Village of Hewlett Harbor 2001—), Audubon Soc. Inc., Phi Delta Phi. Jewish. Avocations: music, photography, swimming, stereo equipment, traveling. Federal civil litigation, Entertainment, Trademark and copyright. Office: Jacobson & Colfin PC 19 W 21st St New York NY 10010-6805 also: 1208 W Broadway Hewlett NY 11557 E-mail: jejesq@aol.com, jeff@thefirm.com

JACOBSON, SANDRA W. lawyer; b. Bklyn., Feb. 1, 1930; d. Elias and Anna (Goldstein) Weinstein; m. Irving Jacobson, July 31, 1955; 1 child, Bonnie Nancy. BA, Vassar Coll., 1951; LLB, Yale U., 1954. Bar: N.Y. 1955, U.S. Supreme Ct. 1960, U.S. Dist. Ct. (so., ea. dists.) N.Y. 1972, U.S. Ct. Appeals (2nd cir.) 1975. Ptnr. Mulligan, Jacobson & Langenus, N.Y.C., 1964-88, Hall, McNicol, Hamilton & Clark, N.Y.C., 1988-92; sole practitioner, 1992—. Lectr. in family law. Contbr. articles to profl. jours. and chpts. to books. Mem.: ABA (family law sect.), N.Y. State Bar Assn. (family law sect., legis. and exec. com., co-chair lawyer specialization 1999—), N.Y. Women's Bar Assn. (pres. 1989—90, matrimonial and family law com. 1984—, chmn. 1986—88, jud. screening com. 1987—88, ethics commn. 1990—), Women's Bar Assn. of State of N.Y. (matrimonial com. 1986—, co-chair 1987—89, chair cts. com. 1987—88, amicus com. 1994—96, CLE com. 1998—99, by-laws 1999—), Assn. of Bar of City of N.Y. (com. matrimonial law 1984—87, com. matrimonial law 2001, chair 1990—93, com. women in the cts. 1986—96, sec. 1987—90, state cts. of superior juridiction 1987—90, women in the profession 1989—92, judiciary 1995—99, family law 1999—2000), Westchester County Bar Assn., Am. Acad. Matrimonial Lawyers (chair lawyer specialization com. 1999—2000, bd. mgrs. N.Y. chpt. 1987—89, bd. mgrs. N.Y. chpt. 1991—93, bd. mgrs. N.Y. chpt. 1995—98, bd. mgrs. N.Y. chpt. 2000—, v.p. 1998—2000, interdisciplinary com., exec. com.), Com. to Improve Availability of Legal Svcs., Ind. Jud. Screening Panel, Westchester Women's Bar Assn., Internat. Acad. Matrimonial Lawyers, Phi Beta Kappa. State civil litigation, Family and matrimonial. Office: Lincoln Bldg Ste 2320 60 E 42d St New York NY 10165

JACOBUS, CHARLES JOSEPH, lawyer, title company executive, writer; b. Ponca City, Okla., Aug. 21, 1947; s. David William and Louise Graham (Johnson) J.; m. Heather Jeanne Jones, June 6, 1970; children: Mary Helen, Charles J. Jr. BS, U. Houston, 1970, JD, 1973. Bar: Tex. 1973; cert. specialist residential and commercial real estate law Tex. Bd. Legal Specialization. Pvt. practice, Houston, 1973-75; staff counsel Tenneco Realty, Inc., 1975-78, gen. counsel Deerfield, Ill., 1979-83; chief legal counsel Speedy Muffler King, 1978-79; v.p. Commerce Title Co., Houston, 1983-85; sr. v.p. Charter Title Co., 1986—; ptnr. Jacobus & Melamed PC, 1988-97; shareholder Jenkens & Gilchrist, 1998-99; pvt. practice Bellaire, Tex., 1999—. Adv. dir. Heritage Bank, Houston; adj. faculty Tex. A&M U.,

1986-90; adj. prof. U. Houston Law Ctr., Houston C.C., Champions Sch. Real Estate; instr. advanced real estate law State Bar Tex., course dir., 1990, Tex. Land Title Assn. Sch. Author: Real Estate Law, 2d edit., 1996, Texas Real Estate, 8th edit., 2001; co-author: Mastering Real Estate Titles and Title Insurance in Texas, 1996, Georgia Real Estate, 1995, Ohio Real Estate, 2d edit., 1990, Calif. Real Estate, 1989, Keeping Current with Texas Real Estate, updated annually, Real Estate Principles, 8th edit., 1999, Real Estate, An Introduction to the Profession, 8th edit., 1999, Texas Title Insurance, updated annually, Texas Real Estate Brokerage and the Law of Agency, 2000; co-author: Real Estate Brokerage Law and Practice; editor: Building Blocks of a Commercial Transaction, 1992, Building Blocks of a Residential Real Estate Transaction, 1994, Texas Real Estate Law Deskbook, 1995; editor-in-chief Tex. Forms Manual. Chmn. Planning and Zoning Commn., Bellaire, Tex., 1976-77; bd. dirs. Tax Increment Fin. Dist., Bellaire, 1984-91; chmn. task force on edn. Tex. Real Estate Commn.; chmn. profl. adv. com. dept. urban and regional planning Tex. A&M U., 1988-89; 1st asst. scoutmaster Boy Scout World Jamboree, Holland, 1995, scoutmaster, Chile, 1999; scoutmaster Nat. Boy Scout Jamboree, 1997, 1st asst. scoutmaster, 2001; mayor City of Bellaire, 1998-2000; sec.-treas. Harris County Mayors and Coun. Assn. 1999. Recipient Peggy Hayes Tchg. Excellence award TLTA, 1993, Don Roose award of excellence in real estate edn., 2001. Mem. ABA (acquisitions editor books and pubs. com., chmn. brokers and brokerage com. 1986-93), Internat. Wine Food Soc. (host Houston chpt. 1993-94), Am. Coll. Real Estate Lawyers, Nat. Assn. Corp. Real Estate Execs. (chpt. v.p.), Am. Land Devel. Assn. (bd. dirs.), Tex. Land Title Assn. (chmn. forms manual com., TREC earnest money contract task force), Tex. Land Title Ins. (chmn. 2001), Houston Real Estate Lawyers Coun., Real Estate Educator's Assn. (pres. 1987-88, Real Estate Educator of Yr. 1986, 2000), Houston Bar Assn. (chmn. real estate sect. 1987-88), Bellaire/S.W. Houston C. of C. (Outstanding Real Estate Educator in Tex. 1986, Outstanding Businessman of Yr. 1990), chmn. Tex. Real Estate Commns. Edn. Task Force, 1999—), U. Tex. Mortgage Lending Inst. (faculty), U. Houston Law Alumni Assn. (bd. dirs.). Universal Order Knights of Vine (master barrister Houston chpt.), Les Amis Escoffier, Amici della Vite. Republican. Roman Catholic. Probate, Real property. Home: 5223 Pine St Bellaire TX 77401-4820 Office: 6800 West Loop S Ste 460 Bellaire TX 77401-4525 E-mail: chuck@chuckjacobus.com

JACOVER, JEROLD ALAN, lawyer; b. Chgo., Mar. 20, 1945; s. David Louis and Beverly (Funk) J.; m. Judith Lee Greenwald, June 28, 1970; children: Aric Seth, Evan Michael, Brian Ethan. BSEE, U. Wis., 1967; JD, Georgetown U., 1972. Bar: Ohio 1972, Ill. 1973, U.S. Ct. Appeals (7th cir.) 1974, U.S. Ct. Appeals (fed. cir.) 1983. Atty. Ralph Nader, Columbus, Ohio, 1972-73, Brinks Hofer, Gilson and Lione, Chgo., 1973—, pres., 2000—. Mem. ABA, Am. Intellectual Property Law Assn. (bd. dirs. 1994-98), Decalogue Soc. Lawyers, Intellectual Property Law Assn. Chgo. (bd. dirs. 1993-94, 98-99, pres. 2000), Intellectual Property Law Assn. Chgo. Ednl. Found. (pres. 1990-93), Am. Techion Soc. (pres. 1994-97). Federal civil litigation, Patent, Trademark and copyright. Office: Brinks Hofer Gilson & Lione Ste 3600 455 N Cityfront Plaza Dr Chicago IL 60611-5599 E-mail: jjacover@brinkshofer.com

JACQUES, RAOUL THOMAS, lawyer; b. Milw., Aug. 7, 1934; s. Arthur Francis and Maude (Mayotte) J.; m. Alice C. Jacques, June 15, 1957 (div. Oct. 1973); children: Marian, Stephen; m. Diana Lynn Hunt, Dec. 20, 1975 (div. Nov. 1983); children: Carina, Michelle, Emilie, Ashley; m. tutsie Silapalikit-Porn, apr. 5, 1987. BS, Marquette U., 1957; LLB, U. Ariz., 1959. Bar: Ariz. 1959, U.S. Dist. Ct. Ariz. 1971. From trust officer to v.p. TransAm. Title (Ariz.), Tucson and Phoenix, 1959-65, 67—; ptnr. MaLean & Jacques, Phoenix, 1965-67; bd. dirs. Land Registrations Inc., Phoenix, Del Webb Corp. Real Estate Adv. Bd. Republican. Roman Catholic. Construction, Real property. Home: PO Box 7296 Phoenix AZ 85011-7296 Office: MacLean & Jacques 40 E Virginia Ave Phoenix AZ 85004-1122

JAFFE, ALAN STEVEN, lawyer; b. Portland, Maine, Nov. 11, 1939; s. Herman and Rose (Simon) J.; m. Elizabeth L. Reiss, Nov. 3, 1943; children: David, Robert, Richard. BS cum laude, Cornell U., 1961; LLB cum laude, Columbia U., 1964. Bar: N.Y. 1964. Assoc. Poletti, Freiden, Prashker and Gartner, N.Y.C., 1964-65; asst. chief counsel N.Y.C. Anti-Poverty Program, 1965-66; ptnr. Proskauer Rose LLP, N.Y.C., 1966—, chmn., 1999—. Bd. dirs. Lincoln Savs. Bank, N.Y.C., 1984-92. Editor Columbia Law Rev., 1962-64. Bd. dirs., v.p. Coun. Jewish Fedns. N.Am., N.Y.C., 1992-99, Jewish Cmty. Rels. Coun., N.Y., 1987-91; bd. dirs., mem. exec. com. Beth Israel Med. Ctr., 1995—, Am. Jewish Joint Distbn. Com., 1991—; bd. govs. Jewish Agy. for Israel, 1999—; pres. Altro Health and Rehab. Svcs., Inc., N.Y.C., 1983-86, pres. UJA Fedn. of N.Y., 1992-95, bd. dirs. 1980—, chmn. bd. domestic affairs, 1988-91; bd. dirs. N.Y.C. Coalition for Homeless, 1995-98; mem. N.Y.C. Sports Devel. Corp., 1995-98. Office: Proskauer Rose LLP 1585 Broadway Fl 27 New York NY 10036-8299

JAFFE, DONALD NOLAN, lawyer; b. East Cleveland, Ohio, Feb. 20, 1938; s. David Baer and Vivian (Kramer) J.; m. Sandra Lois Katz, Aug. 11, 1963; children: Deborah Susan, Charles Edward. AB, Case Western Res. U., 1959, JD, 1961. Bar: Ohio. Law clk. U.S. Ct. Appeals (6th cir.), Cleve., 1962-64; asst. law dir. City of Cleveland Heights, Ohio, 1964-66; trust officer Union Commerce Bank, Cleve., 1966-69; asst. U.S. atty. Dept. Justice, 1969-72; sole practice law, 1972-82; of counsel Persky, Shapiro, Salim, Esper & Arnoff, LPA, 1982—. Acting judge Cleveland Heights, Mcpl. Ct., 1972-75, Shaker Heights Mcpl. Ct., Ohio, 1982-94; arbitrator Am. Arbitration Assn., Ohio State Employment Rels. Bd., Cuyahoga County Common Pleas Ct., BBB; hearing officer Ohio Dept. Edn. Author article in field. Councilman City of Cleveland Heights, 1976; mem. Gallon Club, ARC, Cleve., 1978; pres. No. Ohio coun. Am. Jewish Congress, 1972; trustee Jewish Family Svc. Assn. Cleve. With USAR, 1961—74, col., judge adv. Ohio Mil. Res. USAR, 1986—. Fellow Ohio State Bar Found.; mem. Ohio State Bar Assn. (coun. of dels. 1984-92, 93—, bd. govs. labor and employment law sect.), Cleve. Bar Assn., Ripcon Club, Tau Epsilon Rho (supreme recorder 1979, pres. Cleve. grad. chpt. 1971), Delta Sigma Rho, Pi Sigma Alpha, Kappa Kappa Psi. Avocations: tennis, swimming, jogging, chess, aerobics. Home: 2 Nantucket Ct Cleveland OH 44122-7535 Office: Persky Shapiro & Aruoff 50 Public Sq 1410 Terminal Tower Cleveland OH 44113 E-mail: djaffelaw@aol.com

JAFFE, F. FILMORE, lawyer, retired judge; b. Chgo., May 4, 1918; s. Jacob Isadore and Goldie (Rabinowitz) J.; m. Mary Main, Nov. 7, 1942; children: Jo Anne, Jay. Student, Southwestern U., 1936-39; J.D., Pacific Coast U., 1940. Bar: Calif. 1945, U.S. Supreme Ct. 1964. Practiced law, Los Angeles, 1945-91; ptnr. Bernard & Jaffe, 1947-74, Jaffe & Jaffe, Los Angeles, 1975-91; apptd. referee Superior Ct. of Los Angeles County, 1991-97, apptd. judge pro tem, 1991-97; ret., 1997; atty. in pvt. practice L.A., 1997—. Mem. L.A. Traffic Commn., 1947-48; arbitrator Am. Arbitration Assn., 1968-91; chmn. pro bono com. Superior Ct. Calif., County of Los Angeles, 1980-86; lectr. on paternity; chair family law indigent paternity panel L.A. County Supr. Ct., 2001—. Served to capt. inf. AUS, 1942-45. Decorated Purple Heart, Croix de Guerre with Silver Star, Bronze Star with oak leaf cluster; honored Human Rights Commn. Los Angeles, Los Angeles County Bd. Suprs.; recipient Pro Bono award State Bar Calif., commendation State Bar Calif., 1983. Mem. ABA, Los Angeles County Bar (honored by family law sect. 1983), Los Angeles Criminal Ct. Bar Assn. (charter mem.), U.S. Supreme Ct. Bar Assn., Masons, Shriners State civil litigation, Family and matrimonial, General practice. Office: 433 N Camden Dr Ste 400 Beverly Hills CA 90210-4408 E-mail: filmorejaffe@earthlink.net

JAFFE, MARK M. lawyer; b. Paterson, N.J., Sept. 18, 1941; s. Irving and Bertha (Margolis) J.; m. June A. Fisher, June 19, 1977. BS in Econs., U. Pa., 1962; JD, Columbia U., 1985. Bar: N.J. 1965, La. 1968, N.Y. 1970, U.S. Dist. Ct. (ea. dist.) N.Y., U.S. Ct. Mil. Appeals, U.S. Ct. Appeals (2d and 5th cirs.), U.S. Dist. Ct. N.J., U.S. Supreme Ct. Assoc. Hill, Betts & Nash, LLP, N.Y.C., 1969-72; ptnr. Hill, Betts & Nash, 1972—. Lt. USCGR, 1965-68. Mem. ABA, N.J. Bar Assn., La. Bar Assn., Assn. of Bar of City of N.Y., Am. Judicature Soc., Maritime Law Soc. Admiralty, General civil litigation, General corporate. Home: 377 Rector Pl New York NY 10280-1432 Office: Hill Betts & Nash 99 Park Ave New York NY 10016

JAFFE, PAUL LAWRENCE, judge, lawyer; b. Phila., June 24, 1928; s. Albert L. and Elsie (Peiser) J.; m. Susan Oppenheim, Apr. 16, 1993; children from previous marriage: Marc David, Richard Alan, Peter Edward. B.A., Dickinson Coll., 1947; J.D., U. Pa., 1950. Bar: Pa. Assoc. Wolf, Block, Schorr and Solis-Cohen, Phila., 1950-57; sole practice, 1957-59; mng. ptnr. Mesirov, Gelman, Jaffe, Cramer and Jamieson and predecessor firms, 1959-98; judge Common Pleas Ct. of Phila., 1996-98. Of counsel Mesirov, Gelman, Jaffe, Cramer and Jamieson, 1998-2000, Schnader, Harrison, Segal and Lewis, 2000—. Pres. Reform Congregation Keneseth Israel, 1974-77; trustee Jewish Fedn. Phila.; trustee Moss Rehab. Hosp., pres., 1977-80, chmn. bd., 1980-84, hon. chmn. bd., 1984—; emeritus dir. Albert Einstein Healthcare Network, 1997—; chmn. United Law Network, 1987-89; vice chmn. Phila. Parking Authority, 1992-96. Mem. ABA, Pa. Bar Assn., Phila. Bar Assn., Am. Coll. Real Estate Lawyers, Lawyers Club Phila., Pyramid Club (chmn. bd. govs. 1999—), Banyan Country Club (Palm Beach, Fla.), Union League of Phila. Home: 1820 Rittenhouse Sq Philadelphia PA 19103-5832 Office: 1600 Market St Fl 36 Philadelphia PA 19103-7286 E-mail: pjaffe@aol.com

JAGLOM, ANDRE RICHARD, lawyer; b. N.Y.C., Dec. 23, 1953; s. Jacob and Irene (Moore) J.; m. Janet R. Stampfl, Apr. 12, 1980; children: Peter Stampfl Jaglom, Wendy Stampfl Jaglom. BS in Mgmt., BS in Physics, MIT, 1974; JD, Harvard U., 1977. Bar: N.Y. 1978, U.S. Dist. Ct. (so. and ea. dists.) N.Y. 1978, U.S. Supreme Ct. 1982, U.S. Ct. Appeals (2d cir.) 1987. Assoc. Paul, Weiss, Rifkind, Wharton & Garrison, N.Y.C., 1977-84; mng. ptnr. Stecher Jaglom & Prutzman LLP, 1984-2000; ptnr. Tannenbaum Helpern Syracuse & Hirschtritt LLP, 2000—. Bd. dirs. Cmty. Fund of Bronxville, Eastchester and Tuckahoe, Inc., 1988-94. Computer mktg. and distbn. editor Computer Law Reporter, 1984-90; Am. Law Inst. ABA course of study on product distbn. and mktg., mem. faculty 1983—, chmn., 1987—; contbr. article to law jours.; contbr chpt. to Legal Checklists, 1988—. Trustee bd. edn. Bronxville Union Free Sch. Dist., 1997-2001. Mem. ABA, Bar Assn. City N.Y. (computer law com. 1986-89, sec. 1990-94, com. on tech. and practice of law 1993-96), Am. Inst. Wine and Food (bd. dirs. N.Y. chpt. 1991-99, treas. 1992-99, adv. bd. 2000—. Contracts commercial, General corporate, Intellectual property. Office: 900 3d Ave New York NY 10022-4728 E-mail: jaglom@tanhelp.com

JAHN, KIRSTIN N. lawyer; b. Buffalo; d. Elmer A. and Marilyn A. Jahn. BBA, U. Mass.; JD, U. Buffalo, 1992. Bar: N.Y. 1992, Nev. 1996, Colo. 1998. Pvt. practice, N.Y.C.

JALENAK, JAMES BAILEY, lawyer; b. New Orleans, Sept. 5, 1939; s. Leo R. and Reha (Lichterman) J.; m. Natalie Block, Dec. 27, 1965; children: Margaret Amie Jalenak Wexler, Catherine Ann Jalenak Levit. BA in Politics & Econs. magna cum laude, Yale U., 1961, JD, 1964. Assoc. Paul, Weiss, Rifkind, Wharton & Garrison, N.Y.C., 1964-65; ptnr. Hanover, Walsh, Jalenak & Blair, Memphis, 1965—. Lectr. in law U. Memphis, 1971-76. Sec., gen. counsel Memphis Zool. Soc., also past bd. dirs.; v.p. S.W. coun. Union Am. Hebrew Congregations; chmn. legal com. Henry S. Jacobs Camp; pres. Temple Israel, Memphis, 1992-94; past pres. Memphis Pub. Edn. Fund, Memphis Yale Club; past bd. dirs. Jewish Children's Regional Svc., New Orleans, Memphis Jewish Cmty. Ctr.; past officer, bd. dirs. Plough Towers, Jewish Family Svc.; past chmn. ctrl. area adv. com., supt.'s adv. com., commn. on excellence Memphis City Schs.; v.p. Memphis Jewish Fedn. Recipient Golden Rule award Vol. Ctr. of Memphis, 1994, Cmty. Svc. award Memphis Urban League, Humanitarian of Yr. award NCCJ, 2000. Fellow Tenn. Bar Found.; mem. Memphis Bar Assn. (bd. dirs.), Memphis Rotary (pres. 1998-99), Order of Coif, Phi Delta Phi. Jewish. Avocation: photography. General corporate, Estate planning, Real property. Home: 5260 Sycamore Grove Ln Memphis TN 38120-2242 Office: Hanover Walsh Jalenak Blair 22 N Front St Memphis TN 38103-2162

JALILI, MAHIR, lawyer; b. Mosul, Iraq, Nov. 22, 1944; s. Ahmad and Khadija Jalili. BS, Leeds U., 1967; MEng., Colo. Sch. Mines, 1971; JD, Loyola U.-Chgo., 1976; LLM, Univ. Coll., London. Bar: Ill. 1977, Calif. 1993, Colo. 1994, Eng. 1999. Assoc. Kenyon & Kenyon, N.Y.C., 1977, Graham & James, London, 1977-83; ptnr. Whitman & Ransom, 1983-92, Whitman Breed Abbott & Morgan, L.A., 1993-94. Construction, Immigration, naturalization, and customs, Private international. Office: 211 Piccadilly London WIJ-9HF England

JALLINS, RICHARD DAVID, lawyer; b. L.A., Mar. 21, 1957; s. Walter Joshua and Elaine Beatrice (Youngerman) J.; m. Katherine Sue Pfeiffer, June 12, 1982; children: Stephen David, Rachel Marie. BA, U. Calif., Santa Barbara, 1978; JD, Calif. Western Sch. Law, 1981. Bar: Calif. 1988, U.S. Dist. Ct. (so. dist.) Calif. 1988. Panel atty. Bd. Prison Terms, Sacramento, 1989-96, Appellate Defenders, Inc., San Diego, 1989-91, Calif. Dept. Corrections, Parole Hearings Divsn., Sacramento, 1992-94; dep. commr. Bd. Prison Terms, 1996—. Mem. ABA, San Diego County Bar Assn., Phi Alpha Delta.

JAMAR, STEVEN DWIGHT, law educator; b. Ishpeming, Mich., May 11, 1953; s. Dwight W. and Lorraine (Persgard) J.; m. Shelley June Von Hagen-Jamar, May 19, 1979; children: Alexander S., Eric D. BA, Carleton Coll., 1975; JD cum laude, Hamline U., 1979; LLM with distinction, Georgetown U., 1994. Bar: Minn. 1979, D.C. 1993, U.S. Supreme Ct. 1985. Jud. clk. Minn. Supreme Ct., St. Paul, 1979-80; assoc. Meagher & Geer, Mpls., 1980-86; clin. instr. William Mitchell Coll. of Law, St. Paul, 1987-89; pvt. practice Mpls., 1987-89; vis. asst. prof. law U. Balt., 1989-90; asst. prof. law Sch. Law Howard U., Washington, 1991-94, assoc. prof. law, 1994-96, prof. law, 1996—, dir. legal rsch. and writing program, 1990—. Cons. on environ. legal info. sys. project NASA, 1998—; cons. on global legal info. network to Law Libr. of Congress, 1999—. Co-author: Essential Lawyering Skills: Interviewing, Counseling, Negotiation, and Persuasive Fact Analysis, 1999; contbr. articles to profl. jours. Bd. dirs. Legal Advice Clinics, Hennepin County, Mpls., 1980-89, mem. exec. com., 1986-89, sec.-treas., 1988-89; coach Soccer Assn. Columbia, 1991-96. Rsch. fellow Law Libr. Congress, 2000-01. Mem. Legal Writing Inst. (bd. dirs. 1992-2000, exec com., 1994-98, pres., 1997-98), ABA, ACLU, Am. Soc. Internat. Law, Amnesty Internat., Computer Law Assn., Assn. Legal Writing Dirs. (bd. dirs., exec. com. 1996-97), Sierra Club, Howard County Go Club, Columbia Soccer Club (coach 2001). Avocations: canoe camping, soccer, go, photography, guitar. Office: Howard U Sch Law 2900 Van Ness St NW Washington DC 20008-1106

JAMES, DAVID LEE, lawyer, international advisor, author; b. Chgo., Aug. 23, 1933; s. Roy L. and Ethel (Wells) J.; m. Sheila Feagley, May 26, 1962; children: Pamela, James, Winifred, Paul, Brian, Adam. A.B., Harvard U., 1955; J.D., U. Chgo., 1960; grad. exec. program, Stanford U., 1979. Bar: N.Y. 1961, N.J. 1967, Hawaii 1976, Ill. 1987. With various law firms, N.Y.C., 1960-67; counsel and asst. gen. counsel, asst. sec. Texasgulf Inc., 1967-75; gen. counsel, sec. Dillingham Corp., Honolulu, 1975-77, v.p., gen. counsel, sec., 1977-84, v.p. legal affairs, sec. San Francisco, 1984-85; asst. gen. counsel, asst. sec. Crown Zellerbach Corp., 1985-86; sr. ptnr., sr. corp. atty. Arnstein & Lehr, Chgo., 1987-90, of counsel, 1990-96; chmn. bus. programs East-West Ctr., Honolulu, 1990-92; chief of party and sr. law devel. advisor USAID and Govt. of Indonesia, Jakarta, Indonesia, 1992-93; pres. Bus. Strategies Internat., San Francisco, 1993—, www.bsicorp.net, San Francisco, 1993—. Hon. consul of Malaysia, Hawaii, 1977-84; adv. bd. Internat. and Comparative Law Ctr., Southwestern Legal Found., Dallas, 1976-91; adv. com. Law of Sea Inst., Honolulu, 1977-84; lectr. in law Stanford U. Sch. Law, 1996-98. Author: Doing Business in Asia, 1993, The Executive Guide to Asia-Pacific Communications, 1995; contbg. editor Upside mag.; contbr. various articles on bus. and legal subjects. Bd. dirs. Chgo. Chamber Orch., 1988-90, pres. 1989-90, Jr. Achievement Hawaii, 1976-84, Hawaii Opera Theatre, 1981-84, Friends of East-West Ctr., 1982-84; mem. Morristown (N.J.) Bd. Edn., 1967-68. Served to lt. (j.g.) USNR, 1955-57. Mem. Outrigger Canoe Club (Honolulu), World Trade Club (San Francisco), Harvard Club (N.Y.C.). Office: Bus Strategies Internat 425 Market St Ste 2200 San Francisco CA 94105-2434 E-mail: djames@bsicorp.net

JAMES, GORDON, III, lawyer; b. Montclair, N.J., Feb. 24, 1947; s. Ernest Gordon Jr. and Betty (Wackerman) J.; m. Adelia Louise Medlin (div. Sept. 1989); children: Deidre Leigh, Diana Catherine, Gordon Daniel; m. Gwen Aline Campanile, Jan. 5, 1991 (div. June 1993). BS, U. Tenn., 1969; JD, Vanderbilt U., 1972. Bar: Fla. 1972, U.S. Dist. Ct. (so. dist.) Fla. 1972, D.C. 1973, U.S. Ct. Appeals (11th cir.) 1980, U.S. Dist. Ct. (mid. dist.) Fla. 1985, U.S. Dist. Ct. (no. dist.) Fla. 1986, U.S. Supreme Ct. 1988. Assoc. Bradford, Williams, Kimbrell, et al, Miami, Fla., 1972-76; ptnr. Druck, Grimmett, Norman, Weaver, Scherer, Ft. Lauderdale, 1976-77, Druck, Grimmett, Scherer, James, Ft. Lauderdale, 1977-78, Grimmett, Scherer, James, Ft. Lauderdale, 1978-79, Conrad, Scherer, James & Jenne, Ft. Lauderdale, 1979-95, Heinrich Gordon Hargrove Weihe & James, Ft. Lauderdale, 1995—. Eucharistic lay minister, All Saints Episcopal Ch., 1991—; Gueardian Ad LIet Program Broward County, 1995-. Capt. USAR, 1969-77. Mem. ABA, Fla. Bar Assn. (vice chmn. civil rule of procedure com. 1990-91), Nat. Assn. R.R. Counsel, Am. Bd. Trial Advs. (cert., Ft. Lauderdale chpt. pres. 1998), Def. Rsch. Inst., Fla. Def. Lawyers (pres. 1991-92). Republican. Avocations: fishing, snow skiing, scuba diving, physical and aerobics exercise. General civil litigation, Personal injury, Product liability. Office: Heinrich Gordon Hargrove Weihe & James 500 E Broward Blvd Fort Lauderdale FL 33394-3000 E-mail: jamesiii@heinrichgordon.com

JAMES, JOYCE MARIE, lawyer; b. Cin., Oct. 23, 1951; d. James Andrew and June Eleanor Connelly; m. Daniel K. James; children; Sarah Marie, Susan Barbara. Student, Shimer Coll., 1968-70; BA, U. Minn., 1974; JD cum laude, William Mitchell Coll. Law, 1979. Bar: Minn. 1979, U.S. Dist. Ct. Minn. 1979. Law clk. to presiding justice Minn. Dist. Ct., Stillwater, 1977-79; assoc. Dorsey & Whitney, Mpls., 1979-83, MacIntosh & Commers, Mpls., 1983-84; trust officer U.S. Bancorp, 1984-90, v.p. personal trust, 1991-95, v.p. compliance, 1995—. Adj. prof. William Mitchell Coll. Law, 1995-96. Chairperson legal advice clinics, Mpls., 1985-86; mem. ann. fund com. William Mitchell Coll. Law, 1999—, co-chair, 2000. Mem. ABA (task force legal fin. planning, significant new devels. in probate and trust law com.), YWCA (deferred giving com. 1986), Minn. State Bar Assn. (probate and trust law sect., chmn. community rels. com. 1984-87, pub affairs com. 1987-88, vice chair elder law sect. 1991-92), Minn. Women Lawyers Assn. (pres. 1984-85), Minn. Womens Fund (deferred giving com. 1985), Hennepin and Ramsey County Bar Assn. Avocations: golf, piano, biking, scripting. Estate planning, Probate, Estate taxation.

JAMES, ROBERT WILLIAM, lawyer, government executive; b. Oakland, Calif., July 5, 1922; s. Reginald William and Antoinette C. E. (Balsden) J.; m. Barbara Jean Zaniboni, Feb. 23, 1962; children: Barbara Marie. A.B., U. Calif.-Berkeley, 1946, L.L.B., 1949. Bar: Calif. 1950. Lawyer State of Calif., Sacramento, 1949-64, asst. chief counsel, 1964-75; dep. dir. Dept. Water Resources, State of Calif., Sacramento, 1975-82, acting dep. dir., 1982-83, chief counsel, 1983—. Contbg. author U. Calif. Law Rev., 1948-49. Served with U.S. Army, 1942-45, Europe. Mem. Phi Betta Kappa. Democrat. Roman Catholic. Lodge: Elks. Home: 5601 Haskell Ave Carmichael CA 95608-1203 Office: Dept Water Resources 1416 9th St Sacramento CA 95814

JAMES, STUART FAWCETT, lawyer; b. Daytona Beach, Fla., May 17, 1957; s. George M. and Gertrude (Fawcett) J.; m. Vicki Lawrence, Aug. 4, 1990. B in Polit. Sci., U. Cen. Fla., 1981; JD, Samford U., 1989. Bar: Tenn. 1990, Ga. 1991, U.S. Dist. Ct. (ea. dist.) Tenn. 1990, U.S. Dist. Ct. (no. dist.) Ga. 1992, U.S. Ct. Appeals (6th and 11th cir.) 1992, Ala. 1993. Atty, mng. mem. Manuel & James PLLC, Chattanooga, 1996-2000, The James Firm, 2000—. Assoc. editor Cumberland Sch. Law Rev., 1989. Mem. LAS adv. coun. U. Tenn., Chattanooga. Mem. ABA, Fed. Bar Assn., Tenn. Bar Assn. (chair law office tech./mgmt. sect. 1996, co-chair AIDS awareness com., chmn. computer and tech. com. young lawyers divsn., mem. mock trial com., chair disciplinary diversion project, mem. young lawyers divsn. fellow, Pres.'s Disting. Svc. award 1994), Chattanooga Bar Assn. (pres. 1997, sec.-treas., bd. govs., legis. chair young lawyers sect., chmn., past pres.'s com. 1999, Robert Horton Campbell award), Dem. Leadership Counsel, Kiwanis Club (chmn. rules and regulations com., program chmn.). Episcopalian. Avocations: photography, hiking. General civil litigation, Personal injury, Product liability. Office: Manuel & James James Bldg Ste 702 Chattanooga TN 37402-1804

JAMESON, GENE LANIER, lawyer; b. Dallas, Jan. 18, 1936; s. Joseph Andrew and Minnie (Kittrell) J.; m. Lois Marie Shanahan, July 19, 1958; children: Holly, Scott. BA in Econs., Tex. A&M, 1958; LLB, U. Tex., 1966. Bar: Tex. 1966, U.S. Supreme Ct. 1975, U.S. Ct. Appeals (5th and 11th cirs.) 1981. Assoc. Stubbeman, et al, Midland, Tex., 1966-69; staff atty. 1st Nat. Bank Dallas/1st Internat. Bankshares, 1969-77; assoc. Coke & Coke, Dallas, 1977-79, ptnr., 1979-84, Jones, Day, Reavis & Pogue, Dallas, 1984-91; dir. Donohue, Jameson & Carroll, P.C., 1991—. Served to capt. U.S. Army, 1958-63. Banking, Contracts commercial. Home: 10433 Strait Ln Dallas TX 75229-6537 Office: Donohue Jameson & Carroll PC 2300 Trammell Crow Ctr 1201 Elm St Ste 3400 Dallas TX 75270 E-mail: gjameson@djcpc.com

JAMESON, MICHAEL FRANCIS, lawyer; b. Nashville, Apr. 24, 1963; s. William Kendrick Jameson and Ann Rita Cunningham; m. Tamara Kylene Hart Jameson, Sept. 23, 1995; 1 child, William Kyle. BA, Vanderbilt U., 1985; JD cum laude, U. Tenn., 1990. Bar: Tenn. 1990, U.S. Dist. Ct. (mid., we., and ea. dists.) Tenn. 1992, U.S. Ct. Appeals (6th cir.) 1996. Asst. pub. defender Pub. Defenders Office, 23d Jud. Dist. of Tenn., Charlotte, 1990-91; ptnr. North, Pursell, Ramos & Jameson, Nashville, 1992—. Campaign chmn. Com. to Elect Rob Briley, Nashville, 1998, Com. to Elect Patricia Crotwell, Nashville, 2000. Mem. Tenn. Trial Lawyers' Assn. (young lawyer's divsn. 1992—), Def. Rsch. Inst., Order of Barristers. Democrat. Avocations: political campaigns, acoustic guitar, home improvement. General civil litigation, Insurance, Personal injury. Office: North Pursell Ramos & Jameson Ste 1850 414 Union St Nashville TN 37219-1783

JAMESON, PAULA ANN, lawyer; b. New Orleans, Feb. 19, 1945; d. Paul Henry and Virginia Lee (Powell) Bailey; children: Paul Andrew, Peter Carver. BA, La. State U., 1966; JD, U. Tex., 1969. 010BAr: TEx. 1969, D.C. 1970, Va. 1973, N.Y. 1978, U.S. Dist. Ct. D.C. 1970, U.S. Dist. Ct. (ea. dist.) Va. 1976, U.S. Ct. Appeals (D.C. cir.) 1972, U.S. Ct. Appeals (4th

cir.) 1976, U.S Ct. Appeals (5th cir.) 1978, U.S. Ct. Appeals (2d cir.) 1985, U.S. Supreme Ct. 1973. Asst. corp. counsel D.C. Corp. Counsel's Office, 1970-73; sr. asst. county atty. Fairfax County Atty.'s Office, Fairfax, Va., 1973-77; atty. Dow Jones & Co., Inc., N.Y.C., 1977-79, house counsel, 1979-81, asst. to chmn. bd., 1981-83, house counsel, dir. legal dept., 1983-86; sr. v.p., gen. counsel, corp. sec. PBS, Alexandria, Va., 1986-98; ptnr. Arter & Hadden, Washington, 1998-2000; v.p., gen. counsel Gibson Guitar Corp., Nashville, 2000-01, Jameson Legal & Cons. Svcs., McLean, Va., 2000; pres. Jameson Legal Consulting Svcs. , Laguna Niguel, Calif., 2000—. Mem. FCC WRC-2000 Industry Adv. Com. Mem. ABA, Fed. Comms. Bar Assn., D.C. Bar Assn., Computer Law Assn., Copyright Soc. U.S.A. (past trustee). Democrat. Roman Catholic. Communications, General corporate, Trademark and copyright. E-mail: paulajameson@att.net

JAMIESON, MICHAEL LAWRENCE, lawyer; b. Coral Gables, Fla., Mar. 2, 1940; s. Warren Thomas and Ruth Amelia (Gallman) J.; children: Ann Layton, Thomas Howard; m. Elizabeth Marie Peeples, Dec. 31, 1992. BA in English, U. Fla., 1961, JD with honors, 1964. Bar: Fla. 1964, U.S. Dist. Ct. (mid. dist.) Fla. 1964, D.C. 1998, N.Y. 1999. Teaching asst. U. Fla., 1964; law clk. U.S. Ct. Appeals (5th cir.), 1964-65; assoc. Holland & Knight LLP and predecessor firms, Tampa, Fla., 1965-69; ptnr. Holland & Knight and predecessor firms, 1969—, chmn. bus. law dept., 1992—. Editor-in-chief U. Fla. Law Rev., 1963 Trustee Law Ctr. U. Fla., chmn. bd. dirs., 1986-88; bd. dirs., chmn. Bus. Com. for the Arts Inc., 1989-90; trustee Tampa Bay Performing Arts Ctr. Inc., 1989—, chmn. devel. coun., 1990-91; trustee Cmty. Found. Greater Tampa, 1990-97; chmn. devel. com. Fla. C. of C. Found., 1992-95; mem. Tampa Leadership Conf., Golden Triangle Civic Assn. Recipient Gertrude Brick Law Rev. award, 1963 Fellow Am. Bar Found.; mem. ABA (mem. com on corp. laws, mem. com. on fed. regulation of securities), Am. Law Inst., Hillsborough County Bar Assn., Greater Tampa C. of C. (mem. bd. govs. 1988-91), Com. 100 (mem. policy bd. 1989-92, trustee 1998—), Univ. Club, Tampa Club (bd. dirs. 1985-89, pres. 1987-88), The Down Town Assn., Order of Coif, Phi Kappa Phi. Contracts commercial, General corporate, Securities. E-mail: mjamieso@hklaw.com

JAMIN, MATTHEW DANIEL, lawyer, magistrate judge; b. New Brunswick, N.J., Nov. 29, 1947; s. Matthew Bernard and Frances Marie (Newburg) J.; m. Christine Frances Bjorkman, June 28, 1969; children: Rebecca, Erica. BA, Colgate U., 1969; JD, Harvard U., 1974. Bar: Alaska 1974, U.S. Dist. Ct. Alaska 1974, U.S. Ct. Appeals (9th cir.) 1980. Staff atty. Alaska Legal Svcs., Anchorage, 1974-75, supervising atty. Kodiak, Alaska, 1975-81; contract atty. Pub. Defender's Office State of Alaska, 1976-82; prin. Matthew D. Jamin, Atty., 1982; ptnr. Jamin & Bolger, 1982-85, Jamin, Ebell, Bolger & Gentry, Kodiak, 1985-97; part-time magistrate judge U.S. Cts., 1984—; shareholder Jamin, Ebell, Schmitt & Mason, 1998—. Part-time instr. U. Alaska Kodiak Coll., 1975—; active Theshold Svcs., Inc., Kodiak, 1985—, pres., 1985-92, 95-96, 99-2000. Mem. Alaska Bar Assn. (Professionalism award 1988), Kodiak Bar Assn. General civil litigation, Family and matrimonial, Probate. Office: US Dist Ct 323 Carolyn Ave Kodiak AK 99615-6348 E-mail: matt@jesmkod.com

JAMISON, JUDITH JAFFE, retired judge, lawyer, arbitrator, consultant; b. Phila., Aug. 19, 1924; d. Selig and Mary J.; m. I.I. Jamison, June 23, 1957; 1 child, Sara. BA, Antioch Coll., 1946; student, U. Chgo. Law Sch., 1945-46; JD, Temple U., 1948. Bar: Pa. 1949, U.S. Dist. Ct. (ea. dist.) Pa. 1949, U.S. Ct. Appeals (3d cir.) 1949. Gen. practice, Phila., 1949-51, 91-96; spl. dep., asst. atty. gen. Pa. Dept. Justice, 1956-73; judge Ct. Common Pleas, 1974-90; of counsel Cozen and O'Connor, 1997—. Mem. Supreme Ct. Orphan's Ct. Procedural Rules Commn., Pa., 1985-91, 96-99; advisor Mayor's Commn. on Women, 1976-86; lectr. Pa. Coll. Judiciary, 1978-90. Contbr. articles to law jours. Bd. dirs. Fox Chase Cancer Ctr., Phila., 1980—; dir. Bd. Dirs. City Trusts, Phila., 1990—, Wills Eye Hosp., 1991—; trustee Ctr. for Literacy, Phila., 1990—; dir. Jenkins Law Libr. Recipient Spl. Achievement award Temple Law Alumni-Alumnae Assn., 1984, Legion of Honor, Chapel of the Four Chaplains. Mem. ABA, Nat. Coll. Probate Judges, Nat. Assn. Women Judges, Pa. Bar Assn., Phila. Bar Assn. Democrat. Jewish. Alternative dispute resolution, Estate planning, Probate. Home: 2119 Delancey St Philadelphia PA 19103-6511 Office: Cozen and O'Connor 1900 Market St Philadelphia PA 19103-3527 E-mail: jjamison@cozen.com

JANES, BRANDON CHAISON, lawyer; b. Uvalde, Tex., Oct. 9, 1951; s. Brandon Chaison and Phyllis (Collins) J.; children: Margaret, Michael, Brandon. BBA, Baylor U., 1972; JD, U. Tex., 1976. Bar: Tex. 1976, U.S. Dist. Ct. (we. dist.) Tex. 1978, U.S. Tax Ct. 1981, U.S. Ct. Appeals (5th cir.) 1981, U.S. Supreme Ct. 1981. Assoc., then ptnr. Grambling & Mounce, El Paso, Tex., 1976-80; ptnr. Small, Craig & Werkenthin, Austin, 1981-97, Akin, Gump, Strauss, Haver & Feld, Austin, 1997—. Contbr. articles to profl. jours. Mem. ABA (taxation sect.), State Bar Tex., Tex. Soc. CPAs. Taxation, general, State and local taxation. Home: 901 Forest View Dr Austin TX 78746-4521 Office: Akin Gump Strauss Haver & Feld 816 Congress Ave Ste 1900 Austin TX 78701-4042 E-mail: bjanes@akingump.com

JANIAN, PAULETTE, lawyer; b. Selma, Calif., Oct. 21, 1946; d. Charles and Alice (De Kozan) J.; children: Dennis-Paul, Matthew, Denise, Nicholas. BA, Fresno State U., 1968; JD, Hastings Coll. Law, 1971. Bar: Calif. 1972, U.S. Dist. Ct. (ea. dist.) Calif. 1972. Ptnr. Shepard, Shepard & Janian, Selma, Calif., 1971—; city atty. City of Selma, 1974-83; judge pro tem Fresno County Superior Ct., Calif., 1973. Mem. Fresno County Bar Assn. (sec. 1975, chmn. family law sect. 1995-96), Order of Ea. Star. Mem. Armenian Apostolic Ch. Family and matrimonial, General practice, Probate. Home: 3190 S Fowler Ave Fresno CA 93725-9328 Office: Shepard Shepard & Janian Shepard Shepard & Janian 1814 E Front St Selma CA 93662-3704 E-mail: shepj@PacBell.net

JANICH, DANIEL NICHOLAS, lawyer; b. Chgo., Aug. 8, 1952; s. Nicholas and Antoinette (Colasurdo) J. BA with honors, Marian Coll., 1974; JD, John Marshall Law Sch., 1978; LLM in Taxation, DePaul U., 1986. Bar: Ill. 1978, U.S. Dist. Ct (no. dist.) Ill. 1978, U.S. Ct. Appeals (7th cir.) 1980, U.S.Tax Ct. 1986, U.S. Supreme Ct. 1990. Mem. legal dept. Liberty Mutual Ins. Co., Chgo., 1978-84; instr. law DePaul U., 1984-85; assoc. O'Keefe, Ashenden, Lyons & Ward, 1985-87, Nisen & Elliott, Chgo., 1987-88, Chadwell & Kayser Ltd., Chgo., 1988-90, Masuda, Funai, Eifert & Mitchell, Ltd., Chgo., 1991-97, Altheimer & Gray, Chgo., 1997-98, Freeborn & Peters, Chgo., 1999—. Contbr. articles to profl. jours. Mem. ABA, Chgo. Bar Assn., Ill. State Bar Assn., Am. Arbitration Assn., Delta Theta Phi. Roman Catholic. General civil litigation, General corporate, Pension, profit-sharing, and employee benefits. Home: 1575 Sandpebble Dr Wheeling IL 60090-5920 Office: Freeborn & Peters 311 So Wacker Dr Ste 3000 Chicago IL 60606 E-mail: djanich@freebornpeters.com

JANIGIAN, BRUCE JASPER, lawyer, educator; b. San Francisco, Oct. 21, 1950; s. Michael D. Janigian and Stella (Minasian) Amerian; m. Susan Elizabeth Frye, Oct. 4, 1986; children: Alan Michael, Alison Elizabeth. AB, U. Calif., Berkeley, 1972; JD, U. Calif., San Francisco, 1975; LLM, George Washington U., 1982. Bar: Calif. 1975, U.S. Supreme Ct. 1979, D.C. 1981. Dir. Hastings Rsch. Svcs., Inc., San Francisco, 1973-75; judge adv. in Spain, 1976-78; commr. U.S. Navy and Marine Corps Ct. Mil. Rev., 1978-79; atty. advisor AID U.S. State Dept., Washington, 1979-84; dep. dir., gen. counsel Calif. Employment Devel. Dept., Sacramento, 1984-89; Fulbright scholar, vis. prof. law U. Salzburg, Austria, 1989-90; chmn. Calif. Agrl. Labor Rels. Bd., 1990-95; v.p. Europe, resident dir. Salzburg (Austria) Seminar, 1995-96; U.S. legate European Acad. Scis. and Art, 1996—; Rapporteur World Economic Forum, 1996; of counsel Weintraub Genshlea Chediak Sproul, Sacramento, 1998—. Prof. McGeorge Sch. Law, U. Pacific, Sacramento, 1986—, Inst. on Internat. Legal Studies, Salzburg, summer 1987, London Inst. on Comml. Law, summers 1989, 92-93; vis. scholar Hoover Inst. War, Revolution and Peace, Stanford U., 1991-92; dir. Vienna-Budapest East/West Trade Inst., 1993; vis. prof. law U. Salzburg, 1995-96, prof. internat. bus. mgmt., Golden Gate U., 1998—. Editor: Financing International Trade and Development, 1986, 87, 89, International Business Transactions, 1989, 92, International Trade Law, 1993, 94. Coord. fund raiser March of Dimes, Sacramento, 1987. Capt. USNR, JAGC, 1976-79, mem. Res. Fulbright scholar, 1989-90; decorated Meritorious Achievement medal; recipient USAID Meritorious Honor award, Faculty of Yr. award Golden Gate U., 2001. Mem. Calif. Bar Assn., D.C. Bar Assn., Sacamento Bar Assn. (exec. com. taxation sect. 1988-89, chair, internat. law sect., 1999—), Anthony M. Kennedy Am. Inn of Ct. (barrister 1998-2001), Pub. Internat. Law and Policy Group, Sacramento Met. C. of C. (award for program contbns. and cmty. enrichment 1989), European Acad. Scis. and Art (U.S. Legate 1996—), World Art Forum, Austro-Am. Soc. (v.p. 1996), Navy League (gen. counsel 1997—), Rotary (chair, internat. found. com., 1999—), Comstock Club (dir. 1998-99), Sacramento Capitol Club (dir. 1999-2001), Naval Res. Officers Assn. (life), Marine Meml. Assn., Fulbright Assoc. (life), Knights of Vartan, Phi Beta Kappa. Avocations: cross-country skiing, tennis, bicycling. Home: 1631 12th Ave Sacramento CA 95818-4146 Office: 400 Capitol Mall Fl 11 Sacramento CA 95814-4407 E-mail: bjanigian@weintraub.com

JANKE, RONALD ROBERT, lawyer; b. Milw., Mar. 2, 1947; s. Robert Erwin and Elaine Patricia (Wilken) J.; m. Mary Ann Burg, July 3, 1971; children— Jennifer, William, Emily. B.A. cum laude, Wittenberg U., 1969; J.D. with distinction, Duke U., 1974. Bar: Ohio 1974. Assoc. Jones, Day, Reavis & Pogue, Cleve., 1974-83, ptnr., 1984—. Served with U.S. Army, 1970-71, Vietnam. Mem. ABA (chmn. environ. control com. 1980-83), Ohio Bar Assn., Greater Cleve. Bar Assn., Environ. Law Inst. Environmental. Office: Jones Day Reavis & Pogue N Point 901 Lakeside Ave E Cleveland OH 44114-1190

JANKLOW, MORTON LLOYD, lawyer, literary agent; b. N.Y.C., May 30, 1930; s. Maurice and Lillian (Levantin) J.; m. Linda Mervyn LeRoy, Nov. 27, 1960; children: Angela LeRoy, Lucas Warner. AB, Syracuse U., 1950; JD, Columbia U., 1953. Bar: N.Y. 1953, D.C. 1961, U.S. Dist. Ct. (so. and ea. dists.) N.Y., U.S. Ct. Appeals (2nd cir.), U.S. Supreme Ct. Chmn., CEO Morton L. Janklow Assocs., Inc., 1977-89; of council Janklow & Ashley, LLP, N.Y.C., 1989—; sr. ptnr., now of counsel Janklow & Nesbit Assocs., 1989—. Trustee Managed Accts. Svcs., PaineWebber PACE funds, 1996—; chmn. Janklow & Nesbit (U.K.); bd. dirs. Revlon, Inc., 1997-2000, Orbis Comm., Inc., N.Y.C., 1986-89; bd. dirs., mem. finance com. McCaffrey & McCall, Inc., N.Y.C., 1962-87; chmn. exec. com. Harvey Group, Inc., N.Y.C., 1968-71, Cable Funding Corp., N.Y.C., 1971-73; mem. exec. com. Sloan Commn. Cable Comm., 1970-71, Andrew Wellington Cordier fellow Columbia U. Sch. Internat. Affairs; vis. lectr. Radcliffe Coll., Columbia U. Law Sch., NYU; bus. and fin. adv. bd. NYU Press and NYU Sch. Arts, 1977—; donor, founder Morton L. Janklow Professorship of Lit. and Artistic Property, Columbia U. Sch. Law; life mem., Harlan Fiske Stone fellow of Columbia U. Law Sch.; founder Morton L. Janklow Program for Advocacy in the Arts, Columbia U. Law Sch.; mem. dean's coun. Columbia U. Law Sch., 1992—. Bd. dirs., exec. com., devel. chmn. City Center Music and Drama, 1971-75; bd. dirs. Film Soc., Lincoln Ctr., 1972-75, Am. Cinematheque, 1971-75; bd. govs. Jewish Mus., 1969-75; dir., chmn. Janklow Found.; trustee Mr. and Mrs. Harry M. Warner Found., 1965—, Sidney Sheldon Found.; mem. Council of Friends, Whitney Mus. Am. Art, 1973-82, also mem. com. on paintings and sculptures; ad hoc com. on pub. and merchandising activities Met. Mus. Art; bd. advisors Princeton U. Art. Mus., 1984-89; mem. adv. bd. Guggenheim Mus., 1980-86; adv. council Sch. Arts, NYU; mem. Ind. Com. on Arts Policy; bd. advisors Columbia U. Jour. Art and the Law; assn. of fellows Pierpoint Morgan Libr., N.Y.C.. Served with AUS, 1953-55. Decorated chevalier l'Ordre des Arts et des Lettres de la Republique Française. Mem. ABA, N.Y. Bar Assn., Assn. of Bar of City of N.Y. (membership com. 1967—), N.Y. County Lawyers Assn., Fed. Comms. Bar Assn., Am. Judicature Soc., Coun. on Fgn. Rels., Com. on the Rsch. Librs., N.Y. Pub. Libr. Office: 445 Park Ave New York NY 10022-2606 E-mail: mjanklow@janklow.com

JANNEY, DONALD WAYNE, lawyer; b. Clinton, N.C., Jan. 9, 1952; s. Wayne Columbus and Bernice (Talley) J.; m. Sydney Louise Rhame, May 28, 1977; children: Taylor Columbus, Camden St. Clair. BA, Furman U., 1974; JD, U. Va., 1978. Bar: Ga. 1978, U.S. Dist. Ct. (no. dist.) Ga. 1978, U.S. Ct. Appeals (11th cir.) 1982. Assoc. Troutman Sanders, Atlanta, 1978-85; ptnr. Troutman Sanders and predecessor firm, 1985—. Bd. dirs. State YMCA Ga., Atlanta, 1980-91. Mem. ABA, Ga. Bar Assn., Atlanta Bar Assn., Lawyers Club Atlanta, Phi Beta Kappa. Baptist. General civil litigation, Condemnation. Home: 705 E Morningside Dr Atlanta GA 30324-5220 Office: Troutman Sanders Ste 5200 600 Peachtree St NE Atlanta GA 30308-2216 E-mail: donald.janney@troutmansanders.com

JANNEY, OLIVER JAMES, lawyer, plastics and semiconductor company executive; b. N.Y.C., Feb. 11, 1946; s. Walter Coggeshall and Helen Jennings (James) J.; m. Suzanne Elizabeth Lenz, June 21, 1969; children: Oliver Burr, Elizabeth Flower. BA cum laude, Yale U., 1967; JD, Harvard U., 1970. Bar: Mass. 1970, N.Y. 1971, Fla. 1991. With Walston & Co., Inc., N.Y.C., 19770-73, asst. v.p., 1971-73; assoc. Cleary Gottlieb, Steen & Hamilton, 1973-76; with RKO Gen., Inc., 1976-90, asst. sec., 1977-85, asst. gen. atty., 1978-82, asst. gen. counsel, 1982-85, sec., gen. counsel, 1985-89; exec. v.p., gen. counsel, sec. Uniroyal Tech. Corp., Sarasota, Fla., 1990—. Former pres. River Rd. Assn., Scarborough, N.Y.; vestryman, treas. All Angels by the Sea, Longboat Key, Fla., 1999-2001. Served to 1st lt. USAR, 1969-77. Mem. ABA, N.Y. State Bar Assn., Assn. Bar City N.Y., Am. Corporate Coun. Assn. (bd. dirs. west ctrl. fla. chpt. 1996—), Sleepy Hollow Country Club (Scarborough), Yale Club of NYC. Republican. General corporate, Mergers and acquisitions, Securities. Home: 1684 Peregrine Point Dr Sarasota FL 34231-2331 Office: Uniroyal Tech Corp 2 N Tamiami Trl Ste 900 Sarasota FL 34236-5568

JANOVER, ROBERT H. lawyer; b. N.Y.C., Aug. 17, 1930; s. Cyrus J. and Lillian D. (Horwitz) J.; m. Mary Elizabeth McMahon, Oct. 23, 1966; 1 child, Laura Lockwood. BA, Princeton U., 1952; postgrad., U. Vienna, 1956; JD, Harvard U., 1957. Bar: N.Y. 1957, U.S. Supreme Ct. 1961, D.C. 1966, Mich. 1973. Practice law, N.Y.C., 1957-65; cons. Office of Edn., HEW, Washington, 1965; legis. atty. Office of Gen. Counsel, HEW, 1965-66; asst. gen. atty. Mgmt. Assistance Inc., N.Y.C., 1966-71; atty. Ford Motor Credit Co., Dearborn, Mich., 1971-74; mem. firm Freud, Markus, Slavin, Toohey & Galgan, Troy, 1974-79; pvt. practice Detroit, 1979-82, Bloomfield Hills, Mich., 1982—. Contbr. articles to profl. jours. Bd. dirs. Oakland Citizens League, 1976-96, v.p., 1976-79, pres., 1979-96; bd. dirs. Civic Searchlight, Inc., 1976-96. 1st lt., arty. U.S. Army, 1952-54, Korea. Mem.: ABA, Mich. State Bar, N.Y. State Bar, Detroit Met. Bar Assn., Bar Assn. D.C., Assn Bar of City of N.Y., Am. Inns Ct. (master of the bench 1996—99), Soc. 3d Inf. Divsn., Princeton Club of Mich. (pres. 1991—92), Princeton Club of N.Y., Nassau Club (Princeton, N.J.), Harvard Club (N.Y.C.). General civil litigation, Contracts commercial, General corporate. Home: 685 Ardmoor Dr Bloomfield Hills MI 48301-2415 Office: 100 W Long Lake Rd Ste 200 Bloomfield Hills MI 48304-2774 E-mail: rjdnover@aol.com

JANOWITZ, JAMES ARNOLD, lawyer; b. N.Y.C., Sept. 2, 1946; s. Arnold and Erna (Frankel) J.; m. Katherine Eva Sborovy, Aug. 6, 1967; children: Jessie Elizabeth, William Aaron. BA, Haverford Coll., 1967; JD, NYU, 1971. Bar: N.Y. 1972, U.S. Dist Ct. (so. dist.) N.Y. 1972. Tchr. St. David's Sch., N.Y.C., 1968-72; assoc. Guzik & Boukstein, 1972-73, Reavis & McGrath, N.Y.C., 1973-74, Pryor, Cashman & Sherman, N.Y.C., 1974-76; ptnr. Pryor, Cashman, Sherman & Flynn, 1977—. Adj. prof. Cardozo Law Sch., Yeshiva U., N.Y.C., 1992; bd. dirs. Avenue Entertainment, 1986-99. Editor NYU Jour. Internat. Law and Politics, 1970-71. Mem. N.Y. State Bar Assn., Assn. of Bar of City of N.Y. General civil litigation, Entertainment, Finance. Office: Pryor Cashman Sherman & Flynn 410 Park Ave Fl 10 New York NY 10022-4407

JARBLUM, WILLIAM, lawyer; b. Havana, Cuba, Aug. 29, 1945; came to U.S., 1946; s. Richard S. and Dora F. (Nadel) J.; m. Susan P. Reich, May 24, 1970 (div. 1991); m. Loraine Gage Bassett, Jan. 4, 1992; children: Kimberly, Meredith. Student U. Va., 1962-64; B.A., C.W. Post Coll. of L.I.U., 1967; J.D., Georgetown U., 1970. Bar: N.Y. 1971, U.S. Dist. Ct. (so. and ea. dists.) N.Y. 1972. Assoc., Otterbourg, Steindler, Houston & Rosen, P.C., N.Y.C., 1970-71, Finley, Kumble, Underberg, Persky & Roth, P.C., N.Y.C., 1971-73; ptnr. Persky & Jarblum, P.C., N.Y.C., 1973-75, Fine, Tofel & Saxl, N.Y.C., 1975-77; sole practice, N.Y.C., 1977-79; ptnr. Jarblum Solomon & Fornari, P.C., N.Y.C., 1979-89, Phillips, Nizer, Benjamin, Krim & Ballon, N.Y.C., 1989-94, counsel, Buchalter, Nemer, Fields & Younger, N.Y.C. and L.A. Asst. regional dir. western states Citizens for Humphrey-Muskie, Washington, 1968. Mem. Assn. Bar City N.Y., N.Y. State Bar Assn., N.Y. County Bar Assn. (com. on securities and exchanges). General corporate, Real property, Securities. Home: 6027 Sandhurst Ln # C Dallas TX 75206-4720 also: 9030 Alto Cedro Dr Beverly Hills CA 90210-1805 Office: Buchalter Nemer Fields & Younger 237 Park Ave New York NY 10017-3140 also: Buchalter Nemer Fields & Younger 601 S Figueroa St Los Angeles CA 90017-5704

JARDINE, BRYAN WILSON, lawyer; b. Columbus, Ohio, May 12, 1962; s. John Bryan and Elsa Jean Jardine; m. Mimi Lucille Martin, May 15, 1999. BSFS, Georgetown U., 1984; JD, UCLA, 1990. Bar: Calif. 1990, U.S. Dist. Ct. (no. dist.) Calif. 1991, U.S. Dist. Ct. (cen., ea. and so. dists.) Calif. 1991, U.S. Ct. Appeals (9th cir.) 1995. Assoc. Fulbright & Jaworski LLP, L.A., 1990-94, Gorry & Meyer LLP, L.A., 1994-98; country liaison ABA-CEELI Program, Bucharest, Romania, 1996-97; assoc. Arent Fox Kintner Plotkin & Kahn PLLC, 1998—. Avocations: motorcycling, surfing, travel. Private international, Mergers and acquisitions, Real property. Office: Arent Fox Kintner Plotkin e Blvd N Titulescu Nr 1 BIA7 70000 Bucharest Romania Office Fax: 011-401-211-8771. E-mail: jardineb@arentfox.com

JARVIS, JAMES HOWARD, II, judge; b. Knoxville, Tenn., Feb. 28, 1937; s. Howard F. and Eleanor B. J.; m. Martha Stapleton, June 1957 (div. Feb. 1962); children: James Howard III, Leslie; m. Pamela K. Duncan, Aug. 23, 1964 (div. Apr. 1991); children: Ann, Kathryn, Louise; m. Gail Stone, Sept. 4, 1992. BA, U. Tenn., 1958, JD, 1960. Bar: Tenn. 1961, U.S. Dist. Ct. (ea. dist.) Tenn. 1961, U.S. Ct. Appeals (6th cir.) 1965. Assoc. O'Neil, Jarvis, Parker & Williamson, Knoxville, Tenn., 1960-68, mem., 1968-70, Meares, Dungan, Jarvis, Knoxville, 1970-72; judge Law & Equity Ct., Blount County, 1972-77, 30th Jud. Ct., Blount County, 1977-84, U.S. Dist. Ct. (ea. dist.) Tenn., Knoxville, 1984—, chief judge, 1991-98. Bd. dirs. Maryville (Tenn.) Coll., 1991-98; mem., past chmn. fin. com. St. Andrews Episc. Ch.; past bd. dirs. Detoxification Rehab. Inst. Knoxville; past mem. com. codes of conduct Jud. Conf. U.S. Mem. Tenn. Bar Assn. (bd. govs. 1983-84), Am. Judicature Soc., Tenn. Trial Judges Assn. (pres. mem. exec. com.), Tenn. Jud. Conf. (pres. 1983-84), Blount County Bar Assn., Knoxville Bar Assn., Great Smoky Mountains Conservation Assn., Phi Delta Phi, Sigma Chi (significant Sigma Chi). Republican. Home: 6916 Stone Mill Rd Knoxville TN 37919-7431 Office: Howard H Baker Jr US Courthouse 800 Market St Knoxville TN 37902-2327

JARVIS, JOHN MANNERS, barrister, judge; b. London, Nov. 20, 1947; s. Donald Manners and Brixie Theodora J.; m. Janet Rona Kitson, May 5, 1972; children: Christopher, Fergus. BA, Emmanuel Coll., Cambridge, Eng., 1969; MA, 1972. Bar: Eng., Wales 1970; apptd. Queens counsel 1989; accredited mediator C.E.D.R. Mem. chambers 3 Verulam Bldgs. Gray's Inn, London, 1970—; asst. recorder, 1987-91; recorder, 1991—; dep. high ct. judge, 1998—; joint head chambers, 1999—. Co-author: Lender Liability, 1993; internat. editor: Jour. Banking and Fin. Law and Practice, 1989—; contbr. author: Banks, Liability and Risk, 2d edit. Gov. King's Coll. Sch., Wimbledon, Eng., 1987—. Mem. Comml. Bar Assn. (treas. 1993-95, chmn. 1995-97), Lincoln's Inn (bencher 1997—). Avocations: horse-riding, tennis, skiing, cycling, sailing. Office: 3 Verulam Bldgs Gray's Inn London WC1R 5NT England Fax: 020 7831 8441. E-mail: jjarvis@3vb.com

JARVIS, ROBERT MARK, law educator; b. N.Y.C., Oct. 17, 1959; s. Rubin and Ute (Hacklander) J.; m. Judith Anne Mellman, Mar. 3, 1989. BA, Northwestern U., 1980; JD, U. Pa., 1983; LLM, NYU, 1986. Bar: N.Y. 1984, Fla. 1990. Assoc. Haight Gardner Poor & Havens, N.Y.C., 1983-85, Baker & McKenzie, N.Y.C., 1985-87; asst. prof. law ctr. Nova Southeastern U., Ft. Lauderdale, Fla., 1987-90, assoc. prof., 1990-92, prof., 1992—. Chmn. bd. dirs. Miami Maritime Arbitration Bd., 1993-94; vice chmn. bd. dirs. Miami Internat. Arbitration and Mediation Inst., 1993-94; mem. adv. bd. Carolina Acad. Press, 1996—, Sports Law Reporter, 2000—, hospitalitylawyer.com, 2000—. Co-author: AIDS: Cases and Materials, 1989, 2d edit., 1995, AIDS Law in a Nutshell, 1991, 2d edit., 1996, Notary Law and Practice: Cases and Materials, 1997, Travel Law: Cases and Materials, 1998, Sports Law: Cases and Materials, 1999; author: Careers in Admiralty and Maritime Law, 1993, An Admiralty Law Anthology, 1995; editor: The Law of Cruise Ships, 2000, Maritime Arbitration, 1999; co-editor: Prime Time Law: Fictional Television as Legal Narrative, 1998, Bush v. Gore: The Fight for Florida's Vote, 2001; mem. editl. bd. Washington Lawyer, 1988-94, Jour. Maritime Law and Commerce, 1990-92, 2001—, assoc. editor, 1993-95, editor, 1996-2000, Maritime Law Reporter, 1991-99, Hospitality Law, 1999-2001; mem. adv. bd. Transnat. Lawyer, 1991—; mem. adv. bd. World Arbitration and Mediation Report, 1990—, U. San Francisco Maritime Law Jour., 1992-95; contbg. editor Preview U.S. Supreme Ct. Cases, 1990-95, 99—. Mem.: ABA (vice chmn. admiralty law com. young lawyers divsn. 1992—93, chair 1993—94), Fla. Bar Assn. (admiralty law com. 1988—95, vice chmn. 1991—92, chmn. 1992—93, exec. coun. internat. law sect. 1992—96), Maritime Law Assn. U.S., Assn. Am. Law Schs. (chmn.-elect maritime law sect. 1991—93, chmn. 1993—94), Phi Delta Phi (province pres. 1989—91, coun. 1991—93), Northwestern U. Club South Fla. (v.p. 1992—93, pres. 1993—95), Acacia, Phi Beta Kappa. Democrat. Jewish. Avocations: theatre, running. Office: Nova Southeastern U Law Ctr 3305 College Ave Fort Lauderdale FL 33314-7721

JASCOURT, HUGH D. lawyer, arbitrator, mediator; b. Phila., Mar. 25, 1935; s. Jacquard A. and Gladys Mae (Bregen) J.; m. Resa B. Zall, Nov. 28, 1963; children: Stephen, Leigh. AB, U. Pa., 1956; JD, Wayne State U., 1960. Bar: Mich. 1961, U.S. Supreme Ct. 1965, D.C. 1967. Atty. advisor U.S. Dept. Labor, Washington, 1960-64; asst. dir. employee-mgmt. rels. Am. Fedn. Govt. Employees, 1964-65; atty. advisor Nat. Labor Rels. Bd., 1965-66; exec. dir. Fed. Bar Assn., 1966-67; house counsel Am. Fedn. of State, County, & Mcpl. Employees, 1967-69; sr. labor-law counsel Bd. of Gov. Fed. Reserve Bd., 1969-72; dir. Pub. Employment Rels. Rsch. Inst., 1972-74; asst. solicitor U.S. Dept. of Interior, 1974-82; sr. labor-law counsel U.S. Dept. Commerce, 1982-90; pres. Agency for Dispute Resolutions and Synergistic Rels., Greenbelt, Md., 1991—. Lectr. George

Washington U. Law Sch., Washington, 1970—75; chmn. unfair labor practice panel Prince George County Employee Rels. Bd., Upper Marlboro, Md., 1972—83; mem. Greenbelt (Md.) Employee Rels. Bd. , 1977—; mem. numerous panels including Am. Arbitration Assn., Fed. Mediation and Conciliation Svc., Nat. Mediation Bd., Nat. Assn. Security Dealers, Libr. of Congress, D.C. PERB, N.J. PERC, N.J. Bd. Mediation, SSA-Am., Fedn. Govt. Employees; arbitrator/mediator, 1973—. Author, editor: Trends in Public Sector Labor Relations, 1973, Government Labor Relations, 1979; author: (with others) Labor Relations, 1978-82; Collective Bargaining, 1980; labor rels. editor Jour. Law and Edn., 1972-2001. Pres. Road Runners Club Am., 1962-66, Prince George's County (Md.) Fedn. of Recreational Couns., 1969, Prince George's County Coun. of PTAs, 1989-90; mem. Prince George's County Cmty. Adv. Coun., 1988—; coach U.S. track and field team AAU So. Games, Trinidad, 1964, Internat. Cross Country Championship, Morocco, 1966; v.p. Am. Running and Fitness Assn., 1968-84. Inductee Road Runners Club Am. Hall of Fame, 1986; initial inductee D.C. Road Runners Club Hall of Fame, 1994; named master ofcl. honoree Penn Relays, 2000. Fellow Coll. of Labor and Employment Lawyers; mem. ABA (com. on state and local labor employment and law, chmn. subcom. 1982—, co-chmn. com. on fed. svc. labor and employment law 1985-97, mem. mediation com., sect. on dispute resolution), ASPA, Soc. Fed. Labor Rels. Profls. (bd. dirs. 1992-93), Assn. for Conflict Resolution (charter mem.), Indsl. Rels. Rsch. Assn., Internat. Pers. Mgmt. Assn., Am. Arbitration Assn., Md. Coun. on Dispute Resolution, Am. Arbitration Assn., Nat. Assn. Security Dealers, NJ Bd. Mediation, NJ Employee Relations Commission, Am. Federation Govt. Employees. Office: Agency Dispute Resolution & Synergistic Rels 18 Maplewood Ct Greenbelt MD 20770-1907 E-mail: hugh.d.jascourt@verizon.net

JASEN, MATTHEW JOSEPH, lawyer, state justice; b. Buffalo, Dec. 13, 1915; s. Joseph John and Celina (Perlinski) Jasinski; m. Anastasia Gawinski, Oct. 4, 1943 (dec. Aug. 1970); children: Peter M., Mark M., Christine (Mrs. David K. Mac Leod), Carol Ann, (Mrs. J. David Sampson); m. Gertrude O'Connor Travers, Mar. 25, 1972 (dec. Nov. 1972); m. Grace Yungbluth Frauenheim, Aug. 31, 1973. Student, Canisius Coll., 1936; LLB, U. Buffalo, 1939; postgrad., Harvard U., 1944; LLD (hon.), Union U., 1980; LL.D. (hon.), N.Y. Law Sch., 1981. Bar: N.Y. 1940. Ptnr. firm Beyer, Jasen & Boland, Buffalo, 1940-43; pres. U.S. Security Rev. Bd., Wurttemberg-Baden, Germany, 1945-46; judge U.S. Mil. Govt. Ct., Heidelberg, Germany, 1946-49; sr. ptnr. firm Jasen, Manz, Johnson & Bayger, Buffalo, 1949-57; justice N.Y. Supreme Ct. (8th jud. dist.), 1957-67; judge N.Y. Ct. Appeals, 1968-85; U.S. Supreme Ct. spl. master S.C. v. U.S., 1987-88; spl. master Ill. vs. Ky. U.S. Supreme Ct., 1989-95; of counsel Moot & Sprague, Buffalo, 1986-90; counsel Jasen, Jasen & Sampson, P.C., 1990-99, Jasen & Jasen, P.C., Buffalo, 1999—. Mem. N.Y. State Jud. Screening Com., 1996—. Contbr. articles to profl. jours. Mem. council U. Buffalo, 1963-66; trustee Canisius Coll. Chair of Polish Culture, also, Nottingham Acad. Served to capt. AUS, 1943-46, ETO. Fellow Hilbert Coll.; recipient Disting. Alumnus award SUNY-Buffalo Sch. Law, 1969, Disting. Alumnus award Alumni Assn., 1976, Disting. Alumnus award Canisius Coll., 1978, Edwin F. Jaeckle award SUNY-Buffalo Sch. Law, 1982. Mem. Nat. Conf. Appellate Judges, State U. N.Y. at Buffalo Law Sch. Alumni Assn. (pres. 1964-65), Am., N.Y. State, Erie County bar assns., Am. Law Inst., Am. Judicature Soc., Lawyers Club Buffalo (pres. 1961-62), Nat. Advocates Club, Profl. Businessmen's Assn. Western N.Y. (pres. 1952), Phi Alpha Delta, DiGamma Soc. Roman Catholic (mem. Bishop's Bd. Govs., Buffalo diocese 1951—). Clubs: K.C. (4 deg.). General civil litigation, General corporate, Personal injury. Home: 26 Pine Ter Orchard Park NY 14127-3928 Office: Ste 700 69 Delaware Ave Buffalo NY 14202-3805 E-mail: jjatts@buffnet.net

JASPER, SEYMOUR, lawyer; b. N.Y.C., May 15, 1919; s. Louis and Gussie (Levitch) J.; m. Geulah Eidelsberg, Nov. 24, 1940 (dec.); children: Michael, Ronald, Jeffrey, Idylia; m. Barbara Gray, Feb. 11, 1975. BS, NYU, 1939; JD, Columbia U., 1956. Bar: N.Y. 1956. Assoc. Young, Kaplan & Edelstein, N.Y.C., 1956-59; ptnr. Jasper, Sandler & Lipsay, 1959-62; pvt. practice, 1962—. With USN. Estate planning, Probate. Office: 115 E 87th St New York NY 10128-1136 E-mail: sey1@ren.com

JASSY, EVERETT LEWIS, lawyer; b. N.Y.C., Feb. 4, 1937; s. David H. and Florence A. (Pollak) J.; m. Margery Ellen Rose; children: Katherine Savitt Lennon, Andrew Ralph, Jonathan Scott. AB, Harvard U., 1957, JD, 1960. Bar: N.Y. 1960, D.C. 1975. Assoc. Dewey Ballantine, N.Y.C., 1960-68, ptnr., 1968—, chmn. mgmt. com., 1996—. Mem. ABA, N.Y. State Bar Assn., Assn. of Bar of City of N.Y., The Tax Club, Harmonie Club (bd. govs. 1999-2001), Fairview Country Club, Washington Athletic Club. Avocations: golf, travel. Corporate taxation, Personal income taxation. Home: 20 Tompkins Rd Scarsdale NY 10583-2838 Office: Dewey Ballantine LLP 1301 Avenue Of The Americas New York NY 10019-6022

JASTROCH, LEONARD ANDREW, lawyer; b. Milw., Dec. 31, 1948; s. Edwin Francis and Frances Mary (Brodnan) J.; m. Bonnie Schmidt, Mar. 27, 1993; 1 child, Nina Marie. JD, Marquette U., 1972. Bar: Wis. 1973, U.s. Dist. Ct. (ea. and we. dists.) Wis. 1973, U.S. Supreme Ct. 1976, U.S. Tax Ct. 1982. Sole practice, Waukesha, Wis., 1973-77; sr. ptnr. Jastroch & LaBarbe SC, 1978—. Adj. prof. bus. law Alverno Coll. Bd. dirs. Waukesha Family YMCA. Mem. Wis. Bar Assn., Waukesha Bar Assn., Milw. Bar Assn., Wis. Acad. Trial Lawyers, Assn. Trial Lawyers Am., ABA, Delta Theta Phi. Estate planning, Real property. Home: Hartland WI Office: Jastroch & LaBarge SC 640 W Moreland Blvd Waukesha WI 53188-2433

JAUDES, RICHARD EDWARD, lawyer; b. St. Louis, Feb. 22, 1943; s. Leo August Jr. and Dorothy Catherine (Schmidt) J.; m. Mary Kay Tansey, Sept. 22, 1967; children: Michele, Pamela. BS, St. Louis U., 1965, JD, 1968. Bar: Mo. Supreme Ct. 1968, U.S. Dist. Ct. (ea. dist.), Mo. 1973 U.S. Ct. Appeals (8th cir.) 1973, U.S. Supreme Ct. 1990. With Peper, Martin, Jensen, Maichel & Hetlage, St. Louis, 1973-97, mng. ptnr., 1990-93; lawyer, co-chair labor and employment practice group Thompson Coburn LLP, 1997—; mem. mgmt. com. Thompson Coburn. Bd. dirs. Baldor Electric Co. Vol. Civic Entrepreneurs Orgn., St. Louis, 1990; vol. counsel St. Louis chpt. MS Soc., 1990—, exec. com. Lt. USN, 1968-73; comdr. USNR, ret. Labor. Office: Thompson Coburn One Firstar Plz Saint Louis MO 63101-1693 E-mail: rjaudes@thompsoncoburn.com

JAUVTIS, ROBERT LLOYD, lawyer; b. Bklyn., Oct. 19, 1946; s. Louis and Betty (Slomiansky) J. B.A., U. Rochester, 1968; J.D., Albany Law Sch., 1973; LL.M. in Labor Law, NYU, 1976. Bar: N.Y. 1974, U.S. Ct. Appeals (2d cir.) 1975, U.S. Supreme Ct. 1980. Assoc. Vladeck, Waldman, Elias & Engelhard, P.C., N.Y.C., 1974-78; assoc. Epstein Becker & Green, P.C., N.Y.C., 1978-82, ptnr., 1982— ; moot ct. judge N.Y. Law Sch. Wagner Labor Law Competition, N.Y.C., 1980-82; lectr. Contbr. articles to legal jours. Served with USAR, 1969-74. Mem. ABA, N.Y. State Bar Assn., Assn. Bar City N.Y., Am. Soc. Personnel Adminstrn. (bd. dirs. met. N.Y. chpt. 1983-85). Civil rights, Federal civil litigation, Labor. Office: Epstein Becker & Green PC 250 Park Ave Ste 1200 New York NY 10177-1211

JAVORE, GARY WILLIAM, lawyer; b. San Antonio, Apr. 3, 1952; s. Fred Walter and Glennice Jean (Gilbert) J. BA, Kent (Ohio) State U., 1975; JD, Cleve. State U., 1978. Bar: Tex. 1978, U.S. Dist. Ct. (we. dist.) Tex. 1981, U.S. Ct. Appeals (5th cir.) 1981, U.S. Supreme Ct. 1981. Atty. Bexar County Legal Aid, San Antonio, 1979-81; prin. Johnson, Christopher, Javore & Cochran, 1981—. Bd. dirs. Bexar County Legal Aid, San Antonio, 1986—. Author, speaker legal seminars. Mem. Leadership San Antonio Class XXIV. Fellow Tex. Bar Found., San Antonio Bar Found.; mem. San Antonio Trial Lawyers Assn. (bd. dirs. 1986—, treas. 1991, pres. 1993, Outstanding Young Lawyer award 1986), Greater San Antonio Builders Assn. (cons., exec. bd. 1990—, v.p. assoc. coun. 1993), Tex. Trial Lawyers Assn., Order of Barristers. Avocations: wood carving, tennis, scuba diving. Alternative dispute resolution, Consumer commercial, Construction. Office: Johnson Christopher Javore & Cochran 5802 Northwest Expy San Antonio TX 78201-2851

JAY, WILLIAM WALTON, lawyer; b. N.Y.C., June 29, 1943; s. William Chauncy and Miriam Bell (Samuels) J.; widowed; children: William Robert, Michael Samuel. BA, Emory U., 1965; JD, U. Chgo., 1968; MS in Mgmt., Rensselaer Poly. Inst., 1984. Bar: Ill. 1968, Ariz. 1969, U.S. Dist. Ct. Ariz. 1969, Conn. 1985, N.Y. 1990. Atty. semiconductor products div. Motorola, Inc., Scottsdale, Ariz., 1968-71; pvt. practice, Phoenix, 1971-72; asst. atty. gen. State of Ariz., 1972-74; atty. Kaiser Engrs. div. Kaiser Industries Corp., 1974-75; counsel Naval Sea Systems Command, USN, Pascagoula, Miss., 1975-79; dep. counsel Elec. Boat Corp., Groton, Conn., 1979-99; pvt. practice, 1999—. Chmn. Groton City Dem. Com.; mem. Groton Representative Town Meeting, Groton Town Dem. Com. Served with USN, 1961-65. Mem. ABA (pub. contracts sect.), State Bar Ariz., Nat. Contract Mgmt. Assn. (fellow, lectr., pres. Gulf Coast chpt. 1978, bd. dirs. Gulf Coast chpt. 1979, ctrl. Conn. chpt. 1987, cert. profl. contract mgr.), Shipbuilders Coun. Am. (contracts com. 1982—), Phi Beta Kappa, Pi Sigma Alpha, Phi Delta Phi, Beta Theta Pi. Presbyterian. Lodges: Rotary, Lions. Administrative and regulatory, Contracts commercial, Government contracts and claims. Home: 33 Elderkin Ave Apt C1 Groton CT 06340-4900 Office: 33 Elderkin Ave Ste C1 Groton CT 06340-4900 E-mail: jayw4@prodigy.net, floridafats1@yahoo.com

JEFFARES, PAUL REGINALD, laawyer; b. Glasgow, Scotland, Feb. 14, 1954; s. Reginald Geoffrey and Avis Mary (Leddy) J.; m Sonia Defant, Oct. 7, 1978. BA with honors, U. Sydney, Australia, 1976; LLB, U. New South Wales, Australia, 1978; MBA, AGSM, Sydney, 1996. Bar: solicitor Supreme Ct. of N.S.W., High Ct. of Australia. Solicitor RP Turvey & Son, Sydney, 1980-81, Prudential Assurance, Sydney, 1981-83; gen. counsel Amro Australia Ltd., 1983-88; ptnr. Gadens, 1988-91; head legal for N.S.W., Nat. Australia Bank, 1991-98; ptnr. Ebsworth & Ebsworth, 1998-2000; gen. coun. Duke Energy Int. Asia Pacific, 2000—. Contbr. articles to profl. jours. Fellow Chartered Secs. in Australia; mMem. Australian Corp. Lawyers Assn. (sec.1995-98), Law Soc. of N.S.W. Contracts commercial, Mergers and acquisitions. Office: Duke Energy Int Level Angel Place Pitt St 2000 Sydney NSW 2000 Australia E-mail: pjeffares@duke-energy.com

JEFFERSON, WALLACE B. judge; BA James Madison Coll., JD U. Tex. Cert.: Tex. Bd. Legal Specialization (in civil appellate law). With Groce, Locke & Hebdon, San Antonio, 1988—91; ptnr. Crofts, Callaway & Jefferson, 1991—2001; justice Supreme Ct. Tex., Austin, 2001—. Mem. bd. dirs. San Antonio Pub. Libr. Found., Alamo Area Big Bros./Big Sisters.; mem. edn. com. San Antonio Area Found. Mem.: San Antonio Bar Assn. (pres. 1998—99). Office: 201 W 14th St Austin TX 78701 also: PO Box 12248 Austin TX 78711*

JEFFORDS, EDWARD ALAN, former assistant state attorney general; b. Nov. 28, 1945; s. Roy Ezra and Sylvia Belle (Dickinson) J. AA, Victor Valley Coll., 1967; student, U. Wis. Mgmt. Inst., 1977; BS, USNY-Albany, 1983; JD, Baylor U. Sch. Law, 1985; postgrad, Harvard U., 1991; DHL (hon.), Harington Coll., 1976. Bar: Tex. 1985, U.S. Dist. Ct. (we. dist.) Tex. 1985, U.S. Ct. Appeals (5th cir.) 1985, U.S. Dist. Ct. (so. dist.) Tex. 1986, U.S. Dist. Ct. (no. dist.) Tex. 1988, U.S. Supreme Ct. 1989, D.C. 2001. Editor Auburn (Wash.) Globe-News, 1967-70; fine arts editor Tacoma News-Tribune, 1970-75; exec. dir. Ozark Inst., Eureka Springs, 1976-82; asst. atty. gen. State of Tex., Austin, 1985-92; exec. dir. Pan Am. Ednl. Found., 1989—. Adj. prof. Nat. U. of Costa Rica, 1989-90; trustee Regents Coll. Alumni Assn., USNY, 1990-99; advocate Nat. Coll. Advocacy. Exec. editor Baylor Law Rev., 1984-85. With USAF, 1963-67. Mem.: ABA, ATLA, Travis County Bar Assn., Internat. Acad. Litigators, Trial Lawyers for Pub. Justice, State Bar Coll., State Pro Bono Coll., Tex. Group Legal Ethics, Am. Judicature Assn., Tex. Trial Lawyers Assn., Univ. Club, Million Dollar Adv. Forum, Order of Barrister, Delta Theta Phi. Office: PO Box 2521 Austin TX 78768-2521

JEFFRESS, D. AMES, prosecutor; b. Lexington, Mass., Feb. 24, 1965; d. William Jorace Jr. and Judith Jones Jeffress; m. Christopher Reid Cooper, May 1, 1999. BA, Williams Coll., 1987; diploma, Free U., Berlin, 1989; JD, Yale U., 1992. Bar: Va. 1993, D.C. 1996. Law clk. to Hon. Gerhard Gesell, Washington, 1992-93; counsel U.S. Dept. Def., 1993-94; counsel to dep. atty. gen. U.S. Dept. Justice, 1994-96; asst. U.S. atty. Office of U.S. Atty., 1996—. Mem. Yale Law Sch. Assn. (pres. 1998—). Democrat. Avocation: running marathons. Home: 5405 Potomac Ave NW Washington DC 20016-2553

JEFFREYS, ALBERT LEONIDAS, lawyer; b. Chase City, Va. m. Lee H. Hickson. AB in History and Govt., Fla. So. Coll.; JD, So. Meth. U., 1969. Bar: Tex. 1971. Tech. writer Collins Radio, Dallas, 1959-60; contract negotiator LTV Electro Systems, 1960-71; corp. atty., asst. sec. Earth Resources Co., 1971-73; gen. counsel, asst. sec. Liquid Paper Corp., 1973-80; gen. counsel, dir. of contracts Electrospace Systems, Inc., Richardson, Tex., 1980-81; pvt. practice Richardson and Dallas, 1981—; gen. counsel Ratheal Cos., Garland, Tex., 1991-92; referral counsel to office of econ. devel. City of Dallas, 1999—. Sgt. U.S. Army. Mem. ABA, Tex. Bar Assn., Dallas Bar Assn. General corporate, General practice, Probate. Home: 328 Huffhines St Richardson TX 75081-4113 E-mail: jstrpt@aol.com

JEFFREYS, SIMON BADEN, lawyer; b. London, May 3, 1957; BA with honors, Cambridge U., Eng., 1979. Bar: Supreme Ct. Eng., Wales 1982. Articled clk. McKenna & Co., London, 1980-82; asst. solicitor, 1982-88; ptnr. CMS Cameron McKenna and predecessor firm, 1988—. Author: Hiring and Firing Executives, 1995; co-editor: Employment Precedents and Company Policy Documents, 1996, Transfer of Undertakings, 1997. Mem. Law Soc., Employment Lawyers Assn. Avocation: fly fishing. Labor. Home: 35 The Boundary Tunbridge Wells Kent TN3 OYA England Office: CMS Cameron McKenna Mitre House 160 1 AldersgateSt EC1A 4DD London England E-mail: sbj@cmk.com

JEFFRIES, JOHN CALVIN, JR. law educator; b. 1948; BA, Yale U., 1970; JD, U. Va., 1973. Bar: Va. 1973, D.C. 1974. Law clk. to Hon. Justice Powell U.S. Supreme Ct., 1973-74; asst. prof. U. Va., Charlottesville , 1975-79, assoc. prof. Charlottesville, 1979-81, prof. law, 1981—, Emerson Spies prof., 1986—, acad. assoc. dean, 1994, Arnold H. Leon prof. law, dean Sch. Law. Vis. asst. prof. Stanford U., fall 1977; vis. prof. Yale U., 1981-82, So. Calif. U., fall 1986, 89, 93; prof. FBI Acad., Quantico, Va., 1976—. Author: Justice Lewis F. Powell, Jr.: A Biography, 1994, (with Low) Model Penal Code and Commentaries, 3 vols., 1980, Civil Rights Actions: Section 1983 and Related Statutes, 2d edit., 1994, Federal Courts and the Law of Federal-State Relations, 3d edit., 1994, (with Low and Bonnie) Cases and Materials on Criminal Law, 1982, 2d edit., 1986; editor-in-chief Va. Law Rev. Mem. Am. Law Inst., Va. State Bar (com. for oversight of bar activities). Office: U Va Sch Law Charlottesville VA 22903*

JEFFRIES, MCCHESNEY HILL, JR. lawyer; b. Atlanta, Dec. 25, 1954; s. McChesney Hill Sr. and Alice Elizabeth (Mitchell) J.; m. Virginia Lee Hartley, Aug. 2, 1980; children: Virginia Hartley, McChesney Hill III. BA with high distinction, U. Va., 1977, JD, 1980. Bar: Ga. 1980, U.S. Dist. Ct. (no. dist.) Ga. 1980, U.S. Ct. Appeals (11th cir.) 1980. Assoc. Hurt, Richardson, Garner, Todd & Cadenhead, Atlanta, 1980-85, Long, Aldridge & Norman, Atlanta, 1985-87, ptnr., 1988-95; ptnr., head Capital Markets Group, Alston & Bird, 1995—. Contbr. articles to profl. jours. Mem.: ABA, Ga. Bar Assn. (securities com.), Atlanta Bar Assn. (founding dir. bus. and fin. law sect.), Piedmont Driving Club (Atlanta). Presbyterian. Avocation: sports. General corporate, Mergers and acquisitions, Securities. Home: 4575 Jett Rd NW Atlanta GA 30327-4561 Office: Alston & Bird One Atlantic Ctr 1201 W Peachtree St Atlanta GA 30309-3424 E-mail: hjeffries@alston.com

JEGEN, LAWRENCE A., III, law educator; b. Chgo., Nov. 16, 1934; s. Lawrence A. and Katherine M. (Stibgen) J.; m. Janet M. Holmberg, Aug. 30, 1958; children: Christine M., David L. BA, Beloit Coll., 1956; JD, U. Mich., 1959, MBA, 1960; LLM, NYU, 1963. Bar: Ill. 1959, U.S. Dist. Ct. (no. dist.) Ill. 1959, U.S. Dist. Ct. (so. dist.) Ind. 1962, Ind. 1966, U.S. Tax Ct. 1966, U.S. Ct. Appeals (7th cir.) 1980, U.S. Supreme Ct. 1980. Tax cons. Coopers & Lybrand, N.Y.C., 1960-62; asst. prof. law Ind. U., Indpls., 1962-64, assoc. prof., 1964-66, prof., 1966—, Thomas F. Sheehan prof. tax law and policy, 1982—, prof. philanthropic studies Ctr. Philanthropy, 1992—, external tax counsel, 1997—. Ind. U. rep. to Nat. Assn. Coll. and Univ. Attys.; co-founder Annual Tax Inst. for Colls. and Univs.; bar rev. lectr., vis. prof. in field; spl. counsel Ind. Dept. Revenue, 1963-65, Gov.'s Commn. on Med. Edn., 1970-72; mem. commr.'s adv. com. IRS, 1981-82; advisor Notre Dame Estate Planning Inst.; mem. Ind. Corp. Law Survey Commn.; state tax notes corr. for tax analysts; contbg. editor Inst. Bus. Planning's Tax Planning Svc.; bd. dirs., officer Ind. Continuing Legal Edn. Forum; 1st chmn. bd. dirs. Baccalaureate Edn. Sys. Trust of Ind.; mem. Ind. Gen. Assembly Study Commn.-Ind. Gen. Corp. Act; mem. Ind. Corps. Survey Commn., 1965—; commr. Nat. Conf. Uniform State Laws, 1981-91; dir. N.Am. Wildlife Assn., 1981-90. Author: Indiana Will and Trust Manual, 1967-95; Lifetime and Estate, Personal and Business Planning, 1987; Estate Planning and Administration in Indiana, 1979, numerous other books, articles, chpts. Chmn. bd. dirs. Ind. Bar Ednl. Sys. Tchrs., 1988-89; mem. adv. bd. Ind. U. Ctr. on Philanthropy. Named hon. sec. of state, State of Ind., 1967, 1980, hon. dep. atty. gen., 1968, hon. state treas., 1969, Ford fellow, 1963; recipient Spl Alumni Tch. award, Ind. U. Alumni Assn., 1970, 1976, 1980, 1985, Excellence in Taxation award for improvement tax adminstrn., State of Ind. Quality for Ind. Taxpayers, Inc., 1990, The Thomas Hart Benton Mural medallion, 1993, 3 Sagamore of the Wabash awards, State Ind., Internat. award, Assn. Continuing Legal Administrators for Excellence in Continuing Legal Edn., Pres.'s Cir. Commemorative medallion Ind. U. Disting. Tchg. award, Ind. U. Most Outstanding Law Profl. award (5), Ind. U. Tchg. Excellence award, Ind. U. Tchr. of Significance award. Fellow Am. Bar Found. (life), Am. Coll. Probate Counsel, Am. Coll. Tax Counsel; mem. ABA, FBA, Mid-West Inst. Estate and Tax Planning (adv. bd.), Ind. Bar Assn. (chmn. taxation sect. 1969-70, presdl. citation 1971), Indpls. Bar Assn. (Dr. Morton Finney Jr. Excellence in Legal Edn. award), Ind. Trial Lawyers Assn. (corp. taxation, estate taxation, state and local taxation). Office: Indiana Univ Sch Law 530 W New York St Indianapolis IN 46202-3225 E-mail: profjegen@aol.com

JELINCH, FRANK ANTHONY, lawyer; b. San Jose, Calif., July 22, 1943; s. Frank Anthony and Minnie Leona J.; m. Roberta Katherine Magi, Dec. 27, 1975; 1 child, Michelle. BA cum laude, San Jose Sate U., 1965; JD, U. Calif., Berkeley, 1968. Bar: Calif. 1969, U.S. Dist. Ct. (no. dist.) Calif. 1969, U.S. Supreme Ct. 1972. Ptnr. Jelinch & Rendler, Cupertino, Calif., 1980—. Instr. Lincoln U. Sch. Law, San Jose, 1980; founder Cupertino Nat. Bank. Chmn. San Francisco Shakespeare Festival, 1997-98, Terra Found., San Jose, 1980—; commr. Los Gatos Parks Commn., 1980-88, Cupertino Parks & Recreation, 1996—, chair, 1997, 2001; dir. state bd. Calif. Parks and Recreation Commrs. Assn.; commr. Cupertino Fine Arts Commn., 1990-94; chair Am. Heart Assn. Cardiac Fundraising Drive, 1996; pres. Los Gatos Friends of the Arts; bd. dirs. State Bd. parks Commrs., 2001—, Cupertino Cmty. Svcs. Bd., 2001—. Capt. U.S. Army, 1969-73, Command Judge Advocate, 1st Signal Brigade, USARV, 1971, legal officer Op. Homecoming (Vietnam returning POW's) 1973. Recipient Bronze Star, Oak Leaf Cluster, Army Commendation Medal (1st Oak Leaf Cluster), Vietnam. Mem. ABA (EEOC com.), Sunnyvale-Cupertino Bar Assn. (pres. 1990), Cupertino C. of C. (pres. 1998-99, del. trade delegation to Taiwan 2000), Santa Clara County Bar Assn. (gov. 1990), Calif. State Bar Assn., Santa Clara County Trial Lawyers Assn., U.S. Supreme Ct. Hist. Soc., Phi Alpha Theta, Pi Sigma Alpha. General civil litigation, Insurance, Personal injury. Office: Jelinch & Rendler 20863 Stevens Creek Blvd Cupertino CA 95014-2125

JENKINS, EVERETT WILBUR, JR. lawyer, author, historian; b. Oklahoma City, Nov. 28, 1953; s. Everett Wilbur and Lillie Bell (Ingram) J.; m. Monica Lynn Endsley, June 3, 1978; children: Ryan, Camille, Jennifer, Cristina. BA cum laude, Amherst Coll., 1975; JD, U. Calif., Berkeley, 1978. Bar: Calif. 1979. Dep. county counsel Contra Costa County, Martinez, Calif., 1980-81; dep. city atty. City of Richmond, 1981-84, asst. city atty., 1984—; bd. atty. West County Agy., Richmond, 1981-90; authority atty. Solid Waste Mgmt. Authority West Contra Costa, 1985-87, 88-91. Legal rep. tech. adv. com. Contra Costa County Solid Waste Commn., Martinez, Calif., 1986-87; pub. mem., 1987-88; adv. atty. West Contra Costa Transp. Adv. Com., San Pablo, 1994—; bd. atty. Richmond Housing Authority, 1992-99. Author: Pan-African Chronology, 1996, II, 1998, III, 2001, The Muslim Diaspora, 1999, vol. 2, 2000. Rep. Contra Costa County Hazardous Materials Commn., Martinez, 1987-88; bd. dirs. YMCA of the East Bay, Oakland, 1996—; bd. dirs. West Contra Costa YMCA, Richmond, 1987—, chair program com., 1991-92, vice chair bd. dirs. 1992-96, chair bd. dirs., 1996-98, chair cmty. gifts campaign, 1992-94 (named Rita Davis Vol. of the Yr., 1993); umpire Little League Baseball, 1997—, ASA Softball, 1997—. Mem. ABA, State Bar Calif. (exec. bd. pub. law sect. exec. com. 1987-91, editor Pub. Law News 1988-91, liaison to bd. govs. 1991-92), Continuing Edn. Bar (joint adv. com. 1993-96), Contra Costa County Bar Assn., Charles Houston Bar Assn., Nat. Assn. Sports Officials. Independent. Office: City Atty's Office 2600 Barrett Ave # 330 Richmond CA 94804-1654

JENKINS, GEORGE L. lawyer, entrepreneur; b. Wheeling, W.Va., Jan. 30, 1940; s. George Addison and Mildred Irene (Liggett) J. AB magna cum laude, Kent State U., 1963; JD with honors, U. Mich., 1966. Bar: Ohio 1966. Assoc. Vorys, Sater, Seymour & Pease, Columbus, Ohio, 1966-71, ptnr., 1975—; 1st asst. atty. gen. State of Ohio, 1971-75. Bd. dirs. Fleagane Enterprises, Inc., JMHS, Inc., Impex Logistics, Inc., Nat. Am. Logistics, Inc., ECNext, Inc., CP Techs., Inc., Spata Comm. Corp. Mem. ABA, Ohio Bar Assn., Columbus Bar Assn. (chmn. various coms. 1966—), Columbus Athletic Club, Muirfield Country Club, Desert Mountain Club, others. Democrat. Methodist. Avocations: tennis, jogging, travel, reading, golf. Office: Vorys Sater Seymour & Pease PO Box 1008 52 E Gay St Columbus OH 43215-3161 E-mail: gljenkins@vssp.com

JENKINS, JAMES C. lawyer; b. Logan, Utah, July 16, 1948; BA in Fin., U. Utah, 1972; JD, Gonzaga U., 1976. Bar: Utah 1976, U.S. Dist. Ct. Utah 1976, U.S. Ct. Appeals (10th cir.) 1992, U.S. Tax Ct. 1985, U.S. Supreme Ct. 1981. Ptnr. Olson & Hoggan, P.C., Logan, Utah; Rich county atty., 1978-81; Cache county dep. atty., 1981-95; gen. counsel Bear Lake Spl. Svcs. Dist., Rich County, Utah, 1978-2001. Instr. Utah State U., 1976; trustee Utah Bankruptcy Ct., 1977-80. Chair jud. conduct commn. Utah Jud. Coun., 1996-97, mem. jud. performance and evaluation com., mem.

adv. bd. Utah State Crime Lab. Mem. ABA (trial practice com., litig. sect. 1986-95), Utah State Bar Assn. (pres.-elect 1997-98, pres. 1998-99, law benefit com. 1978-80, law day com. 1989-90, ethics and discipline com. 1992-93, exec. com., litig. com. 1993-95, bd. commrs. 1993-96), Utah Statewide Assn. Pros., Cache County Bar Assn. (sec.-treas. 1978-81) General civil litigation, Personal injury, Real property. Office: Olson & Hoggan PC PO Box 525 88 W Center St Logan UT 84323-0525

JENKINS, JOHN RICHARD, III, lawyer; b. Phila., Apr. 14, 1946; s. John Richard Jr. and Barbara (Ladd) J.; m. Judy Long, June 19, 1971; children: Leigh, John IV, Matthew. BA, UCLA, 1968; JD, U. Tex., 1971; LLM, So. Meth. U., 1977. Bar: Tex. 1971, U.S. Dist. Ct. (no. dist.) Tex. 1972, U.S. Tax Ct. 1972. Cert. Tax Law Tex. Bd. Legal Splization. Assoc. Law, Snakard, Brown & Gambill, Ft. Worth, 1971-72; chief counsel Nu-Way Oil, 1972-73; assoc. Ashley & Welch, Dallas, 1973-78; ptnr. Tanner & Jenkins, 1978-80, McMullen, Porter, Jenkins, Smith, Dallas, 1980-87, Graham Bright & Smith, Dallas, 1987-91; pvt. practice, 1991—. Spkr. estate planning, taxation. Spkr. estate planning, 1980—. Past pres. YMCA, 1988. Mem. ABA, Dallas Bar Assn., Rotary, Masons (past master). Republican. Methodist. Avocation: golf. Corporate taxation, Estate taxation, Taxation, general. Office: 14651 Dallas Pkwy Ste 102 Dallas TX 75240-8395

JENKINS, MELVIN LEMUEL, lawyer; b. Halifax, N.C., Oct. 15, 1947; s. Solomon Green and Minerva (Long) J.; m. Wanda Joyce Holly, May 20, 1972; children— Dawn, Shelley, Melvin, Holly Rae-Ann. B.S., N.C. Agrl. and State U., 1969; J.D., U. Kans., 1972. Bar: Nebr. 1973. US. Dist. Ct. Nebr. 1973. Atty., Legal Aid Soc., Kansas City, Mo., 1972, HUD, Kansas City, 1972-73; regional atty. U.S. Commn. on Civil Rights, Kansas City, Mo., 1973-79; regional dir. U.S. Commn. on Civil Rights, Kansas City, Mo., 1979— . Chmn. A.M. Roundtable, Kansas City, 1981-83; mem. Kansas City Human Relations Commn., 1980; Mem. Mo. Black Adoption Adv. Bd., Kansas City, 1981— ; bd. dirs. Joan Davis Spl. Sch. Mem. Nebr. Bar Assn., ACLU, Nat. Bar Assn., Fed. Bar Assn., ABA, Urban League. African Methodist Episcopalian. Lodge: Masons (master mason for civil rights 1979). E-mail: melvin.1.jenkins@worldnet.att.net. Home: 8015 Sunset Cir Grandview MO 64030-1461 Office: 911 Walnut St Kansas City MO 64106-2017 also: Commission on Civil Rights Central Regional Office 4th & State Ave #908 Kansas City KS 66101

JENKINS, RICHARD ERIK, patent lawyer; b. Newport News, Va., Jan. 12, 1946; s. Willard Erette and Ina Beatrice (Porter) J.; m. Susan Rankin Thurston, Aug. 24, 1968 (div. Nov. 1991); 1 child, Anna. BS, N.C. State U., 1968, M in Stats. and Econs., 1971; JD, U. N.C., 1975. Engr. Celanese Corp., Charlotte, N.C., 1971-72; assoc. atty. Stevens, Davis, Miller & Mosher, Washington, 1975-76, Bell, Seltzer, Park & Gibson, Charlotte, N.C., 1976-78; ptnr. Adams &Jenkins, 1978-80; asst. patent counsel Burlington Industries, Inc., Greensboro, N.C., 1980-84; sr. ptnr. Jenkins & Wilson, Durham, 1984—. Adj. assoc. prof. Duke U., Durham, 1989—, N.C. State U., Raleigh, N.C., 1992—. Trustee N.C. Ctrl. U., Durham, 1992-95; bd. govs. Univ. Club, Durham, 1994-98; bd. dirs. Coun. Entrepreneurial Devel., 1988-90. Mem. AMA, N.C. Bar Assn., Rotary, Hope Valley Country Club, Univ. Club, Carolina Club. Republican. Presbyn. Avocations: golf, yard, reading, sports cars. Intellectual property, Patent. Office: Jenkins & Wilson PA 3100 Tower Blvd Ste 1400 Durham NC 27707-2563

JENKINS, ROBERT ROWE, lawyer; b. Norwalk, Ohio, Aug. 8, 1933; s. Robert Leslie and Millie Leona (Rowe) J.; m. Francis Jean Cline, June 12, 1955 (div. July 1972); children: Diane Elaine, Katherine Eileen; m. Jean Dingus, July 9, 1972. Student, Lebanon Valley Coll., 1951-55; BS in Chemistry, Eastern Coll. (now U. Balt.), 1967; JD, U. Balt., 1975. Bar: Md. 1976, U.S. Dist. Ct. Md. 1976, U.S. Ct. Appeals (4th cir.) 1979, U.S. Supreme Ct. 1979. Atty. Social Security Adminstrn., Balt., 1975-76; trial atty. Nelson R. Kandel, 1976-77; sole practice, 1977-81; ptnr. Jenkins Block & Mering, 1981—. Faculty continuing profl. edn. of lawyers Md. Inst., Balt., 1986—. Ruling elder Faith Christian Fellowship Presbyterian Ch. Am., Balt., 1982—. Served with U.S. Coast Guard, 1955-59. Mem. ABA, Md. Bar Assn., Balt. City Bar Assn., Assn. Trial Lawyers Am., Md. Trial Lawyers Assn., Christian Legal Soc., Nat. Orgn. Social Security Claimant's Rep. (exec. com.). Republican. Avocations: fishing, boating. Administrative and regulatory, Pension, profit-sharing, and employee benefits, Personal injury. Home: 1003 Travers St Cambridge MD 21613-1543 Office: Jenkins Block and Assocs PO Box 739 Cambridge MD 21613 also: PO Box 739 828 Airpax Rd Ste 300 Cambridge MD 21613 also: Ste 300 828 Airpax Rd Cambridge MD 21613 also: 33 W Franklin St Ste 102 Hagerstown MD 21740-4826 E-mail: rjenk5906@aol.com

JENKINS, RONALD WAYNE, lawyer; b. Johnson City, Tenn., Aug. 14, 1950; s. James Herman and Peggy Sue (Hutchison) J.; children: April Chalice, Kimberly Michelle, Robert Herman, Ronald Wayne II. BSEE, U. Tenn., 1972, JD, 1980. Bar: Tenn. 1980, U.S. Supreme Ct. 1986, U.S. Ct. Appeals (6th cir.) 1986, U.S. Dist. Ct. (ea. dist.) Tenn. 1986. Assoc. M. Lacy West, P.C., Kingsport, Tenn., 1980-83, Herndon, Coleman, Brading & McKee, Johnson City, 1984-86, ptnr., 1986—. Editor-in-chief Tenn. Law Rev., 1979. Mem. ABA, Tenn. Bar Assn., Washington County Bar Assn., Nat. Aeronautic Assn., Am. Bd. Trial Advs. (assoc. 1999), Tau Beta Pi (Tenn. col., engring. honor), Eta Kappa Nu (electrical engring. honor). Avocations: agriculture, aviation. General civil litigation, Insurance, Professional liability. Office: Herndon Coleman PO Box 1160 104 E Main St Johnson City TN 37604-5735

JENNINGS, DEAN THOMAS, lawyer; b. Mar. 17, 1951; s. Paul Alyosis and Bonnie Mae (Pace) J.; m. Kathleen Kay Kiefer, June 15, 1973; children: Matthew Thomas, Margaret Jo. BS in English, Iowa State U., 1973; JD, Creighton U., 1976. Bar: Iowa 1976, Nebr. 1982, U.S. Dist. Ct. (so. dist.) Iowa 1976. Tchr., coach Boone H.S., Iowa, 1972-73; ptnr. McGinn, McGinn, Jennings & Springer, Council Bluffs, 1974—. Mem. ABA, Assn. Am. Trial Lawyers, Iowa Bar Assn., Nebr. Bar Assn. State civil litigation, Personal injury, Probate. Office: McGinn McGinn Jennings & Springer 2d Fl 33 W Broadway Council Bluffs IA 51503 E-mail: mmjs@cbiowa.com

JENNINGS, THOMAS PARKS, lawyer; b. Alexandria, Va., Nov. 16, 1947; s. George Christian and Ellen (Thompson) J.; m. Shelley Corrine Abernathy, Oct. 30, 1971; 1 child, Kathleen Eayre. BA in History, Wake Forest U., 1970; JD, U. Va., 1975. Bar: Va. 1975. Assoc. Lewis, Wilson, Lewis & Jones, Arlington, Va., 1975-78; atty. First Va. Banks, Inc., Falls Church, 1978-80, gen. counsel, 1980—, sec., 1993-99, sr. v.p., 1995—. Adj. prof. George Mason U. Sch. Law, Arlington, 1987-88. Trustee Arlington Cmty. Found., 1998—, treas., 2001—; dir. Rixey St. Found., Inc., 1997—; deacon Georgetown Presbyn. Ch., Washington, 1979-82, elder, 1983-85, 95-97, trustee, 1988-90, dir. Bd. Pensions, Presbyn. Ch. USA, 2001—. With U.S. Army, 1970-71. Mem. ABA, Am. Soc. Corp. Secs., Va. State Bar Assn., Va. Bankers Assn. (legal affairs com.), Fairfax County Bar Assn., Am. Corp. Counsel Assn., Washington Met. Area Corp. Counsel Assn. (bd. dirs. 1984-87). Avocations: bridge, kayaking. Banking, Contracts commercial, General corporate. Office: First Va Banks Inc 6400 Arlington Blvd Ste 420 Falls Church VA 22042-2336

JENSEN, D. LOWELL, federal judge, lawyer, government official; b. Brigham, Utah, June 3, 1928; s. Wendell and Elnora (Hatch) J.; m. Barbara Cowin, Apr. 20, 1951; children: Peter, Marcia, Thomas. A.B. in Econs, U. Calif.-Berkeley, 1949, LL.B., 1952. Bar: Calif. 1952. Dep. dist. atty., Alameda County, 1955-66; asst. dist. atty., 1966-69; dist. atty., 1969-81; asst. atty. gen. criminal div. Dept. Justice, Washington, 1981-83, assoc. atty. gen., 1983-85, dep. atty. gen., 1985-86; judge U.S. Dist. Ct. (no. dist.) Calif., Oakland, 1986—. Mem. Calif. Council on Criminal Justice, 1974-81; past pres. Calif. Dist. Atty.'s Assn. Served with U.S. Army, 1952-54. Fellow Am. Coll. Trial Lawyers; mem. Nat. Dist. Atty.'s Assn. (victim/witness commn. 1974-81), Boalt Hall Alumni Assn. (past pres.) Office: US Dist Ct 1301 Clay St Rm 490C Oakland CA 94612-5217

JENSEN, DALLIN W. lawyer; b. Afton, Wyo., June 2, 1932; s. Louis J. and Nellie B. Jensen; m. Barbara J. Bassett, Mar. 22, 1958; children: Brad L., Julie N. BS, Brigham Young U., 1954; JD, U. Utah, 1960. Bar: Utah 1960, U.S. Dist. Ct. Utah 1962, U.S. Ct. Appeals (10th cir.) 1974, U.S. Ct. Appeals D.C. 1980, U.S. Supreme Ct. 1971. Asst. atty. gen. Utah Atty. Gen., Salt Lake City, 1960-83, solicitor gen., 1983-88; shareholder Parsons, Behle & Latimer, Salt Lake City, 1988—; alt. commr. Upper Colo. River Commn., 1983—; mem. Colo. River Basin Salinity Adv. Council, 1975—; spl. legal cons. Nat. Water Commn., Washington, 1971-73; mem. energy law center adv. council U. Utah Coll. Law, 1976—. Mem. editl. bd. Rocky Mountain Mineral Law Found., 1983-85. Author: (with Wells A. Hutchins) The Utah Law of Water Rights, 1965. Contbr. articles on water law and water resource mgmt. to profl. jours. Served with U.S. Army, 1955-57. Mem. LDS Ch. Administrative and regulatory, Natural resources, Real property. Home: 3565 S 2175 E Salt Lake City UT 84109-2902 Office: PO Box 45898 Salt Lake City UT 84145-0898

JENSEN, ERIK MICHAEL, law educator; b. Washington, Aug. 26, 1945; s. Wayne Ivan and Anna Elizabeth (Nelson) J.; m. Helen Burgin, May 4, 1981; 1 child, Addie. SB, MIT, 1967; MA, U. Chgo., 1972; JD, Cornell U., 1979. Bar: N.Y. 1980, U.S. Dist. Ct. (so. dist.) N.Y. 1983, U.S. Ct. Appeals 1983, U.S. Tax Ct. 1981. Law clk. to Hon. Monroe G. McKay, Salt Lake City, 1979-80; assoc. Sullivan & Cromwell, N.Y.C., 1980-83; from asst. prof. law to prof. Case Western Res. U., Cleve., 1983-98, David L. Brennan prof., 1998—. Vis. prof. Cornell U., 1999. Author: (with others) Federal Income Taxation of Oil and Gas Investments, 1989; co-editor Jour. Legal Edn., 1992-98. Adv. coun. Musical Arts Assn. Cleve. Orch., 1984-85. With U.S. Army, 1968-70. Mem. ABA, Cleve. Bar Assn., Am. Polit. Sci. Assn., Internat. Fiscal Assn., Order of Coif (exec. com. 1994—). Home: 3215 Warrington Rd Cleveland OH 44120-3306 Office: Case Western Res U Sch Law 11075 East Blvd Cleveland OH 44106-5409 E-mail: emj@po.cwru.edu

JENSEN, FRODE, III, lawyer; b. Denver, Colo., May 30, 1950; s. Frode and Camille McLean (Anderson) J.; m. Catherine Spotswood Hall, Aug. 16, 1980; children: Christian McLean, Catherine Spotswood Hall, Henry Carter. Grad. Phillips Acad.; BA, Williams Coll., 1972; JD, Columbia U., 1976. Bar: N.Y. 1977, U.S. Dist. Ct. (so. and ea. dists.) N.Y. 1979, Conn. 1985. Law clk. U.S. Dist. Ct. Del., Wilmington, 1976-77; assoc. Davis Polk & Wardwell, N.Y.C., 1978-83; assoc. Cummings & Lockwood, Stamford, Conn., 1983-85, ptnr., 1985-88, Winthrop, Stimson, Putnam & Roberts, Stamford, 1988—. Mem. ABA, Assn. of Bar of City of N.Y., Conn. Bar Assn. Mergers and acquisitions, Securities. Office: Winthrop Stimson Putnam & Roberts PO Box 6760 Stamford CT 06904-6760

JENSEN, JOHN ROBERT, lawyer; b. Rapid City, S.D., Aug. 9, 1946; s. Edwin Robert and Roxina Althier (Hollinger) J.; m. Susan McClelland, Aug. 27, 1977; children: Margaret Marie, Jennifer Jo, Edwin Robert II, James Peder. BA, Calif. State U., Northridge, 1971; JD, Baylor U., 1976. Bar: Tex. 1977, U.S. Dist. Ct. (no. dist.) Tex. 1977, U.S. Ct. Appeals (5th cir.) 1982. Asst. ins. dir. Groesbeck Fin., L.A., 1971-73; v.p. Capital Cons., Dallas, 1973-74; assoc. McConnell & Assocs., Arlington, Tex., 1977; sole practice, 1984—. Author: Checklist for Texas Lawyers, 1979, 2d edit., 1981. Served with U.S. Army, 1966-68, Vietnam. Decorated Army Commedation medal. Mem. Arlington Bar Assn., Baylor Order Barristers, Tex. Bd. Legal Specialization (cert. personal injury trial law), Nat. Bd. Trial Adv. (cert. civil trial adv.), Delta Theta Phi (treas. Baylor chpt. 1976). Lutheran. Federal civil litigation, State civil litigation, Personal injury. Office: Jensen & Jensen 6025 Interstate 20 W Arlington TX 76017-1077

JENSEN, PAUL ROLF, lawyer, real estate investor; b. San Francisco, Nov. 12, 1958; s. Rolf Levald and Ouida (Moore) J.; m. Pamela Balogh, Apr. 3, 1993; children: Peter John, David Christian Rolf. AB, U. Calif., Berkeley, 1981; JD, Whittier Coll., 1990. Bar: Calif. 1991; lic. real estate broker Calif. Dept. Real Estate. Legis. dir. Am. Def. Inst., Washington, 1983-84; campaign advisor U.S. Senator Jeremiah Denton, 1984-86; assoc. atty. Elhai & McIntosh, Hacienda Heights, Calif., 1991; prin. atty. Jensen & Assocs., Newport Beach, 1992-95; ptnr. Jensen & McIntosh, Hacienda Heights, 1995—; gen. counsel Jensen Properties, LLC, Newport Beach, 1997—. Mem. Consumer Attys. Calif., Federalist Soc. (pres. Duke Law Sch. chpt. 1990-91), Consumer Attys. L.A., Bahia Corinthian Yacht Club. Republican. Presbyterian. Avocations: sailing, antiquarian book collecting, travel, wine collecting, fishing. Home: 10304 E Hunter Valley Rd Vienna VA 22181-3012 Office: Jensen McIntosh 1201 S Hacienda Blvd Hacienda Heights CA 91745

JENSEN, WALTER EDWARD, lawyer, educator; b. Chgo., Oct. 20, 1937. A.B., U. Colo., 1959; J.D., Ind. U., 1962, M.B.A., 1964; Ph.D. (Univ. fellow), Duke U., 1972. Bar: Ind. 1962, Ill. 1962, D.C. 1963, U.S. Tax Ct. 1982, U.S. Supreme Ct. 1967. Assoc. prof. Colo. State U., 1964-66; assoc. prof. Ill. State U., 1970-72; prof. bus. adminstrn. Va. Poly. Inst. and State U., beginning 1972, now prof. fin., ins. and law; with Inst. Advanced Legal Studies, U. London, 1983-84; prof. U.S. Air Force Grad. Mgmt. Program, Europe, 1977-78, 83-85; Duke U. legal research awardee, researcher, Guyana, Trinidad and Tobago, 1967; vis. lectr. pub. internat. law U. Istanbul, 1988, Roberts Coll. U. of Bosporous, Istanbul, Uludag Univ., Turkey, 1988; researcher U. London Inst. Advanced Legal Studies, London Sch. Econs. and Inst. Commonwealth Studies, summers, 1969, 71, 74, 76, winter 1972-73; Ford Found. research fellow Ind. U., 1963-64; faculty research fellow in econs. U. Tex., 1968; Bell Telephone fellow in econs. regulated pub. utilities U. Chgo., 1965. Recipient Dissertation Travel award Duke U. Grad. sch., 1968; Ind. U. fellow, 1963, 74, scholar, 1963-64. Mem. D.C. Bar Assn., Ill. Bar Assn., Ind. bar Assn., ABA, Am. Polit. sci. Assn., Am. Soc. Internat. Law, Am. Judicature Soc., Am. Bus. Law Assn., Alpha Kappa Psi, Phi Alpha Delta, Pi Gamma Mu, Pi Kappa Alpha, Beta Gamma Sigma. Contbr. articles to profl. publs.; staff editor Am. Bus Law Jour., 1973— ; vice chmn. assoc. editor for adminstrv. law sect. young lawyers Barrister (Law Notes), 1975-83; book rev. and manuscript editor Justice System Jour: A Mgmt. Rev., 1975— ; staff editor Bus. Law Rev., 1975— . Home: 3358 Glade Creek Blvd 5 Roanoke VA 24012 Office: Va Poly Inst and State U Blacksburg VA 24060

JENTZ, GAYLORD ADAIR, law educator; b. Beloit, Wis., Aug. 7, 1931; s. Merlyn Adair and Delva (Mullen) J.; m. JoAnn Mary Hornung, Aug. 6, 1955; children: Katherine Ann, Gary Adair, Loretta Ann, Rory Adair. BA, U. Wis., 1953, JD, 1957, MBA, 1958. Bar: Wis. 1957. Pvt. practice law, Madison, 1957-58; from instr. to assoc. prof. bus. law U. Okla., 1958-65; vis. instr. to vis. prof. U. Wis. Law Sch., summers 1957-65; asso. prof. to prof. U. Tex., Austin, 1965-68, prof., 1968-98, prof. emeritus, 1998—, Herbert D. Kelleher prof. bus. law, 1982-98, chmn. gen. bus. dept., 1968-74, 80-86. Author: (with others) Business Law Text and Cases, 1968, Business Law Text, 1978, Texas Uniform Commercial Code, 1967, rev. edit., 1975, West's Business Law: Alternate Edition, 7th edit., 1999, Legal Environment of Business, 1989, Texas Family Law, 7th edit., 1992, West's Business Law: Text and Cases, 8th edit., 2001, Fundamentals of Business Law, 5th edit., 2000, Business Law Today, 5th edit., 2000, Business Law Today-Comprehensive Edition, 5th Edit., 2000, Business Law Today-The Essentials, 5th edit., 2000, Business Law Today-Alternate Essentials Edition, 4th edit., 1997; dep. editor Social Sci. Quar., 1966-82, editl. bd., 1982-94; editor-in-chief Am. Bus. Law Jour., 1969-74, adv. editor, 1974—. Served with AUS, 1953-55. Recipient Outstanding Tchr. award U. Tex. Coll. Bus., 1967, Jack G. Taylor Tchg. Excellence award, 1971, 89, Joe D. Beasley Grad. Tchg. Excellence award, 1978, CBA Found. Adv. Coun. award, 1979, Grad. Bus. Coun. Outstanding Grad. Bus. Prof. award, 1980, James C. Scorboro Meml. award for outstanding leadership in banking edn. Colo. Grad. Sch. Banking, 1983, Utmost Outstanding Prof. award, 1989, CBA award for excellence in edn., 1994, Banking Leadership award Western States Sch. Banking, 1995, U. Tex. Civitatis award, 1997; inducted to CBA Hall of Fame, 1999. Mem. Southwestern Fedn. Adminstrv. Disciples (v.p. 1979-80, pres. 1980-81), Am. Arbitration Assn. (nat. panel 1966-96), Acad. Legal Studies in Bus. (pres. 1971-72, exec. com. 1989-94, Faculty award of excellence 1981), So. Bus. Law Assn. (pres. 1967), Tex. Assn. Coll. Tchrs. (pres. Austin chpt. 1967-68, exec. com. 1979-80, state pres. 1971-72), Wis. Bar Assn., Omicron Delta Kappa, Phi Kappa Phi (pres. 1983-84). Home: 4106 N Hills Dr Austin TX 78731-2826 Office: U Tex CBA 5.202 MSIS Dept Austin TX 78712

JERNIGAN, JOHN LEE, lawyer; b. Atlanta, May 29, 1942; s. Alton Lee and Marian (Heidt) J.; m. Virginia McKinney; children: Lee Ashley, Frank McKinney. AB, Davidson Coll., 1964; JD, U. N.C., 1967. Bar: N.C. 1967. Assoc. Smith, Anderson, Blount, Dorsett, Mitchell & Jernigan, Raleigh, N.C., 1969-72, ptnr., 1972—. Bd. adv. U. N.C. Banking Law Inst. Contbr. articles to profl. jours. Bd. visitors Davidson (N.C.) Coll., 1986—; trustee Choate-Rosemary Hall, Wallingford, Conn., 1989-92. Capt. U.S. Army, 1967-69. Fellow N.C. Bar Found.; mem. N.C. Bar Assn. (chmn. bus. law sect. 1985-87, bd. govs. 1989-92, chmn. bar ctr. cabinet 1994-98, pres.-elect 1998-99, pres. 1999-2000, past pres. 2000-2001), Wake County Bar Assn., Cardinal Club (bd. dirs.), So. Conf. Bar Pres., Nat. Conf. Bar Pres., Supreme Ct. Hist. Soc. Episcopalian. Banking, Contracts commercial, General corporate. Office: PO Box 2611 Raleigh NC 27602-2611

JEROME, JOHN JAMES, lawyer; b. N.Y.C., Oct. 17, 1933; s. Eugene George and Gladys Odette (Conterno) J.; ; children by previous marriage: Christopher J., Jennifer T.; m. Maureen M. Murphy, Sept. 19, 1981; children: Mairin Ashling, Emily Campbell. BBA, St. John's U., N.Y.C., 1958, LLB, 1961. Bar: N.Y. 1962, U.S. Dist. Ct. (so. dist.) N.Y. 2d cir., 3d cir., U.S. Supreme Ct., U.S. Dist. Ct. (ea. dist.) N.Y. 1964. Assoc. Milbank, Tweed, Hadley & McCloy, N.Y.C., 1962-70, ptnr., 1970-98; pres. Jerome Advisors, LLC, 1999—. Adj. prof. N.Y. Law Sch., 1978-81. With U.S. Army, 1954-57. Mem. ABA, N.Y. State Bar Assn., Assn. of Bar of City of N.Y. (chmn. com. on bankruptcy and corp. reorgn. 1990-93), Nat. Bankruptcy Conf. Club: Down Town Assn. (N.Y.C.), N.Y. Athletic. Bankruptcy, Contracts commercial, General corporate. Home: 1165 5th Ave New York NY 10029-6931 Office: Jerome Advisors LLC 1270 Ave of the Americans New York NY 10020 E-mail: J.Jerome2@compuserve.com

JESKE, CHARLES MATTHEW, lawyer; b. Bartlesville, Okla., July 16, 1964; s. Arnold Carl and Maudie Marie (Matthews) J.; m. Pamela Kay Paholek, May 20, 1989. BBA in Fin./Acctg., Tex. A&M U., 1986; JD, South Tex. Coll. Law, Houston, 1989. Bar: Tex. 1989, U.S. Dist. Ct. (so. dist.) Tex. 1990, U.S. Ct. Appeals (5th cir.) 1990. Briefing atty. 14th Dist. Ct. of Appeals Tex., Houston, 1989-90, 90-91; sr. assoc. atty. Renneker & Assocs., 1991-96; pvt. practice Jeske & Assocs. PLLC, 1996—, mng. ptnr., 1998—. Contractor, investment analyst Jeske Homes, Bryan, Tex., 1986—. Trustee, officer Meml. Hollow Citizens, Inc., Houston, 1994-96. Mem. ABA, Houston Bar Assn., Tex. A&M U. Former Students Assn., Phi Alpha Delta Alumni Assn. Republican. Lutheran. Avocations: photography, travel. Estate planning, Probate, Estate taxation. Home and Office: 12407 Barryknoll Ln Houston TX 77024-4113 E-mail: cmjeske@usa.net

JESSEE, ROY MARK, lawyer; b. Kingsport, Tenn., Feb. 8, 1966; s. Roy Claude and Myrtle Delight (Robinette) J.; m. Cortney Wynn Williams, June 30, 1990. BA, King Coll., 1988; JD, U. Va., 1991. Bar: Va. 1991, U.S. Dist. Ct. (we. dist.) Va. 1992. Law clk. Ct. of Appeals of Va., Bristol, 1991-92; assoc. atty. Mullins, Thomason & Harris, Norton, Va., 1992-94; shareholder, prin., atty. Mullins, Thomason, Harris & Jessee, 1995-98; shareholder, prin. Mullins, Harris & Jessee, 1998—. Contbr. articles to legal jours. Chmn. Scott County Dem. Party, 1993-95, 95-97. Named one of Outstanding Young Men in Am., 1989. Mem. ABA, Wise County Bar Assn. (pres.-elect 1998, pres. 1999), Am. Judicature Soc., Va. Assn. Def. Attys. Democrat. Baptist. Avocations: running, weight lifting, reading, writing poetry. General civil litigation, Personal injury, Product liability. Home: PO Box 353 112 B Elm St Gate City VA 24251 Office: Mullins Harris & Jessee PO Box 1200 30 Seventh St Norton VA 24273

JESSUP, WILLIAM EUGENE, lawyer; b. Macon, Ga., Aug. 7, 1952; s. Lauren Eugene and Katharine Kimbrough (Hosch) J. BA in English, Emory U., 1974, LLM in Taxation, 1980; JD, U. Ga., 1977. Bar: Ga. 1977, Tenn. 1981, La. 1986, U.S. Dist. Ct. (no. dist.) Ga. 1977, U.S. Dist. Ct. (mid. dist.) Tenn. 1981, U.S. Dist. Ct. (so. dist.) La. 1986, U.S. Dist. Ct. (ea. dist.) Tenn. 1999, U.S. Ct. Appeals (5th cir.) 1977, U.S. Ct. Appeals (6th cir.) 1982, U.S. Supreme Ct. 1982. Assoc. Waller Lansden Dortch & Davis, Nashville, 1981-82; pvt. practice, 1982-85; assoc. Monroe & Lemann, New Orleans, 1984-86; pvt. practice, 1986-88, Atlanta, 1988-94. Contbr. articles to profl. jours. Mem. ABA, State Bar Ga., State Bar Tenn., State Bar La., Rotary, Phi Delta Phi, Alpha Tau Omega. Methodist. Avocations: golf, songwriting, college football. General civil litigation, General practice, Taxation, general. Office: PO Box 4926 Chattanooga TN 37405-0926

JETER, KATHERINE LESLIE BRASH, lawyer; b. Gulfport, Miss., July 24, 1921; d. Ralph Edward and Rosa Meta (Jacobs) Brash; m. Robert McLean Jeter Jr., May 11, 1946. BA, Newcomb Coll. Tulane U., 1943; JD, Tulane U., 1945. Bar: La. 1945, U.S. Dist. Ct. (we. dist.) La. 1948, U.S. Tax Ct. 1965, U.S. Supreme Ct. 1971, U.S. Dist Ct. (ea. dist.) La. 1975, U.S. Ct. Appeals (5th cir.) 1981, U.S. Dist. Ct. (mid. dist.) La. 1982. Assoc. Montgomery, Fenner & Brown, New Orleans, 1945-46, Tucker, Martin, Holder, Jeter & Jackson, Shreveport, 1947-79; ptnr. Tucker, Jeter Jackson and Hickman and predecessor firms, 1980—. Judge pro tem 1st Jud. Dist. Ct., Caddo Parish, La., 1982-83; mem. adv. com. to jt. legis. subcom. on mgmt. of the cmty. Author: (with Fredricka Doll Gute) Historical Profile, Shreveport 1950, 1982, A Man and His Boat, The Civil War and Correspondence of Lieutenant Jonathan H. Carter, 1996; contbr. articles on law to profl. jours. Pres. YWCA of Shreveport, 1963; hon. consul of France, Shreveport 1982-91; pres. Little Theatre of Shreveport, 1966-67, Shreveport Art Guild, 1974-75; mem. task force criminal justice La. Priorities for the Future, 1978; pres. LWV of Shreveport, 1950-51. Recipient Disting. grad. award Tulane U., 1983. Mem. ABA, Am. Law Inst., La. State Law Inst. (mem. coun. 1980—, adv. com. La. Civil Code 1973-77, tem ad hoc com. 1976-77, sr. officer 1993—), Pub. Affairs Rsch. Coun. (bd. trustees 1976-81, 91—, exec. com. 1981-84, area exec. committeeman Shreveport area 1982), La. Bar Assn., Shreveport Bar Assn. (pres. 1986), Nat. Assn. Women Lawyers, Shreveport Assn. for Women Attys., C. of C. of Shreveport (bd. dirs. 1975-77), Order of Coif, Phi Beta Kappa. General corporate. Home: 3959 Maryland Ave Shreveport LA 71106-1021 Office: 401 Edwards St Ste 905 Shreveport LA 71101-5509

JETTE, ERNEST ARTHUR, lawyer; b. Nashua, N.H., Apr. 19, 1945; s. Fernand Ernest and Jeannette M. (Thibodeau) J.; m. Bridget Belton, Sept. 4, 1977; 1 child, Alexandra. BA, Boston Coll., 1967, JD, 1970. Bar: N.H. 1970, U.S. Dist. Ct. N.H. 1971, U.S. Tax Ct. 1972; diplomate Trial Practice Inst. Mng. atty. N.H. Legal Assistance, Nashua, 1970-72; ptnr. Janelle, Nadeau & Jette, 1972-81; dir. Hamblett & Kerrigan, P.A., 1981-93; pvt. practice, 1993—. Lectr. paralegal studies Rivier Coll., Nashua, 1977-78.

Chmn. Nashua Regional Planning Commn., 1981-82; mem. Town of Merrimack (N.H.) Master Plan Com., 1981, dir. Nashua Youth Coun., Inc., 1975-80, pres., 1978-79; dir. NEEDS, Inc., 1972-75; chmn. Heart Sunday, N.H. Heart Assn., 1973; mem. pub. affairs com. N.H. Assn. Commerce and Industry, 1983-93; mem. sch. bd. Bishop Guertin H.S., 1994-96. Capt. U.S. Army, 1970. Mem. ABA (state com. disaster legal assistance 1973-75, litigation, tort and ins. practice sects.), N.H. Bar Assn. (past mem. law related edn., coop. with the cts., profl. responsibility coms.), N.H. Bar Found., N.H. Trial Lawyers Assn., Nashua Bar Assn. (pres. 1990-91), Greater Nashua C. of C. (dir. 1985-96), Four Seasons Property Owners' Assn. (pres. 1977-78), Rotary Club Nashua (dir. 1978-79, pres. 1992-93). General civil litigation, General practice, Personal injury. Home: 9 Westbrook Dr Nashua NH 03060-5314 Office: 7 Concord St Nashua NH 03064-2328 E-mail: e.jette@verizon.net

JETTON, C. LORING, JR. lawyer; b. Pitts., Feb. 10, 1943; s. Clyde Loring and Barbara (Lewis) J.; m. Marion Luyken, Feb. 19, 1966; children: Ada Elizabeth, Christopher Loring. AB, Harvard U., 1964; JD, Columbia U., 1969. Bar: N.Y. 1969, D.C. 1970. Law clk. to Hon. W. Feinberg U.S. Ct. Appeals (2d. cir.), 1969-70; assoc. Wilmer, Cutler & Pickering, Washington, 1970-76, ptnr., 1977—. Lt. U.S. Army, 1964-66. Mem. ABA, D.C. Bar. Antitrust, General civil litigation, Private international. Office: Wilmer Cutler & Pickering 2445 M St NW Ste 500 Washington DC 20037-1487

JEWELL, FRANKLIN P. lawyer; b. Frankfort, Ky., Sept. 26, 1952; s. Wilbert Franklin and Lucille (Perry) J.; m. Rebecca Ann Wright, June 22, 1974; children: Brandon Neil, Amanda Wright. B.A., U. Ky., 1974; J.D., U. Louisville, 1977. Bar: Ky. 1977, U.S. Dist. Ct. (we. dist.) Ky. 1979, U.S. Dist. Ct. (ea.dist.) Ky. 1989. Interviewer, clk. Jefferson Dist. Pub. Defender, Louisville, 1975-77, staff atty., 1977-79, asst. chief juvenile div., 1979-82, chief trial atty. adult div., 1982-88; assoc. Popkin, Stern & Meyer, 1989—; speaker ednl. instns. and seminars. Mem. Kenwood Elem. PTA, Louisville, 1983-84, Parkland Elem. PTA, 1984-85, Klondike Elem. PTA, 1987-89; vice chmn. bd. Shawnee Christian Ch. Recipient awards for advocacy in felony cases, juvenile cases, capital trials, Jefferson Dist. Pub. Defender, 1977-88. Mem. Ky. Bar Assn. (continuing legal edn. award 1981), Louisville Bar Assn. (chmn. subcom. cir. ct. criminal def.), Phi Alpha Delta. Democrat. Office: 200 S 5th St Louisville KY 40202-3215

JEWELL, GEORGE BENSON, lawyer, educator, minister; b. Evanston, Ill., Mar. 26, 1944; s. Benson Murray and Ellen Louise (Mahle) J.; m. Pamela Elaine Peterson, Aug. 12, 1967; children: Jeffrey Benson, Brian Edward. BA, Beloit (Wis.) Coll., 1966; MDiv, Gordon-Conwell Theol. Sem., 1978; JD, Washington U., St. Louis, 1971. Bar: Ill. 1971, Mo. 1972, Mass. 1990, U.S. Dist. Ct. (ea. dist.) Mo. 1973, U.S. Dist. Ct. Mass. 1991, Ind. 1998. Trust adminstr. Ill. Nat. Bank, Springfield, 1971; corp. atty. Ralston Purina Co., St. Louis, 1971-75; assoc. pastor Westminster Presbyn. Ch., Bluefield, W.Va., 1978-81, sr. pastor Cape Girardeau, Mo., 1981-86, Evang. Free Ch., Cape Girardeau, 1986-88; pvt. practice, 1988-89; counsel, dir. gift planning, adj. assoc. prof. bus. law Gordon Coll., Wenham, Mass., 1989-97; dir. legal support svcs. Renaissance Inc., Carmel, Ind., 1997-98, v.p. legal support svcs., v.p. client svcs., 1998-99, v.p., sr. counsel, 1999—. Instr. in bus. law S.E. Mo. State U., Cape Girardeau, 1986; cons. Stone, McGhee, Feuchtenberger & Barringer, Bluefield, 1980-81; mng. editor Washington U. Law Quar. Contbr. chpts. to Life Insurance Answer Book. Deacon Ctrl. Presbyn. Ch., St. Louis, 1974-75; scoutmaster Appalachian coun. Boy Scouts Am., Bluefield, 1979; bd. advisors Sta. KUGT, Cape Girardeau, 1988, Boston Rescue Mission, 1994-97; baccalaureate spkr. Ctrl. H.S., Cape Girardeau, 1988; workshop presenter Congress '93 and Congress '94, Boston; bd. dirs. Young Life of Cape Girardeau. Mem. ABA, Nat. Assn. Coll. and Univ. Attys. (ad hoc com. on income devel. 1990-91, ad hoc com. svcs. small colls. 1991-93, com. profl. devel., 1993-97), Nat. Assn. Estate Planners and Couns., Ind. State Bar Assn. (mem. probate rev. com. 1999—), Mass. Soc. Sons Am. Revolution, Boston Bar Assn. (coll. and univ. com., estate planning com.), Planned Giving Group of New Eng., Christian Fin. Advisors Network (founder), Mo. Bar Assn. (franchise tax subcom. corp. law and bus. orgn. coms.), Evang. Free Ch. Ministerial Assn., Sigma Alpha Epsilon. Avocations: swimming, tennis, sailing. Estate planning, Estate taxation, Personal income taxation. Home: 553 Melark Dr Carmel IN 46032-2312 Office: Renaissance Inc 6100 W 96th St Ste 100 Indianapolis IN 46278-6001

JEWELL, JOHN J. lawyer, mediator; b. Kokomo, Ind., Aug. 31, 1954; s. G.M. and Kathryn (Knepper) J. AB, Ind. U., 1975, JD, MBA, Ind. U., 1979. Bar: Ind. 1979, U.S. Dist. Ct. (so. dist.) Ind. 1979. Assoc. Trimble & Jewell, Evansville, Ind., 1979—. Mem. ABA, Ind. Bar Assn., Evansville Bar Assn., Ind. Jaycees (legal counsel 1983-84, Internat. Senator), Evansville Jaycees (pres. 1982-83). Episcopalian. Consumer commercial, Landlord-tenant, Real property. Home: PO Box 291 Evansville IN 47702-0291 Office: Trimble & Jewell PO Box 1107 Evansville IN 47706-1107

JILES, GARY D. lawyer; b. Newport, Ark., Jan. 27, 1963; s. Randolph and Frances N. Jiles; m. Elisa A. Litchfield, Oct. 26, 1985; children: Katherine E., Trevor G. BSBA in Acctg., U. Ark., Fayetteville, 1985; JD with honors, U. Ark., Little Rock, 1988. Bar: Ark. 1988. Atty., ptnr. Jack, Lyon & Jones, P.A., Little Rock, 1988—. Author: Employment Law Deskbook for Arkansas Employers, 1996—; editor/author newsletter Ark. Employment Law Letter, 1995—. Mem. ABA, Ark. Bar Assn. (treas., sec., chmn. labor and employment law sect., Best of CLE Speaker 1998, 99). Banking, General civil litigation, Labor. Office: Jack Lyon & Jones PA 3400 TCBY Tower 425 W Capitol Ave Little Rock AR 72201-3405 also: Park Pl Office Complex 400 Salem Rd Ste 3 Conway AR 72032-7534 E-mail: gdj@jlj.com

JINNETT, ROBERT JEFFERSON, lawyer; b. Birmingham, Ala., May 9, 1949; s. Bryan Floyd Jr. and Elizabeth Coleman (Borders) J.; m. Doreen S. Ziff, Aug. 2, 1975 (div.); children: Brynn Leigh, Maren Alexandra. BA, Harvard U., 1971; JD, Cornell U., 1975. Bar: N.Y. 1976, U.S. Dist. Ct. (no. dist.) N.Y. 1976, U.S. Dist. Ct. (so. dist.) N.Y. 1978, U.S. Dist. Ct. (ea. dist.) N.Y. 1979, U.S. Supreme Ct. 1988. Law clk. N.Y. State Ct. Appeals, Albany, 1975-77; assoc. Rogers & Wells, N.Y.C., 1977-82, LeBoeuf, Lamb, Greene & MacRae, N.Y.C., 1983-85; ptnr. LeBoeuf, Lamb, Leiby & MacRae, 1986-94, LeBoeuf, Lamb, Greene & MacRae, L.L.P., N.Y.C., 1994, of counsel, 1995—. Pres. LeBoeuf Computing Techs., LLC., N.Y.C., 1996—; sr. cons. Cutter Consortium Distributed Computing Arch./e-Bus. Group. Contbr. articles to profl. jours. Recipient 3d nat. prize Nathan Burkan Meml. Competition, ASCAP, 1974; German Acad. Exch. Svc. fellow U. Heidelberg, Germany, 1971-72. Mem. S.R., Jamestowne Soc. Republican. Episcopalian. Avocation: poetry. Office: LeBoeuf Lamb Greene MacRae 125 W 55th St New York NY 10019-5369 E-mail: Jinnett@llgm.com

JOCHNER, MICHELE MELINA, lawyer; b. Naperville, Ill., May 19, 1966; BA summa cum laude, Mundelein Coll., Chgo., 1987; JD with honors, DePaul U., 1990, LLM in Taxation Law, 1992. Bar: Ill. 1990, U.S. Dist. Ct. (no. dist.) Ill. 1990, U.S. Ct. Appeals (7th cir.) 1996, U.S. Supreme Ct. 1996. Law clk. U.S. Securities & Exch. Commn., Chgo., 1989; legal rsch. asst. to prof. Marlene Nicholson DePaul U. Sch. Law, 1989-91, legal rsch. asst. to assoc. dean Vincent Vitullo, 1989-91; law clk. extern U.S. Dist. Ct. (no. dist.) Ill., Chgo., 1989-90; judicial law clk. Cir. Ct. of Cook County, 1991-92, staff atty., 1992-93, sr. staff atty., 1993-95, acting supr. legal rsch. divsn., 1995-96; staff atty. permanency project child protection divsn. Cir. Ct. Cook County, Chgo., 1996-97; jud. law clk. to Hon. Mary Ann G. McMorrow Ill. Supreme Ct., 1997—. Mem. subcom. money transfers and adminstrv. regulations Ill. Supreme Ct., 1995-96; adj. prof. law John Marshall Law Sch., Chgo., 1994—, judge Herzog moot ct.competition, 1997—; adj. prof. law DePaul U. Coll. Law, 1998—; spkr. in field. Contbr. articles to profl. jours. Recipient Harold A. Shertz award Film, Air & Package Carriers Conf., Alexandria, Va., 1990. Mem. ABA, Ill. Bar Assn. (Lincoln award 2d pl. 1994, 97, 2000, 1st pl. 1996, 99, 2001, mem. and sec. gen. practice sect. coun., chair continuing legal edn. subcom., mem. standing com. legal edn., admission and competence, mem. tradition of excellence award subcom., mem. bench and bar sect. coun., elected assembly mem. 2000), Fed. Bar Assn., Chgo. Bar Assn., U.S. Supreme Ct. Hist. Soc., Order of Coif, Kappa Gamma Pi, Phi Sigma Tau. Avocations: writing fiction, non-fiction.

JOCK, PAUL F., II, lawyer; b. Indpls., Jan. 25, 1943; s. Paul F. and Alice (Sheehan) J.; m. Gail A. Webre, Sept. 16, 1967; children: Craig W., Nicole L. BBA, U. Notre Dame, 1965; JD, U. Chgo., 1970. Bar: Ill. 1970, N.Y. 1990. Ptnr. Kirkland & Ellis, Chgo. and N.Y.C., 1970-2001; v.p., gen. counsel GM Asset Mgmt., N.Y.C., 2000—. V.p. legal affairs Tribune Co., Chgo., 1981. Assoc. editor U. Chgo. Law Rev., 1969-70. Served to lt. USN, 1965-67. Mem. ABA, Chgo. Bar Assn., Assn. of the Bar of City of N.Y. Banking, General corporate, Securities. Address: GM Asset Mgmt 767 Fifth Ave New York NY 10153 E-mail: paul.jock@gm.com

JOELSON, MARK RENE, lawyer; b. Paris, Oct. 23, 1934; came to U.S., 1941, naturalized, 1947; s. Michael and Helen (Streicher) J.; m. Anastasia Whelan, June 4, 1967; children: Helen, Daniel, Marisa. BA, Harvard U., 1955, LLB, 1958; diploma in law, Oxford U., Eng., 1962. Bar: D.C. 1958, U.S. Supreme Ct. 1959. Atty. U.S. Dept. Justice, Washington, 1958-63; assoc., then ptnr. Arent, Fox, Kintner, Plotkin & Kahn, 1963-80; ptnr. Wald, Harkrader & Ross, 1980-85, Morgan, Lewis & Bockius LLP, Washington, 1986-97. Mem. adv. com. internat. investment, tech. and devel. U.S. Dept. State, 1978-87; cons. UN Conf. Trade and Devel., 1977-79; adj. prof. Georgetown U., Washington; panelist N.Am. Free Trade Agreement. Author (with Earl W. Kintner): An International Antitrust Primer, 1974, 2d edit., 2001; editor (with others): Current Legal Aspects of Doing Business in the E.E.C., 1978; editor: Enterprise Law in the 80's, 1980, Joint Ventures in the United States, 1988. Fulbright scholar Oxford U., 1961-62. Mem. ABA (chmn. sect. internat. law and practice 1983-84, del. Internat. Bar Assn. coun. 1984-92), Internat. Bar Assn., Fed. Bar Assn. (pres. D.C. chpt. 1976-77), Washington Inst. Fgn. Affairs, Cosmos Club (Washington). Antitrust, Federal civil litigation, Private international. E-mail: joelsonmr@msn.com

JOFFE, ROBERT DAVID, lawyer; b. N.Y.C., May 26, 1943; s. Joseph and Bertha (Pashkovsky) J.; children by prior marriage: Katherine, David; m. Virginia Ryan, June 20, 1981; stepchildren: Elizabeth DeHaas, Ryan DeHaas. A.B., Harvard U., 1964, J.D., 1967. Bar: N.Y. 1970, U.S. Dist. Ct. (so. and ea. dists.) N.Y. 1971, U.S. Ct. Appeals (2d cir.) 1972, U.S. Supreme Ct. 1973. Maxwell Sch. Africa Pub. Svc. fellow (funded by Ford Found.), Republic of Malawi, 1967-69; state counsel Republic of Malawi, 1968-69; assoc. Cravath, Swaine & Moore, N.Y.C., 1969-75, ptnr., 1975—, dep. presiding ptnr., 1997-98, presiding ptnr., 1999—. Apptd. to bd. dirs. by Pres. Clinton, Romanian Am. Enterprise Fund, 1994—. Be. dirs. Lawyers Com. for Human Rights, The Jericho Project, 1985—97, Fiduciary Trust Co. Internat., The After-School Corp.; chair Harvard Law Sch. Nat. Fund, 1995—97, chair dean's adv. bd., 1997—. Mem. ABA, N.Y. Bar Assn., Assn. of the Bar of the City of N.Y. (chmn. trade regulation com. 1980-83, exec. com. 1995-99, nominating com. 2001—), Coun. on Fgn. Rels., Human Rights Watch/Africa (adv. com.), Harvard Club, Century Assn. Antitrust, Federal civil litigation, Communications. Home: 300 W End Ave Apt 13A New York NY 10023-8156 Office: Cravath Swaine & Moore 825 8th Ave Fl 46 New York NY 10019-7475 E-mail: rjoffe@cravath.com

JOHNS, RICHARD SETH ELLIS, lawyer; b. Eugene, Oreg., Apr. 23, 1946; s. Frank Errol Jr. and Emily Elizabeth (Ellis) J.; m. Eleanor Lee Kuntz, Mar. 8, 1981. BA in English, U. Calif., Santa Barbara, 1968; JD, U. Calif., San Francisco, 1971. Bar: Calif. 1971, Ill. 1972. Instr. law U. Chgo., 1972-73; assoc. Atchison, Topeka & Santa Fe RR, Chgo., 1973-75, Furth, Fahrner, Bluemle & Mason, San Francisco, 1975-84; of counsel Maier, Dimitriou & Ross, 1984; ptnr. Rubenstein, Bohachek & Johns, 1985-88, Kipperman & Johns, San Francisco, 1988—. Contbr. articles to Calif. Law Rev. Bd. dirs. Congregation Beth Shalom, San Francisco, 1982-92, Bay Area sect. Am. Jewish Com., 1984—; leader Family Policy Task Force, 1987-88; guest of Christian Dem. Union, Konrad Adenhauer Stiftung-German-Am. Jewish Exchange Program, Fed. Republic Germany, 1985; dir. Mus. of the City of San Francisco, 1996-97, v.p., 1997—, The San Francisco Old Mint Task Force, 2001-. 1st lt. U.S. Army, 1972-75. Mem. ABA, Calif. Bar Assn., Concordia-Argonaut Club, Ill. State Bar. Federal civil litigation, General civil litigation, Real property. Office: Kipperman & Johns 57 Post St Ste 604 San Francisco CA 94104-5023 E-mail: rsejohns@aol.com

JOHNS, WARREN LEROI, lawyer; b. Nevada, Iowa, June 9, 1929; s. Varner Jay and Ruby Charlene (Morrison) J.; m. Elaine C. Magnuson, July 24, 1955 (div. June 1983); children: Richard Warren, Lynn Cherie Johns-Pence; m. Ruth Page Scott, Sept. 29, 1985. BA, La Sierra U., 1950; MA, Andrews U., 1951; JD, U. So. Calif., 1958. Bar: Calif. 1959, U.S. Dist. Ct. (cen. dist.) Calif. 1959,U.S. Supreme Ct. 1963, Md. 1976, D.C. 1976, U.S. Dist. Ct. Md. 1976, U.S. Dist. Ct. D.C. 1976, U.S. Tax Ct. 1976, U.S. Ct. Appeals (4th cir.) 1976, U.S. Ct. Appeals (10th cir.) 1977, U.S. Ct. Customs and Patent Appeals 1979. Gen. counsel So. Calif. Conf. Seventh-day Adventists, Glendale, 1959-63, Pacific Union Conf. Seventh-day Adventists, Glendale and Sacramento, 1964-69; pvt. practice Sacramento, 1969-75; gen. counsel Gen. Conf. Seventh-day Adventists, Washington, 1975-92, trustee; pvt. practice Brookeville, Md., 1992-98. Mem. adv. bd. Ctr. for Ch./State Studies, De Paul U. Coll. Chgo., 1987-93, spl. counsel to gen. conf., 1992-95; spl. counsel Adventist HealthCare Corp., Columbia Union HealthCare Corp., 1992-97. Author: Dateline Sunday USA, 1967, Ride to Glory, 1999, CreationDigest.com, 2001; founding editor JD, 1978-92, www.creationdigest.com, 2001—. Chmn. bd. dirs., pres. Sacramento Area Econ. Opportunity Coun., 1974. Recipient Frank Yost award Ch. State Coun., Glendale, Alumnus of Achievement award Andrews U., 1981, Alumnus of Yr. award La Sierra U., 1994. Mem. AAAS, ABA (vice-chmn. com. on torts, non-profit, charitable and religious orgns., sect. of tort and ins. practice 1990-91). Democrat. Avocations: sports, photography, book collecting. Alternative dispute resolution, General corporate, General practice. Office: 21320 Georgia Ave Brookeville MD 20833-1132

JOHNSON, ANNE STUCKLY, lawyer, retired; b. Axtell, Tex., Jan. 8, 1921; d. Arnold Joseph and Angeline (Morris) Stuckly; m. Edward James Johnson, Oct. 9, 1943 (dec. 1967); children: edward M., Ronald J., Dennis L., Shawn T., Rozlynn Jan, Anne J'lynn, Kevin J, Karal Ian, Donna Lynn. BA, Baylor U., 1940; MA in Econs., St. Mary's U., 1974, JD, 1980. Bar: Tex. 1980. Claims clk. Social Security Adminstrn., Amarillo, Tex., 1940-42; asst. chief divsn. pers. Pantex Ordnance Plant, 1942-43; chief divsn. pers. Cactus Ordnance Works, Dumas, 1943-44; citations unit supr. Gen. Hdqrs. Far East Command, Tokyo, 1950-51; v.p., treas. Drive-Safe Corp., San Antonio, 1967-69; counseling psychologist ARC, 1968-69, Divsn. Pers. Office, Ft. Sam Houston, 1969, pers. mgmt. specialist, 1969-77; pvt. practice Oliver B. Chamberlin Offices, San Antonio, 1981-86, 1987-93; ret., 1994. Active Am. Heart Assn., 1983—. Mem. ABA, San Antonio Bar Assn., Tex. Bar Assn., Am. Trial Lawyers Assn., Assn. Social Econs., Tex. Trial Lawyers Assn., Phi Alpha Delta, Pi Gamma Mu, Omicron Delta Epsilon. Home: 115 Meadowood Ln San Antonio TX 78216-7323

JOHNSON, BARBARA ELIZABETH, lawyer; b. Des Moines, Aug. 2, 1957; d. William Frederick and Dorothy Jane (Colvin) Spotz; m. Richard Gordon Johnson, Mar. 4, 1984. BS, Grove City (Pa.) Coll., 1979; JD, Coll. of William and Mary, 1984. Bar: Pa. 1984, U.S. Dist. Ct. (we. dist.) Pa. 1984, U.S. Ct. Appeals (3d and Fed. cirs.) 1984. Patent agt. NASA-Langley Rsch. Ctr., Hampton, Va., 1982-84; assoc. atty. The Webb Law Firm, Pitts., 1984-92, shareholder, dir., 1992—. Mng. dir. The Webb law Firm, 2001—; chmn. Obershenk Medallion Trust, Aspen Quality Care, Inc.; bd. dirs. Precision Staffing Svcs., Inc. Mem.: Am. Chem. Soc. (chmn. Pitts. sect. 1995), Pitts. Intellectual Property Law Assn. (pres. 2000—01), Pitts. Chemists Club. Republican. Avocations: piano, writing, baking, automobile repairing. Intellectual property. Office: The Webb Law Firm 436 7th Ave Ste 700 Pittsburgh PA 15219-1827 E-mail: bjohnson@webblaw.com

JOHNSON, BARBARA JEAN, retired judge, lawyer; b. Detroit, Apr. 9, 1932; d. Clifford Clarence and Orma Cecile (Boring) Barnhouse; m. Ronald Mayo Johnson, June 24, 1965; 1 child, Belinda Etezad. BS, U. So. Calif., 1953, JD, 1970. Bar: Calif. 1971. Ptnr. Angela, Burford, Johnson & Tookay, Pasadena, Calif., 1970-77; judge L.A. Mcpl. Ct., 1977-81, L.A. Superior Ct., 1981-97; ret., 1997. Lectr. U. So. Calif. Law Sch. profl. program; adj. prof. Southwestern U. Law Sch. Recipient Ernestine Stahlhut award, 1981. Mem. Calif. Judges Assn., 1977-98, Nat. Assn. Women Judges, 1980-98, Calif. Women Lawyers Assn. (pres. 1976-77), Women Lawyers Assn. L.A. (pres. 1975-76). Home: 1000 Prospect Blvd Pasadena CA 91103-2810

JOHNSON, BENJAMIN F(RANKLIN), III, lawyer; b. Atlanta, Aug. 20, 1943; s. Benjamin Franklin Jr. and Stella Byrd (Darnell) J.; m. Ann Armistead, Aug., 6, 1966; children: Benjamin Franklin IV, James Leslie Armistead. BA, Emory U., 1965; JD, Harvard U., 1968. Bar: Ga. 1968, U.S. Ct. Appeals (5th cir.) 1973, U.S. Ct. Appeals (11th cir.) 1982, U.S. Dist. Ct. (no. dist.) Ga. 1969, U.S. Dist. Ct. (so. dist.) Ga. 1978, U.S. Dist. Ct. (mid. dist.) Ga. 1981. Law clk. to judge Griffin B. Bell U.S. Ct. Appeals (5th cir.), Atlanta, 1968-69; assoc. Alston, Miller & Gaines, 1971-76; ptnr. Alston & Bird and predecessor firm Alston, Miller & Gaines, 1976—. Mem. faculty Stonier Grad. Sch. Banking, Newark, Del., 1982-91. Co-author: Problem Loan Strategies, 1985. Chmn. governing bd. Woodward Acad., College Park, Ga., 1982-95; chmn. bd. trustees Atlanta Leadership Devel. Found., 1994-95; trustee Emory U., 1995, Charles Loridans Found., 1991-95; pres. Rsch. Atlanta, 1988. 1st lt. U.S. Army, 1969-71, Vietnam. Recipient Disting. Alumnus award Woodward Acad., 1981. Mem. Ga. Bar Assn., Atlanta Bar Assn. (chmn. litigation sect. 1980), Atlanta Lawyer's Club, Commerce Club, Ansley Golf Club. Democrat. Avocations: reading, music, politics, exercise. Banking, General civil litigation, Construction. Home: 288 The Prado NE Atlanta GA 30309-3336 Office: Alston & Bird 1 Atlantic Ctr Atlanta GA 30309-3400

JOHNSON, BERNETTE J. state supreme court justice; b. Ascension Parish, La. d. Frank Joshua Jr. and Olivia W. Johnson. BA, Spelman Coll., Atlanta, 1964; JD, La. State U., 1969. Bar: La. Law intern Civil Rights divsn. U.S. Dept. Justice; judge La. Civil Dist. Ct., 1984-94, chief judge, 1994; assoc. justice La. Supreme Ct., New Orleans, 1994—. Legal svc. atty. New Orleans Legal Asst. Corp. Bd. dirs. YMCA, New Orleans; chmn. bd. Learning Ctr., Grand St. Stephen Full Gospel Bapt. Ch. Named Woman of Yr., LaBelle chpt. Am. Bus. Women's Assn., 1994. Office: Supreme Ct Bldg 301 Loyola Ave New Orleans LA 70112-1814*

JOHNSON, BEVERLY J. lawyer, city official; b. Alameda, Calif., Oct. 2, 1958; d. Robert Harold and Jean Ann Follrath; m. Michael Francis Johnson, Feb. 21, 1982; children: Geoffrey Michael, Katherine Ann. MusB, Calif. State U., Hayward, 1980; JD, U. Pacific, 1986. Bar: Calif. 1986, U.S. Dist., 1986, U.S. Cir. Ct. (9th Cir.), 1986, U.S. Supreme Ct., 1996. Law clerk U.S. Atty.'s Office, Sacramento, 1984-85; atty. Law Offices of Wilance Russum, Alameda, 1986-93, Dist. Atty.'s Office, Alameda, 1994-95; prin. Law Offices Beverly J. Johnson, 1997—; mem. city coun. City of Alameda, 1999—. Commr. Alameda Reuse and Redevel. Authority, 1998—, Alameda Housing Authority, 1998—. Trustee Alameda Hosp. Found., 1991—, Children's Learning Ctr., Alameda, 1993—; trustee, bd. dirs. Alameda Edn. Found., 1999—; bd. dirs. Alameda Planning Bd., 1995-98. Mem. U.S. Supreme Ct. Hist. Soc., State Bar Calif., Kiwanis Club Alameda. Avocations: sports, music, art. Office: City of Alameda 2263 Santa Clara Ave Alameda CA 94501-4400 also: 512 Westline Dr Ste 300 Alameda CA 94501-5870 Fax: 510-865-1882. E-mail: Bkillybegs@aol.com

JOHNSON, BRIAN M. lawyer; b. Lexington, Ky., Sept. 18, 1972; s. John L. and Phyllis A. Johnson. BA, Transylvania U., 1994; JD, U. Ky., 1997. Assoc. Greenebaum, Doll & McDonald PLLC, Lexington, 1997—. Mem. Downtown Lexington Corp., 1998. Mem. ABA, Ky. Bar Assn., Fayette County Bar Assn. Avocations: marathons, triathlons, weight lifting. Federal civil litigation, General civil litigation, Estate planning. Office: Greenebaum Doll & McDonald PLLC Ste 1400 333 W Vine St Lexington KY 40507

JOHNSON, BRUCE EDWARD HUMBLE, lawyer; b. Columbus, Ohio, Jan. 22, 1950; s. Hugo Edward and M. Alice (Humble) J.; m. Paige Robinson Miller, June 28, 1980; children: Marta Noble, Winslow Collins, Russell Scott. AB, Harvard U., 1972; JD, Yale U., 1977; MA, U. Cambridge, Eng., 1978. Bar: Wash. 1977, Calif. 1992. Atty. Davis Wright Tremaine LLP, Seattle, 1977—. King County Gov. Access Channel Oversight com., 1996—. Bd. dirs. Seattle Repertory Theatre, 1993—, pres., 1999-01. Mem. ABA (tort and ins. practice sect., media law and defamation torts com. chair 1999-2000). General civil litigation, Constitutional, Libel. Home: 711 W Kinnear Pl Seattle WA 98119-3621 Office: Davis Wright Tremaine LLP 2600 Century Sq 1501 4th Ave Seattle WA 98101-1688

JOHNSON, C. TERRY, lawyer; b. Bridgeport, Conn., Sept. 24, 1937; s. Clifford Gustave and Evelyn Florence (Terry) J.; m. Suzanne Frances Chichy, Aug. 24, 1985; children: Laura Elizabeth, Melissa Lynne, Clifford Terry. AB, Trinity Coll., 1960; LLD, Columbia U., 1963. Bar: Ohio 1964, U.S. Ct. Appeals (6th cir.) 1966, U.S. Dist. Ct. (so. dist.) Ohio 1970. Legal dep. probate ct. Montgomery County, Dayton, Ohio, 1964-67; head probate dept. Coolidge Wall & Wood, 1967-79, Smith & Schnacke, Dayton, 1979-89, Thompson, Hine and Flory, Dayton, 1989-92; head estate planning and probate group Porter, Wright, Morris & Arthur, 1992—. Frequent lectr. on estate planning to various profl. orgns. Contbr. articles to profl. jours. Fellow Am. Coll. Trust and Estate Counsel; mem. Ohio Bar Assn. (bd. govs. estate planning, trust and probate law sect., chmn. 1993-95), Dayton Bar Assn. (chmn. probate com. 1992-94), Ohio State Bar Found. (trustee 1995-2000), Ohio CLE Inst. (trustee 1995-99, chair 1998-99), Dayton Legal Secs. Assn. (hon.), Dayton Racquet Club, Dayton Bicycle Club. Estate planning, Probate, Estate taxation. Home: 8307 Rhine Way Centerville OH 45458-3017 Office: Porter Wright Morris & Arthur 1 S Main St Ste 1600 Dayton OH 45402-2028 E-mail: CTJohnson@porterwright.com

JOHNSON, CAROLYN JEAN, retired law librarian; b. Beaver Dam, Wis., Nov. 7, 1938; d. Henry William and Bernice Mae (Haas) Krueger; m. Robert Edward Johnson, June 19, 1960; children: Eric Steven, Kristin Elizabeth. BS in Edn., Wartburg Coll., 1960. Tchr., various locations, 1960-64, Hennepin County Library, 1972-81; libr. 3M Tech. Libr., St. Paul, 1981-86; law libr. 3M Ctr. Law Libr., 1986-2000; ret., 2000. Mem. Am. Assn. Law Libraries, Minn. Assn. Law Libraries. Lutheran. Avocations: reading, walking, cooking.

JOHNSON, CHARLES OWEN, retired lawyer; b. Monroe, La., Aug. 18, 1926; s. Clifford U. and Laura (Owen) J. BA, Tulane U., 1946, JD, 1969; LLB, Harvard U., 1948; LLM, Columbia U., 1955. Bar: La. 1949. Sole practice, Monroe, 1949-50; mem. law editl. staff West Pub. Co., St. Paul, 1953; atty. Office of Chief Counsel, IRS, Washington, 1955-79, chief Ct. Appeals br. Tax Ct. divsn., 1968-79. Author: The Genealogy of Several Allied Families, 1961. Served with AUS, 1950-52. Mem.: FBA, SAR, S.R. (past pres. D.C. soc.), S.C.V., La. Bar Assn., Nat. Lawyers Club, Nat. Gavel Soc. (past treas., past pres.), Soc. Colonial Wars (past dep. gov. D.C. soc., lt. gov., gov.), Huguenot Soc. S.C., Hereditary Order Descs. Colonial Govs. (past gov. gen.), Soc. Descs. Colonial Clergy (past chancellor gen.), Order Ams. of Armorial Ancestry (past pres.), Soc. Descs. Old Plymouth Colony, Jamestowne Soc., Sons and Daus. of Province and Republic of West Fla. 1763-1810 (past gov.), La. Colonials, Soc. Desc. Jersey Settlers, Huguenot Soc. La. (past pres.), Nat. Soc. Sons and Daus. of Antebellum Planters 1607-1861 (past pres. gen.), City Tavern Club, Army and Navy Club Washington, Order of Scions of Colonial Cavaliers (gov.), Sons and Daus. of Colonial and Antebellum Bench and Bar 1565-1861 (past pres. gen.), Order of Descs. of Colonial Physicians and Chirurgiens (past. pres. gen.), Order First Families of R.I. and Providence Plantations 1636-1647 (past gov. gen.), Va. Hist. Soc., Miss. Hist. Soc., Va. Geneal. Soc., Hereditary Order First Families of Mass. (registrar gen.), Soc. Cin., Mil. Order Stars and Bars (past judge adv. gen.), Order First Families Miss. 1699-1817 (gov. gen. 1967—69), Order Founders and Patriots of Am. (past gov. D.C. and La. soc.), First Families of Ga. (past chancellor gen.), Sons and Daus. of Pilgrims (past treas., 2d dep. gov. gen.), Soc. Colonial New Eng. (past gov. gen. nat. soc.), Sons Union Vets, St. Andrew's Soc. Washington, Royal Soc. St. George, Nat. Soc. Desc. Early Quakers (past nat. presiding clk.), Soc. of 1812 (past pres. D.C. soc.). Home: Apt 809S 2111 Jefferson Davis Hwy Arlington VA 22202-3121

JOHNSON, CHARLES WILLIAM, state supreme court justice; b. Tacoma, Mar. 16, 1951; BA in Econs., U. Wash., 1973; JD, U. Puget Sound, 1976. Bar: Wash. 1977. Justice Wash. Supreme Ct., 1991—. Co-chair Wash. State Minority and Justice Commn. Mem. bd. dirs. Wash. Assn. Children and Parents; mem. vis. com. U. Wash. Sch. Social Work; bd. visitors Seattle U. Sch. Law; liaison ltd. practice bd., co-chair BJA subcom. on juc. svcs.; mem. Am. Inns of Ct., World Affairs Coun. Pierce County. Mem. Wash. State Bar Assn., Tacoma-Pierce County Bar Assn. (Liberty Bell award young lawyers sect. 1994). Avocations: sailing, downhill skiing, cycling. Office: Wash State Supreme Ct Temple of Justice PO Box 40929 Olympia WA 98504-0929*

JOHNSON, CLARK CUMINGS, lawyer, educator; b. Traverse City, Mich., Nov. 19, 1940; s. Harold Eugene and Mary Deilght (Cumings) J.; m. Kerry Jane Spencer, May 1, 1990; children: James, Christopher, Spencer, Sterling, Iris. BA, U. Mich., 1963; JD cum laude, Wayne State U., 1970, MS., 1985; PhD, 1990. Bar: Mich. 1970, U.S. Dist. Ct. (ea. dist.) Mich. 1970, U.S. Supreme Ct. 1974. Asst. atty gen. Mich., 1970-71; ptnr. Schmidt, Nahas, Coburn & Johnson, Mount Clemens, 1971-74; prof. law Detroit Coll. Law, 1974—, assoc. dean, 1984-85. Home: 1687 Quarton Rd Birmingham MI 48009-1037 Office: Detroit Coll Law 130 E Elizabeth St Detroit MI 48201-3454

JOHNSON, CYNTHIA L(E) M(AE), lawyer; b. Detroit, Mar. 1, 1952; d. Robert Alexander and Frances Esedell (Peeples) J.; children: Alexandra, Lauren Gayle. BA, U. Mich., 1973, MPH, 1975, JD cum laude, 1984. Bar: Mich. 1984, U.S. Dist. Ct. (ea. dist.) 1984, U.S. Supreme Ct. 1989; cert. mediator. Health planning asst. Charles R. Drew Postgrad. Sch. Medicine, L.A., 1974; dep. project dir. Mich. Health Maintenance Orgn. Plans, Detroit, 1975; sr. health program analyst N.Y. Health and Hosps. Corp., N.Y.C., 1975-77; health care cons. UAW, Detroit, 1977-84; jud. law clk. Mich. Ct. Appeals, 1984-86, Mich. Supreme Ct., 1986-87; ptnr. Clark, Klein & Beaumont (now Clark Hill, PLC), Detroit, 1987-2000; shareholder Couzens, Lansky, etal, P.C., 2000—. Mem. ABA, Mich. Bar Assn., Detroit Bar Assn., Wolverine Bar Assn., Delta Sigma Theta. General corporate, General practice, Health. Office: Couzens Lansky etal PC 211 W Fort St Ste 1100 Detroit MI 48226-3202 Fax: 313-967-0344. E-mail: cynthiajohnson@couzens.com

JOHNSON, DAVID RAYMOND, lawyer; b. Bartlesville, Okla., Sept. 12, 1946; s. Lloyd Theodore and Mary Pauline (Auten) J.; m. Marion Frances Monroe, May 14, 1977; children: Marc, Meredith. BA, Tulane U., 1968; JD, U. Va., 1971. Bar: Tex. 1971, D.C. 1977, U.S. Dist. Ct. D.C. 1979, U.S. Ct. Appeals (D.C. cir.) 1981, U.S. Supreme Ct. 1982, U.S. Claims Ct. 1984. Assoc. Fulbright & Jaworski, Houston, 1971-72, Washington, 1974-78, ptnr., 1978-87; atty.-advisor Office of Gen. Counsel of Air Force, 1972-74; ptnr. Gibson, Dunn & Crutcher LLP, 1987—. Trustee Washington Episcopal Sch., 1991-93, McLean Sch. Md., 1994-96. Capt. USAF, 1972-74. Mem. D.C. Bar Assn., Phi Beta Kappa, Raven Soc., Order of Coif, Congressional Country Club. Government contracts and claims, Computer, Contracts commercial. Office: Gibson Dunn & Crutcher LLP 1050 Connecticut Ave NW Ste 900 Washington DC 20036-5306

JOHNSON, DAVID WESLEY, lawyer; b. Rochester, N.Y., Mar. 13, 1933; BA, U. Rochester, 1954; LLB, Columbia U., 1959. Bar: N.Y. 1961, U.S. Dist. Ct. (so. dist.) N.Y. 1961, U.S. Dist. Ct. (no. dist.) N.Y. 1971. Counsel, sec., v.p. Textile Banking Co., N.Y.C., 1959-68; legis. counsel CIT Fin. Corp., 1968-70; ptnr. Otterbourg, Steindler, Houston & Rosen, 1970-71, Palmer & Johnson, Tupper Lake, N.Y., 1971-74; pvt. practice, 1974—. Bd. dirs. Adirondack Cmty. Trust Trustee, chmn. bd. North Country C.C., Saranac Lake, N.Y., 1973-82; bd. dirs., pres. High Peaks Hospice, Inc., Saranac Lake, 1988-92; bd. dirs., v.p. Lake Placid (N.Y.) Ctr. for Arts, 1989—, Franklin County Children's Legal Svcs., Inc., pres., 1991—; trustee Nat. History Mus. of the Adirondacks, 1998—; bd. dirs. Adirondack Med. Ctr. Found., 2001—. Mem. Franklin County Bar Assn. (pres. 1979-81), N.Y. State Bar Assn., Lawyers Assn. Textile Industry (bd. dirs., sec.-treas. 1962-71), Assn. Comml. Fin. Attys. (bd. dirs., v.p. 1962-71). General practice. Office: 51 Lake St Tupper Lake NY 12986-1624

JOHNSON, DENNIS ROBERT, lawyer; b. Mpls., Aug. 1, 1946. BS in Bus., U. Minn., 1972, JD, 1975. Bar: Minn. 1975, U.S. Dist. Ct. Minn. 1975. Ptnr. Meshbesher & Spence, Ltd., Mpls., 1975—. Bd. dirs. Minn. Legal Advice Clinics, Mpls., 1978-82. 1st lt. U.S. Army, 1966-69, Vietnam. Mem. Minn. Trial Lawyers Assn. (bd. dirs. 1979—, chmn. legis. com. 1980-84, chmn. edn. com. 1984-86, exec. com. 1984, chmn. fin. com. 1986, treas. 1987, v.p. 1988-89, pres. 1989-90), Minn. State Bar Assn. (mem. med. legal com. 1982—), Assn. Trial Lawyers Am. (sustaining mem.), Cert. Civil Trial Specialists. State civil litigation, Personal injury, Product liability. Office: Meshbesher & Spence Ltd 1616 Park Ave Minneapolis MN 55404-1695

JOHNSON, DON EDWIN, lawyer; b. Decatur, Ill., Jan. 29, 1939; s. B. Edwin and Mary Louise (Pitzer) J.; m. Suzanne Curtis, Aug. 23, 1959; children: Jennifer, Marc Wade. BA cum laude, Millikin U., 1959; LLB, U. Ill., 1961, JD, 1968. Bar: Ill. 1961, U.S. Dist. Ct. (so. dist.) Ill. 1961, U.S. Tax Ct. 1986. Law clk. Ill. Supreme Ct., Springfield, 1961-63; assoc. Hohlt, House & DeMoss, Pinckneyville, Ill., 1961-66; ptnr. Johnson Seibert & Bigham, 1966—; state's atty. Perry County, Ill., 1968-72. Bd. dirs. 1st Nat. Bank, Pinckneyville, First Perry Bancorp, Pinckneyville. Contbr. articles to profl. jours. City atty. DuQuoin, Ill., 1965-68, Pinckneyville, 1983—; bd. dirs. Rend Lake Coll. Found., Ina, Ill., 1981-90; bd. visitors U. Ill. Coll. Law, 1984-88. Fellow Am. Coll. Trust and Estate Counsel, Am. Bar Found., Ill. Bar Found. (chmn. 1986-87); mem. Ill. State Bar Assn. (chmn. fed. tax sect. 1983-84, chmn. mineral law sect. 1984-86, 94-95, 96-97), Energy and Mineral Law Found. (trustee 1985—), Nat. Acad. Elder Law Attys., Pinckneyville C. of C. (pres. 1968), So. Ill. Golf Assn. (pres. 1997—), USGA (sectional affairs com. 1994—), Rotary (pres. 1966, 76), Elks, Scottish Rite, Shriners, Chaine des Rotisseurs, Red Hawk Country Club, Crab Orchard Golf Club, Kelly Greens Golf and Country Club, Delta Sigma Phi. Republican. Presbyterian. Avocations: golf, travel, stamp and coin collecting. Oil, gas, and mineral, Probate, Real property. Home: 605 W South St Pinckneyville IL 62274-1236 Office: Johnson Seibert & Bigham One N Main St Pinckneyville IL 62274 Fax: 618-357-3314. E-mail: JSBAttorneys@Midamer.net

JOHNSON, DONALD EDWARD, JR. lawyer; b. Denver, Sept. 24, 1942; s. Donald Edward and Miriam Bispham (Chester) J.; m. Charlotte Marie Hassett, Aug. 15, 1964; children: Julie Anna, Jenny Marie. Student, Lewis and Clark Coll., 1960-62; BA in History, U. Ariz., 1968; JD, U. Wyo., 1971. Bar: Wyo. 1971, Colo. 1971, U.S. Dist. Ct. Colo. and Wyo. 1971, U.S. Supreme Ct. 1978. Assoc. Hammond and Chilson, Loveland, Colo., 1971-72; dep. dist. atty. 8th Jud. Dist., Loveland and Fort Collins, 1972-80, chief dep. dist. atty., 1977-80; assoc. Allen, Rogers, Metcalk and Vahrenwald, Ft. Collins, 1980-82, ptnr., 1982—. Asst. city atty. City of Loveland, 1971-72; asst. mcpl. judge, Loveland, 1972; instr. bus. law Ames Coll., 1972-74; lectr. Regional Homocide Sch., 1977. Author: Criminal Conspiracy—The Colorado District Attorney's Evidence Manual, 1976; student editor ABA Law Student Jour. Chmn. 45th Republican House Dist., 1977-82; mem. Colo. Rep. Central Com., 1980-85; mem. Loveland Open Space Adv. Bd., 1977-78; bd. dirs. Loveland United Way, 1977-84, pres., 1981-83; bd. dirs. Loveland Midget Athletic Assn., sec., 1974-78; mem. local adv. bd. McKee Med. Ctr., Loveland, 1992—, pres., 1995—; mem. adv. bd. Banner Health Sys., Colo. divsn., 1996—, pres., 1999—; treas. 8th Jud. dist. Victims Assistance Law Enforcement Fund, 1990-96 (8th judicial dist.), mem. nominating commn., 1998—; mem. Larimer County Bench-Bar Commn., 1993-95. Served to sgt. USMC, 1966-68. Mem. ABA (Gold Key award 1970), Larimer County Bar Assn. (pres. 1995-96), Colo. Bar Assn. (bd. govs. 1997-), Wyo Bar Assn., Colo. Trial Lawyers Assn. Episcopalian. State civil litigation, Criminal, General practice. Office: Allen Vahrenwald & Johnson LLC Key Bank Bldg 125 S Howes St 1100 Fort Collins CO 80521

JOHNSON, DONALD RAYMOND, lawyer; b. N.Y.C., June 26, 1960; s. Donald Francis and Jacqueline E. (Barnett) J. BA, Liberty U., 1982, MA, 1984; JD, Washington and Lee U., 1989; postgrad., Va. Polytech. Inst., Yale U., U. Va. Bar: Va. 1989, D.C. 1991, N.Y. 1995, U.S. Dist. Ct. (no., so., and ea. dists.) N.Y., U.S. Dist. Ct. (ea. and we. dists.) Va., U.S. Ct. Appeals (fed. cir.), U.S. Supreme Ct. Pvt. practice, Charlottesville, Va., 1989-96; dir., pres. Internat. Brokerage & Investment Co., 1991-99; dir., v.p. Internat. Investment Svcs., Inc., 1991-2000; pvt. practice N.Y.C., 1995—. Bd. dirs. Excellence in Edn., Charlottesville, 1990-92, Heritage Soc., Charlottesville, 1990-92, World of Life Internat., 2000—; U.S. del. German-Am. Multiplicitorian Seminars; founder Mission, Inc., 2000—. Named one of Outstanding Young Men of Am., Alumnus of the Yr.; recipient numerous awards and honors for ednl., civic, and social activities. Mem. ABA, ATLA. Republican. Baptist. Avocations: running, sailing, tennis. Contracts commercial, General corporate, Private international. Office: 90 Schermerhorn St Brooklyn NY 11201-5028 Fax: (801) 761-5376. E-mail: drjohnson@attglobal.net

JOHNSON, DONALD WAYNE, lawyer; b. Memphis, Feb. 2, 1950; s. Hugh Don and Oline (Rowland) J.; m. Jan Marie Mullinax, May 12, 1972 (div. 1980); 1 child, Scott Fitzgerald; m. Cindy L. Walker, Dec. 10, 1988; children: Trevor Christian, Mallory Faith. Student, Memphis State U., 1968, Lee Coll., 1968-72; JD, Woodrow Wilson Coll. Law, 1975. Bar: Ga. 1975, U.S. Dist. Ct. (no. dist.) Ga. 1975, U.S. Ct. Appeals (5th cir.) 1976, U.S. Ct. Appeals (11th, 9th, DC cirs.) 1984, U.S. Ct. Claims 1978, U.S. Tax Ct. 1978, U.S. Supreme Ct. 1979. Ptnr. Barnes & Johnson, Dalton, Ga., 1975-77, Johnson & Fain, Dalton, 1977-80; pvt. practice, 1975-85, Atlanta, 1985—; city atty. City of Forest Park, Ga., 1996-97. Bd. dirs. Pathway Christian Sch., Dalton, 1978-85, Jr. Achievement of Dalton, 1978-84, Dalton-Whitfield County Day Care Ctrs., Inc.; legal counsel Robertson for Pres. Com., Ga., 1988; bd. chmn. Ga. Family Coun., 1990-97; Rep. chmn. Clayton County, 1993-95; Rep. gen. counsel 3rd Congl. Dist., 1993-95, Clayton County Rep. Com., 1995-96; Rep. candidate for Ga. Senate, 1998. Recipient Power of One award Ga. Family Coun., 1997. Mem. State Bar Ga., Fayette County Bar Assn., Ga. Trial Lawyers Assn., Christian Legal Soc. Mem. Ch. of God. State civil litigation, Personal injury, Workers' compensation. Office: PO Box 187 Fayetteville GA 30214-0187 E-mail: jlfpc@mindspring.com, djohn36755@aol.com

JOHNSON, DOUGLAS WELLS, lawyer; b. May 31, 1949; s. Robert Douglas and Mildred Irene (Fehr) J.; m. Kathryn Ann Hoberg, Oct. 18, 1980. BA, U. Denver, 1971, JD, 1974. Ptnr. Mellman, Mellman & Thorn, Denver, 1974-80; sr. atty. Amoco Corp., Chgo., 1980-91; mgr. real estate Amoco Oil Co., 1991-94; sr. atty. Amoco Corp., 1994-98; chief legal counsel BP Pipelines N.Am., 1998—. U. Denver Alumni scholar, 1967-71. Mem. ABA, Ill. Bar Assn., D.C. Bar Assn., Chgo. Bar Assn., Kappa Delta Pi. Antitrust, Contracts commercial, Franchising. Office: BP Amoco Corp 200 E Randolph St Ste 2102A Chicago IL 60601-6436

JOHNSON, EDWARD MICHAEL, lawyer, consultant; b. Waco, Tex., July 12, 1944; s. Edward James and Anne Margaret (Stuchly) J.; m. Yvonne Margaret Hill, May 7, 1977; children: Hilary Yvonne, Megan Joy, Michael David. BA in Polit. Sci., S.W. Tex. State U., 1967; JD, St. Mary's U., 1970. Bar: Tex. 1971, U.S. Dist. Ct. (we. and so. dist.) Tex. 1972, U.S. Ct. Claims, 1972, U.S. Supreme Ct. 1976. Asst. law libr. Bexar County Law Libr., 1968-69; briefing clk. Judge Preston H. Dial, Jr., 1969-70; briefing atty. U.S. Dist. Judge John H. Wood Jr., San Antonio, 1971-72; asst. U.S. atty. Dept. Justice, 1972-76; sole practice, 1976-81; sr. atty. Wiley, Garwood, Hornbuckle, Higdon & Johnson, 1980-81; pres. McCabe Petroleum Corp., 1981; chmn. bd., CEO, gen. counsel Blue Chip Petroleum Corp., 1981-83; pres., gen. counsel Harvest Investments Corp., 1983-87, also dir.; gen. ptnr. Med. Mobility Ltd. IV, 1984-87; mgr. Med. Mobility Joint Venture, 1984-87; exec. cons. Advance Tax Representation, Inc., 1987-88; gen. ptnr. Harvest Venture Capital Ltd. I, San Antonio, 1986-87; pres., gen. counsel Blue Chip Securities Corp., 1984-87; rep. First Investors Corp., 1987-88; pres., CEO Johnson, Curney, Garcia, Wise & Farmer P.C., 1990-2000. Host radio program The Christian Lawyer, 1990-91, TV program God's Army, 1990-98; mem. adv. bd. Red McCombs Galleria Imports, 1996-98, Network Mktg. Lifestyles Mag., Hovey Motorcars, 1999—. Co-chmn. fund raising Am. Heart Assn., San Antonio, 1982-84; bd. dirs. Am. Cancer Soc., San Antonio, 1982-84; chmn. San Fernando Cathedral Endowment Fund, San Antonio, 1986; mem. Gideons Internat., San Antonio, 1982-86, mem. exec. bd. San Antonio Christian Schs., 1983-84, San Antonio Christian Legal Soc., 1991—, Fed. Bar Licensing Bd., 1976-78; bd. dirs. Tex. Bible Coll., 1984-87, Christian Businessmen's Com., San Antonio, 1981-88, Cornerstone Christian Schs., San Antonio, 1991-92, mem., spkr., pres. Med. Ctr. chpt. 1988-91, mem. Full Gospel Businessmen's Fellowship, 1981-92, pres. 1985-88, field rep., 1988-92; Rep. precinct chmn., 1988-89; bd. dirs. Assn. Spirit Filled Fellowships, 1991-93; pres. God's Army Internat. Found., Inc., 1990-92; gen. counsel, bd. dirs. Four Winds Ministries, Inc., 1992-93; scoutmaster Alamo area coun. Boy Scouts Am., San Antonio, 1973-74; founder, chmn. Christian Businessmen's Focus on the Family, San Antonio, 1984-85. Recipient spl. commendation Dept. Transp. 1973, Dept. Air Force HQ, ATC, 1974, Dept. Treasury, 1974; named Outstanding Asst. U.S. Atty. Dept. Justice, 1974-75, One of Outstanding Young Texans, 1976. Mem. FBA (pres. San Antonio chpt. 1975-76, v.p. 1973-74, sec. 1972-73, treas. 1971-72, Outstanding Chpt. Pres. award 1976), Tex. Bar Assn., San Antio Bar Assn. Republican. Federal civil litigation, Insurance, Securities. E-mail: edjohnson@ecoquestintl.com

JOHNSON, EINAR WILLIAM, lawyer; b. Fontana, Calif., Apr. 6, 1955; s. Carl Wilbur and Judith Priscilla (Orcutt) J.; m. Cynthia Jeanne Bailey, Oct. 9, 1976; children: Brian Mark (dec.), Carl Einar, Gregory Daniel, Christopher James, Shaun Curtis, Bradford Keith. BA in Speech Communications, Brigham Young U., 1980; JD, J. Reuben Clark Law Sch., Provo, Utah, 1983. Bar: Calif. 1983, U.S. Dist. Ct. (cen. dist.) Calif. 1984, U.S. Ct. Appeals (9th cir.) 1986, U.S. Supreme Ct. 1987. Asst. debate coach Brigham Young U., Provo, Utah, 1979-80; fin. committeeman Jed Richardson for Congress, 1980; sales mgr./salesman Ortho Mattress, Orem, Utah, 1979, 81; law clk. Acret & Perrochet, L.A., 1982; jud. clk. U.S. Cts., Salt Lake City, 1983-84; litigation atty. Smith & Hilbig, Torrance, Calif., 1984-90, litigation ptnr., 1990-93; owner, founder Johnson and Assocs., 1993—. Editor Moot Ct. program J. Reuben Clark Law Sch., 1982-83. Contbr. articles to profl. jours. Missionary, leader Ch. of Jesus Christ of Latter Day Saints, Denver, 197476, Sunday sch. tchr., L.A., 1986-89, stake high counselor, 1989-92, 1st counselor ward bishopric, 1992-93, pres. elders quorum, 1993-94, high counselor, 1994-2000, 2nd counselor bishopric, 2000—. Recipient A.H. Christensen award, Am. Jurisprudence awards Bancroft-Whitney, 1981. Mem. ABA, Calif. Bar Assn., L.A. County Bar Assn., Assn. Trial Lawyers Am., Internat. Platofrm Assn., Order Barristers, Kappa Tau Alpha. Republican. Mormon. Avocations: photography, guitar, fishing, house remodeling, automobile restoration. General civil litigation, Labor, Landlord-tenant. Office: Johnson & Assocs 3655 Torrance Blvd Ste 470 Torrance CA 90503-4848

JOHNSON, GARDINER, lawyer; b. San Jose, Calif., Aug. 10, 1905; s. George W. and Izora (Carter) J.; AB, U. Calif., 1926, JD, 1928; m. Doris Louise Miller, Sept. 28, 1935; children: Jacqueline Ann, Stephen Miller. Bar: Calif. 1928; practice San Francisco, 1928— ; ptnr. Johnson & Stanton, 1952-84. Mem. nat. drafting com. Council State Govts., 1944-47, chmn. Gov.'s Conf. Edn., 1955; chmn. Calif. delegation White House Conf. Edn., 1955; mem. Calif. Legislature from 18th Assembly Dist., 1935-47, speaker pro tem, 1940; mem. Rep. State Cen. Com., 1934-46, 50-86; mem. Alameda County Rep. Cen. Com., 1934-47, 59-86; alternate del. Rep. Nat. Conv., 1940, del., 1956, 60, 64, 68, 76; pres. Calif. Rep. Assembly, 1959; mem. Rep. Nat. Com., 1964-68; mem. Citizens Legis. Adv. Commn., 1957-61; bd. dirs. U. Calif. Hosps. Aux., 1960-70, pres., 1956-58; bd. dirs. Florence Crittenton Home, San Francisco, 1960-69, 76—, pres., 1967-69; bd. dirs. Florence Crittenton Assn. Am., 1969-75, v.p., 1973-75; pres. Calif. Hist. Soc., 1968-70; bd. dirs. Spring Opera of San Francisco, 1963-69, Child Welfare League Am., 1976-84; bd. govs. San Francisco Heart Assn., 1963-70, chmn., 1966-69; mem. council Save-the-Redwoods League, 1970—. Fellow Am. Coll. Trial Lawyers; mem. Assn. Trial Lawyers Am., Internat. Bar Assn. (alternate del. 8th Conf. Salzburg 1960), Inter-Am. Bar Assn., ABA (com. state legislation 1957-59, vice chmn. com. pub. contracts 1959), Presidio Soc. (dir. 1981—), Bar Assn. San Francisco (pres. 1958), Phi Beta Kappa, Phi Delta Phi, Kappa Delta Rho. Republican. Episcopalian. Clubs: Pacific-Union, Lawyers (San Francisco), Commonwealth Club Calif. (life, pres. 1958-59). Home: 329 Hampton Rd Piedmont CA 94611-3525 Office: 221 Sansome St San Francisco CA 94104-2307

JOHNSON, GARRETT BRUCE, lawyer; b. Akron, Ohio, Sept. 15, 1946; s. Vincent Hadar and Elizabeth Irene (Garrett) J.; m. Barbara Peters Silver, May 31, 1969; children: Emily Peters, Adam Garrett. A.B., Princeton U., 1968; J.D., U. Mich., 1971. Bar: Ill. 1973, U.S. Dist. Ct. (no. dist.) Ill. 1973, U.S. Ct. Appeals (7th cir.) 1979, U.S. Supreme Ct. 1990. Fellow Max Planck Inst. for Fgn. and Internat. Criminal Law, Freiburg, Germany, 1971-72; assoc. Kirkland & Ellis, Chgo., 1973-78, ptnr., 1978— . Article and book review editor Mich. Law Rev. 1970-71. Humboldt scholar, 1971-72. Federal civil litigation, State civil litigation. Office: Kirkland & Ellis 200 E Randolph St Fl 54 Chicago IL 60601-6636

JOHNSON, GARY THOMAS, lawyer; b. Chgo., July 26, 1950; s. Thomas G. Jr. and Marcia (Lunde) J.; m. Susan Elizabeth Moore, May 28, 1978; children: Christopher Thomas, Timothy Henry, Anna Louisa. AB, Yale U., 1972; Hons. BA, Oxford U., 1974, MA, 1983; JD, Harvard U., 1977. Ba: Ill. 1977, U.S. Dist. Ct. (no. dist.), Ill. 1977, U.S. Ct. Appeals (7th cir.) 1985, U.S. Supreme Ct. 1986, N.Y. 1993. Assoc. Mayer, Brown & Platt, Chgo., 1977-84, ptnr., 1985-94, Jones, Day, Reavis & Pogue, Chgo., 1994—. Mem. Spl. Commn. on Adminstrn. of Justice Cook County, Chgo., 1984-88; v.p. Criminal Justice Project of Cook County, 1987-91; bd. dirs. Lawyers' Com. for Civil Rights Under Law, 1992—, trustee, 1994—, regional co-chair, 1996-2001, co-chair, 2001—; mem. Ill. Supreme Ct. Spl. Commn. on the Adminstrn. of Justice, 1992-94. Bd. dirs. Chgo. Lawyers' Com. for Civil Rights Under Law, 1981-90, Legal Assistance Found., Chgo., 1987-96, pres., 1994-96. Rhodes scholar Oxford U., 1972-74. Fellow Am. Bar Found. (life), Ill. Bar Found. (life); mem. ABA (Ho. of Dels. 1991-97), Am. Judicature Soc. (bd. dirs. 1987-91), Ill. State Bar Assn., Chgo. Bar Assn., Chgo. Coun. Lawyers (pres. 1981-83), Internat. Bar Assn. Democrat. General corporate, Finance, Securities. Office: Jones Day Reavis & Pogue 77 W Wacker Dr Chicago IL 60601-1692

JOHNSON, GEORGE WELDON, lawyer; b. Orleans, Nebr., Oct. 3, 1930; s. Grant O.Q. and Mildred Helen (Baxley) J.; m. Juanita Jane Trotter, June 22, 1952; children: Jeffrey David, Kathy Lynn Johnson Thurston, Nancy Sue Johnson Heck. BS, Ind. U., 1952, JD, 1957. Bar: Ind. 1957, U.S. Dist. Ct. (so. dist.) Ind. 1957, U.S. Tax Ct., 1965, U.S. Supreme Ct. 1965, U.S. Ct. Appeals (7th cir.) 1970. Ptnr. Hilgedag, Johnson, Secrest & Murphy, Indpls., 1957-81; pvt. practice law, 1981-83; ptnr. Johnson & Hall, 1983-84; pres. Johnson, Hall & Lawhead, P.C., 1984-95, Johnson, Lawhead Buth & Pope P.C., Indpls., 1995-2000; sole practitioner, 2000—. 1st lt. USAF, 1952-54. Fellow Indpls. Bar Found. (bd. dirs. 1983-2000, treas. 1990-96, disting. charter), Am. Coll. Trust and Estate Counsel (mem. employee benefits in estate planning com.); mem. ABA, Ind. Bar Assn., Indpls. Bar Assn. (pres. 1982), Indpls. Estate Planning Coun. (pres. 1981-82), Meridian Hills Country Club, Masons, Shriners. Republican. Methodist. Avocations: golf, fishing, travel. Probate, Corporate taxation, Estate taxation. Home: 3274 Bay Rd South Dr Indianapolis IN 46240-2974 Office: 8900 Keystone Xing Ste 1094 Indianapolis IN 46240-7646

JOHNSON, GOODYEAR See O'CONNOR, KARL WILLIAM

JOHNSON, GREGORY SCOTT, lawyer; b. Waukegan, Ill., Sept. 11, 1967; s. Robert Phillip Johnson and Brenda Olsen Hesselgrave; m. Jennifer Joyces Miles, June 23, 1992 (div. Jan. 1996) 1 child, Blake Alexander. BA, La. State U., 1992; JD, Loyola U., New Orleans, 1996. Bar: La. 1997, U.S. Dist. Ct. (ea. dist.) La. 1997. Pvt. practice, New Orleans, 1997—. Registration coord. SELASA, New Orleans, 1998. Republican. Lutheran. Avocations: soccer, computers, reading. Consumer commercial, Family and matrimonial, General practice. Office: 2955 Ridgelake Dr Ste 207 Metairie LA 70112

JOHNSON, HAROLD GENE, lawyer; b. St. Louis, July 20, 1934; s. Edward Henry Johnson and Betty (Burton) Pallister; m. Susan Ann Giesecke, Oct. 10, 1953; children: H. Mark, Deborah S. Johnson Schnitzer, Michael R., Laura A. Johnson Schwent, Mitchell D. BSBA, Washington U., St. Louis, 1961, LLB, 1962. Bar: Mo. 1962, U.S. Dist. Ct. (ea. dist.) Mo. 1964, U.S. Ct. Appeals (8th cir.) 1981. Assoc. Schomburg, Marshall &

Craig, St. Louis, 1962-63, Green & Raymond, St. Louis, 1963-64; ptnr. Johnson & Hayes, 1978-85, Law Offices Mitchell D. Johnson, St. Louis, 1988-93, Johnson & Johnson, 1993—. Judge mcpl. ct. City of Bridgeton, Mo., 1973-85. Served with U.S. Army 1954-56. Recipient Spl. Service award City of Bridgeton, 1985; Honored with ann. presentation of The Judge Harold Johnson award Pro-Life Direct Action League, 1985. Bar: Mo. Bar Assn., Met. Bar St. Louis, St. Louis County Bar Assn. Avocation: woodworking. State civil litigation, General practice, Personal injury. Office: 500 Northwest Plz Ste 715 Saint Ann MO 63074-2222

JOHNSON, JAMES JOSEPH SCOFIELD, lawyer, judge, educator, author; b. Washington, Apr. 28, 1956; s. Richard Carl and Harriette (Benson) J.; m. Sherry Bekki Hall; children: Andrew Joel Schaeffer Johnson. AA with high honors, Montgomery Coll., Germantown, Md., 1980; BA with honors, Wake Forest U., 1982; JD, U. N.C., 1984; ThD with highest honors, Emmanuel Coll. Christian, 1996; PhD with highest honors, Cambridge Grad. Sch., Springdale, Ark., 1996, MSc, M of Liberal Arts, 1999; DASc with highest honors, Emmanuel Coll. Christian Studies, 2000. Bar: Tex. 1985, U.S. Dist. Ct. (no. dist.) Tex. 1986, U.S. Dist. Ct. (ea. dist.) Tex. 1987, U.S. Ct. Appeals (5th cir.) 1989, U.S. Dist. Ct. (we. and so. dists.) Tex. 1990, U.S. Supreme Ct. 2000; bd. cert. bus. bankruptcy law Tex. Bd. Legal Specialization, 1990, 95, 2000, Am. Bankruptcy Bd. Cert., 1992; cert. water quality monitor Tex. Natural Resource Conservation Commn., 1994—. Assoc. various orgns., Dallas, 1985—; pvt. practice law, 1993—. Adj. prof. LeTourneau U., Dallas, 1991—, Dallas Christian Coll., 1995—; lectr. History, Geography, Ecology, Culture, Norwegian Cruise Lines, 1998—; Bibl. langs. instr. Cross Timbers Inst., 2001—. Author: Introduction to Environmental Studies, 1995, 98, Doxological Zoology and Zoogeography, 1998; sr. editl. staff N.C. Jour. Internat. Law and Comml. Regulation, 1983-84; conf. issue editor Harvard Jour. Law & Pub. Policy, 1984; contbr. articles to profl. jours. Protestant chaplain Boy Scouts Am., Goshen, Va., 1976; libr. vol. N.W. Bible Ch., Dallas, 1991-2000; cmty. program dir. Southwestern Legal Founds. Conf. on Internat. and Am. Law, 1991-92; active mem. Pro Bono Coll. State Bar Tex., Dallas, 1992—98; scripture chmn. Gideons Internat., North Dallas, Tex., 1993-94. Recipient award for excellence in biblical studies and biblical langs. Am. Bible Soc., 1982. Mem. Near East Archaeology Soc., Sangre de Cristo Mountain Coun., Creation Rsch. Soc., Evangel. Theol. Soc., Norwegian Soc. Tex., Sons of Norway (historian). Republican. Avocations: reading, writing, birding, traveling, hiking. Bankruptcy, General civil litigation, Environmental. Office: PO Box 2952 Dallas TX 75221-2952

JOHNSON, JAMES MCDADE, lawyer; b. Shreveport, La., Dec. 5, 1939; s. Leslie N. and Nell (McDade) J.; m. Glenda Roth, Jan. 27, 1962; children— Danielle Johnson Soufi, Kimberly Dawn. B.A., La. State U., 1962, J.D., 1964. Bar: La. 1964. First asst. dist. atty. 26th Jud. Dist. La., Minden, 1975-83; ptnr. Campbell, Campbell & Johnson, Minden, 1964—; assoc. nat. legal counsel U.S. Jaycees, Tulsa, 1970-71, nat. legal counsel, 1971-72; mem., Ho. Rep. Dist. 10 La., 1990—. mem. State Ctrl. Democratic Com., 1990—. Chmn. Minden Democratic Exec. Com., La., 1964-74. Named Outstanding Vice Pres. La. Jaycees, 1969. Mem. Assn. Trial Lawyers Am. Episcopalian. Personal injury. Office: Campbell Campbell & Johnson PO Box 834 Minden LA 71058-0834

JOHNSON, JOHN PAUL, lawyer, administrative law judge; b. Omaha, Dec. 4, 1944; s. John and Dorothy (Mullen) J.; m. Suzanne Alice Smiley, July 12, 1974; children: James Thomas, Jennifer Anne. BA, Washburn U., Topeka, 1967; JD, U. Nebr., 1971; postgrad., Fed. Exec. Inst., Charlottesville, Va., 1988. Bar: Nebr. 1972. Claims examiner VA, St. Paul, 1972; staff atty. Bd. Vets. Appeals, Washington, 1973-79, sr. atty., 1979-81; adminstrv. law judge Office of Hearings and Appeals, Des Moines, 1981-88, chief adminstrv. law judge, 1988-93. With U.S. Army, 1968-70 (Vietnam). Decorated Bronze Star; recipient Exceptional Svc. award VA, 1974. Mem. Assn. Adminstr. Law Judges, Nebr. State Bar Assn., Kappa Sigma. Episcopalian. Home: 228 39th St West Des Moines IA 50265-3938 Office: Office Hearings and Appeals 4400 Westown Pky West Des Moines IA 50266

JOHNSON, JOSEPH CLAYTON, JR. lawyer; b. Vicksburg, Miss., Nov. 15, 1943; s. Joseph Clayton and Rose Butler (Levy) J.; m. Cherrian Frances Turpin, Oct. 24, 1970; children: Mary Clayton, Erik Cole. BS, La. State U., 1965, JD, 1969. Bar: La. 1969, U.S. Dist. Ct. (ea. and mid. dists.) La. 1969, U.S. Dist. Ct. (we. dist.) La. 1979, U.S. Ct. Appeals (5th cir.) 1982. Ptnr. Taylor, Porter, Brooks & Phillips, Baton Rouge, 1969—. Mem. civil justice reform act com. U.S. Dist. Ct. (mid. dist.) La., 1995-97, chmn. 1996-97; mem. La. Atty. Disciplinary Bd., 1997-99. Bd. editors Oil and Gas Reporter, 1988—. Pres. Baton Rouge area Am. Cancer Soc., 1987—88; adv. bd. Internat. Oil and Gas Ednl. Ctr., 2000—. With U.S. Army, 1969—75. Recipient John Rogers award, 1999, Ctr. for Am. and Internat. Law. Master: Dean Henry George McMahon Am. Inn of Ct.; mem.: ABA, La. Bar Assn. (mem. ho. of dels. 1979—92, coun. rep. mineral law sect. 1986—94, chmn. mineral law sect. 1992—93), La. State Law Inst. (mineral code com.), Baton Rouge Bar Assn. Republican. Methodist. Oil, gas, and mineral. Office: PO Box 2471 Baton Rouge LA 70821-2471 E-mail: clay@tpbp.com

JOHNSON, JOSEPH H., JR. lawyer; b. Dothan, Ala., July 14, 1925; Student, La. Poly. Inst.; LLB, U. Va., 1949. Bar: Ala. 1949. Of counsel Lange, Simpson, Robinson & Somerville, Birmingham, Ala. Recipient Bernard P. Friel medal for disting. svc. in pub. fin., 1997. Mem. ABA (mem. coun. 1962-66, 68-72, 73-77, chmn. 1981-82, sec. of urban, state and local govt. law), Assn. of Bar of City of N.Y., Birmingham Bar Assn. (chmn. com. on profl. ethics 1978-79), Ala. State Bar, Nat. Assn. Bond Lawyers (pres. 1988-89), Am. Coll. Bond Counsel (bd. dirs. 1998—). Office: Lange Simpson Robinson & Somerville 1700 Regions Bank Bldg # A Birmingham AL 35203-3217 E-mail: jjohn2994@aol.com, jjohnson@langesimpson.com

JOHNSON, KAREN LEE, lawyer; b. Houston, Feb. 29, 1948; d. Bailey Edward and Frances Bette (Pfefferle) J. B.S. in Edn., Tex. Tech. U., 1970, J.D., 1973. Bar: Tex. 1973. Research asst. office legal affairs Tex. Tech. U., Lubbock, 1972-73, staff asst., 1973; univ. legal counsel W. Tex. State U., Canyon, 1973-76; asst. gen. counsel Tex. Edn. Agy., Austin, 1976-78; gen. counsel Tex. State Tchrs.' Assn., Austin, 1978— ; cons. on legal problems in edn. Tex. Jr. Coll. System, 1976-80. Council program chmn. Explorer Scouts, Amarillo, Tex., 1976; mem. Gov.'s Commn. on Juvenile Justice, San Marcus and Austin, 1983; mem. adv. council Windham Sch. Dist., Huntsville, Tex., 1984. Recipient Outstanding Service award Llano Estacado Explorer Scouts, 1976, Windham Sch. System, 1984. Mem. Tex. Bar Assn., Austin Young Lawyers, Nat. Assn. Tchr. Attys., Nat. Orgn. Legal Problems in Edn., Pi Beta Phi. Democrat. Presbyterian. Office: Texas State Tchrs Assn 7701 N Lamar Blvd Ste 518 Austin TX 78752-1025 also: State Bar of Tex PO Box 12487 1414 Colorado St Austin TX 78701-1627

JOHNSON, KATHERINE ANNE, health research administrator, lawyer; b. Medford, Mass., Apr. 20, 1947; d. Lester and Eileen Anne (Henaghan) J. BS, La. State U., 1969; MSA, George Washington U., 1972; JD, Cath. U., 1985. Bar: Md. 1985. Pub. health adviser HHS, Washington, 1970-76; dir. plan implementation SE Colo. Health Sys. Agy., Colorado Springs, 1976-78; sr. mng. assoc. CDP Assocs., Inc., Atlanta, 1978-87, dir. legal affairs, 1986-87; v.p. Cancer CarePoint Inc., 1987; sr. mgr. Salick Health Care, Inc., Bethesda, Md., 1987-89; pvt. practice Potomac, 1989-90; assoc. dir. for adminstrn. San Antonio Cancer Inst., 1990-96; assoc. dir. planning and adminstrn. CTRC Rsch. Found., San Antonio, 1996-97, v.p., 1997-98; COO Inst. Drug Devel., 1997-98; prin. biomed. program devel. consulting, 1998-99; dir. rsch./adminstrn. Am. Coll. Surgeons, 1999—. Spkr. in field. Contbr. articles to profl. jours. Vol. Ct.-Apptd. Spl. Adv. for Abused Children. Mem. Md. Bar Assn., Am. Health Lawyers Assn., Leadership Tex. Class of 1996, Soc. Rsch. Adminstrs. Avocations: skiing, reading, antique collecting. Office: 633 N Saint Clair St Chicago IL 60611-3234 E-mail: kajohns@earthlink.net

JOHNSON, KEVIN BLAINE, lawyer, educator; b. Wichita, Kans., Aug. 28, 1956; s. Howard Blaine and Ruth Signe (Hornlund) J.; m. Karen L. Blucher, Mar. 12, 1994. B.A., Wichita State U., 1978; J.D., Washburn U., 1981. Bar: Kans. 1982, U.S. Dist. Ct. Kans. 1982, U.S. Ct. Appeals (10th cir.) 1991, U.S. Supreme Ct. 1993. Sole practice, Overland Park, Kans., 1981-82; asst. dist. atty. Wyandotte, County, Kans., 1982-84; assoc. Law Office of A. B. Fletcher, Wichita, Kans., 1984-86, Law Office of Stan R. Singleton, Derby, Kans., 1986-88; pvt. practice, Wichita, 1988—; prof. law Kans. Newman Coll., Wichita, 1984-96, Webster U., Wichita, 1995-99; prof. Emporia State U., 1999—. Author: The 11th Kansas Volunteer Cavalry, 1986, A Summer Madness, 1988, A Short Practical Guide to Business Law With Forms, 1990, revised title Business Legal Guide, 1994, At War on the Prairie, 1990, Employer's Legal Guide, 1995, Employee Law Compliance, 2001; contbr. articles to profl. jours. Mem. Wichita Citizen Participation Orgn. Council, 1985-86. Drum instr. Sky Ryders Drum and Bugle Corps, Hutchinson, Kans., 1978-81, bd. dirs., 1988-90; bd. dirs. High Plains Drum Corps, Inc., 1987-90. Mem. Wichita Bar Assn., Kans. Bar Assn. Republican. Lutheran. E-mail: johnsoke@emporia-edu. Bankruptcy, Contracts commercial, General corporate. Home: 2432 N Woodlawn Blvd Derby KS 67037-4212 Office: PO Box 2016 Wichita KS 67201-2016

JOHNSON, KEVIN RAYMOND, lawyer, educator; b. Culver City, Calif., June 29, 1958; s. Kenneth R. Johnson and Angela J. (Gallardo) McEachron; m. Virginia Salazar, Oct. 17, 1987; children: Teresa, Tomás, Elena. AB in Econs. with great distinction, U. Calif., 1980; JD magna cum laude, Harvard U., 1983. Bar: Calif. 1985, U.S. Dist. Ct. (no., ea. and so. dists.) Calif. 1985, U.S. Ct. Appeals (9th cir.) 1985, U.S. Supreme Ct. 1991. From rsch. asst. to Charles Haar prof. Harvard U., Cambridge, Mass., 1982-83, instr. legal writing, 1982; law clk. to Hon. Stephen Reinhardt, U.S. Ct. Appeals (9th cir.), L.A., 1983-84; atty. Heller Ehrman White & McAuliffe, San Francisco, 1984-89; acting prof. law U. Calif., Davis, 1989-92, prof. law, 1992—, assoc. dean for acad. affairs, 1998—, prof. Chicano studies, 2000—01. Instr. civil procedure, complex litigation, immigration law, refugee law, acting dir. clin. legal edn., spring 1992, Latinos and Latines and the Law, 2001; mem. legal del. to El Salvador, 1987. Author: How Did You Get To Be Mexican? A White/Brown Man's Search for Identity, 1999; editor: Harvard Law Review, 1981-83; contbr. articles to profl. jours. Bd. dirs. Legal Svcs. No. Calif., 1996—, exec. com., 1997—, v.p., 2001—; bd. dirs. Yolo County ACLU, 1990-93, chmn. legal com., 1991-93; magistrate merit selection panel U.S. Dist. Ct. for Ea. Dist. Calif.; vol. Legal Svcs. Program, San Francisco, Sacramento, Calif.; mem. Lawyers Com. for Civil Rights of the San Francisco Bay Area, 1991—; various pro bono activies. Recipient Commendation, Calif. State Bar, 1985-90, Cmty. award, 2001. Mem. ABA (coordinators com. immigration 1998—), Calif. Bar Assn. (standing com. legal svcs. for poor 1992-94, gov. com. continuing edn. bar 1993-98, mem. minority affairs com., law sch. admission coun. 1999—), U. Calif. Alumni Assn. (class sec. Class of 1980), Harvard Club San Francisco, Phi Beta Kappa. Democrat. Roman Catholic. Office: U Calif Sch Law King Hall Davis CA 95617

JOHNSON, KRAIG NELSON, lawyer, mediator; b. Landstuhl, Germany, July 8, 1959; came to U.S., 1966; s. Howard Arthur and Joy Anne (Nelson) J.; m. AmberJade F. Leca, Nov. 13, 1993. BA with honors, Eckerd Coll., 1981; M in Internat. Mgmt., Am. Grad. Sch. Internat. Mgmt., Glendale, Ariz., 1982; JD, Baylor U., 1992. Bar: Fla. 1993; cert. mediator and arbitrator Supreme Ct. of Fla. Mktg. mgr. Jack Eckerd Corp., Clearwater, Fla., 1982-85; mktg. systems mgr. NCS, Inc., Houston, 1985-87; dir. ops. Petro, Inc., El Paso, 1987-90; atty. and shareholder Zimmerman, Shuffield, Kiser & Sutcliffe, P.A., Orlando, Fla., 1992—. Editor: Florida Workers' Compensation Practice, 1994; contbr. articles to profl. jours. Mem. internat. trade and investment adv. bd. Econ. Devel. Commn. of Mid-Fla., Orlando, 1997—; mem. Task Force on Title IX, Baylor U. Bd. of Regents, Waco, 1992-93; bd. dirs. Asian-Am. C. of C., Orlando, 1994-95. Fellow Soc. of Antiquaries of Scotland; mem. Am. Immigration Lawyers Assn., St. Andrew's Soc. of Ctrl. Fla. (bd. dirs., v.p. 1996-98, pres. 1998—), Fla. Bar Assn. (sect. on internat. law and litig.), Order of Barristers. Avocations: sailing, flying, shooting sports, Mandarin Chinese and German languages. General civil litigation, Immigration, naturalization, and customs, Private international. Home: 509 N Hampton Ave Orlando FL 32803-5516 Office: Zimmerman Shuffield Kiser & Sutcliffe PA 315 E Robinson St Ste 600 Orlando FL 32801-4308

JOHNSON, LAEL FREDERIC, lawyer; b. Yakima, Wash., Jan. 22, 1938; s. Andrew Cabot and Gudney M. (Fredrickson) J.; m. Eugenie Rae Call, June 9, 1960; children: Eva Marie, Inga Margaret. AB, Wheaton (Ill.) Coll., 1960; JD, Northwestern U., 1963. Bar: Ill. 1963, U.S. Dist. Ct. (no. dist.) Ill. 1964, U.S. Ct. Appeals (7th cir.) 1966. V.p., gen. counsel Abbott Labs., Abbott Park, Ill., 1981-89, sr. v.p., sec., gen. counsel, 1989-94; of counsel Schiff Hardin & Waite, Chgo., 1995—. Mem. Law Sch. bd. Northwestern U. Mem. ABA, Chgo. Bar Assn., Assn. Gen. Counsel. Antitrust, General corporate, Securities. Office: Schiff Hardin & Waite 6600 Sears Tower Chicago IL 60606

JOHNSON, LEONARD HJALMA, lawyer; b. Thomasville, Ga., May 22, 1957; s. Hjalma Eugene and Laura Nell (McLeod) J.; m. Nancy Louise Brock, Dec. 13, 1981; children: Brock Hjalma, Paige McLeod. BSBA, U. Fla., 1978, JD, 1980. Assoc. Dayton, Sumner, Luckie and McKnight, Dade City, 1981-83, Greenfelder and Mander, Dade City, 1983-84; pres. East Coast Bank Corp., Ormond Beach, Fla., 1983-2000; pvt. practice Dade City, 1984-89; ptnr. Johnson, Auvil & Brock, P.A., 1990—; vice chmn. Bank of Madison (Fla.) County, 1985-88, N. Fla. Bank Corp., Madison, 1985-88, Bank at Ormond By-the-Sea, 1983-2000. Vice chmn. Lake State Bank, 1989-96. Bd. dirs. Downtown Dade City Main St. Inc., 1987-96, East Pasco Habitat for Humanity, 1998-99; trustee Dade City Hosp., 1994-96, chmn., 1996; mem. Leadership Fla. Mem. ABA, Fla. Bar Assn., Pasco County Bar Assn. (sec. 1982-83), Young Pres. Orgn. (edn. chmn. Fla. chpt. 1997-98, chpt. chmn. 1998-99), Dade City C. of C., Fla. Blue Key. Republican. Methodist. Banking, General corporate, Real property.

JOHNSON, MARK ANDREW, lawyer; b. Plainville, Kans., Feb. 27, 1959; s. Delton Lee and Margaret Ellen (McCracken) J. BA in Chemistry, Reed Coll., 1982; JD, U. Calif., Berkeley, 1987. Bar: Oreg. 1987, U.S. Supreme Ct. 1991. Jud. clk. U.S. Dist. Ct. Oreg., Portland, 1987-88, Oreg. Ct. of Appeals, Salem, 1988-89; assoc. Gevurtz, Menashe, Larson, Kurshner & Yates, PC, Portland, 1989-93; ptnr. Findling & Johnson LLP, 1993-99; of counsel Bennett Morris & Kaplan, LLP and predecessor, 1999—. Mem. ABA, Nat. Gay and Lesbian Law Assn. (co-chmn. 1994-95), Oreg. Gay and Lesbian Law Assn. (co-chair 1990-92), Oreg. State Bar (pres. 1998-99). Appellate, Family and matrimonial. Office: Hartman Morris & Kaplan LLP 851 SW 6th Ave Ste 1600 Portland OR 97204-1307 E-mail: johnsonm@bennetthartman.com*

JOHNSON, MARK EUGENE, lawyer; b. Independence, Mo., Jan. 8, 1951; s. Russell Eugene and Reatha (Nixon) J.; m. Vicki Ja Lane, June 11, 1983. AB with honors, U. Mo., 1973, JD, 1976. Bar: Mo. 1976, U.s. Dist. Ct. (we. dist.) Mo. 1976, U.S. Ct. Appeals (8th cir.) 1984, U.S. Supreme Ct. 1993. Ptnr. Morrison & Hecker, LLP, Kansas City, Mo., 1976—. Editor Mo. Law Rev., 1974-76. Pres. Lido Villas Assn., Inc., Mission, Kans., 1979-81. Mem. ABA, Mo. Bar Assn., Kansas City Bar Assn., Lawyers Assn. Kansas City, Def. Rsch. Inst., Internat. Assn. Def. Counsel, Mo. Orgn. Def. Lawyers, Carriage Club, Order of Coif, Phi Beta Kappa, Phi Eta Sigma, Phi Kappa Phi, Omicron Delta Kappa. Republican. Presbyterian. Federal civil litigation, State civil litigation. Home: 4905 Somerset Dr Shawnee Mission KS 66207-2230 Office: Morrison & Hecker LLP 2600 Grand Blvd Ste 1200 Kansas City MO 64108-4606

JOHNSON, MARK WAYNE, lawyer; b. Dallas, June 6, 1959; s. W.A. and Wanda Louise (Follis) J.; m. Helene Denise Metz, June 7, 1987; children: Benjamin Gates, Andrew Noah. BS, Belhaven Coll., Jackson, Miss., 1980; JD, U. Miss., Oxford, 1983. Bar: Miss. 1983, U.S. Dist. Ct. (no. and so. dists.) Miss. 1983, U.S. Ct. Appeals (5th cir.) 1990; cert. govt. fin. mgr. Sole practice, Jackson, Miss., 1983-86; investigative auditor Miss. Dept. Audit, 1986-92; budget analyst Office Budget and Fund Mgmt., 1992-2001; dir. acctg. Miss. Sec. of State, 2001—. Owner Possum Press, 1998—; with Madison Hazard Mitigation Coun., 2000—. Contbr. articles to profl. jours. Dir. Miss. Coun. Compulsive Gamblin, 1996-98, adv. bd., 1998—; bd. dirs. Miss. Pub. Employees Credit Union, 1994—. Recipient Spl. Merit award for traffic safety and edn. Nat. Assn. Chiefs of Police, 1987; named one of Outstanding Young Men of Am., 1988. Mem. Miss. Bar. Republican. Avocations: writing, computers. Finance, State and local taxation. Office: Sec of State 202 N Congress St Ste 501 Jackson MS 39201 E-mail: mjohnson@sos.state.ms.us

JOHNSON, NORMA HOLLOWAY, federal judge; b. Lake Charles, La. d. H. Lee and Beatrice (Williams) Holloway; m. Julius A. Johnson, June 18, 1964. B.S., D.C. Tchrs. Coll., 1955; J.D., Georgetown U., 1962. Bar: D.C. 1962, U.S. Supreme Ct. 1967. Pvt. practice law, Washington, 1963; atty. civil divsn. Dept. Justice, 1963-67; asst. corp. counsel Office of Corp. Counsel, 1967-70; judge D.C. Superior Ct., 1970-80, U.S. Dist. Ct. (D.C. dist.), Washington, 1980-97, chief judge, 1997-2001; senior judge U.S. Dist. Ct. (D.C. dist), 2001. Bd. dirs. Judiciary Leadership Devel. Coun. Fellow Am. Bar Found.; mem. Nat. Bar Assn., Fed. Judges Assn., Am. Judicature Soc., Supreme Ct. Hist. Soc., Am. Inns of Ct. (William Bryant inn). Office: US Dist Ct US Courthouse 333 Constitution Ave NW Washington DC 20001-2802

JOHNSON, OLIVER THOMAS, JR. lawyer; b. San Antonio, July 3, 1946; s. Oliver Thomas and Joan Elizabeth (Edwards) J.; m. Susan Caroline Nelson, Nov. 6, 1976; children: Caroline Elizabeth, Thomas Christian. Student, U. Redlands, 1964-65; BA, Stanford U., 1968, JD, 1971. Bar: Calif. 1972, D.C. 1975, U.S. Ct. Internat. Trade 1983, U.S. Supreme Ct. 1991. Atty. office of legal adviser U.S. Dept. State, Washington, 1971-73, spl. asst. to legal adviser, 1973-75; assoc. Covington & Burling, 1975-80, ptnr., 1980—. Co-author: The Registration of Foreign Agents in the United States, 1981, Private Investors Abroad: Problems and Solutions, 1987, The North American Free Trade Agreement: Issues, Options, Implications, 1992, The International Lawyer's Deskbook, 1996; contbr. articles to profl. jours. Bd. dir. U.S.-Azerbaijan Coun., Washington, 1995. Mem. ABA, Am. Soc. Internat. Law (bd. dirs.), Washington Inst. Fgn. Affairs, Inst. Transnat. Arbitration (adv. bd.), Met. Club, Order of Coif. Private international, Public international. Office: Covington & Burling 1201 Pennsylvania Ave NW Washington DC 20004-2401 E-mail: tjohnson@cov.com

JOHNSON, PAUL OREN, lawyer; b. Mpls., Feb. 2, 1937; s. Andrew Richard and LaVerne Delores (Slater) J.; children: Scott, Paula, Amy. BA, Carleton Coll., 1958; JD cum laude, U. Minn., 1961. Bar: Minn. 1961. Atty. Briggs & Morgan, St. Paul, 1961-62, Green Giant Co., Le Sueur, Minn., 1961-66, asst. sec., 1967-74, sec., 1975-79, v.p., gen. counsel, 1971-79, v.p. corporate rels., 1973-79, mem. mgmt. com., 1976-79; gen. counsel H.B. Fuller Co., St. Paul, 1979-84, sr. v.p., sec., 1980-90, mem. mgmt. com., 1981-90. Bd. dirs. The Fulcrum Group, chmn. bd. dirs. Coun. v.p., exec. com. Boy Scouts Am.; bd. dirs. Rep. County Com., 1965; bd. dirs. Minn. State U., 1979-82, v.p., 1980-82; chmn. bd. dirs. Minn. Com. Serving Deaf and Hard of Hearing; bd. dirs. vice chair Minn. Acads. Office: Lexington-Riverside 403-1077 Sibley Meml Hwy Saint Paul MN 55118-3680

JOHNSON, PAUL OWEN, lawyer; b. Ft. Wayne, Ind., Jan. 26, 1919; s. Paul Ephriam and Pauline May (Ebersole) J.; m. Arlyn Marie Munson, Aug. 3, 1945; m. Louise Marie Skoglund, Feb. 11, 1972; children: Roxanne Marie, Dianne Marie. BSL, U. Minn., 1941, LLB, 1943, JD, 1967. Bar: Minn. 1943, U.S. Dist. Ct. Minn. 1948. V.p., counsel United Capital Life Ins., Mpls., 1965-70; assoc. editor Am. Trial Lawyers Jour., 1970-75; ptnr. Johnson & Ildstad, Edina, Minn., 1975—. Bd. dirs. Interchange Investors, Mpls.; corp. counsel Thunderbird Hotel and Conv. Ctr. Corp.; mem. alt. dispute resolution com. Minn. Supreme Ct. Contbr. articles to Minn. Trial Lawyer Jour. Mem. Mayo Found. Lt. comdr. USN, 1941-46, PTO. Mem. ABA, Am. Arbitration Assn. (lectr.), Am. Judicature Soc., Minn. Bar Assn., Am. Trial Lawyers Assn., Minn. Trial Lawyers Assn. (pres. 1957, bd. dirs.), U.S. Naval Inst., Am. Legion (comdr., judge adv. 1980—), Minn. Alumni Assn. (life), U.S. Navy League (nat. dir. 1995), Submarine Vets. U.S. (life, submarine chaser), VFW, Fireside Investors Club, Masons, Shriners, Gamma Eta Gamma. Episcopalian. Avocations: tennis, boating, travel. Alternative dispute resolution, Insurance, Personal injury. Home: 109 Meadow Ln S Minneapolis MN 55416-3404

JOHNSON, PHILIP EDWARD, lawyer; b. Denver, Oct. 17, 1947; s. William Edward Johnson and Margarete Eileen (Brandon) Schmaltz; m. Mary Lou Raders, Jan. 1, 1996; children: Brooke, Brandon, Dara, Bryce. BA, U. Colo., 1969; JD, U. Denver, 1974. Bar: Colo. 1975, U.S. Dist. Ct. Colo. 1975, U.S. Ct. Appeals (10th cir.) 1981. Corp. counsel Tosco Corp., Denver and Los Angeles, 1975-76; assoc., ptnr. Mosley, Wells, Johnson & Ruttum P.C., Denver, 1976-93; ptnr. Bennington, Johnson & Reeve, P.C., 1993—. Bd. dirs. OEA, Inc. Vol. U.S. Peace Corps, Panama, 1969, 70. Avocations: athletics, sailing, traveling. Federal civil litigation, State civil litigation, Real property. Home: 444 Clayton St Denver CO 80206-4231 Office: Bennington Johnson & Reeve PC 370 17th St Ste 2480 Denver CO 80202-1371 E-mail: johnson@bjrlaw.com

JOHNSON, PHILIP LESLIE, lawyer; b. Beloit, Wis., Jan. 24, 1939; s. James Philip and Christabel (Williams) J.; m. Kathleen Rose Westover, May 12, 1979; children: Celeste Marie, Nicole Michelle. AB, Princeton U., 1961; JD, U. South Calif., 1973. Bar: Calif. 1973, U.S. Ct. Appeals (9th cir.) 1975, U.S. Ct. of Military Appeals, 1978, U.S. Supreme Ct. 1980. Pilot U.S. Marine Corps., 1961-70; assoc. Law Office Wm. G. Tucker, L.A., 1973-78; ptnr. Engstrom, Lipscomb & Lack, 1978-92; judge pro tem Calif. State Bar Ct., 1990-95; ptnr. Lillick & Charles, Long Beach, Calif., 1993-99, Shaw, Terhar & LaMontagne, L.A., 2000—. Chmn. aerospace law com. Def. Rsch. Inst. Contbr. articles to profl. jours. Pres., bd. dirs. U. So. Calif. Legion Lex, 1992-93; chmn. com. to nom. alumni trustees Princeton U., 1996-97, mem. exec. com. of alumni coun., 1996-97; chmn. Marine Corps Scholarship Found. L.A. Ball, 1997-99. Mem. ABA, (aviation & space law com., torts & ins. practice section), Princeton Club (So. Calif., bd. dirs.). Avocations: flying, snow skiing, jazz. Aviation, Insurance, Product liability. Home: 5340 Valley View Rd Palos Verdes Peninsula CA 90275-5089 Office: Shaw Terhar & LaMontagne 601 S Figueroa St Fl 37 Los Angeles CA 90017 E-mail: avnlawyer@aol.com

JOHNSON, PHILIP MCBRIDE, lawyer; b. Springfield, Ohio, June 18, 1938; AB with honors, Ind. U., 1959; LLB, Yale U., 1962. Bar: Ill. 1962, D.C. 1983, N.Y. 1984. Ptnr. Kirkland & Ellis, Chgo., 1962-81; chmn. Commodity Futures Trading Commn., Washington, 1981-83; ptnr. Wiley, Johnson & Rein, 1983-84, Skadden, Arps, Slate, Meagher & Flom,

Washington, 1984—; lectr. on commodities regulation U. Va. Law Sch., 1993—. Spkr. panelist on Commodity Exch. Act Fed. Bar Assn., others; mem. adv. com. definition and regulation Commodity Futures Trading Commn., adv. com. state jurisdiction and responsibility; adv. com. regulatory coordination, adv. com. fin. products, adv. com. tech., adv. com. global markets Commodity Futures Trading Commn.; adv. com. Global Markets. Author: Commodities Regulation, 2 vols., 1997, Derivatives: A Manager's Guide to the World's Most Powerful Financial Instruments, 1999; mng. editor Yale U. Law Jour, 1962, Agrl. Law Jour; contbr. articles to legal jours. Mem. ABA (founder, chmn. com. on futures regulation 1975-81, mem. governing coun. sect. on bus. law 1981-83), Futures Industry Assn. (bd. dirs. 1980-81, 86-87), Internat. Bar Assn. (founder, chmn. subcom. on commodities, futures and options law 1986-90), N.Y. Stock Exch. (mem. regulatory adv. com. 1988—). Administrative and regulatory, Securities, Commodities. Office: Skadden Arps Slate Meagher & Flom 1440 New York Ave NW Ste 700 Washington DC 20005-2111 E-mail: pjohnson@skadden.com

JOHNSON, PHILIP WAYNE, judge; b. Greenwood, Ark., Oct. 24, 1944; s. John Luther and Flora (Joyce) J.; m. Carla Jean Newsom, Nov. 6, 1970; children: Betsy, Carl, Jeff, Laura, Philip. B.A., Tex. Tech. U., 1965, J.D., 1975. Bar: Tex. 1975, U.S. Dist. Ct. (no. and we. dists.) Tex. 1976, U.S. Ct. Appeals (5th cir.) 1984, U.S. Supreme Ct. 1984; cert. in civil trial and personal injury trial law, Tex. Bd. Legal Specialization. Assoc. Crenshaw Dupree & Milam, Lubbock, Tex., 1975-80, ptnr., 1980-98; justice Tex. State Ct. of Appeals (7th dist), Amarillo, 1999—. Bd. dirs., pres. Lubbock County Legal Aid Soc., Tex., 1977-79; bd. dirs., chmn. Trinity Christian Schs., Lubbock, 1978-83, 85-89; bd. dirs., pres. S.W. Lighthouse for Blind, Lubbock, 1978-85. Served to capt. USAF, 1965-72. Decorated Silver Star, D.F.C.; Cross of Gallantry (Vietnam). Fellow Am. Bar Found., Tex. Bar Found. (life); mem. ABA, Tex. Bar Assn., Amarillo Bar Assn., Lubbock County Bar Assn. (pres. 1984-85), Phi Delta Phi. Home: 7818 Covington Pkwy Amarillo TX 79121-1940 Office: Seventh Ct of Appeals 501 S Fillmore St Rm 2A Amarillo TX 79101-2449

JOHNSON, PHILLIP EDWARD, lawyer; b. Cleve., Mar. 19, 1950; s. Donald Marquis and Jeannette (Tetinek) Johnson; m. Priscilla Dwinnell, Sept. 12, 1981. B.A., Miami U., Oxford, Ohio, 1972; J.D., Case Western Res. U., Cleve., 1975. Bar: Ohio 1975, U.S. Dist. Ct. (no. dist.) Ohio 1975, Maine 1977, U.S. Dist. Ct. Maine 1977. Assoc. Arter & Hadden, Cleve., 1975-77; assoc. Pierce, Atwood, Scribner, Allen, Smith & Lancaster, Augusta and Portland, Maine, 1977-82, ptnr., 1983-92; pvt. practice, Augusta, Maine, 1992—. Vice chmn. Maine Bd. of Property Tax Review, 1992—. Mem. ABA, Maine State Bar Assn., Main Trial Lawyers Assn (bd. of gov. 1993—), Kennebec County Bar Assn. (pres. 1983-85), Lawyer-Pilots Bar Assn. Republican. Federal civil litigation, State civil litigation. Home: 66 Hemlock Ter Augusta ME 04330-6248 Office: PO Box 29 160 Capitol St Augusta ME 04330-6835

JOHNSON, RICHARD ARLO, lawyer; b. Vermillion, S.D., July 8, 1952; s. Arlo Goodwin and Edna Marie (Styles) J.; m. Diane Marie Zephier, Aug. 18, 1972 (div. Jan. 1979); m. Sheryl Lavonne Mader, June 5, 1981; 1 stepchild, Chadwick O. Wagner; 1 child, Sarah N. BA, U. S.D., 1974, JD, 1976. Bar: S.D. 1977, U.S. Dist. Ct. S.D. 1977. Ptnr. Pruitt, Matthews, Muilenberg & Strange, Sioux Falls, S.D., 1977-92, Strange, Farrell & Johnson, P.C., Sioux Falls, 1992—. Mem. Pub. Defender Adv. Bd., Sioux Falls, 1983-98; mem. S.D. Dental Peer Rev. Com. S.E. Dist. Fellow Am. Acad. Matrimonial Lawyers; mem. ATLA, ABA, S.D. Trial Lawyers Assn., State Bar S.D. (chmn. family law com. 1989-92), Phi Delta Phi (pres. 1976-77), Masons, Shriners. Democrat. Lutheran. Consumer commercial, Criminal, Family and matrimonial. Home: 409 E Lotta St Sioux Falls SD 57105-7109 Office: Strange Farrell & Johnson PC 141 N Main Ave Ste 200 Sioux Falls SD 57104-6429

JOHNSON, RICHARD FRED, lawyer; b. July 12, 1944; s. sylvester Hiram and Naomi Ruth (Jackson) J.; m. Sheila conley, June 26, 1970; children: Brendon, Bridget, Timothy, Laura. BS, Miami U., Oxford, Ohio, 1966; JD cum laude, Northwestern U., 1969. Bar: Ill. 1969, U.S. Dist. Ct. (no. dist.) Ill. 1969), U.S. Dist. Ct. (ctrl. dist.) Ill. 2000, U.S. Ct. Appeals (7th cir.) 1977, U.S. Ct. Appeals (2d cir.) 1980, U.S. Ct. Appeals (9th cir.) 1991, U.S. Ct. Appeals (5th cir.) 1993, U.S. Supreme Ct. 1978. Law clk. U.S. Dist. Ct. (no. dist.) Ill., Chgo., 1969-70; assoc. firm Lord, Bissell & Brook, 1970-77, ptnr., 1977—. Lectr. legal edn. Contbr. articles to profl. jours. Recipient Am. Jurisprudence award 1968. Mem. Chgo. Bar Assn., Union League. Admiralty, Insurance, Personal injury. Home: 521 W Roscoe St Chicago IL 60657-3518 Office: Lord Bissell & Brook 115 S La Salle St Ste 3200 Chicago IL 60603-3902

JOHNSON, RICHARD TENNEY, lawyer; b. Evanston, Ill., Mar. 24, 1930; s. Ernest Levin and Margaret Abbott (Higgins) J.; m. Marilyn Bliss Meuth, May 1, 1954; children: Ross Tenney, Lenore, Jocelyn. AB with high honors, U. Rochester, 1951; postgrad., Trinity Coll., Dublin, Ireland, 1954-55; LLB, Harvard, 1958. Bar: D.C. 1959. Trainee Office Sec. Def., 1957-59; atty. Office Gen. Counsel. Dept. Def., 1959-63; dep. gen. counsel Dept. Army, 1963-67, Dept. Transp., 1967-70; gen. counsel CAB, 1970-73, mem., 1976-77; gen. counsel NASA, 1973-75, ERDA, 1975-76; chmn. organizational integration Dept. Energy Activation, Exec. Office of Pres., 1977; ptnr. firm Sullivan & Beauregard, 1978-81; gen. counsel Dept. Energy, 1981-83; ptnr. Zuckert, Scoutt, Rasenberger & Johnson, 1983-87; prin. Law Offices of R. Tenney Johnson, Esq., Washington, 1987-2001; gen. counsel Assn. of Univs. for Rsch. in Astronomy, 1987—. Lt. USNR, 1951-54. Mem. ABA, Fed. Bar Assn., Cosmos Club, Phi Beta Kappa, Theta Delta Chi. Administrative and regulatory, Aviation, Government contracts and claims. E-mail: marandten@starpower.net

JOHNSON, ROBERT ALAN, lawyer; b. Harrisburg, Pa., June 18, 1944; s. Harry Andrew and Minna Melissa (Ebert) J.; m. Selina Braham Pedersen, Aug. 25, 1979; children: Isabella P., Robert A. Jr. BA, Washington and Jefferson Coll., 1966; JD, Harvard U., 1969. Bar: Pa. 1969. Assoc. Buchanan Ingersoll, Pitts., 1969-76, ptnr., 1977—. Contbr. legal articles to profl. jours. Pres. Bach Choir Pitts., 1979-81; bd. dirs. Pitts. Opera, 1985-94, River City Brass Band, Pitts., 1986-95, Renaissance and Baroque Soc., Pitts., 1994—, Friends of the Music Libr., Carnegie Libr. of Pitts., 1995—, CTC Found., 1999—. Fellow Am. Coll. Tax Counsel, Am. Coll. Employee Benefits Counsel; mem. ABA, Am. Arbitration Assn. (panel arbitrators), Allegheny County Bar Assn., Allegheny Tax Soc. (chmn. 1982-83), Pitts. Tax Club, Duquesne Club. Libertarian. Presbyterian. Avocation: avid collector classical music recs. Non-profit and tax-exempt organizations, Pension, profit-sharing, and employee benefits. Home: 601 St James St Pittsburgh PA 15232-1434 Office: Buchanan Ingersoll 301 Grant St Ste 20 Pittsburgh PA 15219-1410 E-mail: johnsonra@bipc.com

JOHNSON, ROBERT MAX, lawyer; b. Thomas, Okla., Aug. 20, 1942; s. Claude L. and Jesse C. (Stimmel) J.; m. Virginia A. LeForce, May 31, 1964; children: Kelli Brook, Brent Matthew. BS, Okla. State U., 1964; JD, U. Okla., 1967; LLD (hon.), Oklahoma City U., 2001. Bar: Okla. 1967. Shareholder Crowe & Dunlevy, Oklahoma City, 1967—, pres., 1985-87, exec. com., 1992—. Spl. lectr. in land fin. and real estate contracts U. Okla. Coll. of Law, Norman, 1973, 84. Mng. editor: Oklahoma Environmental Law Handbook, 1992-96; contbr. to book: The Law of Distressed Real Estate, 1987; case editor Okla. Law Rev., 1966. Bd. dirs. Redbud Found., Oklahoma City, 1987-96, Myriad Gardens Conservatory, Oklahoma City, 1987-89, Myriad Gardens Found., 1993-96, ARC, 1994-96, Arts Coun. Oklahoma City, 1994—, Am. Heart Assn., 1999—; chmn. Oklahoma City Festival of Arts, 1993-94, Murrah Fed. Bldg. Meml. Task Force, 1995-96, Oklahoma City Nat. Meml. Found., 1996-98, Oklahoma City Nat. Meml. Trust, 1998—. Capt. U.S. Army, 1968-70. Recipient Outstanding Svc. to the Pub. award Okla. Bar Assn., 1998. Fellow Am. Coll. Mortgage Attys. (bd. regents, pres. 1994-95, chmn. exec. com. 1995-96); mem. Am. Coll. Real Estate Lawyers, Oklahoma City Golf and Country Club (bd. dirs. 1981-82, sec. 1982), Order of Coif, Phi Delta Phi (magister 1966-67), Lambda Alpha. Avocations: golf, quail hunting, fly fishing, skiing. Finance, Landlord-tenant, Real property. Home: 1608 Mulholland Dr Edmond OK 73003-4114 Office: Crowe & Dunlevy 1800 Mid Am Tower Oklahoma City OK 73102 E-mail: Johnsonr@crowedunlevy.com

JOHNSON, RODNEY MARCUM, lawyer; b. Dayton, Ohio, Feb. 6, 1947; s. Marvin Clarence and Frances (Marcum) J.; m. Martha Elizabeth Mapp, Sept. 3, 1967 (div. 1974); m. Madolyn Gorman, May 5, 1979; children: Kristine Janeen, Jarrod Marcum, Jason Oliver. AS in Bus. Mgmt., Sinclair C.C., 1968; BS in Bus. Econs., Wright State U., 1975; JD, Cleve. State U., 1978. Bar: Ohio 1979, U.S. Dist. Ct. (so. dist.) Ohio 1980, U.S. Tax Ct. 1980, U.S. Ct. Mil. Appeals 1983, U.S. Supreme Ct. 1983, Fla. 1985, U.S. Dist. Ct. (no. dist.) Fla. 1986; cert. in health law, 2001. Methods engr. Delco Moraine Divsn. GMC, Dayton, 1965-71; sys. analyst D.W. Mikesell, Inc., 1971-74; prin. Johnson Tool Co., Savannah, Ga., 1974-75; pvt. practice Dayton, 1979-81; dist. chief legal counsel Fla. Dept. Health, Pensacola, 1986—. Pro bono legal organizer and advisor Santa Rosa Cmty. Clinic, Inc., 2000—; pro bono legal organizer, advisor and dir. Emerald Coast Wildlife Refuge, Inc., 1994—; commr. Avalon Mulat Fire Protection Dist., 1992—. Lt. comdr. JAGC, USN, 1981-86. Mem. Escambia-Santa Rosa Bar Assn. Avocations: boating, fishing, scuba diving. Office: Fla Dept Health 1295 W Fairfield Dr Pensacola FL 32501-1107 E-mail: rodney_johnson@doh.state.fl.us

JOHNSON, RUFUS WINFIELD, lawyer; b. Montgomery County, Md., May 1, 1911; s. Charles L. and Margaret (Smith) J.; m. Rosena L. Allen, June 21, 1939 (div. May 1971); m. Vaunda Louise Griffith, May 29, 1971; step-children: Yvonne, Jackie, Karen, Rodney, Michelle. AB, Howard U., 1934, postgrad., 1934-36, LLB, 1939. Bar: Calif., Ark., Supreme Ct. Ark., Supreme Ct. Calif., D.C. Dist. Ct., U.S. Ct. Appeals, D.C., U.S. Supreme Ct., Supreme Ct. of South Korea; cert. counsel Judge Advocate Gen. Sch., Washington. Pvt. practice, D.C., Calif., Ark., 1945—. Originator Lawyer's Pro Bono Svc. Ret. lt. col. USAR. Decorated Combat Inf. badge, Purple Heart, Bronze Star with 2 oak leaf clusters, Spl. Citation for Bravery. Mem. VFW (life), Am. Judicature Soc., Am. Acad. Polit. and Social Sci., Mil. Order Purple Heart, Internat. Soc. Poets, Am. Kempo Karate Assn., Sr. Citizens Coalition, Ret. Officers Assn., Am. Legion, Masons, Am. Karate Assn. (5th degree Shorin-Ryu Black Belt), Lions. Baptist. Appellate, Criminal, Military. Home: PO Box 776 Mason TX 76856-0776

JOHNSON, SAKINAH, paralegal; b. Passaic, N.J., Nov. 10, 1971; d. Hosea P. Sr. and Claudette E. Johnson. B in Polit. Sci. magna cum laude, Norfolk State U., 1993. Paralegal Law Offices of Sellinger & Sellinger P.A., Clifton, N.J., 1993-98, Law Offices of Rosemarie Arnold, Ft. Lee, 1998—. Active Mt. Pilgrim Missionary Bapt. Ch., 1991—. Mem. NAACP, Norfolk State U. Alumni (N.J. chpt.), Spartan Alpha Tau. Avocations: exercise, reading, dancing, traveling, time with family and friends. Home: 164 Sherman St Passaic NJ 07055-8408

JOHNSON, SHIRLEY Z. lawyer; b. Burlington, Iowa, Mar. 6, 1940; d. Arthur Frank and Helen Martha (Nelson) Zaiss; m. Charles Rumph, Jan. 19, 1979. BA summa cum laude, U. Iowa, 1962; JD with honors, U. Mich., 1965. Bar: Calif. 1966, D.C. 1976, U.S. Supreme Ct. 1979. Trial atty. antitrust divsn. U.S. Dept. Justice, San Francisco, 1965-72; counsel antitrust subcom. U.S. Senate Jud. Com., Washington, 1973-75; ptnr. Baker & Hostetler, 1976-85; pvt. practice, 1985-98; ptnr., chair antitrust and trade regulations dept. Greenberg Traurig, 1998—. Adv. bd. BNA Antitrust & Trade Regulations Reporter, 2000—; mediator U.S. Dist. Ct., Washington, 1990—. Contbr. articles to profl. jours. Trustee The Textile Mus., Washington, 1991—, v.p. bd. trustees, 1994—. Mem. ABA, Women's Bar Assn. (bd. dirs. 1989-91), Am. Law Inst., Order of Coif, Phi Beta Kappa. Democrat. Avocation: collecting Asian art. Administrative and regulatory, Antitrust, Legislative. Office: Greenburg Traurig 800 Connecticut Ave NW Washington DC 20006-2709 E-mail: Johnson@gtlaw.com

JOHNSON, STEVEN BOYD, lawyer; b. Springfield, Tenn., July 19, 1953; s. Ammon and Dorothy Jean (Anderson) J.; m. Martha Jane Yoakum, 1981 (div. Mar. 1987); 1 child, Eleanor Danielle; m. Betsy Lou Brown, Jan. 4, 1989. BA, Vanderbilt U., 1975; MA, Webster Coll., 1977; JD, U. Memphis, 1979. Bar: Tenn. 1979, U.S. Dsit. Ct. (we., mid. and ea. dists.) Tenn., U.S. Ct. Appeals (6th cir.). Law clk. to Judge Robert M. McRae U.S. Dist. Ct. (we. dist.) Tenn., Memphis, 1980-81; assoc. Apperson, Crump, Duzane & Maxwell, 1981-83; ptnr. Horne & Peppel, 1983-84; mem., ptnr. Butler Vines & Babb, P.L.L.C., Knoxville, 1985—. Assoc. prof. entertainment law U. Memphis, 1980. Co-author: Tennessee Workers Compensation Practice, 1995. Served with USN, 1975-77. Mem. Tenn. Bar Assn., Knoxville Bar Assn., Def. Rsch. Inst., Delta Theta Phi, Omicron Delta Kappa. Republican. Avocations: skiing, water skiing, boating, reading. Insurance, Personal injury, Workers' compensation. Home: 3434 Harbour Front Way Knoxville TN 37922-9422 Office: Butler Vines & Babb PLLC First Am Bank Ctr Ste 810 Knoxville TN 37902

JOHNSON, THOMAS JERALD, lawyer; b. Huron, S.D., Aug. 22, 1953; s. Jerald L. and Kathleen A. J.; m. Susan L. Willroth, Aug. 5, 1978. BA, U. Mont., 1975; JD, U. S.D., 1977. Bar: S.D. 1978, U.S. Dist. Ct. S.D. 1978, U.S. Ct. Appeals (8th cir.) 1979, U.S. Supreme Ct. 1981. Sole practice, Sioux Falls, S.D., 1977-80; ptnr. Quaintance, Swanson & Johnson, Sioux Falls, 1980-85; ptnr. Quaintance & Johnson, 1986-90, Quaintance, Johnson, Nadolski & Starnes, 1991-92; atty. pvt. practice, 1993—; instr. Am. Bankers Assn.; bd. dirs. E. River Legal Services, Sioux Falls, 1979-83. Bd. dirs. Parent to Parent Inc.; chmn. S.D. Bd. Pardons and Paroles. Mem. ABA, Am. Trial Lawyers Assn., S.D. Trial Lawyers Assn., S.D. Bar Assn., Minnehaha County Bar Assn., Alpha Tau Omega. Republican. Lodge: Elks. Contracts commercial, General corporate, Probate. Home: 3060 S Coral Ct Sioux Falls SD 57103-4830 Office: PO Box 899 Sioux Falls SD 57101-0899

JOHNSON, THOMAS STUART, lawyer; b. Rockford, Ill., May 21, 1942; s. Frederick C. and Pauline (Ross) J. BA, Rockford Coll., 1964, LLD, 1989; JD, Harvard U., 1967. Bar: Ill. 1967. Pres. Williams & McCarthy, Rockford, 1967—. Lectr. in field. Contbr. numerous articles to profl. jours. Chmn. bd. trustees Rockford Coll., 1986—89; trustee Eastern Ill. U., 1996—2000, Emanuel Med. Ctr., Turlock, Calif., 1984—86, Swedish Covenant Hosp., Chgo., 1984—86, Lincoln Acad. of Ill., 1999—2000; chmn. bd. dirs. Ill. Inst. Continuing Legal Edn., Chgo., 1984—86; treas. Lawyers Trust Fund of Ill., 1984—86; bd. govs. Regent's Coll., London, 1985—89; bd. dirs., mem. benevolence bd. Covenant Ch. Am., Chgo., 1984—86; chmn. Fegent's Found. for Internat. Edn., London; chancellor Ill. Acad. Lawyers, 1999. With U.S. Army, 1968—70. Fellow Am. Bar Found., Am. Coll. Trust and Estate Counsel; mem. ABA (ho. of dels. 1982-89, chmn. commn. on advt. 1984-88), Ill. Bar Assn. (bd. govs. 1976-82, sec. 1981-82, medal of honor 1997), Winnebago County Bar Assn. (pres. 1990), Am. Judicature Soc. (bd. dirs. 1986-90), Rockford Country Club, Rotary (pres. Rockford 1992-93), Univ. Club Rockford. Republican. General corporate, Estate planning, General practice. Home: 913 N Main St Rockford IL 61103-7068

JOHNSON, THOMAS WEBBER, JR. lawyer; b. Indpls., Oct. 18, 1941; s. Thomas W. and Mary Lucinda (Webber) J.; m. Sandra Kay McMahon, Aug. 15, 1964 (div. 1986); m. Deborah Joan Collins, May 17, 1987 (div. 1990); m. Barbara Joyce Walter, Mar. 13, 1992. BS in Edn., Ind. U., 1963, JD summa cum laude, 1969. Bar: Ind. 1969, Calif. 1970. Law clk. Ind. Supreme Ct., Indpls., 1968-69; assoc. Irell & Manella, L.A., 1969-76, ptnr., 1976-84, Irell & Manella , Newport Beach, Calif., 1984—99; atty. Irell & Manella, of counsel, 2000—. Chair Com. on Group Ins. Programs for State Bar of Calif., San Francisco, 1978-79; adj. prof. law UCLA, 1996—; lectr. for Practicing Law Inst., Calif. Continuing Edn. of the Bar, Calif. Judges Assn., seminars on ins. and bus. litigation. Editor-in-chief: Ind. Law Review, 1968-69; contbr. articles to profl. jours. With USNR, 1959-65. Named Outstanding Grad. Province XII, Phi Delta Phi legal fraternity, 1969. Mem. ABA (lectr. chair ins. coverage litigation com., tort and ins. practice sec. 1995-96), Calif. Bar Assn., Orange County Bar Assn., Masons, Newport Beach Country Club. Republican. Mem. Christian Ch. General civil litigation, Insurance. Office: Irell & Manella 840 Newport Center Dr Ste 400 Newport Beach CA 92660-6323

JOHNSON, VINCENT ROBERT, law educator, educator; b. Latrobe, Pa., Oct. 10, 1953; s. Harry Paul and Anna Ruth (Gozlick) J. BA, St. Vincent Coll., 1975; JD, U. Notre Dame, 1978; LLM, Yale U., 1979; LLD, St. Vincent Coll., 1991. Bar: Pa. 1978, U.S. Ct. Appeals (7th cir.) 1981, Tex. 1985, U.S. Supreme Ct. 1986. Law clk. Hon. Bernard S. Meyer, N.Y.C., Albany, N.Y., 1979-80, Hon. Thomas E. Fairchild, Chgo., 1980-82; asst. prof. St. Mary's U., San Antonio, 1982-85, assoc. prof., 1985-88, prof., 1988—; vis. prof. Vermont Law Sch., 1991, assoc. dean for adminstrn., 2001—; vis. prof. St. Petersburg State U., Russia, 1999, Shandong U., China, 2001. Jud. fellow U.S. Supreme Ct., 1988-89; dir. St. Mary's Inst. on World Legal Problems, Innsbruck, Austria, 1989-2001. Author: Mastering Torts, 1995, 2d edit., 1999; co-author: Studies in American Tort Law, 1994, 2d edit., 1999, Teaching Torts, 1995, 2d edit., 1999; mem. editl. adv. bd. Carolina Acad. Press. Chair Mayor of San Antonio's Task Force on Ethics in Govt., 1997-98. Fulbright sr. scholar, Beijing, China, 1998. Mem. ABA, Am. Law Inst., State Bar Tex. (lawyer advt. com. 1985-88, rules of profl. conduct com. 1996-99), Assn. Am. Law Schs. (chmn. teaching methods sect. 1987-88), Fed. Jud. Fellows Commn., Order of Art and Culture (Innsbruck, Austria), Phi Delta Phi (Teaching Excellence award 1986), Phi Alpha Delta (Disting. Svc. award 1984). Democrat. Roman Catholic. E-mail;. Home: 124 W Gramercy Pl San Antonio TX 78212 Office: St Marys U Sch Law One Camino Santa Maria San Antonio TX 78228-8602 E-mail: johnsonv@law.stmarytx.edu

JOHNSON, WALLACE HAROLD, lawyer; b. Cleve., Oct. 7, 1939; s. Wallace H. and Esther Johnson; m. Donna Simpson, June 9, 1962; children: Kimberly, W. Todd, Vicki, Eric. BA in Polit. Sci., Ohio U., 1961; postgrad., Rutgers U., 1961; JD, U. Toledo, 1965. Bar: Ohio 1965, U.S Dist. Ct. D.C., 1969, U.S. Ct. Claims 1974, U.S. Supreme Ct. 1968, Nebr. 1975, Colo. 1993, Wyo. 1993. Trial atty. organized crime and racketeering sect. U.S. Dept. Justice criminal divsn., Washington, 1965-69; minority counsel subcom. criminal laws and procedures U.S. Dept. Justice, 1969-70, assoc. dep. atty. gen., 1970-72; spl. asst. to Pres. White House, Washington, 1972-73; asst. atty. gen. land and resources divsn. U.S. Dept. Justice, 1973-75; ptnr. Kutok Rock, 1975-90. Gen. counsel, NCBA, 1995-98. Recipient Scholastic Achievement award Bur. Nat. Affairs. Mem. Order of Coif, Phi Beta Delta, Omicron Delta Kappa. Private international, Public international, Natural resources. Home: 3129 Southfork Rd Cody WY 82414-8009 Office: Old Post Office Cody WY 82414

JOHNSON, WALTER FRANK, JR. lawyer; b. Georgiana, Ala., 1945; s. Walter F. and Marjorie Ellen (Carnathan) J.; m. Emily Waldrep, Nov. 23, 1969; children: Brian W., Stacey E. BSBA, Suburn U., 1968; JD, Samford U., 1973. Bar: Ala. 1973, Ga. 1974. Acct. Union Camp Corp., 1968-70; assoc. Hatcher, Meyerson, Oxford and Irvin, Atlanta, 1973-74, Thompson and Redmond, Columbus, Ga., 1974-78, pvt. practice, 1978—. Asst. pub. defender, Columbus, 1978. Mem. ABA, Ala. State Bar, State Bar Ga., Columbus Lawyers Club. Methodist. Bankruptcy, Probate. Home: 3235 Flint Dr Columbus GA 31907-2029 Office: PO Box 6507 3006 University Ave Columbus GA 31907-2106 E-mail: wfjattorney@earthlink.net

JOHNSON, WARREN CHARLES, retired lawyer; b. Wahoo, Nebr., Mar. 22, 1920; s. Wilmer G. and Florence E. (Slama) J.; children: Warren, Lucinda, Lauri, Genevieve. BSBA with high distinction; JD cum laude, U. Nebr. Bar: Nebr. 1948, U.S. Dist. Ct. Nebr. 1948. Assoc. Cline Williams Wright Johnson & Oldfather, Lincoln, Nebr., 1948-50, ptnr., 1951-2000; ret., 2000. Bd. dirs. First Nat. Bank, Lincoln, First Nat. Bank, Fairbury, Nebr., Farmers & Traders Bank, Waco, Nebr., First Nat. Bank, Bradshaw, Nebr., Blue River Bank, McCool Junction, Nebr. Vice-chmn. U. Nebr. Found., 1984-85; pres. S.W. Cmty. Ctr., Lincoln, 1963-67, Nebr. Conf. United Ch. of Christ, 1962-68. Maj. USAAF, 1942-46; PTO. Mem. ABA, Nebr. Bar Assn., Lincoln Bar Assn. (pres. 1966), Masons, Shriners. Republican. Congregationalist. Banking, General corporate, Securities. Home: 6801 Hickory Crest Rd Lincoln NE 68516-2458

JOHNSON, WILLIAM ASHTON, retired lawyer; b. St. Louis, June 26, 1933; s. William Stuart and Adele (Balmer) J.; m. Anne Chartrand, Nov. 11, 1961; children: Mark, Anthony, Jocelyn, Jennifer. BA, St. Louis U., 1955, JD, 1957; postdoctoral, Northwestern U., 1969. Bar: Mo. 1957. Asst. sec. Mercantile Bank NA, St. Louis, 1969-73, asst. trust officer, 1973-76, trust officer, 1976-78, asst. v.p., 1978-83, v.p., 1983-86; sr. atty. trust Mercantile Bancorporation Inc., 1996-2000; ret., 2000. Author St. Louis U. Law Rev., 1971. Served with U.S. Army, 1957-59. Mem. Alpha Sigma Nu. Democrat. Roman Catholic. Home: 4732 Prague Ave Saint Louis MO 63109-2708

JOHNSTON, ALAN COPE, lawyer; b. Evanston, Ill., Mar. 4, 1946; S. Alan Rogers and Eleanor Cope (Smith) J.; m. Kathryn Elizabeth Edwards, June 21, 1969; 1 child, Eliza. BA, Yale U., 1968; JD, Harvard U., 1975. BAR: Calif. 1975, D.C. 1979, u.S. Dist. Ct. (no., ea., ctrl. and so. dists.) Calif., U.S. Dist. Ct. D.C., U.S. Ct. Appeals (9th fed. and D.C. cirs.)., U.S. Supreme Ct. Assoc. Morrison & Foerster, San Francisco, 1975-79, Washington, 1979-81, ptnr. San Francisco, 1981-85, Palo Alto, Calif., 1986—. Lt. USNR, 1969-72. Avocations: sailing, reading. General civil litigation, Intellectual property. Office: Morrison & Foerster 755 Page Mill Rd Palo Alto CA 94304-1018 E-mail: acjohnston@mofo.com

JOHNSTON, COYT RANDAL, lawyer, poet; b. Wheeler, Tex., Nov. 17, 1946; s. Coyt Edward Johnston and Valrea Joyce (Hirons) Chase; m. Sandra Susan Ramos, Sept. 4, 1970 (div. Aug. 1993). BA, Brigham Young U., 1971; JD with honors, U. Tex., 1974. Bar: Tex. 1974. Assoc. Baker & Botts, Houston, 1974-78, Hewett, Johnson, Swanson & Barbee, Dallas, 1979-81; owner Coyt Randal Johnston, 1981-82; atty. Davenport & Brown, 1982-84; shareholder Johnston & Budner, 1984-97; founder, shareholder Johnston & Tobey, 1997—. Mem. Tex. Bd. Legal Specialization, Austin, 1980-83, mem. personal injury adv. commn., 1990—. Author poems. Avocations: water skiing, poetry and song writing, guitar playing. General civil litigation, Personal injury, Professional liability. Office: Johnston & Tobey PC 900 Jackson St Ste 710 Dallas TX 75202-4437

JOHNSTON, DAVID FREDERICK, lawyer; b. Tiffin, Ohio, Sept. 9, 1943; s. Frederick Walter and Aleta Marguerite (Ruehle) J.; m. Ona Lee Graham, June 18, 1966; children: Matthew, Rebecca, Elisabeth, Benjamin. BA in Chemistry, Oreg. State U., 1965; JD, Golden Gate U., 1971. Bar: Calif. 1972, oreg. 1973, U.S. Ct. Mil. Appeals 1974, U.S. Supreme Ct. 1983. Commd. officer U.S. Coast Guard, 1965; sea duty U.S. Coast Guard Cutter Magnolia, 1966-67; staff atty. U.S. Coast Guard, 1971-79; dept.

chief U.S. Coast Guard Marine Safety Office, Norfolk, Va., 1979-82; appeal decision supr. U.S. Coast Guard Hdqrs., Washington, 1982-85; sole practice Portland, Oreg., 1985-86; workers compensation ins. atty. EBI Ins., 1986-95. Author: Suspension and REvocation of Mariner's Licenses, Certificates and Documents, 1984. Elder, Presbyn. Ch., Green Acres Ch., Portsmouth, Va., 1979, Multnomah Ch., Portland, 1986; com. chmn. Clermont Sch., Fairfax County, Va., 1983, bd. co-chair, 1996-99, land use chair, Collins View Neighborhood Assn., Portland, 1999— Mem. Oreg. State Bar, Phi Kappa Phi, Phi Lambda Upsilon. Home and Office: 0550 SW Palatine Hill Rd Portland OR 97219-7830

JOHNSTON, JOCELYN STANWELL, paralegal; b. Evanston, Ill., Feb. 16, 1954; d. Gerald and Dorothy Jeanne (Schoenfield) Stanwell; m. Thomas Patrick Johnston, Nov. 28, 1986. BA, U. Minn., 1981; cert., Phila. Inst. Paralegal Tng., Phila., 1986. Paralegal Fredrikson & Byron PA, Mpls., 1981-84, Reed, Smith, Shaw and McClay, Phila., 1984-85, McCausland, Keen & Buckman, PC, Radnor, Pa., 1985-86, Harris, Guenzel, Meier & Nichols, PC, Ann Arbor, Mich., 1986-87, Conner & Bentley, PC, Ann Arbor, 1987-88, Cichocki & Armstrong, Ltd., Oak Park, Ill., 1988-90, Bishop and Bishop, Oak Brook, 1994-95, Martin, Breen & Merrick, Oak Park, 1994-95, Saitlin, Patzik, Frank & Samotny, Ltd., Chgo., 1995, Bryson R. Cloon, Esquire, Leawood, Kans., 1996—. Mem. Kans. Bar Assn. Democrat. Home: 14501 Marty St Overland Park KS 66223-2300 Office: Bryson R Cloon Esquire 11350 Tomahawk Creek Pkwy Leawood KS 66211-2670 E-mail: johnstont@umkc.edu

JOHNSTON, JOHN STEVEN, lawyer; b. Kansas City, Mo., Dec. 5, 1948; s. Herschel Wayne and Dixie June J.; m. Deb Neal, Feb. 19, 1977; children: Benjamin, Will. BA in Math., William Jewell Coll., 1970; MA in Psychology, U. Mo., 1975, JD, 1980; PhD in Clin. Psychology, U. Minn., 1977. Bar: Mo., 1980, U.S. Dist. Ct. Kans., 1999. Assoc. Linde, Thomson, Fairchild, Langworthy & Kohn, Kansas City, 1980-81, Shook, Hardy & Bacon LLP, Kansas City, 1981-85, ptnr., 1986—, chmn. tort law sect., 1998—. Co-author: Missouri Methods of Practice-Litigation Guide, 1991; contbr. articles to profl. jours. Bd. dirs., exec. com. Big Brothers and Big Sisters, Kansas City, 1989—; bd. dirs. Ozanam Home for Boys, Kansas City, 1990—. Recipient Outstanding Contbn. to Cmty Health award S. Kansas City Mental Health Resource Network, 1975, Michael Coburn award for cmty. svc. Legal Aid of We. Mo., 1999; named to William Jewell Coll. Hall of Fame, 1999. Mem. Kansas City Met. Bar Found. (chmn. civil law and procedure com. 1991, bd. dirs./exec. com. 1995—, chair lawyers for children com. 1998—, pres. 1998, v.p. 2000—, Seventh Annual Pres. award for bar svc. 1993), Mo. Bar Assn. (bd. govs. 1999—), Kansas City Met. Bar Assn. (pres. 1998), Met. Ross T. Roberts Inn of Ct. (master 1995—). General civil litigation. Home: 25004 Timberlake Trl Greenwood MO 64034 Office: Shook Hardy & Bacon LLP 1200 Main St Kansas City MO 64105 Fax: 816-421-4066. E-mail: jjohnston@shb.com

JOHNSTON, LOGAN TRUAX, III, lawyer; b. New Haven, Dec. 9, 1947; s. Logan Truax Jr. and Elizabeth (Josey) J.; m. Celeste Linguere; children: Charlotte Hathaway, Logan Truax IV, Owen Conrad, Oritse J., Gboyega P. BA, Yale U., 1969; JD, Harvard U., 1973. Bar: Ill. 1973, Ariz. 1984, U.S. Ct. Appeals (2d cir.) 1982, U.S. Ct. Appeals (7th cir.) 1973, U.S. Ct. Appeals (9th cir.) 1986, U.S. Ct. Appeals (fed. cir.) 1990, U.S. Supreme Ct. 1991. Assoc. Winston & Strawn, Chgo., 1973-79, ptnr., 1979-83, Phoenix, 1983-89; mng. ptnr. Johnston Maynard Grant & Parker, 1989-97, Johnston & Kelly, Phoenix, 1997—. Spl. asst. state's atty. Du Page County, Ill., Wheaton, 1976-77; cons. Community Legal Svcs., Phoenix, 1984—. Contbg author: Arizona Appellate Handvook, Vol. III. Served with U.S. Army N.G., 1970-76. Mem. ABA, Maricopa County Bar Found., Maricopa County Bar Assn., Ariz. Bar Found., Ariz. State Bar Assn., Phoenis Heroes Endowment Fund. Presbyterian. Avocations: books, movies, golf, hiking, travel. Administrative and regulatory, General civil litigation, Health. Office: Johnston & Dodd PLC 1 N 1st St Phoenix AZ 85004-2357

JOHNSTON, NEIL CHUNN, lawyer; b. Mobile, Ala., Feb. 23, 1953; s. Vivian Gaines and Sara Niel (Chunn) J.; m. Ashley Monroe Hocklander, Dec. 20, 1980; children: Katie, Neil Jr. BA, Southwestern at Memphis (name changed to Rhodes Coll.), 1975; JD, U. Ala., 1978. Atty. Hand, Arendall L.L.C., Mobile, Ala., 1978—. Com. mem. Ala. Law Inst. Com., Tuscaloosa, Ala., 1990; mem. Gov.'s Wetland Mitigation Task Force, 1994. Contbr. articles to profl. jours. Pres. Project CATE Found, Inc., Mobile, 1987—; trustee Nature Conservancy, Ala., 1990-96; mem. Gov.'s Wetland Mitigation Banking Task Force, 1994-96; bd. dirs. Am. Jr. Miss Program, 1996—, Ala. Coastal Fedn. Recipient Ala. Gov.'s award-Water Conservationist, Ala. Wildlife Fedn., 1987, EPA Region IV Wetlands Recognition award, 2000. Mem. ABA (vice-chair forestry com. sect. environment, energy, resc.), Ala. State Bar Assn. (chmn. environ. law sect. 1984-91, corp. banking, bus. law sect. 1993, Mobile Bar Assn., Ala. Forestry Assn., Ala. Law Inst. (mem. com. 1990), Rotary (pres. Mobile 1996-97). Contracts commercial, Environmental, Real property. Office: Hand Arendall LLC 3000 FNB Bldg Royal St Mobile AL 36602

JOHNSTON, OSCAR BLACK, III, lawyer; b. Tulsa, Oct. 1, 1941; s. Oscar Black Jr. and Carol (VanDerwiele) J.; m. Ruth Archdeacon Darrough; children: Eric Oscar, David Darrough. BBA, Baylor U., 1963; JD, U. Tulsa, 1966. Bar: Okla. 1966, U.S. Dist. Ct. (no., ea., we. dists.) Okla., U.S. Ct. Claims, U.S. Ct. Appeals (10th cir.), U.S. Supreme Ct. Asst. U.S. attorney U.S. Dist. Ct. (we. dist.) Okla., 1970-76; ptnr. Logan & Lowry, L.L.P., Vinita, Okla., 1979—. Assoc. editor Tulsa Law Review, 1964-66. Presiding judge divsn. 54 Okla. Temp. Ct. Appeals, 1980-81, judge divsn. XIV, 1991-93; presiding judge panel VI Lawyer-Staffed Ct. Appeals, 1992. Capt. JAGC, U.S. Army, 1966-70. Fellow Am. Bar Found., Okla. Bar Found. (trustee 1988-96, pres. 1995); mem. ABA (sects. litigation, family law and criminal), Fed. Bar Assn. (pres. Oklahoma City chpt. 1975), Craig County Bar Assn. (pres. 1986-88), Okla. Bar Assn. (adminstrn. of justice, bench and bar coms., assoc. editor, mem. bd. editors Okla. Bar Jour. 2000—), Okla. Trial Lawyers Assn., Rotary (pres. Vinita 1983-84), Phi Alpha Delta. Republican. Methodist. General civil litigation, Criminal, Family and matrimonial. Office: Logan & Lowry PO Box 558 Vinita OK 74301-0558 Home: 116 Westwood Ave Vinita OK 74301-2703

JOHNSTON, THOMAS E. prosecutor; BA, JD, W.Va. U. Atty. Schrader, Byrd and Companion, 1994—96; assoc. Flaherty, Sensabaugh and Bonasso, 1996—98; ptnr. Bailey, Riley, Buch and Harmon, Wheeling, W.Va., 1998—2001; U.S. atty. No. Dist. W.Va. U.S. Dept. Justice, 2001—. Office: PO Box 591 Wheeling WV 26003-0011*

JOHNSTON, WILLIAM DAVID, lawyer; b. Aberdeen, Md., Jan. 31, 1957; s. David Irvine and Nancy (Smith) J.; m. Mary Teresa Miller, May 29, 1983; children: Ellen Christine, Amy Elizabeth. AB, Colgate U., 1979; JD, Washington and Lee U., 1982. Bar: Del. 1982, U.S. Dist. Ct. Del. 1983, U.S. Ct. Appeals (3rd cir.) 1991, U.S. Supreme Ct. 1991. Judicial law clk. to chief justice Daniel L. Herrmann Del. Supreme Ct., Wilmington, 1982-83; assoc. Potter, Anderson and Corroon, 1983-85, Young, Conaway, Stargatt and Taylor, Wilmington, 1985-89, ptnr., 1990—. Contbr. articles to profl. jours. Mem. choir, adminstrv. bd. Aldersgate United Meth. Ch., Wilmington, 1970—, chmn. religion and race commn., 1987-89; com. chmn. Boy Scouts of U.S. troop 67, 1982-85, Del. Human Relations Commn., 1986—. Best Brief Worldwide award Am. Soc. Internat. Law, Washington, 1980. Mem. ABA, Internat. Bar Assn., Am. Judicature Soc., Del. State Bar Assn. (award for pub. svc. 1991, pres.-elect 2000-2001, pres. 2001-), Sigma Chi (pres. Colgate U. chpt. 1984-88), Phi Delta Phi, Univ. and Whist Club (bd. govs. 1990—), Rodney Square (Wilmington) Club, Brandywine Country Club, Lincoln (Del.) Club. Methodist. Avocations: running, raquetball, reading, travel, golf. Federal civil litigation, State civil litigation, General corporate. Office: Young Conaway Stargatt and Taylor Rodney Sq N PO Box 391 Wilmington DE 19899-0391*

JOHNSTONE, DEBORAH BLACKMON, lawyer; b. Birmingham, Ala., Jan. 26, 1953; d. T.C. Blackmon and Joan (Thompson) Ryals; m. David Johnstone, July 26, 1968 (div. 1976); children: Pamela, Robin. AS, Jefferson Sch. Nursing, Birmingham, 1976; BA, Birmingham-So. Coll., 1982; JD, Birmingham Law Sch., 1986. Bar: Ala. 1986. Nurse Carraway Med. Ctr., Birmingham, 1976-86; assoc. Emond & Vines, Attys., 1986-88; atty., med.-legal cons. Am. Internat. Group, Burleson, Tex., 1988-90; pvt. practice, 1990—. Founder Burleson Animal Soc., 1998—, pres., 2000—. Mem. ABA, ATLA, ACLU, AAAS, Ala. Trial Lawyers, Ala. State Bar, Tex. Bd. Nurse Examiners, Ala. Bd. Nursing, Consumers Union. Democrat. Roman Catholic. Avocations: history, golf, writing non-fiction, jewelry design. Health, Personal injury, Product liability. Office: 849 E Renfro St Burleson TX 76028-5019 E-mail: deborah@deborahjohnstone.com

JOHNSTONE, DOUGLAS INGE, judge; b. Mobile, Ala., Nov. 15, 1941; s. Harry Inge and Kathleen (Yerger) J.; m. Mary Jayne Baynes (div.); 1 child, Francis Inge. BA, Rice U., 1963; JD, Tulane U., 1966. Bar: Ala. 1966, U.S. Dist. Ct. Ala. 1966, U.S. Ct. Appeals (5th cir.) 1968, U.S. Supreme Ct. 1969. Pvt. practice, Mobile, 1966-84; dist. judge Ala. Dist. Ct., 1984-85, presiding dist. judge, 1985, cir. judge, 1985-99; justice Supreme Ct. Ala., Montgomery, 1999—. Rep. State of Ala., 1974-78. MKem. Jaycees, Mobile, Mobile County Wildlife; bd. advisors Salvation Army, Mobile, 1989—; bd. dirs. Mental Health Assn., Mobile, 1990-92. Capt. U.S. Army, 1963-72. Elected Outstanding Freshman Rep., Capital Prses Corps., 1975; recipient Meritorious Svc. award Mobile County Bd. of Health, 1968, Humanitarian Svc. award Mobile Cerebral Palsy Assn., 1973. Mem. ABA, Am. Judges Assn., Ala. Bar Assn., Mobile Bar Assn., Internat. Acad. Trial Judges. Democrat. Episcopalian. Home: 205 Government St Ste 4500 Mobile AL 36644-0001 Office: Supreme Ct of Ala 300 Dexter Ave Montgomery AL 36104-3741

JOHNSTONE, IRVINE BLAKELEY, III, lawyer; b. Newark, Dec. 21, 1948; s. Irvine Blakeley Jr. and Ruth (Morton) J.; m. Phyllis Nevins, Oct. 16, 1983. BA with honors, Lehigh U., 1972; JD, Duke U., 1975. Bar: N.J. 1975, U.S. Dist. Ct. N.J. 1975, U.S. Ct. Appeals (3d cir.) 1979, N.Y. 1981; cert. civil trial adv. Nat. Bd. Trial Advocacy. Assoc. Riker, Danzig, Scherer & DeBevoise, Newark, 1975-76, Shanley & Fisher, Newark, 1976-80; ptnr. Johnstone, Skok, Loughlin & Lane, Westfield, N.J., 1980—. Mem. bd. of govs. Blair Acad., 1978-84; atty. Rahway Lifers Group (N.J.) State Prison, 1980-85, Planning Bd., Clark, N.J., 1981-82, Bd. of Adjustment, Clark, 1982-84. Mem. ABA, ATLA, Nat. Bd. Trial Advocacy (civil trial advocate), N.J. Bar Assn., Union County Bar Assn., Def. Rsch. Inst., Union County Arbitration Bd. (cert. civil trial atty. N.J. Supreme Ct.), N.J. Trial Lawyers Assn., R.J. Hughes Am. Inns of Ct. (master 1995—). Republican. Presbyterian. Club: Baltusrol (Springfield, N.J.). Avocations: flying, golf, sports. General civil litigation, General corporate, Personal injury. Home: 5 Bartles Rd Lebanon NJ 08833-4606 E-mail: ibj@jsll-lawfirm.com, attys@jsll-lawfirm.com

JOHNSTONE, MARTIN E. state supreme court justice; BA, Western Ky. U.; JD, U. Louisville. Bar: Ky. Judge 3d Magisterial Dist., Ky., 1976-78; dist. judge Jefferson County, 1978-83; chief judge, 1987-93; circuit judge, 1985-87; justice Ky. Ct. Appeals, 1993-96, chief judge pro tem, 1996; justice Ky. Supreme Ct., 1996—, dep. chief justice, 1998—. Recipient Outstanding Trial Judge award Ky. Acad. Trial Attys., 1991. Mem. Louisville Bar Assn. (Judge of Yr. 1981). Office: State Capitol Capitol Bldg Rm 201 700 Capitol Ave Frankfort KY 40601-3410*

JOHNSTONE, PHILIP MACLAREN, lawyer; b. Sharon, Conn., Mar. 24, 1961; s. Rodney Stuart and Frances Louise (Davis) J.; m. Elizabeth Laird McGovern, Sept. 10, 1988. BA in Econs. magna cum laude, Duke U., 1983; JD, U. Pa., 1986. Bar: Mass. 1986, Conn. 1987, U.S. Dist. Ct. Conn. 1988, R.I. 1998. Ptnr. Waller, Smith & Palmer, P.C., New London, Conn., 1997—. Bd. dirs. J Boats, Inc., Newport, R.I., 1987—. Trustee Denison Pequotsepos Nature Ctr., Mystic, Conn., 1998—, Pine Point Sch., Stonington, Conn., 2000—. Mem. ABA, Mass. Bar Assn., Conn. Bar Assn., R.I. Bar Assn. Republican. Episcopalian. Avocations: tennis, golf. General corporate, Estate planning, Real property. Home: 17 Cliff St Stonington CT 06378-1249 Office: Waller Smith and Palmer PC 52 Eugene Oneill Dr New London CT 06320-6324 E-mail: pmjohnstone@wallersmithpalmer.com

JOINER, CHARLES WYCLIFFE, judge; b. Maquoketa, Iowa, Feb. 14, 1916; s. Melvin William and Mary (von Schrader) J.; m. Ann Martin, Sept. 29, 1939; children: Charles Wycliffe, Nancy Caroline, Richard Martin. BA, U. Iowa, 1937, JD, 1939. Bar: Iowa 1939, Mich. 1947. With firm Miller, Huebner & Miller, Des Moines, 1939-47; part-time lectr. Des Moines Coll. Law, 1940-41; faculty U. Mich. Law, 1947-68, assoc. dean, 1960-65, acting dean, 1964-65; dean Wayne State U. Law Sch., Detroit, 1968-72; U.S. dist. judge, sr. judge, 1972—. Assoc. dir. Preparatory Commn. Mich. Constl. Conv., 1961, co-dir. research and drafting com., 1961-62; civil rules adv. com. U.S. Jud. Conf. Com. Rules Practice and Procedure, 1959-70, evidence rules adv. com., 1965-70; rep. Mich. Atty. Gens. Com. Ct. Congestion, 1959-60 Author: Trials and Appeals, 1957, Civil Justice and the Jury, 1962, Trial and Appellate Practice, 1968; Co-author: Introduction to Civil Procedures, 1949, Jurisdiction and Judgments, 1953, (with Delmar Karten) Trials and Appeals, 1971. Mem. charter rev. com. Ann Arbor Citizens Coun.cil, 1959-61; mem. Mich. Commn. Uniform State Laws, 1963-97; Mem. Ann Arbor City Coun.cil, 1955-59. Served tot lt. USAAF, 1942-45. Fellow Am. Bar Found. (chmn. 1977-78); mem. ABA (chmn. com. specialization 1952-56, spl. com. uniform evidence rules fed. cts. 1959-64, adv. bd. jour. 1961-67, spl. com. on specialization 1966-69, ethics com. 1961-70, council mem. sect. individual rights and responsibilities 1967-77, chairperson 1976-77), State Bar Mich. (pres. 1970-71, chmn. joint com. Mich. procedural revision 1956-62, commr. 1964—), Am. Judicature Soc. (chmn. publs. com. 1959-62), Am. Law Student Assn. (bd. govs.), Am. Law Inst., Scribes (pres. 1963-64)

JOLLES, JANET K. PILLING, lawyer; b. Akron, Ohio, Sept. 5, 1951; d. Paul and Marjorie (Logue) Kavanaugh; m. Martin Jolles, Mar. 6, 1987; children: Madeleine Sloan Langdon Jolles, Jameson Samuel Rhys Jolles. BA, Ohio Wesleyan U., 1973; JD, U. Mo., 1976; LLM, Villanova U., 1985. Bar: Pa. 1976, U.S. Tax Ct. 1976, U.S. Dist. Ct. (ea. dist.) Pa. 1976, Ohio 1996. Atty. Schnader, Harrison, Segal & Lewis, Phila., 1976-83; gen. counsel Kistler-Tiffany Cos., Wayne, Pa., 1983-95; lawyer Janet Kavanaugh Pilling Jolles & Assocs., Berea, Ohio, 1996-99; v.p. First Union Trust Co., Wilmington, Del., 1999—. Mem. Estate Planning Coun. Del., Wilmington Tax Group, Phila. Estate Planning Coun., Estate Planning Coun. Cleve., Estate Planning Coun. Del. Mem. ABA, Ohio State Bar Assn., Cleve. Bar Assn., Cuyahoga County Bar Assn., Phila. Bar Assn. (probate sect., tax sect.), Pa. Bar Assn., Berea Women's League, Phi Beta Kappa, Phi Delta Phi. Estate planning, Probate, Estate taxation. Office: 3 Beaver Valley 4th Fl Wilmington DE 19803 E-mail: janet.jolles1@firstunion.com, jjolleslaw@aol.com

JOLLEY, WILLIAM ANDREW, judge; b. Twin Falls, Idaho, Aug. 28, 1918; s. Jervis Joseph and Clara Jane (Shore) J.; m. Cleo Ann Briles, Apr. 1942; children: Leilani Louise, Patricia Ann, Ginger Marion, Jeanne Elizabeth. Student, Nat. Jud. Coll., Reno, 1984-90; State Justice Inst., Nat. Jud. Coll., 1991-92. Engr. refrigeration svcs. self-employed, various locations, 1945-85; mcpl. judge Willamina, Oreg., 1983—. Served with USN, 1936-41, USCG, 1942-43. Named Citizen of Yr., C. of C., Sheridan, Oreg., 1986. Mem. ABA (assoc.), Oreg. Mcpl. Judges Assn. (assoc., bd. mem. 1987-97, editor emeritus bench notes 1995), VFW, Am. Legion, Elks, Kiwanis (lt. gov. 1990-91, treas.-pres. 1978-89). Republican. Avocations: reading, writing, travel, politics, looking on the bright side. Home: PO Box 169 7765 Wheatland Rd N Salem OR 97303-3458

JOLLY, E. GRADY, federal judge; b. 1937; BA, U. Miss., 1959, LLB, 1962. Trial atty. NLRB, Winston-Salem, N.C., 1962-64; asst. U.S. atty. No. Dist. Miss., 1964-67; trial atty. Dept. Justice Tax Div., Washington, 1967-69; pvt. practice Jolly, Miller & Milam, Jackson, Miss., 1969-82; judge U.S. Ct. Appeals (5th cir.), 1982—. Office: US Ct Appeals James O Eastland Courthouse 245 E Capitol St Ste 202 Jackson MS 39201-2414*

JONES, AIDAN DREXEL, lawyer; b. Wilmington, Del., Dec. 17, 1945; s. Richard Leonard and Dorothy Drexel (Walsh) J.; m. Kathleen Dellert, Aug. 19, 1972; 4 children. BA, Wesleyan U., 1967; JD, Georgetown U., 1974. Bar: D.C. 1975, U.S. Supreme Ct. 1984, Md. 1996. Law clk. U.S. Dist. Ct., Washington, 1974-75; assoc. Edward Greensfelder Jr. P.C., 1975-77, Haight, Gardner, Poor & Havens, Washington, 1977-83; ptnr. Finley, Kumble, Wagner, Heine, Underberg, Manley, Myerson & Casey, 1983-87, Laxalt, Washington, Perito & Dubuc, Washington, 1988-90, Washington, Perito & Dubuc, Washington, 1990-91, Graham & James, Washington, 1991-95. Contbr. articles to profl. jours. Mem. nat. alumni com. Wesleyan U., Middletown, Conn., 1987-89, 1967 class agt., 1985-92; trustee River Road Unitarian Ch., 1992-94; co-treas. Sidwell Friends Sch. Parents Assn., 1995-97, v.p., 1997-98, pres. 1998-99. Lt. USN, 1968-71. Mem. ABA (vice chmn. aviation and space law com. 1985-91). Aviation, General civil litigation, Product liability. Office: 1818 N St NW Ste 700 Washington DC 20036-2477

JONES, ALLEN, JR. lawyer; b. Washington, May 24, 1930; s. Allen Sr. and Gladys May (Bunch) J.; m. Gloria Jean Clyma, Nov. 29, 1952 (div. June 1989); children: Victoria, Jennifer, Matthew; m. Cheryl B. Crook, Aug. 11, 1991. BA, Mich. State U., 1952; JD, Georgetown U., 1957. Bar: D.C. 1957, U.S. Supreme Ct. 1961, Md. 1962. Sales rep. Ethyl Corp., Salt Lake City, 1952; sr. atty. Wilkes Artis Chartered, Washington, 1957-2000; of counsel Hamilton and Hamilton, LLP, 2001—. Mem. exec. com., treas. Coun. for Ct. Excellence, Washington, 1988-98; mem. D.C. study devel. coun. Mich. State U., 1999—. Mem. Civil Delay Reduction Task Force, Washington, 1988-92; co-founder Washington Lawyers Against Drugs, 1986-87; mediator Superior Ct. of D.C., 1986—; vice chmn. Children's Hosp. Found., Washington, 1988-92; chmn. Children's Hosp. Telethon, Washington, 1988-89; v.p. Rotary Found. Washington, 2001. Mem. ABA (Ho. of Dels. D.C. chpt. 1986-87), D.C. Bar Assn. (pres. 1986-87, pres. rsch. found. 1984-85), The Barristers (pres. 1982-83), Lawyers Club, Jud. Conf. of D.C., Rotary Club Washington (pres.-elect 1997, pres. 1998-99). Republican. Lutheran. Avocations: golf, biking, hiking. General civil litigation, General corporate, General practice. Home: 703 Penny Ln Stevensville MD 21666-3731 Office: Hamilton and Hamilton LLP Ste 1100 1775 Pennsylvania Ave NW Washington DC 20006-4605 E-mail: aj@hamiltonlaw.com

JONES, B. TODD, lawyer, former prosecutor; s. Paul and Sylvia Jones. Grad., Macalester Coll., 1979; JD, U. Minn., 1983. Mng. ptnr. Greene Espel, Mpls., 1996—97; asst. U.S. atty. for Minn., 1997—98; U.S. atty. Minn. dist. U.S. Dept. Justice, 1998—2001; ptnr. Robins, Kaplan, Miller & Ciresi, Mpls., 2001—. With USMC. Office: Robins Kaplan Miller & Ciresi 2800 LaSalle Plaza 800 LaSalle Ave Minneapolis MN 55402*

JONES, C. PAUL, lawyer, educator; b. Grand Forks, N.D., Jan. 7, 1927; s. Walter M. and Sophie J. (Thorton) J.; m. Helen M. Fredel, Sept. 7, 1957; children— Katherine, Sara H. BBA, JD, U. Minn., 1950; LLM, William Mitchell Coll. of Law, 1955. Assoc. Lewis, Hammer, Heaney, Weyl & Halverson, Duluth, Minn., 1950-51; asst., chief dep. Hennepin County Atty., Mpls., 1952-58; asst. U.S. atty. U.S. Atty.'s Office, St. Paul, 1959-60; assoc. Maun & Hazel, 1960-61; ptnr. Dorfman, Rudquist, Jones, & Ramstead, Mpls., 1961-65; state pub. defender Minn. State Pub. Defender's Office, 1966-90. Adj. prof. law William Mitchell Coll. of Law, St. Paul, 1953-70, prof. law, 1970—, assoc. dean for acad. affairs, 1991-95; adj. prof. U. Minn., Mpls., 1970-90; mem. adv. com. on rules of criminal procedure Minn. Supreme Ct., 1970—. Author: Criminal Procedure from Police Detention to Final Disposition, 1981; Jones on Minnesota Criminal Procedure, 1955, 64, 70, 75; Minnesota Police Law Manual, 1955, 67, 70, 76 Mem. Minn. Gov.'s Crime Commn., St. Paul, 1970s, Minn. Fair Trial-Free Press Assn., Mpls., 1970s, Citizens League, Mpls., 1955—, Mpls. Aquatennial Assn., Mpls., 1955-60, Minn. Coun. on Crime and Justice, 1991—. Recipient Reginald Heber Smith award Nat. Legal Aid and Defender Assn., 1969 Fellow Am. Coll. Trial Lawyers; mem. Am. Bd. Trial Advs., ABA, Minn. State Bar Assn., Hennepin County Bar Assn., Ramsey County Bar Assn., Nat. Legal Aid & Defender Assn. Democrat. Lutheran. Clubs: Suburban Gyro of Mpls., Mpls. Athletic. Lodge: Rotary. Avocations: fishing; hunting; golfing; desert watching. Home: 5501 Dewey Hill Rd Edina MN 55439-1906 Office: William Mitchell Coll Law 875 Summit Ave Saint Paul MN 55105-3030

JONES, CHARLES E. state supreme court justice; BA, Brigham Young U., 1959; JD, Stanford U., 1962. Bar: Calif. 1963, U.S. Dist. Ct. Ariz. 1964, U.S. Ct. Appeals (9th cir.) 1963, Ariz. 1964, U.S. Ct. Appeals (10th cir.) 1974, U.S. Supreme Ct. 1979. Law clk. to Hon. Richard H. Chambers U.S. Ct. Appeals (9th cir.), 1962-63; assoc., ptnr. Jennings, Strouss & Salmon, Phoenix, 1963-96; apptd. justice Ariz. Supreme Ct., 1996, vice chief justice, 1997—. Bd. visitors Brigham Young U. Law Sch., 1973-81, chmn., 1978-81. Named Avocat du Consulat-Gen. de France, 1981—; Alumni Dist. Svc. award Brigham Young U., 1982; recipient Aaron Feuerstein award U. Ariz., 1998. Mem. ABA, State Bar Ariz., Fed. Bar Assn. (pres. Ariz. chpt. 1971-73), J. Reuben Clark Law Soc. (nat. chmn. 1994-97), Maricopa County Bar Assn., Am. Coll. Labor & Employment Lawyers, Pi Sigma Alpha. Office: Ariz Supreme Court 1501 W Washington St Phoenix AZ 85007-3222

JONES, CHRISTOPHER DON, lawyer; b. Longview, Tex., Jan. 23, 1964; s. Donald and Audrey Gale Jones; m. Michelle McCullough, Feb. 16, 1991; children: Catherine Abigail, Christopher Andrew, Michael Adam. BBA, Baylor U., 1987, JD, 1989. Bar: Tex. 1989; cert. personal injury trial law Tex. Bd. Legal Specialization. Assoc. Worsham, Forsythe, Sampels & Wooldrige, Dallas, 1989-92, Misko, Howie & Sweeney, LLP, Dallas, 1992-95, Howie & Sweeney, LLP, Dallas, 1995-96, Erskine, McMahon & Stroup, LLP, Longview, Tex., 1996-97; ptnr. Stroup & Jones, LLP, 1997-2000, Jones & Jones, LLP, Longview, 2000—. Asst. mng. editor Baylor Law Rev., 1989. Mem. Leadership Longview, 1998-99. Named Kiwanian of Yr., Kiwanis Club Dallas, 1993. Mem. ABA, Tex. Bar Assn., Tex. Trial Lawyers Assn. (sustaining). Democrat. Avocations: golf, hunting, running. Labor, Personal injury, Product liability. Office: Jones & Jones LLP 420 N Green St Ste C Longview TX 75601-6443 E-mail: cjones@joneslawyers.com

JONES, CLIFFORD ALAN, lawyer; b. Auston, Tex., Aug. 14, 1953; s. Paul Dale and Marylu (Farnum) J.; m. Lynda Lee Kaid, Jan. 31, 1972. BA in Govt., So. Ill. U., 1974; JD, U. Okla., 1977; MPhil, U. Cambridge, 1995, PhD, 1997. Bar: Okla. 1977, U.S. Dist. Ct. (we. dist.) Okla. 1978, U.S. Ct. Appeals (10th cir.) 1978, U.S. Supreme Ct. 1980, U.S. Ct. Appeals (fed. cir.) 1984, Tex. 1994. Assoc. Fagin, Hewett, Mathews & Fagin, Oklahoma City, 1977-79, 80-81; mem. firm. Bradford, Haswell, Jones, 1981-86,

Clifford A. Jones & Assocs., 1986-96. Vis. asst. prof. law Oklahoma City U., 1979-80, adj. prof. law, 1980; spl. lectr. law U. Okla., Norman, 1979, 81; temporary judge Okla. Ct. Appeals, 1982-83; vis. prof. law and bus. U. Okla., 1996-2001; lectr. Coll. Law U. Fla., 2001—. Author: Private Enforcement of Antitrust Law in the EC, UK and USA, 1999; contbr. articles to profl. jours. Mem. ABA (antitrust and litigation sect.), Assn. Trial Lawyers Am., Okla. Bar Assn. (co-editor Desk Man., antitrust sect., patent trademark adn copyright sect.), Oklahoma County Bar Assn., Internat. Bar Assn. (bus., gen. practice, energy and natural resource law sects.). Antitrust, Appellate, Constitutional. Home: 2230 NW 26th Ave Gainesville FL 32605 E-mail: jonesca@law.ufl.edu

JONES, CRAIG WARD, lawyer; b. Pitts., June 14, 1947; s. Curtis Edison and Margaret (McFarland) J.; m. Sarah Dowding; children: Laura McFarland, Rebecca Long, Nancy Harper. BA, Carleton Coll., 1969; JD, U. Pitts., 1976. Bar: Pa. 1976, U.S. Dist. Ct. (we. dist.) Pa. 1976, U.S. Ct. Appeals (3d cir.) 1981. Ptnr. Reed Smith LLP, Pitts., 1976—. Served to lt. USNR, 1969-73. Mem. Allegheny County Bar Assn. Presbyterian. Federal civil litigation, State civil litigation. Home: 208 Cornwall Dr Pittsburgh PA 15238-2639 Office: Reed Smith LLP Mellon Sq 435 6th Ave Pittsburgh PA 15219-1886

JONES, DALE EDWIN, public defender; b. Rahway, N.J., Oct. 22, 1948; s. Horatio Gates and Audrey Irma (Morgan) J.; m. Karen Anne Woodhall, June 19, 1971; children: Sharon, Michael, Stephan; m. Maria D. Noto, Aug. 2, 1987 (div. 1989); m. Joan E. DiTullio, Oct. 18, 1991; 1 child, Trevor. BA, Rutgers U., 1970, JD, 1973. Bar: N.J. 1973, U.S. Dist. Ct. N.J. 1973, U.S. Supreme Ct. 1977, N.Y. 1983. 1st asst. pub. defender Office Pub. Defender, Newark, 1974-84, dep. pub. defender in charge of capital litigation, 1984-87; asst. pub. defender Office of Pub. Defender, Trenton, N.J., 1987—. Mem. model jury charge com., N.J. Supreme Ct., 1983-88, criminal practice com., Trenton, 1983—, com. media rels., 1987-89, strategic planning com., 1996-98, rules of evidence com., 1998—. Mem. editorial bd. N.J. Lawyer. Mem. ACDL-N.J., Nat. Assn. Criminal Def. Lawyers (cert. criminal atty.), Amnesty Internat. Democrat. office e-mail: jones. Office: Pub Defender Office PO Box 850 Trenton NJ 08625-0850 E-mail: djones2411@aol.com, d@opd.state.nj.us

JONES, DAVID LEROY, lawyer, educator; b. Elkton, Md., Sept. 19, 1947; s. Alvin and Amelia (Carr) J. Student, U.S. Mcht. Marine Acad., 1965-66, Lincoln U., 1968-70; BA cum laude, U. Evansville, 1972; JD, Ind. U., 1976. Bar: Ind. 1976, U.S. Dist. Ct. (so. dist.) Ind. 1976, U.S. Ct. Appeals (7th cir.) 1983. Securities examiner Ind. Sec. State, Indpls., 1972-73; bail commr. Mcpl. Cts., Indpls., 1973-76; ct. commr. Vanderburgh Cir. Ct., Evansville, Ind., 1976-77; county council atty. Vanderburgh County, Ind., 1978-86; formerly ptnr. Frick & Powell, Evansville; formerly assoc. and ptnr. Bowers, Harrison, Kent & Miller, Evansville; ptnr. Jones & Wallace, Evansville, 1987-90; prin. David L. Jones & Assocs., Evansville, 1990—; instr. Am. Inst. Banking, U. Evansville, 1979-85. Atty. Evansville-Vanderburgh Visitors and Conv. Commn., Evansville, 1978-80; bd. dirs. Wish Upon a Star Inc., 1985-86; bd. dirs., judge advocate Vanderburgh County Vet.'s Coun., VFW Post 1114, 1991—, judge adv., 1994—; treas. Vanderburgh County Dem. Ctrl. Com., 1991-92; mem. Evansville YMCA; mem. faculty adv. com. Ind. Vocat. Tech. Coll., 1992—. Served with USNR, 1965-66, USMC, 1966-68, Vietnam. Recipient Interfaith Inter-race award B'nai Brith, 1970, Densmore award Ind. Fedn. for Blind, 1986; named one of Outstanding Young Men in Am., 1973, Boss of Yr. Evansville Legal Secretaries, 1986-87. Mem. Ind. Bar Assn., Evansville Bar Assn., Nat. Fedn. for Blind. Democrat. Mem. United Ch. of Christ. Clubs: U. Evansville Tip-Off (bd. dirs. 1984-85). Home: PO Box 1065 Evansville IN 47706-1065 Office: PO Box 1065 Evansville IN 47706-1065

JONES, DAVID STANLEY, lawyer; b. Columbus, Ohio, July 16, 1948; s. Herbert Morton and Gertrude Olivia (McKeon) J.; m. Mary Elizabeth Lyman, July 8, 1972; children— Colin David, Brian Christopher, Scott Lyman, Megan Elizabeth. B.B.A., U. Notre Dame, 1970; J.D., U. Houston, 1976. Bar: Tex. 1976, U.S. Dist. Ct. (no. dist.) Tex. 1979, (ea. and we. dists.) Tex. 1980, U.S. Ct. Appeals (5th and 11th cirs.) 1981, U.S. Supreme Ct. 1983. trial atty. U.S. Dept. Labor, Office Solicitor, Dallas, 1978-80 ; ptnr. Baldwin, Gilliland & Jones, Dallas, 1984-88; pvt. practice, Dallas, 1988—. Editor U. Houston Law Rev., 1975-76. Mem. State Bar Assn. Tex. (labor law specialist Tex. Bd. Legal Specialization, 1981, author and editor Tex. Practice Guide 1983), ABA (contbr. labor law sect. ann. report 1981-82, 84-88), Fed. Bar Assn. Dallas (pres. elect 1987-88, pres. 1988-89), Dallas Bar Assn., Phi Delta Phi. Roman Catholic. Federal civil litigation, State civil litigation, Labor. Home: 3072 Ponder Dr Dallas TX 75229-5860 Office: PO Box 31 Dallas TX 75221-0031

JONES, DOUGLAS W. lawyer; b. Fort Lauderdale, Fla., 1948; AB, Princeton U., 1970; JD, Harvard U., 1973. Bar: N.Y. 1974. Mem. Milbank, Tweed, Hadley & McCloy LLP, N.Y.C. Mem. ABA, Assn. of the Bar of the City of N.Y. General corporate, Private international, Securities. Office: Milbank Tweed Hadley & McCloy LLP 1 Chase Manhattan Plz Fl 47 New York NY 10005-1413

JONES, E. STEWART, JR. lawyer; b. Troy, N.Y., Dec. 4, 1941; s. E. Stewart and Louise (Farley) J.; m. Constance M., Dec. 28, 1968; children: Christopher, Brady, Erin. BA, Williams Coll., 1963; JD, Albany Law Sch., 1966. Bar: N.Y. 1966, U.S. Dist. Ct. (no. dist.) N.Y. 1966, U.S. Dist. Ct. (so. and ea. dist.) N.Y. 1994, U.S. Dist. Ct. (we. dist.) N.Y. 1987, U.S. Claims Ct. 1991, U.S. Ct. Appeals (2d cir.) 1976, U.S. Supreme Ct. 1976. Asst. dist. atty. Rensselaer County (N.Y.), 1968-70, spl. prosecutor, 1974; ptnr. E. Stewart Jones, Troy, 1974—. Lectr. in field; mem. com. on profl. standards of 3d jud. dept. State of N.Y., 1977-80, mem. 3d jud. screening com., Albany County; mem. merit selection panel for selection and appointment of U.S. magistrate for No. Dist. N.Y., 1981, 91; bd. dirs. Univ. Found. at Albany, trustee Troy Savs. Bank. Contbr. numerous articles to profl. jours. Trustee The Albany Acad., Albany Law Sch.; active Nat. Alumni Coun. Albany Law Sch. With USNG. Fellow: Am. Bar Found., Am. Inns. of Ct., Internat. Acad. Trial Lawyers, Am. Bd. Trial Lawyers, Am. Coll. Trial Lawyers, Am. Bd. Criminal Trial Lawyers (Upstate N.Y. chmn. 1998—), Am. Bd. Profl. Liability Attys. (diplomate), Internat. Soc. Barristers (Upstate N.Y. chmn. 1998—); mem.: N.Y. State Bar Assn. (mem. exec. com. trial lawyers sect. 1977—90, mem. exec. com. trial lawyers sect. 1981—94, mem. spl. com. med. malpractice, other coms., Outstanding Practitioner award 1980), N.Y. State Trial Lawyers Assn. (bd. dirs. 1982—91, dir. emeritus 1991), Capital Dist. Trial Lawyers Assn. (bd. dirs. 1973—76), ABA (numerous coms.), Calif. Attys. for Criminal Justice, Practising Law Inst., Am. Judicature Soc. (sustaining), Rensselaer County Bar Assn., Am. Soc. Law and Medicine, Albany County Bar Assn., N.Y. State Defenders Assn., Am. Arbitration Assn. (nat. panel of arbitrators), Dispute Resolutions, Inc. (nat. panel of arbitrators), Fed. Bar Coun., Upstate Trial Attys. Assn., Inc., Nat. Bd. Trial Advocacy (diplomate), Nat. Assn. Criminal Def. Lawyers, N.Y. STate Assn. Criminal DEf. Lawyers, Am. Bd. Trial Advs. (adv.), Inst. Injury Reduction (founder), Trial Lawyers for Pub. Justice (founder), Civil Justice Found. (founding sponsor), Internat. Acad. Litigators (diplomate), Am. Coll. Barristers (sr. counsel), Schuyler Meadows Club, Troy Country Club, Troy Club, Steuben Athletic Club, Ft. Orange Club, Stone Horse Yacht Club (Harwich Port, Mass.), Williams Club (N.Y.C.). Federal civil litigation, Criminal, Personal injury. Home: 46 Schuyler Rd Loudonville NY 12211-1447 Office: 28 2nd St Troy NY 12180-3986 E-mail: info@esjlaw.com

JONES, E. THOMAS, lawyer; b. Buffalo, July 19, 1950; s. Thomas Kenneth and Marian Arlene (Turk) J.; m. Jennifer Dee Lowery, Oct. 19, 1974; children: Evan Thomas III, Courtney Bree. BA, SUNY, Buffalo, 1972; JD, Cleve. State U., 1981. Bar: N.Y. 1982, U.S. Dist. Ct. (we. dist.) N.Y. 1982, U.S. Ct. Appeals (2d cir.) 1987. Mem. mgmt. staff Marine Midland Bank, Buffalo, 1971-76, M&T Bank, Buffalo, 1976-78, 81-82, Nat. City Bank, Cleve., 1978-81; sole practice Buffalo, 1982—. Hearing officer Buffalo City Ct., 1997—. Committeeman Amherst Rep. Party, N.Y., 1984—; fire fighter Getzville Fire Co., Inc., Amherst, 1988-91; town councilman, Amherst, 1990-91; coach, bd. dirs. Amherst Youth Hockey Assn.; dep. town atty. Town Amherst, N.Y., 1996—. Mem. ABA, Erie County Bar Assn. General civil litigation, General practice, Probate. Home: 1375 N French Rd Amherst NY 14228-1908

JONES, EDGAR ALLAN, JR. law educator, arbitrator, lawyer; b. Bklyn., Jan. 8, 1921; s. Edgar Allan and Isabel (Morris) J.; m. Helen Callaghan, Sept. 15, 1945; children: Linda Marie, Anne Marie, Carol Marie, Edgar Allan III, Denis James, Robert Morris, David Llewellyn, Therese Marie, Catherine Marie, Nancy Marie, Daniel Anthony. BA, Wesleyan U., 1942; LLB, U. Va., 1950. Bar: Va. 1948. Faculty UCLA, 1951—, prof. law, 1958-91, emeritus, 1991—, asst. dean, 1957-58; dir. Law-Sci. Rsch. Ctr., 1963-66; labor dispute arbitrator, mediator, fact finder for pvt. and pub. employers and unions, 1953—. Appeared as judge ABC-TV network programs Accused, 1958-59, Traffic Ct., 1958-61, Day in Court, 1958-64; moderator ednl. TV program Forum West, 1966; author: Mr. Arbitrator, 2000; editor: Law and Electronics: The Challenge of a New Era, 1960; founding editor Va. Law Weekly, 1948-50, NAA Chronicle, 1977-78; contbr. numerous labor law, arbitration and polygraph articles to law revs. Pres. Creddalt Rsch., Inc., 1959-90; dir. Deauville Restaurant, Inc. (Jimmy's 1978-94); pub. mem. Calif. Commn. Manpower Automation and Tech., 1963-67, Calif. Manpower Adv. Com., 1964-67; nat. enforcement commr. WSB, 1951; sec. Californians for Kennedy, 1960. Mem. ABA, Nat. Acad. Arbitrators (pres. 1980-81). Home: PO Box 1347 Pacific Palisades CA 90272-1347 E-mail: tedjones@ucla.edu

JONES, EDITH HOLLAN, judge; b. Phila., Apr. 7, 1949; BA, Cornell U., 1971; JD with honors, U. Tex., 1974. Bar: Tex. 1974, U.S. Supreme Ct. 1979, U.S. Ct. Appeals (5th and 11th cirs.), U.S. Dist. Ct. (so. and no. dists.) Tex. Assoc. Andrews & Kurth, Houston, 1974-82, ptnr., 1982-85; judge U.S. Ct. Appeals (5th cir.), Houston, 1985—. Gen. counsel Rep. Party of Tex., 1981-83. Mem. ABA, State Bar Tex. Presbyterian. Office: US Ct Appeals Bob Casey US Courthouse 515 Rusk St Ste 12505 Houston TX 77002-2605*

JONES, ERIKA ZIEBARTH, lawyer; b. Washington, June 10, 1955; d. Thomas Arthur and Ruth (Helm) Ziebarth; m. Gregory Monroe Jones, June 2, 1978; 1 child, Katherine Anne. AB, Georgetown U., 1976, JD, 1980. Bar: D.C. 1980, U.S. Ct. Appeals (D.C. cir.) 1987, U.S. Supreme Ct. 1987. Atty., regulatory analyst U.S. Office Mgmt. and Budget, Washington, 1980-81; spl. counsel Nat. Hwy. Traffic Safety Adminstrn., 1981-85, chief counsel, 1985-89; of counsel Mayer, Brown and Platt, 1989-90, ptnr., 1991—. Bd. dirs. Immaculata Coll. High Sch., 1985-88. Mem. ABA, D.C. Bar Assn., Phi Beta Kappa. Republican. Roman Catholic. Home: 6612 31st Pl NW Washington DC 20015-2302 Office: 1909 K St NW Washington DC 20006 E-mail: ejones@mayerbrown.com

JONES, FRANK GRIFFITH, lawyer; b. Houston, Sept. 11, 1941; s. A. Gordon and Grace (Griffith) J.; m. Deborah Ann Young, July 5, 1969; children: Russell G., Sarah G., Christopher Y. BS, Rice U., 1963; JD, U. Tex., 1966. Bar: Tex. 1966, U.S. Dist. Ct. (so., no. and ea. dists.) Tex., U.S. Ct. Appeals (5th and 8th cirs.); cert. civil trial specialist. Ptnr. Fulbright & Jaworski, Houston, 1966—, co-ptnr. in charge, 2001—. Fulbright & Jaworski Employment Commn., 1988-92. Chmn. troop com. Boy Scouts Am., Houston, 1986-88; mem. Rice U. Fund Coun., Houston, 1987-93; pres. Baker Coll., Rice U., 1962-63; bd. dirs. Houston Symphony, Holly Hall Retirement Cmty. Lt. (j.g.) USNR, 1967-72. U. Tex. Law Sch. Keeton fellow, 1993—. Fellow Am. Coll. Trial Lawyers (ADR com. 1986-96, chmn. 1992-94, ethics com. 1996—), Internat. Acad. Trial Lawyers; mem. ABA, Am. Bd. Trial Advs., Internat. Assn. Def. Counsel, Houston Bar Assn., Houston Young Lawyers Assn. (pres. 1972-73), Tex. Bar Assn., Tex. Bar Found., Houston Bar Found., Am. Bar Found., Tex. Assn. Civil Trial and Appellate Assocs., Houston Assn. Cert. Civil Trial and Appellate Specialists, Tex. Assn. Def. Counsel, Am. Counsel Assn., Def. Rsch. Inst., Tex. Assn. Cert. Civil Trial Specialists, Products Liability Adv. Coun., Houston City Club, Rotary, Phi Delta Phi (past pres.). Avocations: tennis, travel. General civil litigation, Contracts commercial, Product liability. Office: Fulbright & Jaworski 1301 Mckinney St Houston TX 77010-3095

JONES, FRANKLIN CHARLES, lawyer; b. Hanover, N.H., July 2, 1948; s. Laurence Harry and Dorothy Selma (Covey) J.; m. Jan Lynn Griggs, June 18, 1966; children— Gregory Allen, Matthew Scott, Benjamin Albert, Kathryn Covey. B.A., U. N.H., 1970; J.D., Boston U., 1973. Bar: N.H. 1973, U.S. Dist. Ct. N.H. 1978, U.S. Ct. Appeals (1st cir.) 1978, U.S. Supreme Ct. 1979. Atty. Michael & Wallace, Rochester, N.H., 1973-76; ptnr. Michael & Jones, Rochester, 1976-78, Michael Jones & Wensley, 1979-86, 87— ; instr. Paralegal Studies Program, U. N.H., Durham, 1979-81, Tax Inst., 1981-85. Mem. Rochester Sch. Bd., 1978-84, chmn. bd., 1983-84; chmn. Rochester chpt. ARC, 1976-78; moderator City of Rochester, Ward 4, 1984-86; spl. justice Rochester Dist. Ct., 1986—. Mem. ABA, Nat. Assn. Criminal Def. Lawyers, Assn. Trial Lawyers Am., N.H. Bar Assn. (chmn. com. on econs. of practice law 1982-83, mem. clients indemnity fund com. 1984-88), Rotary (bd. dirs. Rochester). Republican. Roman Catholic. Bankruptcy, General corporate, Real property. Home: 50 Chesley Hill Rd Rochester NH 03839-5501 Office: Michael Jones & Wensley PO Box 1500 Rochester NH 03866-1500

JONES, GEORGE WASHINGTON, JR. lawyer; b. Balt., July 27, 1953; s. George W. and Mattie Alice (Reed) J.; m. Loretta Phylis Pleasant, Aug. 5, 1978; children: Melissa Grace, George Charles, Jessica. BA, U. Chgo., 1975; JD, Yale U., 1978. Bar: D.C. 1980, U.S. Dist. Ct. D.C. 1980, U.S. Ct. Appeals (D.C. cir.) 1983, U.S. Supreme Ct. 1986. Law clk. to judge U.S. Ct. Appeals (7th Cir.), Chgo., 1978-79; assoc. O'Melveny & Myers, Washington, 1979-80; asst. to solicitor gen. U.S. Dept. Justice, 1980-83; assoc. Sidley & Austin, 1983-87, ptnr., 1988—. Mem. ABA, D.C. Bar Assn. (pres. elect 2001-), NBA. Administrative and regulatory, Federal civil litigation, General civil litigation. Office: Sidley & Austin 1501 K St NW Washington DC 20005*

JONES, JAMES ALTON, lawyer; b. Palestine, Tex., Feb. 26, 1956; s. Ralph A. and Jo Nell (Broadway) J. JD magna cum laude, Tulane U., 1983. Bar: Tex. 1985, U.S. Dist. Ct. (so. dist.) Tex. 1985, U.S. Dist. Ct. (no. and eas. dists.) Tex. 1986, U.S. Dist. Ct. (we. dist.) Tex. 1988, U.S. Ct. Appeals (5th cir.) 1985, Minn. 1993, U.S. Dist. Ct. Minn. 1993, U.S. Ct. Appeals (8th cir.) 1993. Law clk. U.S. Ct. Appeals (5th cir.), Houston, 1983-84; assoc. Holtzman & Urquhart, 1984-86, Johnson & Swanson, Dallas, 1986, Figari & Davenport, Dallas, 1986-89; ptnr. Doke & Riley, 1989-92, Sprenger & Lang, Mpls., 1992-95; shareholder Jones & Assocs. P.C., Dallas, 1995—. Instr. legal rsch. and writing Tulane U., 1983. Mem. ABA, State Bar Tex., Dallas Bar Assn., Dallas Assn. Young Lawyers, Order of Coif. Baptist. Avocations: tennis, skiing. Civil rights, Federal civil litigation, Labor. Office: Jones & Associates PC 5015 Tracy St Ste 100 Dallas TX 75205-3400 Fax: 214-219-9309. E-mail: titlvii@anet-dfw.com

JONES, JAMES LEONARD, lawyer; b. Helena, Mont., Sept. 25, 1945; s. Vernon Leonard and Mary Elizabeth (Conn) J.; m. Madilyn Charmaine Bell, June 17, 1967; children— Mathew James, Aaron Christopher, Steven Ryan. B.A., U. Mont., 1967, J.D., 1970. Bar: Mont. 1970, U.S. Dist. Ct. Mont. 1970, U.S. Ct. Appeals (9th cir.) 1973. Law clk. to chief judge U.S. Dist Ct. Mont., Missoula, 1970-71; asst. U.S. atty. U.S. Dept. Justice, Billings, Mont., 1971-74; prin. Anderson, Brown, Gerbase, Cebull & Jones, P.C., Billings, 1974-86, ptnr. Dorsey & Whitney, 1986—. Mem. Yellowstone County Republican Central Com. Served to capt. USAR, 1970. Mem. Mont. Bar Assn. (pres. young lawyers sect. 1974-75), ABA, Yellowstone County Bar Assn., Mont. Assn. Def. Counsel (pres. 1981-82), Def. Research Inst. (state dir. 1983-84), Internat. Assn. Ins. Counsel. Methodist. Federal civil litigation, Insurance, Personal injury. Office: Anderson Brown Gerbase Cebull 315 N 24th St Billings MT 59101-1395 Home: Dorsey & Whitney 1200 First Inerstate Ctr 401 N 31st St Billings MT 59101-1200

JONES, JEFFREY FOSTER, lawyer; b. Phila., Apr. 24, 1944; s. Richard L. and Dorothy A. (Shaw) J.; m. Susan Craft, Aug. 22, 1970; children: Amanda, Michael. BA, Williams Coll., 1966; JD, Harvard U., 1973. Bar: Mass. 1973, U.S. Dist. Ct. Mass. 1974, U.S. Dist. Ct. Appeals (1st cir.) 1974. Law clk. Supreme Jud. Ct., Boston, 1973-74; assoc. Palmer & Dodge, 1974-80, ptnr., 1980-88, mng. ptnr., 1998—. Chmn. bd. Law Firm Resources Project., 1981—. Overseer Boys and Girls Clubs of Boston, 1974-93, sec., bd. dirs., 1993—; trustee Radcliffe Coll., 1995-99, Sterling and Francine Clark Art Inst., 1995-98; bd. dirs. Willow Hill Sch., 1991—. Lt. USN, 1966-70. Mem. ABA, Nat. Assn. Coll. and Univ. Attys., Boston Bar Assn., Mass. Bar Assn., Greater Boston C. of C. (dir. 1998—). Democrat. Avocations: racquetball, golfing, reading. General civil litigation, Education and schools, Public utilities. Office: Palmer & Dodge 1 Beacon St Ste 22 Boston MA 02108-3190

JONES, JENIVER JAMES, lawyer; b. Sutton, W.Va., Sept. 24, 1915; s. Lee Jackson J. and Mary Ida (Lewis) J.; m. Maxine Hickman, Oct. 3, 1939 (dec. Dec. 1993); children: Gary Keith, Glendon Kent, Ronnie Dale; m. Mary Frame, July 30, 1994; stepchildren: Debra Frame Brady, Joseph Brady. Student, Glenville (W. Va.) Coll., 1938; JD, W. Va. U., 1947. Bar: W. Va. 1947. Tchr. Braxton County Bd. Edn., Sutton, W. Va., 1936-43, attendance dir., 1947-48; aircraft inspector Glen L. Martin, Middle River, Md., 1943-45; pvt. practice Sutton, 1948-91, Gassaway, 1991-99. W. Va. Rep. Supreme Ct. nominee, 1988. Mem. Lions Club Internat. (dist. gov. 1963-64, Sutton, W.Va.). Methodist. Avocations: reading, tennis, baseball, golfing. Family and matrimonial, General practice, Real property. Office: Law Offices of Jeniver J Jones HC 62 Box 75 Gassaway WV 26624-9405

JONES, JOHN ARTHUR, lawyer; b. San Antonio, Oct. 9, 1921; s. Charles Garfield and Catherine Magdalene (Smith) J.; m. Margarette Lorraine (Sally) Johnson, Sept. 17, 1949; children: Matthew, Lisa, Malcolm, Darby. AA, U. Fla., 1947, JD with honors, 1949. Bar: Fla. 1949, U.S. Dist. Ct. (so. dist.) Fla. 1952, U.S. Ct. Appeals (5th cir.) 1959, U.S. Supreme Ct. 1978, U.S. Ct. Appeals (11th cir.) 1982. Assoc. Holland & Knight and predecessors, Tampa, Fla., 1949-54, ptnr., 1954—. Faculty Fla. Sch. of Banking, 1969-81. Editor, contbr.: How to Live and Die with Florida Probate, 1972, Practice Under Florida Probate Code, 1976-2000. Served in U.S. Army, 1940-46; lt. col. USAR. Decorated Bronze Star. Fellow Am. Coll. Trust and Estate Counsel; mem. ABA, Fla Bar Assn. (cert. wills, trusts and estates, chmn. real property probate and trust law sect. 1980-81), Hillsborough County (Fla.) Bar Assn., Internat. Acad. Estate and Trust Lawyers, Am. Coll. Real Estate Lawyers, Am. Bar Found., Masons, Shriners, Tampa Club, Univ. Club. Banking, Contracts commercial, Probate. Home: 5027 W San Miguel St Tampa FL 33629-5428 Office: Holland & Knight PO Box 1288 400 N Ashley Dr Ste 2300 Tampa FL 33602-4322 E-mail: jajones@hklaw.com

JONES, JOHN FRANK, retired lawyer; b. Carrington, N.D., Feb. 24, 1922; s. Dwight Frank and Veronica Esther (Sheehy) J.; m. Sally Oppegard; children: Janna Jones Bellwin, John M., Jeramy Ridder, Jill Jones Nester, Julie, Jeffrey, J. David. BS, U. N.D., 1946; MS in Organic Chemistry, U. Wis., 1953; JD, U. Akron, 1956. Bar: Ohio 1956, U.S. Patent Office, U.S. Ct. Appeals. Patent atty. B. F. Goodrich Co., Akron, Ohio, 1956-62; sr. patent atty. Standard Oil Co., Cleve., 1962-70, patent counsel, 1970-81, food and drug atty. Vistron Corp. subs. Standard Oil Co., Cleve., 1968-81, ret., 1981; cons. to Standard Oil Co., Cleve. and Ashland Chem. Co. (div. Ashland Oil Co.), Columbus, Ohio, 1981-95, B.F. Goodrich Co. Served with USAAF, 1943-46. Decorated D.F.C., Air medal. Mem. Am. Chem. Soc., Ohio Bar Assn., ABA, Cleve. Intellectual Property Law Assn., CBI Hump Pilots Assn. Republican. Patentee in chem. and polymer fields; contbr. articles on polymer sci. to profl. jours. Patent, Trademark and copyright. Home and Office: 2724 Cedar Hill Rd Cuyahoga Falls OH 44223-1226

JONES, JOHN HARRIS, lawyer; b. New Blaine, Ark., Apr. 9, 1922; s. Ira Burton and Byrd (Harris); m. Marjorie Crosby Hart, 1983. A.B., U. Central Ark., 1941; postgrad., George Washington U. Law Sch., 1941-42; LL.B., Yale, 1947. Bar: Ark. 1946, U.S. Supreme Ct. 1963. Comms. clk. FBI, 1941-42; practice in Pine Bluff, 1947—; spl. judge Circuit Ct., 1950; spl. chief justice Ark. Supreme Ct., 1997. Chmn. bd. Pine Bluff Nat. Bank, 1964-77, pres., 1966-76; Mem. Ark. Bd. Law Examiners, 1953-59; Republican nominee for U.S. Senate, 1974; Rep. presdl. elector, 1980; v.p., dir. John Rust Found., 1953-60. Served to 1st lt. USAAF, 1943-45. Decorated Purple Heart, Air medal. Mem. Ark. Bar Assn., Jefferson County Bar Assn. (pres. 1959-60). Mem. Christian Ch. (elder 1963-65, trustee 1965-71, 78-84). Clubs: Eden Park (Pine bluff), Little Rock Club. Home: 4001 S Cherry St Pine Bluff AR 71603-7156 Office: 104 S Main St Pine Bluff AR 71601-4320

JONES, JOHN PAUL, probation officer, psychologist; b. Blanchard, Mich., July 23, 1944; s. Lawrence John and Thelma Blanche (Eldred) J.; m. Joan Margaret Bruder, Aug. 18, 1972; children: Jason John, Justin John, Jessica Joan-Margaret. BS, Cen. Mich. U., 1970, MA, 1974; PhD, Wayne State U., Detroit, 1980. Diplomate Am. Bd. Forensic Medicine, Am. Bd. Cert. Forensic Examiners, Am. Bd. Psychol. Specialties, Am. Acad. of Experts in Traumatic Stress; diplomate in psychotherapy; cert. addictions counselor. Mgr. F. W. Woolworth Co., Bay City, Mich., 1970; probation officer Oakland County Cir. Ct., Pontiac, 1970-74, probation officer supr., 1974-78, dir. spl. probation program, 1978-80; chief probation officer County of Oakland, 1980-93; outpatient clin. dir. Auro Med. Ctr., Bloomfield Hills, 1993—. Lectr. Oakland U., Rochester, Mich., 1978-82; lic. psychologist Psychol. Svcs. of Bloomfield Hills, Mich., 1980-82, Family Treatment Ctr., Pontiac, Mich., 1983-84, Associated Profls., Bloomfield Hills, 1984-85, Auro Med. Ctr., Bloomfield Hills, 1985—. Pres. Pontiac Lions Club, 1986-87; study subcom. Oakland County Jail, 1982-84; mem. Oakland County Child Sexual Abuse Task Force, 1982-83. With U.S. Army, 1966-68. Mem. APA (bd. govs.), Internat. Neuropsychol. Assn., Am. Correctional Psychologist Assn., Am. Acad. Experts in Traumatic Stress, Am. Coll. Forensic Examiners (BCFE, BCFM), Am. Psychotherapy Assn., Mich. Corrections Assn., Mich. Assn. Probation Officers Svcs., Mich. Psychol. Assn., Fraternal Order of Police, Cen. Mich. U. Alumni Assn. (bd. dirs. Mt. Pleasant chpt. 1989-93), Mich. Neuropsychol. Soc., Am. Psychol. Assn. Republican. Avocations: travel, horseback riding, reading, fencing. Home: 2915 Masefield Dr Bloomfield Hills MI 48304-1951 Office: Auro Med Ctr Ste 102 1711 S Woodwood Ave Bloomfield Hills MI 48302

JONES, JOSEPH HAYWARD, lawyer; b. Shamokin, Pa., July 9, 1924; s. Joseph H. and Anna Elizabeth (Lippiatt) J.; m. Grace Loretta Hicks, Mar. 17, 1951; children: Elizabeth Christie, Joseph H. Jr., Gregory H. BA, Ursinus Coll., 1947, LLD (hon.), 1987; JD, Dickinson Sch. Law, Carlisle, Pa., 1950; LLM, NYU, 1954. Bar: Pa. 1950, U.S. Supreme Ct. 1959. Ptnr. Williamson, Friedberg & Jones, Pottsville, Pa., 1950—. Mem. Pa. Judicial Reform Commn., 1987. Past pres. Appalachian Trail coun. Boy Scouts Am., Hawk Mountain coun. Boy Scouts Am.; sec., past pres. Schuylkill Econ. Devel. Corp.; pres. Pottsville Area Devel. Corp., 1986; bd. dirs. Salvation Army, Pa. Lawyers Trust Account Bd., 1989-96. Lt. (j.g.) USN, 1942-45, PTO. Recipient Silver Beaver award Boy Scouts Am., Disting. Citizen award Pa. State U., Schuylkill, 1987, Citizen of Yr. award St. David's Soc. Schuylkill and Carbon Counties; named Young Man of Yr., Pottsville Area Jaycees, Vol. of Yr., So. Schuylkill United Fund, 1972. Mem. Pa. Bar Assn. (pres. 1987-88, recipient Pa. Bar medal, chmn. task force legal svcs. to poor 1989-90, recipient ADL torch of Liberty 1997), Pa. Bar Found. (pres.), Masons (33 deg.), Lions (past pres.). General practice, Probate, Taxation, general. Home: 2100 Mahantongo St Pottsville PA 17901-3112 Office: Williamson Friedberg & Jones Ten Westwood Rd Pottsville PA 17901

JONES, LAUREN EVANS, lawyer; b. Lawrence, Kans., Jan. 10, 1952; s. Kevin Rice and Marcia Jo Ann (Peterson) J.; m. Vivien Craig Long, Mar. 26, 1978; children: Dylan Tyler, Hayden Blake, Carson Reed. BA in History, U. Mich., 1973; JD, Duke U., 1977. Bar: R.I. 1978, U.S. Dist. Ct. R.I. 1978, U.S. Ct. Appeals (1st cir.) 1985, U.S. Ct. Appeals (9th cir.) 1994, U.S. Supreme Ct. 1991. Assoc. Lovett, Morgera, Schefrin & Gallogly, Providence, 1979-83; ptnr. Jones & Aisenberg, 1983-89; owner Jones Assocs., 1990—. Mem. Jud. Performance Eval. Commn., 1993—; mem. R.I. Supreme Ct. Com. on Profl. and Civility, 1995-96. Editor R.I. Bar Jour., 1989-95; contbr. articles to profl. jours. Nominee R.I. Supreme Ct., 1993, 95, 96, 97. Mem. R.I. Bar Assn. (exec. com. 1989-2000, sec. 1995, v.p. 1996, pres. elect 1997, pres. 1998-99). Appellate, General civil litigation, Personal injury. Office: Jones Assocs 72 S Main St Providence RI 02903-2907 E-mail: ljones@appeallaw.com

JONES, LAWRENCE TUNNICLIFFE, lawyer; b. Mineola, N.Y., Jan. 20, 1950; s. Carroll Hudson Tunnicliffe and Florence Virginia (Greene) J. BA, U. Va., 1972; JD, U. Richmond, 1975. Bar: Va. 1975, D.C. 1976, N.Y. 1976, U.S. Dist. Ct. (ea. and so. dist.) N.Y. 1976, U.S. Supreme Ct. 1986. Bus. mgr. law review U. Richmond, Va., 1974-75; ptnr. Carroll Hudson Tunnicliffe Jones and Lawrence Tunnicliffe Jones Attys. at law, Mineola, 1976-91; owner, 1992—. Trustee Nassau County Hist. Soc., 1976—, pres., 1983-89; bd. dirs. Friends of Hist. St. George's Ch., Hempstead, N.Y., 1982—, v.p., 1990-92, pres., 1992-94; bd. dirs. St. Mary's Devel. Fund, Garden City, N.Y., 1983-89, pres., 1987-89; pres. coun. Cathedral Sch. St. Paul Alumni Fund, Inc., Garden City, 1984—; bd. govs. Cathedral Sch. St. Mary, Garden City, 1983-86. Recipient Mineola Bus. Person of Yr. award, 2000. Mem. ABA, Nat. Acad. Elder Law Attys., Va. State Bar Assn., N.Y. State Bar Assn., Nassau County Bar Assn., Nassau County Tax and Estate Planning Coun., Univ. Club (N.Y.C.), Univ. Club (L.I., pres. 1986-87, 93-94, bd. dirs. 1983-86, 89—), Mineola C. of C. (dir. 1993—), Garden City Golf Club, Mineola-Garden City Rotary (dir. 1991-94), Garden City Fellowship (pres. 1993-94, dir. 1994—), Cathedral Club (Garden City) (pres. 1993-95), Garden City C. of C. Episcopalian. Avocation: historic building preservation. General practice, Probate, Real property. Home: 158 Cathedral Ave Hempstead NY 11550-1140 Office: Jones & Jones 1000 Franklin Ave Ste 302 Garden City NY 11530-2910

JONES, LINDY DON, lawyer; b. Vernon, Tex., Aug. 20, 1949; s. Earl Irven Jones and Avis June (Koontz) McDowell; m. M. Kathryn Sanders, June 6, 1969; children: Brandi Kim, Megan Dawn, Ty Jeffrey. BBA in Mgmt. with honors, U. Tex., Arlington, 1971; JD, So. Meth. U., 1974. Bar: Tex. 1974, U.S. Ct. Appeals (5th cir.) 1974, U.S. Dist. Ct. (we. dest.) Tex. 1977, U.S. Dist. Ct. (ea. dist.) Tex. 1978, U.S. Dist. Ct. (so. dist.) Tex. 1979. Ptnr. Moseley, Jones, Enoch & Martin and predecessors, Dallas, 1974-81, Moseley, Jones, Allen & Fuquay, Dallas, 1981-86, Jones, Allen & Fuquay, Dallas, 1986—. Pres. Highland Park United Meth. Ch. Mens Club, Dallas, 1979; chmn. bd. dirs. Dickinson Pl. Charitable Corp., Dallas, 1984-86. Recipient hon. life membership Highland Park United Meth. Ch. Mens Club, 1980. Mem. ABA, Dallas Bar Assn. (com. mem. 1974—), State Bar Tex., Delta Theta Phi. Republican. Banking, State civil litigation, Contracts commercial. Home: 8068 Moss Meadows Dr Dallas TX 75231-3915 Office: Jones Allen & Fuquay 8828 Greenville Ave Dallas TX 75243-7160 E-mail: ljones@jonesallen.com

JONES, LUCIAN COX, lawyer; b. Kew Gardens, N.Y., Dec. 22, 1942; m. Ann Waters, Aug. 22, 1964; children— L. Rustin, Norman W., Warren R. A.B., Davidson Coll., 1964; J.D., Columbia U., 1967. Bar: N.Y. 1967. Assoc. Shearman & Sterling, N.Y.C., 1967-68, 70-76, ptnr., 1976-98; lectr.Cameron Sch. Bus. U. N.C., Wilmington, 1998—. Bd. dirs. The Nash Engrng. Co., Trumbull, Conn. 1994—. Served to capt. U.S. Army, 1968-70 Mem. ABA, N.Y. State Bar Assn., Assn. Bar City N.Y. Antitrust, Banking, Contracts commercial. Office: U NC Cameron Sch Bus 601 S College Rd Wilmington NC 28403-3297

JONES, MARY D. court clerk; b. Danbury, Wis., Aug. 12, 1951; d. Eugene F. and Darlene M. Burlingame; m. Larry James Truitt, Nov. 5, 1966 (div. June 1971); children: Jeanne Lynn Truitt Justice, Colleen Regina Truitt Elder; m. Cecil L. Jones, Mar. 5, 1972; children: James A., Andy D.; stepchildren: Gary Wayne Jones, Terri A. Jones. Cert., Muscatine (Iowa) Jr. Coll. With Plastic Factory, Muscatine, 1969-71; sec. Dr. Shoemaker, Kahoka, Mo., 1972-73; rschr. Clark County Abstract, 1973-74; dep. clk., recorder Clark County Cir. Clk. and Recorder's Office, 1974-94; elected officio Cir. Clk. and Recorder, 1995—. Mem. Clark County Dem. Com., Kahoka, 1988, State Dem. Com., Mo., 1995—, Clark County Crime Victim Program, Kahoka, 1997—; mem., past pres. Blackhawk PTO, Kahoka, 1995—; mem., past leader Boy Scouts Am., Kahoka, 1973—. Mem. Mo. Recorder's Assn., Mo. Cir. Clk.'s Assn., Kahoka Hist. Soc. Baptist. Avocations: reading, fishing, listening to radio. Home: 475 N Lincoln St Kahoka MO 63445-1234

JONES, NAPOLEON A., JR. judge; b. 1940; BA, San Diego State U., 1962, MSW, 1967; JD, U. San Diego, 1971. Legal intern, staff atty. Calif. Rural Legal Assistance, Modesto, Calif., 1971-73; staff atty. Defenders, Inc., San Diego, 1973-75; ptnr. Jones, Cazares, Adler & Lopez, 1975-77; judge San Diego Mcpl. Ct., 1977-82, San Diego Superior Ct., 1982-94, U.S. Dist. Ct. (so. dist.) Calif., San Diego, 1994—. Mem. San Diego County Indigent Def. Policy Bd. Bd. visitors Sch. Social Work San Diego State U.; active Valencia Park Elem. Sch. Mem. San Diego County Bar Assn., Earl B. Gilliam Bar Assn., San Diego Bar Found., Nat. Bar Assn., Calif. Bar Assn., Calif. Black Attys. Assn., Nat. Assn. Women Judges, Masons, Sigma Pi Phi, Kappa Alpha Psi. Office: US Dist Ct So Dist Calif US Courthouse 940 Front St Ste 2125 San Diego CA 92101-8912

JONES, NATHANIEL RAPHAEL, federal judge; b. Youngstown, Ohio, May 13, 1926; s. Nathaniel B. and Lillian J. (Rafe) J.; m. Lillian Graham, Mar. 22, 1974; 1 dau., Stephanie Joyce; stepchildren: William Hawthorne, Rickey Hawthorne, Marc Hawthorne, Pamela Haley. A.B., Youngstown State U., 1951, LL.B., 1955, LL.D. (hon.), 1969, Syracuse U., 1972. Editor Buckeye Rev. newspaper, 1956; exec. dir. FEPC, Youngstown, 1956-59; practiced law, 1959-61; mem. firm Goldberg & Jones, 1968-69; asst. U.S. atty., 1961-67; asst. gen. counsel Nat. Adv. Commn. on Civil Disorders, 1967-68; gen. counsel NAACP, 1969-79; judge U.S. Ct. of Appeals, 6th Circuit, 1979-95, sr. judge, 1995—. Adj/ prof. U. Cin. Coll. Law, 1983—; trial observer South Africa, 1985; dir. Buckeye Rev. Pub. Co.; chmn. Con. on Adequate Def. and Incentives in Mil.; mem. Task Force-Vets. Benefits; lectr. South African Judges seminar, Johannesburg. Co-chmn. Cin. Roundtable, Black-Jewish Coalition Cin.; observer Soviet Union Behalf com. on Soviet Jewry; bd. dirs. Interights, USA. Served with USAAF, 1945-47. Mem. Ohio State Bar Assn., Mahoning County Bar Assn., Fed. Bar Assn., Nat. Bar Assn., Am. Arbitration Assn., Youngstown Area Devel. Corp., Urban League, Nat. Conf. Black Lawyers, ABA (co-chmn. com. constl. rights criminal sect. 1971-73), Kappa Alpha Psi. Baptist. Clubs: Houston Law (Youngstown); Elks. Office: US Ct Appeals US Courthouse 100 E 5th St Ste 432 Cincinnati OH 45202-3911*

JONES, PAUL LAWRENCE, lawyer; b. Snow Hill, N.C., Mar. 15, 1948; s. LeRoy and Esther Belle (Harper) J.; m. Asonia Lynette Battle, June 14, 1980; 1 child, Krystle Paulette. B.S., N.C. Agrl. and Tech. State U., 1971; J.D., N.C. Central U., 1974. Bar: N.C. 1975, D.C. 1976, U.S. Tax Ct. 1976, U.S. Ct. Mil. Appeals 1976, U.S. Ct. Claims 1976, U.S. Dist. Ct. (ea. dist.) N.C. 1979, U.S. Supreme Ct. 1982. Atty., asst. clk. U.S. Supreme Ct., Washington, 1974-76; assoc. firm Beech & Pollock, Kinston, N.C., 1979-80; mng. atty. Eastern Carolina Legal Services, Wilson, N.C., 1980-82; ptnr. firm Beech & Jones, Kinston, 1982-88. Mem. N.C. State Banking Commn., Raleigh, 1983; treas. Lenoir County Dem. Com., Kinston, 1983-86; bd. dirs. Lenoir Meml. Hosp.; mem. Lenoir Ind. Devel. Commn. Maj. USAR. Paul Harris fellow. Mem. ABA, N.C. Bar Assn., Assn. Trial Lawyers Am., N.C. Acad. Trial Lawyers, Lenoir County Bar Assn. (pres. 1983), Lenoir County C. of C. (bd. dirs. 1983), Phi Alpha Delta, Kappa Alpha Psi. Mem. Methodist Episcopal Zion Ch. Lodges: Rotary, Masons, Shriners. State civil litigation, Criminal. Home: 1102 N Queen St Kinston NC 28501-3948 Office: 1102 N Queen St Kinston NC 28501-3948

JONES, PHILIP KIRKPATRICK, JR. lawyer; b. Baton Rouge, June 26, 1949; s. Philip Kirkpatrick and Mary Jane (Kincade) J.; m. Serena Catherine Cockayne, Apr. 5, 1980; children: Veronica Cockayne, Nicola Kincade, Clare Kirkpatrick, Philip Carruth Elliot. BA in Govt., Dartmouth Coll., 1971; JD, La. State U., 1974; LLB, diploma in legal studies, Cambridge (U.K.) U., 1976. Bar: La. 1974, U.S. Dist. Ct. (ea. and we. dist.) La. 1980, U.S. Ct. Appeals (5th and 11th cirs.) 1981, U.S. Dist. Ct. (mid. dist.) La. 1987, U.S. Supreme Ct. 1992. Law clk. to John A. Dixon Jr. Supreme Ct. La., New Orleans, 1974-75; staff atty. Presdl. Clemency Bd., Washington, 1975; lectr. U. Singapore, 1977-79; from assoc. to ptnr. Liskow & Lewis, New Orleans, 1980—. 1st lt. USAF, 1975. Republican. Presbyterian. Bankruptcy, Federal civil litigation, Private international. Office: Liskow & Lewis PC 50th Fl One Shell Square New Orleans LA 70139 E-mail: pkjones@liskow.com

JONES, RICHARD MICHAEL, lawyer; b. Chgo., Jan. 16, 1952; s. Richard Anthony and Shirley Mae (Wilhelm) J.; m. Catherine Leona Ford, May 25, 1974. BS, U. Ill., 1974; JD, Harvard U., 1977. Bar: Colo. 1977, U.S. Dist. Ct. Colo. 1977. Assoc. Davis, Graham & Stubbs, Denver, 1977-81; corp. counsel Tosco Corp., 1981-82; asst. gen. counsel Anschutz Corp., 1982-88, gen. counsel, v.p., 1989—. Mem. ABA, Colo. Bar Assn., Denver Bar Assn. General corporate, Oil, gas, and mineral, Private international. Office: Anschutz Corp 555 17th St Ste 2400 Denver CO 80202-3987

JONES, ROBERT EDWARD, federal judge; b. Portland, Oreg., July 5, 1927; s. Howard C. and Leita (Hendricks) J.; m. Pearl F. Jensen, May 29, 1948; children— Jeffrey Scott, Julie Lynn BA, U. Hawaii, 1949; JD, Lewis and Clark Coll., 1953, LHD (hon.), 1995; LLD (hon.), City U., Seattle, 1984, Lewis and Clark Coll., 1995. Bar: Oreg. Trial atty., Portland, Oreg., 1953-63; judge Oreg. Circuit Ct., 1963-83; justice Oreg. Supreme Ct., Salem, 1983-90; judge U.S. Dist. Ct. Oreg., Portland, 1990—. Mem. faculty Nat. Jud. Coll., Am. Acad. Jud. Edn., ABA Appellate Judges Seminars; former mem. Oreg. Evidence Revision Commn., Oreg. Ho. of Reps.; former chmn. Oreg. Commn. Prison Terms and Parole Stds.; adj. prof. Northwestern Sch. Law, Lewis and Clark Coll., 1963—, Willamette Law Sch., 1988—. Author: Rutter Group Practice Guide Federal Civil Trials and Evidence, 1999. Mem. bd. overseers Lewis and Clark Coll., mem. bd. visitors to Northwestern Sch. Law. Served to capt. JAGC, USNR. Recipient merit award Multnomah Bar Assn., 1979; Citizen award NCCJ, Legal Citizen of the Yr. award Law Related Edn. Project, 1988; Service to Mankind award Sertoma Club Oreg.; James Madison award Sigma Delta Chi; named Disting. Grad., Northwestern Sch. Law; Outstanding Profl. Achievement Alumnus award, U.S. Merchant Marine Acad., 1998; Judge Robert E. Jones Oreg. Justice award, Am. Judicature Soc., 1999. Mem. Am. Judicature Soc. (bd. dirs. 1997-2001), State Bar Oreg. (past chmn. Continuing Legal Edn.), Oregon Circuit Judges Assn. (pres. 1967-1968), Oreg. Trial Lawyers Assn. (pres. 1959, chair 9th cir. edn. com. 1996-97). Office: US Dist Ct House 1000 SW 3rd Ave Ste 1407 Portland OR 97204-2944 E-mail: jones@ord.uscourts.gov

JONES, ROBERT GRIFFITH, lawyer, mayor; b. State Coll., Pa., Mar. 25, 1936; s. Edward H. and Dorothy (Griffiths) J.; m. Carolyn E. Hazard, Aug. 29, 1959; Robert Griffith Jr., Chester H. AB, Davidson (N.C.) Coll., 1958; MDiv, Yale U., 1961; PhD, Duke U., 1966; JD, U. Va., 1974. Bar: Va. 1974, U.S. Supreme Ct. 1977. Asst. prof. Davidson (N.C.) Coll., 1964-65; assoc. prof. Lehigh U., Bethlehem, Pa., 1965-71; prof. U. Va., Charlottesville, 1971-74; mayor City of Virginia Beach, Va., 1986-88; chmn. Jones, Marcari, Russotto, Walker & Spencer, P.C., Virginia Beach, 1991—. Adv. bd. mem. Cenit Bank, 1997—. Vice-chmn. Tidewater Transp. Dist. Commn., 1987-88, chmn., 1988; councilman City Council of Virginia Beach, 1982-88, chmn. Va. Beach Econ. Devel. Authority. Mem. ABA, Va. Bar Assn., Virginia Beach Bar Assn. Democrat. Presbyterian. Home: 2716 Robin Dr Virginia Beach VA 23454-1814 Office: 128 S Lynnhaven Rd Virginia Beach VA 23452-7417 E-mail: rgjvbva@aol.com

JONES, ROBERT JEFFRIES, lawyer; b. Atlantic City, Sept. 7, 1939; s. Robert Lewis and Mildred Laura (Jeffries) J.; m. Joan Mary Feichtner, Aug. 17, 1963; children: Christopher, Kendall, Stephen. BA, Colgate U., 1961; LLB with honors, U. Pa., 1964. Bar: Pa. 1965, U.S. Dist. Ct. (ea. dist.) Pa. 1965, U.S. Ct. Appeals (3d cir.) 1965. Assoc. Saul, Ewing, Remick & Saul, Phila., 1964-71, ptnr., 1971—. Mem. steering com. Bond Atty.'s Workshop, Chgo., 1980. Mem. Montgomery County Rep. Com., Norristown, Pa., 1967-71; chmn. Whitpain Twp. Park and Recreation Bd., Blue Bell, Pa., 1980-84; bd. dirs. Phila. YMCA Camps, 1970-76; trustee Colgate U., 1999—; mem. gen. counsel alumni corp., 1993-99, pres. Phila. chpt., 1980-84. Fellow Am. Coll. Bond Counsel (founder); mem. ABA, Phila. Bar Assn. (chmn. tax exempt fin. com. 1985-86), Pa. Bond Lawyers Assn. (founder Harrisburg, Pa. 1987), Pa. Economy League (bd. dirs. 1994—). Avocations: skiing, golf, history. Finance, Municipal (including bonds), Securities. Office: Saul Ewing Remick & Saul 3800 Centre Sq W Philadelphia PA 19102 E-mail: rjjboilerplate@aol.com, rjones@saul.com

JONES, RONALD LEE, lawyer, writer; b. Ames, Iowa, Apr. 11, 1942; s. L. Meyer and Mary Elizabeth (Homer) J.; m. Cynthia Jane Spitzer, Oct. 1, 1994. BA, Ill. Wesleyan U., 1965; cert., Naval Justice Sch., Camp Pendleton, Calif., 1968; JD, Calif. Western Sch. Law, 1972. Bar: Nebr. 1973, U.S. Ct. Appeals (8th cir.) 1973, U.S. Supreme Ct. 1979. Corp. counsel Gene Fuller, Inc., San Diego, 1972-73; asst. gen. counsel Daniel Internat. Corp., Greenville, S.C., 1974-79; v.p., gen. counsel, sec. Royster Co., Norfolk, Va., 1979-83; writer Virginia Beach, 1983—; counsel Peter Kiewit Sons, Inc., Omaha, 1984-87, Occidental Chem. Corp., Dallas, 1988—, The Williams Cos., 1997. Chmn. lawyers coordinating com. Fla. Phosphate Council, Tampa, 1980. Author: Practice Preventive Corporat Law, 1985, How to Counsel Corporate Clients: Ten Reasons Business People Don't Take Legal Advice (And What You Can Do About It), ALI-ABA, 2000; editor (newsletter) Corp. Counsel Reporter, 1985—; contbr. articles to profl. jours. Capt. USMC, 1965-69. Mem. ABA (corp., banking and bus. law sect., constrn. law forum com.), Fertilizer Inst., Am. Mfrs. Assn. Construction, General corporate. Home: 1 Royal Dublin Ln Broken Arrow OK 74011-1127

JONES, SHELDON ATWELL, lawyer; b. Melrose, Mass., Apr. 20, 1938; s. Sheldon Atwell and Hannah Margaret (Andrews) J.; m. Priscilla Ann Hatch, Sept. 10, 1966; children: Sarah Percy, Abigail Atwell. BA, Yale U., 1959; LLB, Harvard U., 1965. Bar: Mass. 1965, U.S. Dist. Ct. Mass. 1967. Assoc. Gaston, Snow, Motley & Holt, Boston, 1965-72; ptnr. Gaston Snow & Ely Bartlett, 1972-87, Dechert Price & Rhoads, Boston, Newport Beach, 1987—. Past sec. H&Q Healthcare Investors, Boston. Contbr. articles to profl. jours. Lt. (j.g.) USN, 1959-62. Mem. ABA (past chmn. subcom. on investment cos., state regulation of securities com.), Mass. Bar Assn., Boston Bar Assn. (past co-chmn. subcom. on investment cos. and investment advisers), Yale Club, Harvard Club. Congregationalist. Avocations: skiing, sailing. General corporate, Securities, Investment. Home: 701 Garrett Dr Corona Del Mar CA 92625 Office: Dechert Price & Rhoads 14th Fl 4675 MacArthur Ct Newport Beach CA 92660 E-mail: sheldon.jones@dechert.com

JONES, STEPHEN, lawyer; b. Lafayette, La., July 1, 1940; s. Leslie William and Gladys A. (Williams) J.; m. Virginia Hadden (dec.); 1 child, John Chapman; m. Sherrel Alice Stephens, Dec. 27, 1973; children: Stephen Mark, Leslie Rachael, Edward St. Andrew. Student, U. Tex., 1960-63; LLB, U. Okla., 1966. Sec. Rep. Minority Conf., Tex. Ho. of Reps., 1963; personal asst. to Richard M. Nixon N.Y.C., 1964; adminstrv. asst. to Congressman Paul Findley, 1966-69; legal counsel to gov. of Okla., 1967; spl. asst. U.S. Senator Charles H. Percy and U.S. Rep. Donald Rumsfeld, 1968; mem. U.S. del. to North Atlantic Assembly NATO, 1968; staff counsel censure task force Ho. of Reps. Impeachment Inquiry, 1974; spl. U.S. atty. No. Dist. Okla., 1979; spl. prosecutor, spl. asst. dist. atty. State of Okla., 1977; judge Okla. Ct. Appeals, 1982; civil jury instrn. com. Okla. Supreme Ct., 1979-81; adv. com. ct. rules Okla. Ct. Criminal Appeals, 1980; now mng. ptnr. Stephen Jones & Assoc., Enid, Okla. Adj. prof. U. Okla., 1973-76; instr. Phillips U., 1982-90; bd. dirs. Coun. on the Nat. Interest Found. Author: Oklahoma and Politics in State and Nation, 1907-62, 1974, Others Unknown: The Oklahoma City Bombing Case and Conspiracy, 1998; co-author: France and China, The First Ten Years, 1964-74, 1991, Vernon's Oklahoma Forms 2d Criminal Practice & Procedure Vols. I, II, 1999; contbr. articles to various jours. Bd. dirs., coun. mem. Nat. Interest Found.; acting chmn. Rep. State Com., Okla., 1982; Rep. nominee Okla. atty. gen., 1974, U.S. Senate, 1990; spl. counsel to Gov. Okla., 1995; apptd. chief def. counsel by U.S. Dist. Ct., Oklahoma City, U.S. vs. Tim McVeigh, Oklahoma City Bombing Case, 1995-97; mem. vestry St. Matthews Episc. Ch., 1974, sr. warden, 1983-84, 89-90. Mem. ABA, Okla. Bar Assn., Garfield County Bar Assn., Beacon Club, Petroleum Club (Oklahoma City). General civil litigation, Criminal, Taxation, general. Office: PO Box 472 Enid OK 73702-0472

JONES, STEPHEN WITSELL, lawyer; b. Honolulu, Aug. 12, 1947; s. Allen Newton Jr. and Maude Estelle (Witsell) J.; m. Judy Kaye Mason, Aug. 13, 1977; children: MaryAnn, Adam, Kathleen. Student, Hendrix Coll., 1965-66; AB with high honors, U. Ill., 1969; JD with highest honors, U. Ark., Little Rock, 1978. Bar: Ark. 1978, U.S. Dist. Ct. (ea. and we. dists.) Ark. 1978, U.S. Ct. Appeals (7th and 8th cirs.) 1978, U.S. Supreme Ct. 1984. Rsch. statistician Ark. Dept. Parks and Tourism, Little Rock, 1971-72, dir. tourist info. ctr., 1972-74; affirmative action specialist Office of the Gov., 1974-75; dir. pers. Ark. Social Svcs. Div., 1975-77; mgmt. info. specialist Ark. Health Dept., 1977-78; assoc. House, Holmes & Jewell, 1978-84; ptnr. House, Wallace, Nelson & Jewell, 1984-86; mng. ptnr. Jack, Lyon & Jones, P.A., 1986—. Adj. instr. div. lifelong edn. U. Ark., Little Rock, 1992-95. Co-author: Employment Law Deskbook for Arkansas Employers, 1997; editor-in-chief U. Ark. Little Rock Law Rev., 1977; editor Ark. Employment Law Letter, 1996—; contbg. author: Employment Discrimination Law, 2d edit., 1983; editor. Bd. dirs. United Cerebral Palsy of Ctrl. Ark., Little Rock, 1978—; bd. dirs. Ark. Ice Hockey Assn., 1992-2000; pres. Ctrl. Ark. Youth Hockey Assn., 2000. With U.S. Army, 1969-71. Recipient Svc. Recognition award United Cerebral Palsy of Ctrl. Ark., 1986, 95. Fellow Coll. Labor and Employment Lawyers, Greater Little Rock C. of C.; mem. ABA (labor/litigation law practice mgmt. sect.), Ark. Bar Assn., Def. Rsch. Inst., Ark. State C. of C. (bd. dirs., chair health com.). Episcopalian. Avocations: photography, golf. Civil rights, Federal civil litigation, Labor. Home: 1724 S Arch St Little Rock AR 72206-1215 Office: Jack Lyon & Jones PA 3400 TCBY Tower 425 W Capitol Ave Little Rock AR 72201-3405

JONES, SYLVANUS BENSON, adjudicator, consultant, lawyer; b. Southport, N.C., Nov. 21, 1928; s. Thomas Henry and Katie Mable J.; m. Karen Ann Charbonneau, Aug. 10, 1970 (div. May 1975); 1 child, Donovan; m. Brenda Castleyoung-Jones, Sept. 9, 1999. Student, Howard U., 1945-48; AD in Fin., Peter's Bus. Coll., Washington, 1955; postgrad., Fgn. Svc. Inst., Arlington, Va., 1956, George Washington U., 1959-60, Bibliothèque de la Sorbonne U. de Paris, Paris, 1962, Georgetown U., Washington, 1962, Am. U., 1966-68. Lic. real estate agt.; lic. gen. contractor, Md.; lic. ins. agt., Md., D.C. Enumerator, IBM computer operator U.S. Census Bur., Suitland, Md., 1950-51; clk. typist, claims div. VA, Washington, 1951-52; rsch. clk. Bur. Security and Consular Affairs, U.S. Dept. State, 1952-53, supr. passport processing sect., 1953-56, from jr. to sr. adjudicator domestic adjudication div., 1956-61, consular affairs officer adv. opinions div., 1961-63, chief pvt. bill staff, office of dep. dir. for ops., 1963-68, chief fraud and investigation unit, 1968-72; adjudicator, gen. cons., 1972—. Editor-in-chief The Washington Press, 1957-63; founder, dir. Mut. Fund Investment Program for Govt. Employees, Washingotn, 1969-73; instr. Tennis U. Puebla (Mex.), 1973-75; editor-in-chief The Annapolis (Md.) Press, 1989—; chmn. ad hoc com. to repeal the utilities tax, Annapolis, 1992—. Contbr. articles to profl. jours; grantee hub cap locking device. Treas. Annapolis City Dem. Ctrl. Com., 1992, 97; Dem. candidate for mayor, Annapolis, 1993, 97, 2001; chmn. trans. adv. bd., Annapolis, 1992-98. Recipient Cert. of Disting. Citizenship, City of Annapolis, 1987, 97, 99, Gov.'s Citation for Outstanding Svc. to Citizens, State of Md., 1997, 99, Red Cross Citizenship award, Trailblazer award U.S. Dept. State, 1998; numerous meritorious svc. awards; Howard U. scholar. Home: 16 Bausum Dr Annapolis MD 21401-4309 E-mail: syl_jones@juno.com

JONES, THEODORE LAWRENCE, lawyer; b. Dallas, Nov. 29, 1920; s. Theodore Evan and Ernestine Lucy (Douthit) J.; m. Marion Elizabeth Thomas, Feb. 29, 1944; children: Suzanne Maas, Scott Evan, Stephen Lawrence, Shannon Ritter. BBA, U. Tex., 1944, JD, 1948; postgrad., So. Meth. U., 1950-52, Am. U., 1965-66. Bar: Tex. 1948, D.C. 1988, U.S. Supreme Ct. 1962; cert. panelist for arbitration and mediation Internat. Ctrs. for Arbitration, 1994—. Assoc. Carrington, Gowan, Johnson & Walker, Dallas, 1948-51; gen. counsel W. H. Cothrum & Co., 1951-54; pvt. practice law, 1955-56; asst. atty. gen., chief ins., banking and corp. div. Atty. Gen. Office, Tex., 1957-60; ptnr. Herring & Jones, Austin, 1960-61; gen. counsel maritime adminstrn. U.S. Dept Commerce, 1961-63; dep. gen. counsel Dept. Commerce, 1963-64, dep. fed. hwy. adminstr., 1964-66; pres. Am. Ins. Assn., N.Y.C., 1967-86; counsel Hunton & Williams, Washington, 1986-99; pvt. practice Floyd, Va., 1999—. Chmn. interdeptl. com. for bilateral agreements for acceptance of nuclear ship, Savannah, 1962-63; lectr. Fgn. Service Inst., 1962-64; alt. U.S. rep. 11th session Diplomatic Conf. on Maritime Law, Brussels, 1962; advisor U.S. del. 6th session Coun., Intergovtl. Maritime Consultative Orgn., London, 1962; mem. maritime subsidy bd. U.S. Dept. Commerce, 1962-63; acting hwy.

beautification coord., 1965-66; del. White House Conf. on Internat. Cooperation; mem. Property-Casualty Ins. Coun., 1976-86, Internat. Ins. Adv. Coun., 1980-87; mem. adv. com. Pension Benefit Guaranty Corp., 1977; mem. Time Newstour, Ea. Europe and Persian Gulf, 1981, Mexico and Panama, 1983, Pacific Rim, 1985; bd. dirs. Nat. Safety Coun., 1967, Ins. Inst. for Hwy. Safety, 1967-86. Contbr. articles to profl. jours. Lt. (j.g.) USNR, 1944-46; lt. commdr. 1962-66. Mem. ABA, D.C. Bar Assn., Fed. Bar Assn. (chmn. nat. spkrs. bur. 1964), Tex. Bar Assn., Am. Judicature Soc., Friars, Phi Delta Phi, Beta Gamma Sigma, Phi Eta Sigma. Democrat. Presbyterian. Home and Office: PO Box 787 2616 Christiansburg Pike NE Floyd VA 24091 Office: Hunton & Williams 1900 K St NW Ste 1100 Washington DC 20006-1110 E-mail: 180jones@earthlink.com

JONES, WILLIAM ALLEN, lawyer, entertainment company executive; b. Phila., Dec. 13, 1941; s. Roland Emmett and Gloria (Miller) J.; m. Margaret Smith, Sept. 24, 1965 (div. 1972); m. Dorothea S. Whitson, June 15, 1973; children— Darlene, Rebecca, Gloria, David. BA, Temple U., 1967; MBA, JD, Harvard U., 1972. Bar: Calif. 1974. Atty. Walt Disney Prodns., Burbank, Calif., 1973-77, treas., 1977-81; atty. Wyman Bautzer et al, L.A., 1981-83, MGM/UA Entertainment Co., Culver City, 1983, v.p., gen. counsel, 1983-86; sr. v.p., corp. gen. counsel, sec. MGM/UA Communications Co., Calif., 1986-91; exec. v.p., gen. counsel, sec. Metro-Goldwyn-Mayer Inc., Santa Monica, 1991-95, exec. v.p. corp. affairs, 1995-97, sr. exec. v.p., 1997—. Bus. mgr. L.A. Bar Jour., 1974-75; bd. dirs. The Nostalgia Network Inc.; mem. bd. of govs. Inst. for Corp. Counsel, 1990-93. Charter mem. L.A. Philharm. Men's Com., 1974-80; trustee Marlborough Sch., 1988-93, Flintridge Preparatory Sch., 1993-96. With USAF, 1960-64. President's scholar Temple U., 1972 Mem. Harvard Bus. Sch. Assn. So. Calif. (bd. dirs. 1985-88). Home: 1557 Colina Dr Glendale CA 91208-2412 Office: Metro Goldwyn Mayer Inc 2500 Broadway Santa Monica CA 90404-3065

JONES, WILLIAM JOHNSON, lawyer; b. Orange, N.J., Aug. 14, 1935; s. William Johnson and Amelia (Opdyke) J.; children— Elizabeth, Jane. A.B., Princeton U., 1957; J.D., Harvard U., 1960. Bar: N.Y. 1961. Asst. dist. atty. N.Y. County, N.Y.C., 1960-66; atty. Western Electric, N.Y.C., 1966-72; gen. atty. N.Y. Telephone, N.Y.C., 1972-75, 78-79; atty. AT&T, N.Y.C., 1975-78, 79-83; gen. solicitor AT&T Techs., Berkeley Heights, N.J., 1983-86, AT&T, Berkeley Heights, 1986-89, AT&T, Basking Ridge, N.J., 1990—. Author: Fifty Years on Fifth, 1957. Mem. ABA, Ctr. Pub. Resources, Ctr. for Litigation Risk Analysis (bd. advs.), Lewis Carroll Soc. Clubs: Princeton (N.Y.), Nassau (Princeton). Antitrust, Environmental, Public utilities. Home: 67 Park Ave # 10-d New York NY 10016-2557 Office: AT&T 295 N Maple Ave Basking Ridge NJ 07920-1002

JONES, WILLIAM REX, law educator; b. Murphysboro, Ill., Oct. 20, 1922; s. Cluade E. and Ivy P. (McCormick) J.; m. Miriam R. Lamy, Mar. 27, 1944; m. Gerri L. Haun, June 30, 1972; children: Michael Kimber, Jeanne Keats, Patricia Combs, Sally Horowitz, Kevin. BS, U. Louisville, 1950; JD, U. Ky., 1968; LLM, U. Mich., 1970. Bar: Ky. 1969, Ind. 1971, U.S. Supreme Ct. 1976. Exec. v.p. Paul Miller Ford, Inc., Lexington, Ky., 1951-64; pres. Bill's Seat Cover Ctr., Inc., 1952-65, Bill Jones Real Estate, Inc., Lexington, 1965-70; asst. prof. law Ind. U., Indpls., 1970-73, assoc. prof., 1973-75, prof., 1975-80; dean Salmon P. Chase Coll. Law. No. Ky. U., Highland Heights, 1980-85, prof., 1980-93, prof. emeritus, 1993—. Vis. prof. Shepard Broad Law Ctr., Nova Southeastern U., Ft. Lauderdale, Fla., 1994-95; mem. Ky. Pub. Advocacy Commn., 1982-93, 97-2000, chmn., 1986-93. Author: Kentucky Criminal Trial Practice, 3d edit., 2001, Kentucky Criminal Trial Practice Forms, 3d edit., 2000. 1st sgt. U.S. Army, 1940-44. Cook fellow U. Mich., 1969-70, W.G. Hart fellow Queen Mary Coll. U. London, 1985. Mem. Order of Coif. Office: No Ky U Nunn Hall Highland Heights KY 41099-1400 E-mail: jonesw@nku.edu, wrexjones@zoomtown.com

JONTZ, JEFFRY ROBERT, lawyer; b. Stuart, Iowa, May 28, 1944; s. John Leo Jontz and Leora Burnette (Pittman) Myers; m. Sharyn Sue Kopriva, June 8, 1968; 1 son, Eric Barrett. BA, Drake U., 1966; JD with distinction, U. Iowa, 1969. Bar: Iowa 1969, Fla. 1971, Ohio 1972, U.S. Dist. Ct. (mid. dist.) Fla. 1971, U.S. Ct. Appeals (5th cir.) 1971, fla. 1972, U.S. Ct. Appeals (11th cir.) 1981, U.S. Tax Ct. 1983. Law clk. to Hon. Charles R. Scott U.S. Dist. Ct. (mid. dist.) Fla., Jacksonville, 1969-70; to Hon. Bryan Simpson U.S. Ct. Appeals (5th cir.), 1970-71; assoc. Jones, Day, Cockley & Reavis, Cleve., 1971-72; asst. U.S. atty. U.S. Dist. Ct. (mid. dist.) Fla., Orlando, 1972-74; pvt. practice, 1974—; ptnr. Young, Turnbull & Linscott, 1974-79, Baker & Hostetler, Orlando, 1979, DeWolf, ward & Morris, Orlando, 1979-84, Jontz, russell & Hull, Orlando, 1985-86, Holland & Knight, 1986-96, Carlton Fields, Orlando, 1996—. Contbr. articles to profl. jours.; mem. editl. bd. Iowa Law Rev., 1968. Chmn. Fed. Judicial Rels. Com., 2001—; Past bd. dirs. The Door Drug Rehab. Ctr. of Ctrl. Fla.; bd. dirs. Fla. Symphony Orch., 1985—93, Jr. Achievement Ctrl. Fla., Inc.; mem. Rollins Coll. Tar Boosters; chmn. bankruptcy com. code enforcement bd. City of Maitland, Fla., 1990—92; chmn bd. adjustment City of Winter Park, 1995—; mem. parents com. Dartmouth Coll., 1995—99; mem. long range planning com. , former county commiteeman Orange County (Fla.) Reps.; past chmn. bd. trustees First Congregational Ch., Winter Park. Recipient Outstanding Individual Cmty. Leadership award Vol. Ctr. Ctrl. Fla., 1991. Mem. Am. Bankruptcy Inst., Ctrl. Fla. Bankruptcy Lawyers Assn., Fla. Bar (ith cir. grievance com. 1979-82, chmn. comml. litigation com. 1981-82, bankruptcy and creditor's rights com. corp. bus. and banking law sect., com. on jud. adminstrn., selection and tenure 1985-86, mem. jud. nominating procedures com. 1995-96, lectr. seminars), Orange County Bar Assn. (chmn. jud. rels. com. 1995—, bankruptcy com.), ABA (mem. comml. transactions litigation com., others), Drake U. Nat. Alumni Assn. (past chmn. ctrl. Fla. chpt., sec., bd. dirs. 1981-93, pres.'s circle coun.), Iowa State Bar Assn., Order of Coif, Winter Park Racquet Club (mem. bd. govs., sec., v.p., pres. 1989-94, 96-98), Tiger Bay Club Orlando, Citrus Club, Omicron Delta Kappa, Tau Kappa Epsilon, Phi Delta Phi. Banking, Bankruptcy, General civil litigation. Office: Carlton Fields PA 450 S Orange Ave Ste 500 Orlando FL 32802 E-mail: jjontz@carltonfields.com, jontz@worldnet.att.net

JORDAN, ALEXANDER JOSEPH, JR. lawyer; b. New London, Conn., Oct. 11, 1938; s. Alexander Joseph and Alice Elizabeth (Mugovero) J.; m. Mary Carolyn Miller, Aug. 8, 1964; children: Jennifer, Michael, Stephanie. BS, U.S. Naval Acad., 1960; LLB, Harvard U., 1968. Ptnr. Gaston & Snow, Boston, 1968-91, Bingham, Dana & Gould, Boston, 1991-93, Nixon Peabody LLP, Boston, 1994—. Mem., past chmn. adv. com. Town of Hingham, Mass., 1989-95, mem. govt. study com., 2000-2001. With USN, 1960-65, capt. USNR, 1965-94, ret. Mem. ABA, Mass. Bar Assn., Boston Bar Assn., U.S. Naval Inst., Naval Res. Assn., Harvard Alumni Assn. (regional dir. 1998-2001), U.S. Naval Acad. Alumni Assn., Harvard Club Hingham (trustee, chmn. com. schs. and scholarships, past pres.), Harvard Club of Boston. General corporate, Finance, Securities. Office: Nixon Peabody LLP 101 Federal St Fl 13 Boston MA 02110-1832

JORDAN, CHARLES MILTON, lawyer; b. Houston, Apr. 3, 1949; s. Milton and Jean J.; m. Jeanette Lutz; children: Nicole, John, Rebecca. BBA, U. Tex., 1971, JD, 1975. Bar: Tex. 1975, U.S. Dist. Ct. (so. dist.) Tex. 1976, U.S. Supreme Ct. 1978, U.S. Ct. Appeals (5th cir.) 1979, U.S. Dist. Ct. (no. dist.) Tex. 1982, U.S. Dist. Ct. (we. and ea. dists.) Tex. 1983. Assoc. Troutman, Earle & Hill, Austin, 1975-76, Simpson & Burwell, Texas City, 1976-78, Smith & Herz, Galveston, Tex., 1978-80; ptnr. Dibrell & Greer, 1980-85, Barlow, Todd, Crews & Jordan PC, Houston, 1986-88, Barlow, Todd, Jordan & Oliver, LLP, Houston, 1988-99, Barlow, Todd, Jordan & Jones, LLP, Houston, 1999—. Commr. Commn. Texas City/Galveston Ports, 1984. 1st lt. USAF, 1971-77. Recipient Outstanding Young Man Am. award, U.S. Jaycees, 1980. Mem. Tex. Bar Assn., Galveston County Bar Assn. (pres. 1981-82, bd. dirs. 1985-88), Tex. Young Lawyers Assn (bd. dirs. 1982-85, Outstanding Dir. award 1983-84), Galveston County Young Lawyers Assn. (pres. 1979-80, Outstanding Young Lawyer award 1981). Federal civil litigation, State civil litigation. Office: Barlow Todd Jordan & Jones LLP 17225 El Camino Real Ste 400 Houston TX 77058-2768 E-mail: cmjpc@subell.net

JORDAN, DANIEL PATRICK, JR. law librarian; b. Bklyn., July 15, 1951; s. Daniel Patrick and Nan (Sinnott) J. BA, Bklyn. Coll., 1975; JD, U. Pacific, 1980; MLS, Pratt Inst., 1982. Ref. librarian Touro Coll., Huntington, N.Y., 1982-83, head pub. services, 1983-86, head law libr., 1986—. Mem. ABA, Calif. Bar Assn., Am. Assn. Law Libraries. Office: Touro Coll Jacob D Fuchsberg Law Ctr 300 Nassau Rd Huntington NY 11743-4346 E-mail: DanJ@tourolaw.edu

JORDAN, DAVID FRANCIS, JR. retired judge; b. Apr. 18, 1928; s. David Francis Jordan and Frances Marion (J.) Edebohls; m. Bess Vukas, Aug. 4, 1956; children: Melissa Marie, David Francis III, Dennis Paul. AB, Princeton U., 1950; JD, NYU, 1953, LLM in Taxation, 1970. Law clk. U.S. Ct. Appeals (2d cir.), 1957-58, chief dep., clk., 1958-59; pvt. practice Smithtown, N.Y., 1959-63; ptnr. O'Rourke & Jordan, Central Islip, 1963-67; asst. dist. atty. Suffolk County, Riverhead, 1969-74; law clk. Supreme Ct., Suffolk County, 1975; investigator N.Y. Supreme Ct. Appellate Divsn. 2d dept., Bklyn., 1976; corp. counsel City of Newburgh, N.Y., 1976-78; acting city mgr., 1978; U.S. magistrate judge Ea. Dist. N.Y., Bklyn., Uniondale, and, Hauppage, N.Y., 1978-94, So. Dist. Calif., San Diego, 1994, So. Dist. Ohio, 1996; mil. judge U.S. Army Judiciary, Washington, 1969-80; legis. analyst Cen. and Ea. European Law Initiative; ret. With JAGC, U.S. Army, 1954-57; col. USAR. Decorated Meritorious Svc. medal. Mem. ABA (vice chair sr. lawyers divsn. jud. com. 1994-97). Home: 15732 Vista Vicente Dr Ramona CA 92065-4323

JORDAN, EDDIE J. former prosecutor; b. Ft. Campbell, Ky., Oct. 6, 1952; BA with honors, Wesleyan U., 1974; JD, Rutgers U., 1977. Bar: Pa. 1977, La. 1982. Law clk. for Hon. Clifford Scott Green U.S. Dist. Ct. (ea. dist.) Pa., Phila.; assoc. Pepper, Hamilton & Scheetz; asst. prof. law So. U., Baton Rouge, 1981-83; asst. U.S. atty. U.S. Dept. Justice, New Orleans, 1984-87; assoc. Sessions & Fishman, 1987-91, ptnr., 1991-92; of counsel Bryan Jupiter, 1992-94; U.S. atty. for ea. dist. La. U.S. Dept. Justice, 1994—2001; lawyer Rodney, Bordenave, Boykin & Ehret, 2001—. Mem. adv. com. on humam rels. City of New Orleans, 1993; mem. various bds. of dirs. Recipient A.P. Tureaud award Louis A. Martinet Legal Soc., 1992. Office: Rodney, Bordenave, Boykin & Ehret 400 Poydras St., Ste. 2450 New Orleans LA 70130*

JORDAN, FRANK J. lawyer; b. New Canaan, Conn., June 13, 1929; s. Michael and Anna (Markva) J.; m. Sheila Filene, June 19, 1960. BS, U.S. Mcht. Marine Acad., 1953; JD, N.Y. Law Sch., 1961. Bar: N.Y. 1961, U.S. Patent and Trademark Office 1961, U.S. Dist. Ct. (so. and ea. dists.) N.Y. 1963, U.S. Supreme Ct. 1967, U.S. Ct. Appeals (fed. cir.) 1968. Atty., Am. Standard, N.Y.C., 1963-65; assoc. Brown and Seward, N.Y.C., 1965-66; atty. Am. Can Co., Greenwich Conn., 1966-68; sole practice, N.Y.C., 1969-79; ptnr. Jordan & Hamburg, N.Y.C., 1979— . Contbr. regular column on patent law to bi-monthly publ. Lt. USN, 1953-55, Korea. Mem. Assn. Bar City N.Y., Internat. Patent and Trademark Assn., N.Y. Patent Law Assn., N.Y. Law Sch. Alumni Assn., U.S. Mcht. Marine Acad. Alumni Assn. Patent, Trademark and copyright. Home: 205 3rd Ave New York NY 10003-2506 Office: Jordan & Hamburg 122 E 42nd St Rm 4000 New York NY 10168-0069

JORDAN, JON BYRON, lawyer; b. Jefferson City, Mo., June 18, 1968; s. Jan Byron and Ivonne Marie Jordan; m. Elizabeth Ann Cintron, June 21, 1997; 1 chld, Taylor Elizabeth. BS in Bus. Mgmt., Fla. State U., 1990; JD cum laude, Loyola U., New Orleans, 1994. Bar: Fla. 1994, D.C. 1997, U.S. Dist. Ct. (so. dist.), Fla., 1995, U.S. Dist. Ct. (middle dist.), Fla., 1996. Assoc. Wicker, Smith, Tutan, O'Hara, McCoy, Graham and Ford, P.A., Miami, Fla., 1995-97; sr. counsel S.E. Regional Office, U.S. SEC, 1997-99; assoc. Baker Botts L.L.P., Washington, 1999—. Contbr. articles to law jours., including Columbia Bus. Law Rev., Northwestern Jour. Internat. Law and Bus., U. Miami Entertainment and Sports Law Rev., Mich. State U. Jour. Internat. Law. Mem. ABA, D.C. Bar (mem. steering com. Corp., Fin. and Securities Law sect., 2000—), Assn. SEC Alumni, Rep. Nat. Lawyers Assn., Phi Delta Phi, Alpha Sigma Nu, Sigma Phi Epsilon. Roman Catholic. Avocations: writing, fishing, golf. General corporate, Public international, Securities. Home: 1801 Crystal Dr Apt 811 Arlington VA 22202-4422 Office: Baker Botts LLP The Warner 1299 Pennsylvania Ave NW Washington DC 20004-2400 Fax: 202-585-1033. E-mail: jon.jordan@bakerbotts.com

JORDAN, ROBERT ELIJAH, III, lawyer; b. South Boston, Va., June 20, 1936; s. Robert Elijah and Lucy (Webb) J.; M. V. Victoria Copeland; children— Janet Elizabeth, Jennifer Anne, Robert Elijah IV. SB, MIT, 1958; JD magna cum laude, Harvard U., 1961. Bar: D.C. bar 1962, Va. bar 1964. Spl. asst. civil rights Office Sec. Def., Washington, 1963-64; asst. U.S. atty. for D.C., 1964-65; exec. asst. for enforcement Office Sec. Treasury, 1965-67; dep. gen. counsel Dept. Army, 1967, acting gen. counsel, 1967-68; gen. counsel of Army, spl. asst. for civil functions to Sec. Army, 1968-71; ptnr. Steptoe & Johnson, Washington, 1971-88, mng. ptnr., 1988-90. Mem. Jud. Conf., D.C. Cir., 1973, 86—; mem. bd. cert. U.S. Cir. Cts. of Appeals Cir. Execs., 1987-88; pres. Langley Sch., 1981-82; mem. civil pro bono com. U.S. Dist. Ct., 1991-92. Contbr. articles to profl. jours. Served to 1st lt. AUS, 1961-63. Recipient Karl Taylor Compton award, 1958, Arthur S. Flemming award, 1970, award for exceptional civilian svc. Dept. Army, 1971; Sloan Found. scholar; Edward J. Noble Found. fellow. Mem. Va. State Bar, D.C. Bar (chmn. ethics com. 1978-83, spl. com. on model rules profl conduct 1983-89, pres. 1987-88), Calif. State Bar, D.C. Bar Found. (pres. 1993-94, 97-98), Atlantic Coun. (bd. dirs. 1993—, exec. com. 1994—, chmn. nominating com. 1997-2001), Tau Beta Pi, Tau Kappa Alpha. Democrat. Antitrust, Federal civil litigation, Oil, gas, and mineral. Home: 5239 Siesta Cove Dr Sarasota FL 34242 Office: 1330 Connecticut Ave NW Washington DC 20036-1795 E-mail: rjordan@steptoe.com

JORDAN, ROBERT LEON, lawyer, educator; b. Reading, Pa., Feb. 27, 1928; s. Anthony and Carmela (Votto) J.; m. Evelyn Allen Willard, Feb. 15, 1958 (dec. Nov. 1996); children: John Willard, David Anthony BA, Pa. State U., 1948; LLB, Harvard U., 1951. Bar: N.Y. 1952. Assoc. White & Case, N.Y.C., 1953-59; prof. law UCLA, 1959-70, 75-91, prof. law emeritus, 1991—, assoc. dean Sch. Law, 1968-69. Vis. prof. law Cornell U., Ithaca, N.Y., 1962-63; co-reporter Uniform Consumer Credit Code, 1964-70, Uniform Comml. Code Articles 3, 4, 4A, 1985-90; Fulbright lectr. U. Pisa, Italy, 1967-68 Co-author: (with W.D. Warren) Commercial Law, 1983, 5th edit., 2000, Bankruptcy, 1985, 5th edit., 1999. Lt. USAF, 1951-53. Office: UCLA Sch Law 405 Hilgard Ave Los Angeles CA 90095-9000

JORDAN, ROBERT LEON, federal judge; b. Woodlawn, Tenn., June 28, 1934; s. James Richard and Josephine (Broadbent) J.; m. Dorothy Rueter, Sept. 8, 1956; children: Robert, Margaret, Daniel. BS in Fin., U. Tenn., 1958, JD, 1960. Atty. Goodpasture, Carpenter, Dale & Woods, Nashville, 1960-61; mgr. Frontier Refining Co., Denver, 1961-64; atty. Green and Green, Johnson City, Tenn., 1964-66; trust officer 1st Peoples Bank, 1966-69; v.p., trust officer Comml. Nat. Bank, Pensacola, Fla., 1969-71; atty. Bryant, Price, Brandt & Jordan, Johnson City, 1971-80; chancellor 1st Jud. Dist., 1980-88; dist. judge U.S. Dist. Ct. (ea. dist.) Tenn., Knoxville, 1988—. Mem. adv. com. U. Tenn. Law Alumni, 1978-80; sec. Tenn. Jud. Conf., 1987-88, mem. exec. com., 1988; del. Tenn. State-Fed. Judicial Coun., 1993—. Bd. dirs., v.p. Tri-Cities estate Planning Coun., Johnson City, 1969; bd. dirs. Washington County Tb Assn., Rocky Mount Hist. Assn., High Rock Camp, Johnson City, Jr. Achievement of Pensacola Inc.; bd. dirs., treas. N.W. Fla. Crippled Children's Assn., Pensacola; chancellor's assoc. U. Tenn. With U.S. Army, 1954-56. Named Boss of Yr. Legal Secs. Assn., Washington, Carter County, Tenn., 1982. Mem. Tenn. Bar Assn., Tenn. Bar Found., Knoxville Bar Assn. (bd. govs. 1999), Washington County Bar Assn. (pres.-elect 1980), Johnson City C. of C., Hamilton Burnett Am. Inn of Ct. (pres. 1993-94), Kiwanis (pres. Met. Johnson City Club 1969, Kiwanian of Yr. award 1986-87). Republican. Mem. Ch. of Christ. Office: Howard H Baker US Courthouse 800 Market St Ste 141 Knoxville TN 37902-2303

JORDEN, DOUGLAS ALLEN, lawyer, zoning hearing officer; b. Ft. Smith, Ark., July 17, 1950; s. James Roy and Gordon P. J.; m. Mary Zoe Arendt, Apr. 23, 1983; children: Michael, Willie, Julia. BA, U. Ark., 1972, JD, 1976. Bar: Ark. 1976, Ariz. 1976, U.S. Dist. Ct. Ariz. 1976, U.S. Ct. Appeals (9th cir.) 1977, Calif. 1992, Colo. 1992, U.S. Supreme Ct. 1996. Assoc. Harold Mott Esq., Phoenix, 1976-78; town atty. Town of Paradise Valley, Ariz., 1978-82; assoc. Fennemore Craig, Phoenix, 1982-84; ptnr. Slavin, Kane & Paterson, 1984-88, Lancy, Scult, McVey, Phoenix, 1988-90, Jorden Law Firm, Phoenix, 1990-92, Kane, Jorden, von Oppenfeld, Phoenix, 1992-98, Jorden & Bischoff, Phoenix, 1998—. Co-author: Arizona Land Use Law, 1988, 3d rev. edit. 1998. Mem. Paradise Valley Village Planning Com. 1988-90; chmn. Phoenix Environ. Quality Commn., 1988-95. Mem. State Bar Ariz. (continuing legal edn. com. 1990-94), Rocky Mt. Land Use Inst. (regional adv. bd. 1992—). Democrat. Methodist. Avocation: hiking. Environmental, Land use and zoning (including planning), Real property. Office: Jorden & Bischoff Ste 205 7272 E Indian Sch Rd Scottsdale AZ 85251-6268 E-mail: djorden@jordenbischoff.com

JORGENSEN, ERIK HOLGER, lawyer; b. Copenhagen, July 19, 1916; s. Holger and Karla (Andersen) J.; children: Jette Friis, Lone Olssen, John, Jean Ann. JD, San Francisco Law Sch., 1960. Bar: Calif. 1961. Atty. pvt. practice, 1961-70; ptnr. Hersh, Hadfield, Jorgensen & Fried, San Francisco, 1970-76, Hadfield & Jorgensen, San Francisco, 1976-88. Author: Master Forms Agreements, Successful Real Estate Sales Agreements, 1991; contbr. articles on law and real estate to profl. jours. Pres. Aldersley, Danish Retirement Home, San Rafael, Calif., 1974-77, REbild Park Soc. Bay Area chpt., 1974-77. Fellow Scandinavian Am. Found. (hon.); mem. ABA, Calif. Assn. Realtors Assn. (hon. life bd. dirs.), San Francisco Lawyers Club, Bar Assn. San Francisco. General practice, Probate, Real property.

JORGENSEN, RALPH GUBLER, lawyer, accountant; b. N.Y.C., Mar. 12, 1937; s. Thorvald W. and Florence (Gubler) J.; m. Patricia June Spivey, June 21, 1971 (dec. Oct. 1997); 1 child, Misty. AB, George Washington U., 1960, LLB, 1962. Bar: D.C. 1963, Md. 1963, N.C. 1972, U.S. Dist. Ct. D.C. 1963, U.S. Ct. Appeals (D.C. cir.) 1963, U.S. Dist. Ct. Md. 1964, U.S. Dist. Ct. (ea. dist.) N.C. 1972, U.S. Dist. Ct. (mid. dist.) N.C. 1977, U.S. Ct. Appeals (4th cir.) 1974, U.S. Tax Ct. 1976, U.S. Ct. Claims 1979, U.S. Supreme Ct. 1971; CPA, Md., Nev., N.C. Sole practice, Washington, Silver Spring, Md., 1963-71, Tabor City, N.C., 1971—. Bd. dirs. Columbus County ARC, N.C., 1974. Mem. ATLA, Am. Assn. Atty.-CPAs, N.C. Bar Assn., N.C. Acad. Trial Lawyers, Alpha Kappa Psi. Democrat. Baptist. Federal civil litigation, State civil litigation, Taxation, general. Home: 101 Pireway Rd Tabor City NC 28463-2021 Office: 116 W 4th St PO Box 248 Tabor City NC 28463-0248 E-mail: R.G.Jorgensen@weblink.net

JORGENSON, MARY ANN, lawyer; b. Gallipolis, Ohio, 1941; BA, Agnes Scott Coll., 1963; MA, Harvard U., 1964; JD, Case Western Res. U., 1975. Bar: Ohio 1975, N.Y. 1982. Ptnr., chair firm's corp. practice Squire, Sanders & Dempsey, 1990—. Office: Squire Sanders & Dempsey LLP 127 Public Sq Ste 4900 Cleveland OH 44114-1284 E-mail: njorgenson@ssd.com

JOSCELYN, KENT B(UCKLEY), lawyer; b. Binghamton, N.Y., Dec. 18, 1936; s. Raymond Miles and Gwen Buckley (Smith) J.; children: Kathryn Anne, Jennifer Sheldon. BS, Union Coll., 1957; JD, Albany (N.Y.) Law Sch., 1960. Bar: N.Y. 1961, U.S. Ct. Mil. Appeals 1962, D.C., 1967, Mich. 1979. Atty. adviser hdqts. USAF, Washington, 1965-67; assoc. prof. forensic studies U. Ind., Bloomington, 1967-76; dir. Inst. Rsch. in Pub. Safety, 1970-75; head policy analysis divsn. Highway Safety Rsch. Inst. U. Mich., Ann Arbor, 1976-81; dir. transp. planning and policy Urban Tech. Environ. Planning Program, 1981-84; prin. Joscelyn and Treat P.C., 1981—93, Joscelyn, McNair & Jeffrey P.C., Ann Arbor, 1993-2001. Cons. Law Enforcement Assistance Adminstrn., U.S. Dept. Justice, 1969-72; Gov.'s appointee as regional dir. Ind. Criminal Justice Planning Agy., 1969-72; vice chmn. Ind. Organized Crime Prevention Coun., 1969-72; commr. pub. safety City of Bloomington, Ind., 1974-76. Editor Internat. Jour. Criminal Justice. Capt. USAF, 1961-64. Mem. NAS, ABA, NRC, D.C. Bar Assn., N.Y. State Bar Assn., Internat. Bar Assn., Transp. Rsch. Bd. (chmn. motor vehicle and traffic law com. 1979-82), Am. Soc. Criminology (life), Assn. for Advancement Automotive Medicine (life), Soc. Automotive Engrs., Acad. Criminal Justice Scis. (life), Assn. Chiefs Police (assoc.), Nat. Safety Coun., Assn. Former Intelligence Officers (life), Product Liability Adv. Coun., Sigma Xi, Theta Delta Chi. General civil litigation, Estate planning, Product liability. Office: Kent B Joscelyn PC PO Box 130589 Ann Arbor MI 48113-0589 E-mail: kbjpc@earthlink.com

JOSEPH, DANIEL MORDECAI, lawyer; b. Paterson, N.J., Aug. 20, 1941; m. Susan Fields, July 30, 1972; 1 child, Nicholas. AB, Columbia U., 1963; LLB, Harvard U., 1966. Bar: N.J. 1967, U.S. Supreme Ct. 1970, D.C. 1974. Law clk. to judge U.S. Ct. Appeals (5th cir.), Dallas, 1966-67; atty. civil div. U.S. Dept. Justice, Washington, 1967-71; asst. gen. counsel EPA, 1971-72; spl. asst. environ. affairs gen. counsel U.S. Dept. Transp., 1972-74; ptnr. Akin, Gump, Strauss, Hauer & Feld, 1974—. Mem. D.C. Bar (rules of conduct rev. com. 1991-2000, chmn. 1996-99, spl. com. on multidisciplinary practice 1999—, legal ethics com. 2000—). Federal civil litigation, Environmental. Office: Akin Gump Strauss Hauer & Feld Ste 400 1333 New Hampshire Ave NW Washington DC 20036-1564

JOSEPH, ELLEN R. lawyer; BA, Barnard Coll., 1960; JD, Columbia U., 1976. Bar: N.Y. 1977. Ptnr. Kaye Scholer LLP, N.Y.C. Mem. ABA (mem. real property law sect.), N.Y. State Bar Assn. (mem. real property law sect.), Assn. Bar City N.Y., Phi Beta Kappa. Stone Scholar. Real property. Office: Kaye Scholer LLP 425 Park Ave New York NY 10022-3506

JOSEPH, GREGORY PAUL, lawyer; b. Mpls., Jan. 18, 1951; s. George Phillip and Josephine Sheha (Nofel) J.; m. Barbara, Jan. 19, 1979. BA summa cum laude, U. Minn., 1972, JD cum laude, 1975. Bar: Minn. 1975, N.Y. 1979, U.S. Dist. Ct. Minn. 1975, U.S. Dist. Ct. (so. and ea. dist.) N.Y. 1979, U.S. Ct. Appeals (8th cir.) 1976, U.S. Ct. Appeals (2d cir.) 1979, U.S. Ct. Appeals (D.C. cir.) 1980, U.S. Supreme Ct. 1983, U.S. Tax Ct. 1987, U.S. Ct. Appeals (7th cir.) 1989, (5th cir.) 1992, (6th cir.) 1999. Pvt. practice, Mpls., 1975-79; assoc. Fried, Frank, Harris, Shriver & Jacobson, N.Y.C., 1979-82, ptnr., 1982-01, chair litigation dept., 2000-01; chmn. Gregory P. Joseph Law Offices, LLC, 2001—. Asst. U.S. spl. prosecutor N.Y.C., 1981—82, Washington, 1981—82; mem. adv. com. on fed. rules of evidence U.S. Judicial Conf, 1993—93; co-chair 3d Circuit Task Force on Selection of Class Counsel, 2001; chair com. of lawyers to enhance the jury process N.Y. State Cts., 1998—99, mem. adv. com. on civil practice, 1999—. Author: Modern Visual Evidence, 1984, Sanctions: The Federal Law of Litigation Abuse, 1989, 3rd edit., 2000, Civil RICO: A Definitive

Guide, 1992, 2nd edit., 2000; co-author: Evidence in America, 1987; editor: Emerging Problems Under the Federal Rules of Evidence, 1983, reporter 2d edit., 1991; co-editor: Sanctions: Rule 11 and Other Powers, 1986, 2d rev. edit., 1988; editorial bd. Moore's Fed. Practice, 1995—; contbr. articles to profl. jours. Fellow Am. Bar Found., Am. Coll. Trial Lawyers (chair downstate N.Y. com. 1996-98, chair fed. rules of civil procedure com. 2000—); mem. ABA (chmn. litig. sect. 1997-98), Am. Law Inst., N.Y. Bar Assn. (chair trial evidence com. 1988-94), Minn. Bar Assn., N.Y. County Lawyers Assn., Assn. of Bar of City of N.Y. (chmn. profl. responsibility com. 1993-96, mem. exec. com. 1999—). Federal civil litigation, State civil litigation. Home: 390 West End Ave Apt 10G New York NY 10024 Office: Law Offices LLC 805 Third Ave Fl 31 New York NY 10022 E-mail: gjoseph@josephnyc.com

JOSEPH, JEFFREY ALAN, lawyer; b. Chgo., Aug. 3, 1947; s. Bryan Kenneth Joseph and Carol Maxine Cummings; m. Valerie Ann Pearson, Sept. 12, 1981; children: Adriana, Bryan. BA, U. Calif., Berkeley, 1969; JD, U. Calif., Davis, 1972. Bar: Calif. 1972, U.S. Dist. Ct. (ea. dist.) Calif. 1972, U.S. Dist. Ct. (so. dist.) Calif. 1973. Dep. atty. Calif. Atty. Gen.'s Office, Sacramento and San Diego, 1972-79, prin. atty. spl. prosecuting unit San Diego, 1979-80; dep. chief counsel Calif. Dept. Transp., 1980—. Arbitrator, mediator San Diego Superior Ct., 1983—, superior judge pro tem, 1992—; adj. prof. law Thomas Jefferson Sch. of Law, San Diego, 1990—; bd. dirs. Assn. Calif. State Attys., 1982-83. Pres. Stella Maris Sch. Bd., La Jolla, Calif., 1996-97. Mem. San Diego County Bar Assn. Roman Catholic. Avocations: music, flute, guitar, basketball, history. Office: Calif Dept Transp Legal Divsn 610 W Ash St Ste 805 San Diego CA 92101-3373

JOSEPH, LEONARD, lawyer; b. Phila., June 8, 1919; s. Harry L. and Mary (Pollock) J.; m. Norma Hamberg, 1942; children: Gilbert M., Stuart A., Janet H. Fitzgerald. BA, U. Pa., 1941; LLB, Harvard U., 1947. Bar: N.Y. 1949. Law clk. to chief judge U.S. Ct. Appeals, Boston, 1947-48; since practiced in N.Y.C.; ptnr. Dewey Ballantine, 1957—. Bd. dirs., exec. com. Legal Aid Soc. N.Y., 1986-89; mem. panel of disting. neutrals CPR Inst. for Dispute Resolution. Bd. editors Harvard Law Rev., 1946-47. Served with AUS, 1943-46. Fellow Am. Bar Found., Am. Coll. Trial Lawyers Antitrust, Federal civil litigation, Public utilities. Office: Dewey Ballantine 1301 Avenue Of The Americas New York NY 10019-6022

JOSEPH, PAUL R, law educator; b. Los Angeles, Apr. 30, 1951; s. Lawrence H. Joseph and Barbara A. (Acoff) Brittin; m. Lynn Wolf, 1990. BA, Goddard Coll., 1973; JD, U. Calif., Davis, 1977; LLM, Temple U., 1979. Bar: Calif. 1977, U.S. Supreme Ct. 1981, U.S. Ct. Appeals (9th cir.) 1982, U.S. Ct. Appeals (11th cir.) 1987. Lectr. law, tchg. fellow Temple U., Phila., 1977-79; asst. prof. Salmon Chase Coll. Law No. Ky. U., Highland Heights, 1979-82, assoc. prof., 1982-84, Nova Southeastern U., Ft. Lauderdale, Fla., 1984-88, prof., 1988—, dir. internat. programs, 1996-98, Goodwin prof., 1999, assoc. dean internat. and external programs, 1999—. Interview team Benjamin Franklin Fellowship Program, Russia, 1992; spkr. on law topics including search and seizure and civil liberties, and the use of computers in legal edn., law and popular culture; lectr. in field. Author: Warrantless Search Law, 1991 (updated yearly); co-editor: Prime Time Law: Fictional Television as Legal Narrative, 1998; mem. editl. bd. Human Rights mag., 1986-95, Legal Studies Forum, 1998-99; columnist Visions mag., 1995; contbr. articles to profl. jours. Mem. Broward County Human Rights Bd., 1986-92, vice chmn., 1987-88, chmn., 1991-92; trustee Goddard Coll., 1981-90, 95-96, vice chmn. bd. dirs., 1985-86, chmn. fin. com., 1986-89, chmn. presdl. search com., 1989-90, chmn. acad. and student affairs com., 1995-96; mem. Broward County Dem. Exec. Com., 1988-92; bd. dirs. Inter-Am. Ctr. for Human Rights, 1997—. Mem. ABA (chair, liaison to state and local individual rights sects. 1991-95, individual rights and responsibilities sect. liaison to spl. com. on the drug crisis 1991-95, standing com. on Gavel awards 1996-99, Gavel awards screening com. 2000-01), ACLU (nat. bd. 1995-97, chmn. Broward County chpt. 1985-86, 90-91, chmn. legal panel 1984-87, Fla. state bd. dirs. 1985-97, chmn. legal programs com. 1986-87, pres. 1990-93, del. to nat. conv. 1987, 89, 91, 95, chair nat. affiliate leadership network 1991-93), Fla. Bar Assn. (faculty affiliate, exec. coun. pub. interest sect. 1990-92, vice-chmn. Broward county fair campaign practices com. 2000—), NSU Criminal Justice Inst. (exec. com. 2000—). Democrat. Avocations: computers, Irish music, travel. Office: Nova Southeastern U Shepard Broad Law Ctr 3305 College Ave Fort Lauderdale FL 33314-7721 E-mail: josephp@nsu.law.nova.edu

JOSEPH, STEVEN JAY, lawyer; b. Baker, Oreg., Sept. 7, 1950; s. Jay Hyrum and Patricia Jean (Cahill) J.; m. Melissa Davis Joseph, Jan. 1, 1978; children: Lindsey Joseph, Logan Joseph. BS, Ea. Oreg. State Coll., 1972; JD, U. Oreg., 1975. Bar: Oreg. 1975, U.S. Dist. Ct. Oreg. 1975. Assoc. Willard K. Carey P.C., LaGrande, Oreg., 1975-76; ptnr. Carey & Joseph P.C., 1976-88, Carey, Joseph & Mendiguren, LaGrande, 1988-95, Joseph & Mendiguren P.C., LaGrande, 1995-96; atty. pvt. practice, 1997—. Pres. La Grande Indsl. Devel. Corp., 1999—. Councilor City of LaGrande, Oreg. 1990-94, 97-98; adv. bd. Salvation Army, 1995-2001; trustee E.O.S.C. Found., 1980-95, pres. 1988-90, East Oreg. U.-East Oreg. U. Found., 2000—, La Grande Sch. Dist. Bd., 2001— Mem. LaGrande-Union County C. of C. (dir. 1982-84), Rotary, Elks. Republican. Avocations: polo, racquetball, skiing, hunting, golf. General civil litigation, Estate planning, Real property. Home: 806 Highland Pl La Grande OR 97850-3216 Office: 901 Washington Ave La Grande OR 97850-2224 E-mail: sjoseph@uwtc.net

JOSEPH, SUSAN B. lawyer; b. N.Y.C., 1958; d. Alfred A. and Bella J. BS in Econ. and Bus. Mgmt., Ramapo Coll. of N.J., 1981; JD cum laude, Seton Hall U., 1985. Bar: N.J. 1985, U.S. Dist. Ct. N.J. 1985, N.Y. 1988, U.S. Dist. Ct. (so. and ea. dist.) N.Y. 1991. Legal asst. Prudential Ins. Co. Am., Newark, 1982-85; assoc. Fox & Fox, 1985-86, Elkes, Maybruch & Weiss, P.A., Freehold, N.J., 1986-87; asst. counsel N.Am. Reins. Corp., N.Y.C., 1987-90; assoc. Mark D. Lefkowitz, Esq., 1991; mgr. GRE Ins. Group, Princeton, N.J., 1991, atty. N.Y.C., 1992-95; cons. Fin. Guaranty Ins. Co., N.Y.C., 1996-97, counsel, 1997—. Vol. campaign Bill Bradley for Senate, 1984, 90; vol. Starlight Found., N.Y.C., 1988—, mem. exec. com. Friends of the Maplewood (N.J.) Lib., 1995; mem Transp. Com., Twp. of Maplewood, 1999—. Mem. N.J. State Bar Assn. (sect. on entertainment and arts law, newsletter editor 1992-93, bd. dirs. 1992-98, founding sec. ins. law sect. 1996-98, vice chair 1998-99, chair 1999-2000). Democrat. Jewish. Avocations: writing, theater, photography. Entertainment, Insurance, Real property. Address: 747 Valley St Maplewood NJ 07040-2664

JOSEPHSON, WILLIAM HOWARD, lawyer; b. Newark, Mar. 22, 1934; s. Maurice and Gertrude (Brooks) J.; m. Barbara Beth Haws, June 18, 1995. A.B., U. Chgo., 1952; J.D., Columbia, 1955; commoner, St. Antony's Coll., Oxford (Eng.) U., 1958-59. Bar: N.Y. 1956, D.C. 1966, U.S. Supreme Ct. 1959. Assoc. Paul, Weiss, Rifkind, Wharton & Garrison, N.Y.C., 1955-58, Joseph L. Rauh, Jr., Washington, 1959; Far East regional counsel ICA, 1959-61; spl. asst. to dir. Peace Corps, 1961-62, dep. gen. counsel, 1961-63, gen. counsel, 1963-66; asso. Fried, Frank, Harris, Shriver & Jacobson, N.Y.C., 1966-67, ptnr., 1968-94, counsel, 1994-99; asst. atty. gen. in charge charities bur. N.Y. State Law Dept., 1999—. Spl. counsel N.Y.C. Human Resources Adminstrn., 1966-67, City Univ. Constrn. Fund, 1967-96, N.Y.C. Bd. Edn., 1968-71, N.Y.C. Employees' Retirement Sys., 1975-86; Nat. Dem. vice presdl. campaign coord., 1972; pres. Peace Corps Inst., 1980—; mem. N.Y. State Gov. Task Force Pension and Investment, 1987-89, N.Y. State His. Records Adv. Bd., 1990-96, N.Y. State Archives Preservation Trust, 1994-96. Bd. editors: Columbia Law Rev, 1953-55. Trustee and treas. St. Antony's Coll. trust, 1994-99. Recipient William A. Jump award exemplary achievement pub. adminstrn., 1965, Disting. Svc. award, Valerie Kantor award, Corp. Social Responsibility award Mex. Am. Legal Def. and Edn. Fund, 1980, 81, 93. Mem. Assn. Bar City N.Y. (spl. com. on Congl. ethics 1968-70), Council on Fgn. Relations. Jewish. General civil litigation, Non-profit and tax-exempt organizations, Probate. Home: 58 S Oxford St Brooklyn NY 11217-1305 Office: Charities Bur NY State Law Dept 120 Broadway Fl 3 New York NY 10271

JOSLYN, ROBERT BRUCE, lawyer; b. Detroit, Jan. 9, 1945; s. Lee Everett, Jr. and Juanita Constance (McGonegal) J.; m. Karen Sue Glenny, July 8, 1967; children: Gwendolyn Constance, Robert Bruce. BA, Fla. State U., 1967; JD, Emory U., 1970. Bar: Mich. 1970. Law clk. Gurney, Gurney & Handley, Orlando, Fla., summer 1969; assoc. Joslyn & Keydel, Detroit, 1970-74; ptnr. Joslyn, Keydel & Wallace, 1975-95; pvt. practice Robert B. Joslyn, PC, St. Clair Shores, Mich., 1996—. Vis. instr. Oakland U., Rochester, Mich., 1974-75; faculty Inst. Continuing Legal Edn., Ann Arbor, Michl, 1975—; guest instr. U. Mich. Law Sch. Co-author: Manual for Lawyers and Legal Assistants: Probate and Trust Administration, 1977, Manual for Lawyers and Legal Assistants: Taxation of Trusts and Estates, 1977, 3d edit., 1980. Active U.S. All Am. Prep. Sch. Swim Team, 1963. Mem. ABA, Detroit Bar Assn. (chmn. taxation com. 1985-87), State Bar Mich. (chairperson probate and estate planning sect. 1992-93), Am. Coll. of Trust and Estate Counsel (state chmn. 1987-92, bd. regents 1994-2001), Internat. Acad. Estate and Trust Law, Fin. and Estate Planning Coun. Detroit (bd. dirs. 1988-92, pres. 1992), Grosse Pointe Yacht Club, Phi Delta Phi, Phi Kappa Psi. Estate planning, Estate taxation, Personal income taxation. Home: 11 Waverly Ln Grosse Pointe Farms MI 48236-3123 Office: 200 Maple Park Blvd Ste 201 Saint Clair Shores MI 48081-2211

JOSSEM, JARED HAYM, lawyer; b. Rochester, N.Y., Sept. 17, 1942; s. Hyb A. A. and Mollie (Fix) J.; m. Carol Ann Ketchledge, Aug. 6, 1967 (dec. July 1989); children: Leah Rose, Joseph Raymond, Adam Abraham; m. Mary Francis Brock, Jan. 6, 1990. BS, Cornell U., 1964; JD, Syracuse U., 1968. Bar: N.Y. 1968, Hawaii 1971, U.S. Ct. Appeals (9th cir.) 1971, U.S. Ct. Appeals (D.C. cir.) 1978, U.S. Supreme Ct. 1976. Field atty. NLRB, Chgo., 1968-70; assoc. Torkildson, Katz, Jossem, Fonseca Jaffe, Moore & Hetherington and predecessor firms, Honolulu, 1970-73, ptnr., 1973— ; spl. dep. atty. gen. State of Hawaii, Honolulu, 1978-85. Pres. Nuuanu Elem. Sch. PTA, 1979-80; trustee Le Jardin Acad., 1983-86; chmn. attys. sect. Aloha United Way, 1981; pres. Honolulu unit Am. Cancer Soc., 1984, crusade chmn., 1982-84, mem. exec. com. Hawaii Pacific div. bd., residential crusade chmn., 1985-90, div. crusade vice-chmn., 1985-90; bd. dirs. Hawaii chpt. ARC, 1982-90; mem. platform and resolutions com., rules com., mem. exec. exec. com., com. Rep. Party Hawaii, 1979-94, chmn. membership com., 1981-83, vice chmn. state cen. com., 1981-85, state chmn., 1991—, small bus. chmn. Reagan-Bush campaign, 1984; chmn., del. White Ho. Conf. on Small Bus., 1986; mem. Rep. Nat. Com., 1991—. Named Advocate of Yr., SBA, Honolulu, 1982. Mem. ABA (labor law sect. com. on practice and procedure before NLRB 1979—), Hawaii State Bar Assn. (chmn. pub. relations com. 1977). Jewish. Clubs: Oahu Country, Waialae Country, Pacific (Honolulu). Lodge: Rotary (bd. dirs. 1986—). Administrative and regulatory, Federal civil litigation, Labor. Office: Verner Liipfert Bernhard McPherson & Hand Chartered 928 Nuuanu Ave Honolulu HI 96817-5190

JOST, RICHARD FREDERIC, III, lawyer; b. N.Y.C., Sept. 25, 1947; s. Richard Frederic Jr. and Gertrude (Holoch) J.; m. Sally Ann Galvin, July 29, 1972; children: Jennifer, Richard IV. BA, Dickinson Coll., 1969; JD, Syracuse U., 1975. Bar: N.Y. 1976, Nev. 1978, U.S. Dist. Ct. Nev. 1979, U.S. Supreme Ct. 1984. Dep. dist. atty. Elko (Nev.) County Dist. Atty.'s Office, 1976-80; dep. atty. gen. Nev. Atty. Gen.'s Office, Carson City, 1980-83; ptnr. Jones & Vargas, Las Vegas, Nev., 1983—. Trustee United Meth. Ch., Carson City, Nev., 1982-83; bd. dirs. Ormsby Assn. Retarded Citizens, Carson City, 1982-83. Served to lt. USNR, 1970-74. Mem. ABA (urban, state and local govt. law sect.), Clark County Bar Assn., Nat. Assn. Bond Lawyers. Democrat. Administrative and regulatory, Municipal (including bonds). Home: 2840 S Monte Cristo Way Las Vegas NV 89117-2951 Office: Jones & Vargas 3773 Howard Hughes Pkwy Las Vegas NV 89109-0949 E-mail: rfj@jonesvargas.com

JOURNEY, DREXEL DAHLKE, lawyer; b. Westfield, Wis., Feb. 23, 1926; s. Clarence Earl and Verna L. Gilmore (Dahlke) Journey Gilmore; m. Vergene Harriet Sandsmark, Oct. 24, 1952; 1 child, Ann Marie. BBA, U. Wis., 1950, LLB, 1952; LLM, George Washington U., 1957. Bar: Wis. 1952, U.S. Dist. Ct. (we. dist.) Wis. 1953, U.S. Supreme Ct. 1955, U.S. Ct. Appeals (4th cir.) 1960, U.S. Ct. Appeals (5th cir.) 1961, U.S. Ct. Appeals (D.C. cir.) 1965, U.S. Ct. Appeals (7th and 9th cirs.) 1967, U.S. Ct. Appeals (1st cir.) 1969, D.C. 1970, U.S. Dist. Ct. D.C. 1970, U.S. Ct. Appeals (2d, 3d, 6th, 8th and 10th cirs.) 1976, U.S. Ct. Appeals (11th cir.) 1981. Counsel FPC, Washington, 1952-66, asst. gen. counsel, 1966-70, dep. gen. counsel, 1970-74, gen. counsel, 1974-77; ptnr. Schiff, Hardin & Waite, 1977—. Mem. mediation program U.S. Dist. Ct. (D.C. cir.), 1989—, early neutral evaluation program, 1989-95; mem. case evaluation program D.C. Superior Ct., 1991—. Author: Corporate Law and Practice, 1975; contbr. articles to profl. jours. Pres. Am. U. Park Citizens Assn., Washington, 1970-72; trustee Lincoln-Wesmoreland Housing Project, Washington, 1978-79. With Mcht. Marine Res., USNR, 1944-46, USNG, 1948-50. Knapp scholar U. Wis., 1952. Mem. ABA, FBA, Energy Bar Assn., Masons, Army and Navy Club, Phi Kappa Phi, Phi Eta Sigma, Theta Delta Chi. Republican. Congregationalist. Administrative and regulatory, FERC practice, Municipal (including bonds). Home: 4540 Windom Pl NW Washington DC 20016-2452 Office: Schiff Hardin & Waite 1101 Connecticut Ave NW Ste 600 Washington DC 20036-4390

JOYCE, JOSEPH JAMES, lawyer, food products executive; b. Chgo., Sept. 28, 1943; s. Edward R. and Mary E. (Jordan) J.; m. Suzanne M. Sheridan, Aug. 26, 1967; children: Joseph, Michael, Peter, Kevin, Edward. BS, Xavier U., 1965; JD, Loyola U., 1968. Bar: Ill. 1968. Mem. Hill, Sherman, Meroni, Gross & Simpson, Chgo., 1968-72; atty. Pepsico, Inc., Purchase, N.Y., 1972-74, trademark counsel, 1974-77, asst. gen. counsel, 1977-86, v.p., asst. gen. counsel, 1986-98, v.p., assoc. gen. counsel, 1998—. Contbr. articles to profl. jours. Bd. mgrs. Lincoln Hall Found., Inc., 1989—. Mem. ABA, Ill. Bar Assn., U.S. Trade Assn., Assn. Internationale pour la Protection de la Propietè Industrielle (bd. dirs.), Licensing Execs. Soc., Westchester-Fairfield Corp. Counsel Assn., Inc., Assn. Inter-Am. de la Propriedad Industrial, IIPA (exec. com. 1989—, bd. dirs.). Roman Catholic. Franchising, Private international, Trademark and copyright. Office: Pepsico Inc Anderson Hill Rd Purchase NY 10577

JOYCE, MICHAEL PATRICK, lawyer; b. Omaha, Oct. 3, 1960; s. Thomas Hunt and Joan Clare (Berigan) J. Student, Miami U., Oxford, Ohio, 1978-79; BSBA, Creighton U., 1982; JD, U. Houston, 1988. Bar: Mo., Kans., U.S. Dist. Ct. (we. dist.) Mo. 1988, U.S. Dist. Ct. Kans. 1989, U.S. Ct. Appeals (8th and 10th cirs.) 1988, U.S. Supreme Ct. 1994. Assoc. mgr. Avco Fin. Svcs. Internat., Inc., Omaha, 1983-85; assoc. Wyrsch, Atwell, Mirakian, Lee & Hobbs, P.C. (formerly Koenigsdorf & Wyrsch, P.C.), Kansas City, Mo., 1988-94; shareholder Wyrsch, Hobbs, Mirakian, & Lee, PC, 1995-97; pvt. practice, 1997-98; pres. The Joyce Law Firm, LLC, Kansas City, Mo., 1998-2000; shareholder Van Osdol, Magruder Erickson & Redmond, PC, 2000—. Adj. prof. U. Mo. Kansas City Sch. Law, 1997—. Asst. editor (newsletter State Bar Tex.) Caveat Vendor, 1987-88. Grad. NITA, 1992; bd. dirs. Creighton U., 1997-99. Mem. ABA, Nat. Assn. Criminal Def. Lawyers, Am. Health Lawyers Assn., Mo. Bar Assn., Mo. Assn. Criminal Def. Lawyers, Kans. Bar Assn., Kansas City Metro Bar Assn., Johnson County Bar Assn., Creighton U. Alumni Assn. (dir. region IV nat. alumni bd. dirs. 1994-96, pres. 1997-99), Creighton U. Alumni Club (pres. Kansas City area 1992-94). Roman Catholic. Avocations: golf, basketball, community service. General civil litigation, Consumer commercial, Criminal. Office: 2400 Commerce Tower 911 Main St Kansas City MO 64105-2009 E-mail: mpjoyce@vomer.com

JOYCE, STEPHEN MICHAEL, lawyer; b. Los Angeles, Mar. 19, 1945; s. John Rowland and Elizabeth Rose (Rahe) J.; m. Bernadette Anne Novey, Aug. 18, 1973; children: Natalie Elizabeth, Vanessa Anne. BS, Calif. State U., Los Angeles, 1970; JD, U. LaVerne, 1976. Bar: Calif. 1976, U.S. Dist. Ct. (cen. dist.) Calif. 1977, U.S. Ct. Claims 1981. Pvt. practice, Beverly Hills, Calif., 1976-93; ptnr. Gold & Joyce, 1982-84. Personal atty. to Stevie Wonder and various other celebrities, 1977—. Contbr. articles to profl. jours. Served to pvt. USAR, 1963-69. Mem. ABA, Calif. Bar Assn., Los Angeles County Bar Assn., Beverly Hills Bar Assn., Los Angeles Trial Lawyers Assn., San Fernando Valley Bar Assn., Calabasas Athletic Club. Democrat. Roman Catholic. Avocation: long distance running. State civil litigation, Entertainment, General practice. Home: 4724 Barcelona Ct Calabasas CA 91302-1403 Office: 15260 Ventura Blvd Ste 640 Sherman Oaks CA 91403-5340 E-mail: enjoyce2@aol.com

JOYE, MARK CHRISTOPHER, lawyer; b. Columbia, S.C., Apr. 28, 1963; s. Reese Irby and Jacquelyn (Day) J.; m. Melissa Beaty, Apr. 7, 1990; children: Mason, Eliza. BA in Polit. Sci., U. N.C., 1985; JD, U. S.C., 1989. Bar: S.C. 1989, U.S. Dist. Ct. S.C. 1991; cert. civil trial advocate Nat. Bd. Trial Advocacy. Atty. Clawson & Staubes, LLC, Charleston, S.C., 1989-92, Joye Law Firm, LLP, North Charleston, 1992—. Mem. Coastal Carolina coun. Boy Scouts Am., 1994—. Mem. ABA, ATLA, S.C. Trial Lawyers Assn., S.C. Bar Assn. (pres. 1998-99, pres.-elect young lawyers divsn. 1997-98, sec.-treas. 1996-97, exec. coun. 1994—, bd. govs. 1999—), Am. Bd. Trial Advs., Charleston County Bar (exec. coun. 1996-97), Million Dollar Advocates Forum, Charleston Lawyers Club (sec. 1994, treas. 1995, pres.-elect 1996, pres. 1997), Atty. Info. Exchange Group, Rotary. Democrat. Presbyterian. Avocations: Hunting, boating, golf, skiing. General civil litigation, Personal injury, Product liability. Office: Joye Law Firm 5861 Rivers Ave Ste 101 North Charleston SC 29406-6044

JOYNER, J(AMES) CURTIS, federal judge; b. Newberry, S.C., Apr. 18, 1948; s. George C. and Joan C. (Glenn) J.; m. Mildred Ann Carter, Apr. 5, 1975; children: Jennifer Christine, Nicole Marie, Jacqlyn Ann. Student, Peirce Jr. Coll., Phila., 1967; BS in Acctg., Ctrl. State U., Wilberforce, Ohio, 1971; JD, Howard U., 1974. Bar: Pa. 1975, U.S. Dist. Ct. (ea. dist.) Pa. 1981. Contr. D.C. Project, Washington, 1972-73; legal publ. specialist Fed. Register, 1974-75; asst. dist. atty. Dist. Atty. Office Chester County, West Chester, Pa., 1975-80, chief dep. dist. atty., 1980-84, 1st asst. dist. atty., 1984-87; judge Ct. of Common Pleas, 15th Jud. Dist., 1987-92, U.S. Dist. Ct. (ea. dist.) Pa., Phila., 1992—. Mem. coun. trustees West Chester U., 1983-2000. Named Trailblazer in Law Enforcement Gov. Thornburgh, 1986; recipient Outstanding Svc. award to law enforcement Pa. Criminal Investigators, 1987, Disting. Law and Justice award County and State Detectives Assn., 1988, Donald K. Anthony Alumni Achievement Hall of Fame Ctrl. State U., 1994. Mem. Fed. Bar Assn. (hon.), Chester County Bar Assn. Avocations: sports, jazz, golf. Office: US Dist Ct Rm 8613 601 Market St Philadelphia PA 19106-1714

JOYNER, WALTON KITCHIN, lawyer; b. Raleigh, N.C., Apr. 1, 1933; s. William Thomas and Sue (Kitchin) J.; m. Lucy Holmes Graves, Sept. 23, 1955; children: Sue Carson Clark, Walton K. Jr., James Y. II. AB in Polit. Sci., U. N.C., 1955, JD with honors, 1960. Bar: N.C.; lic. comml. pilot. Ptnr. Joyner & Howison, Raleigh, 1960-80, Hunton & Williams, Raleigh, 1980—. Sec., treas. N.C. R.R. Co., Raleigh, 1966; bd. dirs. United Title Ins. Co., Raleigh; bd. mgrs. Wachovia Bank, N.C., 1969-98; bd. govs. U.S. Power Squadrons, 1974-81. Assoc. editor U. N.C. Law Rev. Pres. Rehab. and Cerebral Palsy Ctr. Wake County, Raleigh, 1974; trustee St. Mary's Coll., 1990-91; bd. dirs. Peace Coll. Found., 2001—. Mem. ABA, N.C. Bar Assn. (treas. probate sect. 1983), Wake County Bar Assn. (chmn., bd. dirs. 1977), Law Alumni Assn. U. N.C. (bd. dirs.), Order of Coif (cert. mediator), Carolina Country Club (pres. 1983-84, 2000-2001). Presbyterian. Avocation: flying. General corporate, Probate. Home: 620 Marlowe Rd Raleigh NC 27609-7022 Office: Hunton & Williams 1 Hannover Sq PO Box 109 Fl 14 Raleigh NC 27602-0109

JOZWIAK, STEVEN JAY, lawyer; b. N.Y.C., Apr. 19, 1957; s. Leon and Selma Fern (Chaikin) J.; m. Erin Jo Chilbert, Dec. 27, 1994; 1 child, Theodore Samuel. BA, Rutgers Coll., 1979; Diplomate, San Diego U., 1981, Inst. Comparative & Internat. Law Oxford U., 1981; JD, Widener U., 1982; LLM, NYU, 1987. Bar: N.J. 1982, Pa. 1983, N.Y. 1984, U.S. Dist. Ct. N.J. 1983, U.S. Ct. Appeals (3rd cir.) 1986, U.S. Dist. Ct. (ea. dist.) Pa., 1992, U.S. Tax Ct., U.S. Supreme Ct., 2000; CPA N.J. Atty., owner Law Offices of Steven J. Jozwiak, Cherry Hill, N.J., 1986—. Adj. faculty Glassboro State Coll., 1983-84. Contbr. article to profl. jour. Bd. dirs. non-profit health orgs. Recipient Am. Jurisprudence award. Fellow N.J. Soc. CPA's; mem. ABA (mem. com. on tax acctg. problems taxation sect. 1980), Am. Asn. Atty. CPA's (pres. Phila. and greater Del. Valley chpt. 1998-2000), Nat. Assn. Accts., Camden County Bar Assn., Epsilon Delta Epsilon Hon. Fraternity, Phi Delta Phi Law Hon. Fraternity , Sigma Pi. Office: 2201 Route 38 Ste 200 Cherry Hill NJ 08002-4370 E-mail: jozco@aol.com

JUCEAM, ROBERT E. lawyer; b. N.Y.C., June 16, 1940; s. Benjamin T. and Amelia B. (Spatz) J.; m. Eleanor Pam, May 24, 1970; children: Daniel, Jacquelyn, Gregory. AB cum laude, Columbia U., 1961, LLB, 1964, JD, 1972; LLM, NYU, 1966. Bar: N.Y. 1965, U.S. Dist. Ct. (so. and ea. dists.) N.Y. 1966, U.S. Tax Ct. 1968, U.S. Ct. Appeals (2d cir.) 1967, U.S. Supreme Ct. 1971, U.S. Ct. Appeals (5th cir.) 1978, U.S. Ct. Appeals (D.C. cir.) 1980, U.S. Ct. Appeals (11th cir.) 1987, U.S. Ct. Appeals (7th cir.) 1989, U.S. Ct. Appeals (9th cir.) 1999. Law clk. U.S. Dist. Ct., N.Y., 1964-66; assoc. Fried, Frank, Harris, Shriver & Jacobson, N.Y.C., 1966-73, ptnr., 1974—. Bd. dirs. Nat. Network Def. of the Right to Counsel, Inc., 1985-89, Lawyers Com. for Human Rights, 1986-94, Bar Assurance and Reins. Ltd., 1991—, Am. Immigration Law Found., 1987—, pres., 1991-2000, treas., 2000—; gen. counsel U.S. Supreme Ct. Hist. Soc., 1995—, trustee, mem. exec. com., 1999—; mem. arbitration panel U.S. Dist. Ct. (ea. dist.) N.Y., 1986—; mem. comml. and constrn. panels Am. Arbitration Assn., 1972-94; dir. civil rights Washington Lawyers Com., 1996-99; mem. bd. advisors D.C. Bar Found., 1996-2001; treas., bd. dirs. Pro Bono Inst., 1997—. Contbr. articles to legal jours. Trustee Mex.-Am. Legal Def. and Edn. Fund, 1986-90, chmn. program and planning com., 1988-90; adv. com. to task force on racial, gender and minority discrimination U.S. Ct. Appeals for 2d Circuit, 1994-96; bd. dirs. Appleseed Found., Inc., 1997-99; mem. bd. advisors Atlantic Legal Found., 2001—. Recipient Lester Zazuly medal, 1958, Columbia Coll. Alumni Achievement award, 1961, Edward Foxx prize Columbia Coll., 1961, Maldef Corp. Responsibility award, 1993, Valerie J. Kantor award for extraordinary achievement, 1997, Am. Immigration Law Found. hon. fellow and Founder's award, 1989, Lifetime Achievement award Ctr. for Human Rights and Constl. Law, 1993. Fellow Am. Bar. Found. (life), ABA (ho. of dels. 1983—, chmn. com. on immigration sect. litigation 1985-90, immigration pro bono adv. task force, 1992-98, vice chmn., 1995-96, mem. coordinating com. on immigration law 1984-87, chmn. 1989-92, mem. com. environ. controls sect. banking, 1983-86, vice chmn. com. on constrn., sec. gen. practice 1989-90, mem. standing com. lawyers pub. svc. responsibility 1993-96, mem. coun. fund justice & edn. 1994-2000, adv. mem., 2000—, chmn. major gifts com. 1997-98, Pro Bono award 1992); mem. Internat. Bar Assn. (chmn. Sect. Gen. Practice com. bus. migration 1987-88), N.Y. State Bar Assn., Assn. Bar City of N.Y. (com. on trademarks and unfair competition 1983-86,

com. immigration 1986-89, com. on profl. and jud. ethics 1989-92, com. Human Rights Law 1994-96), Nat. Assn. Criminal Def. Lawyers (co-chmn. com. on immigration 1988-90), Am. Judicature Soc. (life), Am. Bar Endowment, Nat. Conf. Bar Presidents (assoc.), Am. Immigration Lawyers Assn. (pres. 1982-83, bd. govs. 1971—, chmn. N.Y. chpt. 1971-72, gen. counsel 1986-91, liaison to ABA commn. on nonlawyer practice 1993-94, editor Ann. Symposium Handbook 1985-88, assoc. editor 1989-90, Edith Lowenstein Meml. award 1981, Pro Bono award 1992), Am. Mgmt. Assn., Fed. Bar Assn., Fed. Bar Coun., N.Y. County Lawyers Assn. (reporter N.Y. Equitable Distribution Law Proposals 1968, bd. dirs. 1996-98), Def. Rsch. Inst., N.Y. Criminal Bar Assn., N.Y. State Trial Lawyers Assn., Assn. Profl. Responsibility Lawyers, Assn. Fed. Def. Lawyers, Cow Neck Peninsula Hist. Soc. (life), Italy and Colonies Philatelic Soc. of Gt. Brit. (life), Jack Knight Soc. (life), L.I. Postal History Soc. (life), Am. Helvetia Philatelic Soc. (life), Am. Philatelic Soc. (life), Internat. Federation Postcard Dealers, City Club (Washington), Columbia Club, India House Club, Continental Club, Alpha Epsilon Pi. Administrative and regulatory, General civil litigation, Insurance. Home: 106 Hemlock Rd Manhasset NY 11030-1214 Office: Fried Frank Harris Shriver & Jacobson 1 New York Plz Ste 2500 New York NY 10004-1901

JUDD, DENNIS L. lawyer; b. Provo, Utah, June 27, 1954; s. Derrel Wesley and Leila (Lundquist) J.; m. Carol Lynne Chilberg, May 6, 1977; children: Lynne Marie, Amy Jo, Tiffany Ann, Andrew, Jacquelyn Nicole. BA in Polit. Sci. summa cum laude, Brigham Young U., 1978, JD, 1981. Bar: Utah 1981, U.S. Dist. Ct. Utah 1981. Assoc. Nielson & Senior, Salt Lake City and Vernal, Utah, 1981-83; dep. county atty. Uintah County, Vernal, 1982-84; ptnr. Bennett & Judd, 1983-88; county atty. Daggett County, Utah, 1985-89, 91-99; pvt. practice Vernal, 1988—; county atty. Daggett County, 2000—; prosecutor City of Naples, Naples, 1996-99; legal counsel Uintah County Sch. Dist., 1996—; city atty. Naples City, Utah, 1999—, Vernal City, 2000—; atty. City of Vernal, 2000—. Mem. governing bd. Uintah Basin applied Tech. Ctr., 1991-95, v.p., 1993-94, pres., 1994-95. Chmn. bd. adjustment Zoning and Planning Bd., Naples, 1982-91, 94—; mem. Naples City Coun., 1982-91; mayor pro tem City of Naples, 1983-91; legis. v.p. Naples PTA, 1988-90; sec. Friends of Utah Field House of Natural History, 2000—; v.p. Uintah Dist. PTA Coun., 1990-92; mem. resolution com. Utah League Cities and Towns, 1985-86, small cities com., 1985-86; trustee Uintah Sch. Dist. Found., 1988-97, vice chmn., 1991-93; mem. Uintah County Sch. Dist. Bd. Edn., 1991-95, v.p., 1991-92, pres., 1992-95; chmn. Uintah County Rep. Conv., 1998. Hinkley scholar Brigham Young U., 1977. Mem. Utah Bar Assn., Uintah Basin Bar Assn., Statewide Assn. Prosecutors, Vernal C. of C. Republican. Mormon. Avocations: hunting, photography, lapidary. Home: 460 E 1555 S Naples UT 84078 Office: 461 W 200 S Vernal UT 84078-3049

JUDELL, HAROLD BENN, lawyer; b. Milw., Mar. 9, 1915; s. Philip Fox and Lena Florence (Krause) J.; m. Maria Violeta van Ronzelen, May 5, 1951 (div.); m. Celeste Seymour Grulich, June 24, 1986. BA, U. Wis., 1936, JD, 1938; LLB, Tulane U., 1950. Bar: Wis. 1938, La. 1950. Mem. Scheinfeld Collins Durant & Winter, Milw., 1938; spl. agt., adminstrv. asst. to dir. FBI, 1939-44; legal attache U.S. Embassy Peru, 1942-44; ptnr. Foley & Judell, LLP, New Orleans, 1950—; v.p., dir. Dauphine Orleans Hotel Corp., 1970—, chmn. bd., 1999—. Mem. Tulane U. Bus. Sch. Coun.; trustee Greater New Orleans YMCA, 1981—; dir. Sizeler Property Investors, Inc., 1986—. Fellow Am. Coll. Bond Counsel (founding); mem. ABA, La. Bar Assn., Nat. Assn. Bond Lawyers (bd. dirs., pres. 1984-85), New Orleans Country Club, Lawn Tennis Club, Met. Club (N.Y.C.). Municipal (including bonds). Office: Foley & Judell 365 Canal St New Orleans LA 70130-1112 E-mail: hjudell@foleyjudell.com

JUDGE, BERNARD MARTIN, editor, publisher; b. Chgo., Jan. 6, 1940; s. Bernard A. and Catherine Elizabeth (Halloran) J.; m. Kimbeth A. Wehrli, July 9, 1966; children: Kelly, Bernard R., Jessica. Reporter City News Bur., Chgo., 1965-66; reporter Chgo. Tribune, 1966-70, city editor, 1974-79, asst. mng. editor met. news, 1979-83; editor, gen. mgr. City News Bur. Chgo., 1983-84; assoc. editor Chgo. Sun-Times, 1984-88; from editor to pub. Chgo. Daily Law Bull., 1988—; pub. Chgo. Lawyer, 1989—; v.p. Law Bull. Pub. Co., Chgo., 1988—. Bd. dirs. Constnl. Rights Found., Chgo., 1992—, chmn. bd. dirs., 1995-97; trustee Fenwick Cath. Prep. H.S., Oak Park, Ill., 1989—. Named to Chgo. Journalism Hall of Fame, 2000. Mem. Sigma Delta Chi. Home: 360 E Randolph St Apt 1905 Chicago IL 60601-7335 Office: Law Bull Pub Co 415 N State St Chicago IL 60610-4631

JUDICE, MARC WAYNE, lawyer; b. Lafayette, La., Oct. 22, 1946; s. Marc and Gladys B. Judice; 1 child, Renee. BS, U. La., 1969; MBA, U. Utah, 1974; JD, La. State U., 1977. Bar: La. 1977; CPA, La.; bd. cert. civil trial law, civil trial advocacy Nat. Bd. Trial Advocacy. Ptnr. Voorhies & Labbe, Lafayette, 1977-85, Juneau, Judice, Hill & Adley, Lafayette, 1985-93, Judice & Adley, Lafayette, 1993—. Bd. dirs. Univ. Med. Ctr., Lafayette, 1991, chmn.; bd. dirs. Home Savs. Bank, Lafayette, 1996—, Women's & Childrens Hosp., Lafayette, 1992-94; bd. trustees Med. Ctr. Southwest La., 1998-2001, chmn. bd. dirs., 1999-2001. Republican. Roman Catholic. Insurance, Personal injury, Professional liability. Office: Judice & Adley 926 Coolidge Blvd Lafayette LA 70503-2434 E-mail: mwj@judice-adley.com

JUDSON, C(HARLES) JAMES (JIM JUDSON), lawyer; b. Oregon City, Oreg., Oct. 24, 1944; s. Charles James and Barbara (Busch) J.; m. Diana L. Gerlach, Sept. 7, 1965; children: Kevin, Nicole. BA cum laude, Stanford U., 1966, LLB with honors, 1969. Bar: Wash. 1969, U.S. Tax Ct. 1970, D.C. 1981. Ptnr. Davis Wright Tremaine, Seattle, 1969—; v.p. Eagle River, Inc. Speaker various convs. and seminars. Author: State Taxation of Fin. Instns., 1981; contbr. articles to profl. jours. Chmn. Bus. Tax Coalition, Seattle, 1987; chmn. lawyers div. United Way, Seattle, 1986, 87, commerce and industry div., 1989-91; trustee Wash. State Internat. Trade Fair, Seattle, 1981-86; bd. dirs. Seattle Prep. Sch., 1986-88; bd. dirs. Olympic Park Inst., 1988—, Yosemite Nat. Insts., 1993—; mem. Assn. Wash. Bus. Tax Com., 1978—; tax advisor Wash. State House Reps. Dem. Caucus; advisor Wash. State Dept. Revenue on Tax and Legis. Matters; mem. Seattle Tax Group, 1983—. Fellow Am. Coll Tax Counsel; mem. ABA (chmn. com. on fin. orgns. tax sect. 1978-82, subcom chmn. state and local tax com. tax sect. 1979—, chmn. excise tax com. 1983-90, interorgn. coordination com. 1985—, chmn. interorgn. tax com. 1991—), Wash. State Bar Assn. (chmn. tax sect. 1984-86, chmn. western region IRS/bar liaison com. 1987-88, mem. rules com. 1991—), Seattle-King County Bar Assn. (mem. tax sect. 1973-86), Seattle C. of C. (tax com. 1982—), Wash. Athletic Club (Seattle), Broadmoor Golf Club (Seattle), Bear Creek Golf Club (Redmond). Avocations: skiing, golf, basketball, wood working, hiking. General corporate, Taxation, general, State and local taxation. Office: Davis Wright Tremaine 2600 Century Sq 1501 4th Ave Seattle WA 98101-1688

JUDSON, PHILIP LIVINGSTON, lawyer; b. Palo Alto, Calif., Oct. 25, 1941; s. Philip MacGregor and Elizabeth Stuart (Peck) J.; m. Dorothy Louisa Lebohner, Sept. 6, 1963 (div. Jan., 1996); children: Wendy Patricia, Philip Lebohner, Michael Lee; m. Danielle DuPuis Kane, May 18, 1996. BA, Stanford U., 1963; JD, U. Calif., Hastings, 1969. Bar: Calif. 1970, Tex. 1999, U.S. Dist. Ct. (no. dist.) Calif. 1970, U.S. Ct. Appeals (9th cir.) 1970, U.S. Dist. Ct. (ctrl. dist.) Calif. 1984, U.S. Dist. Ct. (ea. dist.) Calif. 1985, U.S. Supreme Ct. 1987, D.C. 1988, U.S. Dist. Ct. (so. dist.) Calif. 1989, Tex. 1999, U.S. Dist. Ct. (no. and we. dists.) Tex. 2000. Assoc. Pillsbury, Madison & Sutro, San Francisco, 1969-76, ptnr., 1977-99, Skjerven Morrill MacPherson, LLP, San Jose, Calif., 1999—. Lectr. Practising Law Inst., U. Tex. Advanced Intellectual Property Law Inst. Pres. St. Mark's Sch., San Rafael, 1983-85, founding mem. trustee 1980-86; trustee Marin Acad., San Rafael, 1985-91. 1st lt. U.S. Army, 1963-65. Mem. ABA (antitrust and litigation sects.), San Francisco Bar Assn., Am. Judicature Soc., Austin Intellectual Property Law Assn., Travis County Bar Assn., Order of Coif, Phi Delta Theta. Republican. Episcopalian. Antitrust, Federal civil litigation, State civil litigation. Home: 8004 High Hollow Dr Austin TX 78750-7872 Office: 9600 Great Hills Trl Ste 300W Austin TX 78759-5682 E-mail: phil.daniy.judson@att.net, pjudson@skjerven.com

JUERGENSMEYER, JOHN ELI, lawyer; b. May 14, 1934; s. Irvin Karl and Clara Augusta (johannaber) J.; m. Elizabeth Ann Bogart, Sept. 10, 1963; children: Margaret Ann, Frances Elizabeth. BA, U. Ill., 1955; JD, 1963; MA, Princeton U., 1957; PhD, 1960. Bar: Ill. 1963, U.S. Supreme Ct. 1968. Mem. faculty extension div. U. Ill., 1961-63, 73-74, U. Hawaii, 1958-60; mem. firm Kirkland, Brady, McQueen, Martin & Schnell, Elgin, Ill., 1963-64; founder, sr. ptnr. Juergensmeyer, Zimmerman, Smith & Leahy, 1964-81, Juergensmeyer-Strain & Assocs., Elgin, 1981-95, Juergensmeyer & Assocs., 1995—. Mgr., owner Tollview Office Complex, 1976-95; asst. pub. defender Kane County, 1964-67, asst. states atty., 1976-78; spl. asst. atty. gen. State of Ill., 1978-85; hearing officer Ill. Pollution Control Bd., 1971-74; commr. U.S. Nat. Commn. on Lubraries and Info. Scis., 1982-88; lectr. Inst. for Continuing Legal Edn.; trustee ALA Endowment Fund, 1970-84; assoc. prof. Judson Coll., Elgin, 1963—; bd. dirs. Elgin Nat. Bank. Author: President, Foundations, and the People-to-People Program, 1965; dontbr. articles to profl. jours.; contbr. publs. in field. Chmn. Hiawatha Dist. Boy Scouts Am.; v.p. Elgin Family Svc. Assn., 1967-71, Elgin Sister City Comm., 1990—; sec. Lloyd Morey Scholarship Fund, 1967-73; commr. Elgin Econ.Devel. Commn., 1971-75; chmn. Kane County Rep. Ctrl. Com., 1978-80; adv. bd. Ill. Youth Commn., 1964-68; bd. dirs Wesley Found of U. Ill., 1971-75; pres. adv. bd. Elgin Salvation Army, 1973-75. Served to capt. Intelligence Svc., USAF, 1958-60. Recipient Anti-Pollution Echo award Defenders of the Fox River, Inc., 1971, Cert. Merit, Heart Fund, 1971, Outstanding Young Man award Jr. C. of C., Elgin, 1967; Princeton U. fellow, 1955-56, Merrill Found. fellow, 1956-58. Mem. Assn. Trial Lawyers Am., ABA (local govt. law sect. spl. taxing dists. com. 1978—), Ill. State Bar Assn. (chmn. local govt. com. 1974-75, editor local govt. law newsletter 1973-74, mem. seminar in USSR 1979), Chgo. Bar Assn. (chmn. local govt. com. 1975-76), Kane County Bar Assn. (chmn. legis. com. 1974, chmn. local govt. com. 1992-93), 7th Cir. Bar Assn. (membership com.), Am. Arbitration Assn. (arbitrator), Am. Polit. Sci. Assn. (panel spkr. 1960 convention, mem. Sfrican Politics seminar 1966), Fed. Bar Assn., Midwest Polit.Sci. Assn., Ill. Polit. Sci. Assn. Northwest Suburban Bar Assn. Elgin Bar Assn. (chmn. legal aid 1964-67), Rotary (pres. 1977-78, Paul Harris fellow), Jaycees (legal counsel, bd. dirs. 1965-71), Phi Beta Kappa, Phi Alpha Delta, Alpha Kappa Lambda. Methodist. Club: Union League (Chgo.). Lodges: Masons, Shriners, Rotary (pres. 1977-78). General practice, Municipal (including bonds), Personal injury. Office: Assoc. Prof. Govt. Judson College Elgin IL 60123

JUETTNER, DIANA D'AMICO, lawyer, educator; b. N.Y.C., Jan. 21, 1940; d. Paris T.R. and Dina Adele (Antonucci) D'Amico; m. Paul J. Juettner, June 29, 1963; children: John, Laura. BA, Hunter Coll., 1961; postgrad., Am. U., 1963; JD cum laude, Touro Coll., 1983. Bar: N.Y. 1984, U.S. Dist. Ct. (so. dist.) N.Y. 1984, U.S. Supreme Ct. 1987. Office mgr. Westchester County Dem. Com., White Plains, N.Y., 1976-79; dist. mgr. for Westchester County U.S. Bur. Census, N.Y.C., 1979-80; pvt. practice Ardsley, N.Y., 1984—; prof. law, program dir. for legal studies Mercy Coll., Dobbs Ferry, 1985—, asst. chair dept. law, criminal justice-safety adminstrn., 1994-98, asst. chair social and behavioral scis. divsn., pres. faculty senate N.Y., 1996-98, 2000—, asst. chair social & behavioral scis. divsn., 2000-01. Arbitrator small claims matters White Plains City Ct., 1985-89. Co-author: (booklet) Your Day in Court, How to File a Small Claims Suit in Westchester County, 1976; assoc. editor N.Y. State Probation Officers Assn. Jour., 1990-92; editor-in-chief Jour. Northeast Acad. Legal Studies in Bus., 1996-98; contbr. articles to profl. jours. Councilwoman Town of Greenburgh, N.Y., 1992—; vice chair law com. Westchester County Dem. Com., White Plains, 1987-91; corr. sec. Greenburgh Dem. Town Com., Hartsdale, N.Y., 1986-91; mem. Westchester County Citizens Consumer Adv. Coun., White Plains, 1975-91, chair, 1991; chair Ardsley (N.Y.) Consumer Adv. Commn., 1974-79. Mem. Am. Assn. for Paralegal Edn. (model syllabus task force 1992-95, chair legis. com. 1995-97), N.Y. State Bar Assn. (elder law sect. com. on pub. agy. liaison and legis. 1992-95), Westchester County Bar Assn. (chair paralegal subcom. 1990—, chair bicentennial U.S. Constitution com. 1987-91), Westchester Women's Bar Assn. (v.p. 1989-91, dir. 1994-96, co-chair tech. com. 1996-2000), Women's Bar Assn. State N.Y. (chair profl. ethics com. 1997-98). Avocation: sailing, walking. Probate, Real property. Office: Mercy Coll 555 Broadway Dobbs Ferry NY 10522-1134

JULIAN, JIM LEE, lawyer; b. Osceola, Ark., Dec. 14, 1954; s. John Roland and Lucille Angela (Potts) J.; m. Patricia Lynn Roberts, Jan. 26, 1980; 1 child, Kathryn Elizabeth. BA, Ark. State U., 1976; JD, U. Ark., 1979. Bar: Ark. 1979, U.S. Dist. Ct. (ea. and we. dists.) Ark. 1979, U.S. Ct. Appeals (8th cir.). Assoc. Skillman & Durrett, West Memphis, Ark., 1979-82; staff atty. Ark. Power and Light Co., Little Rock, 1982-84; assoc. House, Wallace & Jewell, 1984-85, ptnr., 1986-89, Chisenhall, Nestrud & Julian, Little Rock, 1989—. Pres. Crittenden County (Ark.) Young Dems., 1980-82; chmn. bd. dirs. Northside YMCA, 1992-96, North Little Rock Boys and Girls Club, 1998—. Mem. ABA, Internat. Assn. Def. Counsel, Ark. Bar Assn., Pulaski County Bar Assn., Ark. Assn. Def. Counsel, Major Sports Assn., North Hills Country Club. Avocation: golf. General civil litigation, Environmental, Insurance. Home: 3711 Lochridge Rd North Little Rock AR 72116-8328 Office: Chisenhall Nestrud & Julian 400 W Capitol Ave Ste 2840 Little Rock AR 72201-3467

JULIANO, JOHN LOUIS, lawyer; b. Oct. 21, 1944; s. John Carmine and Jeannette Helen (Ciotti) J.; m. Maryjane Theresa Groccia, July 4, 1966 (dec.); children: Jennifer, Jonathan. BBA, St. John's U., 1966; JD, Bklyn. Law Sch., 1969. Bar: N.Y. 1970, U.S. Dist. Ct. (ea. and so. dists.) N.Y., U.S. Ct. Appeals (2d cir.), U.S. Supreme Ct. Ptnr. Juliano, Karlson, Weisberg, 1970-72; pvt. practice East Northport, N.Y., 1972—. Pres., dir. Hillside United Van Lines, Inc.; mem. N.Y. State 10th Jud. Grievance Com., 1998—; lectr. Suffolk Acad. Law. Mem. ATLA, N.Y. State Bar Assn. (del., mem. nominating com.), Suffolk County Bar Assn. (pres. 1996-97, v.p. 1995-96, treas. 1994-95, sec. 1993-94, bd. dirs. 1998—), N.Y. State Trial Lawyers Assn., ICC Practitioners, Criminal Bar Assn., Columbian Lawyers Assn. (sec. 1972, treas. 1973, pres. 1974-75), Am. Inns of Ct. Criminal, Family and matrimonial, Personal injury. Address: 39 Doyle Ct East Northport NY 11731-6404

JUNGEBERG, THOMAS DONALD, lawyer; b. Berea, Ohio, June 12, 1950; s. Wilbert Donald and Carolyn Francis (Gaube) J.; m. Kathleen Ann Killmer, Oct. 5, 1973; children: Kimberlee Ann, Allison Lynn, Zebulun Thomas, Nathan Aaron. BA, Kent State U., 1972; JD, Cleve. State U., 1976. Bar: Ohio 1976, Mass. 2001, U.S. Dist. Ct. (no. dist.) Ohio 1977, U.S. Tax Ct. 1980, U.S. Supreme Ct. 1980. Tchr. Berea City Schs., Ohio, 1972-75; staff atty. Palmquist & Palmquist, Medina, 1977-80, Gibbs & Craze, Parma Heights, 1980-81; sole practice Medina, 1981-87; v.p., gen. counsel, corp. sec. Shelby (Ohio) Ins. Co., 1987-95; prin. Lexington (Ohio) Ins. Cons., 1995-96; sole practice Lexington, 1995-96; v.p. legal Reliance Nat., Cleve., 1996-98; asst. v.p., asst. gen. counsel Commerce Ins. Group, Webster, Mass., 1999—. Tchr. First Bapt. Christian Sch., Medina, 1981-84; elder, sec. First Bapt. Ch. of Medina, 1979-86, chmn. First Bapt. Christian Sch., Medina, 1984; bd. govs. Ohio Med. Profl. Liability Underwriting Assn., 1993-95; dir. Inst. Inst. Ind., 1994-95. Mem. Ohio State Bar Assn.Mass. Bar Assn., Am. Corp. Counsel Assn., Gideons Internat. Republican. Avocations: piano, archery. General corporate, Insurance, Labor. Home: 80 Hagstrom Rd North Grosvenordale CT 06255-1522 E-mail: tdjungeberg@aol.com, tjungeb@commerceinsurance.com

JUNKERMAN, WILLIAM JOSEPH, retired lawyer; b. N.Y.C., May 5, 1904; s. Otto J. and Margaret Anne (McCarthy) J.; m. Helen Veronica Barrett, June 28, 1930. AB, NYU, 1925; LLB, Fordham U., 1928. Bar: N.Y. 1929, U.S. Dist. Ct. (so. and ea. dists.) N.Y. 1929, U.S. Ct. Appeals (1st, 2d and 3d cirs.), U.S. Supreme Ct. 1946. Ensign naval aviation USNR, 1925-41; with USN, 1941-46; comdr. ret. ; asst. counsel L.I. State Park Commn., 1929-32; sole practice, N.Y.C., 1932-41; regional atty. CAA, 7th Region, Seattle, 1947-48; mem. Haight, Gardner, Poor & Havens, N.Y.C., 1948-50, gen. ptnr., 1950-80. Spl. master N.Y. Supreme Ct., N.Y. County; abitrator U.S. Dist. Ct. Edn., N.Y. Fellow Am. Coll. Trial Lawyers; mem. Nat. Pilots Assn., Naval Order of U.S., Am. Legion (past comdr.). Clubs: Quiet Birdmen, Wings. Address: 271 Madison Ave Ste 1107 New York NY 10016-1001

JURCYK, JOHN JOSEPH, JR. lawyer; b. Kansas City, Kans., Apr. 15, 1930; s. John Joseph Sr. and Ann (Kordash) J.; m. Rita Menghini, July 13, 1957; children: Jeff, John David, Amy L., Alison C., Ann. E. AB in History, Rockhurst Coll., 1952; JD, U. Kans., 1957. Bar. Kans. 1957, U.S. Dist. Ct. Kans. 1957, U.S. Ct. Appeals (10th cir.) 1957, U.S. Ct. Appeals (8th cir.) 1984, U.S. Supreme Ct. 1970. Law clk. to chief judge U.S. Dist. Ct. Kans., Kansas City, 1957; assoc. McAnany, Van Cleave & Phillips, Kans., 1958-63, ptnr., 1963—, sr. trial lawyer, pres. corp., 1978-89. Mem. nominating commn. 29th Jud. Dist., 1978-79; mem. merit selection panel for magistrate U.S. Dist. Ct. Kans., 1986-89, mem. adv. group Civil Justice Reform Act, 1991-94, mem. 10th Cir. Adv. Com., 1998-2001. Editor-in-chief Kans. Law Rev., 1957. Chmn. Civic Arts Council Kansas City (Kans.), 1965-69, Citizens Commn. on Local Govt. Wyandotte County (Kans.), 1969-70, United Way of Wyandotte County, 1995, 96; chmn. bd. edn. Bishop Ward High Sch., 1968-71; pres. St. Patrick Sch. Bd., Kansas City, Kans., 1979-80; bd. dirs. Kansas City region NCCJ, 1964-72, Kansas City, Kans., YMCA, 1971-76, Cath. Housing Svcs., 1978-2000, pres., 1985-2000; hon. dir. Rockhurst Coll., Kansas City, Mo.; mem. Kans. Citizen Justice Commn., 1997-99. Recipient Exceptional Performance citation Def. Rsch. and Trial Lawyers Assn., 1985. Fellow Am. Coll. Trial Lawyers, Am. Bar Found., Kans. Bar Found. (pres. 1995-96); mem. ABA, Kans. Bar Assn. (numerous coms., Outstanding Svc. award 1986, Disting. Svc. award 2001), Johnson County Bar Assn., Wyandotte County Bar Assn. (pres. 1970-71, editor Advocate 1968-74), Internat. Assn. Def. Counsel, Kans. Assn. Def. Counsel (pres. 1984-85), U. Kans. Law Soc. (bd. govs. 1985-88), U. Kans. Law Alumni Assn. Greater Kansas City (pres. 1966), Kansas City Area C. of C. (sec. 1971-72, bd. dirs., chmn. 1991-92), Cursillo Movement Kansas City (lay dir. 1980-83), Serra Club, Rotary (bd. dirs. Kansas City 1979). Democrat. Roman Catholic. General civil litigation, Non-profit and tax-exempt organizations, Personal injury. Office: McAnany Van Cleave & Phillips PO Box 1300 707 Minnesota Ave Fl 4 Kansas City KS 66101-2703 E-mail: jjjurcyk@mvplaw.com

JUROE, SUSAN E. lawyer; b. Detroit, Jan. 9, 1961; d. James Blickson and Ellen (Emmy) Juroe. BA in Lit., Am. U., 1983; JD, Cath. U., Washington, 1986. Bar: D.C. Atty. Sanders & Assocs., Washington, 1987-89, Paddock & Stone, Washington, 1989-96, Holland & Knight Miller Canfield, Washington, 1996—. Bd. dirs. Nat. Leased Housing, Washington, Housing and Devel. Reporter, Affordable Housing Fin. Mag., Housing Bond Report. Bd. dirs. Cmty. Residences Found., Arlington, VA. Republican. Avocation: breeding and exhibiting paint horses. Home: 1530 33d St Washington DC 20007 Office: Holland & Knight LLP 2100 Pennsylvania Ave NW Washington DC 20037-3295

JUSTICE, WILLIAM WAYNE, federal judge; b. Athens, Tex., Feb. 25, 1920; s. William Davis and Jackie May (Hanson) J.; m. Sue Tom Ellen Rowan, Mar. 16, 1947; 1 dau., Ellen Rowan. LLB, U. Tex., 1942; LLD (hon.), So. Meth. U., 2001. Bar: Tex. 1942. Ptnr. Justice & Justice, Athens, 1946-61; part-time city atty., 1948-50, 52-58; U.S. atty. U.S. Dist. Ct. (ea. dist.) Tex., Tyler, 1961-68, judge, 1968-80, chief judge, 1980-90, sr. judge, 1998—. Subject of book William Wayne Justice, A Judicial Biography (Frank R. Kemerer), 1991. Vice-pres. Young Democrats Tex., 1948; adv. council Dem. Nat. Com., 1954; alternate del. Dem. Nat. Conv., 1956, presdl. elector, 1960. 1st lt. F.A. AUS, 1942-46, CBI. Recipient Nat. Outstanding Fed. Judge award ATLA, 1982, Outstanding Civil Libertarian award Tex. Civil Liberties Union, 1986, Lifetime Achievement award NACDL, 1996, Thurgood Marshall award ABA, 2001. Episcopalian. Office: 903 San Jacinto Blvd Ste 310 Austin TX 78701-2450

KABAK, BERNARD JOSHUA, lawyer; b. Bronx, N.Y., Dec. 22, 1941; s. Samuel Louis and Jeanne (Sirotin) K.; m. Ilana Etta Stern, June 15, 1982. AB, Columbia U., 1963; LLB, Harvard U., 1966; M Urban Planning, Hunter Coll., 1968. Bar: N.Y. 1967, Israel 1975. Sr. atty. N.Y.C. Dept. City Planning, N.Y.C., 1968-73; spl. advisor Ministry of Justice, Jerusalem, Israel, 1974-75; counsel Office of Dep. State Comptroller for N.Y.C., 1976—; counsel Nat. Civic League, Council Mcpl. Performance, 1985—. Contbr. in field. Trustee Lincoln Square Synagogue, N.Y.C., 1986—; divisional chmn. United Jewish Appeal-Fedn. Jewish Philanthropies, N.Y.C., 1973; mem. exec. com. Coalition to Free Soviet Jews, N.Y.C., 1978—. Avocation: silversmith. Home: 393 W End Ave New York NY 10024-6138 Office: Office Dep Comptroller NYC 270 Broadway New York NY 10007-2306

KABAK, DOUGLAS THOMAS, lawyer; b. Elizabeth, N.J., Nov. 19, 1957; s. Aaron and Marilyn Virginia (Johnson) K.; m. Elisabeth Wiggin McDuffie, Oct. 21, 1989; 1 child, Matthew Thomas McDuffie Kabak. BA, Rutgers U., 1979, MBA, MBA, Rutgers U., 1990; postgrad., U. Exeter, Eng., 1980; JD, Seton Hall U., 1982. Bar. N.J. 1982, U.S. Dist. Ct. N.J. 1982. Law clk. Superior Ct. N.J., Elizabeth, 1982-83; assoc. Z. Lance Samay, Morristown, N.J., 1983-86; asst. dep. pub. defender Office Pub. Defender, Elizabeth, 1986—. Legal rep. St. Joseph's the Carpenter Bd. Edn., Roselle, N.J., 1985-87. Dir. St. Joseph the Carpenter Cath. Youth Orgn., Roselle, 1986-88, coach, 1981-88. Mem. KC. Roman Catholic. Home: 16 Indian Spring Rd Cranford NJ 07016-1616 Office: Pub Defender Office 65 Jefferson Ave Ste 3 Elizabeth NJ 07201-2441 E-mail: mckabak@juno.com

KABALA, EDWARD JOHN, lawyer, corporate executive; b. Phila., Mar. 21, 1942; s. Stan and Margaret (Toner) K.; m. Gail L., DEc. 28, 1963; children: Courtenay, Paxson. BS, Pa. State U., 1964; JD, Duquesne U., 1970. Bar: Pa. 1970, U.S. Dist. Ct. (we. dist.) Pa., U.S. Ct. Appeals (3rd cir.) 1970, U.S. Tax Ct. 1970. Indsl. engr. Allegheny Ludlum Steel Co., 1964-67; sr. indsl. engr. Titanium Metals Corp. Am., 1967-68; patent engr. U.S. Steel Corp., 1969; atty., 1970, Houston, Cooper, Speer and German, Pitts., 1970-73; pres. Kabala & Geeseman and predecessor firm, 1973—. Counsel Allegheny Med. Soc.; author, lectr. pensions, estate planning, taxation, fin. planning health care law various univs. and profl. orgns. of physicians, attys., accts., dentists, 1976—; editl. bd. Today's Health Care Mag., 1991—, MD News, 2001—, Best Lawyers in Am., 2001—; bd. dirs., chmn. Cancer Support Network, 1994-96. Author: Defending Your Practice in a Blue Shield Audit, 1992. Bd. dirs. Cancer Support Network, 1992-96, chmn., 1994-96; fund raiser Muscular Dystrophy Assn., 1998—. Recipient Crystal award Cancer Support Network, 1993-95. Fellow Allegheny County Bar Found.; mem. ABA (sect. taxation com. on closely held corps., com. on profl. svc. corps., sec. bus. banking and corp. law com. on employee benefits), Am. Soc. Med. Assn. Counsel, Am. Health Lawyers

Assn., Pa. Bar Assn., Allegheny County Bar Assn., Am. Acad. Hosp. Attys. Estate planning, Health, Pension, profit-sharing, and employee benefits. Home: 4405 Bayard St Pittsburgh PA 15213-1505 Office: 2900 Dominion Twr 625 Liberty Ave Pittsburgh PA 15222 E-mail: ekabala@kglawpgh.com

KACZANOWSKA, LAURIE HYSON SMITH, lawyer; b. Palmerton, Pa., July 7, 1953; d. James Donaldson and Mary Ann (Hyson) Smith; m. Donald James Gerber, Aug. 1976 (div. May 1981); m. Witold-K, Dec. 11, 1993; 1 child, Wit Thomas Kaczanowski. BS, Pa. State U., 1975; MSW, U. Denver, 1981; JD, Northeastern U., 1989. Adminstrv. staff, resource coord., vol. coord., counselor Women in Crisis, Lakewood, Colo., 1977-79; program adminstr. Big Sis. of Colo., Life Choices Program, Denver, 1979-80; legis. coord., lobbyist Common Cause, 1980-81; social work advocate Denver Legal Aid Soc., 1982-86; legis. analyst Nat. Conf. State Legis., Denver, 1987; mediator, intake coord. Harvard Law Sch., Cambridge, Mass., 1988; law clk. Supreme Jud. Ct. State Mass., Boston, 1988-89; legis. staff Rep. Patricia Schroeder, U.S. Congress, Washington, 1989; dir., ptnr. Pfaff & Smith Family Law Clinic, Denver, 1990-91; asst. city atty., sr. atty. unit leader, dir. alternative resolution program Denver City Attys. Office, 1991—. Co-owner, Arte Gallery, Inc.; pres., Apollon, Inc. Mem. Colo. Women's Bar Assn., Colo. Bar Assn., Colo. Lawyers for the Arts, Denver Bar Assn. Presbyterian. Home: 3216 E 6th Ave Denver CO 80206-4407 Office: Denver City Attys Office 303 W Colfax Ave Ste 500 Denver CO 80204-2623 E-mail: lauriesmithk@msn.com

KACZMAREK, CARLA, lawyer; b. Detroit, Sept. 6, 1953; d. Leo Joseph and Charlotte (Schwanke) K.; m. Andrzej Poplawski, Apr. 29, 2000. BS, Eastern Mich. U., 1975; JD, U. Detroit, 1978. Bar: Mich. 1978, Ill. 1979. Law clk. State of Mich. Dept. Mental Health, Detroit, 1977; staff atty. Sr. Citizens Legal Aid Project, Legal Aid and Defenders Assn., State of Mich., 1977-82; ptnr. Kaczmarek P.C., Hamtramck, Mich., 1982—. Bd. dirs. Regina H.S., Harper Woods, Mich., 1997—. Mem. AAUW, Advocates (prs. 1982-83). Avocations: powerboating, waterskiing, fishing. Estate planning, Probate, Estate taxation. Office: Kaczmarek PC 2930 Holbrook St Hamtramck MI 48212-3512

KADEN, LEWIS B. law educator, lawyer; b. 1942; AB, Harvard U., 1963, LLB, 1967. Bar: N.Y. 1970, N.J. 1974. Harvard scholar Emmanuel Coll., Cambridge U., 1963-64; law clk. U.S. Ct. Appeals, 1967; legis. asst. Senator Robert F. Kennedy, 1968; ptnr. Battle, Fowler, Stokes & Kheel, 1969-73; chief counsel to gov. State of N.J., 1974-76; assoc. prof. Columbia U., 1976-79, prof., 1979-84, adj. prof., 1984—, dir. Ctr. for Law and Econ. Studies, 1979-83; ptnr. Davis, Polk & Wardwell, N.Y.C., 1984—. Bd. dirs. Bethlehem Steel Corp.; chmn. U.S. Govt. Overseas Presence Adv. Panel, 1999. Chmn. N.Y. State Indsl. Coop. Coun., 1986-92. Office: Davis Polk & Wardwell 450 Lexington Ave Fl 31 New York NY 10017-3982 E-mail: kaden@dpw.com

KADISH, SANFORD HAROLD, law educator; b. N.Y.C., Sept. 7, 1921; s. Samuel J. and Frances R. (Klein) K.; m. June Kurtin, Sept. 29, 1942; children: Joshua, Peter. B Social Scis, CCNY, 1942; LLB, Columbia U., 1948; JD (hon.), U. Cologne, 1983; LLD (hon.), CUNY, 1985, Southwestern U., 1993. Bar: N.Y. 1948, Utah 1954. Pvt. practice law, N.Y.C., 1948-51; prof. law U. Utah, 1951-60, U. Mich., 1961-64, U. Calif., Berkeley, 1964-91, dean Law Sch., 1975-82, Morrison prof., 1973-91, prof. emeritus, 1991—. Fulbright lectr. Melbourne (Australia) U., 1956; vis. prof. Harvard U., 1960-61, Freiburg U., 1967; lectr. Salzburg Seminar Am. Studies, 1965; Fulbright vis. lectr. Kyoto (Japan) U., 1975; vis. fellow Inst. Criminology, Cambridge (Eng.) U., 1968. Author: (with M.R. Kadish) Discretion to Disobey— A Study of Lawful Departures from Legal Rules, 1973, (with Schulhofer) Criminal Law and Its Processes, 6th edit., 1995, Blame and Punishment—Essays in the Criminal Law, 1987; editor-in-chief Ency. Crime and Justice, 1983; contbr. articles to profl. jours. Reporter Calif. Legis. Penal Code Project, 1964-68; pub. mem. Wage Stblzn. Bd., region XII, 1951-53; cons. Pres.'s Commn. Adminstrn. of Justice, 1966; mem. Calif. Coun. Criminal Justice, 1968-69. Lt. USNR, 1943-46. Fellow Ctr. Advanced Study Behavioral Scis., 1967-68; Guggenheim fellow Oxford U., 1974-75; vis. fellow All Souls Coll. Oxford U. Fellow AAAS (v.p. 1984-86), Brit. Acad. (corr.); mem. AAUP (nat. pres. 1970-72), Am. Assn. Law Schs. (exec. com. 1960, pres. 1982), Order of Coif (exec. com. 1966-67, 74-75), Phi Beta Kappa. Home: 774 Hilldale Ave Berkeley CA 94708-1318 E-mail: shk@law.berkeley.edu

KADUSHIN, KAREN DONNA, law school dean; b. L.A., Sept. 3, 1943; BA, UCLA, 1964; JD, Golden Gate U., 1977. Bar: Calif. 1977, U.S. Dist. Ct. (no. dist.) Calif. 1977. Mem. adj. faculty law Golden Gate U. and U. San Francisco, 1977-84; assoc. Law Offices Diana Richmond, San Francisco, 1978-80; ptnr. Richmond & Kadushin, 1981-83; prin. Kadushin Law Offices, 1983-88; ptnr. Kadushin-Fancher-Wickland, 1989-94; dean Monterey (Calif.) Coll. Law, Monterey, Calif., 1995—. Judge pro tem settlement confs. dept. domestic rels. San Francisco Superior Ct., 1985-95; bd. dirs. Lawyers Mut. Ins. Co. Author: California Practice Guide: Law Practice Management, 1992—. Bd. dirs. Legal Assistance for Elderly, San Francisco, 1983, San Francisco Neighborhood Legal Assistance Found., 1984. Mem. Calif. Women Lawyers, Bar Assn. San Francisco (bd. dirs. 1985-86, pres. 1993, Merit award 1980, 90), Barristers Club (pres. 1982), Monterey County Women Lawyers (treas. 1999-2000, pres. 2001). Office: Monterey Coll Law 404 W Franklin St Monterey CA 93940-2303 Fax: 831-373-0143. E-mail: kdkdean@montereylaw.edu

KAGAN, ROBERT ALLEN, law educator; b. Newark, June 13, 1938; s. George and Sylvia K. AB, Harvard U., 1959; LLB, Columbia U., 1962; PhD, Yale U., 1974. Now prof. polit. sci. and law U. Calif., Berkeley. Office: U Calif Sch Law Boalt Hall Berkeley CA 94720

KAHAN, ROCHELLE LIEBLING, lawyer, concert pianist; b. Chgo., Sept. 5, 1939; d. Arnold Leo and Helly (Ichilson) Liebling; m. Barry D. Kahan, Sept. 22, 1962; 1 child, Kara. BA, Northwestern U., 1959, JD, 1963. Bar: Ill. 1963, Tex. 1977. Atty. Treasury Dept., Chgo., 1964-65, Boston, 1965-66, 68-72, Washington, 1966-67, pvt. practice, Chgo. and Houston, 1972—. Mem. ABA, Tex. Bar Assn., Houston Bar Assn., Houston Tuesday Musical Club (pres.), Treble Clef Club (past pres.), Kappa Beta Pi (past pres.), Mu Phi Epsilon. Avocation: early music. Estate taxation.

KAHARICK, JEROME JOHN, lawyer; b. Johnstown, Pa., Apr. 15, 1955; s. Stanley Joseph and Emily (Solic) K.; m. Carolyn Marie Safko, Aug. 7, 1977; children: Natalie, Allison. BA summa cum laude, U. Pitts., 1977; JD, Duquesne U., 1991. Bar: Pa. 1991, N.Y. 2000, U.S. Dist. Ct. (we. dist.) Pa. 1991, U.S. Dist. Ct. (we. dist.) Mich. 1998, U.S. Dist. Ct. (no. dist.) N.Y. 1998, U.S. Ct. Appeals (3d cir.) 1992, U.S. Supreme Ct., 1997. Sales rep. Met. Life, Johnstown, Pa., 1977-84; owner, stockholder Planned Fin. Svcs., 1984-88; law clk. Wayman, Irvin & McAuley, Pitts., 1988-89; legal analyst Elliott Co., Jeannette, Pa., 1989-92; pvt. practice Johnstown, 1992-95, 97—; asst. pub. defender Cambria County, Pa., 1993-99; ptnr. Weaver and Kaharick, 1995-97; atty. in pvt. practice Johnstown, Pa., 1997—. Exec. production editor Duquesne Law Rev., 1990-91. Mem. ABA, ATLA, N.Y. Bar Assn., Nat. Assn. Criminal Def. Lawyers, Pa. Bar Assn., N.Y. State Bar Assn., Order of Barristers. Republican. Roman Catholic. Civil rights, General civil litigation, Criminal. Office: Lincoln Center 1st Flr 419 Lincoln St Ste 103 Johnstown PA 15901-1906

KAHLENBECK, HOWARD, JR. lawyer; b. Ft. Wayne, Ind., Dec. 7, 1929; s. Howard and Clara Elizabeth (Wegman) K.; m. Sally A. Horrell, Aug. 14, 1954; children: Kathryn Sue, Douglas H. BS with distinction, Ind. U., 1952; LLB, U. Mich., 1957. Bar: Ind. 1957. Ptnr. Krieg, DeVault, Alexander & Capehart, Indpls., 1957—. Sec., bd. dirs. Maul Tech. Corp. (formerly Buehler Corp.), Indpls., 1971-81, Am. Monitor Corp., Indpls., 1971-86, Am. Interstate Ins. Corp. Wis., Milw., 1973-84, Am. Interstate Ins. Co. Ga., Am. Underwriters Group, Inc., Indpls., 1973-86, Pafco Gen. Ins. Co., 1987-88. With USAF, 1952-54. Mem. ABA, Ind. Bar Assn., Indpls. Bar Assn., Alpha Kappa Psi, Delta Theta Phi, Beta Gamma Sigma, Delta Upsilon Internat. (sec., bd. dirs. 1971-83, chmn. 1983-86, trustee found. 1983-98). Lutheran. Contracts commercial, General corporate, Mergers and acquisitions. Home: 6320 Old Orchard Rd Indianapolis IN 46226-1041 Office: Krieg DeVault Alexander & Capehart 2800 Indiana National Bank Tower One Indiana Sq Ste 2800 Indianapolis IN 46204 E-mail: hk@kdac.com

KAHN, ALAN EDWIN, lawyer; b. N.Y.C., Aug. 9, 1929; s. Joseph and Harriet Rose (Rubel) K.; m. Regina Wolf, Aug. 7, 1960 (div. Jan. 1978); 1 child, Jolie Galen; m. Patricia Ann Dugan, June 4, 1978. BBA, CCNY, 1950; JD, Bklyn. Law Sch., 1956. Bar: N.Y. 1956, U.S. Dist. Ct. (so. and ea. dists.) N.Y. 1978, U.S. Tax Ct. 1978; CPA, N.Y. Staff asst.-acct. Feinberg, Jacobs & Furman, N.Y.C., 1956-57; pvt. practice, 1957-96, 98—; prin. Law Office of Alan E. Kahn, 1957-99; sr. ptnr. Kahn, Boyd, Levychin CPAs, 1993; pvt. practice, 1998—. Tax cons. to various nonprofit orgns., N.Y.C., 1977—. Cons. Vol. Lawyers for the Arts, N.Y.C., 1978—. Sgt. U.S. Army, 1951-52. Mem. ATLA (mem. com. 1990—), N.Y. State Bar Assn. (elder law com.), N.Y. State Trial Lawyers Assn. (chmn. subcom. on legis. estate and trusts 1979, spkr. bd. 1990—, mem. com. 1991—, chair 2000—), N.Y. County Lawyers Assn. (taxation com. 1988—, sec. com. on taxation 1996-2000, chair com. on taxation 2000—), Spkr.'s Bur., Assn. Trial Lawyers City N.Y., Jewish Lawyers Guild, N.Y. State Soc. CPAs, Nat. Sculpture Soc. (patron mem.), Odd Fellows (grand adv. bd. N.Y. chpt. 1979-80, gen. counsel grand lodge 1989—), Mchts. Club (bd. govs., asst. treas., treas. and gov. 1992—, award chmn. legal com. 1995—). Democrat. Avocation: collecting prints, paintings and oriental ceramics. State civil litigation, Probate, Personal income taxation. Home: 370 1st Ave New York NY 10010-4923 Office: 99 Wall St New York NY 10005-3101 E-mail: aekwacs@aol.com

KAHN, BRUCE MEYER, lawyer; b. Memphis, Feb. 28, 1952; s. Sidney Louis, Jr. and Maxine March (Meyer) K. B.A., Trinity Coll., 1974; J.D., Tulane U., 1977. Bar: Tenn. 1977. Assoc., Buchignani & Greener, Memphis, 1977-80; ptnr. Goodman, Glazer, Greener, Schneider & McQuiston, Memphis, 1981— ; sec.-treas., dir. Paper Products Co., 1984— . Mem. legal com. B'Nai B'Rith Home and Hosp. for Aged, Memphis, 1981-84, Temple Israel Synagogue, 1984— ; vol. Memphis in May Internat. Festival, 1984— ; chmn. Trinity Coll. Alumni Support Program, 1981-84; v.p. Temple Israel Brotherhood, 1984— . Mem. Memphis and Shelby County Bar Assn., Tenn. Bar Assn., ABA, Tax Watch Group, Greater Memphis Employee Benefits Council. Jewish. Club: Racquet of Memphis. General corporate, Estate planning, Probate. Home: 4995 Normandy Ln Memphis TN 38117-2701 Office: Goodman Glazer Greener Schneider & McQuiston 1500 Commerce Bldg Memphis TN 38103

KAHN, DAVID MILLER, lawyer, educator; b. Port Chester, N.Y., Apr. 21, 1925; m. Barbara Heller, May 9, 1952; children: William, James, Caroline. BA, U. Ky., 1947; LLB cum laude, N.Y. Law Sch., 1950. Bar: N.Y. 1951, U.S. Dist. Ct. (ea. and so. dists.) N.Y. 1953, U.S. Supreme Ct. 1958. Sole practice, White Plains, N.Y., 1951-60; ptnr. Kahn & Rubin, 1960-66, Kahn & Goldman, White Plains, 1967-80; sr. ptnr. Kahn & Landau, White Plains, Palm Beach, Fla., 1980-88, Kahn and Kahn, Fla., N.Y., 1988-95, Kahn, Kahn & Scutieri Esq., Palm Beach Gardens, 1995—. Lectr. N.Y. Law Sch., 1982—; spl. counsel Village Port Chester, N.Y., 1960-63; commr. of appraisal Westchester County Supreme Ct., 1973-77; counsel Chemplex Industries, Inc., BIS Communications Corp., Bilbar Realty Co. Chmn. Westchester County Citizens for Eisenhower, 1950-52; pres. Westchester County Young Reps. Clubs, 1958-60; founder, chmn. bd. dirs. Port Chester-Rye Town Vol. Ambulance Corps, 1968-77; pres. Driftwood Corp., Amagansette, L.I., N.Y., 1984-91. Served with Counter Intelligence Corps USAF, 1942-46. Recipient John Marshall Harlan fellow N.Y. Law Sch., 1990-93, lifetime achievement award Westchester County Bar Assn, 2001. Fellow Am. Acad. Matrimonial Lawyers (bd. govs. N.Y. chpt. 1976-79); mem. ABA, N.Y. State Bar Assn., Westchester County Bar Assn., White Plains Bar Assn., N.Y. Law Sch. Alumni Assn. (bd. dirs. 1970-80), Elmwood C.C. (legal counsel), Eastpointe Country Club. Family and matrimonial, Probate, Real property. Home and Office: 6419 Eastpointe Pines St Palm Beach Gardens FL 33418 also: 175 Main St White Plains NY 10601-3105

KAHN, EDWIN LEONARD, lawyer; b. N.Y.C., Aug. 1, 1918; s. Max L. and Julia (Rich) K.; m. Myra J. Green, Oct. 20, 1946 (dec. 1994); children: Martha L., Deborah K. Spiliotopoulos. AB, U. N.C., 1937; LLB cum laude, Harvard U., 1940. Bar: N.C. 1940, D.C. 1949. Atty., asst. head legislation and regulations div. Office Chief Counsel IRS, 1940-52, dir. tech. planning div., 1952-55; ptnr. Arent, Fox, Kintner, Plotkin & Kahn, Washington, 1955-86, of counsel, ret., 1986—. Lectr. NYU Tax Inst., mem. adv. bd., 1959-70; lectr. tax insts. Coll. William and Mary, U. Chgo., U. Tex. Editor: Harvard Law Rev, 1939-40; editorial adv. bd. Tax Advisor of Am. Inst. CPA's, 1974-86. Bd. dirs. Jewish Community Ctr. Greater Washington, 1972-78; trustee Cosmos Club Found., 1989-93, chmn., 1989-91. With U.S. Army, 1943-46, ETO. Decorated Bronze Star. Fellow Am. Bar Found. (life); mem. ABA (coun. 1963-66, vice chmn. sect. taxation 1965-66), Fed. Bar Assn. (chmn. taxation com. 1967-68), D.C. Bar Assn., Nat. Tax Assn.-Tax Inst. Am. (adv. coun. 1967-69, bd. dirs. 1969-73), Am. Law Inst. (life), Am. Coll. Tax Counsel, J. Edgar Murdock Am. Inn Ct. (master bencher 1988-91), Phi Beta Kappa (life mem. fellows). Jewish. Home: 4104 40th St N Arlington VA 22207-4805 Office: 1050 Connecticut Ave NW Washington DC 20036-5303

KAHN, EDWIN SAM, lawyer; b. N.Y.C., Jan. 22, 1938; m. Cynthia Chutter, May 30, 1966; children: David, Jonathan, Jennifer. BA, U. Colo., 1958; JD, Harvard U., 1965. Bar: Colo. 1965, U.S. Dist. Ct. (Colo.) 1965, U.S. Ct. Appeals (10th cir.) 1965, U.S. Supreme Ct. 1968. Assoc. Holland & Hart, Denver, 1965-70, ptnr., 1970-77; ptnr., shareholder Kelly, Haglund, Garnsey & Kahn, LLC, 1978—. 1st lt. USAF, 1959-62. Fellow Am. Coll. Trial Lawyers; mem. Denver Bar Assn. (pres. 1984-85). Federal civil litigation, State civil litigation, Libel. Home: 2345 Leyden St Denver CO 80207-3441 Office: Kelly Haglund Garnsey & Kahn LLC 1441 18th St Ste 300 Denver CO 80202-1255 E-mail: edkahn@qwest.com

KAHN, ELLIS IRVIN, lawyer; b. Charleston, S.C., Jan. 18, 1936; s. Robert and Estelle Harriet (Kaminski) K.; m. Janice Weinstein, Aug. 11, 1963; children: Justin Simon, David Israel, Cynthia Kahn Nirenblatt. AB in Polit. Sci., The Citadel, 1958; JD, U. S.C., 1961. Bar: S.C. 1961, U.S. Ct. Appeals (5th cir.) 1963, U.S. Ct. Appeals (4th cir.) 1964, U.S. Supreme Ct. 1970, D.C. 1978, U.S. Claims Ct. 1988; diplomate Nat. Bd. Trial Advocacy, Am. Bd. Profl. Liability Attys. (trustee 1989—). Law clk. U.S. Dist. Ct. S.C., 1964-66; prin. Kahn Law Firm, Charleston; adj. prof. med.-legal jurisprudence Med. U. S.C., 1978-87; mem. rules com. U.S. Dist. Ct., 1984-96. Chmn. campaign Charleston Jewish Fedn., 1986-87, pres., 1988-90, S.C. Organ Procurment Agy., 1987-94, chmn. bd. 1989-94, mem. nat. coun. Am. Israel Pub. Affairs Com., 1982-88, Hebrew Benevolent Soc., pres., 1994-96; mem. Hebrew Orphan Soc. Capt. USAF, 1961-64. Fellow Internat. Soc. Barristers; mem. S.C. Bar, ABA, ATLA (state committeeman 1970-74), S.C. Trial Lawyers Assn. (pres. 1976-77), 4th Cir. Jud. Conf. (permanent mem.). Federal civil litigation, State civil litigation, Personal injury. Home: 316 Confederate Cir Charleston SC 29407-7431 Office: PO Box 898 Charleston SC 29402-0898

KAHN, MARK LEO, arbitrator, educator; b. N.Y.C., Dec. 16, 1921; s. Augustus and Manya (Fertig) K.; m. Ruth Elizabeth Wecker, Dec. 21, 1947 (div. Jan. 1972); children: Ann Mariam, Peter David, James Allan, Jean Sarah; m. Elaine Johnson Morris, Feb. 12, 1988. BA, Columbia U., 1942; MA, Harvard U., 1948, PhD in Econs., 1950. Asst. economist U.S. OSS, Washington, 1942-43; tchg. fellow Harvard U., 1947-49; dir. case analysis U.S. WSB, Region 6-B Mich., 1952-53; mem. faculty Wayne State U., Detroit, 1949-85, prof. econs., 1960-85, prof. emeritus, 1985—, dept. chmn., 1961-68, dir. indsl. rels. M.A. program, 1978-85. Arbitrator union-mgmt. disputes. Co-author: Collective Bargaining and Technological Change in American Transportation, 1971; mem. editl. bd. Employee Responsibilities and Rights Jour., 1988-96; contbr. articles to profl. jours. Bd. govs. Jewish Welfare Fedn. Detroit, 1976-82; bd. dirs. Jewish Home for Aged, Detroit, 1978-93, Lyric Chamber Ensemble, Southfield, Mich., 1995-97, Detroit Empowerment Zone Devel. Corp., 1996-99. Capt. AUS, 1943-46. Decorated Bronze Star; recipient Disting. Svc. award U.S. Nat. Mediation Bd., 1987, Am. Arbitration Assn., 1992. Mem. AAUP (past chpt. pres.), Nat. Acad. Arbitrators (bd. govs. 1960-62, v.p. 1976-78, chmn. membership com. 1979-82, pres. 1983-84, chmn. nominating com. 1995-96), Indsl. Rels. Rsch. Assn. (pres. Detroit chpt. 1956, exec. sec. 1979-89, nat. exec. bd. 1985-88), Soc. Profls. in Dispute Resolution (v.p. 1982-83, pres. 1986-87). Home and Office: 15151 Ford Rd Apt 321 Dearborn MI 48126-5027 E-mail: mleokahn@aol.com

KAIER, EDWARD JOHN, lawyer; b. Sewickley, Pa., Sept. 23, 1945; s. Edward Anthony and Mary Patricia (Crimmins) K.; m. Annette Thomas, July 31, 1976; children: Elizabeth Anne, Charles Crimmins, Thomas Edward. AB, Harvard U., 1967; JD, U. Pa., 1970. Bar: D.C. 1970, Pa. 1970, U.S. Dist. Ct. (ea. dist.) Pa. 1971, U.S. Ct. Appeals (3rd and D.C. cirs.) 1971, U.S. Dist. Ct. D.C., 1971. Law clk. to presiding justice U.S. Dist. Ct. for D.C., Washington, 1970-71; assoc. Dechert Price & Rhoads, Phila., 1971-74; ptnr. Kaier and Kaier, 1974-77, Hepburn Willcox Hamilton & Putnam, Phila., 1977—. Pres. Savoy Co., Phila., 1978-80; bd. dirs. Mgrs. Funds, Norwalk, Conn., Mgrs. AMG Funds, Boston. Vice chmn. Rosemont (Pa.) Sch. of Holy Child, 1981-90. Mem. ABA, Phila. Bar Assn. (chmn. office practice com. probate sect. 1987-90, exec. com. 1990-92), Merion Cricket Club, Phila. Club, Phila. Country Club, Avalon Yacht Club (trustee 1987-90, 92-93, treas. 1990-92), Harvard-Radcliffe Club (Phila., sec. 1989—). Republican. Roman Catholic. Avocations: sailing, golf. Estate planning, Probate, Estate taxation. Home: 111 N Lowrys Ln Bryn Mawr PA 19010-1408 Office: Hepburn Willcox Hamilton & Putnam 1100 One Penn Ctr Philadelphia PA 19103 E-mail: ejkaier@hepburnlaw.com, macoejk@aol.com

KAIL, KENNETH STONER, lawyer; b. N.Y.C., Oct. 14, 1955; s. Morton and Adrienne (Stoner) K.; m. Ivy Hwang, Apr. 18, 1986. BS, SUNY, Albany, 1977; JD, U. Pa., 1980. Bar: N.Y. 1981. Law clk. to presiding justice U.S. Ct. Appeals (fed. cir.), Washington, 1980-81; assoc. Simpson Thacher & Bartlett, N.Y.C., 1981-90; of counsel Morrison & Forster, 1990-92, ptnr., 1992-95, Morgan, Lewis & Bockius, LLP, N.Y.C., 1995—. Mem. ABA, N.Y. State Bar Assn. Corporate taxation, Taxation, general, Personal income taxation. Office: Morgan Lewis Bockius LLP 101 Park Ave Fl 33 New York NY 10178-0060 E-mail: kkail@morganlewis.com

KAILAS, LEO GEORGE, lawyer; b. N.Y.C., May 28, 1949; s. George and Evanthia (Skoulikas) K.; m. Merle S. Duskin; children: Arianne, George, Shirley. AB, Columbia U., 1970, JD, 1973. Bar: N.Y. 1974. Assoc. Olwine, Connelly, Chase, O'Donnell and Weyher, N.Y.C., 1973-77; ptnr. specializing in internat., comml.-admiralty litigation Milgrim Thomajan Jacobs & Lee, PC (now Piper & Marbury LLP), 1977-2000, mem. internat. trade and litigation group, until 2000; ptnr. Reitler Brown LLC, 2000—. Mem. ABA, Assn. Bar City N.Y. (chmn. admiralty com. 1985-88). Public international, Commodities. Office: Reitler Brown LLC 800 3d Ave 21st Fl New York NY 10022

KAIMOWITZ, GABE HILLEL, civil rights lawyer; b. N.Y.C., May 5, 1935; s. Abraham and Esther (Bialogursky) K.; children: David, Beth. BS, U. Wis., 1955; MA, U. Cen. Fla., 1988; LLB, NYU, 1967. Bar: N.Y. 1969, Mich. 1971, Fla. 1987, U.S. Dist. Ct. (mid. dist.) Fla., 1987, U.S. Ct. Appeals (6th cir.) 1971, U.S. Ct. Appeals (3d cir.) 1982, U.S. Ct. Appeals (2d cir.) 1983, U.S. Ct. Appeals (11th cir.), 1989 U.S. Ct. Appeals (7th cir.) 1990, U.S. Ct. Appeals (D.C. cir.) 1998. Atty. Ctr. Social Welfare, Politics and Law, N.Y.C., 1967-70; sr. atty. Mich. Legal Services, Detroit, 1971-79; assoc. P.R. Legal Def., N.Y.C., 1980-84; exec. dir. Greater Orlando (Fla.) A. Legal Services, 1985-86; equal opportunity investigator Alachua County, Fla., 1999—. Atty. Attys. Against Am. Apartheid, Fla. and various other civil rights orgns., 1969—; lectr., adj. prof. numerous univs. Contbr. articles to profl. jours.; author poems. Served with U.S. Army, 1956-57, with Res. 1958-60. Smith fellow, 1970-71, Legal Services Corp. fellow, 1979-80. Mem. N.Y. State Bar Assn., Fla. Bar Assn. Jewish. Avocations: writing and editing. Home: 4411 SW 34th St Gainesville FL 32608-2562 Office: PO Box 140119 Gainesville FL 32614-0119 E-mail: gabehk@aol.com

KALAMARAS, JAMES, lawyer; b. N.Y.C., Oct. 29, 1971; s. Nick and Chris Kalamaras. BS, St. John's U., 1993; JD, Quinnipiac Coll., 1996. Bar: N.Y. 1997, Conn. 1997. Ptnr. Siolas & Kalamaras, P.C., N.Y.C., 1998—. Personal injury, Real property. Office: Siolas & Kalamaras PC 55 W 45th St New York NY 10036

KALER, ROBERT JOSEPH, lawyer; b. Boston, July 20, 1956; s. Robert Joseph and Joanne (Bowen) K. BA, Dartmouth Coll., 1978; JD, Am. U., 1981. Bar: D.C. 1981, Mass. 1983, U.S. Dist. Ct. D.C. 1982, U.S. Dist. Ct. Mass. 1984, U.S. Ct. Appeals (D.C. cir.) 1983, U.S. Ct. Appeals (1st cir.) 1984, U.S. Supreme Ct. 1986. Law clk. Sullivan & Cromwell, Washington, 1979-80, U.S. Dept. Justice, Washington, 1980-81; assoc. McKenna, Connor & Cuneo, 1981-83; ptnr. Gadsby & Hannah, Boston, 1983—. Contbr. articles to profl. jours. Mem. ABA, Internat. Bar Assn., Mass Bar Assn. General civil litigation, Private international, Trademark and copyright. Office: Gadsby & Hannah 225 Franklin St Boston MA 02110-2804

KALHA, BALJIT SINGH, lawyer; b. Tokyo, May 13, 1975; s. Ranjit Singh and Babli Kaur Kalha. BA in History with honors, U. Delhi, New Delhi, 1996, LLB, 2000. Bar: Delhi Coun. 2000. Paralegal Titus & Co., New Delhi, 1998-2000, mem. corp. practice law group, 2000—. Bd. dirs. Jeet Associates Plc, New Delhi. Pres. legal cell Lok Bhalai Party, New Delhi, 2000. Mem. Delhi Golf Club, Delhi Gymkhana Club. Avocations: current affairs, politics, hockey, charity. Computer, Insurance, Intellectual property. Home: Kalha House Jaunapur Mehr Delhi New Delhi India Office: Titus & Co R-4/Greater Kailash 1 Delhi New Delhi 110 048 India Fax: 6480300. E-mail: titus@nda.vsnl.net.in

KALIKOW, RICHARD R. lawyer; b. N.Y.C., 1949; BS, Cornell U., 1971; JD, Fordham U., 1974; LLM, NYU, 1979. Bar: N.Y. 1975, Fla. 1979. Mem. Skadden, Arps, Slate, Meagher & Flom, N.Y.C. Real property. Office: Skadden Arps Slate Meagher & Flom 4 Times Sq Fl 24 New York NY 10036-6595

KALISH, ARTHUR, lawyer; b. Bklyn., Mar. 6, 1930; s. Jack and Rebecca (Biniamofsky) K.; m. Janet J. Wiener, Mar. 7, 1953; children: Philip, Pamela. BA, Cornell U., 1951; JD, Columbia U., 1956. Bar: N.Y. 1956, D.C. 1970. Assoc. Paul, Weiss, Rifkind, Wharton & Garrison, N.Y.C., 1956-64, ptnr., 1965-95, of counsel, 1996—. Lectr. NYU Inst. Fed. Taxation, Hawaii Tax Inst., Law Jour. Seminars Contbr. articles to legal jours. Assoc. trustee L.I. Jewish Med. Ctr., New Hyde Park, N.Y., 1978-82, trustee, 1982-95, hon. trustee, 1995-97; trustee emeritus North Shore - L.I. Jewish Health Sys., 1997-98, life trustee, 1998—; bd. dirs. Cmty. Health Program of Queens Nassau Inc., New Hyde Park, 1978-94, pres., 1981-89, chmn. emeritus, 1994-97; bd. dirs. Managed Health, Inc., New Hyde Park, 1990-98, chmn., 1994-95. Fellow Am. Coll. Tax Counsel; mem. ABA, N.Y. State Bar Assn., Assn. Bar City N.Y., Columbia Law Sch. Assn. (bd. dirs. 1990-94). Corporate taxation, Personal income taxation. Home: 2 Bass Pond Dr Old Westbury NY 11568-1307 Office: Paul Weiss Rifkind Wharton & Garrison Ste 1008 1285 Avenue Of The Americas Fl 21 New York NY 10019-6028 E-mail: akalish@paulweiss.com

KALKSTEIN, JOSHUA ADAM, lawyer; b. Phila., Oct. 1, 1943; s. Abraham and Helen (Ponemone) K.; children: Aleta K., Trevor W., Maxim J. AB, Brown U., 1965; JD, U. Pa., 1968. Bar: N.Y. 1968, N.J. 1971, Mass. 1978, U.S. Dist. Ct. N.Y. 1968, U.S. Dist. Ct., N.J. 1971, U.S. Dist. Ct., Mass. 1978, U.S. Ct. of Appeals (3d cir.) 1973, U.S. Ct. Mil. Appeals 1969. Asst. gen. counsel Pfizer Inc., Groton, Conn., 1978—; assoc. Hellring, Lindeman & Landau, Newark, 1972-75; corp. counsel Hooper Holmes Inc., Basking Ridge, N.J., 1975-78. Vis. counsel Harvard U., MIT Ctr. for Exptl. Pharmacology and Therapeutics, Cambridge, 1995—. Bd. dirs. Howland Art Ctr., Beacon, N.Y., 1987-91, Congregation Beth El, New London, Conn., 1995-96, Main Street New London, 2000—; commr. Waterfront Redevel. Commn., Beacon, 1990-91. Lt. USNR, 1969-72. Mem. N.Y. State Bar Assn., N.J. Bar Assn., Mass. Bar Assn. Jewish. Avocations: art collecting, book collecting, golf. Home: 76 Library St Mystic CT 06355-2420 Office: Pfizer Inc Eastern Point Rd Groton CT 06340 E-mail: joshua_a_kalkstein@groton.pfizer.com

KALLGREN, EDWARD EUGENE, lawyer; b. San Francisco, May 22, 1928; s. Edward H. and Florence E. (Campbell) K.; m. Joyce Elaine Kislitzin, Feb. 8, 1953; children: Virginia K. Pegley, Charles Edward. AB, U. Calif., Berkeley, 1951, JD, 1954. Bar: Calif. Assoc., ptnr. Brobeck, Phleger & Harrison, San Francisco, 1954-93, of counsel, 1993—. Bd. dirs. Olivet Meml. Park, Colma, Calif., 1970-98, pres., 1991-98; chair, pres. Five Bridges Found., 1998—; mem. Berkeley City Council, 1971-75; bd. dirs., v.p./treas. Planned Parenthood Alameda/San Francisco, 1984-89. Served to sgt. USMC, 1945-48. Mem. ABA (ho. of dels. 1985-2000, state del. 1997-98, coun. sr. law divsn. 1996-2001, chair 1999-2000), State Bar of Calif. (bd. govs. 1989-92, v.p. 1991-92), Found. of State Bar Calif. (bd. dirs. 1993-98, v.p., 1994-96, chair fellows soc. 1996-98), Bar Assn. San Francisco (pres. 1988, bd. dirs.), San Francisco Lawyers Com. Urban Affairs (co-chair 1983-85), Lawyers Com. Civil Rights Under Law (trustee 1985—), The TenBroek Soc. (chair bd. dirs. 1992-95). Democrat. Contracts commercial, General corporate. Office: Brobeck Phleger & Harrison Spear St Tower 1 Market Plz San Francisco CA 94105-1100 E-mail: ekallgren@brobeck.com

KALLMANN, STANLEY WALTER, lawyer; b. Bklyn., June 6, 1943; s. Silve and Erna (Clesius) K.; m. Carolee A. McDonald, Aug. 23, 1969; children: Alexander, Andrew. BA, Rutgers U., New Brunswick, 1964; LLB, Rutgers U., Newark, 1967. Bar: N.J. 1967, U.S. Dist. Ct. N.J. 1967, N.Y. 1984. Law clk. to judge U.S. Dist. Ct. N.J., Newark, 1967-69; assoc. Stryker, Tams & Dill, 1969-71; asst. U.S. atty. U.S. Atty.'s Office, 1971-75; ptnr. Gennet, Kallmann, Antin & Robinson, Parsippany, N.J., 1975—. Mem. ABA, N.J. Bar Assn. Federal civil litigation, State civil litigation, Insurance. Office: Gennet Kallmann Antin & Robinson 6 Campus Dr Parsippany NJ 07054-4406

KALODNER, HOWARD ISAIAH, legal educator; b. Dec. 16, 1933; BA, Haveford Coll., 1954; LLB, Harvard U., 1957. Bar: Pa. 1958. Law clk. U.S. Supreme Ct., 1958-59; assoc. Schnader, Harrison, Segal & Lewis, Phila., 1960; legal adviser U.S. Dept. State, Washington, 1961-62; spl. asst. to solicitor U.S. Dept. Labor, 1962-64; prof. law NYU, 1964-77; dean Western New Eng. Coll. Law, Springfield, Mass., 1977-94, prof. law, 1977—. Bd. dirs. Inst. Jud. Adminstrn., 1976-78. Home: 55 Riverview Ter Springfield MA 01108-1603 Office: Western New Eng Sch Law 1215 Wilbraham Rd Springfield MA 01119-2689 E-mail: hkalodner@law.wnec.edu

KALOGREDIS, VASILIOS J. lawyer, health care management consultant; b. Mar. 3, 1949; s. John V. and Rose (Simeonidis) K.; m. Stephanie Pahides, May 26, 1974; children: Maria, John. BS in Acctg., Providence Coll., 1971; JD, Villanova U., 1974. Bar: Pa. 1974. Assoc. Beck & Kalogredis, Bala Cynwyd, Pa., 1974-81; ptnr. Kalogredis Law Assocs., Wayne, 1981-95; founder, pres. Kalogredis, Sansweet, Rearden and Burke, Ltd., 1996—. Spkr. in field. Contbr. articles to profl. jours. Pres. St. George Greek Orthodox Ch., Media, Pa., 1980, 86, chmn. bldg. com., 1984-87. Dougherty fellow Villanova U., 1971-74. Mem. ABA, Pa. Bar Assn., Soc. Med.-Dental Cons., Soc. Profl. Bus. Cons., Nat. Health Lawyers Assn. Republican. Contracts commercial, General corporate, Health. Office: Ste 704 987 Old Eagle Sch Rd Wayne PA 19087-1708 E-mail: bkalogredis@ksdbhealthlaw.com

KALOOSDIAN, ROBERT ARAM, lawyer; b. Watertown, Mass., Oct. 29, 1930; s. Paul and Grace (Mugrditchian) K.; m. Marianne Kaloosdian, June 30, 1957; children: Paul, Lori, Sonia. AB, Clark U., 1952; JD, Boston U., 1957, LLM, 1962. Bar: Mass. 1957, U.S. Supreme Ct. 1962. Assoc. Miles, Curran & Malkasian, Boston, 1958-60; pvt. practice Watertown, 1960—; assoc. Kaloosdian, Ciccarelli & Lerman, 1982-99. Corporator Watertown Savs. Bank, 1972—, trustee, 1976—, mem. cmty. reinvestment com. Corporator Mt. Auburn Hosp., Cambridge, Mass., 1978— ; pres. Armenian Nat. Inst., Washington, 1996—. Bd. dirs. Armenian Assembly of Am., 1972-2000, co-chmn., 1974-83, chmn., 1990-92; assoc. dir. State Dept. AID Grant to Lebanon, 1978—; mem. Gov.'s Task Force on Ethinic Heritage, Boston, 1976. With U.S. Army, 1952-54. Recipient Prince of Cilicia award, Catholosate of Antelias, Beirut, 1980, Dist. Svc. award Armenian Assembly, 2000. Mem. ATLA, Middlesex Bar Assn., Mass. Bar Assn. (spl. asst. to pres. 2000), Rotary (pres. 1975-76), Delta Theta Phi. Democrat. Mem. Armenian Apostolic Ch. General practice, Probate, Real property. Home: 25 Fletcher Rd Belmont MA 02478-2014 Office: Kaloosidian & Cicarelli 43 Mount Auburn St Watertown MA 02472-3924 E-mail: kaloosdian@aol.com

KALOW, DAVID ARTHUR, lawyer; b. Queens, N.Y., May 6, 1953; s. Samuel Jay and Joan Elaine (Peirce) K.; m. Janet Lee Samuels, June 18, 1978; children: Margaret Emily, Jacob Richard, Benjamin Charles. BA, U. Chgo., 1974, JD, 1976. Bar: N.Y. 1977, U.S. Dist. Ct. (so. and ea. dists.) N.Y. 1977, U.S. Ct. Appeals (5th cir.) 1983, U.S. Ct. Appeals (2d cir.) 1984, U.S. Ct. Appeals (fed. cir.) 1984, U.S. Supreme Ct. 1987. Assoc. Chadbourne, Parke, N.Y.C., 1976-79, Amster, Rothstein, N.Y.C., 1980-81, Lieberman, Rudolph & Nowak, N.Y.C., 1981-85, ptnr., 1986-96, Kalow, Springut & Bressler, N.Y.C., 1996—. Mem. ABA (com. on sci. and tech., patent, trademark and copyright, computer law). Federal civil litigation, Patent, Trademark and copyright. Office: Kalow Springut & Bressler 380 Lexington Ave # 4300 New York NY 10168-0002 Address: 122 E 42nd St Fl 43 New York NY 10168-4399

KAMERICK, EILEEN ANN, lawyer, financial executive; b. Ravenna, Ohio, July 22, 1958; d. John Joseph and Elaine Elizabeth (Lenney) K.; m. Victor J. Heckler, Sept. 1, 1990; 1 child, Connor Joseph Heckler. AB in English summa cum laude, Boston Coll., 1980; postgrad., Exeter Coll., Oxford, Eng., 1981; JD, U. Chgo., 1984, MBA in Finance and Internat. Bus. with honors, 1993. Bar: Ill. 1984, U.S. Dist. Ct. (no. dist.) Ill. 1985, Mass. 1986, U.S. Ct. Appeals (7th cir.) 1988, U.S. Supreme Ct. 1993. Assoc. Reuben & Proctor, Chgo., 1984-86, Skadden, Arps et al, Chgo., 1986-89; atty. internat. Amoco Corp., 1989-93, sr. fin. mgr. corp. fin., 1993—96, dir. banking and fin. svcs., 1996-97, v.p., treas., 1998-99, Whirlpool Corp., Benton Harbor, Mich., 1997; v.p., gen. counsel GE Capital Auto Fin. Svcs., Barrington, Ill., 1997-98; v.p., CFO BP Am., 1999-2000; exec. v.p. & CFO United Stationers Inc., Des Plaines, Ill., 2000—01; exec. v.p., CFO Bcom3, Chgo., 2001—. Advisor fin. com. Am. Petroleum Inst., 1992; bd. dirs. Heartland Alliance, Vysis. Vol. adv. 7th Cir. Bar Assn., Chgo., 1987—. Mem. Phi Beta Kappa. Roman Catholic. General civil litigation, General corporate, Private international. Home: 2658D N Southport Ave Chicago IL 60614-1228 Office: Bcom3 35 W Wacker Dr Chicago IL 60614

KAMIEN, KALVIN, lawyer; b. Lakewood, N.J., Dec. 11, 1950; s. Joseph and Frieda (Estreich) K.; m. Rhonda Sherry Greenberg, Feb. 7, 1982; children: Joseph Tyler, Joanna Lynn. BA, NYU, 1973; JD cum laude, Bklyn. Law Sch., 1976. Bar: N.Y. 1977, U.S. Dist. Ct. (ea., so. and no. dists.) N.Y. 1977, U.S. Ct. Appeals (2d cir.) 1994. Law asst. appellate divsn. 2d Dept. Supreme Ct., Bklyn., 1976-79; assoc. Max E Greenberg, Trager, Toplitz & Herbst, N.Y.C., 1979-86; ptnr. Max E. Greenberg, Trager, Toplitz & Herbst, 1987—. Bd. dirs. Fieldpoint Community Assn., Irvington, N.Y., 1991—. Recipient Am. Jurisprudence award, 1975. Avocations: tennis, skiing. General civil litigation, Contracts commercial, Construction. Home: 84 Green Way Dr Irvington NY 10533-1844 Office: Max E Greenberg Trager Toplitz & Herbst 100 Church St New York NY 10007-2601 E-mail: kk@megbuildlaw.com

KAMINE, BERNARD S. lawyer; b. Dec. 5, 1943; m. Marcia Phyllis Haber; children: Jorge H., Benjamin H., Tovy H. BA, U. Denver, 1965; JD, Harvard U., 1968. Bar: Calif. 1969, Colo. 1969. Dep. atty. gen. Calif. Dept. Justice, L.A., 1969-72; asst. atty. gen. Colo. Dept. Law, Denver, 1972-74; assoc. Shapiro & Maguire, Beverly Hills, Calif., 1974-76; ptnr. Kamine Ungerer LLP and predecessors, L.A., 1976—. Judge pro tem Mcpl. Ct., 1974-99, Superior Ct., 1989-99; bd. dirs., sec. Pub. Works Stds., Inc., 1996—; arbitrator Calif. Pub. Works Contract Arbitration Com., 1990—, Am. Arbitration Assn., 1976—; mem. adv. com. legal forms Calif. Jud. Coun., 1978-82. Author: Public Works Construction Manual: A Legal Guide for California, 1996; contbr. chpts. to legal texts and articles to profl. jours. Mem. L.A. County Dem. Ctrl. Com., 1982-85; mem. Pacific S.W. regional bd. Anti-Defamation League, 1982—, pres. bd., 1998-00, assoc. nat. commr., 1995—. Col. USAR, 1969-2002. Mem. ABA, Calif. State Bar (chair conf. dels. calendar coordinating com. 1991-92), L.A. County Bar Assn. (chair Superior Cts. com. 1977-79, chair constrn. law subsect. of real property sect. 1981-83), Engring. Contractors' Assn. (bd. dirs. 1985—, affiliate chair 1992-93, affiliate DIG award 1996), Assoc. Gen. Contractors Calif. (L.A. dist. bd. dirs. 1995-00), Am. Constrn. Insps. Assn. (bd. registered constrn. inspectors 1990-97), Beavers, Res. Officers Assn. (pres. chpt. 1977-78), Omicron Delta Kappa. Alternative dispute resolution, Construction, Government contracts and claims. Office: 350 S Figueroa St Ste 250 Los Angeles CA 90071-1201 E-mail: bskamine@post.harvard.edu

KAMINS, BARRY MICHAEL, lawyer; b. Oct. 3, 1943; s. Abe and Evelyn Bertha (Goffen) K.; m. Fern Louise Kamins, Mar. 30, 1968; 1 child, Allyson. BA, Columbia U., 1965; JD, Rutgers U., 1968. Bar: N.Y. 1969, U.S. Dist. Ct. (ea. and so. dists.) N.Y. 1973, U.S. Supreme Ct. 1974. Asst. dist. atty., 1969-73; dep. chief Criminal Ct. Bur., 1971-73; ptnr. Flamhaft, Levy, Kamins & Hirsch, 1973—. Chmn. grievance com. 2d and 11th Jud. Dist., 1994-98; adj. prof. Fordham Law Sch., Bklyn. Law Sch., Bklyn. Law Sch.; adj. prof. in criminal law N.Y. Tech. Coll.; apptd. spl. prosecutor, Kings County, 1990-92; adj. assoc. prof. N.Y. criminal procedure, law sch. Fordham U., 1994—. Author: The Social Studies Student Investigates the Criminal Justice System, 1978, New York Search and Seizure, 1991; contbr. numerous articles on criminal law to profl. jours. Mem. ABA, N.Y. State Bar Assn. (mem. ho. dels., chair com. prof. discipline 1999—), Bklyn. Bar Assn. (past pres., chair jud. com. 1994-98), Kings County Criminal Bar Assn. (past pres.), Nat. Dist. Attys. Assn., Assn. of Bar of City of N.Y. (chair jud. com. 1998—, chairperson oversight com. for criminal def. orgns., 2d appellate divsn. 1997—). Criminal. Office: 16 Court St Brooklyn NY 11241-0102

KAMINS, JOHN MARK, lawyer; b. Chgo., Feb. 7, 1947; s. David and Beulah (Block) K.; m. Judith Joan Sperling, May 5, 1968; children—Robert, Heather. AB with high honors and distinction, U. Mich., 1968, JD, 1970. Bar: Mich. 1971, Fla. 1991. Assoc., Honigman Miller Schwartz and Cohn, Detroit, 1971-75, ptnr., 1976—; lectr. Inst. on Continuing Legal Edn. Pres. Mich. chpt. Leukemia Soc. Am., 1991-92, 93-96, nat. trustee, 1996—, nat. exec. com., 1997—; pres. Goodwill Industries of Greater Detroit Found., 2001, The Leukemia and Lymphoma Soc.; pres. Temple Beth El, Bloomfield Hills, Mich., 1994-96. Mem. Nat. Assn. Bond Lawyers (vice chmn. com. on opinions 1985-86), Mich. Bar Assn. (chairperson, pub. corp. law sect. 1992-93). Jewish. General corporate, Municipal (including bonds), Securities. Home: 1315 Stuyvessant Rd Bloomfield Hills MI 48301-2144 Office: Honigman Miller Schwartz & Cohn 2290 First National Bldg Detroit MI 48226

KAMINSKY, ARTHUR CHARLES, lawyer; b. Bronx, N.Y., Dec. 29, 1946; s. Daniel and Claire (Sternberg) K.; m. Andrea Lynn Polin, Dec. 28, 1969; children: Alexis Kate, Thomas Suradet, Eric Vorapong. BA cum laude with distinction, Cornell U., 1968; JD, Yale U., 1971. Bar: N.Y. 1974, U.S. Dist. Ct. (so. dist.) N.Y. 1975, U.S. Tax Ct. 1977, U.S. Supreme Ct. 1984. Assoc. Paul Weiss Rifkind Wharton & Garrison, 1973-74; ptnr. Taft & Kaminsky, N.Y.C., 1974—; pres. A.C.K. Sports, Inc. (now The Marquee Group, Inc.), N.Y.C., 1977—, Profl. Sports Investors, Inc., N.Y.C., 1982—; mem. selection com. U.S. Olympic Hockey Team, Mpls., 1980. Co-author: One Goal; A Chronicle of the 1980 U.S. Olympic Hockey Team, 1984; weekly columnist N.Y. Times, 1973-77; intern for 3d congl. dist. N.Y. Adlai E. Stevenson Meml., 1967. Dep. campaign mgr. Lindsay for Pres., N.Y.C., 1972; del. credentials com. Dem. Nat. Conv., Miami, 1972; adminstrv. asst. Rep. Michael Harrington, Washington, 1972-73; pres. Plandome Civic Assn., 1981-82; trustee African-Am. Athletic Assn., 1992—. Recipient Outstanding Sr. award Cornell U., 1968, Friends of Edn. award N.Y. State Teachers Union, 1988; named one of the 100 Most Powerful Poeple in Sports, The Sporting News, 1991-92; finalist Thurman Arnold Moot Ct. competition, 1970; inducted charter mem. Jericho H.S. Hall of Fame, 1991. Mem. N.Y. State Bar Assn., Assn. of Bar of City of N.Y., Com. Entertainment and Sports, ABA, New Sch. Soc. Research (lectr.), Sports Lawyers Assn. (lectr.), Quill and Dagger, Friars Club, Plandome Country Club, Phi Beta Kappa (hon.). Democrat. Jewish. Entertainment, Sports. Home: 25 Middle Dr Manhasset NY 11030-1414 Office: The Marquee Group 888 7th Ave Fl 37 New York NY 10106-1698

KAMINSKY, IRA SAMUEL, lawyer; b. Feb. 3, 1936; s. Louis J. and Gertrude (Leff) K.; m. Barbara Handmaker, Feb. 11, 1954; children: Sherry, Louis, Jay, Phillip; m. 2d, Phyllis Levitt, June 24, 1971; 1 child, Glenn. BA, U. Mich., 1957, JD, 1960. Bar: Pa. 1960, U.S. Dist. Ct. (we. dist.) Pa. 1961. Assoc. Kaminsky & Kelly, Johnstown, Pa., 1960-67; of counsel Kaminsky, Thomas, Wharton and Lovette, 1967—. Hearing examiner Pa. Liquor Control Bd., 1970-92; mem. regulatory task force U.S. SBA, 1980-85; mem. com. on fed. assistance for alternative fuels U.S. Dept. Energy, 1982-86. Mem. ABA, Pa. Bar Assn. (ho. dels. 1989—). Bankruptcy, Contracts commercial, Family and matrimonial. Office: 360 Stonycreek St Johnstown PA 15901-1925 E-mail: isk@ktwllaw.com

KAMINSKY, RICHARD ALAN, lawyer; b. Toledo, Nov. 15, 1951; s. Jack and Sally (Kale) K. BA, Johns Hopkins U., 1973; JD, U. Mich., 1975. Bar: Ill. 1976, U.S. Dist. Ct. (no. dist.) Ill. 1976. Assoc. Vedder, Price, Kaufman & Kammholz, Chgo., 1976-83; atty. Borg-Warner Corp., 1983-89; v.p., assoc. gen. counsel CNA Ins. Cos., 1989—. Bd. dirs. DePaul U. Inst. Bus. & Profl. Ethics. Contbr. chpt. to book. Mem. ABA, Chgo. Bar Assn., Ill. State C. of C. General civil litigation, Labor. Home: 47 Williamsburg Rd Evanston IL 60203-1813 Office: CNA Ins Cos Cna Pla Chicago IL 60685-0001

KAMISAR, YALE, lawyer, educator; b. N.Y.C., Aug. 29, 1929; s. Samuel and Mollie (Levine) K.; m. Esther Englander, Sept. 7, 1953 (div. Oct. 1973); children: David Graham, Gordon, Jonathan; m. Christine Keller, May 10, 1974 (dec. 1997); m. Joan Russell, Feb. 28, 1999. AB, NYU, 1950; LLB, Columbia U., 1954; LLD, CUNY, 1978. Bar: D.C. 1955. Rsch. assoc. Am. Law Inst., N.Y.C., 1953; assoc. Covington & Burling, Washington, 1955-57; assoc. prof., then prof. law U. Minn., Mpls., 1957-64; prof. law U. Mich., Ann Arbor, 1965-92, Clarence Darrow disting. univ. prof., 1992—. Vis. prof. law Harvard U., 1964-65; disting. vis. prof. law Coll. William and Mary, 1988; cons. Nat. Adv. Commn. Civil Disorders, 1967-68, Nat. Commn. Causes and Prevention Violence, 1968-69; mem. adv. com. model code pre-arraignment procedure Am. Law Inst., 1965-75. Reporter-draftsman: Uniform Rules of Criminal Procedure, 1971-73; author: (with J.H. Choper, S. Shiffrin and R.H. Fallon), Constitutional Law: Cases, Comments and Questions, 9th edit., 2001; (with W. LaFave, J. Israel and N. King) Modern Criminal Procedure: Cases and Commentaries, 9th edit., 1999, Criminal Procedure and the Constitution: Leading Cases and Introductory Text, 1988; (with F. Inbau and T. Arnold) Criminal Justice in Our Time, 1965; (with J. Grano and J. Haddad) Sum and Substance of Criminal Procedure, 1977, Police Interrogation and Confessions: Essays in Law and Policy, 1980; contbr. articles to profl. jours. Served to 1st lt. AUS, 1951-52. Recipient Am. Bar Found. Rsch. award, 1996. Home: 2910 Daleview Dr Ann Arbor MI 48105-9684 Office: U Mich Law Sch 625 S State St Ann Arbor MI 48109-1215

KAMMER, ROBERT ARTHUR, JR. lawyer; b. Boston, July 31, 1945; s. Robert Arthur and Lorraine B. (Edgar) K.; m. Elizabeth Britton Helmes, Aug. 3, 1968; children: Scott, Betsy. BA, Northwestern U., 1967; JD cum laude, Syracuse U., 1975. Bar: Ill. 1975, U.S. Supreme Ct. 1980, U.S. Dist. Ct. (no. dist.) Ill. 1975, Wis. 1983, U.S. Dist. Ct. (ea. and we. dists.) Wis. 1983. Atty. Lord Bissell & Brook, Chgo., 1975-83, Mulcahy & Wherry, Milw., 1983-86; assoc. gen. counsel, dir. litigation Sentry Ins., Stevens Point, Wis., 1986-99; sr. claims counsel Wausau (Wis.) Ins., 1999; regional litigation mgr. Liberty Mut. Group, Wausau, 1999—. Mem. Lake Bluff (Ill.) Sch. Bd., 1980-83; chmn. bd. dirs. Achievement Ctr. Early Intervention Program, Inc., 1993—; bd. dirs. Portage County Legal Aid Soc., 1994-98. Mem. ABA (vice chmn. TIPS corp. counsel com. 1992-95, co-chmn. litigation mgmt. subcom.), Wis. Bar Assn. (chmn. corp. counsel com. 1988-92), Stevens Point Country Club (bd. dirs. 1998—). Avocations. golf, tennis. State civil litigation, Insurance, Personal injury. Home: 600 7th St Plover WI 54467-2234 Office: Liberty Mut Group 2100 Stewart Ave Ste 200 Wausau WI 54401

KAMMERER, KELLY CHRISTIAN, lawyer; b. N.Y.C., Nov. 29, 1941; s. William Henry and Edith (Langley) K.; m. Nancy Davis Frame, Oct. 2, 1999. BA, U. Notre Dame, 1963; LLB, U. Va., 1968. Bar: Va. 1968, N.Y. 1969, D.C. 1969, Fla. 1969. Peace Corps vol., Colombia, 1963-65; Reginald Heber Smith atty./fellow U. Pa., Washington, 1968-70; atty.-advisor, dep. gen. counsel Peace Corps, 1970-74; atty.-advisor AID, Dept. State, 1975-76, asst. gen. counsel, 1976-78, sr. dep. gen. counsel, 1978-82, legal counselor, 1981-82, dir. congl. rels., 1983-89; mission dir. Kathmandu, Nepal, 1989-93, counselor to the agy., 1994-99; vice chmn., U.S. rep. OECD/DAC, Paris, 1999—. Recipient Disting. Honor award AID, 1979, 83, Equal Opportunity award, 1982; presdl. rank of Disting. Sr. Exec., 1984, 89, Meritorious Sr. Exec., 1997. Mem. Inter-Am. Bar Assn., Soc. Internat. Law. Address: Psc 116 Box Oecd/aid APO AE 09777-5000 also: 11 bis Blvd Jules Sandeau 75016 Paris France

KAMMERER, MATTHEW PAUL, lawyer; b. Cin., Jan. 30, 1965; s. Leo Joseph and Suzanne Mathews Kammerer; m. Lisa Elizabeth Donisi, Nov. 15, 1996; children: Lauren Elizabeth, Margaret Suzanne. BS in Bus., Miami U., 1987; JD, U. Toledo, 1991. Bar: Ohio 1991, Ky. 1992, U.S. Dist. Ct. (so. dist.) Ohio 1992, U.S. Ct. Appeals (6th cir.) 1992. Assoc. Kohnen, Patton & Hunt, Cin., 1991-92, Strauss & Troy, Cin., 1993-98; ptnr. Murdock & Goldenberg, 1998-2000; dir. plan compliance Penco, Inc., 2001—. Field coord. Kearney for coun. campaign, Cin., 1993. Evans scholar. Mem. ABA, Ohio State Bar Assn., Ky. Bar Assn., Cin. Bar Assn., Phi Alpha Delta. Avocations: swimming, golf, skiing. General corporate, Pension, profit-sharing, and employee benefits, Securities. Office: Penco Inc 1313 E Kemper Rd Ste 211 Cincinnati OH 45246 E-mail: matt.kammerer@penco401.com

KAMP, ARTHUR JOSEPH, JR. lawyer; b. July 22, 1945; s. Arthur Joseph and Irene Catherine (Ehrstein) K.; m. Barbara Hays, Aug. 24, 1968; children: Sara, Nathaniel. BA, SUNY, 1968, JD, 1970. Bar: N.Y. 1971, U.S. Dist. Ct. (we. dist.) N.Y. 1971, Va. 1973, U.S. Dist. Ct. (ea. dist.) Va. 1973. Atty. Neighborhood Legal Svcs., Buffalo, 1971; assoc. Diamonstein & Drucker, Newport News, 1972-77; ptnr. Diamonstein, Drucker & Kamp, 1977-84, Kamp & Kamp, Newport News, 1984-87, Kaufman & Canoles, 1987-96, David, Kamp & Frank, L.L.C., 1996—; v.p. Peninsula Legal Aid Ctr., Inc., 1978-92. Mem. ABA, Va. State Bar Assn., Newport News Bar Assn. (past bd. dirs., chmn. legal aid com.), Va. Bar Assn., Va. Peninsula C. of C. (bd. dirs., exec. com., chmn. 1997). Democrat. Chmn. Newport News Planning Commn., 1994-95, commr., 1990-97; mem. bd. visitors Med. Coll. Hampton Rds., 1997—, vice rector, 2001. Lt. USAF, 1971-72. Mem. Va. State Bar Assn., Newport News Bar Assn. (past bd. dirs., chmn. legal aid com.), Va. Peninsula C. of C. (bd. dirs., exec. com., chmn. 1997, gen. counsel 1999—). Democrat. General corporate, Finance, Real property. Office: David Kamp & Frank LLC 301 Hiden Blvd Ste 200 Newport News VA 23606-2939 E-mail: ajkamp@davidkampfrank.com

KAMPELMAN, MAX M. former ambassador, lawyer; b. N.Y.C., Nov. 7, 1920; s. Joseph and Eva (Gottlieb) Kampelmacher; m. Marjorie Buetow, Aug. 21, 1948; children: Anne, Jeffrey, Julie, David, Sarah. AB, NYU, 1940, JD, 1945; MA, U. Minn., 1946, PhD, 1951; PhD (hon.), Hebrew U. of Jerusalem, 1982; LHD (hon.), Hebrew Union Coll., 1984, Georgetown U., 1984; LLD (hon.), Bates Coll., 1986, Bar Ilan U., 1987, Jewish Theol. Sem. of Am., 1988, NYU, 1988, Adelphi U., 1992, Brandeis U., 1993; LHD (hon.), U. Minn., 1987, Yeshiva U., 1990, Fla. Internat. U., 1993. Bar: N.Y. 1947, D.C. 1950, Md. 1956, U.S. Supreme Ct. 1951. Mem. research staff Internat. Ladies Garment Workers Union, N.Y.C., 1940-41; instr. polit. sci. U. Minn., 1946-48; legis. counsel to U.S. Senator Hubert H. Humphrey, Washington, 1949-55; ptnr. Fried, Frank, Harris, Shriver & Kampelman, 1956-85, 89, Fried, Frank, Harris, Shriver & Jacobson, 1989-91, of counsel, 1991—; sr. advisor U.S. Delegation to UN, 1966-67; amb., chmn. U.S. Delegation to Conf. on Security and Cooperation in Europe, Madrid, 1980-83; amb., head U.S. Delegation to Negotiations on Nuclear and Space Arms, 1985-89; counselor of the U.S. Dept. of State, 1987-89. Amb., head U.S. del. Copenhagen meeting of Conf. Human Dimension of the CSCE, 1990, Geneva meeting of Conf. on Nat. Minorities of CSCE, 1991,

Moscow Meeting on Human Dimension of CSCE, 1991; vice chmn. Mayor's Com. on Charter Reform, Mpls., 1947-48; faculty Sch. for Workers U. Wis., summers, 1947-48; faculty polit. economy Bennington Coll., Vt., 1948-50; vis. professorial lectr. dept. govt. Howard U., 1954-56; vis. prof. polit. sci. Claremont Coll., Calif., 1963 Author: Entering New Worlds: The Memoirs of a Private Man in Public Life, 1991, The Communist Party vs The C.I.O.: A Study in Power Politics, 1957, (with Kirkpatrick) The Strategy of deception, 1963, Three Years at the East-West Divide, 1983, Entering New Worlds: The Memoirs of a Private Man in Public Life, 1991; co-author: (with Kirkpatrick) Congress Against the President, 1976; contbr. articles to profl. publs.; moderator Washington Week in Rev. program Eastern Ednl. Network, 1967-70. Pres. Friends of Nat. Zoo, 1958-60, now hon. pres.; hon. vice chmn. Anti-Defamation League B'nai Brith, 1981—, vice chmn., 1977-81; pres. Am. Friends of Hebrew U., 1975-77, chmn. bd., 1977-80, now chmn. emeritus; co-chmn. U.S. Delegation to observe elections in El Salvador, 1984; chmn. Freedom House, N.Y.C., 1983-85, 89-93, now hon. chmn., Jerusalem Found., 1989-93; chmn. adv. com. JINSA; mem. bd. Ethics & Pub. Policy Ctr.; chmn. bd. govs. UN Assn. U.S., 1989—; chmn. emeritus Greater Washington Telecomm. Assn. (WETA-TV); v.p. Helen Dwight Reid Ednl. Found., 1959-85, Jewish Publ. Soc., 1978-85; hon. gov. The Hebrew U. Jerusalem, gov., 1973-85, chmn. Truman Research Inst. for Advancement of Peace, 1983-85; mem. exec. com. Com. on Present Danger, 1976-85; vice chmn. Coalition for a Dem. Majority, 1977-85; overseer Coll. V.I., 1963-80; bd. govs. U. Haifa, 1984-85, Tel Aviv U., 1984-85; bd. advisors Kennedy Inst. Ethics, 1984-85; chmn. Woodrow Wilson Internat. Ctr. for Scholars, 1979-81, trustee, 1979-90, Georgetown U. Inst. for Study of Diplomacy, 1994—; trustee Law Cen. Found. NYU, 1978-85; bd. dirs. Georgetown U., 1978-84, Mt. Vernon Coll., 1972-80, Hebrew Immigrant Aid Soc., 1981-85, Am. Peace Soc., 1973-85, Builders for Peace, 1993—; vice chmn. Internat. Media Fund, 1990-92; bd. dirs. U.S. Inst. Peace, 1985-86, vice chmn., bd. dirs. 1992—; mem. steering com. Action Coun. Peace in Balklans, 1993—; chmn. nat. adv. coun. Am. Jewish Com., 1993— Mem. ABA (mem. standing com. on law and nat. security 1979-85, 90—, mem. exec. bd. East and Ctrl. European Law Inst. 1990), Coun. on Fgn. Rels., Fed. Bar Assn., Bar Assn. D.C., Am. Polit. Sci. Assn. (treas. 1956-58), D.C. Polit. Sci. Assn. (pres. 1955), Cosmos Club. Home: 3154 Highland Pl NW Washington DC 20008-3241 Office: Fried Frank Harris 1001 Pennsylvania Ave NW Washington DC 20004-2505

KAMRATH, ALAN DALE, lawyer; b. Canby, Minn., May 16, 1952; s. Paul Elmer and Verna Marie (Haugen) K.; m. Maria Teresa Victoria Ruiz de Somocurcio, Jan. 20, 1984. B.M.E., Inst. Tech., U. Minn., 1973; J.D., Hamline U., 1977. Bar: Minn. 1977, U.S. Dist. Ct. Minn. 1977, U.S. Patent Office 1976, Can. Patent Office 1977, U.S. Ct. Appeals (8th cir.) 1977. Assoc. Peterson, Wicks, Nemer & Kamrath, P.A., Mpls., 1972—. Mem. Am. Intellectual Property Law Assn., Minn. Intellectual Property Law Assn., Hennepin County Bar Assn., Minn. State Bar Assn., Silver Gavel Honor Soc. Republican. Lutheran. Intellectual property, Patent, Trademark and copyright. Home: 316 Burntside Dr Golden Valley MN 55422-5229 Office: Peterson Wicks Nemer & Kamrath 1407 Soo Line Bldg 105 S 5th St Minneapolis MN 55402-1201

KANAGA, LAWRENCE WESLEY, lawyer; b. Chgo., Dec. 25, 1940; s. Lawrence W. and Virginia (Honold) K.; m. Kareen DiBlanda, Sept. 1, 1962 (div. June 1984); children: Kerry Ann, Matthew Lawrence. BA, Williams Coll., 1962; LLB, Harvard U., 1965. Bar: Conn. 1965, U.S. Dist. Ct. Conn. 1965, U.S. Ct. Appeals (2d cir.) 1968. Assoc. Goldstein & Peck, Bridgeport, Conn., 1965-71; mem. firm Zeldes Needle & Cooper, Bridgeport, 1971-87, Senie, Stock & LaChance, Westport, 1988—; mem. grievance com. U.S. Dist. Ct. Conn., 1984— . Mem. Assn. Trial Lawyers Am., ABA, Conn. Bar Assn. (mem. judiciary com. 1980-83), Conn. Trial Lawyers Assn. Democrat. Federal civil litigation, State civil litigation. Home: 131 Hillside Ave Milford CT 06460-7811 Office: Senie Stock & LaChance 125 Main St PO Box 336 Westport CT 06881-0336

KANAN, GREGORY BRIAN, lawyer; b. El Paso, Tex., Sept. 19, 1949; s. John Emil and Adeline (Bexell) K.; m. Linda M. Lilly, Aug. 22, 1970; children— Jeffery J., Lisa M., Stephanie A. B.A., U. Colo., 1972, J.D., 1975. Bar: Colo. 1975, U.S. Dist. Ct. Colo. 1975, U.S. Ct. Appeals (l0th cir.) 1975. Jud. clk. to chief justice Colo. Supreme Ct., Denver, 1975-76; assoc. Rothgerber, Appel, Powers & Johnson, Denver, 1976-80, ptnr., 1981— ; adj. prof. health law U. Denver; vis. lectr. U. Colo. Sch. Law, Boulder, 1975, 77-78. Chmn. U. Colo. Sch. Law Alumni Reunion, Class of 1975; participant Denver Thursday Night Bar, 1980— . Mem. Denver Bar Assn., Colo. Bar Assn., ABA, Order of Coif. Democrat. Lutheran. Antitrust, Federal civil litigation, State civil litigation. Home: 6375 S Geneva Cir Englewood CO 80111-5437 Office: Rothgerber Appel Powers 1200 17th St Ste 3000 Denver CO 80202-5855

KANDEL, NELSON ROBERT, lawyer; b. Balt., Sept. 15, 1929; m. Brigitte Kleemaier, Feb. 28, 1957; children: Katrin, Christopher, Peter. BA, U. Md., 1951, LLB, 1954. Bar: Md. 1954, U.S. Supreme Ct. 1964, D.C. 1980. Prin. law firm Kandel & Assocs. P.A., Balt., 1957—. With U.S. Army. Mem. Md. Bar Assn., Balt. Bar Assn. Democrat. Lutheran. General civil litigation, Contracts commercial, General practice. Office: The World Trade Ctr Ste 1252 401 E Pratt St Baltimore MD 21202

KANDEL, PETER THOMAS, lawyer; b. Balt. s. Nelson Robert and Brigitte (Kleemaier) K.; m. Marion Hoogstraten, Nov. 18, 1989; children: Andrew, Margaret, James. Student, Johns Hopkins U., 1980-81; BA magna cum laude, Williams Coll., 1984; JD, Yale U., 1987. Bar: N.Y. 1988, Md. 1989, D.C., 1989. Assoc. Jones Day Reavis & Pogue, N.Y.C., 1987-89, Piper & Marbury, Balt., 1990-93; stockholder Kandel & Assocs. P.A., 1993—. Vol. New Haven Legal Assistance, 1985-87. Horace F. Clark prize Williams Coll., 1984. Mem. ABA, Md. Bar Assn., Williams Coll. Alumni Assn. Md. (mem. exec. com.), Phi Beta Kappa, Phi Delta Phi, Delta Phi. Democrat. Lutheran. General civil litigation, General corporate, General practice. Office: Kandel & Assocs PA World Trade Ctr Balt 401 E Pratt St 12th Fl Baltimore MD 21202

KANDEL, WILLIAM LLOYD, lawyer, mediator, arbitrator, educator, writer; b. N.Y.C., Apr. 25, 1939; s. Morton H. and Lottie S. (Smith) K.; m. Joyce Roland, Jan. 27, 1974; 1 child, Aron Daniel (Ari). AB cum laude, Dartmouth Coll., 1961; JD, Yale U., 1964; LLM in Labor Law, NYU, 1967. Bar: N.Y. 1965, U.S. Dist. Ct. (ea., so. and no. dists.) N.Y., U.S. Ct. Appeals (2nd cir.), U.S. Dist. Ct. (no. dist.) Calif. 1988, U.S. Ct. Appeals (3rd cir.), (5th cir.) 2000; cert. mediator. Assoc. Lorenz, Finn & Giardino, N.Y.C., 1964-66; labor atty. NAM, 1966-68; with Singer Co., 1968-79, asst. v.p. pers. dept., 1973-76, mng. counsel pers. office of gen. counsel, 1976-79; assoc. Skadden, Arps, Slate, Meagher & Flom, 1979-85; ptnr. Finley, Kumble, Wagner, Heine, Underberg, Manley, Myerson & Casey, 1985-87, Myerson & Kuhn, N.Y.C., 1987-89, McDermott Will & Emery, 1989-97, Orrick, Herrington & Sutcliffe, 1997-2000; mediator, arbitrator U.S. Dist. Ct. (so. and ea. dists.) N.Y., Surpeme Ct. N.Y., 2001—. Lectr. to Law and bus. groups, 1974—; adj. prof. employment law Fordham U., 1983-86; lectr. Practising Law Inst.'s Ann. Inst. on Employment Law, 1980—, co-chair, 1995, chair, 1996—; mem. adv. panel Am. Arbitration Assn., 1996—; mem. adv. com. employment law City Coun. N.Y., 1996—; vol. mediator U.S. EEO Commn., 2000—, U.S. Dist. Ct. (ea. and so. dists.), 2001—, U.S. Supreme Ct. N.Y. (comml. divsn.), 2001—; mem. panel mediators U.S. Dist. Ct. (ea. and so. dists.) N.Y., Supreme Ct. N.Y., 2001—. Contbg. editor Employee Rels. Law Jour., 1975—; contbr. articles to profl. jours. V.p., bd. dirs. Assn. for Integration Mgmt., 1979-85; bd. dirs. N.Y. chpt. Am. Jewish Com., 1980-82; mem. human resources com. N.Y. YMCA, 1994—. Recipient award of Merit, Nat. Urban Coalition, 1979. Mem. Nat. Assn. Corp. Dirs. Democrat. Jewish. Alternative dispute resolution, Federal civil litigation, Labor. Home and Office: Mediator/Arbitrator 880 Fifth Ave New York NY 10021 E-mail: wlkandel@hotmail.com

KANDRAVY, JOHN, lawyer; b. Passaic, N.J., May 9, 1935; s. Frank and Anna (Chan) K.; m. Alice E. Sullivan, Feb. 17, 1962; children: Elizabeth Ann (Mrs. Joseph P. Cassidy), Katherine Ann. BA, Wesleyan U., Middletown, Conn., 1957; JD, Columbia U., 1960. Bar: N.J. 1960, D.C. 1969, U.S. Supreme Ct. 1973, N.Y. 1982. From assoc. to ptnr. Shanley & Fisher, Newark, 1961-80, ptnr. Morristown, N.J., 1980-99, mng. ptnr., 1983-85, 89-99; ptnr. Drinker Biddle & Shanley LLP, Florham Park, 1999—. Bd. dirs. Tingue, Brown & Co., GAR Internat. Corp.; mem. adv. bd. Ridgewood Savs. Bank of N.J. (divsn. Boiling Springs Savings Bank). Active Gov.'s Mgmt. Commn., State of N.J., 1970; chmn. Planning Bd., Ridgewood, N.J., 1981-85, Zoning Bd. Adjustment, 1979-81; mem. bd. advisors Coll. Bus. Adminstrn., Fairleigh Dickinson U., 1983-87, chmn. bd. advisors, 1985-86; mem. Soc. of Valley Hosp., Ridgewood, 1971—, chmn. bd. trustees Cen. Bergen Comty. Mental Health Ctr., N.J., 1970-73; trustee Palisades Counseling Ctr., Rutherford, 1968-81, The Forum Sch., Waldwick, N.J., 1987—, The Forum Sch. Found., Waldwick, 1978—; trustee The Valley Hosp., Ridgewood, 1992—, chmn. 2001—; trustee Peer Found. for Plastic Surgery and Rehab., Florham Park, 1996—, Valley Health Sys., Inc., Paramus, 1997—, Children's Aid and Family Svcs., Inc., Paramus, N.J., 1998—; lawyers' adv. coun. Rutgers Law Sch., Newark, 1994-98, vis. com., 1994-98. Edward John Noble Found. grant, 1957-60. Mem. ABA, N.J. Bar Assn., Essex County Bar Assn., D.C. Bar Assn., Morris County Bar Assn., Essex Club (gov. 1976-85), Wesleyan U. Alumni Assn. (chmn. 1981-83), Ridgewood Country Club, Park Ave. Club (gov. 1992-97). Republican. Presbyterian. General corporate, Finance, Mergers and acquisitions. Home: 56 Monte Vista Ave Ridgewood NJ 07450-2428 Office: Drinker Biddle & Shanley LLP 500 Campus Dr Fl 4 Florham Park NJ 07932-1047 E-mail: jkandravy@dbr.com

KANE, ALICE THERESA, lawyer; b. N.Y.C., Jan. 16, 1948; AB, Manhattanville Coll., 1969; JD, NYU, 1972; grad., Harvard U. Sch. Bus. Program Mgmt. Devel., 1986. Bar: N.Y. 1973, U.S. Dist. Ct. (so. dist.) N.Y. 1974. Atty. N.Y. Life Ins. Co., N.Y.C., 1972-83, v.p., assoc. gen. counsel, 1983-85, v.p. dept. pers., 1986, sr. v.p., gen. counsel, 1986-89, corp. sec., 1989-94, exec. v.p., gen. counsel, sec., 1992-95, exec. v.p. asset mgmt., 1995-98; exec. v.p. Am. Gen. Investment Mgmt. Corp., 1998—. Mem. ABA (chmn. employee benefits com., tort and ins. practice sect. 1984-85, mem. corp., banking and bus. law sects., tort and ins. practice sects.), NASD, Assn. Life Ins. Counsel (deps. solvency com.). General corporate. Office: Am Gen Investment Mgmt Corp 390 Park Ave 6th Fl New York NY 10022 E-mail: alice_kane@agfg.com

KANE, ARTHUR O. lawyer, consultant; b. Chgo., Jan. 16, 1918; s. Henry L. and Bertha Y. Kane; m. Bernice Estelle Levine, June 14, 1942 (dec. Aug. 1984); m. Esther Steinback, Apr. 21, 1985. AB, U. Chgo., 1937, JD, 1939. Bar: Ill. 1939, U.S. Dist. Ct. (no. dist.) Ill. 1940, U.S. Ct. Appeals 1961. Ptnr. Henry L. Kane & Arthur Kane, Chgo., 1939-63; sole practitioner Kane, Doy & Harrington, 1965-81, pres., CEO, chmn. bd., 1998—. Instr. Ill. Inst. Continuing Legal Edn., Springfield, Ill., 1990. Capt. J.A.G., U.S. Army, 1947-52. Mem. ABA, Workers Compensation Lawyer Assn. Ill. (pres. 1957-58), Ill. Bar Assn. (chair workers compensation com. 1967-68), Chgo. Bar Assn. (chmn. workers compensation com. 1957-61). Avocations: reading, teaching. Workers' compensation. Office: Kane Doy & Harrington Ltd One N LaSalle St Chicago IL 60602

KANE, DONALD VINCENT, lawyer; b. N.Y.C., July 4, 1925; s. Thomas Joseph and Nora O'Kane; m. Margaret Mary Kane, Nov. 25, 1950; children: Mary, Thomas, Donald Jr., Mark, Stephen. JD, St. John's U., 1950. Bar: N.Y. 1950, U.S. Dist. Ct. (so. dist.), U.S. Ct. Appeals (2d cir.) 1953, U.S. V.I. 1981, U.S. Ct. Appeals (3d cir.) 1983. With N.Y.C. Police Dept., 1950-51; with anti-crime com. N.Y.C., 1951-53; with RKO Radio & Picures, 1953-58; pvt. practice, 1958-69, 83—; asst. atty. gen. U.S. Virgin Islands, St. Thomas, 1979-83. With USN submarine svc., 1943-46, WWII. Mem. N.Y. State Defenders Assn. (v.p. 1978-79), Nassau County Criminal Courts Bar Assn. (v.p. 1978), Nassau County Bar Assn. (chmn. criminal courts com. 1977-79). General civil litigation, Criminal, Personal injury. Office: 21 W Columbia St Hempstead NY 11550-2410 Fax: 516-481-0851

KANE, JOELLE K.K.S. lawyer; b. Kealakekua, Hawaii, Nov. 16, 1969; d. Howard Kenji and Mary Jo Segawa; m. Micah Alika Kane, Jan. 14, 1996; children: Ka'ilihiwa Mary Kiyomi, Sunny Hi'ilei Akiko, Ka'ohu Jean Hiroko. BA, U. Wash., 1991; JD, U. Hawaii, 1995. Bar: Hawaii 1995. Law clk. Corp. Counsel Honolulu, 1993; legis. aide Office of Hawaiian Affairs, Honolulu, 1994-95; law clk. First Cir. State Hawaii, 1995-96; sr. assoc. Gallagher & Assocs., 1996-2000; ptnr. Henderson Gallagher & Kane, 2000—. Bd. dirs. WSRSLAA, Honolulu, 1996-98, v.p., 1998-99. Active Office Hawaiian Affairs, Honolulu, 1990—; grass roots organizer Hawaii Rep. Party, Honolulu, 1998—. Mem. ABA, Hawaii State Bar Assn., Hawaii Women Lawyers, Delta Theta Phi, Elks Club. Roman Catholic. Avocations: longboarding, running, gardening. General civil litigation, Construction, Insurance. Home: 45-135 Moamahi Way Kaneohe HI 96744-5329 Office: Henderson Gallagher & Kane 220 S King St Ste 2100 Honolulu HI 96813-4510

KANE, JOHN LAWRENCE, JR. federal judge; b. Tucumcari, N.Mex., Feb. 14, 1937; s. John Lawrence and Dorothy Helen (Bottler) K.; m. Stephanie Jane Shafer, Oct. 5, 1993; children: Molly Francis, Meghan, Sally, John Pattison. B.A., U. Colo., 1958; J.D., U. Denver, 1961, LL.D. (hon), 1997. Bar: Colo. 1961. Dep. dist. atty., Adams County, Colo., 1961-62; assoc. firm Gaunt, Byrne & Dirrim, 1961-63; ptnr. firm Andrews and Kane, Denver, 1964; pub. defender Adams County, 1965-67; dep. dir. eastern region of India Peace Corps, 1967-69; with firm Holme Roberts & Owen, 1970-77, ptnr., 1972-77; judge U.S. Dist. Ct. Colo., Denver, 1978-88, U.S. sr. dist. judge, 1988—. Adj. prof. law U. Denver, U. Colo., 1996—; vis. lectr. Trinity Coll., Dublin, Ireland, winter 1989; adj. prof. U. Colo., 1996. Contbr. articles to profl. jours. Recipient St. Thomas More award Cath. Lawyers Guild, 1983, U.S. Info. Agy. Outstanding Svc. award, 1985, Outstanding Alumnus award U. Denver, 1987, Lifetime Jud. Achievement award Nat. Assn. Criminal Def. Lawyers, 1987, Civil Rights award B'nai B'rith, 1988, Justice Gerald Le Dain award Drug Policy Found., 2000. Fellow Internat. Acad. Trial Lawyers, Am. Bd. Trial Advs. (hon.). Roman Catholic. Office: US Dist Ct C-428 US Courthouse 1929 Stout St Denver CO 80294-1929 E-mail: john_L_Kane@cod.uscourts.gov

KANE, MARGARET MCDONALD, lawyer; b. Long Beach, Calif. d. James LaSalle and Nora Margaret (Foley) McDonald; m. Donald D. Hoytt, Oct. 28, 1967 (div. 1974); children: Lawrence Andrew, Elyse Caron ; m. John J. Kane, May 18, 1985. BA, U. So. Calif., 1967; JD, Southwestern U., 1980. Bar: Calif. 1980, U.S. Dist. Ct. (cen. dist.) Calif. 1981, U.S. Ct. Appeals (9th cir.) 1981. Prin. Silver & Freedman P.C., Los Angeles, 1981—. Mem. Los Angeles County Bar Assn., Century City Bar Assn. Contracts commercial, General corporate, Real property. Office: Silver & Freedman PC 1925 Century Park East Suite 2100 Los Angeles CA 90067-2722 E-mail: mkane@silfre.com

KANE, MARY KAY, dean, law educator; b. Detroit, Nov. 14, 1946; d. John Francis and Frances (Roberts) K.; m. Ronan Eugene Degnan, Feb. 3, 1987 (dec. Oct. 1987). BA cum laude, U. Mich., 1968, JD cum laude, 1971. Bar: Mich., N.Y., Calif. Rsch. assoc., co-dir. NSF project on privacy, confidentiality and social sci. rsch. data sch. law U. Mich., 1971-72, Harvard U., 1972-74; asst. prof. law SUNY, Buffalo, 1974-77; mem. faculty Hastings Coll. Law U. Calif., San Francisco, 1977—, prof. law, 1979—, assoc. acad. dean, 1981-83, acting acad. dean, 1987-88, acad. dean., 1990-93, dean, 1993—; chancellor U. Calif., 2001—. Vis. prof. law U. Mich., 1981, U. Utah, 1983, U. Calif., Berkeley, 1983-84, sch. law U. Tex., 1989; cons. Mead Data Control, Inc., 1971, 74, Inst. on Consumer Justice, U. Mich. Sch. Law, 1972, U.S. Privacy Protection Study Commn., 1975-76; lectr. pretrial mgmt. devices U.S. magistrates for 6th and 11th cirs. Fed. Jud. Ctr., 1983; Siebenthaler lectr. Samuel P. Chase Coll. Law, U. North Ky., 1987; reporter ad hoc com. on asbestos litigation U.S. Jud. Conf., 1990-91, mem. standing com. on practice and procedure, 2001—; mem. 9th Cir. Adv. Com. on Rules Practice and Internal Oper. Procedures, 1993-96; spkr. in field. Author: Civil Procedure in a Nutshell, 1979, 4th edit., 1996, Sum and Substance on Remedies, 1981; co-author: (with C. Wright and A. Miller) Pocket Supplements to Federal Practice and Procedure, 1975—, Federal Practice and Procedure, vols. vol. 7, 3d edit., 2001, 10, 10A and 10B, 3d edit., 1998, vols. 7-7C, 2d edit., 1986, vols. 6-6A, 2d edit., 1990, vols. 11-11A, 2d edit., 1995, (with J. Friedenthal and A. Miller) Hornbook on Civil Procedure, 3d edit., 1999, (with D. Levine) Civil Procedure in California, 6th edit., 1998; mem. law sch. divsn. West. Adv. Editl. Bd., 1986—; contbr. articles to profl. jours. Mem. ABA (mem. bar admissions com. 1995—), Assn. Am. Law Schs. (com. on prelegal edn. statement 1982, chair sect. remedies 1982, panelist sect. on prelegal edn. 1983, exec. com. sect. on civil procedure 1983, 86, panelist sect. on tchg. methods 1984, spkr. new tchrs. conf. 1986, 89, 90, chair sect. on civil procedure 1987, spkr. sects. civil procedure and conflicts 1987, 91, chair planning com. for 1988 Tchg. Conf. in Civil Procedure 1987-88, nominating com. 1988, profl. devel. com. 1988-91, planning com. for workshop in conflicts 1988, planning com. for 1990 Conf. on Clin. Legal Edn. 1989, chair profl. devel. com. 1989-91, exec. com. 1991-93, 2000-02, pres.-elect 2000, pres. 2001), Am. Law Inst. (assoc. reporter complex litigation project 1988-93, coun. 1998—), ABA/Assn. Am. Law Schs. Commn. on Financing Legal Edn., State Bar Mich. Home: 8 Admiral Dr Ste 421 Emeryville CA 94608-1567 Office: U Calif Hastings Coll Law 200 Mcallister St San Francisco CA 94102-4707

KANE, ROBERT FRANCIS, lawyer, former ambassador, consultant; b. Denver, Mar. 15, 1926; s. James Hanley and Helen Mary (Gray) K.; m. Mary Catherine Galligan, Sept. 1, 1951; children: Stephen, Anne Kane Coogan, Thomas, Mary. AA, Coll. San Mateo, Calif., 1948; student, Menlo Coll., 1946-47, U. So. Calif., 1948; JD, U. San Francisco, 1952. Bar: Calif. 1952, U.S. Dist. Ct. (no. dist.) Calif. 1952, U.S. Dist. Ct. (ctrl. dist.) Calif. 1992, U.S. Ct. Appeals (9th cir.) 1952, U.S. Supreme Ct. 1983. Assoc. Bronson, Bronson & McKinnon, San Francisco, 1952-54; ptnr. Roos & Jennings, 1954-55, Ropers, Majeski & Kane, Redwood City, Calif., 1955-61, Kane, Owen & Melbye, Redwood City, 1961-68; judge Superior Ct., 1969-71; justice Calif. Ct. Appeals, San Francisco, 1971-79; dir. Ropers, Majeski, Kohn, Bentley, Wagner & Kane, 1979-94; U.S. Amb. to Ireland, Dublin, 1984-85. Arbitration mediation, spl. master, trial and appellate cons.; lectr. in field; law educator; U.S. arbitrator in treaty dispute with Poland, 1982. Contbr. articles to profl. jours. Bd. dirs. various schs. Served with USN, 1944-66. Recipient Freedoms Found. award, 1980. Fellow Am. Coll. Trial Lawyers; mem. ABA (life fellow found.), Calif. Bar Assn., Internat. Soc. Barristers, Am. Bd. Trial Advs., Internat. Assn. Ins. Counsel, Internat. Acad. Trial Judges, Calif. Acad. Appellate Lawyers. Republican. Roman Catholic. Office: Profl Jud Svcs PO Box 6729 630 N San Mateo Dr San Mateo CA 94401-2328 E-mail: jdgkane@jarsinc.com

KANE, SIEGRUN DINKLAGE, lawyer; b. N.Y.C., Sept. 21, 1938; d. Ralph Dieter and Lisbeth (Adam) Dinklage; m. David H.T. Kane, Jan. 24, 1964; children: David D., Brendon T. BA cum laude, Mt. Holyoke Coll., 1960; LLB, Harvard U., 1963. Bar: N.Y. 1963, U.S. Ct. Appeals (2d cir.) 1964, U.S. Ct Appeals (5th cir.) 1978, U.S. Ct. Appeals (7th cir.) 1984. Ptnr. Kane, Dalsimer, Sullivan, Kurucz, Levy, Eisele & Richard, N.Y.C., 1963-99, Morgan & Finnegan, N.Y.C., 2000—. Bd. mem. Bur. Nat. Affairs Adv. Com., Washington, 1988—; mem. U.S. Patent and Trademark Office Pub. Adv. Com., Washington, 1989-95; lectr. trademarks Practicing Law Inst., N.Y.C., 1980—. Author: Trademark Law: A Practitioner's Guide, 1987, 3d edit., 1997, annual supplements, 1998—; contbr. articles on trademark law to profl. jours. Mem. Briarcliff Zoning Bd. Appeals, Briarcliff Manor, N.Y., 1978-90, Briarcliff Hist. Soc. Bd., Briarcliff Manor, 1986-90. Mem. ABA, Internat. Trademark Assn., N.Y. Patent Law Assn. Avocations: aerobics, tennis, travel. E-mail: skane@morganfinnegan@com. Trademark and copyright. Office: Morgan & Finnegan LLP 345 Park Ave Fl 22 New York NY 10154-0053

KANE-VANNI, PATRICIA RUTH, paleo-educator, lawyer; b. Phila., Jan. 12, 1954; d. Joseph James and Ruth Marina (Ramirez) Kane; m. Francis William Vanni, Feb. 14, 1980; 1 child, Christian Michael. AB, Chestnut Hill Coll., 1975; JD, Temple U., 1985; postgrad., U. Pa. Bar: Pa. 1985, U.S. Ct. Appeals (3d cir.) 1988. Freelance art illustrator, Phila., 1972-80; secondary edn. instr. Archdiocese of Phila., 1980-83; contract analyst CIGNA Corp., Phila., 1983-84; jud. aide Phila. Ct. of Common Pleas, 1984; assoc. atty. Anderson and Dougherty, Wayne, Pa., 1985-86; atty. cons. Bell Telephone Co. of Pa., 1986-87; sr. assoc. corp. counsel Independence Blue Cross, Phila., 1987-96; pvt. practice law, 1996-97; dinosaur educator Acad. Natural Scis., Phila., 1997—. Atty. cons., 1996-99; counsel Reliance Ins. Co., Phila., 1998-2000; cons. Coll. Consortium on Drug and Alcohol Abuse, Chester, Pa., 1986-89; paleo-sci. educator Pa. Acad. Natural Scis., 1997—; paleontology field expdns. include Mont., 1999, 2000, Isle of Wight, Eng., 1999, Bahariya Oasis, Egypt, 2000; spkr. in field. Contbr. articles and illustrations to profl. mags. Judge Del. Valley Sci. Fairs, Phila., 1986, 87, 98, 99; Dem. committeewomen, Lower Merion, Pa., 1983-87; ch. cantor, soloist, mem. choir Roman Cath. Ch.; mem. Phila. Assn. Ch. Musicians, also bd. dirs. Recipient Legion of Honor award Chapel of the Four Chaplins, 1983. Mem. ABA, Pa. Bar Assn., Phila. Bar Assn. (Theatre Wing), Phila. Assn. Def. Counsel, Phila. Vol. Lawyers for Arts (bd. dirs.), Nat. Health Lawyers Assn. (spkr. 1994 ann. conv.), Hispanic Bar Assn., vice pres. Delaware Valley Paleontological Soc., Soc. Vertebrate Paleontology, Pa. Acad. Nat. Scis. (vol.), Delaware Valley Paleontological Soc. (v.p. 1998—). Democrat. Avocations: choral and solo vocal music, portrait painting and illustrating, paleontology. Home: 119 Bryn Mawr Ave Bala Cynwyd PA 19004-3012 E-mail: pkv1@erols.com, pkvanni@sas.upenn.edu

KANNE, MICHAEL STEPHEN, federal judge; b. Rensselaer, Ind., Dec. 21, 1938; s. Allen Raymond and Jane (Robinson) K.; m. Judith Ann Stevens, June 22, 1963; children: Anne, Katherine. Student, St. Joseph's Coll., Rensselaer, 1957-58; BS, Ind. U., 1962, JD, 1968; postgrad., Boston U., 1963, U. Birmingham, Eng., 1975. Bar: Ind. 1968. Assoc. Nesbitt and Fisher, Rensselaer, 1968-71; sole practice, 1971-72; atty. City of Rensselaer, 1972; judge 30th Jud. Cir. of Ind., 1972-82, U.S. Dist. Ct. (no. dist.) Ind., Hammond, 1982-87, U.S. Ct. Appeals, Chgo., 1987—; chmn. U.S. Cts. Design Guide, 1988-95. Lectr. law St. Joseph's Coll., 1975-89, St. Frances Coll., 1990-91; faculty Nat. Inst. for Trial Advocacy, South Bend, Ind., 1978-88. Bd. visitors Ind. U. Sch. Law, 1987—, Ind. U. Sch. Pub. and Environ. Affairs, 1991—; trustee St. Joseph's Coll., 1984—. Served to 1st lt. USAF, 1962-65 Recipient Disting. Service award St. Joseph's Coll., 1973, Disting. Grad. award Nat Cath. Ednl. Assn.; named Outstanding Alumnus Today's Catholic Teacher, 1991. Mem. Fed. Bar Assn., Ind. State Bar Assn. (bd. dirs. 1977-79, Presdl. citation 1979), Jasper County Bar

Assn. (pres. 1972-76), Tippecanoe County Bar Assn., Law Alumni Assn. Ind. U. (pres. 1980). Roman Catholic. Avocations, horseback riding, weightlifting. Office: Charles A Halleck Federal Building 234 N Fourth Street PO Box 1340 Lafayette IN 47902-1340 also: US Ct Appeals 219 S Dearborn St Ste 2722 Chicago IL 60604-1874*

KANNER, GIDEON, lawyer; b. Lwów, Poland, Apr. 15, 1930; came to U.S., 1947; s. Stanley and Claire Kanner; children: Jonathan, Jesse. B of Mech. Engring., The Cooper Union, 1954; JD, U. So. Calif., 1961. Bar: Calif. 1962, U.S. Supreme Ct. 1967. Rocket engr. USN, N.J., 1954-55, Rocketdyne, Calif., 1955-64; assoc. Fadem & Kanner, L.S., 1964-74; prof. law Loyola U., L.A., 1974-90; assoc. Crosby, Heafey, Roach & May, 1990-95; lawyer Berger & Norton, Santa Monica, Calif., 1995—. Cons. Calif. Law Revision Commn., 1968-77, 97—. Co-editor: Nichols on Eminent Domain, Compensation for Expropriation-A Comparative Study, Vol. II, 1990, After Lucas: Land Use Regulation and the Taking of Property Without Compensation, 1993; editor, pub. Just Compensation, 1974—; contbr. articles and revs. to profl. law jours. Recipient Shattuck prize Am. Inst. Real Estate Appraisers, 1973, Harrison Tweed Spl. Merit award for continuing legal edn. Am. Law Inst.-ABA, 1999. Appellate, State civil litigation, Condemnation. Home: PO Box 1741 Burbank CA 91507-1741 Office: Berger & Norton 1620 26th St Ste 200 Santa Monica CA 90404-4059 E-mail: gkanner@bergernorton.com

KANNRY, JACK STEPHEN, lawyer; b. N.Y.C., Oct. 21, 1935; B.C.E., CCNY, 1956; M.I.E., NYU, 1959, M.C.E., 1961; J.D., Fordham U., 1968. Bar: N.Y. 1968, U.S. Ct. Appeals (2d cir.) 1970, U.S. Dist. Ct. (so. and ea. dists.) N.Y. 1970, U.S. Supreme Ct. 1972, U.S. Ct. Claims 1974; lic. profl. engr., N.Y., 1961. Asst. resident engr. Andrews & Clark, N.Y.C., 1957-60; chief contracts engr. Leonard S. Wegman Co., 1961-68; asst. corp. counsel Law Dept. City of N.Y., 1968-70; spl. counsel to City of N.Y., 1970-71, city of Milford, Conn., 1988-91, govt. of Barbados, West Indies, 1985-88; assoc. Corner, Finn, Cuomo & Charles, Bklyn., 1970-73; ptnr. Berman Paley Goldstein & Kannry, LLP, N.Y.C., 1973—. Comml./constrn. arbitrator Am. Arbitration Assn., N.Y.C., 1975—. Contbg. author: Construction Law and the Environment, Hazardous Waste Liability for construction contractors and design profls. in the U.S., 1994; contbr. papers to profl. seminars, contractors, bus. and ednl. orgns. 1st lt. C.E., U.S. Army, 1956-57, 60-61. Mem. Assn. of Bar City of N.Y., N.Y. State Bar Assn., ABA, ASCE, Nat. Soc. Profl. Engrs., Mcpl. Engrs. City of N.Y. Construction, Environmental, Government contracts and claims. Office: Berman Paley Goldstein & Kannry LLP 500 5th Ave Fl 43 New York NY 10110-0375

KANTER, BURTON WALLACE, lawyer; b. Aug. 12, 1930; s. Morris and Beatrice (Wilsker) K.; m. Naomi R. Krakow, June 17, 1927; children: Joel, Janis, Joshua. BA, U. Chgo., 1951, JD, 1952. Bar: Ill. 1952. Cons. U.S. Treasury Dept., 1959-61; atty.-advisor Tax Ct. U.S., 1954-56; mem. Law Office of David Altman, Chgo., 1956-60; ptnr. Altman, Levenfeld & Kanter, Chgo. and San Francisco, 1964-80, Kanter & Eisenberg, Chgo., 1980-87; of counsel Neal, Gerber, Eisenburg, 1987-2000. Bd. dirs. Logic Devices, Inc.; faculty U. Chgo. Law Sch. Editor: Jour. Taxation, Shop Talk, 1963-2000; contbr. articles to profl. jours. Mem. adv. bd. Wharton Real Estate Ctr., U. Pa.; bd. dirs. Chgo. Internat. Film Festival, Midwest Film Ctr. of Sch. Art Inst.; mem. U. Chgo. Tax Policy Coun.; vis. com. U. Chgo. Law Sch. and Art Sch.; trustee Mus. Contemporary Art. Mem. ABA, Ill. Bar Assn., Chgo. Bar Assn., Urban Land Inst. Corporate taxation, Estate taxation, Taxation, general. Office: Ste 2700 333 W Wacker Dr Chicago IL 60606 E-mail: bk6565@aol.com

KANTER, SEYMOUR, lawyer; b. Phila., Feb. 4, 1931; s. William and Elizabeth (Huberman) K.; m. Rhoda Rosen, Aug. 19, 1956; children: Cynthia, Gregg, Lawrence, Brad. BS, Temple U., 1953; LLB, U. Pa., 1956. Bar: Pa. 1957, U.S. Dist. (ea. dist.) Pa. 1957, U.S. Supreme Ct. 1965. Ptnr. Halbert & Kanter, Phila., 1958-74; sr. ptnr. Kanter & Bernstein, 1974—. Contbr. articles to profl. jours. Bd. dirs. Melrose (Pa.) Park Improvement Assn., Pa., 1967-72, Greater Basketball Assn., Melrose, 1966-70. Mem. ABA, Phila. Bar Assn. (chmn. fee disputes com. 1984, 87-91), Acad. of Advocacy (faculty 1981, 84, chmn. free dispute com. 1987, 1988-89), Pa. Bar Assn., Phila. Trial Lawyers Assn., Pa. Trial Lawyers Assn., Assn. Trial Lawyers Am., Pine Tree Rifle Club (sec., treas. 1970-75). Republican. Jewish. Personal injury. Home: Apt 14a5 2401 Pennsylvania Ave Philadelphia PA 19130-3045

KANTOR, HAL HALPERIN, lawyer; b. Chgo., Apr. 4, 1945; s. Philip and Jacqueline (Halperin) K.; m. Linda Schneider, Aug. 25, 1968; children: Lori, Jonathan. BBA, Tulane U., 1967; MBA, U. Calif.-Berkeley, 1969; JD U. Fla., 1972. Bar: Fla. 1972, U.S. Dist. Ct. (mid. dist.) Fla. 1972. Ptnr., Lowndes, Drosdick, Doster, Kantor & Reed P.A., Orlando, Fla., 1972—. Contbr. chpt. to book. Editor-in-chief U. Fla. Law Rev., 1971, The Briefs, 1974. Mem. Mcpl. Planning Bd., Orlando, 1975-79; chmn. Devel. Rev. Com., Orlando, 1975-79, Econ. Devel. Task Force, Orlando, 1980—; bd. dirs. Orlando Regional Med. Ctr., Fla. Symphony Orch.; mem. Leadership Fla. Mem. The Scribes (chmn.), Fla. Planning & Zoning Assn., Fla. Waterworks Assn., Phi Delta Phi. Democrat. Jewish. Club: Citrus. Administrative and regulatory, Public utilities, Real property. Office: Lowndes Drosdick Doster Kantor & Reed PA 215 N Eola Dr Orlando FL 32801-2095

KANTOR, ISAAC NORRIS, lawyer; b. Charleston, W.Va., Aug. 29, 1929; s. Israel and Rachel (Cohen) K.; m. Doris Sue Katz, June 17, 1956; children: Mark B., Cynthia Kantor Kraft, Beth Kantor Zachwieja. BA, Va. Mil. Inst., 1953; JD, W.Va. U., 1956. Bar: W.Va. 1956, U.S. Dist. Ct. (so. dist.) W.Va. 1956, U.S. Ct. Mil. Appeals 1957, U.S. Ct. Appeals (4th cir.) 1978, U.S. Dist. Ct. (no. dist.) W.Va. 1991, U.S. Ct. Fed. Claims 1996. Ptnr Katz Katz and Kantor, Bluefield, W.Va., 1958-70, Katz Kantor Katz Perkins and Cameron, Bluefield, 1970-82, Katz Kantor and Perkins, Bluefield, 1982—. Town atty. Town of Bramwell, W.Va., 1970-75, Town of Petestown, W.Va., 1981-85; bd. dirs. First Cmty. Bank, First Cmty. Bankshares Inc., Bluefield, Va.; mem. vis. com. W.Va. U. Coll. Law, Morgantown, 1986-89; mem. dean's adv. coun. Appalachian Sch. of Law, Grundy, Va., 1998— Parliamentarian W.Va. Dem. Exec. Com., 1964-68; co-chmn. W.Va. Gov.'s Jud. Selection Com., 1988-97; chmn. W.Va. Ethics Commn., 1998-2000; chmn. W.Va. divsn. Am. Cancer Soc., 1990-92, pres. New River Pkwy. Authority, 1996—; mem. adv. bd., chmn. Bluefield State Coll., 1997-2001, chmn. bd. govs. 2001—; chmn. Mercer County W.Va. Dem. Exec. Comm., 1966-70. Capt. JAGC, USAF, 1956-58; mem. USAFR, 1953-61. Paul Harris fellow Rotary Internat., 1999; recipient Citizen of Yr. award Greater Bluefield Jaycees, 1980, Boss of Yr. award, 1992, St. George medal, Nat. Divsnl. award Am. Cancer Soc., 1993. Mem. W.Va. Trial Lawyers Assn. (pres. 1980-81), B'nai B'rith (pres. W.Va. coun. 1975-76), Rotary Internat. Jewish. Avocations: golf, reading, travel, civic activities. Administrative and regulatory, Family and matrimonial, Personal injury. Home: 231 Oakdell Ave Bluefield WV 24701-4840 Office: PO Box 727 Bluefield WV 24701-0727

KANTROWITZ, SUSAN LEE, lawyer; b. Queens, N.Y., Jan. 15, 1955; d. Theodore and Dinah (Kotick) Kantrowitz; m. Mark R. Halperin; 1 child, Jacob Joseph Kantrowitz-Sirotkin. BS summa cum laude, Boston U., 1977; JD, Boston Coll., 1980. Bar: Mass. 1982. Assoc. producer Sta. KOCE-TV, Huntington Beach, Calif., 1980-81; acct. exec. Bozell & Jacobs, Newport Beach, 1981; atty. WGBH Ednl. Found., Boston, 1981-84, dir. legal affairs, 1984-86, gen. counsel, dir. legal affairs, 1986—, v.p., gen. counsel, 1993. Co-author: Legal and Business Aspects of the Entertainment, Publishing and Sports Industries, 1984. Mem. ABA, Mass. Bar Assn., Boston Bar Assn. Entertainment.

KAPELNER, DAVID ISRAEL, lawyer, educator; b. N.Y.C., Oct. 14, 1951; s. Samuel Myron and Rolayne (Kay) K.; B.A. in Math., U. Conn., 1973; M.A. (scholar), Tufts U., 1975; M.B.A., N.Y.U., 1982; JD Suffolk U., 1991. Bar: Mass. 1991, U.S. Dist. Ct. Mass. 1992. Fin. analyst IT&T, 1975-76, economist, 1976-78, mgr. analytical svcs., 1978-79; mgr. econ. analysis Continental Can Co., Stamford, Conn., 1979-80; corp. economist Smith Valve Corp., Westboro, Mass., 1980-84; dir. fin. Princeton Corp., Westboro, Mass., 1984-88; assoc. prof. mgmt. and bus. law Merrimack Coll., North Andover, Mass., 1985—; cons. pub. utility Columbia Group, Canton, Mass., 1988—. adj. instr. fin. and mgmt. Manchester (Conn.) Coll., 1982—, Anna Maria Coll., Paxton, Mass., 1982—, Worcester State Coll. (Mass.), 1982— . Cert. Equal Employment Adv. Council, Affirmative Action Program. Mem. ABA, Mass. Bar Assn., Boston Bar Assn., Worcester County Bar Assn., N.Am. Soc. Corp. Planners, Am. Econ. Assn., Nat. Assn. Bus. Economists, Am. Mgmt. Assn., Stamford Jaycees (past treas.). Home: 45 Manor Rd Shrewsbury MA 01545-2224 Office: Merrimack Coll Dept Mgmt North Andover MA 01820 also: 37 Pierce St Northborough MA 01532-1935

KAPLAN, ALAN MICHAEL, lawyer; b. Chgo., May 2, 1951; s. Milton and Evelyn (Davis) K.; m. Madeline Lewis. BSE, Northwestern U., 1973, MA, 1975; JD, DePaul U., 1980. Bar: Ill. 1980, Ohio 1999, Ky. 1999, U.S. Dist. Ct. (no. dist.) Ill. 1984, U.S. Ct. Appeals (7th cir.) 1988. Atty. NLRB, Washington, 1980-88; assoc. Brydges, Riseborough, Morris, Franke & Miller, Waukegan, Ill., 1988-93, Piper, Marbury, Rudnick & Wolfe, Waukegan, 1993-95; ptnr. Masuda, Funai, Eifert & Mitchell, Ltd., Chgo., 1995—. Contbr. articles to profl. jours. Mem. ABA, Ill. State Bar Assn. Home: 660 Carriage Way Deerfield IL 60015-4537

KAPLAN, ANN LEOPOLD, lawyer; b. Harrisburg, Pa., Sept. 19, 1962; d. Marx S. and Joan (Yaverbaum) Leopold; m. Lawrence David Kaplan, Nov. 26, 1995; 1 child, Jeremy. BA magna cum laude, U. Pitts., 1984; JD, U. Pa., 1987. Bar: Pa. 1987, D.C. 1989. Assoc. Epstein, Becker & Green, P.C., Washington, 1987-96, ptnr., 1996—. Author: (with others) Health Law Handbook, 1993. Mem. young leadership cabinet United Jewish Cmtys., 1996—; mem. exec. coun. women's divsn. Jewish Fedn. Greater Washington, 1999—; chair Capital Polit. Action Com., Washington, 1994. Office: Epstein Becker & Green PC 1227 25th St NW Ste 700 Washington DC 20037-1175

KAPLAN, CARL ELIOT, lawyer; b. N.Y.C., Apr. 17, 1939; s. Lawrence S. and Pearl (Eisenberg) K.; m. Diane L. Garvin, Dec. 16, 1965; children: Lynn, Jonathan. BA, Columbia Coll., 1959; LLB, 1962. Bar: U.S. Dist. Ct. (so. and ea. dists.) N.Y. 1964, U.S. Ct. Appeals (2nd cir.) 1966, U.S. Supreme Ct. 1970. Assoc. Fulbright & Jaworski L.L.P., N.Y.C., 1963-69; ptnr., 1969—. Bd. dirs. Bio Tech. Gen. Corp., Iselin, N.J. Bd. editors: Columbia Law Rev., 1961-62. Mem. ABA, N.Y. Bar Assn., Assn. of Bar City of N.Y., Am. Soc. Corp. Secs., Columbia Club (N.Y.C.), Univ. Club (N.Y.C.), Phi Beta Kappa. Avocations: biking, jogging. General corporate, Finance, Securities. Office: Fulbright & Jaworski LLP 666 5th Ave Fl 31 New York NY 10103-3198 E-mail: ckaplan@fulbright.com

KAPLAN, DAVID LOUIS, lawyer, investment banker; b. Lakeland, Fla., Jan. 10, 1961; s. Donald David and Jane Zelda Kaplan; m. Katherine Ann Gibbons, Jan. 4, 1992. BA, MA, Emory U., 1983; JD, U. Fla., 1986. Bar: Fla. 1987, D.C. 1999, U.S. Supreme Ct. 1992; registered rep., mcpl. fin. prin. Dir. Cegmark Internat., N.Y.C., 1986-87; sr. assoc. Kubicki Draper, Miami, Fla., 1987-94; shareholder, ptnr. Adorno & Zeder, P.A., 1994-97; mng. dir. Prudential Securities, Coral Gables, Fla., 1997—. Chair devel. com. Girl Scouts U.S., 1997; bd. dirs. ARC Zool. Soc. Fla.; exec. bd. dirs. Swithboard Miami; bd. dirs. ARC Greater Miami and The Keys, Fla. Zool. Soc., Switch Bd. Miami. Republican. Jewish. Avocations: riding, sailing, travel, reading. Finance, Municipal (including bonds). Office: Prudential Securities Inc 2800 Ponce De Leon Blvd Coral Gables FL 33134-6913

KAPLAN, EDWARD DAVID, lawyer; b. Newburgh, N.Y., Nov. 18, 1929; s. Sidney L. and Lucille C. (Toback) K.; m. Ursula L. Appel, Aug. 23, 1955; children— Karyn Joyce, Gayle Susan. B.A., Middlebury Coll., 1952; LL.B., Bklyn. Law Sch., 1957, J.S.D., 1957. Bar: N.Y. 1957, U.S. Dist. Ct. (so. dist.) N.Y. 1957, Tex. 1989. Sole practice, Newburgh, N.Y., 1957-68; ptnr. Finkelstein, Kaplan, Levine, Gittlesohn & Tetenbaum, Newburgh, 1968— ; legal counsel N.Y. State Jaycees, 1964-65. Pres. Newburgh Area Indsl. Devel., 1975— ; faculty Tex. Coll. Trial Advocacy, 1985—. Served with U.S. Army, 1952-54, Korea. Recipient Disting. Service award Newburgh Jaycees, 1965. Mem. Assn. Trial Lawyers Am., N.Y. State Trial Lawyers, N.Y. Bar Assn., Pa. Trial Lawyers, Tex. Trial Lawyers, Jaycees, Orange County Bar Assn. (pres. 1983-84). Jewish. Federal civil litigation, State civil litigation, Personal injury. Office: 110 Sprucewood Ln San Antonio TX 78216-6739

KAPLAN, HOWARD GORDON, lawyer; b. June 1, 1941; s. David I. and Beverly Kaplan. BS, U. Ill., 1962; JD, John Marshall Law Sch., Chgo., Ill., 1967. CPA Ill.; bar: Ill. 1967, D.C. 1980, N.Y. 1982, Wis. 1983, U.S. Supreme Ct. 1971. CPA Ill. Acct., Chgo., 1962—67; sr. ptnr. The Kaplan Group Ltd., 1967—, The Kaplan Ptnrs. L.L.P., Chgo., 1975—. Asst. prof. Chgo. City Colls., 1967—78. Contbr. articles to profl. jours. Treas. Ill. Devel. Fin. Authority. Mem.: ABA, Ill. Bar Assn., Chgo. Bar Assn., Bar Assn. 7th Cir., Decalogue Soc., Am. Inst. CPA's, Ill. Soc. CPA's, Cgho. Athletic Assn., Standard Club, Bryn Mawr Country Club (Chgo.), Friars Club (L.A.), B'nai B'rith. Contracts commercial, Probate, Corporate taxation. Office: 180 N La Salle St Fl 28 Chicago IL 60601-2501

KAPLAN, JARED, lawyer; b. Chgo., Dec. 28, 1938; s. Jerome and Phyllis Enid (Rieber) K.; m. Rosellen Engstrom, Dec. 28, 1964 (div. 1978); children: Brian F., Philip B.; m. Maridee Quanbeck, June 2, 1990. AB, UCLA, 1960; LLB, Harvard, 1963. Bar: Ill. 1963, U.S. Dist. Ct. (no. dist.) Ill. 1969, U.S. Tax Ct. 1978. Assoc. Ross & Hardies, Chgo., 1963-69, ptnr., 1970, Roan & Grossman, Chgo., 1970-83, Keck, Mahin & Cate, Chgo., 1983-94, McDermott, Will & Emery, Chgo., 1994—. Bd. dirs. ESOP (Employee Stock Ownership Plan) Assn., Washington, 1987-90, Family Firm Inst., Boston, 1996-99; adv. coun. Ill. Employee-Owned Enterprise, Chgo., 1984-98; chmn. Ill. Adv. Task Force on Ownership Succession and Employee Ownership, 1994-95. Editor in chief: Callaghan's Fed. Tax Guide, 1988; author: Employee Stock Ownership Plans, 1999. Nat. pres. Ripon Soc., Washington, 1975-76; adv. council mem. Rep. Nat. Com., Washington, 1978-80; alt. delegate Rep. Nat. Conv., Detroit, 1980; bd. dirs. Family Firm Inst., 1996-99. Fellow Ill. Bar Found.; mem. ABA (chmn. section of taxation, administrv. practice com. 1978-80), City Club, Chgo. (bd. govs. 1982-92), Univ. Club, Met. Club. Republican. Jewish. Mergers and acquisitions, Pension, profit-sharing, and employee benefits, Corporate taxation. Home: 105 W Delaware Pl Chicago IL 60610-3200 Office: McDermott Will & Emery 227 W Monroe St Fl 44 Chicago IL 60606-5018 E-mail: jkaplan@mwe.com, jkaplan0@aol.com

KAPLAN, JOEL STUART, lawyer; b. Bklyn., Feb. 1, 1937; s. Abraham Larry and Phayne (Moses) K.; m. Joan Ruth Katz, June 19, 1960; children: Andrea Beth, Pamela Jill. BA, Bklyn. Coll., 1958; LLB, NYU, 1961. Bar: N.Y. 1962, U.S. Dist. Cts. (ea. and so. dists.) N.Y. 1964, U.S. Ct. Appeals (2d cir.) 1966, U.S. Supreme Ct. 1979, Fla. 1982, D.C. 1987. Asst. town atty. Town of Hempstead, Nassau County, N.Y., 1962-67; ptnr. Jaspan, Kaplan, Levin & Daniels and predecessors, Garden City, 1970-83; sole practice, 1983-95; counsel Levin Belsky Ross and Daniels, 1995—. Chmn. Hempstead Town Pub. Employment Rels. Bd., 1973-81; Rep. candidate for N.Y. State Senate, 1974. Mem. ABA, N.Y. State Bar Assn., Nassau County Bar Assn., B'nai B'rith (chmn. exec. 2000—). Office: 585 Stewart Ave Ste 700 Garden City NY 11530-4785

KAPLAN, KEITH EUGENE, insurance company executive, lawyer; b. Rahway, N.J., Apr. 6, 1960; s. Eugene Aloysius and Barbara Ann (Dempski) K.; m. Rita Maria Baker, Aug. 8, 1987; children: Matthew Joseph Kaplan, William Alexander Kaplan (dec.). BS, U. Pa., 1982; JD, Temple U., 1992. Bar: Pa. 1992. Underwriter Home Ins. Co., Phila., 1982-85, underwriting supr., 1985-86, product line mgr. N.Y.C., 1987; underwriting dir. Reliance Ins. Co., Phila., 1987-88; asst. v.p. Reliance Nat., 1988-90, N.Y.C., 1990-92, v.p., 1992-96, mng. v.p., 1996-2000, exec. v.p., 2000—. Bd. dirs. Reliance Ins. Co., United Pacific Ins. Co., Reliant Ins. Co., Inter-Ocean Ins. Co. Ltd. Mem. ABA, Phila. Bar Assn., Soc. CPCU, Wharton Club. Home: 1240 Pickering Ln Chester Springs PA 19425-1423 Office: Reliance National 77 Water St New York NY 10005-4499 also: Reliance Ins Co Three Parkway Philadelphia PA 19102

KAPLAN, LEE LANDA, lawyer; b. Houston, Jan. 26, 1952; s. Charles Irving and Ara Celine (Seligman) K.; m. Diana Morton Hudson, Feb. 6, 1982. AB, Princeton U., 1973; JD, U. Tex., 1976. Bar: Tex., U.S. Dist. Ct. (no., we., ea. and so. dists.) Tex., U.S. Ct. Appeals (5th, 11th and Fed. cirs.), U.S Supreme Ct. Law clk. to sr. cir. judge U.S. Ct. Appeals (5th cir.), Houston, 1976-77; assoc. Baker & Botts, L.L.P., 1977-84, ptnr., 1985-94, Smyser Kaplan & Veselka, L.L.P., Houston, 1995—. Mem. Tex. Aerospace Commn., 1994-99. Mem. ABA, State Bar Tex., Houston Bar Assn., Am. Bd. Trial Advs. (assoc.), Am. Intellectual Property Law Assn., Houston Intellectual Property Law Assn. Democrat. Jewish. Avocation: history. Federal civil litigation, State civil litigation, Patent. Office: Smyser Kaplan & Veselka LLP 700 Louisiana St Ste 2300 Houston TX 77002-2728 E-mail: lkaplan@skv.com

KAPLAN, MADELINE, legal administrator; b. N.Y.C., June 20, 1944; d. Leo and Ethel (Finkelstein) Kahn; m. Theodore Norman Kaplan, Nov. 14, 1982. AS, Fashion Inst. Tech., N.Y.C., 1964; BA in English Lit. summa cum laude, CUNY, 1982; MBA, Baruch Coll., 1990. Free-lance fashion illustrator, N.Y.C., 1965-73; legal asst. Krause Hirsch & Gross, Esquires, 1973-80; mgr. communications Stroock & Stroock & Lavan Esquires, 1980-86; dir. adminstrn. Cooper Cohen Singer & Ecker Esquires, 1986-87, Donovan Leisure Newton & Irvine Esquires, N.Y.C., 1987-93, Proskauer Rose Goetz & Mendelsohn, N.Y.C., 1993-95, Kaye Scholer LLP, N.Y.C., 1995—. Mem. adv. bd. Grad. Sch. Human Resources Mgmt. Mercy Coll., 1997—; bd. dirs. Suitability. Contbr. articles to profl. jours. Founder, pres. Knolls chpt. of Women's Am. Orgn. Rehab. Through Tng., Riverdale, N.Y., 1979-82, v.p. edn., Manhattan region, 1982-83; adv. bd. Suitability; vol. Starlight Found. Mem. ASTD, Assn. Legal Adminstrs. (program com.), MBA Alumni Assn. (bd. dirs.), Sigma Iota Epsilon (life). Office: 425 Park Ave New York NY 10022-3506

KAPLAN, MARC J. lawyer; b. Phila., Mar. 12, 1957; s. Ronald L. Kaplan and Sylvia B. (Meyers) Price; m. Mary J. Dulacki, Sept. 16, 1984; children: Alexandra Zoe, Rini Isadora. BA, Duke U., 1979; JD, U. Denver, 1983. Bar: Colo. 1984, Mont. 1999, U.S. Dist. Ct. Colo. 1984, U.S. Ct. Appeals (10th cir.) 1984; cert. civil trial advocate Nat. Bd. Trial Advocacy. Asst. for polit. ops. Dem. Nat. Com., Washington, 1979-80; asst. to spl. asst. to pres. White House, 1980-81; atty. Aisenberg & Kaplan, Denver, 1984-94, Rossi, Cox, Kiker & Inderwish, P.C., Denver, 1994-98; special counsel Gutterman, Carlton & Heckenbach LLP, 1998-2000; pvt. practice Marc J. Kaplan Atty. at Law, LLC, Denver, 2000—. Polit. cons. Washington, 1981, lawyering process adj. prof. U. Denver Coll. of Law, 1990-92, faculty basic civil litig. skills continuing legal edn. of Denver, 1990-92, Colo, Supreme Ct. Greivance Com. Hearing Bd., Denver, 1993-98; mem. Supreme Ct. Colo., com. county and dist. ct. cir. and jud. access issues, 1998-99. Contbr. Colo. Auto Litigator's Handbook. Pres. Duke Club of Denver, 1990-92, chmn. Children of Violence Com., Denver, 1993-94; bd. dirs. United Citizens of Arapahoe Neighborhoods, 1997—. Named Young Polit. Leader U.S. State Dept., Washington, 1979. Mem. ATLA (state del. 1997-99), Colo. Bar Assn. (gov. 1990-93, Pro Bono award 1993), Colo. Trial Lawyers Assn. (pres. 1998-99), Denver and Arapahoe Bar Assn., Thompson G. Marsh Inn of Ct., Faculty of Fed. Advocates. General civil litigation, Family and matrimonial, Personal injury. Office: Atty at Law LLC 2300 15th St Ste 320 Denver CO 80202-1184 E-mail: marc@Kaplan-Law.com

KAPLAN, MARK NORMAN, lawyer; b. N.Y.C., Mar. 7, 1930; s. Louis and Ruth (Hertzberg) K.; m. Helene L. Finkelstein, Sept. 7, 1952; children: Marjorie Ellen, Sue Anne. AB, Columbia, 1951, JD, 1953. Bar: N.Y. 1953. Assoc. Garey & Garey, N.Y.C., 1953; law clk. to Hon. William Bondy U.S. Dist. Ct. for So. Dist. N.Y., 1953-54; assoc. Columbia Law Sch., 1954-55, Wickes, Riddell, Bloomer, Jacobi & McGuire, N.Y.C., 1955-59; from assoc. to sr. ptnr. Marshall, Bratter, Greene, Allison & Tucker, 1959-70; sr. ptnr. Burnham & Co., 1970-71; pres. Drexel Burnham Lambert Inc., 1972-77, also CEO, 1976-77; pres. Engelhard Minerals & Chem. Corp., N.Y.C., 1977-79; mem. firm Skadden, Arps, Slate, Meager & Flom, 1979—. Bd. dirs. Am. Biltrite, Grey Advt., Inc., REFAC Tech. Devel. Corp., DRS Techs. Inc., Volt Info. Sci., Inc., Jim Pattison, Ltd., Internat. Creative Mgmt., Inc., Monte Carlo Grand Hotel, Congoleum Corp., Worldwide Securities Ltd., Smith Barney World Wide Spl. Fund N.V.; vice-chmn. Am. Stock Exch., N.Y.C., 1974, bd. govs., 1975, vice-chmn. bd. govs., 1975-76; trustee Bard Coll.; chmn. audit com. City of N.Y. Co-chmn. audit adv. com. Bd. Edn. of City of N.Y.; chmn. Early Edn. Leadership Group; bd. dirs. New Alternatives for Children. Mem. Coun. Fgn. Rels., Century Assn., Econ. Club N.Y., City Athletic Club. General corporate, Securities. Home: 146 Central Park W New York NY 10023-2005 Office: Skaden Arps 4 Times Sq Fl 24 New York NY 10036-6595 E-mail: mkaplan@skadden.com

KAPLAN, RICHARD ALAN, government official; b. San Francisco; s. Murray M. and Beatrice (Ray) K. AA, Canada Coll., 1973; BA, San Francisco State U., 1975, BA, 1976, MA, 1981. Pvt. practice def. and internat. law rschr., London, 1978-80, Concord, Calif., 1980-83; def. specialist U.S. Govt., Washington, 1983—. Adv. bd. U.S. Congress, Washington, 1982—85; program mgr. Balance Tech. Initiative Office of Sec. of Def., 1988—89; with office of dep. chief of staff Intelligence, Conv. Arms Control Support Group, Strategic Def. Intelligence Working Group, Change Working Group, DIA, 1988—89. Author: An Interdisciplinary Study of the International Law of Armed Conflict, 1981. With U.S. Army, 1968. Recipient Commdrs. award for civilian svc., Dept. of the Army, 1991, Superior Civilian Svc. award, 1991, Civilian award for humanitarian svc., 1992, Superior Civilian Svc. award, 1995, Meritorious Civilian Svc. award, 1996, Commdrs. award for civilian svc., 1996, others. Fellow Inter-Univ. Seminar on Armed Forces and Soc., Internat. Inst. Air and Space Law; mem. Am. Fgn. Law Assn., Internat. Law Assn. (com. on internat. terrorism 1983—, com. on armed conflict 1983—), Internat. Inst. Humanitarian Law, Am. Soc. Internat. Law, Internat. Inst. Strategic Studies, Royal Inst. Internat. Affairs, Royal United Svcs. Instn. for Def. Studies. Home: Apt I 5701 Woodlawn Green Cir Alexandria VA 22309-4609

KAPLAN, SHELDON, lawyer, director; b. Mpls., Feb. 16, 1915; s. Max Julius and Harriet (Wolfson) K.; m. Helene Bamberger, Dec. 7, 1941; children— Jay Michael, Mary Jo, Jean Burton, Jeffrey Lee. BA summa cum laude, U. Minn., 1935; LLB, Columbia U., 1939. Bar: N.Y. 1940, Minn. 1946. Pvt. practice, N.Y.C., 1940-42, Mpls., 1946—; mem. firm

Lauterstein, Spiller, Bergerman & Dannett, N.Y.C., 1939-42; ptnr. Maslon, Kaplan, Edelman, Borman, Brand & McNulty, Mpls., 1946-80. Chmn. Kaplan, Strangis and Kaplan, Mpls., 1980—; bd. dirs. Stewart Enterprises Inc., Creative Ventures Inc. Decisions editor Columbia Law Review, 1939. Served to capt. AUS, 1942-46. Mem. Minn. Bar Assn., Hazeltime Nat. Golf Club, Mpls. Club, Phi Beta Kappa. General corporate, Mergers and acquisitions, Corporate taxation. Home: 2950 Dean Pkwy Minneapolis MN 55416-4446 Office: Kaplan Strangis & Kaplan 5500 Wells Fargo Ctr Minneapolis MN 55402

KAPLOW, LOUIS, law educator; b. Chgo., June 17, 1956; s. Mortimer and Irene (Horwich) K.; m. Jody Ellen Forchheimer, July 11, 1982; children: Irene Miriam, Leah Rayna. BA, Northwestern U., 1977; AM, JD, Harvard U., 1981, PhD, 1987. Bar: Mass. 1983. Prof. law Harvard U., Cambridge, Mass., 1982—, assoc. dean for rsch. and spl. programs, 1989-91. Contbr. articles to profl. jours.; co-author: Antitrust Analysis, 1997; editorial bd. Jour. of Law, Econs. and Orgn., 1989—, Internat. Rev. of Law and Econs., 1988—, Nat. Tax Jour., 1995—, Legal Theory, 1995—. Faculty rsch. assoc. Nat. Bur. Economic Rsch., Cambridge, Mass., 1985—. Mem. Am. Econ. Assn., Nat. Tax Assn. Jewish. Office: Harvard U 1575 Mass Ave Rm 322 Cambridge MA 02138-2801

KAPLOW, ROBERT DAVID, lawyer; b. Bklyn., Feb. 6, 1947; s. Herbert and Geraldine Rhoda K.; m. Lois Susan Silverman, May 22, 1971; children: Julie, Jeffrey. BS, Cornell U., 1968; JD, U. Mich., 1971; LLM, Wayne State U., 1978. Bar: Mich. 1972, U.S. Dist. Ct. (ea. dist.) Mich. 1972, U.S. Tax Ct. 1976, U.S. Ct. Appeals (6th cir.) 1991. Assoc. Milton Y. Zussman, Birmingham, Mich., 1972-75, Rubenstein, Isaacs, Lax & Bordman, Southfield, 1975-89; ptnr. Maddin, Hauser, Wartell, Roth, Heller & Pesses P.C., 1989—. Bd. dirs. Jewish Assn. Retarded Citizens; mem. Fin. and Estate Planning Coun. of Met. Detroit, Inc. Mem. ABA, Mich. Bar Assn., Oakland County Bar Assn., Cornell Club of Mich. General corporate, Estate planning, Personal income taxation. Office: Maddin Hauser Wartell Roth Heller & Pesses PC 28400 Northwestern Hwy Fl 3 Southfield MI 48034-1839 also: PO Box 215 Southfield MI 48037-0215 E-mail: rdk@maddinhauser.com

KAPNER, LEWIS, lawyer; b. West Palm Beach, Fla., May 21, 1937; s. Irving Michael and Mildred Leah (Pikelny) K.; m. Dawn Beth Grossman, Aug. 30, 1964; children: Steven, Kimberly, Michael, Allison. Student, Harvard U., 1956; BA, U. Fla., 1958; postgrad., George Washington U., 1961; JD, Stetson U., 1962; postgrad., Fla. Atlantic U., 1969-73. Bar: Fla. 1962, U.S. Dist. Ct. (so. dist.) Fla. 1963, U.S. Supreme Ct. 1968. Asst. county solicitor, West Palm Beach, 1962-65; ptnr. Kapner & Kapner, 1965-67; gen. counsel Palm Beach County Legis. Del., Tallahassee, 1967; judge Juvenile and Domestic Rels. Ct., West Palm Beach, 1967-73, Cir. Ct. West Palm Beach, 1973-81, chief judge, 1981-83; head marital and family law dept. Montgomery, Searcy & Denney and predecessor firm, West Palm Beach, 1984-88; pvt. practice, 1988—. Faculty Nat. Jud. Coll., Reno, 1980-84, Fla. Jud. Coll., Gainesville, 1979-83, dean, 1982-83; adj. prof. law Nova U., 1982-84; mem. Supreme Ct. Commn. on Matrimonial Law, 1982-85. Contbr. articles to profl. jours. Pres. Internat. Found. Gifted Children, 1972-74; legal com. Am. Jewish Commn., 1998—. With USMC, 1959-60. Fellow ABA (chmn. ad hoc com. on family torts 1987-88), Am. Acad. Matrimonial Lawyers (pres. Fla. chpt. 1983-84, bd. dirs. 1999-2000), Outstanding Fla. Judge in matrimonial law 1982), Fla. Bar Assn. (past chmn. family law sect.), Actors Equity. Republican. Jewish. State civil litigation, Family and matrimonial. E-mail: kapnerl@aol.com

KAPNICK, RICHARD BRADSHAW, lawyer; b. Chgo., Aug. 21, 1955; s. Harvey E. and Jean (Bradshaw) K.; m. Claudia Norris, Dec. 30, 1978; children: Sarah Bancroft, John Norris. BA with distinction, Stanford U., 1977; MPhil in Internat. Rels., U. Oxford, 1980; JD with honors, U. Chgo., 1982. Bar: Ill. 1982, N.Y. 1993. Law clk. to justice Ill. Supreme Ct., Chgo., 1982-84; law clk. to Justice John Paul Stevens U.S. Supreme Ct., Washington, 1984-85; assoc. Sidley, Austin, Brown & Wood, Chgo., 1985-89; ptnr. Sidley & Austin, 1989—. Mng. editor U. Chgo. Law Rev., 1981-82. Trustee Chgo. Symphony Orch., 1995—, governing mem., 1988-95; bd. dirs. Civic Orch. Chgo., chmn. 1999-2001; bd. dirs. Cabrini Green Legal Aid Clinic, 1990-94, chmn. bd., 1991-93; mem., advisor, bd. dirs. Stanford Inst. for Econ. Policy Rsch., 1999—; vestryman Christ Ch., Winnetka, Ill., 2000-03. Marshall scholar, 1978-80; fellow Leadership Greater Chgo., 1989-90. Mem. Order of Coif, Chgo. Club, Econ. Club Chgo., The Lawyers Club Chgo., Phi Beta Kappa. Republican. Episcopalian. General civil litigation, Libel, Mergers and acquisitions.

KAPP, C. TERRENCE, lawyer; b. Pine Bluff, Ark., Oct. 1, 1944; s. Robert Amos and Guenevere Patricia (DeVinne) K.; m. Betsy Langer, May 2, 1987. BA, Colgate U., 1966; JD, Cleve. State U., 1971; MA summa cum laude, Holy Apostles Coll., 1984. Bar: Ohio 1971, U.S. Dist. Ct. (no. dist.) Ohio 1973, U.S. Supreme Ct. 1980, U.S. Tax Ct. 1996. Ptnr. Kapp & Kapp, East Liverpool, Ohio, 1971-84; pvt. practice Cleve., 1984—; ptnr. Marshman, Snyder & Kapp, 1991-93, Kapp Law Offices, Cleve., 1994—. Contbr. articles to profl. jours. Pres., bd. dirs. Lake Erie Nature & Sci. Ctr., Bay Village, Ohio, 1991-92; chair St. John's Cathedral Endowment Trust, Cleve., 1992-94. Mem. ABA (commr. presdl. commn. on non-lawyer practice 1992-96; judge finals nat. appellate adv. competition 1987, nat. chmn. divorce laws and procedures com. Family law sect. 1989-93, vice-chmn. step families com. 1991-93, chmn. alternative funding com. 1992—, taxation com. exec. 1988—, task force on client edn. 1991—, chair nat. symposium on Image of Family law Atty.-Fact or Myth 1993, cert. Outstanding Svc. 1988, 89, 93, 95, domestic rels. taxation problems com. exec. Tax sect., Litigation sect.), Ohio State Bar Assn. (family law com. exec. 1987—, family law curriculum com. Ohio CLE Inst. 1992—), Cuyahoga County Bar Assn. (chair family law sect. 1991-92, bar admissions com. exec. 1986—, cert. grievance com. 1990—, jud. selection com. 1991—, unauthorized practice of law com. 1992—, cert. Outstanding Leadership 1992), Cleve. Athletic Club (pres., bd. dirs.), Bay Men's Club. Roman Catholic. Avocations: sailing, handball, racquet sports. Family and matrimonial. Office: Kapp Law Offices PO Box 40447 Cleveland OH 44140-0447

KAPP, JOHN PAUL, lawyer, physician, educator; b. Galax, Va., Feb. 22, 1938; s. Paul Homer and Jesse Katherine (Vass) K.; m. Emily Lureese Evans, June 23, 1961; children: Paul Hardin, Emily Camille. MD, Duke U., 1963, BS, 1966, PhD in Anatomy, 1967; JD, Wake Forest U., 1990. Bar: N.C. 1990, Va. 1991, Fla. 1991. Intern Med. Coll. Va., Richmond, 1963; resident in surgery Duke U., Durham, N.C., 1964, resident in neurosurgery, 1964-69; asst. prof. neurosurgery U. Tenn., Memphis, 1971-72; attending neurosurgeon Bay Meml. Med. Ctr., Panama City, Fla., 1972-80, Gulf Coast Cmty. Hosp., 1977-80; assoc. prof. neurosurgery U. Miss., Jackson, 1980-83, prof., 1983-85; prof., chmn. dept. neurosurgery SUNY, Buffalo, 1985-87; pvt. practice as lawyer Galax, 1990—. Editor: The Cerebral Venous System and Its Disorders, 1984; contbr. articles to profl. jours. and chpts. to books; patentee arterial pressure control system, prosthetic vertebral body, cranial sensor attaching device. Major U.S. Army, 1969-71. USPHS Neurosurg fellow, 1965-67; recipient Rsch. award Am. Acad. Neurol. Surgery, 1967. Mem. N.C. Acad. Trial Lawyers, N.C. Bar Assn., Va. State Bar Assn. Republican. Methodist. Avocations: hunting, dog training. Personal injury. Office: 2433 Thomas Dr # 104 Panama City FL 32408-5808 E-mail: kappoffice728@cs.com

KAPP, MICHAEL KEITH, lawyer; b. Winston-Salem, N.C., Nov. 28, 1953; s. William Henry and Betty Jean (Minton) K.; m. Mary Jo Chancy McLean, Aug. 13, 1977; 1 child, Mary Katherine. AB with honors, U. N.C., 1976, JD with honors, 1979. Bar: N.C. 1979, U.S. Dist. Ct. (ea. dist.) N.C. 1980, U.S. Ct. Appeals (4th cir.) 1982, U.S. Dist. Ct. (mid. dist.) N.C. 1986, U.S. Supreme Ct. 1988. Law clk. to presiding justice N.C. Ct. Appeals, Raleigh, 1979-80, N.C. Supreme Ct., Raleigh, 1980-81; assoc. Maupin, Taylor & Ellis, 1981-85; ptnr. Maupin, Taylor & Ellis, P.A., 1985—. Research editor U. N.C. Jour. Internat. Law and Comml. Regulation, 1978-79; editor Survey of Significant Decisions of North Carolina Court of Appeals and North Carolina Supreme Court, 1979-81, 2d vol., 1981-82. N.C. teen Dem. advisor, 1983-85; mem. exec. council N.C. Dem. Party, 1983-85; founding dir. N.C. Vol. Lawyers for Arts, Raleigh, 1982-85; counsel Moravian Music Found., Winston-Salem, 1982-85, trustee, 1985-90, pres., 1990-92; counsel Raleigh Little Theatre, 1996-98, bd. dirs., 1998—; bd. dirs. Moravian Ch. Archives, Wiston-Salem, 1984-89, Soc. for Preservation of Historic Oakwood, Raleigh, 1981-83, Carolina Charter Corp., 1990—, dir. 1995—. Morehead scholar U. N.C., 1972. Mem. ABA, N.C. Bar Assn. (chmn. young lawyer div. continuing legal edn. 1980-82, membership 1984-86, bd. govs. 1983-86), N.C. State Bar (ethics com. 1981-91, com. on professionalism 1986-87, jud. dist. councilor 2001—), Wake County Bar Assn. (bd. dirs. 1988-90, pres.-elect 1995, pres. 1996), Kiwanis (Raleigh Kiwanis Found. dir., 1996-98), Raleigh Execs. Club (pres. 1998-99), Phi Beta Kappa, Phi Delta Phi, Pi Lambda Phi. Avocation: historic preservation, hiking, gardening. Administrative and regulatory, General civil litigation, Franchising. Home: 1615 Craig St Raleigh NC 27608-2201 Office: Maupin Taylor & Ellis Highwoods Tower One 3200 Beech Leaf Ct Ste 500 Raleigh NC 27604-1670 E-mail: KKapp@maupintaylor.com

KAPPES, PHILIP SPANGLER, lawyer; b. Detroit, Dec. 24, 1925; s. Philip Alexander and Wilma Fern (Spangler) K.; m. Glendora Galena Miles, Nov. 27, 1948; children: Susan Lea, Philip Miles, Mark William. Bar: Ind. 1948. Assoc. Armstrong and Gause, 1948-49, C.B. Dutton, 1950-51; ptnr. Dutton, Kappes & Overman, 1952-85, of counsel, 1983-85; ptnr. Lewis Kappes Fuller & Eads, Indpls., 1985-89, Lewis & Kappes, Indpls., 1989-92, Lewis & Kappes PC, Indpls., 1993—, Labeco Properties, Creston Group, Indpls.; pres., dir. K&K Realty, Inc. Sec., dir., mem. Ind. Machine Works, Inc., Mooresville, Ind.; instr. bus. law Butler U., 1948-49, chmn. bd. govs., 1965-66, bd. trustees, 1987-90; chmn. Ovid Butler Soc., 1982-83. Life bd. dirs. Crossroads Am. coun. Boy Scouts Am., 1965—, v.p. fin., mem. exec. com., pres., 1977-79, chmn. trustees endowment fund, 1987-92, trustee, 1987—, chmn. Gathering of Eagles dinner, 2000; bd. dirs. Fairbanks Hosp., Indpls., 1986-94, chmn. bd., 1988-91, exec. com., 1987-94, mem. audit and fin. com., 1992-94, life dir. emeritus, 1994—, chmn. nominating com., 1991; trustee Butler U., 1987-90, Children's Mus., Indpls., 1969-88, pres. bd. trustees, 1984-85, bd. disting. advisors, 1990-01, hon. trustee, 2001—; mem. First Meridian Heights Presbyn. Ch., 1933—, chmn. bd. trustees, 1958-61, 69-72, 1996— ruling elder 1982-85, 94-99, deacon, 1950-58; mem. planning com. and dir. 32-Degree Scottish rite Children's Learning ctr., 1997-98, dir., 1998—, chmn. bd., 2000—. Recipient Paul H. Buchanan award of excellence Indpls. Bar Found. Mem. ABA (ho. of dels. 1970-71), Ind. State Bar Assn. (ho. dels. 1959—, chmn. pub. rels. exec. com. 1966-69, sec. 1973-74, bd. mgrs. 1975-77, chmn. law practice mgmt. com. 1991-92), Indpls. Bar Assn. (treas., 1st v.p. 1965, pres. 1970, bd. mgrs. 1968-71, 75-77, chmn. law day com. 1991-92, settlement week com. 1989-95, co-chair Family Law Study Commn., co-chmn. ct. liaison com. 1992-93, family law implementation com. 1993-97, exec. com. bd. mgrs. 1994-96, counsel bd. mgrs. 1994, chmn. sr. lawyers divsn. 1999-2000), Am. Judicature Soc., Indpls. Legal Aid Soc., Indpls. Jr. C. of C. (past 1st v.p., dir. ct. unification implementation com., chmn. 1995-98), Butler U. Alumni Assn. (past pres.), Mich. Alumni Assn., Meridian Hills Country Club, Lawyers Club, Gyro Club (pres. 1966), Masons (worshipful master 1975), Valley Scottish Rite Found. (33d degree, most wise master 1982-84, trustee 1996—, chmn. bd. trustees 1998-99, 2001—, pres. Indpls. Scottish Rite Cathedral Found., dir. 1997—, chmn. 2001—, dir. Indpls. Scottish Rite Found., Shriners, Phi Delta Theta (chpt. advisor 1950-82), Tau Kappa Alpha. Republican. Presbyterian. General corporate, Real property, Taxation, general. Home: 624 Somerset Dr W Indianapolis IN 46260-2924 Office: 1 American Square PO Box 82053 Indianapolis IN 46282-2053 E-mail: pkappes@lewis-kappes.com

KAPS, WARREN JOSEPH, lawyer; b. Bklyn., June 4, 1930; m. Sydelle Tanenbaum, June 29, 1958; children: Lowell, Andrew. AB in Math. and Econs., Rutgers U., 1952, LLB, 1954; LLM, Yale U., 1955. Bar: N.J. 1955, D.C. 1955, U.S. Dist. Ct. N.J. 1955, U.S. Ct. Mil. Appeals 1957, U.S. Tax Ct. 1962, U.S. Ct. Appeals 1962, N.Y. 1964, U.S. Dist. Ct. N.Y. 1965. Law clk. to presiding justice N.J. Supreme Ct., 1954; asst. prof. law U. Ark., 1955-56, U. Md., 1959-60; assoc. Stein & Rosen, N.Y.C., 1960-64, ptnr. N.Y.C. and Ft. Lee, N.J., 1964-75; sole practice Hackensack, N.J., and N.Y.C., 1975-88; ptnr. Kaps & Barto, Hackensack, 1988—. Contbr. articles to profl. jours. Served to capt. JAGC, USAR, 1956-59. Recipient Nathan Burkan Copyright award, Fidelity Union Trust Co. Prize; Bacon scholar, N.J. State scholar; Sterling Grad. fellow. Mem. ABA, N.J. State Bar Assn. (cert. civil trial atty.), Bergen County Bar Assn., Assn. of Bar of City of New York, N.Y. State Bar Assn. E-mial. Alternative dispute resolution, State civil litigation, General corporate. Home: 34 Clover St Tenafly NJ 07670-2804 Office: Kaps & Barto 15 Warren St Hackensack NJ 07601-5436 E-mail: kapsbarto@msn.com

KAPSNER, CAROL RONNING, state supreme court justice; b. Bismarck, N.D. m. John Kapsner; children: Mical, Caithlin. BA in English lit., Coll. of St. Catherine; postgrad., Oxford U.; MA in English lit., Ind. U.; JD, U. Colo., 1977. Pvt. practice, Bismarck, 1977-98; justice N.D. Supreme Ct., 1998—. Mem. N.D. Bar Assn. (bd. govs.), N.D. Trial Lawyers Assn. (bd. govs.), Burleigh County Bar Assn. (past pres.). Office: Supreme Ct State Capitol 600 E Boulevard Ave Dept 180 Bismarck ND 58505-0530 Fax: 701-328-4480. E-mail: ckapsner@ndcourts.com*

KARAIAN, NORMA MAKSOODIAN, lawyer; b. Providence, Sept. 6, 1904; d. Mooseak and Tarvez (Aslanian) Maksoodian; m. Leo J. Karaian, Sept. 5, 1937; children— Lenore, John M., Marilyn A. Karaian Hollisian. LL.B., Boston U., 1925. Bar: Mass. 1927. Mem. Curtis H. Waterman, Elder, Whitman, Weyburn & Crocker, Boston, 1926-41; sole practice, 1942-71; mem. Rackemann, Sawyer & Brewster, Boston, 1971-72, Gaston, Snow, Ely & Bartlett, Boston, 1973— . Mem. ABA, Armenian Law Soc., Mass. Bar Assn., Mass. Conveyancers Assn., Mass. Assn. Women Lawyers (pres. 1954-55), Land Ct. Examiners. Probate, Real property, Trademark and copyright. Home: 289 Common St Watertown MA 02472-4937

KARAN, PAUL RICHARD, lawyer; b. Providence, June 12, 1936; s. Aaron Arnold and Sadye (Persky) K.; m. Susan Clare Brody, Jan. 3, 1964 (dec. Apr. 1986); children: Jennifer Hilary, Steven Lee; m. Linda Doris Adler, July 2, 1987. BA, Brown U., 1957; JD, Columbia U., 1960. Bar: NY 1961, U.S. Dist. Ct. (so. dist.) N.Y. 1962, U.S. Supreme Ct. 1967, U.S. Tax Ct. 1975, U.S. Claims Ct. 1976. Assoc. Demov & Morris, N.Y.C., 1960-65, ptnr., 1966-85, Gordon Altman Weitzen Shalov & Wein, N.Y.C., 1985-2000, Tofel, Karan & Ptnrs., P.C., N.Y.C., 2000—. Contbr. articles to profl. jours. Chmn. Bd. Assessment Rev., Greenburgh, N.Y., 1978-86; mem. Planning Bd., Greenburgh, 1975-78, Bd. Edn., Greenburgh, 1980-83. Fellow Am. Bar Found., Am. Coll. Trust and Estate Counsel (chmn. downstate N.Y. 1996-2001), N.Y. Bar Found.; mem. ABA, N.Y. State Bar Assn. (chmn. trusts and estates law sect. 1990-91), Assn. of Bar of City of N.Y. Avocation: golf. Estate planning, Probate, Estate taxation. Office: Tofel Karan & Ptnrs PC 780 3d Ave New York NY 10017 E-mail: prkaran@tkplaw.com

KARDOS, MEL D. lawyer, educator; b. Phila., Feb. 6, 1947; s. Julius S. and Rose (Klein) K.; children: Lindsay Dara, Matthew Daniel. BS, Temple U., 1970; MEd, Trenton State Coll., 1972; JD, U. Balt., 1975. Bar: Pa. 1975, N.J. 1975, U.S. Dist. Ct. (ea. dist.) Pa. 1975, U.S. Dist. Ct. N.J. 1975, U.S. Supreme Ct. 1984. Asst. pub. defender Bucks County, Doylestown, Pa., 1975-80; ptnr. Kardos & Lynch, Newtown, 1980, Kardos & Heley, Newtown, 1980-87, Kardos, Rickles, Sellers & Hand, Newtown, 1988-. Adj. prof. Temple U., Phila., 1987, Bucks County C.C., 1995. Sec., bd. dirs. Lower Bucks County Pa. chpt. ARC. Mem. ABA, Bucks County Bar Assn., Assn. Trial Lawyers Am., Soc. for Am. Baseball Research. Democrat. Avocations: sports broadcasting, sports, history, politics. General civil litigation, Criminal, Personal injury. Office: Kardos Rickles Sellers & Hand 626 S State St Newtown PA 18940-1509 also: 194 S Broad St Trenton NJ 08608-2405

KARIM, YUMI YAMADA, lawyer; b. Muika-machi, Nigata, Japan, Nov. 15, 1961; came to U.S., 1988; d. Hiroshi and Sadako Yamada; m. Rezaul Karim, May 21, 1988; 1 child, Raisa Yamada. BA, Tsuru U., Tsuru-shi, Yamanashi, Japan, 1984; JD, Touro U., 1995. Bar: N.Y. 1998, U.S. Dist. Ct. (so. and ea. dists.) N.Y. 1998. Tchr. Fujino Jr. H.S., Kanagawa, Japan, 1984-88; asst. mgr. ALC Press USA, Inc., N.Y.C., 1989-90; adminstrv. asst. Sakwa Bank Ltd., 1991-95; assoc. Law Office James C. Nolan, 1995-96; of counsel Law Office Ashok Menon, 1997-98; pvt. practice, 1998—. Mem. ABA, Am. Immigration Lawyers Assn., N.Y. State Bar Assn., New York County Lawyers Assn., Assn. Bar City N.Y. Immigration, naturalization, and customs, Real property, Estate taxation. Home: 213-08 Hillside Ave Queens Village NY 11427 Office: 230 Park Ave Ste 935 New York NY 10169

KARLEN, PETER HURD, lawyer, writer; b. N.Y.C., Feb. 22, 1949; s. S. H. and Jean Karlen; m. Lynette Ann Thwaites, Dec. 22, 1978. BA in History, U. Calif., Berkeley, 1971; JD, U. Calif., Hastings, 1974; MS in Law and Soc., U. Denver, 1976. Bar: Calif. 1974, Hawaii 1989, Colo. 1991, U.S. Dist. Ct. (so. dist.) Calif. 1976, U.S. Dist. Ct. (no. dist.) Calif. 1983, U.S. Dist. Ct. (Hawaii) 1989, U.S. Supreme Ct. 1990. Assoc. Sankary & Sankary, San Diego, 1976; teaching fellow Coll. of Law U. Denver, 1974-75; lectr. Sch. of Law U. Warwick, United Kingdom, 1976-78; pvt. practice La Jolla, Calif., 1979-86; prin. Peter H. Karlen, P.C., 1986—. Adj. prof. U. San Diego Sch. of Law, 1979-84; mem. adj. faculty Western State U. Coll. of Law, San Diego, 1976, 79-80, 88, 92. Contbg. editor Artweek, 1979-95, Art Calendar, 1989-96, Art Cellar Exch. mag., 1989-92; mem. editl. bd. Copyright World, 1988—, IP World, 1997—; contbr. numerous articles to profl. jours. Mem. Am. Soc. for Aesthetics, Brit. Soc. Aesthetics. Intellectual property, Trademark and copyright. Office: 1205 Prospect St Ste 400 La Jolla CA 92037-3613

KARLS, JOHN SPENCER, lawyer, accountant; b. Saginaw, Mich., Feb. 26, 1942; s. Harold M. and Mary Ellen (Spencer) K.; div.; children: Michael Berens, Hilary Marie. BA in Econs., U. Mich., 1964; JD, Harvard U., 1967; LLM in Taxation, NYU, 1973; MS in Acctg., Northwestern U., 1971. Bar: N.Y. 1967, Conn. 1978. Acct. Arthur Young & Co., N.Y.C., 1969-74; sr. tax atty., dir. tax planning Texaco Inc., White Plains, N.Y., 1974-87; tax ptnr. Ernst and Young, N.Y.C., 1987—. Prof. taxation Fordham U. MBA program, N.Y.C., 1988—; lectr. NYU Law Sch. Tax Inst., 1994—. Editor: Effective Tax Strategies for International Corporate Acquisitions: assoc. editor Federal Income Taxation of Oil and Gas; adv. bd. Jour. Internat. Taxation; editl. asst. Oil and Gas: Federal Income Taxation (CCH), 1971-74. Deacon First Congregational Ch., Greenwich, Conn.; pres. I Have A Dream Found. of Stamford, Inc., 1991—; treas. Nat. I Have a Dream Found., 1995—; co-founder first homeless shelter in Fairfield County, Conn., 1983; dir. Kids to Coll. Found., 1997—. Lt. USN, 1967-69. Recipient Elijah Watt Sells Silver medal AICPA, 1971; named Citizen of Yr., Fairfield County, Conn., 1998. Mem. ABA (tax sec. fgn. tax com., chmn.), Tax Execs. Inst., Westchester-Fairfield County Corp. Counsel Assn., YMCA, Harvard (N.Y.C.). Public international, Mergers and acquisitions, Corporate taxation. Home: Harvard Club Box 126 27 W 44th St New York NY 10036-6613 Office: 75 Wall St New York NY 10005-2833

KARLTON, LAWRENCE K. federal judge; b. Bklyn., May 28, 1935; s. Aaron Katz and Sylvia (Meltzer) K.; m. Mychelle Stiebel, Sept. 7, 1958 (dec.); m. Sue Gouge, May 22, 1999. Student, Washington Sq. Coll., 1952-54; LL.B., Columbia U., 1958. Bar: Fla. 1958, Calif. 1962. Acting legal officer Sacramento Army Depot, Dept. Army, Sacramento, 1958-60, civilian legal officer, 1960-62; individual practice law Sacramento, 1962-64; mem. firm Abbott, Karlton & White, 1964, Karlton & Blease, 1964-71, Karlton, Blease & Vanderlaan, 1971-76; judge Calif. Superior Ct. for Sacramento County, 1976-79, U.S. Dist. Ct. (ea. dist.) Calif., Sacramento, 1979-83; formerly chief judge U.S. Dist. Ct., 1983-90, chief judge emeritus, 1990-2000, sr. judge, 2000—. Co-chmn. Central Calif. council B'nai B'rith Anit-Defamation League Commn., 1964-65; treas. Sacramento Jewish Community Relations Council, chmn., 1967-68; chmn. Vol. Lawyers Commn. Sacramento Valley ACLU, 1964-76. Mem. Am. Bar Assn., Sacramento County Bar Assn., Calif. Bar Assn., Fed. Bar Assn., Fed. Judges Assn., 9th Cir. Judges Assn. Club: B'nai B'rith (past pres.). Office: US Dist Ct 501 I St Sacramento CA 95814-7300

KARMALI, RASHIDA ALIMAHOMED, lawyer; b. Uganda, May 12, 1948; came to U.S., 1978; d. Alimahomed and Sakina (Govani) K. BSc, MakerereU., 1971; MSc, Aberdeen U., 1973; PhD, U. Newcastle Upon Tyne, 1976; JD, Rutgers U., 1993. Bar: N.Y. 1994; registered to practice U.S. Patent Office. Fellow Clin. Rsch. Inst., Montreal, 1976-78; rsch. assoc. E. Carolina U., Greenville, N.C., 1978-80, Meml. Sloan-Kettering Inst., N.Y.C., 1980-84; adj. assoc. prof. Cook Coll., New Brunswick, N.J., 1984-90; law clk. N.Y.C., 1991-99; assoc. Pennie & Edmonds, 1997-99; practice in tech. law, 1999—. Bd. dirs. Skin Rsch. Found., N.Y.C. Grantee NIH, Am. Cancer Soc. Mem. ABA, Assn. Bar City N.Y. (com. on patents), Am. Intellectual Property Law Assn. (internat. and fgn. law com.), Licensing Execs. Soc. Antitrust, General civil litigation, Intellectual property. Office: 230 Park Ave Ste 1000 New York NY 10169 E-mail: karmali@aol.com

KARMEL, ROBERTA SEGAL, lawyer, educator; b. Chgo., May 4, 1937; d. J. Herzl and Eva E. (Elin) Segal; m. Paul R. Karmel, June 9, 1957 (dec. Aug. 1994); children: Philip, Solomon, Jonathan, Miriam; m. S. David Harrison, Oct. 29, 1995. BA, Radcliffe Coll.; LLB, NYU, 1962; HHD (hon.), King's Coll., 1998. Bar: N.Y. 1962, U.S. Dist. Ct. (so. and ea. dists.) N.Y. 1964, U.S. Ct. Appeals (2d cir.) 1968, U.S. Supreme Ct. 1968, U.S. Ct. Appeals (3d cir.) 1987. Asst. regional adminstr. SEC, Washington, 1962-69, commr., 1977-80; assoc. Willkie Farr & Gallagher, N.Y.C., 1969-72; ptnr. Rogers & Wells, 1972-77, of counsel, 1980-85; ptnr. Kelley Drye & Warren, 1987-94, of counsel, 1995—. Adj. prof. law Bklyn. Law Sch., 1973-77, 82-85, prof., 1985—, co-dir. Ctr. for Study of Internat. Bus. Law; bd. dirs. Kemper Ins Cos.; trustee Practicing Law Inst.; nat. adjudicatory coun. NASDR, 1998—. Author: Regulation by Prosecution, 1982; contbr. articles to profl. jours. Fellow Am. Bar Found.; mem. ABA, Assn. Bar City N.Y., Am. Law Inst., Fin. Women's Assn. Home: 66 Summit Dr Hastings On Hudson NY 10706-1215 Office: Bklyn Law Sch 250 Joralemon St Brooklyn NY 11201-3700 E-mail: rkarmel@brooklaw.edu

KARNES, EVAN BURTON, II, lawyer; b. Chgo. s. Evan Burton and Mary Alice (Brosnahan) K.; m. Bridget Anne Clerkin, Oct. 9, 1976 (dec. June 1994); children: Kathleen Anne, Evan Burton III, Molly Aileen, Lauren Jean; m. Janet Ann Pioli, Nov. 2, 1996. AB, Loyola U., Chgo., 1975; JD, DePaul U., 1978; grad. civil trial advocacy program, U. Calif., 1979. Bar: Ill. 1978, U.S. Dist. Ct. (no. dist.) Ill. 1978, U.S. Ct. Appeals

(7th cir.) 1978, U.s. Dist. Ct. (no. dist.) Ind. 1995, U.S. Supreme Ct. 1983. Trial atty. Chgo. Milw. St. Paul & Pacific R.R., Chgo., 1978-81; litigation dept. Baker & McKenzie, 1981-87; sr. litigation counsel Levin & Ginsburg Ltd., 1987-89; of counsel Oppenheimer, Wolff & Donnelly, 1989-91; prin. Law Offices of Evan B. Karnes ((& Assocs., 1992-99; mng. ptnr. O'Connor & Karnes, Chgo., 2000—. Bd. dirs. Triad Communications Inc, Albuquerque, chmn. bd., 1988. Trustee Village of Northfield, Ill., 1999—, mem. fin. com., mem. planning and zoning commn., 1990-99, vice chmn., 1994-99. Mem. ABA, ATLA, Ill. Bar Assn., Fed. Bar Assn. (bd. dirs. Chgo. chpt. 1995-99), Chgo. Bar Assn., Def. Rsch. Inst., Nat. Assn. R.R. Counsel (chmn. sci. evidence com. 1995—, nat. exec. com. 1995—, v.p. Midwest region 2000—), Ill. Trial Lawyers Assn., Blue Key (sec. Loyola U. chpg. 1974-75), Phi Sigma Alpha, Phi Alpha Delta. General civil litigation, Contracts commercial. Office: 2 First Nat Plz 20 S Clark St 20th Flr Chicago IL 60603 E-mail: karneslaw@att.net

KARNIEL, YUVAL, lawyer; b. Jerusalem, June 15, 1963; s. Hanania and Ilana Karniel; m. Tamar Olanda Mordahovich, July 2, 1993; 1 child, Adi. LLB, Hebrew U., Jerusalem, 1988, LLD, 1997; LLM, Am. U., Washington, 1990. Legal adviser Police and Communication Minister, Jerusalem, Tel Aviv, 1992-93, 2d TV and Radio Authority, Jerusalem, 1993-95; lectr. Hebrew U., 1996-2000; head communicaion and media law sector Zysman, Aharoni, Gayer & Co., Tel Aviv, 1999—. Mem. Freedom Info. Pub. Commn., Israel, 1994-95, Copyright and Patent Enactment Commn., Israel, 1997—. Contbr. articles to profl. jours. Chmn. Keshev - Protection Democracy in Israel, 1990-2001; mem. Assn. Civic Rights Israel, 1990-2001. Sgt. maj. Israeli Def. Force Air Force, 1981-84. Recipient Outstanding Acad. Achievement award Golda Meir Fund, 1989; grantee New Israel Fund, 1989-90. Mem. Israel Bar Assn., Internet Soc. Communications, General corporate, Intellectual property. Office: Zysman Aharoni Gayer & Co 52A Hayarkon St 63642 Tel Aviv Israel Office Fax: 972-3-7955550. E-mail: mail@zag-law.co.il

KARON, SHELDON, lawyer; b. Superior, Wis., Mar. 1, 1930; s. Bert and Betty Karon; m. Lee Goldwasser, Aug. 6, 1950; children: Maureen Byron, Laurie Feig, Peggy Pattis. BS, Northwestern U., 1952; JD, Harvard U., 1955. Bar: Ill. 1955. Assoc. Jenner & Block, Chgo., 1955-61; ptnr. Friedman & Koven, 1962-75; ptnr., chmn. Karon, Morrison & Savikas, 1975-88, Keck, Mahin & Cate, Chgo., 1988-97; of counsel Foley & Lardner, 1997—. Arbitrator CFR Ctr. for Dispute Resolution, N.Y.C.; mem. Ill. Supreme Ct. Commn. for Jud. Reform, 1993-95. Bd. dirs. Kohl CHildren's Mus., Wilmette, Ill., 1988—, Highland Park (Ill.) Cmty. Edn., 1995—. Fellow Am. Coll. Trial Lawyers; mem. ABA, Ill. State Bar Assn., Chgo. Bar Assn., Fed. Cir. Bar Assn., Am. Arbitration Assn. (chair large complex case panel), Law Club, Legal Club. Alternative dispute resolution, Federal civil litigation, Intellectual property. Office: Foley & Lardner 330 N Wabash Ave Chicago IL 60611-3603 E-mail: skaron@foleylaw.com

KARP, RONALD ALVIN, lawyer; b. Bklyn., Feb. 12, 1945; BA, U. Md., 1967; JD, Washington Coll. Law, 1971. Bar: D.C. 1972, Md. 1972, U.S. Dist. Ct. Md. 1972, U.S. Dist. Ct. D.C. 1972, U.S. Ct. Appeals (D.C. cir.) 1972, U.S. Supreme Ct. 1975. Ptnr. Chalkin & Karp, P.C., Washington, 1971-96; mng. ptnr. Karp, Frosh, Lapidus, Wigodsky & Norwind, P.A., 1996—. Faculty Nat. Coll. Advocacy, Georgetown U., Washington, 1983. Producer, moderator legal programs for NBC Radio, 1974-79, pub. TV programs, 1986—. Trustee McLean Sch. Md., 1985-88; bd. govs. Washington Regional Bd., ADL, 1988—, co-chair, 1996-2000. Mem. ABA (litigation sect.), ATLA (del. D.C. 1986-88), D.C. Bar Assn., Md. Bar Assn., Montgomery County Bar Assn. (chair personal injury sect. 1997-99), Trial Lawyers Assn. Met. Washington D.C. (bd. govs. 1980-82, pres. 1985, Trial Lawyer of Yr. 1988), Am. Bd. Trial Advocates, George Washignton Am. Inn of Ct. (pres. 1994-95). Federal civil litigation, State civil litigation, Personal injury. Office: Karp Frosh et al 1370 Piccard Dr Rockville MD 20850-4304 also: 1133 Connecticut Ave NW Washington DC 20036-4104 E-mail: ronk@karpfrosh.com

KARR, CHARLES, lawyer; b. Coal Hill, Ark., Aug. 3, 1941; s. William Joe and Doris Jane (Coats) K.; m. Suzanne Mary Stoner, Dec. 23, 1962; children: Stephanie, Jennifer, Jeffrey. BA, U. Ark., 1965, LLB, 1967. Bar: Ark. 1968, U.S. Dist. Ct. (we. dist.) Ark. 1979, U.S. Ct. Appeals (8th cir.), 1982, U.S. Supreme Ct. 1985. Law clk. to assoc. justice Ark. Supreme Ct., Little Rock, 1968; dep. pros. atty. Sebastian County, Fort Smith, Ark., 1969-72; pros. atty. 12th Jud. Cir., 1973-78; ptnr. Law Offices Charles Carr, P.A., 1979—. Mem. Criminal Detention Facilities Bd., Pine Bluff, Ark., 1976-78, Gov.'s Commn. on Prisons, Little Rock, 1977; bd. dirs. United Way Fort Smith, Inc., 1977-79, Bost Human Devel. Svcs., Inc., Fort Smith, 1983-88. Mem. ABA (speedy trial com. 1976-77, prosecution discretion com. 1983-84), Assn. Trial Lawyers Am., W.B. Putnam Am. Inn of Ct., Ark. Bar Assn. (chmn. criminal law sect. 1976-77), Ark. Pros. Attys. Assn. (pres. 1977). Democrat. Mem. Ch. of Christ. Personal injury, Product liability, Professional liability. Home: 7415 Westminister Pl Fort Smith AR 72903-4250 Office: Law Offices Charles Karr PA 1st Nat Bank Bldg 602 Garrison Ave Ste 650 Fort Smith AR 72901-2535 E-mail: karrlawfirm@aol.com

KARR, DAVID DEAN, lawyer; b. Denver, Sept. 3, 1953; s. Dean Speece and Jean (Ransbottom) K.; m. Laura A. Foster, Apr. 10, 1982; children: Emily Ann, Bradley Foster. BA, U. Puget Sound, 1975; JD, Loyola U., 1979. Bar: Colo. 1979, U.S. Dist. Ct. 1979, U.S. Ct. Appeals (10th cir.) 1981, U.S. Supreme Ct. 1983. Assoc. Pryor Carney & Johnson, P.C., Englewood, Colo., 1979-84, ptnr., 1984-95, Pryor, Johnson, Montoya, Carney and Karr, P.C., Englewood, 1995—. Mem. ABA (lead atty. pro bono team death penalty project Tex. chpt. 1988—), Colo. Bar Assn. (interprofl. com. 1990—), Arapahoe County Bar Assn.. Denver Bar Assn. Federal civil litigation, Insurance, Personal injury. Home: 5474 E Hinsdale Cir Littleton CO 80122-2538 Office: Pryor Johnson Montoya Carney and Karr PC Ste 1313 6400 S Fiddlers Green Cir Englewood CO 80111-4939

KARSCH, STEPHEN E. store executive, lawyer; b. N.Y.C., Nov. 23, 1939; s. Samuel and Bertha (Delman) K.; m. Phyllis Sloan, Mar. 20, 1965; children— Roxanne C., Michael A. B.S. in Bus. Adminstrn., Am. U., 1961; LL.B., George Washington U., 1964. Bar: D.C., N.Y. Trial atty. SEC, Washington, 1964-66; sr. v.p. Sloan's Supermarkets, Inc., N.Y.C., 1966— ; sr. ptnr. Karsch & Meyer, N.Y.C., 1966— ; pres. Hunts Point Terminal Produce Coop., Bronx, N.Y. Chmn. Citizen Budget Com. Long Beach Sch. Dist., N.Y., 1981-82, active sch. reorgn. com., 1983. Recipient Nat. Retinitis Pigmentosa Found. award, 1980; Man of Yr. award Congregation Beth Shalom, 1982. Mem. N.Y. County Lawyers Assn., Phi Delta Phi. Democrat. Jewish. Contracts commercial, Real property, Securities. Office: Karsch & Meyer 108 Greenwich St New York NY 10006-1821

KARWACKI, ROBERT LEE, judge; b. Balt., Aug. 2, 1933; s. Lee Daniel and Marie Ann (Budzynski) K.; m. Patricia Ann Deal, Nov. 3, 1956 (dec. May 1972); children: Ann Elizabeth, Lee Daniel, John Robert; m. Marion Elizabeth Harper, June 16, 1973. AB, U. Md., 1954; LLB, U. Md., Balt., 1956. Bar: Md. 1956, U.S. Supreme Ct. 1963, U.S. Dist. Ct. Md. 1957, U.S. Ct. Appeals (4th cir.) 1960. Law clk. to Hon. Stephen R. Collins Ct. Appeals Md., Annapolis, 1956-57; assoc. Miles & Stockbridge, Balt., 1957-63, ptnr., 1965-73; asst. atty. gen. State of Md., 1963-65; assoc. judge Cir. Ct. Balt. City, 1973-84, Ct. Spl. Appeals Md., Annapolis, 1984-90, Ct. Appeals Md., Annapolis, 1990-97. Pres. Balt. City Sch. Bd., 1970-72. Sgt. USAR, 1956-62. Recipient Man for All Seasons award St. Thomas More Soc., 1977. Fellow Md. Bar Found.; mem. Lawyer's Roundtable, Wednesday Law Club (pres. 1984). Democrat. Roman Catholic. Avocations: golfing, boating, fishing, hunting.

KARWATH, BART ANDREW, lawyer; b. Davenport, Iowa, July 6, 1966; s. Robert D. and Linda (Bart) K.; m. Karen Elizabeth Lovich, Aug. 20, 1994. BS in pub. affairs, Ind. U., 1988, JD magna cum laude, 1991. Bar: Ind. 1991, U.S. Dist. Ct. (so., no. dist.) Ind. 1991, U.S. Ct. Appeals (7th cir.) 1993, U.S. Supreme Ct. 1998. Law clerk Ct. Appeals of Ind., Indpls., 1991-92, U.S. Dist. Ct. Southern Dist. Ind., Indpls., 1992-94; lawyer Barnes & Thornburg, 1994—. Contbr. articles to profl. jours. Mem. Lawyers for Lugar, Indpls., 1995. Order of Coif Ind. U., 1991; recipient Am. Jurisprudence award Ind. U., 1990, Am. Jurisprudence award Drake U., 1989. Mem. Alpha Sigma Phi. Federal civil litigation, State civil litigation, Pension, profit-sharing, and employee benefits. Office: Barnes & Thornburg 11 S Meridian St Ste 1313 Indianapolis IN 46204-3535

KASARJIAN, LEVON, JR. lawyer; b. Boston, Nov. 27, 1937; s. Levon and Olga Mary (Moses) K.; m. Nancy Elizabeth Sexton, Oct. 12, 1963; children: David, Laurie, Kevin. AB, Harvard Coll., 1959; JD, Boston U., 1962. Bar: Mass. 1962, N.Y. 1974. Trial atty. tax div. U.S. Dept. Justice, Washington, 1963-68; gen. counsel, sec. EDP Resources, Inc., White Plains, N.Y., 1968-74; v.p., corp. counsel Greyhound Capital Corp., Phoenix, 1975-86; sr. v.p., corp. counsel Greyhound Leasing & Fin. Corp., Phoenix, 1986; sr. v.p., corp. counsel Bell Atlantic Systems Leasing Internat., Inc., Phoenix, 1986—. Exec. v.p. Ariz. Assn. for Children and Adults with Learning Disabilities, Phoenix, 1979-82; pres. Valley of the Sun Kiwanis, Phoenix, 1983-84. With U.S. Army, 1962. Recipient Sustained Superior Performance award Tax div. Dept. Justice, Washington, 1967. Methodist. Contracts commercial, General corporate. Office: Bell Atlantic Systems Leasing Internat Inc 11811 N Tatum Blvd Phoenix AZ 85028-1614

KASEMSUP, PUNN JOSEPH, lawyer; b. Bangkok, Thailand, Dec. 29, 1968; s. Preedee and Angkana Agnes Kasemsup; m. Voraphan Arayarangsi, Jan. 19, 1970. LLB, Thammasat U, Bangkok, 1991; LLM, So. Meth. U., 1995. Lawyer Sitthicoke Law Office, Bangkok; legal trainee Walter, Conston, Alexander & Green, P.C., N.Y.C., 1995-96; vis. scholar East Asian Legal Study, Law Sch., U. Wis., Madison, 1996; assoc. Baker & McKenzie, Bangkok, 1996—. Mem. Thailand Bar Assn., Thai Law Soc. Home: 95 Soi Pipat Silom Rd, Bangrak Bangkok 10500 Thailand Office: Baker & McKenzie 990 Rama IV Rd Bangkok 10500 Thailand Fax: 662-636-2111. E-mail: punn.kasemsup@bakernet.com

KASHANI, HAMID REZA, lawyer, computer consultant; b. Tehran, Iran, May 1, 1955; came to U.S., 1976; s. Javad K. BSEE with highest distinction, Purdue U., 1978, MSEE, 1979; JD, Ind. U., 1986. Bar: Ind. 1986, U.S. Dist. Ct. (so. and no. dists.) 1986, U.S. Ct. Appeals (7th cir.) 1986, U.S. Supreme Ct. 1994, U.S. Ct. Appeals (9th cir.) 1996. Rsch. asst. Purdue U., West Lafayette, Ind., 1978-79, 80-81; engr. Cummins Engine Co., Columbus, 1981-82; assoc. faculty Ind. U.-Purdue U., Indpls., 1983-84; sr. software engr. Engineered System Devel., 1985-87; computer cons. Hamid R. Kashani, 1986—; pvt. practice law, 1986—; cons. Good Techs., 1987-90; pres. Virtual Media Techs., Inc., 1998—. Cons. Prism Imaging, Denver, 1990-93, Ind. Bar Assn., 1989-95. Editor: Computer Law Desktop Guide, 1995. Mem., bd. dirs. ACLU, 1997—, Ind. Civil Liberties Union, Indpls., 1987—, mem. legis. com., 1987—, mem. screening com., 1985—, del., 1989, 91, 93, 95, acting v.p. fundraising, 1995-96, v.p. edn., 1996—, chair long-range planning com., 1991-92, 96—, chmn. nominating com., 1997—, pres., 1999—; bd. dirs. ACLU, 1997—. Fellow Ind. U. Sch. Law, 1984; recipient Cert. of Appreciation Ind. Correctional Assn., 1988; named Cooperating Atty. of Yr. Ind. Civil Liberties Union, 1990, 95, 98. Mem. ABA (vice chmn. YLD computer law com. 1990-91, chmn. computer law exec. com. 1991-93, litigation exec. com. 1987-89, 90-93, YLD liaison standing com. on jud. selection, tenure and compensation 1992-94, 95-96, co-chair first amendment rights in the digital age com., vice chair com. on opportunities for minorities and women, YLD liaison to ABA tech. coun. 1992-93, co-chmn. first amendment rights in the digital age com. 1997—, vice chmn. com. on opportunities for minorities women 1997—, vice chmn. nat. info. infrastructure com. sect. sci. and tech. 1993-97, chair privacy info. and civil liberties ABA sect. of individual rights and responsibilities 1998—, mem. standing com. on jud. selection, tenure and compensation 1995-96, chair privacy info. and civil liberties sect. of individual rights and responsibilities 1998—), IEEE (Outstanding Contbns. award 1983), Indpls. Bar Assn. (chmn. articles and bylaws coms. 1994-95), Ind. State Bar Assn. (vice chair computer comms. com. 1995-98, chair computer comms. com. 1998—, chair computer comm. com. 1998—), Eta Kappa Nu, Tau Beta Pi, Phi Kappa Phi, Phi Eta Sigma. Civil rights, Federal civil litigation, Computer. Office: 445 N Pennsylvania St Ste 600 Indianapolis IN 46204-1818 E-mail: hkashani@kashanilaw.com

KASHKASHIAN, ARSEN, lawyer; b. Bristol, Pa., July 23, 1938; s. Arsen and Katherine (Mangiaracina) K.; children: Arsen III, Valerie T. Tomaro, Juliet Kashkashian; m. Elizabeth Ann Greaves, Apr. 29, 1995 (dec. Dec. 24, 1997). BS in Econs., Temple U., 1960, JD, 1963. Bar: Pa. 1964, U.S. Dist. Ct. (ea. dist.) Pa. 1964, U.S. Ct. Appeals (3d cir.) 1964, U.S. Tax Ct. 1970. Assoc. Egnal & Simons, Phila., 1964-66; lawyer ea. divsn. Sears, Roebuck Co., 1966-68; ptnr. Simons, Kashkashian & Kellis, 1968-75, Kashkashian & Kellis, Phila., 1975-85, Kashkashian & Horn, Phila., 1985; owner Kaskashian & Assocs., Bristol, Pa., 1985—. Spl. counsel Redevel. Authority, Phila., 1968-69, Sch. Tchrs. Retirement Fund Pa., 1972-80, Bensalem (Pa.) Twp. Water and Sewer Authority, 1972-78. Inventor, patentee Multiple Credit Card, 1976. Chmn. N.E. Citzens' Planning Coun., Phila., 1972-80. Sgt. First Class, U.S. Army, 1964-65. Named Man of Yr. E. Torresdale Civil Assn., Phila., 1968, Powelton Civil Homeowners Assn., Phila., 1970. Mem. ATLA, Fed. Bar Assn., Phila. Bar Assn., Amigo Club Bucks County, Pa. (chmn. 1996-98). Democrat. Armenian Orthodox. Achievements include representing homeowners association in leading case on urban renewal in U.S. Contracts commercial, Immigration, naturalization, and customs, Real property. Home: 959 Fillmore St Philadelphia PA 19124-2402 Office: Kashkashian & Assocs 1240 Rt 413 Bristol PA 19007

KASISCHKE, LOUIS WALTER, lawyer; b. Bay City, Mich., July 18, 1942; s. Emil Ernst and Gladys Ann (Stuady) K.; m. Sandra Ann Colosimo, Sept. 30, 1967; children: Douglas, Gregg. BA, Mich. State U., 1964, JD, 1967; LLM, Wayne State U., 1971. Bar: Mich. 1968, U.S. Dist. Ct. (southeastern dist.) Mich. 1968; CPA. Acct. Touche Ross & Co., Detroit, 1967-71; atty. Dykema Gossett, 1971—; pres. Pella Window and Door Co., West Bloomfield, Mich., 1990-98. Bd. dirs. Barton Malow Co., Southfield. Author: Michigan Closely Held Corporations, 1986; contbr. articles to profl. jours. Mem. ABA, AICPA, State Bar Mich. (editor column Mich. Bar Jour. 1971-83), Mich. Assn. CPAs, Am. Coll. Tax Counsel Republican. Lutheran. Avocations: mountaineering, skiing, running, squash, golf. General corporate, Corporate taxation, Taxation, general. Home: 3491 N Lakeshore Harbor Springs MI 49740 Office: Dykema Gossett 39577 Woodward Ave Ste 300 Bloomfield Hills MI 48304-5086

KASOWITZ, MARC ELLIOT, lawyer; b. New Haven, June 28, 1952; s. Robert and Felice Beverly (Molaver) K. BA, Yale U., 1974; JD, Cornell U., 1977. Bar: N.Y. 1978, U.S. Dist. Ct. (so. and ea. dists.) N.Y. 1978. Assoc. Rosenman & Colin, N.Y.C., 1977-86, ptnr., 1986-88, Mayer, Brown & Platt, N.Y.C., 1988-93, Kasowitz, Benson, Torres & Friedman LLP, N.Y.C., 1993—. General civil litigation, Contracts commercial, Product liability. Home: 1160 Park Ave Apt 4B New York NY 10128-1212 Office: Kasowitz Benson Torres & Friedman LLP 1633 Broadway New York NY 10019-6022

KASPER, HORST MANFRED, lawyer; b. Dusseldorf, Germany, June 3, 1939; s. Rudolf Ferdinand and Lilli Helene (Krieger) K.; 1 child, Olaf Jan. Diploma in chemistry, U. Bonn, 1963, D. in Natural Scis., 1965; JD, Seton Hall U., 1978. Bar: N.J. 1978, U.S. Patent Office 1977. Mem. staff Lincoln Lab., MIT, Lexington, 1967-69; mem. tech. staff Bell Tel. Labs., Murray Hill, N.J., 1970-76; assoc. Kirschstein, Kirschstein, Ottinger & Frank, N.Y.C., 1976-77; patent atty. Allied Chem. Corp., Morristown, N.J., 1977-79; pvt. practice Warren, 1980-83; with Kasper and Weick, 1983-85, Kasper and Laughlin, 1985—. Contbr. numerous articles to profl. jours.; patentee semicondr. field. Mem. ABA, AAAS, N.J. Bar Assn., Internat. Patent and Trademark Assn., Am. Patent Law Assn., N.J. Patent Law Assn., Am. Chem. Soc., Electrochem. Soc., Am. Phys. Soc., N.Y. Acad. Scis. Private international, Patent, Trademark and copyright. Home and Office: 13 Forest Dr Warren NJ 07059-5832 Office: ul Na Grzgdkach 9 30421 Cracow Poland

KASSEBAUM, JOHN PHILIP, lawyer; b. Oct. 24, 1932; s. Leonard Charles and Helen Nancy (Horn) K.: m. Nancy Josephine Landon, June 8, 1955; children: John Philip, Richard L., William A., Linda J. Johnson; m. Llewellyn Hood Sinkler, Aug. 4, 1979; stepchildren: G. Dana, J. Marshall, Huger II, Llewellyn H. Sinkler. AB, U. Kans., 1953; JD, U. Mich., 1956. Bar: Kans. 1956, U.S. Supreme Ct. 1971, U.S. Ct. Appeals (2d, 4th, 10th, D.C. cirs.), U.S. Tax Ct. 1976, N.Y., 1979. Ptnr. Kassebaum & Johnson, N.Y.C. Bd. dirs. Wichita Eagle-Beacon Pub. Co.. pres. Wyoming-Paris, Ltd. Author: Kassebaum Collection Vol I, 1981. Spl. asst. atty. gen., Kansas, 1970; chmn. Gov.'s Adv. Commn. Kansas Instl. Mgmt., 1961-69, bd. dirs., pres. Wichita Art Mus. Members; chmn. Kans. Assn. for Mental Health; trustee Price R. and Flora A. Reid Charitable Trust; chmn., bd. dirs. Skowhegan (Maine) Sch. Painting and Sculpture; bd. dirs., pres. Carolina Art Assn. and Gibbes Art Gallery, Charleston S.C.; pres. Spoleta Festival U.S. A., Chaleston; treas. Am. Arts Alliance, Washington; bd. dirs. Nat. Inst. for Music Theater; mem. endowment art com. Ulrich Mus. Art, Wichita; chmn. adv. com Spencer Mus. Art, U. Kans. Hon. curator of ceramics Spencer Mus. Art. Mem. ABA (sect. dispute resolution), ATLA, Am. Arbitration Assn., Nat. Inst. Dispute Resolution, Conflict Resolution Edn. Network, Assn. of Bar of City of New York, Kans. Trial Lawyers Assn., Kans. Assn. Def. Counsel, Fedn. Ins. Counsel, Union Club, (NYC), Met Club (Washington), Phi Delta Theta, Omicron Delta Kappa, Phi Delta Phi. Republican. Episcopalian. General civil litigation, Mergers and acquisitions, Product liability. Home: 2065 Pettigrew St Sullivans Island SC 29482-8760 Office: 652 Hudson St Fl 5 New York NY 10014-1619 also: Ste 585 River Park Pl 727 N Waco St Wichita KS 67203-3951

KASSNER, HERBERT SEYMORE, lawyer; b. N.Y.C., Dec. 3, 1931; s. Abraham and Rose (Rosenblatt) K.; m. Sheilah Goodwin, 1957 (div. 1965); children: Andrew, Kenneth; m. Marjorie Fern Golding, 1974 (div. 1992); children: Robin, Jeffrey; m. Linda Rubinstein Finder, 1993. BA (hon.), Franklin and Marshall U., 1952; cert., Hague (Netherlands) Acad. of Internat. Law, 1953; MA, NYU, 1955; LLB (hon.), Harvard U., 1955. Bar: N.Y. 1955, Conn. 1986. Atty. Gallap, Climenko & Gould, N.Y.C., 1955, Otterbourg, Steindler, Huston & Rosen, N.Y.C., 1956; pvt. practice law, 1957-65, 1969; atty. Dryer & Traub, 1966-68, Kassner & Detsky, N.Y.C., 1970-80, Kassner & Haigney, N.Y.C., 1981-90. Instr. Ohio State U., Columbus, 1956-57; asst. prof. Ark. State U., Pine Bluff, 1965. Contbr. articles to profl. jours. on 1st amendment law. Mem. Phi Beta Kappa. Antitrust, Constitutional, Real property. Home: 7221 Montrico Dr Boca Raton FL 33433-6931

KATCHER, RICHARD, lawyer; b. N.Y.C., Dec. 17, 1918; s. Samuel and Gussie (Applebaum) K.; m. Shirley Ruth Rifkin, Sept. 24, 1944; children: Douglas P., Robert A., Patti L. BA, U. Mich., 1941, JD, 1943. Bar: Mich. 1943, N.Y. 1944, Ohio 1946. Assoc. Noonan, Kaufman & Eagan, N.Y.C., 1943-46; from assoc. to ptnr. Ulmer, Berne & Laronge, Cleve., 1946-72; ptnr. Baker & Hostetler, 1972-95. Lectr. in fed. income taxation Case Western Res. U. Sch. Law, Cleve., 1953-69, 71-72; mem. bd. in control of intercollegiate athletics, U. Mich., 2001—. Contbr. articles on fed. tax to profl. jours. Recipient Disting. Alumni Service award U. Mich., 1987, Leadership medal Pres.' Soc. of U. Mich., 1991. Fellow ABA (coun. sect. taxation 1973-76), Am. Coll. Tax Counsel (regent); mem. Am. Bar Retirement Assn. (bd. dirs., v.p. 1986-87, pres. 1987-88), U. Mich. Pres. Soc. (chmn. exec. com. 1987-90), U. Mich. Cleve. Club (pres. 1959, Outstanding Alumnus award 1987), U. Mich. Alumni Assn. (dir. 1994-98, sec. 1997-98). Avocation: tennis. Probate, Corporate taxation, Estate taxation. Home: 26150 Village Ln Apt 104 Beachwood OH 44122-7527 Office: Baker & Hostetler 3200 National City Ctr 1900 E 9th St Ste 3200 Cleveland OH 44114-3475 E-mail: RKatcher@baker-hostetler.com

KATHREIN, REED RICHARD, lawyer; b. Cadillac, Mich., Aug. 14, 1954; s. John Anton and Jean Ann (Reeder) K.; m. Margaret Ann McClellan, Aug. 24, 1980; children: Jonathan, Michael, Eric. Student Universidad Nacional Autonomo de Mexico, Mexico City, 1971, 73; BA, U. Miami, 1974, JD, 1977. Bar: Ill. 1977, Fla. 1978, Calif. 1988. Clk. Racal-Milgo Corp., Miami, Fla., 1976-77; assoc. W. Yale Matheson, Chgo., 1977-79; assoc. Arnstein & Lehr, 1979-85, ptnr., 1985-88; prin. Gold & Bennett, San Francisco, 1988-94; ptnr. Milberg Weiss Bershad Hynes & Lerech LLP, 1994-. Author newsletter Internat. Bus. Council Midamerica Update, 1981-88; editor-in-chief Lawyer of the Americas, 1976-77; co-editor Internat. Sales Handbook, 1987. Mem. ABA (sect. internat. law and practice, chmn. pvt. internat. law com. 1984—), Chgo. Bar Assn. (chmn. internat. and fgn. law com. 1983-84), Ill. Bar Assn. (council mem., internat. and immigration law sect.), Internat. Bus. Coun. MidAm. (vice-chmn. policy com. 1982-86 , bd. dirs. 1983-88, sec. 1985-87, v.p. 1987-88), Nat. Assn. Securities and Comml. Law Attys. (exec. com. 1994-), Consumer Atty. Calif. (bd. govs. 1998-), Phi Kappa Phi., Omicron Delta Kappa, Sigma Alpha Epsilon. Republican. Federal civil litigation, State civil litigation, Private international. Home: 1098 Idylberry Rd San Rafael CA 94903-1144 E-mail: reedk@mwbhl.com

KATSH, SALEM MICHAEL, lawyer; b. N.Y.C., May 5, 1948; s. Abraham Isaac and Estelle (Wachtell) K.; m. Jennette Williams, Sept. 4, 1983; children: Halley Rachel, Emmet Walker. BA, NYU, 1970, JD cum laude, 1972. Bar: N.Y. 1973, U.S. Dist. Ct. (so., ea., no. dists. N.Y.) 1975, U.S. Ct. of Appeals (2d cir.) 1975, U.S. Ct. of Appeals (9th cir.) 1977, U.S. Supreme Ct. 1983, U.S. Ct. Appeals (fed. cir.) 1990, U.S. Dist. Ct. (no. dist.) Calif. 1993. Assoc. Weil, Gotshal & Manges, N.Y.C., 1972-80, ptnr., 1980-97, Shearman & Sterling, N.Y.C., 1997—. Adj. prof. New York Law Sch., 1980-84. Author: (monograph) Industrial Policy and the Law, 1982; (with others) The Limits of Corporate Power, 1981; founder Jour. Proprietary Rights; contbr. articles to profl. jours. Mem. ABA (chmn. nat. inst. com., antitrust law sect. 1986-88), N.Y. State Bar Assn., Order of Coif. General civil litigation, Intellectual property, Patent. Office: 599 Lexington Ave New York NY 10022-6030

KATSORIS, CONSTANTINE NICHOLAS, lawyer, consultant; b. Bklyn., Dec. 5, 1932; s. Nicholas C. and Nafsika (Klonis) K.; m. Ann Kanganis, Feb. 19; children: Nancy, Nicholas, Louis. BS in Acctg., Fordham U., 1953; JD cum laude, 1957; LLM, NYU, 1963. Bar: N.Y. 1957, U.S. Dist. Ct. (so. and ea. dist.) N.Y. 1959, U.S. Tax Ct. 1959, U.S. Ct. Appeals (2nd cir.) 1959, U.S. Supreme Ct. 1961. Assoc. Cahill, Gordon, Reindel & Ohl, N.Y.C., 1958-64; asst. prof. Law Sch. Fordham U., 1964-66, assoc. prof., 1966-69; prof., 1969—; apptd. Wilkinson prof. law, 1991. Cons. N.Y. State Temporary Commn. on Estates, 1964-67; arbitration panelist N.Y. Stock Exchange, 1971—, Nat. Assn. Securities Dealers, 1968—, 1st Jud. Dept., 1972—; pub. mem. Securities Industry Conf. on Arbitration, 1977-97, emeritus pub. mem., 1997—; pvt. judge adjudication ctr. Duke U. Law Sch., 1989—. Contbr. articles to profl. jours. Mem. sch.

bd. Greek Orthodox Parochial Sch. St. Spyridon, 1975-89, chmn. sch. bd., 1983-89. With U.S. Army, 1963. Recipient Cert. Appreciation Nat. Assn. Securities Dealers, 1982, Ellis Is. Medal of Honor award, 1999. Mem. ABA (fed. estate and gift tax com. 1966-68), N.Y. State Bar Assn. (sect. on trust and estates 1969—), Assn. Bar City of N.Y. (trusts, estates and surrogates' cts. com. 1968-70, legal assistance com. 1965-67), Fordham U. Law Alumni Assn. (bd. dirs. 1972—), Fordham U. Law Ref. Alumni Assn. (pres. 1968-64). Republican. Greek Orthodox. Office: 140 W 62nd St New York NY 10023-7407

KATSOS, BARBARA HELENE, lawyer; b. N.Y.C. MA, NYU; JD, U. of City of N.Y.; PhD, NYU. Bar: N.Y., U.S. Dist. Ct. (so. dist.) N.Y., U.S. Dist. Ct. (ea. dist.) N.Y. Pvt. practice, N.Y.C. Contracts commercial, General practice, Private international. Office: Ste 3200 777 3d Ave New York NY 10017

KATSURINIS, STEPHEN AVERY, lawyer; b. Houston, Aug. 4, 1966; s. Ted and JoAnn Katsurinis. BA, Southwestern U., 1988; JD, Franklin Pierce Law Ctr., 1991. Bar: Va. 1992, D.C. 1999, U.S. Ct. Appeals (4th cir.) 1992, U.S. Dist. Ct. (ea. dist.) Va. 1995. Legis. counsel to Rep. Dana Rohrabacher, Washington, 1991-94; policy analyst Dept. of Planning and Budget, Richmond, Va., 1994-95; of counsel Magenheim, Bateman, Houston, 1995-97; staff atty. McGuireWoods LLP, Washington, 1997—. Alt. del. Rep. Nat. Conv., San Diego, 1996; election judge State of Tex., Georgetown, 1986; mem. Alexandria City Rep. com.; Alexandria City chair Bush for Pres., 2000, Earley for Gov., 2001; vice chair Alexandria Electoral Bd., 2001—. Recipient Am. Citizenship award DAR, 1980. Mem. Am. Hellenic Progressive Assn. (chpt. sec. 1990-91), Federalist Soc. for Law and Pub. Policy, Charles Fahy Am. Inn of Cts. (barrister). Republican. Greek Orthodox. Civil rights, Legislative. Office: McGuireWoods LLP # 1200 1050 Connecticut Ave NW Washington DC 20036-5317

KATZ, HADRIAN RONALD, lawyer; b. Cambridge, Mass., Aug. 12, 1949; s. Samuel and Alice (Greenstein) K.; m. Candace Kay Kaufman, Apr. 1, 1977; children: Gwendlyn Rebecca, Jonathan Harold. AB, Harvard U., 1969, JD, 1976; MA, U. Calif., Berkeley, 1973. Bar: D.C. 1977, Mass. 1977, U.S. Dist. Ct. D.C. 1977, U.S. Ct. Appeals (D.C. cir.) 1979, U.S. Supreme Ct. 1983, U.S. Ct. Appeals (6th cir.) 1985, U.S. Ct. Appeals (4th cir.) 1989. Ptnr. Arnold & Porter, Washington, 1976—. Mem. ABA, IEEE, Am. Phys. Soc., Assn. for Computing Machinery, Math. Assn. Am. Democrat. Avocation: computer. Administrative and regulatory, Federal civil litigation, Computer. Home: 1324 Lancia Dr Mc Lean VA 22102-2204 Office: Arnold & Porter 555 12th St NW Washington DC 20004-1206

KATZ, JASON LAWRENCE, lawyer, insurance executive; b. Chgo., Sept. 28, 1947; s. Irving and Goldie (Medress) K.; 2 children. B.A., Northeastern Ill. U., 1969; J.D., DePaul U., 1973. Bar: Calif. 1976, Ariz. 1973, U.S. Ct. Appeals (9th cir.) 1976. Sole practice, Scottsdale, Ariz., 1973-76; v.p., corp. counsel Mission Ins. Group, Inc., Los Angeles, 1976-84; sr. v.p., gen. counsel Farmers Group, Inc., Los Angeles, 1984—, bd. dirs., 1986—; v.p., bd. dirs. Calif. Def. Counsel, 1986-88. Mem. Calif. Bar Assn. (exec. bd. ins. law subcom. 1991-94), Los Angeles County Bar Assn. (mem. exec. bd. corp. law sect. 1993—), Conf. Ins. Counsel (v.p., pres. L.A. chpt. 1981-82), Assn. Calif. Tort Reform (bd. dirs. 1990—), The Ins. Coun. So. Calif. (City of Hope chpt. 1991—). Administrative and regulatory, General corporate, Insurance. Office: Farmers Group Inc 4680 Wilshire Blvd Los Angeles CA 90010-3807

KATZ, JERI BETH, lawyer; b. Washington, Nov. 6, 1964; d. Stanley J. and Paula (Goldberg) K.; m. Daniel Alan Ezra, June 19, 1988 (div. Dec. 1990). BA, U. Md., 1987; JD, Cath. U., Washington, 1990. Bar: Md. 1990, D.C. 1991, U.S. Ct. Appeals (6th cir.) 1991, U.S. Ct. Internat. Trade 1992, Colo. 1994. Assoc. Winston & Strawn, Washington, 1990; ptnr. Law Offices Royal Daniel, 1990-94, Daniel & Katz, L.L.C., Breckenridge, Colo., 1994-98; pvt. practice, 1998—. Mem. jud. performance commn. 5th Jud. Dist., 1998—. Bd. dirs. Snowmass Ski Acad., 1995-98, Breckenridge Resort Chamber, 1998—; mem. Breckenridge Town Coun., 1998-99; chairperson Summit County Transfer of Devel. Rights Commn., 1998—; mem. Breckenridge Planning Commn., 1999—. Mem. Continental Divide Bar Assn. (v.p. 1997-98), Colo. Criminal Def. Bar (rap sheet com. 1998). Administrative and regulatory, State civil litigation, Criminal. Home: PO Box 6602 Breckenridge CO 80424-5200 Office: PO Box 5200 130 Ski Hill Rd Ste 230 Breckenridge CO 80424-6602 E-mail: jbkatz@earthlink.net

KATZ, JEROME CHARLES, lawyer; b. Boston, Sept. 25, 1950; s. Ralph and Thelma M. (Clark) K.; m. Nancy M. Green, Aug. 29, 1976; children: Jonathan Green, Elizabeth Rachel. AB magna cum laude, Duke U., 1972; JD, Columbia U., 1975. Bar: N.Y. 1976, U.S. Dist. Ct. (so. and ea. dists.) N.Y. 1976, U.S. Supreme Ct. 1979, U.S. Ct. Appeals (2d cir.) 1981, U.S. Dist. Ct. (we. dist.) N.Y. 1990. Assoc. Chadbourne & Parke, N.Y.C., 1975-83, ptnr., 1983—. Ct.-apptd. neutral mediator U.S. Dist. Ct. (so. dist.) N.Y., 2001—. Assoc. editor Columbia Jour. Transnat. Law, 1974-75. Harlan Fiske Stone scholar Columbia U., 1974. Mem. ABA, Assn. of the Bar of the City of N.Y., Phi Beta Kappa. Federal civil litigation, General civil litigation, State civil litigation. Home: 77 E 12th St New York NY 10003-5002 Office: Chadbourne & Parke 30 Rockefeller Plz Fl 31 New York NY 10112-0129 E-mail: jkatz@chadbourne.com

KATZ, JOETTE, state supreme court justice; b. Bklyn., Feb. 3, 1953; BA, Brandeis U., 1974; JD, U. Conn., 1977. Bar: Conn. 1977. Pvt. practice, 1977-78; asst. pub. defender Office Chief Pub. Defender, 1978-83; chief legal svcs. Pub. Defender Svcs., 1983-89; judge Superior Ct., 1989-92; assoc. justice Conn. Supreme Ct., Hartford, 1992—; adminstrv. judge Appellate Sys., 1994-2000. Instr. U. Conn. Sch. Law, 1981-84; tchr. ethics and criminal law Quinnipiac Coll. Sch. Law. Mem. Am. Law Inst. (chairperson evidence code drafting com., chairperson adv. com. for appellate rules), Am. Inns Ct. (past pres. Fairfield County br.), Assn. Reproductive Tech. (mem. com.). Office: Conn Supreme Ct Drawer N Sta A 231 Capital Ave Hartford CT 06106-1548

KATZ, JOHN W. lawyer, state official; b. Balt., June 3, 1943; s. Leonard Wallach and Jean W. (Kane) K.; m. Joan Katz, June 11, 1969 (div. 1982); 1 child, Kimberly Erin. BA, Johns Hopkins U., 1965; JD, U. Calif., Berkeley, 1969; DDL (hon.) U. Alaska, 1994. Bar: Alaska, Pa., U.S. Dist. Ct. D.C. 1971, U.S. Ct. Appeals (D.C. cir.), U.S. Tax Ct., U.S. Ct. Claims, U.S. Ct. Mil. Justice, U.S. Supreme Ct. Legis. and adminstrv. asst. to Congressman Howard W. Pollock of Alaska, Washington, 1969-70; legis. asst. to U.S. Senator Ted Stevens of Alaska, Washington, 1971; assoc. McGrath and Flint, Anchorage, 1972; gen. counsel Joint Fed. State Land Use Planning Commn. for Alaska, Anchorage, 1972-79; spl. counsel to Gov. Jay S. Hammond of Alaska, Anchorage and Washington, 1979-81; commr. Alaska Dept. Natural Resources, Juneau, 1981-83; dir. state fed. relations and spl. counsel to Gov. Bill Sheffield of Alaska, Washington and Juneau, 1983-86; dir. state-fed. relations, spl. counsel to Gov. Steve Cowper of Alaska, Washington, 1986-90, Gov. Walter J. Hickel of Alaska, Washington, 1990-94, Gov. Tony Knowles, 1994—; mem. Alaska Power Survey Exec. Adv. Com. of FPC, Anchorage, 1972-74; mem. spl. com. hard rock minerals Govs. Council of Sci. and Tech., Anchorage, 1979-80; guest lectr. on natural resources U. Alaska, U. Denver. Contbr. articles to profl. jours.; columnist Anchorage Times until 1991. Acad. supr. Alaska Externship Program, U. Denver Coll. Law, 1976-79; mem. Reagan-Bush transition team for U.S. Dept. Justice, 1980. Recipient Superior Sustained Performance award Joint Fed. State Land Use Planning Commn. for Alaska, 1978, Resolution of Commendation award Alaska Legis., 1988. Republican. Office: State of Alaska Office of Gov 444 N Capitol St NW Ste 336 Washington DC 20001-1529

KATZ, KENNETH ARTHUR, lawyer, accountant; b. N.Y.C., Apr. 4, 1955; s. Bernard and Shirley Anne (Schachter) K.; m. Gillian Lynn Bagg, Nov. 29, 1986; children: Melissa Lee, Ashley Dawn. AB in Econs. cum laude, Harvard U., 1976; JD, Yeshiva U., 1980; MBA in Pub. Acctg., Pace U., 1987. Bar: N.Y. 1994, U.S. Tax Ct. 1994, D.C. 1995; CPA, N.Y. Legal asst. Law Offices of Jerome A. Wisselman, Manhasset, N.Y., 1980-81, Law Offices of S. Mac Gutman, Forest Hills, 1981-82; asst. contr. Tauck Tours, Inc., Westport, Conn., 1982-84; pvt. practice acct. Eastchester, N.Y., 1984-87; tax specialist KPMG Peat Marwick, White Plains, 1987-88; atty., acct., ptnr. Bernard Katz & Co, P.C., Eastchester, 1988—. Mem. ABA (taxation and internat. law sects.), N.Y. State Bar Assn. (tax sect.), D.C. Bar Assn. (taxation and sect. on corps., fin. and securities law), Westchester County Bar Assn. (tax and trusts and estates coms.), N.Y. State Soc. CPAs, Nat. Tax Assn.-Tax Inst. Am. (com. on internat. pub. fin.), Harvard-Radcliffe Club of Westchester. Avocations: sports, music, personal investing. Corporate taxation, Estate taxation, Personal income taxation. Office: Bernard Katz & Co PC 1 Mayfair Rd Eastchester NY 10709-2701 E-mail: bkatzcopc@aol.com

KATZ, LAURENCE M. legal educator; b. 1940. J.D., U. Md., 1963. Bar: Md. 1963, Fla. 1963. Law clk. presiding justice U.S. Ct. Appeals (4th cir.), 1963-64; assoc. Frank, Bernstein, Conaway and Goldman, Balt., 1964-66; asst. prof. U. Md., 1966-69, assoc. prof., 1969-72, prof., assoc. dean, 1972-78; prof., dean U. Balt., 1978-93, prof., 1993—. Case note editor Md. Law Rev. Mem. Order of Coif. Office: U Balt Sch Law 1420 N Charles St Baltimore MD 21201-5720

KATZ, MARK DAVID, lawyer; b. N.Y.C., Apr. 26, 1949; s. Irving and Belle (Bilinkoff) K.; m. Deborah Jane Exler, Aug. 25, 1974; children: Megan Diane, Craig Edward. BA, SUNY, Buffalo, 1971; JD, Case Western Res. U., 1974. Bar: Ohio, 1974, U.S. Dist. Ct. (no. dist.) Ohio, 1975, U.S. Supreme Ct. 1980, U.S. Ct. Appeals (3d, 6th, 7th and D.C. cirs.). Assoc. Consiglio & Katz, Cleve., 1974-75; trial atty. Dept. Labor, 1975-85; asst. group counsel LTV Steel Co., Inc., 1985-97; assoc. Ulmer & Berne, LLP, 1997—. Mem. ABA, Ohio Bar Assn. Labor. Home: 5043 Boulder Creek Dr Cleveland OH 44139-1379 Office: Ulmer & Berne LLP 1300 E 9th St Cleveland OH 44115 E-mail: mkatz@ulmer.com

KATZ, MARTHA LESSMAN, lawyer; b. Chgo., Oct. 28, 1952; d. Julius Abraham and Ida (Oiring) Lessman; m. Richard M. Katz, June 27, 1976; children: Julia Erin, Meredith Evin. AB, Washington U., St. Louis, 1974; JD, Loyola U., Chgo., 1977. Bar: Ill. 1977, U.S. Dist. Ct. (no. dist.) Ill. 1977, Calif. 1981, U.S. Dist. Ct. (so. dist.) Calif. 1981, U.S. Dist. Ct. (no. dist.) Calif. 1982, Md. 1993, U.S. Supreme Ct. 1993, D.C. 1994. Assoc. Fein & Hanfling, Chgo., 1977-80, Rudick, Platt & Victor, San Diego, 1981-82, 84-91; asst. sec., counsel Itel Corp., San Francisco, 1982-84; ptnr. Katz & Mann, Attys. at Law, 1991-95; with legal dept. U.S. Fidelity and Guaranty Co., 1995-99; mem. intellectual property and tech. practice group Miles & Stockbridge PC, Balt., 1999—. Mem. Greater Balt. com. Tech. Coun. and Bus. Growth and Entrepreneurs Com.; mem. High Tech. Coun. and Ops. Com. Md. Mem. Calif. State Bar Assn., Md. Bar Assn. (spl. tech. com.), Ill. State Bar Assn., Bar Assn. Balt. City, Bar Assn. D.C., Phi Beta Kappa. Jewish. Contracts commercial, Computer, General corporate. Office: 10 Light St Baltimore MD 21202-1435 also: 9881 Brokenland Pkwy Columbia MD 21046-1172 Fax: 410-385-3700. E-mail: mkatz@milesstockbridge.com

KATZ, MICHAEL ALBERT, lawyer; b. Bklyn., May 8, 1942; s. Emanuel and Miriam (Fassler) K.; 1 child, Nathaniel P. BS, Bklyn. Coll., 1963; LLB, NYU, 1966; LLM, George Washington U., 1973. Bar: N.Y. 1966, D.C. 1970, Ill. 1976, N.J. 1995, U.S. Supreme Ct. 1975. Asst. U.S. atty., D.C., 1971-75; trial atty. United Airlines, Chgo., 1975-78; div. counsel ea. divsn. N.Y.C., 1978-81; counsel indsl. rels. Trans World Airlines, Inc., 1981-86, asst. gen. counsel, 1986-91, assoc. gen., counsel, 1991-94; assoc. gen. counsel GAF/ISP Corp., Wayne, N.J., 1994-96; of counsel Pfaltz & Woller PA, Summit, 1996—. Capt. JAGC, U.S. Army, 1967-71, ret. col. res. Decorated Bronze Star. Federal civil litigation, Labor, Military. Home: 94 Canterbury Rd Chatham NJ 07928-1771 Office: GAF/ISP Corp 382 Springfield Ave Ste 217 Summit NJ 07901-2707 E-mail: makatz@worldnet.att.net

KATZ, MICHAEL JEFFERY, lawyer; b. Detroit, May 11, 1950; s. Wilfred Lester and Bernice (Ackerman) K. BE with honors, U. Mich., 1972; JD, U. Colo., 1976; cert. mgmt., U. Denver, 1985, cert. fin. mgmt., 1990. Bar: Colo. 1978. Rsch. atty., immigration specialist Colo. Rural Legal Svcs., Denver, 1976-77, supervising atty. migrant farm lab., 1977-78; ind. contractor Colo. Sch. Fin., 1978-79; sole practice, 1978-86; assoc. Levine and Pitler, P.C., 1986-88; gen. counsel, sec. Grease Monkey Internat., Inc., 1988-92; prin. Katz & Co., 1992—; ptnr. Corprorn, Eyler & Katz LLC, 1999—. Lectr. on incorporating small bus. and real estate purchase agreements Front Range Coll., 1986—, condr. various seminars on real estate and landlord/tenant law, 1980—; of counsel Levine and Pitler, P.C., Englewood, Colo., 1985—. Contbr. Action Line column Rocky Mountain News; contbr. articles to profl. jours. Mem. ATLA, Am. Arbitration Assn. (mem. panel of arbitrators 1989), Denver Bar Assn. (mem. law day com. 1985—, mem. real estate com. 1980—, mem. pro bono svcs. com. 1984—), Colo. Assn. Bus. Intermediaries, U.S. Yacht Racing Assn., Dillon Yacht Club. Avocations: sailing, bicycling, swimming, art collecting, reading. Contracts commercial, General corporate, Real property. Office: 13710 E Rice Pl Aurora CO 80015-1058 Fax: 303-790-0927. E-mail: bizlaw@ix.netcom.com

KATZ, RONALD SCOTT, lawyer; b. Norwich, Conn., Dec. 14, 1946; s. Irving David and Joan (Lebovitz) K.; m. Ann Lisa Mark, Dec. 27, 1969; children: Benjamin, Cynthia. BA, Johns Hopkins U., 1968; JD, Columbia U., 1972. Bar: N.Y. 1972, U.S. Ct. Appeals (2d cir.) 1974, U.S. Ct. Appeals (4th cir.) 1993. Assoc. Golenbock & Barell, N.Y.C., 1972-80, ptnr., 1981-89, Whitman & Ransom, N.Y.C., 1990-93; shareholder, dir. Shack Siegel Katz Flaherty & Goodman PC, 1993—. Mem. ABA, N.Y. State Bar Assn. General corporate, Mergers and acquisitions, Securities. Home: 16 Paxford Ln Scarsdale NY 10583-3318 Office: Shack Siegel Katz Flaherty & Goodman PC PC 530 5th Ave New York NY 10036-5101 E-mail: rkatz@sskfg.com

KATZ, STEVEN MARTIN, lawyer, accountant; b. Washington, Feb. 8, 1941; s. Joseph and Pauline (Weinberg) K.; m. Lauri Gail Berman, Aug. 23, 1964; children: Benjamin, Aaron, Rebecca, Joshua. BS, U. Md., College Park, 1962; JD, George Washington U., 1965. Bar: D.C. 1966, Md. 1971; CPA, Md. Ptnr. Euzent, Katz & Katz, Washington, 1969-72; sr. ptnr. Katz, Frome & Bleecker, P.A., and predecessors, Rockville, Md., 1972-95; pvt. practice, 1995—. Mem. Md. State Grievance Commn., 1991—. Mem. Am. Soc. Atty.-CPAs, Md. Bar Assn., Md. Assn. CPAs, D.C. Bar, Montgomery County Bar Assn., Md. Soc. Accts., Md. State Bar Found. Jewish. General corporate, Estate planning, Probate. Office: 401 E Jefferson St Ste 208 Rockville MD 20850-2613 Fax: 301-294-9484. E-mail: smkatz@intr.net

KATZ, STUART CHARLES, lawyer, jazz musician; b. Chgo., June 9, 1937; s. Jerome H. and Sylvia L. (Singer) K.; m. Penny Schatz, Jan. 23, 1959; children: Steven, Lauren. BA, Roosevelt U., Chgo., 1959; JD with distinction, John Marshall Law Sch., 1964. Bar: Ill. 1964, U.S. Dist. Ct. (no. dist.) Ill. 1965, U.S. Supreme Ct. 1967. Exec. v.p. Heitman Fin. LLC, Chgo., 1972—. Mem. program com. Internat. Coun. Shopping Ctrs., U.S. Law Conf.; jazz pianist and vibraphonist, appeared in concerts with Benny Goodman, Gene Krupa, Bud Freeman. Mem. ABA, Ill. Bar Assn., Chgo. Bar Assn., Mortgage Bankers Am., Chgo. Assn. Realtors, Minn. Real Estate Bd. Jewish. Contracts commercial, Real property. Office: 180 N La Salle St Ste 3600 Chicago IL 60601-2805

KATZ, THOMAS OWEN, lawyer; b. Killeen, Tex., Jan. 15, 1958; s. Herbert D. and Eleanor (Meyerhoff) K.; m. Elissa Ellant, Nov. 6, 1983; children: Joseph, Peyton, Jacob. BS in Econs., U. Pa., 1979; JD, Georgetown U., 1982. Bar: Fla. 1982, U.S. Tax Ct. 1983. Shareholder, chair income tax dept. Ruden, McClosky, Smith, Schuster & Russell, P.A., Ft. Lauderdale, Fla., 1982—. Bd. dirs. Ctr. for Jewish Learning and Leadership, N.Y., 1993—, assoc. chmn., 1997—, Donors Forum S.Fla., 1998—, treas. 2000—, Cmty. Found. of Broward, 2000—; mem. bd. overseers Ctr. Advanced Judaic Studies U. Pa., 2001—. Estate planning, Probate, Taxation, general. Office: Ruden McClosky Smith Sch PO Box 1900 Fort Lauderdale FL 33302-1900 E-mail: tok@ruden.com

KATZEN, SALLY, lawyer, government official; b. Pitts., Nov. 22, 1942; d. Nathan and Hilda (Schwartz) K.; m. Timothy B. Dyk, Oct. 31, 1981; 1 child, Abraham Benjamin BA magna cum laude, Smith Coll., 1964; JD magna cum laude, U. Mich., 1967. Bar: D.C. 1968, U.S. Supreme Ct. 1971. Congl. intern Sente Subcom. on Constl. Rights, Washington, 1963; legal rsch. asst. civil rights div. Dept. Justice, 1965; law clk. to Judge J. Skelly Wright U.S. Ct. Appeals (D.C. cir.), 1967-68; assoc. Wilmer, Cutler & Pickering, Washington, 1968-75, ptnr., 1975-79, 81-93; gen. counsel Coun. on Wage and Price Stability, 1979-80; dep. dir. for policy, 1980-81; adminstr. Office of Info. and Regulatory Affairs, Office of Mgmt. and Budget, Washington, 1993-98; dep. dir. Nat. Econ. Coun., The White House, 1998-99; counsellor to the dir. Office Mgmt. and Budget, 1999-2000, dep. dir. mgmt., 2000-2001. Pub. mem. Adminstrv. Conf. U.S., 1988-93, govt. mem. and vice chair, 1993-95; mem. exec. com. Prettyman-Leventhal Inn of Ct., 1988-90, counselor, 1990-91; mem. Jud. Conf. for D.C. Cir., 1972-91; adj. prof. Georgetown U. Law Ctr., 1988, 90-92. Editor-in-chief U. Mich. Law Rev., 1966-67 Mem. com. visitors U. Mich. Law Sch., 1972—. Fellow ABA (ho. of dels. 1978-80, 89-91, coun. adminstrv. law sect. 1979-82, chmn. adminstrv. law and regulatory practice sect. 1988-89, governing com. forum com. communications law 1979-82, chmn. standing com. Nat. Conf. Groups 1989-92); mem. D.C. Bar Assn., Women's Bar Assn., FCC Bar Assn. (exec. com. 1984-87, pres. 1990-91), Women's Legal Def. Fund (pres. 1977, v.p. 1978), Order of Coif. Home: 4638 30th St NW Washington DC 20008-2127

KATZENBACH, NICHOLAS DEBELLEVILLE, lawyer; b. Phila., Jan. 17, 1922; s. Edward Lawrence and Marie Louise (Hilson) K.; m. Lydia King Phelps Stokes, June 8, 1946; children— Christopher Wolcott, John Strong Minor, Maria Louise Hilton, Anne deBelleville. B.A., Princeton U., 1945; LL.B., Yale U., 1947; Rhodes scholar, Balliol Coll., Oxford (Eng.) U., 1947-49. Bar: N.J. 1950, Conn. 1955, N.Y. 1972. With firm Katzenbach, Gildea & Rudner, Trenton, N.J., 1950; atty.-adviser Office Gen. Counsel Air Force, 1950-52, part-time cons., 1952-56; asso. prof. law Yale Law Sch., 1952-56; prof. law U. Chgo. Law Sch., 1956-60; asst. atty. gen. Dept. Justice, 1961-62; dep. atty. gen., 1962-64; acting atty. gen., 1964; atty. gen., 1965-66; under sec. state, 1966-69; sr. v.p., gen. counsel IBM Corp., 1969-84, sr. v.p. law and external relations, 1984-86, also bd. dirs.; ptnr. Riker, Danzig, Scherer, Hyland & Perretti, Morristown, N.J., 1986-91. Author: (with Morton A. Kaplan) The Political Foundations of International Law, 1961; editor-in-chief: Yale Law Jour, 1947; contbr. articles to profl. jours. Served to 1st lt. USAAF, 1941-45. Decorated Air medal with three clusters; Ford Found. fellow, 1960-61 Mem. AAAS, Am. Law Inst. (mem. coun.), Am. Bar Assn., Am. Judicature Soc., Am. Philos. Soc. Democrat. Episcopalian. General corporate. Home: 33 Greenhouse Dr Princeton NJ 08540-4802 E-mail: nkatzenbac@aol.com

KATZMAN, HARVEY LAWRENCE, lawyer, educator; b. Youngstown, Ohio, Sept. 2, 1948; s. Abraham and Elsie Katzman; m. Elizabeth Viola Ball, Dec. 27, 1980. BA, Ohio No. U., 1971; JD, Glendale U., 1976. Bar: Calif. 1978, U.S. Dist. Ct. (cen. dist.) 1978, U.S. Ct. Appeals (9th cir.) 1979. Pvt. practice, L.A., 1978-97; prof. law Glendale (Calif.) U., 1979—; lawyer La Casella & Katzman, Pasadena, Calif., 1997—. Cons. to newly admitted attys., so. Calif., 1990—; legal advisor Calif. Inst. Baseball Acad., Riverside, 1995—. Mem. L.A. County Bar Assn. (family law com. 1997-99), Delta Theta Phi. Avocations: gardening, baseball, traveling, writing. Bankruptcy, General corporate, Probate. Office: La Casella & Katzman LLP 234 E Colorado Blvd Ste 800 Pasadena CA 91101-2208

KATZMAN, IRWIN, lawyer; b. Windsor, Ont., Can., June 29, 1931; s. Aaron and Rose (Tarnow) K.; m. Helen Frances Blecher, Dec. 20, 1952 (dec. Feb. 1998); children: Barry, Harriet, Kenneth, Rhonda, Aaron; m. Toby Lyman, Aug. 15, 1999. BS, Wayne State U., 1953, MBA, 1963; JD cum laude, Loyola U., L.A., 1974. Bar: Calif. 1974, U.S. Dist. Ct. (cen. dist.) Calif. 1974, U.S. Ct. Appeals (9th cir.) 1980, U.S. Supreme Ct. 1980, U.S. Tax Ct. 1988. Chemist E.I. Dupont de Nemours, Phila., 1953-54; asst. quality mgr. Chrysler Corp., Detroit, 1956-63; mfg. plans mgr. Ford Motor Co., Newport Beach, Calif., 1963-70; prodn. control mgr. Dresser Industries, Huntington Park, 1970-73; purchasing mgr. Hughes Aircraft Co., Inglewood, 1973-74; v.p. First Alliance Mortgage Co., Santa Ana, 1976-77; pvt. practice Anaheim, 1975-94, San Jose, 1995—. Pres. Temple Beth Emet, Anaheim, 1988-90. With U.S. Army, 1953-56. Mem. State Bar of Calif., Orange County Bar Assn., Santa Clara County Bar Assn., Alpha Epsilon Pi (life). Avocations: sailing, golf, amateur radio. Bankruptcy, Family and matrimonial, Personal injury. Office: 8346 Riesling Way San Jose CA 95135-1435

KATZMANN, GARY STEPHEN, lawyer; b. N.Y.C., Apr. 22, 1953; s. John and Sylvia Katzmann. AB summa cum laude, Columbia U., 1973; MLitt, Oxford U., 1976; MPPM, JD, Yale U., 1979. Bar: Mass. 1982, U.S. Dist. Ct. Mass. 1983, U.S. Ct. Appeals (1st cir.) 1983, D.C.. 1984, U.S. Ct. Appeals (2d cir.) 1987, N.Y. 1990, U.S. Ct. Appeals (fed. cir.) 1991. Law clk. to judge U.S. Dist. Ct. (so. dist.) N.Y., N.Y.C., 1979-80; law clk. to Hon. Stephen Breyer U.S. Ct. Appeals (1st cir.), Boston, 1980-81; rsch. assoc. ctr. criminal justice Law Sch. Harvard U., Cambridge, Mass., 1981-83; asst. U.S. atty., chief appellate atty., dep. chief criminal div., chief legal counsel U.S. Atty.'s Office, 1983—; assoc. dep. atty. gen. U.S. Dept. Justice, Washington, 1993-94. Lectr. Harvard U. Law Sch., 1989—; rsch. fellow J.F. Kennedy Sch. Govt., Harvard U., 1997—; participant Yale Law Sch. Sentencing Seminar, 1999—. Author: Inside the Criminal Process, 1991; editor Yale U. Law Jour. Recipient Dir's. Superior Performance award U.S. Dept. Justice, 1993. Mem. ABA, Phi Beta Kappa. Office: US Attys Offci US Courthouse 1 Courthouse Way Ste 9200 Boston MA 02210-3011

KATZMANN, ROBERT ALLEN, federal judge; b. N.Y.C., 1953; AB summa cum laude, Columbia U., 1973; MA in Govt., Harvard U., 1975, PhD in Govt., 1978; JD, Yale U., 1980. Bar: Mass. 1982, U.S. Ct. Appeals (1st cir.) 1983, D.C. 1984, U.S. Dist. Ct. Mass. 1984. Law clk. to judge U.S. Ct. Appeals (1st cir.), Concord, N.H., 1980-81; rsch. assoc. Brookings Instn., Washington, 1981-85, fellow, 1985-99; adj. prof. law, pub. policy Georgetown U., 1984-92, William J. Walsh prof. govt., prof. law, 1992-99; pres. Governance Inst., Washington, 1986-99; acting dir.

govt. studies Brookings Instn., 1998; judge U.S. Ct. Appeals (2nd cir.), 1999—. Vis. prof. polit. sci. UCLA, Washington program, 1990-92; vis. chair, Wayne Morse prof. law and politics U. Oreg., 1992; cons. Fed. Cts. Study Com., 1990. Author: Regulatory Bureaucracy: The Federal Trade Commission and Antitrust Policy, 1980, Institutional Disability, 1986, Courts and Congress, 1997; co-editor: Managing Appeals in Federal Courts, 1988; editor: Judges and Legislators, 1988, The Law Firm and the Public Good, 1995; article and book editor Yale U. Law Jour., 1979-80. Mem. ABA (adminstrv. law sect. vice chair com. on govt. ops. and separation of powers 1991-94, pub. mem. adminstrn. conf., 1992-95), Am. Judicature Soc. (bd. dirs. 1992-98), Am. Polit. Sci. Assn., Assn. Pub. Policy Analysis and Mgmt., Phi Beta Kappa. Office: US Ct Appeals 2d Cir 40 Foley Sq New York NY 10007-1502

KAUCHER, JAMES WILLIAM, lawyer; b. Belleville, Ill., Oct. 20, 1958; s. Robert Frederick and Mary Ellen (Shepard) K.; m. Janine Kaucher, Oct. 24, 1993. BA, U. Colo., 1980; JD, U. Ill., 1983. Bar: Ariz. 1983, U.S. Dist. Ct. Ariz. 1983. Assoc. Evans, Kitchel & Jenckes, Phoenix, 1983-85, Teilborg, Sanders & Parks, Phoenix, 1985-92; ptnr. Cavett and Kaucher, Tucson, 1992-98; dir. Goodwin Raup PC, 1998—. Chmn. human rsch. rev. bd. Humana Hosp., Phoenix, 1989-94. Mem. bioethics com. Northwest Hosp., Tucson, 1993—. Mem. Am. Assn. Health Lawyers, Maricopa Bar Assn., Def. Rsch. Inst., Forum on Health Law, Ariz. Soc. Health Care Risk Mgrs. (bd. dirs. 1989-91), Ariz. Assn. Def. Counsel, Ariz. Mountaineering Club, Am. Alpine Club. Avocations: mountaineering, flying, bicycle racing. Health, Labor, Personal injury. Office: Goodwin Raup PC Ste 2130 One S Church Ave Tucson AZ 85701 E-mail: jamesw@kaucher.com

KAUFFMAN, ALAN CHARLES, lawyer; b. Atlantic City, Aug. 12, 1939; s. Joseph Bernard and Lilyan (Abraham) K.; children: Julie Beth, Debra Amy, Paige Tyler. AB, Rutgers U., 1961; JD, Villanova U., 1964. Bar: Pa. 1964, U.S. Ct. Appeals (3d cir.) 1965, U.S. Dist. Ct. (ea. dist.) Pa. 1965, U.S. Supreme Ct. 1968, Fla. 1985, U.S. Dist. Ct. (so. dist.) Fla. 1985. Pres. Alan C. Kauffman & Assocs., P.A., Boca Raton, Fla. Mem., bd. dirs. Am. Diabetic Assn., Fla. Philharmonic Orch., Caldwell Theater; vice chmn. Fla. Victory Com.; founding chmn. Gold Coast Forum; bd. mem. Fla. Elections Commn. Cmty. Rels. bd. City of Boca Raton; mem. Greater Boca Raton Senate, Palm Beach County Film & TV Bd.; mem. Jewish Adv. Coun. U.S. Senator Connie Mack; Mem. Internat Bd. Weizmann Inst., Rep. Senatorial Inner Circle. Mem. ABA, ATLA, Pa. Bar Assn. (former mem. bd. govs., former trustee), Palm Beach County Bar Assn., Acad. Fla. Trial Lawyers, Phila. Trial Lawyers Assn., Phila. Bar Assn., Fla. Bar Assn., Palm Beach County Film Bd., Boca Roundtable. Antitrust, Federal civil litigation, State civil litigation. Office: Ste 1102 5355 Town Center Rd Boca Raton FL 33486-1023

KAUFFMAN, KREG ARLEN, lawyer; b. Des Moines, May 24, 1950; s. Arlo B. and Helen M. (Crouse) K.; m. Georgia Ann Millhollin, Aug. 11, 1973; children: Katherine Elizabeth, Alex Kreg. BA, U. Iowa, 1972, JD, 1977. Bar: Minn. 1977, U.S. Dist. Ct. Minn., 1978, Iowa 1982, U.S. Dist. Ct. (no. and so. dists.) Iowa 1986, Wis. 1992. Law clk. to presiding justice Minn. 3d Jud. Dist. Ct., Faribault, Minn., 1977-78; assoc. Dunlap, Keith, Finseth, Berndt & Sandberg, Rochester, Minn., 1978-82; asst. atty. gen. State of Iowa, Des Moines, 1982-85; atty. Dingle, Wendland & Kauffman, Ltd., Rochester, 1985-93; prin. Kauffman Law Firm, Rochester, 1993—; legal adviser Delta Chi, Iowa City, 1978-90; civil trial advocate Nat. Bd. Trial Advocates. Bd. dirs. Mayor's Adv. Com. on Alcohol and Drug Abuse, Rochester, 1978-90; active Rochester Brain Injury Cmty. Com., Brain Injury Assn. Minn. Mem. ABA, Minn. Trial Lawyers Assn. (bd. govs., mem. exec. com.), Minn. State Bar Assn. (cert. civil trial specialist), Acad. Cert. Trial Lawyers (treas., sec., past dean), Olmsted County Bar Assn. Home: 734 11th St SW Rochester MN 55902-6339

KAUFFMAN, THOMAS ANDREW, lawyer; b. Indiana, Pa., Apr. 27, 1966; s. Chester T. and Carol Dickerson Kauffman. BA, Pa. State U., 1989; JD, Widener U., 1992. Clk. Commonwealth Ct. of Pa., Harrisburg, 1991-92, Ct. of Common Pleas, Indiana, 1992-93; ptnr. Tomb, Mack & Kauffman, 1993—. Active vol. Big Bros./Big Sisters, Indiana, 1994—; vol., pres. Comty. Living and Learning, Indiana, 1995—. State civil litigation, Criminal, Personal injury. Office: Tomb Mack & Kauffman 52 S 9th St Indiana PA 15701-2664

KAUFMAN, ALBERT I. lawyer; b. N.Y.C., Oct. 2, 1936; s. Israel and Pauline (Pardes) K.; m. Ruth Feldman, Jan. 25, 1959; 1 son, Michael Paul. AA, L.A. City Coll., 1957; BA, U. San Fernando Valley, 1964, JD, 1966. Bar: Calif. 1967, U.S. Ct. Appeals (9th cir.) 1968, U.S. Supreme Ct. 1971, U.S. Dist. Ct. (cen. dist.) Calif. 1967, U.S. Tax Ct. 1971, U.S. Ct. Internat. Trade 1981. Sole practice, Encino, Calif., 1967—; judge pro tem L.A. Mcpl. Ct., 1980—, L.A. Superior Ct., 1991—; family law mediator L.A. Superior Ct., 1980—. Mem. Pacific S.W. regional bd. Anti-Defamation league of B'nai B'rith, 1970-91. Served with USAF, 1959-65, to col. CAP, 1956—. Recipient Disting. Svc. award B'nai B'rith, 1969; Exceptional Svc. award CAP, 1977, 95. Mem. ABA, L.A. County Bar Assn., San Fernando Valley Bar Assn., Consumer Atty. of Calif., Consumer Atty. Assn. L.A. Republican. Clubs: Toastmasters, Westerners 1117 (pres. 1969), B'nai B'rith (pres. 1971-72), Santa Monica Yacht (judge adv.) Civil rights, Family and matrimonial, Personal injury. Office: 17609 Ventura Blvd Ste 201 Encino CA 91316-3825

KAUFMAN, ANDREW LEE, law educator; b. Newark, Feb. 1, 1931; s. Samuel and Sylvia (Meltzer) K.; m. Linda P. Sonnenschein, June 14, 1959; children: Anne, David, Elizabeth, Daniel. A.B., Harvard U., 1951, LL.B., 1954. Bar: D.C. 1954, Mass. 1979, U.S. Supreme Ct. 1961. Assoc. Bilder, Bilder & Kaufman, Newark, 1954-55; law clk. to Justice Felix Frankfurter U.S Supreme Ct., 1955-57; ptnr. Kaufman, Kaufman & Kaufman, Newark, 1957-65; lectr. in law Harvard U., Cambridge, Mass., 1965-66, prof., 1966-81, Charles Stebbins Fairchild prof. law, 1981—, assoc. dean, 1986-89. Author: (with others) Commercial Law, 1971, 82, Problems in Professional Responsibility, 1976, 84, 89, Cardozo, 1998. Treas. Shady Hill Sch., 1969-76; treas. Hillel Found. Cambridge, Inc., 1977-86. Mem. Mass. Bar Assn. (chmn. com. profl. ethics 1982—). Office: Harvard U Law Sch Cambridge MA 02138 E-mail: kaufman@law.harvard.edu

KAUFMAN, ANDREW MICHAEL, lawyer; b. Boston, Feb. 19, 1949; s. Earle Bertram and Miriam (Halpern) K.; m. Michele Moselle, Aug. 24, 1975; children: Peter Moselle, Melissa Lanes, Caroline Raney. BA cum laude, Yale U., 1971; JD, Vanderbilt U., 1974. Bar: Tex. 1974, Ga. 1976, Ill. 1993, U.S. Ct. Appeals (5th and 11th cirs.) 1981. Assoc. Vinson & Elkins, Houston, 1974-76, ptnr., 1982-83, Austin, 1983-92, Dallas, 1992; assoc. Sutherland, Asbill & Brennan, Atlanta, 1976-80, ptnr., 1980-81, Kirkland & Ellis, Chgo., 1993—. Editor in chief Vanderbilt U. Law Rev., 1973-74. Fund raiser alumni fund Yale U., 1971—, mem. alumni schs. com., 1986—; mem. med. ethics com. Seton Hosp., 1988-92; participant Leadership Austin, 1987-88; bd. dirs. United Way, Austin, 1988-92, Sta. KLRU-TV, 1989-93, pub. TV, Ballet Austin, 1986-92; mem. adv. bd. Austin Tech. Incubator, 1989-93, Austin-U. Tex. Entrepreneurs Coun., 1991-92; Dallas bus. com. Arts Leadership Inst, 1992-93; mem. nat. alumni bd. Vanderbilt U. Law Sch., 1994-2000; governing mem. Chgo. Symphony Orch. Mem. ABA (bus. law sect. 1978—, chmn. lease financing and secured transactions subcom. of com. devels. in bus. financing 1993-99, UCC com., legal opinions com., comml. fin. svcs. com.), Tex. Bar Assn., Yale U. Alumni Assn., Order of Coif, Headliners Club, Yale Club, N.Y.C. at Chgo., Knights of the Symphony Austin. Avocation: sailing. Banking, General corporate, Finance. Office: Kirkland & Ellis 200 E Randolph St Fl 54 Chicago IL 60601-6636 E-mail: Andrew.Kaufman@chicago.kirkland.com

KAUFMAN, ARTHUR STEPHEN, lawyer; b. N.Y.C., July 27, 1946; s. Jacob and Helen (Chalphin) K.; m. Susan Werner, Jan. 31, 1971; children: Lewis Scott, Jonathan Charles. AB, Columbia Coll., 1968, JD, 1971. Bar: N.Y. 1972. Assoc. Dewey, Ballantine, Bushby, Palmer & Wood, N.Y.C., 1971-79; ptnr. Shea & Gould, 1980-85, Fried, Frank, Harris, Shriver & Jacobson, N.Y.C., 1985—. General corporate, Finance, Securities. Home: 17 Withington Rd Scarsdale NY 10583-3305 Office: Fried Frank Harris Shriver & Jacobson 1 New York Plz Fl 22 New York NY 10004-1980

KAUFMAN, DAVID JOSEPH, lawyer; b. Harrisburg, Pa., Apr. 7, 1931; s. S. Herbert and Bessie (Claster) K.; m. Virginia Stern, Aug. 30, 1959; children: David J. Jr., James H. BS in Econs. cum laude, Franklin and Marshall Coll., 1952; JD cum laude, U. Pa., 1955. Bar: Pa. 1955. First assoc., to ptnr., then of counsel Wolf, Block, Schorr & Solis-Cohen, Phila., 1957—; chmn., exec. com., 1979, 83. Trustee Abington (Pa.) Meml. Hosp., 1981—, chmn. bd. trustees, 1992-94; pres. Congregation Rodeph Shalom, Phila., 1983-86. Fellow Am. Coll. Trust and Estate Counsel; mem. ABA, Pa. Bar Assn. (chmn. real property, probate and trust sect. 1986-87), Phila. Bar Assn. (chmn. probate sect. 1977). Republican. Estate planning, Probate, Estate taxation. Home: 1770 Oak Hill Dr Huntingdon Valley PA 19006-5817

KAUFMAN, JAMES JAY, lawyer; b. Newark, Jan. 23, 1939; s. Joseph Julius and Ann Gertrude (Quick) K.; m. Patricia Ann Patterson, Sept. 3, 1966; children: Kristine, Jeffrey. BA, Bucknell U., 1960; LLB, JD, Union Coll., Albany, 1964. Bar: N.Y. 1965, U.S. Ct. Appeals (2nd cir.) 1966, U.S. Dist. Ct. (we. and no. dists.) N.Y. 1968, N.C. 1985, Pa. 1985, U.S. Supreme Ct. 1985, U.S. Dist. Ct. (ea. dist.) N.C. 1991, U.S. Ct. Appeals (4th cir.) 1991, U.S. Ct. Appeals (7th cir.) 1992, U.S. Dist. Ct. (mid. dist.) N.C. 1993; certified mediator, Wilmington, Conn. Legal counsel, legis. and adminstrv. asst. Rep. Theodore R. Kupferman, U.S. Congress, Washington, 1965-67; assoc. Houghton, Pappas & Fink, Rochester, N.Y., 1967-70; ptnr. Culley, Marks, 1970-75; sr. ptnr. James J. Kaufman, P.C., Newark, 1975-84, Kaufman & Forsyth, Rochester, 1984-91, Barefoot & Kaufman, Wilmington, N.C., 1991-93, Kaufman, Barefoot & Green, Wilmington, 1993-94; of counsel Hancock & Estabrook, Syracuse, N.Y., 1994-96; sr. ptnr. Kaufman & Green, L.L.P., Wilmington, 1994-2001, Maupin, Taylor & Ellis, P.A., 2001—. V.p. Fed. Bar Coun., 1968; mem. 7th Jud. Dist. Grievance Com., 1983-89; del. U.S./China Joint Session on Trade, Investment and Econ. Law, Beijing, 1987; strategic planning cons., Rochester, 1994-95; panel mem. Commerce Tech. Adv. Bd. on Noise Abatement, Washington, 1968; chmn. noise task force Genesee Region Health Planning, Rochester, 1970-71, mem./counsel noise task force, mem./counsel environ. health planning com., 1972-73. Author: What to Do Before the Money Runs Out—A Road Map for America's Automobile Dealers, 1993; contbr. articles to profl. publs. Justice Town of Arcadia, Newark, 1976-89. Mem. N.Y. State Bar Assn. (mem. spl. com. on environ. law 1974-77, mem. com. on profl. discipline, mem. com. on ct. in cmty. banking com. 1986—), Wayne County Bar Assn. (pres. 1986-87, v.p. 1985-86, chmn. family law sect. 1975-80, chmn. com. on profl. discipline 1975-89), N.C. Bar Assn., Pa. Bar Assn., New Hanover County Bar Assn., Monroe County Bar Assn., Wilmington Inns of Ct. (pres. 1994-97). Republican. Presbyterian. Avocations: boating, scuba diving, fishing. Banking, Contracts commercial, Health. Office: Maupin Taylor & Ellis PA 1985 Eastwood Rd Ste 200 Wilmington NC 28403-7208 E-mail: jkaufman@maupintaylor.com

KAUFMAN, MICHELLE STARK, lawyer; b. N.Y.C., June 11, 1954; d. Maurice E. and Mary (Murray) Stark; m. Daniel M. Kaufman, Oct. 6, 1984; children: Jane Stark, David Stark, Carolyn Stark. BA, Iowa State U., Ames, 1976; JD, U. Mo., Kansas City, 1983. Bar: Mo. 1983, U.S. Dist. Ct. (we. dist.) Mo. 1983. Graphic artist Douglas Stone & Assocs., Newport Beach, Calif., 1976-78; chief news bur. Midwest Records, Kansas City, Mo., 1978-80; ptnr. Stinson, Mag and Fizzell, PC, 1983-95, Sonnenschein Nath & Rosenthal, Kansas City, 1995—. Lectr. U. Mo. Sch. Law, Kansas City, 1984-85; trustee U. Mo.-Kansas City Law Sch. Found., 1992—, exec. com., 1996—, sec., 1998-99, v.p. 1999-2000, pres., 2001—. Bd. dirs. Heart of Am. Family Svcs., Kansas City, 1989-98, vice-chmn., 1991-93, chmn., 1994-95, bd. mem. of the year award, 1995; bd. dirs., sec. Countryside Homes Assn., Kansas City, 1985. Mem. ABA (forum on franchising), Am. Health Lawyers Assn., Mo. Bar Assn., Greater Kansas City C. of C. (chmn. club 1990-96, vice-chmn. 1991-92, chmn. 1992-93, Mo. state affairs com. 1995—, Chmn.'s Club Hall of Fame, 1996), U. Mo. Kansas City Law Alumni Assn. (bd. dirs. 1992-96, pres. 1994-95), Kansas City Tomorrow Alumni Assn. (bd. dirs., pres.-elect 1997-98, pres. 1998-99), Delta Delta Delta (exec. bd. 1979). General corporate, Franchising, Health. Office: Sonnenschein Nath & Rosenthal 4520 Main St Ste 1100 Kansas City MO 64111-7700

KAUFMAN, ROBERT MAX, lawyer, director; b. Vienna, Austria, Nov. 17, 1929; came to U.S., 1939, naturalized, 1945; s. Paul M. and Bertha (Hirsch) K.; m. Sheila Seymour Kelley. BA with honors, Bklyn. Coll., 1951; MA, NYU, 1954; JD magna cum laude, Bklyn. Law Sch., 1957. Bar: N.Y. 1957, U.S. Supreme Ct. 1961. Successively jr. economist, economist, sr. economist N.Y. State Div. Housing, 1953-57; atty. antitrust div. U.S. Dept. Justice, 1957-58; legis. asst. to U.S. Senator Jacob K. Javits, 1958-61; assoc. Proskauer Rose LLP, N.Y.C., 1961-69, ptnr., 1969—. Chmn. bd. Pirelli Cables & Systems, LLC, Pirelli Tires LLC, Old Westbury Funds, Inc.; bd. dirs. Roytex Inc., Meadowbrook Equity Fund, L.L.C.; mem. N.Y. State Legis. Adv. Com. on Election Law, 1973-74; chmn. adv. com. N.Y. State Bd. Elections, 1974-78; chmn. N.Y. State Bd. Pub. Disclosure, 1981-82, U.S. Army Chief of Staff's Spl. Commn. on Honor System, 1988-89, N.Y. Chief Judge's Com. on Availability of Legal Svcs., 1988-90; referee Commn. on Jud. Conduct; spl. master N.Y. Supreme Ct. Appellate Divsn., 1999—; mem. Adminstrv. Conf. U.S. (chair com. regulations), 1988-95; chmn. Fund for Modern Cts., 1990-95; mem. Def. Adv. Com. on Women in the Svcs., 1997-99, vice chair com. on equality mgmt., mem. exec. com. 1998. Co-author: Congress and the Public Trust, 1970, Disorder in the Court, 1973; co-gen. editor: Matthew Bender Treatise on Health Care Law, 4 vols., 1992—. Bd. dirs., mem. exec. com. Lawrence M. Gelb Found., Inc., Lawyers in the Public Interest, 1986-95, Am. Judicature Soc., pres. 1995-97, Citizens Union of N.Y.C., vice chair, 1997-2000, Citizen's Union Found., 1993—; bd. dirs., chmn. exec. com. Cmty. Action for Legal Svcs., Inc., 1976-78; dir., mem. exec. com. Legal Aid Soc., 1985-90, mem. exec. com. Vols. of Legal Svc., 1986-94; mem. platform com. N.Y. Rep. State Com., 1974; mem. jud. selection adv. coms. Senator Javits, 1972-80, and Senator Moynahan, 1977-2000; compensation elected ofcl. N.Y.C. Quadrennial Comm., 1995, 99; mem. distbn. com., vice chair, 2001—, N.Y. Cmty. Trust; bd. dirs. N.Y. Cmty. Funds, James Found.; bd. vis. U.S. Mil. Acad., 1976-79; dir., mem. exec. com., chmn. bd. Times Square Bus. Improvement Dist.; trustee Bklyn. Law Sch. With U.S. Army, 1957-58. Fellow Am. Bar Found., N.Y. State Bar Found.; mem. ABA, Assn. of Bar of City N.Y. (pres. 1986-88, chmn. house com., co-chmn. com. on campaign fin. reform 1997-2001, past chmn. com. on 2d Century; past chmn. exec. com., past chmn. com. profl. responsibility, past chmn. spl. com. on campaign expenditures, past chmn. com. civil rights, past vice chmn. com. grievances, past chmn. delegation to state bar ho. dels.), N.Y. State Bar Assn. (ho. of dels. 1978, 86-90), N.Y. County Lawyers Assn. (past chmn. com. on civil rights), Am. Law Inst. General corporate, Health, Non-profit and tax-exempt organizations. Office: Proskauer Rose LLP 1585 Broadway New York NY 10036-8299 E-mail: kaufman@proskauer.com

KAUFMAN, RONALD C. lawyer; b. Bronx, N.Y., July 24, 1969; s. Ronald S. and Margaret T. K.; m. Sarah Tate. BA, King's Coll., 1992; JD, U. Tulsa, 1997. Bar: Okla. 1997, U.S. Dist. Ct. (no. dist.) Okla. 1998, U.S. Ct. Appeals (10th cir.) 1998. Atty. Bodenhamer & Levinson, Tulsa, 1997—. Mem. ABA (antitrust divsn), Okla. Bar Assn., Tulsa County Bar Assn. Antitrust, Federal civil litigation, Securities. Office: Bodenhamer & Levinson 5310 E 31st St Ste 1100 Tulsa OK 74135

KAUFMAN, STEPHEN EDWARD, lawyer; b. N.Y.C., Feb. 16, 1932; s. Herbert and Gertrude Kaufman; m. Marina Pinto, June 22, 1967; children: Andrew H. and Douglas P. BA, Williams Coll., 1953; LLB, Columbia U., 1957. Bar: N.Y. 1958, U.S. Ct. Appeals (2d cir.) 1958, U.S. Dist. Ct. (so. and ea. dists.) N.Y. 1960, U.S. Supreme Ct. 1963. Asst. U.S. Atty. U.S. Attys. Office, So. Dist., N.Y., 1964-69, chief of criminal div., 1964-69; pres. Stephen E. Kaufman, P.C., N.Y.C., 1976—. Bd. dirs. Smith Barney Mut. Funds. Fellow Am. Coll. Trial Lawyers; mem. ABA, N.Y. State Bar Assn., Assn. of Bar of City of N.Y. Federal civil litigation, State civil litigation. Office: 277 Park Ave New York NY 10172-0003

KAUFMAN, STEVEN MICHAEL, lawyer; b. Spokane, Wash., July 2, 1951; s. Gordon Leonard and Terri (Thal) K.; m. Connie Hoopes, June 7, 1973; children: Kristopher, Shana. BS magna cum laude, U. Utah, 1973; JD cum laude, Gonzaga U., 1977. Bar: Utah 1977, U.S. Dist. Ct. Utah 1977, U.S. Ct. Appeals (10th cir.) 1977, U.S. Supreme Ct. 1985. Founding ptnr. Farr, Kaufman, and Hamilton, 1979-89; mng. ptnr. Farr, Kaufman, Sullivan, Gorman, Jensen, Medsker, Nichols & Perkins, 1989—; judge pro tem, 1981-98; bar commr. Utah State Bar Commn., 1991-98. Chmn. Commn. on Pub. Defenders, Ogden, 1984. Mem. ATLA, ABA, Utah Bar Assn. (pres.-elect 1995-96, pres., 1996-97, bar commr. 1992-98, rep. Utah Jud. Coun. 1998-99), Weber County Bar Assn. (pres. 1981-82), Rex E. Lee Inn of Ct. (master), Utah Jud. Coun. Jewish. Criminal, Family and matrimonial, Personal injury. Home: 5878 S 1050 E Ogden UT 84405-4959 Office: Farr Kaufman Sullivan Gorman Jensen Medsker Nichols & Perkins 205 26th St Ste 34 Ogden UT 84401-3109

KAUFMAN, THOMAS FREDERICK, lawyer, legal educator; b. Buffalo, Sept. 10, 1949; s. Frederick J. and Edna M. (Kilian) K.; children: Alycia, Thomas, Jonathan. BSEE, SUNY, Buffalo, 1971; JD, Georgetown U., 1976; MBA, U. Pa., 2001. Bar: Va. 1976, U.S. Ct. Appeals (6th cir.) 1976, D.C. 1977, U.S. Dist. Ct. D.C. 1981, Md. 1996. Law clk. to chief judge U.S. Ct. Appeals (6th cir.), 1976-77; assoc. Melrod, Redman & Gartlan, Washington, 1977-81, Willkie Farr & Gallagher, Washington, 1981-84, ptnr., 1985-95, Hunton & Williams, Washington, 1995—. Adj. prof. law Georgetown U., Washington, 1986—. Mem. Am. Coll. Real Estate Lawyers. Banking, Real property. Office: Hunton and Williams 1900 K St NW Washington DC 20006-1110 E-mail: tkaufman@hunton.com

KAUGER, YVONNE, state supreme court chief justice; b. Cordell, Okla., Aug. 3, 1937; d. John and Alice (Bottom) K.; m. Ned Bastow, May 8, 1982; 1 child, Jonna Kauger Kirschner. BS magna cum laude, Southwestern State U., Weatherford, Okla., 1958; cert. med. technologist, St. Anthony's Hosp., 1959; J.D., Oklahoma City U., 1969, LLD (hon.), 1992. Med. technologist Med. Arts Lab., 1959-68; assoc. Rogers, Travis & Jordan, 1970-72; jud. asst. Okla. Supreme Ct., Oklahoma City, 1972-84, justice, 1984-94, vice chief justice, 1994-96, chief justice, 1997-98, justice, 1998—. Mem. appellate div. Ct. on Judiciary; mem. State Capitol Preservation Commn., 1983-84; mem. dean's adv. com. Oklahoma City U. Sch. Law; lectr. William O. Douglas Lecture Series Gonzaga U., 1990. Founder Gallery of Plains Indian, Colony, Okla., Red Earth (Down Towner award 1990), 1987; active Jud. Day, Girl's State, 1976-80; keynote speaker Girl's State Hall of Fame Banquet, 1984; bd. dirs. Lyric Theatre, Inc., 1966— , pres. bd. dirs., 1981; past mem. bd. dirs. Civic Music Soc., Okla. Theatre Ctr., Canterbury Choral Soc.; mem. First Lady of Okla.'s Artisans' Alliance Com. Named Panhellenic Woman of Yr., 1990, Woman of Yr. Red Lands Coun. Girl Scouts, 1990, Washita County Hall of Fame, 1992. Mem. ABA (law sch. accreditation com.), Okla. Bar Assn. (law schs. com. 1977—), Washita County Bar Assn., Washita County Hist. Soc. (life), St. Paul's Music Soc., Iota Tau Tau, Delta Zeta (Disting. Alumna award 1988, State Delta Zeta of Yr. 1987, Nat. Woman of Yr. 1988). Episcopalian*

KAUNITZ, KAREN ROSE KOPPEL, lawyer; b. Richmond, Va., July 17, 1951; d. Leopold and Lore (Baer) Koppel; m. Andrew Moss Kaunitz, Sept. 10, 1978; children: Kate Baer, David Koppel. AB, Goucher Coll., 1973; JD, Albany Law Sch., 1976. Bar: N.Y. 1977, Ill. 1978, Fla. 1980, D.C. 1980, Ga. 1982, U.S. Dist. Ct. (no. dist.) N.Y. 1977, U.S. Dist. Ct. (no. dist.) Ga. 1983, U.S. Ct. Appeals (5th cir.) 1980, U.S. Ct. Appeals (9th cir.) 1980, U.S. Ct. Appeals (D.C. cir.) 1980. Gen. counsel N.Y. Farm Bur., Albany, 1976-78; sr. staff atty. Am. Hosp. Assn., Chgo., 1978-82; atty., advisor Ctrs. for Disease Control USPHS/HHS, Atlanta, 1982-84; v.p. legal affairs Meth. Med. Ctr., Jacksonville, Fla., 1984-92; assoc. gen. counsel Bapt. Health Sys., 1992-2000; ret., 2000. Contbr. articles to profl. jours.; chpt. to book. Mem. ABA (health law forum com.), Ga. Bar Assn., Fla. Bar Assn. (health law com.), D.C. Bar Assn., Am. Acad. Hosp. Attys., Am. Soc. Law and Medicine, Nat. Health Lawyers Assn., Phi Beta Kappa. Jewish. Administrative and regulatory, Health, Personal injury. Home: 2966 Forest Cir Jacksonville FL 32257-5618

KAUTTER, DAVID JOHN, lawyer; b. Wilkes-Barre, Pa., Mar. 20, 1948; s. William George and Mary (Flanagan) K.; m. Kathy Jane Price, May 22, 1976; children: Hilary, David Jr. BBA, Notre Dame U., 1971; JD, Georgetown U., 1974. Bar: D.C. 1975, U.S. Dist. Ct. D.C. 1981, U.S. Tax Ct. 1981, U.S. Supreme Ct. 1981. Staff acct. Coopers & Lybrand, Washington, 1971-74; mgr. Arthur Young and Co., 1974-78; legis. asst. Senator John Danforth, 1979-82; ptnr. Arthur Young and Co., 1982-89, dir. Wash. Nat. Tax Group, 1986-89; nat. dir. compensation and benefits tax svcs. Ernst & Young, 1989-98, mem. ptnrs. adv. coun., 1993-96, nat. dir. human resource svcs., 1998-2001, dir. nat. tax, 2001—. Contbr. articles to profl. jours. Mem. ABA, Fed. Bar Assn., AICPA's. Republican. Roman Catholic. Avocation: cabinet making. Legislative, Pension, profit-sharing, and employee benefits, Personal income taxation. Home: 8312 Summerwood Dr Mc Lean VA 22102-2212 Office: Ernst & Young 1225 Connecticut Ave NW Ste 700 Washington DC 20036-2621

KAUTZMAN, JOHN FREDRICK, lawyer; b. Indpls., Aug. 23, 1959; s. Fred L. and Barbara J. (Seeger) K. BA, Ind. U., 1981; JD, Ind. U., Indpls., 1984. Bar: Ind. 1985, U.S. Dist. Ct. (no. and so. dists.) Ind. 1985, U.S. Ct. Appeals (7th cir.) 1992. Law clk. Marion County Pros. Office, Indpls., 1981; bailiff Marion County Cir. Ct., 1981-84, commr., judge pro tempore, 1985-89; assoc. Ruckelshaus, Roland, Hasbrook & O'Connor, 1985-89, ptnr., 1990-98, Ruckelshaus, Roland, Kautzman, Blackwell & O'Connor, Indpls., 1998—. Mem. faculty Ind. Trial Advocacy Coll., 1998—. Contbg. author The Indiana Lawyer newspaper, 1991—. Mem. bd. assocs. Ind. U. Found., Bloomington, 1993—, v.p. 1997-99, pres., 2000—; precinct commiteeman Marion County Rep. Party, Indpls., 1994-96. Mem. ABA, Indpls. Bar Assn. (v.p. 1998, bd. mgrs. 1994-96, 99-2001, young lawyers divsn. chmn. 1988-89, Disting. fellow 1993), Ind. State Bar Assn., Phi Delta Phi. Methodist. Avocations: professional piano, golf. General civil litigation, Criminal, General practice. Office: Ruckelshaus Roland Kautzman Blackwell & Hasbrook Ste 900 107 N Pennsylvania St Indianapolis IN 46204-2424 Fax: (317) 634-8635

KAVALER, THOMAS J. lawyer; b. N.Y.C., Dec. 10, 1948; BA, CCNY, 1969; JD, Fordham U., 1972; LLM, NYU, 1975. Bar: N.Y., U.S. Dist. Ct. (so., ea., we. and no. dists.) N.Y., U.S. Ct. Appeals (2d, 4th, 5th, 6th, 8th, 10th, 11th and fed. cirs.), U.S. Supreme Ct. Law clk. to judge U.S. Dist. Ct. N.Y., N.Y.C., 1972-74; assoc. Cravath, Swaine & Moore, 1974-75, Cahill Gordon & Reindel, N.Y.C., 1975-80, ptnr., 1980—. Served to capt. USAR, 1969-77. Fellow Am. Bar Found., Internat. Acad. Trial Lawyers; mem. Fordham Law Alumni Assn. (pres. 2000—). Federal civil litigation, State civil litigation, Securities. Office: Cahill Gordon & Reindel 80 Pine St Fl 17 New York NY 10005-1790

KAVANAGH, GILES, lawyer, solicitor; b. Belfast, May 2, 1959; s. Joseph and Bernadette K.; m. Anna DeBuisseret, June 29, 1996; children: Tierney, Conall. BA, Cambridge U., 1980, LLM, MA (hon.), 1981. Bar: Eng., Wales 1984; solicitor Supreme Ct. 1998. Barrister, London, 1984-98; solicitor Barlow Lyde & Gilbert, 1998—; pntr., 1999—. Mem. Royal Aeronaut. Soc., Royal Automobile Soc. Aviation. Office: Barlow Lyde & Gilbert Beaufort Ho 15 St Botolph London EC3A 7NJ England Fax: 0207 643 8505. E-mail: gkavanagh@blg.co.uk

KAVANAUGH, JAMES FRANCIS, JR. lawyer; b. New Bedford, Mass., Feb. 20, 1949; s. James Francis and Catherine Mary (Loughlin) K.; m. Cynthia Louise Ward, July 4, 1968; 1 child, James F. III. BA, Coll. of the Holy Cross, 1970; JD magna cum laude, Boston Coll., 1977. Bar: Mass. 1977, U.S. Dist. Ct. Mass., 1978, U.S. Ct. Appeals (1st cir.) 1978, U.S. Supreme Ct. 1990. Law clk. to assoc. justice Mass. Supreme Jud. Ct., Boston, 1977-78; assoc. Burns & Levinson, 1978-82, ptnr., 1983-88, Conn, Kavanaugh, Rosenthal, Peisch & Ford, Boston, 1988—. Adj. lectr., litig. specialist Boston Coll. Law Sch., 1994-99. Editor, contbr. Boston Coll. Law Rev., 1975-77. Mem. ABA, Mass. Bar Assn., Boston Bar Assn., Boston Coll. Law Sch. Alumni Assn. (pres. 1999—). Democrat. Roman Catholic. Clubs: Winchester Country, New Bedford Country. Avocations: golf, skiing, reading fiction and history. Federal civil litigation, General civil litigation, State civil litigation. Office: Conn Kavanaugh Rosenthal Peisch & Ford Ten Post Office Sq Boston MA 02109

KAVOUKJIAN, MICHAEL EDWARD, lawyer; b. Mpls., Apr. 19, 1958; s. Antranik M. and Leikny Dorthea (Oines) K. AB with distinction, Stanford U., 1980; JD cum laude, Harvard U., 1984. Bar: Minn. 1984, N.Y. 1986, U.S. Dist. Ct. Minn. 1985, U.S. Dist. Ct. (so. dist.) N.Y. 1988, Fla. 1999. From assoc. to ptnr. White & Case, N.Y.C. and Miami, Fla., 1985—. Bd. govs. Harvard Law Sch., Cambridge, Mass., 1982—84. Mem.: ABA (chmn. com. estate planning and drafting 1992—94), Minn. State Bar Assn., The Fla. Bar, Assn. of the Bar city of N.Y., Soc. Trust and Estate Practitioners (UK), Harvard Club (N.Y.C., Washington, Boston), Nat. Press Club (Washington), Lincoln's Inn Soc. Republican. Presbyterian. Estate planning, Probate, Estate taxation. Office: White & Case 1155 Avenue Of The Americas New York NY 10036-2787

KAWACHIKA, JAMES AKIO, lawyer; b. Honolulu, Dec. 5, 1947; s. Shinichi and Tsuyuko (Murashige) K.; m. Karen Keiko Takahashi, Sept. 1, 1973; 1 child, Robyn Mari. BA, U. Hawaii, Honolulu, 1969; JD, U. Calif., Berkeley, 1973. Bar: Hawaii 1973, U.S. Dist. Ct. Hawaii 1973, U.S. Ct. Appeals (9th cir.) 1974, U.S. Supreme Ct. 1992. Dep. atty. gen. Office of Atty. Gen. State of Hawaii, Honolulu, 1973-74; assoc. Padgett, Greeley & Marumoto, 1974-75, Law Office of Frank D. Padgett, Honolulu, 1975-77, Kobayashi, Watanabe, Sugita & Kawashima, Honolulu, 1977-82; ptnr. Carlsmith, Wichman, Case, Mukai & Ichiki, 1982-86, Bays, Deaver, Hiatt, Kawachika & Lezak, Honolulu, 1986-95; propr. Law Offices of James A. Kawachika, 1996—. Mem. Hawaii Bd. of Bar Examiners, Honolulu; arbitrator Cir. Ct. Arbitration Program State of Hawaii, Honolulu, 1986—. Chmn. Disciplinary Bd. Hawaii Supreme Ct., 1991-97; mem. U.S. dist. Ct. Adv. Com. on the Civil Justice Reform Act of 1990, 1991—. Mem. ABA, ATLA, Am. Judicature Soc., Hawaii Bar Assn. (bd. dirs. Honolulu chpt. 1975-76, young lawyers sect. 1983-84, 92-93, treas. 1987-88, v.p./pres.-elect 1997-98, pres. 1998-99), 9th Cir. Jud. Conf. (lawyer rep. Honolulu chpt. 1988-90). Avocations: running, tennis, skiing. General civil litigation, Insurance, Personal injury. Office: Pacific Guardian Ctr Mauka Tower 737 Bishop St Ste 2750 Honolulu HI 96813-3216

KAWAGUCHI, MEREDITH FERGUSON, lawyer; b. Dallas, Feb. 5, 1940; d. Hugh William Ferguson and Ruth Virginia (Perdue) Drewery; m. Harry H. Kawaguchi, Apr. 22, 1977. BA, U. Tex., 1962, MA, 1968; JD, So. Meth. U., 1977. Bar: Tex. 1977. Legal examiner gas utilities div. Tex. Railroad Commn., Austin, 1977-84, legal examiner oil and gas div., 1984-89, asst. dir. gas utilities and liquified petroleum gas sect. of legal div., 1989-90, legal examiner legal div., 1990—; cons. in law, lectr. to profl. confs. Author position paper Tex. Energy Natural Resources Adv. Council. Mem., Sorority Adv. Coun., Austin, 1980-88, Japanese-Am. Citizens League, Houston, 1981—, Exec. Women in Tex. Govt., Austin, 1984. Recipient Cert. of Recognition Tex. Railroad Commn., 1982, Outstanding Svc. award, 1987. Mem. ABA, Tex. Bar Assn., Travis County Bar Assn. (oil gas and mineral law sect.), Travis County Women Lawyers Assn., Exec. Women in Tex., Internat. Platform Assn. Home: 5009 Westview Dr Austin TX 78731-4741 Office: Tex Railroad Commn 1701 Congress Ave Austin TX 78701-1402

KAWITT, ALAN, lawyer; b. 1937; JD, Chgo.-Kent Coll. Law, 1965; postgrad. Lawyers Inst., John Marshall Law Sch., 1966-68. Bar: Ill. 1966, U.S. Dist. Ct. (no. dist.) Ill. 1967, U.S. Ct. Appeals (7th cir.) 1971, U.S. Supreme Ct. 1971. Sole practice, 1970—. Lawyer; b. Chgo., 1937. J.D., Chgo.-Kent Coll. Law, 1965; postgrad. Lawyers Inst. John Marshall Law Sch., 1966-68. Bar: Ill. 1966, U.S. Dist. Ct. (no. dist.) Ill. 1967, U.S. Ct. Appeals (7th cir.) 1971, U.S. Supreme Ct., 1971. Sole practice, 1970—. Mem. Am. Arbitration Assn. (arbitrator). Fax: (773) 472-3556. Mem. Am. Arbitration Assn. (arbitrator). Consumer commercial, Insurance, Landlord-tenant. Office: 226 S Wabash Ave Ste 905 Chicago IL 60604-2319 Fax: 773-472-3556

KAY, HERMA HILL, education educator; b. Orangeburg, S.C., Aug. 18, 1934; d. Charles Esdorn and Herma Lee (Crawford) Hill. BA, So. Meth. U., 1956; JD, U. Chgo., 1959. Bar: Calif. 1960, U.S. Supreme Ct. 1978. Law clk. to Hon. Roger Traynor Calif. Supreme Ct., 1959-60; asst. prof. law U. Calif., Berkeley, 1960-62, assoc. prof., 1962, prof., 1963, dir. family law project, 1964-67, Jennings prof., 1987-96, dean, 1992-2000, Armstrong prof., 1996—; co-reporter uniform marriage and div. act Nat. Conf. Commrs. on Uniform State Laws, 1968-70. Vis. prof. U. Manchester, Eng., 1972, Harvard U., 1976; mem. Gov.'s Commn. on Family, 1966. Author: (with Martha S. West) Text Cases and Materials on Sex-based Discrimination, 4th edit., 1996, supplement, 1999; (with D. Currie and L. Kramer) Conflict of Laws: Cases, Comments, Questions, 6th edit., 2001; contbr. articles to profl. jours. Trustee Russell Sage Found., N.Y., 1972-87, chmn. bd., 1980-84; trustee, bd. dirs. Equal Rights Advs. Calif., 1976-99, chmn., 1976-83; pres. bd. dirs. Rosenberg Found., Calif., 1987-88, bd. dirs. 1978—. Recipient Rsch. award Am. Bar Found., 1990, Margaret Brent award ABA Commn. Women in Profession, 1992, Marshall-Wythe medal, 1995; fellow Ctr. Advanced Study in Behavioral Sci., Palo Alto, Calif., 1963. Mem. ABA (sect. on legal edn. and admissions to the bar coun. 1992-99, sec. 1999-2001), Calif. Bar Assn., Bar U.S. Supreme Ct., Calif. Women Lawyers (bd. govs. 1975-77), Am. Law Inst. (mem. coun. 1985-), Assn. Am. Law Schs. (exec. com. 1986-87, pres.-elect 1988, pres. 1989, past pres. 1990), Am. Acad. Arts and Scis., Am. Philosophical Soc., Order of Coif (nat. pres. 1983-85). Democrat. Office: U Calif Law Sch Boalt Hall Berkeley CA 94720-7200 E-mail: kayh@law.berkeley.edu

KAYE, JUDITH SMITH, state supreme court chief justice; b. Monticello, N.Y., Aug. 4, 1938; d. Benjamin and Lena (Cohen) Smith; m. Stephen Rackow Kaye, Feb. 11, 1964; children: Luisa Marian, Jonathan Mackey, Gordon Bernard BA, Barnard Coll., 1958; LLB cum laude, NYU, 1962; LLD (hon.), St. Lawrence U., 1985, Union U., 1985, Pace U., 1985, Syracuse U., 1988, L.I. U., 1989. Assoc. Sullivan & Cromwell, N.Y.C., 1962-64; staff atty. IBM, Armonk, N.Y., 1964-65; asst. to dean Sch. Law NYU, 1965-68; ptnr. Connelly Chase O'Donnell & Weyher, N.Y.C., 1969-83; assoc. judge N.Y. State Ct. Appeals, 1983-93, chief justice, 1993—. Bd. dir. Sterling Nat. Bank. Contbr. articles to profl. jours. Former bd. dirs. Legal Aid Soc. Recipient Vanderbilt medal NYU Sch. of Law, 1983, Medal of Distinction, Barnard Coll, 1987. Fellow Am. Bar Found.; mem. Am. Law Inst., Am. Coll. Trial Lawyers, Am. Judicature Soc. (bd. dirs. 1980-83). Democrat. Office: NY Court of Appeals Court of Appeals Hall 20 Eagle St Albany NY 12207-1009 also: NY Court of Appeals 230 Park Ave Rm 826 New York NY 10169-0007*

KAYE, MARC MENDELL, lawyer; b. Irvington, N.J., Nov. 25, 1959; s. Aaron Morton and Sandra (Hoch) K. AA, BA, Rutgers U., 1980; JD, U. Toledo, 1983. Bar: N.J. 1984, Fla. 1987, D.C. 1991, N.Y. 1998, U.S. Dist. Ct. N.J. 1984, U.S. Supreme Ct. 1992; cert. civil trial atty. 1991. Trial atty. Shevick, Ravich, Koster et al, Rahway, N.J., 1984-85, Greenberg, Margolis et al, Roseland, 1985-86, Brian Granstrand, Fairfield, 1986-90; pvt. practice Livingston, 1986-94, Short Hills, 1994—. Counsel CNA Ins. Co., Fairfield, 1986-90; apptd. arbitrator Union County Arbitrator Program, 1993, Essex County Arbitrator and Mediator Programs, 1995, Millburn Citizen Budget Com., 1998—; adv. coun. mem. Chmn.'s Club Summit Bank, 1989-91. Mem. exec. com. Young Leadership div. United Jewish Appeal, Metrowest, N.J, 1988-91; bd. dirs. Jewish Cmty. Ctr. of MetroWest, 1998—, Opera Music Theatre Internat., 1999—. Mem. N.J. Bar Assn., Essex County Bar Assn. (subcom. chmn. legal med. com. 1992-94), Union County Bar Assn., Fla. Bar Assn., D.C. Bar Assn., Assn. Trial Lawyers Am., N.J. Trial Lawyers Assn., Lions Club (v.p. 1993-95), Prime Ministers Club, Israel Bonds. Avocations: golf, swimming, scuba diving, travel. General civil litigation, Insurance, Personal injury. Office: One N Brook Dr at S Orange Ave Short Hills NJ 07078-3126 E-mail: Kayemarc@hotmail.com

KAYE, RICHARD PAUL, lawyer; b. East Meadow, N.Y., June 11, 1953; s. Maurice and Sarah (Chanin) K.; m. Susan Ann Strickler, April 21, 1985. BA magna cum laude, Clark U., 1975; JD, George Washington U., 1978. Bar: N.Y. 1979, U.S. Dist. Ct. (so. dist.) 1979, (ea. dist) 1982, U.S. Ct. Appeals (2d cir.) 1998. Asst. dist. atty. N.Y. County, State of N.Y., 1978-81; assoc. Burlingham Underwood & Lord, N.Y.C., 1981-83, Danziger Bangser Klipstein Goldsmith Greenwald & Weiss, N.Y.C., 1983-86; ptnr. Carb, Luria, Glassner, Cook & Kufeld, 1986-95, Bangser Klein Rocca & Blum, N.Y.C., 1995-97, Berger & Kaye LLP, N.Y.C., 1997—2001, Ellenoff Grossman Schole & Cyruli, LLP, N.Y.C., 2001—. Arbitrator small claims Civil Ct. City of N.Y.C., 1986-90. Mem. ABA, N.Y. State Bar Assn., Assn. Bar City N.Y., Phi Beta Kappa, Phi Delta Phi. General civil litigation, General corporate, Family and matrimonial. Office: Ellenoff Grossman Schole & Cyruli LLP 370 Lexington Ave New York NY 10017 E-mail: rkaye@egsclaw.com

KAYNE, MICHELE S. lawyer; b. Pequannock, N.J., Apr. 25, 1972; d. Martin Robert and Cecile Sasson Kayne BA in English, cert. tchr. handicapped, Rutgers Coll., 1994; JD, Rutgers U., 1997. Bar: N.J. 1997, U.S. Dist. Ct. N.J. 1997, N.Y. 1998, U.S. Dist. Ct. (so. and ea. dists.) N.Y. 1999. Respite cons. New Horizons in Autism, Cranbury, N.J., 1991-97; jud. clk. N.J. Superior Ct., Chancery N.J., Elizabeth, 1997-98; assoc. Wolff & Samson, P.A., Roseland, N.J., 1998—. Ct.-apptd. mediator N.J. Jud. of Morris County, Morristown, 1999—. Mem. ABA, N.Y. State Bar Assn., N.J. State Bar Assn., Essex County Bar Assn. (employment law divsn. 1998—, young lawyer's divsn.). Avocations: marathon running, ultimate race competition, playing field hockey. Home: 417 3rd Ave Apt 3A New York NY 10016-8189 Office: Wolff & Samson PA 5 Becker Farm Rd Roseland NJ 07068-1727 E-mail: mkayne@wolffsamson.com

KAZANJIAN, JOHN HAROLD, lawyer; b. Newport, R.I., Jan. 25, 1949; s. Powel Harold and Louise T. (Alexander) K.; m. Jane Mitchell Kohlmeyer, Sept. 26, 1981; 1 child, Sara Jane. BA, Providence Coll., 1971; JD, Notre Dame U., 1975. Bar: N.Y. 1976, U.S. Dist. Ct. (so. dist.) N.Y. 1976, U.S. Dist. Ct. (ea. dist.) N.Y. 1977, U.S. Supreme Ct. 1980, U.S. Ct. Appeals (2d crct.) 1986, U.S. Ct. Appeals (fed. crct.) 1991. Assoc. Cadwalader, Wickersham & Taft, N.Y.C., 1975-86; ptnr. Anderson, Kill & Olick, 1986-98, Beveridge & Diamond, N.Y.C., 1999—. Mem. U.S. Naval War Coll. Found., Newport, 1985—. Mem. ABA (sects. on litigation, tort and ins. practice and internat. law), Assn. Bar City N.Y. (chair com. on product liability), N.Y. County Lawyers Assn. (chair com. on ins. law, tort law sect.), Metro. Club. Episcopalian. Avocations: caricatures, cartoons, long distance running. Federal civil litigation, Insurance, Product liability. Office: Beveridge & Diamond 15th Fl 477 Madison Ave New York NY 10022-5802 E-mail: jkazanjian@bd.law.com

KAZANJIAN, PHILLIP CARL, lawyer, business executive; b. Visalia, Calif., May 15, 1945; s. John Casey and Sat-ten Arlene K.; m. Wendy Coffelt, Feb. 5, 1972; 1 child, John. BA with honors, U. So. Calif., 1967; JD with honors, Lincoln U., 1973. Bar: Calif. 1979, U.S. Dist. Ct. (ctrl. dist.) Calif. 1980, U.S. Tax Ct. 1980, U.S. Ct. Appeals (9th cir.) 1980, U.S. Mil. Ct. Appeals 1980, U.S. Supreme ct. 1983. Ptnr. Brakefield & Kazanjian, Glendale, Calif., 1981-87; sr. ptnr. Kazanjian & Martinetti, 1987—. Judge pro tem L.A. County Superior Ct., 1993—; instr. U.S. Naval Acad., Annapolis, Md., 1981; adj. prof. Glendale C.C., 1997—. Author: The Circuit Governor, 1972; editor-in-chief Lincoln Law Rev., 1973. Mem. Calif. Atty. Gen.'s Adv. Commn. on Cmty.-Police Rels., 1973; bd. dirs. L.A. County Naval Meml. Found., Inc., 1981-85; pres., bd. trustees Glendale C.C. Dist., 1981-97, L.A. World Affairs Coun., Town Hall Calif., Rep. Assocs. (dir.), Rep. Lincoln Club; vice chmn. bd. govs. Calif. Maritime Acad., 1986-94. Capt. USNR, 1969-99. Decorated Navy Commendation medal, Navy Achievement medal, knight Order of Knights Templar, 1990; recipient Patrick Henry medal Am. Legion, 1963, Congl. Record tribute U.S. Ho. of Reps., 1974, Centurion award Chief of Naval Ops., 1978; commendatory resolutions Mayor of L.A., L.A. City Coun., L.A. County Bd. Suprs., Calif. State Assembly and Senate, and Govt. of Calif., 1982, Justice award Calif. Law Student Assn., 1973. Mem. ABA (Gold Key 1972), Calif. Bar Assn., L.A. County Bar Assn., Am. Judicature Soc., ATLA, Glendale C. of C. (bd. dirs., Patriot Yr. 1986), Res. Officers Assn. (nat. judge adv., award 1981), Naval Res. Assn. (nat. adv. com.), U.S. Naval Inst., Interallied Confedn. Res. Officers (internat. chmn. 1987-94), Explorers Club, Commonwealth of Calif. Club. Republican. Episcopalian. State civil litigation, Personal injury. Office: Kazanjian & Martinetti 520 E Wilson Ave Ste 250 Glendale CA 91206-4346

KAZEN, GEORGE PHILIP, federal judge; b. Laredo, Tex., Feb. 29, 1940; s. Emil James and Drusilla M. (Perkins) K.; m. Barbara Ann Sanders, Oct. 27, 1962; children: George Douglas, John Andrew, Elizabeth Ann, Gregory Stephen. BBA, U. Tex., 1960, JD with honors, 1961. Bar: Tex. 1961, U.S. Supreme Ct., U.S. Ct. Claims, U.S. Ct. Appeals (5th cir.), U.S. Dist. Ct. (so. dist.) Tex. Briefing atty. Tex. Sup. Ct., 1961-62; founder, first pres. Laredo Legal Aid Soc., 1966-69; assoc. Mann, Freed, Kazen & Hansen, 1965-79; judge U.S. Dist. Ct. (so. dist.) Tex., Laredo, 1979-96; founder, first pres. Laredo Legal Aid Soc., 1966-69; chief judge U.S. Dist. Ct. (so. dist.) Tex., Laredo, 1996—. Mem. Jud. Conf. Com. Criminal Law, 1990-96, chair com., 1996-99; mem. 5th Cir. Jud. Coun., 1991-94, 96—; adj. prof. law St. Mary's U. Sch. Law, 1990—. Pres. Laredo Civic Music Assn.; chmn. St. Augustine-Ursuline Consol. Sch. Bd.; bd. dirs. Boys' Clubs Laredo; trustee Laredo Jr. Coll., 1972-79; bd. dirs., v.p., pres. Econ. Opportunities Devel. Corp., 1968-70; past bd. dirs. D.D. Hachar Found. With USAF, 1962-65. Decorated Air Force Commendation medal; named Outstanding Young Lawyer, Larado Jaycees, 1970. Mem. ABA, Tex. Bar Found., Tex. Bar Assn., Tex. Criminal Def. Lawyers Assn., Tex. Assn. Bank Counsel, Tex. Assn. Def. Counsel, Laredo C. of C. (bd. dirs. 1975-76), 5th Cir. Dist. Judges Assn. (v.p. 1984-85, pres. 1986-88), U. Tex. Law Sch. Alumni Assn. (bd. dirs. 1976-77). Roman Catholic Office: US Dist Ct PO Box 1060 Laredo TX 78042-1060

KEADY, GEORGE CREGAN, JR. judge; b. Bklyn., June 16, 1924; s. George Cregan and Marie (Lussier) K.; m. Patricia Drake, Sept. 2, 1950; children: Margaret Keady Goldberg, Marie E., George Cregan, Catherine A. Keady Dunn, Kathleen V. Student, U. Kans., 1943-44; B.S., Fordham U., 1949; J.D., Columbia U., 1950; LL.D., Western New Eng. Coll., 1973. Bar: Mass. 1950. Since practiced in, Springfield, Mass.; asso. firm Ganley & Crook, 1950-53; assoc. firm Peter D. Wilson, 1953-57; partner firm Wilson, Keady & Ratner, 1958-79; justice Dist. Ct., Springfield, 1979-82; assoc. justice Superior Ct., 1982-93; ret., 1993; freelance mediator and arbitrator, 1993—. Dean Western New Eng. Coll. Law Sch., 1970-73; dir. Western Mass. Bar Rev., 1956-63, Western New Eng. Coll. Bar Rev., 1965-72; chmn. Mass. Continuing Legal Edn., Inc., 1977-80; mem. Mass. Commn. on Jud. Conduct, 1988, chmn., 1990-93. Active United Fund, Springfield, 1950-72, Joint Civic Agys.; chmn. fund drive Am. Cancer Soc., 1962, selectman, Longmeadow, Mass., 1958-68, chmn. selectmen, 1960-61, 63-64, 66-68, moderator, 1968-73; vice chmn. Rep. Town Com., Longmeadow, 1956-60; alt. del. Rep. Nat. Conv., 1960, del., 1964; pres. Hampden Dist. Mental Health Clinic, Inc., 1968-71, Child Guidance Clinic, Springfield, 1962-64; corporator, trustee, chmn. bd. Baystate Med. Center, 1985-87, trustee, 1984-92, 94-99; chmn. bd. Baystate Health System, 1987-90; trustee Western New Eng. Coll., 1978-84, Baypath Jr. Coll., 1972-87, Baystate Health Systems, 1993-98; dir. BHIC, 1993—. Served with AUS, 1943-46. Decorated Bronze star. Mem. Am. Law Inst., Mass. Bar Assn., Hampden County Bar Assn. (exec. com. 1960-79, pres. 1965-67), Supreme Ct. Hist. Soc., Longmeadow Country Club, Phi Delta Phi. Roman Catholic. Home: 16 Meadowbrook Rd Longmeadow MA 01106-1341

KEAN, JOHN VAUGHAN, retired lawyer; b. Providence, Mar. 12, 1917; s. Otho Vaughan and Mary (Duell) K. AB cum laude, Harvard U., 1938, JD, 1941; grad., U.S. Army War Coll., 1970. Bar: R.I. 1942. With Edwards & Angell, Providence, 1941—, ptnr., 1954-87, of counsel, 1987—. Bd. dirs. The Robbins Co., Attleboro, Mass., 1988-2000, Greater Providence YMCA, 1964-76; chmn. Downtown Providence YMCA, 1964-67. Capt. AUS, 1943-46, 50-52, brig. gen. Decorated Legion of Merit. Mem. ABA, R.I. Bar Assn., N.G. Assn., Res. Officers Assn., Assn. U.S. Army, R.I. Army N.G. (brig. gen. 1964-72), Harvard R.I. Club (pres. 1964-66), Soc. Cin. (R.I. hon.), Agawam Hunt Club, Hope Club (v.p., bd. govs. 1996-2000), Providence Art Club, Army and Navy Club (Washington), Sakonnet Golf Club (Little Compton, R.I.). Home: 2 Angell St Providence RI 02903 Office: Edwards & Angell 2800 Financial Plz Providence RI 02903-2499

KEANE, JAMES IGNATIUS, lawyer, consultant; b. Cheverly, Md., Oct. 28, 1944; s. Ignatius James and Anna Mae (Rover) K. BA magna cum laude, Marquette U., 1966; JD, Georgetown U., 1970. Bar: Md. 1971, U.S. Dist. Ct. Md. 1974, U.S. Ct. Appeals (4th cir.) 1974, U.S. Supreme Ct. 1974. Dep. ct. clk. Prince George's County Cir. Ct., Md., 1963-65, law clk., 1968-70; law clk. Md. Ct. Appeals, Annapolis, 1970-71; assoc. DePaul, Willoner & Kenkel P.A., College Park, Md., 1971-73; asst. atty. gen. Md. Atty. Gen.'s Office, Balt., 1973-75; dir. rsch. Aspens Systems Corp., Germantown, Md., 1976-78; dir. litigation svcs. Coopers & Lybrand, L.A. and N.Y.C., 1978-84; nat. dir. legal info. systems, assoc. gen. counsel Arthur Young & Co.; 1984-85; pres. James Keane Co., North Potomac, Md., 1985—; cons. in field of litigation systems. Author: Litigation Support Systems: An Attorney's Guide, 2d edit., 1992; author, editor (with others) Conflicts of Interest, 1984. NDEA fellow, U.Va., 1966-67. Mem. ABA (chmn. various coms., chmn. program on emerging use of tech. in U.S. litigation, Edinburgh, Scotland), Rio. Democrat. Avocation: windsurfing. General civil litigation, Computer, Management consulting. Office: James Keane Co 20 Esworthy Ter North Potomac MD 20878-8724

KEARFOTT, JOSEPH CONRAD, lawyer; b. Martinsville, Va., Sept. 24, 1947; s. Clarence P. and Elizabeth (Kelly) K.; m. Mary Jo Veatch, Feb.10, 1969; children: Kelly, David. BA, Davidson Coll., 1969; JD, U. Va., 1972. Bar: Va. 1972, U.S. Dist. Ct. (ea. and we. dists.) Va. 1973, U.S. Ct. Appeals (4th cir.) 1973, U.S. Tax Ct. 1979, U.S. Ct. Appeals (1st cir.) 1981, U.S. Ct. Appeals (5th cir.) 1982. Law clk. to presiding judge U.S. Dist. Ct. (ea. dist.) Va., Richmond, 1972-73; assoc. Hunton & Williams, 1973-80, ptnr., 1980—. Lectr. NITA program, Washington and Lee U., 1982-83, Va. Com. on Continuing Legal Edn., 1984—; mem. 4th Cir. Jud. conf. Co-author: Virginia Evidentiary Foundations, 1998. Mem. Richmond Bd. Housing, 1977-85, Richmond Dem. Com., 1978-82; trustee Libr. Va. Found., 1994—, William Byrd Cmty. House, 1978-84, chmn., 1982-84; trustee United Way Svcs., Richmond, 1989-95, treas., 1993-95; trustee Libr. Va., 1989-94, vice chmn., 1990-91, chmn., 1991-92; trustee Trinity Episcopal Sch., 1986-94, treas., 1989-92, chmn., 1993-94; mem. Richmond Regional Bd., Thomas C. Sorensen Inst. Polit. Leadership. Mem. ABA, Va. Bar Assn. (Boyd Graves conf., chmn. 1999—), Def. Rsch. Inst., Richmond Bar Assn., Bull and Bear Club, Country Club Va., Order of Coif. Avocations: golf, skiing. Federal civil litigation, State civil litigation. Home: 4436 Custis Rd Richmond VA 23225-1012 Office: Hunton & Williams East Tower Riverfront Pla 951 E Byrd St Richmond VA 23219-4074

KEARNEY, DOUGLAS CHARLES, lawyer, journalist; b. Gloucester, Mass., June 24, 1945; s. Charles Matthew Kearney and Jean (Tarr) Thomas. Student, Brown U., 1963-64; BA, Fla. State U., 1971, JD with high honors, 1973. Bar: Fla. 1974, Calif. 1976, U.S. Ct. Appeals (5th cir.) 1977, U.S. Dist. Ct. (mid. and so. dists.) Fla. 1978, U.S. Ct. Appeals (11th cir.) 1981, U.S. Supreme Ct. 1982, U.S. Dist. Ct. (no. dist.) Tex. 1985, Tex. 1986. Asst. pub. defender Office of Pub. Defender 2d Jud. Cir., Tallahassee, 1973-76; asst. atty. gen. Atty. Gen.'s Office State of Fla., 1977-78, chief antitrust enforcement unit Atty. Gen.'s Office, 1978-79; prin. Law Offices of Douglas C. Kearney, 1979-85; assoc. Brice & Mankoff, P.C., Dallas, 1985-87, mem., 1987-89, Choate & Lilly, P.C., Dallas, 1989-92; prin. Kearney & Assocs., 1992—. Pres. Legal Aid Found. of Tallahassee, Inc., 1984. With U.S. Army, 1965-68, Vietnam. Mem. Fla. Bar Assn., Tex. Bar Assn., Calif. Bar Assn. Episcopalian. Avocations: sailing, tennis, swimming, gardening. Antitrust, Banking, Federal civil litigation. Office: Kearney & Assocs 15105 Cypress Hills Dr Dallas TX 75248-4914

KEARNS, ROBERT WILLIAM, manufacturing engineer, inventor; b. Gary, Ind., Mar. 10, 1927; s. Martin William and Mary Ellen (O'Hara) K.; m. Phyllis Joan McElwee, Aug. 1, 1953 (annulled Oct. 1980); children: Dennis M., Timothy B., Patrick S., Kathleen A., Maureen M., Robert M. Student, U.S. Army Fin. Sch., Ft. Atterbury, Ind., 1945-46; BME, U. Detroit, 1952; MS in Engring. Mechanics, Wayne State U., 1957; cert. Internat. Sch. Nuclear Sci., Argonne Nat. Labs., Chgo., 1958; PhD, Case Inst. Tech., 1964. Registered profl. mech. and elec. engr., Mich.. Rsch. engr. Bendix Rsch. Labs., Detroit, 1952-57; assoc. prof. engring., faculty advisor SPE student br. Wayne State U., 1957-67; commr. Dept. Bldgs. & Safety Engring., 1967-71; prin. investigator for fed. hwy. Nat. Inst. Sci. & Tech., Gaithersburg, Md., 1971-76; trial litigator U.S. Cts.- Auto U.S. Detroit Dist. Ct., 1978—. Eucharistic Minister St. Peters Church Queenstown, MD, 1998—. Inventor intermittent windshield wiper systems; holder numerous patents. Bd. dirs. Vets. of Office of Strategic Svcs. and

William J. Donovan Meml. Found., Inc., 1994—, Office of Strategic Svcs. Soc., 1999—, sr. v.p., 2000—; bd. dirs. Queen Anne's County (Md.) Hist. Soc., 1995—; cand. Comptroller for State of Md., 1998—. With U.S. Army, 1945-47. Mem. OSS Soc. (sr. v.p. 2000—). Roman Catholic. Avocation: violin. Home and Office: Kearns Trust 301 Houghton Lab Ln Queenstown MD 21658-2500

KEARSE, AMALYA LYLE, federal judge; b. Vauxhall, N.J., June 11, 1937; d. Robert Freeman and Myra Lyle (Smith) K. B.A., Wellesley Coll., 1959; J.D. cum laude, U. Mich., 1962. Bar: N.Y. 1963, U.S. Supreme Ct. 1967. Assoc. Hughes, Hubbard & Reed, N.Y.C., 1962-69, ptnr., 1969-79; judge U.S. Ct. Appeals (2d cir.), 1979—. Lectr. evidence N.Y. U. Law Sch., 1968-69 Author: Bridge Conventions Complete, 1975, 3d edit., 1990, Bridge at Your Fingertips, 1980; translator, editor: Bridge Analysis, 1979; editor: Ofcl. Ency. of Bridge, 3d edit, 1976; mem. editorial bd. Charles Goren, 1974— . Bd. dirs. NAACP Legal Def. and Endl. Fund, 1977-79; bd. dirs. Nat. Urban League, 1978-79; trustee N.Y.C. YWCA, 1976-79, Am. Contract Bridge League Nat. Laws Commn., 1975— ; mem. Pres.'s Com. on Selection of Fed. Jud. Officers, 1977-78. Named Women's Pairs Bridge Champion Nat. div., 1971, 72, World div., 1986, Nat. Women's Teams Bridge Champion, 1987, 90, 91. Mem. ABA, Assn. of Bar of City of N.Y., Am. Law Inst., Lawyers Com. for Civil Rights Under Law (mem. exec. com. 1970-79). Office: US Ct Appeals US Courthouse 40 Foley SqRm 2001 New York NY 10007*

KEATING, FRANCIS ANTHONY, II, governor, lawyer; b. St. Louis, Feb. 10, 1944; s. Anthony Francis and Anne (Martin) K.; m. Catherine Dunn Heller, 1972; children: Carissa Herndon, Kelly Martin, Anthony Francis III. A.B., Georgetown U., 1966; J.D., U. Okla., 1969. Bar: Okla. 1969. Spl. agt. FBI, 1969-71; asst. dist. atty. Tulsa County, 1971-72; mem. Okla. Ho. of Reps., 1972-74, Okla. Senate, 1974-81; U.S. atty. No. Dist. Okla., 1981-84; asst. sec. U.S. Treasury Dept., Washington, 1985-88; assoc. atty. gen. Dept. Justice, 1988-89; gen. counsel, acting dep. sec. Dept. Housing and Urban Devel., Washington, 1989-93; gov. State of Okla., 1995—. Mem. Okla. Bar Assn. Office: Office Gov Ste 212 State Capitol Bldg Oklahoma City OK 73105*

KEATING, MICHAEL JOSEPH, lawyer; b. St. Louis, June 8, 1954; s. John David and Patricia Ann (Sullivan) K.; m. Maureen Ann Moder, Aug. 28, 1981; children: Sarah Kathleen, Brendan Michael. AB, Washington U., St. Louis, 1976; JD, St. Louis U., 1979. Bar: Mo. 1979, Ill. 1980. Law clk. Mo. Ct. Appeals, St. Louis, 1979-80, U.S. Dist. Ct. Ea. Dist., St. Louis, 1980-81; assoc. Bryan, Cave, McPheeters & McRoberts, 1981-83; corp. atty. Emerson Electric Co., 1983-85, sr. atty., 1985-87, asst. gen. counsel product liability, 1987—. Author: Designing an Effective Product Liaility Corporate Compliance Program, 1993; contbr. articles to profl. jours. Mem. Am. Law Inst., Mo. Athletic Club, Sigma Alpha Epsilon, Phi Delta Phi, Pi Sigma Alpha. Roman Catholic. Home: 11117 Apache Trl Saint Louis MO 63146-5627 Office: Emerson Electric Co PO Box 4100 8100 W Florissant Ave Saint Louis MO 63136-1494 E-mail: michael.keating@emrsn.com

KEATINGE, ROBERT REED, lawyer; b. Berkeley, Calif., Apr. 22, 1948; s. Gerald Robert and Elizabeth Jean (Benedict) K.; m. Katherine Lou Carr, Feb. 1, 1969 (div. Dec. 1981); 1 child, Michael Towne; m. Cornelia Elizabeth Wyma, Aug. 21, 1982; 1 child, Courtney Elizabeth. BA, U. Colo., 1970; JD, U. Denver, 1973, LLM, 1982. Bar: Colo. 1974, U.S. Dist. Ct. Colo. 1974, U.S. Ct. Appeals (10th cir.) 1977, U.S. Tax Ct. 1980. Ptnr. Kubie & Keatinge, Denver, 1974-76; pvt. practice, 1976; assoc. Richard Young, 1977-86; counsel Durham & Assoc. P.C., 1986-89, Durham & Baron, Denver, 1989-90; project editor taxation Shepard's/McGraw-Hill, Colorado Springs, Colo., 1990-96; of counsel Holland & Hart, LLP, Denver, 1992—. Lectr. law U. Denver, 1982-92, adj. prof. grad. tax program, 1983-94. Author, cons. (CD-ROM) Entity Expert, 1996; co-author: Ribstein and Keatinge on Limited Liability Companies, 1992; contbr. articles to profl. jours. and treatises. Spkr. to profl. socs. and univs. including AICPA, ALI-ABA, U. TEx., 1984—. Recipient Law Week award U. Denver Bur. Nat. Affairs, 1974. Fellow: Am. Coll. of Tax Counsel; mem.: ABA (chmn. subcom. ltd. liability cos. of com. on partnerships 1990—95, chmn. com. on partnerships 2000—, chmn. com. on taxation 1995—99, mem. ho. of dels. 1996—, editl. bd. ABA/BNA Lawyer's Manual on Professional Conduct 1998—, chair 2000—02, ABA/Nat. Conf. Commrs. on Uniform State Laws joint editl. bd. on uninc 1996—, ABA adviser to Uniform Ltd. Liability Co. Act 1995, ABA adviser to Revision of Uniform Ltd. Partnership Act 2001), Colo. Bar Assn. (ethics com., corp. code revision com., co-chmn. ltd. liability co. revision com., taxation sect. exec. coun. 1988—94, sec.-treas. 1991—92, chmn. 1993—94), Denver Bar Assn. Home: 460 S Marion Pky Apt 1904 Denver CO 80209-2544 E-mail: rkeatinge@hollandhart.com

KEATY, ROBERT BURKE, lawyer, writer, business consultant; b. Baton Rouge, July 7, 1949; s. Thomas St. Paul and Alicia (Armshaw) K.; m. Erin Kenny, July 6, 1973; children: Kellen Elizabeth, Kathryn Ellen, Robert Burke II, Kaneil Erin, Rory Bridgette-Anne. BS, U. La., 1971; JD, Tulane U., 1974. Bar: La. 1973, Tex. 1986. Law clk. to judge U.S. Dist. Ct. for Ea. Dist. La., New Orleans, 1974-76. Mem. pres.'s com. Offshore Tng. and Survival Ctr., U. Lafayette, 1988-89; co-chmn. United Giver Fund Jud. Legal, 1994, Bishops Charity Ball Legal Com., 1995. Member dean's adv. com. Tulane U. Law Sch., New Orleans, 1987; mem. dean's exec. adv. com. Coll. Bus. Adminstrn., U. La., Lafayette, 1991. Sears scholar, 1971, Teagle scholar, 1973; recipient Most Outstanding Alumnus award U. La. Coll. Bus., Lafayette, 1991. Fellow La. Bar Found. (lifetime charter mem.). Avocations: reading, woodworking, tennis, fishing, carpentry. E-mail: itsrealhilly@aol.com

KEEDY, CHRISTIAN DAVID, lawyer; b. Worcester, Mass., Jan. 9, 1945; BBA, Tulane U. La., 1967, JD, 1972. Bar: Fla. 1972; bd. cert. in admiralty and maritime law, Fla. Pvt. practice Christian D. Keedy, P.A., Coral Gables, Fla., 1981—. Mem. ABA, Maritime Law Assn. U.S., Southeastern Admiralty Law Inst. (dir. 1982-83), The Fla. Bar (chmn. 1981-82, admiralty law com.), Miami Maritime Arbitration Coun. (dir.). Admiralty, Federal civil litigation, State civil litigation. Office: Christian D Keedy PA 710 S Dixie Hwy Coral Gables FL 33146-2602

KEEFFE, JOHN ARTHUR, lawyer, director; b. Bklyn., Apr. 5, 1930; s. Arthur John and Mary Catherine (Daly) K.; m. Frances Elizabeth Rippetoe, July 24, 1952; children: Virginia Frances, Cynthia Louise, Amy Marie. AB, Cornell U., 1950; JD, U. Va., 1953. Bar: Va. 1953, N.Y. 1956. Asst. U.S. atty. so. dist. State of N.Y., 1955-57; assoc. Rogers, Hoge & Hills, N.Y., 1957-63; of counsel Havens, Wandless, Stitt & Tighe, 1963-65; ptnr. Keeffe & Costikyan, N.Y.C. and Washington, 1965-74, Keeffe Bros., N.Y.C. and Washington, 1974-77; sec., mng. dir. Saud Al-Farhan Inc., N.Y.C., 1979-80; pres., dir. J.A. Keeffe, P.C., Eastchester, N.Y., 1981—. Bd. dirs., sec. The Street Theater, White Plains, N.Y., 1973—. 1st lt. USAF, 1953-55. Mem. ABA, ATLA, N.Y. State Bar Assn., Va. Bar Assn., Westchester County Bar Assn. (dir. 1989-90, chmn. com. on fed. courthouse plans and procedures 1994—), N.Y. State Trial Lawyers Assn., Eastchester Bar Assn. (v.p. 1988-89, pres. 1989-90, dir. 1990—), Rotary (bd. dirs. 1991—, sec. 1991-92, pres.-elect 1992-93, pres. 1993-94, co-chair Eastchester Rotary Gift of Life 1993-94, co-chair dist. 7230 Gift of Life 1995-97). Republican. Congregationalist. Avocations: golf, reading. General civil litigation, General corporate, Estate planning. Home and Office: PO Box 855 Katonah NY 10536-0855

KEEGAN, JOHN E. lawyer; b. Spokane, Wash., Apr. 29, 1943; BA, Gonzaga U., 1965; LLB, Harvard U., 1968. Bar: Wash. 1968, U.S. Ct. Appeals (9th cir.) 1976, U.S. Supreme Ct. Gen. counsel Dept. Housing and Urban Devel., Washington, 1968-70; instr. in bus. sch. and inst. environ. studies U. Wash., 1973-76, instr. land use and environ. law, 1976-78; now ptnr. Davis, Wright & Tremaine, Seattle. Office: Davis Wright Tremaine 2600 Century Sq 1501 4th Ave Seattle WA 98101-1688

KEEGAN, JOHN ROBERT, lawyer, educator; b. Boston, Aug. 22, 1950; s. Francis Harold and Margaret (Huntley) K.; children: Kathleen Elizabeth, Margaret Mary, John Takao. BBA cum laude, Suffolk U., 1972, JD cum laude, 1976; LLM in Taxation, Boston U., 1980; chtd. fin. cons., CLU, Am. Coll., 1985. Bar: Mass. 1977. Group pension adminstr. New Eng. Life Ins. Co., Boston, 1972-75, pension legal specialist, 1975-78, group pension atty., 1978-80, pension atty., 1980-81; asst. counsel Sun Life Assurance Co. of Can., Wellesley Hills, Mass., 1981-83, advanced underwriting officer, 1983-87; assoc. Flynn, Joyce and Sheridan, Boston, 1987, R.W. Joyce PC, Boston, 1988-89; sr. pension atty. New Eng. Life Ins. Co., 1989-90; sr. rsch. atty. The Alexander Consulting Group, 1990-97; sr. cons. Coopers & Lybrand, 1997-98, Pricewaterhouse Coopers, Boston, 1998—. Instr. Bentley Coll., Waltham, Mass., 1981-88, adv. bd. 1984-88; Northeastern U., Boston, 1985-86, Mass. Soc. CPAs, Boston, 1984-87. Mem. editl. bd. Jour. Deferred Compensation, 1996—; contbr. articles to profl. publs. Mem. ABA, Boston Bar Assn. Roman Catholic. Avocations: softball, tennis, skiing. Estate planning, Pension, profit-sharing, and employee benefits.

KEELY, GEORGE CLAYTON, retired lawyer; b. Denver, Feb. 28, 1926; s. Thomas and Margaret (Clayton) K.; m. Jane Elisabeth Coffey, Nov. 18, 1950; children: Margaret Clayton, George C. (dec.), Mary Anne, Jane Elisabeth, Edward Francis, Kendall Anne. BS in Bus, U. Colo., 1948; LLB, Columbia U., 1951. Bar: Colo. 1951. Assoc. Fairfield & Woods, Denver, 1951-58, ptnr., 1958-86, sr. dir., 1986-90, of counsel, 1990-91, ret., 1991; v.p. Silver Corp., 1966-86; mem. exec. com. Timpte Industries, Inc., 1970-78, dir., 1980-89. Mem. Colo. Commn. Promotion Uniform State Laws, 1967—; regional planning adv. com. Denver Regional Coun. Govts., 1972-74; bd. dirs. Bow Mar Water and Sanitation Dist., 1970-74; trustee Town of Bow Mar, 1972-74; trustee, v.p. Silver Found., 1970-90, mem. bd., 1983-90; trustee, v.p. Denver Area coun. Boy Scouts Am., 1985-90; bd. dirs. Pub. Broadcasting of Colo., Inc., 1986-90, Sta. KCFR. With USAF, 1944-47. Fellow Am. Bar Found., Colo. Bar Found.; mem. ABA (ho. of dels. 1977-79), Denver Bar Assn. (life, Merit award 1980), Colo. Bar Assn. (life), Nat. Conf. Commrs. Uniform State Laws (sec. 1971-75, exec. com. 1971-79 , chmn. exec. com. 1975-77, pres. 1977-79, co-chmn. com. U.S.-Can. Transboundary Pollution Reciprocal Access Act 1979-82, chmn. com. Determination of Death Act 1979-80), Am. Law Inst., Cath. Lawyers Guild of Denver (dir. 1965-67), Denver Estate Planning Coun., U. Club of Denver, (dir. 1966-75, pres. 1973-74), Law Club of Denver (pres. 1966-67, Lifetime Achievement award, 1994), Pinehurst Country Club, Hundred Club, Cactus Club, Rotary, Phi Delta Phi, Beta Theta Pi, Beta Gamma Sigma. Banking, General corporate, Mergers and acquisitions. Home: 5220 W Longhorn St Littleton CO 80123-1408

KEENAN, BARBARA MILANO, state supreme court justice; Judge Gen. Dist. Ct., Fairfax County, Va., 1980-82, Circuit Ct., Fairfax County, 1982-85, Court of Appeals of Va., 1985-91; justice Supreme Court Va., Richmond, 1991—. Office: 2101 Parks Ave Ste 501 Virginia Beach VA 23451-4134*

KEENAN, JAMES FRANCIS, lawyer, insurance executive; b. Portland, Maine, Apr. 6, 1939; s. Michael Francis and Ruth Mary (Niles) K.; m. Sandra Annis, July 2, 1966; children— Tina, Michael, Angela, Paige, James, Jr. B.A., Bates Coll., 1961; J.D., Boston U., 1964, LL.M., 1975. Bar: Maine 1964, U.S. Dist. Ct. Maine 1965. Atty. Unionmutual Life Ins. Co., Portland, 1964-68, assoc. counsel, 1968-75, v.p., 1975— ; dir. Unionmutual Charitable Found., Portland, 1980-84. Author: (with Douglas Thornsjo) The Mutual Company, 1972. Trustee Bates Coll., Center Meml. Hosp., Standish, Maine, Sch. Adminstrv. Dist., Buxton, Maine. Fellow Am. Coll. Investment Counsel; mem. Am. Land Title Assn., Assn. Life Ins. Counsel, ABA, Maine Bar Assn. General corporate. Home: RR 1 Box 8450 Sebago Lake ME 04075-9801 Office: UNUM Life Ins Co Unionmutual Life Ins Co 2211 Congress St Portland ME 04122-0003

KEENAN, JOHN FONTAINE, federal judge; b. N.Y.C., Nov. 23, 1929; s. John Joseph and Veronica (Fontaine) K.; m. Diane R. Nicholson, Oct. 6, 1956; 1 child, Marie Patricia BBA, Manhattan Coll., N.Y., 1951; LLD (hon.), Manhattan Coll., 1989; LLB, Fordham U., 1954; LLD (hon.), Mt. St. Vincent Coll., 1989. Bar: N.Y. 1954, U.S. Dist. Ct. (so. dist.) N.Y. 1983. From asst. dist. atty. to chief asst. dist. atty. N.Y. County Dist. Atty.'s Office, 1956-76; spl. prosecutor, dep. atty. gen. City of N.Y., 1976-79; chmn. bd., pres. N.Y.C. Off-Track Betting Corp., 1979-82; criminal justice coord. City of N.Y., 1982-83; judge U.S. Dist. Ct. So. Dist., N.Y.C., 1983—; chief asst. dist. atty. Queens County Dist. Atty.'s Office, N.Y., 1973. Adj. prof. John Jay Coll. Criminal Justice, N.Y.C., 1979-83, Fordham U. Sch. Law, N.Y.C., 1992, 93; mem. Fgn. Intelligence Svc. Ct., 1994-2001, Judicial Panel on Multi-Dist. Litigation, 1998—. Contbr. articles to law jours. Chmn. Daytop Village, Inc., N.Y.C., 1981-83. Served with U.S. Army, 1954-56. Recipient Frank S. Hogan award Citizens Com. Control of Crime in N.Y., 1975, Emory R. Buckner award Federal Bar Coun., 1993; cert. of recognition Patrolmen's Benevolent Assn., 1976; 1st Ann. Hogan-Morgenthau Assocs. award N.Y. County Dist. Atty.'s Office, 1976, Medal of Achievement, 1992; Excellence award N.Y. State Bar Assn., 1978, award N.Y. Criminal Bar Assn., 1979, Disting. Faculty award Nat. Coll. Dist. Attys., 1978, Louis J. Lefkowitz award Fordham Urban Law Jour., 1983, Charles Carroll award Guild Cath. Lawyers, 1994, Ellis Island medal of honor, Nat. Ethnic Coalition of Orgns. Found., Inc., 1998. Mem. Amackassin Club, Skytop Club. Republican. Roman Catholic. Office: US Dist Ct US Courthouse 500 Pearl St Rm 1930 New York NY 10007-1316

KEENE, JOHN CLARK, lawyer, educator; b. Phila., Aug. 17, 1931; s. Floyd Elwood and Marthe (Bussiere) K.; m. Ana Maria Delgado, July 21, 1973; children: Lisa Keene Kerns, John, Suzanna Tonra, Katherine, Peter; stepchildren: Carlos, Rene, Mario, Raul, Silvio Navarro, Carmen Peláez. BA, Yale U., 1953; JD, Harvard U., 1959; M in City Planning, U. Pa., 1966. Bar: Pa. 1960. Assoc. Pepper, Hamilton & Scheetz, Phila., 1959-64; prof. city and regional planning U. Pa., 1968—, chmn., 1989-93, univ. ombudsman, 1978-84, chmn. faculty senate, 1998-99; ptnr. Coughlin, Keene & Assocs., 1981—. Vis. prof. U. Paris X, 1991. Author: (with Robert E. Coughlin) The Protection of Farmland, 1981, Growth Without Chaos, 1987, (with others) Untaxing Open Space, 1976, (with Samuel Hamill) Growth Management in New Jersey, 1989, (with Robert Coughlin and Joanne Denworth) Guiding Growth: Managing Urban Growth in Pennsylvania, 1991, 93, (with Julia Freedgood) Saving American Farmland: What Works, 1997. Trustee ex officio Phila. Mus. Art, 1978-80. Lt. USN, 1953-56. Fulbright fellow Tunisia, 1985. Mem. Am. Inst. Cert. Planners, Merion Cricket Club. Real property. Home: 1527 Montgomery Ave Bryn Mawr PA 19010-1659 Office: U Pa 127 Meyerson Hall Philadelphia PA 19104 E-mail: keenej@pobox.upenn.edu

KEENE, LONNIE STUART, lawyer; b. Milw., Sept. 13, 1954; s. Harold William and Phyllis K. BS, U.S. Mil. Acad., 1976; MPA, Harvard U., 1984; JD, NYU, 1998. Bar: N.Y. Asst. prof., instr. U.S. Mil. Acad., West Point, N.Y., 1984-87; asst. army attache U.S. Embassy, Beijing, 1988-90; mem. policy planning staff U.S. Dept. State, Washington, 1990-94; sr. policy analyst, office sci. & tech. policy The White House, 1994-95; assoc. Linklaters, London, 1998-99, Milbank, Tweed, Hadley & McCloy, London, 1999—. Lt. col. U.S. Army, 1976-95. Decorated Legion of Merit; Olmsted scholar George and Carol Olmstead Found., Beijing, 1981-83. Mem. Coun. Fgn. Rels. (Internat. Affairs fellow 1990-91), Harvard Club N.Y.C. Avocations: golf, art, travel, skiing. General corporate, Mergers and acquisitions, Securities. Office: Milbank Tweed Hadley & McCloy 1 Chase Manhattan Plz New York NY 10005-1413 E-mail: lkeene@milbank.com

KEENEY, STEVEN HARRIS, lawyer; b. Phila., Oct. 1, 1949; s. Arthur Hail and Virginia (Tripp) K.; m. Jean Ashburn, May 10, 1974 (div. Oct. 1986); 1 child, Christian Jeffrey. BA, Trinity Coll., Hartford, Conn., 1971; MA, Hartford Sem. Found., 1973; JD, U. Conn., 1980. Bar: Ky. 1980, U.S. Dist. Ct. (we. dist.) Ky. 1981, U.S. Dist. Ct. (ea. dist.) Ky. 1983. Staff reporter/edn. editor The Hartford Courant, 1971-74; asst. to supt. Hartford Pub. Schs., 1974-77; assoc. Igor Sikorsky & Assocs., Hartford, 1979-80, Brown, Todd & Heyburn, Louisville, 1980-82; ptnr. Barnett & Alagia, 1982-88, Keeney & Willock, Louisville, 1988-90; prin. Amerilaw, 1990-93; pres. LawTech Svcs. Co., 1993—; mng. mem. Trautwein & Keeney PLLC, 1993—. Co-author/editor: Death Benefit: A Lawyer Uncovers A 20 Year Pattern of Seduction, 1993, 94, Reader's Digest Today's Best Non-Fiction Vol. 24, 1994; contbr. articles to profl. jours. Bd. dirs. Hospice of Louisville, Inc., 1984-86; exec. dir. Juvenile Justice Pub. Edn. Project, West Hartford, Conn., 1978-80; pres. bd. dirs. Stage One: Louisville Children's Theatre, 1982-83; founding bd. dirs. Ky. Citizens for Arts, Frankfort, 1983; mem. Lebanon (Conn.) Bd. Edn., 1975-80; campaign mgr. Mazzoli 3d C.D. Ky., Jefferson County, 1982, 84; elder 2d Presbyn. Ch., Louisville, 1984-86. Recipient Disting. Contbn. award Nat. Com. for Prevention of Child Abuse, Ky. chpt., 1982, Disting. Svc. award Conn. Assn. Bds. of Edn., 1976, Profl. Achievement for Gen. Reporting Series award Soc. Profl. Journalists, Sigma Delta Chi, Conn. chpt. 1974. Mem. ABA (editl. com. The Tax Lawyer 1984-89), Assn. Trial Lawyers of Am., Nat. Assn. Criminal Def. Lawyers, Ky. Acad. Trial Atty's., Ky. Bar Assn., Louisville Bar Assn., Million Dollar Advocates Forum, Jefferson Club, Hon. Order of Ky. Cols. Democrat. Presbyterian. Avocations: bibliophile, marksman, golf. Bankruptcy, General civil litigation, General corporate. Office: Trautwein & Keeney PLLC 1 Riverfront Plz Ste 510 Louisville KY 40202-2923 E-mail: steve583fi@aol.com

KEETON, ROBERT ERNEST, federal judge; b. Clarksville, Tex., Dec. 16, 1919; s. William Robert and Ernestine (Tuten) K.; m. Betty E. Baker, May 28, 1941; children: Katherine, William Robert. BBA, U. Tex., 1940, LLB, 1941; SJD, Harvard U., 1956; LLD (hon.), William Mitchell Coll., 1983, Lewis and Clark Coll., 1988. Bar: Tex. 1941, Mass. 1955. Assoc. firm Baker, Botts, Andrews & Wharton (and successors), Houston, 1941-42, 45-51; assoc. prof. law So. Meth. U., 1951-54; Thayer teaching fellow Harvard U., 1953-54, asst. prof., 1954-56, prof. law, 1956-73, Langdell prof., 1973-79; assoc. dean Harvard, 1975-79; judge Fed. Dist. Ct., Boston, 1979—. Commr. on Uniform State Laws from Mass., 1971-79; trustee Flaschner Jud. Inst., 1979-86; exec. dir. Nat. Inst. Trial Advocacy, 1973-76; ednl. cons., 1976-79; mem. com. on ct. adminstrn. U.S. Jud. Conf., 1985-87, mem. standing com. on rules, 1987-90, chmn., 1990-93. Author: Trial Tactics and Methods, 1954, 2d edit., 1973, Cases and Materials on the Law of Insurance, 1960, 2d edit., 1977, Legal Cause in the Law of Torts, 1963, Venturing To Do Justice, 1969, (with Jeffrey O'Connell) Basic Protection for the Traffic Victim: A Blueprint for Reforming Automobile Insurance, 1965, After Cars Crash: The Need for Legal and Insurance Reform, 1967, (with Page Keeton) Cases and Materials on the Law of Torts, 1971, 2d edit., 1977, Basic Text on Insurance Law, 1971, (with others) Tort and Accident Law, 1983, 2d edit., 1989, (with others) Prosser & Keeton, Torts, 5th edit., 1984, Pocket Part, 1988, (with Alan Widiss) Insurance Law, 1988, Judging, 1990, Judging the American Legal System, 1999; also articles. Served to lt. comdr. USNR, 1942-45, PTO, 1945-56. Recipient Wm. B. Jones award Nat. Inst. Trial Advocacy, 1980; recipient Leon Green award U. Tex. Law Rev., 1981, Francis Rawle award Am. Law Inst.-ABA, 1983, Samuel E. Gates litigation award Am. Coll. Trial Lawyers, 1984 Fellow Am. Bar Found., mem., Am. Acad. Arts and Scis., Am. Bar Assn., Mass. Bar Assn., State Bar Tex., Am. Law Inst., Am. Risk and Ins. Assn., Chancellors, Friars, Order of Coif, Beta Gamma Sigma, Beta Alpha Psi, Phi Delta Phi, Phi Eta Sigma. Office: US Dist Ct 1 Courthouse Way Ste 3130 Boston MA 02210-3005

KEHL, RANDALL HERMAN, executive, consultant, lawyer; b. Furstenfeldbruck, Fed. Republic Germany, May 18, 1954; came to U.S., 1955; s. Raymond Herman and Annabelle (Fair) K.; m. Sharon Kay Barnes; children: Lindsey Elizabeth, Jessica Anne, Austin Randall, Ky Randall. BS, USAF Acad., 1976; MBA, U. N.D., 1980; JD, Pepperdine U., 1983. Bar: N.D. 1983, D.C. 1988, U.S. Supreme Ct. 1990. Commd. 2d lt. USAF, 1976, advanced through grades to maj., 1986, chief civil law, 1983-84, chief criminal law, 1984-85; squadron commdr. Alaska Air Command, Anchorage, 1985, chief def. counsel, 1985-86; dep. base atty. Kirtland AFB, Albuquerque, 1986-89; spl. asst. U.S. atty. U.S. Dept. Justice, 1986-89; chief energy litigation Office of USAF JAG, Washington, 1989-90; White House fellow, 1990-91; chmn., CEO POD Assocs., Inc., 1992-97; cons., counsel to DESA-office of sec. of def. U.S. Dept. Def., Albuquerque, 1993; prin. Randall H. Kehl Consulting, 1993-98; chmn. RHK Capital Group Internat., San Antonio, 1997—; pres., CEO Safe Zone Sys., Inc., 1998-99; CEO Optomec, Inc., 2000—. Mem. staff Pres.'s Coun. on Competiveness, 1990-91; vice chmn. White House Working group on Commercialization of Fed. Lab. Tech., 1991; chmn. Candeli, Ltd., Kerorioni, Ltd., Rep. of Georgia, 1992-96; adj. instr. law U. Alaska, 1985-86; bd. dirs., counsel Kirtland Fed. Credit Union, Albuquerque; bd. dirs., sec. Triad Comm., Inc., Albuquerque; chmn. bd. POD Assocs., Inc., 1988-90. Asst. scoutmaster Boy Scouts Am., Minot, N.D., 1977-80; tchr. Officers Christian Fellowship, Minot, 1977-80; civic arbitrator Mediation and Conciliation Svc., 1983-86; mem. pvt. sch. bd. Anchorage, 1984-85; mem. Gov.'s Task Force for Utility Corp. Restructuring, 1987; vice-chmn. N.Mex. Gov.-Elect Transition Team, 1994, Gov.'s Bus. Adv. Coun., 1995—; mem. steering com. Rep. Campaigns, 1995—; co-chmn. N. Mex. Character Counts in the Workplace, 1996—; bd. dirs. Kirtland Partnership Com., 1995—, N.Mex. Ctr. for Civic Values, 1997—; dir. Albuquerque Character Counts, 1998—. Mem. ABA, AMA, Albuquerque Acad. Capital Devel. Com. and Assoc. Trustee, The Forman Sch. (capital devel. com.), Tanoan Country Club, Phi Delta Phi. Republican. Presbyterian. Avocations: swimming, skiing, scuba diving, sailing, golf. Office: Ste 415 5100 John D Ryan Blvd San Antonio TX 78245-3534

KEHOE, DENNIS JOSEPH, lawyer; b. Culver City, Calif., Nov. 12, 1937; s. Ignatius ennis and Anne Theresa (Conroy) K.; m. Jacqueline Mona De Quincy, Aug. 25, 1962; children: Theresa, Suzanne, Patrick, Michael, Kevin. BS in Commerce, U. Santa Clara, 1960; LLB, U. Calif. Hastings Coll. Law, 1963. Bar: Calif. 1964, U.S. Dist. Ct. (no. dist.) Calif. 1964, U.S. Ct. Appeals (9th cir.) 1964, U.S. Supreme Ct. 1980. Asst. county counsel Santa Cruz County, Calif., 1964-66; assoc. Adams, Levin, Kehoe, Bosso, Sachs & Bates and predecessor, Santa Cruz, 1966-70, ptnr., 1970-87; sole practice, 1987—. Mem. Calif. State Bar Assn., Calif. Trial Lawyers Assn., Santa Cruz County Bar Assn. State civil litigation, Condemnation, Personal injury. Home: 607 Cliff Dr Aptos CA 95003-5311 Office: 311 Bonita Dr Aptos CA 95003-4891 E-mail: kehoelaw@yahoo.com

KEINER, CHRISTIAN MARK, lawyer; b. Omaha, Mar. 16, 1953; s. John Frederick Keiner and Geraldine Elizabeth (Smith) Eadie; m. Rosemary Monique White, Nov. 21, 1980; 1 child, Colin MacGregor. BA with high honors, U. Calif., Santa Barbara, 1977; JD with distinction, U. of Pacific, 1980. Bar: Calif. 1980, U.S. Ct. Appeals (9th cir.) 1988, U.S. Supreme Ct. 1991. Assoc. Biddle, Walters, Bukey, Sacramento, 1980-82, Biddle and Hamilton, Sacramento, 1982-92; pvt. practice, 1992-98; ptnr. Girard and Vinson, 1998—. Contbr. articles to law jours. Bd. dirs. Calif.

Found. for Improvement Employer-Employee Rels., Sacramento, 1994-99, Calif. Coun. Sch. Attys., Sacramento, 1996-98; instr., mem. labor-mgmt. adv. com. U. Calif. Davis Ext., Sacramento, 1986-99. Recipient award for adminstrv. law Am. Jurisprudence, 1979. Mem. ABA (pub. law sect.), Sacramento County Bar (adminstv., pub. and employment law sects.), Sacramento Capitol Club, Harry S. Truman Club (pres. 1992), Order of Coif. Democrat. Catholic. Administrative and regulatory, Appellate, Education and schools. Office: Girard and Vinson 1006 4th St 8th Fl Sacramento CA 95814-3326 E-mail: keiner@gandv.com

KEITER, AARON, lawyer; b. Phila., May 26, 1946; s. Joseph and Lisa (Brahen) K.; B.S., Pa. State U., 1968; M.B.A., Widener Coll., 1973; J.D., U. Houston, 1976; m. Eileen Marsha Brown, Sept. 16, 1972; children—Justin Alan, Ashley Rochelle. Trader investment div. Phila. Nat. Bank, 1972-73; admitted to Tex. bar, 1976; tax specialist Coopers & Lybrand, Houston, 1976-77; gen. counsel Jetero Corp., Houston, 1977-79, Allison/Walker Interests, Inc., Houston, 1979-81; partner firm Goldberg & Keiter, Houston, 1981-83; sr. ptnr. Keiter, Blustein, DuBois & Krocker, Houston, 1983-85; ptnr. Keiter & Blustein, P.C., Houston, 1985-88; of counsel Weiner, Strother and Blustein, 1988-89; ptnr. Neely & Keiter, P.C., 1989-91, pvt. practice, 1991-2001 mem. faculty U. Houston Law Sch., 1975-76. Served with U.S. Army, 1968-72; lt. col. Res. Decorated Bronze Star, Air medal, Joint Service Commendation medal (retired); recipient Am. Jurisprudence award, 1974; Sutherland scholar, 1964-66; ROTC scholar, 1966-68. Mem. Am. Bar Assn., State Bar Tex., Houston Bar Assn., Fed. Bar Assn. Republican. Jewish. Club: Houston City. Home: 4545 Mt Vernon Houston TX 77006 Office: 6371 Richmond Ave # 100 Houston TX 77057-5905

KEITH, ALEXANDER MACDONALD, retired state supreme court chief justice, lawyer; b. Rochester, Minn., Nov. 22, 1928; s. Norman and Edna (Alexander) K.; m. Marion Sanford, April 29, 1955; children: Peter Sanford (dec.), Ian Alexander, Douglas Scott. BA, Amherst Coll., 1950; JD, Yale U., 1953. Assoc. counsel, mem. Mayo Clinic, Rochester, 1955-60; state sen. Olmstead County, St. Paul, 1959-63; lt. gov. State of Minn., 1963-67; pvt. practice, Rochester, 1960-73; ptnr. Dunlap Keith Finseth Berndt and Sandberg, 1973-89; assoc. justice Minn. Supreme Ct., St. Paul, 1989-90, chief justice, 1990-98; ret., 1998; of counsel Dunlap & Seeger P.A., Rochester, Minn., 1998—. Sen. del. White House Conf. on Aging, Washington, 1960; U.S. del. UN Delegation for Funding Developing Countries, Geneva, 1966; bd. dirs. Rochester Grad. Edn. Adv. Com., 1988-89, Ability Bldg. Ctr. Inc. 1st lt. USMC, 1953-55, Korea. Named Outstanding Freshman Senator, Minn. Senate, St. Paul. Home: 5225 Meadow Crossing Rd SW Rochester MN 55902-3506 Office: Dunlap & Seeger PA PO Box 549 Rochester MN 55903-0549 Fax: 507-288-9342

KEITH, DAMON JEROME, federal judge; b. Detroit, July 4, 1922; s. Perry A. and Annie L. (Williams) K.; m. Rachel Boone, Oct. 18, 1953; children: Cecile Keith, Debbie, Gilda. BA, W.Va. State Coll., 1943; JD, Howard U., 1949; LLM, Wayne State U., 1956; PhD (hon.), U. Mich., Howard U., Wayne State U., Mich. State U., N.Y. Law Sch., Detroit Coll. Law, W.Va. State Coll., U. Detroit, Atlanta U., Lincoln U., Marygrove Coll., Detroit Inst. Tech., Shaw Coll., Ctrl. State U., Yale U., Loyola Law Sch., L.A., Ea. Mich. U., Va. Union U., Ctrl. Mich. U., Morehouse Coll., Western Mich. U., Tuskegee U., Georgetown U., Hofstra U., DePaul U. Bar: Mich. 1949. Atty. Office Friend of Ct., Detroit, 1952-56; sr. ptnr. firm Keith, Conyers Anderson, Brown & Wahls, 1964-67; mem. Wayne County Bd. Suprs., 1958-63; dist. judge U.S. Dist. Ct. (ea. dist.) Mich., 1967-77, chief judge, 1975-77; judge U.S. Ct. Appeals (6th cir.), Detroit, 1977-95, sr. judge, 1995—. Mem. Wayne County (Mich.) Bd. Suprs., 1958-63; chmn. Mich. Civil Rights Commn., 1964-67; pres. Detroit Housing Commn., 1958-67; commr. State Bar Mich., 1960-67; mem. Mich. Com. Manpower Devel. and Vocat. Tng., 1964, Detroit Mayor's Health Adv. Com., 1969; rep. dist. judges 6th Cir. Jud. Conf., 1975-77; adv. com. on codes of conduct Jud. Conf. U.S., 1979-86; subcom. on supporting pers. Jud. Conf. Com. on Ct. Adminstrn., 1983-87; chmn. Com. on the Bicentennial of Constn. of Sixth Cir., 1985—; nat. chmn. Jud. Conf. Com. on the Bicentennial of Constn., 1987—; mem. Commn. on the Bicentennial of U.S. Constn., 1990; lectr. Howard U., 1972, Ohio State U. Law Sch., 1992, N.Y. Law Sch., 1992; guest lectr. Howard U. Law Sch., 1981; Bicentennial of Constn. lectr. W.Va. State Coll., 1987; keynote speaker Black Law Students Assn., Harvard Law Sch., 1987. Contbr. articles to profl. jours. Trustee Med. Corp. Detroit; trustee Interlochen Arts Acad., Cranbrook Sch., U. Detroit, Mich. chpt. Leukemia Soc. Am.; mem. Citizen's Adv. Com. Equal Ednl. Opportunity Detroit Bd. Edn.; gen. co-chmn. United Negro Coll. Fund Detroit; 1st v.p. emeritus Detroit chpt. NAACP; mem. com. mgmt. Detroit YMCA, Detroit coun. Boy Scouts Am., Detroit Arts Commn; vice chmn. Detroit Symphony Orch.; vis. com. Wayne State U. Law Sch.; adv. coun. U. Notre Dame Law Sch.; bd. dirs. Detroit Bd. Table, NCCJ; deacon Tabernacle Missionary Bapt. Ch.; chmn. Citizen's Coun. for Mich. Pub. Univs. With AUS, World War II. Recipient Mich. Chronicle outstanding Citizen award, 1960. 64. 74, Alumni citation Wayne State U., 1968, Ann. Jud. award, 1971, Citizen award Mich. State U., Disting. Svc. award Howard U., 1972, Jud. Independence award, 1973, Spingarn medal NAACP, 1974, Fed. Judge of Yr. award, Black Law Students Assn., 1974, award for Outstanding Contbns. to Black Community, Nat. Assn. Black Social Workers, 1974, Judge of Yr. award Nat. Conf. Black Lawyers, 1974, Bill of Rights award Jewish Community Coun., 1977, A. Philip Randolph award Detroit Coalition Black Trade Unionists, 1981, Human Rights Day award B'nai B'rith Women's Coun. Met. Detroit, Robert L. Millender award So. Christian Leadership Conf. Mich. chpt., 1982, Afro-Asian Inst. award Histadrut in Israel, 1982, civil rights lectr. award, Creighton U. Ahmanson Law Ctr., 1983, Nat. Human Rels. award Greater Detroit Roundtable of NCCJ, 1984, Knights of Charity award Pontifical Inst. for Mission Extension, 1986, Disting. Pub. Svc. award Mich. Anti-Defamation League of B'nai B'rith, 1987, Nat. Chpt. award, 1988, Black Achievement award Equitable Fin. Cos., 1987, Menorah award Afro-Asian Inst. Histadrut of Israel, 1988, Dr. George Derry award Marygrove Coll. Detroit, One Nation award The Patriots Found./GM, 1989, 1st Ann. Move Detroit Forward award City of Detroit, 1990, Gov's. Minuteman award Rotary Club Lansing, 1991; named 1 of 100 Most Influential Black Ams. Ebony Mag., 1971-92; Damon J. Keith Elementary Sch. named in his honor Detroit Bd. Edn., 1974; Damon J. Keith Ann. Civic and Humanitarian award established in his honor Highland Park YMCA, 1984; 15th Mich. Legal Milestone The Uninvited Ear presented in honor of The Keith Decision, 1991. Mem. ABA (coun. sect. legal edn. and admission to bar), Nat. Bar Assn. (William H. Hastie award Jud. Coun., 8th Ann. equal Justice award), Mich. Bar Assn. (champion of justice award), Detroit Bar Assn. (pres'. award), Nat. Lawyers Guild, Am. Judicature Soc., Alpha Phi Alpha. Baptist (deacon). Club: Detroit Cotillion. Office: US Ct Appeals US Courthouse 231 W Lafayette Blvd Rm 240 Detroit MI 48226-2779*

KEITH, JOHN A.C. lawyer; b. Washington, Aug. 22, 1946; BA, U. Va., 1968, JD, 1974. Bar: Va. 1975, D.C. 1976. Law clk. Hon. Albert V. Bryan, Jr. U.S. Dist. Ct. (ea. dist.) Va., 1974-75; ptnr. Blankingship & Keith, Fairfax, Va. Fellow Am. Bar Found.; mem. ABA, Am. Counsel Assn., Va. State Bar (10th dist. com. 1983-86, chmn. 1985-86, chmn. standing com. on legal ethics 1996-97, bar coun. 1991—, exec. com. 1993—, pres.-elect 1997-98, pres. 1998—), Fairfax Bar Assn. General civil litigation, Personal injury, Real property. Office: Blankingship & Keith PC 4020 University Dr Ste 312 Fairfax VA 22030-6802 E-mail: JKeith@blankeith.com

KEITHLEY, BRADFORD GENE, lawyer; b. Nov. 23, 1951; s. Sanderson Irish and Joan G. (Kenneday) K.; m. Ginger W. Wilhelmi, Mar. 26, 1994; children: Paul Michael, Rachel Austin Bernstein. BS, U. Tulsa, 1973; JD, U. Va., 1976. Bar: Va. 1976, Okla. 1978, D.C. 1979. Atty. Office of Gen. Counsel to Sec. USAF, Washington, 1976-78; ptnr. Hall, Estill, Hardwick, Gable, Collingsworth and Nelson, Tulsa, 1978-84; sr. v.p. gen. counsel Arkla, Inc. (now NorAm Energy Corp. divsn. Reliant Energy, Inc.), Shreveport, La., 1984-90; ptnr. head global oil, gas and power practice team Jones, Day, Reavis and Pogue, Dallas, 1990—. Mem. ABA, Fed. Energy Bar Assn., Va. State Bar, Okla. Bar Assn., D.C. Bar Assn., Am. Gas Assn. (mem. legal sect.), Dallas Petroleum Club. Federal civil litigation, FERC practice, Oil, gas, and mineral. Home: 12652 Sunlight Dr Dallas TX 75230-1856 Office: Jones Day Reavis & Pogue 2727 N Harwood Dallas TX 75201-1515

KELAHER, JAMES PEIRCE, lawyer; b. Orlando, Fla., Oct. 28, 1951; s. Philip James and Neva Cecelia (Peirce) K. BA, U. Cen. Fla., 1973; JD, Fla. State U., 1981. Bar: Fla. 1981, U.S. Dist. Ct. (mid. dist.) Fla. 1982, U.S. Ct. Appeals (11th cir.) 1983, U.S. Supreme Ct.; cert. civil trial law. Assoc. Law Office of Nolan Carter, P.A., Orlando, 1981-83, Law Office of James Kelaher, P.A., Orlando, 1983-87; ptnr. Kelaher & Wieland, P.A., 1987—, Kelaher, Wieland and Hilado, P.A., Orlando, 1996-98, Kelaher Law Offices, P.A., Orlando, 1998—. Contbr. articles to profl. jours. Eagle benefactor Rep. Party. Mem. ABA, ATLA (sustaining), Orange County Bar Assn., Acad. Fla. Trial Lawyers (sec. 1994-95, treas. 1995-96, pres. 1997-98, bd. dirs. coll. diplomates, membership exec. com. bd. trustees Fla. lawyers action group), Ctrl. Fla. Trial Lawyers Assn. (pres. 1992-94). Roman Catholic. Avocations: tennis, golf, snow skiing, fishing. General civil litigation, Personal injury. Office: Kelaher Law Offices 800 N Magnolia Ave Ste 1301 Orlando FL 32803-3255 E-mail: jim@kelaherlaw.com

KELEPECZ, BETTY PATRICE, protective services official, lawyer; b. Santa Monica, Calif., Nov. 13, 1955; d. Andrew J. and Doris L. Giba; m. Steve T. Kelepecz, Sept. 3, 1983. AS, Antelope Valley Coll., 1975; BS in Biology, U. So. Calif., L.A., 1977; JD, Southwestern U., 1990; grad., FBI Nat. Acad., 1992. Bar: Calif. 1990, U.S. Dist. Ct. (ctrl. dist.) Calif. 1991. Microbiologist Rachelle Labs., Long Beach, Calif., 1978-80; police officer I, II, III, background investigator L.A. Police Dept., 1980-85, detective I S.W. Cmty. Police Sta., 1985-86, sgt. I Pacific, 77th and West L.A. patrol divsn., 1986-88, sgt. I ops. South Bur., 1988-89, sgt. II planning and rsch. divsn., 1989-90, lt. I Harbor Cmty. Police Sta., 1990-91, lt. II Ops.-South Bur., 1991, lt. II Office of the Chief of Police, 1991-93, capt. I Harbor Cmty. Police Sta., 1993-95, capt. I Pacific Cmty. Police Sta., 1995-96; owner, ptnr. Law Offices of Pheil & Kelepecz, Long Beach, Calif., 1995-99; capt. II West Traffic divsn. L.A. Police Dept., 1996, capt. III Sci. Investigation divsn., 1996-97, comdr. Cmty. Policing Group, 1997, comdr. Ops.-West Bur., 1997-98, comdr. Pers. Group, 1998—. Spkr., trainer and cons. in field. Recipient Am. Jurisprudence Book award, 1987, Congratulatory cert. Mayor Riordan, 1997, Affirmative Action Assn. Women Recognition for women leaders and pacesetters, 1997, Congress Racial Equality Calif. commendation, 1997; named Outstanding Young Women of Am., 1988. Mem. ABA, FBI Nat. Acad. Assocs., Internat. Assn. Chiefs Police (com. mem. major city chiefs human resources), Nat. Assn. Women Law Enforcement Execs. (past pres., charter), Calif. Bar Assn., L.A. County Bar Assn., L.A. County Police Officer's Assn., L.A. Police Command Officer's Assn. (com. mem.), L.A. Women Police Officer's Assn., Police Exec. Rsch. Forum, Rotary Club Westchester, Delta Theta Phi.

KELFER, MARVIN GERALD (JERRY KELFER), lawyer; b. Chgo., Mar. 6, 1930; s. Morris and Goldye (Kahn) K.; m. Roxana Michael, Apr. 9, 1960; children— Dana, Traci, Leslie. B.B.A., U. Tex., 1951; J.D. magna cum laude, St. Mary's U., 1960. Bar: Tex. 1960, U.S. Supreme Ct. 1980. With Morris Kelfer & Son Furniture Mfg., San Antonio, 1960-62; assoc. Waitz, Bretz & Collins Attys.-at-law, San Antonio, 1962-65; house counsel Travis Savs. & Loans Assn., San Antonio, 1965-68, pres., 1976— , chmn. bd., 1978— ; sole practice, San Antonio, 1968-73; ptnr. Kelfer & Coatney, P.C., Attys.-at-law, San Antonio, 1973-76; sr. mem. Brock & Kelfer, San Antonio, 1983— . Bd. dirs. San Antonio Econ. Found., 1978-84; pres. Temple Beth El, San Antonio, 1984-86; active Reagan/Bush campaign Republican Party, San Antonio, 1980, 84; alt. del. Rep. Nat. Conv., Detroit, 1980; mem. Rep. State Fin. Com., San Antonio, 1980; mem. Bd. Fgn. Scholarships, Washington, 1983-86; U.S. Holocaust Meml. Council. Served with USAF, 1951-55; Labrador. Recipient award for Advt., Freedoms Found., Valley Forge, Pa., 1984. Mem. State Bar Tex., ABA, San Antonio Bar Assn., Tex. Savs. and Loan League (chmn. atty. com. 1977-78, 83-84, bd. dirs. 1984-87 , chmn. nat. rep. com. 1979-80), U.S. League Savs. Instns. (constn. com. 1981), Phi Delta Phi. Jewish. Office: Travis Savs and Loan Assn 9311 San Pedro Ave San Antonio TX 78216-4458

KELLEHER, DANIEL FRANCIS, lawyer; b. Wilmington, Del., May 8, 1935; s. Harry James and Marjorie (Lancaster) K.; children: Hillary, Brendan, Peter; m. Jane Mignanelli, Dec. 27, 1991. AB, St. Marys Sem. and U., 1958; LLB, Georgetown U., 1961. Bar: D.C. 1962, Del. 1962. Ptnr. Theisen, Lank & Kelleher, Wilmington, 1962-72; assoc. judge Del. Family Ct., 1972-78; ptnr. Trzuskowski, Kipp, Kelleher & Pearce PA, Wilmington, 1978—. Atty. Del. State Senate, 1967-68. Bd. dirs. YMCA, 1974-81; active Del. Alcoholism Coun., 1974-81, pres., 1977-80; bd. dirs. Beechwood Sch., 1973-80, pres., 1975-80; trustee, chmn. Del. Childrens Trust Fund, 1985—. Mem. ABA, Del. State Bar Assn., Am. Judicature Soc., Nat. Coun. Juvenile Ct. Judges, Greenville Country Club (Wilmington, v.p. 1980-82). Roman Catholic. Family and matrimonial, General practice, Personal injury. Address: PO Box 429 Wilmington DE 19899-0429 E-mail: dkelleher@tkkp.com

KELLEHER, ROBERT JOSEPH, federal judge; b. N.Y.C., Mar. 5, 1913; s. Frank and Mary (Donovan) K.; m. Gracyn W. Wheeler, Aug. 14, 1940; children: R. Jeffrey, Karen Kathleen Kelleher King. A.B., Williams Coll., 1935; LL.B., Harvard U., 1938. Bar: N.Y. 1939, Calif. 1942, U.S. Supreme Ct 1954. Atty. War Dept., 1941-42; asst. U.S. atty. So. Dist. Calif., 1948-50; pvt. practice Beverly Hills, 1951-71; U.S. dist. judge, 1971-83; sr. judge U.S. Dist. Ct. 9th Cir., 1983—. Mem. So. Calif. Com. Olympic Games, 1964; capt. U.S. Davis Cup Team, 1962-63; treas. Youth Tennis Found. So. Calif., 1961-64. Served to lt. USNR, 1942-45. Recipient Bicentennial Medal award Williams Coll., 2001; enshrined in Internat. Tennis Hall of Fame, 2000. Mem. So. Calif. Tennis Assn. (v.p. 1958-64, pres. 1983-85), U.S. Lawn Tennis Assn. (pres. 1967-68), Internat. Lawn Tennis Club U.S.A., Gt. Britain, France, Can., Mex., Australia, India, Israel, Japan, All Eng. Lawn Tennis and Croquet (Wimbledon), Harvard Club (N.Y./So. Calif.), Williams Club (N.Y.), L.A. Country Club, Delta Kappa Epsilon. Home: 15 St Malo Bch Oceanside CA 92054-5854 Office: US Dist Ct 255 E Temple St Ste 830 Los Angeles CA 90012-3334

KELLER, GLEN ELVEN, JR. lawyer; b. Longmont, Colo., Dec. 21, 1938; s. Glenn Elven and Elsie Mildred (Hogsett) K.; m. Elizabeth Ann Kauffman, Aug. 14, 1960; children: Patricia Carol, Michael Ashby. BS in Bus., U. Colo., 1960; JD, U. Denver, 1964. Bar: Colo. 1964, U.S. Dist. Ct. Colo. 1964, U.S. Ct. Appeals (10th cir.) 1982. Assoc. Phelps, Hall & Keller and predecessor, Denver, 1964-67, ptnr., 1967-73; asst. atty. gen. State of Colo., 1973-74; judge U.S. Bankruptcy Ct., Dist. Colo., 1974-82; ptnr. Davis, Graham & Stubbs LLP, Denver, 1982—. Lectr. law U. Denver, 1977-87; adj. prof., 1987-98, Frank E. Rickston Jr. adj. prof. law, 1998—; mem. ct. adminstrn. com. Jud. Conf. U.S.; dir., mem. fin. com. sch. constrn. Colo. Lawyers' Com., 1997-2000, dir., mem. exec. com., 1999-2000, chmn. task force on sch. discipline, 1999-2000; bd. dirs. Western Stock Show Assoc. Mem. Colo. Bd. Health, 1968-74, pres., 1970-74; pres., dir. The Westernaires, Golden, Colo., Jefferson County R-1 Sch. Bd., 1984-89. Named Colo. Horse Person of Yr., Colo. Horse Coun., 1999. Fellow Am. Coll. Bankruptcy; mem ABA, Colo. Bar Assn., Denver Bar Assn., Nat. Conf. Bankruptcy Judges, Law Club. Republican. Bankruptcy, Federal civil litigation, Contracts commercial. Office: Davis Graham & Stubbs LLP 1550 17th St Ste 500 Denver CO 80202-1202

KELLER, JAMES, state supreme court justice; b. Harlan, 1942; m. Elizabeth Keller; 2 children. Student, Ea. Ky. U.; JD, U. Ky. Pvt. practice; master commr. Fayette Cir. Ct., 1969-76, judge, 1976-99; justice Ky. Supreme Ct., 1999—. Mem. Ky. Bar Assn., Fayette County Bar Assn. Office: Supreme Ct Ky 155 E Main St Ste 200 Lexington KY 40507-1332 E-mail: JamesKeller@mail.aoc.state.ky.us*

KELLER, JOHN WARREN, lawyer; b. Niagara Falls, Aug. 6, 1954; s. Joseph and Edith Lilian (Kilvington) K.; m. Sandra D. Hubbard, Dec. 18, 1981; children: Sean, Christopher. BA, Rider U., 1976; JD, Coll. William and Mary, 1979. Bar: Ky. 1980. Staff atty. Appalachian Rsch. & Def. Fund Ky., Inc., Barbourville, 1979-82; assoc. F. Preston Farmer Law Offices, London, 1982-88; ptnr. Farmer, Keller & Kelley, 1988-91, Taylor, Keller & Dunaway, London, 1991—. Mem. Fla. Adv. Com. on Arson Prevention, 1990—; chair bd. dirs. Appalachian Rsch. & Def. Fund Ky., 1994-96; founder, chmn. bd. dirs. Ky. Lawyers for Legal Svcs. to the Poor; mem. editl. adv. bd. Ky. West Publ. Group, 1997. Contbg. editor: ABA Annotations to Homeowner's Policy, 3rd edit., 1995, ABA Bad Faith Annotations, 2d edit., 2001. Bd. dirs. Christian Ch. in Ky., 1994-98; elder First Christian Ch., London, 1994-97; pres. Access to Justice Found., 1996—. Recipient Access to Justice award Ky. Legal Svcs. Programs, 1995, Outstanding Svc. award Ky. chpt. Nat. Soc. Profl. Ins. Investigators, 2000. Fellow Ky. Bar Found. (bd. dirs. 2000—); mem. ABA (vice chair property ins. law com. 1992-97), Laurel County Bar Assn. (pres. 1992-93), Ky. Bar Assn. (mem. bd. govs. 1996—, donated legal svcs. award 2001), Nat. Soc. Profl. Ins. Investigators (bd. dirs. 2001—), The Honorable Order of Ky Cols. General civil litigation, Insurance. Office: Taylor Keller & Dunaway 1306 W 5th St London KY 40741-1615 E-mail: wkeller@tkdlaw.com

KELLER, SHARON FAYE, judge; Presiding judge Tex. Ct. Criminal Appeals. Office: Tex Ct Criminal Appeals PO Box 12308 Austin TX 78711-2308

KELLER, THOMAS CLEMENTS, lawyer; b. New Orleans, Dec. 20, 1938; s. Charles Agustus and Mary (Chisolm) K. BA, Tulane U., 1960, JD, 1963; LLM, NYU, 1964. Bar: La. 1963. Assoc. Jones, Walker, Waechter, Poitevent, Carrere & Denegre, New Orleans, 1963-70, ptnr., 1970-98, of counsel, 1998-2000, exec. dir., 1998-2000, gen. counsel, 2001—. Cons. Hunt Plywood Co., Inc., 1991—; sec. bd. dirs. McIlhenny Co. Bd. dirs. New Orleans Mus. Art, 1982—, pres., 1988-90; bd. dirs. Met. Arts Found., New Orleans; chmn. pres. coun. Tulane U. Mem. ABA (sect. on taxation 1970—), La. Bar Assn. (chmn. tax sect. 1978), Metropolitan Club (Washington), Knickerbocker Club (N.Y.C.), Pickwick Club (New Orleans). Democrat. Roman Catholic. Estate taxation, Taxation, general, State and local taxation.

KELLEY, FRANK JOSEPH, lawyer, former state attorney general; b. Detroit, Dec. 31, 1924; s. Frank Edward and Grace Margaret (Spears) K.; m. Nancy Courtier; children: Karen Ann, Frank Edward II, Jane Francis. Pre-law cert., U. Detroit, 1948, JD, 1951. Bar: Mich. 1952. Pvt. practice law, Detroit, 1952-54, Alpena, 1954-61; atty. gen. State of Mich., Lansing, 1962-98; pvt. practice, 1998—. Instr. econs. Alpena Community Coll., 1955-56; instr. pub. adminstrn., Alpena County, 1956; atty. city real estate law U. Mich. Extension, 1957-61. Mem. Alpena County Bd. Suprs., 1958-61; pres. Alpena Community Svcs. Coun., 1956; chmn. Gt. Lakes Commn., 1971; Founding dir., 1st sec. Alpena United Fund, 1955; founding dir., 1st pres. Northeastern Mich. Child Guidance Clinic, 1958; pres., bd. dirs. Northeastern Mich. Cath. Family Svc., 1959. Mem. ABA, 26th Jud. Cir. Bar Assn. (pres. 1956), State Bar Mich., Nat. Assn. Attys. Gen. (pres. 1967), Internat. Movement Atlantic Union, Alpha Kappa Psi, KC (4 deg., past legal adv.). Address: 101 S Washington Sq Fl 9 Lansing MI 48933-1731

KELLEY, GEORGE LAWRENCE, JR. lawyer; b. N.Y.C., July 26, 1937; s. George L. and Gertrude (Berger) K.; m. Dana Ruth Murray, Dec. 19, 1970; children— Jessica Wynne, Todd Sterling. A.B., Dartmouth Coll., 1959; J.D., Harvard U., 1962. Bar: N.Y. 1963, Pa. 1976. Vice pres. Hayden Stone, Inc., N.Y.C., 1966-70; asst. gen. counsel INA Corp., Phila., 1970-80; assoc. Erskine, Wolfson & Kelley, P.C., Phila., 1980-82; of counsel Gratz, Tate, Spiegel, Ervin & Ruthrauff, Phila., 1982-88, Leonard, Tillery & Davison, Phila., 1988—; panel mem. Am. Arbitration Assn., Phila., 1982— . Pres., Wynnewood Civic Assn., Pa., 1984-85; co-chmn., founder Concerned Citizens for Rail Transp., Phila., 1981-83. Mem. ABA, Pa. Bar Assn., Phila. Bar Assn. Republican. Unitarian. Clubs: Union League (Phila.); Merion Cricket (Haverford, Pa.). Home: 207 Almur Ln Wynnewood PA 19096-1712 Office: Leonard Tillery & Davison 1530 Chestnut St Philadelphia PA 19102-2739

KELLEY, JEFFREY WENDELL, lawyer; b. Urbana, Ill., June 8, 1949; s. Wendell J. and Evelyn V. (Kimpel) K.; m. Marsha Lynn Adams, Aug. 21, 1971; children: Julie M., Anna E., Adam J., Grant W. BA, Lipscomb Coll., 1971; postgrad., Vanderbilt U., 1971-72; JD, U. Ill., 1975. Bar: Ga. 1975, U.S. Dist. Ct. (mid. and no. dists.) Ga. 1975, U.S. Ct. Appeals (11th cir.) 1982. Assoc. Powell, Goldstein, Frazer & Murphy, Atlanta, 1975-82, ptnr. litigation dept., with bankruptcy splty., 1982—. Speaker in field. Notes and comments editor U. Ill. Law Rev., 1974-75. Mem. ABA (litig. com.), Am. Bankruptcy Inst. (mem. com.), Ga. Bar Assn. (bench and bar com. 1988), Atlanta Bar Assn. (chmn. law day 1980), Lawyers Club Atlanta (rules and judiciary com. 1995). Republican. Avocations: reading, golf, tennis. Bankruptcy, Federal civil litigation, State civil litigation. Office: Powell Goldstein Frazer & Murphy 191 Peachtree St NE Fl 16 Atlanta GA 30303-1740 E-mail: jkelley@pgfm.com

KELLEY, MICHAEL EUGENE, lawyer; b. Creston, Iowa, June 18, 1941; s. Cletus George and Zelphia Ellen (Billingsley) K.; m. Helen Ann Cox Alger, Apr. 14, 1963 (div. Oct. 1974); 1 child, Kurt Allen; m. Georgia Elyse Lunn Aistrope, Oct. 14, 1974; children: Suzanne Elyse Kelley Porter, Michael Keith. AA, S.W. C.C., 1965; BA, Omaha U., 1968; JD, Creighton U., 1971. Bar: Nebr. 1971, Iowa 1971, U.S. Dist. Ct. Nebr. 1971. Trainman, yardmaster Burlington No., Creston, Council Bluffs, Iowa, 1959-71; assoc. Edgar Cook, Atty., Glenwood, 1971-73; pvt. practice, 1973-76; gen. counsel Kearney (Nebr.) Mcpl. Airport Corp., 1976—. Atty. Mills County, Glenwood, 1972-74; city atty. City of Kearney, 1976—; spkr. in field. Mem. Kearney cabinet Kearney Gideons, ch. asst. sec., 1988-90. With USN, 1960-64. Mem. Internat. Mpls. Lawyers Assn. (Nebr. state chair 1995—), Nebr. State Bar Assn., Buffalo County Bar Assn., Nebr. Gideons (mem. state cabinet, ch. asst. sec. 1990-93), Full Gospel Businessmen's Fellowship Internat. (v.p. 1987-89). Avocations: ichthyology, model trains and villages, shotgun sports. Home: 1203 E 34th St Kearney NE 68847-3226 Office: City of Kearney PO Box 1180 Kearney NE 68848-1180

KELLOGG, JAMES CRANE, lawyer; b. Summit, N.J., July 2, 1939; s. James Crane and Elizabeth (Irwin) K.; m. Gail Chambers, Aug. 25, 1962; children: James, Katherine, Elizabeth. AB, Princeton U., 1961; JD, Harvard U., 1964. Bar: N.J. 1965, N.Y. 1966, Fla. 1979. Assoc. Shearman & Sterling, N.Y.C., 1965-70; v.p. Walston & Co., N.Y.C., 1970-73; ptnr. Gifford, Woody, Palmer & Serles, N.Y.C. 1973-85, Townley & Updike,

N.Y.C., 1986—; dir. Prudential Ins. Co., Newark. Pres. Frost Valley YMCA, Claryville, N.Y., 1983—; past pres. Children's Specialized Hosp., Mountainside, N.J.; trustee Ocean Med. Ctr., Point Pleasant, N.J., 1983, Sky Club, Bay Head Yacht Club (trustee N.J. chpt. 1977-83, 86-89). Democrat. Presbyterian Contracts commercial, Estate planning, Real property. Home: 700 Clayton Ave Bay Head NJ 08742-5305

KELLUM, NORMAN BRYANT, JR. lawyer; b. Maysville, N.C. BS , JD, Wake Forest U. Bar: N.C., U.S. Dist. Ct. (ea. dist.) N.C., U.S. Dist. Ct. (mid. dist.) N.C., U.S. Ct. Appeals (4th cir.), U.S. Supreme Ct. Salesman, mgr. The Southwestern Co., Nashville, summers 1962-68; research asst. N.C. Supreme Ct., Raleigh, NC; atty. Norman Kellum Jr., New Bern; ptnr. Beaman & Kellum; pres., majority shareholder Kellum Law Firm and predecessor law firms, New Bern, Jacksonville, Goldsboro, N.C., 1975—. Trustee Meredith Coll., 1988-92, 94-97, 99—, chmn., 1996, 97; bd. visitors Wake Forest U. Sch. Law, 1992-99; mem. Craven Regional Med. Ctr. Found., 1997-2000, pres., 1998, 99; bd. dirs. Craven Regional Med. Authority, 2001—. 1st lt. U.S. Army. Mem. ATLA, N.C. State Bar, N.C. Acad. Trial Lawyers (bd. govs. 1983-87), N.C. Bar Assn., Ea. N.C. Inn Ct. (pres. 1995), Am. Bd. Trial Advs., Wake Forest U. Law Sch. (Alumni of Yr. award 1993). Avocations: travel, boating, golf. Insurance, Personal injury, Product liability. Office: Kellum Law Firm PO Box 866 New Bern NC 28563-0866

KELLY, ANASTASIA DONOVAN, lawyer; b. Boston, Oct. 9, 1949; d. Charles A. and Louise V. Donovan; m. Thomas C. Kelly, Aug. 23, 1980; children: Michael, Brian. BA cum laude, Trinity Coll, 1971; JD magna cum laude, George Washington U., 1981. Bar: D.C. 1982, Tex. 1982. Analyst Air Line Pilots Assn., 1971-74; dir. employee benefits Martin Marietta Corp., Bethesda, Md., 1974-81; assoc. Carrington, Coleman, Sloman & Blumenthal, Dallas, 1981-85, Wilmer, Cutler & Pickering, Washington, 1985-90, ptnr., 1990-95; sr. v.p., gen. counsel, sec. Fannie Mae, Washington, 1995-99; exec. v.p., gen. counsel, sec. Sears, Robuck & Co., 1999—. Named one of Outstanding Young Women of Am., 1980. Mem. Am. Bar Found., Order of Coif. Republican. Roman Catholic. Banking, General corporate. Home: 9 Kensington Dr N Barrington IL 60010-6960 Office: Sears Roebuck & Co 3333 Beverly Rd Hoffman Estates IL 60179-0001

KELLY, DANIEL GRADY, JR. lawyer; b. Yonkers, N.Y., July 15, 1951; s. Daniel Grady and Helene (Coyne) K.; m. Annette Susan Wheeler, May 8, 1976; children— Elizabeth Anne, Brigid Claire, Cynthia Logan. Grad., Choate Sch., Wallingford, Conn., 1969; BA magna cum laude, Yale U., 1973; JD, Columbia U., 1976. Bar: N.Y. 1977, U.S. Dist. Ct. (so. and ea. dists.) N.Y. 1977, Calif. 1986, U.S. Dist. Ct. (cen. dist.) Calif. 1987. Law clk. to judge U.S. Ct. Appeals (2d cir.), N.Y.C., 1976-77; assoc. Davis Polk & Wardwell, 1977-83; sr. v.p. Lehman Bros., 1983-85; sr. v.p., gen. counsel Kaufman & Broad, Inc., L.A., 1985-87; ptnr. Manatt, Phelps, Rothenberg & Phillips, 1987-90, Sidley & Austin, L.A. and N.Y., 1990-99, Davis Polk & Wardwell, N.Y.C. and Menlo Park, Calif., 1999—. Mem. editl. bd. Columbia Law Rev., 1975-76. Finance, Mergers and acquisitions, Securities. Office: Davis Polk & Wardwell 1600 El Camino Real Menlo Park CA 94025-4119 E-mail: dankelly@dpw.com

KELLY, DEE J. lawyer; b. Bonham, Tex., Mar. 7, 1929; s. Dee C. and Era L. (Jones) K.; m. Janice LeBlanc, Dec. 30, 1954; children: Cynthia Kelly Barnes, Dee J., Craig LeBlanc. B.A., Tex. Christian U., 1950; LL.B., George Washington U., 1954. Bar: Tex. 1954. Pvt. practice law, Ft. Worth, 1956-79; founding, sr. ptnr. Kelly, Hart & Hallman, 1979—. Bd. dirs. A.M.R., Justin Industries, Inc. The SABRE Group Holdings, Inc. Trustee Tex. Christian U., 1971—; bd. dirs. Tex. Turnpike Authority, 1967-76, chmn., 1969-76; bd. regents Tex. State U. System, 1969-75; trustee U. Tex. Law Sch. Found.; bd. dirs. Southwestern Legal Found.; trustee Scott and White Meml. Hosp. and Scott, Sherwood and Bridley Found., 1998, U. Tex. Southwestern Moncrief Radiation Ctr.; bd. visitors U. Tex. Cancer Ctr., 1980-87; mem. devel. bd. U. Tex., Arlington, 1975-81, Joint Select Com. on Judiciary, 1988, Task Force on Jud. Selection, 1990, Fed. Jud. Evaluation Com., 1989—; dir. Southwestern Expn. and Livestock Show, 1986—; mem. dean's adv. coun. Tex. Wesleyan U. Sch. Law, 2000—. 1st lt. USAF, 1951-53. Named Disting. Alumni, Tex. Christian U., 1982, George Washington U., 2001, Ft. Worth's Outstanding Bus. Exec., 1993, Ft. Worth's Outstanding Citizen, 2000; recipient Horatio Alger award Horatio Alger Assn. Disting. Ams., 1995, Blackstone award, 1998. Fellow Am. Bar Found.; mem. Tarrant County Bar Assn., Tarrant County Bar Found., Tex. Bar Found. (founding mem.). Avocation: golf. E-mail: dee. General civil litigation, Oil, gas, and mineral. Home: 1315 Hillcrest St Fort Worth TX 76107-1577 E-mail: kelly@khh.com

KELLY, DENNIS MICHAEL, lawyer; b. Cleve., May 6, 1943; s. Thomas Francis and Margaret (Murphy) K.; m. Marilyn Ann Divoky, Dec. 28, 1967; children: Alison, Meredith. BA, John Carroll U., 1961-65; JD, U. Notre Dame, 1968. Bar: Ohio 1968. Law clk. U.S. Ct. Appeals (8th cir.), Cleve., 1968-69; assoc. Jones, Day, Reavis & Pogue, Cleve., 1969-75, ptnr., 1975—. Mem. Ohio Bar Assn., Bar Assn. Greater Cleve. Federal civil litigation, General civil litigation, State civil litigation. Office: Jones Day Reavis & Pogue North Point 901 Lakeside Ave E Cleveland OH 44114-1190

KELLY, EDWARD JOSEPH, lawyer; b. Scranton, Pa., Oct. 31, 1966; s. Edward Joseph and Jane Elizabeth (Lavelle) K. BA, Duke U., 1988; JD, Boston U., 1991; LLM in Internat. Law, Golden Gate U., 2000. Bar: N.Y. 1992, Calif. 2000. Assoc. Blank Rome Comisky & McCauley, Phila., 1990; ptnr. Kelly Rode & Kelly, LLP, Mineola, N.Y., 1991-2000, Harris Corp. Counsel, Redwood Shores, Calif., 2000—. Lectr. in field. Cons. Legal Ctr. for Def. of Life, N.Y.C., 1991—. Emery Worldwide Inc. scholar, 1984-88; Internat. Legal Studies Merit scholar, 2000. Mem. N.Y. State Bar Assn., Bar Assn. San Francisco, Practising Law Inst., Computer Law Assn., Nat. Inst. Trial Advocacy, Guild Cath. Lawyers, N.Y. State Trial Lawyers Inst. Republican. Roman Catholic. Avocations: golf, sailing, weight training. Federal civil litigation, State civil litigation, Personal injury. Home: PMB 924 751 Laurel St San Carlos CA 94070-3113 Office: Harris Corp Microwave Comms Divsn 350 Twin Dolphin Dr Redwood City CA 94065-1408 also: 218 Griffing Ave Riverhead NY 11901-3009 E-mail: eKelly01@harris.com

KELLY, EDWIN FROST, prosecutor; b. Kearney, Nebr., Jan. 3, 1946; s. Edwin F. and Eora Louise (Ludlum) K.; children: Christopher, Summer, Matthew. BA, Wayne (Nebr.) State Coll., 1968; JD, U. Iowa, 1971. Bar: Iowa 1971, U.S. Dist. Ct. (so. dist.) Iowa 1972, U.S. Ct. Appeals (8th cir.) 1975, U.S. Supreme Ct. 1975, U.S. Dist. Ct. (no. dist.) Iowa 1980. Sole practice, Fairfield, Iowa, 1971-73; ptnr. Kelly & Morrissey, 1974-91; fed. prosecutor, asst. U.S. atty. U.S. Dist. Ct. (So. Dist.) Iowa, Des Moines, 1991—. Prosecutor Jefferson County, Fairfield, 1971-83; lectr. Parsons Coll., 1971-72. Author: Iowa Legal Forms; Creditors Remedies, 1983, 2d rev. edition, 1986, 3d rev. edition, 1990. Chmn. Jefferson County Reps., Fairfield, 1984-85, Iowa Rep. Platform Com., 1988; Rep. nominee for Atty. Gen. of Iowa, 1990. Mem. Masons, Midwest Cruising Sailors Assn. (commodore 1999-2000). Methodist. Avocations: private pilot, sailing. Home: 692 48th St Des Moines IA 50312-1955 Office: US Courthouse Annex 110 E Court Ave Des Moines IA 50309-2044 E-mail: ed.kelly@usdoj.gov

KELLY, HUGH RICE, lawyer; b. Austin, Tex., Dec. 16, 1942; s. Thomas Philip and Cecilia Elizabeth (Rice) K.; m. Marguerite Susan McIntosh, Dec. 27, 1971; children: Susan McIntosh, Cecilia Rice. BA, Rice U., 1965; JD, U. Tex., 1972. Bar: Tex. 1972, U.S. Dist. Ct. (so. dist.) Tex. 1974; U.S. Ct. Appeals (5th cir.), U.S. Supreme Ct. 1975. Assoc. Baker & Botts, Houston, 1972-78, ptnr., 1979-84; exec. v.p., gen. counsel Reliant Energy Inc. (formerly Houston Lighting & Power Co.), 1984—. 1st lt. U.S. Army, 1966-69. Fellow Tex. Bar Found., Houston Bar Found.; mem. ABA, State Bar Tex., Houston Bar Assn., Coronado Club. Republican. FERC practice, Administrative and regulatory, General corporate. Home: 1936 Rice Blvd Houston TX 77005-1635 Office: Reliant Energy Inc PO Box 1700 1111 Louisiana Houston TX 77251-1700

KELLY, JOHN BARRY, II, lawyer; b. Washington, Dec. 17, 1942; s. John Barry and Blanche (O'Brien) K.; m. Elizabeth Ann MacDonald, June 26, 1965; children: Christine, John. BA in Am. History, Cath. U. Am., 1965, JD, 1971. Bar: Fla. 1971, Md. 1972, U.S. Dist. Ct. D.C. 1972, U.S. Ct. Appeals (D.C. cir.) 1972, U.S. Dist. Ct. (no. dist.) Fla. 1987; diplomate advanced advocacy Nat. Inst. Trial Advocacy, 1989-90. Investigator U.S. Civil Svc. Com., Alameda, Calif., 1965-66; law clk. U.S. Dist. Ct. D.C., Washington, 1971-72; assoc. Donahue & Ehrmantraut, Rockville, Md., 1972-75; pvt. practice, 1975-78; atty., project mgr. Westat, Inc., 1978-80; trial atty. Tenn. Valley Authority, Knoxville, 1980-85; ptnr. Law Ctr., Pensacola, Fla., 1986-87, Ray, Kievit & Kelly, Pensacola, 1988—. Faculty Fla. Bar (advanced adv. seminars), Gainesville, 1990-94, Labor and Employment Trial Seminar, Fla. Bar, Miami, 1995; spkr. in field. Author: (course book) Labor and Employment Seminars, 1990-95; exec. editor (jour.) Cath. U. Law Rev., 1970. Mem. Leadership Pensacola, Fla., 1992—. Cpl. USMC, 1966-68. Named Gulf Coast's Best Atty., Pensacola (Fla.) News Jour., 1988. Mem. Fla. Bar, D.C. Bar Assn., Escambia/Santa Rosa Bar. Avocations: reading, golfing. Civil rights, General civil litigation, Labor. Office: Kievit Kelly & Odom 15 W Main St Pensacola FL 32501-5927

KELLY, JOHN JAMES, lawyer; b. Rockville Centre, N.Y., July 4, 1949; s. John James Sr. and Eleanor Grace (Vann) K.; m. Clara Sarah Gussin; 1 child, John James III. AB in Govt., Georgetown U., 1971, JD, 1975. Bar: Pa. 1976, D.C. 1979, U.S. Dist. Ct. D.C. 1980, U.S. Claims Ct. 1982, U.S. Ct. Appeals (D.C. cir.) 1980, U.S. Ct. Appeals (fed. cir.) 1982. Law clk. to judge U.S. Dist. Ct., Washington, 1975-77; assoc. Corcoran, Youngman & Rowe, 1977-80, Capell, Howard, Knabe & Cobbs, Washington, 1980-83, Loomis, Owen, Fellman & Howe, Washington, 1983-86, ptnr., 1986-90; v.p., sec., gen. coun. Electronic Industries Alliance, Arlington, Va., 1990-96, exec. v.p., gen. counsel, 1997—; pres. JEDEC Solid State Tech. Assn., 2000—; counsel Howe, Anderson & Steyer, Washington, 1990—. Mem. Jud. Conf., D.C. Cir., Washington, 1983, Jud. Conf. Fed. Cir., Washington, 1988—. Contbr. articles to legal publs. Mem. ABA, D.C. Bar, Pa. Bar Assn., Am. Soc. Assn. Execs. (bd. dirs. legal section 1989-94, chmn. 1992-93), Fed. Bar Assn., Met. Club. Democrat. Roman Catholic. Antitrust, Federal civil litigation, General corporate. Office: Electronic Industries Alliance 2500 Wilson Blvd Arlington VA 22201-3834

KELLY, JOHN MARTIN, lawyer; b. Oshkosh, Wis., Dec. 13, 1948; s. Martin Paul and Ivy Cecile (James) Kelly; m. Teresa Jean Wendland, July 24, 1982. BA, U. Wis., Madison, 1971; JD, Georgetown U., 1974; postgrad. in bus., Harvard U., 1976-77. Bar: Wis. 1974, D.C. 1975. Atty. office chief counsel IRS, Washington, 1974-76; assoc. Dempsey Law Office, Oshkosh, 1977-82, ptnr., 1983—. Mem. ABA, Wis. Bar Assn., D.C. Bar Assn., Winnebago County Bar Assn. General practice, General civil litigation, Personal injury. Office: Dempsey Law Office PO Box 886 Oshkosh WI 54903-0886 E-mail: jmkelly@dempseylaw.com

KELLY, JOHN PATRICK, lawyer; b. Boston, May 9, 1952; s. Patrick and Elizabeth (Glennon) K.; m. Eileen Linda Obuchowski, May 28, 1983; children: John Patrick, Laura Beth, Kevin Sean. AB, Coll. Holy Cross, 1974; JD, Vanderbilt U., 1978. Bar: Mass. 1978, Fla. 1979, U.S. Dist. Ct. (so. dist.) Fla. 1980, U.S. Supreme Ct. 1981; cert. trial lawyer, Fla., litigation specialist, Fla. Law clk. to presiding justice Tenn. Supreme Ct., Nashville, 1978-79; assoc. Fleming, O'Bryan & Fleming, Ft. Lauderdale, Fla., 1979-84, ptnr., 1984-96, Gunster, Yoakley, Valdes-Fauli & Stewart, Ft. Lauderdale, 1996-2000, Lorusso & Loud, Ft. Lauderdale, 2000—. Lectr. Ctr. for Internat. Legal Studies, Kitzbuhel, Austria, 1999. Co-author Florida Business Litigation Manual, 1989-2000. Mem. Fla. Bar Assn. (comml. litigation com., lectr. Continuing Legal Edn. 1988-2000, prof. edn. seminars 1991-2000), Am. Arbitration Assn. (arbitrator), Nat. Futures Assn. (arbitrator), Tower Club, St. Thomas More Soc., Nat. Bd. Trial Advocacy, Phi Beta Kappa. Roman Catholic. Avocations: skiing, scuba diving, photography. Federal civil litigation, State civil litigation, Insurance. Office: Lorusso & Loud Ste #208 2601 East Oakland Park Blvd Fort Lauderdale FL 33306 E-mail: jkelly@businesslitigation.com

KELLY, MARILYN, state supreme court justice; b. Apr. 15, 1938; m. Donald Newman. BA, Ea. Mich. U., 1960, JD (hon.); postgrad., U. Paris.; MA, Middlebury Coll., 1961; JD with honors, Wayne State U., 1971. Assoc. Dykema, Gossett, Spencer, Goodnow & Trigg, Detroit, 1973-78; ptnr. Dudley, Patterson, Maxwell, Smith & Kelly, Bloomfield Hills, Mich., 1978-80; owner Marilyn Kelly & Assocs., Bloomfield Hills, Birmingham, 1980-88; judge Mich. Ct. of Appeals, 1989-96; justice Mich. Supreme Ct., 1997—. Tchr. lang., lit. Grosse Pointe Pub. Schs., Albion Coll., Ea. Mich. U.; past mem. rep. assembly, comms. com., family law coun. Mich. State Bar, now co-chair Open Justice Commn. Active Mich. Dem. Party, 1963—. Recipient Disting Alumni award Ea. Mich. U., Disting. Svc. award Mich. Edn. Assn. Mem. Soc. Irish-Am. Lawyers, Women Lawyers Assn. (past pres.), Oakland County Bar Assn. (past chair family law com.) Office: Mich Supreme Ct 500 Woodward Ave Ste 2000 Detroit MI 48226-3416

KELLY, MARY KATHLEEN, lawyer, researcher; b. Copiague, N.Y., Apr. 30, 1952; d. John Joseph and Catherine Rita Kelly. BA, SUNY, Brockport, 1974; MBA, Rochester Inst. Tech., 1982; JD, U. Buffalo, 1996. Bar: N.Y. 1998. Mgr., counselor Greater Opportunity in Nursing, Rochester, 1974-76; program dir. United Cerebral Palsy, N.Y., 1976-78; br. mgr. Quality Care Nursing Svc., 1978-80; account rep. IBM, 1980-91; case reviewer Ctr. for Helath Dispute Resolution, Pittsford, 1996-97; legal rsch. specialist West Group, Rochester, 1997—; pvt. practice, 1998—. Mem. N.Y. State Bar Assn., Monroe County Bar Assn., Greater Rochester Assn. Women Attys., 19th Ward Commn. Assn. Avocations: painting, piano, theatre, outdoor activities, gardening. Office: Law Offices of Mary K Kelly PO Box 24366 Rochester NY 14624-0366

KELLY, PAUL DONALD, lawyer; b. Rochester, N.Y., Sept. 20, 1955; s. Gerard D. and Ruth A. K.; m. Anne E. Alfieri, Nov. 30, 1985; children: Thomas, Alexander, Raymond, John. BA in English, LeMoyne Coll., 1977; JD, U. Albany, 1980. Bar: N.Y. 1981, U.S. Dist. Ct. (no. dist.) N.Y. 1986, U.S. Dist. Ct. (we. dist.) 1988, U.S. Ct. Claims 1989. Asst. counsel N.Y. State Sen. Mary Goodhue, Albany, 1980-81; asst. pub. defender Monroe County Pub. Defender, Rochester, N.Y., 1981-85; assoc. Davidson, Fink, Cook & Gates, 1985-91; ptnr. Davidson, Fink, Cook, Kelly & Galbraith, 1992—. Mem. Assn. Trial Lawyers Am., N.Y. State Trial Lawyers Assn., Genesee Valley Trial Lawyers Assn. (pres.), N.Y. State Bar Assn., Monroe County Bar Assn. (plaintiff's personal injury sect.). Democrat. Roman Catholic. Avocations: family activities, athletics. General civil litigation, Personal injury. Office: Davidson Fink Cook Kelly & Galbraith 28 Main St E Ste 1700 Rochester NY 14614-1915

KELLY, PAUL JOSEPH, JR. judge; b. Freeport, N.Y., Dec. 6, 1940; s. Paul J. and Jacqueline M. (Nolan) Kelly; m. Ruth Ellen Dowling, June 27, 1964; children: Johanna, Paul Edwin, Thomas Martin, Christopher Mark, Heather Marie. BBA, U. Notre Dame, 1963; JD, Fordham U., 1967. Bar: N.Mex. 1967. Law clk. Cravath, Swaine & Moore, N.Y.C., 1964—67; assoc. firm Hinkle, Cox, Eaton, Coffied & Hensley, Roswell, N.Mex., 1967—71, ptnr., 1971—92; judge U.S. Ct. Appeals (10th cir.), Santa Fe, 1992—. Mem. N.Mex. Bd. Bar Examiners, 1982—85, N.Mex. Ho. of Reps., 1976—81, chmn. consumer and pub. affairs com., mem. judiciary com.; mem. N.Mex. Pub. Defender Bd. Bd. visitors Fordham U. Sch. Law, 1992—; pres. Oliver Seth Inn of Ct., 1993—, Roswell Drug Abuse Com, 1970—71; mem. Appellate Judges Nominating Commn., 1989—92, Eastern N.Mex. State Fair Bd., 1978—83; pres. Chaves County Young Reps., 1971—72; vice chmn. N.Mex. Young Reps., 1969—71, treas., 1968—69; pres. parish coun. Roman Cath. Ch., 1971—76; bd. dirs. Zia coun. Girl Scouts Am., Roswell Girls Club; bd. dirs.. Chaves County Mental Health Assn., 1974—77; bd. dirs. Santa Fe Orch., 1992—93, Roswell Symphony Orch. Soc., 1969—82, treas., 1970—73, pres., 1973—75. Mem.: ABA, Fed. Bar Assn., State Bar N.Mex. (v.p. young lawyers sect. 1969, co-chmn. ins. sub-com. 1972—73, mem. continuing legal edn. com. 1970—73), KC. Office: US Court Appeals 10th Circuit Federal Courthouse PO Box 10113 Santa Fe NM 87504-6113

KELLY, RAYMOND BOONE, III, lawyer; b. Ft. Worth, Oct. 12, 1947; s. Raymond Boone Jr. and Martha (Morehead) K.; children: Alice Katherine, Anne Rowan. BA, Tulane U., 1970; JD, So. Meth. U., 1974. Bar: Tex. 1974. Ptnr. Decker, McMackin & McClane, Ft. Worth, 1974—. V.p., trustee William E. Scott Found., Ft. Worth, 1978—. Bd. dirs., past pres. Goodwill Industries Ft. Worth, 1975-97; bd. dirs. Arts Coun. Ft. Worth and Tarrant County, 1980-91, 95-97, Conf. of S.W. Founds., Dallas, 1986-89, 97-2000, Big Bros./Bis Sisters, Ft. Worth, 1987-94, Intercultura, Inc., Ft. Worth, 1989-96, chmn., 1992-94, Funding Info. Ctr., 1993-97, Ft. Worth Dallas Ballet, 1996-97, Cmty. Found. North Tex., 1996—, All Saints Health Sys., 1997—; trustee Modern Art Mus. Ft. Worth, 1981—, Fort Worth Country Day Sch., 1996—; chmn. All Saints Health Found., 1992—, Goodwill Industries Ft. Worth Found., 1997—, Ft. Worth Club, 1999—. Mem. ABA, State Bar Tex., Tarrant County Bar Assn., Tarrant County Young Lawyers Assn. (v.p., sec. 1976-77), Ft. Worth Club, Exchange Club, Rivercrest Country Club, Steeplechase Club, Ind. Prodrs. Assn. Am., Tex. Oil and Gas Assn. Republican. Episcopalian. Home: 301 Virginia Pl Fort Worth TX 76107-1611 Office: Decker, McMackin & McClane 801 Cherry St Fort Worth TX 76102-3812

KELLY, THOMAS PAINE, JR. lawyer; b. Tampa, Fla., Aug. 29, 1912; s. Thomas Paine and Beatrice (Gent) K.; m. Jean Baughman, July 25, 1940; children: Carla (Mrs. Henry Dee), Thomas Paine III, Margaret Jo (Mrs. Jeffrey Holmes). AB, U. Fla., 1935, JD, 1936. Bar: Fla. 1936, U.S. Dist. Ct. (no. dist.) Fla. 1936, U.S. Ct. Appeals (5th cir.) 1936, U.S. Dist. Ct. (mid. dist.) Fla. 1940, U.S. Dist. Ct. (so. dist.) Fla. 1939, U.S. Ct. Appeals (11th cir.) 1983, U.S. Supreme Ct. 1990. Since practiced in, Tampa; assoc. McKay, Macfarlane, Jackson & Ferguson, 1939-40; ptnr. McKay, Macfarlane, Jackson & Ferguson, 1940-48, Macfarlane, Ferguson, Allison & Kelly, 1948-83, sr. ptnr., 1983-91; of counsel Shear, Newman, Hahn & Rosenkranz, 1992-95; shareholder MacFarlane Ferguson & McMullen, P.A., Tampa, Fla., 1996—. Chmn. Tampa Com. 100, 1960-61; pres. Tampa Citizens' Safety Coun., 1961-62; Bd. dirs. Tampa chpt. ARC, 1955-62, pres., 1958-59; bd. dirs. Boys Clubs Tampa, 1956-67, pres., 1966-67. Col. F.A. AUS, 1940-45. Decorated Silver Star. Fellow Am. Coll. Trial Lawyers, Internat. Acad. Trial Lawyers; mem. Am. Bar Assn., Bar Assn. Hillsborough County, Fla. Bar (chmn. com. profl. ethics 1953-58, chmn. com. ins. and negligence law 1962-63, chmn. fed. rules com. 1969-70) Republican. Home: 5426 Lykes Ln Tampa FL 33611-4747 Office: McFarlane Ferguson & McMullen PO Box 1531 Tampa FL 33601-1531 E-mail: gjs@mocfar.com

KELLY, TIMOTHY WILLIAM, lawyer; b. Apr. 27, 1953; s. George Raymond and Mary Therese (Kelly) K.; m. Mary Teresa Harms, May 24, 1980; children: Ryan Timothy, Colin Patrick, Kaitlynn Elizabeth. BS in Bus. Adminstrn., U. Dayton, 1975, JD, 1978. Bar: Ill. 1978, U.S. Dist. Ct. (cen. and no. dists.) Ill. 1979. Staff counsel Praire State Legal Aid, Bloomington, Ill., 1978-81; felony asst. McLean County Pub. Defenders, 1981-83; assoc. Jerome Mirza & Assocs., 1983-88; asst. prof. polit. sci. Ill. State U., Normal, 1980-83; faculty mem. Ill. Inst. Continuing Legal Edn. Lectr. in field. Contbr. articles to profl. jours. Bd. dirs. Bloomington/Normal Day Care Assn., 1982-83; civil actions arbitrator and mediator McLean County, 1996—. Named one of Top Three Attys. in McLean, Bus. to Bus. Mag., 1997. Fellow Ill. Bar Found.; mem. ATLA, Ill. State Bar Assn. (mem. civil practice and procedure sect. coun. 1992—, chmn. 1998, Allerton house steering com. 1994, 96, 98, tort law sect. coun. 1995—, assembly mem. 1995—), Ill. Trial Lawyers Assn. (mem. bd. mgrs. 1992—, continuing legal edn. com. 1995-96, exec. com. 1996, chmn. ins. law com. 1996-98), Chgo. Bar Assn., McLean County Bar Assn. (sec. 1984-85), McLean County Inns of Ct., IICLE (bd. dirs. 2000—). Democrat. Roman Catholic. Personal injury. Office: 205 N Williamsburg Dr Ste A Bloomington IL 61704-7721 E-mail: twkelly271@aol.com

KELLY, WILLIAM GARRETT, judge; b. Grand Rapids, Mich., Nov. 30, 1947; s. Joseph Francis and Gertrude Frances (Downes) K.; m. Sharon Ann Diroff, Aug. 11, 1979; children: Colleen, Joseph, Caitlin, Meaghan and Patricia. BA, U. Detroit, 1970, JD, 1975. Bar: Mich. 1975, U.S. Dist. Ct. (we. dist.) Mich. 1975. Tchr. Peace Corps, Ghana, Republic of West Africa, 1970-72; asst. prosecutor Kalamazoo (Mich.) Prosecutor's Office, 1975-77; atty. Office of Defender, Grand Rapids, 1977-78; judge 62d B Dist. Ct., Kentwood, 1979—. Mem. faculty Mich. Jud. Inst., Lansing, 1985—, 2d Nat. Conf. on Ct. Tech., Denver, 1988; chmn.-elect Jud. Conf. State Bar Mich., 1990-91, chair, 1991-92; vice chmn. Nat. Conf. Spl. Ct. Judges, 1990-91, chair 1992-93. Bd. dirs. Nat. Ctr. for State Cts., 1994-2000; pres. Kentwood Jaycees, 1979-80. Named one of Five Outstanding Young Men of Mich., Mich. Jaycees, 1982. Mem. ABA (chair nat. conf. spl. ct. judges 1992-93), State Bar Mich., Grand Rapids Bar Assn., Cath. Lawyers Assn. Western Mich. (pres. 1987), Mich. Dist. Judges Assn. (pres. 1989). Roman Catholic. Office: 62d B Dist Ct PO Box 8848 4900 Breton Rd SE Kentwood MI 49518-8848

KELLY, WILLIAM JAMES, III, lawyer; b. St. Louis, July 26, 1967; s. William James Jr. and Lenore (B.) K.; m. Mary McNamara, Dec. 29, 1990; children: Natalie Miles, Katherine Alexandria. BA, Tulane U., 1989; JD, St. Louis U., 1992. Bar: La. 1992, U.S. Dist. Ct. (ea., we. and mid. dists.) La. 1992, U.S. Ct. Appeals (5th cir.) 1994, U.S. Supreme Ct. 1999. Ptnr. Adams and Reese, New Orleans, 1992—. Author articles in field. Bd. govs. La. Civil Svc. League, 2000—. Mem. ABA (labor and employment planning bd. young lawyers divsn. 1994-96), FBA, La. State Bar Assn., Provost Coun. Tulane U., Serra Internat. (pres. 1998-00), Sigma Chi (chpt. advisor 1994-98), Alpha Sigma Nu. Roman Catholic. Avocations: skiing, scuba diving, music collecting. Federal civil litigation, State civil litigation, Labor. Office: Adams and Reese 4500 One Shell Sq New Orleans LA 70139-4501 E-mail: kellywj@arlaw.com

KELLY, WILLIAM WRIGHT, lawyer; b. New Castle, Pa., Aug. 25, 1916; s. Newell Andrew and Emma Price (Shaffer) K.; m. Joy Miller, Jan. 27, 1945; children: William W., Douglas K., Jeffrey B., Richard C. AB, Amherst Coll., 1938; JD, Georgetown U., 1952; MBA, George Washington U., 1963. Bar: D.C. 1952, U.S. Ct. Appeals (D.C. cir.) 1952, U.S. Ct. Mil. Appeals 1952, N.Y. 1974. Commd. ensign U.S. Navy, 1941, advanced through ranks to capt., 1960, ret., 1967; v.p. ops. Mohawk Airlines, Utica, N.Y., 1967-71; pres. Saunders Aircraft Corp., Gimli, Man., Can., 1971-73;

ptnr. Penberthy & Kelly, Utica, 1973-81; pres. Kelly & Walthall, P.C., Utica, 1981—; dir. Bank of Utica, 1979—. Mem. N.Y. State Bar Assn. (real property com.), Oneida County Bar Assn., Phi Delta Phi. Republican. Clubs: Sadaquada Golf (Whitestown, N.Y.) (pres. 1974-77); Fort Schuyler (Utica) (pres. 1983). Lodges: Masons, Shriners. Banking, General corporate, Real property. Office: Kelly & Walthall PC 400 Mayro Bldg 239 Genesee St Ste 400 Utica NY 13501-3451

KELMAN, MARK GREGORY, law educator; b. N.Y.C., Aug. 20, 1951; s. Kurt and Sylvia (Etman) K.; m. Ann Barbara Richman, Aug. 26, 1979; 1 child, Nicholas. JD, Harvard U., 1976. Bar: N.Y. 1977. Dir. criminal justice projects City of N.Y., 1976-77; prof. Stanford U. Law Sch., Calif., 1977—. Author: (novel) What Followed Was Pure Lesley, 1973, AGuide to Critical Legal Studies, 1987; contbr. articles to profl. jours. Mem. Conf. on Critical Legal Studies. Office: Stanford U Law Sch Nathan Abbott Way Stanford CA 94305

KELSO, LINDA YAYOI, lawyer; b. Boulder, Colo., 1946; d. Nobutaka and Tai (Inui) Ike; m. William Alton Kelso, 1968. BA, Stanford U., 1968; MA, U. Wis., 1973; JD, U. Fla., 1979. Bar: Fla. 1980. Assoc. Mahoney, Hadlow & Adams, Jacksonville, Fla., 1979-82, Commander, Legler, Werber, Dawes, Sadler & Howell, Jacksonville, 1982-86, ptnr., 1986-91, Foley & Lardner, Jacksonville, 1992—. Mem. ABA (bus. law sect.), Jacksonville Bar Assn., Phi Beta Kappa, Order of Coif. Avocations: music, gardening, cooking. General corporate, Securities. Office: Foley & Lardner 200 N Laura St Jacksonville FL 32202-3500 E-mail: lkelso@foleylaw.com

KELSO, R. RANDALL, law educator; b. Indpls., Nov. 12, 1955; s. Charles Davidson and Margaret Jane (Tandy) K. B.A., U. Chgo., 1976; J.D., U. Wis., 1979. Instr., U. Miami (Fla.) Sch. Law, 1979-80; assoc. in law Columbia U., N.Y.C., 1980-82; prof. Law South Tex. Coll. Law, Houston, 1983—. Co-author coursebook: Studying Law: An Introduction, 1984. Contbr. articles to profl. publs. Office: South Tex Coll Law 1303 San Jacinto St Houston TX 77002-7013

KELSON, RICHARD B. metal products executive; b. Pitts., Nov. 20, 1946; B in Polit. Sci., U. Pa.; JD, U. Pitts. Atty. Alcoa, Pitts., 1974-77, gen. atty., 1977-83, mng. gen. atty., 1983-84, asst. sec., mng. gen. atty., 1984-89, asst. gen. counsel, 1989-91, sr. v.p. environ. health and safety, 1991-94, exec. v.p. environ., health and safety, gen. counsel, 1994-97, exec. v.p., CFO, 1997—. Bd. dirs. Westvaco Corp. Bd. dirs. Alcoa Found., U. Pitts. Law Sch. Bd. Visitors, Conf. Bd. Coun. Fin. Execs.; mem. Fin. Exec. Inst. the Officers Conf. Group, The Pvt. Sector Coun.'s CFPs; mem. bd. trustees Carnegie Mellon. Mem. ABA. Office: Alcoa 201 Isabella St Pittsburgh PA 15212-5858

KELTNER, ROBERT EARL, lawyer, researcher, business executive; b. Parkersburg, W.Va., Apr. 11, 1940; s. Earl L. and Chloe H. (Hendershot) K.; 1 child, David B. BA, Marietta Coll., 1959; JD, W.Va. U., 1962; PhD, Thomas Edison Coll., 1965. Bar: W.Va. 1962, U.S. Supreme Ct. 1968. Assoc. Redmond, Campbell & Keltner, Parkersburg, 1962-64; sr. ptnr. Keltner & Yankiss, 1964-80. U.S. Appeals agt., Parkersburg, 1966-75; cons. Pacific Test Labs., L.A., 1970—; pres. United Innkeepers Am., Fla., 1973—, Americar Inc., Palm Tree Motels Inc. Mem. ABA, W.Va. State Bar Assn., Wood County Bar Assn., Am. Arbitration Assn., Lawyer Pilots Assn., Internat. Platform Assn., Kiwanis (pres. 1968). Methodist. Address: 4415 N Tamiami Trl Sarasota FL 34234-3863 Office: Keltner & Yankiss 2404 7th Ave Parkersburg WV 26101-5824

KEMP, BARRETT GEORGE, lawyer; b. Dayton, Ohio, Feb. 22, 1932; s. Barrett M. and Gladys M. (Linkhart) K.; children: Becky A., Barrett George II; m. Shirley, 1997. BSC, Ohio U., 1954; JD, Ohio No. U., 1959. Bar: Ohio 1959. With FBI, 1959-61; mem. B.G. Kemp Law Firm, St. Marys, Ohio, 1961—. Law dir. City of St. Marys, 1964-80. Sec., treas. Cmty. Improvement Corp., 1967-79; founder St. Marys Sister City, Inc.; founder, organizer sister city with Ho Kudan-cho, Japan, 1985. Recipient Outstanding Citizen award City of St. Marys, 1973, Builder of Bridges award St. Mary's C. of C., 1995. Mem. Ohio Bar Assn., Auglaize County Bar Assn., Rotary (v.p. 1968, pres. 1969, Lifetime achievement 1997, Four Aves. of Cvs. citation 1999), Masons, Shriners, Scottish Rite. General practice. Office: Ste 203 Cmty First Bank & Trust Bldg Saint Marys OH 45885

KEMP, DANIEL WARREN, lawyer; b. Ironton, Ohio, Oct. 7, 1945; s. Warren Daniel and Evelyn Mary (Ball) K.; m. Judith Elizabeth Renz, Aug. 28, 1965; children: Brian Daniel, Nicole Elizabeth. BA, Ohio U., 1967; JD, U. Cin., 1970. Bar: Ohio 1970. Counsel Cin. Gas & Elec. Co., 1970-81; asst. counsel Armco Inc., Middletown, Ohio, 1981-84, assoc. counsel, 1985-89, corp. counsel, corp. dir., 1989-91; asst. gen. counsel Am. Elec. Power Svc. Corp., Columbus, 1991—. Contbr. articles to profl. jours. Mem. ABA, Ohio Bar Assn., Cin. Bar Assn. (com. chmn. 1976-78), Butler County Bar Assn., Masons. Republican. Presbyterian. Home: 830 Gatehouse Ln Columbus OH 43235-1734 Office: Am Electric Power Svc Corp 1 Riverside Plz Columbus OH 43215-2355

KEMPER, JAMES DEE, lawyer; b. Olney, Ill., Feb. 23, 1947; s. Jack O. and Vivian L. Kemper; m. Diana J. Deig, June 1, 1968; children: Judd, Jason. BS, Ind. U., 1969, JD summa cum laude, 1971. Bar: Ind. 1971. Law clk. U.S. Ct. Appeals (7th cir.), Chgo., 1971-72; mng. ptnr. Ice Miller, Indpls., 1972—. Note editor Ind. U. Law Rev., 1970-71; contbr. articles to profl. jours. Past officer, bd. dirs. Marion County Assn. for Retarded Citizens, Inc., Indpls.; past bd. dirs. Cen. Ind. Easter Seal Soc., Indpls., Crossroads Rehab. Ctr., Inc, Indpls.; pres., bd. govs. Orchard Country Day Sch., Indpls.; mem. bd. Eiteljorg Mus. Native Americans, Butler U. Fellow Ind. Bar Found.; mem. ABA (employee benefit com.), Ind. Bar Assn., The Group, Inc., Midwest Pension Conf., U.S. C. of C. (employee benefit com.), Stanley K. Lacy Leadership Alumni. Health, Pension, profit-sharing, and employee benefits, Corporate taxation. Office: Ice Miller 1 American Sq Indianapolis IN 46282-0020

KEMPF, DONALD G., JR. lawyer; b. Chgo., July 4, 1937; s. Donald G. and Verginia (Jahnke) K.; m. Nancy Kempf, June 12, 1965; children: Donald G. III, Charles P., Stephen R. AB, Villanova U., 1959; LLB, Harvard U., 1965; MBA, U. Chgo., 1989. Bar: Ill. 1965, U.S. Supreme Ct. 1972, N.Y. 1986, Colo. 1992. Assoc. Kirkland & Ellis, Chgo., 1965-70, ptnr., 1971-2000; exec. v.p., chief legal officer Morgan Stanley, N.Y.C., 2000—. Trustee Chgo. Symphony Orch., 1995—, Am. Inns of Ct. Found., 1997—; bd. govs. Chgo. Zool. Soc., 1975—, Art Inst. Chgo., 1984—; bd. dirs. United Charities Chgo., 1985—, chmn. bd., 1991-93. Capt. USMC, 1959-62. Fellow Am. Coll. Trial Lawyers; mem. Am. Econ. Assn., ABA, Chgo. Club, Econ. Club, Univ. Club, Mid-Am. Club, Saddle and Cycle Club (Chgo.), Snowmass (Colo.) Club, Quail Ridge (Fla.) Club, Westmoreland Club. Roman Catholic. Antitrust, General civil litigation, Mergers and acquisitions. Address: Morgan Stanley 1585 Broadway Fl 39 New York NY 10036-8200 E-mail: donald.kempf@morganstanley.com

KENDALL, DAVID E. lawyer; b. Camp Atterbury, Ind., May 2, 1944; BA, Wabash Coll., 1966; MA, Oxford U., England, 1968; JD, Yale U., 1971. Bar: N.Y. 1974, U.S. Ct. Appeals (5th cir.) 1976, D.C. 1978, U.S. Supreme Ct. 1978, Md. 1993. Law clerk to Mr. Justice Byron R. White U.S. Supreme Ct., 1971-72; mem. Williams & Connolly. Adj. prof. Columbia U. Law Sch., 1977-78, Georgetown U. Law Ctr., 1985-95. Note and comment editor Yale Law Jour., 1970-71; author (with Leonard Ross) The Lottery and the Draft, 1970. Rhodes scholar. Mem. N.Y. State Bar Assn. General civil litigation, Criminal. Office: Williams & Connolly 725 12th St NW Washington DC 20005-5901

KENDALL, PHILLIP ALAN, lawyer; b. Lamar, Colo., July 20, 1942; s. Charles Stuart and Katherine (Wilson) K.; m. Margaret Roe Greenfield, May 2, 1970; children: Anne, Timothy. BS in Engring., Stanford U., 1964; JD, U. Colo., Boulder, 1969; postgrad., U. Freiburg (Germany), 1965-66. Engr. Siemens Halske, Munich, 1965; ptnr. Kraemer, Kendall & Benson, Colorado Springs, Colo., 1969—. Gen. counsel Peak Health Care, Inc., Colorado Springs, 1979-87; bd. dirs. Wells Fargo Banks Colorado Springs. Pres. bd. Colorado Springs Symphony Orch. Assn., 1977-80; bd. dirs. Penrose Hosps., Colorado Springs, 1982-88; pres. bd. Citizen's Goals, Colorado, 1984-86; bd. dirs. Legal Aid Found., Denver, 1988-94, chmn., 1991-93; bd. dirs. Colo. Nature Conservancy, 1996—, chair 2001—. Recipient Medal of Distinction-Fine Arts, Colorado Springs C. of C., 1983. Mem. ABA, Colo. Bar Assn. (bd. govs. 1985-88, outstanding young lawyer 1977), El Paso County Bar Assn. (bd. trustees 1983-85), Colorado Springs Estate Planning Coun.(lectr charitable estate planning). Avocations: triathlons, helicopter skiing, marathon swimming, windsurfing, sailing. Estate planning, Probate, Estate taxation. Home: 1915 Wood Ave Colorado Springs CO 80907-6714 Office: Kraemer Kendall & Benson PC 430 N Tejon St Ste 300 Colorado Springs CO 80903-1167 E-mail: pkendall@k2blaw.com

KENDALL, REBECCA O. lawyer, pharmaceutical company executive; BS, Ind. U., 1970, JD, 1975. Bar: Ind. 1975. Lectr. Ind. U. Sch. Bus., 1979-80; counsel Nat. Ins. Assn., 1980-81; atty. Eli Lilly and Co., Indpls., 1981-83, sec., gen. counsel Elanco Products co. divsn., 1983-88, sec., gen. counsel Pharm. divsn., 1988-93, dep. gen. counsel, asst. sec., 1993-95, v.p., gen. counsel, 1995-98, now sr. v.p., gen. counsel, 1998—. Office: Eli Lilly and Co Lilly Corp Ctr Indianapolis IN 46285-0001

KENDALL, ROBERT LOUIS, JR. lawyer; b. Rochester, N.H., Oct. 13, 1930; s. Robert Louis and Marguerite (Thomas) K.; m. Patricia Ann Palmer, Aug. 13, 1955; children: Linda J., Cynthia J., Janet L. AB cum laude, Harvard U., 1952; JD cum laude, U. Pa., 1955; Diploma in Law, Oxford (Eng.) U., 1956. Bar: Pa. 1957, Ga. 1993. Assoc. Schnader, Harrison, Segal & Lewis, Phila., 1956-65, ptnr., 1966-95. Lectr. Temple U. Law Sch., Phila., 1976-77; spl. instr. U. Pa. Law Sch., 1959-62. Contbr. to Antitrust Law Developments, 2d edit. 1984 Bd. dirs. Mann Music Ctr., Inc., Phila., 1971-98, Settlement Music Sch., Phila., Pa., 1984—, Jr. C. of C., Phila., 1962-65; mem. Gladwyne Civic Assn., 1960—, Phila. Orch. Assn., 1983—. Fellow Soc. Values in Higher Edn.; mem. ABA, Pa. Bar Assn., Ga. Bar Assn., Phila. Bar Assn., Atlanta Bar Assn., U. Pa. Law Alumni Assn. (bd. mgrs.), Rotary, Order of Coif (pres. 1979-80), Lawyers Club Atlanta, Harvard Club. Democrat. Episcopalian. Administrative and regulatory, Antitrust, Public utilities. Home: 1208 Hartdale Ln Gladwyne PA 19035-1434 Office: Schnader Harrison Segal 1600 Market St Ste 3600 Philadelphia PA 19103-7287

KENDE, CHRISTOPHER BURGESS, lawyer; b. N.Y.C., Apr. 28, 1948; s. Herbert Alexander and Helga Henrietta (Wieselthier) K.; m. Barbara Gonzales, May 22, 1976. BA, MA, Brown U., 1970; JD, NYU, 1973. Bar: N.Y. 1974, Mass. 1975, D.C. 1988, Calif. 1996, U.S. Dist. Ct. (So. and Ea. dists.) N.Y. 1974, U.S. Ct. Appeals (2nd cir.) 1976, U.S. Ct. Appeals (9th cir.) 1996, U.S. Supreme Ct. 1978. Staff atty. Legal Aide Soc., N.Y.C., 1973-76; assoc. Dewey, Ballantine et al., 1976-78, Hill Betts & Nash, N.Y.C., 1978-82, ptnr., 1982-89, Holtzmann, Wise & Shepard, N.Y.C., 1989-96, Cozen & O'Connor, N.Y.C., 1996—. Contbr. articles to profl. jours. Recipient Silver medal Caisse des Depots, 1984. Mem. ABA, N.Y. County Lawyer's Assn. (past chmn. com. on admiralty and maritime law 1998-99), Maritime Law Assn. (marine ecology com., com. on the CMI), French Maritime Law Assn., India House, Edgartown Yacht Club, Order of Coif, Univ. Club N.Y., The Travellers (Paris), Yacht Club de France, Phi Beta Kappa. Democrat. Presbyterian. Avocations: sailing, motorcycling, tennis, fitness, gardening. Home: 545 W End Ave Apt 2B New York NY 10024-2723 Office: Cozen & O'Connor 45 Broadway New York NY 10006-3007 E-mail: ckende@cozen.com

KENNADY, EMMETT HUBBARD, III, lawyer; b. Houston, Dec. 13, 1957; s. Emmett Hubbard Jr. and Ruth Gail (Lewis) K.; m. Monta Kennady, Sept. 21, 1985; children: Jennings Randolph, Emmett Hubbard IV. BA in Theology, BA in Polit. Sci., Washington and Lee U., 1980; JD, St. Mary's Sch. Law, San Antonio, 1984. Bar: Tex. 1984, U.S. Army Ct. Criminal Appeals 1994, U.S. Ct. Appeals for Armed Forces 1997. Asst. dist. atty. Brazos County Dist. Atty.'s Office, Bryan, Tex., 1985-87; atty. Lawrence, Thornton, Payne, 1987-88; sole practitoner College Station, Tex., 1988—. Mem. staff St. Mary's Sch. Law. Co-author: Medico-Legal Considerations for Dental Practitioner, 1988; contbr. articles to profl. jours. Mem. College Station City Coun., 1992-98, mayor pro tem, 1996-98; mem. Leadership Brazos, Bryan, 1989-90; judge College Station Bd. Adjustment, 1990-91; mem. College Station Capital Improvement Com., 1989-90; bd. dirs. Bryan-College Station Econ. Devel. Bd., 1997-2000, Opera and Performing Arts, College Station, 1997-2001, United Way, Bryan, 1991-96, Arts Coun., College Station, 1990-93. Capt. U.S. Army, 1999. L.B.J. Congl. scholar, 1980. Republican. Baptist. Avocation: flying. Appellate, General civil litigation. Office: 424 Tarrow St College Station TX 77840-7813

KENNARD, JOYCE L. state supreme court justice; Former judge L.A. Mcpl. Ct., Superior Ct., Ct. Appeal, Calif.; assoc. justice Calif. Supreme Ct., San Francisco, 1989—. Office: Calif Supreme Ct 350 Mcallister St San Francisco CA 94102-4783*

KENNARD, RAEBURN GLEASON, lawyer; b. Salt Lake City, May 19, 1946; s. Frankland James and Gladys (Bischoff) K.; m. Nancy Valleau, Aug. 20, 1970 (dec. 1999); children: Elisse, Nathan R., Ashley, Dawn M., Aaron T., Emily; m. Suzanne Southam, Jun 25, 1999. BA in Econs., Brigham Young U., 1970; JD, Duke U., 1973. Bar: Utah 1973. Law clk. U.S. Dist. Ct., Salt Lake City, 1973-74; ptnr. Kirton and McConkie, Salt Lake City, 1974—; sec., gen. counsel Deseret Trust Co., Salt Lake City, 1976—. Mem. ABA (tax sect., exempt orgns. com., religious orgns. sub-com.). Mem. Ch. of Jesus Christ of Latter-day Saints. Non-profit and tax-exempt organizations. Home: 12082 Joey Park Cir Draper UT 84020-8442 Office: 60 E South Temple Ste 1800 Salt Lake City UT 84111-1004

KENNEDY, ANTHONY MCLEOD, United States supreme court justice; b. Sacramento, July 23, 1936; AB, Stanford U., 1958; student, London Sch. Econs.; LLB, Harvard U., 1961; JD (hon.), U. Pacific, 1988, U. Santa Clara, 1988. Bar: Calif. 1962, U.S. Tax Ct. 1971. Former ptnr. Evans, Jackson & Kennedy; prof. constl. law McGeorge Sch. Law, U. of Pacific, 1965-88; judge U.S. Ct. Appeals (9th cir.), Sacramento, 1976-88; assoc. justice U.S. Supreme Ct., Washington, 1988—. Mem. bd. student advisors Harvard Faculty, 1960-61. Fellow Am. Bar Found. (hon.), Am. Coll. Trial Lawyers (hon.); mem. Sacramento County Bar Assn., State Bar Calif., Phi Beta Kappa. Office: US Supreme Ct Supreme Ct Bldg 1 1st St NE Washington DC 20543-0001*

KENNEDY, CHARLES ALLEN, lawyer; b. Maysville, KY, Dec. 11, 1940; s. Elmer Earl and Mary Frances Kennedy; m. Patricia Ann Louderback, Dec. 9, 1961; 1 child, Mimi Mignon. AB, Morehead State Coll., 1965, MA in Edn., 1968; JD, U. Akron, 1969; LLM, George Washington U., 1974. Bar: Ohio 1969. Asst. cashier Citizens Bank, Felicity, Ohio, 1961-63; tchr Triway Local Sch. Dist., Wooster, 1965-67; with office of gen. counsel Fgn. Agr. and Spl. Programs Divsn. USDA, Washington, 1969-71; ptnr. Kauffman, Eberhart, Cicconetti & Kennedy Co., Wooster, 1972-86, Kennedy, Cicconetti, Knowlton & BuyTendyk, LPA, Wooster, 1986—. Mem. ABA, FBA, ATLA, Am. Coll. Barristers, Ohio State Bar Assn., Ohio Acad. Trial Lawyers, Wayne County Bar Assn., Exch. Club, Lions, Elks, Phi Alpha Delta, Phi Delta Kappa. Republican. General civil litigation, State civil litigation, Personal injury. Home: 1770 Burbank Rd Wooster OH 44691-2240 Office: Kennedy Cicconetti & Know Ken 558 N Market St Wooster OH 44691-3406

KENNEDY, CORNELIA GROEFSEMA, federal judge; b. Detroit, Aug. 4, 1923; d. Elmer H. and Mary Blanche (Gibbons) Groefsema; m. Charles S. Kennedy, Jr. (dec.); 1 son, Charles S. III. B.A., U. Mich., 1945, J.D. with distinction, 1947; LL.D. (hon.), No. Mich. U., 1971, Eastern Mich. U., 1971, Western Mich. U., 1973, Detroit Coll. Law, 1980, U. Detroit, 1987. Bar: Mich. bar 1947. Law clk. to Chief Judge Harold M. Stephens, U.S. Ct. of Appeals, Washington, 1947-48; assoc. Elmer H. Groefsema, Detroit, 1948-52; partner Markle & Markle, 1952-66; judge 3d Judicial Circuit Mich., 1967-70; dist. judge U.S. Dist. Ct., Eastern Dist. Mich., Detroit, 1970-79, chief judge, 1977-79; circuit judge U.S. Ct. Appeals, (6th cir.), 1979-99, sr. judge, 1999—. Mem. Commn. on the Bicentennial of the U.S. Constitution (presdl. appointment). Recipient Sesquicentennial award U. Mich. Fellow Am. Bar Found.; mem. ABA, Mich. Bar Assn. (past chmn. negligence law sect.), Detroit Bar Assn. (past dir.), Fed. Bar Assn., Am. Judicature Soc., Nat. Assn. Women Lawyers, Am. Trial Lawyers Assn., Nat. Conf. Fed. Trial Judges (past chmn.), Fed. Jud. Fellows Commn. (bd. dirs.), Fed. Jud. Ctr. (bd. dirs.), Phi Beta Kappa. Office: US Ct of Appeals US Courthouse 231 W Lafayette St Rm 744 Detroit MI 48226-2700*

KENNEDY, DAVID TINSLEY, retired lawyer, labor arbitrator; b. Richmond, Va., Mar. 6, 1919; s. David Tinsley and Lilian Brady (Butcher) K.; m. Jean Elizabeth Stephenson, Nov. 26, 1949 (dec.); children: David T. III, Thomas D., Michael F. JD, U. Va., 1948. Bar: Va. 1948, W.Va. 1949, U.S. Dist. Ct. (so. dist.) W.Va. 1949, U.S. Ct. Appeals (4th cir.) 1963. Atty. Dist. 29 United Mine Workers Am., Beckley, W.Va., 1949-61; ptnr. Kennedy & Vaughan, 1962-98; ret., 1999. Arbitrator Coal Arbitration Svc., Washington, 1970-98; emeritus dir. Raleigh County Nat. Bank, Beckley. Mem. Raleigh County Dem. exec. com., 1980-86, chmn., 1986-90. Lt. col. U.S. Army, 1942-46, PTO. Mem. ABA, W.Va. State Bar, Va. State Bar, Assn. Trial Lawyers Am. Roman Catholic. General practice. Home: 102 Mollohan Dr Beckley WV 25801-2135

KENNEDY, DEBORA A. lawyer; b. Oct. 4, 1942; BA, U. Wash., 1964; JD, U. Wis., 1979. Mng. atty. Wis. Legis. Ref. Bur., Madison, 1998—. Rschr. (book) The Rights of the Critically Ill, 1983. V.p. Vilas Neighborhood Assn., Madison, 1998. Mem. Phi Beta Kappa. Office: Legis Ref Bur 100 N Hamilton St Madison WI 53703-4118

KENNEDY, GEORGE WENDELL, prosecutor; b. Altadena, Calif., Aug. 5, 1945; s. Ernest Campbell Kennedy and Mildred (Onstott) Stuckey; m. Janet Lynn Stites, Aug. 3, 1978; children: Campbell, Britton. BA, Claremont Men's Coll., 1968; postgrad., Monterey Inst. Fgn. Studies, 1968; JD, U. So. Calif., 1971; postgrad., Nat. Coll. Dist. Attys., 1974, F.B.I. Nat. Law Inst., 1989. Bar: Calif. 1972, U.S. Dist. Ct. (no. dist.) Calif. 1972, U.S. Ct. Appeals (9th cir.) 1972. Dep. dist. atty. Santa Clara County, San Jose, Calif., 1972-87, asst. dist. atty., 1987-88, chief asst. dist. atty., 1988-90, dist. atty., 1990—. Author: California Criminal Law Practice and Procedure, 1986. Active NAACP, 1989—, police chiefs' assn. Santa Clara County, San Jose, 1990—; chair domestic violence coun. Santa Clara County, San Jose, 1990-92; bd. dirs. Salvation Army, 1993. Recipient commendation Child Advocates of Santa Clara & San Mateo Counties, 1991, Santa Clara County Bd. Suprs., 1992, Valley Med. Ctr. Found., 1992, 93; elected Ofcl. of Yr. award Am. Electronics Assn., 1998. Mem. Nat. Dist. Attys. Assn. (bd. dirs.), Calif. Dist. Attys. Assn. (bd. dirs. 1988-90, officer 1993-97, pres. 1997-98), Santa Clara County Bar Assn., Rotary Club. Avocation: sailing. Office: 70 W Hedding St 5th Flr West Wing San Jose CA 95110

KENNEDY, HARVEY JOHN, JR. lawyer; b. Barnesville, Ga., Apr. 9, 1924; s. Harvey John and Marisu (Reeves) K.; m. Jean McRitchie King, Apr. 8, 1950; children: Marisu, Jean Gay. LLB, U. Ga., 1949, JD, 1969; diplomate of psychology, Colo. Christian Coll., 1973. Bar: Ga. 1948. Atty. Lamar Electric Membership Corp., Barnesville, Ga., 1948—. County atty. Lamar County, Barnesville, Ga., 1950-52, 58-60; mem. Ga. Indigent Def. Coun., 1958, Ga. Bar Assn. Bd., 1958-59, State Bar of Ga. Bd. Govs. 1980-92; agt. Govt. Appeal Local Bd. 89, 1958; city atty. City of Barnesville, Ga., 1958-65, 83, City of Milner, Ga., 1963-68. Past pres. Barnesville (Ga.) Rotary Club, 1959-60. Capt. U.S. Army, 1942-46, ETO, PTO. Decorated Bronze Star medal and Combat Infantry badge. Mem. ABA, Ga. Trial Lawyers Assn. (v.p. 1972), State Bar Ga., Ga. Assn. Plaintiff's Trial Attys. (v.p. 1968), Towaliga Bar Assn. (pres. 2000-01), Am. Legion (comdr. post #25), Moose (32d degree shriner). Democrat. Presbyterian. Avocations: amateur radio, fishing. Criminal, Family and matrimonial, General practice. Office: PO Drawer B 217 Zebulon St Barnesville GA 30204-1126

KENNEDY, JACK LELAND, lawyer; b. Portland, Oreg., Jan. 30, 1924; s. Ernest E. and Lera M. (Talley) K.; m. Clara C. Hagans, June 5, 1948; children: James M., John C. Student, U.S. Maritime Commn. Acad., Southwestern U., L.A.; JD, Lewis and Clark Coll., 1951. Bar: Oreg. 1951. Pvt. practice, Portland; ptnr. Kennedy & King, 1971-77, Kennedy, King & McClurg, Portland, 1977-82, Kennedy, King & Zimmer, Portland, 1982-98, Kennedy, Watts, Arellano & Ricks L.L.P., Portland, 1998—. Trustee Northwestern Coll. Law, Portland; dir. Profl. Liability Fund, 1979-82. Contbr. articles to legal jours. Mem. bd. visitors Lewis and Clark Coll. With USNR, 1942-46. Recipient Disting. Grad. award Lewis and Clark Coll., 1983. Fellow Am. Coll. Trial Lawyers, Am. Bar Found. (life), Oreg. Bar Found. (charter); mem. ABA (ho. of dels. 1984-88), Oreg. State Bar (bd. govs. 1976-79, pres. 1978-79), Multnomah Bar Assn., City Club, Columbia River Yacht Club. Republican. General civil litigation, Insurance, Personal injury. Office: Kennedy Watts Arellano & Ricks LLP 2850 Pacwest Ctr 1211 SW 5th Ave Portland OR 97204-3713

KENNEDY, JERRY WAYNE, lawyer; b. Murphy, N.C., Nov. 18, 1947; s. Almon T. and Ruby Mae (McCalla) K.; m. Maura Comerford, July 15, 1978. BA, Birmingham So. Coll., 1970; MA, Am. U., 1977; JD, Samford U., 1984; postgrad., Georgetown U., 1983-84. Bar: Ala. 1985, D.C. 1986. Press sec. Rep. Ronnie Flippo, 5th dist. Ala., 1977-80; chief of staff, legis. dir. Rep. Ben Erdreich, 6th dist. Ala., 1982-86; assoc. Heron, Burchette, Ruckert & Rothwell, Washington, 1987-90; of counsel Tuttle & Taylor, 1990-94; owner Kennedy Govt. Rels., 1995—. Adj. prof. Sch. Communication, Am. U., Washington, 1979. Assoc. editor Am. Jour. Trial Advocacy, 1982-82. With USAF, 1970-74. Mem. ABA, Ala. Bar Assn., D.C. Bar Assn., Ala. State Soc. (bd. dirs.), Soc. Profl. Journalists (Sigma Delta Chi), Delta Theta Phi. Democrat. Unitarian. Legislative. Home and Office: Kennedy Govt Rels 313 S Carolina Ave SE Washington DC 20003-4213

KENNEDY, JOHN FORAN, retired lawyer; b. Toronto, Ont., Can., July 25, 1924; came to U.S., 1926, naturalized, 1944; s. Francis Regis and Ellen Susanna (Lunney) K.; m. Carmelita Margaret Stanka, June 20, 1964; 1 son, John Regis Joseph. A.B., Dartmouth Coll., 1949; LL.B., Cornell U., 1952; postgrad. U. Chgo., 1958-60. Bar: Ill. 1954. Mem. trust dept. First Nat. Bank, Chgo., 1952-58; trust officer First Nat. Bank, Lake Forest, Ill., 1959-65; ptnr. Snyder, Clarke, Dalziel, Holmquist & Johnson, Waukegan, Ill., 1966-75; ptnr. Kennedy & Clark, Lake Forest, 1976-82; ptnr. Holmstrom & Kennedy, P.C., 1983-92; cons. various attys. Past pres. Family Service of South Lake County, Ill.; bd. dirs. Lake Forest/Lake Bluff United Way. Served with U.S. Army, 1943-46. Mem. Lake County Bar Assn., Lake Forest C. of C. (past pres.), Phi Alpha Delta. Roman Catholic. Probate, Real property, Estate taxation. Home: 435 Park Ln Lake Bluff IL 60044-2322

KENNEDY, JOHN WILLIAM, lawyer; b. Toronto, Ont., Can., Apr. 26, 1926; s. John and Mary (Strong) K.; m. Mary Alice Millar, Aug. 12, 1952; children: Sandra Kennedy Forster, William I., Mary Lee Kennedy de Vales, Elizabeth. BA, U. Alta., Can., 1950, LLB, 1951. Bar: Alta. 1952, Queen's counsel 1969. Assoc. Smith Clement Partee & Whittaker, Edmonton, Alta., 1951-53; ptnr. Cornie Kennedy, 1953-87; agt.-gen. for China, S.E. Asia, Australia and New Zealand Province of Alta., Hong Kong, 1985—. Chmn. bd. Churchill Devel. Corp., Edmonton, 1980-84. Bd. govs. U. Alta., 1981-85; treas. Edmonton South Progressive Conservative Assn., 1965-84; mem. fin. com. Alta. Progressive Conservative Assn., 1972-84. Served to lt. Royal Can. Navy, 1948-53. Mem. Internat. Bar Assn. (treas. 1982-86, council 1980—), Edmonton Bar Assn., Law Soc. Alta., Can. Bar Assn. (past chmn. comparative law com.), Edmonton Club, Mayfair Golf and Country Club (Edmonton), Centre Club. Office: 1900 Scotia Pl 10060 Jasper Ave Edmonton AB Canada T5J 3V4

KENNEDY, JOSEPH WINSTON, lawyer; b. Marshalltown, Iowa, June 5, 1932; s. Roy Wesley and Julia Harriet (Plum) K.; m. Barbara B. Bowman, July 11, 1954 (div. June 1982); children: Kimberle Ann, Kamella Lucille; m. Paula Terry Smith, Nov. 24, 1984. BS cum laude, McPherson (Kans.) Coll., 1954; JD with honors, George Washington U., 1958. Bar: Kans. 1958, U.S. Dist Ct. Kans. 1958, U.S. Ct. Appeals (10th cir.) 1976, U.S. Supreme Ct. 1970. Spl. agt. Office of Naval Intelligence, Washington, 1954-58; assoc. Morris, Laing, Evans & Brock, Wichita, Kans., 1958-62; ptnr. Morris, Laing, Evans, Brock & Kennedy, 1962—. Chmn. profl. divsn., atty. United Way of the Plains, Wichita, 1990-93. Recipient Best Lawyers in Am. award, 1987, 89-90, 91-92, 93-94, 95-96. Mem. ABA, Kans. Bar Assn. (bd. law examiners 1993—), Wichita Bar Assn. (bd. govs. 1964-66). Federal civil litigation. Office: Morris Laing Evans Brock & Kennedy 200 W Douglas Ave Fl 4 Wichita KS 67202-3013 E-mail: jkennedy@morrislaing.com

KENNEDY, MARC J. lawyer; b. Newburgh, N.Y., Mar. 2, 1945; s. Warren G. K. and Frances F. (Levinson) K.; m. Karen Karatsu; children: Michael L., Kayla R., Shawna D. BA cum laude, Syracuse U., 1967; JD, U. Mich., 1970. Bar: N.Y. 1971. Assoc. Davies, Hardy, Ives & Lawther, N.Y.C., 1971-72, London, Buttenweiser & Chalif, N.Y.C., 1972-73, Silberfeld, Danziger & Bangser, N.Y.C., 1973; counsel Occidental Crude Sales, Inc., 1974-75; v.p., gen. counsel Internat. Ore & Fertilizer Corp., 1975-82; asst. gen. counsel Occidental Chem. Corp., Houston, 1982; v.p., gen. counsel Occidental Chem. Agrl. Products Inc., Tampa, Fla., 1982-87; v.p., gen counsel agrl. products group Occidental Chem. Corp., 1987-91, assoc. gen. counsel Dallas, 1991—. Faculty mentor Columbia Pacific U., Mill Valley, Calif., 1981-88. Contbr. articles to profl. jours. Trustee Bar Harbor Festival Corp., N.Y.C., 1974-87; bd. dirs. Am. Opera Repertory Co., 1982-85; mem. com. planned giving N.Y. Foundling Hosp., 1977-88; Explorer post advisor Boy Scouts Am., 1976-78. Mem. ABA (vice-chmn. com. internat. law liaison young lawyers sect. 1974-75, chmn. sub-com. proposed trade barriers to the importation of products into U.S. 1985-88, vice chmn. corp. counsel com. 1992-93, co-chmn. corp. counsel com. 1993-98), Maritime Law Assn., N.Y. State Bar Assn., Am. Corp. Counsel Assn. Admiralty, General corporate, Private international. Office: Occidental Chem Corp PO Box 809050 Dallas TX 75380-9050

KENNEDY, MICHAEL JOHN, lawyer; b. Spokane, Wash., Mar. 23, 1937; s. Thomas Dennis Kennedy and Evelyn Elizabeth (Forbes) Gordon; m. Pamalee Hamilton, June 14, 1959 (div. July 1968); children: Lisa Marie, Scott Hamilton; m. Eleanore Renee Baratelli, July 14, 1968; 1 child, Anna Rosario. AB in Econs., U. Calif., Berkeley, 1959; JD, U. Calif., San Francisco, 1962. Bar: Calif. 1963, N.Y. 1976, U.S. Ct. Appeals (9th cir. 1963), U.S. Supreme Ct. 1967, U.S. Ct. Appeals (5th cir.) 1975, U.S. Ct. Appeals 2d cir.) 1977, U.S. Ct. Appeals (1st 3d and 4th cirs.) 1979, U.S. Ct. Appeals (3d and D.C. cirs.) 1982. Assoc. Hoberg & Finger, San Francisco, 1962-67; staff counsel Emergency Civil Liberties, N.Y.C., 1967-69; ptnr. Kennedy & Rhine, San Francisco, 1969-76; sole practice N.Y.C., 1976—. Served to 1st lt. U.S. Army, 1963-65. Mem. ABA, N.Y. Criminal Bar Assn., Nat. Assn. Criminal Defenders. Democrat. Roman Catholic. Club: N.Y. Athletic. Civil rights, Criminal, Libel. Home: 1009 5th Ave New York NY 10028-0155 Office: 425 Park Ave New York NY 10022-3506

KENNEDY, THOMAS J. lawyer; b. Milw., July 29, 1947; s. Frank Philip and June Marian (Smith) K.; m. Cathy Ann Cohen, Nov. 24, 1978; children: Abby, Sarah. BA, U. Wisc., 1969, JD cum laude, 1972. Bar: Wis. 1972, U.S. Dist. Ct. (ea. and we. dists.) Wis. 1972, Ariz. 1981, U.S. Dist. Ct. Ariz. 1981, U.S. Ct. Appeals (7th cir.) 1980, U.S. Ct. Appeals (9th cir.) 1981, U.S. Ct. Appeals (D.C. cir.) 1983, U.S. Supreme Ct. 1984, U.S. Ct. Appeals (11th cir.) 1986. Assoc. Goldberg, Previant, Milw., 1972-79, Brynelson, Herrick, Madison, Wisc., 1979-81; ptnr. Snell & Wilmer, Phoenix, 1981-93, Lewis and Roca, Phoenix, 1993-96, Ryley, Carlock and Applewhite, Phoenix, 1996-99, Gallagher & Kennedy, 1999—. Contbg. editor The Developing Labor Laws, 2d, 3d edits., The Fair Labor Standards Act. Mem. ABA, Ariz. State Bar, State Bar Wisc., Maricopa County Bar Assn. Avocations: tennis, reading, hiking. Administrative and regulatory, Labor.

KENNEDY, VEKENO, lawyer; b. Albany, Ga., Feb. 28, 1961; d. Alfred and Algean (Cole) K. BBA, U. San Diego, 1983; JD, Calif. Western Sch. Law, San Diego, 1990. Bar: Calif., U.S. Ct. Appeals (9th cir.), U.S. Dist. Ct. (so. and ctrl. dists.) Calif. Atty. Viviano & Bradley, San Diego, 1991-92, Gibbs, Eppsteiner & Stagg, San Diego, 1993-95, Saxon, Barry, Gardner et al, San Diego, 1995-96; ptnr. Kolod Wager Law Offices LLP, 1997-2001; with Law Offices Vekeno Kennedy, 2001—. Mng. editor California Western Law Rev. and Internat. Law Jour., 1989. Mem. Nat. Assn. Women Lawyers (Outstanding Woman Law Grad. 1990). Roman Catholic. Avocations: theater, golf. General civil litigation, Insurance, Product liability.

KENNELLY, JOHN JEROME, lawyer; b. Chgo., Dec. 11, 1918; s. Joseph Michael and Anna (Flynn) K.; m. Mary Thomson, Mar. 21, 1949. PhB, Loyola U., Chgo., 1939, JD, 1941. Bar: Ill. 1941, U.S. Dist. Ct. (no. dist.) Ill. 1941, U.S. Ct. Appeals (7th cir.) 1946, U.S. Supreme Ct. 1956. Sole practice, Chgo., 1946—. Author: Litigation and Trial of Air Crash Cases, 1969; contbr. articles to profl. jours. Served with USN, 1941-46. Fellow Internat. Acad. Trial Lawyers (past chmn. aviation sect.); mem. AVA (chmn. aviation com. 1981-82), Inter-Am. Bar Assn., Ill. State Bar Assn., Chgo. Bar Assn. (bd. mgrs. 1965-67), Ill. Trial Lawyers Assn. (pres. 1986-69), World Assn. Lawyers, Am. Coll. Trial Lawyers, Internat. Acad. Law and Sci., Internat. Soc. Barristers, Am. Soc. Internat. Law, Am. Bar Found., Butterfield Country Club (Hinsdale, Ill.), Beverly Country Club (Chgo.). Admiralty, Aviation, Federal civil litigation. Office: 111 W Washington St Ste 1449 Chicago IL 60602-2708

KENNEY, JOHN ARTHUR, lawyer; b. Oklahoma City, Aug. 3, 1948; s. Jack H. and Betty Jo (Hill) K.; m. Jane Francis, Sept. 4, 1971; children: John Graham, Lauren Elizabeth. BS in Indsl. Engring. with distinction, U. Okla., 1971, JD, 1975. Bar: Tex. 1975, U.S. Dist. Ct. (so. dist.) Tex. 1976, U.S. Ct. Appeals (5th cir.) 1977, Okla. 1981, U.S. Dist. Ct. Okla. 1981, U.S. Ct. Appeals (10th cir.) 1983. Assoc. Baker & Botts, Houston, 1975-81; shareholder McAfee & Taft, Oklahoma City, 1982—. Temp. judge Okla. Ct. of Appeals, atty. appointed panels, Leadership Oklahoma City, 1993; magistrate judge merit selection com. and civil justice reform act adv. com. U.S. Dist. Ct. (we. dist.) Okla. Bd. advisors dept. indsl. engring.; deacon, past trustee Westminster Presbyn. Ch.; dir., pres. Christmas in April, Oklahoma City. Mem. ABA, Okla. Bar Assn. (adminstrn. of justice com. 1990—), Fed. bar Assn. Okla. City (chpt. pres. 2001-02), Okla. County Bar Assn. (chmn. bench and bar com. 1989-90, Outstanding Mem. 1989, v.p. 1991, bar counsel 1992-96, dir. 1997-98, pres. 1999-2000), Order of Coif, Tau Beta Pi. Federal civil litigation, State civil litigation, Intellectual property. Office: McAfee & Taft Two Leadership Sq 10th Fl Oklahoma City OK 73102

KENNEY, JOHN JOSEPH, lawyer; b. N.Y.C., July 13, 1943; s. Joseph Charles and Regina Elizabeth (Hulbert) K.; m. Charlotte O'Brien, May 23, 1971; 1 child, Alexander Hulbert. BA, St. Michael's Coll., 1966; JD, Fordham U., 1969. Bar: N.Y. 1970, U.S. Dist. Ct. (so. dist.) N.Y. 1973, U.S. Ct. Appeals (2d cir.) 1973, U.S. Dist. Ct. (ea. dist.) N.Y. 1980, U.S. Supreme Ct. 1991. Assoc. Dunnington, Bartholow & Miller, N.Y.C., 1969-71; asst. U.S. atty. U.S. Dist. Ct. (so. dist.) N.Y., 1971-80; assoc. Simpson, Thacher & Bartlett, 1980-81, ptnr., 1981—. Counsel, Village of Bronxville, 1983-86; mem. Planning Bd. of Bronxville, 1992-98, counsel, 1981-83; trustee Hist. Deerfield Inc., 1992-98, Bennington Coll., 1999—; bd. dirs. Citizens Crime Commn., 1998—, Am. Assn. for Internat. Commn. Jurists, 2000—. Recipient John Marshall award U.S. Dept. Justice, 1980. Fellow Am. Coll. Trial Lawyers; mem. ABA, Fed. Bar Coun. (pres. 1994-96), Assn. Bar City N.Y. (chmn. criminal law com. 1992-95), New York County Lawyers Assn. (pres. 1996-97), N.Y. State Bar Assn. (exec. com. 1997-2000). Republican. Roman Catholic. Federal civil litigation, Criminal, Securities. Home: 8 The Byway Bronxville NY 10708-4934 Office: Simpson Thacher & Bartlett 425 Lexington Ave 15th Fl New York NY 10017-3954 E-mail: jjkenney@stblaw.com

KENNICOTT, JAMES W. lawyer; b. Latrobe, Pa., Feb. 14, 1945; s. W.L. and Alice (Hayes) K.; m. Margot Barnes, Aug. 19, 1975 (div. 1977); m. Lynne Dratler Finney, July 1, 1984 (div. 1989). AB, Syracuse (N.Y.) U., 1967; JD, U. Wyo., 1979. Bar: Utah 1979. Prin. Ski Cons., Park City, Utah, 1969—; pvt. practice, 1979-87, 89—; ptnr. Kennicott & Finney, 1987-89; pvt. practice, 1989—. Cons. Destination Sports Specialists, Park City, 1984-99; judge pro tem Utah 3d Dist. Ct., Park City, 1988—; arbitrator Am. Arbitration Assn., 1989-2000. Chmn. Park City Libr. Bd. 1987; bd. dirs. Park City Libr., 1985-91, Park City Handicapped Sports, 1988-94, The Counseling Inst., 1993-97, chmn., 1994-95, treas. 1995-96, mem. program com. Gov.'s Commn. on Librs. and Info. Svcs., 1990-91. Mem. Utah Bar Assn., Am. Arbitration Assn. Avocations: skiing, sailing, hiking, cycling, literature. General civil litigation, Estate planning, Real property. Home and Office: PO Box 2339 Park City UT 84060-2339

KENNY, PHILIP WILLIAM, lawyer; b. Mt. Vernon, N.Y., Nov. 9, 1946; s. Paul James and Ethel Roma (Dooley) K.; m. Ellen Goldberg, Feb. 16, 1974 (div. Nov. 1980); m. Christine Madge Dockum, Nov. 29, 1980; children: Merideth, Jason, Matthew. BA, Fordham U., 1968; JD, N.Y. Law Sch., 1973. Bar: N.Y. 1974. Sole practice, Star Lake, N.Y., 1975-80; atty. Nationwide Ins. Co., Syracuse, 1980-83; assoc. Meiselman, Farber, Poughkeepsie, 1983-84, Grogan & Botti, P.C., Goshen, 1984-86; atty. Office of Ct. Adminstrn., Poughkeepsie, 1986—. Served with U.S. Army, 1968-70. Roman Catholic. Home: 505 Stanton Ter Poughkeepsie NY 12603-1165 Office: Dutchess County Ct Market St Poughkeepsie NY 12601

KENRICH, JOHN LEWIS, retired lawyer; b. Lima, Ohio, Oct. 17, 1929; s. Clarence E. and Rowena (Stroh) Katterheinrich; m. Betty Jane Roehll, May 26, 1951; children: John David, Mary Jane, Kathryn Ann, Thomas Roehll, Walter Clarence. BS, Miami U., Oxford, Ohio, 1951; LLB, U. Cin., 1953. Bar: Ohio 1953, Mass. 1969. Asst. counsel B.F. Goodrich Co., Akron, Ohio, 1956-65; asst. sec., counsel W.R. Grace & Co., Cin., 1965-68, v.p. Splty. Products Group divsn., 1970-71; corp. counsel, sec. Standex Internat. Corp., Andover, Mass., 1969-70; v.p., sec. Chemed Corp., Cin., 1971-82, sr. v.p., gen. counsel, 1982-86, exec. v.p., chief adminstrv. officer, 1986-91, ret., 1991. Trustee Better Bus. Bur., Cin., 1981-90; mem. bus. adv. coun. Miami U., 1986-88; mem. City Planning Commn., Akron, 1961-62; mem. bd. visitors Coll. Law U. Cin., 1988-92; mem. area coun. trustees Franciscan Sisters of Poor Found., Cin., 1989-93; bd. govs. Ohio River Valley chpt. Arthritis Found., 1992-95, 2000—; mem. Com. on Reinvestment City of Cin., 1991-93. 1st lt. JAGC U.S. Army, 1954-56. Mem. Am. Arbitration Assn., Cin. Bar Assn., Beta Theta Pi, Omicron Delta Kappa, Delta Sigma Pi, Phi Eta Sigma. Republican. Presbyterian. General corporate. Home and Office: 504 Abilene Trl Cincinnati OH 45215-2515 E-mail: JKenrich@msn.com

KENT, JOHN BRADFORD, lawyer; b. Jacksonville, Fla., Sept. 5, 1939; s. Frederick Heber and Norma Cleveland (Futch) K.; m. Monett Powers, Dec. 18, 1969; children: Monett, Susan, Sally, Katherine. AB, Yale U., 1961; JD, U. Fla., 1964; LLM in Taxation, NYU, 1965. Bar: Fla., 1964, U.S. Dist. Ct. (mid. dist.) Fla. 1965, U.S. Tax Ct., 1965, U.S. Dist. (so. dist.) Fla., 1981, Neb., 1995, U.S. Ct. Appeals (11th cir.), U.S. Supreme Ct., 1973. Assoc. Ulmer, Murchison, Kent, Ashby & Ball, Jacksonville, 1965-67; ptnr., shareholder Kent, Watts & Durden, P.A. and predecessor firms, 1967-85; shareholder Carlton, Field, Ward, Emmanuel, Smith, Cutler & Kent, 1985-88, Kent, Crawford & Gooding, P.A., Jacksonville, 1988—. Jacksonville Legal Aid Soc. (past bd. dirs.), Fla. Cmty. Coll Found. (past pres., trustee), Children's Home Soc. Fla. NE Divsn. (past pres., bd. dirs.). Mem. Nat. Assn. Theatre Owners Fla. (bd. dirs., officer 1969-2000), Rotary (past officer, Paul Harris Fellow). Banking, Contracts commercial, General corporate. Office: Kent Crawford & Gooding PA 225 Water St Ste 900 Jacksonville FL 32202-5142

KENT, M. ELIZABETH, lawyer; b. N.Y.C., Nov. 17, 1943; d. Francis J. and Hannah (Bergman) K. AB, Vassar Coll. magna cum laude, 1964; AM, Harvard U., 1965, PhD, 1974; JD, Georgetown U., 1978. Bar: D.C. 1978, U.S. Dist. Ct. D.C. 1978, U.S. Ct. Appeals (D.C. cir.) 1978, U.S. Supreme Ct. 1983, U.S. Dist. Ct. Md. 1985. From lectr. to asst. prof. history U. Ala., Birmingham, 1972-74; assoc. Santarelli and Gimer, Washington, 1978; sole practice, 1978—. Mem. Ripon Soc., Cambridge and Washington, 1968-93; rsch. dir. Howard M. Miller for Congress, Boston, 1972; vol. campaigns John V. Lindsay for Mayor, 1969, John V. Lindsay for Pres., 1972, John B. Anderson for Pres., 1980. Woodrow Wilson fellow 1964-65; Harvard U. fellow 1968-69. Mem. ABA, ACLU, D.C. Bar Assn., Women's Bar Assn., D.C. Assn. Criminal Def. Lawyers, Superior Ct. Trial Lawyers Assn., Nat. Women's Polit. Caucus, Phi Beta Kappa. Republican. Avocations: history, politics. Appellate, General civil litigation, Criminal. Home: 35 E St NW Apt 810 Washington DC 20001-1520 Office: 601 Indiana Ave NW Ste 605 Washington DC 20004-2918 E-mail: kentlaw@earthlink.net

KENT, STEPHEN SMILEY, lawyer; b. Reno, July 6, 1952; s. Robert Roe and Muriel (Smiley) K.; m. H. Mayla Walcutt, Dec. 19, 1976; children: Kristopher, Kimberly, Alisa. BS (hons.), U. Nev., 1975; JD, U. of the Pacific, 1980. Bar: Nev. 1980. Law clk. to Hon. William N. Forman, Reno, 1980-81; assoc. Vargas & Bartlett, 1981-86, Beckley, Singleton, Jemison & List, Reno, 1986-89, shareholder, 1989-97, Woodburn & Wedge, Reno, 1997—. Mem. exec. coun. Nev. State Bar Young Lawyers Assn., Reno, 1987-89; mem. fee dispute com. Nev. State Bar, Reno, 1985-88, mem. ins. com., 1986-87. Co-author: (manuals/seminars) Nevada Uninsured Motorist Insurance, 1985, Controlling Damages, 1991, Enforcing Judgments, 1989, Pretrial Discovery, 1988, Default Judgements, 1994, Insurance Coverage Law in Nevada, 1998, Advanced Personal Injury Practice, 2001. Mem. Neighborhood Adv. Coun., Reno, 1992-98. Mem. ABA (litigation sect.), Internat. Assn. Def. Counsel, Nat. Bd. Trial Advocacy (cert. civil trial advocate), Reno Rodeo Assn., Rotary Club Reno. Federal civil litigation, Intellectual property, Personal injury. Home: 2815 Columbus Way Reno NV 89503-1848 Office: Woodburn & Wedge 6100 Neil Rd PO Box 2311 Reno NV 89505-2311 Fax: 775-688-3088. E-mail: skent@woodburnandwedge.com

KENTRIS, GEORGE LAWRENCE, lawyer; b. Detroit, Nov. 3, 1949; s. Michael Nicholas and Mary (Cassimatis) K.; m. Susan Jo Van Dorn, Nov. 18, 1972; children: Emily Joya, Vanessa, Ann Alexia. BA, Ohio State U., 1971; JD, U. Toledo Coll. Law, 1976. Bar: Ohio 1976, U.S. Dist. Ct. (no. dist.) Ohio 1977, U.S. Supreme Ct. 1980, U.S. Ct. Appeals (6th cir.) 1989. Asst. prosecuting atty. Hancock County Ohio Prosecutors Office, Findlay, Ohio, 1977-85; assoc. Noble, Bryant & Needles, 1977-81; pvt. practice, 1981-87, 99—; sr. ptnr. Kentris & Wolph, 1987-92; sr. atty. Kentris & Assocs., 1992-96; sr. ptnr. Kentris, Brown & Powell, 1996-97; pres. Kentris, Brown, Powell & Balega Co., LPA, 1997-98. Franchisee Taco Bell Corp., Ohio, 1982—; officer, dir. Findlay TV Corp., 1991-97. Bd. trustees Am. Cancer Soc. Hancock County, Findlay, 1980-94, pres., 1985-86; mem. Hancock County Rep. Exec. Com., 1982-98, treas., 1984-86; bd. dirs. Jr. Achievement of Hancock Co., Inc., 1991-98, Franchisee Choice Hotels, 1998—; dir. Unified Foodservice Purchasing Coop, LLC, 1999—; rep. Franmac, 2001—. Mem. Findlay/Hancock County Bar Assn. (cert. grievance com. 1987-98, chmn. 1995, sec. 1993, treas. 1980-81). Mem. Greek Orthodox. Avocations: golf, tennis, skiing, softball, sports cars. General civil litigation, Criminal, Personal injury. Office: George L Kentris Atty at Law 431 E Main Cross St Findlay OH 45840-4822 E-mail: gkentris@aol.com

KENWOOD, JOEL DAVID, lawyer; b. Paterson, N.J., June 17, 1951; BA, Stanford U., 1973; JD, Am. U., 1977. Bar: Fla. 1978, D.C. 1985, Colo. 1989; cert. civil trial law and bus. litigation law, civil trial advocacy. Assoc. Jeffer, Walter, Tierney, Dekorte, Hopkinson & Vogel, Palm Beach, Fla., 1978-79, Baskin & Sears, Palm Beach, 1979-82; ptnr. Heeg, Kenwood & Stone PA, Boca Raton, 1982-86, Woods, Oviatt, Gilman, Sturmant & Clarke, Boca Raton, 1987-93; pvt. practice, 1993—. Mem. Fla. Bar Assn. (comml. litigation com. 1984—, copr., banking and bus. law com., jud. nominating procedures com. 1986), Palm Beach County Bar Assn. (chmn. jud. rels. com. 1984-85, chmn. appellate practice com. 1983-84, chmn. legis. liaison com. 1985-86), South Palm Beach County Bar Assn. (bd. dirs. 1983—, sec. 1984-85, treas. 1985-86, v.p. 1986-87, pres. 1988-89). Federal civil litigation, State civil litigation. Office: 6100 Glades Rd Ste 204 Boca Raton FL 33434-4370

KEOUGH, JOSEPH ALOYSIOS, judge; b. Providence, Apr. 8, 1941; s. s. Joseph A. and Mary (Crane) K.; m. Joanne Lee, Oct. 9, 1965; children: Joseph, Maureen, Kathleen, Colleen. BA, Providence Coll., 1962; JD, Suffolk U., 1970. Bar: R.I. 1970, U.S. Dist. Ct. R.I. 1971. Assoc. McGee, Fifford, Farrelly & Keough, Providence, 1970-75; ptnr. Keough, Parker, Gearon & Viner, Pawtucket, R.I., 1975-97; mcpl. ct. judge City of Pawtucket, 1974-97. Dir., sec. First Bank & Trust, Providence; dir. East Greenwich Dairy; pres. Ross Brooks Ent., Pawtucket, 1979—. Exec. sec. R.I. Dem. Com., 1976; del. Dem. Nat. Conv., R.I., 1972; chmn. appeals City of Pawtucket, 1968-74. Burke scholar R.I. Golf Assn., 1958. Mem. Am. Arbitration Assn., Pawtucket County Club (v.p., sec., pres.), Elks, Irish Kings. Roman Catholic. Home: 72 Anawan Rd Pawtucket RI 02861-3327 Office: RI Superior Ct Keough Parker Gearon & Viner 250 Benefit St Providence RI 02903

KEPLINGER, BRUCE (DONALD KEPLINGER), lawyer; b. Kansas City, Kans., Feb. 4, 1952; s. Donald Lee and Janet Adelheit (Viets) K.; children: Mark William, Lisbeth Marie, Kristen Michelle, Kailyn Emily, Courtney Nicole; m. Carol Ann Heinz, Apr. 12, 1991. BA with highest distinction, U. Kans., 1974; JD cum laude, So. Meth. U., 1977. Bar: Kans. 1977, U.S. Dist. Ct. Kans. 1977, Mo. 1980, U.S. Dist. Ct. Mo. 1980, U.S. Ct. Appeals (10th cir.) 1985, U.S. Supreme Ct. 1989. Assoc. Clark, Mize & Linville, Salina, Kans., 1977-79, Blackwell, Sanders et al, Kansas City, Mo., 1979-82; ptnr. Payne & Jones, Overland Park, Kans., 1982-94, Norris, Keplinger & Herman, LLC, Overland Park, 1994—. Master Kansas Inns of Ct.; chmn. Kansas Lawyer Svcs Corp., 1992-01. Contbr. articles to profl. jours. V.p. Friends of Library, Johnson County, Kans., 1980-85; deacon Village Presbyn. Ch., 1982-86. Mem. ABA, Internat. Assn. Def. Counsel, Assn. Def. Trial Attys. (state chmn. 1996—, exec. coun., 1999—), Kans. Bar Assn. (chmn. Kans. lawyer svc. corp. 1992-2001), Mo. Bar Assn., Kans. Assn. Def. Counsel (bd. dirs. 1990—, pres.-elect 1992-93, pres. 1993-94), Def. Rsch. Inst., Rotary Internat., Hallbrook Country Club. Republican. Avocations: reading, golf. Federal civil litigation, State civil litigation, Personal injury. Office: Norris Keplinger & Herman LLC 6800 College Blvd Ste 630 Overland Park KS 66211-1556 E-mail: bkeplinger@k-c-lawyers.com

KEPLINGER, MICHAEL SCOTT, lawyer; b. Martinsburg, W.Va., Mar. 26, 1940; s. Raymond Lester and Bertha Louise (Kidwiler) K.; m. Helen Bunten, Dec. 27, 1963; children: Michael Scott, Gregory Thomas. BS in Chemistry, W.Va. U., 1963; JD, Georgetown U., 1971. Bar: Md. 1972. Computer scientist Nat. Bur. Stds., Washington, 1967-76; asst. exec. dir. Nat. Commn. on New Technol. Uses of Copyrighted Works, 1976-78; spl. legal asst. to register U.S. Copyright Office, 1978-80, chief info. and rev. divsn., 1980-83, policy planning advisor, 1983-84; sr. counselor Office Legis. and Internat. Affairs U.S. Patent and Trademark Office, 1984—. Cons. World Intellectual Property Orgn.; dep. head Del. to Diplomatic Conf. on Certain Copyright and Neighboring Rights Matters, 1996; chief copyright negotiator for Agreement on Trade Related Aspects of Intellectual Property (TRIPS) for the U.S., 1990-95; negotiator for Diplomatic Conf. on Protection of Audiovisual Performers, Dec. 2000. Home: 5001 Nahant St Bethesda MD 20816-2462 Office: US Patent and Trademark Office Washington DC 20034

KEPNER, ANNE JONES, lawyer; b. Norwalk, Conn., Jan. 15, 1969; d. Thomas David Jr. and Elizabeth Call Jones; m. Thomas James Kepner, June 12, 1999. BS in Health Sci., San Jose (Calif.) State U., 1991; JD, U. Calif., San Francisco, 1995. Assoc. Liccardo, Rossi, et al, San Jose, 1996-97, Hoge, Fenton, Jones & Appel, San Jose, 1997—. Mem. Santa Clara Bar Assn. (bd. dirs. 1996-98, pres. barristers sect. 1998-99), Rotary Internat., Valle Monte League. Office: Hoge Fenton Jones and Appel 60 S Market St Ste 1400 San Jose CA 95113-2396

KEPPEL, WILLIAM JAMES, lawyer, educator, writer; b. Sheboygan, Wis., Sept. 25, 1941; s. William Frederick and Anne Elizabeth (Cinealis) K.; m. Polly Holmberg, June 26, 1965; children: Anne Rusert, Timothy, Matthew. BA, Marquette U., 1963; JD, U. Wis., Madison, 1970. Bar: Minn. 1970, U.S. Dist. Minn. 1970, U.s. Ct. Appeals (8th cir.) 1973, U.S. Dist. Ct. (we. dist.) Wis. 1979, U.S. Supreme Ct. 1979, U.S. Ct. Claims 1982. Assoc. Dorsey & Whitney, Mpls., 1970-76, ptnr., 1979-96; assoc. prof. Hamline U. Sch. Law, 1976-79, disting. practitioner in residence, 1996-2000. Instr. U. Minn. Law Sch.; adj. prof. William Mitchell Coll. Law, St. Paul; state adminstrv. law judge, 1977-79, 98—; chmn., dir. Legal Advice Clinics, Ltd.; dir. Legal Assistance of Minn., Inc.; head Hennepin County Pub. Defender's Office for Misdemeanors. Author: (with Mc Farland) Minnesota Civil Practice (4 vols.), 1979, 3d edit., 1999, Administrative Practice

and Procedure, 1999; co-author, editor: Minnesota Environmental Law Handbook, 2nd edit., 1995; contbr. articles and monographs to legal jours. Lt. USN, 1963-67, Vietnam. Mem. ABA, Minn. Bar Assn. Roman Catholic. Administrative and regulatory, Federal civil litigation, Environmental. Home: 10 Luverne Ave Minneapolis MN 55419-2612

KEPPELMAN, NANCY, lawyer; b. Abington, Pa., June 28, 1950; d. H. Thomas and Helene A. (Harrow) Keppelman; m. Michael E. Smerza, Sept. 9, 1978. Student, Oberlin (Ohio) Coll., 1968-70; BA, U. Mich., 1972, JD, 1978; Cert., Inst. for Paralegal Tng., Phila., 1972. Bar: Mich. 1978, U.S. Dist. Ct. (ea. dist.) Mich. 1978, U.S. Tax Ct. 1986. Legal asst. Dykema, Gossett et al, Detroit, 1972-75; assoc. Butzel, Keidan et al, 1978-80, Law Offices of Brook McCray Smith, Ann Arbor, Mich., 1980-82, Miller, Canfield et al, Detroit, 1982-89, Stevenson Assocs., Ann Arbor, 1989-90; shareholder/lawyer Stevenson Keppelman Assocs., 1991—. Condr. seminars in field. Chpt. author, co-editor QDROs, EDROs and Retirement Benefits: A Guide for Michigan Practitioners, 1994; contbr. articles to profl. jours. James B. Angell scholar, U. Mich., 1972. Fellow Mich. State Bar Found.; mem. ABA, State Bar Mich. (mem. taxation coun. 1991-94), Washtenaw County Bar Assn., Women Lawyers Assn. Mich. (bd. dirs., pres. Washtenaw region 1990-93). Avocations: birdwatching, music, hiking. General corporate, Pension, profit-sharing, and employee benefits, Taxation, general. Office: 444 S Main St Ann Arbor MI 48104-2304 E-mail: ska@ic.net

KERIAN, JON ROBERT, retired judge; b. Grafton, N.D., Oct. 23, 1927; s. Cyril Robert and Elizabeth Antoinette (Kadlec) K.; m. Sylvia Ann Larson, Dec. 28, 1959; children: John, Ann. PhB, U. N.D., 1955, LLB, 1957, JD, 1971. Bar: N.D. 1957, U.S. Dist. Ct. N.D. 1958, U.S. Ct. Appeals (8th cir.) 1971, U.S. Supreme Ct. 1963. Pvt. practice law, Grand Forks, N.D., 1958-61; asst. atty. gen. State of N.D., Bismarck, 1961-67; ptnr. Bosard, McCutcheon, Kerian, Schmidt, Minot, N.D., 1967-80; dist. judge State of N.D., 1980-92, surrogate judge, 1993—. History instr. Bismarck State Coll., 1965-67; asst. city atty. City of Minot, 1968-76; atty. Zoning & Planning Commn., Minot, 1969-76; lectr. in field. Contbr. articles to profl. jours.; editor ABA newsletter, The Judges News, 1990—95. Mem. ABA (bd. editors Judges Jour. 1990-95), Western States Bar Conf. (pres. 1982-83), N.D. Bar Assn. (pres. 1979-80), Nat. Conf. State Trial Judges (exec. com. 1983-89). Home: 1800 8th St SW Minot ND 58701-6410 Office: PO Box 340 Minot ND 58702-0340

KERLIN, GILBERT, lawyer; b. Camden, N.J., Oct. 10, 1909; s. Ward Dix Sr. and Jenny (Gilbert) K.; m. Sarah Morrison, Aug. 23, 1941; children: Sarah Kerlin Gray, Gilbert Nye, Jonathan Otis. BA, Harvard U., 1933, LLB, 1936. Bar: U.S. Ct. Appeals (2d cir.) 1937, U.S. Supreme Ct. 1945. Sr. ptnr. Shearman & Sterling, N.Y.C., 1936—. Chmn. bd. dirs. Exmin Corp., Wave Hill Inc.; bd. dirs. Dodge Found. Served to lt. col. USAF, 1942-46. Democrat. Unitarian. Home: Dodgewood Rd Riverdale NY 10471 Office: 153 E 53rd St New York NY 10022-4611 also: Shearman & Sterling 599 Lexington Ave at 53rd St New York NY 10022

KERN, CLIFFORD HAROLD, JR. lawyer; b. New Orleans, Dec. 2, 1915; s. Clifford Harold and Sadie Judith (Schwartz) K.; m. Nettie Cahn Hirsch, June 14, 1947; children— Clifford Harold III, Jay H. LL.B., Tulane U., 1938, J.D., 1969. Bar: La. 1939, U.S. Dist. Ct. (ea. dist.) La. Ptnr. Kuhner & Kern, New Orleans, 1939-46; asst. to pres., treas., sec., v.p. Imperial Shoe Store Inc., New Orleans, 1946-77; assoc. Dresner & Dresner, New Orleans, 1977-92. Pres. Sugar Bowl Football Classic, 1974-75, chmn. bd., 1983-84. Served as lt. comdr., submarine service USN, 1941-46. Elected to Football Hall of Fame, 1977. Mem. La. State Bar Assn., New Orleans Bar Assn., New Orleans C. of C., Mil. Order World Wars, Navy League U.S., Retired Officers Assn. Home: 2100 St Charles Ave Apt 7L New Orleans LA 70130 Office: 210 Baronne St Ste 903 New Orleans LA 70112-4160

KERN, GEORGE CALVIN, JR. lawyer; b. Balt., Apr. 19, 1926; s. George Calvin and Alice (Gaskins) K.; m. Joan Shorell, Dec. 22, 1962; 1 child, Heath. BA, Princeton U., 1947; LLB, Yale U., 1952. Bar: N.Y. 1952. Chief U.S. Info. Ctr., Mannheim, W.Ger., 1947-48; dep. dir. pub. info. Office U.S. Mil. Govt. for Germany, Berlin and Nurnberg, 1948-49; assoc. Sullivan & Cromwell, N.Y.C., 1952-60, ptnr., 1960—. Publ. Cub newspaper, Tehachapi, Calif., 1974—; bd. dirs. McJunkin Corp., Charleston, W.Va. Lt. USN, 1944-46. General corporate, Mergers and acquisitions, Securities. Home: 830 Park Ave New York NY 10021-2757 Office: Sullivan & Cromwell 125 Broad St Fl 28 New York NY 10004-2489

KERN, JOHN WORTH, III, judge; b. Indpls., May 25, 1928; s. John Worth and Bernice (Winn) K.; children: John, Stephen. BA, Princeton U., 1949; LLB, Harvard U., 1952. Bar: D.C. 1953, U.S. Ct. Appeals (D.C. cir.) 1955. With CIA, 1952-54; law clk. to chief judge U.S. Ct. Appeals D.C. Cir. Ct., 1954-55; asst. U.S. atty. D.C. Dist. Dept. Justice, Washington, 1955-59; assoc. Kilpatrick, Ballard & Beasley, 1959-65; with Dept. of Justice, 1965-68; judge D.C. Ct. Appeals, 1968-84, sr. judge, 1987—. Dean Nat. Jud. Coll., Reno, 1984-87. Mem. D.C. Bar. Presbyterian. Office: DC Ct Appeals 500 Indiana Ave NW Washington DC 20001-2138

KERN, TERRY C. judge; b. Clinton, Okla., Sept. 25, 1944; s. Elgin L. Kern and Lora Lee (Miller) Renegar; m. Charlene Heinen, Dec. 26, 1970; children: Lauren, Suzanne, Justin Hunter. BS, Okla. State U., Stillwater, 1966; JD, U. Okla., 1969. Bar: Okla. 1969, U.S. Dist. Ct. (ea. dist.) Okla. 1974, U.S. Dist. Ct. (we. dist.) Okla. 1979, U.S. Dist. Ct. (no. dist.) Okla. 1993, U.S. Ct. Appeals (10th cir.) 1979. Gen. atty. FTC, Washington, 1969-70; ptnr. Fischl, Culp, McMillin, Kern and Chaffin, Ardmore, Okla., 1971-86; founding ptnr., pres. Kern, Mordy and Sperry, 1986-94; dist. judge U.S. Dist. Ct. (no. dist.) Okla., Tulsa, 1994—, chief judge, 1996—. Mem. Jud. Conf. Com. on Security and Facilities; mem. 10th Cir. Jud. coun. ähmn.äBd. dirs. So. Okla. Meml. Hosp., Ardmore, 1982-92, chmn., 1989-91; vice chmn. Ardmore Devel. Authority, 1990; v.p. Perry Maxwell Intercollegiate Assn., Ardmore, 1992—. Served with USAR, 1970-75. Fellow Am. Bar Found., Okla. Bar Found. (pres. 1991, Disting. Svc. award 1992); mem. ABA, Am. Bd. Trial Advocates (Okla. chpt.), Okla. Bar Assn., W. Lee Johnson Inn of Ct. (master of bench), U. Okla. Coll. Law Assn., Fed. Judges Assn., Tulsa City Bar Assn. (bd. dirs.). Democrat. Episcopal. Office: US Dist Courthouse 333 W 4th St Tulsa OK 74103-3839

KERNER, MICHAEL PHILIP, lawyer; b. N.Y.C., July 21, 1953; s. Arthur and Rosalind (Mehr) K. BA, Antioch Coll., 1976; JD, Lewis & Clark U., 1979; LLM in Taxation with honors, Golden Gate U., 1995. Bar: Calif. 1980 (cert. specialist personal and small bus. bankruptcy law), U.S. Dist. Ct. (no. and ea. dists.) Calif. 1983, U.S. Ct. Appeals (9th cir.) 1983, U.S. Tax Ct., 1996. Staff atty. U.S. EPA, Washington, 1979-80, asst. regional counsel region 9 San Francisco, 1980-83; ptnr. Kerner, Weppner & Rosenbaum, 1983-95; prin. Kerner & Assocs., 1996-2000; ptnr. Janin, Morgan & Brenner, 2000—. Bd. dirs. Solano County Legal Assistance, Vallejo, Calif., 1983-86; arbitrator San Francisco Superior Ct., 1991-94. Editor law rev. and law jours. Mem. San Francisco Trial Lawyers Assn., Solano County Bar Assn., Nat. Assn. Consumer Bankruptcy Attys. Democrat. Jewish. Avocations: windsurfing, snowboarding, road and mountain biking. Bankruptcy, Estate planning, Taxation, general. E-mail: mpk@jmblaw.com

KERNOCHAN, JOHN MARSHALL, lawyer, educator; b. N.Y.C., Aug. 3, 1919; s. Marshall Rutgers and Caroline (Hatch) K. AB, Harvard U., 1942; JD, Columbia U., 1948. Bar: N.Y. 1949. Asst. dir. Legis. Drafting Research Fund Columbia U., N.Y.C., 1950-51, acting dir., 1951-52, dir., 1952-69, lectr. law, 1951-52, assoc. prof., 1952-55, prof., 1955-77, Nash prof. law, 1977-89, Nash prof. law emeritus, 1990—, exec. dir. Council for Atomic Age Studies, 1956-59, co-chmn., 1960-62, dir. Ctr. Law & Arts (now Kernochan Ctr. Law Media & Arts), 1986-99; spl. lectr., 1991—; co-dir., 1999—. Chmn. bd. Galaxy Music Corp., 1956-89; cons. Temporary State Commn. to Study Organizational Structure of Govt. of N.Y.C., 1953; bd. dirs. E.C.Schirmer Music Co., Inc.; pres. Gaudia Music & Arts, Inc., 1987—. Author: The Legislative Process, 1980; co-author: Legal Method Cases and Materials, 1980; contbr. articles to profl. jours. Mem. civil and polit. rights com. Pres.'s Commn. on Status of Women, 1962-63; dir. emeritus Vol. Lawyers for the Arts; mem. legal and legis. com. Internat. Confedn. Socs. Authors and Composers. Mem. Assn. Bar City of N.Y. Internat. Lit. and Artistic Assn. (mem. d'honneur, internat. exec. com., mem. U.S.A. group), Copyright Soc. U.S.A. (exec. com. 1986-89), Assn. Tchrs. and Rschrs. in Intellectual Property. Office: Columbia U Sch Law 435 W 116th St New York NY 10027-7297

KERNS, DAVID VINCENT, lawyer; b. Jan. 29, 1917; s. Clinton Bowen and Ella Mae (Young) K.; m. Dorothea Boyd, Sept. 5, 1942; children: David V., Clinton Boyd. BPh, Emory U., 1937; JD, U. Fla., 1939. Bar: Fla. 1939, U.S. Dist. Ct. (mid. dist.) Fla. 1939, (so. dist.) Fla. 1978, (no. dist.) Fla. 1981, U.S. Ct. Appeals (11th cir.) 1981, U.S. Supreme Ct. 1988. Assoc. Sutton & Reeves, Tampa, Fla., 1939-41, Fowler & White, Tampa, 1945-47; ptnr. Moran & Kerns, 1948-49; resident atty. Fla. Road Dept., 1949-53; rsch. asst. Supreme Ct. Fla., 1953-58; dir. Fla. Legis. Reference Bur., 1958-68, Fla. Legis. Svc. Bur., 1968-71, Fla. Legis. Libr. Svcs., 1971-73; gen. counsel Fla. Dept. Adminstrn., 1973-82; mem. Fla. Career Svc. Commn., 1983-86; spl. master Fla. Senate, 1987-96; legal cons. chief inspector gen. Fla. Gov. Office, 1995-98. Contbr. articles to profl. jours. Served with U.S. Army, 1941-45. Mem. Fla. Govt. Bar Assn. (pres. 1956, J. Ernest Webb Meml. award 1982), Fla. Bar (bd. govs. 1978-84), Tallahassee Bar Assn. (spl. dir. 1993-95). Democrat. Methodist. Home: 418 Vinnedge Ride Tallahassee FL 32303-5140

KERR, ALEXANDER DUNCAN, JR. lawyer; b. Pitts., May 6, 1943; s. Alexander Duncan Sr. and Nancy Greenleaf (Martin) K.; m. Judith Kathleen Mottl, May 25, 1969; children: Matthew Jonathan, Joshua Brandon. BS in Bus., Northwestern U., 1965, JD, 1968. Bar: Ill. 1968, Pa. 1969, U.S. Dist. Ct. (ea. dist.) Pa. 1969, U.S. Dist. Ct. (no. dist.) Ill. 1969, U.S. Ct. Appeals (3rd and 7th cirs.) 1969, U.S. Supreme Ct. 1969. Assoc. Clark, Ladner, Fontenbaugh & Young, Phila., 1968-69, 73-74; asst. U.S. atty. U.S. Dept. Justice, Chgo., 1974-79; assoc., ptnr. Keck, Mahin & Cate, Chgo., Oak Brook, Ill., 1979-90; shareholder Tishler & Wald, Ltd., Chgo., 1990—. Staff atty. Park Dist. La Grange, Ill., 1985—; active Ill. St. Andrew Soc., North Riverside, 1982—, pres., 1995-97; vestryman, lay reader, chancellor, chalice bearer Emmanuel Episcopal Ch., 1980-99; mem. Pack 177, Troop 19, Order of the Arrow, Boy Scouts Am., La Grange, 1980—. With USN, 1969-75. Mem. Am. Legion, DuPage Club, Atlantis Divers. Bankruptcy, General civil litigation, General corporate. Home: 709 S Stone Ave La Grange IL 60525-2725 Fax: 708-354-1208. E-mail: adkerrjr@aol.com

KERR, GERALD LEE, III, lawyer, paralegal educator; b. Mpls., July 7, 1944; s. Gerald L. Kerr Jr. BS, U.S. Naval Acad., 1966; JD, Cath. U., 1972; MPA, Golden Gate U., 1976. Bar: D.C., Va. Atty. Kelberg & Childress, Virginia Beach, Va., 1977-78, Gerald L. Kerr III, P.C., Virginia Beach, 1978—. Asst. prof. Tidewater C.C., Virginia Beach, 1977—. Pres., Norfolk Sister City Assn., 1979-81. Served to comdr. JAGC Corps, U.S. Navy, 1966-87. Named to Outstanding Young Men of Am., 1979, 80, 81. Office: 3634 S Plaza Trl Virginia Beach VA 23452-3351

KERRICK, DAVID ELLSWORTH, lawyer; b. Caldwell, Idaho, Jan. 15, 1951; s. Charles Ellsworth and Patria (Olesen) K.; m. Juneal Casper, May 24, 1980; children: Peter Ellsworth, Beth Anne, George Ellis, Katherine Leigh. Student, Coll. of Idaho, 1969-71; BA, U. Wash., 1972; JD, U. Idaho, 1980. Bar: Idaho 1980, U.S. Dist. Ct. Idaho 1980, U.S. Ct. Appeals (9th cir.) 1981. Mem. Idaho Senate, 1990-96, majority caucus chmn., 1992-94, majority leader, 1994-96. Mem. S.W. Idaho Estate Planning Coun. Mem. ABA, Assn. Trial Lawyers Am., Idaho Bar Assn. (3d dist. pres. 1985-86), Idaho Trial Lawyers Assn., Canyon County Lawyers Assn. (pres. 1985). Republican. Presbyterian. Lodge: Elks. Avocations: skiing, photography. Estate planning, Personal injury, Real property. Office: PO Box 44 Caldwell ID 83606-0044

KERSH, DEWITTE TALMADGE, JR. lawyer; b. Balt., June 1, 1930; s. DeWitte Talmadge and Marianna (Snyder) K.; m. Sharon R. Doherty, Aug. 2, 1986; children: DeWitte III, Sarah Anne. BS, Cornell U., 1952, LLB, 1957. Bar: R.I. 1958, N.H. 1991, U.S. Dist. Ct. R.I. 1959, U.S. Dist. Ct. N.H. 1991. Ptnr. Tillinghast, Collins & Graham, Providence, 1965-93; counsel Tillinghast, Licht, Perkins Smith & Cohen, 1993—. Adj. instr. Law Sch. Roger Williams U. Bd. dirs., pres., W.Va. Found. town selection; mem. planning bd. W. Va.; bd. Music Festival, Waterville Valley, NH. Fellow Am. Acad. Matrimonial Lawyers; mem. ABA (family law and elder law sects.), R.I. and N.H. Bar Assns. (pro bono svc. 1987-94), N.H. Family Ct. Bench and Bar (past. pres.), Rotary (pres. 1989-90). Republican. Unitarian. Home: PO Box 346 Waterville Valley NH 03215-0346 Office: Tillinghast Licht et al 10 Weybosset St Providence RI 02903

KERYCZYNSKYJ, LEO IHOR, county official, educator, lawyer; b. Chgo., Aug. 8, 1948; s. William and Eva (Chicz) K.; m. Alexandra Irene Okruch, July 19, 1980; 1 child, Christina Alexandra. BA, BS, DePaul U., 1970, MS in Pub. Svc., 1975; JD, No. Ill. U., 1979; postgrad., U. Ill., Chgo., 1980-82. Bar: Ill. 1981, U.S. Dist. Ct. (no. dist.) Ill. 1981, U.S. Ct. Appeals (7th cir.) 1981, U.S. Tax Ct. 1981, U.S. Ct. Claims 1982, U.S. Ct. Mil. Appeals 1982, U.S. Ct. Appeals (fed. cir.) 1983, U.S. Supreme Ct. 1984. Condemnation awards officer Cook County Treas.'s Office, Chgo., 1972-75, adminstrv. asst., 1975-77, dep. treas., 1977-87, chief legal counsel, 1987-96, dir. fin. svcs., 1988-96; pvt. practice, 1996-98; adv. Office of Profl. Stds. Chgo. Police Dept., 1998—. Adj. prof. DePaul U., Chgo., 1979-95; elected chmn. bd. dirs., 1st Security Fed. Savs. Bank Chgo., 1992-93. Capt. Ukrainian Am. Dem. Orgn., Chgo., 1971. Recipient Outstanding Alumni award Phi Kappa Theta, 1971. Mem. ABA, Ill. State Bar Assn., Ill. Trial Law Assn., Ukrainian Am. Bar Assn., Chgo. Bar Assn., Ill. Assn. County Ofcls., Internat. Assn. Clerks, Recorders, Election Ofcls. and Treas., Shore Line Interurban Hist. Soc. (bd. dirs., legal counsel 1987—, pres. and chmn., 1993-98), Theta Delta Phi. Ukrainian Catholic. Home: 2324 W Iowa St Apt 3R Chicago IL 60622-4720 Office: Office Profl Stds 1130 S Wabash Ave Chicago IL 60605-2372

KESHIAN, RICHARD, lawyer; b. Arlington, Mass., Aug. 11, 1934; s. Hamayak and Takuhe (Malkesian) K.; m. Jacqueline C. Cannilla, Sept. 11, 1965; children: Carolyn D., Richard M. (dec. 1999). BSBA, Boston U., 1956, JD, 1958. Bar: Mass. 1958. Pvt. practice law, Arlington, 1964-71; ptnr. Keshian & Reynolds, P.C., 1971—. Instr. bus law George Washington U., Washington, 1961-63; mem. adv. bd. Coop. Bank Concord, Arlington, 1983-86; corporator Bank Five for Savs., Arlington, 1984-91; bd. dirs., gen. counsel Arlington Coop. Bank, 1978-83. Chmn. Arlington Zoning Bd. Appeals, 1972-76; pres. Arlington C. of C., 1976; v.p. Mass. Fedn. Planning Bds., 1978-85; mem. Arlington Contributory Retirement Bd., 1984—. With USMC, 1958-64; maj. Res. ret. Mem. ABA, Mass. Bar Assn., Am. Arbitration Assn. (arbitrator 1975—), Mass. Conveyancers Assn. (bd. dirs. 1996—, chmn. title standards com. 1996-2000, clk. 1999—), Mass. Assn. Bank Counsel (bd. dirs. 1985—, pres. 1992-95), Middlesex County Bar Assn. Democrat. Congregationalist. Banking, Probate, Real property. Home: 93 Falmouth Rd W Arlington MA 02474-1007 Office: 1040 Massachusetts Ave PO Box 440 Arlington MA 02476-0052 E-mail: keshian@ix.net.com

KESLER, JOHN A. lawyer, land developer; b. Clark County, Ill., Apr. 25, 1923; s. Hal H. and Clara (Hurst) K.; m. Maxine Ruth Weaver, May 13, 1948; children: Nicki Kesler Cotsworth, Bradley Weaver, John A. II. AB, Ind. State U., 1948; JD, Ind. U., 1951. Bar: Ind. 1951, Ill. 1951. Chief dep. prosecutor County Vigo, Terre Haute, Ind., 1954-58; probate commr. Cir. Ct., 1971-74; mem. ho. reps. Ind. Legis., 1969-73; asst. state atty. County Madison, Edwardsville, Ill., 1985-88; pvt. practice law Terre Haute, 1951—. Pres. Wabash Valley Land Developers, Inc., Terre Haute, 1979—. Staff sgt. U.S. Army, 1943-46. Recipient Legion of Honor; recipient Good Govt. award West Vigo Jaycees, 1971, Civic Svc. award U.S. Jaycees, 1957; named Outstanding Pub. Offcl. Terre Haute Jaycees. Mem. Ill. State Bar Assn., Ind. Bar Assn., VFW, Am. Legion, United War Vets. Coun. Vigo County (past commdr.), SAR (pres.), Exchange Club (pres.), Shriners, Grand Soc. Sycamores, Honorable Order of Ky. Cols., Grotto. Democrat. Methodist. Avocations: bowling, geneology, reading. General civil litigation, Criminal, General practice. Home: 76 S Thorpe Pl West Terre Haute IN 47885 Office: 219 Ohio St Terre Haute IN 47807-3420

KESSEL, MARK, lawyer; b. Krasnik, Poland, June 14, 1941; came to U.S., 1948; s. Leo and Erna (Friedman) K.; m. Elaine Keit, Aug. 28, 1966; children: Greer Kessel Hendricks, Robert W. BA with honors in Econs., CUNY, 1963; JD magna cum laude, Syracuse U., 1966. Bar: N.Y., Calif. Assoc. Shearman & Sterling, N.Y.C., 1971-77, ptnr., 1977—, mng. ptnr., 1990-94. Bd. dirs. Heller Fin. Inc., Mus. of City of N.Y. Dir. W.M. Keck Found., L.A., 1985-86; bd. visitors Syracuse U. Coll. Law; ex-officio bd. dirs. San Francisco Psychoanalytic Inst., 1988-90. Capt. JAGC, U.S. Army, 1963-71. Mem. ABA, N.Y. State Bar, Calif. State Bar, Bar Assn. City of N.Y. Avocations: reading, running, tennis. General corporate, Mergers and acquisitions, Securities. Office: Shearman & Sterling 599 Lexington Ave Fl C2 New York NY 10022-6069

KESSLER, ALAN CRAIG, lawyer; b. Washington, Sept. 16, 1950; s. Alfred Milton and Josephine (Taub) K.; m. Gail Elaine Strauss, June 16, 1974; children: Stacy Ilana, Mark Jay, Daniel Jordan. BA with honors, U. Del., 1972; JD with honors, U. Md., 1975. Bar: Pa. 1975, U.S. Dist. Ct. (ea. dist.) Pa. 1975, U.S. Ct. Appeals (3d and 6th cirs.) 1975. Assoc. Dilworth, Paxson, Kalish, Levy & Kauffman, Phila., 1975-77, Berger & Montague, P.C., Phila., 1977-81; ptnr. Mesirov, Gelman, Jaffe, Cramer & Jamieson, 1981-91, Buchanan Ingersoll, P.C., Phila., 1991-99, Wolf, Block, Schorr & Solis-Cohen, 1999—. Instr. Inst. for Paralegal Tng., Phila., 1977-96. Fin. com. Dem. City Com. Phila., 1981-84, dep. counsel, 1980-84; chmn. bd. Bldg. Stds. City of Phila., 1983-84, bd. licenses and inspections rev., 1984-91; mem. City Planning Commn., Phila., 1992-97, Presdl. Transition Team, 1992-93; commr. Lower Merion (Pa.) Twp., 1988-2000, Mayors Commn. Homelessness, 1990—, Mayors Com. on Spl. Svcs. Dist., 1989—; vice-chmn. Pres. Commn. on Risk Assessment and Risk Mgmt., 1993-97; bd. dirs., pres. Randolph Ct. Assn., Phila., 1980-85; bd. dirs., v.p. South St. Neighbors Assn., Phila., 1983-87, Park Towne Pl. Tenants Assn., 1977-79; bd. dirs. Support Ctr. for Child Advs., 1983-94, Phila. Indsl. Devel. Corp.; exec. com. Ctrl. Phila. Devel. Corp., 1989—, Jewish Employment Vocat. Svcs., 1989—, Phila. 2000.; chair Supreme Ct. of Pa. Commn. on CLE, 1999—; mng. trustee Dem. Nat. Com., 1992—, fin. vice-chair, 2000—; bd. govs. U.S. Postal Svc. Mem. ABA, Pa. Bar Assn., Phila. Bar Assn. (exec. bd. dirs. young lawyers sect., legis. liaison com., officer various coms.), Racquet Club, Radnor Valley Country Club. Democrat. Jewish. Antitrust, Federal civil litigation. Home: 204 Daisy Ln Wynnewood PA 19096-1654 Office: Wolf Block Schorr & Solis-Cohen 1650 Arch St Fl 22 Philadelphia PA 19103-2097 E-mail: akessler@wolfblack.com

KESSLER, JEFFREY L. lawyer; b. N.Y.C., Feb. 19, 1954; s. Milton M. and Edith H. Kessler; m. Regina T. Dessoff, May 21, 1977; children: Andrew Zalman, Leora Miriam. BA, JD summa cum laude, Columbia U., 1977. Bar: N.Y. 1978, U.S. Dist. Ct. (so. dist.) N.Y. 1978, U.S. Supreme Ct. 1985. Assoc. Weil, Gotshal & Manges, N.Y.C., 1977-85, ptnr., 1985—. Adj. assoc. prof. Fordham Law Sch., 1988—; founder, bd. advisors study pvt. antitrust litig. Georgetown U., 1983-85. Bd. editors Columbia U. Law Rev., 1976-77; editor-in-chief State Antitrust Practice Statutes, 1999; contbr. numerous articles on antitrust law, sports and policy to profl. jours. Kent scholar, 1975-76, Stone scholar, 1976-77. Mem. ABA (antitrust law sect., vice-chmn. Sherman Act Sect. 2 com. 1989-90, chmn. internat. law com. 1990-94, co-chmn. pub. com. 1994-96, coun. mem. 1996-99), Columbia Coll. Alumni Assn. (bd. dirs. 1996-99), Phi Beta Kappa. Democrat. Jewish. Antitrust, Federal civil litigation, Private international. Office: Weil Gotshal & Manges 767 5th Ave Ste 3406 New York NY 10153-0023 E-mail: jeffrey.kessler@weil.com

KESSLER, JUDD LEWIS, lawyer; b. Newark, Apr. 10, 1938; s. Samuel W. and Ethel S. (Shapiro) K.; m. Marian Osterweis, Jan. 7, 1979 (div. 1986); m. Carol Ann Farris, Oct. 19, 1987; 1 child, Samuel Farris. AB, Oberlin Coll., 1960; LLB, Harvard U., 1963. Bar: N.J. 1963, D.C. 1972, Md. 1989, U.S. Dist. Ct. N.J., U.S. Dist. Ct. D.C., U.S. Dist. Ct. Md., U.S. Ct. Appeals (4th cir.), U.S. Supreme Ct. 1968. Assoc. Toner, Crowley, Woelper and Vanderbilt, Newark, 1963-66; asst. gen. counsel U.S. Agy. for Internat. Devel., Washington, 1966-82; ptnr., chmn. internat. bus. practice group Porter, Wright, Morris & Arthur, 1982—. Author: (with others) Legal Aspects of Exporting, 1986; contbr. articles to profl. jours. Bd. dirs. Congregation Har Shalom, Potomac, Md., 1998—. Recipient Outstanding Career Achievement award U.S. Agy for Internat. Devel. 1982; named Presdl. Appointment to Sr. Fgn. Svc., 1982. Mem. ABA, Am. Arbitration Assn. (mem. internat. panel arbitrators 1997—), Inter-Am. Bar Assn., Inter-Am. Bar Found. (pres., 1994—), Am. Soc. Internat. Law, Fed. Bar Assn. (chmn. internat. sect. 1983-87, nat. coord. Export Legal Assistance Network 1985—, Pres.'s E Excellence Export Svc. award 1997), Cosmos Club. Government contracts and claims, Private international, Public international. Office: Porter Wright Morris & Arthur 1919 Penn Ave NW Washington DC 20006-3434

KESSLER, KEITH LEON, lawyer; b. Seattle, July 18, 1947; s. Robert Lawrence and Priscilla Ellen (Allbee) K.; m. Lynn Elizabeth Eisen, Dec. 24, 1980; children: William Moore, Christopher Moore, Bradley Moore, Jamie Kessler. BA in Philosophy, U. Wash., 1969, JD, 1972. Bar: Wash. 1972, U.S. Dist. Ct. (we. dist.) Wash. 1973, U.S. Dist. Ct. (ea. dist. 1992); U.S. Ct. Appeals (9th cir.) 1973, U.S. Supreme Ct. 1975. Law clk. to Hon. Robert Finley Wash. Supreme Ct., Olympia, Wash., 1972-73; ptnr. Kessler, Tegland & Urmston, Seattle, 1973-75, Kessler & Urmston, Seattle, 1975-76, Kessler, Urmston & Sever, Seattle, 1976-77, Kessler & Sever, Seattle, 1977-79; assoc. Stritmatter & Stritmatter, Hoquiam, Wash., 1980-83; ptnr. Stritmatter, Kessler & McCauley, 1983-93, Stritmatter Kessler, Hoquiam, 1993-97, Stritmatter, Kessler, Whelan, Withey, Hoquiam, 1997—. Chmn. LAW PAC, Seattle, 1991-93; mem. pattern jury instrns. com. Wash. Supreme Ct., 2000—. Editor: Trial Evidence, 1996, author: (with others) Motor Vehicle Accident Litigation Desk Book, 1988, 1995, 97; contbr. chpt. to book. Pres. Kairos Ctr., Aberdeen, Wash., 1984-86; co-founder Grays Harbor Support Group; bd. dir. Wash. State Head Injury Found., Bellevue, Wash., 1993-96. Recipient Founders award Wash. State Head Injury Found., 1990, Silver award United Way, 1992; Named Trial Lawyer of the Year Wash. State Trial Lawyers, 1994. Mem. Am. Bd. Trial

Advocates, (pres. Wash. chpt. 1997), Wash. State Trial Lawyers Assn. (pres. 1990-91), Damage Attys. Round Table, Wash. Trial Attys. Political Forum (chmn. 1993-95), Trial Lawyers for Public Justice (state exec. com. 1994—). Personal injury, Product liability. Office: Stritmatter Kessler Whelan Withey 413 8th St Hoquiam WA 98550-3607 E-mail: keith@skww.com

KESSLER, LAWRENCE W. law educator, lawyer; b. N.Y.C., Sept. 28, 1942; s. Leo and Agatha (Welsch) K.; m. Bonnie B. Blankfeld, June 25, 1968; children— Brett, Nicholas. B.A., Columbia Coll., 1964, J.D., 1967. Bar: N.Y. 1967, Ohio 1974, U.S. Ct. Appeals (2d cir.) 1968, U.S. Dist. Ct. (so. and ea. dists.) N.Y., 1968. Law clk. U.S. Dist. Ct., N.Y.C., 1967-68; trial counsel Fed. Defender div. N.Y. Legal Aid Soc., N.Y.C., 1968-71; assoc. prof. law U. Cin. Coll. Law, 1971-74; assoc. prof. Hofstra Law Sch., Hempstead, N.Y., 1974-80, prof. law, 1980— ; dir. Hofstra Trial Techniques Program; asst. team leader Northwest Regional Intensive Program in Trial Advocacy, Ithaca, N.Y., 1977-78, team leader, Hempstead, 1979, 80, 81, co-dir., team leader, 1982, 83, 84, 85, team mem., Gainsville, Fla., 1980, Cambridge, Mass., 1985. Contbr. articles to profl. jours. Bd. dirs. Ednl. Assistance Ctr. of Long Island, Nassau, N.Y., 1982— , Long Island Advocacy Ctr., 1984— ; chmn. Tri-State Air Com., Cin., 1974; vice chmn. Cin. Environ. Task Force, 1972-73. Home: 100 Country Club Dr Port Washington NY 11050-4551 Office: Hofstra Law Sch 1000 Hempstead Tpke Uniondale NY 11553-1113

KESSLER, RALPH KENNETH, lawyer, manufacturing company executive; b. N.Y.C., May 23, 1943; s. Ralph G. Kessler and Margaret Gilmore; m. Margaret McQueeney, Oct. 12, 1980; children— Daniel, Anne BA, St. John's U., 1965, JD, 1968; LLM, NYU, 1972. Bar: N.Y., U.S. Dist. Ct. (so. and ea. dists.) N.Y., U.S. SEC. SEC trial atty., N.Y.C., 1968-72; assoc. Mudge, Rose et al., 1972-76; sec., asst. gen. counsel Singer Co., Stamford, Conn., 1976-86, v.p., dep. gen. counsel, sec., 1986-88; v.p. legal affairs, sec. TI Group Inc., N.Y.C., 1988-98, sr. v.p. legal affairs, sec., 1998-2000; sr. v.p. legal affairs Smiths Group Inc., Whippany, N.J., 2000—. Home: 86 Mountain Ave New Rochelle NY 10804-4708 Office: Smiths Group Inc 110 Algonquin Pky Whippany NJ 07981

KESSLER, RICHARD PAUL, JR. lawyer; b. Latrobe, Pa., July 11, 1945; s. Richard Paul Sr. and Dorothy Henrietta (Comp) K.; m. Kathleen Jane Parker, June 17, 1973 (dec. May 11, 1996); 1 child, Grace Elizabeth; m. Susan Kessler, Oct. 2000. BA, Fairfield (Conn.) U., 1968; JD, Emory U., 1971. Bar: Ga. 1971, U.S. Dist. Ct. (no. dist.) Ga. 1973, U.S. Ct. Appeals (5th cir.) 1974, U.S. Ct. Appeals (11th cir.) 1981, U.S. Supreme Ct. 1995. Law clk. to presiding justice U.S. Dist. Ct. (no. dist.) Ga., 1971-73; ptnr. Macey, Wilensky, Cohen, Wittner & Kessler, Atlanta, 1973—. Lectr. Practising Law Inst., 1981, 83, Fin. Svc. Corp. Career Conf., Atlanta, 1986, Ga. and Ala. Insts. of Continuing Legal Edn., 1993-95; panelist Credit Union Nat. Assn., Inc. League Attys. Conf., 1980-82, 87, 88-93, ABA, 1990-91; participant Nat. Conf. Commrs. on Uniform State Laws Drafting Com. on U.C.C. Articles, 3, 4, 4A, 1985-90; chair corp. and banking law sect. State Bar Ga., 1995-96. Author: What You Should Know About the New Bankruptcy Code, 1979, Guide to the Bankruptcy Laws: The Bankruptcy Reform Act of 1978, 79, Guide to the Bankruptcy Laws: The Bankruptcy Reform Act of 1978 (Bankruptcy Code) as Amended by the Bankruptcy Amendments and Federal Judgeship Act of 1984, The Bankruptcy Judges, U.S. Trustees and Family Farmer Bankruptcy Act of 1986; contbr. articles to profl. jours. Banking, Bankruptcy, Consumer commercial. Office: Ste 600 285 Peachtree Center Ave NE Atlanta GA 30303-1234 E-mail: rkessler@maceywilensky.com

KESSLER, STEVEN FISHER, lawyer; b. McKeesport, Pa., June 29, 1951; s. Robert and Rae (Alpern) K.; m. Susan Joyce Pearlstein, June 3, 1979; children: Matthew, Katie. BA, U. Pitts., 1973, JD, 1976. Bar: Pa. 1976, U.S. Dist. Ct. (we. dist.) Pa. 1976. Staff atty. Neighborhood Legal Services, McKeesport, Pa., 1976-79; solicitor City of McKeesport, 1980-82; sole practice, McKeesport, 1982—; solicitor McKeesport Housing Corp., 1985—; chmn. bd. dirs. McKeesport Devel. Corp., 1984—. Mem. Am. Arbitration Assn. (panel arbitrators 1981—). Democrat. General practice, Personal injury, Probate. Home: 1337 Foxwood Dr Monroeville PA 15146-4436 Office: 332 5th Ave Mc Keesport PA 15132-2616

KESTENBAUM, HAROLD LEE, lawyer; b. Bronx, N.Y., Sept. 27, 1949; s. Murray Louis and Yetta (Weiner) K.; m. Felice Gail Kravit, Aug. 11, 1973; children: Michelle, Benjamin. BA, Queens Coll., 1971; JD, U. Richmond, 1975. Bar: N.Y. 1976, N.J. 1977, U.S. Dist. Ct. (so. and ea. dist.) N.Y. Assoc. Wayne and Reiss, N.Y.C., 1975-76, Natanson, Reich and Barrison, N.Y.C., 1976-77, Goldstein and Axelrod, N.Y.C., 1977-81; pvt. practice N.Y.C. and L.I., 1981—; chmn. of the bd. Franchise It Corp., Bohemia, N.Y., 1984-89; pres., chief exec. officer Mr. Sign Franchising Corp., 1987-89. Bd. dirs. Sbarro Inc., Travel Network Ltd.; cons. in field. Mem. ABA, N.Y. Bar Assn., N.J. Bar Assn., Nassau County Bar Assn. Republican. Jewish. Avocations: softball, weight training. General corporate, Franchising, Real property. Office: 585 Stewart Ave Ste 700 Garden City NY 11530-4785

KETCHAM, RICHARD SCOTT, lawyer; b. Columbus, Ohio, Jan. 8, 1948; s. Victor Alvin and Dorothy Eloise (Becher) K.; m. Kim Michelle Halliburton, Apr. 7, 1984 (div. 1989); 1 child, Kate Erin; m. Christy M. Canaday, Sept. 9, 1990 (div. 1994). BS, Bowling Green (Ohio) State U., 1970; JD cum laude, Capital U., Columbus, 1974. Bar: Ohio 1974, U.S. Dist. Ct. (so. dist.) Ohio 1979. Asst. pros. atty. Franklin County (Ohio) Pros., Columbus, 1974-79, sr. asst. pros. atty., 1979-84; ptnr. Ketcham & Ketcham, Columbus, 1984—. Mem. task force Legal Aid Referral Project, Columbus Bar Assn. Homeless Project, 1989—. Mem. Gov.'s Task Force on Family Violence, 1984-86. Mem. Nat. Assn. Criminal Def. Lawyers, Ohio Assn. Criminal Def. Lawyers (bd. dirs. 1989—, v.p. CLE, sec.), Ctrl. Ohio Assn. Criminal Def. Lawyers (pres. 1994-95, bd. dirs. 2001—), Ohio State Bar Assn., Columbus Bar Assn. (chmn. criminal law com. 1994-95, 95-96), Franklin County Trial Lawyers. Avocations: fishing, basketball, model railroads, gardening. Criminal. Home: 1937 Elmwood Ave Columbus OH 43212-1112 Office: Ketcham & Ketcham 755 S High St Columbus OH 43206-1908 E-mail: rsketch@msn.com

KETCHAND, ROBERT LEE, lawyer; b. Shreveport, La., Jan. 30, 1948; s. Woodrow Wilson and Attie Harriet (Chandler) K.; m. Alice Sue Adams, May 31, 1969; children: Peter Leland, Marjory Attie. BA, Baylor U., 1970; JD, Harvard U., 1973. Bar: Tex. 1973, Mass. 1973, D.C. 1981. Assoc., ptnr. Butler & Binion, Houston, 1976-85, Washington, 1981-82; shareholder Brodsky & Ketchand, Houston, 1985-88; ptnr. Webster & Sheffield, 1988-90; atty. pvt. practice, 1990-92; ptnr. Short & Ketchand, 1992-2001; dir. Boyer Ewing Inc., 2001—. Founder, chmn. bd. dirs. Rolling Waters, d/b/a Houston Legal Clinic. Pres. Prisoner Svcs. Com. Houston, 1986; deacon South Houston Bapt. Ch., 1976—; gen. counsel, dir. Houston Met. Ministries, 1986-88; dir. Interfaith Ministries Greater Houston, 1996-98; gen. counsel Houston Bus. Roundtable, 1988—. Lt. USNR, 1973-76. Mem. ABA, Tex. Bar Assn., Houston Bar Assn. (chmn. dispute com. 1989-90). Avocations: reading, family. Federal civil litigation, General civil litigation, State civil litigation. Home: 2707 Carolina Way Houston TX 77005-3423 Office: Boyer Ewing Inc 9 Greenway Plz Ste 3100 Houston TX 77046 Fax: 713-871-2024. E-mail: rketchand@BoyerEwing.com

KETCHUM, PATRICIA SUGRUE, lawyer; b. N.Y.C., Jan. 14, 1938; d. Thomas Joseph and Mary Margaret (Ganey) Sugrue; m. A. Bertrand Channon, Apr. 15, 1961 (div. 1982); children: Thomas Sugrue Channon, Aengus Brian Channon; m. Robert H. Ketchum, Sept. 11, 1999. AB, Bryn Mawr Coll., 1958; JD, William and Mary Coll., 1980. Bar: Va. 1980, U.S. Ct. Appeals (4th cir.) 1980, D.C. 1981, U.S. Dist. Ct. (ea. dist.) Va. 1983, U.S. Dist. Ct. (D.C. dist.) 1983. Atty. benefits rev. bd. U.S. Dept. of Labor, Washington, 1980-81; law clk. to presiding justice U.S. Bankruptcy Ct., Alexandria, Va., 1981-83; assoc. Docter, Docter & Salus, P.C., Washington, 1983-85; atty. Adminstrv. Office of The U.S. Cts., 1985—. Mem. ABA (bus. bankruptcy com. bus. law sect.), Va. State Bar Assn., D.C. Bar Assn. Home: 1607 22nd St NW Washington DC 20008-1921 Office: Adminstrv Office US Courts Washington DC 20544

KEYES, GWENDOLYN REBECCA, lawyer, educator; b. Livingston, N.J., Nov. 2, 1968; d. Andrew J. and Ursula Y. Keyes. BS in Fin., Rutgers U., 1990; JD, Emory U., 1993. Bar: Ga. 1993. Asst. solicitor-gen. Dekalb County Solicitor-Gen.'s Office, Decatur, Ga., 1993-94; asst. dist. atty. Fulton County Dist. Atty.'s Office, Atlanta, 1994-97; contract atty., 1997-98; solicitor-gen. Dekalb County Solicitor-Gen.'s Office, Decatur, 1999—. Mem. Supreme Ct.'s Commn. on Equality, Atlanta, 1999—; mem. Leadership DeKalb Ga., 2000; elder First African Presbyn. Ch. Recipient Trail Blazer award Cmtys. Am., Inc., 1998, Justice Robert Benham Cmty. Svc. award. Mem. Nat. Coun. Negro Women, Ga. Assn. Black Women Lawyers, Hispanic Bar Assn., Dekalb Lawyers Assn. (past pres. 1998), Dekalb Bar Assn., Rotary. Democrat. Avocations: reading, tennis. Office: Dekalb County Solicitor-Gen Office 556 N Mcdonough St Decatur GA 30030-3308

KEYS, JERRY MALCOM, lawyer; b. Childress, Tex., Dec. 5, 1947; s. Earl Milas and Mary Maud (Furr) K. BSEE with honors, U. Tex., 1970, JD with honors, 1975. Bar: Tex. 1975, U.S. Dist. Ct. (so. and we. dists.) Tex. 1980, U.S. Ct. Appeals (5th cir.) 1982, U.S. Patent and Trademark Office. Assoc., Pravel & Wilson, Houston, 1975-76; assoc. Brown, Maroney, Rose, Baker & Barber, Austin, Tex., 1975-81; ptnr. Brown, Maroney, Rose, Barber & Dye, Austin, 1981-88; prin. Hagans/Keys PC, Austin, 1988-90; sr. shareholder Thompson & Knight, P.C., 1990-94, Locke Purnell Rain Harrell, P.C., 1994—; ptnr. Locke Liddell & Sapp LLP, 1999; sr. v.p. and gen. counsel, FundsXpress, Inc., 1999-2001; adj. asst. prof. U. Tex., 1979-85; mem. tech. adv. com. Supreme Ct. Tex. 1983-85. Mem. exec. coun. Greater Austin-San Antonio Corridor Coun., 1993—. Mem. Tex. Bar Assn. (profl. efficiency and econ. research com., chmn. office automation subcom. 1982-86), Austin Intellectual Property Law Assn. (pres. 1989-90). Computer, Intellectual property, General corporate.

KHAITAN, GAUTAM, lawyer; b. Calcutta, India, May 6, 1965; s. Om Prakash and Rekha Khaitan; m. Ritu Khetawat; children: Rhea, Karan. B in Communications, Delhi U., LLB, 1992. With Khaitan O.P., New Delhi. Bd. dirs. Global Fiscal Ltd., Shree Krishna Papermills and Industry Ltd., Danfoss Industries Pvt. Ltd., J.K. Drugs and Pharms., Leisure and Allied Indistries Pvt. Ltd. Mem. Delhi High Court Bar Assn., Delhi Bar Council, Fedn. Indian C. of C. and Industry, Internat. Bar Assn., Law Asia. Avocations: music, travel, swimming. Contracts commercial, General corporate, FERC practice. Home: N 12 Panchshila Park New Delhi 110017 India Office: OP Khaitan & Co Khaitan Ho B 1 Defense Colony New Delhi 110024 India

KHEEL, ROBERT J. lawyer; b. New Rochelle, N.Y., May 1, 1943; BA, Cornell U., 1965; MSc, London Sch. Econs., 1966; JD cum laude, U. Mich., 1969. Bar: N.Y. 1969, Fla. 1970, D.C. 1983. Mem. Willkie, Farr & Gallagher, N.Y.C. Contbr. articles to profl. jours. Mem. ABA, N.Y. State Bar Assn., Fla. Bar Assn., D.C. Bar, Assn. of Bar of City of N.Y. General civil litigation. Office: Willkie Farr & Gallagher 1 Citicorp Ctr 787 7th Ave New York NY 10019-6099

KHOREY, DAVID EUGENE, lawyer; b. Pitts., Oct. 5, 1959; s. Eugene George and Margaret (Yanyo) K.; m. Jennifer Ann Robinson, Dec. 29, 1983; children: Christopher David, Katherine Ann, Joanna Dale. BA with honors, U. Notre Dame, 1981; JD, Vanderbilt U., 1984. Bar: Mich. 1984, U.S. Dist. Ct. (we. dist.) Mich. 1984, U.S. Ct. Appeals 1989, U.S. Dist. Ct. (ea. dist.) Mich. 1990, U.S. Supreme Ct. 1999. Assoc. Varnum, Riddering, Schmidt & Howlett, Grand Rapids, Mich., 1984-89, ptnr., 1989—, chair labor practice group, 2000—. Instr. seminars Mich. Inst. of Continuing Legal Edn., Nat. Bus. Inst., Stetson Coll., NACUA Conf. Co-author: Developing Labor Law; mem. editl. bd. State Bar Mich. Mem. ABA (labor sect., com. devels. law under the nat. labor rels. act), State Bar Assn. Mich. (treas., mem. labor and employment tax sect.). Labor. Office: Varnum Riddering Schmidt & Howlett PO Box 352 Bridgewater Pl Grand Rapids MI 49501-0352

KIDDER, FRED DOCKSTATER, lawyer; b. Cleve., May 22, 1922; s. Howard Lorin and Virgina (Milligan) K.; m. Eleanor (Hap) Kidder; children— Fred D. III, Barbara Anne Donelson, Jeanne Louise Haffeman. BS with distinction, U. Akron, 1948; JD, Case Western Res. U., 1950. Bar: Ohio 1950, Tex. 1985, U.S. Dist. Ct. (no. dist.) Ohio 1950, U.S. Dist. Ct. (no. dist.) Tex. 1985. Assoc. Arter & Hadden and predecessors, Cleve., 1950-79, ptnr., 1960-79, Jones, Day, Reavis and Pogue, Cleve., 1980-89, regional mng. ptnr. Tex., 1985-86; gen. counsel Lubrizol Corp., 1989-92, spl. counsel, 1993—. Contbr. articles to profl. jours. Mem. Cleve. Growth Assn., Shaker Heights Citizens Com., Citizens League Cleve.; former pres. Estate Planning Coun.; former co-chmn. bd. trustees Lake Erie Coll.; former bd. trustees, v.p., Alzheimer's Assn., Cleve.; mem., bd. trustees Cleve. Sight Ctr.; past mem. alumni coun. U. Akron; past. corp. coun. Dallas Mus. Art; past pres. Case Western Reserve U. Law Sch. Alumni Assn.; past chmn. Shaker Heights Recreation Bd. Mem. ABA, Nat. Assn. Corp. Secs., Tex. Bar Assn., Ohio State Bar Assn., Estate Planning Coun. (past pres.), Blue Coats, Soc. Benchers (past chmn.), Union Club, Pepper Pike Club (past sec.), The Country Club, Cleve. Skating Club, Order of Coif, Ct. of Nisi Prius (former judge), Phi Eta Sigma, Beta Delta Psi, Phi Sigma Alpha, Phi Delta Theta, Phi Delta Phi. General corporate, Mergers and acquisitions, Securities. Office: The Lubrizol Corp 29400 Lakeland Blvd Wickliffe OH 44092-2298

KIDDER, GEORGE HOWELL, lawyer; b. Boston, June 14, 1925; s. Henry Purkitt and Julia Edwards (Howell) K.; m. Ellen Windom Warren, Aug. 17, 1946 (dec. May 1956); children: Susan Warren, George Howell, Stephen Wells; m. Priscilla Peele Hunnewell, Sept. 3, 1958 (dec. Nov. 1993); children: Priscilla Hunnewell, Timothy Hurd, Peter Arnold; m. Nancy D. Kidder, June 3, 1995. Grad., St. Mark's Sch., Southborough, Mass., 1943; student Navy V-12 program NROTC, Williams Coll., 1943-44; B in Naval Sci., Tufts Coll., 1945; LLB, Harvard, 1950; DD (hon.), Episcopal Div. Sch., 1987. Bar: Mass. 1951. With Office Gen. Counsel CIA, 1952-54, 1950-52; ptnr. Hemenway & Barnes, 1956-97, of counsel, 1997—, assoc. Mem. panel neutral mediators and arbitrators Jud. Arbitration and Mediation Svc./Endispute, 1997—. Trustee Episcopal Ch. Found., Episcopal Divinity Sch., Cambridge, Mass., 1967—86, 1998—, pres. bd. trustees, 1977—86, hon. trustee, 1986—98; chancellor Episcopal Diocese of Mass., 1988—, dir., trustee donations; trustee St. Mark's Sch., 1959—84, pres. bd. trustees, 1974—84; trustee Fenn Sch, Concord, 1956—77, pres. bd. trustees, 1960—73; trustee Concord Acad., 1963—78, pres. bd. trustees, 1971—78; trustee Boston Symphony Orch., 1977—94, pres. bd. trustees, 1987—94, life trustee, 1994—; trustee Children's Med. Ctr. and Children's Hosp. Corp., 1982—97, chmn. bd. dirs., 1992—97; trustee Wellesley Coll., 1962—80, trustee emeritus, 1980—; bd. dirs. Greater Boston Legal Svcs., 1961—87; trustee, mem. exec. com. WGBH Ednl. Found., 1997—; dir. Controlled Risk Ins. Co., Ltd., 1988—99, chmn. bd. dirs., 1991—98; dir. Risk Mgmt. Found. Harvard Med. Instns., Inc., 1988—98, chmn. bd. dirs., 1991—98; trustee Harvard Med. Ctr. Inc., 1989—. Fellow Am. Coll. Probate Counsel; mem. Am. Law Inst., Internat. Acad. Estate and Trust Law; Mem. Tau Beta Pi. General practice, Probate, Estate planning. Home: 110 Spencer Brook Rd Concord MA 01742-5206 Office: 60 State St Boston MA 02109-1800 E-mail: gkidder@hembar.com

KIDWELL, MATHEW CHARLES, lawyer; b. Dartford, Kent, England, May 13, 1964; s. Richard de Villeneuve and Elizabeth Phebe (Clarkson) K. MA with 1st class honors, U. St. Andrews, Scotland, 1987. Bar: Law Soc. Final Examinations Eng. and Wales 1989. Articled clk. Morgan Bruce, Cardiff, Wales, 1989-91; solicitor, 1991-96, Wilde Sapte, London, 1996-99, Vinson & Elkins, London, 1999-2000; of counsel, 2000—. Mem. econ. commn. Europe's B.O.T. expert group UN, Geneva, 1997—. Author: The Guide to Financing Build-Operate-Transfer Projects, 1997. Banking, Oil, gas, and mineral, Mergers and acquisitions. Office: Vinson & Elkins Regis House 45 King William EC4R 9AD London England Fax: 44 20 7618 6001. E-mail: mkidwell@velaw.com

KIDWELL, WAYNE L. state supreme court justice; b. Council, Idaho, 1938; m. Shari Linn; children: Vaughn, Blair. BA, JD, U. Idaho. Bar: Idaho 1964, Hawaii, former U.S. Trust Territories. Past atty. law firms, Idaho and Hawaii; past pvt. practice Idaho and Hawaii; past atty. gen. State of Idaho; past majority leader Idaho Senate; past prosecuting atty. Ada County, Idaho; past assoc. dep. atty. gen. Pres. Reagan adminstrn., past liason Dept. Justice U.S. Govt.; past atty. gen. Republic of Marshall Islands; judge Idaho Supreme Ct. Photographer pvt. shows; one-man shows include galleries in Hawaii. Active numerous civic and profl. orgns. Served USMCR, U.S. Army Mil. Police Corps. Office: Idaho Supreme Ct Supreme Ct Bldg PO Box 83720 Boise ID 83720-3720

KIEHNHOFF, THOMAS NAVE, lawyer; b. Sept. 13, 1949; s. Martin W. and A. Floriene (Nave) K.; m. Tamsen Kathleen Larkin, Aug. 17, 1974; children: John Martin, Daniel Thomas. BA, Washington U., St. Louis, 1971; JD, St. Louis U., 1975. Bar: Colo. 1975, U.S. Dist. Ct. Colo. 1978. U.S. Ct. Appeals, 5th Cir., 1991. Ptnr. McDermott, Kiehnhoff & Meconi (formerly McDermott, Kiehnhoff & Marshall), asst. U.S. atty., Eastern Dist. Tex., 1990-2001, Canon City, Colo., mem. Reavd, Morgan & Quinn, 2001-; lectr. in field. Mem. ABA (vice chair Environmental Crime and Enforcement Com.), Colo. Bar Assn. (com. on availability legal services 1982, sec. gen. and small firm sect. 1985-86, chmn. elect 1986—), Assn. Trial Lawyers Am., Colo. Trial Lawyers Assn. Lutheran. Federal civil litigation, Environmental, Toxic tort.

KIEL, PAUL EDWARD, lawyer; b. Jersey City, Mar. 14, 1957; s. Frank Thomas and Theresa Barbara (Miros) K.; m. Audrey Ann Szotak, Oct. 12, 1985. BA, Rutgers U., 1979; JD, Dickinson Sch. Law, 1982. Bart: N.J. 1983, Pa. 1983, U.S. Dist. Ct. N.J. 1983, U.S. Dist. Ct. (ea. dist.) Pa. 1983. Law clk. to judge Superior Ct. N.J., Elizabeth, 1982-83; assoc. MacDonald, Ryan & Jackel, Ridgewood, N.J., 1983-84, Harwood Lloyd, Hackensack, 1984—. Advisor Explorer Law Post, Hackensack, 1985-98 Mem. ABA, N.J. Bar Assn., Pa. Bar Assn., Bergen County Bar Asn., Phi Beta Kappa, Phi Alpha Theta. Republican. Roman Catholic. State civil litigation, Insurance, Personal injury. Office: Harwood Lloyd 130 Main St Hackensack NJ 07601-7152

KIENER, JOHN LESLIE, judge; b. Ft. Madison, Iowa, June 21, 1940; s. Cyril Joseph and Lucille Olive (Golden) K.; m. Carol Lynn Winston, June 4, 1966; children: Susan, Gretchen. BA cum laude, Loras Coll., 1962; JD, Drake U., 1965. Bar: Iowa 1965, Tenn. 1972, U.S. Supreme Ct. 1974. Practice law, Decorah, Iowa, 1965-68; asst. atty. gen. State of Iowa, 1968-72; ptnr. Cantor & Kiener, 1972-80; city judge City of Johnson City, Tenn., 1975-80, gen. sessions judge, 1980—. Continuing edn. tchr., bus. law East Tenn. State U., 1975—. Contbr. and articles editor in Jonesborough Herald and Tribune. Mem. ABA, Tenn. Bar Assn., Washington County Bar Assn., Rotary, Elks. Republican. Avocations: stamp collecting, genealogy. Home: 2403 Camelot Cir Johnson City TN 37604-2938 Office: Gen Sessions Ct Downtown Ctr Courthouse 101 E Market St Ste 7 Johnson City TN 37604-5722 E-mail: ckiener@preferred.com

KIES, DAVID M. lawyer; b. N.Y.C., Jan. 25, 1944; s. Saul and Lillian (Schultz) K.; m. Emily Bardack, July 6, 1966 (div. 1985); children: Laura, Adam, Abigail; m. Anne Monteith, Oct. 7, 1990 (div. 1998); 1 child, Samuel; m. Kathryn L. Danes, Mar. 11, 2001. AB, Haverford Coll., 1965; JD, NYU, 1968. Bar: N.Y. 1968, U.S. Dist. Ct. (so. dist.) N.Y. 1969, U.S. Ct. Appeals (2d cir.) 1969. Assoc. Sullivan & Cromwell, N.Y.C., 1968-76, ptnr., 1976—, dir. London office, 1992-95; dir. Imclone Systems, Inc. Former trustee Haverford Coll. Root Tilden fellow, NYU Law Sch., 1965. Mem. ABA, N.Y. State Bar Assn., Assn. Bar City of N.Y. Democrat. Jewish. Private international, Mergers and acquisitions, Securities. Office: Sullivan & Cromwell 125 Broad St Fl 28 New York NY 10004-2489

KIESLING, DONALD F., JR. lawyer; b. Ft. Atkinson, Wis., Aug. 27, 1964; s. Donald F. and Kristine L. Kiesling; m. Jean M. Makens, Oct. 24, 1987; children: Thomas, William. BA, St. Norbert Coll., De Pere, Wis., 1987; MPA, U. Wis., Milw., 1994; JD, Marquette U., 1997. Bar: Wis. 1997. Assoc. Godfrey & Kahn, S.C., Milw., 1997—. Mem. ABA, Fedn. Environ. Technologists, State Bar Wis., Milw. Bar Assn. Roman Catholic. FERC practice, Environmental. Office: Godfrey & Kahn SC 780 N Water St Milwaukee WI 53202

KIETDURIYAKUL, KOMKRIT, lawyer; b. Bangkok, Nov. 29, 1968; s. Amnui and Sudarat Kietduriyakul. LLB with honors, Chulalongkorn U., Bangkok, 1990; LLM, Cornell U., 1993, NYU, 1994. Registered barrister, Thailand. Lawyer Sanong Tuchinda, Bangkok, 1990-92; ptnr. Baker & McKenzie, 1994—. Office: Baker & McKenzie Rama 4 Rd 10500 Bangkok Thailand Fax: 662-636-2110-1. E-mail: komkrit.kietduriyakul@bakernet.com

KIHLE, DONALD ARTHUR, lawyer; b. Noonan, N.D., Apr. 4, 1934; s. J. Arthur and Linnie W. (Ljunngren) K.; m. Judith Anne, Aug. 18, 1964; children: Kevin, Kirsten, Kathryn, Kurte. BS in Indsl. Engring., U. N.D., 1957; JD, U. Okla., 1967. Bar: Okla. 1967, U.S. Dist. Cts. (we. and no. dists) Okla. 1967, U.S. Ct. Appeals (10th cir.) 1967, U.S. Supreme Ct. 1971. Assoc. Huffman, Arrington, Scheurich & Kincaid, Tulsa, 1967-71, ptnr., 1971-78; shareholder, dir., officer Arrington Kihle Gaberino & Dunn, 1978-97, pres., 1994-97; shareholder, dir. Gable & Gotwals, 1997-99, advisor, dir., 1999-2001. Dist. chmn. Boy Scouts Am., 1983-85, cubmaster, 1986-88, com. coms., 1988-96, campiree chmn., 1990; mem. Statewide Law Day Com., 1982-86, chmn., 1983-85; trustee Brandon Hall Sch., Atlanta, 1991—, chmn., 1995-99. Lt. U.S. Army, 1957-59. Recipient Silver Beaver award Boy Scouts Am. Mem. ABA, Okla. Bar Assn. (chmn. constl. bicentennial com. 1986-89), Tulsa County Bar Assn., So. Hills Country Club, Q Club (scribe 1991—), Tulsa Club (bd. govs. 1987-94, pres. 1992), Order of Coif, Order of Arrow (vigil), Sigma Tau, Phi Delta Phi, Sigma Chi (Tulsa alumni pres. 1995-97). Republican. General corporate, Oil, gas, and mineral, Securities. Home: 4717 S Lewis Ct Tulsa OK 74105-5135 Office: 1100 ONEOK Plz 100 W 5th St Tulsa OK 74103-4240 E-mail: dkihle@gablelaw.com

KIKEL, SUZANNE, patent agent; b. Pitts., Apr. 4, 1946; d. John George Kikel and Elizabeth Marie Pello; m. John Thomas Stauffer, Oct. 25, 1996. BA in Humanities, U. Pitts., 1972, BS in Mech. Engring., 1981; A in Chemistry, C.C. Allegheny County, Pitts., 1994. Registered patent practitioner U.S. Patent and Trademark Office, 1976. Patent agt. Wean United,

Inc., Pitts., 1974-86, Eckert Seamans Cherin & Mellott, LLC, Pitts., 1986-95; intellectual property coord., patent agt. ECC Internat., Inc., Atlanta, 1995-99; patent agt. Calgon Corp., Pitts., 1999-2000, Pietrallo, Bosick & Gordon, Pitts., 2000—. Mem. Pitts. Intellectual Patent Law Assn., Pitts. Ski Club. Avocations: golfing, tennis, skiing, biking, photography. Office: Pietrallo Bosick and Gordon 38th Flr 1 Oxford Ct Fl Grant38 Pittsburgh PA 15219-1407

KILBOURN, WILLIAM DOUGLAS, JR. law educator; b. Colorado Springs, Colo., Dec. 9, 1924; s. William Douglas and Clara Howe (Lee) K.; m. Barbara Ruth Neff, Sept. 16, 1950; children: Jonathan VI, Katharine Ann. BA, Yale U., 1949; postgrad., Columbia U., 1949-50, LLB, 1953. Bar: Mass. 1962, Oreg. 1953, Minn. 1974. Acct. Arthur Andersen & Co., 1949-50; assoc. Davies, Biggs, Strayer, Stoel & Boley, Portland, Oreg., 1953-56; asst. prof. law U. Mont., 1956-57; assoc. prof. law U. Mo., 1957-59; prof. law, founding dir. grad. tax program Boston U., 1959-71; prof. law U. Minn., 1971-98, prof. emeritus, 1998—. Dir. U. Mont. Tax Inst., 1956; of counsel Palmer & Dodge, Boston, 1964-75, Oppenheimer, Wolff & Donnelly, St. Paul and Mpls., 1980-94; mem. exec. com. Fed. Tax Inst. New Eng., 1966-72; mem. adv. com. Western New Eng. Coll. Tax Inst; vis. prof. law Duke U., 1974-75, U. Tex., 1977, Washington U., St. Louis, 1977; past ednl. advisor Tex. Execs. Inst.; lectr. in 27 states, Mex., The Caribbean, D.C.; expert witness in field. Editor: Estate Planning and Income Taxation, 1957; contbr. articles to profl. jours. Dist. dir. United Fund, Belmont, Mass., chair fair practices com. Recipient numerous tchg. awards; Kent scholar, Stone scholar Columbia U. Law Sch. Mem. ABA (tax sect., corp. stockholder rels. com. 1962-76, chair subcom. inc. 1968-73), Boston Bar Assn. (chair tax sect. 1967-70), Boston Tax Forum, Boston Tax Coun. Avocations: tennis, botany, landscape gardening. Home: 2681 E Lake Of The Isles Pkwy Minneapolis MN 55408-1051

KILBOURNE, GEORGE WILLIAM, lawyer; b. Berea, Ky., Mar. 29, 1924; s. John Buchanan and Maud (Parsons) K.; m. Helen Spooner, Dec. 25, 1945 (div. 1968); m. Carole Marko, June 12, 1970 (div. 1984); children: Stuart (dec.), Charles; m. Anne F. Lavine, Aug. 19, 1996. Student, Berea Coll., 1941-42, Denison U., 1944; BS in Mech. Engring., U. Mich., 1946; JD, U. Calif., Berkeley, 1951. Bar: Calif. 1952, U.S. Dist. Ct. (no. dist.) Calif. 1952, Ind. 1957, U.S. Appeals (9th cir.). Sole practice, Berkeley, 1952-57; assoc. Hays & Hays, Sullivan, Ind., 1957-59, Boyle & Kilbourne, Sullivan, 1961-63, Bernal, Rigney & Kilbourne, Berkeley, 1963-68, Sherbourne & Kilbourne, Pleasant Hill, Calif., 1968-75; sole practice Pleasant Hill and Martinez, Calif., 1975—. Lectr. Lincoln Law Sch., San Francisco, 1956-57, John F. Kennedy Law Sch., Orinda, Calif., 1977-78. Served to 2d lt. USMC, 1942-46, PTO. Episcopalian. Lodge: Elks. Avocations: tennis, bowling, outdoors. Environmental, Personal injury, Toxic tort. Office: 661 Augusta Dr Moraga CA 94556-1035 E-mail: gwkilbourn@aol.com

KILBRIDE, THOMAS L. judge; m. Mary Kilbride; 3 children. BA magna cum laude, St. Mary's Coll., 1978; JD, Antioch Sch. Law, 1981. Practicioner U.S. Dist. Ct., Ill., U.S. Seventh Cir. Ct. Appeals; Supreme Ct. justice Ill. State Supreme Ct., 2000—. Former mem. bd. dirs., former v.p., former pres. Ill. Twp. Attys. Assn. Vol. legal adv. Cmty. Caring Conf., Quad City Harvest Inc.; charter chmn. Quad Cities Interfaith Sponsoring Com.; former mem. Rock Island Human Rels. Com.; former vol. lawyer, charter mem. Ill. Pro Bono Ctr. Mem.: Ill. State Bar Assn., Rock Island County Bar Assn. Office: 1800 Third Ave Rm 202 Rock Island IL 61201*

KILGORE, PETER GEORGE, lawyer, educator; b. Racine, Wis., Jan. 14, 1946; s. Lester Joseph and Helen Mae K.; m. Sharon Ann Hohn, June 7, 1975; children— Timothy, Shannon, Aileen. B.S., U. Wis.-Milw., 1968; J.D., Valparaiso U., 1973; LL.M., Georgetown U., 1976. Bar: Wis. 1973, Fla. 1974, D.C. 1980, U.S. Dist. Ct. D.C. 1980, U.S. Dist. Ct. (so. dist.) Fla. 1976, U.S. Dist. Ct. (ea. dist.) Wis. 1973, U.S. Cts. Appeals (4th and 9th cirs.) 1980, U.S. Supreme Ct. 1980. Atty., advisor to chmn. Occupational Safety and Health Rev. Commn., Washington, 1974-76, asst. gen. counsel, 1977-78; assoc. Alley & Alley, Miami, Fla., 1976-77; ptnr. Kirlin, Campbell & Keating, Washington, 1978; adj. prof. law No. Va. Law Sch., Alexandria, 1984; lectr. labor relations in constrn. Cath. U. Am., Washington, 1985— . Contbg. editor Occupational Safety and Health Law, 1985. Contbr. articles to legal jours. Mem. Com. for Drafting Rules of Procedure under D.C. Human Rights Law, Washington, 1982. Mem. adminstrv. law coms. EEO, 1981— . Mem. ABA (coms. employment and labor relations law, occupational safety and health law, health and environ. rights 1978—), Assn. Trial Lawyers Am. Roman Catholic. Lodge: K.C. Health, Labor. Home: 4836 Dodson Dr Annandale VA 22003-6136 Office: Kirlin Campbell & Keating 1 Farragut Sq NW Washington DC 20006-4003

KILLEEN, MICHAEL JOHN, lawyer; b. Washington, Oct. 5, 1949; s. James Robert and Georgia Winston (Hartwell) K.; m. Therese Ann Goeden, Oct. 6, 1984; children: John Patrick, Katherine Therese, Mary Clare, James Philip. BA, Gonzaga U., 1971, JD magna cum laude, 1977. Bar: Wash. 1977, U.S. Dist. Ct. (we. dist.) Wash. 1979, U.S. Ct. Appeals (9th cir.) 1984, U.S. Supreme Ct. 1990. Jud. clk. Wash. State Ct. Appeals, Tacoma, 1977-79; assoc. Davis Wright Tremaine, Seattle, 1979-85, ptnr., 1985—. Dir. Seattle Goodwill Bd., 1987—, sec., 1998—. Author: Guide to Strike Planning, 1985, Newsroom Legal Guidebook, 1996, Employment in Washington, 1984—. Active Gonzaga Law Bd. Advisors, Spokane, Wash., pres., 1992-96. Recipient Freedom's Light award Washington Newspaper Pub. Assn., 1999. Mem. ABA, Wash. State Bar Assn., King County Bar Assn. (treas. 1987-89, pres. award 1989). Democrat. Roman Catholic. General civil litigation, Communications, Labor. E-mail: mikekilleen@dwt.com

KILLIAN, ROBERT KENNETH, JR. judge, lawyer; b. Hartford, Conn., Jan. 29, 1947; s. Robert Kenneth Sr. and Evelyn (Farnan) K.; m. Candace Korper, Oct. 6, 1979; children: Virginia, Carolyn. BA, Union U., 1969; JD, Georgetown U., 1972. Bar: Conn. 1972, U.S. Ct. Appeals (2nd cir.) 1973, D.C. 1974, U.S. Ct. Appeals (D.C. cir.) 1974. Bur. chief Sta. WTIC-AM-FM-TV, Washington, 1969-72; spl. asst. Senator Abe Ribicoff, 1972-73; ptnr. Gould, Killian, Wynne et al, Hartford, 1972-84; judge Conn. Probate Ct., 1984—; ptnr. Killian & Donohue, 1985-88, Killian Donohue & Shipman LLC, Hartford, 1998—. Spl. counsel Lt. Gov. Conn., Hartford, 1974-78; mem. exec. com. Conn. Probate Assembly, 1987—, pres.-judge, 1997-99; mem. investment adv. coun. State of Conn., 1995-99; mem. Jud. Commn. on Attys.' Ethics, 1990—. Author: Basic Probate in Connecticut, 1990, 6th edit., 1999. Regent, U. Hartford; trustee Hartt Sch. Music; chmn. Conn. chpt. March of Dimes, 1986—; bd. dirs. Yeats Drama Found., 1989—; incorporator St. Francis Hosp. and Med. Ctr. Recipient 1st Pl. award New England Conv. Magicians, 1965; named Conn.'s Outstanding Probate Judge, Conn. Probate Assembly, 1990. Mem. ABA, ATLA, Nat. Coll. Juvenile and Family Ct. Judges, Nat. Conf. Probate Judges, Conn. Bar Assn., Conn. Trial Lawyers Assn., Psychic Entertainer's Assn., Internat. Brotherhood Magicians, Soc. Am. Magicians (chmn. nat. conv. 1977). Democrat. Roman Catholic. Home: 83 Bloomfield Ave Hartford CT 06105-1007 Office: Killian Donohue & Shipman LLC 363 Main St Hartford CT 06106-1885 E-mail: bob@kdslk.com

KILLINGSWORTH, VERNON SCOTT, technology lawyer; b. Cuthbert, Ga., Sept. 22, 1950; s. Lewis Manry Killingsworth and Margery Phillips Dews; m. Patricia M. Killingsworth, Oct. 27, 1979; children: Elizabeth Anne, Laura Catherine. BA, Yale U., 1972, JD, 1975. Bar: Ga. Assoc. Powell, Goldstein, Frazer & Murphy, Atlanta, 1975-82, ptnr., 1982—, co-chair tech. and intellectual property practice, 1997—. Moderator Legal Writing Forum Counsel Connect, 1997-99, High Tech and WWW Forum, Law News Network, 1999. Editl. bd. Internat. Jour. of e-Bus. Strategy Mgmt., 1999—; bd. editors E-Commerce Law Report, Internat. Property Counselor, 1998—; contbr. articles to profl. jours. Bd. govs. Assn. of Yale Alumni, New Haven, 1989-92, assembly del., 1986-89; alumni fellow Davenport Coll., Yale U., New Haven, 1989—. Mem. ABA (com. on cyberspace law), Computer Law Assn., Licensing Execs. Soc., Tech. Assn. of Ga., Yale Club of Ga. (v.p. programs, dir. 1992-93), Druid Hills Golf Club. Democrat. Avocation: writing. Office: Powell Goldstein Frazer & Murphy 191 Peachtree St NE Fl 16 Atlanta GA 30303-1740

KILLORIN, ROBERT WARE, lawyer; b. Atlanta, Nov. 12, 1959; s. Edward W. and Virgina (Ware) K. AB cum laude, Duke U., 1980; JD, U. Ga., 1983. Bar: Ga. 1984, U.S. Dist. Ct. (no. dist.) Ga. 1984, U.S. Ct. Appeals (11th cir.) 1984. Ptnr. Killorin & Killorin, Atlanta, 1984—. Mem. Atlanta Bar Assn., Ga. Def. Lawyers Assn., State Bar Ga. (chair SCOPE com. 1986, young lawyers sect. legis. affairs com. 1989-91, instr. mock trial program 1989—), Ga. C. of C. (govtl. affairs com.), Internat. Assn. Def. Counsel, 11th Cir. Hist. Soc., Assn. Trial Lawyers Am., Nat. Assn. Underwater Instrs., Nat. Speliological Soc., Mil. Order of Carabao, U. Ga. Pres.'s Club, Explorer's Club. Avocations: forestry, scuba diving, basketball, tennis. Antitrust, General civil litigation, Environmental. Office: Killorin & Killorin 5587 Benton Woods Dr NE Atlanta GA 30342-1308

KILLOUGH, STEPHEN PINCKNEY, financial executive, lawyer; b. Terrell, Tex., Nov. 4, 1935; s. Isaac Franklin and Grace Lillian (Yarbrough) K.; m. Deborah Marie Spitler, Mar. 16, 1963; children— Elizabeth Victoria, Richard Carter. B.A. in English and History, Baylor U., 1957; LL.B., J.D., Cumberland Sch. Law of Samford U., 1960. Bar: Tex., 1960, U.S. Ct. Mil. Appeals, 1961, U.S. Ct. Claims, 1962, U.S. Supreme Ct., 1963. City atty. City of Amarillo (Tex.), 1964-66; sole practice Lumpkin, Watson & Smith, Amarillo, 1966-70; assoc. counsel-asst. sec. Fin. Am. Corp., Allentown, Pa., 1970-78; sr. v.p., gen. counsel Mfrs. Hanover Financial Services, Huntingdon Valley, Pa., 1978— ; dir. Ritter Life Ins. Co., Pa., 1978— , Tempco Life Ins. Co., Ariz., 1981— , Mfrs. Hanover Indsl. Banks, Colo., 1982— , Oil and Gas Research, St. Joseph, Mo., 1960. Served to capt. U.S. Army, 1960-64. Baylor U. Scholar, 1953, Mem. Tex. Bar Assn., ABA, Nat. Consumer Fin. Assn. (chmn. real estate subcommittee), Am. Fin. Services Assn. (dir., chmn. real estate adv. group, 1984, vice chmn. law forums 1987, 88). Republican. Episcopalian. Office: Mfrs Hanover Fin Services Inc 3103 Philmont Ave Huntingdon Valley PA 19006-4225

KILROY, WILLIAM TERRENCE, lawyer; b. Kansas City, Mo., May 24, 1950; s. John Muir and Katherine Lorraine (Butler) K.; m. Marianne Michelle Maurin, Sept. 8, 1984; children: Kyle E., Katherine A. BS, U. Kans., 1972, MA, 1974; JD, Washburn U., 1977. Bar: Mo. 1977. Assoc. Shughart, Thomson & Kilroy, Kansas City, Mo., 1977-81, mem., dir., 1981—. Contbr. articles to profl. publs. Mem. Kans. City Citizens Assn., 1980—; pres., bd. govs. Sch. Law Washburn, 1992-94; with Civic Coun. of Greater Kansas City, 1999—; legal coun. Heart of Am. Coun. Boy Scouts Am., 1988-92, mem. exec. com., 1988-95, Cmty. adv. Greater Kans. City Cmty. Found. and Affiliated Trusts, 1993-2000; bd. dirs. Kansas City Neighborhood Alliance, 1998—, Greater Kansas City Crime Commn. Mem. Lawyers Assn. Kansas City, Kansas City Bar Assn. (chmn. civil rights com. 1984), Mo. Bar Assn., ABA (subcom. on arbitration, labor law sect. 1977—), Greater Kansas City C. of C., Univ. Club (pres. 1993-94), Kansas City Country Club. Labor. Office: Shughart Thomson & Kilroy 12 Wyandotte Plz 120 W 12th St Ste 1500 Kansas City MO 64105-1929

KIM, MICHAEL CHARLES, lawyer; b. Honolulu, Mar. 9, 1950; s. Harold Dai You and Maria Adrienne K. Student, Gonzaga U., 1967-70; BA, U. Hawaii, 1971; JD, Northwestern U., 1976. Bar: Ill. 1977, U.S. Dist. Ct. (no. dist.) Ill. 1977, U.S. Ct. Appeals (7th cir.) 1981, U.S. Supreme Ct. 1986. Assoc. counsel Nat. Assn. Realtors, Chgo., 1977-78; assoc. Rudnick & Wolfe, 1978-83, Rudd & Assocs., Hoffman Estates, Ill., 1983-85; ptnr. Rudd & Kim, Hoffman Estates and Chgo., 1985-87; prin. Michael C. Kim & Assocs., Chgo. and Schaumburg, Ill., 1987-88; ptnr. Martin, Craig, Chester & Sonnenschein, Chgo. and Schaumburg, 1988-91, Arnstein & Lehr, Chgo., 1991—. Gen. counsel Assn. Sheridan Condo-Coop Owners, Chgo., 1988—; adj. prof. John Marshall Law Sch., Chgo. Author column Apt. and Condo News, 1984-87; co-author Historical and Practice Notes; contbr. articles to profl. jours. Bd. dirs. Astor Villa Condo Assn., Chgo., 1987-91, treas. 1987-89. Mem. ABA, Chgo. Bar Assn. (chmn condominium law subcom. 1990-92, chmn. real property legis. subcom. 1995-97, vice chmn. real property law com., 1998-99, chmn. real proprty law com. 1999-2000), Ill. State Bar Assn. (real estate law sect. coun. 1990-94, corp. and securities law sect. coun. 1990-92), Asian Am. Bar Assn. Greater Chgo. Area (bd. dirs. 1987-88, 90-91), Cmty. Assns. Inst. Ill. (bd. dirs. 1990-92, pres. 1992), Coll. Cmty. Assn. Lawyers (bd. govs. 1994-98), Univ. Club (Chgo.). Avocations: squash, photography, travel. General civil litigation, Construction, Real property. Office: Arnstein & Lehr 120 S Riverside Plz Ste 1200 Chicago IL 60606-3910

KIMBALL, CATHERINE D. state supreme court justice; Former judge La. Dist. Ct. (18th dist.); now assoc. justice Supreme Ct of La. Office: Supreme Ct of La 301 Loyola Ave New Orleans LA 70112-1814

KIMBALL, JOHN DEVEREUX, lawyer; b. Orange, N.J., Mar. 18, 1949; s. Robert Maxwell and Audrey Josephine (Kerr) K.; m. Astri Jean Baillie; children: children: Astri, Emily, Elizabeth, Andrew. BA, Duke U., 1971; JD, Georgetown U., 1975. Bar: N.Y. 1976. Assoc. Healy & Baillie LLP, N.Y.C., 1975-80, ptnr., 1980—. Adj. prof. law NYU, 1986—. Co-author: Voyage Charters, 1993, Time Charters, 1995; mem. editl. bd. Jour. Maritime Law and Commerce. Mem. ABA, Maritime Law Assn., Assn. of Bar of City of N.Y. Admiralty, Federal civil litigation, Private international. Home: 54 East Ln Madison NJ 07940-2652 Office: Healy & Baillie LLP 29 Broadway New York NY 10006-3201 E-mail: jkimball@healy.com

KIMBALL, SPENCER LEVAN, lawyer, educator; b. Thatcher, Ariz., Aug. 26, 1918; s. Spencer Woolley and Camilia (Eyring) K.; m. Kathryn Ann Murphy, June 12, 1939; children: Barbara Jean (Mrs. Thomas Sherman), Judith Ann (Mrs. William Stillion), Kathleen Louise, Spencer David, Kent Douglas, Timothy Jay; m. Virginia Barrus Johnson, June 4, 1994. BS, U. Ariz., 1940; postgrad., U. Utah, 1946-47; BCL, Oxford (Eng.) U., 1949; SJD, U. Wis., 1958. Bar: Utah 1950, Mich. 1965, Wis. 1968, U.S. Dist. Ct. (we. dist.) Wis. 1968, U.S. Supreme Ct. 1982, U.S. Ct. Appeals (9th cir.) 1986. Assoc. prof. U. Utah Coll. Law, Salt Lake City, 1949-50, dean, 1950-54, prof., 1954-57, rsch. prof. emeritus, 1993—; prof. U. Mich., 1957-68, dir. legal rsch. Law Sch., 1962-67; staff dir. Wis. Ins. Law Revision Project, 1966-79; prof. law, dean U. Wis. Law Sch., 1968-72; exec. dir. Am. Bar Found., Chgo., 1972-82; prof. law U. Chgo., 1972-88, Seymour Logan prof., 1978-88, Seymour Logan prof. emeritus, 1988—. Author: Insurance and Public Policy (Elizur Wright award), 1960, Introduction to the Legal System, 1966, Essays in Insurance Regulation, 1966, Cases and Materials on Insurance Law, 1992; (with Werner Pfenningstorf) The Regulation of Insurance Companies in the United States and the European Communities: A Comparative Study, 1981; editor: (with Herbert Denenberg) Insurance, Government and Social Policy, 1969, (with Werner Pfenningstorf Assicurazioni) Legal Service Plans, 1977; bd. editors: Jour. Ins. Regulation, Internat. Jour. Ins. Law; contbr. articles to profl. jours. Lt. USNR, 1943-46. Recipient Rsch. award Am. Bar Found.; fellow Outstanding Rsch. in Law and Gov't, 1984, Am. Bar Assn. Sect. of Torts and Ins. Practice, Robert B. McKay award Lifetime contbns. to Ins. and Tort Law, 1991. Fellow Am. Bar Found.; mem. ABA, Mich. State Bar, Utah State Bar, Wis. State Bar, Internat. Assn. Ins. Law (hon. pres., past pres. U.S. chpt., mem. presdl. coun.) Phi Beta Kappa, Phi Kappa Phi. Home: 241 N Vine St Apt 1001W Salt Lake City UT 84103-1936 Office: U Utah Coll Law Salt Lake City UT 84112

KIMBERLING, JOHN FARRELL, retired lawyer; b. Shelbyville, Ind., Nov. 15, 1926; s. James Farrell and Phyllis (Casady) K. B of Naval Sci. and Tactics, Purdue U., 1946; AB, Ind. U., 1947, JD, 1950. Bar: Ind. 1950, Calif. 1954. Assoc. Bracken, Gray, DeFur & Voran, 1950-51, Lillick McHose & Charles, and predecessor firms, 1953-63, ptnr., 1963-86, Dewey Ballantine, L.A., 1986-89; ret., 1989. Bd. visitors Ind. U. Sch. Law, 1987—; bd. dirs. Ind. U. Found., 1988—. Lt. (j.g.) USNR, 1951-53. Fellow Am. Coll. Trial Lawyers; mem. ABA (charter mem. litigation sect.), State Bar Calif., L.A. Bar Assn., L.A. Jr. C. of C. (past pres.), Beta Theta Pi, Phi Delta Phi. Democrat. Clubs: California, Chancery, Lincoln. Home: 1180 Los Robles Dr Palm Springs CA 92262-4124 E-mail: jackkim323@aol.com

KIMBROUGH, ROBERT AVERYT, lawyer; b. Sarasota, Fla., Nov. 2, 1933; s. Verman T. and Edith (Averyt) K.; m. Emilie Hudson, Aug. 24, 1957; children: James E., Robert A. Jr. BS, Davidson Coll., 1955; LLB to JD, U. Fla., 1960. Bar: Fla. 1960, U.S. Dist. Ct. Fla. 1962. Pvt. practice, Sarasota, 1960—. Chmn., bd. trustees, Ringling Sch. Art & Design, Sarasota, 1983-85; chmn. Sarasota Welfare Home Inc., 1986-89; pres. Fla. West Coast Symphony, Sarasota, 1986-90. Recipient Champion Higher Edn. in Fla., Ind. Coll. and Univs. of Fla., 1984-85, Alumnus of Yr. award Phi Delta Theta, 1997. Mem. ABA, Fla. Bar, Sarasota County Bar Assn., Sarasota Yacht Club, Kiwanis. Republican. Presbyterian. Avocations: flying, fishing, boating. Home: 7100 S Gator Creek Blvd Sarasota FL 34241-9729 Office: 1530 Cross St Sarasota FL 34236-7015 E-mail: rak@KimbroughKoach.com

KIMMEL, MORTON RICHARD, lawyer; b. N.Y.C., Nov. 10, 1940; s. Benjamin Bert and Sylvia (Alabaster) K.; m. Marcia Harriet LaPotin, Sept. 10, 1967; children: Wayne Douglas, Michelle Wendy, Karen Paige, Larry Keith. BA, Temple U., 1962; JD, George Washington U., 1965. Bar: Del. 1965, D.C. 1966. Law clk. Del. Superior Ct., Wilmington, 1965-66; ptnr. Kimmel, Carter, Roman & Peltz P.A., 1970—. Supr. Del. Justices of the Peace, 1970-72; rep. State Farm Ins. Co., 1968-90, trustee lawyers' fund for client protection, 1985-97; arbitrator and mediator; lectr. in fields of criminal law, ins. law, personal injury law, law office mgmt., trial practice, ethics, professionalism, mediation and arbitration, 1970—. Author: You Can Do It, 1973, Emergency Medicine, 1982, Delaware Arbitration Manual, 1984, The Delaware Bar in the 20th Century, 1994. Mem. ATLA, Am. Bd. Trial Advs., Del. Trial Lawyers Assn., Fedn. Ins. Counsel, Def. Rsch. Inst. (chmn. Del. 1976-77). Democrat. Jewish. Avocations: sports, reading. State civil litigation, Insurance, Personal injury. Office: Kimmel Carter Roman & Peltz PA 913 N Market St Wilmington DE 19801-3019 E-mail: mrkimmel@kcrlaw.com

KIMMITT, ROBERT MICHAEL, executive, banker, diplomat; b. Logan, Utah, Dec. 19, 1947; s. Joseph Stanley and Eunice L. (Wegener) K.; m. Holly Sutherland, May 19, 1979; children: Kathleen, Robert, William, Thomas, Margaret. BS, U.S. Mil. Acad., 1969; JD, Georgetown U., 1977. Bar: D.C. 1977. Commd. 2d lt. U.S. Army, 1969, advanced through grades to maj., 1982, served in Vietnam, 1970-71; maj. gen. USAR, 1999—; law clk. U.S. Ct. Appeals, Washington, 1977-78; sr. staff mem. NSC, 1978-83, dep. asst. to Pres. for nat. security affairs and exec. sec. and gen. counsel, 1983-85; gen. counsel U.S. Dept. Treasury, 1985-87; ptnr. Sidley & Austin, 1987-89; undersec. for polit. affairs Dept. State, 1989-91, ambassador to Germany, 1991-93; mng. dir. Lehman Bros., Washington, N.Y.C., 1993-97; sr. ptnr. Wilmer, Cutler & Pickering, Washington, 1997-00; vice-chmn., pres. Commerce One, Pleasanton, Calif., 2000-01; exec. v.p. AOL Time Warner, Washington, 2001—. U.S. mem. panel of arbitrators Ctr. Settlement of Investment Internat. Disputes, 1988—89. Bd. dirs. Commerce One, Inc., Siemens AG, Allianz Life Ins. Co. N.Am., United Def. Industries, Xign Corp., German Marshall Fund, Atlantic Coun., Mike Mansfield Found., Am. Coun. Germany, Am. Inst. Contemproary German Studies. Decorated Bronze star (3), Purple Heart, Air medal, Vietnamese Cross of Gallantry, German Svc. Cross, German Army Cross in Gold; recipient Arthur Flemming award Downtown Jaycees, 1987, Alexander Hamilton award U.S. Dept. Treasury, 1987, Presdl. Citizens medal, 1991, Def. Disting. Civilian Svc. medal, 1993. Mem. Am. Acad. Diplomacy, Assn. Grads. U.S. Mil. Acad. (trustee 1976-82), Coun. Fgn. Rels. Roman Catholic. Office: AOL Time Warner Ste 800 800 Connecticut Ave NW Washington DC 20006

KIMPORT, DAVID LLOYD, lawyer; b. Hot Springs, S.D., Nov. 28, 1945; s. Ralph E. and Ruth N. (Hutchinson) K.; m. Barbara H. Buggert, Apr. 2, 1976; children: Katrina Elizabeth, Rebecca Helen, Susanna Ruth. AB summa cum laude, Bowdoin Coll., 1968; postgrad., Imperial Coll., U. London, 1970-71; JD, Stanford U., 1975. Bar: Calif. 1975, U.S. Supreme Ct. 1978. Assoc. Baker & McKenzie, San Francisco, 1975-82, ptnr., 1982-90, Nossaman, Guthner, Knox & Elliot, 1990—. Active San Francisco Planning and Urban Rsch., 1978—, The Family, 1987—. Served with U.S. Army, 1968-70. Mem. ABA, San Francisco Bar Assn., Commonwealth Club of Calif., Phi Beta Kappa. Democrat. Episcopalian. Contracts commercial, Private international, Real property. Office: Nossaman Guthner Knox & Elliott 50 California St Fl 34 San Francisco CA 94111-4624

KINAKA, WILLIAM TATSUO, lawyer; b. Lahaina, Hawaii, Apr. 4, 1940; s. Toshio and Natsumi (Hirouji) K.; m. Jeanette Louisa Ramos, Nov. 23, 1968; children: Kimberly H., Kristine N.Y. BA in Polit. Sci., Whittier Coll., 1962; MA in Internat. Rels., Am. U., 1964, JD, 1973. Bar: D.C. 1975, U.S. Ct. Appeals (D.C. cir.) 1975, U.S. Dist. Ct. D.C. 1975, U.S. Tax Ct. 1975, U.S. Ct. Mil. Appeals 1975, Hawaii 1976, U.S. Dist. Ct. Hawaii 1976, U.S. Ct. Appeals (9th cir.) 1976. Career trainee CIA, Langley, Va., 1966; legis. asst. Sen. Hiram L. Fong, Washington, 1966-76; assoc. Ueoka & Luna, Wailuku, Hawaii, 1977-85; pvt. practice law, 1985—; grand jury counsel 2d Cir. Ct., 1985-86. Ct. arbitrator, 1989—; legal cons. Hale Mahaolu Elderly Housing, Kahului, 1976—. Active Dem. Party of Hawaii, Wailuku, 1988-89; pres. Nat. Eagle Scout Assn. of Boy Scouts Am., Wailuku, 1983-91; bd. dirs. Wailuku Main St. Assn., 1988-94, Maui Adult Day Care Ctr., Puunene, pres. 2000—; bd. dirs. Kahului; Maui Coun., Boy Scouts of Am., 1983—; bd. dirs. Maui Youth Intervention Program, Inc., pres. 1993—; bd. dirs. Iao Intermediate Sch. Renaissance Ednl. Found., pres. 1999—; bd. dirs. Iao Intermediate Sch.'s Renaissance Ednl. Found., pres. 1999—. Mem. Hawaii Bar Assn., Maui Bar Assn., Maui Japanese C. of C., Maui C. of C., Nat. Eagle Scout Assn. (pres. Wailuku 1983-91). United Ch. of Christ. Avocations: scouting, gardening, swimming, poetry writing. Consumer commercial, Family and matrimonial, Landlord-tenant. Home: 639 Pio Dr Wailuku HI 96793-2622 Office: 24 N Church St Ste 201 Wailuku HI 96793-1606

KIND, KENNETH WAYNE, lawyer, real estate broker; b. Missoula, Mont., Apr. 1, 1948; s. Joseph Bruce and Elinor Joy (Smith) K.; m. Diane Lucille Jozaitis, Aug. 28, 1971; children: Kirstin Amber, Kenneth Warner. BA, Calif. State U., Northridge, 1973; JD, Calif. Western U., 1976. Bar: Calif. 1976, U.S. Dist. Ct. (ea., so., no. dists.) Calif., 1976, U.S. Cir. Ct. Appeals (9th cir.); lic. NASCAR driver, 1987. Mem. celebrity security staff Brownstone Am., Beverly Hills, Calif., 1970-76; tchr. Army and Navy

Acad., Carlsbad, 1975-76; real estate broker Bakersfield, 1978—; sole practice, 1976—. Lectr. mechanic's lien laws, Calif., 1983—. Staff writer Calif. Western Law Jour., 1975. Sgt. U.S. Army, 1967-70. Mem. ABA, VFW, Nat. Order Barristers, Rancheros Visitadores. Libertarian. State civil litigation, Insurance, Real property. Office: 4042 Patton Way Bakersfield CA 93308-5030

KINDLER, JEFFREY B. lawyer; b. May 13, 1955; JD, Harvard U., 1980. Bar: D.C. 1980. Pres. ptnr. brands McDonald's Corp., 1996-97, exec. v.p., gen. counsel Ill., 1997—; chmn., CEO Boston Mkt., 2000-2001; pres., ptnr. Brands McDonalds Corp., 2001—; chmn., CEO Boston Mkt., 2001—. Office: McDonalds Corp One Kroc Dr Oak Brook IL 60523 E-mail: jeff.kindler@mcd.com

KINDREGAN, CHARLES PETER, law educator; b. Phila., June 18, 1935; s. Charles Peter and Catherine (Delaney) K.; m. Patricia Ann. Patterson, Aug. 18, 1962 (dec. 1998); children: Chad, Helen, Tricia, Brian. BA, LaSalle U., 1957, MA, 1958; JD, Chgo.-Kent Coll. Law, 1966; LLM, Northwestrn U., 1967. Bar: Ill. 1966, Mass. 1968, U.S. Dist. Ct. Mass. 1970. Instr. Va. Mil. Inst., 1960-62, Loyola U., Chgo., 1964-67; prof. law Suffolk U., Boston, 1967—, assco. dean, 1990-94. Author: The Quality of Life, 1969, Malpractice and the Lawyer, 1981, professional Responsibility of the Lawyer, 1995; co-author: Massachusetts Family Law and Practice, 2d edit., 1996-2001, (With M. Inker) Mass. Domestic Relations Rules Annotated, 2001; contbr. articles to law revs., jours. Mem. Hull Bd. Zoning Appeals, Mass., 1969; pres. Beacon Hill PTA, Boston, 1974-75. Mem. ABA (academic rep. to publications bd. family law sect.), Mass. Bar Assn. (task force on model rules of profl. conduct 1982-84, co-chair com. on crisis in probate and family ct.), Suffolk Ctr. for Advanced Legal Studies (dir. 1982-87). Democrat. Roman Catholic. Home: 150 Staniford St Apt 710 Boston MA 02114-2597 Office: Suffolk U Law Sch 120 Tremont St Boston MA 02108-4910

KINDT, JOHN WARREN, lawyer, educator, consultant; b. Oak Park, Ill., May 24, 1950; s. Warren Frederick and Lois Jeannette (Woelffer) K.; m. Anne Marie Johnson, Apr. 17, 1982; children: John Warren Jr., James Roy Frederick. AB, Coll. William and Mary, 1972; JD, U. Ga., 1976, MBA, 1977; LLM, U. Va., 1978, SJD, 1981. Bar: D.C. 1976, Ga. 1976, Va. 1977. Advisor to gov. State of Va., Richmond, 1971-72; asst. to Congressman M. Caldwell Butler, U.S. Ho. of Reps., Washington, 1972-73; staff cons. White House, 1976-77; asst. prof. U. Ill., Champaign, 1978-81, assoc. prof., 1981-85, prof., 1985—. Cons. 3d UN Conf. on Law of Sea; lectr. exec. MBA program U. Ill. Author: Marine Pollution and the Law of the Sea, 4 vols., 1981, 2 vols., 1988, 92, Economic Impacts of Legalized Gambling, 1994; contbr. articles to profl. jours. Caucus chmn., del. White House Conf. on Youth, 1970; co-chmn. Va. Gov.'s Adv. Coun. on Youth, 1971; mem. Athens (Ga.) Legal Aid Soc., 1975-76. Rotary fellow, 1979-80; Smithsonian ABA/ELI scholar, 1981; sr. fellow London Sch. Econs., 1985-86. Mem. Am. Soc. Internat. Law, D.C. Bar Assn., Va. Bar Assn., Ga. Bar Assn. Home: 801 Brookside Ln Mahomet IL 61853-9545 Office: U Ill 350 Commerce W Champaign IL 61820

KING, AUDREY, lawyer, mediator; b. N.Y.C., Jan. 30, 1942; BA, Columbia U., 1968; JD, NYU, 1972. Bar: N.Y. 1973. Atty. Sperry Corp., N.Y.C., 1972-76, GAF Corp., N.Y.C., 1976-78, with consumer affairs dept., dir. mktg. services, 1978-84; v.p. Telephonics Corp., Huntington, N.Y., 1984-89; pvt. practice N.Y.C., 1989—. Adj. faculty mgmt. NYU; lectr. on warranties, mktg., govt. regulations, mgmt.; cons. dispute resolution UN, N.Y.C., 1990—; bd. dirs. N.Y. Law Sch., N.Y.C. Address: 20 Sutton Place South New York NY 10022

KING, BERNARD T. lawyer; b. Gouverneur, N.Y., Feb. 28, 1935; BS, Le Moyne Coll., 1956; JD cum laude, Syracuse U., 1959. Bar: N.Y. 1959. Ptnr. Blitman and King, Syracuse, N.Y. Assoc. editor Syracuse Law Rev., 1958-59; lectr. Labor Studies Program, N.Y. State Sch. Indsl. and Labor Rels., Cornell U., 1974; sec. Onondaga County Indsl. Devel. Agy., 1978-81. Mem., bd. dirs. Syracuse Model Neighborhood Corp., 1972-75, Regents, 1973—, sec., 1983—, bd. trustees, 1984-90. vice chmn., bd. trustees, 1988, LeMoyne Coll., 1974-80, v.p. 1977-79, pres., 1979-80; bd. trustees Manlius Pebble Hill Sch. Corp.; mem. United Way Cen. N.Y., 1971-75, bd. dirs., 1981-87; com. mem. 33rd Congl. Dist. Naval Academise Selection Bd., 1980-83. With USAF, 1961-62, Air NG, 1959-65, Salvation Army. Recipient Disting. Alumni award LeMoyne Coll., 1979, Whitney M. Seymour award Am. Arbitration Assn., 1986. Fellow Am. Bar Found.; mem. ABA (labor law and employment law com. 1963, chmn. labor and employment sect. 1987-88, co-chmn., subcom. B com. on devel. of law under NLRA 1971-76, sect. del. to ho. of dels., mem. joint com. on employee benefits), Soc. Profls. in Dispute Resolution, Panel of Arbitrators, Am. Arbitration Assn. (bd. dirs. 1988), Onondaga County Bar Assn., N.Y. State Bar Assn. (exec. com., labor law sect. 1976—, chmn.-elect 1979, chmn. 1980-81), Am. Judicature Soc., ABA Standing comm. on substance abuse; fel. ABA Coll. Labor and Employment Lawyers, ABA Am. Coll. Employment Benefits. Labor, Pension, profit-sharing, and employee benefits, Personal injury. Office: Blitman and King 500 S Salina St Ste 1100 Syracuse NY 13202-3397

KING, CAROLYN DINEEN, federal judge; b. Syracuse, N.Y., Jan. 30, 1938; d. Robert E. and Carolyn E. (Bareham) Dineen; children: James Randall, Philip Randall, Stephen Randall; m. John L. King, Jan. 1, 1988. A.B. summa cum laude, Smith Coll., 1959; LL.B., Yale U., 1962. Bar: D.C. 1962, Tex. 1963. Assoc. Fulbright & Jaworski, Houston, 1962-72; ptnr. Childs, Fortenbach, Beck & Guyton, 1972-78, Sullivan, Bailey, King, Randall & Sabom, Houston, 1978-79; circuit judge U.S. Ct. Appeals (5th cir.), 1979—, chief judge, 1999—. Trustee, mem. exec. com., treas. Houston Ballet Found., 1967-70; trustee, mem. exec. com., chmn. bd. trustees U. St. Thomas, 1988-98; mem. Houston dist. adv. coun. SBA, 1972-76; mem. Dallas regional panel Pres.'s Commn. White House Fellowships, 1972-76, mem. commn., 1977; bd. dirs. Houston chpt. Am. Heart Assn., 1978-79; nat. trustee Palmer Drug Abuse Program, 1978-79; trustee, sec., treas., chmn. audit com., fin. com., mem. mgmt. com. United Way Tex. Gulf Coast, 1979-85. Mem. ABA, Fed. Bar Assn., Am. Law Inst. (coun. 1991—, chmn. membership com. 1997—), State Bar Tex., Houston Bar Assn. Roman Catholic. Office: US Ct Appeals 11020 US Courthouse 515 Rusk Avenue Houston TX 77002-2694*

KING, DAVID ROY, lawyer; b. N.Y.C., Jan. 5, 1950; s. Joseph S. and Doris (Kagan) K.; m. Eunice Searles, Aug. 22, 1971; children: Mark B., Anna M. BA, U. Pa., 1971; JD, Harvard U., 1974. Bar: Pa. 1974, U.S. Dist Ct. (ea. dist.) Pa. 1974. Assoc. Morgan, Lewis & Bockius LLP, Phila., 1974-81, ptnr., 1981-2000; CEO, Principia Pharms., Inc., 2000; ind. cons., 2001; pres. Delsys Pharms., Inc., 2001—. Computer, Mergers and acquisitions, Securities. Office: 11 Deer Park Dr Ste 202 Monmouth Junction NJ 08852 E-mail: dking@delsyspharma.com

KING, GARR MICHAEL, federal judge; b. Pocatello, Idaho, Jan. 28, 1936; s. Warren I. King and Geraldine E. (Hanlon) Appleby; m. Mary Jo Rieber, Feb. 2, 1957; children: Mary, Michael, Matthew, James, Margaret, John, David. Student, U. Utah, 1957-59; LLB, Lewis and Clark Coll., 1963. Bar: Oreg. 1963, U.S. Dist. Ct. Oreg. 1965, U.S. Ct. Appeals (9th cir.) 1975, U.S. Supreme Ct. 1971. Dep. dist. atty. Multnomah County Dist. Atty.'s Office, Portland, Oreg., 1963-66; assoc. Morrison, Bailey, Dunn, Carney & Miller, 1966-71; ptnr. Kennedy & King, 1971-77, Kennedy, King & McClurg, Portland, 1977-82, Kennedy, King & Zimmer, Portland, 1982-98; judge U.S. Dist. Ct. Oreg., 1998—. Active various pvt. sch. and ch. bds. Served as sgt. USMC, 1954-57. Fellow Am. Coll. Trial Lawyers (regent 1995-98), Am. Bar Found.; mem. ABA, Oreg. Bar Assn., Multnomah County Bar Assn. (pres. 1975), Jud. Conf. 9th Cir. (del.), Northwestern Coll. Law Alumni Assn. (pres.), Multnomah Athletic Club. Democrat. Roman Catholic. Avocations: tennis, reading, gardening. Office: 907 US Courthouse 1000 SW 3rd Ave Portland OR 97204-2930 E-mail: garr-king@ord.uscourts.gov

KING, HENRY LAWRENCE, lawyer; b. N.Y.C., Apr. 29, 1928; s. H. Abraham and Henrietta (Prentky) K.; m. Barbara Hope, 1949 (dec. May 1962); children: Elizabeth King Robertson, Patricia King Cantlay, Matthew Harrison.; m. Alice Mary Sturges, Aug. 1, 1963 (div. 1978); children: Katherine Masury King Baccile, Andrew Lawrence, Eleanor Sturges; m. Margaret Gram, Feb. 14, 1981 AB, Columbia U., 1948; LLB, Yale U., 1951. Bar: N.Y. 1952, U.S. Supreme Ct., other fed. cts. 1952. With Davis Polk & Wardwell, N.Y.C., 1951—, ptnr., 1961—, mng. ptnr., chmn., 1982-96. Mng. editor Yale Law Jour., 1951. Trustee, chmn. bd. Columbia U., 1983-95, chmn. emeritus, 1995—; chmn. bd. Columiba Presbyn. adv. coun.; pres. Assn. Alumni Columbia Coll., 1966-68, Alumni Fedn. Columbia U., 1973-75; chmn. Coll. Fund, 1972-73; pres. Yale Law Sch. Assn., 1984-86, chmn., 1986-88; pres. Cathedral of St. John the Divine, N.Y.C.; bd. dirs. N.Y. Acad. of Medicine, Citizen's Com. for N.Y.C., Inc., Am. Skin Assn., Fishers Island Devel. Co., Episcopal Charities; vestryman Trinity Ch., N.Y.C., 1991-98;trustee Chapin Sch., 1977-89, Columbia U. Press, 1978-92. Recipient Columbia Alumni medal for conspicuous service, 1968, John Jay award, 1992. Fellow Am. Coll. Trial Lawyers; mem. ABA, Coun. on Fgn. Rels., Am. Law Inst., N.Y. State Bar Assn. (pres. 1988-89), Assn. Bar City N.Y., Am. Judicature Soc., Fishers Island Club, Century Assn., Union Club (N.Y.C.), Jupiter Island Club, Blind Brook Club, Fishers Island Yacht Club, Pilgrims, Church Club (N.Y.C.). Antitrust, Federal civil litigation, Private international. Home: 115 E 67th St New York NY 10021-5951 also: 61 Links Rd Hobe Sound FL 33455-2318 also: East End Rd Fishers Island NY 06390 Office: Davis Polk & Wardwell 450 Lexington Ave 27th Fl New York NY 10017-3982 E-mail: hking@dpw.com

KING, JACK A. lawyer; b. Lafayette, Ind., July 29, 1936; s. Noah C. and Mabel E. (Pierce) K.; m. Mary S. King, Dec. 10, 1960; children: Jeffrey A., Janice D., Julie D. BS in Fin., Ind. U., 1958, JD, 1961. Bar: Ind. 1961. Ptnr. Ball, Eggleston, King & Bumbleburg, Lafayette, 1961-70; judge Superior Ct. 2 of Tippecanoe County, Ind., 1970-78; v.p., assoc. gen. counsel Dairyland Ins. Co., 1979; v.p., gen. counsel, asst. sec. Superior Ct. 2 of Tippecanoe County, 1980-85; v.p., counsel Sentry Ctr. West, 1981-85; asst. gen. counsel Sentry Corp., 1979-85; v.p., gen. counsel, asst. sec. Gt. S.W. Fire Ins. Co., 1980-85, Gt. S.W. Surplus Lines Ins. Co., 1981-85; v.p., gen. counsel Dairyland County Mut. Ins. Co. Tex., 1980-85; v.p. legal, asst. sec. Scottsdale Ins. Co., 1985-95; asst. sec. Nat. Casualty Co., 1985-95; v.p. legal, asst. sec. Scottsdale Indemnity Co., 1992-95; sr. v.p., gen. coun. TIG Excess & Surplus Lines, Inc., 1995-96; v.p. Ariz. Ins. Info. Assn., 1988-96; exec. dir. Ariz. Ins. Guaranty Funds, 1998-2001. Bd. dirs. Countrywide Ins. Co.; cons., mediator and arbitrator, 1996-97; exec. com. Ariz. Joint Underwriting Plan, 1980-81; mem. Ariz. Property & Casualty Ins. Commn., 1985-86, vice-chmn., 1986; mem. Ariz. Study Commn. on Ins., 1986-87, Ariz. Task Force on Ct. Orgn. and Adminstrn., 1988-89; adv. com. Ariz. Ho. Rep. Majority Leaders, 1989, Ariz. Dept. Ins. Fraud Unit, 1997-97. Contbr. to The Law of Competitive Business Practices, 2d edit. Bd. dirs. Scottsdale Art Ctr. Assn., 1981-84. Mem. ABA, Ind. Bar Assn., Maricopa County Bar Assn. General corporate, Insurance. Office: 3443 N Central Ave Ste 1000 Phoenix AZ 85012-2222

KING, JAMES FORREST, JR. lawyer; b. Salina, Kans., Jan. 9, 1949; s. James Forrest Sr. and Carolyn (Prout) K.; m. Mary Lou A. Goodwin, May 18, 1985. BA, U. Md., 1970; JD with honors, George Washington U., 1974. Bar: D.C. 1975, U.S. Dist. Ct. D.C. 1976, U.S. Ct. Appeals (D.C. cir.) 1977, U.S. Supreme Ct. 1979, Md. 1982, U.S. Ct. Appeals (4th cir.) 1985. Atty. Law Offices of Washington, 1975-76; ptnr. Reuss, McConville & King, Washington, 1976-80, Reuss, Herndon, McConville & King, Washington, 1980-85; of counsel Herndon, McConville, Brown, Teller & Hessler, 1986-87; ptnr. Law Offices of James Forrest King, 1987—. Commr. D.C. Commn. Human Rights, 1984-90. Mem. Am. Arbitration Assn. (panel mem.), ABA (econs. law practice sect.), D.C. Bar Assn. (co-chmn. div. 6, 1981-84, arbitration bd. 1981-83, employment discrimination panel, 1977-80). Civil rights, Federal civil litigation, Labor.

KING, JAMES LAWRENCE, federal judge; b. Miami, Fla., Dec. 20, 1927; s. James Lawrence and Viola (Clodfelter) K.; m. Mary Frances Kapa, June 1, 1961; children— Lawrence Daniel, Kathryn Ann, Karen Ann, Mary Virginia BA in Edn., U. Fla., 1949, JD, 1953; LHD (hon.), St. Thomas U., 1992. Bar: Fla. 1953. Assoc. Sibley & Davis, Miami, Fla., 1953-57; ptnr. Sibley Giblin King & Levenson, 1957-64; judge 11th Jud. Cir. Dade County, 1964-70; temp. assoc. justice Supreme Ct. Fla., 1965; temp. assoc. judge Fla. Ct. Appeals (2d, 3d and 4th dist.), 1965-68; judge U.S. Dist. Ct. (so. dist.) Fla., Miami, 1970-84, chief judge, 1984-91, sr. judge, 1991—. Temp. judge U.S. Ct. Appeals 5th cir., 1977-78; mem. Jud. Conf. U.S., 1984-87, mem. adv. commn. jud. activities, 1973-76, mem. joint commn. code jud. conduct, 1974-76, mem. commn. to consider stds. for admission to practice in fed. cts., 1976-79, chmn. implementation com. for admission attys. to fed. practice, 1979-85, mem. com. bankruptcy legis., 1977-78; mem. Jud. Conf. U.S., 1984-87; mem. Jud. Coun. 11th Cir., 1989-92; pres. 5th cir. U.S. Dist. Judges Assn., 1977-78; chief judge U.S. Dist. Ct. C.Z., 1977-78; long range planning commn. Fed. Judiciary, 1991-95. Mem. state exec. council U. Fla., 1956-59; mem. Bd. Control Fla. Governing State Univs. and Colls., 1964. Served to 1st lt. USAF, 1953-55 Recipient Outstanding Alumnus award U. Fla. Law Rev., 1980, Lifetime Achievement award Greater Miami Jewish Fedn. Commerce and Professions Attys. Divsn., 1992, 18th Annual Edward J. Devitt Disting. Svc. to Justice award, 2000; The James Lawrence King Fed. Justice Bldg. named in his honor, 1996. Mem. Fla. Bar Assn. (pres. jr. bar 1963-64, bd. govs. 1958-63, Merit award young lawyer sect. 1967), ABA, Am. Law Inst., Inst. Jud. Adminstrn., Fla. Blue Key, Pi Kappa Tau, Phi Delta Phi Democrat Home: 11950 SW 67th Ct Miami FL 33156-4756 Office: US Dist Ct James King Fed Justice Bldg 99 NE 4th St Rm 1127 Miami FL 33132-2139

KING, JENNIFER ELIZABETH, editor; b. Summit, N.J., July 15, 1970; d. Layton E. and Margery A. (Long) K. BS in Journalism, Northwestern U., Evanston, Ill., 1992. Asst. editor Giant Steps Media, Chgo., 1992-93, assoc. editor Corp. Legal Times, 1993-94, dir. confs., 1994-95, mng. editor Corp. Legal Times, 1995-2001, v.p. edit. Corp. Legal Times, 2001—; acting mng. editor Ill. Legal Times, 1996-97; mng. editor U.S. Bus. Litig., 1997. Office: Corporate Legal Times LLC 656 W Randolph St # 500-e Chicago IL 60661-2114

KING, JOSEPHINE YAGER, law educator; b. Homestead, Pa. d. Charles and Maria Yager; m. Benton Davis King; children: Garrett Davis, Loring Brooke. BA, U. Pa.; MA (fellow), Bryn Mawr Coll., PhD, 1950; JD, SUNY, 1965. Bar: N.Y. 1965, U.S. Dist. Ct. (ea. and so. dists.) N.Y. 1976, U.S. Ct. Appeals (2d cir.) 1976. Prof. SUNY Sch. Law, Buffalo, 1965-69, Hofstra U. Sch. Law, Hempstead, N.Y., 1970-75; dep. chief U.S. atty's office appeals div. Eastern Dist. of N.Y., Bklyn., 1975-76; prof. law Pace U., White Plains, N.Y., 1976—, assoc. dean., 1976-78. Lectr. South African Law Schs., 1997. Contbr. articles to profl. jours. in field of constnl. law. Mem. ABA, Am. Law Inst., Phi Beta Kappa, Delta Phi Alpha, Pi Gamma Mu. Address: 11 Menayas Ct Washingtonville NY 10992-2032

KING, LAWRENCE PHILIP, lawyer, educator; b. Schenectady, N.Y., Jan. 16, 1929; s. Louis D. and Sonia K.; children— David J. Kaufman, Deborah J. King. B.S.S., CCNY, 1950; LL.B., NYU, 1953; LL.M., U. Mich., 1957. Bar: N.Y. 1954, U.S. Supreme Ct. 1963. Atty. Paramount Pictures Corp., N.Y.C., 1955-56; asst. prof. law Wayne State U., 1957-59; asst. prof. NYU, 1959-61, assoc. prof., 1961-63, prof., 1963—, Charles Seligson prof. law, 1979—, assoc. dean Sch. Law, 1973-77; of counsel Wachtell, Lipton, Rosen & Katz, N.Y.C. Cons. Commn. to Study Bankruptcy Law U.S., 1970-73, advisor nat. bankruptcy rev. com., 1996-97; assoc. reporter adv. com. on bankruptcy rules U.S. Jud. Conf., 1968-76, reporter, 1979-83, mem. adv. com. on bankruptcy rules, 1983-92; vis. faculty law Hebrew U., Jerusalem, 1971, 87, 94, Haifa U., 1994, 96, 97, 98, 99, Tel Aviv U., 1987, 94, Temple U. Sch. Law, U. Calif. Law Sch., Berkeley; lectr. Bar Ilan U., U. Stockholm, U. Innsbruck, Fed. Ct. Author: (with R. Duesenberg) Sales and Bulk Transfers Under the U.C.C., 1966, supplement, 1999, (with M. Cook) Creditors Rights, Debtor's Protection and Bankruptcy, Cases and Materials, 1985, 2d edit., 1989, 3d edit., 1997; contbr. articles, book revs. to legal jours.; edtor-in-chief: Collier on Bankruptcy, 1964, 15th edit. rev., 1979—; co-editor-in-chief: Collier Bankruptcy Practice Guide, 1981—. Trustee Village of Saltaire (N.Y.), 1980-84, mayor, 1984-86, acting justice, 1988—. Recipient NYU Law Alumni Achievement award, 1976, NYU Law Alumni 25-Yr. Faculty Svc. award, 1984, legal teaching award, 1993, award Bankruptcy Lawyers divsn. UJA-Fedn., 1984, Man of Yr. award Comml. Law League Am., 1969, Disting. Svc. award Am. Coll. Bankruptcy, 1997, Excellence in Edn. award Nat. Conf. Bamkrutpcy Judges, 2000. Mem. ABA, N.Y. State Bar Assn., Assn. of Bar of City of N.Y., Nat. Bankruptcy Conf., Am. Law Inst. Office: NYU Sch Law 40 Washington Sq S New York NY 10012-1005 E-mail: larry.king@nyu.edu

KING, MICHAEL HOWARD, lawyer; b. Chgo., Mar. 10, 1943; s. Warren and Betty (Fine) K.; m. Candice M. King, Aug. 18, 1968; children— Andrew, Julie. B.S. Washington U., St. Louis 1967, J.D. 1970. Bar: Ill. 1970, U.S. Dist. Ct. (no. dist.) Ill. 1970, U.S. Dist. Ct. (ea. dist.) Wis. 1972, U.S. Ct. Appeals (7th cir.) 1974, U.S. Ct. Appeals (5th cir.) 1979, U.S. Supreme Ct. 1975, U.S. Ct. Appeals (3d cir.) 1983, U.S. Tax Ct. 1987, U.S. Ct. Appeals (10th cir.) 1987, U.S. Dist. Ct. (no. dist.) Calif. 1987, U.S. Dist. Ct. Nebr. 1988, U.S. Dist. Ct. (ctrl. dist.) Ill. 1992, U.S. Dist. Ct. (no. dist.) N.Y. 1992, U.S. Ct. Appeals (2nd cir.) 1994. Spl. atty. organized crime, racketeering sect. U.S. Dept. Justice, Washington, 1970-73; asst. U.S. atty. No. Dist. Ill., Chgo., 1973-75; assoc. Antonow & Fink, Chgo., 1976, ptnr., 1977-79; ptnr. Ross & Hardies, Chgo., 1979-95; chmn. Bd. Commr. Office of State Appellate Defender. Co-author Model Jury Instructions in Criminal Antitrust Cases, 1982, Handbook on Antitrust Grand Jury Investigations, 1988. Bd. dirs. Chgo. Youth Ctrs., 1977-82; trustee Cove Sch., 1984-88, the Goodman Theatre, 1993—. Mem. ABA (litigation sect., antitrust sect., criminal practice procedure com.), Ill. Bar Assn., Chgo. Bar Assn. (judiciary com., antitrust com.), Am. Judicature Soc., Fed. Bar Assn., Assn. Trial Lawyers Am., Mid-Am. Club (bd. govs.), Econ. Club, Phi Delta Phi, Alpha Epsilon Pi. Antitrust, Federal civil litigation, Criminal. Home: 2025 Windy Hill Ln Highland Park IL 60035-4233 Office: Ross & Hardies 150 N Michigan Ave Ste 2500 Chicago IL 60601-7567

KING, PAUL MARTIN, lawyer; b. Pitts., Dec. 18, 1946; s. Thomas E. and Alice C. (Myers) K.; m. Mary J. Sargus, Mar. 6, 1976; children— Anne C., M. Elizabeth. B.S. in Bus. Adminstrn., Duquesne U., 1968; J.D., U. Pitts., 1971. Bar: Pa. 1971, U.S. Dist. Ct. (we. dist.) Pa. 1971, U.S. Ct. Appeals (D.C. cir.) 1979. Law clk. Allegheny County Common Pleas Ct., Pitts., 1971-72; atty., sr. atty. PPG Industries, Inc., Pitts., 1972-80, sr. counsel, 1980-82, dir. environ. affairs, 1982— ; adj. prof. law U. Pitts. Contbr. chpts. to books, articles to profl. jours. Mem. ABA (chmn. environ. law com. 1987—), Allegheny County Bar Assn., Chem. Mfrs. Assn. (environ. mgmt. com. 1983-87, chmn. air toxic control policy task group 1986-87). General corporate, Environmental. Home: 220 N Bellefield Ave Apt 601 Pittsburgh PA 15213-1467 Office: PPG Industries Inc 1 Ppg Pl # 1P Pittsburgh PA 15272-0001

KING, ROBERT BRUCE, federal judge; b. White Sulphur Springs, W.Va., Jan. 29, 1940; m. Julia Kay Doak, Apr. 16, 1965. BA, W.Va. U., 1961; JD, W.Va. Coll. of Law, 1968. Bar: W.Va. 1968, U.S. Dist. Ct. (so. dist.) W.Va. 1968, U.S. Ct. Appeals W.Va. 1968, U.S. Ct. Appeals (4th cir.) 1970, U.S. Dist. Ct. (no. dist.) W.Va. 1972, U.S. Supreme Ct. 1974, U.S. Dist. Ct. (ea. dist.) Ky. 1975, U.S. Claims Ct. 1985, U.S. Tax Ct. 1991. Asst. mgr. Sam Snead All-Am. Golf Course, Sharpes, Fla., summer 1965; rsch. asst. State and Cmty. Planning Office, Office of R&D, W.Va. U., Morgantown, 1966-68; law clk. Chief Judge John A. Field, Jr. U.S. Dist. Ct. (so. dist.) W.Va., Charleston, 1968-69; assoc. Haynes and Ford, Lewisburg, W.Va., 1969-70; asst. U.S. atty. So. Dist. of W.Va., Charleston, 1970-74; assoc. Spilman, Thomas, Battle and Klostermeyer, 1975, ptnr., 1976-77, 81; U.S. atty. So. Dist. of W.Va., 1977-81; ptnr. King Allen Guthrie & McHugh, 1981-98; judge U.S. Ct. Appeals (4th cir.), Richmond, Va., 1998—. Mem. Jud. Investigation Commn. of W.Va., 1990-94; vis. com. Coll. of Law of W.Va. U., 1997—. Patrick Duffy Koontz scholar. Fellow Am. Coll. Trial Lawyers, Am. Bar Found.; mem. ABA, W.Va. Bar Assn., Kanawha County Bar Assn., Greenbrier County Bar Assn.,U.S. Golf Assn., W.Va. Golf Assn., W.Va. U. Alumni Assn., W.Va. Law Sch. Assn., Jud. Conf. of 4th Cir. Ct. Appeals, Am. Bd. Trial Advocates (W. Va. chpt. pres. 1986-90), Order of the Coif, Pi Sigma Alpha, Phi Alpha Delta. Presbyterian. Office: Ste 7602 300 Virginia St Charleston WV 25301

KING, ROBERT LUCIEN, lawyer; b. Petaluma, Calif., Aug. 9, 1936; s. John Joseph and Ramona Margaret (Thorson) K.; m. Suzanne Nanette Parre, May 18, 1956 (div. 1973); children: Renee Michelle, Candyce Lynn, Danielle Louise, Benjamin Robert; m. Linda Diane Carey, Mar. 15, 1974 (div. 1981); 1 child, Debra; m. J'an See, Oct. 27, 1984 (div. 1989); 1 child, Jonathan F.; m. Marilyn Collins, June 15, 1991. AB in Philosophy, Stanford U., 1958, JD, 1960. Bar: Calif., N.Y. 1961. Asst. U.S. atty. U.S. Atty's. Office (so. dist.), N.Y.C., 1964-67; assoc. Debevoise & Plimpton, 1960-64, 67-70, ptnr., 1970—, mng. ptnr. L.A., 1989-95. Lectr. Practicing Law Inst., N.Y.C., ABA, Asia/Pacific Ctr. for Resolution of Internat. Bus. Disputes, CPR Inst. for Dispute Resolution. Fellow Am. Coll. Trial Lawyers; mem. ABA, Assn. Bar City N.Y., Calif. Bar Assn. Democrat Avocation: poetry. Alternative dispute resolution, General civil litigation, Construction. Home: 16 Lockwood Rd Scarsdale NY 10583-5302

KING, RONALD BAKER, federal judge; b. San Antonio, Aug. 16, 1953; s. Donald Dick and Elaine (Baker) K.; m. Cynthia Sauer, June 7, 1975; children: Karen Elizabeth, Ronald Baker Jr., Kelsey Ann. BA with high honors, So. Meth. U., 1974; JD with high honors, U. Tex., 1977. Bar: Tex. 1977, U.S. Dist. Ct. (we. dist.) Tex. 1980, U.S. Ct. Appeals (5th cir.) 1981, U.S. Tax Ct. 1985. Briefing atty. Supreme Ct. Tex., Austin, 1977-78; assoc. Foster, Lewis, Langley, Gardner & Banack Inc., San Antonio, 1978-82, ptnr., 1982-88; judge U.S. Bankruptcy Ct. (we. dist.) Tex., 1988—. Mem. Tex. Bar Assn., Nat. Conf. Bankruptcy Judges. Presbyterian. Avocation: basketball. Office: US Bankruptcy Ct PO Box 1439 San Antonio TX 78295-1439

KING, VICTORIA N. lawyer, accountant; b. Louisiana, Mo., Feb. 17, 1953; d. Victor M. and Roseann O. Niemeyer; m. Stanley D. King, July 28, 1979; children: Scott D., Seth D., Spencer D. BS in Acctg., U. Mo., 1974; JD, St. Louis U., 1981. Bar: Mo. 1982, Calif. 1987, Ga. 1995, Fla. 1996; CPA, Mo., Calif., Ga. Govt. auditor Mo. Auditors Office, Jefferson City, 1974; tax audit sr. Price Waterhouse, St. Louis, 1975-78, tax mgr.-in-charge Frankfurt, Germany, 1981-84, tax sr. mgr. L.A., 1984-87; tax/bus. atty. Best, Best & Krieger, Ontario, Calif., 1987-95; tax atty. Chamberlain, Hrdlicka et al, Atlanta, 1995-98, United Parcel Svc., Atlanta, 1998—. Spkr. in field. Mem. Atlanta Archdiocese Bd. Edn., 1999-01; mem. Atlanta Estate

Planning Coun., 1999—; bd. dirs. So. Calif. Blood Bank, 1988-91. Named Woman of Achievement, L.A. C. of C., 1983, Bus. All-Star, Riverside C. of C., 1989. Mem. ABA, Ga. Bar Assn., Calif. Bar Assn., Ga. Soc. CPAs. Roman Catholic. Avocations: travel, gourmet cooking, skiing. Office: United Parcel Svc 55 Glenlake Pkwy NE # B3F4 Atlanta GA 30328-3498 E-mail: vKing@ups.com

KING, WILLIAM H., JR. lawyer; b. Richmomd, Va., Nov. 4, 1940; AB, Dartmouth Coll., 1963; LLB, U. Va., 1967; MA (hon.), Dartmouth Coll., 1992. Bar: Va. 1967, Tex. 1993. Mem. McGuireWoods LLP, Richmond. Fellow Am. Bar Found., Am. Coll. Trial Lawyers; mem. ABA. General civil litigation, Product liability, Toxic tort. Office: McGuireWoods One James Ctr Richmond VA 23219-4030 E-mail: wking@mcguirewoods.com

KINGHAM, RICHARD FRANK, lawyer; b. Lafayette, Ind., Aug. 2, 1946; s. James R. and Loretta C. (Hoenigke) K.; m. Justine Frances McClung, July 6, 1968; 1 child, Richard Patterson. BA, George Washington U., 1968; JD, U. Va., 1973. Bar: D.C. 1973, U.S. Dist. Ct. D.C. 1974, U.S. Ct. Appeals (8th cir.) 1977, U.S. Supreme Ct. 1977, U.S. Ct. Appeals (5th cir.) 1980; registered fgn. lawyer Law Soc. Eng. and Wales, 1994. Editorial asst. Washington Star, 1964-68, 69-70; assoc. Covington & Burling, Washington, 1973-81, ptnr., 1981—, mng. ptnr. London office, 1996-2000. Lectr. law U. Va., Charlottesville, 1977-90; mem. com. issues and priorities new vaccine devel. Inst. Medicine, NAS, 1983-86, Nat. Adv. Allergy and Infectious Diseases Coun. NIH, 1988-92, adv. bd. World Pharms. Report, 1990-96; mem. World Health Org. Coun. Internat. Orgns. Med. Scis. Working Party Comm. in Pharmacovigilance, 1997—; lectr. grad. program in pharmaceutical medicine, U. Wales and Royal Coll. Physicians of London. Articles editor U. Va. law rev., 1972-73; contbr. articles to profl. jours. Treas., mem. parochial ch. coun. St. Peter's Ch. Eaton Sq., London, 1998—2001. Mem. ABA, Brussels Pharm. Law Group, Drug Info. Assn., Food and Drug Law Inst., European Soc. Pharmacovigilance, Food Law Group (U.K.), Soc. Vertebrate Paleontology, European Forum for Good Clin. Practice, Order of the Coif, Reform Club (London). Republican. Episcopalian. Avocation: vertebrate paleontology. Administrative and regulatory, Health. Home: 4821 Dexter St NW Washington DC 20007 E-mail: rkingham@cov.com

KINLIN, DONALD JAMES, lawyer; b. Boston, Nov. 29, 1938; s. Joseph Edward and Ruth Claire (Byrne) K.; m. Donna C. McGrath, Nov. 29, 1959; children: Karen J., Donald J., Joseph P., Kevin S. BS in Acctg., Syracuse U., 1968, MBA, 1970; JD, U. Nebr., 1975. Bar: Nebr. 1976, Ohio 1982, U.S. Supreme Ct. 1979, U.S. Claims Ct. 1982, U.S. Tax Ct. 1982, U.S. Ct. Appeals (5th and fed. cirs.) 1982. Atty. USAF, Mather AFB, Calif., 1976-78; sr. trial atty. Air Force Contract Law Ctr., Wright-Patterson AFB, Ohio, 1978-86, dep. dir., 1986-87; ptnr. Smith & Schnacke, Dayton, 1987-89, Thompson, Hine and Flory L.L.P., Dayton, 1989—. Mem. adv. bd. Fed. Publs. Inc. Govt. Contract Costs, Pricing & Acctg. Report. Contbr. articles to legal jours. Pres. Forest Ridge Assn., Dayton, 1984-96; sec., gen. counsel U.S. Air and Trade Show, 1994-98, chmn., 1998—; bd. dirs. Nat. Aviation Hall of Fame, 1998—. Mem. ABA (chmn. sect. pub. contract law 1993-94, sec., budget and fin. officer sect., coun. mem., chmn. fed. procurement divsn., vice chmn. acct., cost and pricing com., truth in negotiations com., chmn. cost Acctg. stas. subcom.), Fed. Bar Assn., Ohio Bar Assn., Nebr. Bar Assn., Contracts Appeals Bar Assn. (bd. govs. 1998—). Avocation: travel. Administrative and regulatory, Contracts commercial, Military. Office: Thompson Hine & Flory LLP PO Box 8801 2000 Courthouse Pla NE Dayton OH 45401-8801

KINNAN, DAVID EMERY, lawyer; b. Columbus, Ohio, May 15, 1946; BA, Pa. State U., 1968; JD, U. Tex., 1970. Bar: Tex. 1971. Assoc. gen. counsel Shell Oil Co., Houston, 1977—. Served to capt. USAF, 1971-76. Federal civil litigation, General corporate, Oil, gas, and mineral. Office: PO Box PO Box 2463 Houston TX 77252-2463

KINNEY, GREGORY HOPPES, lawyer; b. Anderson, Ind., July 15, 1947; s. Dalton Roth and Effie Eleanor (Hoppes) K. BA, Mich. State U., 1969, M. Labor Rels., 1971; JD, U. Detroit, 1974. Bar: Mich. 1975, U.S. Dist. Ct. (ea. dist.) Mich. 1975, U.S. Ct. Appeals (D.C. cir.) 1975. Labor law editor Bur. Nat. Affairs, Washington, 1974; pension cons. Edward H. Friend & Co., 1975, The Wyatt Co., Detroit, 1976-84; sole practice, 1984-86, Troy, Mich., 1986-99, Decatur, 1999—. General civil litigation, Pension, profit-sharing, and employee benefits. Office: PO Box 243 Decatur MI 49045-0243

KINNEY, RICHARD GORDON, lawyer, educator; b. Chgo., May 8, 1939; s. Michael James Sr. and Blanche Marie (Gill) K.; m. Katherine Choffen, Dec. 26, 1969; 1 child, Richard Greg. BSEE, U. Ill., 1961; JD, U. Chgo., 1964. Bar: Ill. 1964, U.S. Ct. Customs and Patent Appeals 1975, U.S. Supreme Ct. 1970, U.S. Ct. Appeals (fed. cir.) 1982. With patent dept. Zenith Radio Corp., Chgo., 1963-64, Borg-Warner Corp., Chgo., 1968-73; divsn. patent counsel Baxter Travenol Labs., Inc., Deerfield, Ill., 1973-76; prin. Law Offices of Richard G. Kinney, Chgo. and Merrillville, Ind., 1976-95, 98—; pres. Richard G. Kinney, P.C., 1995-98. Roman Catholic. Intellectual property, Patent, Trademark and copyright. Office: Richard G Kinney PO Box 11119 Merrillville IN 46411-1119 E-mail: richardgkinney@hotmail.com

KINNEY, STEPHEN HOYT, JR. lawyer; b. Albuquerque, Feb. 27, 1948; s. Stephen Hoyt and Harriet May (Gadsden) K.; m. Leslie vanLiew, June 10, 1972; 1 child, Erin. BS, MIT, 1970; JD, Harvard U., 1973. Bar: N.Y. 1974, U.S. Dist. Ct. (so. dist.) N.Y. 1974, U.S. Dist. Ct. (ea. dist.) N.Y. 1974, U.S. Dist. Ct. (no. dist.) N.Y. 1978, U.S. Ct. Appeals (2d cir.) 1975, U.S. Supreme Ct. 1982. Programmer, analyst MIT, 1968-70; law clk. N.J. Organized Crime Unit, Trenton, 1972; assoc. Reid & Priest, N.Y.C., 1973-85, sr. atty., 1985-86, ptnr., 1986-98, Thelen Reid & Priest LLP, N.Y.C., 1998—. Author, editor: Outline of Arbitration, 1984; contbr. articles to profl. jours.; creator software. Mem. ABA, N.Y. State Bar Assn., MB Yacht Club (Port Washington, N.Y.). Contracts commercial, Computer, Securities. Office: Thelen Reid & Priest 40 W 57th St Fl 28 New York NY 10019-4097 E-mail: skinney@thelenreid.com

KINTZELE, JOHN ALFRED, lawyer; b. Denver, Aug. 16, 1936; s. Louis Richard and Adele H. Kintzele; children: John A., Marcia A., Elizabeth A.; m. Suzanne Hinsberger; stepchildren: William Karp III, Christopher Karp. BS in Bus., U. Colo., 1958, LLB, 1961. Bar: Colo. bar 1961. Assoc. James B. Radetsky, Denver, 1962-63; pvt. practice law, 1963—. Corp. officer, dir. Kintzele, Inc.; rep. 10th cir. U.S. Ct. of Claims Bar. Chmn. Colo. Lawyer Referral Service, 1978-83, Election commr., Denver, 1975-79, 83-86. Mem. ABA, Colo. Bar Assn., Denver Bar Assn., Am. Judicature Soc. Democrat. Roman Catholic. General civil litigation, Personal injury, Workers' compensation. Home: 10604 E Powers Dr Englewood CO 80111-3957 Office: 1317 Delaware St Denver CO 80204-2704 E-mail: kintzeles@aol.com, jkintlaw@aol.com

KINZLER, THOMAS BENJAMIN, lawyer; b. N.Y.C., June 19, 1950; s. David and Rhoda Lenore (Wolgel) K.; m. Carol Ada Loebel, Aug. 24, 1975; children: Katherine Diane, David James. BA, Columbia Coll., 1971; JD, Boston U., 1975. Bar: N.Y. 1976, U.S. Dist. Ct. (no., so., ea. and we. dists.) N.Y. 1976, U.S. Ct. Appeals (2d cir.) 1976. Assoc. Kreindler, Relkin & Goldberg, N.Y.C., 1975-77, Arthur, Dry & Kalish, N.Y.C., 1977-80, Kelley Drye & Warren LLP, N.Y.C., 1980-85; ptnr. Kelley Drye & Warren, 1985—. Mem. ABA, Assn. of the Bar City of N.Y.C. (products liability com. 1983-86, com. on state legis. 1978-80). Bankruptcy, Federal civil litigation, State civil litigation. Office: Kelley Drye & Warren 101 Park Ave Fl 30 New York NY 10178-0062

KIPP, JOHN THEODORE, lawyer, rancher; b. Guadalajara, Mex., Apr. 19, 1932; (parents Am. citizens); s. Eugene Harvey and Theresa (Greer) K.; 1 child, John Grant. BBA, U. Tex., 1954, JD, 1958. Bar: Tex. 1958, U.S. Dist. Ct. (no. dist.) Tex. 1962, U.S. Supreme Ct. 1964. Assoc. Gardere & Wynne, LLP and predecessor, Dallas, 1958-63, ptnr., 1964-98, of counsel, 1998—. Past chmn. Dallas County chpt. Am. Heart Assn.; trustee, treas. Dallas Hist. Soc. Lt. USN, 1954-56, Korea; mem. USNR (ret.). Mem. State Bar Tex. (chmn. corp. law com. 1973-75, bus. law sect. 1976-77), Dallas Bar Assn. Avocations: hunting, fishing, ranching, photography, golfing. Home: 3823 Hawthorne Ave Dallas TX 75219-2212 Office: Gardere & Wynne LLP 1601 Elm St Ste 3000 Dallas TX 75201-4761

KIRBY, LE GRAND CARNEY, III, lawyer, accountant; b. Dallas, Feb. 25, 1941; s. Le Grand C. and Michie V. (Moore) K.; m. Jane Marie Daniel, June 14, 1958; children: Le Grand C. IV, Kimberli K., Kristina K. BBA, So. Meth. U., 1963, LLB, 1965. Bar: Tex. 1965; CPA, Tex. From staff acct. to ptnr. Arthur Young & Co., Dallas, 1965-80; ptnr., dir. litigation support Arthur Young & Co. (name now Ernst & Young), 1983-2000; dep. chief acct. SEC, Washington, 1980-83; adv. counselm, sec. Fin. Reporting Inst., L.A., 1982—. Mem. ABA (acctg. and law com. 1983—), State Bar Tex. (securities com.), Am. Inst. CPA's, Tex. Soc. CPA's, Nat. Assn. Corp. Dirs. (pres. Dallas chpt. 1985-89), D.C. CPA's. Federal civil litigation, General civil litigation, Securities. Office: Ernst & Young LLP Ste 1500 2121 San Jacinto St Dallas TX 75201-6910

KIRBY, PETER CORNELIUS, lawyer, policy analyst; b. N.Y.C., Mar. 25, 1950; s. Cornelius Carroll and Anne (Pracny) K. B.A., Yale U., 1971; J.D., Harvard U., 1975. Bar: U.S. Dist. Ct. D.C. 1975, U.S. Ct. Appeals (D.C. cir.) 1975. Asst. Law Sch., Harvard U., 1975-76; law clk. U.S. Ct. Appeals (D.C. cir.), 1976-77; counsel Nat. Wildlife Fedn., Washington, 1977-80, Wilderness Soc., Washington, 1980—; mem. faculty Nat. Law Ctr., George Washington U., Washington, 1978-87, Vt. Law Sch., South Royalton, 1979-83; mem. Appalachian Trail Adv. Com., 1979-81. Contbr. numerous articles on natural resources law and policy to profl. jours. Mem. ABA (natural resources section forest resources com., 1984), Soc. Am. Foresters, Scroll and Key, Phi Beta Kappa. Democrat. Roman Catholic. Administrative and regulatory, Environmental, Legislative. Home: 1616 Piedmont Rd NE Apt L-4 Atlanta GA 30324-5270 Office: Wilderness Soc 1447 Peachtree St NE Ste 812 Atlanta GA 30309-3029

KIRCHER, JOHN JOSEPH, law educator; b. Milw., July 26, 1938; s. Joseph John and Martha Marie (Jach) K.; m. Marcia Susan Adamkiewicz, Aug. 26, 1961; children: Joseph John, Mary Kathryn. BA, Marquette U., 1960, JD, 1963. Bar: Wis. 1963, U.S. Dist. Ct. (ea. dist.) Wis. 1963, U.S. Ct. Appeals (7th cir.) 1992. Sole practice, Port Washington, Wis., 1963-66; with Def. Research Inst., Milw., 1966-80, research dir., 1972-80; with Marquette U., 1970—, prof. law, 1980—, assoc. dean acad. affairs, 1992-93. Chmn. Wis. Jud. Council, 1981-83. Author: (with J.D. Ghiardi) Punitive Damages: Law and Practice, 1981, 2d edit (with C.M. Wiseman), 2000; editor Federation of Insurance and Corporate Counsel Quarterly; mem. editorial bd. Def. Law Jour.; contbr. articles to profl. jours. Recipient Teaching Excellence award Marquette U., 1986, Disting. Service award Def. Research Inst., 1980, Marquette Law Rev. Editors' award, 1988. Mem. ABA (Robert B. McKay Professor award 1993), Am. Law Inst., Wis. Bar Assn., Wis. Supreme Ct. Bd. of Bar Examiners (vice chair 1989-91, chair 1992), Am. Judicature Soc., Nat. Sports Law Inst. (adv. com. 1989—), Assn. Internationale de Droit des Assurances, Scribes. Roman Catholic. Office: PO Box 1881 Milwaukee WI 53201-1881

KIRCHMAN, ERIC HANS, lawyer; b. Washington, May 2, 1962; s. Charles Vincent and Erika Ottilie (Knoeppel) K.; m. Hillary Bronkie Hutson, Apr. 19, 1991; children: Erika B., Thomas E. BA, Univ. Md., 1985; JD, Univ. Balt., 1990. Bar: Md. 1990, U.S. Dist. Ct. Md. 1991. Assoc. Hillel Abrams, Rockville, Md., 1990-92; ptnr. Kirchman & Kirchman, Wheaton, 1992—. Of counsel Md. Coun. for Gifted and Talented Children, Inc., Silver Spring, 1994. With U.S. Army Reserve, 1985-98. Mem. ATLA, Md. Criminal Def. Attys. Assn., Montgomery County Bar Assn. General practice. Office: Kirchman & Kirchman 11141 Georgia Ave Ste 403 Wheaton MD 20902-4659

KIRGIS, FREDERIC LEE, law educator; b. Washington, Dec. 29, 1934; s. Frederic Lee Sr. and Kathryn Alice (Burrows) K.; children: Julianne, Paul Frederic. B.A., Yale U., 1957; J.D., U. Calif.-Berkeley, 1960. Bar: Colo. 1961, Va. 1983. Atty. Covington & Burling, Washington, 1964-67; from asst. prof. to prof. law U. Colo., Boulder, 1967-73; prof. law UCLA, 1973-78, Washington & Lee U., Lexington, Va., 1978—, dir. Frances Lewis Law Ctr., 1978-83, dean law sch., 1983-88. Author: International Organizations in their Legal Setting, 1977, 2d edit. 1993, Prior Consultation in International Law, 1983; contbr. articles to profl. jours. Pres. Maury River Soccer Club, Lexington, 1978-85. Served to capt. USAF, 1961-64 Recipient Deak award 1974; research fellow NATO, Brussels, 1978 Mem. Am. Soc. Internat. Law (v.p. 1985-87, sec. 1994—), Am. Law Inst., Internat. Law Assn. (Am. br.), Am. Jour. Internat. Law (bd. editors 1984-96, 98—), State Bar Va., Order of Coif. Democrat. Presbyterian Home: 15 Grey Dove Rd Lexington VA 24450-2269 Office: Washington and Lee U Sch of Law Lexington VA 24450

KIRK, CASSIUS LAMB, JR. retired lawyer, investor; b. Bozeman, Mont., June 8, 1929; s. Cassius Lamb and Gertrude Violet (McCarthy) K. AB, Stanford U., 1951; JD, U. Calif., Berkeley, 1954. Bar: Calif. 1955. Assoc. Cooley, Godward, Castro, Huddleson & Tatum, San Francisco, 1956-60; staff counsel for bus. affairs Stanford U., 1960-78; chief bus. officer, staff counsel Menlo Sch. and Coll., Atherton, Calif., 1978-81; chmn. Eberli-Kirk Properties, Inc. (dba Just Closets), Menlo Park, 1981-94. Faculty Coll. Bus. Adminstrn. U. Calif., Santa Barbara, summers 1967-73; past adv. bd. Allied Arts Guild, Menlo Park; past nat. vice-chmn. Stanford U. Annual Fund. Past v.p. Palo Alto C. of C., pres. Menlo Towers Assn., 2000-. With U.S. Army, 1954-56. Mem. VFW, Stanford Faculty Club, Order of Coif, Menlo Towers Assn. (pres. 2000-01), Phi Alpha Delta. Republican. Home and Office: 1330 University Dr Apt 52 Menlo Park CA 94025-4241

KIRK, DENNIS DEAN, lawyer; b. Pittsburg, Kans., Dec. 13, 1950; s. Homer Standley and Maida Corena (Rouse) K.; 1 child, Dennis Dean II. AA, Hutchinson Cmty. Jr. Coll., 1970; BS with distinction, No. Ariz. U., 1972; JD, Washburn U., 1975. Bar: Kans. 1975, U.S. Dist. Ct. Kans. 1975, D.C. 1977, U.S. Ct. Appeals (D.C. cir.) 1978, U.S. Supreme Ct. 1979, U.S. Ct. Appeals (5th cir.) 1981, U.S. Dist. Ct. Md. 1984, U.S. Tax Ct. 1984, U.S. Claims Ct. 1984, U.S. Ct. Appeals (fed. cir.) 1984, U.S. Ct. Mil. Appeals 1984, Va. 1990, U.S. Ct. Appeals (4th cir.) 1990; lic. pvt. investigator; lic. personal protection specialist. Trial atty. ICC, Washington, 1975-77; assoc. Goff, Sims, Cloud & Stroud, 1977-82; pvt. practice, 1982-90; ptnr. Slocum, Boddie, Murry & Kirk, Falls Church, Va., 1990-93; pvt. practice, 1993—. Pres. Law Facilites, Inc., Washington, 1982—. Vol. parole and probation officer Shawnee County, Kans., 1973-74; citizens adv. task force group Md. Nat. Park and Planning Commn., 1978-80; citizens task force on gen. plan amendments study Fairfax County coun., Va., 1981-82; active Seven Corners Task Force, Fairfax County, 1981-82, chmn. transp. and housing subcoms.; pres. Seven Springs Tenants Assn., College Park, Md., 1976-80, Ravenwood Park Citizens Assn., 1981-82; dir. Greenwood Homes, Inc., Fairfax County Dept. Housing and Cmty. Devel., 1983—; active Gala Com. Spotlight the Kennedy Ctr., Pres. Adv. Com. on the Arts, 1986-87, Mason Dist. Rep. Com., 1981-91, Fairfax County Young Reps., Fairfax County Rep. Com., 1982—; founding chmn., charter mem. Mason Dist. Jaycees, 1984-86; sec., gen. counsel, bd. dirs. U.S. Assocs. for the Cultural Triangle in Sri Lanka, 1983-90; commr. Consumer Protection Commn., Fairfax County, 1982—, chmn., 1996-97; towing adv. bd. Fairfax County, 1993-97; Ravenwood precinct chmn. Rep. Orgn., Falls Church, Va., 1982-90; bd. dirs. PTA Baileys Elem.Magnet Sch., 1995-99, v.p., 1996-97. Named to Honorable Order Ky. Cols. Mem. ABA, NRA (life), Masons (life, Master of Lodge, D.C. Grand Lodge Masons, Valentine Rentzel medal, Am. Fedn. Musicians (life, emeritus), Assn. Former Intelligence Officers, Grand Sword Bearer 1992), Shriners (life), Tall Cedars (life), Scottish Rite (life), Moose, Royal Arch (life), Phi Kappa Phi, Phi Alpha Delta (life, nat. capital area alumni chpt. justice 1984-86, 94-96). Methodist. Avocation: music. Administrative and regulatory, Federal civil litigation, General practice. Home: 6315 Anneliese Dr Falls Church VA 22044-1620 Office: 5201 Leesburg Pike Ste 1108 Falls Church VA 22041-3268 E-mail: kirklaw@fcc.net

KIRK, JOHN MACGREGOR, lawyer; b. Flint, Mich., Mar. 9, 1938; s. R. Dean and Berenice E. (Mac Gregor) K.; m. Carol Lasko, June 8, 1971; children: John M. Jr., Caroline Dwyer. BA, Washington & Lee U., 1960, LLB, 1962; LLM in Taxation, NYU, 1967. Bar: Mich. 1962, U.S. Ct. Mil. Appeals 1966, U.S. Supreme Ct. 1966, U.S. Tax Ct. 1969, U.S. Dist. Ct. (ea. dist.) Mich. 1982, U.S. Ct. Appeals (6th cir.) 1983. Trial atty. tax divsn. U.S. Dept. Justice, Washington, 1967-72; assoc. Boyer & Briggs, Bloomfield Hills, Mich., 1972-74; ptnr. Butler, Long, Gust, Klein & Van Zile, Detroit, 1975-78; mem. Meyer, Kirk, Snyder & Lynch P.L.L.C., Bloomfield Hills, 1978—. Mem., past pres. Friends of Baldwin Pub. Libr., Birmingham, Mich., 1972—. Mem. ABA, State Bar Mich., Oakland County Bar Assn., Detroit Bar Assn., Birmingham Rotary, Walloon Yacht Club (treas., past commodore 1960—). Republican. Presbyterian. Estate planning, Probate, Estate taxation. Home: 4350 Yale Ct Bloomfield Hills MI 48302-1669 Office: Meyer Kirk Snyder and Lynch PLLC 100 W Long Lake Rd Ste 100 Bloomfield Hills MI 48304-2773 E-mail: jkirk@meyerkirk.com

KIRK, JOHN ROBERT, JR. lawyer; b. Stuart, Va., June 21, 1935; s. John Robert and Mary Elise (Mustaine) K.; m. Margarite Conover Kirk; children: Karen Louise, Laura Elise, Rebecca Elizabeth. Student, Rice Inst., 1953-56; BSChemE, U. Tex., 1959; JD, U. Houston, 1966. Bar: Tex. 1966, U.S. Patent and Trademark Office 1967, U.S. Supreme Ct. 1973, U.S. Dist. Ct. (so. dist.) Tex. 1974, U.S. Ct. Claims 1975, U.S. Dist. Ct. (no. dist.) Tex. 1977, U.S. Ct. Appeals (5th cir.) 1980, U.S. Ct. Appeals (11th cir.) 1981, U.S. Ct. Appeals (Fed. cir.) 1983. Patent aty. Jefferson Chem. Co., Houston, 1966-69; mgr. patent divsn., 1969-72; mem. Pravel, Gambrell, Hewitt, Kirk & Kimball, P.C., Houston, 1972-84; ptnr., 1973-84, Baker & Kirk, P.C., 1984-87, Baker, Kirk & Bissex, P.C., 1987-90, Baker & Lindsay, P.C., 1990-93, Jenkens & Gilchrist, 1993—. Dir. Nat. Inventors Hall of Fame Found, Inc., 1979-82, 87-97, treas., 1983-84, v.p., 1984-86, pres., 1986-87; adv. bd. Intellectual Property Law Program U. Houston, 1991, John Marshall Law Sch., 1999—, chair; adv. bd. Gulf Coast Regional Small Bus. Devel. Ctr., 1994—, Tex. Mfg. Assistance Ctr., Inc., 1995—. Lt. USMCR, 1958-60. Fellow Tex. Bar Found. (life), Houston Bar Found. (life), Coll. State Bar (property law sect. 1977-78); mem. ABA (intellectual property law sec. coun. 1990-94, vice chmn. 1994-95, chmn. elect 1995-96, chmn. 1996-97, com. chair 1982-90), Nat. Coun. Intellectual Property Law Assns. (vice chmn. 1986-87, chmn. 1987-88), Commn. of Patents Edn. Roundtable (commr. 1987-95), Houston Intellectual Property Law Assn. (pres.-elect 1989-90, pres. 1990-91, bd. govs. 1986-92), Houston Bar Assn., Licensing Exec. Soc., Nat. Inventive Thinking Assn. (adv. dir. 1990—), Inwood Forest Golf Club, The Houstonian Club, River Bend Golf Club. Republican. Baptist. Intellectual property, Patent, Trademark and copyright. Office: 1100 Louisiana St Ste 1800 Houston TX 77002-5215 E-mail: jkirk@jenkens.com

KIRK, PATRICK LAINE, lawyer; b. South Bend, Ind., May 12, 1948; s. Jerry W. and Vivian E. (Evans) K.; m. Cheryl A. Ensminger, Dec. 30, 1967; children: Kevin P., Travis S. BA, Valparaiso U., 1970, JD, 1973. Bar: N.Y. 1974, U.S. Dist. Ct. (no. dist.) N.Y. 1977, U.S. Supreme Ct. 1986. Ptnr. Grilli & Kirk, Herkimer, N.Y., 1974-89; asst. dist. atty. Herkimer County, 1976-78, chief asst. dist. atty., 1978-86, dist. atty., 1986-91, county judge and county surrogate, 1992—; acting justice Supreme Ct. of N.Y., 1997—. Counsel Herkimer Cen. Sch., 1974-76; asst. counsel Village of Herkimer, N.Y., 1981-89; lectr. Police Tng. Sch., Utica, N.Y., 1979-91, Arson Seminar, 1987, Rape Crisis Tng.; tchr. Herkimer County C.C., 1981; criminal justice com. Nat. Conf. State Trial Ct. Judges. Advisor Law Explorer Post, Herkimer, 1974-76; bd. dirs. Martin Luther Home, Clinton, N.Y., 1980, Herkimer County Drug Task Force; chmn. sect. Mohawk Valley United Fund, Ilion, N.Y., 1985; mem. Arson Task Force, 1986-91. Mem. ABA (N.Y. del. to nat. conf. of spl. court judges 1995), N.Y. State Bar Assn. (jud. adminstrn. com.), Internat. Narcotics Enforcement Officers Assn., Drug Enforcement Assn. N.Y. (v.p. 1990-91), N.Y. State County Judges Assn., N.Y. State Surrogate Judges Assn., Am. Judges Assn., Elks. Republican. Lutheran. Criminal. Home: 840 W German St Herkimer NY 13350-2136 Office: Herkimer County Courthouse Herkimer NY 13350

KIRK, RICHARD DILLON, lawyer; b. Washington, Jan. 23, 1953; s. William Edward and Mary Elizabeth (Dillon) K.; m. Bridget Louise Stillwagon, June 27, 1981; children: Catherine Dillon, Suzanne Grace. AB, Georgetown U., 1975; JD, U. Va., 1978. Bar: Del. 1978, U.S. Dist. Ct. Del. 1980, U.S. Ct. Appeals (3rd cir.) 1984, U.S. Supreme Ct. 1984. Law clk. Del. Supreme Ct., Wilmington, 1978-79; assoc. Richards, Layton & Finger, 1979-82; dep. atty. gen. Del. Dept. Justice, 1982-84; assoc. Morris, James, Hitchens & Williams, 1984-86, ptnr., 1987—. Mem. Del. State Bar Assn. (pres. 1993-94, New Lawyers Disting. Svc. award 1988). Democrat. Roman Catholic. Administrative and regulatory, General corporate, Environmental. Office: Morris James Hitchens & Williams 222 Delaware Ave Wilmington DE 19801-1621 E-mail: rkirk@morrisjames.com

KIRKHAM, JOHN SPENCER, lawyer, director; b. Salt Lake City, Aug. 29, 1944; s. Elbert C. and Emma Kirkham; m. Janet L. Eatough, Sept. 16, 1966; children: Darcy, Jeff, Kristie. BA with honors, U. Utah, 1968, JD, 1971. Bar: Utah 1971, U.S. Dist. Ct. Utah 1971, U.S. Ct. Appeals (10th cir.) 1990, U.S. Supreme Ct. 1991. Assoc. Senior & Senior, Salt Lake City, 1971-73; ptnr. VanCott, Bagley, Cornwall & McCarthy, 1973-92, Stoel Rives LLP, Salt Lake City, 1992—. Mem. exec. bd. Great Salt Lake coun. Boy Scouts Am., 1987—; mem. Utah Statewide Resource Adv. Coun., 1995-97. Mem. Utah Bar Assn., Utah Mining Assn. (bd. dirs. Salt Lake City chpt. 1987—), Rocky Mountain Mineral Law Found. (trustee 1989-92). Republican. Mormon. Environmental, Natural resources, Real property. Office: Stoel Rives LLP 201 S Main St Ste 1100 Salt Lake City UT 84111-4904 E-mail: jskirkham@stoel.com

KIRKLAND, ALFRED YOUNGES, SR. federal judge; b. Elgin, Ill., 1917; s. Alfred and Elizabeth (Younges) K.; m. Gwendolyn E. Muntz, June 14, 1941; children: Pamela E. Kirkland Jensen, Alfred Younges Jr., James Muntz. BA, U. Ill., 1941, JD, 1943. Bar: Ill. 1943. Assoc. Mayer, Meyer, Austrian & Platt, Chgo., 1943; sr. ptnr. Kirkland, Brady, McQueen, Martin & Callahan and predecessor firms, Elgin, 1951-73; spl. asst. atty. gen. State of Ill., 1969-73; judge 16th Cir. Ct. Ill., 1973-74, U.S. Dist. Ct. (no. dist.) Ill., 1974-79, sr. judge, 1979—. Mem. Coun. Practicing Lawyers U. Ill. Law Forum, 1969—, mem. adv. bd., 1972-73, mem. adv. coun. continuing

legal edn., 1959-62; chmn. Ill. Def. Rsch. Inst., 1965-66. Outdoor editor: Elgin Daily Courier-News, Kewanee Star-Courier; fishing editor: Midwest Outdoors Mag. Pres. Elgin YMCA, 1963, chmn. bd. trustees, 1995—. 2d lt. inf. AUS, 1943-46. Fellow Am. Coll. Trial Lawyers, Am. Bar Found.; mem. ABA (ho. of dels. 1967-70), Ill. State Bar Assn. (pres. 1968-69), Chgo. Bar Assn., Kane County Bar Assn. (pres. 1961-62), Elgin Bar Assn. (pres. 1951-52), Am. Judicature Soc. (bd. dirs. 1967—), Ill. Bar Found. (bd. dirs. 1961-69), Ill. Def. Counsel (bd. dirs. 1966-69), Soc. Trial Lawyers, Legal Club Chgo., Law Club Chgo., Internat. Assn. Ins. Counsel, Fed. Ins. Counsel, Assn. Ins. Counsel, Outdoor Writers Assn. Am. (gen. counsel), Assn. Gt. Lakes Outdoor Writers (v.p., bd. dirs.), Ill. C. of C. (bd. dirs. 1969-70), Phi Delta Phi, Sigma Nu. Republican. Congregationalist. Clubs: Elgin Country (pres. 1956), Cosmopolitan Internat. (past pres., judge advocate). Lodges: Elks, Moose. Home: 2421 Tall Oaks Dr Elgin IL 60123-4844 Office: 2421 Tall Oaks Dr Elgin IL 60123-4844

KIRKLAND, JOHN C. lawyer; b. Omaha, Dec. 28, 1963; s. John and Marilou (Witt) K. AB, Columbia U., 1986; JD, UCLA, 1990. Bar: Calif. 1990. Assoc. Cadwalader Wickersham & Taft, L.A., 1990-97; of counsel Weissmann Wolff Bergman Coleman & Silverman, LLP, Beverly Hills, Calif., 1997-2000; ptnr. Brown Raysman Millstein Felder & Steiner LLP, L.A., 2000-01; shareholder Greenberg Taurig LLP, 2001—. Bd. dirs. Oaktree Found., Inc.; exec. mem. Venice Interactive Cmty. Mem. ABA, L.A. County Bar Assn., Beverly Hills Bar Assn. Home: 754 Swarthmore Ave Pacific Palisades CA 90272-4355 Office: 2450 Colorado Ave Ste 400E Santa Monica CA 90404 E-mail: kirklandj@gtlaw.com

KIRKPATRICK, CARL KIMMEL, prosecutor; b. Kingsport, Tenn., Aug. 2, 1936; s. Carl Kimmel and Alice (Rowland) K.; m. Barbara G. Kirkpatrick, Aug. 7, 1992; 1 child, Carl Kimmel III. BA, Vanderbilt U., 1959, JD, 1962. Bar: Tenn. 1962, U.S. Dist. Ct. (ea. dist.) Tenn. 1964. Pvt. practice, Kingsport, 1962-66; asst. dist. atty. 20th Jud. Dist. Sullivan County, Tenn., 1963-64; dist. atty. gen. 2d Jud. Dist. Tenn., 1966-93; U.S. atty. U.S. Dept. of Justice, Knoxville, Tenn., 1993-2001; ret., 2001. Mem. Nat. Dist. Attys. Assn. (bd. dirs. 1983-93), Knoxville Bar Assn., Phi Delta Phi. Democrat. Baptist. Avocations: motorcycle riding, sport shooting, gardening. Office: US Attys Office 800 Market St Ste 211 Knoxville TN 37902-2342

KIRKPATRICK, JOHN EVERETT, lawyer; b. Meadville, Pa., Aug. 20, 1929; s. Francis Earl and Marjorie Eloise (Roudebush) K.; m. Patricia Ann Benkert, Aug. 9, 1952 (div. June 1963); children: Amy Kirkpatrick Fidler, John Scot, Ann Kirkpatrick Mullen; m. Phyllis Jean Daeuble, Aug. 31, 1963. AB, Amherst Coll., 1951; JD, Harvard U., 1954. Bar: Ohio 1955, Ill. 1962. Assoc. Squire, Sanders & Dempsey, Cleve., 1954-61, Kirkland, Ellis, Hodson, Chaffetz & Masters, Chgo., 1962-64; sr. ptnr. Kirkland & Ellis, 1965—. Contbr. articles on tax and estate planning to profl. jours. Mem. Cen. DuPage Hosp. Devel. Commn., Winfield, Ill.; elder 1st Presbyn. Ch., Wheaton, Ill., 1983—. Mem. ABA, Ill. State Bar Assn., Chgo. Bar Assn.,Glen Oak Club (Glen Ellyn, Ill.), Lago Mar Club (Plantation, Fla.). Republican. Clubs: Chgo. Golf (Wheaton), Mid Am. (Chgo.). Avocation: golf. General corporate, Estate planning, Probate. Office: Kirkland & Ellis 200 E Randolph St Fl 54 Chicago IL 60601-6636

KIRKPATRICK, LAIRD CLIFFORD, law educator; b. Mpls., Aug. 8, 1943; s. Clifford and Marjorie (Dietz) K.; m. Carole Schmidt, Aug. 25, 1969; children: Duncan (dec.), Ryan, Morgan. AB cum laude, Harvard U., 1965; JD, U. Oreg., 1968. Instr. U. Mich., Ann Arbor, 1968-69; Reginald Heber Smith fellow OEO, Portland, Oreg., 1969-70; pvt. practice law Eugene, 1970-72; exec. dir., dir. litigation Legal Aid Svc., Portland, 1972-74; asst. U.S. atty. U.S. Atty.'s Office, Eugene, 1978-80; prof. law U. Oreg., 1974—, Hershner prof. jurisprudence, 1993—, assoc. dean, 1986-89; counsel to asst. atty. gen. criminal divsn. U.S. Dept. Justice, 1999-2001; commr. ex-officio U.S. Sentencing Commn., 1999-2001. Chmn. task force on corrections Gov.'s Office, Salem, 1987-88. Author: Evidence Under the Rules, 4th edit., 2000; Oregon Evidence, 3rd edit., 1996, Modern Evidence, 1995, Evidence, 1999, Federal Evidence, 5 vols., 2nd edit., 1994. Mem. Oreg. Criminal Justice Coun., 1987-89. Fellow Am. Bar Found.; mem. ABA (ho. of dels. 1994-96), Am. Law Inst., Am. Judicature Soc. (bd. dirs. 1993-99), Am. Assn. Law Schs. (chair evidence sect. 1998), Oreg. Bar Assn. (Pres.'s award 1991). Office: U Oreg School of Law 1515 Agate St Eugene OR 97403-1221 E-mail: lkirkpat@law.uoregon.edu

KIRNA, HANS CHRISTIAN, lawyer, consultant; b. N.Y.C., Sept. 16, 1956; s. Hans H. and Ingrid D. (Korjus) K.; m. Eileen T. Barrett, June 19, 1993. BA cum laude, Upsala Coll., 1978; MA in Anthropology, New Sch. for Social Rsch., 1982; JD, CUNY, 1986. Indexer H.W. Wilson, Bronx, N.Y., 1986-87; claim counsel Am. Internat. Group, N.Y.C., 1987-94; cons. Willcox, Inc., 1994-97; broker Guy Carpenter, 1997-98; sr. claims analyst Risk Enterprise Mgmt. (Zurich Ins.), 1998-2001; liability counsel Crum & Forster, Morristown, NJ, 2001—. Author: Sam's Strange Friend, 1994; rschr.: (by Dr. Sid Harring) Crow Dog's Case, 1994; artist: prin. works include painting of Christ and 4 disciples, St. Gabriel and Michael's Orthodox Ch., Stroudsburg, Pa.; composer piano pieces. Active Great Neck (N.Y.) Rep. Club, 1980-81, Denville Cmty. Ch., 1996—. Mem. Am. Anthrop. Assn. Avocations: artist, collector of art, antiques, runner. Home: 25 Cypress Dr Denville NJ 07834-1709

KIRNER, PAUL TIMOTHY, lawyer; b. Cleve., July 1, 1947; s. Paul F. and Anna M. (Christy) K.; m. Deborah J. Horvat, July 25, 1970; children: Paul James, Peter S. BS, Marquette U., 1969; JD cum laude, Cleve. State U., 1972. Bar: Ohio 1972, U.S. Supreme Ct. 1976. Assoc. Buckingham & Doolittle, Akron, Ohio, 1972-73, Quandt & Giffels, Cleve., 1973-74, Leary & Schifko, Parma, Ohio, 1974-89, Kirner & Boldt, North Royalton, 1989—. Spl. counsel to atty. gen. State of Ohio, 1982-96. Mem. Cuyahoga County Ctrl. Com., Ohio, 1974—; councilman City of Parma, 1987-99; pres. pro tem Parma City Coun., 1988-99; chmn. Parma Fair Housing Com., 1983-88; pres. St. Anthony's Parish Coun., 1981-84, Athletic Assn. St. Anthony, 1986-93; bd. dirs. St. Ignatius Fathers Club, Cleve., 1987-88. Served to 1st lt. C.E., U.S. Army, 1969-73. Mem. ABA, ATLA, Ohio Trial Lawyers Assn., Ohio State Bar Assn., Cuyahoga County Bar Assn., Cleve. Bar Assn., Parma Bar Assn. (pres. 1979-80, trustee 1980-83, 95-97), Cleve. State U. Coll. Law Alumni (trustee 1969-70), Elks, Lions (treas. Parma 1982-84). Democrat. Roman Catholic. Avocation: photography. Office: 8025 Corporate Cir Cleveland OH 44133-1257 E-mail: pkirner@netway.com

KIRSCH, LAURENCE STEPHEN, lawyer; b. Washington, July 20, 1957; s. Ben and Bertha (Gomberg) K.; m. Celia Goldman, Aug. 19, 1979; children: Rachel Miriam, Max David. BAS, MS, U. Pa., 1979; JD, Harvard U., 1982. Bar: D.C. 1982, U.S. Ct. Appeals (3d cir.) 1983, (5th cir.) 1997, U.S. Dist. Ct. D.C. 1985, U.S. Ct. Appeals (D.C. cir.) 1985, U.S. Supreme Ct. 1987; registered environ. assessor, Calif. 1988. Law clk. to presiding judge Pa. Dist. Ct., Phila., 1982-83; vis. asst. prof. law U. Bridgeport (Conn.) Law Sch., 1983-84; assoc. Cadwalader, Wickersham & Taft, Washington, 1984-90, ptnr., 1991—. Chmn. steering coms. Superfund. Editor-in-chief Indoor Pollution Law Report, 1987-91; mng. editor Harvard Environ. Law Rev., 1981-82; contbr. articles to profl. jours. Mem. ABA, Fed. Bar Assn., AAAS, Air Pollution Control Assn. (indoor air quality com.), Environ. Law Inst., Nat. Inst. Bldg. Scis. (indoor air quality com.), Am. Soc. Testing and Measurement (indoor air quality com.), Phi Beta Kappa. Administrative and regulatory, Federal civil litigation, Environmental. Home: 7212 Longwood Dr Bethesda MD 20817-2122 Office: Cadwalader Wickersham & Taft Ste 700 1333 New Hampshire Ave NW Washington DC 20036-1511 E-mail: lkirsch@cwt.com

KIRSCH, LYNN, lawyer; b. New Orleans, Oct. 31, 1964; d. Henry C. and Therese M. ((Guenther) K. BS in Bus. Mgmt., Fla. State U., Panama City, 1992; JD, U. Ariz., 1995. Bar: Nev. 1995, U.S. Dist. Ct. Nev. 1995, U.S. Ct. Fed. Claims 1997, U.S. Ct. Appeals (9th cir.) 1998, U.S. Supreme Ct. 1999. Law clk. U.S. Atty.'s Office, Phoenix, 1993, Slutes, Sakrison, Evan, Grant & Pelander, Tucson, 1993-94, Lionel, Sawyer & Collins, Las Vegas, 1994; judicial extern Fed. Dist. Ct., Tucson, 1994; rsch. asst. U. Ariz., 1994-95; law clk. Jacob & Fishbein, 1994-95; assoc. Goold, Patterson, DeVore & Rondau, Las Vegas, 1995-97, Curran & Parry, Las Vegas, 1997-99, Bernhard & Leslie, Las Vegas, 1999—. Mem. Justice of the Peace pro-tempore panel, Las Vegas Twp., County of Clark, 1998-2000; alt. mcpl. ct. judge City of Las Vegas, 1999—. Article editor U. Ariz. Law Rev., 1994-95. Mem. Jr. League of Las Vegas, 1998—, league atty., 2000—; mem. State of Nev. Commn. on Postsecondary Edn., 1998—, Social Register of Las Vegas, House of Blues Found. Adv. Bd. Recipient Cert. Appreciation, U.S. Atty.'s Office, Phoenix, 1993, AmJur award Lawyers Coop. Publ., Tucson, 1993. Mem. ABA (litigation sect., assoc. editor The Affiliate 1999-2000), ATLA, State Bar Nev. (chair young lawyers sect. 1999-2000, so. Nev. disciplinary bd., fee dispute arbitration com.), Clark County Bar Assn. (trial by peers com., cmty. svc. com.), Nev. Trial Lawyers Assn., So. Nev. Assn. Women Attys. Avocations: horseback riding, hiking, skydiving. General civil litigation, Construction, Government contracts and claims. Office: Bernhard & Leslie 3980 Howard Hughes Pkwy Ste 550 Las Vegas NV 89109-5905

KIRSCH, STEVEN JAY, lawyer; b. St. Louis, Aug. 31, 1951; BS, U. Mo., 1973; JD, Hamline U., 1976. Bar: Minn. 1976, U.S. Dist. Ct. Minn. 1976, U.S. Ct. Appeals (8th cir.) 1977. Ptnr. Murnane, Conlin, White, & Brandt, St. Paul, 1976—. Adj. prof. law Hamline U., St. Paul, 1979-83; mem. adv. bd. Advanced Legal Edn., 1982—. Author: (novel) Oath of Office, 1988, Minnesota Methods of Practice, 3d edit., 1989. Fellow Am. Coll. Trial Lawyers. Avocations: reading, writing, books, sports. Federal civil litigation, Insurance, Personal injury. Home: 3612 Oak Creek Ter Saint Paul MN 55127-7034 Office: Murnane Law Firm 444 Cedar St 1800 Piper Jaffray Plaza Saint Paul MN 55101 E-mail: skirsch@murnane.com

KIRSCHBAUM, MYRON, lawyer; b. N.Y.C., Nov. 20, 1949; s. Jonas and Doris (Rose) K.; m. Esther Weiner, June 23, 1971; children: Rachel, Shoshana Stein, Yisrael. BA, Yeshiva U., 1971; JD, Harvard U., 1974. Bar: N.Y. 1975, U.S. Dist. Ct. (so. dist.) N.Y. 1975, U.S. Dist. Ct. (no. dist.) Calif. 1989, U.S. Ct. Appeals (2d cir.) 1975, U.S. Ct. Appeals (9th cir.) 1990, U.S. Ct. Appeals (fed. cir.) 1994. Law clk. U.S. Ct. Appeals (2d cir.), N.Y.C., 1974-75; assoc. Kaye, Scholer, Fierman, Hays & Handler, 1975-82, ptnr., 1983—. Editor Harvard Law Rev., 1972-73, case and comment editor, 1973-74. Bd. dirs. Coalition for Soviet Jewry, N.Y.C., 1985—; bd. trustees Rofeh Internat., Boston, 1999—. Mem. ABA, Assn. Bar City N.Y. General civil litigation, Insurance, Securities. Office: Kaye Scholer Fierman Hays & Handler 425 Park Ave New York NY 10022-3506

KIRSHBAUM, HOWARD M. retired judge, arbiter; b. Oberlin, Ohio, Sept. 19, 1938; s. Joseph and Gertrude (Morris) K.; m. Priscilla Joy Parmakian, Aug. 15, 1964; children— Audra Lee, Andrew William B.A., Yale U., 1960; A.B., Cambridge U., 1962, M.A., 1966; LL.B., Harvard U., 1965. Ptnr. Zarlengo and Kirshbaum, Denver, 1969-75; judge Denver Dist. Ct., 1975-80, Colo. Ct. Appeals, Denver, 1980-83; justice Colo. Supreme Ct., 1983-97; arbiter Jud. Arbiter Group, Inc., 1997—, sr. judge, 1997—; adj. prof. law U. Denver, 1970—. Dir. Am. Law Inst. Phila., Am. Judicature Soc., Chgo., Colo. Jud. Inst. Denver, 1979-89; pres. Colo. Legal Care Soc., Denver, 1974-75 Bd. dirs. Young Artists Orch., Denver, 1976-85; pres. Community Arts Symphony, Englewood, Colo., 1972-74; dir. Denver Opportunity, Inc., Denver, 1972-74; vice-chmn. Denver Council on Arts and Humanities, 1969 Mem.: ABA (standing com. pub. edn. 1996—2001), Colo. Bar Assn., Denver Bar Assn. (trustee 1981—83), Soc. Profls. in Dispute Resolution. Avocations: music performance; tennis. Office: Jud Arbiter Group Inc 1601 Blake St Ste 400 Denver CO 80202-1328

KIRSTEIN, PHILIP LAWRENCE, lawyer, investment company executive; b. N.Y.C., May 29, 1945; s. Paul H. and Marie (Erdreich) K. A.B., U. N.C., 1967; J.D., U. Syracuse, 1973; LL.M. in Taxation, NYU, 1974. Bar: N.Y. 1974, Fla. 1974. Assoc., Townley & Updike, N.Y.C., 1974-80; atty. Merrill Lynch Asset Mgmt., LP, N.Y.C., 1980-83, v.p., 1983-84, sr. v.p., gen. counsel, 1984-98; gen. counsel Merrill Lynch Asset Mgmt. Group, 1998—; bd. dirs. N.J. Race for the Cure, 1996—, Jug Tavern Sparta, Inc., ICI Mutual Ins. Co. Mem. Zoning Bd. Appeals, Ossining, N.Y., 1983-85, N.Y.-N.J. Trail Confs., N.Y.C., 1978-82, Mercer County Dem. Com., 1992-97. Served to capt. USNR, 1967-94. Mem. ABA, Fla. Bar Assn., Assn. Bar City N.Y. Democrat. Jewish. General corporate, Securities. Home: 71 Brooks Bnd Princeton NJ 08540-7554 Office: Merrill Lynch Asst Mgmt Group PO Box 9011 800 Scudders Mill Rd Princeton NJ 08540

KIRTLEY, JANE ELIZABETH, law educator; b. Indpls., Nov. 7, 1953; d. William Raymond and Faye Marie (Price) K.; m. Stephen Jon Cribari, May 8, 1985. BS in Journalism, Northwestern U., 1975, MS in Journalism, 1976; JD, Vanderbilt U., 1979. Bar: N.Y. 1980, D.C. 1982, Va. 1995, U.S. Dist. Ct. (we. dist.) N.Y. 1980, U.S. Dist. Ct. D.C. 1982, U.S. Ct. Claims 1982, U.S. Ct. Appeals (4th cir.) 1982, U.S. Ct. Appeals (D.C. cir.) 1985, U.S. Ct. Appeals (10th cir.) 1996, U.S. Ct. Appeals (5th cir.) 1997, U.S. Ct. Appeals (6th cir.) 1998, U.S. Ct. Appeals (6th and 11th cir.) 1998, U.S. Supreme Ct. 1985. Assoc. Nixon, Hargrave, Devans & Doyle, Rochester, N.Y., 1979-81, Washington, 1981-84; exec. dir. Reporters Com. for Freedom of Press, Arlington, Va., 1985-99; Silha prof. media ethics & law U. Minn. Sch. Journalism & Mass Comm., Mpls., 1999—; dir. Silha Ctr. for Study of Media Ethics and Law, 2000—; mem. affiliated faculty U. Minn. Law Sch., 2001—. Mem. adj. faculty Am. U. Sch. Comm., 1988-98; mem. affiliated law faculty U. Minn., 2001—. Exec. articles editor Vanderbilt U. Jour. Transnat. Law, 1978-79; editor: The News Media and the Law, 1985—, The First Amendment Handbook, 1987, 4th edit., 1995, Agents of Discovery, 1991, 93, 95, Pressing Issues, 1998-99; columnist NEPA Bull., 1988-99, Virginia's Press, 1991-99, Am. Journalism Rev., 1995—, W.Va.'s Press, 1997-99, Tenn. Press, 1997-99; mem. editl. bd. Govt. Info. Quar., Comm. Law and Policy. Bd. dirs. Freedom Forum 1st Amendment Ctr., Nashville, Sigma Delta Chi Found., Indpls. Mem. ABA, N.Y. State Bar Assn., D.C. Bar Assn., Va. State Bar Assn., Sigma Delta Chi. Home: 3645 46th Ave S Minneapolis MN 55406-2937 Office: 111 Murphy Hall 206 Church St SE Minneapolis MN 55455-0488 E-mail: kirtl001@tc.umn.edu

KIRVEN, GERALD, lawyer; b. Augusta, Ga., Apr. 26, 1922; s. Ceil LaCoste and Miriam Creber (Gerald) K.; m. Cara Carter Fisken, Sept. 11, 1948; children: James F., Cara M. Kirven Cox, Christine Y., Alfred C., Mary Lea. AB, U. Va., 1944; LLB cum laude, U. Louisville, 1948. Bar: Ky. 1948, U.S. Dist. Ct. (we. dist.) Ky. 1949, Calif. 1953, U.S. Dist. Ct. (ea. dist.) Ky. 1954, U.S. Ct. Appeals (6th cir.) 1954, U.S. Supreme Ct. 1975. Assoc. Bullitt, Dawson & Tarrant, Louisville, 1948-50; law clk. U.S. Dist. Ct. (we. dist.) Ky., 1953; assoc. Middleton, Seelbach, Wolford, Willis & Cochran, Louisville, 1953-80, ptnr., 1958-80; sr. ptnr. Baird, Kirven, Westfall & Talbott, 1980-85; of counsel Greenebaum, Treitz, Brown & Marshall, 1985-93; appointed spl. justice Ky. Supreme Ct., 1990, 92. Instr. law U. Louisville, 1959, 64, 85-91. Bd. dirs., v.p. Arthritis Found., 1960; v.p., bd. dirs. Mental Health Assn., Ky., 1970—, pres., 1980-81; v.p., vice chmn., bd. dirs. Seven Counties Svcs., 1978-81, Living Supports, Inc., 1987-90; vice chancellor Episcopal Diocese of Ky., 1979-94; bd. dirs. Transit Authority River City, 1995—, sec.-treas., 1996—. Lt. comdr. USNR, 1943-46, 50-53. Recipient Disting. Svc. award Arthritis Found., 1961, Alumnus of Yr. award U. Louisville Law Sch., 1993, Vol. of Yr. award Mental Health Coalition, 1998. Mem. ABA, Ky. Bar Assn. (hon. life, sr. counselor), State Bar Calif., Jud. Conf. U.S. 6th Cir. (life), Brandeis Soc. (comty. mem.), Univ. Club, Phi Beta Kappa, Omicron Delta Kappa. Democrat. Episcopalian.

KIRVEN, TIMOTHY J. lawyer; b. Buffalo, May 26, 1949; s. William J. and Ellen F. (Farrell) K.; m. Elizabeth J. Adams, Oct. 31, 1970; 1 child, Kristen B. BA in English, U. Notre Dame, 1971; JD, U. Wyo., 1974. Bar: Wyo. 1974. Ptnr. Kirven & Kirven, PC, Buffalo, 1974—. Author Rocky Mountain Mineral Law, 1982. Mem. Johnson County Libr. Br., Buffalo. Mem. ABA, Wyo. State Bar (pres. 1998-99), Johnson County Bar Assn., KC (grand knight, treas. 1992-96), Western States Bar Conf. (pres. 1998-99), Rotary (pres. Buffalo club 1988-89, youth exch. program chmn. 1993-98). Home: PO Box C Buffalo WY 82834-0060 Office: Kirven & Kirven PC PO Box 640 Buffalo WY 82834-0640

KIRWAN, ALLAN AUGUST, bar executive; b. Washington, July 28, 1945; s. Edward Emmett and Eleanor Godwin (West) K.; m. Diane Pearson, Sept. 23, 1968; children— Kevin John, Nathan Stuart. Student Gordon Mil. Coll., 1965; A.A., DeKalb Coll., 1966; B.A., Oglethorpe U., 1968; M.B.A., U. Ga., 1969. Mgmt. and budget analyst DeKalb County, Decatur, Ga., 1970-76; asst. exec. dir. State Bar Ga., Atlanta, 1976-81, exec. dir., 1981—. Founder, pres. Avondale Community Action, Avondale Estates, Ga., 1982— , editor monthly newsletter, 1982-85; chmn. Avondale Estates Planning and Zoning Bd., 1980-83; co-founder Avondale Estates Gentlemen's Sporting & Philosophical Soc., 1986-88; mayor City of Avondale Estates, commr.; curriculum advisor Dekalb Coll.; mem., chmn. Avondale Devel. Authority, 1986-88. Recipient Outstanding Alumnus award DeKalb Community Coll., 1984, Merit award City of Avondale Estates, 1984, Honor medal., 1988. Mem. Nat. Assn. Bar Execs., Am. Soc. Assn. Execs. Baptist. Clubs: Avondale Community, Avondale Swim and Tennis (pres. 1980). Home: 9 Avondale Avondale Estates GA 30002 Office: State Bar 800 The Hurt Bldg 45 Edgewood Ave SE Atlanta GA 30303-2922

KIRWIN, THOMAS F. prosecutor; U.S. atty. no. dist., Fla. Office: 315 S Calhoun St Ste 510 Tallahassee FL 32301 Office Fax: 850-942-8429*

KISER, JACKSON L. federal judge; b. Welch, W.Va., June 24, 1929; m. Carole Gorman; children: Jackson, William, John Michael, Elizabeth Carol. B.A., Concord Coll., 1951; J.D., Washington and Lee U., 1952. Bar: Va. Asst. U.S. atty. Western Dist. Va., 1958-61; assoc., then ptnr. R.R. Young, Young, Kiser, Haskins, Mann, Gregory & Young P.C., Martinsville, Va., 1961-82; judge U.S. Dist. Ct. (we. dist.) Va., 1982-93, chief judge, 1993-97, sr. judge, 1997—. Mem. Martinsville City Sch. Bd., 1971-77. With JAGC U.S. Army, 1952-55, capt. Res., 1955-61. Mem. Am. Coll. Trial Lawyers (state com.), Va. Bar Assn. (exec. com.), Va. State Bar, Va. Trial Lawyers Assn., 4th Cir. Jud. Conf. (permanent), Martinsville-Henry County Bar Assn., Order of Coif. Office: US Dist Ct PO Box 3326 700 Main St Danville VA 24543-3326

KISHEL, GREGORY FRANCIS, federal judge; b. Virginia, Minn., Jan. 26, 1951; AB, Cornell U., 1973; JD, Boston Coll., 1977. Bar: Minn. 1978, U.S. Dist. Ct. Minn. 1978, U.S. Ct. Appeals (8th cir.) 1978, Wis. 1985, U.S. Dist. Ct. (we. dist.) Wis. 1985. Staff atty. Legal Aid Svc. of N.E. Minn., Duluth, 1978-81; pvt. practice, 1981-86; judge U.S. Bankruptcy Ct., St. Paul, 1986-2000, chief judge, 2000—. Judge U.S. Bankruptcy Ct., Duluth, 1984-86; pro tem mem. bankruptcy appellate panel 8th Cir. Ct., 1996—. Mem. ABA, Nat. Conf. Bankruptcy Judges, Minn. Bar Assn., Polish Geneal. Soc. Minn. (pres. 1996-2000). Office: US Bankruptcy Ct 316 Robert St N Ste 210 Saint Paul MN 55101-1243

KISS, ROBERT, state legislator; s. Matthew J. Sr. and Catherine E. (Schnarr) K.; m. Melinda Ashworth. BA, Ohio State U., 1979, JD, 1982. With firm Gorman, Sheatsley & Co., L.C.; mem. W.Va. Ho. of Dels., 1988-99, chmn. subcom. on ways and means, 1989, vice chair fin. com., chmn. fin. com., 1993, speaker of the house, 1996—. Bd. dirs. Beckley Renaissance, Raleigh County Hospice. Bernard Levy scholar, 1980-82. Mem. Fla. State Bar Assn., Ohio Bar Assn., W.Va. Bar Assn., Raleigh County Bar Assn., Beckley Bus. and Profl. Women's Club. Office: W Va State Legislature Rm 234 M Bldg 1 1900 Kanawha Blvd E Charleston WV 25305

KISSEL, PETER CHARLES, lawyer; b. Watertown, N.Y., Sept. 29, 1947; s. Laurence Haas and Catherine Cantwell (Weldon) Kissel; m. Sharon Darlene Murphy, June 14, 1970. AB, Syracuse U., 1969; JD, Am. U., 1972. Bar: DC 1973, US Court Claims 1976, US Court Appeals (3d cir) 1976, US Supreme Court 1978, US Dist Ct DC 1979, US Ct Appeals (9th cir) 1979, US Ct Appeals (DC cir) 1983, US Ct Appeals (5th cir) 1988. Atty.-advisor Fed. Power Commn., Washington, 1972-74; atty. pub. utilities, 1974-77; assoc. O'Connor & Hannan, Washington, 1977-79, ptnr., 1979-87, Baller Hammett, Washington, 1987-93; ptnr., CFO, Grammer, Kissel, Robbins, Skancke & Edwards (GKRSE), 1993—. Co-bus mgr Energy Law Jour, Washington, 1981, asst editor, 1982—89. Contbr. articles profl jours. Mem Washington adv bd Syracuse Univ, 1995—; bd dirs Episcopal Caring Response to AIDS Inc, 1988—93, vpres, 1990—91, pres, 1992, mem exec comt, 1990—93; mem vestry St Patrick's Episcopal Ch, Washington, 1975—78, chmn ann fundraising campaign, 1987—89; bd dirs PRISM, 1996—97, Waterpower XII Steering Comt, 2000—01. Recipient Spl Award, Fed Power Comn, 1973. Mem.: Fed Bar Asn (vice chmn com on publs 1984—85, chmn com on hydroelectric regulation 1991—92), Nat Hydropower Asn, John Sherman Myers Soc, Bar Asn DC, Syracuse Univ Soc Fellows, Phi Kappa Psi. Democrat. Episcopalian. Avocations: gardening, American history, Irish history. Administrative and regulatory, Appellate, FERC practice. Home: 5604 Utah Ave NW Washington DC 20015-1230 Office: GKRSE 1500 K St NW Ste 330 Washington DC 20005 E-mail: pckissel@GKRSE-law.com

KISSEL, RICHARD JOHN, lawyer; b. Chgo., Nov. 27, 1936; s. John and Anne T. (Unichowski) K.; m. Donna Lou Heidersbach, Feb. 11, 1961; children: Roy Warren, David Todd, Audrey Anne. BA, Northwestern U., 1958; JD, Northwestern U., Chgo., 1961. Assoc. Peterson, Lowrey, Rall, Barber & Ross, Chgo., 1961-65; divsn. counsel Abbott Labs., North Chicago, Ill., 1965-70; mem. Pollution Control Bd., Chgo., 1970-72; adminstrv. asst. Gov.'s Staff, 1972; ptnr. Martin, Craig, Chester & Sonnenschein, 1973-88, Gardner, Carton & Douglas, Chgo., 1988-2000, chmn. mgmt. com., 1996-98, of counsel, 2000—. Adj. prof. U. Ill. Sch. Pub. Health, Chgo., 1973-76; instr. Kent. Sch. Law, Ill. Inst. Tech., Chgo., 1974-78; mem. vis. com. Northwestern U. Law Sch., 1996-99. Recipient Ill. award IAWA, 1996. Contbr. articles to legal jours. Recipient Ill. award IAWA, 1996. Fellow Internat. Soc. Barristers; mem. Ill. State Bar Assn., Chgo. Bar Assn., Ill. State C. of C. (chmn. environ. affairs 1973-76), Com. on Cts. for 21st Century, Knollwood Club (Lake Forest; gov. 1976-82), Lake Forest/Lake Bluff Sr. Citizens Found (bd. mem.). Roman Catholic. Administrative and regulatory, Environmental, Legislative. Office: Gardner Carton & Douglas 321 N Clark St Ste 3000 Chicago IL 60610-4718 E-mail: rkissel@gcd.com

KITCH, EDMUND WELLS, lawyer, educator, private investor; b. Wichita, Kans., Nov. 3, 1939; s. Paul R. and Josephine (Pridmore) K.; m. Joanne Steiner, 1966 (div. 1976); 1 child, Sarah; m. Alison Lauter, Jan. 29, 1978 (div. 2000); children: Andrew, Whitney. BA, Yale U., 1961; JD, U. Chgo., 1964. Bar: Kans. 1964, Ill. 1966, U.S. Supreme Ct. 1973, Va. 1986. Asst. prof. law Ind. U., 1964-65; mem. faculty U. Chgo., 1965-82, prof.,

1971-82; prof., mem. Ctr. Advanced Studies U. Va., Charlottesville, 1982-85, Joseph M. Hartfield prof., 1985—, Sullivan and Cromwell rsch. prof., 1996-99. Vis. prof. Bklyn. Law Sch., 1995; Jack N. Pritzger Disting. vis. prof. of law Northwestern U., 1996; spl. asst. solicitor gen. U.S. Dept. Justice, 1973-74; exec. dir. Adv. Com. on Procedural Reform CAB, 1975-76; reporter Com. on Pattern Jury Instruction, Ill. Supreme Ct., 1966-69; mem. com. on pub.-pvt. sector rels. in vaccine innovation Inst. of Medicine, NAS, 1982-85, mem. com. on evaluation polio vaccine, 1987-88. Author: (with Harvey Perlman) Intellectual Property, 5th edit., 1997; Regulation, Federalism and Interstate Commerce, 1981. Contbr. articles to profl. jours. Mem. Va. Bar Assn., Am. Law Inst., Order of Coif, Phi Beta Kappa. Office: U Va Sch Law 580 Massie Rd Charlottesville VA 22903-1738

KITCHEN, CHARLES WILLIAM, lawyer; b. July 17, 1926; s. Karl K. and Lucille W. (Keynes) K.; m. Mary Applegate, July 22, 1950; children: Kenneth K., Guy R., Anne Kitchen Campbell. BA, Western Res. U., 1948, JD, 1950. Bar: Ohio 1950, U.S. Dist. Ct. Ohio 1952, U.S. Ct. Appeals (6th cir.) 1972, U.S. Supreme Ct. 1981. Ptnr. Kitchen, Derry & Barnhouse Co., LPA, Cleve., 1950-97, sr. ptnr., 1972, ret., 1997; life mem., exec. com. 8th Jud. Dist. Ct., 1988-91. Mem. Regional Coun. on Alcoholism, 1981-86, chmn., 1985-86; bd. dirs. Scarborough Hall, 1992-94. With A.C., U.S. Army, 1944-45. Fellow Internat. Acad. Trial Lawyers, Am. Coll. Trial Lawyers (sr. mem.); mem. ABA (sect. tort and ins. practice, sec. litigation), Am. Arbitration Assn. (panelist 1961-91), Cleve. Assn. Civil Trial Attys. (pres. 1971-72), Ohio Assn. Civil Trial Attys. (pres. 1975-76), Greater Cleve. Bar Assn. (chmn. med.-legal com. 1974-75, chmn. lawyers assistance program 1981-83, chmn. mentor com. 1988-95, jud. campaign com. chmn. 1993-95, ttustee 1984-87), Am. Legion, Order of Coif, Beta Theta Pi, Phi Delta Phi. Presbyterian. Federal civil litigation, State civil litigation. Home: 8755 E Old Spanish Ter Dr Tucson AZ 85710 E-mail: ckitch26@aol.com

KITE, MARILYN S. state supreme court justice, lawyer; b. Laramie, Wyo., Oct. 2, 1947; BA with honors, U. Wyo., 1970, JD with honors, 1974. Bar: Wyo. 1974. Mem. Holland & Hart, Jackson, Wyo., 1979—2000; justice Wyo. Supreme Ct., 2000—. Contbr. articles to profl. jours. Mem. ABA (nat. resources sect., litigation sect.), Wyo. State Bar. Address: Wyo Supreme Ct 2301 Capitol Ave Cheyenne WY 82002*

KITTELSEN, RODNEY OLIN, lawyer; b. Albany, Wis., Mar. 11, 1917; s. Olen B. and Nellie Winifred (Atkinson) K.; m. Pearle M. Haldiman, Oct. 12, 1940; children: Gregory S., James E., Bradley J. PhB, U. Wis., 1939, LLB, 1940. Spl. agt. FBI, Washington, 1940-46; ptnr. Kittelsen, Barry, Ross, Wellington & Thompson, Monroe, Wis., 1946—. Dist. atty. Green County, Monroe, 1947-53; pres. State Bar Wis., Madison, 1976-77, 83-85; dir. Wis. Law Found., Madison, 1992—. Pres. Monroe Police and Fire Commn., 1947—; legal counsel X-FBI Inc., Quantico, Va., 1986—; mem. Am. Coll. Trust and Estate Coun., Chgo., 1983—. Recipient Outstanding Citizen award Monroe Jaycees, 1977, Outstanding Svc. award Albany FFA, 1991, Disting. Svc. award U. Wis. Law Sch., 1995, Disting. Svc. award U. Wis. Law Alumni Assn., 1995. Fellow Am. Bar Found., Wis. Bar Assn. (pres. 1976-77, 83-85, Goldberg award 1990), Wis. Bar Found. (pres. 1985). Email: Kitlaw@KittelsenLaw Office.com. Education and schools, General practice, Probate. Home: 708 26th Ave Monroe WI 53566-1620 Office: 916 17th Ave Monroe WI 53566-2003

KITTLESON, HENRY MARSHALL, lawyer; b. Tampa, Fla., May 13, 1929; s. Edgar O. and Ardath (Ayers) K.; m. Barbara Clark, Mar. 20, 1954; 1 dau., Laura Helen. BS with high honors, U. Fla., 1951, JD with high honors, 1953. Bar: Fla. 1953. Ptnr. Holland & Knight, Lakeland and Bartow, Fla., 1955—. Mem. adv. bd. Fla. Fed. Savs. & Loan Assn., 1974-86; mem. Fla. Law Revision Commn., 1967-76, vice chmn., 1969-71; mem. Gov.'s Property Rights Study Commn., 1974-75, Nat. Conf. Commrs. Uniform State Laws, 1982—. Mem. council U. Fla. Law Center, 1974-77. Served to maj. USAF, 1953-55. Fellow Am. Bar Found.; mem. ABA (chmn. standing com. on ethic and profl. responsibility 1980-81), Am. Law Inst., Am. Coll. Real Estate Lawyers, Fla. Bar (chmn. standing com. profl. ethics 1965-66, tort litigation rev. commn. 1983-84), Blue Key, Sigma Phi Epsilon, Phi Delta Phi, Phi Kappa Phi, Beta Gamma Sigma, Lakeland Yacht and Country Club. Presbyterian. Real property. Home: 5334 Woodhaven Ln Lakeland FL 33813-2656 Office: Holland & Knight PO Box 32092 92 Lake Wire Dr Lakeland FL 33815-1510

KITTRELL, PAMELA R. lawyer; b. Athens, Ga., June 15, 1965; d. John Edison and Anne (Hagins) K. AB summa cum laude, U. Miami, 1987; JD, U. Mich., 1990. Bar: Fla. 1990, U.S. Dist. Ct. (so. dist.) Fla. 1991, D.C. 1992, Colo. 1994, U.S, Ct. Appeals (11th cir.) 1994, U.S. Dist. CT. (mid. dist.) Fla. 1995. Assoc. Stearns, Weaver, Miller, Weissler, Alhadeff & Sitterson, PA, Miami, 1990-93; sr. assoc. Cooney, Mattson, Lance, Blackburn, Richards & O'Connor, P.A., Ft. Lauderdale, Fla., 1994-98. Mem. Fla. Bar (appellate practice and advocacy sec.), Fla. Def. Lawyers Assn. Democrat. Appellate.

KITZES, WILLIAM FREDRIC, lawyer, safety analyst, consultant; b. Bklyn., Nov. 24, 1950; s. David Louis and Rhoda Rachel (Feldman) K; m. Sandra Shimasaki, Apr. 7, 1979: children: Justin, Dana. BA, U. Wis., 1972; JD, Am. U., 1975. Bar: D.C. 1977. Legal advisor on product recalls U.S. Consumer Products Safety Commn., Washington, 1975-77, program mgr., 1977-80, regulatory counsel, 1980-81; v.p., gen. mgr. Inst. for Safety Analysis, Rockville, Md., 1981-83; prin. Consumer Safety Assocs., Potomac, Md., Boca Raton, Fla., 1983—. Cons. Toro Co., Bloomington, Minn., 1987, Vendo Co., Fresno, Calif., 1987, Nat. Assn. Attys. Gens., Washington, 1987, Arctic Cat, Inc., thief River Falls, Minn., 1995—, Global Furniture, Toronto, Ont., 1997, Product Safety Online, Boca Raton, 1997—. Contbg. columnist CCH Product Safety Guide and Products Liability Reporter, 2000—. Counsel Friends of Charlie Gilchrist, Montgomery County, Md., 1983; chmn. Fla. Consumers Coun., 1995—. Recipient silver medal for meritorious svc. U.S. Consumer Products Safety Commn., 1976. Mem. Am. Soc. Safety Engrs., Human Factors Soc., System Safety Soc., Nat. Safety Coun., Internat. Consumer Product Health and Safety Orgn. Personal injury. Home and Office: Consumer Safety Assocs 4501 NW 25th Way Boca Raton FL 33434-2506

KITZMILLER, HOWARD LAWRENCE, lawyer; b. Shippensburg, Pa., May 6, 1930; s. Franklin Leroy and Emma Corrinna (Bedford) K.; m. Shirley Mae Pine, Apr. 4, 1953; children: David Lawrence, Diane May. BA summa cum laude, Dickinson Coll., 1951; JD, Dickinson Sch. of Law, 1954; LLM, George Washington U., 1958. Bar: Pa. 1955, D.C. 1984. Commr. U.S. Ct. Mil. Appeals, Washington, 1958-59; various positions to assoc. gen. counsel FCC, 1959-80; various positions to sr. v.p. and sec. Washington Mgmt. Corp., 1983—. Editor Dickinson Law Rev., 1954. Deacon, elder Westminster Presbyn. Ch., Alexandria, Va.; bd. dirs. S.E. Fairfax Devel. Corp., Fairfax County, Va., 1977-98, also past pres.; various positions including pres., parents adv. coun., bd. assocs., trustee, investment com. Randolph-Macon Coll., Ashland, Va., 1984-95. Capt. JAGC, U.S. Army, 1955-58. Mem. ABA, FBA, City Club Washington, Masons, Phi Beta Kappa. Republican.

KJOS, VICTORIA, lawyer; b. Fargo, N.D., Sept. 17, 1953; d. Orville I. and Annie J. (Tanberg) K. BA, Minot State U., 1974; JD, U. N.D., 1977. Bar: Ariz. 1978. Assoc. Jack E. Evans, Ltd., Phoenix, 1977-78, pension and ins. cons., 1978-79; dep. state treas. State of N.D., Bismarck, 1979-80; freelance cons. Phoenix, 1980-81, Anchorage, 1981-82; asst. v.p., v.p., mgr. trust dept. Great Western Bank, Phoenix, 1982-84; assoc. Robert A. Jensen P.C., 1984-86; ptnr. Jensen & Kjos, P.C., 1986-89; assoc. Allen, Kimerer & LaVelle, 1989-90, ptnr., 1990-91; dir. The Yoga and Fitness Inst., 1994-97. Freelance cons., Phoenix, 1999—; lectr. in domestic rels. Contbr. articles to profl. jours. Bd. dirs. Arthritis Found., Phoenix, 1986-89, v.p. for chpt. devel., 1988-89; bd. dirs. Ariz. Yoga Assn., 1993-95, v.p., 1993-95. Mem. ABA, ATLA, Am. Coll. Sports Medicine, Am. Alliance Health, Phys. Edn., Recreation & Dance, Ariz. Bar Assn. (exec. coun. family law sect. 1988-91), Maricopa Bar Assn. (sec. family law com. 1988-89, pres. family law com. 1989-90, judge pro tem 1989-91), Ariz. Trial Lawyers Assn. Family and matrimonial, Personal injury.

KLAFTER, CARY IRA, lawyer; b. Chgo., Sept. 15, 1948; s. Herman Nicholas and Bernice Rose (Maremont) K.; m. Kathleen Ann Kerr, July 21, 1974; children: Anastasia, Benjamin, Eileen. BA, Mich. State U., 1968, MS, 1971; JD, U. Chgo., 1972. Bar: Calif. 1972. Assoc. Morrison & Foerster, San Francisco, 1972-79, ptnr., 1979-96; dir. corp. affairs legal dept. Intel Corp., 1996—. Lectr. law Stanford Law Sch., 1990-99. Capt. USAR, 1971-78. Mem. Am. Soc. Corp. Secs. (bd. dirs.). Pension, profit-sharing, and employee benefits, Securities.

KLAHR, GARY PETER, lawyer; b. N.Y.C., July 9, 1942; s. Fred and Frieda (Garson) K. Student, Ariz. State U., 1958-61; LL.B. with high honors, U. Ariz., 1964. Bar: Ariz. 1967, U.S. Dist. Ct. Ariz. 1967. Assoc. Brazlin & Greene, Phoenix, 1967-68; sr. ptnr. Gary Peter Klahr, P.C., 1968—. Asst. editor Ariz. Law Rev., 1963-64; contbr. articles to profl. jours. Bd. dirs. CODAMA, 1975-89, pres., 1980-81; bd. dirs. Tumbleweed Runaway Ctr., 1972-76; mem. bd. dirs. Internat. Found. Anti-Cancer Drug Discovery, 1998—, chair exec. com., 1999—; chmn. Citizens Criminal Justice Commn., 1977-78; co-chmn. delinquency subcom. Phoenix Forward Task force; vol. referee Juvenile Ct., 1969; vol. adult probation officer; vol. counselor youth programs Dept. of Corrections, Phoenix; ex-officio mem., spl. cons. Phoenix Youth Commn.; mem. citizen adv. coun. Phoenix Union H.S. Dist., 1985-90, 95-99, co-chmn. 1998-99, elected governing bd., 1991-95, 2000—, v.p., 1992-95, co-chmn. citizens adv. com., 1970-72; mem. rev. bd. Phoenix Police Dept., 1985-94; bd. dirs. Metro Youth Ctr., 1986-87, Svc./Employment/Redevel. (SER) Jobs for Progress, Phoenix, 1985-90, pres., 1986-87; bd. dirs. East McDowell Youth Assn., 1992-94; v.p. local chpt. City of Hope, 1985-86; Justice of the Peace pro tem Maricopa County Cts., 1985-89; juvenile hearing officer Maricopa County Juvenile Ct., 1985-89; v.p., co-founder Cmty. Leadership for Youth Devel. (CLYDE); del. Phoenix Together Town Hall on Youth Crime, 1982. Named 1 of 3 Outstanding Young Men of Phoenix Phoenix Jr. C. of C., 1969; recipient Disting. Citizen award Ariz. chpt. ACLU, 1976. Mem. ACLU (v.p. ctrl. chpt. Ariz. 1990-95, pres. 1995—, mem. state bd.), Ariz. State Bar (past sec., bd. dirs. young lawyers sect., co-chmn. unauthorized practice com. 1988-89, mem. other coms.), Maricopa County Bar Assn. (past sec., bd. dirs. young lawyers sec., vice-chmn. juvenile practice com. 1998-99), Am. Judicature Soc., Jewish Children's and Family Svc., Common Cause, NAACP, Ariz. ConsumersCoun., Phoenix Jaycees, Order of the Coif, Phi Alpha Delta. Democrat. Jewish. Criminal, Juvenile, Personal injury. Office: 2520 N 16th St Phoenix AZ 85006-1401

KLAPER, MARTIN JAY, lawyer; b. Chgo., Feb. 12, 1947; s. Carl and Kate F. (Friedman) K.; m. Julia Warner, Nov. 14, 1973. BS in Bus. summa cum laude, Ind. U., 1969, JD summa cum laude, 1971. Bar: Ind. 1971, U.S. Dist. Ct. (no. and so. dists.) Ind. 1971, U.S. Ct. Appeals (7th cir.) 1972, U.S. Supreme Ct. 1979. Law clk. to justice U.S. Ct. Appeals (7th cir.), 1971-72; ptnr. Ice Miller Donadio & Ryan, Indpls., 1972—. Mem. ABA, Ind. Bar Assn. Civil rights, Labor. Office: Ice Miller Donadio & Ryan PO Box 82001 Indianapolis IN 46282-2001 E-mail: Klaper@iquest.net, Klaper@Icemiller.com

KLAPPER, MOLLY, lawyer, educator; b. Berlin, Germany; came to U.S., 1950; d. Elias and Ciporah (Weber) Teicher; m. Jacob Klapper; children: Rachelle Hannah, Robert David. BA, CUNY, MA, 1964; PhD, NYU, 1974; JD, Rutgers U., 1987. Bar: N.J. 1987, U.S. Dist. Ct. N.J. 1987, N.Y. 1989, U.S. Dist. Ct. (so. and ea. dists.) N.Y. 1989, D.C. 1989, U.S. Supreme Ct. 1991, U.S. Ct. Appeals (2d cir.) 1992; cert. arbitrata, Better Bus. Bur., 2000. Prof. English Bronx C.C., CUNY, 1974-84; law intern U.S. Dist. Ct. N.J., Newark, 1987; law sec. to presiding judge appellate div. N.J. Supreme Ct., Springfield, 1987-88; assoc. Wilson, Elser, Moskowitz, Edelman and Dicker, N.Y.C., 1988-96; adminstrv. law judge Dept. Finance, 1997-2001; adj. prof. law Touro Law Ctr., Huntington, N.Y., 2001—. Small claims ct. arbitrator, 1994-01; mediator N.Y. State Supreme Ct., comml. divsn., 2000—, cert. arbitrator, Better Bus. Bur., 2000—; jud. nominee State Supreme Ct., 2d dist., 1999. Author: The German Literary Influence on Byron, 1974, 2d edit., 1975, The German Literary Influence on Shelley, 1975; contbr. to profl. publs. NEH fellow, 1978; grantee Am. Philos. Soc., 1976. Mem. Assn. Bar of City of N.Y. Avocations: bicycling, skiing, roller skating, walking, hiking. General civil litigation, General corporate, Insurance. Office: 720 Ft Washington Ave New York NY 10040-3708

KLARFELD, PETER JAMES, lawyer; b. Holyoke, Mass., Aug. 19, 1947; s. David Nathan and Gloria (Belsky) K.; m. Mary Myrtle, July 7, 1985; children: Peter Marcus (dec.), Mary Elizabeth, Louis Edward. BA, U. Va., 1969, JD, 1973; MA, U. Chgo., 1970. Bar: Va. 1973, D.C. 1975, U.S. Dist. Ct. D.C. 1977, U.S. Dist. Ct. (ea. dist.) Va. 1977, U.S. Supreme Ct. 1977, U.S. Ct. Appeals (4th cir.) 1978, U.S. Ct. Appeals (3rd & 9th cirs.) 1986, U.S. Ct. Appeals (2d cir.) 1998, U.S. Dist. Ct. (ea. dist.) Wis. 1987, U.S. Dist. Ct. (no. dist.) Calif. 1990. Law clk. to Hon. Robert R. Merhige, Jr. U.S. Dist. Ct. (ea. dist.) Va., Richmond, 1973-74; atty., office of legal counsel U.S. Dept. Justice, Washington, 1974-76; ptnr. Brownstein Zeidman & Lore, 1977-96, Wiley, Rein and Fielding, Washington, 1996—. Editor: Covenants Against Competition in Franchise Agreements, 1992; contbr. articles to profl. jours. Trustee Dalkon Shield Other Claimants Trust, Richmond, 1990-96, chmn., 1991-96. Mem. ABA. Antitrust, General civil litigation, Franchising. Home: 434 E Columbia St Falls Church VA 22046-3501 Office: Wiley Rein & Fielding 1776 K St NW Washington DC 20006-2304 E-mail: pklarfeld@wrf.com

KLASKO, HERBERT RONALD, lawyer, law educator, writer; b. Phila., Nov. 26, 1949; s. Leon Louis and Estelle Lorraine (Baratz) K.; m. Marjorie Ann Becker, Aug. 27, 1977; children: Brett Andrew, Kelli Lynn. BA, Lehigh U., 1971; JD, U. Pa., 1974. Bar: Pa. 1974, U.S. Dist. Ct. (ea. dist.) Pa. 1974, U.S. Ct. Appeals (3d cir.) 1981. Assoc. Fox, Rothschild, O'Brien & Frankel, Phila., 1974-75; ptnr., chmn. immigration dept. Abrahams & Loewenstein, 1975-88, Dechert, Price & Rhoads, Phila., 1988—. Instr., mem. adv. bd. Inst. for Paralegal Tng., Phila., 1974-81; instr. Temple Law Sch. Grad. Legal Studies, Phila., 1984; adj. prof. Villanova U. Law Sch., Pa., 1985-90. Co-author: (with Matthew Bender and Hope Frye) Employer's Immigration Compliance Guide, 1985; bd. editors: Immigration Law and Procedure Reporter. Exec. committeeman, bd. dirs. Jewish Community Rels. Coun., Phila., 1977—; chmn. exec. com., com. on unprosecuted Nazi war criminals Nat. Jewish Community Rels. Adv. Coun., N.Y.C., 1983-90; v.p. Hebrew Immigrant Aid Soc., Phila., 1977—; pres. Coun. of Tenants Assn., Southeastern Pa., 1980-81. Recipient Legion of Honor award Chapel of Four Chaplains, 1977. Mem. ABA (coordinating com. on immigration), Phila. Bar Assn., Am. Immigration Lawyers Assn. (chmn. Phila. chpt. 1980-82, bd. govs. 1980—, nat. sec. 1984-85, 2d v.p. 1985-86, 1st v.p. 1986-87, pres.-elect 1987-88, pres. 1988-89, exec. com. 1984-90, 96-99, gen. counsel, 1996-99, Founders award 1999), Am. Immigration Law Found. (bd. dirs. 1987-90). Avocations: politics, sports, traveling, organizations. Immigration, naturalization, and customs. Office: Dechert Price & Rhoads 4000 Bell Atlantic Tower 1717 Arch St Lbby 3 Philadelphia PA 19103-2713 E-mail: ronald.klasko@dechert.com

KLAUS, CHARLES, retired lawyer; b. Freiburg, Baden, Germany, Feb. 11, 1935; came to U.S., 1939; children: Charles, Kathryn, Richard. BA, Cornell U., 1956, MBA, JD with distinction, 1961; postdoctoral, Case Western Res. U., 1964, Lakeland Community Coll., 1976. Bar: Ohio 1961, U.S. Dist. Ct. (no. dist.) Ohio 1962. Assoc. Baker & Hostetler, Cleve., 1961-71, ptnr., 1972-94, retired, 1995. Past hon. trustee and pres. Cleve. Music Sch. Settlement; past trustee Cleve. Audubon Soc.; past trustee, sec. Cleve. Area Arts Coun., Lake Erie Opera Theatre, N.E. Ohio chpt. Arthritis Found.; former mem. Group Svc. Coun. Welfare Fedn. Cleve.; corp. mem. The Holden Arboretum. Recipient Award of Merit, Cleve. Audubon Soc., 1979. Mem. Millard Fillmore Soc., Rowfant Club (past sec.), Kirtland Country Club (past dir., past sec., Willoughby, Ohio). Contracts commercial, General corporate, Environmental.

KLAUSNER, JACK DANIEL, lawyer; b. N.Y.C., July 31, 1945; s. Burt and Marjory (Brown) K.; m. Dale Arlene Kreis, July 1, 1968; children: Andrew Russell, Mark Raymond. BS in Bus., Miami U., Oxford, Ohio, 1967; JD, U. Fla., 1969. Bar: N.Y. 1971, Ariz. 1975, U.S. Dist. Ct. Ariz. 1975, U.S. Ct. Appeals (9th cir.) 1975, U.S. Supreme Ct. 1975. Assoc. counsel John P. McGuire & Co., Inc., N.Y.C., 1970-71; assoc. atty. Hahn & Hessen, 1971-72; gen. counsel Equilease Corp., 1972-74; assoc. Burch & Cracchiolo, Phoenix, 1974-78, ptnr., 1978-98; judge pro tem Maricopa County Superior Ct., 1990—, Ariz. Ct. Appeals, 1992—; ptnr. Warner Angle Roper & Hallam, Phoenix, 1998—. Bd. dirs. Hunter Contracting Co. Bd. dirs. Santos Soccer Club, Phoenix, 1989-90; bd. dirs., pres. south Bank Soccer Club, Tempe, 1987-88. Antitrust, General civil litigation, Real property. Home: 9146 N Crimson Canyon Fountain Hills AZ 85268 Office: Warner Angel Roper & Hallam 3550 N Central Ave Ste 1500 Phoenix AZ 85012-2112

KLAYMAN, BARRY MARTIN, lawyer; b. Montclair, N.J., Sept. 26, 1952; s. Max M. and Sylvia (Cohen) K.; m. Anna Kornbrot, June 8, 1975; children: Alison Melissa, Matthew Daniel. BA magna cum laude, Columbia U., 1974; JD cum laude, Harvard U., 1977. Bar: Pa. 1977, Del. 1998, U.S. Dist. Ct. (ea. dist.) Pa. 1977, U.S. Dist. Ct. Del. 1998, U.S. Ct. Appeals (3d cir.) 1978. From assoc. to ptnr. Wolf, Block, Schorr & Solis-Cohen LLP, Phila., 1977—. Contbr. articles to profl. jours. Bd. dirs. Akiba Hebrew Acad., 1991—, sec., 1994-95, v.p., 1995-96, 98-2000, treas. 1996-98, pres. 2000—; mem. planning and allocations com. Jewish Fedn. Greater Phila., 1997—, trustee, 2000—, mem. com. on nat. svcs., 1991—, chair, 1998—. Mem. ABA (litig. sect., torts and ins. practice sect.), Del. Bar Assn., Phila. Bar Assn., Pa. Bar Assn., Assn. Trial Lawyers Am., B'nai B'rith Youth Orgn. (bd. dirs. Phila. region 1984—, chmn. 1991-95, mem. internat. youth commn. 1991—, exec. com., 1996—), B'nai B'rith (coun. v.p. 1996-97, mem. Justice Lodge 1992—), Phi Beta Kappa. Federal civil litigation, State civil litigation, Environmental. Office: Wolf Block Schorr & Solis-Cohen LLP 920 King St Ste 300 Wilmington DE 19801-3300 E-mail: bklayman@wolfblock.com

KLECKNER, ROBERT GEORGE, JR. lawyer; b. Reading, Pa., Mar. 14, 1932; s. Robert George and Elizabeth (Endlich) K.; m. Carol Espie, June 15, 1955; children: Anthony Savage, Susan Duffield. BA, Yale U., 1954; LLB, U. Pa., 1959. Bar: Pa. 1960, N.Y. 1964. Pvt. practice, Reading, 1960-63; assoc. Sullivan & Cromwell, N.Y.C., 1963-70; house counsel Goldman, Sachs & Co., 1970-78; cons., 1978-80; house counsel Johnson & Higgins, 1980-97; sr. atty. legal dept. Marsh & McLennan Cos., Inc., 1997; ret., 1997. 1st lt. USAR, 1955-57, Korea. Mem. ABA, Assn. Bar City N.Y., Berks County (Pa.) Bar Assn., Union Club, Univ. Club, Phi Beta Kappa. Republican. Lutheran. Home: 80 East End Ave New York NY 10028-8004

KLEIMAN, BERNARD, lawyer; b. Chgo., Jan. 26, 1928; s. Isadore and Pearl (Wikoff) K.; m. Gloria Baime, Nov. 15, 1986; children: Leslie, David. B.S., Purdue U., 1951; J.D., Northwestern U., 1954. Bar: Ill. 1954. Practice law in assn. with Abraham W. Brussell, 1957-60; dist. counsel United Steel Workers Am., 1960-65, spl. counsel, 1997—, gen. counsel, 1965-97; ptnr. Kleiman, Cornfield & Feldman, Chgo., 1960-75; prin. B. Kleiman (P.C.), 1976-77, Kleiman, Whitney, Wolfe & Elfenbaum, P.C., 1978-99. Mem. collective bargaining coms. for nat. labor negotiations in basic steel, aluminum, tire and can mfg. industries. Contbr. articles to legal jours. Served with U.S. Army, 1946-48. Mem. ABA, Allegheny County Bar Assn. Labor.

KLEIMAN, MARY MARGARET, lawyer; b. Norfolk, Va., May 26, 1959; d. William Edward and Patricia Mae Holste; m. David James Kleiman, June 29, 1991; children: Amanda Grace, Amy Elizabeth. BA in History summa cum laude, Marian Coll., Indpls., 1981; JD cum laude, Ind. U., Indpls., 1984. Bar: Ind. 1985, U.S. Dist. Ct. (no. and so. dists.) Ind. 1985. Bailiff, law clk. Marion County Mcpl. Ct., Indpls., 1983-84; counsel Am. Fletcher Nat. Bank (now Bank One, Ind. N.A.), 1985-88; assoc. Krieg DeVault Alexander & Capehart, 1989-95; ptnr. Krieg Devault Alexander & Capehart, 1995-2000; v.p. and assoc. gen. counsel Federal Home Loan Bank of Indianapolis, 2000—. Bd. dirs. Ind. Bus. Devel. Corp., 1994-97. Contbr. articles to profl. jours. Pro bono atty. Cmty. Orgns. Legal Assistance Project, Indpls., 1994—; vol. com. chair, mem. client programs com. Ind. chpt. Nat. Multiple Sclerosis Soc., 1997—, bd. trustees Ind. chpt., 1999—; mem. mission com. Castleton United Meth. Ch., Indpls., 1993-2000, acolyte coord., mem. worship com., 1998-99, mem. chancel choir, 1999—, chair staff-Parish relations com., 2000—; bd. dirs. Circle Area Comm. Devel. Corp., 2000—, Downtown Area Comm. Devel. Corp., 2000—, Mass. Ave. Comm. Devel. Corp., 2000—, Naval Air Warfare Center Reuse Planning Authority. Recipient Leadership award Nat. Multiple Sclerosis Soc., 1998, Nat. Vol. of Yr. award Nat. Multiple Sclerosis Soc., 1999, Outstanding Vol. award Ind. Ronald McDonald House, 1990; named to Outstanding Young Women in Am., 1981, 87. Mem. ABA, Ind. State Bar Assn., Indpls. Bar Assn. (chair printed forms com. 1987), Phi Delta Phi. Democrat. Avocations: gardening, cross-stitch, reading science fiction, calligraphy. Banking, Contracts commercial, Securities. Office: Federal Home Loan Bank of Indianapolis PO Box 60 Indianapolis IN 46206 E-mail: mkleiman@fhlbi.com

KLEIN, ANDREW MANNING, lawyer; b. New Rochelle, N.Y., Dec. 28, 1941; s. Arthur Manning and Ethelyn (Lappe) K.; m. Christine DeBow, Mar. 14, 1970 (div. Aug. 1990); children: Emily DeBow, Adrienne Manning; m. Mary Manning, Apr. 4, 1992. AB, U. Chgo., 1963, JD, 1966. Bar: N.Y. 1967, D.C. 1980. Assoc. Lovejoy, Wasson, Lundgren & Ashton, N.Y.C., 1966-73; spl. counsel Office of Market Structure, 1973-74, asst. dir. Office of Market Structure and Trading Practices, 1974-75, assoc. dir. Office of Market Structure and Trading Practices, 1975-77, dir. Div. Market Regulation, SEC, Washington, 1977-79; ptnr. Schiff Hardin & Waite, Chgo., 1979-81, Washington, 1981—. Mem. adv. bd. Securities Regulation and Law Report, Bur. Nat. Affairs; contbr. articles to legal jours. With USNG, 1966-67. Mem. ABA (subcom. market regulation, co-chmn. task force on manipulation), Fed. Bar Assn. (exec. coun. securities com.), George Town Club (Washington), University Club (Washington). Administrative and regulatory, General corporate, Securities. Office: Schiff Hardin & Waite 1101 Connecticut Ave NW Ste 600 Washington DC 20036-4390

KLEIN, HARRIET FARBER, judge; b. Elizabeth, N.J., Apr. 30, 1948; d. Melvin Julius and Frances Mildred (Novit) Farber; m. Paul Martin Klein, Sept. 9, 1973; children: Andrew, Zachary. BA with honors, Douglass Coll., New Brunswick, N.J., 1970; JD, Rutgers U., 1973. Bar: N.J. 1973, U.S. Dist. Ct. N.J. 1973. Jud. clk. chancery divsn. Superior Ct. N.J., 1973-74; assoc. Budd, Larner, Kent, Gross, Picillo & Rosenbaum, Newark, 1974-78; ptnr. Greenbaum, Rowe, Smith, Ravin, David & Himmel, Woodbridge, N.J., 1979-98; judge Superior Ct. of N.J., Law Divsn., Essex County, 1998—. Mem. N.J. State Bd. Bar Examiners, 1987-90, reader, 1977-87;

mem. adv. com. on bar admissions N.J. Supreme Ct., 1987-90; mem. Maplewood (N.J.) Juvenile Conf. Com., 1995-98. Mem. ABA, Essex County Bar Assn. (vice-chmn. com. on status of women in law firms 1988-90, vice-chmn. equity jurisprudence com. 1989-90, co-chmn. com. on women in the profession 1990-92), N.J. Bar Assn. (labor and employment law sect., co-chmn. com. on civil and personal rights 1995-98), Order of Barristers, Phi Alpha Theta.

KLEIN, HENRY, lawyer; b. N.Y.C., Oct. 6, 1949; s. Leo Herman and Florence (Silver) K.; m. Ann Laura Hallasey, July 30, 1972; children: Lauren Jennifer, Benjamin Jason. BA, SUNY, Albany, 1971; JD, U. San Diego, 1975. Bar: Calif. 1975, U.S. Ct. Customs and Patent Appeals 1976, U.S. Ct. Appeals (Fed. cir.) 1985, U.S. Dist. Ct. (cen. dist.) Calif. 1986. Trademark atty. U.S. Patent Office, Washington, 1975-77; ptnr. Ladas & Parry, Los Angeles, 1978—. Mem. San Diego Law Rev., 1974-75; editor-in-chief Trademark Soc. Newsletter, 1977. Mem. U. San Diego Civil Legal Clinic, 1974, Civil Rights Research Council, San Diego, 1974, Calif. Pub. Interest Research Group, San Diego, 1975. N.Y. State scholar, 1967-71; Tex. State legal scholar State of Tex., 1972; recipient Am. Jurisprudence award Bancroft-Whitney Co. and Lawyer Co-Op. Pub. Co., Lubbock, Tex., 1972; Patent Trademark Spl. Achievement awards U.S. Dept. Commerce, Washington, 1976, 77. Mem. U.S. Trademark Assn. (v.p. 1976, pres., chmn. 1977), Los Angeles Patent Law Assn., Phi Delta Phi. Republican. Jewish. Patent, Trademark and copyright. Home: 10427 Vivienda St Alta Loma CA 91737-1755 Office: Ladas & Parry 5760 Wilshire Blvd Los Angeles CA 90036-3601

KLEIN, HOWARD BRUCE, lawyer, law educator; b. Pitts., Feb. 28, 1950; s. Elmer and Natalie (Rosenzweig) K.; m. Lonnie Jean Wilets, Dec. 12, 1977; children: Zachary B., Eli H. Student, Northwestern U., 1968-69; BA, U. Wis., 1972; JD, Georgetown U., 1976. Bar: Wis. 1976, Pa. 1981, U.S. Ct. Appeals D.C., 1978, U.S. Dist. Ct. Pa. 1981, U.S. Ct. Appeals (3rd cir.) 1982, U.S. Supreme Ct. 1983. Law clk. to justice Robert Hansen Wis. Supreme Ct., Madison, 1976-77; asst. atty. gen. dept. justice State of Wis., 1977-80; chief criminal divsn. U.S. Atty.'s Office, Phila., 1980-87; ptnr. Blank, Rome & McCauley, 1987-96, chmn. litigation dept., 1991-94; prin. Law Offices of Howard Bruce Klein, 1996—; dir. in house tng. Am. Law Inst.-ABA, 1996—. Regional, nat. instr. Nat. Inst. Trial Advocacy, Phila. and Boulder, Colo., 1987—; lectr. introduction to trial advocacy, evidence Temple U., Phila., 1984—; instr. Atty. Gen. Advocacy Inst., Washington, 1983-87; lectr. pub. corruption and trial advocacy; cons. Pa. Valley Neighborhood Assn., 1984—. Contbr. to profl. jours. Advisor Phila. Police Dept. Reform Commn., 1986—; campaign issues dir. Pa. Atty. Gen. campaign, Phila., 1988, 92; bd. dirs. Citizens Crime Commn. Delaware Valley, Phila. Mem. Fed. Bar Assn. (chmn. criminal law com.), Phila. Bar Assn., Wis. Bar Assn., D.C. Bar Assn., U.S. Attys. Alumni Assn. (co-founder, exec. bd.), Vesper Club (Phila.). Democrat. Jewish. Avocations: swimming, basketball, hiking. E-mial. Federal civil litigation, Criminal. Office: 1700 Market St Ste 2632 Philadelphia PA 19103-3903 E-mail: howbrklein@aol.com

KLEIN, IRVING J. law educator; b. N.Y.C., Nov. 19, 1917; s. Benjamin and Rose (Moses) K.; m. Sylvia Heiser, June 17, 1939 (dec.); children: Linda Klein Diamond, Michael; m. Marta Arias, Feb. 5, 1971. Student U. Mich., 1935-37; BS in Social Sci., CCNY, 1945; JD, Bklyn. Law Sch., 1958. Bar: N.Y. 1958, Fla. 1974, U.S. Dist. Ct. (ea. dist.) N.Y., 1964, U.S. Dist. Ct. (so. dist.) N.Y. 1964, U.S. Dist. Ct. (so. dist.) Fla. 1995, U.S. Ct. Appeals (2d cir.) 1964, U.S. Ct. Appeals (11th cir.) 1996, U.S. Supreme Ct. 1965; cert. cir. ct. of Fla. mediator. From police officer to lt., N.Y.C. Police Dept., 1943-63; asst. dist. atty. Queens County, N.Y.C., 1966-67; from instr. to prof., then prof. emeritus law and police sci. John Jay Coll. Criminal Justice, CUNY, N.Y.C., 1967-91. Author: Law of Evidence for Police, 1973, 2d edit. 1978, Law of Evidence for Criminal Justice Professionals, 1989, 4th edit., 1997, Constitutional Law for Criminal Justice Professionals, 1980, 2d edit., 1986, 3rd edit., 1992, Law of Arrest, Search, Seizure and Liability Issues, 1995. Mem. exec. bd., past. pres. Speech and Hearing Ctr. Queens Coll., N.Y.C., 1959— ; bd. dirs. Roslyn Estates Civic Assn., 1982-84; acting village prosecutor Roslyn Estates, N.Y., 1983-84. Mem. Fla. Bar Assn., Dade County Bar Assn., Am. Acad. for Profl. Law Enforcement, Am. Soc. Criminology. Office: 8261 SW 89th St Miami FL 33156-7331

KLEIN, IRWIN GRANT, lawyer; b. Bklyn., June 6, 1949; s. Melvin Morton and Gladys (Mandel) K.; m. Charlene Elena Perez, July 31, 1988; children: Robert Matthew Perez, Gabriella Margaux Perez. BS, U. Wis., 1971; JD, Vt. Law Sch., 1977. Bar: N.Y., 1977, U.S. Dist. Ct. (so. & ea. dist.) N.Y., 1977, Vt., 1977, U.S. Supreme Ct., 1988. Assoc. atty. Hein, Waters, Klein & Zurkow, Far Rockaway, N.Y., 1977-78; asst. dist. atty. Queens County Dist. Atty., Kew Gardens, 1979-82; ptnr. Hein, Waters & Klein, Cedarhurst, 1982-89, 1991—, Lapp & Klein, Cedarhurst, N.Y., 1989-91. Mem. Vt. Law Rev., N.Y. State Defenders Assn., N.Y. State Bar Assn., Nassau County Bar Assn., Queens County Bar Assn., Phi Delta Phi. General corporate, Criminal, Estate planning. Office: Hein Waters & Klein 123 Grove Ave Cedarhurst NY 11516-2302 E-mail: igkny@earthlink.net

KLEIN, JUDAH BAER, retired lawyer; b. Bklyn., Feb. 9, 1923; s. Kolman Karl and Gladys Ruth (Edelson)) K.; m. Paula Berk, Nov. 8, 1953; 1 child, Caryn Ann. BS, U. Md., 1947; LLB, Bklyn. Law Sch., 1950. Bar: N.Y. 1951, U.S. Dist. Ct. (so. and ea. dists.) N.Y. Ptnr. Klein & Klein, N.Y.C., 1952-58; gen. counsel Paragon Industries Inc., Mineola, N.Y., 1959-70; pvt. practice, 1970-71; asst. chief counsel, sr. v.p. The Title Guarantee Co., N.Y.C., 1972-79; v.p., gen. counsel LTIC Assoc., Inc., 1979-93; ret., 1993. 1st lt. U.S. Army, 1943-46, 51-52. Mem. ABA, Assn. Bar City N.Y., Nassau County Bar Assn., Am. Coll. Real Estate Lawyers, N.Y. State Bar Assn., Masons. Jewish. Insurance, Real property.

KLEIN, LINDA ANN, lawyer; b. N.Y.C., Nov. 7, 1959; d. Gerald Ira Klein and Sandra Florence (Kimmel) Fishman; m. Michael S. Neuren, Sept. 23, 1985. BA cum laude, Union Coll., 1980; JD, Washington & Lee U., 1983. Bar: Ga. 1983, D.C. 1984, U.S. Dist. Ct. (no. and mid. dist.) Ga. 1985, U.S. Ct. Appeals (11th cir.) 1986. Assoc. Nall & Miller, Atlanta, 1983-86, Martin, Cavan & Andersen, Atlanta, 1986-90, ptnr., 1990-93, Gambrell & Stolz, 1993—. Instr. Nat. Ctr. Paralegal Tng., Atlanta, 1986. Mem. ABA (editor Trial Techniques newsletter 1989, vice-chmn. trial techniques com. 1989-90, chair 1991-92, vice chair fidelity and surety com. 1994-97, mem. coun. tort and ins. practice sect. 1998—, chair ann. meeting 1996-97, ho. of dels. 1998—, exec. coun. nat. conf. of bar pres. 1998—, vice chair tort and ins. practice sect. 2001—), State Bar of Ga. (vice chair profl. liability com., chair study com. on rules of practice 1987-94, bd. govs. 1989—, mem. exec. com. 1992-99, sec. 1994-96, pres. 1997-98), Nat. Conf. Bar Pres. (exec. coun. 1998—), Inst. for CLE (chair Ga. br. 1998-2000), Atlanta Bar Assn. (bd. dirs. Atlanta Coun. on Young Lawyers 1986-89, chair commn. on uniform rules of ct. 1986), Coun. of Superior Cts. Judges (ex-officio uniform rules com.), Phi Alpha Delta, Pi Sigma Alpha. General civil litigation, Construction, Personal injury.

KLEIN, MICHAEL D. lawyer; b. Wilkes-Barre, Pa., June 9, 1951; BA magna cum laude, King's Coll., 1973; JD, Dickinson Sch. Law, 1976. Bar: Pa. 1976, U.S. Ct. Appeals (3rd cir.) 1984, U.S. Dist. Ct. (mid. dist.) Pa. 1984, U.S. Dist Ct. (ea. dist.) Pa. 1994. Asst. atty. gen. Commonwealth of Pa., Harrisburg, 1976-82; mgr. corp. affairs, corp. sec. Pa. Am. Water Co., Hershey, 1982-89; ptnr. LeBoeuf, Lamb, Greene & MacRae LLP, Harrisburg, Pa., 1991—. Mem. Pa. Bar Assn., Am. Water Works Assn. Office: LeBoeuf Lamb Greene & MacRae LLP PO Box 12105 Harrisburg PA 17108-2105 E-mail: mklein@llgm.com

KLEIN, PAUL E. lawyer; b. N.Y.C., Apr. 26, 1934; AB, Cornell U., 1956; JD, Harvard U., 1960. Bar: Mich. 1960, Ill. 1965, N.Y. 1967, U.S. Supreme Ct. 1977, U.S. Ct. Appeals (2d cir.) 1980. Atty. Dow Chem. Co., Midland, Mich., 1960-65; assoc. Gunther & Choka, Chgo., 1965-66; atty. Esso Rsch. & Engring. Co., Linden, N.J., 1966-67; sr. mng. editor Matthew Bender & Co., N.Y.C., 1967-72; assoc. gen. counsel N.Y. Life Ins. Co., 1972-80, v.p., assoc. gen. counsel, 1980-84; v.p., counsel Huggins Fin. Svcs., Inc., 1984-86; exec. corp. tax. div. Ernst & Young, 1986-95; pvt. practice White Plains, N.Y., 1995—. Adj. asst. prof. L.I. U., 1972-79, adj. assoc. prof., 1979-80; adj. assoc. prof. acctg. and taxation, Fordham U. at Lincoln Ctr. grad. sch. of bus. adminstrn., 1995—. Former columnist Jour. Real Estate Taxation; writer; editor. Mem. ABA (past chmn. subcom. on life ins. products/ins. cos. com., sect. taxation), Assn. Bar City N.Y. (past chair subcom. on life and health ins. of the com. on ins. law), Assn. Life Ins. Counsel (sec.-treas. 1979-83, bd. govs. 1983-87), N.Y. State Bar Assn. Insurance, Pension, profit-sharing, and employee benefits, Corporate taxation. Office: 58 Midchester Ave White Plains NY 10606-3817 E-mail: pKleinny@earthlink.net, paulklein@excite.com

KLEIN, PETER MARTIN, lawyer, retired transportation company executive; b. N.Y.C., June 2, 1934; s. Saul and Esther (Goldstein) K.; m. Ellen Judith Matlick, June 18, 1961; children: Amy Lynn, Steven Ezra. AB, Columbia U., 1956, JD, 1962. Bar: N.Y. 1962, D.C. 1964, U.S. Supreme Ct. 1966. Asst. proctor Columbia U., 1959-62; asst. counsel Mil. Sea Transp. Svc., Office Gen. Counsel, Dept. Navy, Washington, 1962-65; trial atty. civil div. U.S. Dept. Justice, N.Y.C., 1966-69; gen. atty. Sea-Land Svc., Inc., Menlo Park, N.J., 1969-76, v.p., gen. counsel, sec., 1976-79, Sea-Land Industries, Inc., Menlo Park, 1979-84; assoc. gen. counsel R.J. Reynolds Industries, Inc., Winston-Salem, N.C., 1978-84; sr. v.p., gen. counsel, sec. Sea-Land Svc., Inc. (formerly Sea-Land Corp.), Charlotte, 1984-94, sr. v.p.-law, sec., 1994-95, ret., 1996—. Mem. adv. com. on pvt. internat. law Dept. State, 1974-95; mem. U.S. delegation UN Conf. of Trade and Devel., UN Commn. on Internat. Trade Law, 1975-76, trade regulation adv. bd. Bur. Nat. Affairs, 1986-88; alt. mem. N.Am. coun. London Ct. of Internat. Arbitration, 1988-95. Trustee Jewish Edn. Assn. Met. N.J., 1973-76; trustee Temple B'nai Abraham of Essex County, N.J., 1973—, v.p., 1976-81, pres. 1981-83; mem. Essex County Dems. Com., 1986-88; mem. Livingston Twp. Planning Bd., 1996—, vice chmn. 1997-99, chmn., 2000—. With USN, 1956-59, Antarctica. Mem. ABA, FBA, Am. Maritime Assn. (bd. dirs., chmn. coms. on law and legis. 1974-78), Am. Polar Soc., Navy League U.S. (life), U.S. Naval Inst. (life), N.Y. State Bar Assn., D.C. Bar Assn., Internat. Bar Assn., Maritime Law Assn. Administrative and regulatory, Admiralty, General corporate. Home: 22 Sandalwood Dr Livingston NJ 07039-1409

KLEIN, PETER WILLIAM, lawyer, corporate officer, investment company executive; b. Lorain, Ohio, Sept. 22, 1955; s. Warren Martin Klein and Barbara (Lesser) Pomeroy; m. Jennifer Lynn Ungers, Aug. 3, 1984. Student, U. Sussex, 1975-76; BA, Albion Coll., 1976; JD, Cleve. Marshall Coll. Law, 1981; LLM, NYU, 1982. Bar: Ohio 1981, Ill. 1984. Assoc. Guren, Merritt, Feibel, Sogg & Cohen, Cleve., 1982-84, Siegan, Barbakoff, Gomberg & Gordon, Ltd., Chgo., 1984-86; mng. dir., gen. counsel Trivest Inc., Miami, Fla., 1986-2000; ptnr., gen. counsel Brockway, Moran & Ptnrs., Inc., Boca Raton, 2000—. Mem. ABA (taxation sect., corp. sect., banking and bus. law). General corporate, Securities, Corporate taxation. Home: 3618 Palmetto Ave Miami FL 33133-6221 Office: Brockway Moran & Ptnrs Inc 7th Fl 225 NE Mizner Blvd Fl 7 Boca Raton FL 33432-4078

KLEIN, ROBERT DALE, lawyer; b. Balt., July 29, 1951; s. James Robert and Madeline Margaret (Horak) K.; m. Patricia Kay Purvis, May 6, 1978; children: Morgan Elizabeth, Patrick Jameson, Evan Robert. Student, U. Durham, Eng., 1971-72; BS, MIT, 1973; JD, Columbia U., 1976. Bar: Md. 1976, U.S. Dist. Ct. Md. 1977, U.S. Ct. Appeals (4th cir.) 1978, U.S. Dist. Ct. D.C. 1983, D.C. 1983. Assoc. Piper & Marbury, Balt., 1976-84, ptnr., 1984-87; shareholder Wharton Levin Ehrmantraut Klein & Nash, P.A., 1987—. Mem. Product Liability Adv. Coun., chmn. rules of procedure and practice com., 1991-98, exec. com., 1997-2000; mem. standing com. rules of practice and procedure Ct. Appeals Md. 1994—. Author: Maryland Civil Procedure Forms: Practice, 1984—, annual supplements; editor Def. Line Jour., 1983-84; contbr. articles to profl. jours. Alfred P. Sloan Found. scholar, 1969-73. Mem. ABA, Md. State Bar Assn. (chmn. product liability com. litigaton sect. 1991-95), Balt. Bar Assn. (chmn. com. on long range planning 1986-87, chmn. product liability law com. 1987-88, chmn. spl. com. on video 1983-84, chmn. standing com. on pub. rels. 1984-86), Md. Def. Counsel (bd. dirs. 1984-91, v.p. 1985-86, pres. 1986-87, chmn. product liability law com. 1989-91, chmn. standing com. on the rules of practice and procedure 1992-94), Anne Arundel County Bar Assn., D.C. Bar Assn., Def. Rsch. Inst. (Exceptional Performance award 1987), Chi Phi (sec. Beta chpt.). Roman Catholic. Personal injury, Product liability, Toxic tort. Home: 302 Rugby Cv Arnold MD 21012-2131 Office: Wharton Levin Ehrmantraut Klein & Nash PO Box 551 Annapolis MD 21404-0551 E-mail: rdk@wlekn.com

KLEIN, WILLIAM DAVID, lawyer; b. St. Cloud, Minn., Oct. 30, 1954; s. Wilfred George and Rita Christina (Gottwalt) K.; m. Rebecca Lynn Ready, May 26, 1979; children: Michaela Laine, Caitlin Brianne. BA summa cum laude, St. Olaf Coll., 1976; JD magna cum laude, U. Mich., 1979. Bar: Minn. 1979, U.S. Dist. Ct. Minn. 1979, U.S. Claims Ct. 1983, U.S. Tax Ct. 1985. Law clk. to presiding justice Minn. Supreme Ct., St. Paul, 1979-80; assoc. Gray, Plant, Mooty, Mooty, & Bennett P.A., Mpls., 1980-84, ptnr., 1985—, CFO, 1990-98, chair bus. tax law practice group, 2000—, also bd. dirs. Bd. dirs. Katahdin Inc., chmn. bd., 1992-94. Author: (with others) Case Studies in Tax Planning--Partnerships, 1987, PPC Tax Planning Guide--Partnerships, 1990, S Corporations and Life Insurance, 1992, 2d edit., 1999. Mem.: ABA (chair subcom. revenue rulings, S Corps. com. tax sect. 1996—), Minn. State Bar Assn. (mem. tax coun. 2000—, sec. 2000, treas. 2001), Hennepin County Bar Assn., Mpls. City of Lakes Rotary (bd. dirs. 1999—, pres. Found. 1999—). General corporate, Corporate taxation, Taxation, general. Office: Gray Plant Mooty Mooty & Bennett 33 S 6th St Ste 3400 Minneapolis MN 55402-3796 E-mail: william.klein@gpmlaw.com

KLEINBERG, NORMAN CHARLES, lawyer; b. Phila., July 18, 1946; s. Frank and Mildred Brosnan (Hill) K.; m. Marcia Sue Topperman, Jan. 31, 1971; children: Lauren Blythe, Joanna Leigh. AB, Tufts U., 1968; JD, Columbia U., 1972. Bar: N.Y. 1973, U.S. Supreme Ct., U.S. Ct. Appeals (1st, 2d, 3d and 4th cirs.), U.S. Dist. Ct. (so. and ea. dists.) N.Y., U.S. Tax Ct., U.S. Dist. Ct. (ea. Dist.) Wis., U.S. Dist. Ct. (no. dist.) Calif., U.S. Dist. Ct. (ea. dist.) Mich. Law clk. to judge U.S. Dist. Ct. (so. dist.) N.Y., N.Y.C., 1972-74; assoc. Hughes Hubbard & Reed, 1974-80, ptnr., 1980—. Articles editor Columbia Jour. Law and Social Problems, 1971-72. Served to staff sgt. USAR, 1968-74. Fellow Am. Coll. Trial Lawyers; mem. ABA, Fed. Bar Coun., Assn. Bar of City of N.Y. (com. on state cts. of superior jurisdiction, com. profl. responsibility, com. profl. and jud. ethics., com. on jud., coun. on jud. adminstrn.), Internat. Bar Assn., N.Y. State Bar Assn., Def. Rsch. Inst. Antitrust, General civil litigation, Insurance. Home: 460 E 79th St New York NY 10021-1443 Office: Hughes Hubbard & Reed 1 Battery Park Plz Fl 12 New York NY 10004-1482 E-mail: kleinber@hugheshubbard.com

KLEINBERG, ROBERT IRWIN, lawyer; b. Bronx, N.Y., Sept. 10, 1937; s. Abraham and Lillian (Fox) K.; m. Luise Bitterman, Oct. 27, 1962; children: Andrew, Jeanine. BA, U. Mich., 1958; LLB, Columbia U., 1961. Bar: N.Y. 1962. Mng. dir., gen. counsel Merrill Lynch, Pierce Fenner & Smith, Inc. (subs. Merrill Lynch Capital Mkts. Group), N.Y.C., 1978-80; gen. counsel, exec. v.p. Oppenheimer & Co. Inc., 1980-98, Nat. Fin. Ptnrs. Corp., 1999—. Arbitrator Am. Stock Exch. Mem. ABA, N.Y. State Bar Assn., Nat. Assn. Securities Dealers (arbitrator, dist. com. 12, bd. govs. 1992—, chmn. nat. bus. conduct com. 1993), Securities Industry Assn. (pres. legal and compliance divsn. 1990-91, chmn. bus. com. dist. 10 1991). Home: 1016 5th Ave # 11D New York NY 10028-0132 Office: Oppenheimer & Co Inc Oppenheimer Tower World Fin Ctr New York NY 10281 E-mail: rkleinberg@nfp.com

KLEINFELD, ANDREW J. federal judge; b. 1945; BA magna cum laude, Wesleyan U., 1966; JD cum laude, Harvard U., 1969. Law clk. Alaska Supreme Ct., 1969-71; U.S. magistrate U.S. Dist. Ct. Alaska, Fairbanks, 1971-74; pvt. practice law, 1971-86; judge U.S. Dist. Ct. Alaska, Anchorage, 1986-91, U.S. Ct. Appeals (9th cir.), San Francisco, 1991—. Contbr. articles to profl. jours. Mem. Alaska Bar Assn. (pres. 1982-83, bd. govs. 1981-84), Tanana Valley Bar Assn. (pres. 1974-75), Phi Beta Kappa. Republican. Office: US Ct Appeals 9th Cir Courthouse Sq 250 Cushman St Ste 3-a Fairbanks AK 99701-4665

KLEMANN, GILBERT LACY, II, lawyer; b. New Rochelle, N.Y., July 26, 1950; s. N. Robert and Rosemary Virginia (Gerard) K.; m. Patricia Louise Hild, June 16, 1973; children: Tricia Rosemary, Gilbert Hild. AB, Coll. Holy Cross, 1972; JD, Fordham U., 1975. Bar: N.Y. 1976, U.S. Dist. Ct. (so. and ea. dists.) N.Y. 1976, Conn. 1988, U.S. Supreme Ct. 1991. Assoc. Chadbourne & Parke, N.Y.C., 1975-83, ptnr., 1983-90, of counsel, 2000; sr. v.p., gen. counsel Fortune Brands, Inc. (formerly Am. Brands Inc.), Old Greenwich, Conn., 1991-97, exec. v.p. strategic and legal affairs, 1998, exec. v.p. corp., mem. bd. dirs., 1999; sr. v.p., gen. counsel Avon Products, Inc., N.Y.C., 2001—. Editor Fordham Law Rev., 1974-75. Mem. Conn. Bar Assn., Greenwich (Conn.) Country Club, Nassau Club (Princeton, N.J.), Longboat Key Club (Fla.). Republican. Roman Catholic. Avocation: golf. General corporate, General practice. Home: 25 Hope Farm Rd Greenwich CT 06830-3331 also: 415 L'Ambiance Dr Longboat Key FL 34288 Office: Avon Products Inc 1345 Ave of the Americas New York NY 10105-0196 E-mail: gklemann@law.com

KLEMIN, LAWRENCE R. lawyer; b. New Rockford, N.D., Mar. 31, 1945; s. Lawrence R. Klemin and Carol M. (Cook) Roaldson; m. Rita R. DiPalma, Sept. 2, 1970; children: Laura K., Peter L. BA in English, U. N.D., 1967, JD with distinction, 1978. Bar: N.D. 1978, U.S. Dist. Ct. N.D. 1978, U.S. Ct. Appeals (8th cir.) 1987, U.S. Supreme Ct. 1988. Hearing officer N.D. Employment Security Bur., Bismarck, 1971-75; assoc. Atkinson & Dwyer, 1978-81; ptnr. Atkinson, Dwyer & Klemin, 1981-82, Dwyer & Klemin, Bismarck, 1982-86; pres. Lawrence R. Klemin, P.C., 1986-92, Bucklin & Klemin, P.C., Bismarck, 1992-96, Bucklin, Klemin & McBride, P.C., Bismarck, 1996—. Pres. Title and Escrow Co., Bismarck, 1988-98, Litigation Svcs., Inc., Bismarck, 1995—; state rep. N.D. legis assembly, 1998—; commr. Nat. Conf. of Commrs. on Uniform State Laws, 1999—; mem. state adv. coun. N.D. Office Adminstrv. Hearings, Bismarck, 1993-98; lectr. on real property law Nat. Bus. Inst., 1989—. Author, editor Civil Practice of North Dakota, 1993—. Bd. dirs. N.D. March of Dimes, Bismarck, 1994—; mem. Corpus Christi Parish Coun., Bismarck, 1996—. With U.S. Army, 1967-70, Vietnam. Mem. State Bar Assn. N.D. (chair adminstrv. law com. 1996-98), N.D. Land Title Assn. (legis. com. 1990-99), Bismarck Mandan C. of C. (bd. dirs. 1996-98), Optimist Internat. (bd. dirs. 1985-86), Elks, Eagles, Am. Legion. Roman Catholic. Avocations: antique auto restoration, astronomy, camping. Administrative and regulatory, General civil litigation, Real property. Home: 1709 Montego Dr Bismarck ND 58503-0856 Office: Bucklin Klemin & McBride PC 400 E Broadway #500 PO Box 955 Bismarck ND 58502-0955 E-mail: lklemin@bkmpc.com

KLETT, EDWIN LEE, lawyer; b. Clearfield, Pa., Dec. 8, 1935; s. John L. and Gertrude Elizabeth (Larson) K.; m. Janis Lynn Gibson; children: David, Lauren, Krista, Kirklin, Keenan. BS in Commerce and Finance, Bucknell U., 1957; JD, Dickinson Sch. Law, Carlisle, Pa., 1962. Bar: Pa. 1963, U.S. Dist. Ct. (we. dist.) Pa. 1963, U.S. Dist. Ct. (mid. dist.) Pa. 1995, U.S. Dist. Ct. (ea. dist.) Pa. 2000, U.S. Ct. Appeals (3d cir.) 1967, U.S. Ct. Appeals (6th cir.) 1985, U.S. Supreme Ct. 1983, U.S. Ct. Appeals (11th cir.) 2001. Assoc. Eckert, Seamans, Cherin & Mellott, Pitts., 1962, ptnr., 1969; sr. ptnr., chmn. Klett Rooney Lieber & Schorling P.C., 1989—. Trustee Dickinson Sch. Law, 1982—; mem. civil procedural rules com. Pa. Supreme Ct., 1986-99, vice chair, 1989-92, chair, 1993-99. Mem. Pa. State Transp. Adv. Bd., Harrisburg, Pa., 1985-88, Rep. State Fin. Com., Harrisburg, 1986-91, Allegheny County Rep. Fin. Com., Pitts., 1987-92. Fellow Internat. Acad. Trial Lawyers, Am. Coll. Trial Lawyers (Pa. state com. 1994-99, state chair 1996-98), Am. Bd. Trial Advs., Am. Bar Found., Am. Bar Inst., Pa. Bar Found., Alletheny County Bar Found.; mem. ABA (ho. dels. 1999-2000), Am. Bd. Trial Advs., Acad. Trial Lawyers Allegheny County (bd. govs. 1986-88, pres. 1988—), Am. Judicature Soc., Allegheny County Bar (bd. govs. 1989-92, 99-02, pres. 1999-01). Federal civil litigation, State civil litigation, Securities. Home: 151 Ordale Blvd Pittsburgh PA 15228-1525 Office: Klett Rooney Lieber & Schorling 1 Oxford Ct Fl 40 Pittsburgh PA 15219-1407 E-mail: elklett@klettrooney.com

KLEWANS, SAMUEL N. lawyer; b. Lock Haven, Pa., Mar. 2, 1941; s. Morris and Ruth N. Klewans; children: Richard Bennett, Ruth Elise, Paul Henry, Margo Ilene. AB, U. Pa., 1963; JD, Am. U., 1966. Bar: Va. 1966, U.S. Dist. Ct. (ea. dist.) Va. 1966, U.S. Dist. Ct. D.C. 1967, U.S. Ct. Appeals D.C. 1967, U.S. Ct. Appeals (4th cir.) 1967, U.S. Supreme Ct. 1971. Law clk. U.S. Dist. Ct. (ea. dist.) Va., 1966-67; ptnr. Fried, Fried & Klewans, Springfield, Va., 1970-86; prin. Klewans & Assocs., 1986-91; shareholder, ptnr. Grad, Logan & Klewans, P.C., Alexandria, Va., 1991—. Lectr. No. Va. Inst. Continuing Med. Edn., No. Va. Ctr. Quality and Health Edn. Contbr. articles to profl. jours. 1st lt. JAGC-USAR, 1966-72. General corporate, Health, Corporate taxation. Office: 1421 Prince St Ste 320 Alexandria VA 22314-2805 E-mail: sklew1421@aol.com

KLINE, ALLEN HABER, JR. lawyer; b. Houston, June 17, 1954; s. Allen H. Sr. and Maude Rose (Brown) K.; m. Barbara Ann Byrd, July 24, 1982; children: Allison Ashley, Allen III. BA, U. Denver, 1976; JD, U. Miami, 1979. Bar: Tex. 1980, U.S. Dist. Ct. (so. dist.) Tex. 1980, U.S. Ct. Appeals (5th cir.) 1980, U.S. Ct. Appeals (11th cir.) 1983, U.S. Supreme Ct. 1985; bd. cert. personal injury trial law Tex. Bd. Legal Specialization. Sole practice, Houston, 1980—. Mem. Houston Bar Assn., Coll. of the State Bar of Tex. Club: City Wide (Houston) (life). Avocations: tennis, water, snow skiing. Admiralty, State civil litigation, Personal injury. Office: 440 Louisiana St Ste 2100 Houston TX 77002-4205

KLINE, ARLENE KARIN, lawyer; b. Fort Lauderdale, Fla., Sept. 7, 1972; d. Marvin L. and Trudy L. Lessne; m. Andrew Scott Kline, Dec. 21, 1997. BA, Fla. State U., 1994; JD, Nova Southeastern U., 1996. Bar: Fla. 1997, U.S. Dist. Ct. (so. dist.) Fla. 1997. Title ins. processor Capitol Abstract and Title, Coral Springs, Fla., 1991, Hillsboro Beach Title, Deerfield Beach, 1992; asst. editor Lifetime Books, Inc., Hollywood, 1994, 95; law clk. Broward County Courthouse, Fort Lauderdale, 1996; assoc. Barry M. Silver, P.A., Boca Raton, Fla., 1997-98, Jennifer L. Augspurger P.A., Boca Raton, 1998-2000, Proskauen Rose LLP, Boca Raton, 2000—. Atty. Advocacy Ctr., Hollywood, Fla., 1997; spkr. King's Point Dem. Club, Delray Beach, Fla., 1997; campaign vol. Jack Tobin State Rep., Margate, Fla., 1996. Goodwin fellowship Nova Southeastern U., 1995-96; recipient Courage for Women award NOW, 1997. Mem. Palm Beach County Bar Assn. Democrat. Jewish. Avocations: saltwater aquariums, scuba diving, miniature dollhouses. Federal civil litigation, State civil litigation, General corporate. Office: 2255 Glades Rd Suite 340 West Boca Raton FL 33431

KLINE, JAMES EDWARD, lawyer; b. Fremont, Ohio, Aug. 3, 1941; s. Walter J. and Sophia Kline; m. Mary Ann Bruening, Aug. 29, 1964; children: Laura Anne Kline, Matthew Thomas, Jennifer Sue. BS in Social Sci., John Carroll U., 1963; JD, Ohio State U., 1966; postgrad., Stanford U., 1991. Bar: Ohio, 1966, N.C., 1989, U.S. Tax. Ct., 1983. Assoc. Eastman, Stichter, Smith & Bergman, Toledo, 1966-70; ptnr. Eastman, Stichter, Smith & Bergman (name now Eastman & Smith), 1970-84, Shumaker, Loop & Kendrick, Toledo, 1984-88; v.p., gen. counsel Aeroquip-Vickers, Inc. (formerly Trinova Corp.), 1989-99; exec. v.p. Cavista Corp., 2000—; pres., CEO Cavalear Corp., Sylvania, Ohio, 2000—. Corp. sec. Sheller-Globe Corp., 1977-84; adj. prof. U. Toledo Coll. Law, 1988-94; bd. dirs. Plastic Techs., Inc. Author: (with Robert Seaver) Ohio Corporation Law, 1988. Trustee Kidney Found. of Northwestern Ohio, Inc., 1972-81, pres., 1979-80; bd. dirs. Toledo Botanical Garden (formerly Crosby Gardens), 1974-80, pres., 1977-79; bd. dirs. Toledo Zool. Soc., 1983-96, 99—, pres., 1991-93; bd. dirs. Toledo Area Regional Transit Authority, 1984-90, pres., 1987-88; bd. dirs. Home Away From Home, Inc. (Ronald McDonald House NW Ohio), 1983-88; trustee Toledo Symphony Orch., 1981—, St. John's H.S., 1988-91, Ohio Found. Ind. Colls., 1991-2000; trustee Lourdes Coll., 1988-96, chmn., 1994-96. Fellow Ohio Bar Found.; mem. ABA, Nat. Assn. Corp. Dirs., Ohio Bar Assn. (corp. law com. 1977—, chmn. 1983-86), Toledo Bar Assn., Mfrs. Alliance (chair Law Coun. II 1997-99), Toledo Area C. of C. (trustee 1994—, chmn. 2000-01), Inverness Club, Toledo Club (trustee 1990-97), Stone Oak Country Club, Ottawa Skeet Club, Answer Club. Roman Catholic. General corporate, Securities, Corporate taxation. Home: 216 Treetop Pl Holland OH 43528-8451 Office: Cauista Corp 6444 Monroe St Sylvania OH 43560-1430 E-mail: jkline216@aol.com

KLINE, LOWRY F. lawyer; Sr. v.p., gen. counsel Coca-Cola Enterprises, Atlanta, 1996-97, exec. v.p., gen. counsel, 1997-99, exec. v.p., chief adminstrv. officer, 1999-2001, elected to bd., vice chmn., 2000—, vice chmn., CEO, 2001—. Office: Coca-Cola Enterprises 2500 Windy Ridge Pkwy SE Atlanta GA 30339-5677

KLINE, NORMAN DOUGLAS, federal judge; b. Lynn, Mass., Dec. 28, 1930; s. Samuel and Ida (Luff) K.; m. Betty Toba Feldman, Feb. 27, 1966; children: Sarah, Samuel. AB, Harvard Coll., 1952, postgrad., 1952-53; JD, Boston U., 1959. Bar: Mass. 1959. Pvt. practice, Boston, 1959-60; atty. U.S. Dept. Army, Cleve., 1960; trial atty. FMC, Washington, 1960-72, adminstrv. law judge, 1972-92, chief adminstrv. law judge, 1992—. With U.S. Army, 1953-55. Mem. Fed. Adminstrv. Law Judges Conf. Avocations: classical music, collecting CDs. Office: Fed Maritime Commn 800 N Capitol St NW Washington DC 20573-0001 E-mail: normank@fmc.gov

KLINE, SIDNEY DELONG, JR. lawyer; b. West Reading, Pa., Mar. 25, 1932; s. Sidney D. and Leona Clarice (Barkalow) K.; m. Barbara Phyllis James, Dec. 31, 1955; children: Allison S. McCanney, Leslie S. Davidson, Lisa P. Gallen. BA, Dickinson Coll., 1954, LLD, 1998; JD with honors, The Dickinson Law Sch., 1956, LLD, 1994. Bar: Pa. 1956, U.S. Dist. Ct. (ea. dist.) Pa. 1961, U.S. Supreme Ct. 1967. Assoc. Stevens & Lee, Reading, Pa., 1958-62, ptnr., shareholder, 1963-97, pres., 1977-93, chmn., 1993-97, counsel, 1998—. Bd. dirs. Reading Eagle Co. Pres., United Way of Berks County, Reading, 1972-74, campaign chmn., 1986; bd. dirs. Reading Ctr. City Devel. Fund, 1976-98, pres., 1992-97; trustee Dickinson Sch. Law, 1978—, sec., 1988—; trustee Dickinson Coll., 1979—, chmn., 1990-98; bd. dirs. Greater Berks Devel. Fund, 1998—. Served with U.S. Army, 1956-58. Recipient Doran award United Way Berks County, 1978, Richard J. Caron Cmty. Svc. award Caron Found., 1993, Thun Cmty. Svc. award, 1995. Fellow Am. Coll. Trust and Estate Coun., Nat. Soc. Fund Raising Execs. (Outstanding Vol. Fund Raiser Greater Northeastern Pa. chpt. 1992), Pa. Bar Assn., Berks County Bar Assn., Berkshire Country Club (Reading), Moselem Springs Golf Club (Fleetwood, Pa.), The Club at Pelican Bay (Naples, Fla.). Republican. Lutheran. Banking, Probate, Real property. Office: PO Box 679 111 N 6th St Reading PA 19603-0679 E-mail: sdk@stevenslae.com

KLINE, TIMOTHY DEAL, lawyer; b. Oklahoma City, July 16, 1949; s. David Adam and Ruthela (Deal) K.; m. Alyssa Lipp Krysler, Aug. 29, 1985. BA, U. Okla., 1971, JD, 1976. Bar: Okla. 1976, U.S. Dist. Ct. (we. dist.) Okla. 1977, U.S. Ct. Appeals (10th cir.) 1977; cert. in bus. bankruptcy law and consumer bankruptcy Am. Bankruptcy Bd. of Certification. Law clk. to presiding justice U.S. Dist. Ct. (we. dist.) Okla., Oklahoma City, 1976-80; assoc. Linn, Helms, Kirk & Burkett, 1980-83; ptnr. Kline & Kline, 1983—. Adj. prof. law Oklahoma City U., 1980-84, 90. Mem. Am. Coll. Bankruptcy, Okla. County Bar Assn. (pres. 1998-99), Phi Delta Phi. Democrat. Bankruptcy. Office: Kline & Kline 720 NE 63rd St Oklahoma City OK 73105-6405 E-mail: tkline@klinefirm.org

KLINEDINST, JOHN DAVID, lawyer; b. Washington, Jan. 20, 1950; s. David Moulson and Mary Stewart (Coxe) K.; m. Cynthia Lynn DuBain, Aug. 15, 1981. BA cum laude in History, Washington and Lee U., 1971, JD, 1978; MBA in Fin. and Investments, George Washington U., 1975. Bar: Calif. 1979, U.S. Dist. Ct. (so. dist.) Calif. 1979, U.S. Ct. Appeals (9th cir.) 1987. With comml. lending dept. 1st Nat. Bank Md., Montgomery County, 1971-74; assoc. Ludecke, McGrath & Denton, San Diego, 1979-80; ptnr. Whitney & Klinedinst, 1980-83, Klinedinst & Meiser, San Diego, 1983-86; mng. ptnr. Klinedinst, Fliehman & McKillop, 1986—. Mem. law coun. Washington and Lee U., 1993-97, vice chmn. law campaign, 1991-94, bd. trustees, 2001—; vice chmn. bd. dirs. ARC of San Diego/Imperial, 1991-97; pres. House Corp. Calif. Lamda, Phi Kappa Psi, 1999—. Recipient Disting. Alumnus award Washington and Lee U., 1993. Mem. ABA, Calif. Bar Assn., San Diego Bar Assn., San Diego Def. Lawyers, Washington Soc. (bd. dirs. 1997—), Washington and Lee U. Alumni Assn. (bd. dirs. 1986-90, pres. 1989-90), Washington and Lee U. Club (pres. San Diego chpt. 1980-87), La Jolla Beach and Tennis Club, Fairbanks Ranch Country Club, Phi Kappa Psi. Republican. Episcopalian. Federal civil litigation, State civil litigation. Home: 6226 Via Dos Valles Rancho Santa Fe CA 92067-9999 Office: Klinedinst Fliehman & McKillop 501 W Broadway Ste 600 San Diego CA 92101-3584 E-mail: jdk@kfmlaw.com

KLINEFELTER, JAMES LOUIS, lawyer; b. L.A., Oct. 8, 1925; s. Theron Albert and Anna Marie (Coffey) K.; m. Joanne Wright, Dec. 26, 1957 (div.); children: Patricia Anne, Jeanne Marie, Christopher Wright; m. Mary Lynn S. Klinefelter, Aug. 19, 1971; 1 child, Mary Katherine. BA, U. Ala., 1949, LLB, 1951. Bar: Ala. 1951, U.S. Dist. Ct. (no. dist.) Ala. 1959, U.S. Ct. Appeals (11th cir.) 1983. Regional claims rep. State Farm Mut. Auto Ins. Co., Anniston, Ala., 1951-54; ptnr. Burnham & Klinefelter, 1954—. Mem. adv. com. Supreme Ct. Ala. Mem. Ala. Dem. Exec. Com., 1964—, chmn. legis. rev. com., 1964—; past chmn. Calhoun County Dem. Exec. Com., 1964—; mem. Anniston City Sch. Bd. Lt. (j.g.) USNR, 1943-46. Mem. ABA, Assn. Def. Trial Attys., Ala. Bar Assn. (mem. task force on jud. selection, mem. long-range planning task force), Calhoun County Bar Assn., Ala. Def. Lawyers Assn. (past pres.), Ala. Law Inst. (bd. dirs.), Ala. Sch. Bd. Attys. (past pres.), Internat. Assn. Def. Counsel, Kiwanis (past pres.), Anniston Country Club, Phi Kappa Sigma, Phi Alpha Theta. Avocations: tennis, swimming, reading. General civil litigation, Education and schools, Insurance. Home: 1412 Christine Ave Anniston AL 36207-3924 Office: Burnham & Klinefelter So Trust Nat Bank Bldg PO Box 1618 Anniston AL 36202-1618 E-mail: jlkbkpc@bellsouth.net

KLINGLE, PHILIP ANTHONY, law librarian; b. Bklyn., July 24, 1950; s. Lorin Russell and Therese Margaret (Meehan) K.; m. Rachelle Phyllis Miller, Nov. 20, 1977; children: David Adam, Michael Matthew, Anne Elizabeth. BA, Fordham U., 1971; MA, NYU, 1973; MS, Columbia U., 1976. Asst. reference libr. N.Y. Hist. Soc., N.Y.C., 1973-77; libr. Bklyn. Pub. Libr., 1977-78; reference libr., asst. prof. John Jay Coll. Criminal Justice CUNY, 1978-81; libr. Inst. Jud. Adminstrn. Sch. of Law NYU, 1981-82; sr. law libr. ct. libr. N.Y. State Supreme Ct., S.I., 1982—. Editor: jour. The Literature of Criminal Justice, 1980-81, IJA Report, 1981-82. Mem. ALA, Am. Assn. Law Librs., Law Libr. Assn. Greater N.Y., Libr. Assn. CUNY (mem. exec. coun. 1978-81). Office: NY State Supreme Ct Libr Richmond County Courthouse Staten Island NY 10301

KLIPSTEIN, ROBERT ALAN, lawyer; b. N.Y.C., Sept. 23, 1936; s. Harold David and Hyacinth (Levin) K. AB, Columbia U., 1957, JD, 1960; LLM in Taxation, NYU, 1965. Bar: N.Y. 1960, U.S. Supreme Ct. 1964. Practice of law Saxe Bacon & O'Shea, N.Y.C., 1961—, assoc., 1961, Rosenman, Colin, Kaye, Petschek & Freund, 1962-63; law sec. to justice N.Y. County Supreme Ct., 1963-64; assoc. Bernays & Eisner, 1965-70; ptnr. Eisner, Klipstein & Klipstein, 1971-77, Danziger, Bangser, Klipstein, Goldsmith, Greenwald & Weiss (now Bangser Klein Rocca & Blum), N.Y.C., 1977-92; counsel Sullivan & Donovan, 1992—; arbitrator City of N.Y. Small Claims Ct., 1971—. Arbitrator City of N.Y. Small Claims Ct., 1971—. With U.S. Army, 1960-62. Mem. ABA, N.Y. State Bar Assn., Assn. Bar City of N.Y., N.Y. County Lawyers Assn., Am. Immigration Lawyers Assn., Westchester County Bar Assn., Am. Judges Assn., Univ. Glee Club (N.Y.C.), Phi Alpha Delta. Immigration, naturalization, and customs, Probate, Estate taxation. Home: 401 E 74th St Apt 6G New York NY 10021-3931 Office: Sullivan & Donovan LLP 415 Madison Ave New York NY 10017-1111 E-mail: raklip@aol.com

KLOBASA, JOHN ANTHONY, lawyer; b. St. Louis, Feb. 15, 1951; s. Alan R. and Virginia (Yager) K. BA in Econs., Emory U., 1972; JD, Wash. U., 1975. Bar: Mo. 1975, U.S. Dist. Ct. (ea. dist.) Mo. 1975, U.S. Ct. Appeals (8th cir.) 1976, U.S. Supreme Ct. 1979, U.S. Tax Ct. 1981, U.S. Ct. Appeals (9th cir.) 1990, U.S. Ct. Appeals (10th cir.) 1993. Assoc. Kohn, Shands, Elbert, Gianoulakis & Gilium, St. Louis, 1975-80; ptnr. Kohn, Shands, Elbert, Gianoulakis & Giljum, 1981—. Spl. counsel City of Town and Country, Mo., 1987; spl. counsel City of Des Peres, Mo., 1987, alderman, 1989-91. Mem. ABA, Mo. Bar Assn., Met. St. Louis Bar Assn., Order of Coif, Phi Beta Kappa. Republican. General civil litigation, Family and matrimonial, Probate. Office: Kohn Shands Elbert Gianoulakis & Giljum LLP 1 FirStar Plz Ste 2410 Saint Louis MO 63101-1643 E-mail: jklobasa@ksegg.com

KLODOWSKI, HARRY FRANCIS, JR. lawyer; b. Pitts., June 18, 1954; s. Harry F. and Nancy (Coll) K.; m. Amy Martha Auslander, Nov. 12, 1983; children: Deborah, Daniel. BA, SUNY, Buffalo, 1976, JD, 1979. Bar: Pa. 1979, U.S. Dist. Ct. (we. dist.) Pa. 1979, U.S. Tax Ct. 1979, U.S. Ct. Appeals (3d cir.) 1979. Assoc., then ptnr. Berkman, Ruslander, Pohl, Lieber & Engel, Pitts., 1979-88; prin. Doepken, Keevican & Weiss, P.C., 1988-93, Picadio McCall Kane & Norton, Pitts., 1993-94; pvt. practice, 1994—. Assoc. editor Pitts. Legal Jour., 1979—; contbr. articles to profl. jours. Mem. ABA, Pa. Bar Assn., Allegheny County Bar Assn. (chmn. environ. law sect. 1997), Environ. Law Inst. (assoc.), Air and Waste Mgmt. Assn. (chmn. pub. info. com. 1996—), Rivers Club. Avocations: skiing, racquetball. Administrative and regulatory, General civil litigation, Environmental. Home: 615 Sandy Hill Rd Valencia PA 16059-2731 Office: 330 Grant St Ste 3321 Pittsburgh PA 15219-2202 E-mail: harry@klodowskiilaw.com

KLOESS, LAWRENCE HERMAN, JR. retired lawyer; b. Mamaroneck, N.Y., Jan. 30, 1927; s. Lawrence H. and Harriette Adelia (Holly) K.; m. Eugenia Ann Underwood, Nov. 10, 1931; children: Lawrence H. III, Price Mentzel, Branch Donelson, David Holly. AB, U. Ala., 1954, JD, 1956; grad., Air Command & Staff Coll., 1974, Air War Coll., 1976; grad. Indsl. Coll. of the Armed Forces, Nat. Def. U., 1977. Bar: Ala. 1956, U.S. dist. Ct. (no. dist.) Ala. 1956, U.S. Ct. Appeals (5th cir.) 1957, U.S. Ct. Mil. Appeals 1971, U.S. Supreme Ct. 1971, U.S. Ct. Appeals (11th cir.) 1981. Sole practice, Birmingham, Ala., 1956-60, 62-66; corp. counsel Bankers Fire and Marine Ins. Co., 1961-62; dist. counsel for Ala. Office Dist. Counsel U.S. Dept. Vets. Affairs, Montgomery, 1966-95. Contbr. articles on law to profl. jours. Vice chmn. Salvation Army adv. bd., 1981, mem. bd., 1978-81; mem. nat. conf. bar pres.'s ABA, 1981—; mem. adminstrn. bd. Frazer Meml. United Meth. Ch., 1987-90, 92—; mem. adv. coun. Ret. and Sr. Vol. Program, Montgomery, 1997—; mem. Montgomery Symphony League, 2000—. Col. Judge Adv. Gen. USAFR, 1954-86, ret. Bd. dirs., sec. Air Force Judge Adv. Gen. Sch. Found., 1996—. Decorated Legion of Merit, Meritorious Svc. medal with oak leaf cluster, USAF Commendation medal; named Outstanding Judge Advocate USAFR, 1977, 79. Mem.: ABA (pres. nat. conf. bar 1981—), Ala. State Bar Assn. (chmn. editl. adv. bd. Ala. Lawyer 1975—79, editl. bd. 1970—82, character and fitness com., chmn. law day com. 1973, chmn.citizen edn. com. 1974, mem. adv. com. CLE 1983), Ala. Law Found. (trustee), Montgomery County Bar Assn. (chmn. law day com. 1972, chmn.state bar liason com. 1975, chmn. bd. dirs. 1977, bd. dirs. 1979, chmn. and editor Montgomery County Bar Jour. (ABA Merit award) 1979—80, v.p. 1980, pres. 1981), Fed. Bar Assn. (pres. Montgomery chpt. 1973), Ala. Spl. Camp for Children and Adults (bd. dirs. 1999), Wynlakes Residential Homeowners Assn. (bd. dirs), English Speaking Union (bd. dirs. 1997), Svc. Corps of Ret. Execs. Assn. (bd. dirs. 1996—), Citizens Conf. on Ala. Ct. (exec. com., sponsor new jud. article to state constitution 1973), Citizens Conf. on Criminal and Juvenile Justice (staff mem. 1974), Farrah Law Soc., Res. Officers Assn. of U.S. (chpt. pres. 1978, state pres. 1982), Mystic Soc. (krews of phantom host), Blue-Gray Cols. Assn., The Club, Inc Birmingham, Montgomery Country Club, Capital City Club, Maxwell-Gunter Officers, Montgomery, Air Force Ret. Judge Advocate Assn., Ret. Officers Assn. (life)), Air War Coll. Alumni Assn. (life)), Montgomery Capital Rotary Club (pres. 1979, Paul Harris fellow), Montgomery Rotary Club (v.p. 1996, pres. 1998), Hon. Order Ky. Cols., Sigma Delta Kappa (pres. U. Ala. chpt.), Theta Chi (Outstanding Alumni award 1976). Republican. Home: 7157 Pinecrest Dr Montgomery AL 36117-7413 E-mail: kloess2@aol.com

KLOPPENBERG, LISA A. law educator; b. L.A., Feb. 27, 1962; d. Edwin Francis and Angeline Stella K.; m. Mark Robert Zunich, Apr. 8, 1989; children: Nicholas Steven, Timothy Sean, Kellen Sun-Hee. Diploma (hon.), U.. Kent, Canterbury, Eng., 1983; BA magna cum laude, U. So. Calif., 1984, JD, 1987. Bar: Calif. 1987, DC 1988. Editor-in-chief So. Calif. Law Rev., L.A., 1986-87; law clk. to Hon. Dorothy Nelson U.S. Ct. Appeals (9th cir.), Pasadena, Calif., 1987-88; assoc. Kaye, Scholer, Fierman, Hays & Handler, Washington, 1988-92; law prof. U. Oreg., Eugene, 1992—. Vis. prof. U. San Diego, Trinity Coll., Dublin, Magdalen Coll., Oxford, Eng.; mem. local rules com. U.S. Dist. Ct., Oreg., 1995—. Author: Oregon Rules of Civil Procedure: 1994 Handbook, Oregon Rules of Civil Procedure: 1995-96 Handbook, Oregon Rules of Civil Procedure: 1997-98 Handbook, Oregon Rules of Civil Procedure: 1999-2000 Handbook; contbr. articles, revs. to profl. jours. Bd. dirs. Amigos de los Sobrevivientes, Eugene, 1993-96, Relief Nursery, Eugene, 1999—; pro bono lawyer Guatemalan Human Rights Commn. USA, Washington, 1990-92. Mem. ABA (site evaluator), Am. Judicature Soc., Lane County Bar Assn. (bd. dirs. 1999—), Eugene Inn of Ct. (sec. 1998—), Order of the Coif. Democrat. Roman Catholic. Office: U Oreg Sch Law 1515 Agate St Eugene OR 97403-1919

KLOSK, IRA DAVID, lawyer; b. N.Y.C., Nov. 9, 1932; s. Isidore and Freda (Braunstein) K. B.A., CCNY, 1955; LL.B., Bklyn. Law Sch., 1957. Bar: N.Y. 1958. Sole practice, Bklyn., 1958-81; sr. ptnr. firm Klosk and Ray, Mineola, N.Y., 1981— . Pres. Herricks Citizens Com. Better Schs., N.Y., 1970; mem. Herricks Citizens Budget Adv. Com., 1970, Herricks Sch. Bd., 1971-74; v.p. Hometown Party Mineola, 1979. N.Y. State scholar CCNY, 1951; recipient Richard R. Bowker Meml. award CCNY, 1954, Kupferman-Helm award, 1955. Hon. life mem. N.Y. PTA. Consumer commercial, General corporate.

KLOSOWSKI, THOMAS KENNETH, lawyer; b. Little Falls, Minn., June 22, 1961; s. Melvin and Jacqueline Klosowski. BA summa cum laude, St. Cloud (Minn.) State U., 1983; JD cum laude, U. Minn., 1986. Bar: Minn. 1986, U.S. Dist. Ct. Minn. 1986, U.S. Ct. Appeals (8th cir.) 1987, U.S. Dist. Ct. Colo. 1998. Assoc. Dorsey & Whitney, Mpls., 1986-89; assoc., then ptnr. Cosgrove, Flynn & Gaskins, 1989—. Course dir. Minn. State Bar Assn. product liability courses, 1997; mem. faculty product liability ABA, Boston, 1998. Author: Expert Witneses, Bench and Bar of Minnesota, 1997. Bd. dirs. Playwright's Ctr., Mpls., 1998—. Mem. ABA, Minn. State Bar Assn., Def. Rsch. Inst. Avocations: downhill skiing, hunting. General civil litigation, Product liability. Office: Cosgrove Flynn & Gaskins 2900 333 S 7th St Minneapolis MN 55402

KLOTT, DAVID LEE, lawyer; b. Vicksburg, Miss., Dec. 10, 1941; s. Isadore and Dorothy (Lipson) K.; m. Maren J. Randrup, May 25, 1975. BBA summa cum laude, Northwestern U., 1963; JD cum laude, Harvard U., 1966. Bar: Calif. 1966, U.S. Ct. Claims. 1968, U.S. Supreme Ct. 1971, U.S. Tax Ct. 1973, U.S. Ct. Appeals (Fed. cir.) 1982. Ptnr. Pillsbury Winthrop, San Francisco, 1966—. Tax adv. group to sub-chpt. C J and K, Am. Law Inst.; tchr. Calif. Continuing Edn. of Bar, Practising Law Inst., Hastings Law Sch., San Francisco; bd. dirs., counsel Marin Wine and Food Soc.; exec. v.p., sec. Global Ctr. Inc., 2000-01; vice-chmn. HL Ventures, LLC, 2000—. Commentator Calif. Nonprofit Corp. Law; bd. dirs. Joan Shorenstein Barone Found. for Harvard, The Phyllis J. Shorenstein Fund for the Asian Art Mus. San Francisco; counsel Drum Found. Mem. ABA (tax exempt fin. com.), Calif. State Bar Assn. (tax sect.), San Francisco Bar Assn., Am.-Korean Taekwondo Friendship Assn. (1st dan-black belt), Harvard Club, Northwestern Club, Olympic Club, City Club San Francisco (founding mem.), Bay Club (charter mem.), Harbor Point Racquet and Beach Club, Internat. Wine and Food Soc. (bd. dirs., exec. com., bd. govs. Ams.), Beta Gamma Sigma, Beta Alpha Psi (pres. local chpt.). Corporate taxation. Office: Pillsbury Winthrop 50 Fremont St San Francisco CA 94105-2230

KLOWDEN, MICHAEL LOUIS, lawyer; b. Chgo., Apr. 7, 1945; s. Roy and Esther (Siegel) K.; m. Patricia A. Doede, June 15, 1968; children: Kevin B., Deborah C. AB, U. Chgo., 1967; JD, Harvard U., 1970. Bar: Calif. 1971. From assoc. to ptnr. Mitchell, Silberberg & Knupp, L.A., 1970-78; mng. ptnr. Morgan, Lewis & Bockius, 1978-95; vice chmn. Jefferies Group, Inc. and Jefferies Co., Inc., 1995-96, pres., COO, 1996-2000, vice chmn., 2000—. Bd. dirs. Jefferies Group, Inc., L.A. Trustee U. Chgo., 1986—. General corporate, Real property, Securities. Office: Jefferies Group Inc 11100 Santa Monica Blvd Los Angeles CA 90025-3384 E-mail: mklowden@jefco.com

KMIEC, DOUGLAS WILLIAM, law educator, columnist; b. Chgo., Sept. 24, 1951; s. Walter and Beatrice (Neumann) K.; m. Carolyn Keenan, June 2, 1973; children: Keenan, Katherine, Kiley, Kolleen, Kloe. BA, Northwestern U., 1973; JD, U. So. Calif., L.A., 1976. Bar: Ill. 1976, Calif. 1980, U.S. Supreme Ct. 1986. Assoc. Vedder, Price, et al, Chgo., 1976-78; prof. law Valparaiso U., Ind., 1978-80, Notre Dame U., 1980-99; Caruso family chair in constitutional law Pepperdine U., 1999-01; dean, St. Thomas More prof. Cath. U., Washington, 2001—. Dir. Thomas J. White Ctr. on Law and Govt., 1983-88; dep. asst., atty. gen. Office of Legal Counsel, Dept. Justice, Washington, 1985-87; asst. atty. gen., 1988-89; vis. scholar Stanford U., 1985; spl. asst. to sec. HUD, Washington, 1982-83; disting. chair Dorothy & Leonard Straus, Pepperdine U. Sch. Law, 1995-96, 97-98; mem. pres.'s Commn. on Manufactured Housing, Washington, 1984-85, 89-92; mem. adv. com. Civil Rights Commn., bd. trustees Housing Allowance Program, Ind., 1983-85; state chmn. Scholars for Reagan and Bush, Ind., 1984. Author: Recharting Criminal Procedure, 1984, Zoning and Planning Desk Book, 1986, The Attorney General's Lawyer, 1992, Cease-fire on the Family, 1995, (with Stephen B. Presser) The American Constitutional Order, 1998, Individual Rights and the American Constitution, 1998, The History, Philosophy and Structure of the American Constitution, 1998; host, exec. prodr. Forefront TV series WNIT-TV, 1984-85; radio commentator The American Family Perspective, 1994-96; columnist Chgo. Tribune, 1996-99. Recipient Clark Boardman prize, 1983, 87, 90, Disting. Svc. award HUD, 1983, Disting. Svc. award Dept. Justice, 1987, Edmund J. Randolph award Dept. Justice, 1989; White House fellow, Washington, 1982-83, 40th Anniversary Fulbright Disting. fellow, 1987. Mem. U.S. Supreme Ct. Bar, Ill. Bar Assn., Calif. Bar Assn., Notre Dame Club (Washington). Republican. Roman Catholic. Office: Cath U Sch of Law Washington DC 20064

KMIOTEK-WELSH, JACQUELINE, lawyer; b. Bklyn., Dec. 31, 1959; d. Casimir Edward and Anna Catherine Kmiotek; m. James Winfield Welsh III. BA, St. John's U., N.Y.C., 1981, JD, 1983; MBA, NYU, 1991. Bar: N.Y. 1984, U.S. Dist. Ct. (so. and ea. dists.) N.Y. 1984, U.S. Dist. Ct. (we. dist.) N.Y. 1992, U.S. Supreme Ct. 1989. Asst. counsel N.Y. Job Devel. Auth., 1984-85; assoc. Squadron, Ellenoff, Pleasant & Lehrer, N.Y.C., 1985; assoc. atty. N.Y. Power Authority, 1985-86, atty., 1986-90, sr. atty., 1990-99; prin., 1999—. Fellow N.Y. Bar Found., N.Y. State Bar Assn. (mem. Ho. of Dels. 1993-96, exec. com. young lawyers sect. 1993-97, pub. utility law com. 1994—, chair young lawyers sect., com. profl. svc. project on women subcom. 1994-96, chair young lawyers sect. com. on pub. svcs. and pro-bono project on disaster legal assistance 1994-95, mem. 1995-96, mem. com. 1995—, mem. internat. law and practice sect. com. on U.S.-Can. law 1994—, young lawyer divsn. pub. utility law com.), Am. Bar Found., young Lawyers Divsn.; mem. ABA (fellow young lawyers divsn., liaison pub. contract law sect. 1988-90, exec. com. 1988-89, vice-chmn. 1989-91, chmn. 1991—, young lawyers divsn. pub. utility law com., internat. law exec. com. 1989-91, mem. govt. lawyers exec. com. 1990-91, liaison coord. group on energy law 1990-92, coord. group energy law 1992-95, mem. com. sect. of real property, probate & trust law 1995-97, liaison ABA Jour. 1992-95, mem. Ho. of Dels. 1993-96, vice chair bylaws com. govt. and pub. sector lawyer's divsn. 1993-95, vice chmn. young lawyer divn. publs. com. 1995-96, vice chair women in the profession com. 1994-95, judge awards of achievement com. 1992-95, mem. exec. coun. young lawyer's divsn. 1993-95, 4th dist. rep., mem. membership com. sect. real property probate trust law, 1995-96, liaison, 1995-97, vice chair publ. com. 1995-96, mem. editl. bd. sect. pub. utility comm. transp. law 1996—), Fed. Energy Bar Assn., Phi Alpha Delta. Office: NY Power Authority 1633 Broadway New York NY 10019-6708

KNAB, KAREN MARKLE, lawyer; d. Joseph George and Mary (Kelly) Markle. BA, St. Marys Coll., South Bend, Ind., 1970; JD, U. Chgo., 1975. Bar: Ill. 1975, U.S. Dist. Ct. (no. dist.) Ill. 1981, U.S. Ct. Appeals (7th cir.) 1981. Dep. dir. state cts. Wis. Supreme Ct., Madison, 1977-80; dep. dir. Dept. Revenue, State of Ill., Chgo., 1980-81; dir. family divsn. D.C. Superior Ct., Washington, 1981-84; dir. adminstrn. Pepper, Hamilton & Scheetz, 1984-86, chief adminstrv. officer Phila., 1988-2000; chief oper. officer Shaw Pittman, Washington, 2000—. Cir. exec. U.S. Ct. Appeals

(D.C.) Cir., 1986-88; pres., cons. Knab Assocs., Chgo., 1980-81. Author: Courts of Limited Jurisdiction, 1977, Alternatives to Litigation, 1978; contbr. articles to profl. jours. Mem. Nat. Assn. Trial Ct. Adminstrs., Assn. Legal Adminstrs. Office: Shaw Pittman 2300 N St NW Washington DC 20036 E-mail: karen.knab@shawpittman.com

KNAPP, CHARLES LINCOLN, law educator; b. Zanesville, Ohio, Oct. 22, 1935; s. James Lincoln and Laura Alma (Richardson) K.; m. Beverley Earle Trott, Aug. 23, 1958 (dec. 1995); children: Jennifer Lynn, Liza Beth. BA, Denison U., 1956; JD, NYU, 1960. Bar: N.Y. 1961. Assoc. Paul, Weiss, Rifkind, Wharton & Garrison, N.Y.C., 1960-64; asst. prof. law NYU Law Sch., 1964-67, assoc. prof., 1967-70, prof. law, 1970-88, Max E. Greenberg prof. contract law, 1988-98, Max E. Greenberg prof. emeritus contract law, 1998—, assoc. dean, 1977-82. Vis. prof. law U. Ariz. Law Sch., Tucson, 1973, Harvard U. Law Sch., Cambridge, Mass., 1974-75; vis. prof. law Hastings Coll. Law, San Francisco, 1996-97, disting. prof. law, 1998-2000, Joseph W. Cotchett Disting. prof. law, 2000—. Author: Problems in Contract Law, 1976, (with N. Crystal and H. Prince) 4th edit., 1999; editor-in-chief: Commercial Damages, 1986. Mem. Am. Law Inst., Order Coif, Phi Beta Kappa. Office: Hastings Coll Law 200 Mcallister St San Francisco CA 94102-4707 E-mail: knappch@uchasting.edu

KNAPP, JAMES IAN KEITH, judge; b. Bklyn., Apr. 6, 1943; s. Charles Townsend and Christine (Grange) K.; m. Joan Elizabeth Cunningham, June 10, 1967 (div. Mar. 1971); 1 child, Jennifer Elizabeth; m. Carol Jean Brown, July 14, 1981; children: Michelle Christine, David Michael Keith AB cum laude, Harvard U., 1964; JD, U. Colo., 1967; M in Law in Taxation, Georgetown U., 1989. Bar: Colo. 1967, Calif. 1968, U.S. Supreme Ct. 1983, D.C. 1986, Ohio 1995. Dep. dist. atty. County of L.A., 1968-79; head dep. dist. atty. Pomona br. office, 1979-82; dep. asst. atty. gen. criminal divsn. U.S. Dept. Justice, Washington, 1982-86, dep. assoc. atty. gen., 1986-87, dep. asst. atty. gen. tax divsn., 1988-89, acting asst. atty. gen. tax divsn., 1989, acting dep. chief organized crime sect. criminal divsn., 1989-91, dep. dir., asset forfeiture office criminal divsn., 1991-94; adminstrv. law judge Social Security Adminstrn., 1994—. Editor: California Uniform Crime Charging Standards and Manual, 1975 Vice chmn. Young Reps. Nat. Fedn., 1973-75; pres. Calif. Young Reps., 1975-77; mem. exec. com. Rep. State Ctrl. Com., Calif., 1975-77. Mem. Calif. Bar Assn., D.C. Bar Assn., Dayton Bar Assn. Episcopalian. Avocations: travel; reading. Office: Office of Hearings & Appeals 110 N Main St Ste 800 Dayton OH 45402-1786

KNAPP, JOHN ANTHONY, lawyer; b. Mason City, Iowa, June 14, 1949; s. John Emmett and Lois Jane (Feeney) K.; m. Maureen Ann Jacobs, Dec. 20, 1972; children: Christopher John, Kevin Anthony, Elizabeth Lael. BA, St. John's U., Collegeville, Minn., 1971; JD, U. Iowa, 1974. Bar: Iowa 1974, Minn. 1974, D.C. 1982, U.S. Dist. Ct. Minn. 1974. Asst. revisor of statutes Minn. Legislature, St. Paul, 1974-76; v.p. Hessian, McKasy & Soderberg, Mpls., 1976-85; ptnr. Winthrop & Weinstine, St. Paul, 1985—. Adj. asst. prof. St. Mary's Coll. Grad. Ctr., Mpls., 1985—. Contbr. articles to profl. jours. Mem. ABA, Iowa Bar Assn., Minn. Bar Assn., D.C. Bar Assn., Ramsey County Bar Assn., Min. Govt. Rels. Coun. (pres. 1993-94), Citizens League, Mortgage Bankers Assn. Minn. (chmn. law com. 1984—), Town and Country Club. Mem. Democratic Farmer Labor Party. Roman Catholic. Administrative and regulatory, General corporate, Legislative. Home: 2193 Sargent Ave Saint Paul MN 55105-1130 Office: Winthrop & Weinstine 3200 Minnesota World Trade Ctr 30 7th St E Saint Paul MN 55101-4914 E-mail: jknapp@winthrop.com

KNAPP, WHITMAN, federal judge; b. N.Y.C., Feb. 24, 1909; s. Wallace Percy and Caroline Morgan (Miller) K.; m. Ann Fallert, May 17, 1962; 1 son, Gregory Wallace; children by previous marriage— Whitman Everett, Caroline Miller (Mrs. Edward M. W. Hines), Marion Elizabeth. Grad., Choate Sch., 1927; BA, Yale, 1931; LLB, Harvard U., 1934; LLD (hon.), CUNY City Coll., 1992. Bar: N.Y. 1935. With firm Cadwalader, Wickersham & Taft, N.Y.C., 1935-37; dep. asst. dist. atty., 1937-41; with firm Donovan, Leisure, Newton & Lumbard, 1941; mem. staff dist. atty., 1942-50; chief indictment bd., 1942-44; chief, appeal bur., 1944-50; partner firm Barrett Knapp Smith Schapiro & Simon (and predecessors), 1950-72; U.S. dist. judge So. Dist. N.Y., 1972-87, sr. dist. judge, 1987—. Spl. counsel N.Y. State Youth Commn., 1950-53; Waterfront Commn. N.Y. Harbor, 1953-54; mem. temp. commn. revision N.Y. State penal law and criminal code, 1964-69; chmn. Knapp Commn. to Investigate Allegations of Police Corruption in N.Y.C., 1969-72; gen. counsel Urban League Greater N.Y., 1970-72. Editor: Harvard Law Rev, 1933-34. Sec. Community Council Greater N.Y., 1952-58; pres. Dalton Schs., N.Y.C., 1950-53, Youth House, 1967-68; Trustee Univ. Settlement, 1945-64, Moblzn. for Youth, 1965-70. Mem. ABA, Am. Law Inst., Am. Bar Found., Am. Coll. Trial Lawyers, Assn. Bar City N.Y. (sec. 1946-49, chmn. exec. com. 1971-72). Office: 1201 US Courthouse 40 Foley Sq New York NY 10007-1502

KNAUER, LEON THOMAS, lawyer; b. N.Y.C., July 16, 1932; s. Lawrence R. and Loretta M. (Trainor) K.; m. Traude Kunz, Sept. 11, 1976; children: Robert A., Katrine M. BS in Math., Fordham U., 1954; JD, Georgetown U., 1961. Bar: Conn. 1961, D.C. 1961, U.S. Supreme Ct. 1965. Law clk. U.S. Dist. Ct. (D.C.), 1960-61; assoc. Wilkinson, Barker & Knauer LLP, Washington, 1961-68, ptnr., 1968-82, Wilkinson Barker Knauer, LLP, Washington, 1982—. Instr. Georgetown U. Law Center, 1964-65. Editor: Telecommunications Act Handbook: A Complete Reference for Business, 1996, Telecommunications Act of 1996-A Domestic and International Prospective for Business, 1998. Pres. Catholic Apostolic Mass Media, 1974-76, Knights of Malta, 1979—, Thomas AMarc Soc. of U.S., 1984-85. Lt. USMC, 1954-57. Recipient award for outstanding legal svc. in media area NAACP, 1973, Officer's Cross for legal svcs. to Austria, 1992. Mem. Fed. Comms. Bar Assn. (editor Comms. Bar Jour. 1960-69, treas. 1980-82, mem. exec. com. 1982-84), Washington Golf and County Club, Cosmos Club Washington, Fordham U. Alumni of Washington (pres. 1982-85). Republican. Roman Catholic. Administrative and regulatory, Communications, Private international. Office: 2300 N St NW Ste 700 Washington DC 20037-1122

KNEBEL, DONALD EARL, lawyer; b. Logansport, Ind., May 26, 1946; s. Everett Earl and Ethel Josephina (Hultgren) K.; m. Joan Elizabeth Vest, June 5, 1976 (div. 1980); 1 child, Mary Elizabeth; m. Jennifer Colt Johnson, Sept. 25, 1999. BEE with highest distinction, Purdue U., 1968; JD magna cum laude, Harvard U., 1974. Bar: Ind. 1974, U.S. Ct. Appeals (7th cir.) 1980, U.S. Ct. Appeals (3rd cir.) 1986, U.S. Ct. Appeals (6th cir.) 1987, U.S. Ct. Appeals (fed. cir.) 1988. Assoc. Barnes, Hickam, Pantzer & Boyd, Indpls., 1974-81; ptnr. Barnes & Thornburg, 1981—. Contbr. articles on intellectual property, antitrust and distbn. law to profl. publs. Trustee Indpls. Civic Theatre, 1986-95, chmn., 1988-91, hon. trustee, 1995—; mem. Zionsville (Ind.) Presbyn. Ch. Mem. ABA, Ind. Bar Assn., Indpls. Bar Assn., 7th Cir. Bar Assn., Kiwanis (pres. 1991-92), Columbia Club. Antitrust, Federal civil litigation, Intellectual property. Office: Barnes & Thornburg 11 S Meridian St Ste 1313 Indianapolis IN 46204-3535

KNECHT, WILLIAM L. lawyer; b. Lock Haven, Pa., Jan. 15, 1946; s. Clair N. and Betty R. (Harter) K.; m. Margaret E. O'Malley, June 10, 1972; children: William E., Jennifer M. BA, Pa. State U., 1967; JD, Dickinson Sch. Law, 1970. Bar: Pa. 1970, U.S. Supreme Ct. 1976, U.S. Tax Ct. 1981, U.S. Dist. Ct. (middle dist.) Pa. 1973, Ct. Common Pleas 1970. Assoc. McCormick, Lynn, Reeder, Nichols & Sarno, Williamsport, Pa., 1973-76; ptnr. McCormick, Reeder, Nichols, Bahl, Knecht & Person, 1976-96, McCormick Law Firm, Williamsport, 1996—. Bankruptcy trustee U.S. Justice Dept., Williamsport, Pa., 1978-91. Editor Lycoming Reporter, 1976—. 1st lt. U.S. Army, 1971-73. Mem. ABA, Pa. Bar Assn. (ho. dels. 2000), Lycoming County Law Assn. (exec. com. 1976—), Lycoming Law Assn. (pres. 1995), Ross Club. Republican. United Ch. of Christ. Avocations: stamps and first day cover collecting. Banking, Bankruptcy, Real property. Home: 253 Lincoln Ave Williamsport PA 17701-2237 Office: McCormick Law Firm PO Box 577 835 W 4th St Williamsport PA 17703-0577 E-mail: mcclaw@uplink.net

KNEE, STEPHEN H. lawyer; b. Newark, Oct. 15, 1940; s. Simon E. and Mollie (Liest) K.; m. Carole Leibowitz, Feb. 17, 1984; children: Robert A., David E., Dana R. AB, Duke U., 1962; JD, N.Y.U., 1965. Bar: N.J. 1965, N.Y. 1981, U.S. Ct. Appeals (3rd cir.) 1981, U.S. Supreme Ct. 1969, U.S. Dist. Ct. (so. dist.) N.Y. 1999. Law sec. Superior Ct. of N.J., Paterson, 1965-66; ptnr. Stryker, Tams & Dill, LLP, Newark, 1966-98, Saiber, Schlesinger, Satz & Goldstein, LLC, Newark, 1998—. Author: Buying and Selling Businesses, 1996. Trustee N.J. Shakespeare Festival, 1988—, sec.; trustee Jewish Family Services of Metrowest, 1988—. Mem. ABA (com. on negotiated acquistions, subcom. on uniform securities act of state regulation of securities com.), N.J. Bar Assn. (dir. corp. and bus. law sect. 1979—, chmn. 1984-86, program com. 1991-97), Inst. for Continuing Legal Edn. (past mem. adv. com.), Essex County Bar Assn., Am. Coll. Investment Counsel, Nat. Assn. Bond Lawyers. Bankruptcy, General corporate, Finance. Office: Saiber Schlesinger Satz & Goldstein LLC One Gateway Ctr Newark NJ 07102 E-mail: shk@saiber.com

KNEELAND, MISHELL B. lawyer; b. San Diego, Apr. 23, 1968; BA in Econs., U. Pa., 1990; JD, Georgetown U., 1996. Bar: N.Y. 1997, N.J. 2000, U.S. Dist. Ct. (ea. and so. dist.) N.Y. 1998, U.S. Dist. Ct. N.J. 2000. Analyst Am. Mgmt. Systems, Arlington, Va., 1990-93; law clk. Gladys Kessler, USDJ, D.D.C., Washington, 1996-97; assoc. Dechert Price & Rhoades, N.Y.C., 1997-99, Friedman Kaplan Seiler & Adelman LLP, 1999—. Dir. Washington Legal Clinic for the Homeless, Washington, 1995-96; mentor Cath. Big Sisters, N.Y., 1998—; tutor Friends of Tyler Sch., Washington, 1993-97. Mem. Assn. of the Bar of the City of N.Y. (sec. task force on housing ct. 1997-98), N.Y. County Lawyer's Assn. of Am. Inn of Ct. General civil litigation. Office: Friedman Kaplan Seiler & Adelman LLP 875 Third Avenue New York NY 10022

KNEIPPER, RICHARD KEITH, lawyer; b. Kenosha, Wis., June 18, 1943; s. Richard F. and Esther E. (Beaster) K.; m. Sherry Hayes, Dec. 16, 1977; children: Ryan Hayes, Lindsey Merrill. BS, Washington and Lee U., 1965; JD, Cornell U., 1968. Bar: Tex. 1982, U.S. Dist. Ct. (so. dist.) N.Y. 1968, U.S. Ct. Appeals (2d cir.) 1971. Atty. Chadbourne & Parke, N.Y.C., 1968-81, Jones, Day, Reavis & Pogue, Dallas, 1981-99; chief adminstrv. officer Provider HealthNet Svcs. Inc., 1999—. Mem. adv. com. Nat. Mus. Am., Smithsonian, Nat. Arts Edn. Initiative, Nat. Mus. Am. Art, Smithsonian Instn. Contbr. numerous articles to profl. jours. Bd. trustees The Dallas Parks Found.; mem. profl. adv. group Save Outdoor Sculpture!; chmn. Dallas Adopt-a-Monument; bd. dirs., mem. adv. coun. Appalachian Coll. Assn., Inc., Sch. Visual Arts, U. North Tex.; former mem. new bus. task force, former mem. internat. task force Health Industry Coun. Dallas-Ft. Worth Region. Mem. ABA, N.Y. Bar Assn., Tex. Bar Assn., Tex. Sculpture Assn., Assn. of Bar of City of N.Y. Episcopal. Banking, Mergers and acquisitions, Securities. Office: Provider HealthNet Svcs Inc 15851 Dallas Pkwy Ste 925 Addison TX 75001-6022

KNEISEL, EDMUND M. lawyer; b. Atlanta, Feb. 21, 1946; s. John F. and Mary E. (Moore) K.; m. Leslie A. Jones, June 19, 1976; 1 child, Mary Kathleen. AB, Duke U., 1968; JD, U. Ga., 1974. Bar: Ga. 1974, U.S. Dist. Ct. (no. and mid. dists.) Ga. 1976, U.S. Ct. Appeals (4th, 5th, 6th and 11th cirs.) 1976, U.S. Supreme Ct. 1984. Law clk. to Hon. R.C. Freeman U.S. Dist. Ct. (no. dist.) Ga., Atlanta, 1974-76; assoc. Kilpatrick & Cody, 1976-82; ptnr. Kilpatrick Stockton LLP, 1982—. Mng. editor Ga. Law Rev., Athens, 1973-74; contbr. articles to profl. jours. Lt. USNR, 1968-71. Mem. ABA, Lawyers Club Atlanta, Druid Hills Golf Club. Federal civil litigation, Insurance, Labor. Office: Kilpatrick Stockton LLP 1100 Peachtree St NE Ste 2800 Atlanta GA 30309-4530 E-mail: ekneisel@kilstock.com

KNICKERBOCKER, ROBERT PLATT, JR. lawyer; b. Hartford, Conn., Sept. 23, 1944; s. Robert P. and Audrey Jane (Stempel) K.; m. Kathleen A. Sakal (div. May 1985); children: Sarah, Abigail, Jonathan; m. Barbara Denise Whinnem, Oct. 3, 1987. BA, Cornell U., 1966; JD, U. Conn., 1969. Bar: Conn. 1969, U.S. Dist. Ct. Conn. 1969, U.S. Ct. Appeals (2d cir.) 1970. Law clk. to presiding justice Conn. Supreme Ct., Hartford, 1968-69; ptnr. Day, Berry & Howard, 1969—. Mem. State Implementation Plan Regulation Adv. Commn., 1979-90. Chmn. Town Plan and Zoning Commn., Glastonbury, Conn., 1975-79, Glastonbury Bd. Edn., 1982-86. Mem. Conn. Bar Assn., Greater Hartford C. of C. (state legis. com.). Republican. Episcopalian. Administrative and regulatory, Communications, Nuclear power. Office: Day Berry & Howard Cityplace Hartford CT 06103-3499 E-mail: rpknickerbocker@dbh.com

KNIGHT, JEFFREY LIN, lawyer, corporation executive; b. Evansville, Ind., Sept. 21, 1959; s. Jack T. and Ruth (Rogers) K.; m. Erin Elizabeth Hostettler, Dec. 18, 1982; children: Kathryn Ruth, Abigail Rebekah, Margaret Rachel, Caroline Elizabeth. BS, U. Evansville, 1981; JD, U. Ind., Indpls., 1984. Bar: Ind. 1984. Assoc. Clark, Statham, McCray, Thomas & Krohn, Evansville, 1984-85, Frank, Collins & Stephens, Evansville, 1985-88; v.p., sec., treas., gen. counsel Pacific Press & Shear, Inc., Mt. Carmel, Ill., 1988-90, gen. mgr., 1991-93; sr. v.p., corp. sec., gen. counsel Old Nat. Bancorp, 1993—, sec., gen. counsel, 2000—. Mentor Evansville Vanderburgh Sch. Corp., 1984—87. Mem. Ind. Bar Assn., Evansville Bar Assn., Am. Soc. Corp. Secs., Optimists (sec. 1987-88, v.p. 1988-89). Republican. Baptist. Avocations: golf, tennis. General civil litigation, General corporate, General practice. Home: 330 Largo Ct Evansville IN 47712-7616

KNIGHT, LOUISE OSBORN, lawyer; b. June 17, 1944; d. Newell Sloss and Helen (Willis) Knight. AB, Wellesley Coll., 1966; JD, George Washington U., 1969. Bar: Mo. 1969, D.C. 1970, Pa. 1972, U.S. Dist. Ct. D.C. 1970, U.S. Dist. Ct. (mid. dist.) Pa. 1972, U.S. Ct. Appeals (D.C. cir.) 1976, U.S. Ct. Appeals (5th cir.) 1971, U.S. Ct. Appeals (3d cir.) 1976. Staff atty. Nat. Assn. Broadcasters, 1969—70, asst. gen. counsel, 1970—72; assoc. Kury & Kury, Sunbury, Pa., 1972—74; ptnr. Clement & Knight, Lewisburg, 1974—98; adj. assoc. prof. Bucknell U., 1975—. Chmn. Hearing Com. 3.04, Disciplinary Bd. Pa. Supreme Ct. Contbr. articles to profl. jours. Solicitor Lewisburg Area Sch. Dist., 1975—99, Lewisburg Bur. Zoning Hearing Bd., 1985—99. Mem.: Mo. Bar Assn., D.C. Bar Assn., Pa. Bar Assn., Pa. Sch. Bd. Solicitors Assn. (pres. 1986), Nat. Assn. Women Judges (Pa. conf. state trial judges). Republican. Episcopalian. Federal civil litigation, Family and matrimonial. Home: RR 3 Box 316 Mifflinburg PA 17844-9535 Office: Union County Courthouse 103 South Second St Lewisburg PA 17837

KNIGHT, ROBERT HUNTINGTON, lawyer, bank executive; b. New Haven, Feb. 27, 1919; s. Earl Wall and Frances Pierpont (Whitney) K.; m. Rosemary C. Gibson, Apr. 19, 1975; children: Robert Huntington, Jessie Valle, Patricia Whitney, Alice Isabel, Eli Whitney. Grad., Phillips Acad., Andover, Mass., 1936; B.A., Yale, 1940; LL.B., U. Va., 1947, LLM, 1949. Bar: N.Y. bar 1950. With John Orr Young, Inc. (advt. agy.), 1940-41; asst. prof. U. Va. Law Sch., 1947-49; assoc. firm Shearman & Sterling & Wright, N.Y.C., 1949-55, ptnr., 1955-58; dep. asst. sec. def. for internat. security affairs Dept. Def., 1958-61; gen. counsel Treasury Dept., 1961-62; ptnr. firm Shearman & Sterling, N.Y.C., 1962-80, sr. ptnr., 1980-85, of counsel, 1986—; dep. chmn. Fed. Res. Bank N.Y., 1976-77, chmn., 1977-83. Counsel to bd. United Technologies Corp., 1974-85; dir. internat. bd. Owens-Corning Fiberglas Corp., 1989—; dir. I-Corps, Nat. Leadership Bank, Mercator, Inc., Citizen Exchange Coun.; mem. Intelsat Arbitration Panel, 1971-91. Bd. dirs. Internat. Vol. Services; chmn. bd. dirs. U. Va. Law Sch. Found., 1970-90; bd. dirs. Asia Found.. Served to lt. col. USAAF, 1941-45. Mem. ABA, Fed. Bar Assn., Internat. Bar Assn., Inter-Am. Bar Assn., Assn. of Bar of City of N.Y., N.Y County Lawyers Assn., Internat. Law Assn., Washington Inst. Fgn. Affairs, Council Fgn. Relations, Pilgrims Club, Links Club, World Trade Ctr Club, River Club (N.Y.C.), Army and Navy Club, Met. Club (Washington), Round Hill Club (Greenwich, Conn.), Ocean Club (Ocean Ridge, Fla.), Farmington Club (Va.). Home: 12 Knollwood Dr Greenwich CT 06830-4733 also: 570 Park Ave New York NY 10021-7370 also: 6767 N Ocean Blvd Ocean Ridge FL 33435-3314 Office: 599 Lexington Ave New York NY 10022-6030

KNIGHT, TOWNSEND JONES, lawyer; b. N.Y.C., Aug. 10, 1928; s. Jesse and Marguerite H. (Jones) K.; m. Elise Heck; children: Margaret Knight Dudley, Elise Knight Wallace, Jessica Knight Casoni. BS, Harvard U., 1949; JD, Columbia U., 1952. Bar: N.Y. 1952. Assoc. Curtis, Mallet-Prevost, Colt & Mosle, N.Y.C., 1953-65, ptnr., 1965—. Bd. dirs. Friends Ivory & Sime Trust Co., Friends Ivory & Sime, Inc. Trustee Audrey Cohen Coll., N.Y.C., 1969—, Cold Spring Harbor (N.Y.) Lab., 1970-76, 82-88, 89-95, hon. trustee, 1995—. Mem. ABA, N.Y. State Bar Assn., Assn. of Bar of City of N.Y., Downtown Assn., Harvard Club, Cold Spring Harbor Beach Club. Episcopalian. Avocation: photography. Banking, Private international, Probate. Office: Curtis Mallet-Prevost Colt & Mosle 101 Park Ave Fl 35 New York NY 10178-0061

KNIGHT, W.H., JR. (JOE KNIGHT), dean, law educator; m. Susan Mask; children: Michael Mask, Lauren Mask. BA in Econs., Speech and Polit. Sci., U. N.C., 1976; JD, Columbia U., 1979. Prof. U. Iowa Coll. Law, vice provost, 1997—2000, dean, 2001—, law educator, 2001—. Vis. prof. Washington U., St. Louis, Duke U. Schs. Law; assoc. counsel, asst. sec. Colonial Bancorp, New Haven, Waterbury, Conn. Mem.: ABA, State Farm Mutual Automobile Ins. Co., N.Y. Bar, Am. Law Inst., Nat. Bar Assn., Soc. Am. Law Tchrs., Nat. Conf. on Black Lawyers. Office: U Washington Sch Law 1100 NE Campus Pkwy Seattle WA 98105-6617 Office Fax: 206-616-5305. E-mail: whknight@u.washington.edu, w-knight@uiowa.edu*

KNIGHT, WILLIAM D., JR. lawyer; b. Rockford, Ill., May 18, 1925; s. William D. and Lela Mae (Clark) K. AB, Dartmouth Coll., 1949; JD, Northwestern U., 1952. Bar: Ill. 1953, U.S. Dist. Ct. (no. dist.) Ill. 1957, U.S. Ct. Appeals (7th cir.) 1959. Ptnr., Knight & Knight, Rockford, 1953— . Bd. dirs. Boys Club Assn. of Rockford, 1959-75. Served to 1st lt., inf., U.S. Army, 1943-46. Mem. Ill. Bar Assn., Winnebago County Bar Assn., Internat. Assn. Ins. Counsel, Fedn. Ins. Counsel, Assn. Ins. Attys., Def. Rsch. Inst., Rockford Country Club. Republican. Methodist. Federal civil litigation, State civil litigation, General corporate. Home: 1205 Lundvall Ave Rockford IL 61107-3341 also: 575 S Lake Shore Dr Lake Geneva WI 53147-2126 Office: Knight and Knight 1111 Talcott Bldg 321 W State St Rockford IL 61101-1137

KNOBBE, LOUIS JOSEPH, lawyer; b. Carroll, Iowa, Apr. 6, 1932; s. Louis C. and Elsie M. (Praeger) K.; m. Jeanette M. Sganga, Apr. 3, 1954; children: Louis, Michael, Nancy, John, Catherine. BSEE, Iowa State U., 1953; JD, Loyola U., L.A., 1959. Bar: Calif. 1960, U.S. Supreme Ct. 1963; U.S. Patent and Trademark Office. Tech. staff Bell Telephone Labs., 1953-54; patent engr. GE, Washington, N.Am. Aviation, Downey, Calif., 1956-59; patent lawyer Beckman Instruments, Fullerton, 1959-62; co-founder, ptnr. Knobbe, Martens, Olson & Bear, Newport Beach, 1962—. Lectr. Am. Intellectual Property Law Assn., Computer Law Assn., Inc., L.A. Intellectual Property Law Assn., San Diego Bar Assn., Orange County Patent Law Assn.; adj. prof. Sch. Law U. San Diego, 1987—. Co-author: Attorney's Guide to Trade Secrets, 1972, 2d edit., 1996, How to Handle Basic Patent, 1992; contbg. author: Using Intellectual Property Rights to Protect Domestic Markets, 1986; contbr. articles to profl. jours. Bd. dirs. Orange County (Calif.) Performing Arts Ctr., 1975-83; past pres. Philaharmonic Soc. Orange County; bd. mem., past v.p. Opera Pacific, Orange County; bd. visitors Loyola Law Sch., 2000—. Recipient Jurisprudence award Anti-Defamation League, 1988. Fellow Inst. Advancement Engring.; mem. ABA, IEEE (past chmn. Orange County sect., Centennial medal 1984), Am. Intellectual Property Law Assn., Am. Arbitration Soc. (mem. panel neutrals), State Bar Calif., Orange County Bar Assn. (mem. civil mediation panel), Orange County Patent Law Assn., San Diego Patent Law Assn., Licensing Execs. Soc., Santa Ana North Rotary, First Friday Friars, Pacific Club, Balboa Yacht Club, Phi Kappa Phi, Tau Beta Pi, Eta Kappa Nu. Avocations: boating, still and video photography, travel and exploration in Lake Powell, Death Valley, deserts of Arizona and Baja, California. Intellectual property, Patent, Trademark and copyright. Office: 620 Newport Center Dr Fl 16 Newport Beach CA 92660-8016 E-mail: LKnobbe@kmob.com

KNOLL, JEANNETTE THERIOT, state supreme court justice; b. Baton Rouge; m. Jerold Edward Knoll; children: Triston Kane, Eddie Jr., Edmond Humphries, Blake Theriot, Jonathan Paul. BA in Polit. Sci., Loyola U., 1966, JD, 1969; LLM, U. Va., 1996; studied with Maestro Adler, Mannes Coll. of Music, 1962-63. Criminal defense atty., first asst. dist. atty. Twelfth Jud. Dist. Ct. Avoyelles Parish, 1972-82; gratuitous atty., advisor U.S. Selective Svc., Marksville, La.; judge (3d cir.) U.S. Ct. of Appeal, 1982-93; justice La. Supreme Ct., 1997—. Instr. La. Jud. Coll.; chair CLE La. Ct. of Appeal Judges; mem. vis. com. Loyola U. Sch. of Law, Loyola Music Sch.; bd. dirs. Loyola U. Alumni Assn.; former mem. state bd. of La. commn. on law enforcement and criminal justice. Past pres. Bus. and Profl. Women's Club; Marksville C. of C.; active Am. Legion Aux. Recipient scholarship Met. Opera Assn., New Orleans Opera Guild. Office: La Supreme Ct 301 Loyola Ave New Orleans LA 70112-1814*

KNOPF, BARRY ABRAHAM, lawyer, educator; b. Passaic, N.J., May 11, 1946; s. Edward and Sonia (Sameth) K.; children: Elisa, Scott. Student, Rutgers U., 1968, JD, 1972. Bar: N.J. 1972, U.S. Dist. Ct. N.J. 1972, U.S. Tax Ct. 1975, U.S. Supreme Ct. 1975, U.S. Ct. Appeals (3d cir.) 1981; cert. civil trial atty. Nat. Bd. Trial Advocacy, N.J. Supreme Ct. Assoc. Cohn & Lifland, Saddle Brook, N.J., 1972-75, ptnr., 1975—. Instr. N.J. Inst. for Continuing Legal Edn., 1982—, Nat. Inst. Trial Advocacy, 1989—; adj. faculty Hofstra U. Sch. of Law, 2000. Co-author: Professional Negligence, Law of Malpractice in New Jersey, 1979, 5th edit., 2001, Personal Injury Litigation Practice in New Jersey, 1990, Civil Trial Preparation, Practical skills Series, 1992, 2d edit., 1996, New Jersey Product Liability Law, 1994. V.p. Temple Beth Tikvah, Wayne, N.J., 1985-93, pres. 1993-95. Mem. Morris Pashman Inn of Ct. (barrister 1998—). Federal civil litigation, State civil litigation, Personal injury. Home: 1014 Smith Manor Blvd West Orange NJ 07052-4227 Office: Cohn Lifland Pearlman Herrmann & Knopf Park 80 West 1 Saddle Brook Rochelle Park NJ 07662 E-mail: bak@njlawfirm.com

KNOWLES, MARJORIE FINE, lawyer, educator, dean; b. Bklyn., July 4, 1939; d. Jesse J. and Roslyn (Leff) Fine; m. Ralph I. Knowles, Jr., June 3, 1972. BA, Smith Coll., 1960; LLB, Harvard U., 1965. Bar: Ala., N.Y., D.C. Teaching fellow Harvard U., 1963-64; law clk. to judge U.S. Dist. Ct. (so. dist.), N.Y., 1965-66; asst. U.S. atty. U.S. Atty.'s Office, N.Y.C., 1966-67; asst. dist. atty. N.Y. County Dist. Atty., 1967-70; exec. dir. Joint Found. Support, Inc., 1970-72; asst. gen. counsel HEW, Washington, 1978-79; insp. gen. U.S. Dept. Labor, 1979-80; assoc. prof. U. Ala. Sch. Law, Tuscaloosa, 1972-75, prof., 1975-86, assoc. dean, 1982-84; law prof., dean Ga. State U. Coll. Law, Atlanta, 1986-91, law prof., 1986—. Cons.

Ford Found., N.Y.C., 1973-98, 2000—, trustee Coll. Retirement Equities Fund, N.Y.C., 1983—; mem. exec. com. Conf. on Women and the Constn., 1986-88; mem. com. on continuing profl. edn. Am. Law Inst.-ABA, 1987-93. Contbr. articles to profl. jours. Am. Council Edn. fellow, 1976-77, Aspen Inst. fellow, Rockefeller Found., 1976. Mem. ABA (chmn. new deans workshop 1988), Ala. State Bar Assn., N.Y. State Bar Assn., D.C. Bar Assn., Am. Law Inst. Office: Ga State U Coll Law University Plz Atlanta GA 30303

KNOWLTON, KEVIN CHARLES, lawyer; b. Syracuse, N.Y., Oct. 19, 1957; s. Erwin Leslie and Arlene Grace (Morgan) K.; m. Lois Jean Clair, July 21, 1979; children: Andrew, Keith, Lauren. BA cum laude, Houghton Coll., 1979; JD, Syracuse U., 1982. Bar: Fla. 1982, U.S. Dist. Ct. (mid. dist.) Fla. 1982, U.S. Ct. Appeals (11th cir.) 1982, U.S. Supreme Ct. 1986. Law clk. to judge 2nd Dist. Ct. Appeals, Lakeland, Fla., 1982-85; ptnr. Peterson & Myers P.A., 1985—, mgmt. com. Treas. Phoenix (N.Y.) Rep. Com., 1980-82, Planning Bd., 1980-82, Town of Schroeppel Planning Bd., 1980-82; chmn. bd. dirs. Lakeland Christian Sch.; chmn. pres.'s adv. bd. Houghton Coll.; mem. Fla. Bar 10th Jud. Cir. Grievance Com.; mem. instnl. rev. bd. Lakeland Regional Med. Ctr., mems. ethics com.; chmn. exec. bd. dirs. Lake Morton Cmty. Ch., 1995-99, elder. N.Y. State Regents scholar 1975-79. Mem. ABA, Fla. Bar Assn., Lakeland Bar Assn. (chmn. law day legal forum 1986), Fla. Acad. Healthcare Attys., Am. Health Lawyers Assn., Christian Legal Soc., Houghton Coll. Alumni Assn. (pres. Orlando, Fla. chpt. 1985, 91—), Willson Inn of Ct., Lakeland Yacht and Country Club, Phi Alpha Theta. Avocations: basketball, snow skiing. General civil litigation, Health. Home: 1143 E Highland Dr Lakeland FL 33813-1774 Office: Peterson & Myers PA 100 E Main St Lakeland FL 33801-4655

KNOX, JAMES EDWIN, lawyer; b. Evanston, Ill., July 2, 1937; s. James Edwin and Marjorie Eleanor (Williams) K.; m. Rita Lucille Torres, June 30, 1973; children: James Edwin III, Kirsten M., Katherine E., Miranda G. BA in Polit. Sci., State U. Iowa, 1959; JD, Drake U., 1961. Bar: Iowa 1961, Ill. 1962, Tex. 1982. Law clk. to Justice Tom C. Clark, U.S. Supreme Ct., Washington, 1961-62; assoc., then ptnr. Isham, Lincoln & Beale, Chgo., 1962-70; v.p. law N.W. Industries, Inc., 1970-80; exec. v.p., gen. counsel Lone Star Steel Co., Dallas, 1980-86; sr. v.p. law Anixter Internat. Inc., Chgo., 1986—. Instr. contracts and labor law Chgo. Kent Coll. Law, 1964—69; arbitrator Nat. Ry. Adjustment Bd., 1967—68; ptnr. Mayer, Brown & Platt, Chgo., 1992—96; gen. counsel Arris Group, Inc., 1996—. Mem. ABA, Ill. Bar Assn., Order of Coif, Phi Beta Kappa. General corporate. Office: Anixter Internat Inc 676 N Michigan Ave Ste 2800 Chicago IL 60611-2861 E-mail: jeknoxie@aol.com

KNOX, JAMES MARSHALL, lawyer; b. Chgo., Jan. 12, 1944; s. Edwin John and Shirley Lucille (Collett) K.; m. Janine Foster, July 18, 1964; children: Erik M., Christian S. BA, U. Ill., 1968; MA in Libr. Sci., Rosary Coll., 1973; JD, DePaul Coll. Law, 1979. Bar: Ill. 1979, U.S. Dist. Ct. (no. dist.) Ill. 1979, U.S. Ct. Appeals (7th cir.) 1980. Head reference Northbrook (Ill.) Pub. Libr., 1973-76; asst. dir. hdqrs. Jackson (Miss.) Met. Libr. Sys., 1976-77; assoc. Fishman & Fishman, Ltd., Chgo., 1979-91; prin. Law Office James M. Knox, 1991—. Gen. counsel Deerfield (Ill.) Pub. Libr., 1994—. Commr. Evanston Preservation Commn., 1991-98; sustaining mem. Miss. Hist. Soc. Mem. ABA, Ill. State Bar Assn., Ill. Trial Lawyer's Assn., Chgo. Bar Assn., U. Ill. Alumni Assn. (dir. 1986-91). General practice, Personal injury, Workers' compensation. Home: 1305 Lincoln St Evanston IL 60201-2334 Office: 3700 Three 1st National Plz Chicago IL 60602 E-mail: KawOxford@aol.com

KOBAK, JAMES BENEDICT, JR. lawyer, educator; b. Alexandria, La., May 2, 1944; s. James Benedict and Hope (McEldowney) K.; m. Carol Johnson, June 11, 1966; children: James Benedict III, Katherine Jean, Marcie Ann. BA magna cum laude, Harvard U., 1966; LLB, U. Va., 1969. Bar: U.S. Dist. Ct. (so. and ea. dists.) N.Y. 1972, U.S. Supreme Ct. 1977, U.S. Ct. Appeals (2nd cir.) 1973, (5th cir.) 1982, U.S. Dist. Ct. (no. dist.) Calif. 1983, N.J. 1996. Asst. prof. U. Ala., 1969-70; assoc. Hughes Hubbard & Reed LLP, N.Y.C., 1970-77, ptnr., 1977—. Lectr. in law U. Va., 1986—; adj. assoc. prof. Fordham U., 1986—. Editor: Misuse: Licensing and Litigation, 2000; mem. bd. editors Va. Law Rev., 1967-69, assoc. editor, 1968-69; contbr. articles to profl. jours., mags., treatises and newspapers. Trustee Morristown-Beard Sch., 1995-2001. Mem. ABA (antitrust sect., former chair intellectual property com.), Assn. Bar City N.Y., N.Y. County Lawyers Assn. (bd. dirs. 1988-93, 95-97, 2001—, chmn. trade regulation com. 1987-88, chmn. com. on changing trends in the profession 1990-93, chmn. com. on law reform 1994-98, exec. com. 1996-98, chair libr. com. 1998—), Order of Coif, Am. Law Inst., Adirondack 46ers Club, Keene Valley Country Club (trustee 1995-98), Harvard Club (N.Y.). Antitrust, Federal civil litigation, Trademark and copyright. Home: 206-05 W Shearwater Ct Jersey City NJ 07305 Office: Hughes Hubbard & Reed 1 Battery Park Plz Fl 12 New York NY 10004-1482 E-mail: kobak@hugheshubbard.com

KOBAYASHI, BERT TAKAAKI, JR. lawyer; b. Honolulu, Feb. 4, 1940; s. Bert Takaaki Sr. and Victoria Ruth (Tsuchiya) K.; m. Harriet Sanae Ishimine, Aug. 11, 1962; children: Christopher T., Jonathan A., Matthew H., Jennifer Sanae. Student, U. Hawaii, 1958-62; BA, Gettysburg (Pa.) Coll., 1962; JD, U. Calif., Hastings, 1965. Bar: Hawaii 1965, U.S. Dist. (fed. dist.) Hawaii 1965. Assoc. Chung, Vitousek, Chuck & Fujimana, Honolulu, 1967-69, Kono, Ariyoshi, Honolulu, 1969-71; sr. ptnr. Kobayashi, Sugita & Goda, 1971—. Bd. dirs. First Hawaiian Bank, Honolulu, Bank West Corp., Schuler Homes; exec. com. Bank West Corp. Honolulu; mem. State Jud. Selection Commn., Honolulu, 1985-01, chmn., 1987-89. Mem. ABA, Am. Coll. Trial Lawyers, Hawaii Bar Assn., Assn. Trial Lawyers Am., Am. Bd. Trial Advs., Japah-Hawaii Econ. Coun., Pub. Schools Found. State civil litigation, Construction, Real property. Office: Kobayashi Sugita & Goda 999 Bishop St Ste 2600 Honolulu HI 96813-4430

KOBER, JANE, lawyer; b. Shamokin, Pa., May 17, 1943; d. Jeno Daniel and Angela Agnes (Kogut) DiRienzo; m. Arthur Kober, June 20, 1970 (div. 1975). AB, Pa. State U., 1965; MA, U. Chgo., 1966; JD, Case Western Res. U., 1974. Bar: Ohio, N.Y. Lectr. U. Baghdad, Iraq, 1966-67; editor, cons. Ernst & Young, Washington, 1968-70; law clk. to Hon. William K. Thomas, U.S. Dist. Ct. for No. Dist. Ohio, Cleve., 1974-75; atty., ptnr. Squire, Sanders & Dempsey, Cleve. and N.Y.C., 1975-87; ptnr. Shea & Gould, N.Y.C., 1987-89, LeBoeuf, Lamb, Greene & MacRae, L.L.P., N.Y.C., 1989-98; sole practitioner, 1998—; sr. v.p., gen. counsel, sec. Biopure Corp., Cambridge, Mass., 1998—. Mem. Case Western Res. U. Sch. Law Alumni Assn. (vis. com.). Office: Jane Kober Law Offices 125 W 55th St New York NY 10019-5369 also: Biopure Corp 11 Hurley St Cambridge MA 02141-2110 E-mail: jkober@biopure.com

KOBERT, JOEL A. lawyer; b. Newark, Oct. 4, 1943; BA, Norwich U., 1965; JD, Howard U., 1968. Bar: D.C. 1968, N.J. 1971. Atty. U.S. Dept. Justice, Washington, 1968; ptnr. Courter, Kobert, Laufer & Cohen P.C., Hackettstown, N.J. Active Supreme Ct. Ad Hoc Com. on Legal Svcs. 1982-88, Supreme Ct. Com. on Interests and Trust Accts., 1984-86, Supreme Ct. Com. on Computerization of Ct. System, 1984-86; chmn. bd. trustees Interest on Lawyers Trust Accts., 1988-91. Capt. U.S. Army, 1968-70. Reginald Heber Smith fellow, 1970-71. Fellow Am. Bar Found.; mem. ABA (mem. dist XIII ethics com. 1982-86), D.C. Bar, N.J. State Bar Assn. (treas. 1987, sec. 1988, 2d v.p. 1989, 1st v.p. 1990, pres. elect 1991, pres. 1992, bd. trustees 1981-87, bd. trustees N.J. Lawyer, bd trustees N.J. State Bar Found., 1986-93, mem. ops. com. 1985-91, chmn. com. law adminstrn. and econs. 1981-86, mem. membership com., 1986-87, mem. com. fin. and ops, 1990-93, mem. travel com. 1990-93), N.J. League Mcpl. Attys. Office: Courter Kobert Laufer & Cohen PC 1001 County Road 517 Ste 1 Hackettstown NJ 07840-2709

KOBLENTZ, ROBERT ALAN, lawyer; b. Columbus, Ohio, Aug. 20, 1946; s. Maurice Charles and Martha (Levelle) K.; m. Kathryn Anderson, Oct. 20, 1973; children: Maureen, Robert. BA, Ohio State U., 1967, JD, 1970. Bar: Ohio 1970, U.S. Dist. Ct. (so. dist.) Ohio 1971, U.S. Supreme Ct. 1992; cert. family law specialist. Legal rsch. Bancroft-Whitney Co., San Francisco, 1970-71; atty. Tracy, DeLibera, Lyons & Collins, Columbus, 1971-78, DeLibera, Lyons, Koblentz & Scott, Columbus, 1978-80, Scott, Koblentz & Binau, Columbus, 1980-86; pvt. practice, 1986—. Bd. dirs. Friends of WOSU, Columbus, 1982-88, Opera Columbus, 1984-87, Upper Arlington Civic Assn., Columbus, 1988-90. Mem. ABA, Ohio State Bar Assn. (cert. family rels. specialist, del. family law sect. 1979—), Ohio Acad. Trial Lawyers (chmn. family law sect. 1983), Columbus Bar Assn. (chmn. family law com. 1976-78), Franklin County Trial Lawyers (pres. 1985-86). Family and matrimonial. Office: 35 E Livingston Ave Columbus OH 43215-5762

KOBLENZ, MICHAEL ROBERT, lawyer; b. Newark, Apr. 9, 1948; s. Herman and Esther (Weisman) K.; m. Bonnie Jane Berman, Dec. 22, 1973; children: Adam, Alexander, Elizabeth. B.A., George Washington U., 1969, LL.M., 1974; J.D., Am. U., 1972. Bar: N.J. 1972, D.C. 1973, N.Y. 1980, U.S. Dist. Ct. N.J. 1972, U.S. Dist. Ct. D.C. 1973, U.S. Dist. Ct. (so. dist.) N.Y. 1980, U.S. Ct. Appeals (7th cir.) 1976, U.S. Ct. Claims 1973, U.S. Tax Ct. 1973, U.S. Mil. Ct. Appeals 1974. Atty., U.S. Dept. Justice, Washington, 1972-75; lectr. Am. U., 1975-78; spl. asst. U.S. atty. Office of U.S. Atty., Chgo., 1976-78; atty. Commodity Futures Trading Commn., Washington, 1975-77; spl. counsel, 1977, asst. dir., 1977-78; regional counsel, N.Y.C., 1978-80; assoc. Rein, Mound & Cotton, N.Y.C., 1980-82, ptnr., Mound, Cotton & Wollan (and predecessor firms), 1983—. Contbr. articles to legal jours. Mem. bd. appeals Village of Flower Hill, Manhasset, N.Y., 1983-84, trustee, 1984-86; trustee Village of East Hills, 1988—, Dep. Mayor, 1993-94, Mayor, 1994—; mem. Roslyn Little League, 1991—, bd. dirs., 1992. Recipient Cert. of Appreciation for Outstanding Service U.S. Commodity Futures Trading Commn., 1977. Contracts commercial, General corporate, Securities. Home: East Hills 20 Hemlock Dr Roslyn NY 11576-2303 Office: Mound Cotton & Wollan 1 Battery Park Plz New York NY 10004-1405

KOBRIN, LAWRENCE ALAN, lawyer; b. N.Y.C., Sept. 14, 1933; s. Irving and Hortense (Freezer) K.; m. Ruth E. Freedman, Mar. 5, 1967; children: Jeffrey, Rebecca, Debra. AB in History suma cum laude, Columbia U., 1954, JD, 1957. Bar: N.Y. 1957, U.S. Dist. Ct. (sou. dist.) N.Y. 1958, U.S. Dist. Ct. (ea. dist.) 1958, U.S. Ct. Appeals (2d cir.) 1959, U.S. Supreme Ct. 1966. Assoc. Cahill, Gordon, Reindel & Ohl, N.Y.C., 1958-59, Arthur D. Emil, N.Y.C., 1959-63; ptnr. Emil & Kobrin, 1963-79, Milgrim, Thomajan, Jacobs and Lee, N.Y.C., 1979-83, Cahill Gordon & Reindel, N.Y.C., 1984—. Bd. dirs. Wurzweiler Sch. of Social Work, vice-chmn., 1994-98; dir. UMB Bank and Trust Co., 1978-91; treas. The Jewish Week, N.Y.C., 1992-96, chmn., 1996—. Notes editor Columbia U. Law Rev.; mng. editor Tradition, 1961-64, editl. com. 1964—; contbr. articles to profl. jours. V.p., assoc. treas., chmn. dist. com. Fedn. Jewish Philanthropies, N.Y.C., 1981-84, com. long range planning, 1985-86, com. inner city, 71-76; chmn. Ramaz Sch., N.Y.C., 1978-83; sec. to bd. Bar Ilan U., N.Y.C., 1972-80; pres. The Jewish Ctr., N.Y.C., 1987-90; dir. N.Y.C. UJA-Fedn., chmn. communal planning com., 1988-91, chmn. com. on cmty. couns., 1996-98; v.p. Union Orthodox Jewish Congregations, 1968-74, dir. 1962—; chmn. campus com., 1962-66, chmn. Israel com., 1967-72, chmn. pub. com., 1972-78; pres. Massad Camps, 1971-77; bd. dirs. Am. Friends Pardes, 1991-96, Histadrut Ivrit., 1991—; pres. Ariel Am. Friends of Midrasha and United Instns., 1991-95, chmn., 1995-2001; sec. Beth Din of Am., 1994-96, chmn. exec. com., 1997—, exec. com. Orthodox Caucus, 1995—, Edah, 1999—. Kent scholar, 1954-55, Stone scholar, 1954-55. Mem. Am. Coll. Real Estate Lawyers, Coop. Housing Lawyers Group (exec. com, 1972-80), N.Y. atty. gen. adv. com 1972-80, Assn. Bar City of N.Y. (com. on philanthropic orgns. 1974-79, edn. and law com. 1985-88, com. on legal edn. 1988-91, com. on legal problems of elderly 1991-94), N.Y. County Lawyers Assn. (real property law sec., chmn 1991-93), N.Y. State Bar Assn. (com. coops and condominiusm. com. fgn. investment real estate), Columbia Coll. Alumni Assn. (bd. dirs. 1990—, v.p. 1996-98), Columbia / Barnard Hillel (exec. com., 1998-), The Down Town Assn., Cream Hill Lake Assn., Phi Beta Kappa. General corporate, Non-profit and tax-exempt organizations, Real property. Home: 15 W 81st St New York NY 10024-6022 also: 8 Popple Swamp Rd Cornwall Bridge CT 06754-1135 Office: Cahill Gordon & Reindel 80 Pine St Fl 17 New York NY 10005-1790 E-mail: kobrinl@mindspring.com, lkobrin@cahill.com

KOCH, EDNA MAE, lawyer, nurse; b. Terre Haute, Ind., Oct. 12, 1951; d. Leo K. and Lucille E. (Smith) K.; m. Mark D. Orton. BS in Nursing, Ind. State U., 1977; JD, Ind. U., 1980. Bar: Ind. 1980, U.S. Dist. Ct. (so. dist.) Ind. 1980. Assoc. Dillon & Cohen, Indpls., 1980-85; ptnr. Tipton, Cohen & Koch, 1985-93, LaCava, Zeigler & Carter, Indpls., 1993-94, Zeigler Cohen & Koch, Indpls., 1994—. Leader seminars for nurses, Ind. U. Med. Ctr., Ball State U., Muncie, Ind., St. Vincent Hosp., Indpls., Deaconess Hosp., Evansville, Ind., others; lectr. on med. malpractice Cen. Ind. chpt. AACCN, Indpls. "500" Postgrad. Course in Emergency Medicine, Ind. Assn. Osteo. Physicians and Surgeons State Conv., numerous others. Mem. ABA, ANA, Ind. State Bar Assn., Indpls. Bar Assn., Am. Soc. Law and Medicine, Ind. State Nurses Assn. Republican. State civil litigation, Insurance, Personal injury. Office: Zeigler Cohen & Koch 9465 Counselors Row Ste 104 Indianapolis IN 46240-3816

KOCH, EDWARD RICHARD, lawyer, accountant; b. Teaneck, N.J., Mar. 25, 1953; s. Edward J. and Adelaide M. K.; m. Cora Susan Koch, Apr. 12, 1997; children: Edward Peter, William John. BS in Econs. magna cum laude, U. Pa., 1975; JD, U. Va., 1980; LLM in Taxation, NYU, 1986. Bar: N.J. 1980, U.S. Dist. Ct. N.J. 1980, U.S. Tax Ct. 1981, U.S. Ct. Claims 1981. Staff acct. Touche Ross & Co. (now Deloitte & Touche), Newark, 1975-77; assoc. Winne, Banta & Rizzi, Hackensack, N.J., 1980-82; tax atty. Allied Corp. (now Honeywell Internat. Inc.), Morristown, 1982-87; asst. v.p. ChemBank (now Chase Manhattan), N.Y.C., 1987-90; tax mgr. Paul Scherer & Co. LLP, 1990-97, ptnr., 1998—. Vice chmn. law and legis. com. U.S.A. Track and Field, Indpls., 1985-89, chmn., 1989-2000, chmn. ins. com., 1984-88, bd. dirs., 1989—, treas., 2000—; pres. N.J. Athletics Congress, Red Bank, 1986-90; mem. Jury of Appeals, 1988, U.S. Olympic Men's Marathon Trials, Holy Family Sch. Edn. Coun., 1992-96; Olympic Track and Field ofcl., 1996. Mem. AICPA, N.J. Soc. CPAs, Am. Assn. Attys.-CPAs, N.J. State Bar Assn., N.J. Striders Track Club (chmn. 1981-96). Republican. Roman Catholic. Avocations: running track and field. Corporate taxation, Personal income taxation, State and local taxation. Home: 130 Grant St Haworth NJ 07641-1951 Office: Paul Scherer & Co 335 Madison Ave Fl 9 New York NY 10017-4605 E-mail: ekoch@pscherer.com

KOCH, THOMAS, lawyer; b. Paris, France, Apr. 5, 1963; m. Barbara Koch; children: Tiffany, Noemi. LicIur, U. Zurich, DrIur, 1990. Bar: Zurich 1996, Swiss Supreme Ct. 1996, Dist. and Fed. Cts., Ct. fo Appeals of Canton of Zurich 1996, Dist. and Fed. Cts., Ct. of Appeals of Canton of Schwyz 1998, Dist. and Fed. Cts., Ct. of Appeals of Canton of Thurgau 1999, Dist. and Fed. Cts., Ct. of Appeals of Canton of Basle 2000. Legal sec. Comml. Registry Office of Canton of Zurich, 1992, Zurich Dist. Ct., 1993-96; atty. Fischer & Frei Law Firm, Zurich, 1997-2000, Bill, Isenegger & Ackermann Law Firm, Zurich, 2001—. Dir. Metro Publs. (Switzerland) Ltd., Zurich, Mydn Ltd., Zurich. Author: The compulsory procedure of the Registrar of the Commercial Register, 1997, also articles; eidtor: Yearbook of the Commercial Register, 1992—. Bd. dirs. Swiss Liberal-Conservative Party, Thalwil, Zurich, 1999. 1st lt. arty., NBC, Swiss Army. General civil litigation, General corporate, General practice. Office: Fischer & Frei Gotthardstrasse 61 Zurich 8027 Switzerland Fax: 0041 1 3868899

KOCH, THOMAS FREDERICK, lawyer; b. Hackensack, N.J., Nov. 24, 1942; s. Elmer J. and Evelyn (Zombeck) K.; m. Sally J. Tucker, June 6, 1970; children: Christine E., Donald T. AB, Middlebury Coll., 1964; JD, U. Chgo., 1967. Bar: Vt. 1967, U.S. Dist. Ct. Vt. 1971. Assoc. firm Free and Bernasconi, Barre, Vt., 1970-74; ptnr. Bernasconi & Koch, 1974—. Mem. jud. nominating bd. State of Vt., 1979-81; mem. Vt. Ho. of Reps., 1977-80, 97—, mem. mcpl. corps. and elections, judiciary, house rules and joint rules coms. health and welfare, chair, 2001—, joint com. on health access; moderator Town of Barre, 1984— ; chmn. Vt. Rep. Platform com. 1984. Del. nat. convs. of Assn. of Evang. Luth. Chs., 1978, 84, 86; del. to constrn. conv. of Evang. Luth. Ch. in Am., 1987-94; mem. churchwide assemblies, 1991, 97, 99; mem. New Eng. synod coun. Evangelical Luth. Ch. Am., 1987-94; mem. churchwide assemblies, 1991, 97; scoutmaster Boy Scouts Am., Barre, 1989-93, dist. chmn. 1993-96, 98-2000; mem. exec. bd. Green Mountain coun., 1997—. Mem. Vt. Bar Assn., Washington County Bar Assn., Barre Lions Club (pres. 1977-78). Republican. Probate, Real property. Home: 326 Lowery Rd Barre VT 05641-9090 Office: 107 N Main St PO Box 892 Barre VT 05641-0892 E-mail: tfkoch1@aol.com

KOCHEMS, ROBERT GREGORY, lawyer; b. Cleve., Aug. 6, 1951; s. Roy George and Virginia Mae (Budniak) K.; m. Georgann Ryan; 1 child, Alane Carin. BA cum laude, John Carroll U., 1973; JD, St. Louis U., 1976. Bar: Pa. 1976, U.S. Dist. Ct. (we. dist.) 1978. Sole practice, Mercer, Pa., 1976-81, 88-92; ptnr. Bogaty, McEwen, Sparks, & Kochems, P.C., 1981-87, Nelson, Ryan & Kochems, 1992—. Asst. pub. defender Mercer County, 1977-88; asst. dist. atty., 1988—; sub-com. chairperson Mercer County Juvenile Ct. Adv. Com., 1986-88, chair child death rev. com., 1999—, leader dist. atty.'s child abuse prosecution unit, 1996—; solicitor Mercer County Regional Planning Commn., 1991—. Assoc. editor St. Louis U. Law Jour., 1975-76. Bd. dirs. Transfer Harvest Home Assn., 1986-88; solicitor Mcpl. Corp., 1996—; co-chairperson Mercer County Sexual Assault Response Team, 2000—. Mem. ABA, Pa. Bar Assn., Mercer County Bar Assn. (sec. 1977-79, bench bar com. 1982, 84), KC (adv. 1978-88). Republican. Criminal, Family and matrimonial, Juvenile. Home: PO Box 226 Mercer PA 16137-0226

KOCIUBES, JOSEPH LEIB, lawyer; b. Frankfurt, Fed. Republic of Germany, June 16, 1947; came to U.S., 1949; s. Max and Rachel (Ackerman) K.; m. Peggy Ann Roth, May 18, 1969; children: Lisa Roth, Adam Roth. BA, U. Pitts., 1969; JD, Harvard U., 1974. Bar: Mass. 1974, U.S. Dist. Ct. Mass. 1974, U.S. Ct. Appeals (1st cir.) 1974, U.S. Ct. Appeals (6th cir.) 1987, U.S. Ct. Appeals (4th cir.) 1988, U.S. Supreme Ct. 1981. Asst. to dean Coll. Arts and Sci., U. Pitts., 1969; dir. health and edn. programs North Shore Community Action Program, Beverly, Mass., 1969-71; asst. dir. Project RAP, Beverly, 1971; assoc. Bingham, Dana & Gould, Boston, 1974-81, ptnr., 1981—, mem. mgmt. com., 1984-96; faculty various programs Mass. Continuing Legal Edn., 1989—; trial practice advisor Harvard Law Sch., 1985—. Gen. counsel Civil Liberties Union of Mass.; dir., mem. exec. com. Greater Boston Legal Svcs., 1989—; dir. Vol. Lawyers Project, 1985-95. Fellow Am. Coll. Trial Lawyer, Mass. State Com., Boston Bar Found. (trustee 1997-2000), Am. Bar Found., Mass. Bar Found.; mem. Boston Bar Assn. (v.p. 2000—). E-mail: jlkociubes@bingham.com. Federal civil litigation, State civil litigation. Office: Bingham Dana & Gould 150 Federal St Fl 15 Boston MA 02110-1726

KOEGEN, ROY JEROME, lawyer; b. Spokane, Wash., Mar. 1, 1949; s. Frank J. and Jeanne (Bardsley) K.; m. Ann Martinelli, Aug. 28, 1970; children: Jennifer, Christopher. BA, Gonzaga U., 1971; JD, U. Calif., San Francisco, 1974. Bar: Calif. 1974, Wash. 1979, U.S. Supreme Ct. 1982. Assoc. Wilson, Jones, Morton & Lynch, San Mateo, Calif., 1974-78, Blair & Koegen, Spokane, 1978-80; ptnr. Preston, Thorgrimson, Ellis & Holman, 1980-90, Perkins Coie LLP, Seattle, Spokane, 1990—. Author: Washington Municipal Financing Deskbook, 1992. Chmn. exec. com. Community Alcohol Ctr., Spokane, 1982-84, Century II Park Dist., Spokane, 1982-84; bd. dirs. Nature Conservancy. Mem. ABA, Wash. Bar Assn., Calif. Bar Assn., Nat. Assn. Bond Lawyers, The Nature Conservancy (bd. dirs.). Roman Catholic. Municipal (including bonds), Securities. Office: Perkins Coie LLP 221 N Wall St Ste 600 Spokane WA 99201-0826

KOEHNKE, PHILLIP EUGENE, lawyer, consultant; b. Denver, Sept. 3, 1962; s. Eugene and Lorraine Koehnke; m. Diane Koehnke. BS, Colo. State U., 1985; JD, U. Wash., 1992. Bar: Calif., Colo., U.S. Dist. Ct. (ctrl., so. and no. dists.) Calif., U.S. Supreme Ct. Atty., San Diego, 1992—. Bus. editor U. Wash. Sch. Law Pacific Rim Law and Policy Jour., 1992; contbr. articles to profl. jours. Avocations: running, weightlifting, surfing. General civil litigation, Construction, Securities. Office: Tradeway Securities Group Inc 5875 Avenida Encinas Carlsbad CA 92008-4404

KOELLER, LYNN GARVER, public defender; b. Portsmouth, Ohio, Dec. 4, 1943; d. Stanley Wayne and Ruth Louise (Garver) Paulson; m. Michael Koeller, Sept. 6, 1964 (div. July 1980); children: Kristin Schmid, Mark. BS, U. Dayton, 1977, JD, 1980. Bar: Ohio, 1980, U.S. Dist. Ct., 1980. Assoc. Denny, Malloy & Cox, Dayton, Ohio, 1980-82; asst. pub. defender Montgomery County Pub. Defender Office, 1982-95, chief pub. defender, 1995—. Mem. Dayton Bar Assn. (criminal law com.), Dayton Women's Bar Assn. Montgomery County Criminal Justice Coun., Barbara Jordon/Thurgood Marshall Roundtable. Home: 19983 Forest Ave Apt 5 Castro Valley CA 94546-4569 Office: Office Pub Defender 14 W 4th St Ste 400 Dayton OH 45402-1883

KOELLER, ROBERT MARION, lawyer, director; b. Quincy, Ill., Apr. 8, 1940; s. Marion Alfred and Ruth (Main) K.; m. Marlene Meyer, June 1962; children: Kristin, Katherine, Robert. AB, MacMurray Coll., 1962; LLB, Vanderbilt U., 1965. Bar: Ind. 1968. Asst. gen. counsel Nat. Homes Acceptance Corp., Lafayette, Ind., 1967-70; gen. counsel, sec. Herff Jones Co., Indpls., 1970-74; ptnr. Warren, Snider, Koeller & Warren, 1974-76; sole practice, 1976—; mem. Coons, Maddox & Koeller, 1993-96, Maddox, Koeller Hargett & Caruso, 1996—. Dir. various cos. Mem. ABA, Ind. Bar Assn., Indpls. Bar Assn., Hillcrest Country Club. Republican. Methodist. General corporate, Probate, Securities. Office: Ste 190 7351 Shadeland Station Way Indianapolis IN 46256-3924 E-mail: bkoeller@iquest.net

KOELLING, THOMAS WINSOR, lawyer; b. Jefferson City, Mo., Oct. 10, 1951; s. Oscar Alvin and Helen Louise (Shields) K.;m. Rebecca Ann Nentwig, Nov. 24, 1973; children: Zachary Thomas, Mathew Garret. BS in Criminal Justice Adminstrn., Ctrl. Mo. State U., Warrenburg, 1978; JD, U. Mo., 1981. Bar: Mo. 1981, Colo. 1982, U.S. Dist. Ct. (we. dist.) Mo. 1981, U.S. Dist. Ct. Colo. 1981, U.S. Ct. Appeals (8th cir.) 1982, U.S. Ct. Appeals (10th cir.) 1981, U.S. Supreme Ct. 1992. Assoc. Tinsley, Frantz et al, Lakewood, Colo., 1981-82, Rex Johnson Law Office, Colorado Springs, 1982-85; ptnr. Koelling & Crawford, P.C., Kansas City, Mo., 1985—. Legal advisor Kansas City Ski Club, 1987, Competitors Assn., Kansas City, 1995—; adj. prof. dept. criminal justice and legal studies Mo. Western State Coll., St. Joseph, Mo., 1998—. With USAF, 1972-76. Mem. ABA, Am. Coll. Legal Medicine, Am. Soc. Law, Medicine Ethics, Am. Trial

Lawyers Assn., Mo. Assn. Trial Lawyers, Clay County Bar Assn. Roman Catholic. Avocations: snow skiing, fly fishing, backpacking. Personal injury, Professional liability, Toxic tort. Home: 9617 N Campbell St Kansas City MO 64155-2056 Office: Koelling & Crawford PC 5950 N Oak Trfy Ste 202 Kansas City MO 64118-5164

KOELTL, JOHN GEORGE, judge; b. N.Y.C., Oct. 25, 1945; s. John J. and Elsie (Bender) K. AB summa cum laude, Harvard U., 1967, JD magna cum laude, 1971. Bar: N.Y. 1972, U.S. Dist. Ct. (so. and ea. dists.) N.Y. 1975, U.S. Ct. Appeals (2d cir.) 1975, U.S. Supreme Ct. 1978, U.S. Ct. Appeals (5th and 11th cirs.) 1981, U.S. Ct. Appeals (4th cir.) 1992, U.S. Dist. Ct. (no. dist.) N.Y. 1982. Law clk. to Judge U.S. Dist. Ct. (so. dist.), N.Y.C., 1971-72; law clk. to Justice Potter Stewart U.S. Supreme Ct., Washington, 1972-73; asst. spl. prosecutor Watergate Spl. Prosecution Force, Dept. Justice, 1973-74; assoc. Debevoise & Plimpton, N.Y.C., 1975-78, ptnr., 1979-94; judge U.S. Dist. Ct. (so. dist.), 1994—. Adj. prof. law NYU Law Sch., 1999—. Mem. bd. editors Manual for Complex Litigation 4th edit.; contbr. articles to profl. jours. Mem. ABA (bd. editors jour. 1991-97, vice chmn. securities com. adminstrv. law sect. 1979-81, co-dir. divsn. publs. litigation sect. 1982-84, coun. mem. litigation sect. 1984-87, assoc. editor Litigation jour. 1975-78, exec. editor 1978-80, editor-in-chief 1980-82, chmn. 1st amendment com. 1987-89, chmn. spl. pubs. com. 1989-92, dir. divsn. publs. litigation sect. 1992-93), Coalition for Justice, Assn. Bar N.Y.C. (mem. com. on fed legislation 1976-78, sec. 1978-81, mem. com. profl. and jud. ethics 1981-84, fed. cts. com. 1984-86, chmn. 1986-89, mem. com. on profl. responsibility 1991-94), N.Y. State Bar Assn., N.Y. County Lawyers Assn. (mem. fed. cts. com. 1984-87), Harvard Law Sch. Assn. N.Y. (v.p. 1993-94). Office: US Courthouse 500 Pearl St Rm 1030 New York NY 10007-1316

KOELZER, GEORGE JOSEPH, lawyer; b. Orange, N.J., Mar. 21, 1938; s. George Joseph and Albertina Florence (Graul) K.; m. Patricia Ann Kilian, Apr. 8, 1967; 1 son, James Patrick. AB, Rutgers U., 1962, LLB, 1964. Bar: N.J. 1964, D.C. 1978, N.Y. 1980, Calif. 1993; registered fgn. lawyer, U.K., 2001. Assoc. Louis R. Lombardino, Livingston, N.J., 1964-66, Lum Biunno & Tompkins, Newark, 1971-73, Giordano, Halleran & McOmber, Middletown, N.J., 1973-74; asst. U.S. atty. for N.J. U.S. Dept. Justice, 1966-71; ptnr. Evans, Koelzer, Osborne & Kreizman, N.Y.C. and Red Bank, N.J., 1974-86, Ober, Kaler, Grimes & Shriver, N.Y.C., 1986-92, Lane Powell Spears Lubersky, L.A., 1993-97, Hancock, Rothert & Bunshoft, L.A., 1997-2000, Coudert Bros., L.A., London, 2000—. Adj. prof. Seton Hall U. Sch. Law, 1989-92; mem. lawyers adv. com. U.S. Ct. Appeals (3d cir.) 1985-87, vice chmn., 1986, chmn., 1987; mem. lawyers adv. com. U.S. Dist. Ct. N.J., 1984-92; permanent mem. Jud. Conf. of U.S. Ct. Appeals for 3d cir.; del. jud. conf. U.S. Ct. Appeals for 2d cir., 1987, 88, 89. Recipient Atty. Gen.'s award, 1970. Fellow Am. Bar Found.; mem. ABA (sect. litigation, co-chmn. com. on admirality and maritime litigation 1979-82, 89-90, mem. coun. sect. litigation 1985-88, chmn. 9th ann. meeting sect. litigation 1984, dir. divsn. IV procedural coms. 1982-85, dir. divsn. I adminstrn. 1988-89, mem. nominating com. 1982, 84, 87, advisor standing com. lawyer competence 1986—), Maritime Law Assn. U.S. (ABA relations com., fed. procedure com., vice chmn. com. on maritime fraud and crime 1989-94, chmn. 1994-98, bd. dirs. 1998-2001), State Bar Calif., N.Y. State Bar Assn. (chmn. admiralty com., comml. and fed. litigation sect. 1989-92), Assn. of Bar of City of N.Y. (admirality com. 1987-90), D.C. Bar Assn., Fed. Bar Assn. (mem. fed. practice com. 1994—), Fed. Bar Council, Comml. Bar Assn. (London), Assn. Average Adjustrs Gt. Britain, Assn. Average Adjusters U.S., Assn. Bus. and Trial Lawyers, L.A. World Affairs Coun.; Clubs: Mid-Ocean (Bermuda), Jonathan Club (L.A.). Roman Catholic. Republican. Admiralty, Federal civil litigation, Criminal. Home: 521 S Orange Grove Blvd 100 Pasadena CA 91105-3504

KOENIG, RODNEY CURTIS, lawyer, rancher; b. Black Jack, Tex., Nov. 21, 1940; s. John Henry and Elva Marguerite (Oeding) K.; m. Mary Mishler, May 1, 1993; children: Erik Jason, Jon Todd. BA, U. Tex., 1962, JD with honors, 1969; postgrad., Auburn U., 1965-67. Bar: Tex. 1969, U.S. Dist. Ct. (so. dist.) Tex. 1970, U.S. Ct. Appeals (5th cir.) 1970, U.S. Tax Ct. 1980, U.S. Ct. Mil. Appeals 1986. Ptnr. Fulbright & Jaworski, LLP, Houston, 1969—. Lectr. State Bar Tex., various univs., local estate planning councils; asst. prof. Auburn U., 1965-67 Contbr. articles to profl. jours. Pres. Houston Navy League, 1979-81; commr. Battleship Texas Commn.; Houston Saengerbund; bd. dirs. Houston divsn. Am. Heart Assn., Fayette Heritage Mus.; dir. Advanced Estate Planning and Probate Course, 1988; trustee Luck and Loessin Collection Trust, Luth. Found. of the S.W., treas., exec. com.; active Tex. Luth. U. Corp. With USN, 1962-67; served to capt. JAGC, USNR, 1967-89. Recipient Fed. Republic of Germany Order of Merit, 1994. Fellow Am. Coll. Trust and Estate Counsel, Coll. State Bar Tex. (charter); mem. ABA, Internat. Acad. Estate and Trust Law (academician), Tex. Judge Adv. Res. Officers Assn., German Texan Heritage Soc. (pres. 1997-2000), Res. Officers Assn., Sons of Republic of Tex., Wednesday Tax Forum (past chmn.), German Gulf Coast Assn. (pres. 1989-93), Bach Soc. (bd. dirs.), Houston Early Music (pres. 2000—), Houston Karneval Verein (prince 1994-95), USS San Jacinto Com. (treas.), Houstonian Club, Houston Ctr. Club, Frisch Auf Valley Country Club, Order of Coif, U.S. Naval Order, Phi Delta Phi, Omicron Delta Kappa. Lutheran. Estate planning, Probate, Estate taxation. Home: 2720 University Blvd Houston TX 77005-3440 Office: Fulbright & Jaworski LLP 1301 Mckinney St Fl 51 Houston TX 77010-3031 E-mail: rkoenig@fulbright.com

KOFF, HOWARD MICHAEL, lawyer; b. Bklyn., July 25, 1941; s. Arthur and Blanche Koff; m. Linda Sue Bright, Sept. 10, 1966; 1 son, Michael Arthur Bright. BS, NYU, 1962; JD, Bklyn. Law Sch., 1965; LLM in Taxation, Georgetown U., 1968. Bar: N.Y. 1965, D.C. 1966, U.S. Supreme Ct. 1969, U.S. Ct. Appeals (2d, 3d, 4th, 5th, 7th, 9th and D.C. cirs.), U.S. Dist. Ct. (no. dist.) N.Y. 1981. Appellate atty. tax divsn. U.S. Dept. Justice, Washington, 1965-69; tax supr. Chrysler Corp., Detroit, 1969-70; chief tax counsel Conn. Gen. Life Ins. Co., Hartford, Conn., 1970-77, Rohm & Haus Co., Phila., 1977-78; ptnr., chief tax counsel Dibble, Koff, Lane, Stern and Stern, Rochester, 1978-81; pres. Howard M. Koff, P.C., Albany, N.Y., 1981—. Lectr. tax matters. Editor-in-chief Bklyn. Law Rev., 1964-65; charter mem. editl. adv. bd. Jour. Real Estate Taxation; contbr. articles to legal jours. Chmn. pub. adv. coun. N.Y. State Ethics Commn. Recipient Founders Day award NYU, 1962, Lawyers Coop. award for gen. excellence Lawyers Coop. Pub. Co., 1965. Mem. ABA (past chmn. subcom. on partnerships tax sect.), FBA (past pres. Hartford County chpt.), Albany County Bar Assn., Estate Planning Coun. Ea. N.Y., Albany Area C. of C., Rotary, Colonie Guilderland N.Y. Club. Republican. Corporate taxation, Personal income taxation, State and local taxation. Home: 205 W Bentwood Ct Albany NY 12203-4905 Office: 600 Broadway Albany NY 12207-2205

KOFFLER, WARREN WILLIAM, lawyer; b. N.Y.C., July 21, 1938; s. Jack and Rose (Conovich) K.; m. Barbara Rose Holz, June 11, 1959; m. Jayne Audri Goetzel, May 15, 1970; children: Kevin, Kenneth, Caroline. BS, Boston U., 1959; JD, U. Calif., Berkeley, 1962; LLD, NYU, 1972. Bar: D.C. 1962, N.Y. 1963, U.S. Dist. Ct. D.C. 1963, Fla. 1980, Va. 1981, Pa. 1982. Atty. FAA, Washington, 1964; pvt. practice law, 1964, 78—, Hollywood, Palm Beach, Miami, Fla., 1978—; atty. Fed. Home Loan Bank Bd., Washington, 1964-66; ptnr. Koffler & Spivack, 1967-77. Mem. ATLA, ABA, FBA, Inter-Am. Bar Assn., D.C. Bar Assn., Fla. Bar Assn., Va. Bar Assn., Brit. Inst. Internat. and Comparative Law, Univ. Club (Washington), Bankers Club (Miami), Membership Club PGA Nat. (Palm Beach), City Club (Palm Beach). Administrative and regulatory, Banking, Private international. Office: 11440 Us Highway 1 North Palm Beach FL 33408-3226 also: 1730 K St NW Washington DC 20006-3868 E-mail: wwkvip@msn.com

KOGER, FRANK WILLIAMS, federal judge; b. Kansas City, Mo., Mar. 20, 1930; s. C.H. and Lelia D. (Williams) K.; m. Jeanine E. Strawhacker, Mar. 19, 1954; children: Lelia Jane, Mary Courtney. AB, Kansas City U., 1951, LLB, 1953; LLM, U. Mo., Kansas City, 1966. Staff judge adv. USAF, Rapid City, S.D., 1953-56; ptnr. Reid, Koger & Reid, Kansas City, 1956-61, Shockley, Reid & Koger, Kansas City, 1961-86; U.S. bankruptcy judge U.S. Dept. Judiciary, 1986—; chief judge 8th Cir. Bankruptcy Appellate Panel, 1997—. Adj. prof. law sch. U. Mo., Columbia, 1990—, U. Mo.-Kansas City, 1992—. Author: (manual) Foreclosure Law in Missouri, 1982, Missouri Collection Law, 1983; author, co-editor: Bankruptcy Handbook, 1992; editor: Bankruptcy Law, 1990. Bd. dirs. Jackson County Pub. Hosp., Kansas City, 1974-79, St. Lukes Hosp., Kansas City, 1970—; chair subcom. Jackson County Charter Transition Com., Kansas City, 1978-79. Capt. USAF, 1953-56. Recipient Shelley Peters Meml. award Am. Inst. Banking, Kansas City, 1986. Fellow Am. Coll. Bankruptcy Judges; mem. Nat. Conf. Bankruptcy Judges (dir. 1990-93, sec. 1994-95, pres.-elect 1995-96, pres. 1996-97), Comml. Law League Am. (pres. 1983-84). Avocations: contract bridge, gardening. Office: US Bankruptcy Ct 400 E 9th St Kansas City MO 64106-2607

KOGOVSEK, DANIEL CHARLES, lawyer; b. Pueblo, Colo., Aug. 4, 1951; s. Frank Louis and Mary Edith (Blatnick) K.; m. Patricia Elizabeth Connell, June 30, 1979; 1 child, Ryan Robert. BA, U. Notre Dame, 1973; JD, Columbia U., 1976. Bar: Colo. 1976, U.S. Dist. Ct. Colo. 1976, U.S. Ct. Appeals (10th cir.) 1978, U.S. Supreme Ct. 1983. Ast. atty. gen. Colo. Dept. Law, Denver, 1976-79; campaign mgr. Congressman Kogovsek, Pueblo, 1980, 82; dir. Office Consumer Svcs., Denver, 1981; mem. firm Fish & Kogovsek, 1983-84; sr. assoc. Petersen & Fonda, P.C., Pueblo, 1985-89; mem. firm Kogovsek & Higinbotham, P.C., 1989—; county atty. Pueblo County, 2001—. Mem. ABA, Colo. Bar Assn., Pueblo Bar Assn. Consumer commercial. Home: 584 W Spaulding Ave S Pueblo West CO 81007-1874 Office: 323 S Union Ave Pueblo CO 81003-3429 E-mail: koglaw@aculink.net

KOHL, KATHLEEN ALLISON BARNHART, lawyer; b. Ft. Leavenworth, Kans., Jan. 11, 1955; d. Robert William and Margaret Ann (Snowden) Barnhart. BS, Memphis State U., 1978; JD, Loyola U., New Orleans, 1982. Bar: La. 1982, U.S. Dist. Ct. (ea. dist.) La. 1982, U.S. Dist. Ct. (no. dist.) Tex. 1985, U.S. Ct. Appeals (5th cir.) 1986, U.S. Ct. Appeals (11th cir.) 1988, U.S. Supreme Ct. 1994. Assoc. Garrity & Webb, Harahan, La., 1982; revenue officer IRS, Dallas, 1984; sr. trial atty. EEOC, 1984-86; sr. criminal enforcement counsel U.S. EPA, 1986-91, chief water enforcement sect., office regional counsel, 1991-92, dep. dir. criminal enforcement counsel divsn. Washington, 1992-93, dir. criminal enforcement counsel divsn., 1993-94, sr. criminal enforcement counsel Dallas, 1994—; spl. asst. U.S. atty. U.S. Atty.'s Office, Montgomery, Ala., 1988-89. Vis. instr. Fed. Law Enforcement Tng. Ctr., Glynco, Ga., 1987—; adj. prof. environ. crimes seminar Cornell U. Law Sch., spring 1993, environ. law sch. Law Tex. Wesleyan U., fall 1998; instr. EPA Nat. Acad., 1997—. Vol. instr. New Orleans Police Acad., 1981. Mem. La. Bar Assn. Office: EPA 1445 Ross Ave Ste 1200 Dallas TX 75202-2733

KOHLSTEDT, JAMES AUGUST, lawyer; b. Evanston, Ill., June 1, 1949; s. August Lewis and Deloris (Weichelt) K.; m. Patricia Ann Lang, Oct. 8, 1977; children: Katherine, Matthew, Lindsey, Kevin. BA, Northwestern U., 1971; JD, MBA, Ind. U., 1976. Bar: U.S. Dist. Ct. (no. dist.) Ill. 1976, U.S. Tax Ct. 1978. Tax specialist Peat Marwick, Mitchell & Co., Chgo., 1976-77; assoc. Bishop & Crawford Ltd., Oak Brook, Ill., 1977-83, 1984-85; ptnr. Arnstein, Gluck, Lehr & Milligan, 1985-87, Keck, Mahin and Cate, Oak Brook, 1987-96, McBride Baker & Coles, 1996-2001, mem. mgmt. com., 1997; chair McBride Baker & Coles Trade and Profl. Assn. Practice Group; sr. ptnr. Kohlstedt and Teske LLC, 2001—. Bd. dirs. Nat. Entrepreneurship Found., Bloomington, Ind., 1981-92, Camp New Hope Devel. Bd., Oak Brook, 1983; mem. sch. bd. Lyons Twp. H.S. Dist. 204, La Grange, Ill., 1985-97; pres. Hinsdale (Ill.) Cmty. House Coun., 1991-94; mem. area leadership com. Superconducting Super Collider, 1987-88; mem. citizens adv. com. on edn. to U.S. Congressman Harris Fawell, 1986-93; bd. dirs. Ill. Corridor Partnership for Excellence in Edn., 1988-94; mem. planned giving com. Elmhurst Coll., 1986—; mem. citizens adv. panel U.S. Army ROTC Cadet Command, 1991-94; bd. dirs. Ill. Math and Sci. Acad. Alliance, 1989—; del. White House Conf. Travel and Tourism, 1995; mem. allied adv. bd. midwest chpt. Am. Soc. Travel Agents, 1995; Collegiate Edn. adv. com. Dept. Def., 1995. Recipient Outstanding Young Citizen of Chgo. award 1987. Mem. ABA, Ill. Travel and Tourism Assn., Ill. Bar Assn., DuPage Estate Planning Coun., Oak Brook Jaycees (pres. 1984—, chmn. bd. 1985, trustee 1985-86), Beta Gamma Sigma. Republican. Lutheran. Computer, General corporate, Probate. Office: McBride Baker & Coles 500 W Madison St 40th Fl Chicago IL 60661-2511

KOHN, ALAN CHARLES, lawyer; b. St. Louis, Feb. 14, 1932; s. William Kohn and Rose Kohn (Steinberg) K.; m. Joanne J. Kohn, Aug. 29, 1954; children: Tom, Jim, John. AB, Washington U., 1953, LLB, 1955. Law clk. to assoc. justice Charles E. Whittaker U.S. Supreme Ct., 1957-58; assoc. William Kohn, St. Louis, 1958-59, Coburn, Croft & Kohn, St. Louis, 1959-62, ptnr., 1962-70, Kohn, Shands, Elbert, Gianoulakis & Giljum, St. Louis, 1970—. Adv. Am. Bd. Trial Advs.; mem. Mo. Bd. Law Examiners, 1969-79, pres., 1975-79; mem. U.S. Dist. Ct. (ea. dist.) Mo. Bd. Admissions, 1969-72, chmn., 1970-72; mem. fed. practice com. U.S. Dist. Ct. (ea. dist.) Mo., 1987—. Editor-in-chief Washington U. Law Quarterly, 1955; contbr. articles to profl. jours. Chmn. Mo. Housing Devel. Com., 1975-79; treas. University City (Mo.) Bd. Edn., 1970-71. 1st lt. U.S. Army Security Agy., 1955-57. Fellow Am. Coll. Trial Lawyers; mem. ABA, ABA Found., Am. Law Inst., Mo. Bar Assn., St. Louis Bar Assn., Best Lawyers in Am., Bd. of Trial Advocates (advocate), Order of Coif, Phi Beta Kappa, Omicron Delta Kappa, Phi Eta Sigma. Republican. Avocation: tennis. Federal civil litigation, General civil litigation, State civil litigation. Home: 40 Upper Ladue Rd Saint Louis MO 63124-1630 Office: Kohn Shands Elbert Gianoulakis & Giljum One Mercantile Center 24th Fl Saint Louis MO 63101 E-mail: akohn@kseeg.com

KOHN, IMMANUEL, lawyer; b. Jerusalem, Dec. 6, 1926; came to U.S., 1934; s. Hans and Yetty (Wahl) K.; m. Vera Sharpe, July 22, 1950; children: Gail, Peter, Sheila, Robert. Grad., Deerfield Acad., 1944; B.A. summa cum laude, Harvard U., 1949; LL.B cum laude, Yale U., 1953. Bar: N.Y. 1955, U.S. Dist. Ct. (ea. dist.) N.Y. 1955, U.S. Dist. Ct. (so. dist.) N.Y. 1957, U.S. Ct. Appeals (2d cir.) 1966, U.S. Supreme Ct. 1972. Assoc. Gordon & Reindel, N.Y.C., 1953-62, ptnr., 1962, mem. exec. com., 1972—, chmn. exec. com., 1991—; trustee Inst. Advanced Study, Princeton, NJ, 1997—; nat. Gov. Shaw Festival, Niagara-on-the-Lake, Ontario. Editor, Yale U. Law Jour., 1951-53. Served as ensign U.S. Maritime Service, 1946. Sheldon travelling fellow, 1949-50 Mem. Downtown Assn., Met. Opera Club, Sky Club, Bedens Brook Club (N.J.), Order of Coif, Phi Beta Kappa. Home: 34 Puritan Ct Princeton NJ 08540-2416 Office: Cahill Gordon & Reindel 80 Pine St Fl 17 New York NY 10005-1790

KOHN, SHALOM L. lawyer; b. Nov. 18, 1949; s. Pincus and Helen (Roth) K.; m. Barbara Segal, June 30, 1974; children: David, Jeremy, Daniel. BS in Acctg. summa cum laude, CUNY, 1970; JD magna cum laude, MBA, Harvard U., 1974. Bar: Ill. 1975, U.S. Dist. Ct. (no. dist.) Ill. 1975, U.S. Ct. Appeals (7th cir.) 1976, U.S. Supreme Ct. 1980, N.Y. 1988, U.S. Dist. Ct. (so. dist.) N.Y. 1988. Law clk. to chief judge U.S. Ct. Appeals (2d cir.), N.Y.C., 1974-75; assoc. Sidley & Austin, Chgo., 1975-80, ptnr., 1980—. Exec. com. Adv. Coun. Religious Rights in Eastern Europe and Soviet Union, Washington, 1984-86; bd. dirs. Brisk Rabbinical Coll., Chgo. Contbr. articles to profl. jours. Mem. ABA, Chgo. Bar Assn. Bankruptcy, Federal civil litigation, General practice. Office: Sidley & Austin Bank One Plz 10 South Dearborn Chicago IL 60603 also: 875 3rd Ave New York NY 10022-6225

KOHN, WILLIAM IRWIN, lawyer; b. Bronx, N.Y., June 27, 1951; s. Arthur Oscar and Frances (Hoffman) K.; m. Karen Mindlin, Aug. 29, 1974; children: Shira, Kinneret, Asher. Student, U. Del., 1969-71; BA with honors, U. Cin., 1973; JD, Ohio State U., 1976. Bar: Ohio 1976, U.S. Dist. Ct. (no. dist.) Ohio 1982, Ind. 1982, U. S. Dist. Ct. (no. and so. dists.) Ind. 1982, D.C. 1992, U.S. Supreme Ct., 1992, Ill. 1994; cert. Bus. Bankruptcy Law Am. Bankruptcy Bd. Cert. Ptnr. Krugliak, Wilkins, Griffith & Dougherty, Canton, Ohio, 1976-82, Barnes & Thornburg, Chgo., 1982—. Adj. prof. law U. Notre Dame, Ind., 1984-90. Author: West's Indiana Business Forms, West's Indiana Uniform Commercial Code Forms; contbr. articles to profl. jours. Bd. dirs. Family Svcs., South Bend, 1985-94, Jewish Fedn., Highland Park United Way. Mem. ABA (bus. bankruptcy subcom.), Am. Bankruptcy Inst. (insolvency sect., bd. dirs.), Ill. Bar Assn., Chgo. Bar Assn., Comml. Law League, Am. Bd. Certification (dir., std. com.). Banking, Bankruptcy, Contracts commercial. Office: Barnes & Thornburg 2600 Chase Plz 10 S La Salle St Ste 2600 Chicago IL 60603-1010 E-mail: wkohn@btlaw.com

KOJEVNIKOV, BORIS OLEG, lawyer, foreign legal consultant; b. Rome, Oct. 16, 1950; came to U.S., 1977; s. Oleg Vladimir and Oxana (Artem) K.; m. Irina Maxim Baranova, Aug. 8, 1974; children: Oxana, Oleg. Law Degre, Inst. Fgn. Rels., Moscow, 1972, Cand Legal Scis., 1984. Legal adviser USSR Ministry Fgn. Trade, Moscow, 1972-77, Amtorg Trading Corp., N.Y.C., 1977-82, Comecon, Moscow, 1982-84; dir. legal dept. Chamber Commerce and Industry, 1984-91; v.p. Prosystem GmbH, Vienna, 1991-96; v.p., mem. Golubov & Tiagai, N.Y.C., 1996—; mng. dir. Inhorn GmbH, Vienna, 1999—. Arbitrator Internat. Comml. Arbitration ct., Moscow, 1984—, Internat. Arbitration Ctr., Vienna, 1989-94. Author 4 books; contbr. more than 20 articles to U.S., Russian and German periodicals. Fellow Chartered Inst. of Arbitrators; mem. Assn. Bar City N.Y., U.S.-USSR Trade and Econ. Coun. Inc. (USSR co-chmn. legal com. 1989-91), Canada-USSR Bus. Coun. (USSR co-chmn. legal com. 1989-91), Internat. Chamber of Commerce (USSR coord. ICC-USSR joint task force, 1989-90). Avocations: tennis, squash. Contracts commercial, Private international. Home: 7 Summit St Englewood Cliffs NJ 07632-1443 Office: Golubov & Tiagai PLLC 475 5th Ave Rm 1112 New York NY 10017-6220

KOLBE, KARL WILLIAM, JR. lawyer; b. Passaic, N.J., Sept. 29, 1926; s. Karl William Sr. and Edna Ernestine (Rumsey) K.; m. Barbara Louise Bogart, Jan. 28, 1950 (dec. Aug. 1992); children: Kim E., William B., Katherine B.; m. Patricia L. Coward, Apr. 30, 1994. BA, Princeton U., 1949; JD, U. Va., 1952. Bars: N.Y. 1952, D.C. 1976. Ptnr. Thelen, Reid & Priest, N.Y.C., 1966-92, of counsel, 1993—. Dir. Bessemer Trust Co. (N.A.), N.Y.C.,1977-97, Carolinas Cement Co., 1994-98, World Trade Corp.; vice-chmn. The Friends of Thirteen Inc. Bd. dirs. N.J. Ballet Co., West Orange, 1970-98, Ocean Liner Mus., 1992—. With USN, 1944-46. Mem. ABA (chmn. pub. utility law sect. 1984-85). Republican. Episcopalian. Clubs: Univ. (N.Y.C.); Metro. (Washington). Taxation, general. Home: PO Box 278 111 Old Chester Rd Essex Fells NJ 07021-1625 Office: Thelen Reid & Priest 40 W 57th St New York NY 10019-4097 E-mail: wkolbe@thelenreid.com

KOLE, JANET STEPHANIE, lawyer, writer, photographer; b. Washington, Dec. 20, 1946; d. Martin J. and Ruth G. (Goldberg) K. AB, Bryn Mawr Coll., 1968; MA, NYU, 1970; JD, Temple U., 1980. Bar: Pa. 1980, N.J. 1994. Assoc. editor trade books Simon & Schuster, N.Y.C., 1968-70; publicity dir. Am. Arbitration Assn., 1970-73, freelance photojournalist, 1973-76; law clk. Morgan Lewis & Bockius, Phila., 1977-80; assoc. Schnader, Harrison, Segal & Lewis, 1980-85; ptnr. Cohen, Shapiro, Polisher, Shiekman & Cohen, 1985-95; ptnr., chmn. environ. practice group Klehr, Harrison, Harvey, Branzburg & Ellers, 1995-97; pvt. practice, 1997-2001; chmn. environ. dept. Cooper, Perskie, April, Niedelman, Wagenheim & Levenson, Atlantic City/Cherry Hill, N.J., 2001—. Author: Post Mortem, 1974; editor Environmental Litigation, 1991, 99; contbr. numerous articles to gen. interest publs., profl. jour.; past mem. bd. editors New Am. Rev. Mem. Mayor's Task Force on Rape, N.Y.C., 1972-77; adv. Support Ctr. Child Advs., Phila., 1980—; mem. Phila. Vol. Lawyers for Arts. Fellow Acad. Advocacy, Am. Bar Found.; mem. ABA (co-chair individual and small firm, former co-chair environ. litigation com., former dir., publs., former coun. mem. sect. litigation, dir. publs., former co-divsn. dir. substantive areas litigation, former editor litigation news, former chmn. com. monographs and unpublished papers, com. spl. pubs.), ALTA. Federal civil litigation, State civil litigation, Environmental. Office: 900 Haddon Ave Ste 412 Collingswood NJ 08108-2113

KOLE, JULIUS S. lawyer; b. Chgo., July 27, 1953; s. Jack H. and Ruth (Rakowsky) K.; m. Dorie Elrod, June 27, 1976; children: Ryan, Frederick, Abby. BS in Fin., U. Ill., Chgo., 1975; JD, John Marshall Law Sch., 1978. Bar: Ill. 1978. Asst. pub. defender Cook County Pub. Defender, Chgo., 1978-80; prin. Law Offices of Julius S. Kole, Buffalo Grove, Ill., 1980—. Fellow Ill. State Bar Assn., Lake County Bar Assn. Jewish. Avocations: sports, reading, motorcycling. General corporate, Criminal, Real property. Office: 750 W Lake Cook Rd Ste 135 Buffalo Grove IL 60089-2075

KOLESNYK, OLEG IVANOVICH, lawyer; b. Kyiv, Ukraine, Nov. 2, 1964; s. Ivan Petrovich and Yadviga Andreevna K.; m. Tatiana Andreevna Smorgonskaya Kolysnyk, Aug. 21, 1998. Law degree, Kyiv State U., Ukraine, 1988; student, Leeds U., Eng., 1995. Kyiv bar: 1994—. Atty. Grischenko & Part, Kyiv, Ukraine, 1992-98; cons. Hewett & Co., London, 1995; sr. lawyer Nch Advisors, Kyiv, Ukraine, 1998-99; lawyer Dejure, Ukraine, 1999—. Aviation, Contracts commercial, Corporate taxation. Home: 12 Geroev Dnepra Apt 59 Kyiv 04209 Ukraine Office: Bar Assn of DeJure G Grushevskogo St Kyiv Ukraine

KOLKEY, DANIEL MILES, judge; b. Chgo., Apr. 21, 1952; s. Eugene Louis and Gilda Penelope (Cowan) K.; m. Donna Lynn Christie, May 15, 1982; children: Eugene, William, Christopher, Jonathan. BA, Stanford U., 1974; JD, Harvard U., 1977. Bar: Calif. 1977, U.S. Dist. Ct. (ea. dist.) Calif. 1978, U.S. Dist. Ct. (cen. dist.) Calif. 1979, U.S. Ct. Appeals (9th cir.) 1979, U.S. Dist. Ct. (no. dist.) Calif. 1980, U.S. Supreme Ct. 1983, U.S. Dist. Ct. Ariz. 1992, U.S. Dist. Ct. (so. dist.) Calif. 1994. Law clk. U.S. Dist. Ct. judge, N.Y.C., 1977-78; assoc. Gibson Dunn & Crutcher, L.A., 1978-84, ptnr., 1985-94; counsel to Gov., legal affairs sec. to Calif. Gov. Pete Wilson, 1995-98; assoc. justice Calif. Ct. Appeal, 3rd Appellate Dist., Sacramento, 1998—. Arbitrator bi-nat. panel for U.S.-Can. Free Trade Agreement, 1990—94; commr. Calif. Law Revision Commn., 1992—94, vice chair, 1993—94, chair, 1994; mem. Blue Ribbon Commn. on Jury Sys. Improvement, 1996; adj. prof. McGeorge Sch. Law, 2001—. Contbr. articles to profl. jours. Co-chmn. internat. rels. sect. Town Hall Calif., L.A., 1985—90; chmn. internat. trade legis. subcom., internat. commerce steering com. L.A. Area C. of C., 1983—91, law and justice com., 1993—94; adv. coun., exec. com. Asia Pacific Ctr. for Resolution of Internat. Bus. Disputes, 1991—94; mem. L.A. Com. on Fgn. Rels., 1983—95, Pacific Coun. Internat. Policy, 1999—; gen. counsel Citizens Rsch. Found., 1990—94; assoc. mem. ctrl. com. Calif. Rep. Party, 1983—94. mem. ctrl. com., 1995—98; dep. gen. coun. credentials com.

Rep. Nat. Conv., 1992, alt. Calif. Delegation, 1992, Calif. del., 1996; bd. dirs. L.A. Ctr. for Internat. Comml. Arbitration, 1986—94, treas., 1986—88, v.p., 1988—90, pres., 1990—94. Master Anthony Kennedy Inns. of Ct., 1996-99. Mem. Am. Arbitration Assn. (panel of arbitrators, arbitrator large complex case dispute resolution program 1993-94), Chartered Inst. Arbitrators, London (assoc. 1986-94), Friends of Wilton Park So. Calif. (chmn. exec. com. 1986-94, exec. com. 1986—). Jewish. Office: Calif Ct of Appeal 3d Appellate Dist 914 Capitol Mall Sacramento CA 95814-4802

KOLMIN, KENNETH GUY, lawyer; b. N.Y.C., Oct. 22, 1951; s. Frank William and Edith Kolmin; m. Suzan L. Frumm, Sept. 3, 1978; children—Stephen Todd, Jennifer Dana, Robert Scott. BS summa cum laude, SUNY-Albany, 1973; MS, Syracuse U., 1975, JD cum laude, 1975. Bar: Ill. 1976, U.S. Dist. Ct. (7th dist.) Ill. 1976, U.S. Tax Ct. 1980, U.S. Supreme Ct. 1985; CPA, Ill. Tax cons. Arthur Young and Co., Chgo., 1976-79; atty. Shefsky Saitlin & Froelich, Chgo., 1979-81; ptnr. Rooks Pitts & Poust, Chgo., 1981-84, Schwartz & Freeman, 1984-96, Sonnenschein, Nath & Rosenthal, Chgo., 1996—. Contbr. articles to profl. jours. Mem. ABA, AICPA, Ill. Bar Assn., Ill. Soc. CPAs. General corporate, Securities, Taxation, general. Home: 975 Eastwood Rd Glencoe IL 60022-1122 Office: Sonnenschein Nath & Rosenthal 8000 Sears Tower Chicago IL 60606

KOLODNY, STEPHEN ARTHUR, lawyer; b. Monticello, N.Y., 1940; BA in Bus. Adminstrn., Boston U., 1963, JD, 1965. Bar: Calif. 1966, U.S. Dist. Ct. (cen. dist.) Calif. 1966; cert. family law specialist. Sole practice, L.A., 1966-95; with Kolodny & Anteau, 1995—. Lectr. on family law subjects; adj. prof. U. Houston, ABA Trial Advocacy Inst., 1990—, co-chair, 1998—. Co-author: Divorce Practice Handbook, 1994; author: Evidence ABA Advocate, 1996. Named #1 Family Law Trial Lawyer, Calif. Lawyer Mag., Aug. 1999. Mem. ABA (family law sect., author ABA Advocate), Am. Acad. Matrimonial Lawyers (past pres. So. Calif. chpt., bd. govs.), Am. Coll. Family Trial lawyers (founding dir.), Internat. Acad. Matrimonial Lawyers (bd. govs., past pres. USA chpt.), Calif. State Bar Assn. (cert. family law specialist 1980—, lectr. State Bar panel, CEB programs, mem. family law sect., article author), Los Angeles County Bar Assn. (lectr., mem. and past chmn. family law sect.), Beverly Hills Bar Assn. (lectr., mem. family law sect.). Family and matrimonial. Fax: 310-271-3918. E-mail: kolodny@kolodny-anteau.com

KOLSBY, HERBERT F. lawyer, educator; b. Phila., July 10, 1926; s. Leonard H. and Josephine R. (Refsen) K.; m. Hermine W. Kolsby, Sept. 5, 1948; children: Dana Kolsby Edenbaum, Robert, Paul. JD, Temple U., 1951. Bar: Pa. 1951. Ptnr. Kolsby Gordon Robin & Shore, Phila., 1954—. Prof. law, dir. LLM in trial advocacy Temple U. Sch. Law, Phila., 1991-97. Gen. chmn. Fedn. Jewish Agys., Phila., 1989-90; pres. Temple Adath Israel, Phila., 1993-94. Recipient Justice Michael A. Musmanno award as outstanding trial lawyer Phila. Trial Lawyers Assn., 1993. Fellow Am. Coll. Trial Lawyers, Internat. Acad. Trial Lawyers; mem. Inner Circle Advocats, White Manor Country Club (pres. 1968-69). Democrat. Avocation: golf. Home: 8904 Ventnor Ave Margate City NJ 08402-2443 Office: Kolsby Gordon Robin Et Al 1650 Market St Fl 22D Philadelphia PA 19103-7301

KOMAROFF, STANLEY, lawyer; b. Bklyn, Apr. 1, 1935; s. William Ralph and Fanny (Wein) K.; m. Rosalyn Steinglass, Dec. 25, 1960; children: William Charles, Andrew Steven. BA, Cornell U., 1956, JD, 1958. Bar: N.Y. 1959. Assoc. Proskauer Rose LLP, N.Y.C., 1958-68, ptnr., 1968—, chmn., 1991-99. Mem. rev. and planning coun. N.Y. State Hosp., 1982-92; trustee Beth Israel Med. Ctr., 1984—, vice chair, 1999—; trustee St. Lukes-Roosevelt Hosp. Ctr., Continuum of Health Ptnrs. Inc.; mem. bd. regents L.I. Coll. Hosp., 2001—; bd. dirs. Edmond de Rothschild Found., Club Med, Inc., 1984-95, Overseas Shipholding Group, Inc., Westhampton Beach Performing Arts Ctr.; chmn. ann. fund Cornell U. Law Sch., 1991-93, mem. adv. coun. 1st lt. USAR, 1958. Fellow Am. Bar Found.; mem. N.Y. State Bar Assn., Assn. of Bar of City of N.Y., N.Y. County Lawyers Assn., Order of Coif, Sunningdale Country Club, Phi Kappa Phi. General corporate, Private international, Mergers and acquisitions. Home: 910 Park Ave Apt 5-s New York NY 10021-0255 Office: Proskauer Rose LLP 1585 Broadway New York NY 10036-8299 E-mail: skomaroff@proskauer.com

KONDRACKI, EDWARD ANTHONY, lawyer; b. Camden, N.J., Oct. 10, 1946; s. Edward S. and Helen J. (Roman) K.; m. Mary A. Russo, Aug. 3, 1974; children: Elysia A., Michelle A. BA, Rutgers U., 1968, JD, 1971. Bar: N.J. 1971, U.S. Dist. Ct. N.J. 1971, U.S. Supreme Ct. 1977, U.S. Ct. Appeals (3d cir.) 1980. Law clk. U.S. Dist. Ct., Camden, N.J., 1971-72; assoc. Davis & Reberkenny, Cherry Hill, 1972-75, mem., dir., 1975-99; mem. Law Offices of Edward A. Kondracki, L.L.C., Medford, 2000—. Counsel Evesham Mcpl. Utilities Authority, Bordentown Sewerage Authority, Mt. Holly Mcpl. Utilities Authority, Bordentown City Water Utility, Moorestown Twp. Water & Sewer Utility; mem. Am. Cancer Soc.; chair parents adv. com. Keuka Coll. Mem. ABA, Authorities Assn. N.J. (chmn. legal com. 1981-97), Trial Attys. N.J. (trustee 1985-90), N.J. State Bar Assn., Burlington County Bar Assn. Roman Catholic. State civil litigation, Environmental, Municipal (including bonds). Home: 68 Fawn Ct Medford NJ 08055-8344

KONDRACKI, EDWARD JOHN, lawyer; b. Elizabeth, N.J., Sept. 27, 1932; s. John and Catherine Chudio (Saas) K.; m. Barbara Terese Caruso; children: Carol Ann, Maryanne, Christopher. BSEE, N.J. Inst. Tech., 1959; JD with honors, George Washington U., 1963. Bar: Va. 1964, DC 1964, U.S. Dist. Ct. D.C. 1964, U.S. Dist. Ct. (ea. dist.) Va. 1964, U.S. Dist. Ct. (ctrl. dist.) Calif., U.S. Dist. Ct. (so. dist.) Ala., U.S. Dist. Ct. (no. dist.) Fla., U.S. Dist. Ct. (no. dist.) Ga., U.S. Dist. Ct. (we. dist.) La., U.S. Dist. Ct. (ea. dist.) Mich., U.S. Dist. Ct. (no. dist.) Okla., U.S. Dist. Ct. (ea. dist.) Pa., U.S. Dist. Ct. (no. dist.) N.Y., U.S. Dist. Ct. (ea. dist.) Tex., U.S. Dist. Ct. (no. dist.) Tex., U.S. Ct. Appeals (fed. cir.) 1983, U.S. Ct. Claims 1976, U.S. Ct. Customs and Patent Appeals 1976. Patent atty. Gen. Electric Co., Washington, 1959-63; assoc. Kerkam, Stowell Kondracki & Clarke, P.C. and predecessor, Arlington, Va., 1963-65; dir., prin. Kerkam, Stowell Kondracki & Clarke, P.C., 1965-99; prin. Miles & Stockbridge, McLean, Va., 2000—. Owner, dir. Patmark Paralegal Svcs., 1975-90; treas. SOC Enterprises, 1998-99, chmn., 1999—. Author: Trademarks-Servicemarks, Use, Usage and Protection, 1990, Proper Use of Trademarks and Servicemarks, 1982, Common Pitfalls Encountered in Patenting Inventions, 1983, Copyright Protection of Computer Software, 1989, Intellectual Property, Rights Acquisition and Protection Conference World Trade Assn. N.J., 1989; contbr. article to Voice of Tech. Served with USN, 1951-55. Mem. ABA, Am. Intellectual Property Law Assn., Internat. Assn. Protection Indsl. Property, Fed. Bar Assn., Va. Bar Assn., Internat. Trademark Assn., Washington Patent Lawyers Club, D.C. Bar Assn. (chmn. com. internat. affairs 1973), Gt. Falls Hist. Soc., Marmota Farm Assn., KC, Tau Beta Pi, Eta Kappa Nu, Omicron Delta Kappa, Phi Eta Sigma. Private international, Patent, Trademark and copyright. Office: 1751 Pinnacle Dr Ste 500 Mc Lean VA 22102-3833 Fax: (703) 610-8686. E-mail: ekondracki@milesstockbridge.com

KONDZER, THOMAS ALLEN, lawyer; b. Cleve., Apr. 13, 1950; s. Andrew Francis and Ann (Ziegler) K.; m. Maureen Veronica Walsh, June 2, 1973; 1 child, Joseph Thomas. BBA, John Carroll U., 1972; JD, Case Western Res. U., 1975. Bar: Ohio 1975, U.S. Dist. Ct. (no. dist.) Ohio 1977, U.S. Ct appeals (6th cir.) 1980. Law clk. to presiding justice Ohio Ct. Appeals (8th dist.), Cleve., 1975-77; assoc. Amsdell and Slivka, 1977-81; sole practice, 1981-85; prosecutor Village of Northfield, Ohio, 1981—; ptnr. Kolick and Kondzer, Cleve., 1985—. Lectr. Cleve. State U., 1981-82; coop. counsel Cath. League for Religious and Civil Liberties, Milw., 1981—. Mem. Westlake Civil Service Commn., 1986—. Mem. ABA, Ohio State Bar Assn., Greater Cleve. Bar Assn., North Olmsted C. of C., Order of Coif, Beta Gamma Sigma. Democrat. Roman Catholic. State civil litigation, General practice, Probate. Home: 25668 Melibee Dr Cleveland OH 44145-5455 Office: Kolick and Kondzer 24500 Center Ridge Rd Ste 175 Cleveland OH 44145-5628

KONENKAMP, JOHN K. state supreme court justice; b. Oct. 20, 1944; m. Geri Konenkamp; children: Kathryn, Matthew. JD, U. S.D., 1974. Dep. state's atty., Rapid City; pvt. practice, 1977-84; former and presiding judge S.D. Cir Ct. (7th cir.), 1988-94; assoc. justice S.D. Supreme Ct., Pierre, 1994—. Bd. dirs. Alt. Dispute Resolution Com., Adv. Bd. for Casey Family Program. With USN. Mem. Am. Judicature Soc., State Bar S.D., Pennington County Bar Assn., Nat. CASA Assn., Am. Legion. Office: SD Supreme Ct 500 E Capitol Ave Pierre SD 57501-5070*

KONNOV, SERGEI VLADIMIROVICH, lawyer; b. Orenburg, Russia, Mar. 26, 1968; LLM, Kiev State U., Ukraine, 1991. Bar: Ukraine 1991. Ptnr. Konnov & Sozanovsky, Kiev, 1992-2000. Editor Ukrainian Bus. Law mag., 1993. Mem. ABA (assoc.), Internat. Bar Assn. Communications, General corporate, Intellectual property. Office: Konnov & Sozanovsky 23 Shota Rustaveli St # 5 01023 Kiev Ukraine Fax: 380 44 490-5490. E-mail: skonnov@konnov.com

KOOMEY, RICHARD ALAN, lawyer; b. N.Y.C., Sept. 20, 1932; s. Garo H. and Ruth (Mushekian) K.; m. Cynthia C. Chaffee, Feb. 18, 1961 (div. 1974); children: Jonathan G., Gregory C., Christopher D. AB, Columbia Coll., 1957, MS, 1958; LLB, NYU, 1962. Bar: N.Y. 1962, U.S. Ct. Appeals (3d cir.) 1968, N.C. 1982. Assoc. Chadbourne, Parke, Whiteside & Wolf, N.Y.C., 1966-69; asst. gen. counsel Sperry & Hutchinson Co., 1969-80; gen. counsel Sperry & Hutchinson Furniture Inc., High Point, N.C., 1980-82; of counsel Robert E. Sheehan Assocs., 1982-83, Contino, Ross & Benedict, N.Y.C., 1983-84; dep. gen. counsel Pechiney Corp. and Howmet Corp., Greenwich, Conn., 1984-97; semi retired pvt. practice, 1997—. Adj. prof. law St. John's U. Sch. of Bus., Jamaica, N.Y., 1983-85. Trustee Union Free Sch. Dist. 3, Huntington Station, N.Y., 1966-67. Served to capt. USAF, 1952-56. Mem. N.C. Bar Assn. General corporate, Labor, Pension, profit-sharing, and employee benefits.

KOONCE, NEIL WRIGHT, lawyer; b. Kinston, N.C., July 8, 1947; s. Harold Wright and Edna Earle (Regan) K.; m. Virginia Gayle Evans, Feb. 27, 1993; children: Channing, Carl Younger, Ginny Younger. AB, U. N.C., 1969; JD, Wake Forest U., 1974; postgrad. exec. program, U. Va., 1983. Bar: N.C. 1973, U.S. Dist. Ct. (mid. dist.) N.C. 1975, U.S. Ct. Appeals (4th cir.) 1978, U.S. Supreme Ct. 1981. Atty. Cone Mills Corp., Greensboro, N.C., 1974-81, sr. atty., 1981-85, asst. gen. counsel, 1985-87, gen. counsel, 1987—, v.p., 1989—, v.p., gen. counsel, corp. sec., 1999—. Bd. dirs. Family and Children's Svcs., Greensboro, 1981-89, S.C. Energy Users Com., Columbia, S.C., 1984-89, Carolina Utility Customer's Assn., Raleigh, 1983-90, 94—, N.C. Found. for Rsch. and Econ. Edn., 1986-87, 93—, Electricity Consumers Resource Coun., Washington, 1987, 92—, vice chmn., 1990, chmn., 1991; bd. dirs. N.C. Citizens for Bus. and Industry, Raleigh, 1991-96, Met. YMCA, Greensboro, 1991-95, Salvation Army Boys and Girls Clubs, Greensboro, 1996—, S.C. Mfrs. Alliance, 1998—, N.C. Textile Mfrs. Assn., 1998—. With AUS, 1970-71. Mem. ABA, N.C. Bar Assn., N.C. Textile Mfrs. Assn., Greensboro Bar Assn., Rotary (sec. 1983-86, bd. dirs. 1985-90, pres. 1988). Democrat. Presbyterian. Administrative and regulatory, General corporate, Personal injury. Home: 200 Irving Pl Greensboro NC 27408-6510 Office: Cone Mills Corp 3101 N Elm St Greensboro NC 27408-3184

KOONTZ, LAWRENCE L., JR. state supreme court justice; b. Roanoke, Va, Jan. 25, 1940; BS, Va. Polytech. U., 1962. Asst. commonwealth's atty., Roanoke, 1967-68; judge Va. Juvenile & Domestic Rels. Dist. Ct., 1968-76, Va. Cir. Ct. (23rd cir.), 1976-85, Ct. Appeals of Va., 1985-95, Supreme Ct. of Va., 1995—. Mem. ABA. Office: PO Box 687 Salem VA 24153-0687

KOPELMAN, LARRY GORDON, lawyer; b. Charleston, W.Va., Apr. 20, 1949; s. Leo G. and Ruby Jean (Webb) K.; m. Mary Christine Kessler, June 28, 1975; children— Emily Nicole, Justin Gordon. B.S.E.E., W.Va. U., 1971, J.D., 1975. Bar: W.Va. 1975, U.S. Dist. Ct. (no. and so. dists.) W.Va. 1975, U.S. Ct. Appeals (4th cir.) 1984, U.S. Dist. Ct. D.C. 1986, U.S. Ct. Appeals (D.C. cir.) 1986. Tax analyst W.Va. Tax Dept., Charleston, 1975-76; asst. atty. gen. W.Va. Air Pollution Control Commn., 1976-79; spl. asst. atty. gen., 1979— ; pvt. practice, Charleston, 1979; pres. Larry G. Kopelman, L.C., Charleston, 1984—, Amity Real Estate Ltd., Charleston, 1979—; city atty. Town of Handley, 1980—, Town of Pratt, 1988—. Mem. W.Va. Bar Assn., Kanawha County Bar Assn., W.Va. Trial Lawyers, Assn. Trial Lawyers Am. Republican. Jewish. Club: South Charleston Rotary (pres. 1983-84). Office: 9 Pennsylvania Ave Charleston WV 25302-2313

KOPELMAN, LEONARD, lawyer; b. Cambridge, Mass., Aug. 2, 1940; s. Irving and Frances Estelle (Robbins) K.; m. Carol Hunsberger. B.A. cum laude, Harvard U., 1962, J.D., 1965. Bar: Mass. 1966. Assoc. Warner & Stackpole, Boston, 1965-73; sr. ptnr. Kopelman and Paige, 1974—. Lectr. Harvard U., 1965— ; permanent master Mass. Superior Ct., 1971— ; hon. consul gen. of, Finland, Mass., 1975— ; U.S. del. Soc. for Internat. Devel.; Chmn. Mass. Jud. Selection Com. for the Fed. Judiciary, 1971— ; chief counsel AAUP. Trustee Cathedral of the Pines, 1972; pres. Hillel Found. of Cambridge, Inc., 1973— ; trustee Faulkner Hosp., 1974— , Parker Hill Med. Ctr., 1976—; dir. gen. Consular Corps Coll. NEH grantee, 1975; named one of the 12 most powerful lawyers in Mass. Nat. Law Jour. Mem. ABA (exec. coun. 1969—), Mass. Bar Assn. (chmn. mcpl. law sect.), Am. Judges Assn., Mass. C. of C. (pres. 1974-77), Harvard Faculty Club, Algonquin Club (pres.), Harvard Club, Union Club, Hasty Pudding Club, St. Botolph Club. Private international, Public international, Municipal (including bonds). Home: 33 Yarmouth Rd Chestnut Hill MA 02467-2815 Office: Kopelman and Paige 31 St James Ave Boston MA 02116-4101

KOPF, RICHARD G. federal judge; b. 1946; BA, U. Nebr., Kearney, 1969; JD, U. Nebr., Lincoln, 1972. Law clk. to Hon. Donald R. Ross U.S. Ct. Appeals (8th cir.), 1972-74; ptnr. Cook, Kopf & Doyle, Lexington, Neb., 1974-87; U.S. magistrate judge, 1987-92; fed. judge U.S. Dist. Ct. (Nebr. dist.), 1992—, chief judge, 1999—. Mem. ABA, ABA Found., Nebr. State Bar, Nebr. State Bar Found. Office: US Dist Ct 586 US Courthouse 100 Centennial Mall N Lincoln NE 68508-3859

KOPIT, ALAN STUART, lawyer; b. Cleve., Aug. 26, 1952; s. Irving and Claire (Smira) K.; m. Ivy Jan Stoller. BA summa cum laude, Tufts U., 1974; JD, U. Chgo., 1977. Bar: Ohio 1977, U.S. Dist. Ct. (no. dist.) Ohio 1977, U.S. Ct. Appeals (6th cir.) 1979, U.S. Ct. Appeals (10th cir.) 1991, U.S. Supreme Ct. 1988. Ptnr. Hahn, Loeser & Parks, LLP, Cleve., 1977—. Staff atty. Sta. WKYC-TV3 NBC, Cleve., 1982—; White House fellow spl. asst. to sec. def. The Pentagon, Washington, 1987-88. Mem. Leadership Cleve. Growth Assn., 1985-86; vice chair Cleve. Bicentennial Commn., 1992—; bd. dirs. Adam Walsh Child Resource Ctr., Cleve., 1984-87, Fairmount Theatre of Deaf, Cleve., 1984—, Am. Jewish Com., Cleve., 1985—. Named one of Cleve.'s Most Interesting People, Cleve. Mag., 1984; recipient Sec. of Def. Medal, 1988. Mem. ABA (chairperson young lawyers div. 1986-87, del. ho. of dels. 1987—), Cleve. Bar Assn. (merit svc. award 1978, 79, 81, bd. dirs. 1981-82, 91—, pres. 1996-97), Am. Bar Endowment (bd. dirs. 1987-88), Ohio Bar Assn. (coun. del. 1985-87). Bankruptcy, State civil litigation, Contracts commercial. Home: 2780 Brainard Hills Dr Cleveland OH 44124-4544 Office: Hahn Loeser & Parks 3300 BP America Bldg 200 Public Sq Ste 3300 Cleveland OH 44114-2303 E-mail: askopit@hahnlaw.com

KOPLIK, MARC STEPHEN, lawyer; b. N.Y.C., Aug. 28, 1946; s. Arnold and Lillian (Weiner) K.; m. Deirdre Lee Henderson, May 30, 1970; children: Christopher Henderson, Timothy Henderson. AB cum laude, Brown U., 1968; JD, Yale U., 1971. Bar: N.Y. 1973. Assoc. Debevoise & Plimpton, N.Y.C., 1971-76; founder, mng. ptnr. Henderson & Koplik, N.Y.C., 1982—. Editor Yale Law Jour., 1970-71. Coll. scholar, Frances Wayland scholar. Mem. Assn. Bar City N.Y., N.Y. State Bar Assn., Old Chatham Hunt C. of C. Episcopalian. Club: Yale (N.Y.C.). General corporate, Oil, gas, and mineral, Private international.

KOPP, CHARLES GILBERT, lawyer; b. Hartford, Conn., Jan. 10, 1933; s. Henry and Grace (Goldberg) K.; m. Ann Weiss, June 10, 1962 (div. 1963) BA, Amherst Coll., 1955; JD, U. Pa., 1960. Bar: Pa. 1961. Sr. counsel Wolf, Block, Schorr and Solis-Cohen LLP, Phila., 1960—. Vis. lectr. Villanova (Pa.) Univ., 1981. Contbr. articles to profl. jours. Commr. Delaware River Port Authority, 1986-87; co-chmn. select com. of U.S. Embassy, Bern, Switzerland, 1985; mem. Pa. Gov.'s Spl. Tax Commn., 1980; bd. dirs. Pennsylvanians for Effective Govt., Harrisburg, 1987-99; mem. Pa. Electoral Coll., 1988; mem. adv. bd. region I, Resolution Trust Corp., 1990-93; mem. coun. The Pa. Soc., 1991-98; trustee Thomas Jefferson U. Hosp., 1988—; mem. adv. bd. PNC, Phila., 1992-2000. 1st lt. USAF, 1955-57. Recipient Pop Warner Gold Football award, 1988. Mem. ABA, Pa. Bar Assn., Phila. Bar Assn., The Union League of Phila., Pyramid Club, Squires Golf Club, Vesper Club, Greater Phila. C. of C. (bd. dirs. 1988-96). Republican. Jewish. Administrative and regulatory, Corporate taxation, Taxation, general. Home: 210 W Rittenhouse Sq Apt 3306 Philadelphia PA 19103-5780 Office: Wolf Block Schorr and Solis Cohen LLP 1650 Arch St Fl 22 Philadelphia PA 19103-2003

KOPPENHEFFER, JULIE B. lawyer; b. Lexington, Ky., July 14, 1945; d. Arthur S. and Mae (Bronfeld) Adler; m. Thomas Lynn Koppenheffer, Dec. 22, 1967; children: Michael, Alex. AB, Boston U., 1966, JD, 1969. Bar: Mass. 1969, U.S. Dist. Ct. Mass. 1970, U.S. Supreme Ct. 1976, Tex.1979. Pvt. practice law, Williamstown, Mass., 1974-79; sr. corp. atty. LaQuinta Motor Inn, San Antonio, 1979-83, assoc. gen. counsel, 1983-84; v.p., gen. counsel Texian Inns, San Antonio, 1984—; adj. prof. North Adams State Coll., Mass., 1977-79. Bd. dirs. Encino Park Homeowners Assn., San Antonio, 1984. Mem. Tex. Bar Assn., ABA, San Antonio Bar Assn. (chmn. Corp. Com. 1984-86). Contracts commercial, General corporate, Real property. Home: 20015 Park Bluff St San Antonio TX 78259-1930 Office: The New Texian Co 8000 W Ih 10 Ste 1500 San Antonio TX 78230-3883

KORB, JOAN, lawyer; b. Fond du Lac, Wis., Jan. 22, 1953; d. Allen Dale Korb and Evelyn A. Schmitz-Korb; m. Frederic B. Will, June 19, 1983. BS in Biology, U. Wis., Oshkosh, 1975; JD, John Marshall Sch. Law, Chgo., 1985. Bar: Wis. 1985, Ill. 1985. Asst. corp. counsel Racine County, Racine, Wis., 1985-89, asst. dist. atty., 1990-99, Door County, Sturgeon Bay, 1999—. Commentator on fetal abuse on TV, radio, in newspapers. Author novels. Mem. Mt. Pleasant (Wis.) Zoning Bd. Appeals, 1987-99; pres. Wis. Profl. Soc. on Abuse of Children, Milw., 1998—; treas. Bd. Children Law Sec. of State Bar of Wis., 1998-. Mem. NOW, AAUW (pub. policy chmn. Racine 1995-99), Sierra Club (life). Avocations: teaching about child abuse, reading, SCUBA diving, sailing, travel. Office: Door County Dist Atty's Office 421 Nebraska St Ofc Sturgeon Bay WI 54235-2249

KORB, KENNETH ALLAN, lawyer, educator; b. Boston, Oct. 11, 1932; s. Allan and Mynue (Herbert) K.; m. Jaclyn C. Patricof, June 30, 1962; 1 child, Jason B. BA magna cum laude, Harvard U., 1953, JD cum laude, 1956. Bar: Mass. 1956. Law clk. Supreme Jud. Ct., Mass., 1956-57; assoc. Hutchins & Wheeler, Boston, 1957-60, Kargman & Kargman, Boston, 1960-63; sr. ptnr. Brown, Rudnick, Freed & Gesmer, 1963-89, Posternak, Blankstein & Lund, Boston, 1990-96; ptnr. Perkins, Smith & Cohen, LLP, 1996—. Lectr. Mass. Continuing Legal Edn., Nat. Coun. Savs. Instns., Oxford Club, Cambridge House-Vancouver, Calgary, Toronto, 1997—, Prospecters & Developers Assn. of Can.; sec., bd. dirs., gen. counsel Safety Ins. Co., 1980-99; underwriting mem. Lloyd's of London, 1984—; sec., bd. dirs. Neb-Cell, Inc., 1989-95. Legal columnist The Brookline Citizen, 1990-91; contbr. articles to profl. jours. Internat. pres. Soc. Israel Philatelists, 1974-76, bd. dirs., 1976-80; bd. dirs., treas. Watergate Villas East Condominium U.S.V.I., 1989-95. With USAR, 1956-62. Mem. Mass. Bar Assn. Democrat. Jewish. Kenneth. General corporate, Real property, Securities. Home: 24 Helene Rd Waban MA 02468-1025 Office: 1 Beacon St Boston MA 02108-3107 E-mail: Korb@pscboston.com

KORCHIN, JUDITH MIRIAM, lawyer; b. Kew Gardens, N.Y., Apr. 28, 1949; d. Arthur Walter and Mena (Levisohn) Goldstein; m. Paul Maury Korchin, June 10, 1972; 1 son, Brian Edward. BA with high honors, U. Fla., 1971, JD with honors, 1974. Bar: Fla. 1974, U.S. Ct. Appeal (2d, 5th and 11th cirs.), U.S. Dist. Ct. (so., mid. and no. dists) Fla. Law clk. to judge U.S. Dist. Ct., 1974-76; assoc. Steel, Hector & Davis, Miami, Fla., 1976-81, ptnr., 1981-87, Holland and Knight, Miami, 1987—. Author, exec. editor U. Fla. Law Rev., 1973-74. Mem. U. Fla. Law Ctr. Coun., 1980-83; pres. alumni bd. U. Fla. Law Rev., 1983; bd. dirs. Fla. Film & Rec. Inst., 1982-84. Recipient Trail Blazer award The Women's Com. of 100, 1988. Fellow Am. Bar Found.; mem. ABA (sect. alternative dispute resolution, vice chmn. 1994-95, co-chmn. fed. ct. mediation com. 1995, sect. labor and employment law, sect. litigation), Am. Arbitration Assn. (employment law panel, southeast 1993—, comml. law panel 1993—), CPR Inst. for Dispute Resolution (nat. panelist 1994—), Dade County Bar Assn. (bd. dirs. 1981-82, treas. 1982, sec. 1983, 3d v.p. 1984, 2d v.p. 1985, 1st v.p. 1986, pres. 1987), Nat. Assn. Women Bus. Owners (adv. coun. 1987-88), Nat. Assn. Bank Women (TV panelist greater Miami chpt. 1987), Fla. Bar Assn. (vice chmn. jud. nominating procedures com. 1982, civil procedure rules com. 1984-89, 93-95), Fla. Bar Found. (subcom. legal assistance for poor 1988-90), Rabbinical Assn. Greater Miami (TV panelist Still Small Voice 1987), Dist. XI Health and Human Svcs. Bd. (gov.'s appointee 1993-95, vice chmn. 1993, 94), Greater Miami C. of C. (com. profl. devel. 1988-90), City Club (bd. dirs. 1988-93), Order of Coif, Phi Beta Kappa, Phi Kappa Phi. General civil litigation, Labor, State and local taxation. Office: Holland & Knight PO Box 015441 701 Brickell Ave Ste 3000 Miami FL 33131-2898

KORDONS, ULDIS, lawyer; b. Riga, Latvia, July 9, 1941; came to U.S., 1949; s. Evalds and Zenta Alide (Apenits) K.; m. Virginia Lee Knowles, July 16, 1966. AB, Princeton U., 1963; JD, Georgetown U., 1970. Bar: N.Y. 1970, Ohio 1978, Ind. 1989. Assoc. Whitman, Breed, Abbott & Morgan, N.Y.C., 1970-77, Anderson, Mori & Rabinowitz, Tokyo, 1973-75; counsel Armco Inc., Parsippany, N.J., 1977-84; v.p., gen. counsel, sec. Sybron Corp., Saddle Brook, 1984-88, Hillenbrand Industries Inc., Batesville, Ind., 1989-92; pres. Plover Enterprises, Cin., 1992-95, Kordons & Co., LPA, Cin., 1996—. Lt. USN, 1963-67. Mem. N.Y. Bar Assn., Ohio Bar Assn., Ind. Bar Assn.

KOREN, EDWARD FRANZ, lawyer; b. Eustis, Fla., Aug. 6, 1946; s. Edward Franz Sr. and Frances (Boyd) K.; m. Louise Poole, June 19, 1970; children: Daniel Edward, Susan Louise. BSBA, U. Fla., 1971, JD, 1974. Bar: Fla. 1975, U.S. Dist. Ct. (mid. dist.) Fla. 1977, U.S. Supreme Ct. 1980, U. S. Ct. Appeals (11th cir.) 1981, U.S. Tax Ct. 1985, U.S. Ct. Claims 1986. Instr. tax U. Fla., Gainesville, 1974-75; assoc. Holland & Knight, Lakeland, Fla., 1975-79, ptnr., 1980—, chmn. trusts and estates dept., 1983—. Adj. prof. graduate tax program U. Fla., Gainesville, 1996; adj. prof. grad. estate planning program U. Miami Law Sch., 2000—. Author: Estate and Personal Financial Planning, 1988, 13th edit., 2001; contbr. articles to profl. jours. Capt. U.S. Army, 1971-72. Fellow Am. Coll. Trust and Estates Counsel (mem. bus. planning com., bd. regents 1997—, chmn. estate and gift tax com. 2001—), Am. Coll. Tax Counsel, Am. Bar Found.; mem. ABA (real property, probate and trust law sect., v.p. probate and trust divsn. 2001—, mem. exec. coun. 1995—, chmn. marital deduction com. 1991-95), Fla. Bar Assn. (chmn. real property, probate and trust law sect. 1988-89, chmn. tax sect. 1990-91, active various sects. and coms.), Am. Assn. Attys. and CPAs, Fla. Inst. CPAs, Order of the Coif, Tampa Club, Lakeland Yacht and Country Club, Centre Club. Republican. Presbyterian. Estate planning, Probate, Taxation, general. Home: 114 Hickory Creek Dr Brandon FL 33511-8012 Office: Holland & Knight 92 Lake Wire Dr PO Box 32092 Lakeland FL 33802-2092 E-mail: ekoren@hklaw.com

KORMAN, EDWARD R. federal judge; b. N.Y.C., Oct. 25, 1942; s. Julius and Miriam K.; m. Diane R. Eisner, Feb. 3, 1979; children: Miriam M., Benjamin E. B.A., Bklyn. Coll., 1963; LL.B., Bklyn. Law Sch., 1966; LL.M., NYU, 1971. Bar: N.Y. 1966, U.S. Supreme Ct. 1972. Law clk. to judge N.Y. Ct. Appeals, 1966-68; assoc. Paul, Weiss, Rifkind, Wharton and Garrison, 1968-70; asst. U.S. atty. Eastern Dist. N.Y., N.Y.C., 1970-72; asst. to solicitor gen. of U.S., 1972-74; chief asst. U.S. atty. Eastern Dist. N.Y., 1974-78, U.S. atty., 1978-82; ptnr. Stroock & Stroock & Lavan, N.Y.C., 1982-84; prof. Bklyn. Law Sch., 1984-85; U.S. dist. judge Eastern Dist. N.Y., 1985—, chief judge, 2000—. Chmn. Mayor's Com. on N.Y.C. Marshals, 1983-85; mem. Temporary Commn. of Investigation of State of N.Y., 1983-85. Jewish. Office: US Dist Ct US Courthouse 225 Cadman Plz E Brooklyn NY 11201-1818

KORMES, JOHN WINSTON, lawyer; b. N.Y.C., May 4, 1935; s. Mark and Joanna P. Kormes; m. Frances W. Kormes, Aug. 19, 1978; 1 child, Mark Vincent. BA in Econs., U. Mich., 1955, JD, 1959. Bar: Pa. 1961, D.C. 1961, U.S. Supreme Ct. 1968. With License and Inspection Rev. Bd. Phila., 1972-73; asst. dist. atty. City of Phila., 1973-74; pvt. practice Phila., 1961—. Moot ct. advisor. Mem. staff Re-elect the Pres. Com., 1972, Rizzo for Mayor Com., 1971, 75, Phila. Flag Day Assn., 1965—. Served with USAF, 1956-57. Recipient N.Y. Intercoll. Legis. Assmebly award, 1954, R.I. Model Congress award, 1954, Queens Coll. Speech Guild award; Eminent Wisdom fellow Wisdom Hall of Fame. Fellow Lawyers in Mensa (charter), Triple Nine Soc. (elections officer 1992-93, legal officer, new mem. welcome program officer 1993—, com. to revise constitition 1993—, ombudsman 1994—), Internat. Soc. Phlos. Enquiry (sr. fellow, pub. Best Telicom 1986, 87, legal officer 1986-91, v.p. 1990-91), Wisdom Soc.; mem. Am. Legion (life mem.), Phila. Bar Assn., Phila. Trial Lawyers Assn., N.Y. State Trial Lawyers Assn., Am. Arbitration Assn., Fed. Bar Assn., Pitts. Inst. Legal Medicine, Assn. Trial Lawyers Am., Intertel, Internat. Platform Assn., Cincinnatus soc., Top One Percent Soc., Collegium Soc. 99.5 (charter), Poetic Genius Soc. 99.5 (charter), Masons, Shriners, KP, Lions, Delta Sigma Rho. Republican. State civil litigation, Family and matrimonial, Personal injury. Home: 1070 Edison Ave Philadelphia PA 19116-1342 Office: 2nd Fl 1201 Chestnut St Ste 2 Philadelphia PA 19107-4123

KORN, MICHAEL JEFFREY, lawyer; b. Jersey City, Dec. 22, 1954; s. Howard Leonard and Joyce Ellen (Blumenkranz) K.; m. Pamela Ann VanZandt, May 29, 1983; children: David Harold, Suzanne Faye. BA, U. Va., 1976; JD, U. Fla., 1979. Bar: Fla. 1980, U.S. Dist. Ct. (no. and mid. dists.) Fla., U.S. Ct. Appeals (5th and 11th cirs.). Jud. law clk. Fla. 1st Dist Ct. Appeal, Tallahassee, 1980-81; assoc. Boyer, Tanzler & Boyer, Jacksonville, Fla., 1981-84; pvt. practice, 1984-87; ptnr. Prom, Korn & Zehmer, P.A., 1987-95, Korn & Zehmer, P.A., Jacksonville, 1995—. Rules com. Fla. Appellate Ct., 1991—. Bd. dirs. North Fla. coun. Camp Fire, 1983-86, Jacksonville Jewish Fedn., 1985, v.p., 1994-99, treas., 1999—; bd. dirs. Youth Leadership Jacksonville, 1989-93, Jacksonville Cmty. Coun., 1989-94, 96-98, pres., 1995; Mandarin Cmty. Club, Jacksonville, 1988-91; cmty. adv. bd. WJCT-TV, Jacksonville, 1996—, chmn., 1999-2000; bd. dirs. United Way of N.E. Fla., 1999—; bd. trustees North Fla. Family Housing Found., 1999—. Recipient Young Leadership award Jacksonville Jewish Fedn., 1992. Mem. Fla. Bar (litig, appellate and health law sects.), Jacksonville Bar Assn. (fee arbitration com. 1987-90, CLE chair 1995-99), Acad. Fla. Trial Lawyers. Jewish. Avocations: running, reading, golf. Appellate, General civil litigation, Health. Office: Korn & Zehmer PA Ste 200 6620 Southpoint Dr S Jacksonville FL 32216-0940 Fax: 904-296-0384. E-mail: kzlaw@fdn.com

KORNREICH, EDWARD SCOTT, lawyer; b. Bklyn., Apr. 18, 1953; s. Lawrence and Selma (Rosenblatt) K.; m. Shirley Werner, Feb. 28, 1982; children: Mollie, Davida, Lawrence. BA magna cum laude, Columbia U., 1974; JD, Harvard U., 1977. Appellate atty. Legal Aid Soc., N.Y.C., 1977-79; assoc. atty. Rosenman & Colin, 1979-84; v.p., legal affairs, gen. counsel St. Luke's-Roosevelt Hosp. Ctr., 1984-87; mem. Garfunkel Wild & Travis P.C., Great Neck, N.Y., 1987-90; ptnr. Proskauer Rose LLP, N.Y.C., 1990—. Joint com. on health care decisions near end of life ABA and Hastings Ctr., 1992-95; sr. adv. com. Robert Wood Johnson-N.Y. Acad. Medicine Project. Trustee Postgrad. Ctr. Mental Health, N.Y.C., 1992-99. Mem. Am. Health Lawyers Assn., Assn. of Bar of City of N.Y. (com. on medicine and law 1985-88, chmn. health law com. 1991-94, AIDS com. 1986-97), Phi Beta Kappa. Jewish. Avocations: running (completed N.Y.C. Marathon 1978, 83, 86, 95, 97). Contracts commercial, Health, Non-profit and tax-exempt organizations. Office: Proskauer Rose LLP 1585 Broadway Fl 27 New York NY 10036-8299

KORNSTEIN, MICHAEL ALLEN, lawyer; b. Bklyn., Feb. 7, 1951; s. Samuel and Goldie (Starker) K.; m. Margaret Ann Tomlinson, Jan. 2, 1983; children: Harris, Benjamin, Max. BS, Union Coll., Schenectady, N.Y., 1973; JD, Union U., Albany, N.Y., 1977. Bar: N.Y. 1978, U.S. Dist. Ct. (no. dist.) N.Y. 1978, U.S. Dist. Ct. (so., ea. and we. dists.) N.Y. 1984, U.S. Supreme Ct. 1982. Assoc. Cooper, Erving, Savage, Whalen, Nolan & Heller, 1978-82; ptnr. Cooper, Erving, Savage, Nolan & Heller, LLP, 1983—. Mem. N.Y. State Bar Assn. Democrat. Jewish. Banking, General practice, Real property. Office: Cooper Erving Savage Nolan & Neller LLP 39 N Pearl St Ste 4 Albany NY 12207-2797

KORSINSKY, EDUARD, lawyer; b. Svalva, USSR, May 16, 1971; s. Gersh and Helen Korsinsky. BS in Acctg., Bklyn. Coll., 1992; JD, Bklyn. Law Sch., 1995; LLM, NYU, 1998. Bar: N.Y., N.J. Lawyer, spl. counsel Beatie and Osborn LLP, N.Y.C., 2000—. Patentee in field.

KOSAKOW, JAMES MATTHEW, lawyer; b. New London, Conn., Apr. 12, 1954; s. Leonard Louis and Lois Ann (Rosen) K.; m. Yvonne Manijeh Bokhour, June 4, 1978; 1 child, Jonathan Daniel. BA, Conn. Coll., 1976; JD, Yeshiva U., 1984. Bar: N.Y. 1985, Conn. 1985, D.C. 1985, Fla. 1991, U.S. Dist. Ct. (so. and ea. dists.) 1985, U.S. Tax Ct. 1993. Assoc. Vittoria & Forsythe, N.Y.C., 1986-92, Gregory and Adams, Wilton, Conn., 1992-94; pvt. practice N.Y.C. and Westport, 1994-97; ptnr. Kove & Kosakow, LLC, 1997—; vice-chancellor Cambridge Theol. Seminary, Carthage, Ill., 1996—. Guardian and litem N.Y. County Surrogate's Ct., N.Y.C., 1987—, Norwalk Probate Ct., 1993—; lectr. in field; arbitrator BBB, N.Y.C., 1988-89. Co-author: Handling Federal Estate and Gift Taxes, 6th edit., 2000; asst. editor Insights and Strategies; contbr. articles to profl. jours. Trustee, bd. dirs. Internat. Nursery Sch., Queens, N.Y., 1987-89; mem. estates & trusts specialty group lawyers divsn. United Jewish Appeal-Fedn. Jewish Philanthropies of N.Y., Inc., 1990-94; commr. Wilton Water Commn., 1995-96, Wilton Fire Commn., 1996-2000; ptnr. Creative Philanthropic Resources, 1995—; chmn. membership com. Mid-Fairfield Substance Abuse Coalition, 1995-96; dir. Thee Art Tree Source, Inc., 1995—; adv. com. The Unicorn Archive. Mem. N.Y. Bar Assn. (legis. com., trusts and estates sect. 1987—), Conn. Bar Assn. (elder law com.), Fla. Bar (real property, probate and trust law, out-of-state mem. rels. com. 1994—), Assn. of Bar of City of N.Y., Exch. Club (bd. dirs. Wilton club). Estate planning, Probate, Estate taxation. Office: 25 Ford Rd Westport CT 06880-1261 also: 685 3d Ave 30th Fl New York NY 10013 E-mail: jmk@kovkos.com

KOSARIN, JONATHAN HENRY, lawyer, consultant; b. Bklyn., Aug. 13, 1951; s. Lester and Norma (Higger) K.; m. Gayle C. Skarupa, Nov. 27, 1982. BA in History magna cum laude, Syracuse U., 1973; JD, Bklyn. Law Sch., 1976; LLM in Govt. Contract Law, George Washington U., 1984; postgrad., U.S. Army Command and Gen. Staff Coll., 1990, U.S. Army War Coll., 1997. Bar: N.Y. 1977, D.C. 1978, U.S. Supreme Ct. 1980, U.S. Ct. Claims 1981, U.S. Ct. Appeals (Fed. cir.) 1982. Commd. 2d lt. U.S. Army, 1973, advanced through grades to col., 1997, prosecutor trial counsel Ala., 1977-78, adminstrv. law officer, 1978-79, instr. law, 1979-80, trial atty. contract appeals div. Washington, 1980-84; contracts atty. U.S. Army Hdqrs., Heidelberg, Fed. Rep. Germany, 1985-87; assoc. gen. counsel, dir. procurement law Fed Home Loan Bank Bd., Washington, 1987-89; assoc. counsel USN, 1989-94, dep. counsel, 1994—. Adj. asst. prof. contract law JAG Sch., Charlottesville, Va., 1988-93, adj. assoc. prof., 1993-95, adj. prof., vice chmn., 1995-99, adj. prof., chmn., 1999—; adj. faculty contract law U. Va., 1989—; mem. faculty Fed. Publs. Seminars, 1995—, ESI Internat., 1999—. Vol. info. specialist Smithsonian Instn. Washington, 1993—, pres. Temple Rodef Shalom, Falls, Church, Va., 2000—. Mem. ABA, D.C. Bar Assn., Titanic Hist. Soc., No. Va. Football Ofcls. Assn., Nat. Assn. Sports Ofcls., Phi Alpha Delta, Phi Beta Kappa, Phi Kappa Phi, Phi Delta Kappa. Democrat Office: USN Office Of Gen Counsel Washington DC 20350-0001

KOSIK, EDWIN MICHAEL, federal judge; b. 1925; BA, Wilkes Coll., Wilkes-Barre, Pa., 1949; LLB, Dickinson Sch. Law, Carlisle, Pa. Asst. U.S. atty. Pa. State Workmen's Compensation Bd., 1953-58, chmn., 1964-69; pvt. practice Needle, Needle & Needle, 1958-64; pres. judge 45th Jud. Dist. Ct. Common Pleas, 1979-86; judge U.S. Dist. Ct. (mid. dist.) Pa., Scranton, 1986—, now sr. judge. Office: US Dist Ct US Courthouse PO Box 856 Scranton PA 18501-0856 E-mail: chambers_of_edwin_m._kosik@pamd.uscourts.gov

KOSKO, GEORGE CARTER, lawyer; b. Tampa, Fla., Apr. 14, 1944; s. George and Margaret Elizabeth (Rea) K.; m. Polly Spann, Dec. 7, 1974. B.S., Univ. S.C., 1966, J.D., 1971; postgrad. Nat. Inst. Trial Advocacy, 1972. Bar: S.C. 1971, U.S. Supreme Ct. 1976, D.C. 1981, U.S. Customs Ct. 1976, U.S. Ct. Internat. Trade 1981, Fourth Circuit Court of Appeals Judicial Conference. Ptnr. Kosko, Coffas & Sipes, 1975-82, sr. ptnr., 1976— . Mem. ABA (state reporter aviation com. sect. litigation). S.C. Bar Assn. Clubs: De Bordieu, Palmetto, Sertoma (gov. Wade Hampton dist.), Quiet Birdmen (Columbia). E-mail: george_kosko@scd.uscourts.gov. Home: 21 Lakeview Cir Columbia SC 29206-3222 Office: 4910 Trenholm Rd Columbia SC 29206-4709

KOSKO, SUSAN UTTAL, legal administrator; b. N.Y.C., Oct. 8, 1954; d. Sheldon and Jane Louise (Kaufmann) Uttal; m. James J. Kosko, July 6, 1996. BA, Clark U., 1976; cert. paralegal, Inst. Paralegal Tng., Phila., 1978. Legal asst. Winthrop, Stimson, Putnam & Roberts, N.Y.C., 1978-80; legal coord. Schroder Real Estate Corp., 1980-83; legal asst. supr. real estate svcs. dept. Cravath, Swaine & Moore, 1983-89; sr. legal asst. real estate dept. Rackemann, Sawyer & Brewster, Boston, 1989-90; sr. legal asst. leasing and real estate depts. Goulston & Storrs, 1990-97; contracts adminstr. Cabletron Systems, Inc., Rochester, N.H., 1997-99; v.p. ops. Nonpareil Software, New Durham, 1999—. Mem. Clark U. N.Y. Young Alumni Assn. (steering com.). Democrat. Jewish. Avocations: pottery, piano, photography, cycling, gourmet cooking. Office: Nonpareil Software Inc 39 N Shore Rd New Durham NH 03855-2113 E-mail: skosko@nonpareilsoftware.com

KOSSAR, RONALD STEVEN, lawyer; b. Ellenville, N.Y., May 30, 1948; s. Emanuel and Helen (Panken) K.; m. Sandra Perlman, Aug. 25, 1973. BA cum laude, Boston U., 1970; JD, Am. U., 1973. Bar: N.Y. 1974, D.C. 1974, U.S. Dist. Ct. (no. dist.) N.Y. 1974, U.S. Tax Ct. 1974, U.S. Ct. Appeals D.C. 1974. Tax law specialist Office Asst. Commr. (Tech.), IRS, Washington, 1973-75; sole practice Office of Asst. Commr. (Tech.), IRS, Middletown, N.Y., 1976—. Dir. Newburgh (N.Y.) Realty Corp. Mem. ABA, N.Y. State Bar Assn., Orange County Bar Assn., Middletown Bar Assn., D.C. Bar. Jewish. General corporate, General practice, Real property. Office: 402 E Main St Middletown NY 10940-2516 Office Fax: 845-343-5222. E-mail: rsklaw@warwick.net

KOSTELANETZ, BORIS, lawyer; b. St. Petersburg, Russia, June 16, 1911; came to U.S., 1920, naturalized, 1925; s. Nachman and Rosalia (Dimschetz) K.; m. Ethel Cory, Dec. 18, 1938; children: Richard Cory, Lucy Cory. B.C.S., N.Y. U., 1933, B.S., 1936; J.D. magna cum laude, St. John's U., 1936, LL.D. (hon.), 1981. Bar: N.Y. 1936; CPA, N.Y. With Price, Waterhouse & Co., C.P.A.'s, N.Y.C., 1934-37; asst. U.S. atty. So. Dist. N.Y.; also confidential asst. to U.S. atty, 1937-43; spl. asst. to atty. gen. U.S., 1943-46; chief war frauds sect. Dept. Justice, 1945-46; spl. counsel com. investigate crime in interstate commerce U.S. Senate, 1950-51; ptnr. Kostelanetz Ritholz Tigue & Fink, N.Y.C., 1946-89, of counsel, 1990-94, Kostelanetz & Fink, N.Y.C., 1994—. Instr. acctg. N.Y. U., 1937-47, adj. prof. taxation, 1947-69; Mem. com. on character and fitness Appellate div. Supreme Ct. N.Y., 1st dept., 1974— , chmn., 1985-98. Author: (with L. Bender) Criminal Aspects of Tax Fraud Cases, 1957, 2d edit., 1968, 3d edit., 1980; Contbr. articles to legal, accounting and tax jours. Chmn. Kefauver for Pres. Com. N.Y. State, 1952. Recipient Meritorious Svc. award NYU, 1954, John T. Madden Meml. award, 1969, Pietas medal St. John's U., 1961, medal of honor, 1983, James Madison award, 1988, Torch of Learning award Am. Friends of Hebrew U. Law Sch., 1979, N.Y.U. Presdl. citation, 1990, N.Y. State Bar Assn. Fifty-Yr. Lawyer award, 1990, ABA Sect. Taxation Distinguished Svc. award, 1999. Fellow Am. Coll. Trial Lawyers, Am. Coll. Tax Counsel, Am. Bar Found.; mem. ABA (coun. sect. taxation 1978-81, ho. of dels. 1984-89), Fed. Bar Assn., Internat. Bar Assn., Soc. King's Inn, Ireland (hon. bencher 1995), N.Y. State Bar Assn., N.Y. State CPAs, N.Y. County Lawyers Assn. (v.p. 1966-69, pres. 1969-71, bd. dirs. 1958-64, 66-69, 71-74, chmn. judiciary com. 1965-69), Assn. of Bar of City of N.Y., NYU Sch. Commerce Alumni Assn. (pres. 1951-52), NYU Alumni Fedn. (pres. 1989-92), St. John's U. Law Sch. Alumni Assn. (pres. 1955-57), India House. General civil litigation, Criminal. Home: 37 Washington Sq W New York NY 10011-9181 Office: Kostelanetz & Fink 530 5th Ave Fl 22 New York NY 10036-5101

KOSTELNY, ALBERT JOSEPH, JR. lawyer; b. Phila., July 11, 1951; s. Albert Joseph and Margaret (Naile) K. BA, U. Pa., 1973, MA, 1974; JD, Fordham U., 1979. Bar: N.Y. 1980, U.S. Dist. Ct. (so. dist.) N.Y. 1983, U.S. Ct. Claims 1983, U.S. Supreme Ct. 1983, U.S. Ct. Internat. Trade 1985, U.S. Ct. Appeals (2d cir.) 1985. Atty. N.Y. State Divsn. Human Rights, N.Y.C., 1980-81, sr. atty., 1981-89, acting chief adminstrv. law judge, 1989-91, adjudication counsel to commr., 1990-98, supr. atty., dir. prosecutions unit, 1998—. Mem. ABA, N.Y. State Bar Assn., N.Y. County Lawyers Assn., Assn. Trial Lawyers Am. Republican. Roman Catholic. Office: NY State Div Human Rights One Fordham Plz Bronx NY 10458-5871 E-mail: kostelna@nysnet.net

KOSTYO, JOHN FRANCIS, lawyer; b. Findlay, Ohio, Feb. 9, 1955; s. Albert Robert and Mary Agnes (Welsh) K.; m. Shirley Ann Allgyre, June 9, 1984. BA in Polit. Sci. and Philosophy magna cum laude, John Carroll U., 1978; JD, Case Western Res. U., 1981. Bar: Ohio 1981, U.S. Dist. Ct. (no. dist.) Ohio 1982, U.S. Dist. Ct. (ea. dist.) Mich. 1991, U.S. Supreme Ct. 1991, U.S. Dist. Ct. (so. dist.) Mich. 1992, U.S. Dist. Ct. (we. dist.) Mich. 1992. Assoc. Weasel & Brimley, Findlay, 1981-89; ptnr. Brimley, Kostyo & Elliott, L.P.A., 1989-91, Brimley & Kostyo Co., L.P.A., Findlay, 1991, Brimley, Kostyo & Lather Co., L.P.A., 1991-93, Brimley & Kostyo Co. L.P.A., 1993-99; v.p. Mid-Am. Title Agy., Inc., Findlay, Ohio, 1989—; mem. Kostyo & Clark, PLL, 1999—, Fuller & Henry, Ltd., 2001—. Lectr. contracts and negotiable instruments U. Findlay, 1981-84, sr. lectr. 1984-96. Mem. ABA (corp. banking and bus. law, litigation div.), Ohio Bar Assn., Toledo Bar Assn., William Taft Am. Inn of Ct., Alpha Sigma Nu. Roman Catholic. Clubs: Rockwell Springs Trout. Lodge: Elks, K.C. (4th degree). Avocations: sports, comml. trans., books, theater. State civil litigation, Contracts commercial, General practice. Home: 462 Penbrooke Dr Findlay OH 45840-7472 Office: Fuller & Henry Ltd 1995 Tiffin Ave Ste 312 Findlay OH 45840-6772 also: MidAm Title Agy Inc 100 E Main Cross St Findlay OH 45840-4861

KOSUB, JAMES ALBERT, lawyer; b. San Antonio, Jan. 8, 1948; s. Ernest Pete and Lonie (Doege) K.; divorced; 1 child, James Jr.; m. Jane Stevens Cain, Aug. 11, 1979; children: Kathryn, Nicholas (dec.). Student, East Carolina U., 1970, San Antonio Coll., 1971-72; BS, SW Tex. State U., 1974; JD, St. Mary's U., San Antonio, 1977. Bar: Tex. 1978, U.S. Dist. Ct. (we. dist.) Tex. 1980, U.S. Ct. Appeals (5th cir.) 1981, U.S. Dist. Ct. (so. dist.) 1986, U.S. Supreme Ct. 1988, U.S. Dist. Ct. (no. and ea. dists.) Tex. 1990. Ptnr. Kosub & Langlois, San Antonio, 1978-79, Kosub, Langlois & Van Cleave, San Antonio, 1979-83; mng. ptnr. Kosub & Langlois, 1983-86; sr. ptnr. James A. Kosub, 1986-94; pvt. practice Eldorado, Tex., 1994—. Bd. dirs. Judson Ind. Sch. Bd. Trustees, Converse, Tex., 1975-81, Bexar County Fedn. Sch. Bds., San Antonio, 1977-80. Sgt. USMC, 1966-70. Fellow Tex. Bar Found., San Antonio Bar Found.; mem. ABA (EEOC liaison com. San Antonio chpt. 1987-93), San Antonio Bar Assn. (bd. dirs., 1990-92, sec. 1992-93), Fed. Bar Assn. 5th Cir. Bar Assn., Coll. of State Bar of Tex., State Bar of Tex. (coun. labor and employment sect. 1993-97, sec. 1997-98, vice chair 1998-99, char 1999-2000, past chair 2000-01), Schleicher County C. of C. (pres. 1998-2000), Schleicher County Lions Club. Episcopalian. Avocations: carpentry, gardening, golf. Civil rights, Constitutional, Labor. Office: 105 S Main Eldorado TX 76936-0460

KOTASKA, GARY F. lawyer, partner; b. Flint, Mich., Oct. 20, 1949; s. Joseph Robert and Lillian (Ondrus) K.; m. Kathleen Sharon Marsden, June 10, 1972; children: Jonathan, Robert, Andrew, Kathleen. B.A. in History, Canisius Coll., Buffalo, 1971; J.D. magna cum laude, Bklyn. Law Sch., 1974. Bar: N.Y. 1975, U.S. Dist. Ct. (we. dist.) N.Y. 1975, U.S. Ct. Appeals (2nd cir.) 1986, U.S. Ct. Appeals (11th cir.) 1990. Ptnr. Moot & Sprague, Buffalo, 1974-90, Phillips, Lytle, Hitchcock, Blaine & Huber, Buffalo, 1990—; dir. Naylon Cos., Inc.; United bd. dirs. Battenfield-Am., Buffalo. W.N.Y. United Against Drug & Alcohol Abuse, Inc. Mem. Erie County Bar Assn. Democrat. Roman Catholic. General corporate, Pension, profit-sharing, and employee benefits. Home: 143 Devonshire Rd Buffalo NY 14223-1946 Office: Phillips Lytle Hitchcock Blaine & Huber 3400 Marine Midland Ctr Buffalo NY 14203-2887

KOTLARCHUK, IHOR O. E. lawyer; b. Ukraine, July 31, 1943; came to U.S., 1946, naturalized, 1957; s. Emil and Lidia N. (Maceluch) K. BS in Fin., Fordham U., 1965, JD, 1968; LLM, Georgetown U., 1974, MA in Govt., 1982. Bar: N.Y. 1969, D.C. 1972, Va. 2001, U.S. Ct. Mil. Appeals, U.S. Tax Ct., U.S. Supreme Ct. Sr. trial atty. criminal sect. tax divsn. U.S. Dept. Justice, Washington, 1973-78, civil sect. tax divsn., 1978-80, fraud sect. criminal divsn., 1980-84, internal security sect. criminal divsn., 1984-97; ret., 1999; sr. internat. law enforcement adv. on tax policy/enforcement U.S. Treasury Dept., 2000—. Pres. The Washington Group, 2001—. With U.S. Army, 1969-73, Vietnam; judge advocate gen.; ret. col. USAR. Decorated Bronze star, Legion of Merit. Mem. ABA, N.Y. State Bar Assn., Va. State Bar Assn., Va. Trial Lawyers Assn., D.C. Bar Assn., Res. Officers Assn., Ukrainian Assn. Washington D.C. (pres. 2000-01), Phi Alpha Delta. Ukrainian Catholic. Address: 205 S Lee St Alexandria VA 22314-3307 Office: 109 S Fairfax St Alexandria VA 22314-3307 Fax: 703-548-1861

KOTT, DAVID RUSSELL, lawyer; b. Trenton, N.J., Jan. 22, 1952; s. Maurice G. and Ruth (Shulman) K.; m. Lauren Handler, Aug. 24, 1980; children: Emily R., Adam J. BA, Am. U., 1973; JD, Rutgers U., 1977. Bar: N.J. 1977, U.S. Dist. Ct. N.J. 1977, U.S. Ct. Appeals (3d cir.) 1980, N.Y. 1984, U.S. Dist. Ct. (so. and ea. dists.) N.Y. 1985; cert. civil trial atty. Law clk. to justice N.J. Supreme Ct., Morristown, 1977-78; from assoc. to ptnr. McCarter & English LLP, Newark, 1978—. Sustaining mem. Product Liability Adv. Coun. Fellow Am. Coll. Trial Lawyers; mem. ABA, Am. Bd. Trial Advocates, N.J. Bar Assn., Essex County Bar Assn., Assn. Def. Trial Lawyers Attys., Trial Lawyers N.J., Fedn. Ins. and Corp. Attys., Def. Rsch. Inst., The Newark Club, Club at World Trade Ctr. Republican. Jewish. Federal civil litigation, State civil litigation, Insurance. Office: McCarter & English LLP 4 Gateway Ctr 100 Mulberry St Newark NJ 07102-4004 E-mail: dkott@mccarter.com

KOUBA, LISA MARCO, lawyer; b. Chgo., July 1, 1957; d. Edward Samuel and Phyllis Lavergne Marco; m. Kenneth Edward Kouba, Sept. 24, 1983. BA with honors, U. Ill., 1978; JD cum laude, Loyola U., Chgo., 1981. Bar: Ill. 1981, U.S. Dist. Ct. (no. dist.) Ill. 1981, U.S. Ct. Appeals (6th, 7th, 8th and 10th cirs.) 1982, U.S. Supreme Ct. 1985, U.S. Dist. Ct. (cen. dist.) 1991. Ptnr. Clausen, Miller, Gorman, Caffrey & Witous, PC, Chgo., 1981-97. Editor Loyola Law Jour., 1981. Mem. bd. edn. Elem. Sch. Dist. 101, 1999—; bd. dirs. Mordine & Co. Dance Troupe, 1988; chair Lyons Twp. Legis. Coun., 1996-98. Mem. Ill. Bar Assn., Chgo. Bar Assn. (chair young lawyers sect. on appellate law 1982-83), Appellate Lawyers Assn. (bd. dirs. 1986-88). Appellate, General civil litigation, Insurance.

KOURLIS, REBECCA LOVE, state supreme court justice; b. Colorado Springs, Colo., Nov. 11, 1952; d. John Arthur and Ann (Daniels) Love; m. Thomas Aristithis Kourlis, July 15, 1978; children: Stacy Ann, Katherine Love, Aristithis Thomas. BA with distinction in English, Stanford U., 1973, JD, 1976; LLD (hon.), U. Denver, 1997. Bar: Colo. 1976, D.C. 1979, U.S. Dist. Ct. Colo. 1976, U.S. Ct. Appeals (10th cir.) 1976, Colo. Supreme Ct., U.S. Ct. Appeals (D.C. cir.), U.S. Claims Ct., U.S. Supreme Ct. Assoc. Davis, Graham & Stubbs, Denver, 1976-78; sole practice Craig, Colo., 1978-87; judge 14th Jud. Dist. Ct., 1987-94; arbiter Jud. Arbiter Group, Inc., 1994-95; justice Colo. Supreme Ct., 1995—. Water judge divsn. 6, 1987-94; lectr. to profl. groups. Contbr. articles to profl. jours. Chmn. Moffat County Arts and Humanities, Craig, 1979; mem. Colo. Commn. on Higher Edn., Denver, 1980-81; mem. adv. bd. Colo. Divsn. Youth Svcs., 1988-91; mem. com. civil jury instructions, 1990-95, standing com. gender & justice, 1994-97, chair jud. adv. coun., 1997—, chair com. on jury reform, 1996—; co-chair com. on atty. grievance reform, 1997—; mem. long range planning com. Moffat County Sch., 1990; bd. visitors Stanford U., 1989-94, Law Sch. U. Denver, 1997—; bd. trustees Kent Denver Sch., 1996—. Named N.W. Colo. Daily Press Woman of Yr., 1993; recipient

Trailblazer award AAUW, 1998, Mary Lathrop award, 2001. Fellow Am. Bar Found., Colo. Bar Found.; mem. Am. Law Inst., Rocky Mountain Mineral Found., Colo. Bar Assn. (bd. govs. 1983-85, mineral law sect. bd. dirs. 1985, sr. v.p. 1987-88), Dist. Ct. Judges' Assn. (pres. 1993-94), N.W. Colo. Bar Assn. (Cmty. Svc. award 1993-94). Office: State Jud Bldg 2 E 14th Ave Denver CO 80203-2115

KOURTESIS, NIKOLAOS PANAGIOTIS, lawyer; b. Balt., Oct. 29, 1970; s. Panagiotis and Stella K.; m. Cameron Marlo Robinson, Sept. 26, 1998. BA in Criminal Justice, Am. U., 1991, MS in Justice, 1993; JD, D.C. Sch. of Law, 1997. Bar: Md. 1997, N.J. 1998, U.S. Dist. Ct. N.J., U.S. Dist. Ct. Md. Law clk. Koonz, McKenney, Johnson, Depadis & Lightfoot, Falls Church, Va., 1998; pvt. practice Fort Washington, Md., 1997-98; atty. Robinson Law Firm, Washington, 1998—. Treas. STRIVE, Fairfax, Va. Mem. ABA, Prince George's County Bar Assn., Montgomery County Bar Assn. Criminal, Personal injury. Office: Robinson Law Firm 717 D St NW #400 Washington DC 20004-2023

KOVACHEVICH, ELIZABETH ANNE, federal judge; b. Canton, Ill., Dec. 14, 1936; d. Dan and Emilie (Kuchan) Kovachevich AA, St. Petersburg Jr. Coll., 1956; BBA in Fin. magna cum laude, U. Miami, 1958; JD, Stetson U., 1961, LLD (hon.), 1993. Bar: Fla. 1961, U.S. Dist. Ct. (mid. and so. dists.) Fla. 1961, U.S. Ct. Appeals (5th cir.) 1961, U.S. Supreme Ct. 1968. Rsch. and adminstrv. aide Pinellas County Legis. Del., Fla., 1961; assoc. DiVito & Speer, St. Petersburg, 1961-62; house counsel Rieck & Fleece Builders Supplies, Inc., 1962; pvt. practice, 1962-73; judge 6th Jud. Cir., Pinellas and Pasco Counties, Fla., 1973-82, U.S. Dist. Ct. (mid. dist.) Fla., Tampa, 1982-96, chief judge, 1996—; chmn. St. Petersburg Profl. Legal Project-Days in Court, 1967. Chmn. Supreme Ct. Bicentennial Com. 6th Jud. Circuit, 1975-76. Prodr., coord. TV prodn. A Race to Judgement. Bd. regents State of Fla., 1970-72; legal advisor, bd. dirs. Young Women's Residence Inc., 1968; mem. Fla. Gov.'s Commn. on Status of Women, 1968-71; mem. Pres.'s Commn. on White House Fellowships, 1973-77; mem. def. adv. com. on Women in Service, Dept. Def., 1973-76; Fla. conf. publicity chmn. 18th Nat. Republican Women's Conf., Atlanta, 1971; lifetime mem. Children's Hosp. Guild, YWCA of St. Petersburg; charter mem. Golden Notes, St. Petersburg Symphony; hon. mem. bd. of overseers Stetson U. Coll. of Law, 1986. Recipient Disting. Alumni award Stetson U., 1970, Woman of Yr. award Beta Sigma Phi, 1970, Woman of Yr. award Fla. Fedn. Bus. and Profl. Women, 1981, ann. Ben C. Willard Meml. award, Stetson Lawyers Assn., 1983, St. Petersburg Panhellenic Appreciation award, 1964, Mrs. Charles Ulrick Bay award, St. Petersburg Rotary award, St. Petersburg Quarterback Club award, Pinellas United Fund award in recognition of concern and meritorious effort, 1968, Woman of Yr. award Beta Sigma Phi, 1970, Am. Legion Aux. Unit 14 Pres. award cmty. svc., 1970, Dedication to Christian Ideals award and Man of Yr. award KC Dists. 20-21, 1972, USN Recruiting Command Appreciation award, 1975, Alumni of Yr. award St. Petersburg Jr. Coll., 1994, Cath. Law Person of Yr., Greater Tampa Cath. Lawyer's Guild, 1998, Disting. Svc. award Fla. Coun. on Crime and Delinquency, 1999, J-Ben Watkins award Stetson U. Coll. of Law, 1999, Woman of Achievement award Delta Delta Delta, 2000, Pub. Svc. award William Reece Smith, Jr., 2001, Outstanding Jurist award Hillsborough County, 2000-01. Mem. ABA, Fla. Bar Assn., Pinellas County Trial Lawyers, Assn. Trial Lawyers Am., Am. Judicature Soc., St. Petersburg Bar Assn. (chmn. bench and bar com., sec. 1969). Office: US Dist Ct 801 N Florida Ave Tampa FL 33602-3849

KOVACIC, WILLIAM EVAN, law educator; b. Poughkeepsie, N.Y., Oct. 1, 1952; s. Evan Carl and Frances Katherine (Crow) K.; m. Kathryn Marie Fenton, May 18, 1985. AB with honors, Princeton U., 1974; JD, Columbia U., 1978. Bar: N.Y. 1979. Law clk. to sr. dist. judge U.S. Dist. Ct. Md., Balt., 1978-79; atty. planning office bur. competition FTC, Washington, 1979-82, atty. advisor to commr., 1983; assoc. Bryan, Cave, McPheeters & McRoberts, 1983-86; prof. George Mason U. Sch. Law, Arlington, Va., 1986-99, George Washington U. Law Sch., Washington, 1999—; gen. counsel U.S. FTC, 2001—. Cons. in field; mem. U.S. Senate Judiciary Subcom. on Antitrust and Monopoly, Washington, 1975-76. Contbr. legal articles to profl. jours. Assoc. Father Ford Found. Columbia U. Cath. Campus Ministry, N.Y.C. 1985—. Harlan Fiske Stone fellow Columbia U., 1976-78. Mem. ABA (antitrust law and pub. contract law sects.), Fed. Bar Assn. Roman Catholic. Avocations: hiking, camping, photography. Office: George Washington U Law Sch 720 20th St NW Washington DC 20052-0001 E-mail: wkovacic@main.nlc.gwu.edu

KOVACS, WILLIAM LAWRENCE, lawyer; b. Scranton, Pa., June 29, 1947; s. William Lawrence and Jane Claire (Weiss) K.; m. Mary Katherine Maras, Dec. 2, 1979; children: Katherine Elizabeth, William Lawrence III, Margaret Ellen, Tyler Alexander. BS magna cum laude, U. Scranton, 1969; JD, Ohio State U., 1972. Bar: Pa. 1972, D.C. 1973, U.S. Ct. Appeals (D.C. cir.) 1974, U.S. Supreme Ct. 1976, Va. 1981. Legis. asst., staff atty. Congressman Fred B. Rooney, Washington, 1972-74; chief counsel U.S. Ho. of Reps. Subcom. on Transp. and Commerce, 1975-77; assoc. Liebert, Short, FitzPatrick & Lavin, Phila., 1977-78; environ., litigation atty. Nat. Chamber Litigation Ctr., Washington, 1979; ptnr. Abrams, Kovacs, Westermeier & Goldberg, 1980-84, Kovacs & Bury, Fairfax, Va., 1984-85, Jaeckle, Fleischmann & Mugel, Washington, 1986-87, Eckert, Seamans, Cherin & Mellott, Washington, 1987-89, Dunn, Carney, Allen, Higgins & Tongue, Portland, Oreg., 1990, Keller & Heckman, Washington, 1991-97; pres. Clean States Found., Inc., 1997-98; dir. legal affairs Worldwide Sunshine Makers, Inc., Washington, 1997-98; v.p. environ. tech. and regulatory affairs U.S. C. of C., 1998—. Contbr. articles to profl. jours. Mem. Hazardous Waste Facilities Siting Bd., Richmond, Va., 1984-86; vice chmn., 1984-85, chmn., 1985-86. Mem. ABA (vice chmn. energy resources law com. sect. on torts and ins. practice 1981-83, chmn. 1983-84), U.S. C. of C. (mem. environ. law adv. com. 1986-92). Roman Catholic. Administrative and regulatory, Environmental, Legislative. Home: 9805 Arnon Chapel Rd Great Falls VA 22066-3908 Office: 1615 H St NW Washington DC 20062-0001 E-mail: WKovacs@uschamber.com

KOWALOFF, DOROTHY RUBIN, retired lawyer; b. N.Y.C., May 8, 1917; d. Saul and Fannie (Romanoff) Roberts; m. Meyer Kowaloff, Mar. 18, 1945 (dec.); children: Arthur, Nina. BA, NYU, 1938; LLB, Columbia U., 1940. Bar: N.Y. Sole practice, N.Y.C., 1941-50; pres. Rokor Corp., 1950-67; atty., corp. counsel office Dept. Law, City of N.Y., 1967-86. Lawyer; b. N.Y.C., May 8, 1917; d. Saul and Fannie (Romanoff) Roberts; m. Meyer Kowaloff, Mar. 18, 1945 (dec.); children— Arthur, Nina. B.A., NYU, 1938; LL.B., Columbia U., 1940. Bar: N.Y. Sole practice, N.Y.C., 1941-50; pres. Rokor Corp., 1950-67; atty. corp. counsel office Dept. Law City of N.Y., 1967— . Mem. Women's Bar Assn. City of N.Y., N.Y. State Women's Bar Assn. Mem. Women's Bar Assn. City N.Y., N.Y. State Women's Bar Assn. Office: Corp Counsels Office 100 Church St New York NY 10007

KOZACHOK, STEPHEN K. lawyer; b. Wilkes-Barre, Pa., Jan. 10, 1969; s. Peter Daniel Kozachok and Marjorie Schramm; m. Molli Maier, Oct. 8, 1969; children: Katia Marie, Annika Marie. Diploma of bus. french, U. Catholique de l'Ouest, Angers, France, 1990; BAin Econs. and French, U. Notre Dame, 1992; JD, George Washington U., 1996. Law clk. Minn. Ct. of Appeals, St. Paul, 1996-97; lawyer Dorsey & Whitney, Mpls., 1997—. Mem. ABA, Hennepin County Bar Assn. Private international, Mergers and acquisitions, Securities. Home: 1254 Wellesley Ave Saint Paul MN 55105 Office: Dorsey & Whitney 220 S Sixth St Minneapolis MN 55402

KOZAK, JOHN W. lawyer; b. Chgo., July 25, 1943; s. Walter and Stella (Palka) K.; m. Elizabeth Mathias, Feb. 3, 1968; children: Jennifer, Mary Margaret, Suzanne. BSEE, U. Notre Dame, 1965; JD, Georgetown U., 1968. Bar: Ill. 1968, D.C. 1968. Patent advisor Office of Naval Rsch., Corona, Calif., 1968-69; assoc. Leydig, Voit & Mayer, Ltd. and predecessor firms, Chgo., 1969-74, ptnr., 1974—, chmn. mgmt. com., 1982-91, pres., 2001—. Mem. United Charities Legal Aid Soc., 1989—. Fellow Am. Coll. Trial Lawyers; mem. ABA, Am. Intellectual Property Law Assn., Licensing Execs. Soc., Chgo. Intellectual Property Law Assn., Univ. Club (Chgo.), Law Club (Chgo.), Winter Club (Lake Forest, Ill.), Knollwood Club (Lake Forest). Federal civil litigation, Patent, Trademark and copyright. Office: Leydig Voit & Mayer Ste 4900 2 Prudential Pla Chicago IL 60601 E-mail: jkozak@leydig.com

KOZINSKI, ALEX, federal judge; b. Bucharest, Romania, July 23, 1950; came to U.S., 1962; s. Moses and Sabine (Zapler) K.; m. Marcy J. Tiffany, July 9, 1977; children: Yale Tiffany, Wyatt Tiffany, Clayton Tiffany. AB in Econs. cum laude, UCLA, 1972, JD, 1975. Bar: Calif. 1975, D.C., 1978. Law clk. to Hon. Anthony M. Kennedy U.S. Ct. Appeals (9th cir.), 1975-76; law clk. to Chief Justice Warren E. Burger U.S. Supreme Ct., 1976-77; assoc. Covington & Burling, Washington, 1979-81; asst. counsel Office of Counsel to Pres., White House, 1981; spl. counsel Merit Systems Protection Bd., 1981-82; chief judge U.S. Claims Ct., 1982-85; judge U.S. Ct. Appeals (9th cir.), 1985—. Lectr. law U. So. Calif., 1992. Office: US Ct Appeals 125 S Grand Ave Ste 200 Pasadena CA 91105*

KOZLIK, MICHAEL DAVID, lawyer; b. Omaha, Apr. 20, 1953; s. Otto John and Ella Mae (Slightam) K.; m. Emily C. Cunningham, Sept. 30, 1983; children: John E., Caroline C. BS in Bus., Creighton U., 1975, JD, 1979. Bar: Nebr. 1979, Iowa 2000, U.S. Dist. Ct. Nebr. 1979, U.S. Dist. Ct. Appeals (8th cir.) 1979, U.S. Tax Ct. 1991; CPA, Nebr. Acct. Peat Marwick, Omaha, 1979-84; v.p. fin. Emelco, 1984-86; assoc. Nelson Morrow, 1986-88; shareholder Schmid Mooney, 1988-97, Croker Huck, Omaha, 1997—. Mem. Nebr. CPA Ethics Comm., 1984-85, Nebr. CPA Edn. Comm., 1988—. Contbr. articles to mags. Bd. dirs. Hugh O'Brian Found., Omaha, 1989—, Nebr. ACC Decathlon. Recipient Leadership Omaha award Omaha C. of C., 1989; named One of Ten Outstanding Young Omahans Jaycees, 1990, 92. Mem. Omaha Bar Assn., Nebr. Bar Assn., Optimists (pres. 1989-90, honor award 1990). Republican. Avocations: hunting, fishing, billiards, geneology. Consumer commercial, Contracts commercial, Estate taxation. Home: 727 N 57th St Omaha NE 68132-2033 Address: Croker Huck DeWitt Anderson & Gonderinger 1250 Commerical Federal Tower 2120 S 72nd St Omaha NE 68124-2366 E-mail: mdkozlik@crokerlaw.com

KOZLOWSKI, THOMAS JOSEPH, JR. lawyer, trust company executive; b. Norristown, Pa., July 29, 1950; s. Thomas Joseph Sr. and Mary Elisa (Alvarez) K.; m. Michelle Mary Champagne, Jan. 9, 1971; children: Brian Christopher, Scott Michael, Mark Daniel. BSBA in Acctg., Georgetown U., 1971, JD, 1979; MBA, George Washington U., 1975. Bar: D.C. 1979, Va. 1980; CPA Va. Sr. acct. Touche Ross & Co., Washington, 1972-75; dir. internal audit Pentagon Fed. Credit Union, Arlington, Va., 1975-77; supr. acct. Snyder, Newrath & Co., Washington, 1977-79; v.p., sec. Owens & Co., Inc., Arlington, 1979-86; sr. v.p. fin. Realty Investment Co., Inc., Silver Spring, Md., 1986-89; sr. v.p., treas. The Selzer Group, Inc., N.Y.C., 1989-93; pres. The Collector's Gallery of Va. Inc., Alexandria, 1992-96; exec. v.p., dir. family office group Merrill Lynch Trust Co., Princeton, N.J., 1993—. Bd. dirs. Owens & Co., Alexandria, Va.; mem. bd. advisors Unistates LLC, Alexandria. Editor Jour. Law & Policy in Internat. Bus., 1976-79. Arbiter Fairfax County (Va.) Consumer Protection Commn., 1977-95; treas. Commonweal Found., Inc., Silver Spring, 1986-89; bd. dirs. Resdl. Youth Svcs., Inc., Alexandria, 1981-89, treas., 1982-84, v.p., 1984-85; treas. Coplex Found., N.Y.C., 1989-93; planned giving adv. coun. Pa. State U., 2000—. Fellow D.C. Inst. CPAs; mem. ABA, AICPA, D.C. Bar Assn., Va. State Bar Assn., Inst. Mgmt. Acctg. (cert. mgmt. acctg., cert. disting. performance 1975). Democrat. Roman Catholic. Avocations: reading, photography. Office: Merrill Lynch Trust Co 9 Roszel Rd 1st Fl Princeton NJ 08540

KRACKE, ROBERT RUSSELL, lawyer; b. Decatur, Ga., Feb. 27, 1938; s. Roy Rachford and Virginia Carolyn (Minter) K.; m. Barbara Anne Pilgrim, Dec. 18, 1965; children: Shannon Ruth, Robert Russell, Rebecca Anne, Susan Lynn. Student, Birmingham So. Coll.; BA, Samford U., 1962; JD, Cumberland Sch. Law, 1965. Bar: Ala. 1965, U.S. Tax Ct. 1971, U.S. Supreme Ct. 1971. Individual practice law, Birmingham, Ala., 1965—; pres. Kracke, Thompson & Ellis, 1980—. Editor, Birmingham Bar Bull, 1974—; bd. editors Ala. Lawyer, 1980-86; contbr. articles to profl. jours. Active Dem. Exec. Com., 1970-96; deacon Ind. Presbyn. Ch., Birmingham, 1973-76, elder, 1999—, pres. adult choir, 1968-99, chief adminstrv. officer, 1970-99, pres., treas. Nov. Orgn. Recital Series, 1999—, Housing Agy. Retarded Citizens; pres. Ala. chpt. Nat. Voluntary Health Agys.; mem. exec. com. legal counsel Birmingham Opera Theatre, 1983-95; bd. dirs. Ala. Assn. Retarded Citizens, Jefferson County Assn. Retarded Citizens, 1983-91, pres.-elect, 1994-96, pres. 1996-98, past pres., 1998-2000; coord. com. mem. Nat. Conv. of the ARC of U.S., 1999—; bd. dirs., founding pres. Ala. chpt. Juvenile Diabetes Rsch. Found. Internat., bd. dirs. The ARC of Ala., 1996-98, Found. of ARC, 1998—. With USNR, 1955-61. Mem. Birmingham (exec. com., chmn. law libr., law day 1976, history and archives com.), Ala. Bar Assn., ABA (award merit law day 1976), Am. Judicature Soc., U.S. Supreme Ct. Hist. Soc., Dem. Exec. Com., Ala. Hist. Assn., So. Hist. Assn., The Club, Phi Alpha Delta (pres. chpt. 1964-65), Rotary (pres. Shades Valley club 1988-89, Paul Harris fellow, sec. dist. 6860 1990-91, dist. coord. comm., bd. dir., sec. ednl. found.), Sigma Alpha Epsilon. State civil litigation, Family and matrimonial, Insurance. Home: 4410 Briar Glen Dr Birmingham AL 35243-1743 Office: Kracke Thompson & Ellis Lakeview Sch Bldg 808 29th St S Birmingham AL 35205-1004 E-mail: rkracke@ktlegal.com

KRAEMER, LILLIAN ELIZABETH, retired lawyer; b. N.Y.C., Apr. 18, 1940; d. Frederick Joseph and Edmee Elizabeth (de Watteville) K.; m. John W. Vincent, June 22, 1962 (div. 1964). BA, Swarthmore Coll., 1961; JD, U. Chgo., 1964. Bar: N.Y. 1965, U.S. Dist. Ct. (so. dist.) N.Y. 1967, U.S. Dist. Ct. (ea. dist.) N.Y. 1971. Assoc. Cleary, Gottlieb, Steen & Hamilton, N.Y.C., 1964-71, Simpson Thacher & Bartlett, N.Y.C., 1971-74, ptnr., 1974-99. Mem. vis. com. U. Chgo. Law Sch., 1988-90, 91-94, 97-99. Bd. mgrs. Swarthmore Coll., 1993—; warden St. Francis Episcopal Ch., Stamford, Conn., 2001—. Fellow Am. Coll. Bankruptcy; mem. Lawyers Alliance for N.Y. (bd. dirs. 1996-2001), Assn. of Bar of City of N.Y. (mem. various coms.), Coun. on Fgn. Rels., N.Y. State Bar Assn., Order of Coif, Phi Beta Kappa. Democrat. Avocations: travel, reading, word games. Banking, Bankruptcy. Home: 2 Beekman Pl New York NY 10022-8058 also: 62 Pheasant Ln Stamford CT 06903-4428 E-mail: lkraemer@home.com

KRAEMER, MICHAEL FREDERICK, lawyer; b. N.Y.C., Jan. 21, 1947; s. Jerome W. and Honey (Dunner) K.; m. Ross Shepard, June 21, 1970; 1 child, Jordan Harriet. BA cum laude, Amherst Coll., 1969; JD, U. Pa., 1972. Bar: Pa. 1972, U.S. Dist. Ct. (ea. dist.) Pa. 1972, N.J. 1973, U.S. Dist. Ct. N.J. 1973, U.S. Ct. Appeals (3d cir.) 1974, U.S. Ct. Appeals (2d cir.) 1980, U.S. Ct. Appeals (4th and 7th cirs.) 1981, U.S. Ct. Appeals (6th cir.) 1990, U.S. Ct. Appeals (1st cir.) 2001. Assoc. Astor & Weiss, Phila., 1972-75, Pechner, Sacks, Dorfman, Rosen & Richardson, Phila., 1975-76; ptnr. Kleinbard, Bell & Brecker, 1976-85, White and Williams LLP, Phila., 1985—. Bd. dirs. Ctr. City Residents Assn., Phila., 1976-78; Served to 2d lt. USAR, 1972-73. Recipient Disting. Svc. award Amherst Coll. Alumni Coun., 1994. Mem. Phila. Bar Assn. (profl. responsibility com. 1972-84, labor and employment law com. 1985—), Amherst Alumni Assn. Phila. (pres. 1977-79), Indsl. Rels. Rsch. Assn. Club: Germantown Cricket (Phila.). Labor. Office: White and Williams LLP 1800 One Liberty Pl Philadelphia PA 19103-7395

KRAEUTLER, ERIC, lawyer; b. Newark, Oct. 9, 1954; s. John Howard and Marie (Bevere) K.; m. Jacqueline Maykranz, May 18, 1985; children: Matthew John, Caroline Ann. BA, Princeton U., 1976; JD, U. Va., 1980. Bar: Pa., U.S. Dist. Ct. (ea. dist.) Pa., U.S. Ct. Appeals (3rd cir.), U.S. Ct. Appeals (9th cir.). Assoc. Morgan, Lewis & Bockius, LLP, Phila., 1980-84; asst. U.S. atty. U.S. Atty.'s Office, 1984-87; assoc. Morgan, Lewis & Bockius, LLP, 1987-90; ptnr. Morgan, Lewis & Bockius, 1990—; spl. dep. atty. gen. Commonwealth of Pa., 1992-94. Trustee Princeton Tower Club, 1980—; trustee Nat. Multiple Sclerosis Soc., 1993—, sec., 1994-96, vice chmn., 1996-98, chmn., 1998-2000; mem. Princeton Alumni Coun. 1984-87, Com. of Seventy, 2001—. Mem. ABA, Fed. Bar Assn., Phila. Bar Assn. Presbyterian. Avocation: running. Federal civil litigation, Criminal, Health. Home: 35 Wellesley Rd Swarthmore PA 19081-1232 Office: Morgan Lewis & Bockius LLP 1701 Market St Philadelphia PA 19103-2903 E-mail: ekraeutler@morganlewis.com

KRAFT, C. WILLIAM, JR. federal judge; b. Phila., Dec. 14, 1903; s. C. William and Wilhelmina J. (Doerr) K.; m. Frances V. McDevitt, June 27, 1942; 1 child, C. William III. A.B., U. Pa., 1924, LL.B., 1927, J.D., 1930. Bar: Pa. 1927. Trial lawyer Kraft, Lippincott & Donaldson, Media, Pa., 1928-55; dist. atty. Delaware County, 1944-52; judge U.S. Dist. Ct., Phila., 1955-70, sr. judge, 1970—. Mem. ABA, Pa. Bar Assn. Home and Office: Island House 200 Ocean Lane Dr Apt 602 Key Biscayne FL 33149-1447

KRAFT, CARL DAVID, lawyer; b. Elgin, Ill., July 28, 1952; s. Howard David and Edna Leota Kraft; m. Joan Marie Kaps Evans, May 24, 1975 (div. Jan. 1981); m. Kathleen Susan Webb, Nov. 19, 1983; children: Matthew A., Andrew W. BA, No. Ill. U., 1974; JD, Washington U., St. Louis, 1977. BAr: Mo. 1977, U.S. Dist. Ct. (ea. dist.) Mo., U.S. Ct. Appeals (8th cir.), U.S. Supreme Ct.; cert. civl trial lawyer. Atty. Richard Edwards Law Office, Clayton, Mo., 1977-78, Evans & Dixon, St. Louis, 1978-85; ptnr. Kraft & Harfst, 1985—. Bd. dirs., pres. Luth. Ministries Assn., St. Louis, 1988-95; evaluator, judge, coach H.S. Mock Trial, St. Louis, 1983—; sec. Glendale (Mo.) Luth. Ch. Coun., 1996—. Recipient Vol. Lawyer Svc. award Legal Svcs. Eastern Mo., 1984. Mem. ATLA, Mo. Bar Assn., Mo. Assn. Def. Lawyers. General civil litigation, Family and matrimonial, Insurance. Home: 7642 Westmoreland Ave Saint Louis MO 63105-3807 Office: Kraft & Harfst 12901 N 40 Dr Saint Louis MO 63141-8634

KRAFT, HENRY ROBERT, lawyer; b. L.A., Apr. 27, 1946; s. Sylvester and Freda (Shochat) K.; m. Terry Kraft, July 21, 1968; children: Diana, Kevin. BA in History, San Fernando Valley State Coll., 1968; JD, U. So. Calif., 1971. Bar: Calif. 1972, U.S. Dist. Ct. (ctrl. dist.) Calif. 1985, U.S. Ct. Appeals (9th cir.) 1998, U.S. Dist. Ct. (so. and no. dists.) Calif 1998. Dep. pub. defender San Bernardino (Calif.) County, 1972-78; pvt. practice, Victorville, Calif., 1979-96; city atty., 1987—; of counsel Best Best & Krieger LLP, 1996-98; assoc. Parker, Covert & Chidester, Tustin, Calif., 1999-2000; ptnr. Parker & Covert LLP, 2000—. Atty. City of Barstow, Calif., 1980-97; instr. Victor Valley Coll., Victorville, 1986—. Atty. Barstow Community Hosp., 1980-88. Mem. FBA, San Bernardino Bar Assn. (fee dispute com., jud. evaluation com.), High Desert Bar Assn. (pres., v.p., sec. 1979-81), Calif. Soc. Health Care Attys., League Calif. Cities, Am. Arbitration Assn. (panel neutral arbitrators). Democrat. Jewish. Avocations: bicycling, travel, wine enthusiast. Office: Parker & Covert LLP East Bldg Ste 204 17862 E Seventeenth St Tustin CA 92780-2164 E-mail: edupcc@aol.com

KRAFT, RICHARD LEE, lawyer; b. Lassa, Nigeria, Oct. 14, 1958; m. Tanya Kraft, July 14, 1984; children: Devin, Kelsey. BA in Fgn. Svc., Baylor U., 1980, JD, 1982. Bar: N.Mex. 1982, U.S. Dist. Ct. N.Mex., U.S. Ct. Appeals, U.S. Supreme Ct. Assoc. Sanders, Bruin & Baldock, Roswell, N.Mex., 1982-87, ptnr., 1987-98, Kraft & Stone, LLP, Roswell, 1998-2000; owner The Kraft Law Firm, 2000—. Vol. lawyer Ea. N.Mex. U. Roswell, 1984-98; bd. dirs. Roswell YMCA, 1983-87, Crimestopper, 1991-94; pres. Roswell Mens Ch. Basketball League; participant Roswell Mens Ch. Softball League; asst. chair legal div. United Way Drive, 1990. Recipient Outstanding Contribution award N.Mex. State Bar, 1987. Mem. ABA, N.Mex. Trial Lawyers Assn., N.Mex. Bar Assn. (bd. dirs. young lawyers div. 1983-91, pres. 1986-87, chmn. membership com., bar commr. 1986-87, 91—, pres. 1998-99, Outstanding Young Lawyer award 1990), Chaves County Bar Assn. (chair law day activities, chair ann. summer picnic com., rep. bench and bar com.), Roswell Legal Secs. Assn. (hon.), Roswell C. of C. (participant and pres. Leadership Roswell, exec. dir., bd. dirs. 1991-97), Sertoma (bd. dirs. Roswell club 1989-91). Baptist. General civil litigation, Family and matrimonial, Personal injury. Office: The Kraft Law Firm 400 N Pennsylvania Ave Ste 1250 Roswell NM 88201-4783

KRAHMER, DONALD LEROY, JR. lawyer; b. Hillsboro, Oreg., Nov. 11, 1957; s. Donald L. and Joan Elizabeth (Karns) K.; m. Suzanne M. Blanchard, Aug. 16, 1986; children: Hillary, Zachary. BS, Willamette U., 1981, MM, JD, Willamette U., 1987. Bar: Oreg. 1988. Fin. analyst U.S. Bancorp, Portland, 1977-87; intern U.S. Senator Mark Hatfield, 1978; legis. aide State Sen. Jeannette Hamby, Hillsboro, Oreg., 1981-83, State Rep. Delna Jones, Beaverton, 1983; bus. analyst Pacificorp, Portland, 1987; mgr. mergers/acquisitions Pacificorp Fin. Svcs., 1988-89, dir., 1990; CEO, pres. Atkinson Group, Portland, 1991—; ptnr. Black Helterline, LLP , 1991—. Sec. Marathon Fin. Assocs., Portland, 1989; bd. dirs. Self-Enhancement, Inc.; chmn. Willamette Forum; editor Oreg. Entrepreneur Forum, 1993, chmn. adv. bd., 1995, chmn. bd., 1998; founder co-chmn. Oreg. Emerging Bus. Initiative, 1997—, New Economy Coalition, 2001—; bd. dirs. Portland C.of C., 2002. Treas. Com. to Re-Elect Jeannette Hamby, 1986; bd. dirs. fin. com., devel. com. Am. Diabetes Assn., Portland, 1990-96; founder Needle Bros., 1994; chmn. Atkinson Grad. Sch. Devel. Com., Salem, 1989-92; Bd. Vis. Coll. Law, Willamette U., 1997-2001; adv. bd. Ctr. for Law and Entrepreneurship, U. Oreg. Sch. Law, 1997—; founder Conf. of Entrepreneurship, Salem, 1984, chmn. Entrepreneurship Breakfast Forum, Portland, 1993; chmn., founder Oreg. Conf. on Entrepreneurship and Awards Dinner, 1994-99, sr. v.p., 1999—; exec. com., bd. dirs. Cascade Pacific Coun. Boy Scouts Am., 1998—, chmn. cmty. fund. dir., 1997, chmn. Scoutrageous, 2000; vice-chmn. Govs. Coun. on Small Bus., State of Oreg.; mem. Govs. Econ. Devel. Joint Bds. Working Group, 1999—; mem. ch. couns. Our Savior Luth. Ch., 2000—. Recipient Pub.'s award Oreg. Bus. Mag., 1987, Founders award Willamette U., 1987, award Scripps Found., 1980, Bus. Jour. 40 Under 40 award, 1996, Oreg. State Bar Pres.'s award, 1999. Mem. ABA, Oreg. Bar Assn. (chmn. exec. com., fin. instns. com. sec., exec. com., bus. law sect., chmn. 1999, sec. 1998), Multnomah County Bar Assn., Assn. for Corp. Growth, Oreg. Biosci. Assn., Portland Soc. Fin. Analysts, Japan-Am. Soc. Oreg., Assn. Investment Mgmt. and Rsch., City Club, Software Assn. of Oreg., Oreg. Biotech. Assn., Multnomah Athletic Club (bd. dirs. 2001-), Arlington Club (treas. 2002). Republican. Lutheran. General corporate, Mergers and acquisitions, Securities. Home: 16230 SW Copper Creek Dr Portland OR 97224-6500 Office: Black Helterline LLP 805 SW Broadway Ste 1900 Portland OR 97205

KRAKOWSKI, RICHARD JOHN, lawyer, public relations executive; b. Meppen, Fed. Republic of Germany, Apr. 3, 1946; came to U.S., 1951, naturalized, 1962; s. Feliks and Maria (Chilinski) K. MBA, DePaul U., 1979; JD, John Marshall Law Sch., 1983. Bar: Ill. 1984. Personnel dir. Andy Frain, Inc., Chgo., 1973-78; pub. rels. dir. Chgo. Health Sys. Agy., 1978-84; assoc. firm Mangum, Smietanka & Johnson, Chgo., 1984-87; asst. atty. gen. Ill. Atty. Gen.'s Ofc., 1987-96. Bd. dirs., St. Mary of Nazareth Hosp., Holy Trinity H.S.; lectr. in field. Co-author: Health Care Financing and Policy Making in Chicago and Illinois, 1982. Fundraising and pub. rels. dir. Cabrini-Green Sandlot Tennis Program, Chgo., 1979-83; sustaining mem. Rep. Nat. Com., 1981—; bd. dirs. Internat. Latino Cultural Ctr. Capt. U.S. Army, 1969-72. Mem. ABA, Nat. Advocates Soc., Ill. Bar Assn., Chgo. Bar Assn., Chgo. Coun. Fgn. Rels., Lyric Opera Guild, Art Inst. Chgo., Chgo. Soc. Polish Nat. Alliance, Publicity Club (Chgo.). Roman Catholic. Home: 1350 N Lake Shore Dr Apt 1215 Chicago IL 60610-5143 Office: Cook County Human Resources Divsn 118 N Clark St Ste 824 Chicago IL 60602-1312 E-mail: rjkrak1350@hotmail.com

KRAM, PETER, lawyer; b. Chgo., Nov. 15, 1946; s. Paul Lauer and Nancy Ellen (Dineen) K. BA, St. Louis U., 1968; MA, U. Nev., 1972; JD, U. Puget Sound, 1976. Bar: Wash. 1977, U.S. Dist. Ct. (we. dist.) Wash. 1977, U.S. Ct. Appeals (9th cir.) 1977. Sole practice, Tacoma, 1977-78; ptnr. Lewis, Shillito et al, 1978; assoc. James F. Leggett, 1978-82; ptnr. Leggett & Kram, 1983—. Trustee North End Athletic Assn., Tacoma, 1981-88; mem. Charter Rev. Commn., Tacoma, 1983—. Served to capt. USAF, 1968-72. Mem. ABA, Wash. State Bar (corrections com., public rels. com., fee arbitration com.), Tacoma Price County Bar Assn. (trustee 1996-98). Roman Catholic. Clubs: Lakewood Racquet; Tacoma Lawn Tennis (bd. dirs. 1981). Criminal, Family and matrimonial, Personal injury. Home: 414 Tacoma Ave N Tacoma WA 98403-2739 Office: Leggett & Kram 1901 S I St Tacoma WA 98405-3810

KRAMARIC, PETER STEFAN, lawyer; b. Ljubljana, Yugoslavia, Apr. 29, 1930; came to U.S., 1956; s. Stefan and Ana (Vidic) K.; m. Susan R. Little, Aug. 15, 1959; 1 dau., Karen Louise. Abs. Iur., Law Sch., U. Ljubljana, 1954; LL.B., Yale U., 1960. Bar: N.Y. 1962. Internat. atty. Union Carbide Corp., N.Y.C., 1961-70; gen. counsel internat. Gen. Foods Corp., White Plains, N.Y., 1970-73; dir. office of east-west trade devel. Dept. Commerce, Washington, 1973-74; asst. gen. counsel Am. Home Products Corp., N.Y.C., 1974— , also officer various subs. Mem. ABA, N.Y. State Bar Assn., Pharm. Mfrs. Assn. (legal com.). Republican. Club: Yale (N.Y.C.). General corporate, Private international. Home: 12 Heatherbush Rd Essex Junction VT 05452-3828 Office: Am Home Products Corp 685 3rd Ave # 24th New York NY 10017-4024

KRAMER, ANDREW MICHAEL, lawyer; b. N.Y.C., Nov. 2, 1944; s. Irving and Ida (Kaplan) K.; m. Cheryle Lynn Safran, June 21, 1966; children: Howard, Jennifer; m. Nita Lynne Albert, Mar. 13, 1983; children: Samantha, Stephanie. BA cum laude, Mich. State U., 1966; JD cum laude, Northwestern U., 1969. Bar: Ill. 1969, D.C. 1977, U.S. Ct. Appeals (4th cir.) 1977, U.S. Ct. Appeals (5th cir.) 1972, U.S. Ct. Appeals (6th cir.) 1972, U.S. Ct. Appeals (7th cir.) 1970, U.S. Ct. Appeals (11th cir.) 1982, Ohio 1990. Assoc. firm Seyfarth, Shaw, Fairweather & Geraldson, Chgo., 1969-73, ptnr. Washington, 1974-83, Jones, Day, Reavis & Pogue, Washington and Cleve., 1983—. Exec. dir. Ill. Office Collective Bargaining, Springfield, 1973-74. Contbr. articles to profl. jours. Mem.: ABA, Chgo. Bar Assn., D.C. Bar Assn., Congl. Country Club (Md.), Firestone Country Club, Pepper Pike Club (Cleve.). Civil rights, Federal civil litigation, Labor. Office: Jones Day Reavis & Pogue 51 Louisiana Ave NW Washington DC 20001-2113

KRAMER, DANIEL JONATHAN, lawyer; b. Cin., Dec. 20, 1957; s. Milton and Fradie (Ehrlich) K.; m. Judith L. Mogul, June 10, 1984; children: Ilona, Hannah, Joshua. BA magna cum laude, Wesleyan U., Middletown, Conn., 1980; JD, NYU, 1984. Bar: N.Y. 1985, U.S. Dist. Ct. (so. and ea. dists.) N.Y. 1985, U.S. Ct. Appeals (2d cir.) 1989. Assoc. Cravath, Swaine & Moore, N.Y.C., 1985-86; law clk. to Chief Judge Wilfred Feinberg, U.S. Ct. Appeals for 2d Cir., 1986-87; assoc. Schulte Roth & Zabel LLP, 1987-92, ptnr., 1993—. Mem. pro se discretionary panel U.S. Ct. Appeals for 2d Cir., 1988—. Author: Federal Securities Litigation: Commentary and Forms, A Deskbook for the Practitioner, 1997; contbr. articles to law jours. and newspaper. Bd. dirs. Leukemia Soc., N.Y.C., 1995-98. Mem. ABA, Assn. Bar City N.Y. Federal civil litigation, Professional liability, Securities. Office: Schulte Roth & Zabel LLP 900 3rd Ave Fl 19 New York NY 10022-4774

KRAMER, EDWARD GEORGE, lawyer; b. Cleve., July 15, 1950; s. Archibald Charles and Katherine Faith (Porter) K.; m. Roberta Darwin, June 15, 1974. BS in Edn., Kent State U., 1972; JD, Case Western Res. U., 1975. Bar: Ohio 1975, U.S. Dist. Ct. (no. dist.) Ohio 1975, U.S. Ct. Appeals (6th cir.) 1980, U.S. Supreme Ct. 1980. Assoc. dir. The Cuyahoga Plan of Ohio, Cleve., 1975-76; exec. dir. The Housing Advs., Inc., 1976—; sr. ptnr. Kramer & Assocs., LPA, 1981—. Spl. counsel atty. gen. State of Ohio, Columbus, 1983-95; pres. Atty. Svcs., Inc., 1987—, ASI Info. Sys.; dir. Housing Law Clinic, 1989-95; dir. Fair Housing Law Clinic, 1995—; adj. lectr. Cleve. State U., 1991-94, adj. prof., 1994—; alt. consumer rep., FTC, Washington, 1976-77; cons. HUD, Washington, 1978-80, joint select com. sch. desegregation, Ohio Gen. Assembly, Columbus, 1979; mem. visitors com., Case Western Res. U. Sch. Law, Cleve., 1977-83; mem., chmn. Ford Motor Consumer Appeals Bd., 1989-93; bd. advisors Brownstone Pub. Author: How to Settle Small Claims: A Guide to The Use of Small Claims Courts, 1973, (with others) A Guide to Regional Housing Opportunities, 1979, (with Buchanan) Mobile Home Living: A Guide to Consumers' Rights, 1979; contbr. articles to legal jours. Chmn. Ohio Protection and Advocacy System for Developmentally Disabled, Columbus, 1978-80; trustee Muscle Disease Soc., Cleve., 1979-81; sec. Cuyahoga County Housing and Econ. Devel. com., Cleve., 1983—; mem. Cleve. Mayor's Com. on Employment of Handicapped, 1978-79; mem. fair housing adv. bd. John Marshall Law Sch. Named Disting. Recent Grad. Case Western Reserve U. Law Alumni Assn., 1985; Roscoe Pound fellow. Mem.: ABA (sect. on urban state and local govt. law, com. on housihng and urban devel., forum on constrn. industry), ACLU (litigation com.), ATLA (employment rights sect., chair 2001—, newsletter editor, civil rights sect. sec.), Cleve. Bar Assn. (trustee 1995—98, mem. com. on homeless, chmn. law sch. liaison), Nat. Employment Lawyers Assn., Assn. Am. Law Schs. (com. on clin. legal edn.), Planetary Soc., Am. Coll. Barristers (life)), Ohio State Bar Assn., Trial Lawyers for Pub. Justice (bd. advisors), Am. Arbitration Assn., Million Dollar Adv. Forum, Palm Beach Club (London), Old River Yacht Club, Cleve. Grays, Masons, Tyrian (worshipful master), Order of Ea. Star (James A. Garfield chpt.). Democrat. Mem. United Ch. Christ. Avocations: softball, scuba diving, collecting coins and stamps, chess, reading. Civil rights, Federal civil litigation, Labor. Office: Kramer & Assocs LPA 3214 Prospect Ave E Cleveland OH 44115-2614

KRAMER, EUGENE LEO, lawyer; b. Barberton, Ohio, Nov. 7, 1939; s. Frank L. and Portia I. (Acker) K.; m. JoAnn Stockhausen, Sept. 19, 1970; children: Martin, Caroline, Michael. AB, John Carroll U., 1961; JD, U. Notre Dame, 1964. Bar: Ohio 1964. Law clerk U.S. Ct. Appeals (7th cir.), Chgo., 1964-65; ptnr. Squire, Sanders & Dempsey, Cleve., 1965-91, Roetzel & Andress, A Legal Prof. Assn., Cleve. and Akron, Ohio, 1992-97. Cons. Ohio Constl. Revision Commn., Columbus, 1970-74. Trustee Citizens League Greater Cleve., 1984-90, 93—, Citizens League Rsch. Inst., 1995-97, St. Ann Found., 1990-92, Consultation Ctr. for Diocese of Cleve., 1990-96, Lyric Opera Cleve., 1995—, Regina Health Ctr., 1997—, pres. 2001—; past pres. HELP Found, Inc., HELP, Inc., Cleve., 1981-92, Playhouse Sq. Assn., Cleve., 1980-84; pres. N.E. Ohio Transit Coalition, 1992—; mem. policy com. Build-Up Greater Cleve. Program, 1982-98; mem. Greater Cleve. Growth Assn. Recipient Disting. Leadership award HELP, Inc., 1986, Pioneer achievement award HELP--Six Chimneys, Inc., 1986, Disting. Svc. award Assn. Retarded Citizens, Cuyahoga County, 1990. Mem. ABA, Ohio State Bar Assn. (chmn. local govt. law com. 1986-90), Akron Bar Assn., Cleve. Bar Assn., The Clifton Club (Lakewood, Ohio, bd. dirs. 1986-89), The Union Club of Cleve. Democrat. Roman Catholic. Avocations: music, theater, sports, travel. Municipal (including bonds), State and local taxation. Home and Office: 1422 Euclid Ave Ste 706 Cleveland OH 44115-2001

KRAMER, GERSON BALFOUR, lawyer; b. N.Y.C., June 12, 1925; s. Harry and Dora Bella K.; m. Beryl Joan Alpher, Feb. 10, 1952; children: Phyllis B., Arthur H., Rachel A. AB in Econs. with high honors, Rutgers U., 1951; LLB, George Washington U., 1955. Bar: Md. 1981, U.S. Dist. Ct. D.C. 1955, U.S. Ct. Appeals (D.C. cir.) 1955, U.S. Ct. Appeals (fed. cir.) 1981, U.S. Ct. Claims 1956, U.S. Supreme Ct. 1970. Trial atty. divil divsn. ct. claims sect. Justice Dept., Washington, 1956-66; appeals bd. Dept. Commerce, 1966-67; contract appeals bd. Dept. Transp., 1966-69, chmn., chief adminstrv. judge contract appeals bd., 1969-79; counsel Braude & Margulies PC, 1979—. Contbr. articles to profl. jours. V.p. Franklin Knolls Civic Assn., Md., 1982; sec., treas. Franklin Knolls Swim Assn., 1968-72. With USN, 1943-46. Mem. D.C. Bar Assn. (chmn. divsn. 10 steering com. 1977-81, chmn. procurement law com., sect. on govt. contracts and litigation 1983-86, chmn. ct. and bds. practice com., sect. on govt. contracts and litigation 1986-87), Fed. Bar Assn. (chmn. bd. contract appeals com. 1968-69), Bd. Contract Appeals (sec.-treas. nat. conf. 1969-72, v.p. 1973-74, pres. 1976-77), Selby Bay Yacht Club (comdr. 1987-88), Phi Beta Kappa. Home: 6 Mcalpine Ct Silver Spring MD 20901-4715 Office: Braude & Margulies, PC 888 17th St NW Washington DC 20006-3939

KRAMER, GILDA LEA, lawyer; b. N.Y.C., July 16, 1954; d. William W. and Sylvia (Steinberg) K. BA, Swarthmore Coll., 1976; JD, U. Va., 1979. Bar: D.C. 1979, Pa. 1982, N.J. 1989, D.C. Circuit Ct. 1980, Pa. Circuit Ct. (3d cir.) 1982, U.S. Dist. Ct. (D.C. dist.) 1980, U.S. Dist. Ct. (ea. dist.) Pa. 1982, U.S. Dist. Ct. N.J. 1989. Assoc. Pepper Hamilton & Scheetz, Washington, 1979-81; asst. city solicitor City of Phila., 1981-83, dep. city solicitor, 1983-84; assoc. Schnader, Harrison, Segal & Lewis, Phila., 1984-89; pvt. practice, 1989—. Mem. ABA, Pa. Bar Assn., Phila. Bar Assn. (mem. bd. govs. 1992-94, judge pro tempore 1994—). Democrat. Jewish. Federal civil litigation, State civil litigation, Product liability. Home: 127 Penarth Rd Bala Cynwyd PA 19004-2714 Office: 1500 Walnut St Ste 1100 Philadelphia PA 19102-3506 E-mail: Gilda_Kramer@yahoo.com

KRAMER, KENNETH BENTLEY, federal judge, former congressman; b. Chgo., Feb. 19, 1942; s. Albert Aaron and Ruth (Pokrass) K.; children: Kenneth Bentley, Kelly J. BA magna cum laude in Polit. Sci., U. Ill., 1963; JD, Harvard U., 1966. Bar: Ill. 1966, Colo. 1969. Dep. dist. atty. El Paso County, Colo., Colorado Springs, 1970-72; pvt. practice law, 1972-78; mem. Colo. Ho. of Reps., 1973-78, 96th-99th Congresses from 5th Colo. Dist., 1978-86; asst. sec. Dept. Army, Washington, 1988-89; judge U.S. Ct. of Appeals for Vets. Claims, 1989-2000, chief judge, 2000—. Chmn. com. on vets. benefits ABA, 1990-94. Bd. visitors U.S. Air Force Acad., 1979-86; bd. dirs. Pikes Peak Mental Health Ctr., 1976-78, Mountain Valley chpt. March of Dimes, 1983-85, U.S. Space Found., 1983—; founder U.S. Space Found.; commr. Nat. Coun. on Uniform State Laws, 1977-78. Capt. U.S. Army, 1967-70. Recipient Disting. Civilian Svc. medal. Mem. Phi Beta Kappa. Office: US Ct Appels for Vets Claims Vets Claims 625 Indiana Ave NW Washington DC 20004-2923

KRAMER, KENNETH SCOTT, lawyer; b. Troy, N.Y., Nov. 7, 1957; s. David W. and Judith (Fell) Bernstein. BA, U. Pa., 1979; JD, U. So. Calif., 1982. Bar: Calif. 1982, N.Y. 1984. Assoc. Finley, Kumble, Wagner et al, Beverly Hills and Newport Beach, Calif., 1982-86, Pettit & Martin, Newport Beach and Los Angeles, 1986-89, ptnr., 1990-95, Paone, Callahan, McHolm & Winton, 1995-2000, Drummy, King, White, Parret & Joerger, 2000—. Sec. Pacific Basin Restaurant Concepts Inc., L.A., 1985-90; lectr. Continuing Edn. of Bar, Calif., 1986-87. Chmn. Measure M subcom. Indsl. League of Orange County, 1991; campaign organizer Citizens Against Proposition F, Beverly Hills, 1984. Named one of Outstanding Young Men of Am., 1983. Mem. ABA, Indsl. League Orange County (transp. com. 1990-93). Land use and zoning (including planning), Landlord-tenant, Real property. Office: Drummy King et al Ste 1000 3200 Park Center Dr Costa Mesa CA 92626 also: 355 S Grand Ave Los Angeles CA 90071-1560 E-mail: kkramer@drummyking.com

KRAMER, KENNETH STEPHEN, lawyer; b. Washington, Oct. 5, 1941; m. Audrey Carol Reich, June 13, 1965; children— Beth, Ellen, Aaron. B.S. with high honors, U. Wis.-Madison, 1963; J.D. cum laude, Harvard U., 1966; postgrad. in law George Washington U., 1967-68. Bar: D.C. 1967, U.S. Ct. Claims 1967, U.S. Ct. Appeals (D.C. cir.) 1967, U.S. Ct. Appeals (fed. cir.) 1982, U.S. Supreme Ct. 1976. Law clk. to chief judge U.S. Ct. Claims, Washington, 1966-67; assoc. Fried, Frank, Harris, Shriver & Jacobson, Washington, 1970-75, ptnr., 1975— ; editorial cons. Fed. Contracts Report, Washington, 1968-74. Served as capt. JAGC, U.S. Army, 1967-70. Mem. ABA. Republican. Jewish. General civil litigation, Government contracts and claims. Office: Fried Frank Harris Shriver & Jacobson 1001 Pennsylvania Ave NW Washington DC 20004-2505

KRAMER, MORRIS JOSEPH, lawyer; b. Bklyn., Nov. 18, 1941; s. William J. and Sylvia (Hameroff) K.; m. Linda Garshman, Feb. 11, 1967 (div. 1976); 1 child, Jeremy; m. Nancy Goldstein, Feb. 28, 1978; 1 child, Oliver; m. Barbara Cutler, Sept. 2, 1992. A.B., Dartmouth Coll., 1963; LL.B. Harvard U., 1966. Bar: N.Y. 1966, U.S. Ct. Appeals (2d cir.) 1966, U.S. Dist Ct. (so. dist.) N.Y. 1966, U.S. Dist. Ct. (ea. dist.) N.Y. 1966. Asst. counsel Temporary State Commn. Constl. Conv., N.Y.C., 1966-67; assoc. Cahill, Gordon and Reindel, N.Y.C., 1968-72, Skadden Arps Slate Meagher & Flom, N.Y.C., 1972-75, ptnr. 1975—. General corporate, Securities. Office: Skadden Arps Slate Meagher & Flom 4 Times Sq Fl 24 New York NY 10036-6595

KRAMER, PAUL R. lawyer; b. Balt., June 6, 1936; s. Phillip and Lee (Labovitz) K.; m. Janet Amitin, Sept. 1, 1957; children: Jayne, Susan, Nancy. BA, Am. U., 1959, JD, 1961. Bar: Md. 1961, D.C. 1962, U.S. Supreme Ct. 1965, U.S. Ct. Appeals (6th cir.) 1992, U.S. Dist. Ct. 1963, U.S. Ct. Appeals (4th cir.) 1964, U.S. Ct. Appeals (9th cir.) 1996. Staff atty., dep. dir. Legal Aid Agy. Fed. Pub. Defender's Office, Washington, 1962-63; asst. U.S. atty. Dist. Md., 1963-69; dep. U.S. atty. Md. Balt., 1969-83; exec. bd. Balt. area coun. Boy Scouts Am., 1970-83, adv. counsel to exec. bd., 1983—. Instr. U. Md. Sch. Law, 1975-80; assoc. prof. law Villa Julie Coll., 1976-80; assoc. professorial lectr. George Washington U., 1979; instr. Nat. Coll. Dist. Attys., 1979; permanent mem. 4th cir. fed. jud. conf. Mem. ABA, Fed. Bar Assn. (pres. Md. chpt. 1973-74, nat. dep. sec. 1981-82, nat. sec. 1982-83, nat. cir. v.p. 1973-81, 86-87, cir. officer 4th cir. 1992-93, v.p. 4th cir. 1996—, chmn. nat. cir. v.p. 1978-80, nat. coun. 1973—, jud. selection com. 1971-79, 88—, faculty Fed Practice Inst. 1981-86, strategic long range planning com. 1995-96), Md. Bar Assn. (subcom. litig. dist. ct. 1990—), Balt. Bar Assn. (jud. selection com. 1992—, chair judiciary sub-com. on policy 1993-94, chair criminal law com. 1994-95, grievance commn. Md. 1993—, drug ct. com. 1994-95, dist. ct. com. 1990—), Nat. Assn. Criminal Trial Attys., Md. Trial Lawyers Assn., Md. Criminal Def. Atty.'s Assn., U.S. Atty. Alumni Assn., Masons (past master). Federal civil litigation, State civil litigation, Criminal. Office: Jefferson Bldg Two E Lafayette St Ste 700 Baltimore MD 21202

KRAMER, TIMOTHY EUGENE, lawyer; b. Cleve., Mar. 21, 1943; s. Theodore Eugene and Margaret Agnes (Vargo) Kramer; m. Jacqueline Marie Rini, May 30, 1969; children: Thomas, Kathleen, Anne. BA, John Carroll U., 1965; JD, Case Western Res. U., 1968. Bar: Ohio 1969. Law clk. Cuyahoga County Common Pleas Ct., 1970—72, chief law clk. Ohio, 1972—73; asst. counsel Jacobs, Visconsi & Jacobs Co., Cleve., 1973-78; corp. counsel Revco D.S. Inc., Twinsburg, 1978-93, sr. corp. counsel, 1993-97; legal counsel CVS Pharmacy, 1997-2000, sr. legal counsel, 2000—. Lectr. in field. Served with U.S. Army, 1968-70. Mem. Ohio State Bar Assn. Roman Catholic. General corporate, Landlord-tenant, Real property. Home: 31710 Birch Cir Solon OH 44139-1636 Office: CVS Pharmacy Inc 1920 Enterprise Pkwy Twinsburg OH 44087-2207

KRAMER, WILLIAM DAVID, lawyer; b. Anniston, Ala., Feb. 2, 1944; s. John Robert and Janice Marian (Dye) K.; m. Johanna Scalzi, Dec. 1, 1973; children: Elizabeth Annemarie, David MacLaren. Student, Case Western Res. U., 1959-60; AB in Govt. with honors magna cum laude, Oberlin Coll., 1965; JD, M in Pub. Adminstrn., Harvard U., 1969. Bar: Mass. 1969, D.C. 1973, U.S. Ct. Appeals (D.C. cir.) 1974, U.S. Dist. Ct. D.C. 1976, U.S. Ct. Appeals (10th cir.) 1978, U.S. Ct. Internat. Trade 1983, U.S. Ct. Appeals (fed. cir.) 1983. Assoc. dir. Gov.'s Com. on Law Enforcement and Adminstrn. Criminal Justice, Boston, 1969-71, dep. dir., 1971-73; assoc. Squire, Sanders & Dempsey, Washington, 1973-79, ptnr., 1979-92, Baker Botts LLP, Washington, 1992-2000; mem. Verner, Liipfert, Bernhard, McPherson and Hand, Chartered, 2000—. Mem. internat. law sect. D.C. Bar. Chmn. bd. dirs. Children's Chorus of Washington, 1995-97, mem. adv. bd., 1997—. Mem. Phi Beta Kappa. Administrative and regulatory, Private international, Legislative. Home: 3512 Leland St Chevy Chase MD 20815-3904 Office: Verner Liipfert Bernhard McPherson and Hand Chartered 901 15th St NW Washington DC 20005-2301 Fax: 202-371-6279. E-mail: wdkramer@verner.com

KRAMM, DEBORAH LUCILLE, lawyer; b. Milw. d. Hartzell McDonald and Alice Lucille (Johnson) K.; m. Gary Baiz, June 18, 1988. Student, Trinity Coll., Deerfield, Ill., 1971-73; BS, Bradley U., 1974; JD, New Eng. Sch. of Law, 1977; postgrad., Georgetown U., 1978. Bar: N.Y. 1982, Ill. 1980, Mass. 1978. Trademark atty. U.S. Trademark Office, Washington, 1977-78; assoc. Hume, Clement, Willian, Brinks & Olds, Chgo., 1978-81; atty. Avon Products, Inc., N.Y.C., 1981-84, Tiffany & Co., N.Y.C., 1981-84, v.p., sec., 1984-85; counsel Am. Brands, Inc., Old Greenwich, Conn., 1986-95; of counsel Piper Marbury Rudnick & Wolfe, Chgo., 1996-2000; ptnr. Holland & Knight, Washington, 2000—. N.Y. bd. dirs. Nat. Found. for Advancement for Arts, 1987-91; chmn. Martha Graham Guild, 1988—; trustee Martha Graham Ctr. for Contemporary Dance, Inc., N.Y.C., 1989—. Curt Tiege scholar, 1973. Mem. U.S. Trademark Assn. (bd. dirs. 1984-87), Cosmetic, Toiletry and Fragrance Assn. (chmn. trademark com. 1984). General corporate, Trademark and copyright. Office: Holland & Knight 2100 Pennsylvania Ave NW Washington DC 20037

KRANE, STEVEN CHARLES, lawyer; b. Far Rockaway, N.Y., Jan. 20, 1957; s. Harry and Gloria (Christle) K.; m. Faith Marston, Oct. 1, 1983; children: Elizabeth Jordan, Cameron Marston. BA, SUNY, Stony Brook, 1978; JD, NYU, 1981. Bar: N.Y. 1982, U.S. Dist. Ct. (so. and ea. dists.) N.Y. 1982, U.S. Ct. Appeals (2d and 6th cirs.) 1987, U.S. Supreme Ct. 1987, U.S. Ct. Appeals (1st and 3d cir.) 2000. Ptnr. Proskauer Rose LLP, N.Y.C.; law clk. to Assoc. Judge Judith S. Kaye N.Y. Ct. Appeals, N.Y.C. and Albany, 1984-85. Lectr. in law Columbia U. Sch. Law, N.Y.C., 1989-92; vis. prof. Ga. Inst. of Tech., 1994-96; mem. departmental disciplinary com. Appellate divsn. 1st Jud. dept. Supreme Ct. N.Y., 1996-2000, spl. trial counsel, 1991-93. Editor articles, NYU Jour. Internat. Law and Politics, 1980-81. Securities Inst. NYU fellow, 1980-81; recipient Vol. Counsel award Legal Aid Soc., 1984. Fellow Am. Bar Found., N.Y. Bar Found.; mem. ABA, Westchester County Bar Assn., N.Y. Bar Assn. (com. on stds. of atty. conduct, chmn. 1999-2000, 2001—, com. on profl. ethics 1990-94, spl. com. to rev. the code of profl. responsibility 1992-95, chmn. 1995-99, vice chair spl. com. on future of profession 1997-2000, ho. of dels. 1996—, com. on mass disaster response 1997-2001, com. on multidisciplinary practice and legal profession 1998-99, exec. com. 1998—, mem.-at-large, exec. com. 1998-2000, spl. com. on law gov. firm structure and ops., vice chair 1999—, pres.-elect 2000-01, pres. 2001—, pres. com. on access to justice, co-chair 2000-01, spl. assn. ho. com. chair 2000-2001), Assn. of Bar of City of N.Y. (com. on profl. and jud. ethics 1990-93, chmn. 1993-96, sec 1985-88, com. on profl. responsibility, chmn. subcom. provision legal svcs. 1985-88, com. on fed. cts. 1996-99, com. Marden Meml. lecture 2000—, chmn. del. to N.Y. State Bar Assn. ho. dels. 1997-98, chmn. internat. security affairs 2001—), Am. Law Inst., Phi Beta Kappa, Pi Sigma Alpha. Republican. Avocations: military history, meteorology, Boston Red Sox baseball. Federal civil litigation, Sports. Office: Proskauer Rose LLP 1585 Broadway Fl 27 New York NY 10036-8299 E-mail: skrane@proskauer.com

KRANIS, MICHAEL DAVID, lawyer, judge; b. N.Y.C., Aug. 17, 1955; s. Herbert and Mildred (Swartz) K.; m. Patricia Ann Pagano, Sept. 29, 1989. BA, SUNY, Albany, 1977; JD, Union U., 1980. Bar: N.Y. 1981, U.S. Dist. Ct. (so. and ea. dists.) N.Y. 1983. Law clk. to hon. judge Robert C. William N.Y. Supreme Ct., Monticello, 1980-82; prin. Michael D. Kranis, P.C., Poughkeepsie, N.Y., 1982-88; ptnr. Coombs, Kranis & Wing, 1988-94; sole practitioner, 1995—. Asst. corp. counsel City of Poughkeepsie, 1983-85, hearing officer, 1985—; adj. prof. D.C. C.C., Poughkeepsie, 1984-87; judge Town of Pleasant Valley, N.Y., 1988-97; gen. counsel Grace Smith House, Inc., Poughkeepsie, 1983-95; adj. prof. Marist Coll., 1993. Mem. exec. com. Dutchess County Rep. Com., Pleasant Valley, 1997-2000, Jud. Nominating Com., Dutchess County, 1987, 97-2000; mem. D.C. Republican Com., 1985-87, 97—; mem. Pleasant Valley Planning Bd., 1984-86; bd. dirs., chmn., vice chmn. Task Force for Child Protection, Inc., 1992-2000; mem. bd. dirs. Dutchess County Econ. Devel. Corp., Child Abuse Prevention Ctr., Inc., 2001—. Mem. N.Y. State Bar Assn. (ho. of dels.), Dutchess County Bar Assn. (pres. 1998-99, treas., v.p. 1996, pres.-elect 1997, chmn. fee dispute com., chmn. bar endowment, v.p.), Dutchess County Magistrates Assn., N.Y. State Magistrates Assn., Rotary (pres., bd. dirs. Pleasant Valley chpt. 1985-97, Paul Harris fellow 1987). Family and matrimonial, Personal injury, Real property. Office: 2 Jefferson Pl Poughkeepsie NY 12601

KRANSELER, LAWRENCE MICHAEL, lawyer; b. Newton, Mass., Oct. 28, 1958; s. Arthur Sheldon and Barbara Joan (Siegel) K.; m. Wendy Kranseler; children: Alex, Jenna. BS in Econs., Boston Coll., 1980; MBA, JD, U. Pa., 1984. Bar: Mass. 1985, U.S. Dist. Ct. Mass. 1985. Assoc. Hale and Dorr, Boston, 1984-89; supervising sr. counsel Hasbro, Inc., Pawtucket, R.I., 1989-95, mng. atty., 1995-2000; v.p. Hasbro Inc., 2001—, Hasbro Interactive, Inc., Pawtucket, 1997-2001. Vol. mentor UCAP Mentoring Program. Bd. dirs., treas., chmn. fin. com., mem. exec. com., vol. Big Brother/Big Sister Assn.; fundraising capt. Am. Heart Assn., Combined Jewish Philanthropies; coach Town of Sharon Baseball, Town of Sharon Soccer, Town of Sharon Basketball. Recipient James E. Shaw Meml. award Pres. Boston Coll., 1980. Mem. ABA, Mass. Bar Assn., Boston Bar Assn., Phi Delta Phi. General corporate, General practice, Mergers and acquisitions. Home: 30 Sentry Hill Rd Sharon MA 02067-1522 Office: Hasbro Inc 1027 Newport Ave Pawtucket RI 02861-2500 E-mail: LKranseler@hasbro.com

KRANTZ, SHELDON, lawyer; b. Omaha, June 5, 1938; s. Abraham and Edith (Lewis) K.; m. Susan Dechter, Aug. 30, 1959 (div.); children: Shari Ann, Stuart Jeffrey, Stefanie Louise; m. Carol Rogoff Hallstrom, Dec. 27, 1977 (div.); m. Laurel O. Robinson, Dec. 8, 1992. Bar: Nebr. 1962, Mass. 1969, U.S. Supreme Ct. 1971, Calif. 1988, D.C. 1993. Trial atty. organized crime and racketeering sect. U.S. Dept. Justice, 1962-65; assoc. Monsky, Grodinsky et al, Omaha, 1965-66; staff atty. Pres.'s Commn. on Law Enforcement & Adminstrn. of Justice, 1966-67; exec. dir. Mass. Com. on Criminal Justice, 1967-70; dir. Boston U. Ctr. for Criminal Justice, 1971-79; prof. law Boston U. Sch. Law, 1970-81; dean U. San Diego Sch. Law, 1981-89; vis. prof. Hebrew U., Jerusalem, 1978; vis. fellow Inst. Criminology Cambridge (Eng.) U., 1978; vis. prof. law Am. U., Washington, 1990-92; v.p. Investigative Group, 1989-90; arbitrator Am. Arbitration Assn. 1993—. Author: The Law of Sentencing, Corrections and Prisoners' Rights, 1990; The Law of Corrections and Prisoners' Rights in a Nutshell, 1988. Co-founder, mem. exec. bd. San Diego Law Ctr., 1982-89. Mem. ABA (chair criminal justice sect. 1989-90), Am. Law Inst. Office: U San Diego Law Sch Alcala Pk San Diego CA 92110 also: Piper & Marbury 3251 E Imperial Hwy Brea CA 92821-6722

KRANZDORF, JEFFREY PAUL, lawyer, recording company executive, television producer; b. Phila., Jan. 28, 1955; s. Charles David and Hilda (Eisenberg-Nahama) K.; m. Perri Scott Lovell, Sept. 16, 1979; children: Charles David II, Caitlin Blair. AB, U. So. Calif., 1976; JD, Southwestern U., Los Angeles, 1979; student UCLA Graduate Sch. Mgmt. Bar: Calif. 1979, N.Y. 1989, U.S. Dist. Ct. (cen. dist.) Calif. 1979. Assoc., Davis & Cox, Los Angeles, 1980-81; dir. bus. affairs Am. Variety Internat. Inc., Los Angeles, 1981-82, gen. counsel, mng. dir., 1982-85; v.p., gen. mgr. LaBuick Media, Inc., 1985—, sr. v.p. LaBuick Media, Inc., Silver Eagle Records, Inc., 1988—; sec., dir. Ernie's Record Mart, Nashville, 1981-85; pres. Sun Classic Comm. Group, Inc., 1990-92; sr. v.p. bus. and legal affairs Goldstar Video Corp., 1993—; with U. So. Calif. Entertainment Law Inst., 1980—; internat. licensing cons. Ron V. Brown Internat., Pickwick License A/S Denmark; bus. affairs counsel Franklin Waterman Entertainment, 1993—. Prodr. Howard Keel Live at the Royal Albert Hall, Rockin' the Night Away, Ricky Nelson and Fats Domino Live at the Universal Amphitheatre, Blueberry Hill, A Tribute to Ricky Nelson; prodr., dir. Roy Orbison Live; supervising prodr. The Makeover Show with Jerome Alexander; exec. prodr. Rock U.K.; co-exec. prodr. Party In Progress, 1993—, The New Morton Downey Jr. Show, 1993—. Bd. dirs. Sports Archives, Inc., 1990-91. Entertainment. Office: Franklin-Waterman Entertainment Inc 2644 30th St Santa Monica CA 90405-3009 also: 777 N Palm Canyon Dr Ste 201 Palm Springs CA 92262-5548

KRASNER, DANIEL WALTER, lawyer; b. N.Y.C., Mar. 18, 1941; s. Nathan and Rose Krasner; m. Ruth Pollack, Dec. 20, 1964; children: Jonathan, Lisa, Noah, Rebecca. BA, Yeshiva Coll., 1962; LLB, Yale U., 1965. Bar: N.Y. 1966, U.S. Dist. Ct. (so. dist.) N.Y. 1967, U.S. Dist. Ct. (ea. dist.) N.Y. 1968, U.S. Supreme Ct. 1978, U.S. Ct. Appeals (1st, 2d, 3d, 5th, 6th, 8th-11th dists.). Assoc. Pomerantz Levy Houdek & Block, N.Y.C., 1965-76; sr. ptnr. Wolf Haldenstein Adler Freeman & Herz, 1977—. Vice chmn. Westchester Day Sch., Mamaroneck, N.Y., 1979-86; v.p., trustee Bd. Jewish Edn., N.Y.C., 1981—. Democrat. Avocations: tennis, golf, sailing. Federal civil litigation, Securities. Office: Wolf Haldenstein Adler Freeman & Herz 270 Madison Ave New York NY 10016-0601 E-mail: krasner@whafh.com

KRASNOW, ERWIN GILBERT, lawyer; b. Bklyn., Jan. 8, 1936; s. Charles and Etta (Simowitz) K.; m. E. Judith Levine, Sept. 6, 1960 (dec. July 1994); children: Michael Andew, Catherine Beth; m. Jane Gasperini, Nov. 25, 1995. AB summa cum laude, Boston U., 1958; JD, Harvard U., 1961; LLM, Georgetown U., 1965. Bar: Mass. 1961, U.S. Dist. Ct. Mass. 1961, D.C. 1963, U.S. Ct. Appeals (D.C. cir.) 1963, U.S. Supreme Ct. 1965, U.S. Ct. Appeals (4th cir.) 1978, U.S. Ct. Appeals (5th and 11th cirs.) 1982. Rsch. asst. Harvard U. Law Sch., Cambridge, Mass., 1961; adminstr. asst. to Congressman Torbert H. Macdonald, U.S. Ho. of Reps., Washington, 1962-64; ptnr. Kirkland and Ellis, 1964-76; sr. v.p., gen. counsel Nat. Assn. Broadcasters, 1976-84; ptnr. Verner, Liipfert, Bernhard, McPherson & Hand, 1984—. Vis. prof. Ohio State U., 1974; disting. vis. lectr. Temple U., 1976; adj. prof. Am. U., 1975, Law Ctr., Georgetown U., 1984; professorial lectr. Grad. Sch. Arts and Scis., George Washington U., 1982, 83, adj. prof., 1998; professorial lectr. Sch. Law, Cath. U. Am., 1982; bd. dirs. Broadcast Capital Fund, Inc. (formerly Minority Broadcast Investment Fund), 1978—, treas., 1979-92, vice chmn., 1993—; mem. govt. industry adv. coun. Ctr. for Telecom. Studies, George Washington U., 1980-84; mem. adv. bd. Inst. for Comm. Law, Sch. Law, Cath. U. Am., 1982—; mem. bd. advisors Comm. Media Ctr., N.Y. Law Sch., 1982—; mem. adv. com. comm. law program UCLA, 1983-85. Co-author: A Candidate's Guide to the Law of Political Broadcasting, 1977, 3d edit., 1984, Buying and Building a Broadcast Station, 3d edit., 1987, 199 Ways To Cut Legal Fees and Manage your Lawyer, 1988, Radio Financing: A Guide for Lenders and Investors, 1990, Insider's Guide to Radio Acquisition Contracts, 1992; co-author: FCC Lobbying A Handbook of Insider Tips and Practical Advice, 2001; editor: National Assosication of Broadcasters Legal Guide to FCC Broadcast Rules, REgulations and Policies, 1977; bd. editors Fed. Comm. Bar Jour., 1973-75; mem. editl. ad. bd. Jour. Broadcasting, 1972-85, Telematics and Informatics, 1982—; mem. adv. com. COMM/ENT Law Jour., 1983—; contbr. articles to legal publs. Mem. ABA (vice chmn. agy. adjudication com. 1974-77, chmn. comm. law com. adminstrv. law sect. 1980-81), FBA (pres. Capitol Hill chpt. 1963-64, dep. co-chmn. comm. law com. 1967-69, co-chmn. 1970-71), Fed. Comm. Bar Assn. (exec. com. 1976-79, 84-85, treas. 1984-85), Capitol Hill Bar Assn. (past pres.), Boston U. Alumni Club Washington (pres. 1967-70), Boston U. Nat. Alumni Assn. (bd. dirs. 1966-68, regional v.p. 1971, 73), Phi Beta Kappa. , Communications. Home: 3307 Q St NW Washington DC 20007-2717 Office: Verner Liipfert Et Al 901 15th St NW Ste 700 Washington DC 20005-2327 Business E-Mail: egkrasnow@verner.com

KRASNOW, JORDAN PHILIP, lawyer; b. Malden, Mass., May 14, 1944; s. Louis and Roslyn (Packer) K.; children: Laura, Joshua, Abbey, Abigail. AB, Clark U., 1965; JD magna cum laude, Boston U., 1968. Bar: Mass. 1970. Law clk. to Presiding Justice Mass. Superior Ct., Boston, 1968-69; assoc. atty. Peabody & Arnold, 1969-71, Gaston Snow & Ely Bartlett, Boston, 1971-75, ptnr., 1975-86; officer, dir. Goulston & Storrs, 1986—; co-mng. dir., 1994-97. Lectr. Mass. Continuing Legal Edn., Boston, 1975-85; adv. com. Boston U. Real Estate Program, 1988—; charter mem. Greater Boston Real Estate Bd.-Real Estate Fin., 1989. Mem. Mayor's Adv. Com. Housing Linkage, Boston, 1984; mem. exec. com. Anti Defamation League New Eng.; trustee Roxbury Prep. Charter Sch. Recipient Disting. Achievement award B'nai B'rith Realty Unit, 1995. Fellow Mass. Bar Found.; mem. Mass. Bar Assn., Boston Bar Assn., B'nai Brith (trustee realty unit New Eng. chpt.). Jewish. Avocations: travel, sports. Finance, Land use and zoning (including planning), Real property. Home: 94 Beacon St Apt 2 Boston MA 02108-3329 Office: Goulston & Storrs 400 Atlantic Ave Boston MA 02110-3333 E-mail: jkrasnow@goulstonstorrs.com

KRASS, MARC STERN, lawyer; b. Detroit, June 23, 1949; s. Marvin David and Ruth B. (Stern) K.; m. Susan McAuley; children: Jonathan, Matthew. AB, Oberlin Coll., 1970; postgrad., U. Pitts., 1970-71; JD cum laude, Northwestern U., 1976. Bar: Ill. 1976, U.S. Dist. Ct. (no. dist.) Ill. 1976, U.S. Dist. Ct. (we. dist.) Tex. 1980, Ohio 1981, U.S. Dist. Ct. (so. dist.) Ohio 1982. Assoc. Seyfarth, Shaw, Fairweather & Geraldson, Chgo., 1976-80; assoc. gen. counsel Procter & Gamble Co., Cin., 1980—. Bd. dirs. United Home Care, Inc., Cin., 1983-88, Ctr. for Comprehensive Alcoholism Treatment, Cin., 1988-90. Mem. Cin. Bar Assn. E-mial. Home: 9806 Indian Springs Dr Cincinnati OH 45241-3671 Office: Procter & Gamble Co One Procter & Gamble Pla Cincinnati OH 45202 E-mail: krass.ms@pg.com

KRATT, PETER GEORGE, lawyer; b. Lorain, Ohio, Mar. 7, 1940; s. Arthur Leroy and Edith Ida (Dietz) K.; m. Sharon Amy Maruska, June 15, 1968; children: Kevin George, Jennifer Ivy. BA, Miami U., Oxford, Ohio, 1962; JD, Case Western Res. U., 1966. Bar: Ohio 1966. Atty. Cleve. Trust Co., 1966-74; assoc. counsel AmeriTrust Co., 1974-84, sec., assoc. counsel, 1985-87, sed., sr. assoc. counsel, 1987-92; ret. v.p., mgr. personal trust adminstrn. Huntington Trust Co., 1993-99. Mem. Am. Soc. Corp. Secs., Ohio Bar Assn., Rotary, Lions. Methodist. Avocations: hiking, gardening. Banking, General corporate.

KRAUS, DOUGLAS M. lawyer; b. N.Y.C., Jan. 28, 1949; s. Irving R. and Bebe B. (Baron) K.; m. Alice R. Weigle, Mar. 8, 1970; children— Amy Elizabeth, Jonathan Eric. B.A. magna cum laude, U. Pa., 1970; J.D., U. Chgo., 1973. Bar: N.Y. 1974, U.S. Dist. Ct. (so. and ea. dists.) N.Y. 1974, U.S. Ct. Appeals (2d cir.) 1974, U.S. Ct. Appeals (8th cir.) 1981, U.S. Ct. Appeals (D.C. cir.) 1982, U.S. Ct. Appeals (1st cir.) 1983, U.S. Supreme Ct. 1984. Assoc. firm Skadden, Arps, Slate, Meagher & Flom., N.Y.C., 1973-81, ptnr., 1981— ; chmn., lectr. on bank acquisitions and takeovers Practicing Law Inst., N.Y.C., 1982-84. Assoc. editor, contbr. U. Chgo. Law Rev., 1972-73. Councilman Town of New Castle, Chappaqua, N.Y., 1976-79. Mem. ABA (chmn. nat. inst. 1983), Assn. Bar City N.Y. Banking, Federal civil litigation, Securities. Office: Skadden Arps Slate Meagher & Flom 4 Times Sq Fl 24 New York NY 10036-6595

KRAUS, ROBERT H. lawyer; b. Teaneck, N.J., May 10, 1939; s. Henry and Alice R. (Ziegler) K.; m. Carol A. Gerry, June 10, 1961; children: William R., Karen B., Kathryn L. AB, Rutgers Coll., 1961, JD, 1964. Bar: N.J. 1965, D.C. 1965. Assoc. Lowenstein & Sandler, Newark, 1966-69, Johnstone & O'Dwyer, Westfield, N.J., 1969-70, Shear & Kraus, Scotch Plains, 1971, Leib, Kraus, Grispin & Roth, Scotch Plains, 1972—. Gen. ptnr. Woodland Estates Partnership, RVS/RHK Co., LLC, Scotch Plains, 1987—, Flemington Trade Ctr., LLC, Fanwood Plaza Ptnrs., LLC. Bd. dirs., trustee Fanwood Scotch Plains YMCA, 1976—; trustee Scotch Plains-Fanwood Scholarship Found., 1982-88; chmn. Rotary-Garbe Found., Inc., 1994—. Capt. U.S. Army, 1965-66. Recipient William D. Mason Disting. Svc. award Fanwood-Scotch Plains Jaycees, 1977. Mem. ABA, N.J. Bar Assn., Union Coutny Bar Assn., Scotch Plains-Fanwood Soccer Assn. (gen. mgr., coach 1977-83). Land use and zoning (including planning), Real property, Estate taxation. Home: 96 Forest Rd Fanwood NJ 07023-1305 Office: Leib Kraus Grispin & Roth 328 Park Ave Scotch Plains NJ 07076-1100 E-mail: rkraus@lkgrlaw.com

KRAUS, SHERRY STOKES, lawyer; b. Richmond, Ky., Aug. 11, 1945; d. Thomas Alexander and Callie (Ratliff) Stokes; m. Eugene John Kraus, Aug. 27, 1966. Student, U. Ky., 1962-64; BS, Roosevelt U., 1966; JD cum laude, Albany Law Sch., 1975; LLM in Taxation, NYU, 1981. Bar: N.Y. 1976, U.S. Dist. Ct. (we. dist.) N.Y. 1976, U.S. Tax Ct. 1986. Law clk. U.S. Tax Ct., Washington, summer 1974; law clk. 4th dept. appellate divsn. N.Y. State Supreme Ct., Rochester, 1975-77; assoc. Nixon, Hargrave, Devans & Doyle, 1977-81, 83-84, Harter, Secrest & Emery, Rochester, 1984-86; pvt. practice, 1986—. Faculty grad. tax program Sch. Law, NYU, N.Y.C., 1981-82; prin. tech. adv. to assoc. chief counsel - tech. IRS, Washington, 1983-84; mem. N.Y. State Tax Appeals Adv. Panel on Practice & Procedure, 1998—. Articles editor ABA Tax Articles Periodical, The Tax Lawyer, 1984-88; mng. editor NYU Tax Articles Periodical, NYU Tax Law Rev., 1981-82; lead articles editor Tax Articles Periodical, Albany Law Rev., 1973-75; contbr. articles to profl. jours. David J. Brewer scholar Albany Law Sch., 1973. Mem. ABA, N.Y. State Bar Assn. (tax sect. exec. com. 1984—), Monroe County Bar Assn. (treas. 1990-92), Monroe County Bar Found. (pres. 1994-95), Justinian Soc. Avocations: watercolors, guitar, dulcimer. Corporate taxation, Taxation, general, Personal income taxation. Office: 513 Times Square Bldg Rochester NY 14614-2078

KRAUS, STEVEN GARY, lawyer; b. Newark, Aug. 22, 1954; s. Leon Judah Kraus and Rose (Cohen) Turchin; m. Jane Susan Sukoneck, June 29, 1980; children: Adam. AB, Brandeis U., 1976; JD, Rutgers U., 1979. Bar: N.J. 1979, Pa. 1979, U.S. Dist. Ct. N.J. 1979. Jud. law sec. to assignment judge Charles A. Rizzi, Superior Ct. N.J., Camden, 1979-80; assoc. Kavesh & Basile, Vineland, N.J., 1980-81, Bennett & Bennett, West Orange, 1981-82; pvt. practice, Warren, 1982—. Mem. ABA, N.J. State Bar Assn., Nat. Assn. Subrogation Profls. State civil litigation, Insurance, Personal injury. Home: 17 Regent Cir Basking Ridge NJ 07920-1900 Office: 122 Mount Bethel Rd Warren NJ 07059-5127 E-mail: steven.kraus@subrogationlawyer.com

KRAUSER, SHERRIE L. judge; b. Washington, Sept. 11, 1950; d. Irvin Arthur and Bess Blatkin Lavine; 2 children. BA with honors, U. Md., 1972; JD, Duke U., 1973. Bar: Md. 1973, Pa. 1975, D.C. 1977, U.S. Dist. Ct. Md. 1978, U.S. Ct. Appeals (4th cir.) 1985. Trial atty. honors program, criminal divsn. U.S. Dept. Justice, 1973-74; asst. gen. counsel Pa. Crime Commn., 1975-77; pvt. practice Hyattsville, Md., 1977-79; assoc. county atty. Prince George's County, 1979-89; assoc. judge dist. 5 Dist. Ct. Md., 1989-95; assoc. judge Cir. Ct. for Prince George's County, Md., 1995—. Instr. univ. coll. paralegal program U. Md., 1979-80; instr. Prince George's County Dept. Social Svcs., 1994, Georgetown Law Ctr., 1983—; lectr. in field. Chair com. to establish a family abuse shelter Prince George's County Commn. for Women, 1977-79; bd. dirs. Jewish Social Svc. Agy., 1992-96; judge Cath. U. Moot Ct. Competitions, 1996—; mem. Youth Drug and Violence Prevention Program, 1996—; mem. Cen. Md. regional adv. bd. Md. Alt. Dispute Resolution Commn., 1999. Recipient award for promotion of equal access to the cts. Md. Hispanic Bar Assn., 1996, Md. Women Leading the Way award, 1997, Women of Achievement in Md. History award, 1998. Fellow Md. Bar Found. (life); mem. Am. Judges Assn., Nat. Assn. Women Judges (Md. task force on women in prison 1993—, mem. Md. chpt. 1991—), Women's Bar Assn. Md. (bd. dirs. 1985-86, 89-93, co-chair awards com. 1988-93, co-chair program com. 1988-89, co-chair membership com. 1985-86), Md. State Bar Assn. (sect. litigation 1983—, program com. 1985-89, chair program com. 1986-88, spl. com. on citizenship and law-related edn. 1983-90, planning com. 1988-90), Prince George's County Bar Assn. (bd. dirs. 1983-89, chair litigation sect. 1988-89, chair law-related edn. com. 1983-86, 96-00, chair Law Day com. 1982-83, co-chair Law Day com. 1996-00, ethics com. 1981-85, Pres.'s award for extraordinary contbns. to bar and cmty. 1986), J. Franklyn Bourne Bar Assn., Md. Jud. Conf., Thurgood Marshall Am. Inns of Ct. (master 1998—), Charlotte E. Ray Am. Inns of Ct. (master 1994-96). Office: Prince George's County Cir Ct 14735 Main St Upper Marlboro MD 20772-3065

KRAVER, RICHARD MATTHEW, lawyer; b. Bklyn., Nov. 27, 1946; s. Barnett L. and Pearl (Aronson) K.; m. Harriet Shapiro, Sept. 7, 1970; children— Michael E., Barry S. B.S., NYU, 1968, J.D., Syracuse U., 1971. Bar: N.Y. 1972, Fla. 1975, U.S. Dist. Ct. (so. and ea. dist.) N.Y. 1973, U.S. Tax Ct. 1973, U.S. Ct. Appeals (2d cir.) 1973, U.S. Ct. Appeals (D.C. cir.) 1983, U.S. Supreme Ct. 1976, U.S. Dist. Ct. (no. dist.) N.Y. 1986, U.S. Ct. Appeals (3d cir.) 1986. Assoc. Feldshuh & Frank, N.Y.C., 1972-76; sole practice, N.Y.C., 1977-79; ptnr. Kraver & Martin, N.Y.C., 1979-85, Kraver & Parker, N.Y.C., 1985-88, Kraver & Levy, N.Y.C., 1989—. Mem. ABA, N.Y. State Bar Assn., Fla. Bar Assn. Federal civil litigation, Contracts commercial, General corporate. Home: 153 Albemarle Rd White Plains NY 10605-3303 Office: Kraver & Levy 767 3rd Ave Fl 35 New York NY 10017-2023

KRAVITCH, PHYLLIS A. federal judge; b. Savannah, Ga., Aug. 23, 1920; d. Aaron and Ella (Wiseman) K. BA, Goucher Coll., 1941; LLB, U. Pa., 1943; LLD (hon.), Goucher Coll., 1981, Emory U., 1998. Bar: Ga. 1943, U.S. Dist. Ct. 1944, U.S. Supreme Ct. 1948, U.S. Ct. Appeals (5th cir.) 1962. Practice law, Savannah, 1944-76; judge Superior Ct., Eastern Jud. Circuit of Ga., 1977-79, U.S. Ct. Appeals (5th cir.), Atlanta, 1979-81, U.S. Ct. Appeals (11th cir.), 1981—, sr. judge, 1996—. Mem. Jud. Conf. Standing Com. on Rules, 1994-2000. Trustee Inst. Continuing Legal Edn. in Ga., 1979-82; mem. Bd. Edn., Chatham County, Ga., 1949-55; mem. coun. Law Sch., Emory U., Atlanta, 1985—; mem. vis. com. Law Sch., U. Chgo., 1990-93; bd. visitors, Ga. State U. Law Sch., 1994—; mem. regional rev. panel Truman Scholarship Found., 1992—. Recipient Hannah G. Solomon award Nat. Coun,. Jewish Women, 1978, Trailblazer award Greater Atlanta Hadassah, 2000, James Wilson award U. Pa. Law Alumni Soc., 1992, Kathleen Kessler award Ga. Assn. Women Lawyers, 2001. Fellow Am. Bar Found.; mem. ABA (Margaret Brent award 1991), Savannah Bar Assn. (pres. 1976), State Bar Ga., Am. Judicature Soc. (Devitt award com. 1998—), Am. Law Inst, U. Pa. Law Soc., Nat. Assn. Women Lawyers (Arabella Babb Mansfield award 1999). Office: US Ct Appeals 11th Cir 56 Forsyth St NW # 202 Atlanta GA 30303-2205

KRAVITT, JASON HARRIS PAPERNO, lawyer; b. Chgo., Jan. 19, 1948; s. Jerome Julius and Shirley (Paperno) K.; m. Beverly Ray Niemeier, May 11, 1974; children: Nikola Wedding, Justin Taylor Paperno. AB, Johns Hopkins U., 1969; JD, Harvard U., 1972; diploma in comparative legal studies, Cambridge U., Eng., 1973. Bar: Ill., U.S. Dist. Ct. (no. dist.) Ill. Assoc. Mayer, Brown & Platt, Chgo., 1973-78, ptnr., 1979—, co-chmn., 1998-2001. Adj. prof. law Northwestern U., Evanston, Ill., 1994—, adj. prof. fin. Kellogg Sch. Mgmt., 1998—. Editor: Securitization of Financial Assets, 2d edit., 1996. Bd. dirs. Chgo. Met. YMCA, 1998—, Mus. Contemporary Art, Chgo., 1974-75; dir., chmn. The Cameron Kravitt Found., 1984—. Fellow Am. Coll. Comml. Lawyers; mem. ABA, Chgo. Coun. Lawyers, Chgo. Bar Assn., Econ. Club of Chgo., Execs. Club Chgo. Banking, Contracts commercial, Securities. Home: 250 Sheridan Rd Glencoe IL 60022-1948 Office: Mayer Brown & Platt 190 S La Salle St Ste 3100 Chicago IL 60603-3441 E-mail: jkravitt@mayerbrown.com

KRAVITZ, MARTIN JAY, lawyer; b. Phila., Oct. 3, 1950; s. Louis L. and Shirley (Best) K.; m. Donna Marie Fawcett, Nov. 26, 1978; children: Daniel Jay, Andrew Stephen. BA, U. Denver, 1972; JD, U. Pacific, 1977. Bar: Nev. 1977, U.S. Dist. Ct. Nev. 1977, U.S. Ct. Appeals (9th cir.) 1978, U.S. Supreme Ct. 1985. Law clk. to presiding justice Nev. Supreme Ct., Carson City, 1977-78; jr. ptnr., assoc. Goodman, Oshins, Brown & Singer, Las Vegas, 1978-82, Oshins, Brown, Singer & Wells, 1982-83; ptnr. Brown, Wells, Beller & Kravitz, Las Vegas, 1983-86, Brown, Wells & Kravitz, Las Vegas, 1986-88, Wells, Kravitz, Schnitzer, Sloane & Lindsey, Las Vegas, 1989—; assoc. prof. bus. law Clark County Community Coll., 1979-80. Chmn. lawyers div. United Jewish Appeal, Las Vegas, 1978— ; trustee Clark County Sch. Bd., 1988. Mem. ABA, Am. Trial Lawyers Assn., Clark County Bar Assn. Democrat. Jewish. State civil litigation, Contracts commercial, Personal injury. Office: Wells Kravitz Schnitzer Sloane & Lindsey 520 S 4th St Las Vegas NV 89101-6524

KRAW, GEORGE MARTIN, lawyer, essayist; b. Oakland, Calif., June 17, 1949; s. George and Pauline Dorothy (Herceg) K.; m. Sarah Lee Kenyon, Sept. 3, 1983. BA, U. Calif., Santa Cruz, 1971; student, Lenin Inst., Moscow, 1971; MA, U. Calif., Berkeley, 1974, JD, 1976. Bar: Calif. 1976, U.S. Supreme Ct. 1980, D.C. 1992. Pvt. practice, 1976—; ptnr. Kraw & Kraw, San Jose, 1988—. Mem. ABA, Internat. Soc. Cert. Employee Benefit Specialists, Nat. Assn. Health Lawyers, Inter-Am. Bar Assn., Union Internat. des Avocats. General corporate, Private international, Pension, profit-sharing, and employee benefits. Office: Kraw & Kraw 333 W San Carlos St Ste 1050 San Jose CA 95110-2735

KREBS, ARNO WILLIAM, JR. lawyer; b. Dallas, July 7, 1942; s. Arno W. and Lynette (Linnstaedter) K.; m. Peggy Sharon Stagg, Dec. 17, 1966; 1 child, Kristen; m. Barbara Lyn Craig, Dec. 28, 1973 B.A., Tex. A&M U., 1964; LL.B., U. Tex., 1967. Bar: Tex. 1967, U.S. Dist. Ct. (so. dist.) Tex. 1968, U.S. Ct. Appeals (5th cir.) 1971, U.S. Ct. Appeals (11th cir.) 1981, U.S. Dist. Ct. (we. and no. dists.) Tex. 1981, U.S. Supreme Ct. 1983, U.S. Dist. Ct. (ea. dist.) Tex. 1984. Assoc. Fulbright & Jaworski, Houston, 1967-75, ptnr., 1975—. Contbr. articles to profl. jours. Mem. Internat. Assn. Def. Counsel, Houston Bar Assn., ABA, Tex. Aggie Bar Assn., Tex. Bar Found., Houston Bar Found., Tex. A&M U. 12th Man Found. (pres. 1988), Houston Ctr. Club. Lutheran. State civil litigation, Insurance, Personal injury. Office: Fulbright & Jaworski 1301 Mckinney St Fl 51 Houston TX 77010-3031 also: 2200 Ross Ave Ste 2800 Dallas TX 75201-2750

KREBS, LEO FRANCIS, lawyer; b. Botkins, Ohio, June 9, 1937; s. Eugene L. and Velma L. K.; m. Paula Anne Calvert, Nov. 4, 1961; children: Matthew, Mark, Thomas, Peter. BA, U. Dayton, 1959; JD, Georgetown U., 1965. Bar: Ohio 1966, U.S. Dist. Ct. (so. dist.) Ohio 1966, U.S. Ct. Appeals (6th cir.) 1974, U.S. Supreme Ct. 1975. Legal dep. Montgomery Probate Ct., 1966-68; assoc. Bieser, Greer & Landis, Dayton, Ohio, 1968-74, ptnr., 1974—. Assoc. editor Georgetown Law Rev., 1964-65. Chmn. fin. com. Holy Angels, 1986-98, former chmn., bd. dirs. parish coun.; former bd. dirs. Cath. Social Svcs. Dayton, 1987-90; former mem. Oakwood YMCA Baseball Commn.; coach YMCA baseball. 1st lt. U.S. Army, 1959-62. Fellow Am. Coll. Trial Lawyers, Ohio State Bar Found.; mem. ABA, Ohio State Bar Assn., Ohio Assn. Trial Attys., Dayton Bar Assn., Phi Delta Phi. Avocations: hiking, tennis. General civil litigation, Personal injury, Probate. Office: Bieser Greer & Landis 6 N Main St Ste 400 Dayton OH 45402-1914 E-mail: lfr@bgl.com

KREBS, ROBERT ALAN, lawyer; b. Pitts., Dec. 12, 1958; s. James Arthur and Helen Marie (McGrogan) K.; m. Elizabeth Ann Bedford, Apr. 20, 1985; 1 child, Stephen Vladimir. BA, Pa. State U., 1981; student, U. Exeter, U.K., 1981; JD, Capital U., 1984. Bar: Pa. 1984, D.C. 1989, U.S. Dist. Ct. (ea. dist.) Pa. 1990, U.S. Dist. Ct. (we. dist.) Pa. 1984, U.S. Dist. Ct. (no. dist.) Ohio 1990, U.S. Dist. Ct. (D.C.) 1989, U.S. Ct. Appeals (D.C. cir.) 1989, U.S. Ct. Appeals (3d cir.) 1986, U.S. Supreme Ct. 1988. Assoc. Henderson & Goldberg, Pitts., 1985-87, Messer Shilobod & Crenney, Pitts., 1987-89, Klett Lieber Rooney & Schorling, Pitts., 1989-91, Conte, Melton & D'Antonio, Conway, Pa., 1992—. Articles editor Capital Law Rev., 1983-84. Mem. Pa. Dem. State Com., 37th Dist. (elected 1994, re-elected, 1998), Allegheny County Dem. Com., Pitts., 1991—; vol. Pitts. Ctr. for Grieving Children, 1995, 96. Recipient Am. Jurisprudence award Lawyers Coop. Pub. Co., 1982. Mem. ABA, FBA, D.C. Bar Assn., Pa. Trial Lawyers Assn. (amicus curiae com. 1996-99), Allegheny County Bar Assn. (fed. ct. sect. coun. 1996-99), Capital U. Law Sch. Alumni Assn. (bd. dirs. 1995-2001, v.p. 1996-2001), Western Pa. Trial Lawyers Assn. (bd. govs. 1994—). Democrat. Roman Catholic. Appellate, Consumer commercial, Personal injury. Home: 3235 Comanche Rd Pittsburgh PA 15241-1138 Office: 300 9th St Conway PA 15027-1647 E-mail: cmdlaw@acba.org

KREEK, LOUIS FRANCIS, JR. lawyer; b. Washington, Aug. 24, 1928; s. Louis F. and Esperance (Agee) K.; m. Gwendolyn Schoepfle, Sept. 12, 1970. BS, MIT, 1948; JD, George Washington U., 1952. Bar: D.C. 1952, U.S. Dist. Ct. D.C. 1952, U.S. Ct. Appeals (D.C. cir) 1952, Ohio 1955, N.Y. 1964, U.S. Dist. Ct. (so. and ea. dists.) N.Y. 1964, N.J. 1972. Patent examiner U.S. Patent Office, Washington, 1948-53; patent atty. Pitts. Plate Glass Co., 1953-54, Battelle Meml. Inst., Columbus, Ohio, 1954-56, Merck & Co., Inc., Rahway, N.J., 1956-60; divsn. patent counsel Air Reduction Co., Murray Hill, 1960-63; assoc. Kenyon & Kenyon, N.Y.C., 1963-66; patent atty. Johns-Manville Corp., Manville, N.J., 1967-68; sr. patent atty. Esso Rsch. and Engring. Co., Linden, 1968-73, ICI Ams. Inc, Wilmington, Del., 1973-85; assoc. Oldham, Oldham & Weber Co. (now Oldham & Oldham Co.), Akron, Ohio, 1985-94, of counsel, 1994—. Mem. ABA, Am. Intellectual Property Law Assn., N.Y. Intellectual Property Law Assn. (assoc.), Cleve. Intellectual Property Law Assn. (bd. dirs. 1991-92), Akron Bar Assn., MIT Alumni Assn. (bd. dirs. fund bd. 1977-80, officers conf. com. 1981-84, chmn. 1983), MIT Club Del. Valley (pres. 1978-80), MIT Club NE Ohio (pres. 1986-89), Am. Diabetes Assn. (bd. dirs. Akron chpt. 1989-90), Akron Roundtable (bd. dirs. 1989-90), Kiwanis (pres. 1989-90, lt. gov. 1992-93). Intellectual property, Patent, Trademark and copyright. Home: 2321 Stockbridge Rd Akron OH 44313-4512

KREGER, MELVIN JOSEPH, lawyer; b. Buffalo, Feb. 21, 1937; s. Philip and Bernice (Gerstman) K.; m. Patricia Anderson, July 1, 1955 (div. 1963), children: Beth Barbour, Arlene Roux; m. Renate Hochleitner, Aug. 15, 1975. JD, Mid-valley Coll. Law, 1978; LLM in Taxation, U. San Diego, 1988. Bar: Calif. 1978, U.S. Dist. Ct. (cen. dist.) Calif. 1979, U.S. Tax Ct. 1979, U.S. Supreme Ct. 1995; cert. specialist in probate law, trust law and estate planning law, taxation law, Calif. Life underwriter Met. Life Ins. Co., Buffalo, 1958-63; bus. mgr. M. Kreger Bus. Mgmt., Sherman Oaks, Calif., 1963-78, enrolled agt., 1971—; pvt. practice North Hollywood, 1978—. Mem. Nat. Assn. Enrolled Agts., Calif. Soc. Enrolled Agts., State Bar Calif., L.A. Bar Assn., San Fernando Valley Bar Assn. (probate sect., tax sect.). Jewish. Avocations: computers, travel. Estate planning, Probate, Taxation, general. Office: 11424 Burbank Blvd North Hollywood CA 91601-2301 E-mail: mel@meltaxlaw.com

KREIFELS, FRANK ANTHONY, lawyer, corporate executive; b. Omaha, Nov. 26, 1951; s. Robert Frank and Mary Ellen (Basan) K.; 1 child, Katherine Joy. BBA in Fin., Creighton U., 1974, MBA in Fin. and Acctg., 1975; JD, Hamline U., 1978. Bar: Minn. 1978, U.S. Dist. Ct. Minn. 1978, Nebr. 1983. Staff atty. NCR-Comten Inc., St. Paul, 1978-80; gen. counsel, sec. Agriventure Corp., Foxley & Co., Foxley Cattle Co., Herd Co., Flavorland Industries (and all affiliates), Omaha, 1980-85; mem. Ellsworth Law Firm, Omaha, 1985-87, exec. v.p., chief operating officer, Dale Beggs Devel. Co. (and all affiliates), 1987—; cons. Small Bus. Adminstrn., Omaha, 1974; corp. lobbyist Foxley Cattle Co./Herd Co., Omaha, 1981-85; appointed Neb. state reporter Am. Agrl. Law Update, 1985—. Campaign coord. Nebr. Rep. Com., 1982, 84. Recipient Cert. of Merit, Small Bus. Adminstrn., 1974. Mem. ABA, Am. Corp. Counsel Assn., Am. Agrl. Law Assn., Nebr. State Bar Assn., Phi Alpha Delta. Roman Catholic. Clubs: Omaha Barrister's, Omaha Westroads. Contracts commercial, General corporate, Real property. Office: Montclair Profl Ctr 13057 W Center Rd Omaha NE 68144-3748

KREIG, ANDREW THOMAS, trade association executive; b. Chgo., Feb. 28, 1949; s. Albert Arthur and Margaret Theresa (Baltzell) K. AB, Cornell U., 1970; MSL, Yale U., 1983; JD, U. Chgo., 1990. Bar: D.C. 1991, Mass. 1991, Ill. 1991. Writer, editor Hartford (Conn.) Courant, 1970-84; media dir. Conn. House Spkr., Hartford, 1984; freelance author, journalist, lectr. Hartford and Chgo., 1985-89; law clk. U.S. Dist. Judge Mark L. Wolf, Boston, 1990-91; assoc. Latham & Watkins, Washington, 1991-93; v.p., comms. dir. Wireless Comms. Assn. Internat., Inc., 1993-96, v.p., gen. counsel, 1996, pres., 1997—. Ethics com. Soc. Profl. Journalists, 1987-90. Author: Spiked: How Chain Management, 1987, 2d edit., 1988; editor Spectrum, 1994—; bd. editors Pvt. & Wireless Cable, 1994—, Wireless Internat., 1996—; contbr. articles to profl. jours. V.p. Residences Market Square, Washington, 1993-98; co-chair Fixed Wireless Com. Coalition, 2000—. Ford Found. fellow Yale Law Sch., New Haven, 1982-83. Mem. Fed. Com. Bar Assn. (legis. com.). Home: PH8 701 Pennsylvania Ave NW Washington DC 20004-2608 Office: Wireless Comms Assn Ste 810 1140 Connecticut Ave NW Washington DC 20036-4010 E-mail: president@wcai.com

KREITZMAN, RALPH J. lawyer; b. N.Y.C., Nov. 11, 1945; s. Emanuel M. and Hannah G. (Steinhardt) K.; m. Wendy A. Karpel, Nov. 24, 1968; children: Susan Beth, Emily Meg. BS in Acctg., Rider U., 1967; JD cum laude, Bklyn. Law Sch., 1970. Bar: N.Y. 1971, U.S. Dist Ct. (so. dist.) N.Y. 1971, U.S. Dist. Ct. (ea. dist.) N.Y. 1973, U.S. Ct. of Appeals (2nd cir.) 1975, U.S. Supreme Ct. 1976. Assoc. Hughes Hubbard & Reed LLP, N.Y.C., 1970-80; sr. ptnr. real estate group Hughes Hubbard & Reed LLC, 1980—. Trustee, former chair planning bd., mem. archtl. rev. com. Village of Great Neck. Served with U.S. Army Res., 1968-74. Mem. ABA (real property law sect. and com. on fgn. investment in U.S. real estate), N.Y. State Bar Assn. (real property law sect., com. on comml. leases and com. on financings), Assn. of Bar of City of N.Y. (com. on real property law, former chair leasing subcom.). Private international, Real property, Administrative and r. Office: Hughes Hubbard & Reed LLP 1 Battery Park Plz New York NY 10004-1482 E-mail: kreitzma@hugheshubbard.com

KREIZINGER, LOREEN I. lawyer, nurse; b. Syracuse, N.Y., Apr. 16, 1959; d. David F. and Blanche L. (Heaney) Mosher; m. Kenneth R. Kreizinger, Aug. 30, 1985; 1 child, Katelyn Rose. Grad. in nursing, Crouse-Irving Meml. Hosp., Syracuse, 1981; BS in Bus. with honors, Nova U., 1987, JD, 1990. Bar: Fla. 1990; RN, N.Y., Fla. Nurse ICU and infants neonatal unit, Syracuse, Ft. Lauderdale, Fla., 1979-86; med. malpractice cons. Krupnick, Campbell et al, Ft.Lauderdale, 1986-90, assoc., 1990-92, of counsel, 1992—; pvt. practice, 1992—. Instr. adult intensive care Crouse-Irving Meml. Hosp., 1981-82; adj. prof. Nova U., Ft. Lauderdale, 1994—; seminar instr. legal aspects of nursing Fla. Bd. Nursing, 1990-92; guest spkr. TV talk show Med. Malpractice, 1991. Sec., bd. dirs. Shepherd Care Ministries, Hollywood, Fla., 1993, 94; mem. choir 1st Bapt. Ch. Ft. Lauderdale, 1994—. Mem. ABA (law and medicine com. 1990—), FBA, ATLA (spl. L-Trytophen com. 1991-94), Fla. Bar Assn., Fla. Assn. Women Lawyers, Fla. Acad. Trial Lawyers, Broward County Women Lawyers Assn., Broward County Trial Lawyers Assn., Phi Alpha Delta. Republican. Avocations: sailing, snow skiing, rollerblading. General civil litigation, Personal injury. Office: 515 E Las Olas Blvd Ste 1150 Fort Lauderdale FL 33301-2281

KREMIN, MARK J. lawyer; b. Dayton, Ohio, Dec. 18, 1970; s. Michael Jr. and Beverly Anne Kremin. BA, U. Pitts., 1993; JD, Bklyn. Law Sch., 1997. Bar: N.Y. 1997. Assoc. Burke & Parons, N.Y.C., 1996—. Mem. Maritime Law Assn. U.S., New York County Bar Assn., Bar Assn. City N.Y. Roman Catholic. Admiralty. Home: 413 Pacific St Brooklyn NY 11217 Office: Burke & Parsons 1114 Ave of Americas New York NY 10036

KRESSE, WILLIAM JOSEPH, lawyer, educator, accountant; b. Evergreen Park, Ill., June 12, 1958; s. Robert Alvin and Ellenmary M. (Mulhall) K. BBA, U. Notre Dame, 1980; JD, U. Ill., 1985, MS, 1996, postgrad., 1997—. Bar. Ill. 1985, U.S. Dist. Ct. (no. dist.) Ill. 1985, U.S. Tax Ct. 1987, U.S. Ct. Appeals (7th cir.) 1989, U.S. Supreme Ct. 1989, U.S. Ct. Mil. Appeals 1990, U.S. Ct. Claims 1993. Acct. Deloitte, Haskins & Sells, Chgo., 1980-82; assoc. Hinshaw, Culbertson, Moelmann, Hoban & Fuller, 1985-87; law clk. to sr. judge U.S. Dist. Ct. (no. dist.) Ill., 1987-90; assoc. Ross & Hardies, 1990, Gleason, McGuire & Shreffler, Chgo., 1991-92; pvt. practice, 1992—. Corp. sec. Micro Records Co., Evergreen Park, Ill., 1987—, pres. 1995—; arbitrator arbitration program Cook County (Ill.) Cir. Ct., 1990—; mem. faculty St. Xavier U. Sch. Mgmt., Chgo., 1992-96, asst. prof., 1996—; lectr. U. Ill. Chgo., 1999—; election ctrl. atty. Chgo. Bd. Election Commrs. Author: (with others) Chicago Lawyer's Court Handbook, 1989, 92. Bd. dirs. St. John Fisher Sch. Bd., Chgo., 1988-94, pres., 1993-94; field adv. Met. Tribunal, Archdiocese of Chgo., 1994—; bd. dirs. Hist. Soc. U.S. Dist. Ct. for No. Dist. Ill., 1997—. Mem. ABA, FBA, AICPA, Chgo. Bar Assn. (co-chmn. young lawyer sect. bench/bar rels. com. 1988-89, bd. dirs. young lawyer sect. 1989-91, treas. young lawyer sect. 1991-93), Ill. Bar Assn., 7th Cir. Bar Assn., Hist. Soc. U.S. Dist. Ct. for No. Dist. Ill. (bd. dirs. 1997—), Ill. CPA Soc., Midwest Bus. Adminstrn. Acad., Nat. Lawyers Assn., KC, Elks, Delta Theta Phi. Roman Catholic. Avocations: current events, trivia, politics. General civil litigation, General practice, Probate. Office: 10221 S California Ave Chicago IL 60655-1623 also: St Xavier U 3700 W 103rd St Chicago IL 60655-3105

KRIEGER, FREDERIC MICHAEL, lawyer; b. Wilmington, Del., Apr. 28, 1950; s. Arthur H. and Edythe (Ploener) K.; m. Alice T. Whittelsey, Oct. 28, 1979; children: Daniel Marsh, Anna Caroline. AB, U. Pa., 1972; J.D., Emory U., 1975; student U. Lancaster, Eng., 1970-71. Bar: Ga. 1975, D.C. 1976, Pa. 1978, Ill. 1984, U.S. Dist. Ct. (no. dist.) Ga. 1976, U.S. Dist. Ct. (ea. dist.) Pa. 1978, U.S. Dist. Ct. D.C. 1976, U.S. Ct. Appeals (3d cir.) 1979, U.S. Dist. Ct. (no. dist.) Ill. 1984. Trial atty. SEC, Washington, 1975-78; assoc. firm Morgan, Lewis & Bockius, Phila., 1978-82; ptnr. firm Miller Schreiber & Sloan, Phila., 1982-83; assoc. gen. counsel Chgo. Bd. Options Exchange, 1983— ; adj. faculty Am. U. Law Sch., 1977-78, Cath. U. Law Sch., 1977-78, IIT/Chgo. Kent. Coll., 1986—; lectr. Inst. for Paralegal Tng., Phila., 1982 . Contbr. articles to law jours. Bd. dirs. Friends of Glencoe (Ill.) Pub. Library, 1984; bd. dirs. Glencoe Human Relations Com., 1986—; mem. New Trier Democratic Assn., 1984. Mem. ABA (mem. subcom. on securities markets and market structure, fed. regulation of securities com.). Club: Univ. of Chgo.

KRIEGSMAN, EDWARD MICHAEL, lawyer; b. Bridgeport, Conn., Oct. 29, 1965; s. Irving Martin and Marlene Sonya (Kates) K.; m. Meryl Gail Dennis, June 11, 1989; children: Barry Alan, David Jacob, Rachel Lynn. BS in Biology, MIT, 1986; JD, U. Pa., 1989. Bar: Pa. 1989, U.S. Patent and Trademark Office 1989, Mass. 1990, U.S. Ct. Appeals (Fed. cir.) 1990, U.S. Dist. Ct. Mass. 1992. Assoc. Finnegan, Henderson, Farabow, et al, Washington, 1989-90; ptnr. Kriegsman & Kriegsman, Framingham, Mass., 1990—. Mem. ABA, Am. Intellectual Property Law Assn., Mass. Bar Assn., Fed. Cir. Bar Assn., Boston Patent Law Assn., South Middlesex Bar Assn. Jewish. Avocations: reading, sports. Patent, Trademark and copyright. Home: 103 Richard Rd Holliston MA 01746-1213 Office: Kriegsman & Kriegsman 665 Franklin St Framingham MA 01702 E-mail: kriegspat@aol.com

KRIESBERG, SIMEON M. lawyer; b. Washington, June 4, 1951; s. Martin and Harriet M. K.; m. Martha L. Kahn, Jan. 9, 1994. AB, Harvard U., 1973; M in Pub. Affairs, Princeton U., 1977; JD, Yale U., 1977. Bar: D.C. 1977, U.S. Dist. Ct. D.C. 1978, U.S. Ct. Appeals (D.C. cir.) 1978, U.S. Ct. Internat. Trade 1979, U.S. Ct. Appeals (Fed. cir.) 1981, U.S. Supreme Ct. 1982. Assoc. Leva, Hawes, Symington, Martin & Oppenheimer, Washington, 1977-83; sr. counsel internat. trade Sears World Trade Inc., 1983-85, v.p., gen. counsel, 1985-87; ptnr. Mayer Brown & Platt, 1987—. Professorial lectr. Nitze Sch. Advanced Internat. Studies, Johns Hopkins U., 1991-93; mem. binat. dispute resolution panel under U.S.-Can. Free Trade Agreement, 1990-92; guest scholar Brookings Inst., 1992-93; mem. roster of dispute resolution panelists under NAFTA, 1996—. Mem. editorial adv. com. Internat. Legal Materials, 1991-97; article and book rev. editor Yale Law Jour., 1976-77. Officer or dir. Washington Hebrew Congregation, 1980-94, Jewish Cmty. Coun. Greater Washington, 1986-94, Interfaith Conf. of Met. Washington, 1989—, D.C. Jewish Cmty. Ctr., 1994—, Mid-Atlantic coun. Union Am. Hebrew Congregations, 1994—. Recipient Pro Bono Svc. award Internat. Human Rights Law Group, 1991, Lawrence L. O'Connor medal Sears, Roebuck and Co., 1984. Mem. ABA, Am. Law Inst., Am. Soc. Internat. Law, D.C. Bar. Administrative and regulatory, Private international, Public international. Office: Mayer Brown & Platt 1909 K St NW Washington DC 20006-1152

KRIKORIAN, VAN Z. lawyer; b. Framingham, Mass., Feb. 7, 1960; s. George O. and Agnes A. (Kalousdian) K.; m. Priscilla A. Dodakian, June 1, 1985; children: Ani, Sarah, Lena, George. BA in Internat. Affairs, George Washington U., 1981; JD, Georgetown U., 1984. Bar: Vt. 1985, D.C. 1986, U.S. Tax Ct. 1987, N.Y. 1994, U.S. Ct. Internat. Trade 1996. Law clk. Hon. Jerome Niedermeier U.S. Dist. Ct., Burlington, Vt., 1984-85; assoc. Gravel & Shea, 1985-88; dir. govt. and legal affairs Armenian Assembly Am., Washington, 1988-92; counsellor, dep. rep. to UN Rep. of Armenia, N.Y.C., 1992; counsel Patterson, Belknap, Webb & Tyler, LLP, 1993-98; ptnr. Vedder, Price, Kaufman & Kammhol, 1998—. Adj. prof. comml. law St. Michael's Coll., Winooski, Vt., 1987-88. Contbr. more than 20 articles to profl. jours. Ofcl. U.S. del. to Moscow Conf. on Security and Cooperation in Europe, 1991; vice chair fin. com. Dole for Pres., Washington, 1995. Mem. ABA, Assn. of the Bar of the City of N.Y., D.C. Bar Assn., Vt. Bar Assn., U.S.-Armenian Bus. Coun. (chmn. 1996-2001), Armenian Assembly Am. (trustee, chmn. bd. dirs. 1998—). Private international, Public international. Office: Vedder Price Kaufman & Kammholz 805 3rd Ave New York NY 10022-7513 E-mail: vkrikorian@vedderprice.com

KRINSLY, STUART Z. lawyer, manufacturing company executive; b. N.Y.C., May 19, 1917; m. Charlotte Wolf, Aug. 18, 1944; children: EllinJane, Joan Susan. BA, Princeton U., 1938; LLB, Harvard U., 1941. Bar: N.Y. 1941. Asst. U.S. atty. So. Dist. N.Y., 1942-45; mem. firm Schlesinger & Krinsly, 1945-57; sec. Sun Chem. Corp., N.Y.C., 1957-65, v.p., gen. counsel, 1965-76, sr. v.p., gen. counsel, 1976-78, exec. v.p., gen. counsel, 1978-82, also bd. dirs.; sr. exec. v.p., gen. counsel Sequa Corp., 1982—, also bd. dirs. Mem. Beach Point Club, Princeton Club N.Y. General corporate. Home: 1135 Greacen Point Rd Mamaroneck NY 10543-4612 Office: Sequa Corp 200 Park Ave Fl 44 New York NY 10166-0005

KRISS, ROBERT J. lawyer; b. Cleve., Dec. 15, 1953; BA summa cum laude, Cornell U., 1975; JD cum laude, Harvard U., 1978. Bar: Ill. 1978, U.S. Dist. Ct. (no. dist.) Ill. 1978, U.S. Ct. Appeals (7th cir.) 1983, U.S. Dist. Ct. (no. dist. trial bar) Ill. 1982, U.S. Ct. Appeals (5th cir.) 1984. Ptnr. Mayer, Brown & Platt, Chgo. Presenter in field. Author short story. Chmn. consent degree task force Chgo. Park Dist., 1986-87; bd. dirs. Chgo. Legal Assistance Found., 1996—. Mem. Nat. Inst. Trial Advocacy (faculty midwest regional program 1988-91, 94), Winnetka Caucus (chmn. schs. candidate selection com. 1997). Office: Mayer Brown & Platt 190 S La Salle St Ste 3100 Chicago IL 60603-3441

KRISTOL, DANIEL MARVIN, lawyer; b. July 7, 1936; s. Abraham Louis and Pearl Cecile (Oltman) K.; m. Katherine Fairfax Chinn, Nov. 4, 1968; children: Sarah Douglas, Susan Fairfax. BA, U. Pa., 1958, LLB, 1961. Bar: Del. 1961, U.S. Dist. Ct. Del. 1962. Assoc., ptnr. Killoran & VanBrunt, Wilmington, Del., 1961-76; dir. Prickett, Jones, Elliott & Kristol, 1976-99; ptnr. predecessor Prickett, Ward Burt & Sanders, 1976-99; dir. Richards, Layton & Finger, 1999—. Pub. defender Ct. Common Pleas, Wilmington, 1966-69; asst. solicitor City of Wilmington, 1970-73; spl. counsel Div. Housing State of Del., 1972-87, gen. counsel Del. State Housing Authority, 1973-99. With USAR, 1964-67. Mem. ABA, Del. State Bar Assn. (chmn. real and personal property com. 1974-78, chmn. world peace through law com. 1980-81, chmn. sr. lawyers com. 1999—), Am. Coll. Real Estate Lawyers, Wilmington Country Club, Greenville Country Club, Mill Reef Club (Antigua, W.I.), Wilmington Club. Republican. Jewish. Contracts commercial, Landlord-tenant, Real property. Office: PO Box 551 Wilmington DE 19899-0551 E-mail: kristol@rlf.com

KRITSELIS, WILLIAM NICHOLAS, lawyer; b. Sault Sainte Marie, Mich., Apr. 5, 1931; s. Nicholas William and Theodora G. (Gianacopoulos) K.; m. Elaine John Jennings, Sept. 1, 1963; 1 child, Nicholas William. BA, Mich. State U., 1959; JD, Ohio No. U., 1962. Bar: Mich. 1962, U.S. Dist. Ct. (we. dist.) Mich. 1963, U.S. Supreme Ct. 1966, U.S. Dist. Ct. (ea. dist.) Mich. 1968. Asst. prosecutor Ingham County, Lansing, Mich., 1963-64, chief criminal div., 1964-65; sole practice, 1965—. Pres. Holy Trinity Greek Orthodox Ch., Lansing, 1977; lifetime mem. NAACP, Lansing. Served with USN, 1951-55. Recipient Outstanding Atty. of Yr. award Ingham County Bar Assn., 1992. Fellow State Bar Mich. Found; mem. ABA, Fed. Bar Assn., Mich. Bar Assn. (med.-legal com. 1978-81, negligence com. 1982-85), Assn. Trial Lawyers Am. (lectr. product liability), Mich. Trial Lawyers Assn. (lectr. on construction, R.R. and product liabilty, bd. govs. 1978—), Lansing Trial Lawyers Assn. (pres. 1966-70), Am. Judicature Soc., Lawyers for Pub. Justice, Am. Arbitration Assn., Mich. State Alumni Assn., Mich. State U. Pres. Club. (East Lansing). Federal civil litigation, Insurance, Personal injury. Office: 2827 E Saginaw St Lansing MI 48912-4239 Fax: 517-372-1031

KRITZER, PAUL ERIC, media executive, communications lawyer; b. Buffalo, May 5, 1942; s. James Cyril and Bessie May (Biddlecombe) K.; m. Frances Jean McCallum, June 20, 1970; children: Caroline Frances, Erica Hopkins. BA, Williams Coll., 1964; MS in Journalism, Columbia U., 1965; JD, Georgetown U., 1972. Bar: U.S. Supreme Ct. 1978, Wis. 1980. Reporter, copy editor Buffalo Evening News, 1964, 69, 70; instr. English Augusta (Ga.) Coll., 1968-69; law clk. Office of FCC Commr., Washington, 1971, MCI, Washington, 1972; counsel U.S. Ho. of Reps., 1972-77; assoc. counsel Des Moines Register & Tribune, 1977-80; editor, pub. Waukesha (Wis.) Freeman, 1980-83; legal v.p., sec. Jour. Communications Inc., Milw., 1983—. Bd. dirs. Jour. Communications, Inc., Milw. Trustee Carroll Co., Waukesha, 1981-89; producer Waukesha Film Festival, 1982; bd. dirs. Des Moines Metro Opera, Inc., 1979-80; bd. dirs. Milw. Youth Symphony Orch., 1992-2001, pres. 1994-97; bd. dirs. Milw. Symphony Orch., 1997—; bd. dirs. United Performing Arts Fund, 1994-97. With U.S. Army, 1965-68. Presbyterian. Avocations: bridge, gardening. Home: 211 Oxford Rd Waukesha WI 53186-6263 Office: Jour Communications Inc 333 W State St PO Box 661 Milwaukee WI 53201-0661 Business E-Mail: pkritzer@jc.com

KROENER, WILLIAM FREDERICK, III, lawyer; b. N.Y.C., Aug. 27, 1945; s. William Frederick Jr. and Barbara (Mitchell) K.; m. Evelyn Somerville Bibb, Sept. 3, 1966; children: William F. IV (dec.), Mary Elizabeth, Evangeline Alberta, James Mitchell. AB, Yale Coll., 1967; JD, MBA, Stanford U., 1971. Bar: Calif. 1972, N.Y. 1979, D.C. 1983. Assoc. Davis, Polk & Wardwell, N.Y.C., London, 1971-79, ptnr. N.Y.C., 1979-82, Washington, N.Y.C., 1982-94; gen. counsel Fed. Deposit Ins. Corp., Washington, 1995—. Lectr. Stanford (Calif.) U. Law Sch., 1993-94, George Washington U. Law Sch., Washington, 1994—, Washington Coll. Law, Am. U. Law Sch., Washington, 1996—; chmn. legal adv. group Fed. Interagy. Fin. Exam. Coun., 2001—. Pres. Kroener Family Found.; gov. bd. St. Albans Sch., 1991-95; fin. com. Protestant/Episcopal Cathedral Found.-Wash. Nat. Cathedral, 1992-95; bd. visitors Stanford U. Law Sch., 1983-92, deans adv. coun., 1992-93; nat. chair Stanford Law Fund, 1990-92; dir., gen. counsel Kenwood Citizens Assn., Inc., 1993-94. Mem. ABA, Am. Law Inst., Assn. of Bar of City of N.Y., N.Y. Law Inst., Yale Club, Kenwood Golf Club. Republican. Episcopalian. Home: 6412 Brookside Dr Chevy Chase MD 20815-6649 Office: Fed Deposit Ins Corp 550 17th St NW Washington DC 20429-0001

KROFT, MICHAL, lawyer; b. Pilsen, Czech Republic, Nov. 24, 1969; s. Václav and Ivana K.; m. Olga Slaisová, June 27, 1994; 1 child, Barbara. M, Charles U., Prague, 1993. Assoc. law firm, Pilsen, 1990-93, trainee Prague, 1994-96; sole practice, 1996; ptnr. Weinhold Andersen Legal, 1997—. Lectr. in field. Contbr. articles to profl. jours. Mem. Czech Bar Assn., Slovak Bar Comml. Lawyers. Avocations: reading, cinema, theater, car racing, golf. Patent, Trademark and copyright, Information Technolo. Office: Weinhold Andersen Legal VOS Husova 5 110 00 Prague 1 Czech Republic Fax: 2440 7389. E-mail: michal.kroft@cz.andersenlegal.com

KROLL, ARTHUR HERBERT, lawyer, educator, consultant; b. N.Y.C., Dec. 2, 1939; s. Abraham and Sylvia Kroll; m. Lois Handmacher, June, 1964; children: Douglas, Pamela. BA, Cornell U., 1961; LLB cum laude, St. John's U., 1965; LLM in Taxation, NYU, 1969. Bar: D.C. Assoc. Patterson, Belknap, Webb & Tyler, N.Y.C., 1965-72, ptnr., 1972-90, Pryor, Cashman, Sherman & Flynn, N.Y.C., 1990-95; CEO KST Cons. Group, Inc. Adj. prof. U. Miami Sch. Law, NYU; lectr. numerous confs.; mem. adv. bd. Bur. Nat. Affairs Tax Mgmt., Inc., Practising Law Inst. Tax Adv. Bd., U. Miami Inst. Estate Planning, Bus. Laws, Inc.; mem. adv. com. NYU Ann. Inst. on Fed. Taxation. Author: Executive Compensation, 3 vols., Compensating Executives; monthly newsletter Family Bus. Profl.; mem. bd. contbg. editors and advisers Corporate Taxation; mem. editl. adv. bd. Jour. Compensation and Benefits. Mem. ABA (subcom. exec. compensation), Am. Pension Conf. (mem. steering com.). Pension, profit-sharing, and employee benefits, Probate, Corporate taxation. Office: KST Consulting Group Inc 50 1/2 E 64th St New York NY 10021-7306 E-mail: kstconsultinggroup@worldnet.att.net

KROLL, BARRY LEWIS, lawyer; b. Chgo., June 8, 1934; s. Harry M. and Hannah (Lewis) K.; m. Jayna Vivian Leibovitz, June 20, 1956; children: Steven Lee, Joan Lois Kroll Dolgin, Nancy Maxine Kroll Richardson. A.B. in Psychology with distinction, U. Mich., 1955, J.D. with distinction, 1958. Bar: Ill. 1958. Assoc. firm Jacobs & McKenna, Chgo., 1958-66, Epstein, Manilow & Sachnoff, Chgo., 1966-68, Schiff, Hardin, Waite Dorschel & Britton, Chgo., 1968-69; ptnr. Wolfberg & Kroll, 1970-74, Kirshbaum & Kroll, Chgo., 1972-74; of counsel Jacobs, Williams & Montgomery, Ltd., 1973-74; ptnr. Jacobs, Williams & Montgomery Ltd., 1974-85, Williams & Montgomery Ltd., Chgo., 1985—. Faculty John Marshall Law Sch., Chgo., 1969-73; atty. for petitioner in U.S. Supreme Ct. decision Escobedo vs Ill., 1964, guest lectr. before groups, 1964— ; mem. legal and legis. com. Internat. Franchise Assn., 1976-80 Asst. editor: Mich. Law Rev, 1957-58. Chmn. Park Forest Bd. Zoning Appeals, 1971-78. Served to capt. AUS, 1959-62. Named Outstanding Young Man Park Forest Jr. C. of C., 1966. Mem. Ill. Bar Assn., Chgo. Bar Assn. (chmn. legis. com. 1974-75), Ill. Appellate Lawyers Assn. (treas. 1978-79, sec. 1979-80, pres. 1981-82), Bar Assn. 7th Fed. Circuit, Order of Coif, Tau Epsilon Rho, Alpha Epsilon Pi. Jewish (trustee congregation 1966-70, 72-75, 90—, pres. men's club 1965-66). Appellate, State civil litigation, Insurance. Home: 1440 N State Pky Chicago IL 60610-1564 Office: Williams Montgomery & John Ltd 20 N Wacker Dr Ste 2100 Chicago IL 60606-3005 E-mail: blk@willmont.com

KROLL, MARTIN N. lawyer; b. N.Y.C., Nov. 30, 1937; s. Jack and Ruth (Strassman) K.; m. Rita Evangeline Grossman, Aug. 14, 1965; children: Spencer, Jonathan, Evan. BA, Cornell U., 1959; JD, U. Pa., 1963. Sr. ptnr. Kroll, Levy, Baron & Feinstein, N.Y.C., 1972-80, Snow, Becker, Kroll, Klaris & Kraus, N.Y.C., 1980-86, Kroll, Moss and Kroll, LLP, Garden City, N.Y., 1987—. Receiver Chrysler Bldg., N.Y.C., 1975-77; village atty. Village of East Hills (N.Y.), 1988-95; counsel Town of North Hempstead, 1987—, counsel Econ. Devel. Agy. Town of North Hempstead, 1992—; pres. Jewish Lawyers Assn. of Nassau County, N.Y., 1980. Vice chmn.

Nassau County Republican Party, Westbury, N.Y., 1986—. Recipient Torch of Liberty, B'Nai Brigh-ADL, 1982; named Master Builder Conf. of Jewish Educators, 1990. Mem. ABA, N.Y. State Bar Assn., Nassau County Bar Assn. Federal civil litigation, General civil litigation, Municipal (including bonds). Office: Kroll Moss & Kroll 400 Garden City Plz Garden City NY 11530-3322 E-mail: mkroll100@aol.com

KROLL, SOL, lawyer; b. Russia, Aug. 10, 1918; m. Ruth Saslow; children: Gerald, Judy, Elise, Elliott. LLB, St. John's U., 1942. Bar: N.Y. 1942, U.S. Supreme Ct. 1956. Former U.S. counsel to Assn. Francaise des Socs. D'Assurances Transports; former mem. com. of interfraud task force N.Y. Ins. Dept.; sr. ins. counsel Ward, Kroll, and Jampol, N.Y., L.A., San Diego. County atty. Putnam County, N.Y. Contbr. articles on Am. ins. law to various ins. mags. Mem. ABA, Fed. Bar Assn., N.Y. State Bar Assn., N.Y.C. Bar Assn., Internat. Assn. Ins. Counsel, Industry Adv. Com. on Ins., Ins. Fedn. NY (bd. dirs.). Insurance. Home: 600 Cantitoe St Bedford NY 10506-1107 Office: 110 E 59th St New York NY 10022-1304 Fax: 212-755-9892

KRONE, NORMAN BERNARD, commercial real estate developer, lawyer; b. Memphis, Sept. 13, 1938; s. Irving and Eva (Sauer) K.; m. Norma Lee Moon; children: John, Christine, David. LLB, Stetson U., 1964. Bar: Fla. 1964, Ohio 1987, U.S. Dist. Ct. (mid. dist.) Fla. 1965, U.S. Ct. Appeals (7th cir.) 1968. Atty. Lifsey & Johnston, Tampa, Fla., 1964-65; pvt. practice, 1965-66; property mgmt. atty. Ford Motor Co., Dearborn, Mich., 1966-67; audit mgr. Montgomery Ward & Co., Chgo., 1967-68, corp. real estate mgr., 1968-75; exec. v.p. Momtgomery Ward Properties Corp., 1970-75; from v.p. to sr. v.p. Walgreen Co., Deerfield, Ill., 1975-85; pres., CEO The Hausman Cos., Cleve., 1987-2001; sr. exec. v.p. Henry S. Miller, Grubb & Ellis Comml./Retail Svcs., 1985-87; mng. prin. NK Devel. Ltd., 1996—. Trustee Internat. Coun. Shopping Ctrs., N.Y.C., 1976-79; dir. Myers Industries, Lincoln, Ill., 1976-83; mem. adv. bd. Commerce Exch. Bank, Beachwood, Ohio, 1997—; instr. Intercoun. Shopping Ctrs.-Inst. Profl. Devel.; dean U. Shopping Ctrs.-Internat. Coun. Shopping Ctrs., mem. cert. governance com., endl. adv. com., small ctr. com., chmn. retail adv. com., 1975-76, cert. leasing specialist, 1995-2001; cons. Krone Group, Brokers, 2001—; instr., spkr. in field. Author, editor: The Lease and Its Language, 1996, ICSC Study Lease, 2000; contbr. articles to mags. Acting judge City of Tampa, 1964-66; bd. dirs. Met. Housing and Planning Coun., Chgo., 1977-80, New City YMCA, 1976-78; mem. sch. bd. Palisades Cmty. Sch. Dist., 1968-69; mem. strategic planning com. Met. Chgo. YMCA, 1976-77; 1st pres. Cleve. Pops Orch.; bd. dirs. Walgreen Hist. Found., 1984-87; co-founder, pres., mem. exec. com. Realty Resources (a network of comml. brokerage firms), 1987—. Named Entrepreneur of Yr. Operation Breadbasket, 1977. Mem. Cleve. Bar Assn., Real Estate Inst., Beachwood C. of C. (pres. 1996, exec. com. 1992—), Acacia Country Club (bd. dirs. 1997-99, chmn. planning com. 1998-99, sec. 1998). Avocations: woodworking, golf. Office: The Krone Group 2101 Richmond Rd Beachwood OH 44122-1390 Address: 8650 Hunting Hills Mentor OH 44060 E-mail: nkrone@thekronegroup.com

KRONEY, ROBERT HARPER, lawyer; b. Dallas, May 16, 1939; s. Archie D. and Martha (Harper) K.; 1 child from a preivous marriage, Harper Paul; m. Susan K. Monaghan, Aug. 20, 1994. BS in Geol. Engring., U. Okla., 1962; LLB, U. Tex., Austin, 1964; LLM, So. Meth. U., 1972. Bar: U.S. Dist. Ct. (no. dist.) Tex. 1966. Ptnr. Strasburger & Pride, Dallas, 1966-73, Johnson & Swanson, Dallas, 1973-84, Kroney Mincey Inc., Dallas, 1984—. Adviser, continuing legal edn., So. Meth. U. Served to lt., USAR, 1962-66. Named Cooper Clinic Man of Yr., 2000. Fellow Am. Coll. Trust and Estate Counsel; mem. Dalas Estate Planning Coun. (bd. dirs. 1972, 84), State Bar Tex. (trust editor real estate, probate and trust law newsletter 1972-78), Am. Soc. CLUs (bd. dirs. Dallas chpt. 1976-83, pres. 1982), Tex. Bd. Legal Specialization (estate planning, probate law and tax law). Estate planning, Probate, Estate taxation. Office: Kroney Mincey Inc 1210 Three Forest Plz 12221 Merit Dr Ste 1210 Dallas TX 75251-3287 E-mail: bkroney@ksmdallas.com

KRONGARD, HOWARD J. lawyer; b. Dec. 12, 1940; s. Raphael Harris and Rita (Keyser) K.; children: Kenneth, Mara Lynn. BA, Princeton U., 1961; JD, Harvard U., 1964; postgrad., Cambridge U., 1964-65. Bar: Md. 1965, N.Y. 1967, U.S. Dist. Ct. Md. 1965, U.S. Dist. Ct. (so. dist.) N.Y. 1967, U.S. Ct. Appeals (2d cir.) 1973, U.S. Ct. Appeals (8th cir.) 1980, U.S. Supreme Ct. 1991. Assoc. Piper & Marbury, Balt., 1964, Cravath, Swaine & Moore, N.Y.C., 1965, 66-73; law clk. to Hon. Kenneth B. Keating N.Y. Ct. Appeals, Albany, 1966; assoc., gen. counsel Peat, Marwick, Mitchell & Co., N.Y.C., 1973-86; gen. counsel Deloitte, Haskins & Sells, 1986-89, Deloitte & Touche, LLP, N.Y.C., 1989-95; of counsel Freshfields, Bruckhaus & Deringer, London/N.Y.C., 1996—. Spkr. in field; bd. dirs. Lacrosse Found., Inc., Balt., 1981—, PCX Equities; U.S. rep. to Internat. Lacrosse Fedn.; legal adv. coun. Nat. Legal Ctr. Pub. Interest; pub. gov. Pacific Exch. Named Outstanding Player in U.S.A., U.S. Club Lacrosse Assn., 1968, 74; inducted into Lacrosse Hall of Fame, 1985, N.Y. Sports Hall of Fame, 1994; recipient Ames Briefwriting prize Harvard Law Sch., 1962; Frank Knox Meml. fellow, 1965. Mem. Assn. of Bar of City of N.Y., Harvard Club.

KRONMAN, ANTHONY TOWNSEND, law educator, dean; b. 1945; m. Nancy I. Greenberg, 1982 B.A., Williams Coll., 1968, Ph.D., 1972; J.D., Yale U., 1975. Bar: Minn. 1975, N.Y. 1983. Assoc. prof. U. Minn., 1975-76; asst. prof. U. Chgo., 1976-79; vis. assoc. prof. Yale U. Law Sch., New Haven, 1978-79, prof., 1979—, Edward J. Phelps prof. law, 1985—, dean, 1994—. Editor: (with R. Posner) The Economics of Contract Law, 1979 (with F. Kessler and G. Gilmore) Cases and Materials on Contracts, 1986; past mem. editorial bd. Yale Law Jour.; author: Max Weber, 1983, The Lost Lawyer, 1993. Danforth Found. fellow, 1968-72 Fellow ABA, Am. Acad. Arts and Scis.; mem. Selden Soc., Conn. Bar Assn. (Cooper fellow), Coun. on Fgn. Rels. Office: Yale U Law Sch PO Box 208215 New Haven CT 06520-8215

KROUSE, GEORGE RAYMOND, JR. lawyer; b. Atlantic City, Sept. 30, 1945; s. George R. and Viola (Rogers) K.; m. Susan Naylor, Aug. 7, 1967; children: Geoffrey, Alison. AB cum laude, Brown U., 1967; JD with distinction, Duke U., 1970. Bar: N.Y. 1971, U.S. Ct. Mil. Appeals 1971, U.S. Dist. Ct. (so. and ea. dists.) N.Y. 1975. Assoc. Simpson Thacher & Bartlett, N.Y.C., 1970-71, 75-78, ptnr., 1978—, chmn. cor. dept., 1991—. Articles editor Duke Law Jour. Mem. bd. visitors Sch. Law, Duke U., Durham, N.C., 1986-92, chmn., 1997-2001; mem. nat. devel. coun. Duke U., 1994-2000, dir. Global Capital Markets Ctr. Capt. USAF, 1971-75. Decorated Air Force Commendation medal, Meritorious Svc. medal. Mem. ABA, N.Y. State Bar Assn., Assn. of Bar of City of N.Y. (com. on corps. 1985-88, com. art law 1990-93), Order of Coif, Montclair Golf Club, Cape Cod Nat. Golf Club, Bonita Bay Club. Avocation: golf. General corporate, Finance, Securities. Home: 4 Erwin Park Montclair NJ 07042-3018 Office: Simpson Thacher & Bartlett 425 Lexington Ave 18th Fl New York NY 10017-3954 E-mail: g-krouse@stblaw.com

KRSUL, JOHN ALOYSIUS, JR. lawyer; b. Highland Park, Mich., Mar. 24, 1938; s. John A. and Ann M. (Sepich) K.; m. Justine Oliver, Sept. 12, 1958; children: Ann Lisa, Mary Justine. BA, Albion Coll., 1959; JD, U. Mich., 1963. Bar: Mich. 1963. Assoc. Dickinson Wright PLLP, 1963-71, ptnr., 1971-99, consulting ptnr., 2000—. Asst. editor: U. Mich. Law Rev, 1962-63. Recipient Disting. Alumnus award Albion Coll., 1984; Sloan scholar, 1958-59; Fulbright scholar, 1959-60; Ford. Found. grantee, 1964 Fellow: Am. Bar Found. (life; chmn. Mich. chpt. 1988—89); mem.: ABA (chmn. sect. gen. practice 1989—90, exec. coun. 1984—91, ho. of dels. 1979—, chmn. standing com. on membership 1983—89, tort and ins. practice sect., exec. coun. 1991—94, chmn. fin. com. 1993—94, bd. govs. 1991—99, exec. com. 1993—94, exec. com. 1996—99, treas. 1996—99, editl. bd. ABA Jour. 1996—99, audit com. 2001—), Am. Bar Retirement Assn. (bd. dirs. 1999—), Detroit Bar Assn. (dir. 1971—80, pres. 1979—80), Detroit Bar Assn. Found. (dir. 1971—84, pres. 1979—80), State Bar Mich. (commr. 1973—83, pres. 1982—83), Mich. State Bar Found. (trustee 1982—83, trustee 1985—99, chmn. fellows 1986—87), Fellows of Young Lawyers Am. Bar (bd. dirs. 1977—86, chmn. bd. 1984—86, pres. 1983—84), Am. Judicature Soc. (dir. 1971—79, exec. com. 1973—74), Nat. Conf. Bar Pres. (exec. coun. 1986—89), Am. Bar Endowment (bd. dirs. 1996—99), Am. Bar Ins. Cons. Inc. (bd. dirs. sec. 1988—95), Sixth Cir. Jud. Conf. (life)), Orchard Lake Country Club, Detroit Club, Phi Beta Kappa, Omicron Delta Kappa, Phi Eta Sigma, Delta Tau Delta. Antitrust, General corporate. Home: 7094 Huntington Dr Sawyer MI 49125-9319 Office: Dickinson Wright PLLC 500 Woodward Ave Ste 4000 Detroit MI 48226-3416

KRUCHKO, JOHN GREGORY, lawyer; b. Iowa City, Iowa, Sept. 3, 1948; s. Demitro M. and Caroline (Maloney) K.; m. Susan Lynn Clendaniel, Sept. 15, 1968; 1 child, Jennifer Lynn. B.A., Xavier U., 1970; M.A. in History, U. Cin., 1971, M.A. in Labor Relations, 1972; J.D., Coll. William and Mary, 1975. Bar: Pa. 1975, Md. 1977, D.C. 1983, U.S. Dist. Ct. (ea. and mid. dists.) Pa. 1976, Md. 1978, U.S. Ct. Appeals (4th cir.) 1978, (3d cir.) 1979, U.S. Supreme Ct. 1983. Assoc. Morgan, Lewis & Bockius, Phila., 1975-77, Venable, Baetjer & Howard, Balt., 1977-79; founder, sr. ptnr. Kruchko & Fries, Balt., 1979— . Author: Birth of a Union Local, 1973; The Maryland Employer's Guide to Labor and Employment Law, 1984. Contbr. articles to profl. jours. Chmn. fin. com. Balt. County Victory '84 Reagan/Bush, 1984. Mem. ABA (sect. labor and employment law, subcom. co-chmn. 1980—), Am. Acad. Hosp. Attys., Md. Bar Assn., Pa. Bar Assn. Roman Catholic. Clubs: Center (Balt.); University (Towson, Md.). Labor. Home: 7929 Westpark Dr Ste 202 Mc Lean VA 22102-4238

KRUEGER, HERBERT WILLIAM, lawyer; b. Milw., Apr. 20, 1948; s. Herbert William Sr. and Lily (Kuphall) K.; m. Judith Ann Wanserske, July 20, 1970; children— Kara, Dana, Andrew, Christopher. B.A., U. Wis.-Milw., 1970; J.D., U. Chgo., 1974. Bar: Fla. 1974, Ill. 1975, U.S. Dist. Ct. (no. dist.) Ill. 1975. Instr. in law U. Miami Sch. Law, Coral Gables, Fla., 1974-75; assoc. Mayer, Brown & Platt, Chgo., 1975-80, ptnr., 1981— , head compensation dept., 1984—, mem. mgmt. com., 1989—. Contbg. author Continuing Legal Education Pension Practice and Securities Laws handbooks, Practising Law Inst. handbook Acquiring and Selling Privately Held Companies, Pension Investment Handbook; contbr. articles to profl. jours. State dir. Wis. Coll. Reps., 1969-70; exec. dir. Com. to Reelect Pres., Wis. Young Voters Campaign, 1972; chmn. fiduciary standards com. Ill. Study Commn. on Pub. Pension Investment Policies, 1981-82; mem. nat. adv. bd. NYU Real Estate Inst. Pension Fund Investment in Real Estate Conf. Mem. ABA, Pension Real Estate Assn. (mem. govt. affairs com.). Pension, profit-sharing, and employee benefits. Office: Mayer Brown & Platt 190 S La Salle St Ste 3100 Chicago IL 60603-3441

KRUEGER, JAMES A. lawyer; b. Sept. 21, 1943; s. A.A. and Margaret E. (Hurley) K.; m. Therese Eileen Connors, Aug. 2, 1968; 1 child, Colleen. BA cum laude, Gonzaga U., 1965; JD, Georgetown U., 1968; LLM, NYU, 1972. Bar: Wash. 1969, U.S. Supreme Ct. 1972, U.S. Tax Ct. 1972, U.S. Dist. Ct. (we. dist.) Wash. 1980, U.S. Ct. Appeals (9th cir.) 1982. Mem. staff U.S. senator from Wash., 1967-68; assoc. Kane, Vandeberg & Hartinger, Tacoma, 1972-76; ptnr. Kane, Vandeberg, Hartinger & Walker, 1976-90; shareholder Vandeberg & Johnson PS, 1990—. Spl. dist. counsel Wash. State Bar Assn., 1984-94; adj. prof. law, U. of Puget Sound, 1974-76. Co-author: Representing the Close Corporation, 1979, Partnership Agreements, 1981, Planning for the Small Business Enterprise, 1982, The Partnership Handbook, 1984. Chmn. bd. Cath. Cmty. Svcs. of Pierce and Kitsap Counties, 1983-84; bd. dirs. United Way of Pierce County, 1973-82, 99—. Capt. U.S. Army, 1968-72. Decorated Bronze star. Mem. ABA, Wash. State Bar Assn. (spl. dist. counsel), Tacoma-Pierce County Bar Assn. Roman Catholic. General civil litigation, General corporate, Estate planning. Office: 1201 Pacific Ave Ste 1900 Tacoma WA 98402-4315

KRUMBEIN, CHARLES HARVEY, lawyer; b. Ft. Benning, Ga., Dec. 15, 1944; s. Nathaniel and Amy (Meyers) K.; m. Cynthia J. Nerden, Dec. 17, 1967; children: Jason M., Laura R. BS, Pa. State U., 1966; JD, U. Ga., 1969. Bar: Va. 1970, U.S. Supreme Ct. 1975. Mgmt. trainee Heilig-Meyers Co., Richmond, Va., 1972-80, v.p., corp. counsel, 1980-89; prin. Krumbein and Assocs., 1990—. Mem. Va. adv.bd. U.S. Civil Rights, 1985; nat. commr. Anti-Defamation League of B'nai B'rith, 1986—; mem. Va. Commonwealth U. Dental Sch. Bd., 1999—. Served to capt. U.S. Army, 1970-72, Ger. Mem. So. Home Furnishing Assn. (dir. 1980-90, mem. exec. com. 1986-90), Richmond Retail Mchts. Assn. (pres. divsn. 1982-84), Fishing Bay Yacht Club (Deltaville, Va.). Bankruptcy, General civil litigation, State civil litigation. Office: Krumbein & Assocs 1650 Willow Lawn Dr Ste 300 Richmond VA 23230-3435

KRUMHOLZ, MIMI, human resources administrator; b. N.Y.C., Aug. 7, 1954; d. Jack Walter and Ida Judith (Intrator) Jerome; m. Andrew Jay Krumholz, Aug. 15 1991; children: Matthew, Aaron, Paul. BA in Edn., BS in Psychology, SUNY, 1976; MS in Clin. Psychology, Towson State U., Md., 1982. Paralegal Donovan, Leisure, N.Y.C., 1976-77; human resource mgr. Dynatech Data sys., Springfield, Va, 1977-80; human resource dir. Calif. Milling Corp., L.A., 1980-81, Providence Ctr., Arnold, Md, 1986-88, Dewey, Ballantine, Washington, 1988-90; legal adminstr. Latham & Watkins, 1990—, dir. profl. devel., 1999—, dir. human resources, 2000—. Mem. Assn. Legal Adminstrs, Soc. Human Resources Mgmt., Am. Soc. Training and Devel. Avocations: reading, swimming, writing. Office: Latham & Watkins Ste 1300 1001 Pennsylvania Ave NW Washington DC 20004-2585 E-mail: mimi.krumholz@lw.com

KRUPANSKY, ROBERT BAZIL, federal judge; b. Cleve., Aug. 15, 1921; s. Frank A. and Anna (Lawrence) K.; m. Marjorie Blaser, Nov. 13, 1952. BA, Western Res. U., 1946, LLB, 1948, JD, 1968. Bar: Ohio 1948, Supreme Ct. Ohio 1948, Supreme Ct. U.S 1948, U.S. Dist. Ct. (no. dist.) Ohio 1948, U.S. Ct. Appeals (6th cir.) 1948, U.S. Ct. Customs and Patent Appeals 1948, U.S. Customs Ct. 1948, ICC 1948. Pvt. practice law, Cleve., 1948-52; asst. atty. gen. State of Ohio, 1951-57; mem. Gov. of Ohio cabinet and dir. Ohio Dept. Liquor Control, 1957-58; judge Common Pleas Ct. of Cuyahoga County, 1958-60; sr. ptnr. Metzenbaum, Gaines, Krupansky, Finley & Stern, 1960-69; U.S. atty. U.S. Dist. Ct. (no. dist.) Ohio, Cleve., 1969-70, U.S. dist. judge, 1970-82; judge, now sr. judge U.S. Ct. Appeals (6th cir.), Ohio, 1982—. Spl. counsel Atty. Gen. Ohio, 1964-68; adj. prof. law Case Western Res. U. Sch. Law, 1969-70 2d lt. U.S. Army, pilot USAAC, 1942-46; col. USAF Res. ret. Mem. ABA, Fed. Bar Assn., Ohio Bar Assn., Cleve. Bar Assn., Cuyahoga County Bar Assn., Am. Judicature Soc., Assn. Asst. Attys. Gen. State Ohio. Office: 127 Public Square Rm 5110 Cleveland OH 44114-1201*

KRUPKA, ROBERT GEORGE, lawyer; b. Rochester, N.Y., Oct. 21, 1949; s. Joseph Anton and Marjorie Clara (Meteyer) K.; children: Kristin Nicole, Kerry Melissa. BS, Georgetown U., 1971; JD, U. Chgo., 1974. Bar: Ill. 1974, Colo. 1991, D.C., 1991, Calif. 1998, U.S. Dist. Ct. (no. dist.) Ill. 1974, U.S. Dist. Ct. (ea. dist.) Wis. 1974, U.S. Ct. Appeals (7th cir.) 1976, U.S. Supreme Ct. 1978, U.S. Dist. Ct. (cen. dist.) Ill. 1980, U.S. Dist. Ct. (no. dist.) Calif. 1980, U.S. Dist. Ct. (ctrl. and so. dists.) Calif. 1999, U.S. Ct. Appeals (4th and fed. cirs.) 1982, U.S. Ct. Appeals (6th cir.) 1985, U.S. Ct. Appeals (1st, 2d, 3d, 5th, 8th, 9th, 10th and 11th dists.) 1999. Assoc. Kirkland & Ellis, Chgo., 1974-79, ptnr., 1979—. Author: Infringement Litigation Computer Software and Database, 1984, Computer Software, Semiconductor Design, Video Game and Database Protection and Enforcement, 1984. Mem. bd. trustees Francis W. Parker Sch., 1987-98, pres., 1994-97. Mem. ABA (chmn. sec. com. 1982-88, chmn. div. 1988-90, 98—, coun. 1994-97), Computer Law Assn., U.S. Patent Quar. Adv. Bd., Am. Intellectual Property Law Assn. (chmn. subcom. 1988—), Mid-Am. Club, Chgo. Club. Roman Catholic. Federal civil litigation, Patent, Trademark and copyright. Office: Kirkland & Ellis 200 E Randolph St Fl 54 Chicago IL 60601-6636 E-mail: bob_krupka@kirkland.com

KRUSE, CHARLES THOMAS, lawyer; b. Tulsa, Sept. 26, 1963; s. Joseph Daniel and Judith Sue (Holleman) K.; m. Jennifer Jones, May 20, 1989; 1 child, Charles Thomas Jr. BA, Emory U., 1985; JD, Vanderbilt U., 1989. Bar: Tex. 1989, U.S. Dist. Ct. (so. dist.) Tex. 1990, U.S. Ct. Appeals (5th and 8th cirs.) 1991; bd. cert. civil trial law Tex. Bd. Legal Specialization. Law clk. to Hon. Ricardo H. Hinojosa U.S. Dist. Ct. (so. dist.) Tex., McAllen, Tex., 1989-90; assoc. Fulbright & Jaworski, Houston, 1990-91; ptnr. McDade & Fogler, 1992-95; counsel to ptnr. King & Spalding, 1995-2000; ptnr. Bracewell & Patterson, LLP, 2000—. Contbr. articles and papers to profl. publs. Bobby Jones scholar U. St. Andrews, 1985-86. Fellow Tex. Bar Found., Houston Bar Found.; mem. ABA, Houston Bar Assn., Houston Young Lawyer Assn. Republican. Episcopalian. General civil litigation, FERC practice, Environmental. Home: 10622 S Evers Park Dr Houston TX 77024-5528 Office: Bracewell & Patterson LLP Ste 2900 711 Louisiana St Houston TX 77002 E-mail: tkruse@bracepatt.com

KRUSE, JOHN ALPHONSE, lawyer; b. Detroit, Sept. 11, 1926; s. Frank R. and Ann (Nestor) K.; m. Mary Louise Dalton, July 14, 1951; children: Gerard, Mary Louise, Terence, Kathleen, Joanne, Francis, John, Patrick. BS, U. Detroit, 1950, JD cum laude, 1952. Bar: Mich. bar 1952. Ptnr. Alexander, Buchanan & Conklin, Detroit, 1952-69, Harvey, Kruse, PC, Detroit, 1969—. Guest lectr. U. Mich., U. Detroit, Inst. Continuing Legal Edn.; city atty. Allen Park, Mich., 1954-59; twp. atty., Van Buren Twp., Mich., 1959-61. Co-founder Detroit and Mich. Cath. Radio. Past pres. Palmer Woods Assn.; mem. pres.'s cabinet U. Detroit; mem. product liability adv. coun. Providence Hosp.; bd. dirs. Providence Hosp. Legatus; trustee Ave Maria Coll. Named one of 5 Outstanding Young Men in Mich., 1959, Outstanding Alumnus, U. Detroit Sch. Law, 1989, Humanitarian award Neuromuscular Inst. 1988. Mem. Detroit Bar Assn., State Bar Mich. (past chmn. negligence sect.), Assn. Def. Trial Counsel (bd. dirs. 1966-67), Am. Judicature Soc., Internat. Assn. Def. Counsel, Equestrian Order of the Holy Sepulchre, Cath. Campaign for Am., Gabriel Richard Hist. Soc. (bd. of dirs.) Roman Catholic. Club: Detroit Golf (past pres.). State civil litigation, Insurance, Personal injury. Home: 5569 Hunters Gate Dr Troy MI 48098-2342 Office: 1050 Wilshire Dr Ste 320 Troy MI 48084-1526 E-mail: jkruse@harveykruse.com, johnakruse@home.com

KRUSE, PAMELA JEAN, lawyer; b. Miami, Fla., June 3, 1950; d. Robert Emil and Irma G. Kruse. BS, Mich. State U., 1973, MA, 1975, PhD, 1979; JD, U. Mich., 1985. Bar: Mich. 1986. Grad. asst. Mich. State U., East Lansing, 1976-77, asst. intramural dir., 1977-79, labor rels. rep., 1979-81, asst. dir. labor rels., 1981-82; resident mgr. 719 Oakland, Ann Arbor, Mich., 1982-83; rsch. asst. Law Sch. U. Mich., 1982-85; jud. clk. U.S. Dist. Ct. (we. dist.) Mich., 1985-86; assoc. Clary, Nantz, Wood, Hoffius, Rankin & Cooper, Grand Rapids, Mich., 1986-91; with Village Bike Shops, 1991—. Bd. dirs. Babe Zaharias Golf Tournament, Am. Cancer Soc., 1987-91. Recipient Gold and Silver medals U.S. Pan Am. Team, Winnipeg, Man., Can., 1967, Silver medal U.S. Olympic Team, Mexico City, 1968; holder world records swimming 400 meters freestyle, 1967, 200 meters freestyle, 1967, 440-yard freestyle, 1966; inducted to Greater Fort Lauderdale Sports Hall of Fame, 1979. Mem. ABA, State Bar Mich. (exec. coun. young lawyers sect. 1987-90), Grand Rapids Bar Assn. (chairperson, exec. bd. dirs. young lawyers set. 1987-91), Mich. Pub. Employer Labor Rels. Assn. (bd. dirs. 1981-82, chmn. manual revision com. 1982), Mich. State U. Alumni Assn. (1st v.p., bd. dirs. 1988-89), U.S. Olympians, Phi Delta Kappa, Kappa Alpha Theta. Labor. Office: Village Bike Shop Ltd 450 A Baldwin St Jenison MI 49428

KRUTTER, FORREST NATHAN, lawyer; b. Boston, Dec. 17, 1954; s. Irving and Shirley Krutter. BS in Econs., MS in Civil Engring., MIT, 1976; JD cum laude, Harvard U., 1978. Bar: Nebr. 1978, U.S. Supreme Ct. 1986, N.Y. 1991. Antitrust counsel Union Pacific R.R., Omaha, 1978-86; sr. v.p. law, sec. Berkshire Hathaway Group, 1986—; pres. Republic Ins., Dallas, 2000—. Co-author: Impact of Railroad Abandonments, 1976, Railroad Development in the Third World, 1978; author: Judicial Enforcement of Competition in Regulated Industries, 1979; contbr. articles Creighton Law Rev. Mem. ABA, Phi Beta Kappa, Sigma Xi. Administrative and regulatory, General corporate, Insurance. Office: Berkshire Hathaway Group 4016 Farnam St Omaha NE 68131-3016 E-mail: qedqedfak@aol.com

KRZYZANOWSKI, RICHARD L(UCIEN), lawyer, corporate executive; b. Warsaw, Poland, Mar. 25, 1932; came to U.S., 1967, naturalized, 1972; s. Andrew and Mary K.; children: Suzanne, Peter, Christine. BA, U. Warsaw, 1956; ML, U. Pa., 1960; PhD, U. Paris, 1962. Bar: Pa. With Crown Cork & Seal Co., Inc., Phila., 1967—, dir., exec. v.p. gen. counsel, 1990-2001. Trustee John Paul II Found., Vatican, Rome, Italy; exec. trustee, founder Krzyzanowski Found., Phila. Mem. Int. Bar Assn. (London). General corporate, Private international, Public international. Office: Crown Cork & Seal Co Inc 1 Crown Way Philadelphia PA 19154-4599

KU, ANCHI H. legal assistant; b. Ankara, Turkey, Apr. 12, 1957; came to U.S., 1977; d. Gregory S.L. and Shirley L. Hang; children: Andrew Ku, Amanda Ku. BS, U. Tex., Dallas, 1981; grad., Asian Am. Leadership Conf., Dallas, 1990. Real estate broker Realty World, Richardson, Tex., 1981-83; property mgr. Trammell Crow Co., Dallas, 1985-86; legal asst. Smith, Underwood & Perkins, 1989-95; sr. legal asst. Friedman, Driegert & Hsueh, 1995—. Bd. dirs. Tex. Dept. Human Svcs. Featured interview A World of Difference, Dallas Morning News, 1990. World Cup amb. Dallas Venue, 1994; mem. steering com. Walka Mile in My Shoe, 1993—; mem. adv. coun. Women's Bus. Issues Greater Dallas Chamber, 1994-96; co-chair City of Dallas 14-1 Redistricting Plan, 1990; alt. mem. bd. adjustment, 1990-92; mem. host com. Asian Ams. for Kay Bailey Hutchinson, 1990, 93-94; scheduling co-chair Bartlett mayoral campaign, 1991; asst. campaign dir. Driegert campaign for county Rep. chair, 1992; chair spl. events Rep. Party Dallas County, 1992-93; co-chair Dallas County George W. Bush gubernatorial campaign, 1994; co-chair VIP com. Rep. State Conv., Dallas, 1992; bd. dirs. Dallas Met. YWCA, 1989-92; bd. dirs. Asian Am. C. of C., 1989-94, vice chair, 1991-94. Recipient Pillar of Progress award Dallas Area Rapid Transit, Trinity River Bridge, 1992, Oustanding Cmty. Svc. award West End Pl., Dallas, 1991. Mem. NAFE, Exec. Women in Tex. Govt., Dallas Women Together. Avocations: traveling, photography, community service, politics, children and women's advocacy. Office: Friedman Driegert & Hsueh 8117 Preston Rd Ste 570 Dallas TX 75225-6337

KUBIAK, JON STANLEY, lawyer, auto parts manufacturing company executive; b. Feb. 10, 1935; s. Stanley Michael Kubiak and Sylvia J. Frankowski; m. Mary Ann Rys, May 4, 1963 (dec. 1974); children: Karen Michelle, Kristin Jill; m. Elaine Michaelis, Feb. 26, 1977; 1 child, Mark Stanley. BS in Acctg. cum laude, U. Notre Dame, 1957; JD, 1960. Bar: Ill. 1960, Va. 1995, Mich. 2000, U.S. Dist Ct. (no. dist.) Ill. 1960, U.S. Ct. Appeals (7th cir.) 1961. Budget examiner Chgo. City Coun., 1960; asst. corp. counsel City of Chgo., 1960-61; asst. atty. gen. Ill. State Tollway Commn., Oak Brook, 1961-66; asst. sec. and corp. atty. Maremont Corp., Chgo., 1966-72; sec. and asst. gen. counsel, 1972-78; sec. and gen. counsel, 1979-86; v.p., sec. gen. counsel, dir. Prestolite Electric Inc., Toledo,

1986-94; v.p., gen. counsel The Christian Broadcasting Network, Inc., Va. Beach, 1994-98, Pacific Media Corp., Va. Beach, 1994-98; gen. counsel Freedom Ministries, 2000—, Religious Heritage Am. Found., 2000—. Dir. Starguide Digital Networks, Inc., Reno Nev., Corporate Computer Syss., Inc., Holmdel, N.J., Founders Village, Inc., Chesapeake, Va., Ohmite Mfg. Co., Inc., Skokie, Ill. Sec. 28th Ward Regular Democratic Orgn., Chgo., 1960-68, Freedom Ministries Am., Traverse City, Mich.; vice chmn. Young Dems. Cook County, 1963-67; chmn. 7th Congl. Dist. Young Dems. Ill., 1963-67. Mem. ABA, Ill. State Bar Assn., Va. State Bar Assn., Am. Corp. Counsel Assn. Roman Catholic. Club: Notre Dame of Chgo. (bd. govs. 1977-80). Antitrust, General corporate, Securities. Home: 10021 E San Reno Blvd Traverse City MI 49684 Office: The Christian Broadcasting Network Inc 442 E Front St Traverse City MI 49686

KUBIDA, WILLIAM JOSEPH, lawyer; b. Newark, Apr. 3, 1949; s. William and Catherine (Gilchrist) K.; m. Mary Jane Hamilton, Feb. 4, 1984; children: Sara Gilchrist, Kathleen Hamilton. BSEE, USAF Acad., 1971; JD, Wake Forest U., 1979. Bar: N.C. 1979, U.S. Patent Office 1979, Ind. 1980, U.S. Dist. Ct. (no. dist.) Ind. 1980, U.S. Dist. Ct. (so. dist.) Ind. 1980, U.S. Ct. Appeals (7th cir.) 1981, U.S. Dist. Ct. Ariz. 1982, U.S. Ct. Appeals (9th and fed. cirs.) 1982, Ariz. 1982, Colo. 1990, U.S. Dist. Ct. Colo. 1990, U.S. Ct. Appeals (10th cir.) 1990. Patent and trademark atty. Lundy and Assocs., Ft. Wayne, Ind., 1979-81; patent atty. Motorola, Inc., Phoenix, 1981-85; intellectual property counsel Nippon Motorola, Ltd., Tokyo, 1985-87; ptnr. Lisa & Kubida, Phoenix, 1987-89; engring. law counsel Digital Equipment Corp., Colorado Springs, Colo., 1989-92; of counsel Holland & Hart, Denver, Colorado Springs, 1992-93, ptnr., chmn. intellectual property practice group, 1993-99; ptnr., chmn. patient practice group Hogan & Hartson LLP, Colorado Springs, 1999—. Bd. dirs. Colorado Springs Tech Incubator, 1st lt. USAF, 1971-76. Mem. Am. Intellectual Property Law Assn. (computer software sect.), Japan Am. Soc. Colo. (bd. dirs.), Licensing Exec. Soc. (Pacific Rim subcom.), Country Club Colo., Mensa, Intertel, Phi Delta Phi. Republican. Presbyterian. Computer, Patent, Trademark and copyright. Home: 4165 Regency Dr Colorado Springs CO 80906-4368

KUBY, RONALD LAWRENCE, lawyer; b. Cleve., July 31, 1956; s. Donald Joseph Kuby and Ruth Miller; m. Marilyn Vasta; 1 child, Emma Sojourner. BA, U. Kans., 1979; JD magna cum laude, Cornell U., 1983. Bar: N.Y. 1984. Assoc. Kunstler & Kuby, N.Y.C., 1994-95, Law Office William M. Kunstler, N.Y.C., 1984-94; ptnr. Law Office Ronald L. Kuby, 1996—. Contbr. articles to profl. jours. Mem. adv. bd. police misconduct task force N.Y. Civil Liberties Union, 1999—. Recipient Thurgood Marshall award N.Y. City Bar Assn., 1998. Communist. Office: 740 Broadway Fl 5 New York NY 10003-9518 E-mail: ronkuby@aol.com

KUCZWARA, THOMAS PAUL, postal inspector, lawyer; b. Dec. 21, 1951; s. Stanley Leo and Eleanore (Pawelko) K.; m. Diana Lynn Rychtarczyk, Sept. 8, 1979; 1 child, Paul Stanley. BA, Loyola U., Chgo., 1973; JD, U. S.C., 1976. Bar: Ill. 1976, U.S. Dist. Ct. (no. dist.) Ill. 1982. Assoc. Doria Law Offices, Chgo., 1977-78; asst. corp. counsel City of Chgo., 1978-80; asst. city atty. City of Aurora, Ill., 1980-82; postal insp. U.S. Postal Inspection Svc., Salt Lake City, 1982-85, regional insp. atty. cen. region Chgo., 1985—. Mem. St. Bartholomew's Parish Coun., Chgo., 1978; vol. atty. Lawyers for Creative Arts, 1978. Ill. state scholar, 1969. Mem. Sierra Club, Pi Sigma Alpha. Roman Catholic. Office: US Postal Inspection Svc Ops Support Group 222 S Riverside Plz # 1250 Chicago IL 60606-6100 E-mail: tpkuczwara@uspis.gov

KUDRAVETZ, DAVID WALLER, lawyer; b. Sumter, S.C., Feb. 2, 1948; s. George and Barbara (Waller) K.; m. Eleanor McCrea Snyder, June 21, 1969; 1 child, Julia McCrea. BS, U. Va., 1971, JD, 1974. Bar: Va. 1974, U.S. Tax Ct. 1974; CPA, Va. Assoc. Robert M. Musselman, Charlottesville, Va., 1974; ptnr. Carwile & Kudravetz, 1975-78, McClure, Callaghan & McCallum, Charlottesville, 1979-81, McCallum & Kudravetz, P.C., Charlottesville, 1982—. Instr. fed. income taxation U. of Va. Sch. Continuing Edn., 1975-79. Mem. AICPA, Va. State Bar Assn., Charlottesville-Albemarle Bar Assn., Am. Assn. Atty.-CPAs, Va. Soc. CPAs. Estate planning, Real property, Personal income taxation. Office: McCallum & Kudravetz PC 250 E High St Charlottesville VA 22902-5178 E-mail: DWK@MKPC.com

KUEHN, GEORGE E. lawyer, former beverage company executive; b. N.Y.C., June 19, 1946; m. Mary Kuehn; children: Kristin, Rob, Geoff. BBA, U. Mich., 1968, JD, 1973. Bar: Mich. 1974. Assoc. Hill, Lewis et al, Detroit, 1974-78; ptnr. Butzel, Long et al, 1978-81; exec. v.p., gen. counsel, sec. The Stroh Brewery Co., 1981-99—; shareholder Butzel Long, 2000—. With U.S. Army, 1969-71. General corporate. Office: Butzel Long Ste 900 150 W Jefferson Ave Detroit MI 48226 E-mail: Kuehn@butzel.com

KUELTHAU, PAUL STAUFFER, lawyer; b. West Bend, Wis., Mar. 31, 1912; s. George Herman and Marie Louise (Rix) K.; m. Laura Parish, Aug. 16, 1937; children: Karen Allan, Marline Holmes. AB, U. Wis., 1934, JD, 1936. Bar: Wis. 1936, U.S. Ct. Appeals (10th cir.) 1941, U.S. Ct. Appeals (7th cir.) 1947, Mo. 1953, U.S. Dist. Ct. (ea. dist.) Mo. 1954, U.S. Ct. Appeals (8th cir.) 1962, U.S. Dist. Ct. (so. dist.) Ill. 1964, U.S. Supreme Ct. 1973, U.S. Ct. Appeals (D.C. cir.) 1974. Regional atty. NLRB, various locations, 1939-46, chief counsel to chmn. Washington, 1946-53; assoc. Lewis, Rice, Tucker, Allen & Chubb, St. Louis, 1953-62; ptnr. Moller, Talent, Kuelthau, & Welch, 1962-88. Contbr. articles to profl. jours. Mem. ABA, Mo. Bar Assn., Bar Assn. St. Louis, Indsl. Relations Research Assn. Presbyterian. Labor. Home: 3 Rehabilitation Way Apt 417 Woburn MA 01801-6025

KUH, RICHARD HENRY, lawyer; b. N.Y.C., Apr. 27, 1921; s. Joseph Hellmann and Fannie Mina (Rees) K.; m. Joyce Dattel, July 31, 1966; children: Michael Joseph, Jody Ellen. BA, Columbia Coll., 1941; LLB magna cum laude, Harvard U., 1948. Bar: N.Y. 1948, U.S. Dist. Ct. (so. dist.) N.Y. 1948, U.S. Dist. Ct. (ea. dist.) N.Y. 1967, U.S. Supreme Ct. 1968. Assoc. firm Cahill, Gordon & Reindel, 1948-53; asst. dist. atty. N.Y. County Dist. Attys. Office, 1953-64, dist. atty., 1974; pvt. practice law N.Y.C., 1966-71; ptnr. firm Kuh, Goldman, Cooperman & Levitt, 1971-73, Kuh, Shapiro, Goldman, Cooperman & Levitt, P.C., N.Y.C., 1975-78, Warshaw Burstein Cohen Schlesinger & Kuh, N.Y.C., 1978—. Adj. prof. NYU Law Sch. Author: Foolish Figleaves, 1967; mem. bd. editors: Harvard Law Rev, 1947-48; mem. adv. bd.: Contemporary Drug Problems, 1975— , Criminal Law Bull, 1976— ; contbr. articles to popular and profl. jours. Trustee Temple Israel, N.Y.C., 1975-84, Grace Ch. Sch., 1981-85. With U.S. Army, 1942-45, ETO. Walter E. Meyer Research and Writing grantee, 1964-65 Mem. ABA (chair criminal justice sect. 1983-84, chair spl. com. on evaluation jud. performance 1983-90, ho. dels. 1988-93, mem. jud. evaluation adv. com. Nat. Ctr. State Cts. 1990-91, chair 1st nat. conf. gun violence 1994), Assn. Bar City N.Y., Am. Bar Found., Harvard Law Sch. Assn. N.Y. (trustee 1989-92), Harvard Club (mem. admissions com. 1998-01), Phi Beta Kappa. Democrat. Jewish. Federal civil litigation, State civil litigation, Criminal. Home: 14 Washington Pl New York NY 10003-6609 Office: 555 5th Ave New York NY 10017-2416

KUHL, PAUL BEACH, lawyer; b. Elizabeth, N.J., July 15, 1935; s. Paul Edmund and Charlotte (Hetche) K.; m. Janey Mae Stadheim, June 24, 1967; children: Alison Lyn, Todd Beach. BA, Cornell U., 1957; LLB, Stanford U., 1960. Assoc. Law Offices of Walter C. Kohn, San Francisco, 1961-63, Sedgwick, Detert, Moran & Arnold, San Francisco, 1963-73, ptnr., 1973-99, of counsel, 2000—. Pro tem judge, arbitrator San Francisco Superior Ct., 1989—. Served to lt. USCG, 1961. Mem. ABA, Am. Coll. Trial Lawyers, Am. Bd. Trial Advocates, Def. Rsch. Inst., No. Calif. Assn. Def., Am. Arbitration Assn. (mem. arbitration panel), Mediation Soc., Tahoe Tavern Property Owners Assn. (sec. 1979-81, pres. 1981-83), Lagunitas Country Club (v.p. 1995-97). Avocations: tennis, reading. General civil litigation, Insurance, Personal injury. Home: PO Box 1434 Ross CA 94957-1434 Office: Sedgwick Detert Moran & Arnold 1 Embarcadero Ctr Ste 1600 San Francisco CA 94111-3716 E-mail: beachp.kuhl@sdma.com

KUHLMAN, RICHARD SHERWIN, lawyer, author; b. Chgo., Sept. 4, 1943; s. Milton and Florence (Rosenthal) K.; m. Wendy Sue Kremin, Aug. 13, 1971; children: Andrew Michael, Matthew Foster. BA, U. Ill., 1965; JD, Northwestern U., 1968. Bar: Ill. 1969, U.S. Dist. Ct. (no. dist.) Ill. 1969, U.S. Ct. Appeals (7th cir.) 1969. Former ptnr. Foss, Schuman, Drako & Barnard, Chgo., Gottlieb, Schwartz, Chgo.; with Kuhlman, Perlman, Chgo.; panel atty. fed. defender program U.S. Dist. Ct. (no. dist.) Ill., Chgo. 1969—. Contbr. Real Estate Litigation Handbook, Ill. Inst. for Continuing Legal Education, 1975, articles to profl. jours, bulls., and mags; author: Killer Roads from Crash to Verdict, 1985, Jury Trial, Progress and Democracy, 1981, Killer Roads, 1986, Safe Places, 1989; editor, prin. author: Transportation Negligence, 1981, 4th edition 1986. Chmn. Anti-Defamation League Appeal, Chgo., 1976-77; mem. Leadership Council for Met. Open Communities, 1979. Mem. Ill. State Bar Assn., ABA (TIPS sect., chmn., speaker Nat. Teaching Inst. on Transp. Nelligence 1985-86, chmn. automobile law com. 1986-87), ATLA, Ill. Inst. Continuing Legal Edn. Federal civil litigation, State civil litigation. Office: Kuhlman & Perlman 1 N La Salle St Chicago IL 60602-3902

KUHLMANN, FRED MARK, lawyer, business executive; b. St. Louis, Apr. 9, 1948; s. Frederick Louis and Mildred (Southworth) K.; m. Barbara Jane Nierman, Dec. 30, 1970; children: F. Matthew, Sarah Ann. AB summa cum laude, Washington U., St. Louis, 1970; JD cum laude, Harvard U., 1973. Bar: Mo. 1973. Assoc. atty. Stolar, Heitzmann & Eder, St. Louis, 1973-75; tax counsel McDonnell Douglas Corp., 1975-82, corp. asst. sec., 1977-88, corp. counsel fin. matters, 1982-87, assoc. gen. counsel, 1984-87, staff v.p., 1985-87; exec. v.p. McDonnell Douglas Health Systems Co. div. McDonnell Douglas Corp., Hazelwood, Mo., 1987-88, pres., 1988-89, McDonnell Douglas Systems Integration Co. div. McDonnell Douglas Corp., Hazelwood, 1989-91; v.p., gen. counsel, sec. McDonnell Douglas Corp., St. Louis, 1991-92, sr. v.p. adminstrn., gen. counsel, sec., 1992-95, sr. v.p., gen. counsel, 1995-97; of counsel Bryan Cave, 1997-98; pres. Sys. Svc. Enterprises, 1998—. Bd. dirs. Republic Health Corp., Dallas, 1988-90; mem. governing bd. Luth. Med. Ctr., 1989-95, chmn., 1990-92. Bd. dirs. Luth. Charities Assn., 1982-91, sec. 1984-86, chmn. 1986-89; elder Lutheran Ch. of Resurrection, 1977-80; mem. Regents Coun. Concordia Sem., 1981-84; chmn. cub scout pack 459 Boy Scouts Am., 1984-86; bd. dirs. Luth. High Sch. Assn., 1978-84, 91-97, pres. 1992-97, long range planning com. 1990-92, chmn. alumni assn. 1981; chmn. north star dist. Boy Scouts Am., 1990-93; bd. dirs. Mcpl. Theatre Assn., St. Louis, 1991—; chmn. long range planning com. St. Paul's Luth. Ch., 1988-91, 98-2001, pres., 1996-97; bd. dirs., mem. exec. com. United Way of Greater St. Louis, 1994-97, chmn. Vanguard divsn., 1994-97; mem. amb. coun. Luth. Family and Children's Svcs. of St. Louis, 1998—; bd. dirs. Luth. Charities Found., 1998—; mem. adv. bd. Webster U. Bus. and Tech. Sch., 1999—; mem. bd mgrs. worker benefit plans Luth Ch.-Mo. Synod, 2001—. Recipient Disting. Leadership award Luth. Assn. for Higher Edn., 1981. Mem. ABA, Mo. Bar Assn., Bar Assn. Met. St. Louis, Bellerive Country Club, Phi Beta Kappa, Omicron Delta Kappa. Republican. Avocations: tennis, golf, racquetball. Home: 1711 Stone Ridge Trails Dr Saint Louis MO 63122-3546 Office: Sys Svc Enterprises 77 Westport Plz Ste 500 Saint Louis MO 63146-3126 E-mail: fmkuhlmann@sseinc.com

KUHN, BRIAN LAWRENCE, lawyer; b. Memphis, Feb. 16, 1948; s. Edward William and Mattie (Mahaffey) K.; m. Nancy Brandenburg, June 17, 1970; children: Matthew Lawrence, Andrew Ryan, Anthony Mitchell. BSBA, U. Tenn., 1971, JD, 1974. Bar: Tenn. 1974, U.S. Dist. Ct. (we. dist.) Tenn. 1974. Asst. county atty. Shelby County, Memphis, 1974-81; ptnr. Kuhn, Kuhn & Kuhn, 1980-82; county atty. Shelby County, 1982-94; sr. counsel Ford & Harrison LLP, 1998—. Chief adminstrv. officer, 1981. Bd. dirs. Boys' Clubs of Memphis, 1983—; chmn. bd. trustees, Raleigh United Meth. Ch., Memphis, 1982; parliamentarian, legal adviser, Shelby County Charter Commn., 1984. Mem. ABA, Memphis and Shelby County Bar Assn. (law libr. commn. 1982-92), Tenn. Bar Assn., Kiwanis of La.-Miss.-Tenn. (pres. Memphis, lt. gov., dist. chmn. 1976-80). Office: Ford & Harrison LLP 6750 Poplar Ave Ste 600 Memphis TN 38138 E-mail: bkuhn@fordharrison.com

KUHN, JAMES E. judge; b. Hammond, La., Oct. 31, 1946; s. Eton Percy and Mildred Louise (McDaniel) K.; m. Cheryl Aucoin, Dec. 27, 1969; children: James M., Jennifer L. BA, Southeastern La. U., 1968; JD, Loyola U. of South, 1973. Bar: La. 1973, Colo. 1995, U.S. Supreme Ct. 1978. Asst. dist. atty. 21st Jud. Dist., La., 1980-90, judge, 1990-95, Ct. Appeals (1st cir.), Baton Rouge, 1995—. Instr. history, and polit. sci. Southeastern La. U., Hammond, 1991—; past mem. appellate ct. performance and standards com. La. Supreme Ct.; lectr. in field. Founder For Our Youth; past bd. dirs. La. Coun. Child Abuse, past sec.-treas. Conf. of Ct. Appeal Judges for State of La. Recipient Am. Jurisprudence award Loyola Law Sch. Mem. ABA, La. State Bar Assn. (Professionalism and Quality of Life com.), 21st Jud. Bar Assn., Livingston Parish Bar Assn., Delta Theta Phi. Home: 253 W Oak St Ponchatoula LA 70454-3330

KUHN, VIRGINIA R. lawyer; b. Neillsville, Wis., July 29, 1963; d. Bernard Herman and Ruby Violet K.; m. Michael Joseph Schlecht, Aug. 28, 1993. BA, U. Wis., 1985; JD, Hamline U., 1989. Bar: Minn. 1990. Reference atty. West Pub., St. Paul, 1990-91; atty. advisor Office of Hearings and Appeals, Mpls., 1991-95, sr. atty., 1995—. Lectr. Hennepin C.C., Mpls., 1993-98; coach mock trial team Hamline U., St. Paul, 1998; vol. atty. Legal Aid Svc., St. Paul, 1991-92. Vol. Salvation Army, Mpls., 1995—; bd. dirs. Minn. Stroke Assn., 1999; mentor Homework N'Hoops, Mpls., 1999. Mem. Minn. State Bar Assn., Hennepin County Bar Assn. Democrat. Avocations: reading, skiing, mountain biking, rollerblading. Office: Office of Hearings & Appeals 330 2nd Ave S Ste 650 Minneapolis MN 55401-2225

KUHRAU, EDWARD W. lawyer; b. Caney, Kans., Apr. 19, 1935; s. Edward and Dolores (Hardman) K.; m. Janiece Christal (div. 1983); children: quentin, Clayton; m. Sandy Shreve. BA, U. Tex., 1960; JD, U. So. Calif., 1965. Bar: Calif. 1966, Wash. 1968, Alaska 1977. With Perkins Coie (and predecessor firms), Seattle, 1968—, ptnr., 1973—. Editor-in-chief Wash. Real Property Deskbook; contbr. articles to profl. jours. With USAF, 1955-58. Mem. ABA, Wash. Bar Assn., Am. Coll. Real Estate Lawyers, Pacific Real Estate Inst. (pres., founding trustee), Order of Coif, Seattle Yacht Club, Wing Point Golf and Country Club, Poulsbo Yacht Club. Banking, Finance, Real property. Office: Perkins Coie 1201 3rd Ave Fl 40 Seattle WA 98101-3029 E-mail: kuhre@perkinscoie.com

KUKER, ALAN MICHAEL, lawyer; b. Neptune, N.J., Oct. 7, 1942; s. Max Irving and Ruth (Lewis) K.; m. Belen Castillo. BA, Rutgers U., 1964; JD, Boston U., 1967. Bar: Fla. 1968, U.S. Dist. Ct. (so. dist.) Fla. 1968, U.S. Ct. Appeals (5th cir.) 1968, U.S. Supreme Ct., 1980. With Legal Svcs., South Fla., 1968-72; pvt. practice Miami, Fla., 1973. Contbr. articles to profl. jours. Mem. Fla. Bar Assn., Dade County Bar Assn., Miami Beach Bar Assn. Office: Office of Judge of Compensation Cliams State of Fla 401 NW 2nd Ave 5-321 Miami FL 33128-1740 E-mail: alankuker@hotmail.com

KUKLIN, ANTHONY BENNETT, lawyer; b. N.Y.C., Oct. 9, 1929; s. Norman B. and Deane (Cable) K.; m. Vivienne May Hall, Apr. 4, 1964; children: Melissa, Amanda. AB, Harvard U., 1950; JD, Columbia U., 1953. Bar: N.Y. 1953, D.C. 1970. Assoc. Dwight, Royall, Harris, Koegel & Caskey, N.Y.C., 1955-61, Paul, Weiss, Rifkind, Wharton & Garrison, N.Y.C., 1961-69, ptnr., 1969-95, counsel, 1995—. Lectr. in Law, Columbia Law Sch., 1997—; bd. dirs. Chgo. Title & Trust Co., Chgo. Title Ins. Co., 1986-96. Contbr. articles to legal jours. Mem. ABA (chmn., sec. real property, probate and trust law 1987-88), Internat. Bar Assn. (chmn. div. one 1985-88), N.Y. State Bar Assn. (chmn. sect. real property 1981-82), Assn. of Bar of city of N.Y., Am. Coll. Real Estate Lawyers (pres. 1981-82), Anglo-Am. Real Property Inst. (chmn. 1989), Am. Coll. Constrn. Lawyers. Real property. Home: 22 Pryer Ln Larchmont NY 10538-4022 Office: Paul Weiss Rifkind Wharton & Garrison Ste # 4200 1285 Ave of Ams Fl 22 New York NY 10019-6065

KUKLIN, SUSAN BEVERLY, law librarian, lawyer; b. Chgo., Nov. 25, 1947; d. Albert and Marion (Goodman) K. BA in English and History with honors, U. Ariz., 1969, JD, 1973; MLS, Ind. U., 1970; LLM in Taxation, DePaul U., 1981. Bar: Ariz. 1973, Ill. 1980, Calif. 1984, U.S. Dist. Ct. (no. dist.) Ill. 1980. Asst. city atty. City of Phoenix, 1974-75; dep. county atty. County of Pima, Ariz., 1975-76; polit. sci., law libr. asst. prof. law No. Ill. U., 1976-78; law libr., assoc. prof. U. S.D., 1978-79; dir. law libr., asst. prof. DePaul U., 1979-83; law libr. Santa Clara County, San Jose, Calif., 1983—. Sec. bd. trustees Law Library Santa Clara County. Mem. Am. Assn. Law Libr. (cert. law libr.), Coun. Calif. County Law Libr. (newsletter editor 1983-84), No. Calif. Assn. Law Libr., Phi Beta Kappa, Phi Kappa Phi, Alpha Lambda Delta, Phi Alpha Theta, Phi Delta Phi. Office: Santa Clara County Law Library 360 N 1st St San Jose CA 95113-1004

KULESZA, JOSEPH DOMINICK, JR. lawyer; b. Wilmington, Del., Oct. 18, 1961; s. Joseph Dominick Sr. and Mary Ann (Newell) K.; m. Linda Ann George, July 26, 1986; children: Joseph Dominick III, Thomas D. BA, St. Joseph's U., 1983; paralegal cert., U. Del., 1985; JD, Widener U., 1987. Bar: Del. 1987. Jud. intern Justice of Peace Cts., Wilmington, 1978, law clk., 1983; paralegal Jacobs and Crumplar P.A., 1984-86; asst. supr. Bank of N.Y. (Del.), Newark, 1985-87; pvt. practice Wilmington, 1987—. Mem. ABA, Del. Bar Assn., Del. Trial Lawyers Assn., Delta Theta Phi Democrat. Roman Catholic. Avocations: golf, racquetball, swimming. General civil litigation, Family and matrimonial, General practice. Office: Agostini Levitsky Isaacs & Kulesza 824 N Market St Wilmington DE 19801-3024

KULONGOSKI, THEODORE RALPH, former state supreme court justice; b. Nov. 5, 1940; married; 3 children. BA, U. Mo., 1967, JD, 1970. Bar: Oreg., Mo., U.S. Dist. Ct. Oreg., U.S. Ct. Appeals (9th cir.). Legal counsel Oreg. State Ho. of Reps., 1973-74; founding and sr. ptnr. Kulongoski, Durham, Drummonds & Colombo, Oreg., 1974-87; deputy dist. atty. Mulnomah County, 1992—; atty. gen. State of Oreg., 1993-97; justice Oreg. Supreme Ct., 1997—2001. State rep. Lane County (Oreg.), 1974-77, state senator, 1977-83; chmn. Juvenile Justice Task Force, 1994, Gov.'s Commn. Organized Crime; mem. Criminal Justice Coun.; exec. dir. Met. Family Svc., 1992; dir. Oreg. Dept. Ins. and Fin., 1987-91. Mem. Oreg State Bar Assn., Mo. Bar Assn. E-mail: moberstWhevanet.com. Office: Oreg Supreme Ct PO Box 399 Portland OR 97207

KUMBLE, STEVEN JAY, lawyer; b. July 3, 1933; m. Barbara Kumble (div.); children: Charles Todd, Roger Glenn; m. Peggy Basten Vandervoort. BA, Yale U., 1954; JD, Harvard U., 1959; LLD (hon.), L.I. U., 1990. Bar: N.Y. 1960. Ptnr. Finley, Kumble, Wagner, Underberg, Manley & Casey, N.Y.C., 1968-87; of counsel Summit Rovins & Feldesman, 1988-90; chmn. bd. dirs. Lincolnshire Mgmt., Inc., 1985—. Vice chmn. bd. dirs. L.I. U., Greenvale, N.Y., 1984—, chm., 1982-94; trustee bd. Gov.'s Com. on Scholastic Achievement, N.Y.C., 1981—; mem. adv. bd. Inst. Civil Justice, Rand, 1999—. 1st lt. U.S. Army, 1955-57. Mem. Assn. of Bar of City of N.Y., Phi Beta Kappa, Yale Club. Avocations: skiing, golf. General corporate, Real property. Office: Lincolnshire Mgmt 780 3d Ave 40th Fl New York NY 10017-2024

KUNIYUKI, KEN TAKAHARU, lawyer; b. Honolulu, Nov. 30, 1947; s. Henry Seiya and Emi (Takami) K.; m. Noreen Kanai, Aug. 20, 1971; children: Patricia Satchie, Karen Cheimi. BA, U. Hawaii, 1969, MA, 1970; JD, U. Calif., Berkeley, 1973. Bar: Hawaii 1973, U.S. Dist. Ct. Hawaii 1973, U.S. Ct. Appeals (9th cir.) 1976. Assoc. David Schutter, Honolulu, 1973-74; ptnr. Turk & Kuniyuki, Honolulu, 1974-77, Kuniyuki & Pang, Honolulu, 1978-80; pvt. practice, Honolulu, 1980-81; ptnr. Kuniyuki & Chang, Honolulu, 1981—; arbitrator Hawaii Med. Claims Panel, Honolulu, 1979—, Ct. Annexed Arbitration, Circut Ct. 1st Cir., 1986—. Bd. dirs. ACLU, Hawaii, 1978-80, chmn. litigation com., 1978-81. Mem. Am. Arbitration Assn., Hawaii Chess Fedn. (pres. 1982-83). State civil litigation, Criminal, Personal injury. Office: Kuniyuki & Chang 900 Fort St Suite 310 Honolulu HI 96813

KUNKLE, WILLIAM JOSEPH, JR. lawyer; b. Lakewood, Ohio, Sept. 3, 1941; s. William Joseph and Georgia (Howe) K.; m. Sarah Florence Nesti, July 11, 1964; children: Kathleen Margaret, Susan Mary. BA, Northwestern U., Evanston, Ill., 1963; Jd, Northwestern U., 1969. Bar: Ohio 1969, U.S. Dist. Ct. (no. dist.) Ill. 1969, Ill. 1969, U.S. Ct. Appeals (7th cir.) 1991, U.S. Supreme Ct. 1991. Process control engr. Union Carbide Corp., Cleve., 1964-65, prodn. supr. Greenville, S.C., 1965-66; assoc. Hauxhurst, Sharp, Mollison & Gallagher, Cleve., 1969-70; asst. pub. defender Cook County Pub. Defender, Chgo., 1970-73; asst. states atty. Cook County States Atty., 1973-85; ptnr. Phelan, Cahill & Quinlan, Ltd., 1985-96, Cahill, Christian & Kunkle, LTD., Chgo., 1996—. Chmn. The Ill. Gaming Bd., 1990-93; dep. spl. outside counsel U.S. Ho. Reps., Washington, 1988-89; adj. prof. I.I.T. Chgo. Kent Sch. Law, 1980-84; instr. Nat. Inst. for Trial Advocacy, Chgo., 1978-82, 86; lectr. Nat. Coll. Dist. Attys., Houston, Denver, Chgo., Atlanta, Louisville, 1978-85, Nat. Law Enforcement Inst., San Francisco, Portland, Atlanta, Pitts., Boston, St. Louis, Chgo., 1983-85; 1st asst. states atty. of Cook County, 1983-85; spl. state's atty. 18th Jud. Cir., DuPage County, 1995-99. Contbg. author: Punishment Prosecutor's Viewpoint, 1983, 1989, Trial Techniques Compendium, Nat. College of Dist. Attys. (2d, 3rd, 4th, 5th, 6th eds.). Recipient Disting. Faculty award Nat. Coll. Dist. Attys., 1980, Award for Prosecution Svc. Chgo. Assn. Commerce & Industry, 1981. Fellow Am. Coll. Trial Lawyers, ABA; mem. Internat. Soc. Barristers, Nat. Dist. Attys. Assn. (bd. dirs. 1984-85), Assn. Govt. Attys. in Capital Litigation (pres. 1983-84), Chgo. Bar Assn. (bd. mgrs. 1983-84), Ill. State Bar Assn. (LAWPAC trustee 1989-95), Internat. Assn. Gaming Attys., Chgo. Crime Commn. (bd. dirs.). Republican. Avocations: golf, softball, carpentry, motorcycling. General civil litigation, Criminal, Personal injury. Office: Cahill Christian & Kunkle Ltd 224 S Michigan Ave Ste 1300 Chicago IL 60604-2583

KUNTZ, CHARLES POWERS, lawyer; b. L.A., May 7, 1944; s. Walter Nichols and Katherine (Powers) K.; m. June Emerson Moroney, Dec. 23, 1969; children: Michael Nicholas, Robinson Moroney, Katie Moroney. AB with honors, Stanford U., 1966, JD, 1969; LLM, NYU, 1971. Bar: Calif. 1970, N.Y. 1970, U.S. Dist. Ct. (no. dist.) Calif. 1970, U.S. Ct. Appeals (9th cir.) 1970, U.S. Supreme Ct. 1979. Staff atty. project for urban affairs Office Econ. Opportunity, N.Y.C., 1969-71; dep. pub. defender Contra Costa County Pub. Defender's Office, Martinez, Calif., 1971-75; assoc. Treuhaft, Walker & Brown, Oakland, 1976-78; ptnr. Hirsch & Kuntz, San Rafael, 1979-85; pvt. practice, 1985-89; ptnr. Coombs & Dunlap, Napa, Calif., 1989—. Mem. ABA, Calif. Attys. Consumer Justice, Napa County Bar Assn. General civil litigation, Insurance, Personal injury. Home: 48 Wild Rye Way Napa CA 94558-7014 Office: Coombs & Dunlap 1211 Division St Napa CA 94559-3372 E-mail: ckuntz@coombslaw.com

KUNTZ, JOEL DUBOIS, lawyer; b. Dennis, Mass., Feb. 5, 1946; s. Paul Grimley Kuntz and Harriette (Hunter) Ainsworth; m. Karan Judd, June 29, 1968; children: Matthew Christopher, Kristin Lara. BA, Haverford Coll., 1968; JD, Yale U., 1971; LLM in Taxation, NYU, 1980. Bar: Conn. 1972, Oreg. 1974. Assoc. Stoel, Rives, Boley, Jones & Grey, Portland, Oreg., 1974-79, ptnr., 1979-94; v.p., gen. counsel Entek Internat. LLC, Lebanon, 1994—. Co-author: (with James S. Eustice) Federal Income Taxation of S Corporations, 1982, 3d edit., 1993; (with James S. Eustice, Charles S. Lewis III and Thomas P. Deering) Tax Reform Act of 1986: Analysis and Commentary, 1987; (with Robert J. Peroni) U.S. International Taxation, 1992. Capt. USMC, 1971-74. Mem. Am. Coll. Tax Counsel, Internat. Fiscal Assn. Democrat. General corporate, Corporate taxation, Personal income taxation. Home: 3910 Lakeview Blvd Lake Oswego OR 97035-5549 Address: PO Box 39 Lebanon OR 97355-0039 E-mail: jdkuntz@attglobal.net

KUNTZ, LEE ALLAN, lawyer; b. Nashville, July 9, 1943; s. Irwin and Lucy (Kornman) K.; 1 child, Douglas. BA, Duke U., 1965; LLB, Columbia U., 1968. Bar: N.Y. 1968, U.S. Dist. Ct. (so. dist.) N.Y. 1973, U.S. Tax Ct. 1973. Assoc. Shearman & Sterling, N.Y.C., 1968-76, ptnr., 1976—, mng. ptnr., 1994-98, sr. ptnr. Real Estate Group, 1988-93. Mem. policy com. Shearman and Sterling, 1991-99. Contbr. articles to profl. jours. Bd. visitors Columbia Law Sch., 1998—; dir. Vols. Legal Svcs., 2000—. Mem. ABA, Assn. Bar City N.Y. Real property. Office: Shearman & Sterling 599 Lexington Ave Fl C2 New York NY 10022-6069

KUNTZ, WILLIAM FRANCIS, II, lawyer, educator; b. N.Y.C., June 24, 1950; s. William Francis I and Margaret Evelyn (Brown) K.; m. Alice Beal, May 20, 1978; children: William Thaddeus, Katharine Lowell, Elizabeth Anne. AB, Harvard U., 1972, AM, 1974, JD, 1977, PhD, 1979. Bar: N.Y. 1978. Assoc. Shearman & Sterling, N.Y.C., 1978-86; mem. Milgrim, Thomajan & Lee, 1986-94; ptnr. Seward & Kissel, 1994-2001, The Torys Law Firm, 2001—. Assoc. prof. Bklyn. Law Sch., 1987—. Author: Criminal Sentencing, 1988. Bd. dirs. MFY Legal Svcs., Inc., N.Y.C., 1984-90, Boys Brotherhood Republic, N.Y.C., 1986-90, Habitat for Humanity, N.Y.C., 1987-90; chmn. Resources for Children with Spl. Needs, N.Y.C., 1986-89; mem. N.Y. Civilian Complaint Rev. Bd., 1987—, chmn., 1994. Mem. ABA, N.Y. State Bar Assn., N.Y. County Lawyers Assn. (bd. dirs. 1991-96), Assn. of Bar of City of N.Y. (chmn. mcpl. affairs com. 1992-95, judiciary com.), Bklyn. Bar Assn. (judiciary com. 1995—), Met. Black Bar Assn. Democrat. Roman Catholic. Office: The Torys Law Firm 237 Park Ave New York NY 10017-3142 Business E-Mail: wkuntz@torys.com

KUNTZ, WILLIAM RICHARD, JR. lawyer; b. New Rochelle, N.Y., Oct. 6, 1949; s. William Richard and Mary Margaret (Kerkvliet) K. B.S.E., Princeton U., 1971; JD, U. So. Calif., 1974. Bar: Calif. 1974, U.S. Dist. Ct. (cen. dist.) Calif. Assoc. McKenna & Fitting, Los Angeles, 1974-75, Stroock Stroock & Lavan, Los Angeles, 1975-81; assoc. Hahn, Cazier & Leff, L.A., 1981-82; ptnr. Hahn, Cazier & Smaltz, L.A., 1982-87, Morgan, Lewis & Bockius, 1987-88; v.p., gen. counsel, sec. Chart House Enterprises Inc., Solana Beach, Calif., 1988—. Mem. ABA, State Bar Calif. General corporate, Mergers and acquisitions, Securities. Home: 13536 Kibbings Rd San Diego CA 92130-1242 Office: Chart House Enterprises Inc 640 N La Salle Dr Ste 295 Chicago IL 60610-3754

KUNZ, MICHAEL E. court administrator; b. Bristol, Pa., Feb. 13, 1943; s. Frank John Kunz and Mary Margaret Corrigan; m. Marleen Agnes Senkarik, Aug. 10, 1963; children: Catherine, Mary Ann, Joanne, Lisa. BS, St. Joseph's U., 1970, MBA, 1980. Dep. clk. U.S. Dist. Ct. (ea. dist.) Pa., Phila., 1962-75, chief dep. clk., 1976-79, clk. of the ct., 1979—. Adj. prof. Saint Joseph's U., 1998—. Contbr. articles to profl. jours. Active adv. bd. Coll. Bus. Adminstrn., St. Joseph's U., Phila., 1990—. Recipient Bartholomew A. Sheehan award St. Joseph's U. Law Alumni, 1987, Dir.'s Outstanding Leadership award Adminstrv. Office U.S. Cts., 1992; named for Outstanding Leadership, Fed. Cts. Com. Phila. Bar, 1989. Mem. Am. Judicature Soc., Fed. Cts. Clks. Assn., Capitol Historical Soc., Hist. Soc. USDC, EDPA (sec.). Office: US Dist Ct 2609 US Courthouse Philadelphia PA 19106

KUPCHAK, KENNETH ROY, lawyer; b. Forrest Hills, Pa., May 15, 1942; s. Frank V. and Anne B. (Ruzanic) K.; m. Patricia K. Geer, Jan. 27, 1967; children: Lincoln K., Robinson K. AB, Cornell U., 1964; BS, Pa. State U., 1965; JD in Internat. Affairs, Cornell U., 1971. Bar: Hawaii 1971, U.S. Dist. Ct. Hawaii 1971, U.S. Supreme Ct. 1988. Meteorology staff U. Hawaii, Honolulu, 1968; ptnr. Damon Key Leong Kupchak & Hastert, 1971—, also bd. dirs. Chief minority counsel 8th legis. Hawaii Ho. of Reps., Honolulu, 1974-75, legis. coord. Hawaii State Assn. Counties, Honolulu, 1988; bd. dirs. Fletcher Constrn. Co., N.Am. Ltd., Fletcher Gen. Ltd., Seattle; adj. prof. William S. Richardson Sch. of Law, U. Hawaii, 1993; mem. Honolulu Common Fgn. Rels., 1995—; vice chair bd. counselors Mid-Pacific Inst., 1993-95; bd. trustees Mid-Pacific Inst., 1995—, chmn. personnel com., 1998-99, chmn. edn. com., 2000—; lectr. on constrn. law. Co-author: Fifty State Construction Lien and Bond Laws, 2000, The Design/Build Process, 1997, A State-By-State Guide to Architect, Engineer and Contractor Licensing, 1998, A State-By-State Guide to Construction and Design Law, 1998;contbr. articles to profl. jours. Chair agenda com. C.Z.M. Statewide Adv. Com., Hawaii, 1980—92; pres., bd. dirs. Hawaii Cmty. Svc. Coun., Honolulu, 1982—88; trustee Moanalua Gardens Found., 1985—88, Operation Raleigh (N.C.) U.S.A., 1986—90; bd. dirs. Hawaii Nature Ctr., 1989—; chair Hawaii State Commn. on Korean and Vietnam War Meml., 1992—95. Capt. USAF, 1964—68, Vietnam. Centennial fellow Pa. State U., 1996. Fellow Am. Coll. Constrn. Lawyers; mem. ABA (constrn. industry forum, dispute resolution steering com. 1994—, chair 1998-2000, chair ann. meeting 2001), Hawaii Bar Assn., Internat. Bar Assn., Am. Arbitration Assn. (panel arbitrators), USAF Assn. (v.p. Hawaii chpt. 1994-97), Cornell Law Alumni Assn. (exec. com. 1990-93), Cornell Club Hawaii (bd. dirs., chair scholarship com. 1994-2000), Oahu Country Club, Volcano Golf and Country Club. Avocations: lacrosse, hiking, photography. Construction, Land use and zoning (including planning), Real property. Office: 1600 Pauahi Tower 1001 Bishop St Honolulu HI 96813-3429 E-mail: krk@hawaiilawyer.com

KUPERMAN, FRANCES PERGERICHT, lawyer; b. Cleve., June 4, 1952; d. Joseph and Ann Pergericht; m. Roman G. Kuperman, Feb. 24, 1982; 1 child, Natalie Jill. BA magna cum laude, Case Western Res. U., 1974; JD, Washington U., St. Louis, 1978. Bar: N.H. 1979, Ill. 1981. Law clk. presiding justice U.S. Dist. Ct. No. Dist. Ill., Chgo., 1979-81; assoc. Jenner & Block, 1981-83; asst. regional atty. Dept. Health and Human Svcs., 1983-96, sr. counsel Office of Counsel to the Inspector Gen. Washington, 1996—. Topics editor Washington U. Law Quar., 1977-78. Mem. Phi Beta Kappa. Office: Office of Inspector Gen Dept Health and Human Svcs 330 Independence Ave SW Washington DC 20201-0003 E-mail: kuperman@erols.com

KUPIETZKY, MOSHE J. lawyer; b. N.Y.C., May 17, 1944; s. Jacob Harry and Fanny (Dresner) K.; m. Arlene Debra Usdan, June 22, 1966; children: Jay, Jeff, Jacob. BBA cum laude, CCNY, 1965; LLB, JD magna cum laude, Harvard U., 1968. Bar: N.Y. 1969, Calif. 1970. Law clerk to Hon. William B. Herlands U.S. Dist. Ct., N.Y.C., 1968-69; assoc. Mitchell Silberberg & Knupp, L.A., Calif., 1969-74, ptnr., 1974-80; ptnr., prin. Hayutin Rubinroit Praw & Kupietzky, 1980-87; ptnr. Sidley, Austin, Brown & Wood, 1987—. Bd. dirs. Nat. Inst. Jewish Hospice, Beverly Hills, Calif., 1986-98, L.A. Econ. Devel. Corp.; bd. advisors Graziadio Sch. Bus. and Mgmt. Pepperdine U., L.A., 1996-98. Mem. ABA, Beverly Hills Bar Assn., L.A. County Bar Assn. Contracts commercial, General corporate. Office: Sidley Austin Brown & Wood 555 W 5th St Ste 4000 Los Angeles CA 90013-3000 E-mail: mkupietzky@sidley.com

KUPPERMAN, STEPHEN HENRY, lawyer; b. New Orleans, Sept. 17, 1953; s. Abraham Bernard and Jo-Ellyn (Levy) K.; m. Mara Rothstein, Oct. 18, 1980; children: Zachary Hart, Shane Levi, Jake Benjamin. BA, Duke U., 1974; JD, Tulane U., 1977. Bar: La. 1977, U.S. Dist. Ct. (ea. dist.) La. 1977, U.S. Dist. Ct. (mid. dist.) La. 1978, U.S. Dist. Ct. (we. dist.) La. 1981, U.S. Ct. Appeals (5th cir.) 1977, U.S. Ct. Appeals (11th cir.) 1982, U.S. Supreme Ct. 1980. Assoc. Stone Pigman Walther Wittmann & Hutchinson, New Orleans, 1977-81, ptnr., 1981—. Adj. prof. Tulane Law Sch., 1988—; mem. Tulane Law Rev., 1975-77, adv. bd., 1992—. Articles editor Tulane Law Rev., 1976-77, mem. 1975-76; contbr. articles to law revs., profl. jours. Bd. dirs. Goodwill Industries, 1980-87, mem. adv. bd. 1987-91; bd. dirs. Jewish Family Svcs., New Orleans, 1978-93, treas. 1986, v.p. 1987-88, pres., 1988-90; bd. dirs. Jewish Fedn., New Orleans, 1989-93, 95-2001, treas. 1991-93; mem. adv. bd. Jewish Endowment Found., New Orleans, 1979—, Tulane Continuing Legal Edn. Program, 1983—; mem. adv. bd. B'nai B'rith Anti-Defamation League S. Ctrl. Region, 1987—, vice-chmn., 1991-95, chmn. 1995-99; mem. Young Leadership Cabinet United Jewish Appeal, 1990-92; bd. dirs. Touro Infirmary Found., 1998—, Touro Synagogue, New Orleans, 1991-2000, sec. 1995-97, v.p. 1997-99, Touro Infirmary, 2000—. Mem. ABA, La. Bar Assn. (continuing legal edn. com. 1986-88, disciplinary conduct com. 1995—), New Orleans Bar Assn. (mem. Inn of Ct. 1994—), Fed. Bar Assn. (bd. dirs. New Orleans chpt. 1989-94), Securities Industry Assn., Order of Coif. Democrat. Jewish. Federal civil litigation, State civil litigation, Securities. Office: Stone Pigman Walther Wittmann & Hutchinson 546 Carondelet St Ste 100 New Orleans LA 70130-3588 E-mail: skupperman@stonepigman.com

KURIT, NEIL, lawyer; b. Cleve., Aug. 31, 1940; s. Jay and Rose (Rainin) K.; m. Doris Tannenbaum, Aug. 9, 1964 (div.); m. Donna Chernin, Aug. 24, 1986. BS, Miami U., Oxford, Ohio, 1961; JD, Case Western Res. U., 1964. Bar: Ohio 1964. Prin. Kahn, Kleinman, Yanowitz & Arnson Co., L.P.A., Cleve., 1964—. Co-author Handbook for Attys. and Accts., Jewish Cmty. Fedn. Endowment Fund. Trustee, v.p. Montefiore Home, 1983-87; trustee Jewish Cmty. Fedn. Cleve., 1983-86, 90-95. Mem. ABA, Ohio State Bar Assn. E-mail: nkurit@kkya.com Estate planning, Probate. Home: 2870 Courtland Blvd Cleveland OH 44122-2802 Office: Kahn Kleinman Yanowitz & Arnson Co LPA 2600 Tower at Erieview Cleveland OH 44114

KURLAND, HAROLD ARTHUR, lawyer; b. N.Y.C., Jan. 20, 1952; s. Jordan Emil and Anita (Siegel) K.; m. Christine Rogers, June 28, 1975; children: Thomas Philip, Andrew Rogers. AB, Dartmouth Coll., 1973; JD, Cornell U., 1976. Bar: N.Y. 1977, D.C. 1977, U.S. Dist. Ct. (we. dist.) N.Y. 1977, U.S. Dist. Ct. (no. dist.) N.Y. 1983, U.S. Dist. Ct. (no. dist.) Tex. 1981, U.S. Ct. Appeals (2d cir.) 1980, U.S. Dist. Ct. (D.C. dist.) 1986, U.S. Ct. Appeals (D.C. cir.) 1986, U.S Ct. Appeals (3d cir.) 1988, U.S. Dist. Ct. (mid. dist.) Pa. 1988, U.S. Dist. Ct. (ea. and so. dists.) N.Y. 1991, U.S. Supreme Ct. 1980. Assoc. Nixon, Hargrave, Devans & Doyle LLP (now Nixon Peabody LLP), Rochester, N.Y., 1976-84, ptnr., 1985-2000, Ward Norris Heller & Reidy LLP, Rochester, 2000—. Mediator, arbitrator Am. Arbitration Assn.; mem. adv. com. on civil practice N.Y. Office Ct. Adminstrn., 1988—, co-chair task force on reducing litig. cost and delay, 7th jud. dist., 1996—. Past chmn. bd. dirs. Rochester Philharm. Orch.; bd. dirs. Vol. Legal Svcs. Project. Mem. ABA, N.Y. State Bar Assn., D.C. Bar Assn., Monroe County Bar Assn. (chair judicary com., past. chmn. cts. com., fed. ct. com., exec. com., trustee), Rochester Inn of Ct. (past. pres., master), Am. Bd. Trial Advocates (assoc.). Democrat. Federal civil litigation, State civil litigation, Construction. Home: 154 Council Rock Ave Rochester NY 14610-3335 Office: Ward Norris Heller & Reidy LLP 300 State St Rochester NY 14614 E-mail: hak@wnhr.com

KURNIT, RICHARD ALAN, lawyer, educator; b. N.Y.C., Mar. 22, 1951; s. Shepard and Jean (Zinsher) Kurnit; m. Diane Ruth Katzin, Sept. 9, 1979; 1 child, Katrina. AB magna cum laude, Columbia U., 1972; JD cum laude, Harvard U., 1975. Bar: N.Y. 1976, U.S. Dist. Ct. (so. dist.) N.Y. 1976, U.S. Ct. Appeals (D.C. cir.) 1977, U.S. Ct. Appeals (2d cir.) 1978, U.S. Supreme Ct. 1980, U.S. Dist. Ct. (ea. dist.) N.Y. 1981. Law clk. to Thomas P. Griesa U.S. Dist. Ct. (so. dist.) N.Y., N.Y.C., 1975-76; assoc. Paul, Weiss, Rifkind, Wharton & Garrison, 1976-81; ptnr. Frankfurt Garbus, Kurnit Klein & Selz, 1981—. Instr. advt. law New Sch., N.Y.C., 1981—; lectr. Am. Assn./Advt. Agys., ABA, Am. Promotional Mktg. Assn., ALI, 1985—, Am. Advt. Fedn., 1988—. Author: Libel Claims Based on Fiction, 1985; contbr. articles to profl. jours. and internet related discussions. Vol. atty. Legal Aid Soc., N.Y.C., 1977-81. Recipient Citizens Communications Ctr. award, 1975. Mem. ABA., N.Y.C. Bar Assn. (advt. industry subcom.), Phi Beta Kappa. Intellectual property, Libel, Trademark and copyright. Home: 110 Riverside Dr Apt 16F New York NY 10024-3734 Office: Frankfurt Garbus Kurnit Klein & Selz 488 Madison Ave Fl 9 New York NY 10022-5754

KURRELMEYER, LOUIS HAYNER, retired lawyer; b. Troy, N.Y., July 26, 1928; s. Bernhard and Lucy Julia (Hayner) K.; m. Phyllis A. Damon, June 14, 1952 (div. 1973); children: Ellen Laura, Louis Hayner, Nancy Snow; m. Martina Sophia Kluis, June 14, 1975. AB, Columbia U., 1949, LLB, 1953; MA in Econs., U. N.Mex., 1950. Bar: N.Y. 1953, D.C. 1968. Assoc. Debevoise, Plimpton, Lyons & Gates, N.Y.C., 1953-66; ptnr. Hale Russell & Gray, N.Y.C., 1967-75, counsel, 1976-85; counsel Winthrop, Stimson, Putnam & Roberts, Washington, 1985-96, ret. 1996. Author: The Potash Industry, 1951; contbr. to CPLR Forms and Guidance for Lawyers, 1963. U.S. panelist U.S.-Can. Free Trade agreement, 1989-92; asst. transp. adminstr. City of N.Y., 1966-67; v.p. Emerson Sch., N.Y.C., 1960-64, chmn., 1964-69; bd. dirs. Rice Meml. H.S., South Burlington, Vt., 1992-95; mem. Prudential Com. Fire Dist. No. 1, Shelburne, Vt., 1977-90, chmn., 1977-84; mem. Shelburne Sewer Commn., 1990-93, chmn., 1991-93, interim mgr., 1992-93; bd. commrs. Chittenden County Transp. Authority, 1991-97, treas., 1992-96; mem. Shelburne Selectboard, 1995. Decorated Knight 1st class Royal Swedish Order of North Star. Mem. ABA, D.C. Bar Assn. Home: 364 Clearwater Rd Shelburne VT 05482-7724

KURRUS, THOMAS WILLIAM, lawyer; b. Carmel, N.Y., May 13, 1947; s. Theo Hornsby and Jean Ellen (Cumming) K. BS magna cum laude, U. Fla., 1975, JD, 1979. Bar: Fla. 1980, U.S. Dist. Ct. (no. dist.) Fla. 1980, U.S. Ct. Appeals (5th cir.) 1980, U.S. Dist. Ct. (mid. dist.) Fla. 1981, U.S. Ct. Appeals (11th cir.) 1981, U.S. Ct. Appeals (4th cir.) 1984, U.S. Supreme Ct. 1984. Assoc. Law Firm Larry G. Turner, Gainesville, Fla., 1981-83; ptnr. Turner, Kurrus & Griscti, 1983-88; prin. Law Offices of Thomas W. Kurrus, 1988—. Mem. Fla. Supreme Ct. commn. on jury instructions, 1995. Contbr. articles to profl. jours. Mem. ACLU (Gainesville chpt. legal panel chmn. 1999), Nat. Assn. Criminal Defense Lawyers (Fla. chpt. bd. dirs., chmn. continuing legal edn. com., local legis. liaison, pres. award 1993, appreciation award 1998). Avocations: fishing, art, horses. General civil litigation, Criminal, Personal injury. Office: PO Box 838 Gainesville FL 32602-0838

KURTZ, HARVEY A. lawyer; b. Baraboo, Wis., July 9, 1950; s. Walter R. and Henrietta M. (Hinze) K.; m. Yvonne Larme, Jan. 28, 1978; children: Benjamin L., Leah L. BA, U. Wis., 1972; JD, U. Chgo., 1975. Bar: Wis. 1975, U.S. Dist. Ct. (ea. dist.) Wis. 1980. Atty. Whyte & Hirschboeck S.C., Milw., 1975-89, shareholder, 1981-89; ptnr. Foley & Lardner, 1989—. Mem. ABA, State Bar of Wis. Assn., Milw. Bar Assn. (chmn. employee benefits sect. 1993-94), Greater Milw. Employee Benefit Coun., Wis. Retirement Plan Profls. (pres. 1987-88), Internat. Pension and Employee Benefits Lawyers Assn., Kiwanis, Phi Beta Kappa. General corporate, Pension, profit-sharing, and employee benefits, Corporate taxation. Home: 3927 N Stowell Ave Milwaukee WI 53211-2461 Office: Foley & Lardner Ste 3800 777 E Wisc Ave Milwaukee WI 53202 E-mail: hkurtz@foleylaw.com

KURTZ, JAMES P. administrative law judge; b. Highland Park, Mich., Dec. 5, 1932; s. A.T. and Virginia C. (Riley) K.; m. Barbara A. Gonczy, Feb. 2, 1957; children: Mary T., Christina M., Ann V., J. Peter, Karen M., Eileen M. AB, U. Detroit, 1955, JD, 1958. Bar: Mich. 1958, U.S. Dist. Ct. (ea. dist.) Mich. 1958, U.S. Ct. Appeals (6th cir.) 1964. Supervisory atty. 7th region NLRB, Detroit, 1958-67; ptnr. firm Brennan & Kurtz, 1967-69; adminstrv. law judge Employment rels. commn. State of Mich. Dept. CIS, 1969-2001. Instr. labor and real estate Detroit Coll. Bus., Dearborn, 1968-73; adj. prof. adminstrv. law U. Detroit, 1969-72. Editor-in-chief U. Detroit Law jour., 1957-58; editor procs. Nat. Acad. Arbitrators, 1971-75. Mem. Mich. Bar Assn. (Labor Law sect.). Roman Catholic. Home: RR 1 Craig Beach 401 Erieview Harrow ON Canada N0R 1G0 E-mail: jpkurtz@sympatico.ca

KURTZ, JEROME, lawyer, educator; b. Phila., May 19, 1931; s. Morris and Renee (Cooper) K.; m. Elaine Kahn, July 28, 1956; children: Madeleine, Nettie Kurtz Greenstein. BS with honors, Temple U., 1952; LLB magna cum laude, Harvard U., 1955. Bar: Pa. 1956, N.Y. 1981, D.C. 1982; CPA, Pa. Assoc. Wolf, Block, Schorr & Solis-Cohen, Phila., 1955-56, 57-63, ptnr., 1963-66, 68-77; tax legis. counsel Dept. Treasury, Washington, 1966-68; commr. IRS, 1977-80; ptnr. Paul, Weiss, Rifkind, Wharton & Garrison, 1980-90; prof. law NYU, 1991-2001, dir. grad. tax program, 1995-98. Instr. Villanova Law Sch., 1964-65, U. Pa., 1969-74; vis. prof. law Harvard U., 1975-76; mem. adv. group to commr. IRS, 1976. Editor: Harvard Law Rev, 1953-55; contbr. numerous articles to profl. jours. Pres. Ctr. Inter-Am. Tax Adminstrn., 1980; bd. dirs. Common Cause, 1984-90, chmn. fin. com., 1985-88; bd. dirs. Nat. Capitol Area ACLU, 1990-91; mem. adv. bd. NYU Tax Inst., 1988-97, Little, Brown Tax Practice Series, 1994-96. Recipient Exceptional Service award Dept. Treasury, 1968, Alexander Hamilton award, 1980 Mem. ABA (chmn. tax shelter com. 1982-84), N.Y. Bar Assn. (exec. com. tax sect. 1981-82), Pa. Bar Assn., Phila. Bar Assn. (chmn. tax sect. 1975-76), Assn. of the Bar of the City of N.Y. (chmn. tax coun. 1993-95), Am. Law Inst. (cons. fed. inc. tax project taxation of pass through entities), Am. Coll. Tax Counsel, Beta Gamma Sigma. Corporate taxation, Taxation, general, Personal income taxation. Home: 17 E 16th St New York NY 10003-3116 E-mail: jeromekurtz2@aol.com

KURTZ, PAUL MICHAEL, lawyer, educator; b. Bronx, N.Y., Sept. 22, 1946; s. Louis and Helen (Mechanic) K.p m. Carol Porter, June 6, 1971; 1 child, Benjamin. BA, Vanderbilt U., 1968, JD, 1972; LLM, Harvard U., 1974. Bar: Tenn. 1972, U.S. Ct. Appeals (6th cir.) 1973, U.S. Ct. Appeals (5th cir.) 1977, U.S. Supreme Ct. 1978. Law clk. to chief judge U.S. Ct. Appeals (6th cir.), 1972-73; instr. Boston U. Law Sch., 1973-74, Boston Coll. Law Sch., 1974-75; aasst. prof. law U. Ga., Athens, 1975-78, assoc. prof., 1978-83, prof., 1983-94, assoc. dean, 1991—, J. Alton Husch prof., 1994—. Vis. prof. U. Mo. Law Sch., 1982, Mercer Law Sch., 1984, U. Tex., 1986, Vanderbilt U., 1987; reporter Nat. Conf. of Commrs. on Uniform State Laws, Com. on Interstate Child Support Enforcement, Com. on Status of Children of Aided Conception. Author: Criminal Offenses in Georgia, 1980, Family Law: Cases, Text, Problems, 1986, 2d eidt., 1991; contbr. articles to law revs.; assoc. editor Family Law Quar., 1983—. Mem. Am. Assn. Law Schs. (chmn. sect. family and juvenile law), ACLU, Am. Humane Assn. (bd. dirs. 1998—), Common Cause, Soc. Am. Law Tchrs., Am. Law Inst. (reporter 1995—), Supreme Ct. Hist. Soc., Order of Coif, B'nai B'rith (Ga. state sec., pres. Athens lodge). Democrat. Avocations: reading, travel, bowling, politics. Home: 362 W Cloverhurst Ave Athens GA 30606-4212 Office: U Ga Law Sch Athens GA 30602 E-mail: pkurtz9@home.com, pmkurtz@arches.uga.edu

KURTZBERG, HOWARD, lawyer; b. N.Y.C., Apr. 14, 1958; s. Theodore R. and Charlotte (Taubman) K.; m. Carmelinda Ann Amedo, Nov. 21, 1982; children: Timothy Joseph, Alyssa Lauren. BA, Queens Coll., 1979; JD, Benjamin N. Cardozo Sch. Law, 1982. Bar: N.Y. 1983. Labor rels. asst. L.I. Jewish Med. Ctr., New Hyde Park, N.Y., 1982-83; in-house counsel Rose Assocs., N.Y.C., 1983-84; assoc. gen. counsel Intercontinental Monetary, 1984-89; sr. assoc. Albanese, Albanese & Fiore, Garden City, N.Y., 1989-91; v.p., gen. counsel Inter-Market Fin. Corp., Westbury, 1991-92; pvt. practice Jericho, 1992—. Contracts commercial, Real property, Securities. Office: 380 N Broadway Ste 300 Jericho NY 11753-2109 Fax: 516-932-8353. E-mail: kurtzlaw@aol.com

KURY, FRANKLIN LEO, lawyer; b. Sunbury, Pa., Oct. 15, 1936; s. Barney and Helen (Witkowski) K.; m. Elizabeth Heazlett, Sept. 14, 1963; children: Steven, David, James. Bar: Pa. 1962. Atty. Pa. Dept. Justice, Harrisburg, 1961-62; ptnr. Kury & Kury, Sunbury, 1963-80, Tive, Hetrick & Pierce, Harrisburg, 1981-82, Reed, Smith, Shaw & McClay, Harrisburg, 1983—. Adj. prof. immigration law, Harrisburg, Widener Law Sch., 1999-2000. Mem. Pa. Ho. of Reps., Harrisburg, 1967-72, Pa. Senate, Harrisburg, 1973-80; del. at large Dem. Nat. Conv., San Francisco, 1984; bd. dirs. Hawk Mountain Sanctuary Assn. 1st lt. USAR, 1962-66. Mem. Am. Immigration Lawyers Assn., Pa. Bar Assn. (chmn. environ. sect. 1984, 1st award for Outstanding Contbn. to Profession of Environ. Law Practice 1993), Polish Nat. Alliance. Democrat. Avocation: golf. Administrative and regulatory, Environmental, Real property. Office: Reed Smith Shaw & McClay PO Box 11844 213 Market St Ste 900 Harrisburg PA 17101-2108 E-mail: fkury@reedsmith.llp

KURYK, DAVID NEAL, lawyer; b. Balt., Aug. 24, 1947; s. Leon and Bernice G. (Fox) K.; m. Alice T. Lehman, July 8, 1971; children: Richard M., Robert M., Benjamin A. BA, U. Md., 1969; JD, U. Balt., 1972. Bar: Md. 1972, U.S. Dist. Ct. Md. 1973, U.S. Ct. Mil. Appeals 1973, D.C. 1974, U.S. Ct. Appeals (4th cir.) 1974, U.S. Supreme Ct. 1976, U.S. Ct. Appeals (Fed. cir.) 1982. Assoc. Harold Buchman, Esq., Balt., 1970-76; pvt. practice, 1976—. Mem. editl. bd. Md. Bar Jour., 1973-76. Sgt. USAF, 1967-73. Mem. ABA (products gen. liability and consumer law com. 1976—, com. auto law 1977), Md. State Bar Assn., Bar Assn. Balt. City, ATLA, U. Balt. Alumni Assn., Zeta Beta Tau. Democrat. Jewish. State civil litigation, Contracts commercial, Personal injury. Home: 11200 5 Springs Rd Lutherville MD 21093-3520 Office: Am Bldg 231 E Baltimore St Ste 702 Baltimore MD 21202-3446 E-mail: kuryk@home.com

KURZBAN, IRA JAY, lawyer; b. Bklyn., May 9, 1949; s. Benjamin and Irene (Weiss) K.; m. Magda Montiel Davis, Apr. 15, 1989; children: Kathryn Montiel Davis, Paula Lindsay Davis, Magda Marie Davis, Sadie Bethany Kurzban, Benjamin Kurzban. BA magna cum laude, Syracuse U., 1971; MA, U. Calif., Berkeley, 1973, JD, 1976; hon. fellow, U. Pa. Law Sch., 1987. Bar: Calif. 1976, Fla. 1976, U.S. Dist. Ct. (no. dist.) Calif., 1976, U.S. Dist. Ct. (so. dist.) Fla., 1976, U.S. Ct. Appeals (5th cir.) 1978, U.S. Ct. Appeals (11th cir.) 1981, U.S. Supreme Ct. 1980. Ptnr. Kurzban, Kurzban, Weinger & Tetzeli P.A., Miami, Fla., 1977—; Fla. counsel Nat. Energy Civil Liberties Com., 1979-98; gen. counsel Am. Immigration Lawyers Assn., 1992-93. Adj. prof. immigration and nationality law U. Miami Sch. of Law, 1979—, Nova Southeastern Law Sch., 1982—; instr. polit. sci. U. Calif. Berkeley, 1973; mem. civil justice adv. com. U.S. Dist. Ct. (so. dist.) Fla., 1993-94; mem. certification com. in immigration and univ. law Fla. Bar, 1994-96; lectr. in field. Author: Kurzban's Immigration Law Sourcebook: A Comprehensive Outline and Reference Tool, 7th edit.,

2000; contbr. articles to profl. jours. Founder Berkeley Law Found. Recipient Tobias Simon pro bono svc. award Fla. Supreme Ct., 2002, Trial Lawyer of Yr. award Trial Lawyers for Public Justice, Carol King award Nat. Lawyers Guild, 1996; Polit. Sci. Dept. fellow U. Calif., Berkeley, 1971, Kent fellow Danforth Found., 1974-77, Law and Society fellow U. Calif., Berkeley, 1975-76. Fellow Am. Immigration Law Found. (hon.); mem. Am. ABA (chair refugee legal assistance com. 1983-84, mem. immigration coord. com. 1991-93), Am. Immigration Lawyers Assn. (pres. so. Fla. chpt. 1980-81, nat. pres. 1987, Jack Wasserman award for excellence in federal litigation 1983, Lawyer of the Ams. award 1992), Am. Inns of Ct. Civil rights, Immigration, naturalization, and customs, Public international. Office: Kurzban Kurzban Weinger & Tetzeli PA 2650 SW 27th Ave Miami FL 33133-3003 E-mail: ira@kkwtlaw.com

KURZMAN, ROBERT GRAHAM, lawyer, educator; b. N.Y.C., July 3, 1932; s. Benjamin E. and Betty Kurzman; m. Carol Ellis, Aug. 26, 1956; children: Marc, Nancy, Amy. BA, Hofstra U., 1954; JD, Cornell U., 1957. Bar: N.Y. 1959, U.S. Dist. Ct. (no., so., ea. and we. dists.) N.Y. 1964, U.S. Supreme Ct. 1964. Assoc. Wynn, Blattmachr & Campbell, N.Y.C., 1959-63; ptnr. Leaf, Kurzman, Deull & Drogin, 1963-79, Goldschmidt, Fredericks, Kurzman & Oshatz, 1979-83, Kurzman & Eisenberg and precedessor firms, White Plains, N.Y., 1982—. Adj. prof. law NYU; dir. Stratton Industries, Inc.; acting city ct. judge City of New Rochelle (N.Y.), 1981. Author: (with Rita Gilbert) Paralegals and Successful Law Practice, 1981; contbr. articles to profl. jours. Mem. adv. bd. So. Meth. U. Sch. Law, Estate Planning Inst.; coord. estates and trusts paralegal program Manhattanville Coll., 1974-75; pres. West Putnam coun. Boy Scouts Am., 1981; trustee, pres. Temple Israel; former chmn. New Rochelle Rep. Com. Capt. USAR, 1957-59. Recipient Silver Beaver award Boy Scouts Am., Silver Antelope aawrd; named Man of Yr., New Rochelle B'nai B'rith, 1977. Fellow Am. Coll. Probate Counsel; mem. ABA, N.Y. State Bar Assn., Assn. Bar City N.Y., Masons, Ridgeway Country Club (White Plains), Cornell Club of N.Y.C. (pres.). Family and matrimonial, Probate, Estate taxation. Home: 166 Tewksbury Rd Scarsdale NY 10583-6036 Office: 1 N Broadway White Plains NY 10601-2310 E-mail: rgk166@aol.com

KURZWEIL, HARVEY, lawyer; b. Bklyn., Mar. 23, 1945; s. Martin E. Kurzweil and Muriel (Krause) Kanow; m. Barbara Kramer, Aug. 17, 1969; children: David, Paul (dec.), Emily, Elizabeth. AB, Columbia Coll., 1966, JD, 1969. Bar: N.Y. 1970. Assoc. Dewey, Ballantine, Bushby, Palmer & Wood, N.Y.C., 1969-77, ptnr., 1977-90, Dewey Ballantine, N.Y.C., 1990—, chmn. litigation dept., mem. mgmt. and exec. coms., 1990—. Bd. dirs. Menninger Clinic; trustee Menninger Found.; bd. visitors Columbia Law Sch. Fellow Am. Bar Found.; mem. ABA, N.Y. State Bar Assn., D.C. Bar Assn., Assn. of Bar of City of N.Y. (trade regulation com. 1982-85), Univ. Club, Internat. Acad. of Trial Lawyers Jewish. Avocations: sports cars, reading, gardening, sports. Antitrust, General civil litigation. Home: 1025 5th Ave New York NY 10028 Office: Dewey Ballantine 1301 Avenue Of The Americas New York NY 10019-6022 also: PO Box 389 Saddle River NJ 07458-0389 E-mail: hkurzweil@deweyballantine.com

KUSHNER, GORDON PETER, lawyer; b. Calgary, Alta., Can., Nov. 3, 1966; came to U.S., 1984; s. H. Peter and V. Marlene (Shatilla) K.; m. Patti A. Yakich, Aug. 10, 1991; children: Brantley Peter, Katerina Mari. BA summa cum laude, U. N.D., 1988; JD cum laude, U. Dayton, 1991. Bar: Ohio 1991, U.S. Dist. Ct. (so. dist.) Ohio 1991. Atty. Dinsmore & Shohl, Cin., 1991-94; atty. internat. ops. LensCrafters Internat., Inc., 1994-95; corp. atty. Structural Dynamics Rsch. Corp., Milford, Ohio, 1995-98—; v.p., chief tech. counsel Baan Co. N.V., Herndon, Va., Barneveld, Netherlands, 1998-2000; v.p., gen. counsel Reliacast, Inc., 2000—. Dir. Rite Track Equipment Svcs., Inc., Cin., 1994-95; mem. Vision Coun. of Can., Toronto, Ont., 1994-95; spkr. U. Cin. Law Sch., 1993. Author: (newsletter) Cincinnati Small Business Newsletter, 1993; contbr. articles to profl. jours. Mem. Big Bros. and Big Sisters, Dayton, 1990-91; dir. Housing Network of Hamilton County, Cin., 1993-94; coach Lakota Sports Orgn., West Chester, Ohio, 1997-98; treas. Woodlea WaterMocs Swim Team, 2000—. Recipient Yale in Can. Outstanding Can. award Yale U. Can. Alumni Assn., 1990. Mem. ABA, Ohio Bar Assn., Cin. Bar Assn. (presenter NAFTA seminar 1992), Phi Alpha Delta, Phi Beta Kappa. General corporate, Intellectual property, Private international. Home: 1409 Moore Pl SW Leesburg VA 20175-5820 E-mail: gkushner@reliacast.com

KUSMA, KYLLIKKI, lawyer; b. Tartu, Estonia, Dec. 8, 1943; came to U.S., 1951; d. August and Helji (Traat) K. BA, Ohio U., 1966; MA (VA Rehab. fellow), Ohio State U., 1967; JD, Ohio No. U., 1976; MLT, Georgetown U., 1980. Bar: Ohio 1977, D.C. 1978. Speech and hearing therapist Lima (Ohio) Meml. Hosp., 1967-70, Tipp City (Ohio) Schs., 1970-74; atty.-adv. Office Chief Counsel, IRS, Washington, 1977-81; v.p., assoc. tax counsel Security Pacific Nat. Bank., L.A., 1981-83; ptnr. Brownstein Zeidman & Lore, Washington, 1983-95, Ernst & Young LLP, Columbus, Ohio, 1995—. Instr. Wright State U., 1972-76. Author: (with others) Mortgage-Backed Securities Special Update: REMICs, 1988; contbr. articles to profl. jours. Vol. local civic and polit. activities. Mem. ABA, Ohio Bar Assn., Columbus Bar Assn., Columbus Women Execs. (v.p.), Phi Kappa Phi. Pension, profit-sharing, and employee benefits, Corporate taxation, Personal income taxation. Office: Ernst & Young LLP 1100 Huntington Ctr 41 S High St Columbus OH 43215 E-mail: kyllikki.kusma@ey.com

KUSSEL, WILLIAM FERDINAND, JR. lawyer; b. Norway, Mich., July 30, 1957; s. William F. and Mitzi (Markus) K.; m. Magda G. Villicana, Feb. 25, 2000. BS, St. Norbert Coll., 1979; JD, Southwestern U., 1984. Bar: Calif. 1985, D.C. 1985, Minn. 1986, Wis. 1989, U.S. Dist. Ct. (ea. dist.) Wis. 1993. Law clk. Wis. Cir. Ct., Marinette, 1982; law extern L.A. Dist. Atty.'s Office, 1983; pros. Menominee Indian Reservation, Keshena, Wis., 1986-92; program atty. Menominee Indian Tribe Wis., 1992—; legal counsel Menominee Tribal Gaming Commn., 2000—. Temporary assignment to Menominee Tribal Gaming Commn., 2000—. Mem. Calif. Bar Assn., Minn. Bar Assn., D.C. Bar Assn., Wis. Bar Assn. Avocations: photography, snowmobiling, boating, motorcycling, woodworking. Office: Menominee Indian Tribe Menominee Tribal Gaming Com PO Box 910 Keshena WI 54135 E-mail: wfkussel@kussel.com

KUSTER, LARRY DONALD, lawyer; b. Kewanee, Ill., July 27, 1947; s. Donald Carl and Rosemary Ann (Riggins) K.; m. Mary Catherine Whitmore, July 11, 1970; children— David, Ryan. B.A., Augustana Coll., 1969; J.D with honors, U. Iowa, 1973. Bar: Ill. 1973, U.S. Tax Ct. 1979, U.S. Dist. Ct. (cen. dist.) Ill. 1980, U.S. Ct. Appeals (7th cir.) 1982, U.S. Dist. Ct. (so. dist.) Ill. 1996. Assoc. Rammelkamp, Bradney, Kuster, Keaton, Fritsche & Lindsay, P.C., Jacksonville, Ill., 1973-75, ptnr., 1976— ; arbitrator Am. Arbitration Assn.; lectr. continuing med. edn. seminar sponsored by Springfield Clinic, St. John's Hosp., Springfield, 1986, Lorman Education Svcs., Individuals with Disabilities Education Act in Ill., Professional Development Network, Special Education Law for teh nEw millennium in Ill., Regional Office Of Education #46; moderator continuing legal edn. program Ill. Inst. Continuing Legal Edn., 1985, 86; bd. dirs. Sherwood Eddy Meml. YMCA, 1975-80; bd. dirs. Jacksonville Area C. of C., 1981-84, pres.-elect, 1989; bd. dirs. Jacksonville Area Visitors and Tourism Bur., 1986-91, pres. 1989-90, MacMurray Coll., Jacksonville, 1991—; lectr. Ill. State Bar Assn., Ill. Assn. Sch. Bds., Illini Adminstrs. Inst.; pres. Jacksonville Area C. of C., 1990; mem. Am. Council on Germany, 1982— , City of Jacksonville Heritage Cultural Ctr. Bd., 1986-91; pres. Ill. Assn. Hist. Preservation Commns. 1982; mem. Jacksonville Hist. Preservation Commn., 1979-87, vice chmn., 1981-83, chmn., 1983-84; mem. West Central Ill. Council on World Affairs, pres., 1982-83, Fedn. Ins. and Corp. Coun., 1989—. Mem. Morgan County Bar Assn. (pres. 1977-78), Ill. Bar Assn. (civil procedure and practice council 1976-77, 86-90, sec. workers' compensation sect. 1982-83, vice chmn. 1983-84, chmn. 1984-85). Contbr. articles to profl. jours. General civil litigation, Municipal (including bonds), Personal injury. Home: RR 1 Box 19 Chapin IL 62628-9801 Office: Rammelkamp Bradney 232 W State St Jacksonville IL 62650-2002

KUTTNER, BERNARD A. lawyer, former judge; b. Berlin, Germany, Jan. 13, 1934; arrived in U.S., 1939; s. Frank B. and Vera (Knopfmacher) K.; children: Karen M., Robert D., Stacey M. Gilby. AB cum laude, Dartmouth Coll., 1955; postgrad., U. Va. Law Sch., 1956; JD, Seton Hall U., 1959; postgrad., NYU, 1960. Bar: N.J. 1960, U.S. Supreme Ct. 1964, U.S. Ct. Mil. Appeals 1967, N.Y. 1982, D.C. 1982; cert. civil trial lawyer, N.J. Assoc. Toner, Crowley, Woelper & Vanderbilt, 1959-62; sole practice Newark, 1962-75; corp. counsel Irvington, N.J., 1963-66; judge N.J. State Divsn. Tax Appeals, 1977-79; instr. civil litigation Montclair State Coll., 1979-82. Del. Jud. Conf. N.J. Supreme Ct., 1974-81; vice chmn. Supreme Ct. N.J. Dist. Ethics Com., 1984-85, chmn., 1985-86. Contbr. articles to legal publs. Commr. Essex County (N.J.) Park Commn., 1973-79; appointed bd. on Trial Atty. Certification, N.J. Supreme Ct., 1986-90. Served to lt. comdr. USNR, 1964-74. Mem. ABA (co-editor trial techniques newsletter sect. on tort and ins. practice, chmn. trial techniques com. 1988-89, sect. on litigation), ATLA, Inst. for Ethical Behavior (pres. 1985—), D.C. Bar Assn., Irvington Bar Assn. (pres. 1968-70), Essex County Bar Assn. (chmn. 1973-75, trial and appellate litigation, judiciary com. 1972-75, treas. 1975-79, pres. 1980-81, products liability com. 1981—), Am. Counsel Assn. Jewish. Federal civil litigation, State civil litigation, Personal injury. Office: Kuttner Law Offices 24 Lackawanna Pl Millburn NJ 07041-1618 E-mail: Kuttnerbuck@aol.com

KUYATH, RICHARD NORMAN, lawyer; b. Sacramento, Jan. 25, 1948; s. Norman John and Marie Elizabeth (Engelhardt) Kuyath; m. Laura Ann Brumfield, Aug. 12, 1972; children: Brian James, Bradford David;1 child Matthew Lawrence. BA, U. Minn., 1971; JD, William Mitchell Coll. Law, St. Paul, 1975. Bar: Minn. 1975. Contract specialist FMC Corp., Naval Systems Divsn., Mpls., 1975-80, sr. contract specialist, 1980-87, sr. contract counsel, 1988-89, mgr. contract counsel, 1989—; govt. contract counsel 3M Co., St. Paul, 1989-91, sr. counsel, 1991—. Contbr. articles to profl. jours. Fellow: Am. Bar Found. (vice chair pub. contract law sect. R&D and intellectual property com.); mem.: Nat. Contracts Mgmt. Assn. (cert. assoc. contracts mgr. 1980). Republican. Congregational. Contracts commercial, Government contracts and claims. Home: 6103 Jeffrey Ln Minneapolis MN 55436-1206 E-mail: rnkuyath1@mmm.com

KVINTA, CHARLES J. lawyer; b. Hallettsville, Tex., Feb. 16, 1932; s. John F. and Emily (Strauss) K.; m. Margie N. Brenek, Oct. 9, 1954; children: Charles, Sherri, Kenneth, Christopher. BA in Govt., U. Tex., 1954, LLB, 1959. Bar: Tex. 1959. Atty. Tex. Hwy. Dept., Yoakum, 1959-61; ptnr. Gaus & Kvinta, 1962-67, Kvinta, Young & Frietsch, Yoakum, 1975—, Kvinta & Kvinta Attys., Yoakum, 1986—. Exec. v.p. First State Bank, Yoakum, 1968-74, atty., 1975—; city atty. City of Yoakum, 1980—. Co-founder Bluebonnet Youth Ranch, Yoakum, 1968, bd. trustees, bd. dirs., pres. Yoakum Ind. Sch. Dist.; judge Lavaca County. 1st lt. U.S. Army, 1954-56. Recipient Outstanding Cmty. Svc. award Sons of Hrman, 1984, Outstanding Svc. award Bluebonnet Youth Ranch, 1975, Yoakum Little League, 1982, Yoakum Lions, 1982, Paul Gustwick Outstanding Cmty. Svc. award, 1986, Tex. Rd. Hand award for outstanding support Tex. Hwy. Tex. Dept. Transp. Mem. Tex. Bar Assn., Am. Legion. Democrat. Roman Catholic. General practice, Probate, Real property. Home: 713 Coke St Yoakum TX 77995-4415 Office: Kvinta & Kvinta Attys 403 W Grand Ave Yoakum TX 77995-2617

KYHOS, THOMAS FLYNN, lawyer; b. Cheverly, Md., May 13, 1947. B.A. in Econs., DePauw U., 1969; J.D., Cath. U., 1973. Bar: Md. 1974, D.C. 1974, U.S. Tax Ct. 1974, U.S. Supreme Ct. 1978. sole practice, Washington, 1974— ; pres. First Oxford Corp., Washington, 1976— . Mem. ABA, Md. Bar Assn., D.C. Bar Assn. Taxation, general. Home: 5714 Massachusetts Ave Bethesda MD 20816-1929 Office: 3528 K St NW Washington DC 20007-3503

KYLE, RICHARD HOUSE, federal judge; b. St. Paul, Apr. 30, 1937; s. Richard E. and Geraldine (House) K.; m. Jane Foley, Dec. 22, 1959; children: Richard H. Jr., Michael F., D'Arcy, Patrick G., Kathleen. BA, U. Minn., 1959, LLB, 1962. Bar: Minn. 1962, U.S. Dist. Ct. Minn. 1992. Atty. Briggs & Morgan, St. Paul, 1963-68, 1970-92; solicitor gen. Minn. Atty. Gen. Office, 1968-70; judge U.S. Dist. Ct., 1992—. Pres. Minn. Law Rev., Mpls., 1962. Mem. Minn. State Bar Assn., Ramsey County Bar Assn. Republican. Episcopal. Office: US Dist Ct Federal Courts Bldg 316 Robert St N Saint Paul MN 55101-1495

LABADIE, DWIGHT DANIEL, lawyer; b. Pontiac, Mich., Dec. 16, 1940; s. Francis Edwin and Blanche Burdine (Yoakum) L.; m. Barbara L. Boyden, Sept. 5, 1964; children: Dwight D. Jr., Barbara L., Monique. BA, Kalamazoo Coll., 1963; JD cum laude, Wayne State U., 1971. Bar: Mich. 1971, U.S. Dist. Ct. Mich. 1971. Claim rep. Aetna Casualty Co., Detroit, 1964-68; workmens compensation rep. Chrysler Corp., Highland Park, Mich., 1968-72; assoc. Davidson, Gotshall, Detroit, 1972-78; ptnr. Kohl, Secrest, Wardle, Lynch, Clark & Hampton, Farmington Hills, Mich., 1972-89, Conklin, Benham, Ducey, Ottaway, Listman & Chuhran, Detroit, 1989—, shareholder, 1994—. Atty. Detroit Workers Disability Compensation Council, 1981-83; lectr. Oakland U., Pontiac, 1984. Contbr. articles to profl. jours. Mem. NRA, State Bar Mich. (workers compensation sect., negligence sect.), Econ. Detroit Club, Cruise Club Am. (Chgo.), Grosse Pointe Yacht Club (bd. dirs. 1990—), Clinton River Boat Club. Avocations: boating, sailing, hunting, scuba diving. office phone. Personal injury, Probate, Workers' compensation. Home: 1193 Roslyn Rd Grosse Pointe MI 48236-1349 Office: Conklin Benham Ducey Listman & Chuhran 1740 First National Bldg Detroit MI 48226 E-mail: dlabadie@email.com, dlabadie@conklinbenham.com

LABAY, EUGENE BENEDICT, lawyer; b. El Campo, Tex., July 20, 1938; s. Ben F. and Cecelia M. (Orsak) L.; m. Katherine Sue Ermis, Dec. 29, 1962; children: Michael, Joan, John, Paul, David, Patrick, Steven. BBA, St. Mary's U., San Antonio, 1960; JD, St. Mary's U., 1965. Bar: Tex. 1965, U.S. Dist. Ct. (we. dist.) Tex. 1968, U.S. Dist. Ct. (no. dist.) Tex. 1973, U.S. Dist. Ct. (ea. dist.) Tex. 1986, U.S. Ct. Appeals (5th cir.) 1968, U.S. Ct. Appeals (11th cir.) 1981, U.S. Supreme Ct. 1980. Briefing atty. Supreme Ct. Tex., Austin, 1965-66; assoc. Cox & Smith Inc., San Antonio, 1966-71, ptnr., 1972-83, v.p., 1972-94; pvt. practice, 1994—. Contbr. articles to profl. jours. Served to 1st lt. U.S. Army, 1960-62. Mem. ABA, State Bar Tex. (chmn. sect. internat. law 1979-80), San Antonio Bar Assn., Fed. Bar Assn., Am. Judicature soc., Cath. Lawyers Guild San Antonio, KC (coun. grand knight 1982-83), Phi Delta Phi. State civil litigation, Oil, gas, and mineral, Environmental. Home: 31720 Post Oak Trl Boerne TX 78015-4133 Office: PO Box 15244 112 W Craig Pl San Antonio TX 78212-3416

LABE, ROBERT BRIAN, lawyer; b. Detroit, Sept. 2, 1959; s. Benjamin Mitchell and Gloria Florence (Wright) L.; m. Mary Lou Budman, Nov. 12, 1989; two children: Bridget and Katherine. BA with high honors, Mich. State U., 1981; JD, Wayne State U., 1984; LLM, Boston U., 1985. Bar: Mich. 1984, U.S. Dist. Ct. Mich. 1985, U.S. Tax Ct. 1985. Assoc. Weingarden & Hauer, P.C., Bingham Farms, Mich., 1988-92, shareholder, 1992-94; prin. Robert B. Labe, P.C., Southfield, 1994—. Adj. prof. taxation and estate planning Walsh Coll., Troy, Mich., 1990-92; lectr. and presenter in field. Author: Research Edge-Taxation Guide, 1994, Bus. Succession Planning, 1996, Family Limited Liability Cos. and Limited Partnerships, 1998; mem. publ. adv. bd. Inst. Continuing Legal Edn. U. Mich., 1993—; contbr. articles to profl. jours. Bd. dirs. Oakland Bar, Oakland County Bar Found. Avocations: tennis, spectator sports. General corporate, Estate planning, Estate taxation. Office: Robert B Labe P C 2000 Town Ctr Ste 1780 Southfield MI 48075-1254 E-mail: labelaw1@home.msen.com

LABINGER, LYNETTE J. lawyer; b. L.A., Aug. 7, 1949; d. Harry and Dorothy Labinger; m. Ross A. Eadie, Jan. 21, 1972; 1 child, Loren Labinger Eadie. AB magna cum laude, Mt. Holyoke Coll., 1971; JD cum laude, NYU, 1974. Bar: Mass. 1974, R.I. 1975, U.S. Dist. Ct. R.I. 1975, U.S. Ct. Appeals (1st cir.) 1978, U.S. Supreme Ct. 1980. Law clk. U.S. Dist. Ct. R.I., Providence, 1974-76; assoc. Abedon, Michaelson, Standzler, Biener, Skolnik & Lipsey, 1976-82; ptnr. Roney & Labinger, 1983—. Mem. U.S. Dist. Ct. Bar Examiners, 1981—, Commn. . on Jud. Tenure and Discipline, 1983-86. Bd. dirs., vol. atty. R.I. affiliate ACLU, 1978—; bd. dirs. R.I. Legal Svcs. Inc., 1980-83. Recipient Vol. Atty. award ACLU, 1982, Charles Potter award Planned Parenthood R.I., 1982, NYU Prize, 1974, Alumnae Key award NYU Law Sch., 1974, Sorrentino award Nat. Women's Polit. Caucus, 1988, Civil Libertarian of Yr. award R.I. ACLU, 1989; Root-Tilden scholar, 1971-74. Fellow Am. Coll. Trial Lawyers, R.I. Bar Found. (bd. dirs. 1992—); mem. R.I. Bar Assn., Order of Coif, Phi Beta Kappa. Democrat. Civil rights, Federal civil litigation, Labor. Office: Roney & Labinger 344 Wickenden St Providence RI 02903-4469 E-mail: RoneyLabinger@aol.com

LABOON, ROBERT BRUCE, lawyer; b. St. Louis, June 14, 1941; s. Joseph Warren LaBoon and Ruth (Aab) LaBoon Freling; m. Ramona Ann Hudgins, Aug. 24, 1963; children: John Andrew, Robert Steven. BSc, Tex. Christian U., 1963; LLB cum laude, So. Meth. U., 1965. Bar: Tex. 1965. Ptnr. Locke Liddell & Sapp LLP, Houston, 1965-86, 88—; vice chmn. and gen. counsel Tex. Commerce Bancshares, Inc., 1986-88. Bd. dirs. J.P. Morgan Chase Bank Tex., Tex. Med. Ctr., Tex. Childrens Hosp. Bd. dirs., chair The Greater Houston Partnership, Houston area ARC; trustee The Kayser Found.; mem. bd. visitors M.D. Anderson Cancer Ctr.-U. Cancer Found. Fellow Tex. Bar Found., Am. Coll. of Trust and Estate Counsel; mem. ABA, AM. Law Inst., Tex. Assn. of Bank Counsel, Houston Bar Assn., State Bar Tex., Houston Club, River Oaks Country Club. Banking, General corporate, Securities. Office: Locke Liddell & Sapp LLP 600 Travis St Ste 3500 Houston TX 77002-3095

LABREC, DAVID JOHN, lawyer; b. Mondovi, Wis., Aug. 25, 1948; s. Robert John and Ruth Marie (Miller) LaB.; m. Catherine Ann Gentry, Feb. 14, 1986; 1 child, Megan Elizabeth. BA, U. Tex.-El Paso, 1970; JD, St. Mary's U., 1973. Bar: Tex. 1973, U.S. Supreme Ct. 1977, U.S. Dist. Ct. (no., so., ea. and we. dists.) Tex. 1975, U.S. Ct. Appeals (5th cir.) 1976, U.S. Ct. Appeals (11th cir.) 1981. Sole practice, El Paso, 1973-74; chief trial atty. City of El Paso, 1975-80, 1st asst. city atty., 1978-80; gen. counsel Tex. Mcpl. League, Austin, 1980-85; gen. counsel TML Risk and Ins. Mgmt. Services, Austin 1982-85, Tex. City Atty.'s Assn., 1980-85; 1st asst. city atty. City of Dallas, 1985-87; ptnr. Strasberger & Price, Dallas, 1987—, also chief govtl. law practice group. Editor Tex. City Atty.'s Assn. Mcpl. Law Bull., 1980-85. Bd. dirs. El Paso County March of Dimes Assn., 1979-80; mem. legis. rev. task force City of El Paso, 1976-77. Mem. Nat. Inst. Mcpl. Law Officers (chmn. mcpl. ins. com. 1983, 85-86, chmn. litigation sect. 1986-93), Def. Research Inst. (vice chmn. govtl. liability com. 1983—), El Paso County Young Lawyers Assn. (bd. dirs. 1976-80), Tex. City Attys. Assn. (bd. dirs.), Phi Delta Phi. Insurance, State and federal civil litigation. Home: 6435 Malcolm Dr Dallas TX 75214-3187 Office: Strasberger & Price 901 Main St Ste 4300 Dallas TX 75202-3724

LACEY, DAVID MORGAN, lawyer, school administrator; b. Denison, Tex., Feb. 3, 1950; s. Leon C. and Oneita Mae (Morgan) L.; m. Joy Mae Womack, June 3, 1971; children: Justin Louis, Heather Mae. BA summa cum laude, Harding Coll., 1972; MA, Duke U., 1974; JD with high honors, U. Tex., 1976; MEd, Houston Bapt. U., 1998. Bar: Tex. 1976, U.S. Dist. Ct. (so. dist.) Tex. 1977, U.S. Ct. Appeals (5th cir.) 1977, U.S. Dist. Ct. (ea. dist.) Tex. 1986. Law clk. to U.S. Dist. Judge, Austin, 1976-77; assoc. Baker & Botts, Houston, 1977-84; ptnr. Gilpin, Pohl & Bennett, 1984-88, Driscoll & Lacey, 1989-96; dean student affairs Westbury Christian Sch., Houston, 1998—. Mem. Tex. Law Rev., 1975-76. Pres., Christian Sch. of East Harris County, Houston, 1984-87. Mem. ABA, State Bar Tex., Houston Bar Assn., Order of Coif. Mem. Ch. of Christ. Admiralty, Federal civil litigation, State civil litigation. Home: 14931 Grassington Dr Channelview TX 77530-2307 Office: Westbury Christian Sch 10420 Hillcroft St Houston TX 77096-4796

LACEY, HENRY BERNARD, lawyer; b. Aurora, Colo., Nov. 30, 1963; s. Leonard Joseph and Colleen Trece (Ryan) L. BS, Ariz. State U., 1988, JD, 1991. Bar: Ariz. 1991, Oreg. 1996; U.S. Dist. Ct. Ariz. 1991, U.S. Ct. Appeals (9th cir.) 1992, U.S. Dist. Ct. Oreg. 1999. Jud. law clk. to Hon. Cecil F. Poole U.S. Ct. Appeals 9th Cir., San Francisco, 1991-92; assoc. Kimball & Curry, P.C., Phoenix, 1992-93; atty. Law Office of Henry B. Lacey, 1993-94, Portland, Oreg., 1996-99, Flagstaff, Ariz., 1999—; vis. fellow Natural Resources Law Inst. Northwestern Sch. Law, Lewis and Clark Coll., Portland, 1994-95; chief counsel Colo. Plateau Wildlands Def. Coun., Inc., 2001—. Counsel/environ. group adv. bd. dirs. Coalition to Reform the Ctrl. Ariz. Project, Phoenix, 1993; vol. lawyer Land and Water Fund of the Rockies, Boulder, Colo., 1993—; vol. lawyer Portland Audubon Soc., 1996-99; adj. prof. No. Ariz. U., 2000—; bd. dirs. Brite, Inc., Phoenix, Mountain Air Cmty. Radio, Flagstaff. Gen. counsel Maricopa County, Ariz. Dem. Party, 1992-94. Mem. Order of Coif, Phi Delta Phi. Roman Catholic. Avocations: hiking, bicycling, reading, photography. General civil litigation, Contracts commercial, Natural resources. Office: 120 N San Francisco St Flagstaff AZ 86001 E-mail: henry.lacey@azbar.org

LACH, JOSEPH ANDREW, lawyer; b. Wilkes-Barre, Pa., Oct. 26, 1949; s. Joseph and Catherine (Pavelko) L.; m. Barbara Jean Lach, July 29, 1972; children: Elizabeth Ann, Joseph Robert. BA in Psychology, Lafayette Coll., 1971; JD, Pa. State U., 1977. Bar: Pa. 1977, U.S. Dist. Ct. (mid. dist.) Pa., U.S. Ct. Appeals (3d cir.), U.S. Supreme Ct. Assoc. Lenahan & Dempsey, Scranton, Pa., 1977-81; prin. Hourigan, Klugerr & Quinn, Wilkes-Barre, 1981-94, mng. prin., 1994—. Mem. ethics com. Good Samaritan Regional Med. Ctr., Pottsville, Pa., 1988—, Mercy Hosp., Wilkes-Barre, 1991—; pres. bd. dirs. Wyoming Valley Montessori Sch., Kingston, Pa., 1994—; trustee Mercy Health Care Ctr., Nanticoke, Pa., 1991-95; bd. dirs. Little Flower Manor, Wilkes-Barre, 1996—. Mem. ABA, Pa. Bar Assn. (mem. ho. of dels. 1991—), Psi Chi. Democrat. Roman Catholic. General civil litigation, Personal injury, Product liability. Office: Hourigan Kluger & Quinn 700 Mellon Bank Ctr Wilkes Barre PA 18701

LACHANCE, PAUL ARTHUR, legal educator, consultant; b. Woonsocket, R.I., July 10, 1941; s. Phillippe and Aline (Jalbert) L; m. Joan C. Avanzato, Feb. 8, 1964 (div. 1971); 1 child, Michelle L. B.A.A., Fla. Atlantic U., 1973, M.P.A., 1974. Pub. dir. Sperry Div., Danbury, Conn., 1966-69; instr. Palm Beach Jr. Coll., Lake Worth, Fla., 1973-76; adj. prof. Fla. State U., Tallahassee, 1976-78; asst. prof. law Mesa Coll., Grand Junction, Colo., 1978— ; cons. phychol. stress State of Colo., 1978-81. Bd. dirs. Council of Govt., Region 11, Colo., 1979-83, Arabian Horse Club, Grand Junction, 1978-84, Crime Stoppers, Mesa County, Colo., 1982— , Victim-Outreach Grand Junction, 1979— . Republican. Roman Catholic. Home: 559 31 Rd # 4 Grand Junction CO 81504 Office: Mesa Coll 1175 Texas Ave Grand Junction CO 81501-7605

LACHEEN, STEPHEN ROBERT, lawyer; b. Phila., June 15, 1934; s. Irving H. and Jeannette S. (Silverman) LaC.; m. Arlen Green, July 5, 1955 (div. Apr. 1977); children: Caroline, Amy; m. Helen Hetherington, Apr. 5, 1981; children: Arthur, Christopher, Alexandra. BA, U. Pa., 1953; JD, U. Miami, 1957. Bar: Fla. 1957, Pa. 1958, U.S. Dist. Ct. (ea. dist.) Pa. 1957, U.S. Ct. Appeals (3d cir.) 1975, U.S. Ct. Appeals (4th cir.) 1978, U.S. Ct. Appeals (11th cir.) 1983, U.S. Ct. Appeals (9th cir.) 1983, U.S. Ct. Appeals (2d cir.) 1986, U.S. Supreme Ct. 1977. Pvt. practice, Phila., 1957-72; ptnr. LaCheen, Doner & LaCheen, 1972-82, LaCheen & Alva, Phila., 1982-86, Stephen Robert LaCheen Assocs., Phila., 1986—. Mem. Fed. Criminal Justice Act. Panel, Phila., 1979—, Lawyer Reference Svc. Panel, Phila., 1975—; bd. dirs. Genesis II, Phila.; lectr. in field. Editor The Shingle, 1975—, The Philadelphia Lawyer, 1992; contbr. articles to profl. jours.; author short stories. NEH fellow Yale U., 1978. Mem. ABA, Phila. Bar Assn. (gov. 1982), Pa. Bar Assn., Fla. Bar Assn., Internat. Bar Assn., Am. Bd. Criminal Lawyers (pres. 1997—), Nat. Assn. Criminal Def. Lawyers. Jewish. Criminal. Office: 3100 Lewis Tower Bldg Philadelphia PA 19102 E-mail: slacheen@concentric.net

LACKLAND, JOHN, lawyer; b. Parma, Idaho, Aug. 29, 1939; A.B., Stanford U., 1962; J.D., U. Wash., 1964; master gardener, Colo. State U., 1996. Bar: Wash. 1965, U.S. Dist. Ct. (we. dist.) Wash. 1965, (ea. dist.) Wash. 1973, U.S. Ct. Appeals (9th cir.) 1965, Conn. 1981, U.S. Dist. Ct. Conn. 1983, U.S. Supreme Ct. 1973, U.S. Dist. Ct. (so. dist.) N.Y. 1988. Assoc. firm Lane Powell Moss & Miller, Seattle, 1965-69; asst. atty. gen. State of Wash., 1969-72; asst. chief State of Wash. (U. Wash. div.), 1969-72; v.p., sec., gen. counsel Western Farmers Assn., Seattle, 1972-76, Fotomat Corp., Stamford, Conn., 1976-80; ptnr. Leepson & Lackland, 1981-88, Lackland and Nalewaik, 1988-92; pvt. practices Westport, Conn., 1992-94; prin. Lackland Assocs., Grand Junction, Colo., 1994—. Bd. dirs. Mercer Island (Wash.) Congl. Ch., 1967-70, pres. bd. dirs., 1970; mem. land use plan steering com. City of Mercer Island, 1970-72; bd. dirs. Mercer Island Sch. Dist., 1970-73, v.p. bd. dirs., 1972, pres. 1973; trustee Mid-Fairfield Child Guidance Ctr., 1982-84, Norfield Congl. Ch., 1982-84; bd. dirs. Grand Junction Symphony Orch., 1995-99.

LACKLAND, THEODORE HOWARD, lawyer; b. Chgo., Dec. 4, 1943; s. Richard and Cora Lee (Sanders) L.; m. Dorothy Ann Gerald, Jan. 2, 1970; 1 child, Jennifer Noel. BS, Loyola U., Chgo., 1965; MA, Howard U., 1967; JD, Columbia U., 1975; grad., U.S. Army Ranger Sch., 1968. Bar: N.J. 1975, U.S. Dist. Ct. N.J. 1975, Ga. 1982, U.S. Tax Ct. 1983, U.S. Supreme Ct. 1979, U.S. Dist. Ct. (no. dist.) Ga. 1982, U.S. Dist. Ct. (mid. dist.) Ga. 1985. Assoc. Dewey, Ballantine, Bushby, Palmer & Wood, N.Y.C., 1975-78; asst. U.S. atty. Dist. N.J., Newark, 1978-81; ptnr. Arnall Golden & Gregory, Atlanta, 1981-93, Lackland & Assoc., Atlanta, 1993-95, Lackland & Heyward, Atlanta, 1995-2000, Lackland & Assocs., LLC, Atlanta, 2000—. Adj. prof. law Ga. State U. Law Sch., 1989-99. Assoc. editor Columbia Human Rights Law Rev., 1974-75; contbr. articles to profl. jours. Adv. dir. Atlanta Bus. Devel. Ctr., Minority Bus. Devel. Coun., Atlanta, 1983-91; mem. exec. com. Leadership Atlanta, 1986, 1990-91. Capt. U.S. Army, 1967-71. Decorated Bronze Star with 1 oak leaf cluster, Purple Heart, Air medal. Mem. ABA, N.J. Bar Assn., Ga. Bar Assn., Fed. Bar Assn., Gate City Bar Assn. Democrat. Roman Catholic. General civil litigation, Contracts commercial, General corporate. Home: 4400 Oak Ln Marietta GA 30062-6355 Office: Lackland & Assocs LLC 230 Peachtree St NW Atlanta GA 30303-1562

LACOVARA, MICHAEL, lawyer; b. Bklyn., Oct. 21, 1963; s. Philip Allen and Madeline Estelle (Papio) L.; m. Carla J. Foran, Sept. 9, 1989; children: Claire Elizabeth, Edward Christopher. BA, U. Pa., 1984; MPhil, Cambridge (U.K.) U., 1985; JD, Harvard U., 1988. Law clk. Hon. Stephen Reinhardt, L.A., 1988-89; assoc. Sullivan & Cromwell, N.Y.C., 1989-96, ptnr., 1997-2000, Palo Alto, Calif., 2000—. Bd. dirs. Lower Manhattan Cultural Coun., N.Y.C., 1995—, chair, 1998; trustee Cambridge U. in Am. Thouron Found. fellow, 1984. Mem. ABA, Assn. of Bar of City of N.Y., Phi Beta Kappa. Democrat. Roman Catholic. Home: 2740 Divisadero St San Francisco CA 94123 Office: Sullivan & Cromwell 1870 Embarcadero Rd Palo Alto CA 94303 E-mail: lacovaram@sullcrom.com

LACY, ROBINSON BURRELL, lawyer; b. Boston, May 7, 1952; s. Benjamin Hammett and Jane (Burrell) L. AB, U. Calif., Berkeley, 1974; JD, Harvard U., 1977. Bar: N.Y. 1978, U.S. Dist. Ct. (so. and ea. dists.) N.Y. 1979, U.S. Dist. Ct. (we. dist.) N.Y. 1992, U.S. Ct. Appeals (2d cir.) 1983, U.S. Ct. Appeals (10th cir.) 1990, U.S. Supreme Ct. 1986. Law clk. to judge U.S. Dist. Ct. (so. dist.) N.Y., N.Y.C., 1977-78; law clk. to chief justice Warren Burger U.S. Supreme Ct., Washington, 1978-79; assoc. Sullivan & Cromwell, N.Y.C., 1979-85, ptnr., 1985—. Mem. ABA, Assn. of Bar of City of N.Y., N.Y. State Bar Assn. Bankruptcy, Federal civil litigation. Office: Sullivan & Cromwell 125 Broad St Fl 28 New York NY 10004-2489

LADAR, JERROLD MORTON, lawyer; b. San Francisco, Aug. 2, 1933; AB, U. Wash., 1956; LLB, U. Calif., Berkeley, 1960. Bar: Calif. 1961, U.S. Supreme Ct. 1967. Law clk. to judge U.S. Dist. Ct. (no. dist.) Calif., 1960-61; asst. U.S. atty. San Francisco, 1961-70; chief criminal div., 1968-70; mem. firm MacInnis & Donner, San Francisco, 1970-72; prof. criminal law and procedure U. San Francisco Law Sch., 1962-83; pvt. practice San Francisco., 1970—; ptnr. Ladar & Ladar, San Francisco, 1994—. Lectr. Hastings Coll. Law, Civil and Criminal Advocacy Programs, 1985—; chair pvt. defender panel U.S. Dist. Ct. (no. dist.) Calif., 1980-90; ct. apptd. chair stats. and tech. subcom. Fed. Civil Justice Reform Act Com. (no. dist.) Calif., 1990-95; ct. apptd. mem. Fed. Ct. Civil Local Rules Revision Com. (no. dist.) Calif., 1994—; ct. apptd. chmn. Criminal Local Rules Revision Com. (no. dist.) Calif., 1991-99; mem. continuing edn. of bar criminal law adv. com. U. Calif., Berkeley, 1978-83, 89-2001; panelist, mem. nat. planning com. ABA Nat. Ann. White Collar Crime Inst., 1996—; ct. apptd. mem. Local Disciplinary Rule Draft com., 1998-99 Author: (with others) Selected Trial Motions, Grand Jury Practice, Asset Forfeiture, California Criminal Law and Procedure Practice, 5th edit., 2000, Direct Examination-Tips and Techniques, 1982, Collateral Effects of Federal Convictions, 1997, Insult Added to Injury: The Fallout From Tax Conviction, 1997, Give Me A Break-Finding Federal Misdemeanors, 1998, The Court: We're Here to Seek the Truth; Defense Counsel: Excuse Me, That's Not My Job, 1999, A Day At The Grand Jury, 2000, Daubert at the Gates: Use A Trojan Horse, 2001. Trustee Tamalpais Union High Sch. Dist., 1968-77, chmn. bd., 1973-74; mem. adv. com. Nat. PTA Assn., 1972-78; apptd. mem. criminal justice act com. U.S. Ct. Appeals (9th cir). Fellow Am. Bd. Criminal Lawyers; mem. ABA, San Francisco Bar Assn. (editor in Re 1974-76), State Bar Calif. (pro-tem disciplinary referee 1976-78, vice chmn. pub. interest and edn. com. criminal law sect., mem. exec. com. criminal law sect. 1980-87, editor Criminal Law Sect. News 1981-87, chmn. exec. com. 1983-84), Am. Inns. of Ct. (exec. com. 1994-97), Fed. Bar Assn. (panelist), Nat. Sentencing Inst. (contbr.) Federal civil litigation, State civil litigation, Criminal. Office: 507 Polk St Ste 310 San Francisco CA 94102-3339

LADD, DONALD MCKINLEY, JR. retired lawyer; b. Huntington Park, Calif., Oct. 24, 1923; s. Donald McKinley and Rose (Roberts) L.; B.A., Denison U., 1945; J.D., Stanford U., 1950; m. Eleanor June Martin, June 29, 1951; children— Donald, Richard, Cameron. Admitted to Calif. bar, 1950; asso. firm Anderson McPharlin & Conners, Los Angeles, 1951; legal staff Union Pacific RR, Los Angeles, 1953-56; sr. dep. prosecutor City of Pasadena (Calif.), 1956-58; with Office of Dist. Atty., Santa Clara County, Calif., 1958-88, asst. dist. atty., 1971-88. Served to capt. USMCR, 1943-46, 51-52. Certified criminal law specialist Calif. Mem. Bay Area Prosecutors Assn., Calif. State Bar, Calif. Dist. Attys Assn., Stanford Law Alumni Assn., Blue Key, Omicron Delta Kappa, Phi Alpha Delta. Clubs: Marines Meml., Am. Commons, English-Speaking Union, Brit. Am. Home: 1034 Golden Way Los Altos CA 94024-5057 Office: Office of Dist Atty Santa Clara County 70 W Hedding St San Jose CA 95110-1705

LADD, JEFFREY RAYMOND, lawyer; b. Mpls., Apr. 10, 1941; s. Jasper Raymond and Florence Marguerite (DeMarce) L.; m. Kathleen Anne Crosby, Aug. 24, 1963; children: Jeffrey Raymond, John Henry, Mark Jasper, Matthew Crosby. Student, U. Vienna, Austria; BA, Loras Coll.; postgrad., U. Denver; JD, Ill. Inst. Tech. Bar: Ill. 1973, U.S. Dist. Ct. 1973. V.p. mktg. Ladd Enterprises, Des Plaines, Ill., 1963-66, v.p. mktg. and fin. Crystal Lake, 1966-70; ptnr. Ross & Hardies, Chgo., 1973-81, Boodell, Sears, et al., 1981-86, Bell, Boyd & Lloyd, Chgo., 1986—. Spl. asst. atty. gen. for condemnation State of Ill., 1977-82; chmn. Metra, 1984—. Named Chgo. City Club's 1995 Citizen of Yr. Mem. ABA, Chgo. Bar Assn., Nat. Assn. Bond Lawyers, Ill. Assn. Hosp. Attys., Am. Acad. Hosp. Attys., Crystal Lake Jaycees (Disting. Svc. award), Crystal Lake C. of C. (past pres.), Econ. Club, Legal Club, Union League Club, Bull Valley Golf Club, Woodstock Country Club, Alpha Lambda. Roman Catholic. Avocations: golf, hunting, fishing, tennis, skiing. General corporate, Health, Municipal (including bonds). Office: Bell Boyd & Lloyd 3 First National Pla 70 W Madison St Ste 3300 Chicago IL 60602-4284

LADDAGA, BETH JANE, lawyer; b. Beaufort, S.C., Sept. 29, 1953; d. Philip Covert and Leone (Ford) Goodlove; m. R. Charles May, May 20, 1977 (div. Apr. 1978); 1 child, Amanda; m. Lawrence A. Laddaga, Nov. 12, 1983; 1 child, Rachel. BA, Coll. Charleston, 1993; JD, U. S.C., 1996. Bar: S.C. 1996, U.S. Ct. Appeals (4th cir.) 1996, U.S. Dist. Bar. (no. dist.) Tex. 2000. Assoc. Ness, Motley, Loadholt, Richardson & Poole, Charleston, S.C., 1996—. Contbr. articles to profl. jours. Mem. ABA, ATLA, S.C. Bar Assn., S.C. Trial Lawyers Assn. (products liability subcom.), S.C. Women Lawyers Assn., Roscoe Pound Found., Phi Kappa Phi, Phi Delta Phi. Federal civil litigation, Personal injury, Product liability. Office: Ness Motley Loadholt Richardson & Poole 28 Bridgeside Blvd PO Box 1792 Mount Pleasant SC 29465-1792

LADDAGA, LAWRENCE ALEXANDER, lawyer; b. New Hyde Park, N.Y., Aug. 12, 1957; s. Carmine Michael and Adeline (Lauricella) L.; m. Beth Jane Goodlove, Nov. 12, 1983; children: Amanda May, Rachel. BA cum laude, U. S.C., 1978, JD, 1981. Bar: S.C. 1981, U.S. Dist. Ct. S.C. 1981, U.S. Ct. Appeals (4th cir.) 1981, U.S. Tax Ct. 1982, U.S. Supreme Ct. 1989. Assoc. Wise & Cole, P.A., Charleston, S.C., 1981-83; founding shareholder, sr. ptnr. Laddaga-Garrett PA, 1983—; adj. asst. prof. dept. health adminstrn. and policy Med. U. S.C., 1999—. Bd. dirs., 1st v.p. Charleston chpt. Am. Cancer Soc., 1987-88. Fellow Healthcare Fin. Mgmt. Assn. (advanced mem., bd. dirs. 1991-94, sec., v.p. 1991-95, pres. 1997-98), S.C. Bar Assn. (chairperson health care law com. 1995-97), Charleston County Bar Assn., Am. Health Lawyers Assn., S.C. Hosp. Assn., Order Ky. Cols., Kiwanis, Elks, Masons, Phi Beta Kappa. Contracts commercial, Health. Home: 1391 Madison Ct Mount Pleasant SC 29466-7961 Office: 5300 International Blvd Ste B 203 North Charleston SC 29418 E-mail: LADDAGA@sehealthlaw.com

LAFILI, ELLEN YOST See YOST, ELLEN G.

LAFOLLETTE, ERNEST CARLTON, lawyer; b. Buffalo, Aug. 12, 1934; s. John and Mary Esther (Schramm) LaF.; m. Marcy Eleanore Freeman, June 16, 1979; children: Andre Michael, David Steven; children from previous marriage: karen Yvonne, Brian Clark, Ernest Claud, Leah Ann. BA cum laude, Alfred U., 1956; JD summa cum laude, Syracuse Law Sch., 1959; LLM in Taxation, U. Bridgeport, 1987. Bar: N.Y. 1959, Pa. 1964, Conn. 1978, U.S. Ct. Appeals (2d cir.) 1984, U.S. Supreme Ct. 1985, U.S. Dist. Ct. (so. dist.) N.Y. 1990, U.S. Tax Ct. 1991. Law clk. chief justice N.Y. Supreme Ct., Rochester, 1959; div. atty. GE, King of Prussia, Pa., 1962-70; prof. law Albany Law Sch., 1970-73; supr. attys. NLRB, Washington, 1973-75; labor rels. counsel Norlin Corp., N.Y.C., 1975-78; pvt. practice Fairfield, 1978—. Editor in chief Syracuse Law Sch. Rev., 1959. Capt. U.S. Army. Mem. ABA, ATLA, Conn. Bar Assn., Justinian Soc., Order of Coif. State civil litigation, Labor, Corporate taxation. Office: 1432 Post Rd Fairfield CT 06430-5930 E-mail: esqecl@aol.com

LAFUZE, WILLIAM L. lawyer; b. Washington, Feb. 21, 1946; children: Molly, Betsy, William Jr. BS in Physics, U. Tex., Austin, 1969, JD, 1973; MS in applied Sci., So. Meth. U., 1971; postgrad., U. London, 1973. Rsch. scientist Ctr. for Nuclear Studies, Austin, 1966-69; instr. computer sci. U. Tex., 1968-69, 71-73; assoc. Vinson & Elkins, Houston, 1973-80, ptnr., 1980—. Speechwriter; contbr. articles to profl. jours. Fellow State Bar Tex. (life, intellectual property sect., coun. 1979-83, chmn. 1984-85, consumer law sect., coun. 1981—, computer sect., coun. 1990—), ABA (PTC sect.), ATLA, Houston Bar Assn., Am. Intellectual Property Law Assn. (pres. 1992-93, bd. dirs. 1983, chmn. amicus brief com. 1986-88), U.S. Trademark Assn. (bd. editors Trademark Reporter 1976-78), Nat. Coun. Patent Law Assn. (del. 1982—, bd. dirs. 1987-90), Nat. Inventors Hall of Fame (pres. 1984-85, bd. dirs. 1987—), Licensing Exec. Soc., Tex. Assn. Def. Counsel, MIT Ent. Forum Tex. (bd. dirs.). General civil litigation, Intellectual property. Office: Vinson & Elkins 1001 Fannin 2720 First City Towers Houston TX 77002 E-mail: blafuze@velaw.com

LAGLE, JOHN FRANKLIN, lawyer; b. Kansas City, Mo., Jan. 22, 1938; s. Ernest J. and Hilda B. Lagle; m. Nina E. Weston, Aug. 1, 1959; m. Diana G. Fogle, July 14, 1962 (dec. 1992); children: Robert, Gregory. BBA, UCLA, 1961, JD, 1967. Bar: Calif. 1967, U.S. Dist. Ct. (no. dist.) Calif. 1967. Assoc. Hindin, McKittrick & Marsh, Beverly Hills, Calif., 1967-70, Macco Corp., Newport Beach, 1970, Rifkind & Sterling, Beverly Hills, 1971; mem. Fulop & Hardee, and predecessor firm, 1971-82; ptnr. Leff & Stephenson, 1983; sole practice Los Angeles, 1984; ptnr. Barash & Hill (formerly Wildman, Harrold, Allen, Dixon, Barash & Hill) L. A., 1985-91; pvt. practice L.A., 1992-2000; with Barbosa Garcia, 1998-2000, Hill, Farrer & Burrell, LLP, 2000-01; atty. pvt. practice, 2001—. Arbitrator NASD Regulation, Inc. Contbr. to Practice Under the California Corporate Securities Law of 1978. Served with U.S. Army, 1961-63. Mem. ABA, Arbitration Assn. (arbitrator), Calif. Bar Assn., Los Angeles County Bar Assn. Republican. E-mail: j. General corporate, Real property, Securities. Office: 16750 Marquez Ave Pacific Palisades CA 90272-3240 also: 801 S Grand Ave Los Angeles CA 90017-4613 E-mail: lagle@msn.com

LAGOS, JAMES HARRY, lawyer; b. Springfield, Ohio, Mar. 14, 1951; s. Harry Thomas and Eugenia (Papas) L.; m. Nike Daphne Pavlatos, July 3, 1976. BA cum laude, Wittenberg U., 1970; JD, Ohio State U., 1972. Bar: Ohio 1973, U.S. Dist. Ct. (so. dist.) Ohio 1973, U.S. Tax Ct. 1975, U.S. Supreme Ct. 1976, U.S. Ct. Appeals (6th cir.) 1979. Asst. pros. atty. Clark County, Ohio, 1972-75; with Lagos & Lagos, Springfield, 1975—. Mem. Springfield Small Bus. Coun., past chmn., 1977—, Ohio Small Bus. Coun., 1980—, past chmn., vice chmn.; past pres., v.p. Nat. Small Bus. United, 1982—; del. Small Bus. Nat. Issues Conf., 1984; del. Ohio Gov.'s Conf. on Small Bus., 1984, resource person regulatory and licensing reform com., 1984. Bd. dirs., past pres. Greek Orthodox Ch., 1974—; mem. coun. Greek Orthodox Diocese of Detroit, 1985-86; past chmn. Clark County Child Protection Team, 1974-82; past chmn. Clark County Young Rep. Club, past pres., sec., treas., 1968-76, chmn. Ohio del. to White Ho. Conf. on Small Bus., 1985-86, del. to White Ho. Conf. on Small Bus., 1995. Staff sgt. Ohio Air N.G., 1970-76. Recipient Dr. Melvin Emanuel award West Ctrl. Ohio Hearing and Speech Assn., 1983, Medal of St. Paul the Apostle, Greek Orthodox Archdiocese North and South Am., 1985, Disting. Svc. award Springfield-Clark County, 1977; named one of Outstanding Young Men of Am., 1978, Small Bus. Adv. Yr., U.S. Sma.. Bus. Adminstrn., 1991. Mem. Am. Hellenic Inst. (pub. affairs com. 1979—, bd. dirs.), Am. Hellenic Ednl. Progressive Assn. (pres., past treas.), Rsch. Inst. Small and Emerging Bus. (bd. dirs. 1993—), C. of C. (vice-chmn., treas., bd. dirs.), Jaycees (past chmn. several coms. 1973-89, Spoke award 1974), Ohio State Bar Assn., Clark County Bar Assn. (past sec., exec. com. 1973—), West Ctrl. Ohio Hearing and Speech Assn. (bd. dirs., pres., v.p. 1973-84), Alpha Alpha Kappa, Phi Eta Sigma, Tau Pi Phi, Pi Sigma Alpha. Criminal, Family and matrimonial, Personal injury. Home: 2023 Audubon Park Dr Springfield OH 45504-1113 Office: Lagos & Lagos 1 S Limestone St Ste 1000 Springfield OH 45502-1294 E-mail: lagosth@aol.com

LAGUEUX, RONALD RENE, federal judge; b. Lewiston, Maine, June 30, 1931; s. Arthur Charles and Laurette Irene (Turcotte) L.; m. Denise Rosemarie Boudreau, June 30, 1956; children: Michelle Simone, Gregory Charles, Barrett James. AB, Bowdoin Coll., 1953; LLB, Harvard U., 1956. Assoc. then ptnr. Edwards and Angell Law Firm, Providence, 1956-68; assoc. justice Superior Ct. State of R.I., 1968-86; judge U.S. Dist. Ct., 1986—; chief judge, 1992-99. Exec. counsel to Gov. Chafee, R.I., 1963-65. Rep. candidate for U.S. Senate, 1964; corporator R.I. Hosp., Providence, 1965-01; solicitor Southeastern New Eng. Province United Way, 1957-68. Mem. ABA, Bowdoin Coll. Alumni Council (past v.p., pres.), Am.-French Geneal. Soc. Home: 90 Greenwood Ave Rumford RI 02916-1934 Office: US Dist Ct 1 Exchange Ter Providence RI 02903-1744

LAIDLAW, ANDREW R. lawyer; b. Durham, N.C., Aug. 28, 1946; BA, Northwestern U., 1969; JD, U. N.C., 1972. Bar: Ill. 1972. Chair exec com., mem. Seyfarth, Shaw, Chgo., CEO Chicago. Contbr. articles to profl. jours. Mem. ABA (antitrust and securities law coms. 1982—), Barristers. Contracts commercial. Office: Seyfarth Shaw Mid Continental Plz 55 E Monroe St Ste 4200 Chicago IL 60603-5863

LAIRD, EDWARD DEHART, JR. lawyer; b. Pitts., July 14, 1952; s. Edward D. Sr. and Miriam (Hellman) L.; m. Ellen Armstrong, July 30, 1977; children: Megan, Edward, Peter. BA, SUNY, Oswego, 1974; JD, Western New Eng. Sch. Law, 1977. Bar: N.Y. 1978, U.S. Dist. Ct. (no. dist.) N.Y. 1978, U.S. Dist Ct. (so. dist.) N.Y. 1989, U.S. Dist. Ct. Vt. 1995, U.S. Ct. Appeals (2d cir.) 1985, U.S. Supreme Ct. 1986. Shareholder Carter, Conboy, Case, Blackmore, Maloney and Laird, P.C., Albany, NY, 1977—. Instr. legal rsch. and writing Western New Eng. Sch. Law, Springfield, Mass., 1976-77. Master Am. Inns Ct. Albany Law Sch. chpt.; mem. ABA, N.Y. State Bar Assn., Albany County Bar Assn., Def. Rsch. Inst., Def. Rsch. Inst. of Northeastern N.Y. General civil litigation, Insurance, Personal injury. Office: Carter Conboy Case Blackmore Maloney and Laird PC 20 Corporate Woods Blvd Albany NY 12211-2350

LAITINEN, SARI K.M. lawyer; b. Mikkeli, Finland, 1966; d. Leevi and Liisa Laitinen. Student, U. Jyväskylä, Finland, 1986-87; BA, Hamline U., 1991, JD, 1993. Bar: Minn., D.C. Lay judge, clk. City Ct. of Mikkeli, summers 1990-91; atty. King & Spalding, Atlanta, 1996, Lindquist & Vennum PLLP, Mpls., 1993-95, 96-99, Robins, Kaplan, Miller & Ciresi, LLP, Mpls., 1999—. Mem. staff Hamline Law Rev., 1992. Founding mem. Finnish Trade Steering Com., Mpls., 1997—. Finnish Found. for Econ. Edn. grantee, 1992. Mem. Phi Beta Kappa. Avocations: opera. General corporate, Finance, Securities. Office: Robins Kaplan Miller & Ciresi LLP 2800 LaSalle Plz Minneapolis MN 55402

LAKE, ANN W. law educator; b. Lowell, Mass., May 14, 1919; d. Frank and Aniela (Opielowski) Jablonski; m. Thomas E. Lake, Sept. 5, 1942; children: Beverly Lake Wilkes, Douglas, Warren. BS in Music, Lowell (Mass.) State Coll., 1940; LLB, U. Detroit, 1946, JD, 1968; MEd, Boston State Coll., 1964; MA in History, Boston U., 1967. Bar: Mass. 1946, U.S. Supreme Ct. 1957. Prof. law Boston State Coll., 1964-70, Salem (Mass.) State Coll., 1970-90, prof. emeritus, 1990—; pvt. practice Lowell, Mass. Presenter, lectr. in field. Author: Everywomans Legal Guide; contbr. articles to profl. jours. Tchr., supr. Pape Sch., Savannah, Ga.; clk. U. Lowell Found., Inc., 1977-81. Fellow Am. Bar Found.; mem. ABA (com. mem.), Nat. Assn. Women Lawyers (pres. 1980-81), Nat. Bd. Trial Advocacy, Mass. Coun. Pub. Justice (bd. dirs. 1971-82), Mass. Advocates Soc. (sec. 1958—), Mass. Bar Assn. (bd. dirs. 1971-72, 74-77), Mass. Assn. Women Lawyers (pres. 1971-72), Assn. Mass. State Coll. Alumni (pres. 1961-64), Bar Assn. Norfolk County (council 1977-80), Norfolk Mental Health Assn. (pres. 1972-73), New Eng. Law Inst. (adv. coun. 1971-76), Polish Bus. & Profl. Womens Club (pres. 1977-79). Home: 40 Sawyer Dr Dedham MA 02026-5701

LAKE, I. BEVERLY, JR. state supreme court chief justice; b. Raleigh, N.C., 1934; s. I. Beverly, Sr. and Gertrude L.; m. Susan Deichmann Smith; children: Lynn Elizabeth, Guy, Laura Ann, I. Beverly III. Student, Mars Hill Coll., 1951; BS, Wake Forest U., 1955, JD, 1960. Bar: N.C. Pvt. practice, 1960-69, 76-85; asst. atty. gen. State of N.C., 1969-74, dep. atty. gen., 1974-76; Gov.'s legis. liason, chief lobbyist, 1985; judge Superior Ct., 1985-91; assoc. justice N.C. Supreme Ct., 1992—2000, chief justice, 2001—. Chmn. bd. trustees Ridge Rd. Bapt. Ch., 1968-69; mem. N.C. Senate, 1976-80, chmn. Senate Judiciary Com.; Rep. nominee Gov. N.C., 1979-80; del. Rep. Nat. Convention, 1980; Rep. state fin. chmn., mem. ctr. com., mem. exec. com., 1980-82; N.C. eastern chmn. Reagan-Bush Campaign, 1984; bd. visitors Wake Forest U. Sch. Law, 1995—; bd. vis. Southeastern Bapt. Theol. Sem. Intelligence staff officer U.S. Army, 1956-58; capt. USAR, 1960-68; col. N.C. State Militia, 1989-92. Mem. AMVETS, N.C. Bar Assn., Wake County Bar Assn., Assn. Interstate Commerce Comm. Practitioners, Navy League, Am. Legion, Masons, Shriners, Phi Alpha Delta. Office: NC Supreme Ct PO Box 1841 Raleigh NC 27602-1841*

LAKE, SIM, federal judge; b. Chgo., July 4, 1944; s. Simeon T. Jr. and Helen (Hupka) L.; m. Carol Illig, Dec. 30, 1970; children: Simeon Timothy IV, Justin Carl. BA, Tex. A&M, 1966; JD, U. Tex., 1969. Bar: Tex. 1969, U.S. Dist. Ct. (so. dist.) Tex. 1969, U.S. Ct. Appeals (5th cir.) 1969, U.S. Supreme Ct. 1976. From assoc. to ptnr. Fulbright & Jaworski, Houston, 1969-70, 72-88; judge U.S. Dist. Ct. (so. dist.) Tex., 1988—. Past editor Houston Lawyer. Capt. U.S. Army., 1970-71. Fellow Tex. Bar Found., Houston Bar Assn., State Bar Tex., Am. Law Inst. Office: US Courthouse 515 Rusk Ave Rm 9535 Houston TX 77002-2605

LALLI, MICHAEL ANTHONY, lawyer; b. N.Y.C., Sept. 14, 1955; s. Joseph and Maria (Magnacca) L.; m. Marigrace Ann Esposito, May 19, 1979; children: Elena Marie, Marissa Ann. BA, Fordham Coll., 1976, JD, 1979; LLM, NYU, 1984. Bar: N.Y. 1980, U.S. Dist. Ct. (so. dist.) N.Y. 1981. Assoc. counsel Equitable Life Assurance Soc. U.S., N.Y.C., 1979-85; sr. tax atty. Texaco, Inc., White Plains, N.Y., 1985—. Mem. moot ct. bd. 1977-79. Mem. Fordham Urban Law Jour., 1977-79. Mem. ABA, N.Y. State Bar Assn., Phi Beta Kappa, Pi Sigma Alpha. Roman Catholic. Pension, profit-sharing, and employee benefits, Corporate taxation, Taxation, general. Home: 16 Thomas St Scarsdale NY 10583-1031 Office: Texaco Inc 2000 Westchester Ave Purchase NY 10577-2530

LALLY-GREEN, MAUREEN ELLEN, superior court judge, law educator; b. Sharpsville, Pa., July 5, 1949; d. Francis Leonard and Charlotte Marie (Frederick) Lally; m. Stephen Ross Green, Oct. 5, 1979; children: Katherine Lally, William Ross, Bridget Marie. BS, Duquesne U., 1971, JD, 1974. Bar: Pa. 1974, D.C., U.S. Dist. Ct. (we. dist.) Pa. 1974, U.S. Ct. Appeals (3d cir.) 1974, U.S. Supreme Ct. 1978. Atty. Houston Cooper, Pitts., 1974-75, Commodity Futures Trading Commn., Washington, 1975-

78; counsel Westinghouse Electric Corp., Pitts., 1978-83; adj. prof. law Duquesne U., 1983-86, 2000—, prof. law, 1986-2000; judge Superior Ct, 1998, Superior Ct., 2000—. Fed. dist. ct. arbitrator; mem. criminal procedure rules com. Supreme Ct. Pa., 1994-97; dir. European Union Law Conf., Dublin, 1995-97, Intellectual Law Conf., Italy, 1997; panel Disciplinary Bd. of Commonwealth of Pa.; adj. prof. law Duquesne U., 2000—. Chair Cranberry Twp. Zoning Hearing Bds., Pa., 1983-98; counsel Western Pa. Ptnrs. of Ams., 1987-90, pres. 1993-95, bd. dirs., 1995—; active Elimination of World Hunger Project, 1977-85, Bishop's Com. on Dialogue with Cath. Univs.; co-chair Millenium com. Duquesne U., 1997-2000. Fellow Kellogg Found. (for Ptnrs. of Ams.), 1990-92. Mem. Pa. Bar Assn. (ethics com. 1987-94, commn. on women in the law 1994—, co-chair quality of work life com. 2001), Allegheny County Bar Assn. (women in law com., professionalism com., ethics com., sec. bd. dirs. 1992-2001), Duquesne U. Alumni Assn. (bd. dirs. 1982-89, sec. 1988-89, gov. of bd.), Duquesne U. Law Alumni Assn. (bd. dirs. 1987, treas. 1991, v.p. 1992). Republican. Roman Catholic. Avocations: children's activities, sports. Office: 2420 Grant Bldg 330 Grant St Pittsburgh PA 15219-2202

LAM, WING WO, lawyer; b. Hong Kong; m. Agnes Oi Lun. LLB, U. Hong Kong, 1978, PCLL, 1979. Bar: solicitor Hong Kong 1981, solicitor Eng. and Wales 1984, solicitor and advocate Singapore 1989, solicitor NSW, 1990, notary pub. Hong Kong 1992. Asst. solicitor Deacons, Hong Kong, 1981-86, ptnr., 1986—. Arbitrator Shantou Arbitration Commn., 1997—. Contbr. articles to profl. jours. Mem. Law Soc. Hong Kong (legal edn. co. 1994—), Working Party on Tng. of Trainee Solicitors (chmn. 2000—). Banking, Finance. Office: Deacons Alexandra House Hong Kong China Fax: (852) 2810-0431. E-mail: wingwo.lam@deacons.com.hk

LAMB, KEVIN THOMAS, lawyer; b. Quincy, Mass., Nov. 14, 1956; s. John Philip and Kathleen Elaine (O'Brien) L. BA, Washington and Lee U., 1978, JD, 1982. Bar: Va. 1982, D.C. 1988, Mass. 1990. Law clk. to presiding justice U.S. Bankruptcy Ct. (we. dist.) Va., Lynchburg, 1982-84; atty. U.S. Dept. Justice, Los Angeles, 1984-85; assoc. Jones, Day, Reavis & Pogue, 1985-86, Ballard, Spahr, Andrews & Ingersoll, Washington, 1986-89, Testa, Hurwitz & Thibeault, L.L.P., Boston, 1989-91, ptnr., 1992—. Mem. ABA (com. on cons. fin. svcs., subcom. on securities products, com. on bus. bankruptcy), Am. Bankruptcy Inst. (com. on legis.), Comml. Law League Am. Bankruptcy, Contracts commercial. Office: Testa Hurwitz & Thibeault LLP High St Tower 125 High St Fl 22 Boston MA 02110-2704 E-mail: lamb@tht.com

LAMBE, JAMES PATRICK, lawyer; b. Washington, June 4, 1952; s. John Joseph and Patricia Ann (Job) Lambe; m. Marie Barbara Giardino, May 21, 1977; children: Katherine Mary, Joseph Patrick. AB with distinction, U. Mich., 1974; JD, U. Ill., 1977. Bar: Calif. 1977, U.S. Dist. Ct. (ea. dist.) Calif. 1977, U.S. Ct. Appeals (9th cir.) 1978, U.S. Supreme Ct. 1981, U.S. Dist. Ct. (ctrl. dist.) Calif. 1983, D.C. 1985; cert. specialist in criminal law State Bar Calif. Bd. Legal Specialization; cert. specialist in criminal trial advocacy Nat. Bd. Trial Advocacy. Assoc. Wagner & Wagner, Fresno, Calif., 1978-79, Parichan, Renberg, Crossman & Eliason, Fresno, 1979; claims atty. CIGNA Corp., 1979-85; dep. city atty. City of Fresno, 1985-86; dep. pub. defender County of Fresno, 1986—. Cons., author Continuing Edn. of the Bar, U. Calif./State Bar Calif., Berkeley, 1992—; judge pro tem Fresno County Superior Ct., 2000—; instr. Summer Trial Skills Inst., Calif. Pub. Defenders Assn., San Diego, 2001—. Cons. to books: California Criminal Law Procedure and Practice, update, 1992, 3rd edit., 1996, California Criminal Law Forms Manual, 1995, rev., 2001; co-author: California Criminal Law Procedure and Practice, 4th edit., 1998, California Criminal Law Procedure and Practice, 5th edit., 2000. Mem. Vols. in Parole. Mem.: Calif. Attys. for Criminal Justice, D.C. Bar, Fresno County Bar Assn. (bd. dirs. 1998—99), Nat. Assn. Criminal Def. Lawyers, State Bar Calif. (conf. of dels. 1996—99, criminal law sect. exec. com. 2001—), Phi Alpha Delta. Democrat. Avocation: distance running. Office: Fresno County Pub Defenders Office 2220 Tulare St Ste 300 Fresno CA 93721-2104

LAMBERT, GARY ERVERY, lawyer; b. Providence, Oct. 27, 1959; s. Ervery Eldege and Melitta (Hirsch) L.; m. Lori Keller, Apr. 22, 1995; children: Katherine Elizabeth, Grace Abigail. BS in Chemistry and Biology, Valparaiso (Ind.) U., 1981; JD with honors, Drake U., 1984. Bar: Iowa 1984, Mass. 1986, U.S. Ct. Mil. Appeals 1986, U.S. Dist. Ct. Mass. 1987, U.S. Ct. Appeals (1st cir.) 1987, U.S. Patent and Trademark Office 1993, U.S. Ct. Appeals (fed. cir.) 1996. Litigator Gallagher & Gallagher, P.C., Boston, 1987-89; owner Law Office of Gary Lambert, 1989-93; ptnr. Lambert Assocs., PLLC, 1993—. Intellectual property judge advocate, hdqs. USMC, 1997—. Capt. USMC, 1984-87, Japan. Mem. Boston Bar Assn., Boston Patent Law Assn., Am. Intellectual Property Assn., Marine Corps Res. Officers Assn. (life), NRA (life). Republican. Lutheran. Intellectual property, Patent, Trademark and copyright. Home: 32 Columbia Ave Nashua NH 03064-1601 Office: Lambert Assocs PLLC 92 State St Boston MA 02109-2004

LAMBERT, GEORGE ROBERT, lawyer, real estate broker; b. Muncie, Ind., Feb. 21, 1933; s. George Russell and Velma Lou (Jones) L.; m. Mary Virginia Alling, June 16, 1956; children: Robert Allen, Ann Holt, James William. BS, Ind. U., Bloomington, 1955; JD, IIT Chgo.- Kent Coll. Law, Coll. Law, 1962. Bar: Ill. 1962, U.S. Dist. Ct. (no. dist.) Ill. 1962, Iowa 1984, Pa. 1988, Ind. 1999. V.p., gen. counsel, sec. Washington Nat. Ins. Co., Evanston, Ill., 1970-82; v.p., gen. counsel Washington Nat. Corp., 1979-82; sr. v.p., sec., gen. counsel Life Investors Inc., Cedar Rapids, Iowa, 1982-88; v.p., gen. counsel Provident Mut. Life Ins. Co., Phila., 1988-95; pres. Lambert Legal Consulting, Inc., Wilmington, Del., 1995—; realtor Coldwell Banker, North Palm Beach, Fla., 1996—, Cressy and Everett GMAC Real Estate, South Bend, Ind., 1999-2000; owner, broker Lambert Realty, Granger, 2001—. Alderman Evanston City Coun., 1980-82. Served to lt. USAF, 1955-57. Mem. Ill. State Bar Assn., Ind. Bar Assn., Iowa Bar Assn., Assn. of Life Ins. Counsel (past pres.), Nat. Assn. Realtors, Ind. Assn. Realtors, Greater South Bend-Mishawaka Assn. Realtors, Inc. General corporate, Estate planning, Insurance. Home: 51702 Stoneham Way Granger IN 46530-8493

LAMBERT, JOSEPH EARL, state supreme court chief justice; b. Berea, Ky., May 23, 1948; s. James Wheeler and Ruth (Hilton) L.; m. Debra Hembree, June 25, 1983; children: Joseph Patrick, John Ryan. BS in Bus. and Econs., Georgetown Coll., 1970; JD, U. Louisville, 1974; completed sr. appellate judges seminar, NYU Sch. Law, 1987; Hon. Doctorate, Eastern Ky. U., 1999, Georgetown Coll., 1999. Bar: Ky. 1974. Staff Sen. John Sherman Cooper U.S. Senate, Washington, 1970-71; law clk. to judge U.S. Dist. Ct., Louisville, 1974-75; ptnr. Lambert & Lambert, Mt. Vernon, Ky., 1975-87; justice Supreme Ct. Ky., Frankfort, 1987-98, chief justice, 1998—. Chmn. Jud. Form Retirement Commn., 1996—. Mem. Bd. Regents Eastern Ky. U., Richmond, 1988-92. Recipient Disting. Alumni award U. Louisville Sch. Law, 1988. Mem. Ky. Bar Assn. Republican. Baptist. Office: State Ky State Capitol Bldg Office Chief Justice Rm 231 Frankfort KY 40601 E-mail: cjlambert@mail.aoc.state.ky.us

LAMBERT, LYN DEE, library media specialist, law librarian; b. Fitchburg, Mass., Jan. 5, 1954; m. Paul Frederick Lambert, Aug. 11, 1979; children: Gregory John, Emily Jayne, Nicholas James. BA in History, Fitchburg State Coll., 1976, MEd in History, 1979; JD, Franklin Pierce Law Ct., 1983; MLS, Simmons Coll., 1986. Law libr. Fitchburg Law Libr., Mass. Trial Ct., 1985-96; media specialist libr. Samoset Sch., Leominster, Mass., 1996—. Instr. paralegal studies courses Fisher Coll., Fitchburg, 1989-94, Anna Maria Coll., Paxton, Mass., 1995—, Atlantic Union Coll., Lancaster, Mass., 1995—, pre-law coll. courses Fitchburg State Coll., 1995—; tech. com. City of Leominster Shc., Net Day Participant and trainer/leader, Leominster H.S.., Northwest, Johnny Appleseed, Fall Brook, Southeast and Samoset. Mem. Am. Legion Band, Fitchburg, 1959—, Westminster (Mass.) Town Band, 1965—, Townsend Town Band, 1999—; appt. to Mass. Strategic Plan Com. for delivery of libr. svcs. among multi-type librs. within the commonwealth. Recipient Community Leadership award Xi Psi chpt. Kappa Delta Pi-Fitchburg State Coll. chpt., 1993. Mem. ALA, Am. Assn. Law Librarians (copyright com. 1987-89, publs. rev. com. 1990-92, state, ct. and county law librs. spl. interest sect. publicity com. 1993—), Law Librarians New Eng. (conf. com. 1988), Mass. Libr. Assn. (edn. chair 1991-93, freedom of info. com., legislation com.), New Eng. Libr. Assn., New Eng. Microcomputer Users Group (profl. assoc.), North Cen. Mass. Libr. Alliance (newsletter editor 1990—), Spl. Libr. Assn., Beta Phi Mu, Phi Alpha Delta, Phi Delta Kappa (newsletter editor Montachusett chpt. 1998-2000, pres. Montachusett chpt. 2000—). Avocations: singing, guitar, clarinet, hiking, camping. Office: Samoset Libr Media Ctr 100 Decicco Dr Leominster MA 01453-5161

LAMBERT, SAMUEL WALDRON, III, lawyer, foundation executive; b. N.Y.C., Jan. 12, 1938; s. Samuel W. and Mary (Hamill) L.; m. Louisa Garnsey, Aug. 25, 1962; children: Louisa Kelly, Samuel William, Sarah Hamill. BA, Yale U., 1960; LLB, Harvard U., 1963. BAr: N.J. 1964, U.S. Tax Ct. 1975. Assoc. Albridge C. Smith III, Princeton, N.J., 1964-67; ptnr. Smith, Cook, Lambert & Miller, and predecessors, 1967-80; officer, dir. Smith, Lambert, Hicks & Miller, P.C., 1981-87; ptnr. in charge of office Drinker, Biddle & Reath, 1988-2000, mng. ptnr., 1994-96; chmn. Windham Found., 1997—; ptnr. Drinker, Biddle & Shanley, LLP, Princeton, 2000—, chair personal law dept., 2001—. Bd. dirs. Winslow Found., Bunbury Co., Curtis W. McGraw Found.; capt. Princeton Republican County Com., 1967-69. With USAR, 163-69. Mem. ABA, N.J. Bar Assn., Princeton Bar Assn. (pres. 1976-77). Estate planning, Probate. E-mail: lambersw@dbr.com

LAMBORN, LEROY LESLIE, law educator; b. Marion, Ohio, May 12, 1937; s. LeRoy Leslie and Lola Fern (Grant) L. AB, Oberlin Coll., 1959; LLB, Western Res. U., 1962; LLM, Yale U., 1963; JSD, Columbia U., 1973. Bar: N.Y. 1965, Mich. 1974. Asst. prof. law U. Fla., 1965-69; prof. Wayne State U., 1970-97, prof. emeritus, 1997—. Vis. prof. State U., Utrecht, 1981. Author: Legal Ethics and Professional Responsibility, 1963; contbr. articles on victimology to profl. jours. Mem. Am. Law Inst., Nat. Orgn. Victim Assistance (bd. dirs. 1979-88, 90-91), World Soc. Victimology (exec. com. 1982-94). Home: Apt 2502 1300 E Lafayette St Detroit MI 48207-2924 Office: Wayne State U Law Sch Detroit MI 48202

LAMIA, THOMAS ROGER, lawyer; b. Santa Monica, Calif., May 31, 1938; s. Vincent Robert II and Maureen (Green) L.; m. Susan Elena Brown, Jan. 10, 1969; children: Nicholas, Katja, Jenna, Tatiana, Carlyn, Mignon. Student, U. So. Calif., 1956, BS, 1961; student, U. Miss., 1957-58; JD, Harvard U., 1964. Bar: Calif. 1965, D.C. 1980, N.Y. 1990, U.S. Dist. Ct. (ctrl. dist.) Calif. 1965, U.S. Dist. Ct. D.C. 1980, U.S. Tax Ct. 1982. Assoc. McCutchen, Black, Verleger & Shea, L.A., 1964-66; lectr. in law U. Ife, Ile-Ife, Nigeria, 1966-67, U. Zambia, Lusaka, 1967-68; assoc. Paul, Hastings, Janofsky & Walker, 1968-72, ptnr., 1972-99, mem. exec. com., 1976-80, mng. ptnr. Washington office, 1980-83; pvt. practice N.Y.C., 1999—. Prin., mgr., gen. counsel Cowan Rentals, LLC, 1997—. Mem. ABA (bus. law sect., intellectual prop. law sect.), Internat. Bar Assn., Harvard Law Sch. Assn., Nat. Aquarium Soc. (bd. dirs. 1982-99). Private international, Mergers and acquisitions, Securities. Office: 24 W 55th St Ste 7B New York NY 10019-5320 E-mail: trlamia@lamialaw.com

LAMM, CAROLYN BETH, lawyer; b. Buffalo, Aug. 22, 1948; d. Daniel John and Helen Barbara (Tatakis) L.; m. Peter Edward Halle, Aug. 12, 1972; children: Alexander P., Daniel E. BS, SUNY Coll. at Buffalo, 1970; JD, U. Miami (Fla.), 1973. Bar: Fla., 1973, D.C., 1976, N.Y. 1983. Trial atty. frauds sect. civil div. U.S. Dept. Justice, Washington, 1973-78, asst. chief comml. litigation sect. civil div., 1978, asst. dir., 1978-80; assoc. White & Case, 1980-84, ptnr., 1984—. Mem. Sec. State's Adv. Com. Pvt. Internat. law, Secs. Study Com. on Proposal Hague Conv. on Jurisdiction and the Enforcement of Judgements; arbitrator U.S. Panel of Arbitrators, Internat. Ctr. Settlement of Investment Disputes, 1995—; mem. com. on pvt. dispute resolution NAFTA. Mem. bd. editors Can./U.S. Rev. Bus. Law, 1987-92; mem. editorial adv. bd. Inside Litigation; contbg. editor: Internat. Arbitration Law Rev., 1997—; contbr. articles to legal publs. Mem. Mayor's Commn. on Violence Against Women, 1996-2000; mem. coun. Holy Trinity Parish; bd. dirs. D.C. Appleseed Found.; mem. Frederick Abramson Bd. Found. Fellow Am. Bar Found.; mem. ABA (chmn. young lawyers divsn., rules and calendar com., chmn. house membership com., chmn. assembly resolution com., sec. 1984-85, chmn. internat. litigation com. coun. 1991-94, sect. litigation, ho. dels. 1982—, nomination com. 1984-87, chair 1995-96, past D.C. Cir. mem., standing com. fed. judiciary 1992-95, chmn. com. scope and correlation of work 1996-97, commn. on multidisciplinary practice), Am. Arbitration Assn. (bd., arbitrator, com. on arbitration law, gen. counsel's law com., bd. dirs.), Fed. Bar Assn. (chmn. sect. on antitrust and trade regulation), Bar Assn. D.C. (bd. dirs., sec., found. bd.), D.C. Bar (pres. 1997-98, bd. govs. 1987-93, steering com. litigation sect.), Am. Law Inst. (coun.), Women's Bar Assn. D.C., Am. Soc. Internat. Law, Am. Indonesian C. of C. (bd. dirs.), Am. Uzbekistan C. of C. (bd. dirs., sec., gen. counsel), Am. Turkish Friendship Coun. (bd. dirs., chair), Nat. Women's Forum, Columbia Country Club, Manchester Country Club. Democrat. Administrative and regulatory, Federal civil litigation, Private international. Home: 2801 Chesterfield Pl NW Washington DC 20008-1015 Office: White and Case 601 13th St NW Washington DC 20005-3807 E-mail: clamm@whitecase.com

LAMM, RICHARD DOUGLAS, lawyer, former governor of Colorado; b. Madison, Wis., Aug. 3, 1935; s. Arnold E. and Mary (Townsend) L.; m. Dorothy Vennard, May 11, 1963; children: Scott Hunter, Heather Susan. BBA, U. Wis., 1957; LLB, U. Calif., Berkeley, 1961. Bar: Colo. 1962; CPA, Colo. Accountant, Salt Lake City, 1958, Ernst & Ernst, Denver, 1961-62; atty. Colo. Anti-Discrimination Commn., 1962-63, Jones, Meiklejohn, Kilroy, Kehl & Lyons, Denver, 1963-65; sole practice, 1965-74; mem. Colo. Ho. of Reps., 1966-74, asst. minority leader, 1971-74; gov. Colo., 1975-87; now spl. counsel Berliner, Boyle, Kaplan, Zisser & Walter (formerly O'Connor & Hannan), Denver; dir. Ctr. for Pub. Policy & Contempo U. Denver, 1987—. Asso. prof. law U. Denver, from 1969; chmn. natural resource and environ. mgmt. com. Nat. Gov.'s Assn., 1978-79, mem., from 1979, also mem. exec. com. and environment com., and chmn. task force on synthetic fuels. Pres. Denver Young Democrats, 1963; v.p. Colo. Young Democrats, 1964; mem. Conservation Found., Denver Center Performing Arts Center for Growth Alternatives, Central City Opera House Assn. Served as 1st lt. U.S. Army, 1957-58. Office: Berliner Boyle Kaplan Zisser & Walter 1 United Bank Ctr 1700 Lincoln St Denver CO 80203-4500 Mailing: U Denver Ctr for Pub Policy 2301 S Gaylord St Denver CO 80210-5201

LAMMERS, THOMAS DEAN, lawyer, educator; b. Celina, Ohio, Oct. 19, 1951; s. Calvin Dean and Dorothy (Gilmore) L.; m. Kimberly Sue Stubbs, Mar. 18, 1980. Village solicitor Villages of Ft. Recovery and Montezuma, Ohio, 1978-92, Village of Rockford, 1985-92; ptnr. Purdy and Lammers, Celina, 1980-90, Purdy, Lammers & Schiavone, Celina, 1990—. Adj. prof. bus. law Wright State U., Dayton, Ohio, 1982—; chmn. Celina Civil Svc. Commn., 1986-96. Chmn. Sesquicentennial Com., Celina, 1984; bd. dirs. Tri-County Mental Health Bd., Celina, 1977-83, Mercer County Hospice, Inc., Children's Trust Fund, 1985-95; active Celin Combined Svcs. Appeal, pres., 1989-99. Mem. Ohio Bar Assn. (del. 1984-88, bd. govs. 1994-97), Mercer County Bar Assn. (pres. 1987-89), Rotary (pres. Celina 1984-85), Phi Delta Phi. Democrat. Lutheran. General civil litigation, General corporate, Real property. Home: 328 Johnson Ave Celina OH 45822-1267 Office: Purdy Lammers & Schiavone 113 E Market St # 404 Celina OH 45822-1730

LAMMERT, RICHARD ALAN, corporate lawyer; b. Pitts., Mar. 21, 1949; s. John Albert and Gladys Irene (Miller) L.; m. Susan Christine McLaren, Jan. 30, 1971; children: Ann, Adam. BA, Grove City Coll., 1971; JD, Duquesne U., 1975. Bar: Pa. 1975, N.Y. 1985. Legal asst. Mellon Bank, N.A., Pitts., 1972-75, atty., 1975-76; assoc. counsel Equibank, 1976-80, trust counsel, 1980-81, asst. gen. counsel, sr. v.p., 1981-84; gen. counsel, sr. v.p., sec. M & T Bank Corp, Buffalo, 1984—. Mem. N.Y. State Bar Assn., Allegheny County Bar Assn., Erie County Bar Assn. Republican. Lutheran. Club: Park Country. Banking, General corporate, Securities. Home: 6405 Woodberry Ct East Amherst NY 14051-1547 Office: M & T Bank Corp 1 M & T Plaza Buffalo NY 14240

LAMON, HARRY VINCENT, JR. lawyer, director; b. Macon, Ga., Sept. 29, 1932; s. Harry Vincent and Helen (Bewley) L.; m. Ada Healey Morris, June 17, 1954; children: Hollis Morris, Kathryn Gurley. BS cum laude, Davidson Coll., 1954; JD with distinction, Emory U., 1958. Bar: Ga. 1958, D.C. 1965. Of counsel Troutman Sanders LLP, Atlanta, 1995—. Adj. prof. law Emory U., 1960-79. Contbr. articles to profl. jours. Mem. adv. bd. Metro Atlanta Salvation Army, 1963-97, chmn., 1975-79, life mem., 1997—, mem. nat. adv. bd., 1976-96, chmn. 1991-93, emeritus, 1996—; mem. adv. coun. on employee welfare and pension benefit plans U.S. Dept. Labor, 1975-79; mem. pension and benefits reporter adv. bd. Bur. Nat. Affairs; mem. bd. visitors Davidson Coll., 1979-89; trustee, pres. So. Fed. Tax Inst., Inc., 1965—; trustee Am. Tax Policy Inst., Inc., 1989-96, Embry-Riddle Aero U., 1989-2001, emeritus, 2001—, Cathedral of St. Philip Endowment Fund, Atlanta, 1989—. 1st lt. AUS, 1954-56. Recipient Others award Salvation Army, 1979, Centennial honoree, 1990. Fellow Am. Bar Found. (life), Am. Coll. Trust and Estate Counsel, Am. Coll. Tax Counsel, Internat. Acad. Estate and Trust Law, Ga. Bar Found. (life), Am. Coll. Employee Benefits Counsel (charter); mem. ABA, Atlanta Bar Assn. (life), Am. Bar Retirement Assn. (bd. dirs. 1989-96, pres. 1994-95), Am. Law Inst. (life), Am. Employee Benefits Conf., So. Employee Benefits Conf. (pres., 1972, hon. life mem.), State Bar Ga. (chmn. sect. taxation 1969-70, vice chmn. comm on continuing lawyer competency 1982-89), Am. Judicature Soc., Atlanta Tax Forum, Lawyers Club Atlanta, Nat. Emory U. Law Sch. Alumni Assn. (pres. 1967), Practicing Law Inst., ALI-ABA Inst., CLUs Inst., The Group, Inc. (hon. life), Kiwanis Club Atlanta (hon. mem.; pres. 1974), Peachtree Racket Club (pres. 1986-87), Atlanta Coffee House Club, Capital City Club, Peachtree Club, Cosmos Club (Washington), Phi Beta Kappa (fellow), Omicron Delta Kappa, Phi Delta Phi, Phi Delta Theta (chmn. nat. cmty. svc. day 1969-72, legal commr. 1973-76, province pres. 1976-79, Golden Legion 2001). Episcopalian. Estate planning, Pension, profit-sharing, and employee benefits, Taxation, general. Home: 4415 Paces Battle NW Atlanta GA 30327-3023 Office: Troutman Sanders LLP 600 Peachtree St NE Ste 5200 Atlanta GA 30308-2231 E-mail: HVL9166@aol.com

LAMPERT, MICHAEL ALLEN, lawyer; b. Phila., May 6, 1958; s. Arnold Leonard and Marilyn (Sternberg) L.; m. Angela Gallicchio, Dec. 6, 1987; 1 child, David Max. AB in Econs. cum laude, U. Miami, Coral Gables, Fla., 1979, postgrad., 1980; JD, Duke U., 1983; LLM in Taxation, NYU, 1984. Bar: Fla. 1983, D.C. 1984, Pa. 1984, U.S. Tax Ct. 1984, U.S. Ct. of Appeals for the Armed Forces 1995; U.S. Dist. Ct. (S. Dist. Fla.), 2000, bd. cert. tax lawyer, Fla. Bar. Assoc. Cohen, Scherer, Cohn & Silverman, P.A., North Palm Beach, Fla., 1984-88; instr. div. continuing edn. Fla. Atlantic U., Boca Raton, 1988—; prin. Jacobson & Lampert, P.A., 1988-91; pvt. practice West Palm Beach, 1991—. Mem. editl. bd. Southeastern Tax Alert, 1993-97, Sales and Use Tax Alert, 1997—. Instr., trainer, past chpt. vice-chair, sect. for bd. dirs. ARC, Palm Beach County, Fla.; bd. dirs. Jewish Fedn. Palm Beach County, 1989-91, 97-99, Jewish Family and Children's Svc. Palm Beach County, 1988—, treas., 1991-94, pres., 1997-99; pres. Jewish Residential and Family Svc., Inc., 1997—, T & M Ranch Cmtys., Inc.; commr. Commn. for Jewish Edn.-Palm Beach, 1997-99; mem. nat. planned giving com. Weismann Inst., Israel; v.p. planned giving Am. Soc. for Tech., Palm Beach; pres. T&M Ranch Cmtys., Inc., 2000—. Recipient Young Leadership award, 1988, Safety award ARC, 1989, Cert. of Merit, Am. Radio Relay League, West Palm Beach Club, 1988, Cert. of Appreciation for Leadership, ARC Disaster Svcs., Palm Beach County, 1989, Disaster Svc. award, 1994, Human Resources award, 1993, Tax Law award Legal Aid Soc. of Palm Beach County and Palm Beach County Bar Assn., 1993, Young Leadership award Jewish Fedn. of Palm Beach County, 1998. Mem. Palm Beach Tax Inst. (pres., bd. dirs.), Fla. Bar (exec. coun., tax sect.), Palm Beach County Bar Assn. (chair bus. and corp. continuing legal edn. com. 1989-90, chair legal asst. com. 1988-91, Tax Law award 1993), Legal Aid Soc. of Palm Beach County, Inc. Avocations: aquatics, amateur radio, running. Estate planning, Taxation, general. Office: Ste 900 1655 Palm Beach Lakes Blvd West Palm Beach FL 33401-2211 E-mail: lamperttaxlaw@att.net

LAMPING, WILLIAM JAY, lawyer; b. Detroit, Aug. 27, 1954; s. William Jay and Marilyn Alice (Welsand) L.; m. Kathryn Szczepanik, July 18, 1981; children: Elizabeth, Jacqueline. BS, U. Mich., 1976; JD, Wayne State U., 1979. Bar: Mich. 1979, U.S. Dist. Ct. (ea. dist.) Mich. 1979, U.S. Ct. Appeals (6th cir.) 1981, U.S. Supreme Ct. 1991, U.S. Dist. Ct. (no. dist.) Ohio 1992. Assoc. Kiefer, Allen, Cavanagh & Toohey, Detroit, 1980-82; ptnr. Fieger, Fieger & Lamping, Southfield, Mich., 1982-84; pvt. practice William J. Lamping, P.C., Birmingham, Mich., 1984-86; ptnr. Vestevich, Mallender, DuBois & Dritsas, P.C. and predecessor firms, Bloomfield Hills, Mich., 1986—; arbitrator Better Bus. Bur., Detroit, 1981; Mem. steering com. Ann Arbor Tenants Union, Mich., 1976. Nat. Merit scholar U. Mich., Ann Arbor, 1972. Mem. ABA, Assn. Trial Lawyers Am., Mich. State Bar Assn., Mich. Trial Lawyers Assn., Apple Programmers & Developers Assn. Democrat. Roman Catholic. Lodge: Optimists (bd. dirs. Birmingham club, 1984-91, Chairman's award 1987). Avocations: skiing, computer programming, woodworking. General civil litigation, Contracts commercial, Computer. Home: 4314 Copper Cliff Ct Bloomfield Hills MI 48302-1922 Office: Vestevich Mallender DuBois & Dritsas PC 800 W Long Lake Rd Ste 200 Bloomfield Hills MI 48302-2058

LANAM, LINDA LEE, lawyer; b. Ft. Lauderdale, Fla., Nov. 21, 1948; d. Carl Edward and Evelyn (Bolton) L. BS, Ind. U., 1970, JD, 1975. Bar: Ind. 1975, Pa. 1979, U.S. Dist. Ct. (no. and so. dists.) Ind. 1975, U.S. Supreme Ct. 1982, Va. 1990. Atty., asst. counsel Lincoln Nat. Life Ins. Co., Ft. Wayne, Ind., 1975-76, 76-78; atty., mng. atty. Ins. Co. of N.Am., Phila., 1978-79, 80-81; legis. liaison Pa. Ins. Dept., Harrisburg, 1981-82, dep. ins. commr., 1982-84; exec. dir., Washington rep. Blue Cross and Blue Shield Assn., Washington, 1984-86; v.p. and sr. counsel Union Fidelity Life Ins. Co., Am. Patriot Health Ins. Co., etc., Trevose, Pa., 1986-89; v.p., gen. counsel, corp. sec. The Life Ins. Co. Va., Richmond, 1989-97, sr. v.p., gen. counsel, corp. sec., 1997-98, also bd. dirs.; v.p., chief counsel state rels. Am. Coun. Life Ins., Washington, 1999—. Chmn. adv. com. health care legis. Nat. Assn. Ins. Commrs., 1985-87, chmn. long term care, 1986-87, mem. tech. resource com. on cost disclosure and genetic testing, 1993-98; mem. tech. adv. com. Health Ins. Assn. Am., 1986-89; mem. legis. com.

Am. Coun. Life Ins., 1994-96, mem. market conduct com., 1997-98. Contbr. articles to profl. jours. Pres. Phila. Women's Network, 1980-81; chmn. city housing code bd. appeals Harrisburg, 1985-86. Mem. ABA, Richmond Bar Assn. Republican. Presbyterian. General corporate, Insurance, Legislative. Office: Am Coun Life Ins 1001 Pennsylvania Ave NW Washington DC 20004-2505

LANCASTER, JOAN ERICKSEN, state supreme court justice; b. 1954; BA magna cum laude, St. Olaf Coll., Northfield, Minn., 1977; spl. diploma in social studies, Oxford U., 1976; JD cum laude, U. Minn., 1981. Atty. LeFevere, Lefler, Kennedy, O'Brien & Drawz, Mpls., 1981-83; asst. U.S. atty. Dist. Minn., 1983-93; shareholder Leonard, Street and Deinard, 1993-95; dist. ct. judge 4th Jud. Dist., 1995-98; assoc. justice Minn. Supreme Ct., 1998—. Office: Minn Supreme Ct 25 Constitution Ave Saint Paul MN 55155-1500

LANCASTER, KENNETH G. lawyer; b. Stafford Springs, Conn., Dec. 6, 1949; s. Talbot Augustin and Helen Collier (McRae) L.; m. Margaret Jane Royer, Aug. 25, 1973; children: Kimberly Jane, John Talbot, Christopher Andrew. BA, U. Miami, 1971, JD, 1974. Bar: Fla. 1974, U.S. Dist. Ct. (so. dist.) Fla. 1975, U.S. Dist. Ct. (mid. dist.) Fla. 1976. Adminstr. Met. Dade County, Miami, Fla., 1971-73; assoc. Robert A. Spiegel, Coral Gables, 1973-78; sole practice South Miami, 1978-80; ptnr. Clark, Dick & Lancaster, 1980-87, King & Lancaster PA, South Miami, 1987—. Cons. 1st City Bank Dade County, Miami, 1983-84; dir. U. Miami Bus. Sch. Bd. dirs., pres.-elect U. Miami Hall Fame, Coral Gables, 1984—, mem. endowment com., 1982—; mem. Atty.'s Title Ins. Fund, 1982—. Mem. ABA, Fla. Bar Assn., Dade County Bar Assn. (Disting. Svc. award 1984), Dade County Attys. Real Property Coun., Hurricane Club/U. Miami (bd. dirs. 1984—, pres. 1996-97). Estate planning, Probate, Real property. Home: 10241 SW 141st St Miami FL 33176-7005 Office: King & Lancaster PA 5975 Sunset Dr Ste 703 Miami FL 33143-5198

LANCASTER, RALPH IVAN, JR. lawyer; b. Bangor, Maine, May 9, 1930; s. Ralph I. and Mary Bridget (Kelleher) L.; m. Mary Lou Pooler, Aug. 21, 1954; children: Mary Lancaster Miller, Anne, Elizabeth Peoples, Christopher, John, Martin. AB, Coll. Holy Cross, 1952; LLB, Harvard U., 1955; LLD (hon.), St. Joseph's Coll., 1991. Bar: Maine 1955, Mass. 1955. Law clk. U.S. Dist. Ct. Dist. Maine, 1957-59; ptnr. firm Pierce Atwood, Portland, Maine, 1961—, mng. ptnr., 1993-96; ind. counsel In Re Herman apptd. by spl. divsn. D.C. Ct. Appeals, 1998—. Condr. trial advocacy seminar Harvard U.; lectr. U. Maine; chmn. merit selection panel U.S. Magistrate for Dist. of Maine, 1982, 88; bd. visitors U. Maine Sch. Law, 1991-96, chair, 1991-93; spl. master by appointment U.S. Supreme Ct. in State of N.J. vs. State of Nev. et al, 1987-88; mem. 1st Ctr. Adv. Com. on Rules, 1991-96, legal adv. bd. Martindale Hubbell, Lexis Nexis, 1990—; represented U.S. in Gulf of Maine in World Ct. at The Hague, 1984; U.S. Supreme Ct. apptd. spl. master Commonwealth of Va. vs. State of Md., 2000—. Former mem. Diocese of Portland Bur. Edn. With U.S. Army, 1955-57. Mem. Maine Jud. Coun., Am Coll. Trial Lawyers (chmn. Maine 1974-79, bd. regents 1982-87, treas. 1985-87, pres. 1989-90), Maine Bar Assn. (pres. 1982), Cumberland County Bar Assn., Canadian Bar Assn. (hon.). Republican. Roman Catholic. Federal civil litigation, State civil litigation, Insurance. Home: 162 Woodville Rd Falmouth ME 04105-1120 Office: 1 Monument Sq Portland ME 04101-4033 E-mail: RLancaster@PierceAtwood.com

LANCE, ALAN GEORGE, state attorney general; b. McComb, Ohio, Apr. 27, 1949; s. Cloyce Lowell and Clara Rose (Wilhelm) L.; m. Sheryl C. Holden, May 31, 1969; children: Lisa, Alan Jr., Luke. BA, S.D. State U., 1971; JD, U. Toledo, 1973. Bar: Ohio 1974, U.S. Dist. Ct. (no. dist.) Ohio 1974, U.S. Ct. Mil. Appeals 1974, Idaho 1978, U.S. Supreme Ct. 1996. Asst. pros. atty. Fulton County, Wauseon, Ohio, 1973-74; ptnr. Foley and Lance, Chartered, Meridian, Idaho, 1978-90; prin. Alan G. Lance, 1990-94; rep. Idaho Ho. of Reps., Boise, 1990-94, majority caucus chmn., 1992-94; atty. gen. State of Idaho, 1995—. Capt. AUS, 1974-78. Mem. Nat. Assn. Attys. Gen. (vice chair conf. western attys. gen. 1998, chmn. 1999), Ohio Bar Assn., Idaho Bar Assn., Idaho Trial Lawyers Assn., Meridian C. of C. (pres. 1983), Am. Legion (judge adv. 1981-90, state comdr. 1988-89, alt. nat. exec. com. 1992-94, nat. exec. com. 1994-96, chmn. nat. fgn. rels. commn. 1996-97, ex-officio mem. nat. POW/MIA com. 1996—, nat. comdr. 1999-2000, chair nat. adv. com. 2000-01), Elks. Republican. Avocation: fishing. Home: 1370 Eggers Pl Meridian ID 83642-6528 Office: PO Box 83720 Boise ID 83720-3720

LANCIONE, BERNARD GABE, lawyer; b. Bellaire, Ohio, Feb. 3, 1939; s. Americus Gabe and June (Morford) L.; m. Rosemary C., Nov. 27, 1976; children: Amy, Caitin, Gillian, Bernard Gabe II, Elizabetta Marie. BS, Ohio U., 1960; JD, Capitol U., 1965. Bar: Ohio 1965, U.S. Dist. Ct. (so. dist.) Ohio 1967, U.S. Supreme Ct. 1969, U.S. Ct. Appeals (4th cir.) 1982, U.S. Dist. Ct. (no. dist.) Ohio 1989. Pres. Lancione Law Office, Co., L.P.A., Bellaire, Ohio, 1965-87; mng. atty. Cichon Lancione Co., L.P.A., St. Clairesville, 1982-85; of counsel Ward, Kaps, Bainbridge, Maurer, Bloomfield & Melvin, Columbus, 1987-88; Ohio Asst. Atty. Gen., 1988-91; sole practice, 1991—. Spl. counsel Ohio Atty. Gen's. Office, 1991-95; solicitor Bellaire City (Ohio), 1968-72; asst. prosecutor County of Belmont (Ohio), 1972-76. Pres. Young Dems. Ohio, 1970-72; pack com. chmn. Pack 961, Westerville, Ohio Cub Scouts Am., 1992-93. Mem. ABA, Assn. Trial Lawyers Am., Ohio State Bar Assn., Columbus Bar Assn., Ohio Acad. Trial Lawyers (award of merit 1972). Democrat. Roman Catholic. Bankruptcy, Family and matrimonial, General practice. Home: 1108 Acillom Dr Westerville OH 43081-1104 Office: 647 Park Meadow Rd # E Westerville OH 43081-2878 E-mail: blancion@columbus.rr.com

LAND, CHARLES EDWARDS, lawyer; b. Washington, Nov. 18, 1952; s. Henry Carter Jr. and Marjorie (Nesbitt) L.; m. Margaret Dalton, Feb. 21, 1981; children: Juliet McLure, Charles Edwards Jr. BA, U. Va., 1975, JD, 1978. Bar: Va. 1978, U.S. Dist. Ct. (ea. dist.) Va. 1978. Ptnr. Kaufman & Canoles, Norfolk, Va., 1978—. Mem. ABA, Va. State Bar Assn., Va. Bar Assn. Episcopalian. Real property. Home: 302 Raleigh Ave Norfolk VA 23507-1838 Office: Kaufman & Canoles 1 Commercial Pl Ste 2000 Norfolk VA 23510-2126 E-mail: celand@kaufman.com

LAND, STEPHEN BRITTON, lawyer; b. Norwalk, Conn., Nov. 26, 1954; s. Gay Vallee and Elizabeth Edna (Cooper) L.; m. Jane Elizabeth Drew, June 15, 1974; children: Sarah Britton, John Drew. AB, Harvard U., 1975, JD, MBA, Harvard U., 1979. Bar: N.Y. 1980, U.S. Dist. Ct. (so. and ea. dists.) N.Y. 1980, U.S. Ct. Claims 1980, U.S. Tax Ct. 1980. Assoc. Sullivan & Cromwell, N.Y.C., 1979-87; ptnr. Howard, Darby & Levin, 1987—96, Linklaters, N.Y.C., 1996—. Bd. dirs. Inform, Inc., N.Y.C., 1992-2001. Bd. dirs. Oxfam Am., Boston, 1979-85. Mem. ABA, N.Y. State Bar Assn., Larchmont (N.Y.) Yacht Club. Republican. Presbyterian (elder). Corporate taxation. Home: 29 Mohegan Rd Larchmont NY 10538-1426 Office: Linklaters 1345 Avenue Of The Americas New York NY 10105-0302 E-mail: stephen.land@linklatrs.com, sland@panix.com

LANDAU, FELIX, lawyer; b. Hof/Salle, Germany, June 29, 1947; came to U.S., 1950; s. Fiszel and Ursula (Wahncau) L.; m. Kay Ellen Krutza, Aug. 10, 1979; children: Erik Lloyd, Kelly Anne, Kristine Marie. BS, U. Colo., 1969; MA, U. Northern Colo., 1972; JD cum laude, Gonzaga U., 1982. Bar: Wash. 1983, Wis. 1988. Assoc. Liebman, Conway, Olejniczak and Jerry, S.C., Green Bay, Wis., 1987-90; pvt. practice, Bellevue, Wash., 1990—. Assoc. editor Gonzaga U. Law Rev., 1981-82; author: Accident Investigation - Documenting the Facts, WSTLA Automobile Accident Litigation Deskbook, 2000. Founder, head coach Bellevue Eagles Track and Cross Country Team. Capt. USAF, 1983-87. Mem. ABA, Wash. Bar Assn., Wash. State Trial Lawyers Assn. (Eagle mem., chmn. Eastside roundtable 1995-98), East King County Trial Lawyers Assn., Wis. Bar Assn., Phi Delta Phi. Avocations: sports, golf, basketball, tennis, jogging, coaching USA Track and Field and Cross Country Running. General civil litigation, Family and matrimonial, Personal injury. Office: 14670 NE 8th St Bellevue WA 98007-4127 Business E-Mail: landaulawoffice@aol.com

LANDAU, MICHAEL B. law educator, musician, writer; b. Wilkes-Barre, Pa., July 3, 1953; s. Jack Landau and Florence (Rabitz) Simon. BA, Pa. State U., 1975; JD, U. Pa., 1988. Vis. prof. law Dickinson Sch. Law, Pa. State U., Carlisle; assoc. Cravath, Swaine and Moore, N.Y.C., 1988-90, Skadden, Arps, N.Y.C., 1990-92; assoc. prof. Coll. Law Ga. State U., Atlanta, 1992-99, prof. law, 1999—. Vis. prof. law U. Ga. Law Sch., 1998; guest lectr. Johannes Kepler U., Linz, Austria, summer 1994, 95, 96; vis. scholar Univ. Amsterdam, 2000. Contbr. articles to law jours. on copyright, art, patent, entertainment law. Mem. ABA, N.Y. State Bar Assn., Internat. Bar Assn., Vol. Lawyers for Arts, Am. Fedn. Musicians, Am. Intellectual Property Law Assn., Copyright Soc. U.S. Am., Phi Kappa Phi, Omicron Delta Epsilon. Democrat. Avocations: photography, jazz guitar, jazz piano. Office: Ga State U Coll Law University Pla Atlanta GA 30303 E-mail: mlandau@gsu.edu

LANDAU, PEARL SANDRA, lawyer, real estate broker; b. Toronto, Ont., Can., Nov. 2, 1956; came to U.S., 1983; d. Albie and Carolyn Sylvia Landau. Student, Granton Inst. Tech., 1980; BBA, U. Tex., Arlington, 1994; JD, Tex. Wesleyan U., 1997. Bar: (Tex.) 98; lic. real estate broker Tex. Real estate sales assoc. SCI Comml. Realty, Inc., Dallas, 1984-85, Empire Properties, Inc., Dallas, 1985-87; real estate broker, owner Landau Comml. Real Estate, Irving, Tex., 1987-98; contract atty. Dallas and Ft. Worth, 1998; corp. atty., in-house counsel ACE America's Cash Express, Irving, 1998—. Recipient Pro Bono award Dallas Vol. Atty. Program, 1998. Mem.: ABA, Tex. Bar Assn. (Dallas chpt. vice chair franchise and distbn. law sect. 2001), 5th Fed. Cir. Bar Assn., Dallas Bar Assn., Dallas Area Real Estate Lawyers Group, Am. Corp. Counsel Assn. Jewish. Landlord-tenant, General corporate, Real property. Home: 408 Harwood Circle Euless TX 76039 Office: ACE America's Cash Express 1231 Greenway Dr Ste 800 Irving TX 75038

LANDAU, WALTER LOEBER, lawyer; b. New Orleans, Sept. 9, 1931; s. Walter Loeber and Mae (Wilzin) L.; m. Barbara Jane Gordon, June 23, 1954; children: Donna Hardiman, Blair Tripp, Gordon Loeber. BA, Princeton U., 1953; LLB, Harvard U., 1956. Bar: N.Y. 1956, U.S. Dist. Ct. (so. dist.) N.Y. 1962, U.S. Supreme Ct. 1971. Assoc. firm Sullivan & Cromwell, N.Y.C., 1959-65, ptnr., 1966-98, sr. counsel, 1999—. Trustee Reece Sch., N.Y.C.; mem. Met. Opera Assn.; bd. dirs., treas. Opera Orch. N.Y., bd. dirs. N.Y.C. Opera; bd. dirs., sec. Manhattan Theatre Club. Fellow Am. Bar Found.; mem. ABA, N.Y. State Bar Assn., Assn. Bar City N.Y., Am. Law Inst. Republican. Office: Sullivan & Cromwell 125 Broad St Fl 24 New York NY 10004-2400 E-mail: landaul@sullcrom.com

LANDE, JAMES AVRA, lawyer; b. Chgo., Oct. 2, 1930; s. Theodore and Helen C. (Hamburger) L.; m. Ann Mari Gustavsson, Feb. 21, 1959; children: Rebecca Susanne, Sylvia Diane. BA, Swarthmore Coll., 1952; JD, Columbia U., 1955. Bar: N.Y. 1958, Calif. 1967. Assoc. Rein, Mound & Cotton, N.Y.C., 1957-59; atty. VA, Seattle, 1959-61, Weyerhaeuser Co., Tacoma, 1961-63, Lande Assocs., San Francisco, 1963-67, NASA, Ames Rsch. Ctr., Moffett Field, Calif., 1967-70; house counsel Syntex Corp., Palo Alto, 1970-73; dir. contracts dept. Electric Power Rsch. Inst., 1973-81; corp. atty., dir. contracts Lurgi Corp., Belmont, 1981-82; contracts mgr. Bechtel Corp., San Francisco, 1982-92; sr. contract mgr. Bay Area Rapid Transit Dist., Millbrae, Calif., 1992—. Adj. prof. U. San Francisco Sch. Law, 1972-73; lectr. law U. Santa Clara Sch. Law, 1968-82; pres. Syntex Fed. Credit Union, 1971-72. Served with U.S. Army, 1955-57. Mem. Calif. Bar Assn., Nat. Contract Mgmt. Assn. (past pres., dir. Golden Gate chpt.), Lawyers Club San Francisco. General corporate, Government contracts and claims, Private international. Home: 1330 33rd Ave San Francisco CA 94122-1305 Office: Bay Area Rapid Transit Dist 979 Broadway Millbrae CA 94030-1912

LANDER, GREGG, lawyer; b. Victoria, Tex., Sept. 3, 1965; s. B.E. Leissner Jr. and Reed Johnston. BBA in Mktg., Tex. A&M U., 1989; JD, Calif. Western Sch. Law, 1997. Law clk. Law Office of Kenneth S. Greenfield, San Diego, 1996-97; legal asst. Disney Interactive, Glendale, Calif., 1998; assoc. Bolden & Martin LLP, L.A., 1998-99, Kiesel, Boucher & Larson LLP, Beverly Hills, Calif., 1999—. Mem. ABA, Calif. State Bar Assn., L.A. County Bar Assn., Beverly Hills Bar Assn. Avocations: multimedia, photography, nature. Home: 1546 S Fairfax Ave #1 Los Angeles CA 90019 Office: Kiesel Boucher & Larson LLP 8648 Wilshire Blvd Beverly Hills CA 90211 E-mail: gregglander@email.com

LANDERS, STEVEN E. lawyer; b. N.Y.C., May 23, 1947; BA, Antioch Coll., 1969; JD, Harvard U., 1973. Gen. counsel N.Y. State Exec. adv. com. Sentencing, 1978-79; sec. N.Y. State adv. commn. Adminstrn. Justice, 1981-83; ptnr. Paul, Weiss, Rifkind, Wharton & Garrison, N.Y.C. and Paris. Mem. Internat. Bar Assn., Assn. Bar City N.Y., Am. C. of C. in France (chmn. pres.'s coun. 1995-97). Office: Paul Weiss et al 62 rue Faubourg St Honore 75008 Paris France E-mail: slanders@paulweiss.com

LANDES, ROBERT NATHAN, lawyer; b. N.Y.C., Dec. 24, 1930; s. Joseph William and Gertrude Ann (Sindeband) L.; m. Phyllis Markman, Apr. 16, 1964; children: Lucy Ann Harrop, Kathy Jill Braddock, Jeffrey Mark. A.B., Columbia U., 1952, LL.B. (Harlan Fiske Stone scholar), 1954. Bar: N.Y. 1954. Assoc. Shearman & Sterling, N.Y.C., 1957-61; asst. gen. counsel, v.p. U.S. Industries, Inc., 1961-73; exec. v.p., gen. counsel, sec. McGraw-Hill, 1974-95. Bd. dirs. and vice chmn. Greenwich House, Inc. Editor: Columbia Law Rev, 1953-54; contbr. corp. counsel column N.Y. Law Jour., 1986-87. Bd. trustees Lawyers Com. for Civil Rights Under the Law, 1993—; bd. dirs. Lawyers Alliance for New York; bd. dirs. Town Hall. Served as lt. (j.g.) USNR, 1954-57. Mem. ABA, N.Y. State, N.Y. County Bar Assns., Assn. Bar City N.Y. (com. corp. law 1978-81, sec., corp. law depts, 1985-88, internat. law com. 1981-84), Mag. Pubs. Assn. (chmn. legal affairs com. 1977-82, chmn. AAP lawyers com. 1983-85), Columbia Coll. Alumni Assn. (v.p., bd. dirs. 1974-76, 86-90), Soc. Columbia Grads., (pres., bd. dirs. 1985-88), Columbia Law Sch. Alumni Assn. (treas. 1994—), Vineyards Country Club (Naples, Fla.), Pelham Country Club, (N.Y.), The Club at Pelican Bay (Naples.). Democrat. General corporate, Mergers and acquisitions, Securities. Home: 1192 Park Ave New York NY 10128-1314 Office: 45 Rockefeller Plz Fl 20 New York NY 10111-2099

LANDES, WILLIAM M. law educator; b. 1939. AB, Columbia U., 1960, PhD in Econs., 1966. Asst. prof. econs. Stanford U., 1965-66; asst. prof. U. Chgo., 1966-69; asst. prof. Columbia U., 1969-72; assoc. prof. Grad. Ctr., CUNY, 1972-73; now prof. U. Chgo. Law Sch.; founder, chmn. Lexecon Inc., 1977-98, chmn. emeritus, 1998—; mem. bd. examiners GRE in Econs., ETS, 1967-74. Mem. Am. Econ. Assn., Am. Law and Econ. Assn. (v.p. 1991-92, pres. 1992-93), Mont Pelerin Soc. Author: (with Richard Posner) The Economic Structure of Tort Law, 1987; editor: (with Gary Becker) Essays in the Economics of Crime and Punishment, 1974; editor Jour. Law and Econs., 1975-91, Jour. Legal Studies, 1991—. Office: U Chgo Sch Law 1111 E 60th St Chicago IL 60637-2776 also: Lexecon Inc 332 S Michigan Ave Ste 1300 Chicago IL 60604-4406

LANDFIELD, RICHARD, lawyer; b. Chgo., Jan. 16, 1941; s. Joseph D. and Donna (Mayberg) L.; m. Ilona Kiraldi, Aug. 6, 1965; children: Anne, Katharine, Sarah. BA, Amherst Coll., 1962; LLB cum laude, Harvard U., 1965. Bar: N.Y. 1966, D.C. 1972. Asoc. Breed, Abbott & Morgan, N.Y.C., 1965-66, 69-72, Washington, 1972-75; ptnr. Dunnells, Duvall & Porter, 1975-79, Landfield, Becker & Green, Washington, 1979-89, Breed, Abbott & Morgan, 1989-92, Landfield & Becker, Chartered, 1992-94; shareholder Sanders, Schnabel, Brandenburg & Zimmerman, P.C., 1995-97; ptnr. Berliner, Corcoran & Rowe, L.L.P., 1997—. Bd. dirs. Carlson Holdings Corp., 1984-89; gen. counsel The European Inst.; active numerous Amherst Coll. alumni groups; mem. lawyers com. The Washington Opera, 1984-86, 87—; trustee Holton-Arms Sch., Bethesda, Md., 1984-86, 87-96, chmn. bldgs., grounds com., 1985-91, chmn. fin com., 1993-95, past pres. Parents' Assn., trustee emeritus, 1996—. 1st lt. U.S. Army, 1966-69. Decorated Army Commendation medal; John W. Simpson Law fellow Amherst, 1963. Mem. ABA, N.Y. State Bar Assn., Met. Club (Washington), Kenwood Country Club (Bethesda). Republican. General corporate, Private international, Real property. Home: 5101 Baltan Rd Bethesda MD 20816-2309 Office: Berliner Corcoran & Rowe LLP 1101 17th St NW Ste 1100 Washington DC 20036-4798 E-mail: rlandfield@bcr-dc.com

LANDIN, DAVID CRAIG, lawyer; b. Jamestown, N.Y., Aug. 1, 1946; s. David Carl and Rita Mae (Felthaus) L.; m. Susan Ann Gregory, July 11, 1970; children: Mary Stuart, Alexander Craig, David Reed. BA, U. Va., 1968, JD, 1972. Bar: Va. 1972, Pa. 1991, Tex. 1992, U.S. Supreme Ct. 1979. Ptnr. McGuire, Woods & Battle, Richmond, Va., 1972-95, mgr. of product liability and litigation mgmt. group, 1987-95; gen. counsel Va. Assn. Ind. Schs., 1989—, Coun. for Religion in Ind. Schs., 1990—; ptnr. Hunton & Williams, Richmond, Va., 1995—. Pres. The Landin Cos., 1994—. Chmn. ctrl. Va. chpt. Nat. MS Soc., 1995-96. With USAR, 1968-74. Fellow: Va. Law Found. (pres. 1987—88, DRI Exceptional Performance award 1988); mem.: ABA, Va. Bar Assn. (chmn. young lawyers sect. 1979—80, pres. 1999—2000), Va. Assn. Def. Attys. (pres. 1987—88), Greater Richmond C. of C. (bd. dirs. 1998—2000). Roman Catholic. Avocations: squash, tennis, golf. Federal civil litigation, Environmental, Personal injury. Home: 310 Oak Ln Richmond VA 23226-1639 Office: Hunton & Williams Riverfront Plaza East Tower PO Box 1535 Richmond VA 23218-1535

LANDMAN, ERIC CHRISTOPHER, lawyer; b. N.Y.C., Aug. 1, 1948; s. Louis and Joan (Neill) L.; 1 child, Ian Foster. Grad. Hackley Sch., 1966; BA, George Washington U., 1970; JD, Cath. U. Am., 1973. Bar: N.J. 1973, U.S. Dist. Ct. N.J. 1973, U.S. Supreme Ct. 1983. Assoc. Randall, Randall & McGuire, Westwood, N.J., 1973-74; pvt. practice, Tenafly, Englewood, N.J., 1974-76; assoc. Joseph T. Skelley, Fort Lee, N.J., 1976-79, Davies, Davies, Pojanowski, Mennen & Sandberg, Paterson, N.J., 1979-83, Heilbrunn, Finkelstein, Heilbrunn, Alfonso Goldstein & Pape, P.C., Old Bridge, N.J., 1983-87; ptnr. Toolen, Abbott, Ziznewski & Hollander, Edison, N.J., 1987—; mem. N.J. Supreme Ct. Com. on Model Civil Jury Charges, 1982-88. Bd. dirs., gen. counsel Big Bros./Sisters of Middlesex County, 1983—. Mem. Assn. Trial Lawyers Am., Middlesex County Trial Lawyers Assn., N.J. State Bar Assn., Middlesex County Bar Assn. (trustee 1989—). General civil litigation, State civil litigation, Personal injury.

LANDMEIER, ALLEN LEE, lawyer; b. Elmhurst, Ill., Nov. 24, 1942; s. Vernon O. and Eleanor Marie (Forke) L.; m. Charlotte Landmeier, July 8, 1978; children: Matthew, Mark, Michael. BS in Elec. Engring., Valparaiso U., 1964, JD, 1967. Bar: Ill. 1967, U.S. Dist. Ct. (no. dist.) Ill., U.S. Supreme Ct. 1977. Assoc. Muller & Aichele, 1970-71; mem. Smith, Landmeier, Skaar & Elders PC, Geneva, 1971—; city atty. City of St. Charles, 1977-97. Bd. dirs. Delnor Cmty. Health Sys., 1988-97, St. Charles Ctr. Phys. Rehab., 1991-9 7; chmn. Fox Valley dist. Boy Scouts Am., 1994-96. Served to lt. JAGC, USNR, 1967-70. Recipient Disting. Alumni award St. Charles H.S., 1998, Silver Beaver award Boy Scouts Am., 1999. Fellow Ill. Bar Found.; mem. ABA, Ill. Bar Assn. (state taxation sect. council 1977—, editor newsletter), Kane County Bar Assn. (pres., Cmty. Svc. award 1998), Kane County Bar Found. (pres. 1999-2001). General practice, Real property. Office: 15 N 2nd St Geneva IL 60134-2224 E-mail: a_landmeier@smithlandmeier.com

LANDON, WILLIAM J. intelligence officer; b. Menno, S.D., June 23, 1939; s. Helmuth Samuel and Violet A. (McPherson) Neuharth. LLB, Blackstone Sch. Law, 1962, JD, 1968; AA in Bus. Mgmt., Coastline C.C., 1984; postgrad., Am. Mil. U., 2001—. Criminal investigator Internat. Acad. Police Sci., Oklahoma City, Southwestern Inst. Criminology, Lawton; criminal investigator, intelligence officer ASI divsn. Internat. Investigators and Police, St. John, N.B., Can., 1964-94; intelligence officer, analyst Internat. Investigators & Police, Rapid City, SD, 1990—2001, ret., 2001. Student Am. Mil. U., Manassas Park, Va., 2000—. Sponsor Robin Anne Syperda Benedict meml. scholarship Calif. State U., Fullerton, 1990—. With USMC, 1957-65. Mem. Internat. Assn. Study Organized Crime, Internat. Investigators Police Assn., Internat. Assn. Law Enforcement Intelligence Analysts, Assn. Former Intelligence Officers, Am. Soc. Criminology, Nat. Mil. Intelligence Assn. Avocations: martial arts, classical music, fencing.

LANDRON, MICHEL JOHN, lawyer; b. Santurce, P.R., June 15, 1946; s. Francis Xavier and Francisca (Carretero) Healy; m. Carol McQuade, Apr. 22, 1989; children: Micahel Francis, Ryan McQuade. BA, Lehman Coll., 1968, postgrad., 1969-73; JD, Fordham U., 1977. Bar: N.Y. 1978, U.S. Dist. Ct. (so. dist.) N.Y. 1978, U.S. Dist. Ct. (ea. dist.) N.YU. 1978. Asst. atty. gen. Office of Atty. Gen., N.Y. State Dept. Law, N.Y.C., 1978-80; enforcement atty. N.Y. Stock Exch., 1980-81; pvt. practice, 1981-82, 84—; mem. Leaf, Duell, Drogin P.C., N.Y.C., 1982-84; gen. counsel Rockcom, Inc., 1985-87; adminstrv. law judge City of N.Y., 1987; counsel Berger and Paul, N.Y.C., 1984-85; assoc. area counsel Digital Equipment Corp., 1988-89. Adj. instr. N.Y. Law Sch., Ramapo Coll.; master arbitrator, Am. Arbitration Assn., U.S. Dist. Ct. (ea. dist.) N.Y.; mediator U.S. Dist. Ct. (ea. dist.) N.Y.; guest lectr. Lehman Coll.; cons. in field; arbitrator Civil Ct. N.Y.C., No Fault Ins. Panel State of N.Y., Nat. Assn. Securities Dealers, Inc.; arbitrator, mem. arbitration appeals panel Am. Arbitration Assn. Author: Conflicts of Law, 1992; (with others) Personal Injury: Actions, Defenses and Damages, 1992, Choice of Law; contbr. chpts. to books, articles to profl. jours. Mem. N.Y. State Bar Assn. (com. to cooperate with law revision commn.), Assn. Arbitrators City of N.Y., Am. Judges Assn., KC, Phi Alpha Delta (Disting. Svc. award 1977). Republican. Roman Catholic. Avocations: music, reading, sports. General civil litigation, General practice, Trademark and copyright. Office: Ste 2002 254 Canal St New York NY 10013-3501

LANDSMAN, STEPHEN A. lawyer; b. Chgo., Aug. 28, 1942; s. Sam W. and Jeanne N. (Engerman) L.; m. Beth Landsman; Children: Mark, Scott, Sari. BS in Econs., U. Pa., 1964; JD summa cum laude, U. Mich., 1967. Bar: Ill. 1967, U.S. Dist. Ct. (no. dist.) Ill. 1967, U.S. Ct. Appeals (7th cir.) 1967, U.S. Tax Ct. 1970. Assoc. Mayer, Brown & Platt, Chgo., 1967-69, Rudnick & Wolfe, Chgo., 1969-70, ptnr., 1970—. Contbr. articles to profl. jours. Bd. dirs., treas. St. Joseph Hosp. Assocs., Chgo., 1978-82. Mem. Am. Arbitration Assn., Ill. Bar Assn., Chgo. Bar Assn., Order of Coif. General corporate, Finance, Corporate taxation. Office: Piper Marbury Rudnick & Wolfe 203 N La Salle St Ste 1800 Chicago IL 60601-1210

LANDY, BURTON AARON, lawyer; b. Chgo., Aug. 16, 1929; s. Louis J. and Clara (Ernstein) L.; m. Eleonora M. Simmel, Aug. 4, 1957; children: Michael Simmel, Alisa Anne. Student, Nat. U. Mex., 1948; B.S., Northwestern U., 1950; postgrad. scholar, U. Havana, 1951; J.D., U. Miami, 1952; postgrad. fellow, Inter-Am. Acad. Comparative Law, Havana, Cuba,

1955-56. Bar: Fla. 1952. Practice law in internat. field, Miami, 1955—; ptnr. firm Ammerman & Landy, 1957-63, Paul, Landy, Beiley & Harper, P.A. and predecessor firm, 1964-94, Steel Hector & Davis, 1994-97; ptnr. firm, chmn. emeritus Internat. Practice Group Akerman, Senterfitt & Eidson, P.A., 1997—. Lectr. Latin Am. bus. law U. Miami Sch. Law, 1972-75; also internat. law confs. in U.S. and abroad; mem. Nat. Conf. on Fgn. Aspects of U.S. Nat. Security, Washington, 1958; mem. organizing com. Miami regional conf. Com. for Internat. Econ. Growth, 1958; mem. U.S. Dept. Commerce Regional Export Expansion Council, 1969-74, mem. Dist. Export Council, 1978— ; mem. U.S. Sec. State Adv. Com. on Pvt. Internat. Law; dir. Fla. Council Internat. Devel., 1977—, chmn. 1986-87, 99; mem. U. Miami Citizens Bd., 1977— ; chmn. Fla. del. S.E. U.S.-Japan Assn., 1980-82; mem. adv. com. 1st Miami Trade Fair of Ams., 1978; dir., v.p. Greater Miami Fgn. Trade Zone, Inc., 1978—; mem. organizing com., lectr. 4 Inter-Am. Aviation Law Confs.; bd. dirs. Inter-Am. Bar Legal Found.; participant Aquaculture Symposium Sci. and Man in the Ams., Mexico City, Fla. Gov's Econ. Mission to Japan and Hong Kong, 1978; mem. bd. exec. advisors Law and Econs. Ctr.; mem. vis. com., internat. adv. bd. U. Miami Sch. Bus.; mem. internat. fin. council Office Comptroller of Fla.; founding chmn. Fla.-Korea Econ. Coop. Com., 1982— , Southeast U.S.-Korea Econ. Com., 1985—; chmn. Expo 500 Fla.-Columbus Soc., 1985-87; founding co-chmn. So. Fla. Roundtable-Georgetown U. Ctr. for Strategic and Internat. Studies, 1982-85; chmn. Fla. Gov.'s Conf. on World Trade, 1984— ; founding gen. counsel Fla. Internat. Bankers Assn.; dir., former gen. counsel Fla. Internat. Ins. and Reins. Assn., chmn. Latin Am. Carribbean Bus. Promotion Adv. Counc. to U.S. Sec. of Commerce and Aid Adminstr; appointee Fla. Internat. Trade and Investment Coun.; mem. steering com. Summit of Ams., 1994—, co-chair post summit planning com.; strategic planning com. Mayor Miami Dade County Internat. Trade Commn. Contbg. editor Econs. Devel. Lawyers of the Ams., 1969-74; contbr. numerous articles to legal jours. in U.S. and fgn. countries. Chmn. City of Miami Internat. Trade and Devel. Com., 1984-86; chmn. internat. task force Beacon Coun. of Dade County, Fla., 1985, dir., chmn., 1991—; bd. dirs., exec. com. Internat. Comml. Dispute Resolution Ctr., Miami Internat. Arbitration and Mediation Inst.; chmn. Comml. Dispute Resolution Ctr. for the Ams., Miami, 1995—; apptd. by Gov. of Fla. to Internat. Currency and Barter Commn., 1986; lectr. U. Miami Inter-Ban course for Latin Am. bankers; steering com. Summit of the Americas, Miami, 1994, co-chair post Summit Planning Com., 1994; co-chair mayor Miami-Dade County Strategic Planning for Internat. Trade, 1998—; co-chair strategic planning com. Mayor of Miami Dade County Internat. Trade Commn.; bd. dirs. Trade Mission Ctr. Am., 2000—; mem. internat. adv. com. Enterprise Fla., 2000—. With JACGC, USAF, 1952-54, Korea; to maj. Res. Named Internat. Trader of Yr., Fla. Council Internat. Devel., 1980, Bus. Person of Yr., 1986; recipient Pan Am. Informatica Comunicaciones Expo award, 1983, Lawyer of Americas award U. Miami, 1984, Richard L. McLaughlin award Fla. Econ. Devel. Coun., 1993; named hon. consul gen. Republic of Korea, Miami, 1983-88, State of Fla., 99—, recipient Heung-in medal (Order of Diplomatic Service), 1986, Ministerial Citation, Min. of Fgn. Affairs, 1988; apptd. Hon. consul Ft. Lauderdale, Fla., 1991-98; apptd. Hon. consul gen. State of Fla., 1999—. Fellow ABA Found. (chmn. com. arrangements internat. and comparative law sect. 1964-65, com. on Inter-Am. affairs of ABA 1985-87); mem. Inter-Am. Bar Assn. (asst. sec.-gen. 1957-59, treas. 11th conf. 1959, co-chmn. jr. bar sect. 1963-65, mem council 1969—, exec. com. 1975—, pres. 1982-84, Diploma de Honor 1987, William Roy Vallance award 1989), Spanish Am. Bar Assn., Fla. Bar Assn. (vice chmn. adminstrv. law com. 1965, vice chmn. internat. and comparative law com. 1967-68, chmn. aero. law com. 1968-69), Dade County Bar Assn. (chmn. fgn. laws and langs com. 1964-65), Internat. Ctr. Fla. (World Trade Ctr., pres. 1981-82), World Peace Through Law Ctr., Miami Com. Fgn. Relations, Inst. Ibero Am. Derecho Aero., Am. Soc. Internat. Law, Council Internat. Visitors, Am. Fgn. Law Assn. (pres. Miami 1958), Bar of South Korea (hon. mem.), Greater Miami C. of C. (bd. govs. 1986—), Colombian-Am. C. of C. (bd. dirs. 1986—), Peruvian-Am. C. of C. (bd. dirs.), Norwegian Am. C. of C. (bd. dirs.), Phi Alpha Delta. Alternative dispute resolution, General corporate, Private international. Home: 605 Almeria Ave Coral Gables FL 33134-5602 Office: One SE Third Ave 28th Flr Miami FL 33131 E-mail: blandy@akerman.com

LANDY, LISA ANNE, lawyer; b. Miami, Fla., Apr. 20, 1963; d. Burton Aaron and Eleonora Maria (Simmel) L. BA, Brown U., 1985; JD cum laude, U. Miami, 1988. Bar: Fla. 1988, U.S. Dist. Ct. (so. dist.) Fla. 1988. Atty. Paul, Landy, Beiley & Harper, P.A., Miami, Fla., 1988-94, Steel Hector & Davis, Miami, 1994-97, ptnr., 1996-97, Akerman Senterfitt & Eidson P.A., Miami, 1997—. Bd. dirs. Miami City Ballet, 1992-97, pres., 1996; bd. dirs. Women in Internat. Trade, Miami, 1992—, pres., 1994; bd. dirs. Orgn. Women in Internat. Trade, 1994—, v.p., 1997, 98, pres. 1998-2000; bd. dirs. Women in Tech. Internat. South Fla, The Next Step Youth Cmty. Ctr., Inc. Mem. ABA, Inter-Am. Bar Assn. (asst. sec. 1997-2000). Avocations: sports, arts, fluent in Spanish, French. Contracts commercial, Private international, Trademark and copyright.

LANE, ARTHUR ALAN, lawyer; b. N.Y.C., Dec. 2, 1945; s. George and Delys L.; m. Jane Ficocella, Dec. 30, 1972; 1 child, Eva B. BA, Yale U., 1967; JD, Columbia U., 1970, MBA, 1971. Bar: N.Y. 1971. Assoc. Webster, Sheffield, Fleischmann, Hitchcock & Brookfield, N.Y.C., 1971-72; asst. to divsn. counsel Liggett & Myers, Inc., 1973; assoc. Wickes, Riddell, Bloomer, Jacobi & McGuire, 1974-78, Morgan, Lewis & Bockius, N.Y.C., 1979; ptnr. Eaton & Van Winkle, 1980—94, DeForest & Duer, N.Y.C., 1994-99, Lamb & Barnosky, Melville, 1999—. Mem. ABA, Assn. of Bar of City of N.Y. Avocation: gardening. Banking, General corporate, General practice. Home: 103 Brooksite Dr Smithtown NY 11787-4456 Office: Lamb & Barnosky 534 Broadhollow Rd Melville NY 11747

LANE, BRUCE STUART, lawyer; b. New London, Conn., May 15, 1932; s. Stanley S. and Frances M. (Antis) L.; m. Ann Elizabeth Steinberg, Aug. 10, 1958; children: Sue Ellen, Charles M., Richard I. Student, Boston U., 1948-49; AB magna cum laude, Harvard U., 1952, JD, 1955. Bar: Ohio 1955, D.C. 1966, U.S. Ct. Claims 1960, U.S. Tax Ct. 1961, U.S. Supreme Ct. 1961. Assoc. Squire, Sanders & Dempsey, Cleve., 1955-59; sr. trial atty. tax div. Dept. Justice, Washington, 1959-61; tax atty. Dinsmore, Shohl, Barrett, Coates & Deupree, Cin., 1961-65; sec., asst. gen. counsel corp. and tax matters Communications Satellite Corp., Washington, 1965-69; v.p., gen. counsel Nat. Corp. Housing Partnerships, 1969-70; pres. Lane and Edson P.C., 1970-89; ptnr. Kelley Drye & Warren, 1989-93, Peabody & Brown, Washington, 1993-99, Nixon Peabody LLP, Washington, 1999-2000, sr. cousnel, 2001—. Co-editor-in-chief Housing and Devel. Reporter; author publs. and articles on tax, partnership and real estate. Incorporator, bd. dirs., past pres. D.C. Inst. Mental Health; past chmn. citizens Com. sect. 5 Chevy Chase, Md.; past mem. Montgomery County Hist. Preservation Commn., Md.; mem. chmn. coun. Crow Canyon Archeol. Ctr., Cortez, Colo. Maj. JAG, USAR, 1952-68. Mem. ABA, Am. Law Inst., Am. Coll. Real Estate Lawyers (pres. 1986-87), Anglo-Am. Real Property Inst., Phi Beta Kappa. Alternative dispute resolution, Real property, Corporate taxation. Home: 3711 Thornapple St Chevy Chase MD 20815-4111 Office: Nixon Peabody LLP 401 9th St NW Ste 900 Washington DC 20004-2134

LANE, DOMINICK V. lawyer; b. South Amboy, N.J., Mar. 18, 1961; s. Lister Ray and Marie L. AA in Criminal Justice, San Diego Miramar Coll., 1982; BA in Polit. Sci., U. San Diego, 1985; JD, Calif. Western U., 1988. Bar: Calif. 1989, U.S. Dist. Ct. (so. dist.) Calif. 1989, U.S. Dist. Ct. (ctrl. and no. dists.) Calif. 1990, U.S. Dist. Ct. Ariz. 1996. Assoc. Rutledge, Hathaway, Harris & Newman, L.A., 1990-94; trial atty. Farmers Ins. Co., Aiken, D'Angelo, & Banner, San Diego, 1994-97; trial atty. Richardson, Bambrick, Cermak & Fair, 1997-98, supervising atty. Costa Mesa, Calif., 1998—. Arbitrator San Diego Superior Ct., 1995—. Bd. dirs. Crime Victims Fund, San Diego, 1997; vol. L.A. Mission, 1993-94. Mem. San Diego County Bar Assn. Avocations: music, tennis, golf, travel. Entertainment, Insurance, Trademark and copyright. Office: Richardson Bambrick Cermak & Fair PO Box 25191 Santa Ana CA 92799-5191 Fax: 714-424-0861

LANE, FRANK JOSEPH, JR. lawyer; b. St. Louis, May 10, 1934; s. Frank Joseph and Virginia Laurette (Hausman) L.; m. Margaret Ann Dwyer, Mar. 2, 1957; children: Mary, Stephen, Thomas, Michael. BS in Commerce, JD, St. Louis U., 1956; LLM, Georgetown U., 1960; grad. Parker Sch. Internat. Law, Columbia U., 1970; cert., Coll. Fin. Planning, Denver, 1988. Bar: Mo. 1956, U.S. Dist. Ct. (ea. dist.) Mo. 1956, U.S. Ct. Appeals (8th cir.) 1960, U.S. Supreme Ct. 1959, U.S. Ct. Mil. Appeals, 1957. Ptnr. Goldenhersh, Goldenhersh, Fredericks, Newman & Lane, St. Louis, 1960-64, Lane & Leadlove, St. Louis, 1964-66, Dill & Lane, St. Louis, 1978-79; counsel Ralston Purina Co., 1966-78; pres.'s adv. bd., 1967-69; of counsel Petrolite Corp., St. Louis, 1979-83; v.p., trust officer Gravois Bank, 1983-85; regional v.p., trust officer Merc Bank N.A., 1985-89; of counsel Dill, Wamser, Bamvakais & Newsham PC, 1989—. Instr. internat. law St. Louis U., 1979. Bd. dirs. Met. St. Louis Sewer Dist., 1965-73, chmn., 1968-69; bd. dirs. Webster Groves KC Home Assn., 1999-01; mem. St. Louis Regional Commerce & Growth Assn. environ. com., 1978-82; mem. planned giving com. Am. Heart Assn., St. Louis, 1986-88, St. Louis Soc. for Crippled Children, 1991; bd. dirs. Midwestern Braille Vols., Inc., chmn., 1995—; atty. St. Louis Geneal. Soc., 1996—; pres. Ozark Cmties. Coun. St. Louis County, 1964-65. Capt. U.S. Army JAGC, Pentagon, 1957-60. Mem. Mo. Bar Assn., Met. St. Louis Bar Assn. (chmn. rels. with law schs. com. 1961-62, enrollment com. 1962-63, chmn. office practice com. 1963-64, elected admissions com. 1967), Estate Planning Coun. St. Louis, Rotary (bd. dirs. Crestwood, Mo. chpt. 1988-89), KC (grand knight 1964-66, adv. West County 1983-90, Webster Groves 1991-2001). Republican. Roman Catholic. Avocations: oil painting, golf, travel, investment analysis. Home: 520 Lering Dr Ballwin MO 63011-1588 Office: 9939 Gravois Rd Saint Louis MO 63123-4211 E-mail: frankjlane@gateway.net, frank_j_lane@juno.com

LANE, JAMES EDWARD, lawyer, consultant; b. Stockport, Ohio, Jan. 22, 1921; s. Jesse Benton and Martha Elizabeth (Horn) L.; m. Betty Jayne Bucy, July 28, 1939; children— Betty Jayne, Roberta Lee, James Benton. Student Ohio State U., 1938-43; LLB, William McKinley Sch. Law, Canton, Ohio, 1951; assoc. in mgmt. Ins. Inst. Am., 1970; CPCU, Am. Inst. Property and Liability Underwriters, 1976. Bar: Ohio 1951, U.S. Dist. Ct. (so. dist.) Ohio 1977. Adjuster Allstate Ins. Co., Akron, Ohio, 1958-59, examiner, Cin., 1959-61, dist. claim mgr., Dayton, Ohio, 1961-68; v.p. claims Grange Mut. Casualty Co., Columbus, Ohio, 1968-76, exec. v.p. Ohio and W.Va. Ins. Guaranty Assn., Columbus, 1976-89, then pres.; pvt. practice law, 1976-85; cons., Columbus, 1976— ; lectr. Wright State U., Dayton, 1966, 67; cons. Mut. Reins. Bur., Cherry Valley, Ill., 1981— ; pres. Nat. Conf. of Ins. Guaranty Funds; presenter seminars; mem. speakers bur. Ohio Ins. Inst., Columbus, 1973-76. Pres. Worthington (Ohio) PTA, 1969-70; mem. vestry St. John's Episcopal Ch., Worthington, 1972-77; troop leader Cen. Ohio Dist. council Boy Scouts Am., Worthington, 1972-78. 2d lt. U.S. Army, 1944-46; PTO. Recipient Century award cen. Ohio sect. Boy Scouts Am., 1975-78. Mem. Columbus Bar Assn., Ohio Bar Assn., Ohio Assn. Civil Trial Attys. (legis. chmn. 1974-76; recipient plaque 1976), Def. Rsch. Inst., Columbus Claim Club, Ohio State Claim Club, Nat. Con. Ins. Guaranty Funds (ops. subcom. exec. dir. 1989—), Delta Theta Phi (vice dean Canton chpt. 1950-51). Republican. General practice, Insurance, Personal injury. Home: 6020 Glennvillage Dr Dublin OH 43016-8437

LANE, MATTHEW JAY, lawyer; b. Cin., Mar. 6, 1955; s. Joseph Alan and Adele (Stacks) L.; m. Susan Carol. BA, Emory U., 1977; JD, Northwestern U., 1980. Bar: Ohio 1981, U.S. Dist. Ct. (so. dist.) Ohio 1981, U.S. Ct. Appeals (6th cir.) 1981, Fla. 1982, U.S. Ct. Appeals (11th cir.) 1982. Law clk. to chief judge U.S. Dist. Ct. (so. dist.) Ohio, Cin., 1980-82; v.p., gen. counsel PPI, Inc., North Palm Beach, Fla., 1996—. Legal counsel Juvenile Diabetes Assn., Cin., 1984-92; legal counsel MADD, 1986-92, pres. S.W. Ohio chpt., 1988-91, pres. Palm Beach County chpt., 1993-95; mem. Cin. Bicentennial Commn., 1986-88; bd. trustees Isaac M. Wise Temple, Cin., 1987-89; mem. exec. com. leadership coun. Jewish Fedn. Cin., 1987-92, Big Bros./Big Sisters Devel. Com., 1985-88, Hamilton County Dem. Party, mem. exec. com., county, legis. and jud. selection coms., 1987-92; mem. Palm Beach County Democratic Exec. Com., 1993—; v.p., legal counsel Fetes de Jeunesse, 1984-90. Mem. ABA, Ohio Bar Assn., Fla. Bar Assn., Cin. Bar Assn. (chmn. svc. com.), Phi Beta Kappa. General civil litigation, State civil litigation, General corporate. Home: 2840 Gettysburg Ln West Palm Beach FL 33409-7212 Office: PPI Inc 824 Us Highway 1 North Palm Beach FL 33408-3873

LANE, ROBIN, lawyer; b. Kerrville, Tex., Nov. 28 1947; d. Rowland and Gloria (Benson) Richards; m. Stanley Lane, Aug. 22, 1971 (div. 1979); m. Anthony W. Cunningham, Nov. 22, 1980; children: Joshua Lane, Alexandra Cunningham. BA with honors in Econs., U. Fla., 1969; MA, George Washington U., 1971; JD, Stetson U. Coll. Law, 1978. Bar: Fla. 1979, U.S. Ct. Appeals (11th cir.) 1981, U.S. Supreme Ct. 1986, U.S. Ct. Appeals (D.C. cir.) 1992, U.S. Ct. Appeals (3rd cir.) N.Y. 1993. Mgmt. trainee internat. banking Gulf Western Industries, N.Y.C.; internat. rsch. specialist Ryder Systems, Inc., Miami, Fla., 1973, project mgr., 1974; assoc. Wagner, Cunningham, Vaughan & McLaughlin, Tampa, Fla., 1979-85; pvt. practice law, 1985—; guest lectr. med. jurisprudence Stetson U. Coll. Law, 1982-91, also mem. exec. coun. law alumni bd. Contbr. articles to various revs. Recipient Am. Jurisprudence award-torts Lawyers Co-op. Fla., 1979; Scottish Rite fellow, 1968-69. Mem. ABA, Acad. Fla. Trial Lawyers (mem. com. 1983-84), Assn. Trial Lawyers Am., Fla. Bar Assn., Fla. Women's Alliance, Omicron Delta Epsilon. Labor, Personal injury. Home: 4934 Saint Croix Dr Tampa FL 33629-4831 Office: PO Box 10155 Tampa FL 33679-0155

LANE, WILLIAM ARTHUR, lawyer; b. Nashville, Sept. 16, 1958; s. Thomas Jennings Lane and Nancy Eleanor (Shirley) Boyd; m. Brenda Diane Kinamon, Dec. 5, 1981; children: Charles Thomas, John Ross. BS, Mid. Tenn. State U., 1980; JD, Nashville U., 1984. Bar: Tenn. 1986, U.S. Dist. Ct. (mid. dist.) Tenn. 1986, U.S. Ct. Appeals (6th cir.) 1986, U.S. Supreme Ct. 1990. Pvt. practice law, Smyrna, Tenn., 1987-94, Murfreesboro, 1994—; atty. Travelers Ins. Co., Nashville, 1990-91, U.S.F.&G Ins. Co., Nashville, 1991-92, Willis-Corroon Adminstrv. Svcs. Corp., 1992-94. Mem. Tenn. Bar Assn., Nashville Bar Assn., Assn. Trial Lawyers Am., Masons, Shriners, Sigma Delta Kappa. Baptist. Avocations: golf, hunting, shooting. Criminal, Family and matrimonial, Personal injury. Office: Stahlman Bldg 211 Union St Ste 902 Nashville TN 37201-1559

LANE, WILLIAM EDWARD, lawyer, inventor; b. Chgo., Apr. 29, 1906; s. Edwin J. and Caroline (Eisendrath) Levi. Student, U. Ill., 1925-26, Northwestern U., 1931-32; LLB, Chgo.-Kent Coll. Law, 1929, LLM, 1930, JD, 1969. Bar: Ill. 1929, U.S. Supreme Ct. 1935, U.S. Dist. Ct. (no. dist.) Ill. 1936, U.S. Dist. Ct. Hawaii 1964. Ptnr. Lane & Jacobson, Chgo., 1930-36; pvt. practice, Chgo., 1936-42; ptnr. Lane, Duffy & Connell, Chgo., 1946-58, Lane & Terry, Wilmette, Ill., 1962-83; mem. adv. bd. Atty.'s Title Guaranty Co., Chgo., 1983—; lect. Patentee solar energy. Bd. dirs. Wilmette Vis. Nurse Assn., 1962-64; bd. dirs. New Trier Twp. Family Svc. Ctr., 1962-65. With AUS, 1942-45. Mem. ABA, Ill. Bar Assn., Chgo. Bar Assn., Lake County Bar Assn., Wilmette C. of C. (past pres.), Elks (chmn. bd. trustees 1960-64, exalted ruler 1958-59). Federal civil litigation, State civil litigation, Real property. Office: 1161 Lake Cook Rd Ste B Deerfield IL 60015-5277

LANEY, JOHN THOMAS, III, federal judge; b. Columbus, Ga., Mar. 27, 1942; s. John Thomas Jr. and Leila (Davis) L.; m. Louise Pierce, Nov. 23, 1974; children: Thomas Whitfield, Elizabeth Davis. AB, Mercer U., 1964, JD magna cum laude, 1966. Bar: Ga. 1965, U.S. Dist. Ct. (mid. dist.) Ga. 1966, U.S. Ct. Appeals (5th cir.) 1966, U.S. Ct. Mil. Appeals 1967, U.S. Ct. Appeals (11th cir.) 1981. Assoc. Swift, Pease, Davidson & Chapman, Columbus, 1970-73; ptnr. Page, Scrantom, Harris & Chapman, 1973-86; judge mid. dist. Ga. U.S. Bankruptcy Ct., 1986—. Co-editor-in-chief Mercer Law Rev., 1965-66; contbr. articles to profl. jours. Former pres., dir. Metro. Boys Club of Columbus. Capt. U.S. Army, 1966-70. Mem. ABA (judge adminstrv. divsn. Nat. Conf. Fed. Trial Judges), State Bar Ga. (chmn. gen. practice and trial sect. 1983-84, chmn. state disciplinary bd. 1984-85), Am. Judicature Soc., Nat. Conf. Bankruptcy Judges, Columbus Bar Assn., Inc. (pres. 1985-86), Rotary. Presbyterian. Office: US Bankruptcy Ct 1 Arsenal Pl 901 Front Ave Ste 309 Columbus GA 31901-2797 E-mail: k4bai@worldnet.att.net

LANG, EDWARD GERALD, lawyer; b. Stamford, Conn., Jan. 3, 1948; s. Ira and Bernice (Gelb) L.; m. Pamela Lois Howard, Jan. 8, 1972; children— Samantha, Colin. B.S. in Econs., U. Pa., 1969; J.D., U. Conn., 1973. Bar: Conn. 1973. Ptnr., Lang and Thomas, Middlefield, Conn., 1973— ; atty. Catholic Charities, Middletown, 1982— . Chmn. Middlefield Charter Revision Commn., 1984, 86; bd. dirs. Hartford Ballet, 1982-84; atty. trial referee State of Conn., 1988—. Mem. ABA, Conn. Bar Assn. (bench-bar rules adv. com., 1988—), Middlesex County Bar Assn. Lodge: Lions. Administrative and regulatory, Family and matrimonial, Probate. Home: 183 Cherry Hill Rd Middlefield CT 06455-1223 Office: Box 462 Main St Middlefield CT 06455

LANG, GEORGE EDWARD, lawyer; b. Peekskill, N.Y., Apr. 7, 1932; s. George Louis and Florence (Sheehan) L.; m. Rose Marie Corrao, June 8, 1953; children: G. Vincent Lang, Kathleen M. Lang. AB, U. Notre Dame, 1954, JD, 1955. Bar: Ky. 1955, U.S. Dist. Ct. Ky. 1956. City atty., Munfordville, Ky., 1958-85, Bonnieville, 1958-85; atty. Hart County, Munfordville, 1962-70; hearing officer Ky. Workmen's Compensation Bd., 1971-79; master commr. Hart Cir. Ct., 1984—. Pres. South Ctr. Ky. Broadcasting Co., Munfordville, 1984-88; v.p. Cub Run (Ky.) Industries, 1986-90. Pres. Munfordville Indsl. Found., 1968-90; bd. dirs. Mammoth Cave (Ky.) Devel. Assn., 1972—; chmn. Hart County Dem. Party, Munfordville, 1972-78. Mem. Ctrl. Ky. Wildlife Fedn. (pres. 1962-64), Munfordville Lions Club (pres. 1966-68), Horse Cave Rotary Club (v.p. 1968-69). Roman Catholic. Office: PO Box 366 Munfordville KY 42765-0366 E-mail: glang@scrtc.com

LANG, GORDON, JR. retired lawyer; b. Evanston, Ill., July 27, 1933; s. Gordon and Harriet Kendig Lang; m. Clara Bates Van Derzee, Sept. 26, 1970; children: Elizabeth K., Gordon III, Harriet B. BA, Yale U., 1954; MA in History, U. Ariz., 1958; LLB, Harvard U., 1960. Bar: Ill. 1960. Assoc. Gardner, Carton & Douglas, Chgo., 1960-67, ptnr., 1967-98, ret., 1998. Cons., 1999—. Dir. North Side Boys' Clubs, Chgo., 1961-67, Yale Scholarship Trust Ill., 1966-69, pres., 1967; mem. Assocs. Rush-Presbyn.-St. Luke's Med. Ctr., Chgo., 1962—, Assocs. Northwestern U., Evanston, 1970—; dir. Chgo. Youth Ctrs., 1967—, pres., 1982-84; trustee Chgo. Latin Sch. Found., 1978—, pres., 1995—; trustee Groton (Mass.) Sch., 1982-93; dir. United Way of Chgo., 1984-90, United Way/Crusade of Mercy (Met. Chgo.), 1989-95; apptd. Bush/Cheney elector 2000 presdl. election. 1st lt. USAF, 1955-57. Mem. ABA (sect. bus. law), Ill. State Bar Assn., Chgo. Bar Assn. (mem. corp. law com. 1975-98, mem. fin. instns. com. 1985-98), Chgo. Club (former dir. and sec.), Econ. Club Chgo. (former dir. and sec.), Onwentsia Club, Racquet Club Chgo., Chgo. Commonwealth Club, Yale Club Chgo. (former dir., past pres.). Republican. Episcoplalian. Avocations: golf, skiing, hiking. General corporate, Finance, Securities. Home: 1520 N Astor St Chicago IL 60610-1610 Office: Gardner Carton & Douglas 321 N Clark St Ste 3400 Chicago IL 60610-4795 E-mail: glang@gcd.com

LANG, JOSEPH HAGEDORN, lawyer; b. Cleve., Sept. 30, 1937; s. Carl Frederick and Martha Clotilda (Hagedorn) L.; m. Elsie A. O'Berry, Aug. 8, 1965; children: Joseph H. Jr., Robert Warren, James O'Berry. AA, St. Petersburg Jr. Coll., 1959; BA, Duke U., 1961; JD, U. Fla., 1963. Bar: Fla. 1964, U.S. Dist. Ct. (mid. dist.) Fla. 1965, U.S. Ct. Appeals (5th cir.) 1965, U.S. Supreme Ct. 1975. Assoc. Baynard McLeod & Overton, St. Petersburg, Fla., 1964-69; ptnr. Baynard McLeod & Lang, 1969-80; pres. Baynard McLeod & Lang, P.C., 1980—. Active Police Cmty. Coun., Cmty. Alliance; chmn. bd. dirs. St. Petersburg Jr. Coll., Pinellas County, 1983-97, trustee, 1977-97, chmn., 1982-89, 92-96, chmn. emeritus, 1997—; mem. State Bd. C.C.'s, 1997-2001, vice chmn. 1998-99, chmn., 1999-2000; vice chmn. Pinellas County Workforce Devel. Bd., 1997-99, sec., 1999-2000; bd. dirs. Am. Heart Assn. Pinellas County divsn., 1997—; mem. exec. com. Pinellas County Worknet, 2001—. Named Sch. Adv. Com. Mem. of Yr.; recipient Trustee of Yr. award Fla. Assn. Cmty. Coll., 1993, Bob Graham C.C. Disting. Svc. award, 1994, Trustee Leadership award So. Region, ACCT, 1994, Alumni award St. Petersburg Jr. Coll., 1990. Mem. Fla. Bar Assn., St. Petersburg Bar Assn., St. Petersburg C. of C. (Outstanding Mem. award 1990), Suncoasters Club, Dragon Club, Phi Theta Kappa (Disting. Alumni award 1978). Democrat. Roman Catholic. Probate, Real property. Office: Baynard McLeod & Lang 669 1st Ave N Saint Petersburg FL 33701-3696

LANGARICA O'HEA, LORENZA KRISTIN, lawyer; b. Mexico City, Feb. 24, 1969; d. Mauricio Langarica and Kristin O'Hea. JD, U. Iberoamericana, Mexico City, 1994; diploma, Inst. Tech. Autonoma Mexico, Mexico City, 1995, U. Panamericana, 1999; postgrad., Georgetown U., 2001. Jr. assoc. Cannizzo, Ortiz y Assoc., Mexico City, 1991-98; sr. assoc. Muares, Angoitia, Cortes y Fuentes SC, 1998-2000. Mem. Barra Mexicana de Abogodos. Contracts commercial, General corporate, Land use and zoning (including planning). Office: Mijares Angoitia Cortes Montes Urales 505-3 11000 Mexico City Mexico Office Fax: 525 5201065/75

LANGE, JOSEPH JUDE MORGAN, lawyer; b. San Diego, June 30, 1961; s. Roy Oliver and Edith Ann Lange; m. France-Helen Marina Russman, Mar. 31, 1995; 1 child, Michaela Jeannette. BA in econs. cum laude, UCLA, 1983; JD, Loyola U., 1986. Bar: Calif. 1986, U.S. Dist. Ct. (ctrl. and so. dists.) Calif., U.S. Ct. Claims. Jud. extern Appellate divsn. L.A. Superior Ct., 1984; extern U.S. Dept. Justice, L.A., 1984; law clk. Lewis, D'Amato Brisbois & Bisgara, 1985-87, assoc., 1987-88, Lebovits & David, L.A., 1988-91, ptnr., 1991-93; pvt. practice, 1993—. Mem. ATLA, L.A. County Bar Assn. (fee arbitrator 1997-99), Consumer Attys. Calif., Consumer Attys. L.A., Assn. Bus. Trial Lawyers, Lawyers Against Hunger. Avocations: karate (Black Belt), inline skating, underwater photography, skiing. General civil litigation, Personal injury, Professional liability. Office: 1880 Century Park E Ste 900 Los Angeles CA 90067-1609

LANGEMARK, JESPER, lawyer; b. Gentofte, Copenhagen, May 6, 1969; s. Ole and Tove L.; m. Lotte Klitfod, Apr. 24, 1999; 1 child, Emil. LLM, U. Copenhagen, 1994, London Sch. Econs., 1999. Jr. assoc. Bech-Bruun & Trolle law firm, Copenhagen, Denmark, 1994-97, assoc. Denmark, 1998—2001; ptnr. Vonhaller law firm, Denmark, 2001—; in-house legal counsel COWI Cons. Engrs. AS, Lyngby, Denmark, 1997. Co-author: IT-Law and Security, 1997; contbr. articles to profl. jours. Mem. Copenhagen Bar Asn., Assn. Computer and IT Law. Antitrust, Computer, Intellectual property. Home: Rosenvaengets Allé DK-2100 Copenhagen Oe Denmark Office: Vonhaller Law Firm Fabrikhestervej 10 DK-1437 Copenhagen Denmark E-mail: jl@vonhaller.dk

LANGENHEIM, ROGER ALLEN, lawyer; b. Feb. 21, 1935; s. Elmer L. and Esther L. (Gerkensmeyer) L.; m. Susan C. McMichael, Aug. 31, 1963; children: Ann Elizabeth, Mark Allen, Sara Ann. BS, U. Nebr., 1957, LLB, 1960. Bar: Nebr. 1960, Mo. 1960. Assoc. Stinson, Mag, Thomson, McEvers & Fizzell, Kansas City, Mo., 1960-66; v.p., gen counsel Black, Sivalls & Bryson, Inc., 1966-70; internat. atty. Dresser Industries, Inc., Dallas, 1970-71; group counsel Petroleum & Mineral Group, Houston, 1971-75; gen. counsel Oilfield Products Group, 1975-80; v.p., gen. counsel Magcobar Group, 1980-85; assoc., gen. counsel Dresser Industries, Inc., 1985-87, sr. assoc., gen. counsel, 1987-98, staff v.p., assoc. gen. counsel, 1994-98; gen. counsel Dresser-Rand Co., 2000—. Editor: U. Nebr. Law Rev., 1958-59. Mem. Nebr. Bar Assn., Mo. Bar Assn., Order of Coif. Republican. Roman Catholic. General civil litigation, Contracts commercial, Private international. Home: 6172 Haley Ln Fort Worth TX 76132-3875 E-mail: Rlangenheim@worldnet.att.net

LANGER, BRUCE ALDEN, lawyer; b. N.Y.C., Mar. 17, 1953; s. Samuel S. and Yvette Langer. BA summa cum laude with distinction, Boston U., 1975, JD cum laude, 1978. Bar: N.Y. 1979, U.S. Dist. Ct. (so. and ea. dists.) N.Y. 1979, U.S. Tax Ct. 1979, U.S. Ct. Appeals (2d cir.) 1983, U.S. Supreme Ct. 1985. Law clk. to presiding chief justice U.S. Bankruptcy Ct. (ea. dist.) N.Y., summers 1976-77; with Breed Abbott & Morgan, N.Y.C., 1978-81, White & Case, N.Y.C., 1981-84, Fishman Forman & Landau, N.Y.C., 1984-85, Fishman Forman & Langer, N.Y.C., 1985-86, Paradise & Alberts, N.Y.C., 1986-89; pvt. practice, 1989—. Editor Boston U. Law Rev., 1977-78; contbg. author: Pensions and Investments, 1979; contbr. articles to profl. jours. Harold C. Case Presdl. scholar, 1974-75. Mem. Phi Beta Kappa, Phi Alpha Theta. Bankruptcy, Federal civil litigation, State civil litigation. Office: 5th Fl 488 Madison Ave New York NY 10022

LANGER, CARLTON EARL, lawyer; b. Cleve., Nov. 4, 1954; s. Warren Dexter and Florence (Thompson) L.; m. Rita Lennox, Apr. 30, 1983; children: Christopher Colin, Deanna Faith. BA, Albion Coll., 1976; JD, Cleve. State U., 1979; MBA, Case Western Res. U., 1980. Bar: Ohio 1979, Fla. 1980, U.S. Dist. Ct. (no. dist.) Ohio 1979. Assoc. Vanik, Monroe, Zucco, Donahue & Scanlon, Cleve., 1979-80; atty. Nat. City Bank (subs. of Nat. City Corp.), 1980-83; chief counsel, v.p. and sec. Ohio Citizens Bank (subs. Nat. City Corp.), Toledo, 1983-87; v.p., sr. atty., asst. sec. Nat. City Corp., Cleve., 1987-94, sr. v.p., chief counsel, 1994—. Trustee, asst. sec. Goodwill Industries of Greater Cleve., Inc., 1988—; trustee, sec. Goodwill Industries of Greater Cleve. Found., Inc., 1991—; chmn. Ledgewood Christian Ch., 1998—. Mem. ABA, Ohio Bar Assn., Fla. Bar Assn., Cleve. Bar Assn., Am. Soc. Corp. Secs. (treas. Ohio regional group 1999—). Avocations: woodworking. General corporate, Mergers and acquisitions, Securities. Home: 9000 Kinsman Rd Novelty OH 44072-9638 Office: Nat City Bank 1900 E 9th St Cleveland OH 44114-3484 E-mail: carlton.langer@national-city.com

LANGER, MARSHALL J. lawyer, writer; b. N.Y.C., May 30, 1928; s. Samuel and Edna (Klein) L.; m. Sally Blass, 1955 (div. 1967); children: Andrew, Jeffrey; m. Carole Wien, Jan. 31, 1990. BS in Econ., U. Pa., 1948; JD summa cum laude, U. Miami, Coral Gables, Fla., 1951. Bar: Fla. 1951, U.S. Supreme Ct. Ptnr. Stone, Bittel & Langer, Miami, Fla., 1960-70, Shutts & Bowen, Miami, 1970-75, of counsel Miami and London, 1975—. Adj. prof. law U. Miami, 1965-86. Author: Practical International Tax Planning, 1975, rev. edit., 2000, The Tax Exile Report, 1997; co-author: (6 vols.) Rhoades & Langer: U.S. International Taxation and Tax Treaties, 1980—. Named Outstanding Tax Atty. of Yr., tax sect. Fla. Bar. Assn., 1990. Fellow Am. Bar Found.; mem. Internat. Tax Planning Assn. (mem. exec. com., v.p. U.S. br. 1978-80). Private international, Personal income taxation. Home: 5 Coronation Dr Royal Wstmr St James Barbados Office: Shutts & Bowen 43 Upper Grosvenor St London W1K 2NJ England Fax: 4420.7493.4299. E-mail: mjlanger@aol.com

LANGER, ROBERT MARK, lawyer, educator; b. Norwalk, Conn., Oct. 4, 1948; s. Melvin and Claire (Schnable) L.; m. Shelley Tishler, Dec. 26, 1970; children: Joshua Adam, Jennifer Rebecca. AB, Franklin and Marshall Coll., 1970; JD, U. Conn., West Hartford, 1973. Bar: Conn. 1973, U.S. Dist. Ct. Conn. 1973, U.S. Ct. Appeals (2d cir.) 1975, U.S. Supreme Ct. 1976. Asst. atty. gen. in charge antitrust and consumer protection Conn. Atty. Gen.'s Office, Hartford, 1973-94; ptnr., chmn. antitrust & trade regulation practice group Wiggin & Dana, 1994—. Adj. prof. MBA program U. Conn. Sch. Bus. Adminstrn., 1979—; adv. bd. Bur. Nat. Affairs Antitrust & Trade Regulation Bd. Co-author: Connecticut Unfair Trade Practices Act, 2 vols., 1994; mem. editl. bd. Matthew Bender Antitrust Report; contbr. articles to profl. jours., newspapers. Chmn. Ea. States Antitrust Com., 1988-90, vice-chmn. 1986-88; chmn. James W. Cooper Fellows Program Conn. Bar Found., 2000—. Fellow Am. Bar Found.; mem. ABA (chair state antitrust enforcement com., sect. antitrust law 1992-95, vice-chmn. continuing legal edn. com. sect. antitrust law 1995-96, co-chmn. fed. and state legis. policy task force, sect. antitrust law 1996-97, co-chmn. legis. com., sect. antitrust law 1997-98, vice-chmn. cons. prot. 1998-2000, chmn. cons. prot. 2000—), Corp. Bar Assn. (chmn. antitrust & trade regulation com. 1998—), Conn. Bar Assn. (chmn. antitrust sect. 1979-80), Nat. Assn. Attys. Gen. Multi-State Antitrust Task Force (vice-chmn. 1988-90, chmn. 1990-92). Office: Wiggin & Dana 1 Cityplace 34th Fl Hartford CT 06103-3402 E-mail: rlanger@wiggin.com

LANGER, SIMON HRIMES, lawyer; b. Tel Aviv, Mar. 16, 1952; came to U.S., 1958; AB in Polit. Sci., U. Calif., Berkeley, 1974; MA in Polit. Sci., U. So. Calif., 1975; JD, Calif. Western Sch. Law, 1978; LLM, Columbia U., 1981. Bar: D.C. 1979, Pa. 1980, Calif. 1982, U.S. Dist. Ct. (so., no., ea. and ctrl. dists.) Calif. 1982, U.S. Ct. Appeals (9th cir.) 1982, U.S. Tax Ct. 1986. Atty.-advisor U.S. Internat. Trade Commn., Washington, 1979-80; assoc. Kindel and Anderson, L.A., 1981—83; sr. assoc. Frandzel and Share, Beverly Hills, Calif., 1983—87; ptnr. Stone & Wolfe, L.A., 1987—91, Langer & Spielberger, L.A., 1991—96; internat. legal cons. U.S.-Italy, 1996; gen. counsel Gerant Industries, 1991—95, Powercom Energy & Comm. Access Inc., Calif., 2001—; ptnr. Global Trade & Devel. Group, Washington and Md., 1998—. Internat. legal cons., U.S., Italy, 1996—. Exec. editor Am. Soc. Internat. Law Jour., 1977, editor-in-chief, 1978; contbr. articles to profl. jours. Charles A. Dana Found. fellow, Am. Soc. Internat. Law, 1978-79. Mem. ABA, Pa. Bar Assn., D.C. Bar Assn. E-mila; mpinterntl.aol.com. General corporate, Private international, Public international. Home and Office: 9210 Hazen Dr Beverly Hills CA 90210-1827 E-mail: shlanger@aol.com

LANGFORD, JAMES JERRY, lawyer; b. Birmingham, Ala., May 19, 1933; S. N.B. and Margaret Elizabeth (Fuller) L.; m. Mary Elizabeth Fryant, Mar. 21, 1958; children: Jan Carol Langford Hammett, Joel Fryant L. BS, U. So. Miss., 1955; JD, U. Miss., 1970. Bar: Miss. 1970, U.S. Dist. Ct. (no. and so. dists.) Miss. 1970, U.S. Ct. Appeals (5th cir.) 1971, U.S. Ct. Appeals (11th cir.). Agt. Met. Life Ins. Co., Jackson, Miss., 1957-58; sales rep. Employers Mut. of Wausau, 1958-64; v.p. Reid-McGee Ins. Co., 1964-67; from assoc. to sr. ptnr., mng. ptnr. Wells Marble & Hurst, 1970-97, sr. ptnr., 1997—. Editor-in-chief Miss. Law Jour., 1969-70. 1st lt. U.S. Army, 1955-57. Fellow. Miss. Bar Found.; mem. ABA, Fed. Bar Assn. (pres. Miss. chpt. 1981-82),Fdn. Ins. and Corp. Counsel, Nat. Assn. RR Trial Counsel, Miss. Bar Assn., Miss. Def. Lawyers Assn. (pres. 1992-93), Country Club Jackson, Phi Delta Phi, Omicron Delta Kappa, Pi Kappa Alpha. Presbyterian. Avocations: military history, baseball. General civil litigation, Insurance, Product liability. Home: 12 Plum Tree Ln Madison MS 39110-9620 Office: Wells Marble & Hurst PO Box 131 Jackson MS 39205-0131 E-mail: jlangfordesq@aol.com

LANGTON, JEFFREY H. judge; b. Hamilton, Mont., Apr. 22, 1953; s. Richard L. and N. Louise (Mittower) L.; m. Patricia L. Stanbery, June 17, 1978 (div. Feb. 1999); children: Melanie, Matthew, Stephen, Thomas. BA in history with high honors, U. Mont., 1975, JD, 1978. Bar: Mont. 1978, U.S. Dist. Ct. Mont. 1978. Assoc. Schultz Law Firm, Hamilton, 1978-82; pvt. practice, 1982-92; dist. judge 21st Dist. Ct., 1993—. Bd. clin. visitors Law Sch., U. Mont., Missoula, 1993-99; Mont. Sentence Review Divsn., 1998—, chmn., 2000—; chmn. self represented litigants Mont. Supr. Ct. Commn., 2000— Author: The Victor Story, 1985. Bd. dirs. Victor Heritage Mus., 1990-95. Named Man of Yr. Victor Booster Club, 1988, 93. Mem. ABA (Mont. del. 1994—), Am. Jud. Soc., Mont. Bar Assn., Mont. Judges Assn. Presbyterian. Avocations: Montana history, fly fishing, environmental issues. Home: 2975 Mittower Rd Victor MT 59875-9542 Office: 21st Jud Dist 205 Bedford St Hamilton MT 59840-2853

LANGUM, DAVID JOHN, law educator, historian; b. Oakland, Calif., Oct. 24, 1940; s. John Kenneth and Virginia Anne (deMattos) L.; children: Virginia Eileen, John David, David John, Jr.; m. Frances M. Short, 1996. AB, Dartmouth Coll., 1962; JD, Stanford U., 1965; MA in History, San Jose State U., 1976; LLM in Legal History, U. Mich., 1981, SJD in Legal History, 1985. Bar: Calif. 1966, Mich. 1981, U.S. Supreme Ct. 1972. Rsch. clk. Calif. Ct. Appeals, San Francisco, 1965-66; assoc. Dunne, Phelps & Mills, 1966-68; ptnr. Christenson, Hedemark, Langum & O'Keefe, San Jose, Calif., 1968-78; adj. prof. Lincoln U. Sch. Law, 1968-78; prof. law Detroit Coll. Law, 1978-83; prof. Old Coll. Sch. Law, Reno, 1983-85, dean, 1983-84; prof. Cumberland Sch. Law Samford U., Birmingham, 1985—. Author: Law in the West, 1985, Law and Community on the Mexican Californai Frontier, 1987 (Hurst prize 1988), (with Harlan Hague) Thomas O. Larkin: A Life of Patriotism and Profit in Old California, 1990 (Caroline Bancroft prize, 1991), Crossing Over the Line: Legislating Morality and the Mann Act, 1994, (with Howard Walthall) From Maverick to Mainstream: Cumberland School of Law, 1947-1997, 1997, William M. Kunstler: The Most Hated Lawyer in America, 1999; contbr. articles on law and history to profl. jours. Mem. House of Flag, pro bono litigation, San Francisco, 1973-76; past pres. Victorian Preservation Assn., Santa Clara County, Calif.; pres. ACLU of Ala., 2000—. Mem. Am. Soc. for Legal History (bd. dirs.), Am. History Assn., Western History Assn. (Bolton award 1978). Office: Samford U Cumberland Sch Law 800 Lakeshore Dr Birmingham AL 35229-0002

LANGWORTHY, ROBERT BURTON, lawyer; b. Kansas City, Mo., Dec. 24, 1918; s. Herman Moore and Minnie (Leach) L.; m. Elizabeth Ann Miles, Jan. 2, 1942; children: David Robert, Joan Elizabeth Langworthy Tomek, Mark Burton. AB, Princeton U., 1940; JD, Harvard U., 1943. Bar: Mo. 1943, U.S. Supreme Ct 1960. Practiced in, Kansas City, 1943—; assoc., then mem. and v.p. Linde, Thomson, Langworthy, Kohn & Van Dyke, P.C., 1943-91; pres., mng. shareholder Blackwood, Langworthy & Schmelzer, P.C., Kansas City, Mo., 1991-96; mng. mem. Blackwood & Langworthy, LC, 1996—. Lectr. on probate, law sch. CLE courses U. Mo., Kansas City. Mem. bd. editors Harvard Law Rev., 1941-43; contbr. chpts. to Guardian and Trust, Powers, Conservatorships and Nonprobate Desk Books of Mo. Bar. Mem. edn. appeal bd. U.S. Dept. Edn., 1982-86; commr. Housing Authority Kansas City, 1963-71, chmn., 1969-71; chmn. Bd. Election Commrs. Kansas City, 1973-77; chmn. bd. West Ctrl. area YMCA, 1969—; mem. bd. Mid-Am. region YMCA, 1970-83, vice chmn., 1970-73, chmn., 1973-78; pres. Met. Bd. Kansas City (Mo.) YMCA (now YMCA of Greater Kansas City), 1965, bd. dirs., 1965—, mem. nat. bd. 1971-78, 79-83; bd. dirs. YMCA of the Rockies, 1974—, bd. sec., 1994-99; chmn. bd. trustees Sioux Indian YMCAs, 1983—; bd. dirs. Armed Svcs. YMCA, 1984-85; pres. Met. Area Citizens Edn., 1969-72; chmn. Citizens Assn. Kansas City (Mo.), 1967, bd. dirs., 1995-96; bd. dirs. Project Equality Kans.-Mo., 1967-80, pres., 1970-72, treas., 1972-73, sec., 1973-76; 1st v.p. Human Resources Corp. Kansas City, 1969-71, 72-73, bd. dirs., 1965-73; hon. v.p. Am. Sunday Sch. Union (now Am. Missionary Fellowship), 1965—; vice chmn. bd. trustees Kemper Mil. Sch., 1966-73; U.S. del. YMCA World Coun., Buenos Aires, 1977, Estes Park, Colo., 1981, Nyborg, Denmark, 1985; bd. dirs. Mo. Rep. Club, 1960—; del., mem. platform com. Rep. Nat. Conv., 1960; Rep. nominee for U.S. Congress, 1964; mem. gen. assembly Com. on Representation Presbyn., 1991-97, moderator, 1993-94; commr. to gen. assembly Presbyn. Ch., 1984, mem. gen. assembly com. on location of hdqs. 1984-87; moderator Heartland Presbyn., 1984. Lt. (j.g.) USNR, 1943-46, capt. Res. ret. Mem. ABA, Kansas City Bar Assn. (chmn. probate law com. 1988-90, 99-2000, living will com. 1989-91), Mo. State Bar (chmn. probate and trust com. 1983-85, chmn. sr. lawyers com. 1991-93), Lawyers Assn. Kansas City, Harvard Law Sch. Assn. Mo. (v.p. 1973-74, pres. 1974-75, 85-87), Univ. Club (Kansas City). Presbyterian (elder). Estate planning, Non-profit and tax-exempt organizations, Probate. Home: Claridge Ct Apt 305 8101 Mission Rd Prairie Village KS 66208-5238 Office: 1220 Washington St Ste 300 Kansas City MO 64105-1439 E-mail: Robertlangworthy@aol.com

LANIER, GRADY OLIVER, III, lawyer; b. Murfreesboro, Tenn., Jan. 15, 1944; s. Grady O. and Floy Lillian (Wofford) L.; m. Leslie Ann Scott, Dec. 13, 1969; children— Margaret, Elizabeth, Scott. B.S., Auburn U., 1969; J.D., Cumberland Law Sch., 1973. Bar: Ala. 1973. Staff atty. Ala. Electric Co., Andalusia, Ala., 1973-80; dist. atty. Covington County, Andalusia, Ala., 1980-86 . Mem. Andalusia Indsl. Devel. Bd., 1977-80. Served with USNR, 1963-67. Mem. ABA, Am. Legion. Democrat. Methodist. Club: Lions (pres. 1983-84). Office: 206 S Three Notch St Andalusia AL 36420-3710

LANS, ASHER BOB, lawyer; b. N.Y.C., Dec. 4, 1918; s. Arthur Louis and Sophie (Bob) L.; m. Barbara Eisner , Dec. 5, 1946 (div.); children: Deborah, Stephen, Alan; m. Mary Themo, Nov. 1, 1966 (div.); 1 child, Tracy (dec.); m. Shirley Johnson, June 26, 1967 (div.); 1 child, Andrea Elisabeth; m. Margaret Catherine Clancy, June 12, 1993. AB, Dartmouth Coll., 1938; MA, Columbia U., 1939; LLB, Yale U., 1944. Bar: N.Y. 1945, U.S. Dist. Ct. (so. and ea. dists.) N.Y., U.S. Tax Ct., U.S. Ct. Appeals (2d cir.), U.S. Supreme Ct. Law clk. Trustees of Assoc. G&E Corp., 1942-44; rsch. asst. Yale U., New Haven, 1944; assoc. Coudert Bros., 1945-47; ptnr. Lans, Goldstein, Golenbock & Abrams, N.Y.C., 1948-50; pvt. practice, 1951-57, 69; ptnr. Kramer & Lans, 1958-65, Lans & Fink, N.Y.C., 1966-68, Lans, Feinberg & Cohen, N.Y.C., 1970-84, Summit, Rovins & Feldesman, N.Y.C., 1984-91; of counsel Jackson & Nash, 1991—. Dir., sec. Charbert, Inc. and related cos., N.Y.C., 1964—, J.K. Gallery, Inc., 1994—. Co-author: Studies in World Public Order, 1960; contbr. articles to profl. jours. Mem. Alumni Coun., Dartmouth Coll., Hanover, N.H., 1988-92; elector Spanish Portuguese Synagogue, N.Y.C., 1971—; v.p., bd. dirs. Gramercy Neighborhood Assn., 1993-97, pres., 1997—. Mem. ABA, Yale Club, Nat. Arts Club. Democrat. Jewish. General corporate, Finance, Private international. Home: 24 Gramercy Park S New York NY 10003-1700 Office: Jackson & Nash 330 Madison Ave Rm 1800 New York NY 10017-5001

LANS, DEBORAH EISNER, lawyer; b. N.Y.C., Oct. 26, 1949; d. Asher Bob and Barbara (Eisner) L. AB magna cum laude, Smith Coll., 1971; JD cum laude, Boston U., 1974. Bar: N.Y. 1975, U.S. Dist. Ct. (so. and ea. dists.) N.Y. 1975, U.S. Ct. Appeals (2d cir.) 1975, U.S. Supreme Ct. 1983. Assoc. Lans, Feinber & Cohen, N.Y.C., 1975-80, ptnr., 1980-84, Morrison, Cohen, Singer & Weinstein, N.Y.C., 1984-2000; counsel Morrison, Cohen, Singer & Weinstein LLP, 2000—01, Wasserman, Grubin & Rogers LLP, 2001—. Exec. dir. Mentoring USA. Mem. ABA (bd. editors comml. banking litigation sects 1998—), Am. Arbitration Assn. (comml. panel arbitrators 1984—), Assn. of Bar of City of N.Y. (chmn. young lawyers com. 1981-83, joint com. fee disputes, 1982, judiciary com. 1984-85, exec. com. 1985-89, spl. com. bioethical issues, 1992-94, coun. on judicial adminstrn. 1996—), N.Y. State Bar Assn. (ho. of dels. 1984-87, comml. & fed. litigation sect. com. on judiciary, alternative dispute resolution 1992—, environ. law sect. 1995—, family law sect., co-chair women in cts. com. 1994—), N.Y. Bar Found. Federal civil litigation, State civil litigation. Office: Wasserman, Grubin & Rogers LLP 1700 Broadway New York NY 10019 E-mail: dlans@mentoringusa.org

LANSING, MARK DANIEL, lawyer; b. Albany, N.Y., Feb. 3, 1961; s. Cornelius Hill and Ethel Alice (Haines) L.; m. Nora Ellen Nichols, Oct. 10, 1987. BS, Rensselaer Polytech. Inst., 1983; JD, Union U., 1985; MBA, Rensselaer Poly. Inst., 1998. Bar: D.C., 1989, N.Y., 1985, U.S. Ct. Army Mil. Rev., U.S. Dist. Ct. N.Y., U.S. Supreme Ct. Commd. capt. U.S. Army, 1986; atty. Army Judge Advocate's Gen. Corp., Ft. Ord, Calif., 1986-89; trial atty. tax div. U.S. Dept. Justice, Washington, 1989-93; assoc., then ptnr. Helm Shapiro Anito & McCale P.C., 1993-2001; ptnr. Hiscock & Barclay, Albany, 2001—. Mem. ATLA, N.Y. State Bar Assn., N.Y. State Trial Lawyers Assn., D.C. Bar Assn. Office: Hiscock & Barclay LLP 50 Beaver St Albany NY 12207 E-mail: mlansing@hiscockbarclay.com

LANSNER, DAVID JEFFREY, lawyer; b. N.Y.C., Oct. 13, 1947; s. Seymour L. and Helen (Kulick) L.; m. Carolyn Anne Kubitschek, Apr. 26, 1975; children: Jesse K., Noah K. BA, U. Rochester, 1968; JD, NYU, 1971. Bar: N.Y. 1972, U.S. Dist. Ct. (so. and ea. dists.) N.Y. 1974, U.S. Ct. Appeals (2d cir.) 1975, U.S. Supreme Ct. 1990. Staff atty. Harlem Assertion of Rights, N.Y.C., 1971-72, MFY Legal Svcs., N.Y.C., 1972-75; tng. and staff atty. Legal Aid Soc., Bklyn., 1975-78; dir. family law unit Bronx Legal Svcs., 1978-79; sole practice, N.Y.C., 1979-81; ptnr. Lansner, Himmelstein & McConnell , N.Y.C., 1981-90, Lansner & Kubitschek, 1991—; assoc. counsel N.Y. State Assembly, 1987-2000; instr. Nat. Ctr. Pub. Productivity, N.Y.C., 1980-82. Co-author: Practice Manual for Law Guardians, 1976, Child Abuse and Neglect, 1981. Mem. N.Y. County Lawyers Assn., N.Y. State Bar Assn. Civil rights, Family and matrimonial, Juvenile. Home: 411 9th St Brooklyn NY 11215-4101 Office: Lansner & Kubitschek 325 Broadway New York NY 10007-1112

LANTIER, BRENDAN JOHN, lawyer; b. Rockville Centre, N.Y., July 6, 1948; s. James David and Jane Veronica (O'Connor) L.; m. Karyn Lainis, May 14, 1994. BA, U. Notre Dame, 1970; JD, Syracuse U., 1974. Bar: N.Y. 1975, U.S. Dist. Ct. (so. and ea. dists.) N.Y. 1975, U.S. Supreme Ct. 1979. Asst. dist. atty., dep. bur. chief Kings County Dist. Atty., Bklyn., 1974-83; atty., ptnr. McAloon & Friedman, N.Y.C., 1983—. Mem. N.Y. State Med. Def. Bar Assn. Personal injury. Home: 10 Old Jackson Ave Unit 45 Hastings On Hudson NY 10706-3230 Office: McAloon & Friedman 116 John St Fl 29 New York NY 10038-3498

LANTZ, WILLIAM CHARLES, lawyer; b. Rochester, Minn., July 3, 1946; s. Charles E. and Doris (Greenwood) L.; m. Vickie L. Erickson, May 17, 1972; children: Charles Eric, Andrew William. BA, Hamline U., 1968; JD, U. Minn., 1971. Bar: Minn. 1971. From assoc. to ptnr. Dorsey & Whitney, Rochester, 1975—. Served to lt. JAGC, USNR, 1971-75. Mem. Minn. Bar Assn., Olmsted Bar Assn. Methodist. Contracts commercial, Landlord-tenant, Real property. Home: 807 Sierra Ln NE Rochester MN 55906-4230 Office: Dorsey & Whitney 201 1st Ave SW Ste 340 Rochester MN 55902-3106 E-mail: lantz.chuck@dorseylaw.com

LAPIDUS, STEVEN RICHARD, lawyer; b. N.Y.C., Jan. 14, 1945; s. Leopold and Hortense (Klemons) L.; m. Iris R. Lerner, Mar. 18, 1973; children: Jennifer Lauren, Adam Ross. AB, NYU, 1966; JD, Bklyn. Law Sch., 1969; cert. Nat. Coll. Dist. Attys., U. Houston, 1972. Bar: N.Y. 1970, U.S. Dist. Ct. (so. and ea. dists.) N.Y. 1971, U.S. Ct. Appeals (2d cir.) 1971, U.S. Supreme Ct. 1973. Asst. dist. atty. Office Dist. Atty. Nassau County, N.Y., 1970-73; asst. atty. gen. N.Y. State Dept. Law, N.Y.C., 1973-77; spl. asst. atty. gen. N.Y. State Dept. Law, N.Y.C., 1977-78; ptnr. Lerner Franquinha & Lapidus, N.Y.C., 1977-78; sr. ptnr. Abrams Lerner Kisseloff Kissin & Lapidus, P.C., N.Y.C., 1978—; adj. assoc. prof. Real Estate Inst., NYU, N.Y.C., 1979—; lectr. Practicing Law Inst., N.Y.C., 1988—. With Army NG, 1969-71. Mem. N.Y. State Bar Assn., Coop. Housing Lawyers Group, NYU Club. Jewish. Administrative and regulatory, State civil litigation, Real property.

LAPIN, HARVEY I. lawyer; b. St. Louis, Nov. 23, 1937; s. Lazarus L. and Lillie L.; m. Cheryl A. Lapin; children: Jeffrey, Gregg. BS, Northwestern U., 1960, JD, 1963. Bar: Ill. 1963, Fla. 1980, Wis. 1985; cert. tax lawyer, Fla.; CPA, Ill. Atty. Office Chief Counsel, IRS, Washington, 1963-65; trial atty. Office Regional Counsel, IRS, 1965-68; assoc., then ptnr. Fiffer & D'Angelo, Chgo., 1968-75; pres. Harvey I. Lapin, P.C., 1975-83; mng. ptnr. Lapin, Hoff, Spangler & Greenberg, 1983-88, Lapin, Hoff, Slaw & Laffey, Chgo., 1989-91; ptnr. Gottlieb and Schwartz, 1992-93; prin. Harvey I. Lapin & Assocs., P.C., Northbrook, Ill., 1993—. Instr. John Marshall Law Sch., 1969—; facility adv. lawyers asst. program Roosevelt U., Chgo.; mem. cemetery adv. bd. Ill. Comptroller, 1974-96, 99—; mem. IRS Great Lakes TE/EO Coun., 2001—. Asst. editor Fed. Bar Jour., 1965-67; contbg. editor Cemetery and Funeral Service Business and Legal Guide; contbr. articles to profl. jours. Mem. ABA, Fla. Bar Assn., Wis. Bar Assn., Ill. Bar Assn., Chgo. Bar Assn., (mem. tax exempt orgns. subcom., sect. taxation 1988-90). Jewish. General corporate, Corporate taxation. Office: Harvey I Lapin & Assocs PC PO Box 1327 Northbrook IL 60065-1327

LAPINE, FELIX VICTOR, lawyer; b. Poznan, Poland, Mar. 25, 1941; came to U.S., 1951; s. Otto Karl and Bronislawa Lapping; children: Misha, Edward, Andrei, Maximillian. BA, U. Rochester, 1964; LLB, Syracuse U., 1967, JD, 1969. Bar: N.Y. 1969, U.S. Dist. Ct. (we. and no. dists.) N.Y. 1972, U.S. Ct. Appeals (2d cir.) 1977. Asst. dist. atty. Monroe County, Rochester, N.Y., 1969-72; ptnr. Napier & Lapine, 1972-78; pvt. practice, 1978—. Recipient R.C. Napier award Criminal Def. League, 1992. Mem. Monroe County Bar Assn. (Charles F. Crimi award 1994). Avocation: managing a semi-professional soccer team (finalist U.S. Amateur Cup, 1995). General civil litigation, Criminal. Office: 1 E Main St Ste 711 Rochester NY 14614-1807

LAPORTE, CLOYD, JR. lawyer, retired manufacturing executive; b. N.Y.C., June 8, 1925; s. Cloyd and Marguerite (Raeder) L.; m. Caroline E. Berry, Jan. 22, 1949; children— Elizabeth, Marguerite, Cloyd III. AB, Harvard U., 1946, JD, 1949. Bar: N.Y. 1949. Assoc. mem. firm Cravath, Swaine & Moore, N.Y.C., 1949-56; dir. adminstrn. Metals div. Olin Corp., 1957-66; legal counsel Dover Corp., 1966-93, sec., 1971-93. Dir. Putnam Hosp. Ctr., 2000—. 2d lt. A.C. AUS, WWII. Mem. Harvard Club (N.Y.C.). Home: Gipsy Trail Club Carmel NY 10512

LAPPAS, SPERO THOMAS, lawyer; b. Danbury, Conn., Oct. 20, 1952; s. Tom John and Alexandria (Manolakes) L.; m. Josephine Wahrendorf, Nov. 8, 1981 (div. 1986); 1 child, Thom Spero; m. Julie Marie Waugh, July 12, 1986 (div. 1995); 1 child, Alexandria Julia. BA cum laude, Allegheny Coll., Meadville, Pa., 1974; JD cum laude, Dickinson Sch. Law, Carlisle, Pa., 1977. Bar: Pa. 1977, U.S. Dist. Ct. (mid. dist.) Pa. 1977, U.S. Ct. Appeals (3rd cir.) 1980, U.S. Supreme Ct. 1991. Assoc. Law Office of Arthur Kusic, Harrisburg, Pa., 1977-79; atty. Kusic & Lappas, P.C., 1979-84; pvt. practice, 1984-85; ptnr. Stefanon & Lappas, 1985-88; prin. Law Offices Spero T. Lappas, 1988—. Mem. ATLA, Pa. Bar Assn., Dauphin County Bar Assn., Pa. Assn. Criminal Def. Lawyers, Pa. Trial Lawyers Assn., Mensa, Am. Hellenic Ednl. and Progressive Assn. Civil rights, General civil litigation, Criminal. Office: 205 State St Harrisburg PA 17101-1130 E-mail: lappas@lawyers1.com

LAPUZZA, PAUL JAMES, lawyer; b. Omaha, May 30, 1948; s. Anton T. and Elaine M. (Fitzsenry) LaP.; m. Mary LaPuzza, July 5, 1975; children: Mark James, Tracey Marie. BSBA, Creighton U., 1970, JD, 1972. Bar: Nebr. 1972, U.S. Dist. Ct. Nebr. 1972, U.S. Ct. Appeals (8th cir.) 1975, U.S. Supreme Ct. 1981, U.S. Claims Ct. 1982. Sole practice, Omaha, 1972-78; ptnr. Young & LaPuzza and predecessor, Omaha, 1978—. Co-author: (manual) Phi Kappa Psi, 1984. Served to capt. U.S. Army, 1972. Mem. Nebr. State Bar Assn., Phi Kappa Psi (dept. atty. gen. 1972-78, 82-84, treas. 1986-88, v.p. 1988—, atty. gen. 1978-82), Delta Sigma Rho, Tau Kappa Alpha. Democrat. Roman Catholic. Contracts commercial, General practice, Real property. Home: 9807 Ascot Dr Omaha NE 68114-3847 Office: Young & LaPuzza 1125 S 103rd St Ste 710 Omaha NE 68124-1071

LAQUERCIA, THOMAS MICHAEL, lawyer; b. Bklyn., Apr. 22, 1945; s. Antonio Salvatore and Josephine Maria-Grazia (Livolsi) L.; m. Evelyn Margaret Fernandez, Nov. 2, 1943; children: Thomas Peter, Marc Anthony, Justin Gregory. BA in English, St. Francis Coll., Bklyn., 1966; JD, St. John's U., 1969. Bar: N.Y. 1970, U.S. Dist. Ct. (so. and ea. dists.) N.Y. 1971, U.S. Ct. Appeals (2d dir.) 1971, U.S. Supreme Ct. 1977. With Gen. Accident Group, N.Y.C., 1970-71; staff trial atty.. Kings County Civil Ct., 1970-71; assoc. litigation dept. Post DeMott & Grow, N.Y.C., 1971-74; assoc. Abrams & Martin, P.C., 1974-80; mng. ptnr. Smith & Laquercia LLP, 1980—. Arbitrator small claims night ct. Civil Ct. City N.Y.; counsel Families First Inc., Bklyn. Pres. bd. dirs. Strong Place Day Care Ctr., Inc. Served with USAR, 1969-75. Mem. New York County Lawyers Assn., Def. Assn. N.Y. (bd. dirs.), Assn. Arbitrators Civil Ct. City N.Y., Columbian Lawyers of Bklyn., Columbian Lawyers of First Dept., Nat. Italian-Am. Bar Assn., Alpha Phi Delta, Phi Delta Phi. Roman Catholic. State civil litigation, Insurance, Personal injury. Office: Smith & Laquercia LLP 291 Broadway New York NY 10007-1814 E-mail: sl@smithlaquercia.com

LARDENT, ESTHER FERSTER, lawyer, legal consultant; b. Linz, Austria, Apr. 23, 1947; came to U.S., 1951; d. William and Rose (Seidweber) Ferster; m. Dennis Robert Lardent, July 27, 1969 (div. Dec. 1981). BA, Brown U., 1968; JD, U. Chgo., 1971. Bar: Ill. 1972, U.S. Dist. Ct. Ill. 1972, Mass. 1975, U.S. Dist. Ct. Mass. 1975. Civil rights specialist Office of Civil Rights U.S. HEW, Chgo., 1971-72; staff dir. individual rights ABA, 1972-74; staff atty., supr. Cambridge (Mass.) Problem Ctr., 1975-76; exec. dir. Vol. Lawyers Project Boston Bar Assn., 1977-85; legal and policy cons. Santa Fe and Washington, 1985—; cons. Ford Found., Washington, 1990—. Vis. prof. U. N.Mex. Sch. Law, Albuquerque, 1985; cons. Nat. Vets. Legal Svcs. Program, Washington, 1991—; vis. scholar ethics program Boston U. Sch. Law, 1991-92; reporter ABA/Tulane Law Sch., New Orleans, 1988-90; pres. pro bono inst. Georgetown U. Law Ctr., 1996—. Contbr. articles to profl. jours. Recipient Founders' award Phila. Bar Assn., 1991, Outstanding Pub. Interest Adv. award Nat. Assn. Pub. Interest Law, 1992. Mem. ABA (Ho. of Dels. 1991—, cons. 1974-76, legal cons. postconviction death penalty 1987-96, legal cons. law firm pro bono project 1989-96), Nat. Legal Aid and Defenders Assn. (bd. dirs. 1990—), D.C. Bar (spl. advisor pub. svc. activities review com. 1990—), U. Chgo. Law Sch. (vis. com. 1992—).

LARIMORE, TOM L. lawyer; b. Ft. Worth, Sept. 21, 1937; s. T.R. and Mildred Elizabeth (Angell) L.; m. Bobbie Jeanne Wingo, Dec. 20, 1999; children: Thomas Lee, Robert Karl, Susan Lynne, Natalie Jeanne. BA, Washington and Lee U., 1959; LLB, So. Meth. U., 1962. Bar: Tex. 1962, U.S. Dist. Ct. (no. dist.) Tex. 1965, U.S. Dist. Ct. (so. dist.) Tex. 1975, U.S. Ct. Appeals (5th cir.) 1977. Assoc. Walker & Bishop, Ft. Worth, 1962-66; ptnr. Walker, Bishop & Larimore, 1966-73, Bishop, Larimore, Lamsens & Brown, Ft. Worth, 1973-79; v.p., gen. counsel, sec. Western Co. of N.Am., 1979-80, v.p. law and adminstrn., sec., 1980-86; ptnr. Gandy, Michner, Swindle, Whitaker & Pratt, 1986—. Pres., bd. dirs. YMCA (West), Ft. Worth, 1966-68; sr. warden, vestryman All Saints Episcopal Ch., Ft. Worth, 1973-74, named Churchman of Yr., 1969; pres., bd. dirs. Sr. Citizens Ctrs., Ft. Worth, 1974-78. Fellow Tex. Bar Found.; mem. ABA, Tarrant County Bar Assn. (bd. dirs. 1978-80), Am. Corp. Counsel Ass.n, Ft. Worth Bar Assn. (chmn. dist. admissions com. 1975-77), Ft. Worth C. of C. (bd. dirs. 1985—, chmn. West area coun. 1985-86), Tex. Rsch. League (bd. dirs. 1980-86), Shady Oaks Country Club (Ft. Worth), Rotary (pres., bd. dirs. West Ft. Worth 1974-75, Paul Harris fellow 1982). E-mail: +larimore@whitaker-chalk.com. Federal civil litigation, State civil litigation, General corporate. Home: 11 Lombardy Terr Fort Worth TX 76132 Office: Whitaker Chalk Swindle & Sawyer LLP 301 Commerce St Ste 3500 Fort Worth TX 76102-4186

LARO, DAVID, judge; b. Flint, Mich., Mar. 3, 1942; s. Samuel and Florence (Chereton) L.; m. Nancy Lynn Wolf, June 18, 1967; children: Rachel Lynn, Marlene Ellen. BA, U. Mich., 1964; JD, U. Ill., 1967; LLM, NYU, 1970 Bar: Mich. 1968, U.S. Dist. Ct. (ea. dist.) Mich. 1968, U.S. Tax Ct. 1971. Ptnr. Winegarden Booth Shedd and Laro, Flint, Mich., 1970-75; sr. ptnr. Laro and Borgerson, 1975-86; prin. David Laro, P.C., 1986-92; apptd. judge U.S. Tax Ct., Washington, 1992—. Of counsel Dykema Gossett, Ann Arbor, Mich., 1989-90; pres., CEO, Durakon Industries, Inc., Ann Arbor, 1989-91, chmn., Lapeer, Mich., 1991—; chmn. Republic Bank, 1986—, vice chmn. Republic Bancorp, Inc., Flint, 1986—; instr. Nat. Inst. Trial Advocacy, vis. prof. U. San Diego Law Sch., adj. prof. law Georgetown Law Sch., 1994—; cons. lectr. on tax reform and litigation in Moscow Harvard U., 1997, Ga. State U., 1998. Regent U. Mich., Ann Arbor, 1975-81; mem. Mich. State Bd. Edn., 1982-83; chmn. Mich. State Tenure Commn., 1972-75; commr. Civil Svc. Commn., Flint, 1984—. Mem. Am. Coll. Tax Counsel, State Bar Mich., Phi Delta Phi. Republican. Office: US Tax Ct 400 2nd St NW Rm 217 Washington DC 20217-0002

LAROSE, LAWRENCE ALFRED, lawyer; b. Lowell, Mass., Oct. 26, 1958; s. Alfred M. and Rita B. (Plunkett) L.; m. Janet G. Yedwab, Aug. 12, 1984. BA summa cum laude, Tufts U., 1980; JD magna cum laude, Georgetown U., 1983. Bar: N.Y. 1984. Assoc. Sullivan & Cromwell, N.Y.C., 1983-85, 87-90, Melbourne, Australia, 1985-87, Cadwalader, Wickersham & Taft, N.Y.C., 1990-92, ptnr., 1993-2001, King & Spalding, N.Y.C., 2001—. Vis. fellow Faculty of Law, U. Melbourne, 1986-87. Contbr. articles to profl. publs. Mem. ABA, N.Y. State Bar Assn., N.Y. County Lawyers Assn., Assn. Bar City N.Y., Am. Soc. Internat. Law, Georgetown U. Nat. Law Alumni Bd. (exec. com., sec.), Down Town Assn. in City of N.Y., Phi Beta Kappa. Avocations: art collecting, art history. General corporate, Private international, Mergers and acquisitions. Office: King & Spalding 1185 Ave of the Americas New York NY 10036-4003

LA ROSSA, JAMES M(ICHAEL), lawyer; b. Bklyn., Dec. 4, 1931; s. James Vincent and Marie Antoinette (Tronolone) La R.; m. Dominique Bazin-Thall, Aug. 11, 1998; children: James M., Thomas, Nancy, Susan. B.S., Fordham U., 1953, J.D., 1958. Bar: N.Y. 1958, U.S. Dist. Ct. N.Y. 1961, U.S. Supreme Ct. 1969. Pvt. practice law, N.Y.C., 1958-62, 67-74, 76—; asst. U.S. atty. Eastern Dist. N.Y., Bklyn., 1962-65; ptnr. firm Lefkowitz & Brownstien, N.Y.C., 1965-67, La Rossa, Shargel & Fishetti, N.Y.C., 1974-76, La Rossa, Brownstein & Mitchell, N.Y.C., 1980-82, La Rossa, Axenfeld & Mitchell, N.Y.C., 1982-84, La Rossa, Cooper, Axenfeld, Mitchell & Bergman, N.Y.C., 1984-85, 86-98; now ptnr. Larossa & Ross; participant Debate on Legal Ethics Criminal Cts. Bar Assn. Queens County, N.Y., 1978, Criminal Trial Advocacy Workshop, Harvard U. Law Sch., 1978. Author: White Collar Crimes: Defense Strategies, 1977, Federal Rules of Evidence in Criminal Matters, 1977, White Collar Crimes, 1978. Served to 1st lt. USMC, 1953-55. Recipient Guardian of Freedom award B'nai B'rith, 1979, Career Achievement awardN.Y. Coun. Def. Lawyers, 1996; Ann. honoree N.Y. Criminal Bar Assn., 1999. Mem. ABA, N.Y. State Bar Assn. (Criminal Law Practitioner of Yr. 1990), Fed. Bar Counsel, Assn. Bar City N.Y. Office: LaRossa & Ross 41 Madison Ave New York NY 10010-2202

LARSEN, MICHAEL GREGERS, lawyer; b. Frederiksberg, Denmark, Nov. 6, 1944; s. Gregers Carsten and Else Gregers Larsen. Degree in Law, U. Copenhagen, 1970. Bar: Denmark 1974, Supreme Ct. 1979. Assoc. Poul Schmith Kammeradvokaten, Copenhagen, 1971-78, ptnr., 1978—, legal adv. to Danish Govt., 1992—. Chmn. Fund for Relatives of Knights of Dannebrog, 1993; bd. dirs. Fund of 1982, 1993. Named Knight First Class Order of Dannebrog, 2000. Mem. Bar Supreme Ct. (bd. dirs.) Home: 7 Sveasvej DK 1917 Frederiksberg Denmark Office: Poul Schmith Kammeradvocate 47 Vimmelskaftet DK 1161 Copenhagen Denmark

LARSON, BRYAN A. lawyer; s. Byron Ancedus and Betty Marilyn Stevenett; m. Kathy Larson; children: Aaron, Adam, Conor, Kaden, Sara, Aubrey. BA, Brigham Young U., 1980, JD, 1983. Bar: Utah 1983. Assoc. Christensen, Jensen & Powell, Salt Lake City, 1983-86, McKay, Burton & Thurman, Salt Lake City, 1986-91; ptnr. Larson, Jenkins & Halliday, 1991-95, Larson, Kirkham & Turner, Salt Lake City, 1995-99, Larson, Turner, Fairbanks and Dalby, Salt Lake City, 1999—. Editor newsletter Backtalk, 1995. Mem. ALTA (mem. polit. action com. 1991—), Utah Bar Assn. (com. chmn. 1990-92), Utah Trial Lawyers Assn. (polit. action com. 1991—), Order of Barristers. Mem. LDS Ch. Avocations: boating, snow skiing. Insurance, Personal injury. Office: Larson Turner Fairbanks & Dalby 4516 S 700 E Ste 100 Salt Lake City UT 84107-8319

LARSON, CHARLES W. prosecutor; Grad., Kans. State U., U. Iowa Sch. Law. Magistrate Iowa 5th Judicial Ct., 1973; commr. Iowa Dept. Public Safety, 1973—79; mgr. law enforcement Sanders and Assocs., 1979—82; ptnr. Walker, Larson and Billingsley, Newton, Iowa, 1982—86; U.S. atty. No. dist. Iowa, Cedar Rapids , 1986—93, 2001—. Office: PO Box 74950 Cedar Rapids IA 52407-4950*

LARSON, DAVID ELI, lawyer; b. Dayton, Ohio, Feb. 9, 1945; s. Eli Christian and Myrtle Lorene (Heeren) L.; m. Beverly Jean Farlow, June 17, 1967 (div.); m. Roberta Elizabeth Longfellow, Aug. 25, 1979; children: Jessica Deane Longfellow, Christian David Longfellow. BA, Wittenberg U., 1967; MPA, U. N.C., 1974; JD, Ohio State U., 1979. Bar: Ohio 1979, U.S. Dist. Ct. (so. dist.) Ohio 1980. Cmty. devel. rep. HUD, Colubmus, Ohio, 1970-73, multifamily housing rep., 1975-76; cmty. devel. dir. City of Miamisburg, 1973-75; assoc. Law Clinic of D.W. Bench, Dayton, 1980-83; ptnr. Certo and Larson, Kettering, Ohio, 1983-2000, Altick & Corwin, Kettering, 2000—. Vol. Peace Corps, Turkey, 1968; active Grace United Meth. Ch., Dayton, 1981. Wittenberg alumni scholar Wittenberg U., 1963; study fellow for internat. devel. U. N.C., Chapel Hill, 1969. Mem. Am. Immigration Lawyers Assn., Am. Bankruptcy Law Forum, Ohio State Bar Assn., Dayton Bar Assn. Democrat. Home: 836 Belmonte Park N Dayton OH 45405-4406 Office: Altick & Corwin 1700 One Dayton Ctr One S Main St Dayton OH 45402-2026 E-mail: dlarson836@aol.com, larsond@altickcorwin.com

LARSON, EDWARD, state supreme court justice; m. Mary Loretta Thompson; children: Sarah, John, Mary Elizabeth. BS, Kans. State U., 1954; JD, Kans. U., 1960. Pvt. practice, Hays, Kans., 1960—87; judge Kans. Ct. Appeals, 1987—95; justice Kans. Supreme Ct., Topeka, 1995—. Mcpl. judge City of Hays, 1965—72. 2nd lt. USAF. Office: Kans Supreme Ct 301 W 10th Rm 388 Topeka KS 66612*

LARSON, JERRY LEROY, state supreme court justice; b. Harlan, Iowa, May 17, 1936; s. Gerald L. and Mary Eleanor (Patterson) L.; m. Debra L. Christensen; children: Rebecca, Jeffrey, Susan, David. BA, State U. Iowa, 1958, JD, 1960. Bar: Iowa. Partner firm Larson & Larson, 1961-75; dist. judge 4th Jud. Dist. Ct. of Iowa, 1975-78; justice Iowa Supreme Ct., 1978—. Office: Supreme Ct Iowa PO Box 109 Des Moines IA 50319-0001

LARSON, JOHN WILLIAM, lawyer; b. Detroit, June 24, 1935; s. William and Sara Eleanor (Yeatman) L.; m. Pamela Jane Wren, Sept. 16, 1959; 1 dau., Jennifer Wren. BA with distinction, honors in Economics, Stanford, 1957; LLB, Stanford U., 1962. Bar: Calif. 1962. Assoc. Brobeck, Phleger & Harrison, San Francisco, 1962-68, ptnr., 1968-71, 73—, CEO, mng. ptnr., 1988-92, chmn. of firm, CEO, 1993-96; asst. sec. Dept. Interior, Washington, 1971-73; exec. dir. Natural Resources Com., 1973; counsellor to chmn. Cost of Living Coun., 1973. Faculty Practising Law Inst.; bd. dirs. Sangamo Bio Scis., Inc. Mem. 1st U.S.-USSR Joint Com. on Environment; mem. bd. visitors Stanford U. Law Sch., 1974-77, 85-87, 95-96; pres. bd. trustees The Katherine Branson Sch., 1980-83. With AUS, 1957-59. Mem. ABA, Calif. Bar Assn., San Francisco C. of C. (bd. dirs., chmn. 1996), Bay Area Coun., Calif. Acad. Sci., San Francisco Partnership, Bay Area Life Scis. Alliance, Order of Coif, Pacific Union Club, Burlingame Country Club, Bohemian Club. General corporate, Mergers and acquisitions, Securities. Home: PO Box 349 Ross CA 94957-0349 Office: Brobeck Phleger & Harrison Spear St Tower 1 Market Plz San Francisco CA 94105-1420

LARSON, MARK EDWARD, JR. lawyer, educator, financial advisor; b. Oak Park, Ill., Dec. 16, 1947; s. Mark Edward and Lois Vivian (Benson) L.; m. Patricia Jo Jekerle, Apr. 14, 1973; children: Adam Douglas, Peter Joseph, Alex Edward, Gretchen Elizabeth. BS in Acctg., U. Ill., 1969; JD, Northwestern U., 1972; LLM in Taxation, NYU, 1977. Bar: Ill. 1973, N.Y. 1975, D.C. 1976, Minn, 1982, Tex. 1984, U.S. Dist. Ct. (no. dist.) Ill. 1973, U.S. Dist. Ct. (so. dist.) N.Y. 1975, U.S. Ct. Appeals (2d cir.) 1975, U.S. Ct. Appeals (7th cir.) 1976, U.S. Dist. Ct. D.C. 1977, U.S. Ct. Appeals (D.C. cir.) 1977, U.S. Dist. Ct. Minn. 1982, U.S. Ct. Appeals (8th cir.) 1982, U.S. Tax Ct. 1976, U.S. Supreme Ct. 1976; CPA, Ill. Acct. Deloitte & Touche (formerly Haskins & Sells), N.Y.C., Chgo., 1973-81; atty., ptnr. Larson, Perry & Ward and former firms, Chgo., 1981—; prin. Winfield Fin. Svcs. and affiliates, Dallas and Chgo., 1986—. Adj. faculty U. Minn., Mpls., 1982-83, Aurora (Ill.) U., 1990-98, St. Xavier U., Chgo., 2000—; exec. Fin. Svcs. Inst. Chgo., 1996—. Contbr. articles to profl. jours. Mem. ABA, AICPA, AHLA, Am. Assn. Atty.-CPAs. Private international, Securities, Corporate taxation. Office: 1212 S Naper Blvd Ste 119 Naperville IL 60540-7349 E-mail: larsgen@usa.net

LARSON, SHARON D. lawyer, human resources specialist; b. Seattle, July 2, 1961; d. Harold F. and Ruth E. Larson. AA, Indian River C.C., Ft. Pierce, Fla., 1981; BS in Polit. Sci., Fla. State U., 1983, JD, 1986. Bar: Fla. 1986, U.S. Ct. Appeals (11th cir.) 1987, U.S. Dist. Ct. (no. dist.) Fla. 1995, U.S. Dist. Ct. (mid. dist.) Fla. 1996. Asst. state atty. State Atty.'s Office 19th Jud. Cir., Ft. Pierce, 1986-89; sr. atty. Fla. Dept. Transp., Tallahassee, 1989-90; asst. gen. counsel Fla. Dept. Law Enforcement, 1990-91, Fla. Bd. Bar Examiners, Tallahassee, 1991-93, Fla. Dept. Mgmt. Svcs., Tallahassee, 1993-98, dir. human resource mgmt., 1998—. Guardian ad litem 2d Jud. Cir., Tallahassee, 1996-99; elemn. sch. mentor, Tallahassee, 1999. Mem. Nat. Assn. State Pers. Execs., Soc. for Human Resource Mgmt., Govt. Bar Assn., Tallahassee Women Lawyers. Office: Dept Mgmt Svcs HRM 4050 Esplanade Way Bldg 4040 Tallahassee FL 32399-7016

LARUE, PAUL HUBERT, lawyer; b. Somerville, Mass., Nov. 16, 1922; s. Lucien H. and Germaine (Choquet) LaR.; m. Helen Finnegan, July 20, 1946; children: Paul Hubert, Patricia Seward, Mary Hogan. PhB, U. Wis., 1947, JD, 1949. Bar: Ill. 1955, Wis. 1949, U.S. Supreme Ct. 1972. Grad. asst. instr. polit. sci. dept. U. Wis., 1947-48; mem. staff Wis. Atty. Gen., 1949-50; trial atty., legal advisor to commr. FTC, 1950-55; pvt. practice Chgo.; mem. Chadwell & Kayser, Ltd., 1958-90; ptnr. Vedder, Price, Kaufman & Kammholz, 1990-93; of counsel, 1993-99. Spkr. profl. meetings; mem. Com. Modern Cts. in Ill., 1964; mem. Ill. Com. Constl. Conv., 1968, Better Govt. Assn., 1966-70 Contbr. articles to profl. jours. Mem. lawyers com. Met. Crusade of Mercy, 1967-68, United Settlement Appeal, 1966-68; apptd. pub. mem. Ill. Conflict of Interest Laws Commn., 1965-67. With AUS, 1943-45, ETO; capt. JAGC, USAFR, 1950-55. Fellow Ill. Bar Found. (life); mem. ABA (mem. coun. sect. antitrust law 1980-83, chmn. Robinson-Patman Act com. 1975-78), Ill. State Bar Assn., Chgo. Bar Assn. (chmn. antitrust com. 1970-71), Wis. State Bar, Rotary. Roman Catholic. Antitrust, Alternative dispute resolution, Federal civil litigation. Home and Office: 250 Cuttriss Pl Park Ridge IL 60068 Fax: 847-825-9025. E-mail: phlarue@aol.com

LARVIE, VERONICA I. lawyer; b. Butte, Mont., July 10, 1965; d. Francis Carl Larvie and Nancy Ann Kelly; m. Thomas W. Rinehart, June 11, 1988; 1 child, Jackson Thomas Rinehart. BS in Geology, U. Wyo., 1988, JD, 1995. Registered profl. geologist. Geologist Tri Hydro Corp., Laramie, Wyo., 1988-95; atty. U.S. Dept. of the Interior Office of the Solicitor, Washington, 1995—. Mem. rev. bd. Environ. Justice grant program U.S. EPA, Washington, 1997. Editor Land and Water Law Rev. U. Wyo., 1994-95. Chair com. for better environment City Coll. Park, Md., 1999. Mem. ABA (vice-chair pub. lands 1998—; editor pub. lands and land use newsletter 1998). Home: 4612 Guilford Rd College Park MD 20740-3732 Office: US Dept Interior 1849 C St NW # Ms6412 Washington DC 20240-0001

LARZELERE, KATHY LYNN HECKLER, paralegal; b. Sellersville, Pa., Dec. 4, 1955; d. Harold Tyson and Hannah Ruth (Wile) Heckler; m. Lawrence Sollanek, Nov. 1984 (div.); m. Loel Harry Larzelere, Aug. 27, 1992; 1 stepdaughter, Lindsie M. AAS magna cum laude, Columbus State C.C., 1991. From sales person to dept. mgr. Macy's New York, North Wales, Pa., 1977-83; store mgr. Bathtique, Wilmington, Del., Towson, Md., 1983-86; customer svc. person Marshall Fields, Chgo., 1987; word processor Franklin County Children Svcs., Columbus, Ohio, 1988-89; legal sec., paralegal M. Cohen and Assocs., 1989-94; paralegal Calig and Handelman LPA, 1994-97, Weltman, Weinberg & Reis, Columbus, 1997—. Author: (poetry) American High School Poets, 1973. Ward coord. Amelia Salerno for City Coun., Columbus, 1993; co-chmn. Columbus Christmas in Apr. Home Amb. Com., Columbus Christmas in Apr. Materials and In-Kind Donations Com. Mem. award Phi Theta Kappa. Mem. Nat. Fedn. Paralegal Asns., Paralegal Assn. Cen. Ohio (writer newsletter The Citator, co-chair student outreach com. 1994-95, chair 1995-97, 1st v.p. 1995-97, 2000-2001, pres. 1997-99, mem. adv. bd. 1999-2000, chair student outreach com. 1999-2000), Columbus Bar Assn. (assoc.). Lutheran. Avocations: handcrafts, reading, walking, watercolor painting, counted cross-stitch. Home: 2119 Kingsglen Dr Grove City OH 43123-1252 Office: Weltman Weinberg & Reis 175 S 3rd St Ste 900 Columbus OH 43215-5177 E-mail: klarzele@columbus.rr.com, klarzelere@weltman.com

LASAROW, WILLIAM JULIUS, retired federal judge; b. Jacksonville, Fla., June 30, 1922; s. David Herman and Mary (Hollins) L.; m. Marilyn Doris Powell, Feb. 4, 1951; children: Richard M., Elisabeth H. BA, U. Fla., 1943; JD, Stanford U., 1950. Bar: Calif. 1951. Counsel judiciary com. Calif. Assembly, Sacramento, 1951-52; dep. dist. atty. Stanislaus County, Modesto, Calif., 1952-53; pvt. practice law L.A., 1953-73; bankruptcy judge U.S. Cts., 1973-94; chief judge U.S. Bankruptcy Ct., Central dist., Calif., 1978-90; judge Bankruptcy Appellate Panel 9th Fed. Cir., 1980-82; fed. judge U.S. Bankruptcy Ct., L.A., 1973. Faculty Fed. Jud. Ctr. Bankruptcy Seminars, Washington, 1977-82 Contbg. author, editor legal publs.; staff: Stanford U. Law Review, 1949. Mem. ABA, Am. Coll. Bankruptcy, Am. Bankruptcy Inst., Nat. Conf. Bankruptcy Judges, Los Angeles County Bar Assn., Wilshire Bar Assn., Blue Key, Phi Beta Kappa, Phi Kappa Phi. Home: 11623 Canton Pl Studio City CA 91604-4164

LASCELL, DAVID MICHAEL, lawyer; b. Albion, N.Y., Apr. 11, 1941; s. Walter D. and June (Sargent) L.; m. Donna Lee Hopf, Sept. 5, 1964; children: Daniel, Carrie, Christopher. A.B., Hamilton Coll., 1963; LL.B., Cornell U., 1966. Bar: N.Y. 1966, U.S. Dist. Ct. (we., no. and so. dists.) N.Y. 1966, U.S. Ct. Appeals (3d cir.) 1982, U.S. Ct. Appeals (2d cir.) 1983, U.S. Supreme Ct. 1983. Assoc. Nixon, Hargrave, Devans & Doyle, Rochester, 1966-73, ptnr., 1973—; bd. dirs. United Educators Ins. Risk Retention Group Inc., Sch., Coll. and Univ. Underwriters, Ltd., The Common Fund. Co-author: Trustee Liability Insurance, 1981. Chmn. bd. trustees Wells Coll., Aurora, N.Y., 1975-89; trustee Mt. Vernon Coll., Washington, 1990—; bd. dirs. Rochester Area Colls. Consortium, 1978-81, Nat. Ctr. for Non-Profit Bds., Washington, 1987—, chairperson, 1987—; bd. dirs. Assn. Governing Bds. Colls. and Univs., Washington, 1981—, chmn., 1986-88. Fellow Am. Coll. Trial Lawyers; mem. Am. Law Inst. General civil litigation, Education and schools, Insurance. Office: Nixon Hargrave Devans & Doyle 1051 Clinton Sq Rochester NY 14604-1730

LASCHER, ALAN ALFRED, lawyer; b. N.Y.C., Dec. 8, 1941; s. Morris Julius and Sadie Lillian (Chassen) L.; m. C. Amy Weingarten, July 12, 1969; children: David, Lauren, Alexandra, Carlyn. BS, Union Coll., 1963; LLB, Bklyn. Law Sch., 1967. Bar: N.Y. 1967. Assoc. Kramer, Leven et al, N.Y.C., 1969-75; ptnr. real estate dept. Weil, Gotshal & Manges, 1975—. Mem. law com. N.Y. Real Estate Bd., N.Y.C., 1981—; bd. advisors Chgo. Title Ins. Co., 1995—. Served to sgt. USAF, 1968-69. Named Real Estate Lawyer of Yr. Am. Lawyer, 1982. Mem. Am. Coll. Real Estate Lawyers (mem. Resolution Trust Corp. and Bankruptcy coms.). Real property. Office: Weil Gotshal & Manges 767 5th Ave Fl Concl New York NY 10153-0119

LASHAY, JILL MARIA, lawyer; b. West Chester, Pa., Sept. 24, 1966; d. John M. and Margaret K. Lashay; m. Daniel Gordon Drury, Sept. 20, 1997. BA, George Washington U., 1988, JD, 1991. Bar: Pa., Va. Atty. Reed Smith Shaw & McClay, Washington, 1991-96, Klett Lieber Rooney & Schorling, Pitts., 1996—. Adj. faculty masters degree program Duquesne U., Pitts., 1999—. Author: Home Health Care Law Manual, 1996; contbr. articles to profl. jours. Bd. mem. Cranberry Twp. (Pa.) Libr., 1999. Mem. Am. Wine Soc. Republican. Roman Catholic. Avocations: reading, wine collecting. Office: Klett Lieber Rooney & Schorling One Oxford Ctr Pittsburgh PA 15219

LASHLEY, CURTIS DALE, lawyer; b. Urbana, Ill., Nov. 3, 1956; s. Jack Dale and Janice Elaine (Holman) L.; m. Tamara Dawn Yahnig, June 14, 1986. BA, U. Mo., Kansas City, 1978, JD, 1981. Bar: Mo. 1981, U.S. Dist. Ct. (we. dist.) Mo. 1981, U.S. Tax Ct. 1982, U.S. Ct. Appeals (8th cir.) 1992. Assoc. Melvin Heller, Inc., Creve Coeur, Mo., 1982; ptnr. Domjan & Lashley, Harrisonville, 1983-86; asst. gen. counsel Mo. Dept. Revenue, Independence, 1986-89, assoc. gen. counsel, 1989-92, sr. counsel, 1992—, adminstrv. hearing officer, 1995—; spl asst. atty. gen., 1986—; spl. asst. prosecutor Jackson County, Mo., 1990—. City atty., Adrian and Strasburg, Mo., 1985-86. V.p. Cass County Young Reps., Harrisonville, 1985. Recipient honor Senate Resolution 830 and Mo. Ho. Resolution 2314, 2001, Cert. of Appreciation, Kansas City Bd. Police Commrs., 2001. Mem. ABA, NRA, Kiwanis (treas. Harrisonville chpt. 1985-86, Harrisonville Disting. Svc. award 1985), Phi Alpha Delta. Republican. Presbyterian. Office: Mo Dept Revenue 16647 E 23rd St S Independence MO 64055-1922 E-mail: CurtisL752@excite.com

LASHLEY, LENORE CLARISSE, lawyer; b. N.Y.C., June 3, 1934; d. Leonard Livingston and Una Ophelia (Laurie) L.; children: Donna Bee-Gates, Michele Bee, Maria Bee. BA, CUNY, 1956; MSW, U. Calif., Berkeley, 1970, MPH, 1975; JD, U. Calif., San Francisco, 1981. Bar: Calif. 1981. Atty. W.O.M.A.N., Inc., San Francisco, 1982-84; pvt. practice San Francisco Law Office, 1984-87; dep. dist. atty. Monterey Dist. Atty., Salinas, Calif., 1987-89; trial atty. State Bar of Calif., L.A., 1989; dep. dist. atty. L.A. Dist. Atty., 1989; dep. city atty. Office of City Atty., L.A., 1989—. Chair, bd. dirs. St. Anthony's Dining Room, San Francisco, 1986-87; sec., bd. dirs. NAACP, Monterey, 1987-88; bd. dirs. Childrens Home Soc., Oakland, Calif., 1966-68. Recipient Cert. of Merit, Nat. Assn. Naval Officers, 1987. Mem. L.A. County Bar Assn. (del. to state bar 1992, 93). Roman Catholic. Avocations: running, reading, animal welfare, volunteer work with people with AIDS. Office: City Atty LA 200 N Main St Ste 1700 Los Angeles CA 90012-4110 E-mail: llashle@atty.lacity.org

LASHMAN, SHELLEY BORTIN, retired judge; b. Camden, N.J., Aug. 18, 1917; s. William Mitchell and Anna (Bortin) L.; m. Ruth Horn, Jan. 3, 1959; children: Karen E. Lashman Hall, Gail A. McBride, Mitchell A., Christopher R. BS, William and Mary Coll., 1938; postgrad., Columbia U., 1938, 39; JD, U. Mich., 1946. Bar: N.Y. 1947, N.J. 1968. Judge N.J. Workers Compensation, 1981-2001. With USNR, 1940-70. Mem. Atlantic County Bar Assn., Am. Judges Assn., Atlantic County Hist. Soc., Am. Judicature Soc., Ret. Officers Assn., U.S. Navy League, Fleet Res. Assn., USS Yorktown CV-5 Club, Mil. Order World Wars. Republican. Home: 1209 Old Zion Rd Egg Harbor Township NJ 08234-7667 Home Fax: 609-653-6686

LASKER, MORRIS E. judge; b. Hartsdale, N.Y., July 17, 1917; m. Helen M. Schubach; 4 children. BA magna cum laude, Harvard U., 1938; LLB, JD, Yale U., 1941. Bar: N.Y. 1941. Atty. Nat. Def. Com., U.S. Senate, 1941-42, Battle, Fowler, Jaffin & Kheel, 1946-68; fed. judge U.S. Dist. Ct. (so. dist.) N.Y., 1968-94, U.S. Dist. Ct., Boston, 1994—. Contbr. articles to profl. jours. Hon. trustee, bd. dirs. Vera Inst. Justice. Maj. U.S. Army, 1942-46. Recipient Learned Hand medal Fed. Bar Coun., Edward Weinfeld award N.Y. County Lawyers Assn. Mem. ABA, Assn. of Bar of City of N.Y. (exec. com. 1985-89). Avocations: gardening, reading, history, English and American literature. Office: US Dist Ct US Courthouse 1 Courthouse Way Boston MA 02210-3002

LASKY, DAVID, lawyer, corporate executive; b. N.Y.C., Nov. 12, 1932; s. Benjamin and Rebecca (Malumed) L.; m. Phyllis Beryl Sumper, Apr. 14, 1957; children— Jennifer Lee, Robert Barry. BA, Bklyn. Coll., 1954; LLB, Columbia U., 1957. Bar: N.Y. 1957. Atty. N.Y.C. R.R. Co., 1957-62; with Curtiss-Wright Corp., N.Y.C., 1962—, corp. counsel, 1966-67, gen. counsel, 1967-93, v.p., 1972-80, sr. v.p., 1980-93, sec., 1989-93, pres., 1993-99, chmn., 1995-2000, bd. dirs., 1993—. Bd. dirs. Primex Technologies, Inc. Chmn. zoning bd. appeals, Ramapo, N.Y., 1968-72; dir., v.p. Oak Trail Homeowners Assn., 1987-90. Mem. ABA (chmn. com. corp. gen. counsel 1992-93), Phi Beta Kappa. Contracts commercial, General corporate, Securities. Office: Curtiss-Wright Corp 1200 Wall St W Ste 501 Lyndhurst NJ 07071

LA SORSA, WILLIAM GEORGE, lawyer, educator; b. Lancaster, Pa, Apr. 30, 1945; s. Francis Peter and Madge Marian (Hanson) L.; m. Linda Kay Chappell, Dec. 8, 1973. BA, Marquette U., 1967; JD, U. Tulsa, 1973. Bar: Okla. 1974, U.S. Dist. Ct. (no. dist.) Okla. 1976, U.S. Ct. Appeals (10th cir.) 1976, U.S. Supreme Ct. 1977, U.S. Ct. Mil. Appeals 1985. Asst. dist. atty. Tulsa County Dist. Atty.'s Office, Tulsa, 1974-80; assoc. Howard & Rapp, 1980-81, Gene C. Howard & Assocs., Tulsa, 1981-82; ptnr. Howard, La Sorsa & Widdows, 1982-85, La Sorsa & Weber, Tulsa, 1985-87, La Sorsa, Weber & Miles, P.C., Tulsa, 1987-93; shareholder Corbitt, La Sorsa, Rineer & Zacharias, P.C., 1993-96, Jones, Givens, Gotcher & Bogan, P.C., Tulsa, 1996—; spl. prosecutor Tulsa County Dist. Atty.'s Office, 1996-97. Adj. prof. Tulsa Jr. Coll., 1978-83, Langston U., 1983-84. Capt. U.S. Army, 1969-72, Vietnam; lt. col. USAR, ret. Fellow Am. Bar Found., Okla. Bar Found. (trustee), Tulsa County Bar Found. (charter), ABA (family law sect.); mem. Okla. Bar Assn. (bd. govs. 1994-96, family law sect., exec. com.), ATLA, Okla. Trial Lawyers Assn., Tulsa County Bar Assn., Am. Inns. of Ct. (master emeritus, Hudson-Hall-Wheaton chpt.), Lions Club Internat. (pres. Brookside chpt. 1986-87), Porsche Club Am. (pres. War Bonnet region 1981-82). Republican. Roman Catholic. General civil litigation, Criminal, Family and matrimonial. Office: Jones Givens Gotcher & Bogan PC 15 E 5th St Ste 3800 Tulsa OK 74103-4309 E-mail: blasorsa@jonesgivens.com

LASSAR, SCOTT R. prosecutor; b. Evanston, Ill., Apr. 5, 1950; s. Richard Ernest and Jo (Ladenson) L.; m. Elizabeth Levine, May 22, 1977; children: Margaret, Kate. B.A., Oberlin Coll., 1972; J.D., Northwestern U., 1975. Bar: Ill. 1975. Former dep. chief spl. prosecutions divsn. no. dist. Office U.S. Atty., Chgo.; former ptnr. Keck, Mahin & Cate, Chgo.; now U.S. atty. North Dist. Dept. Justice, Chgo. Office U.S. Atty., Chgo. Office: US Attys Office 219 S Dearborn St Ste 1500 Chicago IL 60604-1700*

LASSEN, STEEN ANKER, lawyer; b. Copenhagen, Oct. 30, 1944; s. Anker and Bente L.; m. Gabriele Salmuth, Sept. 13, 1980; children: Jannek, Luise. JD, U. Copenhagen, 1971; LLM, Harvard U., 1977. Assoc. Sullivan & Cromwell, N.Y., 1977-78; ptnr. Lassen & Ricard, Copenhagen, 1978—. Mem. Danish Bar Assn. (mem. spl. com. intellectual proptery and competition law). Communications, General corporate, Intellectual property. Home: Gyvelvej 6 2942 Skodsborg Denmark Office: Lassen & Ricard Nybrogade 12 1203 Copenhagen K Denmark Fax: 33 32 24 74. E-mail: irlaw@irlaw.dk

LASSON, KENNETH, law educator, author, lawyer; b. Balt., Mar. 24, 1943; s. Nelson Bernard Lasson and Nanette Vera (Macht) Kapustin; m. Barbara Sue Goldstein, Mar. 4, 1974; children: Tamar, Noah, Jeremy. BA, Johns Hopkins U., 1963, MA, 1967; JD, U. Md., 1966. Bar: Md., U.S. Ct. Appeals (4th cir.), U.S. Supreme Ct. Rsch. asst. Constl. Conv. Commn. Md., 1966; teaching fellow, lectr. Johns Hopkins U., 1966-68; asst. to dean Sch. Law, U. Md., 1967-69; asst. to pres. Goucher Coll., 1970-71, lectr. English, 1970-72; asst. prof. polit. sci. and communication arts Loyola Coll., Balt., 1972-78; now prof. law Sch. of Law, U. Balt., vis. scholar Cambridge U., 1985; exec. sec. Md. Sch. Law Revision Commn., 1966-67; editorial and adminstrv. cons. Ralph Nader's Ctr. for Study of Responsive Law, 1969-72; guest scholar Brookings Instn., 1975-77; lectr. U. Md. Sch. Law; vis. faculty Cambridge U., 1985. Md. State Tchrs. scholar, 1960-67; Gilman fellow, 1967; recipient 1981 Bicentennial award Govt. of Sweden, 1982. Author: The Workers/Portraits of Nine American Jobholders, 1971; Proudly We Hail/Profiles of Public Citizens in Action, 1975; Private Lives of Public Servants, 1978; Your Rights and The Draft, 1980; Your Rights as A Vet, 1981; (with William S. Cohen) Getting the Most Out of Washington, 1982; Representing Yourself: What You Can Do Without A Lawyer, 1995, Mousetraps and Muffling Cups, 1986, (with Sheldon Margulies) Learning Law: The Mastery of Legal Logic, Trembling in teh Ivory Tower: Excesses in the Pursuit of Truth and Tenure, 2001; contbr. numerous articles to various publs.; dir. VB/Aberdeen (Scotland) summer program, 1994. Office: U Balt Sch of Law Maryland At Mt Royal Baltimore MD 21201

LASTER, GAIL W. lawyer; BA, Yale U.; JD, NYU. Law clk. to Judge Mary Johnson Lowe U.S. Dist. Ct. (so. dist.) N.Y., 1983-85; staff atty. Pub. Defender Svc. D.C., 1985-90; counsel com. labor and human resources, subcom. labor U.S. Senate, 1990-92; counsel subcom. antitrust, monopolies and bus. rights U.S. Senate on Judiciary, 1992-94; dir. govtl. rels., counsel Legal Svcs. Corp., 1994—; gen. counsel U.S. Dept. Housing and Urban Devel., Washington, 1997—. Office: Dept Housing and Urban Devel 451 7th St SW Washington DC 20410-0002

LASTRA, CARLOS MARIANO, lawyer; b. N.Y.C., Aug. 29, 1967; s. Carlos Gerardo andMercedes (Caridad) L.; m. Sheri Lynn Turnbow, Apr. 5, 1997. BA, U. Miami, 1989, JD, 1992. Bar: Fla. 1992, D.C. 1994, U.S. Ct. Appeals (fed. cir.) 1994, U.S. Ct. Appeals (11th cir.) 1993, U.S. Dist. Ct. (so. dist.) Fla. 1993, U.S. Dist. Ct. (mid. dist.) Fla. 1993. Law clk. Dade Ct. Ct. Judge Leonard M. Rivkind, Miami, 1990; intern Law Offices of Janet Reno, 1991; assoc. atty. Law Offices of Richard H. Ferro, 1992-93; of counsel Ferro & Dickey, 1995-2000; sole practice law, 1993-2000; spl. asst. pub. defender Dade County Pub. Defender's Office, 1996-2000; of counsel James R.C. Dickey, 1997-2000, Brodsy, Greenblatt & Renehan, Chtd., 2000. Mem. ABA, ATLA. Home: 345 Market St W Apt 314 Gaithersburg MD 20878-6446 E-mail: cml@divorce-md.com

LATCHUM, JAMES LEVIN, federal judge; b. Milford, Del., Dec. 23, 1918; s. James H. and Ida Mae (Robbins) L.; m. Elizabeth Murray McArthur, June 16, 1943; children: Su-Allan, Elizabeth M. A.B. cum laude, Princeton U., 1940; J.D., U. Va., 1946. Bar: Va. 1942, Del. 1947. Assoc. Berl, Potter & Anderson, Wilmington, 1946-53, partner, 1953-68; judge U.S. Dist. Ct. Del., Wilmington, 1968-73, chief judge, 1973-83, sr. judge, 1983—. New Castle County atty. Del. Hwy. Dept., 1948-50; asst. U.S. atty., 1950-53; atty. Del. Interstate Hwy. Div., 1955-62, Delaware River and Bay Authority, 1962-68 Chmn. New Castle County Democratic Com., 1953-56, Wilmington City Com., 1959-63. Served to maj. Insp. Gen. Corps AUS, 1942-46, PTO. Mem. ABA, Del. Bar Assn., Va. Bar Assn., Order of Coif, Sigma Nu Phi. Presbyterian. Clubs: Wilmington, Univ. Office: US Dist Ct 844 N King St # 34 Wilmington DE 19801-3519

LATHAM, WELDON HURD, lawyer; b. Bklyn., Jan. 2, 1947; s. Aubrey Geddes and Avril (Hurd) L.; m. Constantia Beecher, Aug. 8, 1948; children: Nicole Marie, Brett Weldon. BA, Howard U., 1968; JD, Georgetown U., 1971; postgrad., George Washington U., 1975-76. Bar: D.C. 1972, U.S. Ct. Appeals (D.C. cir.) 1972, U.S. Ct. Mil. Appeals 1974, U.S. Ct. Claims 1975, U.S. Supreme Ct. 1975, Va. 1981, U.S. Ct. Appeals (fed. cir.) 1988. Mgmt. cons. Checchi & Co., Washington, 1968-71; atty. Covington & Burling, 1971-73; sr. atty. Fed. Energy Adminstrn., 1974; asst. gen. counsel Exec. Office Pres. Office Mgmt. and Budget The White House, 1974-76; atty. Hogan & Hartson, 1976-79; gen. dep. asst. sec. HUD, 1979-81; v.p., gen. counsel Sterling Sys., Inc. (subs. PRC.); exec. asst., counsel to chmn., CEO and assoc. gen. counsel Planning Rsch. Corp., McLean, Va., 1981-86; mng. ptnr. Reed, Smith, Shaw & McClay, 1986-91; sr. ptnr., practice area leader corp. diverse counseling Shaw Pitman, Washington, 1992-2000; sr. ptnr. Holland & Knight, 2000—. Adj. prof. Howard U. Law Sch., Washington, 1972-82; guest prof. U. Va., Charlottesville, 1976-90; mem. Va. Govs. Bus. and Industry Adv. Com. on Crime Prevention, 1983-85, Va. Govs. Regulatory Reform Adv. Bd., 1982-84; chmn. task force SBA, 1982; legal counsel Md. Mondale for Pres. Campaign, 1984; mem. editorial adv. bd. Washington Bus. Jour., 1985-87; gen. counsel Nat. Coalition Minority Bus., 1993—; bd. trustees The Am. Univ., 1999; bd. dirs. Telecomms. Sys., Inc. Columnist Minority Bus. Entrepreneur Mag., 1991—; mem. editl. bd. Washington Bus. Jour., 1985-87. Washington steering com. NAACP Legal Def. Fund, 1975-95, Fairfax County Airports Adv. Com., 1987-88; bd. dirs., gen. counsel Northern Va. Minority Bus. and Profl. Assn., 1985-92; trustee Va. Commonwealth U., Richmond, 1986-90, George Mason U., Fairfax, Va., 1990-94; bd. dirs. Washington Urban League, 1986-90, U. D.C. Found., 1982-87, Washington Coun. Lawyers, 1973, Profl. Svcs. Coun., 1983-88, Minority Bus. Enterprise Legal Def. and Edn. Fund, 1989-91, Wash. Hosp. Ctr. Found., 1996-98; appointee Greater Washington Bd. Trade, Blue Ribbon Task Force on Home Rule, 1985-86, bd. dirs., exec. com., chmn. regional affairs com., corp. sec. Greater Wash. Bd. Trade, 1990-95; adv. bd. First Union Nat. Bank, 1995-99; civilian aide to Sec. of Army, 1995-2000; mem. Small Bus. Adminstrn. Nat. Adv. Coun., 1993—, Burger King Corp. Diversity Action Coun., 1996-98, Md. Econ. Devel. Commn., 1996-98, Gov. Bd. Transition Team, 1995, Dem. Nat. Com., 1996, Platform Drafting Com., 1996; prin. coun. for Excellence in Govt., 1989-95; mayor D.C. Internat. Ins. Adv. Commn., 1994-95; chmn. D.C. Mayors Bus. Adv. Coun., 1994-96; vice-chmn. Dem. Bus. Coun. DNC, 1994-98; co-chmn. UNCF Sportsfest Fundraiser, 1994; hon. vice-chmn. Clinton-Gore Campaign, 1996, Metro. Washington Airports Authority, 1997—; bd. govs. Joint Ctr. Polit. and Econ. Studies, 1998—; corp. adv. coun. Congrl. Black Caucus Found., 1999—; gen. counsels Honors Program Office Sec. Capt. USAF, 1973-74. Recipient SES Effective Mgr. award HUD, 1980, Nat. Assn. for Equal Achievement Opportunity in Higher Edn. award, 1987. Mem. ABA (vice-chmn. subcom. pub. contract law sect. 1988-93), Fed. Bar Assn., Nat. Bar Assn., D.C. C. of C. (gen. counsel 1979), State Va. Bar Assn., Washington Bar Assn.(elected to Hall of Fame, 2001), Bar Assn. D.C., Nat. Contract Mgmt. Assn., Econ. Club Washington. Administrative and regulatory, General corporate, Government contracts and claims. Home: 7004 Natelli Woods Ln Bethesda MD 20817-3924 Office: Holland & Knight LLP 2099 Pennsylvania Ave NW Washington DC 20006-1813

LATHROP, MITCHELL LEE, lawyer; b. L.A., Dec. 15, 1937; s. Alfred Lee and Barbara (Mitchell) L.; m. Lynn Mara Dalton; children: Christin Lorraine Newlon, Alexander Mitchell, Timothy Trewin Mitchell. BSc, U.S. Naval Acad., 1959; JD, U. So. Calif., 1966. Bar: D.C. 1966, Calif. 1966, U.S. Supreme Ct. 1969, N.Y. 1981; cert. arbitrator Nat. Arbitration Forum, ARIAS-US; cert. civil trial specialist Nat. Bd. Trial Advocacy. Dep. counsel L.A. County, Calif., 1966-68; with Brill, Hunt, DeBuys and Burby, L.A., 1968-71; ptnr. Macdonald, Halsted & Laybourne, L.A. and San Diego, 1971-80; sr. ptnr. Rogers & Wells, N.Y.C., San Diego, 1980-86; sr. ptnr., exec. com. Adams, Duque & Hazeltine, L.A., San Francisco, N.Y.C., San Diego, 1986-94, firm chmn., 1992-94; sr. ptnr. Luce, Forward, Hamilton & Scripps, San Diego, N.Y.C., San Francisco, L.A., 1994—. Presiding referee Calif. Bar Ct., 1984-86, mem. exec. com., 1981-88; lectr. law Calif. Judges Assn., Practicing Law Inst. N.Y., Continuing Edn. of Bar, State Bar Calif., ABA, others. Author: State Hazardous Waste Regulation, 1991, Environmental Insurance Coverage, 1991, Insurance Coverage for Environmental Claims, 1992; mem. editl. bd. Def. Counsel Jour., 1997—; editl. bd., Jous. Ins. Coverage. Western Regional chmn. Met. Opera Nat. Coun., 1971-81, v.p., mem. exec. com., 1971—, now chmn.; trustee Honnold Libr. at Claremont Colls., 1972-80; bd. dirs. Music Ctr. Opera Assn., L.A., sec., 1974-80; bd. dirs. San Diego Opera Assn., 1980—, v.p., 1985-89, pres.-elect, 1993, pres., 1994-96; bd. dirs. Met. Opera Assn., N.Y.C.; mem. nat. steering coun. Nat. Actors Theatre, N.Y. Mem. ABA, N.Y. Bar Assn., Fed. Bar Assn., Fed. Bar Council, Calif. Bar Assn., D.C. Bar Assn., San Diego County Bar Assn. (chmn. ethics com. 1980-82, bd. dirs. 1982-85, v.p. 1985), Assn. Bus. Trial Lawyers, Am. Intellectual Property Law Assn., Assn. So. Calif. Def. Counsel, Los Angeles Opera Assos. (pres. 1970-72), Soc. Colonial Wars in Calif. (gov. 1970-72), Order St. Lazarus of Jerusalem, Friends of Claremont Coll. (dir. 1975-81, pres. 1978-79), Am. Bd. Trial Advocates, Judge Advocates Assn. (dir. Los Angeles chpt. 1974-80, pres. So. Calif. chpt. 1977-78), Internat. Assn. Def. Counsel, Brit. United Services Club (dir. Los Angeles 1973-75), Mensa Internat., Calif. Soc., S.R. (pres. 1977-79), Calif. Club (Los Angeles), Valley Hunt Club (Pasadena, Calif.), Met. Club (N.Y.C.), The Naval Club (London), Phi Delta Phi. Republican. General civil litigation, Insurance, Intellectual property. Home: 3355 Valemont St San Diego CA 92106-2430 Office: Luce Forward Hamilton and Scripps 600 W Broadway Fl 26 San Diego CA 92101-3311 also: Citicorp Ctr 153 E 53rd St 26th Fl New York NY 10022-4611 E-mail: mlathrop@luce.com

LATIMER, JOHN THOMAS, law educator; b. Hamilton, Ohio, May 25, 1922; s. Homer H. and Mayme (Hazeltine) L.; m. Eleanor Grace Millikin, Oct. 18, 1948; children: Carolyn E., Bruce M., John H. BS, U. Pa., 1944; JD, U. Cin., 1947. Bar: Ohio 1947. Assoc. Millikin & Fitton, Hamilton, Ohio, 1947-52, ptnr., 1952-73; lectr. law, Miami U., Oxford, Ohio, 1970-73, prof. dept. fin., sch. bus., 1973—, prof. emeritus, 1989—. Mem. Am. Bus. Law Assn. Democrat. Unitarian. Avocation: history. Home: Apt A212 3801 Woodbridge Blvd Fairfield OH 45014-6617 Office: Miami U Sch Bus Dept Fin 3 Upham Hall Oxford OH 45056

LATIMER, STEPHEN MARK, lawyer; b. Bklyn., July 15, 1939; s. Ted and Martha (Goldberg) L.; m. Judith R. Shulman, June 3, 1964 (dec. Mar. 29, 1984); 1 child, Gary. BA, Tufts U., 1961; JD, NYU, 1968. Bar: N.Y. 1968, N.J. 1979, U.S. Dist. Ct. (so. dist.) N.Y. 1970, U.S. Dist. Ct. (ea. dist.) N.Y. 1972, U.S. Dist. Ct. N.J. 1979, U.S. Dist. Ct. (we. dist.) N.Y. 1984, U.S. Dist. Ct. (no. dist.) Tex. 1992, U.S. Ct. Appeals (2d cir.) 1974, U.S. Ct. Appeals (3rd cir.) 1981, U.S. Ct. Appeals (5th cir.) 1986, U.S. Supreme Ct. 1975. Clk. Burke & Parsons, N.Y.C., 1966-67; mng. clk. Otterbourg, Steindler, Houston & Rosen, 1967-68, assoc., 1968-69, Halpern, Schivitz, Scholer and Steingut, N.Y.C., 1969-71; dir. supervised pre-trial release project N.Y. Lawyers Com. for Civil Rights Under Law, 1972-73; dir. cmty. devel. and law reform Bronx Legal Svcs., 1973-79, acting mng. atty., 1974; dir. litigation Camden (N.J.) Regional Legal Svcs., Inc., 1979-81, acting dir., 1981-82; statewide litigation coord. Legal Svcs. of N.J., New Brunswick, 1982-84; sr. litigation atty. Prisoners' Legal Svcs. of N.Y., N.Y.C., 1984-94; asst. dep. pub. defender N.J. Pub. Defender, Newark, 1994-95; ptnr. Loughlin & Latimer, Hackensack, N.J., 1995—. Lectr. Rutgers U. Law Sch., 1975-90. Contbr. articles to profl. jours. Trustee ACLU of N.J., 1982-2001, exec. com. 1984-99, N.J. Assn. Correction, 1986—, Planned Parenthood of Middlesex County, 1981-85. Lt. USN, 1961-66, USNR, 1966-68. Instr. U.S. Marine Acad., Kings Point, N.Y., 1964-66. Mem. N.J. Bar Assn. (vice chmn. individual rights 1998-99, chmn. individual rights, 1999-2001). Civil rights, Criminal. Home: 120 Floyd Ave Bloomfield NJ 07003-5610 Office: Loughlin & Latimer 131 Main St Hackensack NJ 07601-7140 E-mail: slatimer@mindspring.com

LATOVICK, PAULA R(AE), lawyer, educator; b. Detroit, Feb. 17, 1954; d. Raymond and Marjorie Camille (Peters) L.; m. William P. Weiner, Aug. 17, 1985; children: Jeffrey Devon, Robert Stirling. BA in Personnel with high honor, Mich. State U., 1976; JD cum laude, U. Mich., 1980, LLM, 1999. Bar: Mich. 1980, U.S. Dist. Ct. (ea. dist.) Mich. 1980, U.S. Dist. Ct. (we. dist.) Mich. 1981, U.S. Ct. Appeals (6th cir.) 1985. Assoc. Fraser, Trebilcock, Davis & Foster P.C., Lansing, Mich., 1980-86, ptnr., 1986-92, chmn. hiring com., 1987-92, chmn. govt. law dept., 1988-90; assoc. prof. Thomas M. Cooley Law Sch., 1992-97, prof., 1998—, chair property law dept., 2000—. Adj. prof. Thomas M. Cooley Law Sch., Lansing, 1984-86. Head advisor law explorers Boy Scouts Am., Lansing, 1982-84; mem. Capitol Area Women's Network, Lansing, 1984-95; v.p. YWCA, Lansing, 1988, pres., 1989-91, chmn. bldg. com., 1989-91; rec. sec. Friends of Kresge Art Mus., 1992-93, corr. sec., 1993-94, 1st v.p., 1994-95, pres., 1995-96; treas. Cub Scouts Pack 107, Boy Scouts Am., 1998—; co-chair Friends Gtr. Lansing Symphony, 2000-2001; pres. William Donley Elem. Sch. Parent Coun., 2001—. Named One of Outstanding Young Women of Am., 1985. Fellow Mich. State Bar Found.; mem. NOW, Mich. Bar Assn. (mem. young lawyers exec. coun. 1984-86, mem. com. character and fitness dist. F 1991-2000, subcom. chairperson 1994-2000), Women Lawyers Assn. Mich., Ingham County Bar Assn. (chairperson hist. com. 1984-87, mem. young lawyers bd. 1981-84, pres. 1983, mem. com. on jud. qualifications 1990-93, bd. dirs. 1990-92), Thomas M. Cooley Legal Authors Soc., U. Mich. Alumni Assn. (life), Mich. State U. Alumni Assn., Zonta (rec. sec. local club 1985-86, chmn. membership com. 1988-89). Democrat. Roman Catholic. Office: Thomas M Cooley Law Sch 217 S Capitol Ave Lansing MI 48933-1503

LATTA, THOMAS ALBERT, lawyer; b. Tulsa, Nov. 3, 1931; s. Albert Lloyd and Myrtle Irene (Lay) L.; m. Shirley Elaine Glauser, June 20, 1965 (div. 1985); children: Thomas Albert, John Montgomery, Shannon Elaine. Student, Carnegie Mellon U., 1949-52; BA, U. Tex., 1955; JD, U. Tulsa, 1959. Bar: Okla. 1959, Ariz. 1964, D.C. 1965, Calif. 1974. Pvt. practice, San Francisco, 1974, Phoenix, 1975; dir., shareholder Wentworth & Lundin, P.A., 1975-86, San Francisco, 1980-84; of counsel Whitehead, Porter & Gordon LLP, 1997—. Mem. Ariz. Bd. Accountancy, Phoenix, 1979-83. Capt. JAGC, USAR, 1959-60. Avocation: sailing. General corporate, Finance, Securities. Office: Whitehead Porter & Gordon LLP 220 Montgomery St Ste 1850 San Francisco CA 94104-3419 E-mail: tal@wpglaw.com

LAU, EUGENE WING IU, lawyer; b. Canton, China, Sept. 23, 1931; came to U.S., 1939; s. Eugene K. F. and Ann (Leung) L.; m. Dierdre Florence, July 20, 1962; children: Elyse M., Jennifer M. AB, U. Mich., 1953; LLB, Yale U., 1960. Bar: Hawaii 1960, U.S. Supreme Ct. 1965. Dep. Pros. Attys. Office, Honolulu, 1960-63; pvt. practice, 1963-67, 73—; v.p. Hawaii Corp., 1967-73. Del. People to People Legal Del. to China, 1987; mem. Commn. on Manpower and Full Employment, Honolulu, 1965-67. With U.S. Army, 1954-55. Mem. ABA, Hawaii Bar Assn., Punahou Tennis Club (Honolulu). Real property, General civil litigation. Home: 3079 La Pietra Cir Honolulu HI 96815-4736 Office: 1188 Bishop St Ste 1912 Honolulu HI 96813-3308 E-mail: EL923@aol.com

LAUCHENGCO, JOSE YUJUICO, JR. lawyer; b. Manila, Philippines, Dec. 6, 1936; came to U.S., 1962; s. José Celis Sr. Lauchengco and Angeles (Yujuico) Sapota; m. Elisabeth Schindler, Feb. 22, 1968; children: Birthe, Martina, Duane, Lance. AB, U. Philippines, Quezon City, 1959; MBA, U. So. Calif., 1964; JD, Loyola U., L.A., 1971. Bar: Calif. 1972, U.S. Dist. Ct. (cen. dist.) Calif. 1972, U.S. Ct. Appeals (9th cir.) 1972, U.S. Supreme Ct. 1975. Banker First Western Bank/United Calif. Bank, L.A., 1964-71; assoc. Demler, Perona, Langer & Bergkvist, Long Beach, Calif., 1972-73; ptnr. Demler, Perona, Langer, Bergkvist, Lauchengco & Manzella, 1973-77; sole practice Long Beach and L.A., 1977-83; ptnr. Lauchengco & Mendoza, L.A., 1983-92; pvt. practice, 1993—. Mem. commn. on jud. procedures County of L.A., 1979; tchr. Confraternity of Christian Doctrine, 1972-79; counsel Philippine Presdl. Commn. on Good Govt., L.A., 1986. Chmn. Filipino-Am. Bi-Partisan Polit. Action Group, L.A., 1978. Recipient Degree of Distinction, Nat. Forensic League, 1955. Mem. Criminal Cts. Bar Assn., Calif. Attys. Criminal Justice, Calif. Pub. Defenders Assn., Philippine-Am. Bar Assn., U. Philippines Vanguard Assn. (life), Beta Sigma. Roman Catholic. Lodge: K.C. Avocations: classical music, opera, romantic paintings and sculpture, camping, shooting. Federal civil litigation, Criminal, Personal injury. Office: 3545 Wilshire Blvd Ste 247 Los Angeles CA 90010-2388

LAUDERDALE, KATHERINE SUE, lawyer; b. Wright-Patterson AFB, Ohio, May 30, 1954; d. Azo and Helen Ceola (Davis) L. BS in Polit. Sci., Ohio State U., 1975; JD, NYU, 1978. Bar: Ill. 1978, U.S. Dist. Ct. (no. dist.) Ill. 1978, Calif. 1987. Assoc. Schiff, Hardin & Waite, Chgo., 1978-82; dir. bus. and legal affairs Sta. WTTW-TV, 1982-83, gen. counsel, 1983—, also v.p., sr. v.p., gen. counsel legal and bus. affairs, 1993—, acting sr. v.p. Prodn. Ctr., 1994, sr. v.p. new ventures, 1995-99, sr. v.p. network Chgo. implementation, 1999—, sr. v.p. strategic partnerships and gen. counsel, 2000—. Mem. Lawyers Com. for Harold Washington, Chgo. 1983; bd. dirs. Midwest Women's Ctr., Chgo., 1985-94; active Chgo. Coun. Fgn. Rels., 1981—, mem. fgn. affairs com., 1985—; mem. adv. bd. Malcolm X Coll. Sch. Bus., 1996-99. Mem. ABA, Chgo. Bar Assn. (bd. dirs. TV Prodns., Inc. 1986—), Lawyers for Creative Arts (bd. dir. 1984—, v.p. 1998—), ACLU (bd. dirs. 1987-94), Nat. Acad. TV Arts and Scis., NYU Law Alumni Assn. Midwest (mem. exec. bd. 1982—), The Ohio State U. Pres.'s Nat. Adv. Coun. on Pub. Affairs (Chgo. com., 1994—), The U. Chicago Women's Bd., 1996—. Democrat. General corporate, Entertainment. Office: Sta WTTW-TV 5400 N Saint Louis Ave Chicago IL 60625-4680

LAUDERDALE, PAT L. law educator, social scientist; b. Cache, Okla., Oct. 19, 1948; s. T.E. and Almeta (Cantrell) L. M.S. in Psychology, U. Tex., 1969; postgrad. (Woodrow Wilson fellow) Princeton U., 1968; Ph.D. in Sociology, Social Psychology, Stanford U., 1975. Vice-pres. Corad Inc., El Paso, Tex., 1967-69; vis. asst. prof. U. Calif.-Santa Cruz, 1973-74; assoc. prof. U. Minn., Mpls., 1974-80; prof. justice studies, adj. prof. law Ariz. State U., Tempe, 1980— ; rsch. dir. Ctr. for Study of Justice; vis. prof. sociology and law Stanford U., 1987-88, vis. scholar-in-residence sociology, 1994-95; dir. PhD and JD program in Justice, Law and the social sciences, Ariz. State U., 1995-97; rsch. cons. Nat. Inst. Justice. Alumni ambassador Stanford U., 1977-79; mem. Cuban Cultural Ctr., 1979. Recipient Disting. Teaching award U. Minn., 1979; Research and Travel award Cuba, Office of Internat. Programs, 1980; Fulbright Rsch. fellow., Costa Rica, 1984, Fulbright Teaching and Rsch. award, Austria, 1992. Mem. Assn. Am. Indians, Phi Beta Kappa, Omicron Delta Kappa. Author: A Political Analysis of Deviance, 1980; (with James Inverarity) Law and Society, 1983; co-editor: New Directions in the Study of Law, Conflict, and Social Control, 1989, The Struggle for Control, 1993, Law and Society Japanese translation, 1995, Lives in the Balance: A Comparative Perspective on Inequality and Injustice, 1997.

LAUER, ELIOT, lawyer; b. N.Y.C., Aug. 17, 1949; s. George and Doris (Trenk) L.; m. Marilyn Steinberg, June 5, 1977; children: Tamar Rachel, Ilana Jennifer, Michael Jonathan, Samuel Geoffrey. BA, Yeshiva U., 1971; JD cum laude, Fordham U., 1974. Bar: D.C. 1975, N.Y. 1975, U.S. Dist. Ct. (so. and ea. dists.) N.Y. 1975, U.S. Ct. Appeals (2d cir.) 1975, U.S. Supreme Ct. 1984. Assoc. Curtis, Mallet-Prevost, Colt & Mosle, N.Y.C., 1974-82, ptnr., 1982—. Counsel Keren-Or Inc., N.Y.C., 1985—; bd. dirs. Hebrew Acad. Long Beach, N.Y., 1985—, Young Israel Lawrence, Cedarhurst, N.Y., 1984—. Mem.: ABA, Assn. of Bar of City of N.Y., Nat. Futures Assn. (arbitrator 1983—), Fed. Bar Coun. Republican. Federal civil litigation, Criminal. Office: Curtis Mallet-Prevost Colt & Mosle 101 Park Ave Fl 34 New York NY 10178-0061 E-mail: elauer@cm-p.com

LAUFER, JACOB, lawyer; b. Munich, Feb. 28, 1949; came to the U.S., 1951; s. Moritz and Felicja (Pruszanowska) L.; m. Clara G. Schwabe, Jan. 27, 1983; children: Samara, Aviva, Mia. BS, CUNY, 1971; JD cum laude, Fordham U., 1974. Bar: N.Y. 1975, D.C. 1975, U.S. Ct. Appeals (2d cir.) 1975, U.S. Dist. Ct. (so. and ea. dists.) N.Y. 1976, U.S. Ct. Appeals (5th cir.) 1979, U.S. Supreme Ct. 1980, U.S. Ct. Appeals (3d cir.) 1985, U.S. Ct. Appeals (D.C. cir.) 1994. Spl. atty. Organized Crime and Racketeering Sect., U.S. Dept. Justice, 1974-77; asst. U.S. atty. So. Dist. N.Y., N.Y.C., 1977-79; of counsel Bartels, Pykett & Aronwald, White Plains, N.Y., 1979-81; ptnr. Bornstein & Laufer, N.Y.C., 1981-85, Laufer & Karish LLP, N.Y.C., 1986—. Mem., contbr. Fordham Law Rev., 1973-74. Mem. D.C. Bar Assn., Bklyn. Bar Assn., Assn. Bar City of N.Y (com. criminal advocacy 1998—). Democrat. Jewish. Notable cases include: Pavelic & LeFlore vs. Marvel Entertainment Group; and Allen vs. National Video, Inc. Avocation: reading. General civil litigation, Criminal, Entertainment. Office: Laufer@Halberstam LLP 39 Broadway Rm 1440 New York NY 10006-3003 E-mail: jlaufer@lauferhalberstam.com

LAULICHT, MURRAY JACK, lawyer; b. Bklyn., May 12, 1940; s. Philip and Ernestine (Greenfield) L.; m. Linda Kushner, Apr. 4, 1965; children: Laurie Hasten, Pamela Hirt, Shellie Davis, Abigail Herschmann. BA, Yeshiva U., 1961; LLB summa cum laude, Columbia U., 1964. Bar: N.Y. 1965, N.J. 1968, U.S. Supreme Ct. 1976. Legal staff Warren Commn., Washington, 1964; law clk. Hon. Harold R. Medina U.S. Ct. Appeals, 1964-65; assoc. Kaye, Scholer, Fierman, Hays & Handler, N.Y.C., 1965-68; ptnr. Lowenstein, Sandler, Brochin, Kohl & Fisher, Newark, 1968-79, Pitney, Hardin, Kipp & Szuch, Florham Park, 1979—. Mem. N.J. Consumer Affairs Adv. Com., 1991-93; N.J. Commn. on Holocaust Edn., 1991—, chmn. 1992-95; pres. Jewish Edn. Assn., 1981-84, Jewish Fedn. Metro West, 1996-99; chmn. Cmty. Rels. Com., 1988-91, chmn. com. on religious pluralism, 1999—; exec. comm. Coun. of Jewish Fedn., 1996-99; trustee United Jewish Cmtys., 1999—. Recipient Julius Cohn Young Leadership award Jewish Fedn. Metrowest, 1976. Mem. ABA, N.J. State Bar Assn. (dist. X ethics com. 1986-89, bd. editors N.J. Law Jour. 1986-93), N.J. Lawyer Mag. (chmn. 1993-95). Democrat. Avocations: Jewish studies, communal activities. Antitrust, General civil litigation, Intellectual property. Home: 18 Crestwood Dr West Orange NJ 07052-2004 Office: Pitney Hardin Kipp & Szuch PO Box 1945 200 Campus Dr Ste 1 Florham Park NJ 07932-1007 E-mail: mlaulicht@phks.com

LAURIE, ROBIN GARRETT, lawyer; b. Mobile, Ala., June 10, 1956; s. George and Margaret Eloise (Garrett) L.; m. Deborah Dockery; children: Elizabeth Anne, Robin Garrett. AA, Marion (Ala.) Mil. Inst., 1976; BS in Bus., U. Ala., Tuscaloosa, 1978; JD, U.Ala., Tuscaloosa, 1988. Bar: Ala. 1988, U.S. Dist. Ct. (no., mid. and so. dists.) Ala. 1988, U.S. Ct. Appeals (11th cir.) 1988. Ptnr. Balch & Bingham LLP, Montgomery, Ala., 1988—. Lead articles editor Ala. Law Rev., 1986-88. Recipient Outstanding Svc. award Ala. Law Rev., 1988. Mem. ABA, Ala. State Bar, Montgomery County Bar Assn., Montgomery Rotary Club, Order of the Coif. Methodist. Avocations: flying small airplanes, fishing, hunting. Administrative and regulatory, General civil litigation, Public utilities. Office: Balch & Bingham LLP PO Box 78 Montgomery AL 36101-0078 E-mail: rlaurie@balch.com

LAUTENSCHLAGER, PEGGY ANN, prosecutor; b. Fond du Lac, Wis., Nov. 22, 1955; d. Milton A. and Patsy R. (Oleson) L.; m. Rajiv M. Kaul, Dec. 29, 1979 (div. Dec. 1986); children: Joshua Lautenschlager Kaul, Ryan Lautenschlager Kaul; m. William P. Rippl, May 26, 1989; 1 child, Rebecca Lautenschlager Rippl. BA, Lake Forest Coll., 1977; JD, U. Wis., 1980. Bar: Wis., U.S. Dist. Ct. (we. dist.). Pvt. practice atty., Oshkosh, Wis., 1981-85; dist. atty. Winnebago County Wis., 1985-88; rep. Wis. Assembly, Fond du Lac, 1988-92; U.S. atty. U.S. Dept. of Justice, Madison, Wis., 1992—. Apptd. mem. Govs. Coun. on Domestic Violence, Madison, State Elections Bd., Madison; bd. dirs. Blandine House, Inc. Active Dem. Nat. Com., Washington, 1992-93; com. Wis., 1989-92. Named Legislator of Yr., Wis. Sch. Counselors, 1992, Legislator of Yr., Wis. Corrections Coalition, 1992. Mem. Wis. Bar Assn., Dane County Bar Assn., Western Dist. Bar Assn., Fond du lac County Bar Assn., Phi Beta Kappa. Avocations: gardening, house renovation, sports, cooking. Home: 1 Langdon St Apt 211 Madison WI 53703-1326

LAVECCHIA, JAYNEE, judge; b. Paterson, N.J. m. Michael R. Cole. Grad., Douglass Coll., 1976, Rutgers U., 1979. Bar: N.J. 1980. Pvt. law practice; dep. atty. gen. divsn. of law State of N.J., dir. divsn. of law dept. law anf pub. safety, 1984-98, commr. banking and ins., 1998-99; asst. counsel to Gov. Thomas H. Kean Office of Counsel, dep. chief counsel to Gov. Thomas H. Kean; dir., chief admisntrv. law judge Office of Adminstrv. Law, 1989-94; assoc. justice N.J. Supreme Ct., Trenton, 2000—. Chair various N.J. Supreme Ct. Coms. Fellow ABA; mem. Douglss Coll. Alumnae Assn. Office: North Tower 158 Headquarters Pla Morristown NJ 07960*

LAVELLE, BETTY SULLIVAN DOUGHERTY, legal professional; b. Omaha, Nov. 12, 1941; d. Marvin D. and Marie C. Sullivan; children from previous marriage: Clayton B. Dougherty, Lance A. Dougherty; m. James S. LaVelle, 1986; 1 child, Lindsay L. A of Pre-Law, U. Nebr., 1960; student, U. Colo., 1964-66; BA in Philosophy, Metro State Coll., 1979; cert. legal assistant, U. San Diego, 1979. Teaching asst. Metro State Coll., Denver, 1978; paralegal Holland and Hart, 1979-85; litigation paralegal Rothgerber, Appel, Powers and Johnson, 1985-88; pres., cons. Vivant, Inc., Boulder, 1987—; owner, adminstr. Homestead Group Home for Elderly, Longmont, 1987-92; ptnr. LaVelle & McMillan, Boulder, 1989-90; water law and litigation paralegal Moses, Wittemyer, Harrison and Woodruff, P.C., 1990-2001. Mediator domestic relations 20th Jud. Dist., Boulder, 1984-85. Contbr. articles to profl. jours. Vol. legal aid Thursday Night Bar, Denver Bar Assn., 1979-86, paralegal coordinator, panelist, speaker, 1983-85; sr. paralegal Boulder County Legal Svcs., 1988-89; mediator landlord/tenant project City of Boulder, 1983-87; coach, trainer Ctr. for Dispute Resolution, Denver and Boulder, 1984-86; vol. Shelter for Homeless, Boulder, 1988. Recipient cert. U. Denver Coll. Law, 1981, Hoagland award Colo. Bar Assn., 1984. Mem. Colo. Bar Assn., Soc. Profls. in Dispute Resolution, Rocky Mountain Paralegal Assn. (mem. adv. bd. 1980-81, bd. dirs. 1983-85, 94-96, rep. to Colo. Bar Assn. 1994-96, dir. pro bono svcs. 1984-85). Democrat. Avocations: vol. legal services for the indigent, computer applications. Home: 1660 Bradley Ct Boulder CO 80305-7300

LAVELLE, BRIAN FRANCIS DAVID, lawyer; b. Cleve., Aug. 16, 1941; s. Gerald John and Mary Josephine (O'Callaghan) L.; m. Sara Hill, Sept. 10, 1966; children: S. Elizabeth, B. Francis D. Jr., Catherine H. BA, U. Va., 1963; JD, Vanderbilt U., 1966; LLM in Taxation, NYU, 1969. Bar: N.C. 1966, Ohio 1968. Assoc. VanWinkle Buck, Wall, Starnes & Davis, Asheville, N.C., 1968-74, ptnr., 1974—. Lectr. continuing edn. N.C. Bar Found., Wake Forest U. Estate Planning Inst., Hartford Tax Inst., Duke U. Estate Planning Inst. Contbr. articles on law to profl. jours. Trustee Carolina Day Sch., 1981-92, sec., 1982-85; bd. dirs. The Salvation Army, 1986—; bd. dirs. Western N.C. Cmty. Found., 1986—, sec., 1987-90; bd. advs. U. N.C. Ann. Tax Inst., 1981—. Capt. JAG USAF, 1966-67. Mem. ABA, Am. Coll. Trust and Estate Counsel (state chmn. 1982-85, regent 1984-90, lectr. continuing edn.), N.C. Bar Assn. (bd. govs. 1979-82, councillor tax sect. 1979-83, councillor estate planning law sect. 1982-85, v.p. 1997—), N.C. State Bar (splty. exam. com. on estate planning and probate law 1984-90, chmn. 1990-91, cert. 1987), Rotary. Episcopalian. Clubs: Biltmore Forest Country, Asheville Downtown City. Estate planning, Probate, Taxation, general. Home: 45 Brookside Rd Asheville NC 28803-3015 Office: 11 N Market St PO Box 7376 Asheville NC 28802-8506 E-mail: blavelle@vwlawfirm.com

LAVELLE, JOSEPH P. lawyer; b. Scranton, Pa., Sept. 7, 1957; s. Patrick Leo and Anne M. (Antal) L.; m. Kathy A. Mlodzienski, Aug. 14, 1982; children: Remy, Joseph, Taylor. BS in Physics, Wilkes Coll., 1979; JD summa cum laude, U. Pitts., 1982. Bar: D.C. 1982, U.S. Ct. Appeals (Fed. cir.) 1982, U.S. Patent and Trademark Office 1982, U.S. Ct. Appeals (3d, 2d and 6th cir.). Assoc. Howrey & Simon, Washington, 1982-90, ptnr., 1991—. Adj. prof. Georgetown U. Law Ctr., 1995—. Editl. bd. ABA Antitrust Law Developments, III, 1992; contbr. articles to profl. jours.; mng. editor U. Pitts. Law Rev., 1981-82. Mem. ABA, AAAS, Am. Phys. Soc., Order of the Coif. Republican. Antitrust, Federal civil litigation, Patent. Office: Howrey Simon Arnold & White Ste 1 1299 Pennsylvania Ave Washington DC 20004-2420

LAVELLE, WILLIAM AMBROSE, lawyer, judge; b. Athens, Ohio, Jan. 18, 1925; s. Francis Anthony and Belle Elizabeth (Schloss) L.; m. Marion Helen Yanity, Aug. 7, 1954; children: Frank A., John P., Lydia E., Amy M. BBA, Ohio U., 1949; JD, Ohio State U., 1952. Bar: Ohio 1952, U.S. Dist. Ct. (so. dist.) Ohio 1952. Sr. ptnr. Lavelle Law Offices, Athens, Ohio, 1952-91; judge probate/juvenile divsn. Athens County Common Pleas Ct., 1991-94; assigned judge Supreme Ct. of Ohio, 1994; pvt. practice estate planning, trusts, probate, 1994—. Former solicitor City of Nelsonville, Villages of Albany, Chauncey, Coolville, Glouster, Trimble and Zaleski; counsel Margaret Creek Conservancy Dist., L-Ax Water Distbn. Co., Sunday Creek and Hollister Water Assns.; instr. wills, trusts, estate planning Ohio U., Athens, 1991—; mem. commn. on cert. as atty. specialists Supreme Ct. Ohio, 1994. Former chmn. Athens County and Ohio Dem. Party; former mem. Dem. Nat. Com.; chmn. Athens County Bd. Elections, 1967-80; chmn. pers. rev. bd. State of Ohio, 1983-91; trustee, chmn. trustees Ohio U., 1975-81; mem. parish fin. com., parish coun., sch. bd., diocesan bd. lay consultors St. Paul's Cath. Ch., Athens. Served with inf. U.S. Army, 1943-46, ETO, PTO. Mem. ABA, Ohio State Bar Assn. (bd. govs. 1989-92, probate and trust law sect. 1993—, coun. of dels. 1986-89), Athens County Bar Assn. (past pres.), Nat. Acad. Elder Law Attys., Ohio Horse Coun., Tenn. Walking Horse Breeders and Exhibitors Assn., Walking Horse Owners Assn., Athens Symposiarch Club (past pres., Symposiarch of Yr. 1996), Athens Cotillion Club, Athens Country Club, Athens Rotary Club, VFW, Am. Legion, Am. Vets, Sons of Union Vols., Ohio U. Green and White Club, KC (3d and 4th deg.), St. Francis Soc. Avocation: breeding, raising, riding and driving Tennessee Walking Horses. Probate. Home: 39 Cable Ln Athens OH 45701-1304 Office: PO Box 899 Athens OH 45701-0899 Fax: 740-797-1058. E-mail: walavelle@eurekanet.com

LAVENDER, ROBERT EUGENE, state supreme court justice; b. Muskogee, Okla., July 19, 1926; s. Harold James and Vergene Irene (Martin) L.; m. Maxine Knight, Dec. 22, 1945; children— Linda (Mrs. Dean Courter), Robert K., Debra (Mrs. Thomas Merrill), William J. LL.B., U. Tulsa, 1953; grad., Appellate Judges Seminar, 1967, Nat. Coll. State Trial Judges, 1970. Bar: Okla. bar 1953. With Mass. Bonding & Ins. Co., Tulsa, 1951-53, U.S. Fidelity & Guaranty Co., Tulsa, 1953-54; asst. city atty., 1954-55; practice, 1955-60, Claremore, Okla., 1960-65; justice Okla. Supreme Ct., 1965—, chief justice, 1979-80. Guest lectr. Okla. U., Oklahoma City U., Tulsa U. law schs. Republican committeeman, Rogers County, 1961-62. Served with USNR, 1944-46. Recipient Disting. Alumnus award U. Tulsa, 1993. Mem. ABA, Okla. Bar Assn., Rogers County Bar Assn., Am. Judicature Soc., Okla. Jud. Conf., Phi Alpha Delta (hon.) Methodist (adminstrv. bd.). Club: Mason (32 deg.). Home: 2910 Kerry Ln Oklahoma City OK 73120-2507 Office: US Supreme Ct Okla Rm 1 State Capitol Oklahoma City OK 73105

LAVES, ALAN LEONARD, lawyer; b. Austin, Tex., June 17, 1960; s. Benard and Cecile Laves; married 1987; 3 children. BSEE, MIT, 1982; JD with honors, U. Tex., 1985. Bar: Tex. 1985. Assoc. Akin, Gump, Strauss, Hauer & Feld, LLP, Dallas, 1985-94, ptnr., 1994—. Contbr. articles to profl. jours. Banking, Mergers and acquisitions, Securities. Office: Akin Gump Strauss Hauer & Feld Ste 1900 816 Congress Ave Austin TX 78701 Fax: 512-499-6290. E-mail: alaves@akingump.com

LAVES, BENJAMIN SAMUEL, lawyer; b. Bklyn., Aug. 2, 1946; BBA, Temple U., 1968; JD, Am. U., 1971. Bar: N.J. 1971, U.S. Dist. Ct. 1971. Intern Select Com. U.S. Senate, Washington, 1969; atty. Newark-Essex Joint Law Reform Project, N.J., 1971-74; dep. pub. advocate N.J. Dept. Mental Health, Newark, 1974-83, Rate Counsel Pub. Advocate, Newark, 1983-84; pvt. practice West Orange, N.J., 1984—, 1996—. Active Essex County Estate Planning Coun. Bd. dirs. N.J. Maclaw, 1987—. Mem. ABA (gen. practice, econs. law sects.), N.J. State Bar Assn. (real property, probate and trust law sect., taxation sect.), Essex County Bar Assn. (chair computer/Internet com. 1999-00, chmn. gen. practice com. 1987-89), Essex County Estate Planning Coun., Inc., Tax Commn. Estate planning, Probate, Estate taxation. Office: 100 Executive Dr Ste 330 West Orange NJ 07052-3309

LAVIGNE, LAWRENCE NEIL, lawyer; b. Newark, June 30, 1957; s. Daniel S. and Alice M. (Melon) L.; m. Benjie Panesh, Oct. 12, 1980; children: Gabriel A., Derek N. BA, Franklin & Marshall Coll., 1979; JD, Seton Hall U., 1982. Bar: N.J. 1982, U.S. Dist. Ct. N.J. 1982, U.S. Ct. Appeals (3d cir.) 1986, U.S. Supreme Ct. 1986, N.Y. 1989. Assoc. Shanley & Fisher, P.C., Newark, 1982-83; ptnr. Hanlon & Lavigne (and predecessor firm), Edison, N.J., 1983—. Instr. Am. Inst. Paralegal Studies, Mahwah, N.J., 1985-88. Mem. ABA (litigation sect.), N.J. Bar Assn. (product liability com.), Middlesex County Bar Assn., Trial Attys. N.J., N.J. Def. Assn., Assn. Trial Lawyers Am., Somerset Bar Assn., Worrall F. Mountain Inn of Court (barrister 1991-93), Def. Rsch. Inst. Republican. Jewish. Avocations: tennis, music, computers. Federal civil litigation, State civil litigation, Personal injury. Office: Hanlon & Lavigne 523 Raritan Center Pkwy PO Box 6147 Edison NJ 08818 Fax: (732) 346-1501. E-mail: larry@hlt-law.com

LAVIGNE, PETER MARSHALL, environmentalist, lawyer, educator; b. Laconia, N.H., Mar. 25, 1957; s. Richard Byrd and D. Jacquiline (Cobleigh) L.; m. Nancy Gaile Parent, Sept. 20, 1979; 1 child, Rhiannon Genevra Lavigne Parent. BA, Oberlin Coll., 1980; MSEL cum laude, Vt. Law Sch., 1983, JD, 1985. Bar: Mass. 1987. History tchr. Cushing Acad., Ashburnham, Mass., 1983-84; rsch. writer Environ. Law Ctr., Vt., 1985; lobbyist Vt. Natural Resources Coun., Montpelier, 1985; exec. dir. Westport (Mass.) River Watershed Alliance, 1986-88, Merrimack River Watershed Coun., West Newbury, 1988-89; environ. cons. Mass., N.H., Vt., and Oreg., 1990—; N.E. coord. Am. Rivers, Washington, 1990-92; dir. river leadership program River Network, Portland, Oreg., 1992-95, dir. spl. programs, 1995-96; dep. dir. For the Sake of the Salmon, 1996-97; pres. Watershed Cons., 1997-2001; pres., CEO Rivers Found. of the Ams., 2001—. Adj. prof. Antioch New Eng. Grad. Sch., Keene, N.H., 1991-92; mem. Portland Willamette River Task Force, 1997-99; chair adv. bd. Cascadia Times, Portland, 1995-99, Amigos Bravos, Taos, N.Mex., 1993-98; trustee Rivers Coun. Washington, Seattle, 1993-98; bd. dirs. Alaska Clean Water Alliance, 1995-98, acting pres. 1997-98; adv. bd. Glen Canyon Inst., 2000—; Watershed adv. group Natural Resources Law Ctr. U. Colo., 1995-96; coastal resources adv. bd. Commonwealth of Mass., Boston, 1987-91; adj. assoc. prof. Portland State U., 1997—; Watershed Mgmt. Profl. program dir., Portland State U., 1999—; pres. Cascadia Times Rsch. Fund, 1998-99. Co-author: Vermont Townscape, 1987; contbr. articles to profl. jours. Dir. Mass. League of Environ. Voters, Boston, 1988-92; mem. steering com. N.H. Rivers Campaign, 1988-92; co-founder, co-chair New England Coastal Campaign, 1988-92; EMT South Royalton (Vt.) Vol. Rescue Squad, 1982-86; dir., chairperson Vt. Emergency Med. Svcs. Dist. 8, Randolph, 1984-86; co-founder, v.p. Coalition for Buzzards Bay, Bourne, Mass., 1987; housing renewal commn. City of Oberlin, Ohio, 1980-81; mem. properties com. First Unitarian Ch., 1995. Recipient Environ. Achievement award Coalition for Buzzards Bay, 1988; land use rsch. fellow Environ. Law Ctr., Vt. Law Sch., 1984-85; Mellon found. rsch. grantee Oberlin Coll., 1980. Mem. Natural Resources Def. Coun., River Alliance of Wis., River Network, Idaho River United, League of Conservation Voters, Amigos Bravos, Glen Canyon Inst. Democrat. Unitarian-Universalist. Avocations: sea kayaking, mountaineering, woodwork, reading, photography. Home: 3714 SE 11th Ave Portland OR 97202-3724 Office: Rivers Found of Ams 3619 SE Milwaukie Ave Portland OR 97202-3858 Fax: (503) 232-2887. E-mail: watershed@igc.org

LAVIN, BARBARA HOFHEINS, lawyer; b. Buffalo, Feb. 27, 1934; m. Charles V. Lavin, June 19, 1954; children: Laurel, Michael, Peter, Robert. BA, Cornell U., 1955; MA in Tchg., Jacksonville U., 1970; JD, U. Richmond, 1989. Bar: Va. 1991, U.S. Ct. Appeals (4th cir.) 1991, U.S. Dist. Ct. (ea. dist.) Va. 1991, U.S. Bankruptcy Ct. 1991. Asst. prin. Greenwich (Conn.) H.S., 1976; owner, pres. Greenwich Real Estate Co., 1977; owner, broker Lavin Realty, Suffolk, Va., 1978; adj. faculty Tidewater C.C., 1982, Paul D. Camp C.C., Suffolk, 1982; pvt. practice Portsmouth, Va., 1991—. Mediator Va. Mediation Network, 1994—; court apptd. guardian ad litem, Norfolk, Portsmouth, Suffolk, Va. Author: (book) Potential Legal Pitfalls in Elementary Property Transactions in Virginia, 1989; contbr. articles to various publs. Sustaining mem. Jr. League, Soc. Mayflower Descendants; del. Rep. State Conv. Mem. Va. Bar Assn., Portsmouth Bar Assn., Family Law Orgn. Greater Hampton Rds., Portsmouth Bar Assn. (pub. rels. bd. 1996), DAR, Va. Women Attys. Assn. (pres. 1988), Phi Alpha Delta. Republican. Episcopalian. Avocations: figure skating, boating. Alternative dispute resolution, Family and matrimonial, General practice. Office: 301 Columbia St Portsmouth VA 23704-3709

LAVINE, HENRY WOLFE, lawyer; b. Phila., Apr. 21, 1936; s. Samuel Phillips and Sarah Pamela (Leese) L.; m. Meta Landreth Doak, Feb. 20, 1960 (div. Feb. 1980); children: Lisa, Lindsay; m. Martha Putnam Cathcart; children: Samuel Putnam, Gwenn Cathcart. BA, U. Pa., 1957, JD, 1961. Assoc. Squire, Sanders & Dempsey L.L.P., Cleve., 1961-70, ptnr. Washington, 1970-85, mng. ptnr. Washington office, 1985-91, sr. mng. ptnr., 1991—. Dir. Greater Washington Bd. of Trade. Trustee Fed. City Coun., Washington; bd. assocs. Gallaudet U.; mem. The Bretton Woods Com. Mem. Met. Club. General corporate, Private international. Office: Squire Sanders & Dempsey 1201 Pennsylvania Ave NW PO Box 407 Washington DC 20044-0407

LAVORATO, LOUIS A. state supreme court chief justice; s. Charles Lavorato; m. Janis M. Lavorato; children: Cindy, Natalie, Anthony, Dominic. BS in Bus. Adminstrn., Drake U., 1959, JD, 1962. Judge Iowa Supreme Ct., Des Moines, 1986—; sole practice, 1962-79; judge Iowa Dist. Ct., 1979-86; justice Iowa Supreme Ct., 1986—2000, chief justice, 2000—. Office: Iowa Supreme Ct St Capitol Bldg Des Moines IA 50319-0001*

LAW, JOHN MANNING, retired lawyer; b. Chgo., Dec. 5, 1927; s. Fred Edward and Elisabeth (Emmons) L.; m. Carol Lufkin Ritter, May 14, 1955; children: John E., Lucy L., Frederick R., Beth K. Student, U. Chgo., 1944-45, St. Ambrose Coll., 1945; BA, Colo. Coll., 1948; JD, U. Colo., 1951. Bar: Colo. 1951, Ill. 1952, U.S. Ct. Appeals (10th cir.) 1954, U.S. Supreme Ct. 1989. Atty. trust dept. Harris Bank, Chgo., 1951-52; assoc. Dickerson, Morrissey, Zarlengo & Dwyer, Denver, 1952-57; ptnr. Law, Nagel & Clark, 1958-84, Law & Knous, Denver, 1984-93; ret. Mem. law com. Colo. Bd. Law Examiners, 1971-81, Colo. Ofcls. Compensation Commn., 1985-89. Mem. Moffatt Tunnel Commn., Denver, 1966-90. Capt. USNR, 1945-77, ret. Fellow Colo. Bar Found. (charter); mem. ABA (chmn. 1975, mem. com. legal assistance to mil. pers. 1973-77), Colo. Bar Assn. (bd. govs. 1968-71), Denver Bar Assn. (trustee 1971-74), Internat. Soc. Barristers, Denver Country Club. Republican. Presbyterian. Federal civil litigation, State civil litigation, Insurance. Home: 3333 E Florida Ave Unit 35 Denver CO 80210-2541 E-mail: JMLEX2@aol.com

LAW, MICHAEL R. lawyer; b. Rochester, N.Y., Nov. 30, 1947; s. George Robert and Elizabeth (Stoddart) L.; m. Cheryl Heller. BS, St. John Fisher Coll., 1969; JD, U. Louisville, 1975. Bar: N.Y. 1976, U.S. Supreme Ct. 1982. Assoc. Wood, P.C., Rochester, N.Y., 1976-77; pvt. practice, 1977-78; assoc. Sullivan, Peters, et al, 1978-80; ptnr., 1980-81, Phillips, Lytle, Hitchcock, Blaine & Huber, Rochester, 1982—. Bd. dirs. Vol. Legal Svcs. Project, 1995-98. Served with USAR, 1968-74. Mem. ABA (trial law sect., trial techniques com., editor 1986 Trial Techniques, alternate dispute resolution ocm. 1995—), Am. Bd. Trial Advocates, N.Y. State Bar Assn. (trial sect., ins. negigence com.), N.Y. State Trial Lawyers (bd. dirs.), Monroe County Bar Assn. (judiciary com. 1981-88, personal injury com. 1988, chmn. 1999—, profl. responsibility com. 1996—), Genesee Valley Trial Lawyers Assn. (treas. 1992-93, pres.-elect 1993-95, pres. 1995-98). Republican. Roman Catholic. Federal civil litigation, State civil litigation, Personal injury. Home: 3373 Elmwood Ave Rochester NY 14610-3425 Office: Phillips Lytle Et Al 1400 1st Federal Plz Rochester NY 14614-1981 E-mail: mlaw@phillipslytle.com

LAW, THOMAS HART, lawyer; b. Austin, Tex., July 6, 1918; s. Robert Adger and Elizabeth (Manigault) L.; m. Terese Tarlton, June 11, 1943 (div. Apr. 1956); m. Jo Ann Nelson, Dec. 17, 1960; children: Thomas Hart Jr., Debra Ann. AB, U. Tex., 1939, JD, 1942. Bar: Tex. 1942, U.S. Supreme Ct. 1950. Assoc. White, Taylor & Chandler, Austin, 1942; assoc. Thompson, Walker, Smith & Shannon, Ft. Worth, 1946-50; ptnr. Tilley, Hyder & Law, 1950-67, Stone, Tilley, Parker, Snakard, Law & Brown, Ft. Worth, 1967-71; pres. Law, Snakard, Brown & Gambill, P.C., 1971-90; of counsel Law, Snakard & Gambill, P.C., 1990—. Gen. counsel Gearhart Industries, Inc., Ft. Worth, 1960-88, Tarrant County Coll. Dist. Chmn. Leadership Ft. Worth, 1974-90; bd. regents U. Tex. System, 1975-81, vice chmn., 1979-81. Lt. USNR, 1942-46. Recipient Nat. Humanitarian award Nat. Jewish Hosp./Nat. Asthma Ctr., 1983; named outstanding Young Man, City of Ft. Worth, 1950, Outstanding Alumnus, Coll. of Humanities, U. Tex., 1977, Outstanding Citizen, City of Ft. Worth, 1984, Bus. Exec. of Yr., City of Ft. Worth, 1987, Blackstone award for contbns. field of law Ft. Worth Bar Assn., 1990, Disting. Alumnus U. Tex., 1992. Fellow Am. Bar Found., Tex. Bar Found., Am. Coll. Probate Counsel, Tarrant County Bar Found. (founding chmn.); mem. Ft. Worth C. of C. (pres. 1972), Mortar Bd., Phi Beta Kappa, Omicron Delta Kappa, Pi Sigma Alpha, Delta Sigma Rho, Phi Eta Sigma, Delta Tau Delta. Democrat. Presbyterian. Clubs: Ft. Worth (bd. govs. 1984-90), Century II (bd. govs. to 1985), River Crest Country, Exchange (pres. 1972), Steeplechase. Lodge: Rotary (local club pres. 1960). Avocation: numismatics. General civil litigation, Education and schools, Probate. Home: 6741 Brants Ln Fort Worth TX 76116-7201 Office: Law Snakard & Gambill 3300 Burnett Plaza 801 Cherry St Fort Worth TX 76102-3859 E-mail: tlaw@lawsnakard.com, jnlent@juno.com

LAWLESS, WILLIAM BURNS, lawyer, academic administrator; b. Buffalo, June 3, 1922; s. William B. and Margaret H. (Welton) L.; children: Sharon, Barbara, William, Cathy, Gregory, Richard, Robert, Jeannie, Therese, John, Maria, Thomas. JD, Notre Dame U., 1944; AB, U. Buffalo, 1950; LLM, Harvard U., 1950. Bar: N.Y. 1946, U.S. Dist. Ct. (we. dist.) N.Y. 1946, U.S. Tax Ct. 1947, U.S. Supreme Ct. 1956, D.C. 1972, U.S. Dist. Ct. (ea. and so. dists.) N.Y. 1972, U.S. Ct. Appeals (2d cir.) 1972, Mass. 1976, U.S. Ct. Appeals (D.C. cir.) 1978, U.S. Ct. Appeals (7th cir.) 1979. Assoc. Kenefick, Cooke, Mitchell, Bass & Letchworth, Buffalo, 1946-50; ptnr. Williams, Crane & Lawless, 1950-54, Lawless, Offermann, Fallon & Mahoney, Buffalo, 1956-60; justice N.Y. State Supreme Ct. 8th Jud. Dist., 1960-68; dean Notre Dame Law Sch., 1968-71; ptnr. Mudge Rose Guthrie & Alexander, N.Y.C., 1971-75; pvt. practice, 1976—81, Hawkins, Delagreld & Wood, 1971—75; pres. We. State U., Fullerton, Calif., 1982-87; dean Nat. Jud. Coll., 1987-90; pres. Judges Mediation Network, Newport Beach, Calif., 1992—; of counsel Capretz & Assoc., 1994—. Vis. scholar Cambridgge U., Eng., 1990-91; mem. facutly U. Buffalo Law Sch., 1950-59, Notre Dame Law Sch., 1968-71, Fordham U. Law Sch., 1974-81; spl. counsel to Gov. N.Y. State, 1956-58; del., sec. to judiciary com. N.Y. State Constl. Conv., 1967; founder Notre Dame Law Ctr., London, 1968; pub. mem. N.Y. State Joint Legis. Com on Ct. Reorgn., 1973-82; mem. N.Y. State Temporary Commn. on Jud. Conduct, 1974-75; mem. N.Y. State Gov.'s Adv. Panel on Ethical Disclosure Standards, 1974-75; trustee Pace U. Co-author: New York Pattern Jury Instruction, vol. I, 1965, vol. II, 1968; contbr. articles to law revs.; editor-in-chief Notre Dame Lawyer, 1943-44. Bd. dirs. We. State U., Encino, Calif.; corp. city counsel City of Buffalo, 1954-56; pres. Buffalo City Coun., 1956-59. Served to lt. s.g. USNR, World War II, PTO. Mem. ABA, N.Y. State Bar Assn., Am. Law Inst., Am. Coll. Trial Lawyers, Bar N.Y.C., Harvard of N.Y.C. Club, University Club Newport Beach. Office: Judges Mediation Network 5000 Birch St Ste 2500 Newport Beach CA 92660-2151

LAWNICZAK, JAMES MICHAEL, lawyer; b. Toledo, Sept. 11, 1951; m. Christine Nielsen, Dec. 31, 1979; children: Mara Katharine, Rachel Anne, Amy Elizabeth. BA, U. Mich., 1974, JD, 1977. Bar: Mich. 1977, Ill. 1979, Ohio 1989. Law clk. to the Honorable Robert E. DeMascio U.S. Dist. Ct. (ea. dist.) Mich., Detroit, 1977-79; assoc. Levy and Erens, Chgo., 1979-83; assoc. then ptnr. Mayer, Brown & Platt, 1983-88; ptnr. Calfee, Halter & Griswold, LLP, Cleve., 1988—. Contbg. author: Collier on Bankruptcy, 15th rev. edit., 1997—. Mem. Chgo. Bar Assn. (subcom. on bankruptcy 1983-88), Cleve. Bar Assn. (bankruptcy com.). Banking, Bankruptcy, Contracts commercial. Home: 14039 Fox Hollow Dr Novelty OH 44072-9773 Office: Calfee Halter & Griswold 800 Superior Ave E Ste 1400 Cleveland OH 44114-2601 E-mail: jlawniczak@calfee.com

LAWRENCE, JOHN KIDDER, lawyer; b. Detroit, Nov. 18, 1949; s. Luther Ernest and Mary Anna (Kidder) L.; m. Jeanine Ann DeLay, June 20, 1981. AB, U. Mich., 1971; JD, Harvard U., 1974. Bar: Mich. 1974, U.S. Supreme Ct. 1977, D.C. 1978. Assoc. Dickinson, Wright, McKean & Cudlip, Detroit, 1973-74; staff atty. Office of Judge Adv. Gen., Washington, 1975-78; assoc. Dickinson, Wright, McKean, Cudlip & Moon, Detroit, 1978-81; ptnr. Dickinson, Wright, Moon, VanDusen & Freeman, 1981-98, Dickinson Wright PLLC, Detroit, 1998—. Exec. sec. Detroit Com. on Fgn. Rels., 1988—; trustee Ann Arbor (Mich.) Summer Festival, Inc., 1990—; patron Founders Soc. Detroit Inst. Arts, 1979—. With USN, 1975-78. Mem. AAAS, ABA, Am. Law Inst., State Bar Mich., D.C. Bar Assn., Am. Judicature Soc., Internat. Bar Assn., Am. Hist. Assn., Detroit Athletic Club, Econ. Club Detroit, Phi Eta Sigma, Phi Beta Kappa. Democrat. Episcopalian. Banking, Private international, Mergers and acquisitions. Office: Dickinson Wright PLLC 500 Woodward Ave Ste 4000 Detroit MI 48226-3416

LAWRENCE, ROBERT CUTTING, III, lawyer; b. N.Y.C., Aug. 12, 1938; s. Robert Cutting Jr. and Genevieve (Kellogg) L.; m. Mary Stout, Nov. 30, 1963; children: Robert Cutting IV, Kendra Stout. BA in Govt., Cornell U., 1960; LLB, NYU, 1963, LLM in Taxation, 1966. Bar: N.Y. 1964, N.J. 1966; U.S. Ct. Appeals (2d cir.) 1976, U.S. Dist. Ct. (so. dist) N.Y. 1976, U.S. Dist. Ct. N.J. 1976, U.S. Tax Ct. 1969, U.S. Supreme Ct. 1980. Assoc. Cadwalader, Wickersham & Taft, N.Y.C., 1966-74, ptnr., 1974—. Lectr. Cayman Bankers Assn., IBC legal studies and svcs., Mass. continuing legal edn. Inc., World Trade Inst., NYU Inst. on Fed. Taxation, Practicing Law Inst., U. Miami Law Ctr., Heckerling Inst. on Estate Planning, Internat. Acad. Estate and Trust Law, Am. Coll. Trust and Estate Counsel. Author: International Tax and Estate Planning; A Practical Guide for Multinational Investors, 1983, 2d edit., 1989, Lawrence: International Personal Tax Planning Encyclopaedia, 1990; also articles in legal jours.; editl. bd. Journal of International Trust and Corporate Planning, The Chase Journal. Mayor Borough of Shrewsbury, N.J., 1969-74; mem. Shrewsbury Bd. Adjustment, 1968; co-chmn. N.J. subcom. Nat. Rep. Com. for Registration of Minors to Vote, 1972; planned giving group adv. com. mem. Mus. Modern Art; tax coun. mem. Cornell U.; planning com. EastWest Studies. Served to 1st lt. U.S. Army, 1963-65. Named One of The Best Trust & Estate Lawyers in U.S. Town & Country Mag. 1998. Fellow The Am. Coll. Trust and Estate Coun.; mem. ABA (past chmn. internat. and estate planning subcom. tax sect.), N.Y. State Bar Assn. (sect. on trusts and estates law), Assn. of Bar of City of N.Y., Monmouth County Bar Assn., Internat. Acad. Estate and Trust Law (mem. exec. coun. 1986—, v.p.), Am. Coll. Trust and Estate Counsel, N.Y. City Bar Assn. (com. on recruitment 1982-85), Down Town Assn., Nat. Inst. of the Am. Bar Assn., River Club (N.Y.C.), Sea Bright Lawn & Cricket Club, Sea Bright Beach Club (N.J.), The Am. Soc. of the Order of St. John, The Pilgrims of the United States. Republican. Episcopalian. Estate planning, Probate, Estate taxation. Office: Cadwalader Wickersham & Taft 100 Maiden Ln New York NY 10038-4818

LAWSON, BEN F. lawyer, international legal consultant; b. Marietta, Okla., Feb. 7, 1939; s. Woodrow W. and Lennie L. (McKay) L.; m. Diane W. Lawson; children: Nicole, Michael C. BBA, U. Houston, 1965, JD, 1967. Bar: Tex. 1967. Atty. Monsanto/Burmah Oil, Houston, 1967-72; mgr. internat. acquisitions Oxy (formerly Cities Svc. Co.), 1972-78; gen. atty. Damson Oil Corp., 1978-81; gen. counsel, v.p. Newmont Oil Co., 1981-86; pvt. practice internat. law, 1986—. Cons. internat., 1987—. Contbr. numerous articles to profl. jours. Staff sgt. USAF, 1959-65. Fellow Houston Bar Found.; mem. ABA, Am. Corp. Counsel Assn. (chmn. oil and gas com. 1986-87). Republican. Avocations: fishing, antiques. Oil, gas, and mineral, Private international, Mergers and acquisitions. Address: 3027 Bernadette Ln Houston TX 77043-1302 E-mail: customwise@aol.com

LAWSON, JACK WAYNE, lawyer; b. Decatur, Ind., Sept. 23, 1935; s. Alva W. and Florence C. (Smitley) L.; m. Sarah J. Hibbard, Dec. 28, 1961; children: Mark, Jeff. BA in Polit. Sci., Valparaiso U., 1958, JD, 1961. Bar: Ind. 1961, U.S. Supreme Ct. 1970, U.S. Dist. Ct. (no., so. dists.) Ind. 1991, Ind. Supreme Ct., Appellate Cts. 1991. Ptnr. Beckman, Lawson LLP, Ft. Wayne, Ind., 1961-84, sr. ptnr., 1984—. Seminar presenter and writer Ind. CLE Forum, Indpls., 1970—, Nat. Health Lawyers Assn., Washington, 1986. Editor-in-chief Indiana Real Estate Transactions; contbr. articles to profl. jours. Mem. Ft. Wayne C. of C., 1975—; small claims ct. judge, Allen County, Ind., 1963-67. Mem. Am. Coll. Real Estate Lawyers. Republican. Lutheran. Avocations: sailing, teaching religious seminars, antique consulting. General corporate, Land use and zoning (including planning), Real property. Office: Beckman Lawson LLP 800 Standard Federal Plaza PO Box 800 Fort Wayne IN 46801-0800

LAWSON, THOMAS SEAY, JR. lawyer; b. Montgomery, Ala., Oct. 30, 1935; s. Thomas Seay and Rose Darrington (Gunter) L.; m. Sarah Hunter Clayton, May 27, 1961; children: Rose Gunter, Gladys Robinson, Thomas Seay III. AB, U. Ala., 1957, LLB, 1963. Bar: Ala. 1963, U.S. Supreme Ct. 1969. Law clk. to chief judge U.S. Dist. Ct. (no. dist.) Ala., 1963-64; assoc. Steiner, Crum & Baker, Montgomery, 1964-68; ptnr. Capell, Howard, Knabe & Cobbs P.A., 1968-98; asst. dist. atty. 15th jud. cir. of Ala., 1969-70; ptnr. Capell & Howard, P.C., Montgomery, 1999—. Mem. lawyers adv. com. U.S. Ct. Appeals, 5th cir. 1978, 11th cir. 1979-82. Pres. The Lighthouse, 1978-79. Lt. USNR, 1957-60. Fellow Ala. Law Found.; mem. ABA, FBA, Ala. State Bar (pres. young lawyers sect. 1970-71), Montgomery County Bar Assn. (pres. 1980), Am. Judicature Soc., 11th Cir. Hist. Soc. (pres. 1999-2001), Lawyers Adv. Com. U.S. Dist. Ct. (mid. dist.) Ala. (chmn. 2000—), Soc. of Pioneers of Montgomery (pres. 1983), Farrah Law Soc. (pres. 1986-88, Outstanding Alumnus award U. Ala. student chpt. 1989), Montgomery Inn of Ct. (master bencher, bd. dirs. 1989-93, chancellor 1991, pres. 1992-93, emeritus 1994—), Ala. Law Inst. (bd. dirs. 1986—), Ala. Law Sch. Found. (trustee 1985—), Montgomery Country Club, U.S. Dist. Ct. (chmn. lawyers adv. com. mid. dist. 2000). Episcopalian. Administrative and regulatory, Alternative dispute resolution, General civil litigation. Home: 1262 Glen Grattan Dr Montgomery AL 36111-1402 Office: Capell & Howard PC PO Box 2069 150 S Perry St Montgomery AL 36102-2069 E-mail: tsl@chlaw.com

LAWTON, ERIC, lawyer, photographer, visual artist, author; b. N.Y.C., Apr. 9, 1947; s. Leo and Vira L.; m. Gail Schenbaum, July 15, 1989; children: Rebecca Nicole, Alexandra Rose. AB, UCLA, 1969, photographic studies, 1980-81; JD, Loyola U., Los Angeles, 1972. Bar: Calif. 1972, U.S. Dist. Ct. (cen. dist.) Calif. 1974, U.S. Ct. Appeals (9th cir.) 1973, U.S. Supreme Ct. 1976. Assoc. West & Girardi, Los Angeles, 1972-76; pvt. practice, 1976—; of counsel Mahoney, Coppenrath, & Jaffe LLP, 1997—. Guest lectr. UCLA Law Sch., 1986; instr. visual arts dept. UCLA Ext.; AV rating Martindale-Hubbell. One-man shows include L.A. Children's Mus., 1980-81, Am. Film Inst., 1981, Marc Richards Gallery, L.A., 1986, U. Art Gallery Calif. State U. Northridge, 1987, John Nichols Gallery, Santa Paula, Calif., 1988, Gallery at 817, L.A., 1991, Pacific Asia Mus., Pasadena, Calif., 1993, Bergamot Station Arts Ctr., Santa Monica, 2000, L.A. City Hall, Office of the Mayor, 2001; exhibited in group shows at Stockholm Art Fair, Sweden, 1986, Francine Ellman Gallery, 1986-87, Artists' Soc. Internat. Gallery, San Francisco, 1986-87, Fla. State U. Fine Arts Gallery and Mus., Tallahassee, 1988, Silvermine Gallery, Stamford, Conn., 1988, City Hall of West Hollywood, 1988, others; group show P.L.A.N Spring Street Gallery, L.A., 1995, Christie's, Beverly Hills, Calif., 1998, Finegood Gallery, L.A., 1999; spl. film photographer in The Last Day, 1979, Chiva, Getting on in Style, 1980, Child's Play, 1981, others; multi-media prodns. include The Power, 1979, The Tie That Binds, 1981, Large-Screen Visual Montage with performance of Los Angeles Philharm. Orch. at Hollywood Bowl, 1986, Floating Stone performance, Japan Am. Theater, L.A., 1987, Pacific Asia Mus., 1993, Rejoice Performance at Thousand Oaks Performing Arts Ctr., 1998 (multi-media prodr. and digital visual performance), others; represented in permanent collections including Bibliotheque Nationale, Paris, N.Y. Pub. Libr., Skirball Mus., L.A., L.A. Children's Mus., Credit Suisse/First Boston, L.A.Westwood Nat. Bank, Gibralter Savs., L.A., Mobius Soc., L.A., Western Bank, Internat. Photography Mus., Oklahoma City, Condon & Forsyth, others; photographer, co-author The Soul of the World, 1993, The Soul Aflame, 2000; spl. assignment White House photographer, 1983; record album covers include Gyuto Monks, Tibetan Tantric Choir, Jungle Suite, Michael McDonald, A Gathering of Friends, 2001; poster Japanese Boats; contbr. photographs to books, newspapers and mags. including, N.Y. Times Mag., Fortune Mag., Conde Nast Traveler Mag., Comm. Arts. Mag., Am. Photo Mag., Chgo. Tribune, Variety, Gente (Italy), Dukas Femina (Switzerland), The World of Photography (China), Popular Photography, Pan Am Mag., Travel & Leisure Mag., U.S. News Mag., Time, Newsweek, Nat. Geographic, Harper & Row Books, Harcourt Brace Books, Holt, Rinehart & Winston books, John Wiley & Sons Books, others; world-wide advtsg. campaign Iridium, 1998; ann. report Tenn. Valley Authority, 1997; author: (short stories anthologies) Soul Moments, 1997, The Art of Pilgrimage, 1998. Active organizing com., citizens adv. and cultural and fine arts adv. commns. XXIII Olympic Games, Los Angeles, 1983-84; mem Cultural and Fine Arts Adv. Commn, 1983-84. Recipient award Fla. Nat. '88, Artquest awards, 1987, 88, 1st Prize Sierra Mag. Photo Contest, 1990, Award of Excellence for Photography, Communication Arts Mag., 1994, Cert. of Tribute, City of L.A., 2001; named one of top 40 photographers Internat. Photography Congress, 1988, winner Am. Photo Mag. 3rd Ann. Photography Contest, 1994. Mem. ABA, Consumer Atty. Assn. L.A., Consumer Atty. Assn. Calif., L.A. County Bar Assn.., Advt. Photographers Am. Avocations: swimming, music, mountain biking, world traveling, Karate (1st degree black belt). State civil litigation, Construction, Personal injury. Office: Ste 2480 2049 Century Park East Los Angeles CA 90067-3126 E-mail: elawton@mcjlaw.com

LAWYER, VIVIAN JURY, retired lawyer; b. Farmington, Iowa, Jan. 7, 1932; d. Jewell Everett Jury and Ruby Mae (Schumaker) Brewer; m. Berne Lawyer, Oct. 25, 1959; children: Michael Jury, Steven Verne. BS with honors, Iowa State U., 1953; JD with Honors, Drake U., 1968. Bar: Iowa 1968, U.S. Supreme Ct. 1986; cert. tchr. Tchr. home econs. Waukee High Sch., Iowa, 1953-55, Jr. High and High Sch., Des Moines, 1955-61; atty. pvt. practice, 1972-95; chmn. juvenile code tng. sessions Iowa Crime Commn., 1978-79. Coord. workshops, 1980; assoc. Lawyer, Lawyer & Assocs., Des Moines, 1981-98; co-founder, bd. dirs. Youth Law Center, Des Moines, 1977-93; mem. com. rules of juvenile procedure Supreme Ct. Iowa, 1981-87, adv. com. on costs of ct. appointed counsel Supreme Ct. Iowa, 1985-88; trustee Polk County Legal Aid Svcs., Des Moines, 1980-82; mem. Iowa Dept. Human Svcs. and Supreme Ct. Juvenile Justice County Base Joint Study Com., 1984—. Editor: Iowa Juvenile Code Manual, 1979, Iowa Juvenile Vode Workshop Manual, 1980; co-editor: 1987 Cumulative Supplement, 1993, supplement, Iowa Academy of Trial Lawyers Trial Handbook; author booklet in field. Mem. Iowa Task Force permanent families project Nat. Coun. Juvenile and Family Ct. Judges, 1984-88; mem. substance avuse com. Commn. children, Youth and Families, 1985—; co-chair Polk County Juvenile Detention Task Force, 1988; mem. Polk County Citizens Commn. Corrections, 1977. Iowa Dept. Social Svcs. grantee, 1980. Mem. Purple Arrow, Phi Kappa Phi, Omicron Nu. Democrat. Juvenile, Personal injury. Home: 5831 N Waterbury Rd Des Moines IA 50312-1339

LAXON, WILLIAM ALLAN, lawyer; b. Auckland, New Zealand, Jan. 28, 1936; s. William Ash and Alice Margaret Laxon; m. Lorna Delytus Kirk, Nov. 2, 1963; children: Andrew William, Alison Patricia, Iain Allan. LLB, U. Auckland, 1959. Bar: New Zealand; notary public. Ptnr. Brookfields (and predecessor firms), Auckland, 1962-97, cons., 1998—. Bd. dirs. Mount Wellington Trust Hotels Ltd. Author: The Shire Line, 1972, The British India Steam Company Ltd., 1994, Davey and the Awatea, 1997, Crossed Flags, 1997. Chmn. Presbyn. Support, Auckland, 1981-90; pres. Auckland Inst. and Mus., 1989-91. With New Zealand Army, 1955-58. Named MBE, 1988. Mem. Auckland Dist. Law Soc. (convenir libr. com. 1980-88, benevolent fund 1994-97), Northern Club, Auckland Soc. Notaries (councillor). Avocations: shipping history, music, reading, walking. Admiralty, General corporate, , Alternative dispute resolution. Office: Brookfields 19 Victoria St W Auckland New Zealand E-mail: laxon@brookfields.co.nz

LAY, DONALD POMEROY, federal judge; b. Princeton, Ill., Aug. 24, 1926; s. Hardy W. and Ruth (Cushing) L.; m. Miriam Elaine Gustafson, Aug. 6, 1949; children: Stephen Pomeroy (dec.), Catherine Sue, Cynthia Lynn, Elizabeth Ann, Deborah Jean, Susan Elaine. Student, U.S. Naval Acad., 1945-46; BA, U. Iowa, 1948, JD, 1951; LLD (hon.), Mitchell Coll. Law, 1985. Bar: Nebr. 1951, Iowa 1951, Wis. 1953. Assoc. Kennedy, Holland, DeLacy & Svoboda, Omaha, 1951-53, Quarles, Spence & Quarles, Milw., 1953-54, Eisenstatt, Lay, Higgins & Miller, 1954-66; judge U.S. Ct. Appeals (8th cir.), 1966—, chief judge, 1980-92, senior judge, 1992—. Faculty mem. on evidence Nat. Coll. Trial Judges, 1964-65, U. Minn. Law Sch., William Mitchell Law Sch.; mem. U.S. Jud. Conf., 1980-92. Mem. editorial bd.: Iowa Law Rev., 1950-51; contbr. articles to legal jours. With USNR, 1944-46. Recipient Hancher-Finkbine medal U. Iowa, 1980, Disting. Alumni award U. Iowa, 2000. Fellow Internat. Acad. Trial Lawyers; mem. ABA, Nebr. Bar Assn., Iowa Bar Assn., Wis. Bar Assn., Am. Judicature Soc., Assn. Trial Lawyers Am. (bd. govs. 1963-65, Jud. Achievement award), Order of Coif, Delta Sigma Rho (Significant Sig award 1986, Herbert Harley award 1988), Phi Delta Phi, Sigma Chi. Presbyterian. Office: US Ct Appeals 8th Cir 316 Robert St N Ste 560 Saint Paul MN 55101-1461

LAYCOCK, HAROLD DOUGLAS, law educator, writer; b. Alton, Ill., Apr. 15, 1948; s. Harold Francis and Claudia Anita (Garrette) L.; m. Teresa A. Sullivan, June 14, 1971; children: Joseph Peter, John Patrick. BA, Mich. State U., 1970; JD, U. Chgo., 1973. Bar: Ill. 1973, U.S. Dist. Ct. (no. dist.) Ill. 1973, Tex. 1974, U.S. Dist. Ct. (we. dist.) Tex. 1975, U.S. Ct. Appeals (5th and 11th cirs.) 1975, U.S. Supreme Ct. 1976, U.S. Ct. Appeals (6th cir.) 1987, U.S. Ct. Appeals (8th cir.) 1994, U.S. Ct. Appeals (10th cir.) 1997. Law clk. to judge U.S. Ct. Appeals (7th cir.), Chgo., 1973-74; pvt. practice Austin, Tex., 1974-76; asst. prof. U. Chgo., 1976-80, prof., 1980-81, U. Tex., Austin, 1980—, endowed professorships, 1983-88, assoc. dean for acad. affairs, 1985-86, endowed chair, 1988—, assoc. dean for rsch., 1991—. Vis. prof. U. Mich., 1990; reporter com. on motion practice Ill. Jud. Conf., 1977-78. Author: Modern American Remedies, 1985, 2d edit., 1994, The Death of the Irreparable Injury Rule, 1991; mem. bd. advisors Religious Freedom Reporter, 1990—; contbr. articles to law revs. Adv. bd. Consumer Svcs. Orgn., Chgo., 1979-80; exec. bd. Ctr. for Ch./State Studies, DePaul U., Chgo., 1982-87; adv. com. on religious liberty Presbyn. Ch. U.S.A., 1983-88, advisor restatement of restitution, 1984-85, 97—; v.p. St. Francis Sch., 1990-92, bd. dirs., 1990—, pres. 1992-2001; bd. advisors J.M. Dawson Inst. Ch./State Studies, Baylor U., 1990—. Fellow AAAS, Internat. Acad. for Freedom of Religion and Belief; mem. AAUP (mem. com. on status of women in acad. profession 1982-85), Am. Law Inst. (mem. coun. 2001—), Chgo. Coun. Lawyers (v.p. 1977-78), Assn. Am. Law Schs. (chmn., sec. on remedies 1983, 94), chmn., sec. on constitutional law, 2000). Home: 4203 Woodway Dr Austin TX 78731-2034 Office: U Tex Law Sch 727 E Dean Keeton St Austin TX 78705-3224 E-mail: dlaycock@mail.law.utexas.edu

LAYDEN, CHARLES MAX, lawyer; b. Lafayette, Ind., Nov. 10, 1941; s. Charles E. and Elnora M. (Parvis) L.; m. Lynn D. McVey, Jan. 28, 1967; children: David Charles, Kathleen Ann, John Michael, Daniel Joseph. BA in Indsl. Mgmt., Purdue U., 1964; JD, Ind. U., 1967. Bar: Ind. 1967, U.S. Dist. Ct. (no. and so. dists.) Ind. 1967, U.S. Ct. Appeals (7th cir.) 1970. U.S. Tax Ct. 1986. Assoc. Vaughan & Vaughan, Lafayette, 1967-70; ptnr. Vaughan, Vaughan & Layden, 1970-86, Layden & Layden, Lafayette, 1986—. Chmn. profl. div. United Way Lafayette, 1986. Mem. ABA, Ind. Bar Assn., Tippecanoe County Bar Assn. (pres. 1994-95), Am. Bd. Trial Advs. (charter mem. Ind. chpt. 1984—), Ind. Trial Lawyers Assn. (bd. dirs. 1983—). Republican. Roman Catholic. Avocations: photography, classic cars, flying. Federal civil litigation, State civil litigation, Personal injury. Home: 2826 Ashland St West Lafayette IN 47906-1510 Office: Layden & Layden PO Box 909 Lafayette IN 47902-0909

LAYMAN, DAVID MICHAEL, lawyer; b. Pensacola, Fla., July 28, 1955; s. James Hugh and Winifred (Smith) L. BA with high honors, U. Fla., 1977, JD with honors, 1979. Bar: Fla. 1980. Assoc. Gunster, Yoakley, Criser & Stewart, West Palm Beach, Fla., 1980-83, Wolf, Block, Schorr & Solis-Cohen, West Palm Beach, 1983-87, ptnr., 1987-88; shareholder Shapiro and Bregman P.A., 1988-91, Greenberg, Traurig, Hoffman, Lipoff, Rosen & Quentel, P.A., West Palm Beach, Fla., 1991-93, Prom, Korn & Zehmer, P.A., Jacksonville, 1993-94, Mahoney Adams & Criser, P.A., Jacksonville, 1994-96, Greenberg, Traurig, Hoffman, Lipoff, Rosen & Quentel P.A., West Palm Beach, 1996—. Mem. Attys. Title Ins. Fund. Contbg. editor U. Fla. Law Rev.; contbr. articles to profl. jours. Del. Statewide Rep. Caucus, Orlando, Fla., 1986; mem. Blue Ribbon Zoning Rev. Com., West Palm Beach, 1986; bd. dirs., pres. Palm Beach County Planning Congress, 1984-89; trustee South Fla. Sci. Mus., 1994-96; bd. dirs., sec., v.p. Ronald McDonald House, Jacksonville, 1994-96, Cultural Coun. of Greater Jacksonville; bd. dirs. Children's Pl. at Home Safe Inc., 1996—. Named one of Outstanding Young Men in Am., 1980. Mem. ABA, Fla. Bar Assn.

(bd. govs. young lawyers divsn. 1989-91), Palm Beach County Bar Assn. (pres. young lawyers sect. 1987-88), Fla. Blue Key, Palm Beach County Gator Club (pres., bd. dirs.), Omicron Delta Kappa, Sigma Chi, Phi Kappa Phi. Episcopalian. Bus. Landlord-tenant, Real property. Office: 777 S Flagler Dr Ste 300E West Palm Beach FL 33401-6161 E-mail: laymand@gtlaw.com

LAYTON, GARLAND MASON, lawyer; b. Boydton, Va., Aug. 20, 1925; LLB, Smith-Deal-Massey Coll. Law, 1952; LLD, Coll. of William and Mary, 1962. Bar: Va. 1951, U.S. Dist. Ct. (ea. dist.) Va. 1961, U.S. Supreme Ct. 1968. Sole practice, Virginia Beach, Va., 1952—. Of house counsel Layton & Layton Enterprises, Inc. Served with USMC, 1940-45, PTO. Mem. ABA, Fed. Bar Assn., Nat. Lawyers Club, Va. Beach Bar Assn. Democrat. Methodist. Administrative and regulatory, General corporate, Real property. Office: 4809 Baybridge Ln PO Box 5211 Virginia Beach VA 23471-0211

LAZAR, RAYMOND MICHAEL, lawyer, educator; b. Mpls., July 16, 1939; s. Simon and Hessie (Teplin) L; children: Mark, Deborah. BBA, U. Minn., 1961, JD, 1964. Bar: Minn. 1964, U.S. Dist. Ct. Minn. 1964. Spl. asst. atty. gen. State of Minn., St. Paul, 1964-66; pvt. practice Mpls., 1966-72; ptnr. Lapp, Lazar, Laurie & Smith, 1972-86; ptnr., officer Fredrikson & Byron P.A., 1986—. Lectr. various continuing edn. programs, 1972—; adj. prof. law U. Minn., Mpls., 1983-99. Fellow Am. Acad. Matrimonial Lawyers; mem. ABA (chair divorce laws and procedures com. family law sect. 1993-94), Minn. Bar Assn., Hennepin County Bar Assn. (chair family law sect. 1978-79). State civil litigation, Family and matrimonial. Home: 400 River St Minneapolis MN 55401 Office: Fredrikson & Byron PA 1100 Internat Centre 900 2nd Ave S Minneapolis MN 55402-3314 E-mail: rlazar@fredlaw.com

LAZARUS, BRUCE I. restaurant and hotel management educator; b. Pitts. s. Arnold H. and Belle Lazarus. BS, Pa. State U., 1975; JD, U. Pitts., 1980. Bar: Pa. 1980. Ops. analyst ARA Services, Phila., 1976-77; legal intern Pa. Human Relations Commn., Pitts., 1978-79; food service dir. Martin's Run Life Care, ARA Services, Phila., 1980-81; asst. dir. dept. nutrition Bryn Mawr (Pa.) Hosp., ARA Services, 1981-84; assoc. prof. restaurant and hotel mgmt. Purdue U., West Lafayette, Ind., 1984-96, prof. emeritus, 1996—. Council Hotel, Restaurant and Instnl. Edn. (membership com. 1984—, paper rev. com. 1988—). Contbr. articles to profl. pubs. Nat. Inst. Food Service Industry grantee, 1986, Internat. Franchise Assn., 1987; recipient Mary Mathew award for Outstanding Undergraduate teaching Consumer anf Family Svcs., 1993, Purdue Univ. award Outstanding Undergraduate Teaching, 1993. Mem. ABA, Ind. Bar Assn., Pa. Bar Assn., Nat. Restaurant Assn., Phi Kappa Phi. Office: Purdue U 1266 Stone Hall Lafayette IN 47907-1266

LAZARUS, NORMAN F. lawyer; b. Newton, Mass., Oct. 23, 1948; s. Ralph and Barbara J. (Ullian) L.; married; 1 child, Michelle. BA in Polit. Sci., U. R.I., 1970; JD, Suffolk U., 1973. Bar: Mass. 1973, Fla. 1974, U.S. Dist. Ct. Mass. 1974, U.S. Supreme Ct. 1980. Appeals officer U.S. Civil Svc., Washington and Boston, 1973-74; ptnr. Lazarus & Mummolo, Boston, 1975-77; assoc. Daniel F. Featherston, 1977-83; ptnr. Bernstein & Lazarus, 1984-88; of counsel Soble, Van Dam & Berenson, Chestnut Hill, Mass., 1996—; pvt. practice Newton, 1975—. Spl. counsel Mass. Commn. Against Discrimination. 1980-82. Contributed chapters to books. Mem. Lynnfield Town Fin. Com., Mass., 1980-92, mem. long-range planning com. Mass. Bay ARC, Boston, 1981-83; bd. dirs. Peabody chpt. ARC, 1978—; treas. Peabody Ward Civic Assn., 1978. Mem. B'nai B'rith (sec. 1983-84). Democat. Achievements include experience in sexual harassment, employment and discrimination law including a landmark sexual assault and workplace violence case briefed and argued before the full bench of the Supreme Judicial Court. Administrative and regulatory, Civil rights, State civil litigation. Office: 199 Wells Ave Newton MA 02459-3320 Fax: 617-969-2088. E-mail: nglesq@gisnet.com

LAZENBY, ROBERT ALFRED, lawyer; b. Salisbury, N.C., Feb. 4, 1941; s. Alfred Rickert and Caroline Stuart (Rickman) L.; m. Joanne Ruth Van Brunt, Feb. 2, 1963 (div. June 1969); m. Gwen Ellen Whitman, Aug. 2, 1972; children— Robert Todd, Amy Elizabeth, Lori Kristine, Matthew Whitman. B.A., U. Fla., 1963, J.D., 1965. Bar: Fla. 1966, U.S. Dist. Ct. (so. dist.) Fla. 1966, U.S. Ct. Appeals (11th cir.) 1967. Assoc. Frate, Fay, Floyd & Pearson, Miami, Fla., 1966-67; ptnr. High, Stack, Lazenby, Palahach & Lacasa and STack, Lazenby, Palahach & Goldsmith, Coral Gables, Fla., 1967— ; mcpl. judge City of Miami, 1971-72. Mem. Acad. Fla. Trial Lawyers, Acad. Trial Lawyers Am., Dade County Bar Assn., Miami Bar Assn., Coral Gables Bar Assn., Brevard County Bar Assn., Nat. Bd. Trial Advocacy (cert. civil litigation). Democrat. Episcopalian. Clubs: Riviera (Coral Gables); University (Miami).i). Federal civil litigation, State civil litigation. Home: 7722 Ponce De Leon Rd Miami FL 33143-6146 Office: High Stack Lazenby Palahach & Lacasa 3929 Ponce De Leon Blvd Miami FL 33134-7323

LAZERUS, GILBERT, lawyer; b. N.Y.C. s. Jacob and Bessie Lazerus; m. Judith Lazerus, Dec. 25, 1940 (dec.); children: Bruce, June. PhB, Yale U., 1931; JD, Columbia U., 1934. Bar: N.Y. 1934, U.S. Dist. Ct. (so. dist.) N.Y. 1940, U.S. Dist. Ct. (ea. dist.) N.Y., U.S. Supreme Ct. 1940. Assoc. Joseph V. McKee, 1938-45; ptnr. Strook & Strook & Lavan, N.Y.C., 1945-83, of counsel, 1983—. Master arbitrator Dept. Ins., State of N.Y.; adminstrv. law judge Trnasit Dept., City of N.Y.; mem. panel of arbitrators Civil Ct. City N.Y., Am. Arbitration Assn., N.Y. Stock Exch., Am. Stock Exch., Nat. Assn. Security Dealers. Mem. Yale Club (N.Y.C.). Home: 1175 York Ave #95 New York NY 10021 Office: 180 Maiden Ln New York NY 10038

LAZZARO, S. ROBERT E. lawyer, restaurant executive; b. Cleve., Mar. 25, 1953; s. Robert A. and Jan N. Lazzaro. BA, Miami U., Oxford, Ohio, 1975; JD, Dayton U., 1978. Bar: Ohio 1978, U.S. Dist. Ct. Ohio 1978, U.S. Ct. Appeals (8th cir.) 1998, U.S. Ct. Appeals (6th cir.) 1998. Ptnr. Costanzo & Lazzaro, Lakewood, Ohio, 1978—, Madison AVenue Land Co., Lakewood, 1983—. V.p. Glaw Bird, Inc., Cleve., 1983—; acting judge Breren Mcpl. Ct. With USN, 1971-73. Mem. Cuyahoga Bar Assn., Greater Cleve. Bar Assn., Parma Bar Assn., Party Time II Club (pres.), Parma Hts. League. Republican. Roman Catholic. Office: Costanzo & Lazzaro 13317 Madison Ave Cleveland OH 44107-4814

LEA, LORENZO BATES, lawyer; b. St. Louis, Apr. 12, 1925; s. Lorenzo Bates and Ursula Agnes (Gibson) L.; m. Marcia Gwendolyn Wood, Mar. 21, 1953; children— Victoria, Jennifer, Christopher. BS, MIT, 1946; JD, U. Mich., 1949; grad. Advanced Mgmt. Program, Harvard U., 1964. Bar: Ill. 1950. With Amoco Corp. (formerly Standard Oil Co. Ind.), Chgo., 1949—, asst. gen. counsel, 1963-71, assoc. gen. counsel, 1971-72, gen. counsel, 1972-78, v.p., gen. counsel, 1978-89. Trustee Village of Glenview (Ill.) Zoning Bd., 1961-63, Cmty. Found. Collier County; bd. dirs. Chgo. Crime Commn., 1978— , Midwest Council for Internat. Econ. Policy, 1973— , Chgo. Bar Found., 1981— , Chgo. Area Found. for Legal Services, 1981— ; bd. dirs. United Charities of Chgo., 1973—, chmn., 1985—; bd. dirs. Cmty. Foun. of Collier County, 1997—, Naples Bot. Garden, 2000—. Served with USNR, 1943-46. Mem. ABA, Am. Petroleum Inst., Am. Arbitration Assn. (dir. 1980—), Ill. Bar Assn., Chgo. Bar Assn., Assn. Gen. Counsel, Order of Coif, Law Club, Econs. Club, Legal, Mid-Am. (Chgo.), Glen View, Wyndemere, Hole-In-The-Wall, Sigma Xi. Republican. Mem. United Ch. of Christ. Administrative and regulatory, Antitrust, General corporate.

LEACH, RUSSELL, judge; b. Columbus, Ohio, Aug. 1, 1922; s. Charles Albert and Hazel Kirk (Thatcher) L.; m. Helen M. Sharpe, Feb. 17, 1945; children: Susan Sharpe Snyder, Terry Donnell, Ann Dunham Samuelson. B.A., Ohio State U., 1946, J.D., 1949. Bar: Ohio 1949. Clk. U.S. Geol. Survey, Columbus, 1948-49; reference and teaching asst. Coll. Law, Ohio State U., 1949-51; asst. city atty. City of Columbus, 1951, 53-57, city atty., 1957-63, presiding judge mcpl. ct., 1964-66; ptnr. Bricker & Eckler, 1966-88, chmn. exec. com., 1982-87; judge Ohio Ct. Claims, 1988—. Commr., Columbus Met. Housing Authority, 1968-74; chmn. Franklin County Republican Com., 1974-78. Served with AUS, 1942-46, 51-53 Named One of 10 Outstanding Young Men of Columbus, Columbus Jaycees, 1956, 57 Mem. ABA, FBA, Ohio Bar Assn. (coun. of dels. 1970-75), Columbus Bar Assn. (pres. 1973-74, Svc. medal 1993), Am. Judicature Soc., Pres.' Club Ohio State U., Am. Legion, Delta Theta Phi, Chi Phi. Presbyterian. Home: 1232 Kenbrook Hills Dr Columbus OH 43220-4968 Office: Ohio Ct Claims 65 E State St Ste 1100 Columbus OH 43215-4213

LEACHMAN, RUSSELL DEWITT, lawyer; b. Amarillo, Tex., Aug. 8, 1965; s. William D. and Alexia (Hall) L.; m. Margaret Feuille, July 8, 1989; children: William Benton, Richard Boone. BA in Polit. Sci., Tex. Tech. U., 1986, JD, 1990. Bar: Tex. 1990, U.S. Dist. Ct. (we. dist.) Tex. 1992, U.S. Dist. Ct. (no. dist.) Tex. 1994, U.S. Dist. Ct. (ea. dist.) Tex. 1998, U.S. Ct. Appeals (5th cir.) 1994; Bd. cert. criminal law, 1996. Asst. dist. atty. 34th Judicial Dist. Tex., El Paso, 1990-92; atty. Leachman & Escobar LLP, 1992-94, Diamond Rash Gordon & Jackson, El Paso, 1994—. Dir. El Paso Young Lawyers Assn. Mock Trial Competition, El Paso, 1990-95; mem. Ducks Unltd. Area Com., El Paso, 1991—, area chmn., 1999-2000, dist. chmn., 2001—. Mem. Lodge 130 (mason), Phi Gamma Delta, Delta Theta Phi, Delta Phi Epsilon, Phi Rho Pi, Pi Sigma Alpha. Methodist. General civil litigation, Criminal. Office: Diamond Rash Gordon & Jackson PC 300 E Main Dr Fl 7 El Paso TX 79901-1372 E-mail: rdl@diamondrash.com

LEADER, ROBERT JOHN, lawyer; b. Syracuse, N.Y., Oct. 14, 1933; s. Henry John and Dorothy Alberta (Schad) L.; m. Nancy Bruce, Sept. 23, 1960; children: Henry, William, Catherine, Thomas, Edward. AB, Cornell U., 1956; JD, Syracuse U., 1962. Bar: N.Y. 1963. Assoc. Ferris, Hughes, Dorrance & Groben, Utica, N.Y., 1962-64; ptnr. Cole Leader & Elmer, Gouverneur, 1964-66, Case & Leader, Gouverneur, 1966—. Sec. North Country Hosps. Inc., 1972— ; atty. Village of Hermon (N.Y.), 1968— , Town of Gouverneur, 1967-94, Town of Pitcairn (N.Y.), 1974— , Town of Edwards, 1974— , Town of Rossie, 1985—, Town of Fowler, 1978—; corp. counsel Village of Gouverneur, 1973— ; counsel Gouverneur Ctrl. Sch. Dist., 1980—; bd. dirs. Gouverneur Savs. and Loan. Trustee Edward John Noble Hosp., Gouverneur, 1972—, Gouverneur Libr., 1973-83, Governeur Nursing Home Co., Inc., 1972—, past pres., 1979-81, past chmn. bd. trustees, 1979-81; Republican chmn. Town and Village of Gouverneur, 1969-72; del. N.Y. State Jud. conv., 1981—. Served to capt. USAF, 1956-59. Mem. Rotary (pres. 1988-89). Roman Catholic. State civil litigation, Construction, General practice. Home: 187 Rowley St Gouverneur NY 13642-1220 Office: 107 E Main St Gouverneur NY 13642-1408

LEADERCRAMER, DAVID IAN, lawyer; b. London, June 4, 1952; married. Degree in Law, Southampton (ENg.) U., 1973. Bar: Supreme Ct. of Judicature 1976. Mng. ptnr. Ross & Craig, London, 1978—. General civil litigation, Family and matrimonial, Labor. Office: Ross & Craig 12 a Upper Berkeley St London W1H 7PE England Fax: 020 7224 8591. E-mail: david@rosscraig.com

LEAPHART, W. WILLIAM, state supreme court justice; b. Butte, Mont., Dec. 3, 1946; s. Charles William and Cornelia (Murphy) L.; m. Barbara Berg, Dec. 30, 1977; children: Rebecca, Retta, Ada. Student, Whitman Coll., 1965-66; BA, U. Mont., 1969, JD, 1972. Bar: Mont. 1972, U.S. Dist. Ct., U.S. Ct. Appeals (9th cir.) 1975, U.S. Supreme Ct. 1975. Law clk. to Hon. W.D. Murray U.S. Dist. Ct., Butte, 1972-74; ptnr. Leaphart Law Firm, Helena, Mont., 1974-94; justice Mont. Supreme Ct., 1995—. Office: Mont Supreme Ct Justice Bldg 215 N Sanders St Rm 315 Helena MT 59601-4522 also: PO Box 203001 Helena MT 59620-3001*

LEARD, DAVID CARL, lawyer; b. Hartford, Conn., Dec. 9, 1958; BA, Bucknell U., 1981; JD, U. Conn., 1984. Bar: Conn. 1984, U.S. Dist. Ct. Conn. 1985. Assoc. Podorowsky and Wladimer, Hartford, 1985, Manasse, Slaiby & Leard, Torrington, Conn., 1985-88, ptnr., 1989—. Lectr. legal studies Northwestern Conn. Community Coll., Winsted, 1991-92. Contbr. articles to profl. jours. Dir., past pres. Winchester (Conn.) Land Trust, 1988-93; chmn. allocations com. United Way Torrington, 1989—. Mem. Conn. Bar Assn. (workers compensation sect.), Nat. Orgn. Social Security Claimants Reps. General civil litigation, Personal injury, Workers' compensation. Office: Manasse Slaiby & Leard PO Box 1104 Torrington CT 06790-2958

LEARY, THOMAS BARRETT, federal agency administrator; b. Orange, N.J., July 15, 1931; s. Daniel and Margaret (Barrett) L.; m. Stephanie Lynn Abbott, Dec. 18, 1954, June 3, 1991; children: Thomas A., David A., Alison Leary Estep. AB, Princeton U., 1952; JD magna cum laude, Harvard U., 1958. Bar: N.Y. 1959, Mich. 1972, D.C. 1983. Assoc. White & Case, N.Y.C., 1958-68, ptnr., 1968-71; atty.-in-charge antitrust Gen. Motors Corp., Detroit, 1971-77, asst. gen. counsel, 1977-82; ptnr. Hogan & Hartson, Washington, 1983-99; commr. FTC, 1999—. Served to lt. USNR, 1952-55 Mem. ABA (antitrust sect., coun. mem. 1979-83, mem. antitrust adv. bd., BNA antitrust & trade reg. rep., 1981-99. E-mail: tleary2ftc.gov. Office: Fed Trade Commn #526 600 Pennsylvania Ave NW # 526 Washington DC 20580-0002

LEATHERS, RAMSEY BARTHELL, clerk Tennessee Supreme Court; b. Nashville, Oct. 8, 1920; s. John Rucker and Sadie Florence (DeJarnatt) L.; m. Ardis Maurine Freeman, May 8, 1943; children— Ramsey B., Karen Elaine Reddy, Raymond Swen. L.L.B., Cumberland U., 1949. Bar: Tenn. 1949, U.S. Supreme Ct. 1980. Probate master Davidson County Ct., Nashville, 1950-63; clk. Middle Div., Supreme Ct. Tenn., Nashville, 1963— . Served with USAAF, 1941-46. Mem. Nashville Bar Assn., Tenn. Bar Assn. Democrat. Episcopalian. Club: Exchange. Lodges: Masons, Shriners, Elks. Home: 983 Windrowe Dr Nashville TN 37205-3043 Office: 100 Supreme Ct Bldg 7th An Nashville TN 37219

LEAVERTON, MARK KANE, lawyer; b. Lubbock, Tex., Dec. 26, 1949; s. Herbert Walker and Patricia (Kane) L.; m. Vicki Browder, Dec. 21, 1974; children— David, Lindsey. B.B.A. in Bus., Tex. Tech U., 1972; J.D., U. Tex., 1974. Bar: Tex. 1974. Assoc., Stuart Johnston Jr., Dallas, 1975-77; assoc. Stubbeman, McRae, Sealy, Laughlin & Browder, Midland, 1977-80, ptnr., 1980-85; sole practice, Midland, 1985-87; ptnr. Leaverton & Atnipp, Midland, 1987— ; lectr. in law. Contbr. articles to profl. jours. Active, Christmas in April, Midland, 1979— ; chmn. Admissions Com., United Way, Midland, 1982-83, chmn. planning div., 1983-85; teaching dir. Midland Men's Community Bible Study, nat. bd. dirs. Mem. ABA, Tex. Bar Assn., Midland County Bar Assn. Republican. Oil, gas, and mineral. Home: 1308 Brighton Pl Midland TX 79705-2818 Office: 2700 Via Fortuna Ste 150 Austin TX 78746-7007

LEAVITT, JEFFREY STUART, lawyer; b. Cleve., July 13, 1946; s. Sol and Esther (Dolinsky) L.; m. Ellen Fern Sugerman, Dec. 21, 1968; children: Matthew Adam, Joshua Aaron. AB, Cornell U., 1968; JD, Case Western Res. U., 1973. Bar: Ohio 1973. Assoc. Jones, Day, Reavis & Pogue, Cleve., 1973-80, ptnr., 1981—. Contbr. articles to profl. jours. Trustee Bur. Jewish Edn., Cleve., 1981-93, v.p., 1985-87; trustee Fairmount Temple, Cleve., 1982—, v.p., 1985-90, pres., 1990-93; trustee Citizens League Greater Cleve., 1982-89, 92-94, pres., 1987-89; trustee Citizens League Rsch. Inst., Cleve., 1989-98, Great Lakes Region of Union Am. Hebrew Congregations, 1990-93; mem. bd. govs. Case Western Res. Law Sch. Alumni Assn., 1989-92; sec. Kulas Found., 1986-88, 93-99, asst. treas., 1989-92. Mem. ABA (employee benefits coms. 1976—), Nat. Assn. Pub. Pension Attys., Midwest Pension Conf. Jewish. Non-profit and tax-exempt organizations, Pension, profit-sharing, and employee benefits, Personal income taxation. Home: 7935 Sunrise Ln Novelty OH 44072-9404 Office: Jones Day Reavis & Pogue N Point 901 Lakeside Ave E Cleveland OH 44114-1190

LEAVITT, MARTIN JACK, lawyer; b. Detroit, Mar. 30, 1940; s. Benjamin and Annette (Cohen) L.; m. Janice C. McCreary; children: Michael J., Paul J., David A., Dean N., Keleigh R. LLB, Wayne State U., 1964. Bar: Mich. 1965, Fla. 1967. Assoc. Robert A. Sullivan, Detroit, 1968-70; officer, bd. dirs. Law Office Sullivan & Leavitt, Northville, Mich., 1970—, pres., 1979—. Bd. dirs. Tyrone Hills of Mich., Premiere Video, Inc., Menlo Tool Co., Inc., also others. Lt. comdr. USNR, 1965-68. Detroit Edison upper class scholar, 1958-64. Mem. ABA, Mich. Bar Assn., Fla. Bar Assn., Transp. Lawyers Assn., ICC Practitioners, Meadowbrook Country Club, Huron River Hunting and Fishing Club (past pres.), Rolls Royce Owners Club (bd. dirs.). Jewish. Federal civil litigation, General corporate, Labor. Office: Sullivan and Leavitt PC PO Box 5490 Northville MI 48167-5490 E-mail: mjl@sullivanleavitt.com

LEAVITT, MYRON E. state supreme court justice; Justice Nev. Supreme Court, Carson City, 1999—. Office: Supreme Ct 201 S Carson St Carson City NV 89701-4702*

LEAVY, EDWARD, judge; m. Eileen Leavy; children: Thomas, Patrick, Mary Kay, Paul. AB, U. Portland, 1950, LLB, U. Notre Dame, 1953. Dist. judge Lane County, Eugene, Oreg., 1957-61, cir. judge, 1961-76; magistrate U.S. Dist. Ct. Oreg., Portland, 1976-84, judge, 1984-87, cir. judge U.S. Ct. Appeals (9th cir.), 1987-97, sr. judge, 1997—. Office: US Ct Appeals Pioneer Courthouse 555 SW Yamhill St Ste 232 Portland OR 97204-1323*

LEBEDOFF, JONATHAN GALANTER, federal judge; b. Mpls., Apr. 29, 1938; s. Martin David and Mary (Galanter) L.; m. Sarah Sargent Mitchell, June 10, 1979; children: David Shevlin, Ann McNair. BA, U. Minn., 1960, LLB, 1963. Bar: Minn. 1963, U.S. Dist. Ct. Minn. 1964, U.S. Ct. Appeals (8th cir.) 1968. Pvt. practice, Mpls., 1963-71; judge Hennepin County Mcpl. Ct., State Minn., 1971-74; dist. ct. judge State of Minn., 1974-91; U.S. magistrate judge U.S. Dist. Ct., 1991—. Mem. Gov.'s Commn. on Crime Prevention, 1971-75; mem. State Bd. Continuing Legal Edn.; mem. Minn. Supreme Ct. Task Force for Gender Fairness in Cts., mem. implementation com. of gender fairness in cts.. Jewish. Avocations; reading (biographies, history), family, bridge. Office: 300 S 4th St Minneapolis MN 55415-1320

LEBLANC, RICHARD PHILIP, lawyer; b. Nashua, N.H., Aug. 5, 1946; s. Ronald Arthur and Jeanette G. (Chomard) LeB.; m. Doris Julie Lavoie, May 25, 1968; children: Justin D., Renée M., Anne-Marie. AB summa cum laude, Coll. of the Holy Cross, 1968; JD cum laude, Harvard U., 1972. Bar: Maine 1972, U.S. Dist. Ct. Maine 1972. Assoc. Bernstein, Shur, Sawyer & Nelson, Portland, Maine, 1972-75, shareholder, 1976-95, LeBlanc & Young, Portland, 1995—. Mem. Probate Law Revision Commn., Augusta, Maine, 1975-80; mem. probate rules and forms adv. com. Maine Supreme Ct. Pres. United Way Greater Portland, 1982-84; trustee Cleverus H.S., Portland, 1982-88; bd. dirs. Habitat for Humanity, Portland, 1984-91, Cumberland County Affordable Housing Venture, Portland, 1987-94, Maine Spl. Olympics, 1988-94, United Way Found. of Greater Portland, 1997—. Fellow Am. Coll. Trust and Estate Counsel; mem. ABA, Maine Bar Assn., Maine Estate Planning Coun. Democrat. Roman Catholic. Estate planning, Probate, Estate taxation. Home: 142 Longfellow St Portland ME 04103-4027 Office: LeBlanc & Young PO Box 7950 Portland ME 04112-7950

LEBLANG, SKIP ALAN, lawyer; b. Phila., Jan. 14, 1953; s. Morton and Leah LeB.; m. Beth Siegel, Nov. 27, 1977; children: Kaitlyn Alexa, Chelsey Jenna. BA magna cum laude, U. Pitts., 1974; JD, U. San Diego, 1977. Bar: Pa. 1977, U.S. Dist. Ct. (we. dist.) Pa. 1977, D.C. 1980, N.Y. 1980, U.S. Dist. Ct. (so. and ea. dists.) N.Y. 1980. Jud. clk. Pa. Ct. Common Pleas, Pitts., 1977-78; atty. FTC, N.Y.C., 1978-81; asst. corp. counsel law dept. City of N.Y., 1981-84; assoc. Kramer, Dillof, N.Y.C., 1984-87; pvt. practice law 1987—, 1987—. Mem. faculty N.E. regional seat Nat. Inst. Trial Advocacy, Hofstra U., Uniondale, N.Y., 1984-2001; mem. faculty advanced trial program Law Sch., Hofstra U., 1984-93, ABA/USTA Trademark Trial Advocacy Inst., 1993; spkr. in field. Author: Police Misconduct, 1981, Emergency Vehicle Liability, 1981, Sidewalks and Roadways, 1981. Co-dir. Coalition to Save Hempstead Harbor, Sea Cliff, N.Y., 1987-2001, pres., 1998—; mem. Environ. Leaders Network, Hicksville, N.Y., 1988; mem. adv. com. Internat. Environ. Conf., Hofstra U., 1990; pres. Coalition, 1998-2000. Recipient award of merit N.Y. State Gov., 1990. Mem. ATLA, N.Y. State Trial Lawyers Assn., Pa. Bar Assn., Assn. of Bar of City of N.Y., Million Dollar Advocates Forum (elected life mem.). Avocations: family, running, basketball, skiing, fly fishing. General civil litigation, Insurance, Personal injury. Office: 325 Broadway Ste 401 New York NY 10007-1112 Fax: 212-267-5813

LEBOWITZ, JACK RICHARD, lawyer; b. Glens Falls, N.Y., Oct. 3, 1949; s. Harold Louis Lebowitz and Lila Ruth (Gould) Lebowitz Paul; m. Kathleen Maryann Griffin, Feb. 29, 1980; children:Gavin, Anne. BA with honors, Wesleyan U., Middletown, Conn., 1971; JD, Boston U., 1975. Bar: N.Y. 1976, U.S. Dist. Ct. (no. dist.) N.Y. 1977, U.S. Ct. Appeals (2d cir.) 1977, U.S. Supreme Ct. 1980, N.J. 1986. Assoc. Robert J. Kafin Law Offices, Glens Falls, 1975-77; staff counsel N.Y. Pub. Service Commn., Albany, 1977-84, ITT Communications Services, Secaucus, N.J., 1984-86; prin. Law Offices of Jack R. Lebowitz, Glens Falls, N.Y., 1986-87; atty. Miller, Mannix, Lemery & Pratt, P.C., Glens Falls, 1987—. Mem. Competitive Telecommunications Assn. (state affairs com. 1984—), N.Y. State Bar Assn., ABA. Democrat. Jewish. Administrative and regulatory, Environmental, Public utilities. Office: One Broad St Plaza PO Box 765 Glens Falls NY 12801-0765

LECHNER, ALFRED JAMES, JR. judge; b. Elizabeth, N.J., Jan. 7, 1948; s. Alfred J. and Marie G. (McCormack) L.; m. Gayle K. Peterson, Apr. 3, 1976; children: Brendan Patrick, Coleman Thomas, Mary Kathleen. BS, Xavier U., Cin., 1969; JD, U. Notre Dame, 1972. Bar: N.J. 1972, U.S. Dist. Ct. N.J. 1972, N.Y. 1973, U.S. Dist. Ct. (so. and ea. dists.) N.Y. 1974, U.S. Ct. Appeals (2d cir.) 1974, U.S. Supreme Ct. 1975, U.S. Ct. Appeals (3d cir.) 1980. Assoc. Cadwalader, Wickersham & Taft, N.Y.C., 1972-75, MacKenzie, Welt & Duane, Elizabeth, 1975-76, MacKenzie, Welt, Duane & Lechner, Elizabeth, 1976-84; judge Superior Ct. State N.J., 1984-86, U.S. Dist. Ct. N.J., 1986—. Note and comment editor Notre Dame Law Rev., 1972; contbr. articles to profl. jours. Mem. Union County (N.J.) Adv. Bd. Cath. Cmty. Svcs., 1981-83, chmn., 1982. Lt. col. USMCR. Fellow Am. Bar Found.; mem. Assn. Fed. Bar of State N.J., Friendly Sons of St. Patrick (pres. 1982), Union County Club. Office: US Dist Ct Martin Luther King Jr Fed Bldg PO Box 999 Newark NJ 07101-0999

LECKAR, STEPHEN CRAIG, lawyer; b. June 16, 1948; s. Leo and Martha (Kimmel) L.; m. Nancy Jeanne Blumeyer, June 30, 1978 (div. Dec. 1981); m. bonnie G. Erbe, March 7, 1989. BS, Ga. State U., 1970; JD, Duke U., 1973. Bar: GA. 1974, D.C. 1978, Ill. 1979, U.S. Dist. Ct. (no. dist.) Ill., 1979, D.C., 1990, Md. 1992. Legis. asst. Sen. H. Talmadge, Washington, 1973-75; trial atty. Commodity Futures Trading Commn., 1975-78; assoc. Jerome Torshen, Ltd., Chgo., 1978-81; ptnr. Boraks & Leckar, 1981-88; of counsel Cohen & White, 1989-94, Gnessin & Waldman, P.C., Chgo., 1994-97; ptnr. Butera & Andrews, 1997—. Examiner U.S. Bankruptcy Ct., Chgo. 1980; mediator U.S. Dist. Ct. D.C., 1990—; lectr. Ill. Continuing Legal Edn., Chgo., 1980; adv. com. on rules U.S. Ct. of Appeals, Washington, 1998—. Contbr. articles to profl. Jours. Mem. ABA, Ill. Bar Assn., Ga. Bar Assn., D.C. Bar Assn. Democrat. Jewish. Civil rights, Federal civil litigation, Securities. Office: Butera and Andrews 1301 Pennsylvania Ave NW Washington DC 20004-1701

LE CLAIR, DOUGLAS MARVIN, lawyer, educator, judge; b. Montreal, Nov. 13, 1955; s. Lawrence M. and Joan B. Le Clair; m. Debra L. Garland, Oct. 12, 1985. BA, Loyola U., 1977; JD, Southwestern U., 1980; peace officer cert., Mesa C.C. Law Enforcement Acad., 1985; cert. theology, min., Kino Religious Inst., 1994; Juris Canonica Licentiatus, St. Paul U., 1998; M in Canon Law, U. Ottawa (Can.), 1998. Bar: Ariz. 1982, U.S. Dist. Ct. Ariz. 1983, U.S. Ct. Appeals (9th cir.) 1983, U.S. Tax. Ct. 1987, U.S. Ct. Claims 1987, U.S. Supreme Ct. 1987; ordained deacon Roman Cath. Ch., 1995. Pvt. practice, Mesa, Ariz., 1983—; mem. faculty law & acctg. Sterling Sch., Phoenix, 1992-96; judge Tribunal of Diocese, 1998—. Author: Le Clair/Morgan Income Tax Organizer, 1982-83; prodn. editor Computer Law Jour., 1979-80. Res. officer Mesa Police Dept., 1984-92. Named One of Outstanding Young Men Of Am., 1979. Mem. ABA, Ariz. Bar Assn., Maricopa County Bar Assn., Internat. Platform Assn., Southwestern Student Bar Assn. (exec. bd. 1978-79), Southwestern U. Tax Law Soc., Mesa C. of C., Delta Theta Phi, Phi Alpha Theta. General corporate, General practice, State and local taxation. Office: 400 E Monroe St Phoenix AZ 85004-2336

L'ECUYER, ELEANOR CREED, lawyer, retired career officer; b. Boston, June 13, 1922; d. Eugene Wilfred and Eleanor Creed L'Ecuyer. AB, Suffolk U., 1944, JD, 1950, DJS, 1973. Bar Mass. 1951. With USCG, N.Y., Mass., Wash., 1944-46, 56-75; ret., 1975. Decorated Meritorious Svc. medal. Democrat. Roman Catholic. Home: 1010 Am Eagle Blvd #535 Sun City Center FL 33573-5273

LEDBETTER, PAUL MARK, lawyer, writer; b. San Francisco, Oct. 14, 1947; s. John Paul and Joyce (Mayo) L.; m. Jerald Ann Broyles, Sept. 18, 1971; children: Paul Mark, Sarah Broyles. BA in English, Ouachita Bapt. U., 1970; JD, U. Ark., 1973. Bar: Ark. 1974, Tenn. 1995, U.S. Dist. Ct. (ea. dist.) Ark. 1974, U.S. Ct. Appeals (8th cir.) 1974, U.S. Ct. Appeals (6th cir.) 1991, U.S. Dist. Ct. (mid. dist.) Tenn. 1995. From assoc. to ptnr. Frierson, Walker, Snellgrove & Laser, Jonesboro, Ark., 1974-82; regional def. counsel Sq. D. Co., 1980-82; pres. Mark Ledbetter, P.A., Jonesboro, 1982-86; ptnr. Gerber, Gerber & Agee, Memphis, 1986-89, Taylor, Halliburton, Ledbetter & Caldwell, Memphis, 1989—. Author: The Hearing, 1994, The Thayer Class, 1998, The Wait, 2000. Co-founder St. Mark's Episcopal Day Sch., Jonesboro, 1978; mem. vestry St. Mark's Episcopal Ch., 1979; mem. Forum Commn. City of Jonesboro, 1978-80. Conservation Found. grantee, 1976; Rotary Internat. grantee, Japan, 1979. Mem. ATLA, Am. Bd. Trial Advs. (assoc.), Tenn. Bar Assn., Ark. Bar Assn. (mem. tort reform com. 1980, ho. of dels. 1979-80), Ark. Trial Lawyers Assn. (chmn. amicus curiae com. 1980-81, gov. 1980—), Tenn. Trial Lawyers Assn., Jonesboro C. of C. (bd. dirs. 1978-80), Rotary. Federal civil litigation, State civil litigation, Personal injury. Office: Taylor Halliburton Ledbetter & Caldwell 44 N 2nd St Ste 200 Memphis TN 38103-2270 also: Ledbetter & Caldwell 501 Union St Jonesboro AR 72401-2836 E-mail: mark794@aol.com

LEDDY, JOHN THOMAS, lawyer; b. Burlington, Vt., Nov. 29, 1949; s. Bernard Joseph and Johannah Mercedes (Mahoney) L.; m. Louise Anne Thabault, Aug. 25, 1979; children: Michael Joseph, Margaret Thabault. Student, St. Michael's Coll., Winooski Park, Vt., 1967-68; AB, U. Vt., 1972; JD, New Eng. Sch. Law, 1978. Bar: Fla. 1980, Vt. 1981, U.S. Dist. Ct. Vt. 1981, U.S. Cir. Ct. (2d cir.) 1987, U.S. Supreme Ct. 1989, U.S. Ct. Claims 1991. Ptnr. McNeil, Leddy & Sheahan, Burlington, 1978—. Mem. Vt. Lt. Gov.'s Task Force on Pvt. and Pub. Liability, Responsibility and Damages, 1987. Mem. Chittenden County (Vt.) Dem. Com., 1973-77, 81—, treas., 1973-75; mem. Burlington Bd. Aldermen, 1973-75, Vt. Dem. State Com., 1985-87. Mem. Vt. Bar Assn. (profl. responsibility com. 1991—), Fla. Bar Assn., Chittenden County Bar Assn. (pres. 1996-97), ATLA, Vt. Trial Lawyers Assn. (bd. mgrs. 1990-95). Roman Catholic. State civil litigation, General practice. Home: 126 Caroline St Burlington VT 05401-4813 Office: McNeil Leddy & Sheahan 271 S Union St Burlington VT 05401-4572

LEDEBUR, LINAS VOCKROTH, JR. retired lawyer; b. New Brighton, Pa., June 18, 1925; s. Linas Vockroth and Mae (McCabe) L.; m. Conne Ryan, July 3, 1969; children: Gary W., Sally, Nancy, Sandra. Student, Geneva Coll., Beaver Falls, Pa., 1943, 45-46, Muhlenberg Coll., Allentown, Pa., 1943-44; J.D., U. Pitts., 1949. Bar: Pa. 1950. Assoc., then ptnr. Ledebur, McClain & Ledebur, New Brighton, 1950-63; trust mktg. mgr. Valley Nat. Bank Ariz., Phoenix, 1963-72; ptnr. Ledebur & Ledebur, New Brighton, 1972-76; sr. v.p., mgr. state trust div. Fla. Nat. Banks Fla., Inc., Jacksonville, 1976-81; sr. v.p. Fla. Nat. Bank, 1977-81; pres. Northeastern Trust Co. Fla., N.A., Vero Beach, 1982-86; exec. v.p. PNC Trust Co. Fla., N.A., 1986-87; sole practice Beaver, Pa., 1987-96; master in divorce Beaver County, 1990-96; ret., 1996. Instr. bus. law Geneva Coll., 1951-52, 88-90; past pres. Ctrl. Ariz. Estate Planning Coun. Chmn. Beaver County chpt. Nat. Found.-March of Dimes, Pa., 1950-63; chmn. com. corrections Pa. Citizens Assn., 1958-63; bd. dirs., counsel Beaver County Mental Health Assn., 1962-63; bd. dirs. Maricopa County chpt. ARC, Ariz. 1968-72. Served with USMC, 1943-45, 51-53. Mem. ABA, Pa. Bar Assn. Family and matrimonial. Home: 652 Bank St Beaver PA 15009-2728

LEDERBERG, VICTORIA, judge, former state legislator, lawyer; b. Providence, July 7, 1937; d. Frank and Victoria Santopietro; m. Seymour Lederberg, 1959; children: Tobias, Sarah. AB, Pembroke Coll., 1959; AM, Brown U., 1961, PhD, 1966; JD, Suffolk U., 1976, LLD, 1995, Roger Williams U., 2001. Mem. R.I. Ho. of Reps., 1975-82, chmn. subcom. on edn., fin. com., 1975-82; chmn. nat. adv. panel on financing elem. and secondary edn. Washington, 1979-82; mem. R.I. State Senate, 1985-91, chmn. fin. com. subcom. on social svcs., 1985-89, dep. majority leader, 1989-91; prof. psychology R.I. Coll., 1968-93; pvt. practice Providence, 1977-93; justice R.I. Supreme Ct., 1993—, chmn. com. on judicial performance evaluation, 1993—, mem. com. jud. edn., 1993—, chmn. com. on user-friendly cts., 1994-97, chmn. lawday com., 1996-2001; trustee Suffolk U., 2001—. Trustee Brown U., 1983—89, com. on biomed. affairs, 1990—; trustee Roger Williams U., 1980—2001, vice chmn. corp., dir. Sch. Law, Butler Hosp., 1985—93, also sec. of corp., 2000—. USPHS fellow physiol. psychology, 1964-66. Mem. ABA, New Eng. Psychol. Assn., R.I. Bar Assn., Am. Judicature Soc., Nat. Assn. Women Judges, Sigma Xi. Office: 250 Benefit St Providence RI 02903-2719

LEDERER, MAX DONALD, JR. lawyer; b. Plattsburgh, N.Y., June 21, 1960; s. Max Donald and Mary Lilian (Adie) L. BA magna cum laude, Marshall U., Huntington, W.Va., 1982; JD, U. Richmond, 1985. Bar: Pa. 1986, U.S. Army Ct. Mil. Rev. 1986. Commd. 2d lt. U.S. Army, 1982-86, advanced through grades to capt., 1987—; def. counsel Ft. Sill, Okla., 1986-87; command judge advocate CP Red Cloud, Korea, 1987-88; sr. trial counsel Combined Field Army, 1989; chief adminstrv. law div. Combined Field Army- 2d armored div. (forward), 1989-90; command judge adv. Op. Desert Storm 2d armored div. (forward), 1991; officer-in-charge Bremerhaven Legal Ctr., Fed. Republic of Germany, 1991-92; gen. counsel European Stars and Stripes, 1992-96, gen. mgr., 1996-2000; gen. mgr., gen. counsel European and Pacific Stars and Stripes, 2000—. Fellow ABA, Pa. Bar Assn. Avocation: running. Home: 4850 Middleton Dr Lockport NY 14094-1616 Office: 2427 Pondside Ter Silver Spring MD 20906-5752 E-mail: ledererm@stripes.usd.mil

LEDERER, PETER DAVID, lawyer; b. Frankfurt, Germany, May 2, 1930; came to U.S., 1938; s. Leo and Alice Lederer; m. Midori Shimanouchi, Dec. 16, 1966. BA, U. Chgo., 1949, JD, 1957, M in Comparative Law, 1958. Bar: Ill. 1959, U.S. Supreme Ct. 1966, N.Y. 1967. Law and behavioral sci. rsch. fellow U. Chgo. Law Sch., 1958-59; ptnr. Baker & McKenzie, Zurich, Switzerland, 1960-66, N.Y.C., 1966-94, of counsel, 1994—; chmn. bd. dirs. CoverageConnect, Inc. Chmn. bd. dirs. Coverage Connect, Inc. Mem. vis. com. U. Miami Law Sch., Coral Gables, Fla., 1974—, U. Chgo. Law Sch., 1988-91, 2000—; mem. adv. coun. Wildlife Trust, Phila.; dir. Asian-Am. Legal Def. & Edn. Fund, N.Y.C.; chmn. emeritus, bd. dirs. The Midori Found.; pres. bd. trustees The Calhoun Sch., N.Y.C., 1980-83. With AUS, 1951-53. Mem. ABA, Assn. of Bar of City of N.Y., Internat. Nuc. Law Assn. Insurance, Private international. Office: Baker & McKenzie 805 3rd Ave Fl 29 New York NY 10022-7513 E-mail: peterdlederer@att.net

LEDERMAN, BRUCE RANDOLPH, lawyer; b. N.Y.C., Oct. 12, 1942; s. Morris David and Frances Lederman; m. Ellen Kline, Aug. 4, 1979; children: Eric, Jeffrey, Joshua. Cert., U. London, 1963; BS Econs. cum laude, U. Pa., 1964; LLB cum laude, Harvard U., 1967. Bar: U.S. Dist. Ct. (cen. dist.) Calif. 1967. Law clk. to Hon. Irving Hill U.S. Dist. Ct. Cen. Dist., L.A., 1967-68; sr. ptnr. Latham & Watkins, 1968—. Avocations: bicycle riding, real estate investments. Communications, General corporate. Office: Latham & Watkins 633 W 5th St Ste 3800 Los Angeles CA 90071-2007

LEDERMAN, HENRY DAVID, lawyer; b. Bronx, N.Y., Aug. 8, 1949; s. Seymour and May (Barron) L.; m. Nina Alice Chambers, Apr. 19, 1975; children— Michael, Carl, Brian. B.A., U. Md., 1971; J.D., NYU, 1974; Bar: N.Y. 1975, D.C. 1978, Calif. 1977; U.S. Supreme Ct. 1979. Trial atty. Nat. Hwy. Traffic Safety Adminstrn., Washington, 1974-78; assoc. Littler, Mendelson, Fastiff & Tichy, Walnut Creek, Calif., 1978— , v.p., shareholder, 1983— . Mem. ABA, Contra Costa County Bar Assn., Phi Beta Kappa. Avocations: soccer, scrabble, computer programming. Labor. Office: Littler Mendelson et al 2135 N California Blvd Ste 835 Walnut Creek CA 94596-3540

LEDWITH, JOHN FRANCIS, lawyer; b. Phila., Oct. 3, 1938; s. Francis Joseph and Jane Agnes (White) L.; m. Mary Evans, Aug. 28, 1965; children: Deirdre A., John E. AB, U. Pa., 1960, JD, 1963. Bar: Pa. 1965, N.Y. 1984, U.S. Dist. Ct. (ea. dist.) Pa. 1965, U.S. Ct. Appeals (3d cir.) 1965, U.S. Supreme Ct. 1970. Assoc. Joseph R. Thompson, Phila., 1965-71; mem. Schubert, Mallon, Wallheim & deCindis, 1971-81, LaBrum & Doak, Phila., 1981-95, Marshall, Denchey, Warner, Coleman & Goggins, Phila., 1995—. Author: (with others) Philadelphia CP Trial Manual, 1982. Bd. dirs. Chestnut Hill Cmty. Assn., Pa., 1975-76. With USCG, 1963-71. Mem. ABA, Pa. Bar Assn., Phila. Bar Assn., Def. Rsch. Inst., Fedn. Ins. Corp. Coun., Racquet Club (Phila.), Phila. Cricket Club, Avalon Yacht Club (commodore 1982). Republican. Roman Catholic. Federal civil litigation, State civil litigation, Insurance. Office: Marshall Dennehey Warner Coleman & Goggins 1845 Walnut St Philadelphia PA 19103-4708

LEE, BRIAN EDWARD, lawyer; b. Oceanside, N.Y., Feb. 29, 1952; s. Lewis H. Jr. and Jean Elinor (Andrews) L.; m. Eleanor L. Barker, June 5, 1982; children: Christopher Martin, Alison Ruth, Danielle Andrea. AB, Colgate U., 1974; JD, Valparaiso U., 1976. Bar: N.Y. 1977, U.S. Dist. Ct. (so. and ea. dists.) N.Y. 1978, U.S. Ct. Appeals (2nd cir. 1992). Assoc. Marshall, Bellofatto & Callahan, Lynbrook, N.Y., 1977-80, Morris, Duffy, Ivone & Jensen, N.Y.C., 1980-84; sr. assoc. Ivone, Devine & Jensen, Lake Success, N.Y., 1984-85, ptnr., 1985—. Pres., trustee Trinity Christian Sch. of Montville Inc., N.J., 1985—, also track coach. Mem. ABA, N.Y. State Bar Assn., N.Y. County Lawyers Assn., Christian Legal Soc. Republican. Baptist. General civil litigation, Personal injury, Product liability. Home: 292 Jacksonville Rd Pompton Plains NJ 07444-1511 Office: Ivone Devine & Jensen LLP 2001 Marcus Ave New Hyde Park NY 11042-1024 E-mail: brianelee@aol.com, blee@idjlaw.com

LEE, DAN M. retired state supreme court justice; b. Petal, Miss., Apr. 19, 1926; s. Buford Aaron and Pherbia Ann (Camp) L.; m. Peggy Jo Daniel, Nov. 27, 1947 (dec. 1952); 1 child, Sheron Lee Anderson; m. Mary Alice Gray, Sept. 30, 1956; 1 child, Dan Jr. Attended, U. So. Miss., 1946; LLB, Jackson Sch. Law, 1949; JD, Miss. Coll., 1970. Bar: Miss. 1948. Ptnr. Franklin & Lee, Jackson, Miss, 1948-54, Lee, Moore and Countiss, Jackson, Miss., 1954-71; county judge Hinds County, 1971-77; cir. judge Hinds-Yazoo Counties, 1977-82; assoc. justice Miss. Supreme Ct., Jackson, 1982-87, presiding justice, 1987-95, chief justice, 1995-98; ret., 1998; of counsel Dogan & Wilkinson, PLLC, Jackson, 1999. With U.S. Naval Air Corps, 1944-46. Mem. ABA, Hinds County Bar Assn., Miss. State Bar Assn., Aircraft Owners and Pilots Assn., Am. Legion, VFW, Kiwanis Internat. Baptist. E-mail: judgeandr@aol.com

LEE, DENNIS PATRICK, lawyer, judge; b. Omaha, Feb. 12, 1955; s. Donald Warren and Betty Jean (O'Leary) L.; m. Rosemarie Bucchino, July 28, 1979; children: Patrick Michael, Katherine Marie, Megan Elizabeth. BA, Creighton U., 1977, JD, 1980. Bar: Nebr. 1980, U.S. Dist. Ct. Nebr. 1980, U.S. Ct. Appeals (8th cir.) 1980, Iowa 1990. Assoc. Thompson Crounse & Pieper, Omaha, 1980-84; ptnr. Lee Law Offices, 1984-87, Silverman, Lee & Crounse Law Offices, 1987-94, Lee Bucchino & Jones Law Offices, 1994—. Atty. Nebr. State Racing Commn., Lincoln, 1984-87, commr. 1988—, chmn., 1991—; adminstrv. law judge, State of Nebr., 1985-87; lectr. Creighton U., Omaha, 1982-85. Author: Law of Conservatorships, 1981: Legal Aspects of Equine Veterinary Practice, 1984, Planning Opportunities with Living Trusts in Nebraska, 1995; others. Trustee Holy Name Cath. Ch., Omaha, 1980-84; chmn. nat. enforcement officers com. Nat. Assn. State Racing Commrs., Lexington, Ky., 1984-87; commr. Nebr. State Racing Commn., 1988—. Mem. ABA, Nat. Assn. Trial Attys., Comml. Law League Am., Nebr. State Racing Commn. (chmn. 1991), Assn. Racing Commrs. Internat. (treas. 1996-97, v.p. 1997-2000, chmn. and CEO 2000——), Nebr. Bar Assn, Omaha Bar Assn. (chmn. conservatorship com. 1981—), Nebr.-Iowa Referees Assn. (v.p. 1981-88), Omaha C. of C. (Outstanding Young Omahan 1993). Administrative and regulatory, State civil litigation, Consumer commercial. Home: 14767 Burt Dr Omaha NE 68154-1944 Office: Lee & Bucchino 12165 W Center Rd Ste 52 Omaha NE 68144-3974

LEE, DONALD JOHN, federal judge; b. 1927; AB, U. Pitts., 1950; LLB, Duquesne U., 1954. Bar: Pa. Supreme Ct. 1955; U.S. Supreme Ct. 1984. Assoc. George Y. Meyer and Assocs., 1954-57; law clk. to Hon. Rabe F. Marsh Jr. U.S. Dist. Ct., Pa., 1957-58; assoc. Wilner, Wilner and Kuhn, 1958-61; ptnr. Dougherty, Larrimer & Lee, Pitts., 1961-84, 86-88; judge Ct. Common Pleas of Allegheny County, Pa., 1984-86, 88-90, U.S. Dist. Ct. (we. dist.) Pa., Pitts., 1990—. Councilman Borough of Green Tree, 1961-63, solicitor, 1963-84, 86-88; spl. asst. atty. gen. Office of Atty. Gen. Commonwealth of Pa., 1963-74; spl. legal counsel Home Rule Study Commn., Municipality of Bethel Park and Borough of Green Tree, 1973-74, City of Pitts., 1978-80, various municipalities, 1970-86; chmn. Home Rule Charter Transition Com. Bethel Park, 1978. Mem. ad hoc com. Salvation Army. With USN, 1945-47. Mem. ABA, Allegheny County Bar Assn., St. Thomas More Legal Soc., Ancient Order of Hibernians, Woodland Hills Swim Club, Gaelic Arts Soc., Tin Can Sailors. Office: US Dist Ct 7th Grant St Rm 916 Pittsburgh PA 15219

LEE, IN-YOUNG, lawyer; b. In-Cheon, Kyonggi-do, Korea, Dec. 5, 1952; came to U.S. 1978; s. In-Seok and Hyun-Bo (Rim) L.; m. Young-Lae Hong, July 1, 1978; children: Casey K., Brian K. LLB, Seoul Nat. U., Korea, 1975; LLM, Harvard U., 1980; JD, UCLA, 1983. Bar: Ill. 1983, N.Y. 1987, D.C. 1989, U.S. Ct. Internat. Trade. Assoc. Baker & McKenzie, Chgo., 1983-86, Marks & Murase, N.Y.C., 1986-87, Baker & McKenzie, N.Y.C., 1987-91; ptnr. Marks & Murase, 1991-96, McDermott, Will & Emory, N.Y.C., 1996—. Gen. counsel Korean C. of C. and Industry in USA, Inc., 1993—, Assn. Korean Fin. Instns. Am., Inc. Articles editor Pacific Basin Law Jour. Presbyterian. Avocations: fishing, golf. Banking, Contracts commercial, Private international. Office: McDermott Will & Emery 50 Rockefeller Plz Fl 12 New York NY 10020-1600 E-mail: ilee@mwe.com

LEE, JEROME G. lawyer; b. Chgo., Feb. 23, 1924; m. Margo B. Lee, Dec. 23, 1947; children: James A., Kenneth M. BSChemE, U. Wis., 1947; JD, NYU, 1950. Bar: N.Y. 1950, U.S. Supreme Ct. 1964. Assoc. firm Jeffery, Kimball, Eggleston, N.Y.C., 1950-52; assoc. firm Morgan, Finnegan, Durham & Pine, 1952-59; ptnr. Morgan, Finnegan, Pine, Foley & Lee, 1959-86; sr. ptnr. Morgan & Finnegan, 1986-95, of counsel, 1995—. Lectr. in field. Author: (with J. Gould) Intellectual Property Counseling and Litigation, 1988, USPTO Proposals to Change Rule 56 and the Related Rules Regarding a Patent Applicant's Duty of Candour, Patent World, 1992; contbr. articles to legal jours. in patent and trademark litigation splty. Fellow Am. Bar Found.; mem. ATLA, ABA (mem. coun. Intellectual Property Law sect., chmn. com. fed. practice and procedure, chmn. com. Ct. of Appeals Fed. Cir., chmn. com. on ethics and profl. responsibility, stds. com., mem. fed. cir. adv. com. 1992-97), Am. Intellectual Property Law Assn. (bd. dirs. 1984-90, pres. 1991, Am. Judicature Soc., Internat. Fedn. Indsl. Property Attys., Found. for Creative Am. (bd. dirs.), N.Y. Bar Assn., Assn. of Bar of City of N.Y., N.Y. County Bar Assn., N.Y. Patent, Trademark and Copyright Law Assn. (bd. dirs. 1975-80, pres. 1981), others. Federal civil litigation, Patent, Trademark and copyright. Home: 3328 Sabal Cove Ln Longboat Key FL 34228-4157 Office: Morgan & Finnegan 345 Park Ave Fl 22 New York NY 10154-0053

LEE, JOHN JIN, lawyer; b. Chgo., Oct. 20, 1948; s. Jim Soon and Fay Yown (Young) L.; m. Jamie Pearl Eng, Apr. 30, 1983. BA magna cum laude, Rice U., 1971; JD, MBA, Stanford U., 1975. Bar: Calif. 1976. Assoc. atty. Manatt Phelps & Rothenberg, L.A., 1976-77; asst. counsel Wells Fargo Bank N.A., San Francisco, 1977-79, counsel, 1979-80, v.p., sr. counsel, 1980, v.p., mng. sr. counsel, 1981-98, v.p., asst. gen. counsel, 1998—2001. Mem. governing com. Conf. on Consumer Fin. Law, 1989-93. Bd. dirs. Asian Bus. League San Francisco, 1981—, gen. counsel, 1981. Fellow Am. Coll. Consumer Fin. Svcs. Attys., Inc. (bd. regents 1995-96); mem. ABA (chmn. subcom. housing fin., com. consumer fin. svcs., bus. law sect. 1983-90, vice chmn. subcom. securities products, consumer fin. svcs., bus. law sect. 1995-96, chmn. subcom. elec. banking, com. consumer fin. svcs., bus. law sect. 1996-2000, co-chmn. joint subcom. elec. fin. svcs., bus. law sect. 1997-2000, co-chmn. directory com. minority in-house counsel group 1995-98), Consumer Bankers Assn. (lawyers com.), Soc. Physics Students, Stanford Asian-Pacific Am. Alumni/ae Club (bd. dirs. 1989-93, v.p. 1989-91). Democrat. Baptist. Banking, Consumer commercial, Real property. Office: PO Box 1304 San Carlos CA 94070-1304 E-mail: johnjinlee@stanfordalumni.org

LEE, LANSING BURROWS, JR. lawyer, corporate executive; b. Augusta, Ga., Dec. 27, 1919; s. Lansing Burrows and Bertha (Barrett) L.; s. Natalie Krug, July 4, 1943; children: Melinda Lee Clark, Lansing Burrows III, Bothwell Graves, Richard Hancock. BS, U. Va., 1939; postgrad., U. Ga. Sch. Law, 1939-40; JD, Harvard U., 1948. Bar: Ga. 1947. Corp. officer Ga.-Carolina Warehouse & Compress Co., Augusta, 1957-89, pres., CEO; co-owner Ga.-Carolina Warehouse; pvt. practice, Augusta, 1947—. Chmn. bd. trustees James Brice White Found., 1962—; sr. warden Episcopal Ch., also chancellor, lay min.; sr. councillor Atlantic Coun. U.S.; bd. dirs. Med. Coll. Ga. Found. Capt. USAAF, 1942-46. Fellow Am. Coll. Trust and Estate Counsel; mem. Ga. Bar Found., Harvard U. Law Sch. Assn. Ga. (pres. 1966-67), Augusta Bar Assn. (pres. 1966-67), Soc. Colonial Wars Ga., State Bar Ga. (former chmn. fiduciary law sect.), U.S. Supreme Ct. Hist. Soc., U. Va. Thomas Jefferson Soc. Alumni, Internat. Order St. Luke the Physician, Augusta Country Club, Harvard Club Atlanta, President's Club Med. Coll. Ga. General corporate, Estate planning, Probate. Office: First Union Bank Bldg 699 Broad St Ste 904 Augusta GA 30901-1448 E-mail: lawlee@worldnet.att.net

LEE, LEWIS SWIFT, lawyer; b. Dallas, Nov. 19, 1933; '. Lenoir Valentine and Margaret Louise (Clendon) L.; m. Frances Ann Childress, Mar. 16, 1956; children: Frances Ann Lee Webb, Lewis S. Jr., George Childress, Lenoir Valentine Lee II. AB, U. South, 1955; postgrad., Washington & Lee U., 1954-55; MA, Emory U., 1956, LLB (replaced by JD), 1960. Bar: Fla. 1960, U.S. Dist. Ct. (so. and mid. dists.) Fla., U.S. Ct. Appeals (5th and 11th cirs.). Trainee Citizens & So. Nat. Bank, Atlanta, 1956, 58-59; assoc. Adair, Ulmer, Murchison, Kent & Ashby, Jacksonville, Fla., 1960-63; shareholder Ulmer, Murchison, Ashby & Ball, 1963-95; of counsel LeBoeuf, Lamb, Greene & MacRae, LLP, 1996-99, Martin, Ade, Birchfield & Mickler, PA, Jacksonville, 2000, McGuire Woods LLP, Jacksonville, 2001—. Gen. counsel Fla. Rock Industries, Inc., Jacksonville, 1972—, Patriot Transp. Holdings, Inc., Jacksonville, 1989—; dir. Fla. Sch. Book Depository, Jacksonville, 1990—. 1st lt. AUS, 1956-58. Mem. ABA, Jacksonville Bar Assn., Ponte Vedra Inn & Club, Timuquana Country Club, Fla. Yacht Club, The River Club, Haile Plantation Golf & Country Club (Gainesville). Republican. Episcopalian. Avocations: hiking, skiing, swimming, hunting, travel. General corporate, Mergers and acquisitions, Probate. Home: 3733 Ortega Blvd Jacksonville FL 32210-4347 Office: McGuire Woods LLP 50 N Laura St Ste 3300 Jacksonville FL 32202

LEE, MARILYN (IRMA) MODARELLI, library director; b. Jersey City, Dec. 8, 1934; d. Alfred E. and Florence Olga (Koment) Modarelli; m. Alfred McClung Lee III, June 8, 1957 (div. July 1985); children: Leslie Lee Ekstrand, Alfred McClung IV, Andrew Modarelli. BA, Swarthmore (Pa.) Coll., 1956; JD, Western New Eng. Sch. of Law, 1985. Bar: Mass. 1986. Claims rep., supr. region II Social Security Adminstrn., Jersey City, 1956-59; law libr. County of Franklin, Greenfield, Mass., 1972-78; head law libr. Mass. Trial Ct., 1978—. Mem. Franklin County Futures Lab Project (Mass. Cts.), 1994—. Chmn. Franklin County (Mass.) Regional Tech., Turners Falls, 1974-76, Sch. Bldg. Com., 1974-76; mem. Franklin Regional Planning Bd., 1988-98, exec. bd., 1992-95; clk. Franklin County Tech. Sch., 1976-81; vice-chmn. Greenfield Planning Bd., 1987-95; mem. Greenfield Sch. Bldg. Com., 1995—; mem. Greenfield C.C. Found., 1990—, Franklin Regional Transp. Com., 1992—; moderator All Souls Unitarian Ch., 1996-2000, asst. treas., 1997-98, treas., 1998—; mem. alumni coun. Swarthmore Coll., 1994-97. Mem. Mass. Bar Assn., Franklin County Bar Assn. (chmn. lawyer referral com. 1992-94, 97-99, vice-chmn. 1994-97, chmn. libr. com. 1992—), Law Librs. of New Eng. (treas. 1993-97), Am. Assn. Law Librs. (mem. state ct. and county law librs. sect. 1972—, bylaws com. 1996-99, chair bylaws com. 1997-98), Greenfield Charter (commn. clk. 1979-83). Avocations: swimming, gardening. Office: Mass Trial Ct Franklin Law Libr 425 Main St Greenfield MA 01301-3304

LEE, MARK RICHARD, lawyer, educator; b. St. Louis, Jan. 23, 1949; s. Bernard and Leatrice (Lapin) Lee; m. Elaine D. Edelman, June 7, 1980; children: Shira Miriam, Bernard David, Nathan Ross. BA, Yale U., 1967; JD, U. Tex., 1971. Bar: Tex. 1974, U.S. Ct. Appeals (2d, 4th, and 7th cirs.) 1975, U.S. Ct. Appeals(D.C. cir.) 1976. Asst. atty. gen. State of Tex., Austin, 1974-75; atty. antitrust div. U.S. Dept. of Justice, Washington, 1975-76; instr. law U. Miami, 1976-77; prof. law So. Ill. U., Carbondale, 1977—. Vis. lectr. U. Warwick, Coventry, Eng., 1984; cons. Peoria (Ill.) Park Dist., 1978, to Atty. Gen., Springfield, Ill., 1985; vis. prof. law U. San Diego, 1990, 91, 93, 95, 97, 01, Cath. U. of Brussels, 1992, Washington U., 1997, U. Colo., 1998, Georgetown U., 1999, 2000, Am. U., 1999, 2000; mem. Ill. Blue Ribbon Telecommunications Commn., 1990-91; arbitrator Nat. Assn. Securities Dealers, Am. Arbitration Assn., N.Y. Stock Exch. Author: Antitrust Law and Local Government, 1985, (with Gross) Organizing Corporate and Other Business Enterprises, 6th edit., 2000; contbr. articles to profl. jours. Mem. Gov.'s Task Force on Utility Regulation Reform, Springfield, 1982-84. Rsch. scholar Max Planck Inst. for Fgn. and Internat. Pvt. Law, Hamburg, Germany, 1986; Fulbright awardee U. Erlangen-Nurenberg, 1992; recipient Belgian Nat. Fund for Sci. Rsch. award, 1992. Mem. ABA, Order of the Coif, Phi Kappa Phi. Avocations: volleyball, tennis, bridge. Home: 350 Union Grove Rd Carbondale IL 62901-7685 Office: So Ill U Sch Law Carbondale IL 62901 E-mail: markrlee@siu.edu

LEE, PAUL LAWRENCE, lawyer; b. N.Y.C., 1946; AB, Georgetown U., 1969; JD, U. Mich., 1972. Bar: N.Y. 1974. Editor-in-chief Mich. Law Rev., 1971-72; law clk. to Hon. Walter R. Mansfield U.S. Ct. Appeals (2d cir.), 1973-74; spl. asst. to gen. counsel U.S. Treasury Dept., 1977-78, exec. asst. to dep. sec., 1978-79; dep. supt. and counsel N.Y. State Banking Dept., 1980-81; ptnr. Shearman & Sterling, N.Y.C., 1982-94; exec. v.p., gen. counsel Republic N.Y. Corp., 1994-2000; sr. exec. v.p., gen. counsel HSBC USA Inc., 2000—. Office: HSBC USA Inc 452 5th Ave Fl 7 New York NY 10018-2786 E-mail: paul.l.lee@us.hsbc.com

LEE, PAULETTE WANG, lawyer; b. July 25, 1947; d. Paul and Margaret Wang; m. David B.N. Lee, June 17, 1972. BA, UCLA, 1969; MEd, 1971; JD, Southwestern U., Los Angeles, 1976. Bar: Calif. 1976. Asst. sec., asst. gen. counsel Host Internat., Inc., Santa Monica, Calif., 1976-89; asst. gen. counsel Lockheed Air Terminal, Inc., 1989-96; v.p. legal affairs Dick Clark Prodns., Inc., Burbank, Calif., 1996—. Mem. County Bar Assn. General corporate, Real property. Office: Dick Clark Productions Inc 3003 W Olive Ave Burbank CA 91505-4538 E-mail: paulettelee@dickclarkproductions.com

LEE, RICHARD DIEBOLD, law educator, legal publisher, consultant; b. Fargo, N.D., July 31, 1935; s. Sidney Jay and Charlotte Hannah (Thompson) L.; m. Patricia Ann Taylor, June 17, 1957; children: Elizabeth Carol, Deborah Susan, David Stuart. BA with distinction, Stanford U., 1957; JD, Yale U., 1960. Bar: Calif. 1961, U.S. Dist. Ct. (no. dist.) Calif. 1961, U.S. Ct. Appeals (9th cir.) 1961. Dep. atty. gen. Office of Atty. Gen., Sacramento, 1960-62; assoc. McDonough, Holland, Schwartz, Allen & Wahrhaftig, 1962-66, ptnr., 1966-69; asst. dean U. Calif. Sch. Law, Davis, 1969-73, assoc. dean, 1973-76; assoc. prof. law Temple U. Sch. Law, Phila., 1976-77, vis. prof., 1975-76, prof., 1977-89; dir. profl. devel. Baker & McKenzie, Chgo., N.Y.C., 1981-83; dir. Am. Inst. for Law Tng., Phila., 1985-89; dir. profl. devel. Morrison & Foerster, San Francisco, 1989-93; dir. Continuing Edn. of the Bar, Berkeley, 1993-97. Mem. Grad. and Profl. Fin. Aid Coun., Princeton, N.J., 1974-80; trustee Law Sch. Admission Council, Washington, 1976-78; mem. internat. adv. com. Internat. Juridical Org., Rome, 1977-88; mem. bd. advisors Lawyer Hiring and Tng. Report, Chgo., 1983-95; vis. prof. law sch. law Golden Gate U., San Francisco, 1988-89. Author: (coursebook) Materials on Internat. Efforts to Control the Environment, 1977, 78, 79, 80, 84, 85, 87. Co-editor: Orientation in the U.S. Legal System annual coursebook, 1982-92. Contbr. articles to profl. jours. Bd. dirs. Lung Assn. of Sacramento-Emigrant Trails, 1962-69, pres., 1966-68; bd. dirs. Sacramento County Legal Aid Soc., 1968-74, pres., 1971-72; chmn. bd. overseers Phila. Theol. Inst., 1984-88, bd. overseers, 1979-80, 84-88; mem. bd. of council Episcopal Community Services, Phila., 1984-88; trustee Grace Cathedral, San Francisco, 1989—, chair bd. trustees, 1992-95; mem. bd. visitors John Marshall Law Sch., Chgo., 1989-93; trustee Grad. Theol. Union, Berkeley, 1991-2000, vice chair, 1994-99; trustee Coll. of Preachers, Washington Nat. Cathedral, 1999—. Mem. ABA (chmn. various coms., spl. cons. on continuing legal edn. MacCrate Task Force on Law Schs. and the Profession: Narrowing the Gap, 1991-93, standing com. on specialization 1998—), State Bar Calif. (chair standing com. on minimum continuing legal edn. 1990-92, com. mem. 1990-93), Bar Assn. San Francisco (legal ethics com., conf. of delegates 1987—), Profl. Devel. Consortium (chair 1991-93), Am. Law Inst., Yale Club (N.Y.C., San Francisco. Democrat. Episcopalian. Home and Office: 2001 Sacramento St Ste 4 San Francisco CA 94109-3342

LEE, RICHARD H(ARLO), lawyer; b. Glen Falls, N.Y., June 5, 1947; s. Donald D. and Jeanne M. (Uthus) L.; m. Mary Ahearn, June 10, 1972; children: Christine Marie Ahearn Lee, Andrea Elizabeth Ahearn Lee. BS with honors, Mich. State U., 1972; JD magna cum laude, Ariz. State U., 1976. Bar: Ariz. 1977, U.S. Ct. Appeals (6th cir.) 1977, U.S. Dist. Ct. Ariz. 1978, U.S. Ct. Appeals (9th cir.) 1981. Law clk. to Judge George Edwards U.S. Ct. Appeals (6th cir.) Ohio, Cin., 1976-77; assoc. Sparks & Siler, Scottsdale, Ariz., 1977-78, Murphy & Posner, Phoenix, 1979-82, ptnr., 1983-86; assoc. Storey & Ross, 1986-88; prin. McDaniel & Lee, 1989-91, Law Office of Richard H. Lee, Phoenix, 1982—; of counsel Martin & Patterson, Ltd., 1992-98, Martin & Assocs., 1998-99. Comment and notes editor Ariz. State U. Law Jour., 1975-76; bd. editors Maricopa County Lawyer, 1990-91. Chmn. Ariz. Canal Divershion Channel task force City of Phoenix, 1985—86, mem. exec. com., mem. citizens bond com., 1975, chmn. solid waste bond com., 1987—88, mem. bond adv. com., 1988—2000; mem. adv. com. City of Phoenix Neighborhood Orgn. Divsn., 1974—75; vo. VISTA Crow Indian Tribe, Crow Agy., Mont., 1969—71; state committeeman Ariz. Dem.s, Phoenix; bd. dirs. Valley of the Sun Sch. and Habilitation Ctr., 1991—95, treas., 1992—93, chair fin. com., 1993—94. Mem. Ariz. Bar Assn. (chmn. com. on CLE bankruptcy sect. 1985-87, chmn. bankruptcy sect. 1987-88), Maricopa County Bar Assn., Ariz. State U. Coll. Law Alumni Assn. (pres. 1981), Ariz. State U. Alumni Assn. (bd. dirs. 1981-82), Kappa Sigma. Bankruptcy, General civil litigation, Real property. Home: 331 W Orangewood Ave Phoenix AZ 85021-7249 Office: PO Box 7749 Phoenix AZ 85011-7749 E-mail: lee@aybar.org

LEE, TOM STEWART, judge; b. 1941; m. Norma Ruth Robbins; children: Elizabeth Robbins, Tom Stewart Jr. BA, Miss. Coll., 1963; JD cum laude, U. Miss., 1965. Ptrn. Lee & Lee, Forest, Miss., 1965-84; pros. atty. Scott County, 1968-71; judge Scott County Youth Ct., Forest, 1979-82; mcpl. judge City of Forest, 1982; judge U.S. Dist. Ct. (so. dist.) Miss., Jackson, 1984-96, chief judge, 1996—. Asst. editor: Miss. Law Jour. Deacon Sunday sch. tchr. Forest Bapt. ch.; pres. Forest Pub. Sch. Bd., Scott County Heart Assn.; bd. visitors Miss. Coll. Law Sch.; lectr. Miss. Coll. Law, 1993. Capt. USAR. Named one of Outstanding Young Men Am. Mem. Miss. Bar Assn., Scott County Bar Assn., Hinds County Bar Assn., Fed. Bar Assn., Fed. Judge's Assn., 5th Cir. Jud. Coun., CACM com. Jud. Conf., Disting. Svc. award), Ole Miss. Alumni Assn. (pres.), Miss. Coll. Alumni Assn. (bd. dirs.) Am. Legion. Office: US Dist Ct 245 E Capitol St Ste 110 Jackson MS 39201-2414 E-mail: JoyceWorrell@mssd.uscourts.gov-SCA-I

LEE, WILLIAM CHARLES, judge; b. Ft. Wayne, Ind., Feb. 2, 1938; s. Russell and Catherine (Zwick) L.; m. Judith Anne Bash, Sept. 19, 1959; children: Catherine L., Mark R., Richard R. AB, Yale U., 1959; JD, U. Chgo., 1962; LLD (hon.), Huntington Coll., 1999. Bar: Ind. 1962. Ptnr. Parry, Krueckeberg & Lee, Ft. Wayne, 1963-69, chief dep., 1966-69; U.S. atty. No. Dist. Ind., 1970-73; ptnr. Hunt, Suedhoff, Borror, Eilbacher & Lee, 1973-81; U.S. dist. judge U.S. Dist. Ct. (no. dist.) Ind., 1981—. Instr. Nat. Inst. Trial Advocacy; lectr. in field. Co-author: Business and Commercial Litigation in Federal Courts, 1998; author: Volume I Federal Jury Practice and Instructions, 1999; contbr. to numerous publs. in field. Co-chmn. Fort Wayne Fine Arts Operating Fund Drive, 1978; past bd. dirs., v.p., pres. Fort Wayne Philharm. Orch.; past bd. dirs., v.p. Hospice of Fort Wayne, inc.; past bd. dirs. Fort Wayne Fine Arts Found., Fort Wayne Civic Theatre, Neighbors, Inc., Embassy Theatre Found.; past bd. dirs., pres. Legal Aid of fort Wayne, Inc.; past mem. chm. coun., v.p. Trinity English Lutheran Ch. Coun.; past trustee, pres. Fort Wayne Cmty. Schs., 1978-81, pres., 1980-81; trustee Fort Wayne Mus. Art, 1984-90; past bd. dirs., pres. Fort Wayne-Allen County Hist. Soc. Griffin Scholar, 1955-59; chmn. Fort Wayne Cmty. Schs. Scholarship Com.; bd. dirs. Arts United of Greater Fort Wayne, Fort Wayne Ballet. Weymouth Kirkland scholar, 1959-62; named Ind. Trial Judge of Yr., 1988. Fellow Am. Coll. Trial Lawyers, Ind. Bar Found.; mem. ABA, Allen County Bar Assn., Ind. State Bar Assn., Fed. Bar Assn., Seventh Cir. Bar Assn., Benjamin Harrison Am. Inn of Ct., North Side High Alumni Assn. (bd. dris., pres.), Fort Wayne Rotary Club (bd. dirs.), Phi Delta Phi (past bd. dirs., 1st pres.). Republican. Lutheran. Office: US Dist Ct 2145 Fed Bldg 1300 S Harrison St Fort Wayne IN 46802-3495

LEE, WILLIAM CLEMENT, III, lawyer; b. Atlanta, July 17, 1948; s. William Clement Jr. and Barbara Anne (Wilson) L.; m. Mary Reed Evans, Apr. 16, 1982. B.S., U. Ga., 1970, M.S., 1974; J.D., Emory U., 1977. Bar: Ga. 1977, U.S. Patent Office 1980, U.S. Dist. Ct. (no., mid., so. dists.) Ga., U.S. Ct. Appeals (5th, 11th, fed. cirs.), U.S. Claims Ct., U.S. Tax Ct., U.S. Supreme Ct. Sole practice, Bremen, Ga., 1978-80; asst. sec. U. Ga. Research Found., Inc., Athens, 1981-84; patent atty., asst. to v.p. research, U. Ga., Athens, 1980-84; patent staff counsel The Coca-Cola Co., Atlanta, 1984— . Active Peachtree Battle Civic Assn., Historic Oakland Cemetery. Served with U.S. Army Res., 1970-76. Mem. Atlanta Bar Assn., Ga. Bar Assn., ABA, Am. Intellectual Property Law Assn., Licensing Execs. Soc., Am. Corp. Counsel Assn., Am. Judicature Soc., Phi Delta Phi, Delta Tau Delta (Outstanding Alumnus award 1981). General corporate, Patent. Home: 2344 Woodward Way NW Atlanta GA 30305-4048 Office: Coca Cola Co PO Box 1734 Atlanta GA 30301-1734

LEE, WILLIAM JOHNSON, lawyer; b. Jan. 13, 1924; s. William J. and Ara (Anderson) L. Student, Akron U., 1941-43, Denison U., 1943-44, Harvard U., 1944-45; J.D., Ohio State U., 1948. Bar: Ohio 1948, Fla. 1962. Research asst. Ohio State U. Law Sch., 1948-49; asst. dir. Ohio Dept. Liquor Control, chief purchases, 1956-57, atty. examiner, 1951-53, asst. state permit chief, 1953-55, state permit chief, 1955-56; asst. counsel, staff Hupp Corp., 1957-58; spl. counsel City Attys. Office, Ft. Lauderdale, Fla., 1963-65; asst. atty. gen. Office Atty. Gen. State of Ohio, 1966-70; administr. State Med. Bd. Ohio, Columbus, 1970-85. Mem. Federated State Bd.'s Nat. Commn. for Evaluation of Fgn. Med. Schs., 1981-83; mem. Flex 1/Flex 2 Transitional Task Force, 1983-84; pvt. practice law, Ft. Lauderdale, 1965-66; acting municipal judge, Ravenna, Ohio, 1960; instr. Coll. Bus. Adminstrn., Kent State U., 1961-62. chmn. legal aid com. Portage County, Ohio, 1960. Mem. Editl. bd. Ohio State Law Jour., 1947-48; contbr. articles to profl. jours. Mem. pastoral relations com. Epworth United Meth. Ch., 1976; troop awards chmn. Boy Scouts Am., 1965; mem. ch. bd. Melrose Park (Fla.) Meth. Ch., 1966. Served with USAAF, 1943-46. Mem. ATLA, Exptl. Aviation Assn. S.W. Fla., Franklin County Trial Lawyers Assn., Am. Legion, Fla., Columbus, Akron, Broward County (Fla.) bar assns., Delta Theta Phi, Phi Kappa Tau, Pi Kappa Delta. Administrative and regulatory, General practice, Health. Home: Apple Valley 704 Country Club Dr Howard OH 43028-9530

LEE, WILLIAM MARSHALL, lawyer; b. N.Y.C., Feb. 23, 1922; s. Marshall McLean and Marguerite (Letts) L.; m. Lois Kathryn Plain, Oct. 10, 1942; children: Marsha (Mrs. Stephen Derynck), William Marshall Jr., Victoria C. (Mrs. Larry Nelson). Student, U. Wis., 1939-40; BS, Aero. U., Chgo., 1942; postgrad., UCLA, 1946-48, Loyola U. Law Sch., L.A., 1948-49; JD, Loyola U., Chgo., 1952. Bar: Ill. 1952, U.S. Supreme Ct., 1972. Thermodynamicist Northrop Aircraft Co., Hawthorne, Calif., 1947-49; patent agt. Hill, Sherman, Meroni, Gross & Simpson, Chgo., 1949-51, Borg-Warner Corp., Chgo., 1951-53; ptnr. Hume, Clement, Hume & Lee, 1953-72; pvt. practice, 1973-74; ptnr. Lee and Smith (and predecessors), 1974-89, Lee, Mann, Smith, McWilliams, Sweeney & Ohlson, Chgo., 1989—; ind. expert intellectual property Barrington, Ill., 1999—. Cons. Power Packaging, Inc. Speaker and contbr. articles on legal topics. Pres. Glenview (Ill.) Citizens Sch. Com., 1953-57; v.p. Glenbrook High Sch. Bd., 1957-63. Lt. USNR, 1942-46, CBI. Recipient Pub. Svc. award Glenbrook High Sch. Bd., 1963 Mem. ABA (chmn. sect. intellectual property law 1986-87, sect. fin. officer 1976-77, sect. sec. 1977-80, sect. governing coun. 1980-84, 87-88), Ill. Bar Assn., Chgo. Bar Assn., 7th Fed. Cir. Bar Assn., Am. Intellectual Property Law Assn., Intellectual Property Law Assn. Chgo., Licensing Execs. Soc. (pres. 1981-82, treas. 1977-80, trustee 1974-77, 80-81, 82-83, internat. del. 1980—), Phi Delta Theta, Phi Alpha Delta. Republican. Antitrust, Patent, Trademark and copyright. Office: 84 Otis Rd Barrington IL 60010-5128

LEEBRON, DAVID WAYNE, dean, law educator; b. Phila., Feb. 12, 1955; BA, Harvard U., 1976, JD, 1979. Bar: N.Y. 1982, Pa. 1981, Hawaii 1980. Law clk. Judge Shirley Hufstedler, L.A., 1979-80; assoc. Cleary, Gottlieb, Steen & Hamilton, N.Y.C., 1981-83; prof. Sch. Law NYU, 1983-89, Columbia U., N.Y.C., 1989—, dean, Lucy G Moses prof. law, 1996—. Office: Columbia U Sch Law 801 Jerome Greene Hall 435 W 116th St New York NY 10027-7297*

LEECH, NOYES ELWOOD, lawyer, educator; b. Ambler, Pa., Aug. 1, 1921; m. Louise Ann Gallagher, Apr. 19, 1954; children: Katharine, Gwyneth. AB, U. Pa., 1943, JD, 1948. Bar: Pa. 1949. Assoc. Dechert, Price & Rhoads (and predecessors), Phila., 1948-49, 51-53; mem. faculty law sch. U. Pa., 1949-57, prof., 1957-78, Ferdinand Wakeman Hubbell prof. law, 1978-85, William A. Schnader prof. law, 1985-86, prof. emeritus, 1986—. Co-author: The International Legal System, 3d edit., 1988; gen. editor: Jour. Comparative Bus. and Capital Market Law, 1978-86. Mem. Order of Coif, Phi Beta Kappa. Office: U Pa Law Sch 3400 Chestnut St Philadelphia PA 19104-6204

LEEKLEY, JOHN ROBERT, lawyer; b. Phila., Aug. 27, 1943; s. Thomas Briggs and Dorothy (O'Hora) L.; m. Karen Kristin Myers, Aug. 28, 1965 (dec. Mar. 1997); children: John Thomas, Michael Dennis; m. Gerry Lee Gildner, June 5, 1999. BA, Boston Coll., 1965; LLB, Columbia U., 1968. Bar: N.Y. 1968, Mich. 1976. Assoc. Curtis, Mallet-Prevost, Colt & Mosle, N.Y.C., 1968-69, Davis Polk & Wardwell, N.Y.C., 1969-76; asst. corp. counsel Masco Corp., Taylor, Mich., 1976-77, corp. counsel, 1977-79, v.p., corp. counsel, 1979-88, v.p., gen. counsel, 1988-96, sr. v.p., gen. counsel, 1996—. Bd. visitors Columbia U. Law Sch., N.Y.C., 1994-96; mem. Freedom Twp. Bd. Tax Appeals, 1984-85. Mem. ABA (com. long range issues affecting bus. practice 1976-96), Mich. State Bar Assn. Democrat. Roman Catholic. Avocations: Percheron horse breeding, hunting, fishing, outdoor activities. Office: Masco Corp 21001 Van Born Rd Taylor MI 48180-1300

LEEN, DAVID ARTHUR, lawyer; b. Bellingham, Wash., Sept. 28, 1945; s. Gordon William and Margaretta (Verner) L. BA, Beloit Coll., 1968; JD, U. Oreg., 1971. Bar: Wash. 1971, U.S. Dist. Ct. (we. dist.) Wash. 1972, U.S. Ct. Appeals (9th cir.) 1983, U.S. Ct. Claims 1984, U.S. Supreme Ct. 1984. Staff atty. Seattle Legal Services, 1971-76; regional atty. FTC, Seattle, 1976-77, Econ. Devel. Adminstrn., Dept. Commerce, Seattle, 1977-78, Legal Services Corp., Seattle, 1978—; sr. ptnr. Leen & Moore, 1979—. Judge pro tem King County Superior Ct., Seattle, 1980—; lectr. Nat. Bus. Inst., Eau Claire, Wis., 1985—. Author: (with others) Foreclosures, 1986; also articles. Reginald Heber Smith fellow U.Pa., Harvard U., 1971-73. Democrat. E-mila. Real property. Home: 409 Highland Dr Seattle WA 98109-3327 E-mail: David@davidleen.com

LEEPER, HAROLD HARRIS, arbitrator; b. Kansas City, Mo., July 29, 1916; s. Truman Elmer and Bess Mayburn (Harris) L.; m. Maribelle Potts, Sept. 21, 1941; children: Robert Chester, Marilyn Anne. BSBA, U. Mo., 1937; JD, Oklahoma City U., 1956. Bar: Okla. 1957, U.S. Supreme Ct. 1969. Regional pers. officer VA, Oklahoma City, 1946-52; state adminstrv. officer IRS, 1952-56; pers. officer FAA, 1956-63, from hearing officer to chief hearing officer Washington, 1963-71; adminstrv. law judge Social Security Adminstrn., Dallas, 1971-73; freelance labor mgmt. arbitrator, 1974—. Chmn. pers. com. Wesley Rankin Cmty. Ctr., Dallas, 1989—95; pres. Way Back House, Inc., 1975—77, bd. dirs., 1977—80; scoutmaster Boy Scouts Am., S.D., Okla., Va. 1st lt. U.S. Army, 1943—46, lt. col. USAR. Mem. Fed. Bar Assn. (pres. Dallas chpt. 1982-83), Nat. Acad. Arbitrators (regional chmn. 1990-92), Mil. Order World Wars (comdr. D.C. chpt. 1969-70), Mason, Shriner. Democrat. Methodist. Avocations: golf, sailing, flying, church activities. Home and Office: 6256 Glennox Ln Dallas TX 75214-2144

LEESON, SUSAN M. state supreme court judge; Law clerk U.S. 9th Cir. Ct. of Appeals; Tom. C. Clark judicial fellow U.S. Supreme Ct.; prof. polit. sci., assoc. prof. law Willamette U., Salem, Oreg.; judge Oreg. Ct. Appeals, 1993-98; justice Oreg. Supreme Ct., 1998—. Former mem. Oreg. Criminal Justice Coun., Marion-Polk Local Govt. Boundary Commn. Office: Supreme Ct Bldg 1163 State St Salem OR 97310-1331*

LEFCO, KATHY NAN, law librarian; b. Bethesda, Md., Feb. 24, 1949; d. Ted Lefco and Dorothy Rose (Fox) Harris; m. Stephen Gary Katz, Sept. 2, 1973 (div. May 1984); m. John Alfred Price, Nov. 24, 1984 (dec. Jan. 1989). BA, U. Wis., 1971; MLS, U. Wis., Milw., 1975. Rsch. asst. Ctr. Auto Safety, Washington, 1971-73; asst. to dir. Ctr. Consumer Affairs, Milw., 1973-74; legis. libr. Morgan, Lewis & Bockius, Washington, 1976-78; dir. library Mulcahy & Wherry, Milw., 1978; paralegal Land of Lincoln Legal Assistance, Springfield, Ill., 1979-80; reference and interlibrary loan libr. So. Ill. U. Sch. Medicine, 1980; reader svcs. libr. Wis. State Law Library, Madison, 1981-83; ref. libr. Mudge Rose Guthrie Alexander & Ferdon, N.Y.C., 1983-85; sr. legal info. specialist Cravath, Swaine & Moore, 1985-86; asst. libr. Kaye, Scholer, Fierman, Hays & Handler, 1986-89; head libr. Parker Chapin Flattau & Klimpl, 1989-94; dir. libr. svcs. Winston & Strawn, Chgo., 1994—. Author: (with others) Mobile Homes: The Low-Cost Housing Hoax, 1973. Mem. Chgo. Assn. Law Librs., Am. Assn. Law Librs. Democrat. Jewish. Avocations: biking, backgammon, politics. Home: 5445 N Sheridan Rd Apt 808 Chicago IL 60640-7457 Office: Winston & Strawn 35 W Wacker Dr Ste 4200 Chicago IL 60601-1695 E-mail: klefco@winston.com

LEFKOW, MICHAEL FRANCIS, lawyer; b. Dec. 9, 1940; s. Frederick Lord and Marjorie Claiborne (Freeman) L.; 1 child, Duschia; m. Joan Marilyn Humphrey, June 21, 1975; children: Maria, Helena, Laura, Margaret. BA, North Cen. Coll., Naperville, Ill., 1962; JD, Northwestern U., 1966. Bar: Ill. 1966, U.S. Dist. Ct. (no. dist.) Ill. 1967, Colo. 1969, U.S. Ct. Appeals (7th cir.) 1971, U.S. Supreme Ct. 1971, Fla. 1982, U.S. Ct. Appeals (fed. cir.) 1986. Gen. counsel Chgo. Welfare Rights Orgn., 1969-72, Ill. Welfare Rights Orgn., Chgo., 1972-76; pvt. practice, 1977-78, 85—; mng. atty. Prairie State Legal Svcs., Inc., Wheaton, Ill., 1978-79; supervisory trial atty. EEOC, Miami, Fla., 1979-82; asst. regional labor counsel U.S. Postal Svc., Chgo., 1982-85. Spl. commr. U.S. Dist. Ct. (no. dist.) Ill., 1985-87; atty. U.S. Fed. Defender Panel, 1991—. Chpt. v.p. League United Latin-Am. Citizens, Miami, 1979; mem. Social Concerns Com., Episcopal Diocese South Fla., Miami, 1981; mem. vestry St. Luke's Episcopal Ch., Evanston, Ill., 1992-95; mem. Episcopal Vol. Lawyers Network, Diocese Chgo., 1996—; area chair 48th ward Dem. Party and Dem. Coalition, 1996, 48th ward Dem. party, 1996—. Mem. ABA, Chgo. Coun. Lawyers (bd. dirs. 1972-74, 87-89), Plaintiffs Employment Lawyers Assn., Chgo. Bar Assn., (past bd. dirs., vice chair lawyers referral svc. com., 2000-01, chair, 2001—, mem. fin. com.), Nat. Clearinghouse for Legal Svcs., Lake County Bar Assn. Democrat. Episcopalian. Office: 53 W Jackson Blvd Ste 918 Chicago IL 60604-3607 Fax: (312) 427-6053. E-mail: lefkowmf@aol.com

LEFKOWITZ, ALAN ZOEL, lawyer; b. Pitts., Dec. 1, 1932; s. Curtis and Lily Rose Lefkowitz; m. Francine Marcia Kaplan, Feb. 5, 1956; children: Curtis Robert, Gail Ann, David Edward. AB, U. Pitts., 1953; JD, U. Mich., 1955. Bar: Pa. 1956, U.S. Supreme Ct. 1959, U.S. Ct. Appeals (3d cir.), U.S. Dist. Ct. (we. dist.) Pa., U.S. Tax Ct. Assoc. Kaplan, Finkel & Roth, Pitts., 1955-72; mng. ptnr. Kaplan, Finkel, Lefkowitz, Roth & Ostrow, 1972-82, Finkel Lefkowitz Ostrow & Woolridge, Pitts., 1982-88; ptnr., head corp. sect. Tucker Arenberg, P.C., 1988-93; dir. Kabala & Geeseman, 1993-99. Adj. prof. arts and law Heinz Sch. Pub. Policy and Adminstrn./Carnegie Mellon Un.; sec. TPC Comm., Inc., Pitts., 1970-91, Computer Rsch., Inc., Pitts., 1969-92, Star-Tron Tech., Inc., Pitts., 1986-92. Mem. Pitts. Coun. Internat. Visitors; trustee United Jewish Fedn. Pitts., 1964-68, Rodef Shalom Congregation, Pitts., 1962-64, 90-98; bd. dirs., treas., v.p. Jewish Family and Childrens Svcs., Pitts., 1967-68; bd. dirs. Family Resources, 1986X, U.S. Counter-Intelligence Corp. With U.S. Army, 1956-59. Mem. ABA, Internat. Assn. Fin. Planners (Pitts. chpt. v.p. ethics regulation), Internat. Assn. Jewish Lawyers, Pa. Bar Assn., Allegheny County Bar Assn. (former chair arts law sect., former chair, coun. corp. sec., chair securities regulation com., former chair internat. com.), Photoimagers Guild, Acad. Arts and Scis. (photography sect., bd. dirs. 1994X), Silver Eye Ctr. for Photography (trustee, sec.). Avocations: photography, theatre. General corporate, Mergers and acquisitions, Securities.

LEFKOWITZ, HOWARD N. lawyer; b. Utica, N.Y., Oct. 28, 1936; s. Samuel I. and Sarah Lefkowitz; m. Martha Yelon, June 16, 1958; children: Sarah, David. BA, Cornell U., 1958; LLB, Columbia U., 1963. Bar: N.Y. 1963. Ptnr. Proskauer Rose LLP, N.Y.C., 1963—. Tri-bar opinion com. Author: New York LLC and LLP Forms and Practice Manual, Data Trace, 3d edit. 2000; co-author: Transactional Lawyers Deskbook: Advising Business Entities, 2001; editor Columbia Law Rev., 1963. Lt. (j.g.) USN, 1958-61. Kent scholar Columbia U. Law Sch. Fellow: Am. Coll. Investment Counsel; mem.: ABA (mem. ltd. liability entity subcom. of bus. sect. 1993—), Assn. of Bar of City of N.Y. (chmn. com. on corp. law 1990—93, com. on corp. law 1997—2001), N.Y. County Lawyers Assn. (chmn. com. on comm. entertainment and arts-related law 1983—86), Pvt. Investment Fund Forum (sec.). Contracts commercial, Computer, General corporate. Office: Proskauer Rose LLP 1585 Broadway Fl 27 New York NY 10036-8299

LEFKOWITZ, IVAN MARTIN, lawyer; b. Winston-Salem, N.C., Jan. 4, 1952; s. Ernest W. and Matilda C. (Center) L.; m. Fern Deutsch, Apr. 14, 1972; children: Aaron M., Shira B. BBA, U. Cen. Fla., 1973; JD, U. Miami, 1979, LLM Estate Planning, 1980. Bar: Fla. 1979, U.S. Dist. Ct. (mid. dist.) 1980, U.S. Tax. Ct. 1980; CPA, Fla. Sr. acct. Alexander Grant & Co. CPA, Orlando, Fla., 1974-76; assoc. Gray, Harris & Robinson P.A.,

1980-82; pvt. practice, 1982-88; ptnr. Lefkowitz & Miner, P.A., 1988-93; sr. ptnr. Lefkowitz & Bloom, P.A., 1993—. Adj. prof. Am. Coll., Denver, 1984-90, Mgmt. Inst., U. Cen. Fla., Orlando, 1988—; sec., dir. Employee Benefits Coun. Fla., 1987-89, pres., 1990. Mem. dean's exec. coun. U. Ctrl. Fla. Coll. of Bus., 2000—; mem. governing bd. Princeton Hosp., Orlando, 1997—98; mem. Ctrl. Fla. Estate Planning Coun.; treas. Holocaust Meml. Resource and Edn. Ctr. Ctrl. Fla., 2000—01; U. Ctrl. Fla. Found. Orlando, 1981—96; bd. dirs., pres. Nat. Kidney Found. Ctrl. Fla., Orlando and Tampa, 1984—91. Recipient Induction to Coll. of Bus. Adminstrn. Hall of Fame, U. Ctrl. Fla., 2001. Democrat. Estate planning, Pension, profit-sharing, and employee benefits, Corporate taxation. Office: 430 N Mills Ave Orlando FL 32803-5746

LEFKOWITZ, JEROME, lawyer; b. N.Y.C., Mar. 24, 1931; s. Jack and Sue (Horowitz) L.; m. Myrna Judith Weishaut, Aug. 12, 1956; children: Jay, Mark, Miriam, Alan. Student, Jewish Theol. Sem., N.Y.C., 1948-51; BA, NYU, 1952; JD, Columbia U., 1955. Bar: N.Y. 1955, U.S. Dist. Ct. (so. and ea. dists.) N.Y. 1990. Asst. atty. gen. N.Y. State Dept. of Law, Albany, 1958-60; counsel, dep. commissioner N.Y. State Dept. of Labor, N.Y.C., Albany, 1960-67; dep. chmn., mem. N.Y. Pub. Rels. Bd., Albany, 1967-87; adj. faculty Albany Law Sch. Columbia U., N.Y.C., Albany, 1968-89; dep. counsel Civil Svc. Employment Assn., Albany, 1987—. Cons. State of Mich., 1969, State of Hawaii, 1970, State of Pa., 1976, State of Mass., 1978. Author: Public Employee Unionism In Israel, 1971; editor: Public Sector Labor & Employment Law, 1988, 2d edit., 1998, The Evolving Process--Collective Negotiations In Public Employment, 1985. Chmn. community rels. com. Albany Jewish Fedn., 1980-84, 86-87; pres. Massad Hebrew Speaking Camps. Mem. N.Y. State Bar Assn. (chmn. com. on pub. sector labor rels. 1975-79, chmn. com. on legis. 1980-83, chmn. labor law sect. 1991-92). Republican. Avocations: tennis, skiing, reading, history. Home: 54 Maxwell St Albany NY 12208-1639 Office: Civil Svc Employment Assn 143 Washington Ave Albany NY 12210-2303 E-mail: csea16@capital.net

LEGG, BENSON EVERETT, federal judge; b. Balt., June 8, 1947; s. William Mercer Legg and Beverly Mason; m. Kyle Prechtl Legg; children: Jennifer, Charles, Matthew. AB magna cum laude, Princeton U., 1970; JD, U. Va., 1973. Bar: Md. 1973. Law clk. to Hon. Frank A. Kaufman, Balt., 1973-74; assoc. Venable, Baetjer & Howard, 1975-81, ptnr., 1982-91; judge U.S. Dist. Ct., Dist. Md., 1991—. Spl. reporter appeals com. and standing com. on rules of practice and procedure Ct. Appeals Md., 1983-85; faculty mem. nine day intensive trial advocacy program Md. Inst. Continuing Profl. Edn. for Lawyers, Inc., 1987, program on appellate advocacy, 1988; lectr. and panelist in field. Mem. editl. bd. Va. Law Rev., 1973-74; contbr. articles to profl. jours. Bd. dirs. Ctrl. Md. chpt. ARC, 1979-88, past chpt. gen. counsel; mem. adv. bd. Nat. Aquarium in Balt., 1987—; trustee Balt. Zoo. Mem. ABA (bus. torts litigation com. 1987), Md. State Bar Assn., Inc. (chmn. econs. of litigation com. 1981-82), Bar Assn. Balt. City (vice chmn. CLE com. 1986-87, chmn. 1987-88, exec. coun. 1987-88, judiciary com. 1989-90), The Serjeant's Inn Law Club, Order of Coif. Office: US Dist Ct 101 W Lombard St Ste 340 Baltimore MD 21201-2605

LEGG, WILLIAM JEFFERSON, lawyer; b. Enid, Okla., Aug. 20, 1925; s. Garl Paul and Mabel (Gensman) L.; m. Eva Imogene Hill, Dec. 16, 1950; children: Melissa Lou, Eva Diane, Janet Sue. Grad., Enid Bus. Coll., 1943; student, Pittsburg State U., 1944; BBA, U. Tex., Austin, 1946; JD, U. Tulsa, 1954. Bar: Okla. 1954, U.S. Supreme Ct., U.S. Ct. Appeals (10th cir.), U.S. Dist. Ct. (we. dist.) Okla.; ordained Cmty. of Christ, 1964. With aviation sales Phillips Petroleum Co., 1946-48; atty. Marathon Oil Co., 1954-61; pvt. practice Oklahoma City, 1962—; with Andrews Davis Legg Bixler Milsten & Price, Inc. and predecessor firms, 1962—, pres., 83-86, also dir., 1973-77, 80-81, 83-86, 90, sec., 1975-80, 82-83, 90; sr. counsel, 1991—. Adj. prof. law Oklahoma City U., 1975-80; lectr. Okla. U. Law Sch., 1986; bd. dirs., v.p. internat. oil cos., Turkey, Australia, Brunei, 1967-82; bd. dirs., gen. counsel N.J. Natural Resources Co., 1986-91; bd. dirs. Skillpath Seminars, Kansas City, Mo., 1994-98; lectr. energy seminars; rsch. fellow Southwestern Legal Found., Dallas, 1989—, mem. CLE adv. bd., 1998—. Contbr. articles to profl. jours. Mem. legal com. Okla. Gov.'s Energy Adv. Coun., Okla. Blue Ribbon Com. on Natural Gas Well Allowables, 1983; ordained Community of Christ formerly Reorganized Ch. of Jesus Christ of Latter Day Saints, 1964, dist, pres., 1975—80, br. pres., 1986—91, evangelist, 1993—; trustee Am. Inst. Discussion, 1962—88, chmn., 1969—76, now mem. exec. com., counsel; trustee Jenkins Found. Rsch., sec., 1975—81; trustee Restoration Trails Found., 1975, Graceland U., Lamoni, Iowa, 1986—2000, mem. exec. com., chmn. bus. affairs com., 1988—98, mem. investment com., 1998—2000; trustee Met. Lib. Endowment Trust, 1986—99, treas., 1988—99, chmn. investment com. With USN, 1943—46, lt. (j.g.) USNR, 1946—66. Mem. ABA, Okla. Bar Assn. (past com. chmn.), Oklahoma County Bar Assn. (past com. chmn.), Internat. Bar Assn., Internat. Assn. Energy Econs., Econ. Club Okla., Men's Dinner Club, Petroleum Club. Administrative and regulatory, Oil, gas, and mineral, State and local taxation. Home: 3017 Brush Creek Rd Oklahoma City OK 73120-1855 Office: Andrews Davis Legg Bixler Milsten & Price Inc 500 W Main St Ste 500 Oklahoma City OK 73102-2275

LEGH, ROBERT ANDREW, lawyer; b. Johannesburg, South Africa, Feb. 2, 1962; Matriculation, St. Stithians Coll., Johannesburg, 1978; B. Com, U. Witwatersrand, Johannesburg, 1981, LLB, 1983, MBA, 1993. Bar: Rep. South Africa, 1989. Candidate atty. Bowman Gilfillan, Inc., Johannesburg, S. Africa, 1986-88, profl. asst. S. Africa, 1988-89, assoc. ptnr. S. Africa, 1989-92, ptnr. S. Africa, 1992—. Author: Getting the Deal Through, 2000; The Handbook of Competition Regulators, 1999, Getting the Fine Down, 2001. Mem. Internat. Bar Assn., Law Soc. Transuass, The Country Club, Bryanston Country Club, Rand Club. Avocations: reading, traveling, playing golf. Antitrust, Finance, Mergers and acquisitions. Office: Bowman Gilfillan Twin Towers W Sandton City 9th Fl POB 785812 Sandton City 2146 South Africa

LEHAN, JONATHAN MICHAEL, judge; b. Los Angeles, Apr. 25, 1947; s. Bert Leon and Frances (Shapiro) L.; m. Annett Jean Garrett, Aug. 1, 1970; children: Joshua Michael, Melanie Janine. BA, Calif. State U., Fullerton, 1968; JD, Calif. Western Sch. Law, 1971; grad., Nat. Drug Ct. Inst., 2000. Bar: Calif. 1972, U.S. Dist. Ct. (no. dist.) Calif. 1973, U.S. Supreme Ct. 1975. Law clk. to presiding and assoc. justice Calif. Dist. Ct. Appeals, San Bernardino, 1971-73; dep. dist. atty. Mendocino County, Ukiah, Calif., 1973-76, coast asst. dist. atty. Fort Bragg, 1976-83; pvt. practice, 1983-84; ptnr. Lehan & Kronfeld, 1984-90; judge Mendocino County Superior Ct., Ft. Bragg, 1990—. Instr. Barstow C.C., Calif., 1972, Mendocino C.C., Ukiah, 1974-75, Coll. Redwoods, Ft. Bragg, 1981-82; seminar faculty Calif. Jud. Coll., U. Calif., Berkeley, 1993; faculty Calif. Judges Assn. Mid-Year Conf., 1998, ann. conf., 1999, Nat. Drug Ct. Inst., Nat. Ctr. for State Cts., Williamsburg, Va.; contbr. Calif. Drunk Driving Law, Kuwatch, 1995. Bd. dirs. Salmon Restoration Assn., Fort Bragg, Gloriana Opera Co., Mendocino, Mendocino Art Ctr. Editor Calif. Western Sch. Law Law Rev., 1971. Mem. ABA, Mendocino County Bar Assn. (pres. 1989), Phi Delta Phi, Mendocino C. of C. (bd. dirs.). Democrat. Avocations: violinist, violist, Mendocino string quartet. Office: Mendocino Superior Ct 700 S Franklin St Fort Bragg CA 95437-5464 E-mail: judgejon@judgejon.com

LEHMAN, JEFFREY SEAN, dean, law educator; b. Bronxville, N.Y., Aug. 1, 1956; s. Leonard and Imogene (McAuliffe) L.; m. Diane Celeste Becker, May 20, 1979; children: Rebecca Colleen, Jacob Keegan, Benjamin Emil. AB, Cornell U., 1977; M of Pub. Policy, JD, U. Mich., 1981. Bar: D.C. 1983, U.S. Ct. Appeals (fed. cir.) 1984, U.S. Ct. Appeals (D.C. cir.) 1987, U.S. Supreme Ct. 1987. Law clk. to chief judge U.S. Ct. Appeals (1st cir.), Portland, Maine, 1981-82; law clk. to assoc. justice U.S. Supreme Ct., Washington, 1982-83; assoc. Caplin & Drysdale, Chartered, 1983-87; asst. prof. U. Mich. Law Sch., Ann Arbor, 1987-92, prof., 1992-93, prof. law and pub. policy, 1993—, dean, 1994—. Vis. prof. Yale U., 1993, U. Paris II, 1994. Co-author: Corporate Income Taxation, 1994; editor-in-chief: Mich. Law Rev., 1979-80. Foster parent Arlington County Dept. Human Svcs., 1983-87; trustee Skadden Fellowship Found., 1995—. Henry Bates fellow, 1981. Mem. ABA, Am. Law Inst., Order of Coif. Democrat. Jewish. Office: U Mich Law Sch 324 Hutchins Hall 625 S State St Ann Arbor MI 48109-1215 E-mail: jlehman@umich.edu

LEHMAN, LARRY L. state supreme court justice; Judge Wyo. County Ct., 1985-88, Wyo. Dist. Ct. (2nd dist.), 1988-94; justice Wyo. Supreme Ct., Cheyenne, 1994-98, chief justice, 1998—. Office: Supreme Court Bldg 2301 Capitol Ave Cheyenne WY 82002-0001*

LEHMBERG, ROSEMARY, prosecutor; b. Taylor, Tex., Oct. 31, 1949; d. Seth Ward and RoseMary Lehmberg. BA in Natural Sci., U. Tex., 1972; JD, St. Marys U., San Antonio, 1974. Pvt. practice law, Austin, 1975-76; dist. atty. asst., 1976—. Office: Travis County Dist Atty PO Box 1748 Austin TX 78767-1748 also: Office Dist Atty Travis City Adminstrn Bldg 314 W 11th St Ste 200 Austin TX 78701-2112

LEHR, DENNIS JAMES, lawyer; b. N.Y.C., Feb. 7, 1932; s. Irwin Allen and Teeny (Scofield) L.; m. Enid J. Auerbach, June 10, 1956; children—Austin Windsor, Bryant Paul, Amy Lynn BA, NYU, 1954, LLM, 1961; LLB, Yale U., 1957. Bar: N.Y. 1959, D.C. 1967. Atty. Allstate Ins. Co., N.Y.C., 1958-59; atty. Regional Office SEC, 1959-61; assoc. Borden and Ball, 1961-63; atty. Office Spl Counsel Investment Co. Act Matters SEC, Washington, 1963-64; assoc. chief counsel Office Comptroller Currency U.S. Treasury Dept., 1964-67; assoc. Hogan & Hartson, 1967-69, ptnr., 1969-94, of counsel, 1994—. Bd. advs. So. Meth. U. Grad. Sch. Banking; adj. prof. Georgetown Law Sch., 1964-68; legal adv. com. Nat. Ctr. on Fin. Svcs., U. Calif.; lectr. Practicing Law Inst.; adv. coun. Banking Law Inst.; pub. mem. Adminstrv. Conf. of the U.S. Bd. contbrs. Fin. Services Law Report. Contbr. articles to profl. jours. Mem. ABA (coun. mem. sect. bus. law, former chmn. com. on Long Range Issues Affecting Bus. Law Practice, former chmn., com. on devels. in investment svcs, chmn. steering com. on Gavel Awards.). Office: Hogan and Hartson 555 13th St NW Ste 800E Washington DC 20004-1161

LEIB, JEFFREY M. lawyer; b. Detroit, Nov. 21, 1941; s. Samuel W. and Lois (Miller) L.; m. Bryna L. Linden, June 16, 1965; children: Lawrence Jay, Jayme Renee, Jodi Rachelle. BA, Mich. State U., 1964; JD, U. Detroit, 1967. Bar: Mich. 1968, U.S. Dist. Ct. (ea. dist.) Mich. 1968. Asst. prosecutor Oakland County, Pontiac, Mich., 1968-70; legal advisor Oakland Probate Ct., Pontiac, 1970-71; pres. Leib and Leib, P.C., 1971—; pros. atty. Orchard Lake City, Mich., 1975-78; gen. counsel Franks Nursery and Craft, Inc., Detroit, 1978-83, Beech Tool Co., Inc., Detroit. Author, co-chmn. campaign for constl. amendment Taxpayers United for Tax Limitation, 1978; planning commr. West Bloomfield Twp. (Mich.), 1971-83, trustee, councilman, 1984—; vice chmn. West Bloomfield Symphony Orch. 1976-80; bd. dirs. Temple Israel. Mem. Mich. Bar Assn., Oakland County Bar Assn. (chmn. young lawyers sect., chmn. spl. events com., bd. dirs. 1983—), Southfield Bar Assn. (pres. 1981-82) C. of C. (West Bloomfield chpt. pres. 1979-80, Businessman of Yr. award 1980). Jewish. Lodges: Optimist, B'nai B'rith. Personal injury, Probate, Real property. Office: Leib Leib & Kramer PC 26261 Evergreen Rd Southfield MI 48076-4447

LEIBENSPERGER, EDWARD PAUL, lawyer; b. Columbus, Ohio, Dec. 3, 1948; s. William P. and Ruth (Wylie) L.; m. Patricia Karns, Aug. 16, 1969; children— Kristen, Kenneth. B.A. magna cum laude, Muskingum Coll., 1970; J.D. summa cum laude, Ohio State U., 1974. Bar: Mass. 1974, U.S. Dist. Ct. Mass. 1974, U.S. Ct. Appeals (1st cir.) 1974; C.P.A., Ohio. Acct. Ernst & Whinney, Columbus, Ohio, 1970-71; ptnr. Nutter, McClennen & Fish, Boston, 1974— . Bd. dirs. Friends of Eye Research, Inc., Boston, 1984— . Mem. ABA (com. on corporate counsel 1982—), Boston Bar Assn. (spl. com. on profl. ethics 1984). Democrat. Unitarian. Federal civil litigation, Personal injury, Securities. Office: Nutter McClennen & Fish 1 International Pl Fl 15 Boston MA 02110-2699

LEIBOLD, ARTHUR WILLIAM, JR. lawyer; b. Ottawa, Ill., June 13, 1931; s. Arthur William and Helen (Cull) L.; m. Nora Collins, Nov. 30, 1957; children: Arthur William III, Alison Aubry, Peter Collins. AB, Haverford Coll., 1953; JD, U. Pa., 1956. Bar: Pa. 1957. With Dechert, Price & Rhoads, Phila., 1956-69, ptnr., 1965-69, Washington, 1972-97. Gen. counsel Fed. Home Loan Bank Bd. and Fed. Savs. & Loan Ins. Corp., Washington, 1969-72, Fed. Home Loan Mortgage Corp., 1970-72; lectr. English St. Joseph's Coll., Phila., 1957-59 Contbr. articles to profl. publs. Mem. Pres. Kennedy's Lawyers Com. Civil Rights, 1963, Adminstrv. Conf. U.S., 1969-72; bd. dirs. Marymount Coll. Va., 1974-75; Mem. Phila. Com. 70, 1965-74, Fellowship Commn. Mem. ABA (mem. ho. dels. 1967-69, 79-88, treas. 1979-83, mem. fin. com., mem. bd. govs. 1977-83), Fed. Bar Assn. (mem. nat. coun. 1971-80), D.C. Bar Assn., Phila. Bar Assn., Am. Bar Found. (treas. 1979-83), Am. Bar Ret. Assn. (dir. 1978-83), Am. Bar Endowment (bd. dirs. 1984-97, pres. 1995-97), Am. Bar Ins. (bd. dirs. 1999—), Phila. Country Club (Gladwyne, Pa.), Chester River Yacht and Country Club (Chestertown, Md.), Skating Club Phila., Orpheus Club (Phila.), Order of Coif, Phi Beta Kappa. Republican. Roman Catholic. Administrative and regulatory, Banking. Home: 200 River Shore Rd Chestertown MD 21620 Office: Dechert 1775 Eye St NW Ste 1100 Washington DC 20006-2424 E-mail: leibold1@aol.com, aleibold@dechert.com

LEIBOW, RONALD LOUIS, lawyer; b. Santa Monica, Calif., Oct. 4, 1939; s. Norman and Jessica (Kellner) L.; m. Linda Bengelsdorf, June 11, 1961 (div. Dec. 1974); children: Jocelyn Elise, Jeffrey David, Joshua Aaron; m. Jacqueline Blatt, Apr. 6, 1986. AB, Calif. State U., Northridge, 1962; JD, UCLA, 1965. Bar: Calif. 1966, U.S. Dist. Ct. (cen. dist.) Calif. 1966, U.S. Dist. Ct. (no., so. and ea. dists.) Calif. 1971. Spl. asst. city atty. City of Burbank, Calif., 1966-67; from assoc. to ptnr. Meyers, Stevens & Walters, L.A., 1967-71; ptnr. Karpf, Leibow & Warner, Beverly Hills, Calif., 1971-74, Volk, Newman Gralla & Karp, L.A., L.A., 1979-81, Spector & Leibow, L.A., 1982-84, Stroock & Stroock & Lavan, L.A., 1984-94, Kaye Scholer LLP, L.A., 1994—, mng. ptnr., 1996-97. Lectr. law UCLA, 1968-69; asst. prof. Calif. State U., Northridge, 1969-71. Contbr. articles to profl. jours. Pres. Jewish Cmty. Ctr., Greater L.A., 1983-86; vice chair Jewish Cmty. Ctr. Assn. N.Am., N.Y.C., 1988—; vice chair Jewish Fedn. Greater L.A., 1988—, chair planning and allocations com., 1998-2001; internat. bd., exec. com. Starlight Childrens Found., 1997—. Mem. ABA (bus. bankruptcy com.), Phi Alpha Delta. Avocations: writing, tennis, skiing, travel. Bankruptcy, Contracts commercial, Finance. Office: Kaye Scholer LLP 1999 Avenue Of The Stars Fl 16 Los Angeles CA 90067-6022 E-mail: rleibow@kaye.scholar.com

LEIBOWITT, SOL DAVID, lawyer; b. Bklyn., Feb. 18, 1912; s. Morris and Bella (Small) L.; m. Ethel Leibowi, June 18, 1950 (dec. Aug. 1985); m. Babs Lee, Dec. 28, 1986. BA, Lehigh U., 1933; LLB, Harvard U., 1936. Bar: N.Y. 1937, Conn. 1970. Pvt. practice, N.Y.C., 1937-84, Stamford, Conn., 1970-78, Milford, 1978-79; gen. counsel New Haven Clock and Watch Co., 1955-59, pres., 1958-59, Diagnon Corp., 1981-83, vice chmn., 1983-86. Chmn. Card Tech. Corp., 1983-85; dir. Data Card Internat. Corp., Hevant, Eng., 1977-79. Pres. Ethel and David Leibowitt Found.; dir. Am. Com. for Weizmann Inst. Sci.; mediator family law Supreme Ct. State Fla. 15th Jud. Ct., 1990—; arbitrator Am. Arbitration Assn., Fla.; chmn. Israel Cancer Assn. USA; dir. Am. Assocs., Ben-Gurion U., 1999. Recipient Human Rels. award Anti-Defamation League, 1969, Ethel Leibowitt Fund Johns Hopkins U. Sch. Medcine Meml. award Anti-Defamation League, 1971, Tikvah award Israel Cancer Assn., 1995. Mem. ABA, Assn. Bar N.Y.C., N.Y. State Bar Assn., Anti-Defamation League (commr.), Am. Soc. for Technion U. (mem. bd., v.p., Conn. pres.), Lotos Club, Harvard Club (N.Y.C.), Banyon Country Club (West Palm Beach, Fla.). General corporate.

LEIBOWITZ, MARVIN, lawyer; b. Phila., Jan. 24, 1950; s. Aaron and Etheln (Kashoff) L.; m. Faye Rebecca Liepack, Nov. 12, 1983; children: Cheryl Renée, Ellen Paulette. BA, Temple U., 1971, postgrad., 1971-72; JD, Widener U., 1976. Bar: Pa. 1977, N.J. 1977, U.S. Dist. Ct. N.J. 1977, U.S. Dist. Ct. (we. dist.) Pa. 1980. Atty.-advisor SSA, Pitts., 1977-95, sr. atty., 1995—; quality assurance reviewer Office of Program and Integrity Revs., 1997; pvt. practice Pitts., 1979—. Committeeman Phila. Dem. Com., 1973-77. Pa. State Scholar Pa. Higher Edn. Assistance Agy., Harrisburg, 1967-71; recipient U.S. Dept. Health and Human Svcs. Assoc. Commr.'s citation, 1994. Mem. Nat. Treasury Employees Union (regional steward 1982-99, regional v.p. 1999—), Pa. Bar Assn., Allegheny County Bar Assn. Democrat. Jewish. Administrative and regulatory, Bankruptcy, Workers' compensation. Home: 6501 Landview Rd Pittsburgh PA 15217-3000

LEIGHTON, GEORGE NEVES, retired federal judge; b. New Bedford, Mass., Oct. 22, 1912; s. Antonio N. and Anna Sylvia (Garcia) Leitao; m. Virginia Berry Quivers, June 21, 1942; children: Virginia Anne, Barbara Elaine. AB, Howard U., 1940; LLB, Harvard U., 1946; LLD, Elmhurst Coll., 1964; LLD., John Marshall Law Sch., 1973; LLD, Southeastern Mass. U., 1975, New Eng. U. Sch. Law, 1978, R.I. Coll., 1992, So. New Eng. Sch. Law, 2000; LLD (hon.), Loyola U., Chgo., 1989. Bar: Mass. 1946, Ill. 1947, U.S. Supreme Ct. 1958. Ptnr. Moore, Ming & Leighton, Chgo., 1951-59, McCoy, Ming & Leighton, Chgo., 1959-64; judge Cook County Circuit Ct., 1964-69, U.S. Ct. Appeals (1st cir.), 1969-76; U.S. dist. judge U.S. Dist. Ct. (no. dist.) Ill., 1976-86, sr. dist. judge, 1986-87; ret.; of counsel Earl L. Neal & Assocs., 1987—. Adj. prof. John Marshall Law Sch., Chgo., 1965—; commr., mem. character and fitness com. for 1st Appellate Dist., Supreme Ct. Ill., 1955-63, chmn. character and fitness com., 1961-62; joint com. for revision Ill. Criminal Code, 1959-63; chmn. Ill. adv. com. U.S. Commn. on Civil Rights, 1964; mem. pub. rev. bd. UAW, AFL-CIO, 1961-70; Asst. atty. gen. State of Ill., 1950-51; pres. 3d Ward Regular Democratic Orgn., Cook County, Ill., 1951-53; v.p. 21st Ward, 1964; spl. counsel to chmn. bd. Chgo. Transit Authority, 1988. Contbr. articles to legal jours. Bd. dirs. United Ch. Bd. for Homeland Ministries, United Ch. of Christ, Grant Hosp., Chgo.; trustee U. Notre Dame, 1979-83, trustee emeritus, 1983—; bd. overseers Harvard Coll., 1983-89. Capt., inf. AUS, 1942-45. Decorated Bronze Star; recipient Civil Liberties award Ill. div. ACLU, 1961, U.S. Supreme Ct. Justice John Paul Stevens award, 2000, Father Agustus Tolton awardCath. Archdioceses Chgo., 2000; named Chicagoan of Year in Law and Judiciary Jr. Assn. Commerce and Industry, 1964, Laureate, Acad. Ill. Lawyers, 2000. Fellow ABA (chmn. coun. 1976, mem. coun. sect. legal edn. and admissions to bar), Am. Coll. Trial Lawyers; mem. NAACP (chmn. legal redress com. Chgo. br.), John Howard Assn. (bd. dirs.), Chgo. Bar Assn., Ill. Bar Assn. (joint com. mem. for revision jud. article 1959-62, sr. counselor 1996), Nat. Harvard Law Sch. Assn. (mem. coun.), Howard U. Chgo. Alumni Club (chmn. bd. dirs.), Phi Beta Kappa. Office: Earl L Neal & Assocs 111 W Washington St Ste 1700 Chicago IL 60602-2711

LEIKEN, EARL MURRAY, lawyer; b. Cleve., Jan. 19, 1942; s. Manny and Betty G. L.; m. Ellen Kay Miner, Mar. 26, 1970; children: Jonathan, Brian. BA magna cum laude, Harvard U., 1964, JD cum laude, 1967. Asst. dean, assoc. prof. law Case Western Res. U., Cleve., 1967-71; ptnr. Hahn, Loeser, Freedheim, Dean & Wellman, 1971-86, Baker & Hostetler, Cleve., 1986—. Adj. faculty, lectr. law Case Western Res. U., 1971-86. Pres. Shaker Heights (Ohio) Bd. Edn., 1986-88, Jewish Community Ctr., Cleve., 1988-91, Shaker Heights Family Ctr., 1994-97; mem. Shaker Heights City Coun., 2000—. Named one of Greater Cleve.'s 10 Outstanding Young Leaders, Cleve. Jaycees, 1972; recipient Kane award Cleve. Jewish Community Fedn., 1982. Mem. ABA, Greater Cleve. Bar Assn. (chmn. labor law sect. 1978). Federal civil litigation, State civil litigation, Labor. Home: 20815 Colby Rd Cleveland OH 44122-1903 Office: Baker & Hostetler 3200 Nat City Ctr 1900 E 9th St Ste 3200 Cleveland OH 44114-3475

LEINENWEBER, HARRY D. federal judge; b. Joliet, Ill., June 3, 1937; s. Harry Dean and Emily (Lennon) L.; m. Lynn Morley Martin, Jan. 7, 1987; 5 children; 2 stepchildren. AB cum laude, U. Notre Dame, 1959; JD, U. Chgo., 1962. Bar: Ill. 1962, U.S. Dist. Ct. (no. dist.) Ill. 1967. Assoc. Dunn, Stefanich, McGarry & Kennedy, Joliet, Ill., 1962-65, ptnr., 1965-79; city atty. City of Joliet, 1963-67; spl. counsel Village of Park Forest, Ill., 1967-74; spl. prosecutor County of Will, 1968-70; spl. counsel Village of Bolingbrook, 1975-77, Will County Forest Preserve, 1977; mem. Ill. Ho. of Reps., Springfield, 1973-83, chmn. judiciary I com., 1981-83; ptnr. Dunn, Leinenweber & Dunn, Joliet, 1979-86; fed. judge U.S. Dist. Ct. (no. dist.) Ill., Chgo., 1986—. Bd. dirs. Will County Bar Assn., 1984-86, State Jud. Adv. Coun., 1973-85, sec. 1975-76; tchr. legis. process seminar U. Ill., Chgo., 1988—; mem. U. Ill. Inst. Govt. and Pub. Affairs Nat. Adv. Com., 1998—. Bd. dirs. Will County Legal Assistance Found., 1982-86, Good Shepard Manor, 1981—, Am. Cancer Soc., 1981-85, Joliet (Ill.) Montessori Sch., 1966-74; del. Rep. Nat. Conv., 1980; precinct committeeman, 1966-86; mem. nat. adv. com. U. Ill. Inst. Govt. and Pub. Affairs, 1998—. Recipient Environ. Legislator Golden award. Mem. Will County Bar Assn. (mem. jud. adv. coun., 1973-85, sec. 1975-76, bd. dirs. 1984-86), Nat. Conf. Commrs. on Uniform State Laws (exec. com. 1991-93, elected life mem. 1996), The Law Club of Chgo. (bd. dirs. 1996-98). Roman Catholic. Office: US Dist Ct 219 S Dearborn St Ste 1946 Chicago IL 60604-1801

LEIPHAM, JAY EDWARD, lawyer; b. Wilbur, Wash., Dec. 24, 1946; s. Albert Ellsworth and Margaret Lucille (Thomson) L.; m. Arlene R. Fegles, July 31, 1976; children: Hunter, Celeste. BA in Polit. Sci. with high honors, Wash. State U., 1969; JD, U. Chgo., 1972. Bar: Wash. 1973, U.S. Dist. Ct. (we. dist.) Wash. 1973, U.S. Dist. Ct. (ea. dist.) Wash. 1979. Assoc. Hullin, Roberts, Mines, Fite & Riveland, Seattle, 1973-76, Skeel, McKelvy, Henke, Evenson & Betts, Seattle, 1976-79, Underwood, Campbell, Brock, & Cerutti P.S., Spokane, Wash., 1979-80, prin., v.p., 1980-91, chmn. bd. dirs., CEO, 1991-93; prin., v.p., sec. Richter-Wimberley, P.S., 1995—. Mem. ABA, ATLA, Wash. State Bar Assn., Spokane Bar Assn., Wash. State Trial Lawyers Assn., Def. Rsch. Inst., Wash. Def. Trial Lawyers, Phi Beta Kappa, Phi Kappa Phi. Presbyterian. E-mila. General civil litigation, Personal injury. Home: 1028 N Summit Blvd Spokane WA 99201-3042 Office: Richter-Wimberley PS 1300 Seafirst Fin Ctr Spokane WA 99201 E-mail: jayleipham@richter-wimberley.com

LEISURE, PETER KEETON, federal judge; b. N.Y.C., Mar. 21, 1929; s. George S. and Lucille E. (Pelouze) L.; m. Kathleen Blair; Feb. 27, 1960; children: Lucille K. (dec.), Mary Blair, Kathleen K. B.A., Yale U., 1952; LL.B., U. Va., 1958. Bar: N.Y. 1959, U.S. Supreme Ct. 1966, D.C. 1979, U.S. Dist. Ct. Conn. 1981. Assoc. Breed, Abbott & Morgan, 1958-61; asst. U.S. atty. So. Dist. N.Y., 1962-66; partner firm Curtis, Mallet-Prevost, Colt & Mosle, 1967-78; ptnr. Whitman & Ransom, N.Y.C., 1978-84; judge U.S. Dist. Ct. So. N.Y., New York, NY, 1984—. Bd. dirs. Retarded Infants Svcs., 1968-78, pres., 1971-75; bd. dirs. Community Coun. of Greater N.Y., 1972-79, Youth Consultation Svcs., 1971-78; trustee Ch. Club of N.Y., 1973-81, 87-90; mem. jud. ethics com. Jud. Conf., 1990-93, fin disclosure com. 1st lt. USAR, 1953-55. Recipient Ellis Island medal of honor, 2000. Fellow Am. Bar Found., Am. Coll. Trial Lawyers; mem. ABA, Am. Law Inst., Fed. Judges Assn., Am. Judges Assn., D.C. Bar Assn., Fed. Bar Coun. (trustee, v.p. 1973-78), Bar Assn. City of N.Y., Nat. Lawyers Club (hon.). Office: US Dist Ct 1910 US Courthouse 500 Pearl St New York NY 10007-1316

LEITNER, GREGORY MARC, lawyer; b. Chattanooga, Apr. 19, 1957; s. Paul Revers and Suzanne Joy Leitner; m. Sheryl Leitner; children: Gregory Marc, Charlotte Anne, Lauren Elizabeth, Ashley Meredith. BA cum laude, Memphis State U., 1978; JD, U. Tenn., Knoxville, 1980. Bar: Tenn. 1981, U.S. Dist. Ct. (ea. dist.) 1981, U.S. Ct. Appeals (6th cir.) 1983, U.S. Ct. Appeals (11th cir.) 1988. Ptnr. Leitner, Warner, Moffitt, Williams, Dooley, Carpenter et al, Chattanooga, 1986-2001; mem. Husch & Eppenberger, 2001—. Mem. ABA, Tenn. Bar Assn., Pi Sigma Alpha, Phi Delta Phi. Republican. Methodist. Avocations: fishing, politics, international politics, history. General civil litigation, Contracts commercial, Intellectual property. Home: 6259 Forest Trl Signal Mountain TN 37377-2807 E-mail: gleitner@husch.com

LEITNER, PAUL REVERE, lawyer; b. Winnsboro, S.C., Nov. 11, 1928; s. W. Walker and Irene (Lewis) L.; m. Jeannette C. Card, Mar. 16, 1985; children by previous marriage: David, Douglas, Gregory, Reid, Cheryl. AB, Duke U., 1950; LLB, McKenzie Coll., 1954. Bar: Tenn. 1954; cert. civil trial specialist Nat. Bd. Trial Advocacy and Tenn. Commn. on CLE and Specialization. Pvt. practice law, Chattanooga, 1954; assoc. Leitner, Williams, Dooley & Napolitan and predecessor firms, 1952-57; ptnr. Leitner, Warner, Moffitt, Williams, Dooley, Carpenter & Napolitan and predecessor firms, 1957—. Tenn. chmn. Def. Rsch. Inst., 1978-89. Bd. dirs. Family Service Agy., 1957-63, Chattanooga Symphony and Opera Assn., 1986-89, sec., 1987-89; mem. Chattanooga-Hamilton County Community Action Bd.; mem. Juvenile Ct. Commn., Hamilton County, 1955-61, chmn., 1958-59; chmn. Citizens Com. for Better Schs.; mem. Met. Govt. Charter Commn. Served with U.S. Army, 1946-47. Named Young Man of Yr. Chattanooga Area, 1957 Fellow Am. Coll. Trial Lawyers, Tenn. Bar. Found, Chattanooga Bar Found. (founding); mem. ABA, Tenn. Bar Assn., Jaycees (Chattanooga, pres. 1956-57), Fed. Ins. Corp. Counsel, Internat. Assn. Def. Coun., Trial Attys. Am., Tenn. Def. Lawyers Assn. (pres. 1975-76), Am. Bd. Trial Advs. (advocate), U.S. Sixth Cir. Jud. Conf. (life). Methodist. Federal civil litigation, State civil litigation, Personal injury. Home: 3926 Windward Ln Soddy Daisy TN 37379 E-mail: pleitner@leitnerfirm.com

LEMANN, THOMAS BERTHELOT, lawyer; b. New Orleans, Jan. 3, 1926; s. Monte M. and Nettie E. (Hyman) L.; m. Barbara M. London, Apr. 14, 1951 (dec. 1999); children: Nicholas B., Nancy E.; m. Sheila Bosworth Bell, June 1, 2000. A.B. summa cum laude, Harvard U., 1949, LL.B., 1952; M.C.L., Tulane U., 1953. Bar: La. 1953. Assoc. Monroe & Lemann, New Orleans, 1953-58, ptnr., 1958-98; of counsel Liskow & Lewis, 1998—. Bd. dirs. B. Lemann & Bro., Mermentau Mineral and Land Co., So. States Land & Timber Corp., Avrico Inc.; advisory bd. dirs. Riviana Foods. Contbr. articles to profl. publs. Mem. council La. State Law Inst., sec. trust adv. com.; chmn. Mayor's Cultural Resources Com., 1970-75; pres. Arts Coun. Greater New Orleans, 1975-80, bd. dirs.; mem. vis. com. art museums Harvard U., 1974-80; trustee Metairie Park Country Day Sch., 1956-71, pres., 1967-70, New Orleans Philharmonic Symphony Soc., 1956-78, Flint-Goodridge Hosp., 1960-70, La. Civil Service League, pres., 1974-76, New Orleans Mus. Art, 1986-92; bd. dirs. Zemurray Found., Hever Found., Parkside Found., Azby Fund, Azby Art Fund, Greater New Orleans Found., Arts Coun. New Orleans, Musica da Camera. Served with AUS, 1944-46, PTO. Mem. ABA, La. Bar Assn. (bd. govs. 1977-78), New Orleans Bar Assn., Assn. Bar City N.Y., Am. Law Inst., Soc. Bartolus, Phi Beta Kappa. Jewish. Clubs: New Orleans Country, Wyvern (New Orleans). Estate planning, Probate, Estate taxation. Home: 6020 Garfield St New Orleans LA 70118-6039 Office: Liskow & Lewis 701 Poydras St Ste 5000 New Orleans LA 70139-5099 E-mail: tblemann@liskow.com

LEMBO, VINCENT JOSEPH, lawyer; b. Brookline, Mass., Sept. 30, 1950; s. Peter Anthony and Dorothy Marie (Nolan) L.; m. Carol Helen Paciorkowski, July 8, 1973; children: Elisabeth, Julianne, Michael. BA in Polit. Sci., Northeastern U., 1973, MD, 1976. Bar: Mass. 1977. Law clk. R.I. Supreme Ct., Providence, 1977-78; assoc. Lavine & Sutherland, Woonsocket, R.I., 1978-79; assoc. dir. govt. rels. Northeastern U., Boston, 1980-87, legal counsel, 1982—. Asst. sec. bd. trustees, 1984-88, sec. bd. overseers and bd. trustees, 1988—, mem. supervisory com. Credit Union, 1983-95. Mem. Nat. Assn. Coll. & Univ. Attys., Boston Bar Assn., Club Passim (bd. dirs. 2000, Knight of the Holy Sepulchre), Phi Kappa Phi (sec. Northeastern U. chpt. 1987-90). Roman Catholic. Education and schools, Legislative. Office: Northeastern U 360 Huntington Ave Boston MA 02115-5005 E-mail: v.lembo@nvnet.neu.edu

LEMEIN, GREGG D. lawyer; b. Chgo., Feb. 2, 1950; BS with high honors, U. Ill., 1972; MM with distinction, JD magna cum laude, Northwestern U., 1976. Bar: Ill. 1976, U.S. Claims Ct. 1978, U.S. Tax Ct. 1979. Ptnr. Baker & McKenzie, Chgo. Office: Baker & McKenzie 1 Prudential Plz 130 E Randolph St Ste 3700 Chicago IL 60601-6342

LEMLE, ROBERT SPENCER, lawyer; b. N.Y.C., Mar. 6, 1953; s. Leo Karl and Gertrude (Bander) L.; m. Roni Sue Kohen, Sept. 5, 1976; children: Zachary, Joanna. AB, Oberlin Coll., 1975; JD, NYU, 1978. Bar: N.Y. 1979. Assoc. Cravath, Swaine & Moore, N.Y.C., 1978-82; assoc. gen. counsel Cablevision Sys. Corp., Woodbury, N.Y., 1982-84, v.p., gen. counsel, 1984-86, sr. v.p., gen. counsel, sec., 1986-94, exec. v.p., gen. counsel, sec., 1994-2001, vice chmn., gen. counsel, sec., 2001—; vice chmn. Madison Sq. Garden, 1999—. Bd. editors Cable TV and New Media Law and Fin., N.Y.C., 1983-99, bd. dirs. Cablevision Systems Corp., 1988—. Bd. trustees L.I. Children's Mus., 1990—, pres., 1996—; bd. trustees Oberlin Coll., 1996—. Mem. ABA, N.Y. State Bar Assn. Avocation: real estate. General corporate, Entertainment. Office: Cablevision Systems Corp 1111 Stewart Ave Bethpage NY 11714-3581 E-mail: rlemle@cablevision.com

LEMLY, THOMAS ADGER, lawyer; b. Dayton, Ohio, Jan. 31, 1943; s. Thomas Moore and Elzabeth (Adger) L.; m. Kathleen Brame, Nov. 24, 1984; children: Elizabeth Hayden, Joanna Marsden, Isabelle Stafford, Kate Brame. BA, Duke U., 1970; JD with honors, U. N.C., 1973. Bar: Wash. 1973, U.S. Dist. Ct. (we. dist.) Wash. 1973, U.S. Ct. Appeals (9th cir.) 1975, U.S. Supreme Ct. 1980. Assoc. Davis Wright Tremaine, Seattle, 1973-79, ptnr., 1979—. Contbg. editor Employment Discrimination Law, 1984-87, 94—; editor Wash., Oreg., Alaska and Calif. Employment Law Deskbooks, 1987—. Chmn. Pacific Coast Labor Conf., Seattle, 1983; trustee Plymouth Congregational Ch., 1980-84, Seattle Opera Assn., 1991—. Mem. ABA (labor employment law sect. 1975—, subcom. chmn. 1984-90, govt. liaison com. 1982—), Seattle-King County Bar Assn. (chmn. labor sect.), Assn. Wash. Bus. (trustee 1992—, chmn. human resources coun. 1993—, chmn. employment law task force 1987-93), U. N.C. Bar Found. (bd. dirs. 1973-76), Seattle Duke Alumni Assn. (pres. 1979-84), Order of Coif, Wash. Athletic Club (Seattle), Rotary. Republican. Presbyterian. General civil litigation, Labor. Home: 1614 7th Ave W Seattle WA 98119-2919 Office: Davis Wright Tremaine 2600 Century Sq 1501 4th Ave Seattle WA 98101-1688 E-mail: tomlemly@dwt.com

LEMON, WILLIAM JACOB, lawyer; b. Covington, Va., Oct. 25, 1932; s. James Gordon and Elizabeth (Wilson) L.; m. Barbara Inez Boyle, Aug. 17, 1957; children: Sarah E. Lemon Ludwig, William Tucker, Stephen Weldon. BA, Washington & Lee U., 1957, JD, 1959. Bar: Va. 1959. Assoc. Martin, Martin & Hopkins, Roanoke, Va., 1959-61; ptnr. Martin, Hopkins & Lemon, 1962—. Trustee Washington and Lee U., Lexington, Va., 1988-97, North Cross Sch., Roanoke, 1995—; pres. Specific Reading and Learning Difficulties Assn. Shedd Early Learning Ctr., 1985-86, George C. Marshall Found., Lexington, Va., 1997—. With U.S. Army, 1952-54. Mem. Va. Bar Assn., Roanoke Bar Assn. (pres. 1982-83), Va. State Bar, Shenandoah Club. Presbyterian. Avocations: farming, hunting, travel. Health, Probate, Real property. Office: Martin Hopkins Lemon First Union Tower 10 S Jefferson St Ste 1000 Roanoke VA 24011-1314 also: PO Box 13366 Roanoke VA 24033-3366

LEMONS, DONALD W. judge; b. Feb. 22, 1949; Justice Supreme Ct. Va., 2000—. Office: Supreme Ct Bldg 100 N Ninth St Richmond VA 23219 also: PO Box 1315 Richmond VA 23218-1315*

LENAGH, THOMAS HUGH, lawyer, financial advisor; b. Lawrence, Mass., Nov. 1, 1920; s. Frank Albert and Bethia (Coultar) L.; m. Leila Semple Fellner; children: Katherine, Thomas C., Jessie W. BA, Williams Coll., 1941; LLB, Columbia U., 1948. Analyst Cyrus J. Lawrence, N.Y.C., 1953-59; mgr. research service Goodbody & Co., 1959-61; asst. treas. Ford Found., 1961-64, treas., 1964-78; fin. v.p. Aspen Inst., 1978-80; chmn., chief exec. officer Greiner Engring., Los Angeles, 1982-85; chmn. bd. Inrad Corp. Bd. dirs. Gintel Fund, Adams Express, Petroleum & Resources Fund, Inrad Inc., ICN Pharms., Cornerstone Strategic Fund, Progressive Return Fund. Chmn. N.Y. YWCA, N.Y.C., 1975-92. Served with USN, 1941-46, capt. USNR, 1950-53. Mem. Chartered Fin. Analyst, N.Y. Soc. Security Analyst, Conn. Bar Assn. Republican. Club: Williams. Home: 13 Allens Corner Rd Flemington NJ 08822-5620

LENARD, GEORGE DEAN, lawyer; b. Joliet, Ill., Aug. 26, 1957; s. Louis George and Jennie (Helopoulos) L.; m. Nancy Ilene Sundquist, Nov. 11, 1989. BS, Ill. State U., 1979; JD, Thomas Cooley Law Sch., 1984. Bar: Ill. 1984, U.S. Dist. Ct. (no. dist.) Ill. 1984, U.S. Ct. Appeals (6th cir.) 1998, U.S. Supreme Ct. 1990, Mich. 1998, Ariz. 1999, Calif. 2001. Asst. states atty. Will County States Attys. Office, Joliet, 1984-88; pvt. practice law, 1988—. Mem. ABA, ATLA, Nat. Assn. Criminal Def. Lawyers, State Bar Ariz., State Bar Mich., State Bar Calif., Phi Alpha Delta (Isaac P. Christiancy chpt.). Avocation: golf. Constitutional, Criminal. Office: 81 N Chicago St Ste 206 Joliet IL 60432-4383

LENGA, J. THOMAS, lawyer; b. Toledo, Dec. 16, 1942; s. Casimir M. and Rose C. (Sturniolo) L.; children by previous marriage: Christina M., John Thomas Jr., Peter M. BA, U. Toledo, 1965, JD, 1968. Bar: Mich. 1968, Ohio 1968. Capt. JAGC U.S. Army, 1968—72; mem. Dykema Gossett PLLC, Detroit, 1972-96; mem Clark Hill P.L.C., 1996-2000, CEO, 2001—. Mem. com. on std. jury instrns. Mich. Supreme Ct.; advocate Am. Bd. of Trial Advocates. Named Disting. Alumnus, Coll. Law, U. Toledo, 1987. Fellow Internat. Acad. Trial Lawyers; mem. Detroit Bar Assn. (pres. 1989-90), State Bar Mich. (bd. commrs. 1992—, treas. 1995-96, v.p. 1996-97, pres.-elect 1997-98, pres. 1998-99), Internat. Assn. Def. Counsel. General civil litigation, Product liability. Office: Clark Hill PLC 500 Woodward Ave Ste 3500 Detroit MI 48226-3435 E-mail: tlenga@clarkhill.com

LENHART, JAMES THOMAS, lawyer; b. Cambridge, Mass., Nov. 3, 1946; s. James Wills and Martha Agnes (Everly) L.; m. Lynn Dexter Stevens, June 21, 1969; children: Amanda Brooks, James Edward, Abigail Ames. Cert. in History, U. Edinburgh, 1967; AB, Columbia U., 1968, JD, 1972. Bar: N.Y. 1973, D.C. 1974. Clk. to judge U.S. Dist. Ct. (so. dist.) N.Y., 1972-73; assoc. Shaw, Pittman, Potts & Trowbridge, Washington, 1973-79; ptnr. Shaw, Pittman, Potts & Trowbridge (now Shaw Pittman), 1980—. Adj. prof. Cornell Law Sch., 1992-93; instr. Washington Coll. Law of Am. U., Washington, 1976-78. Chair exec. com. Westmoreland Congregational Ch., Washington, 1989, bd. dirs., 1978-79, 83-84. Harlan Fiske Stone scholar Columbia U., 1968-69, 71-72. Mem. ABA, D.C. Bar Assn., Am. Law Inst., D.C. Def. Lawyers Assn., Fed. City Club, The Barristers. Democrat. Mem. United Ch. of Christ. Federal civil litigation, Personal injury, Securities. Office: Shaw Pittman 2300 N St NW Fl 5 Washington DC 20037-1172 E-mail: Thomas.Lenhart@Shawpittman.com

LENOFF, MICHELE MALKA, lawyer; b. Balt., Apr. 10, 1961; d. Israel and Dina (Munz) Drazin; m. Steven Lenoff, Sept. 23, 1984; children: Michael Monroe, Jonathan David, Joseph Nathan, Rachel Lauren. BA cum laude, Bar-Ilan U., Ramat Gan, Israel, 1979; MA in Clin. Psychology, U. Md., 1981; JD cum laude, Nova U., 1986. Bar: Fla. 1987, U.S. Dist. Ct. (so. dist.) Fla. 1991. Therapist Rosewood Hosp., Balt., 1981-82; psycologist Young Adult Inst., N.Y., 1982-83; law clk. Md. Pub. Defender's Office, Balt., 1984; law clk. to presiding justice Fla. Cir. Ct., Ft. Lauderdale, 1985; assoc. McCune & Hiaasen, 1985-88; ptnr. Lenoff & Lenoff P.A., Deerfield Beach, Fla., 1988—; of counsel Law Office of Robert T. Carlilie, 1988-91, G. Ware Cornell Jr., Ft. Lauderdale, Fla., 1988-90. Adj. prof. Howard Community Coll., Columbia, Md., 1981-82; legal rsch. and writing instr. Nova U. Ctr. for the Study of Law, Ft. Lauderdale, 1988-89. Mem. Nova Law Rev., 1985-86. Goodwin fellow Nova U., 1986. Mem. ABA, Fla. Bar Assn. Republican. Jewish. Estate planning, Probate, Real property. Office: Lenoff & Lenoff 1761 W Hillsboro Blvd Ste 405 Deerfield Beach FL 33442-1563

LEON, RICHARD J. lawyer, former government official; b. South Natick, Mass., Dec. 3, 1949; s. Silvano B. and Rita (O'Rorke) L.; m. M-Christine Costa; Nicholas Cavanagh. AB, Holy Cross Coll., 1971; JD cum laude, Suffolk Law Sch., 1974; LLM, Harvard U., 1981. Bar: R.I. 1975, U.S. Ct. Appeals (2d cir.) 1977, U.S. Dist. Ct. R.I. 1976, U.S. Supreme Ct. 1984, D.C. 1991, U.S. Dist. Ct. D.C. 1991, U.S. Ct. Appeals (D.C. cir.) 1991. Law clk. to justices Superior Ct. Mass., 1974-75, to justice R.I. Supreme Ct., 1975-76; spl. asst. U.S. atty. U.S. Attys. Office (so. dist.) N.Y., 1977-78; asst. prof. law St. John's U. Law Sch., 1979-83; sr. trial atty., criminal sect., tax div. U.S. Dept. Justice, Washington, 1983-87, dep. asst. atty. gen. environment and natural resources divsn., 1988-89; ptnr. Baker & Hostetler, Washington, 1989—; dep. chief minority counsel House Select Iran-Contra Com., 1987; active Jud. Conf. D.C. cir., 1991—, Pres. Commn. on White House Fellowships, 1990-93; chief minority counsel House Fgn. Affairs Com. 'October Surprise' Task Force, 1992; mem. admissions and grievances com. U.S. Ct. Appeals D.C. cir., 1994—; spl. counsel house banking com. Whitewater investigation, 1994. Author: (chpt.) Environmental Crime, Lawyers' Desk Book on White Collar Crime, 1991; contbr. articles to legal jours. Bd. trustees Suffolk U., 1990—. Mem. ABA, Order of Barristers, R.I. Bar Assn., Fed. Bar Council, Suffolk Law Sch. Assn. Met. N.Y. (past pres.), Suffolk Law Sch. Assn. Met. Washington (past pres.). Clubs: Harvard of N.Y.C., Harvard of Boston, University (Washington). Republican. Roman Catholic. Office: Baker & Hostetler 1050 Connecticut Ave NW Washington DC 20036-5304

LEON, ROLANDO LUIS, lawyer; b. Ponce, P.R., Oct. 18, 1952; s. Luis Manuel and Patricia (Cruz) L.; m. Janet Williams, May 20, 1994; children: Brandon Alexandre, Bryan Christopher, Lauren Patricia. BA in Govt., U. Tex., Arlington, 1972; JD, Tex. Tech. U., 1975; MS in Pub. Adminstrn., Golden Gate U., 1979. Bar: Tex. 1976, U.S. Ct. Mil. Appeals 1977, U.S Dist. Ct. (we., so. dists) Tex. 1981, U.S. Ct. Appeals (5th cir.) 1985; cert. in personal injury and civil trial law Tex. Bd. Legal Specialization, 1985; cert. civil trial advocacy Nat. Bd. Trial Advocacy, 1990. Ptnr. Thornton, Summers, Biechlin, Dunham & Brown LC, Corpus Christi, Tex., 1980-99; mng. ptnr. Barker, Leon, Fancher & Matthys, LLP, 2000—. Editor: Tex. Tech. U. Law Rev., 1974-75. Lt. USN, 1976-80. Mem. ABA, Tex. Bar Assn., Assn. Trial Lawyers Am. General civil litigation, Insurance, Personal injury. Office: Barker Leon Fancher & Matthys LLP Ste 1200 555 N Carancahua St Corpus Christi TX 78478 E-mail: rleon@blfmlaw.com

LEONARD, ARTHUR SHERMAN, law educator, journalist; b. Bklyn., Jan. 17, 1952; s. Harold A. and Jean (Moverman) L. BS in Indsl. and Labor Rels., Cornell U., 1974; JD cum laude, Harvard U., 1977. Bar: N.Y. 1978, U.S. Dist. Ct. (so. and ea. dists.) N.Y. 1978, U.S. Ct. Appeals (7th cir.) 1981, U.S. Supreme Ct. 1986. Assoc. Kelley Drye & Warren, N.Y.C., 1977-78, Seyfarth, Shaw, Fairweather & Geraldson, N.Y.C., 1979-82; asst. prof. law N.Y. Law Sch., 1982-83, assoc. prof., 1983-88, prof., 1988—. Lectr. in legal issues of AIDS and Lesbian and Gay Rights. Author: Sexuality & The Law: An Encyclopedia of Major Legal Cases, 1993; co-author: AIDS: Law in a Nutshell, 1991, AIDS Law and Policy: Cases and Materials, 2d edit., 1995; editor Lesbian/Gay Law Notes, 1978—; legal reporter, columnist Outweek, N.Y.C., 1989-91, L.G.N.Y., 1995—; contbr. articles to legal jours. Mem. Nat. Gay and Lesbian Task Force; active ACLU; bd. dirs. Jewish Bd. Family & Children's Svcs., N.Y.C., 1994—, Lambda Legal Def. and Edn. Fund, 1983-90, mem. legal com.; bd. dirs. Congregation Beth Simchat Torah, N.Y.C., 1988-90, Madrigal House, Inc., 1995-96; bd. dirs. Ctr. Lesbian and Gay Studies, CUNY, 1996-99; legal cons. World Congress Gay/Lesbian Jewish Orgns.; adminstr. Ind. Dem. Jud. Screen Panel, N.Y. County, 1983; fin. sec. Ind. Suwalk & Vicinity Benevolent Assn., 1990-97, pres., 1997—; nat. bd. Harvard Law Sch. Assn. Com. Gay, Lesbian & Bisexual Alumni, 1993—; mem. ind. Dem. jud. panel N.Y. county, 2001. Mem. ABA (com. rights of gay people, chmn. com. state constitutional rights 1994-96), Assn. of Bar of City of N.Y. (com. labor and employment law 1985-87, chmn. com. sex. and law 1987-90, co-chmn. com. gays and lesbians in legal profession 1991-94, mem. com. AIDS 1987-96), Am. Assn. Law Schs. (chmn. sect. gay/lesbian legal issues 1986, com. curriculum), ACLU, Soc. Am. Law Tchrs. (bd. govs.), Bar Assn. Human Rights of Greater N.Y. (pres. 1984-89). Home: 246 W End Ave Apt 8C New York NY 10023-3621 Office: NY Law Sch 57 Worth St New York NY 10013-2959 E-mail: aleonard@nyls.edu

LEONARD, EDWIN DEANE, lawyer; b. Oakland, Calif., Apr. 22, 1929; s. Edwin Stanley and Gladys Eugenia (Lee) L.; m. Judith Swatland, July 10, 1954; children: Garrick Hillman, Susanna Leonard Hill, Rebecca Leonard McCauley, Ethan York. BA, The Principia, 1950; LLB, Harvard U., 1953; LLM, George Washington U., 1956. Bar: D.C. 1953, Ill. 1953, N.Y. 1957. Assoc. Davis Polk Wardwell Sunderland & Kiendl, N.Y.C., 1956-61; ptnr. Davis Polk & Wardwell, 1961-97, sr. counsel, 1998—. Trustee the Brearley Sch., N.Y.C., 1980-90. Served to 1st lt. JAGC, 1953-56. Mem. ABA, N.Y. Bar Assn., N.Y. County Bar Assn., Assn. of Bar of City of N.Y. (chmn. various coms.). General corporate, Mergers and acquisitions, Securities. Home: 157 Conklin Hill Rd Stanfordville NY 12581-5639 Office: Davis Polk & Wardwell 450 Lexington Ave Fl 31 New York NY 10017-3982 E-mail: deaneleonard@worldnet.att.net

LEONARD, JEFFREY S. lawyer; b. Bklyn., Sept. 14, 1945; m. Maxine L. Bortnick, Dec. 28, 1967; children: Deborah, Jennifer. AB in History, U. Rochester, 1967; JD, U. Ariz., 1974. Bar: Ariz. 1974; U.S. Dist. Ct. Ariz. 1974, U.S. Ct. Appeals (9th cir.) 1974, U.S. Supreme Ct. 1985. Law clk. to judge U.S. Dist. Ct. Ariz., 1974-75. Mem. editl. bd. Ariz. Law Rev., 1973-74. Mem. Order of Coif. Federal civil litigation, State civil litigation. Office: Leonard Collins & Kelly PC Two Renaissance Sq 40 N Central Ave Ste 2500 Phoenix AZ 85004-4405 E-mail: jleonard@lck.net

LEONARD, LOUIS G., III, lawyer; b. Hartford, Conn., Aug. 5, 1972; s. Louis Golden Jr. and Phyllis Leahey Leonard. AB in Classics and Govt. magna cum laude, Georgetown U., 1994; JD in Environ. Law magna cum laude, Boston Coll., 1997. Bar: Mass. 1997. Law clk. to Hon. Douglas P. Woodlock U.S. Dist. Ct., Boston, 1997-98; honors program atty. Office of Solicitor, U.S. Dept. Interior, Washington, 1998—. Lectr. in environ. law and policy polit. sci. dept. Boston Coll., Chestnut Hill, Mass., 1997; pub. defender Boston Coll. Defenders, Newton, Mass., 1996-97. Vol. Clinton Gore Campaign, Washington, 1992; security vol. Dem. Nat. Com., N.Y.C., 1992; mentor Environmentors, Washington, 1998—. Mem. ABA, Order of Coif, Alpha Sigma Nu. Democrat. Roman Catholic. Avocations: swimming, outdoor activities, politics, music, historical biographies. Office: US Dept Interior 1849 C St NW Washington DC 20240

LEONARD, TIMOTHY DWIGHT, judge; b. Beaver, Okla., Jan. 22, 1940; s. Dwight and Mary Evelyn Leonard; m. Nancy Louise Laughlin, July 15, 1967; children: Kirstin Dione, Ryan Timothy, Tyler Dwight. BA, U. Okla., 1962, JD, 1965; student, Mil. Naval Justice Sch., 1966. Bar: Okla. 1965, U.S. Dist. Ct. (no. and we. dists.) Okla. 1969, U.S. Ct. Appeals (10th cir.) 1969, U.S. Supreme Ct. 1970. Asst. atty. gen. State of Okla., 1968-70; mem. Okla. Senate, 1979-88; ptnr. Blankenship, Herrold, Russell et al, Oklahoma City, 1970-71, Trippet, Leonard & Kee, Beaver, 1971-88; of counsel Huckaby, Fleming et al, Oklahoma City, 1988-89; U.S. atty. Western Dist. Okla., 1988-92; judge U.S. Dist. Ct. (we. dist.) Okla., 1992—. Guest lectr., tchr. Oklahoma City U., 1988-89; mem. U.S. Atty. Gen.'s Adv. Com., 1990-92, chmn. office mgmt. and budget subcom., 1990-92. Co-author: 4 Days, 40 Hours, 1970. Rep. Party candidate for lt. gov. of Okla.; minority leader Okla. State Senate, 1985-86; White House mil. aide, Washington, 1966-67; ex officio mem. Okla. State Fair Bd., Oklahoma City, 1987-90; mem. Gov.'s Coun. on Sports and Phys. Edn., Oklahoma City, 1987-89; mem. Donna Nigh Found., Edmond, Okla., 1987-9. Lt. USN, 1965-68. Named Outstanding Legislator, Okla. Sch. Bd. Assn., 1988. Fellow ABA; mem. Okla. Bar Assn., Okla. County Bar, Phi Alpha Delta, Beta Theta Pi. Republican. Presbyterian. Avocations: basketball, running, reading. Office: US Courthouse 200 NW 4th St Ste 5012 Oklahoma City OK 73102-3031

LEONARD, WILL ERNEST, JR. lawyer; b. Shreveport, La., Jan. 18, 1935; s. Will Ernest and Nellie (Kenner) L.; m. Maureen Laniak; children— Will Ernest III, Sherry Elizabeth, Robert Scott, Stephen Michael, Christopher Anthony, Colleen Mary, Leigh Alison. BA, Tulane U., 1956, LLB, 1958; LLM, Harvard U., 1966. Bar: La. 1958, D.C. 1963, U.S. Supreme Ct. 1963. Announcer sta. WVUE-TV, New Orleans, 1958-60; legislative asst. to U.S. Senator Russell B. Long, 1960-65; profl. staff mem. com. fin. U.S. Senate, 1966-68; mem. Internat. Trade Commn. (formerly U.S. Tariff Commn.), 1968-77, chmn., 1975-76; ptnr. Adduci, Mastriani & Schaumberg, LLP, Washington, 2001—. Congl. staff fellow Am. Polit. Sci. Assn., 1965-66 Administrative and regulatory, Private international, Public international. Home: 7324 Bradley Blvd Bethesda MD 20817-2130 Office: Adduci Mastriani & Schaumberg LLP Ste 500 1200 17th St NW Washington DC 20036

LEONHARDT, FREDERICK WAYNE, lawyer; b. Daytona Beach, Fla., Oct. 26, 1949; s. Frederick Walter and Gaetane Larua Leonhardt; m. Victoria Ann Cook, Dec. 27, 1975; children: Ashley Victoria, Frederick Whitaker. BA, U. Fla., 1971, JD, 1974. Bar: Fla. 1974, N.C. 1984, D.C. 1985; cert. real estate lawyer, Fla. Gen. counsel Fla. Ho. of Reps., 1974-75;

ptnr. Cobb, Cole and Bell, Daytona Beach, 1975-79; pres. Leonhardt & Upchurch, 1979-87; ptnr. Holland & Knight, Orlando, Fla., 1987-93, Gray, Harris & Robinson, Orlando, Melbourne, Tallahassee, Clermont, Tampa, Lakeland, 1993—, Tampa, Lakeland, 1993—. Chmn. bd. dirs. Orlando/Orange County Compact, 1989-90, Orlando/Orange County Civic Facilities Authority, 1998—; founder Leadership Daytona Beach; grad. Leadership Fla., mem. bd. regents, 1995—, chmn. state program, 1997-98, chair-elect 1999, chair, 2000—; active Leadership Ctrl. Fla., Leadership Orlando; past chmn. Ctrl. Fla. Sports Commn., bd. dirs., 1992-98; mem. Orange County Civic Facilities Authority, 1998—; bd. dirs. Orlando/Orange County Conv. and Visitors Bur.; founder VCARD; past gen. campaign mgr. Volusia County United Way; bd. dirs. Celebration Health Found., Ctr. for Drug Free Living, Prevent Blindness Fla.; mem. Gov.'s Growth Mgmt. Study Commn.; exec. com. Floridians for Better Transp., 2000—; treas. U. Ctrl. Fla. Found., 2000—; bd. dirs. Econ. Devel. Commn. Mid-Fla., 2001—; mem. adv. bd. Ronald McDonald House. Mem. ABA (chmn. stae and local govt. law sect. 1997-98, editor sect. newsletter 1991-94), Orange and Volusia Counties Bar Assn., Greater Orlando C. of C. (chmn. 1991-92), Daytona Beach Area C. of C. (pres. 1985), Fla. C. of C. (bd. dirs. 1984-90, 93—), Phi Alpha Delta, Delta Chi. Administrative and regulatory, Contracts commercial, Real property. Office: Gray Harris & Robinson PA PO Box 3068 301 E Pine St Ste 1400 Orlando FL 32801-2731 E-mail: fleonhar@grhlaw.com

LEONIE, ANDREW DRAKE, III, judge, lawyer; b. Loma Linda, Calif., Dec. 13, 1952; s. Andrew and Norma Lou Leonie; m. Jamie Lorraine Chism, June 16, 1995; children: Andrew, Aaron, Rachel. BS, Western Ill. U., 1972; MA, U. Ill., 1974; JD, St. Mary's U., 1977; postgrad., Andrews U., 19985. Bar: Tex., U.S. Dist. Ct. (so. dist.) Tex., U.S. Dist. Ct. (no. dist.) Tex., U.S. Supreme Ct. Assoc. Smith, McIlheran, Lauderdale & Jones, Weslaco, Tex., 1977-79; ptnr. Jones, Marsh, Rodriguez, Welch & Leonie, McAllen, 1980-85; asst. atty. gen. Atty. Gen. Tex., Dallas, 1987-94; pvt. practice, 1994-95; judge, family law ct. master 1st Jud. Region Tex., 1995—. Presiding judge City of Lavon, Tex.; mediator Christian Conciliation Svc., McAllen, Tex., 1984—; advisor Tex. Senate Com. on Family Law Issues, 1996; bd. advisors Iverson Inst. Ct. Reporting; mem. transition com. Tex. Atty. Gen. John Cornyn, 1998-99; mem. child support legis. com. Tex. Sunset Commn., 1999. Contbr. article to profl. jour., chpt. to book. Mem. exec. com. Rockwall (Tex.) Rep. Party, 1989-98; commr. planning and zoning commn. City of Rockwall, 1990-92; bd. dirs. Tex. Rural Legal Aid, 1985. Recipient Pro Bono award Rockwall County Bar Assn., 1995. Mem. Am. Jud. Assn., Tex. Bar Assn. (chair mcpl. judges sect.), Dallas Bar Assn. (mem. judiciary com., ethics com. 19945), Hidalgo County Bar Assn. (sec. bd. dirs. 1977-82), Christian Legal Soc., Rotary (pres. Rockwall (Tex., Rotarian of Yr. 1991, Breakfast Club). Republican. Episcopalian. Avocations: running, gardening, religious history. Home: 4617 Lakepointe Ave Rowlett TX 75088-6862 Office: First Jud Region Tex George Allen Civil Cts Bldg 600 Commerce St 7th Fl Dallas TX 75202-4616 E-mail: judgeleonie@airmail.net

LEONTSINIS, GEORGE JOHN, lawyer; b. St. Louis, Feb. 23, 1937; s. John Peter and Lula (Lorandos) L.; m. Patricia Marie Demetrulias, July 9, 1967; children: Anne Marie, Michelle Lynne. BSBA, Washington U., St. Louis, 1958, JD, 1961; LLM, NYU, 1964. Bar: Mo. 1961. Ptnr. Greensfelder, Hemker & Gale, P.C., St. Louis, 1964—. Bd. dirs. Ahepa Apts., St. Louis, 1985-95, Citizens for Modern Transit, St. Louis, 1988-96, Citizen's com. high speed rail Chgo.-St. Louis Corridor, Springfield, Ill., 1992-96. Capt. U.S. Army, 1961-63. Mem. Am. Hellenic Ednl. and Profl. Assn., Racquet Club. Avocation: tennis. Contracts commercial, General corporate, Private international. Office: Greensfelder Hemker & Gale P C 10 S Broadway Saint Louis MO 63102-1712

LEOPOLD, MARK F. lawyer; b. 1950; s. Paul F. and Corinne (S.) L.; m. Jacqueline Rood, June 9, 1974; children: Jonathan, David. BA, Am. U., Washington, 1972; JD, Loyola U., 1975. Bar: Ill. 1975, U.S. Dist. Ct. (no. dist.) Ill. 1975, Fla. 1976, U.S. Ct. Appeals (7th cir.) 1976, U.S. Ct. Appeals (8th cir.) 1979. Assoc. McConnell & Campbell, Chgo., 1975-79; atty. U.S. Gypsum Co., 1979-82, sr. litigation atty., 1982-84, USG Corp., Chgo., 1985-87, corp. counsel, 1987, sr. corp. counsel, 1987-89; asst. gen. counsel G.D. Searle & Co., 1989-93, Household Internat., Inc., Prospect Heights, Ill., 1993—. Mem. adv. bd. Roosevelt U. Legal Asst. Program, 1994-2000; legal writing instr. Loyola U. Sch. Law, Chgo., 1978-79. Pres., bd. dirs. Internat. Policyholders Assn., 1992-93; del. candidate Rep. Nat. Conv., 1996; mem. Lake County Study Commn. II, Waukegan, Ill., 1989-90; commr. Lake County, Waukegan, 1982-84, Forest Preserve, Libertyville, Ill., 1982-84, Pub. Bldg. Commn., Waukegan, 1980-82; chmn. Deerfield Twp. Rep. Cen. Com., Highland Park, Ill., 1984-86, officer, 1981-89; vice chmn. Lake County Rep. Cen. Com., Waukegan, 1982-84; bd. dirs. Am. Jewish Com., Chgo., 1988-91, A Safe Place, Lake County, Ill., 2001—. Recipient Disting. Svc. award Jaycees, Highland Park, 1983. Mem. ABA (antitrust com. 1976—, litigation com. 1980—, torts and ins. practice com. 1989—), Pi Sigma Alpha, Omicron Delta Kappa. Republican. Antitrust, Federal civil litigation, Product liability. Office: Household Internat 2700 Sanders Rd Prospect Heights IL 60070-2701

LEPELSTAT, MARTIN L. lawyer; b. Bklyn., Apr. 10, 1947; s. Larry and Nana (Citrin) L.; m.. Audrey A. Fireman, Jan. 18, 1975; children: Rachel M., Michael H. BBA, CCNY, 1968; JD, Cornell U., 1971; MBA, U. Mich., 1970; LLM, NYU, 1976. Bar: N.J. 1978, N.Y. 1972, Fla. 1972. Tax cons. Touche Ross, N.Y.C., 1971-73; assoc. Weil, Gotshal & Manges, 1973-78, Greenbaum, Rowe, Smith, Woodbridge, N.J., 1978—. Bd. dirs. Winston Towers 300 Assn., Inc., Cliffside Park, N.J., 1978-86. Fellow Am. Coll. of Trust and Estate Counsel, 1991—; mem. ABA (tax and real estate probate com.), N.J. State Bar Assn., Middlesex County Bar Assn. (pres. tax com. 1987-88, pres. probate com. 1986-87, trustee 1988-92), Fla. Bar Assn. Estate planning, Corporate taxation, Estate taxation. Home: 20 Snoden Ln Watchung NJ 07069-6253 Office: Greenbaum Rowe Smith PO Box 5600 Woodbridge NJ 07095-0988 E-mail: mlepelstat@greenbaumlaw.com

LERER, NEAL M. lawyer; b. Chelmsford, Mass., June 20, 1954; m. Rose P. Meegan, July 28, 1991; 1 child, Benjamin Joseph. BA, Brown U., 1976; JD, Duke Law Sch., 1979. Bar: Mass. 1979, U.S. Dist. Ct. Mass. 1980, U.S. Ct. Appeals (1st cir.) 1991. Ptnr. Martin, Magnuson, McCarthy & Kenney, Boston, 1980-96; mng. atty., pvt. practice Chelmsford, Mass., 1996—. Corporator Lowell (Mass.) 5 Cents Savings Bank, 1985—. Co-author: Personal Injury and Death, 1980, Damages in Massachusetts, 1990, Personal Injury Litigation in Massachusetts, 1991, Premises Liability, 1994. Reader Recording for the Blind, Cambridge, Mass., 1987-94; bd. dirs. Goodwin Fund; dir. Town of Chelmsford Scholarship Com. Mem. Mass. Bar Assn., Mass. Bar Found., Greater Lowell Bar Assn., Brown Club of Boston (bd. dirs., co-pres. 1998-2000). General civil litigation, Insurance, Personal injury. Home: 4 Manahan St Chelmsford MA 01824-2844 E-mail: neallerer@aol.com

LERMAN, EILEEN R. lawyer; b. N.Y.C., May 6, 1947; d. Alex and Beatrice (Kline) L. BA, Syracuse U., 1969; JD, Rutgers U., 1972; MBA, U. Denver, 1983. Bar: N.Y. 1973, Colo. 1976. Atty. FTC, N.Y.C., 1972-74; corp. atty. Samsonite Corp. and consumer products divsn. Beatrice Foods, Denver, 1976-78, assoc. gen. counsel, 1978-85, asst. sec., 1979-85; ptnr. Davis, Lerman, & Weinstein, 1985-92, Eileen R. Lerman & Assocs., Denver, 1993—. Bd. dirs. Legal Aid Soc. of Met. Denver, 1979-80. Bd. dirs., vice chmn. Colo. Postsecondary Ednl. Facilities Authority, 1981-89; bd. dirs., pres. Am. Jewish Com., 1989-92; mem. Leadership Denver, 1983. Mem. ABA, Colo. Women's Bar Assn. (bd. dirs. 1980-81), Colo. Bar Assn. (mem. bd. govs.), Denver Bar Assn. (trustee), N.Y. State Bar Assn., Rhone Brackett Inn (pres. 1997-98), Denver Law Club, Rutgers U. Alumni Assn., Univ. Club. State civil litigation, General corporate, Family and matrimonial. Home: 1018 Fillmore St Denver CO 80206-3332 Office: Lerman & Assocs PC 50 S Steele St Ste 820 Denver CO 80209-2813

LERNER, MAX KASNER, lawyer; b. N.Y.C., Dec. 27, 1916; s. Louis Lerner and Beckie Kasner; m. Lila Schachner, Oct. 5, 1943; children: Helene, Beth. LLB, Bklyn. Law Sch., 1939. Bar: N.Y. 1940, U.S. Supreme Ct. 1952. Author: ABA Journal of Limitations Imposed on Radio and TV, 1949. Criminal, Probate, Trademark and copyright. Home: 350 1st Ave New York NY 10010-4902

LESHNER, STEPHEN I. lawyer; b. N.Y.C., Sept. 26, 1951; s. Leo and Gloria (Perlman) L.; m. Mary Ann Relles, Oct. 28, 1978; children: Samuel Joseph, Harry Jacob. BA, SUNY, Stony Brook, 1973; JD, Northeastern U., 1976. Bar: Ariz. 1976, U.S. Dist. Ct. Ariz. 1977, U.S. Ct. Appeals (9th cir.) 1981, U.S. Supreme Ct. 1980. Assoc. Legal Clinic Bates & O'Steen, Phoenix, 1977; ptnr. O'Steen Legal Clinic, 1977-80, Van, O'Steen and Ptnrs., Phoenix, 1980—. Criminal law specialist, Ariz. Bd. Legal Specialization, 1982-95, injury and wrongful death litigation specialist, 1991—; judge pro tem Maricopa County Superior Ct., 1993—. Mem. Assn. Trial Lawyers Am., Ariz. Trial Lawyers Assn. (bd. dirs., pres. 1999), Am. Bd. Trial Advocates, State Bar Ariz. Assn., Nucleus Club (chmn. 1995-96). Personal injury, Product liability. Office: Van O'Steen and Ptnrs 3605 N 7th Ave Phoenix AZ 85013-3638 E-mail: sleshner@vanosteen.com

LESHY, JOHN DAVID, lawyer, legal educator, government official; b. Winchester, Ohio, Oct. 7, 1944; s. John and Dolores (King) L.; m. Helen M. Sandalls, Dec. 15, 1973; 1 child, David Alexander. AB cum laude, Harvard U., 1966, JD magna cum laude, 1969. Trial atty. Civil Rights Divsn. Dept. Justice, Washington, 1969-72; atty. Natural Resources Def. Coun., Palo Alto, Calif., 1972-77; assoc. solicitor energy and resources Dept. Interior, Washington, 1977-80; prof. law Ariz. State U., Tempe, 1980—; spl. counsel to chair Natural Resources Com. U.S. Ho. Reps., Washington, 1992-93; solicitor (gen. counsel) Dept. Interior, 1993-2001. Cons. Calif. State Land Commn., N.Mex. Atty. Gen., Western Govs. Assn., Congl. Rsch. Svc., Ford Found., Hewlett Found.; mem. com. Onshore Oil & Gas Leasing, NAS Nat. Rsch. Coun., 1989-90; vis. prof. Sch. Law U. San Diego, 1990; disting. vis. prof. law U. Calif. Hastings Coll. Law, 2001-02. Author: The Mining Law: A Study in Perpetual Motion, 1987, The Arizona State Constitution, 1993; co-author Federal Public Land and Resources Law, 4th edit., 2000, Legal Control of Water Resources, 3rd edit., 2000; contbr. articles, book chpts. to profl. jours., environ. jours. Bd. dirs. Ariz. Ctr. Law in Pub. Interest, 1981-86, Ariz. Raft Adventures, 1982-92; mem. Gov.'s Task Force Recreation on Fed. Lands, 1985-86, Gov.'s Task Force Environ. Impact Assessment, 1990, City of Phoenix Environ. Quality Commn., 1987-90. Robinson Cox vis. fellow U. Western Australia Law Sch., Perth, 1985, rsch. fellow U. Southampton, Eng., 1986; Ford Found. grantee, Resources for the Future grantee. Democrat. Avocations: piano, hiking, whitewater rafting, photography. Office: Calif Hastings Coll Law 200 McAllister St San Francisco CA 94102-4978 E-mail: leshyj@uchastings.edu

LESK, ANN BERGER, lawyer; b. N.Y.C., Feb. 7, 1947; d. Alexander and Eleanor A. (Dickinson) Berger; m. Michael E. Lesk, June 30, 1968. AB cum laude, Radcliffe Coll., 1968; JD with high honors, Rutgers U., 1977. Bar: N.Y. 1979. Law clk. to justice N.J. Supreme Ct., Mountain, 1977-78; assoc. Fried, Frank, Harris, Shriver & Jacobson, N.Y.C., 1978-84, ptnr., 1984—. Editor-in-chief Rutgers Law Rev., 1976-77. Mem. ABA, New York County Lawyer's Assn. (co-chair, com. Trusts and Estates Section, 1998—; co-chair Com. on Trusts and Estates Legislation and Governmental Affairs, 1995-98), N.Y. State Bar Assn., Assn. of the Bar of City of N.Y. (com. on Trusts, Estates and Surrogates' cts. 1992-95, 2000—; com. on Estate and Gift Taxation, 1997-2000). Estate planning, Probate, Estate taxation. Office: Fried Frank Harris Shriver & Jacobson 1 New York Plz Fl 22 New York NY 10004-1980

LESKO, JANE LYNN, lawyer; b. Willoughby, Ohio, Sept. 5, 1969; d. Andrew M. Jr. and Marcia G. L. BS in Criminal Justice, U. Toledo, 1992; JD, Capital U., 1996. Bar: Ohio, U.S. Dist. Ct. (no. dist.) Ohio 1997. With Army N.G., 1987-93. Mem. Zonta. General civil litigation, General practice, Juvenile. Office: James M Lemieux Co LPA PO Box 243 4717 Park Ave PO Box 1417 Ashtabula OH 44005

LESLIE, ROBERT LORNE, lawyer; b. Adak, Ala., Feb. 24, 1947; s. J. Lornie and L. Jean (Conelly) L.; children: Lorna Jean, Elizabeth Allen. BS, U.S. Mil. Acad., 1969; JD, U. Calif., San Francisco, 1974. Bar: Calif. 1974, D.C. 1979, U.S. Dist. Ct. (no. dist.) Calif. 1974, U.S. Ct. Claims 1975, U.S. Tax Ct. 1975, U.S. Ct. Appeals (9th and D.C. cirs.) 1974, U.S. Ct. Mil. Appeals 1980, U.S. Supreme Ct. 1980. Commd. 2d lt. U.S. Army, 1969, advanced through grades to maj., 1980; govt. trial atty. West Coast Field Office, Contract Appeals, Litigation and Regulatory Law divsns., Office JAG, Dept. Army, San Francisco, 1974-77; sr. trial atty., team chief Office of Chief Trial Atty., Dept. of Amry, Washington, 1977-80; ptnr. McInerney & Dillon, Oakland, Calif., 1980—, 1980—. Lectr. on govt. contracts CSC, Continuing Legal Edn. Program; lectr. in govt. procurement U.S. Army Material Command. Served to col. USAR, ret. Decorated Purple Heart, Silver Star. Mem. ABA, Fed. Bar Assn., Associated Gen. Contractors, The Beavers. Contracts commercial, Construction, Government contracts and claims. Office: McInerney & Dillon Ordway Bldg Fl 18 Oakland CA 94612-3610

LESMAN, MICHAEL STEVEN, lawyer; b. N.Y.C., May 26, 1953; s. Herman and Estelle (Levy) L.; m. Gail R. Grossman, May 26, 1980; children: Adam, Laura. BA magna cum laude, CUNY, 1975; JD, Bklyn. Law Sch., 1982. Bar: N.Y. 1983. From assoc. to supervising atty. Jacobowitz & Lysaght, N.Y.C., 1983-88; atty. of record, mng. atty. Jacobowitz, Garfinkel & Lesman, 1989—. Staff counsel Am. Internat. Cos., N.Y.C., 1989—. Mem. ABA, N.Y. State Bar Assn., N.Y. County Lawyers Assn., Def. Rsch. Inst., N.Y. State Trial Lawyers Assn. State civil litigation, Insurance, Personal injury. Office: Jacobowitz Garfinkel & Lesman 110 William St Fl 17 New York NY 10038-3914 E-mail: michael.lesman@aig.com

LESOURD, NANCY SUSAN OLIVER, lawyer, writer; b. Atlanta, Aug. 22, 1953; d. Carl Samuel and Jane (Meadows) Oliver; m. Jeffrey Alan LeSourd, Oct. 18, 1986; children: Jeffrey Luke, Catherine Victoria. BA in Polit. Sci., Agnes Scott Coll., 1975; MA in History, Edn., Tufts U., 1977; JD, Georgetown U., 1984. Bar: Pa. 1985, D.C. 1986, Va. 1992, Fed. Cir. Ct. Appeals., 1988, U.S. Claims Ct., 1988, U.S. Supreme Ct. Instr. Newton (Mass.) High Sch., 1976-78, The Stony Brook (N.Y.) Sch., 1978-81; assoc. Gammon and Grange, Washington, 1984-88; shareholder Gammon and Grange, P.C., 1988—; mgr. Marshall-LeSourd L.L.C., 1996—. Legal commentator (radio shows) UPI News, Washington, 1985-91, Focus on the Family (Washington corr.), Colorado Springs, Colo., 1987-94; legal columnist Christian Mgmt. Rev., Downers Grove, Ill., 1987-90; spkr. numerous confs. Author: No Longer The Hero, 1992; editor Georgetown Law Jour., 1982-84; contbr. articles to profl. jours.; cons./prodr. three tv movies based on "Christy", 2000—. Bd. dirs. Arlington County Equal Employment Opportunity Commn., 1985; founder and vice-chmn. bd. trustees Ambleside Sch., 1998—. William Robertson Coe fellow SUNY, Stony Brook, 1978. Mem. D.C. Bar Assn., Va. Bar Assn., Christian Legal Society (bd. dirs. 1990-93). Republican. General corporate, Intellectual property, Non-profit and tax-exempt organizations. Home: 2624 New Banner Ln Herndon VA 20171-2659 Office: Gammon and Grange PC 8280 Greensboro Dr Fl 7 Mc Lean VA 22102-3807 E-mail: nol@gandglaw.com

LESSEN, LARRY LEE, federal judge; b. Lincoln, Ill., Dec. 25, 1939; s. William G. and Grace L. (Plunkett) L.; m. Susan Marian Vaughn, Dec. 5, 1964; children: Laura, Lynn, William. BA, U. Ill., 1960, JD, 1962. Bar: Ill. 1962, U.S. Dist. Ct. (ctrl. dist.) Ill. 1964, U.S. Bankruptcy Ct. 1964, U.S. Tax Ct. 1982, U.S. Ct. Appeals (7th cir.) 1981, U.S. Supreme Ct. 1981. Law clk. to presiding justice U.S. Dist. Ct., 1962-64; asst. state's atty. State of Ill., Danville, 1964-67; mng. ptnr. Sebat, Swanson, Banks and Lessen, 1967-85; judge U.S. Bankruptcy Ct., 1973-85, U.S. Magistrate, Danville, 1973-84; chief judge U.S. Bankruptcy Ct., Springfield, Ill., 1985-93; U.S. bankruptcy judge Springfield divsn., 1993—. Mem. ABA, FBA, Sangamon County Bar Assn., Vermilion County Bar Assn, Nat. Conf. Bankruptcy Judges (bd. govs. 1994-97), Am. Bankruptcy Inst., Lincoln-Douglas Inn of Cts. Office: US Bankruptcy Ct 235 U S Courthouse 600 E Monroe St Springfield IL 62701-1626

LESSER, JOAN L. lawyer; b. L.A. BA, Brandeis U., 1969; JD, U. So. Calif., 1973. Bar: Calif. 1973, U.S. Dist. Ct. (cen. dist.) Calif. 1974. Assoc. Irell and Manella LLP, L.A., 1973-80, ptnr., 1980—. Mem. planning com. Ann. Real Property Inst., Continuing Edn. of Bar, Berkeley, 1990-96; speaker at profl. confs. Trustee Windward Sch.; grad. Leadership L.A., 1992; bd. dirs. L.A. chpt. Legion Lex. Mem. Orgn. Women Execs. (past pres., bd. dirs.), Order of Coif. General corporate, Finance, Real property. Office: Irell & Manella LLP 1800 Avenue Of The Stars Los Angeles CA 90067-4276 E-mail: jlesser@irell.com

LESSER, MARGO ROGERS, legal consultant; b. Oklahoma City, Aug. 30, 1950; d. William Wright and Velma June (Clark) Rogers; m. George Robert Lesser, Apr. 25, 1982; children: Scott Robert, Kira Michelle. AB, Cornell U., 1972; JD, Georgetown U., 1975. Bar: D.C. 1975, Mich. 1990, U.S. Ct. Claims 1976, U.S. Tax Ct. 1979, U.S. Ct. Appeals (fed. cir.) 1982, U.S. Supreme Ct. 1979. Law clk. to Hon. judge Oscar Davis U.S. Appellate Ct. Claims, Washington, 1975-76; assoc. Covington & Burling, 1976-81; asst. prof. Wayne State U. Law Sch., Detroit, 1981-88; legal cons. Birmingham, Mich., 1988—. Exec. dir. Ind. Dir. Found., Detroit, 1990-2000. Co-author: Michigan Corporation Law and Practice, 1990, supplements through 2001; assoc. editor Internat. Soc. Barristers Quar., 1988—; contbr. articles to profl. jours. Mem. ABA, Mich. Bar (co-reporter Bus. Corp. Act subcom., law sect. 1986-97, reporter ad hoc limited liability co. rev. com. 1991—). Avocations: family, tennis, sailing. Home and Office: 1044 N Glenhurst Dr Birmingham MI 48009-1111

LESSER, WILLIAM MELVILLE, lawyer; b. N.Y.C., Jan. 26, 1927; s. Sydney Edward and Hattie (Wolf) L.; m. Laura Helen Schwartz, Oct. 3, 1953; children: Robin, Debra, Nancy. BS, NYU, 1949, JD, 1958. Bar: N.Y. 1959, U.S. Dist. Ct. (so. and ea. dists.) N.Y. 1969. Sr. ptnr. Lesser Popick & Rutman, N.Y.C., 1959-96; with Verner Simon LLP, 1996—. Lawyer; b. N.Y.C., Jan. 26, 1927; s. Sydney Edward and Hattie (Wolf) L.; m. Laura Helen Schwartz, Oct. 3, 1953; children: Robin, Debra, Nancy. BS, NYU, 1949, JD, 1958. Bar: N.Y. 1959, U.S. Dist. Ct. (so. and ea. dists.) N.Y. 1969. Sr. ptnr. Lesser Popick & Rutman, N.Y.C., 1959-96; with Verner, Simon LLP, N.Y.C., 1996—. Treas., bd. dirs. Assn. Help Retarded Children, N.Y.C. chpt., 1961-67; chmn. Environ. Control Commn., Town of New Castle, N.Y., 1969-81. Served with USN, 1945-46, PTO. Mem. ABA, Assn. Trial Lawyers Am., N.Y. State Trial Lawyers Assn., Assn. Trial Lawyers City of N.Y., Am. Soc. Law and Medicine. Jewish. Treas., bd. dirs. Assn. Help Retarded Children, N.Y.C. chpt., 1961-67; chmn. Environ. Control Commn., Town of New Castle, N.Y., 1969-81. With USN, 1945-46, PTO. Mem. ABA, ATLA, N.Y. State Trial Lawyers City of N.Y., Am. Soc. Law and Medicine. Jewish. State civil litigation, Insurance, Personal injury. Home: 70 Taconic Rd Millwood NY 10546-1124 Office: Verner Simon LLP 1350 Broadway New York NY 10018-7702

LESTER, ANDREW WILLIAM, lawyer; b. Mpls., Feb. 17, 1956; s. Richard G. and Marion Louise (Kurtz) L.; m. Barbara Regina Schmitt, Nov. 22, 1978; 1 child, Susan Erika. Student, Ludwig-Maximilians Univ., Munich, 1975-76; BA, Duke U., 1977; MS in Fgn. Service, JD, Georgetown U., 1981. Bar: Okla. 1981, D.C. 1985, Tex. 1990, U.S. Supreme Ct. 1992, Colo. 1995. Cons. Dresser Industries, Inc., Washington, 1979-81; assoc. Conner & Winters, Tulsa, 1981-82; asst. atty. City of Enid, Okla., 1982-84; ptnr. various law firms Enid, Oklahoma City, 1984-96; ptnr. Lester, Loving & Davies P.C., Edmond, 1996—. Adj. prof. Okla. City Univ. Sch. of Law; lectr. in field; U.S. magistrate judge Western Dist. Okla., 1988-96; constl. law specialist Ctrl. and East European Law Initiative, ABA, Ukraine, Belarus and Moldova, 1993; adj. scholar Okla. Coun. Pub. Affairs; bd. dirs. St. Mary's Episcopal Sch. Author: Constitutional Law and Democracy, 1994; contbr. book revs. and articles to profl. jours. Intern Office of Senator Bob Dole, Washington, 1977-78; mem. transition team EEOC Office Pres.-Elect Reagan, Washington, 1980-81; chmn. Enid Police Civil Service Commn., 1985-87; bd. dirs. Enid Habitat for Humanity, 1986-88, Booker T. Washington Community Ctr., Enid, 1987-90; mem. Martin Luther King, Jr. Holiday Commn. of Enid, 1988-91; deacon First Bapt. Ch. of Oklahoma City. Fellow Okla. Bar Found.; mem. Okla. Bar Assn., D.C. Bar Assn., Tex. Bar Assn., Colo. Bar Assn., Okla. Assn. Mcpl. Attys. (bd. dirs. 1987-91, 94-98, 2000—, gen. counsel 1987-88, pres. 1988-90), Oklahoma County Bar Assn., Def. Rsch. Inst. (govt. liability com.), Federalist Soc. (vice chmn. civil rights practice group 1996—, pres. Ctrl. Okla. chpt. 1996-99). Republican. Avocations: German language, cartography. Civil rights, General civil litigation, Constitutional. Office: Lester Loving & Davies PC 1505 S Renaissance Blvd Edmond OK 73013-3018 E-mail: alester@lldlaw.com

LESTER, ROY DAVID, lawyer; b. Middletown, Ohio, Jan. 16, 1949; s. Edgel Celsus and Norma Marie (Elam) L.; children: Justin David, Benjamin, Jackson. BS, We. Ky. U., 1970; JD, U. Ky., 1975. Bar: Ky. 1975, U.S. Tax Ct. 1979, U.S. Dist. Ct. (ea. dist.) Ky. 1976, U.S. Supreme Ct. 1979. With Stoll, Keenon & Park, Lexington, Ky., 1975—. [ ]Mem. YMCA (Lexington), Fayette County Bar Assn., Order of Coif, Lexington Country Club. Republican. Contracts commercial, General corporate. Office: Stoll Keenon & Park 201 E Main St Ste 1000 Lexington KY 40507-1380 E-mail: lester@skp.com

L'ESTRANGE, TIMOTHY I. lawyer; b. Sydney, Australia, Nov. 24, 1955; s. Vincent Joseph and Pamela Mary (McGuigan) L.; m. Elizabeth Jill Campbell Lestrange; children: Adelaide, Alistair, Alexandra. B of Commerce, U. New South Wales, Sydney, Australia, 1976, LLB, 1978. Assoc. to justice J.S. Lockhart Fed. Ct. of Australia, Sydney, Australia, 1979-80; ptnr. Allen, Allen & Hemsley, Australia, 1987—, mng ptnr. Australia, 1993-96. Permanent sec. Ct. of Arbitration for Sports, Oceania Divsn., 1996—; bd. mem. Allen, Allen & Hemsley, Sydney, Australia, 2000—. Mem. Internat. Bar Assn., Insolvency Practitioners Assn., Australian Inst. Arbitrators and Mediators. Avocations: golf, rugby union, swimming, walking. Office e-mail: tim.l'estrange@allens.com.au. Antitrust, Alternative dispute resolution, Bankruptcy. Home: Clifton Gardens 3 Morella Rd Sydney 2088 Australia Office: Allen Allen & Hemsley 2 Chifley Tower Sydney 2000 Australia

LETTEN, JAMES, prosecutor; 2 children. Degree, U. New Orleans, 1976; JD, Tulane Law Sch., 1979. With New Orleans Dist. Attys. Office, 1979—82; with Organized Crime and Racketeering Strike Force Dept. Justice, 1982—94; asst. U.S. atty., 1994; interim U.S. atty. ea. dist. La. Office: Itale Boggs Fed Bldg Rm 210 501 Magazine St New Orleans LA 70130 Office Fax: 504-589-4510*

LETTOW, CHARLES FREDERICK, lawyer; b. Iowa Falls, Iowa, Feb. 10, 1941; s. Carl Frederick and Catherine (Reisinger) L.; m. Sue Lettow, Apr. 20, 1963; children: Renee, Carl II, John, Paul. BS in Chem. Engring., Iowa State U., 1962; LLB, Stanford U., 1968; MA, Brown U., 2001. Bar: Calif. 1969, Iowa 1969, D.C. 1972, Md. 1991. Law clk. to Hon. Ben C. Duniway U.S. Ct. Appeals (9th cir.), San Francisco, 1968-69; law clk. to Hon. Warren E. Burger U.S. Supreme Ct., Washington, 1969-70; counsel Council on Environ. Quality, 1970-73; assoc. Cleary, Gottlieb, Steen & Hamilton, 1973-76, ptnr., 1976—. Pres. Busy Way Farms, Inc., 1989—. Contbr. articles to profl. jours. Trustee Potomac Sch., McLean, Va., 1983-90, chmn. bd. trustees, 1985-88. 1st lt. U.S. Army, 1963-65. Mem. ABA, Am. Law Inst., D.C. Bar, Iowa Bar Assn., Order of Coif. Club: University. Federal civil litigation, Environmental. Office: 2000 Pennsylvania Ave NW Washington DC 20006-1801 E-mail: clettow@cgsh.com

LETWIN, JEFFREY WILLIAM, lawyer; b. Pitts., Nov. 26, 1953; s. Myron Harvey and Phyllis Harriet (Unatin) L.; m. Roberta Lee Rosenbloom, July 24, 1983; 1 child, S. Ari; stepchildren: Andrew B. Filipek, Amanda H. Filipek. BA in History and Lit., U. Pitts., 1975; JD, Am. U., 1979. Bar: Pa. 1980, D.C. 1980. Staff atty. Dept. Justice, Washington, 1979-80; assoc. Gilloti, Goldberg & Capristi, Pitts., 1980-83, Finkel, Lefkowitz & Ostrow, Pitts., 1983-85, Rosenberg & Kirshner, Pitts., 1986-94; assoc., v.p. Doepken Keevican & Weiss, 1994—, also bd. dirs. Lectr. Pa. Bar Inst., 1983, 87, 88; mem. Pitts. High Tech. Council, 19855, Enterprise Group, Pitts., 19855; arbitrator N.Y. Stock Exch; solicitor Allegheny County Airport Authority, 19995. Bd. dirs. Holocaust Commn., Pitts., 19835, Jewish Family and Children's Svc., Pitts., 1983-86, Cmty. Coll. Allegheny County Found., Allegheny County Sanitary Authority, 20005; bd. dirs. United Jewish Fedn., Pitts., 1984-86, 985, chmn. young bus. and profl. divsn., 1985-87, chmn. exec. and profl. divsn. 1987-88; mem. Young Leadership Cabinet USA, 1984-87; participant Leadership Pitts., 19895; chmn. Holocaust Commn. of Greater Pitts., 1991-94, Pitts. Israel C. of C. 1991-97; commr. City of Pitts. Planning Commn., 19965; bd. dirs. Pitts. Film Office, 19965, Leadership Pitts., Jewish Assn. on Aging, 19975 ; v.p. C.C. of Allegheny County Edn. Found., 19965; mem. exec. com. United Jewish Fedn., 19975; solicitor Allegheny County Airport Authority, 1999—; bd. dirs. Allegheny County Sanitary Authority, 2000—. Named one of Outstanding Young Men in Am., 1985; recipient Stark Young Leadership award, 1989. Mem. ABA, Pa. Bar Assn., D.C. Bar Assn., Alleghany County Bar Assn. (bus., banking, and comml. sect., continuing legal edn. com.), Nat. Assn. Securities Dealers (arbitrator). Democrat. Jewish. Avocations: golf, tennis, films. General corporate, Real property, Securities. Office: Doepken Keevican 5800 USX Tower Pittsburgh PA 15219

LEVAL, PIERRE NELSON, federal judge; b. N.Y.C., Sept. 4, 1936; s. Fernand and Beatrice (Reiter) L. B.A. cum laude, Harvard U., 1959, J.D. magna cum laude, 1963. Bar: N.Y. 1964, U.S. Ct. Appeals 2d Circuit 1964, U.S. Dist. Ct. So. Dist. N.Y 1966. Law clk. to Hon. Henry J. Friendly, U.S. Ct. Appeals, 1963-64; asst. U.S. atty. So. Dist. N.Y., 1964-68, chief appellate atty., 1967-68; assoc. firm Cleary, Gottlieb, Steen & Hamilton, N.Y.C., 1969-74; ptnr. firm, 1973-75; 1st asst. dist. atty. Office of Dist. Atty., N.Y. County, 1975-76, chief asst. dist. atty., 1976-77; U.S. dist. judge So. Dist. N.Y., N.Y.C., 1977-93; judge U.S. Ct. of Appeals (2d cir.), 1993—. Contbr. articles to profl. jours. Served with U.S. Army, 1959. Mem. Am. Law Inst. (council), Assn. Bar City N.Y., N.Y. County Lawyers Assn. Office: US Courthouse 40 Foley Sq New York NY 10007-1502*

LEVANDER, BERNHARD WILHELM, retired lawyer; b. St. Paul, Mar. 9, 1916; s. Peter Magni and Laura Marie (Lovene) LeV.; m. Dagne E. Anderson, Oct. 14, 1939; children: Kirsten Dawson, Peter A. BA, Gustavus Adolphus Coll., 1937, DL (hon.), 1981; JD, U. Minn., 1939. Bar: Minn. 1939, U.S. Dist. Ct. Minn. 1955, U.S. Ct. Appeals (8th cir.) 1972, U.S. Supreme Ct. 1973. Assoc. S. Bernhard Wennerberg, Center City, Minn., 1939-40, Kelly, LeVander & Gillen, South St. Paul, 1950-52; sole practice Mpls., 1952-57; assoc. Nehls, Anderson, LeVander, Zimpfer & Munson, 1957-64; ptnr. LeVander, Zimpfer & Tierney, 1964-75, LeVander, Zimpfer & Zotaley, P.A., Mpls., 1975—. Past orgn. dir., chmn. Minn. Reps.; chmn. Midwest and Rocky Mountain Rep. Chmns. Assn., 1946-50; pres. Am. Swedish Inst., Mpls. Served to lt. (j.g.) Supply Corps, USNR, 1943-46. Recipient Disting. Service and Significant Attainment in Field of Law award Gustavus Alumni Assn., 1977, Royal Order VASA 1st Class, King of Sweden, 1975. Mem. ABA, Am. Legion. Lutheran. General corporate, Health, Probate. Home: 3550 Siems Ct Saint Paul MN 55112-3671

LEVENSON, ALAN BRADLEY, lawyer; b. Long Beach, N.Y., Dec. 13, 1935; s. Cyrus O. and Jean (Kotler) L.; m. Joan Marlene Levenson, Aug. 19, 1956; children: Scott Keith, Julie Jo AB, Dartmouth Coll., 1956; BA, Oxford U., Eng., 1958, MA, 1962; LLB, Yale U., 1961. Bar: N.Y. 1962, U.S. Dist. Ct. D.C. 1964, U.S. Ct. Appeals (D.C. cir.) 1965, U.S. Supreme Ct. 1965. Law clk., trainee div. corp. fin. SEC, Washington, 1961-62, gen. atty., 1962, trial atty., 1963, br. chief, 1963-65, asst. dir., 1965-68, exec. asst. dir., 1968, dir., 1970-76; v.p. Shareholders Mgmt. Co., L.A., 1969, sr. v.p., 1969-70, exec. v.p., 1970; ptnr. Fulbright & Jaworski, Washington, 1976—. Lectr. Cath. U. Am., 1964-68, Columbia U., 1973; adj. prof. Georgetown U., 1964, 77, 79-81, U.S. rep. working party OECD, Paris, 1974-75; adv. com. SEC, 1976-77; mem. adv. bd. Securities Regulation Inst., U. Calif., San Diego, 1973—, vice chmn. exec. com., 1979-83, chmn., 1983-87, emeritus chmn., 1988—; mem. adv. coun. SEC Inst., U. So. Calif., L.A., Sch. Acctg., 1981-85; mem. adv. com. Nat. Ctr. Fin. Svcs,. U. Calif.-Berkeley, 1985-89; mem. planning com. Ray Garrett Ann. Securities Regulation Inst. Northwestern U. Law Sch.; mem. adv. panel to U.S. compt.-gen. on stock market decline, 1987, panel of cons., 1989-98; mem. audit adv. com. GAO, 1992—. Mem. bd. editl. advisors U. Iowa Jour. Corp. Law, 1978—; Bur. Nat. Affairs adv. bd. Securities Regulation and Law Report, 1976—; bd. editors N.Y. Law Jour., 1976—; bd. advisors, corp. and securities law advisor Prentice Hall Law & Bus., 1991-95; contbr. articles to profl. jours.; mem. adv. bd. Banking Policy Report. Trustee, chair audit com., chair oral history com. SEC Hist. Soc. Recipient Disting. Service award SEC, 1972; James B. Richardson fellow Oxford U., 1956 Mem. ABA (adv. com., fed. regulation securities com., task force rev. fed. securities laws, former chair subcom. on securities activities banks), Fed. Bar Assn. (emeritus mem. exec. com. securities law com.), Am. Law Inst., Practicing Law Inst. (nat. adv. com. 1974, adv. com. ann. securities reg. inst.), AICPA (pub. dir., bd. dirs. 1984-91, fin. com. 1984-91, chmn. adv. coun. auditing standards bd. 1979-80, future issues com. 1982-85), Nat. Assn. Securities Dealers (corp. fin. com. 1981-87, nat. arbitration com. 1983-87, gov.-at-large, bd. govs. 1984-87, exec. com. 1986-87, long range planning com. 1987-90, chmn. legal adv. bd. 1988-93, spl. com. governance and structure 1989-90, numerous adv. coms.), Transparency Internat. USA (bd. dirs.). Banking, Securities. Home: 12512 Exchange Ct S Potomac MD 20854-2431 Office: Fulbright & Jaworski LLP 801 Pennsylvania Ave NW Washington DC 20004-2615 E-mail: alevenson@fulbright.com

LEVETOWN, ROBERT ALEXANDER, lawyer; b. Bklyn., July 20, 1935; s. Alfred A. and Corinne L. (Cohen) L.; m. Roberta S. Slobodkin, Oct. 18, 1959. Student, U. Munich, Fed. Republic Germany, 1954-55; AB, Princeton U., 1956; LLB, Harvard U., 1959. Bar: D.C. 1960, N.Y. 1982, Va. 1984, Pa. 1985. Assoc. Pierson, Ball & Dowd, Washington, 1960-62; asst. U.S. atty., 1962-63; atty. Chesapeake & Potomac Telephone Cos., 1963-66, gen. atty., 1966-68, gen. solicitor, 1968-73, v.p., gen. counsel, 1975-83; exec. v.p., gen. counsel Bell Atlantic, 1983-91, vice chmn., 1991-92, also bd. dirs., 1989-92. Chmn. H.R. com., 1995-99; bd. dirs. Telecom NZ. Mem. ABA (vice chmn. comm. com., pub. utility law sect. 1986-93), Washington Met. Corp. Counsels' Assn. (bd. dirs. 1981-83), Nat. Legal Ctr. (legal adv. coun. 1986-92). Republican. Jewish. Address: PMB 606 10645 N Tatum Blvd #200 Phoenix AZ 85028-3053

LEVI, DAVID F. federal judge; b. 1951; BA, Harvard U., MA, 1973; JD, Stanford U. Bar: Calif. 1983. U.S. atty. ea. dist. State of Calif., Sacramento, 1986-90; judge U.S. Dist. Ct. (ea. dist.) Calif., 1990—. Chmn. task force on race, religious and ethnic fairness U.S. Ct. Appeals (9th cir.), 1994-97, mem. jury com., 1993-95. Adv. com. on Civil Rules, 1994—, chair, 2000—; vis. com. U. Chgo. Law Sch., 1995-98. Mem. Am. Law Inst., Milton L. Schwartz Inn of Ct. (pres. 1992-95). Office: 501 I St Rm 14-230 Sacramento CA 95814-7300

LEVIN, ALLEN JAY, lawyer; b. Bridgeport, Conn., May 27, 1932; s. Simon H. and Adele Miriam (Rossinoff) L.; m. Judith Ann Rubinstein, Aug. 18, 1957 (div. 1987); children: Jennifer Suzanne, Miriam Adele, David Newmark, Michael Aaron; m. Gabrielle Hasson-Azar, Feb. 24, 1995. BA, NYU, 1954; postgrad., Boston U., 1954-55; JD, U. Miami, 1957. Bar: Fla. 1957, Conn. 1958, U.S. Dist. Ct. Conn. 1960, U.S. Dist. Ct. (so. dist.) Fla. 1962, U.S. Dist. Ct. (mid. dist.) Fla. 1969, U.S. Ct. Appeals (11th cir.) 1981, U.S. Supreme Ct. 1972. Small claims ct. judge County of Charlotte, Punta Gorda, Fla., 1962-72; legal counsel Port Charlotte-Charlotte Harbor (Fla.) Fire Control Dist., 1965-86; mcpl. judge City of North Port, Fla., 1973-76, city atty., 1977-87; pvt. practice Charlotte. Legal counsel Charlotte County Habitat for Humanity, Inc. Of counsel Charlotte County Habitat for Humanity Inc. Mem.: ABA, Fla. Bar Assn. (probate law com., real property probate and trust laws sect.), Charlotte County Bar Assn., Port Charlotte-Charlotte County C. of C., Port Charlotte-Charlotte County Bd. of Realtors (assoc.)), Elks, Kiwanis (youth svcs. chmn. Port Charlotte Club 1986—, pres. 1984—85, pres. 1998—99, lt. gov.- elect divsn.18 so. Fla. dist. 1999—2000, lt. gov. 2000—01). Avocation: stamp collecting. Estate planning, Probate, Real property. Home: 125 Graham St SE Port Charlotte FL 33952 Office: 3440 Conway Blvd Ste 1A Port Charlotte FL 33952 E-mail: ajlgal@juno.com

LEVIN, EDWARD M. retired lawyer, retired government administrator; b. Chgo., Oct. 16, 1934; s. Edward M. and Anne Meriam (Fantl) L.; children from previous marriage: Daniel Andrew, John Davis; m. Margot Aronson, Apr. 4, 1993. BS, U. Ill., 1955; LLB, Harvard U., 1958. Bar: Ill. 1958, U.S. Supreme Ct. 1968. Mem. firm Ancel, Stonesifer, Glink & Levin and predecessors, Chgo., 1958, 61-68; draftsman Ill. Legis. Reference Bur., Springfield, 1961; spl. asst. to regional adminstr. HUD, Chgo., 1968-71, asst. regional adminstr. community planning and mgmt., 1971-72; asst. dir. Ill. Dept. Local Govt. Affairs, 1973-77; of counsel Holleb, Gerstein & Glass, Ltd., 1977-79; chief counsel Econ. Devel. Adminstrn., U.S. Dept. Commerce, Washington, 1979-85, 1997-2001; sr. fellow Nat. Gov's. Assn., 1985-86; sr. counsel U.S. Dept. Commerce, Washington, 1987-96; instr. Mgmt. Concepts, Inc., Vienna, 2001—. Lectr. U. Ill., 1972-73, adj. assoc. prof. urban scis., 1973-79; lectr. Loyola U., 1976-79, No. Va. law Sch., 1988. Assoc. editor Assistance Mgmt. Jour., 1990-95; contbr. articles to profl. jours. Mem. Ill. Nature Preserves Com., 1963-68, Northea. Ill. Planning Commn., 1974-77, Ill.-Ind. Bi-State Commn., 1974-77; bd. dirs. Cook County Legal Assistance Found., 1978-79, D.C. Appleseed Ctr., 1994—; mem. Ill. divsn. ACLU, 1965-68, 77-79, v.p., 1977-78; chmn. ABA fed. assistance com., 1995-96. With AUS, 1958-60. Recipient Lincoln award Ill. Bar Assn., 1977, Gold medal U.S. Dept. Commerce, 2000, Corrigan award Econ. Devel. Adminstrn., 2000. Mem. FBA (chmn. fed. grants com. 1991-95), Nat. Grants Mgmt. Assn. (bd. dirs. 1988-92, Pres.'s award 1994), Appleseed Found. (bd. dirs., mem. exec. com. 1994—). Home: 3201 Porter St NW Washington DC 20008-3212 E-mail: elevin111@erols.com

LEVIN, EZRA GURION, lawyer; b. Bklyn., Feb. 10, 1934; s. Harry and Bertha Levin; m. Batya Ann Schaefer, June 19, 1960; children: Zachary Abraham, Ayala Deborah Levin-Kruss. AB, Columbia U., 1955; postgrad., U. Chgo., 1955-56; LLB, Columbia U., 1959. Bar: N.Y. 1961. Assoc., then ptnr. Marshall, Bratter, Greene, Allison & Tucker, N.Y.C., 1961-79; ptnr. Kramer Levin Naftalis & Frankel LLP, 1979—. Bd. dirs. Kaiser Aluminum Corp., MAXXAM, Inc., Houston; adj. prof. sociology Columbia U., 1973-77, 87, 93; adj. faculty U. Conn. Law Sch., 1970-73; vis. prof. U. Wis. Law Sch., 1967, 98. Contbr. articles to profl. jours. Mem.-at-large Jewish Cmty. Rels. Coun., N.Y.C., 1983—, pres., 2001—; trustee N.Y. Citizens Budget Commn., 2000—; vice chmn. Coalition for Soviet Jewry, N.Y.C., 1984-93, co-chair, 1994—; counsel Am. Friends Sarah Herzog Meml. Hosp.-Jerusalem, Inc., N.Y.C., 1975—; sec., bd. dirs. Scholarship, Edn. and Def. Fund for Racial Equality, N.Y.C., 1961-70; founding chair Solomon Schechter High Sch. of N.Y., 1992-96, trustee 1992—. Mem. ABA, Law and Society Assn. Avocation: tennis. General corporate, Mergers and acquisitions, Securities. Office: Kramer Levin Naftalis & Frankel LLP 919 3rd Ave New York NY 10022-3902 E-mail: elevin@kramerlevin.com

LEVIN, FREDRIC GERSON, lawyer; b. Pensacola, Fla., Mar. 29, 1937; s. Abraham I. and Rose (Lefkowitz) L.; m. Marilyn Kapner, June 14, 1959; children: Marci Levin Goodman, Debra Levin Dreyer, Martin, Kimberly Levin Brielmayer. BSBA, U. Fla., 1958, JD, 1961. Bar: Fla. 1961, U.S. Dist. Ct. (no. dist.) Fla., U.S. Ct. Appeals (5th cir.). Assoc. Levin, Middlebrooks, Thomas & Mitchell PA, Pensacola, 1961—. Counsel Fla. Senate, 1981-82. Author: Effective Opening Statements, 1983; contbr. articles to profl. jours. Fellow Acad. Fla. Trial Lawyers (dir. 1977-84), mem. Inner Circle of Advocates, Ala. Trial Lawyers Assn., Tex. Trial Lawyers Assn., Pa. Trial Lawyers Assn. Democrat. Jewish. Personal injury. Home: 533 Deer Point Dr Gulf Breeze FL 32561-4543 Office: Levin Middlebrooks Thomas & Mitchell PA 316 S Baylen St Pensacola FL 32501-5900

LEVIN, HERVEY PHILLIP, lawyer, director; b. Oct. 22, 1942; s. Julius L. and Gertrude (Cohen) L.; m. Madeleine J. Raskin, Sept. 22, 1970; children: Arianne, Nicole, David. BBA, U. Mich., 1964, MBA, 1968; JD, DePaul U., 1969. Bar: Ill. 1969, Tex. 1979, U.S. Dist. Ct. (no. dist.) Ill. 1970, U.S. Ct. Appeals (5th cir.) 1981, U.S. Ct. Appeals (7th cir.) 1971, U.S. Supreme Ct. 1972. Assoc. Potts Randall & Horn, Chgo., 1970-71; assoc., jr. ptnr. Mehlman, Ticho, Addis, Susman, Spitzer, Randall, Horn & Pyes, 1971-75; pvt. practice, 1975-78, Dallas, 1979—. Dir. Leedal Inc., Chgo.; cons. in workers' compensation, occupational disease and gen. practice. Bd. dirs. Solomon Schecter Acad. of Dallas, 1979—, Cong. Shearith Israel, Dallas, 1981-88, Am. Jewish Congress, Dallas, 1980-85, Nat. Assn. Mortgage Planners, 1995—. Named Ky. Col. Mem. ABA (workers compensation com. torts and ins. practices sect., chmn. 1989-90, sr. vice-chair 1990—, coun. mem. torts and ins. practices sect. 1995-98, 99—, ho. of dels. 1999—, various adminstrv. coms., torts and ins. practices sect. 1990—, liaison to Internat. Assn. Indsl. Accident Bds. and Comms. 1989—, cons. labor stds. subcom., house edn. and labor com., U.S. Congress, chmn. solo and small firm practices com. 1994-95), Ill. Bar Assn., Tex. Bar Assn., Dallas Bar Assn., Chgo. Bar Assn. General practice, Real property, Workers' compensation. Office: 6918 Blue Mesa Dr Ste 115 Dallas TX 75252-6140 Fax: 972-733-3269. E-mail: hervey@airmail.net

LEVIN, MARVIN EUGENE, lawyer; b. Antigo, Wis., June 20, 1924; s. Jacob and Lillian (Goldberg) L.; m. Ruth Ganzfried, June 10, 1948; children: Randal Mark, Gregary. BS, U. So. Calif., 1948, JD, 1951. Bar: Calif. 1952. Pvt. practice, L.A., Santa Monica, Calif., 1952-68; sr. ptnr. Levin & Freedman, Santa Monica, 1968-97, of counsel, 1997—. Lectr. in field. Bd. dirs., founding mem. NCCJ, Santa Monica, 1959—, chmn., 1965, So. Calif. regional bd., 1984-92; regional bd. Anti-Defamation League, 1958—, exec. com., 1960-81, 87—; pres. Santa Monica Family YMCA, 1985-86, bd. dirs., 1987—, chmn. endowment com., 1990-; bd. dirs. U. Synagogue, West L.A., Calif., 1970-74. Capt. USAAF, 1943-46. Decorated Air medal with oak leaf cluster; recipient Brotherhood award Santa Monica Bay Area chpt. NCCJ, 1968. Fellow Am. Coll. Trust and Estate Counsel; mem. ABA, State Bar Calif. Assn. (sect. real property, probate, trust law), L.A. County Bar Assn., Santa Monica Bay Dist. Bar Assn. (trustee 1971-74, pres. 1973-74, chmn. sect. real property law 1982-84), Am. Arbitration Assn. (panel of arbitrators 1968—), Rotary Internat. Found. (chmn. world cmty. svc. Santa Monica chpt. 1985-98, chmn, 2001-). Estate planning, Probate, Real property. Office: Levin & Freedman LLP 501 Santa Monica Blvd Ste 601 Santa Monica CA 90401-2488 E-mail: melvin@levinfreedman.com

LEVIN, MURRAY SCOTT, law educator, arbitrator, mediator; b. Dec. 7, 1948; s. Herman Levin and Rita (Tenner) Horwitz; m. Julie Elizabeth Sacks, June 14, 1970; 1 child Paris Anna. BA, U. Wis., 1972, MBA, 1974; JD, U.Kans., 1977. Bar: Mo. 1977. Tchr. Project Head Start, Madison, Wis., 1970—73; assoc. Brown, Korachik & Fingersh, Kans. City, Mo., 1977—79; assoc. prof. bus. law U. Kans., Lawrence, Kans., 1979—; legal cons. Legal Aid of Western Mo., 1980—. Editor (note and comment): (law rev.) U. Kans. Law Rev., 1976—77; editor: (staff) (jour.) Am. Bus. Law Jour., 1988—94;contbr. articles to profl. jours. Mem.: Acad. Legal Studies in Bus., Mo. Bar Assn., Midwest Acad. Legal Studies in Bus. Office: U Kans 118 G Sumerfield Hall Lawrence KS 66045

LEVIN, RICHARD C. lawyer; b. Dallas, June 15, 1945; s. Paul Michael and Yetta Gail (Caplan) L.; m. Kay Robins, June 18, 1982; children: Edward C., Henry A. BA, Tulane U., 1967; JD, Georgetown U., 1970. Bar: Tex. 1975. Law clerk 5th cir. U.S. Ct. Appeals, 1970-71; assoc. Sulivan & Cromwell, N.Y.C., 1971-74, Akin, Gump, Strauss, Hauer & Feld L.L.P., Dallas, 1974-77, ptnr., 1978—. With Dallas Mgmt. com., 1989—; co-head litigation sect. Akin, Gump, Strauss, Hauer & Feld, head antitrust sect., internat. litigation sect.; spkr. in field. Contbr. articles to profl. jours. Former mem. exec. bd. Dallas Opera; former mem. bd. govs. Dallas Symphony; corp. com. Dallas Mus. Fine Arts; former mem., v.p. bd. trustees Hist. Preservation League; former mem. Landmark Com. City Dallas, bd. trustees Arts Magnet Sch.; former mem., dep. vice chmn., mgmt. com. Arts Dist. in Dallas; former chmn. Task Force Multi-Purpose Performing Arts Hall Dallas Opera, Dallas Ballet; bd. dirs. Dallas Opera, Salzburg Music Festival. Mem. Dallas Bar Assn. (coun. mem. Antitrust, Trade Regulation sect. 1987—, internat. law sect. 1990—). Jewish. Avocations: classical music, art, sports. Home: 4408 Saint Johns Dr Dallas TX 75205-3825 Office: Akin Gump Strauss Hauer & Feld 1700 Pacific Ave Ste 4100 Dallas TX 75201-4675

LEVIN, RONALD MARK, law educator; b. St. Louis, May 11, 1950; s. Marvin S. and Lois (Cohn) L.; m. Anne Carol Goldberg, July 29, 1989. BA magna cum laude, Yale U., 1972; JD, U. Chgo., 1975. Bar: Mo. 1975, D.C. 1977. Law clk. to Hon. John C. Godbold U.S. Ct. Appeals, 5th cir., 1975-76; assoc. Sutherland, Asbill & Brennan, Washington, 1976-79; asst. prof. law Washington U., St. Louis, 1979-80, assoc. prof. law, 1980-85, prof. law, 1985-2000, assoc. dean, 1990-93, Henry Hitchcock prof. law, 2000—. Cons. Adminstrv. Conf. U.S., 1979-81, 93-95. Co-author: Administrative Law and Process, 4th edit., 1997, State and Federal Administrative Law, 2d edit., 1998. Chair senate coun. Washington U., 1988-90. Mem. ABA (chair sect. adminstrv. law and regulatory practice 2000—), Assn. Am. Law Sch. (chair sect. adminstrv. law 1993, chair sect. legis. 1995). Home: 7352 Kingsbury Blvd Saint Louis MO 63130-4142 Office: Wash Univ Sch Law Campus Box 1120 Saint Louis MO 63130

LEVIN, SIMON, lawyer; b. Newark, Aug. 4, 1942; m. Barbara Leslie Lasky; children: David, Jennifer Menken, Yale, Michael, Jacob. BS cum laude, Lehigh U., 1964; JD, NYU, 1967, LLM in Taxation, 1974. Bar: N.J. 1967, U.S. Tax Ct. 1971, U.S. Ct. Claims 1972, N.Y. 1980. Assoc. Shanley & Fisher, Newark, 1970, Hannoch Weisman, Newark, 1970-73; ptnr. Robinson, Wayne, Levin, Riccio & La Sala, 1973-88; mem., chmn. tax dept. Sills Cummis Radin Tischman Epstein & Gross, 1988—. Civillian aide to Sec. Army for N.J., 1992-95; mem. N.J. Dept. Treasury Transition Team for Gov. Christine Todd Whitman, 1993-94; mem. Treas. Adv. Group N.J. Dept. of Treasury, 1995—; lectr., panelist numerous orgns. Co-author: Taxation Investors in Securities and Commodities, 1983, 2d edit., 1984, supplement, 1986, Estate Planning and Administration in New Jersey, 1987; contbr. articles to profl. jours. Trustee, mem. exec. com. Jewish Comty. Found., MetroWest, Whippany, N.J., pres., 1979-83; trustee, mem. exec. com. Israel Bond Campaign MetroWest, Livingston, N.J., chmn., 1988-89; trustee Monmouth Healthcare Ctr. Found., 1997—, N.J. Vietnam Vets. Meml. and Edn. Ctr. Found., Holmdel, 1994—. Capt. U.S. Army, 1968-69, Vietnam. Recipient Cohn Leadership award Jewish Fedn. MetroWest, 1982, Endowment Achievement award Coun. Jewish Fedns., 1986, N.J. Meritorious Svc. medal, 1995. Fellow Am. Coll. Tax Counsel; mem. ABA, N.J. Bar Assn. (chmn. commodities sect. 1982-86), Essex County Bar Assn. (chmn. sect. taxation 1974-76), Monmouth County Bar Assn., Phi Delta Phi. Avocations: tennis, skiing, politics, opera, community service. Estate taxation, Taxation, general, State and local taxation. Office: Sills Cummis Radin Tischman Epstein & Gross 1 Riverfront Plz Fl 10 Newark NJ 07102-5401

LEVINE, ALAN, lawyer; b. Middletown, N.Y., Jan. 17, 1948; s. Jacques and Florence (Tananbaum) L.; children: Emily Jane, Malcolm Andrew. BS in Econs., U. Pa., 1970; JD, NYU, 1973. Bar: N.Y. 1974, U.S. Dist. Ct. (so. dist.) N.Y. 1974, U.S. Dist. Ct. (ea. dist.) N.Y. 1980, U.S. Tax Ct. 1980, U.S. Ct. Appeals (2d cir.) 1975. Law clk. U.S. Dist. Ct. (so. dist.) N.Y., N.Y.C., 1973-75; asst. U.S. atty. U.S. Attys. Office, so. dist. N.Y., Dept. Justice, 1975-80; assoc. Kronish, Lieb, Weiner & Hellman, 1980-82, mem., 1982—, mng. ptnr., 1998—. Chmn. bd. dirs. Park Ave. Synagogue, N.Y.C., 1993-98; bd. dirs. Jewish Theol. Sem., 1998, MYF Legal Svcs. Inc., 1990-93; law chmn. N.Y. County Rep. Com., 1991-93. Recipient Atty. Gen. Dirs. award U.S. Dept. Justice, 1980, Torch of Learning award Am. Friends Hebrew U., 1995, Human Rels. award ADL, 2001. Fellow Am. Bar Found., Am. Coll. Trial Lawyers; mem. ABA (ho. of dels. 1983-84, chmn. spl. com. for youth edn. for citizenship, 1988-91, vice chmn. white collar crime com. 1996—), N.Y. State Bar Assn. (chmn. com. on citizenship edn. 1979-84, ho. of dels. 1982-84, award of achievement 1984), Sunningdale Country Club (bd. trustees 1988-90 Scarsdale, N.Y.), Mask and Wig Club (Phila.). Republican. Jewish. Federal civil litigation, Criminal. Home: 1185 Park Ave New York NY 10128-1308 Office: Kronish Lieb Weiner & Hellman 1114 Avenue Of The Americas New York NY 10036-7703

LEVINE, BERNARD BENTON, lawyer; b. New Haven, Aug. 27, 1927; s. Charles and Mildred (Schwartz) L.; m. Joan A. Rapoport, Sept. 7, 1952; children— Stefanie, Kalman, Shelley Levine Kraft. B.A., U. Conn., 1950; LL.B., Boston U., 1953; LL.M. in Taxation, NYU, 1954. Bar: Mass. 1953,

Conn. 1954, Mo. 1955. Assoc. Stinson, Mag, Thomson, McEvers & Fizzell, Kansas City, Mo., 1954-55; ptnr. Warrick, Levine & Greene, Kansas City, 1958-68, Levine & Green, Kansas City, 1968-81; sole practice, Kansas City, 1981— ; instr. real estate, econs. and comml. law; 1985-87. Contbr. articles to legal jour. Bd. govs., past v.p., past bd. dirs. Jewish Geriatric and Convalescent Ctr., Kansas City, Jewish Family and Children's Svcs., Kansas City; bd. govs., past dir. Hyman Brand Hebrew Acad., Overland Park, Kans.; bd. dirs. Jewish Community Ctr., Kansas City, William Jewell Fine Arts Guild, Liberty, Mo., pres.; bd. dirs., mem. campaign cabinet Jewish Fedn., Kansas City. With U.S. Army, 1946-48. Mem. ABA (property and internat. savs. and loan div.), U.S. Savs. and Loan League, Mo. Savs. and Loan League, Mo. Bar Assn., Kansas City Bar Assn., Lawyers Assn. Kansas City, Conn. Bar Assn., Mass. Bar Assn. Real property, Corporate taxation. Home: 121 W 48th St Apt 2102 Kansas City MO 64112-3920 Office: 1101 Walnut 1402 Mercantile Tower Kansas City MO 64106

LEVINE, DAVID ETHAN, lawyer; b. Niagara Falls, N.Y., Feb. 28, 1955; s. Morree Morell Levine and Marbud Juel (Gagen) Prozeller; m. Ann Lee Ruhlin, May 23, 1981. BS in Bus., Miami U., 1977; JD, Capital U., 1981. Bar: N.Y. 1982, U.S. Dist. Ct. (we. dist.) N.Y. 1982. Assoc. Grossman, Levine and Civiletto, Niagara Falls, 1981-89, Cummings and Levine, Niagara Falls, 1989-92; pvt. practice, 1992—. V.p. Buffalo Area Recreational Cyclists, Inc., 1995. Mem. N.Y. State Bar Assn., Erie County Bar Assn., Niagara Falls Bar Assn., Niagara County Sportsman's Assn. Unitarian Universalist. Avocations: skiing, photography, bicycling, camping. Probate, Real property, Workers' compensation. Home: 22 Hemlock Dr Grand Island NY 14072-3315 Office: PO Box 922 669 Main St Niagara Falls NY 14302 E-mail: d.levine2@gte.net

LEVINE, HAROLD, lawyer; b. Newark, Apr. 30, 1931; s. Rubin and Gussie (Lifshitz) L.; children: Brenda Sue, Linda Ellen Levine Gersen, Louise Abby, Jill Anne Levine Lipari, Charles A., Cristina Gussie, Harold Rubin II; m. Cristina Cervera, Aug. 29, 1980. BS in Engring., Purdue U., 1954; JD with distinction, George Washington U., 1958. Bar: D.C. 1958, Va. 1958, Mass. 1960, Tex. 1972, U.S. Patent Office 1958. Naval arch., marine engr. U.S. Navy Dept., 1954-55; patent examiner U.S. Patent Office, 1955-58; with Tex. Instruments, Inc., Attleboro, Mass., 1959-77, asst. sec. Dallas, 1969-72, asst. v.p. and gen. patent counsel, 1972-77; ptnr. Sigalos & Levine, 1977-93; prin. Levine & Majorie LLP, 1994-2000, Levine & Starr LLP, 2001—. Chmn. bd. Vanguard Security, Inc., Houston, 1977—; chmn. Tex. Am. Realty, Dallas, 1977—; lectr. assns., socs.; del. Geneva and Lausanne (Switzerland) Intergovtl. Conf. on Revision, Paris Pat. Conv., 1975-76. Editor George Washington U. Law Rev., 1956-57; mem. adv. bd. editors Bur. Nat. Affairs, Pat., Trdmk. and Copyright Jour.; contbr. chpt. to book and articles to profl. jours. Mem. U.S. State Dept. Adv. Panel on Internat. Tech. Transfer, 1977. Mem. ABA (chmn. com. 407 taxation pats. and trdmks. 1971-72), Am. Patent Law Assn., Dallas Bar Assn., Assn. Corp. Pat. Csl. (sec.-treas. 1971-73), Dallas-Ft. Worth Patent Law Assn., Pacific Indsl. Property Assn. (pres. 1975-77), Electronic Industries Assn. (pres. pat. com. 1972), NAM, Southwestern Legal Inst. on Patent Law (planning com. 1971-74), U.S. C. of C., Dallas C. of C., Kiwanis, Alpha Epsilon Pi, Phi Alpha Delta. Republican. Jewish. Intellectual property, Patent, Trademark and copyright. Office: Levine & Starr LLP Bank Am Pl Tower 101 E Park Blvd Ste 755 Plano TX 75074 Fax: 972-398-6095

LEVINE, HENRY DAVID, lawyer; b. N.Y.C., June 7, 1951; s. Harold Abraham and Joan Sarah (Price) L.; m. Barbara Wolgel, Aug. 28, 1976; children: David, Rachel, Daniel. AB, Yale U., 1972; JD, M in Pub. Policy, Harvard U., 1976. Bar: N.Y. 1977, D.C. 1978, U.S. Supreme Ct. 1980. Assoc. Wilmer, Cutler & Pickering, Washington, 1976-80, Morrison & Foerster, Washington, 1981-83, ptnr., 1983-92, Levine, Blaszak, Block & Boothby LLP, Washington, 1993—. Cons. to GSA on FTS2001, 1994—; chmn. bd. TechCaliber, LLC, 1999—. Editor Telematics, 1984-89. Mem. Nat. Rsch. Coun. Com on High Tech. Bldgs., 1985-88; bd. dirs. Washington Hebrew Congregation, 1996—, Appleseed Found., 2001—. Named one of the twenty-five most powerful people in networking Network World, 1996. Mem. ABA, Fed. Communication Bar Assn., Forum Com. on Comm. Law. Administrative and regulatory, Communications. Home: 5208 Edgemoor Ln Bethesda MD 20814-2342 Office: Levine Blaszak Block & Boothby 2001 L St NW Ste 900 Washington DC 20036-4940 E-mail: hlevine@lb3law.com

LEVINE, HERBERT, lawyer; b. June 5, 1924; s. Barnet and Mollie (Morris) L.; m. Pearl H. Kahn, Mar. 30, 1946; children: Barbara, Susan, Deborah, Steven. BBA, JD, U. Wis., 1950. Bar: Wis. 1950, U.S. Dist. Ct. (ea. dist.) Wis. 1950. Pvt. practice, Milw., 1950-66; assoc. Bernstein, Wessel & Lewis, 1967-75; shareholder Stupar, Schuster & Cooper S.C., 1976-2000; pvt. practice, 2000—. Instr. Am. Inst. Banking, Milw., 1964-88 ; lectr. Marquette U., 1968-79, Milw. Bd. Realtors, 1961. Pres. Bayside PTA, Wis., 1965-66; active Indian Guides, Bayside, Wis., 1972-73. Sgt. USAAF, 1943-46. Mem. Wis. Bar Assn., Milw. Bar Assn. Contracts commercial, General corporate, Real property. Home: 9055 N King Rd Milwaukee WI 53217-1848 Office: 633 W Wisconsin Ave Milwaukee WI 53203-1918 E-mail: ssc@ssclaw.com

LEVINE, HOWARD ARNOLD, state supreme court justice; b. Mar. 4, 1932; m. Barbara Joan Segall, July 25, 1954; children: Neil Louis, Ruth Ellen, James Robert. BA, Yale U., 1953, LLB, 1956; LLD (hon.), Union U., 1994. Bar: N.Y. 1956. Asst. in instrn., research assoc. in criminal law Yale Law Sch., 1956-57; assoc. firm Hughes, Hubbard, Blair, Reed, N.Y.C., 1957-59; practiced in Schenectady, 1959-70; asst. dist. atty. Schenectady County, N.Y., 1961-66, dist. atty., 1967-70; judge Schenectady County Family Ct., 1971-80; acting judge Schenectady County Ct., 1971-80; adminstrv. judge family cts. N.Y. State 4th Jud. Dist., 1974-80; assoc. justice appellate div. 3d dept. N.Y. State Supreme Ct., 1982-93; assoc. judge N.Y. Ct. of Appeals, 1993—. Vis. lectr. Albany Law Sch., 1972-81; mem. N.Y. Gov.'s Panel on Juvenile Violence, N.Y. State Temp. Commn. on Child Welfare, N.Y. State Temp. Commn. on Recodification of Family Ct. Act, N.Y. State Juvenile Justice Adv. Bd., 1974-80; mem. ind. rev. bd. N.Y. State Div. for Youth, 1974-80; mem. rules and adv. com. on family ct. N.Y. State Jud. Conf., 1974-80 Contbr. articles to law revs. Bd. dirs. Schnecatady County Child Guildance Ctr., Carver Community Ctr., Freedom Forum of Schnectady. Mem. ABA, Am. Law Inst., N.Y. State Bar Assn. (chmn. spl. com. juvenile justice), Assn. Family Ct. Judges State N.Y. (pres. 1979-80) Home: 2701 Rosendale Rd Niskayuna NY 12309-1300 Office: County Jud Bldg 612 State St Schenectady NY 12305-2113*

LEVINE, JACK ANTON, lawyer; b. Monticello, N.Y., Dec. 23, 1946; s. Milton and Sara (Sacks) L.; m. Eileen A. Garsh, Sept. 7, 1974; children: Matthew Aaron, Dara Esther. BS with honors, SUNY, Binghamton, 1968; JD with honors, U. Fla., 1975, LLM in Taxation, 1976. Bar: Fla. 1975, U.S. Ct. Appeals (11th cir.) 1981, U.S. Tax Ct., 1982. Tax atty. legis. and regulations divsn. Office chief counsel IRS, Washington, 1977-81; assoc. Holland & Knight, Tampa, Fla., 1981-83, ptnr., 1984—. Lectr. in field. Contbr. articles to profl. jours. Mem. ABA, Fla. Bar Assn. (sect. taxation exec. coun. 1984—, chmn. ptnrship. com. 1985-88, chmn. taxation regulated public utilities com. 1988-92, co-chmn. corps. and tax-exempt orgns. com. 1992—, bd. cert. in tax law 1984—). Democrat. Jewish. Avocations: golf, reading, traveling. Corporate taxation, Taxation, general, Personal income taxation. Home: 10905 Carrollwood Dr Tampa FL 33618-3903 Office: Holland & Knight 400 N Ashley Dr Ste 2300 Tampa FL 33602-4322

LEVINE, JEROME LESTER, lawyer; b. L.A., July 20, 1940; m. Maryanne Shields, Sept. 13, 1966; children: Aron Michael, Sara Michelle. BA, San Francisco State U., 1962; JD, U. Calif., 1965. Bar: Calif. 1966, U.S. Supreme Ct. 1986. Dir. operational svcs., assoc. dir. Western Ctr. on Law and Poverty, L.A., 1968-72; assoc. Swerdlow, Glikbarg & Shimer, Beverly Hills, Calif., 1972-77; ptnr. Lans Feinberg & Cohen, L.A., 1977-79, Albala & Levine, L.A., 1980-83, Neiman, Billet, Albala & Levine, L.A., 1983-90, Levine & Assocs., L.A., 1991-2000, Holland & Knight LLP, L.A., 2000—. Lectr. U. So. Calif. Law Ctr., Loyola U. Sch. Law. Mem. ABA, L.A. County Bar Assn., Beverly Hills Bar Assn., Assn. Bus. Trial Lawyers, Fed. Bar Assn., Nat. Indian Gaming Assn. (co-chmn. law and legis. com.), Internat. Assn. Gaming Lawyers (editl. bd. Indian Gaming Mag.). Federal civil litigation, State civil litigation, General corporate. Office: 633 W 5th St Ste 2100 Los Angeles CA 90071-2017 E-mail: jllevine@hklaw.com

LEVINE, KIMBERLY ANNE, lawyer; b. Bklyn., Aug. 6, 1967; d. Fred Howard and Miriam Carol (Cohen) L. BS, Cornell U., 1989; JD, B.N. Cardozo Sch. Law, N.Y.C., 1993. Bar: N.Y. 1994, U.S. Dist. Ct. (ea. dist.) N.Y. 1996, U.S. Dist. Ct. (so. dist.) N.Y. 1996, U.S. Ct. Appeals (2d cir.) 1999, U.S. Supreme Ct. 1999. Asst. dir. of representation Office of Collective Bargaining, N.Y.C., 1989-91; counsel, asst. to dir. Conf. of Presidents of Major Am. Jewish Orgns., 1995-96; assoc. civil litigation Karp, Silver, Glinkenhouse & Floumanhaft, Far Rockaway, N.Y., 1996-97; assoc. employment litigation Milman & Heidecker, Lake Success, 1997—. Adv. bd. Cornell U. Hillel Alumni Bd., 1995— Advisor Neve Yerushalayim Coll., N.Y.C. and Jerusalem, Israel, 1993—; tutor Bible studies Aish Ha Torah, N.Y.C., 1997—. Recipient Pres.'s prize Met. Squash Rackets Assn., N.Y.C., 1992; named High Ranking Amateur U.S. Squash Rackets Assn., 1990, 91. Fellow Hashevaynu (cons. 1995—); mem. Neve Yerushalayim Coll. Alumni Assn. (Alumni of Yr. 1995). Avocations: tennis, squash, softball. Federal civil litigation, State civil litigation, Labor. Office: Milman & Heidecker 3000 Marcus Ave Ste 3w3 New Hyde Park NY 11042-1009

LEVINE, MARILYN MARKOVICH, lawyer, arbitrator; b. Bklyn., Aug. 9, 1930; d. Harry P. and Fannie L. (Hymowitz) Markovich; m. Louis L. Levine. June 24, 1950; children: Steven R., Ronald J., Linda J. Morgenstern. BS summa cum laude, Columbia U., 1950; MA, Adelphi U., 1967; JD, Hofstra U., 1977. Bar: N.Y. 1978, U.S. Dist. Ct. (so. and ea. dists.) N.Y. 1978, D.C. 1979, U.S. Supreme Ct. 1982. Sole practice, Valley Stream, N.Y., 1978—. Contract arbitrator bldg. svc. industry, N.Y.C., 1982—; panel arbitrator retail food industry, N.Y.C., 1980—; arbitrator N.Y. dist. cts., Nassau County, 1981—; mem. Nat. Acad. Arbitrators, 1992—. Panel arbitrator Suffolk County Pub. Employee Relations Bd., 1979—, Nassau County Pub. Employee Relations Bd., 1980—, Nat. Mediation Bd., 1986—; mem. adv. council Ctr. Labor and Industrial Relations, N.Y. Inst. Tech., N.Y., 1985—; counsel Nassau Civic Club, 1978—. Mem. ABA, N.Y. State Bar Assn., D.C. Bar Assn., Nassau County Bar Assn., N.J. Bd. Mediation (panel arbitrator), Am. Arbitration Assn. (arbitrator 1979—), Fed. Mediation Bd. (arbitrator 1980—). Alternative dispute resolution, Labor. Home and Office: 1057 Linden St Valley Stream NY 11580-2135

LEVINE, MELVIN CHARLES, lawyer; b. Bklyn., Nov. 12, 1930; s. Barnet and Jennie (Iser) L. BCS, NYU, 1952; LLB, Harvard U., 1955. Bar: N.Y. 1956, U.S. Supreme Ct. 1964. Assoc. Kriger & Haber, Bklyn., 1956-58, Black, Varian & Simons, N.Y.C., 1959; sole practice, 1959—. Devel. multiple dwelling housing; dir. Am. ORT; mem. Am. ORT Nat. Campaign Com.; trustee Bramson ORT Coll.; mem. housing ct. adv. coun. N.Y. State Unified Ct. Sys.; mem. ind. dem. jud. screening panel N.Y.C civil ct. judges; mem. Character and Fitness Com., First Jud. Dept. Trustee Jewish Ctr. of the Hamptons. Recipient N.Y. Ort Scholarship Fund Cmty. Achievement award. Mem. N.Y. County Lawyers Assn. (dir., co-chair civil ct. practice sect., civil ct. com., housing ct. com., uniform housing ct. rules com., liaison to Assn. Bar City of N.Y. on selection of housing, civil and criminal ct. judges, com. on jud., task force on tort reform, Civil Ct. Practice Sect. Disting. Svc. award), Assn. Bar of City of N.Y. (adj. mem. jud. com.) Democrat. Jewish. State civil litigation, Landlord-tenant, Real property. Home: 146 Waverly Pl New York NY 10014-3848 Office: 271 Madison Ave Ste 1404 New York NY 10016-1001

LEVINE, RONALD JAY, lawyer; b. Bklyn., June 23, 1953; s. Louis Leon and Marilyn Priscilla (Markovich) L.; m. Cindy Beth Israel, Nov. 18, 1979; children: Merisa, Alisha. BA summa cum laude, Princeton U., 1974; JD cum laude, Harvard U., 1977. Bar: N.Y. 1978, U.S. Dist. Ct. (so. and ea. dists.) N.Y. 1978, D.C. 1980, N.J. 1987, U.S. Supreme Ct. 1982, U.S. Ct. Apeals (2d cir.) 1983, N.J. 1987, U.S. Dist. Ct. N.J. 1987, U.S. Dist. Ct. (we. dist.) N.Y. 1991, U.S. Ct. Appeals (3d cir.) 1991, Pa. 1995. Assoc. Phillips, Nizer, Benjamin, Krim & Ballon, N.Y.C., 1977-80, Debevoise & Plimpton, N.Y.C., 1980-84, Herrick, Feinstein, N.Y.C., 1984-85, ptnr., 1985—. Gen. counsel Greater N.Y. Safety Council, N.Y.C., 1979-81; arbitrator Small Claims Ct. of Civil Ct. of City of N.Y., 1983-85; mem. fee arbitration com. Mercer County, N.J. Mem. Site Plan Rev. Adv. Bd., West Windsor, N.J., 1986, planning bd., 1987. Mem. ABA (litigation sect.), N.Y. State Bar Assn. (chmn. com. on legal edn. and bar admission 1982-92, com. on profl. discipline 1989-90), N.J. State Bar Assn. (product liability com. 1991—, profl. responsibility com. 1992-96), Assn. of Bar of City of N.Y. (coun. jud. adminstrn. 1994-95, com. on profl. responsibility 1980-83, com. on legal assistance 1983-86, product liability com. 1987-91, trustee career devel. awards 1989-90), Phi Beta Kappa. General civil litigation, Environmental, Product liability. Home: 6 Arnold Dr Princeton Junction NJ 08550-1521 Office: Herrick Feinstein 2 Park Ave Fl 20 New York NY 10016-9302

LEVINE, SAMUEL MILTON, lawyer, retired judge, mediator, arbitrator; b. Syracuse, N.Y., Feb. 24, 1929; s. Joseph and Sophie Levine; m. Leona Miller, Sept. 9, 1950; children: Judith, Donald, Gary. BBA, Syracuse U., 1950; JD, Bklyn. Law Sch., 1953. Bar: N.Y. 1953, U.S. Supreme Ct. 1960, U.S. Dist. Ct. (ea. and so. dists.) N.Y. 1962; cert. mediator, arbitrator. Assoc. Law Office of William S. Miller, Esq., N.Y.C., 1954-62, Law Office of Ferdinand I. Haber, Esq., Mineola, N.Y., 1958-62; pvt. practice Nassau County, 1962-65; counsel English, Cianciulli, Reisman & Peirez, 1962-65; supt. of real estate Nassau County, 1965-84; pvt. practice Garden City, N.Y., 1984—. Lobbyist for handicapped; pres. bd. of judges Dist. Ct. Nassau County; lectr. in field. Contbr. articles to profl. jours. Past chmn. Sch. Aid Coun. L.I., Citizens Com. for Elmont Schs., N.Y.; former counsel, trustee Temple Bnai Israel, Elmont; former bd. visitors Pilgrim State Hosp.; treas., counsel N.Y. State Coun. Orgns. for Handicapped; past pres. Nassau County Epilepscy Found.; former chmn. Health and Welfare Coun. Nassau County; former mem. Nassau-Suffolk Health Sys. Agy.; del. White House Conf. on Children and Youth, 1960; candidate N.Y. State Senate, 1964; Dem. candidate Dist. Ct. Judge, 1985; candidate N.Y. State Supreme Ct., 1990; counsel Health Advs., Voice for Handicapped, Fedn. Parent Orgns., League of Voters for Handicapped; del. White House Conf. on Disabilities, 1970; del. White House Conf. on Mental Health, 1999. With U.S. Army, 1948. Recipient Adv. of Yr. award L.I. Coun. Fedn. Parents Orgns., 1978. Mem. Nat. Acad. Elder Law Attys., N.Y. State Bar Assn., Nassau County Bar Assn. (former chmn. social svc. and health law com., legis. com.), Syracuse U. Alumni Club, Kiwanis, Knights of Pythias, B'nai B'rith. Home: 711 Shore Rd Apt 2E Long Beach NY 11561-4707

LEVINE, SANFORD HAROLD, lawyer; b. Troy, N.Y., Mar. 13, 1938; s. Louis and Reba (Semegren) L.; m. Margaret R. Appelbaum, Oct. 29, 1967; children: Jessica Sara, Abby Miriam. AB, Syracuse U., 1959, JD, 1961. Bar: N.Y. 1961, U.S. Dist. Ct. (no. dist.) N.Y. 1961, U.S. Dist. Ct. (we. dist.) N.Y. 1979, U.S. Dist. Ct. (ea. and so. dists.) N.Y. 1980, U.S. Ct. Appeals (2d cir.) 1962, U.S. Supreme Ct. 1967. Law asst. to assoc. judge N.Y. Ct. Appeals, Albany and to justice N.Y. Supreme Ct., 1962-66, N.Y. Ct. Appeals, Albany, 1964; asst. counsel N.Y. State Temporary commn. on Constl. Conv., N.Y.C., 1966-67; assoc. counsel SUNY System, Albany, 1967-70, dep. univ. counsel, 1970-78, acting counsel, 1970-71, acting univ. counsel, 1978-79, univ. counsel and vice chancellor legal affairs, 1979-97, prof. Sch. of Edn., dir. program in edn. and law, 1997—. Adj. prof. Sch. of Edn. State U. N.Y., Albany, 1992-97; mem. paralegal curriculum adv. com. Schenectady County Community Coll., 1975— . Editl. bd. Syracuse U. Law Rev., 1960-61; editl. adv. bd. Jour. Coll. and Univ. Law, 1977-81. Fellow Am. Bar Found., N.Y. Bar Found., State Acad. for Pub. Adminstrn.; mem. ABA (ho. dels. 1987-89), N.Y. State Bar Assn., Albany County Bar Assn., Nat. Assn. Coll. and Univ. Attys. (exec. bd. 1979-82, bd. dirs. 1982-89, pres. 1986-87), Am. Soc. Pub. Adminstrn. Home: 1106 Godfrey Ln Schenectady NY 12309-2712

LEVINE, STEVEN JON, lawyer; b. N.Y.C., Sept. 27, 1942; s. Irving I. and Freda S. (Silverman) L.; m. Linda Jane Silberman, Apr. 23, 1967; 1 child, Lawrence Alan. BS, Syracuse U., 1964; JD, St. John's U., 1966; MA, CCNY, 1973; LLM, NYU, 1978. Bar: N.Y. 1967. Assoc. Augustin J. San Filippo & Steven Jon Levine, PC, predecessor, N.Y.C., 1968-78; mem. Vittoria & Forsythe and predecessor, 1978-93, Levine & Zelman, 1993—. Arbitrator N.Y. County Civil Ct. Panel, 1980-93; asst. csl. N.Y. State Senate Judiciary Com., 1977. Author: of legal column Tomorrow newspapers; co-author: Divorce Q & A: Answers to Questions about Divorce, Equitable Distribution, Maintenance, Custody and Child Support; host weekly radio law program Sta. WVOX, 1990-91; creator, narrator: (audio cassette program) Coping with Separation and Divorce. Committeeman, Bronx County, 1970-76; bd. dirs. Jewish Conciliation Bd. Am., 1973-93. Mem. ABA, N.Y. State Bar Assn., Westchester County Bar Assn., Assn. Bar City N.Y. (sect. vice chmn. matrimonial com. 1977-80), Am. Arbitration Assn. (no-fault, comml. panels 1975-88). Family and matrimonial, General practice, Personal injury. Office: 50 Main St Ph White Plains NY 10606-1901 also: Levine & Zelman 630 5th Ave New York NY 10111-0100

LEVINE, THOMAS JEFFREY PELLO, lawyer; b. Santa Monica, Calif., Mar. 6, 1952; s. Allan Lester and Shirley Elaine (Pello) L.; children: Marissa, Matthew, Molly. Student, U. Denver, 1970-71, Calif. State U., Northridge, 1971-73, Uppsala U., Sweden; BA, Calif. State U., Sacramento, 1974; JD, Southwestern U., 1977; postgrad., Yale U., 1999. Bar: Calif. 1977, U.S. Dist. Ct. (cen. dist.) Calif. 1978. Ptnr. Levine & Levine, L.A., 1977-83; staff atty. Fed. Deposit Ins. Corp., Newport Beach, Calif., 1983-85; v.p., assoc. counsel Imperial Bank, Inglewood, 1985-88; v.p., counsel Community Bank, Pasadena, 1988; gen. counsel, sr. v.p., sec. Calif. Commerce Bank, Banamex USA Bancorp, L.A., 1988-2001; gen. counsel, sr. v.p. Banamex-Citibank, 2001—. Legal affairs com. mem. Calif. Bankers Assn., San Francisco, 1990—; chmn. Am. Bankers Assn. Bank Counsel Com. 1993-97. Dir. Angelino Heights Historic Preservation Assn., L.A., 1985-95; sec., dir. Carroll Ave. Restoration Found., L.A., 1979-87; dir. Wilshire C. of C., L.A., 1982. Mem. L.A. County Bar Assn., Braemar Country Club (bd. govs. 1979-83). Jewish. Avocations: running, golf, Aztec history, historic preservation. Banking, Consumer commercial, Private international. Office: Banamex-Citibank 2029 Century Park E Fl 42 Los Angeles CA 90067-2901

LEVINGS, THERESA LAWRENCE, lawyer; b. Kansas City, Mo., Oct. 24, 1952; d. William Youngs and Dorothy (Neer) Frick; m. Darryl Wayne Levings, May 25, 1974; children: Leslie Page, Kerry Dillon. BJ, U. Mo., 1973; JD, U. Mo., Kansas City, 1979. Bar: Mo. 1979, U.S. Dist. Ct. (we. dist.) Mo. 1979, U.S. Ct. Appeals (8th cir.) 1982, U.S. Ct. Appeals (10th cir.) 1986, U.S. Dist. Ct. (ea. dist.) Mo. 1989. Copy editor Kansas City Star, 1975-78; law clk. to judge Mo. Supreme Ct., Jefferson City, 1979-80; from assoc. to ptnr. Morrison & Hecker, Kansas City, 1980-94; founding ptnr. Badger & Levings, L.C., 1994—. Mem. fed. practice com. U.S. Dist. Ct. (we. dist.), 1990-95; mem. fed. adv. com. U.S. Ct. Appeals (8th cir.), 1994-97. Leadership grad. Kansas City Tomorrow; account exec. United Way; bd. dirs. Jr. League, Housing Info. Ctr. Mem. Mo. Bar (bd. govs. 1990—, pres. 2001-, young lawyers coun. 1982-89, chair 1988-89, Pres. award 1989, Outstanding Svc. award young lawyers coun. 1985, 86), Assn. Women Lawyers Greater Kansas City (pres. 1986-87, Woman of Yr. 1993), Lawyers Assn. Greater Kansas City (bd. dirs. young lawyers sect. 1982-83), Kansas City Met. Bar Assn. (chair civil practice and procedure com. 1988-89, chair fed. practice com. 1990-91). Avocations: antiques, history, cooking. Federal civil litigation, Insurance, Product liability. Office: Badger & Levings LC 1101 Walnut St Kansas City MO 64106-2134*

LEVINSON, CHRISTOPHER GREGORY, legal administrator; b. Encino, Calif., Feb. 27, 1963; s. Irwin and Joette Levinson; m. Lisa S., Sept. 22, 1990; children: Matthew, Jenna. Student, Valley Coll., 1981-82, UCLA, 1982-83. Envir. adminstr. Law Offices of Masry & Vititoe, Westlake Village, Calif., 1983—. Mem. ATLA, Calif. Trial Lawyer Assn., L.A. Trial Lawyer Assn. Office: Masry & Vititoe 5707 Corsa Ave Fl 2 Westlake Village CA 91362-6499 E-mail: levinson@masryvititoe.com

LEVINSON, KENNETH LEE, lawyer; b. Denver, Jan. 18, 1953; s. Julian Charles and Dorothy (Milzer) L.; m. Shauna Titus, Dec. 21, 1986. BA cum laude, U. Colo., 1974; JD, U. Denver, 1978. Bar: Colo. 1978, U.S. Ct. Appeals (10th cir.), 1978. Assoc. atty. Balaban & Lutz, Denver, 1979-83; shareholder Balaban & Levinson, P.C., 1984—, pres., 1994—. Author: A Shadow in the Night, 2001;contbr. articles to profl. jours. Pres., Dahlia House Condominium Assn., 1983-85, bd. dirs., 1991-94; intern Reporters Com. for Freedom of the Press, Washington, 1977; atty. grievance hearing bd., 1988—; jr. varsity volleyball coach Good Shepherd Cath. Sch., 1992-95. Recipient Am. Jurisprudence award Lawyers Co-op, 1977. Mem. Colo. Bar Asn. (profl. liability com. 1991-94), Denver Bar Assn., Denver Law Club. General civil litigation, General practice, Insurance.

LEVINSON, KENNETH S. lawyer, corporate executive; b. Mineola, N.Y., Oct. 27, 1947; s. Max Leonard and Eva (Klamen) L.; m. Laura R. Levinson, Sept. 14, 1969 (div. 1981); 1 child, Barbara Ann Schmidt; m. Jerelyn E. Jarmacz, Feb. 6, 1982; children: Alexander T., Brianna F., Joshua K. BA in Polit. Sci. with distinction, U. Wis., 1969; JD with honors, George Washington U., 1975; LLM in Taxation, Georgetown U., 1978. Bar: D.C. 1975, Va. 1975, U.S. Ct. Claims 1976, U.S. Dist. Ct. (D.C. dist.) 1976, U.S. Tax Ct. 1976, U.S. Ct. Appeals (D.C. cir.) 1976, U.S. Supreme Ct. 1979. Atty., advisor Office Chief Counsel Interpretative div. IRS, Washington, 1975-78, reviewer, asst. br. chief Office Chief Counsel, 1978-79; sr. tax atty. Pepper, Hamilton & Scheetz, 1979-81; v.p., mng. tax dir. Marriott Corp., Bethesda, Md., 1981-85, v.p. internat. project fin., 1985-90; v.p. tax Northwest Airlines, Inc., Eagan, Minn., 1990-92, v.p. tax, risk mgmt., ins. St. Paul, 1992-94, v.p. fin. and planning cargo/charter divsn., 1994-96, v.p. tax, risk mgmt. and ins., 1996—. Adj. prof. Georgetown U. Law Ctr., Washington, 1978-86; asst. sec., v.p. various Marriott Corp. subs., Bethesda, 1981-90; v.p. Wings Holdings, Inc./N.W. Airlines Corp., 1990—; v.p. tax N.W. Airlines, Inc., 1990—, v.p. various subs.; cons. The Chechhi Group, Beverly Hills, Calif., 1989-90; bd. dirs. City Harbour Hotel, Ltd., London. Contbr. articles to profl. jours. Bd. dirs. Minn. Taxpayers Assn., Mpls. Lt. USN, 1969-72. Mem. ABA (subcom. chair 1978-84), D.C. Bar, Va. State Bar, Tax Execs. Inst. (bd. dirs. Minn. chpt. 1999—), Washington Tax Group, Air Transport Assn., Internat. Air Transport Assn. (chair taxation com. 1991-92, 99-2000, vice-chmn. 1999, chmn. ins. com. 1994, 97-99, chair internat. risk mgrs. forum 1995, 98-2001), Nat. Taxpayers Assn. (bd. dirs. 1999—), Minn. Taxpayers Assn. (bd. dirs., exec. com. 1998—). Avocations: golf, art appreciation/collection, boating, equestrian show jumping, skiing. Aviation, Finance.

LEVINSON, PAUL HOWARD, lawyer; b. N.Y.C., Nov. 9, 1952; s. Saul and Gloria (Samson) L.; m. Susan Norine Morley, May 29, 1983; children: Lauren Hope, David Ross. BA in Sociology, Northwestern U., 1973; JD, Columbia U., 1977. Bar: N.Y. 1978; U.S. Dist. Ct. (so. and ea. dist.) N.Y. 1983, U.S. Dist. Ct. (no. dist.) N.Y. 1992; U.S. Ct. Appeals (2d cir.) 1986, U.S. Ct. Appeals (3rd cir. 1987), U.S. Supreme Ct. 1986. Asst. dist. atty., supervising sr. trial atty. Kings County, Bklyn., 1977-84; assoc. Blodnick, Schultz & Abramowitz, P.C., Lake Success, N.Y., 1984-85; ptnr. Leavy, Rosensweig & Hyman and predecessor firms, N.Y.C., 1985-99, McLaughlin & Stern, LLP, N.Y.C., 2000—. Trustee Cmty. Synagogue, Rye, N.Y., 1996—; mem. adv. coun. parks and recreation Village of Rye Brook, N.Y., 1994-97. Harlan Fiske Stone scholar. Mem. ABA, N.Y. State Bar Assn., Assn. of Bar of City of N.Y. (com. on criminal justice ops. and budget 1992-94, com. on criminal cts. 1995—, chmn. sub-com. on the N.Y.C. civilian complaint rev. bd., moderator), Bklyn. Bar Assn. (continuing legal edn. seminars in criminal trial advocacy and matrimonial practice), Columbia Law Sch. Alumni Assn., Northwestern U. Entertainment Alliance East (treas. 1998—, pres. 2000—), Northwestern U. Alumni Assn. Democrat. Jewish. Club: Northwestern U. Alumni of N.Y.C. Avocations: tennis, skiing, swimming. General civil litigation, Criminal, Entertainment. Home: 312 Betsy Brown Rd Rye Brook NY 10573-1901 Office: McLaughlin & Stern LLP 260 Madison Ave 18th Fl New York NY 10016 E-mail: plevinson@mclaughlinstern.com

LEVINSON, PETER JOSEPH, retired lawyer; b. Washington, June 11, 1943; s. Bernard Hirsh and Carlyn Virginia (Krupp) L.; m. Nanette Susan Segal, Mar. 30, 1968; children: Sharman Risa, Justin David. AB in History cum laude, Brandeis U., Waltham, Mass., 1965; JD, Harvard U., 1968. Bar: U.S. Supreme Ct. 1975. Summer supr. Harvard Legal Aid Bur., Cambridge, Mass., 1968; rsch. asst. Harvard Law Sch., 1968-69; tchg. fellow Osgoode Hall Law Sch. York (Can.) U., 1969-70, rsch. assoc., 1969-70, asst. prof., 1970-71; dep. atty. gen. State of Hawaii, 1971-75; vis. fellow Harvard U., 1976-77; ptnr. Levinson and Levinson, Honolulu, 1977-79; spl. asst. to dir. office program support Legal Svcs. Corp., Washington, 1979; cons. Select Commn. on Immigration and Refugee Policy, 1980-81; minority counsel subcom. on immigration, refugees and internat. law com. on judiciary U.S. Ho. of Reps., 1981-85, minority counsel subcom. monopolies and comml. law, 1985-89, minority counsel subcom. econ. and comml. law, 1989-95, counsel com. on judiciary, 1995-2001, ret., 2001. Lawyer; b. Washington, June 11, 1943; s. Bernard Hirsh and Carlyn Virginia (Krupp) L.; m. Nanette Susan Segal, Mar. 30, 1968; children: Sharman Risa, Justin David. AB in History cum laude, Brandeis U., Waltham, Mass., 1965; JD, Harvard U., 1968. Bar: Hawaii 1971, U.S. Supreme Ct. 1975. Summer supr. Harvard Legal Aid Bur., Cambridge, Mass., 1968; research asst. Harvard Law Sch., 1968-69; teaching fellow Osgoode Hall Law Sch., York U. (Can.), 1969-70, research assoc., 1969-70, asst. prof., 1970-71; dep. atty. gen. State of Hawaii, 1971-75; vis. fellow Harvard U., 1976-77; ptnr. Levinson and Levinson, Honolulu, 1977-79; spl. asst. to dir. Office Program Support, Legal Services Corp., Washington, 1979; cons. Select Commn. on Immigration and Refugee Policy, Washington, 1980-81; minority counsel subcom. on immigration, refugees and internat. law com. on judiciary, U.S. Ho. of Reps., Washington, 1981-85, minority counsel subcom. monopolies and comml. law, 1985-89, minority counsel subcom. econ. and comml. law, 1989-95, counsel com. on judiciary, 1995—. Trustee, Hawaii Jewish Welfare Fund, 1972-75, chmn. fund drive, 1972; trustee Temple Emanu-El, Honolulu, 1973-75; mem. alumni admissions council Brandeis U., 1978-82. Recipient award of merit United Jewish Appeal, 1974. Mem. Hawaii State Bar Assn. (chmn. standing com. on continuing legal edn. 1972, chmn. standing com. on jud. adminstrn. 1979), ABA, Am. Judicature Soc. Contbr. articles to profl. jours. Contbr. articles to profl. jours. Trustee Hawaii Jewish Welfare Fund, 1972-75, chmn. fund drive, 1972; trustee Temple Emanu-El, Honolulu, 1973-75; alumni admissions coun. Brandeis U., 1978-82. Recipient Merit award United Jewish Appeal, 1974. Mem. ABA, Am. Judicature Soc. Home: PO Box 5690 Washington DC 20016

LEVINSON, STEVEN HENRY, state supreme court justice; b. Cincinnati, OH, June 8, 1946; BA with distinction, Stanford U., 1968; JD, U. Mich., 1971. Bar: Hawaii 1972, U.S. Dist. Ct. Hawaii 1972, U.S. Ct. Appeals (9th cir.) 1972. Law clk. to Hon. Bernard H. Levinson Hawaii Supreme Ct., 1971-72; pvt. practice Honolulu, 1972-89; judge Hawaii Cir. Ct. (1st cir.), 1989-92; assoc. justice Hawaii Supreme Ct., Honolulu, 1992—. Staff mem. U. Mich. Jour. Law Reform, 1970-71. Active Temple Emanu-El. Mem. ABA (jud. adminstrn. divsn. 1989—), Hawaii State Bar Assn. (dir. young lawyers divsn. 1975-76, dir. 1982-84), Nat. Jud. Coll. (state jud. leader 1991—), Am. Judges Assn., Am. Judicature Soc. Jewish. Office: Supreme Ct Hawaii Aliiolani Hale 417 S King St Honolulu HI 96813-2912

LEVIS, WILLIAM HERST, lawyer; b. Chgo., Oct. 5, 1947; s. Allen and Elaine (Herst) L.; m. Ann Elizabeth Feinstein, Aug. 17, 1969; 1 child, Jonathan Jacob. BA, U. Mich., 1969; JD, U. Ill., 1972. Bar: Colo. 1972, Ill. 1993, U.S. Dist. Ct. Colo. 1972, U.S. Ct. Appeals (10th cir.) 1982. Atty., investigator Colo. Civil Rights Commn., Denver, 1972-73; regional atty. U.S. Com. on Civil Rights, 1973-79; asst. atty. gen. Colo. Dept. Law, 1979-85; spl. counsel Colo. Gen. Assembly, 1983-84; regulatory atty., dir. pub. policy WorldCom, Inc., 1985—. Pres. Knolls West Homeowners Assn., Littleton, Colo., 1973; pres., v.p. Antelope Property Owners Assn., Aurora, Colo., 1981-84. Mem. Fed. Comm. Bar Assn. (co-chmn. mid-west chpt. 1993-94), Colo. Bar Assn., Denver Bar Assn. Home: 10956 E Crestline Pl Englewood CO 80111-3808 Office: WorldCom Inc 707 17th St Ste 4200 Denver CO 80202-3400

LEVIT, JAY J(OSEPH), lawyer; b. Phila., Feb. 20, 1934; s. Albert and Mary Levit; m. Heloise Bertman, July 14, 1962; children: Richard Bertman, Robert Edward, Darcy Francine. AB, Case Western Res. U., 1955; JD, U. Richmond, 1958; LLM, Harvard U., 1959. Bar: Va. 1958, D.C. Ct. Appeals 1961, U.S. Supreme Ct. 1961. Trial atty. U.S. Dept. Justice, Washington, 1960-64; sr. atty. Gen. Dynamics Corp., Rochester, N.Y., 1965-67; ptnr. Stallard & Levit, Richmond, Va., 1968-77, Levit, Mann & Halligan, Richmond, 1978—. Instr. U. Mich. Law Sch., Ann Arbor, 1964-65; adj. assoc. prof. U. Richmond Law Sch., 1974-77; adj. lectr. Va. Commonwealth U., Richmond, 1970-85; lectr. in field. Contbg. editor The Developing Labor Law-Bur. Nat. Affairs, 1974—. Recipient ABA and Bur. Nat. Affairs Books Cert. of Appreciation for significant contbns. to advancement of the law, 1999, 2000. Mem. ABA (labor com.), Va. Bar Assn. (labor and employment com., Chair's award for extraordinary contbns. to labor and employment law sect. 1999), Fed. Bar Assn. (labor and employment com.). Avocations: art collecting, jogging, swimming, travel. General civil litigation, Labor, Pension, profit-sharing, and employee benefits. Home: 419 Dellbrooks Pl Richmond VA 23233-5559 Office: Levit Mann & Halligan 1301 N Hamilton St Richmond VA 23230-3959 also: Levit Mann & Halligan 127 Thompson St Ashland VA 23005-1511 E-mail: levmanhal@mindspring.com

LEVIT, WILLIAM HAROLD, JR. lawyer; b. San Francisco, Feb. 8, 1938; s. William Harold and Barbara Janis Kaiser L.; m. Mary Elizabeth Webster, Feb. 13, 1971; children: Alison Jones Baumler, Alexandra Bradley Kovacevich, Laura Elizabeth Fletcher, Amalia Elizabeth Webster Todryk, William Harold, III. BA magna cum laude, Yale U., 1960; MA Internat. Rels., U. Calif., Berkeley, 1962; LLB, Harvard U., 1967. Bar: N.Y. 1968, Calif. 1974, Wis. 1979. Fgn. service officer Dept. State, 1962-64; assoc. Davis Polk & Wardwell, N.Y.C., 1967-73; assoc. ptnr. Hughes Hubbard & Reed, N.Y.C., L.A., 1973-79; sec. and gen. counsel Rexnord Inc., Milw., 1979-83; ptnr., dir., chair internat. practice group Godfrey & Kahn, 1983—. Substitute arbitrator Iran-U.S. Claims Tribunal, The Hague, 1984-88; lectr. Practicing Law Inst., ABA, Calif. Continuing Edn. of Bar, State Bar of Wis. Contbr. to: Mergers and the Private Antitrust Suit: The Private Enforcement of Section 7 of the Clayton Act, 1977. Bd. dirs. Wis. Humane Soc., 1980-90, pres., 1986-88; bd. dirs. Vis. Nurse Corp., Milw., 1980-90, chmn., 1985-87; bd. dirs. Vis. Nurse Found., 1986-95, chmn., 1989-91; bd. dirs. Aurora Health Care Inc., 1988-93, Wis. Soc. to Prevent Blindness, 1981-91, Columbia Coll. Nursing, 1992—, vice chair, 1998—, Aurora Health Care Ventures, 1993—, chmn., 1998-2000, 2001; adv. bd. Med. Coll. Wis. Cardiovasc. Ctr., 1994—, chmn., 1999—, chmn. Bd. Ad Oversight Supreme Ct. Wis. Office Lawyer Regulation, 2000—; rep. Assn. Yale Alumni, 1976-79, 81-84, 90-93; pres. Yale Club So. Calif., 1977-79; mem. neutral advisor panel and franchise, and ins. panels panels CPR Inst. for Dispute Resolution. Ford Found. fellow U. Pa., 1960-61, NDEA fellow U. Calif., Berkeley, 1961-62. Mem.: ABA, Am. Law Inst., Am. Soc. Corp. Secs. (pres. Wis. chpt. 1982—83, dir. 1981—92), Assn. Bar City N.Y., State Bar Calif. (com. on continuing edn. of bar 1977—79), L.A. County Bar Assn. (ethics com. 1976—79), State Bar Wis. (dir. internat. bus. transactions sect. 1985—92, dist. 2 Wis. Supreme Ct. bd. attys. profl. responsbility com. 1985—94, chmn. 1993—94), Bar Assn. 7th Cir. (1st v.p. 2001), Am. Br. Internat. Law Assn., Am. Arbitration Assn. (comml. panel 1977—, internat. panel 1997—), Nat. Assn. Security Dealers (panel arbitrators 1988—), Chartered Inst. Arbitrators (London), N.Y. Stock Exch. (panel arbitrators 1988—), N.Am. Coun. London Ct. of Internat. Arbitration, Am. Soc. Internat. Law, Inst. Jud. Adminstrn., Milw. Club, Milw. Athletic Club, Town Club, Phi Beta Kappa. Antitrust, Federal civil litigation, State civil litigation. Office: 780 N Water St Ste 1500 Milwaukee WI 53202-3512 E-mail: walevit@gklaw.com

LEVITAN, DAVID M(AURICE), lawyer, educator; b. Tver, Lithuania, Dec. 25, 1915; (parents Am. citizens); m. Judith Morley; children: Barbara Lane Levitan, Stuart Dean Levitan. BS, Northwestern U., 1936, MA, 1937; PhD, U. Chgo., 1940; JD, Columbia U., 1948. Bar: N.Y. 1948, U.S. Dist. Ct. (so. dist.) N.Y. 1948, U.S. Supreme Ct. 1953. Various U.S. Govt. adminstrv. and advisory positions with Nat. Youth Adminstrn., Office Price Adminstrn., War Prodn. Bd., Fgn. Econ. Adminstrn. Supreme Hdqrs. Allied Expeditionary Force, and Cen. European div. Dept. State, 1940-46; cons., sec. joint-com. of 5th and 6th coms., 2d Gen. Assembly, dir. com. of experts for establishing adminstrv. tribunal UN, 1946-47; cons. pub. affairs dept., producer series of pub. affairs programs on TV and radio ABC, 1946-53; pvt. practice N.Y.C., 1948-66; counsel Hahn & Hessen, 1966-68, ptnr., 1968-86, counsel, 1986-96; instr. U. Chgo., 1938-41; adj. prof. public law Columbia U., 1946-65; adj. prof. John Jay Coll. Criminal Justice, CUNY, 1966-75; adj. prof. polit. sci. Post Coll., 1964-66; adj. prof. law Cardozo Sch. Law, 1978-82; pvt. practice, N.Y.C., 1996—. Asst. to Ill. state adminstr. Nat. Youth Adminstrn., chief budget sect., Washington, 1940-41; mgmt. analyst Office of Price Adminstrn., 1941; spl. asst. to chmn. War Prodn. Bd., 1942-43; chief property control divsn. Fgn. Econ. Adminstrn., Washington, 1944-45; with U.S. Group of Control Coun. for Germany at SHAEF, London, 1944; advisor Ctrl. European divsn. U.S. Dept. State, 1945; cons. UN, 1946-47, Sect. Joint Com. 5th and 6th Coms., 1946-47, 2d session of 1st Gen. Assembly, 1946-47; dir. Com. of Experts on Establishment of Adminstrn. Tribunal, 1946-47; cons. pub. affairs dept. ABC, 1946-53. Contbr. articles to legal jours. Mem. Nassau County (N.Y.) Welfare Bd., 1965-69; chmn. Planning Bd., Village of Roslyn Harbor, N.Y., 1965-66; chmn. Bd. of Zoning Appeals, Village Roslyn Harbor, 1967-86. Recipient Demobilization award Social Sci. Rsch. Coun., 1946-48. Fellow Am. Coll. Trust and Estate Counsel; mem. ABA, Am. Polit. Sci. Assn., Am. Soc. Internat. Law, Am. Law Inst., Assn. Bar City N.Y. Constitutional, Probate, Estate taxation. Home: 103 NE 19th Ave Deerfield Beach FL 33441-6106 Office: 40 E 94th St New York NY 10128

LEVITAN, KATHERINE D. lawyer; b. Vienna, Austria, July 8, 1933; came to U.S. 1938, naturalized 1942; d. Otto and Hedweega (Saltzer) Lenz; m. Leonard Levitan, Sept. 12, 1952; children— Joel, Jeffrey, Debbie, Diane. B.A. cum laude, N.Y.U. 1952, J.D. cum laude, 1955, LL.M. in Criminal and Family Law, 1977. Bar: N.Y. 1956, U.S. Dist. Ct. (ea. dist.) N.Y. 1972, U.S. Supreme Ct. 1974. Tchr. bus. law N.Y. Inst. Tech., Old Westbury, 1968-69; assoc. Bennett Reiss, Great Neck, N.Y., 1969-70, Malone and Dorfman, Freeport, N.Y., 1970-71; sole practice, Jericho, N.Y., 1971-80; practice with assocs., Mineola, N.Y., 1980— ; also lectr.; assoc. prof. Hofstra Law Sch. Bd. dirs., legal counsel For Our Children and Us, Inc., Nassau chpt. ACLU, 1975— ; mem. Nassau County Democratic Com., 1969— , law guardian adv. panel 2d dept. Human Rights Adv. Commn. Nassau County; past pres. Nassau chpt. N.Y. Civil Liberties Union. Mem. Nassau Bar Assn. (grievance com., martim com.), Nassau/Suffolk Women's Bar Assn. (past pres., legal counsel), Nassau Civil Liberties Union, L.I. Women's Network, Acad. Matrimonial Lawyers, Contbr. articles to profl. publs. Civil rights, Family and matrimonial, General practice. Home: PO Box 846 New Lebanon NY 12125-0846 Office: 83 Prospect St Huntington NY 11743-3306

LEVITT, PRESTON CURTIS, lawyer; b. Queens Village, N.Y., July 23, 1950; s. Leon and Meryl Barbara (Rosenstock) L.; m. Maddy Charlene Domenitz, July 1, 1973; children— Taryn Audra, Brandon Ross. B.S., Am. U., 1972; J.D., Bklyn. Law Sch., 1975; LL.M., NYU, 1980. Bar: N.Y. 1976, Fla. 1977, U.S. Dist. Ct. (ea. and so. dists.) N.Y. 1976, U.S. Dist. Ct. (so. dist.) Fla. 1980, U.S. Ct. Claims 1980, U.S. Tax Ct. 1976, U.S. Ct. Appeals (5th cir.) 1980. Sr. tax acct. Arthur Young & Co., N.Y.C., 1975-80; mem. firm E.T. Hunter, Hollywood, Fla., 1980-81; sr. ptnr. Brydger & Levitt, P.A., Ft. Lauderdale, Fla., 1981— ; dir. Atlantic Services Group Inc., Ft. Lauderdale; adv. bd. dirs. Regent Bank. Bd. dirs. Vis. Nurses Assn., Fort Lauderdale, 1983— . Mem. Fla. Bar Assn., Broward County Bar Assn., Am. Inst. Banking (bd. dirs. 1981—), Fraternal Order Police, Tau Epsilon Phi. Jewish. General corporate, Probate, Personal income taxation. Office: Brydger & Levitt PA 7770 W Oakland Park Blvd Fort Lauderdale FL 33351-6750

LEVMORE, SAUL, law educator, dean; b. 1953; BA, Columbia Coll., 1973, PhD, 1978; JD, Yale U., 1980; LLD (hon.) , Ill. Inst. Tech. Chgo.-Kent Law Sch., 1995. Bar: Va. 1983. Dean Jonathan Edwards Coll. Yale U., 1979-80; asst. prof. U. Va. , Charlottesville, 1980-84; prof. U. Va., 1984—98, Brokaw prof. of law; William B. Graham prof. law U. Chgo. Law Sch., 1998—, dean, 2001—. Lectr. econs. Yale U., 1976-80, vis. prof., 1986-87; vis. prof. Harvard U., 1990-91, U. Chgo., 1993. Office: U Chgo Law Sch 1111E 60th St Chicago IL 60637*

LEVY, ALAN M. lawyer; b. Milw., Nov. 10, 1940; s. Sam and Emma (Gold) L.; m. Tee Gee Azine, Mar. 3, 1964; children: Shawn, Joshua, Pamela, Jonathan. AB, U. Chgo., 1963, JD, 1965. Bar: Wis. 1965, Ill. 1982, U.S. Ct. Appeals (2d, 5th, 6th, 7th, 8th, 9th and 10th cirs.) 1968, U.S. Dist. Ct. (ea. dist.) Wis. 1965, (no. dist.) Ill. 1982, (so. dist.) Ill. 1969, U.S. Supreme Ct. 1980, U.S. Dist. Ct. (we. dist.) Mich. 2001. Ptnr. Goldberg, Previant, Uelman, Gratz, Miller et al, Milw., 1965-82; sr. legal counsel, dir. plan devel./compliance Central States, S.E. and S.W. Areas Pension Fund, Chgo., 1982-85; assoc. O'Neil, Cannon & Hollman, S.C., Milw., 1985-91, Lindner & Marsack, S.C., Milw., 1991—. Bd. incorporators Commonwealth Mutual Savs. Bank, Milw., 1977-82; adj. prof. labor law U. Wis., Milw., 1974—. Contbr. articles to profl. jours. Chmn. U. Chgo. Alumni Schs. Com., Milw., 1987—; trustee Congregation Emanu-El B'Ne Jeshurun, Milw., 1978-82, 86-92; campaign co-chmn. Urban Day Sch., Milw., 1988; active ACLU, Milw., 1966-82. Named Page scholar, U. Chgo., 1961, Iron Mask, 1961-64. Mem. ABA (labor law sect. 1967—), Wis. Bar Assn. (labor law sect. chmn. 1979-80), Ill. Bar Assn., Iron Mask Soc., U. Chgo. Alumni Assn. of Milw. (chmn. 1996-98), U. Chgo. Alumni Assn. (bd. govs. 1998—). Labor, Municipal (including bonds), Pension, profit-sharing, and employee benefits. Office: Lindner & Marsack SC 411 E Wisconsin Ave Ste 1000 Milwaukee WI 53202-4416 E-mail: alan.levy2@gte.net, alevy@lindner-marsack.com

LEVY, BARBARA JO, lawyer, personal life coach; b. San Antonio, Aug. 3, 1949; d. Rene Harry and Babbette Springer (Heil) L. BA, U. Tex., 1970, JD, 1974; MA in Psychology, Antioch U., 1990; postgrad., Acad. for Coach Tng., 2000-2001. Bar: Wash. 1974, U.S. Dist. Ct. (we. dist.) Wash. 1974. Staff atty. Seattle Legal Svcs., 1974-77; atty. pvt. practice, Seattle, 1978-79; ptnr. Sindell & Levy, Inc., 1979—; prin., owner Radian Life coaching. Instr. U. Tex. Sch. Law, 1973-74; intern Youth Law Ctr.; bd. dirs. Montlake Inst., 1989-93, pres., 1990-92; speaker, presenter seminars and classes regarding civil sexual abuse lawsuits. Co-author: Childhood Sexual Abuse: The Plantiff's Perspective, 1994. Coord. sexual abuse sem. Women's Law Ctr., Seattle, 1982; bd. dirs. Impact Child Abuse, Bellevue, Wash., 1985-86; att. Aradia Women's Health Clinic, Seattle, 1979-83; hospice vol., 1997—. Mem. Wash. State Trial Lawyers Assn., Assn. Trial Lawyers Am., Wash. State Bar Assn., Seattle King County Bar Assn., Wash. Lawyers (CLE com. 1992), N.W. Womens Law Ctr. Insurance, Personal injury, Sexual abuse litigation. Office: Sindell & Levy Inc PS 614 1st Ave Ste 300 Seattle WA 98104-2255

LEVY, BERTRAM LOUIS, lawyer; b. New Orleans, May 11, 1947; s. Louis Keiffer and Barbara Claire (Fox) L.; m. Barbara Jean Weinstock, Aug. 5, 1973; children— Emily Claire Strauss, Caroline Weinstock. B.A. with honors, Vanderbilt U., 1969; J.D., with honors, U. Mich., 1973. Bar: Ga. 1973, Mo. 1977. Assoc. firm Alston, Miller & Gaines, Atlanta, 1973-76, Gallop, Johnson & Neuman, St. Louis, 1977-80; assoc. firm Arnall, Golden & Gregory, Atlanta, 1980-82, ptnr., 1983— ; instr. Nat. Ctr. Paralegal Tng., Atlanta, 1980-81. Contrb. articles to profl. jours. Bd. dirs. and mem. exec. com. 20th Century Art Soc. High Mus., Atlanta, 1982— ; chmn. profl. div. Angel Campaign, Alliance Theater, Atlanta, 1983—; bd. dirs. and presiding bd. chmn. NCCJ, Atlanta, 1984— . Mem. Atlanta Estate Planning Council, ABA, State Bar Ga. (chmn. fiduciary law sect.). Republican. Jewish. Clubs: Capital City, Westwood Country (St. Louis). Estate planning, Probate. Home: 4700 Harris Trl NW Atlanta GA 30327-4410 Office: Arnall Golden & Gregory 55 Park Pl NE Atlanta GA 30303-2529

LEVY, CHARLOTTE LOIS, law librarian, educator, consultant, lawyer; b. Cin., Aug. 31, 1944; d. Samuel M. and Helen (Lowitz) L.; m. Herbert Regenstreif, Dec. 11, 1980; 1 dau., Cara Rachael Regenstreif. B.A., U. Ky., 1966; M.S., Columbia U., 1969; J.D., No. Ky. U., 1975. Bar: Colo. 1979, N.Y. 1985, Ky. 1985, U.S. Ct. Appeals (6th cir.) 1986. Law librarian No. Ky. U., 1971-75; law librarian, assoc. prof. law Pace U., 1975-77; mgr. Fred B. Rothman & Co., Littleton, Colo., 1977-79; law librarian, prof. Bklyn. Law Sch., 1979-85; adj. prof. Pratt Inst. Grad. Sch. Library and Info. Sci., 1982-85; atty. Cabinet for Human Resources, Frankfort, Ky., 1985-87, atty., pres. Vantage Info. Cons., Inc., Lexington, 1983—; cons. to various libraries, pubs. 1st v.p. Ohavay Zion Synagogue; pres. bd. trustees, Syncopated, Inc. Mem. Am. Assn. Law Libraries (cert. law librarian), ABA, Ky. Bar. Assn., Fayette County Bar Assn. Democrat. Jewish. Author: The Human Body and the Law (Am. Jurisprudence Book award in domestic relations 1974, in trusts 1975), 1974, 2d edit., 1983; Computer-Assisted Litigation Support, 1984; mem. editorial bd. No. Ky. U. Law Rev., 1974-75. Home: 200 McDowell Rd Lexington KY 40502-1896

LEVY, DAVID, retired lawyer, insurance company executive; b. Bridgeport, Conn., Aug. 3, 1932; s. Aaron and Rachel (Goldman) L. BS in Econs., U. Pa., 1954; JD, Yale U., 1957. Bar: Conn. 1958, U.S. Supreme Ct. 1963, D.C. 1964, Mass. 1965, N.Y. 1971, Pa. 1972; CPA, Conn. Acct. Arthur Andersen & Co., N.Y.C., 1957-59; sole practice Bridgeport, 1959-60; specialist tax law IRS, Washington, 1960-64; counsel State Mut. Life Ins. Co., Worcester, Mass., 1964-70; assoc. gen. counsel taxation Penn Mut. Life Ins. Co., Phila., 1971-81; sole practice Washington, 1982-87; v.p., tax counsel Pacific Life Ins. Co., Newport Beach, Calif., 1987-2001; ret., 2001. Author: (with others) Life Insurance Company Tax Series, Bureau National Affairs Tax Management Income Tax, 1970-71. Mem. adv. bd. Tax Mgmt., Washington, 1975-90, Hartford Inst. on Ins. Taxation, 1990-97; bd. dirs. Citizens Plan E Orgn., Worcester, 1966-70. With AUS, 1957. Mem. ABA (vice-chmn. employee benefits com. 1980-86, ins. cos. com. 1984-86, torts and ins. practice sect., subcom. chair ins. cos. com. tax sect. 1994—), Assn. Life Ins. Counsel, AICPA, Beta Alpha Psi. Jewish. Insurance, Corporate taxation, Taxation, general.

LEVY, DAVID, lawyer; b. Atlanta, July 7, 1937; s. Meyer and Elsie (Reisman) L.; m. Diane L. Lerner; children: Jeffrey Marc, Robert William, Danielle Beth, Margo Shaw; stepchildren: Mitchell S. Haber, Cort A. Haber. BA, Emory U., 1959, LLB, 1961; LLM, Georgetown U., 1964. Bar: Ga. 1961. Atty. SEC, Washington, 1961-65; assoc., partner Arnstein, Gluck, Weitzenfeld & Minow, Chgo., 1965-71; partner Kaler, Karesh & Frankel, Atlanta, 1971-73; exec. v.p. adminstrn., counsel, dir. Nat. Svc. Industries, Inc., 1973-2001, also bd. dirs.; of counsel King & Spalding, 2001—. Mem. ABA, Ga. Bar Assn. General corporate.

LEVY, DAVID HENRY, lawyer; b. Chgo., Apr. 16, 1951; s. Louis J. and Carolyn A. (Abraham) L. m B in Gen. Studies, Ohio U., 1973; JD, Ill. Inst. Tech/Kent Coll. Law, Chgo., 1976. Bar: Ill. 1976, U.S. Dist. Ct. (no. dist.) Ill. 1976, U.S. Ct. Appeals (7th cir.) 1976. Assoc., Law Offices of John Hirsch, Chgo., 1976-78; assoc. firm Feiwell, Galper Lasky & Berger Ltd., 1978-82, ptnr., 1982-87, Kalcheim, Schatz & Berger, Chgo., 1976—, mng. ptnr., 1996—. Faculty Ill. Inst. Continuing Legal Edn., 1986—; lectr. Young Single Parents Orgn.; guest lectr. Loyola U. Law Sch., Chgo., 1986; spkr. ABA nat. convs., 1993, 95; commentator WCIU-TV, Chgo. Chmn. fundraising com. Lincoln Ctrl. Assn., Chgo., 1982-84, bd. dirs., 1983-86, v.p., 1987, pres., 1988; mem. caucus Village of Northfield, Ill., 1988-92, chmn. platform com., 1992; mem. Lincoln Park Conservation Assn. Mem. ABA (family law sect.), Ill. State Bar Assn. (chmn. Family Law Sect., 1995-96, spkr. 1991-2000, vice chmn. family law sect. 1994-95, sec. 1993-94; mem. Supreme Ct. rules com. 1996—, chmn., 2001-; atty. children/GAL task force 1997; sol. on cable TV programming 1995—), Am. Acad. Matrimonial Lawyers (pres. Ill. chpt. 1993-94, bd. dirs. 1988-2001, nat. bd. govs. 1996-98, chmn. econs. of law practice com., mem. admissions procedures and site selection coms.). Family and matrimonial. Office: Kalcheim Schatz & Berger 161 N Clark St Ste 2800 Chicago IL 60601-3245

LEVY, EUGENE F. lawyer; b. N.Y.C., Nov. 3, 1947; s. Louis and Sara (Bindman) L.; m. Bari Wolfson, Aug. 20, 1972; children: Elizabeth, Douglas. BA, CUNY Queens Coll., 1969; postgrad. Sch. Internat. Affairs, Columbia U., 1969-70; JD, Hofstra U., 1973. Bar: N.Y. 1974, U.S. Dist. Ct. (so. and ea. dists.) N.Y. 1975, U.S. Ct. Appeals (2d cir.) 1975. Trial counsel Legal Aid Soc. City N.Y., 1973-78; assoc. counsel to spkr. N.Y. State Assembly, Albany, 1978-80, counsel to assemblyman, 1980-82, spl. counsel to assemblyman, 1983-85; assoc. counsel to minority leader N.Y. State Senate, 1982-83; spl. counsel to assemblywoman N.Y. State Assembly, 1986-88, 2000—; pvt. practice Kew Gardens, N.Y. Counsel Central Civic Home Care Attendants Assn., 1982—, Pomonok Home Svcs., Inc.

1987—, Metrolare Home Svcs., Inc., 1992—, Everwell Home Health Care Inc., 1993—. Vice chmn. Queens County Dem. Law Com., Forest Hills, N.Y., 1982—. Mem. ABA (sect. labor and employment law), Queens County Bar Assn., Criminal Cts. Bar Assn. (bd. dirs. 1986—), Hofstra U. Law Sch. Alumni Assn. (bd. dirs.). Office: 80-02 Kew Gardens Rd Ste 1010 Kew Gardens NY 11415-3600

LEVY, HERBERT MONTE, lawyer; b. N.Y.C., Jan. 14, 1923; s. Samuel M. and Hetty D. L.; m. Marilyn Wohl, Aug. 30, 1953; children: Harlan A., Matthew D., Alison Jill. BA, Columbia U., 1943, LLB, 1946. Bar: N.Y. 1946, U.S. Dist. Ct. (so. dist.) N.Y. 1946, U.S. Ct. Appeals (2d cir.) 1949, U.S. Dist. Ct. (ea. dist.) N.Y. 1949, U.S. Supreme Ct. 1951, U.S. Ct. Appeals (10th cir.) 1956, U.S. Tax Ct. 1973, U.S. Ct. Appeals (4th cir.) 1988. Assoc. Rosenman, Goldmark, Colin & Kaye, 1946-47, Javits & Javits, 1947-48; staff counsel ACLU, 1949-56; pvt. practice, 1956-64; ptnr. Hofheimer, Gartlir, Hofheimer, Gottlieb & Gross, 1965-69; pvt. practice N.Y.C., 1969—. Bd. dirs. Music Outreach; faculty N.Y. County Lawyers Assn.; past lectr. Practising Law Inst. Author: How to Handle an Appeal (Practicing Law Inst.), 1968, 4th edit., 1999; contbr. articles to profl. jours. Exec. com. on law and social action Am. Jewish Congress, 1961-66; trustee Congregation B'nai Jeshurun, 1987-98, chmn. bd. trustees, 1988-91, gen. counsel bd. trustees, 1991-92. Mem. Fed. Bar Coun. (past trustee), Bar Assn. City N.Y., N.Y. County Lawyers Assn., 1st Amendment Lawyers Assn. Democrat. E-mial. Appellate, General civil litigation, Constitutional. Home: 285 Central Park W Apt 12W New York NY 10024-3006 Office: 60 E 42nd St Ste 4210 New York NY 10165-4299 E-mail: hmlnyc@aol.com

LEVY, MARK ALLAN, lawyer; b. Cambridge, Mass., May 31, 1939; s. Robert A. and Muriel (Goldman) L.; m. Ellen Grob, Oct. 2, 1966; children: Abigail R., Eric V.R. AB, Harvard U., 1961; LLB, Columbia U., 1964, MBA, 1965. Bar: N.Y. 1964, Mass. 1965. Assoc. Parker, Chapin, Flattau & Klimpl, N.Y.C., 1965-68; sr. ptnr. Stroock & Stroock & Lavan, 1968—. Contbr. articles to profl. jours. Former mem. Planning Bd. Town of Greenburgh, N.Y. Mem. N.Y. State Bar Assn., Columbia Law Sch. Alumni Assn. (former dir.). Real property, Corporate taxation, Personal income taxation. Home: 60 Highridge Rd Hartsdale NY 10530-3605 Office: Stroock & Stroock & Lavan 180 Maiden Ln Fl 17 New York NY 10038-4937 E-mail: mlevy@stroock.com

LEW, GINGER, lawyer; b. San Mateo, Calif., Nov. 3, 1948; d. Bing and Suey Bow (Ng) L.; m. Carl Lennart Ehn, Feb. 2, 1984; children: Melissa, Jeremy. BS, UCLA, 1970; JD, U. Calif.-Berkeley, 1974. Bar: Calif. 1974, D.C. 1980. Dep. city atty. City of Los Angeles, 1974-75; asst. regional counsel Dept. Energy, San Francisco, 1975-77, dep. regional counsel, 1977-78, chief counsel, 1978-80; dep. asst. sec. of state for East Asia, Dept. of State, Washington, 1980-81, spl. adviser, 1981-82; ptnr. Stovall, Spradlin, Armstrong & Israel, Washington, 1983-86, Arthur Young Co., Washington, 1986-93; gen. counsel U.S. Dept. Commerce, Washington, 1993—. Recipient Outstanding Achievement award Dept. of State, 1980, Meritorious Svc. award, 1981. Mem. ABA, Asian Pacific Am. Bar Assn. (bd. dirs. 1981-83), Women's Bar Assn., Orgn. of Chinese-Americans, Pi Sigma Alpha. Clubs: Commonwealth (San Francisco); Nat. Lawyers. Office: US Dept Commerce Office Gen Counsel 14th & Constitution Ave NW Washington DC 20230-0001

LEWAND, F. THOMAS, lawyer; b. San Diego, July 24, 1946; s. Barbara (Boening) L.; m. Kathleen Sullivan, Aug. 3, 1968; children: Thomas, Kevin, Kristen, Carrie. BA, U. Detroit, 1968; JD, Wayne State U., 1970. Bar: Mich. 1970, U.S. Dist. Ct. (ea. dist.) 1970. Law clk. to presiding judge U.S. Ct. Appeals (6th cir.), Detroit, 1970; commr. Oakland County, Pontiac, Mich., 1978-80; chief of staff to Gov. J. Blanchard Lansing, 1982-83; ptnr. Jaffe, Raitt & Heuer, Detroit, 1970-92, Bodman, Longley & Dahling, Detroit, 1992—. Trustee Gov. Blanchard Found., Lansing, 1982—, chmn., 2001—; trustee Wayne County Econ. Devel. Corp., 1997—, Isiah Thomas Found., 1998—, Detroit Pub. TV, 1999—, Nat. Conf. on Cmty. and Justice, 1999—; trustee U. Detroit Mercy., 1996—, chmn., 2001—; mem. Nat. Assn. for Cmty. and Justice, 1999—. Campaign mgr. Gov. James J. Blanchard, MIch., 1978; chmn. Mich. Dems., 1989-91. Mem. State Bar Mich., Nat. Assn. Bond Lawyers. General corporate, Government contracts and claims, Municipal (including bonds). Office: Bodman Longley & Dahling 100 Renaissance Ctr Fl 34 Detroit MI 48243-1001

LEWIN, WERNER SIEGFRIED, JR. lawyer; b. San Francisco, Apr. 13, 1954; s. Werner Siegfried and Libby (Lewis) L.; married. BS, Cornell U., 1975; JD, U. Calif., Hastings, 1980. Bar: Calif. 1980. Assoc. Lynch, Loofbornraow et al, San Francisco, 1980-82, Rudy Rapoport & Holden, San Francisco, 1982-86, Hanson, Bridgett, Marcus, Vlahos & Rudy, San Francisco, 1986-87; prin. Werner S Lewin Jr., Esq., Novato, Calif., 1987—. Founder, pres. Attorney Assistance, San Francisco Bay Area, 1987—. General practice. Office: Atty Assistance Co Hdqs 55 Cavalla Cay Novato CA 94949-5341

LEWIS, ADAM MCLEAN, lawyer; b. Hartford, Conn., Dec. 13, 1971; s. J.M. and M.E. Lewis. AB in Philosophy cum laude, Harvard U., 1993; JD, Columbia U., 1997. Bar: N.Y. 1997, Mass. Assoc. Coudert Bros., N.Y.C., 1997—. Finance, Mergers and acquisitions. Home: 254 W 71st St Apt A New York NY 10023 Office: Coudert Bros 1114 Ave of Americas New York NY 10036

LEWIS, ALEXANDER INGERSOLL, III, lawyer; b. Detroit, Apr. 10, 1946; s. Alexander Ingersoll Jr. and Marie T. (Fuger) L.; m. Gretchen Elsa Lundgren, Aug. 8, 1970; children: Jennifer L., Katherine F., Elisabeth M., Alexander Ingersoll IV. BA with honors, Johns Hopkins U., 1968; JD cum laude, U. Pa., 1971. Bar: Md. 1972, U.S. Dist. Ct. Md. 1972, U.S. Ct. Appeals (4th cir.) 1975, U.S. Supreme Ct. 1976, D.C. 1982. Assoc. Venable, Baetjer & Howard, LLP, Balt., 1972-75, 78-80, ptnr., 1981—, head estate and trust practice group, 1993-99, sr. ptnr. estate and trust practice group, 1993—; asst. atty. gen. State of Md., 1975-77. Cons. subcom. on probate rules, standing com. on rules and procedures Md. Ct. Appeals, 1976—; mem. Md. Gov.'s Task Force to Study Revision of Inheritance and Estate Tax Laws, 1987-88; lectr. Md. Inst. Continuing Profl. Edn. Lawyers, 1978-99, Nat. Bus. Inst., 1986-87, 92-99, Cambridge Inst., 1986-90, Nat. Law Found., 1988-99. Contbr. articles to legal jours. Vice chmn. Md. Gov.'s Task Force on Long-Term Fin. Planning for Disabled Individuals, 1990-94. 1st lt. U.S. Army, 1972. Fellow Am. Coll. Trust and Estate Counsel (state laws coord. for Md. 1991-2001); mem. ABA, Md. Bar Assn. (chmn. probate reform and simplification com. estates and trusts coun. 1984-86, sec. 1987-88, chmn. 1989-90, com. on laws 1994-98), D.C. Bar Assn., Bar Assn. City Balt., Balt. Estate Planning Coun., Johns Hopkins Club. Republican. Roman Catholic. Avocations: canoeing, camping, tennis. Estate planning, Probate, Estate taxation. Home: 922 Army Rd Ruxton MD 21204-6703 Office: Venable Baetjer & Howard LLP 1800 Two Hopkins Plz Baltimore MD 21201 E-mail: a.i.lewis@venable.com

LEWIS, ALVIN BOWER, JR. lawyer; b. Pitts., Apr. 24, 1932; s. Alvin Bower Sr. and Ethel Weidman (Light) L.; m. Elizabeth Therese O'Shea; children: Alvin B. III, Judith W., Robert B. II. BA, Lehigh U., 1954; LLB, Dickinson Sch. Law, 1957. Bar: Pa. 1957, U.S. Dist. Ct. (mid. and ea. dists.) Pa. 1958, U.S. Ct. Appeals (3d cir.) 1958, D.C. 1979. Ptnr. Lewis & Lewis, Lebanon, Pa., 1957-66, Lewis, Brubaker, Whitman & Christianson, Lebanon, 1967-76; spl. counsel, acting chief counsel, dir. select com. on assassinations of M.L. King, and J.F. Kennedy U.S. Ho. of Reps., Washington, 1976-77; ptnr. Lewis & Kramer, Phila., 1977-78, Hartman, Underhill & Brubaker, Lancaster, Pa., 1979-95, Sprague & Lewis, Ltd., Lancaster, 1995-99, Stevens & Lee, Lancaster, 1999—. Dist. atty. County of Lebanon, Pa., 1962-70; chmn. Gov.'s Justice Commn., Pa., 1969-74; mem., chmn. Pa. Crime Commn., Pa., 1979-85. Fin. chmn., mem. exec. com. Rep. County Com., Lebanon, 1959-76; chmn. Lancaster City Rep. Com., 1994-98; co-chmn. Lancaster Crime Commn., 2000—; mem. Rep. State Com., 1998-2000; bd. dirs., chmn. adv. com., mem. nominating com. Urban League Lancaster County, 1986-91; elected Rep. State Com., 1998—; co-chmn. Lancaster Crime Commn., 2000; chmn. Lehigh U. Scholar-Athletes Fund Drive, 1990-94; bd. govs. Lancaster County Found. Recipient Furtherance of Justice award Mercyhurst Coll., 1979, Dist. Service award Ho. of Reps. Pa., 1982, Award of Distinction Pa. Senate, 1982, Outstanding Service award Gov. and Atty. Gen. Pa., 1974, Alumni of the Yr. award Lehigh U., 1999. Mem. ABA, Pa. Bar Assn. Lancaster County Bar Assn. (chmn. trial law sect. 1995—), Preservation Fund Pa., Inc., Lebanon County Bar Assn. (pres. 1974-76, bd. dirs. 1982-90), Nat. Dist. Attys. Assn. (bd. dirs. 1966-68), Pa. Dist. Attys. Assn. (officer, pres., bd. dirs. 1964-68), Lancaster County Found. (bd. govs.). Lutheran. Lodge: Masons. Avocations: pilot, small airplanes. Federal civil litigation, State civil litigation, General corporate. Office: Stevens & Lee One Penn Sq Lancaster PA 17602-1594

LEWIS, DAVID JOHN, lawyer; b. Zanesville, Ohio, Feb. 4, 1948; s. David Griff and Barbara Ann (Hoy) L.; m. Susan G. Smith; 1 child, Ann Elizabeth. BS in Fin., U. Ill., 1970, JD, 1973. Bar: Ill. 1973, D.C. 1974. Law clk. to Judge Philip W. Tone U.S. Dist. Ct. For North Dist. Ill., Chgo., 1973-74; assoc. Sidley Austin Brown & Wood, Washington, 1974-80, ptnr., 1980—. Comml. arbitrator Am. Arbitration Assn.; mem. Washington panel CPR Inst. Dispute Resolution. Mem. ABA. Alternative dispute resolution, Federal civil litigation, Product liability. Office: Sidley Austin Brown & Wood 1501 K St NW Washington DC 20005 E-mail: dlewis@sidley.com

LEWIS, DAVID L. lawyer; b. N.Y.C., Aug. 11, 1954; s. Albert B. and Sara Anne (Beresniakoff) L.; m. Carol Hayward, Dec. 21, 1983; children: Alexandra Hayward, Andrew Chase. BA, NYU, 1976; JD, Fordham U., 1979. Bar: N.Y. 1980, U.S. Dist. Ct. (ea. and so. dists.) N.Y. 1980, U.S. Ct. Appeals (2d cir.) 1981, U.S. Supreme Ct. 1983. Counsel to spk. pro tem N.Y. State Assembly, Albany, 1980-83; ptnr. Lewis & Fiore, N.Y.C., 1980—. Assoc. counsel to Senator Ray M. Goodman N.Y. State Senate, 2000, chief counsel, 2001. Columnist Decor mag., 1980-88. Mem. law com. Kings County Dem. Com., Bklyn., 1980—; pres. Bensonhurst Redevel. Corp., Bkyn., 1981-82. Mem. ATLA (author text on plea bargaining and settlement), NADCL (past bd. dirs.), N.Y. State Bar Assn., Assn. Bar City N.Y., N.Y. County Lawyers Assn., N.Y. State Assn. Criminal Def. Lawyers (bd. dirs., past pres.). Jewish. Federal civil litigation, Criminal, Legislative. Office: Lewis & Fiore 225 Broadway Rm 3300 New York NY 10007-3050

LEWIS, DAVID OLIN, lawyer, educator; b. Asheville, N.C., June 2, 1956; s. George Jimmy and Lona (Britt) L.; m. Maureen Maguire, Sept. 18, 1982; children: Dashiell George Maguire Lewis, Bronwyn Maguire Lewis; 1 stepchild, Finn Maguire Cohen. BS in Bus. Adminstrn., U. N.C., Wilmington, 1978; JD, U. N.C., 1981. Bar: N.C., 1981; cert. trial atty. Nat. Bd. Trial Advocacy. Sole practice, Wilmington, 1981-87; lectr. in bus. law U. N.C., 1981-82, asst. prof. bus. law, 1982-87; assoc. Wishart, Norris, Henninger & Pittman, P.A., Raleigh, N.C., 1987-90, ptnr., 1990-93, Bryant, Patterson, Covington & Idol, P.A., Durham, N.C., 1993—. Contbr. articles to profl. jours. DuPont research grantee U. N.C., 1983, 85, faculty devel. grantee U. N.C., 1985. Mem. N.C. Bar Assn., N.C. Assn. Def. Lawyers, Def. Rsch. Ins. Democrat. Avocations: reading, refinishing furniture, travel. General civil litigation, Insurance, Personal injury. Home: 3510 Sheridan Dr Durham NC 27707-4646 Office: Bryant Patterson et al PO Box 341 103 W Main St Durham NC 27702

LEWIS, EDWIN LEONARD, III, lawyer; b. Phila., Nov. 24, 1945; s. Edwin Leonard Jr. and Nancy (Hoffman) L.; m. Elisabeth C. Bacon, Oct. 6, 1984; children: Katharine Bacon, Caroline Huffington. BA, Lafayette Coll., 1967; JD, Temple U., 70. bar: Pa. 1970, Ill. 1995. Assoc. MacElree, Platt & Harvey, West Chester, Pa., 1970-73; asst. gen. counsel Fidelity Mut. Life, Phila., 1973-76; sr. atty. Atlantic Richfield Co.; v.p. law Wells Fargo Alarm Svcs., King of Prussia, Pa., 1983-91; v.p., gen. counsel, sec. Borg Warner Protective Svcs., Parsippany, N.J., 1991-95, Borg Warner Security Corp., Chgo., 1995-97; pres. Atlantic Legal Found., N.Y.C., 1998-2000; v.p., gen. counsel Am. Sci. and Engring., Inc., Billerica, Mass., 2000—. Pub., editor Science in the Courtroom Review, 1998. Capt. M.I., USAR, 1970-76. Mem. Am. Corp. Counsel Assn., Phila. Bar Assn., Nat. Fedn. Ind. Bus. Legal Found. (legal adv. bd. 2000—). Avocations: marathon running, tennis, golf, sailing. General corporate, Mergers and acquisitions, Product liability. Home: 59 Delafield Island Rd Darien CT 06820-6012 Office: Am Sci & Engring 829 Middlesex Turnpike Billerica MA 01821 E-mail: nlewis@as-e.com

LEWIS, ERNEST CROSBY, lawyer; b. Mar. 4, 1934; s. Ernest Van and Nell (Brooks) L.; m. Cleo Brooks, Nov. 4, 1970; children: Lisa, Allyson, Ernest Crosby Jr., Gage. LLB, U. S.C., 1958. Pres. Austin, Lewis and Rogers PA, Columbia, 1958—; mem. S.C. Ho. of Reps., Richland County, 1960-64, Fairfield County, 1983-89. Bd. visitors The Citadel; vice-chmn. S.C. State Bd. Edn. Bd. Trustees Med. Coll. U. S.C., Columbia Coll.; 1st v.p., founding mem. Nat. Assn. S.C. Dem. Chmn.; chmn. S.C. Dem. Party, S.C. Govs. Mansion Commn., 2001—; bd. dirs. S.C. Alliance for Children, Palmetto Trail. Capt. U.S. Army. Mem. ABA, S.C. Bar Assn. Methodist. General civil litigation, General practice, Real property. Office: Austin Lewis and Rogers 508 Hampton St Ste 300 Columbia SC 29201-3352 E-mail: eclewis@alr.com

LEWIS, FELICE FLANERY, lawyer, educator; b. Plaquemine, La., Oct. 5, 1920; d. Lowell Baird and E. Elizabeth (Lee) Flanery; m. Francis Russell Lewis, Dec. 22, 1944. BA, U. Wash., 1947; PhD, NYU, 1974; JD, Georgetown U., 1981. Bar: N.Y. 1982. Dean Liberal Arts and Scis. L.I. Univ., Bklyn., 1974-78; assoc. Harry G. English, 1983-85, 91-01; adj. prof. polit. sci. L.I. Univ., 1983-2000. Author: Literature, Obscenity and Law, 1976; co-editor: Henry Miller, Years of Trial & Triumph, 1962-64, 1978. Constitutional, General practice, Probate. Home: 28 Whitney Cir Glen Cove NY 11542-1316

LEWIS, FRANK B. lawyer; b. N.Y.C., Aug. 12, 1938; s. Saul and Clara (Myers) L. A.B., U. Pa., 1960; J.D., NYU, 1964; LL.M. in Trade Regulations, NYU, 1972. Bar: N.Y. 1965, U.S. Dist. Ct. (so. and ea. dists.) N.Y. 1966. Pvt. practice, N.Y.C., 1965-67; law asst. 1st jud. dept Supreme Ct. State of N.Y., N.Y.C., 1967-79, spl. referee, 1979— . Contbr. to NYU Intramural Law Rev. (Seymour A. Levy Meml. award 1963-64), articles to N.Y. Law Jour. Served with U.S. Army Res, 1960-66. Mem. Assn. of Bar City N.Y. Office: NY Supreme Ct 60 Centre St Rm 324M New York NY 10007-1402

LEWIS, GERALD JORGENSEN, judge; b. Perth Amboy, N.J., Sept. 9, 1933; s. Norman Francis and Blanche M. (Jorgensen) L.; m. Laura Susan McDonald, Dec. 15, 1973; children by previous marriage: Michael, Marc. AB magna cum laude, Tufts Coll., 1954; JD, Harvard U., 1957. Bar: D.C. 1957, N.J. 1961, Calif. 1962, U.S. Supreme Ct. 1968. Atty. Gen. Atomic, La Jolla, Calif., 1961-63; ptnr. Haskins, Lewis, Hugent & Newnham, San Diego, 1963-77; judge Mcpl. Ct., El Cajon, Calif., 1977-79, Superior Ct., San Diego, 1979-84; assoc., justice Calif. Ct. of Appeal, 1984-87; dir. Fisher Scientific Group, Inc., 1987-98, Bolsa Chica Corp., 1991-93, Gen. Chem. Group, Inc., 1996—; of counsel Lathan & Watkins, 1987-97; dir. Invesco Mut. Funds, Denver. Adj. prof. evidence Western State U. Sch. Law, San Diego, 1977-85, exec. bd., 1977-89; dir. Invesco Mutual Funds, 2000—; faculty San Diego Inn of Ct., 1979— , Am. Inn of Ct., 1984— . Cons. editor: California Civil Jury Instructions, 1984. City atty. Del Mar, Calif., 1963-74, Coronado, Calif., 1972-77; counsel Comprehensive Planning Orgn., San Diego, 1972-73; trustee San Diego Mus. Art, 1986-89; bd. dirs. Air Pollution Control Dist., San Diego County, 1972-76. Served to lt. comdr. USNR, 1957-61. Named Trial Judge of Yr. San Diego Trial Lawyers Assn., 1984. Mem. Am. Judicature Soc., Soc. Inns of Ct. in Calif., Confrerie des Chevaliers du Tastevin, Order of St. Hubert (knight comdr.), Friendly Sons of St. Patrick (Irishman of Yr. 2000), The Irisn 50 Aztec Big 50, Bohemian Club, La Jolla Country Club (dir. 1980-83), Prophets, The K Club (County Kildare), Pauma Valley Country Club. Republican. Episcopalian. Home: 6505 Caminito Blythefield La Jolla CA 92037-5806 Office: Latham & Watkins 701 B St Ste 2100 San Diego CA 92101-8197

LEWIS, GUY A. prosecutor; b. Chattanooga; m. Loyda Lewis; 1 child Rose Marie. BS, U. Tennessee, 1983; Juris Doctor, U. Memphis Sch. of Law, 1986. Law clerk Hon. Thomas E. Scott, U.S. Dist. Ct., Fla., Hon. William Cowen. U.S. Ct. Appeals, Federal Circuit , Washington; prosecutor State's Atty.'s Office, 1988—, first asst.; U.S. Atty. So. Dist. Fla. U.S. Dept. Justice, 2000—. Co-counsel trial U.S. vs. Gen. Manuel Noreiga, Matthew Block Prosecution; deputy chief Narcotics Section. Office: 99 NE 4th St Miami FL 33132*

LEWIS, JOHN BRUCE, lawyer; b. Poplar Bluff, Mo., Aug. 12, 1947; s. Evan Bruce and Hilda Kathryn (Kassebaum) L.; m. Diane F. Grossman, July 23, 1977; children: Samantha Brooking, Ashley Denning. BA, U. Mo., 1969, JD, 1972; LLM in Labor and Employment Law, Columbia U., 1978; diploma, Nat. Inst. Trial Advocacy, 1982. Bar: Mo. 1972, U.S. Ct. Appeals (8th cir.) 1973, U.S. Dist. Ct. (ea. dist.) Mo. 1974, U.S. Dist. Ct. (no. dist.) Ohio 1979, Ohio 1980, U.S. Ct. Appeals (6th cir.) 1982, U.S. Dist. Ct. (ea. dist.) Mich. 1983, U.S. Ct. Appeals (3d cir.) 1987, U.S. Supreme Ct. 1987, U.S. Dist. Ct. (no. dist.) Calif. 1987, U.S. Ct. Appeals (7th cir.) 1990. Assoc. Millar, Schaefer & Ebling, St. Louis, 1972-77, Squire, Sanders & Dempsey, Cleve., 1979-85; ptnr. Arter & Hadden, 1985-2001, Baker & Hostetler, Cleve., 2001—. Chair Labor and Employment Law Practice Group, 1987—; lectr. in field. Contbr. articles to legal jours. Mem. Cleve. Council on World Affairs. Mem. ABA (sec. labor and employment law, com. EEO law, comm. law forum), Ohio State Bar Assn. (sec. labor and employment law), Greater Cleve. Bar Assn. (sec. labor law), St. Louis Met. Bar Assn., Am. Law Inst., Def. Rsch. Inst., Selden Soc., Ohio C. of C. (labor adv. com.). Civil rights, Federal civil litigation, Labor. Office: Baker & Hostetler 3200 Nat City Ctr 1900 E 9th St Cleveland OH 44114-3485 Business E-Mail: jlewis@bakerlaw.com

LEWIS, JOHN HARDY, JR. lawyer; b. East Orange, N.J., Oct. 31, 1936; s. John Hardy and Sarah (Ripley) L.; m. Mary Ann Spurgeon, June 25, 1960; children: Peter, David, Mark. AB magna cum laude, Princeton U., 1958; JD cum laude, Harvard U., 1961. Bar: Pa. 1962. Assoc. Morgan, Lewis & Bockius, Phila., 1965-69, ptnr., 1969-99, Montgomery McCracken Walker & Rhoads, LLP, Phila., 1999—. Trustee Blair Acad., Blairstown, N.J. Served to maj. USAF, 1962-65. Fellow Am. Coll. Trial Lawyers. Antitrust, General civil litigation. Home: 1000 Green Valley Rd Bryn Mawr PA 19010-1912 Office: Montgomery McCracken Et Al 123 S Broad St Philadelphia PA 19109-1029

LEWIS, R. FRED, state supreme court justice; b. Beckley, W.Va., Dec. 14, 1947; m. Judith Lewis, 1969; children: Elle, Lindsay. Grad. cum laude, Fla. So. Coll., 1969; JD cum laude, U. Miami, 1972; grad., U.S. Army A.G. Sch.; D (hon.) in Pub. Svc., Fla. So. Coll., 2000. Pvt. practice, Miami; justice Fla. Supreme Ct., 1998—. Contbr. pubs. Continuing Edn. Legal Program. Bd. dirs. Miami Children's Hosp.; inventory atty. The Fla. Bar. Recipient Friends Justice award ABOTA, Jud. Pub. Trust & Confidence award FLREA; NCAA postgrad. grantee, 1969. Mem. Omicron Delta Kappa, Psi Chi, Sigma Alpha Epsilon. Address: 500 S Duval St Tallahassee FL 32399-6556 E-mail: supremecourt@mail.flcourts.org*

LEWIS, RICHARD M. lawyer; b. Gallipolis, Ohio, Dec. 11, 1957; s. Denver E. and Mary Esther (Mobley) L.; m. Cheryl F. Hickman (div.); m. Diane K. Williams, Apr. 26, 1986. BA in Polit. Sci., Ohio State U., 1979; JD, Capital U., 1982. Bar: Ohio 1982, U.S. Dist. Ct. (so. dist.) Ohio 1984, U.S. Supreme Ct. 1986, U.S. Ct. Appeals (6th cir.) 1999; cert. civil trial advocacy Nat. Bd. Trial Advocacy. Pvt. practice law, 1982-83; assoc. Mary Bone Kunze, Jackson, Ohio, 1983-85; pvt. practice law, 1985-86; ptnr. Ochsenbein, Cole & Lewis, 1986-96, Cole & Lewis, Jackson, 1996-2000, The Law Firm of Richard M. Lewis, Jackson, 2001—. Lectr. in field; expert witness. Mem. ABA, Assn. Trial Lawyers Am., Ohio State Bar Assn., Jackson County Bar Assn. (past pres.), Ohio Acad. Trial Lawyers (bd. trustees 1993—, budget com. 1993-94, supreme ct. screening com. 1994, vice-chairperson family law com. 1994-95, chairperson-elect family law com. 1995—, chairperson family law com. 1995-96, exec. com., chair mem. com. 1996-97, co-chair regional CLE seminars 1997, exec. com. 1998-99, chair ADOPT task force 1998). General civil litigation, Family and matrimonial, Personal injury. Home: 603 Reservoir Rd Jackson OH 45640-8714 Office: The Law Firm of Richard M Lewis 295 Pearl St Jackson OH 45640-1748

LEWIS, ROBERT LEE, lawyer; b. Oxford, Miss., Feb. 26, 1944; s. Ernest Elmo and Johnice Georgia (Thirkield) L.; children: Yolanda Sherice, Robert Lee Jr., Dion Terrell, Viron Lamar, William Lovell. BA, Ind. U., 1970, JD, 1973; M in Pub. Service, West Ky. U., 1980. Bar: Ind. 1973, Ky. 1979, U.S. Ct. Claims, U.S. Ct. Internat. Trade, U.S. Tax Ct., U.S. Ct. Mil. Appeals, U.S. Ct. Appeals (fed. cir.), U.S. Supreme Ct. Sole practice, Evansville, Ind., 1973-75, Gary, 1980—; atty., army officer U.S. Army, Ft. Knox, Ky., 1975-78; appellate referee Ind. Employment Security Div., Indpls., 1978-80. Mem. adv. com. Vincennes (Ind.) U., 1983—; bd. dirs. Opportunities Industrialization Ctr., Evansville, 1973-75. Served to sgt. JAGC, USMC, 1962-66, Vietnam, sgt. U.S. Army, 1975-78, lt. col. USAR. Named Ky. Col. Mem. ABA, Ind. Bar Assn., Ky. Bar Assn., Nat. Bar Assn., Ind. Bd. Realtors, Ind. U. Alumni Assn., Phi Alpha Delta. Methodist. Criminal, Family and matrimonial, Personal injury. Home and Office: 2148 W 11th Ave Gary IN 46404-2306

LEWIS, RONALD WAYNE, lawyer; b. Buffalo, May 13, 1943; s. George Weber and Marianne (Parsons) L.; m. Lisa Scruggs; children: Joshua Byron, Kristopher Byron, Katherine Byron, Annalise N. AB, Dartmouth Coll., Hanover, N.H., 1965; MAT in French, Harvard U., 1969; JD, U. Miss., Oxford, 1978. Bar: Miss. 1978, U.S. Dist. Ct. (no. dist.) Miss. 1978, U.S. Ct. Appeals (5th cir.) 1979, U.S. Dist. Ct. (so. dist.) Miss. 1985, U.S. Supreme Ct. 1990, U.S. Claims Ct. 1991. Pvt. practice, Oxford, 1978-81; assoc. Hill, Lewis & Bell, 1981-83, Hill & Lewis, Oxford, 1983-86, Holcomb, Dunbar, Connell, Chaffin & Willard, Oxford, 1986-88; pvt. practice, 1988—. CJA criminal def. tng. coord. No. Jud. Dist., Miss., 1991—, CJA panel rep. to nat. confs., 1995—. Mem. Lafayette County Dem. Exec. Com., Oxford, 1985-96, chmn., 1987-91; bd. dirs. ACLU of Miss., 1989-90, Miss. Assn. for Children with Learning Disabilities, 1990-91; mem. instnl. rev. bd. U. Miss., 1999—. Mem. ABA, ATLA, Nat. Assn. Criminal Def. Lawyers, Miss. Trial Lawyers, Miss. Bar, Lafayette County Bar Assn., Am. Inn. of Ct. Ill. (bencher). Civil rights, Criminal, Labor. Office: PO Box 207 607 S Lamar Blvd Oxford MS 38655-4428

LEWIS, WILLIAM HENRY, JR. lawyer; b. Durham, N.C., Nov. 12, 1942; s. William Henry Sr. and Phyllis Lucille (Phillips) L.; m. Jo Ann Whitsett, Apr. 17, 1965 (div. Sept. 1982); 1 child, Kimberly N.; m. Peyton Cockrill Davis, Nov. 28, 1987. Student, N.C. State U., 1960-63; AB in Polit. Sci., U. N.C., 1965, JD with honors, 1969. Bar: Calif., D.C., U.S. Dist. Ct. (cen. dist.) Calif., U.S. Ct. Appeals (D.C. cir., 2nd and 5th cirs.), U.S. Supreme Ct. Assoc. Latham & Watkins, Los Angeles, 1969-74; exec. officer Calif. Air Resources Bd., Los Angeles and Sacramento, Calif., 1975-78; dir. Nat. Com. on Air Quality, Washington, 1978-81; counsel Wilmer, Cutler & Pickering, 1981-84; ptnr. Morgan, Lewis & Bockius LLP, 1984—, mgr. nat. environ. practice, 1999—. Spl. advisor on environ. policy State of Calif., L.A. and Sacramento, 1975; lectr. Law Sch. U. Va., 1993-97. Bd. dirs. For Love of Children, Inc., Washington, 1985-95, pres., 1987-91; bd. dirs. Advs. for Families, Washington, 1985-87, Hillandale Homeowners Assn., Washington, 1986-87, Thurgood Marshall Ctr. Trust, Washington, 1989-95; mem. EPA Clean Air Act Adv. Com., 1994—; chmn. bd. dirs., co-founder The Montpelier Found., 1998—. Mem. ABA. Federal civil litigation, Environmental. Home: 3900 Georgetown Ct NW Washington DC 20007-2127 also: 18454 Monteith Farm Rd Gordonsville VA 22942-7560 Office: Morgan Lewis & Bockius LLP 1800 M St NW Washington DC 20036-5802

LEWIS, WILMA ANTOINETTE, lawyer, former prosecutor and federal agency admin; b. Santurce, P.R. BA with distinction, Swarthmore Coll., 1978; JD, Harvard U., 1981. Assoc. Steptoe & Johnson, Washington, 1981-1986; asst. U.S. atty. civil divsn. U.S. Atty.'s Office, 1986-1993; assoc. solicitor divsn. gen. law U.S. Dept. Interior, 1993-95, inspector gen., 1995-98; U.S. atty. Washington, 1998-2001; ptnr. Crowell & Moring LLP, 2001—. Mem. civil justice reform act adv. group U.S. Dist. Ct. D.C., mem. adv. com. on local rules; adj. faculty mem. George Washington U. Nat. Law Ctr. Mem. Phi Beta Kappa. Office: Crowell & Moring 1001 Pennsylvania Ave NW Washington DC 20004-2595 E-mail: wlewis@crowell.com

LEWYN, THOMAS MARK, lawyer; b. N.Y.C., July 2, 1930; s. Oswald and Agnes (Maas) L.; m. Ann Salfeld, July 15, 1955; children— Alfred Thomas, Mark Henry. B.A., Stanford, 1952, postgrad., 1952-54; LL.B., Columbia, 1955. Bar: N.Y. 1957. Since practiced in, N.Y.C.; assoc. Simpson, Thacher & Bartlett, 1957-64, ptnr., 1965-75, sr. ptnr., 1976-90, of counsel, 1991—. Bd. dirs. Metro-Goldwyn-Mayer, Inc. Contbr. articles to profl. jours. Served to 1st lt., F.A. AUS, 1955-57. Mem. ABA, Assn. of Bar of City of N.Y., N.Y. State Bar Assn. Home: 911 Park Ave New York NY 10021-0337 Office: Simpson Thacher & Bartlett 425 Lexington Ave Fl 15 New York NY 10017-3954

LEYDIG, CARL FREDERICK, lawyer; b. Denver, Jan. 24, 1925; s. Carl F. and Mae V. (Crowley) L.; m. Patricia L. Schwefer, July 2, 1949; children: Gregory F., Deborah A., Gary W., Suzann M. BS in Chem. Engring., Ill. Inst. Tech., 1945; JD, DePaul U., 1950. Bar: Ill. 1950. Atty. Std. Oil Co. (Ind.), Chgo., 1950-54; assoc., ptnr. Leydig, Voit & Mayer, Ltd. and predecessor firms, 1954-93, of counsel, 1993—. Chmn., Young Reps. of Ill., 1953-55; pres. United Fund of Arlington Heights (Ill.), 1964, 65. Lt. j.g., USNR, 1943-46. Mem. ABA, Am. Intellectual Property Law Assn. (dir. 1979-81), Patent Law Assn. Chgo. (pres. 1980), Am. Coll. Trial Lawyers, Univ. Club, Lawyers Club (Chgo.), Inverness Golf Club (Palatine, Ill.), Fiddlesticks Country Club (Ft. Myers, Fla.). Federal civil litigation, Intellectual property, Patent.

LEYHANE, FRANCIS JOHN, III, lawyer; b. Chgo., Mar. 29, 1957; s. Francis J. and Mary Elizabeth (Crowley) L.; m. Diana M. Urizarri, May 8, 1982; children: Katherine, Francis J. IV, Joseph, Brigid Rose, James Matthew. BA, Loyola U., Chgo., 1977, JD, 1980. Bar: Ill. 1980, U.S. Dist. Ct. (no. dist.) Ill. 1980, U.S. Ct. Appeals (7th cir.) 1986. Assoc. Condon, Cook & Roche, Chgo., 1980-87; ptnr. Condon & Cook, 1988-98, Boyle & Leyhane, Ltd., Chgo., 1998—. Contbr. articles to profl. jours. Mem. Sch. bd. Immaculate Conception Parish, Chgo., 1993-96. Fellow Ill. Bar Found.; mem. Appellate Lawyers Assn. Ill., Ill. State Bar Assn. (mem. assembly 1987-90), Chgo. Bar Assn., Blue Key. Appellate, State civil litigation, Insurance. Office: Boyle & Leyhane Ltd 11 E Adams Set 1600 Chicago IL 60603 E-mail: leyhane329@aol.com

LIBBIN, ANNE EDNA, lawyer; b. Phila., Aug. 25, 1950; d. Edwin M. and Marianne (Herz) L.; m. Christopher J. Cannon, July 20, 1985; children: Abigail Libbin Cannon, Rebecca Libbin Cannon. AB, Radcliffe Coll., 1971; JD, Harvard U., 1975. Bar: Calif. 1975, U.S. Dist. Ct. (cen. dist.) Calif. 1977, U.S. Dist. Ct. (no. dist.) Calif. 1979, U.S. Dist. Ct. (ea. dist.) Calif. 1985, U.S. Ct. Appeals. (2d cir.) 1977, U.S. Ct. Appeals (5th cir.) 1982, U.S. Ct. Appeals (7th cir.) 1976, U.S. Ct. Appeals (9th cir.) 1976, U.S. Ct. Appeals (D.C. cir.) 1978. Appellate atty. NLRB, Washington, 1975-78; assoc. Pillsbury Madison & Sutro LLP, San Francisco, 1978-83, ptnr., 1984-99; sr. counsel Pacific Telesis Group, 1999—. Three Guineas fellow Harvard Law Sch., 1997; dir. Alumnae Resources, San Francisco, 1991-97. Mem. ABA (labor and employment sect.), State Bar Calif. (labor law sect.), Bar Assn. San Francisco (labor law sect.), Radcliffe Club (San Francisco). Labor. Office: Pacific Telesis Group 140 New Montgomery St San Francisco CA 94105-3705

LIBERT, DONALD JOSEPH, lawyer; b. Sioux Falls, S.D., Mar. 23, 1928; s. Bernard Joseph and Eleanor Monica (Sutton) L.; m. Jo Anne Murray, May 16, 1953; children: Cathleen, Thomas, Kevin, Richard, Stephanie. B.S. magna cum laude in Social Scis., Georgetown U., 1950, LL.B., 1956. Bar: Ohio. From assoc. to ptnr. Manchester, Bennett, Powers & Ullman, Youngstown, Ohio, 1956-65; various positions to v.p., gen. counsel and sec. Youngstown Sheet & Tube Co., 1965-78; assoc. group counsel LTV Corp., Youngstown and Pitts., 1979; v.p. and gen. counsel Anchor Hocking Corp., Lancaster, Ohio, 1979-87; pvt. practice, 1987—. Served to lt. (j.g.) USN, 1951-54. Mem. Ohio Bar Assn. (former chmn. sr. lawyers com.), Fairfield County Bar Assn. (mem. alt. dispute resolution com.), Lancaster Country Club, Rotary. Republican. Roman Catholic. Administrative and regulatory, Antitrust, General corporate. Office: 127 W Wheeling St Lancaster OH 43130-3737

LIBERTH, RICHARD FRANCIS, lawyer; b. Bklyn., Mar. 1, 1950; s. S. Richard and Frances J. (Falconer) L.; m. Lisa M. Feenick, June 8, 1974; children: Andrew R., Erica M. BS in Bus. Adminstrn., U. Denver, 1972; JD, Bklyn. Law Sch., 1976. Bar: N.Y. 1977, U.S. Dist. Ct. (so. and ea. dists.) N.Y. 1981, U.S. Dist. Ct. (no. dist.) N.Y. 1991. Staff atty. Mental Health Legal Svcs., Poughkeepsie, N.Y., 1976-78; sr. asst. dist. atty. Rockland County Dist. Attys. Office, N.Y.C., 1978-81; prin. Drake, Sommers, Loeb, Tarshis & Catania, Newburgh, N.Y., 1981—. Atty. Fraternal Order of Police Lodge #957. Dir. Legal Aid Soc. Orange County, Goshen, N.Y., 1982-84, Orange County Cerebral Palsy Assn., Goshen, 1986-89; mem. Rep. Nat. Com., Washington, 1990—; Rep. chmn. Town of Woodbury, 1997-99. Mem. N.Y. Bar Assn., Newburgh Bar Assn. (pres. 1991), Orange County Bar Assn. (v.p. 1995, pres. 1997), Woodbury Lions Club (Central Valley, N.Y.) (past pres.). Avocations: golf, tennis, reading, collecting. General civil litigation, Product liability. Home: 134 Hasbrouck Rd Goshen NY 10924 Office: Drake Sommers Loeb Tarshis & Catania One Corwin Ct Newburgh NY 12550 E-mail: liberth@dsltc.com

LIBERTY, ARTHUR ANDREW, judge; b. Oak Park, Ill., Nov. 7, 1954; s. Arthur and Patricia (Horton) L.; m. Jean Liberty, Nov. 22, 1980; children: Rebecca, Rachael. BS, Excelsior Coll., Albany, 1983; JD with honors, Ill. Inst. Tech., Chgo., 1987. Bar: Ill. 1987, U.S. Dist. Ct. (no. dist.) Calif. 1988, U.S. Dist. Ct. (no. dist.) Ill., 1992, U.S. Dist. Ct. (cen. dist.) Ill., 1995, U.S. Ct. Appeals (7th cir.) 1992, U.S. Ct. Appeals (9th cir.) 1989. Asst. dist. counsel U.S. Immigration and Naturalization Service, San Francisco, Chgo., 1987-88, 91-92; sector counsel U.S. Border Patrol, Livermore, Calif., 1988-91; ptnr. Azulay & Azulay, Chgo., 1992-95; pvt. practice Chgo. and Joliet, Ill., 1995-97; U.S. adminstrv. law judge Office of Hearings and Appeals, Detroit, 1997-98, chief U.S. adminstrv. law judge Evansville, Ind., 1998—. Spl. asst. U.S. atty. ea. dist. Calif., Fresno, 1988-91; instr. law and legal procedure Fed. Law Enforcement Tng. Ctr., Artesia, N.Mex., 1989-91; Assn. President, Hearing Office Chief Judges, 2001-; law & jud. procedure Office Hearings & Appeals Nat. Tng. Cadre, Falls Church, Va., 2001—. Contbr. articles to profl. books. Maj., pilot CAP, comdr. Evansville sr. squadron, 1999—. Mem. Brooks Am. Inns of Ct. (master). Avocations: flying, music, cooking. Office: Office of Hearings and Appeals US Court House Rm 272 101 NW Martin L King Jr Evansville IN 47708-1989 E-mail: aliberty@mail.com

LICATA, ARTHUR FRANK, lawyer; b. N.Y.C., June 16, 1947; BA in English, Le Moyne Coll., 1969; postgrad., SUNY, Binghampton, 1969-71; JD cum laude, Suffolk U., 1976. Bar: Mass. 1977, N.Y. 1985, U.S. Ct. Appeals (1st cir.) 1977, U.S. Dist. Ct. Mass. 1977, admitted Frank B. Murray, Jr. Inns of Ct. 1990-92. Assoc. Parker, Coulter, Daley & White, Boston, 1977-82; pvt. practice Arthur F. Licata P.C., 1982—. Prin. Ardlee Internat. Trading Co., Ea. and Ctrl. Europe and Russia, 1989-99; del. White House Conf. on Trade and Investment in Ctrl. Europe, Cleve., 1995; lectr. Mass. Continuing Legal Edn., Boston, 1982-90, mem. trial adv. com., 1984-88; mem. working group on drinking and drunk driving Harvard Sch. Pub. Health Ctr. for Health Comms., 1986; spkr. Conv. Nat. Fedn. Paralegal Assns., Boston, 1987; del. U.S.-People's Republic of China Joint Session on Trade, Investment and Econ. Law, Beijing, 1987; co-sponsor Estonian legal del. visit to Mass. and N.H. correctional instns., 1990; Boston host former Soviet legal del. visit, 1989; legal advisor Czech Anglo-Am. Bus. Inst., Prague, Czech Republic, 1989—, Russian Children's Fund, 1992-94, Estonia Acad. for Pub. Safety, 1992-94; adv. bd. Ford Found.'s Legal Resource Ctr., Czech Republic, 1994-96; participant U.S.-Russian Investment Symposium; spkr. Conf. on Proposed Tobacco Settlement and Tort Law, Harvard Law Sch., 1997; guest WGBH-Ch 2, TV, Greater Boston With Emily Rooney, 1999; chair seminar Mass. CLE, Boston, 2000. Panel mem. sta. WBZ TV, Boston; contbr. articles to profl. jours. U.S. Del. 6th People to People Juvenile Justice Program to USSR, Moscow, 1989; legal advisor Mass. chpt. MADD, Plymouth County, 1984-87; mem. State Adv. Com. Med. Malpractice, Boston, 1985; bd. dirs. Boston Ctr. for the Arts, 1990-94; mem. profl. adv. bd. Mass. Epilepsy Assn., 1986-93; counsel state coord. commn. MADD, Mass., 1984-86. Recipient Outstanding Citizen award Mothers Against Drunk Driving, 1986, Sacred Angelic Imperial Constanian Order of Saint George awarded by the Duke of Parma, Italy, 2000. Fellow Mass. Bar Found.; mem. ABA, ATLA, Mass. Bar Assn. (bd. dirs., young lawyers sect. 1979-80, 21st Century Club 1984), Mass. Acad. Trial Attys. (bd. dirs. 1991-99, exec. com. 1997-99), Nat. Bd. Trial Advocacy (bd. cert. civil trial advocate 1992— Avocation: travel. General civil litigation, Private international, Personal injury. Office: Fed Res Plz 600 Atlantic Ave 27th Fl Boston MA 02210-2211 Fax: (617) 523-7743. E-mail: Licata@worldnet.att.net

LICHT, RICHARD A. lawyer; b. Providence, Mar. 25, 1948; s. Julius M. Licht and Irene (Lash) Olson; m. Roanne Sragow; children: Jordan David, Jeremy Michael, Jaclyn Rose, Jacob Adam. AB cum laude, Harvard U., 1968, JD cum laude, 1972; LLM in Taxation, Boston U., 1975. Law clk. to chief justice R.I. Supreme Ct., Providence, 1973-74; ptnr. Letts, Quinn & Licht, 1974-84; mem. R.I. Senate, 1975-84, chmn. judiciary com. and rules com., 1984; lt. gov. State of R.I., 1985-89; mng. ptnr. Tillinghast, Licht, Perkins, Smith & Cohen LLP, 1989—. Former chmn. R.I. Commn. on Racial, Religious and Ethnic Harrassment, Dr. Martin Luther King Jr. Holiday Commn., State Energy and Tech. Study Commn. rules com.; chmn. Coun. of State Govt., Intergovtl. Affairs Com., Nat. Focus Team, Bd. Gov. Higher Edn.; bd. regents Elem. and Secondary Edn.; mem. Pub. Telecom. Authority R.I., Univ. R.I. Found., Community Coll. R.I. Found. Bd. dirs., mem. corp. Roger Williams Hosp.; advisor Community Prep. Sch.; corporator Roger Williams Hosp.; trustee Save the Bay, Inc., Emma Pendleton Bradley Hosp.; bd. dirs. Temple Emanuel, Providence, Jewish Fedn. R.I., Samaritans; chmn. Small Bus. Adv. Council, Task Force on Teenage Suicide Prevention, CD Civil Preparedness Adv. Council, Urban League R.I., 1980-82, John Hope Settlement House, 1976-81; chair Am. Cancer Soc. Ball, 1989, Jewish Fedn. R.I. Passage to Freedom, 1989; chair R.I. chpt. Anti-Defamation League; mem. Women and Infants Corp., Dorcas Place, PARI, UNITAM, NCLG task force of Youth Suicide Prevention, Jewish Home for the Aged of R.I., bd. govs. for the handicapped; active YWCA of Greater R.I., Vols. in Action, Inc., Big Sister Assn. of R.I., Big Bros. R.I.; coordinator vols. gubernatorial campaigns Frank Licht, 1968, 70; active Jewish Community Ctr., Providence, 1975-83, East Side Sr. Citizens Ctr., 1975-76, R.I. Youth Guidance Ctr., Inc., 1987, Block Island Conservancy, Inc., Notre Dame Health Care Corp., 1987; Dem. candidate for U.S. Senate, 1988; chmn. ann. campaign Meeting Street Sch., 1990-91, mem. steering com. for capital fund drive, 1989-92; mem. corp. Womens and Infants Hosp.; Dem. candidate U.S. Senate, 2000. Named an Outstanding Young Man of R.I., R.I. Jaycees, 1979; recipient David Ben Gurion award State of Israel Bonds, 1977, Outstanding Pub. Service award Temple Torat Yisrael, 1985, Disting. Services to the Hispanic Community award Casa Puerto Rico, 1985, Hon. Pub. Service award Meeting St. Sch., 1986, Recognition award R.I. Day Care Dirs. Assn., 1986, award of Appreciation Child Care/Human Services, 1986, Govtl. Services award Ocean State Residences for the Retarded, 1987. Mem. R.I. Bar Assn., Hosp. Assn. R.I. (bd. dirs. 1997). Democrat. Office: Tillinghast Licht Perkins Smith & Cohen 10 Weybosset St Providence RI 02903-2818 Fax: 401-456-1210. E-mail: rlicht@tlslaw.com

LICHTENSTEIN, NATALIE G. lawyer; b. N.Y.C., Sept. 17, 1953; d. Abba G. and Cecile (Geffen) L.; m. Willard Ken Tom, June 10, 1979. AB summa cum laude, Radcliffe Coll., 1975; JD, Harvard U., 1978. Bar: D.C. 1978. Atty., advisor U.S. Dept. Treasury, Washington, 1978-80; prin. counsel World Bank, 1980-94, chief counsel East Asia and Pacific divsn. Legal Dept., 1994-99, adviser to v.p. legal, 1999-2001, chief counsel instnl. affairs, 2001—. Adj. prof. Chinese law Georgetown U., Washington, 1982-86. Contbr. articles on Chinese and Vietnamese law to profl. jours. Public international.

LICHTENSTEIN, ROBERT JAY, lawyer; b. Phila., Jan. 23, 1948; s. Irving M. and Marjorie J. (Weiss) L.; m. Sandra Paley, Aug. 14, 1971; children: David P., Kate. BS in Econs., U. Pa., 1969; JD, U. Pitts., 1973; LLM in Taxation, NYU, 1974. Bar: Pa. 1974, U.S. Tax Ct. 1978, U.S. Dist. Ct. (ea. dist.) Pa. 1979, U.S. Ct. Appeals (3rd cir.) 1982, U.S. Ct. Appeals (4th cir.) 1987. Ptnr. Saul, Ewing, Remick & Saul, 1978-88; assoc. Morgan, Lewis & Bockius, Phila., 1974-78, ptnr., 1988—; dir. Maritrans Inc. Instr. Main Line Paralegal Inst., Wayne, Pa., 1984-87, Paralegal Inst., Phila., 1987-90; adj. prof. law Villanova U. Sch. Law, 1991—, U. Pa. Sch. of Law, 1999—. Trustee Temple Brith Achim, King of Prussia, Pa., 1986-91. Mem. ABA, Pa. Bar Assn., Phila. Assn. Democrat. Avocations: skiing, tennis, reading. Pension, profit-sharing, and employee benefits, Corporate taxation, Taxation, general. Office: Morgan Lewis Bockius LLP 1701 Market St Philadelphia PA 19103-2903 E-mail: rlichtenstein@morganlewis.com

LICHTENSTEIN, SARAH CAROL, lawyer; b. East Orange, N.J., May 25, 1953; d. Carl and Hilda Ruth (Warshaw) L. BA, Wellesley Coll., 1975; JD, Columbia U., 1978. Bar: N.Y. 1979, U.S. Dist. Ct. (ea. and so. dists.) N.Y. 1979, U.S. Ct. Appeals (2d cir.) 1981. Assoc. Milbank, Tweed, Hadley & McCloy, N.Y.C., 1978-84, Dreyer and Traub, N.Y.C., 1984-87, ptnr., 1987-93, Shea & Gould, N.Y.C., 1993-94; arbitrator small claims ct. Civ. Ct. of the City of New York, 1988-93; ptnr. Morrison Cohen Singer & Weinstein LLP, N.Y.C., 1994-2000; counsel Lamb & Barnosky, LLP, Melville, N.Y., 2000—. Dir. Eleven Riverside Dr. Corp., 1986-89, 98-2000, pres., 1988-89; mem. panel of chpt. 7 trustees So. Dist. of N.Y., 1993-97; mem. mediation panel U.S. Dist. Ct. So. Dist. N.Y., Bankruptcy Ct. So. Dist. N.Y.; mem. faculty N.E. Deposition Program, Nat. Inst. Trial Advocacy. Contbr. articles to profl. jours. Trustee Stephen Wise Free Synagogue, 1987-90, officer, 1990-98. Wellesley scholar, 1975, Stone scholar Columbia U., 1977-78. Mem. ABA, Suffolk County Bar Assn. Bankruptcy, Federal civil litigation, State civil litigation. E-mail: scl@lambbarnosky.com

LICKE, WALLACE JOHN, lawyer; b. Bemidji, Minn., Jan. 23, 1945; s. George John and Lois (Sanford) L.; m. Martha Miriam Eddy, Dec. 19, 1969; children: Loriann, Paul. BA, U. Minn., 1967, MA, 1970, JD cum laude, 1973. Bar: Minn. 1973, U.S. Dist. Ct. Minn. 1973, U.S. Ct. Appeals (8th cir.) 1981, U.S. Supreme Ct. 1981. Instr. Itasca C.C., Grand Rapids, Minn., 1968—; assoc. Helgesen, Peterson, Engberg & Spector Attys. at Law (now Peterson, Engberg & Peterson), Mpls., 1972-75; sec., gen. counsel Blandin Paper Co. and UPM-Kymmene Inc., subs. UPM-Kymmene a Finnish Co., Helsinki, 1975—. Bd. dirs. Vol. Atty. Program Super Bd., Judy Garland Mus. and Children's Discovery Mus.; chmn. bus. retention and expansion strategies program U. Minn.; mem. panel of arbitrators Am. Arbitration Assn. Mem. bd. editors Minn. Law Rev. Area rep. Minn. awareness project Minn. Internat. Ctr./World Affairs Ctr.; Bd. dirs., pres. hon. bd. dirs. Itasca County Family YMCA, Itasca County Family YMCA, Grand Grand Rapids; bd. dirs., v.p., pres. Itasca County unit Am. Cancer Soc.; bd. dirs., pres. Myles Reif Performing Arts Ctr.; chmn., sec. post com. computer-small bus. explorer post Boy Scouts Am.; adult leader 4-H program Agrl. Extension Svc. U. Minn., St. Paul; mem. Bass Brook Twp. (Minn.) Econ. Devel. Com.; mem. promotion and prospecting com. Itasca Devel. Corp.; trustee Grand Rapids area community found; chmn. coop. solutions adv. bd. Grand Rapids, Minn.; trustee Libr. Found., Cmty. Libr. Found.; class rep. U. Minn. Law Sch. Recipient William Spurgeon III award Boy Scouts Am., 1988; NDEA Title IV fellow, 1967, Paul Harris fellow. Mem. ABA (com. mem.), Fed. Bar Assn., Minn. Bar Assn. (del., planning com.), Itasca County Bar Assn. (past sec., pres.), Minn. 15th Dist. Bar Assn. (com. mem.), Am. Corp. Counsel Assn. (charter), Am. Soc. Corp. Secs., Grand Rapids C. of C. (chmn. com., bd. dirs.), Rotary (bd. dirs., pres., sec. Grand Rapids, dist. rep.), Order of Ski U Mah, Phi Beta Kappa. General corporate, General practice, Labor. Office: Blandin Paper Co 115 SW 1st St Grand Rapids MN 55744-3699 E-mail: john.licke@upm-kymmene.com

LIDAKA, MARIS V. lawyer; b. Memmingen, Germany, Dec. 31, 1949; came to U.S., 1950; s. Rudolfs V. and Veronika A. (Ozolins) L.; m. Lena A. Martin, Oct. 1, 1976; children— Darian Martin, Maris V., Margita M. A.B., Dartmouth Coll., 1972; J.D., DePaul U., 1976. Bar: Ill. 1976, U.S. Dist. Ct. (no. dist.) Ill. 1979. Assoc. Stern, Rotheiser & Dupree, Chgo., 1977— ; atty. Latvian Sr. Assn. of Ill., Inc., Chgo., 1976— . Mem. Ill. Bar Assn., Am.-Latvian Assn. in U.S. Democrat. Lutheran. Personal injury, Probate, Real property. Office: 35 E Wacker Dr Chicago IL 60601-2103

LIDE, VINTON DEVANE, lawyer; b. Greenville, S.C., May 4, 1937; s. Theodore Ellis and Mary Elizabeth (DeVane) L.; m. Carol Jean Keisler, July 8, 1979; children: Wade Patrick, Emily Elizabeth. AB, Davidson Coll., 1959; LLB (now JD), U. Va., 1962. Bar: Va. 1962, S.C. 1962, U.S. Ct. Appeals (4th cir.) 1974, U.S. Ct. Appeals (9th cir.) 2001, U.S. Supreme Ct. 1980. Assoc. Shand & Wilmeth, Hartsville, S.C., 1962-64; ptnr. Shand & Lide, 1964-78; pub. defender Darlington County, 1969-76; exec. asst./legal advisor to gov. S.C., 1978-79; asst. atty. gen. State of S.C., 1978-79; gen. counsel S.C. Dept. Social Svcs., 1979-81; chief counsel, staff dir. Com. on the Judiciary, U.S. Senate, Washington, 1981-85; adminstrv. asst. to U.S. Senator Strom Thurmond, 1985—. Mcpl. ct. judge, Hartsville, 1963—69; U.S. atty. Dist. of S.C., 1985—89. Recipient cert. of Appreciation, Drug Enforcement Adminstrn., U.S. Dept. Justice, 1980. Mem. ABA (ho. dels. 1978-82), S.C. Bar Assn., Va. Bar Assn. Republican. Lutheran. Office: Vinton D. Lide & Assocs LLC 5179 Sunset Blvd Lexington SC 29072 E-mail: lidelaw@aol.com

LIDSKY, ELLA, retired law librarian; b. Wilno, Poland; came to U.S., 1962; d. Leib and Sheina (Izygzon) Cwik; m. Alexander Lidsky, Feb. 20, 1963 (dec. Mar., 1996); 1 son, David Abraham. BA, Pedagogical Inst. Odessa, USSR; MS, Columbia U., 1966, MA, 1973. Cert. Russian and Hebrew lang. tchr. Tchr. high sch., Poland, 1948-51; elem. sch. Israel, 1961-62; asst. cataloger Tchrs. Coll. Columbia U., N.Y.C., 1966-68; cataloger Fairleigh Dickinson U., Teaneck, N.J., 1968-69, asst. dir. tech. services Madison, 1973-84; head cataloger Ramapo Coll., Mahwah, 1971-73; asst. libr. U.S. Ct. Internat. Trade Law Libr., N.Y.C., 1985-2000. Mem. Am. Assn. Law Libraries, Law Librarians of Greater N.Y., N.Y. Tech. Services Librarians, N.J. Law Librarians Assn. Democrat. Jewish. Avocations: music, travel. E-mail: Hella_@msn.com

LIDSTONE, HERRICK KENLEY, JR. lawyer; b. New Rochelle, N.Y., Sept. 10, 1949; s. Herrick Kenley and Marcia Edith (Drake) L.; m. Mary Lynne O'Toole, Aug. 5, 1978; children: Herrick Kevin, James Patrick, John Francis. AB, Cornell U., 1971; JD, U. Colo., 1978. Bar: Colo. 1978, U.S. Dist. Ct. Colo. 1978. Assoc. Roath & Brega, P.C., Denver, 1978-85, Brenman, Epstein, Raskin & Friedlob, P.C., Denver, 1985-86; shareholder Brenman, Raskin & Friedlob, P.C., 1986-94; mem. Friedlob Sanderson Raskin Paulson & Tourtilott, LLC, 1995-98, Norton Lidstone, P.C., Greenwood Village, Colo., 1998—. Adj. prof. U. Denver Coll. Law, 1985-2000; spkr. in field various orgns.; mem. state securities bd. Colo. Dept. Regulatory Agys., 1999—, v. chmn., 2001—, chair 2001-02. Author: Federal and State Securities Regulation for the General Practitioner in Colorado, 2000; editor U. Colo. Law Rev., 1977-78; co-author: Federal Income Taxation of Corporations, 6th edit.; contbg. author: Legal Opinion Letters Formbook, 1996, supplement, 1999; contbr. articles to profl. jours. Served with USN, 1971-75, with USNR, 1975-81. Mem. ABA (Am. Law Inst.), Colo. Bar Assn., Arapahoe County Bar Assn., Denver Assn. Oil and Gas Title Lawyers. Avocation: fluent Spanish language. General corporate, Mergers and acquisitions, Securities. Office: Norton Lidstone PC 5445 Dtc Pkwy Ste 850 Greenwood Village CO 80111-3076 E-mail: hklidstone@nortonlidstone.com

LIEB, L. ROBERT, lawyer, real estate developer; b. Jersey City, July 15, 1941; s. Nathan Philip and Elizabeth (Blum) L.; m. Sherry Young, Sept. 11, 1971; children— Elizabeth Ann, Nathan Young. B.A., U. Buffalo, 1962; LL.B., NYU, 1965. Bar: N.J. 1967, U.S. Dist. Ct. N.J. 1967, N.Y. 1970, U.S. Dist. Ct. (so. and ea. dists.) N.Y. 1970. Law clk. appellate div. Superior Ct. N.J., 1965-66; sr. ptnr. firm Kimmelman, Lieb, Wolf & Samson, West Orange, N.J., 1972-77, chmn. Mountain Devel. Corp., West Paterson, 1978— , Bretton Woods Corp., N.H., 1980-84; chmn. bd. dirs. NorCrown Bank of Roseland, 1987. Served 1st lt. JAGC, USAF, 1966-72. Harry Rudin scholar NYU, 1963-65. Mem. Essex County Bar Assn. Club: Green Brook Country (North Caldwell, N.J.); officer The Children's Inst.. Livingston, N.J.; trustee Passaic County 200 Club, YMCA of the Oranges, Livingston Edn. Found. Office: Mountain Devel Corp 3 Garret Mountain Plz Little Falls NJ 07424-3319

LIEBERMAN, EUGENE, lawyer; b. Chgo., May 17, 1918; s. Harry and Eva (Goldman) L.; m. Pearl Naomi Feldman, Aug. 3, 1947; children: Mark, Robert, Steven. LLB, DePaul U., 1940, JD, 1941. Bar: Ill. 1941, U.S. Supreme Ct. 1963. Mem. firm Jacobs and Lieberman, 1954-60; sr. ptnr. Jacobs, Lieberman and Aling, 1960-74; spl. hearing officer U.S. Dept. Justice, 1967-78; hearing officer Ill. Pollution Control Bd., 1973—; pvt. practice Chgo. Contbr. articles to profl. jours. With U.S. Army, 1942-45.

Recipient 1st in State award Moot Ct. Championship, 1940, gold award Philatelic Exhbn., Taipei, 1981, gold award World Philatelic Exhbn., Melbourne, 1984, Meritorious Svc. medal, bronze arrowhead award, others. Mem. Ill. State Bar Assn. (sr. counselor 1991), Chgo. Bar Assn., Appellate Lawyers Assn., Chgo. Philatelic Soc. (pres. 1964-68), Ill. Athletic Club. Appellate, Environmental, Family and matrimonial. Home: 801 Leclaire Ave Wilmette IL 60091-2065

LIEBERMAN, MARVIN SAMUEL, lawyer; b. N.Y.C., Apr. 26, 1935; s. Abe and Gertrude (Connelly) L.; m. Kathryn Fuhrer, Aug. 10, 1963; children: Kathryn, Willis. BA, Lafayette Coll., 1955; JD, Rutgers U., 1962. Bar: N.J. 1962, U.S. Ct. Appeals (3d cir.) 1965; cert. civil trial atty., N.J. Assoc. Jacob, Alfred & Richardson Levinson, Perth Amboy, N.J., 1962-69; ptnr. Levinson, Conover, Lieberman & Fink, 1969-71, Lieberman & Ryan, Somerville, 1971-83, 88-95, Lieberman, Ryan, Richardson, Welaj & Miller, Somerville, 1983-87, Lieberman, Ryan & Forrest, Somerville, 1995—. With USAF, 1955-58. Mem. ATLA, N.J. Bar Assn., N.J. Trial Lawyers Assn., Middlesex County Trial Lawyers Assn., N.J. Lawyers Assn. Personal injury, Product liability, Workers' compensation. Home: RR 1 Belle Mead NJ 08502-9801 Office: Lieberman Ryan & Forrest 141 W End Ave Somerville NJ 08876-1809 also: 9 Main St Flemington NJ 08822

LIEBERMAN, NANCY ANN, lawyer; b. N.Y.C., Dec. 30, 1956; d. Elias and Elayne Hildegarde (Fox) L.; m. Mark Ellman, Sept. 6, 1997. BA summa cum laude, U. Rochester, 1977; JD, U. Chgo., 1979; LLM in Taxation, NYU, 1981. Bar: N.Y. 1980. Intern White House, Washington, 1975; law clk. Hon. Henry A. Politz U.S. Ct. Appeals (5th cir.), Shreveport, La., 1979-80; assoc. Skadden Arps Slate Meagher & Flom, N.Y.C., 1981-87, ptnr., 1987—. Bd. dirs. Rite Aid Corp. Bd. trustees U. Rochester, 1994—. Mem. ABA, Assn. Bar City N.Y., Coun. Fgn. Rels., Phi Beta Kappa. Republican. Jewish. Contracts commercial, General corporate. Home: 935 Park Ave # 7A New York NY 10028-0212 Office: Skadden Arps Slate Meagher & Flom LLP 4 Times Sq Fl 24 New York NY 10036-6595 E-mail: nlieberm@skadden.com

LIEBERMAN, STEVEN PAUL, lawyer; b. N.Y.C., Apr. 6, 1945; s. Lawrence James and Alice (Levin) L.; m. Enid Marsha Gross, Dec. 24, 1968; children: Amy Greer, Jeffrey Lawrence. BA, George Washington U., 1966; JD, NYU, 1969. Bar: N.Y. 1970. Assoc. Goodstein, Zamore, Mehlman & Krones, N.Y.C., 1970-72; staff atty., asst. sec. Standard Oil Calif., Perth Amboy, N.J., 1972-77; sr. corp. atty. Perkin-Elmer Corp., Norwalk, Conn., 1977-79; asst. gen. counsel, asst. sec. Technicon Instruments Corp., Tarrytown, N.Y., 1979-89; sr. counsel Bayer Corp., 1989-2000. Mem. ABA, Am. Corp. Counsel Assn. (Westchester So. Conn. chpt., internat. law, employment law, antitrust and trade regulation coms.) Antitrust, Computer, General corporate. Home: 187 Winesap Rd Stamford CT 06903-1815 E-mail: spleml3@aol.com

LIEBMAN, EMMANUEL, lawyer; b. Phila., Mar. 26, 1925; s. Morris and Pearl (Zucker) L.; m. Anita Forman, Dec. 24, 1953; children: Judith H. Winslow, Lawrence H. B.S. in Econs., U. Pa., 1950; J.D., Rutgers U., 1954. Bar: N.J. 1954, U.S. Tax Ct. 1955, U.S. Supreme Ct. 1960, D.C. 1972, U.S. Ct. Appeals (3d cir.) 1977. Sole practice, Camden, N.J., 1954-70; pres. Emmanuel Liebman, P.A., Cherry Hill, N.J., 1970-72; pres., chmn. Liebman & Flaster, P.A., Cherry Hill, 1972-86; pres. Emmanuel Liebman, Chartered, Cherry Hill, 1986—; lectr., moderator Inst. Continuing Legal Edn., 1962-87. Served with USNR, 1943-46, PTO. Mem. Camden County Bar Assn. (chmn. com. on fed. tax 1964, 68-70, chmn. retirement plan com. 1986-93), N.J. State Bar Assn. (chmn. com. on bus. taxes 1967-69, 71-73, chmn. state capitol com. 1973-77, chmn. ad hoc com. on financing legal fees 1976-79, exec. coun. 1974-89, chmn. sub chpt. legis. com. 1990-92), ABA (taxation sect., com. personal svc. corps., real property, probate and trust law sect.), D.C. Bar Assn., N.J. State Bar Found. (trustee 1972-87, pres. 1979-83), Am. Judicature Soc., Am. Arbitration Assn. (panelist 1964-88), Camden County Bar Found. (trustee 1986-93). Clubs: Haddon Field (Haddonfield, N.J.); Woodcrest Country (Cherry Hill), St. Andrews Country Club (Boca Raton Fl). Lodge: B'nai B'rith. Probate, Corporate taxation, Personal income taxation. Home: 46 Dublin Ln Cherry Hill NJ 08003-2504 Address: 200 Lake Dr E Ste 204 Cherry Hill NJ 08002-1171

LIEBMAN, LANCE MALCOLM, law educator, lawyer; b. Newark, Sept. 11, 1941; s. Roy and Barbara (Trilinsky) L.; m. Carol Bensinger, June 28, 1964; children: Jeffrey, Benjamin. BA, Yale U., 1962; MA, Cambridge U., 1964; LLB, Harvard U., 1967. Bar: D.C. 1968, Mass. 1976, N.Y., 1995. Asst. to Mayor Lindsay, N.Y.C., 1968-70; asst. prof. law Harvard U., 1970-76, prof., 1976-91, assoc. dean, 1981-84; dean, Lucy G. Moses prof. law Columbia U. Sch. Law, N.Y.C., 1991-96, prof., dir. Parker Sch. Fgn. Law, 1996—, Williams S. Beinecke prof. law, 1998—; dir. Am. Law Inst., 1998—. Successor trustee Yale Corp., 1971-83 Office: Columbia U Sch Law 435 W 116th St New York NY 10027-7297

LIEBMAN, RONALD STANLEY, lawyer; b. Balt., Oct. 11, 1943; s. Harry Martin and Martha (Altgenug) L.; m. Simma Liebman, Jan. 8, 1972; children: Shana, Margot. BA, Western Md. Coll., Westminster, 1966; JD, U. Md., 1969. Bar: Md. 1969, U.S. Dist. Ct. Md. 1970, U.S. Ct. Appeals (4th cir.) 1972, D.C. 1977, U.S. Dist. Ct. D.C. 1982, U.S. Ct. Appeals (D.C. cir.) 1982, U.S. Ct. Appeals (5th cir.) 1985, U.S. Ct. Appeals (2nd cir.) 1988, U.S. Ct. Appeals (9th cir.) 1992, U.S. Dist. Ct. (no. dist.) Calif. 1994, U.S. Supreme Ct. 1995, U.S. Ct. Appeals (7th cir.) 1996, U.S. Dist. Ct. (ea. dist.) Tex. 1999. Law clk. to chief judge U.S. Dist. Ct. Md., 1969-70; assoc. Melnicove, Kaufman & Weiner, Balt., 1970-72; asst. U.S. atty. Office of U.S. Atty., Dept. Justice, 1972-78; ptnr. Sachs, Greenebaum & Tayler, Washington, 1978-82, Patton Boggs, L.L.P., Washington, 1982—. Author: Grand Jury, 1983, Shark Tales, 2000; co-editor: Testimonial Privileges, 1983. Recipient spl. commendation award U.S. Dept. Justice, 1978. Mem. ABA, D.C. Bar Assn., Md. Bar Assn., Sergeants Inn Club (Balt.). Federal civil litigation, State civil litigation, Criminal. Office: Patton Boggs LLP 2550 M St NW Ste 500 Washington DC 20037-1350

LIEGL, JOSEPH LESLIE, lawyer; b. Fond du Lac, Wis., Jan. 20, 1948; s. Melvin Theodore and Verna Lavinia (Jagdfeld) L.; m. Janet L. Meyer, Feb. 1, 1969; children: Matthew, Jeremy. BA with distinction, U. Wis., 1970, JD cum laude, 1973. Bar: Wis. 1973, U.S. Supreme Ct. 1976, Ohio 1978, U.S. Dist. Ct. (no. dist.) Ohio 1978, U.S. Ct. Claims 1978, U.S. Tax Ct. 1978. Assoc. Muchin & Muchin S.C., Manitowoc, Wis., 1973-74; trial atty. U.S. Dept. Justice, Washington, 1974-78; assoc. Jones, Day, Reavis & Pogue, Cleve., 1978-83, ptnr., 1984-96, Coopers & Lybrand, LLP, Detroit, 1996-98; tax counsel McKinsey & Co., Inc., N.Y.C., 1998—. Mem. ABA (taxation sect.), Cleve. Bar Assn. (chmn. tax sect. 1987-88), Cleve. Tax Inst. (chmn. 1994), Internat. Fiscal Assn., Cleve. Tax Club (v.p. 1993-95, pres. 1995-96, past bd. dirs.), Order of Coif, Phi Eta Sigma, Phi Kappa Phi. Avocation: music. Corporate taxation, Taxation, general. Home: 158 Edgemont Rd Scarsdale NY 10583-1717

LIEM, EDWIN T.H. lawyer; b. Jakarta, Indonesia, Mar. 16, 1963; M in Med. Sci., U. Amsterdam, The Netherlands, 1986, M in Netherlands Notarial Law, M in Netherlands Pvt. Law, U. Amsterdam, 1989. Cert. Netherlands law practice, crown appt. civil law notary. Ptnr. Caron & Stevens/Baker & McKenzie, Amsterdam, 1989-96, Wouters Advt. & Notary/Andersen Legal, Amsterdam, 1998-2000. Contbr. articles to profl. jours. Mem. Royal Profl. Orgn. Civil Law Notaries. General corporate, Finance, Mergers and acquisitions. Office: Wouters Adv & Not Andersen Legal Prof WH Keesomlaan 8 1183 DJ Amstelveen The Netherlands Fax: 31 20 8808711. E-mail: edwin.t.h.liem@nl.andersenlegal.com

LIEW, YIK WEE, advocate and solicitor; b. Singapore; LLB, Nat. U. Singapore. Assoc. M/s Wong Partnership, Singapore, 1997—. Mem. Law Soc. Singapore (nfo. tech. com. 1998—). General civil litigation, Computer, Intellectual property. Office: M/s Wong Partnership 80 Raffles Pl #58-01UOB Plz Singapore 048624 Singapore Fax: 2771800. E-mail: lyw@wongpartnership.com.sg

LIFSCHITZ, JUDAH, lawyer; b. N.Y.C., Nov. 28, 1952; s. Morris and Edna (Love) L.; m. Marilyn Feder, Dec. 8, 1974; children: Lisa, Ira, Tamar. BA magna cum laude, Yeshiva U., 1974; JD, George Washington U., 1977. Bar: Md. 1977, U.S. Dist. Ct. D.C. 1980, U.S. Claims Ct. 1980, U.S. Ct. Appeals (D.C. cir.) 1980, U.S. Ct. Appeals (4th cir.) 1982, U.S. Ct. Appeals (fed. cir.) 1985, U.S. Supreme Ct. 1985. Assoc. Hudson, Creyke, Koehler & Tacke, Washington, 1980, Epstein, Becker, Borsody & Green, Washington, 1980-83; ptnr., chmn. govt. contracts dept. Washington Perito & Dubuc, 1983-91; ptnr. Shapiro, Lifschitz and Schram, P.C., 1991—. Washington counsel Nat. Coun. Young Israel, N.Y.C., 1980—; pres. Yeshiva of Greater Washington, 1985-89; bd. dirs. Jewish Community Coun., Washington, 1980—, United Jewish Appeal Fedn., Washington, 1985. Recipient Schofar award Nat. Council Young Israel, 1980. Mem. ABA. Construction, Government contracts and claims. Office: Shapiro Lifschitz & Schram Ste 1050 1101 Pennsylvania Ave NW Washington DC 20004-2500

LIFSCHULTZ, PHILLIP, financial and tax consultant, accountant, lawyer; b. Oak Park, Ill., Mar. 5, 1927; s. Abraham Albert and Frances Rhoda (Siegel) L.; m. Edith Louise Leavitt, June 27, 1948; children: Gregory, Bonnie, Jodie. BS in Acctg., U. Ill., 1949; JD, John Marshall Law Sch., 1956. Bar: Ill. 1956; CPA. Tax mgr. Arthur Andersen & Co., Chgo., 1957-63; v.p. taxes Montgomery Ward & Co., 1963-78; fin. v.p., contr. Henry Crown & Co., 1978-81; prin. Phillip Lifschultz & Assocs., 1981—. Exec. dir. Dodi Orgn., 1987-90; v.p. Altra Travel, Northbrook, Ill., 1975—; v.p. Tax Execs. Inst., Chgo., 1977-78; pres. Great Lakes Shoe Co., Bannockburn, Ill., 1996—. Adv. coun. Coll. Commerce and Bus. Adminstrn., U. Ill., Urbana-Champaign, 1977-78; chmn. Civic Fedn. Chgo., 1980-82; chmn. adv. bd. to Auditor Gen. of Ill., 1965-73; project dir. Exec. Svc. Corps of Chgo., Chgo. Bd. Edn. and State of Ill. projects, 1980-87. With U.S. Army, 1945-46. Mem. Am. Arbitration Assn. (comml. panel 1983-94), Ill. Bar Assn., Chgo. Bar Assn., Am. Inst. CPAs, Ill. CPA Soc., Nat. Retail Merchants Assn. (chmn. tax. com. 1975-78), Am. Retail Fedn. (chmn. taxation com. 1971). Home and Office: 442 Kelburn Rd Apt 123 Deerfield IL 60015-4370 E-mail: papalif@aol.com

LIFTIN, JOHN MATTHEW, lawyer; b. Washington, June 25, 1943; children: Eric, Hilary. AB, U. Pa., 1964; LLB, Columbia U., 1967. Bar: N.Y.. 1967, D.C. 1974, U.S. Dist. Ct. D.C. 1975, U.S. Ct. Appeals (D.C. cir.) 1975, U.S. Supreme Ct. 1980. Assoc. Sullivan & Cromwell, N.Y.C., 1967-71; spl. counsel to chmn. SEC, Washington, 1971-72, assoc. dir. market reg. div., 1972-74; ptnr. Rogers & Wells, 1974-85; pres. Quadrex Securities Corp., N.Y.C., 1985-87; sr. v.p., gen. counsel Kidder, Peabody Group Inc., 1987-96, Prudential Ins. Co. Am., Newark, 1998—. Mem. adv. bd. securities regulation and law reports Bur. Nat. Affairs, Inc., Washington, 1979—; mem. N.Y. Stock Exch. Legal Adv. Com., 2000—. Contbr. articles on securities law to profl. jours. Mem. ABA (former chmn. com. on fed. regulation of securities), Univ. Club. General corporate, Securities. Office: Prudential Ins Co of Am Prudential Plz 751 Broad St Newark NJ 07102-3714

LIGELIS, GREGORY JOHN, lawyer; b. N.Y.C., Mar. 30, 1950; s. John and Roseanne (McCoy) Ligelis; children: Gregory John Jr., Blair Stephanie. BA magna cum laude, Hofstra U., 1972; JD, U. Pa., 1975; postgrad. NYU, 1982—. Bar: N.Y. 1976, U.S. Dist. (so. and ea. dists.) N.Y. 1976, U.S. Ct. Appeals (2d cir.). Ptnr. Robinson & Cole, N.Y.C., 1975—. Mem. Maritime Law Assn. (subcom. Maritime arbitration, marine fin.), ABA, N.Y. County Bar Assn., Met. Club, Washington Club, India House Club. Admiralty, Private international. Home: Fenn Hill Rd PO Box 1283 Washington Depot CT 06793-0283 Office: Robinson & Cole 699 E Main St Stamford CT 06901-2112

LIGHT, ALFRED ROBERT, lawyer, political scientist, educator; b. Dec. 14, 1949; s. Alfred M. Jr. and Margaret Francis (Asbury) L.; m. Mollie Sue Hall, May 28, 1977; children: Joseph Robert, Gregory Andrew. Student, Ga. Inst. Tech., 1967-69; BA with highest honors, Johns Hopkins U., 1971; PhD, U. N.C., 1976; JD cum laude, Harvard U., 1981. Bar: D.C. 1981, Va. 1982. Tax clk. IRS, 1967; lab technician Custom Farm Svcs. Soils Testing Lab, 1968; warehouse asst. State of Ga. Mines, Mining and Geology, 1970; clk.-typist systems mgmt. divsn., def. contract adminstrv. Def. Supply Agy., Atlanta, 1971; rsch. and teaching asst. dept. polit. sci. U. N.C., Chapel Hill, 1971-74; rsch. asst. Inst. Rsch. in Social Sci., 1975-77; program analyst Office of Sec. Sef., 1974; asst. prf. polit. sci., rsch. scientist Ctr. Energy Rsch. Tex. Tech. U., Lubbock, 1977-78; rsch. asst. grad. sch. edn. Harvard U., 1978-79; assoc. Butler, Binion, Rice, Cook & Knapp, Houston, 1980, Bracewell & Patterson, Washington, 1980; Hunton & Williams, Richmond, Va., 1981-89; of counsel, 1989-93, 95-96; assoc. prof. St. Thomas U. Sch. Law, Miami, Fla., 1989-93, prof., 1993—. Interim dean, 1993-94; bd. advisors Toxics Law reporter, Bur. Nat. Affairs, Washington, 1987—. Contbr. articles to profl. jours. Charter mem. West Broward Cmty. Ch. Capt. USAR, 1971-85. Grantee NSF, Inst. Evaluation Rsch., U. Mass., Ctr. Energy Rsch., Tex. Tech. U., 1977-78; recipient Julius Turner award Am. Polit. Sci. Assn., 1977. Mem. ABA (vice-chmn.) tort and ins. practice sect. 1988-97, nat. res. and environ. sect. 1993-95, chmn. 1995-2000), Fed. Bar. Assn., Va. Bar Assn., Richmond Bar Assn., Phi Beta Kappa, Phi Eta Sigma. Democrat. Home: 1042 Woodfall Ct Fort Lauderdale FL 33326-2832 Office: St Thomas U Sch Law 16400 NW 32nd Ave Opa Locka FL 33054-6459 E-mail: alight@stu.edu

LIGHT, ROBERT VANN, lawyer; b. Little Rock, Ark., Dec. 1, 1930; s. Louis Robert and Geneva (Raper) L.; m. Claire De'Ann Whitaker, Aug. 25, 1956 (div. 1969); children— Louis Whitaker, Lynne Ann; m. Cherry Ann Harkey, July 22, 1972. B.S. U. Ark.-Fayetteville, 1952, J.D., 1955. Bar: Ark. 1955, U.S. Dist. Ct. (ea. and we. dists.) Ark. 1955, U.S. Ct. Appeals (8th cir.) 1956, U.S. Supreme Ct. 1960. Assoc., Mehaffy, Smith & Williams, Little Rock, Ark., after 1955, ptnr., 1963; ptnr. law firm Friday, Eldrege & Clark, Little Rock, 1963— . Fellow Ark. Bar Found.; mem. Ark. Bar Assn., ABA, Am. Trial Lawyers Assn., Internat. Soc. Barristers. Federal civil litigation, General civil litigation. Home: 4816 Crestwood Dr Little Rock AR 72207-5438 Office: Friday Eldredge & Clark 2000 First Commercial Bldg Little Rock AR 72201

LIGHT, RUSSELL JEFFERS, lawyer; b. Dallas, Sept. 8, 1949; s. Marion Russell and Isabel (Jeffers) L.; m. Mary Louise Allen, July 20, 1979; children: Erin, Brendan, Justin. BA, So. Meth. U., 1971, JD, 1975. Bar: Tex. 1976. Instr. legal writing So. Meth. U., Dallas, 1975-76; briefing atty. to assoc. justice Ct. of Civil Appeals, Austin, 1976-77; law clk. U.S. Dist. Ct., Ft. Worth, 1977-78; atty. Union Pacific Resources Co., 1978-2001, Burlington, Northern Santa Fe, N.Mex., 2001—. Chmn. air task force of subcom. on environment and health law Am. Petroleum Inst., 1987-89. Author: (poetry) Nirvana, 1971 (recipient Dallas Poetry award 1971); actor, dir. (film) A Child's Garden, 1971 (recipient D.W. Griffith award 1971). Mem. Calif. Coun. Environ. and Econ. Balance, Dallas Bar Environ. Com. Mem. ABA (vice chmn. air com. natural resources sect. 1987-93, environ. controls corp. banking sect. 1987-89), Tex. Mid-Continent Oil and Gas Assn. (environ. law com.), Ft. Worth Petroleum Club, Ridglea Country Club, Ft. Worth Club. General corporate, Environmental. Home: 3705 Streamwood Rd Fort Worth TX 76116-9316 E-mail: russelllight@home.com

LIGHT, WILLIAM RANDALL, lawyer; b. Lynchburg, Va., Sept. 11, 1958; s. John Leftwich and Patricia (Wilson) L.; m. Lisa Burcher, Apr. 27, 1991; children: William Randall II, Madeline Gibson. BA, Emory and Henry Coll., 1980; JD, Nova U. Bar: Va. 1985, U.S. Dist. Ct. (we. dist.) Va. 1985, U.S. Ct. Appeals (4th cir.), U.S. Supreme Ct. Assoc. Killis T. Howard, a profl. corp., Lynchburg, 1984-98; pvt. practice, 1998—. Spl. justice Commonwealth of Va. 24th Jud. Dist., Lynchburg, 1987—; adj. prof. Lynchburg Coll., 1989, 91. Bd. dirs. Lynchburg Mental Health Assn.; vice chmn. Rep. com. City of Lynchburg, 1986-90, acting chmn., 1990-91; vestry St. Paul Episcopal Ch., Ecclesiastical Ct. Episcopal Diocese of Southwestern Va. Maj. Va. Def. Force. Mem. ABA, Lynchburg Bar Assn. (v.p. young lawyers sect. 1984-88, pres. 1989-90), Va. Trial Lawyers Assn., Amherst County-Nelson County Bar Assn., Masons (Master 1991), Phi Alpha Delta. Republican. Episcopalian. Criminal, General practice, Personal injury. Home: 1804 Mobile Rd Lynchburg VA 24503-2434 Office: William R Light PC 1011 Court St PO Box 309 Lynchburg VA 24505-0309 E-mail: wrlightlaw@aol.com

LIGHTSTONE, RONALD, lawyer; b. N.Y.C., Oct. 4, 1938; s. Charles and Pearl (Weisberg) L.; m. Nancy Lehrer, May 17, 1973; 1 child, Dana. AB, Columbia U., 1959; JD, NYU, 1962. Atty. CBS, N.Y.C., 1967-69; assoc. dir. bus. affairs CBS News, 1969-70; atty. NBC, 1970; assoc. gen. counsel Viacom Internat. Inc., 1970-75, v.p., gen. counsel, sec., 1976-80; v.p. bus. affairs Viacom Entertainment Group, Viacom Internat., Inc., 1980-82, v.p. corp. affairs, 1982-84, sr. v.p., 1984-87; exec. v.p. Spelling Entertainment Inc., L.A., 1988-91, CEO, 1991-93; chmn. Multimedia Labs. Inc., 1994-97; CEO, pres. New Star Media Inc., 1997-99, vice chmn., 1999-2000. Lt. USN, 1962-66. Mem. ABA (chmn. TV, cable and radio com.), Assn. of Bar of City of N.Y., Fed. Comm. Bar Assn. General corporate, Entertainment.

LIJOI, PETER BRUNO, lawyer; b. Suffern, N.Y., Sept. 2, 1953; s. Salvatore and Josephine (Gentile) L.; m. Christine Louise Confroy, Aug. 19, 1978; children: Jonathan Peter, Christopher Andrew. BA in History and Econs., Montclair State Coll., 1975; postgrad. in urban planning, Rutgers U., 1975-76; JD, Pace U., 1979; postgrad., Harvard U., 1992. Bar: N.J. 1981, N.Y. 1988. Rsch. intern N.J. Dept. Edn., Trenton, 1976; intern Office U.S. Atty., N.Y.C., 1977-78; energy coord. Rockland County, 1979-80; dep. dir., of counsel Pvt. Industry Coun., Pearl River, N.Y., 1980-91; pvt. practice law Summit, N.J., 1981—; dir., counsel County of Rockland Indsl. Devel. Agy., 1981-95; v.p., gen. counsel Rockland Econ. Devel. Corp., Pearl River, 1990-91. Cons. U.S. Dept. Energy, Washington, 1980; mem. program of instrn. for lawyers Law Sch., Harvard U., 1992; legal counsel and land acquisition mgr. K. Hovnanian Cos. North Jersey, Inc., 1993-95, K. Hovnanian Cos. Northeast, Inc., 1995—; legis. counsel, assemblyman, Eric Munoz N.J. State Legislature. Guest writer The Bond Buyer. Bd. dirs. Rockland County coun. Girl Scouts U.S., 1982-92; pres. Washington Elem. Sch. PTA, Summit, 1986-88; mem. Summit Planning Bd., desegregation grant adv. com. Summit Bd. Edn., 1992—; commr. tax bd. Union County, 1999—. Mem. ABA, N.J. Bar Assn., N.Y. Bar Assn., Union County Bar Assn., Assn. Trial Lawyers Am., Nat. Assn. Bond Lawyers. Roman Catholic. Avocations: running, coaching youth soccer. Environmental, Finance, Real property. Home: 124 Canoe Brook Pkwy Summit NJ 07901-1436 Office: 110 Fieldcrest Ave Edison NJ 08837-3620

LILES, KEVIN WARREN, lawyer; b. Arlington, Tex., Apr. 8, 1971; s. Ken Warren and Julie Hardy Liles. BSME, BSEE and Mktg., Tex. A&M U., 1993; JD, Baylor U., 1997. Bar: Tex. 1997, U.S. Dist. Ct. (so. and ea. dists.) Tex. 1997. Assoc. Fulbright & Jaworski, LLP, Houston, 1997—. Editor-in-chief Baylor Law Rev., 1996-97. General civil litigation. Office: Fulbright & Jaworski LLP 1301 McKinney St Ste 5100 Houston TX 77010

LILIENSTERN, O. CLAYTON, lawyer; b. Houston, Nov. 13, 1943; s. Oscar C. adn Suzanne (Haughton) L.; m. Helen A. Andronis, Jan. 14, 1979; children: Robert, Susan, Kelli, Melanie. AB, U. Ala., 1965; JD, U. Houston, 1968, MBA, 1992; LLM, George Washington U., 1972. Bar: Tex. 1968, U.S. Dist. Ct. (so. dist.) Tex. 1973, U.S. Tax Ct. 1975, U.S. Supreme Ct. 1976, U.S. Dist. Ct. (we. dist.) Tex. 1978, U.S. Dist. Ct. (ea. dist.) Tex. 1987, U.S. Dist. Ct. (no. dist.) Tex. 1988, U.S. Ct. Appeals (5th, 9th, 11th and fed. cirs.); cert. civil trial law Tex. Bd. Legal Specialization. Assoc. Andrews & Kurth, Houston, 1972-79, ptnr., 1979-97, Hicks, Thomas & Lilienstern LLP, Houston, 1997—. Bd. Vocat. Guidance Svc. Inc., chair; bd. dirs. Annunciation Orthodox Sch., 1991-94, 97-2000, Leadership Houston, 1989—. Capt. JAGC, U.S. Army, 1968-72. Decorated Joing Svc. Commendation medal. Fellow Tex. Bar Found., Houston Bar Found.; mem. ABA, State Bar Tex., Houston Bar Assn., A.A. White Soc., U. Houston Law Ctr., U. Houston Law Alumni Assn. (pres. 1982-83, life), Houston Law Rev. Alumni Assn. (pres. 1991-92), Jasons Soc., Briar Club (bd. dirs.) Delta Tau Delta, Omicron Delta Kappa, Phi Alpha Delta. Federal civil litigation, State civil litigation. Home: 4821 Maple St Bellaire TX 77401-5728 Office: Hicks Thomas & Lilienstern LLP 4200 Tex Commerce Tower 700 Louisiana St Houston TX 77002 E-mail: cliliens@hicks-thomas.com

LILLARD, JOHN FRANKLIN, III, lawyer; b. Cheverly, Md., Aug. 2, 1947; s. John Franklin Jr. and Madeline Virginia (Berg) L.; m. Kim Leslie Oliver, June 1, 1991 (div.); 1 child, John F. IV. Bar: N.Y. 1972, D.C. 1974, Md. 1975. Assoc. Donovan, Leisure, Newton & Irvine, N.Y.C., 1971-74; trial atty. civil div. Dept. Justice, Washington, 1976-77; ptnr. Lillard & Lillard, 1977—. Instr. Dale Carnegie Course, 1988-97. Vice chair Village Coun. Friendship Heights, Chevy Chase, Md., 1975-77; candidate U.S. Congress from 5th dist. Md., 1981; chair Am. Solar Energy Assn.; founding mem. 1970 Nat. Adv. Coun. Ctr. for Study of the Presidency, Md. State Adv. Bd. on Spl. Tax Dists., 1976-77, alcoholic beverage adv. bd. Montgomery County, 1977-79; chair 1990 Eisenhower Centennial Meml. Com. Recipient Eastman award Am. Arbitration Assn., 1971. Mem. Md. Bar Assn., Prince George's County Bar Assn., Anne Arundel County Bar Assn., Met. Club (Washington), Tred Avon Yacht Club (Oxford, Md.), Marlborough Hunt Club. Republican. Episcopalian. Federal civil litigation, General practice. Office: 8 Loudon Ln Annapolis MD 21401-1219

LILLEHAUG, DAVID LEE, lawyer; b. Waverly, Iowa, May 22, 1954; s. Leland Arthur and Ardis Elsie (Scheel) L.; m. Winifred Sarah Smith, May 29, 1982; 1 child, Kara Marie. BA summa cum laude, Augustana Coll., Sioux Falls, S.D., 1976; JD cum laude, Harvard U., 1979. Bar: Minn. 1979, U.S. Dist. Ct. Minn. 1979, D.C. 1981, U.S. Ct. Appeals (8th cir.) 1981, U.S. Dist. Ct. D.C. 1982. Law clk. to presiding judge U.S. Dist. Ct. Minn., Mpls., 1979-81; assoc. Hogan & Hartson, Washington, 1981-83, 84-85; issues aide, exec. asst. to Walter Mondale, 1983-84; assoc. Leonard, Street & Deinard, Mpls., 1985-87, ptnr., 1988-93, 98-99; U.S. atty. Dist. of Minn., 1994-98. Candidate U.S. Senate, 1999—. Mondale Policy Forum fellow U. Minn., 1990-91. Mem. ABA, Minn. Bar Assn. (past chair constrn. law sect., Author's award 1990). Lutheran. Avocations: fishing, golf. Home: 6701 Parkwood Ln Edina MN 55436-1735 Office: Lillehaug Law Office 1515 One Financial Plaza Minneapolis MN 55402 E-mail: DLL6701@cs.com

LILLIE, CHARISSE RANIELLE, lawyer, educator; b. Houston, Apr. 7, 1952; d. richard Lyusander and Verneli Audrey (Watson) L.; m. Thomas L. McGill, Jr., Dec. 4, 1982. BA cum laude, Conn. Wesleyan U., 1973; JD, Temple U., 1976; LLM, Yale U., 1982. Bar: Pa. 1976, U.S. Dist. Ct. (ea. dist.) Pa. 1977, U.S. Ct. Appeals (3d cir.) 1980. Law clk. U.S. Dist. Ct. (ea. dist.) Pa., Phila., 1976-78; trial atty., honors program, civil rights divsn. Dept. Justice, Washington, 1978-80; dep. dir. Cmty. Legal Svcs., Phila., 1980-81; asst. prof. law Villanova U. Law Sch., Pa., 1982-83, assoc. prof., 1983-84, prof., 1984-85; asst. U.S. atty. U.S. Dist. Ct. (ea. dist.) Pa., Phila.,

1985-88; with Transp. Authority of Phila., 1988-90; city solicitor law dept. City of Phila., 1990-92; ptnr. litigation dept. Ballard, Spahr, Andrew & Ingersoll, 1992—, exec. com. bd. dirs., 1994—. Mem. 3d Cir. Lawyers Adv. Com., 1982-85; legal coun. Pa. Coalition of 100 Black Women, Phila., 1983-88; bd. dirs. Juvenile Law Ctr., Phila., Pa. Intergovtl. Coop. Authority, Fed. Res. Bank Phila., dep. chmn. bd. dirs., 1997-98, vice chmn. bd. dirs., 1998—; commr. Phila. Ind. City Charter Commn., 1991-94; trustee Women;s Law Project, Phila., 1984-90; mem. Mayor's Commn. on May 13 MOVE Incident, 1985-86. Bd. dirs. Leadership Inc.; chmn. bd. dirs. Juvenile Law Ctr., 997-99; mem. adv. com. Women's Way, Phila., 1986—. Recipient Equal Justice award Cmty. Legal Svcs., Inc., 1991, J. Austin Norris award Barristers Assn., 1991, Outstanding Alumna award Wesleyan U., 1993, Elizabeth Dole Glass Ceiling award ARC, Phila. chpt., 1994, Whitney Young Leadership award Phila. Urban League, 1996; named One of the Top Three Phila. Labor Mgmt. Attys. Phila. Mag., 1994, 99; Davenport fellow, 1973, Yale Sch. fellow, 1981. Mem. ABA, Nat Bar Assn., Fed. Bar Assn. (1st v.p. Phila. chpt. 1982-84, pres. Phila. chpt. 1984-86, 3rd cir. rep. 1991—), Nat. Conf. Black Lawyers (pres. 1970), ABA commn. on race and ethnic diversity in the profession (vice chmn., chmn. 1999—), Am. Law Inst., Phila. Bar Assn. (vice chair bd. govs. 1994, chair, bd. govs. 1995-96), Hist. Soc. U.S. Dist. Ct. (ea. dist.), Pa. (dir. 1983-87), Barristers Assn. (J. Austin Norris award 1983-87). Federal civil litigation, State civil litigation, Labor. Home: 7000 Emlen St Philadelphia PA 19119-2556 Office: Ballard Spahr Andrews Ingersoll 1735 Market St Fl 51 Philadelphia PA 19103-7599

LILLY, JOHN RICHARD, II, lawyer; b. Phila., July 20, 1962; s. John Richard Sr. and Elizabeth Anne (Brown) L.; children: John Richard III, Cameron Lewis. BA, Geoge Washington U., 1987; JD, U. Balt., 1991. Bar: Md. 1992, U.S. Dist. Ct. Md. 1995. Law clk. 7th Jud. Cir. Md., Upper Marlboro, 1991-92; asst. state's atty. State's Atty.'s Office Prince George's County Md., 1992-98; asst. atty. gen. Md. Atty. Gen.'s Office, Balt., 1998-2001; pvt. practice Glen Burnie, Md., 2001—. Adj. prof. U. Balt. Sch. Law, 1999-2000. Comments editor U. Balt. Jour. Environ. Law. Chmn. Oakland Mills Village Bd., Columbia, Md., 1990-92; pres. St. Stephen's Area Civic Assn., Crownsville, Md., 1994-95. Lt. USNR, 1988—. Mem. Anne Arundel Bar Assn. Avocations: tennis, sailing, reading, photography. Criminal, Environmental, Military. Home: 133 Idlewild Rd Severna Park MD 21146 Office: 7439 Baltimore-Annapolis Blvd Glen Burnie MD 21061 E-mail: jrlillyesq@aol.com

LILLY, THOMAS JOSEPH, lawyer; b. Bklyn., Feb. 17, 1931; s. Frank A. and Mary Ellen (Kelly) L.; m. Margaret Mary Doherty, June 28, 1959; children: Thomas J., Mary Jo, Joseph, Sean. BA, St. John's Coll., 1953; JD, Fordham U., 1961; LLM, NYU, 1967. Bar: N.Y. 1962, U.S. Dist. Ct. (ea. and so. dists.) N.Y. 1963, U.S. Ct. Appeals (2d cir.) 1965. Dir. rsch. Office and Profl. Employees Internat. Union AFL-CIO, N.Y.C., 1960-62; asst. U.S. atty. U.S. Dist. Ct. (ea. dist.) N.Y., Bklyn., 1962-66; ptnr. Doran, Colleran, O'Hara, Pollio & Dunne, N.Y.C., 1966-79, Quinn & Lilly, P.C., N.Y.C. and Garden City, N.Y., 1979-89; pvt. practice Garden City, 1989—. Adj. prof. N.Y. State Indsl. and Labor Rels. Sch., Cornell U., 1980-81; arbitrator U.S. Dist. Ct. (ea. dist.) N.Y.; mem. Nassau County Pub. Employment Rels. Bd. With USN, 1953-57. Mem. ABA, N.Y. Bar Assn., Nassau County Bar Assn., Sea Cliff Yacht Club. Civil rights, Labor, Pension, profit-sharing, and employee benefits. Home: 136 8th Ave Sea Cliff NY 11579-1308 Office: 585 Stewart Ave Garden City NY 11530-3302 E-mail: ThomasJLillySr@LillyandAssociates.net

LIMBAUGH, STEPHEN NATHANIEL, JR. state supreme court chief justice; b. Cape Girardeau, Mo., Jan. 25, 1952; s. Stephen N. and Anne (Mesplay) L.; m. Marsha Dee Moore, July 21, 1973; children: Stephen III, Christopher K. BA, So. Meth. U., 1973, JD, 1976; LLM, U. Va., 1998. Bar: Tex. 1977, Mo. 1977. Assoc. Limbaugh, Limbaugh & Russell, Cape Girardeau, 1977-78; pros. atty. Cape Girardeau County, 1979-82; shareholder, ptnr. Limbaugh, Limbaugh, Russell & Syler, 1983-87; cir. judge 32d Jud. Cir., 1987-92; judge Supreme Ct. Mo., Jefferson City, 1992—. Mem. ABA, State Bar Tex., Mo. Bar. Office: Supreme Ct Mo 207 W High St Jefferson City MO 65101-1516

LIMBAUGH, STEPHEN NATHANIEL, federal judge; b. Cape Girardeau, Mo., Nov. 17, 1927; s. Rush Hudson and Bea (Seabaugh) L.; m. DeVaughn Anne Mesplay, Dec. 27, 1950; children— Stephen Nathaniel Jr., James Pennington, Andrew Thomas. BA, S.E. Mo. State U., Cape Girardeau, 1950; JD, U. Mo., Columbia, 1951. Bar: Mo. 1951. Prosecuting atty. Cape Girardeau County, Mo., 1954-58; judge U.S. Dist. Ct. (ea. and we. dists.) Mo., St. Louis, 1983—. With USN, 1945-46. Recipient Citation of Merit for Outstanding Achievement and Meritorious Service in Law, U. Mo., 1982 Fellow Am. Coll. Probate Counsel, Am. Bar Found.; mem. ABA (ho. of dels. 1987-90), Mo. Bar Assn. (pres. 1982-83). Republican. Methodist. E-mail: stephen. Office: US Dist Ct Thomas F Eagleton Courthous 111 S Tenth St Ste 3.125 Saint Louis MO 63102 E-mail: limbaugh@moed.uscourts.gov

LINCKE, KARL HEINRICH, lawyer; b. Bonn, Germany, Mar. 21, 1971; arrived in Spain, 1999; s. Dietrich and Annemarie L.; m. Andrea Henning, Aug. 27, 1999. Abitur, Albert-Einstein-Gymnasium, Bonn, 1991. With AA (Fgn. Affairs), Bonn, 1993, 94, 95, T-Mobil, Bonn, 1996, Deutscher Bundestag, Bonn, 1996-97; atty. Fröhlingsdorf Abogados, Madrid, 1999—. Co-author: Kurswechsel, 1998, Europäische Fallstricke, 2000. Mem. Rechtsanwaltkammer Cologne, Bund der Selbstandigen. Civil rights, Consumer commercial, Mergers and acquisitions. Office: Fröhlingsdorf Abogados Pa de la Castellana 120 53ZQ E-28046 Madrid Spain Fax: (34) 915613123. E-mail: karl_lincke@froehlingsdorfabogados.es

LINDAUER, ERIK D. lawyer; b. Bklyn., Oct. 1, 1956; s. Albert and Dinah (Epner) L.; m. Lisa Diamond, Aug. 16, 1981; children: Jacob, Samuel. BA, SUNY, Albany, 1978; JD, SUNY, Buffalo, 1981. Bar: N.Y. 1982, U.S. Dist. Ct. (ea. dist.) N.Y. 1982, U.S. Dist. Ct. (so. dist.) N.Y. 1982. Assoc. Sullivan & Cromwell, N.Y.C., 1981-89, ptnr., 1989—. Banking, Bankruptcy, Contracts commercial. Home: 37 Seminole Way Short Hills NJ 07078-1216 Office: Sullivan & Cromwell 125 Broad St Fl 28 New York NY 10004-2489

LINDBERG, CHARLES DAVID, lawyer; b. Moline, Ill., Sept. 11, 1928; s. Victor Samuel and Alice Christine (Johnson) L.; m. Marian J. Wagner, June 14, 1953; children: Christine, Breta, John, Eric. AB, Augustana Coll., Rock Island, Ill., 1950; JD, Yale U., 1953; DHL, Augustana Coll., 2000. Bar: Ohio 1954. Assoc. Taft, Stettinius & Hollister, Cin., 1953-61, ptnr., 1961-85, mng. ptnr., 1985-98, of counsel, 1999—. Dir. Cin. Bengals Profl. Football Team, Knowlton Constrn. Co.; chmn. bd. dirs. Schonstedt Instrument Co., 1994-97. Editor Nat. Law Jour., 1979-90. Bd. dirs. Taft Broadcasting Co., Cin., 1973-87, Dayton Walther Corp., 1986-87, Gibson Greeting, Inc., 1991-2000; bd. dirs. Augustana Coll., 1978-87, 91-99, 2000—, sec., 1981-82, vice-chmn., 1982-83, chmn., 1983-86; pres. Cin. Bd. Edn., 1971, 74, Zion Luth. Ch., Cin., 1966-69; chmn. policy com. Hamilton County Rep. Com., 1981-90; mem. exec. com. Ohio Rep. Fin. Com., 1989-90; trustee Greater Cin. Ctr. Econ. Edn., 1976-91, pres., 1987-89, chmn., 1989-91; chmn. law firm divsn. Fine Arts Fund, 1985; trustee Pub. Libr. Cin. and Hamilton County, 1982—, pres., 1989, 96, 01. Mem. Cin. Bar Assn., Greater Cin. C. of C. (trustee 1985, exec. com., vice chmn. govt. and cmty. affairs com. 1989-91), Ohio Libr. Trustees Assn. (bd. dirs. 1986-87), Ohio C. of C. (bd. dirs. 1988-89), Queen City Club (sec. 1989-91), Commonwealth Club, Comml. Club (sec. 1994-96), Cin. Country Club, Optimists. General corporate, Mergers and acquisitions. Office: 1800 Firstar Tower 425 Walnut St Cincinnati OH 45202-3923 E-mail: lindberg@taftlaw.com

LINDE, MAXINE HELEN, lawyer, business executive, private investor; b. Chgo., Sept. 2, 1939; d. Jack and Lottie (Kroll) Stern; B.A. summa cum laude, UCLA, 1961; J.D., Stanford U., 1967; m. Ronald K. Linde, June 12, 1960. Bar: Calif. 1968. Applied mathematician, reseach engr. Jet Propulsion Lab., Pasadena, Calif., 1961-64; law clk. U.S. Dist. Ct. No. Calif., 1967-68; mem. firm Long & Levit, San Francisco, 1968-69, Swerdlow, Glikbarg & Shimer, Beverly Hills, Calif., 1969-72; sec., gen. counsel Envirodyne Industries, Inc., Chgo., 1972-89; pres. The Ronald and Maxine Linde Found., 1989—; vice chmn. bd., gen. counsel Titan Fin. Group, LLC, Chgo., 1994-98. Mem. bd. visitors Stanford Law Sch., 1989-92, law and bus. adv. coun., 1991-94, dean's adv. coun. 1992-94. Mem. Order of Coif, Phi Beta Kappa, Pi Mu Epsilon, Alpha Lambda Delta. General corporate.

LINDENBAUM, SAMUEL HARVEY, lawyer; b. N.Y.C., Mar. 29, 1935; s. Abraham M. and Belle (Axelrad) L.; m. Linda Marion Lewis, June 16, 1957; children: Erica Dale Lindenbaum Tishman, Laurie Ellen. BA cum laude, Harvard U., 1956, JD cum laude, 1959; Fulbright fellow, Oslo U., Norway, 1959-60. Bar: N.Y. 1960. Assoc. Fried, Frank, Harris, Shriver & Jacobson, N.Y.C., 1960-62; mem. Lindenbaum & Young, Bklyn., 1962-74; sr. mem. Rosenman & Colin, N.Y.C., 1974-83, of counsel, 1983—. Bd. overseers Albert Einsteinn Coll. Medicine; chmn. exec. com., Jewish Assn. for Svcs. for the Aged; bd. govs., mem. exec. com., v.p. Real Estate Bd. N.Y.; mem. Counsel Assn. for Better N.Y.; bd. dirs., chmn., exec. com. Am. Friends Israel Mus. Mem. Bklyn. Bar Assn., Harmonie Club, Harvard Club, Friars Club. Home: 998 5th Ave New York NY 10028-0102 Office: Rosenman & Colin 575 Madison Ave Fl 17 New York NY 10022-2511

LINDENMUTH, NOEL CHARLES, lawyer; b. Chgo., Nov. 27, 1940; s. Charles Theodore and Bernice Dorothy (Chowanski) L.; m. Carol Jean Guercio, Nov. 28, 1963 (div. Aug. 1989); children: Eric Jon, Steven Paul; m. Krystyna M. Gajdecki, Apr. 6, 1990; 1 child, Robert E. Gajdecki. JD, Loyola U., Chgo., 1970. Bar: Ill. 1970, U.S. Dist. Ct. (no. dist.) Ill. 1970, U.S. Supreme Ct. 1977, Colo. 1996. Ptnr. Anesi, Ozmon & Rodin, Ltd., Chgo., to 1994, of counsel, 1994-96; pvt. practice Law Office of Gary P. Sandblom, Boulder, Colo., 1996—. Bd. dirs. Opera COlo., 1998—; adv. bd. dirs. U. Colo. Cardiovascular Inst., 2001—. Served with U.S. Army, 1959-62. Mem. ABA, ATLA, Ill. State Bar Assn., Chgo. Bar Assn., N.W. Suburban Bar Assn., Ill. Trial Lawyers Assn. (lectr.), Chgo. Trial Lawyers Club, Am. Soc. Law and Medicine, Ill. Workers Compensation Lawyers Assn., Am. Arbitration Assn. (panel of arbitrators), Colo. Bar Assn., Colo. Trial Lawyers Assn., Boulder County Bar Assn., Park Ridge Club (Ill.), Country Club. Appellate, General civil litigation, State civil litigation. Office: 5390 Manhatten Cir Boulder CO 80303

LINDER, HARVEY RONALD, lawyer, arbitrator, mediator; b. Pitts., July 23, 1949; s. Charles Joseph and Rose (Ruben) L.; m. Reva Rebecca Vertman, Aug. 14, 1971 (div.); children: Zalman F., Seth A. BA, Duquesne U., 1971, JD, 1975. Bar: Pa. 1975, U.S. Dist. Ct. (we. dist.) Pa. 1975, U.S. Supreme Ct. 1979. Legal intern Dist. Atty.'s Office, Pitts., 1974-75; asst. mgr. arbitration U.S. Steel, 1975-80, mgr. labor rels., 1980-81, supt. employee rels. Clairton, Pa., 1981-83; corp. dir. employee rels. U.S. Steel Agri-Chemicals, Atlanta, 1984-86; corp. dir. law and human resources LaRoche Industries Inc., 1986-88, v.p., gen. counsel, 1988-96, Orion Mgmt. Svcs. Inc., 1996-97, SED Internat., Inc., 1997-99. Arbitrator, mediator, 1996—; pres. A.C.I.R.A., 1987-90. Contbr. poetry and photography to Duquesne Literary Mag., 1968-74. Exec. cons. Jr. Achievement, Pitts., 1978-83; head coach Atlanta Jewish Cmty. Ctr., Dunwoody, Ga., 1984—, bd. dirs., 1991—, v.p., 2001—; pres. B'nai Torah Synagogue, 1995-97, Hunter's Woods Homeowners' Assn., Dunwoody, 1986-87; commr. Baseball & Soccer Leagues; bd. dirs. Atlanta Jewish Fedn., 1995-96, Atlanta YAD, 2000. Steel fellow Am. Iron and Steel Inst., 1977-85. Mem. ABA, Allegheny County Bar Assn., Indsl. Rels. Rsch. Assn., Duquesne U. Law Sch. Alumni Assn. (bd. dirs. 1980-84), B'nai B'rith (local v.p. 1975-80), Amer-Israel C. of C. (bd. dirs. 1993—). Democrat. Avocations: coaching, collecting books and sports memorabilia. Alternative dispute resolution, Contracts commercial, General corporate. Home: 7025 Northgreen Dr Atlanta GA 30328-1453

LINDER, IRIS KAY, lawyer; b. Davenport, Iowa, May 3, 1952; d. Forrest Wesley and Josephine Jeanette (Barnett) Shaffer; 1 son, Eric Scott Socolofsky; m. Stephen J. Linder. BS, Mich. State U., 1976; JD, U. Mich., 1980. Bar: Mich. 1980, U.S. Dist. Ct. (we. and ea. dists.) Mich. 1980. Ptnr. Fraser, Trebilcock, Davis & Dunlap, P.C., Lansing., Mich., 1980—. Adj. faculty Cooley Law Sci., 1999—. Co-author: Michigan Usury Manual, 1982; contbr. chpt. to Litigation of the Commercial Case, 1992. Bd. dirs. Capitol Area Girl Scouts USA, 1986-88, Capitol Area Polit. Action Com., 1990-96, chairperson, 1995; bd. dirs. Capitol Enterprise Forum, 1989-95, pres., 1993; mem. planning bd. Ingham County Office for Young Children, 1986-87, Mayor's Parking Adv. Com., 1990-93; group com. chairperson Shared Vision Sys. and Rsch., 1994-96; bd. dirs. Capitol Area United Way, 1994—, Congl. Kehillet Israel, 1995-96, dir.; bd. dirs. Venture Ctr., Inc., 1996—, chair, 1999—; bd. dirs. Infoguys, Inc., 1996-99. Recipient Book award U. Mich. Law Sch., 1980. Mem. ABA, Ingham County Bar Assn., State Bar Assn. Mich., Lansing Regional C. of C. (bus. women's coun. 1984-87, bd. dirs. 1987-92, dir. govt. affairs 1991-92, Tireless award 1992, Small Bus. Advocate of Yr. award 1993), Lansing Assn. Career Women (bd. dirs. 1985-87), Mich. Corp. and Securities Bur. (securities adv. com. 1991—), Athena Found. (bd. dirs. 1986-87). General corporate, Franchising, Securities. Home: 2550 Dustin Rd Okemos MI 48864-2073 Office: Fraser Trebilcock Davis & Foster 1000 Michigan Nat Towers Lansing MI 48933 E-mail: ilinder@fraserlawfirm.com

LINDLEY, JEARL RAY, lawyer; b. Abilene, Tex., Mar. 12, 1934; s. Hardie Lindley and Hope Clement Mourant; m. Annabelle Sim Yee Lindley, May 22, 1954; children: Katheryn Ann, Michael Andrew, Carolyn Elizabeth. BS in Chemistry, N.Mex. State U., 1960; MD, U. Colo., 1964; MS, U. Ill., 1967; JD, South Tex. Coll. of Law, 1997. Asst. clin. prof. of surgery Rush Med. Coll. of Rush U., Chgo., 1969-71, U. Ill. Sch. of Medicine, Chgo., 1969-71; assoc. clin. prof. of surgery Tex. Tech. U. Sch. of Medicine, El Paso, 1976-80; atty., counselor Las Cruces, N.Mex., 1997—. Adj. prof. N.Mex. State U., Las Cruces, 1984-86. Author publs. in field (McNeil Meml. Rsch. award 1967). Bd. dirs. Meml. Gen. Hosp., Las Cruces, 1983, So. N.Mex. Regional Dialysis Ctr., Las Cruces, 1984-89; instr. ACLS, AHA, Las Cruces, 1980-86, ATLS, Am. Coll. Surgeons, Las Cruces, 1980-86; mem. emergency med. svcs. com. Dona Ana Emergency, Las Cruces, 1979, City County Hosp. Bd. Govs., Las Cruces, 1981-83; mem. internat. bd. dirs. N.Mex. State U. Alumni Assn., 1979-81; mem. bd. counselors Citizens Bank, Las Cruces, 1991-93. Named to Outstanding Young Men of Am., 1969, Marine of Yr., Marine Corps League, 1990; commd. Ky. Col., State of Ky., 1989; proclamation of Jearl R. Lindley Day/Mayor of Truth or Consequences, N.Mex., 1990; recipient Disting. Citizen medal Dept. of N.Mex. Marine Corps League, others. Fellow Am. Coll. Surgeons, Internat. Coll. of Surgeons, Southwestern Surg. Congress; mem. Internat. Endovascular Soc., Soc. Clin. Vascular Surgery, AHA, Am. Legion, Marine Corps Assn., Marine Corps Heritage Found., Naval Inst., Marine Meml. Club, Air Force Assn., Marine Corps League (Commandant Dept. of N.Mex. 1990-91, Dept. Commandant's medal 1991, medal with bronze star 1988-90). Republican. Mem. Ch. of Christ. Avocations: shooting, photography, travel in an RV, reading, motorcycling. Home: 4566 Mockingbird St Las Cruces NM 88011-9616

LINDQUIST, YLVA, lawyer; b. Stockholm, July 22, 1961; d. Oscar and Inga-Britt Sjöberg; m. Henrik Lindquist, Oct. 3, 1992; children: Oscar, Astrid. LLM, Stockholm U., 1985. Svc. Stockholm City Ct., 1986-89; assoc. Lagerlöf & Leman, Stockholm, 1989-97, Hammaskiöld & Co., Stockholm, 1998-2000; ptnr., 2000—. Mem. Swedish Bar Assn., Internat. C. of C. (mem. spl. local com. mktg. 1999—). Contracts commercial, General corporate, Mergers and acquisitions. Office: Hammarskiöld & Co Skeppsbron 42 PO Box 2278 SE-10317 Stockholm Sweden Fax: 46-8-57845099. E-mail: ylva.lindquist@hammarskiold.se

LINDSAY, GEORGE PETER, lawyer; b. Bklyn., Feb. 22, 1948; s. Charles Joseph and Marie Antionette (Faraone) L.; m. Sharon Winnett, Sept. 8, 1973; children: William Charles, Kimberly Michelle. BA, Columbia U., 1969; JD, Harvard U., 1973. Bar: N.Y. 1974, Mass. 1985, U.S. Dist. Ct. (so. dist.) N.Y. 1974, U.S. Ct. Appeals (2d cir.) 1975. Assoc. White & Case, N.Y.C., 1973-82; ptnr. Miller, Wrubel & Dubroff, 1982-83, Sullivan & Worcester LLP, N.Y.C., 1983—. Mem. ABA, Assn. Bar City of N.Y., N.Y. State Bar Assn. Banking, Contracts commercial, Finance. Office: Sullivan & Worcester LLP 565 5th Ave New York NY 10017-2413 E-mail: gpl@sandw.com

LINDSAY, REGINALD CARL, judge; b. Birmingham, Ala., Mar. 19, 1945; s. Richard and Louise L.; m. Cheryl E. Hartgrove, Aug. 15, 1970. Cert., U. Valencia, 1966; AB in Polit. Sci. cum laude, Morehouse Coll., 1967; JD, Harvard U., 1970. Bar: Mass. 1971, U.S. Ct. Appeals (1st cir.) 1971. Assoc. Hill & Barlow, 1970-75, 78-79, ptnr., 1979-93; judge U.S. Dist. Ct. Mass., Boston, 1994—. Arbitrator, mem. comml. arbitration panel Am. Arbitration Assn., 1994—; commr. Mass. Dept. Pub. Utilities, Boston, 1975-77; pres. adv. bd. Mus. of Nat. Center of Afro-Am. Artists, 1975-81, v.p., 1981— ; trustee Thompson Islands Edn. Center, Boston, 1975-81; bd. dirs. United Way of Mass. Bay, 1981-84, Morgan Meml. Goodwill Industries, Boston, 1992—, Ptnrs. for Youth with Disabilities, Boston; mem. Nat. Consumer Law Ctr. (bd. dirs.), Mass. Commn. on Jud. Conduct, 1982-88; trustee Newton (Mass.) - Wellesley Hosp. Recipient Ruffin-Fenwick Trailblazer award Harvard Black Law Students Assn., 1994, Amanda V. Houston cmty. svc. award Boston Coll., 1998, Frederick E. Berry Expanding Ind. award Easter Seals, 1999, Heroes Among Us award Boston Celtics, 2001, Leadership award New Eng. Black Law Students Assn., 2001. Mem. ABA, Nat. Bar Found., Mass. Bar Assn., Boston Bar Assn. (coun. 1977—, citation jud. excellence 1999), Pi Sigma Alpha, Phi Beta Kappa. Office: 1 Courthouse Way Ste 5130 Boston MA 02210-3007

LINDSEY, MICHAEL, lawyer; b. Portsmouth, Hampshire, Eng., Dec. 12, 1960; s. John and Joan L.; m. Elizabeth Mary Emmons, Mar. 25, 1988; children: John Gryffudd, Catherine Elena. LLB with honors, U. Birmingham, Eng., 1983. Bar: solicitor Supreme Ct. Articled clk. H.C.L. Hanne & Co. Solicitors, London, 1985-87; solicitor, 1987-88, Morgan Cole, Cardiff, Wales, 1988-99; ptnr., 1999—. Contbr. articles, revs. to profl. jour. Mem. Intellectual Property Inst., Intellectual Property Lawyers Orgn., Chartered Inst. Patent Agents (assoc.). Avocations: cricket, walking, cooking. Intellectual property, Patent, Trademark and copyright. Office: Morgan Cole Bradley Ct Park Pl CF1O 3DP Cardiff CF10 3DP Wales Fax: 029 2038 5409. E-mail: lindsey.emmons@virgin.net, michael.lindsey@morgan-cole.com

LINDSKOG, DAVID RICHARD, lawyer; b. Aug. 4, 1936; s. Gustaf Elmer and Charlotte (Birely) L.; m. Elisabeth Lagg, Jan. 28, 1978; 1 child, Stefanie. BA, Yale U., 1958; LLB, U. Va., 1965. Bar: N.Y. 1966, conseil juridique France 1978, avocat 1992. Assoc. Curtis, Mallet-Prevost, Colt & Mosle, N.Y.C., 1965-72, ptnr., 1973-99; sr. v.p., gen. counsel Leach Holding Corp., Westport, Conn., 1999—. Lt. USNR, 1958-62. Mem. Internat. Bar Assn. Episcopalian. Banking, Construction, Private international. Home: 22 Shore Acre Dr Old Greenwich CT 06870-2130 Office: Leach Holding Corp 315 Post Road West Westport CT 06880

LINE, WILLIAM GUNDERSON, lawyer; b. July 19, 1927; s. William Harrison and Lulu Mae (Gunderson) L.; children: Nancy Line Jacobs, Lindsey Line Natvig, Katherine Line Rasmussen, Julie Ann Line Bailey, Ashley E. Student, Nebr. State Tchrs. Coll., 1943-44; BSL, U. Nebr., 1948, JD, 1950. Bar: Nebr. 1950, U.S. Dist. Ct. Nebr. 1950, U.S. Supreme Ct. 1965. County atty. Dodge County, Nebr., 1955-59; ptnr. Kerrigan, Line & Martin, Fremont, 1962-95. Lectr. Nebr. State Patrol Tng. Camp, Ashland, 1959. Bd. dirs. Nebr. Civil Liberties Union, 1971-75. Mem. Nebr. Bar Assn., Dodge County Bar Assn. (pres. 1967), Phi Alpha Delta. Republican. Episcopalian. Criminal, Family and matrimonial, General practice. Office: PO Box 410 33 W 4th St Fremont NE 68026-0410

LINEBERGER, PETER SAALFIELD, lawyer; b. Akron, Ohio, Mar. 9, 1947; s. Walter F. Jr. and Mary Robinson (Saalfield) L.; children: Katherine Ann, Mary Elizabeth; m. Constance Meyers, Mar. 12, 1988. BA in English, Williams Coll., 1969; JD, Gonzaga U., 1976. Bar: Mont. 1976, Wash. 1994, U.S. Dist. Ct. Mont. 1977, U.S. Dist. Ct. (ea. dist.) Wash. 1994. Legal intern Witherspoon, Kelly, Davenport, Toole, Spokane, 1975; law clk. Mont. Supreme Ct., Helena, 1976; assoc. Landoe, Gary, Bozeman, Mont., 1977-78; ptnr. Landoe, Brown, Planalp, Komers & Lineberger, 1979-83, Lineberger & Davis, Bozeman, 1984-85, Lineberger & Harris, PC, Bozeman, 1986-88, Lineberger, Walsh & McKenna, PC, Bozeman, 1989-94; pvt. practice Peter S. Lineberger, Spokane, 1994—. City atty. Town of West Yellowstone, Mont., 1978-94; chmn. Gallatin County Legal Svcs. Com., Bozeman, 1985-89, chmn. Mont. Child and Family Law Sect., 1993-94. Lt. USNR, 1969-72. Mem. ABA (family law sect. 1987—), Wash. State Bar Assn. (family law sect., exec. com. 1998—, chmn.-elect 2001—), Am. Acad. Matrimonial Lawyers, Gallatin County Bar Assn., Mont. City Attys. Assn. (pres. 1983), Spokane County Bar Assn. (vol. lawyers program adv. com. 1996-2000, chmn. 1998-99). Avocations: fly fishing, skiing. General civil litigation, Family and matrimonial, Real property. Office: US Bank Bldg Ste 1407 422 W Riverside Ave Spokane WA 99201-0306 E-mail: psline@hotmail.com

LINETT, DAVID, lawyer; b. Perth Amboy, N.J., Apr. 9, 1934; s. Jack K. and Anne L.; children: Jon, Peter, Maren. BA, Yale U., 1956; JD, Harvard U., 1959. Bar: D.C. 1959, N.J. 1960. Law sec. to assignment judge Superior Ct. N.J., 1956-60; assoc. Gross, Weissberger & Linett, New Brunswick, N.J., 1960-62, ptnr., 1962-77; prosecutor Somerset County, 1977-82; of counsel Lowenstein, Sandler, Brochin, Kohl et al and predecessor, Roseland and Somerville, 1982-85; ptnr. Gindin & Linett, Bridgewater, 1985—. Chmn. N.J. State Bar Com. on Programs for Law Enforcement Personnel, 1978-80; mem. com. on county dist. cts. N.J. Supreme Ct., 1980-82, mem. Post-Indictment Delay Task Force, 1980, dist. XIII ethics com., 1986-90, chair ethics fin. com., 1990-94, treas., 1992-94. Mem. N.J. Dem. State Com., 1973-77; bd. dirs. Somerset County Resource Ctr. for Women and Their Families, 1982-83; chmn. bd. trustees, Assn. for Advancement of Mentally Handicapped, 1987-89; commr. N.J. Election Law Enforcement Commn., 1987-2000, vice chair, 1996-2000; mem. Ct. House study com., Somerset County Bd. Freeholders, 1979-82. Mem. ABA (corp., real property law sect.), Nat. Dist. Attys. Assn. (nat. treas., exec. com. 1981-82, Pres.'s award for outstanding svc. as chmn. fin. com. 1982), New Brunswick Bar Assn. (pres. 1974), N.J. Bar Assn. (land use sect., real property sect.), Somerset County Bar Assn., Somerset County C. of C. (bd. dirs. 1984-90, Outstanding Citizen of Yr. 1989), Rotary (pres. 1986-87, dist. gov. 1991-92). Banking, General corporate, Real property. Office: PO Box 6135 1170 Rt 22 Bridgewater NJ 08807 E-mail: ginlin@aol.com

LINGELBACH, ALBERT LANE, lawyer; b. N.Y.C., July 19, 1940; s. Robert Lane and Sarah (Lewis) L.; m. Ann Norton, July 31, 1965; children: Albert Lane, Charity Ann. BS, U. Pa., 1962, LLB, 1965. Bar: N.Y. 1967, U.S. Tax. Ct. 1984. Assoc. Jackson & Nash, LLP, N.Y.C., 1965-72, ptnr., 1972—. Co-chmn. Port Washington (N.Y.) Cmty. Chest Fund Drive, 1972-73, bd. dirs. 1973-74, sec. 1974-75, v.p. 1975-76, exec. v.p. 1976-78, pres. 1978-80; elder Roslyn Presbyn. Ch. Mem. ABA (com. on significant new devels. in probate and trust law practice 1983-87), Assn. Bar of City of N.Y. (mem. com. on trusts estates and surrogates ct. 1980-83), N.Y. State Bar Assn., Am. Coll. Trust and Estate Counsel, Estate Planning Coun. N.Y.C. (dir. 1998-2001), Univ. Club (N.Y.C.), Southport (Maine) Yacht Club. Estate planning, Probate, Estate taxation. Home: Ketch Lady Ann PO Box 472 Port Washington NY 11050-0104 Office: Jackson & Nash LLP 330 Madison Ave Fl 18 New York NY 10017-5095

LINGO, ROBERT S(AMUEL), lawyer; b. Homer, Nebr., Mar. 10, 1941; s. Samuel Elmer and Ruth Esther (Ranney) L.; m. Ann Stevens, Oct. 9, 1971; children: Tracy Ann, Robyn Michelle. BS, U. Nebr., Lincoln, 1963, JD, 1966; LLM, George Washington U., 1986. Bar: Nebr. 1966, U.S. Supreme Ct. 1986. Commd. 1st lt. USAF, 1966, advanced through grades to capt.; served as judge adv., 1967-74; atty. advisor U.S. Army, Beltsville, Md., 1974-79, U.S. Army Materiel Command, Alexandria, Va., 1979—2001, ret., 2001. Contbr. articles to publs. Served to lt. col., USAFR, 1966-94. Home: 5218 Dunleigh Dr Burke VA 22015-1644 E-mail: blingo@hqamc.army.mil

LINK, GEORGE HAMILTON, lawyer; b. Sacramento, Mar. 26, 1939; s. Hoyle and Corrie Elizabeth (Evans) L.; m. Betsy Leland; children— Thomas Hamilton, Christopher Leland. AB, U. Calif., Berkeley, 1961; LLB, Harvard U., 1964. Bar: Calif. 1965, U.S. Dist. Ct. (no., ea., ctrl. and so dists.) Calif. 1965, U.S. Ct. Appeals (9th cir.) 1965. Assoc. Brobeck, Phleger & Harrison, San Francisco, 1964-69, ptnr., 1970—, mng. ptnr. L.A., 1973-93, mng. ptnr. firmwide, 1993-96. Chmn. Pacific Rim Adv. Coun., 1992-95. Bd. regents U. Calif., 1971-74; trustee Berkeley Found., Jr. Statesmen Am.; bd. govs. United Way, 1979-81; trustee, v.p. Calif. Hist. Soc., 1987—. Fellow Am. Bar Found.; mem. ABA, Calif. Bar Assn., L.A. Bar Assn., U. Calif. Alumni Assn. (pres. 1972-75), Calif. Club, Bohemian Club, Jonathan Club. Republican. Methodist. Office: Brobeck Phleger & Harrison 550 S Hope St Los Angeles CA 90071-2627 E-mail: glink@brobeck.com

LINK, ROBERT JAMES, lawyer, educator; b. Washington, May 25, 1950; s. Robert Wendell and Barbara Ann (Bullock) L.; m. Cheryl Ann Brillante, Apr. 22, 1978; children: Robert Edward, Holden James. BA, U. Miami, 1972, JD, 1975. Bar: Fla. 1975, U.S. Dist. Ct. (mid. dist.) Fla. 1980, U.S. Ct. Appeals (5th cir.) 1980, U.S. Ct. Appeals (11th cir.) 1981, U.S. Supreme Ct. 1984, U.S. Dist. Ct. (no. dist.) Fla. 1989. Asst. pub. defender City of Miami, Fla., 1975-78, City of Jacksonville, 1978-82; ptnr. Greenspan, Goodstein & Link, Jacksonville, 1982-84, Goodstein & Link, Jacksonville, 1984-85; pvt. practice, 1985-88; assoc. Howell, Liles & Milton, 1988-89; ptnr. Pajcic & Pajcic P.A., 1990—. Guest instr. U. Miami, 1976, U. Fla., 1979-88, Stetson U. Law Sch., 1984, Jacksonville U., 1987-88, U. North Fla., 1991. Atty. legal panel ACLU, Jacksonville, 1982-88. Mem. Fla. Bar Assn. (chmn. com. for representation of indigents criminal law sect. 1980, cert. criminal trial lawyer 1989), Jacksonville Bar Assn. (criminal law sect.), Nat. Assn. Criminal Def. Lawyers (vice-chmn. post conviction com. 1990), Fla. Pub. Defender Assn. (death penalty steering com. 1980-82, instr. 1979-89). Democrat. Methodist. Avocations: sailing, fishing, diving, softball. Criminal, Personal injury, Product liability. Home: 3535 Carlyon St Jacksonville FL 32207-5836 Office: 1900 Independent Dr Jacksonville FL 32202-5023

LINKLATER, WILLIAM JOSEPH, lawyer; b. Chgo., June 3, 1942; s. William John and Jean (Connell) L.; m. Dorothea D. Ash, Apr. 4, 1986; children: Erin, Emily. BA, U. Notre Dame, 1964; JD, Loyola U., 1968. Bar: Ill. 1968, U.S. Dist. Ct. (no. dist.) Ill. 1968, U.S. Ct. Appeals (7th cir.) 1971, U.S. Supreme Ct. 1971, U.S. Ct. Appeals Washington, 1978, U.S. Ct. Appeals Washington 1978, Calif. 1981, U.S. Dist. Ct. (cen. dist.) Calif. 1981, U.S. Tax Ct. 1982, U.S. Dist. Ct. (no. dist.) Calif. 1983, U.S. Dist. Ct. (ea. dist.) Mich. 1989, U.S. Ct. Appeals (6th cir.) 1990, U.S. Dist. Ct. Hawaii, 1992. Atty. Fed. Defender Project, Chgo.; assoc. Baker & McKenzie, 1968-75, ptnr., 1975—. Contbr. articles to profl. jours. Mem. ABA (past co-chmn. com. on internat. criminal law criminal justice sect., mem. criminal practice and procedure com. antitrust sect., mem. criminal justice sect.), FBA, Ill. Bar Assn., 7th Cir. Bar Assn., Chgo. Bar Assn. (bd. mgrs. 1997—, past v.p. jud. candidates evaluation com., chmn. large law firm com., pres. 2000-01), Internat. Inst., Calif. Bar Assn., Colo. Bar Assn., Am. Coll. Trial Lawyers, Am. Bd. Criminal Lawyers, Chgo. Inn of Ct., Wong Sun Soc. San Francisco (internat. proctor), Alpha Sigma Nu. Antitrust, Federal civil litigation, Criminal. Office: Baker & McKenzie 1 Prudential Plz Ste 3000 Chicago IL 60601

LINN, RICHARD, federal judge; b. Bklyn., Apr. 13, 1944; BEE, Rensselaer Poly. Inst., 1965; JD, Georgetown U., 1969. Judge U.S. Ct. Appeals (fed. cir.), Washington, 1999—.

LINSENMEYER, JOHN MICHAEL, lawyer; b. Columbus, Ohio, June 20, 1940; s. John Cyril and Ruth Theresa (Motz) L.; m. Barbara Panish, Aug. 12, 1961; children: Ann Elizabeth Linsenmeyer Nelson, Thomas More, Barbara Mary Linsenmeyer Malone. AB, Georgetown U., 1961, JD, 1964. Bar: Va. 1964, N.Y. 1965, U.S. Supreme Ct.1967, D.C. 1975. Assoc. Cravath, Swaine & Moore, N.Y.C., 1966-75; ptnr. Forsyth, Decker, Murray & Broderick, 1975-80, Morgan, Lewis & Bockius, N.Y.C., 1980—. Columnist Southern Conn. Newspapers, Greenwich, 1984—; contbr. articles to profl. jours. Police officer, sgt. Greenwich Police Dept. Special Div., 1966-87; cons. firearms Presdl. Commn. on the Causes and Prevention of Violence, 1968-69; bd. dirs. Fairfield County Fish and Game Agy., Newtown, Conn., 1973-77. Mem. N.Y. State Bar Assn., N.Y.C. Fed. Cts. Com., N.Y.C. Fed. Bar Coun. Republican. Roman Catholic. Clubs: University (N.Y.C.), Squadron A (N.Y.C.), Rocky Point (Old Greenwich, Conn.), Royal Can. Mil. (Toronto), Can. Club of N.Y. (bd. govs. 1998—). Avocations: hunting, shooting, horses, military history. Federal civil litigation, General civil litigation, Private international. Home: 9 Hendrie Ave Riverside CT 06878-1808 Office: Morgan Lewis & Bockius 43d Fl 101 Park Ave Fl 43D New York NY 10178-0002 E-mail: jlinsenmeyer@morganlewis.com

LINTON, JACK ARTHUR, lawyer; b. N.Y.C., May 29, 1936; s. Paul Phillip and Helen (Feller) L.; m. Nancy A., Sept. 1, 1957; children: Ann Deborah Linton Wilmot, James Paul, John Michael. BA, Albright Coll., 1958; JD, NYU, 1961, LLM in Taxation, 1966. Bar: Pa. 1962, N.Y. 1963, U.S. Tax Ct. 1966, U.S. Dist. Ct. (ea. dist.) Pa. 1978, U.S. Ct. Appeals, 1984. Assoc. DeLong, Dry & Binder, Reading, Pa., 1961-63; asst. ho. counsel Bob Banner Assocs., Inc., N.Y.C., 1963-66; ptnr. DeLong, Dry, Cianci & Linton, Reading, 1967-70, Williamson, Miller, Murray & Linton, Reading, 1970-72, Gerber & Linton, P.C., Reading, 1972-88, Linton, Giannascoli, Barrett & Distasio, P.C., Reading, 1989-97, Linton, Giannascoli, Distasio & Adams, PC, Reading, 1997-98, Linton, Distasio, Adam & Kauffman, PC, Reading, 1998—. Solicitor Reading Parking Authority, 1967-76, City of Reading, 1980-96; bd. dirs. The Group, Inc., Small Bus. Coun. Am., Inc., chmn. polit. action com., 1988—, numerous med. profl. corps., Reading area; lectr. nat. seminars on tax problems for small bus.; co-founder, mem. Estate Planning Coun. Berks County, 1978—. Editor Tax Law Rev., 1965-67; contbr. articles to profl. jours. Pres. Berks County Mental Health Assn., 1968-69, Reading Jewish Community Ctr., 1980-82; mem. Mental Health/Mental Retardation Bd. Berks County, 1974-80; treas., bd. dirs. Reading-Berks Youth Soccer League, 1982-85; bd. dirs. Gov. Mifflin Sch. Dist., Shillington, 1985-93, Exeter Township Sch. Dist., 1999-, v.p., 2000-. Kenneson fellow NYU Sch. Law, 1965-67. Mem. ABA (mem. personal svc. orgn. com., tax sect. 1981—, chairperson task force for repeal top-heavy rules 1987-89, vice chmn. personal svc. orgn. com. 1990-92, chmn. personal svc. orgn. com. 1992-94), Pa. Bar Assn., Berks County Bar Assn. (treas. 1969-72), Berks County C. of C. (mem. nat. affairs com.). Democrat. Jewish. Avocations: sports, reading. Estate planning, Pension, profit-sharing, and employee benefits, Estate taxation. Office: Linton Distasio Adams & Kauffman PC PO Box 461 1720 Mineral Spring Rd Reading PA 19602-2231

LINXWILER, JAMES DAVID, lawyer; b. Fresno, Calif., Apr. 9, 1949; s. George Edwin and Stella Ruth (Schmidt) L.; m. Robyn Kenning, July 12, 1986; children: Elizabeth Ann, John Edwin, Jeffrey David. BA, U. Calif., Berkeley, 1971; JD, UCLA, 1974. Bar: D.C. 1976, U.S. Dist. Ct. Alaska 1976, U.S. Dist. Ct. (D.C. cir.) 1976, Alaska 1977, U.S. Ct. Appeals (9th cir.) 1977, U.S. Supreme Ct. 1988. Lawyer U.S. Dept. Interior, Washington, 1974-76, Cook Inlet Region, Inc., Anchorage, 1976-78, Sohio Petroleum Co., Anchorage, 1978-81; shareholder Guess & Rudd, 1981-2000, mng. shareholder, 2000—. Spkr. seminars on environ. and natural resources law. Contbr. chpts. to book, articles to profl. jours. Chmn. Alaska Coalition Am. Energy Security, 1986-87, Alliance Arctic Nat. Wildlife Refuge Com., 1986-87; bd. dirs. Commonwealth North, 1993-99, pres., 1999-2000. Mem. ABA, FBA, Alaska Bar Assn. (chmn., exec. com. nat. resources sect. 1988-93), D.C. Bar Assn. Democrat. Administrative and regulatory, Oil, gas, and mineral, Environmental. Home: 2407 Loussac Dr Anchorage AK 99517-1272 Office: Guess & Rudd 510 L St Ste 700 Anchorage AK 99501-1959

LIPCON, CHARLES ROY, lawyer; b. N.Y.C., Mar. 20, 1946; s. Harry H. and Rose Lipcon; m. Irmgard Adels, Dec. 1, 1974; children: Lauren, Claudia. BA, U. Miami, 1968, JD, 1971. Bar: Fla. 1971, U.S. Dist. Ct. (so. dist.) Fla. 1971, U.S. Ct. Appeals (5th cir.) 1972, U.S. Supreme Ct. 1976, U.S. Ct. Appeals (D.C. cir.) 1980, U.S. Dist. Ct. (so. dist.) Tex. 1982, U.S. Dist. Ct. (middle dist.) Fla. 2000, U.S. Ct. Appeals (11th cir.) 1994, U.S. Dist. Ct. Colo. 1999, U.S. Dist. Ct. (mid. dist.) Fla. 2000. Pvt. practice, Miami, Fla., 1971—. Lectr. U. Miami Sch. Law. Author: Help for the Auto Accident Victim, 1984, Seaman's Rights in the United States When Involved in An Accident, 1989; pub., editor The Cruise Line Law Reporter; contbr. articles to profl. jours. Named Commodore of High Seas, Internat. Seaman's Union. Mem. ABA, ATLA, Fla. Bar Assn., Fla. Trial Lawyers Assn., Dade County Bar Assn., Dade County Trial Lawyers, Fla. Admiralty Trial Lawyers Assn., Mensa. Admiralty, Federal civil litigation, Personal injury. Office: 2 S Biscayne Blvd Ste 2480 Miami FL 33131-1803 E-mail: sealaw@aol.com

LIPEZ, KERMIT V. federal judge, former state supreme court justice; Former judge Maine Superior Ct.; assoc. justice Supreme Jud. Ct. of Maine, Portland, 1994-98; judge U.S. Ct. Appeals (1st cir.) Maine, 1998—. Office: 156 Federal St Portland ME 04101-4152

LIPFORD, ROCQUE EDWARD, lawyer, corporate executive; b. Monroe, Mich., Aug. 16, 1938; s. Frank G. and Mary A. (Mastromarco) L.; m. Marcia A. Griffin, Aug. 5, 1966; children: Lisa, Rocque Edward, Jennifer, Katherine. BS, U. Mich., 1960, MS, 1961, JD with distinction, 1964. Bar: Mich. 1964, Ohio 1964. Instr. mech. engring. U. Mich., 1961-63; atty. Miller, Canfield, Paddock & Stone, Detroit, 1965-66; asst. gen. counsel Monroe Auto Equipment Co., 1966-70, gen. counsel, 1970-72, v.p., gen. counsel, 1973-77, Tenneco Automotive, 1977-78; ptnr. firm Miller, Canfield, Paddock & Stone, Detroit, 1978—, mng. ptnr., 1988-91. Bd. dirs. La-Z-Boy Inc., Monroe Bank & Trust. Mem.: Mich. Bar Assn., Legatus, Knights of Malta, North Cape Yacht Club, Monroe Golf and Country Club, Otsego Ski Club, Mariner Sands Golf and Country Club, Tau Beta Pi, Pi Tau Sigma. Antitrust, General corporate, Estate planning. Home: 1065 Hollywood Dr Monroe MI 48162-3045 Office: Miller Canfield Paddock & Stone 214 E Elm Ave Ste 100 Monroe MI 48162-2682 E-mail: lipford@mcps.com

LIPOFF, NORMAN HAROLD, lawyer; b. N.Y.C., Dec. 9, 1936; s. Benjamin and Anna (Lippow) L.; m. Nancy B. Bressler, June 12, 1960; children: Ann, Elise. BSBA, U. Fla., 1958, JD with honors, 1961; LLM in Taxation, NYU, 1962. Bar: Fla., 1961. With Carlton, Fields, Ward, Emmanuel, Smith & Cutler, Tampa, Fla., 1962-70; ptnr. Greenberg, Traurig, Hoffman, Lipoff, Rosen & Quentel, Miami, 1970—. Pres. Greater Miami Jewish Fedn.; nat. chmn. United Israel Appeal, 1990-94, Endowment Fund Devel. Coun. of Jewish Fedns.; nat. vice-chmn. United Jewish Appeal, 1978-98; bd. govs. Tel-Aviv U.; bd. govs., exec. com. Jewish Agy. for Israel, 1984-96; citizens bd. U. Miami; bd. dirs. U. Fla. Found.; trustee Law Ctr. Assn., U. Fla. Coll. Law; vice-chmn. Fla. Philharmonic Orch. Governing Coun., 1998-2001. Recipient Pres. Leadership award Greater Miami Jewish Fedn., 1972, Pres. award Tel Aviv U., 1982, Brotherhood award NCCJ, 1988. Mem. ABA (tax sect.), Fla. Bar Assn. (chmn. tax sect. 1972, Outstanding Tax Lawyer in Fla. award 1989). Democrat. Home: Three Grove Isle Dr 1009 Coconut Grove FL 33133 Office: Greenberg Traurig PA 1221 Brickell Ave Ste 21 Miami FL 33131-3224 E-mail: lipoffn@gtlaw.com

LIPPES, GERALD SANFORD, lawyer, business executive; b. Buffalo, Mar. 23, 1940; s. Thomas and Ruth (Landsman) L.; m. Sandra Franger; children: Tracy E., David S., Adam F. Student, U. Mich., 1958-61; JD, U. Buffalo, 1964. Bar: N.Y. 1964. Sr. ptnr. Lippes, Silverstein, Mathias & Wexler, Buffalo, 1964—; sec., dir., gen. counsel Mark IV, Industries, Inc., Amherst, N.Y., 1969-2000. Chmn. Del. Photographic Products, Buffalo, 1970-88, Ingram Micro-D, Buffalo, 1982-86, Abels Bagels, Inc., Buffalo, 1972-75; bd. dirs. Gilbraltar Steel Corp., Buffalo Nat. Health Care Affiliates, Inc., The Wolf Group, Inc., Reciprocal, Inc. Bd. dirs. Buffalo Fine Arts Acad., Kaleida Health Sys.; U. Buffalo Found., U. Buffalo Coun., N.Y. State Arts Coun. Recipient Disting. Alumni award U. Buffalo Law Sch., Nat. Conf. of Christians and Jews Citation award 1997, Jaeckle award SUNY, Buffalo; named Entrepreneur of Yr., 1993. Mem. N.Y. State Bar Assn., Erie County Bar Assn., Am. Soc. Corp. Secs. General corporate, Mergers and acquisitions, Securities. Office: Lippes Silverstein Mathias & Wexler 28 Church St Buffalo NY 14202-3908

LIPPES, RICHARD JAMES, lawyer; b. Buffalo, Mar. 18, 1944; s. Thomas and Ruth (Landsman) L.; m. Sharon Richmond, June 4, 1972; children: Amity, Joshua, Kevin. BA, U. Mich., 1966; JD cum laude, SUNY, Buffalo, 1969. Bar: N.Y. 1970, U.S. Dist. Ct. Md. 1970, U.S. Ct. Appeals (4th cir.) 1970, N.Y. 1971, U.S. Dist. Ct. (we. dist.) N.Y. 1971, U.S. Ct. Appeals (2d cir.) 1971, U.S. Dist. Ct. (no. dist.) N.Y. 1973, U.S. Dist. Ct. (so. dist.) N.Y. 1985. Clk. to presiding justice U.S. Ct. Appeals, Balt., 1970; exec. dir. Ctr. for Justice Through Law, Buffalo, 1971; pvt. practice, U.S. Ct. Appeals, 1971-77; ptnr. Moriarity, Allen, Lippes & Hoffman, 1977-79, Allen & Lippes, Buffalo, 1979—, Moriarity, Allen, Lippes & Hoffman, Buffalo, 1977-79, Allen & Lippes, Buffalo, 1979—. Lectr. SUNY, Buffalo, 1978, 79; lead counsel and spl. environ. counsel for hazardous waste, mass toxic tort cases. Contbr. articles to profl. jours. Chmn. Atlantic chpt. Sierra Club, 1980-83; chmn. Buffalo chpt. Am. Jewish Com., 1986-88; chmn. lawyers com. Niagara Frontier chpt. N.Y. Civil Liberties Union, 1971, chpt. chmn., 1972-74; chmn. Buffalo Environ. Mgmt. Commn., 1987-96; bd. dirs. N.Y. State Preservation League, also gen. coun.; chmn. Buffalo Task Force, 1986-87; pres. Erie County Preservation Coalition, 1998—; also various others. Urban and Environ. Law fellow, 1969. Mem. ABA, N.Y. State Bar Assn., Erie County Bar Assn (former chmn. pub. interest law com. and prepaid legal svcs. com.). Democrat. Environmental, Personal injury. E-mail: rlippes@corcertive.net

LIPPINCOTT, WALTER EDWARD, law educator; b. Bronxville, N.Y., Aug. 15, 1959; s. Walter Edwin and Helen (Patterson) L.; m. Andrea Pratt, July 30, 1983; children: Brittany Marie, Matthew. BS, Roger Williams Coll., 1981; JD, Western New Eng. Coll., 1984; MS, Fla. Inst. Tech., 1995. Bar: Conn. 1984, D.C. 1985. Prosecutor State of Conn. Judicial Dept., Hartford, 1990-93; prof. Naugatuck Valley Cmty. Tech. Coll., Waterbury, Conn., 1993—, U. Conn., Storrs, 1996-97. Lt. col. U.S. Army, 1985-90, USAR, 1990—. Mem. ABA, Conn. Bar Assn., D.C. Bar Assn. Home: 613 Highland Ave Torrington CT 06790-4410

LIPSEY, HOWARD IRWIN, law educator, justice, lawyer; b. Providence, Jan. 24, 1936; s. Harry David and Anna (Gershman) L.; children: Lewis Robert, Bruce Stephen. AB summa cum laude, Providence Coll., 1957; JD, Georgetown U., 1960. Bar: R.I. 1960, U.S. Dist. Ct. R.I. 1961, U.S. Supreme Ct. 1972. Assoc. Edward I. Friedman, 1963-67, Kirshenbaum & Kirshenbaum, 1967-72; ptnr. Abedon, Michaelson, Stanzler, Biener, Skolnik & Lipsey, 1972-83, Lipsey & Skolnik, Esquires, Ltd., Providence, 1983-93; assoc. justice R.I. Family Ct., 1993—. Lectr. trial tactics Nat. Coll. Adv., 1986, U. Bridgeport Law Sch., Yale U., U. Denver Law Sch., Suffolk U. Law Sch., 1987—; adj. prof. U. Houston Law Sch., 1994-98; adj. prof. family law Roger Williams U. Law Sch., 1996-2000. Contbg. author: Valuation and Distribution of Marital Property, 1984; bd. editors Georgetown U. Law Jour. Served to capt. JAGC, USAR, 1960-71. Fellow Am. Coll. Trial Lawyers, Am. Acad. Matrimonial Lawyers; mem. ABA (chair trial advocacy inst. 1994-97, coun. 1995—, chmn. family cts. com., bd. editors: Fairshare, Family Advocate), ATLA, R.I. Bar Assn., B'nai B'rith (Anti-Defamation League). Office: RI Family Ct 1 Dorrance Plz Providence RI 02903-3922 Fax: (401) 458-5360

LIPSKY, BURTON G. lawyer; b. Syracuse, N.Y., May 29, 1937; s. Abraham and Pauline (Leichtner); m. Elaine B. Mannheimer, July 27, 1967; 1 child, Erika S., m. Carol S. Samberg, Feb. 4, 1973; 1 child, Andrew H. BBA, U. Mich., 1959; JD summa cum laude, Syracuse U., 1962. Bar: N.Y. 1962, U.S. Supreme Ct. 1967. Trial atty. U.S. Dept. Justice, Washington, 1962-67; assoc. Kaye, Scholer, Fierman, Hays & Handler, N.Y.C., 1967-72; ptnr. Delson & Gordon, 1972-87, Lipsky & Stout, N.Y.C., 1991-96; pvt. practice, 1996—. Mem. bd. visitors Syracuse U. Coll. of Law, 1989—; sec.-treas., dir. Robert Mapplethorpe Found., Inc., 1988—. Mem. ABA, N.Y. Bar Assn., Order of Coif, Justinian Soc., Am. Contract Bridge League (life master). Estate planning, Corporate taxation, Personal income taxation. Office: 777 3rd Ave New York NY 10017-1302 E-mail: BurtLip@aol.com

LIPSMAN, RICHARD MARC, lawyer, educator; b. Bklyn., Aug. 17, 1946; s. Abraham W. and Ruth (Weinstein) L.; m. Geri A. Russo, 1979; children: Eric, Dara Briana. BBA, CCNY, 1968; JD, St. John's U., Jamaica, N.Y., 1972; LLM in Taxation, Boston U., 1976. Bar: N.Y. 1973, Mass. 1975, U.S. Dist. Ct. (ea. and so. dists.) N.Y. 1977, U.S. Supreme Ct. 1978, U.S. Tax Ct. 1979; CPA, N.Y., Mass. Tax atty. Arthur Young & Co., N.Y.C., 1972-74; assoc. Gilman, McLaughlin & Hanrahan, Boston, 1974-76, Lefrak, Fischer & Meyerson, N.Y.C., 1976-77; ptnr. Tarnow, Landsman & Lipsman, 1978; pvt. practice, 1979—. Adj. faculty Baruch Coll. CUNY, 1984-86, curriculum specialist Rsch. Found. CUNY, 1977-78; adj. faculty Pratt Inst., Bklyn., 1974, Queensboro Coll., Bayside, N.Y., 1978-80. Author, producer book/cassette program Learning Income Taxes, 1978—. Mem. ABA, AICPA, N.Y. State Bar Assn., Assn. of the Bar of the City of N.Y., N.Y. State Soc. CPA's. Jewish. General civil litigation, Private international, Taxation, general.

LIPSON, BARRY J. lawyer, columnist; b. N.Y.C., May 30, 1938; s. Sidney J. and Irene (Abrams) L.; m. Lois J., June 7, 1975; children: Steven J., David J. , Wharton Sch., 1957-59; BS in Econs., U. Pa., 1959; JD, Columbia U., 1962; LLM in Trade Regulation, NYU, 1968; postgrad., Oxford U., 1982, Harvard U., 1984. Bar: N.Y. 1962, Pa. 1970, U.S. Supreme Ct. 1967. Dep. asst. atty. gen. State of N.Y., 1963-64, asst. atty. gen., 1964-67; assoc. counsel, asst. sec. Block Drug Co., Inc. and Reed & Carnick, 1968-69; asst. sec., counsel, trade regulation counsel Koppers Co., Inc., Pitts., 1969-81; v.p., gen. counsel, sec. Elkem Metals Co., Elkem Group, 1982-85; head of corp. divsn. Weisman, Goldman, Bowen & Gross, Pitts., 1985—. Adj. settlement judge U.S. Dist. Ct. (we. dist.) Pa., 1995—, arbitrator, 1995—; arbitrator, master Pa. Ct. Common Pleas, Allegheny County, 1970—; dir. U.S. Chem. Corp., 1972-82; arbitrator, mediator Am. Arbitration Assn., 1978—, Better Bus. Bur., 1986—; mediator Arbitration Forums, Inc., 1993—, EEOC, 1997—; guest lectr. George Washington U., 1979-83; mem. Bus. Roundtable Lawyers Adv. Com., 1978-82; mem. Pa. C. of C. Antitrust Adv. Com., 1978-85; lectr. in field; mem. indsl. functional adv. com. on internat. stds. U.S. Dept. Commerce and Office of U.S. Trade Rep., 1980-88. Mem. editl. bd., columnist Pitts. Legal Jour., 1992—, Pitts. Neighbors, 1993-94, Lawyers Jour., 1999—; columnist Corplaw Commentaries, 1985—, Federally Speaking, 2001—; contbg. editor N.Y. Law Jour., 1965-67, Antitrust Law Jour., 1982, L.A. Daily Jour. Report, 1983, 86, The Practical Lawyer's Manual on Trade Regulation, 1985, Pa. Law Jour.-Reporter, 1985-87, Small Bus. Legal Report, 1986, Pitts. Bus. Times, 1986-87, Antitrust for Bus., 1989, Allegheny Bus. News, 1991-92, Advising Small Bus., 1992—; founding editor Sherman's Summations, 1979-82; interviewee Off the Bench and Off the Cuff, 1987; contbr. articles to profl. jours. Vice-chmn. Pitts. chpt. ACLU, 1977-78, 93-94, bd. dirs., 1972-2000, chmn. legal com., 1975-77; bd. dirs. Pa. ACLU, 1977-84, 91-94, nat. biennial del., 1995; pres. Allegheny County Transit Coun., 1996-97, legis. chair, 1993-94, v.p., 1994-96, chief counsel, 1995-99, exec. com., 1993-99; mem. adv. panel Southwestern Pa. Regional Planning Commn., 1993-98; pres. Beth Samuel, 1990-92; dir. United Synagogue, Western Pa. Region, 1989-97; organizer, mem. steering com. Nat. Conf. Peacemaking and Conflict Resolution, 1996-97. Lt. comdr. JAGC, USNR, 1965-75. Mem.: ABA (chmn. monopolization taskforce 1976—79, chmn., lectr. monopolization program 1978, vice chmn. Sherman Act com. 1979, chmn. monopolization subcom. 1979—82, chmn. antitrust compliance counseling taskforce 1979—82, faculty Nat. Inst. 1980), Allegheny County Bar Asn. (chmn. antitrust and class action com. 1980—82, vice chmn. hqs. comt. 1983—85, chmn. Unauthorized Practice of Law Com. 1998—, founding mem.), Am. Corp. Counsel Asn., Fed. Bar Asn., Boy Scouts Am., Am. Legion, Forty and Eight, Kiwanis, Masons, Royal Arch Masons, Royal and Select Master Masons, Scottish Rite, Odd Fellows, Elks, Shriners, Tall Cedars, Grotto. Antitrust, General corporate, Private international. Home: 102 Christler Ct Moon Township PA 15108-1359 E-mail: blipson@wgbglaw.com

LIPSON, HEATHER JOY, lawyer; b. Phila., Apr. 12, 1971; d. Barry and Barbara Lipson. BA, U. Pitts., 1993; JD, Nova Southeastern U., 1997. Bar: Pa. 1997. Assoc. Anapol, Schwartz, Weiss & Cohan, Phila., 1996—. Mem. Pa. Trial Attys. Assn., Phila. Trial Attys. Assn. Personal injury, Product liability, Toxic tort. Office: Anapol Schwartz Weiss & Cohan 1710 Spruce St Philadelphia PA 19103

LIPTON, LOIS JEAN, lawyer; b. Chgo., Jan. 14, 1946; d. Harold and Bernice (Reiter) Farber L.; m. Peter Carey, May 30, 1978; children: Rachel, Sara. BA, U. Mich., 1966; JD summa cum laude, DePaul Coll. Law, Chgo., 1974; postgrad., Sheffield (Eng.) U., 1966. Bar: Ky. 1974, U.S. Dist. Ct. (we. dist.) Ky. 1974, U.S. Ct. Appeals (6th cir.) 1974, Ill. 1975, U.S. Dist. Ct. (no. dist.) Ill. 1975, U.S. Ct. Appeals (7th cir.) 1976. Staff counsel

Roger Baldwin Found. of ACLU, Inc., Chgo., 1975-79, dir. reproductive rights project, 1979-83; atty. McDermott, Will & Emery, 1984-86, G.D. Searle, Skokie, Ill., 1988-90; sr. atty. AT&T, Chgo., 1990—. Del. White House Conf. on Families, Mpls., 1980. Recipient Durfee award, 1984. Mem. ACLU (v.p.), ABA, Chgo. Coun. Lawyers. Civil rights, Federal civil litigation, State civil litigation. Office: AT&T # R15 222 W Adams St Chicago IL 60606-5017 E-mail: llipton@att.com

LIPTON, PAUL R. lawyer, educator; b. N.Y.C., June 18, 1945; s. Maurice and Lorraine Lipton; m. Marjorie Yourman, June 16, 1968; children: Melissa, Lindsay. BA, Pa. State U., 1967; JD, Washington U., St. Louis, 1970. Bar: N.Y. 1972, Fla. 1973, U.S. Supreme Ct. 1975. Asst. dist. atty. Dist. Atty. of Nassau County, Mineola, N.Y., 1971-72; assoc. Snyder, Young & Stern, Miami, Fla., 1972-78; ptnr. Paul R. Lipton, P.A., 1978-87, Fine, Jacobson, P.A., Miami, 1987-92, Weaver, Kuven, Weaver & Lipton, P.A., Ft. Lauderdale and Miami, 1992-94, Bedzow, Korn, Brown & Lipton, P.A., Miami, 1994-99, Greenberg Traurig P.A., Miami, 1999—. Adj. prof. Nova U. Sch. Law, 1990—; spkr. in field. Bd. dirs. Journey Inst., 1998; co-chair 11th Cir. Commn. on Professionalism, 1998—; com. Fed. Ct. Peer Rev., 1998—. Mem. Fla Bar (standing com. on professionalism), North Dade Bar Assn. (pres. 1980). Avocations: music, writing, riflery, guitar. Federal civil litigation, State civil litigation. Office: Greenberg Traurig PA 1221 Brickell Ave Miami FL 33131-3224

LIPTON, RICHARD M. lawyer; b. Youngstown, Ohio, Feb. 25, 1952; s. Sanford Y. Lipton and Sarah (Kentor) Goldman; m. Jane Brennan, May 24, 1981; children— Thomas, Anne, Martin, Patricia. B.A., Amherst Coll., 1974; J.D., U. Chgo., 1977. Bar: Ill. 1977, D.C. 1978, U.S. Dist. Ct. (no. dist.) Ill. 1979, U.S. Ct. Appeals (D.C. and 7th cirs.) 1979, U.S. Tax Ct. 1977, U.S. Ct. Claims 1979. Law clk. to judge Hall, U.S. Tax Ct., Washington, 1977-79; assoc. Isham, Lincoln & Beale, Chgo., 1979-83; ptnr. Ross & Hardies, Chgo., 1983-86; v.p. Pegasus Broadcasting, Chgo., 1986-88; ptnr. Sonnenschein Nath & Rosenthal, Chgo., 1988—. Contbr. articles to profl. jours. Recipient Order of Coif award U. Chgo. Law Sch., 1977. Fellow Am. Coll. Tax Counsel (regent 1998—); mem. ABA (coun. dir. 1990-93, vice chair taxation sect. 1993-96), Chgo. Bar Assn. (subcom. chair, chair fed. taxation com. 1991-92), Union League Club, Michigan Shores Club, Conway Farms Club. Republican. Corporate taxation, Personal income taxation, State and local taxation. Office: Sonnenschein Nath Rosenthal 233 S Wacker Dr Ste 8000 Chicago IL 60606-6491

LIPTON, ROBERT STEPHEN, lawyer; b. Malone, N.Y., Apr. 19, 1942; BS in Aerospace Engring., U. Mich., 1964; postgrad., U. Wash., 1965-66; JD, Temple U., 1972. Bar: U.S. Patent and Trademark Office 1970, Pa. 1972, U.S. Dist. Ct. (ea. dist.) Pa. 1973, U.S. Ct. Appeals (fed. cir.) 1982. Wind tunnel test engr. The Boeing Co., Seattle, 1965-67, patent adminstr. Phila., 1967-70, patent agt., 1970-72, patent atty., 1972-75; pvt. practice law Media, Pa., 1975-84; ptnr. Lipton, Weinberger & Husick, 1984—. Mem. ABA, Pa. Bar Assn., Delaware County Bar Assn., Phila. Intellectual Property Law Assn., Am. Intellectual Property Law Assn., Am. Helicopter Soc. Contracts commercial, Computer, Patent. Office: Lipton Weinberger & Husick 201 N Jackson St Media PA 19063-2902

LIPUT, ANDREW LAWRENCE, lawyer, educator; b. Trenton, N.J., June 28, 1962; s. Andrew and Bernice Helen L.; m. Jacquelyn Anne Liput, Jan. 11, 1997; children: Mallory, Sloane. BA, Drew U., 1984; JD, Fordham U., 1987. Bar: N.J., 1987, N.Y., 1988, Conn., 1996. V.p., gen. cousel Parssine Group, Inc., NYC, 1988-91; sr. lawyer Hartman, Buhrman & Winnicki, Paramus, NJ, 1991-93; v.p., gen. counsel Marjam Supply Co., Inc., Bklyn., 1993-96; ptnr. Liput, Ricca, Donner LLP, Huntington, 1996—; adj. prof. Felician Coll., Lodi, NJ, 1994-97; assoc. prof. Suffolk C.C., Long Island, NY, 1998—, Briarcliff Coll., Bethpage, 2001—; prof. St. Joseph's Coll., 2001—. Trust officer, Neighborhood Cleaners Assn., N.Y.C., 1998—, Metropolitan Package Store Assn., Westchester, N.Y., 1997—. Author: Long Lost Tales of the Legendary Snarfdoodle, 2001; contbr. articles to profl. jours. Pres., dir. Bridge the Gap!, Long Island, 1999—, councilman, No. Plainfield, N.J., 1988-89. Mem. U.S. Rowing Assn., Aircraft Owners & Pilots Assn., N.Y. State Bar Assn., N.J. State Bar Assn., Conn. Bar Assn. Republican. Avocations: rowing, flying, reading, world travel. General corporate, Labor, Real property. Office: Liput & Speregen PC 790 New York Ave Huntington NY 11743-4499

LISHER, JAMES RICHARD, lawyer; b. Aug. 28, 1947; s. Leonard B. and Mary Jane (Rafferty) L.; m. Martha Gettelfinger, June 16, 1973; children: Jennifer, James Richard II. AB, Ind. U., 1969, JD, 1975. Bar: Ind. 1975, U.S. Dist. Ct. (so. dist.) Ind. 1975, U.S. Supreme Ct. 2000. Assoc. Rafferty & Wood, Shelbyville, Ind., 1976, Rafferty & Lisher, Shelbyville, 1976-77; dep. prosecutor Shelby County Prosecutor's Office, 1976-78; ptnr. Yeager, Lisher & Baldwin, 1977-96; pvt. practice, 1996—. Pros. atty. Shelby County, Shelbyville, 1983-95, pub. defender, 1995—, chief pub. defender, 2000—. Speaker, faculty advisor Ind. Pros. Sch., 1986. Editor: (manual) Traffic Case Defenses, 1982, First Law Office, 1998. Bd. dirs. Girls Club of Shelbyville, 1979-84, Bears of Blue River Festival, Shelbyville, 1982—; pres. Shelby County Internat. Rels. Coun., 1997—. Recipient Citation of Merit, Young Lawyers Assn. Mem. ATLA, Nat. Assn. Criminals, State Bar Assn. (bd. dirs.), Ind. Pub. Defender Assn., Ind. State Bar Assn. (bd. dirs. young lawyer sect. 1979-83, bd. dirs. gen. practice sect. 1996-98, treas. 1997-98, vice-chmn. 1998-99, chmn. 2000-01), Shelby County Bar Assn. (sec.-treas. 1986, v.p. 1987, pres. 1988), Ind. Prosecuting Attys. Assn. (bd. dirs. 1985-95, sec.-treas. 1987, v.p. 1988, pres. 1990), Masons, Elks, Lions. Democrat. Criminal, General practice, Personal injury. Home: 106 Western Trce Shelbyville IN 46176-9765 Office: 407 S Harrison St Shelbyville IN 46176-2170

LISHER, JOHN LEONARD, lawyer; b. Indpls., Sept. 19, 1950; s. Leonard Boyd and Mary Jane (Rafferty) L.; m. Mary Katherine Sturmon, Aug. 17, 1974. BA in History with honors, JD, Ind. U., 1975. Bar: Ind. 1975. Dep. atty. gen. State of Ind., Indpls., 1975-78; asst. corp. counsel City of Indpls., 1978-81; assoc. Osborn & Hiner, Indpls., 1981-86; ptnr. Osborn, Hiner & Lischer, P.C., 1986—. Vol. Mayflower Classic, Indpls., 1981-86; pres. Brendonwood Common Inc.; asst. vol. coord. Marion County Rep. Com., Indpls., 1979-80; vol. Don. Bogard for Atty. Gen., Indpls., 1980, Steve Goldsmith for Prosecutor, Indpls., 1979-83, Sheila Suess for Congress, Indpls., 1980. Recipient Outstanding Young Man of Am. award Jaycees, 1979, 85, Indpls. Jaycees, 1980. Mem. ABA, Ind. Bar Assn., Indpls. Bar Assn. (membership com.), Assn. Trial Lawyers Am., Ind. U. Alumni Assn., Hoosier Alumni Assn. (charter, founder, pres.), Ind. Trial Lawyers Assn., Ind. Def. Lawyers Assn., Ind. U. Coll. Arts and Scis. (bd. dirs. 1983-92, pres. 1986-87), Wabash Valley Alumni Assn. (charter), Founders Club, Pres. Club, Phi Beta Kappa, Eta Sigma Phi, Phi Eta Sigma, Delta Xi Alumni Assn. (Outstanding Alumnus award 1975, 76, 79, 83), Delta Xi Housing Corp. (pres.), Pi Kappa Alpha (midwest regional pres. 1977-86, parliamentarian nat. conv. 1982, del. convs. 1978-80, 82, 84, 86, trustee Meml. Found. 1986-91. Presbyterian. Avocations: reading, golf, jogging, Roman coin collecting. State civil litigation, Insurance, Personal injury. Home: 5725 Hunterglen Rd Indianapolis IN 46226-1019 Office: Osborn Hiner & Lisher PC 8500 Keystone Xing Ste 480 Indianapolis IN 46240-2460

LISI, MARY M. federal judge; BA, U. R.I., 1972; JD, Temple U., 1977. Tchr. history Prout Meml. High Sch., Wakefield, R.I., 1975-76; law clk. U.S. Atty., Providence, 1976, Phila., 1976-77; asst. pub. defender R.I. Office Pub. Defender, 1977-81; asst. child advocate Office Child Advocate, 1981-82; also. pvt. practice atty. Providence, 1981-82; dir. office ct. appointed spl. advocate R.I. Family Ct., 1982-87; dep. disciplinary counsel office disciplinary counsel R.I. Supreme Ct., 1988-90, chief disciplinary counsel, 1990-94; U.S. Dist. judge Dist. Ct., Providence, 1995—, Dist. R.I. (1st cir.), Providence, 1994—. Mem. Select Com. to Investigate Failure of R.I. Share and Deposit Indemnity Corp., 1991-92. Recipient Providence 350 award, 1986, Meritorious Svc. to Children of Am. award, 1987. Office: Fed Bldg and US Courthouse 1 Exchange Ter Ste 113 Providence RI 02903-1744

LISMAN, BERNARD, lawyer; b. N.Y.C., July 21, 1918; s. Samuel and Sarah (Cohen) L.; m. Natalie Kling, June 7, 1942. PhB, U. Vt., 1939; LLB, Harvard U., 1942. Bar: Vt. 1942, U.S. Dist. Ct. Vt. 1948, U.S. Ct. Appeals (2d cir.) 1955, U.S. Supreme Ct. 1964. Ptnr. Lisman & Lisman, Burlington, Vt., 1946-90, of counsel, 1990—. Trustee Vt. Law Sch., 1976-93, trustee emeritus, 1995—; judge Chittenden (Vt.) Mcpl. Ct., 1949-51; mem. Bd. Aldermen, City of Burlington, 1956-58; mem. Vt. Rep. State com., 1956-60. Past pres. Burlington Boys Club, 1961, ARC Chittenden County chpt., 1964, Baird Children's Ctr., 1967, Holbrook Community Ctr., 1965. 1st lt. U.S. Army, 1942-46. Decorated Bronze Star; recipient Disting. Svc. award U. Vt., Burlington, 1984; winner Ames Moot Ct. Competition Harvard U. Law Sch., 1942. Fellow Internat. Acad. Trial Lawyers (bd. dirs. 1985-91); mem. ABA, Vt. Bar Assn., Assn. Trial Lawyers Am. (bd. govs. 1964-65), Vt. Trial Lawyers Assn. (past pres.), Am. Judicature Soc., Phi Beta Kappa. Jewish. Clubs: Ethan Allen, Burlington Country. Lodges: Elks, Masons, Shriners. Avocation: golf. General civil litigation, Estate planning, Personal injury. Home: 16511 Cypress Villa Ln Fort Myers FL 33908 Office: PO Box 728 84 Pine St Burlington VT 05402-4423

LISS, ARTHUR YALE, lawyer; b. Detroit, July 12, 1946; s. George R. and Rose B. Liss; m. Beverly Bein, Jan. 16, 1972; children: Jeremy Seth, Lindsay Audra, Zachary Jonathan. BSBA, Wayne State U., 1968, JD, 1972. Bar: Mich., U.S. Dist. Ct. (ea. dist.) Mich., U.S. Ct. Appeals (6th cir.), U.S. Supreme Ct. Prin. Liss & Assocs., Bloomfield Hills, Mich., 1972—. Dir. Anestesia and Ctrl. Care Rsch. Found., Chgo., 1998—; cons. and lectr. in field. Fellow Million Dollar Advocates Assn.; mem. Mich. Trial Lawyers Assn. (bd. dirs. 1999—), Am. Trial Lawyers Assn. (bd. dirs. 1975—). Avocations: traveling, scuba diving, golf. Office: Liss & Assocs PC 39400 Woodward Ave Ste 200 Bloomfield Hills MI 48304

LISS, NORMAN, lawyer; b. New York, May 7, 1932; m. Sandra Hirsch, Feb. 28, 1959. BS, NYU, 1952, LLB, 1955. Bar: N.Y. 1955, U.S. Dist. Ct. (so. dist.) N.Y. 1961, U.S. Dist. Ct (ea. dist.) N.Y. 1962. Assoc. Booth, Lipton & Lipton, New York, 1956-57, Seymour Detsky, New York, 1957-58; pvt. practice, 1958—. Cons. to Portugal Re-Cultural Events in U.S.; represented Norway in N.Y. proceedings to clear records of sailors arrested during 900th anniversary of Leif Ericson Voyage; jour. chair UJA Trial Lawyers USCG Acad. Law Day, 1987, 89, 94, 98. Contbr. articles to profl. jours. Chmn. Bronx County Bar div. United Jewish Appeal, Hist. Documents Exhbn., Operation Sail, 1986, USCG Acad. Law Day, 1987, 89; chmn. devel. Ellis Island Restoration Commn.; counsel N.Y. State Statue of Liberty Centennial Com., Mayor's Handicapped Citizens Adv. Bd., N.Y.C., Coun. on Arts; mem. Bronx County 350 Commn., N.Y.C. Commn. for Presdl. Conv.; rep., counsel N.Y.C. Com. on Bicentennial of U.S. Constitution; cons. Soc. Congl. Medal of Honor; commd. lt. col. N.Y. Guard Judge Advocate Gen. Unit; bd. dirs. Anti Defamation League; trustee Am. Jewish Hist. Soc. Recipient Disting. Humanitarian award Inst. of Applied Human Dynamics, Meritorious Pub. Svc. award USCG, 1989; named Man of Yr. Am. Jewish Congress, Man of Yr. Kinneret Sch., 1985. Mem. ABA, N.Y. Bar Assn., Bronx County Bar Assn., Am. Arbitration Assn. (panel arbitrators), Assn. Trial Lawyers Am., Law Day Outreach Com., NYU Alumni Assn. (adv. coun.). General civil litigation, Education and schools, General practice. Home: 2727 Palisade Ave Bronx NY 10463-1018 Office: 200 W 57th St New York NY 10019-3211

LIST, ANTHONY FRANCIS, lawyer; b. Phila., Aug. 23, 1942; s. John Joseph and Mary Louise (Docktor) L.; m. Jill Wallace; children: Anthony Francis, Amy Louise. B.S., Mt. St. Mary's Coll., Emmitsburg, Md., 1964; J.D., U. Richmond, 1967. Bar: Pa. 1967, U.S. Ct. Appeals (3d cir.) 1976, U.S. Dist. Ct. (ea. dist.) Pa. 1967, U.S. Dist. Ct. (mid. dist.) Pa. 1972, U.S. Ct. Mil. Appeals 1983. Asst. U.S. atty. Dept. Justice, Phila., 1968-69, spl. asst. to U.S. atty., 1969-72; trial counsel, atty. for trustees Penn Central Transp. Co., Phila., 1969-73; ptnr. Mullray, Ryan & List, Media, Pa., 1973-77, List & List, Media, 1977— Federal civil litigation, State civil litigation, Criminal. Office: List & List PO Box 166 Media PA 19063-0166

LISTER, THOMAS EDWARD, lawyer; b. Columbus, Ohio, Apr. 19, 1948; s. Richard Elwyn and Jean (Nelson) L.; m. Sarah Gray Robinson, July 25, 1970; children: Matthew Thomas, Joshua Capps. BA, DePauw U., 1970; JD, U. Wis., 1973. Bar: Wis. 1973, U.S. Dist. Ct. (we. dist.) Wis. 1973. V.p. Coll. Mktg. and Rsch. Corp., Indpls., 1969-70; staff criminal appeals unit Wis. Dept. Justice, 1971-73; ptnr. Sherman, Stutz & Lister, Black River Falls, Wis., 1973-83; dist. atty. Jackson County, Wis., 1975-80, corp. counsel, 1975-78; mem. firm Stutz & Lister, S.C., 1983—. Guest lectr. U. Wis., Madison, 1988; pres. Wis. Global Tech. Ltd., 1992—; chmn. ThermoSense Co., LLC, 1998—; vice chmn., dir., v.p. legal affairs Hyperformance Materials, Inc., Greensboro, N.C.; corp. dir. Lunda Constrn. Co., Black River Falls, Wis., 2000—. Chmn. S.W. Coun. on Criminal Justice, 1979-82; mem. Wis. Coun. on Criminal Justice, 1982-83, Wis. County Forest Adv. Coun., 1982-84; bd. dirs. Tri-County Cmty. Mental Health, Alcohol and Drug Abuse Bd, 1976-82, Black River Falls Youth Hockey, 1983-84; co-founder, dir. Black River Falls Area Found., 1986-88; chmn. Mayor's Commn. Golf Course Expansion Fundraising, 1988-90, Wazee Lake Recreation Commn., 1991-96; commencement spkr. Black River Falls H.S., 1992; mem. com., presenter All-Am. City Finalist Competition, Charlotte, N.C., 1992; chmn. adminstrv. coun. United Meth. Ch., Black River Falls, 1992-93, bldg. commn., co-chair fundraising, 1992-94; mem. cmty. rels. com. Wis. Dept. Corrections, 1993—. Mem. ABA, ATLA, Wis. Acad. Trial Lawyers (bd. dirs. 1984-90), Wis. Bar Assn., Tri-County Bar Assn. (pres. 1991-92), Black River Falls C. of C. (bd. dirs.), Rotary (bd. dirs., past pres. youth exch. officer), Black River Recreation Assn., Skyline Golf Club (bd. dirs., pres. 1993). State civil litigation, Personal injury, Workers' compensation. Home: N6570 Riverview Dr Black River Falls WI 54615-9207 Office: Stutz & Lister SC PO Box 370 Black River Falls WI 54615-0370

LITMAN, HARRY PETER, lawyer, educator; b. Pitts., May 4, 1958; s. S. David and Roslyn M. (Margolis) L. BA, Harvard U., 1981; JD, U. Calif., Berkeley, 1986. Bar: Calif. 1987, U.S. Ct. Appeals (D.C. cir.) 1987, Pa. 1988, D.C. 1989, U.S. Ct. Appeals (9th cir.) 1990, U.S. Dist. Ct. (so. dist.) Tex. 1992, U.S. Supreme Ct. 1992, U.S. Dist. Ct. (ea. and we. dists.) Pa. 1993, U.S. Ct. Appeals (7th cir.) 1994, U.S. Dist. Ct. (ea. dist.) Va. 1997. Prodn. asst. feature films, N.Y.C., 1980-82; newsman, clk. baseball desk AP, 1982-83, sports reporter, 1983-86; law clk. to Hon. Abner J. Mikva U.S. Ct. Appeals (D.C. cir.), 1986-87; law clk. to Hon. Thurgood Marshall U.S. Supreme Ct., Washington, 1987-88, law clk. to Hon. Anthony M. Kennedy, 1989; asst. U.S. atty., dep. chief appellate sect. Dept. Justice, San Francisco, 1990-92, dep. assoc. atty. gen. Washington, 1992-93, dep. asst. atty. gen., 1993-98; U.S. atty. Western Dist. of Pa., 1998—. Adj. prof. Boalt Hall Sch. Law U. Calif., Berkeley, 1990-92, Georgetown U. Law Ctr., 1996-99, U. Pitts. Law Sch., 1999—. Editor-in-chief Calif. Law Rev., Vol. 73; author various articles. Presdl. scholar, 1976. Mem. Pa. Bar Assn., State Bar Calif., D.C. Bar, Order of Coif. Office: 63 US Courthouse Pittsburgh PA 15219

LITMAN, RICHARD CURTIS, lawyer; b. Phila., May 2, 1957; s. Benjamin Norman and Bette Etta (Saunders) L.; m. Cheryl Lynn Goldstein, May 28, 1989; children: Amanda Rose, Jessica Brooke, Daniel Grant, Victoria Grace. BS, Union Coll., 1973; JD cum laude, U. Miami, 1979; LLM in Patent and Trade Regulation, George Washington U., 1980; M of Forensic Sci., Antioch Sch. Law, 1981. Bar: D.C. 1979, Fla. 1979, Pa. 1979, Va. 1980, Md. 1984, U. Ct. Appeals (fed. cir.), U.S. Patent and Trademark Office, U.S. Supreme Ct. Pvt. practice, Arlington, Va., 1983—. Instr. continuing legal edn.; organizer, dir. James Monroe Bank. Host Great Ideas Radio. com.; Contbr. articles to profl. jours. Fellow Food and Drug Law Inst., 1979-80; named Small Bus. of Yr. Arlington C. of C., 1995. Mem. ABA, Fed. Bar Assn., Am. Acad. Forensic Scis., Am. Intellectual Property Law Assn., Arlington County Bar Assn., Masons (32d degree Scottish Rite), Shriners. Intellectual property, Patent, Trademark and copyright. Office: Litman Law Offices Ltd Patent Law Bldg 3717 Columbia Pike Arlington VA 22204-4255 E-mail: litman@4patent.com

LITMAN, ROSLYN MARGOLIS, lawyer, educator; b. N.Y.C., Sept. 30, 1928; d. Harry and Dorothy (Perlow) Margolis; m. S. David Litman, Nov. 22, 1950; children: Jessica, Hannah, Harry. BA, U. Pitts., 1949, JD, 1952. Bar: Pa. 1952. Practiced in Pitts., 1952—; ptnr. firm Litman Law Firm, 1952—; adj. prof. U. Pitts. Law Sch., 1958—. Permanent del. Conf. U.S. Circuit Ct. Appeals for 3d Circuit; past chair dist. adv. group U.S. Dist. Ct. (we. dist.) Pa., 1991-94, mem. steering com. for dist. adv. group, 1991—; chmn. Pitts. Pub. Parking Authority, 1970-74; mem. curriculum com. Pa. Bar Inst., 1986—, bd. dirs., 1972-82. Bd. dirs. United Jewish Fedn., 1999—, cmty. rels. com., co-chair ch./state com.; bd. dirs. City Theatre, 1999—. Recipient Roscoe Pound Found. award for Excellence in Tchg. Trial Advocacy, 1996, Disting. Alumnus award U. Pitts. Sch. Law, 1996; named Fed. Lawyer of Yr., We. Pa. Chpt. FBA, 1999. Mem. ABA (del., litigation sect., anti-trust health care com.), ACLU (nat. bd. dirs., Marjorie H. Matson Civil Libertarian award Greater Pitts. chpt. 1999), Pa. Bar Assn. (bd. govs. 1976-79), Allegheny County Bar Assn. (bd. govs. 1972-74, pres. 1975, Woman of Yr. 2001), Allegheny County Acad. Trial Lawyers (charter), Order of Coif. Federal civil litigation, State civil litigation, General practice. Home: 5023 Frew St Pittsburgh PA 15213-3829 Office: One Oxford Centre 34th Fl Pittsburgh PA 15219

LITTLE, HAMPTON STENNIS, JR. lawyer, educator; b. Meridian, Miss., Apr. 24, 1934; s. Hampton Stennis and Kathryn (Dale) L.; m. Susan Pilger, July 23, 1965 (div.); children: Kathryn Ann, Michael Stennis. BS, Miss. State U., 1956; JD, U. Miss., 1964; LLM in Taxation, Georgetown U., 1967. Bar: Miss. 1964, Tenn. 1968, U.S. Supreme Ct. 1968, U.S. Tax Ct. 1968. Trial atty. tax civ. U.S. Dept. Justice, Washington, 1964-68; assoc. Boult, Hunt, Cummings & Conners, Nashville, 1968-70; pvt. practice, 1970-80; ptnr. King, Ballow & Little, 1980-84, of counsel, 1984-86; pres. Stennis Little, P.C., 1986-89; ptnr. Blackburn, Little, Smith & Slobey, 1989-92; pres. Little & Smith P.C., 1992-97, Stennis Little, P.C., 1997-98, Little & House P.C., 1998—. Lectr. Vanderbile U. Sch. Law. 1970-83. Contbr. numerous articles to profl. jours. Served to lt. comdr. USNR, 1956-59. Mem. ABA, Miss. State Bar Assn., Nashville Bar Assn. Presbyterian. Pension, profit-sharing, and employee benefits, Corporate taxation, Estate taxation. Office: 315 Deaderick St Ste 2125 Nashville TN 37238-2118

LITTLE, JAMES DAVID, lawyer; b. Laurinburg, N.C., Mar. 9, 1944; s. James A. and Lucille (Quick) L. B.A. in Polit. Sci., U. N.C.-Chapel Hill, 1966; J.D., 1972. Bar: N.C. 1972, U.S. Dist. Ct. (ea. dist.) N.C. 1974, U.S. Ct. Appeals (4th cir.) 1978, U.S. Supreme Ct. 1979, U.S. Ct. Mil. Appeals 1980. Asst. dist. atty. Dist. Atty.'s Office, Fayetteville, N.C., 1972-73; chief pub. defender Pub. Defender's Office, Fayetteville, 1974-76; ptnr. law firm Singleton, Murray, Hefner & Little and predecessor firm, Fayetteville, 1976-80, ptnr., 1980-82; chief counsel N.C. Utilities Commn. Pub. Staff, Raleigh, 1983— ; cons. Nat. Ctr. for Def., 1975-79, N.C. Bar Assn., 1974-76; dir. N.C. Legal Services Corp., Raleigh, 1976-82. Legal cons. Cumberland County Assn. Indian People, 1975-80; mem. N.C. Criminal Code Commn., 1979-82. Mem. N.C. Acad. Trial Lawyers, N.C. Bar Assn., N.C. State Bar Assn., ABA. Democrat. Presbyterian. Office: N C Utilities Commn Pub Staff PO Box 29520 Raleigh NC 27626-0520

LITTLEFIELD, ROY EVERETT, III, association executive, legal educator; b. Nashua, N.H., Dec. 6, 1952; s. Roy Everett and Mary Ann (Prestipino) L.; m. Amy Root; children: Leah Marie, Roy Everett IV, Christy Louise. BA, Dickinson Coll., 1975; MA, Catholic U. Am., 1976, PhD, 1979. Aide U.S. Senator Thomas McIntyre, Democrat, N.H., 1975-78, Nordy Hoffman, U.S. Senate Sergeant-at-arms, 1979; dir. govt. rels. Nat. Tire Dealers and Retreaders Assn., Washington, 1979-84; exec. dir. Svc. Sta. and Automotive Repair Assn., 1984—; exec. v.p. Svc. Sta. Dealers of Am., 1994—. Cons. Internat. Tire and Rubber Assn., 1984; mem. faculty Cath. U. Am., Washington, 1979—. Author: William Randolph Hearst: His Role in American Progressivism, 1980, The Economic Recovery Act, 1982, The Surface: Transportation Assistance Act, 1984; editor Nozzle mag.; contbr. numerous articles to legal jours. Mem. Nat. Dem. Club, 1978—. Mem. Am. Soc. Legal History, Md. Hwy. User's Fedn. (pres.), Nat. Hwy. User's Fedn. (sec.), Nat. Capitol Area Transp. Fedn. (v.p.), N.H. Hist. Soc., Kansas City C. of C., Capitol Hill Club, Phi Alpha Theta. Roman Catholic. Home: 1707 Pepper Tree Ct Bowie MD 20721-3021 Office: 9420 Annapolis Rd Ste 307 Lanham Seabrook MD 20706-3061

LITTON, RANDALL GALE, lawyer; b. Idaho Falls, Idaho, July 13, 1939; s. Ralph John and Inez Evelyn (Petersen) L.; m. Sandra Byrne, Aug. 19, 1961 (div. 1993); children: Sean B., Stephanie L., Emily R.; m. Jo Ann Foerster, July 22, 2000. BSEE, U. Idaho, 1961; LLB, George Washington U., 1965. Bar: Mich. 1965, U.S. Dist. Ct. (ea. dist.) Mich. 1966, U.S. Dist. Ct. (we. dist.) Mich. 1967, U.S. Ct. Appeals (6th cir.) 1971, U.S. Ct. Appeals (8th cir.) 1979, U.S. Ct. Appeals (Fed. cir.) 1984, U.S. Ct. Appeals (7th cir.) 1993, U.S. Supreme Ct. 1993. Examiner U.S. Patent Office, Washington, 1962-64; ptnr. Price, Heneveld, Cooper, DeWitt & Litton, Grand Rapids, Mich., 1965—. Mem. ABA, Mich. Bar Assn. Presbyterian. Avocations: hunting, fishing, skiing. Federal civil litigation, Patent, Trademark and copyright. Office: Price Heneveld Cooper DeWitt & Litton 695 Kenmoor Ave SE Grand Rapids MI 49546-2375 E-mail: rlitton@priceheneveld.com

LITVACK, SANFORD MARTIN, lawyer; b. Bklyn., Apr. 29, 1936; s. Murray and Lee M. (Korman) L.; m. Judith E. Goldenson, Dec. 30, 1956; children: Mark, Jonathan, Sharon, Daniel. BA, U. Conn., 1956; LLB, Georgetown U., 1959. Bar: N.Y. 1964, D.C. 1979. Trial atty. antitrust div. Dept. Justice, Washington, 1959-61, asst. atty. gen., 1980-81; assoc. firm Donovan, Leisure, Newton & Irvine, N.Y.C., 1961-69, ptnr., 1969-80, 81-86, Dewey, Ballantine, Bushby, Palmer & Wood, N.Y.C., 1987-91; vice chmn. bd. The Walt Disney Co., Burbank, Calif., 1991—, also bd. dirs. Bd. dirs. Bet Tzedek. Fellow Am. Coll. Trial Lawyers; mem. ABA, Fed. Bar Coun., N.Y. State Bar Assn. (sec. antitrust sect. 1974-77, chmn. antitrust sect. 1985-86), Va. Bar Assn., Calif. Inst. of Arts (bd. dirs.), Am. Arbitration Assn. (bd. dirs.). Federal civil litigation, General civil litigation. Office: The Walt Disney Co 500 S Buena Vista St Burbank CA 91521-0006

LIU, DIANA CHUA, lawyer; b. N.Y.C., Mar. 23, 1961; d. Donald and Emilie Chua Liu. BA, Johns Hopkins U., 1983; JD, Cornell U., 1986. Bar: Pa. 1986, U.S. Dist. Ct. (ea. dist.) Pa. 1986. Assoc. Montgomery, McCracken, Walker & Rhoads, Phila., 1986-88, Wolf, Block, Schorr and Solis-Cohen, Phila., 1988-94, ptnr., 1994—. Participant legal leadership summit Am. Corp. Counsel Assn., Washington, 1996-97; lectr. law U. Pa. Law Sch., Phila., 1998. Mem. Asian Am. Women's Coalition, Phila., 1986—, pres., 1990; bd. dirs. Big Bro./Big Sister Assn., Phila., 1989—; mem. Johns Hopkins U. Second Decade Soc., Balt., 1993—, nat. chair,

1997. Named 40 under 40 Phila. Bus. jour., 1995. Mem. Nat. Asian Pacific Am. Bar Assn. Ptnrs. Network, Asian Am. Bar Assn. Del. Valley (pres. 1999), Pa. Bar Assn. (ho. of dels. 1991-97), Phila. Bar Assn. (bd. govs. 1996-98) Contracts commercial, General corporate, Real property. Office: Wolf Block Schorr & Solis-Cohen LLP 111 S 15th St Ste 1200 Philadelphia PA 19102-2678

LIVAUDAIS, MARCEL, JR. federal judge; b. New Orleans, Mar. 3, 1925; m. Carol Black (dec.); children: Julie, Marc, Durel. BA, Tulane U., 1945, JD, 1949. Bar: La. 1949. Assoc. Boswell & Loeb, New Orleans, 1949-50, 52-56; ptnr. Boswell Loeb & Livaudais, 1956-60, Loeb & Livaudais, 1960-67, 71-77, Loeb Dillon & Livaudais, 1967-71; U.S. magistrate, 1977-84; judge U.S. Dist. Ct. (ea. dist.) La., New Orleans, 1984-96, sr. judge, 1996—. Mem. Am. Judicature Soc. Office: US Dist Ct C-405 US Courthouse 500 Camp St New Orleans LA 70130-3313

LIVELY, PIERCE, federal judge; b. Louisville, Aug. 17, 1921; s. Henry Thad and Ruby Durrett (Keating) L.; m. Amelia Harrington, May 25, 1946; children: Susan, Katherine, Thad. AB, Centre Coll., Ky., 1943; LL.B., U. Va., 1948. Bar: Ky. 1948. Individual practice law, Danville, Ky., 1949-57; mem. firm Lively and Rodes, 1957-72; judge U.S. Ct. Appeals (6th cir.), Cin., 1972—, chief judge, 1983-88, sr. judge, 1988-97, ret., 1997. Mem. Ky. Commn. on Economy and Efficiency in Govt., 1963-65, Ky. Jud. Advisory Com., 1972 Trustee Centre Coll. Served with USNR, 1943-46. Mem. ABA, Am. Judicature Soc., Order of Coif, Raven Soc., Phi Beta Kappa, Omicron Delta Kappa. Presbyterian.

LIVINGSTONE, WILLIAM EDWIN, III, lawyer; b. Fort Worth, May 22, 1935; s. William Edwin and Margaret (Hall) L.; m. Janice Ann Crow, Aug. 23, 1958; children— William Edwin IV, Carol Roth, Scott Louis. BBA, So. Meth. U., 1957, LLB, 1960. Bar: Tex. 1960. From assoc. to ptnr. Phinney, Hallman, Pulley & Livingstone, Dallas, 1960-73; gen. counsel Dallas Fed. Savs. and Loan Assn., 1973-86; of counsel Jackson, Walker, Winstead, Cantwell & Miller, Dallas, 1986—. Bd. dirs. Greater Dallas Crime Commn., 1980. Served to capt. Air and Army N.G., 1958-65. Mem. ABA, Tex. Bar Assn., Dallas Bar Assn., Tex. Savs. & Loan League (attys. com. 1986—), U.S. League Savs. Assn. (attys. com. 1977—). Banking, Real property. Office: Jackson Walker Winstead Cantwell & Miller 6000 Interfirst Plaza 901 Main St Ste 6000 Dallas TX 75202-3797

LIVOLSI, FRANK WILLIAM, JR. lawyer; b. Stamford, Conn., June 6, 1938; s. Frank Sr. and Rose M. Livolsi. BA, Pa. Mil. Coll., 1962; JD, Fordham U., 1965. Bar: Ct. 1968. Ptnr. Plotkin & Livolsi, Stamford, 1970—. Served to capt. U.S. Army, 1965-67, Vietnam. State civil litigation, General practice. Home: 155 Thornwood Rd Stamford CT 06903-2616 Office: Plotkin & Livolsi 1035 Washington Blvd Stamford CT 06901-2294

LIVOTI, ANTHONY WILLIAM, lawyer; b. Bklyn., Nov. 11, 1967; s. John Dominic and Geraldine Eugenia L.; m. Jill Louise Hanley, Nov. 27, 1993; children: Sophia Louise, A. William Jr. BA in Polit. Sci., The Citadel, 1990; JD cum laude, U. S.C., 1997. Bar: S.C. 1997, U.S. Dist. Ct. S.C. 1997. Assoc. McCutchen Blanton Rhodes & Johnson LLP, Columbia, S.C., 1997—. Articles editor S.C. Law Rev., 1996-97. Lt. USN, 1990-94. Mem. ABA, S.C. Def. Trial Attys., Order of Coif. Republican. Avocations: golf, reading. Civil rights, Federal civil litigation, Insurance. Office: McCutchen Blanton Rhodes & Johnson LLP 1414 Lady St Columbia SC 29201

LLEVAT, JORGE, lawyer; b. Reus, Tarragona, Spain, July 23, 1961; s. Jorge and Nieves (Vallespinosa) L.; m. Pilar Sarrias, Sept. 23, 1992; children: Pilar, Ana, Nieves. Lic., U. Barcelona, Spain, 1984; M in Law, U. Chgo., 1988. Bar: Barcelona 1986, N.Y. 1989. Assoc. Despacho M. Giro, Barcelona, 1986-87; intern Fox & Horan, N.Y.C., 1988; assoc. Baudel, Sales U. & G., Paris, 1989, Cuatrecasas, Barcelona, 1990-96, ptnr., 1997—. Co-author: International Technology Transfer, 1992, Spanish Business Law, 1994. With Spanish Air Force, 1984-86. Mem. ABA, INTA, AIPPI. Computer, Intellectual property, Trademark and copyright. Home: Muntaner 440 08006 Barcelona Spain Office: Cuatrecasas Paseo de Gracia 111 08008 Barcelona Spain E-mail: jorge_llevat@cuatrecasas.com

LLOYD, ALEX, lawyer; b. Atlantic, Iowa, Aug. 13, 1942; s. Norman and Ruth (R.) L.; m. Jacqueline Roe, Aug. 24, 1963; children: Erin, Andrea, John, Peter. BA in Econs., Colby Coll., 1964; LLB, Law Sch., Yale U., 1967. Bar: Conn., U.S. Dist. Ct. (Conn.), U.S. Ct. Appeals (2d cir.), U.S. Tax Ct., U.S. Supreme Ct. Assoc. Shipman & Goodwin, 1967-72, ptnr., 1972—, chmn. mgmt. com., 1985-96. Bd. dirs. Hartford Hosp., Conn. Health System, Inc., Conn. Bar Found., VNA Health Care, Inc., Vis. Nurse and Home Care, Inc. Recipient Charles J. Parker award Conn. Bar Assn., Dist. Svc. award Conn. Legal Svcs. Fellow Am. Bar Found., Conn. Bar Found.; mem. ABA, Am. Soc. of Hosp. Attys., Conn. Bar Assn. Avocations: golf, boating, fishing, raquet sports, piano. General corporate, Health, Corporate taxation. Office: Shipman & Goodwin 1 American Row Hartford CT 06103-2833 E-mail: alloyd@goodwin.com

LLOYD, FRANCIS LEON, JR. lawyer; b. Winchester, Va., Dec. 1, 1955; s. Francis Leon Sr. and Jeannette Marie (Dove) L.; m. Myra Denise DuBose, Sept. 18, 1982. BA in English and French, U. Richmond, 1978; JD, U. Va., 1981. Bar: Va. 1981, Tenn. 1982, U.S. Dist. Ct. (ea. dist.) Tenn. 1982, U.S. Ct. Appeals (6th cir.) 1984. Assoc. Herndon, Coleman, Brading & McKee, Johnson City, Tenn., 1981-86, ptnr., 1987-88; of counsel The Taylor Group, Ltd., 1983; law clk. to judge U.S. Dist. Ct. (ea. dist.) Tenn., Knoxville, 1988-98; assoc. London & Amburn, PC, 1998-99, mem., 1999—. Bd. dirs. Assn. Retarded Citizens Washington County, Inc., Johnson City, 1982-88. Avocations: literature, music, hiking. General civil litigation, Personal injury, Professional liability. Home: 8804 Regent Ln Knoxville TN 37923-1640 Office: London & Amburn PC 1716 W Clinch Ave Knoxville TN 37916-2408 E-mail: fllmail@latlaw.com

LLOYD, JAMES HENDRIE, III, lawyer; b. Phila., Oct. 20, 1943; s. James Hendrie and Margaret Katherine (Koons) L.; m. Blakeslee Ann Benjamin, June 17, 1967; children— Meredith, William. A.B., Princeton U., 1965; M.B.A., U. Pa., 1967; J.D., U. Conn., 1973. Bar: Conn. 1973, U.S. Dist. Ct. Conn. 1973. Planner Capitol Region Planning Agy., Hartford, Conn., 1969-70; ptnr. Updike, Kelly & Spellacy, P.C., Hartford, 1973— . Editor-in-chief Conn. Law Rev., 1972-73. Chmn. Glastonbury Planning and Zoning Commn., 1985-87; vice-chmn. Glastonbury Charter Revision Commn., 1988—. Served to 1st lt. U.S. Army, 1967-69, Vietnam. Decorated Bronze Star. Mem. Hartford County Bar Assn., Conn. Bar Assn., ABA, Am. Planning Assn. Congregationalist. General corporate, Municipal (including bonds), Real property. Home: 105 Farmcliff Dr Glastonbury CT 06033-4186 Office: Updike Kelly & Spellacy 1 State St Ste 15 Hartford CT 06103-3176

LLOYD, JAMES WOODMAN, lawyer; b. Syracuse, N.Y., June 15, 1940; s. William James and Stella Katherine Lloyd. BS, MIT, 1961; LLB, Columbia U., 1964. BAr: N.Y. 1965, U.S. Dist. Ct. (so. dist.) N.Y. 1976, U.S. Ct. Appeals (2d cir.) 1975, U.S. Tax Ct. 1978. Assoc. Davis Polk & Wardwell, N.Y.C., 1968-73, ptnr., 1974-2000, sr. counsel, 2001—. Bd. dirs. Charles A. and Anne Morrow Lindbergh Found. Lt. USN, 1964-67. Fellow Am. Coll. Trust and Estate Counsel; mem. ABA, N.Y. State Bar Assn., Assn. Bar City N.Y., N.Y. Yacht Club. Republican. Estate planning, Probate, Estate taxation. Home: Delafield Island Darien CT 06820 also: 109 Paradise Dr Belvedere Tiburon CA 94920-2518 Office: Davis Polk & Wardwell 450 Lexington Ave Fl 31 New York NY 10017-3982

LLOYD, LEONA LORETTA, judge; b. Detroit, Aug. 6, 1949; d. Leon Thomas and Naomi Mattie (Chisolm) L.; 1 stepson, Joseph Andersen. BS, Wayne State U., 1971, JD, 1979. Bar: Mich. 1981, U.S. Dist. Ct. (ea. dist.) 1981, U.S. Supreme Ct. 1988, U.S. Cir. Ct. (6th cir.) 1983. Speech, drama tchr. Detroit Bd. Edn., 1971-75; instr. criminal justice Wayne State U., Detroit, 1981; sr. ptnr. Lloyd and Lloyd, 1982-92; prin. asst., corp. counsel City Detroit Law Dept., 1992-94; judge 36th Dist. Ct., Detroit, 1994—. Co-author, dir. (gospel musical) Freedom Song, 1991. Wayne State U. scholar, 1970, 75; recipient Fred Hampton Image award, 1984, Kizzy Image award, 1985, Nat. Coalition of 100 Black Women Achievement award, 1986, Community Svc. award Wayne County exec. William Lucas, 1986, Merit Black Law Student Assn. cert. U. Detroit, 1986, Spirit of Detroit award, 1991, Martin Luther King Keep This Dream Alive award, 1995, Special Tribute award State of Mich., 1995, Resolution award County of Wayne, 1995, Appreciation cert. City of Detroit, 1995, Bar Assn. award, 1995, B'nai B'rith Barristers award, 1995, Testimonial Resolution award Detroit City Coun., 1995, Woman of Yr. award African Am. Awards Coun., 1996, African Am. Sheroes award Drusilla Farwell Mid. Sch., 1997, Cmty. Pride award Greater Grace Temple, 2000; named to Black Women Hall of Fame. Mem. ABA, NARAS, Wolverine Bar Assn., Mich. State Bar, Mary McLeon Bethune Assn. Office: 421 Madison St Ste 3067 Detroit MI 48226-2358

LLOYD, ROBERT ALLEN, lawyer; b. Chgo., Aug. 3, 1941; s. Alva Allen and Ann Marie (Goscinski) L.; m. Diane T. Horrell, July 2, 1964; children: Nancy, Lisa, Jennifer. BS in Elec. Engring., U. Ill., 1964; JD, Loyola U., Chgo., 1969. Bar: Ill. 1969, U.S. Dist. Ct. (no. dist.) Ill. 1969, U.S. Ct. Appeals (7th cir.) 1977, U.S. Ct. Appeals (D.C. cir.) 1980. Engr. Teletype Corp., Skokie, Ill., 1964-69; atty., 1969-71, Western Elec., Cicero, 1971-75, Juettner, Pyle, Lloyd & Piontek, Chgo., 1975-97; of counsel Pyle & Piontek, 1998—2000, Greer, Burns & Crain, Chgo., 2000—. Intellectual property, Patent, Trademark and copyright. Office: Pyle & Piontek 221 N La Salle St Chicago IL 60601-1206

LOBB, CYNTHIA JEAN HOCKING, lawyer; b. San Francisco, June 12, 1962; d. Thomas Messinger and Diane (Knight) Hocking; m. Jerry Mark Lobb, Dec. 1, 1990; children: Sean Thomas, Kevin Joseph, Braden McMillan. BA in Polit. Sci., UCLA, 1984; JD, Golden Gate U. Law Sch., U. San Diego Law Sch., 1993. Bar: Ca., 1993. Asst. Congressman W. Dannemeyer, Washington, 1987-88; legal sec. Fulbright & Jaworski, 1988; law clerk MCI Internat. Divsn., Rye Brook, NY, 1990, Kern County Counsel, Bakersfield, Calif., 1991; lawyer Lobb & Cliff, Riverside, 1997-98, Law Office of Cynthia Hocking, Menifee, 1995—. Spanish tchr. Good Shepard Lutheran Sch., Menifee, Calif., 1996-99. Assoc. mem. Calif. Repub. Party, 1980—; mem. Riverside Repub. Women's Federated, Temecula Repub. Women's Federated, Lake Menifee Women's Club, 1998-2000, St. Jeanne's Sch. Bd., 1999-2000; pub. rels. dir. St. Martha's Ch., 1998-2000, Bible sharing leader, 1994-97; bd. mem. Mothers and Others, 1999-2001. Mem. Alpha Delta Chi (named Most Outstanding mem. 1984, Outstanding Young Women of Am., 1985). Republican. Roman Catholic. Avocations: fitness training, jazzercize, scrapbooking, Spanish and French. Home: 23782 Dijon Ct Menifee CA 92584 Office: Lobb & Cliff 1650 Spruce St Ste 500 Riverside CA 92507-2436

LOBEL, MARTIN, lawyer; b. Cambridge, Mass., June 19, 1941; s. I. Alan and Dorothy W. l.; m. Geralyn Krupp, Mar. 15, 1981; children: Devra Sarah, Rachel Melissa, Hannah Krupp. AB, Boston U., 1962; JD, 1965; LLM, Harvard U., 1966. Bar: Mass. 1965, D.C. 1968, U.S. Supreme Ct. 1968. Ptnr. Lobel & Lobel, Boston, 1965-66; asst. prof. law U. Okla., Norman, 1967; congl. fellow Washington, 1968; legis. asst. to Senator William Proxmire, 1968-72; ptnr. Lobel, Novins & Lamont, Washington, 1972—. Lectr. Law Sch. Am. U., Washington, 1972—; resellers referee, U.S. Dist. Ct., Wichita; chmn. Tax Analysts, 1972—. Contbr. artticles to legal jours. Chmn. tax notes/tax analysis. Mem. ABA, Mass. Bar Assn., D.C. Bar Assn. (ch,m. consumer affairs com. 1976-77, chmn. steering com. on antitrust and consumer affairs sect.), Order of Coif, Harvard Club (Washington), Boston U. Club (Washington). Administrative and regulatory, Federal civil litigation, Legislative. Home: 4525 31st St NW Washington DC 20008-2130 Office: Lobel Novins & Lamont 1275 K St NW Ste 770 Washington DC 20005-4048 E-mail: lobel@lnllaw.com

LOBENHERZ, WILLIAM ERNEST, container company/association executive, lawyer; b. Muskegon, Mich., June 22, 1949; s. Ernest Pomeroy and Emajean (Krautheim) L.; m. Carla Rae Krieger; children: Jessica Anne, Rebecca Jean, Christopher William, Andrew William. BBA, U. Mich., 1971; JD cum laude, Wayne State U., 1974. Bar: Mich. 1974. Legal counsel Mich. Legis. Services Bur., Lansing, Mich., 1974-77; legal legis. cons. Mich. Assn. of Sch. Bds., 1977, asst. exec. dir. for legal legis. affairs, 1977-79; asst. v.p. state and congl. relations Wayne State U., Detroit, 1979-81, assoc. v.p. state relations, 1981-82, v.p. govtl. affairs, 1982-87; assoc. Dykema Gossett, Lansing, Mich., 1987-89; pres., CEO, Mich. Soft Drink Assn., 1989—, MSDA Svc. Corp., Lansing, 1997—. Guest lectr. in govtl. affairs, Wayne State U., U. Mich., U. Detroit; referee Mich. Tax Tribunal, 1993-97. Contbr. chpt. Mich. Handbook for School Business Officials, 1979, 2nd edit., 1980; also articles to profl. jours. and mags. Mem. govtl. affairs com. New Detroit Inc., 1984-87, chmn. state subcom. of govtl. affairs com., 1986-87; chmn. ind. schs. campaign Greater Metro Detroit United Fund Torch Dr., 1979, chmn. Colls. and Univs. campaign, 1980; bd. dirs. Mich. Epilepsy Ctr., 1991-97, Coun. for Mich. Pub. Univs., 1991—, Tourism Industry Coalition of Mich., vice-chair, 1998—; mem. Mich. Recycling Partnership, 1997—. Recipient Book award Lawyer's Coop. Pub. Co., 1973, Outstanding Svc. award Mich. Assn. for Marriage and Family Therapy, 1992, 95, Silver scholar key Wayne State U. Law Sch., 1974; named among Top 10 Single Interest Lobbyists, Inside Mich. Politics, 2001. Mem. Mich. Bar Assn., NAACP, Coun. for Advancement and Support of Edn. (Mindpower citation 1982), Mich. Delta Found. (bd. dirs. 1977-97, sec. 1981-84, v.p. 1987-88), Greater Metro Detroit C. of C. (contact interviewer bus. attraction and expansion coun. 1984-86), City Club. Home: 900 Long Blvd # 365 Lansing MI 48911 Office: Mich Soft Drink Assn 634 Michigan National Tower Lansing MI 48933-1707 E-mail: msda@voyager.net

LOBENHOFER, LOUIS F. law educator; b. Denver, Mar. 24, 1950; s. Frederick C. and Betty Lobenhofer; m. Carol E. Clarkson, June 16, 1973; children: Kristina M., Lauren E. AB, Coll. William and Mary, 1972; JD, U. Colo., 1975; LLM, U. Denver, 1979. Bar: Colo. 1975, Tax Ct. 1982. Assoc. law firm Charles H. Booth, Denver, 1975-78; asst. prof. law Ohio No. U., 1979-82, assoc. prof., 1982-85, prof., 1985— . Denver Tax Inst. scholar, 1979. Mem. ABA, Christian Legal Soc., Phi Beta Kappa, Omicron Delta Kappa, Delta Theta Phi. Republican. Roman Catholic. Office: Ohio No U Coll Law Ada OH 45810

LOBL, HERBERT MAX, lawyer; b. Vienna, Austria, Jan. 10, 1932; s. Walter Leo and Minnie (Neumann) L.; m. Dorothy Fullerton Hubbard, Sept. 12, 1960; children: Peter Walter, Michelle Alexandra. AB magna cum laude, Harvard U., 1953, LLB cum laude, 1959, Avocat honoraire, 1993. Bar: N.Y. 1960, U.S. Tax Ct. 1963, French Conseil Juridique 1973; French avocat. mem. Paris bar, 1992, avocat hon., 1993. Assoc. Davis, Polk & Wardwell, N.Y.C., 1959-90, N.Y.C. and Paris, 1963-69, ptnr., 1969-92, sr. counsel, 1993—; assoc. counsel to Gov. Nelson Rockefeller Albany, N.Y., 1960-62. Lectr. law Columbia U., N.Y.C., 1993-95; supervisory bd. mem. CII-HB Internationale, Amsterdam, The Netherlands, 1977-82. Gov. Am. Hosp. Paris, 1981-83, 88-93; bd. trustees Am. Libr., Paris, 1969-81, Nantucket (Mass.) Cottage Hosp., 1996-99, dir. Nantucket Arts Coun., 2000—. Served to 1st lt. UASF, 1954-56. Fulbright scholar U. Bonn, Germany, 1954. Mem. Am. C. of C. (bd. dirs. France 1988-90), Univ. Club, Harvard Club. Address: PO Box 2488 Nantucket MA 02584-2488 also: PO Box 118 Rye NY 10580-0118 also: Davis Polk & Wardwell 450 Lexington Ave New York NY 10017-3911

LOBRETO-LOBO, RAFAEL, law educator; b. Lozana-Pinola, Spain, May 9, 1949; s. Rafael Lobreto-Álvarez and Jovita Lobo-Espoina; m. Pilar Esteban-Zaera, July 24, 1988; 1 child, Rafael. LLM, Oviedo (Spain) U., 1976; grad. as master mariner, Gijon Merchant Marine Acad., Spain, 1975. Mgr. Min. de Fomendo Dept. Merchant Marine, Spain; pres. Sasemar, Spain; mgr. Ramos & Arroyo, Madrid, Peña & Lobeto, Consultants, Madrid; gen. sec. Philippe Coustau Found.; prof. Maritime Law San Pablo CEU U. Recipient Gran Cruz del Merito Naval, Cruz Oficial de la Orden del Merito Civil. Office: Ramos & Arroyo c/Serrano 89 7o 28006 Madrid Spain Office Fax: 91-561-49-03. E-mail: plc.consult@mx4.redestb.es

LOCHBIHLER, FREDERICK VINCENT, lawyer; b. Chgo., Jan. 30, 1951; s. Frederick Louis and Marion Helen (Rutkauskas) L.; m. Darlene Gotfryde Wantuch, Nov. 8, 1952; 1 child, Frederick Karlman. AB in Govt. summa cum laude, U. Notre Dame, 1973; JD with honors, U. Chgo., 1976. Bar: Ill. 1976, U.S. Dist. Ct. (no. dist.) Ill. 1977, U.S. Ct. Appeals (7th cir.) 1980, U.S. Ct. Appeals (8th cir.) 1981, U.S. Supreme Ct. 1982, U.S. Dist. Ct. (ctrl. dist.) Ill. 1983, U.S. Dist. Ct. Ariz. 1991. Assoc. Chapman and Cutler, Chgo., 1976-84, ptnr., 1984—. Mem. Phi Beta Kappa, Order of Coif. Avocations: military history, literature, travel. Federal civil litigation, General civil litigation, Securities. Home: 605 Waukegan Rd #1F Glenview IL 60025 Office: Chapman and Cutler 111 W Monroe St Ste 1700 Chicago IL 60603-4006

LOCHRIDGE, LLOYD PAMPELL, JR. lawyer; b. Austin, Tex., Feb. 3, 1918; s. Lloyd Pampell and Franklyn (Blocker) L.; m. Frances Potter, Jan. 23, 1943; children: Anne, Georgia, Lloyd P. III, Patton G., Hope N., Frances P. AB, Princeton U., 1938; LLB, Harvard U., 1941. Bar: D.C. 1942, Tex. 1945, U.S. Ct. Appeals (5th cir.), U.S. Supreme Ct. Assoc. Law Office Vernon Hill, Mission, Tex., 1945-46; ptnr. Hill & Lochridge, 1946-49, Hill, Lochridge & King, Mission, 1949-59, McGinnis, Lochridge & Kilgore, Austin, 1959—. Mem. adv. bd. Salvation Army, Austin, 1962—; mem. vestry Ch. Good Shepherd, Austin, 1968-73; trustee Austin Lyric Opera, 1986—. Comdr. USNR, 1941-46, ETO. Mem. ABA (bd. govs. 1989-92), State Bar Tex. (pres. 1974-75), Travis County Bar Assn. (pres. 1970-71), Hidalgo County Bar Assn. (pres. 1954-55). Episcopalian. Avocations: tennis, squash, sailing. Federal civil litigation, General civil litigation, Oil, gas, and mineral. Office: McGinnis Lochridge & Kilgore Capitol Ctr 919 Congress Ave Ste 1300 Austin TX 78701-2499 E-mail: llochridge@mcginnislaw.com

LOCKE, JOHN HOWARD, retired lawyer; b. Berryville, Va., Sept. 4, 1920; s. James Howard and Mary Elizabeth (Hart) L.; m. Frances Rebecca Cook, Feb. 23, 1946; children: Anne Locke Evans, Nancy Locke Curlee, Rebecca Locke Leonard. BS, U. Richmond, 1941; LLB, U. Va., 1948. Bar: Va. 1948. Ptnr. Gentry, Locke, Rakes & Moore, Roanoke, Va., ret., 1985. Apptd. Hearing Officer Supreme Ct. Va., 1987; founder, pres. Big Bros., Roanoke, 1960. With USN, 1942-46. Fellow Am. Coll. Trial Lawyers, Internat. Soc. Barristers (pres. 1970); mem. ABA, Va. State Bar, Va. Bar Assn., Roanoke City Bar Assn. (pres. 1970-71), Internat. Assn. Ins. Counsel, 4th Cir. Jud. Conf., Omicron Delta Kappa, Raven Soc., Shenandoah Club (Roanoke, Va.). Presbyterian.

LOCKE, WILLIAM HENRY, lawyer; b. Eagle Pass, Tex., Nov. 14, 1947; s. William Henry and Genevieve (Moss) L.; children: William Henry III, Elizabeth Madeleine. AA with honors, Del Mar Coll., 1967; BA, U. Tex., 1969, JD with honors, 1972. Bar: Tex. 1972; cert. in real estate law. Exec. dir. The Kleberg Law Firm, Corpus Christi, Tex., 1972-99, Graves, Dougherty, Hearon & Moody, Austin, 2000—. Co-dir. advanced real estate law course State Bar of Tex., 1986-87. Author: Seizure of Lender's Collateral Under Drug Enforcement Laws, 1990, Contractual Indemnity in Texas, 1991, Civil Forfeiture Actions, 1993, Shifting of Risk: Contractual Provisions for Indemnity, Additional Insureds, Wavier of Subrogation and Exculpation, 1995, Texas Foreclosure Manual, 1995, Risk Management: Through Contractual Provisions for Indemnity, Additional Insureds Waiver of Subrogation, Releases and Exculpation, 1997, Sales Contracts: A Framework for Risk Allocation, 1998, Due Diligence in the Acquisition of Income Producing Properties, 2000; contbg. author: Texas Construction Law, 1988. Chmn. Corpus Christi Planning Commn., 1984-85, Corpus Christi Airport Zoning Commn., 1985; bd. dirs., sec. Leadership Corpus Christi, 1984-85; pres. Palmer Drug Abuse Program, Corpus Christi, 1985-87, pres., 200001; treas. St. James Episcopal Elem. Sch., 1987-91. Fellow Tex. Bar Found. (life), Tex. Coll. Real Estate Law (dir. 1990-2001), Coll. Law of State Bar Tex.; mem. ABA, Corpus Christi Bar Assn. (pres. 1987-88), Rotary (bd. dirs. Corpus Christi 1987-88, sec. 1989, Disting. Svc. Above Self award 1985, Corpus Christi merit award 1987), Beta Theta Pi. Democrat. Episcopalian. Contracts commercial, Finance, Real property. Fax: 512-478-1976. E-mail: blocke@gdhm.com

LOCKETT, TYLER CHARLES, state supreme court justice; b. Corpus Christi, Tex., Dec. 7, 1932; s. Tyler Coleman and Evelyn (Lemond) L.; m. Sue W. Lockett, Nov. 3, 1961; children: Charles, Patrick. AB, Washburn U., 1955, JD, 1962. Bar: Kans. 1962. Pvt. practice law, Wichita, 1962—; judge Ct. Common Pleas, 1971-77, Kans. Dist. Ct. 18th Dist., 1977-83; justice Supreme Court Kans., Topeka, 1983—. Methodist. Office: Kans Supreme Ct 374 Kansas Judicial Ctr Topeka KS 66612-1502*

LOCKHART, GREGORY GORDON, prosecutor; b. Dayton, Ohio, Sept. 2, 1946; s. Lloyd Douglas and Evelyn (Gordon) L.; m. Paula Louise Jewett, May 20, 1978; children: David H., Sarah L. BS, Wright State U., 1973; JD, Ohio State U., 1976. Bar: Ohio 1976, U.S. Dist. Ct. (so. dist.) Ohio 1977, U.S. Ct. Appeals (6th cir.) 1988, U.S. Supreme Ct. 1993. Legal advisor Xenia and Fairborn (Ohio) Police Dept., 1977-78; asst. pros. atty. Greene County Prosecutor, Xenia, 1978-87; ptnr. DeWine & Schenck, 1978-82, Schenck, Schmidt & Lockhart , Xenia, 1982-85, Ried & Lockhart, Beavercreek, Ohio, 1985-87; asst. U.S. atty. So. Dist. of Ohio, Columbus, 1987-2001, U.S. atty. Dayton, 2001—. Adj. prof. Coll. Law U. Dayton, 1990—, Wright State U., Dayton, 1979—. Co-author: Federal Grand Jury Practice, 1996. Pres. Greene County Young reps., Xenia, 1977-79. With USAF, 1966-70; Vietnam. Mem. Fed. Bar Assn. (chpt. pres. 1994-95), Dayton Bar Assn., Kiwanis (pres. 1983-84, lt. gov. 1986-87), Jaycees (pres. 1976-79), Am. Inns of Ct. (master of bench emeritus). Methodist. Avocations: golf, tennis, hiking, camping. Office: US Attorney Federal Bldg 200 W 3rd St Rm 602 Dayton OH 45402 E-mail: gregory.lockhart@usdoj.gov

LOCKHART, ROBERT EARL, lawyer; b. Fitchburg, Mass., Dec. 16, 1937; s. Earl Perry and Florence (Wuth) L.; m. Barbara Heusner, June 19, 1965; children— Robert, Jr., Andrew. B.B.A., Clark U., 1959; LL.B., Duke U., 1962. Bar: D.C. 1962. Atty., U.S. GAO, Washington, 1963-71; gen. counsel Com. on Post Office and Civil Service, U.S. Ho. of Reps., Washington, 1971— . Office: Post Office & Civil Service 309 Cannon Bldg Washington DC 20515-0003

LOCKYER, BILL, state attorney general; b. Oakland, Calif., May 8, 1941; 1 child, Lisa. BA in Polit. Sci., U. Calif., Berkeley; cert. in sec. tchg., Calif. State U., Hayward; JD, U. of the Pacific. Past tchr., San Leandro, Calif.; Mem. Calif. State Assembly, 1973; state senator State of Calif., 1982; pres. pro tem, chmn. senate rules com., chmn. senate jud. com. Calif. State Senate, 1994-98; atty. gen. State of Calif., 1999—. Active San Leandro Sch. Bd., 1968-73. Past chair Alameda County Dem. Ctrl. Com. Named Legislator of Yr. Planning and Conservation League, 1996, Calif. Jour., 1997, Office: Office Atty Gen Dept Justice PO Box 944255 Sacramento CA 94244-2550

LOCKYER, CHARLES WARREN, JR. corporate executive; b. Phila., Apr. 6, 1944; s. Charles Warren and Mary Alice (Underwood) L.; m. Karen A. Damiani, Jan. 22, 1966; children: Charles Warren III, Larissa A., Daphne M. BA, Fordham U., 1966; MA, Princeton U., 1968, PhD, 1971; JD, Georgetown U., 1995. V.p. Fidelity Bank, Phila., 1970-79; v.p., chief fin. officer Pubco Corp., Glenn Dale, Md., 1980-82; exec. v.p. Perpetual Savs. Bank, F.S.B., Alexandria, Va., 1982-90; pres. Alleco Inc., Cheverly, Md., 191-95; assoc. Fred, Frank, Harris, Schriver & Jacobson, Washington, 1996—. Dir. Gulfstream Land & Devel. Corp., Plantation, Fla., 1980-86. Trustee Jeanes Hosp., Phila., 1973-87; dir. Foulkeways at Gwynedd, Pa., 1975-80; mem. adv. com. classics Princeton U., 1978-83. Woodrow Wilson fellow, 1966. Mem. Phi Beta Kappa. Home: 4409 Glenridge St Kensington MD 20895-4255 Office: Fried Frank Harris Schriver & Jacobson 1001 Pennsylvania Ave NW Washington DC 20004-2505

LOEB, LEONARD L. lawyer; b. Chgo., Mar. 30, 1929; BBA, U. Wis., 1950, JD, 1952. Bar: Wis. 1952, U.S. Supreme Ct. 1960. Sole practice, Milw., 1952—; ptnr. Loeb & Herman. Faculty family mediation inst. Harvard Law Sch.; lectr. family law Marquette U., U. Wis., Madison; cons. revisions Wis. Family Code Wis. Legislature; mem. com. for review of initiatives in child support State of Wis.; Concordia Coll. (Wis.) Paralegal Adv. Bd. Author: Systems Book for Family Law; contbr. articles to profl. jours. Served to col. JAGC, USAF, 1952-53. Fellow Am. Bar Found., Am. Acad. Matrimonial Lawyers (past charter pres. Wis. chpt., pres. nat. chpt.); mem. ABA (past chmn. family law sect., del. to ho. of dels.), Wis. Bar Assn. (pres. 1999-2000), Wis. Bar Found. (bd. dirs.), Milw. Bar Assn. (past chmn. family law sect., past pres.). Family and matrimonial. Office: Loeb & Herman Ste 1125 111 E Wisconsin Ave Milwaukee WI 53202-4868 E-mail: lloeb@loebherman.com

LOENGARD, RICHARD OTTO, JR. lawyer; b. N.Y.C, Jan. 28, 1932; s. Richard Otto and Margery (Borg) L.; m. Janet Sara Senderowitz, Apr. 11, 1964; children: Maranda C., Philippa S.M. AB, Harvard U., 1953, LLB, 1956. Bar: N.Y. 1956, U.S. Dist. Ct. (so. dist.) N.Y. 1958. Assoc. Fried, Frank, Harris, Shriver & Jacobson, predecessor firms, N.Y.C., 1956-64, ptnr., 1967-97; of counsel Fried, Frank, Harris, Shriver & Jacobson, 1997—; dep. tax legis. counsel, spl. asst. internat. tax affairs U.S. Dept. Treasury, Washington, 1964-67. Mem. Commerce Clearing House, Riverwoods, Ill. Editl. bd. Tax Transaction Libr., 1982-94; contbr. articles to profl. publs. Fellow Am. Coll. Tax Counsel; mem. ABA, N.Y. State Bar Assn. (exec. com. tax sect. 1984—, sec. 1994-95, vice chair 1995-97, chair 1997-98), Assn. Bar City N.Y. Taxation, general. Office: Fried Frank Harris Shriver & Jacobson 1 New York Plz New York NY 10004-1980 E-mail: loengri@ffhsj.com

LOESER, HANS FERDINAND, lawyer; b. Kassel, Germany, Sept. 28, 1920; s. Max and Cecilia H. (Erlanger) L.; m. Herta Lewent, Dec. 14, 1944; children— Helen, Harris M., H. Thomas. Student CCNY, 1940-42, U. Pa., 1942-43; LL.B. magna cum laude, Harvard U., 1950. Bar: Mass. 1950, U.S. Supreme Ct. 1968. Asso. firm Foley, Hoag & Eliot, Boston, 1950-55, ptnr., 1956— ; hon. consul-gen. Republic of Senegal; mem. Mass. Bd. Bar Overseers; trustee Vineyard Open Land Found., Martha's Vineyard, Mass.; mem. exec. com. and nat. bd. Lawyers' Com. for Civil Rights Under Law, steering com. and past chmn. Lawyer's Com. for Civil Rights Under Law of Boston Bar Assn.; incorporator Univ. Hosp., Boston, Mt. Auburn Hosp., Cambridge, Mass. Served to capt. U.S. Army, 1942-46. Decorated Bronze Star, Purple Heart; hon. fellow U. Pa. Law Sch., 1978-79, commencement speaker, 1978. Fellow Am. Bar Found., Mass. Bar Found.; mem. ABA, Mass. Bar Assn., Boston Bar Assn. Clubs: Union, Harvard, Cambridge. Administrative and regulatory, General corporate, Private international. Office: Foley Hoag & Eliot 1 Post Office Sq Ste 1700 Boston MA 02109-2175

LOEVINGER, LEE, lawyer, science writer; b. St. Paul, Apr. 24, 1913; s. Gustavus and Millie (Strouse) L.; m. Ruth Howe, Mar. 4, 1950; children: Barbara L., Eric H., Peter H. BA summa cum laude, U. Minn., 1933, JD, 1936. Bar: Minn. 1936, Mo. 1937, D.C. 1966, U.S. Supreme Ct., 1941. Assoc. Watson, Ess, Groner, Barnett & Whittaker, Kansas City, Mo., 1936-37; atty., regional atty. NLRB, 1937-41; with antitrust div. Dept. Justice, 1941-46; ptnr. Larson, Loevinger, Lindquist & Fraser, Mpls., 1946-60; assoc. justice Minn. Supreme Ct., 1960-61; asst. U.S. atty. gen. charge antitrust div. Dept. Justice, 1961-63; commr. FCC, 1963-68; ptnr. Hogan & Hartson, Washington, 1968-85, of counsel, 1986—; v.p., dir. Craig-Hallum Corp., Mpls., 1968-73. Dir. Petrolite Corp., St. Louis, 1978-83; U.S. rep. com. on restrictive bus. practices Orgn. for Econ. Coop. and Devel., 1961-64; spl. asst. to U.S. atty. gen., 1963-64; spl. counsel com. small bus. U.S. Senate, 1951-52; lectr. U. Minn., 1953-60; vis. prof. jurisprudence U. Minn. (Law Sch.), 1961; professorial lectr. Am. U., 1968-70; chmn. Minn. Atomic Devel. Problems Com., 1957-59; mem. Adminstrv. Conf. U.S., 1972-74; del. White House Conf. on Inflation, 1974; U.S. del. UNESCO Conf. on Mass Media, 1975, Internat. Telecomms. Conf. on Radio Frequencies, 1964, 66. Author: The Law of Free Enterprise, 1949, An Introduction to Legal Logic, 1952, Defending Antitrust Lawsuits, 1977, Science As Evidence, 1995; author first article to use term: jurimetrics, 1949; contbr. articles to profl. and sci. jours.; editor, contbr.: Basic Data on Atomic Devel. Problems in Minnesota, 1958; adv. bd. Antitrust Bull., Jurimetrics Jour. Served to lt. comdr. USNR, 1942-45. Recipient Outstanding Achievement award U. Minn., 1968; Freedoms Found. award, 1977, 84 Fellow Am. Acad. Appellate Lawyers; mem. ABA (del. of sci. and tech. sect. to Ho. of Dels. 1974-80, del. to joint conf. with AAAS 1974-76, co-chair 1990-93, liaison 1984-90, 93-98, chmn. sci. and tech. sect. 1982-83, coun. 1986-89, standing com. on nat. conf. groups 1984-90), AAAS, Minn. Bar Assn., Hennepin County Bar Assn., N.Y. Acad. Sci., D.C. Bar Assn., FCC Bar Assn., Broadcast Pioneers, U.S. C. of C. (antitrust coun. 1980-94), Am. Arbitration Assn. (comml. panel), Atlantic Legal Found. (adv. coun.), Cosmos Club (pres. 1990), City Club (Washington), Phi Beta Kappa, Sigma Xi, Delta Sigma Rho, Sigma Delta Chi, Phi Delta Gamma, Tau Kappa Alpha, Alpha Epsilon Rho. Home: 5600 Wisconsin Ave Apt 17D Chevy Chase MD 20815-4414 Office: Hogan & Hartson 555 13th St NW Ste 800E Washington DC 20004-1109 Fax: 202-637-5910. E-mail: loevil@hhlaw.com

LOEW, JONATHAN L. lawyer; b. Chgo., May 24, 1956; s. Andrew and Rita L.; m. Margarite Primozich, Sept. 8, 1950; children: Zachary, Vanessa, Jacob. BA in Philosophy, Ripon Coll., 1978; JD, DePaul U., 1981. Bar: Ill. 1982, U.S. Dist. Ct. (no. dist.) Ill. 1982, U.S. Ct. Appeals (7th cir.) 1991, U.S. Supreme Ct. 1993. Assoc. Maryniak & Steere, Chgo., 1982-83, Berman, Fagel, Haber, Maragos & Abrams, Chgo., 1983-86; assoc., ptnr. Spitzer, Addis, Susman & Krull, 1986-98; ptnr. Katz, Randall, Weinberg & Richmond, 1998—. Contbr. articles to profl. jours. Mem. Chgo. Bar Assn., Appellate Lawyers Assn. Appellate, Contracts commercial. Office: Katz Randall Weinberg & Richmond 333 W Wacker Dr Ste 1800 Chicago IL 60606-1329 E-mail: jloew@krw.com

LOEWY, PETER HENRY, lawyer; b. N.Y.C., Oct. 2, 1955; s. Herbert and Ruth (Berger) L. B.A. summa cum laude, CCNY, 1976; J.D., Rutgers U., 1979. Bar: N.J. 1979, U.S. Ct. Appeals (3rd cir.) N.J. 1980, U.S. Dist. Ct. (ea. and so. dists.) N.Y. 1980, U.S. Ct. Appeals (2d cir.) N.Y. 1980, Fla. 1981, U.S. Dist. Ct. (so. dist.) Fla. 1981, U.S. Ct. Appeals (5th cir.) 1981, Calif. 1983, U.S. Dist. Ct. (cen. dist.) Calif. 1985, U.S. Ct. Appeals (9th cir.) 1985. Assoc. Fragomen Del Rey & Bernsen, N.Y.C., 1978-82, mng. ptnr. West Coast, Los Angeles, 1982-83, ptnr., 1984-85; mng. ptnr. west coast op. Fragomen Del Rey Bersen, San Francisco and Los Angeles, 1985—. Contbg. editor Immigration Law Reports, 1983—. Vice chmn. Community Planning Bd., N.Y.C., 1979-81. Mem. N.Y. State Bar Assn. (immigration com.), N.Y. County Bar Assn. (immigration com.), Internat. Law Soc. (immigration com. 1980—), Assn. Immigration and Nationality Lawyers, Los Angeles County Bar Assn. (immigration com. 1983—), Century City Bar Assn. (immigration and nationality law com. 1985, bd. govs., bd. dirs. 1985—, chmn. immigration and naturalization com. 1985—), Phi Beta Kappa, Phi Alpha Theta. Clubs: 5th Ave. Squash (chmn. bd., dirs. 1982); So. Calif. Squash Racquets Assn. (pres. 1984). Immigration, naturalization, and customs. Office: Fragomen Del Rey & Bernsen # 1050 11400 W Olympic Blvd Ste 1050 Los Angeles CA 90064-1550

LOFSTROM, MARK D. lawyer, educator, communications executive; b. Mpls., May 11, 1953; s. Dennis E. and Dorothy Dee (Schreiber) L. BA in Art History, Carleton Coll., 1979; MBA, Columbia U., 1989; JD, U. Hawaii, 1992. Bar: Hawaii 1992, Minn. 1995. Pub. rels. asst. Honolulu Acad. Arts, 1979, pub. rels. rep., 1980-84, pub. rels. officer, 1984-87; law clk. Kiefer Oshima Chun Fong and Chung, Honolulu, 1990-91; assoc. Cades Schutte Fleming & Wright, 1991-95; pvt. practice Law Offices of Mark D. Lofstrom, Mpls., 1995-97; rep. sales mgr. Guthrie Theater and Minn. Orch., Minn., 1997-99; class counsel Milberg Weiss et al., 1999-2000; atty. Patterson, Thuente et al., Mpls., 2000-01. Instr. internat. bus. law/bus. law for accts. U. Hawaii Coll. Bus., 1995-96; instr. art law U. Hawaii summer session, 1995-96; organizer artists and writers exhbn., 1981; coord. rep. program Carleton Coll. Alumni Assn., Hawaii, 1984-87; co-editor and mktg. assoc. Pacific Telecomms. Coun., 1988-92, intern East-West Ctr., 1992. Editor mag. on preservation; exec. editor U. Hawaii Law Rev., 1991-92; co-editor: (newsletter) Pacific Comm. Coun. Procs., 1990-92; bd. editors Hawaii Bar Jour., 1992-97; contbr. articles on current exhbns., intellectual property, art, and internat. law. Sec., bd. dirs. Arts Coun. Hawaii, 1985-86, chmn. ways and means com., 1986-87, pres. bd. dirs.; bd. dirs. Hawaii Alliance for Arts Edn., 1994-95, chmn.-elect, 1995-97; mem. St. Mathias Twp. Comprehensive Devel. Plan Com., 1997-99; dir. Minn. Stonewall DFL, 2000—; v.p. Rainbow Health Initiative, 2001—. Recipient NCR Stakeholders award, 1988, legal rsch. and writing award Hawaii State Bar Assn. Young Lawyers Div., 1991. Mem. ABA, Hawaii State Bar Assn. (sec. internat. law sect. 1994, chair internat. law sect. 1995-96), Minn. Bar Assn. General corporate, Private international, Trademark and copyright. Office: PO Box 3605 Minneapolis MN 55403-0605

LOFTUS, THOMAS DANIEL, lawyer; b. Nov. 8, 1930; s. Glendon Francis and Martha Helen (Wall) L. BA, U. Wash., 1952, JD, 1957. Bar: Wash. 1958, U.S. Ct. Appeals (9th cir.) 1958, U.S. Dist. Ct. Wash. 1958, U.S. Ct. Mil. Appeals 1964, U.S. Supreme Ct. 1964. Trial atty. Northwestern Mut. Ins. Co., Seattle, 1958-62; sr. trial atty. Unigard Security Ins. Co., 1962-68, asst. gen. counsel, 1969-83, govt. rels. counsel, 1983-89; of counsel Groshong, LeHet & Thornton, 1990-98; mem. Wash. Commn. on Jud. Conduct (formerly Jud. Qualifications), 1982-88, vice-chmn., 1987-88; judge pro tem Seattle Mcpl. Ct., 1973-81; mem. nat. panel of mediators Arbitration Forums, Inc., 1990—. Sec., treas. Seattle Opera Assn., 1980-91; pres., bd. dirs. Vis. Nurse Svcs., 1979-88; pres., v.p. Salvation Army Adult Rehab. Ctr., 1979-86; nat. committeeman Wash. Young Rep. Fedn., 1961-63, vice-chmn, 1963-65; pres. Young Reps. King County, 1962-63; bd. dirs. Seattle Seafair, Inc., 1975; bd. dirs., gen. counsel Wash. Ins. Coun., 1984-86, sec., 1986-88, v.p., 1988-90, Am. Mediation Panel of Mediators, 1990-96; bd. dirs. Arson Alarm Found., 1987-90; bd. visitors Law Sch. U. Wash., 1993—. 1st lt. U.S. Army, 1952-54, col. Res., 1954-85. Fellow Am. Bar Found.; mem. Am. Arbitration Assn. (nat. panel arbitrators 1965—, nat. panel mediators 2000—), Am. Arbitration Forums, Inc. (nat. panel arbitrators 1992), Nat. Assn. Security Dealers (bd. arbitrators 1997—), Am. Mediation Panel, Wash. Bar Assn. (gov. 1981-84), Seattle King County Bar Assn. (sec., trustee 1977-82), ABA (ho. of dels. 1984-90), Internat. Assn. Ins. Counsel, U.S. People to People (del. Moscow internat. law-econ. conf. 1990), Def. Rsch. Inst., Wash. Def. Trial Lawyers Assn., Wash. State Trial Lawyers Assn., Am. Judicature Soc., Res. Officers Assn., Judge Advocate Gen.'s Assn., Assn. Wash. Gens., U. Wash. Alumni Assn., Coll. Club Seattle, Wash. Athletic Club, Masons, Shriners, English Spkg. Union, Ranier Club, Pi Sigma Alpha, Delta Sigma Rho, Phi Delta Phi, Theta Delta Chi. Republican. Presbyterian. Alternative dispute resolution, Insurance, Personal injury. Home: 3515 Magnolia Blvd W Seattle WA 98199-1841 Office: Coll Club Bldg 505 Madison St Ste 300 Seattle WA 98104-1123

LOGAN, DAVID ANDREW, lawyer, educator; b. N.Y.C., Nov. 25, 1949; s. Leslie and Muriel Agnes (Lasky) L.; m. Jeanne Saum Wine, June 20, 1981; 1 child, Benjamin Alexander. B.A., Bucknell U., 1971; M.A., U. Wis.-Madison, 1972; J.D., U. Va., 1977. Bar: D.C. 1979, N.C. 1984, U.S. Dist. Ct. D.C. 1979. Fellow Ctr. Study Pub. Policy and Adminstrn., U. Wis.-Madison, 1971-72; analyst Congl. Research Service, Library of Congress, Washington, 1972-73; law clk-U.S. Dist. Ct. (ea. dist.) Va., 1977-78; assoc. firm Fried, Frank, Harris, Shriver & Kampelman, Washington, 1978-81; asst., then assoc. prof. law Wake Forest U., Winston Salem, N.C., 1981— ; lectr. N.C. bar rev. course, 1983. Author, editor N.C. Tort Practice Handbook, 1983. Bd. dirs. Winston-Salem Civil Liberties Union, 1982-84; chmn. Winston-Salem Human Relations Commn., 1984— . Winner Chief Justice Joseph Brand Excellence in Tchg. awrad, 1986. Mem. Am. Judicature Soc., Pi Sigma Alpha. Democrat. Home: 2121 Royall Dr Winston Salem NC 27106-5226 Office: Box 7206 Reynolda Sta Winston Salem NC 27109

LOGAN, FRANCIS DUMMER, lawyer; b. Evanston, Ill., May 23, 1931; s. Simon Rae and Frances (Dummer) L.; m. Claude Riviere, Apr. 13, 1957; children: Carolyn Gisele, Francis Dummer. B.A., U. Chgo., 1950; B.A. Juris, Oxford U., 1954; LL.B., Harvard U., 1955. Bar: N.Y. 1956, Calif. 1989. Assoc. Milbank, Tweed, Hadley & McCloy, N.Y.C., 1955-64, ptnr. N.Y.C. and L.A., 1965-96, chmn., 1992-96. Mem. vis. com. U. of Chgo. Coll.; bd. dirs. Pasadena Symphony Orchestra. Mem. Calif. State Bar, Coun. on Fgn. Rels., Am. Law Inst., Pacific Coun. on Internat. Policy, N.Y. State Bar. Banking. Home: 1726 Linda Vista Ave Pasadena CA 91103-1132

LOGAN, JAMES KENNETH, lawyer, former federal judge; b. Quenemo, Kans., Aug. 21, 1929; s. John Lysle and Esther Maurine (Price) L.; m. Beverly Jo Jennings, June 8, 1952; children: Daniel Jennings, Amy Logan Sliva, Sarah Logan Sherard, Samuel Price. A.B., U. Kans., 1952; LL.B. magna cum laude, Harvard, 1955. Bar: Kans. 1955, Calif. 1956. Law clk. U.S. Cir. Judge Huxman, 1955-56; with firm Gibson, Dunn & Crutcher, L.A., 1956-57; asst. prof. law U. Kans., 1957-61, prof., dean Law Sch., 1961-68; ptnr. Payne and Jones, Olathe, Kans., 1968-77; judge U.S. Ct. Appeals (10th cir.), 1977-98; pvt. practice Olathe, 1998—. Ezra Ripley Thayer tchg. fellow Harvard Law Sch., 1961-62; vis. prof. U. Tex., 1964, Stanford U., 1969, U. Mich., 1976; sr. lectr. Duke U., 1987, 91, 93; commr. U.S. Dist. Ct., 1964-67; mem. U.S. Judicial Conf. Adv. Com. Fed. Rules of Appellate Procedure, 1990-97, chair, 1993-97. Author: (with W.B. Leach) Future Interests and Estate Planning, 1961, Kansas Estate Administration, 5th edit., 1986, (with A.R. Martin) Kansas Corporate Law and Practice, 2d edit., 1979, The Federal Courts of the Tenth Circuit: A History, 1992; also articles. Candidate for U.S. Senate, 1968. Served with AUS, 1947-48. Rhodes scholar, 1952; recipient Disting. Service citation U. Kans., 1986, Francis Rawle award ABA-ALI, 1990. Mem. ABA, Kans. Bar Assn., Phi Beta Kappa, Order of Coif, Beta Gamma Sigma, Omicron Delta Kappa, Pi Sigma Alpha, Alpha Kappa Psi, Phi Delta Phi. Democrat. Presbyterian. Appellate, General corporate, Estate planning. E-mail: loganlawfirm@world.att.net

LOGAN, SHARON BROOKS, lawyer; b. Nov. 19, 1945; d. Blake Elmer and Esther N. (Statum) Brooks; children: John W. III, Troy Blake. BS in Econs., U. Md., 1967, MBA in Mktg., 1969; JD, U. Fla., 1979. Bar: Fla. 1979. Ptnr. Raymond Wilson, Esq., Ormond Beach, Fla., 1980, Landis, Graham & French, Daytona Beach, 1981, Watson & Assocs., Daytona Beach, 1982—84; prin. Sharon B. Logan, Esq., Ormond Beach, 1984—. Legal adv. to paralegal program Daytona Beach CC, 1984—. Sponsor Ea. Surfing Assn., Daytona Beach, 1983—, Nat. Scholastic Surfing Assn., 1987—; bd. dir. Ctr. for Visually Impaired, 1991—. Recipient Citizenship award, Rotary Club, 1962—63; fellow Woodrow Wilson, U. md., 1967. Mem.: ABA, Fla. Bar Assn. (real property and probate sect., cert. real estate atty. 1996), Volusia County Bar Assn. (bd. dir.), Volusia County Real Property Coun., Inc. (bd. dirs. 1987—, sec. 1987—88, v.p. 1988—89, pres. 1989—90, sec. 1990—91, sec. 1991—97, pres. 1997—98, pres. 1998—), Volusia county Estate Planning Coun., Daytona Beach Area Bd. Realtors, Fla. Supreme Ct. Hist. Soc., Ducks Unlimited, Univ. Ctr. Club (Tallahassee), Beech Mountain Country Club, Md. Club, Ormond Beach C. of C., Halifax Club, Tomoka Oaks Country Club, Daytona Boat Club, Gator Club, Mus. Arts and Scis., Beta Gamma Sigma, Alpha Lamba Delta, Phi Kappa Phi, Omicron Delta Epsilon, Delta Delta Delta (Scholarship award 1964), Sigma Alpha Epsilon. Democrat. Episcopalian. Avocations: golf, cooking, sewing, tennis, aerobics. Office: Sharon B Logan Esq 180 Vining Ct PO Box 4258 Ormond Beach FL 32175-4258

LOHMAN, RICHARD VERNE, lawyer; b. Colorado Springs, Colo., July 19, 1951; s. Edward Verne and Pauline Elizabeth (Hook) L.; m. Barbara Jo Eichhorn, Nov. 3, 1973; children: Kristen Elizabeth, Brett Edward, Bryan Richard. BA in Polit. Sci. with honors, Colo. State U., 1973; JD with distinction, Washburn U., 1976. Bar: Colo. 1976, U.S. Dist. Ct. Colo. 1976, Kans. 1977, U.S. Dist. Ct. Kans. 1977. Assoc. Murphy, Morris & Susemihl, Colorado Springs, 1976-78; spl. county atty. El Paso County Colorado Springs, 1977; ptnr. Murphy, Morris & Susemihl, Colorado Springs, 1978-80, Morris, Susemihl, Lohman & Kent, Colorado Springs, 1980-83, Susemihl, Lohman & McDermott, Colorado Springs, 1983—; bd. dirs. Pikes Peak Legal Svcs., Colorado Springs. Author: Handbook for Caseworkers, 1978, Trial Strategy and Preparation in Divorce Cases, 1985, Marital Agreements and the Colorado Marital Agreement Act, 1986. Mem. Juvenile Justice Task Force, Colorado Springs, 1978; pres. Pikes Peak Children's Advocates, Colorado Springs, 1979. Recipient Appreciation cert. Kans. Bar Assn., 1978, Outstanding Guardian ad litem award Pikes Peak Children's Advocates, 1979, Spl. Recognition award Pikes Peak Children's Advocates, 1981. Fellow Am. Acad. Matrimonial Lawyers; mem. ABA, ATLA, Nat. Assn. Counsel for Children (pres. 1979-80), Colo. Bar Assn. (mem. exec. coun. family law sect.), El Paso County Bar Assn. (cert. appreciation 1983, chmn. mental health com. 1980-81, chairperson family com. 1985-86), Assn. Family & Concilliation Cts., Aircraft Owners and Pilots Assn. Family and matrimonial, Probate. Office: Susemihl Lohman & McDermott 660 Southpointe Ct Colorado Springs CO 80906-3874

LOKEN, JAMES BURTON, federal judge; b. Madison, Wis., May 21, 1940; s. Burton Dwight and Anita (Nelson) L.; m. Caroline Brevard Hester, July 30, 1966; children: Kathryn Brevard, Kristina Ayres. BS, U. Wis., 1962; LLB magna cum laude, Harvard U., 1965. Law clk. to chief judge Lumbard U.S. Ct. Appeals (2d Cir.), N.Y.C., 1965-66; law clk. to assoc. justice Byron White U.S. Supreme Ct., Washington, 1966-67; assoc. atty. Faegre & Benson, Mpls., 1967-70, ptnr., 1973-90; gen. counsel Pres.'s Com. on Consumer Interests, Office of Pres. of U.S., Washington, 1970; staff asst. Office of Pres. of U.S., 1970-72; judge U.S. Ct. Appeals (8th cir.), St. Paul, 1991—. Editor Harvard Law Rev., 1964-65. Mem. Minn. State Bar Assn., Phi Beta Kappa, Phi Kappa Phi. Avocations: golf, running. Office: US Courthouse 300 S 4th St Ste 11W Minneapolis MN 55415-0848*

LOKER, F(RANK) FORD, JR. lawyer; b. Balt., Nov. 15, 1947; s. F. Ford and Catherine (Kenny) L.A.B., Coll. Holy Cross, 1969; postgrad. U. Va., 1969-70; J.D. with honors, U. Md., 1973. Bar: Md. 1973, U.S. Dist. Ct. Md. 1978, U.S. Ct. Appeals (4th cir.) 1977, U.S. Supreme Ct. 1980. Asst. state's atty. Office of State's Atty. Balt., 1973-76; asst. atty. gen. Office Atty. Gen. Md., Balt., 1976-81; assoc. Niles, Barton & Wilmer, Balt., 1981-83, ptnr., 1984-86; ptnr. Whiteford, Taylor & Preston, 1987-93; shareholder Church & Houff, P.A., Balt., 1994—; asst. state reporter Adminstrv. Office Cts. Md.-State Reporter, Annapolis, 1983. Mem. exec. bd. Marian House, Inc., 1987—, Tuscany-Canterbury Assn., Balt., 1982-83, pres., 1984-85. Mem. ABA, Def. Research Inst., Md. State Bar Assn., Md. Assn. Def. Trial Counsel (exec. bd. mem. 1985—, editor The Defense Line, 1985-87, treas. 1992-93, sec. 1993-94), Bar Assn. Balt. City (exec. bd. young lawyers sect. 1984-85), mem. exec. bd., chair continuing legal edn. com. 1984-86). Federal civil litigation, State civil litigation, Personal injury. Office: Church & Houff PA 117 Water St Fl 7 Baltimore MD 21202-1044

LOLLI, DON R(AY), lawyer; b. Macon, Mo., Aug. 9, 1949; s. Tony and Erma Naomi (Gerlich) L.; m. Deborah Jo Mrosek, May 29, 1976; children: Christina Terese, Joanna Elyse, Anthony Justin. BA in Econs., U. Mo., 1971, JD, 1974. Bar: Mo. 1974, U.S. Dist. Ct. (we. dist.) Mo. 1974, U.S. Dist. Ct. (ea. dist) Mo. 1996, U.S. Dist. Ct. Kans. 1998, U.S. Ct. Appeals (8th cir.) 1976, U.S. Ct. Appeals (10th cir.) 1979, U.S. Ct. Appeals (3rd cir.) 1992, U.S. Supreme Ct. 1979, U.S. Tax Ct. 1981. Assoc. Beckett & Steinkamp, Kansas City, Mo., 1974-79; mem. Beckett, Lolli and Bartunek, 1980-96, Swanson, Midgley, LLC, Kansas City, 1997—. Lectr. CLE seminar U. Mo. Sch. Law, Kansas City, 1984, 89. Vol. coach Visitation Sch.; co-chair St. Teresa's Acad. Fundraising. Mem. ABA, Mo. Bar Assn., Kansas City Bar Assn., Lawyers Assn. Kansas City, U. Mo. Alumni Assn., Rotary, Beta Theta Pi (asst. gen. sec. 1997—, Tiedman Inn 1973-74, Merit cert. 1974), Phi Delta Phi (pres.). Roman Catholic. Federal civil litigation, State civil litigation, Family and matrimonial. Home: 645 W 62nd St Kansas City MO 64113-1501 Office: Swanson Midgley LLC Crown Ctr 2420 Pershing Rd Ste 400 Kansas City MO 64108-2505 E-mail: dlolli@swansonmidgley.com

LOMBARD, JOHN JAMES, JR. lawyer, writer; b. Phila., Dec. 27, 1934; s. John James and Mary R. (O'Donnell) L.; m. Barbara Mallon, May 9, 1964; children: John James, William M., James G., Laura K., Barbara E. BA cum laude, LaSalle Coll., 1956; JD, U. Pa., 1959. Bar: Pa. 1960. Ptnr. Obermayer, Rebmann, Maxwell & Hippel, Phila., 1959-84; mgr. personal law sect. Morgan Lewis & Bockius LLP, 1985-90, vice-chair personal law sect., 1990-92, chair, 1992-99; spl. counsel McCarter & English LLP, 2000—. Sec., dir. Airline Hydraulics Corp., Phila., 1969—; adv. com. on decedents estates laws Joint State Govt. Commn., 1992—, mem. subcom. on powers of atty., 1993—; co-chair So. Jersey Ethics Alliance, 1993-97. Co-author: Durable Powers of Attorney and Health Care Directives, 1984, 3d edit. 1994; contbr. articles to profl. jours. Bd. dirs. Redevel. Authority Montgomery County, Pa., 1980-87, Gwynedd-Mercy Coll., Gwynedd Valley, Pa., 1980-89, LaSalle Coll. H.S., Wyndmoor, Pa., 1991-97. Recipient Treat award Nat. Coll. Probate Judges, 1992. Mem. ABA (chmn. com. simplification security transfers 1972-76, chmn. mem. com. 1972-82, mem. coun. real property, probate and trust law sect. 1979-85, sec. 1985-87, divsn. dir. probate div. 1987-89, chair elect 1989-90, chair 1990-91,

co-chair Nat. Conf. Lawyers & Corp. Fiduciaries), Pa. Bar Assn. (ho. of dels. 1979-81), Phila. Bar Assn. (chmn. probate sect. 1972), Am. Coll. Trust and Estate Counsel (editor Probate Notes 1983, bd. regents 1986-91, mem. exec. com. 1988-91, elder law com. 1993—), internat. Acad. Estate and Trust Law (exec. com. 1984-88, 90—), Am. Bar Found., Internat. Fish and Game Assn., Union League Club (Phila.), Ocean City Club (N.J.), Marlin and Tuna Club, Ocean City Yacht Club. Estate planning, Probate, Estate taxation. Office: McCarter & English LLP One Commerce Sq Ste 3600 2005 Market St Philadelphia PA 19103

LOMBARDI, DENNIS M. lawyer; b. L.A., May 15, 1951; s. Peter Joseph and Jean (Nelson) L.; m. Suan Choo Lim, Jan. 9, 1993; children: Alexis Jeanne, Erin Kalani. BA, U. Hawaii, 1974; JD summa cum laude, U. Santa Clara, 1977. Bar: Calif. 1977, U.S. Dist. Ct. Hawaii, 1981. Assoc. Frandzel & Share, Beverly Hills, Calif., 1977-79; pvt. practice Capistrano Beach, 1979-81; ptnr. Case, Bigelow & Lombardi, Honolulu, 1982—. Environmental, Land use and zoning (including planning), Real property. Office: Case Bigelow & Lombardi 737 Bishop St Fl 26 Honolulu HI 96813-3201

LOMBARDI, FREDERICK MCKEAN, lawyer; b. Akron, Ohio, Apr. 1, 1937; s. Leonard Anthony and Dorothy (McKean) L.; m. Margaret J. Gessler, Mar. 31, 1962; children: Marcus M., David G., John A., Joseph F. BA, U. Akron, 1960; LLB, Case Western Res., 1962. Bar: Ohio 1962, U.S. Dist. Ct. (no. and so. dists.) Ohio 1964, U.S. Ct. Appeals (6th cir.) 1966. Prin., shareholder Buckingham, Doolittle & Burroughs, Akron, 1962—, chmn. comml. law and litigation dept., 1989-99. Bd. editors Western Res. Law Rev., 1961-62. Trustee, mem. exec. com., v.p. Ohio Ballet, 1985-93; trustee Walsh Jesuit H.S., 1987-90; life trustee Akron Golf Charities, NEC World Series of Golf; bd. mem. Summa Health Sys. Found., Downtown Akron Partnership, St. Hilary Parish Found. Mem. Ohio Bar Assn. (coun. of dels. 1995-97), Akron Bar Assn. (trustee 1991-94, 97-2000, v.p., pres.-elect 1997-98, pres. 1998-99), Case Western Res. U. Law Alumni Assn. (bd. govs. 1995-98), Case Western Res. Soc. Benchers, Fairlawn Swim and Tennis Club (past pres.), Portage Country Club, Pi Sigma Alpha. Democrat. Roman Catholic. General civil litigation, Contracts commercial, Construction. Office: Buckingham Doolittle & Burroughs 50 S Main St Akron OH 44308-1828 E-mail: flombardi@bdblaw.com

LOMBARDO, MICHAEL JOHN, lawyer, educator; b. Willimantic, Conn., Mar. 25, 1927; s. Frank Paul and Mary Margaret (Longo) L.; children: Nancy C., Claire M. BS, U. Conn., 1951, MS, 1961, JD, 1973. Bar: Conn. 1974, U.S. Dist. Ct. Conn. 1975, U.S. Supreme Ct. 1979, U.S. Ct. Appeals (2d cir.) 1980. Div. controller Jones & Laughlin Steel Corp., Willimantic, 1956-67; adminstrv. officer health ctr. U. Conn., Hartford, 1968-69; dir. adminstrv. svcs. South Central Community Coll., New Haven, 1969-70; asst. dir. adminstrn. Norwich (Conn.) Hosp., 1970-77; asst. atty. gen. State of Conn., Hartford, 1977-92; pvt. practice, Willimantic, 1992—. Adj. asst. prof. U. Hartford, 1961-70; adj. prof. bus. Old Dominion U., 1973-81; adj. lectr. in law and bus. Ea. Conn. State U., 1973-2000, disting. adj. faculty, 1990. Vol. Windham Ctr. (Conn.) Fire Dept. Sgt. U.S. Army, 1945-46, 1st lt. USAFR, 1951-53, col. USAFR, 1953-87, col. USAF ret., 1987. Decorated Air Force Meritorious Svc. medal, 1980; named Disting. Mil. Grad., U. Conn., 1950. Mem. AAUP, VFW, ATLA, Internat. Platform Assn., Retired Officers Assn., Conn. Bar Assn., Windham County Bar Assn., Assn. Trial Lawyers Am., Mensa Internat., Am. Legion, Lions (bd. dirs. Willimantic chpt. 1960-64). State civil litigation, Condemnation, Personal injury. Home: 35 Oakwood Dr Windham CT 06280-1520 E-mail: ecsuprof@aol.com

LONABAUGH, ELLSWORTH EUGENE, retired lawyer; b. San Diego, Feb. 24, 1923; s. Alger Wellman and Marion G. (Bailey) L.; m. Carol W. Marr, Dec. 29, 1949 (div. June 1965); children: Marr, Ellsworth, Carol; m. Jean LaValle Miterenga, Dec. 29, 1967; 1 child, Jason. JD, U. Colo., 1950. Bar: Wyo. 1950, Tex. 1951, U.S. Dist. Ct. (so. dist.) Tex. 1951, U.S. Dist. Ct. (fed. dist.) Wyo. 1953, U.S. Ct. Appeals (10th cir.) 1963, U.S. Supreme Ct. 1971. Assoc. Williams & Thornton, Galveston, Tex., 1951-53; ptnr. Lonabaugh & Lonabaugh, Sheridan, Wyo., 1953-71; sr. ptnr. various law firms, 1971-79, Lonabaugh & Riggs, Sheridan, 1980-98, of counsel, 1998-2001. Mem. uniform state laws commn. State of Wyo., 1963-77; city atty. City of Sheridan, 1957; mem. Wyo. Ho. of Reps., Cheyenne, 1955-56, 67-71. Commr. Wyo. Bar, 1972-74; sr. warden St. Peter's Episcopal Ch., 1962-63; chmn. county ctrl. com. Rep. Party, 1966-70. Staff sgt. U.S. Army, 1942-45, ETO. Decorated Bronze Star; recipient Spl. 76 award Sheridan County Commrs., 1976. Mem. Am. Bar Found. (life), Sheridan County Bar Assn. (pres. 1960-61), Sheridan County C. of C. (pres. 1974-75, named Man of Yr., 1975), Am. Legion, DAV, Sheridan Country Club (sec. 1955-59, Phi Delta Phi, Rotary (pres. local chpt. 1972-73), Elks, Shriners, Sigma Chi (pres. 1946-47). Episcopalian. Avocations: golf, sports. Estate planning, Insurance, Real property. Address: 56 Durango Circle Rancho Mirage CA 92270 Fax: 307-672-2230

LONDON, ALAN E. lawyer; b. Pitts., Mar. 13, 1945; BA, Yale U., 1967, JD, 1972. Bar: Pa. 1972. Ptnr. Reed Smith LLP, Pitts. Mem. Phi Beta Kappa. Office: Reed Smith LLP 435 6th Ave Pittsburgh PA 15219-1886

LONDON, JAMES HARRY, lawyer; b. Balt., Dec. 12, 1949; s. Frank and Coral Marie (Calongne) L.; children: Frank T., Charles J. BS, U. Tenn., 1971, JD, 1974. Bar: Tenn. 1974, U.S. Dist. Ct. (ea. dist.) Tenn. 1974, U.S. Ct. Mil. Appeals 1975, U.S. Tax Ct. 1976. Law clk. to judge Joe D. Duncan State Tenn. Criminal Ct., 1971-74; assoc. Bond, Carpenter & O'Connor, Knoxville, Tenn., 1979-80; ptnr. Hogin, London & Montgomery, 1980-91, London Amburn & Thomforde, Knoxville, 1991—; nominated to White House to be fed. dist. judge, 1991. Mem. hearing com. Bd. of Profl. Responsibility Tenn. Supreme Ct., 1991-95. Chmn. Bd. Deacons Lake Forest Presbyn. Ch., 1984, clk. of Session, 1985; active state and local Rep. politics. Served to capt. JAGC, USAF, 1974-79. Mem. ABA, Tenn. Bar Assn. (chmn. interdisciplinary rels. com. 1995-96), Knoxville Bar Assn. (chmn. citizenship com. 1983-89), Am. Legion (comdr. post #126 1983-85). Avocations: fishing, hunting, tennis. State civil litigation, Insurance, Personal injury. Home: 700 Kenesaw Ave Knoxville TN 37919-6661 Office: London & Amburn PC 1716 W Clinch Ave Knoxville TN 37916-2408

LONDRIGAN, JAMES THOMAS, lawyer; b. Springfield, Ill., Feb. 23, 1925; s. James E. and Sophia (Albright) L.; m. Marilyn Jeanne Brust, Apr. 22, 1950; children— Linda, Janet, Timothy, Lisa, Mary Jeanne. J.D., U. Chgo. Kent Sch. Law, 1949. Bar: Ill. 1950, U.S. Dist. Ct. (so dist.) Ill. 1950. City atty. Springfield, Ill., 1958-60; mem. Ill. Ho. Reps., 1969-76; judge Circ. Ct. Ill., Springfield, 1976-81; justice Appellate Ct. Ill., Springfield, 1981-82; ptnr. Londrigan & Londrigan, Springfield, 1983— . Served with AUS, 1943-45. Democrat. Roman Catholic. Clubs: Sangamo, Island Bay Yacht. State civil litigation, Legislative, Personal injury. Home: 3300 Panther Creek Dr Springfield IL 62707-7841 Office: 3300 Panther Creek Dr Springfield IL 62707-7841

LONERGAN, KEVIN, lawyer; b. Racine, Wis., Oct. 2, 1954; s. Ralph and M. Janet L.; m. Elizabeth Ison, Oct. 10, 1981; children: Lindsey, Kristen, Emily, Marc. BS, USAF Acad., 1976; JD, U. Wis., 1979. Bar: Wis. 1979, U.S. Dist. Ct. (we. dist.), Wis. 1979; cert. Nat. Bd. Trial Advocates. Commd. 2nd lt. USAF, 1976, med. retirement, 1977; asst. dist. atty. Eau Claire County, Eau Claire, Wis., 1979-81; assoc. Thompson, Parke & Heim, Ltd., LaCrosse, 1981-82; ptnr., v.p. Herrling, Clark, Hartzheim & Siddall, Ltd., Appleton, 1982—. Apptd. ct. commr. Outagamie County, 1994—; host (TV program) You and the Law, 1988—; regular guest WHBY "Open Line" Radio show, 1995—. Bd. dirs. Eau Claire Kinship Program, 1981; bd dirs., v.p., pres. Casa Clare Half-Way House, Appleton, 1984-87; mem. United Way Cabinet, 1988, 90. Mem. ATLA, Wis. Acad. Trial Lawyers (bd. dirs. 1991—, treas. 1996, sec. 1997, v.p. 1998, pres.-elect 1999, pres. 2000, past pres. 2001), Outagamie County Bar Assn. (sec. 1992-93, v.p. 1993-94, pres. 1994-95). Roman Catholic. Avocations: family, physical fitness. Insurance, Personal injury, Product liability. Home: 44 N Crestway Ct Appleton WI 54913-9510 Office: Herrling Clark Hartzheim & Siddall 800 N Lynndale Dr Appleton WI 54914-3017 E-mail: LKonergan@HerrlingClark.com

LONG, ANDRE EDWIN, law educator, lawyer; b. San Francisco, Dec. 28, 1957; s. Edwin John and Anna (Suss) L.; m. Michele Jean Dubinsky, Oct. 4, 1986; children: Christian Andre, Katrina Marie. BA, U. Pacific, 1979; MBA, Golden Gate U., 1981; JD, Southwestern U., 1982. Bar: Hawaii 1984, D.C. 1990, U.S. Ct. Appeals (9th cir.) 1984. Legal counsel Pure Water, Ltd., Manama, Bahrain, 1982-84; pvt. practice Honolulu, 1984-85; sr. contracts negotiator Litton Data Systems Corp., Van Nuys, Calif., 1985-87; contracts mgr. Eaton, Am. Nucleonics Corp., Westlake Village, 1987-92; owner, broker A. Long Realty, Ridgecrest, 1989—; asst. prof. contract law Air Force Inst. Tech., Dayton, 1992-99; assoc. counsel Navy Office of Gen. Counsel, China Lake, 1999—. Lectr. Tech. Tng. Corp., 1991-92; instr. Oxnard Coll., 1990-92, George Washington U. Law Sch./ESI Govt. Contract Law Program. Author: U.S. Immigration and Visa Laws Made Simple, 1985, 2d edit., 1991, Government Contract Law, 1995, 96, 98, 99, Negotiating Government Contracts, 1996; editor The Clause, 1995-2000, Contract Mgmt. Jour., 1998-2000. Fellow Nat. Contract Mgmt. Assn. (pres. China Lake chpt. 2001-02); mem. Hawaii Bar Assn., D.C. Bar Assn., Aircraft Owners and Pilots Assn., Bd. Contracts Appeals Bar Assn. (chmn. publs. com. 1995-2000, bd. govs. 1997-2000), Canyon Ranch Assn. (chmn. 2000—). Avocations: scuba diving, snow skiing, sailing, flying. Office: NAWCWD Code 111000D 1 Adminstration Cir Ridgecrest CA 93555 E-mail: longae@navair.navy.mil

LONG, CHARLES THOMAS, lawyer, history educator; b. Denver, Dec. 19, 1942; s. Charles Joseph and Jessie Elizabeth (Squire) L.; m. Susan Rae Kircheis, Aug. 9, 1967; children: Brian Christopher, Lara Elizabeth, Kevin Charles. BA, Dartmouth Coll., 1965; JD cum laude, Harvard U., 1970. Bar: Calif. 1971, U.S. Dist. Ct. (cen. dist.) Calif. 1971, U.S. Ct. Appeals (9th cir.) 1975, D.C. 1980, U.S. Dist. Ct. D.C. 1981, U.S. Ct. Claims 1995. Assoc. Gibson, Dunn & Crutcher, Los Angeles, 1970-77, ptnr., 1977-79, Washington, 1979-83; dep. gen. counsel Fed. Home Loan Bank Bd., 1984-85; ptnr. Jones, Day, Reavis & Pogue, 1985-98; grad. tchg. asst. hist. dept. George Washington U., 1998—. Bar: Calif. 1971, U.S. Dist. Ct. (ctrl. dist.) Calif. 1971, U.S. Ct. Appeals (9th cir.) 1975, D.C. 1980, U.S. Dist. Ct. 1981, U.S. Ct. Fed. Claims 1995. Contbr. articles to profl. jours. Mem. Chesapeake Bay Maritime Mus., Friends of the Nat. Maritime Mus., Greenwich, Eng.; pres. Leigh Mill Meadows Assn., Great Falls, Va., 1980. Served to lt. USNR, 1965-67. Mem. ABA, Calif. Bar Assn., D.C. Bar Assn., Coun. for Excellence in Govt., Women in Housing and Fin., Dartmouth Lawyers Assn., Herrington Harbour Sailing Assn. (sec.-treas. 1996), Soc. for Mil. History, N.Am. Conf. on Brit. Studies, Navy Records Soc. (London), U.S. Naval Inst., Chesapeake Bay Maritime Mus., Friends of the Nat. Maritime Mus. (Greenwich, Eng.), Westwood Country Club (Vienna, Va.), Am. Hist. Assn. Republican. Methodist. Avocations: sailing, photography, computers, naval history.

LONG, CLARENCE DICKINSON, III, lawyer; b. Princeton, N.J., Feb. 7, 1943; s. Clarence Dickinson and Susanna Eckings (Larter) L.; children: Clarence IV, Andrew, Amanda, Victoria, Stephen. BA, Johns Hopkins U., 1965; JD, U. Md., 1971; postgrad., Judge Adv. Gen.'s Sch., 1979-80. Bar: Ct. Appeals Md. 1972, U.S. Dist. Ct. D.C. 1972, U.S. Ct. Mil. Appeals 1975, U.S. Supreme Ct. 1976, N.C. 1978, U.S. Ct. Claims 1982, U.S. Ct. Appeals (fed. cir.) 1990. Asst. state's atty., Balt., 1973-74; trial atty., trial team chief Office Chief Trial Atty. Contract Appeals Divsn., U.S. Army, Washington, 1980-84; chief atty. Def. Supply Svc., 1984-87; trial team chief contract appeals divsn. U.S. Army, 1987-92; sr. atty. Sec. Air Force, Office of Gen. Counsel, 1992—. Contbr. articles on Am. Civil War to various periodicals. Lt. col. U.S. Army. Decorated Silver Star, Soldier's medal, Bronze Star, Purple Heart (2), Meritorious Svc. medal (2), Army Commendation medal (2), Cross of Gallantry with gold star, Combat Infantryman's badge, Legion of Merit. Mem. D.C. Bar Assn., N.C. Bar Assn., BCA Bar Assn. (bd. govs.), Federalist Soc., Grant Monument Assn. (trustee). Federalist Soc. Home: PO Box 640 Bowling Green VA 22427-0640 E-mail: longc@pentagon.af.mil, long2502@aol.com

LONG, GREGORY ALAN, lawyer; b. San Francisco, Aug. 28, 1948; s. William F. and Ellen L. (Webber) L..; m. Jane H. Barrett, Sept. 30, 1983; children: Matthew, Brian, Michael, Gregory. BA magna cum laude, Claremont Men's Coll., Calif., 1970; JD cum laude, Harvard U., 1973. Bar: Calif. 1973, U.S. Dist. Ct. (ctrl. dist.) Calif. 1973, U.S. Ct. Appeals (9th cir.) 1976, U.S. Supreme Ct. 1977, U.S. Ct. Appeals (fed. cir.) 1984. Assoc. Overton, Lyman & Prince, L.A., 1973-78, ptnr., 1978-87, Sheppard, Mullin, Richter & Hampton, L.A., 1987—. Arbitrator L.A. Superior Ct). Fellow Am. Bar Found.; mem. ABA (young lawyers divsn. exec. coun. 1974-88, chmn. 1984-85, ho. of dels. 1983-89, exec. coun. litigation sect. 1981-83), Calif. Bar Assn. (del. 1976-82, 87-88), L.A. County Bar Assn. (exec. com. 1979-82, trustee 1979-82, barristers sect. exec. coun. 1976-82, pres. 1981-82, exec. coun. trial lawyers sect. 1984-88, chair amicus briefs com. 1989-92). Federal civil litigation, State civil litigation. Office: Sheppard Mullin Richter & Hampton 333 S Hope St Bldg 48 Los Angeles CA 90071-1406 E-mail: glong@smph.com

LONG, JAMES JAY, lawyer; b. Pitts., Jan. 23, 1959; s. James E. and Barbara E. (Holsberg) L.; m. Tamara Rae Beer, Sept. 7, 1985. AB, U. Chgo., 1981; JD magna cum laude, U. Minn., 1984. Bar: Ill. 1984, U.S. Dist. Ct. (no. dist.) Ill. 1984, Minn. 1988, U.S. Dist. Ct. Minn. 1989. Atty. Winston & Strawn, Chgo., 1984-87; assoc. Briggs & Morgan, St. Paul, 1987-91, shareholder, 1991—. Contbr. articles to profl. jours. Mem. St. Paul Jaycees (v.p. 1989-90, pres. 1993-94), Order of Coif. Democrat. Avocations: travel, sports, horse racing. Antitrust, General civil litigation, Franchising. Office: Briggs & Morgan 2400 IDS Center 80 S 8th St Ste 2400 Minneapolis MN 55402-2157

LONG, LINDA ANN, lawyer; b. Durham, N.C., Feb. 8, 1952; d. Grover Cleveland and Ellen (Parnell) L. BA, U. Del., 1974; JD, Widener U., 1979. Bar: D.C. 1989. Lobbyist Legis. Svcs., Inc., Dover, Del., 1977-79; campaign staff Connally for Pres., Arlington, Va., 1979-80; exec. dir. Reagan-Bush Com. Del., Wilmington, 1980; asst. for legis. affairs Gov. Pierre S. duPont IV, Dover, 1981; regional rep. pub. affairs Gulf Oil Corp., Phila., 1981-83, dir. GULFPAC, area dir. pub. affairs Pitts., 1983-85; pres. Long Cons. Inc., 1985-89; dir. press & pub. liaison with NASA for Christa McAuliffe Challenger 51-L Mission, 1985-86; atty. Montgomery, McCracken, Walker & Rhoads, Washington, 1989-94, Blank, Rome, Comisky & McCauley, Washington, 1994-96; pvt. practice Wilmington, 1996—. State & fed. legislation regulatory affairs, & non profit adv. to state senate campaigns, Del., 1998; adv. to Del. gubanatorial candidate, 1998—; counsel Pa. House Legis. Redistricting, 1991; gen. counsel Women Execs. in State Govt., 1990-95; counsel Nat. Policy Forum, 1993-96; lectr. Internat. Rep. Inst., election law for Macedonia Parliamentary Party Mem., 1992; del. Internat. Observer Mission-Romania Parliamentary & Presdl. Elections, 1992; mem. comml. space transp. adv. com. U.S. Dept. Transp., 1988-90; bd. dirs., exec. com. Air and Space Heritage Coun., 1987—; loaned exec. pub. affairs dept. NASA, 1984-85; sr. adv. to convention mgr. 1992 Rep. Convention. Mem. Rep. Bus. Coun. Del., 1982-83; cons., asst. to chmn. Rep. Nat. Com., 1986-89, dep. polit. counsel, 1987-89, dep. to gen. counsel, 1992-96, life mem.; me. women's adv. bd. Internat. Rep. Inst.; mem. Gov.'s Commn. Status of Women Spkrs. Bur., 1981-83; mem. Wright Meml. Dinner Com., 1985; dir. contract negotiations-ops. 1989 Am. Bicentennial Presdl. Inaugural Com.; mem. Del. Lawyers for George W. Bush for Pres. Mem. Women in Govt. Rels., Am. Petroleum Inst. (com. pub. rels. 1981-84), Rep. Nat. Lawyers Assn. (bd. dirs. 1993—), U.S. Dept. Transp. Comml. Space Transp. (adv. com. 1988-90), Charter 100, Capitol Hill Club. Administrative and regulatory, Private international, Government relations. Office: 32 Harlech Dr Greenville DE 19807 E-mail: lalong1@aol.com

LONG, MICHAEL THOMAS, lawyer, manufacturing company executive; b. Hartford, Conn., Feb. 22, 1942; s. Michael Joseph and Mary Fagan (Maguire) L.; m. Ann Marie O'Connell, Sept. 9, 1967; children: Michael, Maura, Deirdre. BBA, U. Notre Dame, 1964; JD, U. Conn., 1967, postgrad., 1968. Bar: Conn. 1967. Law clk. U.S. Bankruptcy Ct., U.S. Dist. Ct., Hartford, 1966-68; supr. indsl. rels. Ensigh-Bickford Industries, Inc., Simsbury, Conn., 1968-72, contract adminstr., 1972-74, div. controller, 1974-79, mgr. govt. and legal affairs, 1978-81, gen. counsel, sec., 1981-83, v.p., gen. counsel, sec., 1983—. Bd. dirs. Ensign-Bickford Co.; pres., chief exec. officer Ensign-Bickford Haz-Pros Inc., 1989—; U. Notre Dame Alumni Clubs of Greater Hartford scholarship chmn., 1990—; deputy sherif Hartford Co., 1988-2000. Chmn. Dem. Town Com., Simsbury, 1971-81, Dem. State Ctrl. Com. of Conn., 1992-96, Bradley Internat. Airport Com., Windsor Locks, Conn., 1983—; mem. pub. bldg. com. Town of Simsbury, 1981-85, mem. cultural, parks and recreation com., 1986-87; mem. Simsbury Police Comm., 1999—; mem. Simsbury Jr. Achievement, 1970-74; pres. parish council St. Mary's Ch., Simsbury, 1982-85; chmn. Bradley Internat. Airport Commn., 1983-91. Named Home Town Hero Town of Simsbury, 1987; recipient Man of Yr. award U. Notre Dame Alumni Clubs of Greater Hartford, 1995. Mem. ABA, Conn. Bar Assn., Hartford Bar Assn., Inst. Makers of Explosives (bd. govs. 1987—, chmn. legal affairs com. 1986-93, 95—), Am. Corp. Counsel Assn. (bd. dirs. Hartford chpt. 1988-94), Greater Hartford C. of C. (bd. dirs. 1991-94), Internat. Soc. Explosive Engrs., Simsbury Farms Men's Club (founder 1972), Hop Meadow Country Club. Democrat. Roman Catholic. Home: 9 Metacom Dr Simsbury CT 06070-1851 Office: Ensign-Bickford Industries Inc 100 Gristmill Rd PO Box 7 Simsbury CT 06070-0007 E-mail: mtlong@E-BInd.com

LONG, ROBERT HOWARD, JR. lawyer; b. Granville, N.Y., Sept. 13, 1938; s. Robert Howard and Sarah Rebecca (McCauley) L.; divorced; children: Nicole Long Spangler, Sarah R. Long Zook. BA, Shippensburg U., 1965; JD, Dickinson Sch. Law, Carlisle, Pa., 1968. Bar: Pa., Fla., U.S. Supreme Ct. Ptnr. Rhoads & Sinon LLP, Harrisburg, Pa., 1968—. Del. Rep. Nat. Conv., 1976, 80, 84, 88, 90; panelist Pa. Newsmakers, Harrisburg, 1999; bd. dirs., com. chair Shippensburg Univ. Found., 1990—. Mem. ABA (taxation sect.), Pa. Bar Assn., Masons, Scottish Rite, York Rite, Shriners. Republican. Avocations: current affairs, financial markets, economics, big game hunting. Home: 665 Saint Johns Dr Camp Hill PA 17011-1339 Office: Rhoads & Sinon 1 S Market Sq Fl 12 Harrisburg PA 17101-2132 E-mail: rlong@rhoads-sinon.com

LONG, STEPHEN CARREL MIKE, lawyer; b. Roswell, N.Mex., Sept. 22, 1951; s. R.E. (Mike) and Evelyn Marie (Row) Long; m. Barbara I. Lowe, July 19, 1980; children: Jennifer Lynn, Joel Raymond Matthew. BBA with honors, N.Mex. State U., 1973; JD, U. N.Mex., 1977. Bar: N.Mex. 1977, U.S. Dist. Ct. N.Mex. 1977, U.S. Tax Ct. 1977, U.S. Ct. Appeals (10th cir.) 1977, U.S. Supreme Ct. 1982, U.S. Ct. Mil. Appeals 1982. Pvt. practice, Albuquerque, 1977-82, 85-87; assoc. Wheeler, Nye, McElwee & Martone, 1982-84; v.p. Wheeler, McElwee, Sprague & Long, P.C., 1984-85; pres. Long Law Firm, P.A., 1987-90; dir. Long & Thomas, P.A., 1990-91; pvt. practice Placitas, N.Mex., 1992-94; assoc. Ron Koch, P.A., Albuquerque, 1994-2001, Bill Gordon & Assocs., Albuquerque, 2001—. Staff judge adv. N.Mex. Dept. Mil. Affairs, 1980—92; adj. prof. Wayland Bapt. U., 1999—2000. Author: Consumer Bankruptcy Law in New Mexico, 3d edit., 1991; editor Nat. Resources Jour., 1976-77; staff N.Mex. Law Rev., 1975-76; contbr. articles to profl. jours. Trial coach N.Mex. Law Related Edn. Project, 1983-88, 99-2000; bd. dirs., Christian Legal Aid & Referral Svcs., Inc., Albuquerque, 1982-88; chmn., bd. dirs., Hosanna, Inc., Albuquerque, 1986-94. Served to col., N.Mex. Dept. Mil. Affairs. Mem.: Nat. Assn. Criminal Def. Lawyers, N.Mex. State Bar Assn. (bd. dirs. bankruptcy sect. 1990—94, chmn.-elect 1993), N.Mex. Criminal Def. Lawyers Assn., Delta Theta Phi, Sigma Pi. Republican. Baptist. Avocations: cowboy, team roper. Office: 2501 Yale SE Ste 204 Albuquerque NM 87106 E-mail: stevelong@qwest.net

LONG, THAD GLADDEN, lawyer; b. Dothan, Ala., Mar. 9, 1938; s. Lindon Alexander and Della Gladys (Pilcher) L.; m. Carolyn Frances Wilson, Aug. 13, 1966; children: Louisa Frances, Wilson Alexander. AB, Columbia U., 1960; JD, U. Va., 1963. Bar: Ala. 1963, U.S. Dist. Ct. (no. dist., so. dist., mid. dist.) Ala., U.S. Ct. Appeals (11th cir., 5th cir.), U.S. Supreme Ct. Assoc. atty. Bradley, Arant, Rose & White, Birmingham, Ala., 1963-70, ptnr., 1970—. Adj. prof. U. Ala., Tuscaloosa, 1988—, Samford U., Birmingham, 1999—, Cumberland Law Sch., 1999—. Co-author: Unfair Competition Under Alabama Law, 1990, Protecting Intellectual Property, 1990; mem. editl. bd. The Trademark Reporter; contbr. articles to profl. jours. Chmn. Columbia U. Secondary Schs. Com. Ala. Area, 1975—, Greater Birmingham Arts Alliance, 1977-79; trustee, pres. Birmingham Music Club, 2000—; trustee Oscar Wells Trust for Mus. Art, Birmingham, 1983—, Canterbury Meth. Found., 1993—, sec., 1993—; chmn. Entrepreneurship Inst. Birmingham, 1989; vice chmn., trustee Sons Revolution Found., Ala., 1994—; pres. Birmingham-Jefferson Hist. Soc., 1995-97; trustee Birmingham Music Club Endowment, 1995—; mem. Birmingham Com. Fgn. Rels. Mem. U.S. Patent Bar, Internat. Trademark Assn., Am. Law Inst., Ala. Law Inst., Birmingham Legal Aid Soc., Ala. Bar Assn. (chmn., founder bus. torts and antitrust sect.), Biotechnology Assn. of Ala., Inc. (sec. 1998-2001), U. Va. Law Alumni (chmn. Birmingham chpt. 1984-89), S.R. (pres. 1994-95), Gen. Soc. S.R. (gen. solicitor 1994-2000), Am. Arbitration Assn., Order of the Coif, Omicron Delta Kappa. Republican. Methodist. Avocations: travel, writing, table tennis. Antitrust, General civil litigation, Intellectual property. Home: 2880 Balmoral Rd Birmingham AL 35223-1236 Office: Bradley Arant Rose & White 2001 Park Pl Ste 1400 Birmingham AL 35203-2736 E-mail: thadlong@aol.com

LONG, THEODORE JAMES, lawyer; b. Colgate, Wis., July 29, 1935; s. Harlowe W. and Helen L. (King) L.; m. Betty L. Mielke, Sept. 8, 1962; children: Kristine, Theodore James. BS in Mech. Engring., U. Wis., 1958, LLB, 1961. Bar: Wis. 1961, U.S. Dist. Ct. (we. dist.) Wis. 1962, U.S. Dist. Ct. (ea. dist.) Wis. 1974, U.S. Ct. Appeals (7th cir.) 1981, U.S. Ct. Appeals (fed. cir.) 1982, U.S. Supreme Ct. 1995. Ptnr. Lathrop and Clark, and predecessors, Madison, Wis., 1961—. Chmn. bd. dirs. Meriter Hosp., 1996-98, Meth. Hosp., 1982-86; pres. United Madison Cmty. Found., 1981-83, United Way Dane County, 1973. Served to lt. C.E., U.S. Army, 1958. Mem. ABA, Wis. Bar Assn., Am. Intellectual Property Law Assn., Wis. Intellectual Property Law Assn., Rotary (pres. 1974-75). Congregationalist. Patent, Trademark and copyright. Office: PO Box 1507 Madison WI 53701-1507 E-mail: tjl@lathropclark.com

LONG, THOMAS LESLIE, lawyer; b. Mansfield, Ohio, May 30, 1951; s. Ralph Waldo and Rose Ann (Cloud) L.; m. Peggy L. Bryant, Apr. 24, 1982. AB in Govt., U. Notre Dame, 1973; JD, Ohio State U., 1976. Bar: Ohio 1976, U.S. Dist. Ct. (so. dist.) Ohio 1976, U.S. Dist. Ct. (no. dist.) Ohio 1977, U.S. Ct. Appeals (6th cir.) 1978. Assoc. Alexander, Ebinger, Fisher, McAlister & Lawrence, Columbus, Ohio, 1976-82, ptnr., 1982-85,

Baker & Hostetler, Columbus, 1985—. Mem. ABA, Ohio Bar Assn., Columbus Bar Assn., Fed. Bar Assn., Assn. Trial Lawyer Am. Democrat. Roman Catholic. Club: Capitol (Columbus). Federal civil litigation, State civil litigation, Legislative. Home: 2565 Leeds Rd Columbus OH 43221-3613 Office: Baker & Hostetler 65 E State St Ste 2100 Columbus OH 43215-4260

LONG, VIRGINIA, state supreme court justice; m. Jonathan D. Weiner; 3 children. Grad., Dunbarton Coll. of Holy Cross; JD, Rutgers U., 1966. Dep. atty. gen. State of N.J.; assoc. Pitney, Hardin, Kipp and Szuch; dir. N.J. Divsn. Consumer Affairs, 1975; commr. N.J. Dept. Banking, 1977-78; judge N.J. Superior Ct., 1978-84, Appellate Divsn. N.J. Superior Ct., 1984-95, presiding judge, 1995-99; assoc. justice Supreme Ct. N.J., 1999—. Office: Supreme Ct NJ PO Box 023 Trenton NJ 08625-0970*

LONGHI, PATRICK GEORGE, lawyer, educator; b. Hoboken, N.J., Nov. 10, 1953; s. Charles Joseph and Helen Marie (Robertson) L.; m. Patricia Margaret Meyers, Mar. 11, 1989 (div. Sept. 1994); 1 child, Andrew Patrick. BA, Seton Hall U., 1975; JD, Western State U., Fullerton, Calif., 1980. Bar: Ga. 1984, U.S. Dist. Ct. (no. dist.) Ga.; U.S. Ct. Appeals (11th cir.). Law faculty East Cobb Comm. Sch., Marietta, Ga., 1989-93, Kennesaw (Ga.) State U. Continuing Edn., 1989-93, program chair, lectr., 1993—; panel atty. Cobb County Cir. Defender, Marietta, Ga., 1991—, Fed. Defender Program, Atlanta, 1987-91; prin., 1984—; of counsel Law Firm of Raul G. Lomas, Miami, Fla., 1999—. Program chair, lectr. Inst. for Continuing Legal Edn. in Ga., 1998—. Editor: (program books) Ethics and Malpractice, 1994, 95, 96; dir., writer, host: (ednl. film) Lawyers and the Justice System, 1996 (State Bar award 1996). Rules chmn. Cobb County Rep. Party, Marietta, 1994-98; pres. Cobb County Citizens League, Kennesaw, 1990-94. Mem. Sandy Springs Bar Assn. (bd. dirs. 1989—, pres. 1994-96), State Bar of Ga., Ga. Assn. of Criminal Def. Lawyers. Republican. Roman Catholic. Avocations: writing, travel, reading biographies, nature, current events. General civil litigation, Criminal, Personal injury. Office: 120 Northwood Dr NE Ste 202 Atlanta GA 30342-4643

LONGHOFER, RONALD STEPHEN, lawyer; b. Junction City, Kans., June 30, 1946; s. Oscar William and Anna Mathilda (Krause) L.; m. Elizabeth Norma McKenna; children: Adam, Nathan, Stefanie. BMus, U. Mich., 1968, JD, 1975. Bar: Mich. 1975, U.S. Dist. Ct. (ea. dist.) Mich., U.S. Ct. Appeals (6th cir.), U.S. Supreme Ct. Law clk. to judge U.S. Dist. Ct. (ea. dist.) Mich., Detroit, 1975-76; ptnr. Honigman, Miller, Schwartz & Cohn, 1976—, chmn. litigation dept., 1993-96. Co-author: Mich. Court Rules Practice-Evidence, 1998, Courtroom Handbook on Michigan Evidence, 2001, Michigan Court Rules Practice, 1998, Courtroom Handbook on Michigan Civil Procedure, 2001; editor Mich. Law Rev., 1974-75. Served with U.S. Army, 1968-72. Mem. ABA, Detroit Bar Assn., Fed. Bar Assn., U. Mich. Pres.' Club, Order of Coif, Phi Beta Kappa, Phi Kappa Phi, Pi Kappa Lambda. Federal civil litigation, State civil litigation. Home: 46401 W Main St Northville MI 48167-3035 Office: Honigman Miller Schwartz & Cohn 2290 1st National Bldg Detroit MI 48226 E-mail: rsl@honigman.com, longhofer@mediaone.net

LONGSTRETH, ROBERT CHRISTY, lawyer; b. Phoenix, Oct. 11, 1956; s. Robert Daniel and Marion (Petrovich) L.; m. Veronica Marie Platt, May 7, 1988. BA, Haverford Coll., 1978; JD, Yale U., 1981. Bar: N.Y. 1982, U.S. Ct. Appeals (3d cir.) 1982, U.S. Ct. Appeals (9th and 10th cirs.) 1985, U.S. Ct. Appeals (2d and 11th cirs.) 1986, U.S. Ct. Appeals (D.C. cir.) 1988, D.C. 1988, Calif. 1989, U.S. Dist. Ct. (so. dist.) Calif. 1989, U.S. Supreme Ct. 1989. Law clk. U.S. Dist. Ct., N.J., 1981-83; trial atty. U.S. Dept. Justice, Washington, 1983-87; assoc. Wilmer, Cutler & Pickering, 1987-88, Office of Ind. Counsel Lawrence E. Walsh, Washington, 1988-89, Gray, Cary, Ware & Freidenrich, San Diego, 1989—. Judge pro tem San Diego Superior Ct. Author (with Matthew Bender) Handling Federal Tort Claims, 1988—. Mem. ABA, FBA (past pres. San Diego chpt.), Amnesty Internat., Yale Club San Diego (treas., past pres.), Phi Beta Kappa. Democrat. Episcopalian. Federal civil litigation, Environmental, Insurance. Home: 2225 Pine St San Diego CA 92103-1140 Office: Gray Cary Ware & Freidenrich # 1700 401 B St Ste 2000 San Diego CA 92101-4297 E-mail: rlongstreth@graycary.com

LOONEY, JAMES HOLLAND, lawyer; b. Dallas, May 11, 1944; s. Billy Albert and Helen Dorothy (Holland) L. BA, Tex. Christian U., 1967, MDiv, 1970, postgrad., 1970-71; postgrad. New Orleans Bapt. Theol. Sem., 1970-71; JD, Loyola U., 1978. Bar: La. 1978, U.S. Dist. Ct. (ea. dist.) La. 1978, U.S. Dist. Ct. (mid. dist.) La. 1988, U.S. Ct. Appeals (5th cir.) 1978, U.S. Supreme Ct. 1982. Assoc. Murray, Murray, Ellis, Braden & Landry, New Orleans, 1977-78, Gertler & Gertler, New Orleans, 1978-79; pres. James H. Looney, Covington, Calif., 1979— ; arbitrator small claims div. First City Ct. for City of New Orleans, 1986-87; notary pub. St. Tammany Parish, 1978— ; mem. Criminal Justice Panel, Eastern Dist. La., 1982— ; asst. pub. defender St. Tammany and Washington Parishes, 1987-96; exec. dir. La. Appellate Project, ovington, 1996—. Chmn., Interfaith Com., United Way Greater New Orleans, 1972-74; mem. Links com. Tex. Christian U., 1980—; cubmaster Boy Scouts Am., New Orleans, 1975-77; bd. dirs. Christian Ch. La., 1974-77, Citizens for Quality Nursing Care, 1986-87; mem. La. Interch. Conf., 1972-77; v.p. Greater New Orleans Fedn. Chs., 1971-77; active Children's Ctr., Inc., 1972-77; presenter at various seminars on criminal and apllellate practice. Mem. ABA, La. Bar Assn., Covington Bar Assn., La. Assn. of Criminal Def. Lawyers, Theta Phi. Democrat. Christian Ch. Contbr. Articles to profl. jours. E-mail: looney@appellateproject.org. Federal civil litigation, State civil litigation, Criminal. Home: PO Box 3340 Covington LA 70434-3340

LOONEY, WILLIAM FRANCIS, JR. lawyer; b. Boston, Sept. 20, 1931; s. William Francis Sr. and Ursula Mary (Ryan) L.; m. Constance Mary O'Callaghan, Dec. 28, 1957; children: Willam F. III, Thomas M., Karen D., Martha A. AB, JD, Harvard U. Bar: Mass. 1958, D.C. 1972, U.S. Supreme Ct. 1972, U.S. Dist. Ct. (ea. dist.) Mich. 1986. Law clk. to presiding justice Mass. Supreme Jud. Ct., 1958-59; assoc. Goodwin, Procter & Hoar, Boston, 1959-62; chief civil divsn. U.S. Attys. Office, 1964-65; ptnr. Looney & Grossman, Boston, 1965-94, sr. counsel, 1995—. Asst. U.S. atty. Dist. Mass., 1962-65; spl. hearing officer U.S. Dept. Justice, 1965-68; mem. Mass. Bd. Bar Overseers, 1985-91, vice-chmn., 1990-91; corp. mem. Greater Boston Legal Svcs., Inc., 1994—. Mem. Zoning Bd. of Appeals, Dedham, Mass., 1971-74; bd. dirs. Boston Latin Sch. Found., 1981-85, pres. 1981-84, chmn. bd. dirs., 1984-86; trustee Social Law Libr., 1994-97; chmn. ADR adv. com. U.S. Dist. Ct., 1998—. Fellow Am. Coll. Trial Lawyers (state com. 1996—); mem. Mass. Bar Assn. (co-chmn. standing com. lawyers responsibility for pub. svc. 1987-88, chmn. fed. ct. adv. com. Alternative Dispute Resolution 1998—), Boston Bar Assn. (pres. 1984-85, coun. mem. 1985-90, chmn. sr. lawyers sect. 1992-94, Maguire award for professionalism 1995), Nat. Assn. Bar Pres.'s, Boston Latin Sch. Assn. (pres. 1980-82, life trustee 1982—, Man of Yr. 1985), USCG Found. (bd. dirs. 1987-2000, dir. emeritus 2000—), Norfolk Golf Club, Harvard Club, Harvard U. Alumni Assn. (bd. dirs. 2001—). Democrat. Roman Catholic. Home: 43 Coronation Dr Dedham MA 02026-6230 Office: 101 Arch St Fl 9 Boston MA 02110-1112 E-mail: wlooney@lgllp.com, h.wlooney@socialaw.com

LOOTS, JAMES MASON, lawyer; b. Iowa City, May 24, 1958; s. Robert James and Mary (Ladd) L.; m. Ann Marie Stockmeyer; children: Mason S., Karl R. BSJ, Northwestern U., Evanston, Ill., 1980; JD cum laude, Mich. Law Sch., 1984. Bar: D.C. 1984, U.S. Dist. Ct. D.C. 1985, U.S. Dist. Ct. Md., 1992, U.S. Ct. Appeals (D.C. cir.) 1985, U.S. Tax Ct. 1990, U.S. Ct. Fed. Claims 1998, U.S. Ct. Apeals (4th cir.) 2000. Assoc. Skadden, Arps, Slate, Meagher & Flom, Washington, 1984-89, Jones, Day, Reavis & Pogue, Washington, 1989-92; ptnr. Barrymore & Loots, 1992-95, Perry, Simmons & Loots, Washington, 1995-99, Goldstein & Loots, Washington, 1999—. Treas. Worldly Goods, Inc., Washington, 1988-94; adj. prof. Am. U. Wash. Coll. Law, 1990-96. Editorial Bd. Mich. Law Rev., 1982-84. Vol. VISTA, Baton Rouge, 1980-81; v.p. Bedford Springs (Pa.) Festival, 1987-89; adv. bd. Washington Legal Counsel for the Elderly, 1988-97; mem. D.C. Small Bus. Adv. Bd., 1990-99; chmn. D.C. Commn. Human Rights, 1991-2001; bd. dirs. Capitol Hill Assn. Merchants & Profls., 1994-97. Mem. D.C. Bar Assn. (Pro Bono Lawyer of Year, 1988), Washington Coun. Lawyers. Civil rights, General civil litigation, Labor. Office: Goldstein & Loots Ste 801 1700 K St NW Washington DC 20006 E-mail: jloots@goldlootslaw.com

LOPACKI, EDWARD JOSEPH, JR. lawyer; b. Bklyn., June 4, 1947; s. Edward Joseph and Lillian Jane (Wallace) L.; m. Crystal May Miller, June 21, 1969; children: Edward Joseph III, Elizabeth Jane. BA in sociology, Villanova U., 1971; JD, Vt. Law Sch., 1980. Bar: Fla. 1981, U.S. Dist. Ct. (mid. dist.) Fla. 1983, U.S. Ct. Appeals (11th cir.) 1986. Mgmt. trainee Bankers Trust Co., N.Y.C., 1968-72; counselor N.J. State Employment Svcs., Red Bank, 1972-77; pvt. practice Bradenton, Fla., 1981—. Adj. prof. of law Nova U., Ft. Lauderdale, Fla., 1981, Manatee C.C., Bradenton, Fla., 1994-96; cons. Suncoast Ctr. for Ind. Living, 1999-2001. Mem. Fla. Ind. Living Coun., 1996-2000, dist. VI adv. coun. Fla. Dept. Health and Rehabilitative Svcs., 1988-92, Manatee County Health Care Adv. Bd., 1993—, Manatee County Coun. on Access for the Disabled, 1994—, Suncoast Ctr. for Ind. Living, 1995-99; pres. Cen. Soccer Assn., 1981-82; mem. De Soto Boys Club, 1982-87, sec., 1986-87; chmn. edn. com. Manatee Area c. of C., 1983; mem. Manatee Area Youth Soccer Assn., 1981-82, Manatee Coun. on Aging, 1986-87, Boys' Club Manatee County, 1986-87; bd. dirs. Manatee County G.T. Bray Little League East, 1988-89. Mem. Nat. Orgn. Social Security Claimants Reps., Manatee County Bar Assn. (bd. dirs. 1988-89), KC (advocate 1984-85, 88-91), Lions (pres. Manatee River 1985-86, treas. 1987-88, 90-91, sec. 1988-89, Lion of Yr. award 1988, 94). Democrat. Roman Catholic. Avocations: reading, advocacy for civil rights of people with disabilities. Estate planning, Pension, profit-sharing, and employee benefits, Probate. Home: 6612 27th Avenue Dr W Bradenton FL 34209-7405 Office: 5515 21st Ave W Ste C Bradenton FL 34209-5601 E-mail: LopackiLaw@aol.com

LOPATIN, ALAN G. lawyer; b. New Haven, May 25, 1956; s. Paul and Ruth (Rosen) L.; m. Debra Jo Engler, May 17, 1981; children: Jonah Adam, Asa Louis. BA, Yale U., 1978; JD, Am. U., 1981. Bar: D.C. 1981, U.S. Supreme Ct. 1985. Law clk. FMC, Washington, 1980-81; counsel com. on post office and civil svc. U.S. Ho. of Reps., 1981-82, counsel com. on budget, 1982-86, dep. chief counsel, 1986-87, counsel temp. joint com. on deficit reduction, 1986, dep. gen. counsel com. on post office and civil svc., 1987-90, gen. counsel com. on edn. and labor, 1991-94; pres. Ledge Counsel, Inc., 1995—; exec. dir. Nat. and Cmty. Svc. Coalition, 1995-99; ptnr. Valente Lopatin & Schulze, Washington, 1998—. Mem. presdl. task force Health Care Reform, Washington, 1993. Mem. ABA, D.C. Bar Assn., Nat. Assn. Thrift Savs. Plan Participants (pres. 1999—), Nat. Dem. Club, Yale Club (Washington). Democratic. Jewish. Labor, Legislative, Pension, profit-sharing, and employee benefits. Home: 4958 Butterworth Pl NW Washington DC 20016-4354 Office: Valente Lopatin & Schulze 600 14th St NW Fl 5 Washington DC 20007 E-mail: ledgecnsl@aol.com

LOPEZ, A. RUBEN, lawyer; b. San Juan, P.R., Oct. 1, 1955; s. Angel and Elizabeth (Hernandez) L.; m. Magaly Retamar, Oct. 17, 1993; 1 child, Ruben Eduardo. BA in Psychology, SUNY, Buffalo, 1979; JD, U. Toledo, 1982. Bar: Ohio 1992, U.S. Ct. Appeals (6th cir.) 1998, U.S. Supreme Ct. 1998; cert. death penalty appeals Supreme Ct. Ohio, 1997. Instnl. care asst. Dept. Anti-Addiction Svcs., San Juan, 1984; instnl. social worker Dept. Social Svcs., 1984-86; supr. location Child Support Enforcement Program, 1986-88; chief of benefits Bur. Social Security for Chauffeurs, 1988-90; pvt. practice Cleve., 1992-93; atty. Legal Aid Soc. of Columbus, Ohio, 1993-95; asst. state pub. defender Ohio Pub. Defender Office, Columbus, 1995—. Bd. trustees Ct. Apptd. Spl. Advocates of Franklin County, 1994-96, sec. 1995. Mem. Ohio State Bar Assn. SDA. Avocations: camping, jogging. Appellate, Criminal.

LOPEZ, DAVID, lawyer; b. N.Y.C., May 9, 1942; s. Damaso and Carmen (Gonzalez) L.; m. Nancy Mary Cea, Aug. 29, 1964; children: David, Jonathan. AB, Cornell U., 1963; JD, Columbia U., 1966. Bar: N.Y. 1966. Assoc. firm Leon, Weill & Mahoney, N.Y.C., 1966-67, Bressler & Meislen, N.Y.C., 1967-70; individual practice law, 1970—. Chmn. bd. A.T.I. Adv. Svcs., Inc., 1979—; dir. Nancy Lopez, Inc., Southampton, N.Y. Mem. ABA, N.Y. State Bar Assn., Suffolk County Bar Assn. Federal civil litigation, General corporate, Securities. Office: 171 Edge of Woods Rd PO Box 323 Southampton NY 11969-0323 E-mail: davidlopezesq.com@aol.com

LOPEZ, DAVID TIBURCIO, lawyer, educator, arbitrator, mediator; b. Laredo, Tex., July 17, 1939; s. Tiburcio and Dora (Davila) L.; m. Romelia G. Guerra, Nov. 20, 1965; 1 child, Vianei López Robinson. Student, Laredo Jr. Coll., 1956-58; BJ, U. Tex., 1962; JD summa cum laude, South Tex. Coll. Law, 1971. Bar: Tex. 1971, U.S. Dist. Ct. (so. dist.) Tex. 1972, U.S. Ct. Appeals (5th cir.) 1973, U.S. Dist. Ct. (we. dist.) Tex. 1975, U.S. Ct. Claims 1975, U.S. Ct. Appeals (fed. cir.) 1975, U.S. Supreme Ct. 1976, U.S. Dist. Ct. (ea. dist.) Tex. 1978, U.S. Ct. Appeals (11th cir.) 1981, U.S. Ct. Appeals (9th cir.) 1984; cert. internat. com. arbitrator Internat. Ctr. for Arbitration; mediator tng. Atty.-Mediator Inst. Reporter Laredo Times, 1958-59; cons. Mexican Nat. Coll. Mag., Mexico City, 1961-62; reporter Corpus Christi (Tex.) Caller-Times, 1962-64; state capitol corr. Long News Svc., Austin, Tex., 1964-65; publs. dir. Interam. Regional Orgn. of Workers, Mexico City, 1965-67; nat. field rep. AFL-CIO, Washington, 1967-71, publs. dir. Tex. chpt. Austin, 1971-72; pvt. practice Houston, 1971—. Adj. prof. U. Houston, 1972-74, Thurgood Marshall Sch. Law, Houston, 1975-76; mem. adv. com. nat. Hispanic ednl. rsch. project One Million and Counting Tomas Rivera Ctr., 1989-91; mem. adv. bd. Inst. Transnat. Arbitration; charter mem. Resolution Forum Inc.; mem. adv. bd. South Tex. Ctr. Profl. Responsibility; mem. nat. panel of neutrals JAMS/ENDISPUTE, 1996-2000. Bd. dirs. Pacifica Found., N.Y.C., 1970-72, Houston Community Coll., 1972-75; mem. bd. edn. Houston Ind. Sch. Dist., 1972-75. With U.S. Army. Mem. ABA (co-chair, diversity in litig. com.), FBA, ATLA, Tex. Bar Assn. (com. on pattern jury changes), Houston Bar Assn. (com. on alternative dispute resolution), Internat. Bar Assn., Interam. Bar Assn., Bar of U.S. Fed. Cir., Mex.-Am. Bar Assn., Inter-Pacific Bar Assn., Tex.-Mex. Bar Assn. (chair labor com.), Hispanic Bar Assn., World Assn. Lawyers (chair internat. lab. sect.), Am. Judicature Soc., Indsl. Rels. Rsch. Assn., Sigma Delta Chi, Phi Alpha Delta. Democrat. Roman Catholic. Federal civil litigation, Private international, Labor. Home: 28 Farnham Ct Houston TX 77024 Office: 3900 Montrose Blvd Houston TX 77006-4959 E-mail: dtlopez@lopezlawfirm.com

LOPEZ, MARTIN, III, lawyer; b. Las Cruces, N.Mex., June 20, 1954; s. Abenicio Rafael and Angelina Cordelia (Griego) L.; m. Elizabeth Crawford, Aug. 5, 1978; children: Alisa Angelina Maria, Martin IV. BA, U. N.Mex., 1976; JD, George Washington U., 1979; MPA, U. N.Mex., 1982, MBA, 1989. Bar: N.Mex. 1979, U.S. Dist. Ct. N.Mex. 1980, U.S. Ct. Appeals (10th cir.) 1981, U.S. Supreme Ct. 1982, U.S. Ct. Claims 1983, U.S. Tax Ct. 1984, D.C. 1985, U.S. Ct. Appeals (4th and 9th cirs.) 1996. Legal intern State of N.Mex. Property Tax Dept., Santa Fe, 1977, Pub. Defender Svc., Washington, 1977-78, EEOC, Washington, 1978-79; asst. pub. defender State of N.Mex., Albuquerque, 1979-82, asst. atty. gen., 1982-84; ptnr., dir. firm Lopez & Lopez, P.C., 1984-86; prse. Lopez, Lopez & Jaffe, P.C., 1986-87, Martin Lopez III, P.C., Albuquerque, 1988—. Mem. N.Mex. Bar Examiners, 1998—. Past pres. Alternative House, Inc.; past pres., St. Mary's Sch. Bd., 1990—; v.p., St. Pius X H.S. adv. sch. bd., 1999—; mem. coun. Holary Rosary Parish, 1991-98; mem. citizens' adv. group City of Albuquerque, 1992-94; mem. Leadership Albuquerque, 1994. Recipient Alumni award U. N.Mex., 1972. Mem. ABA, N.Mex. State Bar Assn., N.Mex. Hispanic Bar Assn., N.Mex. Trial Lawyers Assn., Assn. Trial Lawyers Am., Albuquerque Hispano C. of C., Greater Albuquerque C. of C., Albuquerque Jaycees, Socorro County C. of C., Phi Alpha Theta, Pi Alpha Alpha, Phi Alpha Delta. Democrat. Roman Catholic. General civil litigation, Contracts commercial, Criminal. Home: 6124 Carousal Ave NW Albuquerque NM 87120-2171 Office: 1500 Mountain Rd NW Albuquerque NM 87104-1359 E-mail: ML3law@aol.com

LOPEZ-CAMPILLO, JUAN CARLOS, lawyer; b. Havana, Cuba, July 30, 1962; came to U.S., 1971; s. Lino B. Lopez and Gloria Abella; m. Millie Lopez, July 28, 1990; 1 child, Amber. AA with honors, Miami-Dade C.C., 1987; BS, Fla. Internat. U., 1994; JD with honors, St. Thomas U., 1997; LLM, Georgetown U., 1998. Bar: Fla., U.S. Dist. Ct. (mid. dist.) Fla. 1998. Assoc. Jackson, Lewis, Schnitzler & Krupman, Orlando, Fla., 1998—. Sr. articles editor St. Thomas Law Rev., 1996-97. Republican. Roman Catholic. Labor. Office: Jackson, Lewis, Schnitzler & Krupman 390 N Orange Ave Ste 1285 Orlando FL 32801

LORA, GERMAN LINO, lawyer; b. Lima, Peru, Mar. 7, 1973; s. Ricardo Lora and Mercedes Alvarez. BS, U. Lima, 1996; Rsch. Specialist, U. Cath., Lima, 1999; Curso de post Grado en Derecho, U. Salamanca, Spain, 2000. Assoc. KPMG Peru, Lima, 1996—. Prof. U. Lima, 1999-01, U. Garcilazo de la Vega, 2000-01. Avocations: cinema, soccer. Office: KPMG Peru/Av Javier Prado Oeste 203 San Isidro Lima 27 Peru

LORBER, LAWRENCE ZEL, lawyer; b. Bklyn., Jan. 16, 1947; s. Morris and Shirley (Breslow) L.; m. Judith Prins, June 27, 1971; children— Daniel Ari, Rachel Prins. B.A., Bklyn. Coll., 1967; J.D., U. Md., 1970. Bar: D.C. 1970, N.Y. 1971, U.S. Ct. Appeals (D.C. cir.) 1979, U.S. Ct. Appeals (9th cir.) 1980, U.S. Supreme Ct. 1976. Clk. Md. Ct. Appeals, Annapolis, Md., 1971-72; atty. Solicitor's Office, Dept. Labor, Washington, 1972-73; exec. asst. to solicitor of labor, Washington, 1974-75, dep. asst. sec. labor, 1975-77; assoc. Breed, Abbott & Morgan, Washington, 1977-78, ptnr., 1978-89; ptnr. Kelley, Drye & Warren, 1989-91; ptnr. Verner, Liipfert, Bernhard, McPherson & Hand, Washington, 1992—; mem. labor law adv. council Nat. Assn. Mfrs., Washington, 1980— ; mem. EEO task force U.S. C. of C., 1979-81. Author: Fear of Firing, 1984; Sex and Salary, 1985, Fear Itself, 1987 . Trustee, Bklyn. Coll. Found., 1979-82. Served to 1st lt. USAR, 1970-75. Mem. ABA, Fed. Bar Assn., D.C. Bar Assn. Republican. Jewish. Labor, Pension, profit-sharing, and employee benefits. Home: 5816 Midhill St Bethesda MD 20817-6173 Office: Verner Liipfert et al 901 15th St NW Ste 700 Washington DC 20005-2327

LORD, BARBARA JOANNI, lawyer; b. Bay Shore, N.Y., Aug. 7, 1939; d. Theodore and Doris Aileen (Smith) Joanni; m. Robert Wilder Lord, June 24, 1967. BA, U. Miami, 1961; JD, NYU, 1966. Bar: N.Y. 1967, Fla. 1978, U.S. Supreme Ct. 1991. Asst. editor Am. Best Co., N.Y.C., 1961-64; contract analyst Guardian Life Ins. Co., 1964-66; legal trainee N.Y. State Liquor Auth., 1966-67, atty., 1967-70, sr. atty., 1970-80, assoc. atty., 1980—. Mem. ABA, N.Y. State Bar Assn., Fla. Bar Assn., Order Ea. Star. Administrative and regulatory. Office: N Y State Liquor Authority 11 Park Pl New York NY 10007-2801

LORE, STEPHEN MELVIN, lawyer; b. Smithfield, N.C., Nov. 11, 1956; s. Edwin Payne and Miriam Angelea (Lassiter) L.; m. Katharine Sewell, July 27, 1985. BA, Wake Forest U., 1979; JD, U. N.C., 1982. Bar: Ga 1982, U.S. Ct. Appeals (11th cir.) 1982, U.S. Supreme Ct. 2001. Assoc. Freeman & Hawkins, Atlanta, 1982-99; ptnr. Smith, Helms, Mullis & Moore, LLP, 1999—2001, Nelson, Mullins, Riley & Scarborough, L.L.P., 2001—. Mem. ABA, State Bar Ga., Atlanta Bar Assn., Fedn. Ins. and Corp. Counsel, Phi Beta Kappa, Omicron Delta Epsilon. Republican. Presbyterian. Avocations: golf, tennis, gardening. Federal civil litigation, State civil litigation, Personal injury. Home: 2795 Wyngate Dr NW Atlanta GA 30305-2852 E-mail: sml@nmrs.com

LORENTZEN, JOHN CAROL, lawyer; b. Ft. Carson, Colo., Mar. 6, 1955; s. Carol Edward and Marilyn Martha (Jens) L.; m. Penney Louise Fillmer, March 14, 1981; Katherine Penney, Emily Jeanne, David Fillmer. BBA, BA, Drake U., 1977; JD, U. Chgo., 1980. Bar: Ill. 1980, U.S. Dist. Ct. (no. dist.) 1980, U.S. Tax Ct. 1981. Assoc. Winston & Strawn, Chgo., 1980-87, ptnr., 1987; v.p. The Deerpath Group, Lake Forest, Ill., 1987-90, mng. dir., 1990-92; ptnr. Mayer, Brown & Platt, Chgo., 1992-93; capital ptnr. Winston & Strawn, 1993—. Contbr. articles to profl. jours.; creator The Law Sch. Game. Mem. ABA. Avocations: splitting wood, hiking, walking. General corporate, Public utilities, Corporate taxation. Office: Winston & Strawn 35 W Wacker Dr Ste 4200 Chicago IL 60601-1695 E-mail: jlorentz@winston.com

LORIA, MARTIN A. lawyer; b. N.Y.C., Apr. 11, 1951; s. Daniel Bernard and Estelle Miriam (Barasch) L.; m. Carol Berkowitz, June 3, 1973; children: Alyson, Marissa. BA, SUNY, Albany, 1972; JD, Suffolk U., 1975. Bar: Mass. 1975, U.S. Dist. Ct. Mass. 1976, U.S. Supreme Ct. 1979. Atty. New Eng. states counsel Lawyers Title Ins. Corp., Boston, 1979-82; ptnr. Adelson, Golden & Loria, P.C., 1983-2000, Cherwin Theise Adelson & Loria LLP, Boston, 2001—. Mem. ABA, Mass. Bar Assn., Boston Bar Assn., Mass. Conveyancers Assn. (pres. 1991, bd. dirs. 1988-2000), Abstract Club (bd. dirs.). Banking, Real property. Office: Cherwin Theise Adelson & Loria One Internat Place Boston MA 02110 E-mail: mloria@ctallaw.com

LORNE, SIMON MICHAEL, lawyer; b. Hampton, Eng., Feb. 1, 1946; came to U.S., 1952, naturalized, 1961; s. Henry Thomas and Daphne Mary (Brough) L.; AB cum laude, Occidental Coll., 1967; JD magna cum laude, U. Mich., 1970; children: Christopher, Michele, Allison, Nathan James, Katrina. Admitted to Calif. bar, 1971; assoc. firm Munger, Tolles & Olson, L.A., 1970-72, ptnr., 1972-93; gen. counsel U.S. SEC, 1993-96; mng. dir. Salomon Bros. Inc., 1996—; vis. assoc. prof. law U. Pa., 1977-78, acting dir. Ctr. Study of Fin. Instns., 1977-78; lectr. in law, corp. fin. U. So. Calif., 1986-88. Author: Acquisitions and Mergers: Negotiated and Contested Transactions, 1985. Mem. L.A. Mayor's Com. on Internat. Trade Devel., 1979-81; bd. dirs., sec. L.A. Internat. Trade Devel. Corp., 1982-85; mem. adv. com. to U.S. Senator S.I. Hayakawa on Internat. Trade, 1979-82; bd. govs. Econ. Literacy Coun. Calif., 1981-87; mem. Nat. Legal Adv. Commn., Nat. Assn. Security Dealers, 1988-93. Served with USMCR, 1967-68. Mem. L.A. Area C. of C. (exec. com., internat. commerce com., leadership mission to People's Republic of China, 1980), ABA, L.A. County Bar Assn. (exec. com. bus. and corps. law sect., chmn. 1984-85), Calif., Jonathan Club. Republican. Roman Catholic. General corporate, Mergers and acquisitions, Securities.

LORY, LORAN STEVEN, lawyer; b. Phoenix, July 11, 1961; s. Marvin and Lee (Shain) L.; m. Diane Tabachman, Aug. 4, 1984. JD, Thomas Jefferson Sch. Law, 1984. Bar: Calif., U.S. Dist. Ct. (so. dist.) Calif., U.S. Dist. Ct. Ariz. Legal documentation coord. Ernest W. Hahn Co., San Diego, 1984-86; pvt. practice, 1986—. Mem. Juvenile Justice Bar Assn. Avocations: golf, tennis, boating. General civil litigation, Insurance, Juvenile.

LOSCALZO, ANTHONY JOSEPH, lawyer; b. Bklyn., May 13, 1946; s. Frank Anthony and Frances (Puliatti) L.; m. Kathryn Mary Pica, Aug. 4, 1973. BBA, St. John's U., 1967, JD, 1969. Bar: N.Y. 1969, Fla. 1971, U.S. Dist. Ct. (so. and ea. dists.) N.Y. 1973, U.S. Ct. Appeals (2d cir.) 1975, U.S. Supreme Ct. 1975. Ptnr. Loscalzo & Loscalzo, P.C., N.Y.C., 1981—. Mem. ABA, Assn. Trial Lawyers Am., Fla. Bar Assn., N.Y. State Trial Lawyers Assn., N.Y. State Bar Assn. State civil litigation, Personal injury, Workers' compensation. Office: Loscalzo & Loscalzo PC Ste 408 14 E 4th St Apt 408 New York NY 10012-1141 E-mail: aloscalzo@lozcalzolaw.com

LOSEY, RALPH COLBY, lawyer; b. Daytona Beach, Fla., May 26, 1951; s. George Spar and Alix (Colby) L.; m. Molly Isa Friedman, July 7, 1973; children: Eva Merlinda, Adam Colby. Student, Inst. European Studies, Vienna, Austria, 1971; BA, Vanderbilt U., 1973; JD cum laude, U. Fla., 1979. Bar: Fla. 1980, U.S. Dist. Ct. (mid. dist.) Fla. 1980. Assoc. Subin, Shams, Rosenbluth & Moran, Orlando, Fla., 1980-84; ptnr. Katz, Kutter, Haigler, Alderman, Bryant & Yon, P.A., 1984—. Author: Laws of Wisdom, 1994, Your Cyber Rights and Responsibilities: Using the Internet, 1996; contbr. articles to profl. jours. Pres. Sch. of Wisdom, Fla. Mem. Fla. Bar Assn., Orange County Bar Assn., Computer Law Assn. Democrat. Avocations: computers, golf, music, philosophy, reading. Federal civil litigation, State civil litigation, Computer. Home: 1661 Woodland Ave Winter Park FL 32789-2774 Office: Katz Kutter Haigler Alderman Bryant & Yon PA PO Box 4950 Orlando FL 32802-4950 E-mail: ralphl@katzlaw.com

LOTITO, NICHOLAS ANTHONY, lawyer; b. Neptune, N.J., June 19, 1949; s. Nicholas and Grace (Pascazio) L. BA, Emory U., 1971; JD, U. Va., 1975. Bar: Ga. 1975, U.S. Dist. Ct. (no. dist.) Ga., U.S. Ct. Appeals (4th, 5th, 11 cirs.). Atty. FTC, Atlanta, 1975-76; trial atty. Antitrust Div. U.S. Dept. Justice, 1976-82; of counsel Fierer & Westby, 1983-89; ptnr. Davis, Zipperman, Kirschenbaum & Lotito, 1989—. Contbr. articles to profl. jours. Mem. NACDL, ABA (criminal and antitrust sects.), Atlanta Bar Assn. (task force mcpl. ct. reform 1986), Ga. Assn. Criminal Def. Lawyers (past pres., exec. com., chmn. amicus com.), Lamar Inn of Ct. Democrat. Avocations: sports, writing. Antitrust, Criminal. Home: 1055 Alta Ave NE Atlanta GA 30307-2512 Office: Davis Zipperman Kirschenbaum & Lotito 918 Ponce De Leon Ave NE Atlanta GA 30306-4212 E-mail: nick@dzkl.com

LOTSTEIN, JAMES IRVING, lawyer; b. Steubenville, Ohio, Jan. 27, 1944; s. Jack and Dorothy (Nach) L.; m. Paulette L. Gutcheon, June 25, 1972; children: Melissa A., Amanda J. BSBA, Northwestern U., 1965; JD, U. Conn., 1968. Bar: Conn. 1969, U.S. Ct. Appeals (2d cir.) 1971, U.S. Supreme Ct. 1972. From assoc. to ptnr. Hoppin, Carey & Powell, Hartford, Conn., 1969-86; ptnr. Cummings & Lockwood, 1986—, ptnr.-in-charge, 1988-95, chmn. dept. Mid Market Practice Group, 2001—. Author: An Introduction to the Connecticut Business Corporation Act, 1994, Ten Things You Can Do Now to Prepare for the New Connecticut Business Corporation Act, Connecticut Business Corporation Act Sourcebook, New Indemnification Provisions of the Conneticut Business Corporation Act, 1997, Why Choose Connecticut? Advantages of the Connecticut Business Corportion Act Over the Delaware General Corporation Law, 2000. Trustee Conn. Pub. Broadcasting, Inc., Conn. Policy and Econ. Coun., Inc., 1990, exec. com., 1995—, Conn. Pub. Broadcasting, Inc.; mem. Sec. of State's bus. adv. com. State of Conn.; active Am. Coll. Investment Counsel; mem. Econ. Devel. Agy., Canton, Conn., 2001— 1st lt. JAGC, USAR, 1968-74. Mem. ABA (chmn. dirs. and officers task force, mem. corp. laws com. 1992), Conn. Bar Assn. (chmn. mcpl. law and govtl. svc. com. 1981-82, chmn. bus. law sect. 1990-92, co-chmn. Conn. bus. corp. act task force 1993-98). Banking, General corporate, Mergers and acquisitions. Office: Cummings & Lockwood City Pl I Hartford CT 06103

LOTTER, CHARLES ROBERT, corporate lawyer, retail company legal executive; b. 1937; married. BA, St. Johns U., 1959, JD, 1962; LLM, NYU, 1969. With anti-trust div. U.S. Dept. Justice, 1962-65; with Revere Copper & Brass, Inc., 1965-69, Del E. Webb Corp., 1969-70, Louis O. Kelso, 1970-71, J.C. Penney, Dallas, 1971—, sr. v.p., 1987—; sec., gen. counsel, 1987-93; exec. v.p., 1993. V.p., sec. JCP Realty, Inc.; sec. J.C. Penney Properties, Inc., J.C. Penney Funding Corp. With USAFR, 1962-64, lt. USNR, 1964-70. Office: J C Penney Co Inc 6501 Legacy Dr Plano TX 75024-3698

LOTVEN, HOWARD LEE, lawyer; b. Springfield, Mo., Apr. 8, 1959; s. Isadore and Gytel (Tuchmeier) L.; m. Charlotte Lotven. BA, Drake U., 1981; JD, U. Mo., Kansas City, 1984. Bar: Mo. 1984, U.S. Dist. Ct. (we. dist.) Mo. 1984. Pvt. practice, Kansas City, 1984—; asst. prosecutor City of Kansas City, 1985. Prosecutor City of Harrisonville (Mo.), 1989-91, atty., 1989-91; prosecutor City of Napoleon, Mo., 2001—. Mem. B'nai B'rith Dist. II, 1977-97; judge Mo. Sta H.S. Moot Ct. Competition, 1992; Hyde Park Crime Patrol, 1985-91, Hyde Park Assn. Zoning and Planning Commn., 1993-97; vol. Heartland United Way, 1995; trustee Pilgram Chapel, 2001—, Heart of Am. Stand Down, 2001. Mem. ABA, Mo. Bar Assn. (young lawyers coun. 1986-88, lectr. 1987-90, criminal law com. 1989—, gen. practice law com. 1990—, co-chair criminal law com. 1991-92, exec. coun. gen. practice law com. 1993-99, Law Day spkr. 1986, 96, lectr. 1987-90, 92, 97), Kansas City Bar Assn. (mcpl. cts. com., Vol. Atty. Project, 1992—, Vol. Atty. Project award winner 1994, continuing edn. spkr. 2000—), House Rabbit Soc., Delta Theta Phi, Omicron Delta Kappa, others. Democrat. Jewish. Avocation: sports. General civil litigation, Criminal, Municipal (including bonds). Office: PO Box 15055 Kansas City MO 64106-0055

LOTWIN, STANFORD GERALD, lawyer; b. N.Y.C., June 23, 1930; s. Herman and Rita (Saltzman) L.; m. Judy Scott, Oct. 15, 1994; children: Lori Hope, David. BS, Bklyn. Coll., 1951, LLB, 1954, LLM, 1957. Bar: N.Y. 1954, U.S. Supreme Ct. 1961, Pa. 1986. Ptnr. Blank Rome Tenzer, Greenblatt LLP, N.Y.C., 1987—; of counsel Frankfurt, Garbus, Klein & Selz, 1983-87. Served with U.S. Army, 1954-56. Fellow Am. Acad. Matrimonial Lawyers (bd. of mgrs. 1984—); mem. N.Y. State Bar Assn. (family law sect.), N.Y. County Trial Lawyers (lectr. 1980—), Internat. Acad. Matrimonial Attys. Family and matrimonial. Office: 405 Lexington Ave New York NY 10174-0002

LOUBET, JEFFREY W. lawyer; b. Mt. Vernon, N.Y., May 12, 1943; s. Nathaniel R. and Joan (Fleischer) L.; m. Susan Maria Thom, Aug. 29, 1972 (div. Dec. 1997); 1 child, Thom Carlyle; m. Yvonne Phelps, Feb. 26, 1998. BA, Colgate U., 1965; JD, St. John's U., 1968; LLM in Taxation, N.Y. U., 1970. Bar: N.Y. 1968, U.S. Tax Ct. 1969, U.S. Dist. Ct. (so. dist.) N.Y. 1969, N.Mex. 1976, U.S. Dist. Ct. N.Mex. 1977. Assoc. Poletti, Freidin, Prashker, Feldman & Gartner, N.Y.C., 1969-76; ptnr. Modrall, Sperling, Roehl, Harris & Sisk, Albuquerque, 1976-94; counsel Rodey, Dickason, Sloan, Akin & Robb, 1994-2000; pvt. practice, 2000—. Lectr. N.Mex. Estate Roundtable, Albuquerque, 1979—; vis. prof. Estate and Gift Tax U. N.Mex., Albuquerque, 1988-89. Contbr. articles to profl. jours. Mem. Lovelace Respiratory Rsch. Inst. Estate Planning Adv. Coun., 1993—; mem. adv. bd. on charitable giving Albuquerque Cmty. Found., 1995—; bd. dirs. Wheels Mus. Masters World Record Holder, high hurdles and decathlon. Fellow Am. Coll. Trust and Estate Counsel (mem. estate and gift com.); mem. ABA (chair N. Mex. property tax com.), N.Mex. Estate Planning Coun., Greater Albuquerque C. of C. (chair tax task force, 1992, chair state govt. com., 1993), YMCA (mem. bd. dirs.). Avocations: track & field, skiing, fly fishing. Estate planning, Taxation, general, State and local taxation. Home: PO Box 3754 Albuquerque NM 87190-3754 Office: Loubet Law Firm 6301 Indian School Rd NE Albuquerque NM 87110-8103

LOUGHRIDGE, JOHN HALSTED, JR. lawyer; b. Chestnut Hill, Pa., Oct. 30, 1945; s. John Halsted Sr. and Martha Margaret (Boyd) L.; m. Amy Claire Booe, Aug. 3, 1980 (div. Apr. 1995); 1 child, Emily Halsted. AB, Davidson Coll., 1967; JD, Wake Forest U., 1970. Bar: N.C. 1970, U.S. Dist. Ct. 1970, U.S. Ct. Mil. Appeals 1986. Divsn. head, v.p., counsel Wachovia Mortgage Co., Winston-Salem, N.C., 1971-79; sr. v.p., counsel Wachovia Bank, 1980—. Mem. UCC Article 5 drafting com. N.C. Gen. Statutes Commn., 1999. Mem. cabinet, chair profl. divsn. United Way Forsyth County, 1994. Col. JAGC, USAR, 1970-2000. Mem. ABA (corp., banking and bus. law sect. 1970—, internat. law and practice sect. 1999—), N.C. Bar Assn. (internat. law sect. 1984—, fin. instns. com. 1985—, real property sect. 1971—, governing coun. 1988-91, bus. law sect. 1971—, corp. counsel sect. 1989—, governing coun. 1992-98, treas., 1999-00, sec. 2000-2001, vice chair 2001-2002, real property curriculum com. 1990-93, bus. law curriculum com. 1999—), N.C. State Bar, N.C. Coll. of Advocacy, Forsyth County Bar Assn., Am. Corp. Counsel Assn. (v.p., bd. dirs. N.C. chpt. 1988-98, 2001—, comml. law com. 1996—), Mortgage Bankers Assn. of Am. (legal issues com. 1982-92, fin. affiliates com. 1988-92), Res. Officers Assn. (chpt. pres. 1996-97, sec. 1997—), Alumni Assn. (bd. dirs. 2001-2004), Union League (Phila.), Twin City Club (sec. 1990-97, gov. 1994—, pres. 1997-2001), Forsyth Country Club, Phi Delta Phi, Phi Delta Theta. Republican. Presbyterian. Avocations: golf, tennis. Banking, General corporate, Private international. Home: 615 Arbor Rd Winston Salem NC 27104 Office: Wachovia Bank 100 N Main St Winston Salem NC 27101 E-mail: john.loughridge@wachovia.com

LOUIS, PAUL ADOLPH, lawyer; b. Key West, Fla., Oct. 22, 1922; s. Louis and Rose Leah (Weinstein) L.; m. Nancy Ann Edgeworth Lapof, Dec. 28, 1971; children: Louis Benson, IV, Connor Cristina and Marshall Dore (twins). B.A., Va. Mil. Inst., Lexington, 1947; LL.B., U. Miami, Fla., 1950, J.D., 1967. Bar: Fla. 1950, U.S. Dist. Ct. (so. dist.) Fla. Asst. state atty., 1955-57; atty. Beverage Dept. Fla., 1957-60; spl. asst. atty. gen. State of Fla., 1970-71; partner firm Sinclair, Louis, Heath, Nussbaum & Zavertnik (P.A.), Miami, 1960—; mem. Fed. Jud. Nominating Commn., 1977-80; mem. peer rev. com. U.S. Dist. Ct. for So. Dist. Fla., 1983-85. Author: Defamation, How Far Can You Go, Trial and Tort Trends, 1969; contbr.: chpts. to Fla. Family Law, 1967, 72. Founder mem. Palm Springs Gen. Hosp. Scholarship Com., 1968; mem. Dade County Health Facilities Authority, 1979-82; trustee Fla. Supreme Ct. Hist. Soc., 1994—. Served to 1st lt. USAAF, 1943-45, ETO, maj. USAF Res., 1962. Decorated Air medal with five oak leaf clusters, Bronze Star (7), Purple Heart. Mem. ABA, Fla. Bar (bd. cert. civil trial lawyer and marital and family law, bd. govs. 1970-74), Dade County Bar Assn. (dir. 1954-55, 66-69), Am. Judicature Soc., Va. Mil. Inst. Alumni Assn. Democrat. Jewish. Club: Miami, Bath. Home: 4411 Palm Ln Miami FL 33137-3346 Office: 1125 A I duPont Bldg 169 E Flagler St Miami FL 33131-1210

LOUNSBURY, STEVEN RICHARD, lawyer; b. Evanston, Ill., July 26, 1950; s. James Richard and Reba Jeanette (Smith) L.; m. Dianne Louise Daley, Apr. 16, 1983; children: Jimson, Cody, Richard. BA, U. Calif., Santa Barbara, 1973; JD, U. West L.A., 1977. Bar: Calif. 1979, Oreg. 1997, U.S. Dist. Ct. (cen. dist.) Calif. 1979, U.S. Dist. Ct. Oreg. 1999. Pvt. practice, L.A., 1979-83; contract atty. FAA, 1981; trial atty. Hertz Corp., 1983-86; mng. counsel 20th Century Ins. Co., Woodland Hills, Calif., 1986-94; mng. atty. Lounsbury and Assocs., Brea, 1986-94; sr. trial atty. Bollington, Lounsbury and Chase, 1994-99; asst. county counsel Coos County, Coquille, Oreg., 1999—. Arbitrator Orange County Superior Ct., Santa Ana, Calif., 1992-99. Dir. internat. rels. Rotary Internat., Venice-Marina Club, Calif., 1980-81; dir. L.A. Jr. C. of C., 1981-82, chmn. westside com. 1980-81. Mem. ABA, Calif. Bar Assn., Oreg. Bar Assn., Calif. House Counsel (bd. dirs., chmn. membership 1993-94). Avocations: music (flute, choral), travel. Government contracts and claims, Land use and zoning (including planning), State and local taxation. Office: Coos County Office Legal Counsel 250 N Baxter St Coquille OR 97423-1852 E-mail: slounsbury@co.coos.or.us

LOURIE, ALAN DAVID, federal judge; b. Boston, Jan. 13, 1935; AB, Harvard U., 1956; MS, U. Wis., 1958; PhD, U. Pa., 1965; JD, Temple U., 1970. Bar: Pa. 1970. Chemist Monsanto Co., St. Louis, 1957-59; lit. scientist, chemist, patent agt. Wyeth Labs., Radnor, Pa., 1959-64; counsel Smith Kline Beecham Corp., Phila., 1964-90; successively as patent agt., atty., dir. corp. patents, asst. gen. counsel, v.p. corp. patents Smith Kline Beechum Corp.; cir. judge U.S. Ct. Appeals (fed. cir.), Washington, 1990—. Mem. Judicial Conf. Com. on Financial Disclosure, 1990-98; mem. U.S. del. to Diplomatic Conf. on Revision of Paris Conv. for Protection of Indsl. Property, 1982, 84; vice chmn. industry functional adv. com. to U.S. Trade Rep. and Dept. Commerce, 1987-90; chmn. U.S. group of U.S.-Japan Bus. Coun. Task Force on Patents. Bd. visitors Law Sch., Temple U. Mem. ABA, Phila. Patent Law Assn. (pres. 1984-85), Am. Intellectual Property Law Assn. (bd. dirs. 1982-85), Assn. Corp. Patent Counsel (treas. 1987-89), Pharm. Mfrs. Assn. (chmn. patent com. 1981-86), Am. Chem. Soc., Cosmos Club, Harvard Club Washington. Office: US Ct Appeals Fed Cir 717 Madison Pl NW Washington DC 20439-0002

LOVE, GEORGE H., JR. lawyer; b. Latrobe, Pa., Dec. 30, 1943; m. Joann A. Love, Aug. 16, 1969; children: George H. III, Jennifer A. BA, Wabash Coll., 1966; JD, Duquesne U., 1973. Bar: Pa. 1973, U.S. Dist. Ct. (we. dist.) Pa. 1973, U.S. Supreme Ct. 1976. Various positions VA, Pitts., 1970-76, atty. Dist. Counsel's Office, 1977-81, asst. dist. counsel, 1981-95, prin. sr. atty. Regional Counsel's Office, 1995-98, asst. regional counsel, 1998-2001. Cpl. USMC, 1967-68, Viet Nam; lt. JAB, U.S. Navy. Home: RR 4 Box 105B Latrobe PA 15650-9217 Office: PO Box 594 Youngstown PA 15696-0594 E-mail: GHLove1000@aol.com

LOVE, LINDA C. lawyer; b. Valdosta, Ga., Feb. 6, 1954; d. Donald F. Love and Donna A. McClendon; m. Don Williams, Mar. 18, 2001; children: Megan, Lisa. JD, Willamette U., 1981; BA, U. No. Colo., 1976. Bar: Oreg. 1981. Assoc. Olson Law Firm, Salem, Oreg., 1981-83; staff atty. Workers' Compensation Bd., 1983-84; assoc. Churchill, Leonard Law Firm, 1984-86, Francesconi Law Firm, Portland, Oreg., 1986-89; ptnr. Craine & Love, Lake Oswego, 1989-2001, Williams, Dailey, O'Leary, Craine & Love, Portland, 2001—. Pres. Oreg. Workers' Compensation Attys., 1992-94. Contbr. articles to profl. jours. Mem. ATLA, Oreg. Trial Lawyers Assn. (bd. mem. 1993-99, pres. 1997-98), Oreg. Women Lawyers, Oreg. Workers' Compensation Attys. Democrat. Avocations: mountain biking, road biking, downhill skiing, cross country skiing, kayaking. Office: Williams Dailey O'Leary Craine & Love 101 SW Fifth Ave Ste 1900 Portland OR 97204

LOVE, MICHAEL JOSEPH, lawyer; b. Chicopee, Mass., Mar. 1, 1958; BA, U. Mass., 1984; student, Vanderbilt U., 1991-92; JD, U. Denver, 1992. Bar: Tenn., U.S. Dist. Ct. (mid. dist.) Tenn. 1992. Ptnr. Zellar, Cartwright & Love, PLLC, Clarksville, Tenn., 1994-96, Cartwright & Love, Clarksville, 1996—. Gen. editor U. Denver Law Rev. With U.S. Army, 1975-78. Mem. Nat. Assn. Criminal Def. Lawyers (life), Tenn. Bar Assn., Tenn. Assn. Criminal Def. Lawyers (exec. com. criminal def. sect.). Democrat. Civil rights, Constitutional, Criminal. Office: Cartwright & Love PLLC 215 S 2nd St Clarksville TN 37040-3629 E-mail: ml4crimdef@aol.com

LOVE, SCOTT ANTHONY, lawyer; b. Houston, Dec. 30, 1969; s. Robert Allen and Louisa Ann Love. BA in History with honors, U. Houston, 1997, JD, 1993. Bar: U.S. Dist. Ct. (so. dist.) Tex., U.S. Dist. Ct. (ea. dist.) Tex. Law clk. Abraham, Watkins, Nichols & Friend, Houston, 1995-97; assoc. Duckett, Bouligny & Collins, L.L.P., El Campo, Tex., 1997-99, Wojciechowski & Assocs., P.C., Houston, 1999—. Mem. Ducks Unltd., El Campo, 1997—. Mem. Houston Young Lawyers Assn., Houston Bar Assn., Wharton County Bar Assn., Tex. Assn. of Def. Counsel. Republican. Avocations: weight lifting, softball, reading. General civil litigation, Insurance, Personal injury. Home: 3015 Brookdale Dr Kingwood TX 77339-1357 Office: Wojciechowski & Assocs PC PO Box 1567 2 Northpoint Dr Houston TX 77060-3235

LOVE, WALTER BENNETT, JR. lawyer; b. Monroe, N.C., Nov. 14, 1921; s. Wlater B. and Pearl (Hamilton) L.; m. Elizabeth Cannon, Dec. 28, 1951; children: Elizabeth Sheldon Love Sturges, Walter Bennett III, Linda Louise Love Talmadge. BS in Commerce, U. N.C., 1942, JD, 1949, Indsl. Coll. Armed Services, 1972. Bar: N.C. 1949, Fed. bar 1949. Ptnr. Love and Love, Monroe, 1949-52; pvt. practice, 1952-58, 92-99; sr. ptnr. Love and Milliken, 1958-92, attys. for City of monroe; ptnr. Love & Hutlaff PLLP, 1999—. Bd. dirs. Nat. Bd. Am. Cancer Soc., 1969-82, pres. N.C. div., 1984, chmn. bd., 1985; chmn. bd. trustees Cen. United Meth. Ch., 1977-86, 90-92, lay leader, 1986-89, chmn. ch. planning and building com., 1955-80; trustee United Meth. Found. for Western N.C. Conf., 1988—, Union County Found., 1989—; past pres. Union County Hist. Soc.; past sec. bd. trustees Ellen Fitzgeral Hosp. and Union Mem. Hosp.; life mem. bd. adv. The Methodist Home, Inc. Col. USAFR, WWII and Korea. Decorated with Disting. Unit citation. Mem. ABA, N.C. Bar Assn. (estate planning and fiduciary law com. 1988), 20th Jud. Dist. Bar Assn. (past pres.), Union County Bar Assn. (past pres.), Carolinas Genealogical Soc. Clubs: Rolling Hills Country, Tower, Lions (past pres. and zone chmn. Monroe). Estate planning, Probate, Real property. Home: 217 Ridgewood Dr Monroe NC 28112-6365 Office: PO Box 278 Monroe NC 28111-0278

LOVE, WILLIAM EDWARD, lawyer; b. Eugene, Oreg., Mar. 13, 1926; s. William Stewart and Ola A. (Kingsbury) L.; m. Sylvia Kathryn Jaureguy, Aug. 6, 1955; children: Kathryn Love Petersen, Jeffrey, Douglas, Gregory. BS, U. Notre Dame, 1946; MA in Journalism, U. Oreg., 1950, JD, 1952. Bar: Oreg. 1952. Newspaper reporter Eugene Register Guard, 1943-44, 47-52; asst. prof. law, asst. dean Sch. Law U. Wash., Seattle, 1952-56; ptnr. Cake, Jaureguy, Hardy, Buttler & McEwen, Portland, Oreg., 1956-69; pres., chmn., CEO Equitable Savs. & Loan, 1969-82; sr. ptnr. Schwabe, Williamson & Wyatt, 1983—. Chmn. Oreg. Savs. League, 1976; dir. Portland Gen. Electric, 1976-83, Fed. Home Loan Bank of Seattle, 1976-79, 85-96, adv. council Fed. Nat. Mortgage Assn., Washington, 1978-80; exec. dir. Health, Housing, Ednl. & Cultural Facilities Authority, 1990—. Author: (with Jaureguy) Oregon Probate Law and Practice, 2 vols., 1958; contbr. articles to profl. jours. Commr., past chmn. Oreg. Racing Commn., 1963-79; pres. Nat. Assn. State Racing Commrs., 1977-78; commr. Port of Portland, 1979-86, pres. 1983; referee Pac-10 football, 1960-81, Rose Bowl, 1981; active United Way, Boy Scouts Am., Portland Rose Festival, polit. campaigns; mem. adv. coun. Jockey's Guild, Inc., 1990—. Served to lt. (j.g.) USN, 1944-47. Mem. Oreg. Bar Assn., Multnomah County Bar Assn., Arlington Club, Multnomah Athletic Club, Golf Club (Portland). Republican. Home: 10225 SW Melnore St Portland OR 97225-4356 Office: Schwabe Williamson & Wyatt 1211 SW 5th Ave Ste 1800 Portland OR 97204-3713

LOVEALL, GEORGE MICHAEL, lawyer; b. Brazil, Ind., Dec. 3, 1946; s. James Jackson and Jacquelyn (Kerr) L.; B.A., Franklin Coll., 1968; J.D., U. Cin., 1971. Bar: Ind. 1971, U.S. Dist. Ct. (so. dist.) Ind. 1971, U.S. Ct. Appeals (7th cir.) 1980. Ptnr., Loveall and Woods, Franklin, Ind., 1971—. Mem. Ind. Bar Assn., Indpls. Bar Assn., Johnson County Bar Assn. (past pres.), Masons. Republican. Criminal, Family and matrimonial, Personal injury. Home: 300 Carriage Ln Franklin IN 46131-9714 Office: Loveall and Woods 72 E Jefferson St Franklin IN 46131-2321

LOVELESS, GEORGE GROUP, retired lawyer; b. Baldwinsville, N.Y., Sept. 16, 1940; s. Frank Donald and Mayme (Lont) L.; m. Shirley Morrison, Nov. 27, 1965; children: Michael, Peter. BS, Cornell U., 1962, MBA, 1963; JD, U. Md., 1968. Bar: Pa. 1969, U.S. Dist. Ct. (ea. dist.) Pa., U.S. Ct. Appeals (3d cir.). Ptnr. Morgan, Lewis & Bockius LLP, Phila., 1968-2000; ret., 2000. With USAFR, 1963-68. Republican. Presbyterian. Banking, Bankruptcy, General corporate. Home: 11 Rose Valley Rd Media PA 19063-4217 Office: Morgan Lewis & Bockius LLP 1701 Market St Philadelphia PA 19103-2921 E-mail: GGL1@cornell.edu

LOVELL, CARL ERWIN, JR. lawyer; b. Riverside, Calif., Apr. 12, 1945; s. Carl Erwin and Hazel (Brown) L.; m. Danna I. Wale; children: Carl Erwin III, Timothy C., Tishia R., Ashley P., Garrett T. BA, Vanderbilt U., 1966, JD, 1969. Bar: Nev. 1969, D.C. 1971, U.S. Supreme Ct. 1973. Jr. editor Land and Water Law Rev., 1973-89; instr. bus. law U. Nev., Las Vegas, Clark County C.C.; city atty. City of N. Las Vegas, 1970-73; elected city atty. City of Las Vegas, 1973-77; v.p., sec.-treas., legal counsel Circus Circus Hotels, Inc., Las Vegas, 1977-83; sr. ptnr. Lovell, Bilbray & Potter, 1984-89; pvt. practice, 1989—; v.p., dir. Air Nev. Airlines, Inc. Chmn. Nat. Inst. Mcpl. Law Officers Consumer Protection Adv. Com., 1973-77, Nev. Crime Commn. Bd., 1974-77; U.S. rep. to China-U.S. Internat. Trade and Law Talks, Beijing, 1987; arbitrator, AAA, 1989—. Bd. dirs., v.p. BBB, 1983-91; chmn. NCCJ; pres. Clark County Young Dems., 1971-72; bd. dirs. Nat. Kidney Found.; pres., trustee Nev. Donor Network, Inc., 1992-96. With USAF, 1966-68. Mem. ABA, ATLA, Nev. State Bar, Nev. Trial Lawyers Assn., Elks (justice Las Vegas chpt. 1985-88). Administrative and regulatory, General corporate, Personal injury. Office: 2801 S Valley View Blvd Ste 1B Las Vegas NV 89102-0116 E-mail: dcarl@wealthprotectionconcepts.com, lovellachieve4u@earthlink.net

LOVING, SUSAN BRIMER, lawyer, former state official; m. Dan Loving; children: Lindsay, Andrew, Kendall. BA with distinction, U. Okla., 1972, JD, 1979. Asst. atty. gen. Office of Atty. Gen., 1983-87, 1st asst. atty. gen., 1987-91; atty. gen. State of Okla., Oklahoma City, 1991-94; ptnr. Lester, Loving & Davies, Edmond, Okla., 1995—. Master Ruth Bader Ginsburg Inn of Ct., 1995-97. Vice-chmn. Pardon and Parole Bd., 1995; mem. Gov.'s Commn. on Tobacco and Youth, 1995-97; bd. dirs. Bd. for Freedom of Info., Okla. Inc., Legal Aid of West Okla., Okla. Com. for Prevention of Child Abuse; mem. med. steering com. Partnership for Drug Free Okla., Inst. for Child Advocacy, 1996-97. Recipient Nat. Red Ribbon Leadership award Nat. Fedn. Parents, Headliner award, By-liner award Okla. City and Tulsa Women in Comm., First Friend of Freedom award, Freedom of Info., Okla., Dir. award Okla. Dist. Attys. Assn. Mem. Okla. Bar Assn. (past chmn. adminstrv. law sect., mem. ho. dels. 1996—, grievance com. 1999—, chmn. adminstrn. of justice com., chmn. profl. responsibility commn., task force on professionalism and civility 1999—, Spotlight award 1997), Phi Beta Kappa. Administrative and regulatory, Civil rights, General practice. Office: Lester Loving & Davies PLLC 1505 Renaissance Blvd Edmond OK 73013-3018 E-mail: sloving@lldlaw.com

LOVINS, NELSON PRESTON, lawyer; b. Malden, Mass., Mar. 3, 1944; s. Max and Sophie Goldie (Singer) L.; m. Louis Sheinhait, Nov. 19, 1967; children: Kimberly Beth, Brett David. AB, Tufts U., 1965; JD, Suffolk U., 1968; postgrad., Nat. Coll. Criminal Def. Lawyers and Pub. Defenders, 1975. Bar: Mass. 1968, U.S. Dist. Ct. Mass. 1970, U.S. Ct. Claims 1977, U.S. Ct. Appeals (1st cir.) 1980, U.S. Supreme Ct. 2000; cert. fraud examiner. Assoc. Zamparelli & White, Medford, Mass., 1968-71, Lovins, Frazer & Lewin, Boston, 1971-77; ptnr. Lappin, Rosen, Goldberg, 1977-82, Lovins & Diller, Boston, 1982-88, Lovins & Metcalf, Woburn, 1988—. Adj. faculty Mass. Sch. Law. Atty., Suffolk U. Law Sch. Author: Causes of Action Related to Intellectual Property, 1982; mem. editl. bd. Criminal Appellate Procedure in Mass., 1967-68; contbr. articles to profl. jours.

Atty., advisor Winchester (Mass.) Citizens for a Cleaner Environ.; active Temple Isaiah, Lexington, Mass. Mem. Mass. Bar Assn. (21st Century Club 1981, lectr. 1981-82, arbitrator), Nat. Assn. Securities, Brokers and Dealers. General civil litigation, Construction, Insurance. Office: Chestnut Green 10 Cedar St Woburn MA 01801-6364 E-mail: nlovins@aol.com

LOW, ANDREW M. lawyer; b. N.Y.C., Jan. 1, 1952; s. Martin Laurent and Alice Elizabeth (Bernstein) L.; m. Margaret Mary Stroock, Mar. 31, 1979; children: Roger, Ann. BA, Swarthmore Coll., 1973; JD, Cornell U., 1976. Bar: Colo. 1981, U.S. Dist. Ct. Colo. 1981, U.S. Ct. Appeals (10th cir.) 1986. Assoc. Rogers & Wells, N.Y.C., 1977-81, Davis, Graham & Stubbs, Denver, 1981-83, ptnr., 1984—. Editor: Colorado Appellate Handbook, 1984, 94. Pres. Colo. Freedom of Info. Coun., Denver, 1990-92, Colo. Bar Press Com., 1989, appellate practice subcom. Colo. Bar Assn. Litigation Coun., 1994—; bd. dirs. CLE in Colo., Inc., 1993-96; trustee 9 Health Fair, Denver, 1988—; mem. Colo. Sup. Ct. Joint Commn. on Appellate Rules, 1993—. Avocations: skiing, golfing, fly-fishing. Appellate, General civil litigation, Libel. Office: Davis Graham & Stubbs LLP Ste 500 1550 17th St Denver CO 80202 E-mail: andrew.low@dgslaw.com

LOWE, JOHN ANTHONY, lawyer; b. Paterson, N.J., Oct. 3, 1942; s. John William and Jane (Kelly) L.; m. Rose A. Farrell, Jan. 2, 1977; children— Theresa Anne, Katherine. AB, Holy Cross Coll., 1963; JD, Cornell U., 1968. Bar: N.Y. 1968, U.S. Dist. Ct. (no. dist.) N.Y. 1968, U.S. Dist. Ct. (so. dist.) N.Y. 1971, U.S. Dist. Ct. (ea. dist.) N.Y. 1982, U.S. Ct. Appeals (9th cir.) 1982. Assoc. Reavis & McGrath. N.Y.C., 1968-71, ptnr., 1979— ; asst. U.S. atty. So. Dist. N.Y., N.Y.C., 1971-78; faculty Practicing Law Inst., 1977-78; lectr. U.S. Atty. Gen.'s Advocacy Inst., Washington, 1977; arbitrator Civil Ct. of the City of N.Y., 1978— , Nat. Assn. Security Dealers, 1984—. Contbr. articles to mags. Served to lt. (j.g.) USNR, 1963-65. Named Leading Cons. in High Tech. J. Dick & Co., 1983. Mem. Bklyn. Bar Assn., Order of Coif, Friendly Sons St. Patrick, Phi Alpha Delta (treas. 1964-65). Democrat. Clubs: N.Y. Athletic, Westhampton Country, La Ronde Beach. Federal civil litigation, Criminal, Securities. Home: 200 E End Ave New York NY 10128-7831

LOWE, JOHN STANLEY, lawyer, educator; b. Marion, Ohio, May 11, 1941; s. John Floyd and Florence (Andrews) L.; m. Jacquelyn Taft, Jan. 15, 1968; children: Sarah Staley, John Taft. BA, Denison U., 1963; LLB, Harvard U., 1966. Bar: Ohio 1966, Okla. 1980, U.S. Supreme Ct. 1972, Tex. 1989. Adminstrv. officer Govt. of Malawi, Limbe, 1966-69; assoc. Emens, Hurd, Kegler & Ritter, Columbus, Ohio, 1970-75; assoc. prof. law U. Toledo, 1975-78; prof. law U. Tulsa, 1978-87, So. Meth. U., Dallas, 1987—. Vis. prof. U. Tex., Austin, 1983; disting. vis. prof. natural resources law U. Denver, 1987; disting. vis. prof. U. N.Mex., 1996; vis. lectr. U. Dundee, Scotland, 2001. Author: Oil and Gas Law in a Nutshell, 1983, 3d edit., 1995; editor: Cases and Materials on Oil and Gas Law, 1986, 3d edit., 1998; editor Internat. Petroleum Transactions, 1993, 2d edit., 2000, others. Trustee, former sec., mem. exec. com. Rocky Mountain Mineral Law Found. Recipient Outstanding Law Rev. Article award Tex. Bar Found., 1988, 96. Mem. ABA (chair natural resources, energy and environ. law 1992-93), Am. Arbitration Assn., Southwest Legal Found. (vice chair, mem. exec. com. adv. bd. Internat. Oil and Gas Edn. Ctr.), CPR Inst. for Dispute Resolution. Episcopalian. Avocation: sailing. Home: 3526 Greenbrier Dr Dallas TX 75225-5003 Office: So Meth U 3315 Daniel Ave Dallas TX 75275-0001 E-mail: jlowe@mail.smu.edu

LOWE, RALPH EDWARD, lawyer; b. Hinsdale, Ill., Nov. 24, 1931; s. Charles Russell and Eva Eleanor (Schroeder) L.; m. Patricia E. Eichhorst, Aug. 23, 1952; children: John Stuart, Michael Kevin, Timothy Edward. BA, Depauw U., 1953; LLB, U. Ill., 1956. Bar: Ill. 1956, U.S. Dist. Ct. (no. dist.) Ill. 1957, Ga. 1974, U.S. Dist. Ct. (no. dist.) Ga. 1980, S.C. 1990. Assoc. Ruddy & Brown, Aurora, Ill., 1956-58; ptnr. Lowe & Richards, 1959-62, Vincent, Lowe & Richards, Aurora, 1963-71; pvt. practice, Aurora and Atlanta, 1974-85; prin. Lowe & Steinmetz, Ltd., 1985-91; pvt. practice, Aurora, Ill., 1972-74, 92—. Chmn. Inter-Am. Devel. Corp., Ill., 1965-67. Administrative and regulatory, Probate, Real property. Office: 407 W Galena Blvd Aurora IL 60506-3946

LOWE, ROBERT STANLEY, lawyer; b. Herman, Nebr., Apr. 23, 1923; s. Stanley Robert and Ann Marguerite (Feese) L.; m. Anne Kirtland Selden, Dec. 19, 1959; children: Robert James, Margaret Anne. AB, U. Nebr., 1947, JD, 1949. Bar: Wyo. 1949. Ptnr. McAvoy & Lowe, Newcastle, 1949-51, Hickey & Lowe, Rawlins, 1951-55; county and pros. atty., 1955-59; pvt. practice, 1959-67; assoc. dir. Am. Judicature Soc., Chgo., 1967-74; gen. counsel True Oil Co. and affiliates, 1974-98, of counsel, 1998-99. Bd. dirs. Hilltop Nat. Bank, Casper, sec., 1981—; legal adv. divsn. Nat. Ski Patrol Sys., 1975-88; city atty. City of Rawlins, 1963-65; atty., asst. sec. Casper Mountain Ski Patrol, 1988—. Chmn. Casper C. of C. Military Affairs Com., 1995-2000; mem. Wyo. Ho. of Reps., 1952-54; bd. dirs. Vols. in Probation, 1969-82; leader lawyer del. to China, People to People, 1986; mem. Wyo. Vets. Affairs Commn., 1994—, chmn., 1996—; mem. legis. com. United Vets. Coun. Wyo., 1993—; trustee Troopers Found., Inc., 1994—, pres., 1994-99; pres. Casper WWII Commemorative Assn., 1995-96, Navy League Wyo. Coun. (pres. 1997-00); state pres. Wyo., 2000—. Recipient Dedicated Community Worker award Rawlins Jr. C. of C., 1967, Yellow merit star award Nat. Ski Patrol System, 1982, 85, 87, 88, Small Bus. Administrate Vet. Advocate award, 1998, Disting. Svc. award Disabled Am. Vets. Dept., 1994. Fellow Am. Bar Found. (life); mem. VFW (life mem.; post adv. 1991-96, nat. aide-de-camp 1993-94, 98-99, judge adv. dist. 3 Dept. Wyo., 1994—, mil. order of cootie grand judge adv. 1994—), ABA (sec. jud. adminstrn. divsn. lawyers conf., exec. com. 1975-76, chmn. 1977-78, chmn. judicial qualification and selection com. 1986-93, coun. jud. adminstrn. divsn. 1977-78, mem. com. to implement jud. adminstrn. stds. 1978-83, Ho. of Dels. state bar del. 1978-80, 86-87, state del. 1987-93, Assembly del. 1980-83, mem. standing com. on the fed. judiciary 1997-99, ad hoc com. state justice initiatives 1997-99), Am. Judicature Soc. (dir. 1961-67, 85-89, bd. editors 1975-77, Herbert Harley award 1974), Wyo. State Bar (chmn. com. on cts. 1961-67, 77-87), Nebr. State Bar Assn., Ill. State Bar Assn., D.C. Bar, Inter-Am. Bar Assn., Selden Soc., Inst. Jud. Adminstrn., Rocky Mountain Oil and Gas Assn. (legal com. 1976-99, chmn. 1979-82, 90-91), Rocky Mountain Mineral Law Found. (trustee 1980-94), Am. Law Inst. (life), Order of Coif, Delta Theta Phi (dist. chancellor 1982-83, chief justice 1983-93, assoc. justice 1993—; Percy J. Power Meml. award 1983, Gold Medallion award 1990), Casper Rotary Club (pres. 1985-86), Casper Rotary Found. (dir. 1990—, sec. 1990-00). Mem. Ch. of Christ, Scientist. Banking, General corporate, Oil, gas, and mineral. Home and Office: 97 Primrose Casper WY 82604-4018 Office: 5905 Cy Ave Casper WY 82604-4101

LOWENBERG, MICHAEL, lawyer; b. Bklyn., Mar. 6, 1943; s. Leo and Edna (Hanft) L.; m. Julie Goldberg, June 13, 1965; children: Daniel, Frances, Anthony. BA, Bklyn. Coll., 1963; LLB, Harvard U., 1966. Bar: Tex. 1966, U.S. Dist. Ct. (no. dist.) Tex. 1966, U.S. Ct. Appeals (5th cir.) 1967. Assoc. Akin, Gump, Strauss, Hauer & Feld, L.L.P., Dallas, 1966-71; ptnr. Akin, Gump, Strauss, Hauer & Feld, P.C., 1972—. Pres. Dallas Legal Services Found., 1972; chmn. Dallas chpt. Am. Jewish Com., 1973-74. Mem. ABA, Tex. Bar Assn., Bar Assn. of 5th Cir. (past pres., bd. dirs.), Dallas Bar Assn., Dallas Bar Found., Tex. Bar Found., Coll. of State Bar Tex., Def. Rsch. Inst., Tex. Appleseed (bd. dirs.). Democrat. Federal civil litigation, State civil litigation, Contracts commercial. Home: 5321 Drane Dr Dallas TX 75209-5501 Office: Akin Gump Strauss Hauer & Feld 4100 First City Center 1700 Pacific Ave Ste 4100 Dallas TX 75201-4675 E-mail: mlowenberg@akingump.com

LOWENFELD, ANDREAS FRANK, law educator, arbitrator; b. Berlin, May 30, 1930; s. Henry and Yela (Herschkowitsch) L.; m. Elena Machado, Aug. 11, 1962; children: Julian, Marianna. AB magna cum laude, Harvard U., 1951, LLB magna cum laude, 1955. Bar: N.Y. 1955, U.S. Supreme Ct. 1961. Assoc. Hyde and de Vries, N.Y.C., 1957-61; spl. asst. to legal adv. U.S. State Dept., 1961-63, asst. legal advisor for econ. affairs, 1963-65, dep. legal adviser, 1965-66; fellow John F. Kennedy Inst. Politics Harvard U., Cambridge, Mass., 1966-67; prof. law Sch. Law NYU, N.Y.C., 1967—, Charles L. Denison prof. law, 1981-94, Herbert and Rose Rubin prof. internat. law, 1994—. Arbitrator internat. comml. panels ICC. Author: (with Abram Chayes and Thomas Ehrlich) International Legal Process, 1968-69, Aviation Law, Cases and Materials, 1972, 2d edit., 1981, International Economic Law, vol. I, 1975, 3d edit., 1996, vol. II, 1976, 2d edit., 1982, vol. III, 1977, 2d edit., 1983, vol. IV, 1977, 2d edit., 1984, vol. VI, 1979, 2d edit., 1983, Conflict of Laws, Federal, State and International Perspectives, 1986, 2d edit., 1998, International Litigation and Arbitration, 1993, International Litigation: The Quest for Reasonableness, 1996, The Role of Government in International Trade: Essays Over Three Decades, 2000; editor, co-author: Expropriation in the Americas: A Comparative Law Study, 1971; assoc. reporter Am. Law Inst. Restatement on Foreign Relations Law; contbr. articles and book revs. on pub. internat. law, internat. econ. law, air law, conflict of laws, arbitration, history and politics to profl. jours. Mem.: ABA, Assn. of Bar of City of N.Y., Am. Soc. Internat. Law, Am. Arbitration Assn. (arbitrator), Am. Law Inst., Coun. Fgn. Rels., Inst. de Droit, Internat. Acad. Comparative Law, Gray's Inn (assoc.)). Home: 5776 Palisade Ave Bronx NY 10471-1212 Office: NYU Sch Law Sch Law 40 Washington Sq S New York NY 10012-1005 E-mail: andreas.lowenfeld@NYU.edu

LOWENFELS, LEWIS DAVID, lawyer; b. N.Y.C., June 9, 1935; s. Seymour and Jane (Phillips) L.; m. Fern Gelford, Aug. 15, 1965; children: Joshua, Jacqueline. BA magna cum laude, Harvard U., 1957, LLB, 1961. Bar: N.Y. 1961; lic. corp. and securities atty. Ptnr. Tolins & Lowenfels, N.Y.C., 1967—. Adj. prof. Seton Hall U. Law Sch; lectr. Practicing Law Inst., Southwestern Legal Found., U. Minn. Fed. Bar Assn., 1972; pub. gov. Am. Stock Exch., 1993-96. Co-author: Bromberg and Lowenfels on Securities Fraud and Commodities Fraud, 6 vols., 1999; contbr. articles to profl. jours. With USAR, 1957-63. Mem. ABA (fed. regulation of securities com. 1978—, lectr.), N.Y. County Lawyers Assn. (securities and exchanges com. 1974—), Phi Beta Kappa, Harvard Club. Avocations: reading, writing, athletics. General corporate, Securities. Office: Tolins & Lowenfels 747 3d Ave 19th Fl New York NY 10017-1028 E-mail: Lew@TolinsLowenfels.com

LOWENSTEIN, LOUIS, legal educator; b. N.Y.C., June 13, 1925; s. Louis and Ralphina (Steinhardt) L.; m. Helen Libby Udell, Feb. 12, 1953; children: Roger Spector, Jane Ruth, Barbara Ann. B.S., Columbia, 1947, LL.B., 1953; M.F.S., U. Md., 1951. Bar: N.Y. 1953. Pvt. practice law, N.Y.C., 1954-78; Assoc. Judge Stanley H. Fuld, N.Y. Ct. Appeals, 1953-54; assoc., then partner Hays, Sklar & Herzberg, 1954-68; partner Nickerson, Kramer, Lowenstein, Nessen, Kamin & Soll, 1968-78; Simon H. Rifkind prof. emeritus law and fin. Columbia U. Law Sch., 1980—, project dir. Instl. Investor Project, 1988-94; pres. Supermarkets Gen. Corp., Woodbridge, N.J., 1978-79. Bd. dirs. Liz Claiborne, Inc. 1988-96; mem. pub. oversight bd. Panel on Audit Effectiveness, 1998-2000. Author: What's Wrong with Wall Street, 1988, Sense and Nonsense in Corporate Finance, 1991; contbr., co-editor: Knights, Raiders and Targets, 1988; editor in chief Columbia Law Rev., 1951-53. V.p., mem. exec. com. Fedn. Jewish Philanthropies N.Y.; pres. Jewish Bd. Family and Children's Svcs. N.Y., 1974-78; trustee Beth Israel Med. Ctr., N.Y.C., 1975-81; dir. Goddard-Riverside Cmty. Ctr., 1996—; chmn. bd. dirs. Coalition for the Homeless, 1997—. Mem. ABA, Assn. of Bar of City of N.Y., Am. Law Inst. Home: 5 Oak Ln Larchmont NY 10538-3917 Office: Columbia U Law Sch 435 W 116th St New York NY 10027-7297

LOWER, ROBERT CASSEL, lawyer, educator; b. Oak Park, Ill., Jan. 8, 1947; s. Paul Elton and Doris Thatcher (Heaton) L.; m. Jean Louise Lower, Aug. 24, 1968 (dec. Aug. 1985); children: David Elton, Andrew Bennett, James Philip Thatcher; m. Cheryl Bray, July 26, 1986. AB magna cum laude with highest honors, Harvard U., 1969, JD, 1972. Bar: Ga. 1972. Assoc. Alston & Bird, Atlanta, 1972-78, ptnr., 1978—. Adj. prof. Emory U., 1978-85, 92. Contbr. articles to law jours. Co-founder, pres. Ga. Vol. Lawyers for the Arts, Inc., 1975-79; chmn. Fulton County (Ga.) Arts Coun., 1979-87; trustee Woodruff Arts Ctr., 1988-95, Piedmont Coll., Ga. Found. Ind. Colls. Mem. Ga. Bar Assn., Atlanta Bar Assn., Midtown Bus. Assn. (bd. dirs. 1988-90), Author's Ct. Harvard Club (Ga.), Ansley Golf Club, Phi Beta Kappa. Presbyterian. Avocations: running, music, bonsai. General corporate, Health. Home: 935 Plymouth Rd NE Atlanta GA 30306-3009 Office: Alston & Bird 1 Atlantic Ctr Atlanta GA 30309-3400

LOWERY, WILLIAM HERBERT, lawyer; b. Toledo, June 8, 1925; s. Kenneth Alden and Drusilla (Pfanner) L.; m. Carolyn Broadwell, June 27, 1947; children: Kenneth Latham, Marcia Mitchell. PhB, U. Chgo., 1947; JD, U. Mich., 1950. Bar: Pa. 1951, U.S. Supreme Ct. 1955. Assoc. Dechert Price & Rhoads, Phila., 1950-58, ptnr., 1958-89, mng. ptnr., 1970-72; mem. policy com., chmn. litigation dept., 1962-68, 81-84; of counsel Dechert, Phila., 1989—; counsel S.S. Huebner Found. Ins. Edn., 1970-89. Faculty Am. Conf. of Legal Execs., Pa. Bar Inst.; permanent mem. com. of visitors U. Mich. Law Sch. Author: Insurance Litigation Problems, 1972, Insurance Litigation Disputes, 1977. Pres. Stafford Civic Assn., 1958; chmn. Tredyffrin Twp. Zoning Bd., Chester County, Pa., 1959-75; bd. dirs. Paoli (Pa.) Meml. Hosp., 1964-89, chmn., 1972-75; bd. dirs. Main Line Health, Radnor, Pa., 1984-89; permanent mem. Jud. Conf. 3d Cir. Ct. Served to 2d lt. USAF, 1943-46. Mem. ABA (chmn. life ins. com. 1984-85, chmn. Nat. Conf. Lawyers and Life Ins. Cos. 1984-88), Order of the Coif, Royal Poinciana Golf Club (bd. dirs. 1997—, sec. 1997-2000, v.p. 2000—), Phi Gamma Delta, Phi Delta Phi. Federal civil litigation, Health, Insurance. Home: 2777 Gulf Shore Blvd N Apt 4-s Naples FL 34103-4360 Office: Dechert 4000 Bell Atlantic Tower 1717 Arch St Lbby 3 Philadelphia PA 19103-2713

LOWES, ALBERT CHARLES, lawyer; b. Oak Ridge, Mo., Dec. 1, 1932; s. Guy Everett and Lillian Bertina (Tuschhoff) L.; m. Peggy Rae Watson, Aug. 27, 1960; children: Danita Rae, Albert Charles II, Kurt Brandon. Student, Cape State Coll., 1954-56; JD, U. Mo., 1959. Bar: Mo. 1959, U.S. Dist. Ct. (ea. dist.) Mo. 1959, U.S. Ct. Appeals (8th cir.) 1971. With Buerkle, Lowes, Beeson & Ludwig, Jackson, Mo., 1959-84; ptnr. Lowes & Drusch, Cape Girardeau, 1984—. Atty. City of Jackson, 1960-62. Staff sgt. USMC, 1950-54, Korea. Mem. ABA, Mo. Bar Assn., Internat. Assn. Ins. Counsel, VFW (judge adv. dept. Mo.1962-64, 67-68, state judge adv. 1997-98), Masons, Shriners, Elks. Democrat. Lutheran. Avocations: reading, history, legal fields. Criminal, Insurance, Personal injury. Office: Lowes & Drusch 2913 Independence St Cape Girardeau MO 63703-8320

LOWRY, DAVID BURTON, lawyer; b. Bronxville, N.Y., Nov. 6, 1943; s. Burton S. and Virginia Evelyn (Ford) L. BA, U. Ariz., 1966, JD, 1969. Bar: Ariz. 1969, Oreg. 1973. Legal aid atty., Tucson and Coolidge, Ariz. and Hillsboro, Oreg.; asst. atty. gen.; dep. dist. atty. Marion County; dep. pub. defender Mohave County, Ariz.; pvt. practice Portland, Oreg., 1989—. Mem. Oreg. State Bar Assn., Ariz. State Bar Assn., Am. Mgmt. Assn., Assn. Trial Lawyers Am., Alpha Delta Sigma, Phi Alpha Delta, Alpha Sigma Phi. Republican. Civil rights, Pension, profit-sharing, and employee benefits, Personal injury. Home: 13490 SW Genesis Loop Tigard OR 97223-3959

LOWRY, EDWARD FRANCIS, JR. lawyer; b. L.A., Aug. 13, 1930; s. Edward Francis and Mary Anita (Woodcock) L.; m. Patricia Ann Palmer, Feb. 16, 1963; children: Edward Palmer, Rachael Louise. Student, Ohio State U., 1948-50; AB, Stanford U., 1952, JD, 1954. Bar: Ariz. 1955, D.C. 1970, U.S. Supreme Ct. 1969. Camp dir. Quarter Circle V Bar Ranch, 1954; tchr. Orme Sch., Mayer, Ariz., 1954-56; trust rep. Valley Nat. Bank Ariz., 1958-60; pvt. practice, Phoenix, 1960—; assoc. atty. Cunningham, Carson & Messinger, 1960-64; ptnr. Carson, Messinger, Elliott, Laughlin & Ragan, 1964-69, 70-80, Gray, Plant, Mooty, Mooty & Bennett, 1981-84, Eaton, Lazarus, Dodge & Lowry Ltd., 1985-86; exec. v.p., gen. counsel Bus. Realty Ariz., 1986-93; pvt. practice, Scottsdale, Ariz., 1986-88; ptnr. Lowry & Froeb, 1988-89, Lowry, Froeb & Clements, P.C., Scottsdale, 1989-90, Lowry & Clements P.C., Scottsdale, 1990, Lowry, Clements & Powell, P.C., Scottsdale, 1991—. Asst. legis. counsel Dept. Interior, Washington, 1969-70; mem. Ariz. Commn. Uniform Laws, 1972—, chmn., 1976-88; judge pro tem Ariz. Ct. Appeals, 1986, 92-94; mem. Nat. Conf. Commrs. on Uniform State Laws, 1972-97, life mem., 1997—. Chmn. Coun. of Stanford Law Socs., 1968; bd. dirs. Scottsdale Prevention Inst., 1999—; vice chmn. bd. trustees Orme Sch., 1972-74, treas., 1981-83; trustee Heard Mus., 1965-91, life trustee, 1991—, pres., 1974-75; bd. visitors Stanford Sch. Law; magistrate Town of Paradise Valley, Ariz., 1976-83, town councilman, 1998—, mayor, 1998—; juvenile ct. referee Maricopa County, 1978-83. Capt. USAF, 1956-58. Fellow Ariz. Bar Found. (founder); mem. ABA, Maricopa County Bar Assn., State Bar Ariz. (chmn. com. uniform laws 1979-85), Stanford Law Soc. Ariz. (past pres.), Scottsdale Bar Assn. (bd. dirs. 1991—, v.p. 1991, pres. 1992-95), Ariz. State U. Law Soc. (bd. dirs.), Delta Sigma Rho, Alpha Tau Omega, Phi Delta Phi. Estate planning, Probate, Real property. Home: 7600 N Moonlight Ln Paradise Valley AZ 85253-2938 Office: Lowry Clements & Powell PC 2901 N Central Ave Ste 1120 Phoenix AZ 85012-2731 also: 6900 E Camelback Rd Ste 1040 Scottsdale AZ 85251-2444

LOWRY, HOUSTON PUTNAM, lawyer; b. N.Y.C., Apr. 1, 1955; s. Thomas Clinton Falls and Jean Allen (Day) L.; m. Kathryn Santoro Curtiss. BA, Pitzer Coll., 1976; MBA, U. Conn., 1980; JD cum laude, Gonzaga U., 1980; LLM in Internat. Law, U. Cambridge, Eng., 1981. Bar: Conn. 1980, U.S. Dist. Ct. Conn. 1981, U.S. Tax Ct. 1982, U.S. Ct. Mil. Appeals 1982, U.S. Ct. Appeals (1st, 2d, 5th, 11th cirs.) 1982, U.S. Ct. Claims 1984, D.C. 1985, U.S. Ct. Appeals (4th, 6th, 7th, 9th, fed., D.C. cirs.) 1985, U.S. Ct. Appeals (3d, 8th, 10th cirs.) 1986, U.S. Supreme Ct., N.Y. 1989. Law clk. to Judge William M. Acker, Jr. U.S. Dist. Ct., Birmingham, Ala., 1982-83; assoc. Tarlow, Levy & Droney, Farmington, Conn., 1983-88; prin. Tarlow, Levy & Droney, P.C., 1989-93, Brown & Welsh P.C., Meriden, 1993—. Mem. adj. faculty internat. trade law and internat. comml. arbitration U. Conn. Law Sch., 1990-95, 99—. Mem. adv. com. on pvt. internat. law Sec. of State, 1996—. Fellow Chartered Inst. Arbitrators; mem. ABA (various coms.), Conn. Bar Assn. (various coms.), Am. Soc. Internat. Law, Internat. Law Assn., Am. Law Inst., Hon. Soc. Gray's Inn, Hartford Club. General civil litigation, Contracts commercial, Private international. Office: Brown & Welsh PC PO Box 183 530 Preston Ave Meriden CT 06450-4893 E-mail: hplowry@brownwelsh.com

LOWY, GEORGE THEODORE, lawyer; b. N.Y.C., Oct. 6, 1931; s. Eugene and Elizabeth Lowy; m. Pier M. Foucault, Sept. 7, 1957. BA cum laude, LLB cum laude, NYU. Bar: N.Y. 1955, U.S. Dist. Ct. (so. dist.) N.Y. 1958, U.S. Supreme Ct. 1972, U.S. Ct Appeals (2d cir.) 1975. Assoc. Cravath, Swaine and Moore, N.Y.C., 1957-65, ptnr., 1965—. Trustee NYU Law Ctr. Found.; bd. dirs. Equitable Life Assurance Soc. U.S., Eramet, Paris; adj. prof. NYU Law Sch., 1983-88; bd. overseers Brandeis U. Grad. Sch. Internat. Econs. and Fin. Fellow ABA; mem. Am. Law Inst., Assn. of Bar of City of N.Y. (chmn. com. on corp. law), Internat. Bar Assn., Union Internat. des Avocats, Cercle Interallie Paris. Private international, Mergers and acquisitions, Securities. Home: 580 Park Ave New York NY 10021-7313 Office: Cravath Swaine & Moore World Wide Pla 825 8th Ave Fl 43 New York NY 10019-7416 E-mail: glowy@cravath.com

LOYO, LUIS FRANCISCO, lawyer; b. Distrito Federal, Mex., Apr. 25, 1968; s. Hector Loyo and Julieta Rios; m. Anabel Labastida; 1 child, Maria Del Carmen. LLM, U. London, 1995. Atty. Procuraduria Discal de la Fed., Mexico City, Mex., 1991-92; fiscal mgr. Nat. Chamber of Restaurant Industry, 1993; chief spl. projects Dept. Dir. Gen., Fed. Fiscal Audit Treasury, 1994; subdir. fin. Health Dept., 1996; assoc. Basham, Ringe y Correa, 1997. Prof. tax consolidation U. Panamericana, 2000—. Mem. Mex. Bar Assn., Assn. Nacional de Abagados de Empresa, Am. C. of C. Avocations: reading, music, piano. Office: Basham Ringe y Correa Paseo de Los Tamarindos 400 Piso 05120 Mexico E-mail: loyo@basham.com.mx

LUBBEN, CRAIG HENRY, lawyer; b. Fort Lee, Va., Aug. 10, 1956; s. George and Dorothy Marion (Vree) L.; m. Lois Beth Zylstra, June 9, 1979; children: Christina Anne, Brian Craig, Eric George, Kaitlin Louise. BA, Calvin Coll., 1978; JD cum laude, Northwestern U., 1981. Bar: Mich. 1981, U.S. Dist. Ct. (we. dist.) Mich. 1981, U.S. Ct. Appeals (6th cir.) 1984. Ptnr. Miller, Johnson, Snell & Cummiskey, Grand Rapids, Mich., 1981-86, Kalamazoo, 1986—. Pres., Alternative Directions, Grand Rapids, 1985; trustee Grand Rapids Pub. Mus. Assn., 1984-86; pres. Kalamazoo Christian Schs. Devel. Assn., 1988—, Family and Children's Svcs. Kalamazoo, 1993-96. Mem. State Bar Mich. (rep. assemblyperson 1990-92), Kalamazoo County Bar Assn. (pres.-elect 1997-98, pres. 1998-99), Order of Coif. Mem. Christian Reformed Ch. Federal civil litigation, State civil litigation, Contracts commercial. Office: Miller Johnson Snell & Cummiskey Rose St Market Bldg 303 N Rose St Ste 600 Kalamazoo MI 49007-3850

LUBER, THOMAS J(ULIAN), lawyer; b. Louisville, Feb. 16, 1949; s. John J. and Martha E. (Cotton) L.; m. Dorothy Ann Carter, Dec. 19, 1975; children: Katharine Ann, Allison Julia. BS in Acctg., U. Louisville, 1972, JD with honors, 1976; LLM in Taxation, NYU, 1977. Bar: Ky. 1976. Agt. IRS, Louisville, 1972-73; assoc. Fahey & Gray, 1977-79; from assoc. to ptnr. Wyatt, Tarrant & Combs and predecessor firms, 1979—, chmn. tax sect., 1983—. Lectr. U. Louisville, 1978-80; speaker in field; bd. advisors Jour. Multistate Taxation. Contbr. articles to profl. jours. Bd. dirs. Univ. Pediatrics Found., Louisville, Univ. Ob-gyn. Found., Louisville, Assumption High Sch., Louisville. With USAF, 1967-69. Mem. ABA, Ky. Bar Assn. (chmn. tax sect. 1983-84), Louisville Bar Assn., Ky. Inst. Fed. Taxation (mem. planning com. 1981—, chmn. 1984—), Jefferson Club, Big Spring Country Club. Democrat. Roman Catholic. Avocations: hiking, working out. General corporate, Taxation, general, State and local taxation. Home: 2324 Saratoga Dr Louisville KY 40205-2021 Office: Wyatt Tarrant & Combs 2800 Citizens Plz Louisville KY 40202-2898 E-mail: tluber@wyattfirm.com

LUBERDA, GEORGE JOSEPH, lawyer, educator; b. N.Y.C., Apr. 27, 1930; s. Joseph George and Mary Loretta (Koslowski) L. Bar: D.C. 1959, U.S. Ct. Appeals (D.C. cir.) 1959, Mich. 1970, Mo. 1973. Washington rep. Ford Motor Co., Washington, 1955-59; atty. FTC, 1960-64; trial atty. Antitrust Div. Dept. Justice, 1965-69; sr. atty. Bendix Corp., Mich., 1970-71; assoc. Butzel, Long, Gust, Klein & Van Zile, Detroit, 1972; antitrust counsel Monsanto Co., St. Louis, 1973-88; assoc. Herzog, Crebs and McGhee, 1988-93; ptnr. Luberda & Carp, St. Louis, 1993—. Adj. prof. St. Louis U., 1985-96. Mem. Mo. Bar Assn., Bar Assn. Met. St. Louis. Republican. Roman Catholic. Antitrust, General civil litigation, General corporate. Home: 716 Ridgeview Circle Ln Ballwin MO 63021-7810 Office: Luberda & Carp 225 S Meramec Ave Ste 320 Saint Louis MO 63105-3511

LUBET, MARC LESLIE, lawyer; b. Atlanta, Sept. 13, 1946; s. Louis Lubet and Sylvia (Hirsch) Hoppes; m. Carla J Rossi, Mar. 5, 1988. BS in Journalism, U. Fla., 1969; JD, U. Miss., 1974. Bar: Miss. 1974, Fla. 1974, U.S. Dist. Ct. (mid. dist.) Fla. 1974, U.S. Dist. Ct. (no. dist.) Miss. 1974, U.S. Ct. Appeals (5th cir.) 1974, U.S. Supreme Ct. 1977, U.S. Ct. Appeals (11th cir.) 1981. Assoc. Pitts & Eubanks Law Firm, Orlando, Fla., 1974-75, Levine & Cohen, Orlando, 1975-76; sr. ptnr. Lubet & Woodard, 1975-88, Lubet & Blechman, Orlando, 1988-99; prin. Marc L. Lubet, P.A., 1999—. Mediator Citizens Dispute, Orlando, 1980—; arbitrater SEC, 1995-96. Active Margarita Soc., Orlando, 1983—. Fellow Am. Bd. Criminal Lawyers; mem. Orange County Bar (mem. speakers bur. 1980-82, crim. law commn. 1983—), ABA, Fla. Bar Assn., Miss. Bar Assn., Nat. Assn. Criminal Def. Lawyers. Democrat. Jewish. Avocations: racquetball, fishing. Criminal. Office: Marc L Lubet Esq 209 E Ridgewood St Orlando FL 32801-1926 E-mail: lubetlaw@aol.com

LUBIC, ROBERT BENNETT, lawyer, arbitrator, law educator; b. Pitts., Mar. 9, 1929; s. H. Murray and Rose M. (Schwartz) L.; m. Benita Joan Alk, May 18, 1959; children: Wendy, Bret, Robin. AB, U. Pitts., 1950, JD, 1953; LLM in Patent Law, Georgetown U., 1959. Bar: Pa. 1953, U.S. Ct. Appeals (D.C.) cir. 1958, U.S. Supreme Ct. 1958, U.S. Patent Office, 1959, U.S. Dist. Ct. D.C. 1964. Atty., advisor FCC, Washington, 1957-59; pvt. practice, Pitts., 1959-63; asst. prof. law Duquesne U. Law Sch., 1963-65; prof. law Am. U. Law Sch., Washington, 1965-2000, prof. emeritus, 2000—, assoc. dean, 1970-71. Cons. to Embassy Republic of Georgia; pres. Stas. WRGI-AM-FM, Naples and Marco Island, Fla., 1974-77; vis. prof. U. P.R. Law Sch., 1993, Internat. Christian U., Tokyo, 1988-89, East China U. Politics and Law, 1994, U. Warsaw, Poland, 1995, U. Turin, Italy, 1997; CEO, gen. counsel GlobalMedArb LLC, 2000—; mem. panel conciliators and arbitrators of Internat. Ctr. of Investment Settlement Disputes of World Bank; permanent panel arbitrator U.S. Postal Sys., Washington, 1978—, U.S. Dept. Labor, Washington, 1982-87; arbitrator Pub. Employee Rels. Bd. D.C., Washington, 1984—, Pub. Employee Rels. Bd. V.I., 1982—; arbitrator Met. Washington Airports Authority, 2001—; hearing examiner Libr. of Congress, 2001—; dir. Labor Disputes Resolution Seminar, Hamilton, Bermuda, 1982, 83, Nassau, Bahamas, 1983; labor cons. Govt. of Bermuda, 1985; creator, dir. Ea. European Summer Law Program, Moscow and Warsaw, 1979-81, Chinese Am. Summer Law Program, Beijing, Shanghai and Hong Kong, 1984-86; co-dir. Mid. East Summer Law Program, Jerusalem, 1976, 78; arbitrator Met. Washington Airports Authority, 2001—; hearing examiner Libr. of Congress, 2001—. Author short story. With U.S. Army, 1953-55. Recipient Outstanding Tchr. award Am. U. Student Bar Assn., 1981. Mem. ABA, Fed. Comm. Bar Assn., D.C. Bar Assn., Am. Arbitration Assn. Democrat. Jewish. Home: 2813 Mckinley Pl NW Washington DC 20015-1104 Office: GlobalMedArb LLC 2813 McKinley Pl NW Washington DC 20015-1104

LUBIN, DONALD G. lawyer; b. N.Y.C., Jan. 10, 1934; s. Harry and Edith (Tannenbaum) L.; m. Amy Schwartz, Feb. 2, 1956; children: Peter, Richard, Thomas, Alice Lubin Spahr. BS in Econs., U. Pa., 1954; LLB, Harvard U., 1957. Bar: Ill. 1957. Ptnr. Sonnenschein Nath & Rosenthal, Chgo., 1957—, chmn. exec. com., 1991-96. Bd. dirs., mem. exec. com., sec. audit com., nominating and corp. governance com. McDonald's Corp., Molex, Inc.; chmn. audit com. Daubert Industries Inc., Charles Levy Co., Tennis Corp. Am. Former mem. Navy Pier Redevel. Corp., Highland Park Cultural Arts Commn.; life trustee, former chmn. bd. Highland Park Hosp., Ravinia Festival Assn.; trustee, mem. exec. com. Rush-Presbyn.-St. Luke's Med. Ctr.; life trustee Chgo. Symphony Orch.; bd. dirs., v.p. Ronald McDonald House Charities, Inc., Chgo. Found. for Edn.; former dir. Smithsonian Inst., Washington; pres., bd. dir. The Barr Fund; former bd. dirs., v.p., sec. Ragdale Found.; bd. govs. Art Inst. Chgo., Chgo. Lighthouse for the Blind; mem. citizens bd. U. Chgo.; mem. coun. Children's Meml. Hosp.; former bd. overseers Coll. Arts and Sci., U. Pa.; dir. Nat. Mus. Am. History, Washington. Woodrow Wilson vis. fellow Fellow Am. Bar Found., Ill. Bar Found., Chgo. Bar Found.; mem. ABA, Ill. Bar Assn., Chgo. Bar Assn., Law Club Chgo., Chgo. Hort. Soc. (past bd. dirs.), Econ. Club, Comml. Club (former sec.. mem. civic com.), Std. Club, Lakeshore Club, Beta Gamma Sigma. General corporate. Home: 2269 Egandale Rd Highland Park IL 60035-2501 Office: Sonnenschein Nath & Rosenthal 233 S Wacker Dr Ste 8000 Chicago IL 60606-6491

LUBIN, STANLEY, lawyer; b. May 7, 1941; children: David Christopher, Jessica Nicole; m. Barbara Ann Lubin. AB, U. Mich., 1963, JD with honors, 1966. Bar: D.C. 1967, Mich. 1968, U.S. Ct. Appeals (D.C. cir.) 1967, U.S. Ct. Appeals (6th cir.) 1968, U.S. Supreme Ct. 1970, Ariz. 1972, U.S. Ct. Appeals (9th cir.) 1976, U.S. Ct. Appeals (fed. cir.) 1985. Atty. NLRB, Washington, 1966-68; asst. gen. counsel UAW, Detroit, 1968-72; assoc. Harrison, Myers & Singer, Phoenix, 1972-74, McKendree & Tountas, Phoenix, 1975; ptnr. McKendree & Lubin, Phoenix and Denver, 1975-84; shareholder Treon, Warnicke & Roush, P.A., 1984-86; pvt. practice, Law Offices Stanley Lubin, Phoenix, 1986-95, The Law Offices of Stanley Lubin, P.C., 1996-98, Lubin & Enoch, P.C., 1999—. Mem. Ariz. Employment Security Adv. Coun., 1975-77. Co-author: Union Fines and Union Discipline Under the National Labor Relations Act, 1971. Active ACLU, dir. Ariz. chpt., 1974-81; mem. Ariz. State Cen. Com. Dem. Party, 1986-91, 93—, sec., 1991-92, mem. state exec. com., 1986-99, Ariz. Dem. Coun., 1987-99, chmn., 1988-93, Thomas Jefferson Forum, 1987-99, chmn., 1988-93. Mem. ABA, State Bar Ariz., Maricopa County Bar Assn., Indsl. Rels. Rsch. Assn., Ariz. Indsl. Rels. Assn. (exec. bd. 1973—, pres. 1979-80, 84). Administrative and regulatory, Entertainment, Labor. Home: 7520 N 9th Pl Phoenix AZ 85020-4138 Office: 2702 N 3rd St Ste 3020 Phoenix AZ 85004-4607 E-mail: stanley.lubin@azbar.org

LUBLINSKI, MICHAEL, lawyer; b. Eskilstuna, Sweden, Sept. 11, 1951; came to U.S., 1956; s. Walter and Dora L. BA magna cum laude, CCNY, 1972; JD, Georgetown U., 1975. Bar: N.Y. 1976, Calif. 1980, Ct. Internat. Trade 1981, U.S. Dist. Ct. (cen. dist.) Calif. 1981, U.S. Dist. Ct. (so. dist.) N.Y. 1981, U.S. Ct. Appeals (D.C. cir.) 1982, D.C. 2000. Atty. U.S. Customs Service, Washington, 1975-79, U.S. Dept. Commerce, Washington, 1980; assoc. Mori & Ota, L.A., 1980-84, Kelley Drye & Warren LLP, L.A., 1984-85, ptnr., mem. intellectual property practice group, 1986—. Panel moderator Calif. continuing edn. of bar Competitive Bus. Practices Inst., Los Angeles and San Francisco, 1984. Mem. ABA, Calif. Bar Assn., Los Angeles County Bar Assn. (arbitrator 1981-82, chmn. customs law sect. 1986), N.Y. State Bar Assn., D.C. Bar Assn., Phi Beta Kappa. Avocations: travel, movies. Immigration, naturalization, and customs, Trademark and copyright. Office: Kelley Drye & Warren LLP 1200 19th St NW Ste 500 Washington DC 20036-2421 E-mail: mlublinski@kelleydrye.com

LUCAS, STEVEN MITCHELL, lawyer; b. Ada, Okla., Jan. 19, 1948; s. John Dalton and Cherrye (Smith) L.; m. Lori E. Seeberger; children: Steven Turner, Brooke Elizabeth, Sarah Grace. BA, Yale U., 1970; JD, Vanderbilt U., 1973. Bar: D.C. 1973, U.S. Ct. Mil. Appeals 1974, U.S. Dist. Ct. D.C. 1979, U.S. Ct. Appeals (D.C.) 1979, U.S. Supreme Ct. 1979. Assoc. Shaw, Pittman, Potts & Trowbridge, Washington, 1978-82, ptnr., 1983-92; ptnr., head fin. instns. practice Wiley, Rein & Fielding, 1992-93, Winston & Strawn, Washington, 1993-97; pvt. practice, 1997—. Cons. on internat. rels., Rockefeller Found., N.Y.C., 1978, mem. negotiating team Panama Canal Treaty, Washington, 1975-77, legal adviser Dept. Def. Panama Canal negotiations working group. Editor in chief Vanderbilt U. Jour. Transnational Law, 1972-73. Treas., mem. exec. com. St. Anne's Episcopal Ch., Annapolis, Md., 1999—. Capt. JAGC, U.S. Army, 1974-77. Mem. ABA, FBA (chmn. internat. law com. 1978-80, Outstanding Com. Chmn. award 1979), Inter-Am. Bar Assn., Am. Soc. Internat. Law, Army-Navy Country Club (Arlington, Va.), Yale Club (N.Y.C.), Army and Navy Club (Washington). Republican. Episcopalian. Banking, Private international, Securities. Home: 1696 Dunstable Green Annapolis MD 21401-6424 Office: 1730 K St NW Ste 304 Washington DC 20006-3839 E-mail: smlucas@bellatlantic.net

LUCCHINO, FRANK JOSEPH, lawyer, county official; b. Pitts., Mar. 16, 1939; s. Dominic Anthony and Rose Marie (Rizzo) L.; m. Roberta Ann Frank, Aug. 25, 1962; children: F.J., Jennifer, David. BS in Engring., U. Pitts., 1961, LLB, 1964. Bar: Pa. 1965, U.S. Supreme Ct. 1970, U.S. Ct. Appeals (3d cir.) 1976. Assoc. Wirtzman, Sikov & Love, Pitts., 1964-68; ptnr. Lucchino, Gaitens & Hough, Pitts., 1968-80, Grogan, Graffam, McGinley & Lucchino, Pitts., 1980— ; contr. County of Allegheny, Pa., 1980—. Mem. Pitts. City Council, 1974-78; v.p. Buhl Sci. Ctr., Pitts., 1978—; mem. bd. trustees U. Pitts. chmn. Carnegie Science Ctr. Mem. ABA, Pa. Bar Assn., Allegheny County Bar Assn. Democrat. Roman Catholic.

LUCE, GREGORY M. lawyer; Bar: D.C., Va., Md. With Jones, Day, Reavis & Pogue, Washington. Mem. ABA, Am. Health Lawyers Assn. (bd. dirs. 1996—), Va. State Bar (past chair, mem. bd. govs. health law sect.). Administrative and regulatory, Federal civil litigation, Health. Office: Jones Day Reavis & Pogue 51 Louisiana Ave NW Washington DC 20001-2113

LUCE, MICHAEL LEIGH, lawyer; b. Mitchell, S.D., Mar. 2, 1952; s. John Russell and Irene (Merkel) L.; m. Mary Claire Goad, Sept. 7, 1979; children: Juliann Marie, Colin Thomas. B.S., Augustana Coll., Sioux Falls, S.D., 1974; J.D., U. S.D., 1977. Bar: S.D. 1977, U.S. Dist. Ct. S.D. 1977, U.S. Ct. Appeals (8th cir.) 1979. Law clk. to Judge Fred J. Nichol, U.S. Dist. Ct. S.D., Sioux Falls, 1977-78; assoc. Davenport Law Firm, Sioux Falls, 1978-80, ptnr., 1981— . Lead articles editor S.D. Law Rev., 1977. Mem. ABA, S.D. Bar Assn. (com. on rules of evidence), Am. Trial Lawyers Assn., Am. Bd. Trial Attys., S.D. Trial Lawyers Assn., Nat. Sch. Bd. Assn. Counsel Sch. Attys. Democrat. Federal civil litigation, State civil litigation, Insurance. Home: 336 Aspen Cir Sioux Falls SD 57105-6934 Office: Davenport Evans Hurwitz & Smith 513 S Main Ave Sioux Falls SD 57104-6813

LUCERO, CARLOS, federal judge; b. Antonito, Colo., Nov. 23, 1940; m. Dorothy Stuart; 1 child, Carla. BA, Adams State Coll.; JD, George Washington U., 1964. Law clk. to Judge William E. Doyle U.S. Dist. Ct., Colo., 1964-65; pvt. practice Alamosa; sr. ptnr. Lucero, Lester & Sigmund; judge U.S. Ct. Appeals (10th cir.), 1995—. Mem. Pres. Carter's Presdl. Panel on Western State Water Policy. Bd. dirs. Colo. Hist. Soc., Santa Fe Opera Assn. of N.Mex. Recipient Outstanding Young Man of Colo. award Colo. Jaycees, Disting. Alumnus award George Washington U.; Paul Harris fellow Rotary Found. Fellow Am. Coll. Trial Lawyers, Am. Bar Found., Colo. Bar Found. (pres.), Internat. Acad. Trial Lawyers, Internat. Soc. Barristers; mem. ABA (mem. action com. to reduce ct. cost and delay, mem adv. bd. ABA jour., mem. com. on the availability of legal svcs.), Colo. Bar Assn. (pres. 1977-78, mem. ethics com.), San Luis Valley Bar Assn. (pres.), Nat. Hispanic Bar Assn., Colo. Hispanic Bar Assn. (profl. svc. award), Colo. Rural Legal Svcs. (bd. dirs.), Order of the Coif. Office: US Ct Appeals 1823 Stout St Denver CO 80257-1823*

LUCEY, JOHN DAVID, JR. lawyer; b. Phila., May 4, 1930; s. John David and Eleanor (Gallagher) L.; m. Carol Ann Henderson, Oct. 29, 1955; children— John David, Michael Dakin, Timothy Gallagher, Carol Anne. A.B., U. Pa., 1953, LL.B., 1956. Bar: Pa. 1957. Mem. firm LaBrum and Doak, Phila., 1957— ; instr. estate counselling Temple U. Sch. Law, 1977-86; course planner, author, lectr. Pa. Bar Inst., 1967— . Mem. Phila. Bar Assn. (chmn. sect. probate and trust law 1976), Pa. Bar Assn., ABA, Am. Coll. Trust & Estate Counsel. Republican. Roman Catholic. Club: Union League of Phila. Probate, Estate taxation. Home: 1237 Hagys Ford Rd Narberth PA 19072-1103 Office: LaBrum & Doak 1818 Market St Ste 2900 Philadelphia PA 19103-3652

LUCHTEL, KEITH EDWARD, lawyer; b. Milford, Iowa, Sept. 7, 1941; s. Leroy Phillip and Gertrude (Marley) L.; m. Patricia Ann Moss, June 4, 1966; children: Kathleen, Kristina. BS, USAF Acad., 1964; JD, Drake U., 1973. Bar: Iowa 1973. Commd. 2d lt. USAF, 1964, advanced through grades to capt., 1968, resigned, 1970; assoc. Nyemaster Law Firm, Des Moines, 1973-76, ptnr., 1976—. Atty. City of Clive, Iowa, 1978-86. Mem. Order of Coif. Republican. Roman Catholic. Avocations: electronics, golf, reading. Administrative and regulatory, Legislative. Home: 10521 Sunset Ter Clive IA 50325-6548 Office: Nyemaster Goode McLaughlin et al 700 Walnut Ste 1600 Des Moines IA 50309-3899

LUCKEY, ALWYN HALL, lawyer; b. Biloxi, Miss., Oct. 3, 1960; s. Toxie Hall and Joy Evelyn (Smith) L.; m. Jeanne Elaine Carter, Aug. 4, 1984; children: Laurel McKay, Taylor Leah. BA in Zoology, U. Miss., 1982, JD, 1985. Bar: Miss. 1985, U.S. Dist. Ct. (so. and no. dist.) Miss. 1985, U.S. Ct. Appeals (5th cir.) 1985. Assoc. Richard F. Scruggs, Pascagoula, Miss., 1985-88, shareholder, 1988—, Asbestos Group PA, 1988-93; prin. Alwyn H. Luckey, Atty. at Law, Ocean Springs, Miss., 1993—. V.p., bd. dirs. Marine Mgmt., Inc., Ocean Springs, Miss., 1987—. Author: Mississippi Landlord Tenant Law, 1985. Deacon First Presbyn. Ch., Ocean Springs, 1989; chmn. Dole for Pres. com., Jackson County, 1988. Mem. Am. Trial Lawyers Assn., Miss. Bar Assn., Miss. Trial Lawyers Assn., Jackson County Bar Assn., Jackson County Young Lawyers Assn. (v.p.), Ocean Springs Yacht Club, Bienville Club, Treasure Oak Country Club. Avocations: tennis, boating, traveling. Personal injury, Product liability. Office: PO Box 724 Ocean Springs MS 39566-0724

LUCKMAN, GREGG A. lawyer; b. Manhasset, N.Y., Dec. 26, 1967; s. Jerry and Lesley Luckman; m. Dara Susan Weintraub, May 3, 1998. BA in Polit. Sci., Am. U., 1989; JD, Whittier Coll., 1992; MBA in Fin., Hofstra U., 1995. Bar: N.Y. 1992. Legis. asst. Congressman Robert J. Mrazek, Washington, 1988; law clk. Calif. Dept. Health-Food and Drug Divsn., L.A., 1992; lawyer various firms, N.Y.C., 1993-96; pvt. practice law Great Neck, N.Y., 1996-99; ptnr. Schwartz, Schlussel & Luckman, 1999—. Vol. lawyer Vol. Lawyers for the Arts, N.Y.C., 1996—; mentor W.T. Clarke Middle Sch., Westbury, N.Y., 1997—; spkr. Profl. Spkrs. Bur., Roslyn, N.Y., 1998. Recipient Pro Bono award Vol. Lawyers for the Arts, N.Y.C., 1998. Mem. NARAS, ABA, N.Y. State Bar Assn., Nassau County Bar Assn. (spkr. 1996—). Avocations: golf, tennis. General corporate, Entertainment, Real property. Office: Ste 306 1010 Northern Blvd Great Neck NY 11021-5306 Fax: 516-829-3993. E-mail: gregglaw@aol.com

LUDGUS, NANCY LUCKE, lawyer; b. Palo Alto, Calif., Oct. 28, 1953; d. Winston Slover and Betty Jean Lucke; m. Lawrence John Ludgus, Apr. 8, 1983. BA in Polit. Sci. with honors, U. Calif., Berkeley, 1975; JD, U. Calif., Davis, 1978. Bar: Calif. 1978, U.S. Dist. Ct. (no. dist.) Calif. 1978. Staff atty. Crown Zellerbach Corp., San Francisco, 1978-80, Clorox Co., Oakland, Calif., 1980-82, Nat. Semiconductor Corp., Santa Clara, 1982-85, corp. counsel, 1985-92, sr. corp. counsel, asst. sec., 1992-2000, assoc. gen. counsel, asst. sec., 2000—. Contbr. articles to profl. jours. Mem. ABA, Am. Corp. Counsel Assn., Calif. State Bar Assn., Santa Clara County Bar Assn., Phi Beta Kappa. Democrat. Avocations: travel, jogging, opera. Contracts commercial, General corporate, Pension, profit-sharing, and employee benefits. Office: Nat Semiconductor Corp 1090 Kifer Rd # 16135 Sunnyvale CA 94086-5301 E-mail: nancy.lucke.ludgus@nsc.com

LUDWIG, EDMUND VINCENT, federal judge; b. Phila., May 20, 1928; s. Henry and Ruth (Viner) L.; children: Edmund Jr., John, Sarah, David. AB, Harvard U., 1949, LLB, 1952. Assoc. Duane, Morris & Heckscher, Phila., 1956-59; ptnr. Barnes, Biester & Ludwig, Doylestown, Pa., 1959-68; judge Common Pleas Ct., Bucks County, 1968-85, U.S. Dist. Ct. (ea. dist.), Phila., 1985—. Faculty Pa. Coll. of the Judiciary, 1974-85; presenter Villanova (Pa.) U. Law Sch., 1975-80, lectr., 1984-97; vis. lectr. Temple Law Sch., 1977-80; clin. assoc. prof. Hahnemann U., Phila., 1977-85; mem. Pa. Juvenile Ct. Judge's Commn., 1978-85; chmn. Pa. Chief Justice's Ednl. Com., 1984-85; pres. Pa. Conf. State Trial Judges, 1981-82; co-chmn. 3d cir. task force on counsel for ind. litigants in civil cases, 1998. Contbr. articles to profl. jours. Chmn. Children and Youth Adv. Com., Bucks County, 1978-83; mem. Pa. Adv. Com. on Mental Health and Mental Retardation, 1980-85; founder, bd. dirs. Today, Inc., Newtown, Pa., 1971-85, Probation Vols., Bucks County, 1971-81; bd. dirs. New Directions for Women, Del. Valley, 1988—; mem. Pa. Joint Coun. Criminal Justice, Inc., 1979-80; mem. Joint Family Law Council Pa., 1979-85; vice chmn. Human Services Council Bucks County, 1979-81; mem. Com. to Study Unified Jud. System Pa., 1980-82, Pa. Legislative Task Force on Mental Health Laws, 1986-87; chmn. Juvenile Justice Alliance, Phila., 1992—; co-chmn. Doylestown (Pa.) Revitalization Bd., 1993-96; mem. 3d cir. task force on equal treatment in the cts., 1995-97; chmn. Doylestown (Pa.) Hist. Soc., 1995—. Recipient Disting. Svc. award Bucks County Corrections Assn., 1978, Spl. Svc. award Big. Bros., 1989, Humanitarian award United Way Bucks County, 1980, Founder's award Vol. Svcs., 1982, Spl. award Bucks County Juvenile Ct., 1985, Humanitarian award Ctrl. Bucks County C. of C., 1994, Disting. Jurist award John Peter Zenger Soc., 2000; Wasserstein Pub. Interest fellow Harvard Law Sch., 1996-97. Mem. ABA, Pa. Bar Assn. (chmn. com. legal svcs. to disabled 1990-92), Phila. Bar Assn. (pro bono pub. award 1998, Pub. Interest Disting. Svc. award 1998), Fed. Bar Assn. (hon.), Harvard Club (N.Y.C. and Phila., v.p. 1979-80), Harvard Law Sch. Assn. (exec. com. 1993—), Fed. Judges Assn. (bd. dirs. 1998—, mem. chmn. 1999—), U.S. Jud. Conf. (com. on ct. adminstrn. and case mgmt.), Am. Law Inst. Office: 12614 US Courthouse Independence Mall W 601 Market St Philadelphia PA 19106-1713 E-mail: Chambers_of_Judge__Edmund_V._Ludwig@paed.uscourts.gov

LUKENS, JOHN PATRICK, lawyer; b. Washington, Aug. 10, 1944; s. John F. and Patricia A. Lukens; m. Donna Lukens, Sept. 24, 1987; 4 children. BS, U. Idaho, 1970, JD cum laude, 1973. Public defender Clark County Public Defender, Las Vegas, 1974-76; pvt. practice, 1976-87; chief dep. dist. atty. Clark County Dist. Atty., 1987-97. Contbr. articles to profl. jours. Founder Sexual Abuse Investigation Team Clinic at Child Haven, Clark County Child Death Rev. com. With U.S. Army, 1967-69. Recipient award Com. on Victim's Rights, 1989. Criminal, Family and matrimonial, Personal injury. Office: 550 E Charleston Blvd Ste B Las Vegas NV 89104-1303

LUKER, LYNN MICHAEL, lawyer; b. Idaho Falls, Idaho, Aug. 30, 1953; s. Nephi Michael Luker and Betty Ruth (Schild) L.; m. Helen Marie Dahlquist, June 19, 1976; children: Daniel Jacob, Jean Marie, Rebecca Jane, David Alexander, Eric Carlyle, Rachel Elizabeth, Andrew Dahlquist, Emily Ruth. AB, U. Calif., Berkeley, 1977; JD, U. Idaho, 1980. Bar: Idaho 1980, U.S. Dist. Ct. Idaho 1981, U.S. Ct. Appeals (9th cir.) 1984, U.S. Supreme Ct. 1985, Utah 1986. Law clk. to presiding justice Idaho Supreme Ct., Boise, 1980-82; sole practice, 1982-83; assoc. Goioechea Law Office, 1983-85, ptnr., 1985-97; pvt. practice, 1997—. Mem. Idaho Appellate Rules Com., 1986-92; chmn. workers compensation sect. Idaho State Bar, 1993-95, chair, specialist cert. com. worker's compensation, 1995—; mem. Gov.'s Adv. Com. on Worker's Compensation, 1995-98. Editor-in-chief U. Idaho Law Rev., 1979-80. Calif. State scholar, 1974-77, Warren scholar 1979-80. Mem.: Idaho Trial Lawyers Assn. Republican. Mormon. Avocations: family, gardening, photography, German language, scouting. Appellate, Personal injury, Workers' compensation. Office: 1010 N Orchard # 4 Boise ID 83706 E-mail: lmluker@mindspring.com

LUMBARD, ELIOT HOWLAND, lawyer, educator; b. Fairhaven, Mass., May 6, 1925; s. Ralph E. and Constance Y. L.; m. Jean Ashmore, June 21, 1947 (div.); m. Kirsten Dehner, June 28, 1981 (div.); children: Susan, John, Ann, Joshua Abel, Marah Abel. BS in Marine Transp., U.S. Mcht. Marine Acad., 1943-45; BS in Econs., U. Pa., 1949; JD, Columbia U., 1952. Bar: N.Y. 1953, U.S. Supreme Ct. 1959, Pa. 1983. Assoc. Breed, Abbott and Morgan, N.Y.C., 1952-53; asst. U.S. atty. So. Dist. N.Y., 1953-56; assoc. Chadbourne, Parke, Whiteside & Wolff, N.Y.C., 1956-58; ptnr. Townsend & Lewis, 1961-70, Spear and Hill, N.Y.C., 1970-75, Lumbard and Phelan, P.C., N.Y.C., 1977-82, Saul, Ewing, Remick & Saul, N.Y.C., 1982-84; pvt. practice law, 1984-86; ptnr. Haight, Gardner, Poor & Havens, 1986-88; pvt. practice law, 1988-92; ret. Chief counsel N.Y. State Commn. Investigation, 1958-61; spl. asst. counsel for law enforcement to Gov. N.Y., 1961-67; organizer N.Y. State Identification and Intelligence Sys., 1963-67; chair Oyster Bay Conf. on Organized Crime, 1962-67; criminal justice cons. to Gov. Fla. and other states, 1967; chief criminal justice cons. to N.J. Legis., 1968-69; chmn. com. on organized crime N.Y.C. Criminal Justice Coordinating Coun., 1971-74; organizer schs. of criminal justice at SUNY Albany and Rutgers, Newark; mem. departmental disciplinary com. First Dept., N.Y. Supreme Ct., 1982-88; trustee bankruptcy Universal Money Order Co., Inc., 1977-82, Meritum Corp., 1983-89; spl. master in admiralty Hellenic Lines Ltd., 1984-86; chmn. Palisades Life Ins. Co. (former Equity Funding subs. 1974-75); bd. dir. RMC Industries Corp.; chair Am. Maritime History Project, Inc., Kings Point, N.Y., 1996—; lectr. trial practice NYU Law Sch., 1963-65; mem. vis. com. Sch. Criminal Justice, SUNY-Albany, 1968-75; adj. prof. law and criminal justice John Jay Coll. Criminal Justice, CUNY, 1975-86; arbitrator Am. Arbitration Assn. and N.Y. Civil Ct.-Small Claims Part, N.Y. County; mem. Vol. Master Program U.S. Dist. Ct. (so. dist.) N.Y. Contbr. articles to profl. jours. Bd. dirs. Citizens Crime Commn. N.Y.C., Inc., Big Bros. Movement, Citizens Union; trustee Trinity Sch., 1964-78, N.Y.C. Police Found., Inc., 1971-92, chmn., 1971-74, emeritus. Lt. j.g. USNR, 1943-52. Recipient Disting. Svc. award U.S. Merchant Marine Acad. Alumni, 2000. Mem. Assn. Bar City N.Y., N.Y. County Lawyers Assn., ABA, N.Y. State Bar Assn., Maritime Law Assn., Down Town Assn. Club. Republican. Bankruptcy, Federal civil litigation, State civil litigation. Home: 39B Apple Ln Hollis NH 03049-6311

LUNA, BARBARA CAROLE, financial analyst, accountant, appraiser; b. N.Y.C., July 23, 1950; d. Edwin A. and Irma S. (Schub) Schlang; m. Dennis Rex Luna, Sept. 1, 1974; children: John S., Katherine E. BA, Wellesley Coll., 1971; MS in Applied Math., Harvard U., 1973, PhD in Applied Math., 1975. CPA; cert. gen. real estate appraiser Calif. Office Real Estate Appraisers; cert. valuation analyst Nat. Assn. Cert. Valuation Analysts; cert. fraud examiner Assn. Cert. Fraud Examiners, mgmt. cons. Inst. Mgmt. Consultants; accredited sr. appraiser Am. Soc. Appraisers; accredited bus. valuation Am. Inst. CPAs. Investment banker Warburg Paribas Becker, L.A., 1975-77; cons., sr. mgr. Price Waterhouse, 1977-83; sr. mgr. litigation Pannell Kerr Forster, 1983-86; nat. dir. litigation cons. Kenneth Leventhal & Co., 1986-88; ptnr. litigation svcs. Coopers & Lybrand, 1988-93; sr. ptnr. litigation svcs. White, Zuckerman, Warsavsky, Luna & Wolf, Sherman Oaks, Calif., 1993—. Expert witness. Mem. Harvard Bus. Sch. Coun. Wellesley scholar, 1971. Mem. AICPA, Assn. Bus. Trial Lawyers (com. on experts), Am. Soc. Appraisers, Assn. Cert. Valuation Analysts, Calif. Office Real Estate Appraisers, Assn. Cert. Real Estate Appraisers, Appraisal Inst., Assn. Cert. Fraud Examiners, Inst. Mgmt. Cons., Calif. Soc. CPAs (econ.

damages common interest mem. svcs. com., fraud common interest mem. svcs. com., bus. valuation common interest mem. svcs. com.), Am. Bd. Forensic Accts. and Examiners, Harvard-Radcliffe Club So. Calif. (bd. dirs., membership chair). Avocations: golf, swimming. Home: 18026 Rodarte Way Encino CA 91316-4370 E-mail: bluna@lunala.com, bluna@wzwlw.com

LUNA, DENNIS R. lawyer; b. L.A., Aug. 21, 1946; BS in Petroleum Engrng., U. So. Calif., 1968, MS in Petroleum Engrng., 1969, MBA, 1971; JD, Harvard U., 1974. Bar: Calif. 1974; Assoc. firm Baker & Hostetler McCutchen Black, L.A., 1974-81, ptnr., 1981—. Commr. Bd. Recreation and Parks, City of Los Angeles, 1984-89; alt. commr., L.A. Meml. Coliseum Commn., 1987-89; bd. dirs. Econ. Devel. Corp. of L.A. County, 1988—. Commr. Community Redevel. Agy., City of L.A., 1989—, treas., 1990—. Contbr. articles to legal jours. Registered profl. petroleum engr., Calif. Mem. ABA (sect. of corp., banking and bus. law, sect. natural resources law), Calif. State Bar Assn., Soc. Petroleum Engrs. Office: 600 Wilshire Blvd Los Angeles CA 90017-3212

LUND, JAMES LOUIS, lawyer; b. Long Beach, Calif., Oct. 4, 1926; s. G. Louis and Hazel Eunice (Cochran) L.; m. Jo Alvarez, Aug. 5, 1950; 1 son, Eric James. BA in Math., U. So. Calif., 1946; postgrad., Grad. Sch. Annapolis, 1949; JD, Southwestern U., 1955; postgrad. Sch. Law, U. So. Calif., 1956. Bar: Calif. 1955, U.S. Dist. Ct. (cen. dist.) Calif. 1955, U.S. Ct. Appeals (9th cir.) 1955, U.S. Tax Ct. 1955, U.S. Supreme Ct. Spl. agt. U.S. Govt., 1950-52; gen. mgr. Pacific ops., gen. counsel Holmes & Narver, Inc., L.A., 1952-66; exec. v.p. Calif. Fabricators, Oakland and Honolulu, 1966-67; sr. ptnr. James Lund Law Firm, Beverly Hills, Tehran, London and Tokyo, 1967-83; pres., founder Fortres Mgmt. Co.; ptnr. Lund & Lund, 1983—. Chmn. bd. Envirotire, 1998—; dir. Superior Vision Svcs., Inc. Lt. comdr. USNR, 1943-46, 48-50. Mem. ABA, SAR, L.A. County Bar Assn., Internat. Bar Assn., Inter-Am. Bar Assn., Asia Pacific Lawyers Assn., Les Ambassadeurs Club (London). Construction, Private international, Real property. Office: Ste 1555 1901 Avenue Of The Stars Los Angeles CA 90067-6052 E-mail: jlundesq@pacbell.net

LUNDE, ASBJORN RUDOLPH, lawyer; b. S.I., N.Y., July 17, 1927; s. Karl and Elisa (Andenes) L. AB, Columbia U., 1947, LLB, 1949. Bar: N.Y. 1949. Pvt. practice, N.Y.C., 1950-91; with Kramer, Marx, Greenlee & Backus and predecessors, 1950-68, mem., 1958-68; pvt. practice Columbia County, N.Y., 1991—. Bd. dirs., v.p. Orch. da Camera, Inc., 1964—, Sara Roby Found., 1971—; bd. dirs. Clarion Concerts in Columbia County, 1999—; mem. vis. com. dept. European paintings Met. Mus. Art. Fellow Met. Mus. Art (life); mem. ABA, N.Y. State Bar Assn., Assn. Bar City N.Y., Met. Opera Club, East India Club (London). Avocation: art collecting (donor paintings and sculptures to Met. Mus. Art, N.Y.C., Nat. Gallery Art, Washington, Mus. Fine Arts, Boston, Clark Art Inst., Williamstown, Mass., others). Contracts commercial, General corporate, Private international. Home and Office: 135 LaBranche Rd Hillsdale NY 12529-5713

LUNDEEN, BRADLEY CURTIS, lawyer; b. Karlstad, MN, Nov. 16, 1958; s. Curtis W. and LaVonne M. (Oistad) L.; m. Kristina Ogland, May 18, 1984 (div. Dec. 1991); 1 child, Jonathan B. BA, Moorhead State U, 1980; JD cum laude, William Mitchell Coll. Law, 1984. Bar: Minn. 1984, Wis. 1984. Assoc. Gwin, Gilbert, Gwin, Mudge & Porter, Hudson, Wis., 1984, Gilbert, Mudge & Porter, Hudson, 1985; ptnr. Gilbert, Mudge, Porter & Lundeen, 1986-92; lawyer, shareholder Mudge, Porter & Lundeen S.C., 1992-94, Mudge, Porter, Lundeen & Seguin S.C., Hudson, 1995-99, Lundeen Law Ltd., 2000—. Bd. dirs. Hudson Rotary, 1990-91, Bank St. Croix, Hudson, Wis., 1987-94, St. Croix Valley Employers Assn., 1996—; pres. St. Croix Valley Employers Assn., 1999-01. Mem. St. Croix Valley Bar Assn., St. Croix Valley Employers Assn., Masons, Shriners. Lutheran. Avocations: golf, skiing, travel, computers and cooking. Labor, Pension, profit-sharing, and employee benefits, Workers' compensation. Home: 731B Blue Jay Ln Hudson WI 54016-7695 Office: Lundeen Law Ltd PO Box 246 Hudson WI 54446-0246 E-mail: brad@lundeenlawltd.com

LUNDEEN, DAVID F. lawyer; b. Fergus Falls, Minn., Oct. 28, 1932; s. Victor George and Selma Irene (Rostad) L.; m. Mary Dorthea Watson, June 21, 1958; children: Ingrid, Emily Copeland, Eric Jordan. AB, Amherst (Mass.) Coll., 1954; JD, Harvard U., 1957. Bar: Minn. 1957, U.S. Dist. Ct. Minn. 1961, U.S. Dist. Ct. S.D. 1976, U.S. Tax Ct., U.S. Ct. Appeals (8th cir.), U.S. Ct. Appeals (D.C. cir.), U.S. Supreme Ct. Practice, Fergus Falls, Minn., 1960—; assoc. firm Field, Arvesen & Donoho, 1960-61; ptnr. firm Arvesen, Lundeen, Hoff, Svingen, Athens & Russell, 1962—. Sec., dir. Victor Lundeen Co., Fergus Falls, 1971—; lectr. Minn. Continuing Legal Edn. Bd. dirs. Indsl. Devel. Corp. Fergus Falls, 1970s. Served to capt. JAGC, USAR, 1957-60; bd. dirs., sec. Fergus Area Coll. Found., 1986—; founding mem., dir. Fergus Falls 544 Edn. Found., 2000—. Simpson fellow, Harvard U., 1954. Mem. Minn. State Bar Assn. (past pres. tax sect.), 7th Jud. Dist. Bar Assn., Fed. Bar Assn., ABA, Phi Beta Kappa. Club: Rotary (pres. 1970-71). General practice, Probate, Public utilities. Home: 705 W Lakeside Dr Fergus Falls MN 56537-2115 Office: David F Lundeen Law Office 107 N Court St Fergus Falls MN 56537

LUNDGREN, GAIL M. lawyer; b. Tacoma, June 14, 1955; d. Arthur Dean and Vera Martha (Grimm) L. AB cum laude, Vassar Coll., 1977; JD cum laude, U. Puget Sound (now Seattle U. Law Sch.), 1980. Bar: Wash. 1981. Legal intern Reed, McClure, Moceri & Thonn, Seattle, 1979, Burges & Kennedy, Tacoma, 1979-80, Lee, Smart, Cook, Martin & Patterson, P.S., Inc., Seattle, 1980-81, assoc., 1981-92; prin. Law Offices Gail L. Weber, Bothell, 1992-95, Tom Chambers & Assocs., 1995-99; lawyer Law Offices of Kirk Bernard, Seattle, 1999; ptnr. Bernard, Lundgren & Assoc., 1999—. Vestry com. Queen Anne Luth. Ch., 1983-86, v.p. congregation, 1988, 89, mem. worship and music com., 1982-83, 84-86, parish edn. com., 1983-84. Recipient Am. Jurisprudence Book award in Criminal Procedure, Corps. and Bus. Planning, 1980. Mem. ABA, Fed. Bar Asn., Wash. State Trial Lawyers Assn., Order of Barristers, Wash. State Vassar Club (chmn. alumni admissions 1983-85, rep. 1986-92). Democrat. Avocations: scuba diving, tennis, classical music, needlepoint, stitchery. General civil litigation, Personal injury, Product liability. Office: Bernard Lundgren & Assocs PLLC Ste 100 900 Aurora Ave N Ste 100 Seattle WA 98109

LUNDIN, JOHN W. lawyer, urban planner; b. Seattle, Mar. 16, 1943; s. John W. and Margaret (Odell) L.; m. Jane Echols, Mar. 28, 1970; children: J. Ingrid, Jason E. BA, U. Wash., 1965, JD, 1968; M in Urban and Regional Planning, George Washington U., 1975. Bar: Wash. 1968, D.C. 1972, U.S. Dist. Ct. (we. dist.) Wash. 1972, U.S. Dist. Ct. D.C. 1972; U.S. Ct. Appeals (9th cir.) 1973, U.S. Supreme Ct. 1976, U.S. Dist. Ct. (ea. dist.) Wash. 1985. Atty. FAA/Dept. Transp., Washington, 1968-70; with Office of the Asst. Sec., U.S. Dept. Transp., 1970-72; with civil rights divsn. U.S. Dept. Justice, Seattle, 1972-74; sole practice, 1976—. Contbr. articles to law jours. Mem. ABA, Wash. Bar Assn. (chmn. land use and environ. law sect., bd. dirs.), Nat. Assn. Criminal Def. Lawyers, Fed. Bar Assn. Home: 2726 10th Ave E Seattle WA 98102-3924 Office: 710 Cherry St Seattle WA 98104-1925

LUNDSTROM, GILBERT GENE, banker, lawyer; b. Sept. 27, 1941; s. Vernon G. and Imogene (Jackett) L.; m. Joyce Elaine Ronin, June 26, 1965; children: Trevor A., Gregory G. BS, U. Nebr., 1964, JD, 1969; MBA, Wayne State U., 1966. Bar: U.S. Dist. Ct. (1st dist.) Nebr. 1969, Nebr. 1969, U.S. Ct. Appeals (5th cir.) 1970, U.S. Ct. Appeals (10th cir.) 1971, U.S. Ct. Appeals (8th cir.) 1974, U.S. Ct. Appeals (3d cir.) 1986. Ptnr. Woods & Aitken Law Firm, Lincoln, Nebr., 1969-93; pres., CEO, chmn. bd. First Fed. Lincoln Bank, 1994—. Pres., CEO First Lincoln Bancshares Inc., a Delaware Corp.; part-time faculty law sch. U. Nebr.-Lincoln, 1970-74; dir. First Fed. Lincoln Bank, TMS Corp. of Ams., First Fin. Corp.; bd. dirs. Sahara Enterprises, Inc., Sahara Coal Co., Chgo.; dir., vice chmn. Fed. Home Loan Bank Topeka, 1996-98, 99—, dir. City of Lincoln C. of C. Bd. dirs. Folsom Children's Zoo, Lincoln, 1979-83, St. Elizabeth Hosp. Found.; dir. Nat. Coun. Fed. Home Loan Banks, Lincoln C. of C. Fellow Nebr. State Bar Assn.; mem. ABA, ATLA, Lincoln Bar Assn., Nebr. Bar Assn., Newcomer Soc. U.S., Heartland Cmty. Bankers Assn. (bd. dirs.), Country Club of Lincoln, Firethorn County Club, Masons, Scottish Rite (33 degree), Lincoln C. of C. (bd. dirs.) Republican. Methodist. Home: 9519 Firethorn Ln Lincoln NE 68520-1459 Office: First Fed Lincoln 1235 N St Lincoln NE 68508-2083

LUNDY, SHEILA EDWARDS, lawyer; b. Balt., Nov. 29, 1954; d. James Morris and Christine Anne E.; children: Tiffany D., Christopher R. BA, U. Balt., 1978, JD, 1991. Bar: U.S. Ct. Appeals Md. 1992, U.S. Dist. Ct. Md. 1994. Adminstrv. specialist BWI Airport, Md. Aviation Adminstrn., Balt., 1988-91, risk mgmt. specialist, 1991-92; staff atty. Md. Office Atty. Gen., Glen Burnie, 1992-94, asst. atty. gen., 1994—. Faculty The Md. Inst. for Continuing Profl. Edn. of Lawyers, 1999. Mem. Mt. St. Josephs H.S. Mother's Club, Balt., 1997—. Mem. Am. Inns of Ct., Md. Bar Assn. (mem. lawyer counseling com. 1998—), Paca-Brent Joint Inn of Ct., Anne Arundel County Bar Assn. (mem. com. 1994—, bd. trustees 1999), U. Balt. Alumni Assn., Paca-Brent Inn of Ct. (bd. dirs. 1999), Monumental Bar Assn. Democrat. Roman Catholic. Avocations: gardening, reading, old movies.

LUNGREN, JOHN HOWARD, law educator, oil and gas consultant, author; b. Chgo., Feb. 11, 1925; s. Charles Howard and Edna Hughes (Edwards) L.; m. Phyllis Joan Jolidon, Dec. 12, 1953 (div.); 1 son, John Eric; m. Susan Jeanette Whitfield, Sept. 22, 1984. B.A., Beloit Coll., 1948; J.D., Marquette U., 1952; M.A., U. Wis.-Milw., 1974. Bar: Wis. 1952, Ill. 1975, Kans. 1980. Assoc. gen. counsel A. O. Smith Corp., 1964-74; gen. atty. Clark Oil & Refining Corp., 1954-64; prof. law Lewis U., Glen Ellyn, Ill., 1975-80; assoc. prof. law Washburn U. Sch. Law, Topeka, 1980-85; practice, Chgo., from 1977; with Turner & Boisseau Ltd., Wichita, Kans., 1985-88; of counsel Lungren and Whitfield-Lungren, Wichita, 1987—; cons. oil and gas; Kans. rep. legal com. Interstate Oil Compact. Chmn., Milwaukee County Republican Party, 1966-70; justice of peace, Wauwatosa, Wis., 1964-68. Served with USN, 1943-46. Mem. ABA, Ill. Bar Assn., Wis. Bar Assn., Kans. Bar Assn., Wichita Bar Assn.

LUNGSTRUM, JOHN W. federal judge; b. Topeka, Nov. 2, 1945; s. Jack Edward and Helen Alice (Watson) L.; m. Linda Eileen Ewing, June 21, 1969; children: Justin Matthew, Jordan Elizabeth, Alison Paige. BA magna cum laude, Yale Coll., 1967; JD, U. Kans., 1970. Bar: Kans. 1970, Calif. 1970, U.S. Dist. Ct. (ctrl. dist.) Calif., U.S. Ct. Appeals (10th crct.). Assoc. Latham & Watkins, L.A., 1970-71; ptnr. Stevens, Brand, Lungstrum, Golden & Winter, Lawrence, Kans., 1972-91; U.S. Dist. judge Dist. of Kans., Kansas City, 1991—, chief judge, 2001—. Lectr. law U. Kans. Law Sch., 1973—; mem. faculty Kans. Bar Assn. Coll. Advocacy, Trial Tactics and Techniques Inst., 1983-86; chmn. Douglas County Rep. Ctrl. Com., 1975-81; mem. Rep. State Com.; del. State Rep. Convention, 1968, 76, 80; chair com. on ct. adminstrn. and case mgmt. Jud. Conf. of the U.S., 2000—. Chmn. bd. dirs. Lawrence C. of C., 1990-91; pres. Lawrence United Fund, 1979; pres. Independence Days Lawrence, Inc., 1984, 85, Seem-to-be-Players, Inc., Lawrence Rotary Club, 1978-79; bd. dirs. Lawrence Soc. Chamber Music, Swarthout Soc. (corp. fund-raising chmn.); mem. Lawrence Art Commn., Williams Scholarship Fund, Lawrence League Women Voters, Douglas County Hist. Soc.; bd. trustees, stewardship chmn. Plymouth Congl. Ch.; pres. Lawrence Round Ball Club; coach Lawrence Summertime Basketball; Vice chmn. U. Kans. Disciplinary Bd.; bd. govs. Kans Sch. Religion; bd. dirs. Kans. Day Club, 1980, 81. National Merit scholar, Yale Nat. scholar. Fellow Am. Bar Found.; mem. ABA (past mem. litigation and ins. sect.), Douglas County Bar Assn., Johnson County Bar Assn., Wyandotte County Bar Assn., Kans. Bar Assn. (vice chair legislative com., subcom. litigation, mem. continuing legal edn. com.), U Kans. Alumni Assn. (life), Phi Beta Kappa, Phi Gamma Delta, Phi Delta Phi. Avocations: basketball, hiking, skiing. Office: Robt J Dole US Courthouse Ste 517 500 State Ave Rm 517 Kansas City KS 66101-2400

LUNING, THOMAS P. lawyer; b. St. Louis, Oct. 11, 1942; AB magna cum laude, Xavier U., 1964; JD, Georgetown U., 1967. Bar: D.C. 1968, Ill. 1968. Law clk. to Hon. Spottswood W. Robinson III and to ct. U.S. Ct. Appeals (D.C. cir.), 1967-68; atty. Schiff Hardin & Waite, Chgo. Mng. editor Georgetown Law Jour., 1966-67. Mem. ABA, Ill. State Bar Assn., Chgo. Bar Assn., 7th Cir. Bar Assn., Chgo. Coun. Lawyers. Antitrust, General civil litigation, Professional liability. Office: Schiff Hardin & Waite 6600 Sears Tower Chicago IL 60606 E-mail: tluning@schiffhardin.com

LUPERT, LESLIE ALLAN, lawyer; b. Syracuse, N.Y., May 24, 1946; s. Reuben and Miriam (Kaufman) L.; m. Roberta Gail Fellner, May 19, 1968; children: Jocelyn, Rachel, Susannah. BA, U. Buffalo, 1967; JD, Columbia U., 1971. Bar: N.Y. 1971. Ptnr. Orans Elsen & Lupert, N.Y.C., 1971—. Contbr. articles to profl. jours. Mem. ABA, N.Y. State Bar Assn. (trial lawyers sect.), Assn. of Bar of City of N.Y. (com. fed. legislation 1977-80, profl. and jud. ethics com. 1983-86, com. on fed. cts. 1986-89, 95-96), Phi Beta Kappa. Federal civil litigation, State civil litigation, Criminal. Office: Orans Elsen & Lupert 1 Rockefeller Plz New York NY 10020-2102 E-mail: llupert@oelaw.com

LUPINO, JAMES SAMUEL, lawyer; b. Mpls., Oct. 23, 1952; s. Rocco and Marie (Furlong) L.; m. Diane Schaefer, May 14, 1983. BS, Augustana Coll., 1974; JD, Hamline U., 1977. Bar: Fla. 1977, Minn. 1977, U.S. Dist. Ct. (so. dist.) Fla. 1977, U.S. Dist. Ct. Minn. 1977, Colo. 1997. Assoc. Thomson, Nordby & Peterson, St. Paul, 1976-77; counsel Lone Star Industries, Greenwich, Conn., 1977-79; sole practice Coral Gables, Fla., 1980-86; ptnr. Storace & Lupino, Miami, 1986-87, 91-93, Storace, Lupino & Middelthon, Miami, 1987-91, Storace, Lupino, Gregg & Casey, Miami, 1993-95, Hershoff, Lupino, DeFoor & Gregg, Miami, 1995—. Mem. ABA, Fla. Bar Assn., Minn. Bar Assn., Assn. Trial Lawyer Am., Key Largo C. of C (bd. dirs.), Kiwanis, Upper Keys Rotary Club (bd. dirs.). Republican. Roman Catholic. Avocations: family, skiing, scuba, football. Contracts commercial, General corporate, Personal injury. Office: Hershoff Lupino & Mulick LLP 90130 Old Hwy Tavernier FL 33070-2348

LUPKIN, STANLEY NEIL, lawyer; b. Bklyn., Mar. 27, 1941; s. David B. and Sylvia (Strassman) L.; m. Anne Rachel Fischler, June 3, 1962; children: Jonathan Daniel, Deborah Eve. BA, Columbia Coll., 1962; LLB, NYU, 1966. Bar: N.Y. 1966, U.S. Dist. Ct. (so. and ea. dists.) N.Y. 1970, U.S. Ct. Appeals (2d cir.) 1970, U.S. Supreme Ct. 1971. Asst. dist. atty., sr. trial atty., chief indictment bur. N.Y. County Dist. Atty.'s Office, N.Y.C., 1966-71; asst. commr. City of N.Y., 1966-71; 1st dep. commr., commr. Dept. Investigation, N.Y.C., 1978-82; ptnr. Litman, Asche, Lupkin, Gioiella & Bassin, 1982-96; sr. mng. dir., counsel Decision Strategies/Fairfax Internat., L.L.C., 1996—. Mem. faculty Nat. Coll. Dist. Attys., Houston, 1974-75, FBI Nat. Acad., Quantico, Va., 1980-82; chmn. com. on criminal justice ops. Assn. of Bar of City of N.Y., 1982-85. Co-author book: Anatomy of A Municipal Franchise: N.Y.C. Bus Shelter Program, 1973-79, 4 vols., 1981. Trustee, counsel Solomon Schechter Sch. of Queens, Flushing, N.Y., 1974—; mem. secondary schs. com. admissions office Columbia Coll., N.Y.C., 1987-99. With USAR, 1963-69. Mem. NACDL, N.Y. State Bar Assn. (chmn. com. on def. 1985-2000, chmn. com. on prosecution 1977-85, exec. com. criminal justice sect. 1977-2000, Prosecutor of Yr. award 1981), N.Y. State Assn. Criminal Def. Lawyers, N.Y. Criminal Bar Assn., Am. Corp. Counsel Assn., Soc. Columbia Grads. (v.p. 1989-98, dir. 1989—), Internat. Assn. Ind. Pvt. Sector Insps. Gen. Avocations: classical music, Talmudic law. Administrative and regulatory, General civil litigation, Criminal. Office: Decision Strategies/Fairfax Internat LLC 505 Park Ave Fl 7 New York NY 10022-1106

LURENSKY, MARCIA ADELE, lawyer; b. Newton, Mass., May 4, 1948; BA magna cum laude, Wheaton Coll., 1970; JD, Boston Coll. Law Sch., 1973. Bar: Mass. 1973, D.C. 1990, U.S. Dist. Ct. (we. dist.) Wis. 1978, U.S. Dist. Ct. Mass. 1974, U.S. Ct. Appeals (1st cir.) 1974, U.S. Ct. Appeals (3d cir.) 1982, U.S. Ct. Appeals (4th cir.) 1984, U.S. Ct. Appeals (5th cir.) 1995, U.S. Ct. Appeals (8th cir.) 1985, U.S. Ct. Appeals (9th cir.) 1976, U.S. Ct. Appeals (10th cir.) 1995, U.S. Ct. Appeals (11th cir.) 1982, U.S. Ct. Appeals (fed. cir.) 1989, U.S. Claims Ct. 1989, U.S. Supreme Ct. 1979. Atty. U.S. Dept. Labor, Washington, 1974-90, Fed. Energy Regulatory Commn., U.S. Dept. Energy, Washington, 1990—. Mem. Phi Beta Kappa. Office: Fed Energy Regulatory Commn 888 1st St NE Washington DC 20426-0002

LURIE, JEANNE FLORA, lawyer, manufacturing company executive; b. N.Y.C., Aug. 20, 1946; d. Ralph A. and Irene (Chartier) LaFlamme; m. Robert M. Lurie, July 7, 1973; 1 child, Jane Margaret. B.A., Radcliffe Coll., 1968; J.D., Boston U., 1974. Bar: Mass. 1974, Fla. 1976. Assoc. firm Mahoney, Adams, Milam, Surface & Grimsley, Jacksonville, Fla., 1976-82, ptnr., 1982-84; corp. counsel, head legal dept., sec. Clow Corp., Jacksonville, 1984-85; bd. dirs. Jacksonville Area Legal Services, 1979. Mem. program com. Leadership Jacksonville. Mem. Mass. Bar Assn., Fla. Bar Assn. (legal aid com.), ABA (credit union com.), Jacksonville Women's Network (bd. dirs., chmn. membership com. 1980-82), Harvard Club of Jacksonville (v.p., chmn. recruiting). Administrative and regulatory, General corporate. Home: 517 Heyward Cir NW Marietta GA 30064-1405

LURVEY, IRA HAROLD, lawyer; b. Chgo., Apr. 6, 1935; s. Louis and Faye (Grey) L.; m. Barbara Ann Sirvint, June 24, 1962; children: Nathana, Lawrence, Jennifer, Jonathan, David, Robert. BS, U. Ill., 1956; MS, Northwestern U., 1961; JD, U. Calif., Berkeley, 1965. Bar: Calif. 1965, Nev. 1966, U.S. Dist. Ct. (cen. dist.) Calif. 1966, U.S. Tax Ct. 1966, U.S. Ct. Appeals (9th cir.) 1966, U.S. Supreme Ct. 1975. Law clk. to hon. justices Nev. Supreme Ct., Carson City, 1965-66; from assoc. to ptnr. Pacht, Ross, Warne, Bernhard & Sears, Inc., 1966-84; predecessor firm Shea & Gould, L.A.; founding ptnr. Lurvey & Shapiro, 1984—. Lectr. legal edn. programs; mem. Chief Justice's Commns. on Ct. Reform, Weighted Caseloads; mediator family law L.A. Superior Ct. Editor Community Property Jour., 1979-80, Primary Consultant CFL 2d, 1994; columnist Calif. Family Law Monthly; contbr. articles to profl. jours. Former chmn. L.A. Jr. Arts Ctr.; past pres. Cheviot Hills Homeowners Assn.; exec. v.p., counsel Hillel Acad. Sch., Beverly Hills, Calif., 1977—. With U.S. Army, 1957-58. Fellow Am. Acad. Matrimonial Lawyers (pres. So. Calif. chpt. 1991-92, mem. nat. bd. govs. 1992-94), Internat. Acad. Matrimonial Lawyers; mem. ABA (chair family law sect. 1996-97, liaison family law to sr. lawyers' divsn. 1998—, exec. com. 1991-97, governing coun. 1986—, fin. officer 1991-92, chmn. support com., chmn. CLE, chmn. policy and issues com., vice chmn. com. arbitration and mediation, bd. of editors Family Adv. mag., chmn. issues com. sr. lawyer divsn. 2001—), Calif. Bar Assn. (editor jour. 1982-85, chmn. family law sect. 1986-87, exec. com. family law sect. 1982-88, specialization adv. bd. family law 1979-82), L.A. County Bar Assn. (chmn. family law sect. 1981-82, exec. com. family law 1989-92), Beverly Hills Bar Assn. (chmn. family law sect. 1976-77,). State civil litigation, Entertainment, Family and matrimonial. Home: 2729 Motor Ave Los Angeles CA 90064-3441 Office: Lurvey & Shapiro Ste 1550 1333 Beverly Green Drive Los Angeles CA 90035-1018 E-mail: lurvshap@aol.com

LUSKIN, JOSEPH, law educator, researcher; b. N.Y.C., May 30, 1923; s. Harry and Anna (Sklar) L.; m. Mollie Winkler, July 11, 1944; children: Richard Terrence, Elizabeth Karen. Student Bklyn. Law Sch., 1961-62; BBA, CUNY, 1962; MS in Criminal Justice, Auburn U., 1979; M.A., Columbia U., 1971, Ed.D., 1976. Officer Port Authority Police Dept., N.Y.C., 1946-71; state project dir. Am. Justice Inst., Newark, 1971-73; project dir. Police Tng. Commn., Newark, 1973-74; asst. prof. Paterson State Coll., N.J., 1974-75; tenured prof., dir. dept. criminal justice Ala. State U., Montgomery, 1975-92. Pres. Ala. Vols. in Corrections, Montgomery, 1981-83, bd. dirs., 1978-84; bd. dirs. Ala. Office Vol. Citizen Participation, Montgomery, 1980-84. Served with U.S. Army, 1942-46, PTO. Mem. Internat. Assn. Chiefs Police, Am. Soc. Criminology, Am. Criminal Justice Assn. (chpt. adviser 1978-92), Ala. Consortium Criminal Justice Educators (pres. 1978). Lodges: Masons (32 deg.), Shriners.

LUSKIN, ROBERT DAVID, lawyer; b. Chgo., Jan. 21, 1950; s. Bert L. and S. Ruth (Katz) L.; m. Fairlea A. Sheehy, Aug. 23, 1975 (div. Mar. 2000); children: Peter Duncan, Charles Cassimer. BA magna cum laude, Harvard U., 1972, JD magna cum laude, 1979; postgrad., Oxford (Eng.) U., 1972-75. Bar: D.C. 1979, U.S. Ct. Appeals (1st, 2nd, 4th, 5th, 6th, 7th, 8th, 9th, 11th, D.C. and fed. cirs.) 1979, U.S. Supreme Ct., 1983. Law clk. to Hon. Louis F. Oberdorfer U.S. Dist. Ct. for D.C., Washington, 1979-80; spl. counsel organized crime racketeering sect. U.S. Dept. Justice, 1980-82; ptnr. Onek, Klein & Farr, 1982-89, Powell, Goldstein, Frazer & Murphy, Washington, 1989-93, Comey, Boyd & Luskin, Washington, 1993-99, Putton Boggs, LLP, 2000—. Lectr. in law U. Va. Sch. Law, 1992—. Rhodes scholar, 1972-75. Mem. ABA (chmn. RICO Forfeitures and Civil Remedies com. 1986-94, vice chmn. task force on forfeitures), Harvard Law Sch. Assn. Washington (pres.). Federal civil litigation, Criminal. Home: 3415 Prospect St NW Washington DC 20007-3219 Office: Patton Boggs LLP 2550 M St NW Washington DC 20037 E-mail: rluskin@pattonboggs.com

LUSTBADER, PHILIP LAWRENCE, lawyer; b. Balt., May 14, 1949; s. I. William and Evelyn (Kandel) L.; m. Randy R. Tatarka, June 28, 1970; children: Michael Howard, Jamie Robyn. BS, Wharton Sch., U. Pa., 1970; JD summa cum laude, Temple U., 1973. Bar: Pa. 1973, N.J. 1974, U.S. Dist. Ct. (ea. dist.) Pa. 1974, U.S. Dist. Ct. N.J. 1974, U.S. Ct. Appeals (3d cir.) 1975. Assoc. Wolf, Block, Schorr & Solis-Cohen, Phila., 1973-78; counsel Subaru of Am., Inc., Cherry Hill, N.J., 1978-80, asst. v.p., corp. counsel, 1980-83, v.p., gen. counsel, 1983-86, group v.p., gen. counsel and sec., 1987-90, sr. v.p., gen. counsel, sec., 1991-92, Lustbader and Assocs. P.C., Attys. at Law, Phila., 1993-95; pres. Tradewell Discount Investing, LLC, 1996—, Tradewell Holdings, LLC, 1996—; bd. dirs. Subaru of Am., Inc., 1987-90. Exec. editor Temple Law Quar., 1972-73. Mem. ABA. Contracts commercial, Communications, General corporate. Office: Tradewell Discount Investing 45 Broadway Fl 20 New York NY 10006-3007

LUSTENBERGER, LOUIS CHARLES, JR. lawyer; b. Chgo., Mar. 13, 1936; s. Louis Charles and Virginia (Chesrown) L.; m. Anita T. Anderson, June 17, 1961; children: Louis, Gwyn. BA, Williams Coll., 1959; LLB, Harvard U., 1962. Bar: N.Y. 1963, U.S. Dist. Ct. (so. and ea. dist.) N.Y. 1964, U.S. Dist. Ct. (we. dist.) N.Y. 1986, U.S. Ct. Appeals (2d cir.) 1964, U.S. Ct. Appeals (3d cir.) 1989, U.S. Ct. Appeals (5th cir.) 1980, U.S. Supreme Ct. 1978, U.S. Ct. Appeals (10th cir.) 1993, U.S. Dist. Ct. (we. dist.) Mich., 1996, U.S. Ct. Appeals (6th cir.) 1996, U.S. Dist. Ct. (so. dist.) Tex., 1997. Assoc. Donovan, Leisure, Newton & Irvine, N.Y.C., 1962-71, ptnr., 1971-98; ptnr. Orrick, Herrington & Sutcliffe, LLP, 1998—. Sr. warden St. Barnabas Ch., Irvington, N.Y., 1980-82; chmn. Irvington

Zoning Bd., 1989—. Fellow Am. Coll. Trial Lawyers; mem. Assn. of Bar of City of N.Y., N.Y. State Bar Assn., N.Y. County Lawyers Assn., Phi Beta Kappa. Republican. Presbyterian. Federal civil litigation, State civil litigation. Home: 86 Fargo Ln Irvington NY 10533-1202 Office: Orrick Herrington & Sutcliffe LLP 666 5th Ave Rm 203 New York NY 10103-1798

LUSTIG, ROBERT MICHAEL, lawyer; b. Cleve., July 1, 1936; s. Philip and Ruth (Frankel) L.; m. Joan E. Sternberg, Dec. 22, 1963; children—Michael, Karen, Marc. BA., Case Western Res. U., 1957, LLB, 1960. Bar: Ohio 1960, U.S. Dist. Ct. (no. dist.) Ohio 1960, U.S. Tax Ct. 1974, U.S. Ct. Appeals (6th cir.) 1980, U.S. Supreme Ct. 1993. Ptnr., prin. Lustig, Icove & Lustig, Cleve., 1960— . Bd. dirs. City Club Cleve., 1973, 84-86, pres. 1986-87; pres. City Club Forum Found., 1991—. Mem. ABA, Ohio State Bar Assn., Cuyahoga County Bar Assn. (trustee 1977-84), Cleve. Bar Assn. (com. chmn. 1982-83, 92-93), Kiwanis (pres. local lodge 1965-66). Estate planning, Real property.

LUTHEY, GRAYDON DEAN, JR. lawyer, educator; b. Topeka, Sept. 18, 1955; s. Graydon Dean Sr. and S. Anne (Murphy) L.; m. Deborah Denise McCullough, May 26, 1979; children: Sarah Elizabeth, Katherine Alexandra. BA in Letters with highest honors, U. Okla., 1976, JD, 1979; Fellow in Theology, Oxford (Eng.) U., 1976. Bar: Okla. 1979, U.S. Ct. Appeals (10th cir.) 1979, U.S. Dist. Ct. (no., we. and ea. dists.) Okla. 1980, U.S. Supreme Ct. 1982. Assoc. Jones, Givens, Gotcher, Bogan & Hilborne, Tulsa, 1979-84, ptnr., 1984-92, also bd. dirs.; ptnr. Hall, Estill, Hardwick, Gable, Golden & Nelson, 1992—, also bd. dirs. Adj. assoc. prof. U. Tulsa, 1985-87, adj. prof., 1987—; vis. fellow in theology Keble Coll., Oxford (Eng.) U., 1976; presiding judge Okla. Temporary Ct. Appeals, 1992-93; mem. Okla. Supreme Ct. Rules Com., 1992—. Bd. dirs. Tulsa Ballet, 1987-2000; chmn. Tulsa Pub. facilties Authority, 1990-93; tustee Episcopal Theol. Sem. of S.W., 1991-99, exec. com., 1992-99; vice chmn. Univ. Hosps. Authority, 1993-94, chmn. 1994-98, sec., 1998-99; chancellor Episcopal Diocese Okla., 1986-99; mem. bd. visitors Okla. Coll. Arts and Scis., 1997—; mem. State of Okla. Futures Auth., 1998—, chmn., 1999—. Nat. Merit scholar U. Okla., 1973. Fellow Am. Bar Found.; mem. ABA, Okla. Bar Assn. (chmn. continuing legal edn. com. 1989-91), Tulsa County Bar Assn. (bd. dirs. 1983-89, Disting. Svc. award 1988), Am. Law Inst., Am. Inns of Ct. (barrister), Summit Club, Golf Club Okla., Beta Theta Pi, Phi Beta Kappa, Omicron Delta Kappa. Federal civil litigation, State civil litigation, Securities. Office: Hall Estill Hardwick Gable Golden & Nelson 320 S Boston Ave Ste 400 Tulsa OK 74103-3704 E-mail: dluthey@hallestill.com

LUTRINGER, RICHARD EMIL, lawyer; b. N.Y.C., Feb. 4, 1943; s. Emil Vincent Lutringer and Alice Hamilton Rich; m. Dagmar Bonitz, May 1, 1970 (div. 1980); m. Clarinda Higgins, Oct. 11, 1980 (div. 1999); children: Emily, Eric. AB, Coll. of William and Mary, 1964; JD in Internat. Affairs, Cornell U., 1967; MCL, U. Chgo., 1969. Bar: N.Y. 1972, U.S. Dist. Ct. (so. dist.) N.Y. 1972. Assoc. Whitman & Ransom, N.Y.C., 1971-80, ptnr., 1980-94, Morgan, Lewis & Bockius LLP, N.Y.C., 1994—. V.p. N.Y.-N.J. Trail Conf., N.Y.C., 1976-80; pres. German-Am. Roundtable, Inc., 1998—. Mem. ABA, Internat. Bar Assn., Assn. of Bar of City of N.Y. (chmn. com. fgn. and comparative law 1990-93), Am. Fgn. Law Assn. (pres. 1989-93, treas. 1986-89), European-Am. C. of C. (vice-chair trade com. 1992-98), German-Amer. C of C, Inc., Philadelphia (bd. dirs., 1999—), German Am. Law Assn. (bd. dirs. 2000—). Avocations: sailing, hiking, skiing. Contracts commercial, General corporate, Private international. Home: 32 Bridge St Westport CT 06880-6033 Office: Morgan Lewis & Bockius LLP 101 Park Ave New York NY 10178-0060 E-mail: rlutringer@morganlewis.com

LUTTER, CHARLES WILLIAM, JR. lawyer; b. Kenosha, Wis., July 12, 1944; s. Charles William and Eva (Kuyawa) L.; m. Carol Hamilton Ewing, July 13, 1974; children: Charles William III, Scott. BS, U. Wis., 1966; postgrad., U. Tex., 1972; JD, St. Mary's U., 1976. Bar: Tex. 1976, U.S. Dist. Ct. (no. dist.) 1977, U.S. Dist. Ct. (so. dist.) 1981, U.S. Dist. Ct. (we. dist.) 1985, U.S. Ct. Appeals (5th and 11th cir.) 1981. Gen. atty. fin. SEC, Atlanta, 1976-80, chief regulations br. Houston, 1980-83; ptnr. Byrnes & Martin, 1983-84, Martin, Shannon & Drought, Inc., San Antonio, 1984-87; sr. corp. atty. LaQuinta Motor Inns, Inc., 1987-90; v.p., assoc. gen. counsel, sec. United Svcs. Advisors, Inc., 1991-93, v.p., spl. counsel, sec., 1993-95, legal/operational cons., 1995—; counsel to trust and ind. trustees ICON Funds, 1996—, Lindbergh Funds, 1999—, AmeriSen Funds, 2001—; of counsel MGL Cons. Corp., Houston, 2000—. Mem. planning com. Ann. Securities Regulation Conf., SEC, Tex. Securities Bd., State Bar Tex., U. Tex. Law Sch., 1986—; mem. initial exec. com. San Antonio Tech. Adv. Group, 1985-87; mem. target '90 Goals for San Antonio Sci. and Tech. Venture Task Force, 1985-90, exec. com. for forum on entrepreneurship, 1985-87; mem. estate planning coun. Southwest Found. Biomed. Rsch., San Antonio, 1987—; mem. U. Tex. Health Sci. Ctr. Estate Planning Coun., 1998—; arbitrator Nat. Assn. Securities Dealers, N.Y. Stock Exch., Mcpl. Securities Rulemaking Bd. Contbr. articles to profl. jours. Bd. dirs. Boysville, San Antonio, 1989—, mem. exec. com., 1995-99, pres., 1999; scout leader Alamo Area coun. Boy Scouts Am., 1988—. Capt. USAF, 1966-71. Decorated Air medal (6). Mem. ABA, State Bar Tex. (securities and investment banking com. 1984—, ad hoc subcom. on securities activities of banks 1987-89, subcom. on rules of fair practce for Tex. broker-dealers 1990), Internat. Assn. for Fin. Planning (bd. dirs. and regulatory coord. San Antonio chpt. 1987-98), Investment Co. Inst. (SEC rules com. 1993-95), San Antonio Bar Assn., San Antonio Bar Found., U. Wis. Alumni Assn., Air Force Assn., John M. Harlan Soc., Kiwanis, Phi Delta Phi. Administrative and regulatory, General corporate, Securities. Office: 103 Canyon Oaks Dr San Antonio TX 78232-1305 also: care US Global Investors 7900 Callaghan Rd San Antonio TX 78229-2327 also: care MGL Cons Ste 300 100 Grogan's Mill Rd The Woodlands TX 77380

LUTTER, PAUL ALLEN, lawyer; b. Chgo., Feb. 28, 1946; s. Herbert W. and Lois (Muller) L. BA, Carleton Coll., 1968; JD, Yale U., 1971. Bar: Ill. 1971, U.S. Tax Ct. 1986. Assoc. Ross & Hardies, Chgo., 1971-77, ptnr., 1978—. Co-author: Illinois Estate Administration, 1993. Dir. ACLU of Ill., Roger Baldwin Found.; pres., dir. Howard Brown Health Ctr.; chmn.'s coun. Design Industries Found. Fighting AIDS, Chgo. Mem. ABA, Chgo. Bar Assn. Estate planning, Probate, Personal income taxation. Home: 2214 N Magnolia Ave Chicago IL 60614-3104 Office: Ross & Hardies 150 N Michigan Ave Ste 2500 Chicago IL 60601-7567

LUTTIG, J. MICHAEL, federal judge; b. 1954; BA, Washington and Lee U., 1976; JD, U. Va., 1981. Asst. counsel The White House, 1981-82; law clk. to Judge Antonin Scalia U.S. Ct. of Appeals D.C. Cir., 1982-83; law clerk to chief justice Warren Burger Supreme Ct. of U.S., 1983-84, spl. asst. to chief justice Warren Burger, 1984-85; assoc. Davis Polk & Wardwell, 1985-89; prin. dep. asst. atty. gen., office of legal counsel U.S. Dept. of Justice, 1989-90, asst. atty. gen., office of legal counsel, counselor to atty. gen., 1990-91; judge U.S. Cir. Ct. (4th cir.), McLean, Va., 1991—. Mem. Nat. Adv. Com. of Lawyers for Bush, 1988, Lawyers for Bush Com., 1988. Mem. ABA, Va. Bar Assn., D.C. Bar Assn. Office: US Ct of Appeals 4th Cir US Courthouse 401 Courthouse Sq Fl 9 Alexandria VA 22314-5704

LUTZ, JAMES GURNEY, lawyer; b. Cin., Sept. 18, 1933; s. Arthur Harold and Frances (Gurney) L.; children: Monica, Susan. JD, U. Cin., 1960. Bar: Ohio 1960, U.S. Dist. Ct. (so. dist.) Ohio 1961, U.S. Ct. Appeals (6th cir.) 1961, U.S. Tax Ct. 1975, U.S. Supreme Ct. 1975. Ptnr. Barbour, Kinpel & Allen, Cin., 1960-68; chief counsel E.C. Industries Inc., 1968-71; sr. ptnr. Lutz Cornetet & Albrinck, 1971—. Pres., mem. bd. dirs. Motivation Dynamics Inc., Cin., 1978-85. Advisor, staff Hamilton County Vocat. Schs., Cin., 1968; advisor U. Cin. Coll., 1970-75; mem. adv. counsel Wyoming (Ohio) Bd. Edn., 1972-75; mem. bd. Ohio Pvt. Industry Coun., Columbus, 1975; gen. counsel S.W. Ohio Autistic Assn., Cin., 1980—. Mem. ABA, ATLA, Ohio Acad. Trial Lawyers, Ohio State Bar Assn., Cin. Bar Assn. Avocations: psychology, computer science. General civil litigation, Franchising, Personal injury. Office: Lutz Cornetet & Albrinck 130 Tri County Pkwy Cincinnati OH 45246-3289 E-mail: jlutz@lcalaw.com

LUTZ, JOHN SHAFROTH, lawyer; b. San Francisco, Sept. 10, 1943; s. Frederick Henry and Helena Morrison (Shafroth) L.; m. Elizabeth Boschen, Dec. 14, 1968; children: John Shafroth, Victoria. BA, Brown U., 1965; JD, U. Denver, 1971. Bar: Colo. 1971, U.S. Dist. Ct. Colo. 1971, U.S. Ct. Appeals (2d cir.) 1975, D.C. 1976, U.S. Supreme Ct. 1976, U.S. Dist. Ct. (so. dist.) N.Y. 1977, U.S. Tax Ct. 1977, U.S. Ct. Appeals (10th cir.) 1979, N.Y. 1984, U.S. Ct. Appeals (9th cir.) 1990, U.S. Dist. Ct. (no. dist.) Calif. 1993. Trial atty. Denver regional office U.S. SEC, 1971-74; spl. atty. organized crime, racketeering sect. U.S. Dept. Justice (so. dist.) N.Y., 1974-77; atty. Kelly, Stansfield and O'Donnell, Denver, 1977-78; gen. counsel Boettcher & Co., 1987, spl. counsel, 1987-88, ptnr., 1988-93; of counsel LeBoeuf, Lamb, Greene and MacRae, LLP, 1993-94, ptnr., 1995—. Spkr. on broker, dealer, securities law and arbitration issues. Contbr. articles to profl. jours. Bd. dirs. Cherry Creek Improvement Assn., 1980-84, Spalding Rehab. Hosp., 1986-89; chmn., vice-chmn. securities sub sect. Bus. Law Sect. of Colo. Bar, 1990, chmn., 1990-91. Lt. (j.g.) USNR, 1965-67. Mem. ABA, Colo. Bar Assn., Denver Bar Assn., Am. Law Inst., Securities Industry Assn. (state regulation com. 1982-86), Nat. Assn. Securities Dealers, Inc. (nat. arbitration com. 1987-91), St. Nicholas Soc. N.Y.C., Denver Law Club, Denver Country Club, Denver Athletic Club (dir. 1990-93), Univ. Club (Denver), Rocky Mountain Brown Club (founder, past pres.), Racquet and Tennis Club (N.Y.). Republican. Episcopalian. Contracts commercial, Securities. Office: LeBoeuf Lamb Greene MacRae LLP 633 17th St Ste 2000 Denver CO 80202-3620

LUTZKER, ELLIOT HOWARD, lawyer; b. Flushing, N.Y., Feb. 22, 1953; s. Stanley Lawrence and Mildred (Goldberg) L.; m. Jill Leslie Simon, Aug. 24, 1975; children: Stacey, Amanda. BA, SUNY, Stony Brook, 1974; JD, N.Y. Law Sch., 1978. Bar: N.Y. 1979, Fla. 1979, U.S. Dist. Ct. (so. and ea. dists.) N.Y. 1979. Atty. SEC, N.Y.C., 1978-81; assoc. Bachner, Tally, Polevoy, Misher & Brinberg, 1981-85; ptnr. Snow Becker Krauss P.C., 1985—. Mem. ABA (corp., banking law div.). Jewish. Avocations: reading, sports. General corporate, Securities. Home: 15 Kevin Ct Jericho NY 11753-1308 Office: Snow Becker Krauss PC 605 3rd Ave Fl 25 New York NY 10158-0125 E-mail: elutzker@sbklaw.com

LYBECKER, MARTIN EARL, lawyer; b. Lincoln, Nebr., Feb. 11, 1945; s. Earl Edward and Jeanette Frances (Kiefer) L.; m. Andrea Kristine Tollefson, Dec. 27, 1969; children: Carl Martin, Neil Anders. BBA, U. Wash., 1967, JD, 1970; LLM in Taxation, NYU, 1971; LLM, U. Pa., 1973. Bar: Wash. 1970, D.C. 1972, Pa. 1982. Atty. investment mgmt. div. SEC, Washington, 1972-75, assoc. dir. div., 1978-81; assoc. prof. SUNY, Buffalo, 1975-78; ptnr. Drinker Biddle & Reath, Washington, 1981-87, Ropes & Gray, Washington, 1987—. Adj. prof. Georgetown U., Washington, 1974-75, 80-81; vis. assoc. prof. Duke U., Durham, N.C., 1977-78, sr. lecturing fellow in law, 2000—. Contbr. articles to law revs. Fellow U. Pa. Ctr. for Study of Fin. Instns., 1971-72. Mem. ABA (mem. subcom. on investment cos. and investment advisers, mem. subcom. on securities activities of banks, mem. com. on fed. regulation of securities bus. law sect., chairperson com. on devels. in investment svcs. bus. law sect., co-chair com. on long-range planning, mem. subcom. on bank holding co. activities and subcom. on trust and investment svcs. of com. of banking bus. law sect.), Am. Law Inst., Univ. Club Washington. Banking, General corporate, Securities. Home: 2806 Daniel Rd Bethesda MD 20815-3149 Office: Ropes & Gray 1301 K St NW Ste 800E Washington DC 20005-7008 E-mail: mlybecker@ropesgray.com

LYNCH, CRAIG TAYLOR, lawyer; b. Miami, Fla., Apr. 26, 1959; s. Glenn James and Faith Rowland (Folsom) L. BS, Fla. State U., 1981; JD, U. N.C., Chapel Hill, 1986. Bar: N.C. 1986, U.S. Dist. Ct. (we. dist.) N.C. 1986, U.S. Ct. Appeals (4th cir.) 1992. Analyst Ford Motor Co., Charlotte, N.C., 1981-82, zone mgr., 1982-83; assoc. Parker, Poe, Adams & Bernstein, 1986-93, ptnr., 1994—, chmn. recruiting com., 1996—. Author: A Marketing Plan for Basketball, 1981. Vol. Lawyers Program, Charlotte, 1986—. Named to Charlotte Bus. Jour. Forty Under Forty, 1995. Mem. ABA (real property sect.), Nat. Multiple Sclerosis Soc. (co-chair Nat. Chmn.'s Adv. Coun. 2000—, fundraising com. chmn. Mid-Atlantic chpt. 1992-93, bd. dirs. 1993—, chmn. 1995-98, Young Profl. Vol. of Yr. 1993), N.C. State Bar Assn., N.C. Bar Assn., Mecklenburg County Bar Assn., Fla. State U. Alumni Assn. (bd. dirs. 1987—), Fla. State U. Alumni Club Charlotte (pres. 1990-93, mem. comml. bd. realtors local region 1997—), Charlotte Chamber Leadership Sch. (Land Use com., Tower Club Charlotte, Beta Gamma Sigma, Phi Delta Phi. Avocations: photography, running, golf, sports, travel. General civil litigation, Contracts commercial, Real property. Office: Parker Poe Adams & Bernstein LLP Three First Union Ctr 401 S Tryon St Ste 3000 Charlotte NC 28202

LYNCH, J. TIMOTHY, lawyer; b. Feb. 7, 1950; s. Lawrence Thomas and Marion Rita (Schwab) Lynch; m. Karen Lee Seib, May 08, 1976; children: Kelly Lee, Kristy Lauren, Katie Lynn. BS, SUNY, 1972; JD, Albany Law Sch., 1975. Bar: N.Y. 1976, S.C. 1981, U.S. Dist. Ct. (no. dist.) N.Y. 1977, U.S. Dist. Ct. S.C. 1983, U.S. Ct. Appeals (4th cir.); chartered fin. cons. NASD Series 7, CLU. Asst. gen. counsel Security Mut. Life Ins. Co., Binghamton, NY, 1975—79; counsel, v.p. RBC Liberty, Greenville, SC, 1979—. Columnist: jour. Journ. Financial Svc. Profls. Mem.: Assn. Life Ins. Counsel, N.Y. Bar Assn., S.C. Bar Assn., Greenville Bar Assn., Assn. Advanced Life Underwriting. Roman Catholic. Estate planning, Insurance, Pension, profit-sharing, and employee benefits. Office: 2000 Wade Hampton Blvd PO Box 789 Greenville SC 29602-0789

LYNCH, JEFFREY SCOTT, lawyer; b. Dixon, Ill., Oct. 7, 1950; s. Walter Francis and Jacqueline (Olson) L.; m. Nancy Skeen Patterson, Dec. 28, 1971; children— Scott P., Kate O., Elizabeth A. BBA, So. Meth. U., 1971, JD, 1975. Bar: Tex. 1975, U.S. Dist. Ct. (no. dist.) Tex. 1975, U.S. Dist. Cts. (so. and ea. dists.) Tex. 1977, U.S. Dist. Ct. (we. dist.) Tex. 1978, U.S. Tax Ct. 1975, U.S. Ct. Claims 1975, U.S. Ct. Appeals (5th cir.) 1975, U.S. Dist. Ct. (ea. and we. dists.) Ark. 1980, U.S. Ct. Appeals (11th cir.) 1983, U.S. Supreme Ct. 1978. Assoc. Maloney, Milner & McDowell, Dallas, 1975; assoc., ptnr. Vial, Hamilton, Koch & Knox, Dallas, 1975-88; ptnr. Gardere & Wynne, Dallas, 1988—; mem. legal asst. adv. com. El Centro Community Coll., Dallas; instr. So. Meth. U., Dallas, 1975-77, 87. Contbr. chpt. to book. Chmn. bd. deacons Casa Linda Presbyterian Ch., Dallas, 1984; election insp. Gen. Election, Tex., Dallas, 1982. Named one of Outstanding Young Men Am., 1979. Fellow Tex. Bar Found.; mem. Dallas Assn. Young Lawyers (bd. dirs. 1981, treas. 1982, grievance com. 1982—), Am. Bd. Trial Advs. (assoc.), Tex. Bd. Legal Specialization (cert. personal injury and civil trial law). Federal civil litigation, State civil litigation, Personal injury. Office: Lynch & Associates 16475 Dallas Pkwy Ste 300 Addison TX 75001-6230

LYNCH, JOHN EDWARD, JR. lawyer; b. Lansing, Mich., May 3, 1952; s. John Edward and Miriam Ann (Hyland) L.; m. Brenda Jayne Clark, Nov. 16, 1984; children: John E. III, Robert C., David B., Patrick D., Jacqueline E. AB, Hamilton Coll., 1974; JD, Case Western Res. U., 1977. Bar: Conn. 1978, Ohio 1980, U.S. Dist. Ct. (no. dist.) Ohio 1980, U.S. Ct. Appeals (6th cir.) 1980, Tex. 2000. Assoc. Thompson, Weir & Barclay, 1977-78; law clk. U.S. Dist. Judge, Cleve., 1978-80; assoc. Squire, Sanders and Dempsey, 1980-86, ptnr., 1986-96; v.p., gen. counsel, sec. Caliber System, Inc., Akron, Ohio, 1996-98; sr. v.p. gen. couns. BP America, Inc., 1998-99; assoc. gen. counsel Upstream Western Hemisphere BP, 1999—. Master bencher Am. Inns of Ct. Found., 1987-98; mem. civil justice reform act adv. group U.S. Dist. Ct. (no. dist.) Ohio. Del. Hamilton Coll. Alumni Coun., 1992-97, regional chair alumni admissions, 1993—; trustee The Cath. Charities Corp., 1995-97; mem. Cuyahoga County Rep. Exec. Com., Cleve., 1984—; mem. Seton Soc. St. Vincent Hosp. Fund. Roman Catholic. Avocations: golf, jogging. Antitrust, General civil litigation, Construction. Home: 918 Peachwood Bend Dr Houston TX 77077-1555 Office: BP 501 Westlake Park Blvd Houston TX 77079-2604 E-mail: lynchjl@bp.com

LYNCH, JOHN JAMES, lawyer; b. Evergreen Park, Ill., Aug. 22, 1945; s. John J. and Agnes (Daly) L.; m. Kathleen Russell, Aug. 15, 1970; children: Kerry, Elizabeth, Erin. BA, St. Mary of the Lake Sem., 1967; MA in Philosophy, DePaul U., 1970, JD, 1973. Bar: Ill. 1973, U.S. Dist. Ct. (no. dist.) Ill. 1973, U.S. Ct. Appeals (7th cir.) 1976. Assoc. McKenna, Storer, Rowe, White & Haskell, Chgo., 1973-75, Haskell & Perrin, Chgo., 1975-77, ptnr., 1977-2000, Figliulo & Silverman, Chgo., 2000—. Mem. ABA, Ill. State Bar Assn., Chgo. Bar Assn., Fedn. Ins. & Corp. Counsel. General civil litigation, Insurance, Professional liability. Office: Figliulo & Silverman Ten S LaSalle St Ste 3600 Chicago IL 60603 E-mail: jlynch@fslegal.com

LYNCH, JOHN JOSEPH, lawyer; b. Mt. Pleasant, Mich., Jan. 31, 1936; s. Edward N. Lynch and Dorothy K. Botsford; m. Sandra Claire Nunneley, Feb. 4, 1941; children: James, Michael, Patrick, Katherine. BS, John Carroll U., 1960; JD, U. Mich., 1963. Ptnr. Lynch Gallagher Lynch & Martineau, Mt. Pleasant, Mich., 1963—. Arbitrator Am. Arbitration Assn., U.S. Dist. Ct. (we. dist.) Mich., 1980; referee Cir. Ct., Mt. Pleasant, 1963-68. Bd. dir. C.M. Cmty. Hosp., Mt. Pleasant, 1965-80, Broomfield Fund., Mt. Pleasant, 1968-75. With USN, 1955-57. Recipient Plaque Am. Arbitration Assn., 1983, C.M. Cmty. Hosp., 1996. Mem. Mich. Oil and Gas Assn. (legal com.), Assn. Irish Am. Attys. Avocations: fly fishing, hunting, fishing, diving. Administrative and regulatory, Oil, gas, and mineral, Real property. Office: Lynch Gallagher Lynch & Martineau 555 N Main St Mount Pleasant MI 48858-1651

LYNCH, JOHN PETER, lawyer; b. Chgo., June 5, 1942; s. Charles Joseph and Anne Mae (Loughlin) L.; m. Judy Godvin, Sept. 21, 1968; children: Julie, Jennifer. AB, Marquette U., 1964; JD, Northwestern U., 1967. Bar: Ill. 1967, U.S. Ct. Appeals (7th cir.) 1979, U.S. Ct. Appeals (5th cir.) 1976, U.S. Supreme Ct. 1979. Ptnr. Kirkland & Ellis, Chgo., 1973-76, Hedlund, Hunter & Lynch, Chgo., 1976-82, Latham, Watkins, Hedlund, Hunter & Lynch, Chgo., 1982-85, Latham & Watkins, Chgo., 1985—. Mem. vis. com. Northwestern U. Law Sch. Served as lt. USN, 1968-71. Mem. ABA, Ill. Bar Assn., Assn. Trial Lawyers Am., Order of Coif, City Club, Exec. Club, Met. Club. Notes and Comments editor Northwestern U. Law Rev., 1967. Antitrust, Federal civil litigation, Public international. Home: 439 Sheridan Rd Kenilworth IL 60043-1220 Office: Latham & Watkins Ste 5800 Sears Tower Chicago IL 60606

LYNCH, LORETTA E. prosecutor; b. Durham, N.C., May 21, 1959; d. Lorenzo Lynch. Grad., Harvard Coll., 1981; JD, Harvard U., 1984. Litigation assoc. Cahill, Gordon & Reindel, 1984-90; with Office of U.S. Atty. for Ea. Dist. of N.Y., 1990—; chief L.I. offices, 1994-98; chief asst. U.S. States Atty., 1998—; U.S. atty. ea. dist. N.Y. U.S. Dept. Justice, Bklyn., 1999—. Avocations: reading, tennis. Office: Office of US Attorney 147 Pierrepont St Brooklyn NY 11201-2712

LYNCH, LUKE DANIEL, JR. lawyer; b. Bklyn., Mar. 28, 1945; s. Luke Daniel and Marjorie Carol (Thien) L.; m. Nancy G. Ott, Sept. 19, 1970; children: Luke D. III, Bettina Anne. BA cum laude, Yale U., 1966; JD, Harvard U., 1969. Bar: N.Y. 1969, U.S. Dist. Ct. (so. dist.) N.Y. 1970. Assoc. Shearman & Sterling, N.Y.C., 1969-78; spl. asst. U.S. Treasury Dept., Washington, 1978-79, assoc. gen. counsel, 1979-82; gen. counsel Chrysler Corp Loan Guaranty Bd., 1981-82; ptnr. D'Amato & Lynch, P.C., N.Y.C., 1983—. Mem. ABA. Avocation: golf. Banking, General corporate, Insurance. Office: D'Amato & Lynch 70 Pine St Fl 41 New York NY 10270-0110

LYNCH, PATRICK, lawyer; b. Pitts., Nov. 11, 1941; s. Thomas Patrick and Helen Mary (Grimes) L.; m. M. Linda Maturo, June 20, 1964; children: Megan, Kevin, Colin, Brendan, Erin, Brian, Liam, Eamonn, Kilian, Caitlin, Ryan, Declan, Cristin, Mairin, Sean. BA in Philosophy, Loyola U., L.A., 1964, LLB, 1966. Bar: Calif. 1967, U.S. Dist. Ct. (cen., so., no. and ea. dists.) Calif., U.S. Ct. Appeals (9th cir.), U.S. Supreme Ct. Ptnr. O'Melveny & Myers, Los Angeles, 1966—. Panelist PLI Annual Antitrust Law Inst., 1982-2000. Bd. editors Matthew Bender Fed. Litigation Guide Reporter. Fellow Am. Coll. Trial Lawyers; mem. L.A. County Bar Assn. Office: OMelveny & Myers 400 S Hope St Los Angeles CA 90071-2899

LYNCH, ROBERT BERGER, lawyer; b. LaCrosse, Wis., June 10, 1931; s. Jan P. and Eve (Berger) L.; m. Iris D. Healy; children: Jan Fredrick Lynch, Jerry Wayne Coggins. BS, U.S. Merchant Marine Acad., 1955; JD, U. of the Pacific, 1967. Bar: Calif. 1969, U.S. Supreme Ct. 1972. Engr. Aerojet Gen. Corp., Sacramento, 1955-61, proposal mgr., 1961-63, asst. contract adminstrn. mgr., 1963-66, contract adminstrn. mgr., 1967-70; pvt. practice, Rancho Cordova, 1969—. Instr. bus. law Solano C.C., 1977—79, San Joaquin Delta Coll., 1978—79; mediator family law panel Sacramento Superior Ct.; traffic and small claims pro tem judge Sacramento, 1997—2001; presiding judge Mcpl. Ct., Bisbee, Ariz., 2001—. Active various charity fund-raising campaigns in Sacramento, 1966-68; mem. mission com. St. Clements Episcopal Ch., Rancho Cordova, Calif., 1967-68; trustee Los Rios C.C. Dist., Calif., 1971-79; vestryman, reader St. Mark's Anglican Ch., Loomis, Calif., 2000—. With USCG, 1949-51, USNR, 1951-80, N.G., 1988-91, maj. AUS, ret. Mem. IEEE, Calif. Wildlife Fedn., Internat. Turtle Club, Marines Meml. Assn., Am. Legion, Mensa. Family and matrimonial, General practice, Probate. Office: 8752 E Mustang Trl Hereford AZ 85615-9298 E-mail: rblynch@stanbrand.net

LYNCH, SANDRA LEA, federal judge; b. Oak Park, Ill., July 31, 1946; d. Bernard Francis and Eugenia Tyus (Shepherd) L.; married; 1 child. AB in Philosophy, Wellesley Coll., 1968; JD cum laude, Boston U., 1971. Bar: Mass. 1971, U.S. Supreme Ct. 1974-75. Law clk. to Hon. Raymond J. Pettine U.S. Dist. Ct., Providence; asst. atty. gen. Commonwealth of Mass., Boston, 1974; gen. counsel Mass. Dept. Edn., 1974-78; ptnr. Foley, Hoag & Eliot, 1978-95; judge 1st cir. U.S. Ct. Appeals, 1995—. Contbr. articles to profl. jours. Past co-chair leading industries com. Greater Boston C. of C. Recipient Distinguished Alumnae award Boston U. Law Sch., 1993, Wellesley Coll., 1997, Disting. Svc. award Planned Parenthood, 1991. Mem. ABA, Nat. Assn. Women Judges, Mass. Bar Assn., Boston Bar Assn. (pres. 1992-93, Judicial Excellence award 2001), Women's Forum. Office: US Ct Appeals One Courthouse Way Ste 8710 Boston MA 02210-3010

LYNCH, THOMAS WIMP, lawyer; b. Monmouth, Ill., Mar. 5, 1930; s. William Brennan and Mildred Maurine (Wimp) L.; m. Elizabeth J. McDonald, July 30, 1952; children: Deborah, Michael, Maureen, Karen, Kathleen. BS in Geology, U. Ill., 1955, MS in Geology, 1958, JD, 1959. Bar: Ill. 1960, Okla. 1960, U.S. Supreme Ct. 1971, Tex. 1978. Staff atty. Amerada Hess Corp., Tulsa, 1959-72, asst. gen. counsel, 1972-75; mem. Hall, Estill, Hardwick, Gable, Collingsworth & Nelson, 1975; v.p., gen. counsel Tex. Pacific Oil Co., Inc., Dallas, 1975-80, Oryx Energy Co., Dallas, 1980-94; ret., 1994. Adj. prof. law U. Tulsa, 1974; trustee

Southwestern Legal Found., chmn., lectr. ann. Oil and Gas Short course, 1976-92; adv. bd. Oil and Gas Edn. Ctr.; chmn. Oil, Gas and Mineral Law Coun. of State Bar of Tex., 1995-96. Served with USN, 1948-49, U.S. Army, 1951-53. Mem. ABA, Okla. Bar Assn., Tex. Bar Assn., Dallas County Bar Assn. Roman Catholic. General corporate, Oil, gas, and mineral.

LYNCHESKI, JOHN E. lawyer; b. Throop, Pa., Sept. 10, 1945; s. John W. and Laura B. (Oshetski) L.; m. Kathy D. Penhale, Aug. 26, 1967; children: John H., Marc E., Kristin E. BA in Econs., Cornell U., 1967; JD, U. Pitts., 1970. Bar: Pa. 1970, Fla. 1974, U.S. Supreme Ct. 1982, U.S. Ct. Appeals (3d cir.) 1970, U.S. Dist. Ct. (we. and mid. dists.) Pa. 1970. Assoc. Reed Smith Shaw & McClay, Pitts., 1970-71, 74-81; USN judge advocate Gen. Corps, Pensacola, Fla., 1971-74; dir. Manion Alder & Cohen, Pitts., 1981-84, Alder Cohen & Grigsby, Pitts., 1984-89; dir., chmn. labor and employment group Cohen & Grigsby, PC, 1989-99, healthcare group, 1989, exec. com., 1989—. Bd. vis. Robert Morris Coll. Sch. Mgmt., 1997-98; health adv. bd. U. Pitts. Sch. Law, 1996—; steering com. Law Fellows Sch. Law, 1992-98. Pres. Allegheny Beaver United Soccer, Pitts., 1986-94; bd. dirs., legal coun. Jaycees, Pa., 1977-78, pres., Upper St. Clair, 1976-77. Lt. USNR. Mem. Am. Arbitration Assn. (nat. panel), Pa. Bar Assn. (fed.), Fla. Bar Assn. (fed.), Pa. Bar Assn. (labor law com., health care law com.), Fla. Bar Assn. (labor law sect.), Allegheny County Bar Assn. (labor and employment law sect., health law sect.) Am. Health Lawyers Assn. (labor, OHSA & human resources com., chair), Soc. Hosp. Attys. of Western Pa., Pa. Soc. Healthcare Attys., Health Exec. Forum S.W. Pa., Soc. for Human Resource Mgmt., Am. Soc. on Aging, Am. Hosp. Assn. Am. Soc. for Healthcare Risk Mgmt., Am. Coll. Healthcare Administrs., Assisted Living Fedn. Am., Am. Coll. Healthcare Adminstrs. (sec. Pa. chpt.), Am. Soc. for Healthcare Human Resources Adminstrn. (nat. spkrs. bur.), W.Va. Healthcare Human Resources Assn., Federalist Soc., Indsl. Rels. Rsch. Assn., West Pa. chpt. bd. dirs. Pitts. Human Resources Assn., West Pa. Working Together Consortium Health Initiative, Am. Health Lawyers Assn., Alternative Dispute Resolution Svc. (dispute resolver), Bus. Dispute Resolution Alliance, Pa. Govs. Sportsmen's Adv. Coun., Western Pa. Soccer Coaches Assn. (sec., bd. dirs. 1987-95), Pa. Soccer Coaches Assn., Nat. Soccer Coaches Assn., Pa. West Soccer Assn. (bd. dirs., exec. com., dir. classic league), Tri-State Referees Assn, Chartiers County Club (bd. dirs., pres., sec., legal adv., greens chmn.), Sewickley Heights Golf Club. Roman Catholic. Avocations: soccer, golf, hunting, fishing, outdoors. Civil rights, Health, Labor. Office: Cohen & Grigsby PC 11 Stanwix St 15th Flr Pittsburgh PA 15222-1312 also: Ste 309 27200 Riverview Ctr Blvd Bonita Springs FL 34134

LYNN, JAMES TORRENCE, III, lawyer; b. Columbus, Ohio, Dec. 11, 1947; s. James Torrence, Jr. and Barbara Allen Lynn; m. Lynn Louise Bond, Apr. 3, 1971; children: Nancy Bond, James Torrence IV. BA in History, Denison U., 1970; JD, Temple U., 1974. Bar: Pa. 1974, U.S. Dist. Ct. (ea. dist.) Pa. 1976, U.S. Dist. Ct. (ea. dist.) Pa. 1976, U.S. Dist. Ct. (mid. dist.) Pa. 1977, U.S. Ct. Appeals (3d cir.) 1977. Assoc. Obermayer, Rebmann, Maxwell & Hippel, Phila., 1974-79; sr. labor rels. atty. Sperry Corp., Blue Bell, Pa., 1979-80; atty. E.I. DuPont de Nemours & Co., Wilmington, Del., 1980—, mgr. State gov. and Pub. Affairs DuPont External Affairs, 1987-2000; corp. counsel DuPont Legal, 2000—. Bd. dirs. Chem. Industry Coun. N.J., chmn. Pa. Chem. Industry Coun., 1997-99; chmn. Del. Chem. Industry Coun., 1997-2000; bd. dirs. Ohio Chem. Coun.; mem. bd. elected supr. East Marlborough Twp., 1990-97. Mem. Am. Arbitration Assn. (arbitrator), Pa. Bar Assn. Republican. Presbyterian. Labor. Home: 709 Denbigh Chase Kennett Square PA 19348-1532 Office: EI DuPont de Nemours & Co Legal Dept D-7016-2 1007 Market St Wilmington DE 19898

LYNTON, HAROLD STEPHEN, lawyer; b. N.Y.C., Nov. 2, 1909; widowed, Mar. 12, 1990; children: Stephen Jonathan, Richard David, Andrew Edward; m. Hattie Gruenstein Kalish, Jan. 27, 1991. AB magna cum laude, Yale U., 1929; JD cum laude, Harvard U., 1932. Bar: N.Y. 1933, U.S. Supreme Ct. 1947. Ptnr. Kaufman, Gallop, Gould, Climenko & Lynton, N.Y.C., 1934-51, Lynton & Klein and predecessors, N.Y.C., 1951-80, Shea & Gould, N.Y.C., 1980-91, counsel, 1992-94, Dornbush Mensch Mandelstam & Schaeffer, N.Y.C., 1994—; gen. counsel, trustee, mem. adv. bd. Barron Collier Cos., Naples, Fla., 1945—; also bd. dirs. Barron Collier Cos. and predecessors. Capt. AUS, 1943-45. Mem. ABA, N.Y. State Bar Assn., Assn. of Bar of City of N.Y., N.Y. County Lawyers Assn., Yale Club N.Y., Sunningdale Country Club, Phi Beta Kappa. Avocations: travel, theatre, tennis, swimming. General civil litigation, General corporate, Real property. Home: 870 UN Plz New York NY 10017-1807 Office: Dornbush Mensch et al 747 3rd Ave Fl 11 New York NY 10017-2863

LYON, JAMES BURROUGHS, lawyer; b. N.Y.C., May 11, 1930; s. Francis Murray and Edith May (Strong) L. BA, Amherst Coll., 1952; LLB, Yale U., 1955. Bar: Conn. 1955, U.S. Tax Ct. 1970. Asst. football coach Yale U., 1953-55; assoc. Murtha, Cullina LLP (and predecessor), Hartford, Conn., 1956-61, ptnr., 1961-96, counsel, 1996—. Adv. com., lectr. and session leader NYU Inst. on Fed. Taxation, 1973-86; mem. IRS Northeast Key Dist.'s Exempt Orgns. Liaison Group, Bklyn., 1993—. Mem. editl. bd. Conn. Law Tribune, 1988—. Chmn. 13th Conf. Charitable Orgn. N.Y.U. Inst. on Fed. Taxation, 1982; trustee Kingswood-Oxford Sch., West Hartford, Conn., 1961—91, hon. trustee, 1991—, chmn. bd. trustees, 1975—78; exec. com., chmn. Amherst Coll. Alumni Coun., 1963—69; trustee Old Sturbridge Village, Mass., 1974—, chmn. bd. trustees, 1991—93; trustee Ella Burr McManus Trust, Hartford, 1980—99, hon. trustee, 2001—; trustee Ellen Battell Stoeckel Trust, Norfolk, 1994—, Hartford YMCA, 1985—, St. Francis Hosp. Found., 1991—, Watkinson Libr., 1990—, pres., 2001; trustee Wadsworth Atheneum, Hartford, 1968—93, pres., 1981—84, hon. trustee, 1993—; trustee Horace Bushnell Meml. Hall, 1993—, sec., 1996—; corporator Inst. Living, 1981—, Hartford Hosp., 1975—, St. Francis Hosp., Hartford, 1976—, Hartford Pub. Libr., 1979—; bd. dirs. Conn. Policy and Econ. Com., Inc., 1991—98; mem. Conn. adv. com. New Eng. Legal Found., 1991—; mem. adv. com. Florence Griswold Mus., Old Lyme, 1991—; bd. vis. Hartford Art Sch., 1995—; trustee Conn. Hist. Soc., 2000—, Conn. Jr. Republic, Litchfield, 2000—; mem. N.E. regional coun. Nat. Club Assn., 1998—. Recipient Eminent Svc. medal Amherst Coll., 1967, Nathan Hale award Yale Club Hartford, 1982, Disting. Am. award No. Conn. chpt. Nat. Football Found. Hall of Fame, 1983, Community Svc. award United Way of the Capital Area, 1986; honored as a direct descendant of its founder Mary Lyon, Mt. Holyoke Coll., South Hadley, Mass. 1997. Fellow: ABA (exempt orgn. com., co-chmn. subcom. on mus. and other cultural orgns. sect. of taxation 1988—), Am. Coll. Tax Counsel, Phi Beta Kappa; mem.: Am. Law Inst., Conn. State Srs. Golf Assn., Hartford Golf Club, Yale Club, Union Club N.Y.C., Dauntless Club (Essex, Conn.), Wianno Club (Osterville, Mass.), Mory's Assn. (New Haven), Yale Golf Club, Limestone Trout Club (East Canaan, Conn.), Univ. Club Hartford (pres. 1976—77). Corporate taxation, Personal income taxation, State and local taxation. Office: 185 Asylum St Hartford CT 06103-3408 E-mail: jlyon@murthalaw.com

LYON, JOHN DAVID, lawyer, computer products company executive; b. Tulsa, Feb. 16, 1937; s. Buford Carl and Mary Louise (Cochrane) L.; m. Melinda Mitchell, June 16, 1972. B.A. with honors, U. Chgo., 1955; J.D. cum laude, Harvard U., 1960. Bar: N.Y. 1962, Calif. 1974, U.S. Supreme Ct., 1980, N.Mex., 1986. Assoc., Paul, Weiss, Rifkind, Wharton & Garrison, 1960-65; with Tosco Corp. and predecessor firm The Oil Shale Corp., Los Angeles, 1965-83, v.p., gen. counsel, 1979-75, exec. v.p., 1975-83, dir., 1979—, chief operating officer Oil Shale div., 1980-82, chief operating officer Comml. Devel. div., 1982-83; of counsel Katsky & Hunt, Los Angeles, 1984— ; pres. The Cogeneration Co., Los Angeles, 1984-88; pres. Lion Oil Co., 1976-77; sec., bd. dirs. NoRad Corp., Los Angeles, 1986—. Contbr. articles on legal protection of tech., oil shale and alt. energy to legal jours. Chmn. U. Chgo. Pres.'s Fund, Los Angeles, 1982—. Served with USAR, 1960-66. Mem. Calif. Bar Assn., Assn. Bar City N.Y., Lawyer-Pilots Bar Assn., U. Chgo. Alumni Exec. Coun., Quiet Birdmen, U. Chgo. Club (Los Angeles, pres. 1988—). Avocations: flying, writing. Office: Katsky & Hunt 9200 W Sunset Blvd Ste 618 West Hollywood CA 90069-3508

LYON, PHILIP K(IRKLAND), lawyer; b. Warren, Ark., Jan. 19, 1944; s. Leroy and Maxine (Campbell) L.; children by previous marriage: Bradford F., Lucinda H., Bruce P., Suzette P., John P., Martin K., Meredith J.; m. Jayne Carol Jack, Aug. 12, 1982. JD with honors, U. Ark., 1967. Bar: ARk, 1967, U.S. Supreme Ct. 1970, Tenn. 1989. Sr. ptnr., dir. ops. House, Wallace, Nelson & Jewell, P.A., Little Rock, 1967-86; pres. Jack, Lyon & Jones, P.A., Little Rock and Nashville, 1986—. Instr. bus. law, labor law, govt. bus. and collective bargaining U. Ark., Little Rock, 1969-72; lectr. practice skills and labor law, U. Ark. Law Sch., 1979-80; bd. dirs. Southwestern Legal Found., 1978—; host Straightlyonlaw.com, also radio talk show on entertainment and employment law, 2000—; editl. bd. dirs. Entertainment Law and Fin., 1993—. Author: Ark. Employment Law Desk Book, 1997; co-author: Schlei and Grossman Employment Discrimination Law, 2d edit., 1982; editor-in-chief: Ark. Law Rev., 1966-67, bd. dirs., 1978-93, v.p., 1990-92; editor: Ark. Employment Law Letter, 1995-97, Ark. Employment Law Ctr., 1998—. Mem. Ark. State C. of C. (bd. dirs. 1984-88), Greater Little Rock C. of C. (chmn. cmty. affairs com. 1982-84, minority bus. affairs 1985-89). Inaugural fellow Coll. Labor and Employment Lawyers, 1996; recipient Golden Gavel award Ark. Bar. Assn., 1978, Writing Excellence award Ark. Bar Found., 1980. Mem. ABA (select com. liaison office fed. contract compliance programs 1982—, select com. liaison EEOC 1984—, select com. immigration law, co-chair ethics & professionlism com. 2000—, forum com. entertainment and sports industries), Ark. Bar Assn. (chmn. labor law com. 1977-78, chmn. labor law sect. 1978-79, chmn. lawyers helping lawyers com. 1988-94), Tenn. Bar Assn. (labor sect., lawyers helping lawyers com. 1989—), Nashville Bar Assn. (entertainment law com., lawyers concerned for lawyers com., employment law com.), Pulaski County Bar Assn., Country Music Assn., Acad of Country Music, Nashville Entertainment Assn., Nashville Songwriters Assn. Internat., Capitol Club. Civil rights, Entertainment, Labor. Home: 350 Ardsley Pl Nashville TN 37215-3247 also: 17 Heritage Park Cir North Little Rock AR 72116-8528 also: Owl Lyon Ranch HC 70 Box 478 Jasper AR 72641-9744 Office: Jack Lyon & Jones PA 11 Music Cir S Ste 202 Nashville TN 37203-4335 also: Jack Lyon & Jones PA 425 W Capitol 3400 TCBY Tower Little Rock AR 72201 E-mail: pklyon@jljnash.com

LYON, ROBERT CHARLES, lawyer; b. Southampton, N.Y., July 2, 1953; s. Charles and Harriet L.; m. Maureen Griffin, Sept. 1, 1979; children: Christopher Charles, Sean Robert, Katherine Joy. BBA with highest hons., Hofstra U., 1976; JD, So. Meth. U., 1979. Bar: Tex. 1980, U.S. Dist. Ct. (no. dist.) Tex. 1982, U.S. Ct. Appeals (5th cir.) 1984, U.S. Supreme Ct. 1992; bd. cert. personal injury trial law, Tex. Bd. Legal Specialization. Assoc. Lyon & Smith, Mesquite, Tex., 1979-83; ptnr. Lyon & Lyon, Mesquite and Rowlett, 1983-91; pvt. practice Rowlett, 1991—. Sec. Starlight Candles, Ltd., Bloomington, Minn., 1996-2000, TPR Ltd., Edina, 1996-98. Coach soccer, T-ball, baseball Rockwall YMCA, 1987-94; den leader Cub Scouts, Rockwall, 1990-91. Mem. ABA, ATLA, Tex. Trial Lawyers Assn. (assoc. dir. and dir. 1991—), State Bar Tex. (adminstrn. of the rules of evidence com. 1998—), Dallas Trial Lawyers Assn. (bd. dirs. 1990-92, treas. 1992-93, sec. 1993-94, v.p. 1994-95, pres. elect 1995-96, pres. 96-97), Dallas Bar Assn. (judiciary com. and fee dispute com. 1998-2001, legal ethics com. 2000—), Mesquite Bar Assn., Rockwall County Bar Assn. (pres. 1990-91), Patron Ducks Unltd. Democrat. Personal injury, Product liability. Office: 3301 Century Dr # A Rowlett TX 75088-7511 Fax: 972-475-5804. E-mail: attybob@msn.com

LYONS, ALLEN WARD, lawyer, educator; b. Richmond, Calif., Nov. 17, 1947; s. Forrest Ward and Marie Catherine (Rand) L.; m. Marsha Lorane DeBay, Aug. 14, 1971; children— Jessica Lorane, Suzanne Marie, Nathan Allen, Karen Irene. AA, Grays Harbor Coll., 1968; BA, U. Wash., 1970; JD, Willamette U., 1973. Bar: Oreg. 1973. Asst. atty. gen. Oreg. Dept. Justice, Salem, 1973-77; atty. State Accident Ins. Fund, Salem, 1977-81, legal dir., 1981-83, v.p., 1983-84; assoc. counsel Lindsay, Hart, Neil & Weigler, Portland, Oreg., 1984-86; ptnr. Davis, Bostwick, Scheminske & Lyons, Portland, 1986—; adj. prof. law Willamette U., Salem, 1980— . Mem. ABA, Assn. Legal Adminstrs., Workers' Compensation Def. Assn. (exec. mem.), Oreg. Bar Assn., Marion County Bar Assn. Republican. Roman Catholic. Lodge: Rotary. Home: 2745 Bluff Ave SE Salem OR 97302-3104 Office: 11 SW Columbia St Ste 300 Portland OR 97201

LYONS, CHAMP, JR. judge; b. Boston, Dec. 6, 1940; m. Emily Lee Oswalt, 1967; children— Emily Olive, Champ III. A.B., Harvard U., 1962; LL.B., U. Ala., 1965. Bar: Ala. 1965, U.S. Supreme Ct. 1973. Law clk. U.S. Dist. Ct., Mobile, Ala., 1965-67; assoc. Capell, Howard, Knabe & Cobbs, Montgomery, 1967-70, ptnr., 1970-76, Helmsing, Lyons, Sims & Leach, Mobile, 1976-98; legal advisor Hon. Fob James, Jr. Gov. State Ala., 1998; assoc. justice Supreme Ct. of Ala., Montgomery, 1998—. Mem. adv. commn. on civil procedure Ala. Supreme Ct., 1971-98, chmn., 1985-98. Author: Alabama Practice, 1973, 3d edit., 1996; contbr. articles to law jours. Mem. ABA, Ala. Bar Assn., Mobile Bar Assn. (pres. 1991), Am. Law Inst., Ala. Law Inst., Farrah Law Soc., Harvard U. Alumni Assn. (S.E. regional dir. 1988-91, v.p.-at-large 1992-94, 1st v.p. 1994-95, pres. 1995-96). Home: PO Box 1033 Point Clear AL 36564-1033 Office: Supreme Ct of Ala 300 Dexter Ave Montgomery AL 36104-3741

LYONS, GARY GEORGE, lawyer; b. Poughkeepsie, N.Y., Feb. 6, 1951; s. George Grant and Margaret Joan (Hogan) L.; m. Susanne Marie McCarthy, June 21, 1980; children— Matthew, Paul, Andrew. B.A. cum laude, Syracuse U., 1973, J.D., summa cum laude, 1975. Bar: N.Y. 1976, U.S. Dist. Ct. (so. dist.) N.Y. 1976, U.S. Dist. Ct. (ea. dist.) N.Y. 1976. Assoc. Shearman & Sterling, N.Y.C., 1975-81; asst. gen. counsel Nestle Foods Corp., Purchase, N.Y., 1981-87, dep. gen. counsel, 1987—. Mem. ABA, Assn. Bar City N.Y., N.Y. State Bar Assn., Order of Coif. Republican. Roman Catholic. General corporate, Trademark and copyright. Home: 169 Scarborough Rd Briarcliff Manor NY 10510-2005 Office: Nestle Foods Corp 100 Manhattanville Rd Purchase NY 10577-2134

LYONS, PAUL VINCENT, lawyer; b. Boston, July 19, 1939; s. Joseph Vincent and Doris Irene (Griffin) L.; m. Elaine Marie Hurley, July 13, 1968; children: Judith Marie, Maureen Patricia, Paula Anne, Joseph Hurley BS cum laude, Boston Coll., 1960; MBA, NYU, 1962; JD, Suffolk U., Boston, 1968. Bar: Mass. 1968, U.S. Cir. Ct. (1st cir.) 1969, U.S. Supreme Ct. 1991. Div. adminstrn. mgr. Pepsi-Cola Co., N.Y.C., 1962-64; mem. bus. faculty Burdett Coll., Boston, 1964-68; atty. NLRB, 1968-73; assoc. Foley, Hoag & Eliot, 1973-77, ptnr., 1978—. Mem. faculty Boston U., 1972-74. Mem. Town Meeting, Milton, Mass., 1986—, mem. pers. bd., 1994—. Lt. U.S. Army, 1960-62. Mem. ABA, Mass. Bar Assn., Boston Bar Assn. Education and schools, Labor. Office: Foley Hoag & Eliot LLP 1 Post Office Sq Ste 1700 Boston MA 02109-2175 E-mail: plyons@foleyhoag.com

LYONS, WILLIAM HARRY, law educator; b. Fitchburg, Mass., Mar. 5, 1947; s. William Earl and Jeanette Underwood (Weed) L.; m. Karen Virginia Knapp, June 27, 1970; children: Virginia Lynne, Kevin Michael. BA, Colby Coll., Waterville, Maine, 1969; JD, Boston Coll., 1973. Bar: Maine 1973, Mass. 1973, Nebr. 1985, U.S. Dist. Ct. Maine 1974, U.S. Dist. Ct. Nebr. 1986, U.S. Tax Ct. 1986. Assoc. Vafiades, Brountas & Kominsky, Bangor, Maine, 1973-80, ptnr., 1980-81; prof. law U. Nebr., Lincoln, 1981—. Vis. prof. Boston Coll. Law Sch., 1997-98, Vt. Law Sch., spring 2001; planning com. Gt. Plains Fed. Tax Inst., Lincoln, 1982—, program chmn., 1992, pres., 1993; adv. com. Gt. Plains Studies, Lincoln, 1983; prof. in residence IRS, 1987-88. Articles editor The Tax Lawyer, 1982-85; contbr. articles to profl. jours. Tax adviser Lincoln Nonprofit Devel. Corp., Lincoln, 1983—. Recipient Disting. Tchg. award Nebr. U. Found., Lincoln, 1984, Student Bar Assn. U. Nebr.-Lincoln Coll. Law, 1984-85, 97, 99. Fellow Am. Coll. Tax Counsel; mem. ABA (group editor sect. of taxation newsletter 1986-88, chmn. individual investments and workouts com. 1995-97, chmn. important devel. subcom. 2001—), Fed. Bar Assn., Maine State Bar Assn., Nebr. State Bar Assn., Am. Judicature Soc., Delta Theta Phi. Democrat. Home: 5232 S Bristolwood Ln Lincoln NE 68516-1676 Office: U Nebr Coll Law PO Box 830902 Lincoln NE 68583-0902 E-mail: wlyons2@unl.edu

LYTTON, WILLIAM B(RYAN), lawyer; b. St. Louis, Aug. 22, 1948; s. William Bryan and Josephine (Lamy) L.; m. Christine Mary Miller; children— William Bryan IV, Laura Miller. A.B., Georgetown U., 1970; J.D., Am. U., Washington, 1973. Bar: D.C. 1973, U.S. Ct. Appeals (7th cir.) 1975, U.S. Supreme Ct. 1978, Pa. 1979, U.S. Dist. Ct. (ea. dist.) Pa. 1979, U.S. Ct. Appeals (3d cir.) 1979. Legal counsel, legis. asst. U.S. Senator Charles H. Percy, 1973-75; asst. U.S. atty. U.S. Dist. Ct. (no. dist.) Ill., Chgo., 1975-78, U.S. Dist. Ct. (ea. dist.) Pa., 1978-83, dep. chief spl. prosecutions div., 1980, dep. chief criminal div., 1980, chief criminal div., 1980-81, 1st asst. U.S. atty., 1981-83; ptnr. Kohn, Savett, Klein & Graf, P.C., Phila., 1983-87, 87-89; chief counsel, staff dir. Phila. Spl. Investigation Commn., 1985-86; dep. spl. counsellor to Pres. of U.S., Washington, 1987; v.p., gen. counsel GE Aerospace, King of Prussia, Pa., 1989-93; v.p., assoc. gen. counsel Martin Marietta & Lockheed Martin, 1993-95; sr. v.p., gen. counsel Internat. Paper, Purchase, N.Y., 1996—. Contbr. articles to profl. jours. Committeeman Republican Party, Chester County, Pa.; mem. Easttown Twp. Bd. Suprs., 1990-95. Mem. ABA, Am. Corp. Counsel Assn. (bd. dirs. 1997—). Criminal, Libel. Office: Internat Paper Co 400 Atlantic St Stamford CT 06921

LYUBKIN, RINA, lawyer; b. Latvia, May 22, 1973; came to U.S., 1980; d. Samuel and Alexandra Lyubkin; m. Gregg D. Polsky, May 9, 1998. BSBA, BS in Psychology, U. Fla., 1994, JD, 1997. Bar: Fla. Assoc. Lucio, Mandler, Croland et al, Miami, Fla., 1998—. General corporate, Securities. Office: Lucio Mandler Croland 701 Brickell Ave Ste 2000 Miami FL 33131

MACALAGUING, GENE BATALLA, lawyer; b. Alubijid, The Philippines, July 14, 1949; s. Genaro Elarmo Macalaguing and Fortunata Roxas Batalla; m. Eleanor Juanson Salvador, Oct. 18, 1953; children: Mabel Victoria, Maria Aiza, Lowe Thomas. LLB, Silliman U, Dumaguete City, 1974. Bar: The Philippines. Assoc. V.E. del Rosario & Assocs., Makati City, The Philippines, 1978-80, Reyes Santayana Tayao Molo & Alegre, Makati City, 1983—. Contracts commercial, Intellectual property, Probate. Office: 3/F Zaragoza Bldg 102 Gamboa St Legaspi Vill Makati City The Philippines

MACAN, WILLIAM ALEXANDER, IV, lawyer; b. Boston, Nov. 21, 1942; s. William A. and Carol (Whitten) M.; m. Jane Mitchell Ahern, Sept. 3, 1965; children: Sandra Jane, William Andrew. BS, Haverford Coll., 1964; LLB, U. Pa., 1967. Bar: Pa. 1968, U.S. Tax Ct. 1970, N.Y. 1999. Law clk. to judge U.S. Tax Ct., Washington, 1967-69; assoc. firm Morgan, Lewis & Bockius, Phila., 1969-76; ptnr. Morgan, Lewis & Bockius L.L.P., 1976-2000, Allen & Overy, N.Y.C., 2000—. Lectr. legal instns., seminars. Author publs. on tax-oriented equipment leasing, other tax subjects. Mem. ABA. Republican. Presbyterian. Finance, Corporate taxation, Personal income taxation. Office: Allen & Overy 10 E 50th St New York NY 10022 E-mail: william.macan@allenovery.com

MACAULEY, WILLIAM FRANCIS, lawyer; b. Boston, Sept. 12, 1943; s. Bernard Joseph and Mary Louise (Dolan) M.; m. Sheila Rose Hubbard, June 29, 1968; children: Jennifer, Douglas, Leiha, Brian. AB, U. Wash., 1966; JD, Boston U., 1969. Bar: Mass. 1969, U.S. Dist. Ct. Mass. 1970, U.S. Ct. Appeals (1st cir.) 1977, U.S. Dist. Ct. R.I. 1979, U.S. Tax Ct. 1982, U.S. Dist. Ct. Conn. 1983. Assoc. Craig & Craig, Boston, 1970-74; prin. Tyler, Reynolds & Craig, 1975-78; pres. Craig and Macauley, 1979—. Contbr. articles to profl. jours. Trustee Boston U., The Raymond Found., Boston; bd. dirs. YMCA Greater Boston. Mem. ABA, Mass. Bar Assn., Boston Bar Assn. Bankruptcy, Federal civil litigation, State civil litigation. Home: 55 Buttricks Hill Rd Concord MA 01742-5314 Office: Craig and Macauley Profl Corp 600 Atlantic Ave Ste 2900 Boston MA 02210-2215 E-mail: macauley@craigmacauley.com

MACBAN, LAURA VADEN, lawyer; b. Winston-Salem, N.C., Dec. 19, 1963; d. Donald Edward Ridenour and Constance Carrington Whitehead; m. Barry Allistair MacBan, Oct. 7, 1995. Student, U. Calif. (Santa Barbara), 1981-83; BS in Econs. magna cum laude, U. Ariz., 1985, JD cum laude, 1988. Bar: Ariz. 1988. Law clerk Haralson, Kinerk & Morey, Tucson, 1986-87, Bilby & Shoenhair, P.C., Tucson, 1987-88; assoc. Snell & Wilmer, 1988-92, Law Office Robert Hooker, Tucson, 1992-93, Cavett & Kaucher, Tucson, 1993-97; ptnr. MacBan Law Offices, 1997—. Founding mem., v.p. 20/30 Women's Club, Ariz. Chpt., 1987-88. Mem. campaign com. for Jim Kolbe, Tucson, 1988-90; v.p. City Magistrates Merit Selection Commn., Tucson, 1992-97; chairperson Ariz. State Bar Trial Practice Sect., 1998—; pres. Tucson Def. Bar, 1998—. Mem. ABA (exec. coun. 1995—), Ariz. Women Lawyers Assn., Pima County Bar Assn. (social com. 1994-95), Morris K. Udall Inn of Ct. Republican. Episcopalian. General civil litigation, Personal injury, Professional liability. Office: MacBan Law Offices 1 S Church Ave Ste 2040 Tucson AZ 85701-1620

MACCARTHY, TERENCE FRANCIS, lawyer; b. Chgo., Feb. 5, 1934; s. Frank E. and Catherine (McIntyre) MacC.; m. Marian Fulton, Nov. 25, 1961; children— Daniel Fulton, Sean Patrick, Terence Fulton, Megan Catherine B.A. in Philosophy, St. Joseph's Coll., 1955; J.D., DePaul U., 1960. Bar: Ill. 1960, U.S. Dist. Ct. (no. dist.) Ill. 1961, U.S. Ct. Appeals (7th cir.) 1961, U.S. Supreme Ct. 1966. Assoc. prof. law Chase Coll. Law, Cin., 1960-61; law clk. to chief judge U.S. Dist. Ct., 1961-66; spl. asst. atty. gen. Ill., 1965-67; exec. dir. Fed. Defender Program, U.S. Dist. Ct. (no. dist.) Ill., Chgo., 1966—. Mem. nat. adv. com. on criminal rules; 7th cir. criminal jury instrn. com.; chmn. Nat. Defender Com.; chmn. bd. regents Nat. Coll. Criminal Def.; faculty Fed. Jud. Ctr., Nat. Coll. Criminal Def., Nat. Inst. Trial Advocacy, U. Va. Trial Advocacy Inst., Harvard Law Sch. Trial Advocacy Program, Western Trial Advocacy Inst., Northwestern U., U. Ill. Defender Trial Advocacy course, Nat. Criminal Def. Coll., Loyola U. Trial Advocacy Program; lectr. in field Contbr. articles on criminal law to profl. jours. Bd. dirs. U.S.O. Served as 1st lt. USMC, 1955-57 Recipient Nat. Legal Aid and Defender Assn./ABA Reginald Heber Smith award, 1986, Alumni Merit award St. Joseph Coll., 1970, Cert. of Distinction USO, 1977, Harrison Tweed Spl. Merit award Am. Law Inst./ABA, 1987, Bill of Rights award Ga. chpt. ACLU, 1986, William J. Brennan award U. Va., 1989, Alumni Svc. award DePaul U. Coll. Law, 1994, Ann. Significant Contbns. award Calif. Attys. for Criminal Justice, Defender of the Century Fed. Defenders Assn., Inns of Ct. and Ct. of Appeals (7th cir.) Professionalism award; named to Outstanding Young Men of Am., 1970. Mem. ABA (past chmn. criminal justice sect., ho. of dels., bd. govs., Charles English award criminal justice sect.), Ill. Bar Assn., Chgo. Bar Assn., 7th Cir. Bar Assn., Nat. Assn. Criminal Def. Lawyers (Disting. Svc. award 1993), Nat. Legal Aid and Defender Assn., Nat. Coll. Criminal Def. (chair), Union League of Chgo. (pres.). Democrat. Roman Catholic. Office: US Dist Ct No Dist Ill 55 E Monroe St Ste 2800 Chicago IL 60603-5802

MACCHIA, VINCENT MICHAEL, lawyer; b. Bklyn., Dec. 30, 1933; s. Vincent and Lina Rose (Cewli) M.; m. Irene Janet Audino, Feb. 27, 1965; children: Lauren, Michele, Michael. BS, Fordham U., 1955, LLB, 1958; LLM, NYU, 1967. Bar: N.Y. 1958. Assoc. Bernard Remsen Millham & Bowdish, N.Y.C., 1959-60; atty. Equity Corp., 1961-63, Pfizer Inc., N.Y.C., 1964, TWA, N.Y.C., 1964-66; mem. Gifford, Woody, Palmer & Serles, 1966-85, Townley & Updike, N.Y.C., 1985-90; of counsel Smith, Don, Alampi, Scala & D'Argenio, Ft. Lee, N.J., 1990-91; counsel Tenzer, Greenblatt, LLP, N.Y.C., 1991-2000, Diamant, Katz Kahn & Co. LLP, N.Y.C., 2000—. Dir. Hudson Rev., Inc. Mem. editl. staff Fordham Law Rev., 1956-58. With USAR, 1958-64. Mem. ABA, N.Y. State Bar Assn. Republican. Roman Catholic. Home: 4 Greentree Dr Scarsdale NY 10583-7014

MACCIONI, GIOVANNI, lawyer, researcher; b. Siena, Italy, Mar. 6, 1965; Diploma Law, Univ. Siena, Italy, 1990, Fordham Univ., 1998. Bar: Italy, 95. Assoc. Simmons & Simmons, Milan, 1999-2000, Morano & Assocs., Milan, 2000-01. Vis. scholar Columbia U., N.Y., U. Siena, 1996. General corporate, Real property. Home: Corso Sempione no 8 Milan 20154 Italy

MACCOLL, J. A. lawyer; b. Evanston, Ill., July 29, 1948; BA, Princeton U., 1970; JD, Georgetown U., 1973. Bar: Md. 1974, U.S. Dist. Ct. Md. 1974, U.S. Ct. Appeals (4th cir.) 1974. Asst. U.S. atty. Dist. Md., 1978-81; ptnr. Piper & Marbury; v.p., gen. counsel U.S. Fidelity & Guaranty Corp., Balt., 1987-91, sr. v.p., gen. counsel, 1991-95, exec. v.p. dept. human resource, gen. counsel, 1995-98; exec. v.p., gen. counsel The St. Paul Cos., Inc., 1998—. Editor-in-chief Georgetown Law Jour., 1972-73. Office: The St Paul Cos Inc 5801 Smith Ave Baltimore MD 21209-3611

MACCRINDLE, ROBERT ALEXANDER, lawyer; b. Glasgow, Scotland, Jan. 27, 1928; s. Fergus Robertson and Jean (Hill) MacC.; m. Pauline Dilys, Aug. 18, 1959; children: Guy Stephen, Claire. LLB, U. London, 1948; LLM, U. Cambridge, 1952. Called to Bar Eng. and Wales, 1952; created Queen's Counsel, 1963; bar: Hong Kong 1965; conseil juridique France, 1978-91. Barrister Temple, London, 1952-76; Bencher Gray's Inn, 1969—; ptnr. Shearman & Sterling, N.Y.C., 1976-94, of counsel, 1995—. Avocat au Barreau de Paris, 1991—. Flight lt. RAF, 1948-50. Fellow Am. Coll. Trial Lawyers; mem. University Club (N.Y.C.). Club: University (N.Y.C.). Avocation: golf. Contracts commercial, Oil, gas, and mineral. Home: 41 Ave Bosquet Paris 75007 France also: Shearman & Sterling 599 Lexington Ave # 53D St New York NY 10022-6030

MACDONALD, DAVID ROBERT, lawyer, fund administrator; b. Chgo., Nov. 1, 1930; s. James Wear and Frances Esther (Wine) M.; m. Verna Joy Odell, Feb. 17, 1962; children: Martha, Emily, David, Rachel, Rebecca. B.S., Cornell U., 1952; J.D., U. Mich., 1955. Bar: Ill. 1955, Mich. 1955, D.C. 1983. Practiced in Chgo., 1957-74; mem. firm Kirkland, Ellis, Hodson, Chaffetz & Masters, Chgo., 1957-62, ptnr., 1962, Baker & McKenzie, Chgo., 1962-74, 77-81; asst. sec. of Treasury for enforcement, ops. and tariff affairs Dept. Treasury, Washington, 1974-76; undersec. of Navy, 1976-77; dep. U.S. Trade Rep., 1981-83; ptnr. Baker & McKenzie, Chgo., 1983-96. Bd. dirs. Mestek, Inc. (N.Y. Stock Exch.). Pres. David R. Macdonald Found., 1996—. Mem. ABA, D.C. Bar Assn., Chgo. Assn. Commerce and Industry (bd. dirs. 1977-81), Order of Coif, Econ. Club (Chgo.), Cosmos Club (Washington), Grolier Club (N.Y.C.). Home: 6605 Radnor Rd Bethesda MD 20817-6324 Office: 815 Connecticut Ave NW Washington DC 20006-4004

MACDONALD, KIRK STEWART, lawyer; b. Glendale, Calif., Oct. 24, 1948; s. Bruce Mace and Phyllis Jeanne MacDonald. BSCE, U. So. Calif., 1970; JD, Western State U., 1982. Bar: Calif. 1982, U.S. Dist. Ct. (cen. dist.) Calif. 1982, U.S. Ct. Appeals (9th cir.) 1982, U.S. Dist. Ct. (no. dist.) Calif. 1984, U.S. Dist. Ct. (so. dist.) Calif. 1985, U.S. Dist. Ct. (ea. dist.) Calif. 1987. Dist. engr. Pacific Clay Products, Corona, Calif., 1971-76, Nat. Clay Pipe Inst., La Mirada, 1976-82; ptnr. Gill and Baldwin, Glendale, 1982—. Mem. ABA, L.A. County Bar Assn., Water Environ. Assn., Calif. Water Environ. Assn. Avocations: travel, woodworking. General civil litigation, Contracts commercial, Construction. Office: Gill & Baldwin Ste 405 130 N Brand Blvd Glendale CA 91203-2646 E-mail: kirk@gillandbaldwin.com

MACDONALD, THOMAS COOK, JR. lawyer, mediator; b. Atlanta, Oct. 11, 1929; s. Thomas Cook and Mary (Morgan) MacD.; m. Gay Anne Everiss, June 30, 1956; children: Margaret Anne, Thomas William. B.S. with high honors, U. Fla., 1951, LL.B. with high honors, 1953. Bar: Fla. 1953; cert. mediator Supreme Ct. Fla. and U.S. Dist. Ct. (mid. dist.) Fla. Practice law, Tampa, 1953—; mem. firm Shackleford, Farrior, Stallings & Evans, 1953-97; mem. Cook & MacDonald, Tampa, 1997—. Spl. counsel Gov. of Fla., 1963, U. Fla., 1972—; del. 5th cir. Jud. Conf., 1970-81; mem. adv. com. U.S. Ct. Appeals (5th cir.), 1975-78, (11th cir.), 1988-93; mem. Fla. Jud. Qualifications Commn., 1983-88, vice chmn., 1987, chmn., 1988, gen. counsel, 1997—; mem. judicial nominating com. Fla. Supreme Ct., 1995-99. Mem. Fla. Student Scholarship and Loan Commn., 1963-67; bd. dirs. Univ. Cmty. Hosp., Tampa, 1968-78, Fla. West Coast Sports Assn., 1965-80, Hall of Fame Bowl (now Outback Bowl) Assn., 1989-93, Jim Walter Corp., 1979-87; mem. Hillsborough County Pub. Edn. Study Commn., 1965; lic. lay eucharistic min. Episcopal Ch., 1961—; chancellor Episcopal Diocese of S.W. Fla., 1990-93, 2000—, ch. atty. for ecclesiastical ct., 1998-2000; bd. dirs. U. Fla. Found., 1978-86, Shands Tchg. Hosp., U. Fla., 1981-95; counsel Tampa Sports Authority, 1983-94. Recipient George Carr award FBA, 1991, Herbert Goldburg award Hillsborough County Bar Assn., 1995. Fellow Am. Coll. Trial Lawyers (chmn. state com. 1990-91), Am. Bar Found., Fla. Bar (chmn. com. profl. ethics 1966-70, bd. govs. 1970-74, bar mem. Supreme Ct. com. on stds. conduct governing judges 1976, Presdl. award of merit 1995); mem. ABA (com. on ethics and profl. responsibility 1970-76), Am. Law Inst. (life), 11th Cir. Hist. Soc. (trustee 1982-95, pres. 1989-95), U. Fla. Nat. Alumni Assn. (pres. 1973), Phi Kappa Phi, Phi Delta Phi, Fla. Blue Key, Kappa Alpha. Episcopalian. Alternative dispute resolution, General civil litigation, Education and schools. Home: 1904 S Holly Ln Tampa FL 33629-7004 Office: 100 N Tampa St Ste 2100 Tampa FL 33602-5809

MACDOUGALL, MALCOLM EDWARD, lawyer; b. Denver, Jan. 26, 1938; s. Malcolm W. and Helen (Harlow) MacD.; m. Phyllis R. Pomrenke, Dec. 20, 1959; children: Barry Malcolm, Christopher Scott (dec.). BS, Colo. State U., 1959; LLD, U. Colo., 1962. Bar: Colo. 1962, U.S. Dist. Ct. Colo. 1962. Law clk. to judge U.S. Ct. Appeals (10th cir.), Denver, 1962-63; atty. Denver Water Bd., 1963-65; assoc. Saunders, Snyder and Ross, Denver, 1965-68; gen. counsel Golden Cycle Corp., Colorado Springs, Colo., 1968-71; ptnr. Geddes, MacDougall and Worley, P.C., 1971-91; sole practitioner MacDougall Law Office, 1991-99; shareholder MacDougall, Woodridge & Worley, PC, 1999—. Bd. dirs. Park State Bank. Mem. Colo. Bar Assn. Republican. State civil litigation, Real property. Office: Ste 204 530 Communication Cir Colorado Springs CO 80905 E-mail: sandy@waterlaw.tr

MACDOUGALL, PRISCILLA RUTH, lawyer; b. Evanston, Ill., Jan. 20, 1944; d. Curtis Daniel and Genevieve Maurine (Rockwood) MacDougall; m. Lester H. Brownlee, July 5, 1987. BA, Barnard Coll., 1965; grad. with honors, U. Paris, 1967; JD, U. Mich., 1970. Bar: Wis. 1970, Ill. 1970. Asst. atty. gen. State of Wis., 1970-74; instr. Law Sch. and undergrad. campuses U. Wis., 1973-75; staff counsel Wis. Edn. Assn. Council, Madison, 1975—; instr. Columbia Coll., Chgo., 1988—; litigator, writer, speaker, educator women's and children's names and women's rights and employment issues. Mem. ABA, Wis. State Bar (co-founder sect. on individual rights and responsibilities, chairperson, 1973-75, 78-79), Legal Assn. Women Wis. (co-founder). Author: Married Women's Common Law Right to Their Own Surnames, 1972; (with Terri P. Tepper) Booklet for Women Who Wish to Determine Their Own Names After Marriage, 1974, supplement, 1975; The Right of Women to Name Their Children, 1985; contbr. articles to profl. jours. Home: 502 Engelhart Dr Madison WI 53713-4742 Office: 33 Nob Hill Dr Madison WI 53713-2198

MACDOUGALL, WILLIAM RODERICK, lawyer, county official; b. Nevada City, Calif., May 14, 1914; s. William Stewart and Ethel Martha (Hutchison) McDougall; m. Carol Bernie Keane, May 1, 1937; children: Marcia MacDougall Williams, James Stewart. AA, Sacramento City Coll., 1930-32; student U. Calif.-Berkeley, 1933-34; JD, U. of Pacific, 1941. Bar: Calif. 1941, U.S. Dist. Ct. (no. dist.) Calif. 1941, U.S. Supreme Ct. 1950. Library page Calif. State Library, Sacramento, 1932-33; sr. auditor Office of Controller, State of Calif., Sacramento, 1934-37; chief bur. of collections Calif. Social Welfare Dept., Sacramento, 1937-42; gen. counsel County Suprs. Assn. Calif., Sacramento, 1946-70; exec. dir. U.S. Intergovt. Relations Commn., Washington, 1970-75; planning commr. County of Orange, Santa Ana, Calif., 1976-84; chief counsel Calif. Alcoholic Beverage Control Appeals Bd., 1984-92; exec. dir. Calif. County Govt. Edn. Found., 1965-69; chmn. home rule com. Nat. Assn. Counties, 1963-67. Mem. Fed. Public Assistance Adv. Council, 1959-60, Gov.'s Commn. on Met. Problems, Calif., 1960; pres. Laguna Beach Sch. of Art (Calif.), 1983-84. Mem. Am. Planning Assn., Nat. Assn. County and Pros. Attys. (hon.), Calif. County Planning Commrs. Assn. (dir. 1981-84). Republican. Presbyterian.

MACE, STEPHEN ALAN, investment advisor; b. Springfield, Mo., Dec. 30, 1957; s. Leslie Jasper and Virginia Sue (Dunaway) M.; m. Deborah Marie Smith, Dec. 3, 1983; children: Andrew Stephen, Ashley Marie, Alexander Edward. BA, William Jewell Coll., 1979; JD, U. Mo., 1982. Bar: Mo. 1982; CPA, Mo., 1991; CFA Assn. Investment Mgmt. and Rsch., 1998. Tax specialist Coopers & Lybrand, St. Louis, 1982-85; atty. Blumenfeld, Sandweiss, et al, 1985-86; sr. trust officer Boatmen's Nat. Bank, 1986-89; prin. Moneta Group, Inc., 1989-94; portfolio cons. Templeton Portfolio Adv., Carmel, Calif., 1994-2000; mng. dir., gen. counsel Centurion Alliance, Inc., 2000—. Mem. Mo. Bar, Bar Assn. Met. St. Louis, Fin. Planning Assn. (nat. bd. dirs., chair audit com. 1993, mem. practitioner adv. coun. 1991-93), Kiwanis Internat. (charter pres. chpt. 1982-83, Disting. Club Pres. 1983). Republican. Baptist. Avocations: scuba diving, big-game hunting, fly fishing, skiing, tae kwon do (2d degree black belt).

MACH, JOSEPH DAVID, lawyer; b. Bronx, N.Y., Nov. 3, 1944; s. Moses A. and Fanny (Schwartz) M.; m. Joan Maria Blassberg, June 16, 1968; children: Jeffrey Peter, Louis Wilson. BS in Econs., U. Pa., 1965, MS in Acctg., 1966; JD, Harvard U., 1969; LLM in Taxation, NYU, 1974. Bar: N.Y. 1970, U.S. Dist. Ct. (so. and ea. dists.) N.Y. 1971, U.S. Tax Ct. 1972. Assoc. Hellerstein, Rosier & Rembar, N.Y.C., 1969-71, Spear and Hill, N.Y.C., 1971; tax mgr. Richards, Ganly, Fries & Preusch, 1971-74, Main Lafrentz & Co. (now Peat Marwick Main), N.Y.C., 1974-80; dir. tax planning, asst. treas. taxes Becton Dickinson and Co., Franklin Lakes, N.J., 1980-87; v.p. taxes Technicon Instruments Corp., Tarrytown, N.Y., 1987—. Contbg. editor (mag.) The Practical Accountant mag., 1976—; contbr. articles to profl. jours. Mem. Forum Sch. Parent's Assn., Waldwick, N.J. Mem. Am. Inst. CPA's, Tax Execs. Inst., N.Y. State CPA Soc. (pension com. 1975-80), N.J. State Soc. CPA's. Democrat. Jewish. Avocations: opera, family. Pension, profit-sharing, and employee benefits, Corporate taxation. Office: Technicon Instruments Corp 511 Benedict Ave Tarrytown NY 10591-5005

MACHIN, PETER WILLIAM, lawyer; b. Halifax, Yorkshire, England, Apr. 30, 1949; s. Albert William and Elizabeth Evelyn (Foster) M.; m. Catherine Lorina Salmon, Nov. 10, 1979. BA in Jurisprudence, Oxford U., 1970; MA, 1974, BCL, 1975. Bar: solicitor High Ct. Eng. and Wales, Supreme Ct. New South Wales, Victoria, Australian Capital Ter., We. Australia. Atty. Ashursts, London, 1971-74; assoc. Underwood & Co., 1975-77, Gasters, London, 1977-79, Mallesons Stephen Jaques, Perth, Australia, 1979-81; ptnr., 1982-89, N.Y., 1989-91, Sydney, 1991-2001, Minter Ellison, 2001—. Contbr. articles to profl. jours. Mem. Internat. Bar Assn., Rocky Mountain Mineral Law Found., Australian Mining and Petroleum Law Assn., Law Coun. Avocations: travel, food and wine, languages, golf, tennis. Oil, gas, and mineral, Finance, Natural resources. Home: 3209/70 Market St Sydney NSW 2000 Australia Office: Minter Ellison 88 Phillip St Sydney NSW 2000 Australia E-mail: peter.machin@minters.com.au

MACIOCE, FRANK MICHAEL, lawyer, financial services company executive; b. N.Y.C., Oct. 3, 1945; s. Frank Michael and Sylvia Maria (Morea) M.; children: Michael Peter, Lauren Decker, Theodore Kenneth; m. Helen Latourette Duffin, July 9, 1988. BS, Purdue U., 1967; JD, Vanderbilt U., 1972. Bar: N.Y. 1973, U.S. Dist. Ct. (so. dist.) N.Y. 1973, U.S. Ct. Appeals (2d cir.) 1975, U.S. Supreme Ct. 1976. Mem. law dept. Merrill Lynch, Pierce, Fenner & Smith Inc., N.Y.C., 1972-80, v.p., 1978-88, 1st v.p., 1988-2000, Merrill Lynch Investment Mgrs., N.Y.C., 2000—. Mgr. corp. law dept. Merrill Lynch & Co., Inc., N.Y.C., 1980-93, asst. gen. counsel, 1982—; gen. counsel investment banking group, 1993-95, ops., svcs. and tech. counsel, 1995-2000, sec. of audit, compensation and nominating coms. bd. dirs., 1978-83, sec. exec. com., 1981-83; mng. dir. Merrill Lynch Overseas Capital, N.V., Netherlands Antilles, 1980-85; sec., dir. Merrill Lynch Employees Fed. Credit Union, N.Y.C., 1978-82; dir. Merrill Lynch Pvt. Capital Inc., N.Y.C., 1981-87, Teleport Comm. Group Inc., N.Y.C., 1987-92, Enhance Fin. Services Inc, N.Y.C., 1988-92; fin. planning adv. bd. Purdue U., 1996-2000. Served with U.S. Army, 1969-70. Mem. ABA, Assn. of Bar of City of N.Y. Computer, General corporate, Securities. Home: 22 Essex Rd Summit NJ 07901-2802 Office: Merrill Lynch & Co Inc 2 World Fin Ctr Fl 30 New York NY 10080-6100

MACISAAC, RONALD FRANCIS, lawyer; b. Prince Albert, Sask., CAn., Oct. 29, 1925; s. John Francis and Marie (MacNair) M.; children: Carol, Daniel, Elizabeth, Hugh, Melanie, Juliette, Bruce; stepchildren: Frank, Maria, Tara, Brad, Nicola, Peter, Russell, Tami, Monique, Todd, Michelle. LLB, U. Sask., 1948. Bar: B.C. 1949, Grand Cayman Island, 1975. Sr. ptnr. MacIsaac & Mac Isaac, Victoria, B.C., Can., 1949—. Contbr. articles to profl. jours. Mem. Trial Lawyers Assn., Mediator Assn., Holistic Law Assn. Roman Catholic. Office: MacIsaac 2227 Sooke Rd Victoria BC Canada V9B 1W8 E-mail: macmac@macisaacandmacisaac.bc.ca

MACK, JOHN MELVIN, lawyer; b. Chgo., July 31, 1934; s. Louis and Beatrice (Shell) M.; m. Judith Ann Perlow, Aug. 28, 1960; children: Susan Lyn Gutstein, Lawrence Meyer. BA, Northwestern U., 1956; JD, Northwestern U., 1959. Bar: Ill. 1960, U.S. Dist. Ct. (no. dist.) 1962, U.S. Ct. Appeals (7th cir.) 1963, U.S. Supreme Ct. 1974. Asst. state's atty. State's Atty.'s Office, Cook County, Chgo., 1960-64; ptnr. Orner & Wasserman, Chgo., 1964-72, Brody & Gore, Chgo., 1972-80, Holstein, Mack & Assocs., Chgo., 1980-85, Holstein, Mack & Dupree, Chgo., 1985-89, Hosltein, Mack & Klein, 1989-93; of counsel, 1993; arbitrator Am. Arbitration Assn., Chgo., 1970— , Def. Research Inst., Chgo., 1982; lectr. in field. Pres. Caucus Party, Skokie, Ill., 1984, membership chmn., 1982—, chmn. community involvement commn., 1981-86; mem. Skokie Fire and Police Commn., 1978—, chmn. 1995—; chmn. Skokie Human Relations Commn., 1976-78; bd. dirs., v.p. Les Turner Als Found. Apptd. Ill. Supreme Ct. ad hoc com. to proper rules on character and fitness. Served with U.S. Army, 1959. Mem. ABA, Fed. Bar Assn., Ill. State Bar Assn., Chgo. Bar Assn. (vice chmn., chmn. com. on legal edn. 1980-81, vice chmn., chmn. com. on operating of cir. ct. 1981-82, vice chmn., chmn., ins. law com. 1986—), Soc. Trial Lawyers, Assn. Trial Lawyers Am., Ill. Trial Lawyers Assn., Trial Lawyers Club of Chgo. Jewish. General civil litigation, Insurance, Personal injury. Home: 9425 Hamlin Ave Evanston IL 60203-1303 Office: Holstein Mack & Klein 188 W Randolph St Ste 1126 Chicago IL 60601-2998

MACK, JOHN OSCAR, lawyer; b. Columbus, Ohio, May 10, 1932; s. Eugene Henry and Eunice A. (Genthner) M.; m. Cristina Ann Iannone, Nov. 19, 1967; children— John Whitney, Elizabeth Ann, Andrew Laughlin. B.S. in Econs., U. Pa., 1954, LL.B. cum laude, 1961. Bar: Calif. 1962, U.S. Dist. Ct. (no. dist.) Calif. 1962, U.S. Supreme Ct. 1979, U.S. Ct. Appeals (9th cir.) 1981. Assoc. firm Pillsbury, Madison & Sutro, San Francisco, 1961-63; asst. v.p., sec. Bank of Calif. (N.A.), San Francisco, 1963-75, v.p., sec., 1972-75, BanCal Tri State Corp., 1972-75; practice law, San Francisco, 1976— ; sr. mng. ptnr. firm Mack, Hazlewood, Franecke & Tinney, San Francisco, 1978— ; gen. ptnr. Red Hills Investment Co., 1979— . Bd. dirs. Lone Mountain Children's Ctr., 1973-88, pres., 1977-85. Served to lt. USNR, 1954-58. Mem. NRA, Smithsonian Assocs., Phi Delta Theta. Republican. Contracts commercial, General corporate, Real property. Home: 963 Pizarro Ln Foster City CA 94404-2929 Office: Mack Hazlewood et al 221 Pine St Ste 600 San Francisco CA 94104-2705

MACK, JULIA COOPER, judge; b. Fayetteville, N.C., July 17, 1920; d. Dallas L. and Emily (McKay) Perry; m. Jerry S. Cooper, July 30, 1943; 1 dau., Cheryl; m. Clifford S. Mack, Nov. 21, 1957. B.S., Hampton Inst., 1940; LL.B., Howard U., 1951; JD (hon.), U. D.C., 1999. Bar: D.C. 1952. Legal cons. OPS, Washington, 1952-53; atty.-advisor office gen. counsel Gen. Svcs. Adminstrn., 1953-54; trial appellate atty. criminal div. Dept. Justice, 1954-68; civil rights atty. Office Gen. Counsel, Equal Employment Opportunity Commn., 1968-75; assoc. judge Ct. Appeals, 1975-89; sr. judge DC Ct. of Appeals, 1989—. Mem. Am., Fed., Washington, Nat. Bar Assns., Nat. Assn. Women Judges. Home: 1610 Varnum St NW Washington DC 20011-4206 Office: DC Ct Appeals 6th Fl 500 Indiana Ave NW Fl 6 Washington DC 20001-2138

MACK, THEODORE, lawyer; b. Ft. Worth, Mar. 5, 1936; s. Henry and Norma (Harris) M.; m. Ellen Feinknopf, June 19, 1960; children: Katherine Norma, Elizabeth Ellen, Alexandra. AB cum laude, Harvard U., 1958, JD, 1961. Bar: Tex. 1961, U.S. Supreme Ct. 1971, U.S. Ct. Appeals (5th cir.) 1967, U.S. Ct. Appeals (11th cir.) 1981, U.S. Dist. Ct. (no. dist.) Tex. 1961, U.S. Dist. Ct. (we. dist.) Tex. 1968, U.S. Dist. Ct. (so. dist.) Tex. 1968, U.S. Dist. Ct. (ea. dist.) Tex. 1999. Assoc. Mack & Mack, Ft. Worth, 1961-62, ptnr., 1963-70; dir., pres., v.p., treas., ptnr. Renfro, Mack and Hudman, P.C. and predecessors, 1970-93; spl. counsel Brackett & Ellis, P.C. and predecessors, 1993—. Trustee Ft. Worth Country Day Sch., 1976-82; bd. dirs. Beth-El Congregation, 1964-73, 75-78, pres. 1975-77; bd. dirs. Jewish Fedn. Ft. Worth, 1965-72; mem. Leadership Ft. Worth, 1973-74; bd. dirs. Sr. Citizens Ctrs., Inc., 1969-81, Family and Individual Svcs., 1981-84, Presbyn. Night Shelter Tarrant County, Inc., 1992-97; pres. Harvard Law Sch. Assn. Tex., 1976-77. Fellow Tex. Bar Found. (life); mem. Tex. Bar Assn., ABA, Tarrant County Bar Assn., Bar Assn. 5th Cir. Ct., Colonial County Club, Ft. Worth Club, City Club, Harvard Club (N.Y.C., Boston). Democrat. Jewish. Antitrust, Bankruptcy, Federal civil litigation. Home: 2817 Harlanwood Dr Fort Worth TX 76109-1226 Office: 100 Main St Fort Worth TX 76102-3090 Fax: 817-429-8049; 817-870-2265. E-mail: tmack@belaw.com

MACKALL, HENRY CLINTON, lawyer; b. Ft. Lauderdale, Fla., Apr. 6, 1927; s. Douglass Sorrel and Mildred (Parker) M.; m. Mary Margaret Sullivan, June 21, 1952; children: Caroline Clark, Nancy Sorrel, Lucy Parker. BA, U. Va., 1950, LLB, 1952. Bar: Va. 1951. Ptnr. Mackall, Mackall & Gibb, P.C. and predecessors, Fairfax, Va., 1952—. Asst. commr. accounts Fairfax County (Va.), 1963—; spl. commr. in chancery for audit functions for Cir. Ct. Fairfax County, 1976—; substitute judge Fairfax County Ct., Juvenile and Domestic Relations Ct. Fairfax County, 1964-69. Trustee Fairfax Hosp. Assn., 1966-75; with Va. State Bar Client Security Fund Bd., 1976-88, chmn., 1977-78; bd. dirs. F&M Bank, No. Va. Served with AUS, 1945-46. Fellow Am. Coll. Trusts & Estate Counsel, Am. Coll. Real Estate Lawyers, Va. Law Found.; mem. ABA, Va. Bar Assn. (regional v.p. 1963-64), Fairfax County Bar Assn. (pres. 1966-67), Hist. Soc. Fairfax County (pres. 1970-72), Jamestowne Soc. (gov. 1995-97), River Bend Country (pres. 1967-68) (Gt. Falls, Va.), Georgetown Assembly (Washington). Democrat. Episcopalian. Probate, Real property. Home: 1032 Towlston Rd Mc Lean VA 22102-1111 Office: 4031 Chain Bridge Rd Fairfax VA 22030-4103 E-mail: mackmarhen@aol.com, mackgibb@aol.com

MACKEY, LEONARD BRUCE, lawyer, former diversified manufacturing corporation executive; b. Washington, Aug. 31, 1925; s. Stuart J. and Margaret B. (Browne) M.; m. Britta Beckhaus, Mar. 2, 1974; children: Leonard B., Cathleen C., Wendy F. B.E.E., Rensselaer Poly. Inst., 1945; J.D., George Washington U., 1950. Bar: D.C. 1951, N.Y. 1954. Instr. elec. engring. Rensselaer Poly. Inst., Troy, N.Y., 1946-47; patent examiner U.S. Patent Office, Washington, 1947-50; atty. Gen. Electric Co., Schenectady and N.Y.C., 1953-60; dir. licensing, asst. sec. ITT, N.Y.C., 1960-73, v.p., gen. patent counsel, dir. licensing, 1973-90; of counsel Davis Hoxie Faithfull & Hapgood, N.Y.C., 1990-93; cons. licensing and tech. transfer Sarasota, Fla., 1994—. Mem. Recreation Commn., Rye, N.Y., 1966-67; mem. Planning Commn., 1967-70, 72-75, city councilman, 1970-71. Served with USNR, 1943-45; to lt. 1951-53. Mem. ABA (coun. mem., intellectual property law sect. 1989-93), Am. Intellectual Property Law Assn. (bd. mgrs. 1968-70, pres. 1982-83), Licensing Execs. Soc. U.S.A. (pres. 1978), Licensing Execs. Soc. Internat. (pres. 1986), Eta Kappa Nu, Am. Yacht Club (sec. 1968-70), N.Y. Yacht Club, Masons, Apawamis. Republican. Presbyterian. Office: 219 S Orange Ave Sarasota FL 34236-6801

MACKEY, STEVEN R. lawyer; b. Enid, Okla., Nov. 10, 1950; s. Emil R. and Ruby M.; children: Jason, Paige. BS in Bus., Okla. State U., 1972; JD, Notre Dame U., 1976. Bar: Okla. 1976, Tex. 1990. Assoc. Fellers, Snider et al, Okla. City, 1976-77, Sneed, Long et al, Tulsa, Okla., 1980-81; assoc. gen. counsel Weeks Petroleum, Westport, Conn., 1981-83; lawyer pvt. practice, Tulsa, 1983-84; regional atty. Kaiser Aluminum, 1984-85; v.p., gen. counsel, sec. Helmerich & Payne, Inc., 1986—. Bd. dirs. Tulsa chpt. Am. Heart Assn., 1996-99. Capt. U.S. Army, 1977-80. Fellow Tulsa County Bar Found. (pres. 2000-01); mem. Tulsa County Bar Assn. (pres. elect 1998-99, pres. 1999—, Pres. award 1992-93, Disting. Pres. award 1993-94, Golden Rule award 1995). Republican. Methodist. Avocations: Judo (2d degree black belt), reading, running. General corporate, Oil, gas, and mineral, Real property. Office: Helmerich & Payne Inc 1579 E 21st St Ste 748 Tulsa OK 74114-1336

MACKIE, DAVID LINDSAY, lawyer; b. Eng., Feb. 15, 1946; s. Alastair and Rachel (Goodson) M.; m. Phyllis M. Gershon; children: James, Edward, Bella. MA, Oxford U., 1967. Bar: solicitor 1971; Queen's counsel 1998; accredited mediator Ctr. Dispute Resolution. Assoc. Allen & Overy, London, 1971-75; ptnr., 1975—; head of litigation, 1988—. Recorder Crown Ct., 1989—; dep. High Ct. judge, 1998—; dep. chair Royal Cts. Justice Advice Bur., 1997. Fellow Chartered Inst. Arbitrators; mem. Internat. Bar Assn. (chmn. com. product liability, advtsg. and consumer protection 1987-91). Avocation: climbing. Alternative dispute resolution, Public international. Office: Allen & Overy One New Change London EC4M 9QQ England Fax: 0207-330-9999. E-mail: david.mackie@allenovery.com

MACKIEWICZ, EDWARD ROBERT, lawyer; b. Jersey City, July 2, 1951; s. Edward John and Irene Helen (Rakowicz) H. BA, Yale U., 1973; JD, Columbia U., 1976. Bar: N.J. 1976, U.S. Dist. Ct. N.J. 1976, N.Y. 1977, U.S. Dist. Ct. (so. and ea. dist.) N.Y. 1977, D.C. 1978, U.S. Dist. Ct. D.C. 1978, U.S. Ct. Appeals (D.C. cir.) 1978, U.S. Ct. Appeals (3d cir.) 1980, U.S. Supreme Ct. 1980, Md. 1984, U.S. Ct. Claims 1984, U.S. Ct. Appeals (4th cir.) 1986, U.S. Dist. Ct. Md. 1990. Assoc. Carter, Ledyard & Milburn, N.Y.C., 1976-77, Covington & Burling, Washington, 1977-82; counsel for civil rights litigation solicitor's office U.S. Dept. Labor, 1982-83; sr. assoc. Jones, Day, Reavis & Pogue, 1983-85; gen. counsel Pension Benefit Guaranty Corp., 1985-87; of counsel Pierson, Ball & Dowd, 1987-89; ptnr. Reed Smith Shaw & McClay, 1989; gen. counsel Masters, Mates & Pilots Benefit Plans, Linthicum Heights, Md., 1989-92; of counsel Steptoe & Johnson, L.L.P., Washington, 1992-98, ptnr., 1999—. Mem. adv. coun. Sec. of Labor's ERISA, 1991-93; profl. lectr. in law Nat. Law Ctr., George Washington U., 1993—. Mem. Am. Coun. Young Polit. Leaders (del. to Australia 1985), Univ. Club, Yale Club. Bankruptcy, Labor, Pension, profit-sharing, and employee benefits. Home: 3001 Veazey Ter NW Apt 1032 Washington DC 20008-5406 Office: 1330 Connecticut Ave NW Washington DC 20036-1704 E-mail: emackiew@steptoe.com

MACKINNON, CATHARINE ALICE, lawyer, law educator, legal scholar, writer; d. George E. and Elizabeth V. (Davis) MacKinnon. BA in Govt. magna cum laude with distinction, Smith Coll., 1969; JD, Yale U., 1977, PhD in Polit. Sci., 1987. Vis. prof. Harvard U., Stanford U., Yale U., others, Osgoode Hall, York U., Canada, U. Basel, Switzerland; prof. of law U. Mich., 1990—. Long term vis. prof. U. Chgo., 1997—. Author: Sexual Harassment of Working Women, 1979, Feminism Unmodified, 1987, Toward a Feminist Theory of the State, 1989, Only Words, 1993, Sex Equality, 2001; co-author: In Harm's Way, 1997. Office: U Michigan Law School Ann Arbor MI 48109-1215

MACKLIN, CROFFORD JOHNSON, JR. lawyer; b. Columbus, Ohio, Sept. 10, 1947; S. Crofford Johnson, Sr. and Dorothy Ann (Stevens) M.; m. Mary Carole Ward, July 5, 1969; children: Carrie E., David J. BA, Ohio State U., 1969; BA summa cum laude, U. West Fla., 1974; JD cum laude, Ohio State U., 1976. Bar: Ohio 1977, U.S. Tax Ct. 1978. Acct. Touche Ross, Columbus, 1976-77; assoc. Smith & Schnacke, Dayton, 1977-81; ptnr. Porter, Wright, Morris & Arthur, 1983-88; shareholder Smith & Schnacke, 1988-89; ptnr. Thompson, Hine LLP, 1989—; practice group leader personnel and succession planning Thompson, Hine & Flory, 2001—; sole practice Dayton, 1981-82. Adj. faculty Franklin U., 1977; adj. prof. U. Dayton Law Sch., 1981. Contbr. articles to profl. jours. Bd. dirs. Great Lakes Nat. Bank Ohio, 1997, Easter Seals, 1984-86. Served to capt. USMCR, 1969-74. Fellow Am. Coll. Trust and Estate Counsel; mem. ABA, Dayton Bar Assn. (chmn. probate com. 1981-83), Dayton Trust & Estate Planning (pres. 1983-84), Ohio Bar Assn. Presbyterian. Home: 3 Forest Pl Glendale OH 45246-4407 Office: Thompson Hine LLP 2000 Courthouse Pla NE PO Box 8801 Dayton OH 45401-8801

MACLAUGHLIN, HARRY HUNTER, federal judge; b. Breckenridge, Minn., Aug. 9, 1927; s. Harry Hunter and Grace (Swank) MacL.; m. Mary Jean Shaffer, June 25, 1958; children: David, Douglas. BBA with distinction, U. Minn., 1949, JD, 1956. Bar: Minn. 1956. Law clk. to justice Minn. Supreme Ct.; ptnr. MacLaughlin & Mondale, MacLaughlin & Harstad, Mpls., 1956-72; assoc. justice Minn. Supreme Ct., 1972-77; U.S. sr. dist. judge Dist. of Minn., Mpls., 1977—. Part-time instr. William Mitchell Coll. Law, St. Paul, 1958-63; lectr. U. Minn. Law Sch., 1973-86; mem. 8th Cir. Jud. Council, 1981-83. Bd. editors: Minn. Law Rev, 1954-55. Mem. Mpls. Charter Commn., 1967-72, Minn. State Coll. Bd., 1971-72, Minn. Jud. Council, 1972; mem. nat. adv. council Small Bus. Adminstrn., 1967-69. Served with USNR, 1945-46. Recipient U. Minn. Outstanding Achievement award, 1995; named Best Fed. Dist. Ct. Judge in 8th Cir., Am. Lawyer mag., 1983. Mem. ABA, Minn. Bar Assn., Hennepin County Bar Assn., Beta Gamma Sigma, Phi Delta Phi. Congregational. Office: US Dist Ct 684 US Courthouse 110 S 4th St Minneapolis MN 55401-2205

MACLEAN, BABCOCK, lawyer; b. N.Y.C., Jan. 26, 1946; s. Charles Chalmers and Lee Selden (Howe) MacL.; m. Cynthia Gannon, Feb. 15, 1983. BA, Yale U., 1967; MA, Columbia U., 1970; JD, Case Western Res. U., 1975; LLM in Taxation, NYU, 1987. Bar: Ohio 1975, N.Y. 1983. Assoc. Hadley, Matia, Mills & MacLean, Cleve., 1976-77, mem., 1977-83; tax editor Rsch. Inst. Am., N.Y.C., 1983-85; assoc. Robinson Brog, 1985-86, mem., 1987—. Adj. asst. prof. taxation Pace U., N.Y.C., 1983-84; adv. bd. Rsch. Inst. Am., 1992-97. Mem. ABA (sect. taxation), N.Y. State Bar Assn. (sect. taxation), Assn. Bar City N.Y., Yale Club, St. Anthony Club, N.Y. Yacht Club, Seawanhaka Corinthian Yacht Club, St. Andrew's Soc. N.Y., Pilgrims of the U.S. Republican. Episcopalian. Corporate taxation, Taxation, general, Personal income taxation. Home: 77 W 55th St New York NY 10019-4910 Office: Robinson Brog 1345 Avenue Of The Americas New York NY 10105-0144

MACLEOD, WILLIAM CYRUS, lawyer, economist; b. Chgo., Apr. 7, 1952; s. Charles William MacLeod and Sarah Ann (Updyke) MacLeod Simitz; m. Michele Benoit, May 5, 1956; 1 child, Christine Michele. BA, Ripon Coll., 1973; PhD, U. Va., 1975; JD, U. Miami, Coral Gables, Fla., 1979. Bar: Ill. 1979, U.S. Dist. Ct. (no. dist.) Ill. 1979, U.S. Ct. Appeals (7th cir.) 1985. Instr. U. Va., Charlottesville, 1976; cons. Law and Econs. Ctr., Coral Gables, 1976-79; assoc. McDermott Will & Emery, Chgo., 1979-82; atty. advisor FTC, Washington, 1982-83, dir. Chgo. region, 1983—. Contbr. articles to profl. publs. Mem. ABA, Ill. Bar Assn. (mem. antitrust council 1983—), Chgo. Bar Assn. Office: Fed Trade Commission Consumer Protection Bur 6th & Pennsylvania Ave NW Washington DC 20580-0001

MACLIN, ALAN HALL, lawyer; b. DuQuoin, Ill., Dec. 22, 1949; s. John E. and Nora (Hall) M.; m. Joan Davidson (div. Dec. 1981); children: Molly, Tess, Anne; m. Jeanne Sittlow, Nov. 17, 1984. BA magna cum laude, Vanderbilt U., 1971; JD, U. Chgo., 1974. Bar: Minn. 1974, U.S. Dist. Ct. Minn. 1974, U.S. Ct. Appeals (8th cir.) 1974, U.S. Ct. Appeals (5th cir.) 1975. U.S. Supreme Ct. 1978. Asst. atty. gen. Minn. Atty. Gen., St. Paul, 1974-80; chief anti-trust divsn. Briggs & Morgan, 1980—, mem. bd. dirs., 1993-96. Mem. Minn. State Bar Assn. (treas. anti-trust sect. 1978-80, 96-98, chair 1998—), Ramsey County Bar Assn. (sec. jud. com. 1980-82), Phi Beta Kappa. Unitarian. Antitrust, Federal civil litigation, Insurance. Office: Briggs & Morgan 2200 1st St N Saint Paul MN 55109-3210 E-mail: amaclin@briggs.com

MACMILLAN, HOKE, state attorney general; m. Becky Klemt; children: Ryan Klemt, Christopher Klemt. BA, U. Wyo., 1967, JD, 1970. Bar: Wyo., Colo., Nebr., U.S. Ct. Appeals (10th cir.), U.S. Ct. Mil. Appeals, U.S. Supreme Ct. Capt. U.S. Army JAG, 1970—74; mem. Pence and Millett, Laramie, Wyo., 1974—2001, sr. ptnr., 1982—2001; atty. gen. State of Wyo., 2001—. Fellow: Am. Bar Found.; mem.: Wyo. State Bar (pres. 1996—97), Nebr. State Bar, Albany County Bar Assn. Office: Atty Gens Office 123 Capitol Bldg 200 W 24th St Cheyenne WY 82002*

MACMILLAN, PETER ALAN, lawyer; b. Mpls., Apr. 10, 1955; s. John Louis and Celeste Caroline (Eggers) MacM.; m. Karen Christine Johnson, Mar. 19, 1988. BS, Mankato State U., 1977; JD, Hamline U., 1980; postgrad., Sch. Law U. San Deigo, 1980. Bar: Minn. 1980, U.S. Tax Ct. 1980, U.S. Dist. Ct. Minn. 1981, U.S. Dist. Ct. (no. dist.) Tex. 1992, U.S. Ct. Appeals (5th cir.) 1993, U.S. Ct. Appeals (8th cir.) 1995, U.S. Supreme Ct. 1992. Pvt. practice, Robbinsdale, Minn., 1981-84; assoc. Rosenthal & Rondoni, Ltd., Mpls., 1984-85; ptnr. Rosenthal, Rondoni & MacMillan, Ltd., 1985-96, Rondoni, MacMillan & Schneider Ltd., Mpls., 1996—. Chmn. Minn. Jaycees Found. 1987-88, trustee, 1988-92. Mem. ABA, Minn. State Bar Assn., Hennepin County Bar Assn., Assn. Trial Lawyers Am., Am. Judicature Soc., Minn. Trial Lawyers Assn., Min. Def. Lawyers Assn., Def. Rsch. Inst., Jaycees (pres. Robbinsdale chpt. 1986, Jr. chamber internat. senate). Lutheran. Criminal, Personal injury, Workers' compensation. Home: 11282 71st Ave N Osseo MN 55369-7621 Office: Rondoni MacMillan & Schneider Ltd 505 Highway 169 N Ste 175 Plymouth MN 55441-6443

MACRAE, CAMERON FARQUHAR, III, lawyer; b. N.Y.C., Mar. 21, 1942; s. Cameron F. and Jane B. (Miller) MacR.; m. Ann Wooster Bedell, Nov. 30, 1974; children: Catherine Fairfax, Ann Cameron. AB, Princeton U., 1963; LLB, Yale U., 1966. Bar: N.Y. 1966, D.C. 1967, U.S. Dist. Ct. (so. dist.) N.Y. 1975. Atty.-advisor Office of Gen. Counsel to Sec. Air Force, Washington, 1966-69; assoc. Davis, Polk & Wardell, N.Y.C., 1970-72; dep. supt. and counsel N.Y. State Banking Dept., 1972-74; sr. ptnr. LeBeoug, Lamb, Greene & MacRae, 1975—. Dir. Nat. Integrity Life Ins. Co., 2000—. Note and comment editor Yale Law Jour., 1965-66. Trustee, sec. St. Andrew's Dune Ch., 1982—; hon. chmn. Clear Pool Inc., 1990-94. Capt. USAF, 1966-69. Mem. Assn. of Bar of City of N.Y. (past mem. securities regulation com., banking law com.), D.C. Bar Assn., Racquet and Tennis Club, Union Club (N.Y.C.), Meadow Club (v.p., bd. govs.), Bathing Corp. Southampton, Shinnecock Hills Golf Club (Southampton), Cottage Club (Princeton, N.J.), Jupiter Island Club. Republican. Episcopalian. Banking, Contracts commercial, Private international. Office: LeBoeuf Lamb Greene & MacRae 125 W 55th St New York NY 10019-5369 E-mail: c.f.macrae@llgm.com

MACRIS, MICHAEL, lawyer; b. Jackson Heights, N.Y., July 12, 1949; Student, Cornell U.; BA with distinction, Stanford U., 1971; JD, Columbia U., 1974. Bar: N.Y. 1975, Conn. 1976. Mem. Cahill Gordon & Reindel, N.Y.C. Bd. editors Columbia Law Rev., 1973-74; co-editor ERISA & Benefits Law Jour., 1992-99. Harlan Fiske Stone scholar. Fellow Am. Coll. Employee Benefits Counsel (charter); mem. ABA (chmn. com. on fiduciary responsibility, real property, probate and trust law sect. 1993—), Phi Beta Kappa. Pension, profit-sharing, and employee benefits. Office: Cahill Gordon & Reindel 80 Pine St Fl 19 New York NY 10005-1790

MACRITCHIE, KENNETH, lawyer; b. Glasgow, Scotland, Mar. 9, 1956; s. Norman and Daveen MacR.; m. Brenda Kathleen Sinclair, Aug. 31, 1982; children: Rowena Claire, Arabella Jane, Cameron. LLB, U. Glasgow, 1976; BD with 1st class honors, U. Aberdeen (Scotland), 1984. Ptnr. Clifford Chance, Eng., 1991-94, Milbank, Tweed, Hadley & McCloy, Eng., 1994-96, Shearman & Sterling, Eng., 1996—. Banking, Contracts commercial. Office: Shearman & Sterling Broadgate W 9 Appold St London EC2A 2AP England Fax: 020 7655 5500. E-mail: kmarcritchie@shearman.com

MACY, JOHN PATRICK, lawyer; b. Menomonee Falls, Wis., June 26, 1955; s. Leland Francis and Joan Marie (LaValle) M. BA, Carroll Coll., 1977; JD, Marquette U., 1980. Bar: Wis. 1980, U.S. Dist. Ct. (we. and ea. dists.) Wis. 1980, U. S. Ct. Appeals (7th cir.) 1980. Assoc. Hippenmeyer Reilly Arenz Molter Bode & Gross, Waukesha, Wis., 1980-83; ptnr. Arenz Molter Macy & Riffle, S.C., 1983--. Lectr. in field. Mem. ABA, Waukesha County Bar Assn. (chair 1995-96). Republican. Roman Catholic. Land use and zoning (including planning), Municipal (including bonds), State and local taxation. Home: 4839 Hewitts Point Rd Oconomowoc WI 53066-3320 Office: Arenz Molter Macy & Riffle SC 720 N East Ave Waukesha WI 53186-4800

MADDEN, EDWARD GEORGE, JR. lawyer; b. Newark, Feb. 21, 1924; s. Edward and Catherine (Mahon) M.; m. Mary B. Haveron, June 20, 1959; children: Maurica, Margaret, Thomas, Mary, Jane. BS, St. Peter's Coll., 1950; JD, U. Mich., 1953. Bar: N.J. 1954, U.S. Dist. Ct. N.J. 1954, U.S. Ct. Appeals (3d cir.) 1981, U.S. Supreme Ct. 1959. Assoc. McCarter & English, Newark, 1954-56, Donohue & Donohue, Nutley, N.J., 1956-61; ptnr. Troast, Mattson & Madden, Newark, 1961-65, Mattson & Madden, Newark, 1965—. Mem. N.J. State Legislature, 1960-62. With USN 1943-46. Fellow Am. Bar Found.; mem. ABA, N.J. Bar Assn. (trustee, treas. 1972-78), Essex County Bar Assn. (trustee 1971-75), Internat. Assn. Def. Counsel, Transp. Lawyers Assn. Democrat. Roman Catholic. State civil litigation, Insurance, Transportation. Office: 33 Bleeker St Millburn NJ 07041-1414

MADDEN, JEROME ANTHONY, lawyer; b. Memphis, Aug. 24, 1948; s. Bernard Clark and Virginia Ann (Golas) M.; m. Cynthia S. Madden, June 27, 1992; 1 child, Clark John. BA, The Franciscan U. Steubenville, Ohio, 1971; JD summa cum laude, U. Dayton, 1978. Bar: Ohio 1978, D.C. 1979, U.S. Dist. Ct. D.C. 1979, U.S. Ct. Appeals (D.C. cir.) 1980, U.S. Ct. Claims 1984, U.S. Ct. Appeals (Fed. cir.) 1984, U.S. Supreme Ct. 1984, U.S. Ct. Appeals (7th and 11th cirs.) 1987, U.S. Ct. Appeals (4th and 5th cirs.) 1988, U.S. Ct. Appeals (9th cir.) 1991, U.S. Ct. Appeals (2d & 10th cirs.) 1992, U.S. Ct. Appeals (1st cir.) 1993. Law clk. to chief justices O'Neill and Leach Ohio Supreme Ct., Columbus, 1978-79; assoc. Cadwalader, Wickersham & Taft, Washington, 1979-85; sr. trial counsel U.S. Dept. Justice, 1985-91; counsel, then acting sr. counsel, then supervisory counsel FDIC Appellate Litigation Sect., Comml. Litigation Unit, 1991-98; trial atty. U.S. Dept. Justice, Comml. Litigation Br., 1998—. Adj. prof. George Washington U. Sch. Law, Washington, 2000—. Editor-in-chief U. Dayton Law Rev., 1977-78. Served with USMCR, 1970-76. Mem. D.C. Bar Assn. Roman Catholic. Avocation: golf. E-mial. Home: 1502 Powells Tavern Pl Herndon VA 20170-2831 Office: US Dept of Justice 1100 L St NW Washington DC 20005-4035 E-mail: Jerome.Madden@usdoj.gov

MADDEN, JOHN JOSEPH, lawyer; b. N.Y.C., May 27, 1946; s. John L. and Bertha M. (Antonades) M.; m. Mary A. O'Neill, June 19, 1976; children: Elisabeth, Samuel. BA, U. Pa., 1968; JD, Fordham U., 1975. Bar: N.Y. 1976, U.S. Dist. Ct. (so. dist.) N.Y. 1976; avocat a la cour de Paris 1994. Assoc. Shearman & Sterling, N.Y.C., 1975-83, ptnr., 1983—, mng. ptnr. European offices Paris, 1991-95; head Shearman & Sterling Mergers and Acquisitions Group, 1995—, also mem. firm's policy com. Trustee St. David's Sch., N.Y.C., 1981-91. Served to 1st lt. U.S. Army, 1969-71, Vietnam. Mem. ABA, N.Y. Bar Assn., Assn. of Bar of City of N.Y., Internat. Bar Assn., Cercle de l'Union Interalliee (Paris). General corporate, Mergers and acquisitions, Securities. E-mail: jmadden@shearman.com

MADDEN, M. STUART, lawyer, educator; b. Washington, Dec. 1, 1948; s. Murdaugh Stuart and Louise (Mann) M. B.A., U. Pa., 1971; M.A., London Sch. Econs., 1972; J.D., Georgetown U., 1976. Bar: D.C. 1976, U.S. Ct. Appeals (D.C. cir.) 1977, U.S. Ct. Internat. Trade 1982, U.S. Cts. Appeals (5th and 11th cirs.) 1982. Assoc. Reed, Smith, Shaw & McClay, Washington, 1976-78, Weil, Gotshal & Manges, Washington, 1978-80, Santarelli & Gimer, Washington, 1980-83; ptnr. Santarelli & Bond, Washington, 1983-85; distinguished prof. of law Pace U. Sch. Law, White Plains, N.Y., 1986—; vis. prof. William Mitchell Coll. Law, St. Paul, 1985. Assoc. editor Jour. Products and Toxics Liability, 1984—95; Author: Madden and Owen on Products Liability, 3d edit, 2000; contbr. articles to legal jours. Mem. ALI, ABA, Assn. Trial Lawyers Am., Phi Delta Phi. Episcopalian. Insurance, Libel, Personal injury. Home: 2 Westchester Ave #62 White Plains NY 10601 Office: Pace U Sch Law 78 N Broadway White Plains NY 10603-3710 E-mail: smadden@law.pace.edu

MADDEN, NEAL D. lawyer; b. Syracuse, N.Y., May 27, 1946; s. Daniel C. and Thelma (Place) M.; m. Dorothy J. Costie, Aug. 1, 1970; children—Colleen B., Alana E. B.A., Syracuse U., 1968; J.D., U. Chgo., 1971. Bar: N.Y. 1972, U.S. Dist. Ct. (we. dist.) N.Y. 1972. Assoc., Harter, Secrest & Emery, Rochester, N.Y., 1971-79, ptnr., 1980— . Active Genesee Valley Group Health Assn., Rochester, 1975-84; bd. dirs., sec. Nat. Kidney Found. Upstate N.Y., Rochester, 1979-84; bd. dirs., v.p. Ctr. for Environ. Info., Inc., Rochester, 1983-88; bd. dirs. Monroe County Environ. Council, Rochester, 1983-88. Mem. N.Y. State Bar Assn. (chmn. adminstrv. law com. 1982— , exec. com. environ. law sect. 1982—, sect. chmn. 1994—). Environmental, Health, Real property. Office: Harter Secrest & Emery 700 Midtown Tower Rochester NY 14604-2006

MADDEN, PALMER BROWN, lawyer; b. Milw., Sept. 19, 1945; m. Susan L. Paulus, Mar. 31, 1984. BA, Stanford U., 1968; JD, U. Calif., Berkeley, 1973. Bar: Calif. 1973, U.S. Dist. Ct. (no. dist.) Calif. 1973, U.S. Supreme Ct. 1982. Ptnr. McCutchen, Doyle Brown & Enersen, Walnut Creek, 1985-98; prin. ADR Svcs., Alamo, Calif., 1999—. Pres. State Bar Bd. Govs., 2000-2001. Chair bd. govs. Continuing Edn. of the Bar, 1997; judge pro tem Contra Costa Superior Ct., 1991—; pres. Contra Costa Coun., 1995, Kennedy-King Found., 1994; bd. dirs. Episcopal Homes Found., 2001. Mem. Contra Costa County Bar Assn. (pres. 1996-97). Democrat. Episcopalian. General civil litigation. Office: ADR Svcs 3000 Danville Blvd # 543 Alamo CA 94507

MADDEN, PAUL ROBERT, lawyer, director; b. St. Paul, Nov. 13, 1926; s. Ray Joseph and Margaret (Meyer) M.; m. Rosemary R. sorel, Aug. 7, 1974; children: Margaret Jane, William, James Patrick, Derek R. Sorel, Lisa T. Sorel. Student, St. Thomas Coll., 1944; AB, U. Minn., 1948; JD, Georgetown U., 1951. Bar: Ariz. 1957, Minn. 1951, D.C. 1951. Assoc. Hamilton & Hamilton, Washington, 1951-55; legal asst. to commr. SEC, 1955-56; assoc. Lewis and Roca, Phoenix, 1957-59, ptnr., 1959-90, Beus, Gilbert & Morrill, Phoenix, 1991-94, Chapman and Cutler, Phoenix, 1994-97; of counsel Gallagher & Kennedy, 1997—. Bd. dirs. Mesa Air Group, Inc., Phoenix, chmn., 1998-99. Sec. Minn. Fedn. Coll. Rep. Clubs, 1947-48; chmn. 4th dist. Minn. Young Rep. Club, 1948; nat. co-chmn. Youth for Eisenhower, 1951-52; mem. Ariz. Rep. Com., 1960-62; bd. dirs. Found. Jr. Achievement Ctrl. Ariz., Cath. Community Found., Phoenix, Heritage Hills Homeowners Assn., St. Joseph the Worker, past-pres. Attys. for Family-Held Enterprises; past bd. dirs., past chmn. Camelback Charitable Trust; past bd. dirs. The Samaritan Found., Phoenix; past bd. dirs., Ariz. Club, Phoenix, 1990-93; past bd. dirs., past chmn. Found. for Sr. Living; past bd. dirs., vice chmn. Cen. Ariz. chpt. ARC; past bd. dirs., past pres. Jr. Achievement Cen. Ariz., Inc.; mem. nat. bd. vis. U. Ariz. Law Sch. With USNR, 1946-48. Mem. ABA, Ariz. Bar Assn., Maricopa County Bar Assn., Fed. Bar Assn., Maricopa County Bar Assn., Fed. Bar Assn., Fedn. Ins. Counsel, The Barristers Club (Washington, Arizona Club, Phi Delta Phi. General corporate, Insurance, Securities. Home: 1190 Deer Run Rd Prescott AZ 86303 Office: Gallagher & Kennedy PA 2575 E Camelback Rd Phoenix AZ 85016-9225 E-mail: PRM@gknet.com

MADDEN, THOMAS JAMES, lawyer, educator; b. Trenton, N.J., Sept. 13, 1941; s. Jerry A. and Minerva (Quigley) M.; m. Irene Lyons, June 17, 1967; children: Jay, Beth. BEE, Villanova U., 1964; JD with honors, Cath. U., 1968. Bar: N.J. 1968, D.C. 1968, U.S. Patent Office 1968. Atty. adv. Naval Air Sys Command, 1968-69; dep. gen. counsel Dept. Justice Law Enforcement Assistance Adminstrn., 1970-71, gen. counsel, 1972-79; dir. Nat. Adv. Commn. on Criminal Justice Stds. and Goals, 1971-73; adv. U.S. Office Mgmt. and Budget on Fed. Assistance Programs, Washington, 1979-80; gen. counsel Dept. Justice Office Justice Assistance Rsch. and Stats., 1980; from assoc. to ptnr. Kay Scholer, Fierman, Hays and Handler, Washington, 1980-84; ptnr. Venable, Baetjer, Howard & Civiletti, 1984—. Adj. prof. contract law American U., 1980-85; gen. counsel Nat. Criminal Justice Assn., Nat. Coun. Juvenile and Family Ct. Judges; adv. panel on streamlining and codifying fed. acquisition laws Dept. Def., 1991-93; mem. Procurement Round Table, 1998—. Contbr. articles to profl. jours. Pres. U.S. Ct. Fed. Claims Bar Assn., 1999-2000. Recipient Louis Brownlow award Am. Soc. for Pub. Adminstrn., 1982, Disting. Svc. award Dept. Justice, 1973, Wilson Cowen award for disting. svc. to U.S. Ct. Fed. Claims, 1998. Fellow Am. Bar Found.; mem. ABA (chmn. pub. contract law sect. 1988-89, pres. fellows of pub. contract law sect. 1992-93), D.C. Bar Assn., Fed. Bar Assn. (pres. D.C. chpt. 1982-83). Federal civil litigation, General corporate, Government contracts and claims. Office: Venable Baetjer Howard & Civiletti 1201 New York Ave NW Ste 1100 Washington DC 20005-3917

MADDOX, ALVA HUGH, retired state supreme court justice; b. Andalusia, Ala., Apr. 17, 1930; s. Christopher Columbus and Audie Lodella Maddox; m. Virginia Roberts, June 14, 1958; children: Robert Hugh, Jane Maddox. AB in Journalism, U. Ala., Tuscaloosa, 1952, JD, 1957. Bar: Ala. 1957. Law clk. to Judge Aubrey Cates, Ala. Ct. Appeals, Montgomery, 1957-58; field examiner Chief Atty.'s Office, VA, 1958-59; law clk. to Judge Frank M. Johnson, U.S. Dist. Ct., 1959-61; pvt. practice, 1961-65; cir. judge, spl. cir. judge Montgomery Cir. Ct., 1963, asst. dist. atty., 1964; legal advisor to govs. including George C. Wallace, Lurleen B. Wallace, Albert P. Brewer, State of Ala., Montgomery, 1965-69; assoc. justice Supreme Ct. Ala., 1969-2001; ret., 2001. Adv. bd. JUSTEC Rsch. Author: Alabama Rules of Criminal Procedure, 1991, supplements, 1992—. Founder youth jud. program YMCA, Montgomery, 1979, also mem. metro. bd. dirs. 2d lt. USAF, 1952-54, col. USAF Res. ret. Recipient Man of Yr. award YMCA, 1988, Disting. Program Svc. award, 1989, Srs. of Achievement award Montgomery Coun. on Aging, 1999. Mem. ABA, Ala. Bar Assn. (Jud. award of merit 1997), Inst. Jud. Adminstrn., Christian Legal Soc. (bd. dirs.), Federalist Soc. (bd. dirs.), Hugh Maddox Inn of Ct. Montgomery (charter, founding), Ala. Law Inst., Am. Jud. Soc., Kiwanis (past bd. dirs. Montgomery), Am. Inns of Ct. (trustee), Order of Samaritan/U. Ala. Law Sch. Democrat. Baptist. Office: Supreme Ct Ala 300 Dexter Ave Montgomery AL 36104-3741 E-mail: HMaddox@alalinc.net

MADDOX, CHARLES J., JR. lawyer; b. Cameron, Tex., Oct. 8, 1949; s. Charles J. and Mary Jo (Fikes) M.; m. Sandra Peppin, Apr. 29, 1984; children: Elizabeth Asleigh, Kathryn Austin. Student Tex. A&M U., 1968-70; BBA, U. Tex., 1972, JD, 1976. Bar: Tex. 1977, U.S. Dist. Ct. (no., so., ea. and we. dists.) Tex. 1980, U.S. Ct. Appeal (5th and 11th cirs.) 1981, U.S. Supreme Ct. 1982. Staff auditor Walgreen Co., Chgo. and Houston, 1973; asst. atty. gen. State of Tex., Austin, 1977-80; sr. and mng. ptnr. firm Maddox, Perrin Kirkendall, Houston, 1981-91; ptnr. Goldberg & Brown, Houston, 1991-95; prin. Law Offices of Charles L. Maddox, Jr., Missouri City, Tex., 1995—. Sponsor Rep. fund, Washington, 1983—; sustaining mem. Rep. Nat. Com., Washington, 1984—. NSF scholar 1965, Newhause scholar 1968. Mem. Tex. Bar Assn., Houston Bar Assn., Quail Valley Country Club (Missouri City, Tex.), Pla. Club, Govs. Club (Houston), Sigma Iota Epsilon, Alpha Kappa Psi (life, treas. 1971-72). Republican. Presbyterian. Bankruptcy, Federal civil litigation, State civil litigation. Office: Law Offices of Charles J Maddox Jr 3415 Boca Raton Dr Missouri City TX 77459-4408

MADOLE, DONALD WILSON, lawyer; b. Elkhart, Kans., July 14, 1932. Student Kans. State Tchrs. Coll., 1950-51; B.S., U. Denver, 1959, J.D., 1959. Bar: Colo. 1960, U.S. Dist. Ct. Colo. 1960, U.S. Ct. Appeals (10th cir.) 1960, D.C. 1971, U.S. Supreme Ct. 1972, U.S. Ct. Appeals (1st cir.) 1976, U.S. Ct. Appeals (5th cir.) 1977, U.S. Ct. Appeals (6th cir.) 1982, U.S. Ct. Appeals (7th and 9th cirs.) 1975, U.S. Ct. Appeals (11th cir.) 1981. V.p. Mountain Aviation Corp., Denver, 1958-59; trial atty. FAA, Washington, 1960-62; sr. warranty adminstr. Am. Airlines, Tulsa, 1962-63; chief

hearing and reports div., atty. adviser CAB, Washington, 1963-66; ptnr. Speiser, Krause & Madole, Washington, 1966— ; pres. Aerial Application Corp., Burlingame, Calif., 1968-69; v.p., dir. Environ. Power Ltd., Pitts., 1972— ; chm. Gen. Acctg. Office Aircraft Cert. Adv. Com., Washington, 1993; bd. dirs. Equipment Leasing Co., San Antonio, Unitrade Ltd., Washington, Bus. Ins. Mgmt. Inc., Bethesda, Md., Entertainment Capitol Corp., N.Y.C.; gen. counsel Nat. Aviation Club, 1978-80, Internat. Soc. Air Safety Investigators, 1977—; mem. blue ribbon panel on airworthiness Nat. Acad. Sci., 1980; adviser U.S. Govt. del. Internat. Civil Aviation Orgn., 1965; U.S. Govt. rep. Aircraft Inquiry, Montreal, P.Q., Can., 1964. Author: Textbook of Aviation Statutes and Regulations, 1963; International Aspects of Aircraft Accidents, 1963; CAB, Aircraft Accident Investigation, 1964. Mem. chancellor's soc. U. Denver, 1982— . Served to comdr. USNR, 1953-57. Recipient Outstanding Performance award FAA, 1961; Meritorious Achievement award Am. Airlines, 1962; Outstanding Performance awards CAB, 1963-65; Fed. Govt. Outstanding Pub. Service award Jump-Meml. Found., 1966. Fellow Internat. Acad. Trial Lawyers; mem. ABA, Colo. Bar Assn., Fed. Bar Assn., D.C. Bar Assn., Assn. Trial Lawyers Am., Lawyer-Pilots Assn., Am. Law Inst., Phi Delta Phi, Phi Mu Alpha. Clubs: Congl. Country, Nat. Aviation, Nat. Press. Aviation, Federal civil litigation, Personal injury. Home: 23704 Mount Pleasant Landing C Saint Michaels MD 21663-2516 Office: 1216 16th St NW Washington DC 20036-3202

MADORY, RICHARD EUGENE, lawyer; b. Kenton, Ohio, May 14, 1931; s. Harold Richard and Hilda (Strictland) M.; m. Barbara Jean Madory, Sept. 25, 1955; children— Richard Eugene, Terry Dean, Michael Wesly. B.S. in Edn., Ohio State U., 1952; J.D., Southwestern U., 1961. Bar: Calif., 1961, U.S. Ct. Mil. Appeals, U.S. Supreme Ct., U.S. Dist. Ct. (cen. dist.) Calif. With firm Madory, Booth, Zell & Pleiss, Santa Ana, Calif., 1962— , now pres., v.p., sec.-treas. lectr. Continuing Edn. of Bar State of Calif. Served to col. USMC. Fellow Am. Coll. Trial Lawyers; mem. ABA, Orange County Bar Assn., Los Angeles County Bar Assn., So. Calif. Def. Counsel Assn., Am. Bd. Trial Advs., Nat. Bd. Trial Advocacy. State civil litigation, Insurance, Personal injury. Office: 17822 17th St Ste 205 Tustin CA 92780-2152

MADRID, PATRICIA A. state attorney general, lawyer; b. Sept. 25, 1946; BA in English and Philosophy, U. N.Mex., 1969, JD, 1973; cert., Nat. Jud. Coll., U. Nev., 1978. Bar: N.Mex. 1973. Ptnr. Messina, Madrid & Smith, P.A., Albuquerque, 1984-88; atty. gen. State of N.Mex., 1999—. Editor N.Mex. Law Rev., 1972-73. Bd. dirs. Fechin Art Inst., Taos, N.Mex.; dem. nominee Lt. Gov. N.Mex., 1994. Hon. Commdr. award USAF, 1979, award of yr. Albuquerque Bus. and Profl. Women; named Outstanding Young Women of Am., 1980-81; recipient Gov.'s award Outstanding N.Mex. Women, 1993. Mem. Hispanic Women's Coun. of N.Mex. (bd. dirs. 1989), Mex. Am. Legal Def. and Ednl. Fund (bd. dirs. 1989). Office: Atty Gens Office PO Drawer 1508 Santa Fe NM 87504-1508

MADSEN, BARBARA A, state supreme court justice; BA, U. Wash., 1974; JD, Gonzaga U., 1977. Pub. defender King and Snohomish Counties, 1977—82; staff atty. Seattle City Atty.'s Office, 1982—84, spl. prosecutor, 1984—88; judge Seattle Mcpl. Ct., 1988—92; justice Washington Supreme Ct., Olympia, 1993—. Office: Wash Supreme Ct PO Box 40929 Olympia WA 98504-0929*

MADSEN, GEORGE FRANK, lawyer; b. Sioux City, Iowa, Mar. 24, 1933; s. Frank O. and Agnes (Cuhel) M.; m. Magnhild Norstog; 1 child, Michelle Marie. BA, St. Olaf Coll., 1954; LLB, Harvard U., 1959. Bar: Ohio 1960, Iowa 1961, U.S. Dist. Ct. (no. and so. dists.) Iowa, U.S. Ct. Appeals (8th cir.), U.S. Supreme Ct. 1991. Trainee Cargill, Inc., Mpls., 1954; assoc. Durfey, Martin, Browne & Hull, Springfield, Ohio, 1959-61; assoc., then ptnr. Shull, Marshall & Marks, Sioux City, 1961-85; ptnr. Marks & Madsen, 1985-97, Marks, Madsen & Hirschbach, Sioux City, 1998-99, Mayne, Marks, Madsen & Hirschbach, LLP, Sioux City, 1999-2001. Author, editor: Iowa Title Opinions and Standards, 1978; contbg. author: The American Law of Real Property, 1991. Sec., bd.dirs. Sioux City Boys Club, 1969-76; mem. Sioux City Zoning Bd. Adjustment, 1963-65; active Iowa Mo. River Preservation and Land Use Authority, 1992-2001, pres., 1997-2001. Lt. USAF, 1954-56. Fellow Iowa State Bar Found.; mem. ABA, Iowa Bar Assn., Woodbury County Bar Assn., Nat. Wildlife Assn., Mont. Wildlife Assn., Pheasants Forever, Phi Beta Kappa (past pres. Siouxland chpt.), Rotary Internat. Avocations: skiing, hunting, swimming, reading. Contracts commercial, General corporate, Real property. Office: PO Box 3661 Sioux City IA 51102-3661

MADSEN, STEPHEN STEWART, lawyer; b. Spokane, Wash., Oct. 13, 1951; s. H. Stephen Madsen and Sarah Pope (Stewart) Ruth; m. Rebecca Wetherill Howard, July 28, 1984; children: Stephen Stewart Jr., Lawrence Washington, Christina Wetherill, Benton Howard. BA, Harvard U., 1973; JD, Columbia U., 1980. Bar: N.Y. 1981, U.S. Dist. Ct. (so. dist.) N.Y. 1981, U.S. Ct. Appeals (6th cir.) 1983, U.S. Ct. Appeals (8th cir.) 1985, U.S. Ct. Appeals (2d, 7th and D.C. cirs.) 1994, U.S. Supreme Ct. 1996. Law clk. to presiding judge U.S. Ct. Appeals 2d cir., N.Y.C., 1980-81; assoc. Cravath, Swaine & Moore, 1981-88, ptnr., 1988—. Bd. visitors Columbia U. Sch. Law, 1991—; bd. govs. Hill-Stead Mus., 1995—; mem. vestry St. Bartholomew's Ch., 1995—. Mem. ABA, N.Y. State Bar Assn. (exec. com. antitrust law sect. 1998—), New York County Lawyers Assn., London Ct. Internat. Arbitration, Fedn. Bar Coun. Antitrust, General civil litigation. Office: Cravath Swaine & Moore Worldwide Pla 825 8th Ave Fl 38 New York NY 10019-7475

MADU, LEONARD EKWUGHA, lawyer, human rights officer, newspaper columnist, politician, business executive; b. Ibadan, Nigeria, Mar. 17, 1953; came to U.S., 1977; s. Luke E. and Grace (Dureke) M.; m. Jaculine Stephanie Turner, June 4, 1980; children: Christine, Oscar. BA, Marshall U., 1980; JD, U. Tenn., 1988; MA, Am. U. Rsch. assoc. Lamberts Publs., Washington, 1980-82; data specialist Govt. Employees Ins. Co., 1982-85; law intern Knoxville (Tenn.) Urban League, 1986-88; cons. Morris Brown Coll., Atlanta, 1988; staff atty. East Carolina Legal Svc., Wilson, N.C., 1989-90; cons. youth devel. Nat. Crime Prevention Coun., Washington, 1990; contract compliance officer Walters State C.C., Morristown, Tenn., 1990; examiner Dept. of Human Svc., Nashville, 1990-93; human rights officer Human Rights Commn., 1993—; pres. Panafrica, 1994—; CEO Madu and Assoc. Internat. Bus. Cons., 1996—; with Bus. Forum & Banquet, 1994—; 1st v.p. Nashville Multicultural Partnership, Inc., 2000—. Polit. cons. Embassy of Nigeria, Washington, 1995; cons. Embassy of Sierra Leone, Washington, 1995, Healthcare Internat. Mgmt. Co., 1996—, Embassy of Mozambique, 2000—, Embassy of Togo, 2001—; bd. dirs. Peace and Justice Ctr., Nashville; pres. African Conglomerates Internat., Inc. Editor: African Nations Handbook, 1994, Directory of African Universities and Colleges, 1994; editor-in-chief Panafrican Digest, 1994, Panafrican Jour. of World Affairs, 1994; columnist Met. Times, Nashville, 1991—, The African Herald, Dallas, 1995—, U.S./African Voice, Balt., 1995—, African Sun Times, 1995—, The Nigerian and African, 1995—, The African Press, N.Y. Co-chmn. Clergy and Laity Concerned, Nashville, 1992-95; mem. curriculum and character com. Met. Sch. Bd., Nashville, 1994-97; co-coordinator The Haitian Project, 1991-94; vice-chmn. Nigerian Network Leadership awards N.Y., 1996; chmn. Internat. Women's Expo, Knoxville, 1996; co-chair Miss Nigeria Internat. Beauty Pageant, Washington, 1995, Miss Africa Internat. Beauty Pageant, Nashville, 1996, Igbo Union Chieftaincy Coronation Ceremony, Nashville, 1995; chmn. Nigerian Patriotic Front, 1997—; coord. United Nigeria Congress Party, 1997-98, Southeast U.S.; recruiter internat. students Tenn. State U., 1998-99; chmn. bd. dirs. Africa Found., Washington, 2001—. Recipient World Hunger Devel. Program award Marshall U., 1978-79, Hall of Nations scholar Am. U., 1980, 82, Mary Strohbel award United Way, 1994-95, Non-profit Vol. award Nat. Conf. of Christians and Jews, 1994. Mem. NAACP, U.S. Com. on Fgn. Rels., Soc. Profl. Journalists, UN Assn., Orgn. African Natonals (pres. 1994), African C. of C. (pres. 2000—). Avocations: reading, travel, soccer, ping-pong, tennis. Office: Panafrica 1016 18th Ave S Nashville TN 37212-2105

MADVA, STEPHEN ALAN, lawyer; b. Pitts., July 27, 1948; s. Joseph Edward and Mary (Zulick) M.; m. Bernadette A. McKeon; children: Alexander, Elizabeth. BA cum laude, Yale U., 1970; JD, U. Pa., 1973. Bar: Pa. 1973, U.S. Dist. Ct. (ea. dist.) Pa. 1975, U.S. Ct. Appeals (3d cir.) 1976, U.S. Ct. Appeals (11th cir.) 1987, U.S. Supreme Ct. 1985, N.Y. 1990. Asst. defender Defender Assn. Phila., 1973-75, fed. defender, 1975-77, also bd. dirs., 1985—; assoc. Montgomery, McCracken, Walker & Rhoads, Phila., 1977-81, ptnr., 1981—, mem. mgmt. com., 1993—, chmn. litigation sect., 1993—. Bd. dirs. Ferag-Ams., LLC, WRH Mktg. Ams., LLC. Bd. dirs. Ctrl. Phila. Devel. Corp., 1995—, Opera Co. of Phila., 2000—, St. Christopher's Hosp. for Children, 2001—. Fellow Internat. Soc. Barristers, Am. Coll. Trial Lawyers; mem. ABA, Internat. Assn. Def. Counsel, Pa. Bar Assn., Phila. Bar Assn. (fed. cts. com., chmn. commn. on jud. selection and retention), Def. Rsch. Inst., Hist. Soc. Pa., Yale Alumni Assn. (schs. com.), Yale Rowing Assn., Union League of Phila. Democrat. Avocations: tennis, distance running, opera, classical music. Federal civil litigation, Product liability, Toxic tort. Home: 2055 Lombard St Philadelphia PA 19146-1314 Office: Montgomery McCracken Walker & Rhoads 123 S Broad St Fl 24 Philadelphia PA 19109-1099 E-mail: smadva@mmwr.com

MAEMA, WILLIAM IKUTHA, lawyer, consultant; b. Kitui, Kenya, Oct. 19, 1964; s. Peter Claver and Esther Wayua Maema; m. Rose Syomwathi Wambua; children: Eunice, Christine, Lisa. LLB, U. Nairobi, Kenya, 1990; LLM, U. Cambridge, Eng., 1992. Legal asst. Hamilton Harrison & Mathews, Nairobi, 1993-97, ptnr., 1997-2000, Iseme Kamau & Maema Advs., Nairobi, 2000—. Lectr. U. Nairobi, 1992-2000; bd. dirs. Solarnet (NGO), Nairobi. Oda scholar Cambridge Commonwealth Trust, U.K., 1991-92, Pegasus scholar Inner Temple & Clifford Chance, U.K., 1992. Fellow Cambridge Commonwealth Trust; mem. Law Soc. Kenya, Kenya Oxford/Cambridge Soc. Avocations: reading legal fiction, traveling, swimming, collecting souvenier mugs and movies. General corporate, Intellectual property, Trademark and copyright. Home: PO Box 40293 Nairobi Kenya Office: Iseme Kamau & Maema Advs Moi Ave PO Box 11866 Nairobi Kenya Fax: 2542336464. E-mail: wmaema@isemekamau.co.ke

MAES, PETRA JIMENEZ, state supreme court justice; widowed; 4 children. BA, U. N.Mex., 1970, JD, 1973. Bar: N.Mex. 1973. Pvt. practice law, Albuquerque, 1973-75; rep., then office mgr. No. N.Mex. Legal Svcs., 1975-81; dist. judge 1st Jud. Dist. Ct., Santa Fe, Los Alamos, 1981-98; chief judge, 1984-87, 92-95; justice Supreme Ct. N.Mex., 1998—. Active S.W. coun. Boy Scouts Am., mem. dist. coms.; presenter pre cana St. John's Cath. Ch.; bd. dirs. Nat. Ctr. on Women and Family Law; chairperson Tri-County Gang Task Force; mem. Gov.'s Task Force on Children and Families, 1991-92; mem. adv. com. Santa Fe County Jail, 1996. Mem. N.Mex. Bar Assn. (elderly law com. 1980-81, alternative dispute resolution com. 1987-92, code of jud. conduct com. 1992—, juvenile cmty. corrections svcs. com. chairperson), Hispanic Women's Coun. (charter). Office: Supreme Court NMex PO Box 848 Santa Fe NM 87504-0848*

MAFFEI, ROCCO JOHN, lawyer; b. Portland, Maine, Nov. 23, 1949; s. Rocco and Grace Marie (Bartlett) M; m. Susan Marie Farrell, June 23, 1973; children: Rocco Francis, Christopher Matthew. BA in History, Trinity Coll., 1972; JD, U. Maine, 1975. Bar: Maine 1975, Mass. 1975, U.S. Dist. Ct. Maine 1975, Ohio 1977, U.S. Ct. Claim 1980, U.S. Supreme Ct. 1980, Minn. 1981, U.S. Dist. Ct. Minn. 1981. Ptnr. Briggs & Morgan Law Firm, St. Paul, 1980-83, Hart & Bruner Law Firm, Mpls., 1983-85; v.p. gen. counsel Computing Devices Internat., Bloomington, Minn., 1985-98; assoc. gen. counsel Lockheed Martin Tactical Def. Sys., Eagan, 1999-2001; gen. counsel Lockheed Martin Naval Electronics & Surveillance Sys., Akron, Ohio, 2001—. Adj. prof. law William Mitchell Sch. Law, St. Paul, 1982-2000, Air Force Inst. Tech., 1983-2000. Contbr. articles to profl. jours. Capt. USAF, 1975-80; col. USAFR. Fellow Nat. Contract Mgmt. Assn. (bd. advisors, pres. Twin Cities chpt. 1985-86, regional v.p. 1990-91, Charles J. Delaney award 1986); mem. ABA (chmn. com. pub. contract law sect. 1984-88, 93—), Minn. Bar Assn., Huber Hts. Jaycees (Jaycee of Yr. 1978). Republican. Roman Catholic. Avocation: long distance running. General corporate, Government contracts and claims, Private international. Home: 1246 Maxfli Dr Akron OH 44312 Office: Lockheed Martin Tactical Defense Sys PO Box 64525 Saint Paul MN 55164-0525 E-mail: rocco.j.maffei@lmco.com

MAFFEO, VINCENT ANTHONY, lawyer, executive; b. Jan. 22, 1951; s. Michael Anthony and Marie Maffeo; m. Debra Maffeo, Dec. 16, 1972. BA summa cum laude, Bklyn. Coll., 1971; JD, Harvard U., 1974. Bar: N.Y. 1975, Calif. 1982, Ba. 1988, D.C. 1988, Mich. 1994. Assoc. Simpson Thacher & Bartlett, N.Y.C., NY, 1974—77; legal counsel Comms. Sys. divsn. ITT, Hartford, Conn., 1977—79; v.p., gen. counsel Bus. Comms. divsn. ITT, Des Plaines, Ill., 1979—80; asst. counsel western region ITT, 1980—83; group counsel ITT Europe, Inc., 1983—86; v.p. gen. coun. ITT Defense Inc., 1987—91; v.p., gen. coun. ITT Automotive, Inc., 1992—95; sr. v.p., gen. counsel ITT Industries, Inc., 1995—. Lt. Judge Adv. Gen. Corps. USNR, 1975. Mem.: ABA, Calif. State Bar, N.Y.State Bar Assn., Phi Beta Kappa. Office: ITT Industries Inc 4 W Red Oak Ln Ste 2 White Plains NY 10604-3617

MAFFITT, JAMES STRAWBRIDGE, lawyer; b. Raleigh, N.C., Oct. 29, 1942; s. James Strawbridge III and Lois (Handy) M.; children: Amy Maffitt Barkley, Margaret Maffitt Kramer; m. Frances Holton, Aug. 15, 1981. BA, Washington and Lee U., 1964, LLB, 1966. Bar: Va. 1966, Md. 1969. Assoc. Apostolou, Place & Thomas, Roanoke, Va., 1966-67; trust officer Mercantile-Safe Deposit & Trust Co., Balt., 1967-71; from assoc. to ptnr. Cable, McDaniel, Bowie & Bond, 1971-82; ptnr. Maffit & Rothschild, 1982-85, Anderson, Coe & King, Balt., 1986-90, Miles, Stockbridge & Easton, Balt., 1990—. Chmn. Acad. of the Arts, 1994-97, bd. dirs., 1993-99; bd. dirs. United Fund of Talbot County, 1994-98, pres., 1997-98; bd. trustees Grayce B. Kerr Fund, Inc., 1998—. Fellow Md. Bar Found.; mem. ABA (ho. dels. 1986-88), Md. Bar Assn. (bd. govs. 1989-91), Va. Bar. Assn., Balt. City Bar Assn. (pres. 1985-86), Wednesday Law Club, Talbot Country Club, Harbortown Country Club. Republican. Episcopal. Avocations: boating, waterfowl hunting, golf. Contracts commercial, General corporate, Real property. Home: 9498 Martingham Cir Saint Michaels MD 21663-2238 Office: Miles & Stockbridge 101 Bay St Easton MD 21601-2748 also: Miles & Stockbridge 10 Light St Ste 800 Baltimore MD 21202-1407 E-mail: jmaffitt@milesstockbridge.com

MAGEE, THOMAS HUGH, lawyer; b. Rochester, N.Y., Aug. 15, 1943; s. Edward Charles and Jane Kathleen (Cranmer) M.; m. Judith Joy Stone, Oct. 2, 1982; 1 child, Michael Julian. BSME, U. Rochester, N.Y., 1965; JD, Syracuse U., 1973. Bar: N.J. 1974, U.S. Dist. Ct. N.J. 1974, U.S. Ct. Appeals (D.C. cir.) 1975, N.Y. 1981, U.S. Supreme Ct. 1978, U.S. Patent and Trademark Office. Sr. patent counsel RCA Corp., Princeton, N.J., 1973-86, GE/RCA Licensing Operation, Princeton, 1986-88; corp. counsel E.I. duPont de Nemours & Co., Wilmington, Del., 1988—. Lt. USN, 1965-70, Capt. USNR (ret.), 1991. Navy commendation medal with combat V, Vietnam, 1969. Mem. Am. Intellectual Property Law Assn. (com. chair 1974—), Phila. Intellectual Property Law Assn. (com. chmn. 1974—), N.J. Patent Law Assn., Justinian hon. law soc., Phi Alpha Delta. Republican. Presbyterian. Avocations: tennis, handball, coin-collecting. Antitrust, Intellectual property, Patent. Home: 721 Severn Rd Wilmington DE 19803-1724 Office: E I duPont de Nemours & Co Barley Mill Plz BMP 11-1126 Wilmington DE 19880 E-mail: thomas.h.magee@usa.dupont.com

MAGGIO-GONZALES, MARISSA ANN, lawyer, track and field athlete; b. Goshen, N.Y., Apr. 28, 1969; d. Joseph Peter and Helen Anna (Dettloff) Maggio. Student, Villanova U., 1987-89; BBA with honors, U. Tex., 1992; postgrad., Yeshiva U., 1992-93; JD, Emory U., 1995. Bar: Tex. 1997, D.C. 1998. Assoc. Fulbright & Jaworski, L.L.P., Austin, Tex., 1997—. Profl. track and field athlete Atletica 2000/Italian Nat. Team, Milan, 1994—. Administrative and regulatory, Environmental, Sports. Office: Fulbright & Jaworski LLP 600 Congress Ave Ste 2400 Austin TX 78701

MAGGIOLO, ALLISON JOSEPH, lawyer; b. New River, N.C., Aug. 29, 1943; s. Allison and Florence Celeste (Vago) M. Cert., U. Paris-Sorbonne, 1965; AB, Brown U., 1966; JD, U. Louisville, 1975. Bar: Ky. 1976, U.S. Dist. Ct. (we. dist.) Ky. 1981. Ops. mgr., stockbroker Bache & Co., Louisville, 1970-73; ptnr. Reisz, Blackburn, Manly & Treitz, 1976-78, Greenebaum Boone Treitz Maggiolo & Brown, Louisville, 1978-91, Wyatt, Tarrant & Combs, Louisville, 1991—. Workshop panelist Fin. Adv. Coun., 1994; panelist Seminar on Defaulted Bond Issues, 1987-89, Bond Counsel and the Corp. Trustee, 1990-92, Defaults and Workouts, 1993. Author: Indenture Trustee Liability and Defaulted Bond Issues, 1987, Minimizing Indenture Trustee Liability and Defaulted Bond Issues, 1991, Bond Default Resolution, 1993; co-author: The legal Aspects of Doing International Business in Kentucky, 1990. Exec. com. Louisville Com. Fgn. Rels., 1979—, chmn., 1991-96; bd. dirs. Ky. Opera, Louisville, 1978-91, mem. hon. coun., 1991—; bd. dirs. Ky. Show, Louisville, 1980-88. 1st lt. U.S. Army, 1966-69, Vietnam. Decorated Bronze Star. Mem. Internat. Bar Assn., Nat. Assn. Bond Lawyers, Bond Attys. Workshop (planning com. 1991-93), Pendennis Club, Wynn Stay Club, Jefferson Club. Banking, Finance, Municipal (including bonds). Office: Wyatt Tarrant & Combs Citizens Plz Louisville KY 40202-2823

MAGILL, FRANK JOHN, federal judge; b. Verona, N.D., June 3, 1927; s. Thomas Charles and Viola Magill; m. Mary Louise Timlin, Nov. 22, 1955; children: Frank Jr., Marguerite Connolly, R. Daniel, Mary Elizabeth, Robert, John. BS in Fgn. Service, Georgetown U., 1951, LLB, 1955; MA, Columbia U., 1952. Ptnr. Nilles, Hansen, Magill & Davies, Ltd., Fargo, N.D., 1955-86; judge U.S. Ct. Appeals (8th cir.), 1986—. Chmn. fin. disclosure com. U.S. Jud. Conf., 1993-98. Fellow Am. Coll. Trial Lawyers; mem. Cass County Bar Assn. (pres. 1970). Republican. Avocations: tennis, sailing, skiing. Home: 501 7th St S Apt 301 Fargo ND 58103-2761 Office: Quentin N Burdick US Courthouse 655 1st Ave N Ste 320 Fargo ND 58102-4932 Fax: 701 297-7255. E-mail: patricia_mathern@ca8.uscourts.gov

MAGNUSON, PAUL ARTHUR, federal judge; b. Carthage, S.D., Feb. 9, 1937; s. Arthur and Emma Elleda (Paulson) M.; m. Sharon Schultz, Dec. 21, 1959; children— Marlene Peterson, Margaret (dec.), Kevin, Kara. BA, Gustavus Adolphus Coll, 1959; JD, William Mitchell Coll., 1963; DLL (hon.), Wm. Mitchell Coll., 1991. Bar: Minn. 1963, U.S. Dist. Ct. Minn. 1968. Asst. registrar William Mitchell Coll. of Law, 1959-60; claim adjuster Agrl. Ins. Co., 1960-62; clk. Bertie & Bettenberg, 1962-63; ptnr. LeVander, Gillen, Miller & Magnuson, South St. Paul, Minn., 1963-81; judge U.S. Dist. Ct. Minn., St. Paul, 1981—, chief judge, 1994—2001. Jurist-in-residence Hamline U., 1985, Augsberg Coll., 1986, Bethel Coll., 1986, Concordia Coll., St. Paul, 1987, U. Minn., Morris, 1987; instr. William Mitchell Coll. Law, 1984-92, Corcordia Coll., Moorhead, 1988, St. John's U., 1988, Coll. of St. Benedict, 1988; mem. judicial conf. com. on adminstrn. of Bankruptcy System, 1987-96, chmn. 1993-96; mem. judicial conf. com. on Internat. Judicial Rels., 1996—, chair, 1999—; mem. com. on dist. judges edn. Fed. Judicial Ctr., 1998—. Mem. Met. Health Bd., St. Paul, 1970-72; legal counsel Ind. Republican Party Minn., St. Paul, 1979-81 Recipient Disting. Alumnus award Gustavus Adolphus Coll., 1982, First Disting. Svc. award William Mitchell Coll. Law, 1999. Mem. Minn. State Bar Assn., 1st Dist. Bar Assn. (pres. 1974-75), Dakota County Bar Assn., Am. Judicature Soc., Fed. Judges Assn. (bd. dirs. 1993—, treas. 1997-2001, v.p. 2001—). E-mail: PAMagnuson@mnd.uscourts.gov

MAGNUSON, ROGER JAMES, lawyer; b. St. Paul, Jan. 25, 1945; s. Roy Gustaf and Ruth Lily (Edlund) M.; m. Elizabeth Cunningham Shaw, Sept. 11, 1982; children: James Roger, Peter Cunningham, Mary Kerstin, Sarah Ruth, Elizabeth Camilla, Anna Clara, John Edlund, Britta Kristina. BA, Stanford U., 1967; JD, Harvard U., 1971; BCL, Oxford U., 1972. Bar: Minn. 1973, U.S. Dist. Ct. Minn. 1973, U.S Ct. Appeals (8th, 9th, 10th cirs.) 1974, U.S. Supreme Ct. 1978. Chief pub. defender Hennepin County Pub. Defender's Office, Mpls., 1973; ptnr. Dorsey & Whitney, 1972—. Dean Oak Brook Coll. of Law and Govt. Policy, 1995—; chancellor Magdalen Coll., 1999—. Author: Shareholder Litigation, 1981, Are Gay Rights Right, The White-Collar Crime Explosion, 1992, Informed Answers to Gay Rights Questions, 1994; contbr. articles to profl. jours. Elder, Straitgate Ch., Mpls., 1980—. Mem. Christian Legal Soc., The Am. Soc. Writers of Legal Subjects, Mpls. Club, White Bear Yacht Club. Republican. Federal civil litigation, Criminal, Libel. Home: 625 Park Ave Saint Paul MN 55115-1663 Office: Dorsey & Whitney LLP 220 S 6th St Ste 1700 Minneapolis MN 55402-1498

MAGUIRE, RAYMER F., JR. lawyer; b. Orlando, Fla., Oct. 20, 1921; s. Raymer F. Sr. and Ruth (McCullough) M.; m. Sara Corry, Aug. 13, 1951; children: Craig Corry, Raymer F. III, Sara Maguire LeMone, Edmund Corry. BA, U. Fla., 1943, JD, 1948. Bar: Fla. 1948, U.S. Dist. Ct. (so. dist.) 1948, U.S. Supreme Ct. 1969. Assoc. Maguire, Voorhis & Wells, P.A., Orlando, 1948-53, mem., 1953—. Bd. dirs. Sun Bank, N.A.; bd. dirs. and trustee various corps. and trusts. Elder First Presbyn. Ch., 1961—; mem., chmn. community coll. coun. State of Fla., 1976-79, mem. community coll. coordinating bd., 1979-83, vice chmn. 1979-81, chmn. 1981-82; trustee Valencia Community Coll., 1967-86, chmn. 1967-72; bd. dirs. Orange County Hist. Soc., 1982—, pres., 1987-88; chmn. bd. Cen. Fla. chpt. Am. Heart Assn., 1966-67; bd. dirs. Valencia Community Coll. Found., pres., 1974-75; chmn. citizens com. Orange County Sch. Bd. Referendum, 1964. Named in honor of Raymer F. Maguire Jr. Learning Resource Ctr., Valencia Community Coll., 1977. Mem. ABA, Fla. Bar Assn. U. Fla. Alumni Assn. (bd. dirs. 1954—, pres. 1959-60, Disting. Alumnus award 1975), Kiwanis (pres. 1962), U. Fla. Found. Republican. General corporate, Probate.

MAHAR, ELLEN PATRICIA, law librarian; b. Washington, Jan. 15, 1938; d. Richard A. and Lina Mahar. BA, St. Joseph Coll., Emmitsburg, Md., 1959; MLS, U. Md., 1968. Asst. librarian Covington & Burling, Washington, 1971-73, libr. dir., 1978-92; librarian Shea & Gardner, 1974-78; mgr. info. ctr. Assn. Comml. Real Estate, Herndon, Va., 1992-94; head libr. Caplin & Drysdale Chtd., Washington, 1994—. Co-editor: Legislative History of the Securities Act of 1933 and the Securities Act of 1934, 11 vols., 1973. Mem. Am. Assn. Law Libraries, Spl. Libraries Assn., Law Librarians' Soc. Washington. Office: Caplin & Drysdale Chtd 1 Thomas Cir NW Fl 11 Washington DC 20005-5802

MAHER, DAVID WILLARD, lawyer; b. Chgo., Aug. 14, 1934; s. Chauncey Carter and Martha (Peppers) M.; m. Jill Waid Armagnac, Dec. 20, 1954; children: Philip Armagnac, Julia Armagnac. BA, Harvard, 1955, LLB, 1959. Bar: N.Y. 1960, Ill. 1961, Wis. 1996, U.S. Patent Office 1961. Pvt. practice, Boston, N.Y.C., 1958-60; assoc. Kirkland & Ellis, and

predecessor firm, 1960-65, ptnr., 1966-78, Reuben & Proctor, 1978-86, Isham, Lincoln and Beale, 1986-88, Sonnenschein, Nath & Rosenthal, Chgo., 1988—. Gen. counsel BBB Chgo. and No. Ill.; lectr. DePaul U. Sch. Law, 1973-79, Loyola U. Law Sch., Chgo., 1980-84; chmn. policy oversight com. Internet. Vis. com. U. Chgo. Div. Sch., 1986—. 2d lt. USAF, 1955-56. Fellow Am. Bar Found. (life); mem. ABA, Am. Law Inst., Ill. Bar Assn., Wis. State Bar, Chgo. Bar Assn., Internet Soc. (v.p. pub. policy), Chgo. Lit. Club, Union League Club, Tavern Club. Roman Catholic. Computer, Patent, Trademark and copyright. Home: 501 N Clinton St Apt 1503 Chicago IL 60610-8886 Office: Sonnenschein Nath & Rosenthal 233 S Wacker Dr Ste 8000 Chicago IL 60606-6491 E-mail: dwm@sonnenschein.com

MAHER, EDWARD JOSEPH, lawyer; b. Cleve., Sept. 18, 1939; s. Richard Leo and Lucile (Thompson) M.; m. Marilyn K. Maher, Oct. 8, 1966; children: Richard A., David C., Michael E, Colleen Therese. B.S., Georgetown U., 1961, LL.B., 1964; student U. Fribourg, Switzerland, 1959-61. Bar: Ohio 1964, U.S. dist. ct. (no. dist.) Ohio 1964. Assoc., Sweeney, Maher & Vlad, Cleve., 1964-71; sole practice, Cleve., 1971— . Pres. parish council St. Raphael's Ch., Bay Village, Ohio, 1983-84; former adv. bd. Catholic Family and Children's Services; adv. bd. Cath. Youth Orgn., 1973-79, pres., 1975-76; chmn. Elyria Cursillo Ctr., 1974-75; lay del. to Ohio Cath. Conf., Diocese of Cleve., 1973-75; chmn. adv. bd. Cath. Social Services of Cuyahoga County, 1978-79; trustee Cath. Charities Corp., 1977— , treas., 1979, sec., 1981, 1st v.p., 1983, gen. chmn. campaign, 1983, 84, pres., 1985-86; pres. Diocesan adv. bd. Cath. Youth Orgn., 1980-82; team capt. United Way Services Agy. Team Group, 1981, nominating com., 1983; mem. Tabor House, The Consultation Ctr. of the Diocese of Cleve., pres., 1992-94; mem. bd. regents St. Ignotius High Sch., 1997—. Recipient Cardinal Robert Bellarmine S.J. award St. Ignatius High Sch., 1990, Cath. Man of the Year award, 1995. Mem. ABA, Ohio Bar Assn., Cuyahoga County Bar Assn., Cleve. Bar Assn., Cath. Lawyers Guild Cleve. (pres. 1970). Clubs: Irish Good Fellowship (pres.), First Friday of Cleve. (pres. 1990). Insurance, Personal injury, Probate. Office: 1548 Standard Bldg Cleveland OH 44113

MAHER, FRANCESCA MARCINIAK, lawyer, air transportation executive; b. 1957; BA, Loyola U., 1978, JD, 1981. Ptnr. Mayer, Brown & Platt, Chgo., 1981-93; v.p. law, corp. sec. UAL Corp., Elk Grove Village, Ill., 1993-97, v.p., gen. counsel, sec., 1997-98, sr. v.p., gen. counsel, sec., 1998—. Bd. dirs. YMCA Met. Chgo., Lincoln Park Zool. Soc. Mem. Ill. Humane Soc. (pres. 1996-98). Administrative and regulatory, General corporate, Securities. Office: UAL Corp PO Box 66100 Chicago IL 60666-0100

MAHER, JOHN A. lawyer, law educator; b. Bklyn., Dec. 3, 1930; s. John A. and Helen D. (Stack) M.; m. Joan Dawley, July 31, 1954; children: Jeanne M., John A. III, James A., Helen D., Therésè. AB, U. Notre Dame, 1951; LLB, NYU, 1956, LLM in Trade Regulation, 1957; cert. bus. adminstrn., U. Va., 1969; cert. fgn. and comparative law, Columbia U., 1974; LLD (hon.), Pa. State U., 1998. Bar: N.Y. 1957, D.C. 1960, Pa. 1986. Assoc. Healy & Baillie, N.Y.C., 1957-59; staff atty. Swift & Co., N.Y.C, 1959-62; asst. gen. counsel Celanese Corp., N.Y.C., 1962-70; v.p. law Blount, Inc., Montgomery, Ala., 1970-73; prof. Dickinson Sch. of Law, Carlisle, Pa., 1973—, dean, 1989-94, Montague prof. law, 2000—; commr. Pa. Securities Commn., 1997—. Bd. dirs. Atlantic Liberty Savs., Bklyn., vice chmn., 1984-96, chmn., 1996-2001; counsel Eaton & Van Winkle, N.Y.C., 1974-87; trustee Food and Drug Law Inst., Washington, 1984-96; mem. lawyers' adv. com. Pa. Securities Com., 1994-97. Author: Survey of Robinson-Patman Act, 1969; co-author: Export Opportunities and The Export Trading Act of 1982-93; bd. editors Food Drug Cosmetic Law Jour., 1987-84, Jour. Financial Crime (U.K.), 1994—, Internat. Corp. Law Bull. (U.K.), 1998—; contbr. articles to profl. jours. Mem. Pres.'s Adv. Com. on Textile Info., Washington, 1967-68; bd. visitors John Marshall Law Sch., 1995—; N.Am. corr. Amicus Curiae, U.K., 1997—. Served with USNR, 1951-55, ret. lt. comdr., 1974. Food Law Inst. fellow NYU Law Ctr., 1956-57, hon. fellow Soc. for Advancement Legal Studies, U. London, 1997; named to Wall of Fame, U. Notre Dame, 1994. Fellow Am. Bar Found. (life), Pa. Bar Found. (chartered, life); mem. Pa. Bar Assn. (chmn. corp. banking and bus. sect. 1987-89, Ho. of Dels. 1989—, Disting. Svc. award 1988, pres.'s award 1994), Dickinson Sch. Law Gen. Alumni Assn. (Disting. Svc. award and Honor Alumnus 1989). Roman Catholic. Club: Bklyn., Tuesday. Avocations: photography, reading, travel.

MAHER, STEPHEN TRIVETT, lawyer, educator; b. N.Y.C., Nov. 21, 1949; s. William John and Jean Dorothy (Trivett) M.; m. Sharon Leslie Wolfe, Nov. 22, 1981 (dec.); children: Meaghan Wolfe, Caitlin Wolfe. BA, NYU, 1971; JD, U. Miami, Coral Gables, Fla., 1975. Bar: Fla. 1975, U.S. Dist. Ct. (so. dist.) Fla. 1976, D.C. 1979, U.S. Dist. Ct. (no. dist.) Fla. 1979, U.S. Supreme Ct. 1980, U.S. Ct. Appeals (5th and 11th cirs.) 1981, U.S. Dist. Ct. (so. dist.) Fla. 1982, U.S. Dist. Ct. (mid. dist.) Fla. 1983. Assoc. Chonin & Levey, Miami, 1975; staff atty. Legal Svcs. of Greater Miami, Inc., 1975-81; assoc. Finley, Kumble, Wagner et al, Miami, 1981-84; dir. clin. program Sch. of Law U. Miami, Coral Gables, 1984-90, assoc. prof. law Sch. of Law, 1984-92; pvt. practice Stephen T. Maher, P.A., Miami, Fla., 1992—. Mem. Fla. Bar/Fla. Bar Found. Joint Commn. on Delivery Legal Svcs. to the Indigent, Tallahassee, 1990-91, chair, organizer Seventh Adminstrv. Law Conf., Tallahassee, 1990, Conf. on the Fla. Constn., 1995; cons. on in-house legal edn. Contbr. articles to profl. jours. Fellow Fla. Bar Found. (life, bd. dirs. 1984-91); mem. ABA, Fla. Bar (chair adminstrv. law sect. 1993-94, chair coun. of sects. 1996-97), Dade County Bar Assn. Administrative and regulatory, Civil rights, General civil litigation. Home: 1015 Sevilla Ave Miami FL 33134-6328 Office: 1500 Miami Ctr 201 S Biscayne Blvd Miami FL 33131-4332

MAHER ARCODIA, PATRICIA, lawyer; b. Bklyn., June 26, 1954; d. Joseph Francis and Margaret J. (O'Keefe) Maher; m. Charles Arcodia, Sept. 30, 1989; children: Marybeth, Nicole, Juliette. BA, Siena Coll., Loudonville, N.Y., 1976; JD, St. John's U., Jamaica, N.Y., 1983. Bar: Mass. 1983, N.Y. 1985, Md. 1992, Va. 1992, D.C. 1992, U.S. Supreme Ct. 1991. Mng. atty. USF&G, N.Y.C., 1983-93; sr. trial atty. PMA, Hunt Valley, Md., 1993-96; mng. atty. AIG, Towson, 1996—. Roman Catholic. Office: Maher & Assocs 502 Washington Ave Towson MD 21204-4516

MAHON, ELDON BROOKS, federal judge; b. Loraine, Tex., Apr. 9, 1918; s. John Bryan and Nola May (Muns) M.; m. Nova Lee Groom, June 1, 1941; children: Jana, Martha, Brad. BA, McMurry U., 1939; LLB, U. Tex., 1942; LLD (hon.), McMurry U., 1974; HHD (hon.), Tex. Wesleyan U., 1990. Bar: Tex. 1942. Law clk. Tex. Supreme Ct., 1945-46; county atty. Mitchell County, Tex., 1947; dist. atty. 32d Jud. Dist. Tex., 1948-60, dist. judge, 1960-63; v.p. Tex. Electric Service Co., Ft. Worth, 1963-64; mem. firm Mahon Pope & Gladden, Abilene, Tex., 1964-68; U.S. atty. U.S. Dist. Ct. (no. dist.) Tex., Ft. Worth, 1968-72, judge, 1972-89, sr. judge, 1989—. Com. on the budget Judicial Conf. the U.S., 1975-83, 5th cir. judicial coun., 1984-89. Pres. W. Tex. council Girl Scouts U.S.A., 1966-68; former trustee McMurry U.; past bd. dirs. Harris Meth. Hosp. With USAAF, 1942-45. Named an Outstanding Tex. Prosecutor, Tex. Law Enforcement Found., 1957; recipient Disting. Alumnus award McMurry U., 1987. Em. ABA, FBA, Ft.-Worth-Tarrant County Bar Assn. (Silver Gavel award 1998), Am. Judicature Soc., Dist. and County Attys. Assn. Tex. (pres. 1954-55), Tex. Bar Found. (life, Samuel Pessarra outstanding jurist award 1998). Methodist. Office: US Courthouse 501 W 10th St Ste 502 Fort Worth TX 76102-3643

MAHONEY, KATHLEEN MARY, lawyer; b. Methuen, Mass., Oct. 24, 1954; d. Joseph Patrick and Beatrice Evelyn (Blackington) M.; m. Mark Dennis Schmitt, May 26, 1979; children: Alexis Anne Schmitt, Brynne Elizabeth Schmitt. BA, Keene (N.H.) State Coll., 1976; JD, Syracuse (N.Y.) U., 1979. Bar: Minn. 1979, U.S. Dist. Ct. Minn. 1980, U.S. Ct. Appeals (8th cir.) 1985, U.S. Supreme Ct. 1988. Instr. Sch. of Law Hamline U., St. Paul, 1979-80; law clk. to hon. justice Douglas K. Amdahl Minn. Supreme Ct., 1980-81; law clk. to hon. judge Neal P. McCurn U.S. Dist. Ct. (no. dist.) N.Y., Syracuse, 1981-83; spl. asst. atty. gen. Atty. Gen.'s Office State of Minn., St. Paul, 1983-89; assoc. Oppenheimer, Wolff & Donnelly, 1989-91, sr. assoc., 1991-93; ptnr., 1994—; chair labor and employment practice group, 1995-97; mng. ptnr. St. Paul, 1997-2000. Cons. George Banzhaf Co., Milw., 1979-80; adj. prof. Hamline U. Sch. of Law, 1987-89. Mem. Dist. 621 Study Adv. Com., Shoreview, Minn., 1989-91, chair, 1991-93; mem. Turtle Lake Sch. Adv. Com., Shoreview, 1988-96; mem. exec. com., bd. dirs. Voyageurs Regional Nat. Park Assn., 1993-95; mem. Class of '93; bd. dirs. St. Paul Vol. Ctr., 1994-99; leader Girl Scouts Am., 1993-99; mem. Leadership St. Paul.; bd. dirs. Girl Scout Council St. Croix Valley, 2001—. Mem. ABA, Minn. Bar Assn., Ramsey County Bar Assn. Antitrust, Environmental, Labor. Office: Oppenheimer Wolff & Donnelly Plz VII 45 S 7th St Ste 3300 Minneapolis MN 55402

MAI, HAROLD LEVERNE, retired judge; b. Casper, Wyo., Apr. 5, 1928. BA, U. Wyo., 1950, JD, 1952. Bar: Wyo. 1952, U.S. Supreme Ct. 1963. Sole practice, Cheyenne, Wyo., 1953-62, 67-71; judge Juvenile Ct., Cheyenne, 1962-67; U.S. bankruptcy judge, Cheyenne, 1971-93, ret., 1993. Mem. ABA, Wyo. Bar Assn., Laramie County Bar Assn., Nat. Conf. Bankruptcy Judges.

MAIDMAN, STEPHEN PAUL, lawyer; b. Hartford, Conn., Feb. 8, 1954; s. Harry and Roslyn (Mandell) M.; m. Mari Rosenberg, Oct. 13, 1996. AB summa cum laude, Bowdoin Coll., 1976; MBA, U. Pa., 1979, JD, 1980. Bar: Pa. 1980, Mass. 1996, U.S. Dist. Ct. (ea. dist.) Pa. 1980, U.S. Ct. Appeals (3d cir.) 1980, U.S. Dist. Ct. Mass. 1996, U.S. Ct. Appeals (1st cir.) 1996, U.S. Supreme Ct. 1997. Assoc. Drinker, Biddle & Reath, Phila., 1980-81; atty. IBM, Boca Raton, Fla., 1981-84, N.Y.C., 1984-85, staff atty., 1985-87, Rye Brook, N.Y., 1987-88, lab. counsel Poughkeepsie, 1988-92, site counsel Hopewell Junction, 1992-95; pvt. practice, Springfield, Mass., 1996—. Class agt. Bowdoin Coll. Alumni Fund. Mem. Nat. Assn. Criminal Def. Lawyers, Mass. Bar Assn., Mass. Assn. Criminal Def. Lawyers, Hampden County Bar Assn. Avocations: running, black Labradors. E-mail: maidman@!prodigy.net. Criminal, General practice. Home: 7 Chateau Margaux Bloomfield CT 06002-2153 Office: 1145 Main St Ste 417 Springfield MA 01103-2123

MAIER, PETER KLAUS, lawyer, business executive; b. Wurzburg, Germany, Nov. 20, 1929; came to U.S., 1939, naturalized, 1945; s. Bernard and Joan (Sonder) M.; m. Melanie L. Stoff, Dec. 15, 1963; children: Michele Margaret, Diana Lynn. BA cum laude, Claremont McKenna Coll., 1949; JD, U. Calif., Berkeley, 1952; LLM in Taxation, NYU, 1953. Bar: Calif. 1953, U.S. Supreme Ct. 1957; cert. specialist in taxation law, Calif. Atty. tax div. U.S. Dept Justice, Washington, 1956-59; pvt. practice tax law San Francisco, 1959-81. Prof. law Hastings Coll. Law, U. Calif., San Francisco, 1967-95; vis. prof. U. Calif. Boalt Sch. Law, Berkeley, 1988-98, Stanford U. Sch. Law, 1996-98; chmn. Maier & Siebel, Inc., Larkspur, Calif., 1981—; mng. dir. U.S. Trust Co. NA, San Francisco, 1998—; chmn. Fromm Inst. for Lifelong Learning, U. San Francisco, 1997—; pres. John B. Huntington Found., 1996—. Author books on taxation; contbr. articles to profl. jours. Chmn. Property Resources Inc., San Jose, Calif., 1968-77; pres. Calif. Property Devel. Corp., San Francisco, 1974-81. Capt. USAF, 1953-56. Mem. San Francisco Bar Assn. (chmn. sect. taxation 1970-71), Order of Coif. Taxation, general. Home: 2559 Clay St San Francisco CA 94115 Office: Maier & Siebel Inc 1 Embarcadero Ctr 20th Fl San Francisco CA 94111 E-mail: pmaier@ustrust.com

MAILAENDER, KARL PETER, lawyer; b. Stuttgart, Federal Republic of Germany, Oct. 23, 1936; s. Karl Robert and Margarete Marianne M.; m. Eva Maria Runde-Wagner, Sept. 5, 1964; children: Daniela, Peter-Oliver. M in Comparative Jurisprudence, NYU, 1961; JD, Tuebingen U., 1961. Bar: Stuttgart 1965. Asst. prof. Law Sch. Tuebingen U., 1962-63, Munich U., 1963-64; practicing atty. Stuttgart, 1965; ptnr. Haver & Mailander, Attys.-at-Law, 1967—. Chmn. bd. Citibank Germany, Frankfurt, 1967—, MTD Products AG Saarbrücken, 1989—. Author books; contbr. articles to profl. jours. Mem. German Commn. on Control of Concentration in the Media, Potsdam, Constl. Ct. of State of Baden-Württemberg, Stuttgart. Mem. Am. Bar Orgn., German Bar Orgn., Tax Payers Assn. (chmn. bd.). Avocations: golfing, skiing, history in politics. Antitrust, Banking, Mergers and acquisitions. Home: Lenbachstr 53 70192 Stuttgart Baden-Wurttemberg Germany Office: Haver & Mailaender Attys Lenzhalde 83-85 70192 Stuttgart Baden-Wurttemberg Germany Fax: 0049 711 22744 55. E-mail: kpm@baver-mailaender.de

MAILANDER, WILLIAM STEPHEN, lawyer; b. Dover, N.J., July 25, 1958; s. William Stephen and Doris Elizabeth (Post) M.; m. Judith Gay Burrows, May 20, 1989 (div. 1993); m. Rosalind Eager, Dec. 15, 1999. BA, NYU, 1984; JD, Temple U., 1988; MBA, Johns Hopkins U., 2001. Bar: Pa. 1988, N.J. 1991, D.C. 1996; U.S. Ct. Vets. Appeals 1991, U.S. Ct. Appeals (fed. cir.) 1993, U.S. Supreme Ct. 1994. Staff atty. Bd. Vets. Appeals, Washington, 1988-90, Coast Guard Chief Counsel, Washington, 1990-91, VA Gen. Counsel, Washington, 1991-93; asst. gen. counsel Paralyzed Vets. Am., 1993—. Faculty continuing legal edn. seminars, 1993—. Contbr. articles to profl. jours. With USMC, 1976-79. Decorated Navy Achievement medal. Mem. FBA (chair membership vets. law sect. 1993-94, editor newsletter 1996—). Avocations: reading, running. Administrative and regulatory, Federal civil litigation, General corporate. Office: Paralyzed Vets Am 801 18th St NW Washington DC 20006-3517

MAINE, MICHAEL ROLAND, lawyer; b. Anderson, Ind., Feb. 22, 1940; s. Roland Dwight and Vivian Louise (Browning) M.; m. Suzanne Bauman, Aug. 25, 1962; children: Christopher Michael (dec.), Melinda Louise. AB with high distinction, DePauw U.; JD with distinction, U. Mich. Bar: Ind., D.C., U.S. Dist. Ct. (so. dist.) Ind., U.S. Ct. Appeals (7th cir.), U.S. Supreme Ct. Assoc. Baker & Daniels, Indpls., 1964-71, ptnr., 1972—. Contbr. articles to profl. jours. Bd. dirs. Ind. Repertory Theatre, Indpls., 1986—, Cmty. Hosp. N., 1988—91; Japan-Am. Soc. of Ind. Inc., 1988—; pres. Mental Health Assn. Ind., Indpls., 1985; bd. visitors Sch. Law Ind. U.; trustee De Pauw U., Greencastle, 1990—. Capt. USAF, 1965—68. Named Sagamore of Wabash, Gov. Ind., 1986. Fellow: Ind. Bar Found., Indpls. Bar Found.; mem.: Ind. Bar Assn. (chmn. fed. judiciary com. 1986—88), Indpls. Bar Assn. (sec. 1983, pres. 1985, extraordinary svc. award 1985), Kiwanis (lt. gov. Ind. club 1972, pres. Indpls. club 1969), Masons, Order of Coif, Phi Beta Kappa. Lodges: Kiwanis (lt. gov. Ind. club 1972, pres. Indpls. club 1969), Masons. Avocation: golf. General corporate, Labor. Home: 11021 Fall Creek Rd Indianapolis IN 46256-9403 Office: Baker & Daniels 300 N Meridian St Ste 2700 Indianapolis IN 46204-1782

MAINES, JAMES ALLEN, lawyer; b. Tipton, Ind., Oct. 4, 1951; s. Lloyd Leon and Ruth Margaret (James) M. BA in Econs., Taylor U., 1973; JD, U. Fla.-Gainesville, 1976. Bar: Fla. 1976, U.S. Dist. Ct. (no. dist.) Ga. 1976, U.S. Ct. Appeals (5th cirs.) 1976, U.S. Ct. Appeals (11th cir.) 1981. Assoc. Hansell, Post, Brandon & Dorsey, Atlanta, 1976-84; ptnr. Jones, Day, Reavis & Pogue (formerly Hansell & Post), 1984-88, Long, Aldridge & Norman, Atlanta, 1988-98, Paul, Hastings, Janafsky & Walker, Atlanta, 1998—. Mem. faculty Hastings Coll. Trial Advocacy, U. Calif.; lectr. Nat. Inst. Trial Advocacy Mem. ABA (litigation sect. 1976—), Fla. Bar, State Bar Ga., Atlanta Bar Assn. Federal civil litigation, Contracts commercial, Computer. Office: 600 Peachtree St NE Atlanta GA 30308

MAIO, F. ANTHONY, lawyer; b. Passaic, N.J., Mar. 30, 1937; s. Anthony J. and Santina (Sciarra) M.; m. Maureen Margaret McKeown, Dec. 30, 1960; children: Christopher, Duncan, Todd. BSME, Stevens Inst. Tech., 1959; LLB cum laude, Boston Coll., 1968. Bar: Wis. 1968, D.C. 1971. Engr., project mgr. Hazeltine Corp., Greenlawn, N.Y. and Avon, Mass., 1959-64; project mgr. Raytheon Corp., Portsmouth, R.I., 1964-65; atty. Foley & Lardner, Milw., 1968-70, ptnr. Washington, 1971-86, Milw., 1986-97, ptnr., gen. counsel, 1997—. Editor Boston Coll. Law Rev., 1967-68. Dir. Arthritis Found., Milw., 1986-88, ARC, Milw., 1986-94. Mem. Order of Coif, Naples Sailing and Yacht Club (commodore 2001). Avocations: boating, fishing.

MAIOCCHI, CHRISTINE, lawyer; b. N.Y.C., Dec. 24, 1949; d. George and Andreina (Toneatto) M.; m. John Charles Kerecz, Aug. 16, 1980; children: Charles George, Joan Christine. BA in Polit. Sci., MA in Polit. Sci., Fordham U., 1971, JD, 1974; postgrad., NYU, 1977—. Bar: N.Y. 1975, U.S. Dist. Ct. (so. and ea. dists.), N.Y. 1975, U.S. Ct. Appeals (2nd cir) 1975. Law clk. to magistrate U.S. Dist. Ct. (so. dist.) N.Y., N.Y.C., 1973-74; atty. corp. legal dept. The Home Ins. Co., 1974-76; asst. house counsel corp. legal dept. Allied Maintenance Corp., 1976; atty. corp. legal dept. Getty Oil Co., 1976-77; v.p., mgr. real estate Paine, Webber, Jackson & Curtis, Inc., 1977-81; real estate mgr. GK Techs., Inc., Greenwich, Conn., 1981-85; real estate mgr., sr. atty. MCI Telecom. Corp., Rye Brook, N.Y., 1985-93; real estate and legal cons. Wallace Law Registry, 1994-96; sr. assoc. counsel Met. Transp. Authority, 1996-99, dep. gen. counsel, 1999—. Bd. dirs. LWV, Dobbs Ferry, N.Y., 1988. Mem. ABA, Nat. Assn. Corp. Real Estate Execs. (pres. 1983-84, treas. 1985-86, bd. dirs. 1995—, exec. v.p. N.Y. chpt. 2000—), Indsl. Devel. Rsch. Coun. (program v.p. 1985, Profl. award 1987), N.Y. Bar Assn., Women's Bar Assn. Manhattan, The Corp. Bar (sec. real estate divsn. 1987-89, chmn. 1990-92), Jr. League Club, Dobbs Ferry Women's Club (program dir. 1981-92, 94-96, publicity dir. 1992-94). Avocations: sports, theatre, gardening. Real property. Home: 84 Clinton Ave Dobbs Ferry NY 10522-3004 E-mail: cmaiocch@mtahq.org

MAITLAND, GUY EDISON CLAY, lawyer; b. London, Dec. 28, 1942; (mother Am. citizen); s. Paul and Virginia Francesca (Carver) M. BA, Columbia U., 1964; JD, N.Y. Law Sch., 1968. Bar: N.Y. 1969, U.S. Dist. Ct. (so. and ea. dists.) N.Y. 1969, U.S. Ct. Appeals (2d and D.C. cirs.) 1969. Assoc. Burlingham, Underwood & Lord, N.Y.C., 1969-74; admiralty counsel Union Carbide Corp., 1974-76; exec. v.p., gen. counsel, officer Liberian Svcs., Inc., N.Y.C. and Reston, Va., 1976-99; pres. Trust Co. of the Marshall Islands, Inc., 1990—, mng. ptnr., 2000—. Del. UN Conf. on Trade and Devel., Manila, 1979, Belgrade, 1983; participant London Conf. on Limitation of Maritime Liability, 1976; mem. legal com. Internat. Maritime Orgn. (UN) London, 1980—; del. UN Conf. on Law of the Sea, 1976-82, London UN Maritime Law Conf., 1984; co-founder The Admiralty-Fin. Forum, N.Y.C., 1986; mng. ptnr. Internat. Registries, Inc. Contbr. articles on maritime law, U.S. shipping policy. Mem. N.Y. Rep. State Exec. Com., 1974-76; del. Rep. Nat. Conv., Kansas City, 1976; sec. N.Y. Rep. County Com., 1976-87, vice chmn., 1988—, mem. exec. com., 1974-76; co-chmn. Citizens for Reagan, N.Y. State, 1979-80; trustee Am. Mcht. Marine Mus. Found. at U.S. Mcht. Marine Acad., King's Point, Nat. Maritime Hist. Soc., chmn., 2000-01; trustee N.Y. Maritime Coll. at Ft. Schuyler Found., Inc.; bd. dirs. Coast Guard Found.; del. UN Geneva Conf. on Arrest of Vessels, 1999; bd. dirs. Seamen's Ch. Inst., N.Y.C., Ctr. for Seafarers Rights; mem. adv. com. Am. Maritime History Project. Named Outstanding Young Man of Am. U.S. Jaycees, 1975; hon. del Rep. Nat. Conv., Dallas, 1984. Mem. ABA, Assn. of Bar of City of N.Y. (chmn. admiralty com. 1982-85), Maritime Law Assn. U.S. (chmn. com. on intergovtl. orgns. 1987-95), Ctr. for Seafarer's Rights Seamen's Ch. Inst. (bd. dirs. 1995—), Maritime Assn. Port of N.Y. (dir. 1984-87, 98—, pres. 1999-2001). Admiralty. Office: Internat Registries Inc 11495 Commerce Park Dr Reston VA 20191-1507 also: 11495 Commerce Park Dr Reston VA 20191-1507

MAIWURM, JAMES JOHN, lawyer; b. Wooster, Ohio, Dec. 5, 1948; s. James Frederick and Virginia Anne (Jones) M.; m. Wendy S. Leeper, July 31, 1971; children: James G., Michelle K. BA, Coll. Wooster, 1971; JD, U. Mich., 1974. Bar: Ohio 1974, D.C. 1986, Md. 1987, N.Y., 1987. Ptnr. Squire, Sanders & Dempsey, Cleve. and Washington, 1974-90; ptnr., group head Crowell & Moring, Washington, 1990-98; ptnr. Squire, Sanders & Dempsey, 1998-99; chmn., CEO Kaiser Group Internat., Inc., Fairfax, Va., 1999-2000; mng. ptnr. Squire, Sanders & Dempsey, Tysons Corner, 2001—. Bd. dirs. Workflow Mgmt., Inc., Cortez III Svc. Corp., Kaiser-Hill Co., LLC, Kaser Group Holdings Inc. Contbr. articles to profl. jours. Bd. trustees Davis Meml. Goodwill Industries, 1996—. Mem. ABA, D.C. Bar Assn., Leadership Washington. General corporate, Mergers and acquisitions, Securities. Home: 9419 Brian Jac Ln Great Falls VA 22066-2002 Office: Squire Sanders & Dempsey LLP 14th fl 8000 Towers Crescent Tysons Corner VA 22182

MAJOR, ALICE JEAN, lawyer; b. Denver; m. Kent H. Major, Feb. 16, 1997; children: David, Thomas, Kassie, Samantha, Cameron, Eve. BS in Bus., U. Colo., 1984, MBA, 1986; JD, U. Kans., 1987. Bar: Mo. 1987, Kans. 1988, U.S. Dist. Ct. Kans. 1988, Colo. 1990, U.S. Dist. Ct. Colo. 1991, U.S. Ct. Appeals (3d cir.) 1993, U.S. Supreme Ct. 1994. Atty. Legal Aid of Western Mo., Kansas City, 1987-88, Spencer, Fane, Britt & Browne, Kansas City, 1988-91; mcpl. and county atty. City and County of Denver, 1991—. Spkr. Colorado Springs mtg. Colo. County Attys. Assn., 1992. Vol. Denver Dumb Friends League, Denver, 1996—. Recipient miscellaneous ribbons and awards for paintings. Mem. Alfred A. Arraj Inn of Ct. (barrister mem.). Avocations: art, skiing, fishing. Office: City Attys Office City and County of Denver 1437 Bannock St Rm 353 Denver CO 80202-5375

MALAMUD, ALEXANDER, lawyer, consultant; b. Beltz, Moldova, Jan. 4, 1971; came to U.S. s. Yafim and Haya Urman M. BS in Criminal Justice, U. Ariz., 1996; postgrad., UCLA, 1996-2000. CEO, pres. Orient Express, Inc., Bklyn., 1995—. Bus. cons. N.Y. Transporters Assn., 1994; mem. adv. bd. Metro, Inc., Phoenix, 1994-96; cons. Mass. Transp. Mem. N.Y. Transp. Assn. Republican. Avocations: reading books, basketball, practicing law. General corporate, Criminal, Health. Home: 29 Park View Pl Fair Lawn NJ 07410-4353 Office: Orient Express Inc 2752 E 22nd St Brooklyn NY 11235-2845

MALATESTA, MARY ANNE, lawyer; b. Wapakoneta, Ohio, Aug. 7, 1954; d. Leo J. Jr. and Ellen E. Malatesta. BA in English, Ohio State U., 1976; JD, U. Colo., 1979. Bar: Colo. 1979, U.S. Dist. Ct. Colo. 1979, U.S. Ct. Appeals (9th cir.) 1989, U.S. Ct. Appeals (10th cir.) 1990, U.S. Dist. Ct. Ariz. 1992. Dep. dist. atty. 1st Jud. Dist., Golden, Colo., 1979-84; assoc. Tilly & Graves, P.C., Denver, 1985-88, shareholder, 1988-93; asst. atty. gen. Office Atty. Gen. State of Colo., 1994—. Mem. faculty Nat. Inst. Trial Advocacy, South Bend, Ind., 1989-90, asst. team leader, 1990-93, team leader, 1994—; lectr. U. Denver, 1990, 91, 97—; guest faculty U. Colo., 1992—; organizer Victims of Violence seminar; mem. faculty Am. Bd. Trial Advocates seminar, 1992, Domestic Violence Prosecution Tng. Course, 1994, Child Advocates Tng. Course, 1996; master Am. Inns of Ct. Judge William E. Doyle Inn, 1994—, Women's Leadership Forum, 1996—. Founder, mem. Facio ut Des, Denver, 1987-94. Mem. Colo. Bar Assn., Denver Bar Assn. (professionalism com. 1990—, co-chair profes-

sionalism com. 1994-99, professionalism conciliation panel mem. 1999—), Colo. Women's Bar Assn. Avocations: hiking, horseback riding, spectator sports. General civil litigation, Criminal, Product liability. Office: Office of Atty Gen 1525 Sherman St Fl 5 Denver CO 80203-1700

MALDONADO, KIRK FRANCIS, lawyer; b. Omaha, Mar. 7, 1950; s. Manuel and Orpha Mae (Kovar) Maldonado. B.A., U. Nebr.-Omaha, 1975; J.D., Creighton U., 1978; M.L.T., Georgetown U., 1981. Bar: Nebr. 1978, Calif. 1982. Atty., Employee Plans and Exempt Orgns. Divsn. Office of Chief Counsel, IRS, Washington, 1978-81; assoc. Gibson, Dunn & Crutcher, Newport Beach, Calif., 1982-85; prin. Stradling, Yocca, Carlson & Rauth, Newport Beach, 1985-89, prin. Riorday & McKinzie, Costa Mesa, Calif., 1989-2001. Mem. ABA (employee benefits com.), State Bar Calif. Contbr. articles to profl. jours. Fax: 949-790-6301. E-mail: kmaldonado@bazobeck.com. Pension, profit-sharing, and employee benefits. Office: Brobeck Phleger & Harrison LLP 38 Technology Dr Irvine CA 92618

MALEE, THOMAS MICHAEL, lawyer; b. Omaha, May 25, 1947; BA, Carroll Coll., 1970; JD, U. Mont., 1975. Bar: Mont. 1975, U.S. Dist. Ct. Mont. 1975, U.S. Ct. Appeals (9th cir.) 1986, U.S. Supreme Ct. 1988. Staff atty. State of Mont. Legis. Counsel, Helena, Mont., 1975-76; asst. atty. gen. State of Mont. Dept. Revenue, 1976; pvt. practice Seattle, Tacoma area, Wash., 1977-78, Helena, 1979-82, Billings, Mont., 1982—. Mem. State Bar of Mont. (ins. com. 1988—). Roman Catholic. Avocations: skiing, fitness. Federal civil litigation, General civil litigation, Personal injury. Office: 1109 N 22nd St Ste 103A Billings MT 59101-0253

MALEK, HODGE MEHDI, lawyer; b. London, July 11, 1959; s. Ali A. and Irene Elizabeth (Johnson) M.; m. Inez Dies Vegelin Van Claebergen, 1986; children: Yousef, Cyrus, Leila. Diplome, U. Sorbonne, Paris, 1978; MA in Jurisprudence, Oxford U., 1981; B in Civil Law, 1982. Bar: Gray's Inn 1983; Queen's Counsel 1999. Barrister, London, 1983—; customs and excise prosecution list, 1992-99; supplementary treasury panel, 1999; mem. panel Bar Disciplinary Tribunal, 2000—. Co-author: Discovery, 1992, Disclosure, 2001. Atkin scholar Gray's Inn, 1983, Birkenhead scholar Gray's Inn, 1983, Band scholar Gray's Inn, 1984; recipient Lee Essay prize Gray's Inn, 1984. Mem. Comml. Bar assn., Adminstrv. Law Bar Assn., Franco-Brit. Lawyers Soc., Bar Sports Group. Avocations: history, swimming, skiing. Office: 4/5 Gray's Inn Sq Gray's Inn WC1R 5AY London England Fax: 020 7242 7803. E-mail: cyrus.malek@ukgateway.net, hmalek@4-5graysinnsquare.co.uk

MALESKI, CYNTHIA MARIA, lawyer; b. Natrona Heights, Pa., July 4, 1951; d. Richard Anthony and Helen Elizabeth (Palovcak) M.; m. Andrzej Gabriel Groch, Aug. 7, 1982; 1 child, Elizabeth Maria. BA summa cum laude, U. Pitts., 1973; student U. Rouen (France), 1970; JD, Duquesne U., 1976. Bar: Pa. 1976, U.S. dist. ct. (we. dist.) Pa. 1976, U.S. Supreme Ct. 1980, U.S. Ct. Appeals (3d cir.) 1984. Indsl. rels. adminstr. Allegheny Ludlum Industries, Inc., Brackenridge, Pa., 1972-74; law clk. Conte, Courtney, Tarasi & Price, Pitts., 1974, Paul Hammer, Pitts., 1974-76; sole practice Natrona Heights, Pa., 1978-92, 95—; ins. commnr. Penna, 1992—; mem. Gov.'s cabinet, 1992—; v.p., regulatory coun. Highmak Blue Cross/Blue Shield, 1995—; assoc. dir. pers. Mercy Hosp., Pitts., 1976-77, dir. legal affairs, 1977-81, gen. counsel, 1981-92; spl. master Allegheny County Ct. Common Pleas, 1989; bd. dirs. legal adv. bd. Cath. Health Assn., 1980-82; gen. counsel, vice chmn. nat. assembly of reps. Nat. Confedn. Am. Ethnic Groups, 1980— ; health law cons. and lectr. Co-author: The Legal Dimensions of Nursing Practice (Nurses' Book of Month Club award 1982), 1982; contbr. articles to publs. Corp. sec., pres. Duquesne U. Tamburitzans, Pitts.; vice chmn. Czechoslovak room com. Nationality Rooms Program, U. Pitts., 1983; bd. dirs. ARC S.W. Penn. Chpt., 1996—; elected mem. Allegheny County Dem. Com., 1986-89; candidate for del. Dem. Nat. Conv. 20th Pa. Congl. Dist., 1984; chmn. Com. to Re-elect U.S. Congressman Doug Walgren, 1982; Ethnic Com. for Pa. Atty. Gen., 1980, Ethnic Com. for Judge Peter Paul Olszewski, 1983; U.S. del 4th Slovak World Congress, 1981; mem. adv. bd. Children's and Youth Services, Allegheny County, 1984—; mem. Allegheny-Keshi Hist. Soc., 1995—; soloist, speaker various groups, Pitts. Slovakians. Scholar U. Rouen, 1970; Allegheny Ludlum Industries scholar, 1969-73; Andrew Mellon scholar, 1969; tuition scholar U. Pitts., 1969-73; tuition remission grantee Duquesne U., 1975, 76; recipient acad. excellence award Duquesne U., 1976, Disting. Alumnus, 1993; Mem. ABA, Am. Soc. Hosp. Attys., Nat. Health Lawyers Assn., Women Execs. in State Govt. (mem. nat. bd. 1994), Soc. Hosp. Attys. of Hosp. Assn. Pa. (v.p.), Soc. Hosp. Attys. Western Pa., Pa. Bar Assn. (commn. on women, 1996—, exec. women's coun.), Allegheny County Bar Assn., Slavic Edn. Assn. (nat. treas. 1981-86), St. Thomas More Soc. (bd. govs. 1980—), First Cath. Slovak Union, 1st Cath. Slovak Women's Assn., Phi Beta Kappa. Roman Catholic. State civil litigation, General practice, Health. Home: 137 Oak Manor Dr Natrona Heights PA 15065-1949 Office: Ins Dept 1326 Strawberry Sq Harrisburg PA 17120-0046

MALETZ, HERBERT NAAMAN, federal judge; b. Boston, Oct. 30, 1913; s. Reuben and Frances (Sawyer) M.; m. Catherine B. Loebach, May 8, 1947; 1 child, David M. (dec.). AB cum laude, Harvard U., 1935, LLB, 1939. Bar: Mass. 1939, D.C. 1952. Rev. atty. Mktg. Laws Survey, WPA, Washington, 1939-41; mem. staff Truman com. U.S. Senate, 1941-42; trial atty. anti-trust divsn. Dept. Justice, 1946-50; assoc. chief counsel, chief counsel Office of Price Stabilization, 1950-53; law assoc. to Charles P. Clark, 1954-55; chief counsel anti-trust subcom., judiciary com. U.S. House of Reps., 1955-61; trial commr. U.S. Ct. Claims, Washington, 1961-67; judge U.S. Ct. Internat. Trade, N.Y.C., 1967—. Vis. judge with various fed. cts., including U.S. Ct. Customs and Patent Appeals, U.S. Cts. of Appeals for the 1st and 2nd Cirs., U.S. Dist. Cts. for Mass., N.H., Maine, R.I., Ea. Dist. N.Y., Ea. Dist. N.C., Cen. Dist. Calif., So. Dist. Calif.; vis. judge U.S. Dist. Md., Balt., 1987—. Served with AUS, 1942-46; lt. col. Res. E-mail: beverly_daniel2md.uscourts.gov. Office: US Dist Ct Md 101 W Lombard St Baltimore MD 21201-2605

MALIK, JOHN STEPHEN, lawyer; b. Bryn Mawr, Pa., Sept. 15, 1958; s. John and Mary M. (Pisko) M. BA, St. Joseph's U., 1980; JD, Del. Law Sch., 1983. Bar: Del. 1984, Pa. 1984, U.S. Dist. Ct. Del. 1984, N.J. 1985, U.S. Ct. Appeals (3d cir.) 1990, U.S. Supreme Ct. 1989. Adj. faculty Widener U., Wilmington, 1984-86; sole practice, 1985—. Mem. ATLA, Am. Judicature Soc., Nat. Assn. Criminal Def. Lawyers, Del. Assn. Criminal Def. Lawyers, Del. Bar Asns. Democrat. Roman Catholic. Criminal. Office: 100 E 14th St Wilmington DE 19801-3210

MALINA, MICHAEL, lawyer; b. Bklyn., Mar. 20, 1936; s. William and Jean (Kutlowitz) M.; m. Anita May Oppenheim, June 22, 1958; children: Rachel Lynn, Stuart Charles, Joel Martin. AB, Harvard U., 1957, LLB, 1960. Bar: N.Y. 1961, U.S. Dist. Ct. (so. and ea. dists.) N.Y. 1962, U.S. Ct. Appeals (2d, 3d, 4th, 9th, and D.C. cirs.) 1965, U.S. Supreme Ct. 1965, U.S. Tax Ct. 1991. Assoc. Kaye, Scholer, Fierman, Hays & Handler, N.Y.C., 1960-69, ptnr., 1969—. Contbr. articles to profl. jours. Mem. ABA (antitrust sect.), N.Y. State Bar Assn. (chmn. antitrust sect. 1998-99), Assn. Bar City N.Y. (profl. ethics com. 1985-88), Phi Beta Kappa. Democrat. Jewish. Antitrust, Federal civil litigation. Home: 12 Innes Rd Scarsdale NY 10583-7110 Office: Kaye Scholer Fierman Hays & Handler 425 Park Ave New York NY 10022-3506

MALINOWSKI, ARTHUR ANTHONY, lawyer, labor arbitrator; b. Chgo., Apr. 4, 1929; s. Ignatius and Sophie (Data) M. BS in Econs., DePaul U., 1956, JD, 1960; MS in Indsl. Rels., Loyola U., 1958; PhD, Ill. Inst. Tech., 1972; LLM in Labor Law, Chgo. Kent Coll. Law, 1981. Bar: Ill. 1960. Instr. indsl. rels. Loyola U., Chgo., 1963-69, prof., 1969-94; prof. emeritus, 1994—; mem. Ill. Office Collective Bargaining, Chgo., 1973-83. Lectr. dept. econs. Ill. Inst. Tech., Chgo., 1965-68. Mem. Ill. Bar Assn., Indsl. Rels. Rsch. Assn., Nat. Acad. Arbitrators, Knights Malta, Phi Alpha Delta, Alpha Sigma Nu, Pi Gamma Mu, Iota Sigma Epsilon, Beta Gamma Epsilon. Home: 9240 Major Ave Morton Grove IL 60053-1552 Office: Loyola U of Chgo 25 E Pearson Ste 1250 Chicago IL 60611-2147

MALKIN, CARY JAY, lawyer; b. Chgo., Oct. 6, 1949; s. Arthur D. and Perle (Slavin) M.; m. Lisa Klimley, Oct. 27, 1976; children: Dorothy R., Victoria S., Lydia R. BA, George Washington U., 1971; JD, Northwestern U., 1974. Bar: Ill. 1974, U.S. Dist. Ct. (no. dist.) Ill. 1974, N.Y. 2001. Assoc. Mayer, Brown & Platt, Chgo., 1974-80, ptnr., 1981—. Chmn. spl. events com. Mental Health Assn., 1984-85; mem. steering com. Endowment Campaign of the Latin Sch. of Chgo., 1990-91, trustee, 1991-2000, v.p., 1992-98, chmn. capital campaign, 1995-98, nat. trustee, 2000—; mem. exec. com. Friends of Prentice Women's Hosp., 1991-92; bd. dirs. SOS Children's Village Ill., 1992-96; mem. M.S. Weiss fund bd. Children's Meml. Hosp., 1989-93; mem. Graziano Fund bd. Children's Meml. Hosp., 1993-96; mem. steering com. Founder's Coun. Field Mus., 1995—, chmn. steering com., 1999—, trustee, 1999—. Mem. Chgo. Club, Saddle and Cycle Club, Arts Club, Standard Club, Order of the Coif, Phi Beta Kappa. Banking, General corporate, Finance. Home: 233 E Walton St Chicago IL 60611-1510 Office: Mayer Brown & Platt 190 S La Salle St Ste 3100 Chicago IL 60603-3441

MALKIN, JOSEPH M. lawyer; b. N.Y.C., Jan. 26, 1947; BA, Claremont Men's Coll., 1968; JD, Yale U., 1972. Bar: Calif. 1972, U.S. Dist. Ct. (ctrl. dist.) Calif. 1972, U.S. Ct. Appeals (9th cir.) 1973, U.S. Supreme Ct. 1976. Mem. O'Melveny & Myers, San Francisco. Editor Yale Law Jour., 1970-72. Recipient Carter, Ledyard and Milburn prize Yale Law Sch., 1970. Mem. ABA, Bar Assn. San Francisco. Office: O'Melveny & Myers Embarcadero Ctr W Tower 275 Battery St San Francisco CA 94111-3305

MALKIN, MICHAEL M. lawyer; b. New Haven, Nov. 1, 1944; s. Eli B. and Gladys (Pollak) M.; children: Andrea, Lisa, Daniel. BA, U. N.Mex., 1966; JD, NYU, 1969. Bar: N.Y. 1970, U.S. Dist. Ct. (so. dist.) N.Y. 1971, U.S. Dist. Ct. (ea. dist.) N.Y. 1971, U.S. Ct. Appeals (2d cir.) 1972, U.S. Supreme Ct. 1984. Assoc. Weil, Lee & Bergin, N.Y.C., 1970-76, Weil, Guttman & Davis, N.Y.C., 1976-77, ptnr., 1977-82, Weil, Guttman, Davis & Malkin, N.Y.C., 1982-86, Weil, Guttman & Malkin, N.Y.C., 1986-95, Weil, Guttman & Malkin, LLP, N.Y.C., 1995—. Judge Giles Sutherland Rich Moot Ct. Competition, N.Y.C., 1982; arbitrator Civil Ct. of City N.Y., 1984-88. Mem. editl. bd. Trademark Reporter, 1973-75, 88-90, contbg. editor, 1974-75. Mem. N.Y. State Bar Assn., U.S. Trademark Assn., Phi Delta Phi, Alpha Epsilon Pi. Antitrust, Non-profit and tax-exempt organizations, Trademark and copyright. Office: Weil Guttman & Malkin LLP 60 E 42nd St Rm 4210 New York NY 10165-4299 E-mail: m.malkin@worldnet.att.net

MALKIN, MICHELLE LYNN, lawyer; b. Skokie, Ill., Jan. 20, 1973; d. Lee Sanford and Shari Mae (Jelinek) M. BA, So. Ill. U., 1995; JD, Northeastern U., Boston, 1998. Bar: Wash. 1998. Jud. clk. Mass. Ct. Appeals, Boston, 1997; atty. Schwerin Campbell Barnard LLP, Seattle, 1998—. Vol., activity organizer Lesbian Resource Ctr., Seattle, 1999—; vol., mem. com. GSBA Scholarship Com., Seattle, 1998—; intake vol. Gay and Lesbian Advs. and Defenders, Boston, 1996-98; guardian ad litem, Boston, 1997-98. Recipient awards for svc. Mem. ABA, Wash. State Trial Lawyers Assn., Greater Seattle Bus. ASsn. Democrat. Jewish. Avocations: gay and Lesbian politics, theater, films, collectibles. Office: Schwerin Campbell Barnard LLP 18 W Mercer St Ste 400 Seattle WA 98119-3971

MALLEY, ROBERT JOHN, holding company executive, lawyer; b. Buffalo, Dec. 23, 1944; s. Chester John and Mary (Kinmartin) M.; 1 child, Cullen Burdick. Student London Sch. Econs. and Polit. Sci., 1964; BA cum laude, Colgate U., 1966; JD, Columbia U., 1969. Bar: N.Y. 1970. Assoc. Wickes, Riddell, Bloomer, Jacobi & McGuire, N.Y.C., 1969-72; assoc. London, Buttenwieser & Chalif, N.Y.C., 1972-74; v.p., counsel Citibank N.A., N.Y.C., 1975-81; sr. v.p., gen. counsel, sec. State Street Boston Corp., 1981— . Contbr. articles to William and Mary Law Rev. and profl. jours. Served with USAR, 1969-74. Mem. ABA (sect. on corp., banking and bus. law, corp. counsel), Phi Beta Kappa. Club: University (N.Y.C.). Banking, General corporate, Securities. Office: State St Boston Corp 225 Franklin St Boston MA 02110-2804

MALLORY, CHARLES KING, III, lawyer; b. Norfolk, Va., Nov. 16, 1936; s. Charles King Mallory Jr. and Dorothy Pratt (Williams) Swanke; m. Florence Beale Marshall; children: King, Raburn, Anne, Richard. BA, Yale U., 1958; JD, Tulane U., 1961. Bar: La. 1961, Calif. 1965, D.C. 1972. Ptnr. Monroe & Lemann, New Orleans, 1965-72; acting exec. dir. SEC, Washington, 1972; dep. asst. sec. U.S. Dept. Interior, 1973, acting asst. sec., 1974; v.p., gen. counsel Middle South Svcs., Inc., New Orleans, 1975-79; ptnr. Hunton & Williams, Washington, 1979—. Gen. counsel Com. on the Present Danger, 1987-91. Mem. Reagan-Bush Transition Team, Washington, 1980-81, Grace Commn. on Pvt. Sector Survey Cost in the Fed. Govt., Washington, 1983-84. Served to lt. USNR, 1961-65. Mem. ABA, La. Bar Assn., Calif. Bar Assn., D.C. Bar Assn., Fed. Energy Bar Assn., Nat. Assn. Bond Lawyers. Republican. Episcopalian. FERC practice, Legislative, Public utilities. Office: Hunton & Williams 1900 K St NW # 12 Washington DC 20006-1110 E-mail: kmallory@hunton.com

MALLORY, FRANK LINUS, lawyer; b. Calgary, Alta., Can., May 5, 1920; s. Frank Louis and Anna Amy (Allstrum) M.; m. Jean Ellen Lindsey, Jan. 29, 1944; children: Susan Mallory Remund, Ann, Bruce R. AB with distinction, Stanford U., 1941, LLB, 1947. Bar: Calif. 1948. Assoc. Gibson, Dunn & Crutcher, L.A., 1947-54; ptnr. L.A. and Orange County, Calif., 1955-88. Cert. specialist taxation law Calif. Bd. Legal Specialization, 1973-89. Pres. Town Hall of Calif., L.A., 1970, Boys Republic, Chino, Calif., 1962-64; pres. Braille Inst. Am., L.A., 1988-92. Lt. (j.g.) USNR, 1942-46. Mem. ABA, Calif. Bar Assn., Los Angeles County Bar Assn., Orange County Bar Assn., Newport Harbor Yacht Club, Big Canyon Country Club, Transpacific Yacht Club (staff commodore), Order of the Coif, Phi Beta Kappa. Republican. Private international, Probate. Home: 633 Bayside Dr Newport Beach CA 92660-7213 E-mail: flmallory@CS.com

MALLOY, MICHAEL PATRICK, law educator, writer, consultant; b. Haddon Heights, N.J., Sept. 23, 1951; s. Francis Edward and Marie Grace (Nardi) M.; divorced; 1 child, Elizabeth; m. Susie Pieratos, Jan., 1992; children: Michael Emil, Nicholas Charles, Edward Francis, Theodora Marie. BA magna cum laude (scholar), Georgetown U., 1973, PhD, 1983; JD (scholar), U. Pa., 1976. Bar: N.J. 1976, U.S. Supreme Ct. 1991. Rsch. assoc. Inst. Internat. Law and Econ. Devel., Washington, 1976-77; atty. advisor Office Fgn. Assets Control Dept. Treasury, 1977-80, Office of Comptroller of Currency, Washington, 1981; spl. counsel SEC, 1981-82; asst. prof. N.Y. Law Sch., N.Y.C., 1982-83; spl. asst. Office of Gen. Counsel U.S. Dept. Treasury, Washington, 1985; assoc. prof. Seton Hall U. Sch. Law, Newark, 1983-86, prof., assoc. dean, 1986-87; prof. Fordham U. Sch. Law, N.Y.C., 1987-96, dir. grad. studies, 1990-94; prof. U. of Pacific McGeorge Law Sch., 1996—, dir. JD concentration in internat. legal studies, 1999—2001. Law lectr. Morin Ctr. Banking and Fin. Law Studies Boston U. Sch. Law, 1986-90, 95-96, 2001; vis. prof. U. Salzburg, Austria, 2000, Suffolk U. Sch. Law, 2001-2002; cons. bank regulation and pvt. internat. law matters. Author: Corporate Law of Banks (2 vols.), 1988, Economic Sanctions and U.S. Trade, 1990, The Regulation of Banking, 1992, Banking Law and Regulation, 3 vols., 1994, Fundamentals of Banking Regulation, 1998, International Banking, 1998, Banking and Financial Services Law, 1999, Hornbook on Banking Regulation, 1999, U.S. Economic Sanctions: Theory and Practice, 2000; contbr. articles, revs. and comments to profl. jours. Recipient Spl. Achievement award Dept. Treasury, 1982. Mem. Am. Soc. Internat. Law (exec. council 1986-89), Internat. Law Assn. (com. chair Am. br. 1995-97), Am. Assn. Law Schs. (chair-elect sect. fin. insts. and consumer fin. svcs. 2001—), Hegel Soc. Am., L'Association des Auditeurs et Anciens Auditeurs de l'Academie de Droit International de la Haye, Phi Beta Kappa. Office: U of Pacific McGeorge Sch Law 3200 5th Ave Sacramento CA 95817-2705 E-mail: malloympm@aol.com

MALM, ROGER CHARLES, lawyer; b. Hot Springs, S.D., July 8, 1949; s. Harry Milton and Angeline Mae (Johnson) M.; m. Sandra M. Metz, July 15, 1972; children: Andrew, Elliott, Nicholas. BA, St. Olaf Coll., 1971; JD, U. N.D., 1974. Bar: N.D. 1974, Ariz. 1975, Minn. 1980, U.S. Dist. Ct. N.D. 1974, U.S. Dist. Ct. Ariz. 1976, U.S. Ct. Appeals (9th cir.) 1981, U.S. Supreme Ct. 1981, U.S. Ct. Appeals (8th cir.) 1982, U.S. Dist. Ct. Minn. 1985, U.S. Claims Ct. 1985, U.S. Tax Ct. 1988. Ptnr. Brink, Sobolik, Severson, Malm & Albrecht, P.A., Hallock, Minn., 1980—; county atty. Kittson County, 1995—. Pres. N.W. Minn. County Atty.'s Coun. Hospice dir. Kittson County Hospice, Inc., 1984—; bd. dirs. Cmty. Theatre, Hallock, 1987—, Greater Grand Forks Cmty. Theater, 1991-95. Mem. ABA, Ariz. Bar Assn., N.D. Bar Assn., Minn. Bar Assn. (mem. bd. govs. 1993-2000), Am. Acad. Hosp. Attys., Norwest Minn. Atty.'s Coun. (pres.). Lutheran. Avocations: skiing, sailing. General civil litigation, General practice, Health. Office: Brink Sobolik Severson Malm & Albrecht PO Box 790 Hallock MN 56728-0790

MALMSTRÖM, ANDERS C. lawyer; b. Helsingborg, Sweden, Feb. 2, 1969; m. Anna Malmström, May 20, 2000. LLM, U. Lund, Sweden, 1995. Law clk. Adminstrv. Ct. of Västernorrland, HÄrnösand, 1996-98; assoc. Advokatfirma Lindh Stabell Horten, Stockholm, 1998—. Avocations: current affairs, tennis, skiing, sailing, travel. Communications, General corporate, Mergers and acquisitions. Office: Lindh Stabell Horten PO Box 7315 Stockholm 112 20 Sweden Fax: 46 8 796 82 23. E-mail: anders.malmstrom@isnlaw.se

MALONE, DANIEL ROBERT, lawyer; b. El Paso, Tex., Feb. 18, 1960; s. Orba Lee and Margaret Ann (Pounds) M. BBA, Baylor U., 1983, JD, 1986. Bar: Tex. 1986, U.S. Dist. Ct. (we. dist.) Tex. 1988, U.S. Ct. Appeals (5th cir.) 1989. Ptnr., shareholder Malone Law Firm, P.C., El Paso, 1997—. Mem. Baylor Devel. Coun., 1996—. Fellow Tex. Bar Found. (trustee 1993-94); mem. State Bar Tex. (bd. dirs., exec. com. 1992-95), Tex. Young Lawyers Assn. (pres. 1993-94), El Paso Young Lawyers Assn. (pres. 1991-92), El Paso Bar Assn. (bd. dirs. 1999—), Baylor Law Alumni (bd. dirs. 1996-99. Federal civil litigation, State civil litigation, Labor. Home: 712 Wellesley Rd El Paso TX 79902-2422 Office: Malone Law Firm 300 E Main Dr Ste 1100 El Paso TX 79901-1356 E-mail: dmalone@malone-pc.com

MALONE, DAVID ROY, state legislator, university administrator; b. Beebe, Ark., Nov. 4, 1943; s. James Roy and Ila Mae (Griffin) M.; m. Judith Kaye Huff, June 20, 1965 (div. Feb. 1990); 1 child, Michael David. BSBA, U. Ark., 1965, JD, 1969, MBA, 1982. Bar: Ark. 1969, U.S. Dist. Ct. (we. dist.) Ark. 1969, U.S. Tax Ct. 1972, U.S. Ct. Appeals (8th cir.) 1972, U.S. Supreme Ct. 1972. Pvt. practice, Fayetteville, Ark., 1969-72; atty. City of Fayetteville, 1969-72; asst. prof. bus. U. Ark., Fayetteville, 1972-76, asst. dean law, 1976-91; mem. Ark. Ho. of Reps., 1980-84, Ark. Senate, 1984—; exec. dir. U. Ark. Found., 1991—. Chair Senate edn. com., co-chair legis. coun., 1999-2000; bd. dirs. Bank of Elkins, 1976-98, S.W. Edn. Devel. Lab., Austin, Tex., 1988-94; legal adv. coun. So. Regional Edn. Bd., Atlanta, 1991—. Contbr. articles to profl. jours.; bd. dirs. Ark. Law Rev., 1978-92; contbg. author U. Ark. Press, 1989. Mayor City of Fayetteville, 1979-80; mem. Jud. Article Task Force, Little Rock, 1989-91; chair Motor Voter task force, 1994-95; bd. dirs. Music Festival Ark., 1989-91, Washington County Hist. Soc., 1993-96; bd. dirs. Walton Arts Ctr. Found., 1994-2000, chmn., 1994-98; chmn. bd. dirs. Washington County Law Libr., 1970-84; chmn. Ark. Tuition Trust Authority, 1997-99. Recipient Svc. award Ark. Mcpl. League, 1980, Disting. Service award U. Ark., 1988, Lucas Svc. award, Ark. Alumni Assn., 1998. Mem. Ark. Bar Assn. (ho. of dels. 1977-81, award of merit 1980, exec. 1981-82, Outstanding Lawyer-Citizen award 1990), Washington County Bar Assn., Ark. Inst. Continuing Legal Edn. (bd. dirs. 1979-88), Fayetteville C. of C. (bd. dirs. 1984-99), Ark. Genealogy Soc. (bd. dirs. 1990-99). Democrat. Methodist. Avocations: genealogy, stamp collecting. Home: 2848 Club Oak Dr Fayetteville AR 72701-9168 Office: PO Box 1048 Fayetteville AR 72702-1048

MALONE, ERNEST ROLAND, JR. lawyer; b. New Orleans, Nov. 26, 1947; s. Ernest Roland and Geraldine (Stack) M.; m. Mary Harper, June 26, 1971; children: Meredith Harper, Eric Gallatin, R. Chandler. B.S., La. State U., 1970; J.D., Tulane U., 1975. Bar: La. 1975, U.S. Supreme Ct. 1978, U.S. Dist. Ct. (ea. dist.) La. 1975, U.S. Ct. Appeals (5th cir.) 1975, U.S. Dist. Ct. (we. dist.) La. 1976, U.S. Ct. Appeals (6th cir.) 1980, U.S. Ct. Appeals (11th cir.) 1983. Dir., Kullman Firm, New Orleans, 1975— . Contbg. editor: The Developing Labor Law, 1980—. Mem. Preservation Resource Ctr., New Orleans 1980-87, People Assoc. With Children's Hosp., New Orleans, 1982—, Met. Area Com., New Orleans, 1983-87; past chmn. bd. trustees Trinity Episcopal Sch.; past bd. advisors Jr. League of New Orleans. Served to 1st lt. U.S. Army, 1970-72; Vietnam. Decorated Bronze Star. Mem. La. State Bar Assn. (labor law sect. 1980—), ABA (labor and employment law sect. 1976—, litigation sect.), Fed. Bar Assn. (1976-85), New Orleans Bar Assn. Environmental, Labor, Pension, profit-sharing, and employee benefits. Home: 1024 Nashville Ave New Orleans LA 70115-4324 Office: Kullman Firm PO Box 60118 New Orleans LA 70160-0118

MALONE, GAYLE, lawyer, consultant; b. Trenton, Tenn., Sept. 3, 1916; s. Robert Duvall and Sadie Lou (Ingran) M. Mary Beasley, June 22, 1944; children— Gayle, Jr., Cecilia, Robert, Patrick, Christopher. Student George Washington U., 1935-36; B. Law Catholic U. Am., 1940, J.D., 1967; postgrad. U. Miss., 1953-54. Bar: Tenn. 1940, U.S. Supreme Ct. 1957, U.S. Ct. Appeals (6th cir.) 1966. Atty. U.S. Army, Southeast U.S., 1943-46; sole practice, Trenton, 1946-67; mem. Legislature State of Tenn., 1967-71; judge 9th Chancery Div. of Tenn., 1971-73; ptnr. Malone, Holmes & Gossum, Trenton, 1973— ; cons. Brown Shoe Co., St. Louis, 1954-67, Gibson County, Trenton, 1960— , Citizens State Bank, Trenton, 1965— . Bd. dirs. West Tenn. council Boy Scouts Am., 1970. Served as staff sgt. U.S. Army, 1940-42, World War II. Recipient Human Relations award NAACP, 1970, Commitment and Service to Edn. award Trenton Sch. Dist., 1975, 76; named hon. citizen Gibson County, 1978. Mem. Am. Judicature Assn., Assn. Trial Lawyers Am., Tenn. Trial Lawyers Assn., Tenn. Bar Assn. Democrat. Baptist. State civil litigation, Probate, Public utilities. Home: 607 S Lexington St Trenton TN 38382-2138

MALONE, SUE URWYLER, bar association executive; b. Portland, Oreg., Feb. 26, 1940; d. Fred and Frieda (Wyttenberg) U.; m. John S. Malone (div.); 1 child, Margaret Elizabeth. BS, Portland State U., 1962. Asst. exec. sec. Bar Assn. San Francisco, 1963-68, exec. sec. 1968-73; exec. dir. Calif. Judges Assn., San Francisco, 1975-83; exec. dir. Boston Bar Assn., 1983—. Pres. Scott Valley Homeowners Assn., Mill Valley,

Calif., 1981-83. Mem. Nat. Assn. Bar Execs. (exec. com. 1984-86, chair govtl. relations sect. 1982-84, treas. 1987-88, sec. 1988-89), Am. Soc. Assn. Execs. (mem. western council 1981-83), ABA, New Eng. Soc. Assn. Execs., Union (Boston) Club. Office: Boston Bar Assn 16 Beacon St Boston MA 02108-3774

MALONE, WILLIAM GRADY, retired lawyer; b. Minden, La., Feb. 19, 1915; s. William Gordon and Minnie Lucie (Hortman) M.; m. Marion Rowe Whitfield, Sept. 26, 1943; children: William Grady, Gordon Whitfield, Marion Elizabeth, Helen Ann, Margaret Catherine. BS, La. State U., 1941; JD, George Washington U., 1952. Bar: Va. 1952, U.S. Supreme Ct 1971. Statis. analyst Dept. Agr., Baton Rouge, 1941; investigator VA, Washington, 1946-59, legal officer, dep., gen. counsel, asst. gen. counsel, 1959-79; pvt. practice law Arlington, Va., 1979-97. Editor: Fed. Bar News, 1972-73. Pres. Aurora Hills Civic Assn., 1948-49; spl. asst. to treas. Com. of 100, 1979-81, chmn., 1982-83; pres. Children's Theater, 1968-69; trustee St. George's Episc. Ch., 1979— ; chmn. Arlington County Fair Assn., 1979-83. Lt. col. AUS, 1941-46, ETO. Decorated Legion of Merit; recipient Disting. Svc. award, 1979, 3 Superior Performance awards, 1952-72, Outstanding Alumni award George Washington Law Sch., 1978 Mem. Fed. Bar Assn. (pres. D.C. chpt. 1970-71, nat. pres. 1978-79), Va. Bar Assn., Arlington County Bar Assn., Nat. Lawyers Club (dir.), Arlington Host Lions, Ft. Myer Officers Club. Family and matrimonial, Personal injury, Probate. Home: 224 N Jackson St Arlington VA 22201-1253 E-mail: wgmelone@juno.com

MALONEY, MARYNELL, lawyer; b. Hutchinson, Kans., Jan. 14, 1955; d. Robert Edgar and Marian Ellen (Benson) Baker; m. Michael D. Maloney, Nov. 30, 1977; children: Michelle M., Erica O., Dennis Jr. BA, Oberlin Coll., 1975; MA, Trinity U., San Antonio, 1978; JD, St. Mary's U., San Antonio, 1980. Cert. by Tex. bd. of legal specialization. Assoc. Law Offices Pat Maloney, P.C., San Antonio, 1981-82; ptnr., owner Maloney & Maloney, 1982—. Bd. dirs. San Antonio Internat. Keyboard Competition, 1988-90; bd. govs. St. Peters/St. Joseph's Children's Home, San Antonio, 1989-92. Mem. ACLU (bd. dirs. 1990—, v.p. 1995-96, Tex. chpt. 1992—, SACLU 1990—), Am. Trial Lawyers Assn., State Bar Tex., Tex. Trial Lawyers Assn. (assoc. bd. dirs. 1989-90, bd. dirs. 1991—, chair coun. local leadership 1990-92, cert. personal injury trial law), San Antonio Bar Assn., San Antonio Trial Lawyers Assn. (pres. 1991-92). Democrat. Avocations: reading, writing, film. Civil rights, State civil litigation, Personal injury. Office: Maloney & Maloney PC 2000 Milam 115 E Travis San Antonio TX 78205

MALONEY, PAT, SR. lawyer; b. Dallas, Aug. 9, 1924; s. James Edward and Flora Agnes (Kessler) M.; m. Olive Boger, May 20, 1950; children: Patricia, Pat Jr., Michael, Janice, Tim. BJ, U. Tex., 1948, LLB, 1950. Bar: Tex. 1950, U.S. Dist. Ct. (we. dist.) Tex. 1955, U.S. Supreme Ct. 1951; cert. civil law and personal injury trial law, Tex. Bd. Legal Specialization, civil trial advocacy Nat. Bd. Trial Advocacy. 1st asst. trial chief Dist. Atty.'s Office, San Antonio, 1950-53; pvt. practice Law Offices of Pat Maloney P.C., 1953—. Moderator, founder annual seminar Anatomy of a Lawsuit, St. Mary's U., San Antonio; frequent lectr. throughout U.S. in areas of product liability and personal injury law. Author: Winning the Million Dollar Law Suit, 1980; co-author: Trials and Deliberations: Inside the Jury Room, 1992. With USMC, 1942-45, PTO. Recipient Warhorse award So. Trial Lawyers Assn., 1992. Fellow Law Sci. Acad. Am., Am. Bd. Trial Advocates (pres. inner circle of trial advocates) mem. ATLA, Internat. Soc. Barristers, Internat. Acad. Trial Lawyers, San Antonio Trial Lawyers Assn. (co-founder, pres. 1967, 72, bd. dirs. 1967-73,) San Antonio Bar Assn., State Bar of Tex., Tex. Trial Lawyers Assn. (director emeritus) Democrat. Roman Catholic. Achievements include 1977 personal injury verdict awarding his client $26,510,800.00. At that time the largest personal injury verdict in the history of the U.S. He has obtained verdicts and settlements in excess of a million dollars more than fifty times. General civil litigation, Oil, gas, and mineral, Personal injury. Office: 239 E Commerce St San Antonio TX 78205-2931

MALONEY, PATRICK RAYMOND, retired judge; b. Tacoma, Feb. 8, 1928; s. Thomas Emmett and Celia Margaret (Joyce) M.; m. Mary Anne Christnacht, July 2, 1955; children: Martin, Kathleen, John, Michael, James. BSS, Seattle U., 1951; JD, U. San Francisco, 1954. Bar: Calif. 1955, U.S. Dist. Ct. (no. dist.) Calif. 1955, U.S. Dist. Ct. (no. dist.) Tex. 1979, U.S. Ct. Appeals (9th cir.) 1955. Assoc. Lyons & Reisch, South San Francisco, Calif., 1955-57; claims atty. Indsl. Imdemnity Co., San Francisco, 1957-61; sr. counsel State Compensation Ins. Fund, Sacramento, 1961-63; referee, referee in charge Calif. Workments Compensation Appeal Bd., Bakersfield, 1963-72; adminstrv. law judge HHS, San Jose, Calif., 1972-96; ret., 1996. Night law faculty Bakersfield Adult Sch., Calif., 1966-71. Pres. Santa Clara St. Vincent DePaul Assn., San Jose, 1979-81, Peninsula Toastmasters, San Mateo, Calif., 1959. Sgt. U.S. Army, 1950-52. Mem. ABA (adminstrv. law sect. 1963-2000, jud. adminstrv. divsn. 1976-96), Serra Club (pres. 1970-71), K.C. Republican. Roman Catholic. Home: 2244 Glenkirk Ct San Jose CA 95124-1220

MALONEY, ROBERT E., JR. lawyer; b. San Francisco, Sept. 17, 1942; s. Robert E. and Mara A. (Murphy) M.; children: Michael, Sarah, Paul. BA magna cum laude, U. Portland, 1964; JD summa cum laude, Willamette U., Salem, Oreg., 1967. Bar: Oreg., Wash., U.S. Dist. Ct. Oreg., U.S. Dist. Ct. (we. dist.) Wash., U.S. Dist. Ct. (ea. dist.) Wash., U.S. Ct. Appeals (9th cir.). Ptnr. Lane Powell Spears Lubersky, LLP, Portland, 1967—. Bd. dirs., sec. Norm Thompson Outfitters, Inc., Portland; chmn. bd. visitors Willamette U. Law Sch., 1993-95, bd. dirs. emeritus, 1998—; past chair, mem. exec. com. Portland Trial Dept.; lawyers del. 9th Cir. Jud. Conf., 1995-97; pres. adv. coun. U. Portland, 2001—. Bd. dirs., Oreg. chpt. Multiple Sclerosis Soc.; judge pro tem Multnomah County Cir. Ct., 1994-99; bd. dirs. Oreg. Lawyers Against Hunger, 1997-99. Mem. ABA (co-chair products liability com., trial practice com. 1990-94), Nat. Assn. R.R. Trial Counsel, Fedn. Ins. Corp. Counsel, Oreg. Assn. Def. Counsel (bd. dirs. 1987-94, sec. 1991-92, v.p. 1993-94, pres. 1994), Fed. Bar Assn. (exec. com. Oreg. divsn. 1988-96, pres. 1994-95), Multnomah Athletic Club. Republican. Roman Catholic. General civil litigation, Condemnation, Product liability. Office: Lane Powell Spears Lubersky LLP 601 SW Second Ave Ste 2100 Portland OR 97204-3158 Fax: 503-778-2200

MALONEYHUSS, MARY M. lawyer; b. Nov. 3, 1960; BS in Chemistry, U. Rochester, 1982; MS in Chemistry, U. Pitts., 1984; JD, William Mitchell Coll. Law, 1990. Law clk. U.S. Dist. Ct., Wilmington, Del., 1990-91; assoc. Skadden, Arps, Slate, Meagher & Flom, 1991-93, Zeneca Inc., Wilmington, 1994-97; ptnr. Bouchard, Margules, Friedlander & MaloneyHuss, 1998-2000, Wolf Block Schorr & Solis-Cohen LLP, Wilmington, 2000—. Contbr. article to profl. jours. Mem. Del. Natural Areas Adv. Coun. Mem. ABA, ACS, Del. State Bar Assn. Office: Wolf Block Schorr & Solis-Cohen 920 King St Ste 300 Wilmington DE 19801-3300 E-mail: mmaloneyhuss@wolfblock.com

MALOOF, FARAHE PAUL, lawyer; b. Boston, Feb. 10, 1950; s. Farahe and Emily Suzanna (Puchy) M.; divorced; children: Alexandre F., Melissa F. BS, Georgetown U., 1975, JD, 1978. Bar: D.C. 1978, Va. 1981, Md. 1990. Assoc. Corcoran & Rowe, Washington, 1978-82; ptnr. Berliner & Maloney, 1982-84; internat. legal counsel Advocacia Oliveira Ribeiro, Sao Paulo, Brazil, 1984-85; sole practice Washington, 1985-86; prin. Maloof & Assocs., 1986-97; of counsel Haas & Anderson, P.C., McLean, Va., 1997-99; mem. Brinafield Hartnett Maloof & Assocs., P.C., Alexandria, 2000—. Lectr. Am. U., Washington, 1984-85, Internat. Law Inst., Washington, 1986-87. Active Reagan-Bush campaign, Washington, 1984, Frank Wolf re-election campaign, Arlington, Va., 1986, Bush-Quayle campaign, Washington, 1988. Served to cpl. USMC, 1968-70, Vietnam. Mem. ABA, Va. Bar Assn., D.C. Bar Assn. (litigation and corps. sects.), Fed. Bar Assn. (immigration law sect.), Georgetown U. Alumni Assn. (co-chmn. 1983-84). Republican. Roman Catholic. Avocations: tennis, water skiing. General corporate, Immigration, naturalization, and customs, Real property. Home: 1506 Dewberry Ct Mc Lean VA 22101-5629 Office: Brinafield Hartnett Et Al 526 King St Ste 423 Alexandria VA 22314-3143 E-mail: FPMaloof@aol.com

MALOON, JERRY L. trial lawyer, physician, medicolegal consultant; b. Union City, Ind., June 23, 1938; s. Charles Elias and Bertha Lucille (Creviston) M.; children: Jeffrey Lee, Jerry Lee II. BS, Ohio State U., 1960, MD, 1964; JD, Capital U. Law Sch., 1974. Intern Santa Monica (Calif.) Hosp., 1964-65; tng. psychiatry Ctrl. Ohio Psychiat. HOsp., 1969, Menninger Clinic, Topeka, 1970; clin. dir. Orient (Ohio) Devel. Ctr., 1967-69, med. dir., 1971-83; assoc. med. dir. Western Electric, Inc., Columbus, 1969-71; cons. State Med. Bd. Ohio, 1974-80; pvt. practice law Columbus, 1978—; pres. Jerry L. Maloon Co., L.P.A., 1981—. Medicolegal cons., 1972—; pres. Maloon, Maloon & Barclay Co., L.P.A., 1990-95; guest lectr. law and medicine Orient Devel. Ctr. and Columbus Devel. Ctr., 1969-71; dep. coroner Franklin County (Ohio), 1978-84. Dean's coun. Capital U. Law Sch. Capt. M.C., AUS, 1965-67. Fellow Am. Coll. Legal Medicine, Columbus Bar Found.; mem. AMA, ABA, ATLA, Ohio Bar Assn., Columbus Bar Assn., Ohio Trial Lawyers Assn., Columbus Trial Lawyers Assn., Ohio State U. Alumni Assn., U.S. Trotting Assn., Am. Profl. Practice Assn., Ohio State U. Pres.'s Buckeye Club. Health, Personal injury, Professional liability. Home: 2140 Cambridge Blvd Upper Arlington OH 43221-4104 Office: 9155 Moors Pl North Dublin OH 43017 Office Fax: 614-798-8747

MALORZO, THOMAS VINCENT, lawyer; b. Rome, Jan. 10, 1947; s. Vincent T. and Helen Adeline (Grande) M.; m. Catherine Marie Healy, Dec. 28, 1968; children: Amy, Craig, Mary, Thomas Jr. BA, Walsh U., Canton, Ohio, 1969; JD, Cleve. State U., 1979. Bar: Ohio 1979, U.S. Dist. Ct. (no. dist.) Ohio 1980, U.S. Patent Office 1980, Tex. 1981, U.S. Dist. Ct. (no. dist.) Tex. 1981, U.S. Ct. Appeals (7th cir.) 1994, U.S. Dist. Ct. (ea. dist.) Tex., 1998, U.S. Dist. Ct. (so. dist.) Tex., 2000. Environ. regulations analyst Diamond Shamrock Corp., Dallas, 1979-81; ind. counsel, agt. Southwestern Life Ins. Co., 1981-83; staff atty. NCH Corp., Irving, Tex., 1983-89; gen. counsel Wormald US, Inc., Dallas, 1989-90; patent atty. Otis Engring. Corp., Carrollton, Tex., 1990-93; pvt. practice Addison, 1993-95; ptnr. Falk, Vestal & Fish LLP, 1995; pvt. practice Dallas, 1996-97; of counsel Bennett & Weston P.C., 1997—. Asst. prof. law Dallas/Ft. Worth Sch. Law, Irving, Tex., 1990-92. Dist. com. Circle 10 Boy Scouts Am., Dallas, 1985—; first aid team ARC, Cleve., 1972-80. Recipient Dist. Award of Merit, Boy Scouts Am., 1990, Silver Beaver award Boy Scouts Am., 1997. Mem. State Bar Tex. (chmn. trademark com. intellectual property sect. 1989). General civil litigation, General corporate, Intellectual property. Office: Bennett, Weston & LaJone PC 1750 Valley View Ln Ste 120 Dallas TX 75234 E-mail: patents@prodigy.net

MALT, RONALD BRADFORD, lawyer; b. Boston, Aug. 1, 1954; s. Ronald A. and Geraldine (Sutton) M.; m. Sharon Lynn Harford, Feb. 14, 1981; 2 children. AB, Harvard U., 1976, JD, 1979. Bar: Mass. 1979. Assoc. Ropes & Gray, Boston, 1979-86, ptnr., 1987—, mem. policy com., 1993—; dir. Fenway Ptnrs., Inc., N.Y.C., 1999—. Asst. treas. Butler Capital Corp., N.Y.C., 1983—; sec. to adv. bd. Mezzanine Lending Assocs., N.Y.C., 1983—; mem. policy com. Ropes & Gray, Boston, 1993—. Mem. corp. Mass. Gen. Hosp., Boston, 1989—; trustee Butler Found., 1989—, Black River Environ. Improvement Assn., Inc., 1991—. Mem. Republican. Episcopalian. Finance, Mergers and acquisitions. Office: Ropes & Gray One International Pl Boston MA 02110 E-mail: bmalt@ropesgray.com

MAMAT, FRANK TRUSTICK, lawyer; b. Syracuse, N.Y., Sept. 4, 1949; s. Harvey Sanford and Annette (Trustick) M.; m. Kathy Lou Winters, June 23, 1975; children: Jonathan Adam, Steven Kenneth. BA, U. Rochester, 1971; JD, Syracuse U., 1974. Bar: D.C. 1976, U.S. Ct. Appeals (D.C. cir.) 1976, Fla. 1977, U.S. Supreme Ct. 1979, US. Dist. Ct. (ea. dist.) 1983, U.S. Ct. Appeals (6th cir.) 1983, Mich. 1984, U.S. Dist. Ct. (no. dist.) Ind. 1984. Atty. NLRB, Washington, 1975-79; assoc. Proskauer, Rose, Goetz & Mendelsohn, Washington, N.Y.C. and L.A., 1979-83, Fishman Group, Bloomfield Hills, Mich., 1983-85, ptnr., 1985-87; sr. ptnr. Honigman, Miller, Schwartz and Cohn, 1987-94; pres., CEO Morgan Daniels Co., Inc., West Bloomfield, Mich., 1994—; ptnr. Clark Klein & Beaumont, P.L.C., Detroit, 1995-96, Clark Hill, P.L.C., Detroit, 1996—, mem. exec. com., 1999—. Bd. dirs. Mich. Food and Beverage Assn., Air Conditioning Contractors of Am., Air Conditioning Contractors of Mich., Associated Builders and Contractors, Am. Subcontractors Assn., Mich. Mfrs. Assn. Labor Counsel. Gen. counsel Rep. Com. of Oakland County, 1986—; chmn. Constrn. Code Commn. Mich., 1993—; bd. dirs. 300 Club, Mich., 1984-90; pres. 400 Club, 1990-93, chmn., 1993—; mem. Associated Gen. Contractors Labor Lawyers Coun.; mem. Rep. Nat. Com. Nat. Rep. Senatorial Com., Presdl. Task Force, Rep. Labor Coun., Washington; city dir. West Bloomfield, 1985-87; pres. West Bloomfield Rep. CLub, 1985-87; fin. com. Rep. Com. of Oakland County, 1984-93; pres. Oakland County Lincoln Rep. Club, 1989-90; bd. dirs. camping svcs. and human resources com. YMCA, 1989-93, Anti-Defamation League, 1989—; vice chmn. Lawyers for Reagan-Bush, 1984; v.p. Fruehauf Farms, West Bloomfield, Mich., 1985-88; mem. staff Exec. Office of Pres. of U.S. Inquiries/Comments, Washington, 1981-83; exec. v.p., gen. counsel Am. Coun. Competitive Consensus. Fellow Coll. Labor and Employment Attys.; mem. ABA, FBA, Mich. Bar Assn., Fla. Bar Assn. (labor com. 1977—), Rep. Nat. Lawyers Assn., Mich. Bus. and Profl. Assn., Am. Acad. Constrn. and Labor Attys. (exec. dir. 1998—), Am. Subcontractors Assn. (Southeastern Mich., bd. dirs.), Founders Soc. Detroit Bar Assn., Oakland County Bar Assn., B'nai B'rith (v.p. 1982-83, trustee 1987-88, bd. dirs. Detroit Barristers unit 1983-91, pres. 1985-87), Oakpointe Country Club, Detroit Soc. Clubs, Skyline Club, Fairlane Club, Detroit Athletic Club, Renaissance Club, Econ. Club Detroit. Administrative and regulatory, General civil litigation, Labor. Office: Clark Hill PLC 500 Woodward Ave Ste 3500 Detroit MI 48226-3435 also: Morgan Daniels Co Inc 5484 Crispin Way Rd West Bloomfield MI 48323-3402 E-mail: fmamat@aol.com, fmamat@clarkhill.com

MAMURIC, JOSE ROBERTO LOTA, lawyer; b. Manila, Philippines, Feb. 20, 1966; s. Amado Calangan and Normita Lota M.; m. Jocelyn Bautista, Aug. 28, 1993; children: Carlos Miguel, Amanda Jessica, Antonio Luis, Jose Antonio. BBA, Loyola Coll., Balt., 1988; JD, Ateneo de Manila Coll. Law, Philippines, 1992. Jr. assoc. Ponce Enrile Cayetano Reyes & Manalastas, Manila, Philippines, 1997-2000, jr. ptnr. Philippines, 2001—. Corp. sec. Air Liquick Philipplines, Inc., Manila, 1999—; asst. corp. sec. Sun Microsystems Philippines, Inc., Manila, 1999—. Contracts commercial, General corporate, Mergers and acquisitions. Office: Ponce Enrile Reyes Manalast 3/F Vernida IV Bldg Leviste Makati City The Philippines Fax: (632) 8187355. E-mail: jobet@pecabad.com

MANARD, ROBERT LYNN, III, lawyer; b. New Orleans, Sept. 18, 1947; s. Robert Lynn Jr. and Marguerite Manard; m. Brenda Bennett Bohrer, July 7, 1973; children: Robbie, Wendy, Mary Claire. BS, Tulane U., 1969, JD, 1972. Bar: La. 1972, U.S. Dist. Ct. 1972, U.S. Ct. Appeals (5th cir.) La. 1972. Law clk. to Hon. Patrick Shot 4th Cir. Ct. of Appeals, New Orleans, 1972-74; instr. Tulane U. Law Sch., 1973-75; assoc. Hammett, Leake & Hammett, 1974-76; sr. ptnr. Manard & Schoenberger, 1976-81, Manard, McKearn & Ryan, New Orleans, 1981-88, Manard & Minge, New Orleans, 1988-95, Manard & Buck, New Orleans, 1995—. Panelist legal clk. seminar, La. Ct. Appeals, 1975; adv. com. Legal Access, Inc., New Orleans, 1986. Author: (booklet) Proper Techniques in Interviewing Clients, 1974. Bd. dirs. Tulane Legal Asst. Program, New Orleans, 1974-76; mem . deans coun. Tulane U. Law Sch; instr. ARC, Kenner, La., 1966-70. Mem. ATLA, La. Bar Assn., La. Trial Lawyers Assn. (bd. govs.). Democrat. Roman Catholic. Avocations: pole vaulting, running, tennis, golf. Federal civil litigation, State civil litigation, Personal injury. Home: 23 Waverly Pl Metairie LA 70003-2553 Office: 1100 Poydras St Ste 2610 New Orleans LA 70163-2602 E-mail: rocback@aol.com

MANCE, JACK MICHAEL, retired lawyer, insurance company executive; b. Pitts., Oct. 27, 1927; s. Jacob M. and Lucille (Harlovic) M.; m. Leda Mary Dallas, Jan. 25, 1955; children: Lauren Ann Mance Lynd, Craig Michael, Jacqueline Marie Mance Rahm. BA, U. Pitts., 1950; JD, Dickinson Law Sch., 1956. Bar: Pa. 1975, U.S. Dist. Ct. (we. dist.) Pa. 1975. Claims rep. Hardware Muts., Pitts., 1956-57; claim examiner Allstate Ins. Co., 1957-62; claim supr. Ohio Casualty Ins. Corp., Hamilton, 1962-67, claim supr., legal advisor Pitts., 1967-93. Cons. on ins. SErved with U.S. Army, 1946-47, 51-53, Korea. General practice, Insurance. Home: 207 New England Pl Sewickley PA 15143-1029

MANCINO, DOUGLAS MICHAEL, lawyer; b. May 8, 1949; s. Paul and Adele (Brazaitis) M.; m. Carol Keith, June 16, 1973. BA, Kent State U., 1971; JD, Ohio State U., 1974. Bar: Ohio 1974, U.S. Tax Ct. 1977, Calif. 1981, D.C. 1981. Assoc. Baker & Hostetler, Cleve., 1974-80; ptnr. Memel & Ellsworth, L.A., 1980-87, McDermott, Will & Emery, L.A., 1987—. Bd. dirs. Health Net of Calif. Inc. Author: Taxation of Hospitals and Health Care Organizations, 2000, (with others) Hospital Survival Guide, 1984, Navigating the Federal Physician Self-Referral Law, 1998; (with F. Hill) Taxation of Exempt Organizations, 2001; co-author quar. tax column Am. Hosp. Assn. publ. Health Law Vigil, (with L. Burns) Joint Ventures Between Hosps. and Physicians, 1987; contbr. articles to profl. jours. Chmn. bd. dirs. The Children's Burn Found. Mem. ABA (tax, bus., real property, probate and trust sects., chair exempt orgns. com. 1995-97, coun. dir. 1999—), Calif. State Bar Assn. (tax, bus. law sects.), Ohio Bar Assn., Calif. State Bar, D.C. Bar Assn., Am. Health Lawyers Assn. (bd. dirs. 1986-95, pres. 1993-94), Calif. Soc. for Healthcare Attys., Bel Air Country Club, The Regency Club, Calif. Yacht Club. Health, Corporate taxation. Office: McDermott Will & Emery 2049 Century Park E Fl 34 Los Angeles CA 90067-3101 E-mail: dmancino@mwe.com

MANDEL, JOSEPH DAVID, academic administrator, lawyer; b. N.Y.C., Mar. 26, 1940; s. Max and Charlotte Lee (Goodman) M.; m. Jean Carol Westerman, Aug. 18, 1963; children: Jonathan Scott, Eric David. AB, Dartmouth Coll., 1960, MBA with distinction, 1961; JD, Yale U., 1964. Bar: Calif. 1965. Law clk. U.S. Ct. Appeals, 9th cir., L.A., 1964-65; lectr. law U. So. Calif. Law Ctr., 1965-68; assoc. atty. Tuttle & Taylor, 1965-69, mem., 1970-82, 90-91, of counsel, 1984-90; vice chancellor UCLA, 1991—, lectr. in law, 1993; v.p., gen. counsel, sec. Natomas Co., San Francisco, 1983. Mem. Calif. Legal Corps, 1993—; bd. dirs. LRN, The Legal Knowledge Co. Mem. bd. editors Yale Law Jour., 1962-64. Pres. Legal Aid Found., L.A., 1978-79; trustee Southwestern U. Sch. Law, 1982, UCLA Pub. Interest Law Found., 1981-82, L.A. County Bar Found., 1974-79, 82, Coro Found., 1989-92, UCLA Armand Hammer Mus. Art and Cultural Ctr., 1995—, Geffen Playhouse, Inc., 1995-98, Coro So. Calif. Ctr., 1985-92, bd. dirs. pub. coun., 1989-94, cmty. v.p., 1992-94; mem. L.A. Bd. Zoning Appeals, 1984-90, vice-chmn., 1985-86, 89-90, chmn., 1986-87; mem. L.A. City Charter Reform Commn., 1996-99; bd. dirs. Western Justice Ctr. Found., 1989—, v.p., 1992-95, 1st v.p., 1995-97, sr. v.p., 1997-99, pres., 1999—; bd. dirs. Harvard Water Polo Found., 1990-96; bd. advisors Pub. Svc. Challenge Nat. Assn. for Pub. Interest Law, 1990—; bd. govs. Inner City Law Ctr., 1991—; mem. Blue Ribbon Screening Com. to Select Insp. Gen., L.A. Police Commn., 1999; mem. bd. overseers Inst. for Civil Justice, RAND, 1999—. Recipient Maynard Toll award Legal Aid Found. of L.A., 1991, Shattuck-Price award L.A. County Bar Assn., 1993, West Coast Liberty award Lambda Legal Def. and Edn. Fund, 1994, Cmty. Achievement award Pub. Coun., 1996; named One of Calif.'s 100 Most Influential Attys. by Calif. Bus. Jour., 2000. Mem. State Bar Calif. (legal svcs. trust fund commn. 1985-87, chmn. 1985-86), Yale U. Law Sch. Assn. (exec. com. 1983-88, 90-96, v.p. 1986-88, chmn. planning com. 1990-92, pres. 1992-94, chmn. exec. com. 1994-96), mem. alumni Coun. Dartmouth Coll., 1992-95, Dartmouth Coll. Assn. Alumni (exec. com. 1997—), Order of Coif. Democrat. Jewish. Home: 15478 Longbow Dr Sherman Oaks CA 91403-4910 Office: UCLA Office Chancellor 2135 Murphy Hl Los Angeles CA 90095-1405 E-mail: jmandel@conet.ucla.edu

MANDEL, MARTIN LOUIS, lawyer; b. L.A., May 17, 1944; s. Maurice S. and Florence (Byer) M.; m. Duree Dunn, Oct. 16, 1982; 1 child, Max Andrew. BA, U. So. Calif., 1965, JD, 1968; LLM, George Washington U., 1971. Bar: Calif. 1969, U.S. Dist. Ct. (cen. dist.) Calif. 1972, U.S. Ct. Claims 1971, U.S. Tax Ct. 1971, U.S. Supreme Ct. 1972. With office of gen. csl. IRS, Washington, 1968-72; ptnr. Stephens, Jones, LaFever & Smith, L.A., 1972-77, Stephens, Martin & Mandel, 1977-79, Fields, Fehn, Feinstein & Mandel, 1979-83; sr. v.p., gen. counsel Investment Mortgage Internat., Inc., 1983-84; ptnr. Feinstein, Gourley & Mandel, 1984-85, Mandel & Handin, San Francisco, 1985—; gen. counsel L.A. Express Football Club, 1983-85. Instr. corps. U. West L.A., 19873-83. Mem. ABA, L.A. County Bar Assn., L.A. Athletic Club, Phi Delta Phi. General corporate, Entertainment. Office: 1510 Fashion Island Blvd San Mateo CA 94404-1596 E-mail: TMGTalent@aol.com, tmgtalent@msn.com

MANDEL, MAURICE, II, lawyer, educator, mediator; b. Hollywood, Calif. s. Maurice and Wynne Mandel. BSBA, U. So. Calif., 1971, MEd, 1972; JD, Western State U., 1979. Bar: Calif. 1980, U.S. Dist. Ct. (ctrl. dist.) Calif. 1982, U.S. Ct. Appeals (fed. and 9th cirs.) 1983, U.S. Dist. Ct. (we. dist.) Tenn. 1987, U.S. Dist. Ct. Ariz. 1990, U.S. Dist. Ct. (so. dist.) Calif. 1991, U.S. Supreme Ct. 1991, U.S. Ct. Appeals (5th cir.) 1995; cert. level I ski instr. PSIA Nat. Acad. 1998, child specialist 1999, settlement officer, USDC-CDCa. Tchr. Orange County (Calif.) Sch. Dist., 1972-82; pvt. practice law Newport Beach, Calif., 1982—; fed. settlement officer CDCA, 1998—. Instr. Coastline C.C., 1987-95, prof., 1995—, Coastline C.C. Acad. Senate, Coastline C.C. Parlimentarian 1996-99; prof. law Irvine (Calif.) U. Coll. of Law, 1994-98; instr. Orange County Bar Assn. Coll. of Trial Advocacy, 1994—; instr. Orange County Bar Assn. Mandatory Continuing Legal Edn., 1992—, Bear Mountain Calif. Ski Sch., 1996—, Ziet Maros, 1998—; FBA/OCC Mandatory Continuing Legal Edn. provider, 1994—, COURSE Vail Co. Alpine World Cup Finals, 1997, Alpine World Championships, 1999, World Cup, 1999, COURSE St. Anton am Arlberg, Alpine World Championships, 2001, COURSE Ladie's' Norams, Snowbasin, Utah, 2001. Counselor Troy Camp, 1969-72; chmn. Legal Edn. for Youth, 1984-86; active Ctr. Dance Alliance, Orange County, 1986-97; JOC racing dir. So. Cal, 1998-2000; mem. Friends Am. Ballet Theatre, Opera Pacific Guild, Opera Pacific Bohemians, Calypso Soc., World Wildlife Fund., L.A. County Mus. Art, Newport Beach Art Mus., Met. Mus. Art, Laguna Beach Mus. Art, Smithsonian Instn., Friend of Ballet Pacifica, Friends of Joffrey Ballet; assoc. U.S. Ski Team, 1975—; com. assoc. U.S. Olympics, 1988—; 100th Olympics vols., 1996; F.I.S. vol., 1997—, COURSE Alpine World Cup Finals, Vail, Colo., 1997, Alpine World Championships, 1999, 2001; mem. alumni and scholarship com. Beverly Hills H.S.; Opera Pacific Bohemians, Friends of Ballet Pacifica. Recipient cert. of appreciation U.S. Dist. Ct., L.A., 1985, U.S. Dist. Ct. Mediation award O.C., 2000, Thwarted Thwart award Newport Harbor C. of C., 1989, Tovarich award Kirov Ballet, 1989, 92, Perostroika award Moscow Classical Ballet, 1988-89, 94, Skrisivi Nogi award Bolshoi Ballet, 1990, Marinskii Dance award St. Petersburg, 1993; ABT Romeo & Juliet, 1996, Thwarted Thwart award Newport Harbor, 1996; Ziet Maros award Moscow Classical Ballet, 1998, 99, 2000, 2nd Place award JOC Slalom,

1998, 1st place award JOC Slalom, 2000, 2d place award Big Bear Instrs. Giant Slalom, 2000, 1st place award JOC Concourse, 2000, 14th pl. nat. standing JCNA Slalom, 1999. Mem. ABA, ATLA, Assn. Bus. Trial Lawyers, Federal Bar Assn., (founding pres. Orange Country chpt. 1986, nat. del. 1988-90, founder criminal indigent def. panel 1986, mem. numerous other coms., nat. chpt. activity award 1987, nat. membership award 1987, chpt. svc. award 1989, nat. regional membership chmn. 1990, spl. appointee nat. membership com. 1991), Calif. Bar Assn. (Pro Bono awards 1985-89), Pres.'s Coun. (founder 1996—), Orange County Bar Assn. (legal edn. for youth com. 1982-90, chmn, 1985, fed. practice com., sports com., mandatory fee arbitration com. 1985—, lawyer's referral svc. com. 1984-98, Merit award 1986), Orange County Bar Found. (trustee 1984-87), Women Lawyers of Orange County, U.S. Supreme Ct. Hist. Soc., 9th Jud. Cir. Hist. Soc., Am. Inns of Ct., Calif. Trial Lawyers Assn., Calif. Employee Lawyers Assn., Plaintiff Employee Lawyers Assn., Employees Rights Coun., Bar Leaders Coun. Dist. 8, Amicus Publico, U. So. Calif. Alumni Assn., Mensa, Cougar Club of Am., So. Calif. Cougar Club, San Diego Cougar Club, So. Calif. Jaguar Owners Assn. Club: Balboa Yacht. Avocations: skiing, yachting, tennis. Civil rights, Federal civil litigation, Constitutional. Home: PO Box 411 Newport Beach CA 92662 Office: Ste 360 881 Dover Dr Newport Beach CA 92663

MANDELKER, LAWRENCE ARTHUR, lawyer; b. N.Y.C., Dec. 2, 1943; s. Murray and Sally (Levine) M.; m. Carolyn Anne Bareish, Oct. 4, 1970; children: Daniel H., Benjamin E. B.A., Queens Coll., CUNY, 1964; J.D., NYU, 1968. Bar: N.Y. 1968, Pa. 1981, U.S. Dist. Ct. (so. and ea. dists.) N.Y. 1973, U.S. Dist. Ct. (ea. dist.) Wis. 1980, (no. dist.) N.Y., 1995, U.S. Ct. Appeals (2d cir.) 1979, U.S. Ct. Appeals (9th cir.) 1989. Law sec. N.Y.C. Civil Ct., 1970-71, N.Y. State Supreme Ct., 1972; mem. Kantor, Davidoff, Wolfe, Mandelker & Kass, P.C.; mem. com. character and fitness 9th Jud. Dist., Coun., N.Y. State Athletic Commn., 1995—. Bd. dirs. NYU Law Alumni Assocs. Mem. Lewisboro Bd. Assessment Rev., N.Y., 1979—, chmn., 1984—; chmn. Lewisboro Bd. Ethics. Served as staff sgt. USAR, 1968-74. Mem. Assn. Bar City N.Y. (chmn. spl. com. on election law). Federal civil litigation, State civil litigation, Legislative. Home: 206 Todd Rd Katonah NY 10536-2410 Office: Kantor Davidoff Wolfe Mandelker & Kass PC 51 E 42nd St New York NY 10017-5404

MANDELL, JOEL, lawyer; b. Hartford, Conn., July 1, 1939; s. Max Edward and Harriet (Shafer) M.; m. Ellen Solomon, Aug. 23, 1964; children: Peter, Ross, Jason. BA, U. Conn., 1961, JD, 1966. Bar: Conn. 1966, U.S. Dist. Ct. Conn. 1967, U.S. Supreme Ct. 1971. Ptnr. Rosenthal, Clayman & Mandell, Hartford, 1966-72; prin. Levy & Droney, Farmington & West Hartford, Conn., 1972—. Mem. adv. bd. First Am. Title Ins. Co., Hartford, 1984—. Bd. dirs. Farmington Valley Jewish Congregation, Simsbury, Conn., 1980-83; mem. State of Conn. Title Ins. Task Force, 1989-90; selectman Town of Simsbury, 1993—, dept. first selectman, 1999—; mem. Town of Simsbury Charter Revision Commn., 1990-92, Simsbury Housing Authority, 1992-93. Mem.: Conn. Bar Assn. (ho. of dels. 1983—86, real estate exec. com. 1978—2001, emeritus 2001—, chmn. 1995—97), New Eng. Land Title Assn. (panel mem. 1991, panel mem. 2000, bd dirs. 1996—, panel me. 2000—01), Conn. Assn. Real Estate Profls. (panel mem. 1991, real estate exch. panel moderator 1996, real estate exch. panel moderator 2000), Real Estate Exch., KP (chancellor comdr. 1981—82), Am. Legion Simsbury. Real property. Office: Levy & Droney PC 74 Batterson Park Rd Farmington CT 06032-2565 E-mail: joelmandell@home.com, jmandell@ldlaw.com

MANEKER, MORTON M. lawyer; b. N.Y.C., Nov. 14, 1932; s. Arthur and Estelle (Hochberg) M.; m. Roberta S. Wexler, 1985; children: Meryl Colle, Amy Jill, Marion Kenneth. A.B., Harvard U., 1954, LL.B., 1957. Bar: N.Y. State 1957. Assoc. Shearman & Sterling, N.Y.C., 1957-62; trial atty. antitrust div. Dept. Justice, 1962-63; ptnr. Proskauer Rose LLP, N.Y.C., 1963-94; ret., 1994. Trustee Beth Israel Hosp., N.Y.C., 1977—2001. Mem. Am. Law Inst., N.Y. State Bar Assn., Harmonie Club. Jewish. Home: 30 E 65th St New York NY 10021-7013 E-mail: maneker@aol.com

MANEY, MICHAEL MASON, lawyer; b. Taihoku, Japan, Aug. 13, 1936; s. Edward Strait and Helen M. M.; m. Suzanne Cochran, Oct. 22, 1960; 1 child, Michele. B.A., Yale U., 1956; M.A., Fletcher Sch. Law and Diplomacy, Tufts U., 1957; LL.B., U. Pa., 1964. Bar: N.Y. 1966, D.C. 1977. Case officer CIA, 1957-61; law clk. Justice John Harlan, Supreme Ct. U.S., Washington, 1964-65; asso. Sullivan & Cromwell, N.Y.C., 1965-70, ptnr., 1971-77, 81—, mng. ptnr. Washington, 1977-81. Law fellow Salzburg Seminar in Am. Studies, 1967; bd. overseers Fletcher Sch. Law and Diplomacy. Mem. bd. overseers, U. Pa. Law Sch. 1st lt. USAF, 1957-60. Mem. ABA, Am. Law Inst., Am. Coll. Trial Lawyers, N.Y. State Bar Assn., Union Club, Down Town Assn., Madison Beach Club, Madison Country Club, Met. Opera Club, New Haven Country Club. Contracts commercial, General corporate, Private international. Home: 1220 Park Ave New York NY 10128-1733 also: 48 Neptune Ave Madison CT 06443-3210 Office: Sullivan & Cromwell 125 Broad St New York NY 10004-2498 E-mail: maneym@sullcrom.com

MANG, DOUGLAS ARTHUR, lawyer; b. Little Falls, N.Y., Mar. 25, 1942; s. Willard D. and Mary L. (Murray) M.; m. Nora Ladeane Geren; 1 child, Brittany Nandeana. BS, Cornell U., 1964; LLB, Syracuse U., 1967. Bar: N.Y. 1971, Fla. 1971, U.S. Dist. Ct. (no. dist.) Fla. 1977, U.S. Ct. Appeals (5th and llth cirs.) 1981, U.S. Dist. Ct. (mid. dist.) Fla. 1982, U.S. Supreme Ct. 1988. Atty. Mut. Life Ins. Co., N.Y.C., 1971-73; asst. gen. counsel Am. Gen. Capital Mgmt., 1973-77; gen. counsel Fla. Dept. of Ins., Tallahassee, 1977-79; ptnr. Mang & Stowell PA, 1979-86, Mang Law Firm PA, Tallahassee, 1986—. Served to 1st lt. U.S. Army, 1968-70, Vietnam. Mem. Fla. Def. Lawyers Assn., Tiger Bay Club, Fla. Econs. Club, Rotary, Fedn. Regulatory Counsel (regional dir.). Methodist. Avocations: sailing, golf. Administrative and regulatory, Federal civil litigation, Insurance. Office: Mang Law Firm PA 660 E Jefferson St Tallahassee FL 32301-2582 E-mail: dmang@manglaw.com

MANGES, JILL D. lawyer, nurse; b. Knox, Ind., Nov. 8, 1971; d. Jack Laverne and Linda Marie Bell; m. Richard Eugene Manges, Aug. 29, 1998. BSN, Ind. U., South Bend, 1994; JD, Valparaiso U., 1998. Bar: Ind. 1998; RN, Ind. Student nurse extern Pulaski Meml. Hosp., Winamac, Ind., 1994; nurse Koala Hosp., Plymouth, 1995, Porter Meml. Hosp., Valparaiso, Ind., 1996-99; atty. Huelat & Gardner, Michigan City, Ind., 1998-99, Langer & Langer, Valparaiso, 1999-01, Ruman, Clements, Tobin & Holub, Hammond, Ind., 2001—. Mem. ABA, Ind. State Bar Assn., Porter County Bar Assn., Am. Assn. Nurse Attys. Democrat. Avocations: dancing, golf, basketball, walking, swimming. Home: 413 Fair St Valparaiso IN 46383-3664 Office: Ruman Clements Tobin & Holub 5261 Hohman Ave Hammond IN 46320

MANGIA, ANGELO JAMES, lawyer; b. Bklyn., Mar. 12, 1954; AB in Govt. cum laude, Georgetown U., 1975; JD, St. John's U., 1978. Bar: N.Y. 1979, U.S. Dist. Ct. (so. and ea. dists.) N.Y. 1979, U.S. Ct. Appeals (2d cir.) 1985. Asst. atty. Town of North Hempstead, N.Y., 1979-81; assoc. Ain, Libert & Weinstein, Garden City, 1981; atty. Town of North Hempstead, 1982; counsel senate com. on crime State of N.Y., 1983-85, counsel senate com. on banks, 1985-88; chief counsel to majority N.Y. State Senate, 1989-94; managing dir. Sandler, O'Neill & Ptnrs., L.P., N.Y., 1995-2001; exec. v.p. Std. Funding Corp., Woodbury, N.Y., 2001—. Mem. bd. editors N.Y. Law Jour., 1994-96. Recipient Outstanding Work in Field of Criminal Justice Legis. award N.Y. State Bar Assn., 1985, Disting. Svc. award Civil Trial Inst./St. John's Law Sch., 1987, Luther Gulick award for Outstanding Achievement in Pub. Svc. Long Island U., 1992; Toll fellow, 1991. Mem. ABA, Nassau County Bar Assn., Coun. of State Govts. (exec. com., intergovernmental affairs com., internat. task force, legal affairs task force, legis./exec. staff task force 1989-94), Nat. Conf. of State Legislatures. Office: 335 Crossways Park Dr Woodbury NY 11797

MANGINO, MATTHEW THOMAS, lawyer; b. New Castle, Pa., Oct. 3, 1962; s. Thomas Michael and Connie (Frigone) M.; m. Juliann Galmarini, Aug. 6, 1988. BA, Westminster Coll., 1985; JD, Duquesne U., 1988. Bar: Pa. U.S. Dist. Ct. (we. dist.) Pa., U.S. Ct. Appeals (3d cir.), U.S. Supreme Ct. Jud. clk. Hon. Francis X. Caiazza, New Castle, 1988-89; asst. pub. defender County of Lawrence, 1989; pvt. practice, 1990—; dist. atty. Lawrence County, 1998—. Chmn. New Castle Airport Authority, 1990-92; solicitor County of Lawrence, New Castle, 1992-96; instr. Pa. State U., 1992—; legal cons. O.J. Simpson Trial, Sta. WBZY-AM, New Castle, 1995; bd. dirs. Allied Human Svcs.; seminar plan mem. on gang violence Pa. Bar Inst., 1996; guest lectr. Westminster Coll., Slippery Rock U.; participant White House Conf. on Sch. Safety, 1998. Prodr. TV program Gang Violence Curbing the Epidemic, 1996; columnist, New Castle News, 1989-90; prodr. (cable TV) Task Force Program; host TV program Lawrence County's Most Wanted; contbr. chpt. to book, article to profl. jours.; guest numerous TV news programs. Mem. campaign staff Dukakis for Pres., Pitts., 1988; del. Dem. Nat. Conv., Atlanta, 1988; com. mem. Lawrence County Econ. Devel. Corp.; sec. Lawrence County Bd. Assistance, New Castle; bd. dirs. Family Ctr. of Lawrence County, Lawrence County chpt. ARC, Workforce Investment Bd., Youth Coun.; mem. Leadership Lawrence County, 1997, Lawrence County Pride; trustee Western Pa. Youth Devel. Ctrs.; Dem. candidate for Congress, 2000; bd. dirs. Lawrence County Social Svcs.; adv. bd. Lawrence County Learning Ctr.; active Pa. Atty. Gen.'s Task Force on Elder Abuse. Mem. ABA (vice chmn. law and media com. 1996-97), Pa. Bar Assn. (state exec. bd. young lawyers divsn. 1994-97, jud. selection and reform com., co-chair spl. project on gang violence 1996-97), Pa. Dist. Atty.'s Assn., Lawrence County Bar Assn., Lawrence County C. of C. (bd. dirs. 1990), Wolves (bd. dirs., pres. 1996-97), Kiwanis. Roman Catholic. Avocations: golf, writing, reading. Criminal, General practice, Real property. Office: 2nd Fl 315 N Mercer St New Castle PA 16101-2222 E-mail: matthewmangino@aol.com

MANGLER, ROBERT JAMES, lawyer, judge; b. Chgo., Aug. 15, 1930; s. Robert H. and Agnes E. (Sugrue) M.; m. Geraldine M. Delich, May 2, 1959; children: Robert Jr., Paul, John, Barbara. BS, Loyola U., Chgo., 1952, MA, 1983; JD, Northwestern U., 1955. Bar: Ill. 1958, U.S. Dist. Ct. (no. dist.) Ill. 1959, U.S. Supreme Ct. 1976, U.S. Ct. Appeals (7th cir.) 1980. Author: (with others) Illinois Land Use Law, Illinois Municipal Law. Village atty., prosecutor Village of Wilmette, 1965-93; mcpl. prosecutor City of Evanston, 1963-65, adminstrv. law judge, 2000—; chmn. Ill. Traffic Ct. Conf., 1977—; pres. Ill. Inst. Local Govt. Law; mem. home rule attys. com. Ill. Mcpl. League. Mem. ABA (chmn. adv. com. traffic ct. program), Nat. Inst. Mcpl. Law Officers (past pres.), Ill. Bar Assn. (former chmn. traffic laws and ct. com.), Chgo. Bar Assn. (former chmn. traffic ct. seminar, former chmn. traffic laws com.), Caxton Club, Phi Alpha Delta. General practice, Municipal (including bonds).

MANGRUM, RICHARD COLLIN, law educator; b. Dec. 26, 1949; s. Lawrence E. and Ramona D. (Beckstead) M.; m. Barbara Isaac, Aug. 27, 1969 (dec. 1978); children: Charmian, Brett, Wells; m. Ann Walton, July 25, 1980; children: Christian, Rebekah. BA, Harvard U., 1972, SJD, 1983; JD, U. Utah, 1975; BCI, Oxford U., 1978. Bar: Utah 1975, U.S. Dist. Ct. Utah 1975, U.S. Ct. Appeals (10th cir.) 1975, Nebr. 1982, U.S. Dist. Ct. Nebr. 1982, U.S. Ct. Appeals (8th cir.) 1982, U.S. Supreme Ct. 1989. Assoc. Christensen, Gardiner, Jensen, Evans, Salt Lake City, 1975-77; asst. prof. Creighton U. Sch. Law, Omaha, 1979-82, assoc. prof., 1982-85, prof., 1985—. Vis. prof. U. Utah Coll. Law, summer 1985, 97, 2000; vis. scholar U. Edinburgh, Scotland, 1986; A.A. and Ethel Yossend prof. jurisprudence, 1999. Author: Zion in the Courts: A Legal History of the Church of Jesus Christ of the Latter-Day Saints, 1830-1900, 1988; contbr. articles to legal jours. Active Boy Scouts Am., local YMCA, youth sports. Recipient Book award Alpha Sigma Nu, 1989. Mem. Phi Beta Delta, Phi Delta Phi. Mem. Ch. of Jesus Christ of Latter-Day Saints. Home: 5619 S 173rd Ave Omaha NE 68135-2239 Office: Creighton Univ Sch Law 2500 California St Omaha NE 68131-1676

MANIATTY, PHILIP WARD, lawyer; b. Burlington, Vt., Apr. 3, 1952; s. Philip George and Mary Elizabeth (Ward) M.; m. Louise Mercurio, Oct. 27, 1996. BA, U. Vt., 1974; JD, U. Miami, 1977. Bar: Fla. 1977, D.C. 1978, U.S. Dist. Ct. (so. dist.) Fla. Asst. state atty. State Atty'.s Office, 11th cir., Miami, 1977—. Mem. adv. coun. Southeast Fla. Acad. Fire Sci., Miami, 1983-88; bd. dirs. Country Club of Miami Condominium Inc., Hialeah, Fla., 1985-87, pres., 1986-87. Mem. D.C. Bar Assn., Fla. Bar Assn. (chmn. criminal procedure rules com. 1986-87, exec. coun. 1983-94—, chair criminal law sect. 1992-93). Roman Catholic. Avocation: golf. Home: 8541 SW 179th St Miami FL 33157-6035 Office: 1350 NW 12th Ave Miami FL 33136-2102 E-mail: pmaniatty@yahoo.com

MANION, DANIEL ANTHONY, federal judge; b. South Bend, Ind., Feb. 1, 1942; s. Clarence E. and Virginia (O'Brien) M.; m. Ann Murphy, June 29, 1984. BA, U. Notre Dame, 1964; JD, Ind. U., 1973. Bar: Ind., U.S. Dist. Ct. (no. dist.) Ind., U.S. Dist. Ct. (so. dist.) Ind. Dep. atty. gen. State of Ind., 1973-74; from assoc. to ptnr. Doran, Manion, Boynton, Kamm & Esmont, South Bend, 1974-86; judge U.S. Ct. Appeals (7th cir.), 1986—. Mem. Ind. State Senate, Indpls., 1978-82. Office: US Ct Appeals US Courthouse & Federal Bldg 204 S Main St Rm 301 South Bend IN 46601-2122 Home: 20725 Riverlan Rd South Bend IN 46637-1029*

MANIRE, JAMES MCDONNELL, lawyer; b. Memphis, Feb. 22, 1918; s. Clarence Herbert and Elizabeth (McDonnell) M.; m. Nathalie Davant Latham, Nov. 21, 1951 (div. 1979); children: James McDonnell, Michael Latham, Nathalie Manire Willard; m. Nancy Whitman Colbert, Dec. 30, 1995. LL.B., U. Va., 1948. Bar: Tenn. 1948, U.S. Supreme Ct. 1957. Pvt. practice, Memphis, 1948—; city atty., 1968-71; of counsel Waring Cox, 1986—. Editor in chief Va. Law Rev., 1947-48. Served to lt. comdr. USNR, 1941-46. Fellow Am. Coll. Trial Lawyers, Am. Bar Found. (life); mem. Tenn. Bar Assn. (pres. 1966-67), Memphis and Shelby County Bar Assn. (pres. 1963-64, Lawyer's Lawyer award 1995), Tenn. Bar Found. (charter), 6th Circuit Jud. Conf. (life), Raven Soc. Clubs: Memphis Country, Memphis Hunt and Polo General practice. Home: 2927 Frances Pl Memphis TN 38111-2401 Office: Waring Cox PLC 1300 Morgan Keegan Twr 50 N Front St Memphis TN 38103-2126 E-mail: jmanire@waringcox.com

MANLEY, DAVID BOTT, III, lawyer; b. Jacksonville, Fla., June 19, 1953; s. David Bott and Bernadette Claire Manley; m. Gayle Aileen Whitney, Nov. 1, 1978; children: David Jeremiah, Alexandra Ina Claire. BA with honors magna cum laude, U. Ga., 1975, JD, 1982. Bar: Ga. 1983, U.S. Dist. Ct. (no. dist.) Ga. 1983, U.S. Ct. Appeals (11th cir.) 1986. Auditor So. Hostess Sys., Inc., Augusta, Ga., 1975-76; prosecutorial asst. fraud investigator State Ga., Atlanta, 1976-79; assoc. Gadrix & Green, P.C., 1982-83, Lowe, Barham, Eubanks & Lowe, Atlanta, 1983-85; mem. Barham & Manley, 1985-89; dir., ptnr. Campbell Martin & Manley, LLP, 1989—. Corp. counsel Highland Homes, Inc., Dallas and Atlanta, 1990—, Mast Advt. and Pub. Inc., Houston and Nashville, 1991—; corp. sec., counsel Agrisel USA, Inc., Atlanta and Hong Kong, 1998—; mem. Ga. LAw Related Edn. Constorium of Carl Vinson Inst. Govt., U. Ga., 2000—. Pres. U.S. Jaycees, Mt. Park/Lilburn, 1985; cert. coach Lucky Shoals Youth Athletic Assn., Norcross, Ga., 1992-98; bd. dirs Fulton County, Ga. Dept. Family and Children's Svcs. (commendation, bd. resolution for bravery, 1978); svc. provider Parent to Parent of Ga.; mem. Ga. Law-Related Edn. Consortium Carl Vinson Inst. of Govt., U. Ga., 2000—; mem. Dekalb Vol. Lawyers Found., Lawyers Found. Ga. Named Jaycee of Yr., U.S. Jaycees-Mt. Park/Lilburn, Ga., 1984. Mem. ABA, State Bar Ga. (legis. com. corp. and banking law sect. 1987-88, mem. corp. and banking law sect. 1987—, adv. mem. law revision com. 1989-90, mem. trial sect. 1984—, mem. real property sect. 1996—, advocate for spl. needs children 1996—), Nat. Youth Sports Coaches Assn. (continuing mem. 1996—), Sandy Springs Bar Assn. (treas. 1987-88, pres. 1988-89, dir. 1989-90), Omicron Delta Kappa. Avocations: coaching youth sports, model railroading, photography, collecting, travel. General civil litigation, General corporate, Real property. Home: 4390 Flippen Trl Norcross GA 30092-3902 Office: Campbell Martin & Manley LLP 990 Hammond Dr NE Ste 800 Atlanta GA 30328-5510 E-mail: dbmanley@chb-cmm.com

MANLY, SAMUEL, lawyer; b. Louisville, Aug. 8, 1945; s. Samuel III and Nell Thornton (Montgomery) M.; m. Tacie Jarrett Bond, Aug. 8, 1970 (div. 1978); children: Julie Elder, Elizabeth Meriwether. BA cum laude, Yale U., 1967; JD, U. Va., 1970. Bar: Ky. 197l, U.S. Dist. Ct. (we. and ea. dists.) Ky. l972, U.S. Dist. Ct. (so. dist.) Ind. l972, U.S. Dist. Ct. (we. dist.) Mich. 1995, U.S. Ct. Appeals (6th cir.) l972, U.S. Ct. Appeals (10th cir.) 1997, U.S. Supreme Ct. 1997. Pres. Madison House, U. Va., Charlottesville, 1968-70; assoc. Greenebaum Doll & McDonald, Louisville, 1970-76; ptnr. Reisz Blackburn Manly & Treitz, 1976-78; sr. ptnr. Manly & Sears, 1978-81, Manly & Heleringer, Louisville, 1981-84; pvt. practice Law Offices of Samuel Manly, 1984—. Sec., gen. counsel Gibbs-Inman Co., Louisville, 1972-78; contract atty. FDIC, Washington, 1976-84; counsel Winston Products Co., 1988—; dir. defender svcs. U.S. Dist. Ct. (we. dist.) Ky., 1992-94; mem. drug policy com. Ky. Criminal Justice Coun., 1998-2000. Contract atty. Jefferson County, l977-78, City of Louisville, l978-83. Capt. USAR, l967-86. Fellow: Ky. Bar Found. (life); mem.: ABA (com. on products liability, subcom uninsured mfrs. sect. ligitation, com. on self-insurers and risk mgrs. sect. tort and ins. law practice), ATLA, Ky. Bar Assn. (com. on legal ethics 1978—84, com. on legal ethics 1996—98), Louisville Bar Assn., Ky. Assn. Criminal Def. Lawyers (pres. 2001—, bd. dirs., exec. com. 1986—), Nat. Assn. Criminal Def. Lawyers, Ky. Acad. Trial Lawyers, Fed. Bar Assn., Comml. Law League of Am., Am. Judicature Soc., Assn. Fed. Def. Attys., Am. Bankruptcy Inst., Louisville Boat Club. Republican. Avocations: classical music, fishing, golf. General civil litigation, Constitutional, Criminal. Home: 407 S Sherrin Ave Louisville KY 40207-3817 Office: Law Offices of Samuel Manly 239 S 5th St Ste 1606 Louisville KY 40202-3208

MANN, BRUCE ALAN, lawyer, investment banker; b. Chgo., Nov. 28, 1934; s. David I. and Lillian (Segal) M.; m. Naomi Cooks, Aug. 31, 1980; children: Sally Mann Stull, Jonathan Hugh, Andrew Ross. BBA, U. Wis., 1955, SJD, 1957. Bar: Wis. 1957, N.Y. 1958, Calif. 1961. Assoc. Davis, Polk & Wardwell, N.Y.C., 1957-60, Pillsbury, Madison & Sutro, San Francisco, 1960-66, ptnr., 1967-83; adminstrv. mng. dir. L.F. Rothschild Unterberg Towbin, 1983-87; ptnr. Morrison & Foerster, 1987—; sr. mng. dir. W.R. Hambrecht & Co., 1999—. Cons. SEC, 1976; vis. prof. law Georgetown U., 1978; lectr. in field. Author: (with Mattson) California Corporate Practice and Forms, 1999; contbr. articles to profl. jours. Served with USAR, 1957. Mem. Am. Law Inst., Am. Bar Assn. (chmn. fed. regulation of securities com. 1981-83, mem. bus. law sect. coun. 1996-99, standing com. on ethics and profl. responsibility 1997-2000, com. on venture capital 2000—), State Bar Calif., Bar Assn. San Francisco (bd. dirs. 1974-75), Nat. Assn. Securities Dealers (gov. at large 1981-83). Club: The Family. General corporate, Mergers and acquisitions, Securities. Office: Morrison & Foerster 425 Market St Ste 3100 San Francisco CA 94105-2482 E-mail: bmann@mofo.com

MANN, DONEGAN, lawyer; b. Birmingham, Ala., Mar. 6, 1922; s. Ephriam DeValse and Edna Atkins (Donegan) M.; m. Frances Virginia Hindman, Apr. 6, 1957 (dec. May 1993); m. Frances M. Jenkins, Jan. 7, 1995 (dec. Dec. 1997). Student, Birmingham-So., 1940-41; AB, George Washington U., 1947, JD, 1950. Bar: U.S. Dist. Ct. D.C. 1950, U.S. Ct. Appeals (D.C. cir.) 1950, U.S. Ct. Claims 1957, U.S. Supreme Ct. 1961, U.S. Ct. Appeals (fed. cir.) 1982. Acting bur. counsel Civil Aeronautics Bd., Washington, 1953-55; gen. rates atty. GAO, 1955-57; spl. rate counsel Gen. Svcs. Administrn., 1957-60; assoc. Wolf & Case, 1960-66; sr. atty., office gen. counsel. U.S. Dept. Treasury, 1966-79; of counsel Shands & Stupar, 1979-82; pvt. practice, 1984—. Pres. Friends of Historic Great Falls Tavern, Inc., Potomac, Md., 1977-80, bd. dirs., 1980-83. With USN, 1943-46, PTO. Mem. ABA (treas. pub. contracts sect. 1965-66, chmn. awards com. 1975-76, svc. award sr. lawyers' divsn. 1991, counsel sr. lawyers divsn., 1995-97, chmn. guardianship and conservatorship com. 1989-95, sr. lawyers' divsn. task force to reform guardianship laws 1992-94, vice chmn., wills probate and trust com., 1995—, chmn. citizenship com. 1996-97, vice chmn. Law Day and citizenship com. 1997—), FBA, Fed. Energy Bar Assn., D.C. Bar Assn., Montgomery County Hist. Soc. (exec. v.p. 1980-83, bd. dirs. 1984-86). Democrat. Episcopalian. Avocations: fishing, hunting, golf, tennis, gardening. Administrative and regulatory, FERC practice, Taxation, general. Office: 1000 Connecticut Ave NW Ste 204 Washington DC 20036-5337

MANN, J. KEITH, arbitrator, law educator, lawyer; b. May 28, 1924; s. William Young and Lillian Myrle (Bailey) M.; m. Virginia McKinnon, July 7, 1950; children: William Christopher, Marilyn Keith, John Kevin, Susan Bailey, Andrew Curry. BS, Ind. U., 1948, LLB, 1949; LLD, Monmouth Coll., 1989. Bar: Ind. 1949, D.C. 1951. Law clk. Justice Wiley Rutledge and Justice Sherman Minton, 1949-50; pvt. practice Washington, 1950; with Wage Stblzn. Bd., 1951; asst. prof. U. Wis., 1952, Stanford U. Law Sch., 1952-54, assoc. prof., 1954-58, prof., 1958-88, prof. emeritus, 1988—, assoc. dean, 1961-85, acting dean, 1976, 81-82, cons. to provost, 1986-87. Vis. prof. U. Chgo., 1953; mem. Sec. of Labor's Adv. Com., 1955-57; mem. Pres.'s Commn. Airlines Controversy, 1961; mem. COLC Aerospace Spl. Panel, 1973-74; chmn., mem. Presdl. Emergency Bds. or Bds. of Inquiry, 1962-63, 67, 71-72; spl. master U.S. vs. Alaska, U.S. Supreme Ct., 1980-97. Editor book rev. and articles Ind. U. Law Jour., 1948-49. Ensign USNR, 1944-46. Sunderland fellow U. Mich., 1959-60; scholar in residence Duke U., 1972. Mem. ABA, AAUP, Nat. Acad. Arbitrators, Indsl. Rels. Rsch. Assn., Acad. Law Alumni Fellows Ind. U., Order of Coif, Tau Kappa Epsilon, Phi Delta Phi. Democrat. Presbyterian. Home: 872 Lathrop Dr Stanford CA 94305-1053 Office: Stanford U Sch Law Stanford CA 94305-8610 E-mail: jkmann@leland.stanford.edu

MANN, PHILIP ROY, lawyer; b. N.Y.C., Jan. 31, 1948; s. Elias and Gertrude Esther (Levbarg) M. AB, Cornell U., 1968; JD, NYU, 1971, LLM, 1975. Bar: N.Y. 1972, U.S. Dist. Ct. (so. and ea. dists.) N.Y. 1983, U.S. Ct. Appeals (2nd cir.) 1973, U.S. Dist. Ct. (no. dist.) N.Y. 1974, U.S. Ct. Mil. Appeals 1974, U.S. Supreme Ct. 1975, D.C. 1976, U.S. Dist. Ct. (we. dist.) N.Y. 1976, U.S. Tax Ct. 1976, U.S. Ct. Appeals (D.C. cir.) 1978, Conn. 1983, U.S. Dist. Ct. D.C. 1983, U.S. Ct. Claims 1983, U.S. Ct. Appeals (3rd and fed. cirs.) 1983. Assoc. Levin & Weintraub, N.Y.C., 1971-74, Shea & Gould, N.Y.C., 1974-79, ptnr., 1979-84; sole practice, 1984—. Lt. col. J.A., USAR, 1973-2001. Mem. ABA, Fed. Bar Assn. Democrat. Jewish. Bankruptcy, Contracts commercial. Home and Office: 250 E 87th St Apt 26H New York NY 10128-3117

MANN, RICHARD ALLAN, law educator; b. N.Y.C., Dec. 9, 1946; s. Charles and Madeline (Vakshall) M.; m. Karlene Fogelin Knebel. BS in Math., U. N.C., 1968; JD, Yale U., 1973. Bar: N.C. 1975. Asst. prof. law McMasters U., Hamilton, Ont., Can., 1973-74; prof. U. N.C., Chapel Hill , 1974—. Author: Essentials of Business Law, 2001, Business Law and

Regulation of Business, 2001, Business Law, 2000; contbr. articles to profl. jours. Named one of Outstanding Young Men in Am., U.S. Jaycees, 1978. Mem. Am. Bus. Law Assn. (del. 1981-82), Southeastern Regional Bus. Law Assn. (pres. 1980-81). Office: U NC Sch Bus Adminstrn Cb 3490 Chapel Hill NC 27599-0001 E-mail: richard_mann@unc.edu

MANN, ROBERT PAUL, retired lawyer; b. Pitts., July 24, 1929; s. O. Paul and Floy Melinda (Foster) M.; m. Dorothy Neeld, Sept. 4, 1953; children: Robin Duvall Francik, Stewart Neeld Mann. BS, U. Md., College Park, 1951; JD, U. Md., Balt., 1953. Bar: Md. 1954, U.S. Dist. Md. 1965, U.S. Tax Ct. 1976. Pvt. practice, Ruxton, Md., 1956-96; ret., 1996. Trial magistrate, 1957-59. Past pres. Artists Equity, Timonium Rotary, Towson Libr.; active wildlife orgns.; art donor to numerous major mus. Mem. Omicron Delta Kappa, Delta Theta Phi, Sigma Chi. Episcopalian. Probate.

MANN, SAM HENRY, JR. lawyer; b. St. Petersburg, Fla., Aug. 2, 1925; s. Sam Henry and Vivian (Moore) M.; m. Mary Joan Bishop, Sept. 7, 1948; children: Vivian Louise, Sam Henry III, Wallace Bishop. BA, Yale U., 1948; LLB, Fla. U., 1951, JD, 1967. Bar: Fla. 1951, U.S. Dist. Ct. (mid. and so. dists.) Fla. 1951, U.S. Ct. Appeals (5th cir.) 1955, U.S. Ct. Appeals (11th cir.) 1996, U.S. Supreme Ct. 1971. Ptnr. Greene, Mann, Rowe, Stanton, Mastry & Burton, St. Petersburg, 1951-84, Harris, Barrett, Mann & Dew, St. Petersburg, 1984—. Trustee, v.p. Mus. Fine Arts, St. Petersburg, 1980-94, Eckerd Coll., St. Petersburg, 1976-79, Webb Sch., Bell Buckle, Tenn., 1966-75; bd. dirs. Regional Community Blood Ctr., St. Petersburg, 1966—, Fla. Blood Svcs., 1993-94, mem. emeritus 1996—; mem. Disting. Alumni Soc. Webb Sch.; mem., chmn. H. Milton Rogers Heart Found.; bd. dirs., pres. Family and Children's Svc., Inc., 1956-61. Lt. (j.g.) USNR, 1943-48. Fellow Am. Coll. Trial Lawyers, Am. Bar Found., Fla. Bar Found.; mem. ABA, Fla. Bar Assn., Fla. Supreme Ct. Hist. Soc., Am. Counsel Assn., Def. Rsch. Inst., Internat. Assn. Def. Counsel, Pinellas County Trial Lawyers Assn., Nat. Assn. Railroad Trial Counsel, Fla. Def. Lawyers Assn., Assn. Hostp. Attys., Bay Area Vanderbilt, St. Petersburg Bar Assn., Yale and U. Fla. Alumni Assns., Phi Alpha Delta. Republican. Presbyterian. Avocations: RV travel, boating, gardening, workshop. General civil litigation, Personal injury, Probate. Home: 531 Brightwaters Blvd NE Saint Petersburg FL 33704-3713 Office: Harris Barrett Mann & Dew Ste 1500 Southtrust Bank Bldg Saint Petersburg FL 33731-1441

MANNE, HENRY GIRARD, lawyer, educator; b. New Orleans, May 10, 1928; s. Geoffrey and Eva (Shainberg) M.; m. Bobbette Lee Taxer, Aug. 19, 1968; children: Emily Kay, Geoffrey Adam. B.A., Vanderbilt U., 1950; J.D., U. Chgo., 1952; LL.M., Yale U., 1953, J.S.D., 1966; LLD, U. Seattle, 1987, U. Francisco Marroquin, Guatemala, 1987, George Mason U., 2000. Bar: Ill. 1952, N.Y. 1969. Practice in Chgo., 1953-54; assoc. prof. St. Louis U. Law Sch., 1956-57, 59-62; vis. prof. law U. Wis., Madison, 1957-59; prof. George Washington U. Law Sch., 1962-68; Kenan prof. law and polit. sci. U. Rochester, 1968-74; vis. prof. law Stanford (Calif.) Law Sch., 1971-72; disting. prof. law, dir. Law and Econs. Center, U. Miami Law Sch., 1974-80; prof. law Emory U. Law and Econs. Ctr., Atlanta, 1980-86; dean Law Sch., chmn. Law and Econs. Ctr. George Mason U., 1986-96, univ. prof., 1986-99, dean emeritus, 2000—. Vis. prof. law U. Wis., Madison, 1957-59, Stanford (Calif.) Law Sch., 1971-72, U. Chgo. Law Sch., 2000—; dir. Econs. Insts. Fed. Judges, 1976-89. Author: Insider Trading and the Stock Market, 1966, (with H. Wallich) The Modern Corporation and Social Responsibility, 1973, (with E. Solomon) Wall Street in Transition, 1974, Med. Malpractice Guidebook: Law and Economics, 1985; editor: (with Roger LeRoy Miller) Gold, Money and the Law, 1975, Auto Safety Regulation: The Cure or the Problem, 1976; editor: Economic Policy and the Regulation of Corporate Securities, 1968, The Economics of Legal Relationships, 1975; editor: (with James Dorn) Econ. Liberties and the Judiciary, 1987. Served to 1st lt. USAF, 1954-56. Recipient Salvatori award Excellence in Acad. Leadership, 1994; named Cultural Laureate of Va., 1992. Adj. scholar CATO Inst.; fellow Am. Law and Econs. Assn. (hon. life), Mont Pelerin Soc., Order of Coif, Phi Beta Kappa. E-mail: hmanne@mediaone.net

MANNING, CORY E. lawyer; b. Des Moines, Nov. 13, 1970; s. Michael Matt and Donna Kay Manning. BA in Polit. Sci., U. No. Iowa, 1993; JD, U. Iowa, 1997. Bar: S.C. 1997. Assoc. Ness, Motley, Loadnolt, Richardson & Poole, Charleston, S.C., 1997-99; law clk. to Hon. Robert M. Parker U.S. Ct. Appeals (5th cir.), Tyler, Tex., 1999-2000. Contbr. articles to legal jours. Mem. ABA, ATLA. Democrat. Roman Catholic. Product liability, Toxic tort.

MANNING, JEROME ALAN, retired lawyer; b. Bklyn., Dec. 31, 1929; s. Emanuel J. and Dorothy (Levine) M.; m. Naomi Jacobs, Oct. 31, 1954; children: Joy, Stephen, Susan. BA, NYU, 1950, LLB, 1952; LLM, Yale U., 1953. Bar: N.Y. 1953, Fla. 1977. Assoc. Joseph Trachtman, N.Y.C., 1956-61; ptnr. Stroock & Stroock & Lavan, 1961-96; prof. NYU Sch. Law, 1956-96. Editor: NYU Law Rev.; author: Estate Planning, 1980, rev. edit., 1995, Estate Planning for Laymen, 1992. Trustee N.Y.U. Sch. Law. Capt. USAF, 1953-56. Mem. ABA. Estate planning, Probate, Estate taxation. Home: 1835 Franklin St San Francisco CA 94109-3483 E-mail: jmanning@stroock.com

MANNING, KENNETH ALAN, lawyer; b. Buffalo, July 22, 1951; Jack Edwin and Dorothea Ann (Ruhland) M.; m. Diane Louise Garrold, Aug. 11, 1973; children: Michael John, Kathryn Ann. BS in Engring. Sci., SUNY, Buffalo, 1974, JD, 1977. Bar: N.Y. 1978, U.S. Dist. Ct. (we. dist.) N.Y. 1978, U.S. Dist. Ct. (no. dist.) N.Y. 1980, U.S. Ct. Appeals (2d cir.) 1983, U.S. Ct. Appeals (3d cir.) 1988. Confidential law asst. to assoc. justice Appellate Div. 4th Dept., Buffalo, 1977-79; assoc. Phillips, Lytle, Hitchcock, Blaine & Huber, 1979-84, ptnr., 1985—. Vol. Lawyers Project, Erie County, 1985—, Criminal Appeals Program, Erie County, 1988-89; mem. coun. Western N.Y. region NCCJ. Woodburn fellow SUNY, Buffalo, 1973-76. Mem. ABA (TIP sect.), N.Y. State Bar Assn. (ins. negligence sect.), Erie County Bar Assn., Gyro Club (pres. 1988), Park Club, One Hundred Club Buffalo. Avocations: sports, hunting. Federal civil litigation, General civil litigation. Office: Phillips Lytle Hitchcock Blaine & Huber 3400 HSBC Ctr Buffalo NY 14203-2887

MANNING, MICHAEL J. lawyer; b. Wichita, Kans., July 18, 1944; BA, U. Kans., 1966; JD, Washburn U., 1969. Bar: Kans. 1969, D.C. 1970. Mem. Fulbright & Jaworski LLP, Washington. Mem. ABA, Fed. Energy Assn., D.C. Bar, Phi Alpha Delta. FERC practice, Oil, gas, and mineral, Natural resources. Office: Fulbright & Jaworski Market Sq 801 Pennsylvania Ave NW Fl 3-5 Washington DC 20004-2623

MANNINO, EDWARD FRANCIS, lawyer; b. Abington, Pa., Dec. 5, 1941; s. Sante Francis and Martha Anne (Hines) M.; m. Mary Ann Vigilante, July 17, 1965 (div. 1990); m. Antoinette K. O'Connell, June 25, 1993; children: Robert John, Jennifer Elaine. BA with distinction, U. Pa., 1963, LLB magna cum laude, 1966. Bar: Pa. 1967. Law clk. 3d cir. U.S. Ct. Appeals, 1966-67; assoc. Dilworth, Paxson, Kalish & Kauffman, Phila., 1967-71, ptnr., 1972-86, co-chmn. litigation dept., 1980-86, sr. ptnr., 1982-86; sr. prin. Elliott, Mannino & Flaherty, PC, 1986-90; chmn. Mannino Griffith PC, 1990-95; sr. ptnr. Wolf, Block, Schorr & Solis-Cohen, 1995-98; ptnr. Akin, Gump, Strauss, Hauer & Feld LLP, 1998—. Hearing examiner disciplinary bd. Supreme Ct. Pa., 1986-89; lectr. Temple U. Law Sch., 1968-69, 71-72; mem. Phila. Mayor's Sci. and Tech. Adv. Com., 1976-79; mem. adv. com. on appellate ct. rules Supreme Ct. Pa., 1989-95; project mgr. Pa. Environ. Master Plan, 1973; chmn. Pa. Land Use Policy Study Adv. Com., 1973-75; chmn. adv. com., hon. faculty history dept. U. Pa., 1980-85. Author: Lender Liability and Banking Litigation, 1989, Business and Commercial Litigation: A Trial Lawyer's Handbook, 1995, The Civil RICO Primer, 1996; mem. editl. bd. Litigation mag., 1985-87, Comm. Lending Litigation News, 1988—, Bank Bailout Litigation News, 1989-93, Bus. Torts Reporter, 1988-99, Practical Litigator, 1989—, Civil RICO Report, 1991—; contbr. articles to profl. jours. Pres. parish coun. Our Mother of Consolation Ch., 1977-79; bd. overseers U. Pa. Sch. Arts and Scis., 1985-89, chmn. recruitment and retention of faculty com.; commonwealth trustee Temple U., 1987-90, audit, bus. and fin. coms. Named one of Nation's Top Litigators Nat. Law Jour., 1990, Pa.'s Top Ten Trial Lawyers, 1999. Fellow Am. Bar Found., ABA (chmn. various coms.), Am. Law Inst., Hist. Soc. U.S. Dist. Ct. Ea. Dist. Pa. (bd. dirs.), Pa. Bar Assn., Phila. Bar Assn. (gov. 1975), Pa. Soc., Order of Coif, Phi Beta Kappa, Phi Beta Kappa Assocs. Democrat. Antitrust, General civil litigation, Professional liability. Office: Akin Gump Strauss Hauer & Feld LLP One Commerce Sq 2005 Market St Ste 2200 Philadelphia PA 19103-7014 E-mail: emannino@akingump.com

MANNINO, ROBERT, lawyer; b. Phila., July 20, 1968; s. Edward Francis and Mary Ann Mannino. BA, U. Pa., 1991; JD cum laude, Am. U., 1995. Bar: Pa. 1995, N.J. 1995, U.S. Dist. Ct. N.J. 1995, U.S. Dist. Ct. (ea. dist.) Pa. 1996, U.S. Ct. Appeals (3rd cir.) 2000, U.S. Supreme Ct. 2000. Intern U.S. Dept. Justice, Washington, summers 1993-94, U.S. Senate Com. on the Judiciary, Washington, 1994; student atty. D.C. Law Students in Ct., 1994-95; assoc. Lavin, Coleman, et al, Phila., 1995-97, Gollatz, Griffin & Ewing, Phila., 1997—. Com. person Rep. Party, Phila., 1989-91; rsch. asst. Ref. Manual Chpts., U.S. Atty's Manual Criminal Tax Sects., summer 1993; mem. Young Friends of the Phila. Art Mus. Mem. Penn Club N.Y.C., Penn A.C. Rowing Assn. Roman Catholic. General civil litigation, Labor, Product liability. Office: Gollatz Griffin & Ewing 16th Fl Two Penn Center Philadelphia PA 19102

MANNIX, CHARLES RAYMOND, law educator; b. Elizabeth, N.J., Aug. 2, 1950; s. Charles Raymond and Helen Joan (French) M. BA, Duquesne U., 1972, MA, JD, Duquesne U., 1976; MPA, Harvard U., 1998. Bar: Iowa 1976, N.Y. 1996, Va. 1980, D.C. 1980, U.S. Ct. Claims 1976, U.S. Tax Ct. 1976, U.S. Ct. Mil. Appeals 1976, U.S. Ct. Internat. Trade 1976, U.S. Ct. Appeals (4th and 5th cirs.) 1977, U.S. Ct. Appeals (D.C. cir.) 1977, U.S. Dist. Ct. Va. 1980, U.S. Supreme Ct. 1980, U.S. Ct. Appeals (D.C. cir.) 1980, U.S. Ct. Appeals (fed. cir.) 1982, N.Y. 1996. Commd. 2d lt. USAF, 1973, advanced through grade to lt. col., 1982; intern UN Office of Legal Affairs, N.Y.C., 1975; various legal assignments; lectr. USAF Med. Law Cons. Program, 1981-99. Adj. faculty Georgetown U., Washington, 1984-99; assoc. prof. and chmn. dept. med. jurisprudence, asst. prof. mil. medicine, v.p. and gen. counsel Uniformed Svcs. U. Health Scis. Decorated Meritorious Svc. medal with Oak Leaf Cluster, Air Force Commendation medal with Oak Leaf Clusters. Mem. ABA, FBA, ATLA, D.C. Bar Assn., Va. State Bar Assn., Am. Soc. Internat. Law, Am. Soc. Law and Medicine, Am. Arbitration Assn. (arbitrator), Am. Acad. Hosp. Attys., Nat. Assn. Coll. and Univ. Attys., N.Y. State Bar Assn., Bar Assn. of the City of N.Y., Assn. Mil. Surgeons U.S., Harvard Club of N.Y. Home: 10205 Walker Lake Dr Great Falls VA 22066-3558 Office: Uniformed Svcs U Health Scis Gen Coun Jones Bridge Rd Bethesda MD 20815-5737 E-mail: charlesmannix@msn.com

MANOS, CHRISTOPHER LAWRENCE, lawyer, mediator; b. Ft. Bragg, N.C., July 1, 1952; m. B.J. Osmon, June 14, 1974; children: Monica, Kelly. BS, U.S. Mil. Acad., 1974; JD, U. N.D., 1982. Bar: Mont. 1983, U.S. Dist. Ct. (Mont.) 1983, U.S. Ct. Appeals (9th cir.) 1983. Assoc. to ptrn. Moore, O'Connell, Refling & Manos, Bozeman, Mont., 1982-92; ptnr. Biglen & Manos, Bozeman and Big Timber, 1992—. Trainer for mediators The Settlement Ctr. and Alternative Dispute Resolution Assocs., Bozeman and Palo Alto, Calif., 1990—. Contbr. articles to profl. jours. Bd. dirs. Mont. Pub. TV, Bozeman, 1985-92, Mont. Coun. for Internat. Visitors, Bozeman, 1992; mem. Mont. Stat Bar Dispute Resolution Com., Helena, Mont., 1989—. Capt. U.S. Army, 1974-79. Mem. ABA, State Bar of Mont. (pres. 2001-), Soc. of Profls. in Dispute Resolution. Federal civil litigation, State civil litigation. Office: Biglen & Manos PO Box 1188 209 McLeod St Big Timber MT 59011*

MANOS, JOHN M. federal judge; b. Cleve., Dec. 8, 1922; m. Viola Manos; 4 children. BS, Case Inst. Tech., 1944; JD, Cleve.-Marshall Coll. Law, 1950. Bar: Ohio 1950. Asst. plant mgr. Lake City Malleable Iron Co., Cleve., 1946-50; atty. Manos & Manos, 1950-63; law dir. City of Bay Village, 1954-56; industries rep. Cleve. Regional Bd. of Rev., 1957-59; judge Ohio Ct. Common Pleas, Cuyahoga County, 1963-69, Ohio Ct. Appeals, Cuyahoga County, 1969-76; sr. judge U.S. Dist. Ct. (no. dist.) Ohio, Cleve., 1976-91, 1991—. With USN, 1942-45. Named Phi Alpha Delta Man of Yr., 1972, Outstanding Alumnus Cleve.- Marshall Law Alumni Assn., 1976. Mem. ABA, Fed. Bar Assn., Ohio State Bar Assn., Nat. Lawyers Club (hon.), Bar Assn. Greater Cleve., Cuyahoga County Bar Assn., Delta Theta Phi (Man of Yr. 1970). Office: US Dist Ct 201 Superior Ave E Cleveland OH 44114-1201

MANSFIELD, JAMES NORMAN, III, lawyer; b. Chattanooga, Feb. 15, 1951; s. James Norman and Doris June (Hilliard) M.; m. Terry Ann Thomas, Dec. 28, 1975; children: Seth Thomas, James Norman, Scott Michael. BA, U. Tenn., Chattanooga, 1973; MA, La. State U., 1976, JD, 1979. Bar: La. 1979, U.S. Dist. Ct. (we. dist.), La. 1979. Shareholder Liskow and Lewis, Lafayette and New Orleans, La., 1979—. Pres. Raven Soc., Chattanooga, 1973; mem. sch. bd. St. Thomas More H.S. Mem. ABA, La. Bar Assn., La. Min. Law Inst. (adv. coun. mem.), Am. Assn. Profl. Landmen, Lafayette Assn. Petroleum Landmen, Order of Coif. Roman Catholic. Avocations: photography, jogging, fishing. Oil, gas, and mineral, Probate, Real property. Home: 103 Asbury Cir Lafayette LA 70503-3632 Office: Liskow & Lewis PO Box 52008 Lafayette LA 70505-2008

MANSFIELD, KAREN LEE, lawyer; b. Chgo., Mar. 17, 1942; d. Ralph and Hilda (Blum) Mansfield; children: Nicole Rafaela, Lori Michele. BA in Polit. Sci., Roosevelt U., 1963; JD, DePaul U., 1971; student U. Chgo., 1959-60. Bar: Ill. 1972, U.S. Dist. Ct. (no. dist.) Ill. 1972. Legis. intern Ill. State Senate, Springfield, 1966-67; tchr. Chgo. Pub. Schs., 1967-70; atty. CNA Ins., Chgo., 1971-73; law clk. Ill. Apellate Ct., Chgo., 1973-75; sr. trial atty. U.S. Dept. Labor, Chgo., 1975—, mentor Adopt-a-Sch. Program, 1992-95. Contbr. articles to profl. jours. Vol. Big Sister, 1975-81; bd. dirs. Altgeld Nursery Sch., 1963-66, Ill. div. UN Assn., 1966-72, Hull House Jane Addams Ctr., 1977-82, Broadway Children's Ctr., 1986-90, Acorn Family Entertainment, 1993-95; mem. Oak Park Farmers' Market Commn., 1996—; rsch. asst. Citizens for Gov. Otto Kerner, Chgo., 1964; com. mem. Ill. Commn. on Status of Women, Chgo., 1964-70; del. Nat. Conf. on Status of Women, 1968; candidate for del. Ill. Constl. Conv., 1969. Mem. Chgo. Council Lawyers, Women's Bar Assn. Ill., Lawyer Pilots Bar Assn., Fed. Bar Assn. Unitarian. Clubs: Friends of Gamelan (performer), 99's Internat. Orgn. Women Pilots (legis. chmn. Chgo. area chpt. 1983-86, legis. chmn. North Cen. sect. 1986-88, legis. award 1983, 85). Home: 204 S Taylor Ave Oak Park IL 60302-3307 Office: US Dept Labor Office Solicitor 230 S Dearborn St Fl 8 Chicago IL 60604-1505

MANSMANN, CAROL LOS, federal judge, law educator; b. Pittsburgh, Pa., Aug. 7, 1942; d. Walter Joseph and Regina Mary (Pilarski) Los; m. J. Jerome Mansmann, June 27, 1970; children: Casey, Megan, Patrick. B.A., J.D., Duquesne U., 1964, 67; LL.D., Seton Hill Coll., Greensburg, Pa., 1985; PhD (hon.), La Roche Coll., 1990; LLD (hon.), Widener U., 1994, Duquesne U., 1998. Asst. dist. atty. Allegheny County, Pitts., 1968-72; assoc. McVerry Baxter & Mansmann, 1973-79; assoc. prof. law Duquesne U., 1973-82; judge west dist. U.S. Dist. Ct. Pa., 1982-85; judge U.S. Ct. Appeals (3rd cir.), Phila., 1985—. Mem. Pa. Criminal Procedural Rules Com., Pitts., 1972-77; spl. asst. atty. gen. Commonwealth of Pa., 1974-79; co-adminstr. Local Criminal Rules Reorg. Project, 1978-79; chair 2 Bar Assn. CLE programs, 1982; bd. govs. Pa. Bar Inst., Harrisburg, 1984-90; mem. 3d Cir. jud. coun., 1985—; adj. prof. law U. Pitts., 1987-96; mem. U.S. Jud. Conf. on adminstrn. of magistrate-judge sys., 1990-96. Mem. bd. consultors Villanova U. Law Sch., 1985-91; trustee Duquesne U., 1987—, Sewickley Acad., 1988-91. Recipient St. Thomas More award, Pitts., 1983, Phila., 1986, Ann. Dinner award Duquesne U. Law Alumni Assn., 1986, Faculty Alumni award Duquesne U., 1987, Susan B. Anthony award, 2000. Mem. ABA, Nat. Assn. Women Judges, Pa. Bar Assn., Fed. Judges Assn., Am. Judicature Soc., Allegheny County Bar Assn. (gov., bd. govs. 1982-85), Phi Alpha Delta. Republican. Roman Catholic. Office: US Ct Appeals 7th and Grant Sts # 712 Pittsburgh PA 15219-2403

MANSON, KEITH ALAN MICHAEL, lawyer; b. Warwick, RI, Oct. 26, 1962; s. Ronald Frederick and Joan Patricia (Reardon) M.; m. Jennifer Annette Stearns; children: Kristin Elizabeth, Michelle Nicole. BA, R.I. Coll., 1985; cert. computer info. systems, Bryant Coll., 1988; cert. law, U. Notre Dame, London, 1990; JD, Thomas M. Cooley Law Sch., 1991. Bar: Ind. 1991, U.S. Dist. Ct. (no. dist.) Ind. 1991, U.S. Dist. Ct. (so. dist.) Ind. 1991, U.S. Dist. Ct. (so. dist.) Ga. 1992, U.S. Dist. Ct. Mil. Appeals 1991. Spl. asst. U.S. atty. U.S. Dist. Ct. Ga., Brunswick, 1992-93; pvt. practice Fernandina Beach, Fla., 1994—; atty., securities compliance divsn. Prudential Ins. Co., 1997-98; counsel Stonier Transportation Group, Jacksonville Beach, Fla., 1998-99. Cons. The Law Store Ltd. Paralegal Svcs., Fernandina Beach., 1994—, Barnett Bank, Nations Bank, 1998. Contbr. articles to profl. jours. Dist. fin. and mem. chmn. North Fla. coun. Boy Scouts Am., Jacksonville, 1993—; com. mem. sea scout ship 660 St. Peter's Ch., Fernandina Beach, 1994-96; chmn. Scouting for Food Dr., Nassau County, Fla., 1994—. Lt. USN, 1985-86, 90-96. Recipient Nassau Dist. award of merit Boy Scouts Am., 1999, God and Svc. award, 2000; F.C. Tanner Trust, Fed. Products Inc. scholar, Providence, 1981-85, Esterline Corp. scholar, Providence, 1986. Mem. ABA, Ind. Bar Assn., Judge Advocate Assn., Jacksonville Bar Assn., Navy League U.S., Rotary (project mgr. Webster-Dudley Mass. chpt. 1986-88), Am. Legion, Phi Alpha Delta. Avocations: gardening, rugby, sports history, military history, collecting historical items. Consumer commercial, Criminal, Military. Home and Office: 1908 Reatta Ln Fernandina Beach FL 32034-8937 E-mail: mansonjk@netscape.net

MANTEL, ALLAN DAVID, lawyer; b. N.Y.C., June 27, 1951; s. Bernard and Ruth (Weichman) M.; m. Janet Mantel, June 17, 1985; children: Bernard, Elizabeth. BA, NYU, 1973; JD, SUNY, Buffalo, 1976. Bar: N.Y. 1977, U.S. Dist. Ct. (so. and ea. dists.) N.Y. 1977. Assoc. Rosenthal & Herman P.C., N.Y.C., 1977-82; ptnr. Rosenthal, Herman & Mantel, 1983-94, Hofheimer, Gartlir & Gross, LLP, N.Y.C., 1995-98, Stein Riso & Mantel LLP, N.Y.C., 1999—. Mem. adv. bd. Divorce Mag. Fellow Am. Acad. Matrimonial Lawyers (bd. mgrs. 1998-2000, N.Y. chpt. treas. 2001—); mem. ABA (family law sect.), N.Y. State Bar Assn. (equitable distbn. com.), Assn. Bar City N.Y. (matrimonial law com. 1985-88), N.Y. County Lawyers Assn. (matrimonial law and bus. and comml. law com.). Jewish. State civil litigation, Family and matrimonial. Office: Stein Riso & Mantel LLP 405 Lexington Ave New York NY 10174-0002 E-mail: allan.mantel@steinrisomantel.com

MANZO, EDWARD DAVID, patent lawyer; b. N.Y.C., Nov. 23, 1950; s. Edward Joseph and Elvira Helen (Melone) M.; m. Fern Rita Siegel, Oct. 30, 1978 (div. 1984); 1 child, Justin Edward; m. Margaret Ruth Johnson, Oct. 11, 1985; children: Hunter Roy, Kira Nicole. BS in Physics, Poly. Inst. Bklyn., 1972; JD cum laude, SUNY, Buffalo, 1975. Bar: N.Y. 1976, Ill. 1979, U.S. Patent and Trademark Office 1976, U.S. Ct. Appeals (fed. cir.) 1982, U.S. Supreme Ct. 1982. Assoc. Darby & Darby, P.C., N.Y.C., 1975-77; group patent counsel Schlumberger Ltd., 1977-79; ptnr. Cook, Wetzel & Egan, Chgo., 1979-85, 88-90, Jenner & Block, 1985-88; sr. ptnr. Cook McFarron & Manzo, Ltd., Chgo., 1990-99; sr. ptnr., exec. v.p., treas., CFO Cook, Alex, McFarron, Manzo, Cummings & Mehler, Ltd., 1999—. Instr. DePaul U., Chgo., 1989-91. Author (with others): Intellectual Property Law in Illinois, 1988; contbr. articles to profl. jours. Bd. dirs. Concertante di Chgo., 1997—; grantor Edward Manzo Patent Law scholarship DePaul Law Sch., 2001—. Jaeckle Fleishman grantee, 1973. Mem. Am. Intellectual Property Law Assn., Intellectual Property Law Assn. Chgo., Stradivari Soc., Sicilian Am. Cultural Assn. (treas. 1996-98, v.p. 1998-99, pres. 2000—). Avocations: classical piano and guitar, tennis, bridge. Federal civil litigation, Intellectual property, Patent. Home: Lake Forest IL 60045 Office: Cook Alex McFarron Manzo Cummings & Mehler Ltd 200 W Adams St Ste 2850 Chicago IL 60606-5206 E-mail: emanzo@cammcm.com

MAOSA, THOMAS NYAKAMBI, lawyer; b. Kisii, Kenya, 30 Sept. s. Abraham Sure and Susan Jemunto M.; m. Betty Jane Mwaiseje, Sept. 4, 1995; children; Une Boniface, Eric Maosa, Leo Igane, Slyvia Maosa. B of Law, Nairobi U., 1984. Legal asst. Ueihar Shian Advocate, Nairobi, 1985-86; assoc. Oraro & Rather Advocates, Nairobi, 1986-88; ptbr. Maosa & Co. Advocates, Nairobi, 1988—. Def. counsel UN Tribunal on Rowanda, Arusha, 1998—; cons. in field. Mem. Law Soc. Kenya, Tanganyika Law Soc., East African Law Soc. Avocations: tennis, soccer, swimming, bird watching, jogging. Contracts commercial, Insurance, Mergers and acquisitions. Home: Brookside Dr PO Box 42802 Nairoba Kenya Office: Maosa & Co Kimathi PO Box 42802 Nairoba Kenya Fax: 241775. E-mail: maosa@lawyer.com

MAPES, WILLIAM RODGERS, JR. lawyer; b. Cleve., Nov. 29, 1952; s. William R. and Marian (Atkins) M.; m. Patricia Soochan, Sept. 3, 1984. BS in Bus. Adminstrn., Miami U., Oxford, Ohio, 1974; JD, Am. U., 1977. Bar: D.C. 1978, U.S. Ct. Appeals (D.C. cir.) 1979, U.S. Ct. Appeals (fed. cir.) 1980, U.S. Ct. Appeals (5th cir.) 1981, U.S. Supreme Ct. 1982, U.S. Ct. Appeals (3d cir.) 1985, U.S. Ct. Appeals (4th cir.) 1987, U.S. Ct. Appeals (6th cir.) 1988. Ptnr. Ross, Marsh & Foster, Washington, 1978-2000, Duane, Morris & Heckscher, Washington, 2000—. Treas., bd. dirs. Holy Land Christian Ecumenical Found. Mem. ABA (editor nat. resources sect. newsletter 1984-89), Fed. Energy Bar Assn., Univ. Club Washington. Avocations: boating, tennis, cycling. Administrative and regulatory, FERC practice. Home: 6916 Greenvale St NW Washington DC 20015-1437 Office: Duane Morris & Heckscher LLP 1667 K St NW #700 Washington DC 20006-1608 E-mail: wrmapes@duanemorris.com

MARANO, RICHARD MICHAEL, lawyer; b. Waterbury, Conn., June 22, 1960; s. Albert Nicholas and Angeline Domenica (Viotti) M.; m. Eileen N. Barry. BA, Fairfield U., 1982; JD, Seton Hall U., 1985. Bar: Conn. 1985, U.S. Dist. Ct. Conn. 1985, U.S. Tax Ct. 1986, U.S. Supreme Ct. 1990, U.S. Ct. Appeals (2d cir.) 1991; cert. criminal trial advocate. Assoc. Moynahan, Ruskin, Mascolo & Mariani, Waterbury, 1985-87; ptnr. Marano & Diamond, 1987—2001. Bd. of examiners Nat. Bd. Trial Advocacy, 1999—. Author: History of the Order Sons of Italy of Waterbury, Connecticut, 1995, Connecticut Criminal Legal Forms, 1999; co-author: Growing Up Italian and American in Waterbury, 1997; co-editor: Counsel for the Defense, 1991-93, editor, 1993-98; contbr. law articles to Conn. Bar Jour. Bd. dirs. Italian-Am. Dem. Club, Waterbury, 1988—, Ctrl. Naugatuck Valley HELP, 1992—, Anderson Boys Club, 1989— (pres. 1996-98), Waterbury Housing Police Fund, 1992-94, Waterbury Crime Stoppers Inc., 1994-97; pres. Conn. Young Dems., 1981-82; state coord. McGovern for U.S. Presdl. campaign, 1983-84; campaign mgr. Orman for Congress, 1984; commr. Waterbury Pub. Assistance, 1986-88; justice of the peace, Waterbury, 1989-99; gen. counsel Waterbury Dem. Town Com., 1990-96; commr. Waterbury Fire Bd., 1996-98; trustee Our Lady of Lourdes Ch., 1993—; alderman City of Waterbury, 1988-90. Mem. ABA, ATLA, KC,

Conn. Bar Assn., Nat. Assn. Criminal Def. Lawyers (life), Conn. Criminal Def. Lawyers Assn. (pres.-elect 1997-98, pres. 1998-99), Conn. Italian-Am. Bar Assn. (pres. 1993-95), Conn. Trial Lawyers Assn., Waterbury Bar Assn. (bd. dirs. 1993—, pres. 1996-98), New Haven County Bar Assn., Nat. Italian-Am. Bar Assn. (Conn. delegate 1993—), Sons of Italy (pres. lodge # 66 1994-96), Unico Club (pres. Waterbury chpt. 1997-99), Cath. Lawyers Guild, Conn. Acad. Cert. Trial Lawyers, Nat. Eagle Scout Assn. (life), Elks, Alpha Mu Gamma, Pi Sigma Alpha. Roman Catholic. Criminal, General practice, Personal injury. Home: 24 Lake Dr Oxford CT 06478-1172 Office: Marano Law Offices 61 Field St Waterbury CT 06702-1907 E-mail: RichardMarano@aol.com

MARAZITI, JOSEPH JAMES, JR. lawyer; b. Boonton, N.J., May 20, 1940; s. Joseph James and Margaret eileen (Hopkins) M.; m. Claudette A. Awn, June 23, 1968; chidlren: Jacqueline, Michele. BS, Fordham U., 1962; JD, 1965. Bar: N.J. 1965, U.S. Dist. Ct. N.J. 1965, U.S. Ct. Appeals (3rd. cir.) 1980, U.S. Supreme Ct. 1969. Ptnr. Maraziti & Marazati, Boontoon, N.J., 1965-76, Maraziti, Falcon & Healey, LLP, Short Hills, 1976—. Subcom. 21st century task force Gen. Assembly State of N.J.; chmn. N.J. Future; mem. N.J. Com. Tri-State Regional Plan Assn.; founding chair Morris County Bar Assn. Environ. Law Com.; chmn. N.J. State Planning Commn., 1998-. Contbr. articles to profl. jours. Chmn. Morris 2000, 1988-91. Mem. ABA, N.J. Bar Assn. (nat. resources and environ. law sect. 1988—), Environ. Law Inst. Washington. Federal civil litigation, Environmental.

MARBURG-GOODMAN, JEFFREY EMIL, lawyer; b. Taipei, Taiwan, Feb. 20, 1957; s. Samuel and Lisl (Marburg) G. BA, Amherst Coll., 1979; JD, Harvard U., 1983; postgrad., U. Aix-Marseille, France, 1983-84. Bar: N.Y. 1986, U.S. Dist. Ct. (so. and ea. dists.) N.Y. 1988. Assoc. Shearman & Sterling, Paris, 1984, N.Y.C., 1985-89, Patton & Boggs, Washington, 1989-91; legal counsel U.S. AID, U.S. Dept. State, 1991-2000, asst. gen. counsel, 2000—. Mem. nat. steering com. Clinton-Gore '96, Gore 2000, Washington; cons. Gore 2000, Washington. Rotary fellow, 1984. Mem. Harvard Club, Phi Beta Kappa. Avocations: running, weight training, music, theatre, travel. Home: 1401 17th St NW Ph Apt1008 Washington DC 20036-6400 Office: US AID Office Gen Counsel Ronald Reagan Bldg & Interna C Washington DC 20523-0001 E-mail: jmarburg-goodman@usaid.gov

MARCELLINO, STEPHEN MICHAEL, lawyer; b. Bklyn., July 11, 1950; s. Frank Joseph and Marie Leah (Lyda) M.; m. Karen Eileen Kelly, July 24, 1976; children: Bridget, Stephen. BA in English, Fordham U., 1972, JD, 1975. Bar: N.Y. 1976, U.S. Dist. Ct. (so. and ea. dists.) N.Y. 1977,. U.S. Ct. Internat. Trade 1983, U.S. Dist. Ct. (we. dist.) N.Y. 1985, U.S. Ct. Appeals (2d cir.) 1986. Sr. ptnr. Wilson Elser Moskowitz Edelman & Dicker, N.Y.C., 1975—. Mem. N.Y. State Bar Assn., Profl. Liability Underwriting Soc. Roman Catholic. Avocations: basketball, tennis, skiing. General civil litigation, Construction, Insurance. Office: Wilson Elser Moskowitz Edelman & Dicker 150 E 42nd St New York NY 10017-5612 E-mail: marcellinos@wemed.com

MARCELLO, FRANK F. lawyer, educator; b. Chgo., Aug. 11, 1961; s. Fred Anthony and Antoinette Marie (Colombo) M. BS, DePaul U., 1983; MBA, Dominican U., 1996; JD, The John Marshall Law Sch., 1986. Exec. legal coord. Office of Cook County Pub. Defender, Chgo., 1985-87, asst. dep. chief, 1987-89; v.p. exec. counsel Connaught Corp., 1989-93; v.p. sr. counsel Internat. Cons. Group, 1993-96; prof. law Northwestern B.C., 1996—, Dominican U., River Forest, 1996—. Active Joint Civic Com. Italian Ams., Chgo. Mem. ABA, AAUP, Justiniam Soc., Nat. Italian Am. Bar Assn., Sons of Italy Found., Assn. Cath. Colls. and Univs. Office: Dominican U 7900 W Division St River Forest IL 60305 E-mail: ffm@abanet.org

MARCHETTI, KARIN FRANCES, lawyer; b. Shirley, Mass., Nov. 3, 1951; d. Robert Joseph and Patricia (Morico) M.; children: Haley Warden, Henry Warden, Chrisopher W. Kaiser. BA summa cum laude, U. Maine, 1975, JD, 1978. Bar: Mass. 1979, Maine, 1979. Reporter Sta. WGBH-TV, Portland, Maine, 1978-79; news anchorperson Sta. WMTW-TV, Poland Spring, 1977-78; atty., founder Advocates, Inc., Portland, 1979-80; assoc. corp. counsel City of Potland, 1980-83; vol. Peace Corps, Tunisia, South Africa, 1983-84; gen. counsel, clk. Maine Coast Heritage Trust, Northeast Harbor, Maine, 1985—; prin. Land Conservation Legal Svcs., Bernard, 1994—. Mem. faculty Lincoln Inst. Land Policy, Boston, 1987, Maine Bar Assn., Augusta, 1991—; spkr. Land Trust Alliance, Washington, 1988—; spkr., cons. Land Conservation Leadership Program, Conservation Fund, Washington, 1997—; presenter advanced issues in conservation easement stewardship and amending conservation easements. Co-author: Conserving Land with Conservation Easements, 1999. Bd. dirs. Acadia Waldorf Assn., Mt. Desert, Maine, 1997—, Portland Soc. Art, 1976-79. Recipient Alumni scholarship U. so. Maine, 1976. Mem. Maine State Bar Assn., CLE. Avocations: hiking, kayaking, film. Environmental, Land use and zoning (including planning), Non-profit and tax-exempt organizations. Office: Land Conservation Legal Svcs PO Box 100 Bernard ME 04612-0100

MARCKS, RONALD HENRY, lawyer, abrasives and diversified products manufacturing company executive; b. New Haven, Dec. 4, 1931; s. Henry John and Mildred Josephine (Perinchief) M.; A.B., Dartmouth Coll., 1952; LL.B., Harvard U., 1960; m. Barbara Ann Wye, Aug. 17, 1968. Bar: Mass. 1960. Assoc., then ptnr. Goodwin, Procter & Hoar, Boston, 1960-74; chief legal counsel Norton Co., Worcester, Mass., 1974-79, v.p., gen. counsel, sec., 1979— . Served with USNR, 1952-56. Mem. Phi Beta Kappa. Author: (under pseudonym Jens O. Parsson) Dying of Money: Lessons of the Great German and American Inflations, 1974. Office: Norton Co PO Box 15008 Worcester MA 01615-0008

MARCUM, GREGORY WAYNE, lawyer, engineer; b. San Antonio, Apr. 20, 1962; s. James William Marcum and Mary Elizabeth Gay; m. Angela Kay Clary, Oct. 14, 1994; 1 child, Carter Grant. BSME, Tex. A&M U., 1985; JD, U. Houston, 1997. Bar: Tex.; registered profl. engr. Tex. Bldg. studies engr. Northern Telecom, Inc., Dallas, 1985-87; asst. dir. engring. Wadley Med. Ctr., Texarkana, Tex., 1987-90; gen. mgr. engring. GAMA Corp., Riyadh, Saudi Arabia, 1990-91; mech. project engr. Quanex Corp., Houston, 1991-94; assoc. McFall Sherwood & Sheehy, 1997—. Avocation: scuba diving. Office: McFall Sherwood & Sheehy 909 Fannin St Ste 2500 Houston TX 77010

MARCUS, ERIC PETER, lawyer; b. Newark, Aug. 31, 1950; s. John J. and Alice M. (Zeldin) M.; m. Terry R. Toll, Oct. 9, 1983. BA, Brown U., 1972; JD, Stanford U., 1976. Bar: N.Y. 1977, N.J. 1977. Assoc. Kaye, Scholer, Fierman, Hays & Handler LLP, N.Y.C., 1976-84, ptnr., 1985—. Contbr. articles to profl. jours. Mem. Phi Beta Kappa. Banking, Contracts commercial. Office: Kaye Scholer LLP 425 Park Ave New York NY 10022-3506

MARCUS, KENNETH BEN, lawyer; b. Bklyn., June 17, 1952; s. Dolphe Marcus and Jacqueline Foil; m. Gail Elizabeth Hillman, June 27, 1976; children: Joshua B., Richard D. BS, U. Pa., 1972; JD, NYU, 1975. Assoc. Golenbock & Barell, N.Y.C., 1976-78, Paskus, Gordon & Hyman, N.Y.C., 1978-79; ptnr. Carro, Spanbock, Fass, Geller, Kaster & Cuiffo, 1979-89, McCorriston Miho Miller, Honolulu, 1990-99; dir. Starn O'Toole Marcus & Fisher, 1999—. Mem. ABA, Internat. Soc. Hospitality Cons. Avocations: hockey, games, historical simulations. Real property. E-mail: kennethben@mac.com, kmarcus@starnlaw.com

MARCUS, MARIA LENHOFF, lawyer, law educator; b. Vienna, Austria, June 23, 1933; came to U.S., 1938, naturalized, 1944; d. Arthur and Clara (Gruber) Lenhoff; m. Norman Marcus, Dec. 23, 1956; children: Valerie, Nicole, Eric. BA, Oberlin Coll., 1954; JD, Yale Law Sch., 1957. Bar: N.Y. 1961, U.S. Dist. Ct. (so. and ea. dists.) N.Y. 1962, U.S. Ct. Appeals (2d cir.) 1962, U.S. Supreme Ct. 1964. Assoc. counsel NAACP, N.Y.C., 1961-67; asst. atty. gen. N.Y. State, 1967-78; chief litigation bur. Atty. Gen. N.Y. State, 1976-78; adj. assoc. prof. NYU Law Sch., 1976-78; assoc. prof. Fordham U. Law Sch., N.Y.C., 1978-86, prof., 1986—, Joseph M. McLaughlin prof., 1997—. Arbitrator Nat. Assn. Securities Dealers; chair subcom. interrogatories U.S. Dist. Ct. (so. dist.) N.Y., 1983-85. Contbr. articles to profl. jours. Recipient Teacher of Year award, Fordham Law School Students, 2001. Fellow N.Y. Bar Found.; mem. Assn. Bar City of N.Y. (v.p. 1995-96, long range planning com. 1996-2000, exec. com. 1976-80, com. audit 1988-95, labor com. 1981-84, judiciary com. 1975-76, chmn. civil rights com. 1972-75), N.Y. State Bar Assn. (exec. com. 1979-81, ho. dels. 1978-81, com. constitution and by-laws 1984-93), N.Y. Women's Bar Assn. (Pres.'s award 1999). Office: Fordham U Law Sch 140 W 62nd St New York NY 10023-7485

MARCUS, PAUL, law educator; b. N.Y.C., Dec. 8, 1946; s. Edward and Lillian (Rubin) M.; m. Rebecca Nimmer, Dec. 22, 1968; children: Emily, Beth, Daniel. AB, UCLA, 1968, JD, 1971. Bar: Calif. 1971, U.S. Dist. Ct. (cen. dist.) Calif. 1972, U.S. Ct. Appeals (D.C. cir.) 1972, U.S. Ct. Appeals (7th cir.) 1976. Law clk. U.S. Ct. Appeals (D.C. cir.), 1971-72; assoc. Loeb & Loeb, L.A., 1972-74; prof. law U. Ill., Urbana, 1974-83; dean Coll. Law U. Ariz., Tucson, 1983-88, prof., 1988-92; Haynes prof. law Coll. William and Mary, Williamsburg, Va., 1992—, interim dean, 1993-94, 97-98. Reporter, cons. Fed. Jud. Ctr. Commn. Author: The Entrapment Defense, 1989, 2d edit., 1995, The Prosecution and Defense of Criminal Conspiracy, 1978, 4th edit., 1997, Gilbert Law Summary, 1982, 6th edit., 2000, Criminal Law: Cases and Materials, 1982, 4th edit., 1998, Criminal Procedure in Practice, 2001; nat. reporter on criminal law Internat. of Comparative Law, 1978—. Nat. reporter on criminal law Internat. of Comparative Law, 1978—. Office: Coll William & Mary Sch Law Williamsburg VA 23185 E-mail: pxmarc@wm.edu

MARCUS, STANLEY, federal judge; b. 1946; BA, CUNY, 1967; JD, Harvard U., 1971. Assoc. Botein, Hays, Sklar & Herzberg, N.Y.C., 1974-75; asst. atty. U.S. Dist. Ct. (ea. dist.) N.Y., 1975-78; spl. atty., dep. chief U.S. organized crime sect. Detroit Strike Force, 1978-79, chief U.S. organized crime sect., 1980-82; U.S. atty. So. Dist. of Fla., Miami, 1982-85; judge U.S. Dist. Ct. (so. dist.) Fla., 1985-97, U.S. Ct. Appeals (11th cir.), 1997—. Office: US Ct of Appeals 11th Cir 99 NE 4th St Rm 1262 Miami FL 33132-2185*

MARCUSA, FRED HAYE, lawyer; b. Paterson, N.J., Jan. 31, 1946; s. Harry and Alice Marcusa; m. Andrea Disario, June 28, 1986; children; Michael, Daniel. AB, Dartmouth Coll., 1967; JD, U. Pa., 1970. Bar: N.Y. 1971. Assoc. Davis, Polk & Wardwell, N.Y.C., 1970-79; v.p., gen. counsel The Coca-Cola Bottling Co. of N.Y., Inc., 1979-81; ptnr. Kaye, Scholer, Fierman, Hays & Handler, 1981—. General corporate, Private international, Securities. Office: Kaye Scholer Fierman Hays & Handler 425 Park Ave New York NY 10022-3506 E-mail: fmarcusa@kayescholer.com

MARCUSS, STANLEY JOSEPH, lawyer; b. Hartford, Conn., Jan. 24, 1942; s. Stanley Joseph and Anne Sutton (Leone) M.; m. Rosemary Daly, July 6, 1968; children: Elena Daly, Aidan Stanley. BA, Trinity Coll., 1963, Cambridge U., 1965, MA, 1968; JD, Harvard U., 1968. Bar: D.C., N.Y., Conn., U.S. Supreme Ct. Staff atty. office of gen. counsel HUD, Washington, 1968; atty. firm Hogan and Hartson, 1968-73; counsel to internat. fin. subcom. U.S. Senate Com. on Banking, Housing and Urban Affairs, 1973-77; dep. asst. sec. for trade regulation Dept. Commerce, Washington, 1977-78, sr. dep. asst. sec. for industry and trade, 1978-79, acting asst. sec. for industry and trade, 1979-80, acting asst. sec. for trade regulation, 1980; mem. firm Milbank, Tweed, Hadley & McCloy, Washington, 1980-93, Bryan Cave, 1993—. Former adj. prof. Am. U. Law Sch. Author: Effective Washington Representation, 1983; mem. bd. overseers U. Calif. Berkeley Law Jour.; contbr. articles to profl. jours. Former trustee Trinity Coll., Hartford. Marshall scholar. Mem. ABA, D.C. Bar (former chmn., steering com. internat. law div.), Phi Beta Kappa. Home: 4616 29th Pl NW Washington DC 20008-2105

MAREADY, WILLIAM FRANK, lawyer; b. Mullins, S.C., Sept. 13, 1932; s. Jesse Frank and Vera (Sellers) M.; m. Brenda McCanless, Nov. 3, 1979. AB, U. N.C., 1955, JD with honors, 1958. Bar: N.C. 1958, U.S. Dist. Ct. N.C. 1960, U.S. Ct. Appeals (4th cir.) 1962, U.S. Supreme Ct. 1968. Assoc. Mudge, Stern, Baldwin & Todd, N.Y.C., 1958-60, Hudson, Ferrell, Carter, Petree & Stockton, Winston-Salem, N.C., 1960-65; ptnr. Petree, Stockton & Robinson, 1965-92, Robinson, Maready, Lawing & Comerford, 1992-97, Maready, Comerford & Britt, 1997-99; prin. Law Offices of William F. Maready, 1999—. N.C. chmn. Winston-Salem/Forsyth County Bd. Edn., 1968-70, chmn., bd. dirs. and mem. exec. com., N.C. State Port Authority, 1984-97. With Green Berets, U.S. Army, 1952-54. Recipient Disting. Svc. award N.C. Sch. Bds. Assn., Freedom award John Locke Soc., 2000. Fellow Am. Coll. Trial Lawyers, Am. Bar Found.; mem. ABA (chmn. standing com. on aero. law 1979-82, chmn. forum com. on air and space law 1982-86), N.C. Bar Assn. (chmn. litigation sect. 1981-82, adminstrn. of justice com. 1981-82), Nat. Parent Tchr. Assn. (life), Forsyth Country Club, Rotary (Winston-Salem), Order of Coif, Phi Delta Phi, Phi Beta Kappa. Republican. Methodist. Product liability, Professional liability, Toxic tort. Office: 1076 W 4th St Ste 100 Winston Salem NC 27101-2411 E-mail: bmaready@mareadylaw.com

MARGER, EDWIN, lawyer; b. N.Y.C., Mar. 18, 1928; s. William and Fannie (Cohen) M.; m. Kaye Sanderson, Oct. 1, 1951; children: Shari Ann, Diane Elaine, Sandy Ben; m. L. Suzanne Smyth, July 5, 1968; 1 child, George Phinney; m. Mary Susan Hamel, May 6, 1987; 1 child, Charleston Faye. BA, U. Miami, 1951, JD, 1953. Bar: Fla. 1953, Ga. 1971, D.C. 1978. Pvt. practice, Miami Beach, Fla., 1953-67, Atlanta, 1971—. Gen. counsel Physicians Nat. Risk Retention Group, 1988-91, Physicians Reliance Assn., 1988-91, Physicians Nat. Legal Def. Corp., 1988-91; spl. asst. atty. gen. Fla., 1960-61; atty., agt. Republic of Haiti, 1962-67, City of Port-au-Prince for Transp. and Housing, 1962, Dominican Republic for Trade and Industry, 1964-65; of counsel Richard Burns, Miami, 1967—. Contbr. articles to profl. jours. Tchr. Nat. Inst. Trial Advocacy; mem. Miami Beach Social Svc. Commn., 1957; chmn. Fulton County Aviation Adv. Com., 1980—; trustee Forensic Scis. Found., 1984-88; v.p., 1986-88; lt. col., a.d.c. Gov. Ga., 1971-74, 80-84; col., a.d.c. Gov. La., 1977-87; Khan Bahador and mem. exiled King of Afghanistan Privy Council, 1980—. With USAAF, 1946-47. Fellow Am. Acad. Forensic Scis. (chmn. jurisprudence sect. 1977-78, sec. 1976-77, bd. dirs. 1978-79, exec. com. 1983-86); mem. ABA, Fla. Bar Assn. (aerospace com. 1971-83, bd. govs. 1983-87, 90-94, exec. com. 1993-94), State Bar Ga. (chmn. sect. environ. law 1974-75, aviation law sect. 1978, bd. govs. 1999—, stds. of the profession com.), Ga. Trial Lawyers Assn. (mem. stds. of the profession com. 1999—), Nat. Assn. Criminal Def. Lawyers, Ga. Assn. Criminal Def. Lawyers, Assn. Trial Lawyers Am., Am. Judicature Soc., Am. Arbitration Assn. (commn. panel 1978), Inter-Am. Bar Assn. (sr.), World Assn. Lawyers (founding), Lawyer-Pilots Bar Assn. (founding, v.p. 1959-62), VFW, Rotary, Advocates Club. Criminal, Family and matrimonial, Public international. Office: 44 N Main St Jasper GA 30143-1501

MARGOLIN, STEPHEN M. lawyer; b. Chgo., Dec. 23, 1935; s. Albert and Mae Dorothy (Kaufman) M.; m. Pamela B. Miles, March 28, 1998; children: Jocelyn, Holly, Jonathan. BS, U. Ill., 1957; JD, John Marshall Law Sch., 1964. Bar: Ill. 1964, U.S. Dist. Ct. (no. dist.) Ill. 1964. Field agt., lectr. IRS, 1957-62; ptnr. Brainerd, Brydges and Margolin, Chgo., 1965-68; pvt. practice, 1968-77; sr. ptnr. Margolin, Zeitlin & Aronson, 1977—. Contbr. articles to profl. jours. Co-chmn. lawyers divsn. Jewish United Fund, 1982—. Served to 1st lt. U.S. Army, 1958. Mem. ABA (employee benefit com., tax com.), Ill. State Bar Assn. (employee benefit sect.), Midwest Pension Conf., Chgo. Assn. Commerce and Industry (employee benefit subcom. 1981—). Pension, profit-sharing, and employee benefits, Corporate taxation. Office: Chuhak & Tecson PC 225 W Washington St Ste 1300 Chicago IL 60606-3516 E-mail: smargolin@chuhak.com

MARGOLIS, EMANUEL, lawyer, educator; b. Bklyn., Mar. 18, 1926; s. Abraham and Esther (Levin) M.; m. Edith Cushing; m. Estelle Thompson, Mar. 1, 1959; children: Elizabeth Margolis-Pineo, Catherine, Abby Margolis Newman, Joshua, Sarah. BA, U. N.C., 1947; MA, Harvard U., 1948, PhD, 1951; JD, Yale U., 1956. Bar: Conn. 1957, U.S. Dist. Ct. Conn. 1958, U.S. Supreme Ct. 1969. Instr. dept. govt. U. Conn., 1951-53; assoc. Silberberg & Silverstein, Ansonia, Conn., 1956-60, Wofsey Rosen Kweskin & Kuriansky, Stamford, 1960-66, ptnr., 1966-96, of counsel, 1996—. Arbitrator State of Conn., 1984-85; adj. prof. Quinnipiac U. Sch. Law, 1986—. Sr. editor Conn. Bar Jour., 1971-80, 83—, editor-in-chief, 1980-83; contbr. to profl. jours. Mem. nat. bd. ACLU, 1975-79; mem. Westport (Conn.) Planning and Zoning Commn., 1971-75; chmn. Conn. CLU, 1988-95, legal advisor, 1995—; exec. com. Yale Law Sch., 2000—. With U.S. Army, 1944-46. Decorated Purple Heart; recipient First Award for Disting. Svc. to Bar, Conn. Law Tribune, 1987. Fellow Conn. Bar Found. (James W. Cooper fellow 1996); mem. ABA, Conn. Bar Assn. (chmn. human rights sect. 1970-73), Nat. Assn. Criminal Def. Lawyers, Am. Arbitration Assn. (arbitrator 1998—, trial referee 1985—). Civil rights, Federal civil litigation, Criminal. Office: 600 Summer St Stamford CT 06901-1990 Home: 72 Myrtle Ave Westport CT 06880-3512 E-mail: veecha@optonline.net

MARGOLIS, EUGENE, lawyer, government official; b. Bronx, N.Y., Dec. 19, 1935; s. Louis and Minnie (Kaplan) M.; m. Sally Fay Gellman, Sept. 22, 1962; children: Judith Miriam, Linda Aileen, Aaron Keith, Pamela June. BME, Rensselaer Poly. Inst., 1957; JD, Georgetown U., 1960, M in Patent Law, 1962. Bar: N.Y. 1961, U.S. Supreme Ct. 1969; cert. exec. U.S. Office Personnel Mgmt., 1983. Patent examiner U.S. Patent Office, Washington, 1957-60; trial atty. antitrust divsn. U.S. Dept. Justice, 1960-66, N.Y.C., 1966-67; chief consumer protection divsn. N.Y.C. Dept. Law, 1969-71; gen. counsel Mayor's Inderdeptl. Com. on Pub. Utilities, 1972-73; spl. counsel to commr. N.Y.C. Dept. Gen. Svcs., 1974-79; dir. N.Y.C. Office of Energy Conservation, 1975-79; sr. legal adviser U.S. Dept. Energy, Washington, 1979-95, dep. asst. gen. counsel, 1995—. Adj. prof. Cooper Union, 1978-79; adj. assoc. prof. Grad. Sch. CUNY, 1974-80. Mem. editl. bd. Georgetown Law Jour., 1958-60. Chmn. govtl. rels. and grants com. Village of Larchmont, N.Y., 1977-79, mem. cable TV com., 1977-79, mem. tax base com., 1974-79; chmn. Larchmont Dem. Com., 1976-77; vice chmn. Mamaroneck Dem. Com., 1979; mem. Westchester County Dem. Com., 1975-77, 79; bd. dirs. Jewish Cmty. Coun. Greater Washington, 1986-94; mem. adv. bd. Dept. Volunteerism, Commonwealth Va., 1987-91; mem. pub. social policy com. United Jewish Appeal-Fedn. Greater Washnigton, 1988—, mem. No. Va. leadership coun., 1990—; sr. v.p. B'nai Brith Internat., 1996-98, bd. govs., 1992—, Hillel com., 1991-94, com. on cmty. vol. svcs., 1985-89, pres. dist. 5, 1993-94, pres. Va. State Assn., 1986-87, pres. Va. Hillel Found., 1985-86. Recipient Cert. of Appreciation U.S. Dept. Energy, 1984, Sec. of Energy's Award, Outstanding Cmty. Svc. Vol., 1990, Gov. Va.'s Cmty. Svc. and Volunteerism award, 1995. Mem. N.Y. State Bar Assn., ASME, Rensselaer Alumni (sec. chpt. 1976-77), U. Va. Fund Parents, Town and Village Synagogue Men's Club (pres. 1970-71), B'nai Brith (pres. Mcpl. lodge 1976-78, Larchmont-Mamaroneck lodge 1978-80, Masada lodge 1984-85, Internat. Lodge Col. Elliot A. Niles Cmty. Svc. award 1984, Disting. 5 Outstanding Ben Brith award 1988, Outstanding State Pres. award 1987, Hillel award 1986, Cmty. Vol. Svc. award 1984, Va. State Assn. Herman G. Koplen Meml. award 1987, Sherry B. Rose Leadership award 1984), Phi Delta Phi, Pi Delta Epsilon, Tau Epsilon Phi. Jewish. Home: 6504 Sparrow Point Ct Mc Lean VA 22101-1638 Office: US Dept Energy Forrestal Bldg 1000 Independence Ave SE Washington DC 20585-0001 E-mail: eugene.margolis@hq.doe.gov

MARGOLIS, LAWRENCE STANLEY, federal judge; b. Phila., Mar. 13, 1935; m. Doris May Rosenberg, Jan. 30, 1960; children: Mary Aleta, Paul Oliver. BSME, Drexel U., 1957; JD, George Washington U., 1961. Bar: D.C. 1963. Patent examiner U. S. Patent Office, Washington, 1957-62; patent counsel Naval Ordnance Lab., White Oak, Md., 1962-63; asst. corp. counsel D.C., 1963-66; atty. criminal div., spl. asst. U.S. atty. Dept. of Justice, Washington, 1966-68; asst. U.S. atty. for D.C., 1968-71; U.S. magistrate judge U.S. Dist. Ct., Washington, 1971-82; judge U.S. Ct. Fed. Claims, 1982—; chmn. task force on discovery reform U.S. Claims Ct., chmn. alt. dispute resolution. Chmn. Space and Bldg. com., mem. faculty Fed. Jud. Ctr. Editor-in-chief The Young Lawyer, 1965-66, D.C. Bar Jour., 1967-73; bd. editors The Dist. Lawyer, 1978-82. Trustee Drexel U., 1983-89; bd. govs. George Washington U. Alumni Assn., 1978-85, 93-96 Recipient Contbn. award D.C. Jaycees, 1966, Svc. award Boy Scouts Am., 1970, Alumni Svc. award George Washington U., 1976, Disting. Alumni Achievement award George Washington U., 1985, Disting. Alumni Achievement award Drexel U., 1988, Drexel 100 award, 1992, Alternative Dispute Resolution award Ctr. for Pub. Resources, 1988, Alternative Dispute Resolution Svc. award Ct. of Fed. Claims, 1996, Alumni Recognition award George Washington U., 1996. Fellow Inst. Jud. Adminstrn., Am. Bar Found.; mem. ABA (chmn. jud. adminstrn. divsn., Disting. Svc. award 1981), ABA Nat. Conf. Spl. Ct. Judges (chmn., Disting. Svc. award 1978), D.C. Jud. Conf., Bar Assn. D.C. (bd. dirs. 1970-72, jour. editor-in-chief, Contbn. award young lawyers sect. 1983), Fed. Bar Assn., George Washington U. Nat. Law Assn. (pres. D.C. chpt. 1974-76, pres. 1983-84), Univ. Club., Rotary (bd. dirs. Washington 1984-90, pres. 1988-89, dist. gov. 1991-92, Rotarian of Yr. 1984, Rotary Internat. Rep. to the World Bank and Orgn. of Am. States, 1998-99, pres. Rotary Found. 1999-2000), Charles Fahy Am. Inn of Ct. (Nat. Program award, 1997), Phila. Cen. High Sch. Alumni (bd. govs., bd. mgrs. 2001—). Office: US Ct Fed Claims 717 Madison Pl NW Ste 703 Washington DC 20439-0002 E-mail: lawrence_margolis@ao.uscourts.gov

MARGULIES, BETH ZELDES, assistant attorney general; b. Hartford, Conn., Apr. 24, 1954; d. Benjamin and Edith Rose (Herrmann) Zeldes; m. Martin B. Margulies, July 26, 1981; children: Max, Adam. BA in Anthropology, McGill U., Montreal, 1976; JD summa cum laude, U. Bridgeport, 1983; LLM, Yale U., 1985. Bar: Conn. 1983, U.S. Dist. Ct. Conn. 1983, U.S. Ct. Appeals (D.C. cir.) 1988, U.S. Supreme Ct., 1989, U.S. Ct. Appeals (2d cir.) 1992. Asst. atty. gen. Atty. Gen.'s Office State of Conn., Hartford, 1985—. Contbr. articles to profl. jours. Home: 79 High Rock Rd Sandy Hook CT 06482-1623 Office: Atty Gen Office State of Conn 55 Elm St Hartford CT 06106-1746 E-mail: beth.margulies@po.state.ct.us

MARGULIES, MARTIN B. lawyer, educator; b. N.Y.C., Oct. 6, 1940; s. Max N. and Mae (Cohen) M.; m. Beth Ellen Zeldes, July 26, 1981; children: Max Zeldes, Adam Zeldes. AB, Columbia Coll., 1961; LLB, Harvard U., 1964; LLM, NYU, 1966. Bar: N.D. 1968, N.Y. 1974, Mass. 1977, Conn. 1988, U.S. Dist. Ct. Mass. 1977, U.S. Ct. Appeals (2d cir.) 1984, U.S. Supreme Ct. 1995. Asst. prof. law U. N.D., Grand Forks, 1966-69; editor-in-chief Columbia Coll. Today, Columbia U., N.Y.C.,

1969-71; assoc. editor Parade Mag., 1971-72; assoc. prof. law Western New Eng. Law Sch., Springfield, Mass., 1973-76; Bernard Hersher prof. law U. Bridgeport, Conn., 1977-92; prof. law Quinnipiac U., 1992—, Neil H. Cogan Pub. Svc. prof. law, 1997-99. Author: The Early Life of Sean O'Casey, 1970; contbr. articles to profl. jours. Cooperating atty. Conn. Civil Liberties Union, Hartford, 1979—, bd. dirs., 1982-94; bd. dirs. Conn. Attys. for Progressive Legislature, New Haven, 1982: bd. dirs. ACLU, 1987-94, mem. free speech-assn. and poverty constl. rights com., 1988-94; chmn. bd. dirs. Fairfield County Civil Liberties Union, 1982-87, Hampden County Civil Liberties Union, 1976-78; bd. dirs. Civil Liberties Union Mass., Boston, 1975-78, Greater Springfield Urban League, 1976-78, Conn. Civil Liberties Union, 1982-94, ACLU, 1987-94, Ctr. for First Amendment Rights, Inc., 1993—. Recipient Media award N.Y. State Bar Assn., 1972, Gavel award ABA, 1973, Outstanding Tchr. award U. Bridgeport Law Sch., 1986, 87. Mem. Mass. Bar Assn., N.Y. State Bar Assn. Jewish. Home: 79 High Rock Rd Sandy Hook CT 06482-1623 Office: Quinnipiac Univ Sch Law 275 Mt Carmel Ave Hamden CT 06518-1947

MARHOFFER, DAVID, lawyer; b. Chgo., Aug. 4, 1966; s. Dov and Marilyn L. (Edelman) M.; m. Jessica A. Segal, May 29, 1994. BSBA, U. Ariz., 1989; JD, U. Calif., San Francisco, 1994. Bar: Ariz. 1994. Law clk. to hon. judge Edward C. Rapp Maricopa County Superior Ct., Phoenix, 1993; ptnr. Marhoffer Don & Segal PLLC, Scottsdale, Ariz., 1994—. Mem. Am. Jewish Com., Phoenix, 1997—. Hastings coll. grant U. Calif. 1992, 93, 94, Legal Equal Opportunity grant, 1992, 93, 94. Mem. Horace Rumpole Am. Inn of Ct., Scottsdale Bar Assn., Phi Alpha Delta, Sigma Alpha Mu (alumni adv. bd. 1996—). Jewish. Avocations: sports, creative writing, history, literature, philosophy. Contracts commercial, Landlord-tenant, Real property. Office: Marhoffer Don Segal PLLC 7373 N Scottsdale Rd Ste D222 Scottsdale AZ 85253-3506

MARIANES, WILLIAM BYRON, lawyer; b. East Chicago, Ind., Apr. 30, 1955; s. William Charles and Bess (Vambakas) M.; m. Audrey Jean May, Aug. 22, 1981; children: Alexis Elaine, Lia Marie. BA, Northwestern U., 1977; MBA, JD, Emory U., 1981. Bar: Ga. 1981, U.S. Dist. Ct. (no. dist.) Ga., 1981, U.S. Ct. Appeals (5th and 11th cir.) 1981. Assoc. Troutman, Sanders, Lockerman & Ashmore, Atlanta, 1981-89, ptnr., 1989—. Bd. advs. Atlanta Legal Aid Soc., 1987, chmn. intellectual property group, chmn. hiring com. Author and Editor: High Tech Legal Guide, 1985. Loaned exec. United Way of Atlanta, 1982, bd. dirs. 1986—; bd. dirs. United Way Loaned Execs. Assn., 1983-85; fund raiser Atlanta Arts Alliance, 1985; mem. Robert Woodruff Scholarship Selection Com., Atlanta, 1985; bd. dirs. Greek Orthodox Cathedral of the Annunciation, also asst. treas., 1986-89. Recipient Loaned Exec. of Yr. award United Way of Atlanta, 1982, Outstanding Service award, United Way of Atlanta, 1986, Service and Leadership award, Emory U. Sch. Bus. Adminstrn., 1981, . Mem. ABA, Ga. Bar Assn., Atlanta Bar Assn., Order of Am. Hellenic Ednl. Progressive Assn. (sec. 1983-85, v.p. 1985-86, pres. 1986-88, dist. sec. 1989-91, dist. lt. gov. 1991-92), Order of Coif. Avocations: music, athletics. Computer, General corporate, Trademark and copyright. Home: 2692 Cold Water Canyon Dr Tucker GA 30084-2354 Office: Troutman Sanders Lockerman & Ashmore 600 Peachtree St NE Ste 5200 Atlanta GA 30308-2231

MARIANI, MICHAEL MATTHEW, lawyer; b. West Pittston, Pa., Sept. 25, 1950; s. Stephen Francis and Tulia Felicia (DelCorso) M.; m. Patricia Mary Leptak, June 26, 1976; children: Kathryn Elizabeth, Michael Joseph. BS with honors, Wilkes Coll., 1972; JD, St. John's U., Jamaica, N.Y., 1975; LLM, NYU, 1980. Bar: N.Y. 1976, U.S. Dist. Ct. (so. and ea. dists.) N.Y. 1976, U.S. Tax Ct. 1980. Law sec. to presiding judge Surrogate's Ct., New City, N.Y., 1976-80; assoc. Law offices of Edward S. Schlesinger P.C., N.Y.C., 1981-97; sr. v.p., trust counsel Fiduciary Trust Co. Internat., 1997—. Co-author: New York Probate, 1986, supplements 1987-2001; contbr. articles to profl. jours. Trustee Cath. Charities, Diocese of Bklyn., 1981—, treas., 1985-87, v.p., 1987-89, pres., 1989-91; bd. dirs. Mercy Home for Children, Bklyn., 1989-97, adv. bd. mem., 1997—. Recipient Benemerenti medal Pope John Paul II, 1997. Mem. ABA (real property, probate and trust law sects.), N.Y. State Bar Assn. (trusts and estates sects.) Democrat. Estate planning, Probate, Estate taxation. Home: 53-32 215th St Bayside NY 11364-1835 Office: Fiduciary Trust Co Internat 600 Fifth Ave New York NY 10019 E-mail: mmaria@ftci.com

MARICK, MICHAEL MIRON, lawyer; b. Chgo., Nov. 20, 1957; s. Miron Michael and Geraldyne Marilyn (Lid) M.; m. LIsa Amy Gelman, May 17, 1986. BA, Denison U., 1979; JD, Ill. Inst. Tech., 1982. Bar: Ill. 1982, U.S. Dist. Ct. (no. dist.) Ill. 1982, Fla. 1983, U.S. Ct. Appeals (3rd cir.) 1988, U.S. Ct. Appeals (6th cir.) 1992, U.S. Supreme Ct. 1992. Assoc. Hinshaw, Culbertson, Moelmann, Hoban & Fuller, Chgo., 1982-85, Phelan, Pope & John, Chgo., 1985-90; ptnr. Pope & John, 1990-94, Meckler Bulger & Tilson, Chgo., 1994—. Adj. prof. Ill. Inst. Tech./Chgo.-Kent Coll. Law, 1983-84, 87-99; comml. arbitrator Am. Arbitration Assn., Chgo., 1983—. Mem. Ill. Inst. Tech./Chgo.-Kent Law Rev., 1980-82; contbr. articles on ins. law and litigation to profl. jours. Treas., mem. exec. com. 42d Ward Rep. Orgn., 1984-87. Denison U. Econs. fellow, 1978, State of Ill. Gov.'s fellow, 1978; recipient Disting. Svc. award Ill. Inst. Tech./Chgo. Kent Coll. Law, 1996. Mem. ABA (mem. exec. com., com. on legis. action young lawyers divsn. 1983-84, vice chmn. TIPS excess surplus lines and reins. com. 1990-92)), Ill. Bar Assn. (ins. law sect. coun. 1991-96, chair 1994-95, assembly rep. 1993-96), Fla. Bar Assn., Chgo. Bar Assn., Def. Rsch. Inst., Internat. Assn. Def. Counsel, Ill. Inst. Tech./Chgo.-Kent Coll. Law Alumni Assn. (v.p. 1990-94, pres. 1994-95), Trial Lawyers Club, Omicron Delta Upsilon, Pi Sigma Alpha, Alpha Tau Omega. Presbyterian. Federal civil litigation, State civil litigation, Insurance. Home: 3605 Pebble Beach Rd Northbrook IL 60062-3109 Office: Meckler Bulger & Tilson 8300 Sears Tower 233 S Wacker Dr Ste 8300 Chicago IL 60606-6339 E-mail: michael.marick@mbtlaw.com

MARINACCIO, CHARLES LINDBERGH, lawyer, consultant; b. Stratford, Conn., Dec. 10, 1933; BA, U. Conn., 1957; JD with honors, George Washington U., 1962. Bar: Conn. 1962, D.C. 1982. Trial lawyer U.S. Dept. Justice, Washington, 1963-69; advisor supervisory and regulation div. Fed. Res. Bd., 1969-73; dir., exec. sec. law enforcement asstistance adminstrn. U.S. Dept. Justice, 1973-75; gen. counsel banking housing and urban affairs com. U.S. Senate, 1975-84; commr. SEC, 1984-85; ptnr. Kelley, Drye & Warren, 1985-94; ind. cons., 1995—. Apptd. by Pres. Clinton to bd. dirs. Securities Investor Protection Corp.; bd. dirs. AmeriTrade Holding Corp., Omaha. Home and Office: 4911 Massachusetts Ave NW Washington DC 20016-4310

MARING, MARY MUEHLEN, state supreme court justice; b. Devils Lake, N.D., July 27, 1951; d. Joseph Edward and Charlotte Rose (Schorr) Muehlen: m. David Scott Maring, Aug. 30, 1975; children: Christopher David, Andrew Joseph. BA in Polit. Sci. summa cum laude, Moorhead State U., 1972; JD, U. N.D., 1975. Bar: Minn., N.D. Law clk. Hon. Bruce Stone, Mpls, 1975-76; assoc. Stefanson, Landberg & Alm, Ltd., Moorhead, Minn., 1976-82, Ohnstad, Twichell, Breitling, Rosenvold, Wanner, Nelson, Neugebauer & Maring, P.C., West Fargo, N.D., 1982-88, Lee Hagan Law Office, Fargo, 1988-91; pvt. practice Maring Law Office, 1991-96; assoc. justice N.D. State Supreme Ct., Bismarck, N.D., 1996—. Women's bd. mem. 1st Nat. Bank, Fargo, 1977-82; career day speaker Moorhead Rotarians, 1980-83. Contbr. note to legal rev.; note editor N.D. Law Rev., 1975. Mem. ABA (del. ann. conv. young lawyers sect. 1981-82, bd. govs. 1982-83), Minn. Women Lawyers, N.D. State Bar Assn. (bd. govs. 1991-93), Minn. Trial Lawyers Assn., Clay County Bar Assn. (v.p. 1983-84), N.D. Trial Lawyers Assn. (pres. 1992-93), Roman Catholic. Office: ND Supreme Ct Dept 180 600 E Boulevard Ave Fl 1 Bismarck ND 58505-0530*

MARINIS, THOMAS PAUL, JR. lawyer; b. Jacksonville, Tex., May 31, 1943; s. Thomas Paul and Betty Sue (Garner) M.; m. Lucinda Cruse, June 25, 1969; children: Courtney, Kathryn, Megan. BA, Yale U., 1965; LLB, U. Tex., 1968. Bar: Tex. 1968. Assoc. Vinson & Elkins, Houston, 1969-76, ptnr., 1977—. Bd. dirs. Phoenix House of Tex., Inc. Fellow Tex. Bar Found.; mem. ABA (sec. taxation sect. 1986-87), Houston Country Club, Houston Ctr. Club, Coronado Club. Corporate taxation, Personal income taxation. E-mail: tmarinis@velaw.com

MARK, MICHAEL DAVID, lawyer; b. Bklyn., Sept. 16, 1944; s. Irving and Mildred Mark; children: Dana Lynne, Stephanie Lauren. BA, Rutgers U., 1966; JD, U. Tenn., 1969. Bar: Tenn. 1969, N.J. 1970, U.S. Dist. Ct. N.J. 1970, U.S. Supreme Ct. 1973; cert. civil trial atty., N.J. Supreme Ct. 1992. House counsel Liberty Mut. Ins. Co., East Orange, N.J., 1969-71; assoc. Skoloff & Wolfe, Newark, 1971-73; pvt. practice, Union, N.J., 1973—. Past assoc. bd. dirs. United Jersey Bank, Union; Police Benevolent Assn. lawyer City of Linden, N.J., 1980—, Clark Twp., Clark, N.J., 1986; mem. Union-Essex County Early Settlement Panels, Elizabeth and Newark. Mem. Am. Acad. Matrimonial Lawyers (bd. mgrs. 1982—), N.J. Bar Assn., Union County Bar Assn., Union Lawyers Club (past pub. defender). Republican. Avocation: private pilot. General civil litigation, Family and matrimonial, Real property. Office: 2444 Morris Ave Union NJ 07083-5711

MARK, RICHARD STEVE, lawyer, educator, consultant; b. Denver, June 19, 1948; s. Stephen Frank and Hilda (Cavarra) M.; m. Barbara Lester, June l, 1974. BS in Mech. Engring., U. Colo., 1971, JD, 1974; LLM in Taxation, U. Denver, 1977. Bar: Colo. 1974, Tex. 1978, U.S. Dist. Ct. Colo. 1974; CPA. Pvt. practice law, Denver, 1974-77; trust officer United Bank Denver, 1977-79; tax cons. Atlantic Richfield, Dallas, 1979-80; prof. U. Tex., Arlington, 1980— ; dir. Quantum Resources Corp., Denver, 1979-82. Author: Current Updates in Oil Tax, 1984, Royalty Trusts, 1984; co-author: Handbook of Oil and Gas Tax, 1988; contbr. articles to profl. jours. Mem. Coun. Petroleum Accts. (chmn. edn. com. Ft. Worth 1984), ABA (natural resources com. 1988), Tex. Bar Assn., Colo. Bar Assn., Am. Inst. C.P.A.s (edn. com. 1982-84), Ind. Producers Assn. Am. (mem. tax com., editor Journal Petroleum Accounting), Omicron Delta Kappa, Tau Beta Pi. Home and Office: 125 Hunters Hill Ct Argyle TX 76226-9665

MARK, TIMOTHY IVAN, lawyer; b. Hershey, Pa., Oct. 8, 1951; s. Howard Behm and Ethel Mae Beam Mark; m. Janice Leigh Evans, Jan. 5, 1974; children: Andrew James, Amy Elizabeth. BA cum laude, East Stroudsburg U., 1973; JD cum laude, Temple U., 1978. Bar: Pa. 1978, U.S. Dist. Ct. (mid. dist.) Pa. 1978, U.S. Supreme Ct. 1983, U.S. Ct. Appeals (3d cir.) 1983. Law clk. intern U.S. Dist. Ct. (ea. dist.) Pa., Phila., 1978; asst. atty. gen. Com. of Pa., Harrisburg, 1978-79; shareholder Goldberg, Evans and Katzman, 1979-85; ptnr. Evans, Stone and Mark, 1985-87; shareholder Mette, Evans and Woodside, 1987-92, Caldwell & Kearns, Harrisburg, 1992-97; of counsel Thomas Thomas and Hafer, 1997-99; pvt. practice, Hummelstown, Pa., 1999—. Lectr. Pa. Bar Assn., Harrisburg, 1992—. Mem. Pa. Def. Inst. (bd. dirs. 1990-96), Def. Rsch. Inst., Pa. Trial Lawyers Assn., Pa. Bar Assn. Avocations: golfing, reading, computer research. General civil litigation, Insurance, Personal injury. Home and Office: 811 Providence Cir Hummelstown PA 17036-9753

MARKE, JULIUS JAY, law librarian, educator; b. N.Y.C., Jan. 12, 1913; s. Isidore and Anna (Taylor) M.; m. Sylvia Bolotin, Dec. 15, 1946; 1 child, Elisa Hope. BS, CCNY, 1934; LLB, NYU, 1937; BS in Lib. Sci., Columbia U., 1942. Bar: N.Y. 1938. Reference asst. N.Y. Pub. Libr., 1937-42; pvt. practice law N.Y.C., 1939-41; prof. law, law libr. NYU, 1949-83, prof. law emeritus, 1983—, interim dean of librs., 1975-77; Disting. Prof., dir. Law Libr. St. John's U. Sch. Law, 1983-95, disting. rsch. prof. law N.Y., 1995—. Lectr. Columbia Sch. Library Service, 1962-78, adj. prof., 1978-85; cons. Orientation Program Am. Law, 1965-68, Found. Overseas Law Libraries Am. Law, 1968-79, copyright Ford Found., law libraries, Coun. Fgn. Rels., 1990—, Shubert Archives, 1991, others. Author: Vignettes of Legal History, 1965, 2d series, 1977, rev. edit., 2000, Copyright and Intellectual Property, 1967 (with R. Sloane) Legal Research and Law Library Management, rev. edit., 1990, 2001; editor: Modern Legal Forms, 1953, The Holmes Reader, 1955, The Docket Series, 1955—, Bender's Legal Business Forms, 4 vols., 1962; compiler, editor: A Catalogue of the Law Collection at NYU with Selected Annotations, 1953, Dean's List of Recommended Reading for Pre-Law and Law Students, 1958, 84, and others; chmn. editl. bd. Oceana Group, 1977—, Index to Legal Periodicals, 1978—; columnist N.Y. Law Jour., 1970—; contbr. articles to profl. jours. Mem. publs. coun. N.Y.U., 1964-80. Sgt. AUS, 1943-45. Decorated Bronze Star. Mem. ABA, Am. Assn. Law Librs. (pres. 1962-63, Disting. Svc. award 1986), Assn. Am. Law Schs., Coun. of Nat. Libr. Assns. (exec. bd., v.p. 1959, 60), Law Libr. Assn. Greater N.Y. (pres. 1949, 50, chmn. joint com. on libr. edn. 1950-52, 60-61), NYU Law Alumni Assn. (Judge Edward Weinfeld award 1987, mem. exec. bd. 1988—), Columbia Sch. Libr. Svc. Alumni Assn. (pres. 1973-75), Order of Coif (pres. NYU Law Sch. br. 1970-83), NYU Faculty Club (pres. 1966-68), Field Inn, Phi Delta Phi. Home: 4 Peter Cooper Rd Apt 8F New York NY 10010-6746

MARKER, MARC LINTHACUM, lawyer, investor; b. Los Angeles, July 19, 1941; s. Clifford Harry and Voris (Linthacum) M.; m. Sandra Vocom. Aug. 29, 1965; children: Victor, Gwendolyn. BA in Econs. and Geography, U. Calif.-Riverside, 1964; JD, U. So. Calif., 1967. Asst. v.p., asst. sec. Security Pacific Nat. Bank, L.A., 1970-73; sr. v.p., chief counsel, sec. Security Pacific Leasing Corp., San Francisco, 1973-92; pres. Security Pacific Leasing Svcs. Corp., 1977-85, dir., 1977-92. Bd. dirs., sec. Voris, Inc., 1973-86; bd. dirs. Refiners Petroleum Corp., 1977-81, Security Pacific Leasing Singapore Ltd., 1983-85, Security Pacific Leasing Can. Ltd., 1989-92; lectr. in field. Served to comdr., USCGR. Mem. ABA, Calif. Bar Assn., D.C. Bar Assn; Club: Army and Navy. Republican. Lutheran. Banking, Contracts commercial.

MARKEY, BRIAN MICHAEL, lawyer; b. Teaneck, N.J., Feb. 10, 1956; s. Raymond Joseph and Sheila (Barry) M.; m. Virginia M. Lincoln, Oct. 26, 1986. BA cum laude, Rider Coll., 1978; JD, Suffolk U., 1985. Bar: N.J. 1985, U.S. Dist. Ct. N.J. 1985, N.Y. 1988. Assoc. Kohler & Clinch, Hackensack, N.J., 1985-90, Law Office J. Dennis Kohler, Hackensack, 1990-91; pvt. practice law Glen Rock, 1991-94; ptnr. Lincoln & Markey, 1995—. Dir. Glen Rock Savs. Bank. Chmn. Glen Rock Planning Bd. Mem. ABA, N.J. Bar Assn., Glen Rock Independence Day Assn. Roman Catholic. General civil litigation, General practice, Real property. Office: 126 Valley Rd Glen Rock NJ 07452-1796

MARKEY, JAMES KEVIN, lawyer; b. Springfield, Ill., July 15, 1956; s. James Owen and Marjorie Jean (Diesness) M.; m. Allison Markey; children: Lauren, Katherine. BBA with highest honors, U. Notre Dame, 1977; JD cum laude, U. Mich., 1980; MBA, U. Chgo., 1987; LLM in Taxation, DePaul U., 1993. Bar: Ill. 1980; CPA, Ill. Assoc. Chapman & Cutler, Chgo., 1980-81; atty. Quaker Oats Co., 1981-84; corp. counsel Baxter Healthcare Corp., Deerfield, Ill., 1984-90; v.p. law and other positions Motorola, Inc., Schaumburg, 1990-2000; v.p., chief counsel-securities and internat. Kellogg Co., Battle Creek, Mich., 2000—. Mem. ABA, Beta Alpha Psi, Beta Gamma Sigma. Avocations: racquetball, running, bridge. Contracts commercial, General corporate, Mergers and acquisitions. Home: 3541 Sandhill Ln Portage MI 49024 Office: Kellogg Co One Kellogg Sq Battle Creek MI 49016 E-mail: jim.markey@kellogg.com

MARKEY, ROBERT GUY, lawyer, director; b. Cleveland, Ohio, Feb. 25, 1939; s. Nate and Rhoda (Gross) Markey; m. Nanci Louise Brooks, Aug. 25, 1990; children: Robert Guy, Randolph. AB, Brown U., 1961; JD, Case Western Res., 1964. Bar: Ohio 1964. Ptnr. Baker & Hostetler. Republican. Jewish. General corporate, Mergers and acquisitions, Securities. Office: Baker & Hostetler 3200 National City Ctr 1900 E 9th St Ste 3200 Cleveland OH 44114-3475

MARKHAM, CHARLES BUCHANAN, retired lawyer; b. Durham, N.C., Sept. 15, 1926; s. Charles Blackwell and Sadie Helen (Hackney) M. A.B., Duke U., Durham, N.C., 1945; postgrad., U. N.C. Law Sch., Chapel Hill, 1945-46; LL.B., George Washington U., Washington, 1951. Bar: D.C. 1951, N.Y. 1961, N.C. 1980, U.S. Ct. Appeals (2d cir.) 1962, U.S. Ct. Appeals (D.C. cir.) 1955, U.S. Supreme Ct. 1964. Reporter Durham Sun, N.C., 1945; asst. state editor, editorial writer Charlotte News, 1947-48; dir. publicity and research Young Democratic Clubs Am., Washington, 1948-49, exec. sec., 1949-50; polit. analyst Dem. Senatorial Campaign Com., 1950-51; spl. atty. IRS, Washington and N.Y.C., 1952-60; assoc. Battle, Fowler, Stokes and Kheel, N.Y.C., 1960-65; dir. research U.S. Equal Employment Opportunity Commn., Washington, 1965-68; dep. asst. sec. U.S. Dept. Housing and Urban Devel., 1969-72; asst. dean Rutgers U. Law Sch., Newark, 1974-76; assoc. prof. law N.C. Central U., Durham, 1976-81, prof. law, 1981-83; mayor City of Durham, N.C., 1981-85; ptnr. Markham and Wickham, Durham, 1984-86. Trustee Hist. Preservation Soc. Durham, 1982-86; bd. dirs. Stagville Ctr., 1984-86; mem. Gov.'s Crime Commn., Raleigh, 1985; dep. commr. N.C. Indsl. Commn., Raleigh, 1986-93. Editor: Jobs, Men and Machines: The Problems of Automation, 1964 Mem. Carolina Club, Phi Beta Kappa, Omicron Delta Kappa, Phi Delta Phi, Phi Delta Theta. Republican. Episcopalian. Administrative and regulatory, Personal injury, Workers' compensation. Home: 204 N Dillard St Durham NC 27701-3404

MARKMAN, STEPHEN J. judge; b. Detroit, June 4, 1949; s. Julius and Pauline Markman; m. Mary Kathleen Sites, Aug. 25, 1974; children: James, Charles. BA, Duke U., 1971; JD, U. Cin., 1974. Asst. to Rep. Edward Hutchinson, Mich., 1975; legis. asst. to Rep. Tom Hagedorn, Minn., 1976-78; chief counsel, staff dir. subcom. on constn. Senate Com. on Judiciary, 1978-85, dep. chief counsel, 1983; asst. atty. gen. Office Legal Policy, Dept. Justice, Washington, 1985-89; U.S. atty. U.S. Dept. Justice, Detroit, 1989-93; mem. Miller, Canfield, Paddock & Stone, 1993-99; justice Mich. Supreme Ct., Lansing, 1999—. Office: Mich Supreme Ct G Mennen Williams Bldg 525 W Ottawa St Fl 2 Lansing MI 48933-1067*

MARKÓ, JÓZSEF, patent lawyer; b. Jászberény, Hungary, July 20, 1943; s. Jozsef and Eszter (Strosz) M.; married; children: Dora, Noemi. MS in Mech. Engring., U. Agrl. Engring., Budapest, Hungary, 1966, Dr. in Engring., 1984. Designer Inst. of Bldg. Sci., Budapest, 1966-75; patent atty. Danubia Patent and Trademark Attys., 1975—, sr. ptnr., 1990—. Mem. Union of European Practitioners in Indsl. Property (reporter gen.). Intellectual property. Home: Sárospatak ut 30/C Budapest Hungary Office: Danubia Patent/Trademark Bajcsy-Zsilinszky ut 16 Budapest H-1051 Hungary Fax: (36-1) 266 5770. E-mail: majo@danubia.hu

MARKOVITS, RICHARD SPENCER, lawyer, educator, consultant; b. Middletown, N.Y., Mar. 30, 1942; s. William Benjamin and Dorothy Susan (Franzos) M.; m. Inga Schulthes, Mar. 22, 1967; children: Daniel, Stefanie, Benjamin, Julia, Rebecca. B.A., Cornell U., 1965; Ph.D., U. London, 1966; LL.B., Yale U., 1968; M.A. (hon.), Oxford U., 1981. Bar: Tex. 1978. Lectr. econs. Yale U., New Haven, 1966-68; asst. then assoc. prof. Stanford Law Sch., Calif., 1968-75; mem. law faculty Oxford U., Eng., 1981-83; dir. Ctr. for Socio-Legal Studies, Oxford, 1981-83; prof. U. Tex. Law Sch., Austin, 1975-82, Lloyd M. Bentsen prof. law, 1983-85, Marrs McLean prof. law, 1985—; Baker & Botts Regents Research prof., 1988-89; panel mem. NSF, Washington, 1978-80; mem. econ. affairs com. Social Sci. Research Council, London, 1982-83; trustee Law and Soc. Assocs., 1979-80. Contbr. articles to profl. jours.; author collections of essays. Fellow Ctr. for Advanced Studies, Berlin, 1985-86; Guggenheim fellow, 1988. Home: 3112 Wheeler St Austin TX 78705-2816 Office: U Tex Law Sch 727 E 26th St Austin TX 78705-3224

MARKS, ANDREW H. lawyer; b. N.Y.C., May 5, 1951; s. Theodore and Rosalie Ruth (Goldman) M.; m. Susan G. Esserman, Aug. 3, 1975; children: Stephen Matthew, Clifford Michael, Michael David. AB, Harvard U., 1973; JD, U. Mich., 1976. Bar: Fla. 1976, D.C., 1977, Md. 1984, U.S. Ct. Appeals (D.C. cir.). Law clerk for Hon. Charles R. Richey U.S. Dist. Ct. D.C., Washington, 1976-78; exec. asst. to personal rep. of Pres. to Middle East Peace negotiations, 1979-81; assoc. Shea & Gardner, 1978-79, 81-84, ptnr., 1984-86, Crowell & Moring L.L.P., Washington, 1986—. Mem. D.C. Bar (pres. 1998-99, bd. govs. 1989-95, chmn. task force civility in the profession 1993-96), Harvard Club Washington (pres. 1994-96). Insurance, Professional liability. Office: Crowell & Moring LLP 1001 Pennsylvania Ave NW Fl 10 Washington DC 20004-2505

MARKS, JONATHAN BOWLES, lawyer, mediator, arbitrator; b. Dec. 17, 1943; s. Herbert Simon Marks and Rebecca (Bowles) Marks Hawkins; m. Nandita Wagle, Dec. 18, 1971; children: Joshua Benegal, Natasha Bowles. BA cum laude, Harvard U., 1966, JD cum laude, 1972. Bar: Fla. 1972, D.C. 1973, Calif. 1976. Asst. U.S. Atty., Washington, 1973-76; assoc. Munger, Tolles & Rickershauser, L.A., 1976-78, ptnr., 1979; counsel, assoc. dir. planning and evaluation Peace Corps, Washington, 1979-80; gen. counsel Internat. Devel. Coop. Agy., 1980-81; dispute resolution cons., 1981-82; pres. EnDispute, Inc., 1982-94; vice chmn. Jams-EnDispute, 1994-99; prin. MarksADR, LLC, 1999—. Author: Dispute Resolution in America: Processes in Evolution, 1984. Campaign staff Sargent Shriver for V.P., 1972; campaign dir. Calif. for Ct., L.A., 1978. Democrat. Home: 4410 Chalfont Pl Bethesda MD 20816-1804 Office: 800 Connecticut Ave NW Ste 200 Washington DC 20006-2712

MARKS, MERTON ELEAZER, lawyer; b. Chgo., Oct. 16, 1932; s. Alfred Tobias and Helene Fannie (Rosner) M.; m. Radee Maiden Feiler, May 20, 1966; children: Sheldon, Elise Marks Vazelakis, Alan, Elaine Marks Ianchiou. BS, Northwestern U., 1954, JD, 1956. Bar: Ill. 1956, U.S. Ct. Mil. Appeals 1957, Ariz. 1958, U.S. Dist. Ct. Ariz. 1960, U.S. Ct. Appeals (9th cir.) 1962, U.S. Supreme Ct. 1970. Assoc. Moser, Compere & Emerson, Chgo., 1956-57; ptnr. Morgan, Marks & Rogers, Tucson, 1960-62; asst. atty. gen. State of Ariz., Phoenix, 1962-64, counsel indsl. commn., 1964-65; from assoc. to ptnr. Shimmel, Hill, Bishop & Greunder, 1965-74; ptnr. Lewis & Roca, 1974—. Lectr. on pharm., health care, product liability and ins. subjects; Judge Pro Tempore Ariz. Ct. Appeals, 1994; legal columnist Exec. Golfer mag. Contbr. articles to profl. jours. Capt. JAGC, USAR, 1957-64. Fellow Chartered Inst. Arbitrators (London); mem. ABA (tort and ins. practice sect., chmn. spl. com. on fed. asbestos legis. 1987-89, chmn. workers compensation and employers liability law com. 1983-84, dispute resolution sect., internat. law and practice sect.), Am. Bd. Trial Advocates, Acad. Hosp. Industry Attys., Am. Coll. Legal Medicine, Internat. Bar Assn. (sect. on bus. law, product liability, advt., unfair competition and consumer affairs com., internat. litigation com., ins. com., arbitration and alt. dispute resolution com.), Drug Info. Assn., Am.

Soc. Pharmacy Law, State Bar Ariz. (chmn. workers compensation sect. 1969-73), Nat. Coun. Self Insurers, Ariz. Self Insurers Assn., Fedn. Ins. and Corp. Counsel (chmn. pharm. litig. sect. 1989-91, chmn. workers compensation sect. 1977-79, v.p. 1978-79, 81, bd. dirs. 1981-89, mem. products liability sect., mem. reinsurance sect.), Internat. Assn. Def. Counsel, Ariz. Assn. Def. Counsel (pres. 1976-77), Maricopa County Bar Assn., Def. Rsch. Inst. (drug and device com., chmn. workers compensation com. 1977-78), Assn. Internat. de Droit des Assurances (cert. arbitrator), Reinsurance and Ins. Arbitration Soc. (cert. arbitrator), Union Internat. des Avocats. Alternative dispute resolution, Insurance. Office: 8655 E Via De Ventura Ste G-223 Scottsdale AZ 85258

MARKS, MICHAEL J. lawyer, corporate executive; b. 1938. AB, Cornell U., 1960; JD, U. Chgo., 1963. Assoc. Stroock & Stroock & Lavan, 1964-70, Chun, Kerr & Dodd, 1970-72; counsel Kelso, Spencer, Snyder & Stirling, 1972-75; asst. gen. counsel Alexander & Baldwin Inc., Honolulu, 1975-80, v.p., gen. counsel, 1980-84, v.p., gen. counsel, sec., 1984-85, sr. v.p., gen. counsel, sec., 1985—. General corporate. Office: Alexander & Baldwin Inc 822 Bishop St Honolulu HI 96813-3925

MARKS, MURRY AARON, lawyer; b. Carbondale, Ill., July 14, 1933; Student, Northwestern U., 1951-52; BA, Washington U., 1954; attended, U. So. Calif., 1956; JD, Washington U., 1963. Bar: Mo. 1963, U.S. Dist. Ct. (ea. and we. dists.) Mo. 1969, U.S. Ct. Appeals (8th cir.) 1969, U.S. Supreme Ct. 1972, U.S. Tax Ct. 1984. Asst. county counsellor County of St. Louis, 1963-67; ptnr. Elliott, Marks & Freeman, St. Louis, 1967-1971; pvt. practice, 1971—. With U.S. Army, 1954-56. Fellow St. Louis Bar Found.; mem. ABA, ATLA, Nat. Assn. Criminal Def. Lawyers (life), St. Louis County Bar Assn., Mo. Bar Assn., Am. Coll. Legal Medicine, Mo. Assn. Trial Attys., Mo. Assn. Criminal Def. Attys. (bd. dirs. 1986-90), First Amendment Lawyers Assn., Met. Bar Assn. St. Louis (chmn. internet com. 1995—), Lawyers Assn. St. Louis, Trial Lawyers for Pub. Justice, The Roscoe Pound Found. Criminal, Family and matrimonial, Personal injury. Address: 594 Country Club Dr Lake Ozark MO 65049-8939 Office: 7700 Clayton Rd Ste 307 Saint Louis MO 63117-1347

MARKS, RICHARD DANIEL, lawyer; b. N.Y.C., June 21, 1944; s. Morris Andrew and Dorothy (Schill) M.; m. Cheryl L. Hoffman, Nov. 13, 1971. BA, U. Va., 1966; JD, Yale U., 1969. Bar: D.C., U.S. Ct. Appeals (3rd, 4th, 8th, 11th and D.C. cir.), U.S. Supreme Ct. Assoc. Dow, Lohnes & Albertson, Washington, 1972-78, ptnr., 1978-97, Vinson & Elkins, Washington, 1997-2000, Davis Wright Tremaine, Washington, 2000—. Co-author: Legal Problems in Broadcasting, 1974. Trustee U. Va. Coll. Found., 2001—. Capt. U.S. Army, 1970-72. Mem. ABA (chmn. contracting for computer com., sect. for sci. and tech., computer law div., chmn. computer law div. 1994—), Fed. Comms. Bar Assn., Am. Law Inst., Computer Law Assn. (dir. 1999—), Capital Area Assn. Flight Instrs. (pres. 1989-90), UVA Club of Washington (pres. 1991-92). Avocations: aviation, skiing. Communications, Computer, Trademark and copyright. Office: Davis Wright Tremaine LLP 1500 K St NW Ste 450 Washington DC 20005-1272 Business E-Mail: richardmarks@dwt.com

MARKS, RICHARD SAMUEL, lawyer, real estate development executive; b. Milw., May 8, 1937; s. Lewis and Ruth Francis (Brindis) M.; m. Julia F. Newman, Aug. 7, 1962; children: Joseph, Richard, Steven. B.A., U. Wis., 1960, D. Jud. Sci., 1963. Bar: Wis. 1963; cert. property mgr. Prin. Hillmark Corp., Atlanta, 1960—, chief exec. officer Madison, 1979—, chmn. bd., 1979—. Trustee State Wis. Bond Bd., Madison, 1975-76; chmn. State Wis. Investment Bd., Madison, 1976-78. Chmn. State Wis. Small Cities Israel Bonds, Madison, 1975-76; bd. dirs. Metro YMCA, Madison, 1974-76, Madison Jewish Fedn., 1974-77, Atlanta Civic Opera Assn., 1983, 20th Century Art Assn. of High Mus., 1983; bd. dirs. Atlanta Jewish Comty. Ctr., Amalidan Jewish Com. Mem. Young Pres.'s Orgn., World Bus. Council. Clubs: Masons, Shriners, Elks. General corporate. Home: PO Box 19238 Avon CO 81620-9999 E-mail: marks1234@aol.com

MARKS, STEVEN CRAIG, lawyer; b. Miami, Sept. 22, 1960; s. Lawrence Martin and Roberta Barbara (Dilner) M. BA cum laude, U. Fla., 1982; JD cum laude, U. Miami, 1985. Bar: Fla. 1985, U.S. Dist. Ct. (so. dist.) Fla. 1985. Ptnr. Podhurst Orseck, Miami, 1985—. Lectr. in field. Editor-in-chief U. Miami Law Rev., 1985. Mem. ABA (mem. program planning com. for Nat. Inst. on Aviation Litigation 1991—, torts and ins. practice section, mem. editl. bd. The Brief), ATLA (treas. aviation law sect. 1996-97, vice chair aviation and space law com. 1996-97, chair 1998—), Dade County Trial Lawyers, Lawyer-Pilots Bar Assn., Am. Bd. Trial Advocates (treas., 2000—), The Fla. Bar, Acad. Fla. Trial Lawyers, Dade County Bar Assn., Inns. of Court, Order of the Coif, Bar Gravel Law Soc. Aviation, Personal injury, Product liability. Office: Podhurst Orseck & Josefsberg 25 W Flagler St Ste 800 Miami FL 33130-1720 E-mail: info@podhurst.com

MARKS, THEODORE LEE, lawyer; b. N.Y.C., Oct. 18, 1935; s. Irving Edward and Isabel (Goodman) M.; m. Benita Cooper, July 13, 1958; children: Eric, Robert, Jennifer B.S., NYU, 1956, LL.B., 1958. Bar: N.Y. 1959, U.S. Dist. Ct. (so. dist.) N.Y. 1963, U.S. Supreme Ct. 1964, U.S. Ct. Appeals (2d cir.) 1975, U.S. Dist. Ct. (ea. dist.) N.Y. 1978. Assoc. Silver, Bernstein, Seawell & Kaplan, N.Y.C., 1959-65; sole practice, 1965-70; ptnr. Lee, Cash & Marks, 1970-76, Vogel, Marks & Rosenberg, N.Y.C., 1976-79, Bromberg, Gloger, Lifschultz & Marks, N.Y.C., 1979-85, Epstein Becker Borsody & Green, P.C., N.Y.C., 1985-86, Gelberg & Abrams, 1986-87, Morrison Cohen Singer & Weinstein, 1987—. Speaker at meetings of profl. assns. Contbr. articles to profl. jours. Served with Army N.G., 1958-61. Mem. N.Y. State Bar Assn. (mem. real property, banking, corp. and bus. law sects.), N.Y. County Lawyers Assn., Fed. Bar Coun., T&M. General corporate, General practice, Real property. Office: Morrison Cohen Singer & Weinstein LLP 750 Lexington Ave New York NY 10022-1200

MARLAND, MELISSA KAYE, judge; b. Beckley, W.Va., Feb. 16, 1955; d. James Robert and Fannie Evelyn (Cook) M. BA in Polit. Sci., W.Va U., 1976, JD, 1979. Bar: W.Va. 1979, U.S. Dist. Ct. (so. dist.) W.Va. 1979, U.S. Supreme Ct. 1983. Law clk. Pub. Svc. Commn. W.Va., Charleston, 1979-82, hearing examiner, 1982-87, dep. chief adminstrv. law judge, 1987-89, chief adminstrv. law judge, 1989—. Faculty mem. ann. regulatory studies program Nat. Assn. Regulatory Commrs./Inst. Pub. Utilities, Mich. State U., 1994—. Assoc. editor: West Virginia Digest of Public Utility Decisions, vols. 1-7, 1986-91; contbr. articles to profl. jours. Mem. ABA, NAFE, W.Va. State Bar (com. on corp., banking and bus. law 1987—, adminstrv. law com. 1995—), Nat. Assn. Regulatory Commrs. (chmn. subcom. on adminstrv. law judges 1991-95), Phi Beta Kappa, Phi Alpha Delta, Pi Sigma Alpha. Democrat. Avocations: music, reading. Office: Pub Svc Commn WVa 201 Brooks St Charleston WV 25301-1803 E-mail: mmarland@worldnet.att.net

MARLOW, JAMES ALLEN, lawyer; b. Crossville, Tenn., May 23, 1955; s. Dewey Harold and Anna Marie (Hinch) M.; m. Sabine Klein, June 9, 1987; children: Lucas Allen, Eric Justin. BA, U. Tenn., 1976, JD, 1979; postgrad., Air War Coll., Maxwell AFB, Ala., 1990-91, Internat. Studienzentrum, Heidelberg, Germany, 1985-86. Bar: Ga. 1979, D.C. 1980, Tenn. 1980, U.S. Dist. Ct. (mid. dist.) Tenn. 1984, U.S. Ct. Fed. Claims 1987, U.S. Ct. Internat. Trade 1988, U.S. Tax Ct. 1987, U.S. Ct. Mil. Appeals 1980, U.S. Ct. Appeals (fed. cir.) 1987, U.S. Supreme Ct. 1987. Assoc. Carter & Assocs., Frankfurt, Fed. Republic Germany, 1984-85; chief internat. law USAF, Sembach AFB, Germany, 1986-96; pvt. practice Crossville, 1997—. Instr. Ctrl. Tex. Coll., 1997—; asst. prof. Embry-Riddle Aero. U., Kaiserslautern, Fed. Republic Germany, 1985—. Capt. USAF, 1980-84, Lt. Col. USAFR. Mem. Phi Beta Kappa. Avocations: genealogy, basketball, chess, German and Spanish languages. Home and Office: 5746 Highway 127 S Crossville TN 38572

MARLOW, ORVAL LEE, II, lawyer; b. Denver, May 1, 1956; s. Jack Conger and Barbara A. (Stolzenburg) M.; m. Paige Wood, June 8, 1985; children: Lorri Wood, Orval Lee III. BA, U. Nebr., 1978, JD, 1981. Bar: Tex. 1981, U.S. Dist. Ct. (so. dist.) Tex. 1984, U.S. Ct. Appeals (5th cir.) 1984. Assoc. Krist & Scott, Houston, 1981-82; prin. Marlow & Assocs., 1982-83; ptnr. Lendais & Assocs., 1983-91; dir. Morris, Lendais, Hollrah & Snowden, 1992—. Mem. ABA, Internat. Bar Assn., Tex. Bar Assn., Houston Bar Assn., Phi Delta Phi. Lutheran. Avocations: golf, snow skiing, chess. General corporate, Private international, Real property. Office: Morris Lendais Hollrah & Snowden 1980 Post Oak Blvd Ste 700 Houston TX 77056-3881 E-mail: omarlow@mlhs.net

MARONEY, JAMES FRANCIS, III, lawyer; b. Houston, Mar. 24, 1951; s. James Francis and Ellen B. (Cuenod) M.; m. Maureen K. O'Sullivan, May 14, 1983; 1 child, Molly. BA cum laude, U. Tex., 1973, JD, 1976. Assoc. Ray A. Morrison Assocs., Houston, 1977; legal mgr. AMF Tuboscope, Inc., Houston, 1978-82; gen. counsel Koomey, Inc., Houston, 1982-85; pvt. practice, Seguin, Tex., 1985-87; assoc. gen. counsel, chief of litigation TransAm. Natural Gas Corp., Houston, 1987-89; v.p., gen. counsel, sec. Tuboscope Vetco Internat. Corp., Houston, 1989—. Mem. ABA, Houston Bar Assn., Tex. Bar Assn. Roman Catholic. General civil litigation, General corporate. Home: 14807 River Forest Dr Houston TX 77079-6324 Office: Tuboscope Vetco Internat Corp 2835 Holmes Rd Houston TX 77051-1023 Address: 14807 River Forest Dr Houston TX 77079-6324

MARQUARDT, CHRISTEL ELISABETH, judge; b. Chgo., Aug. 26, 1935; d. Herman Albert and Christine Marie (Geringer) Trolenberg; children: Eric, Philip, Andrew, Joel. BS in Edn., Mo. Western Coll., 1970; JD with honors, Washburn U., 1974. Bar: Kans. 1974, Mo. 1992, U.S. Dist. Ct. Kans. 1974, U.S. Dist. Ct. (we. dist.) Mo. 1992. Tchr. St. John's Ch., Tigerton, Wis., 1955-56; pers. asst. Columbia Records, L.A., 1958-59; ptnr. Cosgrove, Webb & Oman, Topeka, 1974-86, Palmer & Marquardt, Topeka, 1986-91, Levy and Craig P.C., Overland Park, Kans., 1991-94; sr. ptnr. Marquardt and Assocs., L.L.C., Fairway, 1994-95; judge Kans. Ct. Appeals, 1995—. Mem. atty. bd. discipline Kans. Supreme Ct., 1984-86. Mem. editorial adv. bd. Kans. Lawyers Weekly, 1992-96; contbr. articles to legal jours. Bd. dirs. Topeka Symphony, 1983-92, 95—, Arts and Humanities Assn. Johnson County, 1992-95, Brown Found., 1988-90; hearing examiner Human Rels. Com., Topeka, 1974-76; local advisor Boy Scouts Am., 1973-74; bd. dirs., mem. nominating com. YWCA, Topeka, 1979-81; bd. govs. Washburn U. Law Sch., 1987—, v.p., 1994-96, pres., 1998—; mem. dist. bd. adjudication Mo. Synod Luth. Ch., Kans., 1982-88. Named Woman of Yr., Mayor, City of Topeka, 1982; Obee scholar Washburn U., 1972-74; recipient Jennie Mitchell Kellogg Atty. of Achievement award, 1999, Phil Leives medal of Distinction, 2000, Atty. of Achievement award Kans. Women Attys. Assn. Fellow Am. Bar Found., Kans. Bar Found. (trustee 1987-89); mem. ABA (mem. ho. dels. 1988—, state del. 1995-99, bd. govs., program and planning com., 1999—, specialization com. 1987-93, chmn. 1989-93, lawyer referral com. 1993-95, bar svcs. and activities, 1995-99, standing com. on comms. 1996-99, bd. govs., 1999—), Kans. Bar Assn. (sec., treas. 1981-85, v.p. 1985-86, pres. 1987-88, bd. dirs. 1983—), Kans. Trial Lawyers Assn. (bd. govs. 1982-86, lectr.), Topeka Bar Assn., Am. Bus. Women's Assn. (lectr., corr. sec. 1983-84, pres. career chpt. 1986-87, named one of Top 10 Bus. Women of Yr., 1985), Law and Organizational Econ. Ctr. (bd. dirs. 2000—). Home: 3408 SW Alameda Dr Topeka KS 66614-5108 Office: 301 SW 10th Ave Topeka KS 66612-1502 E-mail: marquardt@kscourts.org

MARQUARDT, ROBERT RICHARD, lawyer; b. Columbus, Ohio, Aug. 22, 1943; s. Robert Gustave and Ethel M. (Augur) M.; m. Alice Grant, Sept. 9, 1966 (div. 1985); children: Theresa, Robert, Christopher; m. Patricia Moore Peek, Sept. 3, 1989; children: Susan, Katherine. BS in Commerce, Rider U., 1965; MBA, Fairleigh Dickinson U., 1966; JD, U. Ark., 1973; LLM, Temple U., 1977; grad. cert. in dispute resolution, So. Meth. U., 2000. Bar: Iowa 1973, Ark. 1973, U.S. Dist. Ct. (ea. dist.) Ark. 1973, N.J. 1975, U.S. Supreme Ct. 1979. Counsel RCA Corp., Camden, N.J., 1973-77; assoc. counsel Occidental Chem. Corp., Niagara Falls, N.Y., 1977-79, divsn. counsel, 1979-80, counsel, 1980-81, assoc. gen. counsel, 1981-87, v.p., gen. counsel electrochems. and specialty products grp., 1987-91, assoc. gen. counsel, mng. atty., 1991—. Instr. bus. law Niagra U., 1978—82; pres. S.W. Conflict Resolution Network, 2000—01. Chmn. Youngstown (N.Y.) Environ. Com., 1980-84; mil. chmn. UN Operation Horseshoe, Niagara Falls, 1981; staff judge adv. USAFR, 1974-89. Lt. col. USAFR, 1967-89. Recipient United Way award, 1968-76, Corp. award Am. Jurisprudence, 1972; named Judge Adv. of Yr., USAFR, 1980. Antitrust, Contracts commercial, General corporate. Office: 5005 Lbj Fwy Dallas TX 75244-6100 E-mail: robertmarquardt@bigfoot.com

MARQUART, STEVEN LEONARD, lawyer; b. Georgetown, Minn., Feb. 2, 1954; s. Leonard Matthew and Gladys Viola (Myhre) M.; m. Cynthia Lou Smerud, June 21, 1975; children: Stephanie Lynn, Angela Marie, Andrew Steven. BA in Polit. Sci., Moorhead State U., 1976; JD with distinction, U. N.D., 1979. Bar: Minn. 1979, N.D. 1979, U.S. Dist. Ct. N.D. 1979, U.S. Dist. Ct. Minn. 1981, U.S. Ct. Appeals (8th cir.) 1981. Law Clk. U.S. Dist. Ct. N.D., Fargo, 1979-81; assoc. Cahill & Marquart, PA, Moorhead, Minn., 1981-85, ptnr., bd. dirs., 1985. Mem. ABA, Minn. Bar Assn. (cert. civil trial specialist), Def. Rsch. Inst. (chmn. No. Minn. 1987—), N.D. Bar Assn., Order of Coif. Democrat. Roman Catholic. E-mail: smarquart@cahill-marquart.com. Federal civil litigation, State civil litigation, Insurance. Home: 3002 24th Ave S Fargo ND 58103-5014 Office: Cahill & Marquart PA 403 Center Ave Moorhead MN 56560-1900

MARQUESS, LAWRENCE WADE, lawyer; b. Bloomington, Ind., Mar. 2, 1950; s. Earl Lawrence and Mary Louise (Coberly) M.; m. Barbara Ann Bailey, June 17, 1978; children: Alexander Lawrence, Michael Wade. BSEE, Purdue U., 1973; JD, W.Va. U., 1977. Bar: W.Va. 1977, Tex. 1977, U.S. Dist. Ct. (so. dist.) W.Va. 1977, U.S. Dist. Ct. (no. dist.) Tex. 1977, Colo. 1980, U.S. Dist. Ct. Colo. 1980, U.S. Ct. Appeals (10th cir.) 1980, U.S. Supreme Ct. 1984, U.S. Dist. Ct. (no. dist.) Ohio 1988, U.S. Ct. Appeals (DC cir.) 1997, U.S. Dist. Ct. Nebr. 1999. Assoc. Johnson, Bromberg, Leeds & Riggs, Dallas, 1977-79, Bradley, Campbell & Carney, Golden, Colo., 1979-82, ptnr., 1983-84, Stettner, Miller & Cohn P.C., 1984-87, Nelson & Harding, Denver, 1987-88, Heron, Burchette, Ruckert & Rothwell, 1989-90, Harding & Ogborn, 1990-94, Otten, Johnson, Robinson, Neff & Ragonetti, Denver, 1994-2001, Littler Mendelson, P.C., Denver, 2001—. Mem. faculty Am. Law Inst. - ABA Advanced Labor and Employment Law Course, 1986, 87. Mem. ABA (labor, antitrust and litigation sects.), ACLU, Colo. Bar Assn. (co-chmn. labor law com. 1989-92), Denver Bar Assn., 1st Jud. Dist. Bar Assn., Sierra Club, Nat. Ry. Hist. Soc. Democrat. Methodist. Federal civil litigation, Labor, Pension, profit-sharing, and employee benefits. Home: 11883 W 27th Dr Lakewood CO 80215-7000 Office: Littler Mendelson PC 1200 17th St Ste 2850 Denver CO 80202 E-mail: lmarquess@littler.com

MARQUEZ, ALFREDO C. federal judge; b. 1922; m. Linda Nowobilsky. B.S., U. Ariz., 1948, J.D., 1950. Bar: Ariz. Practice law Mesch Marquez & Rothschild, 1957-80; asst. atty. gen. State of Ariz., 1951-52; asst. county atty. Pima County, Ariz., 1953-54; adminstrv. asst. to Congressman Stewart Udall, 1955; judge U.S. Dist. Ct. Ariz., Tucson, 1980-91, sr. judge, 1991—. Served with USN, 1942-45 Office: US Dist Ct US Courthouse Rm 327 405 W Congress Ste 6180 Tucson AZ 85701-5060

MARQUIS, WILLIAM OSCAR, lawyer; b. Fort Wayne, Ind., Feb. 26, 1944; s. William Oscar and Lenor Mae (Gaffney) M.; m. Mary Frances Funderburk, May 11, 1976; children: Lenor, Kathryn, Timothy Patrick, Daniel, Ann. BS, U. Wis., Madison, 1973; JD, South Tex. Coll. Law, 1977. Bar: Wis. 1979, U.S. Dist. Ct. (ea. dist.) Wis. 1982, U.S. Tax. Ct. 1983, U.S. Ct. Appeals (7th cir. 1985). With Wis. Dept. Vet. Affairs, Madison, 1977-79; corp. counsel Barron County, Wis., 1979-80; assoc. Riley, Bruns & Riley, Madison, 1980-81, Jastroch & LaBarge, S.C., Waukesha, Wis., 1981-84; ptnr. Groh, Hackbart & Marquis, 1984-93. Mem. ATLA, Nat. Assn. Criminal Def. Attys., Wis. Trial Lawyers Assn. General civil litigation, Criminal, Personal injury. Office: 322 W State St Milwaukee WI 53203-1306 E-mail: BillMarquisLaw@aol.com

MARQUITZ, KEVIN JOHN, lawyer; b. St. Louis, Apr. 11, 1968; s. John J. and LaVerne M. M. BA in Polit. Sci. and History, Marquette U., 1990; JD cum laude, William Mitchell U., 1996. Bar: Mo. 1997, U.S. Dist. Ct. (ea. dist.) Mo. 1997, Ill. 1998. Assoc. Evans & Dixon, St. Louis, 1997—. Assoc. editor William Mitchell Law Rev., 1995-96. Mem. ABA, Bar Assn. Met.-St. Louis, St. Louis Vol. Lawyers Assn. State civil litigation, Insurance, Personal injury. Office: Evans & Dixon 200 N Broadway Ste 1200 Saint Louis MO 63102

MARR, CARMEL CARRINGTON, retired lawyer, retired state official; b. Bklyn., June 23, 1921; d. William Preston and Gertrude Clementine (Lewis) Carrington; m. Warren Marr II, Apr. 11, 1948; children: Charles Carrington, Warren Quincy III. BA, Hunter Coll., 1945; JD, Columbia U., 1948. Bar: N.Y. 1948, U.S. Dist. Ct. (ea. dist.) N.Y. 1950, U.S. Dist. Ct. (so. dist.) N.Y. 1951. Clk. Dyer & Stevens, N.Y.C., 1948-49; pvt. practice, 1949-53; adviser legal affairs U.S. mission to UN, 1953-67; sr. legal officer Office Legal Affairs UN Secretariat, 1967-68; mem. N.Y. State Human Rights Appeal Bd., 1968-71, N.Y. State Pub. Svc. Commn., 1971-86; cons. Gas. Rsch. Inst., 1987-91. Lectr. N.Y. Police Acad., 1963-67. Contbr. articles to profl. jours. Mem. N.Y. Gov.'s Com. Edn. and Employment of Women, 1963-64; mem. Nat. Gen. Svcs. Pub. Adv. Council, 1969-71; mem., former chmn. adv. coun. Gas. Rsch. Inst.; mem. chmn. tech. pipeline safety standards com. Dept. Transp., 1979-85; former mem. task force Fed. Energy Regulatory Commn. and EPA to examine PCBs in gas supply system; past chmn. gas com. Nat. Assn. Regulatory Utility Commrs.; past pres. Great Lakes Conf. Pub. Utilities Commrs., mem. exec. com.; mem. UN Devel. Corp., 1969-72; bd. dirs. Amistad Rsch. Ctr., New Orleans, 1970—, chmn. bd. dirs., 1981-94; bd. dirs. Bklyn. Soc. Prevention Cruelty to Children, Nat. Arts Stblzn. Fund, 1984-93, hon. bd. mem., 1998, Prospect Park Alliance, 1987-98; bd. visitors N.Y. State Sch. Girls, Hudson, 1964-71; mem. exec. bd. Plays for Living, N.Y.C., 1968-75; pres. bd. dirs. Billie Holiday Theatre, 1972-80; mem. nat. adv. coun. Hampshire Coll.; pres.'s coun. Tulane U., 1988-95. Mem. Phi Beta Kappa, Alpha Chi Alpha, Alpha Kappa Alpha. Republican. Episcopalian.

MARR, DAVID E, lawyer; BA, Colby Coll.; MA, Wesleyan U.; JD with honors, U. Conn. Bar: Conn. 1970, Mass. 1974, U.S. Dist. Ct. Conn. 1971, U.S. Dist. Ct. Mass. 1975, U.S. Ct. Appeals (2d cir.) 1971, U.S. Supreme Ct. 1974, U.S. Tax Ct. 1992. Assoc. Day, Berry & Howard, Hartford, Conn., 1970-73; counsel Honeywell Info. Sys., Inc., Waltham, Mass., 1973-75; pvt. practice Boston, 1975-78, Natick, Mass., 1978—. Editor-in-Chief Law Review, 1970. Author: Employment Law in Connecticut; opinion editor Mass. Lawyers Weekly, 1976-86. Rep. Regional Vocat. Sch.; chmn. Hist. Dist. Com.; bd. dirs. Hist. Soc. and Mus. Mem. ATLA, Mass. Bar Assn. Family and matrimonial, Land use and zoning (including planning), Personal injury. Office: 10 Union St Natick MA 01760-4759

MARRERO, TERESA, lawyer; b. N.Y.C. d. Miquel Angel and Jovita (Otero) Marrero. BA in Bus., Marymount Manhattan Coll., 1988; JD, N.Y. Law Sch., 1991. Bar: N.Y. 1992. Lawyer FCC, Washington, 1991-93; lawyer firm Akin, Gump, 1993-94; lawyer Teleport Comms. Group, N.Y.C., 1994-98, AT&T, Basking Ridge, N.J., 1998—. Mem. ABA. N.Y.C. Bar Assn., N.Y. State Bar Assn., P.R. Bar Assn., Adirondack Hiking Club, Audubon. Avocations: ornithology, birdwatching, bicycling, hiking. Office: AT&T 295 N Maple Ave Rm 1124m1 Basking Ridge NJ 07920-1025

MARSH, WILLIAM DOUGLAS, lawyer; b. Sikeston, Mo., Feb. 22, 1947; s. Ray Carl and Mary Louis (Buchanan) M.; m. Georgia Kay Trigg, June 3, 1967; children: Kristin Elizabeth, Kelly Anne. BSBA, S.E. Mo. State U., 1971; JD, U. Mo., Kansas City, 1973. Bar: Fla. 1974, U.S. Dist. Ct. (no., mid. and so. dists.) Fla. 1974, U.S. Ct. Appeals (5th and 11th cir.) 1974. Shareholder Emmanuel, Sheppard & Condon, Pensacola, Fla., 1973—. Contbr. articles to profl. jours.; reviewer Fla. Torts, 1990. Active numerous polit. campaigns/polit. action groups. 1st lt. U.S. N.G., 1967-73. Mem. ABA (litigation sect., torts and ins. practice sect., com. on auto. law), Assn. Trial Lawyers Am. (diplomate), Acad. Fla. Trial Lawyers (sustaining), Am. Bd. Trial Advocacy (cert. trail lawyer), Fla. Bar Assn. (rules of civil procedure com. 1991—, trial lawyers sect. exec. coun. 1979-88, sec. 1984-85, editor trial sect. newsletter 1982-83, chmn. 1986-87). Democrat. Methodist. Avocation: sailing. Admiralty, Personal injury, Product liability. Office: Emmanuel Sheppard & Condon 30 S Spring St Pensacola FL 32501-5612

MARSHALL, ANTHONY PARR, lawyer; b. N.Y.C., Aug. 7, 1937; s. Joseph Parr and Mildred Yoder (Heimbach) M.; m. Betsy Harbison, Sept. 28, 1963; children: Charles Christopher, Katharine Elizabeth. AB, Princeton U., 1959; JD, Columbia U., 1962. Bar: N.Y. 1963, N.J. 1979, U.S. Supreme Ct. 1968, U.S. Dist. Cts. (so. and ea. dists.) N.Y. 1973, U.S. Dist. Ct. N.J. 1979. Assoc. Davies, Hardy & Schenck, N.Y.C., 1964-68, Goldstein, Judd & Gurfein, N.Y.C., 1968-72, Kirlin, Campbell & Keating, N.Y.C., 1972-73, ptnr., 1973-85; sr. v.p., mgr. estate planning dept. U.S. Trust Co. N.Y., 1985-97; mng. dir. wealth planning strategies group Bankers Trust Co., 1997-2001. Contbr. articles to profl. jours. Past pres., chmn. bd. trustees The Hosp. Chaplaincy, Inc., N.Y.C.; pres. The Fund for the Diaconate of Episcopal Ch. in U.S., N.Y.C.; hon. warden St. Bartholomew's Ch., N.Y.C. Fellow Am. Coll. Trust and Estate Counsel (editor probate notes 1982-83, studies editor 1992-2001), Am. Bar Found.; mem. ABA (past editor probate and property, chmn. coms. on modification, revocation and termination of trusts, tax legislation and regulations, interrelationship of gifts and estates), N.Y. State Bar Assn. (past chmn. com. on fed. legislation, estate and trust adminstrn.), Assn. of Bar of City of N.Y. (pres. estate and fin. planning coun. Ctrl. N.J. 1995-96), Princeton of N.Y.C. Club, Pilgrims Club. Probate, Estate taxation, Personal income taxation. Home: 108 Ocean Blvd Atlantic Highlands NJ 07716-1531 E-mail: tonymarshall@cps.net

MARSHALL, BURKE, law educator; b. Plainfield, N.J., Oct. 1, 1922; A.B., Yale U., 1944, LL.B., 1951, M.A., 1970. Bar: D.C. bar 1952. Assoc., then partner firm Covington and Burling, Washington, 1951-61; asst. atty. gen. U.S., 1961-65; gen. counsel IBM Corp., Armonk, N.Y., 1965-69, sr. v.p., 1969-70; prof. law Yale U. Law Sch., 1970—, Nicholas deB. Katzenbach prof. emeritus. Chmn. Nat. Adv. Commn. SSS, 1967. Author: Federalism and Civil Rights, 1965; co-author: The Mylai Massacre and Its Cover-up, 1975; editor: The Supreme Court and Human Rights, 1982, A

Workable Government?, 1989; contbr. articles, revs. to legal publs. Bd. dirs. Ctr. Community Change, Washington, 1968-98, Robert F. Kennedy Meml., 1969-98, Vera Inst. Justice, N.Y.C., 1965—. Recipient Eleanor Roosevelt award for human rights, 1999. Home: Castle Meadow Rd Newtown CT 06470 Office: Yale U Sch Law 127 Wall St New Haven CT 06511-6636

MARSHALL, CONSUELO BLAND, federal judge; b. Knoxville, Tenn., Sept. 28, 1936; d. Clyde Theodore and Annie (Brown) Arnold; m. George Edward Marshall, Aug. 30, 1959; children: Michael Edward, Laurie Ann. AA, L.A. City Coll., 1956; BA, Howard U., 1958, LLB, 1961. Bar: Calif. 1962. Dep. atty., City of L.A., 1962-67; assoc. Cochran & Atkins, L.A., 1968-70; commr. L.A. Superior Ct., 1971-76; judge Inglewood Mcpl. Ct., 1976-77, L.A. Superior Ct., 1977-80, U.S. Dist. Ct. Central Dist. Calif., L.A., 1980—. Lectr. U.S. Information Agy. in Yugoslavia, Greece and Italy, 1984, in Nigera and Ghana, 1991, in Ghana, 1992. Contbr. articles to profl. jours.; notes editor Law Jour. Howard U. Mem. adv. bd. Richstone Child Abuse Center. Recipient Judicial Excellence award Criminal Cts. Bar Assn., 1992, Ernestine Stalhut award; named Criminal Ct. Judge of Yr., U.S. Dist. Ct., 1997; inducted into Langston Hall of Fame, 2000; rsch. fellow Howard U. Law Sch., 1959-60. Mem. State Bar Calif., Century City Bar Assn., Calif. Women Lawyers Assn., Calif. Assn. Black Lawyers, Calif. Judges Assn., Black Women Lawyers Assn., Los Angeles County Bar Assn., Nat. Assn. Women Judges, NAACP, Urban League, Beta Phi Sigma. Office: US Dist Ct 312 N Spring St Los Angeles CA 90012-4701

MARSHALL, ELLEN RUTH, lawyer; b. N.Y.C., Apr. 23, 1949; d. Louis and Faith (Gladstone) M. AB, Yale U., 1971; JD, Harvard U., 1974. Bar: Calif. 1975, D.C. 1981, N.Y. 1989. Assoc. McKenna & Fitting, Los Angeles, 1975-80; ptnr. McKenna, Conner & Cuneo, Los Angeles and Orange County, Calif., 1980-88, Morrison & Foerster, LLP, Orange County, Calif., 1988—. Mem. ABA (bus. law sect., mem. savs. inst. com., mem. asset securitization com., tax sect., mem. employee benefits com.), Orange County Bar Assn. Club: Center (Costa Mesa, Calif.). Banking, General corporate, Pension, profit-sharing, and employee benefits. Office: Morrison & Foerster LLP 19900 Macarthur Blvd Irvine CA 92612-2445

MARSHALL, JOHN DAVID, lawyer; b. Chgo., May 19, 1940; s. John Howard and Sophie (Brezenk) M.; m. Marcia A. Podlasinski, Aug. 26, 1961; children: Jacquelyn, David, Jason, Patricia, Brian, Denise, Michael, Catherine. BS in Acctg., U. Ill., 1961; JD, Ill. Inst. Tech., 1965. Bar: Ill. 1965, U.S. Tax Ct. 1968, U.S. Dist. Ct. (no. dist.) Ill. 1971; CPA, Ill. Ptnr. Mayer, Brown & Platt, Chgo., 1961—. Bd. dirs. Levinson Ctr. for Handicapped Children, Chgo., 1970-75. Fellow Am. Coll. Probate Counsel; mem. Ill. Bar Assn., Chgo. Bar Assn. (agribus. com. 1978—, trust law com. 1969—, probate practice com. 1969—, com. on coms. 1983—, vice chmn. 1988-89, chmn. 1989-90, legis. com. of probate practice com. 1983—, chmn. and vice chmn. legis. com. of probate practice com. 1983-84, chmn. exec. com. probate practice com. 1982-83, vice chmn. exec. com. 1981-82, sec. exec. com. 1980-81, div. chmn. 78-79, div. vice chmn. 1977-78, div. sec. 1976-77, Appreciation award 1982-83), Chgo. Estate Planning Council. Roman Catholic. Club: Union League (Chgo.). Estate planning, Probate, Estate taxation. Home: 429 Willow Wood Dr Palatine IL 60067-3831 Office: Mayer Brown & Platt 190 S La Salle St Ste 3100 Chicago IL 60603-3441

MARSHALL, JOHN HENRY, lawyer; b. Paterson, N.J., July 31, 1949; s. Henry Leland and Elizabeth Marion (Bates) M.; m. Jan Eastman, May 4, 1979. AB, Dartmouth Coll., 1971; BA, Cambridge U., Eng., 1973; JD, Yale U., 1977. Bar: Vt. 1977, U.S. Dist. Ct. Vt. 1978. Assoc. Downs Rachlin & Martin, St. Johnsbury, Vt., 1977-82, ptnr., 1982—. Mem. Vt. Health Care Authority Adv. Com. Universal Access Plan, 1992. Chmn. Dist. Environ. Commn., St. Johnsbury, 1981-90; mem. Gov.'s Blue Ribbon Commn. on Health Care, 1991; chmn. Vt. Cmty. Found., 2000—; vice chmn. Vt. Pub. TV, 1999—. Served to capt. U.S. Army, 1973-74. Mem. Vt. Bar Assn. (chmn. environ. law com. 1987-92, chmn. health law com. 1994-96. Environmental, Health, Public utilities. Home: PO Box 19 Peacham VT 05862-0019 Office: Downs Rachlin & Martin 90 Prospect St Saint Johnsbury VT 05819-0099

MARSHALL, JOHN PATRICK, lawyer; b. Bklyn., July 3, 1950; s. Harry W. and Mary Margaret (Kelly) M.; m. Cheryl J. Garvey, Aug. 10, 1975; children: Kelly Blake, Logan Brooke. BA, Rutgers U., 1972; JD cum laude, N.Y. Law Sch., 1976. Bar: N.Y. 1977, N.J. 1977, U.S. Dist. Ct. N.J. 1977, U.S. Dist. Ct. (so. and ea. dists.) N.Y. 1978, U.S. Ct. Appeals (3rd cir.) 1982, U.S. Dist Ct. (no. dist.) N.Y. 1991. Assoc. Kelley Drye & Warren, N.Y.C., 1976-84, ptnr., 1985-98. Mem. editl. bd. N.Y. Law Sch. Law Rev., 1975-76, staff mem., 1974-75; contbr. articles to profl. jours. Mem. jud. screening com. N.Y. Dem. Com., N.Y. New Dem. Coalition, 1988; exec. v.p. Humanitarian Found. for Nicaragua, 1991; mem., sec. Respect for Law Found., 1996; mem. Southern Dist. N.Y. Mediation Panel, 1994—; mem. Coun. on Jud. Adminstrn., 1996-98. Fellow Am. Bar Found.; mem. ABA, N.Y. County Lawyers' Assn. (sec. 1984-87, mem. com. on Supreme Ct. 1984-94, mem. legal edn., admission to bar and lawyer placement com. 1983-93), Am. Arbitration Assn. (mem. nat. panel arbitrators N.Y. and N.J. regions 1991—, mem. corp. counsel com. 1993-98), Assn. of Bar of City of N.Y. (sec. judiciary com. 1989-92, mem. com. on arbitration 1994-96, sec. coun. on judical adminstrn. 1996-98). Federal civil litigation, State civil litigation, Private international. Home and Office: 50 Highland Ave Short Hills NJ 07078-2812 E-mail: marshall.highland@prodigy.net

MARSHALL, MARGARET HILARY, state supreme court chief justice; b. Newcastle, Natal, South Africa, Sept. 1, 1944; came to U.S., 1968; d. Bernard Charles and Hilary A.D. (Anderton) M; m. Samuel Shapiro, Dec. 14, 1968 (div. Apr. 1982); m. Anthony Lewis, Sept. 23, 1984. BA, Witwatersrand U., Johannesburg, 1966; MEd, Harvard U., 1969; JD, Yale U., 1976; LHD (hon.), Regis Coll., 1993. Bar: Mass. 1977, U.S. Dist. Ct. Mass., U.S. Dist. Ct. N.H., U.S. Dist. Ct. D.C., U.S. Dist. Ct. (ea. dist.) Mich., U.S. Tax Ct., U.S. Ct. Appeals (1st, 11th and D.C. cirs.), U.S. Supreme Ct. Assoc. Csaplar & Bok, Boston, 1976-83, ptnr., 1983-89, Choate, Hall & Stewart, Boston, 1989-92; v.p., gen. counsel Harvard U., Cambridge, Mass., 1992-96; justice Supreme Jud. Ct. Commonwealth Mass., 1996-99, chief justice, 1999—. Mem. jud. nominating coun., 1987-90, 92; chairperson ct. rules subcom. Alternative Dispute Resolution Working Group, 1985-87; mem. fed. appts. commn., 1993; mem. adv. com. Supreme Judicial Ct., 1989-92, mem. gender equality com., 1989-94; mem. civil justice adv. group U.S. Dist. Ct. Mass., 1991-93; spl. counsel Jud. Conduct Commn., 1988-92; trustee Mass. Continuing Legal Edn., Inc., 1990-92. Trustee Regis Coll., 1993-95; bd. dirs. Internat. Design Conf., Aspen, 1986-92, Boston Mcpl. Res. Bur., 1990-94, Supreme Judicial Ct. Hist. Soc., 1990-94, sec., 1990-94. Fellow Am. Bar Found. (Mass. state chair); mem. Boston Bar Assn. (treas. 1988-89, v.p. 1989-90, pres.-elect 1990-91, pres. 1991-92), Internat. Women's Forum, Mass. Women's Forum, Boston Club, Phi Beta Kappa (hon.). Office: Supreme Jud Ct Pemberton Sq 1300 New Courthouse Boston MA 02108-1701*

MARSHALL, MARILYN JOSEPHINE, lawyer; b. Dayton, Ohio, May 31, 1945; d. Foy Wylie and Inez Virginia (Smith) Gard; m. Alan George Marshall, June 13, 1965; children: Gwendolyn Scott, Brian George. Student, Northwestern U., 1963-65; BA, Stanford U., 1967; cert. in teaching, U. B.C., Vancouver, 1977; JD, Capital Law Sch., Columbus, Ohio, 1985. Bar: Ohio 1985, Fla. 1993, U.S Dist. Ct. (so. dist.) Ohio 1986, U.S. Dist. Ct. (no. dist., mid. dist. and so. dist.) Fla. 1994, U.S. Ct. Appeals (6th cir.) 1986, U.S. Ct. Appeals (11th cir.) 1994. Tchr. Sutherland Secondary Sch., North Vancouver, B.C., 1977-79; instr. Brit. Coll. Inst. Tech., Burnaby, 1979-80; assoc. Crabbe, Brown, Jones, Potts & Schmidt, Columbus, Ohio, 1985-86; clk. to judge U.S. Dist. Ct. (so. dist.) Ohio, 1986-88; clk. to justice Ohio Supreme Ct., 1988-89; assoc. Squire, Sanders & Dempsey, 1989-92; with Columbus City Atty.'s Office, Columbus, Ohio, 1992-93; asst. atty. gen. civil divsn. State of Fla., Tallahassee, 1994-96; pvt. practice, 1996—. Mem. ABA, Ohio Bar Assn., Fla. Bar Assn., Tallahassee Bar Assn., Tallahassee Women Lawyers Assn., Capital U. Law Sch. Alumni Assn. Republican. Avocations: tennis, gardening, music. Office: 254 E 6th Ave Tallahassee FL 32303-6208 E-mail: mjmarshall@aol.com

MARSHALL, RAYMOND CHARLES, lawyer; b. Aquadilia, Puerto Rico, July 23, 1953; m. Piper Kent-Marshall; 1 child, Kyle. BA summa cum laude, Coll. Idaho, 1975; JD, Harvard U., 1978. Bar: Calif. 1978, D.C. 1989. Ptnr. McCutchen Doyle Brown & Enersen, San Francisco. Chmn. Calif. Supreme Ct. Adv. Multi-Jurisdictional Practice. Co-author: Environmental Crimes, 1992; contbr. chpt. to manual; contbr. articles to profl. jours. Bd. dirs. Multiple Sclerosis Soc. Northern Calif. chpt., 1992—; adv. bd. United Negro Coll. Fund Northern Bay Area Chpt., 1992—; bd. trustees Alta Bates Found., 1994—; mem. San Francisco leadership bd. Am. Red Cross Bay Area; adv. coun. mem. San Francisco Sports Coun. Recipient San Francisco Neighborhood Legal Assistance Found. award, 1989, Earl Warren Legal Svcs. award NAACP Legal Def. & Ednl. Found., 1990, Unity award Minority Bar Coalition, 1992, Cmty. Svc. award Wiley Manuel Law Found., 1994, Disting. Jesuit award Anti-Defemation League, 2001. Mem. ABA (met. bar caucus exec. com. 1992-94, vice-chmn. natural resources & energy litigation com. 1989-93, environmental crimes com. 1990-92, nominating com. conf. of minority ptnrs. in maj. corp. law firms 1991, commn. on women in the profession 1994-95, co-chmn. environmental crimes subcom. of white collar crime com. 1994-95), Nat. Bar Assn., Calif. State Bar (bd. govs. 1995—, pres. 1998-99), Charles Houston Bar Assn. Avocations: travel, recreational sports. Office: McCutchen Doyle Brown & Enersen Three Embarcadero Ctr San Francisco CA 94111

MARSHALL, RICHARD TREEGER, lawyer; b. N.Y.C., May 17, 1925; s. Edward and Sydney (Treeger) M.; m. Dorothy M. Goodman, June 4, 1950; children: Abigail Ruth Marshall Bergerson, Daniel Brooks; m. 2d Sylvia J. Kelley, June 10, 1979. BS, Cornell U., 1948; JD, Yale U., 1951. Bar: Tex. 1952, U.S. Ct.. Appeals (5th cir.) 1966, U.S. Ct. Appeals (10th cir.) 1980, U.S. Supreme Ct. 1959; lic. Tex. Dept. Ins. Pvt. practice, El Paso, Tex., 1952-59, 61-79; assoc. Fryer & Milstead, 1952; sr. ptnr. Marshall & Wendorf, 1959-61, Marshall & Volk, El Paso, 1979-81; sr. atty. Richard T. Marshall & Assocs., PC, 1981-85; sr. ptnr. Marshall, Thomas & Winters, 1985-87; sr. atty. Marshall & Winters, 1987-88, Marshall, Sherrod & Winters, 1988-90; pvt. practice El Paso, 1990—. Instr. polit. sci. U. Tex., El Paso, 1961-62; instr. ins. law C.L.U. tng. course Am. Coll.; officer, dir. Advance Funding, Inc., El Paso. Editor El Paso Trial Lawyers Rev., 1973-80; contbr. articles to profl. jours. Mem. ATLA (sec. personal injury law sect. 1967-68, nat. sec. 1969-70, sec.-treas. environ. law sect. 1970-71, vice chmn. family law litigation sec. 1971-72), El Paso Bar Assn., El Paso Trial Lawyers Assn. (pres. 1965-66), Tex. Trial Lawyers Assn.,, Roscoe Pound-Am. Trial Lawyers Found. (commn. on profl. responsibility 1979-82), Nat. Acad. Elder Law Attys., Soc. Cert. Sr. Advisors, Nat. Assn. Charitable Estate Counselors. Estate planning, Personal injury, Probate. Office: 5959 Gateway Blvd W El Paso TX 79925-3331 E-mail: marshall@texseniorlaw.com

MARSHALL, ROBERT WILLIAM, lawyer, rancher; b. L.A., Apr. 12, 1933; s. Kenneth I. and Helen (Putnam) M.; m. Nanette Hollenbeck, June 10, 1965; children: Thomas, Victoria, Rebecca, Kathleen. AB in Pre Law, Stanford U., 1955, JD, 1957. Bar: Calif. 1958, Nev. 1958, U.S. Dist. Ct. (so. dist.) Calif. 1958, U.S. Dist. Ct. Nev. 1958. Assoc. Vargas & Bartlett, Reno, 1958-64, ptnr., 1964-85, sr. ptnr., 1985-94; chmn. of bd. Marshall, Hill, Cassas & de Lipkau, 1994—. Owner Intermountain Cattle Co.; founder Intermountain Pipeline Ltd. Advisor Explorer Boy Scouts Am., Reno, 1971-76, 87-89, scoutmaster Troop 444 Boy Scouts Am., Reno, 1981-85; state chmn. Nev. Young Reps., 1962-64. Mem. ABA, Nat. Cattlemen's Assn., Calif. Bar Assn., Nev. Bar Assn., Washoe County Bar Assn., Rocky Mountain Mineral Law Inst., No. Nev. Indsl. Gas Users (organizer), No. Nev. Large Power Users (organizer), So. Nev. Large Power Users (organizer), Nev. Cattlemen's Assn., Reno Stanford Club (pres. Reno chpt. 1974). Republican. Mormon. Public utilities, Real property. Office: Marshall Hill Cassas & deLipkau 333 Holcomb Ave Ste 300 Reno NV 89502-1665

MARSHALL, SHEILA HERMES, lawyer; b. N.Y.C., Jan. 17, 1934; d. Paul Milton and Julia Angela (Meagher) Hermes; m. James Josiah Marshall, Sept. 30, 1967; 1 child, James J.H. BA, St. John's U., N.Y.C., 1959; JD, NYU, 1963. Bar: N.Y. 1964, U.S. Ct. Appeals (2d, 3d, 5th and D.C. cirs.), U.S. Supreme Ct. 1970. Assoc. LeBoeuf, Lamb, Greene & MacRae, N.Y.C., 1963-72, ptnr., 1973—. Specialist in field. Mem. ABA, N.Y. State Bar Assn., Assn. of Bar of City of N.Y. Republican. Administrative and regulatory, Insurance, Product liability. Home: 1035 Park Ave New York NY 10028-0912 Office: LeBoeuf Lamb Greene & MacRae 125 W 55th St New York NY 10019-5369

MARSHALL, SIRI SWENSON, corporate lawyer; BA, Harvard U., 1970; JD, Yale U., 1974. Bar: N.Y. 1975. Assoc. Debevoise & Plimpton, 1974-79; atty., sr. atty., asst. gen. counsel Avon Products, Inc., N.Y.C., 1979-85, v.p. legal affairs, 1985-89, sr. v.p., gen. counsel, 1990-94, Gen. Mills, Inc., Mpls., 1994-99, sr. v.p. corp. affairs, gen. counsel, 1999—. Bd. dirs. Jafra Cosmetics, Am. Arbitration Assn.; mem. exec. com. Ctr. Pub. resources; bd. trustees Mpls. Inst. Arts. Administrative and regulatory, General corporate. Office: Gen Mills Inc Number One Gen Mills Blvd Minneapolis MN 55426

MARSHALL, VALERIE ANN, lawyer; b. Evansville, Ind., Aug. 26, 1954; d. Arthur E. and Jacqueline J. (Maixner) M. BBA, Stetson U., 1976, JD, 1979. Bar: Fla. 1979. Assoc. Clayton & Landis, Orlando, Fla., 1980-81; in-house counsel Walt Disney World Co., Lake Buena Vista, 1981-83; assoc. Haas, Boehm, Brown, Rigdon & Seacrest, Orlando, 1983-84; jr. ptnr., workers compensation supr. Haas, Boehm, Brown, Rigdon, Seacrest & Fischer, 1984-87; supr. worker's compensation Jeffrey & Thomas, P.A., Maitland, Fla., 1987-89; ptnr. Jeffery, Thomas & Marshall P.A., 1989-90, Jeffery & Marshall, P.A., Maitland, 1991-94, Beers, Jack, Tudhope & Wyatt P.A., Maitland, 1994-99; prin. Valerie A. Marshall, L.L.C., Orlando, 1999—. Mem. ABA, Orange County Bar (vice chmn. worker's compensation com. 1984-86, 89-90), Fla. Bar (workers compensation rules com. 1985-88), Fla. Assn. for Women Lawyers (sec. 1982-84), Cen. Fla. Corp. Counsel Assn. (sec./treas. 1982-83), NOW, Alpha Chi Omega (v.p. 1974-76). Methodist. Avocations: music, writing, cooking, tennis, needlework. Insurance, Workers' compensation. Office: Valerie A Marshall LLC 1106 E Ridgewood St Orlando FL 32803

MARSHALL, WILLIAM TAYLOR, lawyer; b. Dallas; s. Willis A. and Jane T. Marshall; m. Peggy Taylor, May 18, 1973; 1 child, Taylor. BSPA with honors, U. Ark., 1973, MBA with honors, 1975; JD with honors, U. Ark., Little Rock, 1981. Bar: Ark. 1981, U.S. Dist. Ct. (fed. dist.) 1982, U.S. Ct. Appeals (8th cir.) 1982, U.S. Supreme Ct. 1984; CPA, Ark. Fin. analyst Hosp. Affiliates Internat., Nashville, 1975-76, sr. fin. analyst, 1976-78; CFO Hosp. Affiliates Internat./Doctor's Hosp., Little Rock, 1978-81; assoc. House Holmes & Jewell, 1981-83, ptnr., 1983-85, Robinson, Staley, Marshall & Duke, Little Rock, 1985—. Lectr. in field. Contbr. articles to profl. jours. Mem. ABA, AICPAs, Ark. Bar Assn. (cert. tax specialist, health law sect. 1985—), Am. Health Lawyers Assn. General corporate, Health, Corporate taxation. Home: 1900 Beechwood St Little Rock AR 72207-2004 Office: Robinson Staley Marshall & Duke PA 400 W Capitol Ave Ste 2891 Little Rock AR 72201-3463 E-mail: wmarshall@rsmd.com

MARSICO, LEONARD JOSEPH, lawyer; b. Pitts., Sept. 7, 1955; s. Francis A. and Teresa (Constantini) M.; m. Mildred Farrar Williams, Dec. 3, 1983; children: Megan Farrar, John Williams, George Leonard, Robert Francis. BA, U. Va., 1977; JD, U. Pitts., 1980. Bar: Pa. 1980, U.S. Dist. Ct. (we. dist.) Pa. 1980, U.S. Ct. Appeals (3d and 4th cirs.) 1988, U.S. Dist. Ct. (no. dist.) W.Va. 1993, Ohio 1999. Ptnr. Buchanan Ingersoll, Pitts., 1980-88, DKW Law Group, PC, Pitts., 1996—. Staff mem. U. Pitts. Law Rev., 1979-80. Bd. dirs. Greater Pitts. Area Red Cross. Mem. ABA, Allegheny County Bar Assn. Republican. Roman Catholic. Avocations: golf, squash, skiing, sailing. General civil litigation, Contracts commercial. Office: Doepken Keevican & Weiss 58th Fl 600 Grant St Ste 58 Pittsburgh PA 15219-2703 E-mail: lmarsico@dkwlaw.com

MARSTILLER, PHILIP S. lawyer; b. Clarksburg, W.Va., Sept. 4, 1944; s. James Augustus and Marjorie Annon M.; m. Judy Rothwell Philpott, June 1, 1966 (div. Sept. 1983); children: Philip S. Jr., Spencer P.; m. Catherine Profitt Hayden, June 17, 1994. BA, Coll. William & Mary, 1966; LLB, U. Richmond, 1969. Bar: Va. 1969, U.S. Dist. Ct. (ea. and we. dists.) Va. 1969, U.S. Ct. Appeals (4th cir.) 1975, U.S. Supreme Ct. 1980. Asst. commonwealth atty. Henry County Commonwealth Attys. Office, Martinsville, Va., 1969-71; assoc. Mays & Valentine, Richmond, 1972-76; ptnr. Hazel, Thomas, Fiske, Beckhorn & Hanes, 1976-88, Parker, Pollard & Brown, Richmond, 1988-91, Cawthorn, Picard, Rowe & Marstiller, Richmond, 1991-93; pres. Philip S. Marstiller, P.C., 1994—. Adj. prof. law U. Richmond Sch. Law, 1985-89; mem. pres. coun. Coll. William & Mary, Williamsburg, Va., 1994-99; mem. alumni coun. Mercersburg (Pa.) Acad., 1999. Author: The Virginia Alcoholic Beverage Control Board Compliance Manual, 1991. Mem. 2d Presbyn. Ch., Richmond; lobbyist Va. Gen. Assembly, Richmond, 1972-92. Capt. JAGC, 1970-73. Mem. ATLA, ABA (mem. negligence-products liability litig. com. 1975-78), Am. Trial Lawyers Assn., Nat. Assn. Employment Lawyers, Nat. Health Lawyers Assn., Bar Register Preeminent Lawyers Am., Va. Bar Assn., (mem. constrn. litig. com. 1980-82), Va. State Bar (mem. com. legis. 1980, bd. govs. health law section 1984-88), Va. Trial Lawyers Assn. (mem. com. legis. 1975-78, mem. com. employment law 1996), Richmond Bar Assn. (mem. legis. liaison com. 1975-78), 4th Century Club, Deep Run Hunt Club, Farmington Country Club. Democrat. Avocations: Upland bird hunting, duck and goose hunting, fly fishing, long distance running. Labor, Product liability. Office: 16 S 2nd St Richmond VA 23219-3723

MARTENS, DON WALTER, lawyer; b. Darlington, Wis., Mar. 25, 1934; s. Walter W. and Geraldine A. (McWilliams) M.; children: Kim Martens Cooper, Diane Martens Reed. BS in Engring. with hons., U. Wis., 1957; JD with honors, George Washington U., 1963. Bar: Supreme Ct. Calif. 1964, U.S. Ct. Appeals (9th cir.) 1964, U.S. Dist. Ct. (no. and cen. dists.) Calif. 1964, U.S. Supreme Ct. 1973, U.S. Dist. Ct. (so. dist.) Calif. 1977, U.S. Ct. Appeals (fed. cir.) 1982, U.S. Dist. Ct. (ea. dist.) Calif. 1984. Examiner U.S. Patent and Trademark Office, Washington, 1960-63; patent lawyer Standard Oil of Calif., San Francisco, 1963-65; ptnr. Knobbe, Martens, Olson & Bear, Newport Beach, Calif., 1965—. Mem. adv. comm. Fed. Cir. Ct. Appeals, 1991-96, 2000—. Lt. USN, 1957-60. Mem. Orange County Bar Assn. (pres. 1975), Orange County Legal Aid Soc. (pres. 1969), Orange County Patent Law Assn. (pres. 1984), L.A. Patent Law Assn. (pres. 1989), State Bar Calif. (bd. govs. 1984-87, v.p. 1986-87), Am. Intellectual Property Law Assn. (pres. 1995-96), State Bar Intellectual Property Assn. (chmn. 1977), 9th Cir. Jud. Conf. (del. 1985-88, 1995-98), Nat. Inventors Hall of Fame Found. (pres. 1998-99), Nat. Coun. Intellectual Property Law Assn. (chmn. 1998-99), Big Canyon Country Club, Santa Ana Country Club, Rancho La Quinta Country Club. Republican. Roman Catholic. Federal civil litigation, Patent, Trademark and copyright. Office: 620 Newport Center Dr Fl 16 Newport Beach CA 92660-6420 E-mail: dmartens@kmob.com

MART$_8$, MIGUEL TORRENTS, lawyer; b. Barcelona, Spain, Mar. 25, 1959; s. Miguel and Elvira (Torrents) Marti; m. Luisa Jorba, April 27, 1996. LLB, U. Barcelona, Spain, 1983. Ptnr. Martí I Assocs., Barcelona, Spain, 1986—. Mem. Internat. Bar Assn., Internat. Assn. Lawyers, Union Des Avocats Européens. Criminal, Labor, Taxation, general. Office: Marti Assoc S L A V Diagonal 584 pral 08021 Barcelona Spain Fax: 34 93 202 09 14. E-mail: bcn@martinlawyers.com

MARTIN, ALAN JOSEPH, lawyer; b. Berwyn, Ill., Dec. 9, 1959; s. Daniel George and Lillie (Chalupa) M.; m. Dawne Michelle Martin, June 24, 1989; children: Rebecca Marie, Melissa Nicole, Sarah Anne, reid Anthony. BA summa cum laude, U. Ill., 1982; JD, U. Va., 1985. Bar: Ill. 1985, U.S. Dist. Ct. (no. dist.) Ill., 1985, U.S. Ct. Appeals (7th cir.) 1997, U.S. Ct. Appeals (3d cir.) 1999. Analyst office politico-mil. analysis, bur. intelligence and rsch. Dept. State, Washington, 1981; assoc. Isham, Lincoln & Beale, Chgo., 1985-87, Mayer, Brown & Platt, Chgo., 1987—, ptnr., 1993. Mng. and exec. editor Jour. Law and Politics, 1984-85. Counselor terminally ill Mercy Hosp. Hospice, Urbana, Ill., 1980-82; pro bono lawyer, 1985—. Merriam scholar, 1980-82, James, 1982. Mem. ABA, Phi Beta Kappa, Phi Delta Phi. Avocations: racquetball, running, chess. General civil litigation, Insurance, Private international. Home: 1500 White Eagle Dr Naperville IL 60564-9761 Office: Mayer Brown & Platt 190 S La Salle St Ste 3100 Chicago IL 60603-3441

MARTIN, ALICE HOWZE, prosecutor; b. Memphis, Apr. 25, 1956; BSN, Vanderbilt U., 1978; JD, U. Miss., 1981. Bar: Ala., Tenn., Miss. Asst. U.S. atty. U.S. Attys. Office , Memphis, 1983-89; ptnr. Harris Harris & Martin , Florence, Ala., 1992—; U.S. atty. Ala. No. Dist. Mcpl. judge City of Florence, Ala., 1993; bd. dirs. 1st United Meth. Ch., Florence, 1993; adv. bd. mem. Riverbend Mental Health, Florence, 1994. Mem. Ala. Ducks Unltd. Greenwings (chairperson). Avocations: traveling, skeet shooting. Office: 200 Fed Bldg 1800 5th Ave N Rm 200 Birmingham AL 35203-2198*

MARTIN, ALLEN, lawyer; b. Manchester, Conn., Aug. 12, 1937; s. Richard and Ruth Palmer (Smith) M.; m. Bonnie Reid, Sept. 8, 1979; children: Elizabeth Palmer, Samuel Bates. BA, Williams Coll., 1960, Oxford U., 1962; LLB, Harvard U., 1965. Ptnr. Downs, Rachlin and Martin, Burlington, Vt., 1971—. Chmn. bd. dirs. Wicor Ams., 1991—; bd. dirs. IDX Systems Corp.; bd. dirs., chmn. fin. com. Union Mut. Ins. Co., New Eng. Guaranty Ins. Co.; mem. Vt. Jud. Responsibility Bd., vice-chmn., 1978-80. Chmn. Vt. Bd. Edn., 1978-83; chmn. Vt. Rep. Party, 1991-95; mem. Rep. Nat. Com., 1991-95, 97-99; trustee Vt. Law Sch., 2000—. Mem. ABA, Am. Law Inst. (life), Vt. Bar Assn. Republican. E-makl. Home: 283 S Union St Burlington VT 05401-5507 also: Six Chimneys Orford NH 03777 Office: PO Box 190 199 Main St Burlington VT 05401-8309 E-mail: amartin@drm.com

MARTIN, ANDREW AYERS, lawyer, physician, educator; b. Toccoa, Ga., Aug. 18, 1958; s. Wallace Ford and Dorothy LaTranquil (Ayers) M.; children: William Ayers, Malorie Ayers. BA, Emory U., Atlanta, 1980, MD, 1984; JD, Duke U., 1988. Bar: Calif. 1989, La. 1990, D.C. 1991; diplomate Am. Bd. Pathology, Nat. Bd. Med. Examiners; lic. physician, La., Miss., Ark. Intern in pediatrics Emory U./Grady Meml. Hosp., Atlanta, 1984; intern Tulane U./Charity Hosp., New Orleans, 1989-90, resident in

anatomic and clin. pathology, 1990-94; surg. pathology fellow Baylor Coll. Medicine, Houston, 1994-95; law clk. Ogletree, Deakins, Smoak, Stewart, Greenville, S.C., summer 1986, Thelen Marrin Johnson Bridges, L.A., summer 1987, Duke Hosp. Risk Mgmt., 1987-88; assoc. Haight Brown Bonesteel, Santa Monica, Calif., 1988; pvt. practice L.A., 1989; physician/atty. Tulane Med. Ctr./Charity Hosp., New Orleans, 1989-94, Baylor Coll. Medicine/Tex. Med. Ctr., Houston, 1994-95; lab. dir. King's Daus. Hosp., Greenville, Miss., 1995—; asst. clin. prof. pathology Tulane U.; lab. dir., owner Vicksburg Pathology Lab., Bolivar Med. Ctr., Cleveland, Miss.; staff pathologist Delta Regional Ctr., Greenville, N.W. Miss. Regional Medical Ctr., Clarksdale, No. Sunflower County Hosp., Ruteville, Tallahatchie County Hosp., Charleston. Sr. ptnr. Mid-South Pathology Assocs.; med. dir. of labs. Vicksburg Pathology Lab., N.W. Miss. Regional Med. Ctr., Bolivar Med. Ctr., Delta Regional Med. Ctr., North Sunflower County Hosp., 1997—, Tallahatchie (Miss.) County Hosp., N.W. Miss. Regional Med. Ctr., Clarksdale, Lab Corp., Southaven, Miss., Tallahatchie County Hosp.; adj. faculty Moorhead U.; bd. dirs. Martin Bldrs., Inc., Toccoa; mem. AIDS Legis. Task Force for La.; case cons. Office of Tech. Assessment, Washington; tech. cons. and autopsy extra Oliver Stone's "JFK"; adj. clin. faculty Moorhead Coll. Contbr. articles to profl. jours.; author: Reflections on Rusted Chrome (book of poetry). Fellow Coll. Am. Pathologists, Coll. Legal Medicine, La. State Med. Soc. (del. meeting 1992-93). Health. Home: 935 Lakehall Rd Lake Village AR 71653-6096 also: 4104 Alabama Ave Kenner LA 70065-5603 also: 3850 Old Highway 27 Vicksburg MS 39180-8829 Office: Mid-South Pathology Assocs PO Box 5880 Greenville MS 38704-5880

MARTIN, BEVERLY, federal judge; b. Macon, Ga. BA, Stetson U., Deland, Fla., 1976; JD, U. Ga., 1981. Bar: Ga. 1981. Assoc. Martin, Snow, Grant & Napier, Macon, Ga., 1981-84; trial and appellate ct. litigator, sr. asst. atty. gen. and dir. bus. and profl. regulation divsn. Office of Atty. Gen. State of Ga., 1984-94; asst. U.S. atty. mid. dist. Ga., 1994-98; U.S. atty. mid. dist. Ga. U.S. Dept. Justice, 1998-2000; dist. judge U.S. Dist. Ct. for No. Dist. Ga., Atlanta, 2000—. Mem. Ga. Bar Assn., Macon Bar Assn., Am. Judicature Soc., Ga. Assn. Women Lawyers, Lawyers Club of Atlanta. Office: US Dist Ct for No Dist Ga 2388 US Courthouse 75 Spring St SW Atlanta GA 30303

MARTIN, BOE WILLIS, lawyer; b. Texarkana, Ark., Oct. 6, 1940; s. E.H. and Dorothy Annette (Willis) M.; m. Carol J. Edwards, June 12, 1965; children: Stephanie Diane, Scott Andrew. BA, Tex. A&M U., 1962; LLB, U. Tex., 1964; LLM, George Washington U., 1970. Bar: Tex. 1964. Law clk. Tex. Supreme Ct., 1966-67; assoc. Snakard, Brown & Gambill, Ft. Worth, 1967-69, assoc., ptnr., 1971-72; asst. counsel U.S. Senate Labor and Pub. Welfare Com., 1969; legal asst. U.S. Senator Ralph W. Yarborough, 1969-71; assoc., ptnr. Stalcup & Johnson, Dallas, 1972-77; assoc. ptnr. Coke & Coke, 1977-80; ptnr., shareholder Johnson & Gibbs, 1981-96, Bell, Nunnally & Martin, Dallas, 1996—. Vis. prof. law So. Meth. U. Sch. Law, 1972-73, 75, 88-89, 95, 99-2000, U. Tex. Sch. Law, 1977, 79. Contbr. articles to profl. jours. Staff Carter-Mondale Campaign, 1976, 80; cons. to v.p. of U.S., 1977-80; cons. Mondale for Pres. Campaign, 1983-84, Dukakis for Pres. Campaign, 1988, State of Minn., 1990. Capt. U.S. Army, 1964-69. Mem. ABA, Tex. Bar Assn., Dallas Bar Assn. Democrat. Methodist. Home: 4435 Arcady Ave Dallas TX 75205-3604 Office: Bell & Nunnally & Martin 3232 Mckinney Ave Ste 1400 Dallas TX 75204-2426

MARTIN, BOYCE FICKLEN, JR. federal judge; b. Boston, Oct. 23, 1935; s. Boyce Ficklen and Helen Artt M.; m. Mavin Hamilton Brown, July 8, 1961; children: Mary V. H., Julia H.C., Boyce Ficklen III, Robert C. G. II. AB, Davidson Coll., 1957; JD, U. Va., 1963. Bar: Ky. 1963. Law clk. to Shackelford Miller, Jr., chief judge U.S. Ct. Appeals for 6th Circuit, Cin., 1963-64; asst. U.S. atty. Western Dist. Ky., Louisville, 1964; U.S. atty. Western Dist. Ky., 1965; pvt. practice law Louisville, 1966-74; judge Jefferson Circuit Ct., 1974-76; chief judge Ct. Appeals Ky., 1976-79; judge U.S. Ct. Appeals (6th cir.), Cin. and Louisville, 1979-96, chief judge, 1996—. Mem. jud. coun. U.S. Ct. Appeals (6th cir.), 1979-96, chmn., 1996—; mem. Jud. Conf. of U.S., 1996—, exec. com., 1998—. Mem. vestry St. Francis in the Fields Episcopal Ch., Harrods Creek, Ky., 1979-83; bd. visitors Davidson (N.C.) Coll., 1980-86, trustee, 1994-98; trustee Isaac W. Bernheim Found., Louisville, 1981-97, chmn., 1982-95; trustee Blackacre Found., Inc., Louisville, 1983-94, chmn., 1986-94; trustee Hanover (Ind.) Coll., 1982—, vice chmn., 1992-97, chmn., 1998—; mem. exec. bd. Old Ky. Home coun. Boy Scouts of Am., 1968-72; pres. Louisville Zool. Commn., 1971-74. Capt. JAGC U.S. Army, 1958-66. Fellow Am. Bar Found.; mem. Inst. Jud. Adminstrn., Am. Judicature Soc., Fed Bar Assn., ABA (com. effective appellate advocacy Conf. Appellate Judges), Ky. Bar Assn., Louisville Bar Assn. Office: US Ct Appeals 209 US Courthouse 601 W Broadway Louisville KY 40202-2238 Fax: 502-625-3829*

MARTIN, C. D. lawyer; b. Seminole, Okla., Mar. 24, 1943; BS, U. North Tex., 1964; LLB, U. Tex., 1967. Bar: Tex. 1967, N.Mex. 1967, U.S. Dist. Ct. N.Mex., U.S. Dist. Ct. (we. and no. dists.) Tex. Mem., mng. ptnr. Hinkle, Hensley, Shanor & Martin, L.L.C., Midland, Tex., 1986—. Mem. adv. bd. dirs. Norwest Bank Tex., Midland, Wells Fargo Bank Tex., Midland Bank. Mem. Midland Planning and Zoning Commn., 1979-82, chmn., 1982; mem. adv. coun. Sch. Arts and Scis., U. Tex. at Permian Basin; trustee Permian Basin Petroleum Mus.; past dir. U. Tex. Law Sch. Found. Fellow Tex. Bar Found. (life), N.Mex. Bar Found.; mem. ABA, State Bar Tex., State Bar N.Mex., Midland County Bar Assn. (pres. 1984-85), Phi Delta Phi. Contracts commercial, Oil, gas, and mineral, Natural resources. Office: Hinkle Cox Eaton Coffield & Hens PLLC PO Box 3580 Midland TX 79702-3580 E-mail: bud@hinklelawfirm.com

MARTIN, CARLA A. lawyer, veterinarian; b. Anchorage, June 28, 1967; d. Donald Arthur and Eleanor Rulis Young; m. Douglas Lee Martin, Sept. 7, 1991. BS in Biology, Iowa State U., 1991, DVM, 1992; JD, St. Louis U., 1997. Bar: Mo., Ill.; lic. veterinarian Mo. Veterinarian Animal Emergency Clinic, St. Louis, 1992-97; lawyer Lewis, Rice & Fingersh, 1997-98, The May Dept. Stores Co., St. Louis, 1998—. Mem. ABA, Am. Vet. Med. Assn., Am. Vet. Med. Law Assn., Am. Corp. Counsel Assn. Office: The May Dept Stores Co 611 Olive St Ste 1750 Saint Louis MO 63101-1721

MARTIN, CONNIE RUTH, retired lawyer; b. Clovis, N.Mex., Sept. 9, 1955; d. Lynn Latimer and Marian Ruth (Pierce) M.; m. Daniel A. Patterson, Nov. 21, 1987; step-children: David Patterson, Dana Patterson. B in Univ. Studies, Ea. N.Mex. U., 1976, MEd, 1977; JD, U. Mo., Kansas City, 1981. Bar: N.Mex. 1981, U.S. Dist. Ct. N.Mex. 1981. Asst. dist. atty. State of N.Mex., Farmington, 1981-84; ptnr. Tansey, Rosebrough, Gerding & Strother, PC, 1984-93; pvt. practice Connie R. Martin, P.C., 1993-94; domestic violence commr. 11th Judicial Dist. Ct., State of N.Mex., 1993-94; with Jeffrey B. Diamond Law Firm, Carlsbad, N. Mex., 1994-96; assoc. Sager, Curran, Sturges and Tepper PC, Las Cruces, 1996-97, Holt & Babington PC, Las Cruces, 1997-2000; ret., 2000. Dep. med. investigator State of N.Mex., Farmington, 1981-84; instr. San Juan Coll., 1987, N.Mex. State U., 1995; spkr. N.Mex. Jud. Edn. Ctr., 1993-94; chair paralegal program adv. com., 1988, Adv Com., St Francis Clin., Presbyn. Med. Svs., 1994-96; bd. Bar Examiners State of N.Mex., 1989—, vice-chair, 1995-97, chair, 1997-99; asst. bar counsel Disciplinary Bd.; mem. profl. adv. com. Meml. Med. Ctr. Found., 1997-2000, trustee, 1997-2000; mem. So. N.Mex. Estate Planning Coun., 1997-2000. Bd. dirs., exec. com. San Juan County Econ. Opportunity Coun., Farmington, 1982-83; bd. dirs. Four Corners Substance Abuse Coun., Farmington, 1984, N.Mex. Newspapers, Inc.; chmn. Cmty. Corrections-Intensive Supervision Panel, Farmington, 1987-88; jud. selection com. mem. San Juan County, 1991, Chavez County, 1995; nominating com. Supreme Ct./Ct of Appeals, 1991-96; treas. Ft. Morgan United Meth. Ch., 2001—. Recipient Distinguished Svcs. award for Outstanding Young Woman San Juan County Jaycees, 1984. Mem. N.Mex. Bar. Assn. (bd. dirs. elder law sect. 1993-96, peer rev. task force 1994-95, asst. to new lawyers com. 1986-87, local bar com. 1988, bd. dirs. young lawyers divsn. 1989-91, bd. dirs. real property probate and trust sect. 1994-97), San Juan County Bar Assn. (treas. 1985-87, v.p. 1987, pres. 1988), Farmington C. of C. (bd. dirs. 1991-93). Methodist. Avocations: health, fitness, reading. Probate, Real property.

MARTIN, CYNTHIA ANN, lawyer; b. Columbus, Ohio, Nov. 7, 1970; d. Jeffrey James and Catherin Pound; m. Douglas Edward Martin, Aug. 8, 1992. BA in Polit. Sci. Comms., Campbellsville (Ky.) U., 1993; JD, Cumberland Sch. of Law, 1997. Bar: Ala. 1997, U.S. Dist. Ct. (no. and mid. dist.) Ala. 1997, U.S. Ct. Appeals (11th cir.) 1997. Atty. Clark and Scott, P.C., Birmingham, Ala., 1997—. Mem. Birmingham Bar Assn. General civil litigation, Insurance, Personal injury. Office: Clark and Scott PC 3500 Blue Lake Dr Ste 350 Birmingham AL 35243

MARTIN, DALLAS REA, lawyer; b. Kansas City, Kans., Aug. 3, 1954; s. H. Thayne and Frances Colleen (Hay) M.; m. Lianne Marie Taylor, June 2, 1979; 1 child, Elise Taylor. BA in Philosophy with distinction, U. Kans., Lawrence, 1976, JD, 1979. Bar: Kans. 1979, U.S. Dist. Ct. Kans., 1979, U.S. Ct. Appeals (10th cir.) 1979, Colo. 1985, U.S. Dist. Ct. Colo. 1985. Pvt. practice, Olathe, Kans., 1979-81; contracts counsel Midwest Rsch. Inst., Kansas City, Mo., 1981-84; counsel and contracts mgr. Precision Visuals, Inc., Boulder, Colo., 1984-90; mgr. tech. transfer Nat. Renewable Energy Lab., Golden, 1990-94; dir. intellectual property, tech. transfer office U.S. West Advt. Tech., Inc., Boulder, 1994-97; sr. counsel intellectual property First Data Corp., Englewood, Colo., 1997-2000; v.p., gen. counsel, sec. SwitchPoint Networks, Inc., 2001—. Contbr. articles to profl. jours. Bd. dirs. Blue Knights, Inc., Denver, 1997—. Mem. ABA (intellectual property sect. 1991—), Tech. Transfer Soc. (bd. dirs. 1996-98), Licensing Execs. Soc. (co-chair Denver chpt. 2001—). Office: SwitchPoint Networks Inc 6300 S Syracuse Way Englewood CO 80111 E-mail: drmartin@switchpointnetworks.com

MARTIN, DAVID ALAN, law educator; b. Indpls., July 23, 1948; s. C. Wendell and Elizabeth Bowman (Meeker) M.; m. Cynthia Jo Lorman, June 13, 1970; children: Amy Lynn, Jeffrey David. BA, DePauw U., 1970; JD, Yale U., 1975. Bar: D.C. Law clk. to Hon. J. Skelly Wright U.S. Ct. Appeals (D.C. cir.), 1975-76; law clk. to Hon. Lewis F. Powell U.S. Supreme Ct., Washington, 1976-77; assoc. Rogovin, Stern & Huge, 1977-78; spl. asst. bur. human rights and humanitarian affairs U.S. State Dept., 1978-80; from asst. prof. to assoc. prof. U. Va. Sch. Law, Charlottesville, 1980-86, prof., 1986-91, Henry L. & Grace Doherty prof. law, 1991—, F. Palmer Weber Rsch. prof. civil liberties and human rights, 1992-95, 2000—. Cons. Adminstrv. Conf. U.S., Washington, 1988-89, 91-92, U.S. Dept. Justice, 1993-95; gen. counsel U.S. Immigration and Naturalization Svc., 1995-98. Author: Immigration: Process and Policy, 1985, 4th edit., 1998, Asylum Case Law Sourcebook, 1994, 3rd edit., 2001, The Endless Quest: Helping America's Farm Workers, 1994; editor: The New Asylum Seekers, 1988, Immigration Admissions, 1998, Immigration Controls, 1998; contbr. articles to profl. jours. Nat. governing bd. Common Cause, Washington, 1972-75; elder Westminster Presbyn. Ch., Charlottesville, 1982-84, 89-92; bd. dirs. Internat. Rescue Com., 2000—. German Marshall Fund Rsch. fellow, Geneva, 1984-85. Mem. Am. Soc. Internat. Law (Book award 1986), Internat. Law Assn. Democrat. Office: U Va Sch Law 580 Massie Rd Charlottesville VA 22903-1738 E-mail: dmartin@law5.law.virginia.edu

MARTIN, GARY WAYNE, lawyer; b. Cin., Feb. 14, 1946; s. Elmer DeForrest and Nellie May (Hughes) M.; m. Debra Lynn Goldsmith, June 25, 1982; children: Christopher, Jeremy, Joie, Casey. BA, Wilmington Coll., 1967; JD, U. Cin., 1974. Bar: Fla. 1974. Casualty practice leader Fowler White Gillen Boggs Villareal & Banker, Tampa, Fla., 1974—, also bd. dirs. Lt. USNR, 1967-71. Mem. Harbour Island Athletic Club. Republican. Presbyterian. Avocation: tennis. Office: Fowler White Gillen Boggs Villareal & Banker 501 E Kennedy Blvd Ste 1600 Tampa FL 33602-5240 E-mail: gmartin@foulerwhite.com

MARTIN, GEORGE J., JR. lawyer; b. Port Chester, N.Y., June 7, 1942; s. George J. and Eileen Ann (Buckley) M.; m. Joanne L. Frost, Aug. 21, 1965 (div. May 1986); children: Amy Anne, Ryan Frost; m. Anna Marie Cipriati, June 21, 1986; children: Marissa McCreay, Jill McCreay. BA, Georgetown U., 1964, JD, 1967. Bar: N.Y. 1969; conseil juridique, France, 1977-82. From assoc. to ptnr. Mudge Rose Guthrie Alexander & Ferdon, N.Y.C., 1967-95; ptnr. Coudert Bros., 1995—. Mem. Friends Vieilles Maisons Francaises Inc. (dir.-sec.). Roman Catholic. General corporate, FERC practice, Finance. Home: 163 Congress St Brooklyn NY 11201-6103 Office: Coudert Bros 1114 Ave of The Americas New York NY 10036-7710 E-mail: geojmartin@aol.com, marting@coudert.com

MARTIN, GREGORY KEITH, lawyer, mayor; b. Conway, S.C., Nov. 7, 1956; s. George Henry Martin and Julia Ann (Johnson) M. Land. BS in Fin. Mgmt., Clemson U., 1979; JD, U. S.C., 1983. Bar: S.C. 1983. Intern U.S. Senate, 1980; law clk. to presiding judge 15th Jud. Cir. Ct., Conway, 1983; assoc. Johnson & Martin, 1983-88, ptnr., 1988-93, Martin & Smith, Conway, 1993-98; mayor City of Conway, 1995—; pvt. practice, Conway, 1998—. Mem. Conway Planning Commn., 1986-89, chmn., 1989; bd. dirs. Conway-Main St. U.S.A., 1986-90, chmn., 1988; mem. Conway Bd. Appeals, 1987-89, Horry County Bd. Archtl. Rev., 1987-90; mem. Conway City Coun., 1991-94; pres., Horry County Hist. Soc., 1988, 90, mayor pro tem, 1994; mem. adv. bd. Pee Dee Heritage Ctr., 1988—. Mem. ABA, S.C. Bar Assn., Horry County Bar Assn., Sigma Nu, Phi Delta Phi. Methodist. Avocations: tennis, coin collecting. General corporate, Probate, Real property. Home: 706 Elm St Conway SC 29526-4373 Office: PO Box 736 Conway SC 29528-0736

MARTIN, HARRY CORPENING, lawyer, retired state supreme court justice; b. Lenoir, N.C., Jan. 13, 1920; s. Hal C. and Johnsie Harshaw (Nelson) M.; m. Nancy Robiou Dallam, Apr. 16, 1955; children: John, Matthew, Mary. AB, U. N.C., 1942; LLB, Harvard U., 1948; LLM, U. Va., 1982. Bar: N.C. 1948. Pvt. practice, Asheville, N.C., 1948-62; judge N.C. Superior Ct., 1962-78, N.C. Ct. Appeals, Raleigh, 1978-82; justice N.C. Supreme Ct., 1982-92; ptnr. Martin & Martin, Attys., Hillsborough, N.C., 1992—. Adj. prof. U. N.C. Law Sch., 1983-92, Duke U., 1990-91, Dan K. Moore disting. vis. prof., 1992-94; sr. conf. atty. U.S. Ct. Appeals for 4th Cir., 1994-99; chief justice Supreme Ct. ea. bd. of Cherokee Indians, 2000—. With U.S. Army, 1942-45, South Pacific. Mem. U.S. Supreme Ct. Hist. Soc., N.C. Supreme Ct. Hist. Soc. (pres.). Democrat. Episcopalian. Education and schools. Home: 1 Hilltop Rd Asheville NC 28803-3017 Office: Cherokee Supreme Ct PO Box 455 Cherokee NC 28719 Fax: 828-497-5705. E-mail: judgemartin@home.com

MARTIN, HENRY ALAN, public defender; b. Nashville, Sept. 5, 1949; s. James Alvin and Mary Elizabeth (Long) M.; m. Gloria B. Ballard, May 9, 1975; children: Nathan Daniel, Anna Elizabeth. BA, Vanderbilt U., 1971, JD, 1974. Bar: Tenn. 1975, U.S. Dist. Ct. (mid. dist.) Tenn. 1975, U.S. Ct. Appeals (6th cir.) 1976, U.S. Supreme Ct. 1979. Pvt. practice, Nashville, 1975-76; ptnr. Haile & Martin, P.A., 1976-82; assoc. firm Barrett & Ray, P.C., 1982-85; fed. pub. defender U.S. Dist. Ct. (mid. dist.) Tenn., 1985—. Mem. adv. com. on rules criminal procedure U.S. Judicial Conf., 1994-99. CO-author, co-editor trial manual, Tools for the Ultimate Trial, 1985, 2d edit., 1988; contbr. articles to profl. jours. Del., Witness for Peace, Managua, Nicaragua, 1987. Mem. ABA (coun. criminal justice sect. 1993-96), NACDL, Assn. Fed. Defenders (pres. 1995-98), Nashville Bar Assn., Napier Looby Bar Assn., Tenn. Assn. Criminal Def. Lawyers (bd. dirs. 1978-94, pres. 1984-85, Pres.'s award 1984). Democrat. Avocations: jogging, swimming. Home: 3802 Whitland Ave Nashville TN 37205-2432 Office: Fed Pub Defender 810 Broadway Ste 200 Nashville TN 37203-3861 E-mail: henry_martin@fd.org

MARTIN, JAMES WILLIAM, lawyer; b. Turlock, Calif., Dec. 20, 1949; Student, Ga. Inst. Tech., 1967-69; BS, Stetson U., 1971, JD, 1974. Bar: Fla. 1974, U.S. Dist. Ct. (mid. dist.) Fla. 1974, U.S. Ct. Appeals (5th cir.) 1974, U.S. Ct. Appeals (11th cir.) 1987, U.S. Supreme Ct. 1978. Ptnr. Brickley & Martin, St. Petersburg, Fla., 1974-79; pres. James W. Martin, P.A., 1979—. Presenter in field. Author: West's Florida Corporation System, 1984, West's Legal Forms, 3d edit., Non-Profit Corporations, 1991, 92, 93, 94, 96, 97, 98, 99, 2000, 2001, West's Florida Legal Forms, Business Organizations, Real Estate, Specialized Forms, 1990, 91, 92, 93, 94, 95; supplement editor Fla. Jur. Forms, Legal and Bus., 1998, 99; contbr. articles to profl. jours. including Word Perfect mag., ALI-ABA Practical Lawyer, Fla. Bar News, Fla. Bar Jour. City councilman, St. Petersburg, 1982-83; active Leadership St. Petersburg; active charter class Leadership Tampa Bay; founding trustee, sec., counsel Salvador Dali Mus., 1980—; founding dir., sec., counsel Fla. Internat. Mus., 1992-94. Recipient Outstanding Young Man award Jaycees, 1982, Outstanding Contbn. to City award St. Petersburg C. of C., 1980. Mem. Fla. Bar (chmn. coordinating com. tech. 1992-93, probate rules com. 1994-2000), St. Petersburg Bar Assn. (chair probate sect. 1999-00), St. Petersburg C. of C. (gen. counsel 1991-92, arts task force 1987, chmn. parking com., chmn. Urban Solutions coun. 1992-93, chmn. downtown coun. 1993-94), Pres. Club (founder, hon. bd. dirs. 1985-91), Pinellas County Arts Coun. (councilman 1997—). General corporate, Probate, Real property. Fax: 727-823-3479. E-mail: jamesmartinpa@msn.com

MARTIN, JAY GRIFFITH, lawyer; b. Washington, Oct. 13, 1951; s. Drexel Reese and Joyce (Towne) M.; 1 child, Trevor. BBA, So. Meth. U., 1973, MPA, JD, So. Meth. U., 1976. Bar: Tex., D.C., U.S. Ct. Appeals (5th cir.), U.S. Dist. Ct. (so. dist.) Tex., U.S. Dist. Ct. D.C., U.S. Supreme Ct. Counsel Pennzoil Co., Houston, 1976-78, sr. counsel, 1978-81; divsn. counsel The Superior Oil Co., 1981-85; sr. counsel Mobil Natural Gas, 1985-87, gen. counsel, 1987-91; asst. gen. counsel Mobil Oil Corp., Fairfax, Va., 1991-96; ptnr. Andrews & Kurth LLP, Washington, 1996-2000, Phelps Dunbar LLP, Houston, 2000—01, Winstead Sechrest & Minick, Houston, 2001—. Mem. sr. adv. bd. Bus. Laws Inc., Chesterland, Ohio, 1997—; mem. adv. bd. Inst. Transnat. Arbitration, Southwestern Legal Found., 1996—. Author: (book) International Arbitration, 1998, Dispute Resolution for Oil and Gas Practitioners;contbr. articles; mem. adv. bd.: jour. Natural Gas Contracts, 1991—. Chmn. fundraising com. So. Meth. U., Washington, 1996—97, mem. dean's adv. coun. Sch. Law, 1995—; bd. trustees Rocky Mountain Mineral Law Found. Fellow: Tex. Bar Found.; mem.: Tex. Bar Assn., State Bar Tex. (adv. bd. 1985—, chmn. corp. counsel sect. 1990—91), State Bar Coll. of Tex., D.C. Bar Assn. (internat.sect.), Internat. Bar Assn. (sect. energy and natural resources 1994—), Energy Bar Assn. (chmn. antitrust sect. 1986—87, chmn. internat. energy com. 1998—99, chmn. internat. com.), ABA (litig. sect. rep. on ABA coord. com. on energy law 1991—97, sect. pub. utility law 1991—, chmn. natural resources, energy and environ law internat. energy com. 1996—98, exec. coun., budget chmn. sect. on environment, energy and law 1996—, liaison to Fed. Engergy BAr Assn. 1997—, ad hoc mem. of com. 1997—, sr. liaison oversight responsibility for all energy and resource coms. 1998—, vice chmn. sect. on environment, energy and resources' natural gas and), Houston Bar Assn., Assn. Internat. Petroleum Negotiators, Am. Soc. Internat. Law, Rocky Mountain Law Inst. (trustee 1991—), Delta Theta Phi, Fed. Bar Assn. (bd. dirs. 1990—92, chmn. internat. energy com. 1997—, antitrust sect. 1991—98, chmn. 1986—87). Avocations: history, current events and politics, tennis, golf, jogging. FERC practice, Oil, gas, and mineral, General corporate. Home: 3133 Buffalo Speedway Apt 7207 Houston TX 77098-1828 Office: Winstead Sechrest & Minick 910 Travis St Ste 2400 Houston TX 77002 E-mail: jmartin@winstead.com

MARTIN, JAYE LOUISE, lawyer; b. Sigourney, Iowa, June 4, 1959; d. James Leo Martin and Betty Jean Milburn. BS, Iowa State U., 1981; JD, Hamline U., 1993. Bar: Minn. 1993. Program dir. Cmty. Involvement Programs, Mpls., 1983-93; assoc. Gray Plant Mooty, 1993—. Mem. ABA, Am. Health Lawyers Assn., Minn. Bar Assn., Minn. Women Lawyers. Avocations: hiking, gardening, cooking. Office: Gray Plant Mooty 33 S 6th St Ste 3400 Minneapolis MN 55402-3796

MARTIN, JOEL CLARK, lawyer; b. Goshen, N.Y., Mar. 17, 1944; s. Harold Clark and Elma (Hicks) M.; m. Joyce Ellen Barron, Sept. 9, 1973; children: Eric Barron, Abigail Taylor. BA, Harvard U., 1965; JD, U. Chgo., 1977. Bar: Maine 1977, U.S. Dist. Ct. Maine 1977, U.S. Ct. Appeals (1st cir.) 1984. Assoc. Preti, Flaherty & Beliveau, Portland, Maine, 1977-80; ptnr. Petruccelli & Martin, 1980—. Commr. Commn. on Instns. Higher Edn. New England Assn. Sch.s & Colls., 1990-97, chair, 1995-97. Pres., trustee Portland Symphony Orch., 1978-87, adv. trustee, 1988—; mem. standing com. Episcopal Diocese of Maine, 1987-90; chmn. adv. com. on rules of evidence Maine Supreme Jud. Ct., 1990—; rule of law liaison Rep. of Moldova. Mem. ABA (ctrl. and east European law initiative 1999-2001), Maine Bar Assn., Maine Trial Lawyers Assn. Episcopalian. General civil litigation, Contracts commercial, Real property. Home: Spurnink Rd Scarborough ME 04074 Office: Petruccelli & Martin 50 Monument Sq 6th Fl PO Box 9733 Portland ME 04104-5033 E-mail: joelcmartin@hotmail.com, jmartin@petrucellimartin.com

MARTIN, JOHN CHARLES, judge; b. Durham, N.C., Nov. 9, 1943; s. Chester Barton and Mary Blackwell (Pridgen) M.; m. Margaret Rand; children: Lauren Blackwell, Sarah Conant, Mary Susan; step-children: Louise Short, Carl (Trip) Short. BA, Wake Forest U., 1965, JD, 1967; postgrad., Nat. Judicial Coll., Reno, 1979; cert. justice execs. program, U. N.C. Bar: N.C. 1967, U.S. Dist. Ct. (mid. dist.) N.C. 1967, U.S. Dist. Ct. (ea. dist.) N.C. 1972, U.S. Dist. Ct. (we. dist.) N.C. 1975, U.S. Ct. Appeals (4th cir.) 1976. Assoc. Haywood, Denny & Miller, Durham, N.C., 1969-72, ptnr., 1973-77; resident judge Superior Ct. 14th Jud. Dist. N.C., 1977-84; judge N.C. Ct. Appeals, Raleigh, 1985-88, 93—; ptnr. Maxwell & Hutson, P.A., Durham, 1988-92; arbitrator U.S. Dist. Ct. (mid. dist.) N.C., 1988-92. Study com. rules of evidence and comparative negligence N.C. Legis. Research Commn., 1980; mem. N.C. Pattern Jury Instrn. drafting com., 1978-84, N.C. Trial Judge's Bench Book Drafting Com., 1984-87, N.C. News Media-Adminstrn. of Justice Coun., 1987, Appellate Judges' Conf., state/fed. Jud. Coun. N.C., 1985-87, chmn., 1987; bd. visitors Wake Forest U. Sch. Law, 1986—; mem. alumni coun. Wake Forest U., 1993-96, 2001—; mem. N.C. State Jud. Edn. Study Com., 2000—; chmn. N.C. Jud. Stds. Commn., 2001—. Mem. Durham City Coun., 1975—77, chair pub. works com.; panel of arbitrators Duke U. Pvt. Adjudication Ctr., 1988—92. With Mil. Police Corps USAR, 1967—69. Recipient Disting. Svc. award Durham Jaycees, 1976. Mem. ABA, N.C. Bar Assn. (chmn. adminstrn. of justice study com. 1990-92, bench, bar and law sch. com. 1987-91, jud. campaign oversight com. 1990, Lit. Sect. Coun. 1991-94, conv. planning com. 1995—, adminstrn. justice task force 1996-98, appellate rules study com. 1999—, v.p. 1997-98), Durham County Bar Assn. (bd. dirs. 1991-92), Wake County Bar Assn., 10th Jud. Dist. Bar Assn., N.C. Jud. Conf. (v.p. 1999-2000), Hope Valley Country Club, Appalachian State U. Parents Assn. (bd. dirs. 1997—), Phi Delta Phi. Democrat. Methodist. Office: PO Box 888 Raleigh NC 27602-0888 E-mail: mnj@coa.state.nc.us

MARTIN, JOHN SHERWOOD, JR. federal judge; b. Bklyn., May 31, 1935; BA, Manhattan Coll., 1957; LLB, Columbia U., 1961. Bar: N.Y. 1961, U.S. Dist. Ct. (so. dist.) N.Y. 1963, U.S. Supreme Ct. 1966, U.S. Ct. Appeals (2d cir.) 1983. Law clk. to Hon. Leonard P. Moore U.S. Ct. Appeals (2d cir.), 1961-62; asst. U.S. atty. U.S. Dist. Ct. (so. dist.) N.Y., 1962-66; ptnr. Johnson, Hekker & Martin, Nyack, N.Y., 1966-67; asst. to solicitor gen., 1967-69; sole practitioner, 1969-72; ptnr. Martin, Obermaier & Morvillo, 1972-79, Schulte, Roth & Zabel, 1979-80; U.S. atty. U.S. Dist. Ct. for So. Dist. N.Y., N.Y.C., 1980-83; ptnr. Schulte, Roth & Zabel, 1983-90; judge U.S. Dist. Ct. for So. Dist. N.Y., N.Y.C., 1990—. Cons. Nat. Commn. Law Enforcement and the Adminstrn. of Criminal Justice, 1966-67; counsel to commn. to investigate disturbances Columbia U., 1968. Fellow Am. Coll. Trial Lawyers; mem. Assn. Bar City N.Y. Office: US Dist Ct So Dist NY 500 Pearl St New York NY 10007-1316

MARTIN, JOHN WILLIAM, JR. retired lawyer, automotive industry executive; b. Evergreen Park, Ill., Sept. 1, 1936; s. John William and Frances (Hayes) M.; m. Joanne Cross, July 2, 1966; children: Amanda Hayes, Bartholomew McGuire. AB in History, DePaul U., 1958, JD, 1961. Bar: Ill. 1961, D.C. 1962, N.Y. 1964, Mich. 1970. Antitrust trial atty. Dept. Justice, Washington, 1961-62; assoc. Donovan, Leisure, Newton & Irvine, N.Y.C., 1962-70; sr. atty. Ford Motor Co., Dearborn, Mich., 1970-72, assoc. counsel, 1972-74, counsel, 1974-76, asst. gen. counsel, 1976-77, assoc. gen. counsel, 1977-89, v.p., gen. counsel, 1989-99; ret., 1999. Trustee DePaul U., 1998—; bd. dirs. Ctr. Social Gerontology, Inc., Nat. Women's Law Ctr. Contbr. articles to profl. jours. Mem. Assn. Gen. Counsel, Am. Law Inst. Coun., Little Traverse Yacht Club. Republican. Roman Catholic. E-mail: jwmartinjr@netscape.net

MARTIN, KELLY LYNN, prosecutor; b. Stoughton, Mass., June 7, 1973; d. William Benning and Joyce Marie Martin. BA, Am. U., 1995; JD, Cath. U., 1998. Bar: Ill. 1998. Asst. state's atty. Cook County State's Atty.'s Office, Chgo., 1998—. Mem. ABA, Chgo. Bar Assn. Avocations: travel, reading, sports. Home: 535 W Briar Pl Apt 559 Chicago IL 60657

MARTIN, MALCOLM ELLIOT, lawyer; b. Buffalo, Dec. 11, 1935; s. Carl Edward and Pearl Maude (Elliot) M.; m. Judith Hill Harley, June 27, 1964; children; Jennifer, Elizabeth, Christina, Katherine. AB, U. Mich., Ann Arbor, 1958, JD, 1962. Bar: N.Y. 1963, U.S. Ct. Appeals (2d cir.) 1966, U.S. Supreme Ct. 1967. Assoc. Chadbourne Parke Whiteside & Wolff (now Chadbourne & Parke LLP), N.Y.C., 1962-73, ptnr., 1974—. Dir., sec. Carl and Dorothy Bennett Found., Inc.; sec., counsel Copper Devel. Assn., Inc. With U.S. Army, 1958-60. Mem. ABA, N.Y. State Bar Assn., Assn. Bar City of N.Y., St. Andrew's Soc. of N.Y., Met. Opera Guild, Oratamin Club (Blauvelt, N.Y.), Nyack Boat Club, Rockefeller Ctr. Club, Copper Club (N.Y.C.). Estate planning, Probate, Estate taxation. Home: 74 S Highland Ave Nyack NY 10960-3609 Office: Chadbourne & Parke LLP 30 Rockefeller Plz Fl 31 New York NY 10112-0129 E-mail: mmartin@chadbourne.com

MARTIN, MARGARET ANNE See STEELE, ANITA MARTIN

MARTIN, MARK D. state supreme court justice; b. Apr. 29, 1963; s. M. Dean and Ann M. BSBA summa cum laude, Western Carolina U., 1985; JD with honors, U. N.C., 1988; grad., Nat. Jud. Coll., 1993; LLM, U. Va., 1998. Bar: N.C., U.S. Dist. Ct. (ea. and mid. dists.) N.C., U.S. Ct. Appeals (4th crct.). Law clk. to Hon. Clyde H. Hamilton U.S. Dist. Ct., Columbia, S.C., 1988-90; pvt. practice McNair Law Firm, Raleigh, N.C., 1990-91; legal counsel to gov. Office of Gov., 1991-92; superior ct. judge Jud. Dist. 3A, Greenville, N.C., 1992-94; judge N.C. Ct. Appeals, 1994-99; assoc. justice N.C. Supreme Ct., 1999—. Mem. N.C. Dept. Correction Master Plan Adv. Com., 1992; designated hearing officer Commutation Revocation Hearing of Zedie T. Smith, 1992; mem. N.C. Coun. for Women, 1992; legis. and law reform com. Conf. Superior Ct. Judges, 1993-94; co-chair legis liason com. N.C. Jud. Conf., 1995-97; mem. computer com. N.C. Appellate Cts., 1995—; sec. N.C. Jud. Conf., 1997-99; adj. faculty Univ. N.C., Chapel Hill, N.C. Ctrl. Univ. Sch. Law. Office coord. United Way Ann. Combined Campaign, 1991, 92. Recipient Book award, 1987, Order of Long Leaf Pine, 1992, Disting. Alumnus award We. Carolina U., 1995; Lloyd C. Balfour fellow, 1987, N.C. Inst. Polit. Leadership, 1992. Mem. ABA (jud. adminstrv. divsn.), N.C. Bar Assn. (minorities in profession com. 1995—, multidisciplinary practice task force 1999—, v.p. 2000-01), N.C. Assn. Black Lawyers, Wake County Bar Assn., Mortar Bd. Sr. Hon. Soc., Carolina Law Alumni Assn. (bd. dirs.), Internat. Hon. Soc., Alpha Lambda Delta, Phi Kappa Phi, Pi Gamma Mu, Omicron Delta Epsilon, Phi Alpha Delta, Delta Sigma Phi (scholar 1986), Beta Gamma Sigma (hon.). Office: North Carolina Supreme Court PO Box 1841 Raleigh NC 27602-1841*

MARTIN, MICHAEL REX, lawyer; b. Lawton, Okla., Feb. 16, 1952; s. Rex R. and Mary L. (Smith) M.; m. Janet E. Becker, Aug. 25, 1979; children: Katy, Donnie, Melissa. BS in Bus. Adminstrn., Tulsa U., 1974, JD, 1979. Bar: Okla. 1979, U.S. Dist Ct. (we. dist.) Okla. 1984. Ptnr. Musser, Musser & Martin, Enid, Okla., 1981-85, Crowley, Martin & Lovell, Enid, 1985—. Republican. Methodist. General practice. Office: Crowley Martin & Lovell PO Box 3487 Enid OK 73702-3487

MARTIN, PAIGE ARLENE, lawyer; b. Pitts., Nov. 27, 1951; d. James William and Mildred Jean (Toplis) M.; m. Barry Rosenbaum, June 15, 1974 (div. 1977); m. David Kern, Feb. 21, 1988 (div. July 1996). AB, Wellesley (Mass.) Coll., 1973; JD, Case Western Res. U., Cleve., 1978. Bar: Ohio 1978, U.S. Dist. Ct. (no. dist.) Ohio 1978. Assoc. Sindell, Sindell & Rubenstein, Cleve., 1978-83, Spangenberg, Shibley, Traci & Lancione, Cleve., 1983-89; pvt. practice, 1989—. Instr. Cuyahoga Community Coll., Cleve., 1979-80; adj. faculty Case Western Res. U., Cleve., 1984-85; lectr. Assn. Trial Lawyers Assn., Dallas, 1986, Ohio Acad. Trial Attys., Cin., Columbus, 1984, Ohio Legal Ctr. Inst., Sandusky, Ohio, 1985, Cleve. Acad. Trial Attys., 1987. Contbr. chpt. to book. Child advocate CASA program Franklin County. Recipient award of merit Ohio Legal Ctr. Inst., 1985; named to Outstanding Young Women of Am., 1987. Mem. Cleve. Bar Assn. (chair hospice com. 1982-83, Merit Svc. award), Greater Cleve. Bar Assn. (joint med.-legal com. 1983-90, chair 1986-87), Cleve. Acad. Trial Lawyers (dir. 1984-87), Assn. Trial Attys. Am. (diptheria, pertussis, tetnus litigation sect. 1985-87), Ohio State Bar Assn., Ohio Acad. Trial Attys. (constnl. law com. 1989-90). Constitutional, Estate planning, Personal injury. Office: 77 Outerbelt St Columbus OH 43213-1548

MARTIN, QUINN WILLIAM, lawyer; b. Fond du Lac, Wis., Mar. 12, 1948; s. Quinn W. and Marcia E. Martin; m. Jane E. Nehmer; children: Quinn W., William J. BSME, Purdue U., 1969; postgrad., U. Santa Clara, 1969-70; JD, U. Mich., 1973. Bar: Wis. 1973, U.S. Dist. Ct. (ea. dist.) Wis. 1973, U.S. Ct. Appeals (7th cir.) 1973. Sales support mgr. Hewlett-Packard, Palo Alto, Calif., 1969-70; assoc. Quarles & Brady, Milw., 1973-80, ptnr., 1980—. Bd. dirs. Associated Bank Milw., U-Line Corp., Gen. Timber and Land, Inc., Fond du Lac. Chmn. gov. McCallum Trans Com., Wis., U. Mich. Law Sch. Fund; chmn. bd. dirs. Milw. Zool. Soc., Found. for Wildlife Conservation. Mem. ABA, Wis. Bar Assn., Milw. Bar Assn., Milw. Club, Ozaukee Country Club, Chaine des Rottiseurs, Delta Upsilon (sec.), Milw. Alumni Club, Rotary. Antitrust, Contracts commercial, General corporate. Office: Quarles & Brady 411 E Wisconsin Ave Ste 2550 Milwaukee WI 53202-4497

MARTIN, RALPH DRURY, lawyer, columnist; b. Pittsburg, Kans., Mar. 4, 1947; s. Kent Wills and Kathleen (Drury) M.; m. Ruchirawan Meemeskul, Oct. 28, 1982; 1 child, Chanida Kathleen. BA, Tulane U., 1969; JD, Washington U., 1972. Bar: La. 1972, D.C. 1981, Calif. 1992, U.S. Dist. Ct. (mid. dist.) La. 1985, U.S. Dist. Ct. D.C. 1991, U.S. Ct. Appeals (9th cir.) 1979, U.S. Ct. Appeals (D.C. cir.) 1991, U.S. Supreme Ct. 1976. Law clk. to Hon. Frederick J.R. Heebe U.S. Dist. Ct., Ea. Dist. La., New Orleans, 1972-74; spl. asst. to U.S. atty. U.S. Dept. Justice, Washington, 1974-75, trial atty. civil rights div., 1975-80; dep. asst. legal advisor U.S. Dept. State, 1980-82; sr. prosecutor pub. integrity sect. U.S. Dept. Justice, 1982-90; spl. counsel U.S. Dept. State, 1990-91; ptnr. Storch & Brenner, 1991-2000, Dilworth Paxson PLLC, Washington, 2001—. Adj. prof. Washington Coll. Law, The Am. Univ., 1991-92; chmn. Lawyers Com. Effective Assistance of Counsel, 1995—. Comments editor Washington U. Law Quarterly, 1971-72 (honors scholar award 1971). Bd. dirs. Thomas and Bertie T. Smith Arts Found., 1996—, James Madison Project, 1999—. Mem. ABA, Am. Soc. Internat. Law, Nat. Assn. Criminal Def. Lawyers, Univ. Club, D.C. Assn. Criminal Def. Lawyers (v.p. 1995-97), Order of Coif, Stan Musial Soc., E.B. Williams Inn of Ct. (master). General civil litigation, Criminal, Personal injury. Office: Dilworth Paxson PLLC 1200 19th St NW Washington DC 20036 E-mail: rmartin@dilworthlaw.com

MARTIN, RAYMOND WALTER, lawyer; b. Riverside, Calif., Jan. 1, 1952; s. Wilfred W. and Betty Ray (Uhrie) M.; m. Denise A. Mowry, Mar. 22, 1986; children: Justin M., Timothy K., Jeremy T., Sean W. BA, Morningside Coll., Sioux City, Iowa, 1974; JD, U. Denver, 1977. Bar: Colo. 1977, U.S. Dist. Ct. Colo. 1977, U.S. Ct. Appeals (10th cir.) 1978, U.S. Supreme Ct., 1999. Assoc. Rovira DeMuth & Eiberger, Denver, 1977-79; mng. ptnr. Eiberger, Stacy, Smith & Martin, 1979-96; dir. Parcel, Mauro, Hultin & Spaanstra, 1996-98, Freeborn & Peters, Denver, 1998-2000, Wheeler, Trigg & Kennedy, 2000—. Contbr. articles to profl. jours. Trustee, Wheat Ridge United Meth. Ch., 1983. Recipient Jaffa award for highest scholastic average, U. Denver Alumni Assn., 1976, Harold H. Widney Meml. scholar, 1976. Mem. ABA, Colo. Bar Assn., Order of St. Ives. Republican. Methodist. Avocations: golf, skiing. Civil rights, General civil litigation, Labor. Office: Wheeler Trigg & Kennedy 1801 California Ste 3600 Denver CO 80202

MARTIN, RICHARD KELLEY, lawyer; b. Tulsa, June 30, 1952; s. Richard Loye and Maxine (Kelley) M.; m. Reba Lawson, June 12, 1993; children from previous marriage: R. Kyle, Andrew J. BA, Westminster Coll., 1974; JD, So. Meth. U., 1977. Bar: Tex. 1977, U.S. Tax Ct. 1979. Ptnr. Akin, Gump, Strauss, Hauer & Feld, LLP, Dallas, 1977-95, Haynes and Boone LLP, Dallas, 1995—. Bd. dirs. Goodwill Industries, Dallas, 1986-2000, v.p., 1986-91; bd. dirs. Greater Dallas Youth Orchs., 1987-90; bd. dirs., v.p., pres. Big Bros. and Sisters Met. Dallas, 1988-91; bd. dirs. Tejas coun. Girl Scouts U.S., 1997-2001. Mem. Tex. Bar Assn., Salesmanship Club Dallas. Republican. Methodist. Contracts commercial, Real property. Office: Haynes and Boone LLP 3100 NationsBank Plz 901 Main St Ste 3100 Dallas TX 75202-3789 E-mail: martinr@haynesboone.com

MARTIN, ROBERT DALE, lawyer; b. Canton, Ohio, Oct. 1, 1937; s. Charles Leroy and Edith Ruby (Turnbull) M.; m. Carla Jean Kibler, Dec. 27, 1966; 1 child, Kendall Dalene. BA, Ohio U., 1960; JD, U. Akron, 1969, M of Taxation, 1989; MBA, Ashland U., 1995; postgrad., Kent State U., 1998. Bar: Ohio 1969, U.S. Dist. Ct. (no. dist.) 1984, U.S. Ct. Appeals (6th cir.) 1984. Personnel adminstr. Hoover Co., North Canton, Ohio, 1966-67; atty. Allmon and Benson, Carrollton, 1967-69; legal staff asst. Republic Steel Corp., Canton, 1969-71, indsl. rels. counsel, 1971-73, supr. labor rels., 1973-78, asst. supt. indsl. rels., 1978-85; mgr. human resources Republic Engineered Steel Corp., 1985-91; gen. counsel, dir. adminstrn. Office of Summit County Engr., Akron, Ohio, 1991-95; adminstr. bus. and human svcs. Ohio Dept. Transp., New Philadelphia, 1995—. Adj. prof. bus. law Ashland (Ohio) U., 1988; gen. counsel mgmt. consulting Labor Rels. Assocs., Dayton, Ohio, 1991-93; gen. counsel human resource consulting Human Resources Assocs., Dayton, 1993-95. Sgt. U.S. Army, 1960. Mem. Ohio State Bar Assn. (gen. sect. 1970-97, labor/employment law sect. 1995-99, probate/trust sect. 1996-99, corp. law 1996-99), Nat. Assn. Cert. Govt. Fin. Mgmt. Avocations: walking, fishing, reading, fitness. Home and Office: 850 Mcdaniel Ave Minerva OH 44657-1240 Fax: (330) 868-6161

MARTIN, ROBERT DAVID, judge, educator; b. Iowa City, Oct. 7, 1944; s. Murray and G'Ann (Holmgren) M.; m. Ruth A. Haberman, Aug. 21, 1966; children: Jacob, Matthew, David. AB, Cornell Coll., Mt. Vernon, Iowa, 1966; JD, U. Chgo., 1969. Bar: Wis. 1969, U.S. Dist. Ct. (we. dist.) Wis. 1969, U.S. Dist. Ct. (ea. dist.) Wis. 1974, U.S. Supreme Ct. 1973. Assoc. Ross & Stevens, S.C., Madison, Wis., 1969-72, ptnr., 1973-78; chief judge U.S. Bankruptcy Ct. We. Dist. Wis., 1978—. Instr. gen. practice course U. Wis. Law Sch., 1974, 76, 77, 80, lectr. debtor/creditor course, 1981-82, 83, 85, 87, 2001, farm credit seminar, 1985, advanced bankruptcy problems, 1989, 91, 96; co-chmn. faculty Am. Law Inst.-ABA Fin. and Bus. Planning for Agr., Stanford U., 1979; faculty mem. Fed. Jud. Ctr. Schs. for New Bankruptcy Judges, 1985-96; chmn. Ann. Continuing Legal Edn. Wis. Debtor Creditor Conf., 1981—. Author: Bankruptcy: Annotated Forms, 1989; co-author: Secured Transactions Handbook for Wisconsin Lawyers and Lenders, Bankruptcy-Text Statutes Rules and Forms, 1992, Ginsberg and Martin on Bankruptcy, 4th edit., 1996. Chmn., bd. dirs., exec. com. Luth. Social Svcs. for Wis. and Upper Mich., Turnaround Mgmt. Assn., 1997—. Mem. Wis. State Bar, Am. Coll. Bankruptcy, Am. Judicature Soc., Nat. Conf. Bankruptcy Judges (bd. govs. 1989-91, sec. 1993-94, v.p. 1994-95, pres. 1995-96), Nat. Bankruptcy Conf. Office: 120 N Henry Rm 340 PO Box 548 Madison WI 53701-0548

MARTIN, SIVA, lawyer; b. Chgo., Oct. 26, 1925; s. Leon and Goldie (Baronian) M.; m. Mary Kaprelian, Aug. 12, 1952; children: Robert, Jack. BS, Loyola U., 1950; MA, Northwestern U., 1951; JD, DePaul U., 1953. Bar: Ill. 1953. Loan officer Nat. Blvd. Bank, Chgo., 1955-62; v.p. Ill. State Bank, 1962-73; sole practice, 1973—. Dist. chmn. Boy Scouts Am., Chgo., 1957; pres. Chgo. Chpt. Armenian Gen. Benevolent Union, 1978-80. Mem. ABA, Ill. State Bar Assn., Chgo. Bar Assn., Chgo. Mortgage Attys., Northwest Real Estate Bd. Democrat. Mem. Apostolic Ch. Club: Lions. Probate, Real property. Home: 6550 N Kenton Ave Lincolnwood IL 60712-3433 Office: 5860 W Higgins Ave Chicago IL 60630-2036

MARTIN, WALTER, retired lawyer; b. Crookston, Minn., Nov. 7, 1912; s. Frederick and Rosalie (Mertz) M.; m. Catherine Mary Severin, May 1, 1942 (dec. May 1979); children: Frederick H., Jacqueline K., Patricia, Priscilla, Walter Jr., John E. BA, Albion Coll., 1937; JD, U. Mich., 1939. Bar: Mich. 1939, U.S. Dist. Ct. (fed. dist.) 1939, U.S. Ct. Appeals (6th cir.) 1947, U.S. Supreme Ct. 1958. Ptnr. Martin & Martin, Saginaw, Mich., 1939-94; ret., 1994. Fellow Mich. Bar Assn., Saginaw County Bar Assn. (pres. 1958). Lutheran. Avocations: hunting, fishing. Condemnation, Personal injury, Probate. Office: 803 Court St Saginaw MI 48602-4223

MARTIN DE VIDALES, NICOLAS, lawyer; b. Madrid, June 4, 1962; s. Pablo and Pilar (Godino) M. de V.; m. Maria Palomero, Oct. 13, 1990; children: Maria, Luis. Lic. in Law, Icade Law Sch., Madrid, 1985; postgrad. diploma internat. banking law, Clifford Chance-Grindal, Madrid, 1995. Bar: Madrid 1988. Jr. assoc. Estudio Legal, Madrid, 1987-90; sr. advisor Stock Exchange, 1990-92; sr. assoc. Stephenson Harwood, London and Madrid, 1992-95; founding ptnr. Ussia Ruiz Beato & Vidales, Madrid, 1995—. Bd. dirs. Ado Espana S.A., sec., 1999—; bd. dirs. Chocolates Hueso, S.A., sec., 1989; bd. dirs. Soc. Difusion de Informacion de la Bolsa de Valores de Madrid, SA, sec., 1991-92; bd. dirs. Torraspapel, SA, sec., 1997-99; bd. dirs. Sarriopapel y Celculosa SA, sec., 1997-99. Co-author: (book) Setting Up A Business In..., 1995; contbr. articles to profl. jours. With Spanish Army, 1984-86. Mem. Internat. Young Lawyers Assn. Avocations: reading, music, paddle tennis, soccer, writing. Contracts commercial, General corporate, Mergers and acquisitions. Office: Ussia Ruiz Beato & Vidales Hernani 57 E-28020 Madrid Spain E-mail: urbvabogados@retemail.es, nmvidales@airtel.net

MARTINEAU, ROBERT JOHN, law educator; b. May 18, 1934; s. Francis Joseph and Gertrude (Schauer) M.; m. Constance Ann Zimmerman, Dec. 21, 1957; children: Robert John, Renee, Anne, Jeanne. BS, Coll. Holy Cross, 1956; JD, U. Chgo., 1959. Bar: Md. 1960, U.S. Supreme Ct. 1964, Iowa 1969, Mo. 1974, Wis. 1974. Law clk. to chief judge Md. Ct. Appeals, 1959-60; pvt. practice Md., 1960-68; asst. atty. gen., 1964-65; assoc. prof. U. Iowa, 1968-71; prof., 1971-72; cir. exec. U.S. Ct. Appeals (8th cir.), Mo., 1972-74; exec. officer Wis. Supreme Ct., 1974-78; prof. U. Dayton (Ohio), 1978-80; assoc. dean U. Cin., 1980-82; prof. law, 1980-88; disting. rsch. prof., 1988-93; emeritus, 1994—. Acting dean, 1985-86; spl. prof. alw U. Birmingham, Eng., 1987; cons. Fed. Jud. Ctr., 1978, Nat. Ctr. State Cts., 1978-79, 87. Author: Wisconsin Appellate Practice, 1978, Judicial Reform in Wisconsin, in Court Reform in Seven States, 1980, Modern Appellate Practice-Federal and State Civil Appeals, 1983, Fundamentals of Modern Appellate Advocacy, 1985, Cases and Materials on Appellate Justice in England and the United States: A Comparative Analysis, 1990, Drafting Legislation and Rules in Plain English, 1991. Sec. Md. Constnl. Conv. 1967-68; reporter Wis. Supreme Ct. Com. on Discipline of Attys., 1975-77, Wis. Jud. Coun. Com. Appelate Practice and Procedure, 1976-78. Mem. Assn. Am. Law Schs. (mem. Ho. of Reps. 1981-86), ABA (appellate judges conf. com. on appellate skills tng. 1984-85, co-chair, appellate judges conf. com. on appellate practice 1984-86, mem. Ohio Supreme Ct. adv. com. on rules 1988-91), Md. bar Assn. (v.p. 1967), Am. Jud. Soc. (bd. dirs. 1966-68). Democrat. Roman Catholic. Office: U Cin Coll Law Cincinnati OH 45221-0001 E-mail: rjmartineau@jboxford.com

MARTINETTI, RONALD ANTHONY, lawyer; b. N.Y.C., Aug. 13, 1945; s. Alfred Nathan and Frances Ann (Battipaglia) M. Student, U. Chgo., 1981-82; JD, U. So. Calif., 1982. Bar: Calif. 1982; U.S. Dist. Ct. (cen. and no. dists.) Calif. 1982, U.S. Dist. Ct. Ariz., 1992; U.S. Ct. Appeals (9th cir.) 1982. Ptnr. Kazanjian & Martinetti, Glendale, Calif., 1986—. Co-founder Am. Legends Website, 1995, Am. Legends Pub., 1996. Author: James Dean Story, 1995; co-author: Rights of Owners of Lost, Stolen or Destroyed Instruments Under UCC Section3-804: Can They Be Holders in Due Course, 1993; contbr. to Wall St. Jour., Washington Post, Newsday, Balt. Sun, The New Leader, Columbia U. Forum, 1968-76; pub. James Dean Scrapbook, 1996. Vol. trial lawyer Bet Tzedek Legal Svcs., 1987—; vol. arbitrator L.A. Sup. Ct., 1987—; judge pro tem L.A. Superior Ct., 1994—. Mem. Calif. Bar Assn. Roman Catholic. State civil litigation, Labor, Personal injury. Office: Kazanjian & Martinetti 520 E Wilson Ave Glendale CA 91206-4374 Fax: 818-241-2193. E-mail: amlegends@aol.com

MARTINEZ, ALEX J. state supreme court justice; b. Denver, Apr. 1, 1951; m. Kathy Carter; children: Julia, Maggie. Diploma, Phillips Exeter Acad., N.H., 1969; student, Reed Coll., 1969-72; BA, U. Colo., 1973, JD, 1976. Bar: Colo. 1976. Dep. state pub. defender, Pueblo and Denver, 1976-83; county ct. judge Pueblo, 1983-88; dist. ct. judge, 1988-97; justice Colo. Supreme Ct., Denver, 1997—. Supreme Ct. liaison Colo. Criminal Rules Com., Colo. Criminal Jury Instrns.; chmn. Child Welfare Appeals Workgroup, 1997; mem. standing com. Integrated Info. Svcs. Chmn. Pueblo adv. bd. Packard Found., 1993-96; chmn. site-based governing coun. Pueblo Sch. Arts and Scis., 1994-95; mem. site-based governing coun. Roncalli Mid. Sch., 1993-94; bd. dirs. Colo. U. Law Alumni. Mem. Colo. Bar Assn. (regional v.p. 1995-96), Colo. Hispanic Bar Assn., Pueblo Bar Assn. (mem. exec. coun. 1994-96), Pueblo Hispanic Bar Assn. Office: Colo Supreme Ct 2 E 14th Ave Denver CO 80203-2115 E-mail: AJMarti@aol.com*

MARTING, MICHAEL G. lawyer; b. Cleve., Nov. 5, 1948; BA summa cum laude, Yale U., 1971, JD, 1974. Bar: Ohio 1974. Assoc. Jones, Day, Reavis & Pogue, Cleve., 1974-83, ptnr., 1984—. Mem. ABA, Union Club, Cleve. Racquet Club, Kirtland Country Club, Tavern Club (treas., sec., trustee local chpt. 1985-88). Avocations: fly fishing, birdshooting, big game hunting, squash, golf. General corporate, Mergers and acquisitions, Securities. Office: Jones Day Reavis & Pogue N Point 901 Lakeside Ave E Cleveland OH 44114-1190

MARTONE, FREDERICK J. state supreme court justice; b. Fall River, Mass., Nov. 8, 1943; BS, Coll. Holy Cross, 1965; JD, U. Notre Dame, 1972; LLM, Harvard U., 1975. Bar: Mass. 1972, Ariz. 1974, U.S. Dist. Ct. Mass. 1973, U.S. Dist. Ct. Ariz. 1974, U.S. Ct. Appeals (1st cir.) 1973, U.S. Ct. Appeals (9th cir.) 1974, U.S. Supreme Ct. 1977. Law clk. to Hon. Edward F. Hennessey Mass. Supreme Judicial Ct., 1972-73; pvt. practice Phoenix, 1973-85; assoc. presiding judge Superior Ct. Ariz., Maricopa County, judge, 1985-92; justice Supreme Ct. Ariz., 1992—. Editor notes and comments Notre Dame Law Rev., 1970-72; contbr. articles to profl. jours. Capt. USAF, 1965-69. Mem. ABA, Ariz. Judges Assn., Maricopa County Bar Assn., Am. Judicature Soc., State Bar Ariz., Horace Rumpole Inn of Ct. Office: Supreme Ct Arizona 1501 W Washington St Phoenix AZ 85007-3222 E-mail: FMartone@Supreme.sp.state.az.us

MARTONE, PATRICIA ANN, lawyer; b. Bklyn., Apr. 28, 1947; d. David Andrew and Rita Mary (Dullmeyer) M. BA in Chemistry, NYU, 1968, JD, 1973; MA in Phys. Chemistry, Johns Hopkins U., 1969. Bar: N.Y. 1974, U.S. Dist. Ct. (so. and ea. dists.) N.Y. 1975, U.S. Ct. Appeals (2d cir.) 1975, U.S. Ct. Appeals (1st cir.) 1981, U.S. Patent and Trademark Office 1983, U.S. Ct. Appeals (fed. cir.) 1984, U.S. Supreme Ct. 1984, U.S. Dist. Ct. (ea. dist.) Mich. 1985, U.S. Dist. Ct. (no. dist.) Calif. 1995. Tech. rep. computer timesharing On-Line Sys., Inc., N.Y.C., 1969-70; assoc. Kelley Drye & Warren, 1973-77, Fish & Neave, N.Y.C., 1977-82, ptnr., 1983—. Adj. prof. NYU Sch. Law, 1990—, mem. adv. coun. Engelberg Ctr. Innovation Law & Policy, 1996—; participating atty. Cmty. Law Offices, N.Y.C., 1974-78; atty. Pro Bono Panel U.S. Dist. Ct. (so. dist.) N.Y., 1982-84, conf. bd., 2001; lectr. Practising Law Inst., N.Y.C., 1995—, Aspen Law & Bus., 1990-95, Franklin Pierce Law Sch., 1992-97, Lic. Exec. Soc., 1995; chair, bd. dirs. N.Y. Lawyers for the Pub. Interest, 1996-98, vice chair, 1998-2000; dir. Legal Svcs. N.Y.C., 1991-95. Mng. editor NYU Law Sch. Rev. Law and Social Change, 1972-73; contbr. articles to profl. jours. Recipient Founder's Day award NYU Sch. Law, 1973; NSF grad. trainee Johns Hopkins U., 1968-69; NYU scholar, 1964-68. Mem. ABA, Assn. Bar City N.Y. (mem. environ. law com. 1978-83, trademarks, unfair competition com. 1983-86), Fed. Bar Coun., Fed. Cir. Bar Assn., Copyright Soc., Am. Chem. Soc., Licensing Execs. Soc., N.Y. Intellectual Property Law Assn., Univ. Club. Federal civil litigation, Patent, Trademark and copyright. Office: Fish & Neave Fl 50 1251 Ave of the Americas New York NY 10020-1105 E-mail: pmartone@fishneave.com

MARTORI, JOSEPH PETER, lawyer; b. N.Y.C., Aug. 19, 1941; s. Joseph and Teresa Susan (Fezza) M. BS summa cum laude, NYU, 1964, MBA, 1968; JD cum laude, U. Notre Dame, 1967. Bar: D.C. 1968, U.S. Dist. Ct. D.C. 1968, U.S. Dist. Ct. Ariz. 1968, U.S. Ct. Appeals (9th cir.) 1969, U.S. Supreme Ct. 1977. Assoc. Sullivan & Cromwell, N.Y.C., 1967-68, Snell & Wilmer, Phoenix, 1968-69; pres. Goldmar Inc., 1969-71; ptnr. Martori, Meyer, Hendricks & Victor, P.A., 1971-85, Brown & Bain, P.A., Phoenix, 1985-94, chmn. corp. banking & real estate dept., 1994—; chmn. bd. ILX Resorts, Inc. Bd. dirs. Firstar Bank, Phoenix; chmn. ILX Inc., Varsity Clubs Am. Inc. Author: Street Fights, 1987; also articles, 1966-70. Trustee Boys' Clubs Met. Phoenix, 1974-99; consul for Govt. of

Italy, State of Ariz., 1987-97. Mem. ABA, State Bar Ariz., Maricopa County Bar Assn., Lawyers Com.for Civil Rights Under Law (trustee 1976—), Phoenix Country Club, Plaza Club (founding bd. govs. 1979-90). Republican. Roman Catholic. Real property, Corporate taxation, General corporate. Office: ILX Inc 2111 E Highland Ave Ste 210 Phoenix AZ 85016-4786 E-mail: jmartori@ILXresorts.com

MARTUCCI, WILLIAM CHRISTOPHER, lawyer; b. Asbury Park, N.J., Mar. 10, 1952; s. Frank and Evelyn (Gerrity) M.; children: Daniel Robert, William Sessions, John Andrew, James Christopher, Andrew Michael. AB magna cum laude, Rutgers Coll., 1974; JD with honors, U. Ark., 1977; LLM, Georgetown U., 1981. Bar: Mo. 1977. Law clk. to presiding justice Mo. Ct. Appeals, Kansas City, 1977-78; assoc. Spencer, Fane, Britt & Browne, 1981-86, ptnr., 1987-99, Shook, Hardy & Bacon, Kansas City, 2000—. Mem. practice and procedure com. Nat. Labor Relations Act; adj. prof. employment law U. Mo. Law Sch., Kansas City, 1988—, chair minority affairs com. 1992—. Editor-in-chief Ark. Law Rev., 1976-77; contbr. articles to profl. jours. Chmn. adv. coun. Urban League Greater Kansas City Tng. Ctr., chmn. mentor program, 1988—; mem. Kansas City Civic Coun.; mem. Kansas City Tomorrow Leadership Program, 1992-93; adv. bd. Boys and Girls Club Kansas City, Reviving Baseball in the Inner City. Served to lt. JAGC, USN, 1978-81. Mem. ABA, Mo. Bar Assn. (exec. com. continuing legal edn. 1987—, chair 1993—), Kansas City Bar Assn. (chmn. continuing legal edn. 1984-86, mem. exec. com. 1985-87, leadership award 1985, chmn. labor and employment law com. 1988-90, Pres. award 1992, 97), Lawyers Assn. Kansas City (mem. exec. com. young lawyers sect. 1981-82), Nat. Inst. Mcpl. Law Officers (vice-chmn. labor rels. and pers. law com. 1988-90), Kansas City Club, Homestead Country Club, Rotary. Republican. Roman Catholic. Club: Kansas City. Federal civil litigation, General civil litigation, Labor. Home: 1251 W 59th St Kansas City MO 64113-1148 Office: Shook Hardy and Bacon 1 Kansas City Pl 1200 Main St Kansas City MO 64105-2118 E-mail: wmartucci@shb.com

MARVEL, L. PAIGE, federal judge; b. Easton, Md., Dec. 6, 1949; d. E. Warner Marvel and Louise Harrington Harrison; m. Robert H. Dyer, Jr., Aug. 9, 1975; children: Alex W. Dyer, Kelly E. Dyer. BA magna cum laude, Notre Dame Coll., 1971; JD with honors, U. Md., 1974. Bar: Md. 1974, U.S. Dist. Ct. Md. 1974, U.S. Tax Ct. 1975, U.S. Ct. Appeals (4th cir.) 1977, U.S. Supreme Ct. 1980, U.S. Ct. Claims 1981, D.C. 1985. Assoc. Garbis & Schwait, P.A., Balt., 1974-76, shareholder, 1976-85, Garbis, Marvel & Junghans, P.A., Balt., 1985-86, Melnicove, Kaufman, Weiner, Smouse & Garbis, P.A., Balt., 1986-88; ptnr. Venable, Baetjer and Howard LLP, 1988-98; judge U.S. Tax Ct., Washington, 1998—. Bd. dirs. Loyola/Notre Dame Libr., Inc.; mem. U. Md. Law Sch. Bd. Vis., 1995—2001; mem. adv. com. U.S. Dist. Ct. Md., 1991—93. Co-editor procedure dept. Jour. Taxation, 1989-98; contbr. chpts. to books, articles to profl. jours. Active Women's Law Ctr., 1974-85, Md. Dept. Econ. and Community Devel. Adv. Comm., 1978-80. Recipient recognition award Balt. Is Best Program, 1981; named One of Md.'s Top 100 Women, The Daily Record, 1998. Fellow Am. Bar Found., Am. Coll. Tax Counsel (regent 1995-98); mem. ABA (sect. taxation coun. dir. 1989-92, vice-chair com. ops. 1993-95, Disting. Svc. award), Am. Law Inst. (advisor Ali restatement of law third, law governing lawyers), Md. Bar Assn. (chmn. taxation sect. 1982-83, bd. dirs. 1988-90, 96-98, Disting. Svc. award), Md. Bar Found., Balt. Bar Assn. (at-large exec. coun.), Am. Tax Policy Inst. (trustee 1997-98), Serjeant's Inn, Rule Day Club. Avocations: golf, music, travel. Home: 7109 Sheffield Rd Baltimore MD 21212-1628 Office: US Tax Ct 400 2d St NW Washington DC 20217-0001

MARVIN, CHARLES ARTHUR, law educator; b. July 14, 1942; s. Burton Wright and Margaret Fiske (Medlar) M.; m. Elizabeth Maureen Woodrow, July 4, 1970 (div. July 1987); m. Elizabeth Dale Wilson, Mar. 20, 1999; children: Colin, Kristin. BA, U. Kans., 1964; postgrad., U. Toulouse, France, 1964-65; JD, U. Chgo., 1968, M of Comparative Law, 1970. Bar: Ill. 1969. Legal intern EEC, Brussels, 1970; lectr. law U. Kent, Canterbury, Eng., 1970-71; asst. prof. law Laval U., Quebec City, Que., Can., 1971-73; legal adv. constnl., internat. and adminstrv. law sect. Can. Dept. Justice, Ottawa, Ont., 1973-76; assoc. prof. law U. Man., Winnipeg, Can., 1976-77; dir. adminstrv. law project Law Reform Commn., Ottawa, 1977-80; prof. law Villanova (Pa.) U., 1980-83; dir. Adminstrv. Law Reform Project Can. Dept. Justice, 1983-85; prof. law Ga. State U., 1985—, assoc. dean, 1987-89. Legal advisor on adminstrv. code revision to Govt. of Kazakhstan, 1993; law faculty devel. adviser to Bulgaria, 1993; dir. internat. human rights law summer program Regent U. Sch. Law, 1998; lectr., Ivory Coast, 1998; Fulbright prof. Riga Grad. Sch. Law, Latvia, 2000—. Acad. mem. Southwestern Legal Found. Fulbright scholar U. Toulouse, 1964-65, Summerfield scholar U. Kansas, 1961-64, U. Chgo. scholar, 1965-68; Ford Found. Comparative Law fellow, 1968-70. Mem. ABA, Ill. Bar Assn., Chgo. Bar Assn., Am. Soc. Internat. Law, Am. Fgn. Law Assn., Internat. Bar Assn., Internat. Law Assn., Can. Bar Assn., Can. Coun. on Internat. Law, Phi Beta Kappa, Omicron Delta Kappa, Phi Beta Delta, Phi Delta Phi. Office: Ga State U Coll Law PO Box 4037 Atlanta GA 30302-4037 E-mail: lawcam@langate.gsu.edu

MARVIN, MONICA LOUISE WOLF, lawyer; b. San Francisco, Feb. 3, 1947; d. Andrew John and Hazel Louise Wolf; m. Gregory Lewis Marvin, Aug. 17, 1969; children: Brett Lewis, Elizabeth Louise. Student, Pacific U., Forest Grove, Oreg., 1964-66, Sonoma State U., Rohnert Park, Calif., 1966-67; BA in Psychology, Chico (Calif.) State U., 1969; JD, Empire Coll., Santa Rosa, Calif., 1982. Bar: Calif. 1982, U.S. Dist. Ct. Calif. 1982. Assoc. Fitzgerald Fitzgerald and Gowen, Santa Rosa, Calif., 1982-83, Gowen and Marvin, Santa Rosa, 1983-85, Rodeno Robertson & Assocs., Napa, Calif., 1985-86; pvt. practice St Helena, 1986—; of counsel Hardell & Yost, LLP, 2000—. Judge pro tempore Napa County Consol. Cts., Small Claims Divsn., 1991—. Bd. dirs., v.p. Cmty. Resources for Children, Napa, 1991-94; mem. Napa County Commn. on Children, Youth and Family, 1994-97; mem. Napa County Dem. Ctrl. Com., 1994-98; mem. adv. bd. Napa County Vol. Ctr. Ombudsman Program, 1994-95; founder, chair St. Helena C. of C. Jumelage Com., Sister Chamber affiliation with Libourne C. of C. and Industry, France. Mem. State Bar Calif., Napa County Bar Assn. (bd. dirs. 1994), Napa Women Lawyers (past pres., sec. 1987-92), St. Helena C. of C. (bd. dirs. 1992-94), St. Helena Rotary Club (pres. 1999-2000). General corporate, Estate planning, General practice. Office: PO Box 271 Saint Helena CA 94574-0271 E-mail: mwmarvin@napanet.net

MARWEDEL, WARREN JOHN, lawyer; b. Chgo., July 3, 1944; s. August Frank and Eleanor (Wolgamot) M.; m. Marilyn Baran, Apr. 12, 1975. BS in Marine Engring., U.S. Merchant Marine Acad., 1966; JD, Loyola U., Chgo., 1972. Bar: Ill. 1972, U.S. Dist. Ct. (no. dist.) Ill. 1972, U.S. Supreme Ct. 1974. With U.S. Merchant Marines, 1966-70. Mem. ABA (Ho. of Dels. 1989-96), Ill. Bar Assn., Chgo. Bar Assn., Maritime Law Assn. Club: Propellor (Chgo.) (pres. 1982). Avocations: boating, reading, history. Admiralty, Environmental, Transportation. Office: Marwedel Minichello & Reeb PC 10 S Riverside Plz Chicago IL 60606-3708

MARX, PETER A. lawyer; b. N.Y.C., June 14, 1942; s. Robert L. and Helen (Sohn) M.; m. Barbara K. Marx, Dec. 21, 1974; children: Laura, Lisa. BA, Cornell U., 1965, MBA, JD, 1968. Bar: N.Y. 1969, D.C. 1970, Mass. 1980. Atty., advisor U.S. Securites & Exch. Commn., Washington, 1968-71; assoc. Shaw, Pittman, Potts & Trowbridge, 1971-74; v.p., gen. counsel Chase Econometrics and Interactive Data Corp., Waltham, Mass., 1975-85; ptnr. Goulston & Storrs, Boston, 1985-87; prin. The Marx Group, Wellesley, Mass., 1987—. Dir. Info. Industry Assn., Washington, 1980-84, hon. counsel to bd., 1993—; chmn. N.E. Computer Law Forum, 1982-89; adv. bd. CNC Interactive, 1998, LifetecNet.com, 1999—, ForPower.com, 1999—, Eye on Interactive, 1999, WebMediate.com, 2000—, Protegent, Inc., 2001—; host Venture Capital Quest, 1998—; vice-chmn. bd. dirs. Internet Alliance, 1999-2000. Editor: Contracts in the Information Industry, 1988, II, 1990, III, 1995; mem. bd. advisors Computer Law Strategist, 1987-99; info. law editor Info. Mgmt. Rev., 1987-90; host program N.E. Bus. Forum, Sta. WCAB-TV, 1991—; coord. editor The Info. Industry Deal Making Directory, 1994. Mem. ALI-ABA Computer Law Inst. (chmn. 1980-88), New Eng. Corp. Counsel Assn. (chmn. 1981-82). Contracts commercial, Computer, General corporate. Office: The Marx Group 60 Valley Rd Wellesley MA 02481-1448 E-mail: peter@marxgroup.com

MASANOFF, MICHAEL DAVID, lawyer; b. Jersey City, N.J., May 5, 1951; s. Abraham and Rose (Markowitz) M.; m. Faye Ann Sander, Aug. 7, 1977. BA, Am. Internat. Coll., 1972; JD, Hofstra U., 1977. Bar: N.J. 1977, Pa. 1977, U.S. Dist. Ct. N.J. 1977, U.S. Dist. Ct. (ea. dist.) Pa. 1977, U.S. Tax Ct. 1979. Rsch. asst. Tax Analysts & Advocates, Washington, 1976; ptnr. Hill Wallack & Masanoff, Princeton, N.J., 1977—, mng. ptnr, 1978—; sec. Svecia Antigua U.S.A., Inc.; gen. counsel Cabot Med. Corp., 1983—; bd. dirs. Premium Fed. Savs. Bank; mem. loan com. Premium Fed. Savs. Bank, 1989—. Rsch. editor Tax Notes, 1976. Trustee, pres. Village Homeowners Assn., Lawrenceville, N.J., 1980-81. Hofstra Law fellow, 1977; Shalan Found. Tax fellow, 1976. Mem. ABA (loan practices & lender liability com. 1990—), State Bar N.J., Princeton Bar Assn., Mercer County Bar Assn. General corporate, Real property, Corporate taxation. Home: 7900 W Upper Ridge Dr Parkland FL 33067-2360 Address: 202 Carnegie Ctr Fl 2 Princeton NJ 08540-6239

MASERITZ, GUY B. lawyer; b. Balt., June 5, 1937; s. Isadore H. and Gertrude (Miller) M.; m. Sally Jane Sugar, Mar. 30, 1961; children: Marjorie Ellen, Michael Louis. BA, Johns Hopkins U., 1959, MA in Econs., 1961; LLB, U. Md., 1966. Bar: Md. 1966, D.C. 1968, U.S. Supreme Ct. 1975, U.S. Dist. Ct. Md. 1979. Atty. SEC, Washington, 1966-70; asst. gen. counsel securities Am. Life Ins. Assn., 1971-74; atty. eval. sect., chief legis. unit antitrust divsn. U.S. Dept. Justice, 1974-78, spl. asst. U.S. atty. Alexandria, Va., 1978; pvt. practice Columbia, Md., 1978—. Author: U.S. Department of Justice Antitrust Report on Property-Liability Insurance Industry, 1977; contbr. articles to profl. jours. Mem. Howard County (Md.) Charter Revision Commn., 1979; bd. dirs. Howard County YMCA, 1997-99, disting. bd. mem. 1999. With USAR, 1960-66. Mem. Md. Bar Assn., D.C. Bar Assn., Howard County Bar Assn., Greater Howard County C. of C. (dir., gen. counsel 1981-84). Democrat. General corporate, Estate planning, Securities. Office: Hobbits Glen 5040 Rushlight Path Columbia MD 21044-1295 E-mail: consult@maseritzlaw.com

MASI, JOHN ROGER, lawyer; b. Bklyn., Jan. 18, 1954; s. John Roger and Evelyn (Teagno) M.; m. Sherrill Alaine Schlett, June 29, 1985; children: Roger C., Christopher J., Nicholas J. BA, Franklin & Marshall Coll., 1976; JD, Temple U., 1980. Bar: N.J. 1981, Pa. 1981, U.S. Dist. Ct. N.J. 1981. Assoc. Klinger, Nicolette, Mavroudis & Honig, Oradell, N.J., 1982-86, Gern, Dunetz, Roseland, 1986-87; ptnr. J. Roger Masi, Esq., Hackensack, 1987—. Committeeman County Rep., Ridgewood, N.J., 1982-84; mem. Ridgewood Zoning Bd. Adjustment, 1990-94; mem. Commerce and Industry Assn. N.J. Mem. ATLA. Roman Catholic. State civil litigation, General corporate, Personal injury. Office: 55 State St Hackensack NJ 07601-5426

MASIELLO, THOMAS PHILIP, JR. lawyer, risk manager; b. Medford, Mass., Oct. 13, 1961; s. Thomas Philip and Diane Marie (Traina) M.; m. Stephanie Hope Sadwin, Sept. 24, 1994. BA, Johnson (Vt.) State Coll., 1982, BFA, 1983; ARM, Bentley Coll., Waltham, Mass., 1986; JD, New Eng. Sch. Law, Boston, 1992. Bar: Mass. 1993, U.S. Supreme Ct. 1998. With Parker, Colter, Daley & White, 1986-88, Am. Internat. Group Ins. Com., 1988-91, McDonald & Wallace, 1991-92; in risk mgmt. Boston Housing Authority, 1992-95, Cumberland Farms-Gulf Oil, Canton, Mass., 1995-98. Exec. dir. Mass. Mcpl. Workers Compensation Group, Boston. Author Workers Comp Bull., 1996. Mem. ABA, ATLA, Internat. Risk Mgmt. Inst. (self-insurers and risk mgrs. law com.), Boston Bar Assn., Norfolk County Bar Assn., Risk Ins. Mgmt. Soc., Mass. Acad. Trial Attys., Quality Ins. Congress, Phi Alpha Delta. Avocation: adventure travel. Insurance, Personal injury, Workers' compensation. Home: 3 Grantland Rd Wellesley Hills MA 02481-7606 Office: Cumberland Farms/Gulf Oil 777 Dedham St Canton MA 02021-1402

MASIN, MICHAEL TERRY, lawyer; b. Montreal, Jan. 28, 1945; came to U.S., 1954; s. Frank J. and Sonia (Ellmann) M.; m. Joanne Elizabeth Combé, June 4, 1966; 1 child, Courtney. BA, Dartmouth U., 1966; JD, UCLA, 1969. Bar: Calif. 1969, D.C. 1970. Assoc. O'Melveny & Myers, Los Angeles, 1969-76, ptnr. Washington, 1976-91, mng. ptnr. N.Y.C., 1991-93; vice chair, pres. GTE, Irving, Tex., 1993—; vice chmn., pres. Verizon Comms., N.Y.C., 2001—. Bd. dirs. Trust Co. West, L.A., GTE Corp., Stamford, Conn., vice chmn., 1993-95, vice chmn., pres. internat., 1995, The Travelers Group, Inc., Telus Comms. Trustee Carnegie Hall; mem. dean's adv. com. Dartmouth Coll. Mem. Coun. on Fgn. Rels., The Brook, Calif. Club. Republican. Methodist. General corporate, Private international. Office: Verizon Communications 1095 Ave of the Americas 39th Fl Rm 3922 New York NY 10036 E-mail: michael.masin@verizon.com

MASINTER, PAUL JAMES, lawyer; b. New Orleans, June 28, 1961; s. Milton Paul Masinter and Shirley Mae (Rabé) Bradley; m. Audrey Renee Williams, Oct. 10, 1992. BA in Polit. Sci., La. State U., 1984, JD, 1987. Bar: La. 1987, U.S. Dist. Ct. (ea., mid. and we. dists.) La. 1987, U.S. Ct. Appeals (5th cir.) 1990, U.S. Supreme Ct. 1994. Law clk. to assoc. justice Hon. James L. Dennis La. Supreme Ct., New Orleans, 1987-88; assoc. McGlinchey, Stafford, 1988-90, Stone, Pigman, Walther, Wittmann & Hutchinson, New Orleans, 1990-95; ptnr. Stone, Pigman, Walter, Wittmann & Hutchinson, L.L.P., 1996—. Assoc. editor La. Law Rev., 1986-87. Bd. dirs. Save Our Cemeteries, New Orleans, 1993—, treas., 1998, pres., 1999. Mem. ABA (chair newsletter subcom., bus. and corp. litigation com. bus. law sect.), La. State Bar Assn., New Orleans Bar Assn. Democrat. Roman Catholic. Antitrust, General civil litigation, Product liability. Home: 1820 Octavia St New Orleans LA 70115-5660 Office: Stone Pigman Walther Wittmann & Hutchinson 546 Carondelet St Ste 100 New Orleans LA 70130-3588 E-mail: PMasinter@stonepigman.com

MASLEN, DAVID PETER, lawyer; b. Quincy, Mass., Apr. 22, 1948; s. Frederick George and Catherine Elizabeth (Kelly) M.; m. Patricia Ann Ryan, June 17, 1972; children: Pamela Ryan, Julia Kelly. AB, Coll. of Holy Cross, Worcester, Mass., 1972; JD, New Eng. Sch. Law, Boston, 1976; LLM in Taxation, Boston U., 1985. Bar: Mass. 1977, U.S. Dist. Ct. Mass. 1977. Compliance officer U.S. Dept. Labor, Boston, 1975-85; atty. New Eng. Mutual Life Ins. Co., Boston, Burlington, Mass., 1985-87; sr. v.p. Aon Cons., Newburyport, 1987—. Pension, profit-sharing, and employee benefits, Taxation, general. Office: Aon Cons PO Box 926 Newburyport MA 01950-5626 E-mail: david_maslen@aoncons.com, dmaslen@mediaone.net

MASON, MARY ANN, college program director, lawyer, computer consultant; b. Hibbing, Minn., Aug. 31, 1943; d. Thomas James and Ann K. (Starcevich) M.; m. John Burki, July 3, 1965 (div. 1978); 1 child, Thomas; m. Paul Ekman, July 29, 1979; 1 child, Eve. B.A., Vassar Coll., 1965; Ph.D., U. Rochester, 1971; J.D., U. San Francisco, 1976. Bar: Calif. Asst. prof. history Coll. of the Holy Names, Oakland, Calif., 1968-72; asst. prof. history St. Mary's Coll., Moraga, Calif., 1975-77, founder, dir. paralegal program, 1977— . Author: An Introduction to the Use of Computers in the Law, 1984. Contbr. articles to profl. jours. Pres. Albany Democratic Club, Calif., 1969-71. Mem. Calif. State Bar Assn., San Francisco Bar Assn., Contra Costa County Bar Assn., Alameda County Bar Assn., Am. Assn. for Paralegal Edn. Clubs: East Bay (pres. 1978-80), Vassar. Home: 1179 Keith Ave Berkeley CA 94708-1606 Office: Paralegal Program Saint Mary's Coll Moraga CA 94575

MASON, PETER IAN, lawyer; b. Bellfonte, Pa., Mar. 20, 1952; s. Robert Stanley and Abelle (Dinkowitz) M.; m. Margaret Ellen Bremner, July 9, 1983; children: Henry Graham, Ian Peter, Peter Alistair. AB Bard Coll., 1973; JD cum laude, Boston U., 1976. Bar: Ill. 1976, U.S. Dist. Ct. (no. dist.) Ill. 1976, N.Y. 1981. Assoc. Rooks, Pitts, Fullagar and Poust, Chgo., 1976-80, 81-83, Shearman & Sterling, N.Y.C., 1980; ptnr. Freeborn & Peters, Chgo., 1983-97, chmn. oper. com., 1983-96; dir. U.S. Robotics, Inc., Chgo., 1983—, Eagle River Interactive, Inc., 1995—; pres., COO May & Speh, Inc., Downers Grove, Ill., 1997—. Mem. ABA, Ill. State Bar Assn., Chgo. Bar Assn., Young Pres. Orgn. (Chgo. west chpt.), Union League Club, The Chgo. Club. Republican. Episcopalian. General corporate, Mergers and acquisitions, Securities. Office: May & Speh Inc 1501 Opus Pl Downers Grove IL 60515-5727

MASON, STEVEN GERALD, lawyer; b. Dayton, Ohio, Oct. 24, 1963; s. Robert G. and Pauline (Wise) M. BA in Polit. Sci. and History, U. Cen. Fla., 1985; JD, Nova U., 1989. Bar: Fla. 1990, U.S. Dist. Ct. (mid. dist.) Fla. 1990, U.S. Ct. Appeals (11th cir. 1992). Law clk. to Hon. G. Kendall Sharp U.S. Dist. Ct. for Mid. Dist. Fla., Orlando, 1988; felony divsn. atty. Office Pub. Defender, 1989-91; pvt. practice, 1992—. Contbr. to profl. jours. Bd. dirs. Seminole County Humane Soc., Sanford, Fla., 1991-98. Recipient Franklin Graham Defender award, 1990. Mem.: Fla. Bar (cert. criminal trial and criminal appellate specialist), Fla. Assn. Criminal Def. Lawyers, Orange County Bar Assn., Ctrl. Fla. Assn. Criminal Def. Lawyers (sec. 1992—93, amicus com.). Democrat. Avocation: reading. Appellate, Constitutional, Criminal. Office: 1643 Hillcrest St Orlando FL 32803-4809 E-mail: sgmason@bellsouth.net

MASON, THEODORE W. lawyer; b. June 17, 1943; AB, Yale U., 1965; JD, U. Pa., 1972. Bar: Pa. 1972, Fla. 1987. Shareholder Greenberg Traurig, Phila., 1997—2001. Treas., bd. dirs. Nat. Adoption Ctr., Adoption Ctr. Del. Valley, The Hill Top Preparatory Sch. Mem. Nat. Assn. Bond Lawyers (steering com. workshop, enforcement com.). Finance, Municipal (including bonds). Office: Greenberg Traurig LLP 2700 Two Commerce Sq 2001 Market St Philadelphia PA 19103 Fax: 215-988-7801. E-mail: masont@gtlaw.com

MASQUELETTE, PHILIP EDWARD, lawyer; b. Houston, Aug. 9, 1952; s. Philip Abbott and Elizabeth Daggett (Simmons) M.; m. Melissa Simpson Fancher, Nov. 25, 1978; 1 child, Grace Fancher. Student French civilization course Sorbonne, 1972-73; student Institut d'Etudes Politiques de Paris, 1972-73; BA, Tulane U., 1974; JD, U. Houston, 1976. Bar: Tex. 1977, U.S. Tax Ct. 1980, D.C. 1982. Assoc. Dillingham, Masquelette & Boerstler, Houston, 1977-79; officer, bd. dirs. Masquelette & Masquelette P.C., Houston, 1979-84, ptnr., 1984-89, atty. Fed. Deposti Ins. Corp., Midland, Tex., 1989—. Founder, co-chmn. docents Episc. High Sch., Houston, 1984; chmn. Prisoner Svcs. Com. of Houston Met. Ministries, 1987, bd. dirs., 1987. Recipient Svc. award Ch. St. John the Divine, Houston, 1983, 88. Mem. ABA, Houston Bar Assn., D.C. Bar Assn., Tex. Bar Assn., Houston Young Lawyers Assn. (bd. dirs. 1982-83, Outstanding Svc. award 1981-82), Tulane Alumni Coun. of Houston (pres. 1984-86), Tulane Alumni Assn. (Vol. of Yr. award 1987), Sons of Rep. of Tex. Episcopalian. General civil litigation.

MASSAD, STEPHEN ALBERT, lawyer; b. Wewoka, Okla., Dec. 20, 1950; s. Alexander Hamilton and Delores Jean (Razook) M.; m. Amy S. Massad, Jan. 13, 1979; children: Caroline, Sarah, Margaret. AB, Princeton U., 1972; JD, Harvard U., 1975. Bar: Tex. 1975. Assoc. Baker & Botts, Houston, 1975-82, ptnr., 1983—. General corporate, Mergers and acquisitions, Securities. E-mail: stephen.massad@bakerbotts.com

MASSARO, TONI MARIE, dean, law educator; BS, Northwestern U., 1977; JD, Coll. William and Mary, 1980. With Vedder, Price, Kaufman and Kammholz; tchr. law Washington and Lee U., U. Fla.; former prof. law U. Ariz., Tucson, dean, Milton O. Riepe chair constl. law, 1999—. Vis. prof. law Stanford U., U. N.C., Johann Goethe U., Frankfurt, West Germany. Author: Constitutional Literacy: A Core Curriculum for a Multi-Cultural Nation; contbr. numerous articles to law revs. Office: U Ariz James E Rogers Coll Law PO Box 210176 1201 E Speedway Tucson AZ 85721-0176 Fax: 520-621-9140. E-mail: massaro@law.arizona.edu*

MASSEY, KATHLEEN MARIE OATES, lawyer; b. Chgo., Dec. 2, 1955; d. William Robert Jr. and Ethelyn Rose (Calhoun) Oates. Student, U. Claremont-Ferrand, France, 1976-77; BA cum laude, Kalamazoo Coll., 1978; JD, U. Wis., 1981. Bar: Wis. 1981, Minn. 1981, U.S. Dist. Ct. Minn. 1981, U.S. Dist. Ct. (ea. dist.) Wis. 1983. With Larkin, Hoffman, Daily & Lindgren Ltd., Mpls., 1981-87; ptnr. Habush, Habush & Davis, Milw., 1987-90; asst. gen. counsel A.O. Smith Corp., 1992-97; sr. litigation counsel Motorola Inc., Schaumburg, Ill., 1997—. Mem. ABA, Minn. Bar Assn., Wis. Bar Assn., Phi Beta Kappa, Alpha Lambda Delta, Phi Eta Sigma. Insurance, Personal injury.

MASSEY, RAYMOND LEE, lawyer; b. Macon, Ga., Sept. 25, 1948; s. Ford B. and Juanita (Sapp) M.; m. Lynn Ann Thielmeier, Aug. 23, 1967; children: Daniel, Caroline. BA, U. Mo., St. Louis, 1971; JD, U. Louisville, 1974. Bar: Mo. 1974, Ill. 1976, U.S. Dist. Ct. (ea. and we. dists.) Mo. 1974, U.S. Dist. Ct. (so. dist.) Ill. 1976. Assoc. Thompson & Mitchell, St. Louis, 1974-79; ptnr. Thompson & Mitchell (now Thompson & Coburn), 1979—. Mem. Maritime Law Assn. of U.S. (bd. dirs., chmn. ocean and river towing). Admiralty, General civil litigation, Environmental. Home: 3 Wild Rose Dr Saint Louis MO 63124-1465 Office: Thompson Coburn Firstar Plazq Ste 3400 Saint Louis MO 63101-1643

MASSIE, MICHAEL EARL, lawyer; b. Stambaugh, Mich., Aug. 12, 1947; s. Glen E. and Bernice L. (Lambert) M.; m. Vicki L. Colmark, June 11, 1977; children: Christopher, Adam. BA, U. Ill., 1969, JD, 1972. Bar: Ill. 1972, U.S. Dist. Ct. (cen. dist.) Ill. 1989, U.S. Ct. Appeals (7th cir.) 1989. Pvt. practice, Galva, Ill., 1972—. Dir., sec. Community State Bank Galva, 1980—. Fellow Am. Bar Found., Ill. Bar Found.; mem. ABA (chair, coun. mem. gen. practice sect. 1989—), Ill. State Bar Assn. (chmn. gen. practice sect. 1980, chmn. agrl. law com. 1980), Ill. Farm Legal Assistance Found. (chmn. bd. 1985-98). Republican. Avocations: tennis, handball. General practice, Agriculture. Office: 115 NW 3rd Ave Galva IL 61434-1325

MASSUCCO, LAWRENCE RAYMOND, lawyer; b. Waterbury, Conn., Sept. 6, 1947; s. Lawrence Philip and Marion Elizabeth (Bigelow) M.; m. Virginia L. Johnson, Sept. 6, 1969; children— Neil Raymond, Julie Lynn, Kathryn Rose. B.A., U. Vt., 1970; J.D., Suffolk U., 1973. Bar: Vt. 1973, U.S. Dist. Ct. Vt. 1973. Assoc. Kissell Law Offices, Bellows Falls, Vt., 1973-74; ptnr. Kissell & Massucco, Bellows Falls, 1975— ; counsel Bellows Falls Village Corp., 1983— . Pres., v.p., sec. Fall Mountain YMCA, Bellows Falls, 1975— ; chmn. St. Charles Parish Council, Bellows Falls, 1977; pres. Rockingham Townscape, Inc., Bellows Falls, 1977-83;

trustee Connecticut River Watershed Council, 1986—. Mem. ABA, Am. Trial Lawyers Assn., Vt. Bar Assn., Vt. Trial Lawyers Assn.(gov. 1987—), Windham County Bar Assn. Roman Catholic. Lodges: KC (advocate 1980—), Elks. Criminal, Personal injury, Workers' compensation. Office: Kissell & Massucco 90 Westminster St Bellows Falls VT 05101-1547

MASTERS, BARBARA J. lawyer; b. Denver, July 17, 1933; d. Richard P. and Ruth Ann (Savage) Johnson; children: Eliot, Joan. BA, Middlebury Coll., 1955; JD, U. Conn., 1976. Bar: Conn. 1976, U.S. Dist. Ct. Conn. 1976. Assoc. Maruzo & Lucas, Norwich, Conn., 1976-80; pvt. practice, 1980—; prin. Masters and Benson, 1994—. Mem. Conn. Coun. for Divorce Mediation. Bd. dirs. United Comty. Svcs., Norwich, 1980-87, Women's Ctr. Southeastern Conn., New London, 1983-89, Madonna Pl., Norwich, 1989-93; vice-chmn. Lebanon (Conn.) Bd. Fin., 1984-88; mem. People to People del. women lawyers to China, 1986, Norwich Arts Coun., 1989-93; alt. Old Lyme Zoning Bd. Appeals, 1993-97, Old Lyme Dem. Town Com., 1994—; mem. People to People Family Lawyer's Del., Cuba, 2001. Mem. Conn. Bar Assn., New London County Bar Assn. (pres. 1998-99). Unitarian. Avocations: sailing, walking, third world travel. State civil litigation, Family and matrimonial, Real property. Home: 2 Point Rd Old Saybrook CT 06475 Office: 199 W Town St Norwich CT 06360-2106 E-mail: norwichlaw@aol.com

MASTERS, PAUL HOLMES, lawyer; b. Provo, Utah, Sept. 15, 1965; s. Robert William and Carol Jean Masters; m. Tara Lee Gentry, Oct. 14, 1989; children: Benjamin, Andrew, Lydia. BS in Accountancy, Calif. State U., 1991; JD, Brigham Young U., 1997. CPA, Ill., Calif. Sr. acct. Grant Thornton, Sacramento, 1991-94; assoc. Baker & McKenzie, Chgo., 1997—. Mem. AICPA, ABA, Ill. Bar Assn. Mormon. Avocations: rock climbing, canoeing, camping, hiking. Private international, Taxation, general. Office: Baker & McKenzie 130 E Randolph Chicago IL 60601

MASTERSON, KENNETH RHODES, lawyer; b. Memphis, Feb. 22, 1944; s. H. Byron and Mary (Rhodes) M.; children— Michael K., Elizabeth Megel, Grace Megel BA, Westminster Coll., 1966; JD, Vanderbilt U., 1970. Bar: Mo. 1970, Tenn. 1976. Ptnr. Thomason, Crawford & Hendrix, Memphis, 1976-79; v.p. legal Fed. Express Corp., 1980-81, sr. v.p., gen. counsel, 1981-93, sr. v.p., gen. counsel and sec., 1993-96, exec. v.p., gen. counsel and sec., 1996-98, FedEx Corp., Memphis, 1998—. Mem. ABA, Mo. Bar Assn., Am. Corp. Counsel Assn. General corporate. Home: 8679 Classic Dr Memphis TN 38125-8824 Office: FedEx Corp 942 S Shady Grove Rd Memphis TN 38120-4117 Fax: 901-818-7590

MASTERSON, STEPHEN MICHAEL, lawyer, legal association administrator; b. St. Petersburg, Fla., Apr. 14, 1948; s. Bernard Joseph and Stella (Dennis) M.; m. Kathleen Thompson, Dec. 3, 1977; 1 child, Lauren. BA, Fla. State U., 1970; JD, So. Tex. Coll. Law, 1975; LLM, Georgetown U., 1982. Bar: Fla. 1975, U.S. Dist. Ct. (mid. dist.) Fla., 1975, U.S. Ct. Appeals (5th cir.) 1975. Spl. asst. state's atty. Office of State's Atty., Clearwater, Fla., 1975; ptnr. Bauer & Masterson, St. Petersburg, 1975-77, Blews & Masterson, St. Petersburg, 1977-79; judge indsl. claims State of Fla., St. Petersburg, 1979-81; exec. dir. Acad. Fla. Trial Lawyers, Tallahassee, 1982—; adj. prof. Coll. Law Fla. State U., 1987. Author: (with others) Florida Civil Practice Damages, 2d edit. 1980, Florida Criminal Trial Practice Forms, 1980, (with Eleazar and Rice) Florida Criminal Trial Practice, 1982; contbr. articles to profl. jours. Bd. dirs. Young Women's Residence of St. Petersburg, Tallahassee Symphony, Inc.; treas. St. Petersburg Opera Co., Inc. Mem. Assn. Trial Lawyers Am. (state del. 1984—), Fla. Bar (bd. govs. young lawyers sect.). Home: 2664 Egret Ln Tallahassee FL 32312-3242 Office: Acad Fla Trial Lawyers 218 S Monroe St Tallahassee FL 32301-1824

MASTERSON, WILLIAM A. retired judge; b. N.Y.C., June 25, 1931; s. John Patrick and Helen Audrey (O'Hara) M.; m. Julie Dohrmann Cosgrove; children: Mark, Mary, Timothy, Barbara. BA, UCLA, 1953, JD, 1958. Bar: Calif. 1959, U.S. Supreme Ct. 1965.. Assoc. Sheppard, Mullin, Richter & Hampton, L.A., 1952-62, pntr., 1962-79; ptnr. Rogers & Wells, 1979-83, Skadden, Arps, Slate, Meagher & Flom, 1983-87; judge L.A. Superior Ct., 1987-92; justice Ct. Appeal, 1993-2000; ret., 2000. Author, editor: Civil Trial Practice: Strategies and Techniques, 1986. With inf. U.S. Army, 1953-55. Fellow Am. Coll. Trial Lawyers; mem. Order of Coif. Office: PO Box 190 Mendocino CA 95460 E-mail: wmasterson@pobox.com

MASTROMARCO, DAN RALPH, lawyer, consultant; b. Saginaw, Mich., Jan. 18, 1958; s. Victor and Helen (Finkbeiner) M. Student, London Sch. of Econs., Eng., 1982; JD, U. Toledo, 1983; LLM, Georgetown U., 1985. Bar: Mich. 1983, D.C. 1984. Counsel U.S. Senate, Permanent Subcom. on Investigations, Washington, 1983-85; trial atty. Tax div. U.S. Dept. of Justice, 1985-86; asst. chief counsel for tax policy U.S. SBA, 1986-92; dir. tax and fiscal policy Jefferson Group, 1992-94; pres., CEO The Argus Group, 1994—. Coord. Nat. Adv. Coun. for Small Bus., Tax Com., 1986-88; hon. mem. tax com. Small Bus. Legis. Coun., 1986-90; adj. prof. internat. mgmt. program U. Md.; exec. dir. Travel Coun. for Fair Competition; pres. The Prosperity Inst.; exec. dir. Small Bus. Regulators Coun. Author: The Art of Lobbying in Poland, 1995, Out by Its Roots, 1999; contbr. author, editor profl. jours., reports. Mem. Nat. Italian Am. Bar Assn. (trustee scholarship fund, counsel, v.p.), U.S. C. of C. (tax policy com.). Roman Catholic. Office: TAG 333 N Fairfax St Alexandria VA 22314-2632 E-mail: drm@prosperity-institute.org

MASTRONARDI, CORINNE MARIE, lawyer; b. Binghamton, N.Y. d. Joseph Daniel and Frances Marie Mastronardi. BS, Liberty U., 1990; JD, Regent U., 1993. Bar: Fla. 1994, D.C. 1996, Va. 2000. V.p. corp. affairs Va. Metro Protective Svcs., Inc., Virginia Beach, Va.; atty., pres. corp. affairs Pro Rep., Inc., Ft. Lauderdale, Fla.; pvt. practice. Treas. Christian Legal Soc. Republican. General corporate, Family and matrimonial, Sports. Office: PO Box 13176 Chesapeake VA 23325-0176 E-mail: corinne@prorep.com

MASUD, ROBERT, lawyer; b. Havana, Cuba, Jan. 2, 1960; came to U.S., 1963; s. Roberto and Olga (Sanchez) M. B in Bus. Adminstrn., U. Miami, 1982, MBA, 1987; JD, Boston U., 1987; postgrad., Harvard Law Sch., 1991-94. Bar: Fla. 1989, Mass. 1989, U.S. Dist. Ct. Mass 1989, U.S. Ct. Appeals (1st cir.) 1989, U.S. Dist. Ct. (so. dist.) Fla. 1991, U.S. Ct. Appeals (11th cir.) 1992, U.S. Supreme Ct. 1993, U.S. Ct. Appeals (D.C. cir.) 1994, fgn. lawyer, Law Soc. of England. Assoc. Kelley, Drye & Warren, Miami, Fla., 1987-88; founder, operating mgr. Masud & Co., LLC (formerly Masud & Assoc.), Boston, 1989—, Miami, 1992—; founder, prin. Masud & Co., London, 2001—. Spkr. in field. Contbr. to profl. jours. Dep. gen. counsel Mass. Rep. Party, Boston, 1993-94; co-chmn. exploratory com. Dole for Pres., 1995-96; bd. dirs. Assn. Kepha, The Vatican, Rome, 1998-2001, Fondazione Kepha, The Vatican, 2001—. U. Miami scholar, 1977-82. Mem. ABA (vice chmn. arts entertainment sports law com. 1992-95), Inter-Am. Bar Assn., Fla. Bar Assn., Mass. Bar Assn., Boston Bar Assn., Dade County Bar Assn., Alpha Lambda Delta, Phi Eta Sigma. Avocations: skiing, golfing, traveling, racquetball, magic. Finance, Private international, Securities. Office: Masud & Co LLC 60 State St Ste 700 Boston MA 02109-1800

MATAYOSHI, CORALIE CHUN, lawyer, bar association executive; b. Honolulu, June 2, 1956; d. Peter J. and Daisy (Look) Chun; m. Ronald F. Matayoshi, Aug. 8, 1981; children: Scot, Kelly, Alana. BA, U. Calif., Berkeley, 1978; JD, U. Calif., San Francisco, 1981. Bar: Hawaii 1981, U.S. Dist. Ct. Hawaii 1981. Trial atty. U.S. Dept. Justice Antitrust, Washington, 1981-84; assoc. Chun, Kerr, & Dodd, Honolulu, 1984-86; exec. dir. Hawaii Inst. of CLE, 1987-90, Hawaii State Bar Assn., Honolulu, 1990—. Arbitrator Ct. Annexed Arbitration Program, Honolulu, 1992—; adv. bd. Channel 2 TV Action Line, Honolulu, 1993—. Contbr. chapters to books. Bd. dirs. Neighborhood Justice Ctr., 1994-97, mediator, 1997—. Office: Hawaii State Bar Assn 1132 Bishop St Ste 906 Honolulu HI 96813-2814

MATEAS, KENNETH EDWARD, lawyer; b. Aurora, Ill., May 7, 1949; s. Victor Joseph and Lois Rose (Carder) M. BA, U. Ill., 1971; JD, John Marshall Sch. of Law, 1982. Bar: Ill. 1982, D.C. 1982. Assoc. Law Offices of J. Timothy Loats, Aurora, 1982-83, Law Offices of Michael Marsh, Aurora, 1983-84; atty. Kane County States Atty.'s Office, Geneva, 1985; assoc. Law Offices of Gerard Kepple, St. Charles, 1985-89; pvt. practice, Aurora, 1989—. Mem. ABA, Ill. Bar Assn., Nat. Assn. Criminal Def. Lawyers. Republican. Roman Catholic. Lodge: KC. Bankruptcy, Criminal, Family and matrimonial. Office: 408 N Lake St Aurora IL 60506-4106

MATER, MAUD, lawyer; BA in English, Case Western Reserve U., 1969, JD, 1972. Asst. gen. counsel Freddie Mac, McLean, Va., 1976-78, assoc. gen. counsel, 1978-79, v.p., dep. gen. counsel, 1979-82, v.p., gen. counsel, 1982-84, sr. v.p., gen. counsel, sec., 1984-98, exec. v.p., gen. counsel, sec., 1998—. Mem. ABA (com. corp. gen. counsel), FBA, Am. Corp. Counsel Assn. (chair nominating com.), Am. Arbitration Assn. (dir.), Ohio Bar, D.C. Bar, Conf. Bd. Coun. of Chief Legal Officers, Washington Met. Corp. Counsel Assn. Office: Freddie Mac MS # 200 8200 Jones Branch Dr Mc Lean VA 22102-3110

MATERNA, JOSEPH ANTHONY, lawyer; b. Passaic, N.J., June 13, 1947; s. Anthony E. and Peggy Ann Materna; m. Dolores Corio, Dec. 14, 1975; children: Jodi, Jennifer, Janine. BA, Columbia U., 1969, JD, 1973. Bar: N.Y. 1975, Fla. 1977, U.S. Dist. Ct. (ea. and so. dists.) N.Y. 1977, U.S. Supreme Ct. 1977, U.S. Tax Ct. 1978, U.S. Ct. of Claims 1978. Trusts and estates atty. Chadbourne Parke Whiteside & Wolff, N.Y.C., 1973-76, Dreyer & Traub, N.Y.C., 1976-80, Finley Kumble Wagner Heine Underberg & Casey, N.Y.C., 1980-85; ptnr., head trusts and estates dept. Newman Tannenbaum Helpern Syracuse & Hirschtritt, 1985-90, Shapiro Beilly Rosenberg Aronowitz Levy & Fox LLP, N.Y.C., 1990—. Lectr. in field; expert witness in trusts and estate field ct. litigations, N.Y., 1999—. Contbr. articles to profl. jours. Chmn. planned giving com., mem. bd. govs. Arthritis Found. N.Y. Chpt., N.Y.C., 1980—; mem. bd. trustees, corp. treas. Cath. Interracial Coun., N.Y.C., 1992—; mem. bequests and planned gifts com. Cath. Archdiocese of N.Y., N.Y.C., 1988—; corp. sec. Arthritis Found. N.Y. chpt., N.Y.C., 1997—, mem. budget and fin. com., 2001—; mem. Meml. Sloan-Kettering Nat. Trusts and Estates Assocs. Recipient Planned Giving award Arthritis Found.-N.Y. Chpt., N.Y.C., 1994, Discovery Alliance award Arthritis Found.-N.Y. Chpt., N.Y.C., 1995; named Accredited Estate Planner, Nat. Assn. Estate Planners, Marietta, Ga., 1995. Mem. ABA, Fla. Bar (trusts and estate com.), N.Y. State Bar Assn. (com. on estates and trusts), Bar Assn. of the City of N.Y. (com. on surrogate's ct.), N.Y.C. Estate Planning Coun. (lectr., author), N.Y. County Lawyers Assn. (mem. com. on trusts and estates 1979—, com. on profl. ethics, com. on taxation, 2000—), Queen County Bar Assn. (mem. com. trusts and estates 1990—, mem. com. on taxation, mem. com. on profl. ethics), Am. Judges Assn. (civil ct. arbitrator N.Y.C.), Am. Arbitration Assn. (panel of arbitrators), N.Y. State Trial Lawyers Assn., Richmond County Bar Assn. (com. on surrogates ct.), Columbia Coll. Alumni Assn. of Columbia U. (class pres. 1969—). Republican. Roman Catholic. Estate planning, Probate, Estate taxation. Home: 155 Johanna Ln Staten Island NY 10309-3604 Office: Shapiro Beilly Rosenberg Aronowitz Levy & Fox LLP 225 Broadway New York NY 10007-3001

MATHERS, ALLEN STANLEY, judge, arbitrator, consultant; b. Elmhurst, N.Y., Jan. 20, 1949; s. William Albert and Agnes (Przeniczny) M.; m. Mary Elizabeth Breslin, Oct. 1, 1977; children: Matthew Allen, Sarah Anne, Amanda Mary. BA, St. Francis Coll., 1970; JD, St. John's U., Jamaica, N.Y., 1973. Bar: N.Y. 1974, Conn. 1989, U.S. Dist. Ct. (so. and ea. dists.) N.Y. 1974, U.S. Ct. Appeals (2d cir.) 1974, U.S. Supreme Ct. 1983. Assoc. Israelson & Streit, N.Y.C., 1973-80; dir. labor rels. Trans World Airlines, Inc., 1980-82; dir. legal svcs. fund, local 74 Svc. Employees Internat. Union, AFL-CIO, Long Island City, N.Y., 1982—. Village justice Village of Garden City, N.Y., 1997—. Mayor, Village of Garden City; bd. dirs, Arthritis Found. Col., JAG, N.Y. Guard. Mem. ABA, N.Y. State Bar Assn. (spl. com. prepaid legal svcs.), Nassau County Bar Assn., Am. Arbitration Assn., Atlantic Beach Club, Equestrian Order Knights of Holy Sepulchre. Roman Catholic. Home: 30 Kensington Rd Garden City NY 11530-4241 Office: Service Employees Internat Union Local 74 24-09 38th Ave Long Island City NY 11101-3512

MATHERS, PETER ROBERT, lawyer; b. Camden, N.J., Jan. 12, 1955; s. Edward Ronald and Gertrude Louise (Pennypacker) M.; m. Bonnie A. Beavers, Mar. 1, 1997. BS, Rensselaer Poly. Inst., 1976; JD, Yale U., 1979. Bar: D.C. 1979, U.S. Dist. Ct. (D.C. dist.) 1983, U.S. Ct. Appeals (D.C. Cir.) 1983, U.S. Supreme Ct. 1987. Assoc. Kleinfeld, Kaplan & Becker, Washington, 1979-87, ptnr., 1987—. Contbr. articles to profl. jours. Mem. ABA (corp. banking and bus. law sect., food and drug law com.), D.C. Bar Assn., Food and Drug Law Inst., Drug Info. Assn. Administrative and regulatory, Federal civil litigation, Food and drug. Home: 3213 Flushing Meadow Ter Chevy Chase MD 20815-4753 Office: Kleinfeld Kaplan & Becker 1140 19th St NW Washington DC 20036-6601 E-mail: pmathers@kkblaw.com

MATHES, STEPHEN JON, lawyer; b. N.Y.C., Mar. 18, 1945; s. Joseph and Beatrice M.; m. Michele Marshall, Oct. 22, 1972 (div. 1992); children: Aaron, Benjamin; m. Maria McGarry, Dec. 19, 1992; 1 child, Sara. BA, U. Pa., 1967, JD, 1970. Bar: N.Y. 1971, Pa. 1972, U.S. Dist. Ct. (ea. dist.) Pa. 1971. U.S. Ct. Appeals (3d cir.) 1972, U.S. Ct. Appeals (5th cir.) 1985, U.S. Ct. Appeals (4th cir.) 1985, U.S. Ct. Appeals (9th cir.) 2000, U.S. Supreme Ct. 1978. Law clk. U.S. Ct. Appeals (3d cir.), Phila., 1970-71; asst. dist. atty. major felony unit, spl. investigation unit Office of Phil. Dist. Atty., 1975; assoc. Dilworth, Paxson, Kalish & Kauffman, 1971-74, 76-77, sr. ptnr., 1977-91, mem. exec. com., 1987-90, co-chmn. litigation dept., 1987-91; ptnr. Hoyle, Morris & Kerr, 1992—; bd. dirs. The Levitt Found., 1990—, sec., 1991—. Mgmt. com. Hoyle, Morris & Kerr, Phila., 1992-97, 2001—. Bd. dirs., exec. com. Acad. Vocal Arts, 1993-2000, mem. exec. com., chmn. student aid com.; mem. legal and compliance divsn. Securities Industry Assn., 1998—. Mem. ABA, Am. Law Inst., Securities Industries Assn., Pa. Bar Assn., Phila. Bar Assn. (mem. litigation divsn.), Thanatopsis Soc., Racquet Club, Germantown Cricket Club. Federal civil litigation, State civil litigation. Home: 199 Lynnebrook Ln Philadelphia PA 19118-2706 Office: Holye Morris & Kerr One Liberty Pl Ste 4900 Philadelphia PA 19103 E-mail: smathes@hoylemk.com

MATHESON, ALAN ADAMS, law educator; b. Cedar City, Utah, Feb. 2, 1932; s. Scott Milne and Adele (Adams) M.; m. Milicent Holbrook, Aug. 15, 1960; children— Alan, David Scott, John Robert. B.A., U. Utah, 1953, M.S., 1957, J.D., 1959; postgrad. asso. in law, Columbia U. Bar: Utah 1960, Ariz. 1975. Asst. to pres. Utah State U., 1961-67; mem. faculty Ariz. State U., Tempe, 1967—, prof. law, 1970—, dean, 1978-84, 89, 97-98. Bd. dirs. Ariz. Center Law in Public Interest, 1979-81; bd. dirs. DNA Navajo Legal Services, 1984-97. Pres. Tri-City Mental Health Citizens Bd., 1973-74. Served with AUS, 1953-55. Mem. Utah Bar Assn., Ariz. Bar Assn., Maricopa County Bar Assn., Phi Beta Kappa, Order of Coif. Democrat. Mormon. Home: 720 E Geneva Dr Tempe AZ 85282-3737 Office: Ariz State U Coll Law Tempe AZ 85287

MATHESON, DANIEL NICHOLAS, III, lawyer; b. Ft. Worth, Apr. 12, 1949; s. Benjamin Lee Matheson and Ruth (Tankersley) Matheson Flory; m. Jane Allard, May 26, 1974; children— Sarah Austin, Claire Allard, Clayton Nicholas. Student Tulane U., 1967-69; B.A., U. Tex., 1971, J.D., 1974. Bar: Tex. 1974. Assoc. Johnson & Swanson, Dallas, 1974-79, ptnr., Dallas and Austin, 1979-81, 83-93, spl. counsel, 1993—; exec. v.p., gen. counsel Capital Network System, Inc., Austin; dir. State of Tex. Office of State-Fed. Relations, Washington, 1981-82; dir., exec. com. Park Cities Savs. Assn., Dallas, 1985-87. Chmn. So. Govs'. Assn. Staff Adv. Com., Washington, 1982; bd. dirs., chmn., pres. Tex. Lyceum Assn., Austin, 1984-91; bd. regents, chmn. Tex. State U. System, 1989—. Recipient True Texian award Gov. William Clements, 1982. Mem. Tex. Bar Assn. (com. banking law, corp., banking and bus. law sect.), Dallas Bar Assn., Travis County Bar Assn., ABA, Tex. Assn. Bank Counsel. Republican. Methodist. Banking, General corporate, Securities. Home: 2901 Navidad Cv Austin TX 78735-1439

MATHESON, SCOTT MILNE, JR. dean, law educator; b. Salt Lake City, July 18, 1953; s. Scott Milne and Norma (Warenski) M.; m. Robyn Kuida, Aug. 12, 1978; children: Heather Blair, Briggs James. AB, Stanford U., 1975; MA, Oxford U., Eng.; JD, Yale U., 1980. Bar: D.C., 1981, Utah 1986. Assoc. Williams & Connolly, Washington, 1981-85; assoc. prof. law U. Utah, 1985-91; dep. atty. Salt Lake County Attys. Office, 1988-89; vis. assoc. prof. JFK Sch. Govt. Harvard U., Cambridge, Mass., 1989-90; assoc. dean law U. Utah, 1990-93, prof. law, 1991—, dean, 1998—; U.S. atty. Dist. Utah, 1993-97. Adv. com. on rules of evidence Utah Supreme Ct., 1987-93, Utah Constitutional Revision Commn., 1987-93, adv. com. on the local rules of practice, U.S. Dist. Ct. Utah, 1993-97. Contbr. articles to profl. jours. Chmn. U.N. Day for State of Utah, 1991; mem. Univ. Com. on Tanner Lectures on Human Values U. Utah, 1993-2000, Honors Program Adv. Com. U. Utah, 1986-88, Adv. Bd. Hinckley Inst. Politics U. Utah, 1990-93; trustee Legal Aid Soc. of Salt Lake, 1986-93, pres., 1987; trustee TreeUtah, 1992-93; campaign mgr. Matheson for Gov., 1976, 1980; vol. state dir. Clinton/Gore '92. Recipient Up'n Comers award Zions Bank, 1991, Faculty Achievement award Burlington Resources Found., 1993, Disting. Svc. to Fed. Bar award Fed. Bar Assn., Utah chpt., 1998, spl. recognition award Utah Minority Bar Assn., 1999; named one of Outstanding Young Men of Am., 1987, 1988; Rhodes scholar. Mem. ABA, Assn. Am. Law Schs. (chair sect. on mass com. law 1993), Utah State Bar, Salt Lake County Bar Assn. (exec. com. 1986-92), Golden Key Nat. Honor Soc. (hon. 1990), Phi Beta Kappa.

MATHEWS, STANTON TERRY, lawyer; b. May 28, 1952; m. Lisa Diane Earls, Jan. 15, 1977; children: Amy Marie, Adriane Rene, Britton Lafe, Garret Tyler. BA, Brigham Young U., 1976; JD, Western State U. Coll. Law, 1981; cert. in aviation litig., Nat. Jud. Coll., Reno, Nev. Cert. ob-gyn. pediatric malpractice. Pvt. practice law, Laguna Hills, Calif., 1981—. Judge pro tem Orange County Superior Ct. Contbg. to profl. jours. Mem. ATLA, Orange County Bar Assn. (lectr. 1990—), Consumer Attys. of Calif., Diplomate Million Dollar Advocates Forum, Western Trial Lawyers Assn., Orange County Trial Lawyers. Libel, Personal injury. Office: 24012 Calle De La Plata Ste 320 Laguna Hills CA 92653-7624 E-mail: stm@injurytriallaw.com

MATHEWSON, GEORGE ATTERBURY, lawyer; b. Paterson, N.J., Mar. 31, 1935; s. Joseph B. and Christina A. (Atterbury) M.; m. Ann Elizabeth, July 31, 1975' 1 child, James Lemuel. AB cum laude, Amherst Coll., 1957; LLB, Cornell U., 1960; LLM, U. Mich., 1961. Bar: N.Y. 1963. Atty office spl. legal assts., trial atty. FTC, Washington, 1963-65; regional atty. N.Y. State Dept. Environ. Conservation, Liverpool, 1972-73; pvt. practice Syracuse, N.Y., 1967-72, 73—. Adj. instr. bus. law Onondaga Community Coll., Syracuse, 1979-84. Bd. dirs. South Side Businessmen, 1971-72, 88-91, v.p., 1992, pres. 1993; elder Onondaga Hill Presbyn. Ch., 1979, 82-85; dir. Manilus C. of C., 1995, v.p., 1997. Mem. ABA, Fed. Bar Assn., N.Y. State Bar Assn. (state and county bar assn. coms.), Kiwanis (bd. dirs. Onondaga club 1988-89, v.p. 1989, pres. 1989-91). Patentee safety device for disabled airplanes. General civil litigation, General practice, Real property. Office: 224 Fayette St Manlius NY 13104-1804

MATHIAS, JOSEPH MARSHALL, lawyer, judge; b. Frankfort, Ky., Jan. 23, 1914; s. Harry L. and Catherine Snead (Marshall) M.; children: Mark Wellington, Marcia Ann Mathias Wilson, Marilyn Roberta. AB, U. Md., 1935; JD, Southeastern U., 1942. Bar: Md. 1942, U.S. Supreme Ct. 1949, U.S. Dist. Ct. Md. 1963. Ptnr. Moorman and Mathias, 1946-50, Jones, Mathias and O'Brien and predecessor firms, 1950-65; judge Md. Tax Ct., 1959-65; assoc. judge Circuit Ct. of Montgomery County (Md.), 1965-80; chief judge 6th Jud. Circuit of Md., 1980-81; spl. assignments, 1981-83; spl. counsel Beckett, Cromwell & Myers, P.A., 1983-88; of counsel Frank, Bernstein, Conaway and Goldman, 1988-92. Past dir. Nat. Bank Md., Bank So. Md.; former mem. adv. bd. Citizens Bank and Trust Co. Chmn. Bd. Property Rev., Montgomery, Md., 1992—. Served with USN, 1942-46. Recipient cert. of disting. citizenship Gov. of Md., 1981. Mem. ABA, Md. State Bar Assn., Md. Bar Found., Montgomery County Bar Assn., Am. Judicature Soc. Democrat. Roman Catholic. Home: 10011 Summit Ave Kensington MD 20895-3835 E-mail: rwmjmm@erols.com

MATHIS, JOHN PRENTISS, lawyer; b. New Orleans, Feb. 10, 1944; s. Robert Prentess and Lena (Horton) M.; m. Karen Elizabeth McHugh, May 31, 1966; children: Lisa Lynne Mathis Kirkpatrick, Andrew P. BA magna cum laude, So. Meth. U., 1966; JD cum laude, Harvard U., 1969. Bar: Calif. 1970, D.C. 1975, U.S. Ct. Appeals (D.C. cir.) 1972, U.S. Ct. Appeals (5th cir.) 1975, U.S. Ct. Appeals (3d cir.) 1980, U.S. Supreme Ct. 1982. Assoc. Latham & Watkins, L.A., 1969-71; spl. asst. to gen. counsel FPC, Washington, 1971-72; gen. counsel Calif. Pub. Utilities Commn., San Francisco, 1972-74; assoc. Baker & Botts, Washington, 1974-76, ptnr., 1976-92, Hogan & Hartson, Washington, 1992-2000; v.p., assoc. gen. counsel regulatory affairs Edison Mission Energy, 2000—. Mem. ABA (litigation sect., chmn. energy litigation com. 1985-89, div. dir. 1989-90, chmn. legis. com. 1990-94, rep. to coord. group energy law 1992-97), Fed. Energy Bar Assn., Harvard U. Law Sch. Assn. D.C. (past pres.), Congl. Country Club, Met. Club (Washington), Talbot Country Club (Easton, Md.). Republican. Methodist. FERC practice, Nuclear power, Public utilities. Home: 9400 Turnberry Dr Potomac MD 20854-5447 Office: Edison Mission Energy 555 12th St NW Ste 640 Washington DC 20004

MATIA, PAUL RAMON, federal judge; b. Cleve., Oct. 2, 1937; s. Leo Clemens and Irene Elizabeth (Linkert) M.; m. Nancy Arch Van Meter, Jan. 2, 1993. BA, Case Western Res. U., 1959; JD, Harvard U., 1962. Bar: Ohio 1962, U.S. Dist. Ct. (no. dist.) Ohio 1969. Law clk. Common Pleas Ct. of Cuyahoga County, Cleve., 1963-66, judge, 1985-91; asst. atty. gen. State of Ohio, 1966-69, adminstrv. ast. to atty. gen. Columbus, 1969-70; senator Ohio State Senate, 1971-75, 79-83; ptnr. Hadley, Matia, Mills & MacLean Co., L.P.A., Cleve., 1975-84; judge U.S. Dist. Ct. (no. dist.) Ohio, 1991-99, chief dist. judge, 1999—; mem. 6th Cir. Jud. Coun., 1999—. Candidate Lt. Gov. Rep. Primary, 1982, Ohio Supreme Ct., 1988. Named Outstanding Legislator, Ohio Assn. for Retarded Citizens, 1974, Watchdog of Ohio Treasury, United Conservatives of Ohio, 1979; recipient Heritage award Polonia Found., 1988. Mem. Fed. Bar Assn., Club at Key Ctr. Avocations: skiing, gardening, travel. Office: US Dist Ct 201 Superior Ave E Cleveland OH 44114-1201

MATLACK, DON(ALD) (CLYDE), retired lawyer; b. Halstead, Kans., June 18, 1929; s. Orval and Blanche (Harris) M.; m. Ardena Williams, June 10, 1951; children: Lucinda M. Manley, Roxanne Mrasek, Terry C., Rex, Timothy. BBA, Kans. State U., 1951; JD, Washburn U., 1957. Bar: Kans. 1957, U.S. Dist. Ct. Kans. 1957, U.S. Ct. Appeals (10th cir.) 1962, U.S.

Supreme Ct. 1969. Dep. county atty. Sedgwick County, Kans., 1957-59; city atty. City of Clearwater, 1958-96, Bentley, 1960-64, Viola, 1965-79, Belle Plaine, 1975-82, Valley Ctr., 1977-81; ptnr. Matlack & Foote, P.A. and predecessor firms, Wichita, 1977-95; pvt. practice Clearwater, 1995-97; ret., 1997. Mem. Kans. Jud. Study Adv. Commn., 1973-74; legis. liason for Gov. Robert Docking, 1969-74; arbitrator Wichita Small Claims Arbitration Bd., 1973. Co-chmn. Clearwater March of Dimes, 1980, Clearwater Area United Fund, 1980, 83; Dem. precinct committeeman 1964-99; treas. Kans. 5th dist. Dem. Com., 1966-68; Mem. Kans. Civil Service Commn., 1969-70; Kans. state senator, 1965-69; chmn. Docking for Gov. campaigns in Sedgwick County, 1970-72; chmn. and treas. Ardena Matlack for state rep. campaigns 1974, 76, 78, 80, 82; del. Dem. Nat. Conv., 1976; lay leader, trustee, adminstrv. bd. chmn. Clearwater United Meth. Ch.; Mem. Kans. West Conf. com. on Spl. Ministries United Meth. Ch. 1972-80, chmn. 1972-76. Served with USNR, 1951-57. Mem. ABA, Kans. Bar Assn. (profl. econs. com. 1983-84), Wichita Bar Assn. (chmn. legis. com. 1981-82, chmn. domestic relations com. 1979-81, mem. 1979-83, prepaid legal services com., fee disputes com. 1976-80), Assn. Trial Lawyers Am., Kans. Trial Lawyers Assn., Am. Legion (commander 1987-89), Delta Tau Delta, Alpha Kappa Psi. Methodist. Lodges: Masons, Shriners, Lions (Clearwater pres. 1963-64). Home: 448 E Hellar Clearwater KS 67026 E-mail: bellringer@skfc.net

MATRAY, DIDIER F, lawyer; b. Liege, Belgium, June 5, 1951; s. Lambert Matray and France Beck; m: Joelle Gobbels, Aug. 19, 1978; children: Thibaut, Gautier, Bertrand and Sophie. LLB first honor, Liege U., Belgium, 1973. Bar: Liege. Attache State Secretary, regional walloon economy, 1974-75; asst. Prof. Del Marmol, 1976-82; various positions Comm. of Internal Relations, 1987-96; mng. ptnr. Matray, Matray & Hallet, Liege, Belgium, 1973—. Lecturer, U. Liege, Belgium. Chmn. Comm. of the Internat. Relations of the Bar Assoc. ,1994-96. Order of merits, German Federal Rep.; Order of Leopold II, Kingdom of Belgium. Mem. Commn. for Internat. Bus. Practices, Internat. Chamber of Commerce, Paris, France; Cepani(Cente for Study Practice of Nat. and Internat. Arbitration, Brussels; American Assos. of Arbitration, New York; Common Ct. of Justice and Arbitration, Ohada, Ivory Coast; vice-pres. Nat. Com. European Ct. of Arbitration, Alternative dispute resolution, General corporate, Mergers and acquisitions. Office: Matray, Matray & Hallet Rue Des Fories 2 B-4020 Liege Belgium Fax: 32/41252 0857. E-mail: dmatray@matray.be

MATSEN, JEFFREY ROBERT, lawyer; b. Salt Lake City, Nov. 24, 1939; s. John Martin and Bessie (Jackson) M.; m. Susan Davis, July 27, 1973; children: Gregory David, Melinda Kaye, Brian Robert, Jeffrey Lamont, Kristin Sue, Nicole, Brett Richard. BA cum laude, Brigham Young U., 1964; JD with honors, UCLA, 1967. Bar: Calif. 1968, U.S. Supreme Ct., U.S. Tax Ct., U.S. Ct. Appeals (fed. cir.). Atty., L.A., 1968, Newport Beach, Calif., 1971—; mng. ptnr. Jeffrey R. Matsen & Assocs., 1978—. Prof. law Western State U. Coll. Law, Fullerton, Calif., 1969-85; instr. Golden Gate U. Grad. Taxation Program, 1978-84. Author: Business Planning for California Closely-Held Enterprises; contbr. articles to legal jours. Capt., USMCR, 1968-71. Decorated Navy Commendation medal. Mem. State Bar Calif., Order of Coif. General corporate, Estate planning, Taxation, general. Office: 5001 Birch St Newport Beach CA 92660-2116 E-mail: jeff@jrmatsen.com

MATTAR, LAWRENCE JOSEPH, lawyer; b. Buffalo, Apr. 17, 1934; s. Joseph and Anne (Abraham) M.; m. Elaine Kolbe, Aug. 1, 1959; children: Lorraine, Brenda, Anne, Deborah. Grad., Canisius Coll., 1956; JD, SUNY, Buffalo, 1959. Bar: N.Y. 1959, Fla. 1977, U.S. Supreme Ct. 1972. Sole practice, Buffalo, 1959-62; sr. ptnr. Mattar & D'Agostino and predecessors, 1962—. Asst. to county ct. judge, 1961-66; counsel N.Y. State Senate Pub. Utilities Com., 1969-71. Bd. dirs. Better Bus. Bur. Western N.Y.; mem. exec. com. pres.'s coun. Canisius Coll.; mem. ho. of dels. United Way of Buffalo and Erie County; mem. Nat. Maronite Bishops' Adv. Coun., U.s. Congl. Adv. Bd.; Selective Svc. Bd., Western N.Y. Rep.Presdl. Task Force; del. Rep. Jud. Conv. 8th Dist., 1985. Decorated Knight of St. Charbiel, highest honor available to a Maronite Cath.; recipient award for outstanding svc. Buffalo Eye Bank, 1962, Leadership award Lions Club Buffalo, 1963, Citizen's award Erie C.C., 1982, Nat. Tree of Life award Bd. dirs. Jewish Nat. Fund Am., 1987. Mem. Erie County Bar Assn., Erie County Trial Lawyers Assn., N.Y. State Bar Assn., Fla. Bar Assn., N.Y. State Trial Lawyers Assn., Buffalo C. of C., NFL Players Alumni Assn. (assoc.), Di Gamma (life), Rotary Club (sec. 1978-79, dir. 1978-80, trustee, sec., mem. exec. com. Buffalo Rotary Found.), Buffalo Club (Buffalo), Transit Valley Country Club (East Amherst, N.Y.). Roman Catholic. Avocations: golf, skiing. Federal civil litigation, State civil litigation, General corporate. Home: 386 Woodbridge Ave Buffalo NY 14214-1530 Office: Mattar & D'Agostino LLP 17 Court St Ste 600 Buffalo NY 14202-3294

MATTERN, KEITH EDWARD, lawyer; b. Savanna, Ill., Apr. 24, 1931; s. Harvey and Caroline (Miller) M.; m. Sue D. Cuquet, Oct. 12, 1963; children— Scott, David, Melissa. B.S. in Mgmt., U. Ill., 1953; J.D., U. Mo., 1958. Bar: Mo. 1958, U.S. Supreme Ct. 1971. Sole practice, St. Louis, 1958-66; atty. Interco, Inc., St. Louis, 1966-69, asst. gen. counsel, 1969-80, assoc. gen. counsel, 1980-82, gen. counsel, 1982—. Served to capt. USAF, 1953-55. Mem. St. Louis Bar Assn. Roman Catholic. Federal civil litigation, General corporate, Labor. Office: Interco Inc 101 S Hanley Rd Ste 1900 Saint Louis MO 63105-3417

MATTESON, WILLIAM BLEECKER, lawyer; b. N.Y.C., Oct. 20, 1928; s. Leonard Jerome and Mary Jo (Harwell) M.; m. Marilee Brill, Aug. 26, 1950; children: Lynn, Sandra, Holly. BA, Yale U., 1950; JD, Harvard U., 1953. Bar: N.Y. 1954. Clk. to judge Augustus N. Hand U.S. Ct. Appeals, 1953-54; clk. to U.S. Supreme Ct. Justice Harold H. Burton, 1954-55; assoc. firm Debevoise & Plimpton (and predecessors), N.Y.C., 1955-61, ptnr., 1961—, Debevoise & Plimpton (European office), Paris, 1973-78; presiding ptnr. Debevoise & Plimpton, 1988-93. Lectr. Columbia U. Law Sch., 1972-73, 78-80. Trustee Peddie Sch., Hightstown, N.J., 1968-73, Kalamazoo Coll., 1972-77, Miss Porter's Sch., Farmington, Conn., 1977-83, N.Y. Inst. Spl. Edn., 1981—, Salk Inst., La Jolla, Calif., 1993-96, vice-chair, 1994-96, Statue of Liberty Ellis Island Found., 1996—, Hartford Found., 1996—; active USA Bus. and Industry Adv. Com. to the Orgn. for Econ. Coop. and Devel., Paris, 1986-2000; chmn. Worldwide Bus. and Industry Adv. Com., 1994-96; vice chmn. U.S. Coun. for Internat. Bus., 1990-2000, hon. trustee. Mem. ABA, FBA, Internat. Bar Assn., N.Y. State Bar Assn., Assn. of Bar of City of N.Y. (chmn. securities regulation com. 1968-71), Harvard U. Law Sch. Assn. N.Y.C. (trustee 1968-73), Coun. Fgn. Rels., Union Club, Sky Club, Sankaty Head Club, John's Island Redstick, and Windsor Clubs, N.Y. Yacht Club. General corporate, Private international. Office: Debevoise & Plimpton 875 3rd Ave Fl 16 New York NY 10022-6225 E-mail: wbmatteson@debevoise.com

MATTHEW, LEODIS CLYDE, lawyer; b. Eloy, Ariz., June 20, 1949; s. Lester B. and Theressa (Watson) M. BA, Lewis and Clark Coll., 1970, JD, 1973. Bar: Oreg. 1973, D.C. 1977, Calif. 1981. Dep. dist. atty. State of Oreg., Portland, 1973-77; sr. counsel U.S. Congress, Washington, 1977-79; trial atty. internat. trade and comml. litigation Dept. Justice, Washington, 1979-84; ptnr. O'Haire Fiore & von Maur, Frankfurt, Fed. Republic Germany, 1984-88, von Maur, Matthews & Ptnrs., Frankfurt, 1988—; part-time instr. Portland State U., 1974-76. Federal civil litigation, Government contracts and claims, Public international. Office: von Maur Matthews & Ptnrs Myliusstr 23 600 1 Frankfurt on the Main Germany

MATTHEWS, DOUGLAS EUGENE, lawyer, educator, consultant; b. Highland Park, Mich., July 28, 1953; s. Max and Mary Elizabeth (Crane) M. BA with high distinction, Judson Coll., Elgin, Ill., 1982; JD cum laude, U. Wis., 1985, MS in Legal Instns., 1988; LLM, Harvard U., 1991. Bar: Fla. 1986, Ill. 1987, D.C. 1989. Assoc. Gunster, Yoakley, Criser & Stewart, West Palm Beach, Fla., 1986, Zukowski, Rogers, Flood & McArdle, Crystal Lake, 1987; asst. pub. defender McHenry County, Woodstock, Ill., 1988-89; law lectr. No. Ill. U., De Kalb, 1990; asst. prof. St. Thomas U. Sch. Law, Miami, Fla., 1991-94, assoc. prof., 1994-96; adj. prof. law, 1996—; co-founder, v.p. The Grifo Group, Inc., Miami, Fla., 1997—. Past v.p., bd. dirs. Youth Svc. Bur., Woodstock. Mem. Fla. Bar Assn., Ill. Bar Assn., Dade County Bar Assn., Ind. Computer Cons. Assn., Harvard Club of Miami. Democrat. Unitarian. Avocations: gardening, historic preservation. Office: 686 NE 74th St Miami FL 33138-5114 E-mail: matthews@post.harvard.edu

MATTHEWS, ELIZABETH WOODFIN, law librarian, law educator; b. Ashland, Va., July 30, 1927; d. Edwin Clifton and Elizabeth Frances (Luck) Woodfin; m. Sidney E. Matthews, Dec. 20, 1947; 1 child, Sarah Elizabeth Matthews Wiley. BA, Randolph-Macon Coll., 1948, LLD (hon.), 1989; MS in Libr. Sci., U. Ill., 1952; PhD, So. Ill. U., 1972; LLD, Randolph-Macon Coll., 1989. Cert. law libr., med. libr., med. libr. III. Libr. Ohio State U., Columbus, 1952-59; libr., instr. U. Ill., Urbana, 1962-63; lectr. U. Ill. Grad. Sch. Libr. Sci., 1964; libr., instr. Morris Libr. So. Ill. U., Carbondale, 1964-67; classroom instr. So. Ill. U. Coll Edn., 1967-70; med. libr., asst. prof. Morris Libr. So. Ill. U., 1972-74, law libr., asst. prof., 1974-79, law libr., assoc. prof., 1979-85, law libr., prof., 1985-92, prof. emerita, 1993—. Author: Access Points to Law Libraries, 1984, 17th Century English Law Reports, 1986, Law Library Reference Shelf, 1988, 4th edit., 1999, Pages and Missing Pages, 1983, 2d edit., 1989, Lincoln as a Lawyer: An Annotated Bibliography, 1991. Mem. AAUW (pres. 1976-78, corp. rep. 1978-88), Am. Assn. Law Librs., Beta Phi Mu, Phi Kappa Phi. Methodist. Home: 811 S Skyline Dr Carbondale IL 62901-2405 Office: So Ill U Law Libr Carbondale IL 62901

MATTHEWS, PAUL AARON, lawyer; b. Memphis, May 7, 1952; s. Joseph Curtis and Sarah Rebecca (Barret) M.; m. Roberta Bartow, July 29, 1978; children: Sarah Pierrepont, Elizabeth Barret. AB, Duke U., 1974; JD, Vanderbilt U., 1977. Bar: Tenn. 1977, U.S. Dist. Ct. (we. dist.) Tenn. 1977, U.S. Dist. Ct. (ea. dist.) Mich. 1987, U.S. Dist. Ct. (ea. dist.) Tenn. 1991, U.S. Ct. Appeals (6th cir.) 1991, U.S. Dist. Ct. (ea. and we. dists.) Ark. 1995, U.S. Dist. Ct. (mid. dist.) Tenn. 1998, U.S. Dist. Ct. (no. and so. dists.) Miss. 2000, U.S. Supreme Ct. 1998; cert. in bus. bankruptcy law and consumer bankruptcy law, Am. Bd. Certification and Tenn. Comm. on Cont. Legal Edn. and Specialization. Assoc. Armstrong Allen, PLLC, Memphis, 1977-82, ptnr., mem., 1982—. Chief justice Vanderbilt Law Sch. Moot Ct. Bd., Nashville, 1976-77. Co-author: Passport to Tennessee History, 1996; contbg. editor: Martindale-Hubbell Tenn. Law Digest, 1994—99;contbr. articles to profl. publs. Mem. com. chmn. Memphis-in-May Internat. Festival, 1977-79, Tenn. Hist. Commn., 1987-97; bd. dirs. Davies Manor Assn., Brunswick, Tenn., 1994-99, pres. 1996-97; mem. Leadership Memphis Class of 1987, mem. alumni adv. coun., 2000—; trustee Tenn. Hist. Commn. Found., 1998—, Shelby County Hist. Commn., 1997—, vice chmn. 1999, chmn., 2000-01; commr. Tenn. Wars Commn., 1994-97; vestry Ch. of the Holy Communion, 1995-98; trustee St. Mary's Episcopal Sch., 2001—. Recipient Newman award Memphis Heritage, Inc., 1992. Mem. ABA, SAR (Isaac Shelby chpt.), Am. Bankruptcy Inst., Tenn. Bar Assn., Memphis Bar Assn. (mem. publs. coun. 1990-98, bd. dirs. 1999—, mem. jud. practice and procedures com. 2000—), Memphis and Shelby County Mental Health Assn. (pres. 1984-85), Duke U. Alumni Assn. (pres. Memphis chpt. 1986-88), Descendants of Early Settlers of Shelby County (v.p. 1999—), Sigma Alpha Epsilon. Episcopalian. Bankruptcy, General civil litigation, Contracts commercial. Home: 4271 Heatherwood Ln Memphis TN 38117-2302

MATTHIES, MARY CONSTANCE T. lawyer; b. Baton Rouge, Mar. 22, 1948; d. Allen Douglas and Mazie (Poche) Tillman. B.S., Okla. State U., 1969; J.D., U. Tulsa, 1972. Bar: Okla. 1973, U.S. Ct. Appeals (10th cir.) 1974, U.S. Ct. Appeals (8th and D.C. cirs.) 1975, U.S. Supreme Ct. 1976. Assoc., ptnr. Kothe, Nichols & Wolfe, Inc., Tulsa, 1972-78; pres. sr. prin. Matthies Law Firm, P.C., Tulsa, 1978—; guest lectr. U. Tulsa Coll. Law, U. Okla. Sch. Law, Oral Roberts U. Sch. Contbr. articles to profl. jours; mem. staff Tulsa Law Jour., 1971-72. Fellow Am. Coll. of Labor and Employment Lawyers; mem. ABA (mem. spl. subcom. for liaison with EEOC, 1974—, spl. subcom. for liaison with OFCCP, 1979—, mgmt. co-chmn. equal employment law subcoms. on nat. origin discrimination 1974-75, class actions and remedies 1975-80), Okla. Bar Assn. (coun. mem. labor law sect. 1974-80, chmn. 1978-79), Women's Law Caucus, Phi Delta Phi. Presbyterian. Civil rights, Federal civil litigation, Labor. Office: Thompson Bldg 20 E 5th St Ste 310 Tulsa OK 74103-4435 Business E-Mail: mattlawfrm@aol.com

MATTICE, HARRY SANDLIN, JR. prosecutor; b. Chattanooga, Mar. 10, 1954; s. Harry Sandlin Sr. and Kathryn (McCoy) M.; m. Janet Lynn LeVan, Jan 4, 1975; children: Harry Sandlin III, Bryan Christopher, Keven LeVan. BS, U. Tenn., Chattanooga, 1976; JD, U. Tenn., 1981. Bar: Tenn. 1982, U.S. Dist. Ct. (ea. dist.) Tenn. 1982, U.S. Ct. Appeals (6th cir.) 1984, U.S. Tax Ct. 1984, U.S. Claims Ct. 1984, U.S. Ct. Appeals (11th cir.) 1987, U.S. Dist. Ct. (we. dist.) Tenn. 1989. Staff acct. Deloitte, Haskins & Sells , Chattanooga, 1976-78; from assoc. to ptnr. Miller & Martin , 1981—2000; of counsel Baker, Donelson, Bearman & Caldwell, 2000—01; U.S. atty. Ea. Dist. Tenn., 2001—. Pres. Chattanooga Tax Practitioners. Asst. to pres. Chattanooga Goodwill Industries, 1988—; precinct chmn. Hamilton County Rep. Party Coun., Signal Mountain, Tenn., 1989—, treas., 1991—. Mem. Order of Coif, Mountain City Club, Signal Mountain Golf and Country Club, Phi Kappa Phi. Episcopalian. Home: 609 Marr Dr Signal Mountain TN 37377-2280 Office: US Atty 800 Market St Ste 211 Knoxville TN 37902*

MATTIELLI, LOUIS, lawyer; b. Bayonne, N.J., Dec. 15, 1949; s. Domenick and Fannie (LaGatta) M.; m. Maria Mattielli, June 22, 1974; children: Marcus, Alexander, Pamela. BS, St. Peter's Coll., 1971; JD, N.Y. Law Sch., 1974. Bar: N.J., N.Y. Law sec. judge Superior Ct. N.J., Paterson, 1974-75; assoc. gen. counsel Loeb, Rhoades & Co., N.Y.C., 1975-77; asst. gen. counsel Wagner Electric Corp., Parsippany, N.J., 1977-80; assoc. Apruzzese, McDermott, Mastro & Murphy, Liberty Corner, N.J., 1980-81; asst. div. counsel Wagner div. McGraw Edison Co., Parsippany, 1981-82; former gen. ptnr., gen. counsel Mabon, Nugent & Co., N.Y.C., 1982-86; v.p., gen. counsel FL Industries Inc., Livingston, N.J., 1986-90, sr. v.p., gen. counsel, sec., 1990—. Mem. ABA, N.J. State Bar Assn. Roman Catholic. General corporate. Office: The Pullman Co 3 Werner Way # 200 Lebanon NJ 08833-2223

MATTISON, PRISCILLA JANE, lawyer; b. Phila., July 28, 1960; d. Verne Sylvester and Virginia (Dean) M.; m. Bernard M. Resnick, Aug. 4, 1995. BA, Yale U., 1982; cert. in producing, Am. Film Inst., L.A., 1987; JD, U. Pa., 1997. Bar: Pa. 1997, D.C. 1999. Distbn. dir. Michael Blackwood Prodns., N.Y.C., 1985-86; dir. devel., head of casting/head of overseas prodn. Concorde Pictures, L.A., 1987-90; ind. filmmaker, 1990-94; assoc. Harkins Cunningham, Phila., 1997—. Dir., assoc. prodr. numerous films, 1987-90; screenwriter, 1988-94; songwriter, 1983—; photographer; author numerous poems. Sec. Penn Valley (Pa.) Civic Assn., 1998—. Grantee Fulbright Assn., 1982-83. Mem. ABA, Pa. Bar Assn., Phila. Bar Assn., Fulbright Alumni Assn. (bd. dirs. Del. Valley chpt. 1997—). Avocations: travel, photography, writing, songwriting, hiking. Office: Harkins Cunningham 2800 One Commerce Sq 2005 Market St Ste 1800 Philadelphia PA 19103-7075 E-mail: smattison@aol.com

MATTSON, JAMES STEWART, lawyer, wine distribution executive, environmental scientist, educator; b. Providence, July 22, 1945; s. Irving Carl and Virginia (Lutey) M.; m. Carol Sandry, Aug. 15, 1964 (div. 1979); children: James, Birgitta; m. Rana A. Fine, Jan. 5, 1983. BS in Chemistry, U. Mich., 1966, MS, 1969, PhD, 1970; JD, George Washington U., 1979. Bar: D.C. 1979, Fla. 1983, U.S. Dist. Ct. D.C. 1979, U.S. Dist. Ct. (so. dist.) Fla. 1984, U.S. Ct. Appeals (D.C. cir.) 1979, U.S. Ct. Claims 1985, U.S. Supreme Ct. 1985, U.S. Ct. Appeals (11th cir.) 1985, U.S. Ct. Appeals (5th cir.) 1987, U.S. Ct. Appeals (fed. cir.) 1990. Staff scientist Gulf Gen. Atomic Co., San Diego, 1970-71; dir. R & D Ouachita Industries, Inc., Monroe, La., 1971-72; asst. prof. chem. oceanography Rosenstiel Sch. Marine & Atmospheric Sci., U. Miami, Fla., 1972-76; phys. scientist NOAA, Washington, 1976-78; mem. profl. staff & congl. liaison Nat. Adv. Commn. on Oceans and Atmosphere, 1978-80; ptnr. Mattson & Pave, Washington, Miami, Key Largo, 1980-86, Mattson & Tobin, Key Largo, 1987-2000; pres./CEO Great House of Wine, Inc, Sunrise, Fla. and Napa, Calif., 1997—. Adj. prof. law U. Miami, 1983-93; cons. Alaska Dept. Environ. Conservation, 1981-91. Author: (with H.B. Mark) Activated Carbon: Surface Chemistry and Adsorption from Solution, 1971; editor (with others): Computers in Chemistry and Instrumentation, 8 vols., 1972-76; The Argo Merchant Oil Spill: A Preliminary Scientific Report, 1977, (with H.B. Mark) Water Qulity Measurement: Modern Analytical Techniques, 1981; contbr. articles to profl. jours. Candidate dist. 120 Fla. Ho. of Reps., 1994. Fellow Fed. Water Pollution Control Adminstrn., 1967-68; recipient Spl. Achievement award U.S. Dept. Commerce, 1976-77; Regents Alumni scholar U. Mich., 1963. Mem. ABA, Am. Chem. Soc. (chmn. Symposium on Oil Spill Indentification 1971), Order of Coif. Administrative and regulatory, Environmental, Land use and zoning (including planning). Address: PO Box 586 Key Largo FL 33037-0586 E-mail: jmattson@attglobal.net

MATTY, ROBERT JAY, lawyer; b. N.Y.C., July 6, 1948; s. Newton and Beatrice (Mituck) M.; m. Kathy Sirota, May 25, 1974; children— Jeffrey Scott, Lesley Jill. B.A., Queens Coll., 1970; J.D., Am. U., 1974. Bar: Md. 1975, U.S. Dist. Ct. Md. 1975, D.C. 1976, U.S. Dist. Ct. D.C. 1979, N.Y. 1984. Law clk. 7th Jud. Cir. Ct., Upper Marlboro, Md., 1974-75; asst. state's atty. Office Md. State's Atty., Upper Marlboro, 1975-78; asst. public defender Office Public Defender, Upper Marlboro, 1978-79; mng. atty. Robert A. Ades & Assocs., Landover, Md., 1979— . Co-chmn. lawyers div. United Way, Washington, 1981. Mem. Nat. Dist. Attys. Assn., Nat. Assn. Criminal Def. Lawyers, Assn. Trial Lawyers Am., ABA. Democrat. Jewish. State civil litigation, Criminal, Personal injury. Home: 6212 Mazwood Rd Rockville MD 20852-3528 Office: Robert A Ades & Assocs PC 4301 Garden City Dr # 300 Hyattsville MD 20785-2210

MATUG, ALEXANDER PETER, lawyer; b. Chgo., May 25, 1946; s. Alexander J. and Marianne (Paszek) M.; m. Jeanne Marie Buker, Aug. 16, 1969; children: Alexander W., Krista E., Thomas E. BA, St. Mary's Coll., Minn., 1968; JD, Loyola U., Chgo., 1972. Bar: Ill. 1972, U.S. Dist. Ct. (no. dist.) Ill. 1972. Pvt. practice, Palos Heights, Ill., 1972—. Bd. dirs. Am. Heritage, Sertoma, Palos Heights, 1991—; profl. adv. bd. Sertoma Speech and Hearing Ctr., Palos Hills, Ill., 1991—. Mem. Ill. Bar Assn., S.W. Suburban Bar Assn. Roman Catholic. General practice, Probate, Real property. Office: 7110 W 127th St Ste 250 Palos Heights IL 60463-1571

MATUNE, FRANK JOSEPH, lawyer; b. Youngstown, Ohio, Jan. 11, 1948; s. Walter John and Eve (Skiljo) M.; m. Doreen Mary Dolan, June 1, 1974; children: Molly Catherine, John Walter, Kelly Dolan. BA, Ill. Benedictine Coll., 1970; JD, Thomas M. Cooley Law Sch., Lansing, Mich., 1979; LLM, Georgetown U., 1980. Bar: Pa. 1979, Ohio, 1998, U.S. Dist. Ct. (western dist.) Pa. 1982, U.S. Tax Ct. 1980. Tax clk. Bd. Tax Appeals State Mich. Dept. Revenue, Lansing, 1978-79; ptnr. Routman, Moore, Goldstone & Valentino, Sharon, Pa., 1981-98, Nadler, Nadler & Burdman Co., LPA, Youngstown, Ohio, 1998—. Author: Pennsylvania Tax Service, 1987, Federal Tax Service, 1988. Mem. ABA, Ohio Ba Assn., Pa. Bar Assn., Mercer County Bar Assn. (treas. 1983-86). Republican. Roman Catholic. Avocations: sports, classical music. Corporate taxation, Taxation, general, State and local taxation. Home: 798 Lillian Dr Hermitage PA 16148-1571 Office: Nadler Nadler & Burdman Co 20 Federal Plz W Ste 600 Youngstown OH 44503-1424

MATUS, WAYNE CHARLES, lawyer; b. N.Y.C., Mar. 10, 1950; s. Eli and Alma (Platt) M.; m. Marsha Rothblum, Jan. 16, 1982; children: Marshall Scott, Scott Adam. BA, Johns Hopkins U., 1972; JD, NYU, 1975. Law clk. Superior Ct. D.C., 1975-76; assoc. Marshall, Bratter, Greene, Allison and Tucker, N.Y.C., 1976-79, Christy & Viener, N.Y.C., 1979-83, ptnr., 1984-88, Salans Hertzfeld Heilbronn Christy & Viener, N.Y.C., 1999-2001, Leboeuf Lamb Greene & MacRae, N.Y.C., 2001—. Faculty ABA-Am. Law Inst., 1988; neutral mediator Supreme Ct. comml. divsn. 1st jud. dist. State of N.Y. Unified Ct. sys., 1997—; past chmn. global high tech. group Salans Hertzfeld Heilbronn Christy & Viener; co-chmn. intellectual property litigation group LeBoeuf Lamb Greene & MacRae. Mem. Assn. Bar City of N.Y. (com. on computer law 1985-88, chmn. com. on state cts., subcom. on motion practice 1982-84, com. product liability 1994-97), N.Y. State Bar Assn. (com. on class actions and complex civil litigation comml. fed. litigation sect. 1990-99, com. on Internet and litigation 2000—, lectr.), N.Y. Litigators Club (steering com. 1985—), Johns Hopkins U. Alumni Assn. (bd. dirs. met. N.Y. chpt., v.p. 1988—, nat. alumni counsel 1996—). Intellectual property, Computer, General civil litigation. Office: LeBeoeuf Lanb Greene & McRae 125 W 55th St New York NY 10019

MATUSHEK, EDWARD J., III, lawyer; b. Chgo., Feb. 2, 1954; s. Edward J. Jr. and Phyllis A. Matushek; m. Alisa M. Bombassi, Aug. 2, 1980. BA, Ill. Wesleyan U, 1975; JD, John Marshall Law Sch., 1982. Bar: Ill. 1982, U.S. Dist. Ct. (no. dist.) Ill. 1982, U.S. Dist. Ct., Ariz. 1996, U.S. Dist. Ct. (no. dist.) Ind. 2000. Assoc. Haskell & Perrin, Chgo., 1982-89, ptnr., 1989-97, Matushek & Assocs., L.L.C., Chgo., 1998—. Commr. Zoning Bd. Appeals, Village of Tinley Park, Ill., 1985-86, apptd. village trustee, 1986, elected village trustee, 1987-93; bd. dirs. Chgo. Bar Found., 1991-92. Mem. ABA (assembly del., young lawyers div. 1988-90, chair law student outreach commn. 1989-90), Am. Judicature Soc. (bd. dirs. 1992-98), Ill. State Bar Assn., Chgo. Bar Assn. (isntr. Chgo. coalition for law-related edn. 1983-84, chmn. bench-bar rels. com. 1986-87, dir. young lawyers sect. 1987-88, chair young lawyers sect. 1990-91, bd. mgrs. 1992-94, chair CLE com. 2001-2002), Ill. Assn. Def. Trial Counsel, Def. Rsch. Inst. Insurance, Product liability, Toxic tort. Office: Matushek & Assocs LLC One N LaSalle St Ste 3210 Chicago IL 60602

MATZKA, MICHAEL ALAN, lawyer; b. Newark, Oct. 30, 1954; s. John and Liselotte (Heim) M. BS, MIT, 1976; JD, Boston Coll., 1984. Bar: Mass. 1985, U.S. Dist. Ct. Mass. 1985. Assoc. computer systems Index Systems, Inc., Cambridge, Mass., 1976-81; assoc. Sullivan & Worcester, Boston, 1984-92; ptnr. Sullivan & Worcester LLP, 1992-2000, of counsel, 2000—. Mem. ABA. General corporate, Intellectual property, Securities. Office: Sullivan & Worcester LLP 1 Post Office Sq Ste 2300 Boston MA 02109-2129

MAUK, WILLIAM LLOYD, lawyer, investor; b. Pocatello, Idaho, Mar. 15, 1947; s. Jack Lawrence and Doris Lloyd (Shaw) M.; m. Susan Powell Ducker, May 10, 1975; children— Steven Allen and Jonathan Shaw. B.A., U. So. Calif., 1969; M.A., Columbia U., 1971; J.D., Antioch Coll., 1975. Bar: Idaho 1975, U.S. Dist. Ct. Idaho 1975, U.S. Ct. Appeals (9th cir.) 1979. Law clk to assoc. justice Idaho Supreme Ct, Boise, 1975-76; assoc. Eberle, Berlin, Kading, Turbow & Gillespi, Boise, 1976-78; sole practice William L. Mauk, Esq., Boise, 1978-80; ptnr. Skinner, Fawcett & Mauk, Boise, 1980— ; assoc. appellate justice Shoshone-Bannock Tribes, Fort Hall, Idaho, 1977-80; gen. counsel Shoshone-Painte Tribes, Owyhee, Nev., 1980— ; spl. dep. atty.-gen. State of Idaho, 1987—; mem. faculty Nat. Coll. Advocacy. Mem. govs. adv. bd. on worker's compensation, 1985—; mgr. Idaho Indsl. Spl. Indemnity Fund, 1985—; bd. dirs. Idaho Conservation League, Boise, 1976-80; mem. Idaho U.S. Constl. Bicentennial com. Mem. Boise Bar Assn., Idaho Bar Assn., ABA, Idaho Trial Lawyers Assn. (sec., bd. dir. 1978, v.p. 1985-86, pres. 1986-87), Western Trial Lawyers Assn. (bd. dirs. 1987—), Assn. Trial Lawyers Am. (state del. 1987—, membership com. 1987—, v.p. employment law sect. 1988—). Democrat. Unitarian. Contbr. articles to profl. jours. Labor, Personal injury, Workers' compensation. Office: Skinner Fawcett & Mauk 515 S 6th St Boise ID 83702-7634

MAULDIN, JOHN INGLIS, public defender; b. Atlanta, Nov. 6, 1947; s. Earle and Isabel (Inglis) M.; m. Cynthia Ann Balchin, Apr. 15, 1967 (div. Dec. 1985); children: Tracy Rutherford, Abigail Inglis; m. Linda W. Farmer, Nov. 7, 1998. BA, Wofford Coll., 1970; JD, Emory U., 1973. Bar: S.C. 1974, U.S. Ct. Appeals (4th cir.) 1974, U.S. Dist. Ct. S.C. 1975, U.S. Supreme Ct. 1978. Asst. pub. def. Defender Corp. Greenville County, S.C., 1974-76; ptnr. Mauldin & Allison, Greenville, 1977-92; pub. defender Greenville County, S.C., 1992—. Chair S.C. Commn. on Indigent Def., 1993-96; adj. prof. Greenville Tech. Coll., 1975-80; sec., treas. Def. Corp. Greenville County, 1979-92, bd. dirs. Bd. dirs. Speech Hearing & Learning Ctr., Greenville, 1977-90, pres., 1982; bd. dirs. Save Our Sons, 1995—. Named S.C. Atty. Yr. ACLU, S.C., 1986. Mem. Nat. Assn. Criminal Def. Attorneys, Nat. Legal Aid and Defender Assn. (defender policy bd. 1999—), S.C. Trial Lawyers Assn., S.C. Assn. Criminal Def. Lawyers (bd. dirs. 1997-99), S.C. Pub. Defender Assn. (bd. dirs. 1992—), Rotary, Sigma Delta Phi. Democrat. Methodist. Office: PO Box 10264fs Greenville SC 29603

MAULDING, BARRY CLIFFORD, lawyer, director; b. McMinville, Oreg., Sept. 3, 1945; s. Clifford L. and Mildred (Fisher) Maulding; m. Reva J. Zachow, Dec. 27, 1965; children: Phillip B., John C. BA in Psychology, U. Oreg., 1967, JD, 1970. Bar: Oreg. 1970. Sec., gen. counsel Alaska Continental Devel. Corp., Portland, Oreg., 1970—75, Seattle, 1970—75; gen. counsel Alaska Airlines, 1975—84; dir. legal svcs., corp. sec. Univar Corp., 1984—91; v.p., gen. counsel, corp. sec. Prime Source Corp., 1991—. Mem. editl. bd.: law rev. Oreg. Law Rev. Trustee Good Neighbor Found., Seattle. Republican. Contracts commercial, General corporate, Labor.

MAULE, JAMES EDWARD, law educator, lawyer; b. Phila., Nov. 26, 1951; s. Edward Randolph George and Jennie Elisabeth (Zappone) M.; m. Susan Margaret Noonan, June 26, 1982 (div. May 1988); children: Charles Edward, Sarah Margaret; m. Susan K. Garrison, Apr. 7, 1990 (div. 1991). BS cum laude, U. Pa. Wharton Sch., 1973; JD cum laude, Villanova U., 1976; LLM with highest honors, George Washington U., 1979. Bar: Pa. 1976, U.S. Tax Ct. 1986. Atty.-adv. Office Chief Counsel to IRS Legis. and Regulations Divsn., Washington, 1976-78; atty.-adv. judge U.S. Tax Ct., 1978-80; asst. prof. law Dickinson Sch. Law, 1981-83, lectr. and tax program chmn. continuing legal edn., 1981-83; assoc. prof. Villanova Sch. Law, 1983-86, prof., 1986—. Lectr. continuing legal edn. Pa. Bar Inst., Harrisburg, Continuing Legal Edn. Satellite Network, Inc., 1988; lectr. state and local taxes Georgetown U. Law Ctr. Inst., 1992; sr. tax and tech. ptnr. Ctr. Info. Law and Policy, 1993—99; owner JEMBook Pub. Co.; co-owner Starjem LLC. Author: Cases and Materials in Federal Income Taxation, 1981, (21st edit.) , 2001, Materials in Partnership Law and Taxation, 1985, (6th edit.) , 1991, Materials in Partnership Taxation, 1987, (20th edit.) , 2001, Materials in Introduction to Taxation, 1987, (2d edit.) , 1988, Cases and Materials in Introduction to the Taxation of Business Entities, 1992, (9th edit.) , 2001, Materials in Taxation of Fundamental Wealth Transfers , 1986, (2d edit.) , 1988, Materials in Tax Consequences of Disposition of Property, 1983, (3d edit) , 1985, Materials and Problems in Taxation of Property Disposition I, 1987, Materials in Tax Planning for Real Estate, 1986, Materials in Estate and Gift Tax, 1983, (3d edit) , 1985, Materials in Taxation of Real Estate Transactions, 1986, (3d edit.) , 1992, Taxation of Residence Transactions, 1985, S Corporations: State Law and Taxation, 1989; author, author, author, author: S Corporations: State Law and Taxation, 1989, author: Materials and Problems in Computer Applications in the Law, 1990, (6th edit.) , 1995, Materials in Tax Policy, 1990, Materials in Digital Legal Practice Skills, 1996, Materials and Problems in Computer Applications in Tax Law, 1991, (8th edit.) , 1998, Better That 100 Witches Should Live, 1995, (5th edit.) Materials in Decedents Estates and Trusts, 2001; author, author((with A. Clay)): Preparing the 1065 Return, 1992, author: Continuing Legal Edn. Publs., 1981—; contbg. author: Federal Tax Service, Tax Practice Series, —;contbr. articles, chapters to books, monographs; author, developer: Computer Assisted Legal Edn. Programs in Taxation, —, owner, author, editor : computer assisted tax law instruction TaxJEM Inc. , —, cons., prin. author : ABA Section of Taxation Model S Corporation Income Tax Act and Commentary, 1989, author, editor: Report of the Subcommittee on Comparison of S Corporations and Partnerships, 1990, author, editor: author, editor Report of the Subcommittee on Comparison of S Corporations and Partnerships, 1991, case and comment editor : Villanova Law Rev., 1975—76, columnist, mem. editl. bd.: S Corps. Jour., 1987—91, columnist, mem. editl. bd.: Jour. of Ltd. Liability Cos., 1994—98, columnist, mem. editl. bd.: BNA Tax Mgmt., 1994—. Recipient Dist. Author award, BNA Tax Mgmt., 1993; scholar Nat. Merit scholar, 1969—73. Mem. ABA (chair and reporter phaseout Elimination Project, Tax Simplification and Restructuring Com., sect. of taxation, cons., ex-officio mem. subcom. on state law, S Corp. com., chmn. subcom. on comparison of partnerships, mem. task force on pass-through entities, tax sect., former chmn. subcom. manuscripts and unpub. tchg. material, com. tchg. tax), Phila. Bar Assn. (lectr. tax sect. state and local tax CLE program 1991, fed. income taxes 1992—), Ctr. Info. Law and Policy, Order of Coif, Friars Sr. Soc. (Phila), Beta Alpha Psi. Home: 219 Comrie Dr Villanova PA 19085-1402 Office: Villanova U Sch Law Villanova PA 19085 E-mail: maule@law.villanova.edu

MAUPIN, A. WILLIAM, state supreme court justice; children: Allison, Michael. BA, U. Nev., 1968; JD, U. Ariz., 1971. Atty., ptnr. Thorndal, Backus, Maupin and Armstrong, Las Vegas, 1976-93; judge 8th Jud. Dist. Clark County, 1993-97; assoc. justice Supreme Ct. Nev., 1997—. Bd. govs. Nev. State Bar, 1991-95. Recipient highest rating for Retention as Dist. Ct. Judge, 1994, 96, Highest Qualitative Ratings, 1996, Las Vegas Review Jour., Clark County Bar Assn.; highest rating as Supreme Ct. Justice Clark County Bar Assn. and Las Vegas Rev. Jour. judicial poll, 1998, 2000. Mem. Nev. Supreme Ct. (study com. to review jud. elections, chmn. 1995, alternate dispute resolution implementation com. chmn. 1992-96). Office: Nev Supreme Ct 201 S Carson St Carson City NV 89701-4702

MAURENBRECHER, BENEDIKT NIKOLAUS, lawyer; b. St. Gallen, Switzerland, Feb. 1, 1964; s. Karl and Dolores (Karrer) M.; m. Karin Bischof, Aug. 25, 1995; children: Thomas, Jonathan. ML, U. Bern, Switzerland, 1989, PhD summa cum laude, 1994; MBA, INSEAD, Fontainebleau, France, 1999. Bar: Zurich, 1992. Clk. Dist. Ct. Affoltern, Zurich, Switzerland, 1990; atty. Homburger, 1994-98, 2000—; assoc. UBS Warburg, 1999-2000. Dir. Fasimex AG, St. GAllen, 1992-97. Author: Loans at Interest in Swiss Law, 1994; editor (Swiss sect.) Securities Transactions in Europe, 1998; contbg. author: The International Practice of Law. Pres. ZofingerFellowship, Bern, 1998. Soldier Divisional Ct. II, 1994—, Zurich. Mem. Zurich Bar Assn., Swiss Bar Assn. Avocations: traveling, English literature. Office: Homburger Weinbergstrasse 56/58 CH-8006 Zurich Switzerland

MAURO, RICHARD FRANK, lawyer, investment manager; b. Hawthorne, Nev., July 21, 1945; s. Frank Joseph and Dolores D. (Kreimeyer) M.; m. LaVonne M. Madden, Aug. 28, 1965; 1 child, Lindsay Anne. AB, Brown U., 1967; JD summa cum laude, U. Denver, 1970. Bar: Colo. 1970. Assoc. Dawson, Nagel, Sherman & Howard, Denver, 1970-72, Van Cise, Freeman, Tooley & McClearn, Denver, 1972-73, ptnr., 1973-74, Hall & Evans, Denver, 1974-81, Morrison & Forester, Denver, 1981-84; of counsel Parcel & Mauro, P.C., 1984—; pres. Parcel, Mauro & Hultin, P.C., 1988-90; of counsel Parcel, Mauro P.C., 1992-99; pres. Sundance Oil Exploration Co., 1985-88; exec. v.p. Castle Group, Inc., 1992-97, pres., 1998—, Richard F. Mauro, P.C., 1999—; ptnr. Moye, Giles, O'Keefe, Vermeire & Gorrell, 1999—. Adj. prof. U. Denver Coll. Law, 1981-84. Symposium editor: Denver Law Jour., 1969-70; editor: Colorado Corporation Manual; contbr. articles to legal jours. Pres. Colo. Open Space Coun., 1974; mem. law alumni coun. U. Denver Coll. Law, 1988-91. Francis Wayland scholar, 1967; recipient various Am. jurisprudence awards Mem. ABA, Colo. Bar Assn., Denver Bar Assn., Colo. Assn. Corp. Counsel. (pres. 1974-75), Am. Arbitration Assn. (comml. arbitrator), Order St. Ives, Denver Athletic Club (bd. dirs. 1986-89). Contracts commercial, General corporate, Securities. Home: 2552 E Alameda Ave Unit 128 Denver CO 80209-3330 Office: 1225 17th St Fl 29 Denver CO 80202-5534 E-mail: rfmauro@mgorg.com

MAVROUDIS, JOHN M. lawyer; b. N.Y.C., July 24, 1947; s. Michael and Anna (Hariton) M.; m. Anne Drogaris, Dec. 28, 1947; children: Michael, Lauren. JD cum laude, Syracuse Coll. Law, 1972. Bar: N.Y. 1973, N.J. 1975, Fla. 1972. Assoc. Patterson, Belknap & Webb, N.Y.C., 1972-74; sole practice N.Y.C., 1974-77; sr. ptnr. Nicolette & Mavroudis, P.A., Hackensack, N.J., 1978-83, Klinger, Nicolette, Mavroudis & Honig, P.A., 1984-89; sr. ptnr. Mavroudis & Rizzo, 1990—. Trustee The Greek Orthodox Cathedral of St. John the Theologian, N.J., Hellenic Coll. and Holy Cross Greek Orthodox Sch. Theology, Brookline Mass., 1987-91; gen. counsel Greek Orthodox Archdiocese Am., 1997—. Served to capt. USAR. Mem. Bar Assn. City N.Y., Justinian Soc. Editor Syracuse Law Rev., 1972, Archon of the Ecumenical Patriarchate Constantinople, Ellis Island Medal Hon., 1999. Contracts commercial, Real property. Office: 690 Kinderkamack Rd # 300 Oradell NJ 07649-1524

MAX, RODNEY ANDREW, lawyer, mediator; b. Cin., Jan. 28, 1947; s. Howard Nelson and Ruth Max; m. Laurie Gilbert; children: Adam Keith, Jeffery Aaron. Student, Am. U.; BA, U. Fla., 1970; JD cum laude, Cumberland Sch., 1975; grad., Harvard Sch. Negotiation, 1997; postgrad., Pepperdine U., 1999. Bar: Ala. 1975, Fla. 1975, U.S. Ct. Appeals (5th and 11th cirs.) 1975, U.S. Supreme Ct. 1982. From assoc. to ptnr. Najjar Denaburg PC, Birmingham, Ala., 1975-94; ptnr. Sirote & Permutt, PC, 1994—; mem. Jud. Commn. of Jefferson County, 2001—. Ala. adv. com. U.S. Civil Rights Commn., 1985—; CPR regional mediator Inst. for Dispute Resolution; lectr. in field. Officer, bd. dirs. Jewish Cmty. Ctr., Birmingham, 1980—, Family and Child Svcs., Birmingham, 1984—; trustee Temple Emanu-El, sec. 1990-93, v.p., 1992—, 1st v.p., 1997-99, pres., 1999-2001; active Summer Youth Task Force; mem. Camp Birmingham adv. com. Leadership Birmingham, 1989-90, mem. alumni bd., 1990-93; mem. Leadership Ala., 1997-98; bd. dirs., mem. exec. com. NCCJ, 1989—; co-chmn. cmty. affairs com. Operation New Birmingham, pres. exec. com.; bd. dirs. PATH; founder A-Plus; co-chmn. Coalition Against Hate Crimes, 1992—; v.p., mem. exec. com. Mountain Brook City Sch. Found., 1992—; pres. So. Christian Leadership Conf., 2001—. Nominated Citizen of Yr. award Young Bus. Club, 1989; recipient Peggy Spain McDonald award Birmingham Bd. of Edn., 1993, Operation New Birmingham Achievement award, 1996, Better Bus. Bur. Achievement award, 1996, Urban League award, 1998, Brotherhood award NCCJ, 1998, I Have A Dream award of So. Christian Leadership Conf., 1999. Fellow Coll. Atty. Mediators; mem. ABA, ATLA, Ala. Bar Assn. (chmn. task force for alternatives to dispute resolution, co-chmn. increased minority participation, chmn. fee dispute resolution task force), Ala. Trial Lawyers Assn., Ala. Def. Lawyers Assn., Am. Coll. Civil Trial Mediators (bd. dirs., pres.), Am. Arbitration Assn. (arbitrator, mediator, chmn. Ala. adv. coun.), Birmingham Bar Assn. (trustee legal aid 1985-88, mem. exec. bd. 1989-92, sec.-treas. 1993), Am. Acad. Atty. Mediators, Newcomen Soc. U.S., Kiwanis, B'nai B'rith (pres., bd. govts. 1978-85). Democrat. Avocations: sports, politics, children's athletics, religion, internat. relations, interfaith dialogue. Federal civil litigation, State civil litigation. Office: Sirote & Permutt 2311 Highland Ave S Birmingham AL 35205-2972 also: PO Box 55727 Birmingham AL 35255-5727

MAXEINER, JAMES RANDOLPH, lawyer; b. St. Louis, Sept. 7, 1952; s. Philip Arthur and Elaine (Foerster) M.; m. Andrea Dianne Bessac, Aug. 14, 1976. BA, Carleton Coll., 1974; JD in Internat. Legal Affairs, Cornell U., 1977; LLM, Georgetown U., 1981; D in Jurisprudence, U. Munich, Fed. Republic Germany, 1986. Bar: Mo. 1977, D.C. 1978, Ill. 1979, N.Y. 1983, U.S. Dist. Ct. (so. dist.) N.Y. 1983, U.S. Dist. Ct. (ea. dist.) N.Y. 1984, U.S. Ct. Appeals (3d and fed. cirs.) 1985. Trial atty. antitrust div. Dept. Justice, Washington, 1977-80; assoc. Walter, Conston, Alexander & Green P.C. and predecessor firm Walter, Conston & Schurtman P.C., N.Y.C., 1982-88, Kaye, Scholer, Fierman, Hays & Handler, N.Y.C., 1988-92; v.p., assoc. gen. counsel Dun & Bradstreet, Murray Hill, N.J., 1992—. Author: Policy and Methods in German and American Antitrust Law, 1986, Advertising Law in Europe and North America, 1992. Max Rheinstein fellow Max Planck Inst., Munich, 1980-82. Mem. ABA, Am. Fgn. Law Assn. (v.p., editor AFLA newsletter), German Am. Law Assn. (bd. dirs.), Am. Soc. for Legal History, Selden Soc. Lutheran. Antitrust, Computer, Private international. Office: Dun & Bradstreet Inc 1 Diamond Hill Rd New Providence NJ 07974-1218 E-mail: maxeinerj@dnb.com

MAXEY, DAVID WALKER, lawyer; b. Scranton, Pa., May 17, 1934; s. Paul Harold and Margaret (Walker) M.; m. Catharine Eglin, June 6, 1968; children: Paul Eglin, Margaret Wilson. AB, Harvard U., 1956, LLB cum laude, 1960. Bar: Pa. 1961, U. S. Dist. Ct. (ea. dist.) Pa. 1961, U.S. Ct. Appeals (3d cir.) 1963. Assoc. Drinker Biddle and Reath LLP, Phila., 1960-66, ptnr., 1967-2000, chmn. real estate dept., 1970-88, mng. ptnr., 1977-91, co-chmn., 1988-91, of counsel, 2000—. Vis. faculty Villanova (Pa.) U. Law Sch., 1987-95. Contbr. articles to profl. jours. Sec., bd. dirs. Greater Phila. Internat. Network, 1981-94; bd. dirs. Young Audiences Ea. Pa., Phila., 1985-95, Libr. Co., Phila., 1993-2000, sec., 1997-2000; chmn. bd. dirs. Hist. Soc. Pa., Phila., 1991-93; chmn. internat. adv. com. Greater Phila. First, 1994-98; bd. dirs. Gladwyne (Pa.) Libr., 1991-98, pres., 1996-98. Recipient Hughes-Gossett award U.S. Supreme Ct. Hist. Soc., Washington, 1991. Mem. ABA, Pa. Bar Assn., Phila. Bar Assn., Am. Coll. Real Estate Lawyers, Harvard Club Phila. (pres. 1970-72), Merion Cricket Club, Sunday Breakfast Club. Avocation: historical research and publication. Banking, Environmental, Real property. Home: 829 Black Road Rd Gladwyne PA 19035 Office: One Logan Sq 18th and Cherry Streets Philadelphia PA 19103-6996 E-mail: cdmmax@aol.com, maxeydw@dbr.com

MAXFIELD, GUY BUDD, lawyer, educator; b. Galesburg, Ill., May 4, 1933; s. Guy W. and Isabelle B. Maxfield; m. Carol Tunick, Dec. 27, 1970; children: Susan, Stephen, Karen. AB summa cum laude, Augustana Coll., 1955; JD, U. Mich., 1958. Bar: N.Y. 1959. Assoc. White & Case, N.Y.C., 1958-63; prof. law NYU, 1963—. Author: Tennessee Will and Trust Manual, 1982, Federal Estate and Gift Taxation, 7th edit., 1997, Florida Will and Trust Manual, 1984, Tax Planning for Professionals, 1986; contbr. articles to law jours. Trustee Acomb Found., Newark, 1974—. With U.S. Army, 1958-64. Fellow Am. Coll. Tax Counsel; mem. ABA, Am. Law Inst., N.Y. State Bar Assn., Order of Coif, Phi Beta Kappa. Office: NYU Sch Law 40 Washington Sq S New York NY 10012-1099

MAXWELL, BRENDA J. lawyer; b. Detroit, 18 Jan. d. Walter J. and Benjamin M. M.; children: Jonathan, Ethan, Matthew, Alexis. BS, Mich. State U., 1968, MA, 1972; JD, Wayne State U., 1972. Bar: Mich., 1972, D.C., 1978. Gen. counsel bd. dirs. First Independence Nat. Bank, Detroit, 1972-74; defense atty. Legal Aid and Defender Assn., Detrioit, 1974-76; instr. bus. law Wayne Cmty. Coll., 1974-77; ptnr. Maxwell & Smderman, 1976-82; principal atty. Wayne Co. Corp. Counsel, 1987—. Bd. dirs. Legal Aid & Defenders Assn., Detroit, 1998—, Legal Svcs. Corp., Detroit, 1999—. Instr. Ctr. Civic Edn., Detroit, 1995—; bd. dirs. Forster Care Rev. Bd., 1995-97. Mem. ABA (commr.), State Bar Mich., D.C. Bar Assn. Avocations: interior decorating, tennis. Home: 132 Lawrence St Detroit MI 48202-1041 Office: Brenda J Maxwell 26339 Woodward Ave Huntington Woods MI 48070-1331 E-mail: maxwell@worldnet.att.net

MAXWELL, JASON P. lawyer; b. Valparaiso, Ind., May 23, 1973; s. Stanley James and Judith Lynn (Stanton) M. BBA in Fin., U. Miami, 1995; JD, Georgetown U., 1998. Bar: Tex. 1998. Summer assoc. Liddell, Sabb, Zivley, Hill & LaBoon, Dallas, 1997, Fulbright & Jaworski, Dallas, 1997; assoc. Loelxe, Liddell & Sable, 2000—. Mem. Dallas Bar Assn., Dallas Assn. Young Lawyers, Beta Gamma Sigma, Phi Kappa Phi. Republican. Roman Catholic. General corporate, Securities. Office: Locke Liddell & Sapp 2001 Ross Ave Ste 3000 Dallas TX 75201

MAXWELL, JOHN EDWARD, lawyer; b. Waterloo, Iowa, Dec. 31, 1939; s. Nicol Eugene and Elma Lucille (Carr) M.; m. Peggy A. Maxwell, Feb. 14, 1997; children: Julie, Ryan. BA, Wash. State U., 1963, MBA, 1966; JD, Pepperdine U., 1975. Bar: Wash. 1975, Calif. 1975, U.S. Claims Ct. 1990. Sales rep. Exxon Corp., Seattle, 1966-69, analyst L.A., 1969-75; ptnr. Blechschmidt, Bingman & Maxwell, Grandview, Wash., 1975-85; pvt. practice, 1985—. Bd. dirs. Grandview Devel. Corp. Pres. Men's Rep. Club, Grandview, 1977, Campfire Girls Am., Grandview, 1978. Mem. Wash. State Bar Assn. (spl. dist. counsel 1988—), Calif. Bar Assn. (inactive), Yakima County Bar Assn., Ea. Wash. Fed. Bar Assn., Grandview C. of C. (pres. 1977), Rotary (pres. Grandview chpt. 1984-85), Elks. Presbyterian. Avocations: skiing, reading. Bankruptcy, General civil litigation, Family and matrimonial. Home: 117 Ash St Grandview WA 98930-1316 Office: 201 E 2nd St Grandview WA 98930-1347 E-mail: jmaxwell@quicktel.com

MAXWELL, ROBERT EARL, federal judge; b. Elkins, W.Va., Mar. 15, 1924; s. Earl L. and Nellie E. (Rexstrew) M.; m. Ann Marie Grabowski, Mar. 29, 1948; children— Mary Ann, Carol Lynn, Ellen Lindsay, Earl Wilson. LLD (hon.), Davis and Elkins Coll., 1984; LLB, W.Va. U., 1949; LLD (hon.), Davis and Elkins Coll., 1984. Bar: W.Va. 1949. Practiced in, Randolph County, 1949; pros. atty., 1952-61; U.S. atty. for No. Dist. W.Va., 1961-64; judge, then sr. judge U.S. Dist. Ct. (no. dist.) W.Va., Elkins, 1965—; judge Temp. Emergency Ct. of Appeals, 1980-89. Past chmn. budget com. Jud. Conf. U.S.; former mem. exec. com. Nat. Conf. Fed. Trial Judges; former mem. adv. bd. W.Va. U. Mem. bd. advisors W.Va. U., past chmn.; bd. advisors Mary Babb Randolph Cancer Ctr. Recipient Alumni Disting. Svc. award Davis and Elkins Coll., 1969, Religious Heritage Am. award, 1979, Outstanding Trial Judge award W.Va. Trail Lawyers Assn., 1988, Order of Vandalia award W.Va. U., Outstaning Alumnus award, 1992, Tenured Faculty Mem. Recognition award Bd. Govs., Def. Trail Coun., W.Va., 1992, Cert. of Merit, W.Va. State Bar, 1994, Justitia Officium award Coll. of Law, W.Va. U., 1994; fellow W.Va. Bar Found., 1999; Melvin Jones fellow Lions Internat. Found., 2001. Mem. Nat. Conf. Federal Trial Judges, Dist. Judges Assn. 4th Cir. (past pres.), Moose (life), Lions (life), Beta Alpha Beta (merit award), Elkins-Randolph County C. of C. (citizen of yr. 1994). Office: US Dist Ct No Dist PO Box 1275 Elkins WV 26241-1275 E-mail: rmaxwell@neumedia.net

MAXWELL, ROBERT WALLACE, II, lawyer; b. Sept. 6, 1943; s. Robert Wallace and Margaret Maxwell; m. Mamie Lee Payne, June 18, 1966; children: Virginia, Robert, William. BS magna cum laude, Hampden-Sydney Coll., 1965; JD with hons., Duke U., 1968. Bar: Ohio 1968. Assoc. Taft, Stettinius & Hollister, Cin., 1968—75, ptnr., 1975—88, Keating, Muething & Klekamp, Cin., 1988—. Instr. U. Cin. Sch. Law, 1975—76. Elder Wyoming Presbyn. Ch.; bd. dir. Contemporary Arts Ctr. of Cin., Cin. Ballet Co. Mem.: ABA, Am. Assn. Mus. Trustees. Republican. Federal civil litigation, State civil litigation, Labor. Home: 535 Larchmont Dr Cincinnati OH 45215-4215 Office: Keating Muething & Klekamp 1 E 4th St Ste 1800 Cincinnati OH 45202-3752

MAY, ALAN ALFRED, lawyer; b. Detroit, Apr. 7, 1942; s. Alfred Albert and Sylvia (Sheer) M.; m. Elizabeth Miller; children: Stacy Ann, Julie Beth. BA, U. Mich., 1963, JD, 1966. Bar: Mich. 1967, D.C. 1976; former reg. nursing home adminstr., Mich. Ptnr. May and May, PC, Detroit, 1979—. Spl. asst. atty. gen. State of Mich., 1970—; pres., instr. Med-Leg Seminars, Inc., 1978; lectr. Wayne State U., 1974; instr. Oakland U., 1969. Chmn. Rep. 18th Congressional Dist. Com., 1983-87, now chmn. emeritus; chmn. 19th Congressional Dist. Com., 1981-83; mem. Mich. Rep. Com., 1976-84; del. Rep. Nat. Conv., 1984, rules com., 1984; del. Rep. Nat. Conv., 1988, platform com., 1988; former chmn. Mich. Civil Rights Commn.; former mem. Mich. Civil Svc. Commn., 1984-88; trustee NCCJ (exec. bd., vice chmn. nat conf. for cmty. and justice), Temple Beth El Birmingham, Mich., pres. exec. bd.; mem. Electoral Coll.; bd. dirs. ADL, Mich.; bd. dirs. exec. bd., pres., Detroit Region/Nat. Conf. Cmty. and Justice, Charfoos Charitable Found. Mem. Nat. Conf. Cmty. and Justice (exec. bd., vice chmn.), Detroit Bar Assn., Oakland County Bar Assn., Victors Club, Franklin Hills Country Club (past pres., bd. dirs.), President's Club (trustee). State civil litigation, Probate, Workers' compensation. Home: 4140 Echo Rd Bloomfield Hills MI 48302-1941 Office: May & May PC 3000 Town Ctr Ste 2600 Southfield MI 48075-1375

MAY, DENISE EATON, general counsel; b. L.A., Aug. 20, 1960; d. Dewitt Eaton and Delia Quick; m. Roderick W. May, Jr., Oct. 5, 1991; childreN: Shenelle Eaton, Shevonne May, Jacquelynn May. BA, U. Calif., San Diego, 1981; JD, U. Calif., Davis, 1984. Bar: Calif. Legal counsel Office Adminstrv. Law, Sacramento, 1984-85; dep. atty. gen. Calif. Dept. Justice, 1985-97; dep. county counsel Alameda County, Oakland, Calif., 1997-99; gen. counsel Alameda County Retirement Assn., 1999—. Avocations: violin, dance, children's advocacy, environmentalism.

MAY, FRANK BRENDAN, JR. lawyer; b. Bronx, N.Y., Oct. 17, 1945; s. Frank Brendan and Margaret (Borza) M.; m. Mary Frances Fitzsimmons, June 19, 1976; children: David Brendan, Brian Christopher. BA in Econs., NYU, 1973, postgrad., 1973-75; JD, John Marshall Law Sch., Chgo., 1978. Bar: Ill. 1979, U.S. Dist. Ct. (no. dist.) Ill. 1979, U.S. Ct. Appeals (7th cir.), 1979, U.S. Supreme Ct. 1995, lic. Ill. real estate broker 1994. Legal intern criminal div. Cook County State's Atty.'s Office, Chgo., 1977-78; legal intern juvenile div. DuPage County State's Atty.'s Office, Wheaton, 1978; sr. assoc. atty. Lillig, Kemp & Thorness, Ltd., Oak Brook, 1978-81; v.p., gen. counsel Coldwell Banker, 1981-90, Prudential Preferred Properties,

Des Plaines, Ill., 1991-98, Law Offices, Frank B. May, Jr., Wheaton, 1999-2001; sr. corp. atty. Budget Rent a Car Corp., Lisle, 2001—. Arbitrator 18th Jud. Cir. Ct., Dupage County, Ill., 1993—. Dir. Ray Graham Found. for People with Disabilities, 1999—. Sgt. USAF, 1963-67. NYU Coun. scholar, 1971-73; David Davis Meml. scholar, 1970-71. Mem. Ill. State Bar Assn. (real estate sect.), DuPage county Bar Assn. (real estate law com.), Medinah Country Club (mem. legal/bylaws com. 1998-2000, membership com. 1997—, chmn. PGA credentials com. 1999), Ill. Assn. Realtors (mem. large brokers coun. 1996-98, exec. com., fin. com. 1998-, lic. law rewrite task force, nominating com. 1998-99), Realtor Assn. Western Suburbs (legal counsel 1999-2000). Avocations: golf, music, gourmet cooking, wine collector. General civil litigation, General corporate, Real property. Home: 2064 Stonebridge Ct Wheaton IL 60187-7177 Office: Budget Rent a Car Corp 4225 Naperville Rd Lisle IL 60532-3662 Fax: 630-665-7456. Business E-Mail: fmay@budgetgroup.com

MAY, GREGORY EVERS, lawyer; b. Harrisonburg, Va., Sept. 17, 1953; s. Russell J. and Arlene Virginia (Ringgold) M. AB, Coll. of William and Mary, 1975; JD, Harvard U., 1978. Bar: Va. 1978, U.S. Dist. Ct. (ea. dist.) Va. 1979, U.S. Ct. Appeals (4th cir.) 1979, U.S. Claims Ct. 1981, U.S. Tax Ct. 1981, D.C. 1985, N.Y. 1988. Law clk. to Judge Butzner U.S. Ct. Appeals (4th cir.), Richmond, Va., 1978-79; law clk. to Justice Powell U.S. Supreme Ct., Washington, 1979-80; assoc. Hunton & Williams, Richmond, 1980-83, Washington, 1984-86, ptnr., 1986-89, Milbank, Tweed, Hadley & McCloy, Washington, 1989—. Articles editor Harvard Law Rev., 1977-78. Mem. ABA, Va. State Bar, D.C. Bar, N.Y. State Bar. Corporate taxation. Office: Milbank Tweed Hadley & McCloy 1825 I St NW Ste 1100 Washington DC 20006-5492

MAY, JOSEPH LESERMAN (JACK MAY), lawyer; b. Nashville, May 27, 1929; s. Daniel and Dorothy (Fishel) M.; m. Natalie McCuaig, Apr. 12, 1957 (dec. May 1990); children: Benjamin, Andrew, Joshua, Maria; m. Lynn Hewes Lance, June 10, 1994. BA, Yale U., 1951; JD, NYU, 1958; postgrad., Harvard Bus. Sch., 1969. Bar: Tenn. 1959. Prodr. Candied Yam Jackson Show, 1947-51; with CIA, 1951-55; pres. Nuweave Socks, Inc., N.Y.C., 1955-59, May Hosiery Mills, Nashville, 1960-83, Athens Hosiery Mills, Tenn., 1966-83; v.p. Wayne-Gossard Corp., Chattanooga, 1972-83; pvt. practice law Nashville, 1984—. Bd. dirs. Focus 20 Master Trust, Princeton, N.J., World Income Fund, Princeton, Merrill Lynch Growth Fund; dir. Signal Apparel, 1984-89; mem. adv. group Civil Justice Reform Act U.S. Dist. Ct., 1991; mem. adv. bd. Asian Strategies Group, 1994. Bd. dirs. Vanderbilt Cancer Ctr., 1994-99; pres. Jewish Cmty. Ctr., 1969; chmn. Guardianship and Trust Corp., 1994-96, Campus for Human Devel., 2000; mem. AAA panel of neutrals. With USN, 1947-53, U.S. Army, 1954. Mem. Tenn. Bar Assn., Nashville Bar Assn., Am. Arbitration Assn. Panel of Neutrals, Tenn. Hist. Soc. (trustee, pres. 2000), Eagle Scout Assn., Belle Meade Country Club, Shamus Club, Old Oak Club, Yale Club N.Y., Rotary (pres. Nashville 1971). Home: 133 Abbottsford Nashville TN 37215-2442 Office: PO Box 190628 424 Church St Ste 2000 Nashville TN 37219-3304

MAY, JUDY ROYER, lawyer; b. Pottstown, Pa., Nov. 17, 1965; d. Armand Myers and Florence Geraldine Royer; m. Scott Douglas May, Oct. 6, 1995; children: Michael, Ryan. BMus summa cum laude, Susquehanna U., 1987; JD magna cum laude, Villanova U., 1995. Bar: Del. 1995, Pa. 1998, N.J. 1998. Assoc. Potter, Anderson & Corroon, Wilmington, Del., 1995-97, Stevens & Lee, P.C., Wayne, Pa., 1997-99, Stradley, Ronon, Stevens & Young, LLP, Phila., 1999—. Contbr. articles to profl. jours. Mem. ABA, Pa. Bar Assn. Del. Trial Lawyers Assn., Del. State Bar Assn., Chester County Bar Assn. General civil litigation, Contracts commercial, Securities. Office: Great Vly Corp Ctr 30 Valley Stream Pkwy Malvern PA 19355-1407 E-mail: jmay@stradley.com

MAY, LAWRENCE EDWARD, lawyer; b. N.Y.C., Aug. 7, 1947; s. Jack and Ann Marie (Schnell) M.; m. Rosalind Marsha Israel, Feb. 3, 1979; children: Jeremy, Lindsey. BA, UCLA, 1969, JD, 1972. Bar: Calif. 1972, N.Y. 1973. Assoc. Paul, Weiss, Rifkind, Wharton & Garrison, N.Y.C., 1972-76, Levine, Krom & Unger, Beverly Hills, Calif., 1976-79, Weissburg & Aronson, L.A., 1979-81, Valensi & Rose, L.A., 1981-83; prin. Lawrence E. May, P. C., 1983—, 1984—. Bd. dirs. Pub. Counsel, 1989-97; pres., 1995-96. Mem. editorial adv. bd. L.A. Jewish Jour., 1985-91, exec. com. Pacific S.W. Region Anti-Defamation League, 1985—; bd. dirs. L.A. Youth, 1997—. Mem. State Bar Calif., Los Angeles County Bar Assn. (trustee 1987-88, pro bono coun. 1995-98), Beverly Hills Bar Assn. (bd. govs. 1981-90, pres. 1988-89, chmn. bus. law sect. 1984-85). Democrat. Avocations: current events, golf, family activities. General corporate, Estate planning, Real property. Office: Ste 2050 1925 Century Park East Los Angeles CA 90067-2725 E-mail: lmay@maylaw.com

MAYBERRY, ALAN REED, lawyer; b. Akron, Ohio, Mar. 15, 1954; s. Franklin Reed Mayberry and Mark K. (Kissane) Mayberry Alexander Botten; m. Lisa Renee Rush, Dec. 19, 1981; children: Reed Alan, Mason Rush, Clark Carroll. BS in Edn., Bowling Green State U., 1975; JD, U. Toledo, 1978; postgrad., Nat. Coll. Dist. Attys., Nat. Law Inst. Faculty Nat. Advocacy Ctr. Office: Wood County Prosecuting Attys Office 1 Court House Sq Bowling Green OH 43402-2427 E-mail: amayberry@co.wood.oh.us

MAYDEN, BARBARA MENDEL, lawyer; b. Chattanooga, Sept. 18, 1951; d. Eugene Lester Mendel and Blanche (Krugman) Rosenberg; m. Martin Ted Mayden, Sept. 14, 1986. AB, Ind. U., 1973; JD, U. Ga., 1976. Bar: Ga. 1976, N.Y. 1980. Assoc. King & Spalding, Atlanta, 1976-79, Willkie Farr & Gallagher, N.Y.C., 1980, Morgan Lewis & Bockius, N.Y.C., 1980-82, White & Case, N.Y.C., 1982-89; spl. counsel Skadden, Arps, Slate, Meagher & Flom, 1989-95; mem. Bass, Berry & Sims PLC, Nashville, 1996—; lectr. Vanderbilt U. Sch. Law, 1995-97. Mem. bd. visitors U. Ga., Athens, 1986-89; mem. Leadership Nashville, 1999-2000; mem. adv. bd. Women's Fund of the Cmty. Found. of Mid. Tenn., 2001—; bd. dis. YWCA, 2001—, Jewidh Cmty. Ctr., 2001—. Fellow Am. Bar Found. (life); mem. ABA (sec. bus. law sect., chair young lawyers div. 1985-86, house of dels. 1986—, commr. commn. on women 1987-91, commr. commn. opportunities for minorities in profession 1986-87, chmn. assembly resolutions com. 1990-91, select com. of the house 1989-91, membership com. of the house 1991-92, chair com. on rules and calendar 1996-98, bd. govs. 1991-94, chair bd. govs. ops. com., exec. com. 1993-94, mem. task force long range fin. planning 1993-94, com. scope correlation of work 1998—, chair 2001-2002), Nat. Assn. Bond Lawyers (bd. dirs. 1985-86), Bond Attys.' Workshop (chmn. 1986), N.Y. State Bar Assn. (mem. ho. of dels. 1993-95), Assn. of Bar of City of N.Y. (internat. human rights com. 1986-89, 2d century com. 1986-90, com. women in the profession, 1989-92), N.Y. County Lawyers Assn. (com. spl. projects, chair com. rels with other bars), Am. Law Inst. Democrat. Jewish. General corporate, Mergers and acquisitions, Securities. Home: 4414 Herbert Pl Nashville TN 37215-4544 Office: Bass Berry & Sims PLC 315 Deaderick St Ste 2700 Nashville TN 37238-0002 E-mail: bmayden@bassberry.com

MAYER, CARL JOSEPH, prosecutor, lawyer; b. Boston, Apr. 23, 1959; s. Arno Joseph and Nancy Sue (Grant) M. AB magna cum laude, Princeton U., 1981; JD, U. of Chgo., 1986; LLM, Harvard U., 1988. Bar: N.J. 1986, Mass. 1988, N.Y. 1989, D.C. 1989. Writer for Ralph Nader, Washington, 1981-83; law clk. to presiding justice U.S. Dist. Ct., Wilmington, Del., 1986-87; law assoc., prof. Hofstra Law Sch., Hempstead, N.Y., 1989-94; atty. Milberg, Weiss, Bershad, Hynes and Lerach, N.Y.C., 1995-96; spl. counsel N.Y. State Atty. Gen.'s Office, 1999—. Cons. U.S. Senate Com., Washington, 1988-89. Author: Shakedown, 1998; co-author: Public Domain, Private Dominion, 1985; contbr. articles to profl. jours. Town committeeman, Princeton, N.J., 1995-98. NYU fellow, 1988-89. Mem. ABA, N.Y. Bar Assn., N.J. Bar Assn., Mass. Bar Assn. Avocations: marathon running, squash, tennis. Home: 58 Battle Rd Princeton NJ 08540-4902 Office: NY State Atty Gen Office 120 Broadway New York NY 10271-0002 E-mail: carlmayer@aol.com

MAYER, FRANK D., JR. lawyer; b. Dec. 23, 1933; BA, Amherst Coll., 1955; student, Cambridge U.; JD, U. Chgo., 1959. Bar: Ill. 1959. Ptnr. Mayer, Brown & Platt, Chgo. Mem. ABA, Chgo. Bar Assn., Order of Coif, Phi Beta Kappa. Office: Mayer Brown & Platt 190 S La Salle St Ste 3100 Chicago IL 60603-3441 E-mail: fmayer@mayerbrown.com

MAYER, HALDANE ROBERT, federal chief judge; b. Buffalo, Feb. 21, 1941; s. Haldane Rupert and Myrtle Kathleen (Gaude) M.; m. Mary Anne McCurdy, Aug. 13, 1966; children: Anne Christian, Rebecca Paige. BS, U.S. Mil. Acad., 1963; JD, Coll. William and Mary, 1971. Bar: Va. 1971, U.S. Ct. Appeals (4th cir.) 1972, U.S. Dist. Ct. (ea. dist.) Va. 1972, U.S. Ct. Mil. Appeals, U.S. Army Ct. Mil. Rev. 1973, D.C. 1980, U.S. Supreme Ct. 1977, U.S. Ct. Claims 1984. Law clk. U.S. Ct. Appeals (4th cir.), Richmond, Va., 1971-72; atty. McGuire Woods & Battle, Charlottesville, 1975-77; spl. asst. to chief justice U.S. Supreme Ct., Washington, 1977-80; atty. Baker & McKenzie, 1980-81; acting spl. counsel U.S. Merit Systems Protection Bd., 1981-82; judge U.S. Claims Ct., 1982-87, U.S. Ct. Appeals (Fed. cir.), Washington, 1987-97, chief judge, 1997—. Adj. prof. U. Va. Sch. Law, 1975-77, 92-94, George Washington U. Law Sch., 1992-96. Bd. dirs. William and Mary Law Sch. Assn., 1979-85. Served to maj. AUS, 1963-75, lt. col. res. ret. Decorated Bronze Star, two Army Commendation medals, Meritorious Service medal. Mem. West Point Assn. Grads., Army Athletic Assn., West Point Soc. D.C., Omicron Delta Kappa Office: US Ct Appeals for Fed Cir 717 Madison Pl NW Washington DC 20439-0002

MAYER, JAMES HOCK, mediator, lawyer; b. Neptune City, N.J., Nov. 1, 1935; s. J. Kenneth and Marie Ruth (Hock) M.; m. Carol I. Keating, Sept. 20, 1958 (div. Feb. 1981); children: Craig, Jeffrey; m. Patrisha Renk, Mar. 28, 1981 (div. July 2001). AB with distinction, Dartmouth Coll., 1957; JD, Harvard U., 1964. Bar: Calif. 1965, U.S. Dist. Ct (no. dist., so. dist.) Calif. 1965, U.S. Ct. Appeals (9th cir.) 1965, U.S. Supreme Ct. 1974. Assoc. Pillsbury, Madison & Sutro, San Francisco, 1964-72, ptnr., 1973—; ind. mediator, 1992—. Rear adm. USNR, 1957-93. Rufus Choate scholar Dartmouth Coll., 1956-57. Mem. Newcomen Soc., Navy League, Naval Order of U.S., Harvard Club. Alternative dispute resolution, Contracts commercial, General corporate. Office: 12707 High Bluff Dr pmb 200 San Diego CA 92130-2037 E-mail: just-results@msn.com

MAYER, JAMES JOSEPH, retired corporate lawyer; b. Cin., Nov. 27, 1938; s. Cletus Joseph and Berna Mae (Schroeder) M.; m. Margaret Ann Hobbs, Oct. 24, 1964; children: Kimberly, Susanne, Terri. BEE, U. Cin., 1961; JD, No. Ky. U., 1969. Registered profl. engr., Ohio. Bar: Ohio 1969, Ky. 1975. Engr. Cin. Gas & Electric Co., 1961-69, atty., 1969-85, gen. counsel, 1986-91, v.p., gen. counsel, 1991-95, ret., 1995; of counsel Taft, Stetinius & Hollister, Cin., 1995—. With USAFR, 1961-64. Mem. Ohio Bar Assn., Ky. Bar Assn., Cin. Bar Assn., Bankers Club. Republican. Roman Catholic. Avocations: home remodeling, sports, golf. Administrative and regulatory, General corporate, Public utilities. E-mail: mayer@taftlaw.com

MAYER, JOHN WILLIAM, lawyer; b. Houston, Nov. 17, 1941; s. Maurice William and Julie Eldee (Borddofsky) M.; m. M. Ann Jodoin, July 30, 1972; children: Norbert, Kristin, Mara. BA in Econs., Vanderbilt U., 1963; JD, U. Chgo., 1966; postgrad. Nat. Jud. Coll., 1984. Bar: Ill. 1966, U.S. Ct. Mil. Appeals 1971, Colo. 1987, Ala. 1987. Assoc. Lorenz & Stamler, Newark, 1963-66; estate tax atty. IRS, Chgo., 1966-67; commd. 2d lt., USAF, 1967, advanced through grades to lt. col., 1980; judge advocate USAF, 1967-87; dep. dist. atty., 15th Jud. Dist. Ala., Montgomery, 1987-90; dep. atty. gen. State of Ala., 1990-91; chief dep. dist. atty. 15th Jud. Dist. Ala., Montgomery, 1991-98, pvt. practice, 1998—; adj. prof. Jones Coll. of Law, 1998—. Nat. Honor scholar U. Chgo., 1963; recipient Nat. Pub. Defender's award, Chgo., 19 66. Mem. ABA (chmn. mil. judges com. 1984—), Assn. Trial Lawyer's Am., Zeta Beta Tau, Phi Delta Phi, Standard Club. Jewish.

MAYER, NEAL MICHAEL, lawyer; b. N.Y.C., Dec. 4, 1941; s. Joseph Henry and Cele (Brodsky) M.; m. Jane Ellen Greenberg, Aug. 24, 1963; children: Andrew Warren, Amy Lynn, Rebecca Ann, Jenny Leigh. BA in History with honors, Kenyon Coll., 1963; JD, Georgetown U., 1966. Bar: D.C. 1967, U.S. Dist. Ct. D.C. 1967, U.S. Ct. Appeals (D.C. cir.) 1967, U.S. Customs Ct. 1967, U.S. Supreme Ct. 1970, U.S. Ct. Appeals (5th cir.) 1975. Assoc. Coles & Goertner, Washington, 1966-71, ptnr., 1971-82; sr. ptnr. Hoppel, Mayer & Coleman, 1982—. Trustee Kenyon Coll., 1995—. Mem. ABA, D.C. Bar Assn., Maritime Adminstrv. Bar Assn. (pres. 1979), Assn. for Transp. Law, Logistics and Policy, Propeller Club of U.S. (Washington), Kenyon Coll. Alumni Assn. (pres. 1993-94). Administrative and regulatory, Admiralty, Transportation. Office: Hoppel Mayer & Coleman 1000 Connecticut Ave NW Washington DC 20036-5302 E-mail: nmayer@hmc-law.com

MAYER, RENEE G. lawyer; b. Elizabeth, N.J., Apr. 17, 1933; d. Harry and Bertha Sheinblatt Miller; m. Joseph C. Mayer, June 19, 1955; children: Douglas, Julia, Amy, Andrew. BS, Cornell U., 1955; JD, Hofstra U., 1978. Bar: N.Y. 1979, U.S. Dist. Ct. (ea. dist.) N.Y. 1979, U.S. Ct. Appeals (2d cir.) 1983, U.S. Supreme Ct. 1982. Assoc. atty. Meyer, English & Cianciulli, Mineola, N.Y., 1978-79; pvt. practice, 1979-89; ptnr. Riebesehl, Mayer, Keegan & Horowitz, Garden City, 1989-97; pvt. practice law Mineola, 1997-2001, Port Washington, 2001—. Mem. N.Y. State Bar Assn., Nassau Lawyers Assn. Long Island, Inc. (pres. 1996-97, first vice chancellor conf. of continuing legal edn.), Nassau County Women's Bar Assn. (pres. 1985-86), Nassau County Bar Assn. (dir. 1984-87, asst. dean acad. law 1987-91), Cornell Club (bd. govs. 1980-90), Democratic Com. (zone leader, Port. Washington, N.Y., 1980-93). Avocations: reading, theatre, travel. Family and matrimonial. Home and Office: 7 Leeds Dr Port Washington NY 11050-4116

MAYERLE, THOMAS MICHAEL, lawyer; b. Grand Rapids, Minn., Jan. 5, 1948; s. James Raphael and Frances (Kosher) M.; m. Susan Terry Potter, Oct. 9, 1976; children— Jennifer Leigh, Scott Michael, Robert Michael. A.B., Dartmouth Coll., 1970; J.D. magna cum laude, U. Minn., 1973. Bar: Minn. 1973, U.S. Ct. Appeals (D.C. cir.) 1973. Law clk. to justice U.S. Ct. Appeals (D.C. cir.), Washington, 1973-74; ptnr. Faegre & Benson, Mpls., 1974— . Note and articles editor Minn. Law Rev., 1972-73. Mem. Minn. State Bar Assn., Hennepin County Bar Assn., Order of Coif. Construction, Landlord-tenant, Real property. Home: 5905 Chapel Dr Minneapolis MN 55439-1716 Office: Faegre & Benson 2200 Norwest Ctr 90 S 7th St Ste 2200 Minneapolis MN 55402-3901

MAYERSON, SANDRA ELAINE, lawyer; b. Dayton, Ohio, Feb. 8, 1952; d. Manuel David and Florence Louise (Tepper) M.; m. Scott Burns, May 29, 1977 (div. Oct. 1978); 1 child, Katy Joy. BA cum laude, Yale U., 1973; JD, Northwestern U., 1976. Bar: Ill. 1976, U.S. Ct. Appeals (7th cir.) 1976, U.S. Dist. Ct. (no. dist.) Ill. 1977, U.S. Dist. Ct. Md. 1989, U.S. Ct. Appeals (5th cir.) 1994. Assoc. gen. counsel JMB Realty Corp., Chgo., 1979-80; assoc. Chatz, Sugarman, Abrams et al, 1980-81; ptnr. Pollack, Mayerson & Berman, 1981-83; dep. gen. counsel AM Internat., Inc., 1983-85; ptnr. Kirkland & Ellis, 1985-87; ptnr., chmn. bankruptcy group Kelley Drye & Warren, N.Y.C., 1987-93; ptnr., chmn. N.Y. bankruptcy group McDermott, Will & Emery, 1993-99; ptnr. Holland and Knight, 1999—. Examiner Interco chpt. 11, 1991. Bd. dirs. Jr. Med. Rsch. Inst. coun. Michael Reese Hosp., Chgo., 1981-86; mem. met. div. Jewish Guild for Blind, 1990-92; mem. nat. legal affairs com. Anti-Defamation League, 1990—; mem. lawyers' exec. com. United Jewish Appeal. Fellow Branford Coll., Yale U., 1993—. Mem. ABA (bus. bankruptcy com. 1976—, sec. 1990-93, chair avoiding powers subcom. 1993-96, chair claims trading subcom. 1997—), Ill. State Bar Assn. (governing council corp. and securities sect. 1983-86), Chgo. Bar Assn. (current events chmn. corp. sect. 1980-81), 7th Cir. Bar Assn., Yale Club (N.Y.C.). Democrat. Jewish. Bankruptcy, General corporate. Office: Holland and Knight 195 Broadway Fl 24 New York NY 10007-3100

MAYNARD, ELLIOTT, state supreme court justice; b. Williamson, W.Va. BS in Psychology, Fla. So. Coll., 1967; JD, W.Va. U., 1974. Judge W.Va. Cir. Ct. 30th Jud. Cir., 1982-97; justice W.Va. Supreme Ct. Appeals, Charleston, 1997—. Prosecuting atty., Mingo County, 1976, 80. Mng. dir. Tug Valley C. of C., 1968-70; active Boy Scouts Am.; dist. chmn. Mingo-Pike Dist., Chief Cornstalk Dist.; bd. dirs. Buckskin Coun. With USAF, 1961-66. Recipient Silver Beaver award Boy Scouts Am. Office: State Capital State Ct Appeals Bldg 1 Rm E306 Charleston WV 25305*

MAYNARD, JOHN RALPH, lawyer; b. Mar. 5, 1942; s. John R. and Frances Jane (Mitchell) Maynard Kendryk; m. Meridee J. Sagadin, Sept. 10, 1995; children: Bryce James, Pamela Ann. BA, U. Wash., 1964; JD, Calif. Western U., San Diego, 1972; LLM, Harvard U., 1973. Bar: Calif. 1972, Wis. 1973. Assoc. Whyte & Hirschboeck, Milw., 1973-78, Minahan & Peterson, Milw., 1979-91, Quarles & Brady, Milw., 1991-2000, Davis & Kuelthau, Milw., 2000—. Bd. dirs. Am. Heart Assn., 1979-82, Transitional Living Svcs., Inc., 2000—; pres. Milw. Chamber Orch., 2000—; mem. Wis. Adv. Coun. to U.S. SBA, 1987-89. Lt. USN, 1964-69. Mem. ABA, Harvard Club (Wis.), Milw. Yacht Club. Contracts commercial, General corporate, Estate planning. Home: 809 E Lake Forest Ave Milwaukee WI 53217-5377 Office: Davis & Kuelthau 111 E Kilbourn Ste 1400 Milwaukee WI 53202

MAYNARD, ROBERT HOWELL, retired lawyer; b. San Antonio, Feb. 15, 1938; s. William Simpson Sr. and Lillian Isabel (Tappan) M.; m. Joan Marie Pearson, Jan. 6, 1962; children: Gregory Scott, Patricia Kathryn, Alicia Joan, Elizabeth Simms. BA, Baylor U., 1959, LLB, 1961; LLM, Georgetown U., 1965. Bar: Tex. 1961, D.C. 1969, Ohio 1973. Trial atty. gen. litigation sect. lands div. U.S. Dept. Justice, Washington, 1964-65; spl. asst. to solicitor U.S. Dept. Interior, 1965-69; legis. asst. U.S. Senate, 1969-73; ptnr., dept. head Smith & Schnacke, Dayton, Ohio, 1973-83; dir. Ohio EPA, Columbus, 1983-85; ptnr., environ. policy and strategy devel., tech. law Vorys, Sater, Seymour and Pease, 1985-2000; ret., 2000; pres. Tappan Woods LLC, 2001—. Trustee Ohio Found. for Entrepren. Edn., Business Technology Ctr., 1994-2000, Episcopal Cmty. Svcs. Found., 1990-96, Industry & Tech. Coun. Ctrl. Ohio, Johnson's Island Preservation Soc. USNR, 1962-65. Episcopalian. Administrative and regulatory, Environmental, Natural resources. Office: Vorys Sater Seymour & Pease PO Box 1008 52 E Gay St Columbus OH 43215-1008

MAYNE, WILEY EDWARD, lawyer; b. Sanborn, Iowa, Jan. 19, 1917; s. Earl W. and Gladys (Wiley) M.; m. Elizabeth Dodson, Jan. 5, 1942; children— Martha (Mrs. F.K. Smith), Wiley Edward, John. S.B. cum laude, Harvard, 1938; student, Law Sch., 1938-39; J.D., State U. Iowa, 1939-41. Bar: Iowa bar 1941, U.S. Supreme Ct. 1950. Practiced in, Sioux City, 1946-66, 75—; mem. Shull, Marshall, Mayne, Marks & Vizintos, 1946-66, Mayne and Berenstein, 1975-87, Mayne & Mayne, 1988-99, Mayne, Marks, Madsen and Hirschbach, 1999—. Spl. agt. FBI, 1941-43; Mem. 90th-93d Congresses, 6th Dist. Iowa; mem. judiciary com., agr. com. Commr. from Iowa Nat. Conf. Commrs. Uniform State Laws, 1956-60; chmn. grievance commn. Iowa Supreme Ct., 1964-66; del. FAO, 1973; chmn. Woodbury County Compensation Bd., 1975-80 Chmn. Midwest Rhodes Scholar Selection Com., 1964-66; pres. Sioux City Symphony Orch. Assn., 1947-54, Sioux City Concert Course, 1982-85; vice chmn. Young Republican Nat. Fedn., 1948-50; bd. dirs. Iowa Bar Found., 1962-68. Served to lt. (j.g.) USNR, 1943-46. Fellow Am. Coll. Trial Lawyers; mem. ABA (ho. of dels. 1966-68), Iowa Bar Assn. (pres. 1963-64), Sioux City Bar Assn., Internat. Assn. Def. Counsel (exec. com. 1961-64), Harvard Club (N.Y.C.), Sioux City Country Club, Masons (Scottish Rite/33 deg.). Federal civil litigation, State civil litigation, Insurance. Home: 2728 Jackson St Sioux City IA 51104 Office: Pioneer Bank Bldg 701 Pierce St Ste 300 Sioux City IA 51101 Fax: 712-252-1535. E-mail: maynelaw@pionet.net

MAYO, GEORGE WASHINGTON, JR. lawyer; b. Waycross, Ga., Dec. 23, 1946; s. George Washington Sr. and Perrie R. (Ling) M.; m. Katherine Louise Boland, Nov. 15, 1977; children— Regan L.B., Taylor L.B. A.B., Emory U., 1967; J.D., U. Va., 1973. Bar: Va. 1973, D.C. 1974. Assoc., Hogan & Hartson, Washington, 1973-80, ptnr., 1980—. Contbr. articles to prof. jours. Bd. dirs. Vietnam Vets. Meml. Fund, Inc., 1978—, Earth Conservation Corps., 1990—, coll. coun. of advisors Emory U., 1994—, Deafness Rsch. Found., 1997-2001. Served to 1st lt., U.S. Army, 1969-71, Vietnam. Mem. ABA, D.C. Bar Assn., Order of Coif. Democrat. Methodist. Club: Met. (Washington), City (Washington). E-mail: gwmayo@hhlaw.com Administrative and regulatory, Federal civil litigation, General practice. Home: 26 Holly Leaf Ct Bethesda MD 20817-2652 Office: Hogan & Hartson 555 13th St NW Ste 800E Washington DC 20004-1161 E-mail: gwmayo@hhlaw.com

MAYORA-ALVARADO, EDUARDO RENE, lawyer, law educator; b. Guatemala, Guatemala, Apr. 20, 1957; s. Eduardo Alfredo Mayora-Dawe and Adelaida (Alvarado) De Mayora; m. Alicia Bascunana, June 18, 1983; children: Javier Eduardo, Santiago, Jose Andres, Sebastian. JD, U. Rafael Landivar, Guatemala, 1980; LLM, Georgetown U., U.S.A., 1982; Diploma (2) in Principles Econ. Sci., U. Francisco Marroquin, Guatemala, 1991, LLD, 1997. Bar: Guatemala, 1980; cert. notary. Assoc. Mayora & Mayora, Guatemala, 1980-81, ptnr., 1982—, mem. tax adminstrn. bd., 1998-2000; prof. bus. law and principles of law U. Francisco Marroquin, 1984-87, prof. bus. law and principles of law Sch. of Econs., 1986-88, prof. constitutional law, dean Sch. of Law, 1989-2000, prof. principles of pvt. and pub. law, 1993; bd. dirs. Financiera de Inversion, S.A., 1988-96. Alt. dir. Seguros Alianza S.A., Guatemala, 1988-94; trustee U. Francisco Marroquin, 1989—; vis. prof. Pontificia U. Catolica, Porto Alegre, Brazil, 1994, Montpellier U. Sch. Law, France, 1995. Co-author: El Desafio Neoliberal, 1992; author; (essay) El Drama De La Arena Movedisa, 1993 (Charles Stillman award 1993); contbr. to profl. jours. Mem. Guatemala Bar Assn. (author articles Bar Law Jour. 1990—m v.p. ethics bd. 1985-86), Assn. De Amigos Del Pais, Fundacion Para La Cultura (v.p. 1994), Inst. Guatemalteco De Derecho Notarial, Phi Delta Phi, Guatemala Country Club. Roman Catholic. Avocations: reading, sailing, golf. E-mail: mayorae@intelnet.net.gt; mayora&mayora@gua.gbm.net. Office: Mayora & Mayora15 Calle 1-04 Plz Centrica 3er Nivel #301 Zona 10 Guatemala City Guatemala also: PO Box 661447 Miami FL 33266-1447 E-mail: mayorae@intelnet.net.gt

MAYORKAS, ALEJANDRO, lawyer, former prosecutor; b. Cuba; With Patterson, Belknap, Webb & Tyler, L.A., 1986-89; asst. U.S. atty., 1989-99; chief office's gen. crimes sect., 1996-98; U.S. atty. cen. dist. Calif. U.S. Dept. Justice, 1999—2001; ptnr. O'Melveny & Myers, L.A., 2001—. Tchr. trial advocacy Loyola Law Sch., 1997-98. Office: O'Melveny & Myers 400 S Hope St Los Angeles CA 90071-2899*

MAYR, ANDREAS W. lawyer; b. Linz, Austria, Sept. 13, 1966; s. Wolfgang and Herta M.; m. Eva-Maria Parzer. Mag.iur, U. Salzburg, Austria, 1990, Dr.iur, 1995; LLM, Columbia U., 1991. Assoc. Ré, Parser & Ptnrs., N.Y.C., 1991-92, Heller Löber Bahn & Ptnr., Vienna, 1993-96, Skadden Arps Slate Meagher, Frankfurt, Germany, 1996-99, Vienna, 1996-99; ptnr. Huegel & Ptnrs., 1999-2000, CMS Strommer Reich-Rohrwig Karasek Hainz, Vienna, 2000—. Fulbright scholar Columbia U., 1991. Mem. EASE (legal com.), Vienna Stock Exch. (ATX com. 1998—). Avocation: modern art. Mergers and acquisitions, Securities, Venture capital. Home: Westbahnstrasse 21/6 Vienna A1070 Austria Office: CSM Strommer Reich-Rohrwig Ebendorferstrasse 3 Vienna A1010 Austria Fax: 001-1-403-9000. E-mail: andreas.mayr@cmslegal.at

MAYSON, PRESTON B., JR. retired lawyer; b. Spartanburg, S.C., June 18, 1932; s. Preston Brooks and Sophie Rowena (Morgan) M.; m. Sara Dudley Heaton, June 16, 1955; children: Brooks, James. BS, U.S. Mil. Acad., West Point, 1955; MD, George Washington U., 1962; JD, Washington and Lee U., 1991. Bar: Va. Diplomate Am. Bd. Radiology. Physician Letterman Hosp., San Francisco, 1962-66, 93rd Evacuation Hosp., Vietnam, 1966-67, Walter Reed Army Hosp., Washington, 1967-70, Radiology Assocs., Roanoke, Va., 1970-88; law student Washington & Lee U., Lexington, 1988-91; sr. atty. Woods, Rogers & Hazlegrove, Roanoke, 1991-95; pres. Preston B. Mayson, PC, 1995-2000; ret., 2000. Decorated Bronze Star medal. Mem. ABA, Va. State Bar Assn., Va. Trial Lawyers Assn. Presbyterian. Avocation: oil painting. E-mail: pdoctorlaw@aol.com

MAZO, MARK ELLIOTT, lawyer; b. Phila., Jan. 12, 1950; s. Earl and Rita (Vane) M.; m. Fern Rosalyn Litman, Aug. 19, 1973; children: Samantha Lauren, Dana Suzanne, Ross Elliott, Courtney Litman. AB, Princeton U., 1971; JD, Harvard U., 1974. Bar: D.C. 1975, U.S. Dist. Ct. D.C. 1975, U.S. Claims Ct. 1975, U.S. Ct. Appeals (D.C. cir.) 1976, U.S. Supreme Ct. 1979. Ptnr. Hogan & Hartson, L.L.P., Washington and Paris, 1990—. Contbr. articles to profl. jours. White House intern Exec. Office of Pres., Washington, 1972. Capt. USAR, 1971-79. Mem. ABA, Harvard Law Sch. Assn., D.C. Bar Assn., Columbia Country Club, Princeton Club (N.Y.C.), Colonial Club, City Club, Phi Beta Kappa. Republican. Contracts commercial, Private international, Mergers and acquisitions. Home: 3719 Cardiff Rd Chevy Chase MD 20815-5943 Office: Hogan & Hartson LLP 555 13th St NW Ste 800E Washington DC 20004-1161 also: Hogan & Hartson Cariddi Mee Rue 12 rue de la Paix 75002 Paris France E-mail: memazo@hhlaw.com

MAZZAFERRI, KATHERINE AQUINO, lawyer, bar association executive; b. Phila., May 14, 1947; d. Joseph William and Rose (Aquino) M.; m. William Fox Bryan, May 5, 1984 (div.); 1 child, Josefa Mazzaferri Bryan. BA, NYU, 1969; JD, George Washington U., 1972. Bar: D.C., 1972. Trial atty. EEOC, Washington, 1972-75; dir. litigation LWV Edn. Fund, 1975-78; dep. asst. dir. for advt. practices FTC, 1978-80, asst. dir. for product liability, 1980-82, asst. dir. for advt. practices, 1982; exec. dir., v.p. pub. svcs. activities corp. D.C. Bar, 1982—. Bd. dir. regulatory analysis project U.S. Regulatory Coun.; mediator D.C. Mediation Svc., 1982; vis. instr. Antioch Law Sch., Washington, 1985; mem. Bd. of Women's Bar Assn. Found., 1990-93; mem. FBA Meml. Found., 1991-96. Recipient Superior Service award FTC, 1979 Mem. ABA (rep. of the homeless project steering com. 1988-90), D.C. Bar , Womens Legal Def. (pres. 1972-73, bd. dirs. 1971-75, 76-79), FBA Meml. Found. Home: 5832 Lenox Rd Bethesda MD 20817-6070 Office: DC Bar 1250 H St NW Lbby 6 Washington DC 20005-5906

MCADAMS, JOHN P. lawyer; b. Phila., June 5, 1949; s. Eugene P. and Mary (Miller) McA.; m. Anne Christina Connelly, Sept. 5, 1970; children: Emily Lane, Anne Connelly. BA, U. N.C., 1971; JD, Wake Forest U., 1976. Bar: Fla. 1976, N.C. 1976, U.S. Dist. Ct. (mid. dist.) Fla. 1977. Assoc. Carlton, Fields, Ward, Emmanuel, Smith & Cutler, Tampa, Fla., 1976-82, ptnr., 1982—. Contbg. editor: The Developing Labor Law, 1983, Employee Duty of Loyalty, 1995; contbr. articles to profl. jours. Pres. Hillsborough Cmty. Mental Health Ctr., Tampa, 1983; trustee City of Temple Terrace (Fla.) Pension Plan, 1985-89; pres. Hyde Park Preservation, Inc., Tampa, 1993, Child Abuse Coun., Inc., 2001; bd. dirs. Tampa Lighthouse for the Blind, 1997, Child Abuse Coun., Inc., 1998. Mem. ABA, ABA Equal Rights & Responsibilities Com., Fla. Bar Assn. (exec. coun. labor sect. 1987-89). Republican. Episcopalian. Labor. Home: 820 S Delaware Ave Tampa FL 33606-2915 Office: Carlton Fields PO Box 3239 Tampa FL 33601-3239

MCAFEE, WILLIAM JAMES, lawyer; b. Bronx, N.Y., June 18, 1962; s. James J. and Marie A. (Theyson) McA.; m. Helen W. Wagner, Oct. 12, 1962; children: Rebecca A., Ryan P. BA, AA, U.C.F., 1984; JD, Stetson U., St. Petersburg, Fla., 1987. Bar: Fla. 1987, U.S. Dist. Ct. (so. dist.) Fla. 1988, U.S. Dist. Ct. (mid. dist.) Fla. 1989. Asst. states atty. County of Palm Beach, West Palm Beach, Fla., 1987-88; assoc. Schuler & Wilkerson, 1988-89, Slawson & Burman, West Palm Beach, 1989-90; ptnr. Wagner, Johnson & McAfee, 1990—, Ricci Hubbaro Leopold Frankel Farmer & McAfee, West Palm Beach. Contbr. articles to profl. jours. Mem. Fla. Acad. Trial Lawyers (pres. young lawyers sect. 1989-92, frequent lectr.). Avocations: family, fishing, exercise, yard work, karate. Insurance, Personal injury. Office: Ficci Hubbaro Leopolo Frankel Farmer & McAfee PO Box 2946 1645 Palm Beach Lakes Rd West Palm Beach FL 33402 E-mail: wmcagee@riccihubbard.com

MCALHANY, TONI ANNE, lawyer; b. Decatur, Ind., May 1, 1951; d. Robert Keith and Evelyn L. (Fisher) McA. BA, Ind. U., 1973; JD, Valparaiso U., 1976. Bar: Mich. 1976, Ind. 1982, Ill. 1986, U.S. Dist. Ct. (no. dist.) Ind. 1989. Asst. prosecutor Ottawa County Prosecutor's Office, Grand Haven, Mich., 1976-81; assoc. Hann, Doss & Persinger, Holland, 1981-82, Romero & Thonert, Auburn, Ind., 1982-85; ptnr. Dahlgren & McAlhany, Berwyn, Ill., 1985-88, Colbeck, McAlhany & Stewart, Angola, Ind. & Coldwater, Mich., 1988-98. Atty. Angola Housing Authority, 1989-98. Bd. dirs. Child and Family Svcs., Ft. Wayne, Ind., 1983, Fillmore Ctr., Berwyn, 1986-88, Altrusa, Coldwater, 1989-92. Mem. ATLA, State Bar Mich., State Bar Ind., State Bar Ill., Mich. Friend of the Ct. Assn., Referees Assn. Mich., Branch County Bar Assn., Steuben County Bar Assn. Avocations: traveling, horseback riding. Family and matrimonial, General practice, Personal injury. E-mail: tmcalhany@hotmail.com

MCALLISTER, KENNETH WAYNE, lawyer; b. High Point, N.C., Jan. 3, 1949; s. John Calhoun and Ruth Welch (Buie) McA.; children: Katherine Owen, Kenneth Grey. B.A., U. N.C., 1971; J.D., Duke U., 1974. Bar: N.C. 1974, U.S. Dist. Ct. for Middle dist. N.C. 1974, U.S. Ct. Appeals for 4th circuit 1980, U.S. Supreme Ct. 1980. Ptnr. firm Fisher, Fisher & McAllister, High Point, 1974-81; former U.S. atty. for middle dist. N.C. U.S. Dept. Justice, Greensboro, 1981-86; sr. exec. v.p., gen. counsel Wachovia Corp., Winston-Salem, N.C. Bd. of visitors Wake Forest U. Sch. of Law, 1988-96, U. N.C. at Chapel Hill, 1989-93, Duke U. Law Sch., 1996—. Pres. High Point Drug Action Coun., 1977-78; chmn. High Point Rep.Com., 1976-78, 88-89; mem. adv. bd. Salvation Army, High Point, 197-79; bd. dirs. Sch. of Nursing Found., U. N.C., Chapel Hill, 1993-99; vice chair Attys. Gen. Adv. Com. U. S Atty., 1985-86; govs. commn. Bus. Laws and the Economy, 1994—; bd. govs. Presbyn. Homes, 1997—, chmn. 2000—; permanent mem. Fourth Cir. Jud. Conf. John Motley Morehead scholar Morehead Found., 1967; Arthur Priest scholar Phi Delta Theta, 1971 Fellow Am. Bar Found.; mem. N.C. Bar Assn. (bd. govs. 2000—), Piedmont Triad Airport Authority (bd. dirs. 1998-2001), High Point Country Club, Phi Beta Kappa. Republican. Presbyterian. Home: 220 Cascade Dr High Point NC 27265-9685 Office: Wachovia Corp 100 N Main St Winston Salem NC 27101-4047

MCALPIN, KIRK MARTIN, lawyer; b. Newark, Sept. 14, 1923; s. Aaron Champion and Margaret (Martin) McA.; m. Sarah Frances Morgan, Dec. 14, 1951; children: Kirk Martin Jr., Philip Morgan, Margaret Champion Margeson. LLB, U. Ga., 1948; postgrad., Columbia U., 1949. Bar: Ga. 1949. Asst. solicitor gen. Ea. Jud. Cir. Ct. Ga., 1951; assoc. Bouhan, Lawrence, Williams, Levy & McAlpin, Savannah, Ga., 1952-53, ptnr., 1954-63; sr. ptnr. King & Spalding, Atlanta, 1963-86; pvt. practice Savannah, 1987-97, Atlanta, 1998—. Chmn. Inst. Continuing Legal Edn., 1980-81, Inst. Continuing Jud. Edn. in Ga., 1981-84, Jud. Council Ga., 1979-82. Pres. Atlanta Legal Aid Soc., 1971. Fellow Am. Bar Found., Am. Law Inst., Am. Coll. Trial Lawyers, Internat. Acad. Trial Lawyers, Internat. Soc. Barristers; mem. ABA (Jr. Bar Conf. chmn. 1958-59, chmn. gen. practice sect. 1972-73, chmn. sr. lawyers div. 1986-87, ho. of dels. 1960-90, state del. 1970-90, bd. govs. 1973-76), State Bar Ga. Assn. (chmn. Young Lawyers 1953-54, bd. govs. 1953-63, pres. 1979-80), Atlanta Bar Assn., Savannah Bar Assn. (v.p. 1960-61), Nat. Conf. Bar Pres. (exec. com. 1981-83), Ga. Def. Lawyers Assn., Ga. Trial Lawyers Assn., Am. Trial Lawyers Assn., Fed. Bar Assn., Am. Judicature Soc., Assn. R.R. Trial Counsel, Soc. of Cin., Sons Colonial Wars, St. Andrews Soc., Capital City Club, Piedmont Driving Club, Oglethorpe Club, Phi Delta Phi, Sigma Alpha Epsilon. Episcopalian. Administrative and regulatory, General civil litigation, Personal injury. Office: 77 E Andrews Dr NW Apt 352 Atlanta GA 30305-1392 Fax: 404-467-0619

MCAMIS, EDWIN EARL, lawyer; b. Cape Girardeau, Mo., Aug. 8, 1934; s. Zenas Earl and Anna Louise (Miller) McA.; m. Malin Eklof, May 31, 1959 (div. 1979); 1 child, Andrew Bruce. AB magna cum laude, Harvard U., 1956, LLB, 1959. Bar: N.Y. 1960, U.S. Dist. Ct. (so. dist.) N.Y. 1962, U.S. Supreme Ct. 1965, U.S. Ct. Appeals (2d and 3d cirs.) 1964, U.S. Ct. Appeals (D.C. cir.) 1981. Assoc. law firm Webster, Sheffield & Chrystie, N.Y.C., 1959-61, Regan Goldfarb Powell & Quinn, N.Y.C., 1962-65, Lovejoy, Wasson, Lundgren & Ashton, N.Y.C., 1965-69, ptnr., 1969-77, Skadden, Arps, Slate, Meagher & Flom, N.Y.C., 1977-90, spl. ptnr., pro bono, 1990-93; adj. prof. law Fordham U., 1984-85, Benjamin N. Cardozo Sch. Law, N.Y.C., 1985-90. Bd. dirs. Aston Magna Found. for Music, Inc., 1982-93, Cmty. Rsch. Initiative N.Y., 1988-89; mem. Lambda Legal and Edn. Fund, 1991-95. With U.S. Army, 1961-62. Mem. ABA, Selden Soc. Federal civil litigation, State civil litigation. Home: 4110 Kiaora St Coconut Grove FL 33133-6350

MCANDREW, PAUL JOSEPH, JR. lawyer; b. Kalona, Iowa, Mar. 8, 1957; s. Paul Joseph and Virginia (Krowka) McA.; m. Lola Maxine Miller, Mar. 1, 1975; children: Stephanie, Susan, Rose, Paul Joseph III, Bridget. BA with honors, U. Iowa, 1979, JD with high distinction, 1983. Bar: Iowa 1983, U.S. Dist. Ct. Iowa 1985, U.S. Claim Ct. 1985, U.S. Ct. Appeals (8th cir.) 1999, U.S. Supreme Ct. 2000. Law clk. to chief judge U.S. Dist. Ct. (so. dist.) Iowa, Des Moines, 1983-85; ptnr. Meardon, Sueppel, Downer & Hayes, Iowa City, 1985-99, Paul J. McAndrew Law Firm, Iowa City, 1999—. Claimant's counsel rep. Iowa Workers' Compensation Adv. Com., 2000—. Recipient Hancher-Finkbine award, 1979. Mem. ABA, ATLA (1st v.p. workers' compensation sect. 2000), Iowa Bar Assn. (chmn. worker's compensation sect. 1993-95), Iowa Trial Lawyers Assn. (rep. bd. govs. 1993—, workers' compensation sect. 1997—), Johnson County Bar Assn., Iowa Assn. Workers Compensation Attys. (rep. bd. govs. 1993—), Work Injury Litigation Group (Iowa rep. to nat. bd. govs. 1997—). Democrat. Roman Catholic. Avocations: jogging, biking, golf, travel. Personal injury, Workers' compensation. Home: 620 Scott Park Dr Iowa City IA 52245-5140 Office: Paul McAndrew Law Firm 2590 Holiday Rd Ste 100 Coralville IA 52241 Fax: 319 887 1693

MCANDREW, THOMAS JOSEPH, lawyer; b. Providence, Oct. 19, 1945; s. Joseph L. and Amelia L. (Bonhotel) McA.; m. Luise Mary Fogarty, June 13, 1970; children: John Maxwell, Mercedes, Hope, Marya, Cornelia. BA, Providence Coll., 1968; JD, Georgetown U.-Am. U.-George Washington U., 1971; LLM, Georgetown U., 1973. Bar: R.I., 1971, U.S. Dist. Ct. R.I., 1972, D.C. 1972, U.S. Ct. Claims, 1972, U.S. Tax Ct., 1971, U.S. Custom and Patent Ct., 1971, U.S. Ct. Mil. Appeals, 1971, U.S. Ct. Appeals (1st cir.), 1971, U.S. Ct. Appeals (D.C.), 1971, U.S. Supreme Ct., 1974, Comm. of Mass., 1985. Trial atty. Civil Aeros. Bd., Washington, 1971-72; legal asst. to John H. Fanning NLRB, 1972-73; labor rels. officer dept. edn. State of R.I., Providence, 1973-74, dep. asst. commr. edn., 1974-79, adminstr. labor rels., 1979-80; with Powers & McAndrew, Inc., 1980-87; pvt. practice, 1987—. Adj. prof. law U. R.I., Kingston; lectr. in field. Contbr. articles to profl. jours. Treas., trustee John E. Fogarty Found., Providence, 1974—; mem. adv. bd. NIH Fogarty Internat. Ctr., Bethesda, Md., 1998—; mem. Providence Com. on Fgn. Rels., Providence. Mem. ABA (com. on labor law) FBA, ATLA, Am. Arbitration Assn. (adv. coun.). Avocations: golf, tennis, walking. Alternative dispute resolution, Construction, Labor. Home: 6 Wingate Rd Providence RI 02906-4910 Office: Ste 205 One Turks Head Place Providence RI 02903 Fax: 401-455-0882

MCANENY, EILEEN S. lawyer; b. Phila., May 31, 1952; d. William Patrick and Mary (DiBono) M.; m. Michael D. Gallagher, June 14, 1980; 1 child, Nicholas. BA cum laude in Polit. Sci., Rosemont Coll., Pa., 1974; JD, Villanova U., Pa., 1977. Bar: Pa. 1977. Assoc. LaBrum and Doak, Phila., 1977-80; sr. assoc. German, Gallagher & Murtaugh, 1980-81; sr. atty. SmithKline Beckman Corp., 1981-86; gen. counsel SmithKline Bio-Sci. Labs., Ltd., 1986—. Lectr. in law. Contbr. articles to profl. and popular jours. Mem. ABA (health law, corp. banking and bus. law sect., antitrust, corp. gen. div.), Nat. Health Lawyers Assn., Am. Clin. Labs. Assn., Am. Corp. Counsel Assn. (product liability com.), Pa. Bar Assn., Phila. Bar Assn., Am. Clin. Labs. Assn., Delta Epsilon Sigma. General corporate, Health, Mergers and acquisitions. Home: 1106 Ivymont Rd Bryn Mawr PA 19010-1627 Office: Smith Kline Beckman Corp One Franklin Plaza PO Box 7929 Philadelphia PA 19101-7929

MCANIFF, EDWARD JOHN, lawyer; b. N.Y.C., June 29, 1934; s. John Edward and Josephine (Toomey); m. Jane Reiss, June 11, 1960; children: John E., Maura T., Anne T. Annick, Jane A., Peter J., Kathleen A. AB magna cum laude, Holy Cross Coll., 1956; LLB cum laude, NYU, 1961. Bar: N.Y. 1962, Calif. 1963, D.C. 1976. Law clk. to Justice A.T. Goodwin Supreme Ct. Oreg., Salem, 1961-62; ptnr., of counsel O'Melveny & Myers, L.A., 1962—. Adj. prof. Sch. Law Stanford U., 1974-75, 94-98, Boalt Hall Law Sch., 1992-95, UCLA Law Sch., 1996—; vis. prof. U. Oreg. Law Sch., 1999—; fgn. law counsel Freehill, Hollingdale & Page, Sydney, 1981-82; bd. dirs. Mellon Fin. Corp. Bd. dirs. L.A. Master Chorale, 1979-81, 87—, chmn., 1996—; dir., exec. com. Perf. Art Ctr. Los Angeles County, 1992—; bd. dirs. Music Ctr. Found., 1992—. Capt. USNR, 1956-87. Republican. Banking, Mergers and acquisitions, Securities. Office: O Melveny & Myers 400 S Hope St Ste 1717 Los Angeles CA 90071-2899 E-mail: tmcaniff@omm.com

MCARDLE, ERIN DOUGHERTY, lawyer; b. Dec. 22, 1969; JD, U. Memphis, 1994. Bar: Tenn. Atty. D. Ragsdale Law Offices, Memphis, 1993-96, Moffatt & McArdle, Bristol, Tenn., 1993-96. Mem. Tenn. Bar Assn., N.E. Tenn. Young Lawyers Assn. (v.p.). Office: PO Box 1115 Bristol TN 37621-1115

MCATEE, DAVID RAY, lawyer; b. Rosebud, Tex., Nov. 20, 1941; s. Lee Ray and Florine (Davis) McA.; m. Carole Kay Pendergraft, Jan. 28, 1967; children— David Ray, Kristin Carole. B.B.A. with honors, Baylor U., 1964; LL.B., U. Tex., 1967. Bar: Tex. 1967; U.S. Dist. Ct. (no. dist.) Tex. 1968, (so. dist.) Tex., 1994; U.S. Ct. Appeals (5th cir.) 1969, (11th cir.) 1981; U.S. Tax Ct., 1993. Briefing atty. Supreme Ct. Tex., Austin, 1967-68; ptnr. Thompson & Knight, Dallas, 1968-90; ptnr. Gibson Dunn & Crutcher, Dallas, 1990-95; with Akin, Gump, Strauss, Hauer & Feld, L.L.P., Dallas, 1995—. Founder, bd. dirs. No. Hills Neighborhood Assocs., Inc., 1974-76; pres., bd. dirs. Montessori Sch. of Park Cities, 1975-78; mem. Goals for Dallas Com., City of Dallas Citizens Safety Adv. Com., 1975-77; chmn. City of Dallas Thoroughfare Com., 1979-81; mem. City of Dallas Plan Commn., 1979-83, vice-chmn., 1981-83. Mem. Dallas Bar Assn. (legal ethics com. 1979-81), Tex. Bar Assn. (legal ethics com. 1975-81), ABA (antitrust sect.). Democrat. Methodist. Antitrust, Federal civil litigation, State civil litigation. Office: Akin Gump Strauss Hauer & Feld 1700 Pacific Ave Ste 4100 Dallas TX 75201-4675

MCAULIFFE, ROSEMARY, lawyer; b. New Rochelle, N.Y., May 24, 1927; d. William J. and Rose B. (Payne) McA. BA, Regis Coll., 1949; JD, New Eng. Sch. Law, 1954; MEd, Boston State Coll., 1971, Cert. advanced grad studies, 1981. Bar: Mass. 1956, U.S. Dist. Ct. Mass. 1957, U.S. Supreme Ct. 1961. Pvt. practice law, Boston, 1956—. Tchr. City of Boston, 1965-93. Prodr. (weekly TV show) The Legal Line, Boston Pub. Access Answer Channel. Active World Affairs Coun., Boston, 1980-95; sec. Italian Hist. Assn. Mass., 1988—. Mem. Mass. Bar Assn., Am. Acad. Trial Lawyers, Mass. Assn. Women Lawyers (v.p.). General practice. Home and Office: 61 Prince St Boston MA 02113-1829

MCAULIFFE, STEVEN JAMES, federal judge; b. 1948; BA, Va. Mil. Inst., 1970; JD, Georgetown U., 1973. Capt. appellate coun. U.S. Army Judge Advocate Gens. Corps, 1973-77; asst. atty. gen. Office N.H. Atty. Gen., 1977-80; ptnr. Gallagher, Callahan, Gartrell, P.A., Concord, N.H., 1980-92; fed. judge U.S. Dist. Ct. (N.H. dist.), 1992—. Trustee Univ. System of N.H., 1986-94; bd. dirs. N.H. Med. Malpractice Stabilication Res. Fund Trust, 1987-92, Office Pub. Guardian, 1980-92, Challenger Ctr. for Space Sci. Edn.; active N.H. Dem. Leadership Coun., 1988-92. Capt. U.S. Army, 1970-77, USAR, 1977-80, N.H. Army NG, 1980-88. Fellow N.H. Bar Found.; mem. ABA, N.H. Bar Assn. (pres. 1991-92, pres.-elect 1990-91, v.p. 1989-90, mem. ex-officio N.H. Supreme Ct. com. profl. conduct 1989-90, mem. ethics com. 1984-86), Nat. Conf. Bar Pres., Merrimack County Bar Assn., D.C. Bar Assn., U.S. Supreme Ct. Hist. Soc., N.H. Jud. Coun. (vice-chmn. 1991-92), Aircraft Owners and Pilots Assn., N.H. Hist. Soc., Concord Country Club. Office: US Dist Ct 55 Pleasant St Concord NH 03301-3904

MCBARNETTE, BRUCE OLVIN, lawyer, corporate executive; b. N.Y.C., Oct. 7, 1957; s. Olvin R. and Yvette Fay (Francis) McB. BA, Princeton U., 1980; JD, NYU, 1983. Bar: N.Y. 1985, Hawaii 1987, D.C. 1989. Atty. Natural Resources Def. Coun., N.Y.C., 1984, U.S. Judge Adv.Gen.'s Corp., Aberdeen Proving Grand, Md., 1988-89, Schofield, Hawaii, 1985-88; legis. asst. U.S. Ho. of Reps., Washington, 1989; counsel impeachment trial com. U.S. Senate, 1989-90; sr. counsel Fed. Nat. Mortgage Assn., 1990-93; pres. Summit Connections, Inc., 1993—. Faculty George Washington U.; dir. devel. Charlies Pl., 1998—. Coord. Achieve Speakers Bur., Washington, 1990. Capt. U.S. Army, 1985-88. Mem. ABA (contbg. author newsletter for mil. pers.), SAG, D.C. Bar Assn., N.Y. Bar Assn., Hawaii Bar Assn. Democrat. Episcopalian. Avocation: track and field. Banking, Military, Securities. Home: 248 Willow Ter Sterling VA 20164-1628 Office: Summit Connections Inc 248 Willow Ter Sterling VA 20164-1628

MCBRIDE, BEVERLY JEAN, lawyer; b. Greenville, Ohio, Apr. 5, 1941; d. Kenneth Birt and Glenna Louise (Ashman) Whited; m. Benjamin Gary McBride, Nov. 28, 1964; children: John David, Elizabeth Ann. BA magna cum laude, Wittenberg U., 1963; JD cum laude, U. Toledo, 1966. Bar: Ohio 1966. Intern Ohio Gov.'s Office, Columbus, 1962; asst. dean women U. Toledo, 1963-65; assoc. Title Guarantee and Trust Co., Toledo, 1966-69; spl. counsel Ohio Atty. Gen.'s Office, 1975; assoc. Cobourn, Smith, Rohrbacher and Gibson, 1969-76; v.p., gen. counsel, sec. The Andersons, Maumee, Ohio, 1976—. Exec. trustee, bd. dirs. Wittenberg U., Springfield, Ohio, 1980-83; trustee Anderson Found., Maumee, 1981-93; mem. Ohio Supreme Ct. Task Force on Gender Fairness, 1991-94, Regional Growth Partnership, 1994—; chmn. Sylvania Twp. Zoning Commn., Ohio, 1970-80; candidate for judge Sylvania Mcpl. Ct., 1975; trustee Goodwill Industries, Toledo, 1976-82, Sylvania Cmty. Svcs. Ctr., 1976-78, Toledo-Lucas County Port Authority, 1992-99, vice chair Fla. CPA; chair St. Vincent Med. Ctr., 1992-99; founder Sylvania YWCA Program, 1973; active membership drives Toledo Mus. Art, 1977-87. Recipient Toledo Women in Industry award YWCA, 1979, Outstanding Alumnus award Wittenberg U., 1981. Fellow Am. Bar Found.; mem. ABA, AAUW, Ohio Bar Assn., Toledo Bar Assn. (pres., treas., chmn., sec. various coms.), Toledo Women Attys. Forum (exec. com. 1978-82), Pres. Club (U. Toledo exec. com.). Home: 5274 Cambrian Rd Toledo OH 43623-2626 Office: The Andersons 480 W Dussel Dr Maumee OH 43537-1690

MCBRIDE, KENNETH EUGENE, lawyer, title company executive; b. Abilene, Tex., June 8, 1948; s. W. Eugene and I. Jean (Wright) McB.; m. Peggy Ann Waller, Aug. 7, 1969 (div. 1980); m. Katrina Lynne Small, June 1, 1985; children: Katherine Jean, Kellie Elizabeth. BA, Central State U., 1971; JD, Oklahoma City U., 1974. Bar: Okla. 1974. Assoc. Linn, Helms & Kirk, Oklahoma City, 1974-76; city atty. City of Edmond (Okla.), 1976-77; v.p., gen. counsel Am. First Land Title Ins., Oklahoma City, 1977-81; pres. Am. First Abstract Co., Norman, Okla., 1981-90, Lawyers Title of Oklahoma City, Inc., 1990—; CEO Am. Eagle Title Ins. Co., 1994—. Pres. Okla. Land Title Assn., 1987-88, LT Exch. Corp., 1996—. Bd. dirs. Norman Bd. Adjustment, 1982-85, Leadership Okla., Inc., 1986-94, pres., 1989-90, 93-94. Fellow Okla. Bar Found.; mem. ABA, Okla. Bar Assn. (bd. dirs. Real Property Sect. 1992-94), Oklahoma County Bar Assn., Oklahoma City Met. Assn. Realtors (bd. dirs. 1995-96), Oklahoma City Real Property Lawyers Assn., Leadership Norman Alumni. Democrat. Presbyterian. Avocation: sailing. General corporate, Real property. Office: Lawyers Title Oklahoma City Inc 1141 N Robinson Ave Oklahoma City OK 73103-4929

MCBRIDE, MICHAEL FLYNN, lawyer; b. Milw., Mar. 27, 1951; s. Raymond Edward and Marian Dunne McBride; m. Kerin Ann O'Brien, Mar. 23, 1991; children: Raymond Erin, Barbara Marian. BS in Chem. and Biology, U. Wis., 1972, JD, 1976; MS in Environ. Engr. Sci., Calif. Inst. Tech., 1973. Bar: Wis. 1976, D.C. 1976. Assoc. LeBoeuf, Lamb, Greene & MacRae, Washington, 1976-84, ptnr., 1985—. Mem. Energy Bar Assn., Assn. for Transp. Law, Logistics and Policy (v.p., energy tranps., law inst. com. 1990, co-chmn. 1991—, pres. 1994-95, editor ATLLP Jour.), Chantilly Nat. Golf and Country Club. Avocations: golf, reading, travel. Federal civil litigation, FERC practice, Nuclear power. Home: 6648 Byrns Pl Mc Lean VA 22101-4419 Office: LeBoeuf Lamb Greene & MacRae LLP 1875 Connecticut Ave NW Washington DC 20009-5728 E-mail: mfmcbrid@llgm.com

MCBRIDE, MILFORD LAWRENCE, JR. lawyer; b. Grove City, Pa., July 16, 1923; s. Milford Lawrence and Elizabeth B. (Douthett) McB.; m. Madeleine Coulter, Aug. 6, 1947; children: Marta, Brenda, Trip, Randy, Barry. AB, Grove City Coll., 1944; BS, N.Y.U., 1944; JD, U. Pa., 1949. Bar: Pa. 1949, U.S. Dist. Ct. (we. dist.) Pa. U.S. Supreme Ct. Ptnr., McBride & McBride, Grove City, 1949-77, sr. ptnr., 1992—; ptnr. McBride and McNickle, Grove City, 1977-92; dir. Integra Fin. Corp., 1988-93; trustee Grove City Coll., 1995—. Served to 1st lt. USAAF, 1943-46. Mem. Mercer County Bar Assn. (state treas. 1970-77), ABA, Am. Bar Found. Republican. Clubs: Oakmont Country, University (Pitts.). General corporate, Probate, Real property. Office: 211 S Center St Grove City PA 16127-1508

MCBROOM, THOMAS WILLIAM, SR. aviation educator, lawyer; b. Atlanta, Mar. 29, 1963; s. William Ralph and Ethel Irene (Bradley) McB.; m. Susan H.; 1 child, Thomas William Jr. B in Mech. Engring., Ga. Tech., 1985, MS in Mech. Engring., 1987; JD, MBA, Ga. State U., 1992; postgrad., Embry-Riddle Aero. U. Registered prof. engr., Ga.; cert. ins. agt.-life, accident and sickness, property, casualty & surety Ga.; bar: Ga. 1993, D.C. 1994, U.S. Tax Ct. 1993, U.S. Supreme Ct. 1996; lic. comml. pilot and flight instr., registered mediator and arbitrator Ga. Mfg. engr. AT & T Techs., Norcross, Ga., 1985-86; energy systems engr. Atlanta Gas Light Co., 1987-89, sales engr., 1989-90, dir. power systems markets, 1991-94, sr. corp. planning analyst, 1994-95, mgr. major accounts, 1995-97, dir. major accts., 1997-99; atty., cons. Newnan, Ga., 1999—; pilot ground instr. Delta Air Lines, Atlanta, 2000—; project mgr. Aviation Consulting, AIR, Inc., 2001—. Mem. Grad. Leadership Coweta, 1996, Grad. Coverdell Rep. Leadership Inst., 1997; vice chmn. state ho. dists. Coweta County Rep. Com., 1997-99, vice chair legis. dists., 1999; state com. Ga. Rep. Party, 1997-99. With USAR, 1997—, Capt. JAGC. Mem. Ga. Bar Assn., Coverdell Leadership Inst., Phi Delta Phi (exchequer 1991). Military, Probate. Home: 15 Culpepper Way Newnan GA 30265-2217

MCBRYDE, JOHN HENRY, federal judge; b. Jackson, Oct. 9, 1931; m. Betty Vinson; children: Rebecca McBryde Dippold, Jennifer, John Blake. BS in Commerce, Tex. Christian U., 1953; LLB, U. Tex., 1956. Bar: Tex. 1956, U.S. Ct. Appeals (5th cir.) 1958, U.S. Dist. Ct. (no. dist.) 1958, U.S. Dist. Ct. (ea. dist.) 1989, U.S. Supreme Ct. 1972. Assoc. Cantey, Hanger, Johnson, Scarborough & Gooch, Ft. Worth, 1956-62; ptnr. Cantey & Hanger and predecessor firm, 1962-69, McBryde, Bennett and predecessor firms, Ft. Worth, 1969-90; judge U.S. Dist. Ct. (no. dist.) Tex., 1990—. Fellow Am. Bar Found. (life), Tex. Bar Found. (life), Am. Coll. Trial Lawyers. Office: US Dist Ct US Courthouse 501 W 10th St Ste 401 Fort Worth TX 76102-3642

MCBRYDE, NEILL GREGORY, lawyer; b. Durham, N.C., Jan. 11, 1944; s. Angus M. and Priscilla (Gregory) McB., m. Margaret McPherson, Aug. 1, 1970; children: Margaret Courtauld, Neill Gregory Jr. AB cum laude, Davidson Coll., 1966; JD with high honors, U. N.C., 1969. Bar: N.C. 1969., Ga. 1972. Assoc. King & Spalding, Atlanta, 1971-76; ptnr. Fleming, Robinson, Bradshaw & Hinson, Charlotte, N.C., 1977-81, Helms, Mulliss & Johnston, Charlotte, 1981-86, Smith Helms Mulliss & Moore, Charlotte, 1986-90, Moore & Van Allen PLLC, Charlotte, 1990—. Lectr. in field, conducter workshops in field. Author, editor: First Union National Bank of North Carolina Will Book, 1986; contbr. to profl. jours. Elder and Deacon Myers Park Presbyn. Ch., Charlotte, 1980-86, 92-95, 2001-04; dir. sec. Presbyn. Home for Aged, Charlotte, 1978-82; trustee Charlotte Latins Schs., Inc., 1980-86, 87-93; immediate past chmn., trustee Mint Mus. Charlotte. Fellow Am. Coll. Trust and Estate Counsel (mem. bd. regents, immediate past pres.), Am. Coll. Tax Counsel; mem. ABA, Ga. Bar Assn., N.C. Bar Assn. (probate and fiduciary law sect.), Order of Coif, Phi Beta Kappa, Omicron Delta Kappa. Republican. Avocations: tennis, golf, fishing. General corporate, Estate planning, Mergers and acquisitions. Office: Moore & Van Allen PLLC Nations Bank Corp Ctr 100 N Tryon St Fl 47 Charlotte NC 28202-4003

MCBURNEY, CHARLES WALKER, JR. lawyer; b. Orlando, Fla., June 6, 1957; s. Charles Walker McBurney and Jeane (Brown) Chappell. BA, U. Fla., 1979, JD, 1982. Bar: Fla. 1982, U.S. Dist. Ct. (mid. dist.) Fla. 1983, U.S. Ct. Appeals (11th cir.) 1984. Assoc. Mathews, Osborne, McNatt, Gobelman & Cobb, Jacksonville, Fla., 1982-84; asst. state's atty. State's Atty.'s Office, 1984-90, civil atty., 1987-88, sr. trial atty., 1988-90; ptnr. Fischette, Owen, Held & McBurney, 1990—. Dir. Serious or Habitual Juvenile Offender Program, 1986. Bd. dirs. Civic Round Table, 1988-92, treas., 1988-89, pres. 1989-90; chmn. com. congl. campaigns, Jacksonville, 1982, 84, 88; mem. Mayor's Bicentennial Constnl. Commn., 1989-91; dir. Internat. Devel. Commn. for Jacksonville, 1993—, treas., 1995-97; bd. dirs. Am. Heart Assn. N.E. Fla., 1990-92. Mem. ABA, Jacksonville Bar Assn. (chmn. bankruptcy sect. 1998-2000), Jacksonville Bankruptcy Bar Assn. (bd. dirs. 1999—), Nat. Dist. Attys. Assn., Comml. Law League (So. region exec. coun. 1998—, treas. 2000—), Fla. Jaycees (legal counsel 1987-88, most outstanding local pres. award 1987), Jacksonville Jaycees (pres. 1986, Jaycee of yr. 1984), Jacksonville C. of C. (bd. govs. 1987, govtl. affairs com. 1998—), Summit Civitan (judge adv. 1991-93, ctrl. civitan 1991—, bd. dirs.), Masons, Bull Snort Club (pres. 1995-96, 99-2000, chmn. bd. 1996-97, 1998-99), C. of C. (trustee 1996-98, govtl. affairs com. 1998—), N.E. Fla. Alumni Assn. (v.p. 1998-2000), James Madison Inst., Jacksonville Hist. Soc., Phi Beta Kappa. Republican. Presbyterian. Criminal, Juvenile. Home: 6326 Christopher Creek Rd E Jacksonville FL 32217-2485 Office: Fishette Owen Held & McBurney Riverplace Tower Ste 1916 Jacksonville FL 32207

MCCABE, CHARLES KEVIN, lawyer, author; b. Springfield, Ill., Nov. 2, 1952; s. Charles Kenneth and Betty Lou (Williams) McC. BS in Aero. and Astronautical Engring. magna cum laude, U. Ill., 1975; JD, U. Mich., 1978. Bar: Ill. 1978, U.S. Dist. Ct. (no. dist.) Ill. 1978, U.S. Ct. Appeals (7th cir.) 198o. Engring. co-op. student McDonnell Aircraft, St. Louis, 1972-74; chief aerodynamicist Vetter Fairing Co., Rantoul, Ill., 1974-75; with Lord, Bissel & Brook, Chgo., 1978—. Author: Qwiktran: Quick FORTRAN, 1979, FORTH Fundamentals, 1983, Steam Locomotive Fundamentals, 1999; co-author: 32 BASIC Programs, 1981; contbr. articles on aviation, computers to various mags., 1974—. Pres., dir. Ill. Railway Mus, 1992—. Nat. Merit scholar U. Ill., Urbana, 1970. Mem. Chgo. Bar. Assn. Aviation, Insurance, Personal injury. Office: Lord Bissell & Brook 115 S La Salle St Ste 3200 Chicago IL 60603-3902

MCCABE, MICHAEL J. insurance executive; b. Denver, June 19, 1945; s. Joseph J. and Mary J. (Kane) McC.; m. Catherine Corrine Marquette, July 21, 1978; children: Brian Michael, Shannon Marquette. BS, U. Notre Colo., 1967; JD, Cath. U. Am., 1971. Bar: D.C. Air transport econ. analyst U.S. Civil Aeronautics Bd., Washington, 1967-71; Washington counsel Allstate Ins. Co., 1971-74, of counsel Ill., 1974-82, asst. v.p. bus. planning, 1982-84, v.p. corp. planning, 1984-89, group v.p., gen. atty., 1989-95; v.p., gen. counsel Allstate Corp.; sr. v.p., gen. counsel Allstate Ins. Co., 1999—. Bd. advisors No. Ill. U. Sch. Bus., DeKalb, 1986—. Chmn. Gateway Found. Mem. ABA, Fed. Bar Assn., D.C. Bar Assn., Planning Forum, Sigma Chi, Pi Alpha Delta. Democrat. Roman Catholic. Office: Allstate Ins Co 2775 Sanders Rd Northbrook IL 60062

MCCABE, THOMAS EDWARD, lawyer, business consultant; b. Washington, Jan. 22, 1955; s. Edward Aeneas and Janet Isabel McCabe; m. Kelly Marie McCarthy; children: Edward Charles, Benjamin Patrick, Adrienne Marie, Therese Eileen, Luke Stevens, Nicholas Joseph. AB, Georgetown U., 1977; MBA, JD, U. Notre Dame, 1981. Bar: D.C. 1982, U.S. Dist. Ct. D.C. 1983, U.S. Ct. Appeals (D.C. cir.) 1983, Va. 1989, U.S. Supreme Ct. 1990. Law clk. U.S. Dist. Ct. Judge Hon. Charles R. Richey, Washington, 1981-82; assoc. Reavis & McGrath, 1982-84, Venable Baetjer Howard & Civiletti, Washington, 1984-85, McCarthy & Durrette, Washington, 1985-88; ptnr. McCarthy & Burke, 1988-91; sr. v.p., dir. corp. devel., gen. counsel, sec. GRC Internat., Inc., Vienna, 1992-2001; pres., CEO Storetrax.com, Inc., Bethesda, Md., 2001—. Republican. Roman Catholic. General corporate, Government contracts and claims, Securities. E-mail: tmccabe@tmccabe.net

MCCAFFREY, CARLYN SUNDBERG, lawyer; b. N.Y.C., Jan. 7, 1942; d. Carl Andrew Lawrence and Evelyn (Back) Sundberg; m. John P. McCaffrey, May 24, 1967; children: John C., Patrick, Jennifer, Kathleen. Student, Barnard Coll., 1963; AB in Econs., George Washington U., 1963; LLB cum laude, NYU, 1967, LLM in Taxation, 1970. Bar: N.Y. 1974. Law clk. to presiding justice Calif. Supreme Ct., 1967-68; teaching fellow law NYU, N.Y.C., 1968-70, asst. prof. law, 1970-74; assoc. Weil, Gotshal & Manges, 1974-80, ptnr., 1980—. Prof. in residence Rubin Hall NYU, 1971-75; adj. prof. law NYU, 1975—, U. Miami, 1979-81; lectr. in field. Contbr. articles to profl. jours. Mem. ABA (chmn. generation-skipping transfer tax 1979-81, 93—, real property pro ate and trust law sect.), N.Y. State Bar Assn. (exec. com. tax sect. 1979-80, chmn. estate and gift tax com. 1976-78, 95—, life ins. com. 1983-85, trusts and estates sect.), Assn. of Bar of City of N.Y. (matrimonial law com., chmn. tax subcom. 1984-86, Am. College Trusts & Estates Counsel (bd. regents 1992—, mem. exec. com. 1995—, v.p. 2001). Family and matrimonial, Probate. Home: PO Box 232 Waccabuc NY 10597-0232 Office: Weil Gotshal & Manges 767 5th Ave Fl Concl New York NY 10153-0119 E-mail: Carlyn.mccaffrey@weil.com

MCCAFFREY, JUDITH ELIZABETH, lawyer; b. Providence, Apr. 26, 1944; d. Charles V. and Isadore Frances (Langford) McC.; m. Martin D. Minsker, Dec. 31, 1969 (div. May 1981); children: Ethan Hart Minsker, Natasha Langford Minsker. BA, Tufts U., 1966; JD, Boston U., 1970. Bar: Mass. 1970, D.C. 1972, Fla. 1991. Assoc. Sullivan & Worcester, Washington, 1970-76; atty. FDIC, 1976-78; assoc. Dechert, Price & Rhoads, 1978-82, McKenna, Conner & Cuneo, Washington, 1982-83; gen. counsel, corp. sec. Perpetual Savs. Bank, FSB, Alexandria, Va., 1983-91; ptnr. Powell, Goldstein, Frazer & Murphy, Washington, 1991-92, McCaffrey & Raimi, P.A., 1992—. Contbr. articles to profl. jours. Mem. Leadership Collier, 1998. Mem. ABA (chairperson subcom. thrift instns. 1985-90), Fed. Bar Assn. (exec. com., banking law com. 1985-91), D.C. Bar Assn. (bd. govs. 1981-85), Fla. Bar Assn. (chmn. fin. svcs. com. 1999-2000), Women's Bar Assn. D.C. (pres. 1980-81), Collier County Women's Bar Assn. (pres. 1997-98). Episcopalian. Avocations: golf, travel, sailing, reading. Banking, Finance, Securities. Home: PO Box 2081 Naples FL 34106-2081 Office: McCaffrey & Raimi PA 5811 Pelican Bay Blvd Ste 206-A Naples FL 34108-2710

MCCALEB, JOE WALLACE, lawyer; b. Nashville, Dec. 9, 1941; s. J.W. McCaleb and Majorie June (Hudson) DePriest; m. Glenda Jean Queen, June 26, 1965. BA, Union U., 1964; JD, Memphis State U., 1970; MSEL cum laude, Vt. Law Sch., 1995. Bar: Tenn. 1971, U.S. Dist. Ct. (mid. dist.) Tenn. 1977, U.S. Ct. Appeals (6th cir.) 1984, U.S. Supreme Ct. 1978. Law clk. to presiding justice Tenn. Supreme Ct., Memphis, 1970-71; staff atty. Tenn. Dept. of Pub. Health Bur. Environ. Svcs., Nashville, 1971-77; pvt. practice Hendersonville, Tenn., 1977-94, 96—. Chmn. Hendersonville Recycling Com., 1990-91. Mem. ATLA, Tenn. Bar Assn., Sierra Club (chmn. local chpt. 1980-81, chmn. mid.-Tenn. group 1989-90, 93-94, chmn. water quality com., co-chmn. forestry com.), Tenn. Environ. Coun. (v.p. 1987-88, conservation adv. 1991-92), Defenders of Wildlife, Tenn. Forest Def. Coun., Save Our Cumberland Mountains. Democrat. Avocations: wilderness backpacking, photography, forestry, environmental protection. Administrative and regulatory, Federal civil litigation, Environmental. Home and Office: 100 Colonial Dr Hendersonville TN 37075-3205

MCCALL, DONN JAY, lawyer; b. Alliance, Nebr., May 27, 1949; s. Richard Lee and Virginia Mae (Louks) McC.; m. Anita Jo Kiser, Aug. 10, 1974; 1 child, Brendan Kiser. B.S. in Bus. Adminstrn., U. Wyo., 1971, J.D., 1976; postgrad. in history Georgetown U., 1971-72. Bar: Wyo. 1976, U.S. Dist. Ct. Wyo. 1976, U.S. Ct. Appeals (10th cir.) 1976. Law clk. Silverstein & Mullens, Washington, summer 1974; legal intern Wyo. Atty. Gen., Cheyenne, 1975-76; staff atty. to chief justice Wyo. Supreme Ct., Cheyenne, 1976-79; assoc. Brown & Drew (formerly Brown, Drew, Apostolos, Massey & Sullivan), Casper, Wyo., 1979-84, ptnr., 1985—; faculty seminars. Active United Way of Natrona County, Casper, 1983; Democratic precinct committeeman, Laramie County Cheyenne, 1978-79; pres. U. Wyo. Young Democrats Laramie, 1970-71. Recipient Am. Jurisprudence Book award U. Wyo., 1975; Watt Bros. scholar U. Wyo., 1973-76, honor scholar, 1967-71. Mem. Wyo. State Bar Assn., ABA, Natrona County Bar Assn., Am. Judicature Soc., U. Wyo. Alumni Assn., Casper C. of C., Potter Law Club, Sigma Alpha Epsilon (activities chmn. 1968-69), Alpha Kappa Psi, Phi Epsilon Phi, Omicron Delta Kappa, Beta Gamma Sigma, Iron Skull. Democrat. Mem. First United Methodist Ch. Banking, Bankruptcy, Contracts commercial. Office: Brown & Drew 123 W 1st St Ste 800 Casper WY 82601-2486

MCCALL, JACK HUMPHREYS, JR. lawyer; b. Nashville, Jan. 10, 1961; s. Jack Humphreys Sr. and Patricia Jean (Holmes) McC.; m. Jennifer Lynn Ashley, Oct. 4, 1992; 1 child, Margaret Ashley. BA, Vanderbilt U., 1983; JD, U. Tenn., 1991. Bar: Tenn. 1992, U.S. Ct. Appeals (10th cir.) 1993. Clk. Hon. Gilbert S. Merritt, Chief Judge U.S. Ct. Appeals 6th Cir., Nashville, 1991-92; assoc. Farris, Warfield & Kanaday, 1992-94, Hunton & Williams, Knoxville, Tenn., 1994—. Adj. prof. U. Tenn. Coll. Law, Knoxville, 1997—; adv. bd. Knoxville Legal Aid Soc. Pro Bono Project, 1999—. Contbr. chpt. to book and articles to profl. jours. Mem. alumni adv. coun. U. Tenn. Coll. Law, Knoxville, 1992-95. Capt. U.S. Army, 1983-88. Recipient Loevinger prize ABA Sect. of Sci. and Tech., 1992, Bruno Bittker award ABA Standing Com. World Order Law, 1993, Pro Bono Lawyer award Knoxville Legal Aid Soc., 1999. Mem. Nashville Bar Assn. (elder law com. chair young lawyers divsn. 1993-94), Knoxville Bar Assn. Barristers (com. chair young lawyers sect. 1995-97), Nat. Assn. Real Estate Investment Trusts. Lutheran. Avocations: history, writing, genealogy, languages, travel. General corporate, Finance, Securities. Office: Hunton & Williams 900 S Gay St Ste 2000 Knoxville TN 37902-1861 E-mail: nmccall@hunton.com

MC CALLUM, CHARLES EDWARD, lawyer; b. Memphis, Mar. 13, 1939; s. Edward Payson and India Raimelle (Musick) McC.; m. Lois Ann Gowell Temple, Nov. 30, 1985; children: Florence Andrea, Printha Kyle, Chandler Ward, Sabra Nicole Temple. BS, MIT, 1960; JD, Vanderbilt U., 1964. Bar: Mich., Tenn. 1964. Assoc. Warner Norcross & Judd LLP, Grand Rapids, Mich., 1964-69, ptnr., 1969—, mng. ptnr., 1992-97. Rep. assemblyman State Bar Mich., 1973-78; dir. TerraLex, 2001—, Rsch. and Tech. Inst. West Mich., 1986-96, chmn., 1989-91; lectr. continuing legal edn. programs; chmn., bd. dirs. Butterworth Ventures, 1987-96; mem. West Mich. World Trade Week Com., 1988-99, chmn., 1990-91; mem. Mich. Dist. Export Coun., 1990-99, chmn., 1992-97. Chmn. Grand Rapids Area Transit Authority, 1976-79, mem., 1972-79; regional v.p. Nat. Mcpl. League, 1978-86, mem. coun., 1971-78; pres. Grand Rapids Art Mus., 1979-81, 96-98, trustee, 1976-83, 94-99; chmn. Butterworth Hosp., 1979-87, trustee, 1977-87; chmn. Butterworth Health Corp., 1982-89, dir., 1982-97, vice chmn., 1989-91, sec., 1991-97; vice chmn. Citizens Com. for Consolidation of Govt. Svcs., 1981-82; mem. nat. alumni bd. Vanderbilt U. Sch. Law, 1998-2001; chmn. Priority Health, 1995—, bd. dirs., 1995—. Woodrow Wilson fellow, 1960-61; Fulbright scholar U. Manchester, Eng., 1960-61. Fellow Coll. Law Practice Mgmt.; mem. ABA (com. on law firms bus. law sect. 1982-94, chmn. com. on law firms 1994-98, coun. mem. bus. law sect. 1998—, mem. fed. regulation of securities com., mem. internat. bus. law com., com. on multijurisdictional practice 2000—), Am. Bar Found., Am. Law Inst., Tenn. Bar Assn., Mich. Bar Assn. (mem. coun. bus. law sect. 1983-89, sect. chmn. 1988-89, ex-officio coun. bus. law sect. 1989—, chmn. takeover laws subcom. 1986-88, co-chmn. internat. bus. law com., internat. law sect. 1988-89), Grand Rapids Bar Assn., Internat. Bar Assn., Grand Rapids C. of C. (pres. 1975, bd. dirs. 1970-76), Univ. Club, Peninsular Club, Order of Coif, Sigma Xi. General corporate, Private international, Mergers and acquisitions. Home: 110 Bittersweet Ln NE Ada MI 49301-9552 E-mail: mccallce@wnj.com

MCCAMPBELL, ROBERT GARNER, prosecutor; b. Oklahoma City, Nov. 23, 1957; s. Stanley Reid and Joan Fontane (Garner) McC. BA in History with honors, Vanderbilt U., 1980; JD, Yale U., 1983. Bar: Okla. 1983. Assoc. Crowe & Dunlevy, Oklahoma City, 1983-87; asst. U.S. atty. Western Dist. Okla. , 1987-94; chief fin. fraud unit Western Dist. Okla., 1990-94, interim U.S. atty., 2001—; dir. Crowe & Dunlevy , 1994—2001. Dir. Ctr. for Advancement of Sci. and Tech., 1995, chmn., 1999—. Mem. ABA, Phi Beta Kappa. Republican. Episcopalian. Office: US Atty 210 W Park Ave Ste 400 Oklahoma City OK 73102*

MCCANN, CLIFTON EVERETT, lawyer; b. Des Moines, July 11, 1950; s. George Lockhart and Evelyn Elizabeth (Miller) McC.; m. Marcia Ellen Morrow, Feb. 19, 1984; children: Gregory Lockhart, Jeanna Lauren. BA in Psychology, No. Ill. U., 1972; JD, Columbus Sch. Law, 1977; LLM in Intellectual Property, George Washington U., 1985. Bar: Va. 1978, U.S. Patent Office 1979, U.S. Ct. Appeals (fed. cir.) 1982, U.S. Supreme Ct. 1983, D.C. 1984. Assoc. Beveridge, DeGrandi & Kline, Washington, 1978-83; ptnr. Lane, Aitken & McCann, 1983-2000, Venable, Baetjer, Howard & Civiletti, LLP, Washington, 2000—. Counsel intellectual property Am. Mensa, Ltd., Fort Worth, 1984—. Mem.: ABA (chair fed. litigation sub-com. on patent claim interpretation 1996—99, chair com. on intellectual property litigation 1999—), Va. Bar Assn., D.C. Bar Assn. (chmn. trademark com. of the patent, trademark and copyright sect. 1985—89), Bar Assn. D.C. (steering com. patent, trademark, copyright sect. 1996—97), Am. Intellectual Prperty Law Assn., Patent Lawyers Club (Washington), Delta Theta Phi. Federal civil litigation, Patent, Trademark and copyright. Home: 5508 Grove St Chevy Chase MD 20815-3410 Office: Venable Baetjer Howard & Civiletti 1201 New York Ave NW Ste 1000 Washington DC 20005-6197

MCCANN, JOSEPH LEO, lawyer, former government official; b. Phila., Aug. 27, 1948; s. Joseph John and Christina Mary (Kirwan) McC.; m. Aida Laico Kabigting, Dec. 6, 1986; 1 child, Angela Kathleen. BA, St. Charles Sem., Phila., 1970, postgrad., 1970-71; MA, Temple U., 1975, JD, 1977. Bar: Pa. 1977, U.S. Dist. Ct. (ea. dist.) Pa. 1977, U.S. Dist. Ct. (mid. dist.) Pa. 1978, U.S. Ct. Appeals (3d cir.) 1978, D.C. 1986, U.S. Supreme Ct. 1986, Md. 1987, U.S. Ct. Appeals (Fed. cir.) 1988, U.S. Ct. Internat. Trade 1988. Law clk. to chief justice Pa. Supreme Ct., Phila., 1977-78; dep. atty. gen. Pa. Dept. Justice, Harrisburg, 1978-80; sr. atty. U.S. GAO, Washington, 1980-96; sr. asst. gen. counsel GSA, 1996-99; pres., counsel, headmaster The Kabigting-Kirwan Meml. Nonprofit Corp., 1997-2000; atty., 2001—. Mem. Pa. Bar Assn., Phila. Bar Assn., Md. State Bar Assn. Roman Catholic. Home and Office: 204 Bookham Ln Gaithersburg MD 20877-3789 E-mail: amccann@mindspring.com

MCCANN, MAURICE JOSEPH, lawyer; b. St. Louis, July 26, 1950; s. James M. and Marie V. (Del Commune) M.; m. Suzanne Marie Grob, Dec. 29, 1990; 1 child, Mathew Maurice. BS, So. Ill. U., 1972, MA, 1974, PhD, 1976, JD, 1986. Bar: Ill. 1986, Mo. 1987, U.S. Dist. Ct. (ea. dist.) Mo. 1987, U.S. Dist. Ct. (so. dist.) Ill. 1988, U.S. Ct. Appeals (7th cir.) 1998. Teaching asst. So. Ill. U., Carbondale, 1972-76; asst. dir. Vermillion County Comprehensive Employment and Tng. Act, Danville, Ill., 1976; prof. John A. Logan Coll., Carterville, 1977; adj. prof. St. Louis U., 1977-78; exec. dir. Jackson County Comprehensive Employment and Tng. Act, Murphysboro, Ill., 1978-81, Jackson County YMCA, Carbondale, 1982-83; ptnr. McCann & Foley, Murphysboro, 1986-88; pvt. practice law, 1988—. Atty. Murphysboro Fire Protection Dist., Jackson County, 1988—; instr. dept. fin. So. Ill. U., 1988—, instr. dept. higher edn., 1994-96. Author: A Prelude to McCarthyism, 1974, Truman Administration and Federal Aid to Education, 1976, The Black Sox Scandal, 1986. Mem. Found. for Restoration of Ste. Genevieve, Mo., 1984; bd. dirs. So. Ill. Spl. Olympics, Carbondale, 1983-86; commr. Murphysboro Pk. Dist., 1990-92. Harry S. Truman scholar Truman Libr., Independence, Mo., 1975. Mem. ABA, Ill. Bar Assn., St. Louis Bar Assn., Mo. Bar Assn., Jackson County Bar Assn. Roman Catholic. Probate. Home: 42 Brian Ave Murphysboro IL 62966-6189 Office: 1331 Walnut St Murphysboro IL 62966-2026

MC CARTAN, PATRICK FRANCIS, lawyer; b. Cleve., Aug. 3, 1934; s. Patrick Francis and Stella Mercedes (Ashton) McC.; m. Lois Ann Buchman, Aug. 30, 1958; children: M. Karen, Patrick Francis, III. AB magna cum laude, U. Notre Dame, 1956, JD, 1959. Bar: Ohio 1960, U.S. Ct. Appeals (6th cir.) 1961, U.S. Ct. Appeals (3rd cir.) 1965, U.S. Ct. Appeals (D.C. cir.) 1980, U.S. Ct. Appeals (5th cir.) 1981, U.S. Ct. Appeals (4th cir.) 1989, U.S. Ct. Appeals (7th cir.) 1992, U.S. Supreme Ct. 1970. Law clk. to Hon. Charles Evans Whittaker, U.S. Supreme Ct., 1959; asso. Jones, Day, Reavis & Pogue, Cleve., 1961-65, ptnr., 1966-93, mng. ptnr., 1993—. Trustee U. Notre Dame, 2000—, chair, 2000—; trustee Cleve. Clinic Found.; chair Greater Cleve. Roundtable; mem. standing com. on rules of practice and procedure, Jud. Conf. of U.S. Fellow Am. Coll. Trial Lawyers, Internat. Acad. Trial Lawyers; mem. ABA, 6th Cir. Jud. Conf. (life), Coun. on Fgn. Rels., U.S.-Japan Bus. Coun., Ohio Bar Assn., Bar Assn. Greater Cleve. (pres. 1977-78), Musical Arts Assn. (trustee), Greater Cleve. Growth Assn. (chmn. 1997-2000). Roman Catholic. E-mai. Federal civil litigation, State civil litigation, General corporate. Office: Jones Day Reavis & Pogue North Point 901 Lakeside Ave E Cleveland OH 44114-1190 E-mail: pmccartan@jonesday.com

MCCARTER, LOUIS EUGENE, lawyer; b. Enid, Okla., Mar. 15, 1940; s. Louis Eugene and Bertha Marguerite (Krittenbrink) McC.; m. Janet Ann Korn, May 25, 1968; children— Scott Louis, Kathryn Nicole. B.A., U. Okla., 1962; LL.M., U. Tex., 1965. Bar: Tex. 1965, U.S. Dist. Ct. (ea. and so. dists.) Tex. 1975, U.S. Ct. Mil. Appeals 1966. Assoc., Vinson & Elkins, Houston, 1968-75, ptnr., 1975—. Served to capt. JAGC, U.S. Army, 1965-68; Vietnam. Decorated Bronze Star, Army Commendation medal. Mem. ABA, Tex. Bar Assn., Tex. Bd. Legal Specialization, Am. Bd. Trial Advs., Internat. Assn. Def. Counsel, Ctr. Club, Houston Country Club. E-mail: lmccarter@velaw.com. Admiralty, General civil litigation, Personal injury. Office: Vinson & Elkins 3300 First City Tower 1001 Fannin St Ste 3300 Houston TX 77002-6706

MCCARTER, W. DUDLEY, lawyer; b. St. Louis, Dec. 20, 1950; s. Willard Dudley and Vera Katherine (Schneider) McC.; m. Elizabeth Dunlop, June 14, 1986; children: Katherine, Elizabeth, Emily. BA, Knox Coll., 1972; JD, U. Mo., 1975. Bar: Mo. 1975, U.S. Dist. Ct. (ea. dist.) Mo. 1976, U.S. Ct. Appeals (8th cir.) Mo. 1977. Assoc. Mann & Poger, St. Louis, 1975-76, Suelthaus & Krueger, St. Louis, 1976-80; ptnr. Suelthaus & Kaplan, P.C., 1980-92, Behr, McCarter & Potter P.C., St. Louis, 1992—. Atty. for the City of Creve Coeur, Mo., 1992—. Author editor: Missouri Civil Litigation Handbook, 1992; author Jour. of the Mo. Bar, St. Louis Bar Jour. and Mo. Law Rev. Recipient W. Oliver Rasch award, 1985, 1989, Outstanding Young Lawyer award St. Louis County Bar Assn. 1983. Fellow ABA; mem. The Missouri Bar (pres. 1993-94). General civil litigation, Construction. Office: Behr McCarter & Potter PC 7777 Bonhomme Ave Ste 1810 Saint Louis MO 63105-1911

MCCARTER, WILLIAM KENT, lawyer; b. Brookville, Pa., Aug. 2, 1936; s. Leon Evermond and Mabel Lucille (Manners) McC.; m. Susan Ann Jordan, June 25, 1966; children— Sean Arthur, Mark James. B.S. in Social Sci., John Carroll U., 1960, M.A., 1962; J.D., Cleve. Marshall Law Sch., 1967. Bar: Ohio 1967, U.S. Dist. Ct. (no. dist.) Ohio 1968, U.S. Supreme Ct. 1971. Mem. firm McCarter & Weaver, Mentor, Ohio, 1967-68, McCarter & Weaver, Willoughby, Ohio, 1968— ; instr. law Cleve. State U., 1967-69, Am. Savs. & Loan Inst., Cleve., 1974-75. Contbr. articles to profl. jours. Mem. Lake County Bar Assn. Democrat. State civil litigation, Family and matrimonial, General practice. Home: 9079 Blue Jay Ln Mentor OH 44060-1803

MCCARTHY, CHARLES FRANCIS, JR. lawyer; b. Springfield, Mass., Dec. 9, 1926; s. Charles Francis and Maude Veronica (Clayton) McC.; m. Dorothy Bray, June 14, 1952 (dec. June 1987); children: Richard J., Linda A. Moylan, Robert P. AB, St. Michael's Coll., 1949; JD, Boston Coll., 1951. Bar: Mass. 1952, U.S. Dist. Ct. Mass. 1953. Assoc. Ganley, Crook & Smith, Springfield, Mass., 1954-67, Laming, Smith & Auchter, Springfield, 1967-80; of counsel Bacon & Wilson, P.C. and predecessor firms, 1980-94; ret., 1994. Clk. Ellis Title Co., Inc., Springfield, 1988-94. Democrat. Roman Catholic. Home: 48 Palmyra St Springfield MA 01118-2027

MCCARTHY, J. THOMAS, lawyer, educator; b. Detroit, July 2, 1937; s. John E. and Virginia M. (Hanlon) McC.; m. Nancy Irene Orrell, July 10, 1976 BS, U. Detroit, 1960; JD, U. Mich., 1963. Bar: Calif. 1964. Assoc. Julian Caplan, San Francisco, 1963-66; prof. law U. San Francisco, 1966—; vis. prof. law U. Calif., Berkeley, 1976-77, Davis, 1979-80. Cons. in field; mem. Trademark Rev. Commn., 1986-88. Author: McCarthy on Trademarks and Unfair Competition, 6 vols., 4th edit., 1996, McCarthy on Rights of Publicity and Privacy, 1987, 2d edit., 2000, McCarthy's Desk Encyclopedia of Intellectual Property, 2d edit., 1995; mem. editl. bd. Trademark Reporter. Recipient Jefferson medal N.J. Intellectual Property Assn., 1994, Ladas award Brand Names Ednl. Found., 1997, Pattishall medal Brand Names Found., 2000. Mem. Am. Intellectual Property Law Assn. (Watson award 1965, Centennial award in Trademark law 1997), Internat. Assn. for Advancement of Teaching and Rsch. in Intellectual Property, Am. Law Inst. (adv. com. on restatement of law of unfair competition), IEEE.

MCCARTHY, KEVIN JOHN, lawyer; b. N.Y.C., Apr. 8, 1941; s. Vincent Patrick and Mary (H.) McC.; m. Marianne Pitts, Nov. 5, 1966; children: Mary Rita, Kevin, Colin. BS, U. Md., 1963; JD, U. Md., Balt., 1966. Bar: Md. 1966, U.S. Dist. Ct. Md. 1966, U.S. Ct. Appeals (4th cir.) 1966, U.S. Supreme Ct. 1972, D.C. 1976, U.S. Dist. Ct. D.C. 1976, U.S. Ct. Appeals (D.C. cir.) 1976, Fla. 1998. Law clk. Cir. Ct. for P.G. County, Upper Marlboro, Md., 1964-66; assoc., ptnr. Sasscer, Clagett & Channing, 1966-76; ptnr. O'Malley, Miles & McCarthy, 1976-86, McCarthy, Bacon & Costello, Landover, 1986—. Arbitrator Am. Arbitration Assn., Washington, 1972—. Contbg. author: Maryland Civil Patter Jury Instructions, 1975, 2d edit., 1984, 3d edit., 1993. Named The Best Lawyers in Am., Woodward/White. Fellow Am. Bar Found., Md. Bar Found.; mem. Internat. Assn. Ins. Counsel, Fedn. Ins. and Corp. Counsel, Def. Rsch. Inst., Am. Trial Lawyers Assn., Md. Trial Lawyers Assn., Assn. Def. Trial Attys., Million Dollar Advocates Forum, Trial Lawyers for Pub. Justice. Avocations: golf, racquetball, coaching soccer and lacrosse. General civil litigation, Personal injury, Product liability. Office: McCarthy & Costello 4640 Forbes Blvd Lanham Seabrook MD 20706-4323 E-mail: Kevin@McCarthyCostello.com

MCCARTHY, ROBERT EMMETT, lawyer; b. Bklyn., May 26, 1951; s. John Joseph and Leona Mary (Hart) McC.; m. Elizabeth Anne Naumoff, May 20, 1978; children: John Philip, Emily Jane. BS in Fgn. Studies, Georgetown U., 1973, MS in Fgn. Studies, JD, 1978. Bar: N.J. 1978, U.S. Dist. Ct. (ea. and so. dists.) N.Y. 1979. Assoc. Patterson, Belknap et al, N.Y.C., 1978-84; gen. counsel MTV Networks Inc., 1984-86; v.p., counsel/communications Viacom Internat., 1986-87; exec. v.p. Nelson Vending Tech., Ltd., 1987-89; exec. v.p., gen. counsel Cateret Savs. Bank FA, Morristown, N.J., 1989-91; cons. McCarthy Comms., Elizabeth, 1991-95; sr. v.p., gen. counsel Time, Inc., N.Y.C., 1996—. Cons. UN Ctr. on Transnat. Corps., N.Y.C., 1979; exec. dir. Spl. Master Reapportionment of N.Y., 1982; term mem. Council Fgn. Relations, N.Y.C., 1980-84. Founder, pres. Elizabeth (N.J.) Dem. Assn., 1980; coordinator Florio for Gov., Union County, N.J., 1981. Mem. ABA, N.Y. State Bar Assn., N.J. State Bar Assn., N.Y. County Lawyers Assn., Assn. Bar City N.Y. Roman Catholic. E-mail: robert. Communications, General corporate, Entertainment. Home: 3 Woods Ln Chatham NJ 07928-1760 Office: Time Inc 33rd Fl 1271 Avenue Of The Americas New York NY 10020-1300 E-mail: mccarthy@timeinc.com

MCCARTHY, THOMAS JAMES, JR. lawyer; b. Pulaski, Va., Nov. 24, 1943; s. Thomas James and Jane (Osborne) McC.; m. Sally Stockdale, July 25, 1987. BA in Econs., Washington and Lee U., 1967; JD, U. Va., 1970. Bar: Va. 1970, U.S. Dist. Ct. (we. dist.) Va. 1974, U.S. Supreme Ct. 2000. Asoc. Gilmer, Sadler, Ingram Sutherland & Hutton, Pulaski, 1970-75, ptnr., 1975—; county atty. Pulaski County, 1983—. Adminstrv. hearings officer Commonwealth of Va., 1983—; commr. of accts. Pulaski County, 1989—. Bd. dirs. New River C.C., 1980-88, 96—, vice chair, 1981-88, 2000—, mem. found. bd., 1989-91. Col. JAGC, U.S. Army Res., ret., 1997. Decorated Legion of Merit, Meritorious Svc. medal, Army Commendation medal. Mem. Va. Bar Assn., 27th Jud. Cir. Bar Assn. (pres. 1978-81), Pulaski County Bar Assn., Sigma Chi, Phi Alpha Delta. Democrat. Episcopalian. Home: PO Box 818 Pulaski VA 24301-0818 Office: Gilmer Sadler et al 65 E Main St Pulaski VA 24301-5013

MCCARTHY, THOMAS O. lawyer; b. Denver, Aug. 3, 1947; s. Thomas E. and Edna D. (Davis) McC.; m. Sharon K., June 22, 1974; children: Jennifer, Julianne. BSEE cum laude, U. Mo., 1970, JD, 1972. Bar: Mo. 1973, U.S. Supreme Ct. 1994, U.S. Ct. Appeals (8th cir.) 1974, U.S. Dist. Ct. (ea. dist.) Mo. 1974. Mng. ptnr. McMahon, Berger, Hanna, Linihan, Cody & McCarthy, St. Louis. Bd. dirs. BJC Healthsys., St. Louis, 1997—, Mo. Bapt. Med. Ctr., St. Louis, 1996—, Humane Soc. Mo. Mem. St. Louis Bar Assn. (chmn. labor law com. 1985-86, labor and employment sect., litigation sect.). Avocations: hunting, skiing. Home: 13522 Weston Park Dr Saint Louis MO 63131-1044 Office: McMahon Berger Hanna Linihan Cody & McCarthy 2730 N Ballas Rd Ste 200 Saint Louis MO 63131-3039

MCCARTHY, WILLIAM JOSEPH, lawyer, financial service executive; b. Bklyn., Feb. 13, 1923; s. William Joseph and Louise Ann (Malonson) M.; m. Carol E. Martin, Jan. 22, 1949 (dec. Jan. 1987); children: Christian, Mark, Margaret, Kelley, Mary. BS, Georgetown U., 1944, LLB, 1947; MBA, N.Y.U., 1965. Bar: D.C. 1947, U.S. Ct. Appeals (2d cir.) 1948, N.Y. 1947. Assoc., Hill, Rivkins & Middleton, 1947-49, Sullivan, Donovan, Heenehan & Hanrahan, 1949-52, Hawkins, Delafield & Wood, 1952-56; dep. U.S. mem. Validation Bd. for German Dollar Bond, 1956-60; mcpl. analyst Shearson, Hammill & Co., N.Y.C., 1960-62, sr. analyst, 1962-68, v.p., 1970, dir. new issue svc., 1962-72; mcpl. bond rsch. div., Moody's Investors Svcs., Inc., N.Y.C. 1972-75; v.p., mgr. mcpl. rsch. Blyth, Eastman, Dillon & Co., NYC, 1975-80; v.p. pub. finance Fitch Investors Svc., Inc., N.Y.C., 1980-90; cons., 1990-97. Active North East Yonkers Taxpayers Assn. (pres. 1970-71), Mohegan Heights Homeowners Assn. Mem. Soc. Mcpl. Analysts (pres. 1983), Assn. for Mcpl. Leasing & Fin. (dir. 1982-83), N.Y. Mcpl. Analysts (chmn. 1967-68), The Money Marketeers, Mun. Forum of N.Y., Met. Econ. Assn., Mcpl. Bond Club, KC. Republican. Roman Catholic. Home: 36 Shawnee Ave Yonkers NY 10710-5121

MC CARTNEY, RALPH FARNHAM, lawyer; b. Charles City, Iowa, Dec. 11, 1924; s. Ralph C. and Helen (Farnham) McC.; m. Rhoda Mae Huxsol, June 25, 1950; children: Ralph, Julia, David. J.D., U. Mich., 1950; B. Sci., Iowa State U., 1972. Bar: Iowa 1950. Mem. firm Miller, Heuber & Miller, Des Moines, 1950-52, Frye & McCartney, Charles City, 1952-73, McCartney & Erb, Charles City, 1973-78; judge Dist. Ct. Iowa, 1978-87; chief judge 2d Judicial Dist., 1987-92; sr. judge Ct. Appeals, 1992—. Mem. jud. coordinating com. Iowa Supreme Ct. Chmn. Supreme Ct. Adv. Com. on Adminstrn. of Clks. Offices; mem. Iowa Ho. of Reps., 1967-70, majority floor leader, 1969-70; mem. Iowa Senate, 1973-74. Bd. regents U. Iowa, Iowa State U., U. No. Iowa, Iowa Sch. for Deaf, Iowa Braille and Sight Saving Sch. Served with AUS, 1942-45. Mem. Iowa Judges Assn. No e-mail. Appellate. Home: 1828 Cedar View Dr Charles City IA 50616-9129 Office: Cty Chambers Courthouse Charles City IA 50616

MCCARTY, WILLIAM MICHAEL, JR. lawyer; b. Trenton, N.J., 1938; AB, Am. U., Dickinson Coll., 1964; JD, Dickinson Sch. Law, 1967. Bar: Vt. 1967, U.S. Dist. Ct. Vt. 1967, U.S. Ct. Appeals (2d cir.) 1973, U.S. Supreme Ct. 1978. Assoc. Fitts & Olson, Brattleboro, Vt., 1967-71; sole practice, 1971-76; ptnr. McCarty & Rifkin, Brattleboro, Wilmington, Vt., 1976-80; sr. ptnr., pres. McCarty Law Offices, P.C., 1980—. Presenter in various fields; dir. various corps. Mem. Brattleboro Zoning Bd. Adjustment, 1968-75; trustee Vt. Legal Aid, 1970-82, pres., 1979-80; pres. Brattleboro Winter Carnival, 1971-72; rep. Windham Regional Planning & Devel. Com., 1968-70, chmn. ch. coun., bench bar com., 1992-97, moderator Congl. Ch., 1990-94. With USMC, 1956-60. Mem. ABA, ATLA, Am. Bd. Trial Advocates, Vt. Bar Assn., Windham County Bar Assn. (pres. 1991-93, chair bench bar com. 1989-97), Am. Jud. Soc., Am. Law Student Assn. (nat. v.p., bd. govs.), Nat. Coun. Sch. Attys., Vt. Trial Laywers Assn. (outstanding litigation achievement award 1994), Am. Bd. Trial Advocates (advocate, Vt.), Inns of Ct., Vt. Criminal Def. Attys. Assn., Brattleboro C. of C. (bd. mgrs. 1971-72), U.S. Supreme Ct. Hist. Soc. (Vt. state chair 1999-2001). Republican. General civil litigation, Family and matrimonial, Personal injury. Office: 76 High St Brattleboro VT 05301-6074

MCCASLIN, LEON, lawyer; b. Royal, Ark., Oct. 3, 1931; s. Robert O. and Gladys M. (Williamson) McC.; widowed; children: Robyn, Marcus, Jennifer, David, Ted. BS in Sci., U. Oreg., 1956; LLB, LaSalle Extension U., 1968. Bar: U.S. Dist. Ct. (no. dist.) Calif. 1968, U.S. Dist. Ct. (ea. dist.) Calif. 1969, U.S. Ct. Appeals (9th cir.) 1973, U.S. Tax Ct. 1974, U.S. Dist. Ct. (cen. dist.) Calif. 1980. Police officer Marysville Police Dept., Calif., 1956-59; adjuster CalFarm Ins. Co., Yuba City, 1959-68; sole practice, 1968—; ptnrshp. McCaslin & McCaslin LLP, 1999—. Dist. claims mgr. CalFarm Ins. Co., 1968-69; dep. dist. atty. Yuba City, 1970-74. Past pres., bd. dirs. Sutter Buttes Regional Theatre; treas. Sutter County Dem. Cen. Com., Buttes Area Counsel. Mem. ABA, Calif. Bar Assn., Assn. Trial Lawyers Am., Calif. Trial Lawyers Assn. Am. Arbitration Assn., Am. Judicature Soc., Ducks Unltd., Lambda Chi Alpha. Club: Toastmasters. Lodges: Masons, Shriners, Elks. Avocations: travel, marathon running, tennis, reading. Criminal, Personal injury, Workers' compensation. Office: 1408 Live Oak Blvd # A Yuba City CA 95991-2970

MCCAULEY, CLEYBURN LYCURGUS, lawyer; b. Houston, Feb. 8, 1929; s. Reese Stephens and Elizabeth Ann (Burleson) McC.; m. Elizabeth Kelton McKoy, June 7, 1950; children: Stephens Francis, Lillian Elizabeth, Cleyburn, Lucy Annette. BS, U.S. Mil. Acad., 1950; MS in Engring. Econ., Statistical Quality Control and Indsl. Engring., Stanford U., 1959; JD, Coll. William and Mary, 1970. Bar: D.C. 1971, Va. 1970, Tex. 1970, U.S. Ct. Claims 1971, U.S. Tax Ct. 1971, U.S. Supreme Ct. 1973. Commd. 2d lt. U.S. Air Force, 1950, advanced through grades to lt. col., 1971, ret., 1971; pvt. practice law, Washington, 1975—. Mem. Fed. Bar Assn., Va. Bar Assn., Tex. Bar Assn., D.C. Bar Assn., IEEE, AIAA, Am. Soc. Quality Control, Phi Alpha Delta. Banking, General corporate, Corporate taxation. Home: 402 S 3rd St Wilmington NC 28401-5102

MCCAULEY, DAVID W. lawyer, educator; b. Wheeling, W.Va., June 29, 1958; s. David A. and Patricia S. (Clark) McC.; children from previous marriages: Ashley Lynn, Connor Bryan. BA, U. W.Va., 1980, JD, 1983. Bar: W.Va. 1983, U.S. Dist. Ct. (no. and so. dists.) W.Va. 1983. Assoc. Coleman & Wallace, Buckhannon, W.Va., 1983-86; guardian ad litem child abuse, neglect 26th Judicial Dist., 1983—; ptnr. Coleman & Wallace, 1986-94. City atty. City of Buckhannon, 1983—; instr. bus. law W.Va. Wesleyan Coll., Buckhannon, 1983-94, asst. prof., 1994-2000, sr. lectr., 2000—, dir. MBA program, 1994-99, gen. legal counsel, 1993—; spkr. W.Va. Mcpl. League Conv., 1989; presenter sexual harrassment workshops. Sec. Upshur-Buckhannon Main St. Project, 1987-89, pres., 1989-90; bd. dirs., legal counsel W.Va. Strawberry Festival, 1986-99—; bd. dirs. Upshur County United Way, Buckhannon, 1986-89, v.p., 1987; v.p. Buckhannon-Upshur Work Adjustment Ctr., 1990—. Mem. ABA, Internat. Municipal Lawyers Assn., W.Va. Bar Assn., W.Va. State Bar Assn., Upshur County Bar Assn. (pres. 1990-93), W.Va. Trial Lawyers Assn., W.Va. U. Alumni Assn., Mountaineer Athletic Club (Upshur County chpt.), Lions (pres. Buckhannon club 1988), Nat. Assn. of Bus. Schs. and Programs. Avocation: sports. General civil litigation, Construction. Home: 10 Meade St Buckhannon WV 26201-2630 Office: WVa Wesleyan Coll PO Box 121 Buckhannon WV 26201-0121 E-mail: mccauley@wvwc.edu

MCCLAIN, WILLIAM ANDREW, lawyer; b. Sanford, N.C., Jan. 11, 1913; s. Frank and Blanche (Leslie) McC.; m. Roberta White, Nov. 11, 1944. AB, Wittenberg U., 1934; JD, U. Mich., 1937; LLD (hon.), Wilberforce U., 1963, U. Cin., 1971; LHD, Wittenberg U., 1972. Bar: Ohio 1938, U.S. Dist. Ct. (so. dist.) Ohio 1940, U.S. Ct. Appeals (6th cir.) 1946, U.S. Supreme Ct. 1946. Mem. Berry, McClain & White, 1937-58; dep. solicitor, City of Cin., 1957-63, city solicitor, 1963-72; mem. Keating, Muething & Klekamp, Cin., 1972-73; gen. counsel Cin. br. SBA, 1973-75; judge Hamilton County Common Pleas Ct., 1975-76; judge Mcpl. Ct., 1976-80; of counsel Manley, Burke, Lipton & Cook, Cin., 1980—; adj. prof. U. Cin., 1963-72, Salmon P. Chase Law Sch., 1965-72. Mem. exec. com. ARC, Cin., 1978—; bd. dirs. NCCJ, 1975—. Served to 1st lt. JAG, U.S. Army, 1943-46. Decorated Army Commendation award; recipient Nat. Layman award, A.M.E. Ch., 1963; Alumni award Wittenberg U., 1966; Nat. Inst. Mcpl. Law Officers award, 1971, Ellis Island Medal of Honor, 1997. Fellow Am. Bar Found.; mem. ABA, FBA, Am. Judicature Soc., Cin. Bar Assn., Ohio Bar Assn., Nat. Bar Assn., Friendly Sons St. Patrick, Bankers Club, Masons (33d degree), Alpha Phi Alpha, Sigma Pi Phi. Republican. Methodist. Home: 2101 Grandin Rd Apt 904 Cincinnati OH 45208-3346

MCCLARD, JACK EDWARD, lawyer; b. Lafayette, La., May 13, 1946; s. Lee Franklin and Mercedes Cecile (Landry) McC.; m. Marilyn Kay O'Gorman, June 3, 1972; 1 child, Lauren Minton. BA in Hist., Rice U., 1968; JD, U. Tex., 1974. Bar: Va. 1974, D.C. 1981, N.Y. 1985, Tex. 1996, U.S. Dist. Ct. (ea. and we. dists.) Va. 1974, U.S. Dist. Ct. D.C. 1981, U.S. Dist. Ct. (so. and ea. dists.) N.Y. 1985, U.S. Dist. Ct. (ea. dist.) Tex. 1998, U.S. Ct. Appeals (4th cir.) 1978, U.S. Ct. Appeals (D.C. cir.) 1980, U.S. Ct. Appeals (5th cir.) 1993. Assoc. Hunton & Williams, Richmond, Va., 1974-81, ptnr., 1981—. Contbr. articles to profl. jours., books. Served to lt. (j.g.) USN, 1968-71. Mem. ABA, Va. Bar Assn., Richmond Bar Assn., Va. defense Attys. Assn., 5th Cir. Bar, John Marshall Inns of Ct. Democrat. Episcopalian. Avocations: bridge, gardening, wine. Federal civil litigation, State civil litigation, Construction. Home: 100 Trowbridge Rd Richmond VA 23233-5724 Office: Hunton & Williams Riverfront Plz E Tower 951 E Byrd St Richmond VA 23219-4074 E-mail: jmcclard@hunton.com

MCCLAUGHERTY, JOE L. lawyer, educator; b. June 1, 1951; s. Frank Lee and Elease (Terrell) McC. BBA with honors, U. Tex., 1973, JD with honors, 1976. Bar: Tex. 1976, N.Mex. 1976, U.S. Dist. Ct. N.Mex. 1976, U.S. Ct. Appeals (10th cir.) 1976, U.S. Supreme Ct. 1979, Colo. 1988. Assoc. Rodey, Dickason, Sloan, Akin & Robb, P.A., Albuquerque, 1976-81, ptnr., dir., 1981-87, resident ptnr. Santa Fe, 1983-87, mng. ptnr., 1985-87; ptnr. Kemp, Smith, Duncan & Hammond, P.C., 1987-92, mng. ptnr., 1987-92; ptnr. McClaugherty & Silver, P.C., Santa Fe, 1992—. Adj. prof. law U. N.Mex., Albuquerque, 1983—; faculty Nat. Inst. Trial Advocacy, so. regional, So. Meth. U. Law Sch., 1983—, Rocky Mt. regional, U. Denver Law Sch., 1986—, nat. session U. Colo. Law Sch., 1987; faculty Hastings Ctr. for Trial and Appellate Advocacy, 1985—; bd. dirs. MCM Corp., Raleigh, N.C., Brit.-Am. Ins. Co., Ltd., Nassau, The Bahamas, 1985-91. Mem. N.Mex. Bar Assn. (bd. dirs. trial practice sect. 1976-85, chairperson 1983-84, dir. young lawyers divsn. 1978-80), N.Mex. Assn. Def. Lawyers (pres. 1982-83, bd. dirs. 1982-85). Federal civil litigation, State civil litigation, Personal injury. Office: McClaugherty & Silver PC PO Box 8680 Santa Fe NM 87504-8680

MCCLELLAN, CRAIG RENE, lawyer; b. Portland, Oreg., June 28, 1947; s. Charles Russell and Annette Irene (Benedict) McC.; m. Susan Armistead Nash, June 7, 1975; children: Ryan Alexander, Shannon Lea. BS in Econs., U. Oreg., 1969; JD magna cum laude, Calif. We. U., 1976. Bar: Calif. 1976, U.S. Dist. Ct. (so. dist.) Calif. 1976, U.S. Dist. Ct. (ea., ctrl., no. dists.) Calif. 1991, U.S. Supreme Ct. 1991. Compliance specialist Cost of Living Coun. and Price Commn., Washington, 1972-73, dir. Oil Policy subcom., 1973; ptnr. Luce, Forward, Hamilton & Scripps, San Diego, 1976-87; owner McClellan & Assocs., 1987—. Chmn. annual fundraising auction KPBS, 1984. Capt. USMC, 1969-72. Fellow Am. Coll. Trial Lawyers; mem. Assn. Trial Lawyers Am., Am. Bd. Trial Advocates, Am. Inns of Ct. (master), Calif. State Bar Assn., San Diego County Bar Assn., Calif. Trial Lawyers Assn. (bd. govs. 1985-87), San Diego Trial Lawyers Assn. (bd. dirs. 1983-90), Nat. Forensics League, Phi Gamma Delta, Phi Alpha Delta. Presbyterian. Avocations: reading, running, tennis, chess, civic activities. Personal injury, Product liability. Office: McClellan & Assocs 1144 State St San Diego CA 92101-3529 E-mail: mcclellan9@aol.com

MCCLELLAN, JANET ELAINE, law educator; b. Salina, Kans., June 30, 1951; d. William Francis and Ethel Mary (Rinebold) McC. BA in Govt., Adminstrn., Park Coll., Parkville, Mo., 1976; MPA, U. Dayton (Ohio), 1978; postgrad., U. Kans., 1982-86. Police officer City of Leavenworth, Kans., 1970-71; narcotics agt. Kans. Bur. Investigation, Topeka, 1971-73; asst. to chief Police Dept., Ellensberg, Wash., 1973-76, dir. juvenile divsn. Centerville, Ohio, 1976-79, watch comdr. Douglas, Wyo., 1978-79; dir. criminal justice adminstrn. Park Coll., 1979—. Directing advisor Tau Lambda Alpha Epsilon and Alpha Phi Omega, Park Coll., 1980-98; cons. Probation-Parole Dept., Kansas City, Mo., 1979-80, Police Dept., Leavenworth, 1981-82, Sheriff's Dept., Liberty, Mo., 1984-86; corrections adminstr. Kans. Dept. of Correction, 1988-96; police chief Pawnee Rock, Kans., 1996-98; prof. criminal justice, 1998—. Author: mystery book series including K.C. Bomber, 1996, Murder in Cloud City, 2000, Penn Valley Phoenix, 1997, River Quay, 1998, Chimney Rock Blues, 1999, Windrow Garden, 1999; contbr. articles to profl. jours.; reviewer criminal justice textbooks, jours., reviewing editor book Introduction to Criminal Justice, 1984, Modern Police Management, Criminal Justice and Public Policy. Chmn. S.W. Montgomery County Youth Commn., Dayton, Ohio, 1977-79; bd. dirs. Synergy Youth Half-way House, Parkville, 1980-86. Mem. Internat. Assn. Chiefs of Police, Am. Soc. Criminology, Am. Criminal Justice Soc., Am. Correctional Assn., Mo. Polit. Sci. Assn., Am. Soc. Pub. Adminstrn., Mo. Acad. Sci., Pi Gamma Mu, Pi Sigma Alpha, Delta Tau Kappa. Democrat. Office: Southwestern Oreg CC 1988 Newmark Ave Coos Bay OR 97420-2911 E-mail: jmcclell@southwestern.cc.or.us

MCCLINTOCK, THOMAS LEE, lawyer; b. Lake Bluff, Ill., July 5, 1948; s. Harold B. and Sarah O. (Durbin) M.; children: Ryan Arthur, Andrew Smith, Max Thomas. AA, Ill. Valley C.C., 1968; BS, No. Ill. U., 1970, MBA, 1971; JD, Valparaiso U., 1974. Bar: Ill. 1974, U.S. Dist. Ct. (no. dist.) Ill. 1975, U.S. Supreme Ct. 1977. Intern Ill. Defender Project, Ottawa, 1973; asst. states atty. LaSalle County, 1974-79; ptnr. McClintock & Steele, LaSalle, Ill., 1979-83, McClintock, Steele & Barry, LaSalle, 1983-84, Aplington, Kaufman, McClintock, Steele & Barry, Ltd., LaSalle, 1984—. Dem. candidate for State's Atty., 1980. Named among Outstanding Young Men of Am., Jaycees, 1980-84. Fellow Phi Beta Lambda (Ill. Bus. Exec. award 1971); mem. ATLA, Ill. State Bar Assn., Ill. Trial Lawyers Assn., Sigma Iota Epsilon. Methodist. State civil litigation, Criminal, Personal injury. Home: 207 Shooting Park Rd Peru IL 61354-1966 Office: 160 Marquette St La Salle IL 61301

MCCLOSKEY, JAY P. former prosecutor; Asst. U.S. atty. Dept. Justice, Bangor, Maine, U.S. atty. Portland, 1993—2001.

MCCLOW, ROGER JAMES, labor lawyer; b. St. Johns, Mich., July 23, 1947; s. Jack Gordon and Madalene V. (Mahaffy) McC.; m. Suzanne Terese Posler, July 13, 1978. BA in Polit. Sci. with distinction, U. Mich., 1969; JD magna cum laude, Wayne State U., 1976. Bar: Mich. 1977, U.S. Dist. Ct. (ea. dist.) Mich. 1977, U.S. Ct. Appeals (6th cir.) 1985, U.S. Ct. Appeals (8th cir.) 1987, U.S. Supreme Ct. 1988. Assoc. Miller, Cohen, Martens & Sugerman, Detroit, 1977-81, Klimist, McKnight & Sale, P.C., Southfield, Mich., 1981-83; ptnr. Klimist, McKnight, Sale, McClow & Canzano, P.C., 1983—. Bd. dirs. Hemid (Sr. Citizen's Agy.), Detroit, 1982—; tutor Children's Ctr., Detroit, 1990-93; vol. Hospice Legal Aid, Detroit, 1991—, Patient Advocate Found., 1998—; mem. gun safety com. Alliance for Greater, Safer Detroit, 1993-95. Recipient Outstanding Vol. Svc. award Children's Ctr. Detroit, 1993. Mem. State Bar Mich. (coun. mem., labor law and employment sect. 1992-96), Detroit Bar Assn., Oakland County Bar Assn., Assn. Trial Lawyers Am., Mich. Trial Lawyers Assn., Indsl. Rels. Rsch. Assn., Phi Sigma Alpha. Democrat. Avocations: antiques, tennis, historic home restoration, landscaping. Labor, Pension, profit-sharing, and employee benefits, Personal injury. Office: Klimist McKnight Sale McClow & Cazano 400 Galleria Officentre Ste 117 Southfield MI 48034-2161 E-mail: rjmcclow@aol.com

MCCLURE, JAMES FOCHT, JR. federal judge; b. Danville, Pa., Apr. 6, 1931; s. James Focht and Florence Kathryn (Fowler) McC.; m. Elizabeth Louise Barber, June 14, 1952; children: Holly McClure Kerwin, Kimberly Ann Pacala, Jamee McClure Sealy, Mary Elizabeth Hudec, Margaret McClure Persing. AB, Amherst Coll., 1952; JD, U. Pa., 1957. Bar: D.C. 1957, Pa. 1958, U.S. Dist. Ct. D.C. 1957, U.S. Dist. Ct. (ea. and mid. dist.) Pa. 1958, U.S. Ct. Appeals (3d cir.) 1959. Atty., advisor Dept. State, Washington, 1957-58; assoc. Morgan, Lewis & Bockius, Phila., 1958-61; atty. Merck & Co., Inc., N.Y.C., 1961-65; ptnr. McClure & McClure, Lewisburg, Pa., 1965-77, McClure & Light, Lewisburg, 1978-84; pres., judge Ct. Common Pleas, 17th Jud. Dist. Pa., 1984-90; sr. dist. judge U.S. Dist. Ct. (mid. dist.) Pa., Williamsport, Pa., 1990—. Dist. atty. Union County, Lewisburg, 1974-75. Pres. bd. sch. dirs. Lewisburg Area Sch. Dist., 1969-74. Cpl. U.S. Army, 1952-54. Mem. Pa. Bar Assn., Union County Bar Assn., Bucknell U. Golf Club, Susquehanna Valley Chorale, Order of Coif, Phi Beta Kappa. Republican. Presbyterian. Office: US Dist Ct 240 W 3rd St Ste 406 Williamsport PA 17701-6466 E-mail: gary_palmer@unc.edu

MCCLURE, MICHELLE DEVONDRIA, lawyer; b. Charlotte, N.C., July 9, 1972; d. Robert and Brenda (Wentz) McC. BA, Stanford U., 1994; JD, U. N.C., 1997. Bar: N.C. 1998. Assoc. atty. Martin & McClure, Elon College, N.C., 1998, Stefan R. Latorre, P.A., Charlotte, 1998—. Mem. ABA, ATLA, N.C. Assn. Women Attys., N.C. Bar Assn., N.C. Assn. Black Lawyers, Mecklenburg County Bar Assn. Avocations: traveling, reading, cooking, exercising, movies. Home: PO Box 37125 Charlotte NC 28237-7125 Office: Stefan R Latorre PA 2629 Central Ave Charlotte NC 28205 E-mail: dm7972@aol.com

MCCLURE, ROGER JOHN, lawyer; b. Cleve., Nov. 22, 1943; s. Theron R. and Colene (Irwin) McC. BA, Ohio State U., 1965, JD cum laude, 1972; MA, Northwestern U., 1966. Bar: U.S. Ct. Appeals (D.C. cir.) 1974, U.S. Supreme Ct. 1978, Va. 1973, Md. 1973, Ohio, U.S. Ct. Appeals (4th, 5th & 10th cirs.). Asst. atty. gen. State of Ohio, Columbus, 1972; trial atty. FTC, Washington, 1972-76; sr. assoc. Law Offices of A.D. Berkeley, 1976-81; pvt. practice Alexandria, Va., 1981—; pres. Roger J. McClure, PC, 1987—; del. Va. Gen. Assembly, 1992—, co-chmn. militia and police com., 1998—. Adj. prof. Acad. of Multidisciplinary Practice, Mich. State U., 2001—; host talk show Sta. WRC Radio, 1987-93, 99-2001, Sta. WPGC, 1993-94. Bd. editors Ohio State U. Law Rev., 1970-72; contbr. articles to profl. jours.; contbg. reviewer and author: Conspectus, Estate and Wealth Strategies Planning. Bd. dirs. No. Va. Cmty. Found., 1995—. With U.S. Army, 1967-69. Decorated Bronze Star; Masters Fellow Esperti Peterson Inst., 1996—. Mem. D.C. Bar Assn. (real estate steering com. 1982-84, chmn. antitrust divsn. 1975-76), No. Va. Apt. Assn. (bd. dirs. 1988-92, 1st v.p. 1987-88, pres. 1988-89), Nat. Network Estate Planning Attys., Dulles Area Transp. Assn. (bd. dirs.), Wolf Trap Found. (adv. coun.), Washington Nat. Cathedral. Avocation: sailing. Estate planning, Real property, Estate taxation. Office: 500 N Washington St Alexandria VA 22314-2314 E-mail: rmcclure@ix.netcom.com

MCCLURE, WILLIAM PENDLETON, lawyer; b. Washington, May 25, 1925; s. John Elmer and Helen Newsome (Pendleton) McC.; children: Marilyn Alexander, Helen Pendleton, Elizabeth Ruffin, Melinda Geoghegan. BS, U. Pa., 1949; JD, George Washington U., 1951, LLM, 1954; postgrad., The Hague (Netherlands) Acad. Internat. Law, 1952. Bar: D.C. 1951. Sr. ptnr. McClure & Trotter, Washington, 1952-91, McClure, Trotter & Mentz, Washington, 1991-93, McClure, Trotter & Mentz, chartered, Washington, 1993-95; ptnr. White & Case, 1995—. Chmn. D.C. div. Crusade Against Cancer, Am. Cancer Soc., 1966, 67. Served from pvt. to 1st lt., inf. U.S. Army, 1943-46, PTO. Mem. Am. Bar Assn., Bar Assn. D.C., Am. Judicature Soc., Order of Coif, Phi Delta Phi, Phi Delta Theta. Clubs: Metropolitan (Washington), Columbia Country (Washington), Nat. Press (Washington). Corporate taxation, Estate taxation. Home: 26201 Prescott Rd Clarksburg MD 20871-9163 Office: 601 13th St NW Ste 600 S Washington DC 20005-3807

MCCOBB, JOHN BRADFORD, JR. lawyer; b. Orange, N.J., Oct. 14, 1939; s. John Bradford and Dorothea Joyce (Hoffman) M.; m. Maureen Kelly, Oct. 6, 1973; 1 dau., Carrie Elizabeth. A.B., Princeton U. cum laude, 1961; J.D., Stanford U., 1966; LL.M., NYU, 1973. Bar: Calif. 1967. Assoc., IBM, Armonk, N.Y., 1966-1974, gen. counsel, Tokyo, 1974-77, lab. counsel, Endicott, N.Y., 1977-79, sr. atty., White Plains, N.Y., 1979-81, regional counsel, Dallas, 1981-83; counsel, sec. IBM Instruments, Inc., Danbury, Conn., 1983-87; area counsel European Labs, Hursley, England, 1987-90; counsel govtl. programs IBM, Washington, 1990-97. Trustee Princeton-in-Asia, Inc., 1970-86 . Princeton-in-Asia-teaching fellow at Chinese Univ. of Hong Kong, 1963-65. Mem. ABA, State Bar of Calif., Phi Beta Kappa. Contbr. articles to profl. jours. Antitrust, Computer, Private international.

MCCOID, NANCY KATHERINE, lawyer; b. Tacoma, July 30, 1953; d. Francis Patnck and Kathleen Grace McCoid; m. Tom Mash, Aug. 25, 1989; 1 child, Kelly Elizabeth. BS in Psychology summa cum laude, U. Wash., 1976; MA in Psychology summa cum laude, Western Wash. U., 1979; JD with high honors, U. Wash., 1983. Bar: Wash., U.S. Dist. Ct. (we. dist.) Wash., U.S. Ct. Appeals (9th cir.), U.S. Supreme Ct. Law clk. divsn. I Ct. Appeals, Seattle, 1983-85; assoc. Merrick, Hofstedt & Lindsey, 1985-90, shareholder, 1991—. Mentor to 1st-yr. law students U. Wash., Seattle, 1990—; arbitrator King County Superior Ct., Seattle, 1991—; mem. healthcare panel counsel Tenet, 1996—; spkr. in field. Vol. atty. Bar Assn. Pro Bono Program, Seattle, 1991—, Fed. Pro Bono Program, Seattle, 1992; mem. Gov. Gary Locke's Transition Team. Mem. Am. Law Firm Assn. (health practices com., employment law com.), Wash. State Bar Assn. (com. on profl. liability 1995—, vol. spkr. 1998), Wash. Def. Trial Lawyers (com. on profl. liability 1995—), Def. Rsch. Inst. (com. on profl. liability 1990—), King County Bar Assn. (com. on professionalism 1995, gender bias com., com. on jud. evaluation 1998, pres.'s coun. mem.), Order of Coif. Avocations: jazz, theater, gardening, traveling. General civil litigation, Personal injury, Professional liability. Office: Merrick Hofstedt & Lindsey 710 9th Ave Seattle WA 98104-2099

MCCOLLUM, JAMES FOUNTAIN, lawyer; b. Reidsville, N.C., Mar. 24, 1946; s. James F. and Dell (Frazier) McC.; m. Susan Shasek, Apr. 26, 1969; children: Audra Lynne, Amy Elizabeth. BS, Fla. Atlantic U., 1968; JD, Fla. State U., 1972. Bar: U.S. Ct. Appeals (5th cir.) 1973, Fla. 1972, U.S. Ct. Appeals (11th cir.) 1982. Assoc. Kennedy & McCollum, 1972-73; prin. James F. McCollum, P.A., 1973-77, McCollum & Oberhausen, P.A., 1977-80, McCollum, Oberhausen & Tuck, L.L.P. (and predecessor firm), Sebring, Fla., 1977—. Bd. dirs. Comml. Bancorp, Inc., Comml. Bank Highlands County; pres. Highlands Devel. Concepts, Inc., Sebring, 1982—; sec. Focus Broadcast Comm., Inc., Sebring, 1982-87; mng. ptnr. Highlands Investment Service. Treas. Highlands County chpt. ARC, 1973-76; vestryman St. Agnes Episcopal Ch., 1973—, chancellor, 1978—; mem. Fla. Sch. Bd. Atty.'s Assn., 1974—, bd. dirs., 1989-97, pres., 1995-96; mem. Com. 100 of Highlands County, 1975-83, bd. dirs., 1985-87, chmn., 1991-92; chmn. Highlands County High Speed Rail Task Force; chmn. bd., treas. Ctrl. Fla. Racing Assn., 1976-78; chmn. Leadership Sebring: life mem., past pres. Highlands Little Theatre, Inc.; bd. dirs. Palms of Sebring Nursing Home, 1988-90, Palms Estate Mobile Home Park, Sebring Airport Authority, 1988-90, treas., 1988, chmn. indsl. com., 1988, vice-chmn., 1989-90, chmn., 1990-91, Highlands County High Speed Rail Task Force, 1986-89; bd. dirs. Highlands County Family YMCA, 1985-93, pres. Sebring br., 1992-93, chmn. bldg. com., 1992-94; bd. dirs. Good Shepherd Hospice, Inc., v.p., 2000—. Recipient ARC citation, 1974, Presdl. award of appreciation Fla. Jaycees, 1980-81, 82, 85, Outstanding Svc. award Highlands Coun. of 100, 1988, Most Valuable Player award Highlands Little Theatre, Inc., 1986, Zenon Significant Achievement award, 1991; named Jaycee of Year, Sebring Jaycees, 1981, Outstanding Local Chpt. Pres., U.S. Jaycees, 1977. Outstanding Service award Highlands Council of 100, 1988. Mem. ABA, ATLA, Comml. Law League Am., Am. Arbitration Assn. (comml. arbitration panel), Nat. Assn. Retail Credit Attys., Fla. Bar (jour. com.), Highlands County Bar Assn. (past chmn. legal aid com.), Fla. Sch. Bd. Attys. Assn. (dir. 1989—, v.p. 1993-94, pres. 1994-95), Greater Sebring C. of C. (dir. 1982-89, pres. 1986-87, chmn. transp. com. 1986—, Most Valuable Dir. award 1986, 87), Fla. Jaycees (life mem. internat. senate 1977—), Lions (bd. dirs. 1972-73, v.p. 1994-95, Disting. award 1984). Republican. Episcopalian. Probate, Real property. Office: 129 S Commerce Ave Sebring FL 33870-3602

MCCOLLUM, SUSAN HILL, lawyer; b. Ogden, Utah, Aug. 16, 1955; d. George Junior and Marion Ella (Watson) Hill; m. Thomas David McCollum, Jan. 16, 1982. AAS in Radiol. Tech., Weber State Coll., 1975, BS in Acctg., 1979; JD, Brigham Young U., 1982. Bar: Utah 1982, U.S. Dist. Ct. Utah 1982, Calif. 1983, U.S. Ct. Appeals (9th cir.) 1984, U.S. Dist. Ct. (cen. dist.) Calif. 1985. X-ray technician Drs. West & McKay, Ogden, 1975-77; tax examiner IRS, 1977-79; assoc. Craig P. Orrock P.C., Salt Lake City, 1982-83, Hollister & Brace, Santa Barbara, Calif., 1983—. Mem. Santa Barbara County Bar Assn. (dir. 1994-2000, officer 1996-99, pres. 1999, chair Probate & Estate Planning Sec., 2001, Atty. of Yr. 1999), Santa Barbara Women Lawyers (pres. 1990-92), Phi Delta Phi. Mem. LDS Ch. , Estate planning, Probate. Office: Hollister & Brace 1126 Santa Barbara St PO Box 630 Santa Barbara CA 93102-0630 E-mail: shmccollum@hbsb.com

MCCONKIE, OSCAR WALTER, lawyer; b. Moad, Utah, May 26, 1926; s. Oscar Walter and Margaret Vivian (Redd) M.; m. Judith Stoddard, Mar. 17, 1951; children: Oscar III, Ann, Daniel, Gail, Clair, Pace Jefferson, Roger James, Edward. BS in Polit. Sci., U. Utah, 1949, JD, 1952. Bar: Utah 1952, U.S. Ct. Appeals (10th cir.) 1952, U.S. Supreme Ct. 1981, U.S. Ct. Appeals (8th cir.) 1994. County atty. Summit County (Utah), 1959-63; instr. bus. law Stevens Henager Coll., Salt Lake City, 1952-67; ptnr. Kirton & McConkie, 1967—. Author: The Kingdom of God, 1962, God and Man, 1963, The Priest in the Aaronic Priesthood, 1964, Angels, 1975, Aaropnic Priesthood, 1977, She Shail Be Called Woman, 1979. Mem. Utah Ho. of Reps., 1955-57; pres. Utah State Senate, 1965-66; chmn. Utah Bd. Edn., 1983-85. With USN, 1944-46. Mem. Utah Bar Assn., Salt Lake City County Bar Assn. Democrat. Mem. LDS Ch. General practice, Legislative. Home: 1954 Laird Dr Salt Lake City UT 84108-1823 Office: 1800 Eagle Gate Tower 60 E South Temple Salt Lake City UT 84111-1004 E-mail: omcconkie@kmclaw.com

MCCONNAUGHEY, GEORGE CARLTON, JR. retired lawyer; b. Hillsboro, Ohio, Aug. 9, 1925; s. George Carlton and Nelle (Morse) McC.; m. Carolyn Schlieper, June 16, 1951; children: Elizabeth, Susan, Nancy. B.A., Denison U., 1949; LL.B., Ohio State U., 1951, J.D., 1967. Bar: Ohio 1951. Sole practice, Columbus; ptnr. McConnaughey & McConnaughey, 1954-57, McConnaughey, McConnaughey & Stradley, 1957-62, Laylin, McConnaughey & Stradley, 1962-67, George, Greek, King, McMahon & McConnaughey, 1967-79, McConnaughey, Stradley, Mone & Moul, 1979-81, Thompson, Hine & Flory (merger McConnaughey, Stradley, Mone & Moul with Thompson, Hine & Flory), Cleve., Columbus, Cin., Dayton and Washington, 1981-93; ret. ptnr. Thompson Hine LLP, Columbus, 1993—. Bd. dirs. N.Am. Broadcasting Co. (Sta. WMNI, WBZX and WEGE Radio); asst. atty. gen. State of Ohio, 1951-54. Pres. Upper Arlington (Ohio) Bd. Edn., 1967-69, Columbus Town Meeting Assn., 1974-76; chmn. Ohio Young Reps., 1956; U.S. presdl. elector, 1956; trustee Buckeye Boys Ranch, Columbus, 1967-73, 75-81, Upper Arlington Edn. Found., 1987-93; elder Covenant Presbyn. Ch., Columbus. With U.S. Army, 1943-45, ETO. Fellow Am. Bar Found., Ohio Bar Found., Columbus Bar Found.; mem. ABA, Ohio Bar Assn., Columbus Bar Assn., Am. Judicature Soc., Scioto Country Club, Athletic Club, Rotary, Masons. Home: 1993 Collingswood Rd Columbus OH 43221-3741 Office: Thompson Hine LLP One Columbus 10 W Broad St Ste 700 Columbus OH 43215-3435

MCCONNELL, DAVID KELSO, lawyer; b. N.Y.C., July 12, 1932; s. David and Caroline Hanna (Kelso) McC.; m. Alice Schmitt, Dec. 26, 1953; children: Elissa Anne McConnell Henebry, Kathleen Anne, David Willet. BCE, CCNY, 1954; LLB, Yale U., 1962. Bar: Conn. 1962, U.S. Dist. Ct. Conn. 1963, U.S. Ct. Appeals (2d cir.) 1964, U.S. Ct. Appeals (3d cir.) 1966, U.S. Sup. Ct. 1970, U.S. Dist. Ct. (ea. dist.) Pa. 1971, Pa. 1975, N.Y. 1986. Asst. counsel N.Y.N.H. & H. R.R., New Haven, 1962-65, counsel, 1966-68; asst. atty. gen. U.S. V.I., 1965-66; asst. gen. atty. Pa. Cen. Transp. Co., New Haven, 1969-70, asst. gen. counsel Phila., 1970-71, sr. reorganization atty., 1971, adminstrv. officer, spl. counsel to trustees, 1971-76, gen. atty., 1977-78; asst. to chmn., CEO The Penn Cen. Corp., N.Y.C., 1979-80, corp. sec., 1980-82; v.p., gen. counsel Gen. Cable Co., Greenwich, Conn., 1982-85; pvt. practice Stamford, 1985-86, Pelham, N.Y., 1989-91, Greenwich, Conn., 1991-98. Of counsel McCarthy, Fingar, Donovan, Drazen & Smith, White Plains, N.Y., 1986-89. Dep. supr., councilman Town of Pelham, N.Y., 1986-90, budget officer, 1996; dep. mayor, trustee Village of Pelham, 1992-95, village atty., 1995-96; clk. of session, elder, trustee, deacon Huguenot Meml. Ch., Pelham N.Y. With U.S. Navy, 1954-59, USNR, 1959-79. Mem. Conn. Bar Assn., Assn. of Bar of City of N.Y., Yale U. Law Sch. Assn. (exec. com. 1988-91), N.Y. State Bar Assn., The Corinthians (mem. afterguard, dir, The Corinthians Assn., trustee, pres., treas. The Corinthians Endowment Fund), St. Andrews Soc. N.Y. (bd. mgrs. 1986-89, 96-99, chmn. bd. mgrs. 1988-89), Rotary Club of Pelhams, N.Y. (pres. 1993-94), Rotary Club of Newport, R.I. (dir. 2001—). General corporate, General practice, Municipal (including bonds). Home: 68 1/2 Roseneath Ave Newport RI 02840-3849 E-mail: dkmccon@earthlink.net

MCCONNELL, EDWARD BOSWORTH, legal organization administrator, lawyer; b. Greenwich, Conn., Apr. 3, 1920; s. Raymond Arnott and Anna Bell (Lee) McC.; m. Jeanne M. Rotton (dec. 1984); children: Annalee, Marilyn, Edward, Barbara, William; m. Florence M. Leonard, (dec. 1991); stepchildren: Susan L. Little, William R. Leonard, Molly M. Leonard. AB, U. Nebr., 1941, LLB, 1947; MBA with distinction, Harvard U., 1943. Bar: Nebr. 1947, N.J. 1950. Mem. faculty Rutgers U. Sch. Bus. Adminstrn., Newark, 1947-53; assoc. firm Toner, Speakman and Crowley, 1949-50; adminstrv. asst. and law sec. to Chief Justice of N.J., 1950-53; adminstrv. dir. Cts. of N.J., Trenton, 1953-73; also standing master Supreme Ct., 1953-73; pres. Nat. Center for State Cts., Williamsburg, 1973-90, bd. dirs., 1980-90, pres. emeritus, 1990—, cons. on ct. mgmt., 1990—. Mem. U.S. Dept. Justice Coun. on Role of Cts. in Am. Soc., 1978-83; mem. adv. com. Dispute Resolution Policy Study, Social Sci. Rsch. Inst., U. So. Calif., 1975-79, Civil Litigation Rsch. Project, U. Wis. and U. So. Calif., 1979-83, nat. judg. edn. program to promote equality for men and women in the cts., 1980—; mem. Nat. Inst. Criminal Justice Task Force, Urban Consortium, 1979-83; participant Access To Justice Colloquium, European Univ. Inst., Florence, Italy, 1979; nat. adv. coun. Ctr. Adminstrn. Justice, Wayne Stae U., 1973-77; nat. project com. State Jud. Info. Sys. Project SEARCH Group, 1973-76; lectr. Inst. of Local and State Govt. Wharton Sch. U. Pa., 1955-65, Appellate Judges Seminar, Inst. Jud. Adminstrn., NYU, 1962-75; vis. expert UN Asia and Far East Inst., Tokyo, 1971; mem. Cts. Task Force Nat. Adv. Commn. Criminal Justice Standards and Goals, 1971-73; nat. adv. com. D.C. Ct. Mgmt. Project, 1966-70; trustee Inst. Ct. Mgmt., 1969-73, 84-86; chmn. Nat. Conf. Ct. Adminstrv. Officers, 1956; mem. nat. task force on gender bias in cts. Nat. Assn. Women Judge's 1985-90; mem. adv. bd. Nat. Ctr. for Citizen Participation in Admisntrn. of Justice, 1984-90; mem. Nat. Commn. Trial Ct. Performance Standards, 1991-95. Mem. adv. com. on article III Commn. on the Bicentennial of the Constitution, 1989-91; adv. com. Judicary Leadership Coun., 1990-95. Maj. C.E., AUS, 1943-46. Decorated Bronze Star medal; recipient Warren E. Burger award for greatest contbn. to improvement of ct. adminstrn. Inst. for Ct. Mgmt.., 1975, Herbert Lincoln Harley award for efficient adminstrn. justice Am. Judicature Soc., 1973, Glenn R. Winters award for outstanding service in jud. adminstrn. Am. Judges Assn., 1974, Tom C. Clark award for outstanding contbns. to field of ct. adminstrn. Nat. Conf. Met. Cts., 1983, Award of Merit Nat. Assn. Ct. Mgmt., 1987, Spl. award, Nat. Assn. Women Judges, 1989, Paul C. Reardon award for disting. svc. Nat. Ctr. for State Cts., 1991, Alumni Achievement award U. Nebr., 1991, Robert B. Yegge award ABA Jud. Divsn. Lawyers Conf., 1997. Fellow Nat. Acad. Pub. Adminstrn. (mem. panel on evaluation budget decentralization project of fed. cts. 1989-91, chmn. panel long range planning in fed. cts. 1991-92, mem. panel for study of fed. trial ct. adminstrv. structure 1995-96); mem. ABA (fellow-at-large, coun. mem. 1960-66, 71-80, house of dels., 1977-80, chmn. com. on oversight and goals 1975-76, chmn. com. on jud. compensation jud. adminstrn. div. 1984-89, chmn. jud. adminstrn. div. 1976-77, sect. of litigation task force on excess litigiousness in Am. 1986-88, task force on reduction of litigation cost and delay, jud. adminstrn. dir. 1984-94, chmn. 1991-94, mem. long range planning com. 1989-94), N.J. Bar Assn., Nebr. Bar Assn., Warren E. Burger Soc., Kingsmill (Va.) Golf, Tennis and Yacht Clubs (pres. 2001), Order of Coif (hon.), Delta Upsilon, Sigma Delta Phi, Phi Delta Phi. E-mail: ebm80@aol.com

MCCONNELL, MICHAEL THEODORE, lawyer; b. San Francisco, June 18, 1954; s. Lawrence V. and Ann (Poland) McC. BS, U. Oreg., 1977; JD, U. Denver, 1980. Bar: Colo., Wyo., U.S. Dist. Ct. Colo., U.S. Ct. Appeals (10th cir.), U.S. Supreme Ct., U.S. Dist. Ct. Wyo. Ptnr. Long & Jaudon, Denver, 1980—. Fellow Am. Coll. Trail Lawyers; mem. ABA, Colo. Bar Assn., Denver Bar Assn., Colo. Def. Lawyers Assn. Appellate, General civil litigation, Professional liability. Office: Long & Jaudon 1600 Ogden St Denver CO 80218-1414 E-mail: mmcconnell@L-J.com

MCCONNICO, STEPHEN E. lawyer; b. Jacksonville, Tex., Apr. 8, 1950; s. Charles Kit and Ruth (Nettle) McC. BA, U. Tex., 1972; JD, Baylor U., 1976. Bar: Tex. 1976. Briefing atty. Tex. Supreme Ct., Austin, 1976-77; assoc. Andrews & Kurth, Houston, 1977-81; ptnr. Scott, Douglass & Mcconnico, Austin, 1981—. Mem. Tex. Supreme Ct. Adv. Com., Austin, 1982-93. Mem. Austin Dem. Forum, 1984. Fellow Am. Coll. Trial Lawyers, Internat. Acad. Trial Lawyers, Internat. Soc. Barristers, Am. Bar Found., Tex. Bar Found.; mem. ABA, Travis County Bar Assn. (bd. dirs. 1986), Tex. Young Lawyers Assn., Austin Young Lawyers Assn. (outstanding young lawyer 1984), Am. Bd. Trial Advocates (pres. Austin chpt. 1994—, Tex. bd. dirs. 1993-94), Headliners Club, Westwood Club. General civil litigation, Personal injury. Home: 1403 Hardouin Ave Austin TX 78703-2516 Office: Scott Douglass & McConnico 600 Congress Ave Ste 1500 Austin TX 78701-2589

MC CORD, JOHN HARRISON, lawyer, educator; b. Oceanside, N.Y., Dec. 22, 1934; s. John Francis and Elsie (Powers) McC.; m. Maureen Ursula Maclean, Dec. 30, 1961; children: John F.X., Paul V., David G., Maureen E. AB, Fordham Coll., 1957; JD magna cum laude, St. John's U., 1960; LLM, U. Ill., 1965. Bar: N.Y. 1960, Ill. 1964. Atty. U.S. Dept. Justice, Washington, 1960-61; mem. faculty U. Ill. Coll. Law, Champaign, 1964—, prof. law, 1965—, assoc. dean for acad. affairs., 1990-92; of counsel Meyer Capel PC, 1998—. Acad. cons. Ill. Inst. Continuing Legal Edn., 1968-72; vis. prof. law U. N.C., 1975, U. Hawaii, 1976 Author: (with Keeton and O'Connell) Crisis in Car Insurance, 1967, Buying and Selling Small Businesses, 1969, (with O'Byrne) Deskbook for Illinois Estate Planners, 1969, Closely Held Corporations, 1971, (with O'Neill, Pearlman and Stroud) Buying, Selling and Merging Businesses, 1975, (with Lowndes and Kramer) Estate and Gift Taxes, 3d edit, 1974, (with McKee) Federal Income Taxation-A Summary Analysis, 1975, (with Kramer) Problems for Federal Estate and Gift Taxes, 1976, Estate and Gift Tax Reform, 1977, Estate and Gift Tax Summary, 15th edit. 1993, Estate, Gift and Generation-Skipping Taxes, 1999; editor: Dimensions and Academic Freedom, 1969, With All Deliberate Speed: Civil Rights Theory and Reality, 1969, Ill. Law Forum, 1965-69; contbr. articles to profl. jours.; author computer programs for estate planning, 1984—. Served to capt. JAGC, USAF, 1961-64. St. Thomas More fellow St. John's U., 1960. Fellow Am. Coll. Trust and Estate Counsel; mem. ABA (com. CLE and chief reporter for study outline on buying, selling and merging businesses sect. fed. tax 1969-73, com. estate and gift taxes 1973-84, chmn. subcom. gross estate issues 1976-78, subcom. tax reform 1978-84), Ill. Bar Assn. (exec. coun. fed. tax sect. 1966-73, chmn. sect. 1971-72, exec. coun. bus. planning sect. 86-91), Champaign County Bar Assn., Am. Arbitration Assn. (nat. panel arbitrators 1969-90), Eastern Ill. Estate Planning Coun. (pres. 1970-71), U. Miami Inst. Estate Planning (adv. coun. 1979-87), Assn. Am. Law Schs. (fed. taxation roundtable coun. 1969-72), Ill. Inst. CLE (bd. dirs. 1991-2000, estate planning adv. com. 2000—), U.S. Navy League, Order of Coif. Home: 104 E Sherwin Dr Urbana IL 61802-7133 Office: U Ill Coll Law Champaign IL 61820 E-mail: jmccord@law.uiuc.edu

MCCORKINDALE, DOUGLAS HAMILTON, lawyer, publishing company executive; b. N.Y.C., June 14, 1939; s. William Douglas and Kathleen (Miles) McC.; m. Nancy Walsh, Dec. 24, 1991; children by previous marriage: Laura Ann, Heather Jean. BA, Columbia U., 1961, LLB cum laude (Harlan Fiske Stone scholar), 1964. Bar: N.Y. 1964. Assoc. Thacher Proffitt & Wood, N.Y.C., 1964-70, ptnr., 1970-71; gen. counsel, sec. Gannett Co., Inc., 1971-72, v.p., gen. counsel, sec., 1972-77, sr. v.p. fin. and law, 1977-79, sr. v.p., chief fin. officer, 1979-83, pres. diversified media div., 1980-83, exec. v.p., 1983, vice chmn., CFO Va., 1984—, chief adminstrv. officer, 1986—, vice chmn., pres., 1997—, CEO Va., 2000—, chmn., pres., CEO, 2001—. Bd. dirs. Continental Airlines Inc., Lockheed Martin Corp., The Global Govt. Plus Fund Inc., Prudential Global Genesis Fund Inc., Prudentual Natural Resources Fund Inc., Prudential Multi-Sector Fund Inc.; trustee Prudential Equity Income Fund, Prudential Allocation Fund, Prudential Mcpl. Bond Fund, Mut. Ins. Co. Ltd. Mem. ABA (chmn. com. Exch. Art of 1934 1971-73), Newspaper Assn. Am., Pine Valley Golf Club, Mid Ocean Club, Burning Tree Club. General corporate, Mergers and acquisitions, Securities. Office: Gannett Co Inc 1100 Wilson Blvd Arlington VA 22234-0001*

MC CORMACK, FRANCIS XAVIER, lawyer, former oil company executive; b. Bklyn., July 9, 1929; s. Joseph and Blanche V. (Dengel) Mc C.; m. Margaret V. Hynes, Apr. 24, 1954; children: Marguerite, Francis Xavier, Sean Michael, Keith John, Cecelia Blanche, Christopher Thomas. AB cum laude, St. Francis Coll., Bklyn., 1951; LLB, Columbia U., 1954. Bar: N.Y. 1955, Mich. 1963, Calif. 1974, Pa. 1975. Assoc. Cravath, Swaine & Moore, N.Y.C., 1956-62; sr. atty. Ford Motor Co., 1962-64, asst. gen. counsel, 1970-72; v.p., gen. counsel, sec. Philco-Ford Corp., 1964-72; v.p., gen. counsel Atlantic Richfield Co., 1972-73, sr. v.p., gen. counsel, 1973-94. Editor Columbia U. Law Rev., 1954. Decorated commendatore Ordine al Merito (Italy); Stone scholar Columbia U., 1954. Mem. Calif. Club, Chancery Club, Annandale Golf Club. Home and Office: 975 Singingwood Dr Arcadia CA 91006-1924

MCCORMACK, HOWARD MICHAEL, lawyer; b. Bklyn., Aug. 26, 1932; s. Michael Francis and Sarah Catherine (Russell) McC.; m. Patricia Anne Riley, Aug. 24, 1957; children: Sean M., Maureen A. MacDougall. AB cum laude, Coll. Holy Cross, Worcester, Mass., 1954; LLB, Fordham U., N.Y.C., 1961; LLM in Internat. Law, NYU, 1965. Bar: N.Y. 1962, U.S. Dist. Ct. (so. and ea. dists.) N.Y. 1963, U.S. Ct. Appeals (2d cir.) 1964, U.S. Ct. Appeals (4th cir.) 1977, U.S. Supreme Ct. 1966, U.S. Dist. Ct. Md. 1975, U.S. Dist. Ct. (so. dist) Tex. 1983, U.S. Ct. Appeals (5th cir.) 1984, U.S. Ct. Mil. Appeals 1994. Acct. exec. C.R. Black Jr. Corp., N.Y.C., 1958-61; ptnr. Zock, Petrie, et al., 1961-71; maritime counsel Bethlehem Steel Corp., 1972-79; ptnr. Healy & Baillie LLP, 1979—; adj. prof. law Fordham U. Adj. prof. law Touro Law Sch. Contbr. articles to profl. publs. Lt. (j.g.) USN, 1954-57; comdr. JAGC, USNR, ret. Mem. Maritime Law Assn. U.S. (pres. 1998-2000). Avocations: tennis, golf, wine studies. Admiralty, Federal civil litigation, Insurance. Office: Healy & Baillie LLP New York NY 10006 E-mail: hmccormack@healy.com

MCCORMACK, JOHN ROBERT, lawyer; b. Middletown, Conn., Mar. 30, 1962; s. John Francis and Ann Jane (Monarca) McC.; m. Cristina Dorthea Dwyer, Sept. 27, 1986; children: Kevin, Cara. BS, Univ. Conn., 1984; JD, Stetson Univ., 1990. Assoc. Kelly & McKee, P.A., Tampa, Fla., 1990-92; ptnr. Wiggins & McCormack, Clearwater, 1992-94; sole practitioner J. Robert McCormack, P.A., 1994-00; ptnr. Persante & McCormack, P.A., 2000—. Editor: Labor and Employment in Florida, 1990, Critical Issues in Labor and Employment Labor, 1990. Mem. ABA (labor and employment law sect.), Fla. Bar Labor and Employment Law Sect., Barney Masterson Inn of Ct. (treas. 1998-99), Clearwater Bar Employment Law Com. (co-chair 1997-99). Administrative and regulatory, Labor. Office: Persante & McCormack P A 2555 Enterprise Rd Bldg 15 Clearwater FL 33763

MCCORMACK, MICHAEL, state supreme court justice; b. Omaha, July 20, 1939; JD, Creighton U., 1963. Asst. pub. defender, Douglas County, Nebr., 1963-66; pvt. practice Omaha, 1966-97; justice Nebr. Supreme Ct., 1997—. Office: State Capitol Bldg Rm 2218 Lincoln NE 68509 also: PO Box 98910 Lincoln NE 68509*

MCCORMACK, WILLIAM ARTHUR, lawyer; b. Rochester, N.Y., Sept. 18, 1951; s. Austin Francis and June Ann (Doyle) McC. AB in Polit. Sci. magna cum laude, St. Louis U., 1973; cert., Sorbonne, Paris, 1974; JD, Georgetown U., 1977. Bar: Tex. 1978, D.C. 1979. Assoc. Crutcher, Hull, et al., Dallas, 1978-82, Hughes & Luce, Dallas, 1982-83, ptnr., 1983—, mem. mgmt. com., exec. com., sect. head, 1993-97, mgn. ptnr., chm., 1997—. Bd. dirs. Engles Capital Corp., McCormack Corp.; speaker and author on legal topics. Contbr. articles to profl. jours. Bd. dirs. Alliance Francaise Found., Dallas, Jesuit Found., Dallas Epilepsy Found., pres., 1992, Dallas Citizens Coun.; bd. advisors Jesuit Prep., Bishop Dunne H.S., Bus. Com. for the Arts, Dallas; coun. mem., exec. comm. circle ten coun. Boy Scouts Am.; leadership coun. Dallas Chamber. Mem. ABA, State Bar Assn. Tex. (chmn. minority com.), Dallas Bar Assn. (chmn. legal ethics com., mem. minority commn.), Pi Sigma Alpha, Alpha Sigma Nu. Roman Catholic. Office: Hughes and Luce 1717 Main St Ste 2800 Dallas TX 75201-4685

MCCORMICK, DAVID ARTHUR, lawyer; b. McKeesport, Pa., Oct. 26, 1946; s. Arthur Paul and Eleanor Irene (Gibson) McC. BA, Westminster Coll., 1967; JD, Duquesne U., 1973; MBA, U. Pa., 1975. Bar: Pa. 1973, D.C. 1978, U.S. Ct. Appeals (3d cir.) 1977, U.S. Ct. Appeals (4th and D.C. cirs.) 1980, U.S. Supreme Ct. 1980. Asst. commerce counsel Penn Cen. R.R., Phila., 1973-76; assoc. labor counsel Consol. Rail Corp., 1976-78; atty. Dept. Army, Washington, 1978—. Author various geneal. and hist. works; contbr. articles to profl. jours. Mem. ATLA, Pa. Bar Assn., Phila. Bar Assn., D.C. Bar Assn., Assn. Transp. Practitioners, Soc. Cin. (Del. chpt.), SAR (Pitts. chpt.), Am. Legion, Res. Officers Assn., Masons, Phi Alpha Delta, Theta Chi. Presbyterian.

MCCORMICK, HOMER L., JR. lawyer; b. Frederick, Md., Nov. 11, 1928; s. Homer Lee McCormick and Rosebelle Irene Biser; m. Jacquelyn R.; children: Deidre Ann and Thomas Lee. Student, George Washington U., 1946-48; AB, San Jose State U., 1951; JD, U. Calif., San Francisco, 1961. Bar: Calif. 1961, U.S. Dist. Ct. Ctrl. Dist. Calif. 1972, U.S. Dist. No. Calif. 1961, U.S. Dist. Ct., So. Dist. Calif. 1976, U.S. Dist. Ct. of Appeals (9th cir. 1961), U.S. Tax Ct. 1977, U.S. Ct. Claims 1977, U.S. Supreme Ct. 1977. Atty. Holiway Jones State of Calif., 1961-63; atty. assoc. Rutan & Tucker, Santa Ana, Calif., 1963-66, atty. ptnr., 1966-70, atty., sr. ptnr. Costa Mesa, 1970-88, dept. head pub. law, 1974-88, mng. ptnr., 1984-88; founding ptnr., sr. ptnr. McCormick, Kidman & Behrens, 1988—. Arbitrator Am. Arbitration Assn., 1966-88; judge pro tem Orange County Superior Ct., 1975, 81, 84; spkr., lectr. Cal. Continuing Edn. of the Bar, 1976-88; profl. designation Internat. Right of Way Assn.; elected mem. Cal. Condemnation Lawyers, 1994—. Contbg. author: Real Property Remedies, 1982; contbr. articles to profl. jours. Mem. bd. govs. Bus. Com. Arts, Orange County Philharm. Soc. Lt. USMCR, 1951-56; pilot, Korea. Named Alumnus of Year Hastings Law Sch., 1992. Mem. ABA (com. chair 1991), Am. Bd. Trial Adv. (pres. O.C. chpt. 1973), Orange City Atty. Assn. (pres. 1972), Fed. Bar Assoc., Consumer Attys. Calif., Am. Judicature Soc., Orange County Bar Assn. (com. chair 1991-92), Orange County Bus. Trial Lawyers, Order Coif, Thurston Soc., Hastings Alumni Assn. (pres. 1973), Springs Country Club, Delta Theta Pi. Republican. Episcopalian. Avocations: boating, fishing, flying, golf, foreign travel. General civil litigation, Condemnation, Real property.

MCCORMICK, HUGH THOMAS, lawyer; b. McAlester, Okla., Nov. 24, 1944; s. Hugh O. and Lois (McGucken) McC.; m. Suzanna G. Weingarten, Dec. 5, 1975; 1 child, John B. BA, U. Mich., 1968; JD, Rutgers U., 1977; LLM in Taxation, Georgetown U., 1980. Bar: N.Y. 1977, D.C. 1979, Maine 1981. Atty. office chief counsel interpretative divsn. IRS, Washington, 1977-81; assoc. Perkins, Thompson, Hinkley & Keddy, Portland, Maine, 1981-83, LeBoeuf, Lamb, Leiby & MacRae, N.Y.C., 1983-88, counsel, 1989-91; ptnr. LeBoeuf, Lamb, Greene & MacRae, L.L.P., 1992—. Dir. Ins. Tax. Conf., 1993—, sr. v.p., 2000—. Mem. bd. contbrs. and advisors Jour. of Taxation of Investments; contbr. articles to profl. jours. Trustee U.S. Team Handball Found., N.J., 1985-95. Fellow Am. Bar Found.; mem. ABA (chmn. com. on taxation of ins. cos. 1989, chmn. subcom. sect. of taxation 1989-96, mem. torts and ins. practice sect., sect. on taxation), D.C. Bar Assn., Assn. of Bar of City of N.Y. Democrat. Insurance, Corporate taxation. Home: 555 Pelham Manor Rd Pelham NY 10803-2525 Office: LeBoeuf Lamb Greene MacRae LLP 125 W 55th St New York NY 10019-5369 E-mail: hmccormi@llgm.com

MCCORMICK, JOHN HOYLE, lawyer; b. Pensacola, Fla., July 30, 1933; s. Clyde Hoyle and Orrie Brooks (Frink) McC.; m. Patricia McCall, Dec. 27, 1974. BS, U. Fla., 1955; JD, Stetson U., 1958. Bar: Fla. 1958. Ptnr. McCormick, Drury & Scaff, Jasper, Fla., 1958-74; county atty., 1973—; sr. ptnr. McCormick, Drury & Scaff, Jasper, 1974-91; pvt. practice, 1991—. County judge, Hamilton County, Fla., 1960-72; local counsel So. Ry. System, 1968—, CSX, Ry., 1972—; atty. Hamilton County Devel. Authority, 1970-91; bd. dirs. 1st Fed. Savs. Bank Fla.; bd. dirs., v.p., atty. Hamilton County Bank. Mayor City of White Springs, Fla., 1959; pres. Hamilton County C. of C., Jasper, 1961. Mem. Phi Delta Phi. Democrat. Methodist. Lodges: Masons. Avocations: gardening, motorhome camping, college football. Banking, Government contracts and claims, Probate. Home: 403 2nd Ave NW Jasper FL 32052-6687 Office: 215 2nd St NE Jasper FL 32052-6616 Address: PO Drawer O Jasper FL 32052-0695

MCCORMICK, MICHAEL JERRY, judge; b. Fort Lewis, Wash., Oct. 17, 1945; s. Thaddeus Charles and Geraldine (Fogle) McC.; m. Katleen Karen Kelley, Sept. 2, 1967; children: Patrick Kelley, Karen Michelle. BA, U. Tex.-Austin, 1967; JD, St. Mary's U., 1970. Bar: Tex. 1970. Briefing atty. Tex. Ct. Criminal Appeals, 1970-71; asst. dist. atty. Travis County, Tex., 1971-72; exec. dir. Tex. Dist. and County Attys. Assn., Austin, 1972-80; judge Tex. Ct. Criminal Appeals, 1981—, chief presiding judge, 1988-2000, sr. judge, 2001—. Dir. Tex. Ctr. for Judiciary, 1983; vice-chmn. Tex. Commn. on Sentencing, 1984; mem. Tex. Jud. Budget Bd., 1983; co-chair Tex. Jud. Coun., 1997—. Author: Branch's Annotated Penal Code, 3d edit., Criminal Forms and Trial Manual, 10th edit., Tex. Justice Court Deskbook, Tex. Constables Civil Process Handbook. Pres. Joslin (Tex.) P.T.A., 1981-82. Served with U.S. Army, 1966-72. Named Rosewood Gavel Outstanding Jurist, St. Mary's U. Sch. Law, 1984, Disting. Law Grad., 1992. Mem. State Bar Tex., Tex. Dist. and County Attys. Assn.

MCCORMICK, TIMOTHY BRIAN BEER, lawyer; b. Northampton, Mass., May 16, 1959; s. Brian Beer and Margaret Ann McCormick; m. Lee Hillary Kadis, Sept. 2, 1979 (div. June 1991); m. Virginia Lee Kostner, June 30, 1991 (div. May 1995); 1 child, Cameron A.; m. Jill Ann Knowland, Apr. 23, 1997; 1 child, Britton K. BA, U. Calif., Berkeley, 1984; JD, Am. U., 1987. Bar: Calif. 1987, U.S. Dist. Ct. (no. dist.) Calif. 1987, U.S. Ct. Appeals (9th cir.) 1987, U.S. Dist. Ct. (ea. dist.) Calif., 1991, U.S. Dist. Ct. (ctrl. dist.) Calif. 1994. Staff asst. Office of Lt. Gov., Sacramento, 1982-83; cons. Calif. Rep. Party, 1984; rsch. asst. Nat. Right to Work Found., Springfield, Va., 1985-86; assoc. Graham & James, San Francisco, 1987-93, McPharlin & Mahl, San Jose, Calif., 1993-94; ptnr. McPharlin & Sprinkles, 1994-95; v.p., assoc. coun. Fidelity Nat. Title Ins. Co., Walnut Creek, Calif., 1995-2000; prin. McCormick Dispute Resolution Svcs., Piedmont, 1996—; prin. cons. Libris Solutions, Oakland, 2000—. Judge pro tem Santa Clara County Superior Ct., 1993—. Comments editor Administrv. Law Jour., 1986-87. Treas., Hom for Mayor, San Francisco, 1995; mem. Rep. State Cen. Com. of Calif., 1983-85, 2000—, assoc. mem., 1985-2000, mem. exec. com., 1983-84; gen. coun. Asian Am. Polit. Edn. Found., 1992—; mem. Alameda County Rep. Ctrl. Com., 2000—; Rep. candidate 16th Dist. Assembly, 2000. Mem. ABA (litigation sect.), Santa Clara County Bar Assn., Bar Assn. San Francisco, Engring. and Utility Contractors Assn. (legis. com. 1991-95, co-chair, 1994-95). Avocations: skiing, bicycling, cooking, scuba diving. General civil litigation, Insurance, Real property. Home: 235 Park View Ave Piedmont CA 94610-1041 E-mail: din3500psi@scubadiving.com

MCCOTTER, JAMES RAWSON, lawyer; b. May 19, 1943; s. Charles R. and Jane M. (Ballentine) McC.; M. Carole Lee Hand, Sept. 5, 1965; children: Heidi M., Sage B. BA, Stanford U., 1965; JD, U. Colo., 1969. Bar: Colo 1969, D.C. 1970, U.S. Dist. Ct. Colo. 1969, U.S. Ct. Appeals (10th and D.C. cirs.) 1970, U.S. Ct. Appeals (5ht cir.) 1972, U.S. Supreme Ct. 1974, Tex. 1996. Law clk. U.S. Ct. Appeals (10th cir.), Denver, 1969-70; assoc. Covington & Burling, Washington, 1970-75, Kelly, Stansfield & O'Donnell, Washington, 1975-76, ptnr., 1977-86; assoc. gen. counsel Pub. Svc. Co., Colo., 1986-88, sr. v.p. gen. counsel, corp. sec., 1988-93; of counsel LeBoeuf, Lamb, Greene & MacRae, Denver, 1993-94; v.p. law and adminstrn. El Paso Natural Gas Co., Tex., 1994-96, v.p. dep. gen. counsel, 1997-99; sr. v.p., dep. gen. counsel El Paso Energy Corp., 1999—. Editor in chief U. Colo. Law Rev., 1968-69 (Outstanding Achievement award 1969). Bd. dirs. Sewall Rehab. Ctr., Denver, 1979-84, Opera Colo., 1987-95; dir., vice chmn. Denver Civic Ventures, Inc., 1988-94; mem. law alumni bd. U. colo., 1988-91; bd. dirs. Colo. Coun. on Econ. Edn., Found. for Denver Ctr. for Performing Arts complex, 1991-94, World Trade Ctr. El Paso/Juárez, 1996-99, Nat. Conservancy N. Mex., 1996—, El Paso YMCA, 1997-99, El Paso Symphony Orch., 1997-99. Recipient Disting. Achievement award U. Colo. Law Sch., 1989; named to Outstanding Young Men Am., U.S. Jaycees, 1971; Storke scholar U. Colo., Boulder, 1967. Mem. ABA, Colo. Bar Assn. (adminstrv. law com. 1979-84), Fed. Energy Bar Assn. (chmn. com. on environment 1982-83), Tex. Bar Assn., Univ. Club, Denver Country Club, Order of Coif, El Paso C. of C. (mem. exec. com. 1996-99). Episcopalian. Public utilities. Home: 204 Travis St Apt 2D Houston TX 77002-1775 Office: El Paso Energy Corp PO Box 2511 El Paso TX 77252-2511

MCCOY, FRANCIS TYRONE, law educator; b. N.Y.C., Oct. 15, 1922; s. Francis Thomas and Gladys (Parker) M.; m. Mary Caldwell Watson, June 28, 1975. B.A., U. Fla., 1944, M.A., 1947, J.D., 1955. Bar: Fla. 1955. Faculty mem. U. Fla. Coll. Law, Gainesville, 1955— , prof., 1971— . Contbr. articles to profl. jours. Served to lt. U.S. Army, 1943-45. Mem. 8th Jud. Cir. Fla. Bar (sec. 1956—), Phi Beta Kappa (hon.). Episcopalian. Home: 2841 SW 1st Ave Gainesville FL 32607-3001 Office: Coll of Law U Fla Gainesville FL 32611

MCCOY, JERRY JACK, lawyer; b. Pitts., Aug. 4, 1941; s. Norris and Martha (Jack) McC.; m. Alexandra Armstrong; children: MadeleineRena, Allison Norah, Jonathan Howard. BS, W.Va. U., 1963; LLB, Duke U., 1966; LLM in Taxation, N.Y.U., 1967. Bar: D.C. 1968, N.Y. 1967. Assoc. Silverstein & Mullens, Washington, 1968-72, ptnr., 1973-92; of counsel Reid and Priest, N.Y.C., Washington, 1992-94; sole practitioner Washington, 1994—. Adj. law faculty U. Miami, Fla., 1983—, Law Ctr. Georgetown U., 1996—. Co-author: Family Foundation Handbook, 2001; exec. editor Tax Mgmt., Estates Gifts and Trusts series, Washington, 1972-92; co-founder, co-editor Charitable Gift Planning News, Dallas, 1983—; contbr. articles to profl. jours. Mem. ABA, Am. Law Inst., Am. Coll. Trust and Estate Counsel (chair com. on charitable planning and exempt orgns.), Am. Coll. Tax Counsel. Democrat. Jewish. Estate planning, Non-profit and tax-exempt organizations, Estate taxation. Home: 3560 Winfield Ln NW Washington DC 20007-2368 Office: PO Box 66491 Washington DC 20035-6491

MCCOY, REAGAN SCOTT, oil company executive, lawyer; b. Port Arthur, Tex., Nov. 25, 1945; s. William Murray and Elizabeth (Gilbert) McC.; m. Pat Kowalski, June 21, 1969; 1 child, Traci. BCE, Ga. Inst. Tech., 1968; JD, Loyola U., 1972. Bar: Tex. 1972, La. 1978; registered prof. engr., Tex., La. Structural engr. McDermott Inc., New Orleans, 1966-72, data processing mgr. London, 1972-76, cons. engr. New Orleans, 1976-79; adminstrv. mgr. Concord Oil Co., San Antonio, 1979-81, v.p., 1981—. Mem. World Affairs Coun., Tex. Luth. U. Bus. Sch. Adv. Com. Treas. Countryside San Pedro Recreation Club, 1981-82; bd. dirs. Countryside San Pedro Homeowners Assn., 1984-86; v.p. Bluffview Homeowners Assn., 1998-99, pres., 1999—; pres. San Antonio Baylor U. Parents League, 1995-96; mem. Tex. State Bd. Pub. Accountancy, 1997—; bd. dirs. Consumer Credit Counseling Svc. Greater San Antonio, 2000—. Fellow Tau Beta Pi; mem. ABA, NSPE, ASCE, Am. Assn. Profl. Landmen (San Antonio chpt. treas. 1990-91, v.p. 1991-93, pres. 1993-94), La. State Bar Assn., Tex. State Bar, San Antonio Bar Assn. (natural resources com. treas. 1986-87, vice chmn. 1987-88, chmn. 1988-89), Tex. Soc. Profl. Engrs., La. Soc. Profl. Engrs., So. Tex. Assn. Divsn. Order Analysts (v.p. 1993, pres. 1994, 98, bd. dirs. 1999—), Fin Execs. Inst. (treas. 1991-92, sec. 1992-93, v.p. 1993-94, pres. 1994-95, bd. dirs. 1995-97), Soc. Mining Engrs., Real Estate Fin. Soc. (bd. dirs. 1986-89, v.p. 1987-88, pres. 1988-89, 98-2000, pres. coun.), Adminstrv. Mgmt. Soc. (pres. 1985-86, 89-90), Plz. Club, Sonterra Club, Tex. Ind. Producers and Royalty Owners Assn., Am. Petroleum Inst. (South Tex. chpt. pres. 1997-2000). Presbyterian. Avocations: water sports, reading, woodworking. Home: 14103 Bluff Manor Dr San Antonio TX 78216-7976 Office: Concord Oil Co 105 S Saint Marys St Ste 1500 San Antonio TX 78205-2898

MCCRACKEN, GREGORY WILLIAM, lawyer; b. Long Beach, Calif., Aug. 4, 1962; s. William Meredith and Dulcie Ann (Ramsey) McC.; m. Marsha Jo Dasenbrock, Apr. 3, 1993. AB, U. Calif., Davis, 1985; JD, U. Pacific, 1993; MUP, U. Ill., 2000. Bar: Calif. 1993, U.S. Dist. Ct. (ea. dist.) Calif. 1993, U.S. Ct. Appeals (9th cir.) 1994, U.S. Supreme Ct. 1997, Ill. 2000, Conn. 2001, U.S. Dist. Ct. Conn. 2001. Regulatory affairs analyst Enseco-Calif. Analytical Lab., West Sacramento, Calif., 1990-91; law clk. PLF, Sacramento, 1991-92; summer assoc. Boutin, Lassner, Gibson & Delehant, 1992, assoc. atty., 1993-94; atty. Pacific Legal Found., 1994-95; assoc. atty. Murphy, Pearson, Bradley & Feeney, 1995-98; assoc. atty., planner Robinson & Cole, Hartford, Conn., 2000—. Editor (law jour.) The Transnational Lawyer, 1992-93. Mem. ABA, Am. Planning Assn., Calif. Bar Assn., Ill. State Bar Assn., Conn. Bar Assn., Phi Beta Kappa, Phi Kappa Phi, Order of Coif. Republican. Administrative and regulatory, Land use and zoning (including planning), Real property. Home: 552 Fern St West Hartford CT 06107 Office: Robinson & Cole LLP 280 Trumbull Street Hartford CT 06103-3597 Fax: 860-275-8299. E-mail: gmccracken@rc.com

MCCRACKEN, STEVEN CARL, lawyer; b. Artesia, Calif., Oct. 29, 1950; s. Glenn A. and Helen V. (Fears) McCracken; m. Susan Lee Waggener, July 29, 1979; children: Casey James, Scott Kevin. BA magna cum laude, U. Calif., Irvine, 1972; JD, U. Va., 1975. Bar: Calif. 1975, U.S. Dist. Ct. (cen. dist.) Calif. 1975, U.S. Ct. Appeals (9th cir.) 1976, U.S. Dist. Ct. (no. dist.) Calif. 1977, D.C. 1979, U.S. Supreme Ct. 1985, U.S. Dist. Ct. (so. dist.) Calif. 1990. Assoc. Gibson, Dunn & Crutcher, L.A., 1975-82, ptnr. Irvine, Calif., 1983-94; v.p., sec. and gen. counsel Callaway Golf Co., Carlsbad, 1994-96, exec. v.p., gen. counsel and sec., 1996-97, exec. v.p. licensing, chief legal officer, sec., 1997-2000, sr. exec. v.p., chief legal officer, sec., 2000—. Lawyer rep. Ninth Cir. Jud. Conf., 1989-91. Editor Va. Law Rev., 1973-75, mng. bd. 1974-75, bd. editors The Computer Lawyer, 1984-96. Mem. ABA (antitrust sect.), Orange County Bar Assn. (bd. dirs. 1988-90, chmn. fed. ct. com. 1988-89, chmn. bus. litigation sect. 1990, sec. 1991, treas. 1992, pres.-elect 1993, pres. 1994). Democrat. Antitrust, Federal civil litigation, General civil litigation. Office: Callaway Golf Co 2180 Rutherford Rd Carlsbad CA 92008-8815

MCCREARY, FRANK E., III, lawyer; b. Santa Monica, Calif., Mar. 25, 1943; s. Frank Elijah and Irma (Holland) McC.; m. Jacqueline Moehlman, Feb. 15, 1969; children: Jennifer Claire, Frank Ward. BA, Cornell U., 1965; LLB with honors, U. Tex., 1968. Bar: Tex. 1968. Ptnr. Vinson & Elkins, Houston, 1970—. Trustee United Way of Tex. Gulf Coast, Houston, 1988-90; bd. dirs. Vol. Ctr., Houston, 1987-99. Capt. U.S. Army, 1968-70, Vietnam. Mem. Nat. Assn. Bond Lawyers, Tex. Law Rev. Assn., Houston Bar Found. Administrative and regulatory, Banking, Municipal (including bonds). Office: Vinson & Elkins 2300 First City Tower 1001 Fannin St Ste 3300 Houston TX 77002-6706

MCCRERY, DAVID NEIL, III, lawyer; b. Ames, Iowa, Mar. 7, 1957; s. David Neil Jr. and Judith Ann (Purlee) McC.; m. Katherine Marie Meridith, June 9, 1979; children: Evelyn Judith, David Neil IV. BS in Agrl., U. Ill., 1979; JD, So. Ill. U., Carbondale, 1993. Bar: Ill. 1993, U.S. Dist.Ct. (ctrl. dist.) Ill. 1993. Dist. mgr. Ralston Purina Co., St. Louis, 1979-83; farmer, businessman McCrery Farms, Monmouth, Ill., 1984-90; grad. rsch. asst. So. Ill. U. Sch. Law, 1991-93; pvt. practice McCrery Law, Galesburg, Ill., 1993—. Judge Knox County Teen Ct., 1997-99. Assoc. del. U.S.-Can. Gt. Lakes Conf., 1984; assoc. bd. dirs. Warren County Soil and Water Dist., Monmouth, 1986; bd. dirs., v.p. West Ctrl. Ill. Legal Assistance, 1996-98; bd. dirs. Head Start Ops. for Presch. Edn.-HOPE, 1996-98, Galesburg Youth Athletic Club, 1994-98; mem. Ill. Agr. Leadership Program, 1986-87; session mem. Galesburg 1st Presbyn. Ch., 1999—. Recipient Outstanding State Dir. award Monmouth Jaycees, 1988. Mem. Knox County Bar Assn. Presbyterian. Avocations: hunting, fishing, collecting antiques, travel, mission work. Criminal, Family and matrimonial, Personal injury. Home: 105 N Carlysle Ave Abingdon IL 61410-1403 Office: 153 E Main St Galesburg IL 61401-4612 E-mail: mccreryd@hotmail.com

MCCROHON, CRAIG, lawyer; b. Harvey, Ill., Oct. 17, 1961; s. Maxwell and Nancy McCrohon. BA, Harvard U., 1984; postgrad., London Sch. Econs., 1988; JD, MBA, U. Pa., 1989. Bar: Ill. 1989, U.S. Dist. Ct. (no. dist.) Ill. 1989. Partner McBride, Baker & Coles, Chicago. Editor: Let's Go: USA, 1983. Mem. Cook County Transition Team-Econ. Devel., 1995. Mem.: Chgo. Bar Assn. (chmn. com. on consumer fin. svcs. 1991—92), Ill. C. of C. (working group econ. devel. com. 1992), Tech. Execs. Roundtable (pres.). Banking, Computer, General corporate. Home: 2 E 8th St Apt 2708 Chicago IL 60605-2134 Office: McBride Baker and Coles 500 W Madison Chicago IL 60606

MCCRORY, ALDOUS DESMOND, lawyer; b. Rome, June 18, 1969; s. Bobbie (Dorsey) McC. BA, Emory U., 1991; JD, U. Notre Dame, 1994. Bar: Ga. 1994, U.S. Dist. Ct. (no. dist.) Ga. 1994. Atty. The McCrory Firm, Rome, 1994—. Bd. dirs. Boys and Girls Club Rome, 1997, Habitat for Humanity, Rome, 1996—, Exch. Club Family Resource Ctr., 1996—. Mem. Greater Rome C. of C. (bd. dirs. 1994—), 100 Black Men of Rome Inc. (chair fin. com. 1996-97), Emory U. Alumni Assn. (bd. govs. 1996—). Baptist. General corporate, Estate planning, Real property. Home: PO Box 164 Rome GA 30162-0164

MCCRUM, ROBERT TIMOTHY, lawyer; b. Pitts., Nov. 4, 1958; s. Robert Terrence and Gertrude Callanan McCrum; m. Andrea Nourie, Mar. 19, 1960; children: Megan, Kelsey, Brian, Colleen, Shane. BA in Geology, Franklin & Marshall Coll., 1980; JD, Lewis & Clark Coll., 1983. Atty. U.S. Dept. Interior, Washington, 1984-86; ptnr. Crowell & Moring LLP, 1986—, vice chmn. natural resources and environ. group. Co-author: RCRA Hazardous Waste Handbook, 1996, Superfund Manual, 1997, Natural Resources Law Manual, 1995. Mem. Bush-Cheney Transition Adv. Com., 2000-2001. Mem. ABA (chmn. mining com. sect. environment, energy and resources 1997-99), Rocky Mt. Mineral Law Found. (bd. trustees). Republican. Roman Catholic. Avocation: prestidigitation. Environmental, Natural resources. Office: Crowell & Moring LLP 1001 Pennsylvania Ave NW Washington DC 20004-2505

MCCULLOUGH, EDWARD EUGENE, patent agent, inventor; b. Baldwin, N.D., June 4, 1923; s. Elmer Ellsworth and Emma Izelda (Nixon) McC. BA, U. Minn., 1957; postgrad., Utah State U., 1965. Machine designer Sperry Rand Corp., Mpls., 1952-58; patent adminstr. Thiokol Corp., Brigham City, Utah, 1958-86, patent cons., 1986; pvt. practice, 1986—. Patentee 34 U.S. patents including instruments for making perspective drawings, apparatus for forming ignition surfaces in solid propellant motors, passive communications satellite or similar article, flexible bearings and process for their manufacture, rocket nozzel support and pivoting system, cavity-shaping machine, others. Pianist Aldersgate Meth. Ch., Brigham City, 1959—. Staff Sgt. U.S. Army, 1949-52. Decorated two battle stars. Avocations: philosophy, music composition, hiking in the mountains. Patent. Home: PO Box 46 Brigham City UT 84302-0046 E-mail: ed@burgoyne.com

MCCULLOUGH, FRANK WITCHER, III, lawyer; b. New Orleans, Dec. 13, 1945; s. Frank Witcher Jr. and Kathleen Elizabeth (Van Pelt) McC.; m. Barry Jean Bock, Mar. 7, 1981; children: William David Oat, Frank Witcher IV, Elizabeth Layton. BA, Stetson U., 1967; JD, W.Va. U., 1970. Bar: W.Va. 1970, Tex. 1970, U.S. Dist. Ct. (so. dist.) W.Va. 1970, U.S. Dist. Ct. (so. dist.) Tex. 1972, U.S. Ct. Appeals (5th cir.) 1972, U.S. Supreme Ct. 1980, U.S. Dist. Ct. (no. dist.) Calif. 1983, U.S. Dist. Ct. (we. dist.) Tex. 1987, U.S. Dist. Ct. (ea. dist.) Tex. 1993. Indsl. rels. specialist Continental Oil Co., Houston, 1970-72; asst. U.S. atty. U.S. Atty.'s Office, 1972-75; assoc. Baker & Botts, 1975-76, Austin, 1985-89; ptnr. Weiner Strother & Lamkin, Houston, 1983-85; regional counsel GATX Leasing Corp., 1976-78; ptnr. Walsh Squires Tompkins & McCullough, 1978-82; shareholder Sheinfeld, Maley & Kay, Austin, 1989-2001, Diamond McCarthy Taylor & Finley, Austin, 2001—. Spl. commr. Harris County, Houston, 1982; mem. Bellaire (Tex.) Bd. Adjustment, 1982; bd. dirs. Big Bros. and Big Sisters of Austin, 1991-94. Mem. State Bar Tex. (grievance com. 1979-87, 95—), chmn. unauthorized practice law com. 1984-87), Austin Country Club, SAR. Republican. Episcopalian. General civil litigation, Consumer commercial. Home: 6707 Bridge Hill Cv Austin TX 78746-1338 Office: Diamond McCarthy Taylor & Finley Ste 400 6504 Bridgepoint Pkwy Austin TX 78730

MCCULLOUGH, RALPH CLAYTON, II, lawyer, educator; b. Daytona Beach, Fla., Mar. 28, 1941; s. Ralph C. and Doris (Johnson) McC.; m. Elizabeth Grier Henderson, Apr. 5, 1986; children from previous marriage: Melissa Wells, Clayton Baldwin. B.A., Erskine Coll., 1962; J.D., Tulane U., 1965. Bar: La. 1965, S.C. 1974. Assoc. Baldwin, Haspel, Maloney, Rainold and Meyer, New Orleans, 1965-68; asst. prof. law U. S.C., 1968-71, asso. prof., 1971-75, prof. 2, 1975—, chair prof. of advocacy, 1982—, asst. dean Sch. Law, 1970-75, instr. Med. Sch., 1970-79, adj. prof. law and medicine Med. Sch., 1979—; adj. prof. medicine Med. U. S.C., 1984—; of counsel Finkel & Altman, 1978—. Adj. prof. pathology Med. U. S.C., 1985—; asst. dean U. S.C. Sch. Law 1970-75. Author: (with J.L. Underwood) The Civil Trial Manual, 1974, 7th supplement, 1987, The Civil Trial Manual II, 1984, 87, (with Myers and Felix) New Directions in Legal Education, 1970, (with Finkel) S.C. Torts II, 1986, III, 1990, IV, 1995; co-reporter S.C. Criminal Code, 1977, S.C. Study Sentencing, 1977. Trustee S.C. dist. U.S. Bankruptcy Ct., 1979— ; exec. dir. S.C. Continuing Legal Edn. Program.; bd. visitors Erskine Coll.; reporter S.C. Jury Charge

Commn., 1991-95. Mem. ABA, La. Bar Assn., S.C. Bar (sec. 1975-76, exec. dir. 1972-76, award of service 1978), New Orleans Bar Assn., Am. Trial Lawyers Assn., Am. Law Inst., Southeastern Assn. Am. Law Schs. (pres.), S.C. Trial Lawyers Assn. (bd. govs. 1984-88), Phi Alpha Delta. Republican. Episcopalian. Club: Forest Lake. Home: PO Box 1799 Columbia SC 29202-1799 Office: U SC Sch Law Columbia SC 29208-0001

MC CUNE, BARRON PATTERSON, retired federal judge; b. West Newton, Pa., Feb. 19, 1915; s. James Patterson and Lyda Barron (Hammond) McC.; m. Edna Flannery Markey, Dec. 23, 1943; children: Edward M., James H., Barron Patterson. AB, Washington and Jefferson Coll., 1935; LLB, U. Pa., 1938. Bar: Pa. bar 1939. Practiced in, Washington, 1939-64; judge 27th Jud. Dist. Ct. Common Pleas, 1964-71, U.S. Dist. Ct., Western Dist. Pa., Pitts., 1971-95, sr. fed. judge; ret., 1995. Trustee emeritus Washington and Jefferson Coll.; bd. dirs. emeritus Washington (Pa.) Hosp. Served with USNR, 1942-45. Home: 144 Lemoyne Ave Washington PA 15301-3636

MCCUNE, PHILIP SPEAR, lawyer; b. Spokane, Wash., Sept. 14, 1965; s. Calmar A. McCune and Katrina Y. Spear; m. Joey Leigh Hankins, Jan. 15, 1993; children: Emma Sophia, Jackson Spear. BA magna cum laude, Dartmouth Coll., 1987; JD cum laude, U. Mich., 1991. Bar: Wash. 1991, U.S. Dist. Ct. (we. dist.) Wash. 1991, U.S. Ct. Appeals (9th cir.) 1992, U.S. Dist. Ct. (ea. dist.) Wash. 1993, U.S. Dist. Ct. Utah 1998. Law clk. Hon. John C. Coughenour chief judge U.S. Dist. Ct. (we. dist.) Wash., Seattle, 1991-93; assoc. Heller, Ehrman, White and Maculliffe, 1993-97; ptnr., founder Summit Law Group, 1997—. Author: The Forest Practices Act, Washington Environmental Law and Practice, 1997; sr. editor U. Mich. Jour. Law Reform, 1989-91; contbr. articles to profl. jours. Young leaders Seattle Art Mus., 1996-98; bd. dirs. Cmty. Svc. for the Blind, Seattle, 1997—, bd. dir. Friends of Ind. Schs. and Better Edn.; jr. bd. Seattle Repatory Theater, 1999—; pres. bd. dirs. Am. Friends St. Michaels U. Sch. Named Washington Law and Politics Rising Star, 2002. Mem. ABA, Washington State Bar Assn., King County Bar Assn., Wash. Athletic Club, U. Mich. Law Sch. Barristers. Avocations: hiking, running. General civil litigation, Environmental, Land use and zoning (including planning). Office: Summit Law Group 1505 Westlake Ave N Ste 300 Seattle WA 98109-6211 E-mail: philm@summitlaw.com

MCCURLEY, CARL MICHAEL, lawyer; b. Denton, Tex., July 15, 1946; s. Carl and Geneva McC.; m. Mary Jo Trice, June 5, 1983; 1 child, Melissa Renee. BA, N. Tex. State U., 1968; JD, So. Meth. U., 1972. Bar: Tex. 1972, U.S. Dist. Ct. (no. dist.) Tex. 1972, U.S. Dist. Ct. (ea. dist.) Tex. 1974, U.S. Supreme Ct. 1977. Ptnr. McGuire, Levy & McCurley , Irving, Tex., 1972-82, Koons, Fuller, McCurley & Vanden Eykel, Dallas, 1982-92, McCurley, Kinser, McCurley & Nelson, 1992—. Contbr. articles to profl. jours. Mem. Family Law Council (chmn. 1991-93), Dallas Bar Assn., Am. Acad. Matrimonial Lawyers (treas. 1990-93, v.p. 1993-96, pres.-elect 1997, pres. 1998), Internat. Acad. Matrimonial Lawyers. Family and matrimonial. Home: 4076 Hanover Ave Dallas TX 75225-7009 Office: McCurley Kinser McCurley & Nelson 5950 Sherry Ln Ste 800 Dallas TX 75225-6533

MCCURLEY, MARY JOHANNA, lawyer; b. Baton Rouge, Oct. 3, 1953; d. William Edward and Leora Elizabeth (Block) Trice; m. Carl Michael McCurley, June 6, 1983; 1 stepchild, Melissa Reneé Rockenbach. BA, Centenary Coll., 1975; JD, St. Mary's U., 1979. Bar: Tex. 1979; cert. family law. Assoc. Martin, Withers & Box, Dallas, 1979-82, Raggio & Raggio, Inc., Dallas, 1982-83; ptnr. Bruner, McColl, McColloch & McCurley, 1983-87; assoc., ptnr. Selligson & Douglass, 1987-90; jr. ptnr. Koons, Fuller, McCurley & VanderEykel, 1990-92; ptnr. McCurley, Kinser, McCurley & Nelson, 1992—. Contbr. articles to profl. jours. Adv. Women's Service League, Dallas, 1993—. Mem.: Am. Acad. Matrimonial Lawyers (treas. Tex. chpt. 1993—95, sec. 1995—96, pres. 1997, nat. bd. dirs., bd. govs. 2000, nat. sec. 2000—01, pres. Tex. chpt. 1997—98), Dallas Bar Assn. (chair family law sect. 1985), Tex. State Bar Assn. (family law coun., sec. 2001, treas. 2001, vice-chair 2001), Tex. Acad. Family Law Specialist, Dallas Bar Assn. Methodist. Avocations: golf, travel, jogging, horseback riding. Family and matrimonial. Home: 4076 Hanover Ave Dallas TX 75225-7009 Office: McCurley Kinser McCurley & Nelson LLP 5950 Sherry Ln Ste 800 Dallas TX 75225-6533 Fax: 214-273-2470. E-mail: marjo@mkmn.com

MCCURN, NEAL PETERS, federal judge; b. Syracuse, N.Y., Apr. 6, 1926; LL.B., Syracuse U., 1952, J.D., 1960. Bar: N.Y. 1952. Ptnr. Mackenzie Smith Lewis Mitchell & Hughes, Syracuse, 1957-79; judge U.S. Dist. Ct. (no. dist.) N.Y., 1979-88; chief judge U.S. Dist. Ct. (no. dist.), N.Y., 1988-93; sr. judge, 1993—. Del. N.Y. State Constl. Conv., 1976; mem. 2d Cir. Jud. Council. Pres. Syracuse Common Coun., 1970-78. Mem. ABA, N.Y. State Bar Assn. (chmn. state constn. com.), Onondaga County Bar Assn. (past pres.), Am. Coll. Trial Lawyers, Am. Judicature Soc. (bd. dirs. 1980-84). Office: US Dist Ct 100 S Clinton St Rm 33 Syracuse NY 13261-6100

MCCURRY, BRUCE, lawyer; b. Carthage, Mo., July 7, 1947; s. James B. and Fern (Denney) M.; m. Vicki Fletcher, June 3, 1972; children— Kyle, Jeff. B.S., U. Mo., 1969, J.D., 1972. Bar: Mo. 1973, U.S. Ct. Appeals (8th cir.) 1977, U.S. Supreme Ct. 1978. Ptnr. Dickey, Allemann, Chaney & McCurry, Springfield, Mo., 1972— . Mem. ABA, Greene County Bar Assn. (bd. dirs. 1982—), Motor Carrier Lawyers Assn. Methodist. Administrative and regulatory, State civil litigation, General corporate. Office: Dickey Allemann Chaney & McCurry 910 Plaza Springfield MO 65804

MCCUSKER, PAUL DONALD, lawyer, educator; b. Niagara Falls, N.Y., Sept. 23, 1921; s. Alexander J. and Catherine (Barron) McC.; m. Joan Gross, Aug. 28, 1948; children: Karen, Mary, Paul Alexander, Ian. BA, Holy Cross Coll., 1943; JD, Cornell U., 1949, U. Rome, Italy, 1952. Bar: N.Y. 1949. Counselor of embassy U.S. Fgn. Svc., Dept. State, Washington, 1950-69; prin. officer UN, N.Y.C., 1969-82; ptnr. Garrity & McCusker, 1982-94. Adj. prof. L.I. U., 1982-99. Served with AUS, 1943-46. Fulbright fellow, Italy, 1949-50. Mem. Am. Soc. Internat. Law. Club: Rotary. Home and Office: 32 Glenmore Dr Durham NC 27707-3980

MCCUTCHAN, GORDON EUGENE, retired lawyer, insurance company executive; b. Buffalo, Sept. 30, 1935; s. George Lawrence and Mary Esther (De Puy) McC.; m. Linda Brown; children: Lindsey, Elizabeth. BA, Cornell U., 1956, MBA, 1958, LLB, 1959. Bar: N.Y. 1959, Ohio 1964. Pvt. practice, Rome, 1959-61; atty., advisor SEC, Washington, 1961-64; ptnr. McCutchan, Druen, Maynard, Rath & Dietrich, 1964-94; mem. office of gen. counsel Nationwide Mut. Ins. Co., Columbus, Ohio, 1964-94, sr. v.p., gen. counsel, 1982-89, exec. v.p., gen. counsel, 1989-94; exec. v.p. Law and Corp. Svcs., Nationwide Ins. Enterprise, 1994-98; ret., 1998. Trustee, bd. govs. Franklin U., 1992-97; trustee Ohio Tuition Trust Authority, 1992-97. Mem. Columbus Bar Assn., Ohio Bar Assn., Am. Corp. Counsel Assn., Assn. Life Inst. Counsel (bd. govs. 1990-94), Fedn. Ins. and Corp. Counsel, Am. Coun. Life Ins. (chair legal sect. 1992-93). Home: 2376 Oxford Rd Columbus OH 43221-4011 E-mail: tunkpa@columbus.rr.com

MCDANIEL, DONALD HAMILTON, lawyer; b. Washington, Apr. 26, 1948; s. Roy Hamilton and Mildred Dean (Borden) McD.; m. Eva Styron, Dec. 29, 1973; children: Sharon, Michelle. BS, La. State U., 1970; JD, U. Miss., 1973. Bar: Miss. 1973; bd. cert. tax atty., 1987—; bd. cert. estate planning & adminstrn. atty. Atty. IRS, Washington, 1974-77; tax law specialist Bourgeois Bennett Thokey, New Orleans, 1977-81; ptnr. McCloskey Dennery Page, 1981-85, Lemle & Kelleher, New Orleans, 1985—. Author: Estate Planning in Louisiana, 1991. Trustee St. Martins Episcopal Sch., New Orleans, 1993, East Jefferson Hosp. Found., New Orleans, 1995, United Meth. Found., New Orleans, 1995. Mem. ABA, La. State Bar Assn. (chmn. com. on trusts, estates and immovable property 1997—), Miss. State Bar Assn., New Orleans Estate Planning Coun. Avocations: golf, fishing. Estate planning, Estate taxation, Taxation, general. Office: Lemle & Kelleher LLP 601 Poydras St Ste 2100 New Orleans LA 70130-6021

MCDANIEL, JAMES EDWIN, lawyer; b. Dexter, Mo., Nov. 22, 1931; s. William H. and Gertie M. (Woods) McD.; m. Mary Jane Crawford, Jan. 22, 1955; children: John William, Barbara Anne. AB, Washington U., St. Louis, 1957, JD, 1959. Bar: Mo. 1959. Assoc. firm Walther, Barnard, Cloyd & Timm, 1959-60, McDonald, Barnard, Wright & Timm, 1960-63, ptnr., 1963-65; ptnr. firm Barnard, Timm & McDaniel St. Louis, 1965-73; ptnr. firm Barnard & Baer, 1973-82; ptnr. Lashly & Baer, 1982—, prosecuting atty., 1968—. City atty. City of Glendale, Mo., 1996—; bd. dirs. Eden. Theol. Sem.; lectr. Latvian U., Riga, Inst. Fgn. Rels., Banking in Am., 1992-93. Leader legal del. Chinese-Am. Comparative Law Study, People's Republic China, 1988, Russian-Am. Comparative Law Study, USSR, 1990; trustee, past chmn., past treas. 1st Congl. Ch. St. Louis. With USAF, 1951-55. Fellow Am. Bar Found. (life), St. Louis Bar Found. (life); mem. ABA (bd. govs. 1997-2000, ho. of dels. 1976-80, 84-92, 97-2000, state del. 1986-92, chmn. lawyers conf., jud. adminstrn. divsn. 1992-95, 8th cir. rep. standing com. on fed. jud. 1995-98, mem. standing com. on jud. qualification, tenure and compensation 1996-97), The Mo. Bar (pres. 1981-82, bd. govs. 1974-83), Mo. Assn. Def. Counsel, Bar Assn. Met. St. Louis (pres. 1972), Internat. Assn. Ins. Counsel, Assn. Def. Counsel St. Louis (past pres.), Phi Delta Phi. General civil litigation, Insurance, Labor. Home: 767 Elmwood Ave Saint Louis MO 63122-3216 Office: Lashly & Baer 714 Locust St Saint Louis MO 63101-1699

MCDANIEL, JARREL DAVE, lawyer; b. Clovis, N. Mex., Oct. 17, 1930; s. Raymond Lee and Blanch (Booth) McD.; m. Anne Louise McAllister; children: Jarrel Dave Jr., Julia Anne. A.A., Riverside Coll., 1951; B.A., U. Tex., 1956, LL.B., 1957. Bar: Tex. 1957. Assoc. Vinson & Elkins, Houston, 1957-69, ptnr., 1969-96; of counsel Sheinfeld, Maley & Kay, 1997-2001; sr. counsel Akin, Gump, Strauss, Hauer & Feld, L.L.P., 2001—. Author, lectr. in field. Served with USAF, 1950-54. Mem. ABA, Am. Coll. Bankruptcy, State Bar Tex., Am. Bankruptcy Inst., Tex. Bd. Legal Specialization in Bankruptcy (mem. adv. com. 1976-99, chair 1999—). Roman Catholic. Clubs: Houston Ctr. Bankruptcy, General civil litigation, Contracts commercial. Home: 1217 Potomac Dr Houston TX 77057-1919 Office: Akin Gump Strauss Hauer & Feld LLP 711 Louisiana St Ste 1900 Houston TX 77002 E-mail: jmcdaniel@akingump.com

MCDANIEL, JOHN MARK, lawyer; b. Decatur, Ala., Nov. 5, 1951; s. John Lester and Helen Juanita McD.; m. Henri Butler, Jan. 19, 1973; children: Henri Jo, John Benjamin. BS, Athens Coll., 1972; JD, Birmingham Sch. of Law, 1976. Bar: Ala. Ptnr. McDaniel & McDaniel, Huntsville, Ala., 1976—; prosecuting atty. Town of New Hope, 1976-83. Pres. McDaniel Media, Inc., Huntsville, 1995—; legal counsel Congressman Cramer, Huntsville, 1991—; trial counsel Gov. Hunt, Montgomery, Ala., 1994; spl. atty. gen., Montgomery, 1984, 90; legal advisor to dir. emergency mgmt., State of Ala., Montgomery, 1984-87; assoc. prof. Faulkner U., Huntsville, 1976—; instr. People's Law Sch., Huntsville, 1993—, Athens State Coll., 1998; adv. bd. Jones Sch. of Law, Montgomery, 1984-87. Bd. dirs. Boys Club, Huntsville, 1994-97, Huntsville Stars, 1995—, Indsl. Devel. Named to County Sports Hall of Fame, Huntsville, 1996, Alumni of Yr., Athens State Coll., 1993. Mem. ABA, Ala. State Bar (pres. criminal law sect. 1985-86), Madison County Bar, Mensa. Mem. Ch. of Christ. Avocations: jogging.

MCDANIEL, PAUL R. law educator, lawyer; b. Sabetha, Kans., Jan. 28, 1936; s. Paul T. McDaniel and Marie (Sutton) McDaniel Welch; div.; children: Alysa M., Kyle W.; m. Virginia Lambert Mason, May 31, 1997. BA, U. Okla., 1958; JD, Harvard U., 1961. Bar: Okla. 1961, Mass. 1979. Assoc. firm Crowe & Dunlevy, Oklahoma City, 1961-67; atty. adviser Office of Tax Legis. Counsel, Washington, 1967-69; acting assoc. tax legis. counsel U.S. Dept. Treasury, 1969; spl. asst. tax matters U.S. Sen. Albert Gore, 1969-70; prof. law Boston Coll., Newton, Mass., 1970-87; ptnr. Hill & Barlow, Boston, 1987—93; prof. law N.Y.U., 1993—. Author: (with Ault, McMahon and Simmons) Federal Income Taxation, 4th edit., 1998, Federal Income Taxation of Business Organizations, 3d edit., 1998, Federal Wealth Transfer Taxation, 4th edit., 1999, (with Ault) Introduction to United States International Taxation, 4th edit., 1998, (with Surrey) International Apsects of Tax Expenditures, A Comparative Study, 1985, Tax Expenditures, 1985; contbr. numerous articles on taxation to profl. jours. Chmn. Gov.'s Adv. Task Force on Dept. Revenue, Boston, 1982-83; mem. Sec. of State's Adv. Task Force on Securities Regulations, 1982-83. Recipient Meritorious Service award Dept. Treasury, 1969. Mem. ABA, Mass. Bar Assn., Nat. Tax Assn.-Tax Inst. Am., Internat. Fiscal Assn., Internat. Inst. Pub. Fin. Education and schools, Corporate taxation, Personal income taxation. Home: 35 Lincoln St Andover MA 01810-2954

MCDANIELS, WILLIAM E. lawyer; b. Needham, Mass., July 1, 1941; BA, Williams Coll., 1963; JD, Georgetown U., 1966. Bar: D.C. 1967, Md. 1983. Grad. fellow criminal law, litigation U. Pa., Phila., 1966-68; pub. defender Phila. Pub. Defender's Office, 1966-68; adj. prof. evidence, criminal law, advanced criminal procedure Georgetown U. Law Ctr., Washington, 1970-87; mem. Williams & Connolly, 1968—. Instr. Nat. Inst. Trial Advocacy, 1975—. Fellow Am. Coll. Trial Lawyers; mem. ABA, Md. State Bar Assn, D.C. Bar. General civil litigation, Criminal, Intellectual property. Office: Williams & Connolly 725 12th St NW Washington DC 20005-5901

MCDAVID, JANET LOUISE, lawyer; b. Mpls., Jan. 24, 1950; d. Robert Matthew and Lois May (Bratt) Kurzeka; m. John Gary McDavid, June 9, 1973; 1 child, Matthew Collins McDavid. BA, Northwestern U., 1971; JD, Georgetown U., 1974. Bar D.C. 1975, U.S. Ct. Appeals (fed. cir.) 1975 (D.C. cir. 1976), U.S. Supreme Ct. 1980, U.S. Ct. Appeals (5th cir.) 1983, (9th cir.) 1986. Assoc. Hogan & Harston, Washington, 1974-83, ptnr., 1984—. Gen. counsel ERAmerica, 1977-83; mem. antitrust task force Dept. Defense, 1993-94, 96-97; mem. antitrust coun. U.S. C. of C., 1994—; advisor Bush adminstrn. transition team, 2001. Contbr. articles to profl. jours. Participant Clinton and Bush adminstrn. transition team FTC. Mem. ABA (antitrust sect., vice chmn. civil practice com. 1986-89, sect. 2 com. 1989-90, chmn. franchising com. 1990-91, coun. mem. 1991-94, program officer 1994-97, vice chair 1997-98, chair-elect 1998-99, chair 1999-2000, immediate past chair, governing com. of forum on franchising 1991-97), ACLU, U.S. C. of C. (antitrust coun. 1995—), Washington Coun. Lawyers, D.C. Bar Assn., Fed. Bar Assn., Womens Legal Def. fund. Democrat. Antitrust, Federal civil litigation, Franchising. Office: Hogan & Hartson 555 13th St NW Ste 800E Washington DC 20004-1161

MCDERMITT, EDWARD VINCENT, lawyer, educator, writer; b. Hagerstown, Md., Nov. 29, 1953; s. Edward Bernard and Genevieve Natalie (Gallo) McD.; m. Jane Langmead Springmann, June 28, 1986; children: Edward S., Maureen K. BA, Georgetown U., 1975, MA, 1978; JD, U. Santa Clara, 1980; LLM, U. Pa., 1984. Bar: D.C. 1981, U.S. Dist. Ct. D.C. 1981. Rsch. asst. U. Santa Clara, Calif., 1980; pvt. practice Washington, 1981—; assoc. Law Offices of Miller & Loewinger, 1982; rsch. asst. U. Pa., Phila., 1983-84. Adj. asst. prof. Yale Gordon Coll. Liberal Arts, U. Balt., 1991—, vis. asst. prof., 1996, adj. assoc. prof. U. Md. Univ. Coll., 1998—, lectr. law Columbus Sch. Law, Cath. U. Am., 1999—; mng. ptnr. J-L-S Svcs., Washington, 1985—, Early and Valuable Memorabilia, Md., 1985—; congl. intern to rep. Pat Schroeder, Washington, 1975; vol. atty. ACLU Nat. Capital area, Washington, 1982—; lectr. writing The Writer's Ctr., 1987—; participant program instrn. lawyers Harvard Law Sch., 1989—. Author: Overruled, Mr./Ms. Writer: An Argument in Favor of Accuracy in Depiction, How to Write an Uncommonly Good Novel, 1990, Return to Berlin, 1996, Toward a New Social (Democratic) Contract, 2000, John Marshall: Farmer Extraordinaire and the Seeds of Corporate Capitalism, 2001. Vol. McGovern for Pres. campaign, Washington and Md., 1972, United Farmworkers Union, Washington, 1973-77, Urban Coalition Basketball League, Washington, 1977-78, Sarbanes re-election campaign, Md., 1982. Mem. D.C. Bar (cons., mem. lawyer/tchr. partnership program 1987—), Superior Ct. Trial Lawyers Assn., Washington Writers Group, Internat. Platform Assn., Assn. for Practical & Profl. Ethics, Pi Sigma Alpha. Roman Catholic. Avocations: photography, poetry, fiction writing, military history, bridge. Civil rights, Constitutional, Criminal. Home and Office: 8000 Wildwood Dr Silver Spring MD 20912-7425

MCDERMOTT, JOHN H(ENRY), lawyer; b. Evanston, Ill., June 23, 1931; s. Edward Henry and Goldie Lucile (Boso) McD.; m. Ann Elizabeth Pickard, Feb. 19, 1966; children: Elizabeth A., Mary L., Edward H. BA, Williams Coll., 1953; JD, U. Mich., 1956. Bar: Mich. 1955, Ill. 1956. Assoc. McDermott, Will & Emery, Chgo., 1958-64, ptnr., 1964-99, of counsel, 2000—. Bd. dirs. Patrick Industries Inc. 1st lt. USAF, 1956-58. Mem. ABA, Ill. Bar Assn., Chgo. Bar Assn. Clubs: Commerical of Chgo., Econ. of Chgo., Legal Chgo. (pres. 1981-82), Law Chgo. (pres. 1986-87). Banking, General corporate, Securities. Home: 330 Willow Rd Winnetka IL 60093-4130 Office: McDermott Will & Emery 227 W Monroe St Ste 3100 Chicago IL 60606-5096 E-mail: mcdermott330@cs.com

MCDERMOTT, KEVIN R. lawyer; b. Youngstown, Ohio, Jan. 26, 1952; s. Robert J. and Marion D. (McKeown) McD.; m. Cindy J. Darling, Dec. 11, 1976; children: Ciara, Kelly. AB, Miami U., Oxford, Ohio, 1974; JD, Ohio State U., 1977. Bar: Ohio 1977, U.S. Dist. Ct. (so. dist.) Ohio 1978, U.S. Dist. Ct. (no. dist.) Ohio 1988, U.S. Dist. Ct. (we. dist.) Mich. 1993, U.S. Supreme Ct. 1990, U.S. Ct. Appeals (3rd cir.) 1996, U.S. Ct. Appeals (6th cir.) 1988. Assoc. ptnr. Murphey Young & Smith, Columbus, Ohio, 1977-88; ptnr. Squire Sanders & Dempsey, 1988-90, Schottenstein Zox & Dunn, Columbus, 1990—. Adv. bd. mem. Capital U. Legal Asst. Program, Columbus, Ohio, 1988—. Bd. pres. Easter Seal Soc. Ctrl. Ohio, Columbus, 1992-94, bd. mem. 1988-92; pres. Upper Arlington Civic Svc. Commn., Columbus, Ohio, 1988-93. General civil litigation, Constitutional, Securities. Office: Schottenstein Zox & Dunn 41 S High St Ste 2600 Columbus OH 43215-6109

MCDERMOTT, THOMAS JOHN, JR. lawyer; b. Santa Monica, Calif., Mar. 23, 1931; s. Thomas J. Sr. and Etha Irene (Cook) McD.; m. Yolanda Amante Jatap; children: Jodi Friedman, Kimberly E., Kish S. BA, UCLA, 1953, JD, 1958. Bar: Calif. 1959. Ptnr. Gray, Binkley and Pfaelzer, L.A., 1964-67, Kadison, Pfaelzer, Woodward, Quinn and Rossi, L.A., 1967-87, Rogers & Wells, L.A., 1987-93, Bryan Cave, L.A., 1993-95, Manatt, Phelps & Phillips, LLP, L.A., 1995-99, Shanks and Herbert, San Diego. Served with U.S. Army, 1953-56, Korea. Fellow Am. Coll. Trial Lawyers; mem. ABA, Assn. Bus. Trial Lawyers (pres. 1980-81, mem. exec. com. 9th cir. jud. conf. 1993—, chair 1997), State Bar Calif. (chair litigation sect. 1993-94), UCLA Law Alumni Assn. (pres. 1961-62), Order of Coif. Federal civil litigation, General civil litigation, State civil litigation. Office: Shanks & Herbert Ste 330 4350 La Jolla Village Dr San Diego CA 92122

MCDEVITT, CHARLES FRANCIS, retired state supreme court justice, lawyer; b. Pocatello, Idaho, Jan. 5, 1932; s. Bernard A. and Margaret (Hermann) McD.; m. Virginia L. Heller, Aug. 14, 1954; children: Eileen A., Kathryn A., Brian A., Sheila A., Terrence A., Neil A., Kendal A. LLB, U. Idaho, 1956. Bar: Idaho 1956. Ptnr. Richards, Haga & Eberle, Boise, 1956-62; gen. counsel, asst. sec. Boise Cascade Corp., 1962-65; mem. Idaho State Legislature, 1963-66; sec., gen. counsel Boise Cascade Corp., 1965-67, v.p. sec., 1967-68; pres. Beck Industries, 1968-70; group v.p. Singer Co., N.Y.C., 1970-72, exec. v.p., 1973-76; pub. defender Ada County, Boise, 1976-78; co-founder Givens, McDevitt, Pursley & Webb, 1978-89; justice Idaho Supreme Ct., 1989-97, chief justice, 1993-97; ptnr., founder McDevitt & Miller, LLP, 1997—. Served on Gov.'s Select Com. on Taxation, Boise, 1988-89; mem. State Select Com. on Campaign Ethics and Campaign Finances, State Select Com. on Legis. Compensation. Chair Idaho Jud. Coun., 1993-97, Cts. Advisors Coun., 1994-98; mem. Multi-State Tax Com. Home: 4940 Boise River Ln Boise ID 83716-8816 Office: McDevitt & Miller LLP 537 W Bannock St Ste 215 Boise ID 83702-5759 E-mail: chas@McDevitt.org

MCDEVITT, RAY EDWARD, lawyer; b. San Francisco, Nov. 15, 1943; s. Edward Anthony and Margaret Ann (Peterson) McD.; m. Mary Rolfs, July 1, 1967; children— Jessica, Devon. B.A., Stanford U., 1966, J.D., 1969; Diploma in Law, Oxford U., 1973. Bar: Calif., 1970, U.S. Supreme Ct., 1975. Teaching fellow Stanford U., 1969; law clk. Calif. Supreme Ct., 1970; atty. EPA, 1973-75, assoc. gen. counsel, 1975-76; ptnr. Hanson, Bridgett, Marcus, Vlahos & Rudy, San Francisco, 1976—; adj. prof. Sch. Law U. San Francisco, 1994—. Mem. ABA, Calif. Bar Assn., Order of Coif. Environmental, Municipal (including bonds), Real property. Office: 333 Market St Ste 2300 San Francisco CA 94105-2124

MCDIARMID, ROBERT CAMPBELL, lawyer; b. N.Y.C., July 13, 1937; s. Norman Hugh and Dorothy (Shoemaker) McD.; m. Ruth Sussman, 1963 (div. 1996); children: Jennifer, Alexander Samuel; m. Frances Enseki Francis, 1996. BS in Mech. Engring., Swarthmore Coll., 1958; MS in Engring. Physics, Cornell U., 1960; LLB, Harvard U., 1963. Bar: D.C. 1964, Va. 1964, U.S. Supreme Ct. 1967, U.S. Ct. Appeals (4th, 6th and 9th cirs.) 1965, U.S. Ct. Appeals (3d, 5th and 10th cirs.) 1966, U.S. Ct. Appeals (7th, 8th and D.C. cirs.) 1967, U.S. Ct. Appeals (2d cir.) 1970, U.S. Ct. Appeals (1st cir.) 1979, U.S. Ct. Appeals (11th cir.) 1981. Assoc. Weaver & Glassie, Washington, 1963-64; trial atty. civil divsn. appellate sect. Dept. Justice, 1964-68; asst. to gen. counsel Fed. Power Commn., 1968-70; assoc. Law Office of George Spiegel, 1970-73; ptnr. Spiegel & McDiarmid, 1973—. Mem. alumni coun. Swarthmore Coll., 1986-89. Mem. ABA, Va. State Bar, Bar Assn. D.C., D.C. Bar, Energy Bar Assn. (exec. com. 1982-83, bd. dirs. 1997-2000). Democrat. Mem. Soc. of Friends. Antitrust, Federal civil litigation, FERC practice. Home: 3625 Fulton St NW Washington DC 20007-1452 Office: Spiegel & McDiarmid 1350 New York Ave NW Ste 1100 Washington DC 20005-4798 E-mail: robert.mcdiarmid@spiegelmcd.com

MCDONALD, ALAN ANGUS, federal judge; b. Harrah, Wash., Dec. 13, 1927; s. Angus and Nell (Britt) McD.; m. Ruby K., Aug. 22, 1949; children: Janelle Jo, Saralee Sue, Stacy. BS, U. Wash., 1950, LLB, 1952. Dep. pros. atty. Yakima County, Wash., 1952-54; assoc. Halverson & Applegate, Yakima, 1954-56; ptnr. Halverson, Applegate & McDonald, 1956-85; judge U.S. Dist. Ct. (ea. dist.) Wash., 1985-95, sr. judge, 1995—. Fellow Am. Coll. Trial Lawyers; mem. Yakima C. of C. (bd. dirs.). Clubs: Yakima Country, Royal Duck (Yakima). Office: US Dist Ct PO Box 2706 Yakima WA 98907-2706

MCDONALD, ALAN THOMAS, lawyer; b. Aug. 16, 1949; s. James Francis and Jennie Eloise (Thomits) McDonald; m. Joyce Ann Martin, Feb. 28, 1981. BSCE, Rutgers U., 1971; JD, U. Houston, 1973; LLM in Patent and Trade Regulation Law, George Washington U., 1976. Bar: Tex. 1974, Pa. 1977, Va. 1980, U.S.C. Ct. Customs and Patent Appeals 1974. Patent examiner U.S. Patent and Trademark Office, Arlington, Va., 1974—75;

patent atty. PPG Industries, Inc., Pitts., 1975—78, Reynolds Metals Co., Richmond, Va., 1978—97, Honda of Am. Mfg., Inc., 1998—. Mem. adminstrv. bd. Dutilh United Meth. Ch., Cranberry, Pa., 1977—78; sunday sch. tchr. Providence United Meth. Ch., Chesterfield County, Va., 1981—84, mem. adminstrv. bd., 1985—, chmn. fin. com., 1988—90; mem. coun. on ministries Reveille United Meth. Ch., 1994—95. Mem.: ABA, Am. Intellectual Property Law Assn., Mensa (vice local sec. Richmond chpt. 1981—82, adminstr. 1980—81), Phi Delta Phi. Republican. Achievements include patents for method for producing slubbed yarn. Home: 23920 N Darby Coe Rd Milford Center OH 43045-9775

MCDONALD, BRADLEY G. lawyer; m. Ann Gilbert, Sept. 2, 1964; 1 child, Perry. BA, U. Okla.; JD, Georgetown U., 1961. Bar: D.C. 1961, U.S. Ct. Appeals (D.C., 11th and 4th cirs.), U.S. Supreme Ct. With McDonald & Karl, Washington. Lawyer; b. Okla.; m. Ann Gilbert, Sept. 3, 1964; 1 child, Perry. BA, U. Okla.; JD, Georgetown U., 1961. Bar: D.C. 1961, U.S. Ct. Appeals (D.C. cir.), U.S. Ct. Appeals (11th cir., 4th cir,) U.S. Supreme Ct. Nat. Alumni Adv. Coun. U. Okla.; mem. Arlington Com. of 100; bd. dirs. McLean Montessori, , Sigma Nu Ednl. Found.; trustee, treas. Randolph-Macon Acad. Served to 1st lt. USMC, 1956-58. Named to Legion of Honor, Delta Epsilon, Sigma Nu; recipient 1st Regent's Alumni award U. Okla. Mem. nat. alumni adv. coun. U. Okla; mem. Arlington Com. of 100; bd. dirs. McLen Montessori; trustee, treas. Randolph-Macon Acad. 1st lt. USMC, 1956-58. Recipient 1st Regent's Alumni award U. Okla. Mem. Sigma Nu (mem. Ednl. Found.), Delta Epsilon. General practice.

MCDONALD, CASSANDRA BURNS, lawyer; b. Aberdeen, Md., Aug. 28, 1963; d. Charles Franklin and Elizabeth (Connor) Burns; 1 child, Christopher. AB, Dartmouth Coll., Hanover, N.H., 1985; JD, Cornell U., 1990. Bar: Conn. 1991, U.S. Dist. Ct. Conn. 1992, U.S. Dist. Ct. (ea. and so. dists) N.Y. 1992. Atty. Cummings & Lockwood, Stamford, Conn., 1990-94, 96—. 1st v.p. The Links, Inc., Fairfield County, 2000—; mem. Women's Leadership Conf., Conn., 1998—. Mem. ABA, Conn. Bar Assn., Nat. Bar Assn., Lawyers for Children Am., Inc., Dartmouth Lawyers Assn., Dartmouth Alumni, Black Alumni Dartmouth, Delta Sigma Theta. Baptist. Avocations: travel, reading, tennis. General civil litigation, Environmental, Product liability. Office: Cummings & Lockwood 4 Stamford Plz Stamford CT 06904-0120 E-mail: cmcdonald@cl-law.com

MCDONALD, CHARLES EDWARD, lawyer; b. El Paso, Tex., Nov. 13, 1957; s. Carlos and Armida (Adauto) McD.; 1 child, Miranda Lee. BA in Philosophy, U. St. Thomas, Houston, 1980; JD, South Tex. Coll. Law, 1985. Bar: Tex. 1985, U.S. Ct. Appeals. (5th cir.) 1991, U.S. Supreme Ct. 1992. Prin. Law Office Charles E. McDonald, El Paso, 1985-2000, McDonald and Assocs, El Paso, 2000—. Comms. liaison Coleman Reelection Congl. Campaign, El Paso, 1984, 86. Mem. ATLA, Tex. Trial Lawyers Assn., State Bar Tex., El Paso County Bar Assn. (ethics com. 1997-98, rules com. 1997-98, clin. law coun. 1997-98), Nat. Assn. Cave Divers. Roman Catholic. Avocations: cave diving, chess, traveling, foreign language (Spanish). Civil rights, General civil litigation, Professional liability. Office: 4150 Rio Bravo St Ste 136 El Paso TX 79902-1013 E-mail: charles.mcdonald@prodigy.net

MCDONALD, FRANCIS MICHAEL, judge trial referee, retired state supreme court justice; b. Waterbury, Conn., Jan. 22, 1931; s. M. Francis and Margaret (Kelly) McD.; m. Mary Kelly, Jan. 28, 1956; children: Michael, Mary Ann, John K. AB, Holy Cross Coll., 1953; LLB, Yale U., 1956. Bar: Conn. 1956. Spl. agt. FBI, Washington, 1956-57; asst. U.S. atty. Dist. of Conn., New Haven, 1958-60; asst. prosecutor Cir. Ct., Waterbury, 1961-68; state's atty., 1968-84; judge Superior Ct., 1984-96; assoc. justice Conn. Supreme Ct., Hartford, 1996-99, chief justice, 1999-2001, judge trial referee Conn., 2001—. Avocations: fishing, skiing, fly tying. Home: 257 Christian Rd Middlebury CT 06762-2908

MCDONALD, JOEL MATTHEWS, lawyer; b. Tylertown, Miss., Nov. 13, 1962; s. William Irvin and Emma Jean McD. BS in Acctg., U. Ala., 1984; JD, U. Va., 1987. Bar: D.C., Ga. Assoc,. King & Spalding, Washington, 1987-89, Gibson, Dunn & Crutcher, London N.Y.C. Washington, 1990-93; deputy dir. U.S. Treasury Tax Adv. Program, Moscow, 1994-95; resident dir. Harvard U., Russian Tax Reform Project, 1996-97; of counsel Salans, Herzfeld & Heilbronn, 1998, ptnr., 1999—. Contbr. articles to profl. jours., chpts. to books. Methodist. Office: Salans Hertzfeld Heilbronn 14-18 Gresham St London EC2V 7NN England

MCDONALD, MICHAEL SCOTT, lawyer; b. Ft. Stockton, Tex., Feb. 6, 1962; s. Roland R. and Harriett L. McD.; m. Sara; children: Matthew, Michael. BA, U. Tex., El Paso, 1984; JD, U. Tex., Austin, 1987. Bar: Tex. 1987, U.S. Ct. Appeals (5th and 10th cirs.), U.S. Dist. Ct. (all dists.) Tex. With Littler Mendelson, Dallas; shareholder Littler, Mendelson. Co-author, editor: Chapter 9, The 1999 National Employer; The Texas Employer; contbg. editor Covenents Not to Compete-A State by State Survey, 1995—, Employee Duty of Loyalty, 1995—, Trade Secrets - A State by State Survey, 1998—; contbr. articles to profl. jours. Mem. ABA (litigation sect., labor and employment law sect.), Tex. Bar Assn. (labor and employment law sect.), Tex. Assn. Bus. (employee rels. chair Dallas chpt.), Dallas Bar Assn. (employment law sect., chmn. 2000, exec. com. 1994-2001). General civil litigation, Labor. Office: Littler Mendelson 2001 Ross Ave Ste 2600 Dallas TX 75201-2931

MCDONELL, NEIL EDWIN, lawyer; b. Johnson City, N.Y., May 30, 1952; s. Alexander Edwin McDonell and Loretta Arlene Terry; m. Margaret Lynn Moline, June 18, 1978; children: Adam, Aaron. AB in Philosophy and English Lit., U. Mich., 1974; PhD in Philosphy, Harvard U., 1979; JD, Columbia U., 1983. Bar: N.Y. 1984. Asst. prof. philosophy Middlebury (Vt.) Coll., 1979-80; assoc. Battle Fowler, N.Y.C., 1983-89, Marks & Murase, N.Y.C., 1989-92, ptnr., 1992-96, Dorsey & Whitney LLP, N.Y.C., 1996—. Editor-in-chief Columbia Jour. Tranational Law, 1982-83, bd. dirs., 1989—; contbr. articles to profl. jours. Mem. ABA (internat., sci., tech., and antitrust sects.), N.Y. State Bar Assn., Internat. Trade Commn. Trial Lawyers Assn., Harvard Club, Phi Beta Kappa. Avocations: literature, history, poetry. Alternative dispute resolution, General civil litigation, Private international. Office: Dorsey & Whitney LLP 250 Park Ave New York NY 10177-0001

MCDONNELL, MICHAEL R. N. lawyer; b. Paterson, N.J., Sept. 24, 1940; s. Thomas Edward and Margaret (Chapline) McD.; m. Nina Carlotta Gray, Jan. 5, 1980; children— Amy Kathleen, Andrew Gray; children by previous marriage— Michael R.N., James Egan. B.S., U.S. Mil. Acad., 1962; J.D., Stetson U., 1970. Bar: Fla. 1970, U.S. Dist. Ct. (so. and mid. dists.) Fla. 1972, U.S. Dist. Ct. (no. dist.) Fla. 1976, U.S. Supreme Ct. 1974, U.S. Ct. Appeals (5th cir.) 1975; cert. civil trial lawyer Fla. Bar. Hearing officer Div. Adminstrv. Hearings, State of Fla., Tallahassee, 1977-79; pres. McDonnell & Berry (name now McDonnell Trial Lawyers), Naples, Fla., 1981— ; pres., dir., lectr. Am. Trial Forum, Naples, 1983-84. Contbr. articles to legal jours. Pres., Voters League of Collier County, Naples, 1982. Served to capt. U.S. Army, 1962-66. Mem. Assn. Trial Lawyers Am., Acad. Fla. Trial Lawyers. Republican. Episcopalian. Club: Naples Athletic. State civil litigation, Criminal, Personal injury. Office: McDonnell Trial Lawyers 720 Goodlette Rd N Ste 304 Naples FL 34102-5656

MCDONNELL, WILLIAM JOHN, lawyer; b. South Amboy, N.J., June 9, 1950; s. William Thomas and Joan Alyce (Donnelly) McD.; m. Bridget Griggs, May 26, 1950 (div. July 1982); children: Neal G., Amy C.; m. Sharon Larkin, Oct. 1, 1952. BA in History, Fairfield U., 1972; JD, St. Mary's U., 1976. Bar: N.J. 1976. Ptnr. Tabman, Downs, McDonnell, 1976-78, Alan J. Karcher, PA (name changed to Karcher, McDonnell), 1978-90, Karcher, McDonnell merger Donington, Karcher, 1990-91; pvt. practice Sayreville, N.J., 1991-95, South Amboy, 1996—. Legis. aide N.J. State Assemlby, Trenton, 1980-86. Mem. ATLA, ATLA of N.J., Elks (sec. # 2555 1994), S.A. Irish Am. Assn. (grand marshall). Democrat. Roman Catholic. Avocation: boating. State civil litigation, Criminal, General practice. Home: 22 Whittney Ct East Brunswick NJ 08816-3688 Office: 110 N Broadway South Amboy NJ 08879-1706

MCDONOUGH, LAWRENCE, lawyer; b. Wichita, Kans., Jan. 11, 1942; s. Ross F. and Mary Virginia (Cleary) M.; m. Katharine Angley, Jan. 16, 1965; children: Mary Anne, Mark. BA, Wichita U., 1964; JD, Washburn U., 1968. Bar: Kans. 1968, U.S. Dist. Ct. Kans. 1968, U.S. Ct. Appeals (10th cir.) 1971, Ariz. 1979, U.S. Dist. Ct. Ariz. 1979, U.S. Ct. Appeals (9th cir.) 1989. Ptnr. Jochems, Sargent & Blaes, 1968-77; gen. counsel Gates Learjet Corp., Wichita, 1977-87, gen. counsel, sec., 1987. Mem. bd. dirs. So. Ariz. div. Am. Heart Assn., Tucson Symphony Soc.; sect. chmn. campaign drive United Way, Tucson, 1979; chmn. adv. bd. Salpointe Cath. High Sch., Tucson, 1988—. Mem. ABA, Kans. State Bar Assn., Ariz. State Bar Assn., Pima County Bar Assn. Roman Catholic. Avocation: automobiles. Contracts commercial, General practice, Real property. Office: Kimble Gothreau & Nelson 5285 E Williams Cir Tucson AZ 85711-4426

MCDONOUGH, PATRICK JOSEPH, lawyer; b. Los Angeles, Oct. 11, 1943; s. Thomas John and Cecilia Veronica (Roach) McD.; m. Susan Ann Singletary, Dec. 30, 1967; 1 child, Colleen Marie. BA, Calif. State U., Northridge, 1967; JD, Loyola U., Los Angeles, 1971. Bar: Calif. 1971, U.S. Dist. Ct. (cen. dist.) Calif. 1971. Assoc. counsel. Auto Club So. Calif., Los Angeles, 1971-77, sec., assoc. counsel, 1977-86; sr. v.p., gen. counsel, prin. Johnson & Higgens Calif., 1986-96; sr. v.p., Pacific region legal dept. mgr. J & H Marsh & McLennan, 1996-99; dir. Stirling Cook Brown Holdings, Ltd., Encino, Calif., 1999—; ptnr. Troop Steuber Pasich Reddick & Tobey, L.A., 2000—. Active United Way Koko Challenge, 1993-99; bd. visitors Loyola Law Sch., 1994—; mem. adv. bd. Georgetown U. Law Ctr. Corp. Counsel Inst., 1999—. Mem. ABA, Calif. State Bar Assn. (ins. law com. 1993-95, 97), L.A. Bar Assn. (chmn. corp. law sect. 1987-88, Outstanding Corp. Coun. 1992), Univ. of Calif. Law Ctr., Inst. of Corp Counsel (chmn. 1986-87, bd. govs. 1982—), Am. Corp. Counsel Assn. So. Calif. (bd. dirs. 1985-87), Assn. Calif. Tort Reform (bd. dirs. 1986—), L.A. Bar Found. (bd. dirs. 1993-94), Town Hall Calif. Roman Catholic. Avocations: boating, sailing, fishing. General corporate, Insurance, Legislative. Office: 2029 Century Park East Los Angeles CA 90067 Fax: (818) 342-9438. E-mail: pjmcdonough@trooplaw.com

MCDONOUGH, RUSSELL CHARLES, retired state supreme court justice; b. Glendive, Mont., Dec. 7, 1924; s. Roy James and Elsie Marie (Johnson) McD.; m. Dora Jean Bidwell, Mar. 17, 1946; children: Ann Remmich, Michael, Kay Jensen, Kevin, Daniel, Mary Garfield. JD, George Washington U., 1949. Bar: Mont. 1950. Pvt. practice, Glendive, Mont., 1950-83; judge Gen. Jurisdiction State of Montana, 1983-87; justice Mont. Supreme Ct., Helena, 1987-93, ret., 1993. City atty. City of Glendive, 1953-57; county atty. Dawson County, Mon., 1957-63; del. Mont. Constl. Conv., Helena, 1972. 1st lt. AC, U.S. Army, 1943-45, ETO. Decorated DFC. Mem. Mont. Bar Assn. Roman Catholic. Home: PO Box 60 Circle MT 59215-0060

MCDONOUGH, SANDRA MARTIN, lawyer, administrator; b. Albany, N.Y., Feb. 5, 1939; d. Stevens John and Louise Jane (Minshall) Martin; 1 child, Lora Elizabeth Couture. BA, Regents Coll., Albany, 1979; JD, U. Bridgeport, 1982. Bar: Conn. 1982, U.S. Dist. Ct. 1983; lic. airline transport pilot, flight instr. Rsch. assoc. Yale U., New Haven, 1958-61; svc. rep. Conn. Blue Cross, 1962-67; project dir. Bridgeport Hosp. (Conn.), 1967-68; dir. patient accounts Park City Hosp., Bridgeport, 1968-74; adminstr., pres. Med. Personnel Pool, Fairfield, Conn., 1975-90; sole practice Fairfield and Stratford, 1982—. Adult advisor Safe Rides of Fairfield, 1984-86; N.E. region legal officer Civil Air Patrol, 1988-98. Mem. NTSB Bar Assn. (founding mem., v.p. 1990—), Lawyer-Pilots Bar Assn., Conn. Bar Assn. (exec. com. family law sect.), Regents Coll. Alumni Assn. (trustee Regents Coll. 1983-87), Mensa. Republican. Episcopalian. Aviation, Family and matrimonial, Real property. Office: 3333 Main St Stratford CT 06614-4820

MCDOUGALL, GERALD DUANE, lawyer; b. Hammond, Ind., Sept. 18, 1931; s. John and Carol Maxine (Lind) McD.; m. Ingrid Rosina Kempf, Jan. 26, 1960 (dec. 2000); children: Manfred, James. JD, Mercer U., 1971. Bar: U.S.V.I. 1972, Colo. 1973, Germany 1973, Tex. 1985. Atty. US V.I. Dept. Labor, St. Thomas, 1971-72; pvt. practice, Denver, 1972-74, 76-84, Heilbronn, Neckar, Germany, 1974-76, Amarillo, Tex., 1985—. Precinct committeeman Rep. Ctrl. Com., Denver, 1978-84. Sgt. U.S. Army, 1951-54, ETO, 61-67, Vietnam. Mem. Nat. Assn. Criminal Defense Lawyers, Tex. Bar Assn., Tex. Criminal Defense Lawyers Assn., Amarillo Bar Assn., State Bar Coll. State civil litigation, Criminal, Government contracts and claims. Home: 7910 Merchant Dr Amarillo TX 79121-1028 Office: PO Box 50898 Amarillo TX 79159-0898 E-mail: gmcdougal@tcac.net

MCDOWELL, KAREN ANN, lawyer; b. Ruston, La., Oct. 4, 1945; d. Paul and Opal Elizabeth (Davis) Bauer; m. Gary Lee McDowell, Dec. 22, 1979. BA, U. La., Monroe, 1967; JD, U. Mich., 1971; diploma, John Robert Powers Sch., Chgo., 1976, Nat. Inst. Trial Advocacy, 1990. Bar: Ill. 1973, Colo. 1977, U.S. Dist. Ct. (so. dist.) Ill. 1973, U.S. Dist. Ct. Colo. 1977. Reference libr. assoc. Ill. State Library, Springfield, 1972-73; asst. atty. gen. State of Ill., 1973-75; pvt. practice Boulder, Colo., 1978-79, Denver, 1979—. Mem. So. Poverty Law Ctr.; mem. hate violence task force Colo. Lawyers Com. Mem.: ABA, DAR, Am. Assn. Retired Persons, Colo. Bar Assn. (legal fee arbitration com.), Denver Bar Assn., Colo. Women's Bar Assn. (editor newsletter 1982—84), Am Inns of Ct., Survivors United Network Profls. (exec. com. 1992), Sovereign Colonial Soc., Survivors United Network (legal coord. 1992—93), Alpha Lambda Delta, Sigma Tau Delta, Mensa (local sect. Ann Arbor, Mich. 1968), Toastmasters Internat. (Able Toastmaster Bronze 1992), Colonial Order of Crown, Ams. of Royal Descent, Colonial Dames, Nat. Soc. Magna Carta Dames, Phi Alpha Theta. Avocations: philately, chess, needlework, dinosaurs, Horatio Alger stories. Family and matrimonial. Office: 1525 Josephine St Denver CO 80206-1406

MCDOWELL, MICHAEL DAVID, lawyer, utility executive; b. Lewisburg, Pa., May 10, 1948; s. David Leonard and Mary Ellen (Scallan) McD.; m. Martha LaMantia, Aug. 4, 1973; 1 child, Daniel Joseph. BS in Bus. Mgmt., U. Dayton, 1970; JD, U. Pitts., 1973. Bar: Pa. 1973, U.S. Ct. Appeals (3d cir.) 1974, U.S. Dist. Ct. (we. dist.) Pa. 1975, U.S. Supreme Ct. 1977. Asst. U.S. atty. Dept. Justice, Lewisburg, Pa., 1973-75; assoc. Hirsch, Weise & Tillman, Pitts., 1975-76, Plowman & Spiegel, Pitts., 1976-80; counsel Dravo Corp., 1980-86, sr. counsel, 1987; sr. atty. Allegheny Energy Svc. Corp. (formerly West Penn Power Co.), Greensburg, Pa., 1987-2000; dir. human resources Allegheny Energy Supply Co., Monroeville, 2001—. Mem. panel of arbitrators Am. Arbitration Assn., 1978-94, Pa. Bur. Mediation, 1983—, Pa. Labor Rels. Bd., 1985—. Contbr. articles to profl. jours. Mem. nat. panel consumer arbitrators Better Bus. Bur., 1986—, sr. arbitrator, 1989—. Recipient Dravo Corp. Editl. Achievement awards, 1982, 83, 85, 86; nominated as one of Outstanding Young Men Am., 1983, 84. Mem. ABA (ho. of dels. 1985-91, exec. coun. sect. labor and employment law 1983-85, exec. coun. young lawyers divsn. 1982-84, chmn. YLD labor law com. 1981-83, fellow 1985—), Pa. Bar Assn. (ho. of dels. 1980-94, chmn. spl. rules subcom. disciplinary bd. study com. 1983-93, com. on legal ethics and profl. responsibility 1983—, arbitrator lawyer dispute resolution program 1987—, house com. on rules and calender 1991-94, Outstanding Young Lawyer award 1984, Spl. Achievement award 1986), Allegheny County Bar Assn. (profl. ethics com. 1980-94, bd. govs. 1979, 85-91, asst. sec.-treas. 1979, chmn. young lawyers sect. 1978, coun. professionalism 1988-90, by-laws com. 1990—, award for outstanding leadership and valuable contbns. to bar 1979), Am. Corp. Counsel Assn., Phi Alpha Delta (justice 1972-73, cert. Outstanding Svc. 1973). Republican. Roman Catholic. General civil litigation, Labor, Public utilities. Office: Allegheny Energy Supply Co LLC 4350 Northern Pike Monroeville PA 15146-2841

MCELDOWNEY, TODD RICHARD, lawyer; b. Rhinelander, Wis., Apr. 7, 1955; s. Russell James and Donna Jo (Stoll) McE. BS with highest honors, U. Wis., Stevens Point, 1977; JD, Marquette U., 1980. Bar: Wis. 1980, U.S. Dist. Ct. (ea. dist.) Wis. 1980, U.S. Dist. Ct. (we. dist.) Wis. 1980. With O'Melia, Eckert, McEldowney & Mangerson, Rhinelander, 1981-85; ptnr. O'Melia & McEldowney, S.C., 1985-89, O'Melia, Schiek & McEldowney, S.C., Rhinelander, 1989—. Commr., Rhinelander Basketball League, 1976—; mem., sec., Rhinelander Police and Fire Commn., 1982—; mem. Oneida County Hwy. Safety Commn., Rhinelander, 1983—. Mem. Def. Rsch. Inst., Wis. Acad. Trial Lawyers, Am. Jud. Soc., Oneida-Vilas-Forest County Bar Assn., Optimists Club (pres. local club 1981—), Lions Club, Rhinelander Basketball Assn. (pres. 1991-). State civil litigation, Family and matrimonial, Personal injury. Home: 705 Lake Shore Dr Rhinelander WI 54501-2310 Office: O'Melia Schiek & McEldowney PO Box 797 Rhinelander WI 54501-0797 E-mail: Todd@Schieklaw.com

MC ELHANEY, JOHN HESS, lawyer; b. Milw., Apr. 16, 1934; s. Lewis Keck and Sara Jane (Hess) McE.; m. Jacquelyn Masur, Aug. 4, 1962; children— Scott, Victoria. B.B.A., So. Meth. U., 1956, J.D., 1958. Bar: Tex. bar 1958. Pvt. practice law, Dallas, 1958—; pntr. Locke, Liddell & Sapp, L.L.C., 1976—. Lectr. law So. Meth. U., 1967-76 Contbr. articles to legal jours. Trustee St. Mark's Sch. Tex., 1980-86. Fellow Am. Coll. Trial Lawyers; mem. Am. Bd. Trial Advs., ABA, Tex. Bar Assn., So. Meth. U. Law Alumni Assn. (pres. 1972-73, dir. 1970-73), Town and Gown Club (pres. 1981-82). Presbyterian. Federal civil litigation, General civil litigation, Libel. Home: 5340 Tanbark Dr Dallas TX 75229-5555 Office: Locke Liddell & Sapp 2200 Ross Ave Ste 2200 Dallas TX 75201-6776

MCELHINNY, HAROLD JOHN, lawyer; b. San Francisco, Jan. 5, 1947; s. Harold James and Margaret I. (Mahoney) McE.; m. Mary Ellen McElhinny, June 22, 1968; children: Hannah, Jennifer, William. BA in Polit. Sci., U. Santa Clara, 1970; JD, U. Calif., Berkeley, 1975. Bar: Calif. 1976, U.S. Supreme Ct. 1983. Vol. Peace Corps., Tripoli, Libya, 1968-69; juvenile counselor Santa Clara County (Calif.) Juvenile Hall, 1969-72; law clk. U.S. Dist. Ct., Hartford, Conn., 1975-76; ptnr. Morrison & Foerster, San Francisco, 1976—. Mem. ABA, Calif. Bar Assn., State Bar Calif. (rev. dept. 1986-89, chmn. 1988), San Francisco Bar Assn., Am. Intellectual Property Law Assn., Assn. Bus. Trial Lawyers (bd. govs. 1992-97, pres. 1997). Democrat. Roman Catholic. Office: Morrison & Foerster 425 Market St Fl 30 San Francisco CA 94105-2482 E-mail: hmcelhinny@mofo.com

MCELLIGOTT, JAMES PATRICK, JR. lawyer; b. Chgo., Jan. 11, 1948; s. James Patrick and Helen Cecelia (Hogan) McE.; children: Michael Sean, Andrew David; m. Trina Reff, Aug. 25, 1985. BA, U. Ill., Urbana, 1970; JD, Harvard U., 1973. Bar: Va. 1974, U.S. Dist. Ct. (ea. and we. dists.) Va. 1974, U.S. Ct. Appeals (4th cir.) 1974, U.S. Supreme Ct. 1979. Research asst. U. Ill., 1970; assoc. McGuire, Woods & Battle, Richmond, 1973-79; ptnr. McGuire Woods, 1979—. Mem. exec. com. Va. Home for Boys, Richmond, 1976-92, pres. bd. govs., 1981-83; mem. Leadership Metro Richmond-Met. C. of C., 1984-85; bd. dirs. ARC Greater Richmond Chpt., 1990-96, chmn., 1994-95. Recipient Clara Barton award ARC Richmond Chpt., 1997. Mem. ABA, Va. Bar Assn. (exec. com., chmn. pub. rels. com. 1978-82, producer pub. svc. message 1973, Hot Spot award 1973), Coll. of Labor and Employment Lawyers, Richmond Bar Assn., Fed. Bar Assn. (pres. Richmond chpt. 1986), Nat. Sch. Bds. Assn., Coun. of Sch. Attys., Coll. Labor and Employment Lawyers, Phi Beta Kappa, Phi Kappa Phi, Omicron Delta Epsilon. Federal civil litigation, Labor, Pension, profit-sharing, and employee benefits. Home: 203 Cyril Ln Richmond VA 23229-7740 Office: McGuire Woods LLP One James Ctr Richmond VA 23219-3229 E-mail: jmcelligott@mcguirewoods.com

MCELVEEN, JUNIUS CARLISLE, JR. lawyer; b. Rogersville, Tenn., Feb. 17, 1947; s. Junius Carlisle and Martha Kathleen (Harrison) McE.; m. Mary Wallace Pyles, Sept. 22, 1973; children: Kathryn Carlisle, Sarah Elizabeth. BA cum laude, U. Va., 1969, JD, 1972. Bar: Va. 1972, Calif. 1975, U.S. Dist. Ct. (ea. dist.) Va. 1976, D.C. 1978, U.S. Ct. Appeals (4th cir.) 1978, U.S. Ct. Appeals (Fed. cir.) 1986, U.S. Ct. Appeals (11th cir.) 1990. Rsch. assoc. Atlantic Richfield, Washington, 1972; assoc. Pender & Coward, Norfolk, Va., 1976-77, Seyfarth, Shaw, Washington, 1977-80, ptnr., 1981-83, Jones, Day, Reavis & Pogue, Washington, 1983—. Mem. adv. com., reproductive hazards in the workplace Office of Tech. Assessment, Washington, 1984-86; mem. adv. council Ctr. Environ. Health, U. Conn., 1986-95; mem. editorial bd. The Occupational and Environ. Medicine Report, 1986—, Human and Ecol. Risk Assessment, 1998—. Contbr. articles to legal jours. Elder Kirkwood Presbyn. Ch., Springfield, Va., 1984-86. Served as lt. USN, 1972-75. Mem. ABA, Va. State Bar, State Bar Calif., Phi Beta Kappa, Phi Delta Phi (sec. local chpt. 1971-72, Outstanding Grad. award 1972). E-mial. Federal civil litigation, Environmental, Labor. Home: 318 S Pitt St Alexandria VA 22314-3712 Office: Jones Day Reavis & Pogue 51 Louisana Ave NW Washington DC 20001 E-mail: jcmcelveen@jonesday.com

MCELVEIN, THOMAS IRVING, JR. lawyer; b. Buffalo, Apr. 19, 1936; s. Thomas I. and Edith Marian (Bowen) McE.; m. Ernesta F. McElvein, June 26, 1965; children: Christopher, Andrew, Kathryn. BA, Antioch Coll., 1959; JD, Yale U., 1962. Bar: N.Y. 1962, U.S. Dist. Ct. (we. dist.) N.Y. 1969. Atty. Village Akron, N.Y., 1963-99, spl. project atty., 2000—. Mem. N.Y. State Bar Assn., Erie County Bar Assn. General corporate, Estate planning, Municipal (including bonds). Home: 295 Nottingham Ter Buffalo NY 14216-3125 Office: 1500 Liberty Bldg Buffalo NY 14202-3612

MCENROE, MICHAEL LOUIS, lawyer; b. July 31, 1951; s. C. Louis and Mary C. (Cain) McE. BA magna cum laude, Loras Coll., 1973; JD, Creighton U., 1976. Bar: Ill. 1976, Iowa 1977, U.S. Dist. Ct. (no. dist.) Iowa 1977, U.S. Dist. Ct. (so. dist.) Iowa 1988, U.S. Supreme Ct. 1992. Assoc. McMahon & Cassel, Algona, Iowa, 1977-78; ptnr. McMahon, Cassel, Algona, McEnroe, McCarthy & Gotsdiner PC, 1998—; judicial magistrate 3rd Judicial Dist. State of Iowa, Algona, 1981-89. Mem. Ill. State Bar Assn., Iowa State Bar Assn. (agrl. law com. 1986-90, exec. coun. young lawyers sect. 1986-88, gen. practice com. 2000—), Iowa Assn. Trial Lawyers, Blackstone Inn of Ct., Polk County Bar Assn., Delta Epsilon Sigma. Democrat. Roman Catholic. Consumer commercial, General practice, Agriculture. Home: 700 S 32nd Ct West Des Moines IA 50265-5701 Office: McEnroe McCarthy & Gotsdiner PC 1701 48th St Ste 100 West Des Moines IA 50266-6723 E-mail: mmencoe@dwx.com

MCERLEAN, CHARLES FLAVIAN, JR. lawyer; b. Detroit, Nov. 23, 1938; s. Charles F. and Theodora L. McErlean; children: James, Laura, Kelly. BS, Georgetown U., 1960; JD, U. Notre Dame, 1963. Bar: Ill. 1963, Ind. 1963, D.C. 1964, U.S. Supreme Ct. 1966. Assoc. Mayer, Brown & Platt, Chgo., 1963; asst. gen. counsel United Airlines, 1967—. Bd. dirs. Sacred Heart of Mary High Sch., Rolling Meadows, Ill. 1978-81, The Need Found., La Grange, Ill., 1991-98. Served to lt. USNR, 1963-67. Mem ABA, D.C. Bar Assn., Georgetown Club. Republican. Avocations: woodworking, golf, computers. General corporate, Finance, Pension, profit-sharing, and employee benefits. Office: United Air Lines Inc PO Box 66100 Chicago IL 60666-0100

MCEVILLY, JAMES PATRICK, JR. lawyer; b. Phila., July 30, 1943; s. James P. and Virginia Frances (Madden) McE.; m. Joan Elizabeth O'Connor; children: James III, Christopher (dec.), Sara, Michael. BS, St. Joseph's U., 1965; JD, Temple U., 1971. Bar: Pa. 1971, U.S. Dist. Ct. (ea. dist.) Pa. 1972, U.S. Ct. Appeals (3d cir.) 1975, U.S. Supreme Ct. 1982. Law clk to president judge Phila. Mcpl. Ct., 1971-73; assoc. Galfand, Berger, Lurie & March, Phila., 1973-76; asst. dist. atty. Phila. Dist. Atty., 1976-79; prin. McEvilly & Assocs., Feasterville, Pa., 1979—. Editor Temple U. Law Rev., 1971. Mem. Pa. Trial Lawyers Assn., Phila. Bar Assn., Trial Lawyers Am. Criminal, General practice, Personal injury. Home: 1401 Silo Rd Yardley PA 19067-4240 Office: 1200 Bustleton Pike Ste 1B Trevose PA 19053-4108

MCEVOY, SHARLENE ANN, law educator; b. Derby, Conn., July 6, 1950; d. Peter Henry Jr. and Madaline Elizabeth (McCabe) McE. BA magna cum laude, Albertus Magnus Coll., 1972; JD, U. Conn., West Hartford, 1975; MA, Trinity Coll., Hartford, 1980, UCLA, 1982, PhD, 1985. Bar: Conn., 1975. Pvt. practice, Derby, 1984—; asst. prof. bus. law Fairfield (Conn.) U. Sch. Bus., 1986—; adj. prof. bus. law, polit. sci. Albertus Magnus Coll., New Haven, 1978-80, U. Conn., Stamford, 1984-86; acting chmn. polit. sci. dept. Albertus Magnus Coll., 1980; assoc. prof. law Fairfield U., 1992-98, prof. bus. law, 1998—. Chmn. Women's Resource Ctr., Fairfield U., 1989-91. Staff editor Jour. Legal Studies Edn., 1989-94; reviewer Am. Bus. Law Assn. jour., 1988—, staff editor, 1995—; sr. articles editor N.E. Jour. of Legal Studies in Bus., 1995-96. Mem. Derby Tercentennial Commn., 1973-74; bd. dirs. Valley Transit Dist., Derby, 1975-77, Justice of Peace, City of Derby, 1975-83; alt. mem. Parks and Recreation Commn., Woodbury, 1995-99; mem., treas. Woodbury Dem. Town Com., 1995-96, corr. sec. 1996-98; v.p. N.E. Acad. Legal Studies in Bus., 2001—. Recipient Best Paper award N.E. Regional Bus. Law Assn., 1990, Best Paper award Tri-State Regional Bus. Law Assn., 1991; Fairfield U. Sch. Bus. rsch. grantee 1989, 91, 92, Fairfield U. rsch. grantee, 1994. Mem. ABA, Conn. Bar Assn., Acad. Legal Studies in Bus., Mensa (coord. SINISTRAL spl. interest group 1977—). Democrat. Roman Catholic. Avocations: running, chess, tennis, swimming. Office: 198 Emmett Ave Derby CT 06418-1258 E-mail: samcevoy@mail.fairfield.edu

MCFADDEN, FRANK HAMPTON, lawyer, business executive, former judge; b. Oxford, Miss., Nov. 20, 1925; s. John Angus and Ruby (Roy) McF.; m. Jane Porter Nabers, Sept. 30, 1960; children— Frank Hampton, Angus Nabers, Jane Porter. B.A., U. Miss., 1950; LL.B., Yale U., 1955. Bar: N.Y. 1956, Ala. 1959. Assoc. firm Lord, Day & Lord, N.Y.C., 1955-58, Bradley, Arant, Rose & White, Birmingham, Ala., 1958-63, partner, 1963-69; judge U.S. Dist. Ct. No. Dist. Ala., 1969-73, chief judge, 1973-81; sr. v.p., gen. counsel Blount, Inc., Montgomery, Ala., 1982-91, exec. v.p. adminstrn. and govt. affairs, 1991, exec. v.p. legal affairs, 1991-93, exec. v.p., gen. counsel, 1993-95; mem. Capell & Howard, P.C., 1995—. Chmn. Blount Energy Resource Corp., Montgomery, 1983-88. Mem. jud. panel CPR Inst. for Dispute Resolution, 1985—. Served from ensign to lt. USNR, 1944-49, 51-53. Fellow Am. Coll. Constrn. Lawyers; mem. Am. Corp. Counsel Assn. (bd. dirs. 1984-93, chmn. 1989). Alternative dispute resolution, General civil litigation, Construction. Office: Capell & Howard PC 150 S Perry St Montgomery AL 36104-4227

MCFALL, DONALD BEURY, lawyer; b. Charleston, W.Va., Aug. 2, 1941; s. Henry Tucker and Elizabeth Katharine (Beury) McF.; m. Donna Glenn Binion, May 27, 1972; children: Katharine Atkinson, Mary Crawford. BA, Washington and Lee U., 1964, JD, 1969. Bar: Va. 1969, Tex. 1969, U.S. Supreme Ct. 1979, U.S. Dist. Ct. (we., so. and ea. dists.) Tex. 1969. Asst. U.S. atty. U.S. Dept. justice, Houston, 1970-71; assoc. Butler & Binion, 1971-77, ptnr., 1977-85, McFall, Sherwood & Sheeny, Houston, 1985-2000. Trustee Humana Hosp., Shaprstown, Houston, 1984-85; bd. dirs. Planned Parenthood of Houston and S.E. Tex., 1978-88; trustee Woodberry Forest Sch., Orange, Va., 1984-90, Washington and Lee U., 1997—. Capt. U.S. Army, 1964-66. Fellow Tax Bar Found., Am. Coll. Trial Lawyers, Internat. Soc. Barristers; mem. Intenrat. Assn. Def. Counsel, Va. State Bar Assn., Tex. State Bar Assn., Fedn. Ins. and Corp. Counsel, Am. Bd. Trial Advocates (advocate). Federal civil litigation, State civil litigation, Personal injury. Office: McFall Glidden Sherwood & Breitbell 4800 Texaco Heritage Plz 1111 Bagby St Houston TX 77002 Fax: 713-655-8889. E-mail: dmcfall@mcfallglidden.com

MCFARLAND, KAY ELEANOR, state supreme court chief justice; b. Coffeyville, Kans., July 20, 1935; d. Kenneth W. and Margaret E. (Thrall) McF. BA magna cum laude, Washburn U., Topeka, 1957, JD, 1964. Bar: Kans. 1964. Sole practice, Topeka, 1964-71; probate and juvenile judge Shawnee County, 1971-73; dist. judge, 1973-77; assoc. justice Kans. Supreme Ct., 1977-95, chief justice, 1995—. Mem. Kans. Bar Assn., Women Attys. Assn. Topeka. Office: Kans Supreme Ct Kans Jud Ctr 301 W 10th St Topeka KS 66612 Fax: (785) 291-3274

MCFARLAND, ROBERT EDWIN, lawyer; b. St. Louis, July 25, 1946; s. Francis Taylor and Kathryne (Stephens) McF.; m. Jeannine M. Ghekiere, Feb. 26, 1982. BA, U. Mich., 1968, JD, 1971. Bar: Mich. 1971, U.S. Dist. Ct. (ea. dist.) Mich. 1971, U.S. Ct. Appeals (6th cir.) 1974, U.S. Supreme Ct. 1975, U.S. Ct. Appeals (D.C. cir.) 1978, N.Mex. 2001. Law clk. to chief judge Mich. Ct. Appeals, 1971-72; assoc. William B. Elmer, St. Clair Shores, Mich., 1972-74, James Elsman, Birmingham, 1974-75; ptnr. McFarland, Schmier, Stoneman & Singer, Troy, 1975-77; sr. ptnr. McFarland & Bullard, Bloomfield Hills, 1977-90, McFarland & Niemer, Farmington Hills, 1990-91; shareholder Foster, Swift, Collins & Smith, P.C., 1992—, mem. exec. com., 1995—. Chmn. bd. govs. Transp. Law Jour., U. Denver Coll. Law, 1981-83. Mem. bd. control Intercollegiate Athletics, U. Mich., 1966-68; mem. rulemaking study com. Mich. Pub. Svc. Commn., 1983-84, Motor Carrier Adv. Bd., 1984-88. Capt. USAR, 1971-80. Mem. ABA, Transp. Lawyers Assn. (officer 1998—, Disting. Svc. awad 1997), Assn. Transp. Law, Logistics and Policy, State Bar Mich. (vice-chmn. transp. law com. adminstrv. law sect. 1990—, sect. coun. adminstrv. law sect. 1994, 99), Am. Judicature Soc. Administrative and regulatory, Labor, Transportation. Office: Foster Swift Collins & Smith PC 32300 Northwestern Hwy Ste 230 Farmington MI 48334-1571 E-mail: rmcfarland@fosterswift.com

MCFARLANE, WALTER ALEXANDER, lawyer, educator; b. Richlands, Va., May 4, 1940; s. James Albert and Frances Mae (Padbury) McF.; m. Judith Louise Copenhaver, Aug. 31, 1962. BA, Emory and Henry Coll., 1962; JD, U. Richmond, 1966. Bar: Ba. 1966, U.S. Supreme Ct. 1970, U.S. Ct. Appeals (4th cir.) 1973, U.S. Ct. Appeals (D.C. cir.) 1977, U.S. Dist. ct. (ea. dist.) Va. 1973. Asst. atty. gen. Office Va. Atty. Gen., Richmond, 1969-73, dep. atty. gen., 1973-90; exec. asst., chief counsel, dir. policy Gov.'s Office Commonwealth of Va., 1990-94, supt. Dept. Correctional Edn., 1994—. Acting dir. Dept. Juvenile Justice, 1997; prof. adj. staff U. Richmond, 1978—; chmn. transp. law com. Transp. Rsch. Bd., Nat. Rsch. Bd. Nat. Acads. Sci. and Engring., Washington, 1977-85, 88-94, chmn. legal affairs com., 1978-85, chmn. environ., archeological and hist. com., 1985-90; mem. State Water Commn., 1994-96, mem., Coun. of State Govts. Henry Toll Fell., 1988; Legal Task Force, 1988—. Contbr. articles to profl. jours. Mem. exec. com., bd. govs. Emory and Henry Coll., 1985-98; pres. Windsor Forest Civic Assn., Midlothian, Va., 1975-76; bd. dirs. Greater Midlothian Civic League, 1980-86, v.p., 1980; instr. water safety ARC, 1962-87; chmn. bldg. com. Mt. Pisgah United Meth. Ch., 1980-85, pres. men's club, 1980-81; bd. dirs. cen. Va. chpt. Epilepsy Assn. Va., 1988-91, Woodland Pond Civic Assn., 1988-89; mem. State Criminal Justice Svcs. Bd., 1994—. Capt. JAGC, USAF, 1966-69. Recipient J.D. Buscher Disting. Atty. award Am. Assn. State Hwy. and Transp. Ofcls., 1983, John C. Vance legal writing award Nat. Acads. Sci. and Engring., 4th ann. outstanding evening lectr. award Student Body, U. Richmond, 1980. Mem. Chesterfield Bar Assn., Richmond Bar Assn. (bd. dirs. 1989-93), Richmond Scottish Soc. (bd. dirs. 1980-82), Emory and Henry Coll. Alumni Assn. (chpt. pres. 1971-73, regional v.p. 1974-77, pres. 1981-83), Meadowbrook Country Club (bd. dir. 2001-). Home: 9001 Widgeon Way Chesterfield VA 23838-5274 Office: 101 N 14th St Richmond VA 23219-3684

MCFERRIN, JAMES HAMIL, lawyer; b. Mobile, Ala., July 26, 1960; BS in Criminal Justice, U. Ala., 1982; JD, Cumberland Sch. of Law, 1987. Bar: Ala. 1987, U.S. Dist. Ct. (no. dist.) Ala. 1987. Pvt. practice, Birmingham, Ala., 1987—. Legal dir. Behavioral Health Systems, Birmingham, 1991—, Risk Reduction, Inc., Birmingham, 1991—; mem. task force Birmingham Area C. of C., 1992; mem. task force on utilization rev. State of Ala.; cons., com. chair Ala. Supreme Ct.; nat. bd. dirs. Workplace Injury Litigation Group. Author: Informed Consent: A New Standard For Proximate Cause, 1987; rsch. editor Cumberland Law Rev. Recipient Dean's scholarship Cumberland Law Sch., 1984-87, Book awards Am. Jurisprudence, 1984-87. Mem. Am. Trial Lawyers Assn. (state capt. worker's compensation), Nat. Employment Assn., Ala. Bar Assn., Ala. Trial Lawyers Assn., Birmingham C. of C. General civil litigation, Health, Workers' compensation.

MCGAFFEY, JERE D. lawyer; b. Lincoln, Nebr., Oct. 6, 1935; s. Don Larsen and Doris (Lanning) McG.; m. Ruth S. Michelsen, Aug. 19, 1956; children: Beth, Karen. BA, BSc with high distinction, U. Nebr., 1957; LLB magna cum laude, Harvard U., 1961. Bar: Wis. 1961. Mem. firm Foley & Lardner, Milw., 1961—, ptnr., 1968—. Dir. Smith Investment Co., Northwestern Mut. Trust Co., Lord Balt. Corp., Wis. Gas Co., 1978-2000. Author works in field. Chmn. bd. dirs. Helen Bader Found.; former chmn. bd. dirs. Aurora Health Care; vice chmn. legis. Milw. Met. Assn. Commerce; former chmn. Wis. Taxpayers Alliance, sec., treas., 1994—; chmn. bd. advisors U. Wis. Nursing Sch., Milw. Mem. ABA (chmn. tax sect. 1990-91, ho. dels. 1995-2000), AICPA, Wis. Bar Assn., Wis. Inst. CPAs, Am. Coll. Tax Counsel (chmn. 1996-98), Am. Coll. Trust and Estate Counsel (chmn. bus. planning com. 1994-97, regent 2000—), Am. Law Inst., Univ. Club (Milw.), Milw. Club, Milw. Country Club, Harvard Club N.Y.C., Univ. Club Washington, Phi Beta Kappa, Beta Gamma Sigma, Delta Sigma Rho. General corporate, Corporate taxation, Estate taxation. Home: 12852 NW Shoreland Dr Mequon WI 53097-2304 Office: Foley & Lardner 777 E Wisconsin Ave Ste 3600 Milwaukee WI 53202-5302 E-mail: jkmcgaffey@foleylaw.com

MCGAHEY, JOHN PATRICK, lawyer; b. Toledo, Mar. 29, 1941; s. Edwin Patrick and Ann Lillian (Liner) McG.; m. Kathleen C. Hanley, June 25, 1966; children— Mary K., John P. Jr., Kevin P. A.B., Marquette U., 1963; J.D., Northwestern U.-Ill., 1966. Bar: Ill. 1966, U.S. Dist. Ct. (no. dist.) Ill. 1967, U.S. Ct. Appeals (7th cir.) 1969. Ptnr. Wilson, Elser, Moskowitz, Edelman & Dicker. Mem. Chgo. Bar Assn., Ill. Bar Assn., Northwest Suburban Bar Assn. Chgo. Athletic Assn. Republican. Roman Catholic. Clubs: Oak Park, Plum Grove. Lodge: K.C. State civil litigation, Insurance, Personal injury. Home: 505 Balmoral Ln Palatine IL 60067-4629 Office: Wilson Elser Moskowitz Edelman & Dicker La Salle Bank Bldg 135 S La Salle St Chicago IL 60603-4159

MCGAHREN, EUGENE DEWEY, JR. lawyer; b. Oct. 4, 1926; s. Eugene D. and Cecelia (Paulson) McGahren; m. Elizabeth M. Connellan, Oct. 19, 1957; children: Eugene, Thomas, Kevin, Brian, Paul, Peter. AB, Columbia U., 1949; JD, Columbia U., 1952; LLM, NYU, 1960. Bar: N.Y. 1955. Assoc. Willkie Farr & Gallagher, N.Y.C., NY, 1954—56, McGovern, Vincent & Connelly, N.Y.C., 1956—60; asst. divsn. counsel Sperry Corp., 1960—69, divsn. counsel, 1969—72, asst. gen counsel, 1972—80, staff v.p., assoc. gen. counsel, 1980—87; pvt. practice, 1988—. Arbitrator Am. Arbitration Assn., 1988—, N.Y. Stock Exchange, 1988—, NASD, 1988—; adminstrv. law judge, N.Y.C., 1993—. V.p. Lincoln Park Taxpayers Assn., Yonkers, NY, 1974—78. Contracts commercial, General corporate, Government contracts and claims.

MCGANNEY, THOMAS, lawyer; b. San Mateo, Calif., Mar. 12, 1938; s. Daniel James and Mary Irene (West) McG.; m. Mildred Kalik; children— Jennifer, Abigail, Melanie, Juliana. B.A., Stanford U., 1959; LL.B., Harvard U., 1962. Bar: N.Y. 1963, U.S. Dist. Ct. (so. and ea. dists.) N.Y. 1965, U.S. Ct. Appeals (2d cir.) 1966, (3d cir.) 1969, (10th cir.) 1970, U.S. Supreme Ct. 1971, U.S. Ct. Appeals (9th cir.) 1990. Law clk. U.S. Dist. Ct., So. Dist. N.Y., 1962-64; assoc. White & Case, N.Y.C., 1964-72, ptnr., 1973— ; adj. prof. NYU Law Sch., 1984-86. Mem. Am. Coll. Trial Lawyers, N.Y. State Bar Assn., ABA, Fed. Bar Council, Assn. Bar City N.Y. Federal civil litigation, Securities. Office: White & Case Bldg Ll 1155 Avenue Of The Americas New York NY 10036-2787

MCGARRY, ALEXANDER BANTING, lawyer; b. Detroit, July 27, 1940; s. Patrick Joseph and Marne Elizabeth (Banting) McG.; m. Diane Lee Fisher, Feb. 10, 1940; children— Erin Kathleen, Molly Anne, Megan Catherine. B.S., Drake U., 1962; J.D., U. Minn., 1965. Bar: Minn. 1965, Mich. 1966, U.S. Supreme Ct. 1978. Asst. pros. atty. Oakland County (Mich.), 1967-69; assoc. Condit, Denison, Devine, Porter & Bartush, Bloomfield Hills, Mich., 1969-71; ptnr. Condit & McGarry, Birmingham, Mich. and sucessor Condit, McGarry & Schloff, P.C., 1971— . Chmn. City of Troy Irish Heritage Group and Bicentennial, 1976; mem. citizens adv. com. Troy Sch. Bd., 1978; chmn. Oakland County Health & Welfare, 1995—; mem. City of Rochester Hills Traffic Safety Adv. Bd., 1989-95. Recipient Disting. Service award Oakland County, 1970; named Master of the Bench, Oakland A.I.C. Mem. State Bar Mich., Oakland County Bar Assn. (dir., chair health and welfare com. 1993—, Disting. Svc. award 1994, Professionalism award 1998), Assn. Trial Lawyers Am., Inc. Soc. Irish Am. Lawyers (dir.), Cath. Lawyers Soc., Minn. Bar Assn. Lodges: Ancient Order Hibernians (state pres. 1972-76, nat. dir. 1976-78, nat. chmn. Notre Dame Fund 1978-82, Hibernian of Yr. 1980). General civil litigation, Criminal, Family and matrimonial. Office: 6905 Telegraph Rd Ste 215 Bloomfield Hills MI 48301-3159

MCGARRY, RICHARD LAWRENCE, lawyer; b. Flushing, N.Y., Jan. 12, 1960; s. Richard J. and Loretta (McCarthy) McG.; m. Lynda R. Jones, Dec. 21, 1987; children: Abraham A. Eichelberger, Chelsea Eichelberger St. Clair, David B. Eichelberger. BS, Hampden Sydney Coll., 1982; JD, Washington and Lee U., 1989. Bar: Va. 1989, U.S. Dist. Ct. (we. dist.) Va., U.S. Supreme Ct., 1993. Assoc. Jeffrey H. Krasnow and Assocs., Roanoke, Va., 1989-93; ptnr. Johnson & McGarry, P.C., Charlottesville, 1993-94; pvt. practice Roanoke, 1994—. Bd. dirs. Roanoke Valley SPCA. Mem. Va. Trial Lawyers Assn., Assn. Trial Lawyers Am., Roanoke Bar Assn., Va. Bar Assn. General civil litigation, Personal injury, Product liability. Office: PO Box 21565 2320 Electric Rd SW Roanoke VA 24018 E-mail: rick.mcgarry@att.net

MCGAUGHEY, JERRY JOSEPH, lawyer, educator; b. Vincennes, Ind., Dec. 8, 1937; s. Robert William and Vera Elizabeth (Leinbach) McG.; m. Barbara F. O'Neill, June 15, 1978; 1 child, L. Scott. AA, Vincennes U., 1957; BS in Bus., Ind. U., 1959, LLB, 1962. Bar: Ind. 1963, U.S. Dist. Ct. (so. dist.) Ind. 1963, U.S. Supreme Ct. 1973. Law clk. to presiding justice Ind. Supreme Ct., Indpls., 1963-64; ptnr. Hornbrook, Stratton & McGaughey, Petersburg, Ind., 1964-70; prosecuting atty. 83rd Jud. Ct., Petersburg, 1970-82; dept. head abstracting and bus. law Vincennes U., Ind., 1982-86; prosecuting atty. 12th Jud. Ct., Vincennes, 1987—; bd. dir. First Nat. Bank Spurgeon, Ind., 1965-72. Com. mem. Ind. Criminal Law Study Commn., Indpls., 1971-76; bd. dirs. Ind. Criminal Justice Planning Agy., Dist. 8, Evansville, 1972-80, Ind. Prosecuting Attys. Coun., Indpls., 1975-77, Rotary (pres. local chpt. 1970-71). Republican. Office: Knox County Courthouse Vincennes IN 47591

MCGAVIC, MITZIE W. court clerk; b. July 19, 1958; d. Harold E. and Margaret O. White; m. William E. McGavic, Jr., Apr. 30, 1983. Student, Charron-Williams Bus. Sch., Tampa, Fla., 1977. Sec., 1977-83; sec. to supr. DeSoto County Sch. Bd., Arcadia, Fla., 1983-85; jud. asst. State of Fla., 1985-97; clk. of ct., 1997—. Mem. adv. bd. DeSoto Domestic Violence Prevention Bd. Mem. Elks (sec. 1997—), Rotary Club (treas. 1999—). Office: Clk of Ct 115 E Oak St Arcadia FL 34266-2401

MCGEE, JAMES FRANCIS, lawyer; b. N.Y.C., Sept. 19, 1950; s. James F. and Elizabeth J. (Mooney) M.; m. Annamarie Saunders, Feb. 13, 1988; children: James, Brooke Nicole. BS, U. Penn., 1972; JD, Western State U., Fullerton, Calif., 1980. Bar: Calif. 1980. Founder McGee & Assocs., Newport Beach, Calif., 1980—. Chmn. Laguna Beach Bd. Adjustment, 1985-87, Laguna Beach Architecture Review Bd., 1985-87; pres. Junior All Am. Football, 1997—; pres. Pelican Hill Cmty. Assn., 1995—; pres. Newport Coast Cmty. Assn., 1997—, chmn. annexation com., 1998—; chief Indian Guides Chumash Tribe, 1996-99; chief Newport Beach-Costa Mesa YMCA Indian Guides Dolphin Nation, 1997-99. Recipient 20-30 Internat. So. Calif. Man of Yr., 1985. Mem. ABA, ATLA, Calif. Bar Assn., Orange County Bar Assn., Calif. Trial Lawyers Assn., Orange County Trial Lawyers Assn. Avocations: sports, flying, public speaking. Construction, Environmental, Real property. Office: 23 Corp Plaza Ste 230 Newport Beach CA 92660

MC GIFFERT, DAVID ELIOT, lawyer, former government official; b. Boston, June 27, 1926; s. Arthur Cushman and Elizabeth (Eliot) McG.; m. Enud De Kibedi-Varga, Jan. 21, 1966; children: Laura, Carola.; m. Nelse Greenway, Apr. 9, 1983. Student, U. Calif.-Berkeley, 1944; B.A., Harvard U., 1949, LL.B., 1953; postgrad., Cambridge (Eng.) U., 1950. Bar: D.C. 1954. With firm Covington & Burling, Washington, 1953-55, 57-61, ptnr., 1969-77, 81—. Lectr. law U. Wis., 1956; asst. to sec. def. for legis. affairs Dept. Def., 1962-65, undersec. army, 1965-69, asst. sec. for internat. security affairs, 1977-81 Served with USNR, 1944-46. Mem. Am. Bar Assn., Council Fgn. Relations, Alpha Delta Phi. Club: Metropolitan (Washington). Home: 3819 Veazey St NW Washington DC 20016-2230 Office: Covington & Burling PO Box 7566 1201 Pensylvania Ave NW Washington DC 20044-7566

MCGILL, GILBERT WILLIAM, lawyer; b. Glen Cove, N.Y., Mar. 28, 1947; BS, L.I. U., 1972; JD, Hofstra U., 1975. Bar: N.Y. 1975, U.S. Dist. Ct. 1976, U.S. Supreme Ct. 1979. Pvt. practice, Huntington, N.Y., 1975-76; ptnr. Dunne & McGill, Huntington and Sea Cliff, 1976-81; pvt. practice Sea Cliff, 1981—. Citizens adv. com. North Shore Schs., Glen Head, N.Y., 1977-79, mem. local waterfront revitalization com. Town of Oyster Bay, 1988—; chmn. legal adv. com. Sea Cliff Civic Assn., 1978-79; adv. com. North Shore Republican Club, Glen Head, 1979-81; trsutee Sea Cliff Village Libr., 1980-86; trustee Angelo J. Melillo Ctr. for Mental Health, 1986—, pres., 1986—. Mem. ABA, N.Y. State Bar Assn., Nassau County Bar Assn., Nassau County Lawyers Assn., North Shore Lawyers Assn. (chmn. 1977-78), Sea Cliff Bus. Assn. (pres. 1979-85), Rotary (pres. Glen Head 1983-84, 97-99). General practice. Office: 203 Glen Cove Ave Sea Cliff NY 11579-1437

MCGILL, JOHN GARDNER, lawyer; b. Columbus, Ohio, Mar. 2, 1949; s. James Dawn and Madolin Rose (Gardner) McG.; m. Jacqueline Frances Runfola, Oct. 10, 1970; children: Sean, Kevin, Brian, Brendan. BS in Fgn. Svc., Georgetown U., 1971; JD, U. Denver, 1976. Bar: Colo. 1976, Ohio 1977, Ga. 1988. Counsel United McGill Corp., Columbus 1977-81, v.p., sec., dir., Groveport, Ohio, 1981-86; sec., treas., dir. Groveport, Ohio, 1986-87; ptnr. Varner, Stephens, Wingfield, McIntyre & Humphries, Atlanta, 1987-89; pvt. practice law, Atlanta, 1989—. Contbr. articles to legal jours. Pres. Montessori Soc. Lancaster Ohio, 1978. Mem. ABA (banking and bus., internat. law and pub. contract sects.; forum com. on constrn. industry), Ohio Bar Assn., Am. Arbitration Assn. (arbitrator constrn. and internat. panels), Lawyer-Pilot Bar Assn., Lawyer's Club Atlanta. Democrat. Avocations: pilot, scuba diving. Aviation, General civil litigation, Construction. Office: 333 Rhodes-Haverty Bldg 134 Peachtree St NW Atlanta GA 30303-1802

MCGINLEY, JAMES DUFF, lawyer; b. Pasadena, Calif., Apr. 8, 1959; m. Maribeth Walton McGinley, Apr. 28, 1984. BA, Calif. State U., Long Beach, 1981; JD, Pepperdine U., 1991. Bar: Calif. 1992, U.S. Dist. Ct. (ctrl. and ea. dists.) Calif. 1992. Assoc. Sedgwick, Detert, Moran & Arnold, L.A., 1990-94; ptnr. Hiepler & Hiepler, Oxnard, Calif., 1994—. Chmn. Mealey's Publ. HMO Liability Conf. Contbr. articles to Pepperdine Law Rev. Civil Justice Program leader Leadership Glendale, Calif., 1997. Lt. col. USMCR, 1981—. Decorated USN and USMC Commendation medal, 1998. Mem. Ventura County Bar Assn., Pepperdine U. Alumni Assn. (pres. 1997-99), Million Dollar Advocates Forum (Achievements award). General civil litigation, Health, Product liability. Office: Hiepler & Hiepler 500 Esplanade Dr Ste 1550 Oxnard CA 93030-0576

MCGINTY, BRIAN DONALD, lawyer, author; b. June 22, 1937; s. Donald Bruce and Natalia Vallejo (Haraszthy) M. AB, U. Calif., Berkeley, 1959, JD, 1962. Bar: Calif. 1963. Assoc. Twohig, Weingarten & Haas, Seaside, Calif., 1962-63; ptnr. Weingarten & McGinty, 1963-70; sole practice Monterey, 1970-73, San Francisco, 1973-83; writer, editor Mathew Bender & Co., San Francisco, Oakland, Calif., 1984-93. Author: Haraszthy at the Mint (Famous Calif. Trials Series), 1975, The Palace Inns, 1978, We the People, 1987, Strong Wine: The Life and Legend of Agoston Haraszthy, 1998; contbg. author: The Craft of the Essay, Historical Times Illustrated Encyclopedia of the Civil War, Portrait of America, 5th edit., 1990, California Real Estate Law and Practice, California Forms of Pleading and Practice, California Legal Forms, California Insurance Law, California Probate Law and Practice, California Public Agency Law and Practice, California Wills and Trusts; editor: Napa Wine (Rounce and Coffin Club award 1975), 1974; contbr. numerous articles to profl. jours. Recipient Excellence in Writing award Nat. Hist. Soc., 1976, Editor's award for Hist. Scholarship, Sonoma County Hist. Soc., 1999. Mem. Calif. Hist. Soc. Estate planning, Real property.

MCGIVERIN, ARTHUR A. former state supreme court chief justice; b. Iowa City, Nov. 10, 1928; s. Joseph J. and Mary B. McG.; m. Mary Joan McGiverin, Apr. 20, 1951; children: Teresa, Thomas, Bruce, Nancy. BSC with high honors, U. Iowa, 1951, JD, 1956. Bar: Iowa 1956. Pvt. practice law, Ottumwa, Iowa, 1956; alt. mcpl. judge, 1960-65; judge Iowa Dist. Ct.

8th Jud. Dist., 1965-78; assoc. justice Iowa Supreme Ct., Des Moines, 1978-87, chief justice, 1987-2000, sr. judge, 2000—. Mem. Iowa Supreme Ct. Commn. on Continuing Legal Edn., 1975. Served to 1st lt. U.S. Army, 1946-48, 51-53. Mem. Iowa State Bar Assn., Am. Law Inst. Roman Catholic. Avocation: golf. Office: Wapello County Courthouse Ottumwa IA 52501

MCGIVNEY, JOHN JOSEPH, lawyer; b. Boston, Oct. 31, 1956; s. William A. and Mary Angela (Wall) McG. AB magna cum laude, Boston Coll., 1978, JD cum laude, 1981. Bar: Mass. 1981, U.S. Dist. Ct. Mass. 1982, U.S. Ct. Appeals (1st cir.) 1983, U.S. Supreme Ct. 1990. Assoc. Burns & Levinson, Boston, 1981-87, ptnr., chief appellate sect., 1988-96; ptnr. Rubin and Rudman, 1997—. Sec. Lynnfield (Mass.) Dem. Town Com., 1974-75, chmn., 1976-77. Mem. Mass. Acad. Trial Attys., Mass. Def. Lawyers Assn. (bd. dirs.), Algonquin Club of Boston. General civil litigation, Private international, Product liability. Home: 47 Doncaster Cir Lynnfield MA 01940-2255

MCGLAMRY, MAX REGINALD, lawyer; b. Wilcox County, Ga., Sept. 12, 1928; s. Edgar Lee and Allie Bea (Faircloth) McG.; m. Jean Louise Hilyer, Dec. 28, 1950; children: Sharon Kay McGlamry Hendrix, Michael Lee. BS, Auburn U., 1948; LLB cum laude, Mercer U., 1952, JD cum laude, 1970. Bar: Ga. 1953, U.S. Dist. Ct. (mid. dist.) Ga. 1954, U.S. Ct. Appeals (5th cir.) 1964, U.S. Supreme Ct. 1972, U.S. Ct. Appeals (11th cir.) 1981, U.S. Ct. Appeals (4th cir.) 1985, U.S. Dist. Ct. (no. dist.) Calif. 1988, U.S. Dist. Ct. (no. dist.) Ga. 1989. Pvt. practice, Columbus, Ga., 1953-64; from ptnr. to officer Swift, Pease, Davidson & Chapman (name changed to Page, Scranton, Harris, McGlamry, & Chapman, P.C.), 1964-85; ptnr. Pope, Kellogg, McGlamry, Kilpatrick & Morrison, 1985-90, Pope, McGlamry, Kilpatrick & Morrison, LLP, Columbus, 1990-2000; pres. Max R. McGlamry, P.C., 2000—. Exec. com. Muscogee County Dem. Orgn., Columbus, 1956-60; bd. dirs. Columbus Jr. C. of C. Ens. USN, 1948-49. Am. Coll. Trust & Estate Counsel fellow, 1973, Lawyers Found. Ga. fellow, 1983. Mem. ABA, ATLA, State Bar Ga., Ga. Trial Lawyers Assn., Assn. U.S. Army, Ga. Golfers Sr. Assn., Urban League of Greater Columbus, Inc., Columbus Lawyers Club (pres. 1964-65), Lions (Columbus chpt. pres. 1967-68), Chattahoochee River Club, Green Island Country Club, Phi Kappa Phi, Alpha Epsilon Delta, Phi Alpha Delta, Pi Kappa Alpha. Democrat. Methodist. Avocations: golf, fishing. General civil litigation, Personal injury, Product liability. Home: 6941 Wethersfield Rd Columbus GA 31904-3317 Office: Max R McGlamry PC PO Box 4481 Columbus GA 31904-0481

MCGLONE, MICHAEL ANTHONY, lawyer; b. New Orleans, Jan. 6, 1951; s. James Godfrey and Dorothy (Barta) McG.; m. Suzanne Blanchard, Nov. 27, 1976; children: Kevin, Kathleen, Meghan. BBA cum laude, Loyola U., New Orleans, 1972, JD, 1975. Bar: La. 1975, U.S. Dist. Ct. (ea. dist.) La. 1975, U.S. Ct. Appeals (5th and 11 cirs.) 1975, U.S. Dist. Ct. (we. dist.) La. 1978, U.S. Dist. Ct. (mid. dist.) La. 1979, U.S. Supreme Ct. 1981. Law clk. to Hon. Herbert W. Christenberry U.S. Dist. Ct., New Orleans, 1975-76; ptnr. Lemle and Kelleher, 1976—. Mem. ABA, ALA, FBA (bd. dirs. New Orleans chpt. 1986—, pres. 1995-96), La. Bar Assn., Southeastern Admiralty Law Inst., New Orleans Bar Assn., Maritime Law Assn., St. Thomas More Inn of Ct. (master barrister), Alpha Sigma Nu, Beta Gamma Sigma. Democrat. Roman Catholic. Admiralty, Federal civil litigation, Personal injury. Home: 4708 N Turnbull Dr Metairie LA 70002-1447 Office: Lemle and Kelleher 601 Poydras St New Orleans LA 70130-6029 E-mail: MMcGlone@lomw.com

MCGLOTHLIN, MICHAEL GORDON, lawyer; b. Richlands, Va., Oct. 31, 1951; s. Woodrow Wilson and Sally Ann (Cook) McG.; m. Sandra Lee Keen, Oct. 1, 1983; children: Michael Alexander, Robert Aaron. BA, U. Va., 1974; JD, Coll. William and Mary, 1976. Bar: Va. 1977, U.S. Dist. Ct. (we. dist.) Va. 1978. Ptnr. McGlothlin, McGlothlin & McGlothlin, Grundy, Va., 1977-79; commonwealth atty. Buchanan County, Grundy, 1980-83; ptnr. McGlothlin & Wife, Grundy, 1984—; atty.for Buchanan County, 1984-89; bd. dirs. Gt. Southwest Home Commn., vice chmn., 1983—. Mem. adv. bd. Clinch Valley Coll.; sec. Buchanan County Dem. Party. Mem. ABA, Va. State Bar Assn., Buchanan County Bar Assn. (pres. 1984), Kiwanis (sec. Buchanan County Dem. Com.), Phi Alpha Delta, Phi Sigma Kappa. Presbyterian. Criminal, General practice, Personal injury. Home and Office: PO Box 810 Grundy VA 24614-0810

MCGLYNN, JOSEPH MICHAEL, lawyer; b. Detroit, Jan. 15, 1937; s. Frank J. and Germaine J. (Ackermann) McG.; m. Kathryn A. Montie, June 23, 1962; children: Julianne McGlynn Cress, Timothy, Kevin, Kathleen. BS in Acctg., U. Detroit, 1958, JD, 1960. Bar: Mich. 1961, U.S. Dist. Ct. (ea. dist.) Mich. 1961, U.S.Supreme Ct. 1971. Pvt. practice law, Detroit, 1961-67; ptnr. McGlynn, Dettmer & Spaulding and predecessor firms, 1967-74, Welday, Rosenthal, Reilly & McGlynn, Southfield, 1974-75, Welday, Klyman, Fortescue, Burau, McGlynn, Southfield, 1975-82, Brown, McGlynn, Charters & Thomas, Bloomfield Hills, 1982-87, Powers, Chapman & Deagostino, P.C., 1987—. Editor U. Detroit Law Jour., 1958-60. Active Fin. and Estate Planning Coun., Detroit, Oakland County Estate Planning Coun.; treas. Voluntas Dei Inst., Inc. With USAR, 1960—66. Recipient 1st prize Nathan Burkan Meml. Competition, 1959. Mem.: State Bar Mich., Oakland County Bar Assn., Delta Sigma Pi, Alpha Sigma Nu (hon.)), Beta Gamma Sigma (hon.)). Roman Catholic. General corporate, Probate, Real property. Office: Powers Chapman & DeAgostino 3001 W Big Beaver Rd Ste 704 Troy MI 48084-3193 E-mail: jmcglynn@powerschapman.com

MCGOLDRICK, JOHN LEWIS, lawyer; b. Plainfield, N.J., Mar. 2, 1941; s. John Leslie and Sarah (Walker) McG.; m. Ann Chapman Puffer, Oct. 1, 1966; children: Scott Runyon, Jennifer Winslow. BA cum laude, Harvard U., 1963, LLB, 1966. Bar: N.J. 1966, N.Y. 1985. Assoc. McCarter & English, Newark, 1966-73, ptnr., 1974-95; exec. v.p., pres. Med. Devices Group, gen. counsel Bristol-Myers Squibb Co., N.Y.C., 1995—. Vice-chmn., bd. dirs. N.J. Transit Corp., Newark; dir. Bristol-Myers Squibb Found., Advanced Med. Tech. Assn.; com. mem. Harvard Bd. Overseers. Chmn. zoning bd. Borough of Princeton, N.J.; trustee Essex-Newark Found. Legal Svcs. N.J., Newark YMCA-YWCA; adv. bd. United Negro Coll. Fund. Fellow Am. Coll. Trial Lawyers, Am. Bar Found., Am. Acad. Appellate Lawyers; mem. ABA, World Econ. Forum, Legal Svcs. N.J. (bd. dirs.), N.J. Bar Assn., N.Y. Bar Assn., Essex County Bar Assn., Mercer County Bar Assn., Internat. Bar Assn., Assn. Bar City of N.Y., Assn. Fed. Bar N.J. (former pres., mem. adv. bd.), Am. Law Inst., Assn. Gen. Counsel, Chief Legal Officers Roundtable, Coun. of Chief Legal Officers (The Conf. Bd. Inc.), CPR Inst. for Dispute Resolution (mem. exec. com.), Am. Arbitration Assn. (nat. panel), Aspen Inst. on the World Economy, Regional Plan Assn. (dir.), Harvard Clubs (N.Y.C. and N.J.), Harvard Law Sch. Assn. N.J. (former pres.). Home: 25 Vandeventer Ave Princeton NJ 08542-6937 Office: Bristol-Myers Squibb Co 345 Park Ave New York NY 10154-0004

MCGONAGLE, JOHN JOSEPH, JR. lawyer, economist; b. Ft. Pierce, Fla., Dec. 16, 1944; s. John Joseph and Catherine (Pukinskas) McG.; m. Carolyn M. Vella, Aug. 11, 1971. B.A., Yale U., 1966; J.D., cum laude, U. Mich. 1969; LL.M. in Urban Legal Studies with highest honors, George Washington U., 1971; M.A. in Bus. and Applied Econs., U. Pa., 1980. Bar: N.J. 1969, D.C. 1970, N.Y. 1972, U.S. Supreme Ct. 1974, Pa. 1979. Staff atty. VISTA, Washington, 1969-71; assoc. Casey, Lane & Mittendorf, N.Y.C., 1971-72; assoc. Williams, Caleri, Miller & Otley, Passaic, N.J., 1972-73; resident counsel Mudge, Rose, Guthrie & Alexander, Washington, 1973-76; sr. staff counsel INA Corp., Phila., 1976-80; v.p., gen. counsel Union Fidelity Life Ins., Trevose, Pa., 1980-81; v.p. Helicon Group Ltd., Allentown, Pa., 1981—. Author: Master Guide to Organization, Capitalization and Guide to Control of Corporations, 1985, Business Agreements-A Complete Guide to Oral and Written Contracts, 1982, Managing the Consultant, 1981; (with Carolyn M. Vella) Incorporating—A Guide For Small Business Owners, 1984, Competitive Intelligence in the Computer Age, 1987, Improving Business Planning with Competitive Intelligence, 1988, Outsmarting The Competition, 1990, In The Spotlight, 1990; contbr. articles to profl. jours. V.p., trustee Soc. for Advancement of Behavioral Economists, 1984-86; mem. Air Force Task Force, Pres. Reagan's Pvt. Sector Survey on Cost Control, 1982-84; vice chmn. Warwick Twp. Planning Commn., Jamison, Pa., 1978-81. Mem. ABA (chmn. com. 1979-81). Contracts commercial, General corporate, Government contracts and claims. Office: Helicon Group Ltd PO Box 2764 Lehigh Valley PA 18001-2764

MCGONEGLE, TIMOTHY JOSEPH, lawyer; b. Ft. Dodge, Iowa, Aug. 22, 1952; s. Eugene Francis and Margaret Ann (Chambers) McG.; m. Barbara Jo Sullivan, Oct. 6, 1979; children: Melissa Jo, Erin Kathleen, Matthew Sullivan. AA, Iowa Cen. Coll., 1972; BA, U. Iowa, 1974; JD, Loyola U., Chgo., 1977. Bar: Ill. 1977, (trial bar) Ill. 1978, U.S. Dist. Ct. (no. dist.) Ill. 1977, U.S. Dist. Ct. (cen. dist.) Ill. 1978, U.S. Ct. Appeals (7th cir.) 1978, U.S. Supreme Ct. 1981, U.S. Tax Ct. 1984, U.S. Ct. Appeals (Fed. cir.) 1987. Law clk. to presiding justice Ill. Supreme Ct., Chgo., 1977-78, Ill. Appellate Ct., Chgo., 1978; assoc. O'Brien, Carey, McNamara, Scheuneman & Campbell Ltd., 1978-82; ptnr. Ashcraft & Ashcraft Ltd., 1982-91; of counsel Andrew J. Maxwell, 1992-94, Ashcraft & Ashcraft Ltd., Chgo., 1994-2000, Schain, Burney, Ross & Citron, Ltd., Chgo., 2000—. Instr. legal writing Loyola U., Chgo., 1978-81, appellate advocacy Loyola U., 1984-87. Bd. dirs. Graceland West Cmty. Assn., Chgo., 1983-88, treas., 1985-91, legal counsel, 1988-92; vol. clinic atty. Chgo. Vol. Legal Svcs. Found., 1982—; elected Hawthorne Scholastic Acad. Local Sch. Coun., 1993-95, chair, 1994-95; vice chair parent involvement com. Hawthorne Scholastic Acad. PTA, mem. exec. com., 1988-90; den leader Boy Scouts Am., 1998—. Mem. ABA (sect. litigation 1978-91), Fed. Bar Assn., Ill. State Bar Assn. (sect. civil practice and procedure 1977-86), Chgo. Bar Assn. (investigator jud. evaluation com. 1983-86, hearings divsn. 1987-89). Federal civil litigation, General civil litigation, State civil litigation. Office: Schain Burney Ross & Citron Ltd 222 N LaSalle St Ste 1910 Chicago IL 60601 E-mail: TMcGonegle@aol.com, TMcGonegle@Sainlaw.com

MCGOVERN, DAVID CARR, lawyer; b. Taunton, Mass., Sept. 3, 1946; s. James Edward and Dorothea Elizabeth (Carr) McG.; m. Pamela Lee Compton, Mar. 22, 1975; 1 child, William David. AB, Coll. of Holy Cross, 1968; JD, U. Va., 1979. Bar: Calif. 1980, U.S. Dist. Ct. (ctrl. dist.) Calif. 1980, U.S. Dist. Ct. (so. dist.) Calif. 1981. Assoc. Rosenfeld, Meyer and Susman, Beverly Hills, Calif., 1979-81; ptnr. Engstrom, Lipscomb and Lack, L.A., 1981-90, Haight, Brown and Bonesteel LLP, L.A., 1990—. Bd. dirs. United Cerebral Palsy/Spastic Children's Found., L.A., 1985-94; men's com. John Tracy Clinic Women's Aux., L.A., 1988-94; founding mem. Friends of John Tracy Clinic, L.A., 1996—. Mem. ABA, State Bar Calif., Aviation Ins. Assn. Avocations: running, reading, coaching youth sports, travel. Aviation, General civil litigation, Product liability. Home: 7812 W 80th St Playa Del Rey CA 90293-7905 Office: Haight Brown and Bonesteel LLP 6080 Ctr Dr Ste 800 Los Angeles CA 90045-1574 Fax: (310) 215-7300. E-mail: dmcgovern@hbblaw.com

MCGOVERN, DAVID TALMAGE, lawyer; b. N.Y.C., Apr. 3, 1928; s. Coleman Benedict and Doris (Mangam) McG.; m. Margery White, June 28, 1958; children: Alexandra, Justine. BS, Yale U., 1950; LLB, Columbia U., 1955. Bar: N.Y. 1955. Assoc. Shearman & Sterling, N.Y.C., 1955-67, ptnr. Paris, 1967—. Chmn., trustee Am. U. Paris. 1st lt. U.S. Army, 1951-53. Named to French Legion of Honor, 1983. Mem. Am. C. of C. in France (pres. 1979-82, bd. dirs.). General corporate, Private international. Office: Shearman & Sterling 599 Lexington at 53rd St New York NY 10022

MCGOVERN, FRANCES, retired lawyer; b. Akron, Ohio, Apr. 18, 1927; d. Bernard Francis and Pauline A. (Menegay) McG. AB, U. Akron, 1948; LLB, Case Western Res. U., 1949. Bar: Ohio 1949, U.S. Dist. Ct. (no. dist.) Ohio 1951, U.S. Supreme Ct. 1963, U.S. Ct. Appeals (6th cir.) 1975. Pvt. practice, Barberton, Ohio, 1949-52; assoc. Motz, Morris, Wilson & Quine, Akron, 1952-55; ptnr. Quine & McGovern, 1955-60, 63-65; atty. Ohio Edison Co., 1965-78, sr. atty., 1978-88, assoc. gen. counsel, 1988-89. Author: Written on the Hills-The Making of the Akron Landscape, 1996. Mem. Ohio Gen. Assembly, 1955-60, chmn. judiciary com., 1959-60; mem., chmn. Ohio Pub. Utilities Commn., 1960-63; mem. Dept. Labor Employment Security Bd., Washington, 1963-68; vice chmn. Charter Commn. Summit County, 1969-70; del., mem. platform com. Dem. Nat. Conv., 1960, del. 1964; trustee N.E. Ohio Coll. Medicine, Rootstown, 1979-81, U. Akron, 1973-82; pres. United Way, 1987-89, also bd. dirs.; sec. Employee Spl. Svcs. Commn., 1974-91; bd. dirs. Med. Edn. Found. of N.E. Ohio U. Coll. Medicine, 1982-97, Archbishop Hoban H.S., 1984-90; bd. dirs. U. Akron Found., 1973-97, Summit County Hist. Soc., 1997—, Progress Through Preservation, 1996—, Access, 1999—; trustee emeritus NEOUCOM Found., 1997—; chmn. county charter com. Akron Regional Devel. Bd., 1990-92; active League Women Voters, Akron Edn. Found., 1993-96, Summit 2000. Recipient Achievement award Kappa Kappa Gamma, 1962, Akron Beacon Jour., 1968, Disting. Svc. award United Way, Akron, 1969, Disting. Alumni award U. Akron, 1989, others. Mem. Akron Bar Assn. (St. Thomas More award 1997). Democrat. Roman Catholic. Administrative and regulatory, General corporate, Public utilities.

MCGOVERN, PETER JOHN, law educator; b. N.Y.C., Dec. 6, 1938; s. John Phillip and Helen Marie (Gaisser) McG.; m. Catherine Bigley, Aug. 31, 1963; children: Brian Peter, Sean Daniel. AB, Notre Dame U., 1961; JD, Fordham U., 1964; EdD, U. S.D., 1980. Bar: N.Y. 1964, S.D. 1972, Ind. 1983, Ill. 1990, U.S. Supreme Ct. 1968. Atty. criminal divsn. Dept. Justice, 1971-72; prof. law U. S.D., Vermillion, 1972-83; from asst. dean to assoc. dean U. S.D. Sch. Law, 1972-77, dir. programs and planning, 1979-83; dean Valparaiso (Ind.) U. Sch. Law, 1983-85, St. Thomas U. Sch. Law, Fla., 1985-87, John Marshall Law Sch., Chgo., 1987-90, prof. law, 1990—. Dir. Ctr. for Internat. Bus. and Trade Law, 2000; dir. continuing legal edn. State Bar S.D., 1972-83; past chmn. S.D. Family Law Com.; bd. dirs. Legal Svcs. of Greater Gary Inc. Past pres. Vermillion Area Arts Coun., Nat. Anti-Vivisection Soc.; bd. dirs. Lawyer for Creative Arts, 1990-92. Lt. comdr. JAGC, USN, 1965-71. Recipient Legal Writing award Fed. Bar Assn., 1969. Fellow Ind. Bar Found.; mem. ABA, State Bar Ind., Am. Acad. Alternative Dispute Resolution Attys. (bd. dirs.). Democrat. Roman Catholic. Home: 440 N Wabash Ave Apt 4706 Chicago IL 60611-7679 Office: John Marshall Law Sch 315 S Plymouth Ct Chicago IL 60604-3968 E-mail: mcgover@jmls.edu

MC GOVERN, WALTER T. federal judge; b. Seattle, May 24, 1922; s. C. Arthur and Anne Marie (Thies) McG.; m. Rita Marie Olsen, June 29, 1946; children: Katrina M., Shawn E., A. Renee. B.A., U. Wash., 1949, LL.B., 1950. Bar: Wash. 1950. Practiced law in, Seattle, 1950-59; mem. firm Kerr, McCord, Greenleaf & Moen; judge Municipal Ct., Seattle, 1959-65, Superior Ct., Wash., 1965-68, Wash. Supreme Ct., 1968-71, U.S. Dist. Ct. (we. dist.) Wash., 1971-87, chief judge, 1975-87, sr. judge, 1987—. Mem. subcom. on supporting personnel Jud. Conf. U.S., 1981-87, chmn. subcom., 1983, mem. adminstrn. com., 1983-87, chmn. jud. resources com., 1987-91. Mem. Am. Judicature Soc., Wash. State Superior Ct. Judges Assn., Seattle King County Bar Assn. (treas.), Phi Delta Phi. Club: Seattle Tennis (pres. 1968). Office: US Dist Ct US Courthouse 5th Fl 1010 5th Ave Ste 215 Seattle WA 98104-1189

MCGOWAN, PATRICK FRANCIS, lawyer; b. N.Y.C., July 23, 1940; s. Francis Patrick and Sonia Veronica (Koslow) M.; m. Patricia Neil, June 6, 1964; children: Susan Claire, Kathleen Anne. BA, Rice U., 1962; JD, U. Tex., Austin, 1965. Bar: Tex. 1965, U.S. Ct. Appeals (5th cir.) 1969, U.S. Tax Ct. 1972, U.S. Supreme Ct. 1970, U.S. Ct. Appeals (11th cir.) 1981, U.S. Ct. Appeals (fed. cir.) 1993. Briefing atty. Tex. Supreme Ct., Austin, 1965-66; ptnr. Strasburger & Price, Dallas, 1966-98, Akin, Gump, Strauss, Hauer & Feld, Dallas, 1998—. Pres., chmn. bd. Tex Lex, Inc., 1991-98; faculty I.P. Law Instit. Ctr. Am. and Internat. Law, 2001. Contbr. numerous articles on interent trademark, copyright and franchise law. Bd. advisors Dallas Ft. Worth Sch. Law. Fellow Coll. State Bar Tex. (faculty Franchising Inst. 1987, Intellectual Property Inst. 1992, S.W. Legal Found. Patent Law Inst. 1992, Practising Law Inst. 1996); mem. ABA (forum com. on franchising, trademark and unfair competition com., patent, trademark and copyright law sect.), State Bar Tex. (intellectual property sect., com. continuing legal edn.), Dallas Bar Assn. (dir. intellectual property law sect. 1994—, chmn. I.P. Basics seminar 1999, sect. vice chmn. 2001), ALFA Internat. Tel. Symposium, Internat. Anti-Counterfeiting Assn., Tex. Law Rev. Editors Assn., Phi Delta Phi. Federal civil litigation, Patent, Trademark and copyright. Office: Akin Gump 1700 Pacific Ave Ste 4100 Dallas TX 75201-4675 E-mail: pmcgowan@akingump.com

MCGRATH, CHRISTOPHER THOMAS, lawyer; b. Inwood, N.Y., Nov. 25, 1958; s. John J. and Dolores Marie McG.; m. Monica Jean DiPalma, Sept. 15, 1984; children: Kristin Marie, Kelli Anne, Katelynn. BS cum laude, St. John's U., Jamaica, N.Y., 1980; JD, U. Dayton, 1983. Bar: N.Y. 1984, U.S. Dist. Ct. (so. and ea. dists.) N.Y. 1984, U.S. Supreme Ct. 1987; bd. cert. civil trial advocacy Nat. Bd. Trial Advocacy. Assoc. Sullivan & Liapakis, N.Y.C., 1983-89, ptnr., 1989-99, Sullivan, Papain, Block, McGrath & Cannavo P.C., N.Y.C., 1999—. Lectr. N.Y. State Bar Assn., N.Y. State Trial Lawyers Assn., Assn. Trial Lawyers Am. Chmn. humanitarian award Nassau County 4th Precinct Police, 1985—. Mem. Assn. Trial Lawyers Am., N.Y. State Trail Lawyers Assn., Nassau County Bar Assn. (bd. dirs., chair med. legal com. 1997-98, chair jud. com. 1999—), N.Y. State Bar Assn., Kiwanis (pres.-elect Hewlet, N.Y., disting. past pres. Peninsula chpt. 1988-89). Republican. General civil litigation, State civil litigation, Personal injury. Home: 1348 Hewlett Ln Hewlett NY 11557-2208 Office: Sullivan Papain Block McGrath Cannavo PC 120 Broadway New York NY 10271-0002 also: 55 Mineola Blvd Mineola NY 11501-4220 E-mail: cmcgrath@traillaw1.com

MCGRATH, J. NICHOLAS, lawyer; b. Hollywood, Calif., Feb. 12, 1940; children: Nicholas Gerald, Molly Inez. BA with honors, Lehigh U., 1962; LLB magna cum laude, Columbia U., 1965. Bar: D.C. 1966, Calif. 1969, U.S. Supreme Ct. 1970, Colo. 1971. Law clk. U.S. Ct. Appeals (D.C. cir.), 1965-66; law clk. to assoc. justice Thurgood Marshall U.S. Supreme Ct., Washington, 1967-68; pvt. practice Aspen, 1971—. Chmn. grievance com. Colo. Supreme Ct., 1989, mem. 1984-89. Mem. bd. editors Columbia Law Review, 1964-65. Mem. planning commn. Town of Basalt, Colo., 1992—93, town trustee, 1993—94; lectr. nat. and state CLE programs on ethics, litigations, and land use subjects; pres. Basalt Children's Recreation Fund, Inc., 1994—, Basalt Soccer Club, 1997—99. Mem. Colo. Bar Assn. (v.p. 1991-92), Pitkin County Bar Assn. (pres. 1977). Democrat. State civil litigation, Land use and zoning (including planning), Real property. Home: 415 Elk Cir Basalt CO 81621-8202 Office: 600 E Hopkins Ave Ste 305 Aspen CO 81611-2933 E-mail: jnm@jnmpc.com

MCGRATH, JOHN JOSEPH, law educator; b. N.Y.C., Mar. 7, 1953; s. John J. and Anne G. (Fox) McG.; m. Catherine Bridget Burns, Aug. 21, 1983. B.A., L.I. U., 1975; Ph.D., A.B.D., Fordham U., 1985. Pvt. investigator Pincertons Inc., N.Y.C., 1976-77; lectr. Nassau Police Acad., Mineola, N.Y., 1979; legal adminstr. Law Office of Bernard Kenny, N.Y.C., 1977-80; prof. dept. law and criminal justice, Mercy Coll., Dobbs Ferry, N.Y., 1980— , asst. dir. Peace Officer Tng. Program, 1983— , debate moderator, 1980— . Mem. Ancient Order Hiberians (historian 1975-83), Criminal Justice Educators Assn., Brehon Law Soc. N.Y. Roman Catholic. Office: Dept Law Mercy Coll 555 Broadway Dobbs Ferry NY 10522-1134

MCGRATH, KATHRYN BRADLEY, lawyer; b. Norfolk, Va., Sept. 2, 1944; d. James Pierce and Kathryn (Hoyle) Bradley; children: Ian M., James D. AB, Mt. Holyoke Coll., 1966; JD, Georgetown U., 1969. Ptnr. Gardner, Carton & Douglas, Washington, 1979-83; dir. div. investment mgmt. SEC, 1983-90; ptnr. Morgan, Lewis & Bockius, LLP, 1990—. Named Disting. Exec. Pres. Reagan, 1987. Mem. Fed. Bar Assn. (exec. council securities law com.). Office: Morgan Lewis & Bockius LLP 1800 M St NW Washington DC 20036-5802

MCGRATH, MIKE, lawyer; b. Rapid City, S.D., Aug. 22, 1947; s. John E. and Jean F. (Funk) McG.; m. Joy L. Rasmusson, May 22, 1971; children— Patrick John, Christopher Paul. B.S., U. Mont., 1970; J.D., Gonzaga U., 1975. Bar: Wash. 1975, Mont. 1977, U.S. Ct. Appeals (9th cir.) 1980, U.S. Supreme Ct. 1980. Legal intern Spokane Legal Services, Spokane, 1973-75; atty. Washoe County Legal Services, Reno, Nev., 1975-76, Bradbury & Bliss, Anchorage, 1976; asst. atty. gen. State of Mont., Helena, 1977-82; county atty. Lewis and Clark County, Helena, 1983—2001; atty. gen. State of Mont., 2001- . Chmn. rules com. Mont. Dem. Party, 1983—; pres. Mont. Legal Services Assn., 1984-85, 95-96, bd.dirs. 1980—; bd. dirs. Mountain chpt. Nat. Com. for Prevention of Child Abuse, 1985-90, Big Bros. and Sisters, Helena, 1977-83; bd. dirs. Friendship Ctr. Helena, 1989—, pres., 1995-97. Served with USAF, 1970-72. Mem. Mont. Bar Assn., Nat. Dist. Attys. Assn., Mont. County Attys. Assn. (pres. 1996-97). Democrat. Home: 514 Hayes Ave Helena MT 59601-6106 Office: 215 N Sanders 3d Fl PO Box 201401 Helena MT 59620*

MCGRATH, THOMAS J. lawyer, writer, film producer; b. N.Y.C., Oct. 8, 1932; m. Mary Lee McGrath, Aug. 4, 1956 (dec.); children: Maura Lee, J. Connell; m. Diahn Williams, Sept. 28, 1974; 1 child, Courtney C. B.A., NYU, 1956, J.D., 1960. Bar: N.Y. 1960. Assoc. Milbank, Tweed, Hadley & McCloy, N.Y.C., 1960-69; ptnr. Simpson, Thacher & Bartlett, 1970-95; retired, 1995. Lectr., writer Practicing Law Inst., 1976—, Am. Law Inst. ABA, 1976-81; bd. dirs. Fast Food Devel. Corp. Author: Carryover Basis Under Tax Reform Act, 1977; contbg. author: Estate and Gift Tax After ERTA, 1982; producer: feature film Deadly Hero, 1977. Bd. dirs. N.Y. Philharm.; pres. Am. Austrian Found., Tanzania Wildlife Fund. With U.S. Army, 1953-54, Korea. Fellow Am. Coll. Trust and Estate Coun.; mem. ABA, N.Y. State Bar Assn., Assn. Bar City N.Y. Estate planning, Probate, Estate taxation. Home: 988 5th Ave New York NY 10021-0143 Office: Simpson Thacher & Bartlett 425 Lexington Ave New York NY 10017-3954 E-mail: mcgrathtwf@aol.com, mcgraththomasj@aol.com

MCGRATH, WILLIAM ARTHUR, lawyer; b. Hackensack, N.J., Jan. 31, 1941; s. Donald Marble and Elinor (Peck) M.; m. Diane Gurley, Apr. 25, 1965 (div. Nov. 1976); children: Philip M., Christian P.; m. Clair Farmer, Aug. 7, 1994. BS, Calif. U., Long Beach, 1963; J.D., U. Pacific, 1972. Bar: Colo. 1972, U.S. Dist. Ct. Colo. 1972. Pvt. practice, Breckenridge, Colo., 1972-82, Aurora, Colo., 1982-84; ptnr. McGrath & Callan, P.C., Breckenridge, 1975-80, McGrath & Lavenhar, Esq., Denver, 1984-85, prin. William A. McGrath & Assocs., Denver, 1985-88; pvt. practice real estate cons., San Diego, 1988—; pvt. practice arbitration, mediation, alternate dispute resolution tng. and program design, cons., Sacramento, 1993—; vocat. instr. Colo. Mountain Coll., 1972-80. Mem. ABA, Colo. Trial Lawyers Assn., Colo. Assn. Realtors. Republican. Episcopalian. E-mail: wmcgrathppl@aol.com. State civil litigation, General practice, Real property. Home: 3300 Capital Center Dr Apt 66 Rancho Cordova CA 95670-7974

MCGRATH, WILLIAM JOSEPH, lawyer; b. Cleve., July 6, 1943; s. William Peter and Marie Agnes (Wolf) McG.; m. Mary Ann Ostrenga; children: William Peter, Geoffrey Walton, Megan Joy. ABcl, John Carroll U., 1965; MA, Loyola U., 1967; JD, Harvard U., 1970. Bar: Ill. 1970. Assoc. McDermott, Will & Emery, Chgo., 1970-75, ptnr., 1976—, mem. mgmt. com., 1993-98, mem. exec. com., 1994-97. Vice chmn. investment com. Glencoe Capital LLC, 1997—; bd. dirs. Tomy Am., Inc., Torrance, Calif. Trustee Boys and Girls Club Found., 1983; bd. dirs. Ctr. for Econ. Policy and Analysis, 1989—. Mem. ABA, Evanston Golf Club, Union League (Chgo.), Chgo. Club, Met. Club. Chgo. Democrat. Roman Catholic. General corporate, Mergers and acquisitions, Securities. Home: 943 Edgemere Ct Evanston IL 60202-1428 Office: McDermott Will & Emery 227 W Monroe St Ste 3100 Chicago IL 60606-5096

MC GRAW, DARRELL VIVIAN, JR. state attorney general; b. Mullens, W.Va., Nov. 8, 1936; s. Darrell Vivian and Julia (ZeKany) McG.; m. Jorea Marple; children: Elizabeth, Sarah, Darrell, Elliott. AB, W.Va. U., 1961, JD, 1964, MA, 1977. Bar: W.Va. 1964. Gen. atty. Fgn. Claims Settlement Commn., U.S. Dept. State, 1964; counsel to gov. State of W.Va., 1965-68; pvt. practice Charleston, Shepherdstown and Morgantown, 1968-76; judge W.Va. Supreme Ct. Appeals, Charleston, 1977-88, chief justice, 1982, 83; atty. gen. State of W.Va., 1993—. Served with U.S. Army, 1954-57. Fellow W.Va. U., Nat. Ctr. Edn. in Politics/Ford Found. Fellow Am. Polit. Sci. Assn., Rotary. Democrat. Office: Office of Atty Gen 1900 Kanawha Blvd E Rm E-26 Charleston WV 25305-0009

MCGRAW, PATRICK ALLAN, lawyer; b. Radford, Va., Aug. 26, 1942; s. Delfrod Armstrong and Virginia Elizabeth (Ramsey) McGraw; m. Martha Jane Schrock, June 22, 1968; children: Katherine Martha, Michael Patrick. AB, Kenyon Coll., 1963; JD, Harvard U., 1966. Bar: Ohio 1966, US Dist Ct (no dist) Ohio 1967, US Supreme Ct 1978, US Ct Appeals (6th cir) 1983. Assoc. Fuller and Henry, Toledo, 1967-72, ptnr., 1972-84; prin. The Toledo Group, Inc., 1985-96; supr. Ohio Civil Rights Comn., 1996—. Asst atty gen State of Ohio, 1992—95. Trustee Bell and Beckwith Liquidation, Toledo, 1983—97, Knoxville Col, Tenn., 1981—83. With USAR, 1966—72. Mem.: ABA, Am Judicature Soc, Ohio State Bar Asn, Cleveland Bar Asn, Toledo Bar Asn, Kenyon Col Alumni Asn (pres 1980), Phi Beta Kappa. Democrat. E-mail: mpmcgraw@att.net

MCGRAW, PATRICK JOHN, judge; b. Detroit, Feb. 3, 1956; s. John William and Elizabeth Kay (Foley) McG.; m. Susan Elaine Borowiak, Jan. 14, 1978; children: Kelly Elizabeth, Ryan Patrick, Brandon David, Kyle Elaine. BS, Cen. Mich. U., 1979; JD, Cooley Law Sch., 1982. Bar: Mich. 1982. Ptnr. McGraw, Martin & Heyn, P.C., Saginaw, Mich., 1982-99; judge Probate Ct. 10th Jud. Cir., 1999—. Lectr. ACLS Legal Implications, Saginaw, 1985; instr. Ctrl. Mich. U., Mt. Pleasant, Mich., 1986-90; spkr. Sponsor of Malpractice Issues Delta Coll. and Saginaw Valley State Coll., 1986—. Atty. Sch. Program, Saginaw, 1986—; mem. YMCA; bd. trustees Saginaw Twp., 1988—; sch. coun. mem. Saginaw Nouvel Cath. Cen. High Sch., 1988—; apptd. Mich. Bd. of Counseling, 1994—. Mem. ABA, ATLA, Mich. Bar Assn., Saginaw County Bar Assn., Mich. Soc. Hosp. Attys., Mich. Def. Trial Counsel, Phi Alpha Delta. Avocations: black belt karate, hunting, fishing, racquetball. E-mial. Home: 5220 Overhill Dr Saginaw MI 48603-1727 Office: Saginaw County Govtl Bldg 111 S Michigan Ave Saginaw MI 48602-2019 E-mail: pmcgraw@saginawcounty.com

MCGRAW, WARREN RANDOLPH, state supreme court chief justice; b. Wyoming County, W.Va., May 10, 1939; m. Peggy Shufflebarger; children: W. Randolph, H. Suzanne, Rebecca L. AB, U. Charleston, 1960; postgrad., W.Va. U.; JD, Wake Forest U., 1963. Bar: W.Va. 1963. Trial atty. U.S. Dept. Justice, Washington; legal svc. atty.; elected W.Va. Ho. of Dels., 1968, 70, W.Va. Senate, 1972, 76, 80; elected prosecuting atty. Wyoming County, 1996; justice W.Va. Supreme Ct. Appeals, 1998—. Instr. W.Va. U. Ext. Agy.; W.Va. del. Dem. Nat. Conv., 1972, 74; mem. Del. and Senatorial Dist. Exec. Coms.; del. State Dem. Jud. Conv. and State Dem. Conv.; elected pres. W.Va. Senate, 1980, 82; co-chmn. Crime Commn.; mem. Nat. Conf. Lt. Govs. Featured on Nat. Pub. TV series Bill Moyers Journal. Trustee 1st United Meth. Ch., Pineville; participant Marshall U.'s Taft Lectr. Series; elected W.Va. del. Dem. Nat. Conv., 1972, 74, Wyo. County Bd. Edn., 1986, 44th pres. W.Va. Sen., 1980, 82; del. State Dem. Jud. Conv., State Dem. Conv.; past pres. Jaycees; mem. Nat. Conf. Lt. Govs., Heart Fund, Wyoming County Cancer Fund, Del. and Sen. Dist. Exec. Coms.; past chmn. Wyoming County Dem. Exec. Com.; co-chmn. Crime Commn. Named one of nation's Outstanding Legislators, Rutgers U.; recipient Friend of Edn., Margaret Baldwin award W.Va. Edn. Assn. Mem. Wyo. Bar Assn., Raleigh County Bar Assn., Rotary Internat. Office: Bldg 1 Rm E-302 Capitol Complex Charleston WV 25305*

MCGREGOR, RUTH VAN ROEKEL, state supreme court justice; b. Le Mars, Iowa, Apr. 4, 1943; d. Bernard and Marie Frances (Janssen) Van Roekel; m. Robert James McGregor, Aug. 15, 1965. BA summa cum laude, U. Iowa, 1964, MA, 1965; JD summa cum laude, Ariz. State U., 1974. Bar: Ariz. 1974, U.S. Dist. Ct. Ariz. 1974, U.S. Ct. Appeals (9th cir.), U.S. Supreme Ct. 1982. Assoc. Fennemore, Craig, von Ammon, Udall & Powers, Phoenix, 1974-79, ptnr., 1980-81, 82-89; law clk. to justice Sandra Day O'Connor U.S. Supreme Ct., Washington, 1981-82; judge Ariz Ct. Appeals, 1989-98, vice chief judge, 1993-95, chief judge, 1995-98; justice Ariz. Supreme Ct., 1998—. Mem. disciplinary commn. Ariz. Supreme Ct., 1984-89, City of Mesa jud. adv. bd., 1997—. Mem., newsletter editor Charter 100, Phoenix, 1981—; bd. dirs., mem. Ctr. for Law in Pub. Interest, Phoenix, 1977-80. Mem. ABA (chmn. state memberships 1985—), Ariz. Bar Assn. (disciplinary com. 1984—), Ariz. Judges Assn. (exec. com. 1990—, sec. 1991-92, v.p. 1992-93, pres. 1993-94), Nat. Assn. Women Judges (chair first time attendees com. 1990-91, 1994 conv. com.; exec. com. 1995—). Democrat. Lutheran. Lodge: Soroptomists. Office: Arizona Supreme Court 1501 W Washington St Phoenix AZ 85007-3231*

MCGUANE, FRANK L., JR. lawyer; b. White Plains, N.Y., July 10, 1939; s. Frank L. and Dorothy P. (McGrath) McG.; m. Carla L. Miller, June 26, 1993; children: Lauri Elizabeth, Molly Elizabeth. BA, U. Notre Dame, 1961; JD, U. Cin., 1968. Bar: Colo. 1968, U.S. Dist. Ct. Colo. 1968, U.S. Ct. Appeals (10th cir.) 1970, U.S. Supreme Ct. 1971. Shareholder McGuane and Malone, P.C., Denver, 1981-95; pres. Frank McGuane & Assocs., P.C., 1995—; ptnr. McGuane & Hogan, LLP, 1997—. Mem. faculty Nat. Inst. for Trial Advocacy, 1987—; lectr. in field. Author: Domestic Relations-Colorado Methods of Practice, 1983; co-author: Colorado Family Law and Practice, 1999; contbr. articles to profl. jours. Chmn. Denver area chpt. Nat. Eagle Scout Assn. Boy Scouts Am,. 1980-82. With USMC, 1961-63. Fellow Am. Acad. Matrimonial Lawyers (jour. editor 1990-95, 2000—, bd. govs. 1988-95, pres. Colo. chpt. 1988-89), Internat. Acad. Matrimonial Lawyers (founding fellow, bd. govs. 1997—); mem. ABA, Colo. Bar Assn. (chmn. family law sect. 1977-78), Denver Bar Assn., Arapahoe County Bar Assn., Douglas-Elbert County Bar Assn., Pitkin County Bar Assn., Am. Coll. Family Trial Lawyers (diplomate), Cath. Lawyers Guild. Family and matrimonial. Office: The Galleria 720 S Colorado Blvd Ste 910N Denver CO 80246-1935 E-mail: flm@mcguanehogan.com

MCGUCKIN, JOHN HUGH, JR. lawyer; b. Bryn Mawr, Pa., Nov. 8, 1946; AB magna cum laude, Harvard Coll., 1968, JD, 1971. Bar: Mass. 1971, Calif. 1973. Assoc. Orrick, Herrington, Rowley & Sutcliffe, 1972-79; sr. counsel legal divsn. Bank Am., 1979-81; exec. v.p., gen. counsel UnionBanCal Corp./Union Bank Calif., N.A., San Francisco, 1981—, UnionBanCal Corp., 1998—. Adj. instr. Hastings Coll. Law U. Calif., 1980-82; judge pro tem San Francisco Superior Ct. Contbr. articles to profl. jours. Mem. ABA, State Bar Calif. (v.p., treas., bd. govs., chmn. subcom. duties and liabilities trustees probate and trust law sect. 1985-86, legal svcs. trust fund commn. 1989-90, minimum CLE com.), Calif. Bankers Assn. (legal affairs com. 1988-90), Bar Assn. San Francisco (chmn. probate and trust law sect. 1985, exec. com., vice chmn. corp. law dept. sect. 1985-87), Phi Beta Kappa. General corporate. Office: Union Bank Calif NA 400 California St Ste 1200 San Francisco CA 94104-1320

MCGUFFEY, CARROLL WADE, JR. lawyer; b. Decatur, Ga., Dec. 1, 1951; s. Carroll Wade and Dorothy (Landers) McG.; m. Virginia Elizabeth Miller, Aug. 12, 1972; children: Carroll Wade, III, Michelle Elizabeth, Jennifer Lanier. BBA, U. Ga., 1973, JD cum laude, 1976. Bar: Ga. 1976, Fla. 1977, U.S. Dist. Ct. (mid. dist.) Ga. 1976, U.S. Supreme Ct. 1980. Capt. Chief Claims Tort Litigation Div. USAF, Eglin AFB, Fla., 1976-80; assoc., ptnr. Savell and Williams, Atlanta, 1980-90; mng. ptnr., CEO Goodman McGuffey Aust & Lindsey LLP, 1990—. Lectr. in field. Editor: Employers Guide to Workers Compensation in Georgia, Employee Leasing: An Employer's Guide. Ward capt. Athens Mayoral Campaign (Ga.), 1975; commr., dir. Stone Mountain Dixie Youth Baseball, 1982-87; cubmaster Boy Scouts Am., 1986-88, scoutmaster, 1988-90, troop chmn., 1991-92, dist. chmn., 1993-95; mgr., coach Murphy Candler Girls Softball Assn., 1996—. Recipient Dist. Award of Merit, Boy Scouts Am., 1995. Mem. ABA, Fla. Bar Assn., Atlanta Bar Assn. (workers compensation seminar chmn. 1993, 97, fundraising chmn. Kid's Chance Found. Race, 1992, workers compensation section, bd. dirs. 1994-01, sec.-treas. 1997, chair-elect 1998, chair 1999), Ga. Def. Lawyers Assn. (trial acad. instr. 1987), Def. Rsch. Inst., Ind. Ins. Agts. of Ga. (hon. life, young agents com.), Ga. Mental Health Assn. (bd. dirs. 1987). Methodist. Clubs: Athens Boat (dir. 1982-90), Lawyers (Atlanta), UGA Pres. Club. Insurance, Personal injury, Workers' compensation. E-mail: wmcguffey@gmal.com

MCGUIRE, EDWARD DAVID, JR. lawyer; b. Waynesboro, Va., Apr. 11, 1948; s. Edward David and Mary Estelle (Angus) McG.; m. Georgia Ann Charuhas, Aug. 15, 1971; children: Matthew Edward, Kathryn Ann. BS in Commerce, U. Va., 1970; JD, Coll. William and Mary, 1973. Bar: Va. 1973, D.C. 1974, Md. 1990, Pa. 1995, U.S. Dist. Ct. (ea. dist.) Va. 1974, U.S. Dist. Ct. D.C. 1974, U.S. Dist. Ct. Md. 1990, Ct. Appeals (4th cir.) 1974, U.S. Ct. Appeals (D.C. cir.) 1974, U.S. Supreme Ct. 1993. Assoc. Wilkes and Artis, Washington, 1973-78; gen. corp counsel Mark Winkler Mgmt., Alexandria, Va., 1978-80; sr. contracts officer Amtrak, Washington, 1980-81; sr. real estate atty., asst. corp. sec. Peoples Drug Stores, Inc., Alexandria, 1981-88; of counsel Cowles, Rinaldi & Arnold, Ltd., Fairfax, Va., 1989-91; sr. assoc. Radigan, Rosenberg & Holmes, Arlington, 1991; pvt. practice, Annandale, 1992-97; sr. assoc. Stein, Sperling, Bennett, DeJong, Driscoll, Greenfeig Metro, Rockville, Md., 1997-99; of counsel Hodes, Ulman, Pessin & Katz, P.A., Annandale, 1999-2000; atty. pvt. practice, Alexandria, Va., 2000—; mng. dir., personal trust adminstr. Riggs Bank, N.A., Washington, 2000—. Co-author: Legacy: Plan, Protect and Preserve Your Estate, 1995, Generations: Planning Your Legacy, 1998. Bd. dirs. Dist. XVI Va. Student Aid Found., 1978-85, George Washington dist. Boy Scouts Am., 1986; active William and Mary Law Sch. Assn., bd. dirs., 1983-96, pres., 1987-88, treas., 1990-91. Capt. JAGC, USANG, 1973-79. Mem. ABA, Va. Bar Assn., Va. State Bar, D.C. Bar, Md. State Bar Assn., Fairfax Bar Assn., Am. Trial Lawyers Am., Arlington County Bar Assn., Va. Trial Lawyers Assn., No. Va. Estate Planning Coun., William and Mary Alumni Soc. (bd. dirs. D.C. chpt. treas. 1992-94), U. Va. Club of Washington (schs. com. chmn. 1995—, v.p. outreach 1997-99, pres.-elect 1998-99, bd. dirs. 1996-99), Rotary (treas. Springfield chpt. 1985-86, sec. 1986-87, pres.-elect 1987, chmn. World Affairs Conf. 1985-88, bd. dirs. 1984-88, 96-97, Dist. 7610 youth leadership awards chmn. 1994-97, Outstanding Rotarian award 1985). Greek Orthodox. Avocations: racquetball, coaching youth sports. General civil litigation, Estate planning, Real property. Home and Office: 31 W Myrtle St Alexandria VA 22301-2422

MCGUIRE, EUGENE GUENARD, lawyer; b. Apr. 1, 1945; s. Edward Joseph and Carmen Isabel (Guenard) McG.; m. Pamela Jean Cottam, Sept. 14, 1969; children: Lauren Lambert, Christopher Cottam. BArch, Cornell U., 1967; JD, Columbia U., 1970. Bar: N.Y. 1971, U.S. Dist. Ct. (so. dist.) N.Y. 1972, U.S. Dist. Ct. (ea. dist.) N.Y. 1972, U.S. Ct. Appeals (2d cir.) 1974, Conn. 1988. Assoc. Winthrop, Stimson, Putnam & Roberts, N.Y.C., 1970-79; counsel Texasgulf, Inc., 1979-81, sr. counsel, asst. sec., 1981-90, sec., asst. gen. counsel, 1990-94; sr. counsel, asst. sec. Elf Aquitaine Inc., 1983-90, sec., asst. gen. counsel, 1990-94, sec., gen. counsel, 1995-97, v.p., sec., gen. counsel, 1998—. V.p.-law Elf Techs., Inc., N.Y.C., 1987-94, 96-98. Mem. Am. Corp. Counsel Assn., Assn. Bar of City of N.Y., Am. Yacht Club (Rye, N.Y.), Cornell Club (N.Y.). Quaker. Antitrust, General corporate, Securities. Office: Elf Aquitaine Inc 444 Madison Ave Fl 20 New York NY 10022-6903

MCGUIRE, JOHN THOMAS, lawyer, educator; b. Bronx, N.Y., Oct. 12, 1966; s. Thomas John and Irene McGuire. BA in History magna cum laude, MA in History, U. Scranton, 1988; JD cum laude, U. Buffalo, 1991; PhD in Am. History, Binghamton U., 2001. Bar: N.Y. 1991. Trial atty. U.S. Dept. of Justice, Washington, 1991-95; atty. AARP, 1996-97; pvt. practice Vestal, N.Y., 1997—; adj. prof. SUNY-Oneonta, 2000—. Bd. dirs. Broome and Chenango Legal Aid, Inc., Binghamton. Reviewer American Jewish History, 1998, Left History, 2001; editor: Binghamton Jour. of History, 1998—99; author: A Catalyst for Reform: The Women's Joint Legislative Conference and Its Fight for Labor Legislation in New York State, 1918-1933, Making the Democratic Party a Partner: Eleanor Roosevelt the WJLC and the Women's Division of the New York State Democratic Party, 2001, A Sense of Shame, 2001. Del. Grad. Student Employee's Union, Vestal, N.Y., 1999—; bd. dirs. Broome County Peace Action, Binghamton, 1999—; negotiator GSEU, 2000-01. James A. Finnegan fellowship, 1987. Mem. N.Y. State Bar Assn., Am. Hist. Assn., Orgn. of Am. Historians, Phi Alpha Theta (pres. 1999-01), Alpha Sigma Nu Home: 422 Clubhouse Rd Vestal NY 13850-3727 Office: SUNY Oneonta NY 13820 E-mail: johnmcguireus@yahoo.com

MCGUIRE, PAMELA COTTAM, lawyer; b. Aug. 25, 1947; d. Robert D. and Marion E. (Swift) Cottam; m. Eugene G. McGuire, Sept. 14, 1969; children: Lauren Lambert, Christopher Cottam. BA, Vassar Coll., 1969; MS in Urban Planning, Columbia U., 1973, JD, 1973. Bar: N.Y. 1974, U.S. Dist. Ct. 9ea. dist.) N.Y. 1974, U.S. Dist. Ct. (so. dist.) N.Y. 1974, U.S. Ct. Appeals (2d cir.) 1974. Law clk to presiding judge U.S. Dist Ct. (ea. dist.) N.Y., Bklyn., 1973—74; asst. U.S. atty. U.S. Atty.'s Office, 1974—75; staff counsel Moreland Commn., N.Y.C., 1975—76; assoc. Hughes, Hubbard & Reed, 1976—77; from staff counsel to sr. v.p., gen. counsel, sec. PepsiCo., Inc., Purchase, 1977—98; sr. v.p., gen. counsel, sec. The Pepsi Bottling Group, Inc., 1998—. Fellow, Woodrow Wilson Found., 1973. Administrative and regulatory. Office: Pepsi Bottling Group Inc 1 Pepsi Way Somers NY 10589

MCGUIRE, WILLIAM B(ENEDICT), lawyer; b. Newark, Feb. 14, 1929; children: Joan Ellen, Ralph R., James C., Keith P., Grant W. BS, Fordham U., 1950; JD, Seton Hall U., 1958; LLM in Taxation, NYU, 1963. Bar: N.J. 1958, U.S. Dist. Ct. N.J. 1958, U.S. Supreme Ct. 1971, U.S. Ct. Appeals (3d cir.) 1980, N.Y. 1982. Chief acct. Hanover Fire Ins. Co., N.Y.C., 1950-58; sr. ptnr. Lum, Blunno & Tompkins, Newark, 1958-83, Tompkins McGuire Wachenfeld & Barry LLP, Newark, 1984—, mng. ptnr. Asst. prosecutor Essex County, N.J., 1964-65; bd. dirs. Ind. Coll. Fund of N.J.; trustee St. Barnabas Corp., St. Barnabas Med. Ctr. and Irvington Gen. Hosp.; mem. Essex County Ethics Com., 1974-77; mem. com. to review State Commn. of Investigation, 1982. Fellow Am. Coll. Trial Lawyers, Am. Bar Found. (state chmn.), Am. Bd. Trial Advocates, Internat. Acad. Trial Lawyers, Internat. Soc. Barristers; mem. ABA, N.J. State Bar Assn. (trustee 1982-89, sec. 1989-90, treas. 1990-91, 2d v.p. 1991-92, 1st v.p. 1992-93, pres.-elect 1993-94, pres. 1994-95), N.J. State Bar Found. (pres. 1988-89), Essex County Bar Assn. (pres. 1975-76), Internat. Assn. Ins. Counsel, Fedn. Ins. Counsel, Def. Rsch. Inst., Maritime Law Assn., U.S. Am. Arbitration Assn., Trial Attys. N.J., Assn. Fed. Bar N.J. (pres. 1985-88), Essex County Country Club (pres. 1983), Newark Club. Roman Catholic. Federal civil litigation, State civil litigation, Insurance. Office: Tompkins McGuire Wachenfeld & Barry LLP 4 Gateway Ctr 100 Mulberry St Newark NJ 07102-4007

MCGUIRL, MARLENE DANA CALLIS, law librarian, educator; b. Hammond, Ind., Mar. 22, 1938; d. Daniel David and Helen Elizabeth (Baludis) Callis; m. James Franklin McGuirl, Apr. 24, 1965. AB, Ind. U., 1959; JD, DePaul U., 1963; MALS, Rosary Coll., 1965; LLM, George Washington U., 1978; postgrad., Harvard U., 1985. Bar: Ill. 1963, Ind. 1964, D.C. 1972. Asst. DePaul Coll. of Law Libr., 1961-62, asst. law libr., 1962-65; ref. law librarian Boston Coll. Sch. Law, 1965-66; libr. dir. D.C. Bar Libr., 1966-70; asst. chief Am.-Brit. Law Divsn. Libr. of Congress, Washington, 1970, chief, 1970-90, environ. cons., 1990—; counsel Cooter & Gell, 1992-93; adminstr. Washington Met. Transit Authority, 1994—. Libr. cons. Nat. Clearinghouse on Poverty Law, OEO, Washington, 1967-69, Northwestern U. Nat. Inst. Edn. in Law and Poverty, 1969, D.C. Office of Corp. Counsel, 1969-70; instr. law librarianship Grad. Sch. of U.S. Dept. of Agr., 1968-72; lectr. legal lit. Cath. U., 1972; adj. asst. prof., 1973-91; lectr. environ. law George Washington U., 1979—; judge Nat. and Internat. Law Moot Ct. Competition, 1976-78, 90—; pres. Hamburger Haven, Inc., Palm Beach, Fla., 1981-91, L'Image de Marlene Ltd., 1986-92, Clinique de Beautè Inc., 1987-92, Heads & Hands Inc., 1987-92, Horizon Design & Mfg. Co., Inc., 1987—; dir. Stoneridge Farm Inc., Gt. Falls, Va., 1984—. Contbr. articles to profl. jours. Mem. Georgetown Citizens Assn.; trustee D.C. Law Students in Ct.; del. Ind. Democratic Conv., 1964. Recipient Meritorious Svc. award Libr. on Congress, 1974, letter of commendation Dirs. of Pers., 1976, cert. of appreciation, 1981-84. Mem. ABA (facilities law libr. Congress com. 1976-89), Fed. Bar Assn. (chpt. council 1972-76), Ill. Bar Assn., Women's Bar Assn. (pres. 1972-73, exec. bd. 1973-77, Outstanding Contbn. to Human Rights award 1975), D.C. Bar Assn., Am. Bar Found., Nat. Assn. Women Lawyers, Am. Assn. Law Libraries (exec. bd. 1973-77), Law Librarians Soc. of Washington (pres. 1971-73), Exec. Women in Govt. Home: 3416 P St NW Washington DC 20007-2705

MCGUNNIGLE, GEORGE FRANCIS, judger; b. Rochester, N.Y., Feb. 22, 1942; s. George Francis and Mary Elizabeth (Curran) McG.; m. Priscilla Ann Lappin, July 13, 1968; children: Cynthia A., Brian P. AB, Boston Coll., 1963; LLB, Georgetown U., 1966; LLM, George Wash. U., 1967. Bar: Conn. 1971, Minn. 1972, U.S. Dist. Ct. D.C. 1967, U.S. Dist. Ct. Conn. 1971, U.S. Dist. Ct. Minn. 1972, U.S. Ct. Appeals (2d cir.) 1971, U.S. Ct. Appeals (8th cir.) 1977, U.S. Supreme Ct. 1986. Asst. U.S. atty. Office of U.S. Atty., Bridgeport, Conn., 1971-72; assoc. Leonard, Street and Deinard, Mpls., 1972-73, ptnr., 1974-2000; judge Fourth Jud. Dist., 2001—. Mem. adv. bd. Minn. Inst. Legal Edn., Mpls., 1986—; mem. bd. editors Bus. Torts Reporter, N.Y.C., 1988—; panelist Minn. Inst. Legal Edn., 1991, moderator, 1989; panelist Leadership Mpls. Pvt. Sector Day Greater Mpls. C. of C., 1987; co-chmn. Minn. Inst. Legal Edn., 1987. Editor: Business Torts Litigation, 1992. Bd. dirs. Cath. Charities, 1997—, Minn. chpt. Arthritis Found., Mpls., 1986-92, 94—, mem. exec. com., 1988-92, 2001—. Lt. JAGC, USN, 1967-71. Recipient Nat. Vol. Svc. citation Arthritis Found., 1992. Mem. ABA (litigation sect., chmn. bus. torts litigation com. 1988-91, divsn. dir. 1991-92, 97-98, coun. 1992-95, sect. of dispute resolution coun. 2000-01). Avocations: reading, boating. E-mal. Federal civil litigation, General civil litigation, State civil litigation. Office: Fourth Judicial Disteinard C-1251 Hennepin County Govt Ctr Minneapolis MN 55487-0422 E-mail: george.mcgunnigle@co.hennepin.mn.us

MCGURK, EUGENE DAVID, JR. lawyer; b. Phila., Feb. 27, 1951; s. Eugene David and Mary Rose (O'Donnell) McG.; m. Kathleen Mary Murphy, Dec. 28, 1973 (dec. Aug. 1978). BA, LaSalle Coll., 1973; JD summa cum laude, Widener U., 1978. Bar: Pa. 1978, N.J. 1978, U.S. Dist. Ct. (ea. dist.) Pa. 1978, U.S. Dist. Ct. N.J. 1978, U.S. Ct. Appeals (3rd cir.) 1981, U.S. Supreme Ct. 1982. Mgmt. analyst Mng. Dirs. Office, Phila., 1974-76; adminstr. Dept. Commerce, 1976-78; asst. city solicitor law, sr. trial atty. City of Phila., 1978-81; with Raynes, McCarty, Binder, Ross & Mundy, Phila., 1981-87, ptnr., 1987—. Guest lectr. Thomas Jefferson U. Med. Sch., 1983, 84, Del. Law Sch., 1980, U. Pa. Dental Sch., Phila., 1985-90, Med. Coll. Pa., Phila.; vis. instr. Dept. Community and Preventive Medicine, 1983-91, Am. Soc. Law and Medicine, 1987—; lectr. internat. law studies program U. Nairobi, Kenya, summer 1990; adj. faculty Sch. Law Widener U., 1993—. Articles editor Del. Jour. Corp. Law, 1977-78; mem. disciplinary bd. hearing commn. Pa. Supreme Ct., 1993-98, chmn., 1995-97. Mem. Camden County Bd. Elections, 1970; bd. of overseers Widener U. Sch. Law, Wilmington, Del., 1985—. Recipient award Fed. Bar Assn., 1978, Mayoral award City of Phila., Am. Judisprudence award, 1978. Mem. ABA, Assn. Trial Lawyers Am., Pa. Bar Assn., N.J. Bar Assn., Camden County Bar Assn., Phila. Bar Assn. (bench bar com. 1982, profl. responsibility com. 1982), Widener U. Sch. Law Alumni Assn. (bd. dirs. 1980—, v.p. 1982-85, pres. 1985-92), Phila. Ctr. City Proprietors Assn. (legis. chair, bd. dirs. 1986-90, adv. coun. legis. liaison 1990—), Phi Kapp Phi, Phi Alpha Delta (scholastic award Read chpt. 1978). Federal civil litigation, General civil litigation, State civil litigation. Office: Raynes McCarty Binder Ross & Mundy PA 1845 Walnut St Ste 2000 Philadelphia PA 19103-4767 also: 116 White Horse Pike Haddon Heights NJ 08035-1928

MCHALE, CATHERINE A. lawyer; b. Chgo., Aug. 20, 1964; d. Edward Michael and Nancy Ruth (Martin) McH. BA, Fordham U., 1992; MDiv, Harvard U., 1996; JD, Columbia U., 1999. Press attaché Karl Lagerfeld N.A., N.Y.C., 1988-90; tutor The Learning Ctr., 1990-92; curatorial asst. Peabody Mus., Cambridge, Mass., 1993-95; asst. to dir. Harvard Native Am. Program, 1995-96; cons. The Drawing Ctr., N.Y.C., 1996-97; with Sonnenschein Nath & Rosenthal, 1999—, Kay Collyer & Boose, N.Y.C. Author book chpt., poems, articles. Vol. The Repatriation Found., N.Y.C., 1997-99, Vol. Lawyers for the Arts, N.Y.C., 1997-99; mentor Mock Trial Program, N.Y.C., 1999; vol. N.Y. Cares, 2000—. Charlotte Newcombe scholar, 1989, Vera Bellus scholar, 1994, Harland Fiske Stone scholar, 1999. Mem. Am. Acad. Religion, Soc. for Study of Native Am. Religious Traditions. Democrat. Avocations: reading, skiing, cooking. Office: Kay Collyer & Boose 1 Dag Hammarskjold Plaza New York NY 10017

MCHALE, MICHAEL JOHN, lawyer; b. N.Y.C., Apr. 14, 1960; s. Michael Joseph and Mary Beatrice (Graddy) McH. BA, U. of the South, 1982; JD, Samford U., 1985. Bar: Ala. 1986, U.S. Dist. Ct. (no., mid. and so. dists.) Ala. 1986, U.S. Ct. Appeals (11th cir.) 1986, Fla. (cert. admiralty and maritime law) 1991, U.S. Dist. Ct. (mid. and so. dists.) Fla. 1991, U.S. Dist. Ct. (no. dist.) Fla. 1997, U.S. Supreme Ct. 1991; cert. admiralty and maritime lawyer Fla. Bar Bd. of Legal Specialization, mediator, arbitrator Fla. Supreme Ct. Assoc. Wagner, Nugent, Johnson, Roth, Romano, Eriksen & Kupfer, West Palm Beach, Fla., 1989-92; ptnr. Whalen & McHale, 1992-95, Daves, Whalen, McHale & Considine, West Palm Beach, 1995-98; sole practitioner Jensen Beach, 1998—; of counsel Deorchis, Corsa & Hillenbrand LLP, Miami, 1998—. Author: Strategic Use of Circumstantial Evidence, 2nd edit., 1991, Evaluating and Settling Personal Injury Claims, 1992, supplement through present, Making Trial Objections, 1993, supplement through present, Expert Witnesses: Direct and Cross Examination, 1993, supplement through present; editor, author: Litigating TMJ Cases, 1993 and yearly supplements. Named one of Outstanding

Young Men of Am., 1988. Mem. ABA (mem. admiralty com.), ATLA, Am. Acad. Fla. Trial Lawyers, Maritime Law Assn. U.S. (procter), Southeastern Admiralty Law Inst., Fla. Bar (admiralty law com. editl. bd., admiralty and maritime cert. com.), Palm. Beach Bar Assn., Martin County Bar Assn., Sigma Nu Phi. Avocation: vessel building. Admiralty, Federal civil litigation, Contracts commercial. Home: 1905 NE River Ct Jensen Beach FL 34957-6423 Office: Deorchis Corsa & Hillenbrand LLP 2650 Biscayne Blvd Miami FL 33137-4531 Fax: 305-571-9250

MCHUGH, JAMES JOSEPH, lawyer; b. Phila., Sept. 15, 1961; s. James Joseph and Helene Anne (Kiernan) McH.; m. Colette Marie Taylor, May 20, 1989; children: Albert Taylor, James Joseph III, Cole Michael. BSME, Drexel U., 1985; JD magna cum laude, Villanova (Pa.) Law Sch., 1992. Bar: Pa. 1992, N.J. 1992, U.S. Dist. Ct. (ea. dist.) Pa., U.S. Dist. Ct. N.J. Ptnr. McHugh Plumbing & Heating, Phila., 1984-89; project mgr. Fluidics Mech Contractors, 1989-92; assoc. Pepper, Hamilton & Scheetz, 1992-94, Beasley, Casey & Erbstein, Phila., 1994—. Author, editor case notes. Mem. adv. com. Penn Pub. Svc. Program, Sch. Law, U. Pa. Named to Order of the Coif, Villanova Law Sch., 1992. Mem. ATLA, Pa. Bar Assn., Phila. Bar Assn. Civil rights, Libel, Personal injury. Home: 65 Brooks Rd Moorestown NJ 08057-3855 Office: Beasley Casey & Erbstein 1125 Walnut St Philadelphia PA 19107-4918 E-mail: jjm@tortlaw.com

MCHUGH, WILLIAM F. legal educator; b. Stamford, Conn., June 23, 1933; s. William Thomas and Dorothy Amelia (Hanson) M.; m. Donna Hubbard, Apr. 10, 1960; children— William, Holly, Brian. B.A. in English Lit., Colgate U., 1956; J.D., Union U., Albany, N.Y., 1959. Bar: N.Y. 1960. Law clk. N.Y. State Supreme Ct., 1960-61; assoc. counsel Cornell U., Ithaca, N.Y., 1962-64; assoc. counsel SUNY, 1964-71; prof. law Am. U., Washington, 1971-73; prof. law Fla. State U., Tallahassee, 1973— ; cons. and lectr. in law; dir. Ctr. Employment Relations and Law. Named Prof. of Yr., Fla. State U. Law Sch., 1976. Mem. N.Y. State Bar Assn., Nat. Assn. Coll. and Univ. Attys., Am. Assn. Law Schs., Soc. Profls. in Dispute Resolution. Episcopalian. Author: Contract Law for Electrical Contractors; contbr. articles to profl. jours. Office: Fla State U Coll Law Tallahassee FL 32306

MCILVAINE, JAMES ROSS, lawyer; b. Youngstown, Ohio, July 22, 1944; s. Earl Eugene and Caroline E. (Clawson) McI.; m. Carol Beth Boyer, June 24, 1967; children: Andrew S., Katherine Erin. BA, Muskingum Coll., 1966; JD cum laude, Ohio State Coll., 1969. Bar: Ohio 1969, U.S. Dist. Ct. (no. dist.) Ohio 1971. Assoc. Oestricher, Seamon, Newman & Knoll, Akron, Ohio, 1969-70; asst. prosecuting atty. Summit County Prosecutor's Office, 1970-71; ptnr. Palecek, McIlvaine, Paul & Hoffman, Co., Wadsworth, 1971—. Mem. citizen's adv. bd. Medina County Correctional Facility Study, 1983; founding trustee Wedsworth City Schs. Performing Arts Found., 1994—; mem. bd. edn. Wadsworth City Sch., 1988—; trustee Wadsworth-Rittmann Hosp., 1999—; bd. dirs. Medina County Law Libr., 1979—83, Wadsworth chpt. ARC, 1981—94. Mem. ATLA (state del. 1985-87, bd. govs. 1987-88), Ohio Acad. Trial lawyers (Editor profl. newsletter 1982-84, chair reginal trial sems. 1980-81, sec. 1981-83, lectr. criminal law sem. 1981, ins. law sem. 1980, 84, 86, negligence law sem. 1984, 86, 88, chair student advocacy divsn. 1976-78, pres. 1984-85, trustee, bd. dirs. 1976-83), Medina County Bar Assn. (pres. 1983, dir., chmn. common pleas ct. rules com., lectr. sms. 1986, 87), Ohio State Bar Assn., Wadsworth Area C. of C. (bd. dirs. 1995—, v.p. 1997-98, pres. 1998-99), Lions. State civil litigation, Family and matrimonial, Personal injury. Office: Palecek McIlvaine Paul & Hoffmann Co LPA 200 Smokerise Dr Ste 200 Wadsworth OH 44282-0031

MCINERNEY, GARY JOHN, lawyer; b. Grand Rapids, Mich., Oct. 4, 1948; s. James Martin and Marjorie (Dumas) McI.; m. Linda McInerny, June 14, 1996; children: Ryan, John, Patrick, Kevin, Molly. BA, Notre Dame U., 1970, JD, 1973. Bar: Mich. 1973, U.S. Dist. Ct. (we. and ea. dists.) Mich. 1973, U.S. Supreme Ct. 1976. Assoc. Varnum, Riddering et al, Grand Rapids, 1973-74; ptnr. Murphy, Burns et al, 1974-86; pres. Gary J. McInerney, P.C., 1986—. Bd. dirs. Mich. Blue Cross/ Blue Shield. Pres. Cath. Social Services, Grand Rapids; v.p. Kent County Legal Aid Soc., Grand Rapids; mem. devel. bd. St. Mary's Hosp., Grand Rapids; 5th congl. dist. chmn. Sesquicentenniel commn. State of Mich., 1984-86; Dem. nominee 5th dist. U.S. Congress, 1984. Mem. Am. Trial Lawyers Assn., Mich. Trial Lawyers Assn., Mich. Bar Assn. (criminal jurisprudence, med. legal, atty. arbitration coms.), Kent County Bar Assn., Grand Rapids Bar Assn., Grand Rapids C. of C. (pres. 1985-86). Roman Catholic. Clubs: Kent Country, Peninsular (Grand Rapids). Federal civil litigation, State civil litigation, General corporate.

MCINTYRE, ANITA GRACE JORDAN, lawyer; b. Louisville, Jan. 29, 1947; d. Blakely Gordan and Shirley Evans (Grubbs) Jordan; m. Kenneth James McIntyre, Oct. 11, 1969; children: Abigail, Jordan Kenneth. BA, Smith Coll., 1969; JD, U. Detroit, 1975. Bar: Mich. 1975, U.S. Dist. Ct. (ea. dist.) Mich. 1975, U.S. Dist. Ct. (we. dist.) Mich. 1979, U.S. Ct. Appeals (6th cir.) 1979. Ptnr. Rollins White & Rollins, Detroit, 1975-79; vis. assoc. prof. Detroit Coll. Law, 1979-81; assoc. Tyler & Canham, Detroit, 1981-82; prin. Anita G. McIntyre, P.C., Grosse Pointe, Mich., 1982-87, 91—; of counsel Nederlander Dodge & Rollins, Detroit, 1987-90; assoc. Damm & Smith, P.C., 1990-91. Hearing panel chmn. Atty. Discipline Bd., 1985—. Editor, author (case notes) U. Detroit Jour. Urban Law, 1975; contbr. articles to profl. jours. Sec. Berry Subdivsn. Assn., Detroit, 1975-77; pres. Smith Coll. Club Detroit, 1982-86; mem. parents bd. U. Liggett Sch., Grosse Pointe, Mich., 1991-95; chmn. polit. action com. Jr. League Detroit, 1998-99. Mem. State Bar Mich., Wayne County (Mich.) Probate Bar Assn., Wayne County Juvenile Trial Lawyers Assn., Edgmont Park Assn. (sec.), Jr. League Detroit (chair pub. affairs com. 1998-2001, vice chair Mich. state pub. affairs com. 1999-2001, chair, 2001—). Episcopalian. Avocations: skiing, swimming, needle point. General civil litigation, Family and matrimonial, Real property. Office: 15324 Mack Ave Ste 201 Detroit MI 48224-3397 E-mail: agmcintyr@cs.com

MCINTYRE, DOUGLAS CARMICHAEL, II, congressman; b. Lumberton, N.C., Aug. 6, 1956; s. Douglas Carmichael and Thelma Riley (Hedgpeth) McI.; m. Lola Denise Strickland, June 26, 1982; children: Joshua Carmichael, Stephen Christopher. BA, U. N.C., 1978, JD, 1981. Bar: N.C. 1981, U.S. Dist. Ct. (ea. dist.) N.C. 1984, U.S. Dist. Ct. (mid. dist.) N.C. 1985., U.S. Ct. Appeals (4th cir.) 1987, U.S. Supreme Ct., 1987. Assoc. Law Office Bruce Huggins, Lumberton, 1981-82, McLean, Stacy, Henry & McLean, Lumberton, 1982-86; ptnr. Price & McIntyre P.A., 1987-89; prin. McIntyre Law Firm, P.A., 1989-96; congressman U.S. Ho. of Reps., 1997—. Mem. law-focused edn. adv. com. N.C. Dept. Pub. Instrn., 1986-87; mem. U.S. Ho. Com. on Agr., 1997—, Nat. Security Com., 1997—; co-chmn. Coalition Task Force on Edn., 1997-98, Congrl. Task Force on Promotion of Fatherhood, Rural Health Care Coalition, 1999—, Democratic Task Force on Children, 1999-2000, Coalition Task Force on Bus. and Tech.; mem. President's Summit on Am.'s Future, 1997. Del. Dem. Nat. Conv., N.Y.C., 1980, N.C. Dems., Raleigh, 1974—; pres. Robeson County Young Dems., Lumberton, 1982; sec.-treas. 7th Congl. Dist. Young Dems., N.C., 1983, chmn., 1984; 2d vice chmn. 7th Congl. Dist. Dems. So. N.C., 1986-89, 1st vice chmn., 1989; mem. state adv. bd. North Carolinians Against Drug and Alcohol Abuse, Raleigh, 1984-85; chmn. Morehead Scholarship Selection Com., Robeson County, 1985-94; deacon, elder, clk. of session Presbyn. Ch.; active Boy Scouts Am., Lumberton, 1983; mem. N.C. Commn. on Children and Youth, 1987-89, N.C. Commn. on the Family, 1989-91; mem. Young Life Lumberton com., 1987-89; chmn. Robeson County U.S. Constn. Bicentennial com., 1986-87; mem. lawyers' adv. com. to N.C. Commn. on Bicentennial of U.S. Constn., 1986-89; bd. dirs. Robeson County Group Home, Lumberton, 1984-87, Lumberton Econ. Advancement for Downtown, Inc., 1987-90, pres., 1988-89, 89-90; chmn. legis. affairs com. C. of C., 1991, 92, 93, bd. dirs., 1992-94; mem. N.C. Mus. of History Assocs., 1987-89; mem. regional selection com. Gov.'s Award for Excellence in Teaching Social Studies, 1991. Morehead Found. scholar, 1974-78; named one of Outstanding Young Men in Am., 1981, 84, 85, 88; Outstanding Young Dem. Robeson County Young Dems., 1984-85; one of State's Outstanding Young Dems. Young Dems. N.C., 1984, 85; recipient Algernon Sydney Sullivan award U. N.C., 1978, Outstanding Young North Carolinian award N.C. Jaycees, 1988, Outstanding Young North Carolinians, Heart Robeson Jaycees, 1988, Nat. Bicentennial Leadership award for Individual Achievement Coun. for Advancement of Citizenship and Ctr. for Civic Edn., Washington, 1987, Gov.'s Outstanding Vol. Svc. award, 1989, Thomas Jefferson award Food Distbrs. Internat., 1998, Guardian of Small Bus. award, Nat. Fedn. Independent Bus., 1997-99, Nat. Rural Health Legislative award, 1999, Outstanding Health Svc. award Cmty. Ptnrs. Health Net, 2000, Spirit of Enterprise award, U.S. C. of C., 1997-98, Super Hero award Nat. Assn. Cmty. Health Ctrs., 2001, Quality Pub. Svc./Pub. Edn. and Health Care award Am. Fedn. Tchrs., 2001. Mem. ABA (exec. com. citizenship edn. com. 1985-87, nat. cmty. law week com. 1982-83), Internat. Platform Assn., N.C. Bar Assn. (chmn. youth edn. and constn. bicentennial com. 1986-87, youth edn. com., exec. coun. young lawyers divsn. 1986-87), Robeson County Bar Assn. (founder, chmn. citizenship edn. com. 1982-94, law day com.), 16th Jud. Dist. Bar Assn., N.C. Acad. Trial Lawyers, N.C. Coll. Advocacy, Christian Legal Soc. (state adv. bd. 1986-90, state pres. 1987), Lumberton C. of C. (bd. dirs. 1992-94), Order of Old Well, Lumberton Rotary Club (bd. dirs. 1995-96), Phi Beta Kappa, Phi Eta Sigma. Avocations: tennis, snow skiing, softball, dancing, Bible study. Home: 1701 N Chestnut St Lumberton NC 28358-3839 Office: 228 Cannon Washington DC 20515-3307 E-mail: congmcintyre@mail.house.gov

MCKAY, JOHN, lawyer; b. Seattle, June 19, 1956; s. John Larkin and Kathleen (Tierney) M. BA, U. Wash., 1978; JD, Creighton U., 1982. Bar: Wash. 1982, U.S. Dist. Ct. (we. dist.) Wash. 1982, U.S. Supreme Ct. 1990, U.S. Ct. Appeals (9th cir.) 1990, D.C. 1999. Ptnr. Lane Powell Spears Lubersky, Seattle, 1982-92, Cairncross & Hempelmann, Seattle, 1992-97; pres. Legal Svcs. Corp., Washington, 1997—2001; U.S. atty. We. dist. Wash. U.S. Dept. Justice, 2001—. White House fellow, Washington, 1989-90. Mem. ABA (bd. govs. 1991-94), Wash. State Bar Assn. (pres. young lawyers divsn. 1988-89). Republican. Roman Catholic. Avocations: soccer, golf. General civil litigation. Office: US Atty 601 Union St Ste 5100 Seattle WA 98101-3903*

MCKAY, JOHN DOUGLAS, lawyer; b. Wheeling, W.Va., Feb. 27, 1960; s. Douglas and Margaret Ann McK.; m. Jennifer Hall, June 13, 1987; children: John Wallace, Megan Diane, Hannah Nadine. BA with distinction, U. Va., 1982; JD, U. Maine, 1985. Bar: W.Va. 1985, Maine 1985, U.S. Dist. Ct. (so. dist.) W.Va. 1985, U.S. Dist. Ct. Maine 1985, U.S. Ct. Appeals (1st cir.) 1986, Va. 1988, U.S. Ct. Appeals (4th cir.) 1988, U.S. Dist. Ct. (we. dist.) Va. 1988, Colo. 1997, Fla. 1999. Assoc. Petruccelli, Cohen, Erler & Cox, Portland, Maine, 1985-88, Taylor & Zunka, Ltd., Charlottesville, Va., 1988-91; ptnr. McKay & Cattano PLC, 1991-97; prin. McKay Law Offices, 1997—. Founder, editor (legal newsletter) Equine Law & Bus. Letter, 1990-95; contbr. articles to profl. jours. Elder Presbyn. Ch. Recipient Best Adv. award U. Maine Sch. of Law, 1988. Mem. Va. State Bar (7th dist. disciplinary com. 1994-2000), W.Va. State Bar, Charlottesville-Albemarle Bar Assn. (bd. dirs. 1994-96), Thomas Jefferson Inn of Ct. (past pres). General civil litigation, Contracts commercial, Communications. Office: McKay Law Offices 205 E High St PO Box 2018 Charlottesville VA 22902-2018

MCKAY, JOHN JUDSON, JR. lawyer; b. Anderson, S.C., Aug. 13, 1939; s. John Judson and Polly (Plowden) McK.; m. Jill Hall Ryon, Aug. 3, 1961 (div. Dec. 1980); children: Julia Plowden, Katherine Henry, William Ryon, Elizabeth Hall; m. Jane Leahey, Feb. 18, 1982; children: Andrew Leahey, Jennifer McFaddin. AB in History, U. S.C., 1960, JD cum laude, 1966. Bar: S.C. 1966, U.S. Dist. Ct. S.C. 1966, U.S. Ct. Appeals (4th cir.) 1974, U.S. Supreme Ct. 1981, U.S. Dist. Ct. (so. dist.) Ga. 1988, U.S. Ct. Appeals (11th cist.) 1990. Assoc. Haynsworth, Perry, Bryant, Marion & Johnstone, Greenville, S.C., 1966-70; ptnr. Rainey, McKay, Britton, Gibbes & Clarkson, P.A. predecessor, 1970-78; sole practice Hilton Head Island, S.C., 1978-80; ptnr. McKay & Gertz, P.A., 1980-81, McKay & Mullen, P.A., Hilton Head Island, 1981-88, McKay & Taylor, Hilton Head Island, 1988-91; pvt. practice, 1991—. Editor-in-chief U. S.C. Law Rev., 1966; contbr. articles to legal jours. E-mail: jmckay@mckaylawfirm.com. Served to lt. (j.g.) USNR, 1961-64; lt. comdr. Res. (ret.). Mem. ABA, S.C. Bar Assn. (pres. young lawyers sect. 1970, exec. com. 1971-72, assoc. mem. grievance and disciplinary com. 1983-87), S.C. Bar, Beaufort County Bar Assn., Hilton Head Bar Assn., Assn. Trial Lawyers Am., S.C. Trial Lawyers Assn., S.C. Bar Found. (pres. 1977), Blue Key, Wig and Robe, Phi Delta Phi. Episcopalian. Clubs: Poinsett (Greenville). Federal civil litigation, State civil litigation, Personal injury. Home: 17 Foxbriar Ln Hilton Head Island SC 29926 Office: 203 Watersedge Hilton Head Island SC 29928-3541

MCKAY, MICHAEL DENNIS, lawyer; b. Omaha, May 12, 1951; s. John Larkin and Kathleen (Tierney) McK.; m. Christy Ann Cordwin, Apr. 22, 1978; children: Kevin Tierney, Kathleen Lindsay, John Larkin. BA in Polit. Sci. with distinction, U. Wash., 1973; JD, Creighton U., 1976. Bar: Wash. 1976, U.S. Dist. Ct. (we. dist.) Wash. 1978, U.S. Dist. Ct. (ea. dist.) Wash. 1982, U.S. Ct. Appeals (9th cir.) 1982, U.S. Supreme Ct. 1993. Sr. dep. pros. atty. King County, Seattle, 1976-81; ptnr. McKay & Gaitan, 1981-89; U.S. atty. we. dist. Wash., 1989-93; ptnr. Lane Powell Spears Lubersky, 1993-95, McKay Chadwell PLLC, Seattle, 1995—. Bd. dirs. Mental Health North, Seattle, 1982-85, St. Joseph Sch. Bd., 1984-87, Our Lady of Fatima Sch. Commn., 1994-97, Creighton U., 1988-90; mem. stadium adv. bd. Seattle Kingdome, 1987-89; mem. U.S. Atty. Gen. Adv. Com., 1991-93, vice chmn., 1992; mem. Washington Citizens' Commn. on Salaries for Elected Officials, 1997—; vice chmn., 1999—; vice chmn. Seattle Expert Rev. Panel, 1999; co-chair Washington State George W. Bush Campaign, 2000. Mem. Creighton U. Alumni Assn. (pres. 1988-90, nat. alumni bd. 1988-92), Wash. Athletic Club, Columbia Tower Club. Republican. Roman Catholic. Avocations: swimming, golf. Federal civil litigation, State civil litigation, Criminal. Office: McKay Chadwell PLLC 701 5th Ave Seattle WA 98104-7097 E-mail: mckay@mckay-chadwell.com

MCKAY, MONROE GUNN, federal judge; b. Huntsville, Utah, May 30, 1928; s. James Gunn and Elizabeth (Peterson) McK.; m. Lucile A. Kinnison, Aug. 6, 1954; children: Michele, Valanne, Margaret, James, Melanie, Nathan, Bruce, Lisa, Monroe. B.S., Brigham Young U., 1957; J.D., U. Chgo., 1960. Bar: Ariz. 1961. Law clk. Ariz. Supreme Ct., 1960-61; assoc. firm Lewis & Roca, Phoenix, 1961-66, ptnr., 1968-74; assoc. prof. Brigham Young U., 1974-76, prof., 1976-77; judge U.S. Ct. Appeals for 10th Cir., Denver, 1977-91, chief judge, 1991-94, sr. judge, 1994—. Mem. Phoenix Community Council Juvenile Problems, 1968-74; pres. Ariz. Assn. for Health and Welfare, 1970-72; dir. Peace Corps, Malawi, Africa, 1966-68; bd. dirs., pres. Maricopa county Legal Aid Soc., 1972-74. Served with USMCR, 1946-48. Mem. Ariz. Bar Assn. Mem. LDS Ch. Office: US Ct Appeals 10th Cir Fed Bldg 125 S State St Ste 6012 Salt Lake City UT 84138-1181*

MCKEAGUE, DAVID WILLIAM, judge; b. Pitts., Nov. 5, 1946; s. Herbert William and Phyllis (Forsyth) McK.; m. Nancy L. Palmer, May 20, 1989; children: Mike, Melissa, Sarah, Laura, Elizabeth, Adam. BBA, U. Mich., 1968, JD, 1971. Bar: Mich. 1971, U.S. Dist. Ct. (we. dist.) Mich. 1972, U.S. Dist. Ct. (ea. dist.) 1978, U.S. Ct. Appeals (6th cir.) 1988. Assoc. Foster, Swift, Collins & Smith, Lansing, Mich., 1971-76, ptnr., 1976-92, sec.-treas., 1990-92; judge U.S. Dist. Ct., Western Dist. Mich., Lansing, 1992—. Adj. prof. Thomas M. Cooley Law Sch., Mich. State U. Detroit Coll. Law. Nat. com. U. Mich. Law Sch. Fund, 1980-92; gen. counsel Mich. Rep. Com., 1989-92; adv. coun. Wharton Ctr., Mich. State U., 1996—. Mem. FBA (bd. dirs. Western Mich. chpt. 1991—), Mich. Bar Assn., Am. Inns of Ct. (pres. Mich. State U. Detroit Coll. of Law chpt. 1999-01), Country Club Lansing (bd. govs. 1988-92, 96—), The Federalist Soc. for Law and Pub. Studies (lawyers divsn. Mich. chpt. 1996—). Roman Catholic. Office: US Dist Ct 315 W Allegan St Lansing MI 48933-1500

MCKEE, CATHERINE LYNCH, law educator, lawyer; b. Boston, June 7, 1962; d. Robert Emmett and Anne Gayle (Tanner) Lynch; m. Bert K. McKee Jr., Dec. 25, 1990; children: Timothy Kingston, Shannon Lancaster. BA in Biol. Sci., U. Calif. Berkeley, 1984; JD, U. San Diego, 1988. Bar: Calif. 1988, U.S. Dist. Ct. (cen., so. and ea. dists.) Calif. 1989, U.S. Ct. Appeals (9th cir.) 1989. Assoc. Parkinson, Wolf, Lazar & Leo, L.A., 1988-89, McCormick & Mitchell, San Diego, 1989-91; prof., mock trial coach, paralegal program dir. Mt. San Antonio Coll., Walnut, Calif., 1994—. Certification review hearing officer, Orange County, 1994—; legal counsel Imperial Valley Lumber Co., Valley Lumber and Truss Co., 1998—; coach nat. champion C.C. mock trial team, 2000. Contbr. weekly newspaper column, 1993-99; prodr., star videos An Attorney's Guide to Legal Research on the Internet, 1998, 99; co-author: Jeff and Catherine's World's Best List of Legal (and Law-related) Internet Sites. Chair scholarship com. U. Calif. Alumni Assn., Diamond Bar area, 1995—; capt. auction team SCATS Gymnastics, 2000—. Named Cmty. Person of Yr. Diamond Bar C. of C., 1995. Mem. State Bar Calif. (probation monitor 1993—), Ea. Bar Assn. L.A. (trustee 2000—), Am. Inns of Ct., Calif. Assn. Lanterman-Petris-Short Hearing Officers. Avocations: weight lifting, photography, reading. Office: Mount San Antonio Coll 1100 N Grand Ave Walnut CA 91789-1341 E-mail: cmckee@mtsac.edu

MCKEE, FRANCIS JOHN, medical association consultant, lawyer; b. Bklyn., Aug. 31, 1943; s. Francis Joseph and Catherine (Giles) McK.; m. Antoinette Mary Sancis; children: Lisa Ann, Francis Dominic, Michael Christopher, Thomas Joseph. AB, Stonehill Coll., 1965; JD, St. John's U., 1970. Bar: N.Y. 1971. Assoc. Samuel Weinberg, Esquire, Bklyn., 1970-71, Finch & Finch, Esquire, Long Island City, N.Y., 1971-72; staff atty. Med. Soc. of State of N.Y., Lake Success, 1972-77; prin. Francis J. McKee Assocs., Clinton, 1984—; exec. dir. Suffolk Physicians Rev. Orgn., East Islip, 1977-81, N.Y. State Soc. Surgeons, Inc., Clinton, 1981-2000, N.Y. State Soc. Orthopaedic Surgeons, Inc., Clinton, 1981-2000, Upstate N.Y. chpt. ACS, Inc., Clinton, 1981-2000, N.Y. State Ophthalmol. Soc., 1984-92, N.Y. State Soc. Obstetricians and Gynecologists, 1985-2001, Orthopac of N.Y., 1986-2000, Nat. Com. for the Preservation Orthopaedic Practice, New Hartford, N.Y., 1989-2000; L.I. Ophthalmological Soc., 1994-2000. Coun. Suffolk County Med. Soc., Hauppauge, N.Y., 1977-81. With U.S. Army, 1966-68. Mem. N.Y. State Bar Assn., Oneida County Bar Assn., Am. Soc. Assn. Execs., Am. Assn. Med. Soc. Execs., Nat. Health Lawyers Assn., Skenandoa Club, Am. Legion. Republican. Roman Catholic. Home and Office: 19 Mulberry St Clinton NY 13323-1532 Fax: (315) 859-1137. E-mail: Frank4Mets@aol.com

MCKEE, ROGER CURTIS, retired federal judge; b. Waterloo, Iowa, Feb. 11, 1931; s. James A. and Leonace (Burrell) McK.; m. Roberta Jeanne Orvis, Sept. 3, 1954; children: Andrea Jane, Brian Curtis, Paul Robert. BA, State Coll. of Iowa, 1955; MA, U. Ill., 1960; JD, U. San Diego, 1968. Bar: Calif. 1970, U.S. Dist. Ct. (so. dist.) Calif. 1969, U.S. Ct. Appeals (9th cir.) 1971. Telegrapher, agt. Ill. Cen. R.R., 1950-55; tng. asst. No. Ill. Gas Co., Aurora, 1959-60; with indsl. rels. dept. Convair div. Gen. Dynamics Corp., San Diego, 1960-68; contract adminstr. and supr. Datagraphix div. Gen. Dynamics Corp., 1968-69, asst. counsel, 1969-70; ptnr. Powell & McKee, 1970-75, Millsberg, Dickstein & McKee, San Diego, 1975-83; magistrate judge U.S. Dist. Ct. for So. Dist. Calif., 1983-97; presiding magistrate judge, 1993-97. Bd. trustees So. Calif. Presbyn. Homes, L.A., 1979-81; moderator Presbytery of San Diego, 1980. Capt. USNR, 1949-85. Mem. Calif. Bar Assn., Fed. Magistrate Judges Assn., Navy League U.S., Naval Res. Officers Assn., Res. Officers Assn., Dixieland Jazz Soc. (bd. dirs. San Diego chpt. 1984—). Republican. Fax: (858) 277-0444. E-mail: rcmckee10@cs.com

MCKEE, THEODORE A. federal judge; b. 1947; B.A., SUNY, Cortland, 1969; J.D. magna cum laude, Syracuse U. Coll. of Law, 1975. Dir. of minority recruitment & admissions SUNY, Binghamton, 1969-72; atty. Wolf, Block, Schorr & Solis-Cohen, Phila., 1975-77; asst. U.S. atty., Eastern Dist. PA, 1977-80; asst. U.S. atty., Eastern Dist. Gen. Crimes Unit, Narcotics and Firearms Unit, then Polit. Corruption Unit; lecturer Rutgers U. Coll. of Law, 1980-91; dep. city solicitor Law Dept., Phila., 1980-83; gen. counsel Phila. Parking Auth., 1983; judge Ct. of Common Pleas, 1st Jud. Dist, PA, 1984-94, judge major felony program, 1986, judge orphans' ct. divsn., 1992; judge U.S. Ct. Appeals (3d cir.), Phila., 1994—. Bd. dirs. Diagnostic and Rehab. Ctr. of Phila. Trustee Edna McConnell Clark Found.; mem. adv. bd. City Yr. for Phila. Mem. ABA, Nat. Bar Assn., Am. Law Inst., Barristers' Assn. Phila., Temple Inn of Ct., Crime Prevention Assn. (bd. dirs.). Office: 601 Market St Rm 20614 Philadelphia PA 19106-1715

MCKEEVER, JOSEPH FRANCIS, III, lawyer; b. Weymouth, Mass., July 21, 1950; s. Joseph Francis Jr. and Virginia Agnes McK.; m. Janice Danielle Kearney, Oct. 17, 1970. BA, George Washington U., 1972, JD, 1978. Bar: D.C. 1978, U.S. Supreme Ct. 1989. Editor Congl. Rsch. Svc. Libr. Congress, Washington, 1974-78; law clk. Honorable Harry Wood U.S. Ct. Claims, 1978-79, Honorable Wilson Cowen U.S. Ct. Claims, Washington, 1979-80; atty. Sutherland, Asbill & Brennan, 1980-85; ptnr. Davis & Harman LLP, 1985—. Author, editor: Annuities Answer Book, 1999; contbr. articles to profl. jours. Mem. ABA (chair sect. on taxation com. on ins. cos. 2000—). Avocations: gardening, bicycling. Corporate taxation. Home: 2812 34th Pl NW Washington DC 20007-1405 Office: Davis & Harman LLP Willard Office Bldg 1455 Pennsylvania Ave NW Washington DC 20004-1008

MCKELVEY, JUDITH GRANT, lawyer, educator, university dean; b. Milw., July 19, 1935; d. Lionel Alexander and Bernadine R. (Verdun) Grant. B.S. in Philosophy, U. Wis., 1957, J.D., 1959. Bar: Wis. 1959, Calif. 1968. Atty. FCC, Washington, 1959-62; adj. prof. U. Md., Europe, 1965; prof. law Golden Gate U. Sch. Law, San Francisco, 1968-99, dean, 1974-81. Mem. State Jud. Nominees Evaluation Commn., 1981-82. Contbr. to: Damages Book, 1975, 76. Bd. dirs. San Francisco Neighborhood Legal Assistance Found. Fellow Am. Bar Found.; mem. ABA, Wis. Bar Assn., Calif. Bar Assn., San Francisco Bar Assn. (dir. 1975-77, chmn. legis. com., sec.-treas., pres.-elect 1980-83, pres. 1984), Calif. Women Lawyers (1st pres.), Law in a Free Soc. (exec. com.), Continuing Edn. of Bar (chmn. real estate subcom., mem. joint adv. com.), Legal Svcs. to Children Inc. (pres. 1987-89), San Francisco Neighborhood Legal Assistance Found. (dir. and exec. com. 1985-87), Lawyers Com. for Urban Affairs (dir. and exec. com. 1985-87, co-chairperson 1988-90). Office: Golden Gate U Sch Law 536 Mission St San Francisco CA 94105-2921

MCKENDRY, JOHN H., JR. lawyer, educator; b. Grand Rapids, Mich., Mar. 24, 1950; s. John H. and Lois R. (Brandel) McK.; m. Linda A. Schmalzer, Aug. 11, 1973; children: Heather Lynn, Shannon Dawn, Sean William. BA cum laude, Albion Coll., 1972; JD cum laude, U. Mich., 1975. Bar: Mich. 1975. Assoc., then ptnr. Landman, Latimer, Clink & Robb, Muskegon, Mich., 1976-85; ptnr. Warner, Norcross & Judd, 1985—. Dir. debate Mona Shores High Sch., Muskegon, 1979-90; adj. prof. of taxation (employee benefits), Grand Valley State U., 1988—; debate instr. Muskegon C.C., 1999-2001. Pres. local chpt. Am. Cancer Soc., 1979; bd. dirs. West Shore Symphony, 1993-2000, v.p. 1995-97, pres., 1997-99; bd. dirs. Cath. Social Svcs., 1998—; chair profl. divsn. United Way, 1994, 98. Recipient Disting. Service award Muskegon Jaycees, 1981; named 1 of 5 Outstanding Young Men in Mich., Mich. Jaycees. 1982; named to Hall of Fame, Mich. Speech Coaches, 1986, Diamond Key Coach Nat. Forensic League, 1987. Mem. ABA, Mich. Bar Assn., Muskegon County Bar Assn. (dir. 1992-98, pres. 1996-97), Muskegon C. of C. (bd. dirs. 1982-88), Mich. Interscholastic Forensic Assn. (treas. 1979-86), Optimists (pres. 1992). Republican. Roman Catholic. Pension, profit-sharing, and employee benefits. Home: 1575 Brookwood Dr Muskegon MI 49441-5276 Office: Warner Norcross & Judd LLP PO Box 900 400 Terrace Pla Muskegon MI 49443-0900 E-mail: mckendjh@wnj.com

MCKENNA, FREDERICK GREGORY, lawyer, consultant; b. Chgo., Oct. 4, 1952; s. Frederick Hilary and Jean Elizabeth (Henneberry) McK.; m. Cornelia Ann Burns, Nov. 17, 1984; children: Kieran Padraig, Conor Burns. BA with honors, Coll. Holy Cross, 1974; JD, Georgetown U., 1978; postgrad., U. Nev., Las Vegas, U. Denver. Bar: D.C. 1978, Md. 1981, Nev. 1986, U.S. Supreme Ct. 1987, Colo. 1993. Assoc. Joseph, McDermott et al, Washington, 1979-82, Hudson & Creyke, Washington, 1982-85; sr. counsel Reynolds Elec. & Engring. Co., Inc., Las Vegas, 1985-90; dep. gen. counsel EG&G Rocky Flats, Golden, Colo., 1990-92, v.p., gen. counsel, 1992-96; ptnr. Hall & Evans, Denver, 1996—. Mem. Community Svc. Commn., Md., 1984-85. Mem. ABA, D.C. Bar Assn. (D.C. procurement com.), Mensa. Republican. Roman Catholic. Avocation: history. Environmental, Government contracts and claims. Home: 5954 Wood Sorrel Way Littleton CO 80123-6758 Office: Hall & Evans 1200 17th St Ste 1700 Denver CO 80202-5817

MCKENNA, MATTHEW MORGAN, lawyer; b. Washington, Apr. 29, 1950; s. James Aloysius and Rebecca (Rial) McK.; m. Nancy Fitzpatrick, Sept. 11, 1976; children: Matthew, James, Christine, Connor. BA, Hamilton Coll., 1972; JD, Georgetown U., 1975, LLM, 1978. Bar: N.Y. 1977. Clk. to Hon. Fred B. Ugast, Superior Ct., Washington, 1975-76; assoc. Olwine, Connelly, N.Y.C., 1976-79; assoc. Winthrop, Stimson, Putnam & Roberts, N.Y.C., 1979-83, ptnr., 1984-93; v.p. taxes PepsiCo, Purchase, N.Y., 1993-97, sr. v.p., treas. 1998-2001, sr. v.p. fin. 2001-; adj. prof. Sch. Law, Fordham U., N.Y.C., 1983-94. Trustee Merrill Lynch Found., 1986-95, Mt. St. Mary's Coll., Emmitsburg, Md., 1994—. Mem. ABA (tax sect.), N.Y. State Bar Assn. (chmn. com. on fgn. activities of U.S. taxpayers), Assn. Bar City N.Y. (com. internat. taxation). Corporate taxation. Home: 35 Valley Rd Bronxville NY 10708-2226 Office: PepsiCo 700 Anderson Hill Rd Purchase NY 10577-1444

MCKENNA, WILLIAM FRANCIS, lawyer; b. Meriden, Conn., May 14, 1910; s. Francis Joseph and Alice Nancy (Downes) McK.; m. Catherine Agnes Donahue, June 25, 1935 (dec.); children: William Francis (dec.), Daniel Joseph. PhB, Yale U., 1930, JD, 1932. Bar: Conn. 1932, Md. 1940, U.S. Dist. Ct. D.C. 1950, U.S. Ct. Appeals (D.C. cir.) 1951, U.S. Ct. Mil. Appeals 1953, U.S. Supreme Ct. 1938. Assoc. Buckley, Creedon & Danaher, Hartford, Conn., 1932-35; atty., counsel pub. loans sect. RFC, Washington, 1935-42; chief airports br. War Assets Adminstrn., 1945-47; counsel U.S. Senate Com. on Banking and Currency, 1947-57; assoc. Ford Motor Co., 1957-58; house counsel Nat. Assn. Mut. Savs. Banks, N.Y.C., 1958-59, dir.-counsel Washington, 1959-63; gen. counsel, v.p., sec. Nat. Savs. and Loan League, 1963-75; assoc. Housley, Goldberg & Kantarian PC, 1976-86; pvt. practice Silver Spring, Md., 1986—. Adminstr. asst. to U.S. Senator William Benton, Washington, 1950, counsel U.S. Congl. Joint Com. on Def. Prodn., 1950-51; commdg. officer USNR Law Co. 5-11, Washington, 1956-57, 64-65; chmn. exec. com. Knickerbocker Fed. Savs. and Loan Assn., N.Y.C., 1980. Editor: (periodical) Nat. League Legal Bull., 1973—75; co-author, editor: Frank J. McKenna 1884-1967, 1968. Pres. Conn. Dem. in D.C., 1939-40; lector, server St. Matthews Cathedral, Washington, 1968-86; extraordinary minister St. Michaels Roman Cath. Ch. Silver Spring, 1986, liturgy com., 1982-99. Capt. USNR, 1943-45, PTO. Mem. Inter-Am. Bar Assn., D.C. Bar Assn., Assn. Former Senate Aides, Holy Name Soc., Univ. Club, Exchequer Club (chancellor 1962-63), Phi Beta Kappa. Home and Office: 8004 Park Crest Dr Silver Spring MD 20910-5415

MCKENZIE, JAMES FRANKLIN, lawyer; b. Mobile, Ala., May 3, 1948; s. Frank L. McKenzie and Mary K. (Crow) McKenzie O'Neal; m. Randy Jo Jones, June 25, 1977; children: Katherine J., J. Alistair. BA magna cum laude, U. W. Fla., 1970; JD with honors, U. Fla., 1973. Bar: Fla. 1973, U.S. Dist. Ct. (no. dist.) Fla. 1973, U.S. Ct. Appeals (5th cir.) 1975, U.S. Ct. Appeals (11th cir.) 1982, U.S. Supreme Ct. 1988. Lectr. bus. law U. Fla., Gainesville, 1972-73; assoc. Levin, Warfield et al, Pensacola, Fla., 1973-76; ptnr. Myrick & McKenzie, PA, 1976-82, McKenzie & Taylor, PA, Pensacola, 1982—. Contbr. chpts. to books, articles to profl. jours. Pres. N.W. Fla. Easter Seal Soc., Pensacola, 1975; bd. dirs. Five Flags Sertoma Club, 1977; trustee Fla. Lawyers Action Group, Tallahassee, 1996-97; adv. bd. Lupus Soc., N.W. Fla., 1992. Mem. ABA, ATLA (pres. club), Acad. Fla. Trial Lawyers (bd. dirs. 1986-93, 2000—, exec. com. 1990-91, coll. diplomates, Silver Eagle award 1989, ABCD award 1991), 1st Cir. Acad. Trial Lawyers (founding mem., pres. 1984), Fla. Bar Assn. (cert. in civil trial law), Escambia-Santa Rosa Bar Assn., Nat. Bd. Trial Advocacy (cert. civil trial advocacy), Civil Justice Found. (founding sponsor), Million Dollar Advocates Forum, Order of Coif, Pensacola Country Club, Phi Kappa Phi, Omicron Delta Kappa, Phi Delta Phi, Phi Delta Phi. Republican. Methodist. General civil litigation, Insurance, Personal injury. Home: 12 Tristan Way Pensacola Beach FL 32561-5121 Office: McKenzie & Taylor PA 905 E Hatton St Pensacola FL 32503-3931 E-mail: jfm01@bellsouth.net

MCKENZIE, ROBERT ERNEST, lawyer; b. Cheboygan, Mich., Dec. 7, 1947; s. Alexander Orlando and Edna Jean (Burt) McK.; m. Theresia Wolf, Apr. 26, 1975; 1 child, Robert A. BA in Personnel Adminstrn., Mich. State U., 1970; JD with high honors, Ill. Inst. Tech., 1979. Bar: Ill. 1979, U.S. Dist. Ct. (no. dist.) Ill. 1979, U.S. Tax Ct. 1979, U.S. Ct. Appeals (7th cir.) 1979, U.S. Supreme Ct. 1984; lic. pvt. pilot. Revenue officer IRS, Chgo., 1972-78; ptnr. McKenzie & McKenzie, 1979-2000, Arnstrin & Lehr, 2000—. Lectr. Tax Seminars Inst., Chgo., 1984—. Author: Representation Before the Collection Divison of the IRS, 1989; co-author: Representing the Audited Taxpayer Before the IRS, 1990; contbr. articles to profl. jours. Mem. tax adv. com. Nat. Bankruptcy Rev. Commn., 1997; del. Rep. Nat. Conv., Detroit, 1980, Ill. State Rep. Conv., Peoria, 1980. Served with U.S. Army, 1970. Recipient scholarship Mich. State U., 1966-70, State of Mich., 1966-70, Silas Strawn scholarship ITT, 1977. Mem. ABA (chmn. employment tax com. tax sect. 1992-94, co-chmn. bankruptcy task force 1997-98, coun. tax sect. 1998-2001), Chgo. Bar Assn. (chmn. com. devel. tax com. 1996-97), N.W. Suburban Bar Assn., Fed. Bar Assn. (tax com.), Rotary (pres. Norridge club 1985-86). Avocation: genealogy. Corporate taxation, Personal income taxation. Office: Ste 1200 120 S Riverside Plz Chicago IL 60606 E-mail: remckenzie@arnstein.com

MCKEON, THOMAS JOSEPH, lawyer, broadcaster, detective; b. Indpls., Feb. 3, 1948; s. Thomas Michael and Mary Rose (Luzar) McK. BA, Ind. U., 1970; JD cum laude, Ind. U.-Indpls., 1974. Bar: Ind. 1974, U.S. Dist. Ct. (so. dist.) Ind. 1974, U.S. Supreme Ct. 1979. Assoc. Nisenbaum & Brown, Indpls., 1974-76, Osborn & Hiner, Indpls., 1976-82; counsel Am. Family Ins., Indpls., 1982— ; asst. counsel Radio Earth Internat. Inc., Radio Earth Curacao, Netherlands Antilles, 1985—. Author: Post Traumatic Stress Disorder: Real or Imagined, 1986, Repetition Strain As A Compensable Injury, 1987; contbr. articles to profl. jours. Mem. ABA, Assn. Trial Lawyers Am. (assoc.), Ind. Bar Assn., Ind. Def. Lawyers Assn. Inc., Ind. Trial Lawyers Assn., Indpls. Bar Assn., Def. Research & Trial Lawyers Assn., Am. Corp. Counsel Assn., Ind. Assn. Pvt. Detectives, San Diego Turtle and Tortoise Soc., Ind. Arson and Crime Assn. Communications, Insurance, Arson, fraud. Office: 7330 Shadeland Sta Indianapolis IN 46256-3919

MCKEONE, KERI MARIE, lawyer; b. Lansing, Mich., Aug. 12, 1969; d. Gerald Joseph McKeone and Patricia Anne Ballard; m. David Eric Katchman, Nov. 15, 1997. BA, U. Mich., 1992; JD, Mich. State U., 1996. Bar: Mich. 1996. Atty. GKN Automotive, Inc., Auburn Hills, Mich., 1997; staff atty. Entertainment Publs., Inc., Troy, 1998—. Mem. State Bar Mich. Avocation: tennis. Contracts commercial, General corporate, Intellectual property. Home: 3325 Thomas Ave Berkley MI 48072 Office: Entertainment Publs Inc 2125 Butterfield Rd Troy MI 48084

MCKEOWN, H. MARY, lawyer, educator; b. West Palm Beach, Fla., Sept. 17, 1952; d. Honore Stephen McKeown and Margaret Berg McKeown Growney; m. Jon Henry Barber, Sept. 18, 1981; children: Sean Patrick, Mary Kathleen. AA, St. Petersburg Jr. Coll., Fla., 1970; BA in Polit. Sci. and Sociology, U. South Fla., 1972; JD cum laude, Samford U., 1976. Bar: Fla. 1976, U.S. Dist. Ct. (mid. dist.) Fla. 1977, U.S. Ct. Appeals (5th and 11th cirs.) 1981, U.S. Supreme Ct. 1992. Asst. state atty. 6th Jud. Ct., Clearwater, Fla., 1976-90; ptnr. Growney, McKeown & Barber, St. Petersburg, 1976—. Adj. prof. Stetson Coll. of Law, St. Petersburg, 1990—. Chairperson Child Welfare Std. and Tng. Coun., 1995-98; mem. Health and Human Svcs. Bd., nominee qualifications review com. Dist. 5, 1992—; mem. Study Commn. Child Welfare, 1990-91; Suncoast Girl Scout leader, 1991—. Recipient Victim Advocacy award Pinellas County Victims Rights Coalition, 1984, Law and Order award Elks, Pinellas County, 1991. Mem. ABA, ATLA, Acad. Fla. Trial Lawyers, Fla. Bar Assn., St. Petersburg Bar Assn., Phi Alpha Delta. Personal injury. Office: 7455 38th Ave N Saint Petersburg FL 33710-1228

MCKEOWN, MARY MARGARET, federal judge; b. Casper, Wyo., May 11, 1951; d. Robert Mark and Evelyn Margaret (Lipsack) McK.; m. Peter Francis Cowhey, June 29, 1985; 1 child, Megan Margaret. BA in Internat. Affairs and Spanish, U. Wyo., 1972; JD, Georgetown U., 1975. Bar: Wash. 1975, D.C. 1982. Assoc. Perkins Coie, Seattle, 1975-79, Washington, 1979-80; White House fellow U.S. Dept. Interior and White House, 1980-81; ptnr., mem. exec. com. Perkins Coie, Seattle, 1981-98, mng. dir. strategic planning and client rels., 1990-95; judge U.S. Ct. Appeals for 9th Circuit, from 1998, San Diego. Trustee The Pub. Defender, Seattle, 1982-85; rep. 9th Cir. Judicial Conf., San Francisco, 1985-89, mem. gender bias task force, 1992-93. Author: Girl Scout's Guide to New York, 1990; contbr. chpt. to book and articles to profl. jours. Nat. bd. dirs. Girl Scouts U.S., N.Y.C., 1976-87; bd. dirs. Family Svcs., Seattle, 1982-84; mem. exec. com. Corp. Coun. for the Arts, Seattle, 1988-98; bd. gen. counsel Downtown Seattle Assn., 1986-89; mem. exec. com. Wash. Coun. Internat. Trade, 1994—; bd. mem. YMCA Greater Seattle, 1998—. Recipient Rising Stars of the 80's award Legal Times Washington, 1983, 100 Young Women of Promise, Good Housekeeping, 1985; named Washington's Winningest Trial Lawyers Washington Journal, 1992; Japan leadership fellow, 1992-93, Top 50 Women Lawyers, Nat. Law Jour., 1998; featured in article Newsweek, July 10, 2000. Fellow ABA (ho. of dels. 1990—); Fed. Bar Assn. (trustee western dist. Wash. 1980-90), Wash. Bar Assn. (chmn. jud. recommendations 1989-90), Seattle-King County Bar Assn. (trustee, sec. 1984-85, Outstanding Lawyer award 1992), Legal Found. Wash. (trustee, pres. 1989-90), Washington Women Lawyers (bd. dirs., pres. 1978-79), Nat. Assn. Iolta Programs (bd. dirs. 1989-91), White House Fellows Found. (bd. dirs. 1998—, pres. 2000-01). Avocations: travel, classical piano, hiking, gourmet cooking, tennis. Office: US Ct Appeals 401 West A St Ste 2000 San Diego CA 92101-7908

MCKIBBEN, HOWARD D. federal judge; b. Apr. 1, 1940; s. James D. and Bernice McKibben; m. Mary Ann McKibben, July 2, 1966; children: Mark, Susan. BS, Bradley U., 1962; MPA, U. Pitts., 1964; JD, U. Mich., 1967. Assoc. George W. Abbott Law Office, 1967-71; dep. dist. atty. Douglas County, Nev., 1969-71, dist. atty., 1971-77; dist. ct. judge State of Nev., 1977-84; judge U.S. Dist. Ct. Nev., Reno, 1984—. Mem. Nev. Bar Assn., Am. Inns of Ct. (pres. Nev. chpt. 1986-88). Methodist. Avocations: tennis, golf, racquetball. Home: PO Box 588 Verdi NV 89439-0588 Office: US Dist Ct 400 S Virginia St Ste 804 Reno NV 89501-2197

MCKIM, SAMUEL JOHN, III, lawyer; b. Pitts., Dec. 31, 1938; s. Samuel John and Harriet Frieda (Roehl) McK; children: David Hunt, Andrew John; m. Eugenia A. Leverich. AA cum laude, Port Huron Jr. Coll., 1959; BA cum laude, U. Mich., 1961, JD cum laude, 1964. Bar: Mich. 1965, U.S. Dist. Ct. (so. dist.) Mich. 1965, U.S. Ct. Appeals (6th cir.) 1969, U.S. Supreme Ct. 1994. Assoc. Miller, Canfield, Paddock and Stone, PLC, Detroit, Bloomfield Hills, 1964-71, sr. mem., 1971—, head state and local tax sect., 1985—, chmn. tax dept., 1989-94, mng. ptnr., 1979-85, chmn., mng. ptnr., 1984-85. Mem. tax coun. State Bar Mich., 1981-94, chmn. state and local tax com. real property sect., 1982-90; adj. prof. law sch. Wayne State U., 1993-99. Assoc. editor Mich. Law Rev. Bd. dirs., past chmn. Goodwill Industries of Greater Detroit, 1970-2000; dir. Goodwill Industries Found., 1982-95; elder Presbyn. Ch., Stevens min.; coun. mem. at large Detroit area coun. Boy Scouts Am., 1987—. Fellow Am Coll. Tax Counselors; mem. ABA, Mich. Bar Assn., Detroit Bar Assn., Barrister's Soc., Ostego Ski Club, Port Huron Golf Club, Order of Coif, Nomads Club, Phi Delta Phi. General corporate, State and local taxation. Home: 32778 Friar Tuck Ln Beverly Hills MI 48025-2500 Office: Miller Canfield Paddock & Stone 150 W Jefferson Ave Ste 2500 Detroit MI 48226-4416

MCKINNEY, JAMES DEVAINE, JR. lawyer; b. Muscatine, Iowa, Dec. 13, 1931; s. James D. and Jeffie Lillian (Eblen) McK.; m. Betty A. Guy, June 10, 1966; children: James D. III, Cynthia Dee, Jennifer Jean. BA, U. Iowa, 1956, LLB, 1958. Bar: Iowa 1958, D.C. 1960, U.S. Ct. Appeals (D.C. cir.) 1961, U.S. Supreme Ct. 1962. Trial atty. FPC, Washington, 1958-60; assoc. Law Offices Charles E. McGee, 1960-65, Ross, Marsh & Foster, Washington, 1965-68, ptnr., 1968—. Mem. ABA, D.C. Bar Assn., Energy Bar Assn. (exec. com. 1979-82), Met. Club, Washington Golf and Country Club. Administrative and regulatory, Appellate, FERC practice. Home: 6105 Lee Hwy Arlington VA 22205-2110 Office: Ross Marsh & Foster 2001 L St NW Washington DC 20036-4910 E-mail: rmfmckinne@aol.com

MCKINNEY, JANET KAY, law librarian; b. Kansas City, Mo., Feb. 15, 1959; d. Charles Durward and Helen Jean (Bost) Freeman; m. Larry Emmett McKinney, July 11, 1981. BA, Avila Coll., 1981; MA in Libr. Sci., U. Mo., 1989; MA in Religious Studies, Ctrl. Bapt. Theol. Sem., 1997. Circulation libr. Midwestern Bapt. Theol. Sem., Kansas City, 1981-84, acquisitions libr., 1984-85, reference libr., 1985-90; environ. divsn. libr. Black & Veatch, 1990-91; dir. collection resources U. Mo. Leon E. Bloch Law Libr., 1991-2000; computer svcs. libr. Shook, Hardy & Bacon, 2000—. Mem. ALA, Am. Assn. Law Librs. (com. on rels. with info. vendors 1994-96, editl bd. Tech. Svcs. Law Libr. 1994-96, tech. svcs. spl. interest sect. chair 1999-2000, treas pvt. law librs. spl. interest sect. 2001—, index to fgn. legal periodicals adv. com. 2001—), Mid-Am. Assn. Law Librs. (newsletter adv. mgr. 1993-94, treas. 1997-99), Southwestern Assn. Law Librs., N.Am. Serials Interest Group, Spl. Librs. Assn. (chpt. employment com. chmn. 1990-91, chpt. treas. 1991-94, chpt. pres. 1995-96), Kansas City Assn. Law Librs. (v.p., pres. 2000). Office: Shook Hardy & Bacon LLP 1200 Main St Kansas City MO 64105 E-mail: jmckinney@shb.com, mckinneyj1@msn.com

MCKINNEY, LARRY J. federal judge; b. South Bend, Ind., July 4, 1944; s. Lawrence E. and Helen (Byers) McK.; m. Carole Jean Marie Lyon, Aug. 19, 1966; children: Joshua E., Andrew G. BA, MacMurray Coll., Jacksonville, Ill., 1966; JD, Ind. U., 1969. Bar: Ind. 1970, U.S. Dist. Ct. (so. dist.) Ind. 1970. Law clk. to atty. gen. State of Ind., Indpls., 1969-70, dep. atty. gen., 1970-71; ptnr. Rodgers and McKinney, Edinburgh, Ind., 1971-75, James F.T. Sargent, Greenwood, 1975-79; judge Johnson County Cir. Ct., Franklin, 1979-87, U.S. Dist. Ct. (so. dist.) Ind., Indpls., 1987—, chief judge, 2001—. Presbyterian. Avocations: reading, jogging. Office: US Dist Ct 204 US Courthouse 46 E Ohio St Indianapolis IN 46204-1903

MCKINSTRY, RONALD EUGENE, lawyer; b. Bakersfield, Calif., Aug. 11, 1926; s. Melville Jack and Lillian Agatha (Saner) McK.; m. Shirley Danner, June 19, 1948; children: Michael R., Jill I. McKinstry Epperson, Jeffrey A., Carol A. McKinstry Sundquist. BS, U. Wash., 1950, JD, 1951. Bar: Wash. 1951, U.S. Ct. Claims 1970, U.S. Ct. Appeals (D.C. cir.) 1981, U.S. Supreme Ct. 1982. Assoc. Evans, McLaren, Lane, Powell & Beeks, Seattle, 1951-55, Bogle, Bogle & Gates, Seattle, 1955-61; ptnr. Bogle & Gates, 1962-91, chmn. litigation dept., 1970-91; sr. trial ptnr. Ellis Li & McKinstry, 1992—. Apptd. spl. master by U.S. Dist. Ct. (we. dist.) Wash., 1976-81, apptd. settlement mediator, 1980— Editor-in-chief Washington Civil Procedure Before Trial Deskbook, 1981, Supplement to Deskbook, 1986; contbr. articles to profl. jours. Attends Christ Meml. Ch., Poulsbo, Wash. With USN, 1944-46, PTO. Recipient Svc. award Western Ctr. for Law and Religious Freedom, 1990. Fellow Am. Coll. Trial Lawyers (regent 1978-82); mem. ABA, Internat. Assn. Def. Counsel (mem. exec. com. 1974-78, voted Best Lawyers in Am., 1983—), CPR Panels of Disting. Legal Neutrals, AAA Club Wash. (mem. exec. com. 1983-98). Mem. Christ Meml. Ch. Avocations: golf, travel. Federal civil litigation, General civil litigation, Environmental. Office: Ellis Li & McKinstry Two Union Square 601 Union St Ste 4900 Seattle WA 98101-3906 E-mail: rmckinstry@ellisi.com

MCKINSTRY, TAFT AVENT, lawyer; b. Versailles, Ky., July 17, 1947; d. John O. and Betty (Avent) McKinstry; m. J. Douglas Rood, Aug. 10, 1974. BA, U. Ky., 1969, JD, 1972. Bar: Ky. 1972, U.S. Dist. Ct. (ea. dist.) Ky. 1972, U.S. Ct. Appeals (6th cir.) 1972. Ptnr. Fowler, Measle & Bell, Lexington, Ky., 1972—. Mem. staff Ky. Law Jour., 1970-72. Bd. dirs., treas. Bluegrass Trust Antique Show, 1982-83, atty., 1983-85; treas. Lexington Jr. League Horse Show, 1979-80; bd. dirs. Living Arts & Sci. Ctr., 1976-82, atty., 1986-88; mem. Lexington-Fayette County Hist. Commn., 1974-77. Re cipient Sullivan medallion U. Ky., 1969. Mem. Lexington-Fayette County Bar Assn. (bd. govs. 1982-84, sec. 1973-74), Jr. League of Lexington. Republican. Episcopalian. Bankruptcy, Consumer commercial, Contracts commercial. Office: Fowler Measle & Bell Kincaid Tower 6th Fl 300 W Vine St Ste 650 Lexington KY 40507-1660

MCKITTRICK, NEIL VINCENT, lawyer; b. Framingham, Mass., June 21, 1961; s. Harold Vincent and Dorothy Frances (Alexander) McK.; m. Karen Beth Hoffman, May 30, 1987; children: Kerry Alexandra, Brian Hoffman, Robert Hoffman. AB magna cum laude, Brown U., 1983; JD, U. Va., 1987. Bar: Mass. 1988, U.S. Dist. Ct. Mass. 1989, U.S. Ct. Appeals (1st cir.) 1989, U.S. Supreme Ct. 1999. Law clk. to Hon. Frank M. Johnson Jr. U.S. Ct. Appeals (11th cir.), Montgomery, Ala., 1987-88; assoc. Hill & Barlow, Boston, 1988-95, mem., 1995—; pub. defender Suffolk County (Mass.) Bar Advocate, 1990-91; asst. dir. White House sec. rev. U.S. Dept. Treasury, 1994-95; case conf./mediator Boston Mcpl. Ct. Alternative Dispute Resolution Program, 1997—. Mem. steering com. Lawyers' Com. Civil Rights Under Law, 1998—. Editor U. Va. Law Rev., 1985-87. Recipient Arc Mass. Disting. Citizens award, 1996, Charles River Arc Gala Benefit award, 2001, Bldg. a Dream Benefit award, 2001; Dillard fellow U. Va., 1985-86. Mem. ABA (Pro Bono Publico award 2001), Mass. Bar Assn. (Access to Justice Pro Bono Publico award 2001), Fed. Bar Assn. (exec. com. 1997—, treas. 2000-01), Boston Bar Assn. (lawyers' com. civil rights, steering com., 1998—), Order of the Coif, Phi Beta Kappa, Theta Delta Chi. General civil litigation, Criminal, Personal injury. Office: Hill & Barlow One International Pl Boston MA 02110 E-mail: nmckittrick@hillbarlow.com

MCKNIGHT, FREDERICK L. lawyer; b. Kansas City, Mo., Nov. 28, 1947; s. Harry A. and Donna Ruth (Breining) McK.; m. Linda Jean McKnight, June 20, 1970; children: Justin Teague, Cristin Ruth. AB honors, Princeton U., 1969; JD, U. Calif., Berkeley, 1972. Bar: Calif. 1973, N.Y. 1973. Regional mng. ptnr. Jones Day Reavis & Pogue, L.A., 1997—. Adv. com. Jones, Day, Reavis & Pogue, Cleve., 1991—, Calif. regional mng. ptnr., 1997—. Bd. dirs. Econ. Devel. Corp., L.A., 1992—, St. Vincent Med. Ctr. Found., L.A., 1994—. Fellow Am. Coll. of Trial Lawyers; mem. Assn. Bus. Trial Lawyers. Office: Jones Day Reavis & Pogue 555 W 5th St Ste 4600 Los Angeles CA 90013-1025 E-mail: fmcknight@jonesday.com

MCKOWEN, LAURIE GARRIGAN, lawyer; b. Washington, June 29, 1956; d. Daniel P. and Catherine M. (Carroll) Garrigan; m. James Anthony McKowen, Aug. 30, 1986 (div. Dec. 1993); children: James Andrew, Ryan D., Patrick S. BA, Radford Coll., 1978; JD, W.Va. U., 1981. Bar: W.Va. 1981, U.S. Dist. Ct. (so. and no. dists.) W.Va. 1981, U.S. Ct. Appeals (4th cir.) 1988. Asst. atty. gen. W.Va. Office Atty. Gen., Charleston, 1981-82; law clk. U.S. Dist. Ct. (so. dist.) W.Va., 1982-83; assoc. Preiser & Wilson, 1983-87; ptnr. Hunt & Wilson, 1987-90; mem. Masters & Taylor, 1990—. Vice pres., treas. W.Va. Heady Injury Found. Inst., W.Va., 1984-91. Mem. W.Va. Trial Lawyers Assn. (med. negligence com. 1983—), Assn. Trial Lawyers of Am., Kanawha County Bar Assn., W.Va. Bar Assn., Phi Kappa Phi, Omicron Delta Kappa, Pi Gamma Mu, Alpha Lamda Delta. Personal injury. Office: Masters & Taylor LC 4th Flr/Peoples Bldg 181 Summers St Charleston WV 25301-2134

MCKUSICK, VINCENT LEE, former state supreme court justice, lawyer, arbitrator, mediator; b. Parkman, Maine, Oct. 21, 1921; s. Carroll Lee and Ethel (Buzzell) McK.; m. Nancy Elizabeth Green, June 23, 1951; children: Barbara Jane McKusick Liscord, James Emory, Katherine McKusick Ralston, Anne Elizabeth. AB, Bates Coll., 1943; SB, SM, MIT, 1947; LLB, Harvard U., 1950; LLD, Colby Coll., 1976, Nasson Coll., 1978, Bates Coll., 1979, Bowdoin Coll., 1979, Suffolk U., 1983; LHD, U. So. Maine, 1978, Thomas Coll., 1981. Bar: Maine 1952. Law clk. to Chief Judge Learned Hand, 1950-51; to Justice Felix Frankfurter, 1951-52; partner Pierce, Atwood, Scribner, Allen & McKusick and predecessors, Portland, Maine, 1953-77; chief justice Maine Supreme Jud. Ct., 1977-92; of counsel to Pierce Atwood (formerly Pierce, Atwood, Scribner, Allen, Smith, & Lancaster), Portland, Maine, 1992—. Mem. adv. com. rules civil procedure Maine Supreme Jud. Ct., 1957-59, chmn., 1966-75, commr. uniform state laws, 1968-76, sec. nat. conf., 1975-77; mem. Conf. Chief Justices, 1977-92, bd. dirs., 1980-82, 91-92, pres.-elect, 1989-90, pres., 1990-91; dir. Nat. Ctr. for State Ctrs., 1988-89, chmn.-elect, 1989-90, chmn., 1990-91; spl. master U.S. Supreme Ct. Conn. v. N.H., 1992-93, La. v. Miss., 1994-96, Kans. v. Nebr., 1999—; master Mass. S.J.C. Liquidation Am. Mutual Liability Ins. Co., 1995-96; leader Am. Judges Del. to China, 1983, USSR, 1988, U.S. State Dept. Rule of Law Del. to Republic of Ga., 1992; mem. permanent com. Oliver Wendell Holmes Devise, 1993—.

Author: Patent Policy of Educational Institutions, 1947, (with Richard H. Field) Maine Civil Practice, 1959, supplements, 1962, 67, (with Richard H. Field and L. Kinvin Wroth) 2d edit., 1970, supplements, 1972, 74, 77; also articles in legal publs. Trustee emeritus Bates Coll.; mem. adv. com. on pvt. internat. law U.S. State Dept., 1980-85, Fed.-State Jurisdiction com., Jud. Conf. of U.S., 1987-89. With AUS, 1943-46. Recipient The Maine prize U. Maine Sys., 1993, Benjamin E. Mays award Bates Coll., 1994, Big M award Maine State Soc. Washington, 1995, Paul C. Reardon award Nat. Ctr. for State Ctrs., 1999. Fellow Am. Bar Found. (bd. dirs. 1977-87), Am. Philos. Soc. (coun. 1990-96, 97—); mem. ABA (chmn. fed. rules com. 1966-71, bd. editors jour. 1971-80, chmn. 1976-77, mem. study group to China 1978, ho. dels. 1983-87, coun. sr. lawyers divsn. 1997—), Maine Bar Assn., Cumberland County Bar Assn., Am. Arbitration Assn. (bd. dirs. 1994—), Am. Judicature Soc. (dir. 1976-78, 92-98), Am. Law Inst. (coun. 1968—), Maine Jud. Coun. (chmn. 1977-92), Inst. Jud. Adminstrn., Supreme Ct. Hist. Soc. (trustee 1994—), Rotary Club (hon., past pres. Portland club), Portland Yacht Club, Phi Beta Kappa, Sigma Xi, Tau Beta Pi. Republican. Unitarian. Home: 1152 Shore Rd Cape Elizabeth ME 04107-2115 Office: 1 Monument Sq Portland ME 04101-1110 E-mail: judgemac@aol.com, vmckusick@pierceatwood.com

MCLAIN, CHRISTOPHER M. lawyer; b. San Luis Obispo, Calif., July 21, 1943; s. James Latane and Marjorie Patricia (McNalley) McL.; m. Barbara McFarland, Nov. 23, 1968; children: Beth, Brian, Amy. BS in Bus. Adminstrn., U. Calif.-Berkeley, 1965, JD, 1968. Assoc. Knox, Goforth & Ricksen, Oakland, Calif., 1968-69, Donahue, Gallagher, Thomas & Woods, Oakland, 1969-73, ptnr., 1973-83; sec., counsel Lucky Stores, Inc., Dublin, 1984-89, v.p., 1985-89; ptnr. Sonnenschein, Nath & Rosenthal, San Francisco, 1989-90; sr. v.p., gen. counsel, sec. Transam. Corp., 1990-94; of counsel Sonnenschein Nath & Rosenthal, 1994-95; sr. v.p., gen. counsel, sec. Crown Vantage Inc., Oakland, Calif., 1995-99; ptnr., sr. v.p., gen. counsel Sequoia Assocs., LLC, Menlo Park, 1999—. Mem. ABA, State Bar Calif., Alameda County Bar Assn., San Francisco Bar Assn., Am. Soc. Corps. Secs. Avocation: skiing. General corporate. Office: Sequoia Assocs LLC Bldg 2 Ste 140 3000 Sand Hill Rd Menlo Park CA 94025

MCLAIN, SUSAN LYNN, legal educator; b. Chestertown, Md., May 6, 1949; d. Joseph Howard and Margaret Ann (Hollingsworth) McL.; m. Donald Howard Pohl, July 5, 1974 (div. 1977); m. Bryson Leitch Cook, May 21, 1977; 1 child, Joseph Bryson Cook. BA, U. Pa., 1971; JD, Duke U., 1974. Bar: Md. 1974, U.S. Dist. Ct. Md. 1975. Assoc. Piper & Marbury, Balt., 1974-76; John S. Bradway grad. fellow Duke U., Durham, N.C., 1976-77; asst. prof. U. Balt., 1977-80, assoc. prof. law, 1980-83, prof. law, 1983—; reporter on evidence Md. Trial Judge's Bench Book, 1981—; spl. con. to Md. Ct. Appeals, 1988—. Author: Maryland Evidence: State and Federal (2 vols.), 1987; contbr. chpt. to book, articles to profl. jours. Recipient Best Full-Time Faculty Mem. award Student Bar Assn., U. Balt., 1984. Mem. ABA (sect. patent, trademark and copyright law, 1982—, chmn. subcom. 1983-84, sect. litigation trial evidence com. 1982-86), Md. Bar Assn. (sect. litigation fed. bar cts. com. 1982—, co-chmn. 1982-83, chmn. com. and subcom. ednl. fed. practice program 1982-84). Republican. Episcopalian. Home: 5 Fawn Ridge Ct Reisterstown MD 21136-5654 Office: U Balt Law Sch 1420 N Charles St Baltimore MD 21201-5720

MCLAIN, WILLIAM ALLEN, lawyer; b. Chgo., Oct. 19, 1942; s. William Rex and Wilma L. (Raschka) McL.; divorced; children: William A., David M., Heather A.; m. Kristine R. Zierk. BS, So. Ill. U., 1966; JD, Loyola U., Chgo., 1971. Bar: Ill. 1971, U.S. Dist. Ct. (no. dist) Ill. 1971, U.S. Ct. Appeals (7th cir.) 1971, Colo. 1975, U.S. Dist. Ct. Colo. 1975, U.S. Ct. Appeals (10th cir.) 1975. Law clk. U.S. Dist. Ct. (no. dist.) Ill., Chgo., 1971-72; assoc. Sidley & Austin, 1972-75; ptnr. Welborn, Dufford, Brown & Tooley, Denver, 1975-86; pres. William. A. McLain PC, 1986—; ptnr. McLain & Singer, Denver, 1990—. Mem. Dist. 10 Legis. Vacancy Commn., Denver, 1984-86. Served with U.S. Army, 1966-68. Recipient Leadership and Scholastic Achievement award Loyola U. Alumni Assn., 1971. Mem. Colo. Bar Assn. (lobbyist 1983-85), Denver Bar Assn., Colo. Assn. Commerce and Industry (legis. policy coun. 1983-88), Colo. Mining Assn. (state and local affairs com. 1978-88), Inst. Property Taxation, Mt. Vernon Country Club, Roundup Riders of the Rockies Club, Masons, Shriners, Scottish Rite, York Rite. Republican. Legislative, State and local taxation. Home and Office: 3962 S Olive St Denver CO 80237-2038

MCLANE, DAVID GLENN, lawyer; b. Dallas, Jan. 17, 1943; s. Alfred Ervin and Dixie Marie (Martin) McL.; m. Sally Ruth Payne, Apr. 5, 1963; children: Cynthia Lynn, Kathleen Michelle, Michael Scott; m. Beverly Anne Bledsoe, Feb. 5, 1983; children: Morgan Elizabeth, Nicholas Martin, Elizabeth Clark. BA, So. Meth. U., 1963, LLB, 1966. Bar: Tex. 1966, U.S. Supreme Ct. 1971. Briefing atty. Supreme Ct. Tex., 1966-67; assoc., then ptnr. Gardere Wynne Sewell LLP (and predecessor firm), Dallas, 1967—. Lectr. in field. Author: Texas Corporations - Law and Practice, 1984; editor: Incorporation Planning in Texas, 1977. Bd. dirs. urban Svcs. br. YMCA, Dallas, 1977-84, Dallas Symphony assn., 1980-93; mem. Dallas County AIDS Planning Commn. Task Force, 1988; pres. Coun. Dallas Theol. Sem., 1994—; exec. bd. Law Sch. So. Meth. U., 1997—; mem. ministry coun. Josh McDowell Ministries, 1997—. Mem. ABA, Tex. Bar Assn., Dallas Bar Assn., S.W. Benefits Assn. (bd. dirs. 1975-80, prs. 1978-79), So. Meth. U. Law Alumni Assn. (sec., bd. dirs. 1981-85, Vol. of Yr. award 1984), So. Meth. U. Alumni Assn. (bd. dirs. 1972-77). Presbytrian. General corporate, Pension, profit-sharing, and employee benefits, Securities. Office: 3000 Thanksgiving Tower Dallas TX 75201 E-mail: dmclane@gardere.com

MCLANE, FREDERICK BERG, lawyer; b. Long Beach, Calif., July 24, 1941; s. Adrian B. and Arlie K. (Burrell) McL.; m. Lois C. Roberts, Jan. 28, 1967; children: Willard, Anita. BA, Stanford U., 1963; LLB, Yale U., 1966. Bar: Calif. 1967, U.S. Dist. Ct. (cen. dist.) Calif. 1967. Assoc. prof. law U. Miss., Oxford, 1966-68; assoc. O'Melveny & Myers, L.A., 1968-74, ptnr., 1975—. Com. of counsel HUD, Los Angeles, 1979-84; lectr. in field. Pres., bd. dirs. Legal Aid Found., L.A., 1974-83; deacon Congl. Ch., Sherman Oaks, Calif., 1979-83; vice-chair L.A. Music Ctr., Unified Fund, 1992-94; bd. dirs. Calif. Sci. Ctr. Found., 1991-2000. Mem. ABA (banking com., fed. regulation of securities com.), Calif. Bar Assn. (fin. insts. com., uniform comml. codes), L.A. Bar Assn., Order of Coif, Calif. Club (L.A.), L.A. Country Club (bd. dirs.), Lakeside Golf Club (L.A.). Democrat. Avocations: golf, walking, reading. General corporate, Mergers and acquisitions, Securities. Office: O'Melveny & Myers 400 S Hope St Los Angeles CA 90071-2899 E-mail: fmclane@omm.com

MCLAREN, RICHARD WELLINGTON, JR. lawyer; b. Cin., May 15, 1945; s. Richard Wellington and Edith (Gillett) McL.; m. Ann Lynn Zachrich, Sept. 4, 1971; children: Christine, Richard, Charles. BA, Yale U., 1967; JD, Northwestern U., 1973. Bar: Ohio 1973, Ill. 1997, U.S. Dist. Ct. (no. dist.) Ohio 1973, U.S. Dist. Ct. (no. dist.) Ill. 1997, U.S. Ct. Appeals (6th cir.) 1978, U.S. Ct. Appeals (7th cir.) 1997, U.S. Ct. Appeals (fed. cir.) 1997, U.S. Supreme Ct. 1981. Assoc. Squire, Sanders & Dempsey, Cleve., 1973-82, ptnr., 1983-87; prin., counsel Ernst & Whinney, 1988-89; assoc. gen. counsel Ernst & Young, 1989-93; prin. counsel Centerior Energy Corp., 1994-96; prin. Welsh & Katz, Ltd., Chgo., 1997—. 1st lt. U.S. Army, 1967-70. Mem. ABA (litigation, intellectual property and corp. law), FBA, Am. Judicature Soc., Ohio Bar Assn., Ill. Bar Assn. Federal civil litigation, General civil litigation, General corporate. Home: 638 S Monroe St Hinsdale IL 60521-3926 Office: 120 S Riverside Plz Fl 22D Chicago IL 60606-3913 E-mail: rwmclaren@welshkatz.com

MCLAUGHLIN, EDWARD FRANCIS, JR. lawyer; b. Boston, Aug. 18, 1920; s. Edward Francis and Helen Celia McLaughlin; m. Elizabeth Drake, Apr. 14, 1945; children: Edward F., Patricia A. (deceased), Paul R. (deceased), Robert D., Richard J., Elizabeth A. AB in Bus., Dartmouth Coll., 1942; LLB, Northeastern U., 1949. Bar: Mass. 1949, U.S. Dist. Ct. Mass. 1950, U.S. Ct. Appeals (1st cir.) 1950, U.S. Supreme Ct. 1963. Asst. U.S. atty. U.S. Dept. Justice, Boston, 1950-53; assoc. Sullivan & Worcester, 1953-61; lt. gov. Commonwealth of Mass., 1961-63; gen. counsel Metropolitan Transit Authority, Mass. Bay Transportation Authority, 1962-70; assoc. Herrick & Smith, 1970, ptnr. 1971-86, Nutter, McClennen & Fish, LLP, Boston, 1986-90, of counsel, 1990-2000; asst. dist. atty. Commonwealth of Mass., Barnstable, Mass., 2000—. Dir. nat. coun. Northeastern U., Boston, 1979—. Councillor Boston City Coun., Mass., 1954—61, pres., 1959—60; del. Dem. Nat. Conv., L.A., Calif. Lt. USN, 1942—45. Named Outstanding Alumnus Northeastern U., 1974. Fellow Mass. Bar Assn. Roman Catholic. Avocations: sports, political activities, reading. General civil litigation, Condemnation, Criminal. Office: The Commonwealth of Mass Office of District Atty PO Box 455 Barnstable MA 02630-0455 Fax: 508-362-8221

MCLAUGHLIN, JOHN SHERMAN, lawyer; b. Pitts., Apr. 1, 1932; s. John H. and Dorothy I. (Schrecongost) McL.; m. Suzanne Shaver, June 5, 1971; children— Dorothy, Sarah, Martha. AB, Harvard U., 1954, LLB, 1957. Bar: Pa. 1958, U.S. Supreme Ct. 1967. Assoc. Reed, Smith, Shaw & McClay, Pitts., 1957-71, ptnr., 1971—. Trustee Harmarville Rehab. Ctr., Inc., 1980-87; pres., trustee Western Pa. Sch. for the Deaf, 1985—; pres. Pa. NG Assn., 1976-78; justice of peace Borough of Edgewood, 1963-73; trustee Winchester Thurston Sch., 1987-94, emeritus trustee, 1994—; life trustee Carnegie Libr. of Pitts., Carnegie Inst., 1994—, Carnegie Mus. Art, 1997—; dir. Pitts. Symphony, 1985-95, adv. 1996-99. Lt. col. Air NG, 1957-79. Mem. Am. Law Inst., Am. Coll. Trust and Estate Counsel, Allegheny County Bar Assn., Duquesne Club, Rolling Rock Club (Ligonier, Pa.). General practice, Probate. Office: Reed Smith Shaw & McClay 435 6th Ave Ste 2 Pittsburgh PA 15219-1886 E-mail: jmclauglin@reedsmith.com

MCLAUGHLIN, JOSEPH MICHAEL, federal judge, law educator; b. Brooklyn, N.Y., Mar. 20, 1933; s. Joseph Michael and Mary Catherine (Flanagan) McL.; m. Frances Elizabeth Lynch, Oct. 10, 1959; children: Joseph, Mary Jo, Matthew, Andrew. A.B., Fordham Coll., 1954, LL.B., 1959; LL.M., NYU, 1964; LL.D., Mercy Coll., White Plains, N.Y., 1981; LLD, Fordham U., 1998. Bar: N.Y. 1959. Assoc. Cahill, Gordon, N.Y.C., 1959-61; prof. law Fordham U., 1961-71, dean Sch. of Law, 1971-81, adj. prof., 1981—; judge U.S. Dist. Ct. Eastern Dist. N.Y., Bklyn., 1981-90; judge to sr. judge U.S. Ct. Appeals (2nd Cir.), N.Y.C., 1990—. Adj. prof. St. John's Law Sch., N.Y.C., 1982-97 ; chmn. N.Y. Law Revision Commn., Albany, 1975-82 Author: (with Peterfreund) New York Practice, 1964, Evidence, 1979; also articles Served to capt. U.S. Army, 1955-57, Korea Mem. ABA, Assn. of Bar of City of N.Y., N.Y. State Bar Assn. Roman Catholic. Club: Lotos Office: US Courthouse US Ct Appeals 40 Foley Sq Rm 2402 New York NY 10007-1502

MCLAUGHLIN, JOSEPH THOMAS, lawyer; b. Boston, Mar. 30, 1944; s. James Francis and Madeline Louise (Hickman) McL.; m. Christine E. Mullen, Sept. 2, 1967; children: Amy Melissa, Caitlin Christine, Ian Michael. BA magna cum laude, Boston Coll., 1965; JD, Cornell U., 1968. Bar: Mass. 1969, N.Y. State 1968, U.S. Supreme Ct. 1974. Research asst. Brit. Council of Archaeology, Winchester, Eng., 1964, site supr., 1966; legis. asst. Rep. Thomas P. O'Neill, Washington, 1967; research asst. Cornell U., 1967-68; law clk. to chief justice Mass. Superior Ct., 1968-69; assoc. Shearman & Sterling, N.Y.C., 1969-76, ptnr., 1976-97; exec. v.p., legal and regulatory affaais Credit Suisse First Boston, 1997—2001; chmn. Credit Suisse First Boston Found. Trust, 2001—. Adj. prof. Fordham Law Sch., 1981—; vis. prof. Cornell Law Sch., 1995—. Author: Federal Class Action Digests, 1974, 1976; contbr. articles to profl. jours. Exec. dir. Brooklyn Heights Draft Counseling Svc., 1970-74, Presbyn. Task Force for Justice Counseling Svc., 1973-75; v.p., bd. dirs. Brooklyn Heights Assn., 1973-77; bd. dirs. Willoughby Settlement House, Inc., Ingersoll-Willoughby Cmty. Ctr., Inc., 1970-75, United Neighborhood Houses, 1976-78, Good Shepherd Svcs., Resources for Children with Spl. Needs, Inc., Internat. House, Bklyn. Mus. Art. Mem. ABA, Assn. of Bar of City of N.Y. (mem. com. on profl. discord 1986—, chmn. com. to promote diversity in the legal profession), N.Y. State Bar Assn. (chmn. com. on marijuana and drug abuse 1972-75), Am. Law Inst., Am. Arbitration Assn., N.Y. Lawyers for Pub. Interest (chmn. bd. dirs.) ABAC (com. on promoting settlements), Heights Casino Club. Banking, Federal civil litigation, Private international. Home: 89 Remsen St Brooklyn NY 11201 Office: 11 Madison Ave New York NY 10010 E-mail: joseph.mclaughlin@csfb.com

MCLAUGHLIN, MICHAEL JOHN, retired insurance company executive; b. Cambridge, Mass., Feb. 14, 1944; s. Michael John and Evelyn Katherine (Quinn) McL. A.B., Boston Coll., 1965; J.D., N.Y. U., 1968. Bar: N.Y., Mass. With N.Y. Life Ins. Co., 1968—, sr. v.p. info. systems and services dept., 1982-88, sr. v.p., 1988-91, sr. v.p., dep. gen. counsel, 1991-95, sr. v.p., gen. counsel, 1995-2000. Mem. ABA, N.Y. State Bar Assn. E-mail: mmclau2260@aol.com

MCLAUGHLIN, PHILIP T. state attorney general; b. Nashua, N.H., Jan. 23, 1945; s. Philip J. and Pauline (Reilly) McL.; m. Janice Livingston, 1968; children: Matthew, Timothy, Emily, Katherine, Philip. AB in History, Holy Cross coll., 1967; MPA, U. R.I., 1971; JD, Boston Coll., 1974. Bar: N.H. 1974. Atty. Belknap County, N.H., 1979-81; ptnr. McLaughlin, Hemeon & Lahey, P.A., Laconia, 1981-97; atty. gen. State of N.H., 1997—. Past pres. Lakes Region Mental Health Ctr., Laconia; mem. Laconia City Coun., 1976-80; del. N.H. Constl. Conv., 1984; mem. Laconia Sch. Bd., 1985-94, also chair; mem. prof. conduct com. N.H. Supreme Ct., 1983-92, 94-97. Lt. USN, 1969-71. Office: Atty Gen Office 33 Capitol St Concord NH 03301-6397

MCLAUGHLIN, T. MARK, lawyer; b. Salem, Mass., Apr. 20, 1953; s. Terrence E. and Mary E. (Donlon) McL.; m. Sandra L. Roman, Oct. 16, 1982; children: Daniel, Kathleen, Eileen. BA in Econs., U. Notre Dame, 1975, JD, 1978. Bar: Ill. 1978, U.S. Dist. Ct. (no. dist.) Ill. 1978, U.S. Dist. Ct. (cen. dist.) Ill. 1992, U.S. Dist. Ct. (ea. dist.) Wis. 1992, U.S. Ct. Appeals (7th cir.) 1982, U.S. Ct. Appeals (11th cir.) 1982, U.S. Ct. Appeals (8th cir.) 1998. Assoc. Mayer, Brown & Platt, Chgo., 1978-84, ptnr., 1985—. Adj. faculty law Loyola U., Chgo., 1983, 86-90. Bd. dirs. no. Ill. affiliate Am. Diabetes Assn., Chgo., 1985-94. Mem. ABA (franchising forum com. antitrust law sect.), Phi Beta Kappa. Antitrust, Federal civil litigation, Franchising. Office: Mayer Brown & Platt 190 S La Salle St Ste 3100 Chicago IL 60603-3441 E-mail: mmclaughlin@mayerbrown.com

MCLAUGHLIN, THOMAS JEFFREY, lawyer; b. Columbus, Ohio, Nov. 30, 1946; s. Robert Fred and Ruth Eileen (Ridenour) McL. BAAE, Ohio State U., 1969, MS, 1969; JD, Harvard U., 1975. Bar: Wash. 1975, U.S. Supreme Ct., U.S. Ct. Appeals (6th, 7th, 9th and D.C. cirs.), U.S. Dist. Ct. (we. dist.) Wash., U.S. Dist. Ct. (so. dist.) Fla., U.S. Dist. Ct. (ea. dist.) Mich., U.S. Dist. Ct. (we. dist.) Pa., U.S. Dist. Ct. (no. dist.) Ill., U.S. Dist. Ct. D.C. Engr. Boeing Co., Seattle, 1969-72; assoc. Perkins Coie, Seattle, 1975-81, ptnr., 1981—. Mem. Wash. State Bar Assn., ABA, Seattle-King County Bar Assn. Aviation, General civil litigation, Product liability. Home: 2600 2nd Ave Apt 1201E Seattle WA 98121-1239 Office: Perkins Coie 1201 3rd Ave Fl 40 Seattle WA 98101-3029

MCLEAN, DAVID LYLE, lawyer; b. Longview, Wash., May 5, 1941; s. David Edward and Helen Margaret (Andrews) McL.; m. Sheila Marsha Avrin, Apr. 27, 1968; children— Alexandra Andrews, David Benjamin Avrin. AB, Princeton U., 1963; LLB, Yale U., 1966. Bar: N.Y. 1967, D.C. 1980, U.S. Dist. Ct. (so. dist.) N.Y. 1968, U.S. Dist. Ct. (ea. dist.) N.Y. 1969, U.S. Ct. Appeals (2d cir.) 1969, U.S. Supreme Ct. 1973. Assoc. Sullivan & Cromwell, N.Y.C., 1967-73; assoc. gen. counsel Coopers & Lybrand, N.Y.C., 1973-76, dep. gen. counsel and prin., 1976-96, gen. counsel, 1996-98, dep. gen. counsel Pricewaterhouse Coopers LLP, 1998—. Treas, Bellamy for State Senate campaigns 1970-76. Served with USMCR, 1966-72. Mem. ABA, Assn. Bar City N.Y., Princeton Club N.Y. Democrat. Contbr. articles to legal jours. Federal civil litigation, General corporate, Securities. Office: Pricewaters Coopers LLP 1301 Avenue Of The Americas New York NY 10019-6022

MCLEAN, R. BRUCE, lawyer; b. N.Y.C., Nov. 15, 1946; BS with honors, Ind. U., 1968, JD cum laude, 1971. Bar: Ind. 1971, D.C. 1974. Atty. appellate ct. branch Nat. Labor Rels. Bd., 1971-73; chmn. Akin, Gump, Strauss, Hauer & Feld L.L.P., Washington. Bd. visitors Ind. U. Sch. Law, 1989—, vice chair, 1998—. Mem. ABA, Fed. Bar Assn., D.C. Bar, Order Coif, Phi Alpha Delta. Office: Akin Gump Strauss Hauer & Feld LLP Ste 400 1333 New Hampshire Ave NW Washington DC 20036-1564 E-mail: bmclean@akingump.com

MCLEAN, ROBERT ALEXANDER, lawyer; b. Memphis, Oct. 24, 1943; s. Albert A and Harriet Spencer (Pond) McLean; m. Sydney Ross, July 16, 1977; children: Robert Alexander, Ross Andrew. BA with honors, Rhodes Coll., 1965; MA, Princeton U., 1968, PhD, 1974; JD, U. Memphis, 1978. Bar: Tenn 1979, US Dist Ct (we dist) Tenn 1979, US Dist Ct (ea dist) Wis 1985, US Ct Appeals (5th cir) 1986, US Dist Ct (ea and we dists) Ark 1990, US Ct Appeals (8th cir) 1990, US Ct Appeals (10th cir) 1991, US Ct Appeals (6th cir) 1998, US Supreme Ct 1998. Asst. prof. Russian lit. U. Calif., Santa Cruz, 1971-76; staff atty. FCA, Washington, 1979-81; assoc. Wildman, Harrold, Allen, Dixon & McDonnell, Memphis, 1981-88, ptnr., 1988-89, McDonnell Boyd, Memphis, 1989-94; mem. McDonnell Dyer, PLC, 1994-95; spl. counsel Wolff Ardis, P.C., 1995-96, shareholder, 1997; mem. Farris Mathews Branan Bobango & Hellen, PLC, 1997—; asst. city atty. Germantown, Tenn., 1981—. Adj asst prof Russian lang Rhodes Col, Memphis, 1982—86. Translator: (book) Mozart and Salieri, 1973; mem: journal Univ Memphis Law Rev, 1977—78. Mem session Germantown Presby Ch, Tenn., 1988—, chmn fin comt, 1989—94. Fellow Charlotte Elizabeth Procter, Princeton Univ, 1968, Fulbright, USSR, 1969, Regents, Univ Calif, Santa Cruz, 1975. Mem.: ABA, Tenn Bar Asn, Memphis Bar Asn. Republican. Avocations: golf, quail hunting, tennis. General civil litigation, Environmental, Private international. Home: 8820 Somerset Ln Germantown TN 38138-7375 Office: Farris Matthews et al Ste 2000 One Commerce Sq Memphis TN 38103 E-mail: envtlatty@aol.com

MCLEMORE, GILBERT CARMICHAEL, JR. lawyer; b. Savannah, Ga., Dec. 15, 1942; s. Gilbert Carmichael and Jeannie Elizabeth (Gulley) McL.; m. Susan Ellen Hair, Nov. 21, 1965; children: Kimberly Bates, Gilbert Carmichael, Erin Frances. AB in Polit. Sci., U. N.C., 1965; JD, U. Ga., 1970. Bar: Ga. 1970, U.S. Dist. Ct. (so. dist.) Ga. 1970. Assoc. Fendig, Dickey, Fendig & Whelchel, Brunswick, Ga., 1970-74, ptnr., 1974-77, Fendig, McLemore, Taylor & Whitworth, Brunswick, 1981—. Bd. dirs. Glyn County chpt. ARC; bd. dirs. Humane Soc. South Coastal Ga. Served to lt. USNR, 1965-67. Mem. Glynn County Bar Assn. (treas. 1072-73, v.p. 1973-74, pres. 1974-75), Brunswick-Golden Isles Estate Planning Coun. (pres. 1980-81), Brunswick-Golden Isles C. of C. (chmn. com. 1975), Rotary. Democrat. Methodist. Banking, Probate, Real property. Home: 545 Old Plantation Rd Jekyll Island GA 31527-0718 Office: PO Box 1996 Brunswick GA 31521-1996 E-mail: bmclemore@fendiglaw.com, gcmclemore@earthlink.net

MCLENDON, SUSAN MICHELLE, lawyer, nurse; b. N.Y.C., Mar. 5, 1964; d. James U. McLendon, Sr. BSN, Binghamton U., 1986; JD, Hofstra U., 1990. Bar: N.J. 1991, D.C. 1998, N.Y. 2000; RN, N.Y., 1986. Asst. regional counsel Social Security Adminstrn., Office Gen. Counsel, N.Y.C., 1990-98; nurse All Care Nursing Corp., 1998—, pvt. practice law, 2000—; nurse North Shore Health Sys., Roosevelt, N.Y., 2000—. Mentor Practicing Attys. for Law Students, N.Y.C., 1992-94. Fundraiser Race for the Cure, March Dimes, UNICEF. General corporate, Entertainment, Health.

MCLEOD, WALTON JAMES, lawyer, state legislator; b. Walterboro, S.C., June 30, 1937; s. Walton James Jr. and Rhoda Lane (Brown) M.; m. Julie Edwina Hamiter, Feb. 15, 1969; 1 child, Walton James IV. BA, Yale U., 1959; LLB, U. S.C., 1964. Bar: S.C. 1964, U.S. Supreme Ct. 1974. Law clk. to Chief Judge Clement Haynsworth U.S. Ct. Appeals (4th cir.), Richmond, Va., 1964-65; assoc. Pope and Schumpert, Newberry, S.C., 1965-67; asst. U.S. Atty. Columbia, 1967-68; gen. counsel S.C. Dept. Health & Environ. Ctrl., 1968-94, spl. counsel, 1994-96; dep. S.C. atty. gen., 1987-88. Magistrate Newberry County, Little Mountain, S.C., 1973-81; mcpl. judge Town of Little Mountain, 1981-83, mayor, 1983-89, 93-96; mem. S.C. Ho. of Reps., Columbia, 1996—. Author: Legal Perspectives of Environmental Health, 1973; co-author: Environmental Quality Law, 1975, Hospital Franchising Law and Regulation, 1979. Pres. Newberry (S.C.) Jaycees, 1967; bd. dirs. S.C. Housing Fin. & Devel. Authority, Columbia, 1977-96; chair Ctrl. Midlands Coun. Govts., Columbia, 1981-82; trustee S.C. State Mus., Columbia, 1981-85. Lt. (j.g.) USN, 1959-61, served to Capt. USNR, 1961-92, ret. Recipient Outstanding Jaycee award Newberry Jaycees, 1967, Howell Excellence award Naval Res. Law Program, Washington, 1991; named Outstanding Freshman Rep. of Yr. Carolina Hist. Found. Soc., Inc., 1997. Fellow S.C. Bar Found.; mem. S.C. Magistrates Assn. (pres. 1976-77, Disting. Jud. Svc. award 1975, 77), Judge Advs. Assn. (nat. pres. 1991-92), S.C. Res. Officers Assn. (state pres. 1981-82, Res. Officer of Yr. 1998), S.C. Soc. (pres. 1990-93). Democrat. Luth. Avocations: jogging, reading. Home: 308 Pomaria St Little Mountain SC 29075-9003 Office: SC House of Reps PO Box 11867 Columbia SC 29211-1867 Fax: 803-345-0770

MCLURKIN, THOMAS CORNELIUS, JR. lawyer; b. L.A., July 28, 1954; s. Thomas Cornelius and Willie Mae (O'Connor) McL.; m. Charmaine Bobo. BA, U. So. Calif., 1976, MPA, 1980, PhD in Pub. Adminstrn., 1998; JD, U. LaVerne, 1982. Bar: Calif. 1984, U.S. Dist. Ct. (ctrl. dist.) Calif. 1984, U.S. Dist. Ct. Hawaii 1984, U.S. Ct. Appeals (9th cir.) 1984, U.S. Dist. Ct. (ea., no. and so. dists.) Calif. 1985, U.S. Tax Ct. 1988, U.S. Ct. Mil. Appeals 1989, U.S. Army Ct. Mil. Rev. 1993, U.S. Supreme Ct., 1995. Law clk. dept. water and power City of L.A., 1979-82; jud. clk. cen. dist. U.S. Dist. Ct., L.A., 1982-83; law clk. Office City Atty., 1983-84, dep. city atty., 1984—. Author (with others): Facts in American History, 1968, 2nd edit. 1989, Eagle Scout, 1970. Mem. L.A. World Affairs Coun., 1980—, Smithsonian Assocs.; bd. dirs. L.A. Area coun. Boy Scouts Am., Hillsides Homes for Children; provisional patron Tournament of Roses Assn., Pasadena, 1994—; mem. Verdugo Hills Area coun. Boy Scouts Am. Mem. ABA, ALA, ASPA, Los Angeles County Bar Assn., Assn. Trial Lawyers Am., Langston Law Assn. L.A., U. So. Calif. Gen. Alumni Assn. (bd. govs. exec. bd. 1986-90), U. So. Calif. Black Alumni Assn.-Ebonics (pres. 1988-89), U. So. Calif. Pres.'s Cir., Elks, Am. Legion, Phi Alpha Delta, Kappa Alpha Psi. Republican. United Methodist. Avocations: sailing, tennis, volunteer work, American and world history. Office: LA City Atty Office 200 N Main St Ste 1700 Los Angeles CA 90012-4110 E-mail: tmclurk@atty.lacity.org

MCMAHON, JAMES CHARLES, lawyer; b. Bklyn., Dec. 4, 1951; s. James Charles and Rosemary Margaret (Gilroy) McM.; m. Nancy M. Neble, Oct. 30, 1984; children: Deirdre Kathleen Wright, Laura Elizabeth, Elizabeth Jane. BA, Boston Coll., 1973; JD, Fordham U., 1977. Bar: N.Y. 1978, Mass. 1996, U.S. Supreme Ct. 1996. Assoc. Winthrop Stimson Putnam & Roberts, N.Y.C., 1977-78, Brodsky, Linett, Altman, Schechter & Reicher, N.Y.C., 1978-82; ptnr. Brodsky, Altman & McMahon, LLP, 1982—, mng. ptnr., 1988—. Exec. sec., counsel N.Y. Movers Tariff Bur., Inc., N.Y.C., 1984—; gen. counsel Mass. Movers Assn., Woburn, 1986—, Commonwealth Transp. Compensation Corp., Andover, Mass., 1992—, Transport Health Plan, Woburn, 1994—, N.Y. State Movers and Warehousemen's Assn., N.Y.C., 1984—, Nat. Moving and Storage Assn., Fairfax, Va., 1988-98. Mem. editl. bd. Fordham Urban Law Jour., 1976. Recipient Disting. Svc. award Mass. Movers Assn., 1992. Mem. N.Y. State Bar Assn. (labor and employment law sect.), Assn. Bar City N.Y. (transp. com. 1997—), Assn. Comml. Fin. Attys., Transp. Lawyers Assn., Assn. for Transp. Law, Logistics and Policy, N.Y. Athletic Club. Democrat. Roman Catholic. Antitrust, Labor, Transportation. Home: 196 Pinesbridge Rd Ossining NY 10562-1428 Office: Brodsky Altman & McMahon 342 Madison Ave Rm 1930 New York NY 10173-1900 also: 10 State St Woburn MA 01801-6820 E-mail: jmcmahon@mcmahonlaw.com

MCMAHON, JOHN JOSEPH, lawyer; b. N.Y.C., Aug. 23, 1949; s. John Joseph and Elizabeth Mary (Rowland) McM.; m. Susan Bernice Mullen, Dec. 2, 1978 (div. 1993); children: John Joseph IV, Christopher Jordon, James Matthew; m. Susan L. Arseneault, Dec. 26, 1993. BA in History, Fordham U., 1971, JD, 1974; MA in Human Devel., Salve Regina U., 1980. Bar: N.Y. 1975, U.S. Ct. Mil. Appeals 1975, R.I. 1978, U.S. Dist. Ct. R.I. 1978. Trial, def. counsel U.S. Marine Corps., Judge Adv. Div., Quantico, Va., Newport, R.I., 1974-79; staff judge adv. HQ 2nd MAB, 4th Marine Div. U.S. Marine Corps Res., Camp Edwards, Mass., 1979-81; state prosecutor Dept. of Atty. Gen., Providence, 1979-84, 86—, dep. chief criminal divsn., 1993; ptnr. Faerber & McMahon, Newport, 1985; exec. officer Trans. Co., 6th MTBN U.S. Marine Corps. Res., 1981-84, comdg. officer, 1985-86; exec. officer Marine Res. Unit Naval War Coll., Newport, 1997-99. Planner, participant sumposium on utilization of paralegals, Law Ctr. Roger Williams Coll. and R.I. Paralegal Assn., 1988; adj. faculty Community Coll. R.I., 1988, Nat. Advocacy Ctr., Columbia, Solar, 2000—; lectr. Roger Williams Coll., 1985; dir., juvenile prosecutor uit Dept. of Atty. Gen., Criminal Div., Providence, 1982-84; mem. Delinquency Prevention Task Force, Providence, 1983, Juvenile Probation Standards Task Force, Providence, 1983-84; mem. exec. com. Atty. Gen.'s Task Force on Sexual & Violent Phys. Abuse of Children, 1990—, chair legis. subcom. Counselor St. Joseph's Catholic Youth Orgn., Newport, 1980-81; team capt. Cath. Charities, 1974-79. Mgr. Newport Am. Little League, 1989-92, bd. dirs., 1991-92; bd. dirs. R.I. Childen's Advocacy Ctr., 1992—, R.I. Rape Crisis Ctr., 1993—, Sherwood Neighborhood Assn., 1997—, Portsmouth Pop Warner, 1998-2000; paralegal advisory bd. mem. Roger Williams U., chmn. new instructors com. Served to lt. col. USMCR. Named Jr. Officer of Yr., U.S. Navy Base, Newport, 1979. Mem. ABA, Nat. Dist. Atty. Assn. (acting state dir. 1986—), Fed. Bar Assn. (v.p. R.I. chpt. 1980-81), N.Y. Bar Assn., R.I. Bar Assn. (criminal bench-bar com. 1983—), Marine Corps Res. Criminal, Juvenile, Military. Home: 108 Sherwood Dr Portsmouth RI 02871-3800 Office: Dept Atty Gen 150 S Main St Providence RI 02903-2907 E-mail: JMcMAHON@riag.state.ri.us

MCMAHON, ROBERT ALBERT, JR. lawyer; b. New Orleans, July 23, 1950; s. Robert Albert and Marie Rose (Kennedy) McM.; m. Cynthia Ann Steffan, June 29, 1979; children: Angela, Jennifer, Robyn. BA cum laude, U. Southwestern La., 1972; JD, Loyola U., 1975. Bar: La. 1975, U.S. Dist. Ct. (ea. dist.) La. 1977, U.S. Ct. Appeals (5th cir.) 1978, U.S. Dist. Ct. (mid. dist.) La. 1985, U.S. Dist. Ct. (ea. dist.) Tex. 2000, U.S. Supreme Ct. 1989, U.S. Dist. Ct. (we. dist.) La. 1991. Atty. Brown & Hull, Metairie, La., 1975-76, Stewart Title La., New Orleans, 1976, Duplechin & Assocs., Gretna, La., 1977-80, Zelden & Zelden, New Orleans, 1980-81; ptnr. Bernard, Cassisa, Elliott & Davis, Metairie, La., 1982—. Vol. New Orleans Pro Bono Project, 1991—. Mem. New Orleans Pachyderm Club, 1992—, NRA-Inst. for Legis. Action, Washington, 1991—; chief YMCA Indian Guide/Princess Program, Metairie, 1988-89. Recipient scholarship U. New Orleans, 1968, U. Southwestern La., 1968. Mem. Def. Rsch. Inst., La. Assn. Def. Counsel, Maritime Law Assn. U.S., Jefferson Bar Assn., La. State Bar Assn.(ho. dels. 1993—), Hibernians, Phi Kappa Theta. Republican. Roman Catholic. Avocations: military history, hunting, tennis, golf. Admiralty, Insurance, Product liability. Office: Bernard Cassisa Elliott & Davis 1615 Metairie Rd Metairie LA 70005-3926 E-mail: mcmahonr@bernard-assisa.com

MCMAHON, THOMAS JOHN, retired lawyer, educator; b. Syracuse, N.Y., June 17, 1929; s. Thomas Denis and Margaret (Ryan) McM.; m. Alcida Rose Levesque, June 2, 1956; children— Sharon Rose, Alcida Marie, Michelle Ann, Thomas Paul. A.B. magna cum laude, Holy Cross Coll., 1951; J.D., Georgetown U., 1957. Bar: D.C. 1957, N.Y. 1957, Conn. 1960, Pa. 1964, Mass. 1971, U.S. Supreme Ct. 1963, U.S. Claims Ct. 1982, U.S. Ct. Mil. Appeals, U.S. Tax Ct., U.S. Ct. Appeals (1st, 2d, 3d, D.C. and fed. cirs.), U.S. Dist. Ct. Mass. 1971, U.S. Dist. Ct. Conn., U.S. Dist. Ct. (ea., no., we., so. dists.) N.Y., U.S. Dist. Ct. (we. dist.) Pa., U.S. Dist. Ct. D.C., U.S. Ct. Internat. Trade 1964, U.S. Temp. Ct. Emergency Appeals 1985. Assoc. firm Shearman & Sterling, N.Y.C., 1957-59, Keogh & Candee, Norwalk, Conn., 1959-60; atty. Am. Cyanamid Co., Stamford, Conn., 1960-63, Gulf Oil Corp., Pitts., 1963-69, Gillette Co., Boston, 1969-74; prof. Suffolk U. Law Sch., Boston, 1974-96; prof. emeritus, 1996—. Served to lt. (j.g.) USNR, 1951-54, to capt. JAGC. Mem. Boston Patent Law Assn. (chmn. copyright com. 1980-85). Republican. Roman Catholic. Home: PO Box 28 Walpole MA 02081-0028 Office: Suffolk U Law Sch Beacon Hill Boston MA 02114

MCMAHON, THOMAS MICHAEL, lawyer; b. Evanston, Ill., May 11, 1941; s. Robert C. and Kathryn D. (Dwyer) McM.; m. M. Ann Kaufman, July 11, 1964; children— Michael, Patrick. Student, U. Notre Dame, 1959-61; BA, Marquette U., 1963; JD magna cum laude, Northwestern U., 1970. Bar: Ill. 1970. Mgr. legal adv. sect. Ill. EPA, Springfield, 1970-72; assoc. Sidley & Austin, Chgo., 1972-75, ptnr., founder nat. environ. group, 1975-2000, sr. counsel, 2001—. Lectr. in field; mem. City of Evanston Environ. Control Bd., 1981-83. Author: The Superfund Handbook, 1989, International Environmental Law and Regulation, 1992, Legal Guide to Working with Environmental Consultants, 1992, The Environmental Manual, 1992. Lt. USN, 1963-67. Decorated Republic of Vietnam Campaign medal. Mem. ABA (vice-chmn. alternative dispute resolution com., past vice-chmn. environ. quality com., environ. aspects of bus. trans. com., internat. environ. law com., lectr. confs., teleconfs. and satellite seminars), Order of Coif. Alternative dispute resolution, General corporate, Environmental. Office: Sidley & Austin Bank One Plz Chicago IL 60603-2000 E-mail: tmcmahon@sidley.com

MCMAHON, THOMAS PATRICK, lawyer, state official; b. Detroit, Jan. 19, 1946; s. Patrick Joseph and Vivian Estelle (Kolfs) McM. B.A. magna cum laude, Mich. State U., 1968; J.D. cum laude, U. Mich., 1970; postgrad. Nat. Jud. Coll., 1980. Bar: Mich. 1971, U.S. Ct. Mil. Appeals 1972, U.S. Dist. Ct. (ea. dist.) Mich. 1971, Colo. 1976, U.S. Dist. Ct. Colo. 1976, U.S. Ct. Appeals (10th cir.) 1980, U.S. Supreme Ct. 1981. Assoc. Davis, Graham & Stubbs, Denver, 1976-78; asst. atty. gen. antitrust sect. Colo. Dept. Law, Denver, 1978-81, chief antitrust unit, 1981— ; lectr. in field. Contbr. articles to legal jours. Served as capt. JAGC, USAF, 1971-75. Weymouth Kirkland Found. scholar, 1968-70; U. Mich. Law Sch. scholar, 1968-70. Mem. Barristers Soc., Order of Coif, Phi Eta Sigma. Democrat. Roman Catholic.

MCMANAMAN, KENNETH CHARLES, lawyer; b. Fairfield, Calif., Jan. 25, 1950; s. Charles James and Frances J. (Holys) McM.; m. Carol Ann Wilson, Apr. 15, 1972; children; Evan John, Kinsey Bridget, Klerin Rose. BA cum laude, S.E. Mo. State U., 1972; JD, U. Mo., Kansas City, 1974; grad., Naval Justice Sch., Newport, R.I., 1975; MS in Bus. Mgmt. summa cum laude, Troy State U., Montgomery, Ala., 1978; LLM in Advanced Litigation, Nottingham-Trent U., 2001. Bar: Mo. 1975, U.S. Dist. Ct. (we. dist.) Mo. 1975, Fla. 1976, U.S. Dist. Ct. (No. and mid. dists.) Fla. 1976, U.S. Dist. Ct. Mil. Appeals 1977, U.S. Ct. Appeals (5th and 8th cirs.) 1977, U.S. Dist. Ct. (ea. dist.) Mo. 1978, U.S. Supreme Ct. 1978, D.C. 1991; cert. mil. judge spl. and gen. ct. martials; diplomate Am. Bd. Forensic Examiners. Ptnr. O'Loughlin, O'Loughlin & McManaman, Cape Girardeau, Mo., 1978—; prof. bus. law Troy (Ala.) State U., 1976-78, S.E. Mo. State U., Cape Girardeau, 1978-84, prof. criminal justice, 1998; prof. leadership Sch. Law William Woods U., 1998—; prof. bus. mgmt., Sch. Law, Cert. to Teach Trial Advocacy Nat. Inst. Trial Advocacy; prof. Sch. Law. Mem. Cape Cirardeau County Coun. on Child Abuse, 1980-89; membership dir. S.E. Mo. Scouting coun. Boy Scouts Am., 1980-82; mem. Cape Girardeau County Mental Health Assn., 1982-92; active local and state Dem. Party, del. Nat. Dem. Conv., San Francisco, 1984, chmn. County Dem. Com., 1984-96; mem. 8th Congl. Dist. Dem. Com., 1984-86, 27th State Dem. Senatorial Com., 1984-86, ward committeeman, 1984-94; bd. dirs. Area wide Task Force on Drug and Alcohol Abuse, 1984-87; sponsor drug edn./prevention program in schs.; bd. dirs. Cape County chpt. Nat. Kidney Found., 1988-93; pres. Jackson Area Soccer Assn., 1987-93. Capt. JAGC, USNR, 1994—. Recipient Robert Chilton award City of Jackson for Leadership, Integrity and Responsibility, 1995-97; named One of Outstanding Young Men Am., 1981, 82, 84, 85, Outstanding Pub. Svc. award Cape Girardeau Police Dept. Mem. ABA (Mo. del. young lawyers divsn. 1982-83), Mo. Bar Assn. (chmn. trial advicacy task force 1983), Mo. Bar (young lawyers sect. coun. rep. dist. 13 1980-85), Fla. Bar Assn., Kansas City Bar Assn., Assn. Trial Lawyers Am., Fed. Bar Assn., Nat. Coll. Dist. Attys., Cape Girardeau County Bar Assn. (founder, pres. young lawyers sect. 1981-82), Cape County Bar Assn. (sec. 1999, treas. 2000, v.p. 2001), Naval Res. Assn. (v.p. Southeast Mo/So. Ill. chpt. 1980-85), S.E. Mo. State Alumni Coun., Sigma Chi (numerous awards), Sigma Tau Delta, Pi Delta Epsilon. Roman Catholic. Bus. General practice, Workers' compensation. Home: 1162 Trail Ridge Dr Jackson MO 63755-3507 Office: O'Loughlin O'Loughlin McManaman 1736 N Kingshighway St Cape Girardeau MO 63701-2190 E-mail: oomk@midwest.net, kcmcm@prodigy.net

MCMANIS, JAMES, lawyer; b. Haverhill, Mass., May 28, 1943; s. Charles and Yvonne (Zinn) McM.; m. Sara Wigh, Mar. 30, 1968. BA, Stanford U., Palo Alto, Calif., 1964; JD, U. Calif., Berkeley, 1967. Bar: Calif. 1967, U.S. Dist. Ct. (no. dist.) Calif. 1967, U.S. Ct. Appeals (9th cir.) 1967, U.S. Supreme Ct. 1971. Dep. dist. atty. Santa Clara County Dist. Atty., 1968-71; mem. McManis, Faulkner & Morgan, San Jose, Calif., 1971—. Spl. master tech. equities litigation, 1987—; spl. examiner State Bar Calif., 1995-98; prof. law Lincoln U. Law Sch., San Jose, 1972-82; lectr. Calif. Continuing Edn. of Bar, 1989-90; instr. U. Calif. Law Sch., 1992-96, Stanford U. Sch. Law, 1994-99. Pres. Santa Clara County Bar Assn. Law Found., 1996, dir., 1987—. Fellow Am. Coll. Trial Lawyers; mem. ABA, State Bar Calif., Calif. Trial Lawyers Assn., Santa Clara County Bar Assn., Boalt Hall Alumni Assn. Avocations: history, books, travel, running. General civil litigation, Criminal, Intellectual property. Office: McManis Faulkner & Morgan Inc 160 W Santa Clara St Fl 10 San Jose CA 95113-1701 Fax: 408-279-3244. E-mail: jmcmanis@mfmlaw.com

MC MANUS, EDWARD JOSEPH, federal judge; b. Keokuk, Iowa, Feb. 9, 1920; s. Edward W. and Kathleen (O'Connor) McM.; m. Sally A. Hassett, June 30, 1948 (dec.); children: David P., Edward W., John N., Thomas J., Dennis Q.; m. Esther Y. Kanealy, Sept. 15, 1987. Student, St. Ambrose Coll., 1936-38; B.A., U. Iowa, 1940, J.D., 1942. Bar: Iowa 1941. Gen. practice of law, Keokuk, 1946-62; city atty., 1946-55; mem. Iowa Senate, 1955-59; lt. gov. Iowa, 1959-61; chief U.S. judge No. Dist. Iowa, 1962-85, sr. U.S. judge, 1985—. Del Democratic Nat. Conv., 1956, 60. Served as lt. AC USNR, 1942-46. Office: US Dist Ct 329 US Courthouse 101 1st St SE Cedar Rapids IA 52401-1202

MCMANUS, JAMES WILLIAM, lawyer; b. Kansas City, Mo., Aug. 1, 1945; s. Gerald B. and Mary M. (Hagan) McM.; m. Julie C. Waters, Feb. 17, 1973. BA, Rockhurst Coll., 1967; JD, St. Louis U., 1971. Bar: Mo. 1971, U.S. Dist. Ct. (we. dist.) Mo. 1972, U.S. Ct. Appeals (8th cir.) 1974, U.S. Supreme Ct. 1979, U.S. Ct. Appeals (10th cir.) 1984, U.S. Dist. Ct. Kans., 1995. Law clk. to presiding justice U.S. Dist. Ct. (we. dist.) Mo., 1971-73; assoc. Shughart, Thomson & Kilroy, P.C., Kansas City, 1973-76, dir., 1977-94; counsel Dysart, Taylor, Lay, Cotter & McMonigle, P.C., 1994—. Course lectr. med. jurisprudence U. Health Scis., Coll. Osteo. Medicine, Kansas City, 1994. Mem. adv. coun. St. Joseph Health Ctr., 1989—. Mem. ABA, Mo. Bar Assn., Kansas City Lawyers Assn., Kansas City Met. Bar Assn. (chmn. alternate dispute resolution com. 1996-97, vice chmn. 1994-95, chmn. med. malpractice com. 1989), Mo. Orgn. Def. Lawyers, St. Louis Alumni Assn. (pres. 1984-92), St. Louis U. Law Sch. Alumni Assn. Federal civil litigation, General civil litigation, Personal injury. Home: 6824 Valley Rd Kansas City MO 64113-1929 Office: Dysart Taylor Lay Cotter & McMonigle PC 4420 Madison Ave Kansas City MO 64111-3407 E-mail: jmcmanus@dysarttaylor.com

MCMICHAEL, DONALD EARL, lawyer; b. Denver, Aug. 8, 1931; s. Earl L. and Charlotte F. McM.; m. Zeta Hammond, July 6, 1955; children: Lauren A. McMichael Burnett, Thomas D., Susan E. McMichael Markle. AB, Dartmouth Coll., 1953; LLB, U. Colo., 1956. Bar: Colo. 1956, U.S. Dist. Ct. Colo. 1956, U.S. Ct. Appeals (10th cir.) 1956. Assoc. Holme Roberts & Owen, 1956-58; pres. Corp. Ins. Assocs., 1958-70; dir. trust devel. Ctrl. Bank Denver, 1970-72; ptnr. Brenman, Sobol & Baum, Denver, 1972-74, McMichael, Sell & Agresti (formerly McMichael, Multz & Lipton), Denver, 1974-99; pvt. practice, 1999-2000; of counsel Schmidt & Horen, 2000—. Chmn. Denver Ctrl. YMCA, 1971-73. Capt. USAR, 1956-64. Named Layman of Yr. Denver Ctrl. YMCA, 1973, named to Denver Metro YMCA Hall of Fame, 1989. Mem. Colo. Bar Assn., Denver Bar Assn., Denver Estate Planning Coun. (sec. 1971-73). Republican. Methodist. General corporate, Estate planning, Probate. Office: 6325 W Mansfield Ave Unit 234 Denver CO 80235-3015 E-mail: dmcmic@aol.com

MCMILLAN, LEE RICHARDS, II, lawyer; b. New Orleans, Aug. 26, 1947; s. John H. and Phoebe (Skillman) McM.; m. Lynne Clark Pottharst, June 27, 1970; children: Leslie Clark, Hillary Anne, Lee Richards III. BS in Commerce, Washington and Lee U., 1969; JD, Tulane U., 1972; LLM in Taxation, NYU, 1976. Bar: La. 1972. Assoc. Jones, Walker, Waechter, Poitevent, Carrere & Denegre, New Orleans, 1976-79, ptnr., 1979—, sect. head, corp. and securities sect., 1987-90, 94—, exec. com., 1990-94, 96-99, 2001—, chmn. exec. com., 1991-94, 96-98, 2001—. Vice-chmn. Mech. Equipment Co., Inc., New Orleans, 1980-86, chmn. bd., 1986—, pres. 1989-99; mem. The Bus. Coun. Greater New Orleans, 1998—, exec. com., 1999—; bd. dirs. The Chamber/New Orleans and the River Region, 1996-98; bd. trustees Alton Ochsner Med. Found., 1995—. Trustee New Orleans Mus. Art., 1989-95; bd. dirs. Bur. Govt. Rsch. New Orleans, 1987-93, Louise S. McGehee Sch., New Orleans, 1982-88, co-chmn. capital fund dr., 1984-86, pres. bd. dirs., 1986-88; bd. govs. Isidore Newman Sch., New Orleans, 1991-95. Lt. JACG USNR, 1972-75. Mem. ABA (com. on negotiated acquisitions 1986-94), La. State Bar Assn. (chmn. corp. and bus. law sect. 1985-86, mem. com. on bar admissions 1986-87), Young Pres. Orgn., Washington and Lee U. Alumni Assn. (bd. dirs. 1995-99). Republican. Episcopalian. Avocation: sailing. Banking, Mergers and acquisitions, Securities. Office: Jones Walker Waechter Poitevent Carrere & Denegre 201 Saint Charles Ave Ste 5100 New Orleans LA 70170-5101

MCMILLAN, M. SEAN, lawyer; Diploma, U. Munich, 1963; cert., Internat. Sch., Copenhagen, Denmark, 1962; SB, U. So. Calif., 1967; JD, Qarvard U., 1970. Bar: Calif. 1971. Spl. projects dir. Mass. Gen. Hosp., Boston, 1967-70; ptnr. Keatinge, Libbott, Bates & Loo, Los Angeles, 1970-74, Loo, Merideth & McMillan, Los Angeles, 1974-85, Bryan Cave LLP, Los Angeles/Santa Monica, 1986—. Editor: Harvard Internat. Law Jour., 1968-70.. Mem. Assn. Computing Machinery, ABA, Am. Soc. Internat. Law, Phi Beta Kappa, Phi Kappa Phi. Computer, General corporate, Private international. Office: Bryan Cave LLP 120 Broadway Ste 300 Santa Monica CA 90401-2386

MCMILLEN, ROBERT STEWART, lawyer; b. Yonkers, N.Y., Feb. 25, 1943; s. David Harry and Blodwyn Elizabeth (Evans) McM; m. Dorothea Anne Murray, July 2, 1966; children: Elissa London, Tara Evans. BS, U. Rochester, 1964; JD cum laude, Albany Law Sch. Union U., 1969. Bar: N.Y. 1969, U.S. Dist. Ct. (no. dist.) N.Y. 1969. Assoc. Clark, Bartlett & Caffry, Glens Falls, N.Y., 1969-73; ptnr. Caffry, Pontiff, Stewart, Rhodes & Judge, 1974-80; prin. Bartlett, Pontiff, Stewart & Rhodes, P.C., 1981—. Sr. law examiner N.Y. State Bd. Law Examiners, Albany, 1986-2001, bd. mem. 2001—; bd. dirs. Cmty. Title Agy., Inc., Glens Falls, 1984—, pres., 1984-99, v.p., sec., 1999—. Editor-in-chief Albany Law Rev., 1968-69. Bd. dirs., officer Voluntary Action Ctr. of Glens Falls Area, Inc., 1970-97; bd. dirs., treas. Arts and Crafts Ctr. of Warren County, Inc., Glens Falls, 1984-94; mem. Warren County Rep. Com., Queensbury, N.Y., 1979-2001; alt. or del. Rep. Jud. Nomination Com. 4th Jud. Dist. N.Y., 1977—. Recipient Disting. Svc. award Voluntary Action Ctr. of Glens Falls Area, Inc., 1990. Mem. ABA, N.Y. State Bar Assn. (mem. com. profl. ethics 1990-99, 2000—), Warren County Bar Assn. (bd. dirs. 1979-82, treas. 2001—), Adirondack Regional C. of C. (bd. dirs. 1997-2000, vice chmn. 1999-2000, counsel 2000—), Rotary. Avocations: travel, downhill skiing, boating. General corporate, Pension, profit-sharing, and employee benefits, Real property. Home: 147 Assembly Point Rd Lake George NY 12845-5201 Office: 1 Washington St Glens Falls NY 12801-2963

MCMILLIAN, THEODORE, federal judge; b. St. Louis, Jan. 28, 1919; m. Minnie E. Foster, Dec. 8, 1941. BS, Lincoln U., 1941, HHD (hon.), 1981; LLD, St. Louis U., 1949; HHD (hon.), U. Mo., St. Louis, 1978. Mem. firm Lynch & McMillian, St. Louis, 1949-53; asst. circuit atty. City of St. Louis, 1953-56; judge U.S. Ct. Appeals (8th cir.), 1978—. Judge Circuit Ct. for City St. Louis, 1956-72, Mo. Ct. Appeals eastern div., 1972-78; asso. prof. adminstrn. justice U. Mo., St. Louis, 1970— ; asso. prof. Webster Coll. Grad. Program, 1977; mem. faculty Nat. Coll. Juvenile Justice, U. Nev., 1972— Served to 1st lt. Signal Corps U.S. Army, 1942-46. Recipient Alumni Merit award St. Louis U., 1965, ACLU Civil Liberties award, 1995, Disting. Lawyer award Bar Assn. Met. St. Louis, 1996, Salute to Excellence Civil Rights award St. Louis Am., 1997; named Disting. Non-Alumnus U. Mo.-Columbia Law Sch., 1999. Mem. Am. Judicature Soc., Am. Bd. Trial Advs. (hon. diplomate), Lawyers Assn. Mo., Mound City Bar Assn., Phi Beta Kappa, Alpha Sigma Nu. Office: Thomas F Eagleton Court House Ste 25 162 111 S 10th St Saint Louis MO 63102

MCMILLIN, JAMES CRAIG, lawyer; b. Oklahoma City, June 27, 1949; s. Lawrence Harold and Rose Lee (Jeffrey) McM. BA, U. Okla., 1971; JD, NYU, 1976. Bar: N.Y. 1977, Okla. 1997, U.S. Dist. Ct. (so. and ea. dists.) N.Y. 1977, D.C. 1979, U.S. Supreme Ct. 1980, U.S. Dist. Ct. (no. dist.) Calif. 1981, U.S. Dist. Ct. (we. dist.) Okla. 1996, U.S. Dist. Ct. (no. dist.) Okla. 2000, U.S. Ct. Appeals (2d cit.) 1981, U.S. Ct. Appeals (7th cir.) 1982, U.S. Ct. Appeals (11th cir.) 1993. Assoc. Donovan, Leisure, Newton & Irvine, N.Y.C., 1976-79; ptnr. Liddle, McMillin & Henze, 1979-80, Werbel, McMillin & Carnelutti PC, N.Y.C., 1981-96; counsel McAfee & Taft, Oklahoma City, 1996—. With U.S. Army, 1971-73. Root-Tilden scholar, 1971, 73-76. Mem. ABA, Fed. Bar Coun., N.Y. State Bar Assn., Okla. State Bar Assn., D.C. Bar Assn., Assn. Bar City N.Y. Democrat. Antitrust, Federal civil litigation, Securities. Office: McAfee & Taft 211 N Robinson Ave Ste S-1000 Oklahoma City OK 73102-7103 E-mail: james.mcmillin@mcafeetaft.com

MCMORROW, MARY ANN G. state supreme court justice; b. Chgo., Jan. 16, 1930; m. Emmett J. McMorrow, May 5, 1962; 1 dau., Mary Ann. Student, Rosary Coll., 1948-50; JD, Loyola U., 1953. Bar: Ill. 1953, U.S. Dist. Ct. (no. dist.) Ill. 1960, U.S. Supreme Ct. 1976. Atty. Riordan & Linklater Law Offices, Chgo., 1954-56; asst. state's atty. Cook County, 1956-63; sole practice, 1963-76; judge Cir. Ct. Cook County, 1976-85, Ill. Appellate Ct., 1985-92, Supreme Ct. Ill., 1992—. Faculty adv. Nat. Jud. Coll., U. Nev., 1984. Contbr. articles to profl. jours. Mem. Chgo. Bar Assn., Ill. State Bar Assn., Women's Bar Assn. of Ill. (pres. 1975-76, bd. dirs. 1970-78), Am. Judicature Soc., Northwestern U. Assocs., Ill. Judges Assn., Nat. Assn. Women Judges, Advocates Soc., Northwest Suburban Bar Assn., West Suburban Bar Assn., Loyola Law Alumni Assn. (bd. govs. 1985—), Ill. Judges Assn. (bd. dirs.), Cath. Lawyers Guild (v.p.), The Law Club of the City of Chgo., Inns of Ct. Office: Supreme Ct of Ill 160 N La Salle St Chicago IL 60601-3103

MCNABOE, JAMES FRANCIS, lawyer; b. Newark, July 24, 1945; s. Frank A. and Eleanor (Baran) McN.; m. Constance G. Ilardi, Nov. 8, 1986. AB, Seton Hall U., 1966; JD, Rutgers U., 1969; student, Northwestern U., Chgo., 1966-67. Bar: N.J. 1969, U.S. Supreme Ct. 1979, N.Y. 1982, U.S. Ct. Appeals (3d cir.) 1982, U.S. Dist. Ct. (ea. dist.) N.Y. 1982, U.S. Dist. Ct. (so. dist.) N.Y. 1997; cert. civil trial atty. N.J., 1982. Law clk. Hoffman & Humphreys, Wayne, N.J., 1969, Hon. Bertram Polow, Morristown, 1969-70, Hon. Scott M. Long Jr., 1970-71; assoc. Evans, Hand, Allabough & Amoresano, West Paterson, N.J., 1971-81, Schwartz & Andolino, Livingston, 1981-85; sole practice Hackensack, 1986-87; assoc. Golden, Rothschild, Spagnola and DiFazio, Somerville, 1987-88, ptnr., 1989-90; assoc. Sheft & Sheft, Jersey City, 1991-92; trial counsel Caron, Greenberg & Fitzgerald, Rutherford, N.J., 1993-96; mng. atty. Sehr Cortner McNaboe Colliau & Jordan, West Orange, 1996—. Mem. ABA, N.J. State Bar Assn., Def. Rsch. Inst., Trial Attys. N.J. Democrat. Roman Catholic. State civil litigation, Insurance, Personal injury. Home: 29 Chestnut Rd West Orange NJ 07052-2632 Office: 200 Executive Dr Ste 160 West Orange NJ 07052-3303

MCNALLY, SUSAN FOWLER, lawyer; b. Portsmouth, Va., Jan. 10, 1957; d. Joseph D. and Marie C. Fowler; m. James Edward McNally, Mar. 23, 1985. BA, U. Pacific, 1978; JD, UCLA, 1981. Bar: Calif. 1981, U.S. Dist. Ct. (cen. dist.) Calif. 1982, U.S. Ct. Appeals (9th cir.) 1982. Assoc. Hahn, Cazier & Smaltz, Los Angeles, 1982-85, Gilchrist & Rutter, Santa Monica, Calif., 1985-88, ptnr., 1989—. Speaker in field. Mem. ABA (real property, probate and trust sect., comml. leasing com., vice chair emerging issues com.), Calif. Bar Assn. (real property sect.), Los Angeles County Bar Assn. (real property sect.), Santa Monica Bar Assn., Women Lawyers Assn Calif., Women Lawyers Assn. L.A., Irish Am. Bar Assn., CREW-L.A. (chair membership com. 1993-94, dir., gen., co-chmn. vols. and resources com. 2000), Bldg. Owners and Mgrs. Assn. Avocations: hiking, bicycling, skiing, running. Contracts commercial, General corporate, Real property. Office: Gilchrist & Rutter 1299 Ocean Ave Ste 900 Santa Monica CA 90401-1000

MCNAMARA, ANNE H. lawyer, corporate executive; b. Shanghai, Republic of China, Oct. 18, 1947; came to U.S. 1949; d. John M. and Marion P. (Murphy) H. AB, Vassar Coll., 1969; JD, Cornell U., 1973. Bar: N.Y. 1973, Tex. 1981. Assoc. Shea, Gould, Climenko & Casey, N.Y.C., 1972-76; from asst. corp. sec. to corp. sec. Am. Airlines, Inc., Dallas, 1976-88, v.p. pers. resources, 1988; sr. v.p., gen. counsel Am. Airlines (AMR Corp.), 1988—. Bd. dirs. Louisville Gas & Electric Co., LG&E Energy Corp., Sabre Group Holdings, Inc. Antitrust, General corporate, Securities. Office: Am Airlines Inc Dallas/Fort Worth Airport PO Box 619616 Dallas TX 75261-9616

MCNAMARA, DENIS MICHAEL, lawyer; b. Arapuni, New Zealand, May 27, 1948; s. Terrence Anthony and Patricia McNamara; m. Priscilla Cathrine Williams, Aug. 10, 1973; children: Siobhan, Liam. LLB with honors, Auckland (New Zealand) U. Bar: barrister and solicitor High Ct. of New Zealand. Ptnr. Simpson Grierson, 1969—. Bd. dirs. numerous corps. Bd. dirs. New Zealand Pacific Econ. Co-op Coun., 2000—, others. Mem. Inter Pacific Bar Assn., Int. Bar Assn., Internat. Soc. Hospitality Cons., Inst. of Dirs. Avocations: golf, sailing, travel. General corporate, Private international, Mergers and acquisitions. Office: Simpson Grierson 92-96 Albert St Auckland New Zealand Fax: +64 9 307 0331. E-mail: dennis.mcnamara@simpsongrierson.com

MCNAMARA, J(OHN) DONALD, retired lawyer, business executive; b. Bridgeport, Conn., Feb. 28, 1924; s. John T. and Agnes (Keating) McN.; m. Shirley Addison Holdridge, Nov. 5, 1960. BA, Dartmouth Coll., 1945; MA in Govt., Harvard U., 1947, LLB, 1950. Bar: N.Y. 1951, Conn. 1951. Assoc. Hall, Haywood, Patterson & Taylor, N.Y.C., 1951-53, 55-56; asst. U.S. Atty. U.S. Dist. Ct. (so. dist.) N.Y., 1953-55; assoc. Wickes, Riddell, Bloomer, Jacobi & McGuire, N.Y.C., 1956-57; assoc., then ptnr. Nottingham & McEniry (and successor), 1957-59; sec., gen. counsel Interpub. Group of Cos., Inc., 1960-79, dir., 1965-85, sr. v.p., 1966-73, exec. v.p., 1973-79, pres., 1980-85, mem. exec. com., 1967-85, mem. fin. com., 1980-85. Chmn. U.S. Nat. Tennis Championships, 1965. Served to lt. (j.g.) USNR, 1943-46. Mem. River Club, Univ. Club, Met. Opera Club (bd. dirs. 1999—), Ekwanok Country Club (bd. govs. Manchester, Vt. 1991-95), Dorset (Vt.) Field Club (bd. govs. 1996-99, pres. 1997-98), West Side Tennis Club (pres. Forest Hills, N.Y. 1964-66, 79-80). Home: 350 E 57th St New York NY 10022-2953 also: River Rd Manchester VT 05254

MCNAMARA, MICHAEL JOHN, lawyer; b. Hutchinson, Minn., July 1, 1948; s. John Oliver and Lucille Violet (Wedell) M.; m. Kathleen Elizabeth Dahl; children: Jennifer, Kelly. BA, U. Utah, 1976; JD, U. Minn., 1980. Bar: Minn. 1981, U.S. Dist. Ct. Minn. 1981, U.S. Ct. Appeals (8th cir.) 1982, U.S. Supreme Ct. 1988, Wis. 1992. Pvt. practice, Mpls., 1981—. Panel arbitrator Am. Arbitration Assn., Hennepin County Dist. Ct.; panelist No-Fault Arbitrators Minn. Supreme Ct. Contbr. articles to profl. jours. Sgt. U.S. Army, 1968-71, Vietnam. Nat. Merit scholar. Mem. FBA, ATLA, The Federalist Soc., Internat. Platform Assn., Minn. State Bar Assn., Minn. Trial Lawyers Assn., Hennepin County Bar Assn. (mem. spkrs. bur.). Avocations: jogging, biking, hiking. General civil litigation, General corporate, Criminal. Office: Henderson Howard et al 6200 Shingle Creek Pkwy Ste 385 Minneapolis MN 55430-2176

MCNAMARA, PATRICK JAMES, lawyer; b. Bethpage, N.Y., Mar. 27, 1959; s. James Francis and Kathleen (Marrinan) McN.; m. Kimberly McNamara, Dec. 7, 1991; children: James Patrick, Emma Kathleen. BA in History, Rutgers U., New Brunswick, N.J., 1981, MA in Polit. Sci., 1985; JD, Rutgers U., Camden, N.J., 1987. Bar: N.J. 1987, U.S. Dist. Ct. N.J. 1987, Pa. 1987. Legal sec. to Hon. Neil F. Deighan Jr., Appellate Divsn. N.J. Superior Ct., 1987-88; with Giordano, Halleran & Ciesla, Middletown, N.J., 1988-91; ptnr. Carpenter, Bennett and Morrissey, Newark, 1991-94, Scarinci & Hollenbeck, Secaucus, N.J., 1994—. Gen. counsel Nat. Assn. Fruits, Flavors & Syrups, Inc., 1995—, Chem. Sources Assn., 1998—, Soc. of Flavor Chemists, 2001-. Assoc. editor Food Exec. mag., 1997, Food Product Design mag., 1999; contbr. author to profl. jours. Mcpl. atty. Township of Aberdeen, 1992-95; spl. counsel Twp. of Aberdeen, 1996-97, Fredon Twp. Zoning Bd. of Adj., 1999-, Borough of S. River, 2001-; lead counsel City of Elizabeth Planning Bd., 1999—. Rutgers U. Grad. fellow Eagleton Inst. Politics, 1984-85. Mem. N.J. State Bar Assn. (environ. law sect.), Environ. Law Inst., N.J. Group Small Chem. Businesses, Rutgers Alumni Assn. (bd. dirs.). Avocations: sports, travel, golf, politics. Administrative and regulatory, Environmental, Real property. Office: Scarinci & Hollenbeck 500 Plaza Dr PO Box 3189 Secaucus NJ 07096-3189 Fax: 201-348-3877. E-mail: patrick@njlegalink.com

MCNAMARA, ROBERT M., JR. lawyer; b. Ohio; m. Patti Devenney; children: Brendan, Caitlin. BA, Mt. Carmel Coll., 1967; AB, John Carroll U., 1968; JD, Georgetown U., 1973. Law clk. to Hon. George C. Edwards, Jr. U.S. Ct. Appeals (6th cir.), Cin.; dep. dir. enforcement Commodity Futures Trading Commn.; gen. counsel Peace Corps.; legis. counsel U.S. Senate Judiciary com.; asst. U.S. atty. U.S. Senate Watergate Com., asst. majority counsel; asst. gen. counsel enforcement Dept. Treasury; gen. counsel CIA, 1997—. Adj. prof. law Georgetown U. Law Ctr. Symposium editor: Am. Criminal Law Rev. Office: CIA Office of Gen Counsel Washington DC 20505-0001

MCNAMEE, STEPHEN M. federal judge; b. 1942; B.A., U. Cinn., 1964; M.A., J.D., U. Ariz., 1969. U.S. atty. Dist. of Ariz., Phoenix, 1985-90; chief judge U.S. Dist. Ct. Ariz., 1990—. Office: US Dist Judge Sandra Day O'Connor US Ct 401 W Washington St SPC 60 Phoenix AZ 85003-2158

MCNEELY, JAMES LEE, lawyer; b. Shelbyville, Ind., May 4, 1940; s. Carl R. and Elizabeth J. (Orebaugh) McN.; m. Rose M. Wisker, Sept. 5, 1977; children: Angela, Susan, Meg, Matt. AB, Wabash Coll., 1962; JD, Ind. U., 1965. Bar: Ind. 1965, U.S. Dist. Ct. (so. dist.) Ind. 1965, U.S. Ct. Appeals (7th cir.) 1970. Assoc. Pell & Matchett, Shelbyville, 1965-70; ptnr. Matchett & McNeely, 1970-74; sole practice, 1974-76; sr. ptnr. McNeely & Sanders, 1976-86, McNeely, Sanders & Stephenson, Shelbyville, 1986-89, McNeely, Sanders, Stephenson & Thopy, Shelbyville, 1989-96, McNeely, Stephenson, Thopy & Harrold, Shelbyville, 1997—. Guest lectr. Franklin Coll., Ind., 1965-72; judge Shelbyville City Ct., 1967-71. Chmn. Shelbyville County Rep. Cen. Com., 1968-88; bd. dirs. Ind. Lung Assn., 1972-75, Crossroads Council Boy Scouts Am., 1982; bd. dirs., pres. Shelbyville Girls Club. Named Sagamore of the Wabash, gov. Otis Bowen, 1977, gov. Robert Orr, 1986, 88, gov. Evan Bayh, 1996. Fellow Ind. Bar Found. (patron, sec. 1999-2000, chair elect 2000-01); mem. ABA, Ind. Bar Assn. (sec. 1985-87, bd. dirs. 1976-78, chair-elect Ho. Dels. 1994-95, chair 1995-96, v.p. 1996-97, pres.-elect 1997-98, pres. 1998-99), Shelby County Bar Assn. (pres. 1975), Ind. Lawyers Commn. (pres., dir.), Fed. Merit Selection Commn. (adv. mem. 1988-92, chmn. 2001—), Shelbyville Jaycees (Distinguished Service award 1969, Good Govt. award 1970), Wabash Coll. Nat. Assn. Wabash Men (dir. 1983-89, sec. 1989-91, v.p. 1991-93, pres. 1993-95, Man of Yr. 1995), Kappa Sigma Alpha Pi chpt. (Hall of Fame 1995). Methodist. Lodges: Lions, Elks, Eagles. Avocations: golf, travel. State civil litigation, Insurance, Labor. Home: 1902 E Old Rushville Rd Shelbyville IN 46176-9569

MCNEIL, MARK SANFORD, lawyer; b. Shawnee, Okla., Feb. 4, 1950; s. Irving Jr. and Sylvia Louise (Sanford) McN.; m. Cathy Marleen Yandell, Sept. 7, 1974; children: Elizabeth, Laura. Assoc. Lillick McHose & Charles, San Francisco, 1974-76; rsch. asst. Kyoto (Japan) U., 1976-77; internat. law cons. Amita & Hirokawa, Osaka, Japan, 1976-77, Ono Law Office, Osaka, 1976-77; internat. counsel Medtronic, Inc., Mpls., 1978-84; mgr. contract adminstrn. Cray Rsch., Inc., 1985, internat. counsel, 1986-88, dir. internat. contracts, 1988-91, dir. corp. contacts, 1991; assoc. Briggs and Morgan, P.A., 1995-97. Adj. prof. William Mitchell Coll. Law, St. Paul, 1989-91. Bd. dirs. Midwest China Ctr. Mem. ABA, Minn. Bar Assn. (chmn. internat. bus. law sect. 1986-87), Hennepin County Bar Assn., Corp. Counsel Assn., Minn. World Trade Assn. (bd. dirs. 1996—, pres. 1998-99). Avocations: photography, music, fiction writing, rafting. Computer, General corporate, Private international. Home: 514 5th St E Northfield MN 55057-2220 Office: Lindquist and Vennum PLLP 4200 IDS Ctr Minneapolis MN 55402 E-mail: mmcneil@lindquist.com

MCNEILL, THOMAS RAY, lawyer; b. Pitts., June 2, 1952; s. Thomas William McNeill and Mary (Shiveley) Hiss; m. Patsy Lynch, June 25, 1977; children: Elizabeth, Kathleen, Thomas. BSBA, U. Fla., 1974; JD, Emory U., 1977. Bar: Ga. 1977, U.S. Dist. Ct. (no. dist.) Ga. 1977. Assoc. Powell, Goldstein, Frazer & Murphy, LLP, Atlanta, 1977-84, ptnr., 1984—, mgr. corp. dept., 1993-95, bd. ptnrs., 1998—. Mem. Ga. Bar Assn., Emory U. Alumni Assn. (pres. exec. com. Atlanta chpt. 1988-89, Law Sch. coun. 1990-2000), Soc. of Internat. Bus. Fellows, Beta Gamma Sigma. Finance, Franchising, Mergers and acquisitions. Office: Powell Goldstein Frazer & Murphy 191 Peachtree St NE Ste 1600 Atlanta GA 30303-1700 E-mail: tmcneill@pgfm.com

MCNEIL STAUDENMAIER, HEIDI LORETTA, lawyer; b. Preston, Iowa, Apr. 7, 1959; d. Archie Hugo and Heidi (Waltert) McN.; m. L. William Staudenmaier III; children: Kathleen Louise McNeil Staudenmaier, Jacob William Staudenmaier. BA in Journalism and Broadcasting with distinction, U. Iowa, 1981, JD with distinction, 1985. Bar: Ariz. 1985, U.S. Dist. Ct. Ariz. 1985, U.S. Ct. Appeals (9th cir.) 1985, U.S. Ct. Appeals (10th cir.) 1990. Sports journalist The Daily Iowan, Iowa City, 1977-81, Quad City Times, Davenport, Iowa, 1981-82; ptnr. Snell & Wilmer, Phoenix, 1985—. Judge pro tem, Maricopa County, Phoenix, 1992—, Ariz. Ct. Appeals, 1998—. Mem. ABA (mem. domestic violence commn. 1995-98, Ho. of Dels. 1995-98, 2001—, chair young lawyers career issues com. 1992-93, mem. affiliate assistance program com. 1992-93, dir. 1993-94, spl. projects coord. 1994-95, bus. law sect., mem. editl. bd. bus. Law Today), Internat. Assn. Gaming Attys., Ariz. Bar Assn. (Indian law sect. exec. coun. and chair, 1995-99, young lawyers exec. coun. 1991-94), Maricopa County Bar Assn. (bd. dirs. 1991—, young lawyers divsn. 1987-93, pres. 1991-92, 99-2000), Ariz. Women Lawyers, Phoenix Assn. Def. Counsel, Native Am. Bar Assocs., Phi Beta Kappa, Phi Eta Sigma. Lutheran. Avocations: running, golf, skiing, hiking, bicycling. General civil litigation, Native American.

MCNIDER, JAMES SMALL, III, lawyer; b. Richmond, Va., Aug. 23, 1956; s. James Small Jr. and Phoebe Warwick (Johnston) McN.; m. Anna Mary Van Buren, Apr. 30, 1983; children: Anna Lee, Mary Tyler, James S. IV, Elle Page. BS, Washington & Lee U., 1978, JD, 1981. Bar: Va. 1981, U.S. Tax Ct. 1981, U.S. Dist. Ct. (ea. dist.) Va. 1986. Assoc. Kaufman & Canoles, Norfolk, Va., 1981-85, Willcox & Savage, Norfolk, 1985-87, ptnr., 1987-95, James S. McNider, III P.L.C., Hampton, Va., 1995—. Author: (with others) ABA Sales and Use Tax Handbook, 1988. Mem. ABA, Va. Bar Assn. (chmn. tax sect. 1993-94), Princess Anne Country Club, Omicron Delta Kappa. Episcopalian. Avocations: pvt. pilot, tennis, golf. General corporate, Corporate taxation, State and local taxation. Home: 808 Park Pl Hampton VA 23669-4152 Office: PO Box I Hampton VA 23669-0256 E-mail: jmcnider@ualaw.com

MCNITT, DAVID GARVER, lawyer; b. Lewistown, Pa., Sept. 26, 1949; s. Garver M. and H. Faith (Harbeson) McN.; m. Mary Ellen Davis, Oct. 2, 1971; 1 child, David. BS, Juniata Coll., 1971; JD, Hamline U., 1976; cert. U. Exeter, Eng., 1976. Bar: Pa. 1977, U.S. Tax Ct. 1977, U.S. Dist. Ct. (ea. dist.) Pa. 1978, U.S. Ct. Appeals (3rd cir.) 1986, U.S. Supreme Ct. 1985. Sales assoc. Fin. Planning Assocs., Harrisburg, Pa., 1971-72; account supr. FMBAS, Inc., Camp Hill, Pa., 1972-74; tax acct. Stradley, Ronan, Stevens & Young, Phila., 1977; shareholder, dir. Cramp, D'Iorio, McConchie & Forbes, P.C., Media, Pa., 1977-87, George J. Lavin Jr. Assocs., Phila., 1987-90; counsel to the firm Lesser & Kaplin, P.C., Blue Bell, Pa., 1990-93; shareholder, dir. David G. McNitt, Esq. P.C., Media, Pa., 1993—; guest lectr. Wharton Sch., U. Pa., Phila., 1982-84, 87; adj. prof. Del. Law Sch. at Widener U., Wilmington. Mem. ABA, Pa. Bar Assn., Nat. Assn. Coll. and Univ. Attys. Republican. Mem. Society of Friends. Bankruptcy, General corporate, Securities. Home and Office: David G McNitt Esq PC 103 Lafayette Bldg Media PA 19063

MCNULTY, MARK ANDREW, lawyer, state official; b. Jersey City, N.J., Nov. 10, 1944; s. Daniel Edward and Grace Marie (Bender) McN.; m. Barbara Anne Woznicki, Aug. 9, 1969; children: Christine Anne, Joanne Lynne. BS, St. Peters Coll., Jersey City, N.J., 1966; JD, Seton Hall U., 1973. Bar: Del. 1973, U.S. Dist. Ct. Del. 1974, U.S. Ct. Appeals (D.C. cir.) 1976. Tchr. West New York Dept. Edn., N.J., 1966-73; pvt. practice, Dover, Del., 1974; asst. pub. defender Del. Office of Pub. Defender, Dover, 1974-75; chief counsel Del. Dept. Transp., Dover, 1975-85, exec. asst. Del. Dept. Transp., 1985-88; dir. Del. Transp. Auth., 1988-93; spl. counsel State of Del., Dover, 1993—; acting sec. Dept. Transp., 1992-93; dir. NICKI Internat., Houston, Tex. Parish council Holy Cross, Dover, 1982-84. Mem. ABA, Assn. Trial lawyers Am., Hwy. Rsch. Council, Am. Assn. State Hwy and Transp. Offls.), Maple Dale Country Club, K.C. Roman Cathloic. Office: Del Dept Transp PO Box 778 Dover DE 19903-0778

MCNULTY, PAUL J. prosecutor; BA, Grove City Coll.; JD, Capital U. Counsel U.S. House Com. on Standards of Official Conduct, Washington, 1983—85; dir. legal svcs. Legal Svcs. Corp., 1985—87; minority counsel House Judiciary Subcom. Crime, 1987—90; dep. dir. Office Policy Devel., dir. Office Policy and Comms. U.S. Dept. Justice, Washington, 1990—93; counsel Shaw, Pittman, Potts and Trowbridge, 1993—95, U.S. Ho. Reps. Com. on Judiciary, Washington, 1995—99; prin. assoc. dep. atty. gen. U.S. Dept Justice, 2001; chief counsel, dir. legis. ops. Office of Majority Leader U.S. Ho. Reps., Washington, 1999—2001; U.S. atty. Ea. Dist. Va. U.S. Dept. Justice, 2001—. Office: 2100 Jamieson Ave Alexandria VA 22314*

MCPHERSON, JAMES WILLIS, JR. retired lawyer; b. Kalamazoo, Mich., Oct. 25, 1920; s. James Willis and Helen Evringham (Rose) McP.; m. Bea Shaheen, Mar. 25, 1949; children— Marena Lee, Cheryl Ann McPherson Loden, James W. III. Student Kent State U., 1940-41, 42, 46; LL.B., George Washington U., 1949; postgrad. Ohio State U., 1949. Bar: Ohio 1949, D.C. 1949, U.S. Dist. Ct. (no. dist.) Ohio 1949, U.S. Supreme Ct. 1964. U.S. capitol police officer, Washington, 1947-49; ptnr. McPherson & Hite, Hartville, Ohio, 1949-95; ret., 1995; ct. referee Stark County Domestic Ct., Canton, Ohio, 1956-59, solicitor Village of Hartville, 1958-70; asst. U.S. atty. gen. State of Ohio, 1969; dir., agt. Ohio Bar Title Ins. Co., Dayton, 1974— . Central committeeman Republican Party, Canton; bd. dirs. Stark County Civic Opera, Canton, 1977-79; bd. dirs., contbr. Hartville Area Cmty. Charitable Trust Assn. Served with USMC, 1942-45, PTO. Fellow Ohio State Fellow Found.; mem. Internat. Bar Assn., ABA, Ohio Bar Assn., Stark County Bar Assn. (exec. com. 1977-79, bd. dirs. 1977-79), Alpha Tau Omega, Delta Theta Phi. Republican. Club: Congress Lake (Hartville, Ohio). Lodges: Masons, Lions, Scottish Rite. Family and matrimonial, Probate, Real property. Office: McPherson & Hite 140 Sunnyside St SW Hartville OH 44632-8933

MCQUIGG, JOHN DOLPH, retired lawyer; b. Abilene, Tex., Oct. 19, 1931; s. John Lyman and Dorothy Elinor (King) McQ.; m. Sandra Elainea Duke, Oct. 18, 1969 (div. 1989); 1 child, John Revel. BA, Denison U., 1953; LLB, U. Tex., 1962. Bar: Fla. 1962, U.S. Supreme Ct. 1971. Account exec. San Antonio Light, 1957-59; assoc. Shackleford, Farrior, Stallings & Evans, 1962-66, ptnr. Fla., 1966-73; pres. John McQuigg, P.A., 1973-80; shareholder Fowler, White, Gillen, Boggs, Villareal & Banker, P.A., 1980-92; of counsel Stephen Rosen, P.A., 1993; pvt. practice, 1994-2000; ret., 2000. Arbitrator, U.S. Dist. Ct., 2000—. Judge Compensation Claims pro hac vice, 1993; bd. dirs. Fla. Gulf Coast R.R. Mus., Inc., Am. Assn. Pvt. Railroad Car Owners; pres. Fla. Coalition R.R. Passengers, 1990-99. 1st lt. USAF, 1953-57. Mem. ABA, Fla. Bar, Tampa Club. Episcopalian. Alternative dispute resolution, General civil litigation, Workers' compensation.

MCRAE, CHARLES R. (CHUCK MCCRAE), state supreme court presiding justice; BA, Marietta Coll., 1962; JD cum laude, Miss. Coll. Sch. Law, 1970. Trial atty., Pascagoula, Miss., 1970—90; spl. chancellor, cir. ct. judge Jackson, Forrest and Lincoln Counties, 1990; justice Miss. Supreme Ct, Jackson, 1991—. Mem.: ABA, Miss. Trial Lawyer's Assn. (life)), ATLA, Magnolia Bar Assn., Fed. Bar Assn., Am. Judicature Soc. Office: Supreme Court Carroll Gartin Bldg Jackson MS 39205*

MCRAE, HAMILTON EUGENE, III, lawyer; b. Midland, Tex., Oct. 29, 1937; s. Hamilton Eugene and Adrian (Hagaman) McR.; m. Betty Hawkins, Aug. 27, 1960; children: Elizabeth Ann, Stephanie Adrian, Scott Hawkins BSEE, U. Ariz., 1961; student, USAF Electronics Sch., 1961-62; postgrad., U. Redlands, Calif., 1962-63; JD with honors and distinction, U. Ariz., 1967; LHD (hon.), Sterling Coll., 1992; vis. fellow, Darwin Coll. and Martin Ctr., Cambridge (Eng.) U., 1996-97. Bar: Ariz. 1967, U.S. Supreme Ct. 1979; cert. real estate specialist, Ariz. Elec. engr. Salt River Project, Phoenix, 1961; assoc. Jennings, Strouss & Salmon, 1967-71, ptnr., 1971-85, chmn. real estate dept., 1980-85, mem. policy com., 1982-85, mem. fin. com., 1981-85, chmn. bus. devel. com., 1982-85; ptnr. and co-founder Stuckey & McRae, 1985—; co-founder, chmn. bd. Republic Cos., 1985—. Magistrate Paradise Valley, Ariz., 1983-85; juvenile referee Superior Ct., 1983-85; pres., dir. Phoenix Realty & Trust Co., 1970—; officer Indsl. Devel. Corp. Maricopa County, 1972-86; instr. and lectr. in real estate; officer, bd. dirs. other corps.; adj. prof. Frank Lloyd Wright Sch. Architecture, Scottsdale, Ariz., 1989—; instr. Ariz. State U. Coll. Architecture and Environ. Design; lead instr. ten-state-bar seminar on Advanced Real Estate Transactions, 1992; evaluation com. for cert. real estate specialist Ariz. Bar, 1994-96; mem. real estate adv. commn. Ariz. Bar, 1996—. Exec. prodr. film documentary on relief and devel. in Africa, 1990; contbr. articles to profl. jours. Elder Valley Presbyn. Ch., Scottsdale, Ariz., 1973-75, 82-85, 96-98, chair evangelism com. 1973-74, corp. pres., 1974-75, 84-85, trustee, 1973-75, 82-85, chmn. exec. com., 1984, mem. mission com. 1993—, chmn. 1998; trustee Upward Found., Phoenix, 1977-80, trustee, Valley Presbyn. Found., 1982-83, Ariz. Acad., 1971—; trustee, mem. exec. com. Phi Gamma Delta Ednl. Found., Washington, 1974-84; trustee Phi Gamma Delta Internat., 1984-86; bd. dirs. Archon, 1986-87, Hall of Fame, 1999; founder, trustee, pres. McRae Found., 1980—; founder Hall of Fame, Ariz., 1999; bd. dirs. Food for Hungry Inc. (Internat. Relief), 1985-95, exec. com., 1986-95, chmn. bd. dirs., 1987-92; chmn. bd. dirs. Food for Hungry Internat., 1993-95, pres. adv. coun., 1995—, mem. building com., 1999—; trustee, mem. exec. com. Ariz. Mus. Sci. and Tech., 1984—, 1st v.p., 1985-86, pres., 1986-88, chmn. bd. dirs., 1988-90, exec. com. 1984-90, exhibits com. 1990—, strategic planning com., 1999—, svc. recognition 1999; Lambda Alpha Internat. Hon. Land Econs. Soc, 1988-98; sec.-treas. Ariz. State U. Coun. for Design Excellence, 1989-90, bd. dirs. 1988-99, pres. 1990-91, trustee 1999—; mem. Crisis Nursery Office of the Chair, 1988-89, Maricopa Community Colls. Found., 1988—, sec. 1990-91, 2d v.p. 1993-94, 1st v.p. and pres. elect 1994-95, pres. 1995-96, mem. Elsner scholarship com., 1999—, web site com., 1999, capital campaign cabinet, 1995-96, 98-99, mem. of chair, 1998-99, mem. nominating com., 1997—, deferred gifts com., 1999—, strategic planning com., 2000—, Phoenix Cmty. Alliance, 1988-90, Interchurch Ctr. Corp., 1987-90, Western Art Assocs., bd. dirs., 1989-91, Phoenix Com. on Fgn. Rels., 1988-99, U. Ariz. Pres.'s Club, 1984—, chmn., 1991-92; bd. dirs. Econ. Club of Phoenix, 1987— , sec.-treas., 1991-92, v.p., 1992-93, pres. 1993-94; bd. dirs. Ctrl. Ariz. Shelter Svcs., 1995—, bd. dir., Ariz. Community Found., 1996—, invest. com., 1996—, chair, 2000, exec. com. 1997—, treas. 1997—, chair nominating com. 1997-98, vice chair bd. dirs., 1999—, chair devel. com., 1999—, advancement com., 1999—, chair, 1999—, fin. and adminstrn. com. 1999—; founding mem. Alliance linking poverty and homelessness, 1996-98, bd. dirs., 1996-98, mem. exec. com., 1996-98, co-chair long range planning com., 1997-98; mem. adv. bd. Help Wanted USA, 1990-92; vol. fund raiser YMCA, Salvation Army, others; bd. dirs. Frank Lloyd Wright Found., 1992—, chair fin. com. 1997-98, chmn. bd. dirs., 1998—; mem. Taliesin Coun., 1985—; bd. dirs. Taliesin Arch., 1992-98, Taliesin Conservation Com. (Wis.), 1992—; founding mem. Frank Lloyd Wright Soc., 1993—; mem. fin. com. Kyl for Congress, 1985-92, bd. dir. campaign bd. Kyl for U.S. Senate, 1993-94, 99—; Senator Kyl Council, 1995—; campaign com. Symington for Gov. '90, 1989-90, mem. gubernatorial adv. bd., 1990-91; mem. Gov.'s Selection Com. for State Revenue Dir., 1993; mem. bond com. City of Phoenix, 1987-88; mem. Ariz. State U. Coun. of 100, 1985-89, investment com., 1985-89; bd. govs. Twelve Who Care Hon Kachina, 1991; mem. adv. coun. Maricopa County Sports Authority, 1989-93; mem. Ariz. Coalition for Tomorrow, 1990-92; founding mem., bd. dirs. Waste Not Inc., 1990-94, pres., 1990-92, chmn., 1992-94, adv. bd. 1996—; bd. dirs. Garden Homes at Teton Pines Home Owners Assn., 1996—; selected as bearer for the Olympic Torch Relay Team, 1996; adv. bd. KAET TV PBS (Channel 8). 1st lt. USAF, 1961-64. Recipient various mil. awards; 1st place award Ariz. Bar exam, 1967; named to Ariz. Hall of Fame, 1999. Mem. ABA, AIEE, AIME, Ariz. Bar Assn., Maricopa County Bar Assn., U. Ariz. Alumni Assn., Nat. Soc. Fund Raising Execs. (Philanthropy award Ariz. chpt. 1991, 97), Clan McRae Soc. N.Am. Phoenix Exec. Club, Internat. Platform Assn., Am. Friends of the U. Cambridge (Eng.), Jackson Hole Racquet Club, Teton Pines Country Club, Tau Beta Pi. Republican. General civil litigation, General corporate, Taxation, general. Address: Republic Cos 11811 N Tatum Blvd Ste 1005 Phoenix AZ 85028-1617 E-mail: repcos@aol.com

MCRAE, ROBERT MALCOLM, JR. federal judge; b. Memphis, Dec. 31, 1921; s. Robert Malcolm and Irene (Pontius) McR.; m. Louise Howry, July 31, 1943; children: Susan Campbell, Robert Malcolm III, Duncan Farquhar, Thomas Alexander Todd. BA, Vanderbilt U., 1943; LLB, U. Va., 1948. Bar: Tenn. 1948. Practice in, Memphis, 1948-64; judge Tenn. Circuit Ct., 1964-66, U.S. Dist. Ct. (we. dist.) Tenn., Memphis, 1966-94, chief judge, 1979-86, sr. judge, 1987-94, inactive sr. judge, 1995—; mem. Jud. Council 6th Cir., 1982-85, Jud. Conf. Commn. Adminstrn. Criminal Law, 1979-86, Jud. Conf. U.S., 1984-87; ret. Pub.: Oral History of the Desegregation of the Memphis City Schools (1954-74), 1997. Pres. Episcopal Ch. men of Tenn., 1964-65. Mem. Dist. Judges Assn. 6th Circuit (pres.). Home: 1914 Poplar Ave Apt 902 Memphis TN 38104

MCREYNOLDS, MARY ARMILDA, lawyer; b. Carthage, Mo., Sept. 2, 1946; d. Allen and Virginia Madeliene (Hensley) McR. BA, Mt. Holyoke Coll., 1968; JD, Georgetown U., 1971; LLM, Harvard U., 1973. Bar: D.C. 1971, U.S. Ct. Appeals (D.C. cir.) 1971, U.S. Ct. Appeals (2d cir.) 1975, U.S. Ct. Appeals (4th cir.) 1979, U.S. Ct. Appeals (1st, 5th, 6th, 9th 10th cirs.) 1980, U.S. Supreme Ct. 1980, U.S. Ct. Appeals (11th cir.) 1981, U.S. Ct. Appeals (3rd, 7th, 8th cirs.) 1983, U.S. Ct. Appeals (fed. cir.) 1988. Law clk. U.S. Ct. Appeals for D.C. cir., 1971-72; assoc. Wilmer, Cutler & Pickering, Washington, 1973-77; sr. trial atty. civil divsn. fed. program br. U.S. Dept. Justice, 1977-79, mem. appellate staff, 1979-81; ptnr. McReynolds & Mutterperl, Washington, 1981-83, Wilner & Scheiner, Washington, 1983-89, Haley, Bader & Potts, 1989-92; prin. Law Offices of Mary A. McReynolds, P.C., 1992—. Bd. dirs., gen. counsel Washington Bach Consort, 1977-81, 1985-92, pres. 1981-82, 89-90; pres. Calla, 1993—. Contbr. articles to profl. jours. Bd. dirs., gen. counsel Washington Bach Consort, 1977-81, 85-92, pres. 1981-82, 89-90; pres. Calla, 1993—. Mem.

ABA, Fed. Comms. Bar Assn., Kenwood Club, City Tavern Club. Episcopalian. Administrative and regulatory, Federal civil litigation, Communications. Home: 2101 Connecticut Ave NW Apt 26 Washington DC 20008-1754 Office: Ste 300 1701 Pennsylvania Ave NW Washington DC 20006 E-mail: marymcreynolds@aol.com

MCREYNOLDS, STEPHEN PAUL, lawyer; b. Sacramento, Oct. 16, 1938; s. Leslie N. and Mary C. McR.; m. Chodi D. Greeno, Sept. 29, 1970. A.B., U. Calif., Davis, 1969; J.D., U. Calif., 1972. Bar: Calif. 1972. Sole practice, Sunnyvale, Calif., 1972—. Served with U.S. Navy, 1956-62. Mem. Mensa Internat. General practice. Office: 1111 W El Camino Real # 329 Sunnyvale CA 94087-1056

MCSHANE, ROSEMARY, lawyer; b. Tucson, May 4, 1950; d. John B. and Jean Ann Jacobson McShane; m. James Allen Dator, Sept. 4, 1981; 1 child, McShane Allen Dator. BA, U. Hawaii, 1973; JD, William S. Richardson Sch. Law, 1981. Pvt. practice, Honolulu, 1981-82; lawyer corp. counsel, family support divsn. City and County of Honolulu, 1983-89; lawyer dept. atty. gen., social svcs. divsn. State of Hawaii, Honolulu, 1989-93; adminstr., head hearings officer dept. atty. gen. Office Child Support Hearings, State of Hawaii, 1993-95; atty., divsn. head dept. corp. counsel, family support div. City and County of Honolulu, 1995—. Contbg. author: (book) Our Rights, Our Lives, 3d edit., 1996, (manual) Hawaii Divorce Manual, 3d edit., 1996. Mem. Hawaii Women Lawyers (bd. dirs. 1995-97, 99—, v.p. 1997-98, pres. 1998-99), Hawaii State Bar Assn., William S. Richardson Sch. Law Alumni Assn. Office: Dept Corp Counsel Family Support Divsn # 703 204 Makee Rd Honolulu HI 96815-3978

MCSHERRY, WILLIAM JOHN, JR. lawyer, consultant; b. N.Y.C., Oct. 28, 1947; s. William John Sr. and Mary Elizabeth (Dunphy) McS.; m. Elizabeth Ann Crosby, June 8, 1974; children: Brendan, Sean, Rory. AB cum laude, Fordham U., 1969; JD cum laude, Harvard U., 1973. Bar: N.Y. 1974, U.S. Dist. Ct. (so. dist.) N.Y. 1975, U.S. Ct. Appeals (2d cir.) 1977. Assoc. Spengler, Carlson, Gubar, Brodsky & Frischling, N.Y.C., 1973-78, ptnr., 1979-88, Bryan, Cave, McPheeters & McRoberts, N.Y.C., 1989-91, Battle Fowler LLP, N.Y.C., 1991—. Exec. dir. U.S. Football League, N.Y.C., 1985-86; chmn. litigation dept. Battle Fowler, 1992-96; pres., bd. dirs. Playtex Mktg. Corp.; bd. dirs. Questron Tech., Inc. Author: (with others) Tender Offer Regulation: The Federal SEC's Challenge and New York State's Response. Derivatives Risk and Responsibility, 1996, Attorney Client Privilege in tge Second Circuit, 1998. Mem. Zoning Bd. Appeals, Village of Larchmont, N.Y., 1988-91, dep. mayor, 1992-98, bd. trustees, 1991-98. Served with USAR, 1970-75. Mem. ABA (litigation, antitrust, entertainment and sports, corp. banking and bus. law sects., subcom. litigation 1940 Act; vice-chair com. alt. dispute resolution), Assn. of Bar of City of N.Y. (mem. 1979-82 com. state cts. superior jurisdiction, 1987-90, com. arbitration and alternative dispute resolution, mem. sports law com. 1998—), Fed. Bar Council, Council N.Y. Law Assocs. (bd. dirs., treas. 1975), Phi Beta Kappa. Roman Catholic. Avocations: community involvement, sports, writing. Federal civil litigation, State civil litigation, Entertainment. Home: 2 Summit Ave Larchmont NY 10538-2930 Address: 75 E 55th St New York NY 10022-3205

MC SWAIN, ANGUS STEWART, JR. retired law educator; b. Bryan, Tex., Nov. 26, 1923; s. Angus Stewart and Lois (Pipkin) McS.; m. Betty Ann McCartney, June 3, 1956; 1 child, Angus Earl. BS in Civil Engring., Tex. A. and M. U., 1947; LLB, Baylor U., 1949; LL.M., U. Mich., 1951. Bar: Tex. 1949. Mem. faculty Baylor U. Law Sch., 1949—, prof. law, 1956—, dean, 1965-84, ret., 1994. Mem. panel arbitrators Fe. Mediation and Conciliation Service. Author: (with Wendorf) Cases and Materials on Texas Trusts and Probate, 1965, Supplementary Cases and Materials on Property, 1965, 78, (with Norvell and Simpkins) Cases and Materials for Texas Land Practice, 1968. Served to 1st lt., C.E. AUS, 1943-46. Mem. ABA, Tex.Bar Assn. (chmn. family law sect. 1967-69, chmn. com. on standards of admission 1972-73, 77-79), Tau Beta Pi, Phi Alpha Delta Home: 4600 Kenny Ln Waco TX 76710-2059

MCTURNAN, LEE BOWES, lawyer; b. N.Y.C., Sept. 13, 1937; s. Lee M. and Alice (Light) McT.; m. Susan Cassady, Aug. 2, 1969; children: John M., Sarah D. AB magna cum laude, Harvard U., 1959; diploma in law, Oxford (Eng.) U., 1961; JD, U. Chgo., 1963. Bar: Ill. 1965, U.S. Dist. Ct. (no. dist.) Ill. 1965, U.S. Ct. Appeals (7th cir.) 1966, U.S. Supreme Ct. 1969, Ind. 1978, U.S. Dist. Ct. (so. dist.) Ind. 1978, U.S. Dist. Ct. (no. dist.) Ind. 1987. Law clk. to hon. justice U.S. Supreme Ct., Washington, 1963-64; assoc. Sidley & Austin, Chgo., 1964-69, ptnr., 1970-78, Hackman, McClarnon & McTurnan, Indpls., 1978-88, McTurnan & Turner, Indpls., 1989—. Assoc. spl. counsel procs. on chief justice R.I. Commn. Jud. Tenure and Discipline, Providence, 1985; mem. Local Rules Adv. Com. for So. Dist. Ind., 1995-2000. Adminstrv. bd. Meridian St. United Meth. Ch., 1987-90. Mem. ABA, Ind. Bar Assn., Ill. Bar Assn., Indpls. Bar Assn., 7th Cir. Bar Assn., Law Club of Indpls. (pres. 1998-90), Legal Club of Chgo., Columbia Club, Woodstock Club, Lit. Club, Rotary. Republican. Avocations: running, reading, gardening. Antitrust, Federal civil litigation, General civil litigation. Home: 9907 Summerlakes Dr Carmel IN 46032 Office: McTurnan & Turner 2400 Market Tower 10 W Market St Indianapolis IN 46204-2954

MCVEY, LANE LEROY, lawyer; b. Wilmington, Del., Oct. 7, 1947; s. Francis Lane and Evelyn Christine (Irons) M.; m. Elaine Marie Noonan, June 14, 1969; 1 child, Cristin Marie. B.A., Va. Poly. Inst., 1969; J.D., Georgetown U., 1975. Bar: Va. 1975, D.C. 1976, Calif. 1992. Law clk. to Chief Judge U.S. Ct. Claims, Washington, 1975-76; assoc. Sellers, Conner & Cuneo, 1976-79; ptnr. Wager & McVey, 1979-80, McKenna & Cuneo, Washington and San Diego, 1980—. Contbr. articles to law jours. Editor Georgetown Law jour., 1974-75. Served with U.S. Army, 1969-71. Mem. ABA, Omicron Delta Epsilon. Government contracts and claims. Office: McKenna & Cuneo 750 B St San Diego CA 92101-8114

MCWHIRTER, BRUCE J. lawyer; b. Chgo., Sept. 11, 1931; s. Sydney and Martha McWhirter; m. Judith Hallett, Apr. 14, 1960; children: Cameron, Andrew. BS, Northwestern U., 1952; LLB, Harvard U., 1955. Bar: DC 1955, Ill 1955, US Ct Appeals (7th cir) 1963, US Supreme Ct. Assoc. Lord, Bissell & Brook, Chgo., 1958-62; from assoc. to sr. ptnr. Ross & Hardies, 1962-95, of counsel, 1996—. Editor: (book) Donnelley SEC Handbook, 1972—87;contbr. articles to profl jours. With U.S. Army, 1955—57. Mem.: ABA, Chicago Bar Asn, Harvard Law Soc Ill, Lawyers Club Chicago, Harvard Club (New York City), Phi Beta Kappa. Democrat. Home: 111 Sheridan Rd Winnetka IL 60093-1539 Office: Ross & Hardies 150 N Michigan Ave Ste 2500 Chicago IL 60601-7567 E-mail: jbmcw@aol.com

MCWILLIAMS, JOHN LAWRENCE, III, lawyer; b. Phila., Dec. 21, 1943; s. John Lawrence Jr. and Elizabeth Dolores (Chevalier) McW.; m. Paula Ann Root, July 19, 1969 (dec.); children: John Lawrence, IV, Robert Root, Anne Elizabeth, David Stanford, Peter Farrell; m. Kathleen Nolan Pradella, Apr./ 3, 1993. BS, St. Joseph's U., 1965; JD, Seton Hall U., 1969. Bar: N.J. 1969, N.Y. 1975, U.S. Supreme Ct. 1975, Fla. 1977. Trial atty., regional office SEC, N.Y.C., 1969-72; assoc. Mudge Rose Guthrie & Alexander, 1972-77; mem. Freeman, Richardson, Watson & Kelly, P.A., Jacksonville, Fla., 1977-89, chmn., pres., 1984-89; ptnr. Squire, Sanders & Dempsey, 1989-98, Livermore, Freeman & McWilliams, P.A., Jacksonville, 1998—. Trustee Mcpl. Svc. Dist. Ponte Vedra Beach, 1981-85, chmn. bd. trustees, 1984-85; treas. Ponte Vedra Cmty. Assn., 1980-82; mem. Leadership Jacksonville, 1981, mem. steering com., 1982; dir. Jacksonville Country Day Sch., 1985-87; pres. Jacksonville Beaches Ponte Vedra Unit Am. Cancer Soc., 1988-90; bd. dirs. Sawgrass Property Owners Assn., Inc., 2000—. Mem. Nat. Assn. Bond Lawyers, The Fla. Bar, Jacksonville C. of C. Republican. Roman Catholic. Clubs: Ponte Vedra, Sawgrass, River. State and local taxation, Securities, Municipal (including bonds). Home: 3040 Timberlake Pt Ponte Vedra Beach FL 32082-3726 Office: Livermore Freeman & McWilliams PA 1301 Riverplace Blvd Ste 1825 Jacksonville FL 32207-9029

MCWILLIAMS, JOHN MICHAEL, lawyer; b. Annapolis, Md., Aug. 17, 1939; s. William J. and Helen (Disharon) McW.; m. Frances Edelen McCabe, May 30, 1970; children: M. Edelen, J. Michael Jr., James McC. B.S., Georgetown U., 1964; LL.B., U. Md., 1967; LLD (hon.), U. Balt., 1993. Bar: Md. 1967, U.S. Supreme Ct. 1970, U.S. Ct. Internat. Trade 1991, U.S. Ct. Mil. Appeals 1992; cert. mediator NASD. Law clk. Chief Judge Roszel C. Thomsen, U.S. Dist. Ct. Md., 1967-68; assoc. Piper and Marbury, Balt., 1968-69; asst. atty. gen. State of Md., 1969-76; gen. counsel Md. Dept. Transp., 1971-76; sr. ptnr. Tydings and Rosenberg, Balt., 1977-97; pres. McWilliams Dispute Resolution, 1997—. Permanent mem. 4th Cir. Jud. Conf.; mem. panel of disting. neutrals CPR Inst. for Dispute Resolution, 1994—; mem. Md. Alt. Dispute Resolution Commn. Asst. editor Law Rev., U. Md., 1967; mem. nat. bd. advisors Ohio State Jour. Dispute Resolution; mem. editl. adv. bd. The Daily Record. Chmn. Md. adv. coun. to Nat. Legal Svcs. Corp., 1975-78; mem. Gov.'s Commn. to Revise Annotated Code of Md., 1973-78; transition dir. Md. Gov.-Elect Harry Hughes, 1978-79; mem. Md. Indsl. Devel. Financing Authority, 1980; mem. Greater Balt. Com., 1979-94; mem. exec. com. Econ. Devel. Coun. Greater Balt., 1979-83; vice chmn. bd. Washington/Balt. Regional Assn., 1980-83; mem. Md. Econ. and Cmty. Devel. Adv. Commn., 1983-87; chmn. bd. Md. Econ. Devel. Corp., 1984-89. Served to 1st lt. U.S. Army, 1958-60. Fellow Am. Bar Found. (bd. dirs. 1986-88, 91-93), Internat. Acad. Mediators (v.p. 1998—), Coll. Comml. Arbitrators (sec. 2000—), Md. Bar Found. (dir. 1980-82); mem. ABA (pres. 1992-93, mem. ho. of dels. 1976—, chmn. 1986-88, chmn. Md. del. 1976-86, bd. editors jour. 1986-88, 91-93) Md. Bar Assn. (pres. 1981-82), Nat. Conf. Bar Pres. (exec. council 1982-85), Bar Assn. Balt. City, Am. Law Inst., Am. Judicature Soc. (dir. 1974-81, exec. com. 1975-77), Am. Acad. Judicature Edn. (dir. 1977), Md. Law Rev. (trustee 1980-83), Md. Inst. Continuing Edn. Lawyers (trustee 1980-83), Inst. Internat. Bus. Law and Practice (corr.), Md. Club, Rule Day Club. Democrat. Roman Catholic. Alternative dispute resolution. Home: 3 Merryman Ct Baltimore MD 21210-2815 Office: 26 South St Baltimore MD 21202-3215 E-mail: mcw@triallaw.com

MCWILLIAMS, ROBERT HUGH, federal judge; b. Salina, Kans., Apr. 27, 1916; s. Robert Hugh and Laura (Nicholson) McW.; m. Catherine Ann Cooper, Nov. 4, 1942 (dec.); 1 son, Edward Cooper; m. Joan Harcourt, Mar. 8, 1986. A.B., U. Denver, 1938, LL.B., 1941. Bar: Colo. bar 1941. Colo. dist. judge, Denver, 1952-60; justice Colo. Supreme Ct., 1961-68, chief justice, 1969-70; judge U.S. Ct. Appeals (10th cir.), Denver, 1970—, now sr. judge. Served with AUS, World War II. Mem. Phi Beta Kappa, Omicron Delta Kappa, Phi Delta Phi, Kappa Sigma. Republican. Episcopalian. Home: 137 Jersey St Denver CO 80220-5918 Office: Byron White US Courthouse 1823 Stout St Rm 216 Denver CO 80257-1823

MEACHAM, BONNIE JEAN MARINELLI, lawyer; b. Detroit, Jan. 18, 1941; d. Roy Duffield and Eva Mae (Gordon) Meacham; m. Libero Marinelli, Jr., Jan. 20, 1967; 1 dau., Karen Ann. B.A., Vanderbilt U., 1963, LL.B., 1966. Bar: Tenn. 1966. Legis. atty. Tenn. Legis. Council, Nashville, 1966-67; procurement analyst U.S. Army, Ft. Sheridan, Ill., 1968; legis asst. U.S. Ho. Reps., Washington, 1968-69; sr. atty.-advisor Bd. Vets. Appeals, VA, Washington, 1970— . Editorial asst. Race Relations Law Reporter, 1964-67; problem editor Moot Ct. Vanderbilt U. Law Sch., 1965. Recipient VA Adminstrs. award, 1974. Mem. Gamma Phi Beta (1st v.p. 1962). Office: Bd Veterans Appeals 811 Vermont Ave NW Washington DC 20420-0001

MEAD, IRENE MARIE, b. Gary, Ind., Aug. 3, 1952; d. Robert R. and Marian F. (Eister) M.; m. Thomas R. Broadbent, Sept. 5, 1981. BSCE, Mich. State U., 1975; JD cum laude, T.M. Cooley Law Sch., 1980. Bar: Mich. 1980, U.S. Dist. Ct. (we. dist.) Mich. 1980, U.S. Ct. Appeals (6th cir.) 1985, U.S. Dist. Ct. (ea. dist.) Mich. 1986; registered profl. engr., 1980. Transp. engr. Mich. Dept. Transp., Lansing., 1975-80, litigation coord., 1981-83; rsch. atty. Mich. Ct. Appeals, Lansing, 1980; sole practice Haslett, Mich., 1981-83; asst. atty. gen. Office Mich. Atty. Gen., Lansing, 1983-88, asst. dep. atty. gen. legal ops., 1988-97, asst. in charge Liquor Control Divsn., 1997—. Adj. prof. civil engring. Mich. State U., East Lansing, 1980-83; cons. engring., spl. project, Hwy. Safety Office, Mich. State U., East Lansing. Mem. ABA, Soc. for Women in Transp. (founding pres. 1977-78), Women in State Govt., Ingham County Bar Assn. (exec. council young lawyers sect. 1980-81). Home: 7088 Manitou Way Grand Ledge MI 48837-9338 Office: Mich Atty Gen Liquor Control Divsn PO Box 30005 Lansing MI 48909-7505 E-mail: meadi@ag.state.mi.us

MEAD, MATTHEW HANSEN, prosecutor; Graduate, Trinity U., U. Wyo. Sch. Law. Deputy Co. Atty. Cambell Co. Atty Office , Wyo., 1987—90; Asst. US Atty. and Special Asst. US Atty. Dist. of Wyo., 1991—95; ind. practice, 1995—97; ptnr. Mead and Phillips, 1997—2001; US Atty. Dist. of Wyo., 2001—. Office: US Attorney 2120 Capitol Rm 4002 Cheyenne WY 82001*

MEADER, JOHN DANIEL, judge; b. Ballston Spa, N.Y., Oct. 22, 1931; s. Jerome Clement and Doris Luella (Conner) M.; m. Joyce Margaret Cowin, Mar. 2, 1963; children: John Daniel Jr., Julia Rae, Keith Alan. BA, Yale U., 1954; JD, Cornell U., 1962. Bar: N.Y. 1963, U.S. Dist. Ct. (no. dist.) N.Y. 1963, U.S. Ct. Appeals (2d cir.) 1966, U.S. Supreme Ct. 1967, U.S. Ct. Mil. Appeals 1973, Ohio 1978, U.S. Dist. Ct. (no. dist.) Ohio 1979, Fla. 1983, U.S. Ct. Appeals (4th cir.) 1992, U.S. Ct. Appeals (fed. cir.) 1993. Sales engr. Albany (N.Y.) Internat. Corp., 1954-59; asst. track coach Cornell U., 1959-62; asst. sec., asst. to pres. Albany Internat. Corp., 1962-65; asst. atty. gen. State of N.Y., Albany, 1965-68; ops. counsel, attesting sec. GE, Schenectady, 1968-77; gen. counsel, asst. sec. Glidden div. SCM Corp., Cleve., 1977-81; chmn. bd., pres. Applied Power Tech. Co., Fernandina Beach, Fla., 1981-84; pres. Applied Energy, Inc., Ballston Spa, 1984-88; judge N.Y. State Workers Compensation Bd., Albany, 1988—. Dir. Saratoga Mut. Fire Ins. Co. Author: Labor Law Manual, 1972, Contract Law Manual, 1974, Patent Law Manual, 1978. Candidate U.S. Ho. of Reps., 29th Dist. N.Y., 1964, N.Y. Supreme Ct., 1975, 87, 93. Col. JAGC, USAR, 1968—, dep. staff judge adv. 3d U.S. Army & Cen. Command, 1984. Nat. AAU High Sch. 1000 Yard Indoor Track Champion, 1949, Nat. AAU Prep. Sch. 440 and 880 Yard Indoor Track Champion, 1950, Nat. AAU Outstanding Performer award, Melrose Games Assn., 1950, Heptagonal Track 880-Yard Champion 1954. Mem. ABA, N.Y. State Bar Assn., Fla. Bar, Amelia Island Plantation Club, Cyprus Temple Club, Yale Club Jacksonville (pres.), Masons. Republican. Presbyterian. Home: 271 Round Lake Rd Ballston Lake NY 12019-1714 Office: NY State Workers Compensation Bd 100 Broadway Albany NY 12241-0001 E-mail: john.meader@wcb.state.ny.us

MEADOR, DANIEL JOHN, law educator; b. Selma, Ala., Dec. 7, 1926; s. Daniel John and Mabel (Kirkpatrick) M.; m. Janet Caroline Heilmann, Nov. 19, 1955; children: Janet Barrie, Anna Kirkpatrick, Daniel John. BS, Auburn U., 1949; JD, U. Ala., 1951; LLM, Harvard U., 1954; LLD (hon.), U. S.C., 1998. Bar: Ala. 1951, Va. 1961. Law clk. to Justice Hugo L. Black U.S. Supreme Ct., 1954-55; assoc. firm Lange, Simpson, Robinson & Somerville, Birmingham, Ala., 1955-57; faculty U. Va. Law Sch., Charlottesville, 1957-66, prof. law, 1961-66; prof., dean U. Ala. Law Sch., 1966-70; James Monroe prof. law U. Va., Charlottesville, 1970-94, prof. emeritus, 1994—; asst. atty. gen. U.S., 1977-79; dir. grad. program for judges, 1979-95. Fulbright lectr., U.K., 1965-66; vis. prof. U.S. Mil. Acad., 1984; chmn. Southeastern Conf. Assn. Am. Law Schs., 1964-65; chmn. Cts. Task Force Nat. Adv. Commn. on Criminal Justice, 1971-72; dir. appellate justice project Nat. Ctr. for State Cts., 1972-74; mem. Adv. Coun. on Appellate Justice, 1971-75, Coun. on Role of Cts., 1978-84; bd. dirs. State Justice Inst., 1986-92; exec. dir. commn. on structural alternatives Fed. Ct. Appeals, 1998-99. Author: Preludes to Gideon, 1967, Criminal Appeals-English Practices and American Reforms, 1973, Mr. Justice Black and His Books, 1974, Appellate Courts: Staff and Process in the Crisis of Volume, 1974, (with Carrington and Rosenberg) Justice on Appeal, 1976, Impressions of Law in East Germany, 1986, American Courts, 1991, 2000 (with J. Bernstein) Appellate Courts in the United States, 1994, His Father's House, 1994, Unforgotten, 1999, (with Rosenberg and Carrington) Appellate Courts: Structures, Functions, Processes, and Personnel, 1994; editor: Hardy Cross Dillard: Writings and Speeches, 1995; editor Va. Bar News, 1962-65; contbr. articles to profl. jours. 1st lt. U.S. Army, 1951-53; col. JAGC, USAR ret. Decorated Bronze Star.; IREX fellow German Dem. Republic, 1983 Mem. ABA (chmn. standing com. on fed. jud. improvements 1987-90), Ala. Bar Assn., Va. Bar Assn. (exec. com. 1983-86), Am. Law Inst., Am. Judicature Soc. (bd. dirs. 1975-77, 80-83), Soc. Pub. Tchrs. Law, Am. Soc. Legal History (bd. dirs. 1968-71), Order of Coif, Raven Soc., Phi Delta Phi, Omicron Delta Kappa, Kappa Alpha. Presbyn. Office: U Va Sch Law 580 Massie Rd Charlottesville VA 22903-1738

MEADOWS, JOHN FREDERICK, lawyer; b. Manila, Mar. 7, 1926; s. Grover Cleveland and Millie M.; m. Karen Lee Morris, Nov. 17, 1962; children: Ian Joseph, Marie Irene. AA, U. Mich., 1944; BA (Freshman Alumni Scholar, 1943), U. Calif., Berkeley, 1948; LLB, Boalt Hall, 1951. Bar: Calif 1952, U.S. Dist. Ct. (no. dist.) Calif. 1952, U.S. Ct. Apls. (9th cir.) 1952, U.S. Sup. Ct. 1958. Assoc. Wallace, Garrison, Norton & Ray, San Francisco, 1952-56; atty. advisor Maritime Adminstrn, U.S. Dept. Commerce, Washington, 1956; trial atty., Admiralty and Shipping Sect. U.S. Dept Justice, West Coast Office, San Francisco, 1956-64, atty. in charge, 1964-72; sr. resident ptnr. Acret & Perrochet, 1972-76; sr. ptnr. Meadows, Smith, Lenker, Sterling & Davis, 1976-93, Long Beach, Calif., 1976-93, Seattle, 1976-93; mng. ptnr. west coast Kirlin, Campbell, Meadows & Keating, N.Y.C., 1993; ptnr. Jedeikin Meadows & Schneider, San Francisco, 1994. Cons. maritime law, UN; lectr. seminar Taipei, Taiwan, 1968. Author: Preparing a Ship Collision Case for Trial, 1970, Ship Collision Cases: Technical and Legal Aspects; Investigation and Preparation for Suit, 1997, contbr. articles to legal publs.; assoc. editor: Am. Maritime Cases. Lt. M.I. AUS, 1944-46. Mem. ABA, Maritime Law Assn., San Francisco Bar Assn. Republican. Roman Catholic. Admiralty, Federal civil litigation, Insurance. Home: 205 The Uplands Berkeley CA 94705-2818 Office: 333 Pine St 5th Floor San Francisco CA 94104-1958 Fax: 415-421-5658. E-mail: jmeadows@jmslex.com

MEADOWS, PAUL MANVERS, lawyer; b. Melbourne, Victoria, Australia, Oct. 17, 1956; s. John Bernard and Evelyn M.; m. Patricia Anne Cross, May 28, 1989; children: John, Richard, Alexandra. BA, LLB, Melbourne U., Australia, 1979. Cert. solicitor. Solicitor Rigby & Fielding, Melbourne, 1981-83, Arthur Robinson & Hedderwicks, Melbourne, 1984-86, sr. assoc., 1987-88, ptnr., 1989—; solicitor Linklaters & Paines, London, 1986-87. Avocations: golf, tennis, cricket, hiking, reading. Antitrust, Alternative dispute resolution. Office: Arthur Robinson & Hedderwic 530 Collins St Melbourne VIC 3000 Australia Fax: 03 96144661

MEANS, ELIZABETH ROSE THAYER, financial consultant, writer, lawyer; b. N.Y.C., Aug. 29, 1960; d. Cyril Chesnut and Rosaline (Limtiuco y Sy) M. Student, Sch. of Am. Ballet-Lincoln Ctr, N.Y.C., 1970-75, Harvard Coll., 1980, Tufts U., 1981, Fletcher Sch. Law/Diplomacy, 1983-84; BS, Chatham Coll., 1983; cert. in comparative law, Heidelberg U., 1988; JD, Samford U., 1989; LLM in Internat. Banking Law, Boston U., 1990. Bar: Mass. 1991, Pa. 1991; cert. for piloting, seamanship and small boat handling USCG Aux. Dancer The N.Y.C. Ballet Co., 1971, Balanchine Cast for PBS The Nutcracker Suite, N.Y.C., 1971; docent The Hammond Castle Mus., Gloucester, Mass., 1982-85; asst. mgr. The Gallery, Rockport, 1977-83; cons. The Galleries, Ltd., Wellesley, 1988; legal intern U. Ala. Health Svcs. Found., Birmingham, 1988-89; loan officer UN/UNFCU, N.Y.C., 1984-86; overnight counselor Germaine Lawrence Sch., Arlington, Mass, 1989-90; contracts mgr. for Eastern Region Unisys Corp., Berkeley Heights, N.J., 1990-92; fin. cons. Innovatech, Lexington, Mass., 1992-93, 94-95; contract analyst Guy Carpenter & Co., Inc., N.Y.C., 1994; gen. counsel Mojo Working Prodns., 1996. Chair Cordell Hull Speakers' Forum, Birmingham, 1988-89; alumnae class sec. Chatham Coll. Class of 1980s, Pitts., 1983-87, 97—. Clk. of vestry The Ch. of the Resurrection, N.Y.C., 1993-95, mem. vestry, 1995-97; overnight counselor The Germaine Lawrence Sch., Arlington, Mass., 1989-90. Recipient Cert. of Appreciation 1990 Alumni award Cumberland Sch. Law, 1990; named to Nat. Dean's List, 1989-90. Mem. DAR (Cape Ann chpt. const. week chair 1993-94, Mass. const. week chair 1995-97, N.Y.C. chpt. jr. com. mem. Sons and Daus. Gala Ball 1996), The Federalist Soc. (Cumberland chpt. treas. 1988-89, adv. bd. 1983, sec. 1987-88), Clan Menzies Soc. N.Am., Clan Menzies Soc. Scotland, Princeton Club, Thayer Families Assn., Daus. Union Vets. of Civil War 1861-65: Hudson Valley-N.Y. Metro Tent, Mass. Soc. Mayflower Descs., Baronial Order Magna Charta, Dames of Ct. of Honor, Nat. Soc. Magna Charta Dames and Barons, Nat. Soc. Col. Daus. Seventeenth Century (Rensselaerswyck chpt.), Nat. Soc. First Families of Minn., Soc. of the Friends of St. George's and Descs. of Knights of the Garter, Soc. of Desc. of Knights of the Most Noble Order of the Garter, Hugenot Soc. Am., Order of Wash., N.Y. State Continental Soc. Daus. of Indian Wars 1607-1900, St. Georges Soc. N.Y., First Families Ohio, Colonial Order the Crown, The Sovereign Colonial Soc. Ams. of Royal Descent, The Plantagenet Soc., Nat. Soc. Descs. of Early Quakers, Nat. Soc. Colonial Daus. of the 17th Century. Republican. Episcopalian. Avocations: lobstering, sailing, fishing, swimming, bicycling. Address: Brier Neck 13 Salt Island Rd Gloucester MA 01930-1972 Fax: 516-829-5799. E-mail: meansert@email.msn.com

MEARS, PATRICK EDWARD, lawyer; b. Oct. 3, 1951; s. Edward Patrick and Estelle Veronica (Mislik) M.; m. Geraldine O'Connor, July 18, 1981. BA, U. Mich., 1973, JD, 1976. Bar: N.Y. 1977, Ill. 1996, Ind. 1997, U.S. Dist Ct. (so. and ea. dists) N.Y. 1977, Mich. 1980, U.S. Dist. Ct. (we. and ea. dists.) Mich. 1980, U.S. Ct. Appeals (6th cir.) 1983, Ill. 1996, Ind. 1997, U.S. Dist. Ct. (no. dist.) Ill. 1998, U.S. Dist. Ct. (no. dist.) Ind. 1998. Assoc. Milbank, Tweed, Hadley & McCloy, N.Y.C., 1976-79; ptnr. Warner, Norcross & Judd, Grand Rapids, Mich., 1980-91; sr. mem. Dykema Gossett PLLC, memnd Rapids, 1991—. Adj. prof. Grand Valley State U., Allendale, Mich., 1981-84; dir. Children's Law Ctr., 1994, Grand Rapids Ballet, 1994-99, East Grand Rapids Pub. Sch. Found., 1994-98. Author: Michigan Collection Law, 1981, 2d edit., 1983, Basic Bankruptcy Law, 1986, Bankruptcy Law and Practice in Michigan, 1987, 95, Revised Article 9 of the UCC in Michigan, 2001; contbg. author Collier Bankruptcy Practice Guide; contbr. articles to profl. jours. Chmn. legis. com. East Grand Rapids PTA, 1992-94. Fellow Am. Coll. Bankruptcy, Mich. State Bar Found.; mem. ABA (chmn. loan practices and lender liability com. ABA real property sect. 1997—), Mich. State Bar Assn. (mem., sec. coun. real property sect. 1993-97, chair Uniform Comml. Code com. Bus. Law sect. 2000—), Am. Bankruptcy Inst., Am. Law Inst., Fed. Bar Assn. (chmn. bankruptcy sect. We. Mich. chpt. 1992-94, newsletter editor 1998—, pres.-elect 2000-01), Grand Rapids Rotary, Peninsular Club (Grand Rapids), East Hills Athletic Club, Urban Inst. Contemporary Art (bd. dirs.). Bankruptcy, Consumer commercial. Office: Dykema Gossett PLLC 300 Ottawa Ave NW Ste 700 Grand Rapids MI 49503-2306 E-mail: pmears@dykema.com

MEBANE, DAVID CUMMINS, lawyer; b. Toledo, Dec. 18, 1933; s. Donald Cummins and Frances (Malm) M.; children: Margery, Suezanne. BBA, Ariz. State U., 1957; LLD, U. Wis., 1960. Bar: Wis. 1960. Atty., trust officer First Wis. Nat. Bank, Oshkosh, 1963-67; assoc. Hayes Law Offices, Ripon, Wis., 1967; dep. dist. atty., Madison, 1967-70; asst. atty gen. Wis. Dept. Justice, Madison, 1971-73, dep. atty. gen., 1973-75; U.S. atty. U.S. Dept. Justice, Madison, 1975-77; corp. atty. Madison Gas and Electric Co., 1977-79, gen. counsel, 1979-85, v.p., 1985-87, sr. v.p., gen. counsel, dir., 1987-91, pres. and COO, 1993, pres., COO, CEO, 1994, chmn. pres. CEO, 1994—; bd. dirs. Mad. Gas and Electric, 1st Fed. Savs. Bank, Madison, 1st Capital Investment Corp., Madison, 1st Fed. Capital Corp., La Crosse. Mem. Rep. Nat. Com., Washington; chmn. Wis. Racing Commn. Served with JAGC, USAF, 1960-63. Mem. ABA, State Bar Wis., Dane County Bar Assn., Exchange Club (Madison). Home: 1122 Sunridge Dr Madison WI 53711-3365 Office: Madison Gas and Electric Co PO Box 1231 Madison WI 53701-1231

MEBANE, JULIE SHAFFER, lawyer; b. San Antonio, Mar. 13, 1957; d. John Cummins and Mildred (Hill) M.; m. Kenneth Jerome Stipanov, Jan. 21, 1984; children: Thomas Kenneth Stipanov, Kristen Hill Stipanov. BA in Polit. Sci., UCLA, 1978, JD, 1981. Bar: Calif. 1981, U.S. Dist. Ct. (so. dist.) Calif. 1981. Assoc. Gray, Cary, Ames & Frye, San Diego, 1981-85, Sheppard, Mullin, Richter & Hampton, San Diego, 1986-90, Scalone, Stipanov, Yaffa & Mebane, San Diego, 1990-94, Stipanov & Mebane, San Diego, 1994—. Panelist Calif. Continuing Edn. of the Bar, 2000. Mem. ABA, San Diego County Bar Assn., Nat. Assn. Women Bus. Owners (bd. dirs. San Diego chpt. 1996-97), San Diego Lawyers Club, UCLA Alumni Assn. (gen. counsel, bd. dirs. 1992-96), San Diego Tennis and Racquet Club, Bruin Club (San Diego), Phi Beta Kappa, Kappa Alpha Theta. Democrat. Avocations: sports, travel. General corporate, Intellectual property, Real property. Office: Stipanov & Mebane 501 W Broadway Ste 520 San Diego CA 92101-3544 E-mail: mebane@stipmed.com

MECHAM, GLENN JEFFERSON, lawyer, mayor; b. Logan, Utah, Dec. 11, 1935; s. Everett H. and Lillie (Dunford) M.; m. Mae Parson, June 5, 1957; children: Jeff B., Scott R., Marcia, Suzanne. BS, Utah State U., 1957; JD, U. Utah, 1961; grad., Air Command and Staff Coll., 1984, Air War Coll., 1984. Bar: Utah 1961, Supreme Ct. U.S., U.S. Ct. Appeals (10th cir.), U.S. Dist. Ct. Utah, U.S. Ct. Claims. Gen. practice law, 1961-65; atty. Duchesne County, Utah, 1962, City of Duchesne, 1962; city judge Roy City, Utah, 1963-66; judge City of Ogden, 1966-69, mayor, 1992-2000. Lectr. law and govt. Stevens-Henager Coll., Ogden, 1963-75; asst. U.S. atty., 1969-72; ptnr. Mecham & Richards, Ogden, Utah, 1972-82; pres. Penn Mountain Mining Co., South Pacific Internat. Bank, Ltd.; mem. Bur. Justice Stats. Adv. Bd., U.S. Dept. Justice, U.S. Conf. Mayors; chmn. Marina Capital Inc. Chmn. Ogden City Housing Authority, Marine Capitol, Inc.; chmn. bd. trustees Utah State U., Space Dynamics Lab.; mem. adv. coun. Fed. Home Loan Bank; pres. Utah League Cities and Towns, 1981-82; vice chmn. Wasatch Front Reg. Coun. Col. USAF, 1957. Recipient Disting. Svcs. award Utah State U., Weber State U. Mem ABA, Weber County Bar Assn. (pres. 1966-68), Utah Bar Assn., Am. Judicature Soc., Weber County Bar Legal Svcs. (chmn. bd. trustees 1966-69), Utah Assn. Mcpl. Judges (sec.), Ogden-Weber C. of C. (Order of the Big Hat), Sigma Chi, Phi Alpha Delta. General corporate, Education and schools, Real property. Home: 1715 Darling St Ogden UT 84403-0556

MEDALIE, RICHARD JAMES, lawyer; b. Duluth, Minn., July 21, 1929; s. William Louis and Mona (Kolad) M.; m. Susan Diane Abrams, June 5, 1960; children: Samuel David, Daniel Alexander. B.A. summa cum laude, U. Minn., 1952; cert., U. London, 1953; A.M., Harvard U., 1955, J.D. cum laude, 1958. Bar: D.C. 1958, N.Y. 1963. Law clk. to Hon. George T. Washington U.S. Ct. Appeals, Washington, 1958-59; asst. solicitor gen. U.S., 1960-62; assoc. Kaye, Scholer, Fierman, Hays & Handler, N.Y.C., 1962-65; dep. dir. Ford Found. Inst. Criminal Law and Procedure, Georgetown U. Law Ctr., 1965-68; ptnr. Friedman & Medalie and predecessors, Washington, 1968-98; pres. Pegasus Internat., 1970—; exec. dir. The Appleseed Found., 1993-94, chmn. bd., 1993—, pres., 1995-98; of counsel Brock Silverstein LLC, N.Y.C., 1995—; pvt. practice, Washington, 1998—. Adj. prof. adminstrv. and criminal law Georgetown U. Law Center, 1967-70; Mem. D.C. Law Revision Commn., 1975-87, chmn. Criminal Law Task Force, mem. exec. com., 1978-82; panel comml. arbitrators Am. Arbitration Assn., 1964— ; vice chmn. Harvard Law Sch. Fund, 1981-84, chmn. nat. maj. gifts, 1984-86, dep. chmn., 1986-87, chmn. 1987-89; v.p., bd. dirs. Trial Lawyers for Pub. Justice, Washington, 1998—. Author: From Escobedo to Miranda: The Anatomy of a Supreme Court Decision, 1966; co-author: Federal Consumer Safety Legislation, 1970; co-author, editor: Commercial Arbitration for the 1990s, 1991; co-editor: Crime: A Community Responds, 1967; staff: Harvard Law Rev., 1956-58; case editor, 1957-58; contbr. articles to legal jours. Bd. dirs. alumni assn. Expt. in Internat. Living, Brattleboro, Vt., 1961-64, pres., 1962-63. Fulbright scholar, 1952-53; Ford fellow, 1954-55. Mem. ABA (program chair 1984, 90, chair legis. subcom. 1986-89, ADR/arbitration com., rep. on adv. com. nat. conf. Emerging ADR Issues in State and Fed. Cts. 1991, vice chair 1991-94, arbitration com. litigation sect., co-chair nat. conf. Critical Issues in Arbitration 1993), D.C. Unified Bar, Assn. Bar City of N.Y., Am. Law Inst., D.C. Estate Planning Coun.; fellow Am. Bar Found., Harvard Law Sch. Assn. D.C. (pres. 1976-77, nat. v.p. 1977-78), Harvard Alumni Assn. (law sch. dir. 1991-95), Cosmos Club, Harvard Club of Washington, Phi Beta Kappa, Phi Alpha Theta. Home: 3113 Macomb St NW Washington DC 20008-3325 Office: 1750 K St NW Ste 1200 Washington DC 20006-2303 E-mail: medalie@compuserve.com

MEDALIE, SUSAN DIANE, lawyer, management consultant; b. Boston, Oct. 7, 1941; d. Samuel and Matilda (Bortman) Abrams; m. Richard James Medalie, June 5, 1960; children: Samuel David, Daniel Alexander. BA, Sarah Lawrence Coll., 1960; MA, George Washington U., 1962, Cert. Pubs. Spec., 1977; JD, Am. U., 1986. Bar: Pa., 1987, D.C., 1987. Pres. Medalie Cons., Washington, 1980—; dep. dir. U.S. Holocaust Meml. Coun., 1980-82; assoc. pub. Campaigns & Elections, 1983-84; legis. analyst Subcom./House Energy and Commerce, 1985; ea. regional dir. Josephson Found. for Adv. Ethics, L.A., 1986-88; asst. dean for external affairs George Washington U. Nat. Law Ctr., Washington, 1988-90; exec. dir. Internat. Soc. Global Health Policy, Washington and Paris, 1990-93; pvt. practice, Washington, 1993-2000; exec. dir. Women's Campaign Fund, 2000—. Corp. liaison First Hosp. Corp., Norfolk, Va., 1986-88; assoc. producer and cons. Prof. Arthur Miller's "Headlines on Trial" (NBC), N.Y.C., 1987-91. Editor/pub.: Getting There mag., 1977-80; sr. editor: Am. Univ. Law Rev., Washington, 1984-86. Nat. dep. fin. dir. Edward M. Kennedy for Pres. Com., Washington, 1979-80; del. D.C. Ward 3 Dem. Ctrl. Com.; mem. exec. bd., D.C. Bar rep. D.C. Coalition Against Drugs and Violence, 1997-2000; bd. dirs., mem. exec. com. Women's Campaign Fund, 1999-2000. Mem. ABA, D.C. Bar. Education and schools, Nonprofit and tax-exempt organizations. Office: Womens Campaign Fund 1734 15th St NW Washington DC 20005 E-mail: susanmedalie@wcfonline.org

MEDEIROS, MATTHEW FRANCIS, lawyer; b. Little Compton, R.I., Apr. 30, 1945; s. Manuel S. and Marie F. (Goulart) M.; m. Sarah Judith Medjuck, July 26, 1970. AB, Brown U., 1967; JD, NYU, 1970. Bar: R.I. 1970, Mass. 1985, U.S. Dist. Ct. R.I. 1971, D.C. 1971, U.S. Dist. Ct. D.C. 1971, U.S. Ct. Appeals (1st cir.) 1972, U.S. Ct. Appeals (D.C. cir.) 1972, U.S. Supreme Ct. 1974. Summer assoc. Lewis & Roca, Phoenix, 1969; law clk. to chief judge U.S. Dist. Ct. R.I., 1970-71; assoc. Covington & Burling, Washington, 1971-76; on leave with Neighborhood Legal Svcs. Program, 1973; ptnr. Edwards & Angell, Providence, 1977-87, Flanders & Medeiros Inc., Providence, 1987-2000, Little, Bulman, Medeiros & Whitney, P.C., 2000—. Chmn. planning com. 1st Cir. Jud. Conf., 1980-81; mem. jud. screening coms. U.S. Bankruptcy Judge and U.S. Magistrate, 1981-82; mem. adv. com. for U.S. Ct. Appeals (1st cir.), 1983-88; adj. prof. fed. trial practice So. New Eng. Sch. Law, 1986-88; editor: NYU Law Rev., 1969-70; bd. dirs. Associated Alumni Brown U., 1969-71; bd. dirs. R.I. br. ACLU, 1977-79. Mem. ABA, Am. Bd. Trial Advocates, Fed. Bar Assn. (pres. R.I. chpt. 1978-80), R.I. Bar Assn. Antitrust, Federal civil litigation, General civil litigation. Office: Little Bulman Medeiros & Whitney 72 Pine St Providence RI 02903

MEDINA, OMAR F. lawyer; b. Santa Clara, Cuba, Oct. 7, 1959; came to U.S., 1961; s. Omar Pedro and Zulima Carmen M.; m. Deborah Eileen Ticknor, Aug. 7, 1981; children: Dominic, Justine, Xavier. BA in English, Ea. Ky. U., 1981; JD, U. Fla., 1985. Bar: Fla. 1988, U.S. Dist. Ct. (mid. dist.) Fla., U.S. Ct. Appeals (11th cir.), U.S. Dist. Ct. (so. dist.) Tex., U.S. Dist. Ct. (ea. dist.) Ohio. Pvt. practice Law Offices Omar F. Medina, Tampa, Fla., 1988-92, sr. atty., 1997—; ptnr. Medina, Pihsei & Dowell, 1992-96. Vice chmn. jud. nominating com. 13th Jud. Cir. State of Fla., Tampa, 1995—. Mem. NACDL, Acad. Fla. Trial Lawyers. Avocations: private pilot, tae kwon do. Criminal, Personal injury, Workers' compensation. Office: 505 S Magnolia Ave Tampa FL 33606-2256

MEDVECKY, THOMAS EDWARD, lawyer; b. Bridgeport, Conn., Apr. 22, 1937; s. Stephen and Elizabeth P. Medvecky; m. Patricia Conneally, Aug. 25, 1967; 1 son, Thomas Edward, II. A.B., Bowdoin Coll., 1959; LL.B., St. John's U., 1962. Bar: Conn. 1962. Assoc., Louis Katz, Danbury, Conn., 1963-68; sole practice, Bethel, Conn., 1968— ; asst. town counsel Town of Bethel, 1963-67; assoc. dir. State Nat. Bank Conn. Mem. budget com. Danbury (Conn.) Community Chest, 1966-68. Served with USAR, 1962-68. Recipient Am. Jurisprudence award 1962. Mem. ABA, Conn. Bar Assn., Danbury Bar Assn. Democrat. Lutheran. General practice, Probate, Real property. Office: 99 Greenwood Ave PO Box 272 Bethel CT 06801-0272

MEDVIN, ALAN YORK, lawyer; b. N.Y.C., Sept. 13, 1947; s. Murray and Leona (Alpert) M.; m. Harriet A. Kass, July 11, 1976; children—Michelle K., Michael J. A.B., Colgate U., 1969; J.D., Rutgers U., 1972. Bar: N.J. 1972, U.S. Dist. Ct. N.J. 1972, U.S. Supreme Ct. 1981. Assoc., Horowitz, Bross & Sinins, Newark, 1972-75; ptnr. Horowitz, Bross, Sinins, Imperial & Medvin, 1976-83, Medvin & Elberg, Newark, 1983—; adj. prof. law Rutgers U., 1987. Fellow Roscoe Pound Found.; mem. Assn. Trial Lawyers Am. (state del. 1980, pres. N.J. affiliate, mem. bd. govs.), Am. Arbitration Assn., N.J. State Bar Assn. (Outstanding Profl. Achievement award 1982), Essex County Bar Assn., Mercer County Bar Assn. Democrat. Jewish. Federal civil litigation, State civil litigation, Personal injury. Home: 165 Bertrand Dr Princeton NJ 08540-2949 Office: Medvin & Elberg 1 Gateway Ctr Newark NJ 07102-5315

MEEHAN, MICHAEL JOSEPH, lawyer; b. St. Louis, Aug. 28, 1942; s. Joseph Michael and Frances (Taylor) M.; m. Sharon Kay McHenry (div. 1988); m. Patricia Ann Shive, July 8, 1989 (dec. 1999). BS in Engring., U.S. Coast Guard Acad., 1964; JD with high distinction, U. Ariz., 1971. Bar: Ariz. 1971, U.S. Ct. Appeals (6th, 8th, 9th and 10th cirs.), U.S. Supreme Ct. 1975. Law clk. Assoc. Justice William H. Rehnquist, U.S. Supreme Ct., 1972; assoc. Molloy, Jones & Donahue, P.C., Tucson, 1971-75, shareholder, 1975-93; chmn. exec. com., head trial dept., 1986-93; founder Meehan & Assocs., Tucson, 1993-2001; ptnr. Quarles & Brady/Striech Long, 2001—. Mem. fed. appellate rules adv. com. Jud. Conf. U.S., 1994-99. Author chpt. on appellate advocacy: State Bar of Arizona Appellate Practice Handbook. Fellow Am. Acad. Appellate Lawyers (treas.); mem. ABA (sect. on litig., sect. on intellectual property), Ariz. Bar Assn. (exec. coun., past chair appellate practice sect. 1995-99). Republican. Lutheran. Avocation: golf. Federal civil litigation, Communications, Securities. Office: Quartes & Brady 1 S Church Ave Ste 1700 Tucson AZ 85701-1621 E-mail: mmeehan@quarles.com

MEEHAN, PATRICK L. prosecutor; BA, Bowdoin Coll., 1978; JD, Temple U., 1986. Assoc. Dilworth, Paxon, Kalish and Kauffman; sr. counsel, exec. dir. U.S. Sen. Arlen Specter; dist. atty. Delaware County, Pa., 1986—2001; U.S. atty. Ea. Dist. Pa. U.S. Dept. Justice, 2001—. Office: 615 Chestnut St Philadelphia PA 19106*

MEHLE, ROGER W. federal agency administrator; b. Long Beach, Calif., Dec. 28, 1941; BS, U.S. Naval Acad., 1963; MBA, NYU, 1972; JD, Fordham U., 1976. Mng. dir. The First Boston Corp., N.Y.C., 1969-79; sr. v.p., dir. Dean Witter Reynolds, Inc., 1979-81; asst. sec. for domestic fin. Dept. Treasury, Washington, 1981-83; exec. v.p., mng. dir. PaineWebber, Inc., N.Y.C., 1983-84; banking and securities atty. Washington, 1985-94; chmn. Fed. Ret. Thrift Investment Bd., 1985-94; exec. dir. Fed. Retirement Thrift Investment Bd., 1994—. Office: Fed Ret Thrift Investment Bd 1250 H St NW Washington DC 20005-3952

MEHLMAN, MARK FRANKLIN, lawyer; b. L.A., Dec. 18, 1947; s. Jack and Elaine Pearl (Lopater) M.; m. Barbara Ann Novak, Aug. 20, 1972; children: David, Jennifer, Ilyse. BA, U. Ill., 1969; LLB, U. Mich., 1973. Bar: Ill. 1973; U.S. Dist. Ct. (no. dist.) Ill. 1973. Assoc. Sonnenschein, Nath & Rosenthal, Chgo., 1973-80, mem. policy and planning com., 1989—. Trustee Groveland Health Svcs., Highland Park (Ill.) Hosp., 1991-97; trustee, treas., exec. com. Spertus Inst. Jewish Studies, Chgo., 1992-97, vice chmn. bd. trustees, 1996—; vice-chmn. regional bd. Anti-Defamation League, 1987-89, hon. life mem. nat. commn., 1993—. Fellow Am. Bar Found.; mem. ABA (chmn. mortgages and other debt financing subcom. 1991-95, supervisory coun. 1997—), Am. Coll. Real Estate Lawyers (bd. govs. 2000—, chmn. MDP com. 2000—, chmn. mem. selection com. 2000-01), Nat. Conf. Lawyers and CPAs, Ango-Am. Real Property Inst., Legal Club of Chgo., Lake Shore Country Club, Standard Club, Exec. Club of Chgo. Contracts commercial, Finance, Real property. Office: Sonnenschein Nath & Rosenthal 233 S Wacker Dr Ste 8000 Chicago IL 60606-6491

MEHRPOO, NIKOO NIKKI, lawyer, educator; b. Tehran, Iran, June 13, 1972; came to U.S., 1980; d. Rahim and Sharin Mehrpoo. BA, Calif. State U., Northridge, 1994; JD, Pepperdine U., 1997. Bar: Calif. 1997, U.S. Dist. Ct. (cen. dist.) Calif. 1998, U.S. Ct. Appeals (9th cir.) 1998. Assoc. Reeves and Hanlon, PLC, Pasadena, Calif., 1998—; prof. L.A. C.C., 1998—. Mem. Am. Immigration Lawyers Assn. Avocations: reading, movies. Family and matrimonial, Immigration, naturalization, and customs. Office: Reeves and Hanlon PLC 2 N Lake Ave # 950 Pasadena CA 91101

MEHTA, EILEEN ROSE, lawyer; b. Colver, Pa., Apr. 1, 1953; d. Richard Glenn and Helen (Wahna) Ball; m. Abdul Rashid Mehta, Aug. 31, 1973. Student, Miami U., 1971-73; BA with distinction, Fla. Internat. U., 1974; JD cum laude, U. Miami, 1977. Bar: Fla. 1977, U.S. Dist. Ct. (so. dist.) Fla. 1977, U.S. Ct. Appeals (11th cir.) 1981. Law clk. to presiding judge U.S. Dist. Ct. (so. dist.) Fla., Miami, 1977-79; asst. atty. County of Dade, 1979-89; shareholder Fine Jacobson Schwartz Nash Block & England, Fla., 1989-94; ptnr. Eckert Seamans Cherin & Mellott, 1994-98, Bilzin Sumberg Dunn Price & Axelrod, Miami, 1998—. Lectr. in field; v.p., bd. dirs. Mehtatron Enterprises, Inc., Miami, Shalimar Homes Inc., Anderson, S.C. Miami U. scholar, 1971-73. Mem. Fla. Bar Assn., Dade County Bar Assn. Appellate, Government contracts and claims, Land use and zoning (including planning). Office: Bilzin Sumberg Dunn Price & Axelrod 2500 First Union Fin Ctr Miami FL 33131

MEIGS, JOHN FORSYTH, lawyer; b. Boston, Dec. 4, 1941; s. Charles H. Meigs and Florence S. Truitt; children: Amy, Perry, John. BA, Yale U., 1964; LLB, U. Pa., 1969. Bar: Pa. 1969, U.S. Supreme Ct. 1977. Assoc. Saul, Ewing, Remick & Saul (now Saul Ewing LLP), Phila., 1969-76, ptnr., 1976—, co-chair, estates and trusts, 1997—. Co-chair estates and trusts Saul Ewing LLP, 1997—. Contbr. articles to profl. jours. Trustee Independence Seaport Mus., 1978—, Woodmere Art Mus., 1987—; mem. Com. of 70, 1976—. Mem. ABA, Pa. Bar Assn., Phila. Bar Assn. Episcopalian. General corporate, Estate planning, Probate. Home: 6 Norman Ln Philadelphia PA 19118-3617 Office: Saul Ewing LLP 3800 Centre Sq W Philadelphia PA 19102 E-mail: jmeigs@saul.com

MEIGS, WALTER RALPH, lawyer, dry dock and shipbuilding company executive; b. Macon, Ga., Sept. 7, 1948; s. Ralph and Alice (Lee) M.; B.A., Birmingham So. Coll., 1970; J.D., U. Ala., 1973, postgrad., 1982; postgrad. Auburn U., 1974; m. Gloria Sharmon Eddins, Sept. 17, 1977; children—Nancy Sharmon, Stephen Walter, Christopher. Admitted to Ala. bar, 1973; law clk. Jud. br. State of Ala., 1973-74; assoc. firm Hubbard, Waldrop and Jenkins, Tuscaloosa, Ala., 1974-75; house counsel Ala. Dry Dock and Shipbldg. Co., Mobile., 1975— , asst. sec., 1978— , asst. v.p. adminstrn., 1981—; corp. sec., counsel Addsco Industries Inc., 1985—; gen. counsel, Atlantic Land Corp., 1992—. Bd. dirs. Mobile Pre-sch. for Deaf, Mobile chpt. ARC. Mem. ABA, Ala. State Bar Assn., Mobile Bar Assn., Maritime Law Assn., Propeller Club U.S., Mobile C. of C., Leadership Mobile, Ala. Forestry Assn., Am. Forestry Assn., Ala. Hist. Soc., So. Hist. Soc. Methodist (adminstrv. bd.). Club: Kiwanis. Administrative and regulatory, Real property, Maritime. Home: 155 Provident Ln Mobile AL 36608-1417 Office: Atlantic Land Corp PO Box 190 Mobile AL 36601-0190

MEISTER, RONALD WILLIAM, lawyer; b. Bklyn., Mar. 19, 1947; s. Marvin and Helen Selma (Schwartz) M.; m. Jane M. Sovern; children: Beth Rose, Sarah Miriam, David Henry. BA summa cum laude, Yale U., 1967, JD, 1970. Bar: D.C. 1970, U.S. Ct. Appeals Armed Forces 1971, U.S. Ct. Appeals (1st cir.) 1972, N.Y. 1975, U.S. Dist. Ct. (so. and ea. dists.) N.Y. 1975, U.S. Ct. Appeals (2d cir.) 1975, U.S. Ct. Claims 1977, U.S. Supreme Ct. 1977, U.S. Ct. Internat. Trade, 1994. Assoc. Paul, Weiss, Rifkind, Wharton & Garrison, N.Y.C., 1974-80; ptnr. Kornstein, Meister & Veisz, 1980-84, Meister Leventhal & Slade, N.Y.C., 1984-93, Eaton & Van Winkle, N.Y.C., 1993—95, Cowan, Liebowitz & Latman, N.Y.C., 1995—. Contbr. articles to profl. jours. Served to lt. JAGC, USNR, 1970-74. Mem. Fed. Bar Coun., Am. Law Inst. Federal civil litigation, State civil litigation, Criminal. Office: Cowan Liebowitz & Latman 1133 Ave of Americas New York NY 10036-6710 E-mail: rwm@cll.com

MELAMED, ARTHUR DOUGLAS, lawyer; b. Mpls., Dec. 3, 1945; s. Arthur Charles and Helen Beatrix (Rosenberg) M.: m. Carol Drescher Weisman, May 26, 1983; children: Kathryn Henrie, Elizabeth Allyn. B.A., Yale U., 1967; J.D., Harvard U., 1970. Bar: D.C. 1970, U.S. Ct. Internat. Trade 1985, U.S. Ct. Appeals (9th cir.) 1971, U.S. Ct. Appeals (2d cir.) 1975, U.S. Ct. Appeals (D.C. cir.) 1978, U.S. Ct. Appeals (8th cir.) 1981, U.S. Ct. Appeals (fed. cir.) 1985, U.S. Ct. Appeals (4th cir.) 1989, U.S. Ct. Appeals (10th cir.) 1993, U.S. Supreme Ct. 1981. Law clk. U.S. Ct. Appeals for 9th Circuit, 1970-71; assoc. Wilmer, Cutler & Pickering, Washington, 1971-77, ptnr., 1978-96, 2001—; prin. dep. asst. atty. gen. U.S. Dept. Justice, 1996-2000, acting asst. atty. gen. antitrust divsn., 2000-2001. Vis. prof. Georgetown U. Law Ctr., 1992-93, adj. prof., 1993-94. Contbr. articles to profl. jours. Class agt. Alumni Fund Yale U.; D.C. area chair Yale campaign, 1993-97; mem. social scis. coun. com. Yale U., 1989-94; trustee Nat. Child Rsch. Ctr., 1990-93, Sidwell Friends Sch., 2000—. Mem. ABA, D.C. Bar Assn., Am. Law Inst., Yale Club (N.Y.C.), Kenwood Country Club. Antitrust, Federal civil litigation. Home: 6405 Shadow Rd Bethesda MD 20815-6613 also: Wilmer Cutler & Pickering 2445 M St NW Washington DC 20036 E-mail: dmelamer@wilmer.com

MELAMED, CAROL DRESCHER, lawyer; b. N.Y.C., July 12, 1946; d. Raymond A. and Ruth W. (Schwartz) Drescher; children from previous marriage: Stephanie Weisman, Deborah Harper; m. Arthur Douglas Melamed, May 26, 1983; children: Kathryn, Elizabeth. AB, Brown U., 1967; MAT, Harvard U., 1969; JD, Cath. U. Am., 1974. Bar: Md. 1974, D.c. 1975, U.S. Ct. Appeals (D.C. dir.) 1975, U.S. Dist. Ct. D.C. 1981, U.S. Supreme Ct. 1982. Tchr. English Wellesley (Mass.) H.S., 1968-69; law clk. U.S. Ct. Appeals (D.C. cir.), Washington, 1974-75; assoc. Wilmer, Cutler & Pickering, 1975-79; assoc. counsel The Washington Post, 1979-95, v.p. govt. affairs, 1995—. Mem. Phi Beta Kappa. Office: The Washington Post 1150 15th St NW Washington DC 20071-0002

MELDMAN, CLIFFORD KAY, lawyer; b. Milw., July 27, 1931; s. Edward H. and Rose (Bortin) M.; children: Mindy, David, Linda, James, Noah. JD, Marquette U., 1956. Bar: Wis. 1956. Ptnr. Meldman & Meldman, Milw., 1956-73; pres. Meldman & Meldman S.C., 1973-98; pvt. practice, 1956—. Contbr. articles to profl. jours., also editor. Mem.: Am. Acad. Matrimonial Lawyers (Wis. chpt., pres. 1982), Milw. Bar Assn. (bd. dirs. 1984—86, pres. 1986—87, chmn. family law sect.), Wis. Bar Assn. (chmn. family law sect.). Family and matrimonial. Home and Office: 170 W Cherokee Cir Milwaukee WI 53217-2716

MELDMAN, ROBERT EDWARD, lawyer; b. Milw., 05 Aug. s. Louis Leo and Lillian (Gollusch) M.; m. Sandra Jane Setlick, July 24, 1960; children: Saree Beth, Richard Samuel. B.S., U. Wis., 1959; LL.B., Marquette U., 1962; LL.M. in Taxation, NYU, 1963. Bar: Wis. 1962, Fla. 1987, Colo. 1990, U.S. Ct. Fed. Claims, U.S. Tax Ct. 1963, U.S. Supreme Ct. 1970. Practice tax law, Milw., 1963—; pres. Meldman, Case & Weine, Ltd., 1975-85; dir. tax div. Mulcahy & Wherry, S.C., 1985-90; shareholder Reinhart, Boerner, Van Deuren, Norris & Rieselbach, S.C., 1991—. Adj. prof. taxation U. Wis., Milw., 1970-2000, mem. tax adv. coun., 1978-2000; adj. prof. Marquette U. Sch. of Law, Milw., 2001—; sec. Profl. Inst. Tax Study, Inc., 1978—; bd. dirs. Wis. Bar Found., 1988-94; exec. in residence Deloitte & Touche Ctr. for Multistate Taxation, U. Wis., Milw., 1996-2000. Co-author: Federal Taxation Practice and Procedure, 1983, 86, 88, 92, 98, 2001, Practical Tactics for Dealing with the IRS, 1994, A Practical Guide to U.S. Taxation of International Transactions, 1996, 97, 2000, Federal Taxation Practice and Procedure Study Guide/Quizzes, 1998, A Quizzer Study Guide for Federal Taxation Practice and Procedure, 1998; editor Jour. Property Taxation; mem. editl. bd. Tax Litigation Alert, 1995-2000; contbr. articles to legal jours. Mem. IRS Midwest Citizen Advocacy Panel, 2001—. Recipient Adj. Taxation Faculty award UWM Tax Assn., 1987; named Outstanding Tax Profl. 1992 Corp. Reports Wis. Mag. and UWM Tax Assn. Fellow Am. Coll. Tax Coun.; mem. ABA, Fed. Bar Assn. (pres. Milw. chpt. 1966-67), Milw. Bar Assn. (chmn. tax sect. 1970-71), Wis. Bar Assn. (bd. dirs. tax sect. 1964-78, chmn. 1973-74), Internat. Bar Assn., The Law Assn. for Asia and the Pacific (chair tax sect. 2000—, dep. chair bus. law sect.), Marquette U. Law Alumni Assn. (bd. dirs. 1972-77), Milw. Athletic Club, Wis. Club, B'nai B'rith (trustee, Ralph Harris Meml. award Century Lodge 1969-70), Phi Delta Phi, Tau Epsilon Rho (chancellor Milw. chpt. 1969-71, supreme nat. chancellor 1975-76, v.p. Wis. chpt., tech. 1992-2000). Jewish (trustee congregation 1972-77). Private international, Corporate taxation, Personal income taxation. Home: 7455 N Skyline Ln Milwaukee WI 53217-3327 Office: 1000 N Water St Ste 2100 Milwaukee WI 53202-3197 E-mail: rmeldman@reinhartlaw.com

MELI, SALVATORE ANDREW, lawyer; b. N.Y.C., Sept. 18, 1947; s. Andrew and Marie (Ruggiero) M.; m. Barbara Ann Chiesa, Aug. 16, 1970. BA, St. John's U., Jamaica, N.Y., 1969, JD, 1975. Bar: N.Y. 1976, Fla. 1976, U.S. Dist. Ct. (ea. and so. dist.) N.Y. 1976. Sole practice, Flushing, N.Y., 1976-78; ptnr. Muratori & Meli, Flushing and Lake Worth, Fla., 1978-97; sole practice, 1997—. Lectr. Lawyers in the Classroom program, N.Y.C., 1977-81; mem. adv. bd. Title Ins. Co., Queens, N.Y., 1985—. Recipient Regents Scholarship, N.Y. State Bd. Regents, 1965. Mem. ABA, N.Y. State Bar Assn., Fla. Bar Assn., Queens County Bar Assn. Probate, Real property.

MELIN, ROBERT ARTHUR, lawyer; b. Milw., Sept. 13, 1940; s. Arthur John and Frances Madgalena (Lanser) M.; m. Mary Magdalen Melin, July 8, 1967; children: Arthur Walden, Robert Dismas, Nicholas O'Brien, Madalyn Mary. BA summa cum laude, Marquette U., 1962, JD, 1967. Bar: Wis. 1966, U.S. Dist. Ct. (ea. dist.) Wis. 1966, U.S. Ct. Appeals (7th cir.) 1966, U.S. Ct. Mil. Appeals 1967, U.S. Surpeme Ct. 1975. Law clk. U.S. Dist. Ct. Eastern Dist., Wis., 1966; instr. bus. law U. Ga., Hinesville, 1968; lectr. bus. law U. Md., Asmara, 1970; lectr. law Halle Salassie I. U. Law Faculty, Addis Ababa, Ethiopia, 1971-72; with Walther & Halling, Milw., 1973-74, Schroeder, Gedlen, Riester & Moerke, Milw., 1974-82; ptnr. Schroeder, Gedlen, Riester & Melin, 1982-84, Schroeder, Riester, Melin & Smith, Milw., 1984—. Author: Evidence in Ethiopia, 1972; contbg. author Ann. Survey African Law, 1974; contbr. numerous articles to legal jours. Rep. Class of 2000, West Point Parent Assn. Wis., 1996-99, 99—, exec. bd., 1997-98, 98—; lectr. charitable solicitations and contracts Philanthropy Monthly 9th Ann. Policy Conf., N.Y.C., 1985; chmn. Milw. Young Dems., 1963-64. Capt. JAGC, AUS, 1967-70. Mem. ABA, Wis. Acad. Trial Lawyers, Wis. Bar Assn., Milw. Bar Assn., Am. Legion, Friends Ethiopia, Delta Theta Phi, Phi Alpha Theta, Pi Gamma Mu. Roman Catholic. Federal civil litigation, State civil litigation, Non-profit and tax-exempt organizations. Home: 8108 N Whitney Rd Milwaukee WI 53217-2752 Office: 135 W Wells St Milwaukee WI 53203-1807

MELLEM, ROGER DUANE, lawyer; b. Eugene, Oreg., Feb. 23, 1950; s. Duane and Carolyn Mellem. BA, Evergreen State Coll., 1973, U. Oreg., 1973; MSL, Yale U., 1980; JD, U. Oreg., 1982. Law clk. U.S. Dist. Ct., Portland, Oreg., 1982-84; assoc. Foster Pepper & Shefelman PLLC, Seattle, 1985-91, mem., 1992—. Mem. Wash. adv. bd. Pacific Crest Outward Bound Sch., 1989—. Democrat. Lutheran. Avocation: mountaineering. Federal civil litigation, State civil litigation, Securities. Office: Foster Pepper & Shefelman PLLC 34th Fl 1111 3d Ave Bldg Seattle WA 98101

MELLEN, FRANCIS JOSEPH, JR. lawyer; b. Williamsport, Pa., Dec. 19, 1945; s. Francis Joseph and Mary Emma (Oberst) M.; m. Mary Wilder Davison, Aug. 2, 1975 (div. 1987); m. Beverly Joan Glascock, Sept. 2, 2000; children: Elizabeth, Catherine, Robert, Christine. BA, U. Ky., 1967, MA, 1971; JD, Harvard U., 1973. Bar: N.Y. 1974, Ky. 1975, U.S. Dist. Ct. (so. dist.) N.Y. 1974, U.S. Dist. Ct. (ea. dist.) Ky. 1977, U.S. Dist. Ct. (we. dist.) Ky. 1978, U.S. Ct. Appeals (2d cir.) 1975, U.S. Ct. Appeals (6th cir.) 1982. Assoc. atty. Rogers & Wells, N.Y.C., 1973-75, Wyatt, Grafton & Sloss, Louisville, 1975-80; ptnr. Wyatt, Tarrant & Combs, 1980—. Coauthor: Kentucky Mineral Law, 1986, Kentucky Forms and Transactions, 1991. Contbr. articles to profl. jours. Mem. spl. study com. for Uniform Commercial Code, Ky. Legis. Rsch. Comsn., Frankfort, 1984-91; bd. dirs. Leadership Louisville Found., counsel, 1996-98, 2000-01; bd. dirs. Stage One: The Louisville Children's Theatre, 1995-2001, v.p., 1997-98, pres., 1998-2000; bd. dirs. Louisville-Jefferson County A.W.A.R.E. Coalition, 1994-98. Mem. ABA, Am. Arbitration Assn. (panel), Ky. Bar Assn. (ho. dels. 1986-92), Louisville Bar Assn. (chmn. com. profl. responsibility 1992-94), Jefferson Club, Filson Club, Am. Mensa. Republican. General corporate, Mergers and acquisitions. Home: 2944 Lexington Rd Louisville KY 40206-2934 Office: Wyatt Tarrant & Combs 2800 Citizens Plz Louisville KY 40202 E-mail: fmellen@wyattfirm.com

MELLER, ROBERT LOUIS, JR. lawyer; b. Mpls., Apr. 24, 1950; s. Robert Louis and June Louise (Grenacher) M. B.A., Carleton Coll., 1972; J.D., Cornell U., 1975. Bar: Minn., 1975, U.S. Dist. Ct. (no. dist.), 1975. Atty. Best & Flanagan, Mpls., 1977—, ptnr., 1982—. Mem. ABA, Minn. State Bar Assn., Mpls. Club, Phi Beta Kappa, Sigma Xi. Republican. Episcopalian. Federal civil litigation, State civil litigation. Home: 1800 Major Dr N Minneapolis MN 55422-4153 Office: Best and Flanagan 4000 US Bank Pl 601 2nd Ave S # D Minneapolis MN 55402-4303

MELLON, THOMAS EDWARD, JR. lawyer; b. Phila., July 24, 1947; s. Thomas Edward and Honor (McCormick) M.; m. Marilyn Joan Scott, Dec. 28, 1968; children: Thomas E. III, Christopher Scott, Ryan Scott. BS, St. Joseph's U., 1969; JD, Georgetown U., 1972; LLM, Harvard U., 1974. Bar: Pa. 1973, D.C. 1973, U.S. Dist. Ct. (ea. dist.) Pa. 1974, U.S. Ct. Appeals (3d cir.) 1973, U.S. Supreme Ct. 1980. Law clerk to judge U.S. Ct. Appeals, Phila., 1972-73; asst. U.S. atty. Ea. Dist. Pa., Phila., 1974-80, chief narcotics unit, 1977-78, chief criminal div., 1978-80; atty. gen. Advocacy Inst., Washington, 1978-80; ptnr. Grim and Grim, Perkasie, Pa., 1980-81; asst. solicitor Bucks County, Doylestown, Pa., 1984-87; founding ptnr. Mellon & Mellon, Doylestown, 1982-89; mem. hearing com. Supreme Ct. Disciplinary Bd., Phila., 1984—. Counsel Dem. Party Bucks County, 1982-89, chmn., 1989—; active Dem. State Exec. Com., Harrisburg, Pa., 1984. Recipient Outstanding U.S. Atty. award for Ea. Dist. Pa., Atty. Gen. U.S., 1980. Mem. ABA, Assn. Trial Lawyers Am., Pa. Bar Assn., Bucks County Bar Assn. Roman Catholic. Criminal, General practice, Personal injury. Office: Mellon Webster & Mellon 87-89 Broad St Doylestown PA 18901

MELLUM, GALE ROBERT, lawyer; b. Duluth, Minn., July 5, 1942; s. Lester Andrew and Doris Esther (Smith) M.; m. Julie Murdoch Swanstrom, July 23, 1966; children: Eric Scott, Wendy Jane. BA summa cum laude, U. Minn., 1964, JD magna cum laude, 1968. Bar: Minn. 1968. Assoc. Faegre & Benson, Mpls., 1968-75, ptnr., 1976—, mem. mgmt. com., 1986-98. Planning com. Garret Corp. and Securities Law Inst., Northwestern U. Law Sch., 1984—; adv. bd. Quali Tech Inc., Chaska, Minn., 1985-98, bd. dirs.; bd. dirs. The Tesseract Group, Inc., Mpls.; corp. sec. Excelsior-Henderson Motorcycle Mfg. Co., Belle Plaine, Minn., 1997-2000. Hockey chmn. LARC Bd., Mpls., 1980-85. Mem. ABA (fed. securities regulation com.), Minn. Bar Assn., Hennepin County Bar Assn. (securities regulation com.). Republican. Lutheran. Avocations: tennis, golf, snow and water skiing, handball, boating. General corporate, Mergers and acquisitions, Securities. Home: 4889 E Lake Harriet Pky Minneapolis MN 55409-2222 Office: Faegre & Benson 2200 Wells Fargo Ctr 90 S 7th St Ste 2200 Minneapolis MN 55402-3901 E-mail: gmellum@faegre.com

MELLUM, WENDY, lawyer; b. Mpls., Sept. 2, 1969; d. Gale Robert and Julie (Swanstrom) Mellum. BA, U. Wis., 1992; JD, U. Minn., 1996. Atty. Lifetouch Inc., Bloomington, Minn., 1996; law clk. State of Minn. 6th Jud. Dist., Duluth, 1997-98; assoc. Magle Law Firm, 1998; assoc. atty. Wagner Falconer & Judd, Ltd., Mpls., 1998—. Mem. ABA, Minn. State Bar Assn., Minn. Women Lawyers, Vol. Lawyers Network. Office: Wagner Falconer & Judd Ltd 80 S 8th St Ste 3500 Minneapolis MN 55402-2214 E-mail: wymellum@aol.com

MELNIK, SELINDA A. lawyer; b. Ft. Worth, Aug. 22, 1951; d. Mitchell Mandel Melnik and Sylvia (Hoffman) Goldberg. BA, Temple U., 1972; M of City and Regional Planning, Rutgers U., 1974; JD summa cum laude, N.Y. Law Sch., 1984. Bar: N.Y. 1985, Del 2001, U.S. Dist. Ct. (so. and ea. dists.) N.Y. 1985, U.S. Dist. Ct. Del. 2001, U.S. Ct. Appeals (D.C. cir.) 1993, Ct. Internat. Trade 1993. Program assoc. to John D. Rockefeller III, 1974-78; cons. to various orgns. U.S., internat., 1975—; sr. policy analyst Planned Parenthood, 1978-79; dir. Ms. and Free to Be Founds., 1979-81; assoc. Milbank, Tweed, Hadley & McCloy, N.Y.C., 1984-87, LeBoeuf, Lamb, Leiby, MacRae, N.Y.C., 1987-90; ptnr. Dechert, Price & Rhoads, 1991-93; internat. counsel Rogers & Wells, 1993-96; pres. Internat. Counsel, NYC, 1996-2000; ptnr. Smith, Katzenstein & Furlow LLP, Wilmington, Del., 2000—. Founder, 1st pres. Internat. Women's Insolvency and Restructring Confederation, cons. internat. law, trade Cross Border Insolvency and Bankruptcy Prevention Planning, 1987—; cons. fgn. govts. internat. trade and insolvency law; writer, lectr. internat. trade and insolvency law. Mem. ABA, Internat. Bar Assn. (chair membership, chair com. on creditor's rights & insolvency, rep. to UN Commn. on Status of Women), Internat. Lawyers Club, N.Y. State Bar Assn., Internat. Women's Insolvency and Restructuring Confedn. (chair), Order of Coif. Bankruptcy, Contracts commercial, Private international. Office: Smith Katzenstein & Furlow 800 Delaware Ave Wilmington DE 19801-1322 E-mail: samelnik@aol.com

MELTON, BARRY, lawyer, musician; b. N.Y.C., June 14, 1947; s. James Gerald and Terry Melton; m. Barbara Joy Langer; children: Kingsley, Kyle. Bar: Calif. 1982, U.S. Dist. Ct. (no. dist.) Calif. 1982, U.S. Dist. Ct. (cen. dist.) Calif. 1983, U.S. Ct. Appeals (9th cir.) 1983, U.S. Dist. Ct. (ea. dist.) Calif. 1985, U.S. Supreme Ct. 1988. Pvt. practice, San Francisco, 1982-94; pub. defender Yolo County, Woodland, Calif. Musician, pub. Seafood Music, San Francisco, 1965—; pro-tem judge San Francisco Mcpl. Ct., 1987-94. Musician, composer various mus. recs., 1965—. Mem. State Bar Calif. (cert. criminal law specialist 1993—, vol. legal svc. awards 1983-87), Calif. Attys. Criminal Justice, Calif. Pub. Defenders Assn. (bd. dirs. 1999—). Criminal, Juvenile. Office: Yolo County Pub Defender 814 North St Woodland CA 95695-3538 E-mail: melton@counterculture.net, thefish@counterculture.net

MELTON, HOWELL WEBSTER, SR. federal judge; b. Atlanta, Dec. 15, 1923; s. Holmes and Alma (Combee) M.; m. Margaret Catherine Wolfe, Mar. 4, 1950; children— Howell Webster, Carol Anne. JD, U. Fla., 1948. Bar: Fla. 1948. With Upchurch, Melton & Upchurch, St. Augustine, 1948-61; judge 7th Jud. Circuit of Fla., 1961-77, U.S. Dist. Ct. (mid. dist.) Fla., Jacksonville, 1977-91, sr. judge, 1991—. Past chmn. Fla. Conf. Cir. Judges, 1974; past chmn. coun. bar pres.'s Fla. Bar. Trustee Flagler Coll., St. Augustine. Served with U.S. Army, 1943-46. Recipient Disting. Service award St. Augustine Jaycees, 1953 Mem. ABA, St. Johns County Bar Assn., Jacksonville Bar Assn., Fed. Bar Assn., Fla. Blue Key, Ponce de Leon Country Club, St. Augustine Fla. Officers Club, Masons, Phi Delta Theta, Phi Delta Phi. Methodist. Office: US Dist Ct PO Box 52957 Jacksonville FL 32201-2957

MELTON, ROBERT EARL, lawyer; b. Dawson Springs, Ky., Jan. 4, 1938; s. Lonnie E. and Margaret L. (Blaine) M.; m. Flois C. Anderson, Dec. 23, 1964; 1 child, Robert Earl Jr. B.A. Western N. Mex. U., 1961; postgrad., 1961-62; J.D., U. N.Mex., 1969. Bar: N.Mex., 1969, U.S. Dist. Ct. (N.Mex.), 1969, U.S. Tax Ct., 1971, U.S. Ct. Appeals (10th Cir.) 1973, U.S. Supreme Ct. 1984. Various positions Kennecott Copper Corp., Santa Rita, N.Mex., 1956-66; asst. city atty. City Albuquerque, 1969-71; atty. Roy F. Miller Jr., Albuquerque, 1971-73; atty., ptnr. Miller & Melton, Albuquerque, 1973-75, atty., sec. treas., 1975-78; atty., pres. Melton & Puccini, P.A., Albuquerque, 1978— ; sec., gen. counsel Amateur Trap shooting Assn. Am., 1984— . Bd. dirs., sec. Pediatric Pulmonary Assn. Am., Albuquerque, 1976-82, Children's Lung Assn. Am., Albuquerque, 1981-82; active in Sojourners, Ft. Mc Clellan, Ala., 1963, Jr. C. of C., Silver City, N. Mex., 1964-65. Served to 1st lt. U.S. Army, 1962-64, USAR, 1964-70 Mem. ABA, Albuquerque Bar Assn., N.Mex. Trial Lawyers Assn., N. Mex. Estate Planning Council. Republican. Lodge: Masons. Office: Melton & Puccini PA Suite 1800 Western Bank 505 Marquette NW Albuquerque NM 87102

MELTZER, BERNARD DAVID, law educator; b. Phila., Nov. 21, 1914; s. Julius and Rose (Welkov) M.; m. Jean Sulzberger, Jan. 17, 1947; children: Joan, Daniel, Susan. A.B., U. Chgo., 1935, J.D., 1937; LL.M., Harvard U., 1938. Bar: Ill. 1938. Atty., spl. asst. to chmn. SEC, 1938-40; assoc. firm Mayer, Meyer, Austrian & Platt, Chgo., 1940; spl. asst. to asst. sec. state, also acting chief fgn. funds control div. div. State 1941-43; asst. trial counsel U.S. stafff Internat. Nuremberg War Trials, 1945-46; from professorial lectr. to disting. svc. prof. law emeritus U. Chgo. Law Sch., 1946—; counsel Vedder, Price, Kaufman & Kamnholz, Chgo., 1954-55, Sidley and Austin, Chgo., 1987-89. Hearing commr. NPA, 1952-53; labor arbitrator; spl. master U.S. Ct. Appeals for D.C., 1963-64; bd. publs. U. Chgo., 1965-67, chmn., 1967-68; mem. Gov. Ill. Adv. Commn. Labor-Mgmt. Policy for Pub. Employees in Ill., 1966-67, Ill. Civil Service Commn., 1968-69; cons. U.S. Dept. Labor, 1969-70 Author: Supplementary Materials on International Organizations, 1948, (with W.G. Katz) Cases and Materials on Business Corporations, 1949, Labor Law Cases, Materials and Problems, 1970, supplement, 1972, 75, 2d edit., 1977, supplements, 1980, 82 (with S. Henderson), 3d edit. (with S. Henderson), 1985, supplement, 1988; also articles. Bd. dirs. Hyde Park Community Conf., 1954-56, S.E. Chgo. Commn., 1956-57. Served to lt. (j.g.) USNR, 1943-46. Mem. ABA (co-chmn. com. devel. law under NLRA 1959-60, mem. spl. com. transp. strikes), Ill. Bar Assn., Chgo. Bar Assn. (bd. mgrs. 1972-73), Am. Law Inst., Coll. Labor and Employment Lawyers, Am. Acad. Arts and Scis., Order of Coif, Phi Beta Kappa Home: 1219 E 50th St Chicago IL 60615-2908 Office: U Chgo Law Sch 1111 E 60th St Chicago IL 60637-2776

MELTZER, JAY H. lawyer, retail company executive; b. Bklyn., Mar. 30, 1944; s. Solomon G. and Ethel L. (Kraft) M.; m. Bonnie R. Rosenberg, June 27, 1965; children: Wendy, Elizabeth, Jonathan. A.B., Dartmouth Coll., 1964; JD, Harvard U., 1967. Bar: N.Y. 1968, Mass. 1978, U.S. Dist. Ct. Mass. 1979. Law clk. to U.S. dist. judge, 1967-68; assoc. firm Shearman & Sterling, N.Y.C., 1968-72; with Damon Corp., Needham Heights, Mass., 1972-84, gen. counsel, sec., 1973-84, v.p., 1979-84; v.p., corp. counsel The TJX Cos., Inc., Framingham, Mass., 1984-87, v.p., gen. counsel, sec., 1987-89, sr. v.p., gen. counsel, sec., 1989—. Dir. coun. Better Bus. Bur., 1990-93. Mem. ABA, Am. Soc. Corp. Secs., Am. Corp. Counsel Assn. (bd. dirs. N.E. chpt. 1991-2000), Retailers Assn. Mass. (bd. dirs., exec. com., sec.), New Eng. Corp. Counsel Assn. (bd. dirs.). Contracts commercial, General corporate, Securities. Office: TJX Cos Inc 770 Cochituate Rd Framingham MA 01701-4672 E-mail: jay_meltzer@tjx.com

MELTZER, ROBERT CRAIG, lawyer, educator; b. Chgo., July 31, 1958; s. Franklyn Richard and Zelma (Cohen) M. BA, U. Colo., 1980; cert., Inst. de Internat., Strasbourg, France, 1984; JD, No. Ill. U., DeKalb, 1985; postgrad., U. Salzburg, Austria, 1985. Bar: Ill. 1985, U.S. Dist. Ct. (no. dist.) Ill. 1985, U.S. Ct. Appeals (7th cir.) 1988, U.S. Supreme Ct. 1989. Law clk. Hurwitz & Abramson, Washington, 1980, Mayer, Brown & Platt, Chgo., 1983; lawyer UN WHO, Geneva, Switzerland, 1985; assoc. Robert C. Meltzer & Assocs., Chgo., 1986-91, Katz, Randall & Weinberg, Chgo., 1991-93, Arnstein & Lehr, Chgo., 1993-98, Grotefeld & Denenberg, Chgo., 1998-99; pres. Visanow.com., Inc., 1999—. Creator online immigration processing. Contbr. articles to profl. jours.; editor The Globe, Springfield, Ill., 1984-99. Pro bono lawyer Fed. Bar Assn., Chgo., 1985-98. Recipient Medal of Appreciation, Ministry of Justice, Beijing, 1996. Mem. Ill. State Bar Assn. (internat. and immigration law sect. 1985—, pres. internat. law sect. 1990-91, Editor's award 1989, 94), Am. Immigration Law Assn. Avocations: history, racquet sports, golf, arts, music. Immigration, naturalization, and customs, Private international. Home: 71 E Division St Chicago IL 60610 Office: Visanow.com Inc 33 N La Salle St # 300 Chicago IL 60602-2603 E-mail: meltzer@visanow.com

MELTZER, ROGER, lawyer; b. N.Y.C., Jan. 31, 1951; s. Irwin Samuel and Beula (Jacobs) M.; m. Robin Hirtz, July 20, 1975; children: Justin, Martin, Elizabeth. BA cum laude, Harvard U., 1973; postgrad., Tulane U., 1974-75; JD cum laude, NYU, 1977. Bar: N.Y. 1978, D.C. 1979. Assoc. Cahill, Gordon & Reindel, N.Y.C., 1977-84, ptnr., 1984—, mem. exec. com., 2000—. Mem. ABA, Order of the Coif. General corporate, Securities. Office: Cahill Gordon & Reindel 80 Pine St Fl 17 New York NY 10005-1790

MEMEL, SHERWIN LEONARD, lawyer; b. Buffalo, Mar. 28, 1930; s. Maurice and Nellie (Munshen) M.; m. Iris C. Gittleman, Aug. 17, 1952; children: Jana Sue, Steven Keith, David Scott, Mara Jean. BA, UCLA, 1951, JD with honors, 1954. Bar: Calif. 1955, U.S. Ct. Appeals (9th cir.) 1955, U.S. Dist. Ct. (cen. dist.) Calif. 1959, U.S. Supreme Ct. 1963, D.C. 1979. Sr. ptnr. health law practice group Manatt, Phelps & Phillips, LA, 1987—. Chmn. bd. Pac. Pub. Radio Sta. KLON; past instr. health law USC Sch. Pub. Adminstrn.; past instr. health UCLA; cons. and lectr. in field. Co-author: (with R. Barak) Real Estate Issues in the Health Care Industry, 1996; contbr. articles to profl. jours. Chmn. LA Arts Council, 1986-87; vice-chmn. Dem. Bus. Council, Washington, 1985-86; past pres. Calif. Bd. Med. Quality Assurance. Recipient Disting. Service award Fedn. Am. Hosps., 1970. Mem. ABA (com. health law), Am. Hosp. Assn. (life, Award of Honor 1971), Am. Soc. Law and Medicine, Am. Health Lawyers Assn., Calif. Soc. for Healthcare Attys. (life, pres. 1983), Calif. Bar Assn., D.C. Bar Assn., L.A. County Bar Assn. Administrative and regulatory, Health, Legislative. Office: Manatt Phelps & Phillips 11355 W Olympic Blvd Los Angeles CA 90064-1614

MENAKER, FRANK H., JR. lawyer; b. Harrisburg, Pa., Aug. 23, 1940; s. Frank H. and Romaine (Sadler) M.; m. Sharon Ann Lynch, Feb. 21, 1981; children: Denise L., Jamie E.; children by previous marriage: David C., Michelle R. BA, Wilkes Coll., 1962; JD, Am. U., 1965. Bar: D.C. 1966, Md. 1975, U.S. Supreme Ct. 1975. Formerly staff counsel Office Gen. Counsel, GAO, Washington; v.p., gen. counsel Martin Marietta Corp., 1981-95, Lockheed Martin, 1995-96, sr. v.p., gen. counsel, 1996—. Spl. counsel U.S. Commn. on Govt. Procurement, 1971. Mem. ABA (mem. sect. pub. contract law, former chair), Md. Bar Assn., Wash. Met. Corp. Counsel Assn. (bd. dirs. 1988-95). General corporate, Government contracts and claims, Mergers and acquisitions. Office: Lockheed Martin 6801 Rockledge Dr Bethesda MD 20817-1877

MENASHE, ALBERT ALAN, lawyer; b. Portland, Oreg., Apr. 24, 1950; s. Solomon A. and Faye F. (Hasson) M.; m. Laura L. Richenstein, July 23, 1972 (div. Oct. 1979); 1 child, Shawn Nathan; m. Sandra J. Laniado, June 28, 1980 (div. Jan. 1994). B.S. in Polit. Sci., U. Oreg., 1971; J.D., Willamette U., 1976. Bar: Oreg. 1977, U.S. Dist. Ct. Oreg. 1977, U.S. Ct. Appeals (9th cir.) 1977, U.S. Supreme Ct. 1980. Assoc. Bullivant, Wright, et al, Portland, 1976-79; ptnr. Samuels, Samuels, et al, Portland, 1979-80; sr. ptnr., shareholder Gevurtz, Menashe, Larson, Yates, & Howe, PC, Portland, 1981— ; arbitrator Multnomah County Circuit Ct., Portland, 1983— ; lectr. family law Lewis and Clark Law Sch., Portland, 1980— , Willamette U. Coll. Law, 1986; frequent speaker on family law, 1979—; pro tem judge County of Clackamas, Oreg. Served to 1st lt. U.S. Army, 1971-73. Mem. Am. Arbitration Assn. (mem. family dispute panel 1979—), Assn. Family Conciliation Cts., Am. Acad. Matrimonial Lawyers (pres. Oreg. chpt. 1996-97), Am. Acad. Matrimonial Law, Oreg. State Bar Assn., Multnomah County Bar Assn. (pres. 1997-98), Washington County Bar Assn., Oreg. Trial Lawyers Assn., ABA, Phi Kappa Phi. Democrat. Jewish. Family and matrimonial. Home: 3000 SW Montgomery Dr Portland OR 97201-1681 Office: Gevurtz Menashe Larson Yates & Howe PC 1515 SW 5th Ave Ste 808 Portland OR 97201-5447

MENCER, GLENN EVERELL, federal judge; b. Smethport, Pa., May 18, 1925; s. Glenn Hezekiah and Ruth Leona (Rice) M.; m. Hannah Jane Freyer, June 24, 1950; children— Ruth Ann, Cora Jane, Glenn John B.B.A., U. Mich., 1949, J.D., 1952. Bar: Pa. 1953, U.S. Dist. Ct. (we. dist.) Pa. 1953, U.S. Supreme Ct. 1958. Sole practice, Eldred, Pa., 1953-64; dist. atty. McKean County, 1956-64; judge 48th Jud. Dist. Ct., Smethport, 1964-70, Commonwealth Ct. of Pa., Harrisburg, 1970-82, U.S. Dist. Ct., Erie, Pa., 1982—. Served with U.S. Army, 1943-45, ETO Mem. Fed. Judges Assn., Pa. Bar Assn., McKean County Bar Assn. Republican. Methodist. Lodge: Masons (33 degree) Home: 30 W Willow St Smethport PA 16749-1524 Office: US Dist Ct Fed Courthouse PO Box 1820 Erie PA 16507-0820

MENDALES, RICHARD EPHRAIM, lawyer; b. N.Y.C., Mar. 12, 1950; s. Arnold and Helen Shirley (Milk) M.; m. Christine Piejak, Dec. 16, 1993. AB, U. Chgo., 1969, AM, 1970; JD, Yale U., 1981. Bar: N.Y. 1982, U.S. Dist. Ct. (so. and ea. dist.) N.Y. 1982. Research asst. Mus. of Sci. and Industry, Chgo., 1973-74; quality claims analyst Social Security Adminstrn., 1975-78; assoc. Cravath, Swaine & Moore, N.Y.C., 1981-84, Skadden, Arps, Slate, Meagher & Flom, N.Y.C., 1984-88; assoc. prof. U. Miami Sch. Law, Coral Gables, 1988-95, prof., 1995-99; jud. fellow Adminstrv. Office U.S. Cts., 1999-2000; of counsel Crowell & Moring, LLP, Washington, 2000—. Ford Found. fellow, 1969-73. Mem. ABA, AAAS, Assn. Internat. des Jeunes Avocats, Am. Hist. Assn. Democrat. Avocations: hist. research and writing, photography. Bankruptcy, Contracts commercial, Private international. Home: 2601 Park Center Dr Apt C802 Alexandria VA 22302-1408 Office: Crowell & Moring LLP 5k Law 1001 Pennsylvania Ave Washington DC 20004-2595 E-mail: rmendales@cromor.com

MENDELOWITZ, MICHAEL SYDNEY, solicitor; b. Liverpool, Eng., June 8, 1952; s. Arnold and Rachel (Levinsohn) M.; m. Kim Merle Momberg, July 20, 1980; children: Jonathan, Alice. BA, U. Witwatersrand, Johannesburg, South Africa, 1974, LLB, 1976; BCL, Oxford U., Eng., 1979. Advocate of Supreme Ct. of South Africa, 1977, barrister of Mid. Temple, 1981, solicitor Supreme Ct. of Eng. and Wales, 1989. Barrister, Johannesburg, 1983-87; asst. Barlow Lyde & Gilbert, London, 1987-90, ptnr., 1990—. Co-author: Insurance Disputes, 1999, Insurance Handbook, 2000; editor, co-author: Reinsurance Practice and the Law, 1993; contbr. articles to profl. jours. Mem. Internat. Assn. for Ins. Law (asst. sec., gen. adminstrn.), British Ins. Law Assn., U.K. Environtl. Law Assn., Chartered Ins. Inst. Avocations: family, music, skiing. General civil litigation, Insurance, Toxic tort. Office: Barlow Lyde & Gilbert Beaufort Ho 15 Saint Botolph St London EC3A 7NJ England Fax: 44-20-7643-8500. E-mail: mmendelowitz@blg.co.uk

MENDELSOHN, MARTIN, lawyer; b. Bkyln., Sept. 6, 1942; s. Syman and Gertrude M.; m. Syma Barbara Rossman, Aug. 15, 1964; children: Alice S., James D. BA, Bklyn. Coll., 1963; LLB, George Washington U., 1966. Bar D.C. 1967, U.S. Ct. Appeals (D.C. cir.) 1967, U.S. Supreme Ct. 1970, U.S. Ct. Appeals (3d cir.) 1971, U.S. Ct. Appeals (7th cir.) 1973, Ill. 1973, U.S. Ct. Appeals (9th cir.) 1987, U.S. Tax Ct. 1988, U.S. Ct. Appeals (2d cir.) 1988, U.S. Ct. of Appeals (5th cir.) 2000. With Gen. Counsel's Office, HEW, Washington, 1966-67; legal svcs., 1967-70, Pa., 1971-72, Ill., 1973-75; counsel Legal Svcs. Corp., Washington, 1976; adminstrv. asst. U.S. Congress, 1977; chief spl. litigation U.S. Dept. Justice, 1977-79, dep. dir. office spl. investigations, 1979-80; counsel House Judiciary Com., 1980; pvt. practice Washington, 1980-88; ptnr. Dilworth, Paxon, Kalish &

Kauffman, 1989-91, Verner, Liipfeert, Bernhard, McPherson & Hand, 1991—. Author: (with Aaron Freiwald) The Last Nazi, 1994. Mem. ABA, D.C. Bar Assn., Order of Merit (officer). Jewish. Private international, Public international, Legislative. Home: 5705 Mckinley St Bethesda MD 20817-3638 Office: 901 15th St NW Ste 700 Washington DC 20005-2327

MENDELSON, ALAN CHARLES, lawyer; b. San Francisco, Mar. 27, 1948; s. Samuel Mendelson and Rita Rosalie (Spindel) Brown; children: Jonathan Daniel, David Gary; m. Agnès Marie Barbariol. BA with great distinction, U. Calif., Berkeley, 1969; JD cum laude, Harvard U., 1973. Bar: Calif. 1973. Assoc. Cooley Godward LLP, San Francisco, 1973-80, ptnr. Palo Alto, 1980-2000, mng. ptnr. Palo Alto office, 1990-95, 96-97; sec. gen. counsel Amgen Inc., Thousand Oaks, Calif., 1990-91; acting gen. counsel Cadence Design Sys., Inc., San Jose, 1995-96; sr. ptnr. Latham & Watkins, Menlo Park, 2000—. Co-chair Latham and Watkins Venture and Tech. Group, 2001-; bd. dirs. Valentis Inc., Axys Pharms., Inc., Aviron, USSearch.com, Inc., iScribe, Inc., Connectix Corp.; mem. mgmt. com. Cooley Godward, LLP; chmn. Cos. Practice Group, 1990—, Life Sci. Group, 1998-2000. Chmn. Piedmont (Calif.) Civil Svc. Commn., 1978-80; den leader Boy Scouts Am., Menlo Park, Calif.; fundraiser Crystal Springs Upland Sch., Hillsborough, Calif., Harvard Law Sch. Fund, Berkeley, Lucille Packard Children's Hosp.; coach Menlo Park Little League, 1982-86; pres., mem. exec. com., bd. dirs. No. Calif. chpt. Nat. Kidney Found., 1986-98. With USAR, 1969-75. Recipient Disting. Svc. award Nat. Kidney Found., 1992; named U. Calif. Berkeley Alumni scholar, 1966, Scaife Found. scholar, 1966, One of 100 Most Influential Attys. in U.S. Nat. Law Jour., 1994, 97, 2000 (Best Lawyers in Am., 1993-2000). Mem. Bohemian Club, Phi Beta Kappa. Jewish. General corporate, Intellectual property, Securities. Home: 76 De Bell Dr Atherton CA 94027-2253 Office: Latham & Watkins 135 Commonwealth Dr Menlo Park CA 94025 E-mail: alan.mendelson@lw.com

MENDELSON, STEVEN EARLE, lawyer; b. Los Angeles, Mar. 24, 1948; s. Robert Alexander and Nell Earle (Jacobs) M.; children: Carolyn, Laurel. BA, U. Calif., Santa Cruz, 1971; JD, Golden Gate U., 1975. Bar: Calif. 1975, U.S. Dist. Ct. (no. dist.) Calif. 1975. Assoc. Law Offices Robert A. Mendelson, Los Angeles, 1975-76, Law Offices Paul A. Eisler, San Francisco, 1976-77; sole practice Oakland, Calif., 1977-84; ptnr. Mendelson & Mendelson, 1985—. Founding sponsor Civil Justice Found., 1986. Mem. Assn. Trial Lawyers Am., Calif. Trial Lawyers Assn. (speaker), Alameda Contra Costa Trial Lawyers Assn., Calif. Applicant Atty's Assn., Am. Back Soc. (workshop dir., speaker, bd. dirs. com. on programs and interprofl. relations, incorporator, legal counsel 1981—). Personal injury, Toxic tort. Office: Mendelson & Mendelson 120 11th St Oakland CA 94607-4806

MENDENHALL, HARRY BARTON, lawyer; b. Oct. 31, 1946; BA, Colo. Coll., 1968; JD, U. Colo., 1971. Bar: Colo. 1971. Ptnr. Mendenhall & Malouff, R.L.L.P., Rocky Ford, Colo., 1971—. Mem. nominating com. Colo. Supreme Ct., Denver, 1986-91; pres. Colo. Lawyer Trust Account Found., Denver, 1995-97. Mem. Colo. Bar Assn. (pres. 1999-2000). Estate planning, Probate, Real property. Office: Mendenhall & Malouff 805 Chestnut Ave Rocky Ford CO 81067-1224 E-mail: bmendenhall@rmi.net

MENDOZA, ENID DUANY, lawyer; b. Havana, Cuba, Oct. 21, 1951; came to U.S., 1960; m. Sergio Gonzalez de Mendoza; children: Sergio A., Beatriz C. BA in History, Princeton U., 1973; MA in Journalism, Marquette U., 1979; JD, U. Miami, 1990. Bar: Fla. 1991. Summer intern to Hon. William H. Hoeveler, Miami, Fla., 1988; assoc. Steel Hector & Davis, 1991-92, Colson, Hicks, Eidson & Matthews, Miami, 1992-96; ptnr. Colson, Hicks, Eidson, Colson, Matthews, Martinez & Mendoza, 1997—. Bd. govs. Anne Bates Leach Hosp., Miami, 1998—; mem. edn. com. Greater Miami C. of C., Miami, 1985-86; mem. exec. com. Leadership Miami, 1986; bd. trustees Ransom Everglades Sch., 1993—, Hispanic Women's Leadership Alliance, Miami, 1994-96; mem. alumni com. Princeton U., chairperson, 1981—. Mem. Fla. Bar Found. (legal assistance com. 1996-99), Miami Rowing Club (guardian ad litem 1987—). Democrat. Roman Catholic. Avocation: crew member women's masters team. Office: Colson Hicks 200 S Biscayne Blvd Ste 4700 Miami FL 33131-2351 E-mail: enid@colson.com

MENEFEE, SAMUEL PYEATT, lawyer, anthropologist; b. Denver, June 8, 1950; s. George Hardiman and Martha Elizabeth (Pyeatt) M. BA in Anthropology and Scholar of Ho. summa cum laude, Yale U., 1972; diploma in Social Anthropology, Oxford (Eng.) U., 1973, BLitt, 1975; JD, Harvard U., 1981; LLM in Oceans, U. Va., 1982, SJD, 1993; MPhil in Internat. Rels., U. Cambridge, Eng., 1995. Bar: Ga. 1981, U.S. Ct. Appeals (11th cir.) 1982, Va. 1983, La. 1983, U.S. Ct. Mil. Appeals 1983, U.S. Ct. Internat. Trade 1983, U.S. Ct. Claims 1983, U.S. Ct. Appeals (10th cir.) 1983, U.S. Ct. Appeals (fed., 1st, 3d, 4th, 5th, 6th, 7th, 8th and 9th cirs.) 1984, D.C. 1985, Nebr. 1985, Fla. 1985, U.S. Supreme Ct. 1985, U.S. Ct. Appeals (D.C. cir.) 1986, Maine 1986, Pa. 1986. Assoc. Phelps, Dunbar, Marks, Claverie & Sims, New Orleans, 1983-85; of counsel Barham & Churchill PC, 1985-88; sr. assoc. Ctr. for Nat. Security Law U. Va. Sch. Law, 1985—, fellow Ctr. for Oceans Law and Policy, 1982-83, sr. fellow, 1985-89, Maury fellow, 1989—, adv. bd., 1997—. Vis. lectr. U. Cape Town, 1987; vis. asst. prof. U. Mo.-Kansas City, 1990; law clk. Hon. Pasco M. Bowman, U.S. Ct. Appeals (8th cir.), 1994-95; vis. prof. Regent U., 1996-97, scholar-at-large, 1997—, prof., 1998—; adv. The Am. Maritime Forum/The Mariners' Mus., 1997-98; lectr. various nat. and internat. orgns.; mem. ICC Consultative Task Force on Comml. Crime, 1996—. Author: Wives for Sale: An Ethnographic Study of British Popular Divorce, 1981, Contemporary Piracy and International Law, 1995, Trends in Maritime Violence, 1996; co-editor: Materials on Ocean Law, 1982; contbr. numerous articles to profl. jours. Recipient Katharine Briggs prize Folklore Soc., 1992; Bates traveling fellow Yale U., 1971, Rhodes scholar, 1972; Cosmos fellow Sch. Scottish Studies U. Edinburgh, 1991-92, IMB fellow, ICC Internat. Maritime Bur., 1991—, Piracy Reporting Ctr. fellow, Kuala Lampur, 1993—, Huntington fellow The Mariners Mus., 1997. Fellow Royal Anthrop. Inst., Am. Anthrop. Assn., Royal Asiatic Soc., Royal Soc. Antiquaries of Ireland, Soc. Antiquaries (Scotland), Royal Geog. Soc., Soc. Antiquaries; mem. ABA (vice-chmn. marine resources com. 1987-90, chmn. law of the sea com. subcom. naval warfare, maritime terrorism and piracy 1989—, mem. law of the sea com. steering com. 1996—, mem. working group on terrorism), Southeastern Admiralty Law Inst. (com. mem.), Maritime Law Assn. (proctor, com. mem., chmn. subcom. law of the sea 1988-91, vice chmn. com. internat. law of the sea 1991— , chair working group piracy 1992—, UNESCO study group, 1998—), Marine Tech. Soc. (co-chmn. marine security com. 1991—), Selden Soc., Am. Soc. Internat. Law, Internat. Law Assn. (com. mem., rapporteur Am. br. com. EEZ 1988-90, rapporteur Am. br. com. Maritime Neutrality 1992, observer UN conv. on Law of the Sea meeting of States Parties 1996, chmn. Am. br. com. on Law of the Sea 1996—), rapporteur joint internat. working group on uniformity of the law of piracy 1998—, (Com. Maritime Internat.), Am. Soc. Indsl. Security (com. mem.), U.S. Naval Inst., USN League, Folklore Soc., Royal Celtic Soc., Internat. Studies Assn., Royal Scottish Geog. Soc., Royal African Soc., Egypt Exploration Soc., Arctic Inst. N.Am., Internat. Studies Assn., Am. Hist. Soc., Internat. Assn. Rsch. on Peasant Diaries (nat. editor 1996—), Nat. Eagle Scout Assn., Raven Soc., Jefferson Soc., Fence Club, Mory's Assn., Elizabethan Club, Yale Polit. Union, Leander Club, Cambridge Union, United Oxford and Cambridge Univ. Club, Yale Club (N.Y.C.), Paul Morphy Chess Club, Pendennis Club, Round Table Club (New Orleans), Phi Beta Kappa, Omicron Delta Kappa. Republican. Episcopalian. Avocations: anthropology, archaeology, social history, crew, hill walking. Office: U Va Ctr Nat Sec Law 580 Massie Rd Charlottesville VA 22903-1738

MENENDEZ, MANUEL, JR. judge; b. Tampa, Fla., Aug. 2, 1947; s. Manuel and Clara (Marin) M.; m. Linda Lee Stewart, Aug. 31, 1969; children: Jennifer Kay, Christine Marie. AA, U. Fla., 1967, BA, 1969, JD with Honors, 1972. Bar: Fla. 1972, U.S. Dist. Ct. (mid. dist.) Fla. 1973, U.S. Ct. Appeals (5th cir.) 1973, U.S. Ct. Claims 1974, U.S. Tax Ct. 1974, U.S. Ct. Customs and Patent Appeals 1974, U.S. Supreme Ct. 1976, U.S. Ct. Appeals (11th cir.) 1983, U.S. Ct. Appeals (D.C. cir.) 1984. Asst. U.S. atty. Dept. Justice, Jacksonville, Fla., 1973-77, chief asst. U.S. atty. Tampa, 1978-83; assoc. Law Office Jack Culp, Jacksonville, 1977-78; ptnr. Culp & Menendez, P.A., 1978; county judge jud. br. State of Fla., Tampa, 1983-84, cir. judge jud. br., 1984—; chief judge 13th Cir., 2001. Dept. head, faculty mem. Fla. Coll. of Advanced Jud. Studies; faculty mem. pre-bench program Fla. New Judges Coll., 1993; faculty mem. Fla. Bar Prosecutor-Pub. Defender Advocacy Tng. Program, 1989-91, 94—; mentor judge coord. 13th Cir. Ct., 1995—; co-chair edn. steering com. Fla. Cir. Judge's Conf., 1996. Exec. editor U. Fla. Law Rev., 1971-72. Mem. adv. bd. Salvation Army, 1988-91. Recipient Pub. Service Meritorious Achievement award West Tampa Civic Clubs Assn., 1983. Mem. ABA, Fla. Bar Assn. (mem. criminal procedure rules com. 1988-94, chmn. 1991-92, chmn. rules and jud. adminstrn. com. 1995-96), Fed. Bar Assn. (v.p. Jacksonville chpt. 1974-75, pres. Tampa Bay chpt. 1980-85), Hillsborough County Bar Assn. (media law com. 1984—, trial lawyers sect. 1985—, Liberty Bell award selection com. 1991-93, jud. evaluation com. 1993, Outstanding Jurist award 1998-99), Am. Judicature Soc., Am. Judges Assn., Am. Inns of Ct. (master of bench, pres. 1991—), U. Fla. Alumni Assn., U. Fla. Law Ctr. Assn., First U.S. Calvary Regiment Rough Riders Inc., Propellor Club, Tampa Gator Club. Avocations: fishing, golf, Univ. Fla. athletics, coaching little league sr. girls softball. Office: Hillsborough County Courthouse 419 N Pierce St Ste 375 Tampa FL 33602-4025

MENGEL, CHRISTOPHER EMILE, lawyer, educator; b. Holyoke, Mass., Sept. 11, 1952; s. Emile Oscar and Rose Ann (O'Donnell) M.; m. Ellen Christine Creager, Dec. 6, 1991; children: Meredith Anne, Celia Claire; step-children: Cara Elizabeth Creager, Kristen Michele Creager. Student, U. Notre Dame, 1970-71; BA, Holy Cross Coll., 1974; JD, Detroit Coll. Law, 1979. Bar: Mich. 1979, U.S. Dist. Ct. (ea. dist.) Mich. 1989, U.S. Ct. Appeals (6th cir.) 1990. Tchr. Holyoke Pub. Schs., 1974-76; assoc. Fried & Sniokaitis P.C., Detroit, 1980-82; prof. Detroit Coll. Law, 1982-85; pvt. practice Detroit, 1982-91; mng. ptnr. Berkley, Mengel & Vining, PC, 1992—. Mem. coun. St. Ambrose Parish, Grosse Pointe Park, Mich., 1985-88, pres. 1986-87. Matthew J. Ryan scholar, 1970; recipient Disting. Brief award Thomas M. Cooley Law Rev., 1996. Mem. ABA, Mich. Bar Assn., Detroit Bar Assn. Democrat. Roman Catholic. Avocations: baseball, sailing, photography. Appellate, State civil litigation, General practice. Home: 1281 N Oxford Rd Grosse Pointe MI 48236-1857 Office: Berkley Mengel & Vining PC 3100 Penobscot Bldg Detroit MI 48226 E-mail: cmengel@flash.net

MENGLER, THOMAS M. dean; b. May 18, 1953; BA in Philosophy magna cum laude, Carleton Coll., 1975; MA in Philosophy, U. Tex., 1977, JD, 1981. Bar: Ill., Tex., D.C., U.S. Ct. Appeals (5th, 7th and 10th cirs.), U.S. Dist. Ct. (we. dist.) Tex. Law clk. to Hon. James K. Logan U.S. Ct. Appeals for 10thCir., Olathe, Kans., 1980-81; assoc. atty. Arnold & Porter, Washington, 1982-83; asst. atty. gen. Office of Atty. Gen. of Tex., Austin, 1983-85; asst. prof. law U. Ill. Coll. Law, Champaign, 1985-89, assoc. prof., 1989-91, prof. law, 1991—, assoc. dean for acad. affairs, 1992-93, dean, 1993—. Contbr. numerous articles to profl. jours. Mem. ABA, Ill. State Bar Assn., Order of Coif, Phi Beta Kappa. Office: U Ill Coll Law 202 Law Bldg 504 E Pennsylvania Ave Champaign IL 61820-6909*

MENKE, WILLIAM CHARLES, lawyer; b. Cin., Aug. 30, 1939; s. William Garhardt and Margaret Philomena (Mercurio) M.; m. Mary Lou Lapan, Jan. 7, 1967; children: William Leo II, Lorelei Louise. BS, U. Detroit, 1961; MBA, Ind. No. U., 1972; JD, U. Detroit, 1976. Bar: Ohio 1977, U.S. Ct. Appeals (6th cir.) 1977; Masters Lic., USCG. Sr. engr. GE Co., Cin., 1964-67; v.p., gen. mgr. Preventicare Systems, Inc., Dearborn, Mich., 1967-71; dir. Comshare, Inc., Ann Arbor, 1971-76; CEO William C. Menke & Assocs., Inc., New Richmond, Ohio, 1976—. Chmn. Strategic Eight Cons. Group, 1996—, Luerum, Inc.; adj. prof. U. Cin., 1994—; bd. dirs. New Richmond Nat. Bank, Geocel Corp., Lucrum, Inc.; city atty. City of New Richmond, 1979-81; monthly columnist Cin. Bus. Record, 1994—. Lt. (j.g.) USN, 1961-64. Fellow Lawyers in Mensa; mem. ABA, Assn. Trial Lawyers Am., Ohio State Bar, Pres.'s Forum (chmn.), Mensa, KC. Republican. Roman Catholic. General corporate, Corporate taxation. Home: 6336 Sylvan Dr Gladwin MI 48624-9002 Office: William C Menke & Assocs Inc 6336 Sylvan Dr Gladwin MI 48624-9002 E-mail: wcmenke@aol.com

MENTZ, BARBARA ANTONELLO, lawyer; b. Kansas City, Mo., July 4, 1944; d. John Francis and Eleanor Barbara (Vagnino) Antonello; m. Lawrence Mentz, Nov. 10, 1973; children: Kathleen Elizabeth, Lawrence Goodwin. BA in Econs., U. Kans., 1965; JD magna cum laude, U. Notre Dame, 1973. Bar: N.Y. 1974, U.S. Dist. Ct. (so. and ea. dists.) N.Y. 1974, U.S. Ct. Appeals (2d cir.) 1974, U.S. Supreme Ct. 1977, U.S. Ct. Appeals (9th cir.) 1981, U.S. Ct. Appeals (3d cir.) 1983, N.J. 1985, U.S. Dist. Ct. N.J. 1986. Various positions with ins. cos., Chgo., 1965-68, Kansas City, Mo., 1968-70; assoc. Sullivan & Cromwell, N.Y.C., 1973-77, Forsyth, Decker, Murray and Hubbard, N.Y.C., 1977-79; ptnr. Hall, McNicol, Hamilton & Clark, 1979-86; sr. litig. counsel CBS, 1986-88; assoc. gen. counsel, prin. Deloitte & Touche USA LLP, N.Y.C., 1988—. Contbr. articles to profl. jours., chpt. to supplements, publs. Mem. ABA (antitrust sect. 1979-90), Nat. Futures Assn. (panel of arbitrators 1985—), Assn. Bar City of N.Y. (prof. discipline com. 1983-86, antitrust and trade regulation com. 1988-91). Antitrust, Federal civil litigation, Securities. Home: 140 W 86th St Apt 2B New York NY 10024-4067 Office: Deloitte & Touche USA LLP 1633 Broadway New York NY 10019-6708 E-mail: bmentz@deloitte.com

MENTZ, HENRY ALVAN, JR. federal judge; b. New Orleans, Nov. 10, 1920; s. Henry Alvan and Lulla (Bridewell) M.; m. Ann Lamantia, June 23, 1956; children: Ann, Carli, Hal, Frederick, George BA, Tulane U., 1941; JD, La. State U., 1943. Bar: La. 1943, U.S. Dist. Ct. (ea. dist.) La. 1944. With legal dept. Shell Oil, New Orleans, 1947-48; pvt. practice Hammond, 1948-82; judge U.S. Dist. Ct. (ea. dist.) La., New Orleans, 1982—, sr. judge, 1992—. Editor: Combined Gospels, 1976 Pres. La. Soc. Music and Performing Arts, 1994-97, L.A. Civil Svc. League, 1979-81; bd. dirs. Southea. La. U. Found., Salvation Army; chmn. Tulane U. 50th Anniversary Reunion for 1991. Decorated 2 Battle Stars, Bronze Star; recipient Disting. Svc. award AMVETS, 1950. Mem. SAR, Royal Soc. St. George (pres.), Boston Club New Orleans, Delta Tau Delta. Republican. Episcopalian. Home: 2105 State St New Orleans LA 70118-6255 Office: US Dist Ct C-114 US Courthouse 500 Camp St New Orleans LA 70130-3313

MENTZ, LAWRENCE, lawyer; b. N.Y.C., Nov. 5, 1946; s. Joseph Walter and Audrey Cecilia (Armstrong) M.; m. Barbara Antonello, Nov. 10, 1973; children: Kathleen Elizabeth, Lawrence Goodwin. BS in Physics, Rensselaer Poly. Inst., 1968; JD, U. Notre Dame, 1973. Bar: N.Y. 1973; Washington 1974. Assoc. Condon & Forsyth, N.Y.C., 1973-80, ptnr., 1981-89, Biedermann, Hoenig, Massamillo & Ruff, N.Y.C., 1990—; counsellor at law. Speaker Worldwide Airlines Customer Rels. Assn. Conf., Singapore, 1983, 2d Cir. Speakers Bur., Com. on BiCentennial of U.S. Constn., 1987; arbitrator U.S. Dist. Ct. (ea. dist.) Bklyn., 1986—; bd. dirs. Black Mountain Mgmt. Inc. With USNR, 1969-70. Mem. ABA, Fed. Bar Coun., N.Y. State Bar Assn. (exec. com. sect. on comml. and fed. litigation, fed. judiciary com., 1993, com. Supreme Cts.), Assn. of Bar of City of N.Y. (com. on aeronautics law, task force on N.Y. Constl. Conv., com. on state legis.), Wings Club. Roman Catholic. Avocations: swimming, running, philately. Aviation, Federal civil litigation, Insurance. Office: Biedermann Hoenig Massamillo & Ruff 90 Park Ave New York NY 10016-1301 E-mail: lmentz@bhmr.com

MEOLA, JANICE GRACE, lawyer; b. Newark, Jan. 10, 1966; d. William Frank and Rose Marie Meola. BS in Fin., Pa. State U., 1988; JD, U. N.C., Chapel Hill, 1991. Bar: N.J., U.S. Dist. Ct. N.J. Jud. clk. Superior Ct. of N.J., Jersey City, 1991-92; litigation assoc. Bumgardner, Hardin & Ellis, Springfield, N.J., 1992-94; environ. counsel CNA Ins. Cos., Cranbury, 1994-96; assoc. counsel Suburban Propane, L.P., Whippany, 1996-98, counsel, 1998-99, gen. counsel, sec., 1999—. Mem. ABA, Am. Corp. Counsel Assn., Am. Soc. of Corp. Secs., Propane Gas Def. Assn. Office: Suburban Propane LP PO Box 206 240 Route 10 Whippany NJ 07981-0206

MERANUS, LEONARD STANLEY, lawyer; b. Newark, Jan. 7, 1928; s. Norman and Ada (Binstock) M.; m. Jane B. Holzman, Sept. 20, 1989; children: Norman, James M., David. LittB, Rutgers U., 1948; LLB, Harvard U., 1954. Bar: Ohio 1954. Assoc. Paxton & Seasongood, cin., 1954-59, ptnr., 1959-85, pres., 1985-89; ptnr. Thompson, Hine and Flory, 1989-96, ptnr.-in-charge Cin. office, 1989-91, mem. firm mgmt. com., 1991-93, of counsel, 1998—; adj. prof. law U. Cin. Coll. Law, 1998-2000. Chmn. bd. dirs. Jewish Hosp., 1982-86; trustee Andrew Jergens Found., 1962-97. Mem. ABA, Ohio Bar Assn., Cin. Bar Assn., Am. Arbitration Assn. (chmn. comml. arbitration adv. com., Ohio panel large, complex arbitration cases). General corporate, Mergers and acquisitions, Real property. Office: Thompson Hine LLP 312 Walnut St Ste 14 Cincinnati OH 45202-4089

MERCER, EDWIN WAYNE, retired lawyer; b. Kingsport, Tenn., July 19, 1940; s. Ernest LaFayette and Geneva (Frye) M. BBA, Tex. Tech U., 1963; JD, S. Tex. Coll. Law, 1971. Bar: Tex. 1971, U.S. Dist. Ct. (no. dist.) Tex 1975, U.S. Supreme Ct. 1976, U.S. Ct. Appeals (5th Cir.) 1979. Pvt. practice, Houston, 1971-73; gen. counsel, corp. sec. Alcon Labs., Inc., Ft. Worth, 1973-81; ptnr. Gandy Michener Swindle Whitaker Pratt & Mercer, 1981-84; v.p., gen. counsel, corp. sec. Pengo Industries, Inc., 1984-90, also bd. dirs. Bd. dirs. Soc. for Prevention Blindness, 1979—. Mem. ABA, State Bar Tex., Houston Bar Assn., Ft. Worth-Tarrant County Bar Assn., Coll. State Bar Tex., South Tex. Coll. Law Alumni Assn., Tex. Tech U. Ex-Assn., Ft. Worth Club, Delta Theta Phi, Phi Delta Theta. Methodist. General corporate, Public international.

MERCER, RICHARD JAMES, lawyer; b. New London, Conn., Oct. 2, 1950; s. James Wilson and Marianne (Wieczorek) M.; m. Ann Holly Gutting, Oct. 9, 1970 (div. 1977); m. Harriet Allston Jopson, May 1, 1982; 1 child, James. BBA, Old Dominion U., 1972; JD, Coll. William and Mary, 1975; LLM in Taxation, Boston U., 1977, LLM in Banking, 1986. Assoc. Epstein & Epstein, Norfolk, Va., 1975, Bernard A. Kaplan, Boston, 1975-76; sole practice, 1976-78, 1979-80; ptnr. Shagory & Shagory, Boston, 1978-79, Alpert, Thurman & Mercer, Boston, 1980-82; assoc. counsel First Nat. Bank Boston, 1983-85, asst. v.p., assoc. counsel, 1985-86, sr. counsel, 1986—. Town coordinator George Bush Presdl. Campaign, Weston, 1980. Mem. ABA, Boston Bar Assn., Am. Arbitration Assn. (arbitrator 1978), Mass. Bar Assn., Va. Bar Assn. Republican. Episcopalian. Banking, Federal civil litigation, State civil litigation. Office: First Nat Bank Boston 100 Federal St Boston MA 02110-1802

MERCER, WILLIAM W. prosecutor; BA, U. Mont.; MPA, Harvard U.; JD, George Mason U. Counselor to asst. atty. gen., sr. policy analyst Office of Policy Devel. U.S. Dept. Justice, 1989—94, asst. U.S. atty. Dist. Mont., 1994—2001, U.S. atty., 2001—. Office: PO Box 1478 Billings MT 59103*

MERCORELLA, ANTHONY J. lawyer, former state supreme court justice; b. N.Y.C., Mar. 6, 1927; s. Sante and Josephine (Bozzuti) M.; m. Maria G. Delucia, June 16, 1956; children: Anne Mercorella Flynn, Susan Mercorella Creavin, Robert, Carole Crinieri. BA, L.I. U., 1949; LLD, Fordham U., 1952. Bar: N.Y. Law asst. City Ct., City of N.Y., 1955-62; chief law asst. Civil Ct., City of N.Y., 1962-65; mem. N.Y. State Assembly, 1965-72; councilman City Coun., City of N.Y., 1973-75; judge Civil Ct., City of N.Y., 1975-79; justice Supreme Ct., N.Y.C., 1980-84; ptnr. Wilson, Elser, Moskowitz, Edelman & Dicker, 1984—. Currently arbitrator and mediator in various dispute resolution systems. With USN, 1945-46, Europe, Pacific. Mem. ABA (del. N.Y. State Bar Assn.), N.Y. State Bar Assn., Assn. of Bar of City of N.Y., Bronx County Bar Assn. (pres. 1971), Columbian Lawyers Westchester County (pres. 1984). Office: Wilson Elser Moskowitz Edelman & Dicker 150 E 42nd St New York NY 10017-5612 E-mail: mercorellaa@wemed.com, ajmmediate@aol.com

MERHIGE, ROBERT REYNOLD, JR. lawyer; b. N.Y.C., Feb. 5, 1919; s. Robert Reynold and Eleanor (Donovan) M.; m. Shirley Galleher, Apr. 24, 1957; children: Robert Reynold III, Mark Reynold. LLB, U. Richmond, 1942, LLD (hon.), 1976; LLM, U. Va., 1982; LLD (hon.), Washington and Lee U., 1990, Wake Forest U., 1994. Bar: Va. 1942. Ptnr. Bremner Merhige Montgomery & Baber, Richmond, 1945-67; judge U.S. Dist. Ct., 1967—; resigned, 1998; assoc. Hunton & Williams, Richmond, 1998—. Guest lectr. trial tactics Law Sch. U. Va., Ewald disting. prof. law, 1987-88; adj. prof. Law Sch. U. Richmond, 1973-87; appeal agt. Henrico County Draft Bd., 1954-67; mem. NCAA spl. com. on discipline rules; profl.-in-residence, Zambia, Africa, 1994. Co-author: Virginia Jury Instructions. Mem. Richmond Citizens Assn. Served with USAAF, World War II. Decorated Air medal with four oak leaf clusters; recipient Amara Civic Club award, 1968, Spl. award City of Richmond, 1967; named Citizen of the Yr., 3d Dist. Omega Psi Phi, 1972, Citizen of the Yr., Richmond Urban League, 1977, Richmonder of Yr. Style mag., 1984, 87, Citizen of Yr., 1986; recipient Disting. Alumni award U. Richmond, 1979, Disting. Svc. award Nat. Alumni Coun., U. Richmond, 1979, Herbert T. Harley award Am. Judicature Soc., 1982, Athenian Ciitizen medal, 1979, Torch of Liberty award Anti-Defamation League of B'nai Brith, 1982, T.C. Williams Sch. of Law Disting. Svc. award, 1983, Pres.'s award Old Dominion Bar Assn., 1986, William J. Brennan award, 1986, Merit Citation award NCCJ, 1987, William B. Green award for professionalism U. Richmond, 1989, Marshall-Wythe medallion (William & Mary Faculty award), 1989, Lewis F. Powell, Jr. award for Professionalism and Ethics, Am. Inns of Ct., 1999; named one of 100 Most Influential Richmonders of Last Century by Style Mag. and Valentine Mus., 2000. Fellow Va. Law Found.; mem. Va. Bar Assn., Richmond Bar Assn. (pres. 1963-64, multi-dist. litigation panel 1990—, Hill-Tucker award 1991), Am. Law Inst. (faculty), Va. Trial Lawyers Assn. (chmn. membership com. 1964-65, Disting. Svc. award 1977), Jud. Conf. U.S., John Marshall Inns of Ct. (founding mem.), FedNet (dispute resolution), Nat. Patent Bd. (cert. panelist), Nat. Arbitration Forum (arbitrator), Omicron Delta Kappa (Hunter W. Martin profl. award 1998). Alternative dispute resolution, General civil litigation, Intellectual property. Office: Hunton & Williams Riverfront Plz East Tower 951 E Byrd St Richmond VA 23219-4074 E-mail: MerhigeR@Hunton.com

MERKEL, CHARLES MICHAEL, lawyer; b. Nashville, Nov. 2, 1941; s. Charles M. and Lila K. Merkel; m. Donna White, Jan. 7, 1967; children: Kimberly Dale, Charles M. III. BA, U. Miss., 1964, JD, 1966; LLM in Taxation, Georgetown U., 1969. Bar: Miss. Trial atty. U.S. Dept. Justice, Washington, 1966-70; ptnr. Dunbar & Merkel, Clarksdale, Miss., 1970-73, Holcomb Dunbar Connell & Merkel, Clarksdale, 1973-82, Merkel & Cocke, Clarksdale, 1982—. Pres. Miss. chpt. Am. Bd. Trial Advs., 1989.

Bd. dirs. Lula Rich Edn. Found., Clarksdale, 1983-89. Carrier scholar U. Miss. 1959-63. Fellow Miss. State Bar Found.; mem. ATLA, Am. Bd. Trial Advocates, Am. Coll. Trial Lawyers, Miss. Trial Lawyers Assn. (sec. 1985-87). Episcopalian. Avocations: hunting, tennis, skiing. Federal civil litigation, Personal injury, Product liability. Home: 101 Cypress Ave Clarksdale MS 38614-2603 Office: Post Office Drawer 16689 2506 Lakeland Dr Ste 500 Jackson MS 39236

MERKER, STEVEN JOSEPH, lawyer; b. Cleve., Feb. 21, 1947; s. Steven Joseph and Laverne (Zamenik) M.; m. Janet L. Whyatt; children: Steven, Rena, Ashley, Matthew. BS, Case Inst. Tech., 1968; MS, U. Fla., 1973. Bar: Ohio 1976, U.S. Dist. Ct. (no. dist.) Ohio, 1976, U.S. Dist. Ct. Colo. 1979, U.S. Ct. Appeals (10th cir.) 1979, U.S. Supreme Ct. 1989. Assoc. Jones, Day, Reavis & Pogue, Cleve., 1976-78, Davis, Graham & Stubbs, Denver, 1978-82, ptnr., 1983-96, chmn. labor and employment group, 1989-96; chmn. litigation and labor and employment groups Merrick, Calvin & Merker, LLP, 1996-97; ptnr. Dorsey & Whitney LLP, Denver, 1997—, mng. ptnr. Denver office, 2000—. Mem. Tenth Cir. Adv. Com., 1997-2000. Legal counsel Coloradans for Lamm-Dick campaign, Denver, 1982, Nancy Dick for U.S. Senate Com., Denver, 1984, Cantrell for Dist. Atty., Jefferson County, Colo., 1984; bd. dirs. Very Spl. Arts, Colo., 1994—. Capt. USAF, 1969-72. Mem. ABA, Colo. Bar Assn., Denver Bar Assn. Federal civil litigation, State civil litigation, Labor. Office: Dorsey & Whitney LLP 370 17th St Ste 4400 Denver CO 80202-5644 E-mail: werker.steve@dorseylaw.com

MERKIN, DAVID, reference librarian; b. Bklyn., Sept. 16, 1958; s. William and Doris (Beart) M.; m. Martine Merkin, Aug. 28, 1983; 1 child, Jennifer. BA, Bklyn. Coll., 1980; cert. in paralegal studies, L.I. U., 1982; MLS, Pratt U., 1997. Clk. Bklyn. Pub. Libr., 1975-77, Shearman & Sterling, N.Y.C., 1981-83, libr. asst., 1983-85, asst. reference libr., 1985-93, reference libr., 1993—. Mem. Am. Assn. Law Librs., Law Libr. Assn. of Greater N.Y.C. (co-chmn. pro bono com. 1996—). Jewish. Avocations: swimming, bicycle riding, kite flying, bowling, baseball. Office: Shearman & Sterling 599 Lexington Ave Fl C2 New York NY 10022-6069

MERKIN, WILLIAM LESLIE, retired lawyer; b. N.Y.C., Apr. 30, 1929; s. Jules Leo Merkin and Rae (Levine) Lesser; children: Monica Jo, Lance Jeffrey, Tiffany Dawn. BA, U. Tex., Austin, 1950; JD, St. Mary's U., San Antonio, 1953. Bar: Tex. 1953, U.S. Ct. Mil. Appeals 1954, U.S. Dist. Ct. (we. dist.) Tex. 1957, U.S. Ct. Appeals (5th cir.) 1969, U.S. Supreme Ct. 1970. Pvt. practice, El Paso, Tex., 1956-71; sr. ptnr. Merkin & Gibson, 1972-78, Merkin, Hines & Pasqualone, El Paso, 1978-90; ret. Lectr. U. Tex.-El Paso, 1978—; cons. in field. Served to capt. JAGC, U.S. Army, 1953-56. Mem. Tex. State Bar Assn., Soc. Profls. in Dispute Resolution, Am. Trial Lawyers Assn., Tex. Trial Lawyers Assn., Common Cause, Internat. Wine and Food Soc. (pres. 1979-80), Am. Arbitration Assn. (part-time arbitrator), Nat. Assn. Securities Dealers (part-time arbitrator), Del Norte Club (El Paso), B'nai B'rith (pres. 1961-62), Phi Delta Phi. General civil litigation, State civil litigation, General practice. Home: 1442 Seacoast Dr Imperial Beach CA 91932-3183

MERMELSTEIN, JULES JOSHUA, lawyer, township commissioner; b. Phila., Apr. 25, 1955; s. Harry and Ellen Jane (Greenberg) M.; m. Ruth Susan Applebaum, Aug. 18, 1974; children: Hannah Leona, Benjamin Isaac. BA, Temple U., 1977; JD, Am. U., 1979; MEd, Beaver Coll., 1994. Bar: Pa. 1980, U.S. Dist. Ct. (ea. dist.) Pa. 1980, U.S. Ct. Appeals (3d cir.) 1982, U.S. Supreme Ct. 1983. Ptnr. Mermelstein & Light, Norristown and Hatboro, Pa., 1980-83; v.p., gen. counsel Am. Ins. Cons., Feasterville, 1983; staff atty. Hyatt Legal Svcs., Phila., 1983-84, mng. atty., 1984-85; pvt. practice Phila./Montgomery County, 1985-93; tchr., social studies coord. The Bridge, 1997-99; ednl. cons. Interim House, 1998-2000. Prof. law, St. Matthew Sch. Law, Phila., 1985-87; adj. prof. criminal justice Glassboro State U., N.J., 1988; faculty polit. sci. dept. Temple U., 1989; atty. Levin & Assocs., Wyncote, Pa., 1998-99, Levin & Assocs., Wyncote, Pa., 1999—. Editor: The Montco Democrat, 1990-92. Vol. atty. ACLU, Phila., 1980-93; chmn. Tikkun Olam (Repair the World) Com., 1989-92, 98-2000; area rep. Montgomery County Dem. Exec. Com., 1982-85, 88-94; treas., 1994-98, candidate coord., 1982, nominee for dist. atty., 1983, committeeman, 1973-77, 82-85, 88-92, campaign mgr. Talbot for state legis., 1988; Upper Dublin chmn. Dukakis-Bentsen, 1988, chair Upper Dublin Dem. Com., 1990-91, commr. Upper Dublin Twp., 1992—; Dem. candidate Pa. State Legis., 2000; bd. dirs. Reconstructionist Congregation Or Hadash, Ft. Washington, Pa., 1988-92, 96-2000, 2001—, confirmation tchr., 1994—. Jewish. Appellate, State civil litigation, Constitutional. Home: 18 Northview Dr Glenside PA 19038-1318 E-mail: JulesMermelstein@hotmail.com

MERRIAM, DWIGHT HAINES, lawyer, land use planner; b. Norwood, Mass., Apr. 20, 1946; s. Austin Luther and Lillian Diana (Olsen) M.; m. Cynthia Ann Hayes, May 21, 1966 (div. June 1992); children: Sarah Ann Leilani, Jonathan Hayes; m. Susan Manning Standish, May 6, 1995; children: Alexander Harlan, Lucy Caroline. BA cum laude, U. Mass., 1968; M in Regional Planning, U. N.C., 1974; JD, Yale U., 1978. Bar: Conn. 1978, Mass. 1980, U.S. Dist. Ct. Conn. 1981, U.S. Dist. Ct. Hawaii 1984, U.S. Supreme Ct. 1990, U.S. Ct. Appeals (4th cir.) 1993. Land use planner Charles E. Downe, Newton, Mass., 1968; assoc. Byrne, Buck & Steiner, Farmington, Conn., 1978, Robinson, Robinson & Cole, Hartford, 1979-83; ptnr. Robinson & Cole LLP, 1984—. Adj. prof. law Western New Eng. Coll., 1978-86, U. Conn., 1982, 84-87, Vt. Law Sch., 1994—; instr. planning U. Bridgeport, 1981-83, U. Conn., 1986-92; mem. faculty Nat. Coll. Dist. Attys., 1983-87, Nat. Jud. Coll., 1994; mem. faculty Am. Law Inst.-ABA Land Use Inst., 1988—; instr. city and regional planning Memphis State U., 1989, 94; speaker in field. Co-author: The Takings Issue, 1999; co-editor: Inclusionary Zoning Moves Downtown, 1985; contbr. more than 100 articles and book revs. to profl. jours. Bd. dirs. Conn. chpt. Appleseed Found., 1997-2000, Am. Boat Builders and Repairers Assn., 1995—, Growth Mgmt. Inst., Washington, 1992—, Housing Edn. Resource Ctr., 1984-88, Housing Coalition for Capitol Region, Inc., 1984-86; bd. dirs. Conn. Fund for Environment, 1981-85, legal adv. com., 1985-88, legal adv. bd., 1978-81; mem. Environment 2000 environ. plan adv. bd. Conn. Dept. Environ. Protection, 1987-91; assoc. Environ. Law Inst., 1987—; mem. housing task force Conn. Dept. on Aging, 1981; mem. Gov.'s Housing Task Force, Conn., 1980-81. With USN, 1968-75, Vietnam; capt. USNR, 1975-99. Fellow Am. . Cert. Planners (pres. 1988-90); mem. ABA, Conn. Bar Assn. (exec. com. zoning and planning sect. 1985-87, 91—), Am. Planning Assn. (bd. dirs. 1988-90, chmn. planning and law divsn. 1984-86, exec. com. planning and law divsn. 1978-88, chmn. legis. com. Conn. chpt. 1978-80, editl. adv. bd. 1984-92), Internat. Mcpl. Law Assn. (chmn. sect. on zoning, planning and land devel. 1988-89, sect. vice-chmn. 1987), Assn. State Floodplain Mgrs., Am. Coll. Real Estate Lawyers. Democrat. Unitarian. Avocations: sailing, skiing. Environmental, Land use and zoning (including planning), Real property. Home: 80 Latimer Ln Weatogue CT 06089 Office: Robinson & Cole LLP 280 Trumbull St 27th Fl Hartford CT 06103-3597

MERRICK, GLENN WARREN, lawyer; b. Ft. Devens, Mass., Oct. 5, 1954; s. Clyde Douglas and Gloria Pauline (Alix) M. BA magna cum laude, U. Colo., 1976; JD with high honors, U. Tex., 1979. Bar: Colo. 1979, D.C. 1979, U.S. Ct. Appeals (5th and 10th cirs.) 1980, Tex., 1986. Law clk. to presiding judge U.S. Ct. Appeals (5th cir.), Austin, Tex., 1979-80; assoc. Davis, Graham & Stubbs, Denver, 1980-85, ptnr., 1985-95; founder, ptnr. Merrick, Calvin & Merker LLP, 1995-97; shareholder, dir. Brega & Winters P.C., 1997—. Mem. faculty Nat. Bus. Inst., Denver, 1985—; chmn. 1st and 2d Ann. Real Estate Reorgn. and Foreclosure Conf., Denver, 1987-88; adj. prof. law U. Denver, 1988—; lectr. Internat. Practicum Inst., 1990-91. Contbr. articles to profl. jours. Counsel Am. Bd. Spine Surgery, Am. Coll. Spine Surgery, Colo. Open Space Coun., Denver, 1984—85, Concerned Friends and Relatives of Nursing Home Residents, Ft. Collins, 1984—85, Urban League of Met. Denver, 1989; spkr., author Rocky Mountain Mineral Law Found. Spl. Inst., Denver, 1986. Fellow: Am. Coll. Bankruptcy; mem.: ABA, Am. Bankruptcy Inst., Law League Am., Colo. Bar Assn., Denver Bar Assn., Comml. Law League Am., Chancellors, Phi Beta Kappa, Phi Delta Phi. Republican. Roman Catholic. Club: Law (Denver). Avocations: running, golf, skiing. Bankruptcy, Federal civil litigation, Consumer commercial. Home: 5360 Preserve Dr Littleton CO 80121-2109 Office: Davis Graham & Stubbs 1030 World Trade Ctr 1675 Broadway Denver CO 80202-4675 E-mail: gmerrick@brega-winters.com

MERRILL, ABEL JAY, lawyer; b. Balt., Mar. 25, 1938; s. Yale and Evelyn (Cordish) M.; m. Susan Stein, June 15, 1963; children: Adam L., Julie F. BA, Colgate U., 1959; LLB, U. Md., 1964. Bar: Md. 1964. Law clk. U.S. Ct. Appeals, Balt., 1964-65; assoc. Gordon, Feinblatt & Rothman, 1965-70; atty. pvt. practice, Annapolis, Md., 1970-78, 83—; prin. Blumenthal, May, Downs & Merrill, 1979-83; mem. firm Merrill & Cruttenden, P.A. Mem. inquiry com. Atty. Grievance Commn. Md., 1975-85, character com. Ct. of Appeals, 1987-88; mem. pension oversight bd. Anne Arundel County, Md. Fellow Am. Coll. Probate Counsel; mem. ABA, Md. Bar Assn., Anne Arundel County Bar Assn. Estate planning, Probate, Estate taxation. E-mail: abelj@merillaw.com

MERRILL, GEORGE VANDERNETH, lawyer, investment executive; b. N.Y.C., July 2, 1947; s. James Edward and Claire (Leness) M.; m. Janice Anne Humes, May 11, 1985; children: Claire Georgina, Anne Stewart. Student, Phillips Exeter Acad., 1960-64; AB magna cum laude, Harvard U., 1968, JD, 1972; MBA, Columbia U., 1973. Bar: N.Y. 1973, U.S. Dist. Ct. (so. and ea. dists.) N.Y. 1974, U.S. Ct. Appeals (2d cir.) 1974. Assoc. Cleary, Gottlieb, Steen & Hamilton, N.Y.C., 1974-77, Hawkins, Delafield & Wood, N.Y.C., 1977-79; v.p. Irving Trust Co., 1980-82, Listowel, Inc., N.Y.C., 1982-84, bd. dirs., exec. v.p., 1984-93; v.p. instl. portfolio mgmt. Shawmut Investment Advisors, 1993-95; also co-mgr. Shawmut Growth & Income Equity Mut. Fund; v.p. instl. portfolio mgmt. Fleet Investment Advisors, 1995-96, also co-mgr. Galaxy Growth & Income Equity Mut. Fund.; v.p. trust and instl. portfolio mgmt., mem. Fla. equity com. No. Trust Corp., Chgo., 1996-2000; v.p., sr. personal investment officer Bank of N.Y., N.Y.C., 2000—. Bd. dirs. Pres. Arell Found., N.Y.C., 1985-93, also bd. dirs., pres. Northfield Charitable Corp., N.Y.C., 1986-93; v.p., sec. Brougham Prodn. Co., N.Y.C., 1986-89, bd. dirs., sr. v.p., sec., 1990-93; v.p., sec. Marinetics Inc., N.Y.C., 1988-90, sr. v.p., sec., 1991-93, also bd. dirs., 1989-93; v.p. Sci. Design and Engring. Co., Inc., N.Y.C., 1987-88, bd. dirs., exec. v.p., 1989-93. John Harvard scholar; recipient Detur award Harvard U., 1968. Mem. ABA, Am. Mgmt. Assn., Nat. Cum Laude Soc., The Brook, Union Club (N.Y.C.), Down Town Assn., Racquet and Tennis Club, Somerset Club (Boston), Signet Soc. (Cambridge), Pilgrims of U.S. General corporate, Estate planning, Finance. Home: 2 Pierce Rd Riverside CT 06878 Office: The Bank of NY 5th Fl 1290 Ave of the Americas New York NY 10104 E-mail: gmerrill@bankofny.com

MERRILL, THOMAS WENDELL, lawyer, law educator; b. Bartlesville, Okla., May 3, 1949; s. William McGill and Dorothy (Glasener) M.; m. Kimberly Ann Evans, Sept. 8, 1973; children: Jessica, Margaret, Elizabeth. BA, Grinnell Coll., 1971, Oxford U., 1973; JD, U. Chgo., 1977. Bar: Ill. 1980, U.S. Dist Ct. (no. dist.) Ill. 1980, U.S. Ct. Appeals (5th cir.) 1982, U.S. Ct. Appeals (7th cir.) 1983, U.S. Ct. Appeals (9th and D.C. cirs.) 1984, U.S. Supreme Ct. 1985. Clk. U.S. Ct. Appeals (D.C. cir.), Washington, 1977-78, U.S. Supreme Ct., Washington, 1978-79; assoc. Sidley & Austin, Chgo., 1979-81, counsel, 1981-87, 90—; dep. solicitor gen. U.S. Dept. Justice, 1987-90; prof. law Northwestern U., Chgo., 1981—, John Paul Stevens prof., 1993—. Contbr. articles to profl. jours. Rhodes scholar Oxford U., 1971; Danforth fellow, 1971. Home: 939 Maple Ave Evanston IL 60202-1717 Office: Northwestern U Sch Law 357 E Chicago Ave Chicago IL 60611-3059

MERRITT, BRUCE GORDON, lawyer; b. Iowa City, Oct. 4, 1946; s. William Olney and Gretchen Louise (Kuever) M.; m. Valerie Sue Jorgensen, Dec. 28, 1969; children: Benjamin Carlyle, Alicia Marie. AB magna cum laude, Occidental Coll., 1968; JD magna cum laude, Harvard U., 1972. Bar: Calif. 1973, D.C., 1996, N.Y. 1996. Assoc. Markbys, London, 1972-73, Nossman, Krueger & Marsh, L.A., 1973-79, ptnr., 1979-81; asst. U.S. Atty., L.A., 1981-85; ptnr. Hennigan & Mercer, 1986-88, Debevoise & Plimpton, L.A., 1989-95, N.Y., 1996—. Lay reader St. James Ch. Fellow Am. Coll. Trial Lawyers; mem. Calif. State Bar Assn. (exec. com. litigation sect. 1992-95), L.A. County Bar Assn. (del. state bar conf. 1984-86), Phi Beta Kappa, Harvard Club (N.Y.C.). Episcopalian (lay reader St. James Ch.). Federal civil litigation, State civil litigation. Home: 200 E 90th St Apt 27A New York NY 10128-3528 Office: Debevoise & Plimpton 919 3d Ave New York NY 10022-3904 E-mail: bgmerritt@debevoise.com

MERRITT, GILBERT STROUD, federal judge; b. Nashville, Jan. 17, 1936; s. Gilbert Stroud and Angie Fields (Cantrell) M.; m. Louise Clark Fort, July 10, 1964 (dec.); children: Stroud, Louise Clark, Eli. BA, Yale U., 1957; LLB, Vanderbilt U., 1960; LLM, Harvard U., 1962. Bar: Tenn. 1960. Asst. dean Vanderbilt U. Law Sch., 1960-61, lectr., 1963-69, 71-75, assoc. prof. law, 1969-70; assoc. Boult Hunt Cummings & Conners, Nashville, 1962-63; city atty. City of Nashville, 1963-66; U.S. Dist. atty. for (mid. dist.) Tenn., 1966-69; ptnr. Gullett, Steele, Sanford, Robinson & Merritt, Nashville, 1970-77; judge U.S. Ct. Appeals (6th cir.), 1977-2001, chief judge, 1989-98, sr. judge., 2001—. Exec. sec. Tenn. Code Commn., 1977. Mng. editor: Vanderbilt Law Rev, 1959-60; contbr. articles to law jours. Del. Tenn. Constl. Conv., 1965; chmn. bd. trustees Vanderbilt Inst. Pub. Policy Studies. Mem. ABA, Fed. Bar Assn., Tenn. Bar Assn., Nashville Bar Assn., Vanderbilt Law Alumni Assn. (pres. 1979-80), Am. Law Inst., Order of Coif. Episcopalian. Office: US Ct Appeals Customs Ho 701 Broadway Ste 303 Nashville TN 37203-3967*

MERRITT, RAYMOND WALTER, lawyer; b. N.Y.C., July 16, 1938; s. Raymond C. and Mildred M.; m. Carol A. Brmer, Apr. 29, 1939; children— Raymond William, Kimberly. A.B., Coll. of Holy Cross, 1960; LL.M., Columbia U., 1963. Bar: N.Y. 1963. Mem. firm Willkie, Farr & Gallagher N.Y.C., 1963— . Editor: New York Corporate Handbook, 1983. Trustee Loyola Found., Washington, Internat. Ctr. Photography. General corporate, Real property, Securities. Home: 511 E 20th St New York NY 10010-7522 Office: Willkie Farr & Gallagher 1 CitiCorp Ctr 787 7th Ave Lbby 2 New York NY 10019-6018

MERRITT, THOMAS BUTLER, lawyer; b. Toledo, Apr. 3, 1939; s. George Robert and Bernice (Gerwin) M.; m. Mary Jane Bothfeld, July 23, 1966; children— Thomas Butler, Haidee Soule, Theodore Bothfeld AB magna cum laude, Harvard U., 1961, LLB cum laude, 1966. Bar: Mass. 1966, U.S. Supreme Ct. 1974, N.H. 1994. With N.Y. State Dept. Civil Svc., Albany, 1961-62; intern Office of Legal Advisr U.S. Dept. State, Washington, 1965; law clk. to assoc. justice Arthur E. Whittemore Supreme Jud. Ct. Mass., Boston, 1966-67; assoc. Nutter, McClennen & Fish, 1967-69, Palmer & Dodge, Boston, 1969-73; asst. counsel to Gov. Mass., 1973; reporter of decisions Supreme Jud. Ct. Mass., Boston, 1974-94; pvt. practice Hollis, N.H., 1994—. Contbr. articles to profl. jours. Mem. Conservation Comm. Town of Sherborn, Mass., 1969-74, chmn., 1972-74; mem. corp. Tenacre Country Day Sch., Wellesley, Mass., 1972-84, trustee, 1973-78; planning bd. Town of Hollis, N.H., 1995-98. 1st lt. U.S. Army, 1962-63, capt. USAR, 1963-69. Mem. Mass. Bar Assn., N.H. Bar Assn., Fed. Bar Assn., Am. Law Inst., Am. Soc. Internat. Law, Internat. Law Assn. (Am. br.), Nat. Assn. Reporters of Jud. Decisions (pres. 1983-84), Union Club, Harvard Club of Boston, Harvard Faculty Club (Cambridge). Episcopalian. Public international. Office: 5 Hutchings Dr PO Box 1646 Hollis NH 03049-1646

MERSEL, MARJORIE KATHRYN PEDERSEN, lawyer; b. Manila, Utah, June 17, 1923; d. Leo Henry and Kathryn Anna (Reed) Pedersen; AB, U. Calif., 1948; LLB, U. San Francisco, 1948; m. Jules Mersel, Apr. 12, 1950; 1 son, Jonathan. Admitted to D.C. bar, 1952, Calif. bar, 1955; Marjorie Kathryn Pedersen Mersel, atty., Beverly Hills, Calif., 1961-71; staff counsel Dept. Real Estate State of Calif., Los Angeles, 1971—. Active L.A.-Guangzhou Sister City. Mem. Beverly Hills Bar Assn., L.A. County Bar Assn., Trial Lawyers Assn., So. Calif. Women Lawyers Assn. (treas. 1962-63), L.A.-Guangzhou Sister City Assn., Beverly Hills C. of C., World Affairs Coun., Current Affairs Forum, Am. Bar Assn., L.A. Athletic Club, Sierra Club. Home: 13007 Hartsook St Sherman Oaks CA 91423-1616 Office: Dept Real Estate 107 S Broadway Ste 8107 Los Angeles CA 90012-4402

MERSKY, ROY MARTIN, law educator, librarian; b. N.Y.C., Sept. 1, 1925; s. Irving and Rose (Mendelson) Mirsky; m. Rosemary Bunnage; children: Deborah, Lisa, Ruth. BS, U. Wis., 1948, JD, 1952, MALS, 1953. Bar: Wis. 1952, U.S. Supreme Ct. 1970, Tex. 1972, U.S. Ct. Appeals (5th cir.) 1981, N.Y. 1983. U.S. govt. documents cataloger U. Wis. Law Libr., 1951-52; reference asst. Madison (Wis.) Free Libr., 1952; pvt. practice law Wis., 1952-54; readers adv., reference and catalog libr., mcpl. reference libr. at City Hall, Milw. Pub. Libr., 1953-54; chief readers and reference svc. Yale Law Libr., 1954-59; dir. Wash. State Law Libr., 1959-63; exec. sec. Jud. Coun. Commn. Wash. Court Report, State of Wash., 1959-63; prof. law, law libr. U. Colo., Boulder, 1963-65; prof. law, dir. rsch. U. Tex., Austin, 1965-84, William Stamps Farish Centennial prof. law, 1984—, adj. prof. Grad. Sch. Libr. and Info. Sci., 1976—. Vis. prof. law, dir. law libr. N.Y. Law Sch., N.Y.C., 1982-84; M.D. Anderson Found. vis. prof. law Queen Mary and Westfield Coll., U. London, 1994; interim dir. Jewish Nat. and Univ. Libr., Hebrew U., 1972-73; vis. fellow Australian Nat. U. Fac. of Law, Canberra, 1999; cons. to legal pubs. and law schs.; panelist various confs.; lectr. in field. Author: A Treasure in Jerusalem, 1974, (with J. Myron Jacobstein Dunn) Fundamentals of Legal Research, 7th edit., 1998, (with Jacobstein Dunn) Legal Research Illustrated, An Abridgement of Fundamentals of Legal Research, 7th edit., 1998, (with Albert P. Blaustein) The First One Hundred Justices: Statistical Studies on the Supreme Court of the United States, 1978, (with Gary R. Hartman and Suzanne F. Young) A Documentary History of the Legal Aspects of Abortion in the United States, 1990, 96 (with Jacobstein Dunn and Bonnie Koneski-White) Reports on Successful and Unsuccessful Nominations, 1992, 94, 96; contbr. articles to profl. jours., chpts. to books; editor numerous books in field. Bd. dirs. Ctrl. Tex. chpt. ACLU, pres., 1969; bd. dirs. Human Rights Documentation Exch., 1998—, pres.-elect, 2000-01; mem. bd. advisors Anti-Defamation League, Austin, 1974-78; bd. dirs. Hillel Found., 1980-83; bd. dirs. Tex. Com. for Humanities, 1978-80, chair, 1980-82, conf. facilitator, 1982. With U.S. Army, 1944-46, ETO. Decorated Bronze Star. Fellow Am. Bar Found., Coll. Law Practice Mgmt., Tex. Bar Found.; mem. ABA (various coms.), AAUP (chmn. nominating com. 1979-80), Am. Law Inst., Assn. Am. Law Schs. (various coms.), Internat. Assn. Lawyers and Jurists (bd. govs. Am. sect. 1980-95), Nat. Bar Assn., Am. Assn. Law Librs. (chair various coms.), Am. Soc. Info. Sci. (pres. Tex./Okla. chpt. 1992-93), Scribes (bd. dirs. 1974-95, book awards com. 1978-95, pres. 1991-93, chair Scribes Law Review Competition award com. 1993—), Soc. Am. Law Tchrs. (bd. govs. 1979-88, nominations com. 1984), ALA (rsch. librs. group 1987, libr. edn. divsn.), Am. Soc. Indexers, Internat. Assn. Law Librs. (U.S. adv. coun.), Internat. Fedn. Libr. Assns., Nat. Librs. Assn. (pres. 1980-81), Spl. Libr. Assn., State Bar Tex. (com. Tex. Bar Jour. 1983-90), State Bar Wis. (bd. mem. nonresident lawyers divsn. 1992-98), Nat. Assn. Coll. and Univ. Attys., Tex. Assn. Coll. Tchrs., Tex. Humanities Alliance (bd. dirs. 1986-88), Tex. Supreme Ct. Hist. Soc. (bd. trustees 1988—), Order of Coif (mem. triennial book award com.). Home: 6412 Cascada Dr Austin TX 78750-8157 Office: U Tex Sch Law Tarlton Law Libr 727 E Dean Kelton St Austin TX 78705-3224

MERSMAN, RICHARD KENDRICK, III, lawyer; b. Des Moines, Sept. 14, 1949; s. Richard K. Jr. and Mary Jane Mersman; children: Richard K. IV, Thomas R. BA, Tulane U., 1971, JD, 1975. Bar: Mo. 1976. Atty. Boyce & Mersman, St. Louis, 1976-81; gen. counsel Mason Group, Inc., 1981-90; CFO The Forsythe Group, 1990-92; atty. The Stolar Partnership, 1992-2001; COO, Forsythe Investments, LLC, Aspen, Colo., 2001—. Roman Catholic. Avocations: golf, soccer coaching. Finance, Land use and zoning (including planning), Real property. Office: Forsythe Investments LLC 455 Gold Rivers Rd Basalt CO 81621

MERTENS, EDWARD JOSEPH, II, lawyer; b. N.Y.C., Dec. 11, 1949; s. Edward Joseph and Loretta (Clark) M.; m. Laurie Shea, Apr. 6, 1968; children— Mary, Susan, Edward. B.A., U. N.H., 1975; J.D., Franklin Pierce Law Ctr., Concord, N.H., 1978. Bar: N.H., U.S. Dist. Ct. N.H. Ptnr. Shea, Mertens, Sager & Sager, P.A., Wolfeboro, N.H., 1978— . Bd. dirs. Wolfeboro Ctr. of Hope, 1984. Mem. Assn. Trial Lawyers Am., N.H. Trial Lawyers Assn. (past gov.). Personal injury. Home: Main St Wolfeboro NH 03894 Office: Shea Mertens Sager & Sager PO Box 1508 Wolfeboro NH 03894-1508

MERZ, MICHAEL, federal judge; b. Dayton, Ohio, Mar. 29, 1945; s. Robert Louis and Hazel (Appleton) M.; m. Marguerite Logan LeBreton, Sept. 7, 1968; children: Peter Henry, Nicholas George. AB cum laude, Harvard U., 1967, JD, 1970. Bar: Ohio 1970, U.S. Dist. Ct. (so. dist.) Ohio 1971, U.S Supreme Ct. 1974, U.S. Ct. Appeals (6th cir.) 1975. Assoc. Smith & Schnacke, Dayton, Ohio, 1970-75, ptnr., 1976-77; judge Dayton Mcpl. Ct., 1977-84; magistrate U.S. Dist. Ct. (so. dist.) Ohio, 1984—. Adj. prof. U. Dayton Law Sch., 1979—; mem. rules adv. com. Ohio Supreme Ct., 1989-96. Bd. dirs. United Way, Dayton, 1981-95; trustee Dayton and Montgomery County Pub. Libr., 1991—, Montgomery County Hist. Soc., 1995—, Ohio Libr. Coun., 1997-2000. Mem. ABA, Fed. Bar Assn., Am. Judicature Soc., Fed. Magistrate Judges Assn. (trustee 1997-2000), Ohio State Bar Assn., Dayton Bar Assn. Republican. Roman Catholic. Office: US Dist Ct 902 Federal Bldg 200 W 2nd St Dayton OH 45402-1430

MERZON, JAMES BERT, lawyer; b. Fresno, Calif., Aug. 3, 1942; s. Bert A. and Pauline D. (Normart) M.; children— Robin, John, Maria, Andrew. B.A., Fresno State Coll., 1964; J.D., UCLA, 1968. Bar: Calif. 1968, U.S. Dist. Ct. (no., ea., cen. and so. dists.) Calif. 1969, U.S. Ct. Appeals (9th cir.) 1972, U.S. Ct. Claims 1974. Ptnr. Ogle, Gallo, and Merzon, Morro Bay, Calif., San Luis Obispo, Calif., 1969— ; dir. Vault Corp., Westlake Village, Calif. Co-founder, bd. dirs. Meals On Wheels, Morro Bay, 1972-79, Big Bros., Morro Bay, 1972-75; bd. dirs. Santa Lucia Council Boy Scouts Am., 1974-76; chmn. Parks and Recreation Commn., Morro Bay, 1973-79. Named Boss of Yr., County Legal Secs. Assn., 1975. Mem. Calif. Bar Assn., ABA, San Luis Obispo County Bar Assn. (pres.). Episcopalian. Lodges: Elks, Lions. Construction, Probate, Real property. Office: Ogle Gallo and Merzon 770 Morro Bay Blvd Morro Bay CA 93442-1918

MESCHKOW, JORDAN M. lawyer; b. Bklyn., Mar. 25, 1957; s. Gerald Meschkow and Florence Y. (Katz) Silverman; m. Susan G. Scher, Aug. 10, 1980; children: Sasha Hayley, Alisha Sadie. BS in Biology, SUNY, Stony Brook, 1979; JD, Chgo. Kent Coll. Law, 1982. Bar: Ariz. 1982, Fla. 1983; registered U.S. Patent and Trademark Office 1983. Assoc. James F. Duffy, Patent Atty., Phoenix, 1982; ptnr. Duffy & Meschkow, 1983-84; sole practice, 1984-92; sr. ptnr. Meschkow & Gresham, P.L.C., 1992—. Frequent talk radio guest and spkr. at seminars on patent, trademark and

copyright law. Contbr. article series to profl. jours.; patentee in field. Exec. bd. City of Phoenix Fire Pub. Awareness League, 1996—. Mem. Am. Intellectual Property Law Assn., State Bar Ariz. (intellectual property sect. 1982—), State Bar Fla. Avocations: gardening, motorcycling, bicycling, skating, swimming. Intellectual property, Patent, Trademark and copyright. Office: 5727 N 7th St Ste 409 Phoenix AZ 85014-5818 E-mail: JM@patentmg.com

MESERVE, RICHARD ANDREW, lawyer; b. Medford, Mass., Nov. 20, 1944; s. Robert William and Gladys Evangeline (Swenson) M.; m. Martha Ann Richards, Sept. 20, 1966; children: Amy, Lauren. BA, Tufts U., 1966; JD, Harvard U., 1975; PhD in Applied Physics, Stanford U., 1976. Bar: Mass. 1975, D.C. 1980, U.S. Supreme Ct. 1982. Law clk. Mass. Supreme Jud. Ct., Boston, 1975-76; law clk. to presiding justice U.S. Supreme Ct., Washington, 1976-77; legal counsel Pres. Sci. Adviser, 1977-81; ptnr. Covington & Burling, 1981-99; chmn. U.S. Nuclear Regulatory Commn., 1999—. Chmn. com. to assess safety and tech. issues at Dept. Energy reactors, NAS, 1987-88, chmn. com. on fuel economy of automobiles and light trucks, 1991-92, chmn. com. on declassification of info. for Dept. Energy's environ. programs, 1994-95; co-chmn. AAAS-ABA Nat. Conf. Lawyers and Scientists, 1988-94; mem. adv. bd. Sec. Energy, 1996-99; bd. dirs. Carnegie Instn., Washington; mem. bd. overseers for arts and scis. Tufts U. Fellow AAAS (bd. dirs.), Am. Phys. Soc., Am. Acad. Arts and Scis. (coun. and exec. com.); mem. Phi Beta Kappa, Sigma Xi. Democrat. Administrative and regulatory, General civil litigation, Environmental. Home: 708 Berry St Falls Church VA 22042-2402 Office: Office of Chmn NRC Washington DC 20555-0001

MESHBESHER, RONALD I. lawyer; b. Mpls., May 18, 1933; s. Nathan J. and Esther J. (Balman) M.; m. Sandra F. Siegel, June 17, 1956 (div. 1978); children: Betsy F., Wendy S., Stacy J.; m. Kimberly L. Garnaas, May 23, 1988; 1 child, Jolie M. BS in Law, U. Minn., 1955, JD, 1957. Bar: Minn. 1957, U.S. Supreme Ct. 1966. Prosecuting atty. Hennepin County, Mpls., 1958-61; pres. Meshbesher and Spence Ltd., 1961—. Lectr. numerous legal and profl. orgns.; mem. adv. com. on rules of criminal procedure Minn. Supreme Ct., 1971-91; cons. on recodification of criminal procedure code Czech Republic Ministry of Justice, 1994. Author: Trial Handbook for Minnesota Lawyers, 1992; mem. bd. editors Criminal Law Advocacy Reporter; mem. adv. bd. Bur. Nat. Affairs Criminal Practice Manual; contbr. numerous articles to profl. jours. Mem. ATLA (bd. govs. 1968-71), ABA, Minn. Bar Assn., Internat. Acad. Trial Lawyers, Am. Coll. Trial Lawyers, Am. Bd. Trial Advs., Am. Bd. Criminal Lawyers (v.p. 1983), Am. Acad. Forensic Scis., Nat. Assn. Criminal Def. Lawyers (pres. 1984-85), Minn. Trial Lawyers Assn. (pres. 1973-74), Minn. Assn. Criminal Def. Lawyers (pres. 1991-92, Disting. Svc. award 2001), Trial Lawyers for Pub. Justice, Calif. Attys. for Criminal Justice. Avocations: biking, photography, travel, flying. General civil litigation, Criminal, Personal injury. Home: 2010 Sugarwood Dr Orono MN 55356-9339 Office: Meshbesher & Spence 1616 Park Ave Minneapolis MN 55404-1695

MESKILL, THOMAS J. federal judge; b. New Britain, Conn., Jan. 30, 1928; s. Thomas J. M.; m. Mary T. Grady; children— Maureen Meskill Heneghan, John, Peter, Eileen, Thomas. B.S., Trinity Coll., Hartford, Conn., 1950, LL.D., 1972; J.D., U. Conn., 1956; postgrad., Sch. Law, NYU; LL.D., U. Bridgeport, 1971, U. New Haven, 1974. Bar: Conn. 1956, Fla. 1957, D.C. 1957, U.S. Ct. Appeals (2d cir.) 1975, U.S. Supreme Ct. 1971. Former mem. firm Meskill, Dorsey, Sledzik and Walsh, New Britain; mem. 90th-91st Congresses 6th Conn. Dist.; gov. Conn., 1971-75; judge U.S. Ct. Appeals (2d cir.), New Britain, Conn., 1975—, chief judge, 1992-93, now sr. judge. Pres. New Britain Council Social Agys.; Asst. corp. council City of New Britain, 1960-62, mayor, 1962-64, corp. counsel, 1965-67; mem. Constl. Conv., Hartford, 1965. Served to 1st lt. USAF, 1950-53. Recipient Disting. Svc. award Jr. C. of C., 1964, Jud. Achievement award ATLA, 1983, Learned Hand medal for Excellence in Fed. Juridprudence, Fed. Bar Coun., 1994. Mem. Fla. Bar Assn., Con. Bar Assn. (Henry J. Naruk Jud. award 1994), Hartford County Bar Assn., New Britain Bar Assn., KC. Republican. Office: US Ct Appeals 114 W Main St New Britain CT 06051-4223

MESSA, JOSEPH LOUIS, JR. lawyer; b. Phila., Mar. 24, 1962; s. Joseph Louis and Virginia (Ciaffoni) M. BS, Tulane U., 1984; JD, Temple U., 1988. Bar: Pa. 1988, N.J. 1988, U.S. Dist. Ct. N.J. 1988, U.S. Dist. Ct. (eastern dist.) Pa. 1998, U.S. Ct. Appeals (3d cir.) 1996. Assoc. Duane Morris & Heckscher, Phila., 1988-90; ptnr. Ominsky & Messa, 1990-2000, Messa & Assocs., P.C., Phila., 2001—. Ward leader Rep. Party, Phila. 1985—, city com., 1985—, exec. com., 1985—. Mem. ATLA, ABA, Pa. Trial Lawyers (cons., seminar presenter, liability com.), Phila. Trial Lawyers, N.J. Trial Lawyers, Pa. Bar Assn., N.J. Bar Assn., Phila. Bar Assn., Burlington County Bar Assn., Camden County Bar Assn., Million Dollar Advocates Forum. Roman Catholic. Avocations: physical fitness, bodybuilding, waterskiing, boating, traveling. Personal injury, Product liability, Professional liability. Office: Messa & Assoc Inc 1700 Twp Logan Sq 18th & Arch Sts Philadelphia PA 19103 E-mail: jlmessajr@aol.com

MESSEMER, GLENN MATTHEW, lawyer; b. Hartford, Conn., Jan. 7, 1947; s. Joseph M. and Mary S. Messemer. BSBA, Georgetown U., 1968; JD, U. Conn., 1971. Bar: Conn. 1972. Staff atty. Kaman Corp., Bloomfield, Conn., 1972-74; asst. sec., 1974-79; asst. v.p., 1979-81; v.p., gen. counsel, 1981—. Prof. bus. law Sch. Bus. Adminstrn., U. Hartford (Conn., 1974-80; legal counsel Am. Helicopter Soc.; arbitrator Am. Arbitration Assn., 1978-82. Bd. dirs., trustee, regent U. hartford, 1993—. Served with M.I., U.S. Army, 1969-75. Mem. ABA, Conn. Bar Assn. (founding; exec. com., sec.), Hartford County Bar Assn. Clubs: Hartford Golf, Hartford, Masons. Contracts commercial, Private international, Labor. Office: Kaman Corp 1332 Blue Hills Ave Bloomfield CT 06002

MESSERSMITH, LANNY DEE, lawyer; b. Laverne, Okla., Oct. 3, 1942; s. Harry D. and Vivian D. (Bowers) M.; m. Christine Diane Smith, Sept. 28, 1974; 1 child, Nicholas Ryan. BA, U. N.Mex., 1966, JD, 1969; DCL (hon.), Holy Cath. Apostolic Ch., 1975. Bar: N.Mex. 1969, U.S. Ct. Claims 1978, U.S. Supreme Ct. 1981. Asst. dist. atty. 1st Dist. State of N.Mex., Santa Fe, 1969-70, asst. atty. gen., 1974-76; assoc. Rhodes & McCallister, Albuquerque, 1970-72; ptnr. McCallister, Messersmith & Wiseman, 1972-74, Lanny D. Messersmith, PA, Albuquerque, 1974-85, Messersmith, Eaton & Keenan, Albuquerque, 1985-89, Schuler, Messersmith, Daley & Lansdowne, Albuquerque, 1989—. Cons., hon. consul Govt. of Fed. Republic of Germany, 1981—. Mem. Albuquerque Com. on Fgn. Rels., 1988—, Sister Cities, 1988—. Mem. N.Mex. Bar Assn. (bd. dirs. internat. com.), Albuquerque Bar Assn., N.Mex. Retail Assn. (pres. 1987), Albuquerque UN Assn. (bd. dirs. 1985), Albuquerque Country Club, Masons (scholarship chmn. Albuquerque chpt. 1984-87), Shriners, Rotary Internat. Avocations: sailing, reading. Federal civil litigation, Private international, Probate. Home: 7904 Woodridge Dr NE Albuquerque NM 87109-5258 Office: Schuler Messersmith Daly & Lansdowne 4300 San Mateo Blvd NE Ste B380 Albuquerque NM 87110-8401 E-mail: mesersmith@aol.com

MESSICK, WILEY SANDERS, retired lawyer; b. Troy, Ala., Mar. 5, 1929; s. Verbia Travis and Mary (Carter) M.; m. Betty Dotson, June 18, 1955; children: Mary Tallant, Sandy McClanahan, Carter Messick. BS, U. Ala., 1950, LLB, 1953; LLM, Georgetown U., 1956. Bar: Ala. 1953, U.S. Supreme Ct. 1956. Mem. legal dept. Sonat, Birmingham, Ala., 1954; asst. to cong. George Andrews U.S. Ho. of Reps., Washington, 1955-56; counsel Small Bus. Com. U.S. Senate, 1956-61; exec. sec., adminstrv. asst. Senator John Sparkman, 1961-67; regional adminstr. SBA, Atlanta, 1967-81, dep. regional adminstr., 1981-91, dep. dist. dir., 1991-93, acting regional adminstr., 1993-94; ret., 1994. Arbitrator Am. Arbitration Assn.; chmn. Atlanta Fed. Exec. Bd., 1987. 1st lt. USAF, 1950-52, col. USAFR. Recipient Disting. Svc. award SBA, 1970, EEO award, 1980, Legion Merit, USAF, 1981. Mem. Rotary. Democrat. Presbyterian. Fax: 770-886-6717. E-mail: messick@mindspring.com

MESSINA, BONNIE LYNN, lawyer; b. Lima, Ohio, Mar. 17, 1961; m. Dominick Messina. BA, We. Md. Coll., 1983; JD magna cum laude, U. Balt., 1991. Bar: Md. 1991. Claim adjuster The Hartford, Hunt Valley, Md., 1983-86, claim supr., 1986-88; assoc. Venable, Baetjer & Howard, Balt., 1991-94; sr. counsel U.S. Fidelity & Guaranty Co., 1994-98, St. Paul Fire & Marine Ins. Co., Balt., 1999, group claims counsel, 1999—. Assoc. editor U. Balt. Law Rev., 1990-91. Mem. jud. selection com. Women's Law Ctr., Balt., 1993-2000; mentor U. Balt. Sch. of law, Balt., 1993-97. Recipient Am. Jurisprudence award Balt., 1989, 90 (2). Mem. ABA, Md. State Bar Assn., Balt. County Bar Assn., Md. Assn. Def. Trial Counsel, Def. Rsch. Inst., Inc. General civil litigation, Insurance. Office: St Paul Fire & Marine Ins Co Ins Co 5801 Smith Ave Baltimore MD 21209-3652

MESSING, SARA VIRGINIA DRICK, lawyer; b. Williamsport, Pa., June 8, 1941; d. Jacob Ralph and Sara Belva (Bitting) Drick; m. Aaron I. Messing, Oct. 30, 1966; children: Benjamin, Jacob. BA, Ohio Wesleyan U., 1963; LLB, Albany Law Sch., 1966. Bar: N.J. 1967, U.S. Ct. Appeals (3d cir.) 1967, U.S. Supreme Ct. 1975; cert. civil trial atty., N.J. Sr. trial atty. Doreen M. Ryan, Ewquire, Cranford, N.J., 1966—. Charter mem., vol. lawyer Garden State Theatre Organ Soc., Inc., 1973—. Mem. Morris County Bar Assn., Order of Ea. Star, Alpha Xi Delta. Personal injury. Home: 37 Birch St West Orange NJ 07052-4533 Office: Law Offices of Doreen M Ryan 65 Jackson Dr Cranford NJ 07016-3516

MESSINGER, SHELDON L(EOPOLD), law educator; b. Chgo., Aug. 26, 1925; s. Leopold J. and Cornelia (Eichel) M.; m. Mildred Handler, June 30, 1947; children— Adam J., Eli B. Ph.D. in Sociology, UCLA, 1969. Assoc. rsch. sociologist Ctr. Study Law and Soc. U. Calif., Berkeley, 1961-69, rsch. sociologist, 1969-70, prof. criminology, 1970-77, prof. law jurisprudence and social policy program, 1977-88, Elizabeth J. Boalt prof. law, 1988-91, prof. law emeritus, 1991—, prof. grad. sch., 1995-97, vice chmn., 1961-69, acting dean criminology, 1970-71, dean criminology, 1971-75, chmn. program, 1983-87. Author, co-author numerous books, articles. Mem. Coun. U. Calif. Emeriti Assns. (chair-elect 1999-2000, chair 2000-01). Home: 860 Indian Rock Ave Berkeley CA 94707-2051 Office: U Calif Sch Law Boalt Hall Berkeley CA 94720 E-mail: slm@uclink.berkeley.edu

MESSITTE, PETER JO, judge; b. Washington, July 17, 1941; s. Jesse B. and Edith (Wechsler) M.; m. Susan P. Messitte, Sept. 5, 1965: children: Zachariah, Abigail. BA cum laude, Amherst Coll., 1963; JD, U. Chgo., 1966. Bar: Md. 1969, D.C. 1969, U.S. Ct. Appeals (4th cir.) 1977, U.S. Supreme Ct. 1973, U.S. Ct. Appeals (DC cir.) 1982, U.S. Ct. Appeals (5th cir.) 1983. Assoc. Zuckert, Scoutt & Rasenberger, Washington, 1968-71; solo practice Chevy Chase, Md., 1971-75; mem. Messitte & Rosenberg, P.A., 1975-81; prin. Peter J. Messitte, P.A., 1981-85; assoc. judge Cir. Ct. for Montgomery County Rockville, Md., 1985-93; judge U.S. Dist. Ct. Md., Greenbelt, 1993—. Mem. internat. jud. rels. com. Jud. Conf. U.S. Bd. dirs. Cmty. Psychiat. Clinic, Montgomery County, Md., 1974-85, v.p. 1980-85; Peace Corps vol. , Sao Paulo, Brazil, 1966-68; Md. del. Dem. Nat. Conv., N.Y.C., 1980. Recipient teaching citations Fed. Deposit Ins. Corp. Bank Exam. Sch., 1975, 79, Am. Inst. Banking, 1978, Elizabeth Scull award for Outstanding Svc. to Montgomery County, Md., 1993, Spl. citation Divorce Roundtable Montgomery County, 1993, Contbr. Mental Health Cmty. Psychiat. Clinic, 1986. Fellow Md. Bar Found. (H. Vernon Eney award for contbn. to adminstrn. of justice 2001); mem. ABA, FBA, Inter-Am. Bar Assn., D.C. Bar Assn., Md. Bar Assn., Montgomery County Bar Assn. (Century of Svc. award 1999), Am. Law Inst., Fed. Judges Assn. (4th jud. cir.), Charles Fahy Inn of Ct. (master 1987-88), Montgomery County Inn of Ct. (pres. 1988-90), Jud. Inst. Md. (bd. dirs. 1989-93). Jewish. Office: US Courthouse 6500 Cherrywood Ln Greenbelt MD 20770-1249

MESSNER, ROBERT THOMAS, lawyer, banking executive; b. McKeesport, Pa., Mar. 27, 1938; s. Thomas M. and Cecilia Mary (McElhinny) M.; m. Anne Margaret Lux, Dec. 3, 1966; children: Megan Anne, Michael Thomas. A.B., Dartmouth Coll., 1960; LL.B., U. Pa., 1963. Bar: Pa. 1965. With firm Rose, Schmidt & Dixon, Pitts., 1965-68; with G.C. Murphy Co., McKeesport, 1968-86, corp. sec., 1974—, gen. counsel, 1975-86, v.p., 1976-86; v.p., gen. counsel, corp. sec. Dollar Bank, Pitts., 1986—. Dir. G.C. Murphy Found. Bd. dirs. McKeesport YMCA, Downtown Pitts. YMCA, Mon-Yough Heritage Found., 1981-83, Braddock's Field Hist. Soc., 1994—; mem. adv. bd. Pa. Human Rels. Commn., 1968, 69; Rep. candidate for Pa. Legis., 1986, fin. adv. bd. Wilkinsburg, Pa., 1988—. 1st lt. U.S. Army, 1963-65. Decorated Commendation medal. Mem. ABA, Pa. Bar Assn. (chmn. corp. law dept. com.), Allegheny County Bar Assn. (coun. on corp., banking and bus. law), Am. Soc. Corp. Secs. (pres. Pitts. regional group, dir.), Am. Mgmt. Assn., Pa. Assn. Savs. Instns. (chmn. legal com. 1989—), Am. Corp. Counsel Assn., Theta Delta Chi. Clubs: Dartmouth Western Pa., Rivers. Banking, Consumer commercial, General corporate. Home: 1061 Blackridge Rd Pittsburgh PA 15235-2719 Office: Dollar Bank Three Gateway Ctr Pittsburgh PA 15222

MESTRES, RICARDO ANGELO, JR. lawyer; b. N.Y.C., Aug. 12, 1933; s. Ricardo Angelo and Anita (Gwynne) M.; m. Ann Farnsworth, June 18, 1955; children: Laura, Ricardo III, Lynn, Anthony. AB, Princeton U., 1955; LLB, Harvard U., 1961. Bar: N.Y. 1962, U.S. Supreme Ct. 1970. Assoc. Sullivan & Cromwell, N.Y.C., 1961-67, ptnr., 1968-2000, chmn., sr. ptnr., 1995-2000, sr. counsel, 2001—. Trustee Unitarian Ch. All Souls, N.Y.C., 1973-79, 84-87; trustee Phillips Exeter Acad., 1989-99, pres. bd. trustees, 1993-99. Served to lt. USN, 1955-58. Mem. ABA, N.Y. State Bar Assn., Assn. Bar City N.Y. (corp. law, securities regulation law and state legis. coms.), Am. Law Inst., Coun. Fgn. Rels., Links Club, Mill Reef Club (Antigua), Phi Beta Kappa. Clubs: Downtown Assn., Links (N.Y.C.); Mill Reef (Antigua). General corporate, Mergers and acquisitions, Securities. Office: Sullivan & Cromwell 125 Broad St Fl 28 New York NY 10004-2489

METCALFE, WALTER LEE, JR. lawyer; b. St. Louis, Dec. 19, 1938; s. Walter Lee and Carol (Crowe) M.; Cynthia Williamson, Aug. 26, 1965; children— Carol, Edward. AB, Washington U., St. Louis, 1960; JD, U. Va., 1964. Bar: Mo. 1964. Ptnr. Armstrong, Teasdale, Kramer & Vaughan, St. Louis, 1964-81; sr. ptnr. Bryan Cave LLP, 1982—, now chmn. Bd. dirs. Washington U., Danforth Found., St. Louis RCGA, Pulitzer Found. for Arts; dep. chmn. Fed. Res. Bd. St. Louis. Mem. ABA, Mo. Bar Assn., St. Louis Bar Assn., Bogey Club (pres.), Noonday Club. Episcopalian. General corporate. Home: 26 Upper Ladue Rd Saint Louis MO 63124-1675 Office: Bryan Cave 211 N Broadway 1 Metropolitan Sq Ste 3600 Saint Louis MO 63102-2750

METZ, CRAIG HUSEMAN, legislative administrator; b. Columbia, S.C., Aug. 26, 1955; s. Leonard Huseman and Annette (Worthington) M.; m. Karen Angela McCleary, Aug. 11, 1984; 1 child, Preston Worthington. BA, U. Tenn., 1977; JD, U. Memphis, 1986; cert., U.S. Ho. of Reps. Rep. Leadership Parliamentary Law Sch., 1987. Bar: S.C., D.C., U.S. Ct. Claims, U.S. Supreme Ct., U.S. Ct. Appeals (4th cir.). Canvass coord., liaison Campaign to Re-elect Congressman Floyd Spence, 1978; del., chmn. Shelby County Del. to 1983 Tenn. Young Rep. Fedn. Conv.; vice chmn. Shelby County Young Reps., 1983-84, chmn., 1984-85; Shelby County adminstr., asst. to Tenn. state exec. dir. Reagan-Bush Campaign, 1984; field rep. Campaign to Re-elect Congressman Floyd Spence, 1986; spl. asst. to Congressman Floyd Spence, 1986-88; counsel com. on labor and human resources U.S. Senate, 1988-90; commr.'s counsel U.S. Occupational Safety and Health Rev. Commn., Washington, 1990-91; spl. asst. to asst. sec. for legis. and congl. affairs; dep. asst. sec. for congl. liaison U.S. Dept. Edn., Washington, 1991-93; asst. dir. Divsn. Congl. Affairs AMA, 1993; chief of staff Congressman Floyd Spence, 1993—2001; adminstr. Office of the Second Congl. Dist. of S.C., U.S. House of Rep. , Washington, D.C., 2001—. Judge nat. writing competition U.S. Constn. Bicentennial, S.C. 1987-88; mem. Ch. of the Ascension and Saint Agnes, Washington. Recipient award of merit Rep. Party of Shelby County, 1985, Outstanding Leadership award Shelby County Young Reps., 1985. Mem. Rep. Nat. Lawyers Assn. (state chmn. S.C. chpt. 1987-90), Freedoms Found. Valley Forge, Va. Hist. Soc., Assn. for Preservation Va. Antiquities, Va. Geneal. Soc., U. South Caroliniana Soc., Palmetto Trust for Historic Preservation, Lowcountry Heritage Soc., Orangeburg County Hist. Soc., Nat. Trust for Hist. Preservation (assoc. Capital region), SAR, St. David's Soc., St. Andrew's Soc. Washington, Mil. Soc. War of 1812, Vet. Corps Arty. State of N.Y., Gen. Soc. War of 1812, Mil. Order Loyal Legion of U.S., Order of St. John (Hospitaller), SCV, Mil. Order Stars and Bars, Sons and Daus. Colonial and Antebellum Bench and Bar 1565-1861, Sons of the Revolution, Ky. Col., Nat. Cathedral Assn., U. Tenn. Nat. Alumni Assn., Sigma Alpha Epsilon, Phi Alpha Delta (v.p. McKellar chpt., Outstanding Svc. award 1983). Republican. Episcopalian. Home: 8505 Westown Way Vienna VA 22182-2513 Office: 2405 Rayburn Bldg Washington DC 20515-4002

METZ, JEROME JOSEPH, JR. lawyer; b. Cin., Dec. 25, 1950; s. Jerome Joseph Sr. and Loretta Ellen (Donnellon) M.; m. Deborah Carolyn Hundemer, July 2, 1976; children: Andrew Thomas, Matthew Jerome, Angela Christina. BA, Xavier U., 1976; JD, U. Cin., 1980. Bar: Ohio 1980, U.S. Dist. Ct. (so. dist.) Ohio 1980, U.S. Ct. Appeals (6th cir.) 1980. Law clk. to judge U.S. Dist. Ct. (so. dist.) Ohio, Cin., 1980-82; assoc. Hartsock, Harris & Schneider, 1982-83, Porter, Wright, Morris & Arthur, Cin., 1983-89, ptnr., 1990—. Trustee Winton Place Devel. Corp., Cin., 1982-91, sec., 1987-91. Vice pres. Mercy Montessori Parents Assn., 1990-91, pres., 1991-92, past pres., 1992-93. Mem. ABA, Ohio Bar Assn., Cin. Bar Assn. Democrat. Roman Catholic. Bankruptcy, Federal civil litigation, State civil litigation. Office: Porter Wright Morris & Arthur 250 E 5th St Ste 2200 Cincinnati OH 45202-4199

METZ, LARRY EDWARD, lawyer; b. Phila., Mar. 20, 1955; s. Harry Franz and Joan (Nye) M.; m. Mariko Tomisato, Mar. 26, 1980; children: Marla Jo, Christina Jill. BA, U. Fla., 1976; JD with high honors, Fla. State U., 1983. Bar: Fla. 1983, U.S. Dist. Ct. (so., mid. and no. dists.) Fla. 1984, U.S. Ct. Appeals (11th cir.) 1984, U.S. Supreme Ct. 1987. Assoc. Fleming, O'Bryan & Fleming, Ft. Lauderdale, Fla., 1983-86; atty. Westinghouse Electric Corp., Coral Springs, 1986-88; pvt. practice Ft. Lauderdale, 1988-91, Coral Springs, 1991-93; assoc. Herzfeld & Rubin, Miami, 1993-96, ptnr. Ft. Lauderdale, 1996-99; assoc. Unger, Acree, Weinstein, Marcus, Merrill, Kast & Metz, P.L., Orlando, Fla., 1999-2000; ptnr. Unger, Acree, Weinstein, Marcus, Merrill, Kast & Metz, PL, 2000—. Area leader, sign co-chmn., spkr. George Bush for Pres. Broward County (Fla.) Victory Com., 1988; pres. Broward County Regional Rep. Club, 1991, 95; mem. exec. com. Broward County Rep. Party, 1988-91, 93-96, Lake County Rep. Party, 1999—; Rep. nominee U.S. Ho. Reps. 19th dist., Fla., 1992; mem. Fla. Guardian Ad Litem program, 1991-97; mem. Cmty. Ch. Howey-in-the-Hills, Fla., 1999—, chmn. stewardship and finance com., 2000—. Capt. USMC, 1976-82. Recipient Outstanding Mem. of Yr. award Broward Lawyers Care, 1989, 90. Mem. ABA, Order of Coif, Marine Corps League (judge advocate North Lake Detachment, Fla. 2000—). General civil litigation, Personal injury, Product liability. Office: Unger, Acree Weinstein et al 701 Peachtree Rd Orlando FL 32804-6847 E-mail: Lmetz@ungerlawfirm.com

METZER, PATRICIA ANN, lawyer; b. Phila., Mar. 10, 1941; d. Freeman Weeks and Evelyn (Heap) M.; m. Karl Hormann, June 30, 1980. BA with distinction, U. Pa., 1963, LLB cum laude, 1966. Bar: Mass. 1966, D.C. 1972, U.S. Tax Ct. 1988. Assoc., then ptnr. Mintz, Levin, Cohn, Glovsky and Popeo, Boston, 1966-75; assoc. tax legis. counsel U.S. Treasury Dept., Washington, 1975-78; shareholder, dir. Goulston & Storrs, P.C., Boston, 1978-98; stockholder Hutchins, Wheeler & Dittmar, P.C., 1998—. Lectr. program continuing legal edn. Boston Coll. Law Sch., Chestnut Hill, Mass., spring 1974; mem. adv. com. NYU Inst. Fed. Taxation, N.Y.C., 1981-87; mem. practitioner liaison com. Mass. Dept. Revenue, 1985-90; spkr. in field. Author: Federal Income Taxation of Individuals, 1984; mem. adv. bd. Corp. Tax and Bus. Planning Review, 1996—; mem. editl. bd. Am. Jour. Tax Policy, 1995-98; contbr. articles to profl. jours., chpts. to books. Bd. mgrs. Barrington Ct. Condominium, Cambridge, Mass., 1985-86; bd. dirs. University Road Parking Assn., Cambridge, 1988—; trustee Social Law Libr., Boston, 1989-93. Mem. ABA (tax sect., vice-chair publs. 2000—, mem. coun. 1996-99, chmn. subcom. allocations and distbns. partnership com. 1978-82, vice chmn. legis. 1991-93, chmn. 1993-95, com. govt. submissions, vice liaison 1993-94, liaison 1994-95, North Atlantic region, co-liaison 1995-96, N.E. region, regional liaison meetings com.), FBA (coun. on taxation, chmn. corp. taxation com. 1977-81, chmn. com. partnership taxation 1981-87), Mass. Bar Assn., Boston Bar Assn. (coun. 1987-89, chmn. tax sect. 1989-91), Am. Coll. Tax Counsel (bd. regents 1999—), Boston Estate Planning Coun. (exec. com. 1975, 79-82). Avocation: vocal performances (as soloist and with choral groups). Corporate taxation, Estate taxation, Taxation, general. Office: Hutchins Wheeler & Dittmar PC 101 Federal St Boston MA 02110-1817

METZGER, BARRY, lawyer; b. Newark, June 11, 1945; s. William and Dorothy (Bagoon) M.; m. Jacqueline Sue Ivers, June 26, 1966; children: Darren Thomas, Rebecca Lynne. AB magna cum laude, Princeton U., 1966; JD cum laude, Harvard U., 1969. Bar: D.C. 1970. Asst. to Prin. Ceylon Law Sch., Colombo, 1969-71; dir. Asian programs Internat. Legal Ctr., N.Y.C., 1971-74; ptnr. Coudert Brothers, 1974-76, 99—; resident in Hong Kong, 1976-84; Sydney, 1984-89; London, 1989-95; gen. counsel Asian Devel. Bank, Manila, 1995-99. Mem. New South Wales Atty. Gen.'s Commn. on Comml. Dispute Resolution, Com. for Econ. Devel. Australia; arbitrator ICC Ct. Arbitration.; v.p. Internat. Legal Aid Assn., 1972-80; pres. Harvard Legal Aid Bur., 1968-69; trustee Princeton-in-Asia; dir. Partnership for Transparency Fund; chmn. Asian Affairs Com. Assn. Editl. advisor: Internat. Fin. Law Rev.; editor: Legal Aid and World Poverty, 1974; contbr. articles to profl. jours. Sheldon Meml. fellow, 1969, vis. fellow Stanford Law Sch., 1999. Mem. ABA, Counalan Foreign Relations, Internat. Bar Assn. Democrat. Banking, Private international, Public international. Home: 153 W 93rd St Apt Z New York NY 10025 Office: Coudert Brothers 1114 Avenue Of The Americas New York NY 10036-7703 E-mail: metzgerb@coudert.com

METZGER, JEFFREY PAUL, lawyer; b. Oct. 13, 1950; s. John E. and Ellen J. M; m. Stephanie Ann Stahr, Dec. 27, 1977. BA magna cum laude, Amherst Coll., 1973; JD, Georgetown U., 1976. Bar: D.C. 1977. Legis. asst. U.S. Senator Joseph Biden, Jr., Del., 1973; assoc. Collier, Shannon, Rill and Scott, Washington, 1976-79, Cole and Groner PC, Washington, 1979-82; trial atty. comml. litigation br. civil divsn. U.S. Dept. Justice, 1982-85; mem. prof. staff Pres.'s Blue Ribbon Commn. on Def. Mgmt., 1985-86; asst. gen. counsel Unisys Corp., McLean, Va., 1986-88, v.p., assoc. gen. counsel, 1989—. Mem. ABA. E-mail: jmetz10771@aol.com

METZGER, JOHN MACKAY, lawyer; b. Princeton, N.J., Mar. 8, 1948; s. Bruce Manning and Isobel Elizabeth (Mackay) M.; m. Sandra Kay Wellington, May 8, 1999. BA cum laude, Harvard U., 1970; JD, NYU, 1973; postgrad., London Sch. Econs., 1973-74. Bar: Pa. 1976, N.J. 1976, U.S. Dist. Ct. N.J. 1976, U.S. Tax Ct. 1977, D.C. 1978, U.S. Ct. Appeals (fed. cir.) 1982. Tax adminstr. N.J. Div. Taxation, Trenton, 1976-86, 88—; atty. McCarthy & Schatzman PA, Princeton, 1986-88. Mem. N.J. Econ. Devel. Coun., 1987-90. Contbr. articles to profl. jours. Pres., trustee Friends of N.J. State Libr., 2000—. Mem. ABA, Am. Soc. Internat. Law, Harvard Club of N.Y.C., N.J. Hist. Soc., Supreme Ct. Historical Soc. Republican. Home: 52 Coriander Dr Princeton NJ 08540-9434 Office: 50 Barrack St Trenton NJ 08695-0269 E-mail: MetzgerEsq@aol.com

METZGER, ROBERT STREICHER, lawyer; b. St. Louis, Sept. 27, 1950; s. Robert Stanley and Jean Harriet (Streicher) M.; m. Stephanie Joy Morgan, Nov. 16, 1980; children: Michael, Kristen, Marisa. BA, Middlebury Coll., 1974; JD, Georgetown U., 1977. Bar: Calif. 1978, D.C. 1978. Legis. aide U.S. Rep. Robert F. Drinan, Washington, 1972-73; legis. asst. U.S. Rep. Michael J. Harrington, 1973-75; rsch. fellow Ctr. for Sci. and Internat. Affairs Harvard U., Cambridge, Mass., 1977-78; assoc. Latham & Watkins, L.A., 1978-84, ptnr., 1984-90, Kirkland & Ellis, L.A., 1990-93, Troop, Meisinger, Steuber & Pasich and predecessor, L.A., 1993-97, Gibson, Dunn & Crutcher LLP, L.A., 1997—. Chmn. Aerospace & Govt. Practice Group, 1997—; cons. Congl. Rsch. Svc., Washington, 1977-78. Contbr. articles to profl. jours. Mem. ABA (litigation pub. contracts sect.), Internat. Inst. for Strategic Studies, Jonathan Club. Federal civil litigation, Computer, Government contracts and claims. Office: Gibson Dunn & Crutcher LLP 333 S Grand Ave Los Angeles CA 90071-3197

METZGER, YALE HYDER, lawyer, educator; b. Adrian, Mich., Oct. 20, 1959; s. John Andrew and Shirley Jane Metzger; m. Susan E. Richmond, May 19, 1995. BA in Justice, U. Alaska, 1987; JD cum laude, Gonzaga U., 1995. Bar: Alaska 1995, U.S. Dist. Ct. Alaska 1996. Law clk. to magistrate judge U.S. Dist. Ct., 1995-96; atty. in pvt. practice Anchorage, 1995—. Mem. paralegal edn. adv. com. U. Alaska, Anchorage, 1989—; adj. prof. U. Alaska, Anchorage, 1996—. With USAF, 1982-85. Mem. ATLA, Whittier Boat Owners' Assn., S.Am. Explorers Club, Anchorage Inn of Ct. (sec. 1999-2000, treas. 2000-01). Avocations: exploration of Amazon rainforest in Ecuador, sailing in Prince William Sound, SCUBA diving, hunting big game in Alaska and Africa. Office: 425 G St Ste 510 Anchorage AK 99501-2160

METZINGER, TIMOTHY EDWARD, lawyer; b. L.A., Aug. 21, 1961; s. Robert Cole and Mary Jean (Cusick) M.; m. Cynthia Lee Stanworth, Nov. 16, 1991. BA, UCLA, 1986; JD, U. San Francisco, 1989. Bar: Calif. 1989, U.S. Dist. Ct. (ctrl., so., ea. and no. dists.) Calif. 1989, U.S. Ct. Appeals (9th cir.) 1989, U.S. Supreme Ct. 1994. Assoc. Bronson, Bronson & McKinnon, L.A., 1989-93; ptnr. Price, Postel & Parma, Santa Barbara, Calif., 1993—. Editor Santa Barbara Lawyer, 1999—. Bd. dirs. Santa Barbara County Bar Assn. Mem. Santa Barbara County Bar Assn. (bd. dirs., CFO), Santa Barbara Mus. Natural History (bd. advisors), Santa Barbara Barristers Club (pres.), Order of Barristers, Am. Inns. Ct. Avocations: diving, moutaineering, sailing. General civil litigation, Contracts commercial, Environmental. Office: Price Postel & Parma 200 E Carrillo St Ste 400 Santa Barbara CA 93101-2190

METZNER, CHARLES MILLER, federal judge; b. N.Y.C., Mar. 13, 1912; s. Emanuel and Gertrude (Miller) M.; m. Jeanne Gottlieb, Oct. 6, 1966. A.B., Columbia U., 1931, LL.B., 1933. Bar: N.Y. 1933. Pvt. practice, 1934; mem. Jud. Council State N.Y., 1935-41; law clk. to N.Y. supreme ct. justice, 1942-52; exec. asst. to U.S. atty. Gen. Herbert Brownell, Jr., 1953-54; mem. firm Chapman, Walsh & O'Connell, 1954-59; judge U.S. Dist Ct. (so. dist.) N.Y., 1959—. Mem. Law Revision Commn. N.Y. State, 1959; chmn. com. adminstrn. magistrates system U.S. Jud. Conf., 1970-81; chmn. Columbia Coll. Coun., 1965-66. Pres. N.Y. Young Republican Club, 1941; Trustee Columbia U., 1972-84, trustee emeritus, 1984—; bd. dirs. N.Y.C. Ctr. Music and Drama, 1969-74. Recipient Lawyer Div. of Joint Def. Appeal award, 1961, Columbia U. Alumni medal, 1966, Founders award Nat. Coun. U.S. Magistrates, 1989. Mem. ABA, Am. Law Inst., Fed. Bar Coun. (cert. Disting. Jud. Svc. 1989).

MEYER, CHARLES MULVIHILL, lawyer; b. Cin., Dec. 31, 1951; s. Charles Louis and Camilla Kathryn (Mulvihill) M.; children: Philip, Katherine, Evan. AB in English, Boston Coll., 1974, JD, 1977. Bar: Mass. 1977, Ohio 1978, Fla. 1978, Ky. 1993, U.S. Dist. Ct. (so. dist.) Ohio 1978, U.S. Ct. Appeals (6th cir.) 1990. Law clk. City of Boston Law Dept., 1976-77; assoc. Curhan & Curhan, Boston, 1977-78, Waite, Schneider, Bayless & Chesley, Cin., 1978-81, Santen & Hughes, Cin., 1981—. Instr. Great Oaks Vocat. Schs., Cin., 1983-86, Cin. Tech. Coll., Cin., 1984-85; legal advisor St. James Day Care Ctr., Cin., 1985—, Sec. Cin. Opera Guild, 1983-85. Mem. ABA, Ohio Bar Assn., Cin. Bar Assn. Roman Catholic. Club: Boston Coll. of Cin. (pres. 1979-80). Avocation: long distance running. Bankruptcy, Contracts commercial, Real property. Office: Santen & Hughes 312 Walnut St Fl 31 Cincinnati OH 45202-4024

MEYER, FERDINAND CHARLES, JR. lawyer; b. San Antonio, Sept. 30, 1939; Student, Tulane U.; BBA, U. Tex., 1961, LLB, 1964. Bar: Tex. 1966, U.S. Dist. Ct. (we. dist.) Tex. 1969, U.S. Ct. Appeals (5th cir.) 1971, U.S. Supreme Ct. 1975, U.S. Ct. Appeals (11th cir.) 1979, D.C. 1986. V.p., gen. counsel CSW Svcs.; ptnr. Matthews & Branscomb, San Antonio; v.p. asst. gen. counsel CSW Corp., 1986-88; v.p., gen. counsel Ctrl. & S.W. Corp., 1988-90, sr. v.p., gen. counsel, 1990-98, gen. counsel, 1990-2000, exec. v.p., gen. counsel, 1998-2000. Instr. trial advocacy St. Mary's Sch. Law, 1980-86. Capt. USAR. Fellow Am. Coll. Trial Lawyers, Tex. Bar Found.; mem. ABA, Am. Bd. Trial Advs. (adv.), State Bar Tex., Dallas Bar Assn., San Antonio Bar Assn., Internat. Assn. Def. Counsel, Phi Alpha Delta. General corporate, Public utilities. Office: PO Box 7616 Dallas TX 75209-7616

MEYER, G. CHRISTOPHER, lawyer; b. Fremont, Nebr., Mar. 27, 1948; s. Gerald William and Mildred Ruth (Clausen) M.; m. Linda Haines, Dec. 27, 1969; children: Kate, Stacy, Jon, Robert. Student, Grinnell (Iowa) Coll., 1966-69; BA, U. Kans., 1970; JD, U. Pa., 1973. Bar: Ohio 1973, U.S. Dist. Ct. (no. dist.) Ohio 1975, U.S. Ct. Appeals (6th cir.) 1982. Assoc. Squire, Sanders & Dempsey, L.L.P., Cleve., 1973-82, ptnr., 1982—. Mem. ABA, Ohio State Bar Assn., Greater Cleve. Bar Assn. Bankruptcy, Contracts commercial, General corporate. Office: Squire Sanders & Dempsey LLP 4900 Key Tower 127 Public Sq Cleveland OH 44114-1304 E-mail: cmeyer@ssd.com

MEYER, GRACE TOMANELLI, lawyer; b. Bklyn., Aug. 7, 1935; d. Cosmo and Grace (Giabia) Tomanelli; m. Heinz Meyer, May 26, 1956; children: Kenneth, Carolyn, Christa, Karla. BA, Ramapo Coll. of N.J., 1975; JD, Seton Hall U., 1978. Bar: N.J. 1978, U.S. Supreme Ct. 1983, N.Y. 1988. Adminstrv. sec. U.S. Atomic Energy Commn., N.Y.C., 1955-58; assoc. lawyer Beattie & Padovano, Montvale, N.J., 1978-80; counselor Grace T. Meyer Law offices, River Vale, 1980—. Adj. prof. Ramapo Coll., 1980, 81, Nyack Coll., 1994, 95; facilitator Pressing Onward, Pascack Bible Ch., Hillsdale, 1991—. Contbr. various articles to profl. jours. Honored for pro bono work by Bergen County Legal Svcs., 1993. Mem. N.J. Bar Assn., Bergen County Bar Assn., Christian Legal Soc., Rutherford Inst., Concerned Women for Am., Am. Family Assn. Republican. Avocations: writing, counseling, walking, arts and crafts. Estate planning, Family and matrimonial, Real property. Office: Grace T Meyer Law Offices 669 Westwood Ave Ste H River Vale NJ 07675-6336

MEYER, IRWIN STEPHAN, lawyer, accountant; b. Monticello, N.Y., Nov. 14, 1941; s. Ralph and Janice (Cohen) M.; children: Kimberly B., Joshua A. BS, Rider Coll., 1963; JD, Cornell U., 1966. Bar: N.Y. 1966; CPA, N.J. Tax mgr. Lybrand Ross Bros. & Montgomery, N.Y.C., 1966-71; mem. Ehrenkranz, Ehrenkranz & Schultz, 1971-74; prin. Irwin S. Meyer, 1974-77, 82-96; mem. Levine, Honig, Eisenberg & Meyer, 1977-78, Eisenberg, Honig & Meyer, 1978-81, Eisenberg, Honig, Meyer & Fogler, 1981-82, Janow & Meyer, LLC., 1997—. With U.S. Army, 1966-71. Mem. ABA, N.Y. Bar Assn., Am. Assn. Atty.-CPA, N.Y. Assn. Atty.-CPA, N.J. Soc. CPA. Estate taxation, Taxation, general, Personal income taxation. Office: 1 Blue Hill Plz Ste 1006 Pearl River NY 10965-3100 E-mail: jmeyerllc@aol.com

MEYER, LAWRENCE GEORGE, lawyer; b. East Grand Rapids, Mich., Oct. 2, 1940; s. George and Evangeline (Boerma) M.; children from previous marriage: David Lawrence, Jenifer Lynne; m. Linda Elizabeth Buck, May 31, 1980; children: Elizabeth Tilden, Travis Henley. BA with honors, Mich. State U., 1961; JD with distinction, U. Mich., 1964. Bar: Wis., 1965, Ill. 1965, U.S. Supreme Ct. 1968, D.C. 1972. Assoc. Whyte, Hirschboeck, Minahan, Hardin & Harland, Milw., 1964-66; atty. antitrust div. U.S. Dept. Justice, Washington, 1966-68; legal counsel U.S. Senator Robert P. Griffin, Mich., 1968-70; dir. policy planning FTC, 1970-72; ptnr. Patton, Boggs & Blow, Washington, 1972-85, Arent, Fox, Kintner, Plotkin & Kahn, Washington, 1985-96, Gadsby & Hannah, 1996-2001; pvt. practice Washington, 2001—. Contbr. articles on antitrust and trial practice to law jours.; asst. editor. U. Mich. Law Rev., 1960-61. Bd. dirs. Hockey Hall of Fame, Toronto, 1993-99, Woodrow Wilson House, 1997—. Recipient Disting. Svc. award FTC, 1972. Mem. ABA, D.C. Bar Assn., Wis. Bar Assn., Ill. Bar Assn., U.S. Senate Ex S.O.B.s Club, City Tavern Club, Sulgrave Club, Congl. Country Club. E-mail: lawlgm.com. Administrative and regulatory, Antitrust, Federal civil litigation. Home: 8777 Belmart Rd Potomac MD 20854-1610

MEYER, MARK ALAN, lawyer; b. N.Y.C., Dec. 19, 1946; s. Paul and Tilly M. BA, Fairleigh Dickinson U., 1968; JD, St. Johns U., 1971; LLM, Harvard U., 1972. Bar: N.Y. 1972, U.S. Dist. Ct. (so. and ea. dists.) N.Y. 1973, U.S. Ct. Appeals (2d cir.) 1973, U.S. Supreme Ct. 1977. Instr. law Boston U., 1971-72; asst. dist. atty. N.Y. County Dist. Atty., 1972-74; assoc. Golenbock & Barell, 1975-77, Solinger & Gordon, 1977-82; ptnr. Goldschmidt, Oshatz, Powsner & Saft, N.Y.C., 1982-85, Spitzer & Feldman PC, 1985-87, Hall, Dickler, Lawler, Kent & Friedman, N.Y.C., 1987-94, Herzfeld & Rubin PC, N.Y.C., 1995—. Lawyer; b. N.Y.C., Dec. 19, 1946; s. Paul and Tilly Meyer. BA, Fairleigh Dickinson U., 1968; JD, St. Johns U., 1971; LLM, Harvard U., 1972. Bar: N.Y. 1972, U.S. Dist. Ct. (so. and ea. dists.) N.Y. 1973, U.S. Ct. Appeals (2nd cir.) 1973, U.S. Supreme Ct. 1977. Instr. law Boston U., 1971-72; asst. dist. atty. N.Y. County Dist. Atty., 1972-74; assoc. Golenbock & Barell, 1975-77, Solinger & Gordon, 1977-82; ptnr. Goldschmidt, Oshatz, Powsner & Saft, N.Y.C., 1982-85, Spitzer & Feldman, P.C., 1985-87, Hall, Dickler, Lawler, Kent & Friedman, N.Y.C., 1987-94, Herzfeld & Rubin P.C., 1995—; chmn. bd. Fingermatrix, Inc., N. White Plains, N.Y., 1983-90; spl. counsel to Pres. Ion Iliescu of Romania and Pres. Mircea Snegur of Moldova, 1991-95; assoc. prof. law U. Crestina Dimitrie Cantemir, Bucharest, Romania; vice chmn. Romanian Presdl. Tax Reform Commn., 1999—. Chmn. Am.-Romanian Cultural Found., 1995—. Mem. Assn. of Bar of City of N.Y. (mem. com. on Ea. European affairs), Romanian-Am. C. of C. (chmn. 1990—). Avocations: art, photography. Chmn. Am-Romanian Cultural Found., 1995—. Mem. Assn. of Bar of City of N.Y. (com. on European affairs), Romanian-Am. C. of C. (chmn. 1990—). Avocations: art, photography. Private international. Home: 35 Overlook Rd Dobbs Ferry NY 10522-3209 Office: Herzfeld & Rubin PC 40 Wall St Fl 56 New York NY 10005-2349

MEYER, MARTIN ARTHUR, lawyer; b. Saratoga Springs, N.Y., Mar. 17, 1934; s. Edward and Ann Rita (Mintzer) M.; m. Lynn Greenberg, Apr. 16, 1961; 1 child, Steven. BA, Union Coll., 1955; LLB, Columbia U., 1958. Bar: N.Y. 1959, U.S. Dist. Ct. (no. dist.) N.Y. 1959, U.S. Ct. Appeals (2d cir.) 1978, U.S. Tax Ct. 1966. Assoc. McPhillips, Fitzgerald & McCarthy, Glens Falls, N.Y., 1958-60; ptnr. McPhillips, Fitzgerald & Meyer, 1961-70, McPhillips, Fitzgerald, Meyer & McLenithan, Glens Falls, 1971-88, McPhillips, Fitzgerald & Meyer, Glens Falls, 1989-96, of counsel, 1997-98. Atty. City of Glens Falls, 1970-74. Bd. govs. Glens Falls Hosp., 1976-88; mem. Glens Falls Civic Ctr. Commn., 1977-79; mem. bd. edn. City of Glens Falls, 1984-89; past mem., pres. and trustee Congregation Shaaray Tefila, Glens Falls, 1961-81; pres. Glens Falls Area Coun. Chs.; N.Y. State Dem. committeeman, 1969-70. Mem. ABA, N.Y. State Bar Assn. (trial lawyers sect. mem. exec. com. 1986-96, chmn. 1995-96), B'nai B'rith. State civil litigation, Personal injury, Probate. Home: 22 Roosevelt Ave Glens Falls NY 12801-2532

MEYER, MARTIN JAY, lawyer; b. Wilkes-Barre, Pa., Aug. 1, 1932; s. Max and Rose (Wruble) M.; m. Joan Rosenthal, Aug. 24, 1954; children: Leah, Gary. BA, Wilkes Coll., 1954; postgrad., U. Miami, 1956-57; LLB, Temple U., 1959. Bar: Pa. 1960, U.S. Dist. Ct. (mid. dist.) Pa. 1961, U.S. Ct. Appeals (3d cir.) 1966, U.S. Supreme Ct. 1978. Assoc. Mack, Kasper & Meyer, Wilkes-Barre, 1961-66, Mack & Meyer, Wilkes-Barre, 1966-68, ptnr., 1968-80; sr. ptnr. Meyer & Swatkoski, Kingston, Pa., 1980—. Chmn. disciplinary hearing com. Pa. Supreme Ct.; apptd. spl. trial master State Ct., 1995; apptd. cert. mediator U.S. Dist. Ct. (mid. dist.) Pa., 2000; mem. Million Dollar Advocates Forum. Contbr. articles to profl. jours. Chmn. Muscular Dystrophy Assn., 1960; co-chmn. March of Dimes, 1962; trustee Temple Israel Wilkes-Barre; bd. dirs. Jewish Home Scranton, Family Svc. Assn.; arbitrator U.S. Arbitration and Mediation of N.E., Inc., Am. Arbitration Assn., Million Dollar Advocates Forum. With U.S. Army, 1955-56. Fellow Pa. Bar Found.; mem. DAV, ATLA, Am. Arbitration Assn., Pa. Soc., Pa. Bar Assn. (former co-chmn., adoption com. family law sect., alt. dispute resolution com.), Nat. Conf. Bar Pres.'s, Pa. Trial Lawyers Assn. (lectr.), Luzerne County Bar Assn. (pres. 1984-85), Elks (trustee), Masons (32 degree), B'nai Brith (pres. 1967), Tau Epsilon Rho. Republican. Family and matrimonial, General practice, Personal injury. Office: 405 3rd Ave Kingston PA 18704-5802 Fax: 570-288-1003. E-mail: mslawyers@earthlink.net

MEYER, MAX EARL, lawyer; b. Hampton, Va., Oct. 31, 1918; s. Earl Luther and Winifred Katherine (Spacht) M.; m. Betty Maxwell Dodds, Sept. 22, 1945; children— Scott Maxwell, Ann Culliford. AB, U. Nebr., 1940, JD, 1942. Bar: Nebr. 1942, Ill. 1946. Assoc. firm Lord, Bissell & Brook, Chgo., 1945-53, ptnr., 1953-85; chmn. Chgo. Fed. Tax Forum, 1965, U. Chgo. Ann. Fed. Tax Conf., 1972; mem. Adv. Group to Commr. of IRS, 1967. Lectr. in field Bd. dirs. Music Acad. of the West, chmn. 1993-94. Mem. ABA (mem. council tax sec. 1969-72), Ill. Bar Assn. (mem. council tax sect. 1973-76), Nebr. Bar Assn., Chgo. Bar Assn. (chmn. taxation com. 1959-61), Am. Coll. Tax Counsel Republican. Presbyterian. Clubs: Legal, Law (Chgo.); Valley Club of Montecito, Birnam Wood Golf. Lodge: Masons. General corporate, Mergers and acquisitions, Taxation, general.

MEYER, MICHAEL BROEKER, lawyer, consultant; b. Boston, July 12, 1946; s. Edward Carl and Marjory (Morse) M.; m. Barbara Rachel Beatty, June 23, 1977; children: Douglas Beatty, Lucy Beatty. BA, Harvard U., 1967; JD cum laude, Boston Coll., 1973. Bar: Mass. 1973, U.S. Dist. Ct. Mass. 1974, U.S. Ct. Appeals (1st cir.) 1978, U.S. Ct. Appeals (D.C. cir.) 1978, U.S. Supreme Ct. 1978. Law clk. to chief justice Mass. Superior Ct., Boston, 1973-74; staff atty. Mass. Defenders Com., New Bedford, 1974-75; asst. atty. gen. Mass. Atty. Gen., Boston, 1975-79; cons., prin. Analysis & Inference, Inc., Boston, 1979-86; ptnr. Meyer, Connolly, Sloman & Macdonald, Boston, 1986—. Editor-in-chief Environ. Affairs Law Rev., 1972-73. Contbr. articles to profl. jours. Served to capt. USMC, 1967-70. Decorated Bronze Star. Mem. ABA, Mass. Bar Assn., Am. Arbitration Assn., Boston Bar Assn., Order of Coif. Home: 33 Beverly Rd Newton MA 02461-1112 Office: Meyer Connolly Sloman & Macdonald 12 Post Office Sq Fl 5 Boston MA 02109-3917

MEYER, PAUL I. lawyer; b. St. Louis, Jan. 5, 1944; AB magna cum laude, Harvard U., 1966, JD cum laude, 1969. Bar: Calif. 1970. Atty. Latham & Watkins, San Diego. Capt. USMCR, 1970-73. Mem. ABA (Profl. Merit award 1970), San Diego County Bar Assn., Phi Beta Kappa. Real property, Landlord-tenant, Sports. Office: Latham & Watkins 701 B St Ste 2100 San Diego CA 92101-8197 E-mail: Paul.Meyer@LW.com

MEYER, PHILIP GILBERT, lawyer; b. Louisville, June 26, 1945; s. Henry Gilbert and Adele (Gutermuth) M.; m. Jackie Darlene Watson, Jan. 30, 1971 (div. Apr. 1976); m. Sylvia Saunders, Oct. 9, 1976. BBA, U. Mich., 1967; JD, U. Tex., 1970. Bar: Tex. 1970, Mich. 1971, U.S. Tax Ct. 1972, U.S. Dist. Ct. (ea. dist.) Mich. 1971, U.S. Ct. Appeals (6th cir.), 1972, U.S. Dist. Ct. (no. dist.) Ohio 1976, U.S. Dist. Ct. (we. dist.) Mich. 1993, U.S. Dist. Ct. (no. dist.) Ill. 1998. Law clk. Wayne County Cir. Ct., Detroit, 1970-72; atty. Leonard C. Jaques, 1972; assoc. Christy & Robbins, Dearborn, Mich., 1972-73; ptnr. Foster, Meadows & Ballard, Detroit, 1973-79; of counsel Christy, Rogers & Gantz, Dearborn, 1979-81, Rogers & Gantz, Dearborn, 1981-86; prin. Philip G. Meyer and Assocs., Farmington Hills, 1986—. Adj. prof. U. Detroit Sch. Law, 1979. Mem. ABA (com. vice chmn. rules and procedure 1982-88), Maritime Law Assn. U.S., Mich. Bar Assn. (vice chmn. admiralty sect. 1978), Tex. Bar Assn., Detroit Bar Assn. (vice chmn. admiralty com. 1991-93, chmn. admiralty sect. 1993-95), Propeller-Port of Detroit Club (pres. 1984-85). Republican. Home: 5905 Independence Ln West Bloomfield MI 48322-1854 Office: Ste 113 30300 Northwestern Hwy Farmington Hills MI 48334-3212

MEYER, THEODORE JAMES, lawyer; b. Des Moines, Aug. 20, 1948; s. Clarence Gustav and Martha Sophie (Anderson) M.; m. Barbara Jean Bicket, Aug. 29, 1970 (div. 1980); 1 child, Julia Ann. Bar: Minn. 1973, U.S. Dist. Ct. Minn. 1979. Assoc. Oppenheimer, Wolff, Foster, Shepard & Donnelly, St. Paul, 1973-79, ptnr.; counsel Oppenheimer Wolff & Donnelly; adj. prof. William Mitchell Coll. Law, St. Paul, 1976-80. Treas. Ind. Republican Party, Falcon Heights, Minn., 1978-84; mem. council St. Michael's Luth. Ch., Roseville, Minn., 1983-84. Mem. ABA, Minn. State Bar Assn. (sec. real property sect. 1983, vice chmn. real property sect. 1984), Ramsey County Bar Assn. Club: St. Paul Athletic. Real property. Home: 1755 Saint Marys St Saint Paul MN 55113-5722 Office: Oppenheimer Wolff & Donnelly 1700 1st St SW Saint Paul MN 55112-3315

MEYER, WILLIAM LORNE, lawyer; b. Long Beach, Calif., Oct. 25, 1946; s. Harris Embury and Dorothy (Dinning) M.; m. Virginia Bell, Sept. 7, 1974; children: William Dinning, Lauren Elizabeth. BA, Vanderbilt U., 1968; JD, Emory U., 1975. Bar: Ga. 1975. Assoc. Smith, Gambrell & Russell and predecessor firm, Atlanta, 1975-82, ptnr., 1982—. Served to lt. USNR, 1968-72. Mem. Nat. Assn. Bond Lawyers, Nat. Health Lawyers Assn., ABA, State Bar Ga., Atlanta Bar Assn., Atlanta C. of C., Order of Coif. General corporate, Municipal (including bonds), Securities. Home: 4756 Woodvale Dr NW Atlanta GA 30327-4554 Office: Smith Gambrell & Russell 3333 Peachtree Rd NE Ste 1800 Atlanta GA 30326-1070

MEYERS, JERRY IVAN, lawyer; b. McKeesport, Pa., Mar. 26, 1946; s. Eugene J. and Gladys Claire (Rubenstein) M.; m. Judith Drake Aughenbaugh, June, 26, 1971; 1 child, Lindsey Drake. BA in Philosophy and Rhetoric, U. Pitts., 1972; JD cum laude, U. Miami, 1975. Bar: Pa. 1975, U.S. Dist. Ct. (we. dist.) Pa. 1975. Assoc. Berger & Kapetan, Pitts., 1975-78; ptnr. Meyers, Rosen, Louik & Perry P.C., 1978—. Mem. Assn. Trial Lawyers Am., Pa. Trial Lawyers Assn. (past pres. western Pa. chpt., bd. govs. legis. policy com., med.-legis. com.), Acad. Trial Lawyers Allegheny County. Personal injury. Office: Meyers Rosen Louik & Perry PC The Frick Building Ste 200 Pittsburgh PA 15219-6002 E-mail: meyers@meyersmedmal.com

MEYERS, KAREN DIANE, lawyer, educator, corporate officer; b. Cin., July 8, 1950; d. Willard Paul and Camille Jeannette (Schutte) M.; m. William J. Jones, Mar. 27, 1982. BA summa cum laude, Thomas More Coll., 1974; MBA, MEd, Xavier U., 1978; JD, U. Ky., Covington, 1978. Bar: Ohio 1978, Ky. 1978; CLU; CPCU. Clk. to mgr. Baldwin Co., Cin., 1970-78; adj. prof. bus. Thomas More Coll., Crestview Hill, Ky., 1978—; asst. sec., asst. v.p., sr. counsel The Ohio Life Ins. Co., Hamilton, 1978-91; prin. KD Meyers & Assocs., 1991; v.p. Benefit Designs, Inc., 1991-96, Little, Meyers, Garretson & Assocs., Ltd., Cin., 1996—; adj. prof. Meame U., 1998—. Bd. dirs. ARC, Hamilton, 1978-83, vol., 1978—; bd. dirs. YWCA, Hamilton, 1985-91; v.p. Benefit Designs Inc., 1991—. Gardner Found. fellow, 1968-71; recipient Ind. Progress award Bus. & Profl. Women, 1990. Fellow Life Mgmt. Inst. Atlanta; mem. ABA, Soc. Chartered Property Casualty Underwriters (instr. 1987—), Cin. Bar Assn., Butler County Bar Assn., Ohio Bar Assn., Ky. Bar Assn. Roman Catholic. Avocations: aerobics, jogging, crafts. General corporate, Insurance. Home: 7903 Hickory Hill Ln Cincinnati OH 45241-1363

MEYERS, PAMELA SUE, lawyer; b. Lakewood, N.J., June 13, 1951; d. Morris Leon and Isabel (Leibowitz) M.; m. Gerald Stephen Greenberg, Aug. 24, 1975; children: David Stuart Greenberg, Allison Brooke Greenberg. AB with distinction, Cornell U., 1973; JD cum laude, Harvard U., 1976. Bar: N.Y. 1977, Ohio 1990. Assoc. Stroock & Stroock & Lavan, N.Y.C., 1976-80; staff v.p., asst. gen. counsel Am. Premier Underwriters, Inc., Cin., 1980-96; legal counsel Citizens Fed. Bank, Dayton, Ohio, 1997-98; gen. counsel, sec. Mosler Inc., Hamilton, 1998—. Bd. dirs. Hamilton County Alcohol and Drug Addiction Svc. Bd., 1996-2000, Adath Israel Synagogue, 1999—. Mem. Cin. Bar Assn., Harvard Club of Cin. (pres. 1998-99, bd. dirs. 1993-2000), Phi Beta Kappa. Jewish. Avocations: piano, reading, golf. Contracts commercial, General corporate, Mergers and acquisitions. Home: 3633 Carpenters Creek Dr Cincinnati OH 45241-3824 Office: Mosler Inc 8509 Berk Blvd Hamilton OH 45015-2213 E-mail: meyersp@moslerinc.com

MEYERS, WILLIAM VINCENT, lawyer, educator; b. Washington, Jan. 14, 1940; s. Theodore Albert and Alice Mae (Vincent) M.; m. Karen Anne, June 10, 1961; children: Michelle, William Vincent, Jason, Michael. BA, U. Md., 1961; JD, Georgetown U., 1964. Bar: Md. 1964, D.C. 1965, U.S. Supreme Ct. 1978. Assoc. Nylen & Gilmore, Hyattsville, Md., 1964-68, ptnr., 1968-75; pres., mng. officer Meyes, Rodbell and Rosenbaum P.A., Riverdale, Md., 1975—. Atty. Bd. Suprs. of Elections for Prince George's County (Md.), 1969-78; gen. counsel Bank Md., 1978-84, bd. dirs., 1978-84; chmn. County Exec.'s Task Force on Alternative Funding Sources, 1982; co-founding dir., vice-chmn., gen. counsel Cmty. Band Md., 1988-96, chmn. 1996-2001; bd. dirs., gen. counsel, vice-chmn. Cmty Bankshare Md., Inc., 1988-96, chmn. bd., CEO, 1996-2001; lectr. on alcoholic beverage law, estate planning and legis. lobbying to civic groups; trustee Md. Client Security Trust Fund, 1993—; mem. Gov.'s Task Force on Jud. Nominating Commns., 1995, Md. Econ. Devel. Commn., 1995—; bd. dirs. F&M Bank, Md., 2001—. Edtl. bd. Georgetown Law Jour., 1963-64. Bd. dirs. Greater Laurel Area C. of C.; chmn. bus. polit. action com. Prince George's County, 1982-87; bd. dirs. Prince George's Hosp. Ctr. Found. Inc., 1992—, vice-chmn., 1993-99, chmn., 1999—; mem. Md. Port Commn., 2000—; chmn., pres. Govt. House Found. Inc., 1996— Mem. ABA, D.C. Bar Assn., Prince Georges County Bar Assn., Md. State Bar Assn., Am. Judicature Soc., Md. Bar Found., Prince George's C. of C.

(life; pres. 1980-81, award of Excellence 1980, Outstanding Svc. award 1982, 83, Pres.'s award 1983), Balt. Corridor C. of C. (bd. dirs. 1979-84), Congressional Country Club, U. Md. Prince George's County Alumni Assn. (former pres.). Administrative and regulatory, General corporate, Estate planning. Home: 12211 Drews Ct Rockville MD 20854-1135 Office: 6801 Kenilworth Ave Ste 400 Riverdale MD 20737-1331

MEYERSON, CHRISTOPHER CORTLANDT, law scholar; b. Princeton, N.J., July 7, 1962; s. Dean and Beatrice Meyerson; m. Megumi Kawaguchi; 1 child, Kenneth. BA in Govt. magna cum laude, cert. in L.Am. studies, MA in History, Harvard U., 1985; MPhil in Polit. Sci., Columbia U., 1993, JD, 2001; LLM, Kyoto (Japan) U., 1994; JD, Columbia U., 2001. Intern Bur. Inter-Am. Affairs, Office Policy Planning/Coord. U.S. State Dept., Washington, summer 1982; rsch. asst. Harvard U., 1982-83; intern, rschr. macro econ. rsch. dept. Banco Itau, São Paulo, 1983-84; human rights intern Coalition for Homeless, N.Y.C., summer 1988; legal intern gen. counsel Mus. Modern Art, summer 1989; law clk. Office of Chief Counsel for Internat. Commerce U.S. Commerce Dept., Washington, summer 1991; editl. asst. Kyoto Comparative Law Ctr., summer 1994, 95; vis. scholar Associated Kyoto Program, 1996. Summer assoc. Venable, Baetjer, Howard & Civiletti, Washington, 1998; law clk. Office of Chief Counsel for Import Adminstrn., U.S. Commerce Dept., Washington, 1999-2000. Contbr. articles to bus. jours., Columbia Internat. Affairs Online. Mem. Am. Soc. Internat. Law, Soc. Legislation Comparee, Am. Polit. Sci. Assn. (presenter papers ann. meetings), Internat. Studies Assn. (Internat. Polit. Economy Jr. Scholar award 2000, presenter papers ann. meetings), Assn. for Asian Studies (presenter papers ann. meetings), Assn. Japanese Bus. Studies (Young Scholar 1996), Internat. House of Japan. Episcopalian. Home: 7306 Summit Ave Chevy Chase MD 20815-4030

MEYERSON, STANLEY PHILLIP, lawyer; b. Apr. 13, 1916; s. Louis A. and Ella Meyerson; m. Sherry Maxwell, Nov. 30, 1996; children: Marianne Martin, Camilla Meyerson, Margot Ellis, Stanley P. AB, Duke U., 1937, JD, 1939. Bar: S.C. 1939, N.Y. 1940, Ga. 1945, U.S. Supreme Ct. Ptnr. Johnson Hatcher & Meyerson, Atlanta, 1945-55, Hatcher, Meyerson, Oxford & Irvin, Atlanta, 1955-78, Westmoreland, Hall, McGee, Oxford & Meyerson, Atlanta, 1978-88, McGee & Oxford, Atlanta, 1988—. Former adj. prof. Ga. State U.; dir., officer various corps. Contbr. articles to legal jours. Co-founder West Paces Ferry Hosp., Atlanta, Annandale at Suwanee for the Handicapped; trustee Hudson Libr., Inc., Highlands, NC; del. Moscow Conf. Law and Bilateral Econ. Rels., 1990; trustee MetroGroup, Atlanta. Lt. comdr. USNR, 1943—45. Mem. ABA (former mem. professionalism com.), Duke U. Alumni Assn. (former pres. Atlanta chpt.), Ga. Bar Assn. (former chmn. tax com.), Atlanta Bar Assn. (former sec.) General corporate, Entertainment, Estate planning. Home (Summer): PO Box 1541 300 Satulah Rd Highlands NC 28741

MEZVINSKY, EDWARD M. lawyer; b. Ames, Iowa, Jan. 17, 1937; m. Marjorie Margolies; 11 children. BA, U. Iowa, 1960; MA in Polit. Sci., U. Calif., Berkeley, 1963, JD, 1965. State rep. Iowa State Legislature, 1969-70; U.S. congressman 1st Dist., Iowa, 1973-77; U.S. rep. UN Commn. on Human Rights, 1977-79; chmn. Pa. Dem. State Com., 1981-86. Author: A Term to Remember; contbr. articles to law jours. Mem. Pa. Bar Assn., Bar of the Supreme Ct. of U.S., Omicron Delta Kappa. General practice, Private international, Public international. Office: 815 N Woodbine Ave Narberth PA 19072-1430

MEZZULLO, LOUIS ALBERT, lawyer; b. Balt., Sept. 20, 1944; m. Judith Scales, Jan. 2, 1970. BA, U. Md., 1967, MA, 1976; JD, T.C. Williams Law Sch., 1976. Bar: Va. 1976. Sales rep. Humble Oil (name now Exxon), Richmond, Va., 1970-72; acctg. Marcoin, Inc., 1972-73; pvt. practice bookkeeping, tax preparation, 1973-76; assoc. McGuire, Woods, Battle and Boothe, 1976-79; dir. Mezzullo & McCandlish, 1979-2000; mem. Mezzullo & Guare, PLC, 2000—. Contbr. articles to profl. jours. Bd. dirs. Richmond Symphony; former pres. Southampton Citizens Assn., Richmond, 1986. Served with USAR, 1969-75. Mem. ABA (tax sect.), Internat. Acad. Estate and Trust Law, Am. Coll. Trust and Estate Counsel, Am. Coll. Tax Counsel, Va. State Bar (tax sect.), Va. Bar Assn., Am. Bar Found., Va. Law Found., Estate Planning Coun. Richmond, Trust Adminstrs. Coun., Willow Oaks Country Club. General corporate, Estate planning, Corporate taxation. Home: 2961 Westchester Rd Richmond VA 23225-1842 Office: Mezzullo & Guare PLC 6802 Paragon Pl Ste 100 Richmond VA 23230 E-mail: lmezzullo@mezzulloguare.com

MICALE, FRANK JUDE, lawyer; b. Pitts., Jan. 10, 1949; s. Frank Jacob and Catherine Anna (Wagner) M.; m. Jane Sincler Czak. BA, Duquesne U., 1971, JD, 1977. Bar: Pa. 1977, U.S. Dist. Ct. (we. dist.) Pa. 1977, U.S. Ct. Appeals (3rd cir.) 1978. U.S. Supreme Ct. 1986; cert. Nat. Bd. Trial Advocacy. Law clk. to judge U.S. Ct. Appeals (3rd cir.), 1977-78, U.S. Dist. Ct. (we. dist.) Pa., 1978-79; assoc. Egler & Reinstadtler, Pitts., 1979-80; dep. atty. gen., sr. dep. atty. gen. in charge torts litigation sect. western region Office of Atty. Gen. Commonwealth of Pa., 1980-92; pvt. practice, 1992—. Mem. ABA, Am. Arbitration Assn., Pa. Bar Assn., Allegheny County Bar Assn., Acad. Trial Lawyers Allegheny County. General civil litigation, Personal injury, Product liability. Home: 5521 Claybourne St Pittsburgh PA 15232-1634 Office: 200 One Williamsburg Pl Warrendale PA 15086 E-mail: frankmac@msn.com

MICHAEL, DOUGLAS CHARLES, law educator; b. Omaha, Dec. 8, 1957; s. B.B. and Arleen M. (Heinz) M.; m. Susan Lindsey, Jan. 11, 1986; children: Stuart Douglas, Amanda Lindsey. AB, Stanford U., 1979; MBA, U. Calif., Berkeley, 1982, JD, 1983. Bar: Calif. 1984, D.C. 1988. Staff atty. SEC, Washington, 1983-85, commr.'s counsel, 1985-87; assoc. Arnold and Porter, 1987-89; asst. prof. U. Ky. Coll. Law, Lexington, 1989-93, assoc. prof., 1993-97, prof., 1997—. Vis. prof. law U. Fla., 2000. Contbr. articles to legal jours.; author: Legal Accounting: Principles and Applications, 1997. Mem. ABA, Am. Bankruptcy Inst., Order of Coif. Home: 4625 Hickory Creek Dr Lexington KY 40515-1509 Office: U Ky Coll Law Lexington KY 40506-0001 E-mail: michaeld@pop.uky.edu

MICHAEL, JAMES HARRY, JR. federal judge; b. Charlottesville, Va., Oct. 17, 1918; s. James Harry and Reuben (Shelton) m. Barbara E. Puryear, Dec. 18, 1946; children: Jarrett Michael Stephens, Victoria von der Au. BS, U. Va., 1940, LLB, 1942. Bar: Va. 1942. Sole practice, Charlottesville; ptnr. Michael & Musselman, 1946-54, J.H. Michael, Jr., 1954-59, Michael & Dent, 1959-72, Michael, Dent & Brooks Ltd., 1972-74, Michael & Dent, Ltd., 1974-80; assoc. judge Juvenile and Domestic Rels. Ct., Charlottesville, 1954-68; judge U.S. Dist. Ct., 1980-95, sr. judge, 1996—; mem. Va. Senate, 1968-80. Exec. dir. Inst. Pub. Affairs, U. Va., 1952; chmn. Council State Govts., 1975-76, also mem. exec. com.; chmn. So. Legis. Conf., 1974-75. Mem. Charlottesville Sch. Bd., 1951-62; bd. govs. St. Anne-Belfield Sch., 1952-76. Served with USNR, 1942-46; comdr. Res. ret. Wilton Park fellow Wilton Park Conf., Sussex, Eng., 1971 Fellow Am. Bar Found.; mem. ABA, Va. Bar Assn. (v.p. 1956-57), Charlottesville-Albermarle Bar Assn. (pres. 1966-67), Am. Judicature Soc., 4th Jud. Conf., Va. Trial Lawyers Assn. (Va. disting. svc. award 1993), Assn. Trial Lawyers Am., Raven Soc., Sigma Nu Phi, Omicron Delta Kappa. Episcopalian (lay reader). Office: US Dist Ct 255 W Main St Rm 320 Charlottesville VA 22902-5058

MICHAEL, M. BLANE, federal judge; b. Charleston, S.C., Feb. 17, 1943; AB, W.Va. U., 1965; JD, NYU, 1968. Bar: N.Y. 1968, U.S. Dist. Ct. (so. and ea. dists.) N.Y. 1968, W.Va. 1973, U.S. Ct. Appeals (4th cir.) 1974, U.S. Dist. Ct. (no. dist.) W.Va. 1975, U.S. Dist. Ct. (so. dist.) W.Va. 1981. Counsel to Gov. W.Va. John D. Rockefeller IV, 1977-80; atty. Jackson & Kelly, Charleston, W.Va., 1981-93; fed. judge U.S. Ct. Appeals (4th cir.), 1993—. Active 4th Cir. Jud. Conf. Mem. ABA, W.Va. Bar Assn., Kanawha County Bar Assn., Phi Beta Kappa. Office: US Circuit Judge Robert C Byrd US Courthouse 300 Virginia St E Rm 7404 Charleston WV 25301-2504

MICHAEL, ROBERT ROY, lawyer; b. Washington, Dec. 28, 1946; s. Colin Lamar and Mary Elva (Wilson) M.; m. Carolyn Ann Sandberg, Dec. 20, 1975; children: Shawn Robert, Erika Rae, Andrew Jon. BA, George Washington U., 1968, JD, 1971. Bar: Md. 1972, D.C. 1972, U.S. Dist. Ct. Md. 1972, U.S. Dist. Ct. D.C. 1972, U.S. Ct. Appeals (4th cir.) 1972, U.S. Supreme Ct. 1973. Assoc. A.D. Massengill, Esq., Gaithersburg, Md., 1972-73, Massengill & Jersin, Gaithersburg, 1973-74; ptnr. Massengill, Jersin & Michael, 1974-77; pres. Robert R. Michael, Chartered, Bethesda, Md., 1977-84; ptnr. Shadoan & Michael L.L.P., Rockville, 1984—. Lectr. continued profl. edn. of lawyers Md. Inst., Balt., 1984—, continuing legal edn., Rockville, 1984—, continuing legal edn. of Montgomery and Prince George's Counties; lectr. various schs. and bar assns., 1983—. Author: Videotape Depositions, 1987, Comparative Liability; co-author: Automobile Accident Deskbook; co-editor: The Annual Review of Maryland Case Law, 1983; contbr. Product Liability in Maryland, articles to profl. jours. Mem. legis. taskforce product liability, Annapolis, 1980; trustee Redland Bapt. Ch.; founder Trial Lawyers for Pub. Justice, 1982. Named Sect. Chmn. of Yr., Montgomery County, 1986-87. Mem. ABA, ATLA (gov. 1984-86, del. 1982-83), Md. Trial Lawyers Assn. (pres. 1982-83, lectr.), Montgomery County Bar Assn. (jud. selections com. chmn. 1990-91, exec. com. 1991-93, trial cts. jud. nominating commn., 1992-94, adminstrn. of Justice Comm., 1993-94, pres. 1995), Montgomery County Bar Assn. Found. (pres. bar leaders 1996-97), Am. Bar Assn. Found., Assn. Plaintiffs Trial Lawyers Met. Washington, Civil Justice Found. (trustee 1987-89), Md. State Bar (jud. selections com. 1988-94, litigation sect. coun. 1989—, chair 1997—), Am. Inns Ct. (exec. com. 1988—, chpt. LXI program chmn. 1988-89, organizer, pres. 1990, bd. govs., founder Montgomery chpt. program chair 1989-90, pres. 1990-91), Nat. Inst. Advocacy (lectr.), Am. Bd. Trial Advocates, Am. Coll. Trial Lawyers, Internat. Acad. Trial Lawyers. Democrat. Baptist. Personal injury, Product liability, Professional liability. Home: 8921 Brink Rd Gaithersburg MD 20882-1013 Office: Shadoan & Michael LLP 108 Park Ave Rockville MD 20850-2694

MICHAELIS, KAREN LAUREE, law educator; b. Milw., Mar. 30, 1950; d. Donald Lee and Ethel Catherine (Stevens) M.; m. Larry Severtson, Aug. 2, 1980 (div. Aug. 1982); 1 child, Quinn Alexandra Michaelis. BA, U. Wis., 1972, BS, 1974; MA, Calif. State U., L.A., 1979; MS, U. Wis., 1985, PhD, 1988, JD, 1989. Bar: Wis., U.S. Dist. Ct. (we. dist.) Wis. Asst. prof. law Hofstra U., Hempstead, N.Y., 1990-93; assoc. prof. law Ill. State U., Normal, 1993-95; asst. prof. law Wash. State U., Pullman, 1995—. Author: Reporting Child Abuse: A Guide to Mandatory Requirements for School Personnel, 1993, Theories of Liability for Teacher Sexual Misconduct, 1996, Postmodern Perspectives and Shifting Legal Paradigms: Searching For A Critical Theory of Juvenile Justice, 1998; Student As Enemy: A Legal Construct of the Other, 1999; editor Ill. Sch. Law Quarterly, 1993-95; mem. editl. bd. Nat. Assn. Profs. of Ednl. Adminstrn., 1994-95, Planning and Changing, 1993-95, Jour. Sch. Leadership, 1991-99, People & Education: The Human Side of Edn., 1991-96. Mem. ABA, State Bar of Wis., Nat. Coun. Profs. Ednl. Adminstrn. (program com. 1994-95, morphet fund com. 1993—), Nat. Orgn. Legal Problems in Edn. (publs. com. 1993—, program com. 1995, exec. bd.), Edn. Law Assn. (bd. dirs. 1998-2000, co-chair publs. com. 1998—). Office: Wash State U Dept Ed Leadership & Co Psy Pullman WA 99164-0001

MICHAELS, BEVERLY ANN, lawyer; b. Elizabeth, N.J., Dec. 12, 1929; d. Samuel and Pauline Dorothy (Shapiro) Kreisberg; m. Martin M. Michaels, Sept. 8, 1951; children: Steven Scott, Edward Alan, Julie Cara. BA, Syracuse U., 1951, JD, 1953. Bar: N.Y. 1953, U.S. Dist. Ct. (no. dist.) N.Y. 1957, U.S. Dist. Ct. Hawaii 1985, U.S. Ct. Appeals (2nd cir.) 1963, U.S. Supreme Ct. 1980. Assoc. Sidney H. Greenberg, Esq., Syracuse, N.Y., 1953-55; pvt. practice, 1955-56; ptnr. Michaels & Michaels, 1956—. Lectr., adj. prof. Syracuse U., 1975-83; appointee 5th jud. dist. grievance com. 1988-94. Bd. dirs. Planned Parenthood, 1972-77, pres. 1975-76; del. Nat. and Regional Conv., 1975-76; jud. candidate Onon. County Family Ct., Syracuse, 1978; bd. dirs. Legal Svcs. Cen. N.Y., v.p., 1989-95. Mem. ATLA, Onondaga County Bar Found. (pres. 1990-92), Onondaga County Trial Lawyers Assn., Onondaga Bar Assn. (bd. dirs. 1981-83, chmn. judiciary com. 1988-90), N.Y. State Bar Assn., N.Y. State Trial Lawyers Assn., N.Y. Womens Bar Assn. (sec. 1980), Zonta Internat., Order of Eastern Star. Democrat. General civil litigation, Estate planning, Personal injury. Office: Michaels & Michaels State Tower Bldg 109 S Warren St Ste 902 Syracuse NY 13202-1703

MICHAELS, GARY DAVID, lawyer; b. Pitts., Apr. 27, 1955; s. Edgar Wolfe and Norma Flora (Barker) M.; m. Joan Marie Kelly, June 9, 1984; children: Jeffrey Thomas, Abbey Rose. BA, U. Pa., 1977; JD, George Washington U., 1980. Bar: D.C. 1980, U.S. Dist. Ct. D.C. 1981, U.S. Ct. Appeals (D.C. cir.) 1981, U.S. Ct. Appeals (4th cir.) 1985, U.S. Supreme Ct. 1985, U.S. Ct. Appeals (1st cir.) 1987. Assoc. Troy, Malin & Pottinger, Washington, 1981-82, Ballard, Spahr, Andrews & Ingersoll, Washington, 1982-84, Krivit & Krivit P.C., Washington, 1984-98, Fed. Comm. Commn., Washington, 1998—. Bd. dirs. Hinkel-Hofmann Supply Co. Inc., Pitts., 1976—. Mem. The George Washington Law Rev., 1978-80. Vol. legal staff Gary Hart Presdl. Campaign, Washington, 1983, field coord. N.H. and Pa., 1984; bd. dirs. Van Ness South Tenants Assn., Inc., 1986-88, v.p., 1987, pres., 1988, of counsel, 1989-90. Mem. ABA, D.C. Bar Assn. Democrat. Jewish. Administrative and regulatory, Federal civil litigation, Communications. Home: 11922 Coldstream Dr Potomac MD 20854-3602 Office: Fed Comm Commn 445 12th St SW Washington DC 20554-0001 E-mail: gmichael@fcc.gov

MICHAELS, KEVIN RICHARD, lawyer; b. Buffalo, Feb. 9, 1960; s. Richard Ronald and Marlene Constance (Mnich) M.; m. Beatrice Mary Szeliga, Jan. 15, 1983; 1 child, Jaena René. BS in Govt., U. Houston, 1987; JD, South Tex. Coll. Law, 1992. Bar: Tex. 1992, U.S. Dist. Ct. (so. dist.) Tex. 1996. Ct. coord. Harris County Dist. Clk., Houston, 1985-88; paralegal O'Quinn, Kerensky, McAninch & Laminack, 1988-92, atty., 1992-97, Davis & Shank, P.C., Houston, 1997-99; sole practitioner, 2000—. Recipient Commendation medal U.S. Army, 1984, Oak Leaf Cluster, 1985, Good Conduct medal, 1985. Mem. ATLA (Tex. gov. New Lawyers div. 1994-97), Houston Bar Assn., Tex. Trial Lawyers Assn., Tex. Bar Assn. Avocations: golf, camping. Federal civil litigation, State civil litigation. Office: 11767 Katy Fwy Ste 730 Houston TX 77079

MICHAELS, RICHARD EDWARD, lawyer; b. Chgo., June 10, 1952; s. Benjamin and Lillian (Borawski) Mikolajczewski; m. Karen Lynn Belau Michaels, May 17, 1980; children: Jonathan R., Timothy R., Matthew R. BS in Commerce summa cum laude, DePaul U., 1973; JD, Northwestern U., 1977. Bar: Ill. 1977, U.S. Dist. Ct. (no. dist.) Ill. 1977, U.S. Ct. Appeals (7th cir.) 1977; CPA, Ill. Acct. Touche Ross & Co., Chgo., 1973-74; assoc. Schuyler, Roche & Zwirner and predecessor firm Hubachek & Kelly Ltd., 1977-83; ptnr. Schuyler, Roche & Zwirner, 1983—, pres., 1994—. Mem. Northwestern U. Law Rev., 1976-77. Mem. mission bd. St. Andrew's Luth. Ch., Park Ridge, Ill., 1983-87, chmn. visitation com., 1989, vice chmn. congregation, 1990-92, chmn. congregation, 1992-94. Mem. ABA, Internat. Bar Assn., Ill. Bar Assn., Chgo. Bar Assn., DePaul U. Alumni Assn., DePaul U. Boosters, Chgo. Athletic Assn., Northwestern Club, C.A.A. Club, Beta Gamma Sigma, Pi Gamma Mu, Beta Alpha Psi. Lutheran. Avocations: photography, golf. Antitrust, General corporate, Private international. Home: 808 Elm St Park Ridge IL 60068-3312 Office: Schuyler Roche & Zwirner 130 E Randolph St Ste 3800 Chicago IL 60601-6342 E-mail: rmichaels@srzlaw.com

MICHAELSON, BENJAMIN, JR. lawyer, director; b. Annapolis, Md., May 30, 1936; s. Benjamin and Naomi Madora (Dill) M.; m. Frances Means Blackwell, Apr. 12, 1986; children: Benjamin, Robert Wendell. BA, U. Va., 1957; JD, U. Md., 1962. Bar: Md. 1962, U.S. Dist. Ct. Md. 1976. Assoc. Goodman, Bloom & Michaelson, Annapolis, Md., 1962-63; atty. pvt. practice, 1963-73, 77-81; sr. ptnr. Michaelson & Christhilf, 1973-77; ptnr. Michaelson & Simmons, 1982-86, Michaelson & Newell, Annapolis, 1987-88, Michaelson, Krause & Ferris, Annapolis, 1988-91; atty. pvt. practice, 1991-2000; of counsel McNamee, Hosea, Jernigan & Kim, 2000—. Pres. Michaelson Title & Escrow Co., 1993-2001; gen. counsel, dir. Annapolis Fed. Savs., 1965-94 Counsel Anne Arundel County (Md.) Bd. Edn., 1966-76; mem. vestry St. Anne's Episcopal Ch., Annapolis, 1997—, sr. warden, 1999—. Lt. U.S. Army, 1957-59. Fellow Am. Coll. Mortgage Attys.; mem. Md. Bar Assn. (chmn. real property, planning and zoning sect. coun. 1982-84, grievance commn. inquiry panel 1976-85, vice chmn. 1983-85, grievance commn. rev. bd. 1985-88), Anne Arundel County Bar Assn., Jaycees (Md. state legal counsel 1964-65, nat. dir. 1965-66, Outstanding Young Men Am. 1995), Sailing Club Chesapeake (commodore 1982), Rotary (pres. 1975-76, Paul Harris fellow), Delte Thete Phi. Republican. Episcopalian. Banking, Probate, Real property. Home: 1612 Winchester Rd Annapolis MD 21401 Office: 705 Melvin Ave Ste 102 Annapolis MD 21401-1534

MICHAELSON, MARTIN, lawyer; b. Boston, Apr. 12, 1943; s. Eliot D. and Charlotte (Selib) M.; m. Anne Taylor, Aug. 30, 1987; children: Andrew M., Daniel M.; stepchildren: Rachel T., Hannah T. BA, U. Chgo., 1965; JD, Boston Coll., 1968. Bar: N.Y. 1968, D.C. 1973, U.S. Supreme Ct. 1973, Mass. 1983, U.S. Dist. Ct. N.Y. 1969, D.C. 1973, U.S. Ct. Appeals (1st, 2d, 3d, 4th, 6th and 9th cirs.). Atty. Cravath, Swaine & Moore, N.Y.C., 1968-71; legis. asst. Congressman Robert F. Drinan, Washington, 1971-73; atty. Hogan & Hartson, 1973-76, ptnr., 1976-83, 89—. Dep. gen. counsel Harvard U., Cambridge, Mass., 1983-88, univ. counsel, 1989, lectr. Harvard Grad. Sch. of Education, 1999. Columnist Trusteeship mag. Administrative and regulatory, General civil litigation, General corporate. Office: Hogan & Hartson Columbia Square 555 13th St NW Ste 800E Washington DC 20004-1161 E-mail: mmichaelson@hhlaw.com

MICHAELSON, PETER LEE, lawyer; b. N.Y.C., Aug. 29, 1952; BS in Elec. Engring. and Econs., Carnegie-Mellon U., 1974, MSEE, 1975; JD, Duquesne U., 1979; LLM in Trade Regulation, NYU, 1985; postgrad., Harvard U., 1993, 96, 97, 96, 97, 99. Bar: Pa. 1979, N.J. 1980, U.S. Patent and Trademark Office 1980, U.S. Dist. Ct. N.J. 1980, U.S. Ct. Claims 1980, U.S. Ct. Mil. Appeals 1980, U.S. Tax Ct. 1980, U.S. Ct. Appeals (3d cir.) 1981, U.S. Ct. Appeals (fed. cir.) 1983, N.Y. 1986, U.S. Supreme Ct. 1986, Alaska 2000. Electronics project engr. Control Systems Research, Inc., Pitts., 1975-76; electronics devel. engr. Aluminum Co. Am., Alcoa Tech. Ctr., Prodn. Equip. Lab., Pitts., 1976-77, Rockwell Internat. Corp., Pitts., 1977-79; corp. patent atty., mem. patent and legal staff Bell Telephone Labs., Holmdel, N.J., 1979-82; patent atty. Pennie & Edmonds, N.Y.C., 1982-84; founding, sr. ptnr. Michaelson & Wallace, Counsellors at Law, Red Bank, N.J., Ventura, Calif., 1984—. Mem. disting. panel neutrals tech. ICANN domain names and Y2K panels CPR Inst. Dispute Resolution, N.Y.C.; approved mediator/arbitrator in intellectual property and ICANN domain name and keyword disputes World Intellectual Property Orgn., Geneva; arbitrator ICANN domain name and keyword disputes, arbitrator/mediator on-line disputes eResolution, Montreal, Que., Canada; arbitrator ICANN domain name disputes Nat. Arbitration Forum, Mpls.; arbitrator London Ct. Internat. Arbitration, N.Am. Coun., Internat. C.of C., Paris, Internat. Ct. Arbitration, U.S. Coun. for Internat. Bus., N.Y.C.; mediator N.J. Superior Ct.; mem. CPR Inst. Dispute Resolution; master Justice Marie Garibaldi Am. Inn of Ct. for Alternative Dispute Resolution; sponsoring mem. Am. Arbitration Assn.; mem. Ctr. for Effective Dispute Resolution (CEDR), London. Contbr. articles to profl. jours. Mem. Sch. Budget Adv. Com., Rumson, N.J., 1981-85, Zoning Bd. of Adjustment, Rumson, 1988-93. Mem.: AIPPI, Am. Arbitration Assn. (arbitration-tech. panel, N.Y.C.), Am. Intellectual Property Law Assn., N.J. Intellectual Property Law Assn., Chartered Inst. Arbitrators, Soc. Profls. in Dispute Resolution. Alternative dispute resolution, Patent, Trademark and copyright. Home: 15 Holly Tree Ln Rumson NJ 07760-1950 Office: Michaelson & Wallace 328 Newman Springs Rd Parkway 109 Office Ctr PO Box 8489 Red Bank NJ 07701-8489 E-mail: pmichaelson@mandw.com

MICHALAK, EDWARD FRANCIS, lawyer; b. Evanston, Ill., Sept. 6, 1937; s. Leo Francis Michalak and Helen Sophie (Wolinski) Krakowski. BSBA, Northwestern U., 1959; LLB, Harvard U., 1962. Bar: Ill. 1962. Assoc. McDermott, Will & Emery, Chgo., 1963-69, ptnr., 1969—. Served to sgt. USAR, 1962-68. Mem. Ill. Bar Assn., Chgo. Bar Assn., Beta Gamma Sigma, Beta Alpha Psi. Roman Catholic. Avocations: golf, opera. Corporate taxation, Personal income taxation. Home: 3455 Harrison St Evanston IL 60201-4953 Office: McDermott Will & Emery 227 W Monroe St Ste 3100 Chicago IL 60606-5096 E-mail: emichalak@mwe.com

MICHALIK, JOHN JAMES, legal educational association executive; b. Bemidji, Minn., Aug. 1, 1945; s. John and Margaret Helen (Pafko) M.; m. Diane Marie Olson, Dec. 21, 1968; children: Matthew John, Nicole, Shane. BA, U. Minn., 1967, JD, 1970. Legal editor Lawyers Coop. Pub. Co., Rochester, N.Y., 1970-75; dir. continuing legal edn. Wash. State Bar Assn., Seattle, 1975-81, exec. dir., 1981-91; asst. dean devel. and cmty. rels. Sch. of Law U. Wash., 1991-95; exec. dir., CEO Assn. Legal Adminstrs., Vernon Hills, Ill., 1995—. Fellow Coll. Law Practice Mgmt.; mem. Am. Soc. Assn. Execs., Am. Mgmt. Assn., Nat. Trust Hist. Preservation, Coll. Club Seattle. Lutheran. Office: Assn Legal Adminstrs #325 175 E Hawthorn Pkwy Ste 325 Vernon Hills IL 60061-1460

MICHAL-SMITH, SUSAN, lawyer; b. Louisville, May 22, 1953; d. Stanley Edward and Evelyn Lee (Glazer) Smith; m. Steven Linder, Sept. 5, 1982 (div. Mar. 1992); 1 child, Stuart Linder. BA summa cum laude, U. Cin., 1975; JD, Emory U., 1978. Bar: D.C., Ga. Atty. Somers & Altenbach, Atlanta, 1978-79, IRS, Washington, 1980-88; sr. atty. U.S. GAO, 1988—. Instr. Office of Legal Edn. Inst., Dept. of Justice, Washington, 1986-89. Mem. D.C. Bar Assn., State Bar Ga. Assn., Phi Beta Kappa. Office: US GAO 441 G St NW Washington DC 20548-0001

MICHEL, CLIFFORD LLOYD, lawyer, investment executive; b. N.Y.C., Aug. 9, 1939; s. Clifford William and Barbara Lloyd (Richards) M.; m. Betsy Shirley, June 6, 1964; children: Clifford Fredrick, Jason Lloyd, Katherine Beinecke. AB cum laude, Princeton U., 1961; JD, Yale U., 1964. Bar: N.Y. 1964, U.S. Dist. Ct. (so. dist.) N.Y. 1968, U.S. Ct. Appeals (2d cir.) 1967, U.S. Supreme Ct. 1972. Assoc. Cahill Gordon & Reindel, N.Y.C., 1964-67, Paris, 1967-69, N.Y.C., 1969-71, ptnr. Paris, 1972-76, N.Y.C., 1976-2001, sr. counsel, 2001—. Bd. dirs. Alliance Capital Mgmt. Mut. Funds, Placer Dome Inc. Bd. dirs. Jockey Hollow Found., Michel Found., St. Mark's Sch., Morristown Meml. Hosp., Meml. Health Found., Atlantic Health Sys. Mem. ABA, FBA, N.Y. State Bar Assn., New York County Lawyers Assn., Am. Soc. Internat. Law, Racquet and Tennis Club, River Club, The Links, Shinnecock Hills Golf Club, Somerset Hills

Country Club, Essex Hunt Club, Sankaty Head Golf Club (Mass.), Golf de Morfontaine (France), Travellers Club (Paris), Loch Lomond Club (Scotland), Nantucket Golf Club, Mayacama Golf Club. Republican. General corporate, Private international, Securities. Office: Cahill Gordon & Reindel 80 Pine St Fl 17 New York NY 10005-1790

MICHEL, PAUL REDMOND, federal judge; b. Philadelphia, Pa., Feb. 3, 1941; s. Lincoln M. and Dorothy (Kelley) M.; m. Sally Ann Clark, 1965 (div. 1987); children: Sarah Elizabeth, Margaret Kelley; m. Elizabeth Morgan, 1989. BA, Williams Coll., 1963; JD, U. Va., 1966. Bar: Pa. 1967, U.S. Supreme Ct., 1970. Asst. dist. atty. Dist. Atty's Office, Phila., 1967-71, dep. dist. atty. for investigations, 1972-74; asst. spl. prosecutor Watergate investigation Dept. Justice, Washington, 1974-75, dep. chief pub. integrity sect., Criminal div. and prosecutor "Koreagate" investigation, 1976-78, assoc. dep. atty. gen., 1978-81, acting dep. atty. gen., 1979-80; asst. counsel intelligence com. U.S. Senate, 1975-76, counsel and adminstrv. asst. to Sen. Arlen Specter, 1981-88; judge U.S. Ct. Appeals (Fed. cir.), Washington, 1988—. Instr. appellate practice and procedure George Wash. U. Nat. Law Ctr., 1991—, appellate advocacy John Marshall Law Sch., Chgo. 2d lt. USAR, 1966-72. Office: US Ct Appeals Fed Cir 717 Madison Pl NW Washington DC 20439*

MICHELI, CHRISTOPHER MICHAEL, lawyer; b. Sacramento, Mar. 14, 1967; s. Paul Lothar and Vima Nina (de Marchi) M.; m. Liza Marie Hernandez, Sept. 4, 1994; 2 children: Morgan, Francesca. Student, George Washington U., 1985-86; BA in Polit. Sci. and Pub. Svc., U. Calif., Davis, 1989; JD, McGeorge Sch. Law, 1992. Bar: Calif. 1992, U.S. Dist. Ct. (no. and cen. dists.) 1993, (ea. dist.) 1992, U.S. Ct. Appeals (D.C. and 9th cirs.) 1993. Assoc. Bell & Hiltachk, Sacramento, 1992-93; gen. counsel Calif. Mfrs. Assn., 1993-94; atty., legis. advocate Carpenter, Snodgrass & Assocs., 1994—. Mem. editl. adv. bd. State Income Tax Alert, Ga., 1997—, Interstate Tax Report, 1997—, Sacramento Lawyer, 1995-99; legis. com. Inst. Govtl. Advocates, Sacramento, 1994-95; adv. bd. Franchise Tax Bd., Sacramento, 1996—. Columnist The Daily Recorder, 1994—; contbr. articles to newspapers and profl. jours. Bd. dirs. Jesuit H.S. Alumni Assn., Sacramento, 1992—; soccer referee and coach Del Dayo Sch., Carmichael, Calif., 1994—. William D. James Found. scholar, 1989. Mem. ABA, State Bar Calif., Sacramento County Bar Assn., Phi Delta Phi. Democrat. Roman Catholic. Avocations: politics, martial arts, travel, soccer. Administrative and regulatory, Legislative, State and local taxation. Home: 3335 Sunnybank Ln Carmichael CA 95608-5913 Office: Carpenter Snodgrass Assocs 1201 K St Ste 710 Sacramento CA 95814-3973 E-mail: cmicheli@carpentersnodgrass.com

MICHELSTETTER, STANLEY HUBERT, lawyer; b. Milw., July 8, 1946; s. Donald Lee and Gloria (Menke) M.; m. Joyce Bladow, Apr. 29, 1972; children: Chad S., Chris E. BA in Math., U. Wis., 1968, JD, 1972. Bar: Wis. 1972, U.S. Dist. Ct. (we. dist.) Wis. 1972. Staff atty. Wis. Employment Rels. Commn., Milw., 1972-80; pvt. practice, 1980—; adminstrv. law judge, equal rights div. adminstrat. Wis. Dept Industry, Labor & Human Rels., 1992-93. Chmn. North Shore Rep. Club, Milw., 1984-86. Served to 2d lt. Wis. N.G., 1968-74. Mem. Wis. Bar Assn. (chmn. 1993), Milw. Bar Assn., Nat. Acad. Arbitrators, Indsl. Rels. Rsch. Assn. (bd. dirs. 1987—), Rotary. Republican. Jewish. Alternative dispute resolution, General practice, Labor. Home: 1500 W Green Brook Rd Milwaukee WI 53217-1515 Office: 1749 N Prospect Ave Milwaukee WI 53202-1966 also: PMB 37 5185 Broadway Gary IN 46409-2708 E-mail: stan@expcpc.com

MICHENER, JOHN ATHOL, lawyer; b. St. Louis, Mar. 17, 1947; s. Athol John and Anne Everett (Purnell) M.; m. Kibble Lee Jackson, June 19, 1970; children: Christopher Athol, Amelia Morgan, Dorian Everett. BA, Vanderbilt U., 1969; JD, U. Mo., Columbia, 1974. Bar: Mo. 1974, U.S. Dist. Ct. (ea. dist.) Mo. 1975, U.S. Ct. Appeals (8th cir.) 1985. Assoc. Evans & Dixon, St. Louis, 1974-81, ptnr., 1982—. Recipient Lon O. Hocker Meml. Trial Lawyer award Mo. Bar Found. 1980. Mem. 22d Jud. Cir. Bar Com. State civil litigation, Personal injury, Product liability. Office: Sandberg Phoenix and Von Gontard One City Centre 15th Fl Saint Louis MO 63101 E-mail: jam@spvg.com

MICHENFELDER, ALBERT A. lawyer; b. St. Louis, July 21, 1926; s. Albert A. and Ruth Josephine (Donahue) M.; m. Lois Barbara Sullivan, Sept. 03, 1949 (div. May 2, 1967); children: Michael J., Ann C. Michenfelder Yancey, Elizabeth D. Michenfelder Brown; m. Ramona Jo Dysart, July 12, 1968 (dec. Jan. 2, 1998); 1 child, Julie D. Michenfelder Wolfe. B of Naval Sci., Marquette U., 1946; LLB, St. Louis U., 1950. Bar: Mo. 1950, U.S. Dist. Ct. (ea. dist.) Mo. 1950, U.S. Supreme Ct. 1975. Assoc. Flynn & Challis, St. Louis, 1950-54; pvt. practice, 1954-55; of counsel Husch & Eppenberger LLC. Mem. 21st Cir. Jud. Commn., St. Louis, 1981-87. Contbr. articles to profl. jours. City atty. City of Webster Groves, Mo., 1966-79; mem. John Marshall Club, St. Louis. Lt. (j.g.) USNR, 1944-47. Mem. Mo. Bar Assn., Bar. Assn. Met. St. Louis, St. Louis County Bar Assn. (pres. 1966), Westborough Country Club. Republican. Avocations: golf, tennis. Appellate, General civil litigation, Land use and zoning (including planning). Office: Husch & Eppenberger LLC 231 S Bemiston Clayton MO 63105-1914 Fax: (314) 727-2824. E-mail: al.michenfelder@husch.com

MICHIE, DANIEL BOORSE, JR. lawyer; b. Phila., July 28, 1922; s. Daniel Boorse and Mae (Mueller) M.; m. Barbara F. Maddox, Aug. 29, 1970. BS, Harvard U., 1943; LLB, U. Va., 1948. Bar: Pa. 1949. Lawyer, Phila., 1949-94; assoc. Harry J. Alker (Esq.), 1949, Kephart & Kephart, 1950-51, Fell & Spalding, 1952-53, ptnr., 1954-68, Fell, Spalding, Goff & Rubin, 1969-82, Fell & Spalding, 1982-94; of counsel Richard W. Stevens, Esq., Jenkintown, Pa., 1994-2001; spl. master U.S. Ct. Appeals (3d cir.), 1970—; solicitor Twp. Abington, Pa., 1958-78. Pres. Phila. Council Internat. Visitors, 1957-60, chmn., 1979-81; pres. Phila. Crime Commn., 1960-63, Phila. Fellowship Commn., 1970-71; chmn. Pa. Adv. Com. on Probation, 1966-92, Bd. Phila. Prisons, 1968-71 Pres. Nat. Assn. Citizens Crime Commns., 1961-62, Unitarian Universalist Svc. Com., 1969-72; regional co-chmn. NCCJ, 1967-71, nat. bd. govs., 1971-80, nat. trustee, 1968-98, nat. exec. bd., 1981-88, nat. advisor, 1998—; vice chmn. Southeastern Pa. chpt. ARC, 1978-82; bd. dirs. Urban League Phila., 1981-83; bd. dirs. Valley Forge coun. Boy Scouts Am., 1955-84, adv. bd., 1984-96, adv. coun. Cradle of Liberty coun., 1996-2001; mem. St. Andrew's Soc., counselor, 1989-95; mem. Friendly Sons of St. Patrick, counselor, 1989-98. Lt. USNR, 1943-46. Mem. ABA (chmn. organized crime com. 1964-65), Phila. Bar Assn. (gov. 1970-72), Pa. Bar Assn. (ho. of dels. 1971-2000), Am. Coll. Real Estate Lawyers, Fed. Bar Assn., Am. Judicature Soc., Navy League (dir. Phila. 1967-73, v.p. 1973-76, pres. 1976-78, nat. dir. 1977-83). Republican. Unitarian Universalist (ch. pres. 1961-62, dist. pres. 1966-69). General corporate, Probate, Real property. Home and Office: PO Box 522722 Marathon Shores FL 33052-2722

MICKEL, JOSEPH THOMAS, lawyer; b. Monroe, La., Nov. 12, 1951; s. Toufick and Ruth Ella (Phelps) M.; m. Carlene Elise Nickens, Dec. 10, 1981 (div.); children: Thomas, Matthew. BA, La. State U., 1975; postgrad., Tulane U., 1977-78; JD, So. U., 1979. Bar: La. 1979, U.S. Dist. Ct. (mid. dist.) La. 1981, U.S. Ct. Appeals (5th cir.) 1981, U.S. Dist. Ct. (we. dist.) La. 1983, U.S. Ct. Mil. Appeals 1985, U.S. Supreme Ct. 1985. Staff atty. Pub. Defenders Office, Baton Rouge, 1979-80; assoc. Law Offices of Michael Fugler, 1981; asst. dist. atty. La. 4th Jud. Dist. Atty.'s Office, Monroe, 1982-89; ptnr. Bruscato, Loomis & Street, 1984-85; Asst. U.S. Atty. Western Dist., U.S. Atty.'s Office, Lafayette, 1989—. Adj. prof. Northeast La. U., Monroe, 1988; mem. U.S. Dept. Justice Organized Crime Drug Task Force, 1992-93; instr. Acadiana Law Enforcement Tng. Acad., U. Lafayette La., 1995—; asst. bar examiner, com. on bar admissions Supreme Ct. State of La. Elder Presbyn. Ch., 1995—. Republican. Avocations: trapshooting, skeetshooting, bird hunting, fishing. Home: PO Box 91961 Lafayette LA 70509-1961 Office: US Atty Office 800 Lafayette St Ste 2200 Lafayette LA 70501-6865 E-mail: joseph.nickel@usdoj.gov

MIDDLEBROOK, STEPHEN BEACH, lawyer; b. Hartford, Conn., 1937; BA, Yale U., 1958, LLB, 1961. Bar: Conn. 1961. Counsel Aetna Life and Casualty Co., Hartford, Conn., 1969-71, asst. gen. counsel, 1971-78, corp. sec., 1973-83, v.p., gen. counsel, 1981-88, sr. v.p., gen. counsel, 1988-90, sr. v.p., exec. counsel, 1990-94; spl. counsel Day, Berry & Howard, 1995—. Vis. fellow Rand, Santa Monica, Calif., 1994. General corporate, Insurance. Office: Day Berry & Howard City Place I Hartford CT 06103-3499 E-mail: sbmiddlebrook@dbh.com

MIDDLEDITCH, LEIGH BENJAMIN, JR. lawyer, educator; b. Detroit, Sept. 30, 1929; s. Leigh Benjamin and Hope Tiffin (Noble) M.; m. Betty Lou Givens, June 27, 1953; children: Leigh III, Katherine Middleditch McDonald, Andrew B. BA, U. Va., 1951, LLB, 1957. Bar: Va. 1957. Assoc. James H. Michael, Jr., Charlottesville, Va., 1957-59; ptnr. Battle, Neal, Harris, Minor & Williams, 1959-68; legal adviser U. Va., 1968-72; ptnr. McGuire, Woods, Battle & Boothe (now McGuire Woods LLP), 1972-99, of counsel, 2000—; v.p. McGuire Woods Cons. LLC, 2001—. Lectr. Grad. Bus. Sch., U. Va., Charlottesville, 1958-94, lectr. Law Sch., 1970-90. Co-author: Virginia Civil Procedure, 1978, 2d edition, 1992; contbr. articles to profl. jours. Chmn. U. Va. Health Svcs. Found., 1988-97; bd. mgrs. U. Va. Alumni, 1994—, pres., 2000-01; bd. dirs., chmn. Va. Health Care Found., 1997-98; trustee Claude Moore Found., 1991—; mem. Va. Health Planning Bd., 1989—; bd. visitors U. Va., 1990-91; trustee Thomas Jefferson Meml. Found., Monticello, 1994—. Fellow Am. Bar Found., Va. Bar Found., Am. Coll. Tax Counsel; mem. ABA (bd. govs. 1999—), Va. State Bar (coun., chmn. bd. govs. various sects.), Charlottesville-Albemarle Bar Assn. (pres. 1979-80), U. Va. Law Sch. Alumni Assn. (pres. 1979-81), U.S. C. of C. (bd. dirs. 1998—), Va. C. of C. (pres. 1988-90), Omicron Delta Kappa. Episcopalian Estate planning, Non-profit and tax-exempt organizations, Probate. Office: McGuire Woods LLP PO Box 1288 Charlottesville VA 22902-1288

MIDDLETON, JACK BAER, lawyer; b. Phila., Jan. 13, 1929; s. Harry C. and Mildred Cornell (Baer) M.; m. Ann Dodge, Aug. 22, 1953; children: Susan D., Jack B. Jr., Peter C. AB, Lafayette Coll., 1950; JD cum laude, Boston U., 1956. Bar: N.H. 1956, U.S. Dist. Ct. Vt. 1988, U.S. Ct. Appeals (1st cir.) 1957, U.S. Supreme Ct. 1972. Assoc. McLane, Graf, Raulerson & Middleton, Manchester, N.H., 1956-62, ptnr., dir., 1962—. Spl. justice Merrimack (N.H.) Dist. Ct., 1964-87; bd. dirs. Greater Manchester Devel. Corp., 1983-95; commr. Uniform State Laws, 1971-74; trustee New Eng. Law Inst., 1977-80. Author: (with others) Summary of New Hampshire Law, 1964, Compendium of New Hampshire Law, 1969, Trial of a Wrongful Death Action in New Hampshire, 1977; editor Boston U. Law Rev., 1954-56; contbr. articles to legal jours. Mem. Mt. Washington Commn., 1969—, Bedford (N.H.) Sch. Bd., 1960-66; mem. adv. bd. Merrimack Valley Coll.; trustee, sec. Mt. Washington Obs., 1957—; chmn. bd. trustees White Mountain Sch., 1976-79; campaign chmn. United Way Greater Manchester, 1987, bd. dirs., 1986-92, chmn., 1990-91; bd. dirs. N.H. Pub. Radio, 1988-91; bd. govs. N.H. Pub. TV, 1994—, chmn., 1997-99. Sgt. USMCR, 1950-52. Fellow Am. Coll. Trial Lawyers (chmn. N.H. sect. 1988-90), Am. Bar Found. (life); mem. ABA (ho. dels. 1984—, bd. govs. 1996—, sec.-elect 1998-99, sec. 1999—), New Eng. Bar Assn. (bd. dirs. 1977-88, pres. 1982-83), N.H. Bar Assn. (pres. 1979-80), N.H. Bar Found. (bd. dirs. 1979-92, chair 1983-90), Nat. Ctr. State Cts. (dir. 1999—), Nat. Conf. Bar Found. (trustee 1985-92, pres. 1989-90), Nat. Conf. Bar Pres. (exec. coun. 1987-95, pres. 1993-94), N.H. Bus. and Industry Assn. (bd. dirs. 1988—, sec. 1990—), Manchester C. of C. (bd. dirs. 1967-89, chmn. 1984-85), New Eng. Coun. (bd. dirs. 1991—), New Eng. Legal Found. (bd. dir. 2001-). Appellate, General civil litigation, Personal injury. Office: McLane Graf Raulerson & Middleton 900 Elm St Ste 1001 Manchester NH 03101-2029

MIDDLETON, JAMES BOLAND, retired lawyer; b. Columbus, Ga., Aug. 19, 1934; s. Riley Kimbrough and Annie Ruth (Boland) M.; 1 child, Cynthia. BA in Psychology, Ga. State U., 1964; JD, Woodrow Wilson Coll. Law, 1972. Bar: Ga. 1972, U.S. Patent Office. Draftsman, paralegal and office mgr. to patent atty., Atlanta, 1955-68; draftsman, paralegal and office mgr. Jones & Thomas, 1968-72, assoc., 1972-76; pvt. practice intellectual property Decatur, Ga., 1976-98; ret., 1998. Mem. editl. bd. Atlanta Lawyer, 1973-82, assoc. editor, 1978-81, editor-in-chief, 1981-82. Dir. arts coun. Unitarian-Universalist Congregation Atlanta, 1989-91; bd.d irs. Unitarian-Universalist Endowment Fund, 1993-96, vice chair, 1994-95, sec., 1995-96; bd. dirs., sec. Decatur Arts Alliance, 1990-94. With U.S. Army, 1957-59. Mem. ABA, Am. Intellectual Property Law Assn., Am. Arbitration Assn. (comml. panel 1983-94), DeKalb Bar Assn., State Bar Ga. (editl. bd. jour. 1985-92, patent trademark and copyright sect. 1972-2000, chmn. 1982-83, pub. rels. com. 1982-88), Fed. Cir. Bar Assn. Intellectual property.

MIERZWA, JOSEPH WILLIAM, lawyer, legal communications consultant; b. Chgo., Nov. 21, 1951; s. Joseph Valentine and Betty Ann (Ray) M.; m. Rolana Conley, May 18, 1974. BA, U. Kans., 1981, JD, 1985. Bar: Kans. 1985, U.S. Dist. Ct. Kans. 1985. Pvt. practice, Prairie Village, Kans., 1985-86; gen. counsel Hyatt Legal Svcs., Kansas City, Mo., 1986-87; corp. counsel NLS Corp., Inc., Lakewood, Colo., 1988; owner, mgr. Joseph W. Mierzwa Cons., 1988-92; pres. Prose Assocs., Inc., Highlands Ranch, Colo., 1991—. Cons. Nat. Legal Shield, Lakewood, 1988-92, Reader's Digest Assn., Pleasantville, N.Y., 1988—, Hyatt Legal Svcs., Cleve., 1988-94, Media Resources Internat., 1992-94, others; editor OverDrive Sys., Inc., Cleve., 1990-95. Author: The 21st Century Family Legal Guide, 1994. Mem. ABA, Kans. Bar Assn. Avocations: cooking, travel, creative writing. General practice. Office: 8989 S Spring Hill Dr Hghlnds Ranch CO 80129-4349 E-mail: paibooks@aol.com

MIGHELL, KENNETH JOHN, lawyer; b. Schenectady, N.Y., Mar. 17, 1931; s. Richard Henry and Ruth Aline (Simon) M.; m. Julia Anne Carstarphen, Aug. 24, 1961; children: Thomas Lowry, Elizabeth Anne. BBA, U. Tex., 1952, JD, 1957. Bar: Tex. 1957. Assoc. Scurry, Scurry, Pace & Wood, Dallas, 1957-61; asst. U.S. Atty. Justice Dept., 1961-77; 1st asst. No. Dist. Tex., 1972-77; U.S. Atty. No. Dist., Tex., 1977-81; ptnr. Cowles & Thompson, Dallas, 1981-96, of counsel, 1996—. Chmn. bd. mgmt. Downtown Dallas YMCA, 1974-76; pres. Dallas Area Am. Lung Assn., 1985-87; bd. dirs. YMCA Met. Dallas, 1987—; chmn. adv. bd. Southwestern Law Enforcement Inst., 1994-98; mem. SW Legal Found. (CLE adv. com. 1999—). With USN, 1952-54; capt. USNR, 1954-78. Mem. FBA, Dallas Bar Assn. (bd. dirs. 1984-89, chmn. 1989, v.p. 1990-91, pres. 1993) Dallas Bar Found. (trustee 1994—, vice chmn. 1999-2000, chmn. 2001—), State Bar Tex. (bd. dirs. 1994-95), Nat. Assn. Former U.S. Attys. (pres. 1995). Democrat. Methodist. Alternative dispute resolution, General civil litigation, Personal injury. Office: Cowles & Thompson 901 Main St Ste 4000 Dallas TX 75202-3793 E-mail: kmighell@cowlesthompson.com

MIHM, MICHAEL MARTIN, federal judge; b. Amboy, Ill., May 18, 1943; s. Martin Clarence and Frances Johannah (Morrissey) M.; m. Judith Ann Zosky, May 6, 1967; children— Molly Elizabeth, Sarah Ann, Jacob Michael, Jennifer Leah BA, Loras Coll., 1964; JD, St. Louis U., 1967. Asst. prosecuting atty. St. Louis County, Clayton, Mo., 1967-68; asst. state's atty. Peoria County, Peoria, Ill., 1968-69; asst. city atty. City of Peoria, 1969-72; state's atty. Peoria County, Peoria, 1972-80; sole practice, 1980-82; U.S. dist. judge U.S. Govt., 1982—; chief U.S. dist. judge U.S. Dist. Ct. (ctrl. dist.) Ill., 1991-98. Chmn. com. internat. jud. rels. U.S. Jud. Conf., 1994—96, mem. exec. com., 1995—97, mem. com. jud. br., 1987—93, mem. com. internat. jud. rels., 1998—; mem. Supreme Ct. Fellows Commn., 2000—; adj. prof. law John Marshall Law Sch., 1990—. Past mem. adv. bd. Big Brothers-Big Sisters, Crisis Nursery, Peoria; past bd. dirs. Salvation Army, Peoria, W.D. Boyce council Boy Scouts Am., State of Ill. Treatment Alternatives to Street Crime, Gov.'s Criminal Justice Info. Council; past vice-chmn. Ill. Dangerous Drugs Adv. Council; trustee Proctor Health Care Found., 1991—. Recipient Good Govt. award Peoria Jaycees, 1978 Mem. Peoria County Bar Assn. Roman Catholic. Office e-mail: michael. Office: US Dist Ct 204 Federal Bldg 100 NE Monroe St Peoria IL 61602-1003 E-mail: mihm@ilcd.uscourts.gov

MIKAMI, JIRO, lawyer; b. Tokyo, Aug. 29, 1972; s. Yoichi and Kazuko Mikami; m. Tami Hirota, May 4, 1973; 1 child, Nana. BL, U. Tokyo, 1995. Bar: Japan 1997. Assoc. atty. Nagashima Ohno & Tsunematsu, Tokyo, 1997—. General corporate, Finance, Real property. Office: Nagashima Ohno & Tsunematsu Kioicho Bldg, 3-12 Kioicho Tokyo 102-0094 Japan Office Fax: 81-3-5213-2271

MIKELS, RICHARD ELIOT, lawyer; b. Cambridge, Mass., July 14, 1947; s. Albert Louis and Charlotte Betty (Shapiro) M.; m. Deborah Gwen Katz, Aug. 29, 1970; children: Allison Brooke, Robert Jarrett. BS in Bus. Adminstrn., Boston U., 1969, JD cum laude, 1972. Bar: Mass. 1972, U.S. Dist. Ct. Mass. 1974, U.S. Ct. Appeals (1st cir.) 1978. Legal examiner ICC, Washington, 1972-74; ptnr. Riemer & Braunstein, Boston, 1974-80; ptnr., chmn. comml. law sect. Peabody & Brown, 1980-88; mem., chmn. comml. law sect. Mintz, Levin, Cohn, Ferris, Glovsky and Popeo, P.C., 1988—. Contbr. articles to profl. jours. Tng. adv. com. Jewish Vocat. Svc., Boston, 1991, 95, 96, bd. dirs., 1995-99, vice chair microenterprise adv. com. 1997; vice-chair lawyers com. Combined Jewish Philanthropies, 1994, 95. Fellow Am. Coll. Bankruptcy; mem. ABA, Am. Bankruptcy Inst. (bd. dirs. 2000—), Assn. Comml. Ins. Attys., Comml. Law League Am., Mass. Bar Assn., Boston Bar Assn., Boston U. Law Alumni Assn. (mem. exec. com., v.p. exec. com. 1999-2000, pres. exec. com. 2000-01). Office: Mintz Levin Cohn Ferris Glovsky & Popeo PC 1 Financial Ctr Fl 39 Boston MA 02111-2657

MIKESELL, RICHARD LYON, lawyer, financial counselor; b. Corning, N.Y., Jan. 29, 1941; s. Walter Ray and Clara Ellen (Lyon) M.; m. Anna May Creese, Mar. 16, 1973; 1 child, Joel. BSChemE, U. Calif., Berkeley, 1962; LLB, Duke U., 1965; BA in Liberal Studies, UCLA, 1977. Bar: U.S. Supreme Ct. 1971, Ohio 1965, Calif. 1967, U.S. Ct. Appeals (9th cir.) 1982, U.S. Ct. Appeals (2d cir.) 1993, U.S. Patent Office 1967. Patent atty. Procter & Gamble, Cin., 1965-66, Rocketdyne divsn. N.Am. Aviation, L.A., 1966-69; pvt. practice law, 1969-81; prin. Law Offices of R.L. Mikesell, 1981—. Fin. counselor L.A. Police Dept., 1986—; arbitrator Am. Arbitration Assn., L.A., 1980—. Pres. San Fernando Valley Fair Housing Coun., L.A., 1969-72, Valley Women's Ctr., L.A., 1990; line res. officer L.A. Police Dept., 1969-72. Named Res. Officer of Yr. L.A. Police Dept., 1990, 98; recipient 1st Place award Nat. SPAM Recipe Contest, 1998. Avocation: high power rifle shooting. General civil litigation, Patent, Real property. Office: 14540 Hamlin St Ste B Van Nuys CA 91411-4147 E-mail: richlyon@worldnet.att.com

MIKVA, ABNER JOSEPH, lawyer, retired federal judge; b. Milw., Jan. 21, 1926; s. Henry Abraham and Ida (Fishman) M.; m. Zoe Wise, Sept. 19, 1948; children: Mary, Laurie, Rachel. JD cum laude, U. Chgo., 1951; DL (hon.), U. Ill., Am. U., Northwestern U., Tulane U.; DHL (hon.), Hebrew U.; DHL (Hon.), U. Wis.; DL (hon.), Ill. Inst. Tech., Santa Clara U. Bar: Ill. 1951, D.C. 1978. Law clk. to Hon. Sherman Minton U.S. Supreme Ct., 1951; ptnr. Devoe, Shadur, Mikva & Plotkin, Chgo., 1952-68, D'Ancona, Pflaum, Wyatt & Riskind, 1973-74; lectr. Northwestern U. Law Sch., Chgo., 1973-75, U. Pa. Law Sch., 1983-85, Georgetown Law Sch., 1986-88, Duke U. Law Sch., Durham, N.C., 1990-91, U. Chgo. Law Sch., 1992-93; mem. Ill. Gen. Assembly from 23d Dist., 1956-66, 91st-92d Congresses from 2d Dist. Ill., 94th-96th Congresses from 10th Dist. Ill.; mem. ways and means com., judiciatry com. ways and means com., judiciary com.; chmn. Dem. Study Group; resigned, 1979; from judge to chief judge U.S. Circuit Ct. Appeals D.C., 1979-94, chief judge, 1991-94; counsel to the President The White House, Washington, 1994-96. Vis. prof., Walter Schaefer chair in pub. policy U. Chgo., 1996-98; vis. prof. U. Ill. Coll. Law, 1998-2000, U. Chgo., 2000—. Author: The American Congress: The First Branch, 1983, The Legislative Process, 1995, An Introduction to Statutory Interpretation, 1997. With USAAF, WWII. Sr. fellow Inst. Govt. & Pub. Affairs U. Ill., 1998-2000; recipient Page One award Chgo. Newspaper Guild, 1964, Best Legislator award Ind. Voters Ill., 1956-66, Alumni medal U. Chgo., 1996, Paul Douglas Ethics in Govt. award, 1998; named one of ten Outstanding Young Men in Chgo., Jr. Assn. Commerce and Industry, 1961. Fellow AAAS; mem. ABA, Chgo. Bar Assn. (bd. mgrs. 1962-64), D.C. Bar Assn., Am. Law Inst., U.S. Assn. Former Mems. Congress, Order of Coif, Phi Beta Kappa. Home: 5020 S Lake Shore Dr Ph 8 Chicago IL 60615-3253 E-mail: amikva@law.uchicago.edu

MILBOURNE, WALTER ROBERTSON, lawyer; b. Phila., Aug. 27, 1933; s. Charles Gordon and Florie Henderson (Robertson) M.; m. Georgena Sue Dyer, June 19, 1965; children: Gregory Broughton, Karen Elizabeth, Walter Robertson, Margaret Henderson. A.B., Princeton U., 1955; LL.B., Harvard U., 1958. Bar: Pa. 1959. Assoc. firm Pepper, Hamilton & Sheetz, Phila., 1959-65, Obermayer, Rebmann, Maxwell & Hippel, Phila., 1965-67, ptnr., 1968-84, Saul, Ewing, Remick & Saul, 1984-2000, of counsel, 2001—. Bd. dirs. Pa. Lumbermen's Mut. Ins. Co., Phila. Reins. Corp.; co-chmn. Nat. Conf. Lawyers and Collection Agys., 1979-90; chmn. bus. litigation com. Def. Rsch. Inst., 1986-89, mem. law instsn. com., 1989-95. Chmn. mental health budget sect. Phila. United Fund, 1967-70; pres. Found. Internat. Assn. Def. Counsel, 1997—. Served with Army N.G., 1958-64. Fellow Am. Coll. Trial Lawyers (mem. internat. com. 1992-96); mem. ABA, Pa. Bar Assn., Phila. Bar Assn., Internat. Assn. Def. Counsel (exec. com. 1985-88, pres. IADC Found. 1997—), Merion Cricket Club, Idle Hour Tennis Club (pres. 1968-68, Phila. Lawn Tennis Assn. (pres. 1969-70). Republican. Federal civil litigation, State civil litigation, Insurance. Home: 689 Fernfield Cir Wayne PA 19087-2002 Office: Saul Ewing Remick & Saul 3800 Centre Sq W Philadelphia PA 19102 E-mail: Waltermilb@aol.com

MILES, JUDITH ELLEN, lawyer, educator; b. Washington, Oct. 22, 1943; d. Louis Morton and Sylvia L. (Livingston) Bernstein; m. Harry Lehman Miles, Aug. 20, 1967; children— Gary David, Sarah Lynn. B.A., Sarah Lawrence Coll., 1965; J.D. magna cum laude, Western New Eng. Coll., 1977. Bar: Mass. 1977, U.S. Dist. Ct. Mass. 1978. Intern dist. atty. for northwestern dist. Commonwealth of Mass., 1976-77; assoc. firm Richard M. Howland, P.C., Amherst, Mass., 1977-79; law clk. Mass. Appeals Ct., Springfield and Boston, 1979-80, criminal staff atty., 1980-85, sr. criminal staff atty., 1985—; adj. prof. law Western New Eng. Coll., Springfield, 1980— . Assoc. editor Mass. Law Rev., 1981-88 . Recipient Am. Jurisprudence awards 1974-75, 76, 77. Mem. Mass. Ender Bias Study Com., 1987—. Mem. ABA, Mass. Assn. Law Related Edn. (lectr. 1982—), Mass. Bar Assn., Women's Bar Assn. Mass (v.p. 1984-85), Mass. Assn. Women Lawyers, Mass. Trial Lawyers Assn., Hampshire County Bar Assn., Franklin County Bar Assn., Hampden County Bar Assn. Democrat. Home: 389 Federal St Montague MA 01351-9531 Office: Mass Appeals Ct 80 State St Springfield MA 01103-2010

MILES, WENDELL A. federal judge; b. Holland, Mich., Apr. 17, 1916; s. Fred T. and Dena Del (Alverson) M.; m. Mariette Bruckert, June 8, 1946; children: Lorraine Miles, Michelle Miles Kopinski, Thomas Paul. AB, Hope Coll., 1938, LLD (hon.), 1980; MA, U. Wyo., 1939; JD, U. Mich., 1942; LLD (hon.), Detroit Coll. Law, 1979. Bar: Mich. Ptnr. Miles & Miles, Holland, 1948-53, Miles, Mika, Meyers, Beckett & Jones, Grand Rapids, Mich., 1961-70; pros. atty. County of Ottawa, 1949-53; U.S. dist. atty. Western Dist. Mich., Grand Rapids, 1953-60, U.S. dist. judge, 1974—, chief judge, 1979-86, sr. judge, 1986—. Cir. judge 20th Jud. Cir. Ct. Mich., 1970-74; instr. Hope Coll., 1948-53, Am. Inst. Banking, 1953-60; adj. prof. Am. constl. history Hope Coll., Holland, Mich., 1979— ; mem. Mich. Higher Edn. Commn.; apptd. Fgn. Intelligence Surveillance Count, Washington, 1989—. Pres. Holland Bd. Edn., 1952-63. Served to capt. U.S. Army, 1942-47. Recipient Liberty Bell award, 1986. Fellow Am. Bar Found.; mem. ABA, Mich. Bar Assn., Fed. Bar Assn., Ottawa County Bar Assn., Grand Rapids Bar (Inns of Ct. 1995—), Am. Judicature Soc., Torch Club, Rotary Club, Masons. Office: US Dist Ct 236 Fed Bldg 110 Michigan St NW Ste 452 Grand Rapids MI 49503-2363 E-mail: miles@miwd.uscourts.gov

MILGRIM, ROGER MICHAEL, lawyer; b. N.Y.C., Mar. 22, 1937; s. Isreal and Iola (Lash) M.; m. Patricia Conway, July 10, 1971; children: Justin. BA, U. Pa., 1958; LLB, NYU, 1961, LLM, 1962. Bar: N.Y., U.S. Supreme Ct. Assoc. Baker & McKenzie, Paris, 1963-65, Nixon Mudge et al, N.Y.C., 1965-68; mem. Milgrim Thomajan & Lee P.C., 1968-92; ptnr., chmn. intellectual property group Paul, Hastings, Janofsky & Walker LLP, 1992—, chmn. litigation dept., 1999-2000. Adj. prof. sch. law NYU, N.Y.C., 1974—; bd. dirs. Colfexip Stena Offshore S.A., 1999—; bd. advisors, UniStates, LLC, 2001—. Author: Milgrim on Trade Secrets, 1968, supplement, 2001, Milgrim on Licensing, 1990, supplement, 2001. Trustee Coll. Wooster, 1994-97, Bklyn. Hosp., 1982-91; bd. dirs. Fulbright Assn., 1998—, chmn. Fulbright Prize com., 1999—. Mem. Knickerbocker Club, Phila. Cricket Club. Republican. General corporate, Intellectual property, Private international. Home: 301 E 52nd St New York NY 10022-6319 Office: Paul Hastings Janofsky & Walker LLP 75 E 55th New York NY 10022-3205 E-mail: rogermilgrim@paulhastings.com

MILLAR, RICHARD WILLIAM, JR. lawyer; b. L.A., May 11, 1938; LLB, U. San Francisco, 1966. Bar: Calif. 1967, U.S. Dist. Ct. (cen. dist.) Calif. 1967, U.S. Dist. Ct. (no. dist.) Calif. 1969, U.S. Dist. Ct. (so. dist.) Calif. 1973, U.S. Supreme Ct. Assoc. Iverson & Hogoboom, Los Angeles, 1967-72; ptnr. Eilers, Stewart, Pangman & Millar, Newport Beach, Calif., 1973-75, Millar & Heckman, Newport Beach, 1975-77, Millar, Hodges & Bemis, Newport Beach, 1979—. Fellow: Am. Bar Found.; mem.: ABA (litigation sect. trial practice com., ho. of dels. 1990—), Calif. Bar Assn. (lectr. CLE), Orange County Bar Assn. (sec. 1999, treas. 2000, pres. 2002, chmn. bus. litig. sect. 1981, chmn. judiciary com. 1988—90, dir. charitable fund 2000), Balboa Bay Club, Bohemian Club (San Francisco), Pacific Club, Palm Valley Country Club (Palm Desert, Calif.). Federal civil litigation, State civil litigation. Home: 71 Hillsdale Newport Beach CA 92660 Office: Millar Hodges & Bemis One Newport Pl Ste # 900 Newport Beach CA 92660 E-mail: millar@mhblaw.net

MILLARD, JOHN ALDEN, lawyer; b. Buenos Aires, Argentina, Nov. 4, 1940; s. Alden Shultz and Lois (Guthrie) M.; m. Carey Barbara French, Sept. 7, 1966; children— John Alden, James Guthrie, Alexander French. B.A., Harvard U., 1963, LL.B., 1967. Bar: N.Y. 1968. Assoc., Shearman & Sterling, N.Y.C., 1967-75, ptnr., 1976— . Served with U.S. Army, 1963-64. Mem. Assn. Bar City N.Y. Banking, General corporate.

MILLARD, NEAL STEVEN, lawyer; b. Dallas, June 6, 1947; s. Bernard and Adele (Marks) M.; m. Janet Keast, Mar. 12, 1994; 1 child, Kendall Layne. BA cum laude, UCLA, 1969; JD, U. Chgo., 1972. Bar: Calif. 1972, U.S. Dist. Ct. (cen. dist.) Calif. 1973, U.S. Tax Ct. 1973, U.S. Ct. Appeals (9th cir.) 1987, N.Y. 1990. Assoc. Willis, Butler & Schiefly, Los Angeles, 1972-75; ptnr. Morrison & Foerster, 1975-84, Jones, Day, Reavis & Pogue, Los Angeles, 1984-93, White & Case, L.A., 1993—. Instr. Calif. State Coll., San Bernardino, 1975-76; lectr. Practising Law Inst., N.Y.C., 1983-90, Calif. Edn. of Bar, 1987-90; adj. prof. USC Law Ctr., 1994—. Citizens adv. com. L.A. Olympics, 1982-84; trustee Altadena (Calif.) Libr. Dist., 1985-86; bd. dirs. Woodcraft Rangers, L.A., 1982-90, pres., 1986-88; bd. dirs. L.A. County Bar Found., 1990-2000, pres., 1997-98; mem. Energy Commn. of County and Cities of L.A., 1995-99; bd. dirs. Inner City Law Ctr., 1996-99; mem. jud. procedures commn. L.A. County, 1999—, chair, 2000—. Mem. ABA, Calif. Bar Assn., N.Y. State Bar Assn., L.A. County Bar Assn. (trustee 1985-87), Pub. Counsel (bd. dirs. 1984-87, 90-93), U. Chgo. Law Alumni Assn. (pres. 1998—), USC Inst. for Corporate Counsel (advisory bd. 1998—), Calif. Club, Phi Beta Kappa, Pi Gamma Mu, Phi Delta Phi. Banking, Private international, Real property. Office: White & Case 633 W 5th St Ste 1900 Los Angeles CA 90071-2087 E-mail: nmillard@whitecase.com

MILLARD, RICHARD STEVEN, lawyer; b. Pasadena, Calif., Feb. 6, 1952; s. Kenneth A. and Kathryn Mary (Paden) M.; m. Jessica Ann Edwards, May 15, 1977; children: Victoria, Elizabeth, Andrew. AB, Stanford U., 1974; JD magna cum laude, U. Mich., 1977. Bar: Calif. 1977, Ill. 1985. Assoc. Heller, Ehrman, White & McAuliff, San Francisco, 1977-81, Mayer, Brown & Platt, Chgo., 1982-83, ptnr., 1984-99, Weil, Gotshal & Manges, Menlo Park, Calif., 1999—. Mem. ABA, Order of Coif. General corporate, Finance, Securities. Office: Weil Gotshal & Manges 2882 Sand Hill Rd Menlo Park CA 94025-7064 E-mail: richard.millard@weil.com

MILLBERG, JOHN C. lawyer; b. New London, Conn., Jan. 4, 1956; s. Melvin Roy and Dorothy (Van Zandt) M.; m. Lori Bruce, Oct. 18, 1981; children: Kathryn Faye, Rebecca Ann, Melvin Roy III. BA, Bowling Green State U., 1977; JD, Wake Forest U., 1980. Bar: Tex. 1980, U.S. Dist. Ct. (so. dist.) Tex. 1981, U.S. Ct. Appeals (5th and 11th cirs.) 1981, N.C. 1986, U.S. Dist. Ct. (ea., mid. and we. dists.) N.C. 1986, U.S. Ct. Appeals (4th cir.) 1986, S.C. 2000. Assoc. Crain Caton James & Womble, Houston, 1981-85; assoc., dir. Maupin, Taylor, Ellis & Adams, Raleigh, N.C., 1985-94; mng. ptnr. Millberg & Gordon, 1994—. Mem. bar candidate com. N.C. Bd. Law Examiners, 1988-90. Scholar Wake Forest U. Sch. Law, 1977-80. Mem. N.C. Assn. Def. Attys. (exec. com.), Nat. Assn. R.R. Trial Counsel. General civil litigation, Insurance, Personal injury. Office: Millberg & Gordon 1030 Washington St Raleigh NC 27605-1258

MILLENDER, BEATRICE PENNIE, magistrate judge; b. Detroit, June 4, 1952; d. Robert Lee and Louise J. Millender. Student, Olivet (Mich.) Coll., 1970-71; BA in Psychology, So. U., Baton Rouge, La., 1974; MA in Vocat. Rehab. Counseling, Wayne State U., 1976; JD, Detroit Coll. Law, 1987. Bar: Mich. Instnl. social worker State of Mich. Dept. Health, Mt. Clemens, 1975-78; intake supr. City of Detroit/Youth Incentive Entitlement, 1978-79; staff asst. U.S. Congressman, 1981-84; atty. NLRB, Detroit, 1987-90; mem. Mich. Employment Security Bd. of Rev., 1993-97, chair, 1990-92; magistrate 36th Dist. Ct., 1997—; jud. intern to Hon. Claudia House Morcom Wayne County Cir. Ct., 1985; jud. intern to Hon. Dennis W. Archer Mich. Supreme Ct., 1986; project dir. vocat. edn. task force New Detroit, Inc., 1980-81. Bd. dirs. Robert L. Millender Sr. Meml. Fund Inc., 1970—, Sugar Law Ctr. for Econ. Justice, 1995-97, Mich. Appellate Defender Commn., 1984-87. Recipient Harold E. Bledsoe award for acad. excellence, 1985, Detroit Area Peacemaker award Wayne State U. Ctr. Peace and Conflict Studies, 1992. Mem. NAACP, Mich. Bar Assn. (chair civil liberties com. 1995-97), Assn. Black Judges Mich., Nat. Congress of Black Polit. Women (Shirley Chisholm Woman of Yr. award 1997), Nat. Assn. Unemployment (exec. bd. 1991-96) Avocations: reading, fishing, water aerobics. Office: 36th Dist Ct 421 Madison St Detroit MI 48226-2382

MILLER, ALFRED MONTAGUE, lawyer; b. Augusta, Ga., Jan. 5, 1940; s. Dessie Ford and May Belle (Power) M.; m. Lynthia Wofford, Aug. 25, 1962 (div. 1979); children— William Montague, Stephen Mathews; m. Peggy Elaine Mays, July 26, 1980. B.B.A., U. Ga., 1961, J.D., 1963. Bar: Ga. 1962, Superior Ct. Ga. 1962, U.S. Dist. Ct. (so. dist.) Ga. 1963, U.S. Ct. Appeal (11th cir.) 1981, U.S. Supreme Ct. 1978. Ptnr. Fulcher, Fulcher, Hagler, Harper and Reed, Augusta, 1963-71, Dye, Miller, Tucker and Everitt, P.A., Augusta, 1971—90, of counsel 1990-; pres. Club Car, Inc., 1990-2001; dir. First Bank of Ga., 2001-. Fellow Ga. Bar Found., Am. Coll. Trial Lawyers; mem. Am. Judicature Soc., ABA, Lawyers-Pilot Bar Assn., State Bar Ga. (bd. govs. 1977-85), Augusta Bar Assn. (pres. 1985), Internat. Assn. Def. Counsel, Beta Gamma Sigma, Chi Phi (pres. 1960-61), Phi Delta Phi. Presbyterian. Federal civil litigation, State civil litigation, Personal injury. Home: 4384 Deer Run Evans GA 30809-4440 Office: Tucker Everitt Long Brewton & Lanier PO Box 2426 Augusta GA 30903-2426 E-mail: mill4384@aol.com

MILLER, ALLEN TERRY, JR. lawyer; b. Alexandria, Va., Sept. 19, 1954; s. Allen Terry and Eleanor Jane (Thompson) M.; m. Maureen Ann Callaghan, June 22, 1985; children: Brendan Allen, Patrick Joseph, Brigit Eleanor. BA, U. Va., 1977; JD, Seattle U., 1982. Bar: Wash. 1982, U.S. Dist. Ct. (we. dist.) Wash. 1982, U.S. Ct. Appeals (9th cir.) 1985, U.S. Dist. Ct. (ea. dist.) Wash. 1986, U.S. Dist. Ct. (no. dist.) N.Y. 1990, U.S. Dist. Ct. (we. dist.) Mich. 1990, U.S. Supreme Ct. 1990, U.S. Ct. Appeals (2d and 6th cirs.) 1991. Legis. asst. Congressman Paul N. McCloskey Jr., Washington, 1978-79; asst. atty. gen. State of Washington, Olympia, 1982-92; prin. Connolly, Tacon & Meserve, 1992—. Adj. prof. environ. law Seattle U., 1991—. Commr. Olympia Planning Commn., 1987-92, vice-chair, 1991, chair, 1992; mem. North Capitol Campus Heritage Pk. Devel. Assn., 1989—, sec., 1989-90, pres., 1991—; pres. Olympia Chorale and Light Opera Co., 1984-85; mem. St. Michael's Sch. Bd., 1993-96, chair, 1994-96; bd. dirs. South Sound YMCA, 1996—, Olympia Symphony, 1999—, Olympia Sch. Dist. Found., 1998—; pres. bd. dirs. United Way Thurston County, 1998—, pres. 2000-01; pres. Olympia Yashiro Sister City Assn., 2001—. Recipient Merit award Am. Planning Assn., 1989, 92, Citizen of Yr. award Thurston County, 1998. Mem. ABA, Wash. Bar Assn. (mem. environ. law sect. 1984—, ct. rules com. 1985-89, jud. recommendation com. 1991-94, legis. com. 1994-97, ct. improvement com. 1997-2000), Thurston County Bar Assn., Leadership Thurston County, Olympic-Thurston C. of C. (trustee 1996-00, pres.-elect 1997, pres. 1998), Rotary. Democrat. Roman Catholic. Avocations: mountaineering, kayaking, tennis, piano. Environmental, Land use and zoning (including planning), Real property. Home: 1617 Sylvester St SW Olympia WA 98501-2228 Office: Heritage Bldg. 5th and Columbia Olympia WA 98501-1114

MILLER, ARTHUR HAROLD, lawyer; b. Plainfield, N.J., Sept. 21, 1935; s. Leon Daniel and Bertha Zelda (Madoff) M.; m. Lynn Fieldman, Aug. 24, 1958; children: Jennifer, Jonathan. BA, Princeton U., 1957; JD, Columbia U., 1960. Bar: N.J. 1961, U.S. Supreme Ct. 1965, N.J. 1969. Assoc. Wachtel & Michaelson, N.Y.C., 1961-65, Netter, Lewy, Dowd, N.Y.C., 1965-67, Dannenberg Hazen & Lake, N.Y.C., 1967-69; ptnr. Clarick, Clarick & Miller, New Brunswick, N.J., 1971-78, Miller, Miller & Tucker PA, New Brunswick, 1979—. Chmn. Middlesex County Legal Svcs. Corp., New Brunswick, 1975-83. Active Sch. Bd. Highland Park, N.J., 1981-84. Mem. N.J. Bar Assn. (chmn. availibility legal svcs. com. 1983-85, lawyer referral com. 1986-88), MIddlesex County Bar Assn. (pres. 1993-94, lawyer achievement award 1996), Middlesex County Bar Found. (pres. 1997-98), Middlesex County C. of C. (trustee and legal counsel 1990-93). Democrat. Jewish. Bankruptcy, State civil litigation, General corporate. Home: 145 N 9th Ave Highland Park NJ 08904-3627 Office: Miller Miller & Tucker 96 Paterson St New Brunswick NJ 08901-2109 E-mail: amiller@millerandmiller.com

MILLER, ARTHUR MADDEN, lawyer, investment banker; b. Greenville, S.C., Apr. 10, 1953; s. Charles Frederick and Kathryn Irene (Madden) M.; m. Roberta Beck Connolly, Apr. 17, 1993; children: Isabella McIntyre Madden, Roberta Beck Connolly. AB in History, Princeton U., 1973; MA in History, U. N.C., 1976; JD with distinction, Duke U., 1978; LLM in Taxation, NYU, 1982. Bar: N.Y. 1979, U.S. Dist. Ct. (so. dist.) N.Y. 1979. Assoc. Mudge Rose Guthrie Alexander & Ferdon, N.Y.C., 1978-85; v.p. pub. fin. Goldman, Sachs & Co., 1985—. Mem. adv. bd. Mary Baldwin Coll., Staunton, Va., 1982-86; trustee Princeton U. Rowing Assn., N.J., 1980—, pres., 1986-95; trustee Rebecca Kelly Dance Co., N.Y.C., 1984-86; mem. Power Ten, N.Y., steward, 1992-95. Mem. ABA (tax sect. com. on tax exempt financing 1985—), Nat. Assn. Bond Lawyers (lectr. 1985—), Pub. Securities Assn. (cons. 1985—), Practising Law Inst. (lectr. 1980, editor/author course materials 1980—), Bond Attys. Workshop (editor/author course material 1983—, lectr. 1983—), Princeton Club. Municipal (including bonds), Securities, Personal income taxation. Office: Goldman Sachs & Co 85 Broad St New York NY 10004-2456 E-mail: arthur.miller@gs.com

MILLER, BENJAMIN K. retired state supreme court justice; b. Springfield, Ill., Nov. 5, 1936; s. Clifford and Mary (Luthyens) M. BA, So. Ill. U., 1958; JD, Vanderbilt U., 1961. Bar: Ill. 1961. Ptnr. Olsen, Cantrill & Miller, Springfield, 1964-70; prin. Ben Miller-Law Office, 1970-76; judge 7th jud. cir. Ill. Cir. Ct., 1976-82, presiding judge Criminal div., 1977-81, chief judge, 1981-82; justice Ill. Appellate Ct., 4th Jud. Dist., 1982-84, Ill. Supreme Ct., Springfield, 1984-2001, chief justice, 1991-93, ret., 2001. Adj. prof. So. Ill. U., Springfield, 1974—; chmn. Ill. Cts. Commn., 1988-90; mem. Ill. Gov.'s Adv. Coun. on Criminal Justice Legis., 1977-84, Ad Hoc Com. on Tech. in Cts., 1985—. Mem. editorial rev. bd. Illinois Civil Practice Before Trial, Illinois Civil Trial Practice Pres. Cen. Ill. Mental Health Assn., 1969-71; bd. govs. Aid to Retarded Citizens, 1977-80; mem. Lincoln Legals Adv. Bd., 1988—. Lt. USNR, 1964-67. Mem. ABA (bar admissions com. sect. of legal edn. and admissions to bar 1992—), Ill. State Bar Assn. (bd. govs. 1970-76, treas. 1975-76), Sangamon County Bar Assn., Ctrl. Ill. Women's Bar Assn., Am. Judicature Soc. (bd. dirs. 1990-95), Abraham Lincoln Assn. (bd. dirs. 1988-98). Address: 1918 Jeanette Ln Springfield IL 62702

MILLER, BRIAN CHARLES, lawyer; b. Tulsa, Okla., May 13, 1973; s. Charles R. and Peggy Z. M. BA, BSChemE, Rice U., 1994; JD, U. Tex., 1997. Bar: Tex. 1997, U.S. Dist. Ct. (so. dist.) Tex. 1998, (ea. dist.) Tex. 2001. Lawyer Hunt, Hermansen, McKibben & Villarreal, Corpus Christi, Tex., 1997—2000, Howrey, Simon, Arnold & White, Houston, 2000—. Humor columnist, assoc. editor The Daily Texan, 1994-97. Player Corpus Christi Adult Hockey League, 1998—. Scholarships U. Tex. Sch. of Law, 1994-97. Mem. ABA, State Bar of Tex. (litigation sect.), C.C. Young Lawyers Assn. Civil rights, Insurance, Libel. Office: Howrey Simon Arnold & White 750 Bering Dr Houston TX 77057

MILLER, CARL THEODORE, lawyer; b. Lewistown, Pa., July 17, 1953; s. Clifford R. Jr. and Pauline (Baker) M.; m. Lisa Williams, June 4, 1977; children: Emily Elizabeth, Timothy Stephen, Karen Lynn. AB, Coll. William and Mary, 1975, JD, 1978. Bar: Ky. 1979, U.S. Dist. Ct. (we. dist.) Ky. 1979. Assoc. Greenebaum Doll & McDonald, Louisville, 1978-80; atty. Ky. Ct. Appeals, Frankfort, 1980-83, Ky. Supreme Ct., Frankfort, 1983—. Speaker workshops, Louisville, Denver and Frankfort. Pres. council and congregation Calvary Luth. Ch., Louisville, 1980-82; mem. fin. com. Hopeful Luth. Ch., Florence, Ky., 1984—, ch. council, 1987—. Mem. ABA (jud. adminstrn. div.), Ky. Govt. Bar Assn., Com. Appellate Staff Attys., Ky. Bar Assn., No. Ky. Bar Assn. Avocation: sports. Home: 108 Beech Dr Covington KY 41017-2305 Office: Ky Supreme Ct 204 W State St Frankfort KY 40601-3421

MILLER, CARROLL GERARD, JR. (GERRY MILLER), lawyer; b. San Antonio, Dec. 12, 1944; s. Carroll Gerard Sr. and Glyn (Roddy) M.; m. Sylvia Louise Mertins, Mar. 7 1971 (dec. 1982); children: Glyn Marie Bennett, Roddy Gerard, Gina Louise. AS, Del Mar Coll., 1965; BS, U. Houston, 1967; JD, Tex. Tech. U., 1970. Bar: Tex. 1970, Colo. 1987, D.C. 1989, U.S. Dist. Ct. (so. dist.) Tex. 1971, U.S. Ct. Appeals (5th cir.) Tex. 1973, U.S. Supreme Ct. 1974, U.S. Ct. Appeals (D.C. 1986); bd. cert. in criminal law. Assoc. Allison, Madden, White & Brin, Corpus Christi, Tex., 1970-71; asst. city atty. City of Corpus Christi, 1971; asst. dist. atty. Nueces County Dist. Attys. Office, Corpus Christi, 1971-73; asst. city atty. civil div. City of Corpus Christi, 1973-74; atty. Corpus Christi Police Dept.-City of Corpus Christi, 1974-77; pvt. practice Corpus Christi, 1973—. Adj. prof. Bee County Coll., Beeville, Tex., 1973-74, Tex. A & I U., Corpus Christi, 1975-76. Past treas. and diaconate First Presbyn. Ch., Corpus Christi; bd. dirs., incorporator Iron Curtain Outreach; 20/20 coun. Open Doors. Mem. SAR, SCV, Assn. Trial Lawyers Am., Tex. Criminal Def. Lawyers Assn., Nat. Criminal Def. Lawyers Assn., Coll. State Bar Tex., Sons of Republic Tex., Crime Stoppers, Inc. (past dir.), Bay Yacht Club (dir.). Republican. Avocations: sailing, scuba diving, photography, astronomy. Criminal, Personal injury. Home: 1209 Sandpiper Dr Corpus Christi TX 78412-3821 Office: 1007 Kinney St Corpus Christi TX 78401-3009 E-mail: lawgmiller@aol.com

MILLER, CHARLES HAMPTON, lawyer; b. Southampton, N.Y., Jan. 25, 1928; s. Abraham E. and Ethel (Simon) M.; m. Mary Fried, Aug. 26, 1956; children: Cathy Lynn, Steven Scott, Jennifer Lee. BA, Syracuse U., 1949; LLB, Columbia U., 1952. Bar: N.Y. 1952, Republic of Korea 1954, U.S. Ct. Appeals (2d cir.) 1958, U.S. Supreme Ct. 1969, U.S. Ct. Appeals (3d cir.) 1972, U.S. Ct. Appeals (7th cir.) 1973, U.S. Ct. Appeals (9th cir.) 1995; cert. mediator and early neutral evaluator (so. and ea. dists.) N.Y., 1994, mediator Supreme Ct. N.Y. County, 1996; arbitrator Ea. dist. N.Y., 1993. Asst. counsel Waterfront Commn., N.Y. Harbor, 1954-56; asst. atty. U.S. Atty. for So. Dist. N.Y., 1956-58; assoc. Cole & Deitz, N.Y.C., 1958-61, Marshall Bratter Greene Allison & Tucker, N.Y.C., 1961-64, ptnr., 1964-82, Hess Segall Guterman Pelz Steiner & Barovick, N.Y.C., 1982-86, Loeb & Loeb LLP, N.Y.C., 1986-2000, counsel, 2000—. Mem. faculty Continuing Legal Edn., Columbia U. Law Sch., 1976-82. With U.S. Army, 1952-54. Fellow Am. Bar Found.; mem. Assn. Bar City of N.Y. Federal civil litigation, General civil litigation, State civil litigation. Home: 171 Ralph Ave White Plains NY 10606-3813 Office: Loeb & Loeb LLP 345 Park Ave Fl 18 New York NY 10154-1895 E-mail: cmiller@loeb.com

MILLER, CHARLES MAURICE, lawyer; b. L.A., Sept. 7, 1948; BA cum laude, UCLA, 1970; postgrad., U. So. Calif., L.A., 1970-71; JD, U. Akron, 1975. Bar: Ohio 1975, Calif. 1978, U.S. Dist. Ct. (cen. dist.) Calif. 1978, U.S. Ct. Appeals (9th cir.) 1978, U.S. Supreme Ct. 1981. Gen. atty. U.S. Immigration & Naturalization Svc., U.S. Dept. Justice, L.A., 1976-79; ptnr. Miller Law Offices, 1979—. Adj. prof. law U. West L.A., 1989-90. Co-editor: The Visa Processing Guide: Process and Procedures at U.S. Consulates and Embassies, 8th edit., 2000; articles editor U. Akron Law Rev., 1974-75. Mem. Calif. Bd. Legal Specialization, San Francisco, 1988-89. Mem. Bar of Calif. (chmn. immigration splty. 1988-89, commr. immigration splty. 1987-90), Am. Immigration Law Found. (bd. trustees 1995-98), Am. Immigration Lawyers Assn. (bd. dirs. 1998-2001, mem. bd. govs., chair So. Calif. chpt. 1993-94, INS headquarters liaison com. 1997-98, co-chair mentor program 1990-91, co-chair visa office liaison 1991-92, vice chair 1994-95, co-chair consular rev. task force 1993-95, Jack Wasserman Meml. award for excellence in immigration litigation 1995). Immigration, naturalization, and customs. Office: Miller Law Offices 12441 Ventura Blvd Studio City CA 91604-2407

MILLER, CHRISTINE ODELL COOK, judge; b. Oakland, Calif., Aug. 26, 1944; m. Dennis F. Miller; 2 children. BA in Polit. Sci., Stanford U., 1966; JD, U. Utah, 1969. Bar: D.C., Calif.; cert. profl. gemologist. Law clk. to Hon. David T. Lewis U.S. Ct. Appeals (10th cir.), Salt Lake City; trial atty. Dept. Justice, U.S. Ct. Claims; team leader atty. FTC; atty. Hogan & Hartson, Washington; spl. counsel Pension Benefit Guaranty Corp.; dep. gen. counsel U.S. Ry. Assn.; ptnr. Shack & Kimball, Washington; judge U.S. Ct. Fed. Claims, 1982—. Comment editor Utah law Rev. Scholar U. Utah Coll. Law. Mem. D.C. Bar Assn., Calif. State Bar, Order of Coif, Univ. Club (bd. govs.), Cosmos Club. Avocations: running, weight trainer. Office: US Ct Fed Claims 717 Madison Pl NW Ste 617 Washington DC 20439-0002

MILLER, CLIFFORD JOEL, lawyer; b. L.A., Oct. 31, 1947; s. Eugene and Marian (Millman) M. BA, U. Calif., Irvine, 1969; JD, Pepperdine U., 1973. Bar: Calif. 1974, Hawaii 1974, U.S. Dist. Ct. Hawaii 1974. Ptnr. Rice, Lee & Wong, Honolulu, 1974-80, Goodsill Anderson Quinn & Stifel, Honolulu, 1980-89, McCorriston Miller Mukai MacKinnon, Honolulu, 1989—. Mem. ABA, Calif. Bar Assn., Hawaii Bar Assn., Am. Coll. Real Estate Lawyers. Avocations: sailing, volleyball, swimming, history. General corporate, Private international, Real property. Office: McCorriston Miller Mukai MacKinnon 5 Waterfront Plz 500 Ala Moana Blvd Ste 400 Honolulu HI 96813-4920 E-mail: cmiller@m4law.com

MILLER, DAVID ANTHONY, lawyer; b. Linton, Ind., Oct. 6, 1946; s. Edward I. and Jane M. (O'Hern) M.; m. Carol E. Martin, Aug. 9, 1970; 1 child, Jennifer Rose. Student, Murray State U., 1965; BS, Ind. State U., 1969; JD, Ind. U., Indpls., 1973. Bar: Ind. 1973, U.S. Dist. Ct. (so. dist.) Ind. 1973, U.S. Supreme Ct. 1981, U.S. Ct. Appeals (7th cir.) 1982. Dep. atty. gen. State of Ind., Indpls., 1973-76, dir. consumer protection divsn. office atty. gen., 1976-93, asst. atty. gen., 1977-80, chief counsel office atty. gen., 1981-93; prin. Hollingsworth, Meek, Miller and Minglin, 1993—. Bd. dirs. Greater Indianapolis Republican Fin. Com. Youth dir. Emmanuel Luth. Ch., Indpls., 1981-85, exec. dir., 1988-90; chmn. bd. Chambers Found., 1994—; pres. bd. Lutheran H.S., 1996—. Mem. ABA, Ind. State Bar. Assn., Indpls. Bar Assn., Ind. State U. Alumni Assn., Columbia Club, Lambda Chi Alpha. Republican. Avocations: numismatics, golfing. Administrative and regulatory, Contracts commercial, Legislative. Home: 6454 Forrest Commons Blvd Indianapolis IN 46227-7105 Office: 7550 S Meridian St Ste A Indianapolis IN 46217

MILLER, DOUGLAS ANDREW, lawyer, educator; b. Chgo., May 10, 1959; s. Walter William and Jean (Johnson) M.; m. Birgitte Jorgensen, Aug. 4, 1984. BS, Boston Coll., 1981; JD, Ill. Inst. Tech. Chgo., 1986. Bar: Fed. Trial, Ill., U.S. Dist. Ct. (no. dist.) Ill. Assoc. Bresnahan, Garvey, O'Halloran & Colman, Chgo., 1986-90; ptnr. Williams & Montgomery, Ltd., 1990—. Adj. prof. law Loyola U., Chgo., 1997—. Contbr. articles to profl. jours. Mem. ABA, Ill. State Bar Assn. (civil practice sect., torts sect.), Chgo. Bar Assn. (vice-chmn. bench and bar com., trial techniques sect., ins. law sect.), Ill. Assn. of Def. Trial Counsel. Avocation: distance running. State civil litigation, Insurance, Personal injury. Office: Williams & Montgomery Ltd 20 N Wacker Dr Ste 2100 Chicago IL 60606

MILLER, DWIGHT WHITTEMORE, lawyer; b. Worcester, Mass., July 8, 1940; s. Fred Hamilton and Jeanette (Lewis) M.; m. Mary Francisco, June 22, 1963; children— Rebecca, David. A.B., Colgate U., 1962; J.D., Boston Coll., 1965. Bar: Vt. 1965, MO. 1969, Law clk. U.S. Dist. Ct. Vt., 1965-66; sole practice, Brattleboro, Vt., 1966-68; with Monsanto Co., St. Louis, 1968-72; gen. counsel Stromberg Carlson Communications, Inc., St. Louis, 1972-75, Pott Industries, Inc., St. Louis, 1975-85; gen. solicitor Mo. Pacific R.R., St. Louis, 1985-86, Union Pacific R.R., 1991—; ptnr. Thompson & Mitchell, St. Louis, 1987-91; Mem. ABA, Order of Coif. Unitarian. General corporate, Environmental. Office: 210 N 13th St Saint Louis MO 63103-2329

MILLER, ELIZABETH H. lawyer, educator; b. Pomona, Calif., Oct. 3, 1970; d. John M. and Diane E. Hawkins; m. Eric S. Miller, May 28, 1995. BA, UCLA, 1992; JD, Yale U., 1995. Jud. clk. U.S. Ct. Appeals (2d cir.), Brattleboro, Vt., 1995-96; atty. Mornson & Foerster, San Francisco, 1996-98, Dinse, Knapp & McAndrew, Burlington, Vt., 1998—; tchr. C.C. of Vt., 1999—. Office: Dinse Knapp McAndrew 209 Battery St Burlington VT 05401-5261

MILLER, FRANK LOUIS, lawyer; b. N.Y.C., July 15, 1967; s. Theodore Norman and Margaret (L'Engle) M.; m. Felicity Rosalind Toube, June 13, 1999. BS, U. Ill., 1989; MBA, JD, NYU, 1995. Bar: N.Y. 1996; solicitor Eng. and Wales, 2000. Fin. analyst IBM Corp., Mt. Pleasant, N.Y., 1989-92; law clk. to Hon. John G. Koeltl N.Y.C., 1995-96; assoc. Wachtell Lipton Rosen & Katz, 1996-98, Freshfields Bruckhaus Deringer, London, 1999—. Office: Freshfields Bruckhaus Deringer 65 Fleet St London EC4Y 1HS England

MILLER, GAIL FRANKLIN, lawyer; b. Mansfield, Ohio, Mar. 24, 1938; d. James William and Dorothy (Franklin) M.; m. Carolyn Jean Baker, Sept. 26, 1964; children: Geoffrey Franklin, Bryan Alexander. BA, Columbia U., 1960; JD, U. Mich., 1963. Bar: Ohio 1963. Mem. Dinsmore & Shohl, Cin., 1963—. Past pres. zoning chmn. Clifton Town Meeting, past squadron comdr. Civil Air Patrol. Mem. Ohio Bar Assn., Cin. Bar Assn., Columbia U. Alumni Club Cin. (trustee 1965—). Avocations: aviation, antique autos. Contracts commercial, Real property. Home: 545 Evanswood Pl Cincinnati OH 45220-1526 Office: Dinsmore & Shohl 255 E 5th St 1900 Chemed Ctr Cincinnati OH 45202

MILLER, GALE TIMOTHY, lawyer; b. Kalamazoo, Sept. 15, 1946; s. Arthur H. and Eleanor (Johnson) M.; m. Janice Lindvall, June 1, 1968; children: Jeremy L., Amanda E., Timothy W. AB, Augustana Coll., 1968; JD, U. Mich., 1971. Bar: Mich. 1971, Colo. 1973, U.S. Dist. Ct. Colo. 1973, U.S. Ct. Appeals (10th cir.) 1979, U.S. Supreme Ct. 1997. Trial atty. FTC, Washington, 1971-73; assoc. Davis Graham & Stubbs LLP, Denver, 1973-77, ptnr., 1978—, chmn. exec. com., 1998—. Bd. dirs. Sr. Housing Options, Inc., 1980-93, Colo. Jud. Inst., 1999—; chair Colo. Lawyers Com., 1989-91, bd. dirs., 1987—, Individual Lawyer of Yr., 1994. Recipient Cmty. Svc. award Colo. Hispanic Bar Assn., 1996. Mem. ABA (antitrust sect. task force on model civil antitrust jury instrns.), Colo. Bar Assn. (chair antitrust sect. 1996-98), Denver Bar Assn. Democrat. Lutheran. Antitrust, Federal civil litigation, State civil litigation. Office: Davis Graham & Stubbs LLP 1550 17th St Ste 500 Denver CO 80202

MILLER, GARY C. lawyer; b. Little Rock, May 23, 1955; s. William Scott, Jr. and Margaret Imogene (Puckett) M.; m. Mary Catherine Miller, Oct. 23, 2000; children: Daniel, Sarah. BA in Econs. and Managerial Studies, Rice U., 1977; JD, U. Tex., 1980. Bar: Tex. 1980, U.S. Dist. Ct. (so. dist.) Tex. 1981, U.S. Dist. Ct. (no. and we. dists.) Tex. 1991, U.S. Dist. Ct. (ea. dist.) Tex. 1993, U.S. Ct. Appeals (5th cir) 1980, U.S. Supreme Ct. 1995. Atty. Wood, Campbell, Moody & Gibbs, Houston, 1980-83, Gibbs & Ratliff, Houston, 1983-85, Mayor, Day, Caldwell & Keeton, Houston, 1985—. Contbr. articles to profl. jours. Chmn. Westminster Weekday Sch., Houston, 1993-96; chmn., bd. trustees Westminster United Methodist Ch., Houston, 1996-98. Mem. ABA (bus. in bankruptcy com., bus. & corp. litigation com.), Houston Bar Assn., Phi Beta Kappa, Order of the Coif. Bankruptcy, Federal civil litigation, General civil litigation. Office: Mayor Day Caldwell & Keeton 700 Louisiana St Ste 1900 Houston TX 77002-2725 E-mail: gmiller@mdck.com

MILLER, GARY H. lawyer; b. New Orleans, Mar. 11, 1957; s. Leo Jr. and Suzanne Robinowitz (Meltzer) M.; m. Ellen Baldwin Hoffman, Oct. 18, 1986; children: Matthew Hilliard, Katherine Elise. BA magna cum laude, New Eng. Coll., 1979; JD cum laude, Tulane U., 1982. Assoc. Jones Walker, New Orleans, 1982-89, ptnr., 1990—. Mem. moot ct. bd. Tulane U. Sch. Law, 1980-82; lectr in field. Bd. dirs. Golden Retriever Club Greater New Orleans, Inc., 1980, Burtheville Cmty. Assn., Inc., 1997—; class agt. New England Coll. Mem. La. Bar Assn. (treas. consumer protection, lender liability and bankruptcy sect. 1990-91, chmn. consumer protection, lender liability and bank sect. 1991-92), Phi Tau Beta. Democrat. Jewish. Avocations: Retriever and obedience training, fishing, hunting, guitar. Contracts commercial, Intellectual property, Real property. Office: Jones Walker 201 Saint Charles Ave Ste 5200 New Orleans LA 70170-5100 E-mail: fisher31157@msn.com, gmiller@joneswalker.com

MILLER, GAY DAVIS, lawyer; b. Florence, Ariz., Dec. 20, 1947; d. Franklin Theodore and Mary (Belshaw) Davis; m. John Donald Miller, May 15, 1971; 1 child, Katherine Alexandra. BA, U. Colo., 1969; JD, Am. U., 1975. Bar: D.C. 1975. Atty., spl. asst. to gen. counsel, sr. counsel corp. affairs Inter Am. Devel. Bank, Washington, 1975-78, 83—; atty. Intelsat, 1978-80. Articles editor Am. U. Law Rev., 1974-75; contbn. author: The Inspection Panel of the World Bank: A Different Complaints Procedure, 2001. Bd. dirs. Hist. Mt. Pleasant, Inc., Washington, 1985-86, Washington Bridle Trails Assn., 1992—. Mem. ABA, Am. Soc. Internat. Law, Inter Am. Bar Assn., Women's Bar Assn. General corporate, Public international, Labor. Office: Inter Am Devel Bank 1300 New York Ave NW Washington DC 20577-0001 E-mail: gaym@iadb.org

MILLER, GEORGE DEWITT, JR. lawyer; b. Detroit, Aug. 20, 1928; s. George DeWitt and Eleanor Mary Miller; m. Prudence Brewster Saunders, Dec. 28, 1951; children: Margaret DeWitt, Joy Saunders. BA magna cum laude, Amherst Coll., 1950; JD with distinction, U. Mich., 1953. Bar: Mich. 1953, U.S. Dist. Ct. (so. dist.) Mich. 1953, U.S. Ct. Appeals (6th cir.) 1960, U.S. Tax Ct. 1960. Assoc. Bodman, Longley & Dahling, Detroit, 1957-61, ptnr., 1962—. Trustee, mem. Matilda R. Wilson Fund, 1993—, pres., 1998—; trustee Maplegrove Ctr./Kingswood Hosp., Henry Ford Health Sys., 1995—. Capt. USAF, 1953-56. Recipient Commendation medal. Fellow Mich. State Bar Found.; mem. ABA, State Bar Mich., Detroit Bar Assn., Detroit Athletic Club, Orchard Lake Country Club, Order of Coif, Phi Beta Kappa. Episcopalian. Avocations: yacht racing, shooting, gardening. Estate planning, Probate, Estate taxation. Home: 320 Dunston Rd Bloomfield Hills MI 48304-3415 Office: Bodman Longley & Dahling 100 Renaissance Ctr Ste 34 Detroit MI 48243-1001

MILLER, GEORGE SPENCER, lawyer; b. Kansas City, Mo., July 6, 1947; s. Lloyd George and Kathleen Margaret (Youngberg) M.; m. Avilda Earl Fisher, Feb. 25, 1967; children— Mary Alicia, Tyra Elizabeth, George Spencer. A.A., Fla. Coll., 1964; B.A., William Jewell Coll., 1969; J.D., U. Mo.-Kansas City, 1973. Bar: Mo. 1973. U.S. Dist. Ct. (we. dist.) Mo. 1975, U.S. Ct. Appeals (8th cir.) 1978. Assoc., ptnr. Morris & Foust, Kansas City, 1975-81; ptnr. Miller & Dougherty, Kansas City, 1981— . Served to maj. JAG, USMCR, 1970— . Mem. Assn. Trial Lawyers Am., Mo. Trial Lawyers Assn. Lon O. Hocker Meml. Trial Lawyers award 1978), Def. Research Inst., Kansas City Bar Assn., Clay County Bar Assn. Republican. Mem. Church of Christ. Federal civil litigation, State civil litigation, Personal injury. Home: 3617 NE Wild Plum Ln Kansas City MO 64119-2248 Office: Miller & Dougherty 1100 Main St Ste 2170 Kansas City MO 64105

MILLER, GORDON DAVID, lawyer; b. Huntington, N.Y., May 6, 1940; s. Gordon Stanley and Marie Christine (Smith) Miller; m. Leueen Mary O'Connor, Aug. 06, 1966; children: Christine Victoria, Heather Leueen, Winston Gordon Malachie. AB cum laude, Colgate U., 1962; LLB, Harvard U., 1965; LLM, NYU, 1974. Bar: N.Y. 1966, U.S. Dist. Ct. (so. and ea. dists.) N.Y. 1968. Sr. atty. N.Y. Life Ins. Co., N.Y.C., 1966—69; assoc. Winthrop Stimson Putnam & Roberts, 1969—70; atty. Pfizer Inc., 1970—73; legal officer, asst. sec. Internat. Nickel Co. Inc., 1973—85; assoc. Bruce Clark & Assocs., 1985—88; asst. corp. counsel City of New York, 1988—. Mem. exec. com. Colgate U. Ann. Fund, 1970—84; bd. dirs. Colgate U. Alumni Corp., 1976—80, chmn. nom. com., 1978—80. Recipient Maroon citation, Colgate U. Alumni Corp., 1977. Mem.: N.Y. County Lawyers Assn., Harvard Club. Antitrust, Labor. Home: 360 1st Ave New York NY 10010-4912 Office: Office of Corp Counsel 100 Church St New York NY 10007

MILLER, GREGORY R. lawyer; Chief asst. U.S. atty. Dept. Justice, Tallahassee, U.S. atty., 1993-98; asst. U.S. atty. Dept Justice, 2000—; assoc. Fowler, White, Gillen, Boggs, Villareal and Banker, PA, 1998-2000. Office: US Atty's Office 111 N Adams St Tallahassee FL 32301

MILLER, HAROLD ARTHUR, lawyer; b. St. Marie, Ill., Aug. 18, 1922; s. Arthur E. and Luletta (Noé) M.; m. Michele H. Rogivue, Nov. 21, 1947; children: Maurice H., Jan Leland, Marc Richard. BS in Acctg., U. Ill., 1942, JD, 1950. Bar: Ill. 1950, U.S. Dist. Ct. Ill. 1950, U.S. Tax Ct. 1950. Fgn. svc. officer U.S. State Dept., Paris, France, 1945-48; ptnr. Filson, Williamson & Miller, Champaign, Ill., 1950-60, Williamson & Miller, Champaign, 1960-72, Miller & Hendren, Champaign, 1972—. Atty. Christie Clinic Found., Champaign, 1960—; atty. pub. schs. dists., Champaign & Vermilion Counties, Ill., 1960—; atty. for municipalities in Champaign County, Ill., 1970—. Author: Estate Planning for Doctors, 1961, Intervivos Trusts Alternative to Probate, 1996. Bd. dirs., officer Urbana Ill. Sch. Dist., 1957-69; chmn., trustee Parkland Coll., Champaign, 1971-91; founding bd. mem. CCDC Found., Champaign-Urbana Ednl. Found., Moore Heart Found., Christie Found.; life mem. PTA. With inf. U.S. Army, 1942-45, ETO. Mem. ABA, Am. Judicature Soc., Ill. and Local Bar Assns., Ill. Trial Lawyers Assn., Alpha Kappa Psi. Presbyterian. Education and schools, Estate planning. Office: Miller & Hendren Attys 30 E Main St #200 Champaign IL 61820-3629 E-mail: ham@mhlawoffice.com

MILLER, HARVEY R. lawyer, bankruptcy reorganization specialist; b. Bklyn., Mar. 1, 1933; married Grad., Columbia U. Law Sch., 1959. Ptnr. Weil Gotshal and Manges LLP, N.Y.C. Adj. prof. law NYU Law Sch.; lectr. law Columbia U. Law Sch. Office: Weil Gotshal & Manges LLP 767 5th Ave Fl 29 New York NY 10153-0023 E-mail: harvey.miller@weil.com

MILLER, HENRY FRANKLIN, lawyer; b. Phila., May 19, 1938; s. Lester and Bessie (Posner) M.; m. Barbara Ann Gendel, June 20, 1964; children: Andrew, Alexa. AB, Lafayette Coll., 1959; LLB, U. Pa., 1964. Bar: Pa. 1965. Law clk. U.S. Dist. Ct. Del., Wilmington, 1964-65; assoc. Wolf, Block, Schorr & Solis-Cohen, Phila., 1965-71, ptnr., 1971—. Pres. Soc. Hill Synagogue, Phila., 1978-79, Big Brothers/Big Sisters Assn. of Phila., 1980-81, Jewish Family & Children's Agy., Phila., 1986-88. 1st lt. U.S. Army, 1959-60. Mem. Am. Coll. Real Estate Lawyers. Avocations: swimming, hiking, cycling, reading. Construction, Real property. Office: Wolf Block Schorr & Solis-Cohen 1650 Arch St Fl 21 Philadelphia PA 19103-2029 E-mail: hmiller@wolfblock.com

MILLER, HERBERT H. lawyer; b. Balt., May 24, 1921; s. Louis Miller and Rebecca Platt; m. Irene R. Rosen, Aug. 27, 1944; children: Rose, Marjorie, Fran. JD cum laude, U. Balt., 1942; ABA in Acctg., Balt. Coll. of Commerce, 1947. Bar: Md. 1943, U.S. Dist. Ct. Md. 1944, U.S. Supreme Ct. 1986; notary pub., Md. Law clk. Rubenstein and Rubenstein, Balt., 1938-39, Joel J. Hochman, Balt., 1939-40, Feikin & Talkin, Balt., 1940-42; atty. Sherbow, Harris & Medwedeff, 1942-43, Harris & Medwedeff, Balt., 1943-45; pvt. practice Balt. and Towson, Md., 1946—. Mem. inquiry panel Atty. Grievance Com. Md., Balt. County, 1985—; panel chmn. Health Claims Arbitration, Balt., 1994—. Bd. trustees Balt. Coll. Commerce, 1948-52, Beth El Congregation, Balt. County, 1990-94; youth advisor B'nai B'rith, Balt., 1943-88, mem. B'nai B'rith Youth Orgn., pres., 1940-42. Mem. Md. State Bar Assn., Balt. City Bar Assn., Balt. County Bar Assn., Mensa Internat. (arbitrator Md.). Avocations: reading, handyman work, walking. General corporate, Probate, Real property. Office: 200 E Joppa Rd Ste 205 Towson MD 21286-3107

MILLER, JAMES MONROE, lawyer; b. Owensboro, Ky., Apr. 20, 1948; s. James Rufus and Tommie (Melton) M.; m. Patricia Kirkpatrick, Nov. 28, 1975; children: Marian Elizabeth, James Graham. Student, George Washington U., 1966-67; BE, U. Ky., 1970, JD, 1973. Bar: Ky. 1973, U.S. Dist. Ct. Ky. 1973, U.S. Ct. Appeals (6th cir.) 1976, U.S. Supreme Ct. 1976. Law clk. to chief judge U.S. Dist. Ct. (we. dist.) Ky., Louisville and Owensboro, 1973-74; ptnr. Sullivan, Mountjoy, Stainback & Miller, P.S.C., Owensboro, 1974—. Mem. Leadership Ky., 1988, Leadership Owensboro, 1986; bd. dirs. Wendell Foster Ctr. Endowment Found., Inc., Owensboro; sec., trustee Owensboro-Daviess County Pub. Library, Owensboro; chmn. subcom. on sch. system merger Strategies for Tomorrow, Owensboro; v.p. legal Owensboro-Daviess County C. of C.; bd. dirs., sec. Owensboro-Daviess County Indsl. Found., Inc. Mem. ABA, Ky. Bar Assn. (chmn. Law Day/Spkrs. Bur. com. 1989-91), Daviess County Bar Assn., Ky. Coun. on Higher Edn. (chmn. programs com. 1991-93, chmn. 1993-96), Coun. Postsecondary Edn., Gov.'s Higher Edn. Rev. Commn. (chmn. 1993), Gov.'s Task Force on Tchr. Edn. Democrat. Methodist. Avocations: fishing, hunting, hiking, golf, skiing. General corporate, General practice, Public utilities. Home: 1920 Sheridan Pl Owensboro KY 42301-4525 Office: Sullivan Mountjoy Stainback & Miller PSC PO Box 727 100 Saint Ann St Owensboro KY 42303-4144

MILLER, JAMES ROBERT, lawyer; b. McKeesport, Pa., Aug. 2, 1947; s. Robert Charles and Ethel Margaret (Yahn) M.; m. Kathleen Ann Galka, June 6, 1975; children: Jesse J., Cassidy A. BA, NYU, 1969; JD, Duquesne U., 1972. Bar: Pa. 1972, U.S. Dist. Ct. (we. dist.) Pa. 1974, U.S. Ct. Appeals (3d cir.) 1978, U.S. Ct. Appeals (11th cir.) 1989, U.S. Supreme Ct. 1990. Law clerk to Hon. James C. Crumlish, Jr. Commonwealth Ct. of Pa., Phila., 1972-74; shareholder Dickie, McCamey & Chilcote, Pitts., 1974—. Mem. ABA, Am. Coll. Trial Lawyers, Pa. Bar Assn., Acad. Trial Lawyers. Avocation: sports. General civil litigation, Personal injury, Product liability. Office: Dickie McCamey & Chilcote Two PPG Pl Ste 400 Pittsburgh PA 15222

MILLER, JANISE LUEVENIA MONICA, lawyer; b. Atlanta, Dec. 25, 1956; d. James Thomas and Vera Luevenia (Brown) M.; 1 child, Brandyn Matthew Cooper. BA, Spalding U., 1976; JD, John Marshall Law Sch., 1979. Bar: Ga. 1982, U.S. Ct. Appeals (11th cir.) 1989. Mental health law specialist Ga. Legal Svcs., Atlanta, 1987-88; atty., paralegal Rogers & Sparks, 1980-82; staff counsel Ga. Dept. Med. Assistance, 1982-83; assoc. atty. Cuffie, Mitchell & Assocs., 1983-84, Cuffie & Assocs., Atlanta, 1984-85; pvt. practice, 1985-86; of counsel Albert A. Mitchell & Assocs., 1987-92, A.A. Mitchell & Assocs., Atlanta, 1987-92; pvt. practice, 1993—. Judge pro hac vice Atlanta Mcpl. Ct. 1989-91. Assoc. editor Nexus, 1980. Chairperson, pres. United Schleroderma Found., Atlanta, 1991-92. Fellow Ga. Bar Found.; mem. State Bar of Ga., Ga. Assn. of Black Women Attys. (Svc. award 1986), Atlanta Bar Assn. (chairperson, seminar com. 1987-88, sec./treas. criminal law sect. 1988-89), Nat. Bar Assn. (chairperson Gertrude Rush Dinner 1992), Gate City Bar Assn. (pres. 1987, editor newsletter 1992). Democrat. Roman Catholic. Avocations: reading, writing, swimming, cooking. General civil litigation, Criminal, Family and matrimonial. Office: PO Box 11229 Atlanta GA 30310-0229 E-mail: JLMMIL@aol.com

MILLER, JOHN EDDIE, lawyer; b. Wayne, Mich., Nov. 14, 1945; s. George Hayden and Georgia Irene (Stevenson) M.; m. Nancy Carol Sanders, Jan. 7, 1968; children: Andrea Christine, Matthew Kit. BA, Baylor U. , 1967; JD, U. Memphis, 1973; LLM, U. Mo., 1980. Bar: Mo. 1974, U.S. Dist. Ct. (we. dist.) Mo. 1974, Tex. 1982. Asst. prof. Central Mo. State U., Warrensburg, 1973-74; sole practice Sedalia, Mo., 1974-79; sr. contract adminstr. Midwest Research Inst., Kansas City, 1979-81, Tracor Inc., Austin, Tex., 1981-84; contract negotiator Tex. Instruments, 1984-86; sr. contract adminstr. Tracor Aerospace Inc., 1986-87, Radian Corp., Austin, 1987-96; counsel., asst. co. sec. Radian Internat. LLC, 1996—. Corp. sec. Radian Southeast Asia (SEA) Ltd., Bangkok, 1995—, dir. Radian Southeast Asia (SEA) Ltd., Bangkok, 1996—; corp. sec. Radian Internat. Overseas Mgmt. Co., 1996—; instr. bus. law State Fair Community Coll., Sedalia, 1974-79, Austin Community Coll., 1983-84. Bd. dirs. Legal Aid Western Mo., 1977—79, Boy's Club, Sedalia, 1974—79. Served with U.S. Army, 1968—71. Mem.: Mo. Bar Assn. (internat. law com., patent, trademark and copyright law com., tech. law com.), Tex. Bar Assn. (intellectual property law sect., internat. law sect., computer law sect.), U.S. Tennis Assn., Phi Alpha Delta. Computer, Intellectual property, Private international. E-mail: johnemiller@excite.com

MILLER, J(OHN) KENT, lawyer, educator; b. Chanute, Kans., Mar. 9, 1944; s. Ernest William and Margery (Olson) M.; m. Toni R. Taff, June 5, 1965 (div. Apr. 1975); children: Gentry, Callan; m. Leslie J. Jaffe, Sept. 14, 1979; children: Todd, Morgan. BS, U. Kans., 1966; JD, U. Denver, 1970. Bar: Colo. 1970, U.S. Dist. Ct. Colo. 1970, U.S. Supreme Ct. 1975. Mng. ptnr. Anderson, Campbell & Langesen, Denver, 1970-83; v.p. Gerash, Robinson, Miller & Miranda, 1984-87; pres. Miller & McCarren, PC, 1988-94, of counsel, 1994—. Adj. prof. U. Denver Sch. Law, 1990—. Author: (with others) Annual Survey Colorado Law, 1982-2000; author (2 vols.) Colorado Personal Injury Practice, 1989, 2d edit. (4 vols.), 2000. Mem. ABA, ATLA, Am. Bd. Trial Advs. (adv.), Colo. Trial Lawyers Assn. (bd. dirs. 1984-87), Denver Bar Assn., Colo. Bar Assn., Def. Rsch. Inst., Colo. Def. Lawyers Assn. Avocations: squash, skiing, performance driving. Insurance, Personal injury, Professional liability. Office: Miller & McCarren PC 2150 W 29th Ave Ste 500 Denver CO 80211-3844

MILLER, JOHN LEED, lawyer; b. Geneva, May 7, 1949; s. John Axel and Martha Mary (Masilunis) M.; m. Roosy Yanti, Jan. 2, 2001. BA, Northwestern U., 1971; JD, U. Chgo., 1975. Bar: Ill. 1975, U.S. Dist. Ct. (no. dist.) Ill., U.S. Ct. Appeals (7th and 8th cirs.). Assoc. counsel Profl. Ind. Mass-Mktg. Adminstrs., Chgo., 1975-76; legis. counsel to minority leader Ill. Ho. of Reps., Chgo. and Springfield, Ill., 1977-80, chief legal counsel, 1980, chief counsel to spkr., 1981-83; ptnr. Shaw and Miller, Chgo., 1981-84, Theodore A. Woerthwein, Chgo., 1984-85, Woerthwein & Miller, Chgo., 1985—. Statewide chmn. Ill. Young Voters for the Pres., 1972; dir. Ill. Ho. Rep. campaign com., 1976, 78, cons., 1982; pres. Newberry Pla. Condominium Assn., 1989-94. With ISNG, 1969-75. James scholar, 1970. Mem. Lawyers for the Creative Arts, Primitive Art Soc. Chgo. (treas. 1984-86, v.p. 1987, pres. 1988-89), Indonesia-Am. Assn. Ill. (bd. dirs.), Adventurers Club, Phi Eta Sigma, Phi Beta Kappa. Lutheran. General corporate, Legislative. Home: 1030 N State St Apt 9D Chicago IL 60610-5484 Office: Woerthwein & Miller PO Box A 3612 Chicago IL 60690-3612

MILLER, JOHN RANDOLPH, lawyer; b. Balt., Oct. 1946; s. Alan Randolph and Martha Virginia (Mercer) M.; m. Margaret Rose McGrane, July 20, 1969; children— John Randolph, Joseph Alan. A.B., Duke U., 1968, J.D., 1975. Bar: N.C. 1975, U.S. Dist. Ct. (we. and mid. dists.) N.C. Ptnr. Robinson, Bradshaw & Hinson, P.A., Charlotte, N.C., 1975—. Author: North Carolina Construction Law, 7th edit., 1990. Co-author Architect-Engineer Liability Under North Carolina Law 3d edit, 1991; editorial asst. Law and Contemporary Problems, 1974; article editor Duke Law Jour., 1975. Mem. Duke U. Delvl. Council, 1993—. Served to lt. USN, 1969-72. Angier Biddle Duke scholar, 1964. Mem. ABA, N.C. Bar Assn., Am. Arbitration Assn. (panel arbitrators 1986—), Order of Coif, Phi Delta Phi, Sigma Pi Sigma, Pi Mu Epsilon. Democrat. Episcopalian. Club: Tower (Charlotte). Construction, Securities. Home: 1644 Myers Park Dr Charlotte NC 28207-2670 Office: Robinson Bradshaw & Hinson PA 1900 Independence Ctr 101 N Tryon St Charlotte NC 28246-0100

MILLER, JOHN T., JR. lawyer, educator; b. Waterbury, Conn., Aug. 10, 1922; s. John T. and Anna (Purdy) M.; children: Kent, Lauren, Clare, Miriam, Michael, Sheila, Lisa, Colin, Margaret. AB with high honors, Clark U., 1944; JD, Georgetown U., 1948; Docteur en Droit, U. Geneva, 1951; postgrad., U. Paris, 1951. Bar: Conn. 1949 (inactive), D.C. 1950, U.S. Ct. Appeals (2d, 3d, 5th, 10th, 11th and D.C. cirs.), U.S. Supreme Ct. 1952. With Econ. Cooperation Adminstn. Am. Embassy, London, 1950-51; assoc. Covington & Burling, 1952-53, Gallagher, Connor & Boland, 1953-62; pvt. practice Washington, 1962—. Adj. prof. law Georgetown U. Law Ctr., Washington, 1959—; mem. Panel on Future of Internat. Ct. Justice. Co-author: Regulation of Trade, 1953, Modern American Antitrust Law, 1948, Major American Antitrust Laws, 1965; author: Foreign Trade in Gas and Electricity in North America: A Legal and Historical Study, 1970, Energy Problems and the Federal Government: Cases and Material, 8th edit., 1996, Deregulating the Interstate Natural Gas and Electric Power Industries, 2000; contbr. articles, book revs. to legal publs. Trustee Clark U., 1970-76; bd. trustees De Sales Sch. of Theology, 1993-97; bd. advisors Georgetown Visitation Prep. Sch., 1978-94, bd. trustees, 1994-96, emeritus trustee, 1996—; former fin. chmn. troop 46 Nat. Capital Area coun. Boy Scouts Am.; pres. Thomas More Soc. Am., 1996-97. 1st lt. U.S. Army, 1943-46, 48-49. Decorated Bronze Star; recipient 10 yr. teaching award Nat. Jud. Coll., 1983. Mem. ABA (coun., chmn. adminstrv. law sect. 1972-73, ho. dels. 1991-93), AAUP, D.C. Bar Assn., Fed. Energy Bar Assn. (pres. 1990-91), Congl. Country Club, Army and Navy Club (bd. govs. 2000—), DACOR, Prettyman-Leventhal Am. Inn of Ct. (master 1988-99, pres. 1995-96), Sovereign Mil. Order of Malta (knight). Republican. Roman Catholic. Administrative and regulatory, Antitrust, FERC practice. Home: 4721 Rodman St NW Washington DC 20016-3234 Office: 1001 Connecticut Ave NW Washington DC 20036-5504 E-mail: jtmillerjr@erols.com

MILLER, J(OHN) WESLEY, III, lawyer, writer; b. Springfield, Mass., Oct. 3, 1941; s. John Wesley Jr. and Blanche Ethel (Wilson) M. AB, Colby Coll., 1963; AM, Harvard U., 1964, JD, 1981. Bar: Mass. 1984, U.S. Dist. Ct. Mass. 1984, U.S. Supreme Ct. 1993. Instr. English Heidelberg Coll., Tiffin, Ohio, 1964-69, U. Wis., 1969-77; real estate broker, 1977-84. Founder Miller-Wilson Family Papers, U. Vt., Madison (Wis.) People's Poster and Propaganda Collection, St. Hist. Soc. Wis. Author: History of Buckingham Junior High School, 1956, The Millers of Roxham, 1958, Giroux Genealogy, 1958, Symphonic Heritage, 1959, Community Guide to Madison Murals, 1977, Aunt Jennie's Poems, 1986, Blanche and John's Fernbank: A Wilbraham Camping Experience, 2001 ; founding editor: Hein's Poetry and the Law Series, 1985—; editor: The Curiosities and Law

of Wills, 1989, The Lawyers Alcove, 1990, Famous Divorces, 1991, Legal Laughs, 1993, Coke in Verse, 1999, The Law and Lawyers Laid Open, 2002; founding editor: Law Libr. Microform Consortium Arts Law Letters Collection, 1991—; exhibitor A Salue to Street Art, State Hist. Soc. wis., 1974; represented in permanent collections U. Vt., Colby Coll. Archives, State Hist. Soc. Wis., Boston Pub. Libr., Pierpont Morgan Libr.; contbr. The Poems of Ambrose Philips, 1969, Dictionary of Canadian Biography, 1980, Collection Building Reader, 1992, Oxford English Dictionary, 1995—; contbr. numerous articles on Am. street lit., bibliography, ethics, history, edn., law, religion, librarianship, mgmt. of archives, gay studies. Recipient Cmty. Activism award Bay State Objectivist, 1993, 94, 95; fellow Wisdom Hall of Fame, 2000, Samuel Victor Constant fellow, 2001. Mem. MLA, Am. Philol. Assn., Milton Soc., New Eng. Historic Geneal. Soc., Vt. Hist. Soc., Wis. Acad. Scis., Arts & Letters, Social Law Library, Pilgrim Soc., Ancient and Hon. Arty. Co., Mayflower Soc., Soc. Colonial Wars, Sons and Daus. of the Victims of Colonial Witch Trials, Mensa, Springfield Renaissance Group. Office: 5 Birchland Ave Springfield MA 01119-2708

MILLER, JOSEPH BAYARD, lawyer; b. Highland, La., Feb. 25, 1920; s. Harrison Coleman and Jeannette (Donaldson) M.; m. Gloria Berthelot, Dec. 31, 1950; children: Joseph Bayard Jr., Melinda May. BA in Arts and Scis., Tulane U., 1939, LLB, 1941. Bar: La. 1941, U.S. Dist. Ct. (ea. dist.) La. 1941, U.S. Ct. Appeals (5th cir.) 1941, U.S. Supreme Ct. 1969. Assoc. Milling, Godchaux, Saal & Milling, New Orleans, 1941-47; ptnr. Milling, Benson, Woodward, Hillyer, Pierson & Miller, 1948—. Bd. dirs. Continental Land & Fur Co., Inc., New Orleans. Maj. USAAF, 1942-46, PTO. Mem. New Orleans Country Club, City Energy Club. Episcopalian. Avocations: hunting, fishing, horses. General corporate, Oil, gas, and mineral, General practice. Home: 7399 Agate St New Orleans LA 70124-3512 Office: Milling Benson Woodward Hillyer Pierson & Miller 909 Poydras St Ste 2300 New Orleans LA 70112-1010

MILLER, KEITH ALLAN, judge, lawyer; b. Jacksonville, N.C., Aug. 21, 1953; s. Paul V. Miller and Ruth E. Vanderpool; m. Ivanna D. Long, Dec. 24, 1981; children: Esther, Gail, Joel, Jared, Isaac. BS in Phys. Scis., Pacific Union Coll., Angwin, Calif., 1978; JD, Syracuse U., 1990; postgrad., Willamette U., 1991-94. Bar: Oreg. 1992, U.S. Ct. Vet. Appeals 1992, U.S. Supreme Ct. 1999. Orchadist Miller Farms, Umqua, Oreg., 1981-85; pvt. practice atty. Sublimity, 1992-95, Sweet Home, 1996—; peer ct. judge Linn County Cts., 1998—. Dir. guardian ad-litem program ABA, Chgo., 1983. Columnist Horse Cents, 1993. Dir. John Anderson for Pres., Douglas County, Oreg., 1980, Multiple Sclerosis Soc. Douglas County, Roseburg, Oreg., 1980; organizer, pres. Dallas Mobile Home Pk. Renters Assn., 1992-94; Dem. candidate Oreg. State Rep. Dist. 34, 1992, 94. Petty officer USN, 1979-80. Scholar Am. United Separation Ch. and State, 1985. Mem. Oreg. Criminal Def. Lawyers Assn. Democrat. Avocations: auto restoration, stamp collecting, boat building. Office: 1262 Main St Sweet Home OR 97386-1608 Fax: 541-367-4209

MILLER, KERRY LEE, lawyer; b. West Palm Beach, Sept. 11, 1955; s. Clyde Howard and Alice (Hummel) M.; m. Myrna Patricia Garza, June 9, 1979; children: Alexander James, Eric Anthony. BA, George Mason U., 1977; JD, Cath. U., 1981. Bar: D.C. 1981, Va. 1982, U.S. Dist. Ct. (D.C. dist.) 1982, U.S. Ct. Appeals (D.C. and 4th cirs.) 1982, U.S. Ct. Appeals (fed. cir.) 1989, U.S. Ct. Claims 1989, U.S. Supreme Ct. 1989, U.S. Dist. Ct. (ea. and we. dists.) Va. 1993. Asst. gen. counsel Office Gen. Counsel U.S. Govt. Printing Office, Washington, 1981-87, assoc. gen. counsel contracts and procurement, 1987-99; adminstrv. law judge Bd. Contract Appeals U.S. Govt. Printing Office, 1999—. Mem. Fed. Bar Assn. (mem. chpt. coun. Capitol Hill chpt.), Bd. Contract Appeals Judges Assn., Computer Law Assn., Contract Appeals Bar Assn. Office: US Govt Printing Office Office Bd Contract Appeals 732 N Capitol St NW Washington DC 20401-0001 E-mail: kmiller@gpo.gov

MILLER, KIRK EDWARD, lawyer, health foundation executive; b. San Jose, Calif., June 9, 1951; BA in Polit. Sci., U. Calif., Riverside, 1973; JD, Syracuse U., 1976. Bar: Colo. 1976, Calif. 1980, Tex. 1993. Assoc. Hughes & Dorsey, Denver, 1977-78; v.p., assoc. gen. counsel Am. Med. Internat., Inc., Dallas, 1979-88, v.p., sec., gen. counsel, 1988-91; with McGlinchey Stafford Lang, 1991-94; sr. v.p., sec., gen. counsel Kaiser Found. Health Plan, Inc., Kaiser Found. Hosps., Inc., Oakland, Calif., 1994—. Instr. Syracuse U., 1975-76. Mem. ABA (co-vice chair com. health care fraud and abuse 1995-96). Office: Kaiser Found Health Plan 1 Kaiser Plz Oakland CA 94612-3610

MILLER, LESLIE ANNE, lawyer; b. Franlin, Ind., Nov. 4, 1951; d. G. Thomas and Anne (Gaines) Miller; m. Richard B. Worley, Feb. 14, 1987. AB cum laude, Mt. Holyoke Coll., South Hadley, Pa., 1973; MA in Polit. Sci., Eagle Inst. Politics Rutgers U., New Brunswick, N.J., 1974; JD, Dickinson Sch. of Law, Carlisle, Pa., 1977; LLM with honors, Temple U., 1994. Bar: Pa. 1977, U.S. Dist. Ct. (ea. dist.) Pa. 1977, U.S. Ct. Appeals (3d cir.) 1980, U.S. Dist. Ct. (ea. dist.) Pa. 1987. Assoc. LaBrum & Doak, Phila., 1977-81, ptnr., 1982-86, Goldfein & Joseph, Phila., 1986-95, McKissock & Hoffman, P.C., Phila., 1995—. Bd. dirs. WHYY-TV, 1996—; del. Third Circuit Jud. Conf., 1981, 82, 85; mem. Jud. Inquiry and Rev. Bd., 1990-94, chair, 1993-94; mem. faculty trial advocacy program Dickinson Sch. Law, 1992, 94; mem. hearing com., disciplinary bd. Supreme Ct. Pa., 1996—; mem. faculty Acad. Advocacy Temple U., 1994—; judge pro tem Ct. of Common Pleas. Mem. acad. ball com. Phila. Orch., 1986-87, 89-91, 95-96, mem. acad. music com. 1998—; mem. Open Space Task Force Com., Lower Merion Twp., Pa., 1990, bd. dirs., 1990-94, mem. counsel, 1990, Lower Merion Conservancy, 1995-97, 2000—, others; bd. dirs. Med. Coll. Pa., 1985-96, sec., 1987-92, chair presdl. search com., 1993, chair presdl. inauguration, 1987, chair com. on acad. affairs, 1989-95, chair dean's search com., 1994-95, chair nomenclature com., 1996; bd. dirs. Med. Coll. Hosps., 1991-96, Allegheny Health Edn. and Rsch. Found., 1993-96, Hahnemann U. Med. Sch., 1994-96, Pa. Ballet, 1994—, St. Christopher's Hosp. for Children, 1991-94, vice chair, 1990-94; bd. dirs. Phila. Free Libr., 1997—; trustee Mt. Holyoke Coll., 2000—; bd. govs. Dickinson Sch. Law, Pa. State U., 2001—. Recipient Mary Lyon award, Mt. Holyoke Alumni Assn., 1985, Alumnae Medal of Honor, 1988, Hon. Alumnae award, 1989, Pres.'s award Med. Coll. Pa., 1993, Sylvia Rambo award Dickinson Sch. of Law, 1997, Star award Forum of Exec. Women, 1998, Ann Alpern award PBA Women in the Profession, 1999, Sandra Day O'Connor award Phila. Bar Assn., 1999, Outstanding Leadership in Support of Legal Svcs. award Pa. Legal Svcs., 1999; named to Pa. Honor Roll of Women, 1996, Disting. Dau. of Pa., Gov. Tom Ridge, 1999. Fellow Am. Bar Found., Pa. Bar Found.; mem. ABA, Phila. Bar Assn. (mem. exec. com. divsn. young lawyers 1982-85, mem. bicentennial com 1986-87, bd. govs. 1990-93, mem. gender bias task force 1993-97, chair com. on jud. selection and retention 1987-89, vice chair 1985-87, investigative divsn. 1982-85, chair Andrew Hamilton Ball 1989, trustee Phila. Bar Found. 1990-97, co-chair century three commn. 1995-97, others), Pa. Bar Assn. (found. ho. dels. life fellow, bd. govs. 1980-83, 84-87, 91-93, chair young lawyers divsn. 1982-83, mem. long range planning com. 1985-87, mem. com. on professionalism, 1987-91, vice chmn. jud. inquiry and rev. bd. study com. 1989-91, sec. 1984-87, chair ho. dels. 1991-93, chair commn. on women in the profession 1993-95, v.p. 1996-97, pres. 1998-99, immediate past pres. 1999—, apptd. mem. ct. jud. discipline 1999), Pa. Bar Inst. (mem. faculty, course planner), Phila. Assn. Def. Counsel (mem. exec. coun. 1987-90, 94, mem. joint trial demonstration with Phila. Trial Lawyers Assn. 1993), Def. Rsch. Inst. (spkr. toxic torts seminar 1983), Phila. Bar Edn. Advocacy Women Litigators (course planner, mem. faculty 1995), Women's Assn. Women's Alternatives (bd. dirs. 1983-94, vice chair 1985-94), Phila. Forum Exec. Women, Pa. Women's Forum, Com. of Seventy, Mt. Holyoke Alumnae Assn. (bd. dirs. 1986-89). Democrat. Lutheran. Avocations: collecting Am. antiques, gardening, running. General civil litigation, Personal injury. Office: McKissock & Hoffman PC 1700 Market St Ste 3000 Philadelphia PA 19103-3933 E-mail: millesq@aol.com

MILLER, LOUIS H. lawyer; b. Lampeter, U.K., Apr. 22, 1945; m. Diane Matuszewski, Dec. 31, 1973; children: Margaret, Anthony. BA in History, Rutgers Coll., 1967; JD, Temple U., 1970. Bar: N.J. 1970, U.S. Dist. Ct. N.J. 1970, U.S. Supreme Ct. 1996. Law clk. to Judge Thomas Beetel Hunterdon County Ct., Flemington, N.J., 1970-71; law clk. to Judge Baruch Seidman Superior Ct. N.J. Chancery, Trenton, 1971-72; assoc. Jefferson, Jefferson & Vaida, Flemington, 1972-75; ptnr. Vaida & Miller, 1975-78; pvt. practice, 1978-81, 88—; judge Superior Ct. N.J., 1981-88; of counsel Levinson Axelrod Wheaton & Grayzel, 1990-97. Spl. dep. atty. gen. N.J. Hunterdon County Prosecutor Office, Flemington, 1972-73; condemnation commr. Appt. Superior Ct. N.J., Flemington, 1988—, N.J. Assembly spkrs. commr.; commr. N.J. State Commn. Investigation, Trenton, 1993-97; arbitrator U.S. Fed. Dist. Ct. N.J., 1989—. Twp. committeeman Alexandria Twp. Com., R.D. Milford, N.J., 1978-81. Mem. Am. Judges Assn., Am. Judicature Soc., N.J. State Bar Assn. (mem. dist. ethics com. 1980-81, mem. mcpl. ct. practice com. 1996—), Hunterdon County Bar Assn., Consular Law Soc., Welsh Am. Geneal. Soc., Welsh North Am. C. of C. (bd. dirs.). Republican. Avocations: paleontology, traveling, hiking. Criminal, Family and matrimonial, Personal injury. Office: PO Box 850 40 Main St Flemington NJ 08822-1411 E-mail: millerlh@earthlink.net

MILLER, MAX DUNHAM, JR. lawyer; b. Des Moines, Oct. 17, 1946; s. Max Dunham and Beulah (Head) M.; m. Melissa Ann Dart, Jan. 10, 1969 (div. July 1975); 1 child, Ann Marie Victoria; m. Caroline Jean Armendt, Sept. 19, 1981; children: Alexander Bradshaw, Benjamin Everrett. BS with high honors, Mich. State U., 1968; postgrad., George Washington U., 1970-71; JD, U. Md., 1975. Bar: Md. 1976, U.S. Dist. Ct. Md. 1976, U.S. Ct. Appeals (4th cir.) 1981, U.S. Supreme Ct. 1982. Engr. U.S. Dept. of Def., Aberdeen Proving Ground, Md., 1968-72; law clk. to presiding judge Md. Cir. Ct., Higinbothom in Bel Air, 1975-76; asst. county atty. Harford County, Bel Air, 1976-79; assoc. Lentz & Hooper P.A., Balt., 1979-81; ptnr. Miller, Olszewski & Moore, P.A., Bel Air, 1981-94; prin. Law Offices of Max D. Miller, P.A., 1994—. County atty. Harford County, Md., 1983-88. Mem. Md. Bar Assn., Assn. Trial Lawyers Am., Md. Trial Lawyers Assn., Harford County Bar Assn., Phi Kappa Phi, Phi Eta Sigma. Avocations: golf, sailing, canoeing, bicycling, ice and roller hockey. General civil litigation, General corporate, Real property. Home: 308 Whetstone Rd Forest Hill MD 21050-1332 Office: 5 S Hickory Ave Bel Air MD 21014-3732

MILLER, MICHAEL PATIKY, lawyer; b. Huntington, N.Y., Apr. 16, 1944; s. George J. and Alida (Patiky) Miller; m. Dorothy Denn, Dec. 25, 1966; children: Lauren M. Golubtchik, Jonathan M., Rachel Miller Lazarus. AB, Rutgers U., 1965; JD, NYU, 1968. Bar: N.J. 1968, U.S. Dist. Ct. N.J. 1968, Calif. 1975, U.S. Dist. Ct. (no. dist.) Calif. 1975, U.S. Tax Ct. 1977, U.S. Ct. Appeals (9th cir.) 1977, U.S. Ct. Appeals (fed. cir.) 1984, U.S. Dist. Ct. (cen. dist.) Calif. 1982, U.S. Supreme Ct. 1983, U.S. Claims Ct. 1986. Atty. Electric Power Research Inst., Palo Alto, Calif., 1974-77; assoc. Weinberg, Ziff & Kaye, 1977-78; ptnr. Weinberg, Ziff & Miller, 1978—, mng. ptnr., 1991-98; lectr. on tax and estate planning U. Calif. Extension, 1980—. Author: Creditor Rights in Proceedings Outside Estate Adminstrn., 1995, rev., 1999, Estate Planning for Foreign Nationals in Silicon Valley, 2000; co-author: Decedents Estate Practice, 2001, Trust Administration, 2d edit., 2001; contbg. author: California Wills and Trusts, 1991, Estate Planning for Unmarried Couples, 1998, California Trust Administration, 1999; contbr. chpts. in books and articles to profl. jours. Treas. No. Calif. region United Synagogue Am., 1985-89, pres., 1992-95. Capt. U.S. Army, 1969-74, Vietnam, Ethiopia. Recipient Lion of Judah award, 1984, Cert. Merit U. Judaism, 1992. Mem. ABA (chmn. region VI pub. contract law sect. 1975-78, commn. tax practice in small law firms, com. on taxation of trusts, estates, taxation sect. 1986—), N.J. State Bar, State Bar of Calif. (commr. tax law adv. commn. 1989-92, 93-95, chair 1994-95, mem. bd. legal specialization 1994-95), Santa Clara County Bar Assn. (chmn. estate planning, probate and trust sect. 1982, trustee 1983-84), Silicon Valley Bar Assn. (pres. 2000—). Probate, Estate taxation, Personal income taxation. Office: Weinberg Ziff & Miller 400 Cambridge Ave Palo Alto CA 94306-1507

MILLER, MILTON ALLEN, lawyer; b. L.A., Jan. 15, 1954; s. Samuel C. and Sylvia Mary Jane (Silver) Miller; m. Mary Ann Toman, Sept. 10, 1988; 1 child Mary Ann. AB With distinction and honors in Econs., Stanford U., 1976; JD with honors, Harvard U., 1979. Bar: Calif. 1979, U.S. Dist. Ct. (cen., no. and so. dists.) Calif., U.S. Ct. Appeals 99th cir.) 1979, U.S. Supreme Ct. 1989. Law clk. U.S. Ct. Appeals (9th cir.), Sacramento, 1979—80; assoc. Latham & Watkins, L.A., 1979—87, ptnr., 1987—. Author: (non-fiction) Attorney Ethics; editor (articles): (law rev.) Harvard Law Rev., 1978—79. Mem.: ABA, ATLA, Calif. State Bar Assn. (mem. com. on profl. responsibility), L.A. County Bar Assn. (chmn. profl. responsibility and ethics com.), Am. Cancer Soc. (L.A. chpt.), Phi Beta Kappa. Federal civil litigation, General civil litigation, Insurance. Office: Latham & Watkins 633 W 5th St Ste 4000 Los Angeles CA 90071-2005

MILLER, MORRIS HENRY, lawyer; b. Thomasville, Ga., June 14, 1954; s. Gibbes Ulmer and Marianne (Morris) M.; m. Anita Carol Payne, Mar. 23, 1985; children: Morris Payne, Rose Elizabeth, David Gibbes, Paul Louis Henry, John Henry. BS in Acctg. summa cum laude, Fla. State U., 1976; JD, U. Va., 1979. Bar: Fla. 1979. Assoc. Holland & Knight, Tampa, Fla., 1979-84, ptnr. Tallahassee, 1984—, chmn. health law practice, 1989—. Founder, chair PENmd.com. Dist. fin. chmn. Gulf Ridge coun. Boy Scouts Am., 1988-89, mem. pack com., cubmaster Pack 23, Suwannee River Area coun., 1995-98, scoutmaster Troop 182, 1997-99, scoutmaster Troop 10, 2000—, dist. nominating com.; mem. Leadership Tampa, 1986, Leadership Tampa Bay, 1989; bd. dirs. John G. Riley House Mus. Ctr. for African-Am. History and Culture, 1999—, Tallahassee YMCA, 1994—, chmn. long range planning com., 1997; founder, chmn. Tampa Bus. Com. for Arts, Inc., 1988-89; elder Presbyn. Ch. Mem. ABA (health law sect.), Fla. Bar Assn. (chmn., vice chmn. computer law com. 1983-89, Fla. corp. law revision com. 1986-89, health law sect.), Tallahassee Bar Assn., Tallahassee Area C. of C. (strategic plan implementation com., Tallahassee trustees), Fla. Acad. Hosp. Attys. (chair govtl. hosp. com.). Computer, General corporate, Health. Office: Holland & Knight 315 S Calhoun St Ste 600 Tallahassee FL 32301-1897

MILLER, NORMAN RICHARD, lawyer; b. Oak Ridge, Tenn., Apr. 4, 1948; s. Francis J. and Sylvia R. Miller; m. Carol Golden, Aug. 15, 1971; children: Russell, Adam, Jordan. BA with distinction, Northwestern U., 1970; JD, Harvard U., 1973. Law clk. to Judge Latham Castle U.S. Ct. Appeals (7th cir.), Chgo., 1973-74; ptnr. Akin, Gump, Strauss, Hauer & Feld, Dallas, 1980-90, Cox & Smith Inc., San Antonio, 1990-93, Kirkpatrick & Lockhart LLC and predecessor, 1995—. Trustee Temple Shalom, 1982-84. Hon. Woodrow Wilson fellow. Mem. ABA, State Bar Tex., Dallas Bar Assn., Phi Beta Kappa. General corporate, Mergers and acquisitions, Securities. Office: 1717 Main St Ste 3100 Dallas TX 75201-4681

MILLER, PAUL J. lawyer; b. Boston, Mar. 27, 1929; s. Edward and Esther (Kalis) M.; children— Robin, Jonathan; m. Michal Davis, Sept. 1, 1965; children— Anthony, Douglas B.A., Yale U., 1950; LL.B., Harvard U., 1953. Bar: Mass. 1953, Ill. 1957. Assoc. Miller & Miller, Boston, 1953-54; assoc. Sonnenschein Nath & Rosenthal, Chgo., 1957-63, ptnr., 1963—. Bd. dirs. Oil-Dri Corp. Am., Chgo. Trustee Latin Sch. of Chgo., 1985-91. 1st lt. JAGC, U.S. Army, 1954-57. Fellow Am. Bar Found.; mem. Tavern Club, Saddle and Cycle Club, Law Club, Phi Beta Kappa. Avocation: sailing. Contracts commercial, General corporate, Securities. Office: Sonnenschein Nath & Rosenthal 233 S Wacker Dr Ste 8000 Chicago IL 60606-6491 E-mail: pjm@sonnenschein.com

MILLER, PETER ALEXANDER, lawyer; b. N.Y.C., Jan. 29, 1943; s. Oscar and Shulamith (Ourlicht) M.; m. Karen Riber Apple, June 4, 1968; 1 dau., Georgia Alexander. B.A., B.S., U. Hartford, 1967; postgrad., U. Iowa, 1968; J.D., U. Ark., 1979. Bar: Ark. 1980. Producer, United Artists, N.Y.C., 1969-72; editor Arkansas Sun, Heber Springs, 1976-79; producer Media Resources, Little Rock, Ark., 1979-81; ptnr. Kaplan, Brewer & Miller, Little Rock, 1980— . Author: Disfarmer; Portraits, 1977. Mem. ABA, Ark. Bar Assn., Assn. Trial Lawyers Am. State civil litigation, Libel, Personal injury. Home: 2106 S Gaines St Little Rock AR 72206-1319 Office: Miller Law Firm 111 Center St Ste 1620 Little Rock AR 72201-4446

MILLER, RALPH WILLIAM, JR. lawyer; b. Chgo., Mar. 9, 1931; s. Ralph William and Pearl Mae (Bauer) M.; m. Jean Lois Gromer; children: Darlene Miller Martinez, Ralph William, Dean. BS, Northwestern U., 1952, JD, 1955. Bar: Ill. 1956, U.S. Dist. Ct. (no. dist.) Ill. 1987, U.S. Ct. Appeals (7th cir.) 1987, U.S. Supreme Ct. 1995. With firm Taylor, Miller, Magner, Sprowl & Hutchings, 1946-55; pvt. practice, Elgin, Ill., 1957-58, Elmhurst, Ill., 1980-81, Oak Brook, Ill., 1986—; asst. counsel Jewel Cos., Inc., Melrose Park, Ill., 1958-67, ins. atty., 1967-71, sr. atty., 1971-72, gen. atty., 1972-74, v.p. regulatory rsch. and planning Jewel Food Stores div., 1974-80, also gen. counsel, 1975-80; of counsel Law Offices of Francis M. Discipio, 1988-95, Law Offices of Francis J. Discipio, 1995—; mem. Indsl. Commn. State of Ill., Chgo., 1981-86. . Mem. Gov.'s Agreed Bill Process Com. for Workers' Compensation in Ill., 1979-81. With U.S. Army, 1955-57. Mem. ABA, Ill. Bar Assn. (chmn. ins. program com. 1971-73), Chgo. Bar Assn. (chmn. food, drug and consumer product safety com. 1975-76), DuPage County Bar Assn., Ill. Def. Counsel, Def. Rsch. Inst., Nat. Conf. Weights and Measures, Workers Compensation Lawyers Assn., Dupage County Estate Planning Coun., Industry Com. Packaging and Labeling (chmn. 1977-79), Food Mktg. Inst. (chmn. metric com. 1978-80), Am. Nat. Metric Council (chmn. retailers sector, vice-chmn. legal adv. com. 1978-80), Ill. State C. of C. (chmn. workers compensation com. 1973-78). E-mail: 630-953-8534. Home: 936 Spring Rd Elmhurst IL 60126-4928 Office: 2021 Midwest Rd Ste 200 Oak Brook IL 60523-1370

MILLER, RANDAL J. lawyer, educator; b. Joliet, Ill., Apr. 16, 1952; s. William D. Jr. and Joyce N. Miller; m. Mary Kaluzny, Oct. 4, 1980; children: Randal J. Jr., Hayley K., Hannah S. AA, Joliet Jr. Coll., 1973; BS, Lewis U., Lockport, Ill., 1975; JD, John Marshall Law Sch., Chgo., 1978. Bar: Ill. 1978, U.S. Dist. Ct. (no. dist.) Ill. 1982, U.S. Ct. Appeals (7th cir.) 1982. Real estate and trust atty. Heritage Bank, Crest Hill, Ill., 1978-79; asst. state's atty. County of Will, Joliet, 1979-86, asst. pub. defender, 1986-89; ptnr. Dunn, Martin & Miller, Ltd., 1991—. Adj. prof. Joliet Jr. Coll., 1980-84, U. St. Francis, Joliet, 1988—. Cons. atty. Reflex Sympathetic Dystrophy Assn., Chgo., 1996—. Mem. exec. com. Will County Rep. Orgn., Joliet, 1985-90. Mem. Ill. State Bar Assn. (assemblyman 1991-97, standing com. supreme ct. rules 1997—), Will County Bar Assn. (bd. dirs. 1992-95, pres. 1999-2000), Masons. Avocations: music, collectibles, fine art. State civil litigation, Personal injury, Workers' compensation. Home: 2604 Glasgow St Joliet IL 60435-1335 Office: Dunn Martin & Miller Ltd 15 W Jefferson St Ste 300 Joliet IL 60432-4301

MILLER, RAYMOND VINCENT, JR. lawyer; b. Providence, July 1, 1954; s. Raymond Vincent and Mary Eunice (Mullen) M.; m. Elizabeth Ann White, May 31, 1980; children: Travis, Charles. BA, U. R.I., 1976; JD cum laude, U. Miami, 1981. Bar: Fla. 1981, U.S. Dist. Ct. (so. dist.) Fla. 1981, U.S. Ct. Appeals (11th cir.) 1986, U.S. Dist. Ct. (mid. dist.) Fla. 1987. Area supr. job devel. and tng. div. R.I. Dept. Econ. Devel., Providence, 1977-78; assoc. Thornton & Herndon, Miami, Fla., 1981-83, Britton, Cohen et al, Miami, 1983-85, Edward A. Kaufman, P.A., Miami, 1985-88; ptnr. Kaufman, Miller, Dickstein & Grunspan, 1988-2000; shareholder Gunster, Yoakley & Stewart, P.A., 2000—. Mem. ABA, Fla. Bar Assn., Nat Order Barristers, Soc. Bar and Gavel, Acad. Fla. Trial Lawyers (chair comml. law sect. 1993-95). Federal civil litigation, State civil litigation, Personal injury. Office: Gunster Yoakley & Stewart PA 2 S Biscayne Blvd Ste 3400 Miami FL 33131 E-mail: RMiller@gunster.com

MILLER, RICHARD ALLAN, lawyer; b. N.Y.C., Oct. 28, 1947; s. Harold B. and Helen (Schwartz) M.; m. Karen R. Mangold, July, 5, 1970; children: David, Matthew. BA, SUNY, Buffalo, 1969; MA, Ohio State U., 1970; JD, NYU, 1973. Bar: N.Y. 1974, U.S. Dist. Ct. (so. and ea. dists.) N.Y. 1974, U.S. Ct. Appeals (2d cir.) 1977, U.S. Supreme Ct. 1980. Assoc. Paul Weiss et al, N.Y.C., 1973-75; asst. dist. atty. N.Y. County, 1975-77; ptnr. Newman, Tannenbaum et al, 1980-91, Katten Muchin & Zavis, N.Y.C., 1992-96, White & Case, 1996—. Staff counsel Presdl. Task Force on Market Mechanisms, 1987-88; speaker Internat. Conf. Futures Money Mgmt., 1990-92. Editor, pub. Futures & Derivatives L. Rpt., 1981—, Securities Arbitration Commentator, 1988—. Mem. Assn. of the Bar of the City of N.Y. (chair futures regulations com.). Jewish. Avocation: golf. Administrative and regulatory, Federal civil litigation, Securities. Home: 22 Roosevelt Rd Maplewood NJ 07040-2116 Office: White & Case 1155 Ave Americas New York NY 10036 E-mail: rmiller@whitecase.com

MILLER, RICHARD ALLEN, lawyer; b. East Chicago, Ind., Nov. 22, 1945; s. Ernest R. and Sophie D. (Kurmis) M.; m. Patricia Annette Bratton, July 26, 1969 (div. May 1974); 1 child, Jason Todd; m. Kathleen Patrice Sills, Jan. 3, 1976; children: Andrew Christian, Caroline Grace. BS, Ind. U., 1967; JD, Valparaiso U., 1973. Bar: Ind. 1974, U.S. Dist. Ct. (no. dist.) Ind. 1974, U.S. Supreme Ct. 1985, U.S. Ct. Appeals (7th cir.) 1987, U.S. Claims Ct. 1990. Assoc. Owen W. Crumpacker & Assocs., Hammond, Ind., 1974-76, Benjamin, Greco & Gouveia, Gary, 1976-77; ptnr. Greco, Gouveia, Miller & Pera, 1978-79, Greco, Gouveia, Miller, Pera & Bishop, Merrillville, Ind., 1979-85, Gouveia & Miller, Merrillville, 1985—. Spl. counsel City of Hammond, 1974-76; trial counsel Ind. Toll Rd. Com., South Bend, 1981-82, Ind. Dept. Highways Toll Rd. Div., Granger, 1982-87; spl. asst. U.S. Rep. Peter J. Visclosky, Gary and Washington, 1985-86. Author: Indiana Rules of Evidence Applying to Expert Testimony, 1991. Campaign mgr. Visclosky for U.S. Congress, 1st Congl. Dist., Ind., 1983-88; dist. coordinator Nat. Bicentennial Competition on U.S. Constitution and Bill of Rights, 1st Congl. Dist., Ind., 1987-88. Mem. Ind. Bar Assn., Assn. Trial Lawyers Am., Ind. Trial Lawyers Assn. Democrat. Lutheran. Avocations: fly fishing, walking dog. General civil litigation, Condemnation, Personal injury. Home: 10313 Marlou Dr Munster IN 46321-4339 Office: Gouveia & Miller 433 W 84th Dr Merrillville IN 46410-6173 E-mail: rambeaulaw@aol.com

MILLER, RICHARD MARK, lawyer; b. Feb. 12, 1952; s. Abraham and Phyllis (Isaacson) M.; m. Beverly Elaine Sparks, Aug. 7, 1976 (div. 1992); m. Cathryn Alexandra Mitchell, Oct. 3, 1993; children: Jeffrey Brian, David Gregory, Scott Alan, Jenifer Marlena. BA, Bklyn. Coll., 1973; JD, SUNY, Buffalo, 1976. Bar: N.Y. 1977, N.J. 1977, U.S. Dist. Ct. (so. and ea. dists.) N.Y. 1977, U.S. Dist. Ct. N.J. 1977. Gen. counsel Amswiss Internat. Corp., Jersey City, 1976-78; assoc. gen. counsel Loeb Rhoades, Hornblower, N.Y.C., 1978-79, Shearson Loeb Rhoades, 1979-80; assoc. counsel Bausch & Lomb Inc., Rochester, N.Y., 1980-83, counsel, 1983-85; sr. atty. Cheseborough Pond's Inc., 1985-87; corp. counsel Prince Sports Group, Inc. (formerly Prince Mfg., Inc.), Princeton, N.J., 1987-90, gen. counsel, 1990-93; cons. Proskauer Rose Goetz & Mendelsohn, N.Y.C., 1993-94; counsel Stark & Stark, Princeton, 1994-96; prin. Miller & Mitchell,

1996—. Chmn. Internat. Trade Network; mem. Internat. Trade Adv. Commn., Mercer County C.C. Contracts commercial, General corporate, Mergers and acquisitions. Home: 29 Crusher Rd Hopewell NJ 08525-2201 Office: Miller & Mitchell PC 863 State Rd Princeton NJ 08540 E-mail: rmiller@millermitchell.com

MILLER, RICHARD SHERWIN, law educator; b. Boston, Dec. 11, 1930; s. Max and Mollie Miller; m. Doris Sheila Lunchick, May 24, 1956; children: Andrea Jayne Armitage, Matthew Harlan. BSBA, Boston U., 1951, JD magna cum laude, 1956; LLM, Yale U., 1959. Bar: Mass. 1956, Mich. 1961, Hawaii 1977. Pvt. practice law, Boston, 1956-58; assoc. prof. law Wayne State U., Detroit, 1959-62, prof., 1962-65, Ohio State U., Columbus, 1965-73, dir. clin. and interdisciplinary program, 1971-73; prof. U. Hawaii, Honolulu, 1973-95, prof. emeritus, 1995—, dean, 1981-84. Vis. prof. law USIA/U. Hawaii, Hiroshima U. Affiliation Program, Japan, fall 1986, Victoria U., Wellington, N.Z., Spring 1987; del. Hawaii State Jud. Conf., 1989-92; cons. Hawaii Coalition for Health, 1997—. Author: Courts and the Law: An Introduction to our Legal System, 1980; editor: (with Roland Stanger) Essays on Expropriations, 1967; editor-in-chief: Boston U. Law Rev., 1955-56; contbr. articles to profl. jours. Mem. Hawaii Substance Abuse Task Force, 1994-95; arbitrator Hawaii Ct. Annexed Arbitration Program, 1995-99; bd. dirs. Drug Policy Forum Hawaii, 1996—; mem. Save our Star-Bulletin Com., 1999-2001. 1st lt. USAF, 1951-53. Sterling-Ford fellow Yale U., 1958-59; named Lawyer of Yr. Japan-Hawaii Lawyers Assn., 1990; recipient Cmty. Svc. award Hawaii Med. Assn. Alliance, 1999. Mem. ABA, Hawaii State Bar Assn., Hawaii ACLU, Am. Inn of Ct. IV (emeritus founding mem., master of the bench), Am. Law Inst., Honolulu Cmty-Media Coun. (pres. 1994-98, v.p. 1998-2000, treas. 2000—). Office: U Hawaii Richardson Sch Law 2515 Dole St Honolulu HI 96822-2328

MILLER, ROGER JAMES, lawyer; b. Yankton, S.D., Oct. 6, 1947; s. Kenneth LeRoy and Bernice Mildred (Peterson) M.; m. Kristine Olga Christensen, June 12, 1971; children: David, Adam, Luke. BS, U. Nebr., 1970, JD, 1973. Bar: Nebr. 1973, U.S. Dist. Ct. Nebr. 1973, U.S. Ct. Appeals (5th, 8th and 10th cirs.) 1973, U.S. Ct. Appeals (D.C. cir.) 1974, U.S. Dist. Ct. (no. dist.) Calif. 1984. Assoc. Nelson & Harding, Lincoln, Nebr., 1973-74, ptnr. Omaha, 1974-84, McGrath, North, Mullin and Kratz, P.C., Omaha, 1984—. Adv. bd. Douglas County Rep. Party, Omaha, 1984. Mem. ABA (labor law sect., litigation sect.), Nebr. Bar Assn. Republican. Methodist. Avocations: golf, skiing, reading. Labor. Home: 13626 Seward St Omaha NE 68154-3823 Office: McGrath North Mullin & Kratz PC 222 S 15th St Omaha NE 68102-1680 E-mail: rmiller@mnmk.com

MILLER, ROGER WAYNE, court reporter; b. Tahoka, Tex., Apr. 14, 1953; s. Wayne Howard and Wyenema Miller; m. Leah Anne Fowlkes; children: Kathryn Mackenzie, Collin Lee. Student, Stenograph Inst. Tex., Abilene, 1973; LLD (hon.), Northwood Inst., Cedar Hills, Tex., 1995. Cert. shorthand reporter, Tex., N.Mex. Freelance ct. reporter Curtis D. Ruff & Assocs., Lubbock, Tex., 1973; ct. reporter U.S. Dist. Ct., 1973-87; ct. reporter, officer Stanley, Harris, Rice, Dallas, 1987-92, Keith & Miller, El Paso, 1992—, Fuller & Parker, Dallas, 1996—; litigation support officer Am. LegalTech, El Paso and Dallas, 1994—. Mem. adv. bd. Educorp Internat., 1987-90, Rapidtext, Inc., 1988—; mem. profl. ct. reporting adv. bd. Coll. of Richardson, Tex., 1990; mem. profl. adv. bd. ct. reporting divsn. El Paso C.C., 1991, 92; numerous presentations in field. Contbr. articles to law jours. Mem. jr. livestock com. State Fair Tex., 1988-90; asst. coach Coppell (Tex.) Little League, 1990; active Indian princess program YMCA, 1988-90, Indian guides program 1991. Scholar in his name at Stenograph Inst. Tex., 1986—; Hall of Fame fellow Acad. Profl. Reporters. Mem. U.S. Ct. Reporters Assn. (nat. bd. dirs. 1983-87), Nat. Ct. Reporters Assn. (cert. of proficiency, registeree merit, profl. and dilomate reporter, nat. bd. dirs., pres. 1987-94), Tex. Ct. Reporters Assn. (bd. dirs. 1985-86, Disting. Svc. award 1994), EPCCRA, DCRA. Avocations: hiking, travel, reading. Home: 5880 Via Cuesta Dr El Paso TX 79912-6608 Office: Keith & Miller 100 N Stanton St Ste 1320 El Paso TX 79901-1448

MILLER, RONALD STUART, lawyer; b. Chgo., Sept. 28, 1931; s. Manuel and Ruth (Romack) M.; m. Patricia Ann Murphy, Dec. 14, 1962; children: Michelle Ann, Lynn Elizabeth. BS, U. Ill., 1953, LLB, 1955. Bar: Ill. 1955, N.Y. 1960. Assoc. Devoe, Shadur & Mikva, Chgo., 1961-65; ptnr. Miller, Shakman & Hamilton, 1965—. Trustee, bd. dirs. Lawyers Com. for Civil Rights, Washington, 1977— ; mem. Ill. Speakers Task Force, Springfield, 1984. Bd. visitors U. Ill. Law Sch., Champaign, 1984-90, pres., 1988; bd. advisors DePaul Law Sch., Chgo., 1987-94. Mem. ABA, Ill. Bar Assn., Chgo. Bar Assn., Chgo. Coun. Lawyers, Legal Club Chgo. Jewish. General corporate, Real property, Securities. Home: 330 W Diversey Pkwy Chicago IL 60657-6231 Office: Miller Shakman & Hamilton 208 S La Salle St Ste 1100 Chicago IL 60604-1184

MILLER, SAM SCOTT, lawyer; b. Ft. Worth, July 26, 1938; s. Percy Vernon and Mildred Lois (MacDowell) M.; m. Mary Harrison FitzHugh, May 10, 1969. BA, Mich. State U., 1960; JD, Tulane U., 1964; LLM, Yale U., 1965. Bar: La. 1965, N.Y. 1966, Minn. 1969. Assoc. Simpson Thacher & Bartlett, N.Y.C., 1965-68; sr. counsel Investors Diversified Services, Mpls., 1968-73; ptnr. Ireland Gibson Reams & Miller, Memphis, 1973-74; gen. counsel Paine Webber Group, Inc., N.Y.C., 1974-87, sr. v.p., 1976-87; ptnr. Orrick, Herrington & Sutcliffe, 1987—. Adj. prof. NYU Law Sch., 1986-90; vis. lectr. Yale Law Sch., 1980-85, Inst. for Internat. Econs. and Trade, Wuhan, China, 1983, U. Calif., 1986; trustee Omni Mut., Inc., 1988-; ombudsman Kidder Peabody Group, 1988-, Charles Schwab & Co., 1991-, Gruntal & Co., 1995-. Contbr. articles to profl. jours.; editor-in-chief: Tulane Law Rev, 1964-65; bd. editors Securities Regulation Law Jour., 1982—. Bd. dirs. Guthrie Theatre Found., Mpls., 1971-74; bd. dirs. Minn. Opera Co., 1971-74, Yale U. Law Sch. Fund., 1981—; bd. govs. Investment Co. Inst., 1980-87. Fellow Fgn. Policy Assn.; mem. ABA (chmn. subcom. market regulation 1985-93, vice chmn. com. fed. regulation of securities 1995-98, chmn. subcom. electronic comm. 1999—), Assn. Bar City N.Y. (treas. and mem. exec. com. 1994-96, chmn. broker-dealer investment co. and regulations subcom. 1982-83), Internat. Bar Assn., Securities Industry Assn. (chmn. fed. regulation com. 1976-78), Down Town Assn., Knickerbocker Club, Order of Coif, Omicron Delta Kappa. Democrat. Baptist. Administrative and regulatory, General corporate, Legislative. Office: Orrick Herrington & Sutcliffe 666 5th Ave Rm 203 New York NY 10103-1798

MILLER, SHELDON LEE, lawyer; b. Detroit, Apr. 19, 1936; s. Jack and Rose (Steinberg) M; m. Elaine Jo Schweitzer, Dec. 17, 1961; children: Randall, Lisa. Grad., Wayne State U., 1958, LLB, 1961. Bar: Mich. 1962, U.S. Dist. Ct., U.S. Ct. Appeals (6th cir.), U.S. Supreme Ct. 1971. Ptnr. Lopatin, Miller, P.C., Detroit. Served with U.S. Army, 1954-56. Mem.: ATLA (pres. Detroit chpt., nat. v.p. 8485, bd. govs. 1977—, parliamentarian 1982—83, sec. 1983—84, v.p. 1984—85, Champion of Justice award 1998), Mich. Trial Lawyers Assn. (pres. 1975—76), Wayne County Mediation Tribunal Assn. (founder, bd. dirs. 1978—92). Democrat. Jewish. Federal civil litigation, State civil litigation, Personal injury. Office: Lopatin Miller PC 3000 Town Ctr Ste 1700 Southfield MI 48075-1188 E-mail: slm1936@aol.com

MILLER, STACY LORRAINE, lawyer; b. Bklyn., May 12, 1972; d. Emmanuel and Joyce Miller. BS in Indsl. and Labor Rels., Cornell U., 1994; JD, Northeastern U., 1997. Bar: Mass. 1997. Assoc. Morgan Brown & Joy LLP, Boston, 1997—. Mem. ABA, Boston Bar Assn., Women's Bar Assn., Alpha Kappa Alpha (parliamentarian 1999). Avocations: dancing, reading. Labor. Office: Morgan Brown & Joy 1 Boston Pl Ste 1616 Boston MA 02138

MILLER, STEPHEN RALPH, lawyer; b. Chgo., Nov. 28, 1950; s. Ralph and Karin Ann (Olson) M.; children: David Williams, Lindsay Christine. m. Sheila L. Krysiak, Feb. 2, 1998. BA cum laude, Yale U., 1972; JD, Cornell U., 1975. Bar: Ill. 1975. Assoc. McDermott, Will & Emery, Chgo., 1975-80, income ptnr., 1981-85, equity ptnr., 1986—, mgmt. com. mem., 1992-95. Mem. spl. task force on post-employment benefits Fin. Acctg. Standards Bd., Norwalk, Conn., 1987-91. Contbr. articles to profl. jours. Mem. Chgo. Coun. on Fgn. Rels., 1978—, mem. devel. com., 1997—, chair mem. devel. subcom., 1999—; trustee police pension bd., Wilmette, Ill., 1992-98; trustee Seabury We. Theol. Sem., Evanston, Ill., 1994—, chancellor, 1996-97, chair trusteeship com., 2000—. Mem.: ABA, Yale Club Chgo., Hundred Club Cook County, Lawyers' Club of Chgo. Avocations: sailing, water skiing, cross-country skiing. Pension, profit-sharing, and employee benefits. Office: McDermott Will & Emery 227 W Monroe St Ste 3100 Chicago IL 60606-5096 E-mail: smiller@mwe.com

MILLER, STEVEN SCOTT, lawyer; b. N.Y.C., May 28, 1947; s. Stanley Irwin and Corinne (Mass) M.; m. Nina Catherine Augello, Apr. 24, 1983. BA cum laude, U. Pa., 1967; JD cum laude, NYU, 1970. Bar: N.Y. 1971, U.S. Dist. Ct. (so. and ea. dists.) N.Y. 1972, U.S. Ct. Appeals (2d cir.) 1974. Law clk. to judge U.S. Dist. Ct. (so. dist.) N.Y., N.Y.C., 1970-71; assoc. Proskauer Rose Goetz & Mendelsohn, 1971-78, Rosenman & Colin, N.Y.C., 1978-81, ptnr., 1981-92; v.p., asst. gen. counsel Chase Manhattan Bank (formerly Chemical Bank), 1992—. Editor NYU Law Rev., 1968-70. Mem. N.Y. State Bar Assn., NYU Law Sch. Alumni Assn. (pres. 2000—). Federal civil litigation, General civil litigation, State civil litigation. Home: 135 E 83rd St New York NY 10028-2408 Office: Chase Manhattan Bank 1 Chase Manhattan Plz Fl 26 New York NY 10081-0001

MILLER, STEWART RANSOM, lawyer; b. Dallas, June 11, 1945; s. Giles Edwin and Betty Jane (Stewart) M.; m. Alice B. Miller, Aug. 30, 1997; children: Rhett, Ross, Christi, Melissa, Anna. BA, Austin Coll., 1968; JD, U. Tex., 1970. Bar: Tex. 1970, U.S. Dist. Ct. (ea. dist.) Tex. 1971, U.S. Dist. Ct. (no. dist.) Tex. 1972, U.S. Dist. Ct. (so. dist.) Tex. 1989, U.S. Dist. Ct. (we. dist.) Tex. 1992, U.S. Tax Ct. 1977, U.S. Ct. Appeals (5th cir.) 1977, U.S. Ct. Appeals (9th cir.) 1995, U.S. Supreme Ct. 1977, U.S. Dist. Ct. (no. dist.) Okla. 1987; cert. comml. real estate law specialist, consumer bankruptcy law specialist. Assoc. Wade & Thomas, Dallas, 1970-71, Sammons Enterprises Inc., Dallas, 1971-78; ptnr. The Miller & Miller Firm, PLLC, 1978-99, Legal Svcs. of North Tex. Inc., Dallas, 1999—. Dir. Legal Security Life Ins. Co., Dallas, 1971-78. Mem. Charter Commn. Town of Highland Park; bd. dirs., sec. Aberrant Behavior Ctr. Inc., Dallas, 1978-85, Behavioral Rsch. Ctr. cInc., Dallas, 1980-85. Mem. State Bar Tex., Dallas Bar Assn., Dallas Bus. Assn. (past pres.), Nat. Assn. Consumer Advocates. Episcopalian. Bankruptcy, Federal civil litigation, Real property. Home: 9310 Esplanade Dr Dallas TX 75220-5038 Office: 1515 Main St Dallas TX 75201-4845 E-mail: stewartm@lsnt.org, srm@stewartmillerlaw.com

MILLER, SUZANNE MARIE, state librarian, educator; b. Feb. 25, 1954; d. John Gordon and Dorothy Margaret (Sabatka) M.; 1 child, Altinay Marie. B.A. in English, U. S.D., 1975; M.A. in Library Sci., U. Denver, 1976, postgrad. in law, 1984. Librarian II U. S.D. Sch. of Law, Vermillion, 1977-78; law libr. U. LaVerne, Calif., 1978-85, instr. in law, 1980-85; asst. libr. tech. svcs. McGeorge Sch. Law, 1985-99, prof. advanced legal rsch., 1994-99; state librarian S.D. State Library, Pierre, S.D., 1999—. Co-author (with Elizabeth J. Pokorny) U.S. Government Documents: A Practical Guide for Library Assistants in Academic and Public Libraries, 1988; contbr. chpt. to book, articles to profl. jours. Recipient A. Jurisprudence award Bancroft Whitney Pub. Co., 1983. Mem. ALA, S.D. Libr. Assn., Am. Assn. Law Librs., So. Calif. Assn. Law Libs. (arrangements com. 1981-82), Mountai Plains Libr. Assn., No. Calif. Assn. Law Librs. (mem. program com., inst. 1988), Western Pacific Assn. Law Librs. (sec. 1990-94, pres. elect 1994-95, pres. 1995-96, local arrangements chair 1997), Mt. Plains Libr. Assn. Roman Catholic. Home: 505 N Grand Ave Pierre SD 57501-2014 Office: SD State Library 800 Governors Dr Pierre SD 57501-2235 E-mail: suzanne.miller@state.sd.us

MILLER, THOMAS EUGENE, lawyer, writer; b. Bryan, Tex., Jan. 4, 1929; s. Eugene Adam and Ella Lucille (Schroeder) M. BA, BS, Tex. A&M U., 1950; MA, U. Tex., 1956, JD, 1966; postgrad., U. Houston, 1956-58, U. Calif., 1983. Bar: Tex. 1966. Rsch. technician M.D. Anderson Hosp., Houston, 1956-58; claims examiner trainee Social Security Adminstrn., New Orleans, 1964; trademark examiner U.S. Patent and Trademark Office, Washington, 1966; editor Bancroft-Whitney Co., San Francisco, 1966-92. Author: (under pseudonym Millard Thomas) Home From 7-North, 1984; contbr. to numerous legal publs. Contbg. mem. Dem. Nat. Com., 1981—; mem. Celebrate Bryan Com. Mem. ABA, World Lit. Assn., World Inst. Achievement, United Writers Assn. India, Nat. Trust for Hist. Preservation, Tex. Bar Assn., African Wildlife Found., World Wildlife Fund, Internat. Platform Assn., Nat. Writers Assn., Scribes, Acad. Polit. Sci., Press Club, Commonwealth Club, Rotary Club (Paul Harris fellow), Menninger Soc., Tex. A&M U. Faculty Club, Phi Kappa Phi, Psi Chi, Phi Eta Sigma. Methodist. Home: 101 N Haswell Dr Bryan TX 77803-4848

MILLER, THOMAS J. state attorney general; b. Dubuque, Iowa, Aug. 11, 1944; s. Elmer John and Betty Maude (Kross) M.; m. Linda Cottington, Jan. 10, 1981; 1 child, Matthew. B.A., Loras Coll., Dubuque, 1966; J.D., Harvard U., 1969. Bar: Iowa bar 1969. With VISTA, Balt., 1969-70; legis. asst. to U.S. rep.John C. Culver, 1970-71; legal edn. dir. Balt. Legal Aid Bur., also mem. part-time faculty U. Md. Sch. Law, 1971-73; pvt. practice McGregor, Iowa, 1973-78; city atty., 1975-78, Marquette, Iowa; atty. gen. of Iowa, 1979-91, 95—; ptnr. Faegre & Benson, Des Moines, 1991-95. Pres. 2d Dist. New Democratic Club, Balt., 1972. Mem. Am. Bar Assn., Iowa Bar Assn., Common Cause. Roman Catholic. Office: Office of the Atty Gen 1305 E Walnut St Des Moines IA 50319-0112*

MILLER, WARREN LLOYD, lawyer; b. Bklyn., July 18, 1944; s. Allan and Ella Miller; m. Jana Lee Morris, May 13, 1978; children: Lindsey Beth, Alan Gregory, William Brett. BA with high honor, Am. U., 1966; JD with honors, George Washington U., 1969. Bar: Va., 1969, D.C., 1969, U.S. Supreme Ct., 1981. Law clk. to Hon. Edward A. Beard Superior Ct. D.C., 1968-69; asst. U.S. atty. for D.C., 1969-74; ptnr. Stein, Miller & Brodsky, 1974-85; pres. Warren L. Miller, P.C., 1986—; of counsel Reed, Smith, Shaw & McClay, 1986-93. Lectr. Georgetown U. Law Sch., 1970-71, Am. U., 1971-72; guest spkr. various TV programs and legal forums; mem. Jud. Conf. D.C. Cir., 1984—; pres. Asst. U.S. Attys. Assn. of D.C., 1983-84. Contbr. articles to profl. jours. Parliamentarian credentials and rules coms. Rep. Nat. Conv., 1984, commr. D.C. Law Revision Commn., 1987-91 (apptd. by Pres. Reagan); commr. U.S. Commn. for Preservation of Am.'s Heritage Abroad, 1992— (apptd. by Pres. Bush, reapptd. by Pres. Clinton 1996, 99), now chmn. (apptd. by Pres. Bush) 2001—; bd. dirs. Found. for Buchenwald and Mittelbau-Dora Memls., 1994—; spkr. ceremonies commemorating 50th anniversary of liberation of Buchenwald Concentration Camp, Buchenwald, Germany, 1995; spkr. U.S. Holocaust Meml. Mus., 1995; fundraiser for Rep. Nat. Com. and Pres. Bush, 1988-92; co-chmn. dinner for V.P. Bush, 1988; vice-chmn. Pres.'s Dinner, 1989; co-chmn. Pres.'s Club, Washington, 1990-92; chmn. fundraiser for U.S. Senator Christopher Bond, 1992, 97; chmn., fundraiser U.S. Senator John Warner, 1996; vice-chmn., fundraiser Senator Bob Dole, 1996; co-chmn., fundraiser Gov. George W. Bush Presdl. Exploratory Com., 1999, mem. host com., fundraiser for Gov. George W. Bush, 2000. Mem. Congl. Country Club (Bethesda, Md.), Phi Delta Phi, Omicron Delta Kappa, Pi Gamma Mu. Office: 2300 N St NW Washington DC 20037-1122

MILLER, WILLIAM HARLOWE, JR. lawyer; b. Mineola, N.Y., Apr. 22, 1939; s. William Harlowe and Martha Owen (Clarke) M.; m. Jean McKenzie Piersol, Oct. 1, 1966; children: William Harlowe III, Thomas P. Grad., Phillips Exeter Acad., 1957; AB, Princeton U., 1961; JD, Syracuse U., 1966. Bar: N.Y. 1967, Conn. 1970. Assoc. Humes, Andrews, Botzow & Wagner, N.Y.C., 1966-71, ptnr., 1972-93, Walter, Conston, Alexander & Green, P.C., 1993-2000, Davidson, Dawson & Clark, LLP, N.Y.C., 2001—. Trustee Greens Farms Acad., Westport, Conn., 1983-94. Served to lt. USNR, 1961-63. Mem. Conn. Bar Assn., Norwalk (Conn.) Yacht Club (bd. dirs. 1972-91), N.Y. Yacht Club. Probate, Real property, Personal income taxation. Home: 4 Valley Rd Wilson Point South Norwalk CT 06854 Office: Davidson Dawson & Clark LLP 330 Madison Ave New York NY 10017 also: 30 Center St Darien CT 06820-4529

MILLER-LERMAN, LINDSEY, state supreme court justice; b. L.A., July 30, 1947; BA, Wellesley Coll., 1968; JD, Columbia U., 1973; LHD (hon.), Coll. of St. Mary, Omaha, 1993. Bar: N.Y. 1974, U.S. Dist. Ct. (so. dist.) N.Y. 1974, U.S. Ct. Appeals (2d cir.) 1974, Nebr. 1976, U.S. Dist. Ct. (ea. dist.) N.Y. 1975, U.S. Dist. Ct. Nebr. 1976, U.S. Ct. Appeals (8th cir.) 1979, U.S. Supreme Ct. 1982, U.S. Ct. Appeals (6th cir.) 1984, U.S. Ct. Appeals (10th cir.) 1987. Law clk. U.S. Dist. Ct., N.Y.C., 1973-75; from assoc. to ptnr. Kutak Rock, Omaha, 1975-92; judge Nebr. Ct. Appeals, Lincoln, 1992-98, chief judge, 1996-98; justice Nebr. Supreme Ct., 1998—. Contbr. articles to profl. jours. Bd. dirs. Tuesday Musical, Omaha, 1985—. Office: Nebr Supreme Ct State Capitol Rm 222 Lincoln NE 68509

MILLET, JOHN PORATH, lawyer; b. Detroit, Feb. 3, 1943; s. John Pettigrew and Doris Frieda (Porath) M.; m. Cecelia Fay McCallister, Apr. 14, 1973; children: Karen Anne, John Christopher. BBA, N. Tex. State U., 1966; JD, So. Meth. U., 1969. Bar: Tex. 1969, U.S. Dist. Ct. (no. dist.) Tex. 1971. Fellowship prof. bus. law U. North Tex., 1969-70; examining atty. Fidelity Title Co., Dallas, 1970-72; atty., plant mgr., 1973-75; atty., plant mgr. Chgo. Title Co., Dallas, 1975-76; sr. v.p. USLIFE Title Co., San Antonio, 1976-83; v.p., chief title officer Dallas & Tex. Title Companies, Dallas, 1984-85; exec. v.p., Dallas Title Co., 1985-87, v.p. ops. Comml. Title Co./Lawyers Title of San Antonio, 1987—; exec. v.p. Am. Title Co. Dallas, 1987-90. Instr. law Eastfield Coll., Dallas, 1975-76; instr. Tex. Land Title Sch. Mem. Tex Bar Assn. Republican. Methodist. Club: Early Ford V-8. Real property. Home: 13310 Serenity Ln San Antonio TX 78232-4883 Office: Lawyers Title San Antonio 100 Sandau Rd Ste 100 San Antonio TX 78216-3635

MILLHONE, JAMES NEWTON, lawyer; b. Omaha, Feb. 14, 1937; s. Paul Lambert and Margaret (Griffith) M.; m. Mary Ann Whitted, Sept. 4, 1961; 1 son, John Taber. B.A., Parsons Coll., 1958; J.D., U. Mich., 1961. Bar: Iowa 1961. Instr., Presbyn. Ch., Alexander, Egypt, 1961-63; ptnr. Stephens & Millhone, Clarinda, Iowa, 1963—80; county atty. Page County, Clarinda, 1967-69; ptnr. Millhone & Anderson, PC, 1991-; tchr. Iowa Western Coll., Clarinda, 1966-70; cons. Profl. Structures, Inc., Clarinda, 1966-75; mem. Iowa Bd. Law Examiners, 1978—87, chmn., 1983—87. Contbr. articles to legal jours. Bd. dirs. Tarkio Coll. (Mo.), 1976-82, Clarinda Found., 1989-, Clarinda A's, 1981— , Clarinda Arts Council, 1966—80; mem., pres. Clarinda Devel. Corp., 1976. Mem. Page County Bar Assn. (pres. 1966), Iowa State Bar Assn. (jud. adminstrn., criminal law legal heritage coms.), Clarinda C. of C. (v.p.). Republican. Presbyterian. General practice, Probate, , Estate planning. Office: 101 E Main St Clarinda IA 51632-2110 E-mail: millandelaw@clarindaheartland.net

MILLICHAP, PAUL ANTHONY, lawyer; b. London, Jan. 29, 1952; came to U.S., 1956; s. Joseph Gordon and Mary Irene (Fortey) M.; m. Joan Christine Haigler, May 17, 1980; 1 child, Christopher Spencer. B.A., U. Va., 1974; J.D., DePaul U., 1978. Bar: Ill. 1978, U.S. Dist. Ct. (no. dist.) Ill. 1978, U.S. Ct. Appeals (7th cir.) 1983. Student research asst. Children's Meml. Hosp., Chgo., 1964-69, pharmacology dept. Northwestern U. Med. Sch., Chgo., 1970; clin. research asst. J. Gordon Millichap, M.D., Chgo., 1974-78; law clk. gen. law div. Ill. Atty. Gen.'s Office, Chgo., 1978, asst. atty. gen., 1978-84; assoc. Brydges, Riseborough, Morris, Franke & Miller, 1984-86, assoc., Vedder, Price, Kaufman & Kammholz, 1986—. Recipient Am. Jurisprudence award DePaul U. Sch. Law, 1976. Mem. ABA, Ill. State Bar Assn. Episcopalian. Office: Vedder Price Kaufman & Kammholz 222 N La Salle St Ste 2600 Chicago IL 60601-1100

MILLIGRAM, STEVEN IRWIN, lawyer; b. N.Y.C., July 16, 1953; s. Harry William and Judith Edith (Soffen) M.; m. Evan L. Greenberg; children: David Michael, Brian Harry; stepchildren: Caitlin Anderson, Kyle Smith. BA, SUNY, Buffalo, 1976; JD, Pace U., 1981. Bar: N.Y. 1982, U.S. Dist. Ct. (ea. and so. dists.) N.Y. 1982, N.J. 1982, U.S. Dist. Ct. N.J. 1982, U.S. Dist. Ct. (no. dist.) N.Y. 1993. Asst. dist. atty. County of Bronx, N.Y., 1982-86; assoc. Meiselman, Farber, Packman & Eberz, Poughkeepsie, 1986-91, Drake, Sommers, Loeb, Tarshis and Catania, P.C., Newburgh, 1991-96, ptnr., 1996—. Founding atty. Bedford (N.Y.) Mt. Kisco Youth Ct., 1984-85; lectr. Nat. Bus. Inst., 1991, 92, Practising Law Inst., 1993. Contbg. author: Trial Advocacy in New York, 1991, Civil Trial Procedures in New York, 1991, Winning the Slip and Fall Case, 1993. Mem. ABA, Assn. Trial Lawyers Am., N.Y. State Trial Lawyers Assn., N.Y. State Bar Assn., Fed. Bar Council, Pace U. Alumni Assn., Orange County Bar Assn. (bd. dirs., chmn. law day com.). Jewish. State civil litigation, Insurance, Personal injury. Home: 178 Rye Hill Rd Monroe NY 10950-3023 Office: Drake Sommers Loeb Tarshis and Catania One Corwin Ct Newburgh NY 12550 E-mail: smilligram@dsltc.com

MILLIMET, ERWIN, lawyer; b. N.Y.C., Oct. 7, 1925; s. Maurice and Henrietta (Cohen) M.; m. Mary Malia; children: Robert, James, Rachel, Sarah. BA magna cum laude, Amherst Coll., 1948; LLB cum laude, Harvard U., 1951. Bar: N.Y. 1952. Formerly sr. ptnr., chmn. exec. com. Stroock & Stroock & Lavan, N.Y.C.; ret., 1991. Mem. faculty Grad. Sch. Mgmt., U. Mass. Mem. bd. visitors U. San Diego Law Sch.; active Nat. Support Group for Africa; founder Citizens for Am., Washington, 1984; mem. Rep. Presdl. Task Force. Mem. N.Y. State Bar Assn., Assn. of Bar of City of N.Y., Fed. Bar Assn., Rep. Club (N.Y.C. and Washington), Phi Beta Kappa. General corporate, Mergers and acquisitions, Securities. E-mail: riverbend@iopener.net

MILLISOR, KENNETH RAY, lawyer; b. Belle Center, Ohio, Jan. 31, 1937; s. Darrel R. and Clara Sue (Miller) M.; m. Annette M. Seifert Ross, June 7, 1985. BA, Ohio Wesleyan U., 1959; JD, Ohio State U., 1960. Bar: Ohio 1960, U.S. Dist. Ct. (no. dist.) Ohio, 1965, U.S. Ct. Appeals (6th cir.) 1965, U.S. Ct. Appeals (D.C. cir.) 1975, U.S. Supreme Ct. 1970. Ptnr. Poetzel & Andress, Akron, Ohio, 1960-74, Millisor & Nobil, Akron and Cleve., 1975—. Past v.p. Akron Area coun. Boy Scouts Am.; active United Way. Mem. ABA, Ohio Bar Assn., Cleve. Bar Assn., Order of Coif, Shoreby Club. Democrat. Labor. Home: Vratenahl Pl II Unit 10A Bratenahl OH 44108-1161 Office: Millisor & Nobil Co 9150 S Hills Blvd Ste 300 Cleveland OH 44147-3599 E-mail: kmillisor@millisor.com

MILLMAN, BRUCE RUSSELL, lawyer; b. Bronx, N.Y., June 4, 1948; s. Meyer and Garie (Solomon) M.; m. Lorrie Jan Liss, Aug. 12, 1973; children: Noemi, Avi. AB, Princeton U., 1970; JD, Columbia U., 1973. Bar: N.Y. 1974, U.S. Dist. Ct. (ea. and so. dists.) N.Y. 1975, U.S. Ct. Appeals (2d dir.) 1978, U.S. Supreme Ct. 1978. Assoc. Rains & Pogrebin and predecessors Rains, Pogrebin & Scher, Mineola, N.Y., 1973-79, ptnr., 1980—. Arbitrator Nassau County Dist. Ct., Mineola, 1981-83. Contbr. New York Employment Law, 1995, Labor and Employment Law for the Corporate Counselor and General Practitioner, 1994, Updating Issues in Employment Law, 1986, Public Sector Labor and Employment Law, 1988.

Bd. dirs. West Side Montessori Sch., N.Y.C., 1984-90, sec., 1985-87, pres., 1987-90. Harlan Fiske Stone scholar Columbia U. Law Sch., N.Y.C., 1971, 73. Mem. ABA, N.Y. State Bar Assn. (chair labor and employment law sect. 1997-98), Nassau County Bar Assn., Indsl. Rels. Rsch. Assn. (bd. dirs. L.I. chpt. 1984—, pres. 1995-96). Civil rights, Education and schools, Labor. Home: 60 Riverside Dr New York NY 10024-6108 Office: Rains & Pogrebin PC 210 Old Country Rd Ste 12 Mineola NY 11501-4288 also: 375 Park Ave New York NY 10152-0002 E-mail: bmillman@rainslaw.com

MILLMAN, JODE SUSAN, lawyer; b. Poughkeepsie, N.Y., Dec. 28, 1954; d. Samuel Keith and Ellin Sadenberg (Bainder) M.; m. Michael James Harris, June 20, 1982; children: Maxwell, Benjamin. BA, Syracuse U., 1976, JD, 1979. Bar: N.Y. 1980, U.S. Dist. Ct. (so. and ea. dists.) N.Y. 1982, U.S. Supreme Ct. 1983. Asst. corp. counsel City of Poughkeepsie, 1979-81; assoc. Law Office of Lou Lewis, Poughkeepsie, 1981-85; pvt. practice, 1985—. Staff counsel City of Poughkeepsie Office of Property Devel., 1990—; gen. mgr. WCZX-Communicatons Corp. Author: (children's books) Birthday Wishes and Rock'n Roll Dreams, The Firebird Ballet, Goldie Lox and the Three Behrs; contbg. author: Kaminstein Legislative History of the Copyright Law, 1979. Pres. Dutchess County (N.Y.) Vis. Bur., 1980-82; bd. dirs. Poughkeepsie Ballet Theater, 1982, Jewish Comty. Ctr., 1988; mem. assigned counsel program Dutchess County Family Ct., 1985—; trustee Greater Poughkeepsie Libr. Dist., 1991-94, Poughkeepsie Day Sch., 1995—. Mem. N.Y. State Bar Assn., Dutchess County Bar Assn. (grievance com. 1994—), Mid-Hudson Women's Bar Assn. Democrat. Jewish. General corporate, Entertainment, Family and matrimonial. Office: 97 Cannon St Poughkeepsie NY 12601-3303 E-mail: jodem54@aol.com

MILLNER, DIANNE MAXINE, lawyer; b. Columbus, Ohio, Mar. 21, 1949; d. Charles Nelson and Barbara Rose Millner. A.A., Pasadena City Coll., 1970; A.B.,U. Calif.-Berkeley, 1972; J.D., Stanford U., 1975. Bar: Calif. 1975, U.S. Dist. Ct. (no. dist.) Calif. 1975. Assoc. Pillsbury, Madison & Sutro, San Francisco, 1975-80; ptnr. Alexander, Millner & McGee and predecessor firm Alexander, Burris, Millner & McGee, San Francisco, 1980-91, Steefel, Levitt & Weiss, 1991—; legal intern Calif. Supreme Ct., San Francisco, 1974; bar exam. grader State Bar Calif., San Francisco, 1976-78. Bd. dirs. Youth for Service, San Francisco, 1977-80. NEH summer fellow, 1978. Mem. William Hastie Lawyers Assn. (bd. dirs. 1980-82), Nat. Bar Assn. (women lawyers div. Presdl. award 1980), Charles Houston Bar Assn., Bar Assn. San Francisco, Black Women Lawyers No. Calif., Black Writers Workshop, Phi Beta Kappa. Bankruptcy, General corporate, Real property. Office: Steefel Levitt 29th Fl One Embarcadero Ctr San Francisco CA 94111

MILLS, CHARLES GARDNER, lawyer; b. Griffin, Ga., Feb. 29, 1940; s. Charles G. and Marguerite (Powell) M. AB, Yale U., 1962; JD, Boston Coll., 1967. Bar: N.Y. 1967, U.S. Dist. Ct. (so. and ea. dists.) 1972, U.S. Ct. Appeals (2d cir.) 1975, U.S. Supreme Ct., 1977, U.S. Ct. Claims 1991, U.S. Ct. Vets. Appeals 1996, U.S. Ct. Appeals (fed. cir.) 1997, U.S. Dist. Ct. (no. dist.) N.Y. 1999. Assoc. Smart & McKay, N.Y.C., 1967-68, Smart & Mills, N.Y.C., 1969-71, Eaton & VanWinkle, N.Y.C., 1971-82, Payne, Wood & Littlejohn, Glen Cove and Melville, N.Y., 1982-91; pvt. practice, Glen Cove, 1991—. With U.S. Army, 1962-64, ETO. Mem. Assn. Bar City N.Y., Nassau County Bar Assn., Rotary (pres. Glen Cove Club 1989-90), Am. Legion (comdr. Locust Valley, N.Y. post 1988-90, comdr. Nassau County com. 1995-96, N.Y. Judge Advocate, 1998—), Soc. Colonial Wars, SCV, Order of the Arrow. Republican. Roman Catholic. Civil rights, Federal civil litigation, Libel. Office: 56 School St Glen Cove NY 11542-2512

MILLS, JON, dean, law educator; b. Miami, Fla., July 24, 1947; s. Herb J. and Marguerite (Sweat) M.; m. Beth Bechard; 1 child, Marguerite. BA, Stetson U., 1969, LLD, 1986; JD, U. Fla., 1972. Mem. Fla. Ho. of Reps., 1978-88, majority leader, 1986-87; speaker Fla. Ho. of Reps. , 1987-88; ptnr. McGalliard, Mills, DeMontomollin, Monaco & Sieg; of counsel Schutts and Bowen; mem. faculty U. Fla., Gainesville, 1973—80, prof. law, 1988—, interim dean, 1999—2001, dean, 2001—. Mem. Fla. Constitution Revision Commn., 1997-98 Co-author: Voting Rights and Democracy, 1996; contbr. articles to profl. jours. 1st lt. USAR. Decorated Order of Coif; recipient Allen Morris award, 1979-80, Outstanding Legis. award Fla. Health Care Assn., 1982; named Rep. of Yr. Assn. Retarded Citizens Fla., 1981. Mem. ABA, Fla. Bar Assn., Pi Kappa Alpha, Fla. Blue Key. Methodist. Home: 2727 NW 58th Blvd Gainesville FL 32606-8516 Office: U Fla Coll Law 230 Bruton-Geer Hall Gainesville FL 32611 also: PO Box 117625 Gainesville FL 32611*

MILLS, KEVIN PAUL, lawyer; b. Detroit, Oct. 1, 1961; s. Raymond Eugene and Helene Audrey M.; m. Holly Beth Fechner, June 15, 1986. BA, Oberlin Coll., 1983; JD, U. Mich., 1987. Bar: Mich. 1988. High sch. tchr., asst. dir. summer environ. inst. The Storm King Sch., Cornwall-on-Hudson, N.Y., 1983-84; staff atty. E. Mich. Environ. Action Coun., Birmingham, Mich., 1987-90; assoc. Tucker & Rolf, Southfield, 1988-89; sr. atty., pollution prevention program dir. Environ. Def., Washington, 1990—. Low-level radioactive waste cons. State Mich., Lansing, 1988; founder Pollution Prevention Alliance, 1991, co-founder Great Printer's Project, 1992, co-founder Clean Car Campaign, 1999, staff to co-chair eco-efficiency Pres. Coun. Sustainable Devel., 1993-95, Auto Pollution Prevention adv. group, 1994-98, EPA Auto Mfr. CSI, 1994-97; mem. adv. bd. Nat. Pollution Prevention Roundtable, 1996—; mem. adv. com. Working Group on Cmty. Right-to-Know, 1997—; mem. Nat. Adv. Coun. on Environ. Policy and Tech., 1997—. Bd. dirs., v.p. Ea. Mich. Environ. Action Coun., Birmingham, 1985-87; pres. Environ. Law Soc., Ann Arbor, Mich., 1986-87. Recipient Outstanding Achievement award Environ. Def., 2000. Mem. State Bar Mich. Environmental, Transportation. Office: Environ Def 1875 Connecticut Ave NW Washington DC 20009-5728

MILLS, LAWRENCE, lawyer, business and transportation consultant; b. Salt Lake City, Aug. 15, 1932; s. Samuel L. and Beth (Neilson) M. BS, U. Utah, 1955, JD, 1956. Bar: Utah 1956, ICC 1961, U.S. Supreme Ct. 1963. With W.S. Hatch Co. Inc., Woods Cross, Utah, 1947-89, gen. mgr., 1963-89, v.p., 1970-89, also dir. Bd. dirs. Nat. Tank Truck Carriers, Inc., Washington, 1963—, pres., 1974-75, chmn. bd., 1975-76; mem. motor carrier adv. com. Utah State Dept. Transp., 1979—; keynote speaker Rocky Mountain Safety Suprs. Conf., 1976; mem. expedition to Antartica, 1996, Titanic Expedition, 1996. Contbr. articles to legal and profl. jours. and transp. publs. Del. to County and State Convs., Utah, 1970-72; v.p. Utah Safety Coun., 1979-82, bd. dirs., 1979—, pres., 1983-84; mem. Utah Gov's Adv. Com. on Small Bus.; capt. Easter Seal Telethon, 1989, 90; state vice chmn. High Frontier, 1987—; mem. adv. com. Utah State Indsl. Commn., 1988—, chmn. com. studying health care cost containment and reporting requirements 1990—; mem. expdn. to Antarctica, 1996, Titanic '96 expedition., Iceland and Greenland, 2001. Recipient Safety Dir. award Nat. Tank Carriers Co., 1967, Outstanding Svc. and Contbn. award, 1995, Trophy award W.S. Hatch Co., 1975, Disting. Svc. award Utah State Indsl. Commn., 1992, Outstanding Svc. award Utah Safety Coun., 1994. Mem. Salt Lake County Bar Assn., Utah Motor Transport Assn. (dir. 1967—, pres. 1974-76, Outstanding Achievement Award 1989), Utah Hwy. Users Assn. (dir. 1981—), Indsl. Rels. Coun. (dir. 1974—), Salt Lake City C. of C., U.S. Jaycees (life Senator 1969—, ambassador 1977—, pres. Utah Senate 1979-80, Henry Giessenbier fellow 1989), Nat. Petroleum Coun., Utah Associated Gen. Contractors (assoc. 1975-77, 88—), Silver Tank Club, Hillsdale Coll. President's Club, Traveler's Century Club. Administrative and regulatory, Transportation. Home: HC 11 Box 329 Kamiah ID 83536-9410 Office: PO Box 1495 Kamiah ID 83536-1495

MILLS, MICHAEL PAUL, state supreme court justice; b. Charleston, S.C., Aug. 25, 1956; s. Paul H. and Shirley (Dulaney) M.; m. Mona Robinson, Aug. 2, 1976; children: Alysson, Chip, Rebekah, Penn. AA, Itawamba C.C., Fulton, Miss., 1976; BA, U. Miss., 1978, JD, 1980; LLM, U. Va., 2001. Bar: Miss. 1980, U.S. Ct. Appeals (fed. cir.) 1986, U.S. Ct. Appeals (5th cir.) 1980, U.S. Supreme Ct. 1990. Pvt. practice, Miss., 1980-95; legis. Miss. Ho. of Reps., Jackson, 1983-95, chmn. jud. com., 1992-95; mem. Nat. Conf. Commrs. on Uniform State Laws, 1993—; justice Miss. Supreme Ct., Jackson, 1995—. Home: PO Box 38 Fulton MS 38843-0038

MILLS, RICHARD HENRY, federal judge; b. Beardstown, Ill., July 19, 1929; s. Myron Epler and Helen Christine (Greve) M.; m. Rachel Ann Keagle, June 16, 1962; children: Jonathan K., Daniel Cass. BA, Ill. Coll., 1951; JD, Mercer U., 1957; LLM, U. Va., 1982. Bar: Ill. 1957, U.S. Dist. Ct. Ill. 1958, U.S. Ct. Appeals 1959, U.S. Ct. Mil. Appeals 1963, U.S. Supreme Ct. 1963. Legal advisor Ill. Youth Commn., 1958-60; state's atty. Cass County, Virginia, Ill., 1960-64; judge Ill. 8th Jud. Cir., 1966-76, Ill. 4th Dist. Appellate Ct., Springfield, Ill., 1976-85, U.S. Dist. Ct. (cen. dist.) Ill., Springfield, 1985—. Adj. prof. So. Ill. U. Sch. Medicine, 1985—; mem. adv. bd. Nat. Inst. Corrections, Washington, 1984-88, Ill. Supreme Ct. Rules Com., Chgo., 1963-85. Contbr. articles to profl. jours. Pres. Abraham Lincoln coun. Boy Scouts Am., 1978-80. With U.S. Army, 1952-54, Korea, col. res.; maj. gen. Ill. Militia. Recipient George Washington Honor medal Freedoms Found., 1969, 73, 75, 82, Disting. Eagle Scout Boy Scouts Am., 1985. Fellow Am. Bar Found.; mem. ABA, Nat. Conf. Fed. Trial Judges (chmn. 1999-00), Ill. Bar Assn., Chgo. Bar Assn., Cass County Bar Assn. (pres. 1962-64, 75-76), Sangamon County Bar Assn., 7th Cir. Bar Assn., Am. Law Inst., Fed. Judges Assn., Army and Navy Club (Washington), Sangamo Club, Masons (33 degree), Lincoln-Douglas Am. Inn of Ct. 150 (founding, pres. 1991-93). Republican. Office: US Dist Ct 600 E Monroe St Ste 117 Springfield IL 62701-1659

MILLS, THOMAS C. H. lawyer; b. Long Beach, Calif., Dec. 14, 1949; s. William Donald and Roberta Mae (Fogg) M. Student Brown U., 1968-70; BA Stanford U., 1972; JD, Hastings Coll. of Law, 1976. Bar: Calif., 1977, N.Mex., 1981. Staff atty. Office of San Francisco City Atty., 1977-78, State Bar Calif., San Francisco, 1978-81; gen. counsel N.Mex. Energy and Minerals Dept., Santa Fe, 1981-83; assoc. Stephenson Carpenter, Crout & Olmsted, Santa Fe, 1983-86; ptnr. Potter & Mills, Santa Fe, 1986—; bd. dirs. Sante Fe Econ. Devel. Corp., 1986-89, v.p., 1988-89; bd. dirs. TRADE, Inc., 1986-93, pres., 1989-90. Mem. Santa Fe Planning Commn., 1982-86, chmn., 1984; mem. Los Alamos Nat. Lab. Community Council, 1986-93; chmn. Sante Fe Group, 1990-91; mem. N.Mex. First., Inc., 1987—, mem. exec. com., chmn., 1993-94; bd. dirs. Quality N.Mex., 1993-95; gov. appointee to N.Mex. Fin. Authority, 1992-96; mem. Ctr. Study of Cmty. Cmty. Bldg. Inst., Santa Fe, 1995-96; bd. dirs. Cornerstones Cmty. Partnerships, Inc., 1997-2000, Leadership NMex, 2001. Mem. Am. Planning Assn., Urban Land Inst., Bar Assn. Sante Fe, Indsl. Devel. Execs. Assn. Democrat. Episcopalian. Club: Stanford of N.Mex. (pres. 1983-85, bd. dirs. 1983-88). Administrative and regulatory, Contracts commercial, Real property. Home: PO Box 269 Santa Fe NM 87504-0269 Office: Potter & Mills 126 E De Vargas St Santa Fe NM 87501-2702

MILLS, WILLIAM MICHAEL, lawyer; b. McAllen, Tex., Dec. 11, 1950; s. Clarence Young and Margaret Jo (Smith) M.; m. Kathy Jo Kirkpatrick, Feb. 6, 1982; children: Gregory Cy, Lucas William, Nathaniel Michael. BA with honors, U. Tex., 1973, JD, 1976. Bar: Tex. 1976, U.S. Dist. Ct. (so. dist.) Tex. 1977, U.S. Supreme Ct. 1980, U.S. Ct. Appeals (5th and 11th cirs.) 1981. Assoc. Atlas & Hall, McAllen, 1976-82, ptnr., 1982—. Mem. ABA, Hidalgo County Bar Assn. (bd. dirs. 1985-87), Tex. Assn. Def. Counsel, Phi Beta Kappa, Phi Delta Phi. Federal civil litigation, State civil litigation, Insurance. Home: 321 Tulip Ave Mcallen TX 78504-2951 Office: Atlas & Hall 818 Pecan Blvd Mcallen TX 78501-2418

MILLSTEIN, LEO LEE, lawyer; b. China, Apr. 3, 1947; came to U.S., 1966; s. Benjamin and Jessie M.; m. Linda Sue Finkelman, Feb. 17, 1979. B.S. in Aero. Engring., Purdue U., 1970; J.D., George Washington U., 1975. Bar: D.C. 1975, U.S. Dist. Ct. D.C. 1975. Counsel corp. devel. Comm. Satellite Corp., Washington, 1974-84; ptnr. Rothblatt & Millstein, Washington, 1984-85, Dyer, Ellis, Joseph & Mills, Washington, 1985-89; dep. gen. counsel Internat. Telecomm. Satellite Orgn., 1989-99, dir. corp. reconstructuring, 1999-2000; v.p., gen. counsel, corp. sec. Merant plc, 2000—; mgr. Whitman Assocs., Inc., Washington, 1983—. Mem. ABA, D.C. Bar Assn. E-mail: leo.millstein@merant.com. Communications, General corporate, Private international. Home: 2934 Garfield St NW Washington DC 20008-3536 Office: 9420 Key West Ave Rockville MD 20850

MILLSTONE, DAVID J. lawyer; b. Morgantown, W.Va., 1946; AB, Johns Hopkins U., 1968; JD, U. W.Va., 1971. Bar: Ohio 1971. Ptnr. Squire, Sanders & Dempsey LLP, Cleve. Co-author: (book) Wage Hour Law--How to Comply, 2001; editor: (manual) Ohio and Fed. Employment Law Manual, 2001. Mem. ABA (internat. coord. labor and employment practice). Education and schools, Labor. Office: Squire Sanders & Dempsey 4900 Key Tower 127 Public Sq Ste 4900 Cleveland OH 44114-1304 E-mail: dmillstone@ssd.com

MILMED, PAUL KUSSY, lawyer; b. Newark, Oct. 15, 1944; s. Leon Sidney and Bella (Kussy) M.; m. Debra R. Anisman, Oct. 23, 1988; children: Laura, Julia. AB, Amherst Coll., 1966; MSc, U. London, 1968; EdM, Harvard U., 1969; JD, NYU, 1975. Bar: N.J. 1975, N.Y. 1976, U.S. Ct. Appeals (2d cir.) 1975, U.S. Dist. Ct. N.J. 1975, U.S. Dist. Ct. (so. dist.) N.Y. 1976, U.S. Dist. Ct. (ea. dist.) N.Y. 1994. Law clk. Hon. Alan B. Handler N.J. Superior Ct. Appellate Divsn., Newark, 1975-76; assoc. Weil, Gotshal & Manges, N.Y.C., 1976-83; asst. U.S. atty. U.S. Atty.'s Office, So. Dist. N.Y., 1983-93, chief environ. protection unit, 1990-93; of counsel White & Case, 1993—. Ct.-apptd. mediator U.S. Dist. Ct., So. Dist. N.Y., 1996—. Rsch. editor NYU Rev. of Law and Social Change, 1974-75; editl. adv. bd. Fordham Environ. Law Jour., 1993—; contbr. articles to profl. jours. Mem. bd. trustees The Town Sch., N.Y.C. Mem. ABA, Assn. Bar City of N.Y. Avocation: photography. Alternative dispute resolution, General civil litigation, Environmental. Home: One Gracie Terr New York NY 10028 Office: White & Case 1155 Avenue Of The Americas New York NY 10036-2787 E-mail: pkm@post.harvard.edu

MILMOE, PATRICK JOSEPH, lawyer; b. Oct. 2, 1939; s. Hugh A. Milmoe and Mary Francis (O'Connell) Steenken; m. Carolyn Mann, Nov. 30, 1963; children: Mary Kaye Chrysicas, Caroline Pugh, Hugh. BA, Coll. William and Mary, 1959; JD, U. Va., 1962. Bar: N.Y. 1962, Va. 1962, Fla. 1989. With Davis & Polk, N.Y.C., 1965-72; ptnr. Hunton & Williams, Richmond, Va., 1972-2001. Chmn. DARE Marina, Inc., Grafton, Va., 1992—, States Roofing Corp., Norfolk, Va., 1994—, Virginia Beach Marlin Club, Inc., 1980—. Trustee Village of Atlantic Beach, N.Y., 1965-72; bd. dirs. St. Joseph's Villa, Richmond, Va., 1985-91, Hanover Tavern Found., 1998-2001. Capt. U.S. Army, 1963-65. Mem. Am. Coll. Real Estate Lawyers. Avocations: boating, fishing. Office: Hunton & Williams Riverfront Plz East Tower 951 E Byrd St Ste 200 Richmond VA 23219-4074 E-mail: pmilmoe@hunton.com

MILONE, FRANCIS MICHAEL, lawyer; b. Phila., June 18, 1947; s. Michael Nicholas and Frances Theresa (Fair) M.; m. Maida R. Crane, Nov. 25, 1991; children: Michael, Matthew. BA, LaSalle Coll., 1969; MS, Pa. State U., 1971; JD, U. Pa., 1974. Bar: Pa. 1974, U.S. Dist. Ct. (ea dist.) Pa. 1974, U.S. Dist. Ct. (mid. dist.) Pa. 1979, U.S. Dist. Ct. (ea. dist.) Mich. 1983, U.S. Ct. Appeals (3d cir.) 1978, U.S. Ct. Appeals (4th and 5th cirs.) 1979, U.S. Supreme Ct. 1979. Assoc. Montgomery, McCraken, Walker & Rhoads, Phila., 1974-77; ptnr. Morgan, Lewis & Bockius, 1977—. Mem. ABA (labor and litigation sects.), Pa. Bar Assn., Phila. Bar Assn. Federal civil litigation, State civil litigation, Labor. Home: 912 Field Ln Villanova PA 19085-2003 Office: Morgan Lewis & Bockius 1701 Market St Philadelphia PA 19103-2903 E-mail: fmilone@morganlewis.com

MILSTEIN, EDWARD PHILIP, lawyer; b. N.Y.C., Apr. 20, 1949; s. Paul and Sylvia Milstein; m. Andrea Kay Wintner, Aug. 16, 1970; children—Scott, Erika. B.A., NYU, 1970; J.D., Bklyn. Law Sch., 1974. Bar: N.Y. 1975, U.S. Dist. Ct. (so. and ea. dists.) N.Y. 1975, U.S. Ct. Appeals (2d cir.) 1975, U.S. Supreme Ct. 1978, N.J. 1983. Assoc. Lipsig, Sullivan & Liapakis, P.C., N.Y.C., 1975-80, ptnr., 1980— . Mem. Assn. Trial Lawyers Am., ABA, N.Y. County Lawyers Assn., Acad. Sci., N.Y. Acad. Medicine, Am. Soc. Medicine and Law, N.Y. State Bar Assn., N.J. Bar Assn., Bergen County Bar Assn., N.Y. County Trial Lawyers Assn. Personal injury. Home: 30 Mountain Rd Tenafly NJ 07670-2214 Office: 157 Engle St Englewood NJ 07631-2508

MILSTEIN, ELLIOTT STEVEN, law educator, academic administrator; b. Oct. 19, 1944; s. Samuel M. and Mildred K. Milstein; m. Bonnie Myrun, Oct. 1, 1967 (div. Oct. 1992); 1 child, Jacob. BA, U. Hartford, 1966, LLD (hon.) , 1997; JD, U. Conn., 1969; LLM, Yale U., 1971; LLD (hon.) , Nova Southeastern U., 2001. Bar: conn. 1969, D.C. 1972, U.S. Dist. Ct. Conn. 1969, U.S. Ct. Appeals (D.C.) 1972. Lectr. law U. Conn. Clin. Program, 1969-70; staff counsel New Haven Legal Assistance Assn., 1971-72; asst. prof. law, dir. clin. programs Washington Coll. Law Am. U., 1972-74, assoc. prof., dir. clin. programs, 1974-77, prof., dir. clin. programs, 1977-88, interim dean, 1988-90, dean, 1990—. Prof. law, Washington Coll. Law Am. U., 1995—; co-dir. Nat. Vets. law Ctr., 1978-84; cons. Calif. Bar Bd. of Bar Admissions, Nat. Conf. Bar Examiners, law tng. Practising Law Inst., N.Y.C.; chmn. D.C. Law Students in Ct. Program, 1982-83; mem. Law Tchrs. for Legal Svcs. Bd. dirs. Alliance for Justice, 1996-97. Ford Urban Law fellow, 1971-72. Mem. ABA (skills tng. com. 1983-85, govt. rels. com. 1992—), ACLU, Soc. Am. Law Tchrs., Assn. Am. Law Schs. (chmn. sect clin. edn. 1982, accreditation com. 1984-86, chmn. standing com. clin. edn. 1993—, exec. com. 1996—, pres.-elect 1999, pres. 2000)., Democrat. Home: 3216 Brooklawn Ct Bethesda MD 20815-3941 Office: Am U Washington Coll Law 4801 Massachusetts Ave NW Washington DC 20016-8196

MILSTEIN, RICHARD CRAIG, lawyer; b. N.Y.C., July 16, 1946; s. Max and Hattie (Jacobson) Worchel; children: Brian Matthew, Rachel Helanie. AA with honors, Miami-Dade Jr. Coll., 1966, AB cum laude, U. Miami, Fla., 1968, JD, 1973. Bar: Fla. 1974, U.S. Dist. Ct. Fla. 1974, U.S. Ct. Appeals (5th cir.) 1974, U.S. Supreme Ct. 1977, U.S. Ct. Appeals (11th cir.) 1982. Assoc., August, Nimkoff & Pohlig, Miami, Fla., 1974-76; mng. ptnr. Jepeway, August, Gassen & Pohlig, Miami, 1976-78, August, Gassen, Pohlig & Milstein, Miami, 1978-80, August, Pohlig & Milstein, P.A., Coral Gables, Fla., 1980-83; sr. ptnr. Milstein & Wayne, Coral Gables, 1983-85; ptnr. Tescher & Milstein, PA, Coral Gables, 1986-90, Akerman, Senterfitt & Eidson, P.A. 1990—. Co-founder Dade County Vol. Lawyers for Arts; mem. Met. Dade County Ind. Rev. Panel, 1984-86; councilor Metro Dade County Cultural Affairs Coun., 1986-91; sec./treas. Ops. SafeDrive, 1988; bd. dirs. South Fla. Mediation Ctr., 1982-89, chmn. bd. dirs., 1985-86; bd. dirs. Ptnrs. for Youth, 1981-91, Bet Shira Congregation, 1986—, pres., 1985-86, South Fla. Inter-Profl. Council Inc., 1986-87, v.p., 1985-86, sec. 1984-85, bd. dirs., 1983—; bd. dirs. Dance Umbrella Inc., 1983-87, Miami Coalition Inc., 1988-94; Fla. bar elder law sect., chair U. Miami, 1996-97; chair Dade County Cultural Alliance, 1993—. Fellow Am. Coll. Trust and Estate Counsel, Nat. Acad. Elder Law, Nat. Coun. Aging; mem. ABA, Am. Trial Lawyers Assn., Dade County Bar Assn. (dir. 1980-83, treas. 1983-84, sec. 1984-85, v.p. 1985-87, pres.-elect 1987-88, pres. 1988-89,), Coral Gables Bar Assn., Fla. Bar Assn. (professionalism com. guest lectr. real property and probate sect., Pro Bono awards 1986), Acad. Fla. Trial Lawyers (City of Miami Beach transition team), U. Miami Law Alumni (pres. 1997—), Phi Theta Kappa, Delta Theta Mu, Omicron Delta Kappa, Phi Alpha Theta, Kappa Delta Pi, Phi Kappa Phi, Alpha Kappa, Zeta Epsilon Nu. Democrat. Family and matrimonial, General practice, Probate. Home: North Bay Island 720 NE 69th St Apt 26S Miami FL 33138-5759 Office: Akerman Senterfitt & Eidson One SE 3rd Ave Fl 28 Miami FL 33131

MILTON, CHAD EARL, lawyer; b. Brevard County, Fla., Jan. 29, 1947; s. Rex Dale and Mary Margaret (Peacock) M.; m. Ann Mitchell Bunting, Mar. 30, 1972; children: Samuel, Kathleen, Kelsey. BA, Colo. Coll., 1969; JD, U. Colo., 1974; postgrad., U. Mo., 1976-77. Bar: Colo. 1974, Mo. 1977, U.S. Dist. Ct. Colo. 1974, U.S. Dist. Ct. (we. dist.) Mo. 1977. Counsel Office of Colo. State Pub. Defender, Colo. Springs, 1974-76; pub. info. officer, counsel Mid-Am. Arts Alliance, Kansas City, Mo., 1977-78; claims counsel Employers Reinsurance Corp., 1978-80; sr. v.p. Media/Profl. Ins., 1981-2000; sr. v.p. nat. practice leader, intellectual property & media Marsh, 2000—. Reporter, photographer, editor Golden (Colo.) Daily Transcript, 1970; investigator, law clk. Office of Colo. State Pub. Defender, Denver, Golden, 1970-74; participant Annenberg Project on the Reform of Libel Laws, Washington, 1987-88; adj. prof., comm. and advt. law Webster U., 1989-93; lectr. in field. Pres. bd. dirs. Folly Theater, 1992-94. Mem. ABA (chair intellectual property law com. of the torts and ins. practice sect., forum com. on comm. law, ctrl. and Ea. European law initiative), Mo. Bar Assn., Kansas City Met. Bar Assn., Libel Def. Resource Ctr. (editorial bd., exec. com.). Avocations: tennis, golf, skiing, sailing, antique maps. Insurance, Libel, Trademark and copyright. Home: 8821 Alhambra St Shawnee Mission KS 66207-2357 Office: Marsh 2405 Grand Blvd Kansas City MO 64108-2510 E-mail: chad.e.milton@marsh.com

MILTON, JOSEPH PAYNE, lawyer; b. Richmond, Va., Oct. 24, 1943; s. Hubert E. and Grace C. Milton; children: Michael Payne, Amy Barrett, David King; m. Cela Cabler Milton, Apr. 8, 1989. BS in Bus. Adminstrn., U. Fla., 1967, JD, 1969. Bar: Fla. 1969, U.S. Ct. Appeals (5th cir.) 1971, U.S. Supreme Ct. 1972, U.S. Ct. Appeals (11th cir.) 1981. Assoc. Toole, Taylor, Moseley & Gabel, Jacksonville, 1969-70; ptnr. Toole, Taylor, Moseley, Gabel & Milton, 1971-78, Howell, Liles, Braddock & Milton, Jacksonville, 1978-89, Milton & Leach, Jacksonville, 1990-95, Milton, Leach & D'Andrea, Jacksonville, 1996—. Mem. Mayor's Blue Ribbon Task Force; mem. Law Ctr. Coun., U. Fla. Coll. Law, 1972-78, mem. alumni coun., 1995—; campaign chmn. N.E. Fla. chpt. March of Dimes, 1973-74, v.p., 1974-75; pres. Willing Hands, 1974-75; chmn. attys.' divsn. United Way, 1977; pres. Civic Round Table of Jacksonville, 1980-81; mem. exec. com. Jacksonville Area Legal Aid, Inc., 1982-83; chmn. pvt. bar involvement com. Legal Aid Bd. Dirs., 1982-83. Recipient Outstanding Svc. award for individual contbns. in support of legal svcs. for the poor, 1981. Fellow: Am. Bar Found., Internat. Soc. Barristers, Southeastern Admiralty Law (com., dir. Port, Jacksonville 1996—99), Soc. Lawyers for Pub. Svc.; mem.: ATLA, Fla. Chpt. Am. Bd. Trial Advs. (treas. 1999, mem. exec. com. 1997—), Am. Bd. Trial Advs. (charter, pres. Jacksonville chpt. 1997, FLABOTA bd. mem. 1997—, treas. 1999, pres.-elect 2000, nat. bd. mem. 1999—, chpt. selected as Best in Nation 1997, Jacksonville chpt. Trial Lawyer of Yr. 2000, selected as Fla. Trial Lawyer of Yr. 2000), Jacksonville Bar Assn. (pres. 1980—81, young lawyers sect. 1974—75, Lawyer of Yr. award 1999), Fla. Bar (bd. cert civil trial lawyer, bd. cert. admiralty and maritime law , grievance com. 1975—77, chmn. grievance com. 1976, 4th jud. cir. nominating commn. 1980—82, mem. exec. coun. for trial sect. 1982—89, voluntary bar liaison com. 1982—83, chmn.-elect 1986—87, chmn. 1987, chmn. 1988, bd. govs. 1988, charter mem. admiralty and maritime law bd. cert. 1996—2000, chmn. 1998, chmn. 4th

jud. cir. professionalism com. 1998—, recipient Outstanding Professionalism Program 1999, 2001), Fla. Coun. Bar Assn. Pres. (exec. com. 1982—88, v.p. 1984, pres. 1985—86), Jacksonville Assn. Def. Counsel (pres. 1981—82, lectr. CLE programs, guest lectr. U. Fla. Nat. Assn. R.R. Trial Counsel), Nat. Assn. R.R. Trial Counsel (exec. com. 1979—, v.p. southeastern region 1984—86, pres.-elect 1989—90, pres. 1990—91), Maritime Law Assn. U.S. (mem. com. professionalism 1996—), Acad. Fla. Trial Lawyers, Am. Judicature Soc., San Jose Country Club, Univ. Club, Gulf Life Tower Club, Country Club Sapphire Valley (N.C.). Republican. Admiralty, General civil litigation, Personal injury. Home: 4655 Corrientes Cir N Jacksonville FL 32217-4329 Office: Milton Leach & D'Andrea 815 S Main St Ste 200 Jacksonville FL 32207-8181

MIMMS, THOMAS BOWMAN, JR. lawyer; b. Atlanta, Oct. 11, 1944; s. Thomas Bowman and Alice Buehl Mimms; m. Alison Hayward, July 22, 1967; children: Karen Mimms Swift, Christina Mimms Couret. BA, U. N.C., 1965; JD, Columbia U., 1969. Bar: Fla. 1969, Ga., 1999, U.S. Dist. Ct. (mid. dist.) Fla. 1972, U.S. Supreme Ct. 1973, U.S. Ct. Appeals (11th cir.) 1981 Ga. Supreme Ct., 2000. Assoc. atty. Fleming O'Bryan, Fort Lauderdale, Fla., 1969-72; shareholder Macfarlane Ferguson & McMullen, Tampa, 1972-99. Fellow Am. Bar Found.; mem. Fla. Bar Assn. (exec. coun. bus. law sect. 1987-99, chair bus. law legislation com. 1995-99, chair bus. law bankrupty/UCC com. 1988-89, chair fin. instns. com. 1993-94), Tampa Bay Bankruptcy Bar Assn. (pres. 1992-93), Columbia U. Alumni Club (dir. 1991-99). Democrat. Episcopalian. Bankruptcy, Contracts commercial, Real property. Office: Mimms Enterprises 85A Mill St Ste 100 Roswell GA 30075-4952 E-mail: legal@mimms.org

MINARDI, RICHARD A., JR. lawyer; b. Mobile, Ala., Aug. 15, 1943; s. Richard A. and Martha F. (Beck) M.; m. Frances Archer Guy, Oct. 21, 1989. BA, Yale U., 1965, LLB, 1968. Bar: Va. 1969. Assoc. McGuire Woods & Battle, Richmond, Va., 1968-71; ptnr. Staples, Greenberg Minardi & Kessler, 1971-86, Mays & Valentine, Richmond, 1986-2000, Troutman Sanders LLP, Richmond, 2001—. Mem. ABA, Va. Bar Assn., Richmond Bar Assn. General corporate, Securities, Corporate taxation. Home: 211 Santa Clara Dr Richmond VA 23229-7152 Office: Mays & Valentine PO Box 1122 Richmond VA 23218-1122 E-mail: rick.minardi@troutmansanders.com

MINCHEW, JOHN RANDALL, lawyer; b. Washington, July 31, 1957; s. John Richard and Lucile Elizabeth (Shaw) M. AB, Duke U., 1980; JD, Washington & Lee U., 1984; Cert. in Jurisprudence, Oxford U., 1982. Bar: Va. 1984, U.S. Dist. Ct. (ea. dist.) Va. 1985, U.S. Ct. Appeals (4th cir.) 1985, U.S. Supreme Ct. 1997. Jud. clk. Supreme Ct. Va., 1984-85; mng. ptnr. Loudoun County Office, Walsh, Colucci, Stackhouse, Emrich & Lubeley, P.C., Leesburg, Va., 1998—. V.p., dir. devel. The Minchew Corp., Fairfax, Va., 1985—; chmn. Loudoun County Econ. Devel. Commn., 1996-98; pres. Va. Shelter Corp. Adminstrv. editor: Washington & Lee Law Rev., 1984. Pro bono caseworker Legal Aid Soc. Roanoke Valley, Lexington, Va., 1982-84. Mem. ABA, Va. State Bar (mem. Commn. on Unauthorized Practice of Law 1994-98), Fairfax Bar Assn., Loudoun Bar Assn. (pres. 1995-96), Phi Delta Phi. Avocations: scuba diving, aviation, rugby. Condemnation, Land use and zoning (including planning), Real property. Home: 330 W Market St Leesburg VA 20176-2601 Office: Walsh Colucci Stackhouse Emrich & Lubeley PC 1 E Market St Ste 3 Leesburg VA 20176-3014 Fax: 703-737-3633

MINER, ROGER JEFFREY, federal judge; b. Apr. 14, 1934; s. Abram and Anne M.; m. Jacqueline Mariani; 4 children BS, SUNY; LLB cum laude, N.Y. Law Sch., 1956; postgrad., Bklyn. Law Sch., Judge Advocate Gen.'s Sch., U. Va.; LLD (hon.), N.Y. Law Sch., 1989, Syracuse U., 1990, Albany Law Sch./Union U., 1996; attended, Emory U. Bar: N.Y. 1956, U.S. Ct. Mil. Appeals 1956, Republic of Korea 1958, U.S. Dist. Ct. (so. and ea. dists.) N.Y. 1959. Ptnr. Miner & Miner, Hudson, N.Y., 1959-75; corp. counsel City of Hudson, 1961-64; asst. dist. atty. Columbia County, 1964, dist. atty., 1968-75; justice N.Y. State Supreme Ct., 1976-81; judge U.S. Dist. Ct. (no. dist.) N.Y., 1981-85, U.S. Ct. Appeals (2d cir.), Albany, N.Y., 1985—, now sr. judge. Adj. assoc. prof. criminal law State U. System, N.Y., 1974-79; adj. prof. law N.Y. Law Sch., 1986-96, Albany Law Sch. Union U., 1997—; lectr. state and local bar assns.; lectr. SUNY-Albany, 1985; N.Y. Law Sch. Bd. Trustees, 1991-96; mem. jud. coun. 2d Cir., 1992-96; chmn. 2d Cir. Com. on Hist. and Commemorative Events, 1989-94; Cameras in the Courtroom Com., 1993-96, No. Dist. Hist. Com., 1981-85; State, Fed. Jud. Coun. of N.Y., 1986-91, chmn., 1990-91; Jud. Conf. of U.S. com. on fed.-state jurisdiction, 1987-92; trustee Practicing Law Inst. Mng. editor N.Y. Law Sch. Law Rev.; contbr. articles to law jours. 1st lt. JAGC, U.S. Army, 1956-59, capt. USAR ret. Recipient Dean's medal for Disting. Profl. Svc., N.Y. Law Sch., Disting. Alumnus award, Charles W. Froessel award for Valuable Contbn. to Law. Albany Jewish Fedn. award, Abraham Lincoln award, Community Svc. award Kiwanis, others; named Columbia County Man. of Yr., 1984, Ellis Island medal of Honor. Mem. ABA, N.Y. State Bar Assn., Assn. of Bar of City of N.Y., Columbia County Bar Assn., Am. Law Inst., Am. Judicature Soc., Fed. Judges Assn., Fed. Bar Coun., Am. Soc. Writers on Legal Subjects, Assn. Trial Lawyers Am., Columbia County Magistrates Assn., Supreme Ct. Hist. Soc., Columbia County Hist. Soc., N.Y. Law Sch. Alumni Assn. (hon. mem., bd. dirs.), B'nai Brith, Elks (past exalted ruler). Jewish. Office: US Ct Appeals 445 Broadway Ste 414 Albany NY 12207-2926

MINES, MICHAEL, lawyer; b. Seattle, May 4, 1929; s. Henry Walker and Dorothy Elizabeth (Bressler) M.; m. Phyllis Eastham, Aug. 24, 1957; children: Linda Mines Elliott, Sandra, Diane Paull, Michael Lister. BA, U. Wash., 1951, JD, 1954. Bar: Wash. 1954, U.S. Dist. Ct. (we. dist.) Wash. 1957, U.S. Dist. Ct. Mont. 1970, U.S. Ct. Appeals (9th cir.) 1961, U.S. Supreme Ct. Assoc. Skeel, McKelvy, Henke, Evenson & Uhlman, Seattle, 1956-66, ptnr., 1966-68, Hullin, Roberts, Mines, Fite & Riveland, Seattle, 1968-75, Skeel, McKelvy, Henke, Evenson & Betts, Seattle, 1975-79, Betts, Patterson & Mines, 1978—. Moderator Wash.-No. Idaho conf. United Ch. of Christ, 1975-76; trustee Plymouth Housing Group, 1991-97; chair adult edn. bd. Plymouth Congl. Ch., Seattle, 1998-2001. With U.S. Army, 1954-56. Mem. ABA, Wash. State Bar Assn., Seattle-King Bar Assn., Am. Coll. Trial Lawyers (state chair 1984-85), Internat. Acad. Trial Lawyers (bd. dirs. 1991-96), U. Wash. Law Sch. Alumni Assn. (trustee, pres. bd. dirs. 1995-97). Federal civil litigation, State civil litigation, Insurance. Home: 2474 Crestmont Pl W Seattle WA 98199-3714 Office: Betts Patterson Mines PS One Convention Ctr Ste 1400 700 Pike St Seattle WA 98101-3927 E-mail: mpmines@aol.com, mmines@bpmlaw.com

MINISI, ANTHONY S. lawyer; b. Sept. 18, 1926; s. Anthony F. and Leonora (Petoia) M.; m. Rita Marie Hentz, Jan. 8, 1949; children: Claire, Anthony J., Joseph J., Brian A. BS, U. Pa., 1948, JD, 1952. Player N.Y. Giants NFL, 1948; law clk. to presiding judge Ct. of Common Pleas #6, Phila., 1952-54; counsel Wolf, Block, Schorr and Solis-Cohen, 1954—. Past pres., vice chmn. Robert E. Maxwell Meml. Football Club, Eastern Assn. Intercoll. Football Ofcls. Past chmn. Com. of Seventy, Phila.; former mem., past pres. Bd. of Edn., Tredyffrin/Easttown Joint Sch. Dist.; mem., chmn. bd. supr. Easttown Twp.; past v.p. Cmty. Svcs. Planning Coun., Phila.; trustee U. Pa.; trustee, mem. exec. com. U. Pa. Health Sys.; chmn. Clin. Care Assocs. U. Pa. Health Sys.; former mem., vice-chmn. Pa. State Bd. Law Examiners. Served to maj. USAR. Mem. ABA (ho. of dels.), Pa. Bar Assn., Phila. Jr. Bar Assn. (past pres.), Def. Lawyers Am., Assn. Trial Attys. Am., Phila. Bar Assn. (bd. of govs., past chmn.), Phila. Trial Lawyers Assn., Fed. Bar Assn., Lawyers Club (past pres.), Justinian soc., Union League (Phila.). Republican. Roman Catholic. Federal civil litigation, State civil litigation, Family and matrimonial. Office: Wolf Block Schorr & Solis-Cohen SE Corner 15th & Chestnut Sts Philadelphia PA 19102

MINKEL, HERBERT PHILIP , JR. lawyer; b. Boston, Feb. 11, 1947; s. Herbert Philip and Helen (Sullivan) M. BA, Holy Cross Coll., 1969; JD, NYU, 1972. Bar: Mass. 1973, N.Y. 1976, U.S. Dist. Ct. Mass. 1973, U.S. Dist. Ct. (so. dist.) N.Y. 1976. Law clk. U.S. Dist. Ct. Mass., Boston, 1972-73; assoc. Milbank, Tweed, Hadley & McCloy, N.Y.C., 1973-79; ptnr. Fried, Frank, Harris, Shriver & Jacobson, 1979-94; mem. adv. com. on bankruptcy rules Jud. Conf. U.S., 1987-93; sr. ptnr. Minkel and Assocs., N.Y.C., 1994—. Adj. assoc. prof. NYU Law Sch., 1987-94. Contbg. author: American Bankers Assn. Bankruptcy Manual, 1979; contbg. editor: 5 Collier on Bankruptcy, 15th edit., 1979-96; contbr. articles to profl. jours. Bd. advisors Internat. Yacht Restoration Sch., Newport, R.I., Spl. Olympics, Spl. Smiles. Root-Tilden scholar NYU, 1969-72. Mem. ABA, Nat. Bankruptcy Conf., Assn. Bar City of N.Y. Bankruptcy. Home: 68 Bumps River Rd Osterville MA 02655-1525 Office: Minkel and Assocs Ste 2217 1270 Avenue Of The Americas New York NY 10020-1801 also: 112 Revere St Boston MA 02114

MINKOWITZ, MARTIN, lawyer, former state government official; b. Bklyn., 1939; s. Jacob and Marion (Kornblau) M.; m. Carol L. Ziegler; 1 son from previous marriage, Stuart Allan. AA, Bklyn. Coll., 1959, BA, 1961; JD, Bklyn. Law Sch., 1963, LLM, 1965. Bar: N.Y. 1963, U.S. Supreme Ct. 1967, U.S. Tax Ct. 1974, all four U.S. Dist. Cts. N.Y. Ptnr. Minkowitz, Hagen & Rosenbluth, N.Y.C., 1964-76; gen. counsel State of N.Y. Workers' Compensation Bd., 1976-81; dep. supt. and gen. counsel State of N.Y. Ins. Dept., 1981-88; instr. CUNY, 1975; ptnr. Stroock & Stroock & Lavan, N.Y.C., 1988—. Adv. bd. Coll. Ins., 1987-90; adj. prof. law N.Y. Law Sch., N.Y.C., 1982—; lectr. ABA, N.Y. C. of C., Practicing Law Inst., N.Y. State Bar Assn., Nat. Assn. Ins. Commrs., Nat. Conf. Ins. Legis.; hearing officer N.Y.C. Transp. Dept., 1970-75; cons. City Coun. N.Y.C. 1969. Author: (with others) Rent Stabilization and Control, 1973; (with others) Handling the Basic Workers' Compensation Law Case, 1996; co-author: Workers Compensation, Insurance and Law Practice-The Next Generation, 1989; commentaries to McKinney's Consol. Laws, 1982—; mem. editl. bd. Jour. Occupl. Rehab. U. Rochester, 1991—; contbr. articles to profl. jours. Bd. dirs., sec. Kingsbay YM-YWHA, Bklyn., 1978-99, elected dir. emeritus, 1999—; pres. bd. dirs. Shore Terrace Co-op., Bklyn., 1982-83; co-chmn. exec. bd., met. coun., nat. v.p. Am. Jewish Congress, N.Y.C., 1983-91; bd. dirs. Met. Coord. Coun. on Jewish poverty, 1993—, Nat. Conf. for Cmty. and Justice (bd. dir. N.Y. divsn. 1994—, nat. bd. trustees 1995—, chair N.Y. divsn. 1998—). Recipient cert. meritorious svc. Bklyn. Law Sch., Outstanding Pub. Svc. award Ind. Ins. Agt. Assn., citation outstanding performance State of N.Y. Workers' Compensation Bd., Disting. Leadership award N.Y. Claims Assn., City of Peace award State of Israel Bonds, Brotherhood award NCCJ. Fellow N.Y. State Bar Found.; mem. N.Y. County Lawyers Assn. (chmn. unlawful practice of law com. 1982-86, mem. profl. ethics com. 1985-91, chair worker's compensation com. 1988-91, bd. dirs. 1997-2001, chair profl. ethics com. 2001—), N.Y. State Bar Assn. (mem. ho. of dels., chmn. unlawful practice of law com. 1981-83, mem. com. on profl. ethics 1981-84, chmn. com. profl. discipline 1988-92, Sustaining Mem. of Yr. award 1995), Soc. Ins. Receivers, Bklyn. Law Sch. Alumni Assn. (v.p. bd. dirs. 1984-92, pres. elect 1993-94, pres. 1995-96). Office: Stroock Stroock & Lavan 180 Maiden Ln Fl 17 New York NY 10038-4937 E-mail: mminkowitz@stroock.com

MINNEY, MICHAEL JAY, lawyer; b. Lancaster, Pa., Aug. 15, 1948; s. Jay W. and Mary Jane (Erisman) M.; m. Barbara Ann Dunlap, June 28, 1975; 1 child, Michael Jayson. Student, U.S. Mil. Acad., 1967; BA, Ohio Wesleyan U., 1970; JD, Villanova U., 1973. Bar: Pa. 1973, U.S. Dist. Ct. (ea. dist.) Pa. 1974, U.S. Supreme Ct. 1977, U.S. Ct. Appeals (3d cir.) 1979. Ptnr. Minney, Mecum & Kohr, Lancaster, 1975-78, 1978-84; sole practice, 1973-75, 84—. Regional council Govs. Justice Commn., Harrisburg, Pa., 1975-78; commr. Pa. Commn. on Sentencing, Harrisburg, 1979-81. Candidate U.S. House of Reps., 16th Dist., Pa., 1974, 76; bd. dirs. United Cerebral Palsy, Lancaster, 1976-84, pres. 1983-84; mem., prin. Bring Back Baseball to Lancaster. Named one of Outstanding Young Men of Am., 1976. Mem. Lancaster County Bar Assn., Pa. Bar Assn., James Buchannan Found. for the Preservation of Wheatland (treas, 1998-99, v.p. 2001—). Republican. Lutheran. Clubs: Hamilton, Conestoga Country (Lancaster). Lodge: Elks. Avocations: running, golf, photography. Criminal, Real property. Home: 1011 Woods Ave Lancaster PA 17603-3126 Office: 145 E Chestnut St Lancaster PA 17602-2740

MINNICK, BRUCE ALEXANDER, lawyer; b. New London, Conn., Apr. 16, 1943; s. Robert Wood Minnick and Nedra Louise (Alexander) Wiesman; m. Judith Anita Saxon, Sept. 23, 1967 (div. 1981); children: Audra Anne, Lisa Michelle; m. Charlotte Ann Springfield, Apr. 10, 1983 (div. 1991); 1 child, Matthew Alexander; m. Debra C. Williams, July 3, 1997; 1 stepchild, Brandy Michelle Williams. AA, Broward Community Coll., 1970; BS with honors, Fla. State U., 1971, JD, 1977. BarL Fla. 1978, U.S. Dist. Ct. (no. dist.) Fla. 1979, U.S. Dist. Ct. (mid. and so. dists.) Fla. 1982, U.S. Supreme Ct. 1981, U.S. Ct. Appeals (11th cir.) 1982, U.S. Tax Ct. 1983, U.S. Ct. Claims 1983, U.S. Dist. Ct. (ea. dist.) Mich. 1990. Staff dir., counsel rules com. Fla. Ho. Reps., Tallahassee, 1976-78; v.p., gen. counsel Fla. Credit Union League, 1978-80; asst. atty. gen. dept. legal affairs State of Fla., 1981-86; ptnr. Mang, Rett & Collette, P.A., 1986-93, Mang, Rett & Minnick PA, Tallahassee, 1994-95; pvt. practice Bruce A. Minnick PA, 1996—. Chief adv. Fla. Commn. on Ethics, 1995-96; lectr. state agys., 1982—, Fla. Bar, 1986—; v.p. for fin., gen. counsel UCompass.com, Inc.. Mem. Leon County Dist. Adv. Com., 1980-82, 92-94; mem. exec. com. Leon County Dems., 1984-2000.—. Mem. ABA (labor sect., local govt. and law sect.), Fla. Bar Assn. (chmn. com. labor sect. 1987-91, mem. exec. coun. labor sect. 1989-93, founding chmn. Fed. Ct. practice com. 1990-92, del. to 11th Cir. Jud. Conf. 1990-92, com. chmn. govt. lawyer sect. 1991-2000—, rep. mem. pub. rels. com. 1991-93), Tallahassee Bar Assn., Fa. Govt. Bar Assn., Fla. Women Lawyers Assn., Fed. Bar Assn. (pres.-elect Tallahassee chpt. 1995, pres. 1996), Govs. Club, Univ. Ctr. Club, Golden Eagle Country Club, Phi Alpha Delta. Christian Scientist. Avocations: golf, astronomy, writing. Civil rights, Labor, Securities. Home: 9017 Eagles Ridge Dr Tallahassee FL 32312-4046 Office: 3116 Capital Cir NE PO Box 15588 Tallahassee FL 32317-5588 Fax: 850-385-8414. E-mail: minnicklaw@prodigy.net

MINNICK, MALCOLM DAVID, lawyer; b. Indpls., July 5, 1946; s. Malcolm Dick and Frances Louise (Porter) M.; m. Heidi Rosemarie Klein, May 24, 1972. BA, U. Mich., 1968, JD, 1972. Bar: Calif. 1972, U.S. Dist. Ct. (cen. dist.) Calif. 1972, U.S. Ct. Appeals (9th cir.) 1984, U.S. Dist. Ct. (no. dist.) Calif. 1986, U.S. Supreme Ct. 1986. Assoc. Lillick McHose & Charles, Los Angeles, 1972-78; ptnr. Lillick & McHose, 1978-91, Pillsbury Winthrop LLC, San Francisco, 1991—. Group mgr. Creditors Rights and Bankruptcy Group, 1993-98; panelist Calif. Continuing Edn. of Bar, L.A., 1982-86, 88, Practicing Law Inst., 1992, 93, 94, Banking Law Inst., 1999, 2000; bd. govs. Fin. Lawyers Conf., L.A., 1981-84; mem. exec. com. Lillick & McHose, 1982-85. Co-author: Checklist for Secured Commercial Loans, 1983. Pres. Ross Sch. Found., 1997-98. Mem. ABA (corp., banking and bus. law sect.), Calif. Bar Assn. (Uniform Comml. Code com. 1983-86), L.A. County Bar Assn. (exec. com. comml. law and bankruptcy sect. 1987-90), Bar Assn. San Francisco (comml. law and bankruptcy sect.), L.A. Country Club, Univ. Club (bd. dirs. 1983-86, pres. 1985-86). Avocation: golf. Banking, Bankruptcy, Contracts commercial. Office: Pillsbury Winthrop LLC 50 Fremont St San Francisco CA 94105-2230 E-mail: dminnick@pillsburywinthrop.com

MINOR, CLARA MAE, election judge; b. Altapass, N.C., Dec. 3, 1931; d. David Wilkerson Sullins, and Carrie Mae Schism; m. Lawrence Alfred Minor, Oct. 27, 1950; children: Lawrence, Charles, Beverly, John. Grad. h.s., Canton, Ohio, 1949. Sales clk. JC Penney Co., Canton, 1973-80; presiding judge Stark County Election Bd., 1983—. Pres., mem. PTA, Hubbard, Ohio, 197-72. Mem. DAR, Daus. Am. Colonists, Daus. War of 1812. Republican. Methodist. Avocations: reading, collector ladies antique watches and compacts.

MINSKY, BRUCE WILLIAM, lawyer; b. Queens, N.Y., Sept. 28, 1963; m. Jill R. Heinter, May 1992; children: Aryeh Hanan, Elisheva Yael, Calev Betzalel, Refael Akiva. BA in Polit. Sci., Boston U., 1985; JD, Southwestern U., 1988; LLM in Am. Banking, Boston U., 1989. Bar: Calif. 1988, Conn. 1989, N.Y. 1990, U.S. Dist. Ct. (ea. and so. dist.), U.S. Ct. Appeals. Assoc. Quirk & Bakalor, N.Y.C., 1989-91; house counsel, v.p. Banco Popular N.Am., 1991—, Banco Poplur N. Am., 1999. Atty. Monday Night Law Pro Bono Svcs., N.Y.C. Mem. Assn. of Bar of City of N.Y. (mem. young lawyers com. 1993-95). Avocations: music, sports, literature. Banking, General corporate, General practice. Office: 7 W 51st St New York NY 10019-6910

MINTER, ALAN HUNTRESS, lawyer; b. San Antonio, Feb. 21, 1939; s. Merton Melrose Minter and Katherine Logan Huntress; m. Patricia West, May 31, 1964; children: Katherine Ruth, Patricia West. Student, Brown U., 1957-59; BA, U. Tex., 1962, JD, 1965. Bar: Tex., U.S. Supreme Ct., U.S. Tax Ct., U.S. Ct. Claims, U.S. Ct. Mil. Appeals, U.S. Ct. Customs and Patent Appeals, U.S. Ct. Appeals (5th cir.), U.S. Dist. Ct. (no., we., ea., so. dists.) Tex. Asst. atty. Atty. Gen.'s Office, State of Tex., Austin, 1965-71; pvt. practice, 1971—. Mem. nat. adv. com. Deganawidah Quetzalcoatl U., Davis, Calif., History Aviation Collection U. Tex., Austin; bd. dirs. Young Man's Bus. League, Austing, 1972, St. Andrew's Episcopal Sch. Austin, 1973-76, Tex. Hist. Found., 1983-85, Les Patrons Paramount Theatre Performing Arts, 1978-82; mem. ad hoc hist. zoning com. City of Austin, 1973; mem. citizen adv. com. Tex. Constl. Revision Com., 1973; bd. dirs. Austin Heritage Soc., 1974-81, chmn. properties com., 1975-76, co-chmn. properties com., 1976-77, 2d v.p., 1978-79; mem. steering com. Tex. Heritage Coun. Tex. Hist. Found., 1977-80, 81-83, v.p. edn., 1978-80; mem. adv. coun. Winedale Hist. Ctr. U. Tex., 1978-87, treas., 1984-85; vice-chmn. City Austin Tex. Libr. Commn., 1980-81, chmn., 1981-84; trustee Elisabet Ney Mus. Assn., 1980-81. Fellow Tex. Bar Found.; mem. ABA (vice chmn. 1981-85, hist. preservation and easement com. real property, probate and trust law sect.), ATLA, SCV, Comml. Law League Am., State Bar Tex., Sheriff's Assn. Tex. (assoc.), Tex. Old Fts. and Missions Restoration Assn., Old Trail Drivers Assn. Tex., State Assn. Tex. Pioneers, Sons Republic Tex., Travis County Bar Assn. (bd. dirs. chmn. estate planning and probate law sect. 1994-2001, bd. dirs. estate planning and probate law sect. 1995-96, bd. dirs. bankruptcy law sect. 2001—), Order Alamo, Order Sons Hermann State Tex., German Club, Phi Alpha Delta. Avocations: hunting, fishing, travel, reading, writing. Home: 1602 W Lynn St Austin TX 78703-3446

MINTON, HARVEY STEIGER, lawyer; b. Columbus, Ohio, Dec. 16, 1933; s. Harvey Alan and Elsie (Steiger) M.; m. Jane Rickey Grimm, July 21, 1956; children: Harvey Randall, Jennifer Thelma. BS, Ohio State U., 1956, JD, 1962. Bar: Ohio 1956, N.Y. 1985. Atty. Shumaker, Loop & Kendrick, Toledo, 1962-65; asst. atty. Owens Ill., 1965-82; sec., pres. Sun Master (subs. Corning), N.Y.C., 1983-84; v.p. Leeward Capital, Columbus, Ohio, 1985-87; gen. counsel, sr. ptnr. Harvey S. Minton & Assocs., Worthingon, 1987--. Pres. bd. trustees Toledo Symphony, 1973-76; chmn. Law Week, Toledo, 1964, jail action, Toledo, 1973; mem. Worthington Zoning Bd. Appeals, 1992. Capt. USAF, 1958-59. Mem. Rotary (named Man of the yr. 1988). Republican. Presbyterian. Bankruptcy, General corporate, Estate planning. Home: 617 Hartford St Worthington OH 43085-4119 Office: 6641·N High St Worthington OH 43085-4038

MINTON, KENT W. lawyer; b. Independence, Mo., May 16, 1955; s. Roy V. and Donabelle M. Minton; m. Karen S. MacDonald, Oct. 21, 1989; children: Kathy, Megan, Abby. BS, Ctrl. Mo. State U., 1976; postgrad., U. Tulsa, 1979-80; JD, U. Mo., Kansas City, 1982. Bar: Mo. 1982, U.S. Dist. Ct. (we. dist.) Mo. 1982, U.S. Ct. Claims 1986. Assoc. Paxton, Block et al, Independence, 1982-83, Holliday & Holliday, Kansas City, 1983-85; ptnr. Raymond, Raymond & Minton, 1985-96, Stewart, Cook, Constance, Stewart & Minton LLC, Independence, 1996—. Bd. dirs. Comprehensive Mental Health Svcs. Found., Independence. Contbr. chpt. to book. Mem. Mo. Bar (trust law revision subcom.), Kansas City Metro Bar Assn. (probate com.). State civil litigation, Estate planning, Probate. Office: Stewart Cook Constance Stewart & Minton LLC 501 W Lexington Ave Independence MO 64050-3648

MINTZ, JEFFRY ALAN, lawyer, consultant; b. N.Y.C., Sept. 15, 1943; s. Aaron Herbert and Lillian Betty (Greenspan) M.; m. Susan Politzer, Aug. 22, 1979; children: Jennifer, Melanie, Jonathan. AB, Tufts U., 1964; LLB, Rutgers U., 1967; postgrad., U. Pa. Law Sch., 1968-70. Bar: D.C. 1968, N.Y. 1970, U.S. Supreme Ct. 1972, N.J. 1973, Pa. 1983; registered mediator, N.J. Law clk. to judge U.S. Ct. Appeals, New Orleans, 1967-68; asst. defender Defender Assn. Phila., 1968-70; asst. counsel NAACP Legal Def. and Ednl. Fund, N.Y.C., 1970-74; dir. Office Inmate Advocacy, N.J. Dept. Pub. Adv., Trenton, 1974-81; pvt. practice Haddonfield and Medford, N.J, 1982; ptnr. Stein & Shapiro, Medford, 1982-83, Cherry Hill, N.J., 1983-84, Mesirov, Gelman, Jaffe, Cramer & Jamieson, Cherry Hill, Phila., 1984-90, Schlesinger, Mintz & Pilles, Mt. Holly, N.J., 1990-92; pvt. practice, 1992—. Trustee Congregation M'Kor Shalom, Cherry Hill, 1990-97; mem. Burling County and Mt. Laurel Dem. Coun. Com., 1993-95; chair Moorestown Dem. Com., 1995-2001. Mem. ABA, ATLA, N.J. Bar Assn. (del., gen. coun. 1986-88, 89-91), D.C. Bar Assn., Camden County Bar Assn., Burlington County Bar Assn. (trustee 1989-92), Assn. Trial Lawyers N.J. (bd. govs. 1990-95), Barrister, Burlington Am. Inn. of Ct. (founding mem. dist. fee arbitration com., vice chair, 1999-2000, chair 2000-01). Jewish. General civil litigation, Personal injury. Home: 22 Lexington Ct Mount Laurel NJ 08054-3701 Office: 129 High St Mount Holly NJ 08060-1401 E-mail: mhlaw@eticomm.net

MINTZ, JOEL ALAN, law educator; b. N.Y.C., July 24, 1949; s. Samuel Isaiah and Eleanor (Streichler) M.; m. Meri-Jane Rochelson, Aug. 25, 1975; children: Daniel Rochelson, Robert Eli. BA, Columbia U., 1970, LLM, 1982, JSD, 1989; JD, NYU, 1974. Bar: N.Y. 1975, U.S. Dist. Ct. (so. and ea. dists.) N.Y. 1982, U.S. Ct. Appeals (2d cir.) 1982. Atty. enforcement div. EPA, Chgo., 1975-76, chief atty. case devel. unit, 1977-78, policy advisor to regional adminstr., 1979; sr. litigation atty. Office Enforcement, EPA, Washington, 1980-81; asst. prof. environ. law Nova U. Law Ctr., Ft. Lauderdale, Fla., 1982-85, assoc. prof., 1985-87, prof., 1987—. Author: State and Local Government Environmental Liability, 1994, Enforcement At the EPA: High Stakes, 1995; author: (with others) Environmental Law, 4th edit., 2000, State and Local Taxation and Finance In A Nutshell, 2nd edit., 2000; contbr. articles to legal jours. and treatises. Mem. ABA, Environ. Law Inst. Assocs., Fla. Bar (assoc.), Internat. Coun. Environ. Law,

Internat. Union for Conservation of Nature (commn. on environ. law), Assn. Am. Law Schs. (exec. com., state and local govt. law sect.), Phi Alpha Delta. Avocations: reading, fitness walking, canoeing. Home: 2060 NE 209th St Miami FL 33179-1628 Office: Nova Southeastern U Law Ctr 3305 College Ave Fort Lauderdale FL 33314-7721 E-mail: mintzj@nsu.law.nova.edu

MINZNER, PAMELA BURGY, state supreme court justice; b. Meridian, Miss., Nov. 19, 1943; BA cum laude, Miami U., 1965; LLB, Harvard U., 1968. Bar: Mass. 1968, N.Mex. 1972. Pvt. practice, Mass., 1968-71, Albuquerque, 1971-73; adj. prof. law U. N.Mex., 1972-73, asst. prof., 1973-77, assoc. prof., 1977-80, prof. law, 1980-84; judge N.Mex. Ct. Appeals, 1984-94, chief judge, 1993-94; justice N.Mex. Supreme Ct., Santa Fe, 1994—, chief justice, 1999-01. Mem. faculty Inst. Preparativo Legal U., N.Mex. Sch. Law, 1975, 79; participant NEH Summer Seminar for Law Tchrs. Stanford Law Sch., 1982, U. Chgo. Law Sch., 1978. Author: (with Robert T. Laurence) A Student's Guide to Estates in Land and Future Interests: Text, Examples, Problems & Answers, 1981, 2d edit. 1993. Mem. ABA, State Bar N.Mex. (co-editor newsletter 1979-83, bd. dirs. 1978-79, 83-84, sect. on women's legal rights and obligations), Gamma Phi Beta. Democrat. Avocations: reading, bridge, movies. Office: NMex Supreme Ct Supreme Ct Bldg 237 Don Gaspar Santa Fe NM 87504-0848

MIRA, JOSEPH LAWRENCE, lawyer; b. Huntington, N.Y., Aug. 14, 1966; s. Salvatore Joseph and Carol Ann Mira; m. Tina Marie Lovelace, June 4, 1994. BS, So. Meth. U., 1988; JD, Tulane U., 1997. Bar: Tex. 1997, U.S. Dist. Ct. (no. dist.) Tex. 1997. Program mgr. Space Ordinance Sys., Canyon Country, Calif., 1988-90; contracts mgr. Dallas Area Rapid Transit, 1990-94; assoc. Fernandez & Knebel, P.C., Dallas, 1997—. Mem. Dallas Bar Assn., Dallas Assn. Young Lawyers, Phi Gamma Delta (bd. chpt. advisors Dallas 1994). Republican. Baptist. Avocations: golf, hunting, tennis. General civil litigation, Construction, Real property. Home: 4201 Polstar Dr Plano TX 75093 Office: Fernandez & Knebel PC 1717 Main St Ste 2100 Dallas TX 75201

MIRABILE, THOMAS KEITH, lawyer; b. May 11, 1948; s. Joseph Anthony and Marie Johanna (Reynolds) M.; m. Margaret Sue Hughes, Feb. 11, 1981; children: Adrian, Joseph. BA, No. Ill. U., 1972; MA, Northeastern Ill. U., 1974; JD, Oklahoma City U., 1975. Bar: Okla. 1976, Ill. 1977, U.S. Dist. Ct. (we. dist.) Okla. 1976, U.S. Ct. Appeals (10th cir.) 1980, U.S. Tax Ct. 1977, U.S. Supreme Ct. 1983, U.S. Ct. of Claims 1985. Prof. sociology Oklahoma City U., 1976-77; prof. bus. Edmond, Okla., 1977-82; ptnr. Mirabile and Assocs. P.C., Oklahoma City, 1977—; prof. Sch. Law, Grad. Sch. Bus. U. Cen. Okla., 1986-95; prof. Grad. Sch. Webster U., 1991—. Vis. faculty DePaul U., Chgo. Mem. Ill. Bar Assn., Okla. Bar Assn. Federal civil litigation, Immigration, naturalization, and customs, Securities. Home: 1507 Johnstown Ct Wheaton IL 60187-7524 Office: Mirabile and Assocs PC 6250 N River Rd Ste 3000 Rosemont IL 60018-4209

MIRIKITANI, ANDREW KOTARO, lawyer; b. N.Y.C., Aug. 25, 1955; s. Carl Mamoru and Hisa (Yoshimura) M. BA magna cum laude, U. So. Calif., 1978; JD, U. Santa Clara, 1982. Bar: Hawaii 1984, U.S. Dist. Ct. Hawaii 1984, U.S. Ct. Appeals (9th cir.) 1984. Law clk. to chief judge James S. Burns Intermediate Ct. of Appeals, State of Hawaii, Honolulu, 1985-86; atty. Case, Kay & Lynch, 1986-87; mem., vice-chmn. Honolulu City Coun., 1990—; atty. Char Hamilton Campbell & Thom, Honolulu, 1988-92. V.p. Am. Beltwrap Corp. Honolulu, 1986—. Editor Santa Clara Law Rev., 1982; patentee in field. Trustee Carl K. Mirikitani Meml. Scholarship Fund, Honolulu, 1984—; pres. East Diamond Head Community Assn., Honolulu, 1988-89; chmn. Waialae-Kahala Neighborhood Bd., Honolulu, 1988-89; bd. dirs. Legal Aid Soc. of Hawaii, 1988-90, Protection ad Advocacy Agy., Honolulu, 1989; del. Dem. Party of Hawaii, Honolulu, 1990-92; pres. Save Diamond Head Beach, Honolulu, 1993—; mem. Nat. Women's Polit. Caucus, Hawaii Women's Polit. Caucus. Recipient award Am. Soc. for Pub. Adminstrs., 1997, Outstanding Pub. Svc. Media Program award, Nat. Achievement award Nat. Assn. of Counties, 1997. Mem. ABA, Hawaii Bar Assn., am. Trial Lawyers Assn., Hawaii Women Lawyers Assn., Advocates for Pub. Interest Law, Alpha Mu Gamma, Phi Beta Kappa. Democrat. General civil litigation, Insurance, Legislative. Office: City Council Honolulu Hale Honolulu HI 96813

MIRSKY, ELLIS RICHARD, lawyer; b. San Diego, Nov. 22, 1947; s. Jacob Joseph and Lucille (Albert) M.; m. Renee Grundstein, Apr. 18, 1970; children— Jason, Lauren. B.Engring., CCNY, 1969, M.Engring., 1971; J.D., Fordham U., 1976. Bar: N.Y. 1977, U.S. Dist. Ct. (so. and ea. dists.) N.Y. 1978, U.S. Supreme Ct. 1986. Engr., Curtiss-Wright Corp., Woodridge, N.J., 1969-73, Ebasco Services, Inc., N.Y.C., 1973-75; assoc. Rosenman Colin Freund Lewis & Cohen, N.Y.C., 1975-83; asst. gen. counsel Combustion Engring., Inc., Stamford, Conn., 1983-87, head litigation dept., 1985-87, v.p. chief, litigation dept., 1987—; adv. com. products liability Practicing Law Inst., 1988—. Mem. bd. editorial advisors Bus. Laws Inc., 1988—. NSF grantee, 1968. Mem. Assn. Bar City of N.Y., ASME (assoc.), Engrs. Club (trustee 1976), Fedn. Ins. and Corp. Counsel. General civil litigation, Insurance. Home: 10 Cupsaw Ct Nanuet NY 10954-3506 Office: Combustion Engring Inc 900 Long Ridge Rd Stamford CT 06902-1128

MIRVAHABI, FARIN, lawyer; b. Tehran, Iran; d. Ali and Azar Mirvahabi; children: Bobby Naemi, Jimmy Naemi. Degree in Law, Tehran U., Iran, 1968; M of Comparative Law, Georgetown U., 1972; LLM, George Washington U., 1976; JSD, NYU, 1978; diploma, The Hague Acad. Internat. Law, 1983. Bar: Va. 1989, U.S. Dist. Ct. (ea. and we. dists.) Va. 1990, D.C. 1990, U.S. Dist. Ct. D.C. 1990, U.S. Supreme Ct. 1997. With Gold & Cutner, N.Y.C., 1979-80; in-house counsel IRA Engring. and Constrn., Tehran, London, 1981-82; legal advisor Bank Markazi, Tehran, 1981-82; practiced law The Hague, The Netherlands, 1982-87; arbitrator Iran Air-Pan Am Arbitration Tribunal, Paris, 1984-87; legal cons. Rooney, Barry & Fogerty, Washington, 1987-88; atty. sole practice, Washington, 1989—. Law prof. No. Va. Law Sch., Alexandria, 1989-90; instr. Paralegal Inst., Arlington, Va., 1988-89; prof. Tehran U., 1982; panelist Am. Arbitration Assn.; guest speaker in field; life dep. gov. Am. Biog. Inst. Rsch. Assn., 19995—. Contbr. numerous articles to profl. jours. Named Maxplank fellow Maxplank Inst. of Internat. Law, 1986; recipient Clyde Eagleton award NYU, 1977, Woman of Yr. medallion honoring Cmty. Svc. and Profl. Achievement, 1995. Mem. ABA, Internat. Bar Assn., Arbitration Forum Inc., D.C. Bar Assn. (panelist client-atty. arbitration bd. 1990—), D.C. Bar & Lawyers Assn., Trial Lawyers Assn., Va. Bar Found., Am. Soc. Internat. Law, Am. Film Inst. The Kennedy Ctr. Avocations: reading, writing, Broadway shows, picnic, swimming. Private international, Public international. Office: 1730 K St NW Ste 304 Washington DC 20006-3839

MISHKIN, BARBARA FRIEDMAN, lawyer; b. Phila., Feb. 19, 1936; d. Maurice Harold and Gertrude (Sanders) F.; m. Martin S. Thaler, Mar. 22, 1958 (div. 1970); children: Diane Sanders, Paul Sanders, David Emile, Amy Suzanne; m. Mortimer Mishkin, May 27, 1971. AB, Mount Holyoke Coll., 1957; MA, Yale U., 1958; JD, Am. U., 1981. Bar: D.C. 1982, U.S. Supreme Ct. 1989, U.S. Ct. Appeals (4th cir.) 1995. Research psychologist NIMH, Bethesda, Md., 1968-69; spl. asst. to chief judge U.S. Ct. Appeals (D.C. cir.), Washington, 1970-71; spl. asst. to scientific dir. Nat. Inst. Child Health, Bethesda, 1971-74; asst. staff dir. Nat. Commn. for the Protection of Human Subjects, Washington, 1974-78; staff dir. Ethics Adv. Bd. HEW, 1978-80; dep. dir. Pres.' Commn. on Ethics in Medicine and Research, 1980-83; assoc. Hogan and Hartson, 1983-89, counsel, 1990-93; ptnr. Hogan & Hartson, 1994—. Cons. Ctr. for Law and Health Scis., Boston, 1970-73; cons., lectr. Johns Hopkins U. Sch. of Medicine, Balt., 1971-73; bd. dirs. Bon Secours Health Systems, Inc., Columbia, Md., 1984-90. Contbr. numerous articles on health law, med. ethics and biomed. research to jours. in field. Mem. policy bd. Legal Counsel for the Elderly, Washington, 1984-88, vice chair, 1988-90; trustee Mt. Holyoke Coll., 1985-90; mem. Mayor's Adv. Task Force on Hospice Licensure, Washington, 1985-87; bd. dirs. Hebrew Home Greater Washington, 1987-91. Mem. ABA (chair sect. on health and environment 1988-92, chair com. on regulating rsch. 1996-98), D.C. Bar Assn. (subcom. rights of the elderly and the handicapped 1985-92, Pro Bono Atty. Yr. 1988), AAAS (com. on sci. freedom and responsibility 1986-92, AAAS/ABA Nat. Conf. Lawyers and Scientists 1992, ABA co-chair 1993-97), Am. Soc. Law, Medicine and Ethics (bd. dirs. 1995-98). Home: 5610 Wisconsin Ave Apt 402 Chevy Chase MD 20815-4429 Office: Hogan & Hartson Columbia Sq 555 13th St Washington DC 20004 E-mail: bfmishkin@hhlaw.com

MITBY, JOHN CHESTER, lawyer; b. Antigo, Wis., Jan. 7, 1944; s. Norman Peter and Luvern T. (Jensen) M.; m. Julie Kampen, June 10, 1972; children: Tana, Jenna. BS, U. Wis., 1966, LLB, 1971. Bar: Wis. 1971, Colo. 1992. Ptnr. Axley, Brynelson, LLP, Madison, Wis., 1973—. Lectr. U. Wis. Law Sch.; mem. adv. bd. U. Wis. Golf Course, 1991-96. Served to capt. C.E., U.S. Army, 1966-68. Mem.: ATLA, ABA, Acad. Trial Lawyers, Am. Bd. Trial Advs., Am. Soc. Hosp. Attys., Am. Soc. Law and Medicine, Nat. Acad. Elder Law Attys. Inc. (adv. bd.), Wis. Bar Assn. (past chmn. litigation sect.), Western Dist. of Wis. Bar Assn., Dane County Bar Assn., Nakoma Country Club (Madison). Federal civil litigation, State civil litigation, General practice. Home: 726 Oneida Pl Madison WI 53711-2958 Office: Axley Brynelson LLP PO Box 1767 2 E Mifflin St Madison WI 53703-2889 E-mail: jmitby@axley.com

MITCHAM, BOB ANDERSON, lawyer, judge; b. Atlanta, July 16, 1933; s. George Anderson and Pearl (Bing) M.; m. Lupe M. Vazquez, Dec. 6, 1969; children: Robert Anderson, Tamara Lynn, Matthew Vazquez, Micah Marissa Vasquez. BS, Fla. So. Coll., 1959; JD, Stetson U., 1962. Bar: Fla. 1963, U.S. Dist. Ct. (mid. dist.) Fla. 1963, U.S. Ct. Appeals (5th cir.) 1965, U.S. Ct. Appeals (11th cir.) 1983, U.S. Supreme Ct. 1988. Ptnr. Mitcham & Honig, Tampa, Fla., 1963-66, Mitcham, Leon & Guito, Tampa, 1966-68; pvt. practice, 1968-82; ptnr. Mitcham, Weed & Barbas, 1982—90. Cir. judge, Tampa, 1990—; lectr. Oxford U., Eng., 1981, U. London, 1987. Contbr. articles to profl. jours. Pres. Young Dem. of Fla., Tampa, 1968; active Davis Island Baptist Church. With USAF, 1952-59. Perry Nichols Trial scholar, 1961. Mem. Criminal Def. Lawyers Hillsborough County (pres. 1981-82), Hillsborough County Bar Assn. (dir. 1981-85), Ybor City C. of C. (dir. 1981-82, chmn. Super Bows XVIII). Republican. Criminal.

MITCHELL, BURLEY BAYARD, JR. state supreme court chief justice; b. Oxford, N.C., Dec. 15, 1940; s. Burley Bayard and Dorothy Ford (Champion) M.; m. Mary Lou Willett, Aug. 3, 1962; children: David Bayard, Catherine Morris. BA with honors, N.C. State U., 1966, DHL (hon.), 1995; JD, U. N.C., 1969; LLD (hon.), Campbell U., 1998. Bar: N.C. 1969, U.S. Ct. Appeals (4th cir.) 1970, U.S. Supreme Ct. 1972. Asst. atty. gen. State of N.C., Raleigh, 1969-72, dist. atty., 1973-77, judge Ct. Appeals, 1977-79, sec. crime control, 1979-82; justice Supreme Ct. N.C., Raleigh, 1982-94; chief justice Supreme Ct. of N.C., Raleigh, 1995-99; ptnr. Womble Carlyle Sandridge and Rice, 1999—. Served with USN, 1958-62, Asia. Recipient N.C. Nat. Guard Citizen Commendation award, 1982 Mem. ABA, VFW, N.C. Bar Assn., Mensa, Am. Legion, Phi Beta Kappa. Democrat. Methodist. Home: 4301 City of Oaks Wynd Raleigh NC 27612-5316 Office: First Union Cptl Ctr Ste 2100 PO Box 831 Raleigh NC 27602-0831

MITCHELL, CAROL ANN, lawyer; b. New Bedford, Mass., Sept. 2, 1957; d. John E. and Edith A. (Mogensen) M. AB, Vassar Coll., 1979; JD, William and Mary Coll., 1982. Bar: D.C. 1983, U.S. Ct. Appeals (Fed. cir.) 1988, U.S. Ct. Internat. Trade 1986. Atty.-advisor Benefits Rev. Bd., Washington, 1982-83; import compliance specialist Internat. Trade Adminstrn. U.S. Dept. Commerce, 1983-85; assoc. Collier, Shannon & Scott, 1985-90, Akin, Gump, Strauss, Hauer & Feld, Washington, 1990-91, Dewey, Ballantine, Washington, 1991-94; of counsel Steptoe & Johnson, 1994—. Mem. Vassar Club. Administrative and regulatory, Immigration, naturalization, and customs, Private international. Office: 1330 Connecticut Ave NW Washington DC 20036-1704 E-mail: cmitchel@steptoe.com

MITCHELL, CHARLES EDWARD, lawyer, arbitrator; b. Seymour, Ind., July 7, 1925; s. Edward Charles Mitchell and Lula Belle (Thompson) Browning; m. Julia Viola Sarjeant, Sept. 15, 1951; children: Charles Leonard, Albert Bascom. Student, Morehouse Coll., Atlanta, 1943-44, 46-47, NYU, 1949; JD, Temple U., Phila., 1954. Bar: D.C. 1970, U.S. Ct. Appeals (3d cir.) 1971, Pa. 1972, U.S. Supreme Ct. 1973, U.S. Ct. Appeals (6th cir.) 1984; cert. labor arbitrator, Am. Arbitration Assn., Fed. Mediation and Conciliation Svc. Tchr. City of Phila., 1954-55; mgmt. trainee Office of Dir. of Fin., Budget Bur., Phila., 1955-56; legal asst. Office of Phila. Dist. Atty., 1956-60; claims rep., claims authorizer U.S. HEW, Social Security Adminstrn., Phila., 1960-64; atty., examiner NLRB, 1964-72; mgmt. labor counsel E.I. duPont de Nemours & Co., 1972-92; pvt. practice, 1993-99. Mem. labor panel Am. Arbitration Assn.; mem. roster of arbitrators Fed. Mediation and Conciliation Svc. 1st class seaman USN, 1944-46. Mem. ABA (mgmt. mem. sect. labor and employment law, practice and procs. com. 1973-92), Fed. Bar Assn. (pres. Del. chpt. 1974-76, nat. chpt. del. 1973-78), Indsl. Rels. Rsch. Assn. (v.p. 1970-72), Phila. Bar Assn. Democrat. Episcopalian. Avocations: golf, tennis, chess, bridge, travel. E-mail: cemitchell5500ap@aol.com

MITCHELL, LANSING LEROY, retired federal judge; b. Sun, La., Jan. 17, 1914; s. Leroy A. and Eliza Jane (Richardson) M.; m. Virginia Jumonville, Apr. 18, 1938; children— Diane Mitchell (Mrs. Donald Lee Parker), Lansing Leroy. B.A., La. State U., 1934, LL.B., 1937. Bar: La. 1937. Pvt. practice, Pontchatoula, 1937-38; spl. agt. FBI, 1938-41; atty. SEC, 1941-42; asst. U.S. atty. Eastern Dist. La., 1946-53; also engaged in pvt practice; ptnr. Deutsch, Kerrigan & Stiles., New Orleans, 1953-66; U.S. dist. judge Eastern Dist. La., 1966—. Chmn. nat. security com. New Orleans C. of C., 1963-66; vice chmn. New Orleans Armed Forces Day, 1964, 65, New Orleans Heart Fund campaign, 1959-60; mem. New Orleans Municipal Auditorium Adv. Com., 1957-61, New Orleans Municipal Com. Finance, 1955-67, Small Bus. Adv. Council La., 1963-66; pres. Camp Fire Girls Greater New Orleans, 1965-67; La. chmn. Lawyers for Kennedy-Johnson, 1960. Served to lt. col. AUS, 1942-46; col. Res. (ret.). Decorated Royal Order St. George Royal Order Scotland. Mem. ABA, Inter-Am. Bar Assn., La. Bar Assn., New Orleans Bar Assn., Maritime Law Assn. U.S., Judge Adv. Assn., Soc. Former Spl. Agts. FBI, Am. Legion, Mil. Order World Wars, V.F.W., Navy League, Assn. U.S. Army (pres. La. 1964-65, pres. New Orleans 1961-64, v.p. 4th Army region 1963-66), Soc. Mayflower Descendants in State of La. (assoc.), Scabbard and Blade, SAR, S.R., Soc. War 1812 La., Pi Kappa Alpha, Phi Delta Phi, Theta Nu Epsilon. Clubs: Mason (33 degree, New Orleans) (Shriner), Press (New Orleans), Southern Yacht (New Orleans), Bienville, Pendennis (New Orleans). Office: US Dist Ct C-508 US Courthouse 500 Camp St New Orleans LA 70130-3313

MITCHELL, LAURA ANN, lawyer; b. Miles City, Mont., Oct. 21, 1952; d. Wilmer Ashford and Avis Jean (Baldwin) M.; m. John Walker Ross, Nov. 21, 1981. BA in Polit. Sci. with high honors, U. Mont., Missoula, 1975; JD with honors, George Washington U., 1978. Bar: Mont. 1978. Law clk. to presiding justice U.S. Dist. Ct. for Mont., Billings, 1978-79; assoc. Crowley, Haughey, Hanson, Toole & Dietrich, Billings, 1979-83; ptnr. Crowley, Haughey, Hanson, Toole & Dietrich, 1983-97; atty. pvt. practice, Billings, 1997—. Mem. adv. panel spl. projects Mont. Arts Council, 1980-82; bd. dirs. Billings Preservation Soc., 1988-93, St. Labre Indian Edn. Assn., 1988-94. Mem. Am. Judicature Soc., ABA, Mont. Bar Assn., Yellowstone County Bar Assn. Presbyterian. Avocations: gardening, reading. Contracts commercial, Labor, Real property. Office: 611 O'Malley Billings MT 59101

MITCHELL, P. SUSAN, lawyer; b. Morrow, Ohio, Dec. 4, 1956; d. Stewart and Loyd M. Mitchell; children: S. David, Susan Martha, James D. ADN, Wake Tech. Coll., Raleigh, N.C., 1985; BSN, Atlantic Christian Coll., Wilson, N.C., 1987; JD, N.C. Ctrl. U., Durham, 1997. Bar: N.C. 1998; RN, N.C. Nurse, clk. Rex Hosp., Raleigh, 1983-88; nurse, emergency dept. Duke U. Med. Ctr., Durham, 1988-94, U. N.C. Hosps., Chapel HIll, 1992-98; atty. Law Offices of P. Susan Mitchell, Durham, 1998—. Served with USAF, 1977-79. Office: Law Office of P Susan Mitchell PO Box 747 Durham NC 27702-0747

MITCHELL, ROBERT BERTELSON, JR. lawyer; b. Grand Forks, N.D., Nov. 26, 1952; s. Robert Bertelson and Laura Mae (Fleming) M.; m. Grayce Adele Anderson, Aug. 30, 1975; children: Carrie Jane, Emily Elspeth. BA, U. N.D., 1974, Oxford U., Eng., 1976; JD, Yale U., 1979. Bar: Wash. 1980, U.S. Dist. Ct. (we. dist.) Wash. 1980, U.S. Ct. Appeals (9th cir.) 1985. Law clk. to judge U.S. Ct. Appeals (8th cir.), Fargo, N.D., 1979-80; assoc. Preston, Thorgrimson, Ellis & Holman, Seattle, 1980-85, ptnr., 1986—. Mem. Mcpl. League Seattle and King County, 1980-2001; elder Bethany Presbyn. Ch., Seattle, 1986-91. Rhodes scholar Oxford U., 1974. Mem. ABA, Am. Judicature Soc., Wash. State Bar Assn., King County Bar Assn. Appellate, General civil litigation, Intellectual property. Home: 2303 NW 96th St Seattle WA 98117-2547 Office: Preston Gates Ellis LLP 701 5th Ave Seattle WA 98104-7078 E-mail: robm@prestongates.com

MITCHELL, ROBERT EVERITT, lawyer; b. Port Washington, N.Y., June 14, 1929; s. Everitt and Alice (Fay) M.; m. Anne Nordquist, Nov. 2, 1957; children: Anne C. Mitchell Coneys, Maura A. Kelly, Michael E. BS, U. Mich., 1952; JD, Georgetown U., 1956. Bar: N.Y. 1957, U.S. Dist. Ct. (so. dist). N.Y. 1958, U.S. Supreme Ct. 1966. Assoc. Sullivan & Cromwell, N.Y.C., 1956-63; v.p., sec., gen. counsel Lambert & Co. Inc., 1963-65; ptnr. Campbell & Mitchell, Manhasset, N.Y., 1965-80; asst. gen. counsel J.P. Stevens & Co. Inc., N.Y.C., 1980-82, gen. counsel, 1982-88; pvt. practice Peconic, N.Y., 1988—. Atty. Village Baxter Estates, Port Washington, 1967-83; Counsel Mobilized Community Resources, Roslyn, N.Y., 1969-80; asst. scout master Troop 1001 Boy Scouts Am., Port Washington, 1976-79; justice Village Sands Point, N.Y., 1966-85. Served to lt. USNR, 1952-55. Mem. ABA. Republican. Roman Catholic. Clubs: Manhasset Bay Yacht (Port Washington) (commodore 1972-73); N.Y. Yacht (N.Y.C.), Shelter Island Yacht. Avocations: sailing, fishing, camping, platform tennis, music. Antitrust, General corporate, Securities. Home and Office: 3905 Wells Rd Peconic NY 11958-1738 E-mail: commodoreA@aol.com

MITCHELL, RONNIE MONROE, lawyer, educator; b. Clinton, N.C., Nov. 10, 1952; s. Ondus Corneilius and Margaret Ronie (Johnson) M.; m. Martha Cheryl Coble, May 25, 1975; children: Grant Stephen, Mitchell, Meredith Elizabeth Mitchell. BA, Wake Forest U., 1975, JD, 1978. Bar: N.C. 1978, U.S. Dist. Ct. (ea. dist.) N.C. 1978, U.S. Ct. Appeals (4th cir.) 1983, U.S. Supreme Ct. 1984. Assoc. atty. Brown, Fox & Deaver, Fayetteville, N.C., 1978-81; ptnr. Harris, Sweeny & Mitchell, 1981-91, Harris, Mitchell & Hancox, 1991-96, Harris & Mitchell, 1997-98, Harris, Mitchell, Burns & Brewer, 1998-2000, Mithchell, Brewer, Richardson, Adams, Burns and Boughman, 2000—. Adj. prof. law Norman Adrian Wiggins Sch. of Law, Campbell U; bd. dirs. Mace, Inc. Contbr. chpts. to books. Chmn. Cumberland County Bd. Adjustment, 1985-92, Cumberland County Rescue Squad, 1986-93; bd. dirs. Cumberland County Rescue Squad, Fayetteville, 1983-91. Recipient U.S. Law Week award Bur. Nat. Affairs, 1978. Mem. ABA, ATLA, Twelfth Judicial Dist. Bar Assn. (pres. 1988-89), N.C. Bar Assn. (councillor Young Lawyers divsn. 1982-85), N.C. Legis. Rsch. Commn. (family law com. 1994), Cumberland County Bar Assn. (mem. family law com., N.C. State Bar Bd. legal specialization), N.C. Acad. Trial Lawyers, Fayetteville Ind. Light Infantry Club, Dem. Men's Club (pres. 1993-94), Moose, Masons. Home: RR 1901 Water Oaks Dr Fayetteville NC 28301-9125 Office: Mitchell Brewer Richardson Adams Burns and Boughman 308 Person St Fayetteville NC 28301-5736

MITCHELL, ROY SHAW, lawyer; b. Sherwood, N.Y., Jan. 16, 1934; s. Malcolm Douglas and Ruth Landon (Holland) M.; m. Nancy Elizabeth Bishop, Aug. 27, 1955; children: Mark E., Jeffrey B., Jennifer R. BS, Cornell U., 1957; JD with honors, George Washington U., Washington, D.C., 1959. Bar: D.C. 1959, Ohio 1960, Va. 1967, U.S. Ct. Fed. Claims 1963, U.S. Supreme Ct. 1965. Atty. Squire, Sanders & Dempsey, Cleve., 1960-61, Hudson & Creyke, Washington, 1961-67, Lewis, Mitchell & Moore, Vienna, 1967-87, Morgan, Lewis & Bockius LLP, Washington, 1987-99; pres., CEO constrn. claims group Hill Internat., Inc., 1999—. Vice-chmn. Ameribanc Savs. Bank, Annandale, Va., 1980-95; trustee Ameribanc Investors Group, Annandale, 1980-95. Co-author: (with others) Handbook of Construction Law and Claims, 1982, 89; contbr. numerous articles to profl. jours. Fellow ABA (pub. contract law sect.), Am. Coll. Construction Lawyers, Va. Bar Assn., D.C. Bar Assn. Presbyterian. Avocation: boating. Construction, Government contracts and claims, Private international. Home: 5 Jefferson Run Rd Great Falls VA 22066-3200 Office: Constrn Claims Group Hill Internat Inc 1225 Eye St NW Ste 601 Washington DC 20005-5961 E-mail: roymitchell@hillinti.com

MITCHELL, SALLY E. lawyer, city official, former mayor; b. San Mateo, Calif., Aug. 31, 1952; d. Edward Francis Jr. and Edna Virginia Mitchell; m. Mell Lazarus, May 13, 1995; stepchildren: Margery White, Suesan Pawlitski, Cathleen Carr. Student, Foothill Coll., Los Altos Hills, Calif., 1970-71, Canada Coll., Redwood City, Calif., 1972-73, Golden Gate U., San Francisco, 1974-75; LLB, San Mateo Law Sch., 1980. Bar: Calif. 1980. Atty. Rockhill & Schaiman, Redwood City, Calif., 1982-85, The Boccardo Law Firm, San Jose, 1985-89, Law Offices of Sally E. Mitchell, Redwood City, 1989—. Mayor City of San Carlos, 1988-89, 92-93, 96-97. Address: 600 Elm St San Carlos CA 94070-3018

MITCHELL, WILEY FRANCIS, JR. lawyer; b. Franklin County, N.C., July 23, 1932; s. Wiley Francis and Nancy Irene (Edwards) M.; m. Marshale Moody, May 31, 1953; children: Katherine, Frances. BA, Wake Forest U., 1953, JD, 1954. Bar: N.C. 1954, D.C. 1962, Va. 1986. Assoc. Joyner & Howison, Raleigh, N.C., 1954-60; ptnr. Joyner, Howison & Mitchell, 1960-62; gen. atty. So. R.R. Co., Washington, 1062-68, gen. solicitor, 1968-83; sr. gen. solicitor Norfolk-So. Corp., 1983-89, gen. counsel litigation, 1989-94, sr. gen. counsel, 1995—2001; of counsel Willcox & Savage, Va., 2001—. Coun. mem. City of Alexandria, Va., 1967-76, vice-mayor, 1970-76; active Va. Senate, 1976-88, asst. minority leader, 1978-88; chmn. joint House/Senate Rep. Legis. Caucus, 1987-88, Rep. exec. com., Va., 1987-89; bd. trustees Va. Marine Sci. Mus., 1992—; trustee Va. Nature Conservancy, 1992—. With USAR, 1948-70. Mem. ABA, Alexandria C. of C. (George Washington Leadership award 1984), Hampton Rds. C. of C. (bd. dirs. 2001—). Republican. Baptist. Home: 437 Goodspeed Rd Virginia Beach VA 23451-2206 E-mail: twodeacs@aol.com, wmitchell@wilsav.com

MITCHELL, WILLIAM GRAHAM CHAMPION, lawyer, business executive; b. Raleigh, Dec. 24, 1946; s. Burley Bayard and Dorothy Ford (Champion) M.; children: William Graham, Margaret Scripture. AB, U. N.C., 1969, JD with highest hons., 1975. Bar: N.C. 1975, U.S. Dist. Ct. (ea., mid. and we. dists.) N.C. 1976, U.S. Ct. Appeals (4th cir.) 1978. Ptnr.

Womble, Carlyle, Sandridge & Rice, Winston-Salem, 1975-87; sr. v.p. for external affairs RJR Nabisco, Atlanta, 1987-89; exec. v.p. R.J. Reynolds Tobacco Co., Winston-Salem, 1988-89; ptnr. Howrey & Simon, Washington, 1990-94; spl. counselor to chmn. bd. True North Comm., Inc., Chgo., 1996; chmn. bd., CEO Global Exch. Carrier Co., Leesburg, Va., 1997-00; pres., CEO Global Comms. Techs. Inc., Reston, 1999-2000; chmn. bd., CEO Convergence Equipment Co., Manassas, 1999-2000; chmn. bd. Qfactor Inc., Bethesda, Md., 2000-01; exec. v.p., gen. mgr. Verisign Inc., Mountainview, Calif., 2001—. Bd. dirs. Fed. Agrl. Mortgage Corp., Washington. Mem. Pres.'s Adv. Com. on Trade Policy and Negotiations, Indsl. Policy Adv. Com., Washington, 1991—; exec. com. Nat. Assn. Mfrs., Washington, 1988-89, Nat. Fgn. Trade Coun., 1988-89; chmn. Tobacco Inst., Washington, 1988-89; bd. dirs. Washington Performing Arts Soc., 1988-92; bd. advisors Dem. Leadership Coun., 1988—; founding trustee Progressive Policy Inst., 1988—; vice chmn. fin. Bush Campaign. Mem. ABA (vice chmn. antitrust sect., pvt. litigation com. 1987-89, chmn. subcom. of FTC com. 1986), Georgetown Club, City Club of Washington, Forsyth Country Club, Order of the Coif. Antitrust, Mergers and acquisitions, Product liability. E-mail: champ@qfactor.com, Wgchamp@aol.com

MITCHEM, JAMES E. lawyer; b. Denver, July 3, 1949; s. Allen P. and K. Irene (Egan) M.; m. Rose M. Flanigan, Dec. 13, 1975; children: Margaret, Rachael. AB, Brown U., 1971; JD, U. Denver, 1974. Bar: Colo. 1974, U.S. Dist. Ct. Colo. 1974, U.S. Ct. Appeals (10th cir.) 1976, U.S. Supreme Ct. 1986. Ptnr. Mitchem and Mitchem, Denver, 1974-95, Mitchem & Flanigan, Englewood, 1995—. Author: The Lawyer's Duty to Report Ethical Violations, vol. 18, no. 10, Colorado Lawyer, 1989. Mem. ABA, Colo. Bar Assn. (chmn. com. on law and tech. 1984-86), Denver Bar Assn., Am. Arbitration Assn. (panel of arbitrators). Federal civil litigation, General civil litigation, Real property. Home: 5929 S Akron Cir Englewood CO 80111-5215 Office: 5445 Dtc Pkwy Ste P4 Englewood CO 80111-3059

MITLAK, STEFANY (LYNN), lawyer; b. N.Y.C., Oct. 1, 1958; d. Irwin and Karel Sondra (Sperling) Cooperman; m. Bruce H. Mitlak, Sept. 20, 1987. BS, U. Mich., 1980; JD, Western New Eng. Coll., 1983; LLM, Boston U., 1989. Bar: R.I. 1984, Mass. 1985, Md. 1986, Ind. 1996. Spl. asst. atty. gen. Atty. Gen.'s Office State of R.I., Providence, 1984-85; assoc. McCormack & Putziger, Boston, 1985-90, Fitch, Wiley, Richlin & Tourse, Boston, 1990-92; spl. asst. corp. counsel pub. facilities dept. City of Boston, 1992-95; assoc. Johnson, Smith, Densborn, Wright & Heath, Indpls., 1995-96; devel. atty. Simon Group, 1996—. Fundraiser Women's Polit. Caucus, Providence, 1984-85; chairwoman bldg. and licensing com. Neighborhood Assn. of the Back Bay, Boston, 1992. Avocations: swimming, skiing. Real property.

MITTMAN, LAWRENCE, lawyer; b. Mar. 17, 1951; s. Joseph and Esther (Yarmark) Mittman; m. Ellyn Roth, Aug. 27, 1978; children: Wesley, Jordan. BA, Yeshiva Coll., 1972; JD, Columbia U., 1975. Bar: N.Y. 1976. Assoc. Weil, Gotshal & Manges, N.Y.C., NY, 1975—79; ptnr. Battle Fowler, 1979—. Bankruptcy, Contracts commercial, General corporate. Office: Battle Fowler 75 E 55th St New York NY 10022-3205

MITZNER, MICHAEL JAY, lawyer; b. Paterson, N.J., July 4, 1944; s. Louis B. and Dora (Sandler) M.; m. Jere Peg Herzog, Dec. 23, 1967; children— Dawn Lee, Scott Clinton. AB, NYU, 1965; JD, Harvard U., 1968. Bar: N.J. 1968, U.S. Dist. Ct. N.J. 1968, U.S. Supreme Ct., 1972, N.Y. 1981. Law clk. appellate div. N.J. Superior Ct., Asbury Park, N.J., 1968-69; asst. prosecutor Union County Prosecutor's Office, Elizabeth, N.J., 1969-75; ptnr. Mitzner & Pizzi, P.A., Fanwood, N.J., 1975—; twp. atty. Twp. of Scotch Plains (N.J.), 1979-82, mcpl. prosecutor, Scotch Plains, 1983-85, 89—; mcpl. prosecutor Borough of Fanwood (N.J.), 1977—, Twp. of Berkeley Heights, 1989-90. Editor: Criminal Law, 1976. Bd. dirs. Watchung Hills Soccer Assn. (N.J.), 1983-85; coach Watchung Soccer League, 1979-85, Watchung Little League, 1979-85, Watchung Recreation Basketball League, 1983-85. Mem. Nat. Dist. Attys. Assn., N.J. Inst. Municipal Attys., Somerset Bar Assn., N.J. Bar Assn., Union County Bar Assn. Republican. Jewish. Criminal, General practice, Personal injury. Home: 115 Hill Hollow Rd Watchung NJ 07069-6441 Office: Mitzner & Pizzi PA 141 South Ave PO Box 157 Fanwood NJ 07023-0157

MIXTER, CHRISTIAN JOHN, lawyer; b. Basel, Switzerland, Mar. 13, 1953; s. Keith Eugene and Beatrice Maria (Ruf) M.; m. Linna M. Barnes, Dec. 17, 1977; children: Sara Elizabeth Barnes Mixter, Laura Ellen Barnes Mixter. BA, Ohio State U., 1974; JD, Duke U., 1977. Bar: N.Y. 1978, D.C. 1981. Assoc. Davis Polk & Wardwell, N.Y.C. and Washington, 1977-87; assoc. counsel Office Ind. Counsel (Iran/Contra), Washington, 1987-91; asst. chief litigation counsel Enforcement divsn. SEC, 1991-97, chief litigation counsel, 1997-2000; ptnr. Morgan, Lewis & Bockius LLP, 2000—. Mem. ABA (bus. law and litig. sects.), Assn. Bar City N.Y., Phi Beta Kappa, Order of the Coif. Administrative and regulatory, Federal civil litigation, Securities. Office: Morgan Lewis & Bockius LLP 1800 M St NW Washington DC 20036-5869 E-mail: cmixter@morganlewis.com

MIYASAKI, SHUICHI, lawyer; b. Paauilo, Hawaii, Aug. 6, 1928; s. Torakichi and Teyo (Kimura) M.; m. Pearl Takeko Saiki, Sept. 11, 1954; children: Joy Michiko, Miles Tadashi, Jan Keiko, Ann Yoshie. BSCE, U. Hawaii-Honolulu, 1951; JD, U. Minn., 1957; grad., Army War Coll., 1973. Bar: Minn. 1957, Hawaii 1959, U.S. Supreme Ct. 1980. Examiner U.S. Patent Office, 1957-59; dep. atty. gen. State of Hawaii, 1960-61; mem., dir., sec./treas. Okumura Takushi Funaki & Wee, Honolulu, 1961-90; pvt. practice, 1991—; atty. Hawaii Senate, 1961, chief counsel ways and means com., 1962, chief counsel judiciary com., 1967-70; civil engr. Japan Constrn. Agy., Tokyo, 1953-54; staff judge adv., col. USAR, Ft. DeRussy, Hawaii, 1968-79. Local legal counsel Jaycees, 1962; lectr. Nat. Assn. Pub. Accts. Hawaii Chpt. Ann. Conf., 1990, 94, Mid Pacific Inst. Found., Honolulu, 1990, Econ. Study Club of Hawaii, 1990, Meiji Life Ins. Co. Japan, 1992, Cent. YMCA, 1992, City Bank Honolulu, 1997. Legis. chmn. armed services com. C. of C. of Hawaii, 1973; instnl. rep. Aloha council Boy Scouts Am., 1963-78; exec. com., sec., dir. Legal Aid Soc. Hawaii, 1970-72; state v.p. Hawaii Jaycees, 1964-65; dir., legal counsel St. Louis Heights Community Assn., 1963, 65, 73, 91—; dir., legal counsel Citizens Study Club for Naturalization of Citizens, 1963-68; advisory bd. Project Dana Honolulu, 1991—, vice chair, 1991, 92; bd. dirs. Omote Senke Found., 1999—; life mem. Res. Officers Assn. U.S. Served to 1st lt. AUS, 1951-54. Decorated Meritorious Service medal with oak leaf cluster. Mem. ABA, Hawaii Bar Assn., U.S. Patent Office Soc., Hawaii Estate Planning Council, Rotary, Central YMCA Club, Waikiki Athletic Club, Army Golf Assn., Elks, Phi Delta Phi. Estate planning, Corporate taxation, Estate taxation. Office: 1001 Bishop St Ste 1030 Honolulu HI 96813-3408

MIZRAHI, ELAN S(HAI), lawyer; b. Bklyn., Mar. 31, 1970; s. Eli and Bonita Jean Mizrahi. BA in Polit. Sci., U. Ariz., 1992; JD, Ariz. State U., 1996. Bar: Ariz. 1997, U.S. Dist. Ct. Ariz. 1998, U.S. Ct. Appeals (9th cir.) 1999, U.S. Supreme Ct. 2001. Assoc. Jennings, Haug & Cunningham, PLLC, Phoenix, 1997—. Mem. Jewish Fedn. Greater Phoenix, U.S. Maccabiah and Scottsdale Blues Rugby Football Clubs. Mem. AIPAC, Tempe Old Devils Rugby Football Club. Appellate, General civil litigation, Insurance. Office: Jennings Haug & Cunningham PLLC 2800 N Central Ave Ste 1800 Phoenix AZ 85004-1049

MLSNA, KATHRYN KIMURA, lawyer; b. Yonkers, N.Y., Apr. 23, 1952; d. Eugene T. and Grace (Watanabe) Kimura; m. Timothy Martin Mlsna, Oct. 4, 1975; children: Lauren Marie, Matthew Christopher, Michael Timothy. BA, Northwestern U., 1974, JD, 1977. Bar: Ill. 1977, U.S. Dist. Ct. (no. dist.) Ill. 1977. Dept. dir. McDonald's Corp., Oak Brook, Ill., 1977—. Speaker in field. Contbr. chpt. to book. Bd. dirs. Japanese Am. Svc. Com.; mem. adv. bd. intellectual property DePaul U. Sch. Law, 1999—. Mem. ABA, Ill. Bar Assn., Chgo. Bar Assn., Asian Am. Bar Assn. (bd. dirs. 1996-98), Promotion Mktg. Assn. Am. (v.p. 1988-92, chmn., pres. 1992-93, chmn. integrated mktg. com. 1993-94, chmn. assn. alliance com., co-chair legal and govtl. affairs com.), Northwestern U. Alumni Assn. (officer, bd. dirs. 1994-98). Entertainment, Intellectual property. Office: McDonald's Corp 1 Mcdonalds Plz Oak Brook IL 60523-1911

MLYNIEC, WALLACE JOHN, law educator, lawyer, consultant; b. Berwyn, Ill., July 10, 1945; s. Casimir Adele and Adeline Mary Mlyniec. BS, Northwestern U., 1967; JD, Georgetown U., 1970. Bar: D.C. 1971, Alaska 1971, U.S. Dist. Ct. D.C. 1971, U.S. Ct. Appeals (D.C. cir.) 1971, U.S. Supreme Ct. 1974. Exec. dir. ABA stds. U.S. Cir. Jud. Conf. on ABA Stds., Washington, 1971-73; dir. Juvenile Justice Clinic Georgetown U., 1973—, prof. law, 1973—. Lupo-Rico prof. clin. legal studies, 1998—; coord. clin. edn, 1986-89, assoc. dean, 1989—; cons. Nat. Adv. Com. on Juvenile Justice, Washington, 1979-80; cons. pvt. and pub. agys. on juvenile and criminal justice, 1974—; chmn. Juvenile Justice Adv. Group, D.C., 1980-82; mem. Nat. Resource Ctr. on Child Abuse and Neglect. Recipient Stuart Stillar Found. award, 1994; Meyer Found. grantee, 1980-82; Swedish Bicentennial fellow, 1985; disting. vis. scholar in pediat. law, Loyola U. Law Sch., Feb. 2001. Mem. ABA (mem. adv. com. on family ct. rules 1984, chair com. on juvenile justice 1998—), Am. Assn. Law Schs. (mem. com. on polit. interference 1983-84, chair 1991, standing com. on clin. edn., William Pincus award 1996), D.C. Bar Assn. (chmn. juvenile justice sect. 1973).

MOAKES, JONATHAN, lawyer; b. Preston, Eng., Mar. 30, 1960; s. Willis and Enid Margaret Moakes; m. Sally Jane Stubington, Sept. 14, 1996; 1 child, Andrew David. BA, Queens Coll., Cambridge, Eng., 1981, MA, 1984. Bar: Supreme Ct. Eng. and Wales. Articled clk. Baker & McKenzie, London, 1982-84, solicitor, 1984-88, Halliwell Landau, Manchester, Eng., 1988-89, ptnr. Eng., 1989—. Author: Encyclopaedia of Information Technology Law, 1988, International Information Technology Law, 1997. Mem. Licensing Execs. Soc. (N.W. br. 1992-97). Avocations: skiing, tennis, hill walking, playing the violin, sailing. Antitrust, Computer, Intellectual property. Office: Halliwell Landau St James Ct 1 Brown St Manchester M2 2JF England Office Fax: 0044 161 835 2994. E-mail: jmoakes@halliwells.co.uk

MOATES, G. PAUL, lawyer; b. May 26, 1947; s. Guy Hart and Virginia Rose (Mayolett) Moates. BA, Amherst Coll., 1969; JD, U. Chgo., 1975. Bar: Ill. 1975, D.C. 1976, U.S. Ct. Appeals (D.C. cir.) 1976, U.S. Supreme Ct. 1980, U.S. Ct. Appeals (6th cir.) 1984, U.S. Ct. Appeals (3d cir.) 1991, U.S. Ct. Appeals (7th cir.) 1993. Assoc. Sidley & Austin, Washington, 1975—82, ptnr., 1982—. Contbr. articles to profl. jours. Mem.: ABA, Ill. Bar Assn., D.C. Bar Assn. Administrative and regulatory, Antitrust, Transportation. Office: Sidley Austin Brown & Wood 1501 K Street NW Washington DC 20005

MOBLEY, JOHN HOMER, II, lawyer; b. Shreveport, La., Apr. 21, 1930; s. John Hinson and Beulah (Wilson) M.; m. Sue Lawton, Aug. 9, 1958; children: John Lawton, Anne Davant. AB, U. Ga., 1951, JD, 1953. Bar: Ga. 1952, U.S. Dist. Ct. D.C. Ptnr. Kelley & Mobley, Atlanta, 1956-63, Gambrell & Mobley, Atlanta, 1963-83; sr. ptnr. Sutherland, Asbill & Brennan, 1983—. Chmn., Cities in Schs. of Ga.; bd. dirs. Cities in Schs. Capt. JAGC, USAF, 1953-55. Mem. ABA, D.C. Bar, State Bar Ga., Atlanta Bar Assn., Am. Judicature Soc., Atlanta Lawyers Club, Atlanta Athletic Club, Atlanta Country Club, Commerce Club, Piedmont Driving Club, Georgian Club, N.Y. Athletic Club, Met. Club of Washignton, Phi Delta Phi. Municipal (including bonds). Home: 4348 Sentinel Post Rd NW Atlanta GA 30327-3910 Office: Sutherland Asbill & Brennan 999 Peachtree St NE Ste 2300 Atlanta GA 30309-3996 E-mail: jhmobley@sablaw.com

MOCK, RANDALL DON, lawyer; b. Oklahoma City, Aug. 9, 1943; s. J. Haskell and M. Louise M.; m. Sally Merkle, June 4, 1966; children: Adam Peterson, Caroline Louise. BBA, U. Okla., 1965, JD, 1968; LLM in Taxation, NYU, 1970. Bar: Okla. 1968, U.S. Tax Ct. 1970, U.S. Supreme Ct. 1974; CPA. With Mock, Schwabe, Waldo, Elder, Reeves & Bryant, Oklahoma City. Sec., chmn. Okla. Attys. Mut. Ins. Co. Editor: Oklahoma Law Review, Tax Law Review; co-author: Oklahoma Corporate Forms. Pres. Oklahoma City Estate Planning Coun., 1987-88, dir., 1980-88; pres. Oklahoma City Tax Lawyers Group, 1973; bd. dirs., mem. exec. com. Met. YMCA; trustee Westminster Sch., Okla. Med. Rsch. Found. Fellow Am. Coll. Tax Counsel; mem. Okla. Bar Assn. (sect. taxation), Beacon Club (pres., bd. dirs.), Order of Coif. General corporate, Estate planning, Taxation, general. Office: Mock Schwabe Waldo Elder Reeves & Bryant 14th Fl Two Leadership Sq 211 N Robinson Ave Oklahoma City OK 73102-7109 E-mail: rmock@mswerb.com

MODEROW, JOSEPH ROBERT, lawyer, package distribution company executive; b. Kenosha, Wis., 1948; Grad., Calif. State U., Fullerton, 1970; JD, Western State U., 1975. Bar: Calif. 1975, U.S. Dist. Ct. (cen. dist.) Calif. 1975, U.S. Supreme Ct. 1982. Sr. v.p. legal and pub affairs, sec., gen. counsel, dir. United Parcel Svc., Inc., Atlanta, 1986—. General corporate. Office: United Parcel Svc Inc 55 Glenlake Pkwy NE Atlanta GA 30328-3498

MODISETT, JEFFREY A. lawyer, state attorney general, business executive; b. Windfall, Ind., Aug. 10, 1954; s. James Richard and Diana T. Modisett; m. Jennifer Ashworth, June 9, 1990; 2 children: Matthew Hunter Ashworth, Haden Nicholas. BA, UCLA, 1976; MA, Oxford (Eng.) U., 1978; JD, Yale U., 1981. Bar: Ind., Calif., D.C. Clk. to Hon. R. Peckham U.S. Dist. Ct. (no. dist.) Calif., San Francisco, 1981-82; asst. U.S. atty. Office U.S. Atty. (ctrl. dist.) Calif., L.A., 1982-88; issues dir. Evan Bayh for Gov., Indpls., 1988; exec. asst. to gov. State of Ind., 1989-90; prosecutor Marion County, 1991-94; sr. counsel Ice Miller Donadio & Ryan, 1995-96; atty. gen. State of Ind., 1997-2000; dep. CEO, gen. counsel Dem. Nat. Conv., 2000; co-CEO TechNet, Palo Alto, Calif., 2000—; ptnr. Manatt Phelps & Phillips LLP. Chmn. Gov. Commn. for Drug Free Ind., Indpls., 1989—, Gov. Coun. on Impaired & Dangerous Driving, Indpls., 1989—; pres. Family Advocacy Ctr., Indpls., 1991-94, Hoosier Alliance Against Drugs, Indpls., 1993-96; dir. Cmty. Couns. of Indpls., 1991-93; chmn. Ind. Criminal Justice Inst., Indpls., 1989-90, dir., 1989—; vice chmn. Juvenile Justice and Youth Gang Study Com., Indpls., 1992-94; legal analyst Sta. WTHR-TV, Indpls., 1995-96. Author: Prosecutor's Perspective, 1991-94; editor-in-chief Yale Jour. Internat. Law, 1980-81. Co-chair Ind. State Dem. Coordinated Campaign, Indpls., 1996. Recipient Spl. Enforcement award U.S. Customs, 1988, Child Safety Adv. award Automotive Safety for Children, 1997, STAR Alliance Impact award, 1998, Spirit of Ind. award Am. Lung Assn., 1999; named Top Lawyer, Indpls. Monthly mag., 1993; named to Sagamore of Wabash, State of Ind., 1995. Mem. Ind. Bar Assn., Indpls. Bar Assn. Avocation: bicycling.

MODLIN, HOWARD S. lawyer; b. N.Y.C., Apr. 10, 1931; s. Martin and Rose Modlin; m. Margot S. Modlin, Oct. 18, 1956; children: James, Laura, Peter. AB, Union Coll., Schenectady, 1952; JD, Columbia U., 1955. Bar: N.Y. 1956, D.C. 1973. Assoc. Weisman, Celler, Spett & Modlin, P.C., N.Y.C., 1956-61, ptnr., 1961-76, mng. ptnr., 1976-95, pres., 1996—. Sec., dir. Gen. DataComm Industries, Inc., Middlebury, Conn.; dir. Am.-Book-Stratford Press, Inc., N.Y.C., Fedders Corp., Liberty Corner, N.J., Trans-Lux Corp., Norwalk, Conn. Chmn. bd. dirs. Daus. of Jacob Geriat. Ctr., Bronx, N.Y. Mem. ABA, Assn. of Bar of City of N.Y., D.C. Bar Assn. Contracts commercial, General corporate, Securities. Office: Weisman Celler Spett & Modlin PC 445 Park Ave New York NY 10022-2606

MOELING, WALTER GOOS, IV, lawyer; b. Quantico, Va., Feb. 16, 1943; s. Walter Goos III and Dorothy (Tritle) M.; m. Nell Frances Askew, Aug. 27, 1965; children: Charles H., Christine E. BA, Duke U., 1965, JD, 1968. Bar: Ga. 1968. Assoc. Powell, Goldstein, Frazer & Murphy, Atlanta, 1968-75, ptnr., 1975—. Bd. dirs. So. Banking Law and Policy Conf., 1989-96, Southeastern Conf. for Bank Dirs., 1996—, Children's Rehab. Ctr., Atlanta, 1982—, Gatchell Home, Atlanta, 1983—; bd. dirs. Frazer Ctr., 1989—, chmn. bd. dirs., 1993. Mem. ABA (mem. banking com. 1986—), Ga. C. of C. (bd. dirs. 1998-2000), Ga. Bar Assn., Ga. Bankers Assn. (assoc., chairperson bank counsel sect. 1992-95, bd. dirs. 1998-2000), Cmty. Bankers Assn. (assoc.), Capital City Club, Willow Point Country Club. Democrat. Unitarian. Avocations: golf, fly-fishing. Banking, General corporate, Finance. Office: Powell Goldstein Frazer & Murphy 191 Peachtree St NE Ste 16 Atlanta GA 30303-1740 E-mail: wmoeling@pgfm.com

MOELLER, FLOYD DOUGLAS, lawyer; b. Safford, Ariz., Aug. 16, 1949; s. Floyd Albert and Helen Lou (Posey) M.; m. Tyra Brown, Dec. 18, 1970; children: Kristin, Sam, John, Susan. BS in Police Sci., Brigham Young U., 1972, JD, 1977; MS in Mgmt., Lesley Coll., 1985, MA in Counseling Psychology, 1987; LLM in Tax, Washington Sch. Law, 1992. Bar: N.Mex. 1978, U.S. Dist. Ct. N.Mex. 1978, U.S. Dist. Ct. Ariz. 1978, U.S. Ct. Appeals (10th cir.) 1979 , U.S. Tax Ct. 1981, U.S. Supreme Ct. 1981, Navajo Nation, Hopi Tribe, Jicarilla Apache Tribe, White Mountain Apache Tribe, So. Ute Tribe, Ute Mountain Tribe, So. Paiute Coun., Ft. Belknap Indian Ct., Gila River Indian Ct., Mescalaro Apache Ct., S.W. Inter Tribal Ct. Appeals. Assoc. Wade Beavers & Assocs., Farmington, N.Mex., 1978-79; ptnr. Nunn & Moeller, 1979; sole practice, 1979-80, 87—; ptnr. Moeller & Burnham, 1980-87. Mem. exec. com. Better Bus. Bur. of 4 Corners, 1978, bd. dirs., 1978—; bd. dirs. Farmington Pub. Library Bd., 1979-86, San Juan Med. Found., San Juan Pub. Library Found., Halvorson House; chmn. local troop coms. Boy Scouts Am., Farmington, 1985—. Capt. USMC, 1972-75. Named diplomat Nat. Bd. Trial Advocacy, 1986. Mem. ABA, J. Reuben Clark Law Soc., Nat. Panel Consumer Arbitrators, Am. Arbitration Assn., N.Mex. Trial Lawyers Assn., N.Mex. State Bar Assn. (CLE, fee arbitration coms. 1985, pres. trial practice sect. 1988), Navajo Nat. Bar Assn., San Juan County Bar Assn., 4 Corners Inn of Ct. Republican. Mormon. Avocations: reading, poetry, gardening, knot tying. General civil litigation, General practice, Personal injury. Office: PO Box 15249 Farmington NM 87401-5249 Fax: (505) 362-0818. E-mail: dmoeller@acrnet.com

MOERBEEK, STANLEY LEONARD, lawyer; b. Toronto, Ont., Can., Nov. 12, 1951; came to U.S., 1953; s. John Jacob and Mary Emily Moerbeek; m. Carol Annette Mordaunt, Apr. 17, 1982; children: Sarah, Noah. BA magna cum laude, Calif. State U., Fullerton, 1974; student, U. San Diego-Sorbonne, Paris, 1977; JD, Loyola U., 1979. Bar: Calif. 1980; cert. in internat. bus. transactions, bankruptcy and bus. rehab., and civil trial practice. From law clk. to assoc. McAlpin Doonan & Seese, Covina, Calif., 1977-81; assoc. Robert L. Baker, Pasadena, 1981-82, Miller Bush & Minnott, Fullerton, 1982-83; prin. Law Office of Stanley L. Moerbeek, 1984—. Judge pro tem Orange County Superior Ct., Calif., 1984—; notary pub., lt. gov. 9th cir. law student divsn. ABA, 1979. Mem. Heritage Found., Washington, 1989—. Calif. Gov.'s Office scholar, 1970; recipient Plaque of Appreciation, Fullerton Kiwanis, 1983. Mem. Calif. Assn. Realtors (referral panel atty. 1985—), Orange County Bar Assn. (Coll. of Trial Advocacy 1985), Calif. C. of C., Phi Kappa Phi. Roman Catholic. Avocations: history, politics, sports. General civil litigation, Personal injury, Real property. Office: 1370 N Brea Blvd Ste 210 Fullerton CA 92835-4128 E-mail: slmlaw@netzero.net

MOFFATT, MICHAEL ALAN, lawyer; b. Indpls., Feb. 22, 1964; s. James L. Kelso and Peggy A. Tackett; m. Nancy Norman, Sept. 23, 1989; children: Patricia Margaret, Michael Alan, Nicole Elizabeth, Michelle Ann. BA in Polit. Sci., Depauw U., 1986; JD, Ind. U., 1989. Bar: Ind. 1989, U.S. Dist. Ct. (so. and no. dists.) Ind. 1989, U.S. Ct. Appeals (7th cir.) 1991, U.S. Supreme Ct., 1999. Law clk., assoc. White & Raub, Indpls., 1987-94; assoc. Wooden McLaughlin & Sterner, 1994-95, Barnes & Thornburg, Indpls., 1995-2000, ptnr., 2001; shareholder Ogletree Deakins, Nash, Smoak and Stewart, P.C., 2001—. Lectr. litigation, paralegal program, Ind. U./Purdue U., Ind. CLE Forum & labor/employment seminars. Contbr. articles to legal jours. Co-chmn. Keep Am. Beautiful, Greencastle, Ind., 1986, bd. dirs., sec., 1990—94; mem. devel. control com. Geist Harbors Property Owner's Assn., Indpls., 1993—94, cons., 1994, pres., 1997—99; bd. dirs., tournament chair Fall Creek Little League, 2001—; cons. pediatric ethics com. Meth. Hosp., Indpls., 1990—92; winners cir. mentor U.S. Auto Club. Mem.: ABA (labor and employment sect.), Fed. Bar Assn., Ind. Bar Assn., Indpls. Bar Assn. (exec. coun. labor sect. 1999, vice chmn. 2000, chmn. 2001), Exch. Club (pres.-elect 1997—98, pres. 1998—99, past pres. 1999—2000). Avocations: golf, basketball, softball. General civil litigation, Labor. Office: Ogletree Deakins Nash Smoak & Stewart PC One Indiana Sq Ste 2300 Indianapolis IN 46204 Business E-Mail: mike.moffatt@odnss.com

MOFFETT, J. DENNY, lawyer; b. Atlanta, Sept. 20, 1947; s. James Denny Moffett Jr. and Dorothy (Mckenzie) McCall; m. Mary F. Ray, June 6, 1987; children: David, Jenny. BA, U. Okla., 1969; JD with honors, George Washington U., 1972, LLM in Taxation, 1974. Bar: Okla. 1972, U.S. Tax Ct. 1973, Wyo. 2001. Legis. asst. U.S. Senate, Washington, 1973-74; ptnr. Conner & Winters, Tulsa, 1974-90, McKenzie, Moffett, Elias & Books, Tulsa, Oklahoma City, 1990-97, Moffett & Assocs., P.C., Tulsa, 1997—. Adj. faculty U. Tulsa Law Sch., 1978; arbitrator Nat. Assn. Securities Dealers. Commr. Ark.-Okla. River Compact Commn., 1990-94; pres. Nicholas Club Tulsa, 1984; endowment com. Trinity Episcopal Ch., 1990—. 2d lt. U.S. Army, 1972-74; bd. dirs. Am. Cancer Soc., Tulsa, 1991-94. Mem. Am. Arbitration Assn., Tulsa Tax Club (pres. 1981, 94). Republican. Bankruptcy, General corporate, Taxation, general. Home: 2132 E 32nd Pl Tulsa OK 74105-2222 Office: Moffett & Assocs PC 1722 S Carson Ave Ste 3203 Tulsa OK 74119

MOFFETT, T(ERRILL) K(AY), lawyer; b. Becker, Miss., July 11, 1949; s. Elmer C. and Mary Ethel (Meek) M.; m. Rita C. Millsaps, Mar. 11, 1972; 1 child, Tara Leigh. BS, U.S. Mil. Acad., 1971; MA in Polit. Sci., U. Hawaii, 1974; JD, U. Miss., 1979. Bar: Miss. 1979, Ala. 1998. Grad. tchr. Am. govt. U. Miss., Oxford, 1977-80; ptnr. Moffett and Thorne, Tupelo, Miss., 1980-88; owner Moffett Law Firm, 1988—; pros. atty. City of Tupelo, 1989-99. Rep. candidate for U.S. Congress 1st Miss. Dist., 1978, 80; 1st dist. coord. Reagan for Pres., 1980; co-chmn. Lee County George Bush for Pres. Com., 1988, 92; mem. Lee County Rep. Exec. Com., 1980—; chmn. Tupelo Rep. Exec. Com., 1988—; active 1st Bapt. Ch., Tupelo; bd. dirs. Sav-A-Life Tupelo, Inc. Capt. U.S. Army, 1971-76; brig. gen. USAR, 2000—, Miss. Army NG, 1999—. Harvard fellow, 1995-96.

Mem. ABA, Miss. State Bar Assn., Lee County Bar Assn., Ala. State Bar Assn., Civitan, Masons, Habitat for Humanity, Phi Sigma Alpha. Avocations: music, hunting, tennis, travel. General civil litigation, Family and matrimonial, General practice. Home: 1761 N Parc Cir Tupelo MS 38804-9753 Office: Moffett Law Firm PO Drawer 1707 330 N Broadway St Tupelo MS 38802-3926

MOGELMOSE, HENRIK, lawyer; b. Kerteminde, Denmark, Mar. 13, 1958; s. Lise-Lotte Mogelmose, June 1989; children: Louise, Julie. Law degree, U. Aarhus, Denmark, 1983; LLM, U. Chgo., 1991. Bar: Denmark 1988, N.Y. 1992. Fgn. assoc. Skadden, Arps, Slate, Meagher & Flom, N.Y.C., 1991-92; ptnr. Kromann Reumert, Copenhagen, 1992—. Mem. ABA, Danish Bar Assn., Internat. Bar Assn. General corporate, Finance, Mergers and acquisitions. Home: Vermehrensvej 3 DK-2930 Klampenborg Denmark Office: Kromann Reumert Raadhuspladsen 14 DK-1550 Copenhagen Denmark Fax: 45-70-12-13-11. E-mail: HM@Kromannreumert.com

MOGOL, ALAN JAY, lawyer; b. Balt., July 29, 1946; s. Jesse and Kitty (Stutman) m.; m. Ellen Epstein, June 19, 1969; children: Andrew Stephen, Jonathan David. BA with distinction, U. Va., 1968, JD, 1971. Bar: Md. 1972, U.S. Dist. Ct. Md. 1972, U.S. Ct. Appeals (4th cir.) 1972, U.S. Supreme Ct. 1978. Assoc. Ober, Kaler, Grimes & Shriver, Balt., 1971-77, ptnr., 1978—. Chmn. bus. dept. Ober, Kaler, Grimes & Shriver, Balt., 1980-81, 84-85, 91-97, chmn. equipment leasing practice group, 1998—; lectr. on continuing edn. Md. Inst. Continuing Profl. Edn. for Lawyers, 1988-92, trustee, 1990-93; spkr. seminars Nat. Health Lawyers Assn., Washington, 1986-87, Rocky Mountain Mgmt., Denver, 1987, Med. Imaging Expo., 1995, Washington, 1995. Co-author: In Structuring the Secured Loan Agreement, 1991, Commercial Finance Guide, 1997, Equipment Leasing, 1999; contbr. articles to profl. jours. and local newspapers. Bd. dirs. Transitional Living Coun., Balt., 1972-92; bd. trustees Md. Inst. of Continuing Profl. Edn. for Lawyers, 1990-93. Fellow Md. Bar Found., Inc.; mem. ABA, Equipment Leasing Assn. Am. (lawyers com. 1986-89, program com. 1986-91, speaker seminars), Md. Bar Assn. (uniform comml. code com. 1988—, chmn. 1991-93, vice chmn. bus. sect. 1995-96, chmn. bus. sect. 1996-97). Avocation: tennis. Contracts commercial, General corporate. Office: Ober Kaler Grimes & Shriver 120 E Baltimore St Ste 800 Baltimore MD 21202-1643 E-mail: ajmogol@ober.com

MOHAMMED, SOHAIL, lawyer, consultant; b. Hyderabad, A. Pradesh, India, Aug. 12, 1963; came to U.S., 1980; s. Ahsanuddin and Syeda (Tahira) M.; m. Ashraf Mohammed, Nov. 20, 1994; 1 child, Omair. BS in Elec. Engring., N.J. Inst. Tech., 1988; JD, Seton Hall U., 1993. Bar: Pa. 1993, U.S. Ct. Appeals 1995, N.J. 1993, Wash. 1995. Elec. engr. GEC-Marconi Electronic Sys. Corp., Totowa, N.J., 1988-97; pvt. practice Clifton, 1993—. Mem. City Clifton (N.J.) Cultural Awareness Com., 1995—. Recipient Highest Acad. Achievement award Bur. Nat. Affairs, 1993. Mem. ABA (young lawyers divsn. scholarship, 1996), N.J. Bar Assn. (profl. achievement award, 1997), N.J. State Bar Young Lawyer Divsn. (exec. bd., 1994—). Muslim. Avocations: tennis, jogging, auto racing, reading. Immigration, naturalization, and customs, Municipal (including bonds), Real property. Office: 1030 Clifton Ave Clifton NJ 07013-3522

MOHR, ANTHONY JAMES, judge; b. L.A., May 11, 1947; s. Gerald Leonard and Rita Lenore (Goldstein) M. BA in Govt. cum laude with honors, Wesleyan U., 1969; JD, Columbia U., 1972; diploma with honors, 1975. Bar: Calif. 1972, U.S. Dist. Ct. (cen. dist.) Calif. 1973, U.S. Ct. Appeals (9th cir.) 1974, D.C. 1976, U.S. Supreme Ct. 1981. Law clk. to judge U.S. Dist. Ct. (cen. dist.) Calif., 1972-73; assoc. Alschuler Grossman, Stein & Kahan, 1973-75; pvt. practice L.A., 1976-94; judge L.A. Mcpl. Ct., 1994-97, L.A. Superior Ct., 1997—. Faculty atty. asst. tng. program UCLA, 1982-97, bd. dirs. internat. student ctr., 1986—, Performing Tree, 1997—. Mem. editl. bd. Calif. Bar Jour., 1979-80, L.A. Lawyer Mag., 1989-94; contbr. articles to profl. jours. Del. White House Conf. on Youth, 1971; faculty Ctr. Jud. Edn. and Rsch, 1997—; nat. adv. coun. Ctr. for Study of Presidency, 1974-99; mem. L.A. Dist. Atty.'s Adv. Coun., 1976-82; hearing officer L.A. County Employees Ret. Assn., 1986-94. Mem. ABA, Calif. Judges Assn., Beverly Hills Bar Assn. (bd. govs. 1975-80, chmn. litig. sect. 1983-85, chair resolutions com. 1991-92, ex. officio bd. dirs. 1998-99, Dist. Svc. award 1992), Assn. of Bus. Trial lawyers (bd. govs. 2001—), Barristers of Beverly Hills Bar Assn. (pres. 1979-80), Am. Judicature Soc. (dir. 1982-83), L.A. County Bar Assn., Phi Beta Kappa, Phi Delta Phi. Office: LA Superior Ct 600 S Commonwealth Ave Los Angeles CA 90005 E-mail: amohr@lasc.cv.la.ca.us

MOJOCK, DAVID THEODORE, lawyer; b. Uniontown, Pa., Nov. 9, 1945; s. Charles Angelo and Mary Ann (Fabbri) M.; m. Colleen E. Creany, Aug. 10, 1968; children— David T., Angela, Todd, Eric. BS, Duquesne U., 1967, JD, 1972. Bar: Pa. 1972, U.S. Dist. Ct. (we. dist.) Pa. 1972, U.S. Ct. Appeals (3d cir.) 1976. Assoc. Cauley, Birsic & Conflenti, Pitts., 1972; law clk. presiding justices Ct. Common Pleas, Lawrence County, New Castle, Pa., 1973; assoc. Gamble & Verterano, New Castle, 1974-76; ptnr. Gamble, Verterano, Mojock, New Castle, 1976-81; ptnr. Gamble, Verterano, Mojock, Piccione & Green, New Castle, 1981-91, Gamble, Mojock, Piccione Palmer & Green, 1991-95, Gamble, Mojock, Piccione, Acker & Palmer, 1995— . Contbr. article to Scapel and Quill. Bd. dirs. Cath. Social Svcs., New Castle, 1981-83, Vis. Nurse Assn., New Castle, 1983-87, Allied Human Svcs. Assn., New Castle, 1983— . With U.S. Army, 1969-71. Mem. ATLA, Pa. Bar Assn., Pa. Trial Lawyers Assn., Lawrence County Bar Assn., Allegheny County Bar Assn., KC (grand knight 1976-77, legis. chmn. state coun. 1980-82, state advocate 1994-96). Democrat. Roman Catholic. State civil litigation, Insurance, Personal injury. Home: 811 Highland Ave New Castle PA 16101-2319 Office: Gamble Mojock Piccione et al 25 N Mill St Ste 500 New Castle PA 16101-3723

MOK, BARBARA WAI KUN, lawyer; b. Hong Kong, Nov. 26, 1957; d. Keith K.H. Mok and Louise Y.M. Ho; m. Raymond W.M. Lo, Nov. 24, 1998; 1 child, Audrey S.Y. Lo. LLB, U. Hong Kong, 1980; Postgrad. Cert. Laws, 1981, LLM, 1988. Asst. solicitor Gallant Y.T. Ho & Co., Hong Kong, 1983-86; ptnr., 1986-90; cons. Victor Chu & Co., Hong Kong, 1991-92; ptnr., 1992-99, Jones, Day, Reavis & Pogue, Hong Kong, 1999—. Vis. atty. Pillsbury, Madison & Sutro, LLP, San Francisco, 1986. Mem. Inter-Pacific Bar Assn., Internat. Bar Assn., Law Soc. Hong Kong, Law Soc. Eng. Home: Apt 12N 28 Scenic Villa Dr Pokfulam Hong Kong Office: Jones Day Reavis & Pogue 29 F Ent Bldg 30 Queen's Rd Ctrl Hong Kong China Fax: (852) 2868-5871. E-mail: bmok@jonesday.com

MOLDOFF, WILLIAM MORRIS, retired lawyer; b. Phila., Jan. 1, 1921; s. David and Pauline (Arcusin) Moldoff; m. Doris Elaine Johnson (dec.); children: Phillip Douglas, Laura Ellen, Janet Susan Sayers, Allan William. BA, U. Iowa, 1943; JD cum laude, U. Miami, 1950; LLM, U. Mich., 1955. Law editor Lawyers Coop. Pub. Co., Rochester, N.Y., 1952-54, 57-60; instr. Ohio Northern U. Coll. of Law, 1955-57; proofreader N.Y. Codes, Rules and Regulations State of N.Y., 1960, adminstrv. asst. to exec. dep. Sec. of State, 1961-63; pvt. practice Nassau, N.Y., 1963-66; veterans claims examiner, rating bd. Vets. Adminstrn. Regional, N.Y.C., 1966-85; ret., 1985. Lt (jg) USNR, 1943—46. Republican. Jewish. Home: 2 Phillips St #151 Nassau NY 12123-0151

MOLER, ELIZABETH ANNE, lawyer; b. Salt Lake City, Jan. 24, 1949; d. Murray McClure and Eleanor Lorraine (Barry) M.; m. Thomas Blake Williams, Oct. 19, 1979; children: Blake Martin Williams, Eleanor Bliss Williams. BA, Am. U., 1971; postgrad., Johns Hopkins U., 1972; JD, George Wash. U., 1977. Bar: D.C. 1978. Chief legis. asst. Senator Floyd Haskell, Washington, 1973-75; law clk. Sharon, Pierson, Semmes, Crolius & Finley, 1975-76; profl. staff mem. com. on energy and natural resources U.S. Senate, 1976-77, counsel, 1977-86, sr. counsel, 1987-88; commr. FERC, 1988-93, chair, 1993-97; dep. sec. Dept. of Energy, 1997-98, acting sec., 1998; ptnr. Vinson & Elkins, 1998-99; sr. v.p. Exelon Corp., 2000—. Mem. ABA, D.C. Bar Assn. Democrat. Office: Suite 115 701 Pennsylvania Ave NW Washington DC 20004-1008 Home: 1537 Forest Ln Mc Lean VA 22101-3317

MOLHO, ISAAC, lawyer; b. Jerusalem, Jan. 30, 1945; s. Raphael and Rachel Molho; m. Irene Shlomit Shimron, 1967; children: Hadar Valero, Vered. LLB, Hebrew U., Jerusalem, 1969. Apprentice to Erwin S. Shimron, Jerusalem, 1968-70; assoc. Proskauer Rose LLP, N.Y.C., 1971-72, Shimron, Novick, Levitt, Jerusalem, 1972-75; ptnr. Shimron, Novick, Levitt, Molho, 1975-78; mng. ptnr. E. S. Shimron I. Molho, Persky & Co., 1978—. Bd. dirs. Triumph Internat., Ltd. Hon. consul Republic of Austria, Jerusalem, 1979—; bd. dirs., dep. chmn. Jerusalem Internat. YMCA, 1980-2001; mem. bd. govs. Hebrew U., Jerusalem, 1990-2001; mem. internat. coun. Jerusalem Found., 1992-2001; mem. Prime Minister's envoy to Palestinian Leadership and Chmn. Yasser Arafat, Jerusalem, 1996-99; chief Israeli negotiator Palestinian Authority Hebron and Wye Agreements, 1996-99; bd. dirs. Israel Mus., 1999-2001. Capt. Israel Def. Forces, 1963-65. Decorated Silbernes Ehrenzeichen (Austria), 1994. Mem. Israel Bar Assn., Internat. Orgn. Jewish Jurists. Avocation: tennis. Communications, General corporate, Intellectual property. Office: ES Shimron I Molhy Persky & Co Tech Pk Bldg 1 Manahat 91487 Jerusalem Israel Office Fax: 972-2-649-0659. E-mail: officejm1@smplaw.co.il

MOLINARO, THOMAS J. lawyer; b. Cleve., June 4, 1952; s. Albert J. and Marilyn M.; m. Betty E., Oct. 22, 1989; children: Daniel, Paul, Marisa, Anna. BS, U. Wis., 1976; JD, U. Wis. Law Sch., 1979. Bar: Wis., U.S. Dist. Ct. (we. and ea. dists.) Wis. Law clk. Wis. Ct. Appeals, Waukesha, 1979-80; assoc. Crooks, Law & Connell, Wausau, 1980-83; ptnr. Brady, Hoover & Molinaro, 1983-85, Brady & Molinaro, Wausau, 1986-92; sole practice law, 1993—. Bd. dirs. Marathon Civic Corp., Wausau, 1988-94, Wausau Area Youth Soccer Assn., 1990-94; membership com. YMCA, Wausau, 1988-90. Mem. ATLA, Wis. Bar Assn., Marathon County Bar Assn. Avocations: antique collecting and restoration, skiing, soccer. Family and matrimonial, Personal injury, Workers' compensation. Office: 215 Grand Ave Wausau WI 54403-6220

MOLINARO, VALERIE ANN, lawyer; b. N.Y.C, Oct. 21, 1956; d. Albert Anthony and Rosemary Rita (Zito) M.; m. Howard Robert Birnbach; 1 child, Michelle Annalise Birnbach. BA with honors, SUNY, 1978; JD, MPA, Syracuse U., 1980. Asst. counsel. New York State Housing Finance Agy., N.Y.C., 1980-82; assoc. counsel, asst. secy. N.Y. State Urban Devel. Corp., 1982-85; assoc. Mudge Rose Guthrie Alexander & Ferdon, 1985-87, Bower & Gardner, N.Y.C., 1988, Hawkins, Delafield & Wood, N.Y.C., 1988-91; of counsel McKenzie McGhee, 1991-98; assoc. Battle Fowler, 1998-2000, Garfunkel Wild & Travis PC, Gt. Neck, N.Y., 2000—. Author: Am. Bar Assn. Jour., 1981 Mem. N.Y.C. Comm. on Status of Women, 1995—. Mem. ABA, N.Y. State Bar Assn., (tax exempt fin. com.), Assn. Bar City of N.Y., Nat. Assn. Bond Lawyers, N.Y.C. Commn. on the Status of Women (legis. chmn.). Office: Garfunkel Wild & Travis 111 Great Neck Rd Great Neck NY 11021 E-mail: vmolinaro@gotlaw.com

MOLINEAUX, CHARLES BORROMEO, lawyer, arbitrator, columnist, poet; b. N.Y.C., Sept. 27, 1930; s. Charles Borromeo and Marion Frances (Belter) M.; m. Patricia Leo Devereux, July 2, 1960; children: Charles, Stephen, Christopher, Patricia, Peter, Elizabeth. BS cum laude, Georgetown U., 1950; JD, St. Johns U., 1959. Bar: N.Y. 1959, Mass. 1981, D.C. 1988. From assoc. to ptnr. Nevius, Jarvis & Pilz and successor firms, N.Y.C., 1959-77; ptnr. Gadsby & Hannah, 1978-80; v.p., gen. counsel Perini Corp., Framingham, Mass., 1980-87; pvt. practice Washington, 1987—. Adj. faculty Internat. Law Inst., Washington, 1989—. Author numerous poems. Committeeman Rep. Party, Nassau County, N.Y., 1965-71, Fairfax County, Va., exec. com., 1969; adv. bd. Inst. for Transnat. Arbitration, Southwestern Legal Found. 1st lt. U.S. Army, 1954-56. Fellow Am. Bar Found.; mem. ASCE, Am. Arbitration Assn. (constrn. ADR task force 1994—), Chartered Inst. Arbitrators, Fedn. Internat. Engrs.-Conseils (Assoc. Gen. Contractors del. constrn. contract com., Louis Prangey award for svc. to profession cons. engring. 1996), Del. Hist. Soc., London Ct. Internat. Arbitration, Fellowship Cath. Scholars. Roman Catholic. Construction, Private international. Home: 8321 Weller Ave Mc Lean VA 22102-1717 Office: 8201 Greensboro Dr Ste 1000 Mc Lean VA 22102 also: 46 Essex St London WC2R 3GH England E-mail: cmlnx@aol.com

MOLINS, MARCEL J. lawyer; b. Barcelona, Spain, Nov. 1, 1936; s. Pedro and Rosa (Viaplana) M.; m. Martina Molins, Aug. 5, 1963; children: Thomas, Nicole. JD, Barcelona U., 1958; LM, Northwestern U., 1964; JD, Loyola U., Chgo., 1966. Assoc. Baker & McKenzie, Chgo., 1964-70, ptnr., 1970—. Chmn. adv. bd. Instituto Cervantes, Chgo., 1996—. Recipient medalla merito civil Spanish Govt., Madrid, 1997. Office: Baker & McKenzie 130 E Randolph Dr 1 Prudential Plaza Chicago IL 60601 E-mail: marcel.j.molins@bakernet.com

MOLITOR, STEVEN JOHN, lawyer; b. May 19, 1962; BA, Franklin and Marshall Coll., 1984; JD, Cornell U., 1987. Bar: N.Y. 1988, Pa. 1996. Assoc. Morgan, Lewis & Bockius LLP, N.Y.C. and Phila., 1992-95, ptnr., 1995—. Office: Morgan Lewis & Bockius LLP 101 Park Ave Fl 44 New York NY 10178-0060 also: 1701 Market St Philadelphia PA 19103-2903 E-mail: smolitor@morganlewis.com

MOLJORD, KARE I. lawyer; b. Kristiansand, Norway, Mar. 28, 1953; 2 children. LLB, U. Oslo, 1978. Bar: Norway 1999. Assoc. judge, Oslo, 1982-84; atty. KPMG Audit Co., Norway, 1984-87, Bugge, Arentz-Hansen & Rasmussen, 1987-89; ptnr. Advokatfirmaet de Besche & Co., Oslo, 1989-2001, Arntz3n de Besche, Oslo, 2001—. Chmn. Paintbox AS, Norway, 1999—; bd. dirs. various cos. Author: Pledge of Real Estate, 1982; contbr. articles to profl. jours. Chm. Nat. Acctg. Adv. Bd., Oslo, 1989-92. Served to 2s lt. Norwegian Army, 1978-79. Mem. Internat. Fin. Assn., Norwegian Bar Assn. Avocations: bridge, golf. General corporate, Mergers and acquisitions, Corporate taxation. Office: Arntzen de Besche AS PO Box 1424-Vika N-0115 Oslo Norway E-mail: kare.i.moljord@ArntzenDeBesche.no

MOLLER, STEPHEN HANS, solicitor; b. Rochester, U.K., Aug. 13, 1965; s. Hans and Helen M.; m. Rachael Beaumont. BA in Law and Politics, Durham U., U.K., 1987. Solicitor of Supreme Ct. Ptnr. Simmons & Simmons, London, 1997—. Mem. City of London Law Soc. Banking, Securities. Office: Simmons & Simmons One Ropemaker St London EC2Y9SS England E-mail: stephen.moller@simmons-simmons.com

MOLLING, CHARLES FRANCIS, lawyer; b. Grafton, Wis., Jan. 5, 1940; s. Frank Joseph and Gertrude Catherine (Tillmann) M.; m. Gretchen Arlene Lundberg, Sept. 27, 1961. BA magna cum laude, U. Mo., 1973; JD, Loyola U., Chgo., 1977. Bar: Colo. 1977, Ill. 1977, U.S. Dist. Ct. Colo. 1979, U.S. Dist. Ct. (no. dist.) Ill. 1979, U.S. Ct. Appeals (7th and 10th cirs.) 1979, U.S. Ct. Claims 1979. Claims and bond underwriting positions various ins. cos., Milw. and other locations, 1961-76; assoc. state counsel Pioneer Title Ins. Co., Denver, 1976-77; assoc. Boatright & Deuben, Wheat Ridge, Colo., 1977-78, McNeela & Griffin, Chgo., 1979; ptnr. Boatright Molling & Ripp, Wheat Ridge, 1980-88; pvt. practice law Denver, 1988—. Author: Public Trustee Foreclosures in Colorado--A Systems Approach, 1983; (computer software) MicroLawyer, 1985. Cpl. USMC, 1960-61. Mem. Colo. Bar Assn., 1st Jud. Dist. Bar Assn., Nat. Lawyers Assn., POETS. Avocations: computers, photography. Contracts commercial, General corporate, Real property. Office: 4704 Harlan St Ste 300 Denver CO 80212-7418 E-mail: cmolling@lawyernet.com, cmolling@escapees.com

MOLNAR, LAWRENCE, lawyer; b. Czygand, Hungary, Apr. 14, 1927; came to U.S., 1954; s. Alexander and Marie (Vavra) M.; m. Virginia Hampton Broome, July 16, 1999. Juris Utriusque Candidatus, Charles U., Prague, Czechoslovakia, 1951; JD, NYU, 1962; LLM, LLD (hon.), Charles U., 1991. Bar: N.Y. 1962, U.S. Dist. Ct. (so. and ea. dists.) N.Y. 1970, Czech Republic, 1991. With U.S. Intelligence, Berlin, 1951-54, Lansen, Naeve Corp., N.Y., 1955-56; asst. mgr. export traffic Intra-Mar Shipping Corp., 1957-58; mgr. export traffic Melchior, Armstrong, Ridgefield, N.J., 1958-59; assoc. Hamburger, Weinschenk, N.Y.C., 1963-69; ptnr. Hamburger, Weinschenk, Molnar & Fisher, 1969—. Mem. ABA, Assn. of Bar of City of N.Y., Consular Law Soc. (v.p. 1980—), Fgn. Law Assn., Queens Bar Assn. Estate planning, Private international, Probate. Office: Hamburger Weinschenk Molnar & Fisher 36 W 44th St New York NY 10036-8102

MOLO, STEVEN FRANCIS, lawyer; b. Chgo., June 30, 1957; s. Steven and Alice (Babinski) M.; m. Mary Wood, Dec. 31, 1986; children: Alexander, Madeline, Julia, Allison. BS, U. Ill., 1979, JD, 1982. Bar: Ill. 1982. Asst. atty. gen. criminal pros. and trial divsn., Chgo., 1982-86; assoc. Winston & Strawn, 1986-89, ptnr., 1989—, mem. exec. com., 2000—. Adj. prof. Loyola U. Law Sch., Chgo., 1988-93,. Northwestern U. Law Sch., Chgo., 1989—; mem. faculty Nat. Inst. Trial Advocacy, Chgo., 1989—; lectr. on trial advocacy, appellate advocacy, and evidence to various orgns. Co-author: Corporate Internal Investigations, 1993, updated annually, 1993—; bd. editors Bus. Crimes Bull: Litigation and Compliance, 1994—; contbr. articles to legal jours. Spl. counsel Ill. Jud. Inquiry Bd., 1986-90; spl. reapportionment counsel Cook County Judiciary, 1988-89, spl. reapportionment counsel to Rep. leadership Ill. Ho. of Reps. and Senate, 1991-92. Named World's Leading White Collar Crime Lawyers, Euromoney PLC, 1995, Leading Ill. Attys. Comml. Litigation and Criminal Law, 1996, Crain's Chicago Bus. "40 Under 40" Chicago Leaders, 1997, Best Lawyers in Am., 2000. Mem. ABA, FBA, Ill. Bar Assn., Chgo. Bar Assn., Theodore Roosevelt Assn., Chgo. Athletic Assn., Econ. Club Chgo., Tavern Club, Chgo. Inn of Ct. (master of bench, pres. 1997-98), Saddle & Cycle Club, Gilda's club Chgo. (presdl. gov. bd. 1999—). Federal civil litigation, General civil litigation, Criminal. Office: Winston & Strawn 35 W Wacker Dr Ste 4200 Chicago IL 60601-1695

MOLONEY, STEPHEN MICHAEL, lawyer; b. L.A., July 1, 1949; s. Donald Joseph and Madeline Marie (Sartoris) M.; m. Nancy Paula Barile, Jan. 15, 1972; children: Michael, John, Kathleen. Student, St. John's Sem., Camarillo, Calif., 1967-69; BS, U. Santa Clara, 1971, JD, 1975. Bar: Calif. 1975, U.S. Dist. Ct. (cen. dist.) Calif. 1976, U.S. Supreme Ct. 1990. Assoc. Gilbert, Kelly, Crowley & Jennett, L.A., 1975-80, from ptnr. to sr. ptnr., 1980—. Arbitrator, settlement officer Los Angeles Superior Ct., 1985—. Contbr. articles to profl. jours. Dir. Calif. Def. Polit. Action Com., Sacramento, 1991—. With USAR. Recipient Svc. award to Pres. of So. Calif. Def. Counsel, Def. Rsch. Inst., Chgo., 1992. Mem. Assn. So. Calif. Def. Counsel (pres. 1992-93), Calif. Def. Counsel (dir. 1991—), L.A. County Bar Assn. (vols. in parole, 1976-77, exec. com. alternative dispute resolution com. 1992-96), Oakmont Country Club, La Quinta Resort and Club. Democrat. Roman Catholic. Avocations: politics, golf, reading, travel. Construction, Labor, Personal injury. Office: Gilbert Kelly Crowley & Jennett 1200 Wilshire Blvd Ste 6 Los Angeles CA 90017-1908 E-mail: smm@gilbertkelly.com

MOLONEY, THOMAS E. lawyer; b. Rockville Ctr., N.Y., Jan. 9, 1949; BS, U. Dayton, 1971; JD, U. Notre Dame, 1974. Bar: Ohio 1974. Prin. Am. Energy Svcs., Inc., Columbus, Ohio. Office: Am Energy Svcs Inc 1105 Schrock Rd Ste 602 Columbus OH 43229-1174

MOLONEY, THOMAS JOSEPH, lawyer; b. Bklyn., Oct. 14, 1952; s. Thomas J. and Grace (Nelson) M.; m. Molly K. Heines, Dec. 26, 1976. AB, Columbia U., 1973; JD cum laude, NYU, 1976. Bar: N.Y. 1977, U.S. Dist. Ct. (so. dist.) N.Y. 1977, U.S. Dist. Ct. (ea. dist.) N.Y. 1978, U.S. Ct. Appeals (2d cir.) 1981. Assoc. Cleary, Gottlieb, Steen & Hamilton, N.Y.C., 1976-84, ptnr., 1984—. Bd. dirs. N.Y. Lawyers for Pub. Interest, N.Y.C., 1986-91; mediator U.S. Bankruptcy Ct. for So. Dist. N.Y., 1995. Asst. counsel Gov.'s Jud. Nominating Com., N.Y.C., 1981-85; chmn. bus. adv. coun. Washington Irving H.S., 1994—. Mem. ABA, Am. Bankruptcy Inst., Assn. of Bar of City of N.Y. (bankruptcy, corp. reorganization coms. 1983-86, chair com. legal assistance 1995-97), Order of Coif. Avocations: chess, golf, dance, travel, wine. Bankruptcy, Federal civil litigation, State civil litigation. Office: Cleary Gottlieb Steen & Hamilton 1 Liberty Plz Fl 38 New York NY 10006-1470

MOLONY, MICHAEL JANSSENS, JR. lawyer, arbitrator, mediator; b. New Orleans, Sept. 2, 1922; s. Michael Janssens and Marie (Perret)M.; m. Jane Leslie Waguespack, Oct. 21, 1951; children: Michael Janssens III (dec.), Leslie, Megan, Kevin, Sara, Brian, Ian, Duncan. JD, Tulane U., 1950. Bar: La. 1950, D.C. 1979, U.S. Dist. Ct. (ea. and mid. dists.) La. 1951, U.S. Ct. Appeals (5th cir.) 1953, U.S. Supreme Ct. 1972, U.S. Dist. Ct. (we. dist.) La. 1978, U.S. Ct. Appeals (11th and D.C. cirs.) 1981. Ptnr. Molony & Baldwin, New Orleans, 1950; assoc. Jones, Flanders, Waechter & Walker, 1951-56; ptnr. Jones, Walker, Waechter, Poitevent, Carrere & Denegre, 1956-75, Milling, Benson, Woodward, Hillyer, Pierson & Miller, New Orleans, 1975-91, Chaffe, McCall, Phillips, Toler & Sarpy, New Orleans, 1991-92, Sessions & Fishman, New Orleans, 1993-2000, Molony Law Firm, New Orleans, 2000—. Instr., lectr. Med. Sch. and Univ. Coll. Tulane U., 1953-59; mem. Eisenhower Legal Com., 1952. Bd. commrs. Port of New Orleans, 1976-81, pres., 1978; mem. bd. rev. Assoc. Br. Pilots, 1990—; bd. dirs. La. World Expn. Inc., 1974-84; bd. dirs., exec. com. New Orleans Tourist and Conv. Commn., 1971-74, 78, chmn.; family attractions com. 1973-75; chmn. La. Gov.'s Task Force on Space Industry, 1971-73; chmn. La. Gov.'s Citizens' Adv. Com. Met. New Orleans Transp. and Planning Location of new Miss. River Bridge, 1971-77; mem. La. Gov.'s Task Force Natural Gas Requirements, 1971-72; mem. La. Gov.'s Proaction Comm. for Higher Edn., 1995; mem. Goals Found. Coun. and ex-officio mem. Goals Found., Met. New Orleans, 1969-73; vice chmn. Port of New Orleans Operation Impact, 1969-70, mem. Met. Area Com., New Orleans, 1970-84; trustee Pub. Affairs Rsch. Coun. La., 1970-73, mem. exec. com. Bus./Higher Edn. Coun., U. New Orleans, 1980-94, bd. dirs., 1980-2000, dir. emeritus, 2000—, v.p., 1986-88, pres., 1988-90, chmn. Task Force on Pub. Higher Edn. Funding, 1990-95, chmn. govtl. affairs, 1995-2000, Task Force on Edn./Econ. Devel. Alliances, 1993-95; mem. Mayor's Coun. on Internat. Trade and Econ. Devel., 1978; mem. Mayor's Transition Task Force Econ. Devel., 1994; bd. dirs. La. Partnership for Tech. and Innovation, 1989—, Acad. Sacred Heart, 1975-77, Internat. House, 1985-86, adv. coun., 1985—; bd. dirs. U. New Orleans Found., 1991—; mem. vis. com. Sch. Bus. Adminstrn., Loyola U., New Orleans, 1981-2001, trustee Loyola U., 1985-91, vice chmn. bd. trustees, 1990-91; mem. Dean's Coun. Tulane U. Law Sch., 1988-96, vice chmn. bldg. com., 1991-95; bd. dirs., mem. exec. com. Internat. Trade Mart, chmn. internat. bus. com., 1983-85, World Trade Ctr.-New Orleans (bd. dirs. 1983—, mem. Port Activity com. 1985-91, transp. com. 1991-95, 2000, 2001, govt. affairs com. 1996-99); chmn. Task Force on Internat. Banking, 1982; mem. Mayor's Task Force on Drug Abuse, 1989-90, vice comdr. La. Commandery, Mil. Order Fgn. Wars, 2000—. Capt. PTO, 1942-46, JAGDR, USAAF, 1950-. Recipient Leadership award AIAA, 1971, Yenni award Loyola U., New Orleans, 1979, New Orleans Times

Picayune Loving Cup, 1986, First Citizen of the Learning Soc. Dean's award UNO Met. Coll., 1992; also various civic contbn. awards; co-recipient Silver Anvil award New Orleans chpt. Pub. Rels. Soc. Am., 1991. Fellow Coll. Labor and Employment Lawyers; mem. ABA (labor and employment law and litigation sects., com. equal opportunity law, chmn. regional com. liaison with equal opportunity commn., office of fed. contract compliance programs), D.C. Bar Assn., Fed. Bar Assn., La. Bar Assn. (past sec.-treas., bd. govs. 1957-60, editor jour. 1957-59, sec. spl. supreme ct. com. on drafting code jud. ethics), New Orleans Bar Assn. (dir legal aid bur. 1954, chmn. standing com. legis. 1968, vice chmn. standing com. pub. rels. 1970-71), Am. Judicature Soc., La. Law Inst. (asst. sec.-treas. 1958-70), Am. Arbitration Assn. (bd. dirs., 1995-98, chmn. reg. adv. coun., chmn. reg. adv. coun. employment law cases, mem. panel large complex employment and comml. arbitration/mediation cases, Whitney North Seymour Sr. award 1991), So. Inst. Mgmt. (founder), AIM, U.S. C. of C. (urban and regional affairs com. 1970-73), La. C. of C. (bd. dirs. 1963-66), New Orleans and River Region C. of C. (v.p. met. devel. and urban affairs 1969, past chmn. labor rels. coun., bd. dirs. 1970-78, pres.-elect 1970, pres. 1971, dir., exec. com. 1972, ex officio mem., bd. dirs. 1979—), Bienville Club, Pickwick Club, Plimsoll Club, Serra Club, So. Yacht Club, Sigma Chi (pres. alumni chpt. 1956). Roman Catholic. Alternative dispute resolution, General civil litigation, Labor. Home: 3039 Hudson Pl New Orleans LA 70131-5337 Office: Molony Law Firm 201 Saint Charles Ave Ste 3500 New Orleans LA 70170-3500 Fax: 504-582-1553. E-mail: mjm@mmolony.law.com

MONAGHAN, PETER GERARD, lawyer; b. Belfast, Ireland, July 12, 1949; came to U.S., 1961; s. William Liam and Elizabeth (Eccles) M.; m. Barbara Marion Farrenkopf, Sept. 24, 1972; children: Brian Patrick, Kevin James, Allison Mary. BS, Fordham U., 1970; JD, St. John's U., Jamaica, N.Y., 1977. Bar: N.Y. 1978, U.S. Dist. Ct. (so. dist.) N.Y. 1978, U.S. Dist. Ct. (ea. dist.) N.Y. 1979, U.S. Supreme Ct. 1986. Claims examiner Royal Ins. Co., N.Y.C., 1970-76; assoc. Kroll, Edelman, Elser and Dicker, 1976, Bower and Gardner, N.Y.C., 1977-83, ptnr., 1984-91, Bartlett, McDonough, Bastone & Monaghan, LLP, Mineola, N.Y., 1992—. Cubmaster Boy Scouts Am., Bayside, N.Y., 1985-89. Capt. U.S. Army Res., 1970-78. Mem. ABA, Queens County Bar Assn., N.Y. State Bar Assn. (trial lawyers sect. com. on med. malpractice 1988—), Assn. of Trial Lawyers of Am., Nassau-Suffolk Trial Lawyers Assn., Nassau County Bar Assn. Federal civil litigation, State civil litigation, General practice. Office: Bartlett McDonough Bastone & Monaghan LLP 300 Old Country Rd Mineola NY 11501-4198

MONAGHAN, THOMAS JUSTIN, former prosecutor; J.D., U. Nebr. Law School. Adjunct faculty College of St. Mary, Nebr., 1985—91; partner Monaghan, Tiedman & Lynch, Omaha; U.S. atty. Dept. Justice, 1993—2001.*

MONAHAN, MARIE TERRY, lawyer; b. Milford, Mass., June 26, 1927; d. Francis V. and Marie I. (Casey) Terry; m. John Henry Monahan, Aug. 25, 1951; children: Thomas F., Kathleen J., Patricia M., John Terry, Moira M., Deirdre M. AB, Radcliffe Coll., 1949; JD, New Eng. Sch. Law, 1975. Bar: Mass. 1977, U.S. Dist. Ct. Mass. 1978, U.S. Supreme Ct. 1982. Tchr. French and Spanish Holliston (Mass.) High Sch., 1949-52; pvt. practice Newton, Mass., 1977—. Mem. Mass. Assn. Women Lawyers (pres. 1986). Avocations: reading, travel. State civil litigation, Family and matrimonial, Probate. Home and Office: 34 Foster St Newton MA 02460-1511

MONCHARSH, PHILIP ISAAC, lawyer; b. N.Y.C., May 27, 1948; s. Bernard J. and Betty R. (Chock) M.; m. Karen L. Fellows, Nov. 1, 1981; children: Rachael, Anna. BA, Yale U., 1970; JD, Columbia U., 1973. Bar: Calif. 1973, U.S. Dist. Ct. (cen. dist.) Calif. 1979, U.S. Ct. Appeals (9th cir.) 1981. Trial dep. L.A. County Pub. Defender, L.A., 1973-78; assoc. Strote & Whitehouse, Beverly Hills, Calif., 1978-81, Ghitterman, Hourigan, et al, Ventura, 1981-86, Heily & Blase, Ventura, 1986-87; of counsel Hecht, Diamond & Greenfield, Pacific Palisades, 1988; ptnr. Benton, Orr, Duval & Buckingham, Ventura, 1988-89, Rogers & Sheffield, Santa Barbara, Calif., 1989—. Arbitrator, judge pro tem Superior and Mcpl. Cts., Ventura and Santa Barbara, 1986—. Pres. Ojai Valley (Calif.) Land Conservancy, 1988-94. Mem. Calif. Trial Lawyers Assn., Santa Barbara Trial Lawyers Assn., Ventura Trial Lawyers Assn., L.A. Trial Lawyers Assn., Assn. Trial Lawyers Am., Consumer Attys. of Calif., Consumer Attys. of L.A., Yale Club Santa Barbara, Ventura and San Luis Obispo Counties (pres.). Avocations: hiking, backpacking, travel. General civil litigation, Insurance, Personal injury. Office: Rogers & Sheffield 427 E Carrillo St Santa Barbara CA 93101-1401 E-mail: pmoncharsh@rogerssheffield.com

MONDUL, DONALD DAVID, patent lawyer; b. Miami, Fla., Aug. 24, 1945; s. David Donald and Marian Wright (Heck) M.; children: Alison Marian, Ashley Megan; m. Anna Marie Towle, Oct. 12, 1996. BS in Physics, U.S. Naval Acad., 1967; MBA, Roosevelt U., 1976; JD, John Marshall Law Sch., 1979. Bar: Ill. 1979, Fla. 1980, Tex. 1998; U.S. Patent Office 1980; U.S. Ct. Appeals (fed. cir.) 1982; U.S. Supreme Ct. 1990. Commd. ensign USN, 1967, advanced through grades to comdr., 1977; mktg. rep. Control Data Corp., Chgo., 1977-79; patent atty. Square D Co., Palatine, Ill., 1979-81; group patent counsel Ill. Tool Works Inc., Chgo., 1981-87; assoc. Cook, Wetzel & Egan, 1987-89; ptnr. Foley & Lardner, Chgo. and Milw., 1989-95; sr. patent atty. IBM, East Fishkill, N.Y., 1995-96; gen. patent counsel Ericsson, Inc., Richardson, Tex., 1996-99; pvt. practice Dallas, 1999—. Patentee in methods and apparatus for multiplying plurality of numbers, N numbers, determining the product of two numbers, air baffle appartus, electrical encoding device. Commander, USNR, 1967-87. Patent. Office: 6631 Lovington Dr Dallas TX 75252-2519 E-mail: dmondul@aol.com

MONE, MICHAEL EDWARD, lawyer; b. Brockton, Mass., May 15, 1942; s. Edward Patrick and June Elizabeth (Kelliher) M.; m. Margaret E. Supple, Sept. 11, 1965; 1 child, Michael Edward. BA, Middlebury Coll., 1964, LLB (hon.), 2000; JD, Boston Coll., 1967; LLB (hon.), Suffolk U., 1999. Bar: Mass. 1967, U.S. Dist. Ct. Mass. 1968, U.S. Ct. Appeals (1st cir.) 1968. Trial atty. Schneider & Reilly, Boston, 1967-73, ptnr., 1969-73; trial lawyer Esdaile, Barrett & Esdaile, 1973—, ptnr., 1976—. Instr. Boston Coll. Law Sch., 1981. Chmn. Zoning Bd. Appeals, Brockton, 1976-78. Fellow Am. Coll. Trial Lawyers (bd. regents 1995—, sec. 1997-98, pres. 199-2000); mem. ABA, ATLA (bd. govs. 1975-78), Mass. Bar Assn. (pres. 1993-94), Mass. Acad. Trial Lawyers (pres. 1981-84, joint bar com. on jud. nominations 1986-90). Federal civil litigation, State civil litigation, Personal injury. Office: Esdaile Barrett & Esdaile 75 Federal St Boston MA 02110-1913

MONE, PETER JOHN, lawyer; b. Brockton, Mass., Apr. 8, 1940; s. Edward Patrick and June E. (Kelliher) M.; m. Sharon Lee Bright, Oct. 9, 1965; children: Kathleen, Peter. AB, Bowdoin Coll., 1962; JD, U. Chgo., 1965. Ptnr. Baker & McKenzie, Chgo., 1968—. Active Winnetka Caucus, Ill., 1984-85. Capt. U.S. Army, 1966-67, Vietnam. Decorated Purple Heart, Bronze Star, Air medal. Fellow Am. Coll. Trial Lawyers, Internat. Acad. Trial Lawyers; mem. Soc. Trial Lawyers, Chgo. Trial Lawyers Club, Internat. Assn. Def. Counsel, Skokie Country Club. Democrat. Roman Catholic. Avocations: photography, golf, paddle tennis, softball. General civil litigation, Product liability, Professional liability. Home: 1035 Sunset Rd Winnetka IL 60093-3622 Office: Baker & McKenzie 1 Prudential Plz 130 E Randolph St Ste 3100 Chicago IL 60601-6342 E-mail: pjm4840@home.com, peter.j.mone@bakernet.com

MONE, SHEILA, lawyer; b. Brockton, Mass., Mar. 16, 1959; d. William Kerr and Mary Louise (Lane) Mone. BS cum laude, Providence Coll., 1992; JD, New Eng. Sch. Law, Boston, 1996. B1r: Mass. 1996. Assoc. Esdaile, Barrett & Esdaile, Boston, 1996—. New Eng. Sch. Law scholar, 1996. Mem. ATLA, Mass. Bar Assn., Boston Bar Assn. Office: Esdaile Barrett & Esdaile 75 Federal St Boston MA 02110-1913

MONGE, JAY PARRY, lawyer; b. N.Y.C., Mar. 15, 1943; s. Joseph Paul and Dorothy Emma (Oschmann) M.; m. Julia T. Burdick, 1966 (div. 1994); children: Justin Parry, Lindsay Newton; m. Elizabeth Ann Tracy, 1994. AB, Harvard U., 1966; LLB, U. Va., 1969. Bar: Ill. 1969, N.Y. 1981. Assoc. Mayer, Brown & Platt, Chgo., 1969-75, ptnr., 1976-79, N.Y.C., 1980-99, mng. ptnr., 1981-94, ptnr. Charlotte, NC, 2000—. Contbr. legal commentaries Ill. Inst. Continuing Legal Edn., 1974, 78, 81, 84, 87, 93, 96, 2001. Trustee Wagner Coll., 1996—. Mem. ABA, Assn. Bar City N.Y., Chgo. Club, Onwentsia Club, Sky Club, Westchester Country Club, Charlotte City Club, Carmel Country Club. Banking, General corporate, Finance. Office: Mayer Brown & Platt Bank of Am Corp Ctr 100 N Tryon St Charlotte NC 28202 E-mail: jmonge@mayerbrown.com

MONIHAN, MARY ELIZABETH, lawyer; b. Cleve., Mar. 22, 1957; d. Michael Reilley and Donna (Warner) Monihan. BS in Econs., John Carroll U., 1979; JD, Cleve. State U., 1984. Bar: Ohio 1984, U.S. Dist. Ct. (no. dist.) Ohio 1985, U.S. Supreme Ct. 1989. Atty. in office of counsel Ameritrust Co. Nat. Assn., Cleve., 1984-85; assoc. Jones, Day, Reavis & Pogue, 1985-89, Squire, Sanders & Dempsey, Cleve., 1989-95; ptnr. Spieth, Bell, McCurdy & Newell, Co., L.P.A., 1995—. Pres. Estate Planning Coun. Cleve., 1994-95. Pres., vol. Coun. Cleve. Orch., 1998-2001; trustee Assn. Major Symphony Orch. Vols., 1997-99; trustee Women's Com. of the Cleveland Orch., 2000—. Mem. ABA, Am. Coll. Trust & Estate Counsel, Ohio Bar Assn., Cleve Bar Assn., Jr. Com. Cleve. Orch. (pres. 1997-99). Estate planning, Probate, Estate taxation. Office: Spieth Bell McCurdy & Newell Co LPA 925 Euclid Ave Ste 2000 Cleveland OH 44115-1407 E-mail: memonihan@spiethbell.com

MONK, CARL COLBURN, lawyer, academic administrator; b. Sept. 11, 1942; BA in Polit. Sci., Okla. State U., 1965; JD, Howard U., 1971. Bar: D.C. 1971, N.Y. 1973. Assoc. Simpson, Thacher & Bartlett, N.Y.C., 1971-74; from asst. prof. to assoc. prof. Washburn U., Topeka, 1974-78, from assoc. dean to dean, prof., 1976-88, disting. prof. law, 1988—. Dep. dir. Assn. Am. Law Schs., Washington, 1988-90, exec. dir., 1992—; vis. scholar Bklyn. Law Sch., 1985-86; vis. prof. law W.S. Richardson Sch. Law U. Hawaii Manao, 1990-91; lit. cons., expert witness U. Wis., 1992; expert witness Whittier Coll. Sch. Law; cons. accreditation stds. Sch. Law U. Bridgeport, 1992. Contbr. articles to profl. jours. Bd. dirs. Kans. Civil Liberties Union. Office: Assn Am Law Schs Ste 800 1201 Connecticut Ave NW Washington DC 20036-2656 E-mail: cmonk@aals.org

MONOHAN, EDWARD SHEEHAN, IV, lawyer; b. Frankfort, Ky., Feb. 12, 1940; s. Edward Sheehan III and Mary (Lally) M.; m. Marilyn Louise Diebold, Aug. 31, 1963; children: Meredith, Edward, Patrick, Megan. BSChemE, Purdue U., 1962; JD, Georgetown U., 1965. Bar: D.C. 1966, Ky. 1966, Ohio 1990, U.S. Supreme Ct. 1975. Assoc. Vest & Ware, Covington, Ky., 1967-74; ptnr. Ware & Monohan, Florence, 1974-80, Monohan, Hertz & Blankenship, Florence, 1993-2000, Monohan & Blankenship, Florence, 2000—. Pres. Boone County Bar Assn., Florence, 1980-81. City councilman City of Crestview Hills, Ky., 1972-78. Mem. Ky. Bar Assn., Ky. Trial Lawyers Assn., No. Ky. Bar Assn., Louisville Bar Assn., Am. Inns of Ct. (master), Rotary (pres. 1981, 2001). Republican. Roman Catholic. Avocations: sailing, jogging, reading, French. General civil litigation, Estate planning, Real property. Home: 21 Winding Way Crestview Hills KY 41017-2227 Office: Monohan & Blankenship 7711 Ewing Blvd Ste 100 Florence KY 41042-1814 Fax: 859-283-5155. E-mail: ed@kyattys.com

MONORIEFF, DOROTHY, retired paralegal; b. Portland, Oreg., June 6, 1926; d. Charles Welsey Monorieff and Grace Lillian Fisher. BA, UCLA, 1947; MS, U. So. Calif., 1958, cert. paralegal, 1988. Tchr., Stratford, Calif., 1948, Piru, 1948-52, Torrance, 1952-87; paralegal Ball, Hunt et al, 1989-95; ret., 1995. V.p. Torrance Tchrs. Assn., 1956; club sec., precinct capt. Dems., Culver City, Calif., 1956. Mem. Malibu Art Assn. (Cert. Appreciation 1997). Avocations: watercolor, oil painting, piano, books, cooking. Home: 10915 Rose Ave Apt 20 Los Angeles CA 90034-5380

MONROE, CARL DEAN, III, lawyer; b. Birmingham, Ala., Sept. 15, 1960; s. Carl D. and Martha Jo M. BA, Birmingham-So. Coll., 1982; JD, Georgetown U., 1985. Bar: Ala. 1986, U.S. Ct. Appeals (11th cir.) 1988. Scheduler Siegelman for Atty. Gen., Montgomery, 1986; legal rsch. aide Office of Sec. of State State of Ala., 1986; asst. atty. gen., adminstrv. asst. Office of Atty. Gen., 1987-89; atty.-advisor Office Gen. Counsel, U.S. Dept. Energy, Washington, 1989—. Mem. panel of judges Georgetown Law Ctr. Moot Ct., 1991, 92, CIA Environ. Roundtable; lectr. waste mgmt. Johns Hopkins U., natural resources George Washington U. Mem. panel of judges Ala. YMCA Youth Legislature, Montgomery, 1979, 87, 88, 89; office coord. blood dr. ARC, Montgomery, 1987, 88; com. mem. Georgetown Alumni Admissions, Washington, 1986-91; mem. Nat. Trust for Hist. Preservation. Mem. ABA (author environ. law sect. newsletter Looking Ahead), Acad. Polit. Sci., Ala. Bar Assn., Birmingham-So. Alumni (alumni leader 1986—), Smithsonian Assocs., Phi Beta Kappa. Democrat. Presbyterian. Avocations: water skiing, tennis, horseback riding. Home: 1200 N Nash St Apt 264 Arlington VA 22209-3620 E-mail: dean.monroe@hq.doe.gov

MONROE, KENDYL KURTH, retired lawyer; b. Clayton, N.Mex., Sept. 6, 1936; s. Dottis Donald and Helen (Kurth) M.; m. Barbara Sayre, Sept. 12, 1956; children: Sidney, Dean, Loren. AB, Stanford U., 1958, LLB, 1960. Bar: N.Y. 1961, Calif. 1961. Assoc. Sullivan & Cromwell, N.Y.C., 1960-67, ptnr., 1968-94. Chmn. TEB Charter Svcs., Inc., Teterboro, N.J., El Valle Escondido Ranch Ltd. Co., Seneca, N.Mex., Highland Forests, Keeseville, N.Y., Eklund Assn. Clayton, N.Mex.; bd. dirs. Clan Munro Assn., Great Falls, Va., N.Y. Chamber Soloists, N.Y.C. Bd. dirs. Pub. Health Rsch. Inst., N.Y.C., N. Mex. First, Albuquerque, N. Mex. Water Dialogue, Gallup, Clayton (N.Mex.) Health Systems, Inc.; mem. bd. advisors N. Mex. Pilots' Assn.; chmn. adv. coun. The Mandala Ctr., Des Moines; mem. adv. com. Cornerstones Cmty Partnerships, Santa Fe. Mem. State Bar Calif., Assn. of Bar of City of N.Y., N.Mex. Amigos, Met. Club (N.Y.C.). Real property, Securities, Corporate taxation. Home: 189 Sayre Rd Seneca NM 88415 E-mail: kkmonroe@ptsi.net

MONROE, MURRAY SHIPLEY, lawyer; b. Cin., Sept. 25, 1925; s. James and Martha (Shipley) M.; m. Sally Longstreth, May 11, 1963; children: Tracy, Murray, Courtney, David. BE, Yale U., 1946, BS, 1947; LLB, U. Pa., 1950. Bar: Ohio 1950, U.S. Dist. Ct. (so. dist.) Ohio 1954, U.S. Dist. Ct. (mid. dist.) Tenn. 1981, US. Dist. Ct. (mid. dist.) N.C. 1974, U.S. Dist. Ct. (mid. dist.) Pa. 1986, U.S. Dist. Ct. (ea. dist.) Pa. 1960, U.S. Dist. Ct. (we. dist.) Mo. 1974, U.S. Dist. Ct. Mass. 1978, U.S. Dist. Ct. (ea. dist.) La. 1979, U.S. Dist. Ct. (no. dist.) Ill. 1980, U.S. Ct. Appeals (4th cir.) 1984, U.S. Ct. Appeals (6th cir.) 1969, U.S. Supreme Ct. 1977, U.S. Ct. Appeals (3d cir.) 1990. Assoc. Taft, Stettinus & Hollister, Cin., 1950-58, ptnr., 1958-96; of counsel, 1997—. Mem. lawyers com. Nat. Ctr. for State Cts., 1985-96; faculty Ohio Legal Ctr. Inst., 1970-93. Contbr. articles to profl. jours. Trustee, treas. The Coll. Prep. Sch., 1972-76; trustee The Seven Hills Schs., 1982-88, chmn. bd., 1982-85. 2d lt. USNR, 1943-46. Recipient award Seven Hills Schs., 1985. Fellow Ohio Bar Found.; mem. ABA (speaker symposiums), Ohio Bar Assn. (coun. dels. 1977-82, bd. govs. antitrust sect. 1960-95, dir. emeritus 1995—, chmn. bd. govs. 1973-75, Merit award 1976, speaker symposiums), Bankers Club (Cin.), Cin. Country Club, Met. Club, Tau Beta Pi. Republican. Episcopalian. Avocations: sailing, tennis. Antitrust, Federal civil litigation.

MONSON, JOHN RUDOLPH, lawyer; b. Chgo., Feb. 4, 1941; s. Rudolph Agaton and Ellen Louise (Loeffler) M.; m. Susan Lee Brown, May 22, 1965; children: Elizabeth Louisa, Christina Lee, Donald Rudolph. BA with honors, Northwestern U., 1963; JD with distinction, U. Mich., 1966. Bar: Ill. 1966, N.H. 1970, Mass. 1985. Atty. assoc. Chapman & Cutler, Chgo., 1966-68, Levenfeld, Kanter, Baskes & Lippitz, Chgo., 1968-70, Nighswander, Martin & Mitchell, Laconia, N.H., 1970-71; mem., ptnr. Wiggin & Nourie, P.A., Manchester, 1972—, pres., 1991-94. Sec., gen. counsel Rock of Ages Corp., 1996-2000. Mem. N.H. Fish and Game Commn., Concord, 1980-94, chmn., 1983-93; sr. bd. dirs. Brown-Monson Found., 1991—; incorporator Cath. Med. Ctr., 1988-95, Optima Health, 1994-99; commr. N.H. Land and Cmty. Heritage Commn., 1998-2000. Fellow Am. Coll. Trust and Estate Counsel, Safari Club Internat. (v.p. 1999-2001, dir.-at-large 1997-99, treas. 2001—). Republican. Avocations: skiing, hunting, running. General corporate, Estate planning. Home: 24 Wellesley Dr Bedford NH 03110-4531 Office: Wiggin & Nourie PA 20 Market St Manchester NH 03101-1931

MONTAGUE, H. DIXON, lawyer; b. Midland, Tex., Feb. 7, 1952; BA, Tulane U., 1974; JD, U. Miss., 1977. Bar: Miss. 1977, Tex. 1978. Ptnr. Vinson & Elkins L.L.P., Houston. General civil litigation, Condemnation. Office: Vinson & Elkins LLP 2500 First City Tower 1001 Fannin St Ste 3300 Houston TX 77002-6706

MONTAGUE, ROBERT LATANE, III, lawyer; b. Washington, Sept. 18, 1935; s. Robert Latane and Frances Breckinridge (Wilson) M.; m. Prudence Darnell, June 20, 1964; children: Anne Steele Mason Montague, Robert Latane IV. BA, U. Va., 1956, LLB, 1961. Bar: Va. 1961, D.C. 1966, U.S. Supreme Ct. 1966. Asst. atty. gen., Ky., 1961-64; pres. Historic Alexandria Found., 1968-70; chmn. Alexandria Environ. Policy Commn., 1970-74; pres. Conservation Coun. Va., 1978-80; chmn. Alexandria Commn. on Bicentennial of U.S. Constitution, 1987-91, Alexandria Historical Restoration and Preservation Commn., 1988—; trustee Assn. for Preservation of Va. Antiquities, 1990-96. Chmn. Bd. of Vis. of Gunston Hall, 1987-92; del. Moscow Conf. on Law and Econ. Coop., 1990. Comdr. USNR, 1956-79. Mem. Va. Bar Assn., Va. State Bar (chmn. environ. law sect. 1973-74), Alexandria Bar Assn. Office: 1007 King St Alexandria VA 22314-2922

MONTEDONICO, JOSEPH, lawyer; b. Washington, May 30, 1937; s. Joseph and Linda (Love) M.; m. Lynne Morrell, Nov. 12, 1979; 1 child, Maria. BA, U. Md., 1962, JD, 1965. Bar: Md. 1965, D.C. 1965, U.S. Dist. Ct. D.C. 1965, U.S. Dist. Ct. Md. 1965. Law clk. to justice, Rockville, Md., 1965-66; assoc. Donahue, Ehrmantraut Mitchell, 1966-78; ptnr. Donahue, Ehrmantraut, Montedonico, Washington, 1978-88, Montedonico & Mason, Rockville, 1988-91, Montedonico, Hamilton & Altman, PC, Chevy Chase, Md., 1991—. Cons., lectr. in field. Author: Medical Malpractice and Health Care Care, 1987; (with others) Anesthesia Clinics, 1987, Surgical Pathology, 1989. With U.S. Army, 1956-58. Named one of Best Lawyers in Am., Washingtonian Mag., 1989-96, one of Best Lawyers in Washington. Mem. Am. Bd. Trial Lawyers (pres. D.C. chpt.), Inns of Ct., Md. Bar Assn., D.C. Bar Assn. Republican. Avocations: scuba, skiing, photography. General civil litigation, Health, Personal injury. Office: Montedonico Hamilton & Altman 5454 Wisconsin Ave Ste 1300 Chevy Chase MD 20815-6919 E-mail: jm@mha.law.com

MONTGOMERIE, BRUCE MITCHELL, lawyer; b. South Bend, Ind., Feb. 9, 1946; s. Ralph H. and Dorothy (Larson) M.; m. Kathleen Ann McIntyre, June 21, 1969 (dissolved); m. Claire Desrosier, Nov. 28, 1985. BA, DePauw U., 1968; JD, MIA, Columbia U., 1972; LLM in Taxation, NYU, 1975. Bar: N.Y. 1973. From assoc. to ptnr. Milbank, Tweed, Hadley & McCloy, N.Y.C., 1972-83; ptnr. Willkie, Farr & Gallagher, 1983—. Mem. N.Y. State Bar (tax sect. exec. com. 1982-90), Nat. Assn. Real Estate Investment Trusts (bd. govs. 1983-85). Real property, Corporate taxation. Home: 17 Windabout Dr Greenwich CT 06831-3702 Office: Willkie Farr & Gallagher 787 7th Ave New York NY 10019-6018 E-mail: bmontgomerie@willkie.com

MONTGOMERY, BETTY DEE, state attorney general, former state legislator; BA, Bowling Green State U.; JD, U. Toledo, 1976. Former criminal clk. Lucas County Common Pleas Ct.; asst. pros. atty. Wood County, Ohio, 1977-78, pros. atty., 1981-88, City of Perrysburg, 1978-81; mem. Ohio Senate, 1989-94; atty. gen. State of Ohio, Columbus, 1995—. Mem. Wood County Bar Assn. Office: Attorney Generals Office State Office Tower 30 E Broad St Columbus OH 43215-3414*

MONTGOMERY, CHARLES HARVEY, lawyer; b. Spartanburg, S.C., Jan. 28, 1949; s. Dan Hugh and Ann Louise (Gasque) M.; m. Renée Jean Gubernot, Mar. 27, 1971; children: Charles Scott, Marie Renée. BA, Duke U., 1971; JD, Vanderbilt U., 1974. Bar: N.C. 1974, U.S. Dist. Ct. (ea. dist.) N.C. 1974, U.S. Supreme Ct. 1979, U.S. Dist. Ct. (mid. dist.) N.C. 1991; cert. family law specialist, N.C., 1995. Assoc. Jordan Morris & Hoke, Raleigh, N.C., 1974-75; atty. Wake County Legal Svcs., 1975-76; pvt. practice, 1977; ptnr. Montgomery & Montgomery, Cary, N.C., 1978-79, Sanford Adams McCullough & Beard, Raleigh, 1979-86, Adams McCullough & Beard, Raleigh, 1986-88, Toms Reagan & Montgomery, Cary, 1989-92, Toms & Montgomery, Cary, 1992-93; pvt. practice, 1993—. Bd. dirs. Br. Bank and Trust, Cary; pres. Family Law Mediation, Inc. Councilman Town of Cary, 1977-81, 83-87; vice-chmn. Wake County Dem. party, Raleigh, 1991-92; commr. Wake County, Raleigh, 1992; bd. dirs. East Cen. Cmty. Legal Svcs., Inc., 1997—, State Capitol Found., 1994—. Mem. ABA, N.C. Bar Assn. (chmn. pub. info. com. 1994-96, dir. family law coun. 1994-97), Wake County Bar Assn. (bd. dirs. 1999—), N.C. Acad. Trial Lawyers (chair family law sect. 1996-98). Methodist. Avocation: sailing. State civil litigation, Family and matrimonial, Land use and zoning (including planning). Office: PO Box 1325 590 New Waverly Pl Ste 110 Cary NC 27512-1325 E-mail: charles@montylaw.com

MONTGOMERY, JAMES EDWARD, JR. lawyer; b. Champaign, Ill., Feb. 8, 1953; s. James Edward Sr and Vivian M.; m. Linda C.; children: James III, Anne, Heather, Leslie. AB Polit. Sci., Duke U., 1975; JD, So. Meth. U., 1978. Bar: Tex., 1978, Md., 1994; U.S. Dist. Ct. (ea. dist.) Tex. 1978, U.S. Dist. Ct. (we. dist.) Tex., 1985, U.S. Dist. Ct. (so. dist.) Tex. 1986, U.S. Dist. Ct. (no. dist.) Tex. 1987, U.S. Dist. Md., 1994; U.S. Ct. Appeals (5th cir.) 1979; U.S. Supreme Ct., 1993. Assoc. Strong, Pipkin, Nelson & Parker, Beaumont, Tex., 1978-81; owner Sibley & Montgomery, 1981-85; assoc. Law Offices of Gilbert Adams, 1985; prin. James E. Montgomery, 1985-88; ptnr. Montgomery & Koniusczy, 1988-89; assoc. Sawtelle, Goode, Davidson & Troilo, San Antonio, 1989-91; shareholder Davidson & Troilo, 1991-94; pres. Montgomery & Assocs., 1994-97; ptnr. Soules & Wallace, P.C., 1997—. Editor: Fifth Cir. Reporter, 1983-86. Bd. dirs. Boys and Girls Clubs of San Antonio, 1995-97; dist. chmn. Boy Scouts, San Antonio, 1994. Mem. ABA, State Bar of Tex., San Antonio Bar Assn., Rotary (pres. Alamo Hts. chpt. 1997-98), 5th Cir. Bar Assn. (bd. dirs. 1983-86), Jefferson County Bar Assn. (treas. 1986). Avocations: tennis, skiing, golf, reading. General civil litigation, Contracts commercial, Product liability. Office: Soules & Wallace PC Frost Bank Tower 100 W Houston St Ste 1500 San Antonio TX 78205-1433

MONTGOMERY, JOHN WARWICK, law educator, theologian; b. Warsaw, Oct. 18, 1931; s. Maurice Warwick and Harriet (Smith) M.; m. Joyce Ann Bailer, Aug. 14, 1954; children: Elizabeth Ann, Catherine Ann; m. Lanalee de Kant, Aug. 26, 1988; 1 adopted child, Jean-Marie. Baron of Kiltartan and Lord of Morris. AB in Philosophy with distinction, Cornell U., 1952; BLS, U. Calif., Berkeley, 1954, MA, 1958; BD, Wittenberg U., 1958, MST, 1960; PhD, U. Chgo., 1962; Docteur de l'Université, mention Théologie Protestante, U. Strasbourg, France, 1964; LLB, LaSalle Extension U., 1977; diplôme cum laude, Internat. Inst. Human Rights, Strasbourg, 1978; MPhil in Law, U. Essex, Eng., 1983; D in Civil and Canon Law (hon.), Inst. Religion and Law, Moscow, 1999; LLM, Cardiff U., Wales, 2000. Bar: Va. 1978, Calif. 1979, D.C. 1985, Wash. 1990, U.S. Supreme Ct. 1981, Eng. 1984; lic. real estate broker Calif.; cert. law librarian; diplomate Med. Library Assn.; ordained to ministry Luth. Ch., 1958. Librarian, gen. reference service U. Calif. Library, Berkeley, 1954-55; instr. Bibl. Hebrew, Hellenistic Greek, Medieval Latin Wittenberg U., Springfield, Ohio, 1956-59; head librarian Swift Libr. div. and Philosophy, mem. federated theol. faculty U. Chgo., 1959-60; assoc. prof., chmn. dept. history Wilfred Laurier U. (formerly Waterloo Luth. U.), Ont., Can., 1960-64; prof., chmn. div. ch. history, history of Christian thought, dir. European Seminar program Trinity Evang. Div. Sch., Deerfield, Ill., 1964-74; prof. law and theology George Mason U. Sch. Law (formerly Internat. Sch. of Law), Arlington, Va., 1974-75; theol. cons. Christian Legal Soc., 1975-76; dir. studies Internat. Inst. Human Rights, Strasbourg, France, 1979-81; founding dean, prof. jurisprudence, dir. European program Simon Greenleaf U. Sch. Law, Anaheim, Calif., 1980-88; lic. disting. prof. theology and law, dir. European program Faith Evang. Luth. Sem., Tacoma, 1989-91; from prin. lectr. to reader in law Luton U., Eng., 1991-93, prof. law and humanities, dir. Ctr. Human Rights Eng., 1993-97, emeritus prof. Eng., 1997—; disting. prof. apologetics, law, and history of Christian thought, v.p. acad. affairs U.K. and Europe Trinity Coll. and Theol. Sem., Newburgh, Ind., 1997—; disting. prof. law Regent U., Va., 1997-99; sr. counsel European Ctr. Law and Justice, 1997-2001; founding dir. Internat. Acad. of Apologetics, Evangelism and Human Rights, Strasbourg, France, 1997—. Vis. prof. Concordia Theol. Sem., Springfield, Ill., 1964-67, DePaul U., Chgo., 1967-70; hon. fellow Revelle Coll., U. Calif., San Diego, 1970; rector Freie Fakultaten Hamburg, Fed. Republic Germany, 1981-82; lectr. Rsch. Scientists Christian Fellowship Conf. St. Catherines Coll., Oxford U., 1985, Internat. Anti-Corruption Conf., Beijing, China, 1995; Pascal lectr. on Christianity and the Univ., U. Waterloo, Ont., Can., 1987; A. Kurt Weiss lectr. biomed. ethics U. Okla., 1997; adj. prof. Puget Sound U. Sch. Law, Tacoma, 1990-91; founding dir. Internat. Acad. Apologetics, Evangelism and Human Rights, Strasbourg, France, 1997—; Worldwide Adv. Conf. lectr. Inns of Ct. Sch. Law, London, 1998; law and religion colloquium lectr. U. Coll. London, 2000; numerous other invitational functions. Author: The Writing of Research Papers in Theology, 1959, A Union List of Serial Publications in Chicago Area Protestant Theological Libraries, 1960, A Seventeenth-Century View of European Libraries, 1962, 1962, Chytraeus on Sacrifice: A Reformation Treatise in Biblical Theology, 1962; author, author(rev. edit.): The Shape of the Past: An Introduction to Philosophical Historiography, 1962, author: The Is God Dead Controversy, 1966; author: (with Thomas J.J. Altizer) The Altizer-Montgomery Dialogue, 1967, Crisis in Lutheran Theology, 2 vols., 1967, author: Es confiable el Christianismo?, 1968, Ecumenicity, Evangelicals, and Rome, 1969, Where is History Going?, 1969, History and Christianity, 1970, Damned Through the Church, 1970, The Suicide of Christian Theology, 1970, Computers, Cultural Change and the Christ, 1970, In Defense of Martin Luther, 1970, La Mort de Dieu, 1971; author: (with Joseph Fletcher) Situation Ethics: True or False?, 1972, The Quest for Noah's Ark, 1972, author: Verdammt durch die Kirche, 1973, Christianity for the Toughminded, 1973, Cross and Crucible, 2 vols., 1973, Principalities and Powers: The World of the Occult, 1973, author: How Do We Know There is a God?, 1973, Myth, Allegory and Gospel, 1974, God's Inerrant Word, 1974, Jurisprudence: A Book of Readings, 1974, author: The Law Above the Law, 1975, Cómo Sabemos Que Hay un Dios?, 1975, Demon Possession, 1975, The Shaping of America, 1976, Faith Founded on Fact, 1978, Law and Gospel: A Study for Integrating Faith and Practice, 1978, author: Slaughter of the Innocents, 1981, The Marxist Approach to Human Rights: Analysis & Critique, 1984, Human Rights and Human Dignity, 1987, Wohin marschiert China?, 1991, Evidence for Faith: Deciding the God Question, 1991, Giant in Chains: China Today and Tomorrow, 1994, Law and Morality: Friends or Foes?, 1994, Jésus: La Raison Rejoint L'Histoire, 1995; author: (with C.E.B. Cranfield and David Kilgour) Christians in the Public Square, 1996; author: Conflicts of Law, 1997, The Transcendent Holmes, 2000, The Repression of Evangelism in Greece, 2001, Christ Our Advocate, 2001; editor: Lippincott's Evangelical Perspectives, 7 vols., 1970-72, 1970—72, International Scholars Directory, 1973, Simon Greenleaf Law Rev., 7 vols., 1981—88, Global Jour. Classical Theology, 1998—; contbg. editor: Christianity Today, 1965—84, New Oxford Review, 1993—95; films Is Christianity Credible, 1968, In Search of Noah's Ark, 1977, Defending the Biblical Gospel (11 videocassette series), 1985, writer Christianity on Trial, 1987—93;contbr. articles to acad., theol., legal encys. and jours., chapters to books. Nat. Luth. Ednl. Conf. fellow, 1959-60; Can. Council postdoctoral sr. research fellow, 1963-64; Am. Assn. Theol. Schs. faculty fellow, 1967-68; recipient Angel award Nat. Religious Broadcasters, 1989, 90, 92; named Lord of Morris. Fellow Trinity Coll. (Newburgh, Ind.), Royal Soc. Arts (Eng.), Victoria Inst. (London), Acad. Internat. des Gourmets et des Traditions Gastronomiques (Paris), Am. Sci. Affiliation (nat. philosophy sci. and history sci. commn. 1966-70); mem. ALA, European Acad. Arts, Scis. and Humanities (corr. mem., Paris), Acad. Lit. France (titulary mem.), Lawyers' Christian Fellowship (hon. v.p. 1995—), Nat. Conf. U. Profs., Calif. bar Assn. (human rights commn. 1980-83), Internat. Bar Assn., World Assn. Law Profs., Mid. Temple and Lincoln's Inn (barrister mem.), Am. Soc. Internat. Law, Union Internat. des Avocats, Nat. Assn. Realtors, Tolkien Soc. Am., N.Y. C.S. Lewis Soc., Am. Hist. Assn., Soc. Reformation Rsch., Creation Rsch. Soc., Tyndale Fellowship (Eng.), Stair Soc. (Scotland), Presbyn. Hist. Soc. (North Ireland), Heraldry Soc., Soc. of Genealogists, Irish Geneaol. Soc., Am. Theol. Libr. Assn., Bibliog. Soc. U. Va., Evang. Theol. Soc., Internat. Wine and Food Soc., Soc. des Amis des Arts (Strasbourg), Chaine des Rôtisseurs (commandeur), Athenaeum (London), Wig and Pen (London), Players' Theatre Club (London), Sherlock Holmes Soc. London, Soc. Sherlock Holmes de France (hon.), Club des Casseroles Lasserre (Paris), Ordre des chevaliers du Saint-Sepulcre Byzantin (commandeur), Heralory Soc., Soc. Genealogist, Irish Geneal. Soc., Phi Beta Kappa, Phi Kappa Phi, Beta Phi Mu. Office: Church Lane Cottage 3-5 High St Lidlington Bedfordshire MK43 0RN England also: 2 rue de Rome 67000 Strasbourg France E-mail: 106612.1066@compuserve.com

MONTGOMERY, JULIE-APRIL, lawyer; b. Chgo., June 17, 1957; d. Constance Louise Montgomery. BS, U. San Francisco, 1978; MBA, Roosevelt U., 1979; JD, NYU, 1983, LLM in Taxation, 1985. Bar: Ill. 1983, U.S. Dist. Ct. (no. dist.) Ill. 1983, N.Y. 1990, U.S. Supreme Ct. 1995. Legis. advisor Ill. State Senator Charles Chew, Chgo., 1983-84; staff atty. Ill. Indsl. Comm., 1984; sole practice, 1985-86; asst. corp. counsel City of Chgo. Office of Corp. Counsel, 1986—. Co-author Ill. Inst. Cont. Legal Edn. States and Local handbook, 1990; contbr. articles to profl. jours. Instr. Minority Legal Edn. Resources Inc., Chgo., 1983—; vol. March of Dimes Chgo., 1995—; shelter vol. children's program Chgo. Christian Indsl League, 1996—. Mem. ABA, Ill. State Bar Assn. (state local tax sect. 1996—), Ill. Cert. Pub. Accts. Soc. (state and local tax sect. 1995—), Chgo. Bar Assn. (state and local tax sect. 1986—, chmn. com. 1994-95), Phi Alpha Delta, Phi Chi Theta, Alpha Sigma Nu. Lutheran. Avocations: cross-stitching, collecting Betty Boop, puzzles, movies, history. Administrative and regulatory, State civil litigation, State and local taxation. Office: City of Chgo Corp Counsel 30 N La Salle St Ste 1040 Chicago IL 60602-2503

MONTGOMERY, WILLIAM ADAM, lawyer; b. Chgo., May 22, 1933; s. John Rogerson and Helen (Fyke) M.; m. Jane Fauver, July 28, 1956 (div. Dec. 1967); children: Elizabeth, William, Virginia; m. Deborah Stephens, July 29, 1972; children: Alex, Katherine. AB, Williams Coll., 1955; LLB, Harvard U., 1958. Bar: D.C. 1958, Ill. 1959, U.S. Ct. Appeals (7th cir.) 1959, U.S. Supreme Ct. 1977. Atty. civil div., appellate sect. Dept. Justice, Washington, 1958-60; assoc. Schiff Hardin & Waite, Chgo., 1960-68, ptnr., 1968-93; v.p., gen. counsel State Farm Ins. Cos., Bloomington, Ill., 1994-97, sr. v.p., gen. counsel, 1997-99; ptnr. Schiff Hardin & Waite, Chgo., 1999—. Author: (39 corp. practice series) Tying Arrangements, 1984, also articles. Fellow Am. Coll. Trial Lawyers; mem. ABA (coun. antitrust sect. 1989-92), Chgo. Bar Assn., Seventh Cir. Bar Assn. (pres. 1988-89), Lawyers Club Chgo., Econ. Club Chgo. Avocations: skiing, woodturning. Antitrust, Federal civil litigation, General civil litigation. Office: Schiff Hardin & Waite 6600 Sears Tower Chicago IL 60606 E-mail: wmontgomery@schiffhardin.com

MONTROSS, W. SCOTT, lawyer; b. Milw., Apr. 16, 1947; s. William Phillips and Gay (Altenhofen) M.; m. Janice Townsend, May 25, 1968; children— Eric, Christine. B.B.A., U. Mich., 1969; J.D., Ind. U., 1971. Bar: Ind. 1971, U.S. Dist. Ct. (so. dist.) Ind. 1971, U.S. Ct. Appeals (7th cir.) 1973, U.S. Dist. Ct. (so. dist.) Wis. 1978, U.S. Dist. Ct. (so. dist.) Ohio 1983. Assoc., Townsend, Hovde & Townsend, Indpls., 1971-76, ptnr. Townsend, Hovde, Townsend & Montross, Indpls., 1976-84; ptnr. Townsend, Hovde and Montross, 1984-96; ptnr. Townsend & Montross, 1996—. Contbr. articles to profl. jours. Fellow Am. Coll. Trial Lawyers, Indpls. Bar Found., Ind. Coll. Trial Lawyers; mem. Assn. Trial Lawyers Am., ABA, Am. Bd. Trial Advocates, Am. Judicature Soc., Am. Assn. Automotive Medicine, Am. Arbitration Assn., Ind. Trial Lawyers Assn. (lifetime bd. dirs., treas. 1984, sec. 1985, 1st v.p., 1986, pres.-elect 1987, pres. 1988). Clubs: Crooked Stick. Federal civil litigation, State civil litigation, Personal injury. Office: Townsend & Montross 230 E Ohio St Indianapolis IN 46204-2160

MOODY, WILLARD JAMES, SR. lawyer; b. Franklin, Va., June 16, 1924; s. Willie James and Mary (Bryant) M.; m. Betty Glenn Covert, Aug. 21, 1948; children: Sharon Paige Moody Edwards, Willard J. Jr., Paul Glenn. AB, Old Dominion U., 1946; LLB, U. Richmond, 1952. Bar: Va. 1952. Pres. Moody, Strople & Kloeppel Ltd., Portsmouth, Va., 1952—. Commr. Chancery, Portsmouth, 1960—, Accounts, 1960—. Del. Va. Ho. of Reps., Portsmouth, 1956-68; senator State of Va., 1968-83; chmn. Portsmouth Dems., 1983—. Recipient Friend of Edn. award Portsmouth Edn. Assn., 1981. Mem. ABA, Va. Bar Assn., Portsmouth Bar Assn. (pres. 1960-61, lectr. seminars), Va. Trial Lawyers Assn. (pres. 1968-69), Hampton Roads C. of C. (bd. dirs. 1983-86), Portsmouth C. of C. (bd. dirs. 1960-61), Inner Circle Advs., VFW, Cosmopolitan Club, Moose. General civil litigation, Labor, Personal injury. Home: 120 River Point Cres Portsmouth VA 23707-1028 Office: Moody Strople & Kloeppel Ltd 500 Crawford St Portsmouth VA 23704-3844

MOOG, MARY ANN PIMLEY, lawyer; b. Havre, Mont., May 29, 1952; d. Orville Leonard and Della Mae (Cole) Pimley; m. Daren Russell Moog, Apr. 15, 1978; children: Eric John, Keith Cole, Trygg Orville. BS, Mont. State U., 1975; JD, U. Mont., 1981; LLM, NYU, 1983. Bar: Mont. Law clk. Mont. Supreme Ct., Helena, 1981-82; assoc., ptnr., staff atty. Bosch, Kuhr, Dugdale, Martin & Kaze, Havre, 1984—. Recipient Am. Jurisprudence Book award Lawyers Coop. Publ. Co., 1980-81, Tax award Prentice Hall, Inc., 1981, Northwestern Union Trust Co. award, 1981. Mem. ABA, Mont. Bar Assn., 12th Jud. Bar Assn. (pres. 1987-88), Phi Delta Phi. Democrat. Roman Catholic. Avocations: sports, arts and crafts, photography. Estate planning, Estate taxation, Personal income taxation. Home: 925 Wilson Ave Havre MT 59501-4331 Office: Bosch Kuhr Dugdale Martin & Kaze PO Box 7152 Havre MT 59501-7152

MOOL, DEANNA S. lawyer; AB in Econs., U. Ill., 1987, JD, 1990. Bar: Ill. 1990, Ind. 1990. Atty. Locke Reynolds Boyd & Weisell, Indpls., 1990-92; gen. counsel Ill. House Minority Leader, Springfield, 1992-94, Speaker's Office, Ill. Ho. of Reps., Springfield, 1994-95, Ill. Dept. Pub. Health, Springfield, 1995—. Mem. U. Ill. Alumni Assn. (bd. dirs. 1995—). Office: Ill Dept Pub Health 535 W Jefferson St Springfield IL 62761-0002 E-mail: dmool@idph.state.il.us

MOON, RONALD T. Y. state supreme court chief justice; b. Sept. 4, 1940; m. Stella H. Moon. B in Psychology and Sociology, Coe Coll., 1962, LLD, 2001; LLB, U. Iowa, 1965. Bailiff, law clk. to Chief Judge Martin Pence U.S. Dist. Ct., 1965-66; dep. prosecutor City and County of Honolulu, 1966-68; assoc. Libkuman, Ventura, Ayabe, Chong & Nishimoto (predecessor firm Libkuman, Ventura, Moon & Ayabe), Honolulu, 1968-72, ptnr., 1972-82; judge 9th div. 1st cir., Cir. Ct., State of Hawaii, 1982-90; assoc. justice Supreme Ct., State of Hawaii, 1990-93, chief justice, 1993—. Adj. prof. law U. Hawaii, 1986, 87, 88; lectr., guest spkr. numerous events. Mem. ABA, Hawaii Bar Assn., Assn. Trial Lawyers Am., Am. Bd. Trial Advocates (pres. 1986-93, nat. sec. 1989-91), Am. Inns of Cts. IV (bencher 1983—), Am. Judicature Soc., Hawaii Trial Judges' Assn., Conf. Chief Justices (bd. dirs.). Office: Supreme Ct Hawaii 417 S King St Honolulu HI 96813-2902 E-mail: cjrmoon@yahoo.com

MOONEY, JEROME HENRI, lawyer; b. Salt Lake City, Aug. 7, 1944; s. Jerome Henri and Bonnie (Shepherd) M.; m. Carolyn Lasrich, Aug. 10, 1965 (div. Dec. 1978); 1 child, Dierdre Nicole; m. Kaitlyn Cardon, Sept. 23, 1995. BS, U. Utah, 1966, JD, 1972. Bar: Utah 1972, Calif. 1998, U.S. Ct. Appeals (10th cir.) 1974, U.S. Supreme 1984, U.S. Ct. Appeals (7th cir.) 1999. Sole practice, Salt Lake City, 1972-75, 79-83; sr. ptnr. Mooney, Jorgenson & Nakamura, 1975-78, Mooney & Smith, Salt Lake City, 1983-87, Mooney & Assoc., Salt Lake City, 1987-94, Mooney Law Firm, Salt Lake City, 1995-98, Larsen & Mooney Law, Salt Lake City, 1999—. Bd. dirs. Mooney Real Estate, Salt Lake City. Mem. Gov.'s Coun. on Vet. Affiars, Salt Lake City, 1982-89; trustee Project Realty, Salt Lake City, 1976—, P.E.A.C.E.; SAMHSA sponsor Project Reality, 1994—; vice chair State Mil. Acad. Assoc. USANG, 1992-93. Mem. ABA (criminal justice sect. U.S. Sentencing Commn. com.), Utah Bar Assn. (chmn. criminal bar sect. 1987-88), Nat. Assn. Recording Industry Profls., Utah NG Assn. (trustee 1976), 1st Amendment Lawyers Assn. (v.p. 1986-88, pres. 1988-89), Nat. Assn. Criminal Def. Lawyers, Families Against Mandatory Minimums (adv. coun.), VFW. Democrat. Jewish. Avocations: sailng, computers. Criminal, Entertainment. Home: 128 I St Salt Lake City UT 84103-3418 Office: 50 W Broadway Ste 100 Salt Lake City UT 84101-2066 E-mail: JerryM@MooneyLaw.com

MOONEY, MICHAEL EDWARD, lawyer; b. Beloit, Wis., Jan. 21, 1945; s. William C. and Edith (Slothower) M. BA in Econs., St. Norbert Coll., 1966; JD, Boston Coll., 1969. Bar: Mass. 1969, Maine 1969, U.S. Tax Ct. 1975, U.S. Ct. Internat. Trade 1986. Assoc. Nutter, McClennen & Fish, LLP, Boston, 1969-77, sr. ptnr., 1978—, now mng. ptnr. V.p., exec. dir. Fed. Tax Inst. New Eng.; spkr., lectr. numerous seminars. Co-editor: Considerations in Buying or Selling a Business, 1985; mem. bd. editors Accounting for Law Firms, 1988—. Bd. dirs. Lincoln and Therese Filene Found., Boston, Alliance Francaise of Boston, 1987-97, Artery Bus. Com., Internat. Bus. Ctr. New Eng., 1986-89; clk. U.S.S. Constn. Bicentennial Salute, Inc. Fellow Am. Coll. Tax Counsel; mem. Boston Bar Assn. (chmn. tax highlights com. 1986-95, mem. fin. com. 1990-92), Boston Tax Forum, Boston Ptnrs. in Edn. (lawyers fund com.). General corporate, Corporate taxation, Personal income taxation. Office: Nutter McClennen & Fish 1 International Pl Boston MA 02110-2699 E-mail: mem@nutter.com

MOONEY, THOMAS ROBERT, lawyer; b. Montclair, N.J., June 16, 1933; s. Thomas Edward and Ruth Evelyn (Meurling) M.; m. Mary Frances Davis, Aug. 23, 1958; children: Terrance Kevin, Rebecca Lee Poyner, Thomas Edward. BA in Econs., Fla. So. Coll., Lakeland, 1956; LLB, JD, Stetson U., 1961. BAr: Fla. 1961, Ga. 1962, U.S. Dist. Ct. (mid. dist.) 1964, U.S. Supreme Ct. 1965. Claims adjuster State Farm Mut. Ins. Co., Atlanta, 1961-63; atty. Maguire, Voorhis & Wells, P.A., Orlando, Fla., 1963-64, Meyers & Mooney, P.A., Orlando, 1964-94, Meyers, Mooney Stanley & Hollingsworth, Orlando, 1994—. Chair Workers Compensation Ednl. Conf., Fla., 1980-81. Chmn. bd. dirs. Epilepsy Assn. Ctrl. Fla., Orlando, 1964-67; bd. dirs. Children's Home Soc., Orlando, 1970-75, chmn., 1970-72. 1st lt. U.S. Army, 1956-58, Korea. Mem. ATLA, ABA, Fla. Bar Assn., Ga. Bar Assn., Acad. Fla. Trial Lawyers (chair workers compensation sect. 1985), Fla. Workers Advocates (bd. dirs. 1992—). Democrat. Methodist. Avocations: skiing, golf, travel, hiking, rafting. Personal injury, Workers' compensation. Office: Meyers Mooney Stanley & Hollingsworth P A 17 Lake Ave Orlando FL 32801-2730

MOORE, ANDREW GIVEN TOBIAS, II, investment banker, law educator; b. New Orleans, Nov. 25, 1935; m. Ann Elizabeth Dawson, June 5, 1965; children— Cecily Elizabeth, Marianne Dawson. B.B.A., Tulane U., 1958, J.D., 1960. Bar: La. 1960, Del. 1963. Law clk. to chief justice Del., Dover, 1963; assoc. firm Killoran & Van Brunt, Wilmington, Del., 1964-70, partner, 1971-76; partner firm Connolly, Bove & Lodge, Wilmington, 1976-82; justice Del. Supreme Ct., 1982-94; sr. mng. dir. Wasserstein Perella & Co., Inc., N.Y.C., 1994—. Mem. Del. Bar Examiners, 1975-82; mem. Del. Gen. Corp. law com., 1969-83; chmn. joint com. Del. Bar Assn.-Del. Bankers Assn., 1978-79; chmn. Del. Jud. Proprieties Com., 1983-94, Del. Bench and Bar Conf., 1988-94; trustee Del. Bar Found., 1984-94; faculty Tulane Inst. European Legal Studies, Paris Inst., 1990-96, 99; adj. prof. law Georgetown U. Law Ctr., Widener U. Sch. Law, U. Iowa Coll. Law; guest lectr. law Columbia U., Tulane U., U. Toronto, Can., U. Tex., Villanova U., Washington U., St. Louis, U. Iowa, George Mason U., DeVrije U. van Brussel, Cath. U. Louvain La Neuve; mem. pres.'s coun. Tulane U., 1990-96; chmn. Tulane Corp. Law Inst., 1988-95; Lehmann disting. vis. prof. law Washington U., St. Louis, 1994, 96; Mason Ladd disting. vis. prof. U. Iowa, 1995; disting. vis. prof. law St. Louis U., 1995, 96, 99; bd. dirs. Am. Lawyer Media, Inc. Trustee Del. Home and Hosp. for Chronically Ill, Smyrna, 1966-70, chmn., 1966-69; mem. New Castle County Hist. Rev. Bd., Wilmington, 1974-82; mem. Del. Cts. Planning Com., 1982-94; dean's coun. Tulane U. Law Sch., 1988-96; bd. visitors Walter F. George Sch. Law, Mercer U., 1985-91, chmn., 1988-90. With JAGC, USAF, 1960-63. Mem. ABA, La. Bar Assn., Del. Bar Assn. (v.p. 1976-77, exec. com. 1982-83), Am. Judicature Soc. (bd. dirs. 1982-86), Order Barristers, Phi Delta Phi, Delta Theta Phi (hon.), Omicron Delta Kappa Democrat. Presbyterian. Office: Dresdner Kleinwort Wasserstein Inc 1301 Ave of the Americas New York NY 10019

MOORE, ARTHUR WILLIAM, retired lawyer; b. Erie, Pa., Feb. 10, 1920; s. Arthur Gordon and Barbara P. (Dillon) M.; m. Geraldine Marie O'Brien, Apr. 5, 1943; children: Christopher A., Mary Judith Moore Salva. BS in Econs., U. Pa., 1941; LLB, Georgetown U., 1948. Bar: Ohio 1949, D.C. 1950, U.S. Tax Ct. 1966, U.S. Supreme Ct. 1974. Ptnr. Taggart, Cox, Moore & Hays, Wooster, Ohio, 1949-70; pvt. practice, 1970-82; resident prin. lawyer Buckingham, Doolittle & Burroughs LPA, 1982-92, of counsel, 1992-93; ret., 1993. Sec. Wooster Products, Inc., 1954-82, Magni Power Co., Wooster, 1954-82, Magni-Fab Ga. Inc., Thomaston, Ga., 1978-88, also bd. dirs. Bd. dirs., trustee YMCA, Wooster, 1975-83; tax appeals bd. City of Wooster, 1983-93; chmn. Wooster chpt. ARC, 1984-86. Maj. AUS, 1942-46, ETO. Decorated Bronze Star; recipient Pope John Benemerenti medal Cath. Ch., 1978. Mem. ABA, Ohio State Bar Assn., Wayne County Bar Assn. (pres. 1975), Kiwanis (pres. 1956, lt gov. 1958). Roman Catholic. Avocation: golf. General corporate, Probate, Taxation, general. Home: 6360 Pelican Bay Blvd #PH3C Naples FL 34108 Office: Buckingham Doolittle & Burroughs PA 3397 Oak Hill Rd Wooster OH 44691-9085

MOORE, BRADFORD L. lawyer; b. Brownfield, Tex., Feb. 9, 1952; s. Billie Buell and Jimmy (Green) M.; m. Carmelita Chaffin, June 20, 1971; children: April V., Ashli F. BA, Tex. Tech U., 1974, JD, 1977. Bar: Tex. 1978, U.S. Dist. Ct. (no. dist.) Tex. 1978, U.S. Dist. Ct. (we. dist.) Tex. 1987, U.S. Supreme Ct. 1987. V.p. McGowan & McGowan PC, Brownfield, 1978-90; pvt. practice, 1990—; mayor city of Brownfield, 1998-2000. Pres. Brownfield Little Girls Basketball, 1987-90. Recipient award for outstanding representation of abused children Tex. Dept. Human Svcs., 1984. Mem. Brownfield Bar Assn. (social chmn. 1980—), Rotary (sgt.-at-arms Brownfield 1980-81, pres. 1997-98), Kiwanis (pres. Brownfield 1984-86). General civil litigation, Contracts commercial, General corporate. Office: PO Box 352 Brownfield TX 79316-0352

MOORE, CHRISTOPHER MINOR, lawyer; b. L.A., Oct. 12, 1938; s. Prentiss Elder and Josephine (French) M.; m. Gillian Reed, Sept. 29, 1965; children: Stephanie Kia Conn, Carrie Christine McKay. AB, Stanford U., 1961; JD, Harvard U., 1964. Dep. county counsel L.A. County Counsel, 1965-66; ptnr. Moore & Lindelof, L.A., 1966-69, Burkley & Moore, Torrance, Calif., 1969-74; pvt. practice Law Offices of Christopher Moore, 1974-81; ptnr. Burkley, Moore, Greenberg & Lyman, 1981-90; prin. Christopher M. Moore & Assoc., 1990-2000, Moore, Bryan & Schroff, Torrance, 2000—. Mem. bd. edn. Palos Verdes (Calif.) Peninsula Unified Sch. Dist., 1972-77. Fellow Am. Coll. Trust and Estate Counsel, Am. Acad. Matrimonial Lawyers; mem. L.A. Yacht Club, Palos Verde Golf Club. Avocations: sailing, golf. Estate planning, Family and matrimonial, Probate. Office: Moore Bryan & Schroff Ste 490 21515 Hawthorne Blvd Torrance CA 90503-6525 E-mail: chris@cmoorelaw.com

MOORE, EDWARD WARREN, lawyer; b. Odessa, Tex., July 21, 1959; s. Edward Warren and Gloria (Schroeter) M.; m. JoAnne Bisso; children: Peggy, Barbara. BS in Econs., Princeton U., 1981; JD, So. Meth. U., 1984. Bar: Tex. 1984, U.S. Dist. Ct. (no. dist.) Tex. 1984, U.S. Ct. Appeals (5th cir.) 1984, U.S. Ct. Appeals (10th cir.) 1985. Assoc. Ravkind, Kuehne & Biesel, Dallas, 1984-85; ptnr. Kuehne & Moore, 1984-96; pvt. practice, 1996-2000; mng. ptnr. Moore & Anderson. Vol. Park Cities YMCA, Ronald McDonald Ho. Mem. AAAS, ABA (litigation sect., trial practice sect. and com., product liability, antitrust, intellectual property sect.), ATLA (toxic, environ. and pharm. litigation sect., comml. litigation sect.), State Bar Tex., Dallas Bar Assn., Tex. Trial Lawyers Assn., Dallas Country Club. Methodist. General civil litigation, Intellectual property, Product liability. Home: 3832 Villanova St Dallas TX 75225-5219 E-mail: eddymoor@sprynet.com

MOORE, FRANCIS XAVIER, lawyer; b. Bklyn., May 12, 1933; s. Michael Joseph and Catharine Agnes (Shea) M.; m. Harriet Joan Rogers; children: Christine Mari, Ann-Therese, Francis X. Jr., Tara Louise-Colby, Timothy Rogers. BS, Fordham U., 1955, LLB, LLD, 1960. Bar: N.Y. 1961, N.J. 1961, U.S. Dist. Ct. N.J. 1961, U.S. Dist. Ct. N.Y. (so. and ea. dist.)1961, U.S. Supreme Ct. 1976. Cert. chem. breath test experts, DUI def. lawyer. Ptnr. Meyer, Ferrara, Moore, N.Y.C., 1960; assoc. Durand, Ivins, Carton, Asbury Park, N.J., 1960-63; dep. atty. gen. State of N.J., Trenton, 1963-64, N.J. spl. rep. to U.S. Senate subcom. organized crime Washington, 1964-65; ptnr. Sorenson and Moore, Atlantic Highlands, N.J., 1965-68, McGowan, Saling, Bolglo, Moore, Eatontown, 1968-76, Moore, Coogan, Feldman, Red Bank, 1976-80; prin., sr. ptnr. Francis X. Moore and Assocs., 1980—. Mem. N.J. Sup. Ct. Improvement, Trenton, 1984-92, N.J. State Bar Mcpl. Comm., New Brunswick, N.J., 1994—, Nat. Coll. Driving Under Influence Defense Regent, Houston, 1992—. Author: Defense of Drunk Driving, 1990, (manual) National College-Defense, 1996; contbr.

articles to profl. jours. Anchor Club scholar N.Y.C. Police Dept., 1948, Hayden grant Planatarium Fordham U., 1951; recipient Honor Legion award N.J. Police Depts., Woodbridge, N.J., 1994. Mem. ABA, N.J. State Bar Assn., N.J. Criminal Defense Lawyers, Monmouth Bar Assn. (trustee 1962—, pres. 1975-76), Kiwanis Internat. (local chpt., past pres.), Friendly Sons St. Patrick (local chpt., past pres.), 200 Club (local chpt., bd. dirs.) Roman Cath. Avocations: card, coin, and stamp collections. Appellate, Criminal, General practice. Office: Francis X Moore PA 1806 Rt 35 S Ocean NJ 07712 E-mail: FXM_LAW1@aol.com, jaymond@absolutelynotguilty.com

MOORE, HUGH JACOB, JR. lawyer; b. Norfolk, Va., June 29, 1944; s. Hugh Jacob and Ina Ruth (Hall) M.; m. Jean Garnett, June 10, 1972; children: Lela Miller, Sarah Garnett. BA, Vanderbilt U., 1966; LLB, Yale U., 1969. Bar: Tenn. 1970, U.S. Dist. Ct. (mid. dist.) Tenn. 1970, U.S. Supreme Ct. 1973, U.S. Ct. Appeals (6th cir.) 1973, U.S. Dist. Ct. (ea. dist.) Tenn. 1973, U.S. Dist. Ct. (we. dist.) Tenn. 1982, U.S. Ct. Claims 1993. Law clk. U.S. Dist. Ct. (mid. dist.) Tenn., Nashville, 1969-70; trial atty. civil rights divsn. U.S. Dept. Justice, Washington, 1970-73; asst. U.S. atty. Eastern Dist. of Tenn., Chattanooga, 1973-76; assoc. Witt, Gaither & Whitaker, P.C., 1976-77, shareholder, 1977—, also bd. dirs. Mem. Commn. Women and Minorities Profession Law; mem. hearing com. Bd. Profl. Responsibility Supreme Ct. Tenn.; mem. mediation and arbitration panel U.S. Dist. Ct. (ea. dist.) Tenn.; cert. arbitrator, cert. mediator Tenn. Rule 31 Nat. Assn. Securities Dealers; cert. artbitrator N.Y. Stock Exch., Nat. Arbitration Forum; mem. adv. commn. on rules of civil and appellate procedure Tenn. Supreme Ct., chmn., 1999—. Contbr. articles to profl. jours. Bd. dirs. Adult Edn. Coun., Chattanooga, 1976-81, pres., 1977-79; bd. dirs. Chattanooga Symphony and Opera Assn., 1981-87, Riverbend Fesitval, 1983-85, 91—, pres., 1995-97, Landmarks Chattanooga, 1983-84, Cornerstones, 1995-98, Orange Grove Sch., 1996—; mem. alumni coun. McCallie Sch., 1980-85; trustee St. Nicholas Sch., 1983-89, chmn., 1986-88. Fellow Am. Coll. Trial Lawyers, Tenn. State Com., Tenn. Bar Found., Chattanooga Bar Found.; mem. ABA (mem. bd. editors jour. Litigation News 1983-90), Tenn. Bar Assn., Am. Bar Found., Chattanooga Bar Assn. (mem. bd. govs. 1985-87), Mountain City Club, Rotary. Methodist. Federal civil litigation, General civil litigation, Criminal. Home: 101 Ridgeside Rd Chattanooga TN 37411-1830 Office: Witt Gaither & Whitaker 1100 SunTrust Bank Bldg Chattanooga TN 37402 E-mail: hmoore@wgwlaw.com

MOORE, JAMES E. state supreme court justice; b. Laurens, S.C., Mar. 13, 1936; s. Roy Ernest and Marie (Hill) M.; m. Mary Alicia Deadwyler, Jan. 27, 1963; children: Erin Alicia, Travis Warren. BA, Duke U., 1958, JD, 1961. Bar: S.C. 1961, U.S. Dist. Ct. S.C. 1961. Pvt. practice, Greenwood, S.C., 1961-76; cir. judge 8th Jud. Cir. S.C., 1976-91; assoc. justice S.C. Supreme Ct., 1992—. State supreme court justice; b. Laurens, S.C., Mar. 13, 1936; s. Roy Ernest and Marie (Hill) M.; m. Mary Alicia Deadwyler, Jan. 27, 1963; children— Erin Alicia, Travis Warren. B.A., Duke U., 1958, J.D., 1961. Bar: S.C. 1961, U.S. Dist. Ct. S.C. 1961. pvt. practice, Greenwood, S.C., 1961-76; cir. judge 8th Jud. Cir. S.C., Greenwood, 1976-1991; Assoc. Justice S.C. Supreme Ct., 1992—; Mem. S.C. Ho. of Reps., Columbia, 1968-76. Mem. S.C. Bar Assn., ABA, Am. Judicature Soc. Baptist. Mem. S.C. Ho. of Reps., Columbia, 1968-76. Mem. ABA, S.C. Bar Assn., Am. Judicature Soc. Baptist. Home: 148 Amherst Dr Greenwood SC 29649-8901 Office: PO Box 277 Greenwood SC 29648-0277

MOORE, JOHN CORDELL, retired lawyer; b. Winchester, Ill., July 20, 1912; s. John Clayton and Winifred (Peak) M.; m. Pauline Ruyle, July 29, 1939 (dec. 1979); m. Wilma K. Smith Jackson, Aug. 1981. A.B., Ill. Coll., 1936, LL.D., 1967; LL.B., Georgetown U., 1949, J.D., 1967; postgrad. in geology, Am. U., 1955-57. Bar: Tenn., U.S. Supreme Ct. Rep. Universal Credit Co., St. Louis, 1937-39; tchr. Capitol Page Sch.; also clk. to mem. Ho. of Reps., 1939-41; examiner Metals Res. Co., 1941-42; exec. dir. Fgn. Liquidation Commn. for S. and C. Am., Balboa, C.Z., 1946-47; with Office Alien Property, Dept. Justice, 1947-50; asst. dir. property mgmt. Interior Dept., 1950-52, dir. security for dept., 1952-61; adminstr. Oil Import Adminstrn., 1961-65, asst. sec. for mineral resources, 1965-69; ret. U.S. rep. oil and energy com. OECD, Paris, 1965-69; former dir. Clark Oil, Milw. Served to comdr. USNR, 1942-46; capt. Res. Mem. Am. Legion, Scott County (Winchester, Ill.) Hist. Soc. (life), Delta Theta Phi, Elks, Army-Navy Club, Jacksonville Country Club.

MOORE, KAREN NELSON, judge; b. Washington, Nov. 19, 1948; d. Roger S. and Myrtle (Gill) Nelson; m. Kenneth Cameron Moore, June 22, 1974; children— Roger C., Kenneth N., Kristin K. A.B. magna cum laude, Radcliffe Coll., 1970, J.D. magna cum laude, Harvard U., 1973. Bar: D.C. 1973, Ohio, 1976, U.S. Ct. Appeals (D.C. cir.) 1974, U.S. Supreme Ct. 1980, U.S. Ct. Appeals (6th cir.) 1984. Law clk. Judge Malcolm Wilkey, U.S. Ct. Appeals (D.C. cir.), 1973-74; law clk. Assoc. Justice Harry A. Blackmun, U.S. Supreme Ct., Washington, 1974-75; assoc. Jones, Day, Reavis & Pogue, Cleve., 1975-77; asst. prof. Case Western Res. Law Sch., Cleve., 1977-80, assoc. prof., 1980-82, prof., 1982-95; judge U.S. Ct. Appeals (6th cir.), Cleve., 1995—; vis. prof. Harvard Law Sch., 1990-91. Mem. Harvard Law Rev., 1971-73. Contbr. articles to legal publs. Trustee Lakewood Hosp., Ohio, 1978-85, Radcliffe Coll., Cambridge, 1980-84. Fellow Am. Bar Found.; mem. Am. Law Inst., Harvard Alumni Assn. (bd. dirs. 1984-87), Phi Beta Kappa. Office: US Ct Appeals 6th Cir 328 US Courthouse 201 Superior Ave E Cleveland OH 44114-1201

MOORE, KENNETH CAMERON, lawyer; b. Chgo., Oct. 25, 1947; s. Kenneth Edwards and Margaret Elizabeth (Cameron) M.; m. Karen M. Nelson, June 22, 1974; children: Roger Cameron, Kenneth Nelson, Kristin Karen. BA summa cum laude, Hiram Coll., 1969; JD cum laude, Harvard U., 1973. Bar: Ohio 1973, U.S. Dist. Ct. Md. 1974, U.S. Ct. Appeals (4th cir.) 1974, D.C. 1975, U.S. Dist. Ct. (no. dist.) Ohio 1976, U.S. Ct. Appeals (6th cir.) 1977, U.S. Ct. Appeals (D.C. cir.) 1979, U.S. Supreme Ct. 1980. Law clk. to judge Harrison L. Winter U.S. Ct. Appeals (4th cir.), Balt., 1973-74; assoc. Squire, Sanders & Dempsey, Washington, 1974-75, Cleve., 1975-82, ptnr., 1982—, mem. fin. com., 1990—, profl. ethics ptnr., 1996—. Chmn. Ohio Fin. Com. for Jimmy Carter presdl. campaign, 1976; del. Dem. Nat. Conv., 1976; chief legal counsel Ohio Carter-Mondale Campaign, 1976; trustee Hiram Coll., 1997—, mem. exec. com., 1999, chair audit com., 1999, vice chair bd. trustees, 2000—, chair faculty affairs subcom. of edn. policy com., 2000—. With AUS, 1970-76. Mem. ABA, Fed. Bar Assn., Ohio Bar Assn., Cleve. Bar Assn., Cleve. City Club. Federal civil litigation, State civil litigation, Environmental. Home: 15602 Edgewater Dr Cleveland OH 44107-1212 Office: Squire Sanders & Dempsey 4900 Society Ctr 127 Public Sq Ste 4900 Cleveland OH 44114-1304

MOORE, MARIANNA GAY, law librarian, consultant; b. La Grange, Ga., Sept. 12, 1939; d. James Henry and Avanelle (Gay) M. AB in French, English, U. Ga., 1961; MLS, Emory U., 1964; postgrad., U. Ga., 1965-66, U. Ill., 1967-68. Asst. law libr. U. Ga., Athens, 1964-66; asst. libr. Yavapai Coll. Libr., Prescott, Ariz., 1969-72; libr. U. Ill. Law Libr., Urbana, 1966-68; law libr. Leva, Hawes, Symington, Washington, 1972-75; libr. project coord. Wash. Occupational Info. Svc., Olympia, 1976-80, Wash. State Health Facilities Assn., Olympia, 1981-82; mgr. Wash. State Ret. Tchrs. Assn., 1982-83, exec. dir., 1984-89, Wash. State Retired Tchrs. Found., Olympia, 1986-89; law libr. Solano County Law Libr., Fairfield, Calif., 1989—. Libr. LIBRARY/USA N.Y. World's Fair, N.Y.C., 1965; consulting law libr. Dobbins, Weir, Thompson & Stephenson, Vacaville, Calif., 1989—; law libr. cons. Coconino County Law Libr., Flagstaff, Ariz., 1968-70. Author: Guide to Fin. Aid for Wash. State Students, 1979; tng. package to introduce librs. to Wash. State Info. Svc., 1980; indexer for Calif. Coun. of County Law Libr.'s publ. For Your Information, 1999—; contbg. author Solano County Bar Assn. pub. VOIR DIRE. Bd. dirs. Thurston County Sr. Ctr., Olympia, 1976-84, Thurston-Mason Nutrition Program, Olympia, 1977-79, Wash. Soc. Assn. Execs., Edmonds, 1987-89. Mem. Am. Assn. Law Librs., No. Calif. Assn. Law Librs., Calif. Coun. of County Law Librs. Avocations: reading, tatting, travel, music, calligraphy, cats. Office: Solano County Law Libr Hall of Justice 600 Union Ave Fairfield CA 94533-6324 E-mail: mmoore@solanocounty.com

MOORE, MARILYN PAYNE, lawyer; b. Summit, N.J., Sept. 2, 1970; d. Ervin Carroll and Rosemary M. BA in Polit. Sci., Spanish and Sociology, Rice U., 1992; JD, U. Houston, 1995. Bar: Tex. 1995. Assoc. corp. and securities sect. Bracewell & Patterson LLP, Houston, 1995-97; assoc. internat. and corp. and securities sects. Baker & McKenzie, Dallas, 1997—. Dir. John C. Ford Program, Dallas, 1998—. Contbr. articles to profl. jours. Ct. appointed adv. abused children Child Advs., Inc., Houston, 1995-97. Mem. ABA (mem. internat. and bus. sects. 1996—), Dallas Bar Assn. (mem. internat. sect., mem. corp. sect.), Women in Internat. Trade Tex. Avocations: traveling, writing, tennis, horseback riding. General corporate, Private international, Securities. Office: Baker & McKenzie 2001 Ross Ave Ste 2300 Dallas TX 75201-2984

MOORE, MCPHERSON DORSETT, lawyer; b. Pine Bluff, Ark., Mar. 1, 1947; s. Arl Van and Jesse (Dorsett) M. BS, U. Miss., 1970; JD, U. Ark., 1974. Bar: Ark. 1974, Mo. 1975, U.S. Patent and Trademark Office 1977, U.S. Dist. Ct. (ea. dist.) Mo. 1977, U.S. Ct. Appeals (8th, 10th and fed. cirs.). Design engr. Tenneco, Newport News, Va., 1970-71; assoc. Rogers, Eilers & Howell, St. Louis, 1974-80; ptnr. Rogers, Howell, Moore & Haferkamp, 1981-89, Armstrong, Teasdale, Schlafly & Davis, St. Louis, 1989-95, Polster, Lieder, Woodruff & Lucchesi, St. Louis, 1995—. Engr. City of Ladue, Mo., 1998-2000. Bd. dirs. Legal Svcs. Ea. Mo.; mem. Ladue Zoning and Planning Commn., 1998—. With USAR, 1970-76. Mem. ABA, Bar Assn. Met. St. Louis (chmn. young lawyers sect. 1981-82, sec. 1984-85, v.p. 1985-86, chmn. trial sect. 1986-87, pres. 1988-89), Ark. Bar Assn., St. Louis Bar Found. (sec. 1984-85, v.p. 1988-89, pres. 1989-90), The Mo. Bar (chmn. patent, trademark and copyright law com. 1992-94, co-chmn. 1994-95), St. Louis County Bar Assn., Women Lawyers Assn., Am. Intellectual Property Law Assn., Mound City Bar Assn., Phi Delta Theta Alumni (treas. St. Louis chpt. 1987-88, sec. 1988-89, v.p. 1989-90), Racquet Club (St. Louis). Federal civil litigation, Patent, Trademark and copyright. Home: 33 Deerfield Rd Saint Louis MO 63124-1412 Office: Polster Lieder Woodruff & Lucchesi 763 S New Ballas Rd Ste 160 Saint Louis MO 63141-8750

MOORE, MICHAEL T. lawyer; b. Mullins, S.C., Feb. 21, 1948; s. Claude Richard and Melinda Doris (Stone) M.; m. Leslie Jean Lott, Nov. 12, 1978; children: Michael T. Jr., Emmett Russell Lott. BA, U. Fla., 1970, JD, 1974. Assoc. Burlingham, Underwood & Lord, N.Y.C., 1974-77, Hassan, Mahassni, Burlington, Underwood & Lord, Jeddah, Saudi Arabia, 1977-79; ptnr. Holland & Knight, Miami, Fla., 1982—, bd. dirs., 1986—, exec. ptnr. Miami office, 1993—. Bd. dirs. Marine Arbitration Bd., Inc., Miami, 1985—; pres. The Marine Coun., 1989-90. Editor-in-chief Southern District Digest, 1980-82; contbr. articles to profl. jours. Mem. Orange Bowl Com.; bd. dirs. United Way Greater Miami, 1994—, U.S. Sailing Ctr., YMCA; chmn. Alexis de Tocqueville Soc.; mem. Miami River Coordinating Com.; trustee St. Stephens Sch.; chancellor St. Stephens Episc. Ch., 2000—; mem. Coral Gables (Fla.) Youth Adv. Bd.; chmn. bd. dirs. Fla. Guard Found. Mem. ABA, Maritime Law Assn. U.S., Fla. Bar Assn., Dade County Bar Assn. (bd. dirs. 1981—, Outstanding Young Lawyer award 1982), Adms. of the Fleet of Fla. (pres.). Republican. Admiralty, Personal injury, Transportation. Home: 3515 Anderson Rd Miami FL 33134-7050 Office: Holland & Knight 701 Brickell Ave Flr 30 PO Box 15441 Miami FL 33131-5441

MOORE, MIKE, state attorney general; m. Tisha Moore; 1 child, Kyle. Grad., Jackson County Jr. Coll., 1972; BA, U. Miss., 1974, JD, 1976. Asst. dist. atty. State of Miss., 1977-78, dist. atty., 1979, atty. gen., 1988—. Office: Office of Atty Gen PO Box 220 Jackson MS 39205-0220*

MOORE, MITCHELL JAY, lawyer, law educator; b. Lincoln, Nebr., Aug. 29, 1954; s. Earl J. and Betty Marie (Zimmerlin) M.; m. Sharon Lea Campbell, Sept. 5, 1987. BS in Edn., U. Mo., Columbia, 1977, JD, 1981. Bar: Mo. 1981, U.S. Dist. Ct. (we. dist.) Mo. 1981, Tex. 1982, U.S. Ct. Appeals (8th cir.) 1998. Sole practice, Columbia, Mo., 1981—. Coordinating atty. student legal svcs. ctr. U. Mo., Columbia, 1983-89. Mem. Columbia Substance Abuse Adv. Commn., 1989—; bd. dirs. Planned Parenthood of Ctrl. Mo., Columbia, 1984-86, Opportunities Unltd., Columbia, 1984-86, ACLU of Mid-Mo., 1991-98; Libertarian candidate for Atty. Gen. of Mo., 1992, 2000, for 9th congl. dist. U.S. Ho. of Reps., 1994, 96, for Mo. State Rep. 23d dist., 1998, for Atty. Gen. Mo., 2000; mem. Probation and Parole Citizens Adv. Bd., 1997-99. Mem. Boone County Bar Assn., Assn. Trial Lawyers Am., Phi Delta Phi. Libertarian. Unitarian. Avocations: softball, camping. Criminal, Family and matrimonial, Personal injury. Office: 1210 W Broadway Columbia MO 65203-2126 E-mail: mmoore259@home.com

MOORE, RICHARD WAYNE, prosecutor; b. Bartow, Fla., Dec. 5, 1952; s. James Ferrell and Mary Etta (Carlisle) M.; m. Elizabeth Ann Mitchell, Sept. 1, 1984; children: Michaelan Susan, John Mark. BS summa cum laude, Spring Hill Coll., 1974; JD, Samford U., 1977. Bar: Ala. 1977, U.S. Dist. Ct. Ala. 1977. Assoc. Marr & Friedlander, Mobile, Ala., 1977-79; ptnr. Sherling, Drinkard & Moore, 1979-81; assoc. Gibbs & Craze, Cleve., 1981-85; sr. litigation counsel U.S. Atty.'s Office, Mobile, 1985—. Atlantic fellow in Pub. Policy U.K., Oxford, Eng., 1997. Mem. Mobile County Bar Assn., Paul Brock Mobile Inn of Ct. Anglican. Avocations: fox hunring. Office: U S Attys Office So Dist of Alabama 69 S Royal St Mobile AL 36602

MOORE, ROBERT MADISON, food industry executive, lawyer; b. New Orleans, June 21, 1925; s. Clarence Greer and Anna Omega (Odendahl) M.; m. Evelyn Eileen Varva, Apr. 11, 1953; children: Eileen Alexandria Moore Wynne, John Greer. BBA, Tulane U., 1947; JD, U. Va., 1952; LLM (Food Law Inst. fellow), NYU, 1953. Bar: La. 1956, Calif. 1972. Asst. to pres., gen. counsel Underwear Inst., N.Y.C., 1953-55; pvt. practice law New Orleans, 1955-56; asst. gen. atty., dir. Legal services, sec. and gen. atty. Standard Fruit & Steamship Co., 1957-72; v.p., gen. counsel Castle & Cooke Foods, 1972-81, Castle & Cooke, Inc., 1973-81, sr. v.p. law and govt., 1981-82; pres. Internat. Banana Assn., 1983-98; acting exec. dir. Pan Am. Devel. Found., 1999. Dir. Ferson Optics of Del., Inc., 1958-69, Baltime Securities Corp., Pan American Devel. Found. Asst. atty. gen., La., 1958-63. Served with AUS, 1943-46. Mem. ABA, Calif. Bar Assn., La. Bar Assn., SAR (sec. 1960-61), KM, Cosmos Club, Phi Delta Phi, Alpha Tau Omega. Democrat. Roman Catholic. Home: 3323 R St NW Washington DC 20007-2310 E-mail: rmevmoore@aol.com

MOORE, ROY F. lawyer; b. Detroit, June 13, 1950; s. Roy Flint Jr. and Doris Ellen (Murphy) M. BA with distinction, Wayne State U., 1975, JD, 1979. Bar: Mich. 1979, U.S. Dist. Ct. (ea. dist.) Mich. 1979, U.S. Tax Ct. 1985. Mgmt. asst. Moore Signs, Inc., Detroit, 1968-77; freelance labor cons., 1977-79; assoc. James A. Brescoll, PC, Mt. Clemens, 1980-83, Wright & Goldstein PC, Birmingham, 1983-88, mng. ptnr., 1986-88; pvt. practice, 1988-95; v.p., gen. counsel Federated Capital Corp., Farmington Hills, 1995—. Tutor Psi Chi, Detroit, 1973; rsch. asst. conflict resolution Wayne State U., Detroit, 1974; rsch. asst. legal philosophy, 1977. Patron Detroit Inst. Arts Founders Soc., 1983—. Mem. ABA (comml., banking and fin. transactions litigation com. 1984—), Mich. Bar Assn., Fed. Bar Assn., Detroit Bar Assn., Macomb Bar Assn., Phi Beta Kappa. Lutheran. Contracts commercial, General corporate, Finance. Office: 30955 Northwestern Hwy Farmington Hills MI 48334-2580 E-mail: rmoore@federatedcapital.com

MOORE, ROY S. judge; m. Kayla Moore; children: Heather, Roy, Caleb, Micah. BS, U.S. Mil. Acad., 1969; JD, U. Ala., 1977. Dep. dist. atty. Etowah County, Ala., 1977—82; pvt. practice Gadsden, 1982—92; cir. judge 16th Judicial Cir., 1992—2001; chief justice Ala. Supreme Ct., 2001—. Republican. Baptist. Office: Ala Supreme Ct 300 Dexter Ave Montgomery AL 36104-3741*

MOORE, STANLEY RAY, lawyer; b. Dallas, July 20, 1946; s. Elzey and Heloise (Dillon) M.; m. Sherri Boren; children: Natalie, William, Julie, Colin, Brendan, Rosie. BSME, So. Meth. U., 1969, JD, 1973. Bar: Tex. 1973, U.S. Dist. Ct. (no. dist.) Tex. 1974. Assoc. Clegg, Cantrell, Crisman, Dallas, 1973-75; ptnr. Crisman & Moore, 1975-80, Schley Cantrell & Moore, Dallas, 1980-83, Schley, Cantrell, Kice & Moore, Dallas, 1983-87, Johnson & Wortley, P.C., Dallas, 1987-94, Jenkens & Gilchrist, Dallas, 1995—. Patentee in field. Foster parent Hope Cottage, Dallas, 1982-90; fund raiser Am. Heart Assn., YMCA, rep. Orgn. Recipient Outstanding Leadership commendation ASME, 1969. Mem. ABA, Dallas Bar Assn. Patent, Trademark and copyright. Home: 1 Victoria Cir Rowlett TX 75088-6059 Office: Jenkens & Gilchrist 1445 Ross Ave Ste 3200 Dallas TX 75202-2785 E-mail: smoore@jenkens.com

MOORE, STEPHEN JAMES, lawyer; b. Kansas City, Mo., Aug. 9, 1947; s. James Andrew and Frances Clare (Kennedy) M. BSBA, Rockhurst Coll., 1969, BA, 1975; JD, U. Mo., Kansas City, 1977, LLM, 1997. Bar: Mo. 1978, U.S. Dist. Ct. (we. dist.) Mo. 1978, U.S. Ct. Appeals (8th cir.) 1980, U.S. Ct. Appeals (10th cir.) 1981, U.S. Ct. Fed. Claims 1991, U.S. Ct. Appeals (6th cir.) 1997. Law intern Mo. Atty. Gen.'s Office, Kansas City, 1976-77, asst., 1978; assoc. Popham, Conway, Sweeny, Fremont & Bundschu PC, 1978-84, Freilich, Leitner & Carlisle, PC, Kansas City, 1985, Herrick, Feinstein, Kansas City, 1985-86, Freilich, Leitner, Carlisle & Shortlidge, Kansas City, 1986-90; ptnr. Freilich, Leitner & Carlisle, Kansas City, Dallas, L.A., 1987-2000, Aspen, Colo., 1997-2000, Peters, Moore & Jones, LLC, Kansas City, Mo., 2001—. Adj. prof. law U. Mo., Kansas City, 1995—. Mem. Friends of Art, Nelson-Atkins Mus. Art, Kansas City, 1988—, Smithsonian Inst., Washington, 1985—, Nat. Trust for Historic Preservation, Washington, 1988—, Libr. of Congress Assocs., The Federalist Soc., Nat. Audubon Soc. Mem. ABA, Assn. Trial Lawyers Am., Kansas City Metro Bar Assn., Sports Car Club Am., Am. Mus. Nat. History, Porsche Club Am., Lake Ozarks Yacht Assn., Boat Owners Assn. U.S., Ancient Order of Hibernians, Delta Theta Phi, Tau Kappa Epsilon. Roman Catholic. Avocations: vintage sportscars, boating. Land use and zoning (including planning), Municipal (including bonds), Real property. Home: 5840 McGee St Kansas City MO 64113-2132 Office: Peters Moore & Jones LLC 916 Traders on Grand Bldg 1125 Grand Ave Kansas City MO 64106 E-mail: moore@pmj-law.com

MOORE, THOMAS RONALD (LORD BRIDESTOWE), lawyer; b. Duluth, Minn., Mar. 27, 1932; s. Ralph Henry and Estelle Marguerite (Hero) M.; m. Margaret C. King, Sept. 10, 1955; children: Willard S., Clarissa, Charles R.H. BA magna cum laude, Yale U., 1954; JD, Harvard U., 1957. Bar: N.Y. 1958, U.S. Supreme Ct. 1965. Instr. Harvard Law Sch., 1956-57; with Dewey Ballantine, N.Y.C.; ptnr. Breed, Abbott & Morgan, Finley Kumble & Wagner, N.Y.C., Hawkins, Delafield & Wood, N.Y.C.; Law Offices of Thomas R. Moore. Lectr. on law Cornell Law Sch., NYU, Practising Law Inst., N.Y.C., Las Vegas, New Orleans; lectr. Oxford, N.Y.C., San Antonio, Tampa, L.A., Moscow, Charlottesville, Washington, Kansas City. Author: Plantagenet Descent, 31 Generations from William the Conqueror to Today, 1995; co-author: Estate Planning and the Close Corporation; editor-in-chief Gastronome; bd. editors: The Tax Lawyer; contbr. articles to profl jours., popular press and TV commentaries. Bd. dirs. exec. com. Citymeals on Wheels; pres. bd. dirs. Nat. Soc. to Prevent Blindness, 1973-81, chmn., 1981-83, now hon. pres.; sec.-treas., trustee A.D. Henderson Found., Del.; trustee, Fla.; bd. dirs. Phoenix Theatre Inc., Inst. Aegean Prehistory, Found. Future of Man, Am. and Internat. Friends of Victoria and Albert Mus., London; conservator N.Y. Pub. Libr.; trustee Found. for Renaissance of St. Petersburg (Russia), Malcolm Wiener Found., Lawrence W. Levine Found. Recipient Coat of Arms and created Knight of St. John, Queen Elizabeth II, Order of Crown of Charlemagne, Order of Plantagenet, Order of Barons of Magna Charta, Descendants Knights of the Garter, Key to Kansas City, Mayor of Kansas City, Mo., 1989, Thomas R. Moore Disting. Pub. Servant award, Nat. Soc. to Prevent Blindness; scholar Yale, 1954. Mem. ABA, N.Y. State Bar Assn. (exec. com.), Assn. of Bar City of N.Y., Confrerie de la Chaine des Rotisseurs (nat. pres., dir., exec. com. world coun. Paris), Chevalier du Tastevin, Nat. Wine Coalition (bd. dirs. 1989—), The Pilgrims, St. George Soc., St. Andrews Soc., Robert Burns Soc., Downtown Assn., Univ. Club, Church Club, Delta Sigma Rho. Republican. Episcopalian. General civil litigation, Estate planning, Taxation, general. Office: 730 5th Ave Ste 900 New York NY 10019-4105

MOORE, THURSTON ROACH, lawyer; b. Memphis, Dec. 10, 1946; s. Richard Charlton Moore and Halcyon Hall (Roach) Lynn; m. Corell Luckhardt Halsey, Sept. 26, 1998. BA with distinction, U. Va., 1968, JD, 1974. Bar: Va. 1974. Rsch. analyst Scudder, Stevens & Clark, N.Y.C., 1968-71; ptnr. Hunton & Williams, Richmond, Va., 1974—. Bd. dirs. Met. Advantage Corp., Richmond. Mary Morton Parsons Found. Charlottesville, Va., The Nature Conservancy, Charlottesville, chmn. Va. chpt.; trustee Va. Aerospace Bus. Roundtable, Hampton, 1989—, Va. Ea. Shore Sustainable Devel. Corp., 1995-2000. Mem. ABA (bus. law sect., chmn. ptnrs. com. 1992-96, mem. fed. regulation security com., bus. law coun.), Va. Bar Assn., Va. State Bar. Office: Hunton & Williams Riverfront Plz E Tower 951 E Byrd St Richmond VA 23219-4074

MOORHEAD, WILLIAM DAVID, III, lawyer, corporate executive; b. Knoxville, Tenn., Aug. 13, 1952; s. William David an dVirginia (Wood) M.; m. Thelma Rogena Murray, Sept. 4, 1976; children: John Murray, Virginia Salima. BBA, U. Ga., 1973, JD, 1976. Bar: Tenn. 1976, U.S. Dist. Ct. (ea. dst.) Tenn. 1976, Ga. 1977, U.S. Tax Ct. 1977, U.S. Ct. Claims 1985, U.S. Supreme Ct. 1985. Assoc. Stophel, Caldwell 7 Heggie, Chattanooga, 1976-77; ptnr. Murray & Moorhead, Americus, Ga., 1977-80, Vansant, Corriere & Moorhead, P.C., Albany, 1981-85; propr. William D. Moorhead III, P.C., 1991—. Pres. Continental Consol. Corp., Albany, 1983-87, W.D. Moorhead & Co., Albany, 1984-87; sec., gen. coun. Daylight Industries Inc., Atlanta, 1989-90, pres. 1990-91; pres. Medication Mgmt. Inc., 1997—. De. Ga. Dem. Com., 1978; chmn. edn. task force, Albany C. of C., 1989-90, bd. trustees Deerfield-Windsor Sch., 1993-2000; mem. Ctrl. Bapt. Ch., Albany, 1982—, deacon, 1992—, chmn., 1996-99. Vassar Wooley scholar, 1973-76. Mem. Tenn. Bar Assn., Ga. Bar Assn., Dougherty County Bar Assn., Albany Estate Planning Coun. (v.p. 1982-83). Baptist. General corporate, Probate, Estate taxation. Home: 3509 Old Dawson Rd Albany GA 31707-1555 Office: William D Moorhead III PC 314 W Residence Ave Albany GA 31701-2319 E-mail: wdm3@bellsouth.net

MORALES, JULIO K. lawyer; b. Havana, Cuba, Jan. 17, 1948; came to U.S., 1960; s. Julio E. and Josephine (Holsters) M.; m. Suzette M. Dussault, May 31, 1970 (div. 1978); children: Julio E., Karel A.; m. Barbara A. Miller, July 14, 1979 (div. 1988); 1 child, Nicolas W. BA, Carroll Coll., 1969; JD, U. Mont., 1972. Bar: Mont. 1972, U.S. Dist. Ct.

Mont. 1972, U.S. Ct. Mil. Appeals 1972, U.S. Ct. Appeals (9th cir.) 1980. Law clk. to presiding justice Mont. Supreme Ct., Helena, 1972; sole practice Missoula, Mont., 1973-78, 88—; sr. ptnr. Morales & Volinkaty, 1978-88; pvt. practice law Morales Law Office, 1988—. Author: Estate Planning for the Handicapped, 1975. Pres. Rockmont, Inc., Missoula, 1985-2001. Served to 2d lt. U.S. Army, 1972. Named Boss of the Yr., Missoula chpt. Mont. Assn. Legal Secs., 1988. Mem. ABA (dist. rep. 1975-79, exec. coun. young lawyer divsn. 1977-79), Mont. Bar Assn. (chmn. law day 1974, 75, 77), Am. Judicature Soc., Assn. Trial Lawyers Am., World Assn. Lawyers, Missoula Soccer Assn. (pres. 1983-85), Mont. Sailing Assn. (bd. dirs. 1994—), Nat. Exch. Club (bd. dirs. Yellowstone dist. 1987-88, pres. 1990-91), Missoula Exch. Club, Elks (officer 1999-2001, exalted ruler 2001—), Phi Delta Phi. Roman Catholic. Avocations: sports, coaching youth, boating, skiing, golf. Personal injury, Probate, Workers' compensation. Office: PO Box 9311 430 Ryman St Missoula MT 59802-4249 E-mail: jmorales@dsnetworks.net

MORAN, HAROLD JOSEPH, retired lawyer; b. N.Y.C., Feb. 21, 1907; s. Thomas J. and Leonore M.F. (Geoghegan) M.; A.B. cum laude, Holy Cross Coll., 1928; LL.B., Fordham U., 1932; J.D., 1968; m. Geraldine D. Starkey, July 12, 1956. Admitted to N.Y. bar, 1934; practiced in N.Y.C., 1934-42, Bklyn., 1949-57, Malverne, N.Y., 1977— ; law dept. Title Guarantee & Trust Co., Bklyn., 1945-48; sr. atty. real property bur. N.Y. State Law Dept., Albany, 1957-63, N.Y.C., 1963-77, ret., 1977; spl. dep. atty. gen. election frauds, 1973. Title closer City Title Co., Bklyn., 1949-52; U.S., P.R. mortgage loan examiner Cadwalader, Wickersham & Taft, N.Y.C., 1952-56, 63— , 9th Fed. Savs. & Loan Assn., N.Y.C., 1971— ; instr. law St. John's U. Sch. Commerce, Jamaica, N.Y., 1956-57. Served with AUS, 1942-45. Knight Holy Sepulchre. Mem. Am. Bar Assn., Bar Assn. Nassau County, Am. Judicature Soc., N.Y. County Lawyers Assn., Catholic Lawyers Guild. Democrat. Roman Catholic. Club: Southward Ho Country.

MORAN, JAMES BYRON, federal judge; b. Evanston, Ill., June 20, 1930; s. James Edward and Kathryn (Horton) M.; children: John, Jennifer, Sarah, Polly; stepchildren: Katie, Cynthia, Laura, Michael. AB, U. Mich., 1952; LLB magna cum laude, Harvard U., 1957. Bar: Ill. 1958. Law clk. to judge U.S. Ct. of Appeals (2d cir.), 1957-58; assoc. Bell, Boyd, Lloyd, Haddad & Burns, Chgo, 1958-66, ptnr., 1966-79; judge U.S. Dist. Ct. (no. dist.) Ill., Chgo., 1979—. Dir. Com. on Ill. Govt., 1960-78, chmn., 1968-70; vice chmn., sec. Ill. Dangerous Drug Adv. Coun., 1967-74; dir. Gateway Found., 1969— ; mem. Ill. Ho. of Reps., 1965-67; mem. Evanston City Council, 1971-75. Served with AUS, 1952-54. Mem. Chgo. Bar Assn., Chgo. Council Lawyers, Lawyers Club, Phi Beta Kappa. Home: 117 Kedzie St Evanston IL 60202-2509 Office: US Dist Ct 219 S Dearborn St Ste 2050 Chicago IL 60604-1800 E-mail: jbm117@aol.com

MORAN, RACHEL, lawyer, educator; b. Kansas City, Mo., June 27, 1956; d. Thomas Albert and Josephine (Portillo) M. AB, Stanford U., 1978; JD, Yale U., 1981. Bar: Calif. 1984. Assoc Heller, Ehrman, White & McAuliffe, San Francisco, 1982-83; prof. law U. Calif., Berkeley, 1984—, Robert D. and Leslie-Kay Raven prof. law, 1998—. Vis. prof. UCLA Sch. Law, 1988, Stanford (Calif.) U. Law Sch., 1989, N.Y.U. Sch. of Law, 1996, U. Miami Sch. Law, 1997, U. Tex. Law Sch., 2000; chair Chicano/Latino Policy Project, 1993-96. Contbr. numerous articles to profl. jours. Recipient Disting. Tchg. award U. Calif. Mem. ABA, Assn. of Am. Law Schs. (mem. exec. com.), Am. Law Inst., Calif. Bar Assn., Phi Beta Kappa. Democrat. Unitarian. Avocations: jogging, aerobics, reading, listening to music. Office: U Calif Sch Law Boalt Hall Berkeley CA 94720

MORAVSIK, ROBERT JAMES, lawyer; b. Jersey City, Sept. 21, 1942; s. Charles B. and Marie A. (Hoppe) M.; children: Barry, Athena (dec.), Shane; m. Anne B. Wyman, July 29, 1984. BS in Aero. Engring., Tri-State U., 1962; MMS, Stevens Inst. Tech., 1969; JD, Seton Hall U., 1978. Bar: N.J. 1978, U.S. Dist. Ct. N.J. 1978, U.S. Supreme Ct. 1986, N.Y. 1988. Sr. engr. Curtiss Wright Corp., Fairfield, N.J., 1963-66; mgr. Fisher Stevens Inc., Totowa, 1966-78, v.p., gen. counsel, 1978-87; v.p., gen. counsel, sec. Biosearch Med. Products, Inc., Somerville, 1987—; sr. v.p., gen. counsel, sec. Hydromer, 1998—. Councilman Boro of Ringwood, N.J., 1974; pres. Par Troy Condominium Assn., Parsippany, N.J., 1984—. Mem. ABA, N.J. Bar Assn., Am. Corp. Counsel Assn. Computer, General corporate, General practice. Fax: 908-526-3633. E-mail: bob@moravsik.net, rjmoravs@hydromer.com

MORD, IRVING CONRAD, II, lawyer; b. Mar. 22, 1950; s. Irving Conrad and Lillie Viva (Chapman) M.; m. Julia Ann Russell, Aug. 22, 1970 (div. Apr. 1980); children: Russell Conrad, Emily Ann; m. Kay E. McDaniel, Aug. 31, 1985; children: Kurt August, Clayton Troy. BS, Miss. State U., 1972; JD, U. Miss., 1974. Bar: Miss. 1974, U.S. Dist. Ct. (no. dist.) Miss. 1974, U.S. Dist. Ct. (so. dist.) Miss. 1984. Counsel to bd. suprs. Noxubee County, Miss., 1976-80, Walthall County, 1980—, Bd. Edn., Walthall County, 1982—. County pros. atty. Noxubee County, Miss., Macon, 1974-80, Walthall County, Tylertown, 1982-88, 91-96; mem. local workforce investment bd., 2000—. Bd. dirs. East Miss. Coun., Meridian, 1978-80, Trustmark Nat. Bank, Tylertown, 1986—; v.p. Macon coun. Boy Scouts Am., 1978, mem. coun., 1979; county crusade chmn. Am. Cancer Soc., Macon, 1976-78, county pres., 1979; chmn. fund dr. fine arts complex Miss. State U., Macon, 1979; Walthall County family master, 1996—, Walthall County Youth referee, 1996—; mem. Local Workforce Investment Bd., 2000—. Recipient Youth Leadership award Miss. Econ. Coun., 1976. Mem. Miss. Assn. Bd. Attys. (v.p. 1985, pres. 1986), Miss. Assn. Sch. Bd. Attys., Miss. State Bar, Am. Judicature Soc. (Torts award 1972), Nat. Fed. Ind. Bus., Miss. State U. Alumni Assn., Walthall County C. of C., Phi Kappa Tau (bd. govs. 1976-80, grad. coun. 1972—, pres. grad. coun. 1977-80, pres. house corp. 1977-80, Alumnus of Yr. Alpha Chi chpt. 1979), Rotary (sec.-treas. 1977, v.p. 1978, pres. Macon 1979, pres. Tylertown club 1986-87), Phi Delta Phi. E-mila. Office: 729 Beulah Ave Tylertown MS 39667-2709 E-mail: icmord@telapex.com

MOREIRA, BARBARA LYNE, lawyer; b. N.Y.C., May 27, 1966; d. Antone F. and Barbara A. Moreira. BA, Boston Coll., 1988, JD, 1996. Bar: Mass. 1997, U.S. Dist. Ct. Mass. 1998. Law clk. to Judge Karen Jenneman, Orlando, Fla., 1996-97; assoc. Peabody & Brown, Boston, 1997-98, Kearns & Rubin, Boston, 1998—. Mem. ABA, Boston Bar Assn. Bankruptcy, General civil litigation, Labor. Office: Kearns & Rubin 60 State St Boston MA 02109

MORELLI, CARMEN, lawyer; b. Oct. 30, 1922; s. Joseph and Helen (Carani) Morelli; m. Irene Edna Montminy, June 26, 1943; children: Richard A., Mark D., Carl J. BSBA, Boston U., 1949, JD, 1952. Bar: Conn. 1955, U.S. Dist. Ct. Conn. 1958. Asst. prosecutor Town of Windsor, 1957—58; mem. Conn. Ho. of Reps., 1959—61; atty. Town of Windsor, 1961; rep. Capitol Regional Planning Agy., 1965—72. Mem. Windsor Town Com., 1957—82, chmn., 1964—65, treas., 1960—64, mem. planning and zoning commn., 1965—74, mem. charter revision com., 1963—64; rep. Presdl. Task Force. Served with USN, 1943—45. Mem.: ABA, conn. Bar Assn., Hartford Bar Assn., Am. Arbitration Assn., Windsor Bar Assn. (pres. 1979), Windsor C. of C. (v.p. 1978), Elks, Rotary (sgt. arms, sec. 1989—90, pres. 1990—91). Roman Catholic. General practice, Personal injury, Probate. Home: 41 Farmstead Ln Windsor CT 06095-1834 Office: 66 Maple Ave Windsor CT 06095-2926

MOREN, CHARLES VERNER, lawyer, judge; b. Webster, Wis., Jan. 29, 1920; s. John Arthur and Jennie Marie (Anderson) M.; m. Sylvia Jene Smith, Mar. 15, 1946 (div.); m. Donna Rae McFarland, Sept. 22, 1982; children— Marie, Leslie, Stephen, James, John, Daniel. B.A., U. Minn., 1942, LL.B., 1948. Bar: Minn. 1948, Wash. 1954, U.S. Dist. Ct. (we. dist.) Wash. 1956. Trial atty. Mpls. St. Ry. Co., 1948-50; sole practice, Anoka, Minn., 1951-52; assoc. Bundlie, Kelley, Finley & Maun, St. Paul, 1952-53; asst. city atty. City of Seattle, 1954-55; atty. Gen. Ins. Co., Seattle, 1955-56; ptnr. Keller, Rohrback, Waldo, Moren & Hiscock, Seattle, 1957-75, Moren Lageschulte & Cornell, Seattle, 1975-88, Moren Cornell & Hansen, 1988—; city atty. City of Lake Forest Park, Wash., 1963-65, judge mcpl. ct., 1970-90. Co-founder City of Lake Forest Park, Seattle, 1963, Served to lt. USN, 1942-46, PTO. Mem. ABA, Minn. Bar Assn., Wash. State Bar Assn., Am. Arbitration Assn., Assn. Trial Lawyers Am., Full Gospel Businessmens Fellowship (bd. dirs. Seattle chpt. 1975-78). Republican. State civil litigation, Personal injury. Home: 134 Ravens Ridge Rd Sequim WA 98382-3829 Office: Moren Cornell & Hansen 11320 Roosevelt Way NE Seattle WA 98125-6228

MORENO, FERNANDO, lawyer, educator; b. Santurce, P.R., Oct. 17, 1934; s. Esteban and Maria (Salas) M.; m. Rosario Gonzalez, Dec. 21, 1957; children: Rosario, Esteban, Marie, Fernando. BA, U. P.R., 1955, postgrad. in pub. adminstrn., 1955-56, JD magna cum laude, 1973; LLM in Ocean and Coastal Law, U. Miami, 1982, PhD, 1998. Bar: P.R. 1974, U.S. Dist. Ct. P.R. 1974, U.S. Ct. Appeals (1st cir.) 1974. Treas. Gonzalez R. Investment Corp., P.R., 1958-79, dir., 1958-83; lectr. Sch. Law, U.P.R., 1973-79; law lectr. marine sci. program U. Miami, 1982—. Office mgr., personnel dir., in-house counselor at law, dir. Gonzalez Rodriguez Investment Corp., Catalan Gonzalez & Co., Inc., Indsl. Gonzalez, Inc., Santurce, 1958-79. Mem. U. P.R. Law Rev., 1971-73, chmn. San Juan Mail Users Coun., 1968. Mem. ABA, P.R. Bar Assn., P.R. Philatelic Soc. (founder 1952, pres. 1967-68), Sigma Xi. Home: 1811 SW 99th Pl Miami FL 33165-7552 E-mail: fmoreno@rsmas.miami.edu

MORGAN, DANIEL LOUIS, lawyer, educator; b. Newark, Oct. 17, 1952; s. A. Henry and Eunice (Neubauer) M. BA in History, Tufts U., 1974; JD, U. Conn., 1977; LLM, Georgetown U., 1981. Bar: Conn. 1977, D.C. 1978. Atty., advisor, chief counsel IRS, Washington, 1977-81; assoc. Tucker, Flyer & Lewis P.C., 1981-85, prin., 1985-99; ptnr. Venable, Baetjer & Howard, LLP, 2000—. Adj. prof. Cath. U. Law Sch., Washington, 1984-96; profl. lectr. in law George Washington U. Law Sch., 1997—; charter fellow Am. Coll. Employee Benefits Counsel. Co-author: The 401(K) Handbook, 1991, Employees and Independent Contractors, 1990; adv. bd. Jour. Taxation of Employee Benefits; mem. bd. contbrs. Employee Benefits for Non-Profits; contbr. articles to profl. jours. Fellow Am. Coll. Employee Benefits Counsel (charter); mem. ABA (chmn. tax sect. com. on employment taxes 1986-88), D.C. Bar Assn. (sect. taxation and employee benefits com., chmn. employee benefits com. 1998-2000). General corporate, Pension, profit-sharing, and employee benefits, Taxation, general. Office: Venable, Baetjer & Howard LLP 1201 New York Ave Ste 1000 Washington DC 20005-3917

MORGAN, DENNIS RICHARD, lawyer; b. Jan. 3, 1942; s. Richard and Gladys Belle (Brown) Morgan. BA, Washington and Lee U., 1964; JD, U. Va., 1967; LLM in Labor Law, NYU, 1971. Bar: Ohio 1967, Va. 1967, U.S. Ct. Appeals (4th cir.) 1968, U.S. Ct. Appeals (6th cir.) 1971, U.S. Supreme Ct. 1972. Law clk. to chief judge U.S. dit. Ct. (ea. dist.) Va., 1967—68; mem. Marshman, Snyder & Seeley, Cleve., 1971—72; dir. labor rels. Ohio Dept. Adminstrv. Svcs., 1972—75; asst. city atty. Columbus, Ohio, 1975—77; dir. Ohio Legis. Reference Bur., 1979—81; assoc. Clemans, Nelson & Assocs., 1981; pvt. practice, 1978—92. Lectr. in field; guest lectr. Cen. Mich. U., 1975; judge moot ct. Ohio State U. Sch. Law, 1981, 83, grad. divsn., 73, 74, 76; guest lectr. Baldwin-Wallace Coll., 1973; legal counsel Dist. IV Comms. Workers Am., 1982—88; pers. dir. Pub. Utilities Commn., Ohio, 1989—91; asst. atty. gen. State of Ohio, 1991—. Negotiator Franklin County United Way, 1977—81; regional chmn. ann. alumni fund-raising program U. Va. Sch. Law; mem. Greater Hilltop Area Commn., 1989—; pres. Woodbrook Village Condominium Assn., 1985—; trustee Hilltop Civic Coun., Inc., 1997—99; vice-chmn. Franklin County Dem. Party, 1976—82; dem. com. person Ward 58, Columbus, 1973—95; chmn. rules com. Ohio State Dem. Conv., 1974; co-founder, trustee Greater West Side Dem. Club; bd. dir. Hilltop Civic Coun., Inc., 1997—99. Capt. U.S. Army, 1968—70. Recipient Am. Jurisprudence award, 1967; scholar Robert E. Lee Rsch., 1965. Mem.: ABA, Indsl. Rels. Rsch. Assn., Fed. Bar Assn., Am. Judicature Soc., Columbus Metropolitan club (charter), Pi Sigma Alpha. Roman Catholic. Administrative and regulatory, Labor, Legislative. Home: 1261 Woodbrook Ln # G Columbus OH 43223-3243

MORGAN, DONALD CRANE, lawyer; b. Detroit, Sept. 17, 1940; s. Donald Nye and Nancy (Crane) M.; m. Judith Munro, June 23, 1962; children: Wendy, Donald. BA, Ohio Wesleyan U., 1962; JD, U. Mich., 1965. Bar: Mich. 1966, U.S. Dist. Ct. (ea. dist.) Mich. 1966, U.S. Ct. Appeals (6th cir.) 1967, U.S. Supreme Ct. 1971. Ptnr. Kerr, Russell and Weber, Detroit, 1965-87; of counsel Draugelis & Ashton, Plymouth, Mich., 1988-93; pvt. practice, 1993—. Twp. atty. Plymouth Twp., 1970-85, Northville Twp., 1972-85; city atty. City of Plymouth, 1995-98; mediator Wayne County Mediation Tribunal, Detroit, 1981—, Oakland County Mediation Tribunal, Pontiac, Mich., 1992—; hearing panelist Mich. Atty. Discipline Bd., 1981—. Chmn. Wayne County II congl. Dist. Rep. Party, 1979-81; bd. dirs. Growth Works, Inc., treas., 1992-95, pres. 1995-99; ruling elder 1st Presbyn. Ch., Plymouth, 1976-79, 90-93; local bd. 222 mem. U.S. Selective Svc. Sys.; mem. spl. grants and agy. admissions com. United Way Cmty. Svcs. Paul Harris fellow, 1980. Mem. ABA, Mich. Def. Trial Counsel, State Bar of Mich. (rep. assembly 1979-85, 89-95, chmn. medicolegal problems com. 1995-96), Oakland County Bar Assn., Detroit Assn. Def. Trial Counsel, Plymouth Rotary (pres. 1985-86), Plymouth Rotary Found., Inc. (sec. 1996-98, dir. 1995, 99—), Phi Alpha Delta, Sigma Alpha Epsilon, Pi Sigma Alpha. Republican. Presbyterian. Avocations: reading, travel, sports. General civil litigation, General corporate, Real property. Home: 1440 Woodland Pl Plymouth MI 48170-1569 Office: 134 N Main St Plymouth MI 48170-1236 E-mail: morganlaw@aol.com

MORGAN, HENRY COKE, JR. judge; b. Norfolk, Va., Feb. 8, 1935; s. Henry Coke and Dorothy Lea (Pebworth) M.; m. Margaret John McGrail, Aug. 18, 1965; children: A. Robertson Hanckel Jr., Catherine Morgan Stockwell, Coke Morgan Stewart. BS, Washington and Lee U., 1957, JD, 1960; LLM in Jud. Process, U. Va., 1998. Bar: Va. 1960, U.S. Dist. Ct. (ea. dist.) Va. 1961, U.S. Ct. Appeals (4th cir.) 1964. Asst. city atty. City of Norfolk, 1960-63; ptnr. Pender & Coward, Virginia Beach, Va., 1963-92; vice chmn., gen. counsel Princess Anne Bank, 1986-92; judge U.S. Dist. Ct. (ea. dist.) Va., 1992—. Served with U.S. Army, 1958-59. Episcopalian. E-mail: henry. Office: US Dist Ct Eastern Dist Va Walter E Hoffman US Courthouse 600 Granby St Ste 183 Norfolk VA 23510-1915 E-mail: morgan@vaec.uscourts.gov

MORGAN, KERMIT JOHNSON, lawyer; b. Henderson, Iowa, Feb. 13, 1914; s. Samuel Jr. and Jennie Amelia Morgan; m. Georgina R. Morgan, Oct. 12, 1940 (dec. 1958); children: Georgina Morgan Street, Wilson S.; m. Ortrud Impol, Dec. 9, 1960. BA, U. Iowa, 1935; JD, U. So. Calif., 1937. Bar: Calif. 1939. Pvt. practice, L.A., 1940-45, 71-80; ptnr. McBain & Morgan, 1945-65, McBain, Morgan & Roper, L.A., 1965-71, Morgan & Armbrister, L.A., 1980-91; pvt. practice, Santa Monica, Calif., 1991—. Mem. ABA, Am. Bd. Trial Advs. (diplomate, nat. pres. 1973, pres. L.A. 1972, 77), Assn. Def. Trial Attys. (bd. dirs. 1982-85), Internat. Assn. Ins. Counsel, Hon. Order of Blue Goose, Calif. State Bar, Assn. Def. Trial Attys., Assn. So. Calif. Def. Counsel (bd. dirs. 1966-67), L.A. Bar Assn., Wilshire Bar Assn. Republican. Congregationalist. Avocation: golf. Insurance, Personal injury. Home: 2108 Stradella Rd Los Angeles CA 90077-2325 Office: 2850 Ocean Park Bld Santa Monica CA 90405

MORGAN, MARY ANN, lawyer; b. Orlando, Fla., Mar. 12, 1955; d. Charles Clayburn and Eileen Louise (Mutzbauer) M.; m. Patrick Thomas Burke, Dec. 12, 1992. BS in Criminology, Fla. State U., 1978, JD, 1986. Bar: Fla. 1986, U.S. Dist. Ct. (mid. dist.) Fla. 1986, U.S. Supreme Ct. Investigator Auditor Gen.'s Office State of Fla., Orlando, 1979-83; staff analyst criminal justice com. Fla. Ho. of Reps., Tallahassee, 1985-86; ptnr. Billings, Cunningham, Morgan & Boatwright, Orlando, 1986—. Chmn. renovation com. Orange County Hist. Mus., Orlando, 1995—; spkr. Physician/Lawyer Drug Awareness Program, Orange County Schs., Orlando, 1997. Mem. ABA, ATLA, Fla. Bar Assn. (spkrs. bur. 1997, chair grievance com. 1993-96, vice chair 9th jud. cir. fee arbitration com.), Orange County Bar Assn. (exec. coun. 1991—, chmn. renovation com. 1995—, del. ABA 1989, 90, pres. young lawyers sect. 1990-91, pres. 2001—), Acad. Fla. Trial Lawyers, Ctrl. Fla. Assn. for Women Lawyers (bd. dirs. 1990-92), Fla. State U. Alumni Assn. (bd. dirs. 1996—), Orange County Legal Aid Soc. (bd. dirs. 1997—, pres.-elect 1998-99, pres. 1999—), Nat. Assn. Women Lawyers, Am. Inns of Ct., Tiger Bay Club, Million Dollar Advs. Club. Avocations: waterskiing, golf, boating. General civil litigation, Personal injury. Office: Billings Cunningham Morgan & Boatwright 330 E Central Blvd Orlando FL 32801-1921

MORGAN, RICHARD GREER, lawyer; b. Houston, Dec. 23, 1943; s. John Benjamin (stepfather) and Audrey Valley (Brickwede) Haus; children: Richard Greer, Jonathan Roberts. AB in History, Princeton U., 1966; JD, U. Tex., 1969. Bar: Tex. 1969, D.C. 1970, Minn. 1976, U.S. Ct. Appeals (D.C. cir.) 1970, U.S. Ct. Appeals (5th and 9th cirs., temporary emergency ct. appeals) 1976. Atty., advisor to commr. Lawrence J. O'Connor, Jr. Fed. Power Commn., Washington, 1969-71; assoc. Morgan, Lewis & Bockius, 1971-75; ptnr. O'Connor & Hannan, 1975-89, Lane & Mittendorf, Washington, 1989-97; mng. ptnr. Shook, Hardy & Bacon, L.L.P., Houston, 1997—. Bd. dirs. Hexagon, Inc.; instr. law seminars; lectr. in field. Author: Gas Lease and Royalty Issues, Natural Gas Yearbook, 1989, 90, 91, 92; contbr. articles on energy law to profl. jours. Bd. dirs. Mighty Spl. Music Makers, U. Tex. Law Sch. Found. Mem. ABA, Fed. Bar Assn., Energy Bar Assn. (bd. dirs.), D.C. Bar Assn., Princeton Alumni Coun., Princeton Alumni Assn. Houston, Energy Law Found. (pres.). Contracts commercial, Nuclear power, Oil, gas, and mineral. Office: Shook Hardy and Bacon LLP 600 Travis St Ste 1600 Houston TX 77002-2911

MORGAN, ROBERT HALL, lawyer; b. San Jose, Calif., Oct. 14, 1950; s. William Robert and Willa June (Hall) M.; m. Susan Kay Meyer, June 16, 1972; children: Robert Scott, Ryan William, Cory Benjamin, Nathan Thomas, Katherine Linn. BA, U. Oreg., 1974; MBA, U. Santa Clara, 1975, JD summa cum laude, 1978. Bar: Calif. 1978, U.S. Dist. Ct. (no. dist.) Calif. 1978. Legal extern Supreme Ct. Calif., San Francisco, 1978; pvt. practice law, 1978—; counsel Better Bus. Bur. Santa Clara Valley, Ltd., San Jose, 1980-86. Bd. dirs. Youth Sci. Inst., 1987-92, pres. 1990-92; bd. dirs. Triton Mus. of Art, 1998—; prin. Morgan Law Offices. Mem. Santa Clara County Bar Assn., Assn. Trial Lawyers Am. Democrat. Federal civil litigation, State civil litigation, Probate. Office: Morgan Law Offices 1501 The Alameda San Jose CA 95126-2311

MORGAN, TIMI SUE, lawyer; b. Parsons, Kans., June 16, 1953; d. James Daniel and Iris Mae (Wilson) Baumgardner; m. Rex Michael Morgan, Oct. 28, 1983; children: Tessa Anne, Camma Elizabeth. BS, U. Kans., 1974; JD, So. Meth. U., 1977. Bar: Tex. 1977, U.S. Dist. Ct. (no. dist.) Tex. 1978, U.S. Ct. Appeals (5th cir.) 1979, U.S. Tax Ct. 1980; cert. tax law specialist. Assoc. Gardere & Wynne, Dallas, 1977-79, Akin, Gump, Strauss, Hauer & Feld, Dallas, 1979-83, ptnr., 1984-86; of counsel Stinson, Mag & Fizzell, 1986-88; sole practice, 1988—. Adj. lectr. law So. Meth. U., 1989-90, 92-98. Bd. dirs. Dallas Urban League Inc., 1987-91. Mem. State Bar Tex. (mem. taxation sect.), Dallas Bar Assn., So. Meth. U. Law Alumni Coun. (sec. 1985-86), Order of Coif, Beta Gamma Sigma. Republican. Episcopalian.

MORGANROTH, FRED, lawyer; b. Detroit, Mar. 26, 1938; s. Ben and Grace (Greenfield) M.; m. Janice Marilyn Cohn, June 23, 1963; children: Greg, Candi, Erik. BA, Wayne State U., 1959, JD with distinction, 1961. Bar: Mich. 1961, U.S. Dist. Ct. (ea. dist.) Mich. 1961, U.S. Ct. Claims 1967, U.S. Supreme Ct. 1966; trained matrimonial arbitrator. Ptnr. Greenbaum, Greenbaum & Morganroth, Detroit, 1963-68, Lebenbom, Handler, Brody & Morganroth, Detroit, 1968-70, Lebenbom, Morganroth & Stern, Southfield, Mich., 1971-78; pvt. practice, 1979-83; ptnr. Morganroth & Morganroth P.C., 1983-94, Morganroth, Morganroth, Alexander & Nye, P.C., Birmingham, Mich., 1994-98, Morganroth, Morganroth, Jackman & Kasody, PC, Bloomfield Hills, 1999—. Mem. ABA (family law sect. 1987—), Mich. Bar Assn. (hearing panelist grievance bd. 1975—, Oakland County family law com. 1988—, vice chmn. 1992-93, chair 1993—), State Bar Mich. (mem. family law coun. of family law sect. 1990—, treas. 1993-94, chmn.-elect 1994-95, chmn. 1995-96), Detroit Bar Assn., Oakland Bar Assn. (cir. ct. mediator 1984—), Am. Arbitration Assn. (Oakland County family law com. 1985—, vice chmn. 1992-93, chmn. 1993-94, trained matrimonial arbitrator), Detroit Tennis Club (Farmington, Mich., pres. 1978-82), Charlevoix Country Club. Jewish. Avocations: comml. pilot, golfing. Alternative dispute resolution, Family and matrimonial. Home: 30920 Woodcrest Ct Franklin MI 48025-1435 Office: 40701 Woodward Ave Ste 250 Bloomfield Hills MI 48304 E-mail: fmmman1@aol.com

MORGANROTH, MAYER, lawyer; b. Detroit, Mar. 20, 1931; s. Maurice Jack Morganroth and Sophie (Reisman) Blum; m. Sheila Rubinstein, Aug. 16, 1958; children: Lauri, Jeffrey, Cherie. JD, Detroit Coll. Law, 1954. Bar: Mich. 1955, U.S. Dist. Ct. Mich. 1955, Ohio 1958, U.S. Dist. Ct. (no. dist.) Ohio 1958, U.S. Ct. Appeals (6th cir.) 1968, U.S. Supreme Ct. 1971, N.Y. 1983, U.S. Dist. Ct. N.Y. 1985, U.S. Tax Ct. 1985, U.S. Ct. Appeals (4th cir.) 1985, U.S. Ct. Claims 1986, U.S. Ct. Appeals (2d cir.) 1986, U.S. Ct. Appeals (fed. cir.), U.S. Ct. Appeals (8th cir.) 1994. Sole practice, Detroit, 1955—, N.Y.C., 1983—; ptnr. Morganroth & Morganroth, 1989—. Cons. to lending instns.; lectr. on real estate NYU, 1980—, bus. entities and structures Wayne State U., 1981—; trial atty. in fed. and state jurisdictions, nationwide. Served with USN, 1948-50. Mem. ABA, FBA, N.Y. State Bar Assn., Southfield Bar Assn., Oakland Bar Assn., Assn. Trial Lawyers Am., Assn. Trial Lawyers Mich., Am. Judicature Soc., U.S. Supreme Ct. Hist. Soc., Nat. Criminal Def. Assn., West Bloomfield (Mich.) Club, Fairlane Club (Dearborn, Mich.), Knollwood Country Club, Edgewood Athletic Club (pres. 1963-65). Democrat. Jewish. Federal civil litigation, General civil litigation, Criminal. Office: 3000 Town Ctr Ste 1500 Southfield MI 48075-1186 also: 156 W 56th St Ste 1101 New York NY 10019-3800

MORGANTI, PETER ANTHONY, paralegal; b. Port Chester, N.Y., Oct. 19, 1946; s. Anthony P. and Marie (Sikora) M.; m. Victoria Frances Morganti, July 24, 1977. BA, Loyola U., 1968; MA, Ball State U., 1974; cert. paralegal, Mercy Coll., 1983. Paralegal Dist. Attys' Office, Bronx, N.Y., 1988—. Chmn. Sr. Citizen Commn., Port Chester, 1982; mem. Tamarack Tower Found., Port Chester, 1992; mem. paralegal adv. group Bronx C.C. Mem. Manhattan Paralegal Assn. (v.p. 1995-97, pres. 1997—). Home: 67 Halstead Ave Port Chester NY 10573-2745 Office: Bronx Dist Attys Office 215 E 161st St Bronx NY 10451-3511 E-mail: morgantip@aol.com

MORGENS, WARREN KENDALL, lawyer; b. Oklahoma City, May 25, 1940; s. Alvin Gustav and Helen Alene (McFarland) M. Student, Westminster Coll., Fulton, Mo., 1958-60; BSBA, Washington U., St. Louis, 1962, JD, 1964. Bar: Mo., 1964, U.S. Supreme Ct. 1968, D.C., 1981. Atty. gen. counsel's office SEC, Washington, 1968-69; asst. atty. gen. State of Mo., St. Louis, 1969-72; ptnr. Park, Craft & Morgens, Kansas City, Mo., 1973-76; pvt. practice law, 1976-81; mng. atty. Hoskins. King, McGannon & Hahn, Washington, 1981-85; spl. ptnr. Barnett & Alagia, 1985-89; of counsel Anderson, Hibey, Nauheim & Blair, 1989-93; pvt. practice, 1993—. Bd. dirs. George Washington Nat. Bank, Alexandria, Va., Cmty. Nat. Bank & Trust, Staten Island, N.Y., 1986-87, George Washington Banking Corp., George Washington Fin. Corp., Washington and France. Patron Nat. Symphony, Washington, 1966-68, 81-85, Washington Performing Arts Soc., 1989—, Kansas City Philharmonic, 1974-80, Supreme Ct. Hist. Soc., Washington, 1982—, The Williamsburg (Va.) Found., 1982—. Named one of Outstanding Young Men Am., 1977. Mem. Mo. Bar Assn., D.C. Bar Assn., Univ. Club (St. Louis). Republican. Presbyterian. Avocations: hiking, sailing, fishing, golf. General corporate, Private international, Securities. Office: 1805 Crystal Dr Ste 201 Arlington VA 22202-4402

MORGENSTERN, CONRAD J. lawyer; b. Cleve., Apr. 25, 1924; m. Renee Saltzman, Nov. 4, 1951; children: Jonathan D., Margo Cohen, Richard L., Beth Ann Kuhel. AB, Western Res. U., 1948; LLB, Case Western Res. U., 1949, JD, 1965. Bar: Ohio 1949, Tex. 1985. Pres. Morgenstern & Assocs., Cleve., 1949-87; U.S. trustee Ohio and Mich., 1987-92; sr. v.p. Brown, Gibbons, Lang & Co., 1993—. Founder, sec., bd. dir., gen. legal counsel Midwestern Nat. Life Ins. Co., 1963-75; acting judge Shaker Heights (Ohio) Mcpl. Ct., 1975-87, 92—; pres. Kanwood Cons. Group Ltd., 1998—. Ct. mem. jud. scanning and selection com. Citizens League Cleve., 1975—, moot ct. appellate trial judge Case Western Res. U. Sch. Law; trustee MetroHealth Sys., 1996—; foreman Cuyahoga County Grand Jury, 1997. Mem. Ohio Bar Assn., Greater Cleve. Bar Assn. (unauthorized practice law com., civil liberties com.), Cuyahoga County Bar Assn. (profl. ethics com., grievance com., ins. com., judicial selection com., scanning com., jt. bar assn. judicial seclection com., bankruptcy com. fed. ct. com.), Am. Arbitration Assn. (panelist chmn.). Avocations: tennis, world travel. Bankruptcy, Federal civil litigation, State civil litigation. Office: Brown Gibbons & Co Inc 1111 Superior Ave E Ste 700 Cleveland OH 44114-2507 also: 113 Saint Clair Ave NE # 900 Cleveland OH 44114-1214

MORGENSTERN, ROBERT TERENCE, lawyer; b. N.Y.C., Aug. 23, 1944; s. Carl G. and Jean C. (Madden) M.; m. Nancy G. Golden, June 29, 1968; children: Cynthia, John, Kathryn, Brian. BA, Villanova U., 1966, JD, 1969. Bar: N.J. 1969, U.S. Supreme Ct. 1986; cert. civil trial atty. Assoc. Dolan & Dolan, Newton, N.J., 1969-74, officer, dir., 1975—. Mem. ABA, Assn. Trial Lawyers Am., N.J. Fedn. Planning Officials, Sussex County Bar Assn., N.J. State Bar Assn. (trustee), Rotary. Roman Catholic. State civil litigation, Personal injury, Probate. Home: 44 Deire Dr Sparta NJ 07871-1134 Office: Dolan & Dolan PA 53 Spring St & 1 Legal Ln PO Box D Newton NJ 07860-0605

MORGENTHALER-LEVER, ALISA, lawyer; b. St. Louis, June 3, 1960; d. Gerald Thomas and Mary Louise (Neece) M. BA, S.W. Mo. State U., 1982; JD, Cornell U., 1985. Bar: N.Y. 1986, D.C. 1988, Calif. 1990. Law clk. City of Springfield, Mo., 1981; atty. bd. govs. Fed. Res. Sys., Washington, 1984, staff atty., 1985-86; assoc. Kirkpatrick & Lockhart, 1986-88, Stroock & Stroock & Lavan, Washington, 1988-89; ptnr. Christensen, Miller, Fink, Jacobs, Glaser, Weil & Shapiro, L.A., 1989—. Bd. dirs. L.A. Retarded Citizens Found. Mem. ABA, Calif. Bar Assn. (del. to com. on adminstrn. justice), D.C. Bar Assn., N.Y. Bar Assn., L.A. County Bar Assn., Beverly Hills Bar Assn., Century City Bar Assn., Women Lawyers Assn. of L.A. (bd. dirs.), 3019 Third St. Owners Assn. (bd. dirs.), Order of Omega, Phi Alpha Delta, Rho Lambda, Phi Kappa Phi, Pi Sigma Alpha, Gamma Phi Beta. Banking, General civil litigation. Office: Christensen Miller Fink Jacobs Glaser Weil & Shapiro 2121 Ave Of Stars Fl 18 Los Angeles CA 90067-5010 E-mail: amorgenthaler@chrismill.com

MORGENTHAU, ROBERT MORRIS, prosecutor; b. N.Y.C., July 31, 1919; s. Henry Jr. and Elinor (Fatman) M.; m. Martha Pattridge (dec.); children: Joan, Anne, Elinor, Robert P., Barbara; m. Lucinda Franks, Nov. 19, 1977; children: Joshua, Amy. Grad., Deerfield (Mass.) Acad., 1937; BA, Amherst Coll., 1941, LLD (hon.), 1966; LLB, Yale U., 1948; LLD (hon.), N.Y. Law Sch., 1968, Syracuse Law Sch., 1976, Albany Law Sch., 1982, Colgate U., 1988. Bar: N.Y. 1949. Assoc. firm Patterson Belknap & Webb, N.Y.C., 1948-53, ptnr., 1954-61; U.S. atty. So. Dist. N.Y., 1961-62, 62-70; dist. atty. New York County, 1975—. Former pres. N.Y. State Dist. Attys. Assn.; lectr. London Sch. Econs., 1993. Chmn. Police Athletic League; Dem. candidate for Gov. of N.Y., 1962; bd. dirs. P.R. Legal Def. and Edn. Fund; trustee Baron de Hirsch Fund, Federated Jewish Philanthropies, Temple Emanu-El, N.Y.C.; chmn. Gov.'s Adv. Com. on Sentencing, 1979; counsel N.Y. State Law Enforcement Coun.; mem. N.Y. exec. com. State of Israel Bonds; chmn. A Living Meml. to the Holocaust-Mus. of Jewish Heritage. Lt. comdr. USNR, 1941-45. Recipient Emory Buckner award Fed. Bar Coun., 1983, Yale Citation of Merit, 1982, Fordham-Stein prize, 1988, Thomas Jefferson award in law U. Va., 1991, Brandeis medal U. Louisville, 1995, Omanut award Yeshiva U., 1995, Trumpeter award Nat. Consumers League, 1995, Frank S. Hogan award N.Y. State Dist. Atty's. Assn., 2000, Lone Sailor award USN Meml. Found., 2000; Matheson-Morgenthau Disting. Professorship in Law named in his honor, Va. Law Sch. Fellow Am. Bar Found.; mem. ABA, N.Y. State Bar Assn. (award for Excellence in Pub. Svc. 2001), Assn. of the Bar of the City of N.Y., N.Y. County Lawyers Assn. (Disting. Pub. Svc. award 1993), Amherst Alumni Assn. (hon. pres. 2001), Phi Beta Kappa. Office: Office Dist Atty 1 Hogan Pl New York NY 10013-4311

MORIARTY, GEORGE MARSHALL, lawyer; b. Youngstown, Ohio, Sept. 16, 1942; s. George Albert Moriarty and Caroline (Jones) Bass; m. Elizabeth Bradley Moore, Sept. 11, 1965 (div. 1986); children: Bradley Marshall, Caroline Walden, Sarah Cameron; m. Phyllis A.N. Thompson, May 2, 1998. BA magna cum laude, Harvard U., 1964, LLB magna cum laude, 1968. Bar: Mass. 1969, U.S. Dist. Ct. Mass. 1973, U.S. Ct. Appeals (1st cir.) 1976, U.S. Ct. Appeals (D.C. cir.) 1984, U.S. Claims Ct. 1983, U.S. Supreme Ct. 1976, U.S. Ct. Appeals (2d cir.) 1997. Law clk. to Hon. Bailey Aldrich U.S. Ct. Appeals (1st cir.), Boston, 1968-69; law clk. to Hon. Warren Burger, Hon. Hugo Black, Hon. Potter Stewart, Hon. Byron White U.S. Supreme Ct., Washington, 1969-70; spl. asst. to Hon. Elliot L. Richardson, Dept. Health, Edn. & Welfare, 1970-71, exec. asst., 1971-72; assoc. Ropes & Gray, Boston, 1972-77, ptnr., 1977—. Trustee Boston Athenaeum, Brigham & Women's Hosp., Ptnrs. Cmty. HealthCare, Inc. Mem. ABA, Am. Law Inst., Boston Bar Assn., Somerset Club, Tavern Club, Met. Club. Federal civil litigation, General civil litigation, State civil litigation. Office: Ropes & Gray 1 Internat Pl Boston MA 02110

MORIARTY, HERBERT BERNARD, JR. lawyer; b. Memphis, June 5, 1929; s. Herbert Bernard and Kathleen (Prindaville) M.; m. Mary Louise Chaffee; 6 children. B.A., Vanderbilt, U., 1950, J.D., 1952. Bar: Tenn. 1952, U.S. Supreme Ct. 1956, U.S. Ct. Mil. Appeals 1956. Commr. Shelby County, 1960-66; mem. firm Moriarty & Moriarty, Memphis, gen. ptnr., 1960—; mem. Tenn. State Legislature, 1959-60, Dem. exec. com., 1959-65; lectr. ABA, Am. Law Inst., 1980. Pres., Muscular Dystrophy Assn., 1957-62; dir. Goodwill Industries, 1960-66; chmn. NCCJ, Memphis, 1962, life bd. dirs., 1963— . Served to capt. JAGC USAF, 1952-54. Recipient Disting. Service award, U.S. Jaycees, Memphis, 1963, Disting. Merit Citation, NCCJ, 1968. Mem. ABA, Tenn. Bar Assn., Shelby County Bar Assn., Memphis Bar Assn., Young Lawyers Assn. Memphis (v.p. 1957-58), Am. Legion (adj. Memphis Post 1 1959), Sigma Chi, Delta Theta Phi. Democrat. Roman Catholic. Clubs: University, University (Memphis). Lodge: Kiwanis (bd. dirs. East Memphis chpt. 1974-75). Federal civil litigation, State civil litigation, Environmental. Home: 714 S Prescott St Memphis TN 38111-4217 Office: Moriarty & Moriarty 848 Thistledown Dr Apt 4 Memphis TN 38117-5039

MORISSET, MASON DALE, lawyer; b. Portland, July 10, 1940; s. Gordon Dale and Georgia Adell (Frazier) M.; m. Karen Winberg, Aug. 29, 1970; children— Brian, Colleen, Catharine. B.Mus., Lewis and Clark Coll., Portland, 1963; M.A., U. Wash., 1965; J.D., U. Calif.-Berkeley, 1968. Bar: Wash. 1968, U.S. Dist. Ct. (ea. dist.) Wash. 1975, U.S. Dist. Ct. (we. dist.) Wash. 1969, U.S. Dist. Ct. (no. dist.) Calif., U.S. Tax Ct. 1978, U.S. Ct. Appeals (9th cir.) 1972. Ptnr. Ziontz, Pirtle, Morisset, Ernstoff & Chestnut, Seattle, 1968-86, Pirtle, Morisset, Schlosser & Ayer, 1986—. Chmn. Planning Commn., Clyde Hill, Wash., 1980-86, Bd. Adjustment, Clyde Hill, 1986; mayor City of Clyde Hill, 1986—. Federal civil litigation, Land use and zoning (including planning). Home: Fieldstone Ln NE Bainbridge Island WA 98110-4282

MORONEY, LINDA L. S. lawyer, educator; b. Washington, May 27, 1943; d. Robert Emmet and Jessie (Robinson) M.; m. Clarence Renshaw II, Mar. 28, 1967 (div. 1977); children: Robert Milnor, Justin W.R. BA, Randolph-Macon Woman's Coll., 1965; JD cum laude, U. Houston, 1982. Bar: Tex. 1982, U.S. Ct. Appeals (5th cir.) 1982, U.S. Dist. Ct. (so. dist.) Tex. 1982, U.S. Supreme Ct. 1988. Law clk. to assoc. justice 14th Ct. Appeals, Houston, 1982-83; assoc. Pannill and Reynolds, 1983-85, Gilpin, Pohl & Bennett, Houston, 1985-89, Vinson & Elkins, Houston, 1989-92. Adj. prof. law U. Houston, 1986-91, dir. legal rsch. and writing, 1992-96, civil trial and appellate litigation and mediation, 1996—. Fellow Houston Bar Found.; mem. ABA, State Bar Tex., Houston Bar Assn., Assn. of Women Attys., Tex. Women Lawyers, Order of the Barons, Phi Delta Phi. Episcopalian. Alternative dispute resolution, General civil litigation, Education and schools. Home and Office: 4010 Whitman St Houston TX 77027-6334

MORONEY, MICHAEL JOHN, lawyer; b. Jamaica, N.Y., Nov. 8, 1940; s. Everard Vincent and Margaret Olga (Olson) M.; children: Sean, Megan, Matthew. BS in Polit. Sci., Villanova U., 1962; JD, Fordham U., 1965; Police Sci. (hon.), U. Guam, 1976. Bar: Hawaii 1974, U.S. Dist. Ct. Hawaii 1974, U.S. Ct. Appeals (9th cir.) 1974, Guam 1976, U.S. Dist. Ct. (Guam dist.) 1976, U.S. Ct. Claims 1976, U.S. Tax Ct. 1976, U.S. Ct. Mil. Appeals 1977, U.S. Supreme Ct. 1977, High Ct. Trust Ters. 1977, U.S. Dist. Ct. (No. Mariana Islands) 1983. Spl. agt. FBI, Memphis and Nashville, 1965-67, Cleve. and Elyria, Ohio, 1967-71; spl. agt., prin. legal advisor FBI, U.S. Dept. Justice, Honolulu, 1971-97; v.p. Merrill Corp., 1997-2000; mgr. Investigative Svcs. Worldwide, 2000—; mng. dir. Paradise Meml. Park, LLC, Honolulu, 2000—; pres., mgr. ISW, LLC, 2000—. Bar examiner and applications rev. com. Supreme Ct. Hawaii, 1980—; pres. Hawaii State Law Enforcement Assn., 1985-86; mem. and del. to congress Gov.'s Task Force on Hawaii's Internat. Role, 1988; mem. Charter Commn., City and County of Honolulu, 1998-2000; mem. Consular Corps of Hawaii, 1997-2000; regent Harris Manchester Coll., Oxford U., 2000—. Gov.'s task force, del. gov.'s congress on Hawaii's Internat. Role, 1988—; apptd. hon. consul gen. Republic of Palau, Pres. Kunio Nakamura, 1999. Recipient Govs. Award for outstanding contbns. to law enforcement Govt. of Guam, 1974, 76, cert. of appreciation Supreme Ct. Hawaii, 1981, Honolulu Police Commn., 1984, 86; named Fed. Law Enforcement Officer of Yr., State of Hawaii, 1992, Outstanding Career award in law enforcement and commitment to Hawaii State Law Enforcement Ofcls. Assn., 1998. Mem. ABA, Hawaii Bar Assn., Guam Bar Assn., Inst. Jud. Adminstrn., Hawaii State Law Enforcement Ofcls. Assn., Hilo Yacht Club, Oahu Country Club, Plaza Club, Rotary Club Honolulu. Address: 7858 Makaaoa Pl Honolulu HI 96825-2848 Office: Paradise Meml Park LLC 1154 Fort Street Mall Ste 300 Honolulu HI 96813-2712 Fax: 808-599-5004. E-mail: mmoro007@aol.com

MOROS, NICHOLAS PETER, railroad executive, lawyer; b. N.Y.C., Oct. 18, 1947; s. Nicholas F. and Mary M. (Sulima) M.; m. Susan Ann Girouard, Aug. 28, 1971; 1 child, Alexander N. BA, Manhattan Coll., 1969; JD cum laude, Boston Coll., 1972. Bar: N.Y. 1973, Minn. 1976, Tex. 1985. Assoc. Dewey, Ballantine, Bushby, Palmer & Wood, N.Y.C., 1972-75; staff atty. Burlington No. R.R. Co., St. Paul, 1975-83, gen. counsel, Fort Worth, 1983-86, sr. asst. v.p. Coal & Taconite, 1986, v.p., 1987—. Editor Environ. Affairs Law Rev., 1971-72. Advisor, Boy Scouts Am., St. Paul, 1977-78; bd. dirs. Theatre Arlington, Tex., 1984—. Mem. ABA, Minn. Bar Assn., Tex. Bar Assn., Tarrant County Bar Assn., Ramsey County Bar Assn., N.Y. State Bar Assn., Nat. Coal Coun., Petroleum Club (Ft. Worth), Colonial Country Club. Republican. Roman Catholic. Administrative and regulatory, Antitrust, General corporate. Home: 1801 SW Highland Rd Portland OR 97221-2731 Office: Burlington No RR Co 3700 Continental Plaza 777 Main St Fort Worth TX 76102-5304

MORPHONIOS, DEAN B. lawyer; b. Miami, Fla., Apr. 27, 1956; s. Alexander George and Ellen (James) M.; m. Joan Julien, Aug 7, 1982; children: Kimberly Anne, Matthew James. BA, Fla. Internat. U., Miami, 1979; JD, Fla. State U., 1983. Bar: Fla. 1983, U.S. Dist. Ct. (so. dist.) Fla. 1985, U.S. Dist. Ct. (mid. and no. dists.) 1988, U.S. Ct. Appeals, U.S. Supreme Ct. 1989. Assoc. gen. counsel Fla. Police Benevolent Assn., Tallahassee, 1983-84; pvt. practice Miami, 1984-86; asst. state atty. State Attys. Office/2d Jud. Cir., Tallahassee, 1986-88; assoc. Kitchen Judkins Simpson & High, 1988-97; pvt. practice, 1997—. Mem. Bench Bar Com., Tallahassee, 1996—, Conflict Rev. Com., Tallahassee, 1996—. Mem. Fla. Assn. Criminal Defendant Attys. (pres. Tallahassee chpt. 1994-95). Republican. Criminal, Family and matrimonial. Office: 610 N Duval St Tallahassee FL 32301-1135 E-mail: dmorphon@yahoo.com

MORPHY, JAMES CALVIN, lawyer; b. Pitts., Jan. 16, 1954; s. Robert Samson and Autumn (Phillips) M.; m. Priscilla Winslow Plimpton, July 11, 1981; children: Calvin, Katherine, Victoria. BA, Harvard U., 1976, JD, 1979. Bar: N.Y. 1980. Assoc. Sullivan & Cromwell, N.Y.C., 1979-86, ptnr., 1986—, mng. ptnr. com., 1992—, mng. ptnr. M&A group, 1995—. Author (contbg.): (treatise) New York and Delaware Business Entities: Choice Formation, Operation, Financing, and Acquisition, 1997, Transactional Lawyer's Deskbook, 2001. Trustee Greenwich (Conn.) Acad. Mem. ABA (com. on fed. securities law 1992—), Assn. Bar of City of N.Y., Wianno Club (bd. govs.), Greenwich Country Club, Harvard Club N.Y., Wianno Yacht Club, Phi Beta Kappa. Mergers and acquisitions, Securities. Office: Sullivan & Cromwell 125 Broad St Fl 28 New York NY 10004-2489

MORRIONE, MELCHIOR S. management consultant, accountant; b. Bklyn., Dec. 31, 1937; m. Joan Finnerty, June 22, 1968; children: Karyn Morrione Frick, Nicole. BBA magna cum laude, St. John's U., 1959. CPA, N.J., N.Y. Tax ptnr. Arthur Andersen, N.Y.C., 1959-91; mng. dir. MSM Consulting LLC, Woodcliff Lake, N.J., 1992—. Lectr. in field. Contbr. articles to profl. jours. With U.S. Army, 1960-61. Mem. CPAs, N.Y. State Soc. CPAs, N.J. Soc. CPAs, Internat. Fiscal Assn., Internat. Tax Assn., Ridgewood Country Club. Republican. Roman Catholic. Avocations: golf, tennis. Office: MSM Consulting LLC 11 Ginny Dr Woodcliff Lake NJ 07677-8115 E-mail: morrione@att.net

MORRIS, EDWARD WILLIAM, JR. lawyer; b. Medford, Oreg., Apr. 12, 1943; s. Edward William and Julia Loretta (Sullivan) M.; m. Margaret Ellen McKenna, 1976; children: John McKenna, Elizabeth Anne. BS, Fordham Coll., 1965, JD, 1971. Bar: N.Y. 1973. Dir. Drug Products Co., Inc., Union City, N.J., 1968-71; asst. arbitration dir. N.Y. Stock Exch., N.Y.C., 1971-73, arbitration dir., 1973-74, asst. sec., arbitration dir., 1974-89, v.p. arbitration, 1989-91, chief hearing officer, 1991—. Dir. Stock Clearing Corp., N.Y.C.; mem. Securities Industry Conf. on Arbitration, N.Y.C., 1977— ; lectr. in field. Served to sgt. U.S. Army, 1965-68, Vietnam. Mem. ABA, Am. Arbitration Assn. (comml. law com. 1983—), Assn. Bar City N.Y. (retail fin. svcs. com. 1989—), N.Y. County Lawyers Assn. (sec. com. on arbitration 1983—), High Mountain Golf Club, N.Y. Roadrunners Club. E-mial. Securities. Home: 67 Arlton Ave Allendale NJ 07401-1331 Office: NY Stock Exch Inc 2 Broad St New York NY 10005-1974 E-mail: emorris@nyse.com

MORRIS, FRANCIS EDWARD, lawyer; b. N.Y.C., June 7, 1942; s. J. Frank and Kathleen (O'Connell) M.; m. Carole A. Comstock, May 31, 1969; children— Brian F., Gillian C. S.B., Holy Cross Coll., Worcester, Mass., 1963; LL.B., Harvard U., 1966; M.E., Stevens Inst. Tech., 1971. Bar: N.Y. 1967, N.J. 1980. Mem. patent staff Bell Telephone Labs, Murray Hill, N.J., 1966-71; assoc. Pennie & Edmonds, N.Y.C., 1971-76, ptnr., 1976— . Presenter in the field. Mem. Bar Assn. City N.Y., Am. Arbitration Assn., ABA, IEEE, Assn. Computing Machinery, N.Y. Patent Law Assn., N.J. Patent Law Assn., N.Y. State Bar Assn. Roman Catholic. Computer, Patent. Office: Pennie & Edmonds Ste 603 1155 Avenue Of The Americas Fl 17 New York NY 10036-2720

MORRIS, GARY WAYNE, lawyer; b. El Paso, Tex., Jan. 14, 1945; s. Harold W. and Ruth (Ingram) M.; m. Janet S. Young; children: Patricia, Jennifer, Michael, John. BA, Point Loma Nazarene U., Pasadena, 1967; JD, U. Loyola, 1970. Assoc. Hart & Mieras, L.A., 1971-74, ptnr., 1974-96, Hart, Mieras, Morris & Peale, Pasadena, Calif., 1996—. Presenter (audio cassette) Living Trust, 1992. Sec. L.A. Dist. Adv. Bd., Pasadena, 1976—; trustee Point Loma Nazarene U., San Diego, 1994—. Recipient Pres.'s award Optimist Club, 1975, Alumnus award Point Loma Nazarene U. Pasadena, 1980. Mem. State Bar Calif., Christian Legal Soc., L.A. County Bar Assn. Republican. Avocations: sandrail, fishing, tennis. General corporate, Estate planning, Real property. Office: Hart Mieras Morris & Peale Ste 300 255 E Santa Clara Arcadia CA 91066

MORRIS, JAMES MALACHY, lawyer; b. Champaign, Ill., June 5, 1952; s. Walter Michael and Ellen Frances (Solon) M.; m. Mary Delilah Baker, Oct. 17, 1987; children: James Malachy Jr., Elliot Rice Baker, Walter Michael, Nicholas Aidan. Student, Oxford U. (Eng.), 1972; BA, Brown U., 1974; JD, U. Pa., 1977. Bar: N.Y. 1978, U.S. Dist. Ct. (so. and ea. dists.) N.Y. 1978, Ill. 1980, U.S. Tax Ct. 1982, U.S. Supreme Ct. 1983; admitted to Barristers Chambers, Manchester, Eng., 1987. Assoc. Reid & Priest, N.Y.C., 1977-80; sr. law clk. Supreme Ct. Ill., Springfield, 1980-81; assoc. Carter, Ledyard & Milburn, N.Y.C., 1981-83; sole practice, 1983-87; counsel FCA, Washington, 1987—; acting sec., gen. counsel FCS Ins. Corp., McLean, Va., 1990-98. Cons. Internat. Awards Found., Zurich, 1981—, Pritzker Architecture Prize Found., N.Y.C., 1981—, Herbert Oppenheimer, Nathan & VanDyck, London, 1985—. Contbr. articles to profl. jours. Mem. ABA, Ill. Bar Assn., N.Y. State Bar Assn., N.Y. County Lawyers Assn., Assn. Bar City N.Y., Brit. Inst. Internat. and Comparative Law, Lansdowne Club (London), Casanova (Va.) Hunt Club. General corporate, General practice, Probate. Office: PO Box 1407 Mc Lean VA 22101-1407

MORRIS, NORVAL, criminologist, educator; b. Auckland, New Zealand, Oct. 1, 1923; s. Louis and Vera (Burke) M.; m. Elaine Richardson, Mar. 18, 1947; children: Gareth, Malcolm, Christoper. LLB, U. Melbourne, Australia, 1946, LLM, 1947; PhD in Criminology (Hutchinson Silver medal 1950), London Sch. Econs., 1949. Bar: called to Australian bar 1953. Asst. lectr. London Sch. Econs., 1949-50; sr. lectr. law U. Melbourne, 1950-58, prof. criminology, 1955-58; Ezra Ripley Thayer teaching fellow Harvard Law Sch., 1955-56, vis. prof., 1961-62; Boynthon prof., dean faculty law U. Adelaide, Australia, 1958-62; dir. UN Inst. Prevention Crime and Treatment of Offenders, Tokyo, Japan, 1962-64; Julius Kreeger prof. law and criminology U. Chgo., 1964—, dean Law Sch., 1975-79. Chmn. Commn. Inquiry Capital Punishment in Ceylon, 1958-59; mem. Social Sci. Rsch. Coun. Australia, 1958-59; Australian del. confs. div. human rights and sect. social def. UN, 1955-66; mem. standing adv. com. experts prevention crime and treatment offenders. Author: The Habitual Criminal, 1951, Report of the Commission of Inquiry on Capital Punishment, 1959, (with W. Morison and R. Sharwood) Cases in Torts, 1962, (with Colon Howard) Studies in Criminal Law, 1964, (with G. Hawkins) The Honest Politicians Guide to Crime Control, 1970, The Future of Imprisonment, 1974, Letter to the President on Crime Control, 1977, Madness and the Criminal Law, 1983, Between Prison and Probation, 1990, The Brothel Boy and Other Parables of the Law, 1992, The Oxford History of the Prison, 1995, Maconochie's Gentlemen, 2001. Served with Australian Army, World War II, PTO. Decorated Japanese Order Sacred Treasure 3d Class. Fellow Am. Acad. Arts and Scis. Home: 1207 E 50th St Chicago IL 60615-2908 Office: U Chgo Law Sch 1111 E 60th St Chicago IL 60637-2776 E-mail: norval_morris@law.uchicago.edu

MORRIS, ROLAND, lawyer; b. Phila., Feb. 18, 1933; s. Edward S. and Leslie H. (Hun) M.; m. Sally J. Fageol, Jan. 29, 1955; children— Roland, Deirdre L.E., Heather H. B.A., Princeton U., 1955, LL.B., U. Pa. 1960. Bar: Pa. 1960, U.S. Dist. Ct. (ea. dist.) Pa. 1961, U.S. Ct. Appeals (3d cir.) 1961, U.S. Supreme Ct. 1975. Assoc. firm Duane, Morris & Heckscher, Phila., 1960-66, ptnr., 1966-71, adminstrv. ptnr., 1971-83, mng. ptnr., 1983— ; gen. counsel Hosp. Assn. Pa., Milk Distbrs. Assn. of Phila. Area, Inc., N.J. Milk Industry Assn., Inc., Northeast Ice Cream Assn., Inc.; spl. counsel Del. River Port Authority and Port Authority Transit Corp., Gen. Assembly Pa.; dir., gen. counsel Mellon PSFS; gen. counsel, dir. Galliker Dairy Co. Gen. counsel, trustee, vice-chmn. Phila. Coll. Pharmacy and Sci., 1980-83, chmn., 1983— ; v.p. bd. dirs. Legal Aid Soc. Phila., 1972-75; pres. bd. dirs. Big Bro. Assn. Phila., 1975-78; chmn. bd. dirs. Salvation Army, 1978-81; trustee Dolfinger-McMahon Found., Magee Meml. Hosp. bd. dirs. Phila. Urban Coalition, Citizens Crime Commn. Phila.; mem. adv. bd. United Way. Mem. ABA, Pa. Bar Assn., Phila. Bar Assn. Democrat. Episcopalian. Clubs: Union League; Merion Cricket. Administrative and regulatory, Antitrust, Health. Office: Duane Morris & Heckscher 1880 John F Kennedy Blvd Fl 10 Philadelphia PA 19103-7424

MORRIS, ROY LESLIE, lawyer, electrical engineer, venture capitalist; b. N.Y.C. BE, SUNY, Stony Brook, 1975; EE, SM, MIT, 1978; JD, George Washington U., 1984; MBA, Wharton U., 1995. Bar: D.C. 1984, U.S. Patent Office. Mem. tech. staff Bell Telephone Labs., Holmdel, N.J., 1978-80; sr. staff engr. FCC, Washington, 1981-83; assoc. regulatory counsel MCI Communications, 1983-87; dep. gen. counsel Allnet Comms., 1988-95; dir. pub. policy and regulatory affairs Allnet/Frontier Comms., 1989-96; mng. ptnr. RoyLyn L.L.C., Arlington, Va., 1996—; v.p. govt. affairs and revenue devel. US ONE Comms., McLean, 1996-97; mng. ptnr. Strategic Tech. Investors LLC, Arlington, 1998—; pres. MIT Enterprise Forum, Washington/Balt., 1998—. Ednl. counselor MIT; adj. prof. Capitol Coll., Laurel, Md., 1998—. Contbr. numerous articles to profl. publs. Mem. ABA, IEEE, MIT Enterprise Forum, Sigma Xi, Tau Beta Pi. Administrative and regulatory, Communications, Finance. Address: Strategic Tech Investors LLC 4001 9th St N Ste 306 Arlington VA 22203-1957

MORRIS, SANDRA JOAN, lawyer; b. Chgo., Oct. 13, 1944; d. Bernard and Helene (Davies) Aronson; m. Richard William Morris, May 30, 1965 (div. Jan. 1974); children: Tracy Michelle, Bretton Todd; m. William Mark Bandt, July 12, 1981; 1 child, Victoria Elizabeth. BA, U. Ariz., 1965; JD, Calif. Western U., 1969. Bar: Calif. 1970, U.S. Dist. Ct. (so. dist.) Calif. 1970; diplomate Am. Coll. Family Trial Lawyers. Ptnr. Morris & Morris, APC, San Diego, 1970-74; sole practice, 1974—. Mem. Adv. Commn. on Family Law, Calif. Senate, 1978-79. Contbr. articles to profl. jours. Pres. San Diego Community Child Abuse Coordinating Coun., 1977; mem. human rsch. rev. bd. Children's Hosp., San Diego, 1977-92. Fellow Am. Acad. Matrimonial Lawyers (chpt. pres. 1987-88, nat. bd. govs. 1987-89, 93-94, parliamentarian 1989-91, treas. 1994-97, v.p. 1997-2000, 1st v.p. 2000-2001, pres. elect 2001-), Internat. Acad. Matrimonial Lawyers; mem. ABA (family law sect exec. com. marital property 1982-83, 87-94, faculty mem. Trial Advocacy Inst., 2001—), State Bar Calif. (cert. family law specialist 1980—), Lawyers Club San Diego (bd. dirs. 1973), San Diego Cert. Family Law Specialists (chair 1995-96). Republican. Jewish. Avocations: skiing, travel. Family and matrimonial. Office: 3200 4th Ave Ste 101 San Diego CA 92103-5716

MORRIS, THOMAS BATEMAN, JR. lawyer; b. Columbus, Ohio, Aug. 11, 1936; s. Thomas Bateman and Margaret (O'Shaughnessy) M.; m. Ann Peirce, Feb. 23, 1963; children: Lauren, Thomas III, Richard. AB, Princeton U., 1958; JD, Harvard U., 1962. Bar: Pa. 1962. Sr. ptnr. Dechert Price & Rhoads, Phila., 1962—, chmn., 1990-96. Bd. dirs. PNC Bank N.A., Phila., Berwind Corp., Phila., Asten Johnson, Inc., Charleston, S.C., Envirite Corp., Plymouth Meeting, Pa., Peirce-Phelps, Inc., Phila., Harmac Med. Products, Inc., Buffalo, The Contributionship Cos. Co-chmn. Greater Phila. First, 1996—; trustee Princeton U., 1975-80; bd. trustees Thomas Jefferson U., 1989—. Hon. Consul King of Belgium, Phila., 1974-89. Mem. ABA, Pa. Bar Assn., Phila. Bar Assn. (chmn. city tax policy com.), Internat. Bar Assn. (chmn. com. on structure and ethics of law practice), Phila. Club, Phila. Cricket Club, Princeton Club, Sunnybrook Golf Club, Pine Valley Golf Club. Home: 8320 Seminole St Philadelphia PA 19118-3932 Office: Dechert Price & Rhoads 4000 Bell Atlantic Tower Philadelphia PA 19103-2793 E-mail: tmorris@dechert.com

MORRISON, FRANCIS HENRY, lawyer; b. Springfield, Mass., July 3, 1947; s. Frank Henry Jr. and Rita Jean (Conley) M.; m. Sally Murphy, Sept. 26, 1970; children: Brian Conley, Matthew J. A.B., Coll. of Holy Cross, 1969; J.D. with distinction, Duke U., 1975. Bar: Conn. 1975, U.S. Dist. Ct. Conn. 1975, U.S. Dist. Cts. (so. and ea. dists.) N.Y. 1975, U.S. Ct. Appeals (2d cir.) 1976. Assoc. Day, Berry & Howard, Hartford, Conn., 1975-81, ptnr., 1981—; corp. counsel Town of West Hartford (Conn.), 1983-85; spl. master U.S. Dist. Ct. Conn., 1983—; med. malpractice com. various hosps., Con., 1983-85. pres. parish council Ch. of St. Helena, West Hartford, 1987-90; trustee Kingswood Oxford Sch. Served to lt. USNR, 1969-72. Note and comments editor Duke Law Jour., 1974-75. Fellow Am. Coll. Trial Lawyers; mem. Am. Bd. Trial Advocates (charter Conn. chpt., cert. as a Civil Trial Specialist by Nat. Bd. Trial Advocacy 1991), ABA, Hartford County Bar Assn., Def. Rsch. Inst., Fed. Insurance and Corp. Counsel, Conn. Def. Lawyers Assn. (pres. 1991-92). Democrat. Roman Catholic. Avocations: travel, golf. Insurance, Intellectual property, Product liability. Home: 57 Pheasant Hill Dr West Hartford CT 06107-3328 Office: Day Berry & Howard Cityplace Hartford CT 06103

MORRISON, JOHN HORTON, lawyer; b. Sept. 15, 1933; BBA, U. N.Mex., 1955; BA, U. Oxford, 1957; JD, Harvard U., 1962. Bar: Ill. 1962, U.S. Supreme Ct. 1966. Assoc. Kirkland & Ellis, Chgo., 1962-67, ptnr., 1968-99. Named Hon. Officer Most Excellent Order Brit. Empire, 1994; Rhodes scholar. Mem. ABA, Internat. Arbitration (arbitrator, mediator London Ct.), Internat. Bar Assn., Am. Arbitration Assn. (internat., large complex case and Chgo. panels), Am. Assn. Rhodes Scholars (pres. 1998—), Chgo. Bar Assn., Chgo. Internat. Dispute Resolution Assn. (dir.). office e-mail: john. Antitrust, Alternative dispute resolution, Federal civil litigation. Home: 2717 Lincoln St Evanston IL 60201-2042 E-mail: jhmobe@aol.com, morrison@kirkland.com

MORRISON, JOHN MARTIN, lawyer; b. McCook, Nebr., June 18, 1961; s. Frank Brennor and Sharon Romain (McDonald) M.; m. Catherine Helen Wright, Aug. 17, 1991; children: Allison Kay, Amanda Grace. BA, Whitman Coll., 1983; JD, U. Denver, 1986. Bar: Mont. 1987, U.S. Dist. Ct. Mont. 1988, U.S. Ct. Appeals (9th cir.) 1989, U.S. Supreme Ct. 1996. Legis. asst., legal counsel U.S. Senate, Washington, 1987-88; ptnr. Morrison Law Offices, Helena, Mont., 1988-93, Meloy & Morrison, Helena, 1994-2000; elected ins. and securities commr. Mont. State Auditor, 2001—. Elected commr. securities Mont. State Auditor, 2000—. Author: Mavericks: The Lives and Battles of Montana's Political Legends, 1997; contbr. articles to profl. jours. Alt. del. Dem. Nat. Conv., N.Y.C., 1980; del. Dem. Nat. Platform Com., 1992 Recipient Lewis F. Powell/ACTL/Bur. of Nat. Affairs Advocacy awards, 1986. Mem. ATLA, Mont. Bar Assn., Mont. Trial Lawyers Assn. (past pres., bd. dirs. 1991-2000), Western Trial Lawyers Assn. (bd. govs. 1990-95), Trial Lawyers Pub. Justice (chair 1989-90), Nat. Assn. Ins. Commn., Nat. Assn. Securities Administrs. Avocations: skiing, fly fishing, mountain climbing, river rafting, running. General civil litigation, Insurance, Personal injury. Office: Meloy & Morrison 80 S Warren St Helena MT 59601-5700 E-mail: johnmorrison@mcn.net

MORRISSEY, GEORGE MICHAEL, judge; b. Chgo., Aug. 12, 1941; s. Joseph Edward and Mary Bernice (Shields) M.; m. Mary Kay McCarthy, Jan. 3, 1976; children: Meghan Catherine, Colleen Mary. BS, Ill. Inst. Tech., 1963; JD, De Paul U., 1971. Bar: Ill. 1972, U.S. Dist. Ct. (no. dist.) Ill. 1978, U.S. Supreme Ct. 1981. Auditor Touche Ross & Co., Chgo., 1963-68; pvt. practice Evergreen Park and Worth, Ill., 1972-77; chief 5th Mcpl. Dist. Cook County Pub. Defender, Chgo., 1978-90; assoc. judge Cook County Cir. Ct., 1991—. Mem. spl. commn. on adminstrn. of justice in Cook County, Chgo., 1984-91. Mem. commn. on future of Ill. Inst. Tech., Chgo., 1976-77; bd. trustees Oak Lawn (Ill.) Library, 1979-85; bd. dirs. Crisis Ctr. for South Suburbia, Worth, 1979—. Served with U.S. Army, 1963-69. Mem. Chgo. Bar Assn. (jud. retention com., bar pres. com.), S.W. Bar Assn. (past pres.), Coalition of Suburban Bar Assn. (past pres.), Alpha Sigma Phi. Roman Catholic. Clubs: Columbia Yacht (commodore 1976-78) (Chgo.), Chgo. Yachting (commodore 1982). Lodge: Elks. Office: Cir Ct of Cook County 2600 Richard J Daley Ctr Chicago IL 60602

MORRONE, CORRADO LUCIO, lawyer; b. Cosenza, Italy, Feb. 14, 1967; s. Vincenzo Morrone and Emma Natalina De Paola; m. Marina Sarchiola, Sept. 20, 1997; 1 child, Gianvincenzo. Degree in law cum laude, LUISS U., Rome, 1991. Mem. Studio Legale Guarino, Rome, 1991—. Asst. prof. LUISS U., 1996—. Contbr. articles to profl. publs. Mem. Italian Assn. Adminstrv. Lawyers. Avocations: hunting, shuffleboard, jogging. Office: Studio Legale Guarino Piazza Borghese 3 00176 Rome Italy Fax: 39 06 686 76 27. E-mail: guarino@uni.net

MORROW, EMILY RUBENSTEIN, lawyer, estate planner; b. Poughkeepsie, N.Y., Sept. 14, 1952; d. Lewis W. and Erica (Beckh) Rubenstein; m. Paul L. Morrow; 1 child, Lillian. BA summa cum laude, Oberlin Coll., 1974; JD, U. Buffalo, 1977. Bar: N.Y. 1978, Ill. 1979, Vt. 1982. Law clk. to presiding justice N.Y. State Supreme Ct., Syracuse, N.Y., 1977-78; assoc. Altheimer & Gray, Chgo., 1978-80; sr. tax counsel Cen. Carolina Bank, Durham, N.C., 1980-82; assoc. Pierson, Affolter & Wadhams, Burlington, Vt., 1982-86; ptnr. Dinse, Erdmann & Clapp, 1986—. Adj. prof. bus. law Trinity Coll., Burlington, 1983-84; adj. prof. comml. law St. Michaels Coll., Burlington, 1984-85; bd. dirs. Shelburne Farms; chmn. Howard Bank, Burlington. Mem. editorial adv. bd. Vt. Woman Pubs., Burlington, 1986-89. Bd. govs. Med. Ctr. Hosp. of Vt., Burlington, 1985-94; bd. dirs. Chittenden County United Way, Burlington, 1985-88; chmn. Vt. Whey Pollution Abatement Authority, Cabot, 1985-86; spl. asst. to pres. Vermona Land Trust. Mem. ABA (real property com., probate and trust law com., taxation com.), Vt. Bar Assn., Chittenden County Bar Assn., Internat. Assn. Fin. Planners, Am. Coll. Trust and Estate Counsel, Phi Beta Kappa. Avocations: skiing, swimming, reading, sailing. General corporate, Estate planning, Probate. Office: Dinse Knapp & McAndrew 209 Battery St Burlington VT 05401-5261 E-mail: emily@vlt.org

MORROW, JOHN E. lawyer; b. L.A., Mar. 17, 1943; s. Charles Henry and Lillian (Harmon) M.; m. Sue C. Taylor, June 28, 1989. BS, U. Southern Calif., 1965; JD, U. Chgo., 1968; postgrad., U. Munich, 1969. Bar: Calif. 1969, Ill. 1971. Law clk. to judge U.S. Dist. Ct. (cen. dist.) Calif., 1969-70; ptnr. Baker & McKenzie, Chgo., 1970-73, 75-76, 83—, Zurich, Switzerland, 1974-75, Hong Kong, 1976-82. Mem. ABA (subcom. on internat. bus. law com. corp. sect.). Finance, Private international, Mergers and acquisitions. Office: Baker & McKenzie One Prudential Plz 130 E Randolph St Fl 32 Chicago IL 60601-6207 E-mail: john.e.morrow@bakernet.com

MORROW, THOMAS CAMPBELL, lawyer; b. Cin., July 5, 1948; s. Worcester Beach Morrow & Alice Patricia (Faust) Bardon; children: Courtney Ann, Thomas Richard, John Campbell. BA, U. Cin., 1971; JD, U. Balt., 1975. Bar: Md. 1975, Fla. 1975, U.S. Dist. Ct. Md. 1979, U.S. Supreme Ct. 1979, U.S. Dist. Ct. (so. dist.) Fla. 1981, U.S. Ct. Appeals (4th cir.) 1981. Chief, adminstrv. services State's Atty.'s Office, Balt., 1972-75; asst. state's atty. Balt. County, 1975-78; asst. atty. gen. Md., Balt., 1978-79; asst. state atty. 11th Jud. Cir., Miami, Fla., 1979-80; assoc. Weinberg & Green, Balt., 1980-84, ptnr., 1984-87 ptnr. Soudry & Morrow, Balt., 1987, Morrow & Hassani, P.A., 1988-96; atty. pvt. practice, 1997—. Bd. dirs. Montessori Soc. Central Md., 1982, Kingsville Civic Assn., 1982-83. Mem. ABA, Assn. Trial Lawyers Am., Fed. Bar Assn., Md. Bar Assn., Md. Criminal Def. Attys. Assn., Heuisler Honor Soc. Federal civil litigation, State civil litigation, Criminal. Home: 2701 Boston St Baltimore MD 21224-4729 Office: 15 E Chesapeake Ave Towson MD 21286-5306

MORROW, WILLIAM CLARENCE, judge, lawyer, mediator; b. Austin, Tex., Aug. 9, 1935; s. Theodore Faulkner and Gladys Lee (Ames) M.; m. Sheila Beth Pfost, June 29, 1973; children: Scott Fitzgerald Morrow, Elizabeth Ann Rettig; 1 stepchild, Shana Lynn Barbee. BA, Baylor U., 1957; JD, So. Meth. U., 1962. Bar: Tex. 1962. Trial atty. SEC, Ft. Worth, 1963-65; former ptnr. Cotton, Bledsoe, Tighe, Morrow & Dawson, Lynch, Chappell, Alsup & Midland; v.p. Magnatex Corp., Midland, 1980-86; v.p., gen. cousnel, sec. Elcor Corp., 1986-88; county judge Midland County, Tex., 1999. Mem. Midland City Coun., 1992-95, mayor pro tem, 1994-95; former vice chmn. Tex. Rehab. Commn.; pres. Found. Mental Health and Mental Retardation Permian Basin; pres. United Way of Midland, 1985, Indsl. Found. Midland, 1987; trustee Midland Cmty. Theatre, 1980—, chmn., 1995-96; elder First Presbyn. Ch., Midland. Mem. Coll. of State Bar Tex., Tex. Bar Assn., Midland County Bar Assn., Tex. Coll. of Probate Judges, Phi Delta Phi. Home: 3110 Gulf Ave Midland TX 79705-8205 Office: 200 W Wall Ste 006 Midland TX 79701-4512

MORSE, JACK CRAIG, lawyer; b. Evanston, Ill., Aug. 11, 1936; s. Leland Robert and Pauline (Pettibone) M.; children by past marriage: David Leland, Katherine Malia. BA, Beloit Coll., 1958; JD, Northwestern U., 1965. Bar: Hawaii 1967, U.S. Dist. Ct. Hawaii 1969, U.S. Ct. Appeals (9th cir.) 1977. Legal staff Bishop Estate, Honolulu, 1966-68; dep. atty. gen. State of Hawaii, Honolulu, 1968-71; ptnr. Saunders & Morse, Honolulu, 1971-73; assoc. Chuck & Wong, Honolulu, 1974-75; officer, dir. Morse, Nelson & Ross, Honolulu, 1976-85; mem. Hawaii Med. Claim Conciliation Panel, Honolulu, 1977—, chmn., 1980—; mem. panel of arbitrators First Judicial Cir., Hawaii, 1986—. Lt. USN, 1959-62. Hardy scholar Northwestern U., 1962. Mem. Am. Judicature Soc., Assn. Trial Lawyers Am., Omicron Delta Kappa. Federal civil litigation, State civil litigation, Personal injury. Office: 700 Richards St Ste 1706 Honolulu HI 96813-4619

MORSE, MARVIN HENRY, judge; b. Mt. Vernon, N.Y., July 19, 1929; s. Frank Irving and Lillian (Seeger) M.; m. Betty Anne Hess, Dec. 27, 1953; children: Martin Albert, Michael Howard, Lee Anne. AB, Colgate U., 1949; LLB, Yale U., 1952. Bar: N.Y. 1952, Ky. 1956, Md. 1964, U.S. Supreme Ct. 1960, U.S. Ct. Appeals (6th cir.), U.S. Dist. Ct. (we. dist.) Ky., U.S. Ct. Mil. Appeals, U.S. Ct. Claims, U.S. Ct. Appeals (D.C. cir.), U.S. Ct. Appeals (fed. cir.), U.S. Dist. Ct. (no. dist.) Tex., U.S. Dist. Ct. Hawaii. Pvt. practice, Louisville, 1956-62; asst. advisor Office of Gen. Counsel Dept. Navy, Washington, 1962-65; asst. counsel Office of Gen. Counsel Office Sec. Def., 1965-68; asst. gen. counsel GSA, 1968-70, U.S. Postal Svc., Washington, 1970-73; adminstrv. law judge Fed. Energy Regulatory Commn., 1973-75, Postal Rate Commn., Washington, 1975-77, CAB, Washington, 1977-80; dir. adminstrv. law judges Office Pers. Mgmt., 1980-82; chief adminstrv. law judge SBA, 1982-87, asst. adminstr. hearings and appeals, 1985-87; adminstrv. law judge Exec. Office of Immigration Rev. Dept. Justice, 1987—. Mem. Adminstrv. Conf. of U.S., 1980-84, govt. mem., 1985-86, 87-95, liaison mem.; faculty and faculty coord. The Nat. Jud. Coll., 1977, 79-80. Author: (with S. Groner) ABA Handbook chpt. on adminstrv. law, 1981. Trustee Washington area chpt. Am. Digestive Disease Soc., 1976-87. With JAGC, USAF, 1952-56, to col. USAFR, ret. 1979. Decorated USAF Legion of Merit; recipient Disting. Svc. award Am. Digestive Disease Soc., 1980. Mem. ABA (exec. com. 1977-82, 84-87, chmn. 1980-81, conf. adminstrv. law judges, del. ho. of dels. 1984-87, lawyers in govt. com. 1985-86, jud. selection, tenure and compensation com. 1987-93, govt. pub. sect. lawyers divsn., coun. 1996—), Fed. Bar Assn. (nat. coun. 1976—, chmn. career svc. sect. 1983-86, chmn. judiciary sect. 1986-88, sect. coord. 1988-90, sec. 1991-92, del. to ABA ho. of dels. 1992-93, 97-99, v.p. 1993-94, pres.-elect 1994-95, pres. 1995-96), Am. Law Inst., Fed. Adminstrv. Law Judges Conf. (exec. com. 1975-77, 82-96, 2000-01), Nat. Assn. Adminstrv. Law Judges (hon.), Fed. Am. Inn of Ct. (coun. 1990-92, pres. 1992-94). Home: 11221 Potomac Crest Dr Potomac MD 20854-2743 Office: US Dept Justice 5107 Leesburg Pike Falls Church VA 22041-3234 E-mail: marvin.morse@usdoj.gov

MORSE, SAUL JULIAN, lawyer; b. Jan. 17, 1948; s. Leon William and Goldie (Kohn) M.; m. Anne Bruce Morgan, Aug. 21, 1982; children: John Samuel, Elizabeth Miriam. BA, U. Ill., 1969, JD, 1972. Bar: Ill. 1973, U.S. Dist. Ct. (so. dist.) Ill. 1976, U.S. Ct. Appeals (7th cir.) 1983, U.S. Supreme Ct. 1979, U.S. Tax Ct. 1982. Law clk. State of Ill. EPA, 1971-72, Ill. Commerce Commn., 1972, hearing examiner, 1972-73; trial atty. ICC, 1973-75; asst. minority legal counsel Ill. Senate, 1975, minority legal counsel, 1975-77; mem. Ill. Human Rights Commn., 1985-91; dir., treas., chair grievance com. Ill. Comprehensive Health Ins. Plan; gen. counsel Ill. Legis. Space Needs Commn., 1978-92; pvt. practice Springfield, Ill., 1977-79; ptnr. Gramlich & Morse, 1980-85; prin. Saul J. Morse and Assocs., 1985-87; ptnr. Morse, Giganti and Appleton, 1987-92; v.p., gen. counsel Ill. State Med. Soc., 1992—. Lectr. in continuing med. edn., 1986-90; counsel symposia; adj. asst. prof. med. humanities So. Ill. Sch. Medicine; pres. Springfield Profl. Baseball, LLC. Bd. dirs. Springfield Ctr. for Ind. Living, 1984-89, Ill. Comprehensive Health Ins. Plan Bd., United Cerebral Palsy Land of Lincoln, United Way Cen. Ill., Inc., 1991-97; treas. City of Leland Grove, Ill., 1999; dir. Hope Sch.; mem., bd. dirs. Springfield Jewish Fedn., 1992-95, mem. bd. dirs. Hope Sch., Springfield; mem. task force on transp. Rep. Nat. Com., 1979-80, Springfield Jewish Comty. Rels. Coun., 1976-79, 82; mem. spl. com. on zoning and land use planning Sangamon County Bd., 1978; treas. City of Leland Grove, 1999—; exec. com. AMA and State Med. Socs. Litigation Ctr., 1999—. Named Disabled Adv. of Yr., Ill. Dept. Rehab. Svcs., 1985; recipient Chmn.'s Spl. award Ill. State Med. Soc., 1987, Susan S. Suter award as outstanding disabled citizen of Ill., 1990. Mem. ABA (vice-chmn. medicine and law com. 1988-90, tort and ins. practice sect., forum com. on health law), Am. Assn. Health Lawyers, Am. Soc. Law and Medicine, Ill. State Bar Assn. (spl. com. on reform of legis. process 1976-82, spl. com. on the disabled lawyer 1978-82, young lawyers sect. com. on role of govt. atty. 1977-80, chmn. 1982, sect. coun. adminstrv. law, vice-chmn. 1981-82), Sangamon County Bar Assn., Am. Soc. Med. Assn. Counsel, Phi Delta Phi. Health, Insurance, Legislative. Home: 1701 S Illini Rd Springfield IL 62704-3301 Office: Ill State Med Soc 600 S 2nd St Ste 200 Springfield IL 62704-2578 E-mail: morse@ismie.com

MORTIMER, ANITA LOUISE, minister; b. Jefferson City, Mo., July 2, 1950; m. Ross Maitland Snell and Viola Alice (Leigh) M.; children: Caleb Ross, Hannah Erin (dec.). BA, Graceland Coll., 1973; JD, Washburn U., 1976; MA in Religion with honors, Park Coll., 1992. Bar: Kans. 1976, U.S. Dist. Ct. Kans. 1976, Mo. 1980, U.S. Dist. Ct. (we. dist.) Mo. 1980, U.S. Ct. Appeals (8th cir.) 1980, U.S. Supreme Ct. 1980; ordained to ministry Reorganized Ch. of Jesus Christ of Latter-day Saints, 1993. Tng. cons. Orgn. to Counter Sexual Assault, Mo., Iowa, Kans., Ill., 1979-80; asst. dist. atty. Wyandotte County, Kansas City, Kans., 1976-80; asst. U.S. atty. U.S. Dept. Justice, Mo., 1980-97; min. Reorganized Ch. of Jesus Christ Latter-day Saints Ch., 1998—. Appointee Organized Crime and Drug Enforcement Task Force, 1988; cons. Govs. Task Force on Rape Prevention, Mo., 1979-80; instr. Nat. Coll. Dist. Attys., 1980, various camps and retreats, family-related topics, various seminars for fed. agts.; bd. dirs. SHARE, Inc. Contbr. articles to profl. jours. Bd. dirs. Met. Orgn. to Counter Sexual Assault, Kansas City, 1976-80, Outreach Internat., 1995-99, Graceland Ctr. for Profl. Devel., 1994—; apptd. to Presdl. Com. on Status of Women, 1979-80; trustee Independence (Mo.) Regional Health Ctr., 1990-94; mem. Ctr. Stake Strategic Planning Commn. RLDS, 1989-90; apptd. chair World Ch. Task Force on Singles' Ministry RLDS, 1990—; chair del. caucus RLDS World Conf., 1992, 94, 96, 98, 00; trustee Graceland Coll., 1994-2000, chair, 1998-2000; mem. Friends of the Zoo. Named to Honorable Order of Ky. Cols., Gov., 1980. Mem. ABA, Mo. Bar Assn., Assn. Women Lawyers, Kansas City Met. Bar Assn.; Alumni Assn. Graceland Coll. (bd. dirs. 1987, pres. 1988), John Whitmer Hist. Soc. Clubs: MOCSA (Kansas City), Friends of Art. Office: Peace and Justice Ministries Community of Christ PO Box 1059 Independence MO 64051-0559 E-mail: amortimer@cofchrist.org

MORTIMER, WENDELL REED, JR. judge; b. Alhambra, Calif., Apr. 7, 1937; s. Wendell Reed and Blanche (Wilson) M.; m. Cecilia Vick, Aug. 11, 1962; children: Michelle Dawn, Kimberly Grace. AB, Occidental Coll., 1958; JD, U. So. Calif., L.A., 1965. Bar: Calif. 1966. Trial atty. Legal div. State of Calif., L.A., 1965-73; assoc. Thelen, Marrin, Johnson & Bridges, 1973-76, ptnr., 1976-93; pvt. practice San Marino, Calif., 1994-95; judge L.A. Superior Ct., 1995—, mem. complex litigation panel, 2000—. With U.S. Army, 1960-62. Mem. ABA, Internat. Acad. Trial Judges, Los Angeles County Bar Assn., Calif. Judges Assn., Am. Judicature Soc., Am. Judges Assn., Legion Lex., ABOTA, San Marino City Club, Pasadena Bar Assn., Balboa Yacht Club. Home: 1420 San Marino Ave San Marino CA 91108-2042

MORTON, FRED J. lawyer; b. El Paso, Tex., Nov. 13, 1935; s. R.a.D. and Julianne (More) M.; m. Anne Adele Reynolds, July 19, 1960; children: Chris, Anne, John, Robert, Peter, Mary Virginia, Thomas, Mary Katherine. BA, U. Tex., El Paso, 1957; LLB, U. Tex., Austin, 1958. Bar: Tex. 1958. Asst. U.S. atty., El Paso, 1961-65; U.S. commr. cts., 1966-71. Trustee, Southwestern Children's Home Trust, El Paso, 1983—; pres. El Paso County Hist. Soc., 1967. Fellow U. Tex. law sch. Ctr. for Pub. Policy Dispute Resolution, 1996. Mem. Tex. Bar Assn., El Paso Trial Lawyers Assn. (pres. 1972), El Paso Bar Assn. (pres. 1985), Sigma Alpha Epsilon, Phi Delta Phi. Democrat. Roman Catholic. Alternative dispute resolution, General civil litigation, Real property. Home: 1101 Montana Ave El Paso TX 79902-5509 E-mail: fandamorton@aol.com

MOSBACKER, MERVYN, prosecutor; b. Cuidad Victoria, Mex. JD, U. Tex., 1982. Prosecutor Cameron County Dist. Atty.'s Office; asst. U.S. atty. Brownsville; U.S. atty. so. dist. Tex. U.S. Dept. Justice, 1999—. Office: US Courthouse PO Box 61129 Houston TX 77208-1129

MOSCHOS, DEMITRIOS MINA, lawyer; b. Jan. 8, 1941; s. Constantine Mina and Vasiliky (Strates) M.; m. Celeste Thomaris, Sept. 28, 1975; children: Kristin M., Thomas W. BA magna cum laude, U. Mass., 1962; JD magna cum laude, Boston U., 1965; grad. basic courses, U.S. Army JAG Sch., Charlottesville, va., 1966. Bar: Mass. 1965, U.S. Dist. Ct. Mass. 1975, U.S. Ct. Mil. Appeals 1966. Exec. asst. to city mgr., spl. legal counsel City of Worcester, 1968-75, asst. city mgr., spl. legal counsel, 1975-80; assoc. Mirick, O'Connell, Worcester, 1980-81, ptnr., 1982—. Lectr. labor rels. Worcester State Coll., 1975-88, Clark U., 1978—; chmn. Worcester Housing Com., 1968-78, Worcester Energy Com., 1978-80; mem. Mass. Joint Labor Mgmt. Com., 1978-80. Drafter adminstrv. codes; contbr. articles to profl. jours. Past pres. archdiocesan coun. Greek Orthodox Archdiocese of Am.; bd. dirs. Worcester Mcpl. Rsch. Bur., Worcester Regional C. of C. Capt. JAGC, U.S. Army, 1966-68. Decorated Army Commendation medal; recipient Alumni Acad. Achievement award Boston U. Law Sch., 1965; named Outstanding Young Man of Worcester County, Worcester County Jaycees, 1969, named in resolution of commendation Worcester City Coun., 1980. Mem. ABA, Mass. Bar Assn. (Comty. Svc. award 1987), Worcester Bar Assn. (former chmn. labor sect.), Tatnuck Country Club. Greek Orthodox. Administrative and regulatory, Education and schools, Municipal (including bonds). Office: Mirick O'Connell 100 Front St Ste 1700 Worcester MA 01608-1426

MOSELEY, JAMES FRANCIS, lawyer; b. Charleston, S.C., Dec. 6, 1936; s. John Olin and Kathryn (Moran) M.; m. Anne McGehee, June 10, 1961; children: James Francis Jr., John McGehee. AB, The Citadel, 1958; JD, U. Fla., 1961. Bar: Fla. 1961, U.S. Supreme Ct. 1970. Pres. Moseley, Warren, Prichard & Parrish, Jacksonville, Fla., 1963—. Chmn. jud. nominating com. 4th Jud. Cir., 1978-80 Assoc. editor: American Maritime Cases; contbr. articles on admiralty, transp. and ins. law to legal jours. Pres. Jacksonville United Way, 1979; chmn. bd. dirs. United Way Fla., 1992-93, S.E. regional coun. United Way, 1992-96; trustee Jacksonville Cmty. Found.; chmn. bd. trustees Jacksonville Pub. Libr.; trustee Libr. Found., sec., 1987-91; trustee CMI Am. Found.; chmn. Jacksonville Human Svcs. Coun., 1989-91; chmn. bd. trustees United Way N.E. Fla., 1995-97; bd. govs. United Way Am., 1996—. Recipient Meritorious Pub. Svc. award/medal U.S. Dept. Transp./USCG, 1998. Fellow Am. Coll. Trial Lawyers, Am. Bar Found.; mem. Jacksonville Bar Assn. (pres. 1975), Fla. Coun. Bar Pres. (chmn. 1979), Maritime Law Assn. U.S. (exec. com. 1978-81, chmn. navigation com. 1981-88, v.p. 1992-96, pres. 1996-98), Comm. Maritime Internat. (titulary), Com. on Collision (Lisbon Rules), Fed. Ins. Corp. Counsel (chmn. maritime law sect.), Internat. Assn. Def. Counsel (chmn. maritime com. 1989-91), Am. Inns of Ct. (master of bench), Assn. of Citadel Men (bd. mem. 1989-93, exec. com. 1994, Man Yr. award 1992, Palmetto award/medal 2001), Citadel Inn of Ct. (sr. bencher), Deerwood Club, River Club, India House (N.Y.C.), Army Navy Club (Washington), St. John's Dinner Club (pres. 1988). Admiralty, Federal civil litigation, Insurance. Home: 7780 Hollyridge Rd Jacksonville FL 32256-7134 Office: Moseley Warren Prichard & Parrish 1887 West Rd Bay St Jacksonville FL 32216-4542

MOSENSON, STEVEN HARRIS, lawyer; b. Phila., Dec. 3, 1956; BS, NYU, 1978, M of Pub. Adminstrn., 1979; JD, Yeshiva U., 1982. Bar: N.Y. 1983, U.S. Ct. Appeals (2d cir.) 1983, U.S. Dist. Ct. (so. and ea. dists.) N.Y. 1983, U.S. Ct. Internat. Trade 1985, U.S. Supreme Ct. 1986. Assoc. Baden Kramer Huffman & Brodsky, N.Y.C., 1982-85; asst. corp. counsel N.Y.C. Law Dept., 1985-89; gen. counsel United Cerebral Palsy Assns. of N.Y. State, Inc., N.Y.C., 1989—. Pres. bd. dirs. Bklyn. Heights Ctr. for Counseling, Inc., 1992—; bd. dirs. Walden, N.Y. Local Devel. Corp., 1998—; mem. Walden Cmty. Coun., 1998—. Mem. N.Y. State Bar Assn. (chmn. com. on issues affecting people 1997—), Guardianship Assn. of N.Y. State, Inc. (v.p. 1995—). Office: United Cerebral Palsy Assns of NY 330 W 34th St Fl 13 New York NY 10001-2488 Fax: 212-356-0746. E-mail: mosenson@aol.com

MOSER, C. THOMAS, lawyer; b. Seattle, Aug. 10, 1947; s. Carl Thomas and Helen Louise (Felton) M.; m. Deborah J. St. Clair, Sept. 25, 1976; children: Nicole, Lauren. BA, Cen. Wash. U., 1972; M in Pub. Adminstrn., George Washington U., 1974; JD, Gonzaga U., 1976. Bar: Wash. 1977; U.S. Dist. Ct. (we. dist.) Wash. 1977, U.S. Dist. Ct. (ea. dist.) Wash. 1980, U.S. Ct. Appeals (9th cir.) 1980, U. S. Supreme Ct. 1981. Dep. pros. atty. Skagit County Pros. Atty., Mount Vernon, Wash., 1976-77, chief civil dep., 1979-80, pros. atty., 1980-86, San Juan County Pros. Atty., Friday Harbor, 1977-79; pvt. practice Mount Vernon, 1987—. Hearing examiner pro tem Skagit County, 1992—. Author: Gonzaga Law Review, 1975. Bd. dirs. Wash. Environ. Coun., Seattle, 1971-72, Padilla Bay Found., Skagit County, Wash., 1988; bd. trustees Wash. Assn. County Ofcls., Olympia, 1983; exec. bd. North Pacific Conf. Evang. Covenant Ch., vice sec. 1991-96; bd. trustees Skagit Valley Coll., 2000—. Sgt. U.S. Army, 1967-69, Korea. Recipient Silver Key award ABA Student Law Div., 1976, Legion of Honor award Internat. Order DeMolay, Kansas City, Mo., 1982, Chevalier award 1982. Mem. ATLA, Nat. Coll. Advocacy (advocate), Wash. State Trial Lawyers Assn. (bd. govs. 1990-92, 96-97), Wash. Assn. Pros. Attys. (bd. dirs. 1983-85), Skagit County Bar Assn. (pres. 1995-96), Kiwanis Club Mt. Vernon, Affiliated Health Svc. (ethics com.), Christian Legal Soc. Democrat. Evangelical. Avocations: skiing, golf, jogging, woodworking. Criminal, Land use and zoning (including planning), Personal injury. Office: 411 Main St Mount Vernon WA 98273-3837

MOSER, M(ARTIN) PETER, lawyer; b. Balt., Jan. 16, 1928; s. Herman and Henrietta (Lehmayer) M.; m. Elizabeth Kohn, June 14, 1949; children— Mike, Moriah, Jeremy AB, The Citadel, Charleston, S.C., 1947; LLB, Harvard U., 1950. Bar: Md. 1950, U.S. Supreme Ct., U.S. Ct. Appeals (4th cir.). Asst. states atty. City of Balt., 1951, 53-54; assoc. Blades Rosenfeld, Balt., 1950, 53-54; ptnr. Frank, Bernstein, Conaway & Goldman and predecessor firms, 1955-90, co-chmn. firm, 1983-86; counsel, 1991-92; of counsel Piper Marbury Rudnick & Wolfe LLP, 1992—. Instr. U. Balt. Law Sch., 1954-56, 86, U. Md. Law Sch., 1986-87. Contbr. articles to profl. jours. Del., chmn. local govt. com. Md. Constl. Conv., 1967-68; mem. Balt. City Planning Commn., 1961-66, Balt. Regional Planning Council, 1963-66, Md. Commn. to Study Narcotics Laws, 1965-67, Mayor's Task Force on EEO, 1966-67, Met. Transit Authority Adv. Council, 1962, Com. to Revise Balt. City Planning Laws, 1962, Com. to Revise Balt. City Charter Provision on Conflicts of Interest, 1969-70; mem. Citizens Adv. Com. on Dist. Ct., chmn., 1971, Dist. Adv. Bd. for Pub. Defender System for Dist. 1, 1973-85; mem. Atty. Grievance Commn. of Md., 1975-78, chmn. 82-86; chmn. Md. State Ethics Commn., 1987-89; bd. dirs. Sinai Hosp., 1983—, Lifebridge Health Sys., 1998—, Ct. of Appeals Comm. to Study the Model Rules, 1983-86. Served with JAGC, U.S. Army, 1951-53 Fellow Am. Bar Found. (v.p.), Md. Bar Found., Balt. Bar Found.; mem. ABA (ho. of dels. 1978—, treas. 1993-96, bd. govs. 1984-87, 92-96, ethics com. 1981-84, 87-90, 96—, chmn. 1981-82, 87-90, 98-99, scope and cor. com. 1987-92, chmn. 1990-91, sec. bus. law coun. 1999—), Md. State Bar Assn. (pres. 1979-80), Balt. Bar Assn. (pres. 1971-72), Am. Law Inst. (adv. coun. gov. lawyers 1987-99), Wednesday Law Club, Lawyers' Round Table Club, Hamilton St. Club. Democrat. Jewish. General corporate, Estate planning, Health. Office: Piper Marbury Rudnick & Wolfe LLP 6225 Smith Ave Baltimore MD 21209-3600

MOSES, ALFRED HENRY, lawyer, diplomat, writer; b. Balt., July 24, 1929; s. Leslie William and Helene Amelia (Lobe) M.; m. Carol Whitehill, Nov. 24, 1955; Barbara, Jennifer, David, Amalie. BA, Dartmouth, 1951; postgrad., Woodrow Wilson Sch., Princeton U., 1951-52; JD, Georgetown U., 1956. Bar: D.C. 1956. Assoc. Covington & Burling, Washington, 1956-65, ptnr., 1965-94, 97—; spl. advisor, spl. counsel Pres. Jimmy Carter, 1980-81; amb. to Romania, Am. Embassy, Bucharest, 1994-97; Pres. Spl. Emissary for Cyprus, 1999-2001. Legal advisor minority rights Dem. Nat. Com., Washington, DC Commn. on Urban Renewal; lectr. Am. Law Inst., ABA , New Orleans, Am. Inst. CPAs, ABA, Washington, Georgetown U. Law Ctr., Tax Exec. Inst., Washington, Tulane Tax Inst., New Orleans; guest lectr. on non-legal subjects at Coun. of Europe, Yale U., Princeton U., Dartmouth Coll.; commr. Pub. Housing, Fairfax County, Va., 1971-72. Contbr. articles, commentaries to internat. jours. and press. Co-chmn. legal div. United Givers Fund, Washington, 1975-76; mem. Coun. Fgn. Rels., N.Y.C., 1977—; bd. dirs. Paralysis Cure Rsch. Found., 1978-81; trustee Phelps Stokes Fund, N.Y.C., 1978-84; pres. Nat. Children's Island, Washington, 1975-76; pres. Golda Meir Assn., 1986-88, nat. chmn., 1988-93; trustee Jewish Publ. Soc., 1989-94, Haifa U., 1988-90; pres. Am. Jewish Com., 1991-94; mem. bd. regents Georgetown U., 1986-92. Mem. ABA, D.C. Bar Assn., Met. Club. Democrat. Jewish. General civil litigation, General corporate, Real property. Home: 7710 Georgetown Pike Mc Lean VA 22102-1431 Office: 1201 Pennsylvania Ave NW Washington DC 20004-2401

MOSES, BONNIE SMITH, lawyer, educator; b. Phila., Jan. 20, 1955; d. D. Ralph and Mercedes McKinley (Harrison) S.; m. Richard Moses, July 8, 1978; children: Michelle Irene, Jacquelyn Elyse. BS in Psychology summa cum laude, pa. State U., 1975; JD, Temple U., 1978, LLM in Taxation, 1981. Bar: Pa. 1978, U.S. Dist. Ct. (ea. dist.) Pa. 1978, U.S. Ct. Appeals (3d cir.) 1980, U.S. Tax Ct. 1981, U.S. Supreme Ct. 1986. Law clk. Ct. Common Pleas, Phila., 1978-79; assoc. Leonard M. Sagot Assocs., 1979-80, mng. assoc. Jenkintown, Pa., 1980-84; ptnr. Dessen, Moses & Sheinoff, Phila., 1984—. Adj. prof. bus. law Arcadia U., Glenside, Pa., 1982—. Contbr. articles to law jours. Vol. ARC, Elkins Park, Pa., Keneseth Israel Synagogue Sisterhood; bd. dirs. Big Sisters Phila., chair pers., bd. dirs. Phila. Jewish Archives, sec., chair nom. com., bd. dirs. Jewish Heritage Program; mem. mentoring com., Leadership Coun. Phila.; vol. Lawyers for the Arts; mentor, Women's Law Caucus, Temple U. Law Sch. Fellow Pa. Bar Assn.; mem. ABA, AAUW, NAFE, Pa. Bar Assn., Phila. Bar Ass.n, Montgomery County Bar Assn., Am. Prepaid Legal Svcs. Inst. (chair 2001 conf.), Law Alumni Temple U., Ogontz Campus Alumni Assn., Phi Beta Kappa, Phi Kappa Phi (9th Annal Woman of Vision award). Family and matrimonial, General practice, Probate. Office: Dessen Moses & Sheinoff 1814 Chestnut St Philadelphia PA 19103 E-mail: bmoses@dms-lawyer.com

MOSHER, SALLY EKENBERG, lawyer, musician; b. N.Y.C., July 26, 1934; d. Leslie Joseph and Frances Josephine (McArdle) Ekenberg; m. James Kimberly Mosher, Aug. 13, 1960 (dec. Aug. 1982). MusB, Manhattanville Coll., 1956; postgrad., Hofstra U., 1958-60, U. So. Calif., 1971-73, JD, 1981. Bar: Calif., 1982. Musician, pianist, tchr., 1957-74; music critic Pasadena Star-News, 1967-72; mgr. Contrasts Concerts, Pasadena Art Mus., 1971-72; rep. Occidental Life Ins. Co., Pasadena, 1975-78; v.p. James K. Mosher Co., 1961-82, pres., 1982—, Oakhill Enterprises, Pasadena, 1984—; assoc. White-Howell, Inc., 1984-94; real estate broker, 1984-96. Harpsichordist, lectr., composer, 1994—; pub. Silver Wheels Pub., ASCAP. Musician (CD recs.) William Byrd: Songs, Dances, Battles, Games, 1995, From Now On: New Directions For Harpsichord, 1998; author: People and Their Contexts: A Chronology of the 16th Century World; contbr. articles to various publs. Bd. dirs. Jr. League Pasadena, 1966-67, Encounters Concerts, Pasadena, 1966-72, U. So. Calif. Friends of Music, L.A., 1973-76, Calif. Music Theatre, 1988-90, Pasadena Hist. Soc., 1989-91, I Cantori, 1989-91; bd. dirs. Pasadena Arts Coun., 1986-92, pres., 1989-92, chair adv. bd., 1992-93; v.p., bd. dirs. Pasadena Chamber Orch., 1986-88, pres., 1987-88; mem. Calif. 200 Coun. for Bicentennial of U.S. Constn., 1987-90; mem. Endowment Adv. Commn., Pasadena, 1988-90; bd. dirs. Foothill Area Cmty. Svcs., 1990-95, treas., 1991, vice chair, 1992-94, chair, 1994-95; sec., bd. dirs. Piano Spheres, 2001—. Manhattanville Coll. hon. scholar, 1952-56. Mem. ABA, Calif. Bar Assn., Assocs. of Calif. Inst. Tech., Athenaeum, Kappa Gamma Pi, Mu Phi Epsilon, Phi Alpha Delta. Home: 1260 Rancheros Rd Pasadena CA 91103-2759 Fax: 626-795-3146. E-mail: sally@cyberverse.com

MOSICH, NICHOLAS JOSEPH, Lawyer; b. San Pedro, Calif., July 2, 1951; s. Nicholas Andrew and Barbara Yvonne (Chutuk) M.; m. Susanne Melinda Wolf, Dec. 18, 1976 (dec. Jan. 1998); children: Nicholas Daniel, Andrea Michelle. BA, Santa Clara U., 1974; JD, Pepperdine U., 1977. Bar: Calif. 1977, U.S. Dist. Ct. (so. dist.) Calif. 1979, U.S. Dist. Ct. (cen. dist.) Calif. 1980. Assoc. Forgy & Inadomi, Santa Ana, Calif., 1978-83, ptnr., 1983-92. Bd. dirs. Young Men's Christian Assn., Santa Ana, 1980-87. Mem. ABA, Orange County Bar Assn., Assn. Trial Lawyers Am. Republican. Roman Catholic. State civil litigation, Insurance, Real property. Office: 2204 E 4th St Ste 100 Santa Ana CA 92705-4071

MOSK, RICHARD MITCHELL, lawyer; b. L.A., May 18, 1939; s. Stanley and Edna M.; m. Sandra Lee Budnitz, Mar. 21, 1964; children: Julie, Matthew. AB with great distinction, Stanford U., 1960; JD cum laude, Harvard U., 1963. Bar: Calif. 1964, U.S. Supreme Ct. 1970, U.S. Ct. Mil. Appeals 1970, U.S. Dist. Ct. (no., so., ea., and cen. dists.) Calif 1964, U.S. Ct. Appeals (9th dist.) 1964. Staff Pres.'s Commn. on Assassination Pres. Kennedy, 1964; rsch. clk. Calif. Supreme Ct., 1964-65; ptnr. Mitchell, Silberberg & Knupp, L.A., 1965-87; prin. Sanders, Barnet, Goldman, Simons & Mosk, PC, 1987-2000. Spl. dep. Fed. Pub. Defender, L.A., 1975-76; instr. U. So. Calif. Law Sch., 1978; judge Iran-U.S. Claims Tribunal, 1981-84, 97—, substitute arbitrator, 1984-97; mem. L.A. County Jud. Procedures Commn., 1973-82, chmn., 1978; co-chmn. Motion Picture Assn. Classification and Rating Adminstrn., 1994-2000; mem. panel Ct. Arbitration for Sport-Geneva. Contbr. articles to profl. jours. Mem. L.A. City-County Inquiry on Brush Fires, 1970; bd. dirs. Calif. Mus. Sci. and Industry, 1979-82, Vista Del Mar Child Ctr., 1979-82; trustee L.A. County Law Libr., 1985-86; bd. govs. Town Hall Calif., 1986-91; mem. Christopher Commn. on L.A. Police Dept., 1991; mem. Stanford U. Athletic Bd., 1991-95. With USNR, 1964-75. Hon. Woodrow Wilson fellow, 1960; recipient Roscoe Pound prize, 1961. Fellow Am. Bar Found.; mem. ABA (coun. internat. law sect. 1986-90), FBA (pres. L.A. chpt. 1972), L.A. County Bar Assn., Beverly Hills Bar Assn., Internat. Bar Assn., Am. Arbitration Assn. (comml. panel, large complex case panel, entertainment panel, internat. panel), Hong Kong Internat. Arbitration Ctr. (mem. panel 1986—), Am. Film Mktg. Assn. (arbitration panel), B.C. Internat. Arbitration Ctr. (mem. panel), World Intellectual Property Orgn. (mem. arbitration panel), Ctr. Pub. Resources (arbitration panel), Ct. Arbitration Sport-Geneva (arbitration panel, NASD arbitration panel), Calif. Tribal Labor Panel, Phi Beta Kappa. Alternative dispute resolution, Private international, Public international. Office: Ste 700 1901 Avenue Of The Stars Los Angeles CA 90067-6078

MOSK, SUSAN HINES, lawyer; b. Pitts., Dec. 14, 1946; d. William James and Catherine Elizabeth (Cook) Hines; m. Stanley Mosk, Aug. 27, 1982 (div. Jan. 1995). B in Music Edn., Fla. State U., 1968, M in Music Edn., 1970; JD, U. Calif., San Francisco, 1990. Bar: Calif. 1990, U.S. Dist. Ct. (no. dist.) Calif. 1990, U.S. Ct. Appeals (9th cir.) 1990. Assoc. Payne, Thompson & Walker, San Francisco, 1990-94; of counsel Knecht, Haley, Lawrence & Smith, 1994-95; prin. Law Offices of Susan H. Mosk, 1995—, Mosk Mediation and Negotiation, San Francisco, 2000—. Commr. Jud. Nominees Evaluation Commn., 1992-96; mem. BASF judiciary com., 1997-2000; arbitrator San Francisco MTA, 2001—. Author/editor: Rainmaking Guide to Corporate Counsel, 1993. Mem. steering com. Women's Leadership Coun. for U.S. Senator Diane Feinstein, 1992—; chair No. Calif. Women's Cabinet for Kathleen Brown Gubernatorial Campaign, San Francisco, 1994; co-chair fin. Willie L. Brown Mayoral Campaign, 1995; program chair San Francisco Mayor's Summit for Women, 1998, chair, 1999. Mem. State Bar of Calif., Calif. Women Lawyers (bd. govs. 1992-94, 1st v.p. 1993-94), Queen's Bench. Democrat. Avocations: music, skiing, traveling, reading. Family and matrimonial, Labor, Real property. E-mail: SMOSK@pacbell.net

MOSKOWITZ, STUART STANLEY, lawyer; b. N.Y.C., Aug. 27, 1955; s. Arthur Appel and Rebecca (Gordon) M. BS magna cum laude, SUNY, Albany, 1977; JD with honors, Union U., Albany, 1981; LLM, NYU, 1990. Bar: N.Y. 1982, U.S. Tax Ct. 1983, U.S. Dist. Ct. (so. dist.) N.Y. 1985. Law clk. to presiding judge U.S. Tax Ct., Washington, 1981-83, U.S. Ct. Appeals for 2d cir., N.Y.C., 1983-84; sr. counsel IBM, Armonk, N.Y., 1984—. Research asst. fin. SUNY Sch. of Bus., Albany, 1976-77, corp. law Albany Law Sch., 1980-81; instr. acctg. Ednl. Opportunities Program SUNY, Albany, 1977-78. Tax counselor for elderly Am. Assn. Ret. Persons, Westchester County, N.Y., Corp. Lawyers of Svc. to the Elderly, Westchester County Legal Svcs., N.Y. Mem. ABA, Order of Justinian. Contracts commercial, General corporate, Securities. Home: 153 Princeton Dr Hartsdale NY 10530-2010 Office: IBM New Orchard Rd Armonk NY 10504 E-mail: smoskowi@us.ibm.com

MOSLEY, DEANNE MARIE, lawyer; b. Meridian, Miss., Oct. 24, 1969; d. James Alton and Betty Anne (Rutledge) Mosley. B in Pub. Adminstrn., U. Miss., 1991, JD, 1994. Bar: Miss. 1994, U.S. Dist. Ct. Miss. 1994, U.S. Supreme Ct. 1997. Assoc. Hamilton & Linder, Meridian, Miss., 1994-95, Langston Frazer Sweet & Freese, Jackson, 1995-98; spl. asst. atty. gen. State of Miss., 1999—. Instr. Ctr. for Legal Studies, Golden, Colo., 1998—. Editor: A Guide to Women's Legal Rights in Mississippi, 1998. Mem. Miss. Supreme Cts. Gender Fairness Task Force, Jackson, 1998—. Mem. Miss. Bar Assn. (mem. disciplinary rules and procedures adv. com. 1998—, bd. dirs. young lawyers divsn. 1998—), Miss. Women Lawyers Assn. (treas., bd. dirs.), Jackson Young Lawyers Assn. (publ. editor 1997-98), Ctrl. Miss. Ole Miss Alumni Assn. (bd. dirs. 1998—). Administrative and regulatory, Government contracts and claims. Office: Contract Rev Bd 301 N Lamar St Jackson MS 39201-1404

MOSMAN, MICHAEL W. prosecutor; BA, Utah State U.; JD, Brigham Young U. Assoc. Miller, Nash, Portland, Oreg., 1986—88; asst. U.S. atty. Dist. Oreg. U.S. Dept. Justice, 1988—2001, U.S. atty. Dist. Oreg., 2001—. Office: 1000 SW 3rd Ave Ste 600 Portland OR 97204-2902*

MOSS, BILL RALPH, lawyer; b. Amarillo, Tex., Sept. 27, 1950; s. Ralph Voniver and Virginia May (Atkins) M.; 1 child, Brandon Price. BS with honors, West Tex. State U., 1972, MA, 1974; JD, Baylor U., 1976; cert. regulatory studies program, Mich. State U., 1981. Bar: Tex. 1976, U.S. Dist. Ct. (no. dist.) 1976, U.S. Tax Ct. 1979, U.S. Ct. Appeals (5th cir.) 1983. Briefing atty. Ct. Appeals 7th Supreme Jud. Dist. Tex., Amarillo, 1976-77; assoc. Culton, Morgan, Britain & White, 1977-80; hearings examiner Pub. Utility Commn. Tex., Austin, 1981-83; asst. gen. counsel State Bar Tex., 1983-87; founder, owner Price & Co. Publs., 1987-97; asst. gen. counsel Tex. Ethics Commn., 1997—. Instr., lectr. West Tex. State U., Canyon, Ea. N.Mex. U., Portales, 1977-80; spkr. in field. Active St. Matthew's Episcopal Ch.; election inspector State of Tex., 1998—. Mem. ABA, Tex. Bar Assn., Nat. Orgn. Bar Counsel, Internat. Platform Assn., Alpha Chi, Lambda Chi Alpha, Omicron Delta Epsilon, Phi Alpha Delta, Sigma Tau Delta, Pi Gamma Mu. Administrative and regulatory, Professional liability, Ethics. Home: 506 Explorer St Lakeway TX 78734-3447 Office: Sam Houston Bldg 201 E 14th St Fl 10 Austin TX 78701 E-mail: bill_moss@ethics.state.tx.us

MOSS, ERIC HAROLD, lawyer; b. N.Y.C., July 7, 1947; s. Jack and Ruth (Schaffer) M.; m. Linda Beth Schwartz, Oct. 17, 1970; children: Stacey Lynn, Darren Irwin. BA, CCNY, 1968; JD, NYU, 1972. Bar: N.Y. 1972, U.S. Dist. Ct. (so. and ea. dists.) N.Y. 1975, U.S. Dist. Ct. (no. and we. dists.) N.Y. 1983, U.S. Ct. Appeals (2d cir.) 1975, U.S. Ct. Appeals (10th cir.) 1979, U.S. Supreme Ct. 1975. Assoc. Phillips, Nizer, Benjamin, Krim & Ballon, N.Y.C., 1972, Arum, Friedman & Katz, N.Y.C., 1972-75, LeBoeuf, Lamb, Leiby & MacRae, N.Y.C., 1975-83; pvt. practice, Great Neck and Armonk, N.Y., 1983—; v.p. U.S. Tele-Comm., Inc., 1987—, also bd. dirs.; sec., bd. dirs. Nu-Tech Industries, Inc., 1988. Mem. ABA (litigation sect. com. securities litigation torts and ins. sect. com. on trial techniques). Club: Windmill (Armonk). Bankruptcy, Federal civil litigation, State civil litigation. Home: 24 Evergreen Row Armonk NY 10504-2210

MOSS, FRANK EDWARD, lawyer, former senator; b. Salt Lake City, Sept. 23, 1911; s. James E. and Maud (Nixon) M.; m. Phyllis Hart, June 20, 1934; children— Marilyn, Edward, Brian, Gordon. B.A. magna cum laude, U. Utah, 1933, LL.D., 1975; J.D. cum laude, George Washington U., 1937; Ph.D. (hon.), So. Utah U., 1974. Bar: D.C. 1937, Utah 1938, U.S. Dist. Ct., U.S. Supreme Ct., U.S. Ct. Appeals. City judge, Salt Lake City, 1941-50; county atty. Salt Lake County, 1951-59; U.S. senator from Utah, 1959-77; ptnr. Moss & Hyde, Salt Lake City, 1951-55, Moss & Cowley, Salt Lake City, 1956-58, Moss, Frink & Franklin, Washington, 1977-78, Moss & Wilkins, Salt Lake City, 1979-83; of counsel Schnader, Harrison, Segal & Lewis, Washington, 1979-86. Mem. bd. dirs. Utah Cancer Soc. Served to col. USAAF, ETO. Recipient Goddard award Nat. Space Club, 1976; Good Guy award Better Govt. Assn., 1976, Disting. Pub. Service award Consumer Fedn. Am., 1976, John F. Kennedy award Nat. Assn. Aeros. and Astronautics, 1975; Disting. Alumni award George Washington U., 1963. Mem. ABA, D.C. Bar Assn., Utah Assn. Counties (state pres.), Nat. Dist. Attys. Assn. (nat. pres.), Utah Assn. UN (bd. dirs.), Air Res. Assn. (nat. v.p.), Am. Judicature Soc., Smithsonian Instn. (bd. regents), African Art Mus. (trustee, chmn.), Am. Legion, VFW, Amvets, Nat. Soc. Sons Utah Pioneers, Army and Navy Club. Club: Bonneville Knife and Fork. Lodge: Lions. Home: 426 S 1000 E Salt Lake City UT 84102-3036

MOSS, GIUDITTA CORDERO, lawyer; b. Milan, Dec. 7, 1961; d. Franco and Maria Teresa Cordero; m. Arvid Moss, 1992; 1 child, Marcus Cordero. Degree in law, Law Faculty Rome, 1984; PhD in Law, Acad. Scis., Moscow, 1995; JD, Law Faculty Oslo, 1999. Bar: Italy 1989, Norway 1999. Atty. Fiat SpA, Turin, Italy, 1985-89, Norsk Hydro asa, Oslo, 1989-96; asst. prof. Law Faculty Oslo, 1999—; atty. Advokatfirmaet Hjort DA, Oslo, 1999—. Author: (books) Avtonomia Volie v Praktike mezhdunarondnovo arbitrazja, 1995, International Commercial Arbitration: Party Autonomy and Mandatory Rules, 1999. Recipient Willoughby prize, 1998. Alternative dispute resolution, Private international, Mergers and acquisitions. Office: Advokatfirmaet Hjort DA Akersgate 2 Oslo 0105 Norway E-mail: g.c.moss@hjort.no

MOSS, STEPHEN B. lawyer; b. Jacksonville, Fla., July 14, 1943; s. Rudy and Betty (Sobel) M.; m. Rhoda Goodman, Nov. 24, 1984; children: Kurt, Shannon. BA, Tulane U., 1964; JD, Samford U., 1968. Bar: Fla. 1968, U.S. Dist. Ct. (so. dist.) Fla., U.S. Tax Ct. From assoc. to ptnr. Heiman & Crary, Miami, Fla., 1971-74; pvt. practice law So. Miami, 1974-75; ptnr. Glass, Schultz, Weinstein & Moss P.A., Coral Gables, 1975-78, Ft. Lauderdale, 1978-80, Holland & Knight, Ft. Lauderdale, 1980—. Mem. pro bono com. 17th Jud. Cir., 2000; co-chair Broward County Child Welfare Initiative, 2001. Capt. U.S. Army, 1968-70, Vietnam. Named Outstanding Kiwanian, Miami, 1974; Olympic torchbearer, 1996. Fellow ABA, Fla. Bar Found.; mem. Fla. Bar Assn., Legal Aid Svc. of Broward County (bd. dirs. 2000), Greater Ft. Lauderdale C. of C. (gen. counsel 1991-92, chmn. bd. dirs., bd. govs. 1995, 99—, Chmn.'s award 1991, 2000), Tower Club, Tower Forum (pres. 1993-94, bd. dirs. 2001—). Democrat. Jewish. Avocations: running, softball, hiking. Land use and zoning (including planning), Probate, Real property. Office: Holland & Knight LLP 1 E Broward Blvd Fl 13 Fort Lauderdale FL 33301-1845 E-mail: smoss@LKlaw.com

MOSS, STEPHEN EDWARD, lawyer; b. Washington, Nov. 22, 1940; s. Morris and Jean (Sober); m. Sharon S. Moss; children: Aubrey, Hilary. BBA, Baldwin-Wallace Coll., 1962; JD with honors, George Washington U., 1965, LLM, 1968. Bar: D.C. 1966, Md. 1971. Assoc. Cole & Groner, Washington, 1965-70; pvt. practice law Bethesda, Md., 1971-80; pres. Stephen E. Moss, P.A., 1981-89, Moss, Strickler & Weaver, Bethesda, 1990-94, Moss, Strickler & Sachitano, P.A., Bethesda, 1995—. Lectr. in family law and trial practice. Fellow Am. Acad. Matrimonial Lawyers (cert.), Internat. Acad. Matrimonial Lawyers; mem. Montgomery County Bar Assn. Inc. (chmn. family law sect. 1980), Md. Bar Found., Inc. (cert. mediator). General civil litigation, Family and matrimonial, General practice. Office: Moss Strickler & Sachitano PA 4550 Montgomery Ave Ste 700 Bethesda MD 20814-3304 E-mail: smoss@mss-law.com

MOSS, THOMAS E. prosecutor; Grad., U. Idaho; JD, U. Idaho Coll. Law. Prosecuting atty. Bingham County Dist. Ct., 1967—71, 1979—99; ptnr. Moss, Cannon and Romrell, Blackfoot, Idaho; U.S. atty. Dist. of Idaho, 2001—. Mem.: Idaho Ho. of Reps. Office: PO Box 32 Boise ID 83707-0032 Office Fax: 208-334-9375*

MOSSINGHOFF, GERALD JOSEPH, patent lawyer, educator; b. St. Louis, Sept. 30, 1935; m. Jeanne Carole Jack, Dec. 29, 1958; children: Pamela Ann Jennings, Gregory Joseph, Melissa M. Ronayne. BSEE, St. Louis U., 1957; JD with honors, George Washington U., 1961. Bar: Mo. 1961, D.C. 1965, Va. 1981. Project engr. Sachs Electric Corp., 1954-57; dir. congl. liaison NASA, Washington, 1967-73, dep. gen. counsel, 1976-81; asst. sec. Commerce, commr. patents and trademarks U.S. Patent Office, 1981-85; pres. Pharm. Rsch. and Mfrs. Am., Washington, 1985-96; Cifelli prof. intellectual property law George Washington U., 1996—; sr. counsel Oblon, Spivak, McClelland, Maier & Neustadt, Arlington, Va., 1997—. Amb. Paris Conv. Diplomatic Conf.; adj. prof. George Mason U. Law Sch. Recipient Exceptional Svc. medal NASA, 1971, Disting. Svc. medal, 1980, Outstanding Leadership medal, 1981, Jefferson medal, 2000; Disting. Alumnus George Washington U., 1996; granted presdl. rank of meritorious exec., 1980; Disting. Pub. Svc. award Sec. of Commerce, 1983 Fellow Am. Acad. Pub. Adminstrn.; mem. Reagan Alumni Assn. (bd. dirs.), Cosmos Club, Knights of Malta, Order of Coif, Eta Kappa Nu, Pi Mu Epsilon. Health, Patent. Home: 1530 Key Blvd Penthouse 28 Arlington VA 22209-1532 Office: Oblon Spivak McClelland Maier & Neustadt 1755 Jefferson Davis Hwy Fl 4 Arlington VA 22202-3509

MOST, JACK LAWRENCE, lawyer, consultant; b. N.Y.C., Sept. 24, 1935; s. Meyer Milton and Henrietta (Meyer) M.; children: Jeffrey, Peter; m. Irma Freedman Robbins, Aug. 8, 1968; children: Ann, Jane. BA cum laude, Syracuse U., 1956; JD, Columbia U., 1960. Bar: N.Y. 1960, U.S. Dist. Ct. (so. and ea. dists.) N.Y. 1963. Assoc. Hale, Grant, Meyerson and O'Brien, N.Y.C., 1960-66; dep. assoc. dir. OEO, Exec. Office of The Pres., Washington, 1965-67; asst. to gen. counsel C.I.T. Fin. Corp., N.Y.C., 1968-70; corp. counsel PepsiCo, Inc., Purchase, N.Y., 1970-71; v.p. legal affairs Revlon, Inc., N.Y.C., 1971-76; asst. gen. counsel Norton Simon,

Inc., 1976-79; ptnr. Rogers Hoge and Hills, 1979-86, Finkelstein Bruckman Wohl Most & Rothman LLP, N.Y.C., 1986-97, mng. ptnr., 1990-93, Ferster Bruckman Wohl Most & Rothman LLP, 1997-98; ptnr. Goetz, Fitzpatrick, Most & Bruckman LLP, 1999—. Corp. sec. Requa, Inc., Flowery Beauty Products, Inc., 1987—. Contbr. articles to profl. jour. and mags. Bd. dirs. Haym Salomon Home for the Aged, 1978-91, pres., 1981-91; bd. dirs. The Jaffa Inst. for Advancement Edn., 1994-95; bd. dirs. Jewish Fellowship of Hemlock Farms, 1995-2001, treas., 1996-98, sec. 1998-99; bd. dirs., 1992—, pres. Haym Salomon Found., 1992-99; mem. bd. advisors Touro Coll. Health Scis., 1989-90. Mem. ABA (food, drug and cosmetic law com., trademark and unfair competition com.), N.Y. State Bar Assn. (food, drug and cosmetics sect.), YRH Owners Corp. (bd. dirs., pres. 1989-92), Lords Valley Country Club (bd. govs. 1984-90, 1st v.p. 1987-88, 2d v.p. 1989-90), Zeta Beta Tau, Omicron (trustee Syracuse chpt. 1988-91). Jewish. Administrative and regulatory, General corporate, Trademark and copyright. Home: 429 E 52nd St New York NY 10022-6430 Office: Goetz Fitzpatrick Most & Bruckman LLP One Penn Plz New York NY 10119 E-mail: jmost@goetzfitz.com

MOSTOFF, ALLAN SAMUEL, lawyer, consultant; b. N.Y.C., Oct. 19, 1932; s. Morris and Ida (Goldman) M.; m. Alice Tamara Popelowskuy, July 31, 1955; children: Peter Alexander, Nina Valerie. BS, Cornell U., 1953; MBA, NYU, 1954; LLB, N.Y. Law Sch., 1957. Bar: N.Y. 1958, D.C. 1964. Assoc. Olwine Connelly Chase O'Donnell & Weyher, N.Y.C., 1958-61; atty. SEC, Washington, 1962-66, asst. dir., 1966-69, assoc. dir., 1969-72, dir. divsn. investment mgmt. regulation, 1972-76; ptnr. Dechert Price & Rhoads, 1976-2000, Dechert, Washington, 2000—. Adj. prof. Georgetown U. Law Ctr., 1972-82; mem. Fin. Acctg. Standards Adv. Bd., 1982-86; adv. bd. Investment Lawyer, Mutual Fund Dirs. Edn. Coun. Mem. ABA, Assn. of Bar of City of N.Y., Fed. Bar Assn. (chmn. exec. coun. securities regulation com. 1990-92), Am. Law Inst. General corporate, Securities. Home: 6417 Waterway Dr Falls Church VA 22044-1325 Office: Dechert 1775 I St NW Washington DC 20006-2402 E-mail: allan.mostoff@dechert.com

MOTE, CLYDE A, lawyer; b. Vernon, Tex., Feb. 12, 1926; s. Neven and Lona (May) M.; m. Jean Henderson, Apr. 26, 1952; children— Terron, Bruce, Douglas. J.D., Baylor U., 1950. Bar: Tex. 1950, Okla. 1960. Ptnr. Cummings & Mote, Abilene, Tex., 1950-52; asst. city atty. City of Lubbock, Tex., 1952-54; ptnr. Napier & Mote, Lubbock, 1954-59; atty. Amoco Prodn. Co., Houston, 1959-86, regional atty., New Orleans Region, 1986—. Served to sgt. U.S. Army, 1943-46, ETO. Mem. Am. Petroleum Inst. (subcom. on exploration and prodn. law), Interstate Oil Compact Commn., Phi Alpha Delta. Republican. Baptist. General corporate, Oil, gas, and mineral. Home: 244 N Bay Dr Bullard TX 75757-8917 Office: Amoco Prodn Co PO Box 50879 New Orleans LA 70150-0879

MOTES, CARL DALTON, lawyer; b. May 31, 1949; s. Carl Thomas and Orpha Jeanette (McGauley) M.; m. Maria Eugenia Aguirre, Apr. 19, 1975. AA with honors, St. Johns River Jr. Coll., 1969; BA, Fla. State U., 1971, JD with honors, 1974. Bar: Fla. 1974, U.S. Dist. Ct. (cen., no. and so. dists.) Fla. 1975, U.S. Ct. Appeals (11th cir.) 1980. Assoc. Maguire, Voorhis & Wells P.A., Orlando, Fla., 1975-79, ptnr., 1979-97, Motes & Sears P.A., Winter Park, 1998-99, Motes & Carr, P.A., Orlando, 1999—; asst. to pres. Fla. Bar, Tallahassee, 1974-75. Dir. Legal Aid Soc., Orlando, 1979-83, pres., 1983-84; lectr. at various Bar Assns. and ednl. insts. Mem. editl. bd. Jour. Trial Advocate Quar., 1981-91, chmn., 1989-91; contbr. articles to profl. jours. Active in Planning & Zoning Bd., Altamonte Springs, Fla., 1977-79, Capital Funds Project Rev. Com., Cen. Fla., 1983; bd. dirs. Cen. Fla. coun. Boy Scouts Am., mem. exec. bd., v.p. adminstrn. 1993-94. Mem. Internat. Assn. Def. Counsel, Fla. Def. Lawyer's Assn. (bd. dirs. 1989-94, sec., treas. 1991-92, pres.-elect 1992-93, pres. 1993-94), Fla. Bar, Fed. of Ins. and Corp. Coun., Orange County Bar Assn. (sec. 1979-80, exec. coun. 1980-83, named Outstanding Mem. 1981-82, Outstanding Com. Chmn. 1977), Fla. State U. Coll. Law Alumni Assn. (bd. dirs. 1975-78, pres. 1979), Def. Rsch. Inst. (state chair 1994), Phi Delta Phi. Republican. Federal civil litigation, State civil litigation, Professional liability. Office: Motes & Carr PO Box 3426 Orlando FL 32802-3426 Fax: 407-897-6949. E-mail: carl@moteslaw.com

MOTLEY, CONSTANCE BAKER (MRS. JOEL WILSON MOTLEY), federal judge, former city official; b. New Haven, Sept. 14, 1921; d. Willoughby Alva and Rachel (Huggins) Baker; m. Joel Wilson Motley, Aug. 18, 1946; 1 son, Joel Wilson, III. AB, NYU, 1943; LLB, Columbia U., 1946. Bar: N.Y. bar 1948. Mem. Legal Def. and Ednl. Fund, NAACP, 1945-65; mem. N.Y. State Senate, 1964-65; pres. Manhattan Borough, 1965-66; U.S. dist. judge So. Dist. N.Y., 1966-82, chief judge, 1982-86, sr. judge, 1986—. Author: Equal Justice Under Law, 1998. Mem. N.Y. State Adv. Council Employment and Unemployment Ins., 1958-64. Mem. Assn. Bar City N.Y. Office: US Dist Ct US Courthouse 500 Pearl St New York NY 10007-1316 E-mail: constance_motley@nysd.uscourts.gov

MOTLEY, SUSAN DENARA, lawyer; b. Dallas, Aug. 13, 1970; d. William Thomas Jr. and Judith Faye Motley; m. Leopoldo Hernandez, Dec. 16, 9189; children: Sophia, Briana, Rebecca. BA magna cum laude, Coll. of Charleston, 1993; JD, U. Tex., 1997. Bar: Tex. 1997, U.S. Dist. Ct. (no. dist.) Tex. 1997, U.S. Dist. Ct. (so. dist.) Tex. 1998. Assoc. Gillespie, Rozen, Tanner & Watsky, P.C., Dallas, 1997—. Asst. dir. children's nursery Christ Temple, Irving, Tex., 1998. Mem. Nat. Employment Lawyers Assn., Dallas Young Lawyers Assn. Democrat. Pentecostal. Avocations: reading, skating, snow skiing. Labor. Office: Gillespie Rozen Et Al 2777 Stemmons Fwyy Dallas TX 75207

MOTZ, DIANA GRIBBON, federal judge; b. Washington, July 15, 1943; d. Daniel McNamara and Jane (Retzler) Gribbon; m. John Frederick Motz, Sept. 20, 1968; children: Catherine Jane, Daniel Gribbon. BA, Vassar Coll., 1965; LLB, U. Va., 1968. Bar: U.S. Dist. Ct. Md. 1969, U.S. Ct. Appeals (4th cir.) 1969, U.S. Supreme Ct. 1980. Assoc. Piper & Marbury, Balt., 1968-71; asst. atty. gen. State of Md., 1972-81, chief of litigation, 1981-86; ptnr. Frank, Bernstein, Conaway & Goldman, 1986-91; judge Md. Ct. of Special Appeals, Md., 1991-94, U.S. Ct. Appeals (4th Cir.), 1994—. Mem. ABA, Md. Bar Assn., Balt. City Bar Assn. (exec. com. 1988), Am. Law Inst., Am. Bar Found., Md. Bar Found., Lawyers Round Table, Fed. Cts. Study Com., Wranglers Law Club. Roman Catholic. Office: 101 W Lombard St Ste 920 Baltimore MD 21201-2611

MOTZ, JOHN FREDERICK, federal judge; b. Balt., Dec. 30, 1942; s. John Eldered and Catherine (Grauel) M.; m. Diana Jane Gribbon, Sept. 20, 1968; children: Catherine Jane, Daniel Gribbon AB, Wesleyan U., Conn., 1964; LLB, U. Va., 1967. Bar: Md. 1967, U.S. Ct. Appeals (4th cir.) 1968, U.S. Dist. Ct. Md. 1968. Law clk. to Hon. Harrison L. Winter U.S. Ct. Appeals (4th cir.), 1967-68; Assoc. Venable, Baetjer & Howard, Balt., 1968-69; asst. U.S. atty. U.S. Atty.'s Office, 1969-71; assoc. Venable, Baetjer & Howard, 1971-75, ptnr., 1976-81; U.S. atty. U.S. Atty.'s Office, 1981-85; judge U.S. Dist. Ct. Md., 1985-94, chief judge, 1994—. Trustees Friends Sch., Balt., 1970-77, 1981-88, Sheppard Pratt Hosp., 1987-97, 99—. Mem.: ABA, Md. State Bar Assn., Am. Bar Found., Am. Law Inst., Am. Coll. Trial Lawyers (mem. bd. editors. Manual of Complex Litigation (4th), mem. Judicial Panel on Multidist. Litigation). Republican. Mem. Soc. of Friends. Office: US Dist Ct 101 W Lombard St Rm 510 Baltimore MD 21201-2605

MOUL, WILLIAM CHARLES, lawyer; b. Columbus, Ohio, Jan. 12, 1940; s. Charles Emerson and Lillian Ann (Mackenbach) M.; m. Margine Ann Tessendorf, June 10, 1962; children: Gregory, Geoffrey. BA, Miami U., Oxford, Ohio, 1961; JD, Ohio State U., 1964. Bar: Ohio 1964, U.S. Dist. Ct. (so. dist.) Ohio 1965, U.S. Ct. Appeals (2d cir.) 1982, U.S. Ct. Appeals (6th cir.) 1984, U.S. Ct. Appeals (3d cir.) 1985. Assoc., ptnr. George, Greek, King, McMahon & McConnaughey, Columbus, 1964-79; ptnr. McConnaughey, Stradley, Mone & Moul, 1979-81; ptnr.-in-charge Thompson, Hine & Flory, 1981-89, exec. com., 1989-98. Chmn. Upper Arlington Civil Svc. Commn., Ohio, 1981-86. Mem. ABA, Ohio State Bar Assn. (labor sect. bd. dirs. 1983—), Columbus Bar Assn. (chmn. ethics com. 1980-82), Lawyers Club Columbus (pres. 1976-77), Athletic Club, Scioto Country Club, Wedgewood Country Club, Masons. Lutheran. Federal civil litigation, State civil litigation, Labor. Home: 2512 Danvers Ct Columbus OH 43220-2822 Office: Thompson Hine & Flory 10 W Broad St Ste 700 Columbus OH 43215-3435

MOULDS, JOHN F. federal judge; m. Elizabeth Fry, Aug. 29, 1964; children: Donald B., Gerald B. Student, Stanford U., 1955-58; BA with honors, Calif. State U., Sacramento, 1960; JD, U. Calif, Berkeley, 1963. Bar: U.S. Supreme Ct., U.S. Dist. Ct. (no. dist.) Calif., U.S. Dist. Ct. (ea. dist.) Calif. 1968, U.S. Ct. Claims 1982, U.S. Ct. Appeals (9th cir.) 1967, Calif. Rsch. analyst Calif. State Senate Fact-Finding Com. on Edn., 1960-61; adminstrv. asst. Senator Albert S. Rodda, Calif., 1961-63; staff atty. Calif. Rural Legal Assistance, Marysville, 1966-68, dir. atty. Marysville field office and Sacramento legis. adv. office, 1968-69; staff atty. Sacramento Legal Aid, 1968-69; ptnr. Blackmon, Isenberg & Moulds, 1969-85, Isenberg, Moulds & Hemmer, 1985; magistrate judge U.S. Dist. Ct. (ea. dist.) Calif., 1985—, chief magistrate jdge, 1988-97. Moot ct. and trial practice judge U. Calif. Davis Law Sch., 1975—, U. of Pacific McGeorge Coll. Law, 1985—; part-time U.S. magistrate judge U.S. Dist. Ct. (ea. dist.) Calif., 1983-85; mem. 9th Cir. Capital Case Com., 1992—, U.S. Jud. Conf. Com. on the Magistrate Judge Sys., 1992—, Adv. Com. to the Magistrate Judges' Divsn. Adminstv. Office of U.S. Jud. Conf., 1989—. Author: (with others) Review of California Code Legislation, 1965, Welfare Recipients' Handbook, 1967; editor: Ninth Circuit Capital Punishment Handbook, 1991. Atty. Sacramento Singlemen's Self-Help Ctr., 1969-74; active Sacramento Human Relations Commn., 1969-75, chair, 1974-75; active community support orgn. U. Calif. at Davis Law Sch., 1971—; mem., atty. Sacramento Community Coalition for Media Change, 1972-75; bd. dirs. Sacramento Country Day Sch., 1982-90, Sacramento Pub. Libr. Found., 1985-87; active various polit. orgns. and campaigns, 1960-82. Mem. ABA, Fed. Bar Assn., Nat. Coun. Magistrates (cir. dir. 1986-88, treas. 1988-89, 2d v.p. 1989-90, 1st v.p. 1990-91), Fed. Magistrate Judges Assn. (pres.-elect 1991, pres. 1992-93), Calif. State-Fed. Jud. Coun. Conf. (panelist capital habeas corpus litigation 1992), Fed. Jud. Ctr. Training Conf. for U.S. Magistrate Judges (panel leader 1993), Milton L. Schwartz Inns of Ct. Office: 8240 US Courthouse 501 I St Ste 8-240 Sacramento CA 95814-7300

MOULTON, HUGH GEOFFREY, lawyer, retired business executive; b. Boston, Sept. 18, 1933; s. Robert Selden and Florence (Bracq) M.; m. Catherine Anne Clark, Mar. 24, 1956; children: H. Geoffrey, Cynthia C. Moulton Bassett. B.A., Amherst Coll., 1955; LL.B., Yale U., 1958; postgrad. Advanced Mgmt. Program, Harvard U., 1984. Bar: Pa. 1959. Assoc. Montgomery, McCracken, Walker-Rhoads, Phila., 1958-66, ptnr., 1967-69; v.p., counsel Dolly Madison Industries, Inc., 1969-70; sec. Alco Std. Corp., Valley Forge, Pa., 1970-72, v.p. law, 1973-79, v.p., sec., gen. counsel, 1979-83, sr. v.p., gen. counsel, 1983-92, exec. v.p., chief adminstrv. officer, gen. counsel, 1992-94; exec. v.p. Alco Std. Corp. now IKON Office Solutions Inc., 1994-96, Unisource Worldwide, Inc., 1997-99; ret., 1999. Pres. Wissahickon Valley Watershed Assn., Ambler, Pa., 1975-78, treas., 1978—; mem. Pa. Coun. for Econ. Edn., bd. dirs., 1985-95; trustee Beaver Coll., 1991—, chair, 1998—. Mem. Am. Corp. Counsel Assn. (bd. dirs. Delaware Valley chpt. 1984-88, pres. 1986-87), Nature Conservancy (trustee Pa. chpt. 1991—, chmn. 1993—), Sunnybrook Golf Club (Plymouth Meeting, Pa.), Cape Cod Nat. Golf Club (Harwich, Mass.), Lemon Bay Golf Club (Englewood, Fla.). Home: 300 Williams Rd Fort Washington PA 19034-2015 Address: Solutions Inc 300 Williams Rd Fort Washington PA 19034 E-mail: hgmoulton@att.net

MOULUN, RENEE, lawyer; b. Mexico City, May 6, 1962; came to the U.S., 1962; d. Roberto Moulun and B.J. Willits; m. Bart Anderson Brush; 1 child, Hanna. BA, U. Hawaii, 1986; JD, Lewis & Clark U., 1996. Bar: Oreg. 1996. Natural resources specialist Oreg. Water Resources Dept., Salem. Dean's fellow Northwestern Sch. Law, Lewis & Clark U., Portland, 1993-96. Mem. Oreg. Bar Assn. (exec. com. nat. resources sect. 1998—), N.W. Environ. Def. Ctr., Phi Beta Kappa. Home: 9416 SW 4th Ave Portland OR 97219-4819

MOURSUND, ALBERT WADEL, III, lawyer, rancher; b. Johnson City, Tex., May 23, 1919; s. Albert Wadel and Mary Frances (Stribling) M., Jr.; m. Mary Allen Moore, May 8, 1941; children: Will Stribling, Mary Moore Moursund. LLB, U. Tex., 1941. Bar: Tex. 1941, U.S. Ct. Appeals (5th cir.) 1964, U.S. Dist. Ct. (so. dist.) Tex. 1964, U.S. Dist. Ct. (we. dist.) Tex. 1964, U.S. Tax Ct. 1972. Pvt. practice law, Johnson City, 1946-63; mem. Moursund & Moursund Johnson City, Round Mountain and Llano, Tex., 1963-80; ptnr. Moursund, Moursund, Moursund & Moursund, 1980—, county judge Blanco County, Tex., 1953-59; chmn. bd. Arrowhead Bank, 1963—, Cattleman's Nat. Bank, Round Mountain; bd. dirs., pres. Arrowhead Co., Arrowhead West, Inc., Tex. Am. Moursund Corp., S.W. Moursund Corp., Ranchlander Corp. Mem. Parks and Wildlife Commn., 1963-67, Tex. Ho. reps., 1948-52. With USAAF, 1942-46. Mem. ABA, Tex. Bar Assn., Hill County Bar Assn. (past pres.), Blanco Country Hist. Soc. (charter), Masons, Woodmen of World. General practice. Office: Moursund Moursund Moursund & Moursund PO Box 1 Round Mountain TX 78663-0001

MOUSEL, CRAIG LAWRENCE, lawyer; b. St. Louis, July 22, 1947; s. George William and Charlotte (Howard) M.; m. Polly Deane Burkett, Dec. 21, 1974; children: Donna, Dennis, D'Arcy. AB, U. So. Calif., 1969; JD, Ariz. State U., 1972. Bar: Ariz. 1973, U.S. Dist. Ct. Ariz. 1973, U.S. Ct. Appeals (9th cir.) 1973, U.S. Dist. Ct. (cen. dist.) Calif. 1984, Colo. 1993; registered lobbyist, Ariz. Adminstrv. asst. to Hon. Sandra O'Connor Ariz. State Senate, Phoenix, 1971-72; asst. atty. gen. Ariz. Atty. Gen.'s Office, 1973-75; ptnr. Sundberg & Mousel, 1975—. Spl. counsel City of Chandler, 1991 Hearing officer Ariz. State Personnel Bd., 1976-80, spl. appeals counsel, 1978—; hearing officer Ariz. Outdoor Recreation Coordinating Commn., 1975; dep. state land commr. Ariz. State Land Dept., 1978; precinct capt. Rep. Com.; mem. Ariz. Kidney Found., Orpheum Theatre Found., Phoenix Zoo Curators Club; sponsor Phoenix Art Mus.; varsity baseball coach Valley Luth. H.S., 1995-97, St. Mary's H.S., 2000; asst. baseball coach St. Mary's H.S., 1997-99. Fellow Ariz. Bar Found.; mem. ABA, ATLA, Ariz. Bar Assn., Maricopa County Bar Assn., Sports Lawyers Assn., Internat. Platform Assn., Ariz. Club, Am. Baseball Coaches Assn., Nat. High Sch. Baseball Coaches Assn., Ariz. Baseball Coaches Assn., USC Ptnrs. Alumni Group, U. So. Calif. Alumni Assn., Ariz. State U. Alumni Assn., Ariz. State Coll. Law Alumni Assn. Administrative and regulatory, General corporate, Entertainment. Office: Sundberg & Mousel 934 W Mcdowell Rd Phoenix AZ 85007-1730 E-mail: mousel@mindspring.com

MOUSSA, RHONDA K. lawyer; b. Praidence, R.I., July 17, 1971; d. Dhofo S. and Samia M.; m. Daniel R. Gillies, Sept. 12, 1998. BA in Polit. Sci., Columbia U., 1993; JD, NYU, 1996. Bar: N.Y. 1997, N.J. 1997. Atty. Kelley Drye & Warren, N.Y.C., 1996-97, Watson Farley & Williams, N.Y.C., 1997—. General corporate, Finance. Home: 330 E 39th St Apt 25P New York NY 10016 Office: Watson Farley & Williams 380 Madison Ave New York NY 10017-2513

MOW, ROBERT HENRY, JR. lawyer; b. Cape Girardeau, Mo., Dec. 10, 1938; s. Robert H. Sr. and Anne Elise (Beck) M.; m. Jody K. Boggs, Aug. 29, 1987; children: Robert M., Brynn A., W. Brett, Rebecca M., W. Kirk, Allison M. Student, Westminster Coll., 1956-57; AB with distinction, U. Mo., 1960; LLB magna cum laude, So. Meth. U., 1963. Bar: Tex. 1963, U.S. Dist. Ct. (no. dist.) Tex. 1965, U.S. Dist. Ct. (so. dist.) Tex. 1969, U.S. Dist. Ct. (ea. and we. dists.) Tex. 1976, U.S. Ct. Claims 1973, U.S. Ct. Appeals (5th cir.) 1972, U.S. Ct. Appeals (11th cir.) 1981, U.S. Ct. Appeals (fed. cir.) 1994, U.S. Supreme Ct. 1978. Assoc. Carrington, Johnson & Stephens, Dallas, 1963-69; ptnr. Carrington, Coleman, Sloman & Blumenthal, 1970-85, Hughes & Luce, LLP, Dallas, 1985—. Editor-in-chief Southwestern Law Jour., 1962-63. Trustee First Bapt. Acad., chair, 1999—. Served to 1st lt. U.S. Army, 1963-65. Fellow Am. Coll. Trial Lawyers; mem. Dallas Assn. Def. Counsel (chmn. 1976-77), Tex. Assn. Def. Counsel (v.p. 1981-82), Am. Bd. Trial Advocates (pres. Dallas chpt. 1983-84). Republican. Baptist. Federal civil litigation, State civil litigation, Professional liability. Office: Hughes & Luce LLP 1717 Main St Ste 2800 Dallas TX 75201-4685 E-mail: mowb@hughesluce.com

MOWELL, GEORGE MITCHELL, lawyer; b. Balt., July 31, 1951; s. George Robert and Polly (Sattler) M.; m. Patricia Edith Forbes, Sept. 23, 1978; children: Rachel Elizabeth, George Robert. BA, Washington Coll., Chestertown, Md., 1973; JD, U. Balt., 1977. Bar: Md. 1978, U.S. Dist. Ct. Md. 1981, U.S. Bankruptcy Ct. 1982. Claims authorizer Social Security Adminstrn., Balt., 1973-79; law clk. to presiding justice Kent County Cir. Ct., Chestertown, 1979-81; ptnr. Boyer & Mowell, 1981-87, Mowell, Nunn & Wadkorsky, Chestertown, 1987-98, Wadkovsky & Mowell, Chestertown, 1998—. Atty. Kent County Planning Commn., Chestertown, 1982—, Betterton Planning Commn., 1987—, Town of Rock Hall, 1987—; panel atty Public Defenders Office, 1981—, Md. Vol. Lawyers, 1981—; mem. adv. bd. Farmers Bank of Md., 1994-99. Bd. dirs. Kent County Heart Assn., Chestertown, 1983-84; mem. Galena Planning Commn., 1997—. Mem. ABA, Md. Bar Assn. (com. on laws 1984-87), Kent County Bar Assn. (sec. 1985-86, treas. 1987-88, v.p. 1988-89, pres. 1990-93), Balt. Bar Assn., Md. Trial Lawyers Assn., Elks. Democrat. Episcopalian. Family and matrimonial, General practice, Land use and zoning (including planning). Home: 140 Deer Field Dr Chestertown MD 21620-2482 Office: Wadkovsky & Mowell 107 Court St Chestertown MD 21620-1507 Fax: 410-778-9325

MOY, MARY ANASTASIA, lawyer; b. Melrose Park, Ill., Aug. 13, 1964; d. Kenneth Kwok and Chuk Ying (Tsang) M. BA cum laude, Wellesley Coll., 1986; JD, U. Pa., 1989. Bar: N.Y. 1991, D.C. 1993, U.S. Dist. Ct. (so. and ea. dists.) N.Y. 1992. Law clk. to Hon. Glenn E. Mencer U.S. Dist. Ct. (we. dist.), Pitts., 1989-90; assoc. Thelen, Reid & Priest, N.Y.C., 1990-93, Ladas & Parry, N.Y.C., 1993-98, 1999-2000; ptnr. Bristol-Myers Squibb Co., 2000—. Assoc. counsel N.Y. State Gov.'s Jud. Screening Com. for 1st Jud. Dept., 1991-92. Articles editor U. Pa. Jour. of Internat. Bus. Law, 1988-89. Mem. Asian Am. Bar Assn. of N.Y., Internat. Trademark Assn. Republican. Avocations: opera, music, dance, travel. Federal civil litigation, Trademark and copyright. Office: Bristol-Myers Squibb Co 345 Park Ave New York NY 10154

MOYA, PATRICK ROBERT, lawyer; b. Belen, N.Mex., Nov. 7, 1944; s. Adelicio E. and Eva (Sanchez) M.; m. Sara Dreier, May 30, 1966; children: Jeremy Brill, Joshua Dreier. AB, Princeton U., 1966; JD, Stanford U., 1969. Bar: Calif. 1970, Ariz. 1970, D.C. 1970, U.S. Dist. Ct. (no. dist.) Calif. 1970, U.S. Ct. Claims 1970, U.S. Tax Ct. 1970, U.S. Ct. Appeals (D.C. cir.) 1970, U.S. Supreme Ct. 1973. Assoc. Lewis and Roca, Phoenix, 1969-73, ptnr., 1973-83; sr. ptnr. Moya, Bailey, Bowers & Jones, P.C., 1983-84; ptnr., mem. nat. exec. com. Gaston & Snow, 1985-91; ptnr. Quarles & Brady, LLP, 1991—, mem. nat. exec. com., 2000—. Instr. sch. of law Ariz. State U., 1972; bd. dirs. homebid.com, inc., 1999-2000; BIGE Real Estate, Inc., 2000-. Mem. Paradise Valley Bd. Adjustment, 1976-80, chmn., 1978-80; mem. Paradise Valley Town Coun., 1980-82; bd. dirs. Phoenix Men's Arts Coun., 1973-81, pres., 1979-80; bd. dirs. The Silent Witness, Inc., 1979-84, pres., 1981-83; bd. dirs. Enterprise Network, Inc., 1989-94, pres., 1991-92; bd. dirs. Phoenix Little Theatre, 1973-75, Interfaith Counseling Svc., 1973-75; precinct committeeman Phoenix Rep. Com., 1975-77; dep. voter registrar Maricopa County, 1975-76; mem. exec. bd. dirs. Gov.'s Strategic Partnership for Econ. Devel.; pres. GSPED, Inc.; mem. of Steering Com. for Sonora-Ariz. Joint Econ. Plan; mem. Gov.'s Adv. Com., Ariz. and Mex., Ariz. Corp. Commn. Stock Exch. Adv. Coun., Ariz. Town Hall. Mem. ABA, Nat. Hispanic Bar Assn., Los Abogados Hispanic Lawyers Assn., Nat. Assn. Bond Lawyers, Ariz. Bar Assn., Maricopa County Bar Assn., Nat. Mgmt. Com., Paradise Valley Country Club, Univ. Club. General corporate, Mergers and acquisitions, Securities. Office: Quarles & Brady LLP One Renaissance Sq Two North Central Ave Phoenix AZ 85004-2391

MOYER, THOMAS J. state supreme court chief justice; b. Sandusky, Ohio, Apr. 18, 1939; s. Clarence and Idamae (Hessler) M.; m. Mary Francis Moyer, Dec. 15, 1984; 1 child, Drew; stepchildren: Anne, Jack, Alaine, Elizabeth. BA, Ohio State U., 1961, JD, 1964. Asst. atty. gen. State of Ohio, Columbus, 1964-66; pvt. practice law, 1966-69; dep. asst. Office Gov. State of Ohio, 1969-71, exec. asst., 1975-79; assoc. Crabbe, Brown, Jones, Potts & Schmidt, 1972-75; judge U.S. Ct. Appeals (10th cir.), 1979-86; chief justice Ohio Supreme Ct., 1987—. Sec. bd. trustees Franklin U., Columbus, 1986-87; trustee Univ. Club, Columbus, 1986; mem. nat. council adv. com. Ohio State U. Coll. Law, Columbus. Recipient Award of Merit, Ohio Legal Ctr. Inst.; named Outstanding Young Man of Columbus, Columbus Jaycees, 1969. Mem. Ohio State Bar Assn. (exec. com., council dels.), Columbus Bar Assn. (pres. 1980-81), Critchon Club, Columbus Maennerchor Club. Republican. Avocations: sailing, tennis. Office: Ohio Supreme Ct 30 E Broad St Fl 3 Columbus OH 43266-0001

MOYLAN, JAMES JOSEPH, lawyer; b. Forest Hills, N.Y., Feb. 3, 1948; s. James Gerard and Jessie Cora (Geary) M.; m. Barbara Chesrow, Aug. 29, 1970; children: James, C., Joseph O., Alicia G. BSBA, U. Denver, 1969, JD, 1971. Bar: Colo. 1972, D.C. 1972, Ill. 1975, U.S. Dist. Ct. Colo. 1972, U.S. Supreme Ct. 1975. Trial atty. SEC, Washington, 1972-75; assoc. gen. counsel Chgo. Bd. Options Exch., Ill., 1975-77; assoc. Abramson & Fox, Chgo., 1977-80; ptnr. Bowen, Knepper & Moylan Ltd., 1980-82, Moylan & Early, Ltd., Chgo., 1983-84; prin. James J. Moylan and Assocs., Ltd., 1984-95; ptnr. Arnstein & Lehr, 1995-2000, Tressler, Soderstrom, Maloney & Priess, Chgo., 2000—. Adj. prof. law IIT Chgo. Kent Coll. Law, 1976—; former pub. dir. MidAm. Commodity Exch. divsn. Chgo. Bd. Trade, Chgo. Contbr. articles to profl. jours. Mem.: ABA (sect. corp., banking and bus. law, sect. litigation), Ill. State Bar Assn. (sect. coun. mem.), Chgo. Bar Assn., D.C. Bar Assn., Theta Chi (grand chpt. 1993—2000, funds bd. 2000—). Republican. Roman Catholic. General corporate, Securities, Commodities. Fax: 312-627-1717. E-mail: jmoylan@mail.tsmp.com

MOYNIHAN, JOHN BIGNELL, retired lawyer; b. N.Y.C., July 25, 1933; s. Jerome J. and Stephanie (Bignell) M.; m. Odilia Marie Jacques, Nov. 13, 1965; children: Blair, Dana. BS, Fordham U., 1955; JD, St. John's U., N.Y.C., 1958. Bar: Tex. 1961, U.S. Supreme Ct. 1965, U.S. Dist. Ct. (we. dist.) Tex. 1968, U.S. Ct. Appeals (5th cir.) 1973. Sole practice, Brownsville, Tex., 1961-62; asst. city atty. City of San Antonio, 1962-63;

sole practice San Antonio, 1963-65; estate tax atty. IRS, 1965-73; dist. counsel EEOC, 1974-79; asst. U.S. atty. Office U.S. Atty., 1980-87, sr. litigation counsel, 1987-94; sole practice, 1995-98; ret., 1998. Chmn. reform and renewal com., San Antonio Roman Cath. Archdiocese, 1968. Served with U.S. Army, 1958-60; lt. col. USAFR (ret.), 1986. Mem. San Antonio Bar Assn. (chmn. state and nat. legis. com. 1972-73, Meritorious Svc. award 1968), Fed. Bar Assn. (bd. dirs. San Antonio chpt. 1983—, pres. elect 1986, pres. 1987), KC (pres. 1967). Civil rights, Federal civil litigation, Labor. Home: 11011 Whispering Wind St San Antonio TX 78230-3746 E-mail: djmoynihan@aol.com

MRACHEK, LORIN LOUIS, lawyer; b. Fairmont, Minn., Jan. 5, 1946; s. Louis L. and Kathleen (Loring) M.; m. Elizabeth Moss, Aug. 31, 1968; children: Kathleen Elizabeth, Louis Moss. BA with honors, Fla. State U., 1968; MBA, JD, Columbia U., 1974. Bar: Fla. 1974, Va. 1977, U.S. Ct. Mil. Appeals 1977, U.S. Supreme Ct. 1978; cert. in civil trial law and bus. litigation Fla. Bar Bd. Certification; cert. in bus. bankruptcy law Am. Bd. Bankruptcy Certification; cert. in civil trial advocacy Nat. Bd. Trial Advocacy. Commd. 2d lt. USMC, 1969, advanced through grades to capt., 1974, chief def. counsel Marine Corps. Recruit Depoit, 1975-77, resigned, 1977; spl. asst. to gen. counsel U.S. Ry. Assn., Washington, 1977-78; shareholder Gunster, Yoakley, Valdes-Fauli & Stewart, P.A., West Palm Beach, Fla., 1978-2000; founding shareholder Page, Mrachek, Fitzgerald & Rose, 2000—. Editor-in-chief Columbia Jour. Law and Social Problems, 1973-74; contbr. articles to profl. jours. Fellow Am. Coll. Trial Attys.; mem. ABA, Am. Bankruptcy Inst., So. Fla. Bankruptcy Bar Assn. Avocations: running, tennis, golf. Bankruptcy, General civil litigation. Office: 505 S Flagler Dr Ste 200 West Palm Beach FL 33401-5941 E-mail: lmrachek@pm-law.com

MUCCI, GARY LOUIS, lawyer; b. Buffalo, Nov. 12, 1946; s. Guy Charles and Sally Rose (Battaglia) M.; m. Carolyn Belle Taylor, May 4, 1991. BA cum laude, St. John Fisher Coll., 1968; JD, Cath. U., 1972. Bar: N.Y. 1972. Law clk. to Hon. John T. Curtin U.S. Dist. Ct., Buffalo, 1972-74; assoc. atty. Donovan Leisure Newton & Irvine, N.Y.C., 1974-75, Saperston & Day P.C., Buffalo, 1975-80, sr. ptnr., 1980—. Chmn. bd. Buffalo Philharm. Orch., 1985-86; pres. Hospice Buffalo, 1986-87; mem. N.Y. State Coun. on the Arts, 1987; chmn. Citizens Com. on Cultural Aid, Buffalo, 1992—; trustee St. John Fisher Coll. Recipient Brotherhood award NCCJ, Buffalo, 1983; named Man of Yr. William Paca Soc., 1984. Mem. Erie County Bar Assn., N.Y. State Bar Assn. Antitrust, General corporate, Real property. Home: 27 Tudor Pl Buffalo NY 14222-1615 Office: Saperston & Day PC 3 Fountain Plz Ste 1100 Buffalo NY 14203-1486

MUCCIA, JOSEPH WILLIAM, lawyer; b. N.Y.C., May 31, 1948; s. Joseph Anthony and Charlotte (Mohring) M.; m. Margaret M. Reynolds, June 29, 1985. BA magna cum laude, Fordham U., 1970, JD, 1973. Bar: N.Y. 1974, U.S. Dist. Ct. (so. dist.) N.Y. 1974, U.S. Dist. Ct. (ea. dist.) N.Y. 1980, U.S. Ct. Appeals (2d cir.) 1974, U.S. Ct. Appeals (D.C. cir.) 1980, U.S. Supreme Ct. 1980. Assoc. Cahill Gordon & Reindel, N.Y.C., 1973-82; ptnr. Corbin Silverman & Sanseverino, 1983—. Assoc. editor Fordham Law Rev., 1972-73. Mem. ABA (litigation sect.), N.Y. County Lawyers Assn., Fed. Bar Coun., N.Y. State Bar Assn. (com. litigation sect.), Phi Beta Kappa, Pi Sigma Alpha. Federal civil litigation, State civil litigation, Securities. Office: Corbin Silverman & Sanseverino 805 3rd Ave New York NY 10022-7513 E-mail: jmuccia@csslaw.com

MUCHIN, ALLAN B. lawyer; b. Manitowoc, Wis., Jan. 10, 1936; s. Jacob and Dorothy (Biberfeld) M.; m. Elaine Cort, Jan. 28, 1960; children: Andrea Muchin Leon, Karen, Margery Muchin Goldblatt. BBA, U. Wis., Manitowoc, 1958, JD, 1961. Gen. counsel IRS, Chgo., 1961-65; assoc. Altman, Kurlander & Weiss, 1965-68, ptnr., 1968-74; co-mng. ptnr. Katten Muchin & Zavis, 1974-95, chmn. bd., 1995—. Bd. dirs. Chgo. Bulls, Chgo. White Sox, Alberto-Culver Co., Acorn Investment Trust; bd. visitors U. Wis. Law Sch.; trustee Noble St. Charter Sch. Pres. Lyric Opera Chgo., 1993—; mem. adv. com. Am. Com. for Weizmann Inst. of Sci., Chgo., 1991—. Mem. Econ. Club Chgo., Comml. Club Chgo. Avocations: travel, tennis, reading. Office: Katten Muchin Zavis 525 W Monroe St Ste 1600 Chicago IL 60661-3693

MUCHOW, DAVID JOHN, lawyer, consultant; b. Holliston, Mass., Aug. 25, 1944; s. Albert J. and Mildred E. (Gerni) M.; m. Marilee Nietmann, July 10, 1971; children: Heather, Scott. B.S., Sch. Fgn. Svc., Georgetown U., 1966, J.D., 1971; postgrad., Cornell U. Law Sch., 1966-68. Bar: Fla. 1972, U.S. Supreme Ct. 1977, D.C. 1979, Va. 1988. Staff asst. to Congressman James Haley, Washington, 1962-66; with Office Mgmt. and Budget, 1968-69; staff Nat. Security Coun., 1969-70; assoc. Smathers & Herlong, 1970-73; trial atty., spl. asst. to atty. gen. U.S. Dept. Justice, 1973-76; gen. counsel, corp. sec. Am. Gas Assn., Arlington, Va., 1976-98, spl. counsel, 1998—; exec. v.p. New Century Land Renewal, LLC, 1998—; gen. counsel Bus. Coun. for Sustainable Energy; sr. cons. Nat. Rufal Utilities Coop. Fin. Corp. Trustee Eastern Mineral Law Found., Morgantown, W.Va. Co-editor: Energy Law and Transactions; co-author: Regulation of the Gas Industry. Recipient Spl. Achievement award Dept. Justice, 1975. Mem. ABA (vice-chmn. gas com. pub. utility law sect.), Am. Corp. Counsel Assn. (chmn. legal reform task force). Home: 4449 N 38th St Arlington VA 22207-4551

MUDD, JOHN O. lawyer; b. 1943; BA, Cath. U., 1965, MA, 1966; JD, U. Mont., 1973; LLM, Columbia U., 1986; JSD of Law, 1994. Bar: Mont. 1973. Pntr. Mulroney, Delaney, Dalby & Mudd, Missoula, Mont., 1973-79; lectr. U. Mont., 1973-74, 75-76, prof. law, dean, 1979-88; ptnr. Garlington, Lohn & Robinson, Missoula, 1988-1999; sr. v.p. Providence Svcs., 2000—. Pres. Mid-Continent Assn. Law Schs., 1982-83. Editor: Mont. Law Rev., 1972-73. Bd. dirs. St. Patrick Hosp., 1985-90, Providence Svcs. Corp., 1992-97, Ascension Health, 1999—; elected Dem. candidate U.S. Senate, 1994; chmn. Mont. Commn. Future of Higher Edn., 1980-81. With U.S. Army, 1967-73. Mem. ABA, Am. Judicature Soc. (bd. dirs. 1985-89), State Bar Mont. General civil litigation, Labor, Legislative.

MUDD, PHILIP JOHN, lawyer; b. Huddersfield, Yorkshire, Eng., Jan. 19, 1959; s. George Cecil and Jane M.; m. Janice Sylvia Williamson; children: Christopher, Jonathan. LLB with honors, Bristol U., 1980. Bar: Law Soc. Eng. and Wales. Ptnr. Walker Morris, Leeds, Eng., 1985—; mng. ptnr., 1998—. Contbr. articles to profl. jour. Fellow Assn. Bus. Recovery Profls.; mem. Insolvency Lawyers Assn. Avocations: music, sailing, skiing. Banking, Bankruptcy. Office: Walker Morris Kings Ct 12 King St L51 2HL Leeds Yorkshire England Fax: 0113 2459412. E-mail: pjm@walkermorris.co.uk

MUECKE, CHARLES ANDREW (CARL MUECKE), federal judge; b. N.Y.C., Feb. 20, 1918; s. Charles and Wally (Roeder) M.; m. Claire E. Vasse; children by previous marriage: Carl Marshall, Alfred Jackson, Catherine Calvert. B.A., Coll. William and Mary, 1941; LL.B., U. Ariz., 1953. Bar: Ariz. 1953. Rep. AFL, 1947-50; reporter Ariz. Times, Phoenix, 1947-48; since practiced in; with firm Parker & Muecke, 1953-59, Muecke, Dushoff & Sacks, 1960-61; U.S. atty. Dist. Ariz., 1961-64, U.S. dist. judge, 1964—, now sr. judge. Mem. Phoenix Planning Commn., 1955-61, chmn., 1960; chmn. Maricopa County Dem. Party, 1961-62. Maj. USMC, 1942-45, USMCR, 1945-60. Mem. Fed. Bar Assn., Ariz. Bar Assn., Maricopa Bar Assn., Dist. Judges Assn. Ninth Circuit, Phi Beta Kappa, Phi Alpha Delta, Omicron Delta Kappa.

MUELLER, DIANE MAYNE, lawyer; b. Milw., Aug. 8, 1934; d. George and Ann (Matuszewski) Markussen; widowed; 1 child, Paul Wilhite; m. Milton W. Mueller, Jan. 1, 1990. AB, Valparaiso U., 1956; MSW, Fla. State U., 1963; JD summa cum laude, DePaul U., 1974. Bar: Ill. 1974, U.S. Dist. Ct. (no. dist.) Ill. 1974, U.S. Dist. Ct. (ea. dist.) Wis. 1977, N. Mex., 1996. Assoc. Seyfarth, Shaw, Fairweather & Geraldson, Chgo., 1974-82, ptnr., 1982-86; asst. group counsel LTV Steel Co., Cleve., 1986-93, sr. atty., 1993-95. Adj. prof. Northwestern U. Sch. Law, 1984-86. Mem. Chgo. Club, Chgo. Yacht Club, Exec. Club of Chgo. (chmn. bd. 1984-85, mem. adv. bd. 1986-96), Econ. Club Chgo., Albuquerque Petroleum Club. General corporate. Home: 1216 Rock Rose Rd Albuquerque NM 87122-1115

MUELLER, MARK CHRISTOPHER, lawyer; b. Dallas, June 19, 1945; s. Herman August and Hazel Deane (Hatzenbuehler) M.; m. Linda Jane Reed. BA in Econs., So. Meth. U., 1967; MBA in Acctg., 1969, JD, 1971. Bar: Tex. 1971, U.S. Dist. Ct. (no. dist.) Tex. 1974, U.S. Tax Ct. 1974; CPA, Tex. Acct. Arthur Young & Co., Dallas, 1967-68, A.E. Krutilek, Dallas, 1968-71; pvt. practice law, 1971—; assoc. L. Vance Stanton, 1971-72. Instr. legal writing and rsch. So. Meth. U., Dallas, 1970-71, instr. legal acctg., 1975; mem. unauthorized practice of law com. Supreme Ct. Tex. Leading articles editor Southwestern Law Jour., 1970-71. Mem. NRA, Tex. Bar Assn., Tex. State Rifle Assn., Tex. Soc. CPA's, Dallas Bar Assn., SAR, Sons Republic Tex., Sons of Union Vets. of Civil War, Sons Confederate Vets., Mil. Orer Stars and Bars, Order of Coif, Dallas Hist. Soc., Dallas County Pioneer Assn., Rock Creek Barbeque Club, Masons, Shriners, York Rite, Grotto, Scottish Rite (32 degree Knight Commdr. Ct. of Honor), Beta Alpha Psi, Phi Delta Phi, Sigma Chi. State civil litigation, General practice, Real property. Home: 7310 Brennans Dr Dallas TX 75214-2804 Office: 6510 Abrams Rd Ste 565 Dallas TX 75231-7292

MUELLER, ROBERT SWAN, III, federal official, lawyer; b. N.Y.C., Aug. 7, 1944; s. Robert Swan Jr. and Alice (Truesdale) M.; m. Ann Standish, Sept. 3, 1966; children: Cynthia, Melissa. BA, Princeton U., 1966; MA, NYU, 1967; JD, U. Va., 1973. Bar: Mass., U.S. Dist. Ct. Mass., U.S. Ct. Appeals (1st cir.), Calif., U.S. Dist. Ct. (no. dist.) Calif., U.S. Ct Appeals (9th cir.). Assoc. Pillsbury, Madison & Sutro, San Francisco, 1973-76; asst. U.S. atty. U.S. Atty.'s Office, No. Dist. Calif., 1976-80; chief unit spl. prosecutions, Calif. no. dist. U.S. Atty.'s Office, 1980-81, chief criminal div., 1981-82, chief criminal div. Mass. dist. Boston, 1982-85, 1st asst. U.S. atty. in Boston, 1985, U.S. atty. for Mass. dist., 1986-87, dep. U.S. atty. for Mass. dist., 1987-88; ptnr. Hill and Barlow, 1988-89; asst. to atty. gen. for criminal matters U.S. Dept. Justice, Washington, 1989-90, asst. atty. gen. for criminal div., 1990-93; lawyer Hale & Dorr, 1993—95; US atty, Calif no. dist U.S. Dept of Justice , 1998—2001, acting dep. U.S. Atty. Gen., 2001; dir. FBI, 2001—. Capt. USMC, 1967-70; Vietnam. Decorated Bronze Star, Purple Heart, Vietnamese Cross of Gallantry. Office: FBI J Edgar Hoover Bldg 935 Pennsylvania Ave NW Washington DC 20535-3404*

MUGRIDGE, DAVID RAYMOND, lawyer, educator, writer; b. Detroit, Aug. 6, 1949; s. Harry Raymond and Elizabeth Lou (Aldrich) M.; m. Sandra Lee Jackson, June 25, 1988; children: James Raymond, Sarah Lorraine. BA, U. of Ams., Puebla, Mex., 1970; MA, Santa Clara U., 1973; JD, San Joaquin Coll. of Law, 1985. Bar: Calif. 1986, U.S. Dist. Ct. (ea. dist.) Calif. 1986, U.S. Ct. Appeals (9th cir.) 1987, U.S. Supreme Ct. 1996; cert. specialist in criminal law. Staff atty. to presiding justice 5th Dist. Ct. Appeals, Fresno, Calif., 1985-87; assoc. Law Office of Nuttall, Berman, Magill, 1987-88; pvt. practice, 1988—. Tchr. Fresno City Coll., 1988-96; tchr. Spanish for legal profession, Fresno, 1994; tchr. Fresno Pacific U., 1997—; arbitrator Fresno County Bar Assn., 1988—; judge pro-tem juvenile, traffic and small claims Fresno County Superior Ct., 1988—. Contbg. author: Practical Real Estate Law, 1995,99. Mem. Calif. Attys. for Criminal Justice, Calif. State Bar Assn. (cert. specialist in criminal law). Republican. Roman Catholic. Avocations: fishing, travel, photography, hiking. Appellate, Criminal, Personal injury. E-mail: mugridge@juno.com

MUHLBACH, ROBERT ARTHUR, lawyer; b. Los Angeles, Apr. 13, 1946; s. Richard and Jeanette (Marcus) M.; m. Kerry Eldene Mahoney, July 26, 1986. BSME, U. Calif., Berkeley, 1967; JD, U. Calif., San Francisco, 1976; MME, Calif. State U., 1969; M in Pub. Adminstrn., U. So. Calif., 1976. Bar: Calif. 1976. Pub. defender County of Los Angeles, 1977-79; assoc. Kirtland & Packard, Los Angeles, 1979-85, ptnr., 1986—. Chmn. Santa Monica Airport Commn., Calif., 1984-87, chmn., bd. dirs. Hawthorne Airport Cmty. Assn. Inc. Served to capt. USAF, 1969-73. Mem. ABA, AIAA, Internat. Assn. Def. Counsel, Am. Bd. Trial Advs. Federal civil litigation, Insurance, Personal injury. Office: Kirtland & Packard Ste 2600 1900 Avenue Of The Stars Los Angeles CA 90067-4507 E-mail: ram@kirtland-packard.com

MUIR, J. DAPRAY, lawyer; b. Washington, Nov. 9, 1936; s. Brockett and Helen Cassin (Dapray) M.; m. Louise Rutherfurd Pierrepont, July 16, 1966. A.B., Williams Coll., 1958; J.D., U. Va., 1964. Bar: Md., Va., D.C. 1964, U.S. Supreme Ct. 1967. Asst. legal advisor for econ. and bus. affairs U.S. Dept. State, 1971-73; ptnr. Ruddy & Muir, LLP, Washington. Mem. U.S. del. to Joint U.S./USSR Comml. Commn., 1972; chmn. D.C. Securities Adv. Com., 1981-84, mem. 1985-88. Bd. editors Va. Law Rev, 1963-64; contbr. articles to profl. jours. Mem. bd. dirs. Trust Mus. Exhbns. Lt. (j.g.) USNR, 1958-61. Mem. D.C. Bar (chmn. internat. law div. 1977-78, chmn. environ., energy and natural resources div. 1982-83, Met. Club (Washington), Chevy Chase (Md.) Club, Am. Arbitration Assn. (panel of comml. arbitrators 1997—). General corporate, Securities. Home: 3104 Q St NW Washington DC 20007-3027 Office: 1730 K St NW Ste 304 Washington DC 20006

MUIR, MALCOLM, federal judge; b. Englewood, N.J., Oct. 20, 1914; s. John Merton and Sarah Elizabeth Muir; m. Alma M. Brohard, Sept. 6, 1940 (dec. 1985); children: Malcolm, Thomas, Ann Muir, Barbara (dec.), David Clay. B.A., Lehigh U., 1935; LL.B., Harvard U., 1938. Sole practice, Williamsport, Pa., 1938-42, 45-49, 68-70; mem. firm, 1949-68; judge U.S. Dist. Ct. (mid. dist.) Pa., 1970—. Active charitable orgns., Williamsport, 1939-70 Mem. ABA, Pa. Bar Assn. (pres.-elect 1970) Avocation: reading. Office: US Dist Ct Ste 401 240 W 3rd St Williamsport PA 17701-6438

MUKAMAL, STEVEN SASOON, lawyer; b. Bagdad, Iraq, Aug. 5, 1940; s. Abraham and Mary (Murad) M.; m. Nancy Barst, Aug. 3, 1963 (div. Mar. 1983); children: Wendy, Betsy, Thomas; m. Kathleen Nanowsky, Nov. 25, 1983; children: Theodore Douglas, Andrew John. BA, Mich. State U., 1962; JD, Bklyn. Law Sch., 1965. Bar: N.Y. 1966, U.S. Dist. Ct. (so. dist.) N.Y. 1967, (ea. dist.) N.Y., U.S. Ct. Appeals (1st, 2nd and 3rd cirs.) 1968, U.S. Supreme Ct. 1975. Sr. ptnr. Barst & Mukamal, N.Y.C., 1965—. Pres. Immigration Info. Sys., Hong Kong, L.I.C. Mortgage Corp., Around the Clock Realty Corp., 33-00 No. L.I.C. Assocs., The Factory L.P.; bd. dirs. The A Cons. Team Inc. Author: U.S. Immigration Laws: Working, Living, and Staying in America, 1993, translated into Chinese and Japanese, 1993; mem. editorial bd. Transnational Immigration Lawyer Reporter, 1978—; contbr. articles to profl. jours. Exec. dir., spl. immigration counsel Nat. Com. for Furtherance of Jewish Edn., 1980—, v.p., 1996—; mayor Village of Woodsburg, N.Y., 1975-78. Recipient Internat. Humanitarian award Nat. Com. for Furtherance of Jewish Edn., 1981. Mem. Am. Immigration Lawyers Assn. (chair com. cert. 1991, life mem. bd. dirs., lectr. 1970—, chmn. ann. conf. 1967-81, treas. 1974-75, 1st v.p. 1975-76, 2d v.p. 1976-77, pres. 1977-78), Coun. on Fgn. Rels. Avocations: tennis, art, thoroughbred horse racing and breeding, human motivation. Immigration, naturalization, and customs. Office: Barst & Mukamal 2 Park Ave Rm 1902 New York NY 10016-9396

MUKASEY, MICHAEL B. federal judge; b. 1941; AB, Columbia U., 1963; LLB, Yale U., 1967. Assoc. Webster Sheffield Fleischmann Hithcock & Brookfield, 1967-72, Patterson, Belknap, Webb & Tyler, 1976-88; asst. U.S. atty. U.S. Dist. Ct. (so. dist.) N.Y., 1972-76, dist. judge, 1988—. Lectr. in law Columbia Law Sch. Contbr. articles to profl. jours. Office: US Dist Ct US Courthouse 500 Pearl St New York NY 10007-1316

MULCAHY, CHARLES CHAMBERS, lawyer, educator; b. Milw., Oct. 5, 1937; s. Thomas Lawrence and Mary (Chambers) M.; m. Judith Ann Schweiger, June 29, 1963; children: Mary Mulcahy Muth, Meg Mulcahy Ekmark, Beth. BS, Marquette U., 1959, JD, 1962. Bar: Wis. 1962, Fla. 1987. Atty., pres. Mulcahy & Wherry, Milw., 1966-91; atty. Whyte Hirschboeck Dudek S.C., 1991—. Adj. prof. Marquette U. Law Sch., Milw., 1975-90; hon. consul Belgium, Milw., 1985—; pres. Pub. Policy Forum, 1992-94; bd. dirs. Wis. Mfrs. and Commerce, 1988-95; mem. Wis. Coun. on Mcpl. Collective Bargaining, 1993—; bd. dirs. Med. Coll. Wis., 1980—, Greater Milw. Com., 1976—. Author: Public Employer Managers Manual, 1968; co-editor: Public Employment Law , 1974, 2nd edit., 1979, 3rd. edit., 1988. County supr. Milw. County, 1964-76; pres. Milw. Tennis Classic, 1975—; chmn. War Meml. Corp., 1976-84; pres. Wis. World Trade Ctr., 1987-91 (Meritorious Svc. award 1991). With USAF, 1962-68. Recipient County Achievement award Nat. Assn. Counties, 1976, Human Rels. award Nat. Conf. on Cmty. and Justice, 1998, Annual Svc. award Nat. Sports Law Inst., 1998, Bill Letwin Tennis award, 1998, O' Neill award Nat. Sports Law Inst., 1998. Mem. Milw. County Hist. Soc. (pres. 1980-81), Marquette Law Alumni Assn. (pres. 1971-72). Republican. Roman Catholic. Avocations: tennis, history, reading, travel. General corporate, Labor. Home: 1820 E Fox Ln Fox Point WI 53217-2858 Office: Whyte Hirschboeck Dudek SC 111 E Wisconsin Ave Ste 2100 Milwaukee WI 53202-4861 E-mail: cmulcahy@whdlaw.com

MULHERN, EDWIN JOSEPH, lawyer; b. Bklyn., Mar. 8, 1927; s. Edward Thomas and Jennie (Keenan) M.; m. Maureen P. Purcell, Oct. 2, 1964; children: Edwin T., Deborah J., Kevin T. BBA, St. John's U., 1950, LLB, 1954. Bar: N.Y. 1954, U.S. Dist. Ct. (ea. and so. dists.) N.Y. 1954, U.S. Supreme Ct. 1960. Sr. acct. Susquehanna Mills Inc., N.Y.C., 1947-53; chief acct. Rockwood Chocolate Co., Bklyn., 1953-54; trial atty. Allstate Ins. Co., Freeport, N.Y., 1954-57; claims rep. State Farm Ins. Co., Hempstead, N.Y., 1957-58; sole practice, Bellmore, N.Y., 1958-70, Mineola, N.Y., Carle Place, N.Y., 1970—; mem. joint grievance com. for 10th jud. dist. (N.Y.), 1981-89. Pres. Christian Bros. Boys' Assn., 1975-82; bd. dirs. Legal Aid Soc. of Nassau County, 1980—. Served with USAAF, 1945-46. Mem. ABA, N.Y. State Bar Assn., Nassau Bar Assn. (bd. dirs. 1981-83, chmn. admissions com. 1979, chmn. grievance com. 1980-82), Suffolk County Bar Assn., Nassau Lawyers Assn. (pres. 1975, exec. dir. 1993—, Man of Yr. 1981), Criminal Cts. Bar Assn. of Nassau County (pres. 1976), Criminal Cts. Bar Assn. of Suffolk County, Am. Assn. Trial Lawyers. Clubs: University of L.I. (Hempstead), K.C. (new Hyde Park, N.Y.). Criminal, Family and matrimonial, Personal injury. Office: 1 Old Country Rd Ste 145 Carle Place NY 11514-1801

MULHERN, PATRICK J. lawyer, banker; b. N.Y.C., Mar. 17, 1928; s. John J. and Beatrice (Gilholly) M.; m. Joan F. Cassidy, June 14, 1952; children— Eileen, John, Barbara. B.S., Fordham U., 1952, J.D., 1955. Bar: N.Y. 1955, U.S. Dist. Ct. (so. dist.) N.Y. Assoc. counsel Shearman & Sterling, 1955-66; v.p. cashier's adminstrn. Citibank N.A., N.Y.C., 1966-79, sr. v.p. Office of Gen. Counsel, 1979-80, sr. v.p., gen. counsel, 1980—. Served with U.S. Army, 1946-47. Mem. Assn. Bar City of N.Y., Am. Soc. Corp. Secs., ABA, Fed. Bar Assn. Clubs: University (N.Y.C.); Unqua Corinthian Yacht (Massapequa, N.Y.). Lodges: K.C., Kiwanis. Office: Citicorp 399 Park Ave New York NY 10022-4614

MULL, GALE W. lawyer; b. Hillsdale, Mich., Sept. 8, 1945; s. Wayne E. and Vivian M. (Bavin) M.; m. Holly Ann Allen, Aug. 2, 1969 (div. Nov. 1983); 1 child, Carter B.; m. Jeanne Anne Haughey, Aug. 18, 1985. BA, Mich. State U., 1967; MA in Sociology, Ind. U., 1969; JD, Emory U., 1972. Bar: Ga. 1972, U.S. Dist. Ct. (no. dist.) Ga. 1972, U.S. Ct. Appeals (5th cir.) 1973, U.S. Ct. Appeals (11th cir.) 1981. Instr. sociology Clemson (S.C.) U., 1968-69, Spelman Coll., Atlanta, 1969-70; pvt. practice, 1972-75; ptnr. Mull & Sweet, 1975-81; pres. Gale W. Mull, P.C., 1981—. Bd. dirs. BOND Community Fed. Credit Union, Atlanta, 1975-81; directing atty. Emory Student Legal Services, Atlanta, 1975-91; Sociology instr. Clemson U., Clemson, S.C., 1968-69, Spelman Coll., Atlanta, Ga., 1969-70. Pres. Inman Park Restoration, Inc., Atlanta, 1972-74, BASS Orgn. for Neighborhood Devel., Inc., 1974-78; mem. Housing Appeals Bd., Atlanta, 1982-88; mem. Mayor's Task Force on Prostitution, 1984-86; bd. dirs. ACLU Ga., 1981-92, sec. bd. dirs., 1983-85, cooperating atty., 1972—; vestry St. John's Episcopal Ch., 1992-99, sr. warden, 1998-99; bd. dirs. St. John's Episcopal Day Sch., 1992-97, Bethlehem Ministries, 1997—, Trinity Towers, Inc., 1999-2000. Mem. ABA, Ga. Bar Assn., Atlanta Bar Assn., Lawyers Club Atlanta. Club: Quail Unltd. (bd. dirs., sec. 1984-86). Criminal, Family and matrimonial, General practice. Office: 990 Edgewood Ave NE Atlanta GA 30307-2581

MULLANAX, MILTON GREG, lawyer; b. Galveston, Tex., Mar. 16, 1962; s. Milton Gayle and Sharon Kay (Sanders) M.; m. Susan Lynn Griebe, Apr. 19, 1986; children: Adrienne Irene, Mason Glenn. BA in History, U. Tex., Arlington, 1987; JD, U. Pacific, 1991. Bar: Calif., 1991, Nev., 1992, Tex., 1993, Colo., 1993, Minn., 1994, D.C., 1993; U.S. Dist. Ct. (ea. dist.) Calif. 1991, U.S. Dist. Ct. Nev., 1993, U.S. Dist. Ct. (no. dist.) Tex. 1996. Congrl. intern U.S. Rep. Richard K. Armey, Arlington, Tex., 1985; senate aide U.S. Sen. Phil Gramm, Dallas, 1985-86; legis. aide State Rep. Kent Grusendorf, Austin, Tex., 1987; law clk. Criminal Divsn. U.S. Atty., Sacramento, 1989-90; legal researcher Nev. Atty. Gen., Carson City, 1991-92, dep. atty. gen., 1992-94; pvt. practice Fort Worth, Tex., 1995—. Vol. Reagan/Bush 1984, Dallas/Ft. Worth, 1984, Rep. Nat. Conv., Dallas, 1984, Armey for Congress, Arlington, 1984, Vol. Lawyers of Washoe County, Reno, Nev., 1993-94. Mem. ABA, ATLA, Tarrant County Bar Assn., State Bar of Tex. Avocations: sports, politics, reading, shortwave radio. General civil litigation, Estate planning, General practice. Office: 500 W 7th St Ste 1212 Fort Worth TX 76102-4734

MULLANEY, THOMAS JOSEPH, lawyer; b. N.Y.C., Feb. 9, 1946; s. James Joseph and Dorothy Mary (Fulling) M.; m. Christine E. Hampton, Aug. 16, 1969; children: Richard, Jennette. BA, Fordham U., 1967; JD, U. Va., 1970; LLM, NYU, 1977. Bar: Va. 1970, N.Y. 1971, U.S. Dist. Ct. (so. and ea. dists.) N.Y. 1972, U.S. Ct. Appeals (2d cir.) 1972, U.S. Supreme Ct. 1975. Assoc. Brown, Wood, Ivey, Mitchell & Petty, N.Y.C., 1970-79, Law Offices of John M. Kenney, Garden City, N.Y., 1979-84; ptnr. Abrams, Thaw & Mullaney, N.Y.C., Farmingdale, 1985-91; dir., sr. counsel law dept. Merrill Lynch & Co., Inc., N.Y.C., 1991—. Capt. JAGC, U.S. Army, 1971-74. Mem. Va. State Bar Assn., N.Y. State Bar Assn. Republican. Roman Catholic. Federal civil litigation, State civil litigation, Securities. Home: 104 Huntington Rd Garden City NY 11530-3122 Office: 222 Broadway Fl 14 New York NY 10038-2510 E-mail: tmullaney@exchange.ml.com

MULLARE, T(HOMAS) KENWOOD, JR. lawyer; b. Milton, Mass., Jan. 19, 1939; s. Thomas Kenwood and Catherine Marie (Leonard) M.; m. Joan Marie O'Donnell, May 27, 1967; children: Jennifer M. Cedrone, Tracy K., Jill M., Joyce M. AB, Holy Cross Coll., 1961; LLB, Boston Coll., 1964. Bar: Mass. 1964. Atty. New Eng. Electric System, 1964-69; v.p., gen. counsel, sec. AVX Corp., N.Y.C., 1970-73; v.p., gen. counsel, clk. Tyco Labs., Inc., Exeter, N.H., 1974-77; v.p., gen. counsel, sec. SCA Svcs., Inc., Boston, 1978-83; spl. counsel Houghton, Mifflin Co., 1984-85, v.p., dir. bus. software divsn., 1985-92; pres. North River Capital Co., Inc., Norwell,

Mass., 1990—; gen. counsel, sec. Aztec Tech. Ptnrs., Inc., Braintree, 1999—. Bd. dirs. Friendship Home, Inc. Mem. regional adv. bd. Commonwealth of Mass. Dept. Mental Retardation, 1994-97; bd. dirs. Barque Hill Assn., Norwell, 1980-84, pres., 1981-83; pres. Ch. Hillers, Norwell, 1983-84; bd. dirs. South Shore Assn. for Retarded Citizens, Weymouth, Mass., 1993-98, chmn., 1995-97. Mem. Boston Bar Assn. General corporate, Intellectual property, Mergers and acquisitions. Home: 31 Barque Hill Dr Norwell MA 02061-2815 Office: Aztec Tech Ptnrs Inc Ste 220 50 Braintree Hill Office Park 20 Braintree MA 02184-8724

MULLARKEY, MARY J. state supreme court chief justice; b. New London, Wis., Sept. 28, 1943; d. John Clifford and Isabelle A. (Steffes) M.; m. Thomas E. Korson, July 24, 1971; 1 child, Andrew Steffes Korson. BA, St. Norbert Coll., 1965; LLB, Harvard U., 1968; LLD (hon.), St. Norbert Coll., 1989. Bar: Wis. 1968, Colo. 1974. Atty.-advisor U.S. Dept. Interior, Washington, 1968-73; asst. regional atty. EEOC, Denver, 1973-75; 1st atty. gen. Colo. Dept. Law, 1975-79, solicitor gen., 1979-82; legal advisor to Gov. Lamm State of Colo., 1982-85; ptnr. Mullarkey & Seymour, 1985-87; justice Colo. Supreme Ct., 1987—, chief justice, 1998—. Recipient Alumni award St. Norbert Coll., De Pere, Wis., 1980, Alma Mater award, 1993. Fellow ABA Found., Colo. Bar Found.; mem. ABA, Colo. Bar Assn., Colo. Women's Bar Assn. (recognition award 1986), Denver Bar Assn., Thompson G. Marsh Inn of Ct. (pres. 1993-94). Office: Supreme Ct Colo Judicial Bldg 2 E 14th Ave Denver CO 80203-2115*

MULLEN, GRAHAM C. federal judge; b. 1940; BA, Duke U., 1962, JD, 1969. Bar: N.C. 1969. Ptnr. Mullen, Holland, Cooper, Morrow, Wilder & Sumner, 1969-90; judge U.S. Dist. Ct. (we. dist.) N.C., Charlotte, 1990—. Lt. USN, 1962-66. Mem. N.C. Bar Assn. (bd. govs. 1983-88), Mecklenburg County Bar Assn. Office: US Courthouse 401 W Trade St Rm 230 Charlotte NC 28202-1619 E-mail: gmullen@ncwd.net

MULLEN, J. THOMAS, lawyer; b. Evanston, Ill., Aug. 27, 1940; BSE, Princeton U., 1963; JD cum laude, U. Mich., 1967. Bar: Ill. 1967. Ptnr. Mayer, Brown & Platt, Chgo.; ptnr.-in-charge London office, 1974-78. Bd. dirs. Legal Assistance Found. Chgo., 1979-85. Mem. ABA, Chgo. Bar Assn., Chgo. Coun. Lawyers. Office: Mayer Brown & Platt 190 S La Salle St Ste 3100 Chicago IL 60603-3441 E-mail: tmullen@mayerbrown.com

MULLEN, PETER P. lawyer; b. N.Y.C., Apr. 8, 1928; m. Cecilia Kirby; 5 children. AB cum laude, Georgetown U., 1948; LLB, Columbia U., 1951. Bar: N.Y. 1951. Ptnr. Skadden, Arps, Slate, Meagher & Flom LLP, N.Y.C., 1961-98, exec. ptnr., 1981-94, of counsel, 1998—. Co-chmn. Cardinal's Com. Laity Archdiocese N.Y., 1992—; bd. dirs., sec., treas., Eye Surgery, Inc. Formerly mem., pres. Bd. Edn. Pub. Schs., Bronxville, N.Y., 1979-81; chmn. Skadden Fellowship Found., 1988—; bd. dirs., vice-chmn. Lawrence Hosp., Bronxville, 1984-89; bd. dirs. Project Orbis, Georgetown U., Washington, 1982-99, chmn., 1985-92; bd. dirs. Legal Aid Soc., 1987-93, Vols. Legal Svcs., Inc., 1988-99, United Way Bronxville, 1985-93, Practicing Attys. Law Students, 1988-99; trustee Lawyer's Commn. Civil Rights Under Law, 1984-99; chmn. Gregorian U. Found., 1989—; bd. dirs., exec. com. Vatican Obs. Found., 1993. Named Man of Yr. Cath. Big Bros., 1987; recipient John Carroll award Georgetown U., 1984, John Carroll Medal Merit, 1988, Thomas More award Lawyers Com. Cardinal's Com. of the Laity, 1996, Elizabeth Ann Seton award Nat. Cath. Edn. Assn., 1998. Mem. Am. Bar Assn., N.Y. State Bar Assn. (com. securities regulation 1980-83), Assn. Bar City N.Y. (com. corp. law 1964-67, com. admissions 1965-68, com. securities regulation 1970-73), Soc. Friendly Sons St. Patrick (N.Y., pres. 1989-90), Knight Malta. Office: Skadden Arps Slate et al LLP 4 Times Sq New York NY 10036-6522

MULLENBACH, LINDA HERMAN, lawyer; b. Sioux City, Iowa, Dec. 25, 1948; d. Verner Wilhelm and Margaretta Victoria (Grant) Herman; m. Hugh James Mullenbach, Aug. 22, 1970; children: Erika Lynn, Linnea Britt. BS in Speech, Northwestern U., 1971, MS in Speech, 1972, JD, 1979. Bar: Ill. 1979, U.S. Dist. Ct. (no. dist.) Ill. 1979, D.C. 1983, U.S. Dist. Ct. D.C. 1983, U.S. Ct. Appeals (7th, D.C. and fed. cirs.), 1983, U.S. Supreme Ct. 1984. Assoc. Jenner & Block, Chgo., 1979-83, Dickstein, Shapiro & Morin, Washington, 1983-85, prin., 1985-87, ptnr., 1988-93; v.p., assoc. gen. counsel Zurich Small Bus. and Zurich Comml. Legal Divsn., Balt., 1994-99; asst. gen. counsel, v.p. Corp. Law Divsn. Zurich U.S., 1999-2001; asst. gen. counsel, v.p. corp. law divsn. Zurich N.Am., 2001—. Mem. ABA (litigation sect.), D.C. Bar Assn., Women's Bar Assn. D.C., Women's Legal Def. Fund, Assn. Trial Lawyer Am., Mortar Bd., Zeta Phi Eta. Federal civil litigation, Criminal, Labor. Home: 8201 Killean Way Potomac MD 20854-2728

MULLENDORE, JAMES MYERS, lawyer; b. Charlottesville, Va., Mar. 21, 1946; s. James M. and Elaine (Gregg) M.; m. Kristine B. Mullendore; children: Margaret E., Sean T. BS, W.Va. U., 1968; JD, U. Va., 1975. Bar: Mich. 1975, U.S. Dist. Ct. (we. dist.) Mich. Ptnr. Frye, Mullendore & Carr, Greenville, Mich., 1975-88; & Carr & Mullendore, 1988—. Pres., v.p. Greenville Bd. Edn., 1976-82; ofcl. Mid-Am. Football Conf., 1985-86, Big Ten Football Conf., 1987—; bd. dirs. United Way Greenville, 1978-83; chmn. controlled substances adv.com. State Mich.; bd. dirs. Danish Festival Inc, 1997-2000. Mem. ABA, Assn. Trial Lawyers Am., Mich. Trial Lawyers Assn. (pres. 1982-83), U.S. Football League (ofcl. 1983), Greenville Area C. of C. (chmn. bd. dirs.), Rotary (v.p. 1983-84). Congregationalist. Criminal, Family and matrimonial, Personal injury. Home: 13337 Oakcrest Ave Gowen MI 49326-9708 Office: PO Box 10 132 S Lafayette St Greenville MI 48838-1934

MULLER, FREDERICK ARTHUR, legal editor, publisher; b. Center Moriches, N.Y., Dec. 18, 1937; s. Frederick Henry and Estelle May (Reeve) M.; m. Ellen Ruth Willard, Sept. 8, 1962; children: John F., Matthew R. BA, U. Rochester, N.Y., 1960; JD, U. Chgo., 1963. Bar: Ill. 1963, N.Y. 1964, U.S. Ct. Mil. Appeals 1965, U.S. Dist. Ct. (we. dist.) N.Y. 1971. Law clk. to judge N.Y. State. Ct. Appeals, 1968-69, 72; assoc. Hodgson, Russ, Andrews, Woods & Goodyear, Buffalo, 1969-72; asst. consultation clk. N.Y. State Ct. Apls., 1973-82; dep. state reporter State of N.Y., 1982-90, state reporter, 1990—; cons. staff atty. N.Y. State Ct. on Judiciary, 1973; chmn. supervisory com. Stewart AFB Fed. Credit Union, 1964-65. Editor N.Y. State Official Style Manual, 1985, 87, 92, 96, 97. Mem. budget and allocations com. United Way Northeastern N.Y., Inc., 1975-80, bd. advisors law sch. U. Chgo., 1988—. Served with JAGC USAF, 1964-67. Mem. ABA (com. on appellate style manual 1987—), Am. Judicature Soc. (bd. dirs. 1996-97), Am. Assn. Law Librs. (task force citation formats 1994-95), Assn. Reporters of Jud. Decisions (sec. 1988-89, v.p. 1989-90, pres. 1990-91), N.Y. State Bar Assn., U. Chgo. Club (chmn. alumni schs. com., 1984-89, bd. dirs. 1986—), Phi Beta Kappa, Phi Delta Phi. Baptist. Home: 211 Milford Ln Mc Cormick SC 29835-2428

MULLER, KURT ALEXANDER, lawyer; b. Chgo., June 21, 1955; s. Jack and Janet (Kasten) M.; m. Sylvia Saltoon, Apr. 6, 1986; 1 child, Marissa Grace. BS, U. Wis., Parkside, 1977; JD, John Marshall Law Sch., 1986. Bar: Ill. 1986, U.S. Dist. Ct. (no. dist.) Ill. 1986, Ariz. 1987, U.S. Dist. Ct. (ea. dist.) Wis. 1989. Creative dir. Brand Advt., Chgo., 1977-80; dep. sheriff Cook County, 1978-86; broker Gerstenberg Commodities, 1980-83; assoc. Gordon & Glickson, P.C., 1986-87, Michael Harry Minton, P.C., Chgo., 1987-90; pvt. practice, 1990-92; ptnr. Law Offices of Richter-Muller, P.C., 1992-95; lawyer, CEO The Muller Firm, Ltd., 1995—. Author: In Consideration of Divorce: Giving Credit (and Debits) to Dissolution, 1991, 3d edit., 1998; contbr. The Jewish American Prince Handbook, 1986; contbr. articles to profl. jours. and newspapers; host (CBS radio show) Kurt Muller's Uncommon Law; monthly columnist for Chgo. Social: Ask Muller. Mem. ABA, ACLU, Nat. Smoker's Alliance, Chgo. Bar Assn., Masons. Avocations: interior design, films, theater, writing. E-mail: www. mullaw.com. Alternative dispute resolution, Family and matrimonial, Juvenile. Office: 200 N Dearborn St Apt 4602 Chicago IL 60601-1628 Fax: 312-855-9362

MULLIGAN, ELINOR PATTERSON, lawyer; b. Bay City, Mich., Apr. 20, 1929; d. Frank Clark and Agnes (Murphy) P.; m. John C. O'Connor, Oct. 28, 1950; children: Christine Fulena, Valerie Clark, Amy O'Connor, Christopher Criffan O'Connor; m. William G. Mulligan, Dec. 6, 1975. BA, U. Mich., 1950; JD, Seton Hall U., 1970. Bar: N.J. 1970. Assoc., Springfield and Newark, 1970-72; pvt. practice, Hackettstown, N.J., 1972; ptnr. Mulligan & Jacobson, N.Y.C., 1973-91, Mulligan & Mulligan, Hackettstown, 1976—. Atty. Hackettstown Planning Bd., 1973-86, Blairstown Bd. Adjustment, 1973-95; sec. Warren County Ethics Com., 1976-78, sec. Dist. X and XIII Fee Arbitration Com., 1979-87, mem. and chair, 1987-91, mem. dist. ethics com. XIII, 1992—; mem. spl. com. on atty. disciplinary structure N.J. Supreme Ct., 1981—; lectr. Nat. Assn. Women Judges, 1979, N.J. Inst. Continuing Legal Edn., 1988—. Contbr. articles to profl. jours. Named Vol. of Yr., Attys. Vols. in Parole Program, 1978. Fellow Am. Acad. Matrimonial Lawyers (1st woman pres. N.J. chpt. 1995-96); mem. ABA, Warren County Bar Assn. (1st woman pres. 1987-88), N.J. State Bar ASsn., N.J. Women Lawyers Assn. (v.p. 1985—), Am. Mensa Soc., Union League Club (N.Y.C.), Baltusrol Golf Club (Springfield, N.J.), Panther Valley Golf and Country Club (Allamuchy, N.J.), Kappa Alpha Theta. Republican. State civil litigation, Family and matrimonial, Probate. Home: 12 Goldfinch Way Hackettstown NJ 07840-3007 Office: 933 County Road 517 Hackettstown NJ 07840-4654 E-mail: llp-nj@mindspring.com

MULLIGAN, JOHN THOMAS, lawyer; b. Phila., Dec. 28, 1934; s. Martin A. and Mary Katherine (Glennon) M.; m. Marie A. Pinter, Aug. 22, 1959; children— Mary T., Lisa M. B.S. in Polit. Sci., St. Joseph's U., 1956; J.D. cum laude, U. Pa., 1959. Bar: N.Y. 1960, Pa. 1963, U.S. Dist. Ct. (so. and ea. dists.) N.Y. 1962, U.S. Dist. Ct. (ea. dist.) Pa. 1964, U.S. Tax Ct. 1962, U.S. Ct. Appeals (3d cir. 1965), U.S. Supreme Ct. 1965. Assoc. Dewey, Ballantine, Bushby, Palmer & Wood, N.Y.C., 1959-62; sr. atty. Western Electric Co., N.Y.C., 1962-63; ptnr. Lord & Mulligan, Media, Pa., 1963— ; solicitor Marple Twp., Broomall, Pa., 1970-71, Haverford Twp., Havertown, Pa., 1972-73, Radnor-Haverford-Marple Sewer Authority, Wayne, Pa., 1974-83; panel mem. Fed. Ct. Arbitration, Phila., 1977— . Mem. Haverford Twp. Adult Sch., Haverford, Pa., 1965-66; fin. chmn. Haverford Twp. Democratic Com., Havertown, 1965-70. Recipient Commendation U.S. Dist Ct. (ea. dist.) Pa. 1983. Mem. Assn. Trial Lawyers Am., ABA, Pa. Trial Lawyers Assn., Pa. Bar Assn., N.Y. State Bar Assn., Delaware County Bar Assn., Assn. Bar City of N.Y. Democrat. Roman Catholic. Clubs: Llanerch Country (Havertown, Pa.) (sec. 1977-81); Atlantic City Country (Northfield, N.J.); Overbrook Country (Bryn Mawr, Pa.). Federal civil litigation, State civil litigation, Environmental. Home: 2728 N Kent Rd Broomall PA 19008-2013 Office: Lord and Mulligan 218 W Front St Media PA 19063-3101

MULLIGAN, MICHAEL DENNIS, lawyer; b. St. Louis, Mar. 9, 1947; s. Leo Virgil and Elizabeth (Leyse) M.; m. Theresa Baker, Aug. 7, 1971; children: Brennan, Colin. BA in Biology, Amherst Coll., 1968; JD, Columbia U., 1971. Bar: Mo. 1971, U.S. Dist. Ct. (ea. dist.) Mo. 1972, U.S. Ct. Appeals (8th cir.) 1982, U.S. Tax Ct. 1985. Law clk. to judge U.S. Dist. Ct. (ea. dist.) Mo., 1971-72; assoc. Lewis, Rice & Fingersh, L.C., St. Louis, 1972-80, ptnr., 1980—. Mem. editl. bd. Estate Planning Mag., 1985—. Served as cpl. USMC, 1968-70. Fellow Am. Coll. Trust and Estate Counsel; mem. ABA (mem. real property, probate and trust, and taxation sects.), Mo. Bar Assn. (mem. probate and trust, taxation sects.). Probate, Estate taxation. Office: Lewis Rice & Fingersh LC 500 N Broadway Ste 2000 Saint Louis MO 63102-2147 E-mail: mmulligan@lewisrice.com

MULLIN, PATRICK ALLEN, lawyer; b. Newark, Jan. 13, 1950; s. Gerard Vincent and Frances Regina (Magnanti) M. BA, William Paterson U., 1972, MEd, 1974; JD, NYU, 1979, LLM in Taxation, 1990; postgrad., Harvard Law Sch., 1979; Gerry Spence's Trial Lawyers Coll., Duboise, Wyo., 1997. Bar: N.J. 1979, D.C. 1980, N.Y. 1990; cert. criminal trial atty. N.J. Supreme Ct. Law clk. to Hon. Dickinson R. DeBevoise, U.S. Dist. Ct. N.J., Trenton, 1979-80; assoc. Charles Morgan Assocs., Washington, 1980-81; pvt. practice, Hackensack, N.J., 1988—. Mem. Practitioners Adv. Group U.S. Sentencing Commn. Mem. ABA. Roman Catholic. Avocations: jogging, martial artist. Criminal, Taxation, general. Address: 25 Main St # 200 Hackensack NJ 07601-7015 also: 305 Madison Ave Ste 449 New York NY 10165-0006 Fax: 201-487-2840. E-mail: pmullin@bellatlantic.net

MULLINIX, EDWARD WINGATE, lawyer; b. Balt., Feb. 25, 1924; s. Howard Earle and Elsie (Wingate) M.; m. Virginia Lee McGinnes, July 28, 1944; children: Marcia Lee Ladd, Edward Wingate. Student, St. John's Coll., 1941-43; JD summa cum laude, U. Pa., 1949. Bar: Pa. 1950, U.S. Supreme Ct. 1955; cert. BBB Auto Line arbitrator. Assoc. Schnader Harrison Segal & Lewis LLP, Phila., 1950-55, ptnr., 1956-92, now sr. coun. Mem. adv. bds. Antitrust Bull., 1970-81, BNA Antitrust and Trade Regulation Report, 1981-94; mem. Civil Justice adv. group U.S. Dist. Ct. (ea. dist.) Pa., 1998—; mem. Civil Justice Reform Act of 1990 adv. group U.S. Dist. Ct. (ea. dist.) Pa., 1991-98; co-chmn. Joint U.S. Dist. Ct./Phila. Bar Assn. Alternative Dispute Resolution Com., 1990—; cons. on revision of local civil rules U.S. Dist. Ct. (ea. dist.) Pa., 1995—; mem. adv. com. U. Pa. Law Sch. Ctr. on Professionalism, 1988-92; judge pro tem Day Forward and Commerce Case Mgmt. programs, chmn. adv. com. Commerce program ct. Common Pleas of Phila. County; atty. advocate, mem. steering com. in elderly-victim-assistance program Phila. Dist. Atty.'s Office; faculty participant Pa. Bar Inst., and other CLE programs. Trustee Sta. KYW-TV Project Homeless Fund, 1985-86. Served with USMCR, 1943-44; to lt. (j.g.) USNR, 1944-46. Fellow Am. Bar Found. (life), Am. Coll. Trial Lawyers (emeritus, mem. complex litig. com. 1980-91, vice-chmn. com. 1981-83); mem. ABA (spl. com. complex and multidist. litig. 1969-73, co-chmn. com. 1971-73, coun. litig. sect. 1976-80), Pa. Bar Assn., Phila. Bar Assn., Hist. Soc. U.S. Dist. Ct. (ea. dist.) Pa. (bd. dirs. 1984—, pres. 1991-94), Juristic Soc., Order of Coif, Union League (Phila.), Socialegal Club (Phila.). Aronimink Golf Club (Newtown Sq., Pa.). Republican. Presbyterian. Home: 251 Chamounix Rd Saint Davids PA 19087-3605 Office: 1600 Market St Ste 3600 Philadelphia PA 19103-7286 E-mail: ewm@shsl.com

MULLINS, MARGARET ANN FRANCES, lawyer, educator; b. Jersey City, Feb. 3, 1953; d. William Francis Sr. and Ada Louise (Pellizzari) M.; m. Robert Laurence Tortoriello, Sept. 29, 1979; children: Lauren, Christopher, Kenneth. AB, Coll. of St. Elizabeth, 1975; JD, Seton Hall U., 1978. Bar: N.J. 1978, U.S. Dist. Ct. N.J. 1978, U.S. Ct. Appeals (3d cir.) 1982, U.S. Supreme Ct. 1982, N.Y. 1984, D.C. 1985, U.S. Ct. Appeals (D.C. cir.) 1986. Assoc. Edwin C. Eastwood Jr., North Bergen, N.J., 1978-79; asst. prosecutor Essex County Prosecutor's Office, Newark, 1980-82, Passaic County County Prosecutor's Office, Paterson, N.J., 1982-86; mem. faculty Seton Hall U. Sch. Law, Newark, 1987—. Mem. ABA, N.J. Bar Assn., N.Y. State Bar Assn. Republican. Roman Catholic. Home: 112 Heller Way Montclair NJ 07043-2512

MULLINS, ROGER WAYNE, lawyer; b. Bluefield, Va., Feb. 6, 1944; s. Robert Ford and Gladys Mae (Stacy) M.; m. Lois Nan Barnett, Apr. 3, 1977; children: Stacey Marie, Alison Lea. BS, U. Ala., 1968, JD, 1971. Bar: Va. 1971, U.S. Dist. Ct. (we. dist.) Va. 1974, U.S. Ct. Appeals (4th cir.) 1980. Jr. ptnr. McClintock & Mullins, Tazewell, Va., 1971; commonwealth atty. State of Va., County of Tazewell, 1977-80; pvt. practice Tazewell, 1981-84, 88—; pres. Mullins & Henderson, 1984-87. Served with USAF, 1962-66. Mem. Tazewell County Bar Assn. (pres. 1977), Va. State Bar, Va. Trial Lawyers Assn. (bd. govs. 1976—, v.p. 1984, pres. 1988). Democrat. Disciples of Christ. General practice. Home: 604 Summit St Bluefield VA 24605-9417 Office: PO Box 923 Tazewell VA 24651-0923

MULLMAN, MICHAEL S. lawyer; b. N.Y.C., Sept. 17, 1946; s. Herbert and Harriet (Weissman) M.; m. Ellen Mullman, 1975; children: Jeremy, Cassie. BA in Polit. Sci. cum laude, Union Coll., Schenectady, N.Y., 1968; JD, Columbia U., 1971. Bar: N.Y. 1972, U.S. Ct. Appeals (2d cir.), U.S. Dist. Ct., 1975. Atty. Paskus, Gordon & Hyman, N.Y.C., 1976-80; ptnr. Schonwald, Schaffzin & Mullman, 1980-89, Tenzer Greenblatt LLP, N.Y.C., 1989-99; adminstrv. ptnr. in charge N.Y. Blank Rome Tenzer Greenblatt LLP, 2000—, mem. distbn. com., mgmt. com. Bd. editors Columbia Jour. Law and Soc. Problems, articles edition, 1970-71. Nott scholar Union Coll., 1967, Harlan Fiske Stone scholar Sch. Law Columbia U., 1971. Mem. Bar Assn. N.Y.C., Phi Beta Kappa. Avocations: tennis, skiing, gardening. General corporate, Mergers and acquisitions, Real property. Office: Blank Rome Tenzer Greenblatt LLP The Chrysler Bldg 405 Lexington Ave New York NY 10174-0002

MULROY, THOMAS ROBERT, JR. lawyer; b. Evanston, Ill., June 26, 1946; s. Thomas Robert and Dorothy (Reiner) M.; m. Elaine Mazzone, Aug. 16, 1969. Student, Loyola U., Rome, 1966; BA, U. Santa Clara, Calif., 1968; JD, Loyola U., Chgo., 1972. Bar: Ill. 1973, U.S. Dist. Ct. (no. dist.) Ill. 1973, U.S. Ct. Appeals (7th cir.) 1973. Asst. U.S. atty. No. Dist. Ill., Chgo., 1972-76; ptnr. Jenner & Block, Chgo. 1976—, chmn. products liability group; adj. prof. Northwestern U. Sch. Law, Chgo., 1978-85, Loyola U. Sch. Law, 1983—, DePaul U. Sch. Law, Chgo., Nova U. Ctr. for Study of Law. Editor: Annotated Guide to Illinois Rules of Professional Conduct; contbr. articles to profl. jours.; bd. dirs. Loyola U. Trial Advocacy Workshop, 1982—, Legal Assistance Found., Ill. Inst. for Continued Legal Edn.; chmn. inquiry panel Ill. Atty. Registration and Disciplinary Commn., spl. counsel, 1989—. Mem. Chgo. Crime Commn., 1978—. Mem. ABA, (torts and ins. pratcie, chmn. rules and evidence com.), Am. Judicature Soc., Fed. Trial Bar, Legal Club Chgo., Law Club, 7th Fed. Cir. Bar Assn., Chgo. Bar Assn., Ill. Assn. Def. Trial Counsel, Ill. Bar Assn. Clubs: Univ., Execs. of Chgo., Union League. Federal civil litigation, State civil litigation, Product liability. Office: Jenner & Block 1 E Ibm Plz Fl 42 Chicago IL 60611-3586

MULVEY, W. MICHAEL, lawyer, court administrator; b. Salem, Mass., May 2, 1945; s. William Keane and Mary Angela (MacDuffie) M.; m. Debra Anne Dalton, July 1984; children— Courtney K., Meredith M., Wynne M. B.A., Villanova U., 1967; J.D., Del. Sch. Law, 1975. Bar: Pa. 1976, U.S. Dist. Ct. (ea. dist.) Pa. 1976, U.S. Ct. Appeals (3d cir.) 1983. Court adminstr. Phila. Ct. Common Pleas, 1971-78, mental health master, 1978— ; sole practice law, Phila., 1978-81; assoc. Sagot and Jennings, Phila., 1981-85; ptnr. Ritner, Mulvey & Flanagan, Phila., 1985— ; instr. basic legal practices course, 1978, civil practices course Pa. Bar Inst., 1980. Bd. dirs. Sparrowhawk, Ltd., Phila., 1982— . Mem. Assn. Trial Lawyers Am., Pa. Trial Lawyers Assn., Phila. Trial Lawyers Assn., Phila. Bar Assn., LAWPAC. Democrat. Roman Catholic. State civil litigation, Personal injury, Workers' compensation. Office: Ritner Mulvey and Flanagan The Exchange Suite 600 1411 Walnut St Philadelphia PA 19102

MUND, GERALDINE, judge; b. L.A., July 7, 1943; d. Charles J. and Pearl M. BA, Brandeis U., 1965; MS, Smith Coll., 1967; JD, Loyola U., 1977. Bar: Calif. 1977. Bankruptcy judge U.S. Ctrl. Dist. Calif., 1984—, bankruptcy chief judge, 1997—. Past pres. Temple Israel, Hollywood, Calif.; past mem. Bd. Jewish Fedn. Coun. of Greater L.A. Mem. ABA, L.A. County Bar Assn. Office: 21041 Burbank Blvd Woodland Hills CA 91367-6606

MUNDHEIM, ROBERT HARRY, law educator; b. Hamburg, Germany, Feb. 24, 1933; m. Guna Smitchens; children: Susan, Peter. BA, Harvard U., 1954, LLB, 1957; MA (hon.), U. Pa., 1971. Bar: N.Y. 1958, Pa. 1979. Assoc. Shearman & Sterling, N.Y.C., 1958-61; spl. counsel to SEC Washington, 1962-63; vis. prof. Duke Law Sch., Durham, N.C., 1964; prof. law U. Pa., Phila., 1965—. Univ. prof. law and fin., 1980-93, dean, 1982-89, Bernard G. Segal prof. law, 1987-89; co-chmn. Fried, Frank, Harris, Shriver & Jacobson, N.Y.C., 1990-92; exec. v.p., gen. counsel Salomon Inc., 1992-97; sr. exec. v.p., gen. counsel Salomon Smith Barney Holdings, Inc., 1997-98; of counsel Shearman & Sterling, 1999—; gen. counsel U.S. Dept. Treasury, Washington, 1977-80, trustee and pres. Am. Acad. in Berlin, 2000—; dir. Ctr. for Study of Fin. Instns., U. Pa.; pres. Appleseed Found.; trustee New Sch. U.; bd. dirs. eCollege, Salzburg Seminar, The Kitchen, Benjamin Moore & Co.; gen. counsel Chrysler Loan Guarantee Bd., 1980; mng. dir., mem. mgmt. bd. Salomon Bros. Inc., N.Y.C., 1992-97; overseer Curtis Inst. Fin., 2000—. Author: Outside Director of the Publicity Held Corporation, 1976; American Attitudes Toward Foreign Direct Investment in the United States, 1979; Conflict of Interest and the Former Government Employee: Re-thinking the Revolving Door, 1981; chmn. adv. bd. Jour. Internat. Econ. Law, 1996-97. Trustee SEC Hist. Soc. With USAF, 1961-62. Recipient Alexander Hamilton award U.S. Dept. Treasury, 1980, Harold P. Seligson award Practicing Law Inst., 1988, Francis J. Rawle award, ABA-ALI, 1992, Anti-Defamation League Human Rels. award, 1999. Mem. Am. Law Inst. (mem. coun., mem. exec. com.), Nat. Assn. Securities Dealers (gov.-at-large, vice-chmn.), San Diego Securities Regulation Inst. (chmn.), Am. Acad. in Berlin (pres. 2000—). Office: Shearman & Sterling 599 Lexington Ave Fl 16 New York NY 10022-6069

MUNDY, GARDNER MARSHALL, lawyer; b. Roanoke, Va., July 19, 1934; s. Gardner Adams and Betty (Marshall) M.; m. Jean Stephens, Nov. 13, 1956 (div. 1979); children: Stephens M., Liza I.; m. Jenice Hamrick, June 21, 1980 (div. 1998); children: G. Marshall Jr., Natalie J.; m. Monika Ferguson, Aug. 28, 1999. BA, Va. Mil. Inst., 1956; LLB, U. Va., 1962. Bar: Va. 1962, U.S. Dist. Ct. (we. dist.) Va. 1962, U.S. Ct. Appeals (4th cir.) 1962. Ptnr. Woods, Rogers & Hazlegrove, Roanoke, 1962-71, Mundy & Garrison, Roanoke, 1973-76, Mundy & Strickland, Roanoke, 1976-82; pvt. practice, 1982-86; ptnr. Mundy, Rogers & Frith, 1986—. 1st lt. U.S. Army, 1957-59. Fellow Am. Coll. Trial Lawyers, Am. Bd. Trial Advocates (pres. Western Va. chpt. 1990-91), Am. Bar Found., Va. Bar Found.; mem. ABA, Va. State Bar Assn. (chmn. bd. govs. litig. sect. 1985-86, bd. govs. sr. law sect. 2000—), Roanoke Bar Assn. (bd. dirs. 1986-90, pres. 1990-91), Shenandoah Club, Roanoke Country Club, Coral Beach and Tennis Club (Bermuda). Presbyterian. Avocations: tennis, skiing, cooking, growing roses. General civil litigation, Family and matrimonial, Personal injury. Home: 1542 Electric Rd Roanoke VA 24018-1106 Office: Mundy Rogers & Frith 1328 3rd St SW Roanoke VA 24016-5219 Fax: 540-982-1362. E-mail: gmundy@mrf-law.com

MUNGIA, SALVADOR ALEJO, JR. lawyer; b. Tacoma, Feb. 19, 1959; s. Salvador Alejo Sr. and Susie (Tamaki) M. BA, Pacific Luth. U., 1981; JD, Georgetown U., 1984. Bar: Wash. 1984, U.S. Dist. Ct. (we. dist.) Wash. 1985, U.S. Ct. Appeals (9th cir.) 1986, U.S. Supreme Ct. 1992. Law clk. to Justice Fred Dore Wash. State Supreme Ct., Olympia, 1984-85; law clerk to Hon. Carolyn R. Dimmick U.S. Dist. Ct. (we. dist.) Wash., Seattle, 1985-86; assoc. Gordon, Thomas, Honeywell, Malanca, Peterson & Daheim, Tacoma, 1986-91, ptnr., 1991—. Adj. prof. Pacific Luth. U., 1993-94. Vol. atty. ACLU, Tacoma, 1986—, bd. dirs., 1987-92; commr. Tacoma Human Rights Commn., 1990-96; bd. dirs. Legal Aid for Washington, 1992-96, life bd. dirs., 1997—. Mem. ABA, Wash. State Bar Assn., Fed. Bar Assn. Western Wash., Tacoma-Pierce County Bar Assn. (pres. 1999),

Pierce County Young Lawyers Assn. (trustee 1988-90), Wash. Alpine Club, Tacoma Lawn Tennis Club, Tacoma Club. Avocations: mountain climbing, skiing, tennis, running. Federal civil litigation, State civil litigation. Home: 615 N C St Tacoma WA 98403-2810 Office: Gordon Thomas Honeywell Malance Peterson & Daheim PO Box 1157 Tacoma WA 98401-1157 E-mail: smungs@gth-law.com

MUNIC, MARTIN DANIEL, lawyer; b. Duluth, Minn., Feb. 16, 1959; s. Robert Solomon and Pearl (Daniels) M.; m. Barbara Stimson, May 30, 1993; 1 child, Sophia Miriam. BA, Drake U., 1981; JD, U. Minn., 1984. Bar: Minn. 1984, U.S. Dist. Ct. Minn. 1986, U.S. Ct. Appeals (8th cir.) 1989. Law clk. to Hon. Harry H. MacLaughlin U.S. Dist. Ct., Mpls., 1984-86; assoc. Tanick & Heins, 1986-89, Opperman Heins & Paquin, Mpls., 1989-92; asst. county atty. Hennepin County Atty.'s Office, 1993—. Bd. dirs. Loan Assistance Repayment Program Minn., 1991-96, pres., 1991-94; arbitrator Nat. Futures Assn., Nat. Assn. Securities Dealers. Contbr. articles to profl. jours. Vol. atty. Minn. Civil Liberties Union, Mpls., 1988—92; alt. Dem.-Farmer-Labor State Conv., 1990, del., 1994; bd. dirs. Minn. NARL, 1995—99, PAC, 1998—. Recipient William O. Douglas award U. Minn., 1984, Edward J. Devitt award, 1983. Mem. Minn. Justice Found. (bd. dirs. 1983-84, 88-92, pres. bd. dirs. 1989-91), Minn. Assn. Parliamentarians, Nat. Assn. Parliamentarians, Hennepin County Bar Assn., Order of Coif, Phi Beta Kappa. Jewish. Avocations: baseball, cross-country skiing. Office: Hennepin County Atty Office A2000 Government Ctr Minneapolis MN 55487-0001 E-mail: martin.munic@co.hennepin.mn.us

MUNNEKE, GARY ARTHUR, law educator, consultant; b. Dec. 29, 1947; s. Leslie Earl and Margaret Frances (Fortsch) M.; children: Richard Arthur, Matthew Frederick. BA in Psychology, U. Tex., 1970, JD, 1973. Bar: Tex. 1973, Pa. 1987. Asst. dean, dir. placement U. Tex., Austin, 1978-80; asst. prof., asst. dean Del. Law Sch. Widener U., Wilmington, 1980-84, assoc. prof., 1984-87; pres. Legal Info. Sys., 1987-92; prof. Sch. Law Pace U., 1988—. Contbr. articles to profl. jours. Fellow Am. Bar Found., Coll. Law Practice Mgmt.; mem. ABA (chmn. standing com. on profl. utilization and career devel. 1981-85, chmn. law practice mgmt. sect. 1998-99, chmn. law practice mgmt. sect. pub. bd. 1992-95, articles editor Legal Econs. mag. 1984-86), State Bar Tex. Presbyterian. Office: Pace U Sch Law 78 N Broadway White Plains NY 10603-3710

MUNSEY, STANLEY EDWARD, lawyer; b. Brunswick, Maine, Mar. 12, 1934; s. Maynard Edward and Estelle Mary (Martin) M.; m. Elena Opal Munsey, Dec. 22, 1954; children: Stanley, Edward, Michele E. BA, Millsaps Coll., 1961; JD, Tulane U., 1964. Bar: Miss. 1965, Ala. 1970. With land dept. Shell Oil Co., New Orleans, 1964-66; pvt. practice Picayune, Miss., 1966-67; exec. dir. Muscle Shoals (Ala.) Coun. Local Govts., 1967-71; ptnr. Rosser & Munsey, Tuscumbia, Ala., 1971-85; sr. ptnr. Munsey & Ford, 1986-87; & Munsey, Ford & Heflin, 1987-98, Stanley E. Munsey & Assocs. P.C., Tuscumbia, 1998—. Chmn. N. Ala. Health Systems Agy., 1981-82; vice chmn. Ala. Statewide Health Coordinating Council, 1981-82. With AUS, 1953-58. Mem. ABA, Miss. Bar Assn., Ala. Bar Assn., Miss. Trial Lawyers Assn., Ala. Trial Lawyers Assn., Assn. Trial Lawyers Am. (mediator svcs.). Presbyterian. General civil litigation, State civil litigation, General practice. Office: PO Box 496 Tuscumbia AL 35674-0496

MUNSON, HOWARD G. federal judge; b. Claremont, N.H., July 26, 1924; s. Walter N. and Helena (O'Halloran) M.; m. Ruth Jaynes, Sept. 17, 1949; children: Walter N., Richard J., Pamela A. B.S. in Economics, U. Pa., 1948; LL.B., Syracuse U., 1952. Bar: N.Y. With Employers' Assurance Corp., Ltd., White Plains, N.Y., 1949-50; mem. firm Hiscock, Lee, Rogers, Henley & Barclay, Syracuse, 1952-76; judge U.S. Dist. Ct. No. Dist. N.Y., 1976—. Mem., pres. Syracuse Bd. Edn.; bd. dirs. Sta. WCNY-TV; chmn. ethics com. Onondaga County Legislature. Served with U.S. Army, 1943-45, ETO. Decorated Bronze Star, Purple Heart. Mem. Am. Coll. Trial Lawyers, Nat. Assn. R.R. Trial Counsel, Am. Arbitration Assn., Justinian Soc., Alpha Tau Omega, Phi Delta Phi. Office: US Dist Ct US Courthouse P O Box 7376 Syracuse NY 13261-7376

MUNSON, NANCY KAY, lawyer; b. Huntington, N.Y., June 22, 1936; d. Howard H. and Edna M. (Keenan) Munson. Student, Hofstra U., 1959-62; JD, Bklyn. Law Sch., 1965. Bar: N.Y. 1966, U.S. Supreme Ct. 1970, U.S. Ct. Appeals (2d cir.) 1971, U.S. Dist. Ct. (ea. and so. dists.) N.Y. 1968. Law clk. to E. Merritt Weidner, Huntington, 1959-66; sole practice, 1966—. Mem. legal adv. bd. Chgo. Title Ins. Co., Riverhead, N.Y., 1981—; bd. dirs., legal officer Thomas Munson Found. Trustee Huntington Fire Dept. Death Benefit Fund; pres., trustee, chmn. bd. Bklyn. Home Aged Men Found.; bd. dirs. Elderly Day Svcs. on the Sound, Huntington Rural Cemetery Assn., Inc. Mem. ABA, N.Y. State Bar Assn., Suffolk County Bar Assn., Bklyn. Bar Assn., NRA, DAR (trustee Ketewamoke chpt.), Soroptimists (past pres.). Republican. Christian Scientist. General practice, Probate, Real property. Office: 197 New York Ave Huntington NY 11743-2711

MUNSON, PETER KERR, lawyer; b. Sherman, Tex., Dec. 5, 1944; s. William Ben and Martha M. (deGolian) M.; m. Kathleen Cook, Aug. 30, 1969; children— Peter, Brian, Christopher. B.B.A., U. Notre Dame, 1967; J.D., U. Tex., 1970. Bar: Tex. 1970, U.S. Dist. Ct. (ea. dist.) Tex. 1970, U.S. Ct. Appeals (5th cir.) 1970; cert. specialist in family law, Tex. Sr. mem. Munson, Munson & Pierce, Grayson County, Tex. 1970— ; Gov's. appointee Commn. on Uniform State Laws, State of Tex., 1985-91, 97—. Chmn. adv. bd. Sherman-Denison Salvation Army, 1983— ; chmn. parish council St. Mary's Ch., Sherman, 1982-83; scoutmaster, dist. commr. Boy Scouts Am.; adv. bd., past chmn. Salvation Army; bd. dirs. Grayson County United Way, Sherman, 1973— . Ford Found. grantee, 1969. Mem. North Tex. Bar Assn., Tex. Council Sch. Bd. Attys. Roman Catholic. General corporate, Family and matrimonial, Real property. Office: Munson Munson Cardwell & Pierce 123 S Travis St Sherman TX 75090-5928

MUNZER, STEPHEN IRA, lawyer; b. N.Y.C., Mar. 15, 1939; s. Harry and Edith (Isacowitz) M.; m. Patricia Eve Munzer, Aug. 10, 1965; children: John, Margaret. AB, Brown U., 1960; JD, Cornell U., 1963. Bar: N.Y. 1964, U.S. Supreme Ct. 1974, U.S. Dist. Ct. (so. and eas. dists.) N.Y., U.S. Ct. Appeals (3d cir.). Formerly ptnr. Pincus Munzer Bizar & D'Alessandro, 1978-83; atty., real estate investor Munzer & Saunders, LLP, 1984—. Pres. Simcor Mgmt. Corp., N.Y.C., 1984—. Lt. USNR, 1965-75. Mem. Assn. of Bar of City of N.Y., N.Y. State Bar Assn., City Athletic Club, Washington Club. Jewish. Avocations: golf, skiing. Federal civil litigation, General civil litigation, Real property. Home: 99 Battery Pl New York NY 10280-1320 also: 170 Shearer Rd Washington CT 06793-1013 Office: 609 5th Ave New York NY 10017-1021

MUOKA, ALEXANDER NDUKA, lawyer; b. Lagus, Nigeria, Aug. 13, 1971; s. Alexander Nuannu and Esther Nneka M. LLB, Lagus State U., Nigeria, 1990; BL, Nigerial Law Sch., Nigeria, 1991; LLM, U. Lagus, Nigeria, 1994. Nigerian Bar; International Bar. Legal officer Abiola Holdings Ltd., Lagus, Nigeria, 1991-92; counsel Tunde Odanye & Co., Nigeria, 1992-96, head of chambers Nigeria, 1997; principal ptnr. A Muoka & Co., Nigeria, 1997—. Dir. Ingortech Business Network, Nigeria, 1999—. Author: (book) The Office of the Company Secretary, 1990. Mem. Intellectual Property Law Assn. of Nigeria (treas. 1998—). Avocations: reading, writing poetry, chess, music, traveling. General corporate, Intellectual property, Real property. Office: A Muoka & Co PO Box 3360 No 9 Turton Street 3d Fl Sabo-Yaba Lagus Nigeria Fax: 234-1-2693975. E-mail: amuoka_co@hotmail.com

MURAI, RENE VICENTE, lawyer; b. Havana, Cuba, Mar. 11, 1945; came to the U.S., 1960; s. Andres and Silvia (Muñiz) M.; m. Luisa Botifoll, June 12, 1970; 1 child, Elisa. BA, Brown U., 1966; JD cum laude, Columbia U., 1969. Bar: Fla. 1970, N.Y. 1972, U.S. Supreme Ct. 1977. Atty. Reginald Heber Smith Fellow Legal Svcs. Greater Miami, Fla., 1969-71; assoc. Willkie, Farr & Gallagher, N.Y.C., 1971-73; ptnr. Paul, Landy & Beiley, Miami, 1973-79; shareholder Murai, Wald, Biondo & Moreno, 1979—. Acting chmn. bd. dirs. PanAm. Bank, Miami; dir. Cuban Am. Bar Assn., 1982-96, pres., 1985; vice chmn., lectr. Internat. Conf. for Lawyers of the Ams., 1982, chmn. and lectr., 1984; mem. panel grievance com. Fla. Bar, 1983-86. Mng. editor Columbia Law Rev., 1967-69. Bd. dirs., sec. Archtl. Club of Miami, 1978-86; bd. dirs. Dade Heritage Trust, 1979-82, Facts About Cuban Exiles, Inc., 1982—, pres., 1989, Legal Svcs. of Greater Miami, Inc., 1980-90, pres. 1986-88, ARC, 1984-90, exec. com., 1988-90, Mercy Hosp. Found., 1985-91, United Way, 1989-95, dir. Dade Cmty. Found., 1988-93, chair grants com., 1991-93; chmn. adminstrn. of justice com. Fla. Bar Found., 1996-98, bd. dirs., 1991-2000, chmn. audit and fin. com., 1993-98, sec., 1997-98, pres. 1999-2000; mem. task force leadership Dade County Ptnrs. for Safe Neighborhoods, 1994-95, Code Enforcement Bd. City of Coral Gables, 1982-86, Bd. Adjustment, 1987-89, city mgr. selection com., 1987, charter rev. commn., 1980; trustee U. Miami, 1994-96; bd. dirs. Miami Children's Hosp., 1999—. Mem. ABA, Cuban-Am. Bar Assn., Dade County Bar Assn. (dir. 1987-88), Greater Miami C. of C., Spain-U.S. C. of C., Miami City Club (bd. dirs. 1997—, pres. 2000—). Democrat. Roman Catholic. Avocation: sports. Banking, Contracts commercial, General corporate. Home: 3833 Alhambra Ct Coral Gables FL 33134-6229 Office: Murai Wald Biondo & Moreno PA 25 SE 2nd Ave Ste 900 Miami FL 33131-1600 E-mail: rmurai@mwbm.com

MURANE, WILLIAM EDWARD, lawyer; b. Denver, Mar. 4, 1933; s. Edward E. and Theodora (Wilson) M.; m. Rosemarie Palmerone, Mar. 26, 1960; children: Edward Wheelock, Peter Davenport, Alexander Phelps. AB, Dartmouth Coll., 1954; LLB, Stanford U., 1957. Bar: Wyo. 1957, Colo. 1958, D.C. 1978, U.S. Supreme Ct. 1977. Assoc. then ptnr. Holland & Hart, Denver, 1961-69; dep. gen. counsel U.S. Dept. Commerce, Washington, 1969-71; gen. counsel FDIC, 1971-72; ptnr. Holland & Hart, Denver, 1972—. Pub. mem. Adminstrv. Conf. of the U.S., Washington, 1978-81. Bd. dirs. Ctr. for Law and Rsch., Denver, 1973-76, Acad. in the Wilderness, Denver, 1986—; trustee Colo. Symphony Orch., 1994-2000; mem. bd. visitors Stanford U. Law Sch. Capt. USAF, 1958-61. Fellow Am. Coll. Trial Lawyers; mem. ABA (ho of dels. 1991-96), U. Club, Cactus Club. Republican. Avocations: fishing, classical music. Administrative and regulatory, General civil litigation, Libel. Office: Holland & Hart 555 17th St Ste 2700 Denver CO 80202-3950

MURASE, JIRO, lawyer; b. N.Y.C., May 16, 1928; B.B.A., CCNY, 1955; J.D., Georgetown U., 1958, LL.D. (hon.), 1982. Bar: D.C. 1958, N.Y. 1959. Sr. ptnr. Marks & Murase L.L.P., N.Y.C., 1971-97, Bingham, Dana & Murase, N.Y.C., 1997—. Legal counsel Consulate Gen. of Japan; mem. Pres.'s Adv. Com. Trade Negotiations, 1980-82; mem. Trilateral Commn., 1985—; apptd. mem. World Trade Coun., 1984-94; adv. com. internat. investment, tech. and devel. Dept. State, 1975. Editorial bd.: Law and Policy in Internat. Bus. Trustee Asia Found., 1979-83, Japanese Ednl. Inst. N.Y.; bd. dirs. Japan Soc., Japanese C. of C. in N.Y., Inc.; bd. regents Georgetown U.; adv. coun. Pace U., Internat. House Japan; pres. Japanese-Am. Assn. N.Y., Inc., 1996-98—, Japan Ctr. Internat. Exch., 2001—. Recipient N.Y. Gov.'s citation for contbns. to internat. trade, 1982; named to Second Order of Sacred Treasure (Japan), 1989. Mem. ABA, Assn. of Bar of City of N.Y., N.Y. State Bar Assn., N.Y. County Lawyers Assn., Maritime Law Assn., Consular Law Soc., Fed. Bar Coun., Am. Soc. Internat. Law, World Assn. Lawyers, Japanese-Am. Soc. Legal Studies, Am. Arbitration Assn., Lic. Execs. Soc., U.S. C. of C. Clubs: Nippon (dir.); Ardsley Country; N.Y. Athletic; Mid-Ocean (Bermuda). Office: Bingham Dana Murase 399 Park Ave New York NY 10022-4614

MURCHISON, DAVID RODERICK, lawyer; b. Washington, May 28, 1948; s. David Claudius and June Margaret (Guilfoyle) M.; m. Kathy Ann Kohn, Mar. 15, 1981; children: David Christopher, Benjamin Michael. BA cum laude, Princeton U., 1970; JD, Georgetown U., 1975. Bar: D.C. 1975, Fla. 1993. Legal asst. to vice chmn. CAB, Washington, 1975-76, enforcement atty., 1976-77; sr. atty. Air Transport Assn., 1977-80, asst. v.p., sec., 1981-85; sr. assoc. Zuckert, Scoutt and Rasenberger, 1980-81; v.p., asst. gen. counsel Piedmont Aviation, Inc., Winston-Salem, N.C., 1985-88; v.p., gen. counsel, sec. Braniff, Inc., Dallas, 1988-89, chief exec. officer Orlando, 1990-94; fed. adminstrv. law judge Office of Hearings and Appeals, Charleston, W.Va., 1994-96, chief adminstrv. law judge Mobile, Ala., 1996-99, adminstrv. law judge, 1999—. Lectr. continuing legal edn. program Wake Forest U., Winston-Salem, 1988. Contbr. articles to legal jours. Lt. USNR, 1970-72. Mem. ABA, Met. Club Washington. Republican. Roman Catholic. Administrative and regulatory, General corporate, Legislative. Office: Office Hearings and Appeals 3605 Springhill Bus Park Mobile AL 36608-1239

MURCHISON, HENRY DILLON, lawyer; b. Alexandria, La. Feb. 27, 1947; s. Julian Truett and Annie Laurie (Liddell) M.; m. Darla Aymond, Sept. 29, 1984. B.S., La. Tech. U., 1969; J.D., La. State U., 1974. Bar: Texas 1974, La. 1974, U.S. Dist. Ct. (we. dist.) Tex. 1974, U.S. Ct. Appeals (5th cir.) 1974, U.S. Dist. Ct. (we., cen., and ea. dist.) La. 1977, U.S. Tax Ct. 1977, U.S. Supreme Ct. 1977. Assoc. Baer, Cryon, Keen & Kelley, Houston, 1974-76; gen. counsel Jetero Corp. Houston, 1976-77; ptnr. Stafford, Randow et al, Alexandria, 1977-78, Craven, Scott & Murchison, Alexandria, 1978-79, Davis & Murchison, Alexandria, 1979-84, Broadhurst, Brook, Mangham & Hardy, New Orleans, 1984— ; dir. Security 1st Nat. Bank, Alexandria, First Nat. Bancshares of La. Dist. chmn. La. Republican Com., 1982. Mem. Alexandria-Pineville C. of C. (dir. 1982-83), New Orleans River Region C. of C. Presbyterian. Lodge: Kiwanis (program chmn. 1982). Banking, General corporate, Real property. Office: Brook,Morial,Cassibry,Fraiche & Pizza 400 Poydras Suite 2500 New Orleans LA 70130

MURDOCH, DAVID ARMOR, lawyer; b. Pitts., May 30, 1942; s. Armor M. and N. Edna (Jones) M.; m. Joan Wilkie, Mar. 9, 1974; children: Christina, Timothy, Deborah. AB magna cum laude, Harvard U., 1964, LLB, 1967. Bar: Pa. 1967, U.S. Dist. Ct. (we. dist.) Pa. 1967, U.S. Ct. Mil. Appeals 1968, U.S. Supreme Ct. 1990, U.S. Ct. Appeals (3d cir.) 1991. Assoc. Kirkpatrick & Lockhart, LLP, Pitts., 1971-78, ptnr., 1978—. Mem. adv. bd. Ctr. for Internat. Legal Edn., U. Pitt., 1997—. Co-author: Business Workouts Manual. V.p., bd. dirs. Avonworth Sch. Dist., 1977-83; mem. bd. dirs. Pitts. Expt., 1988-93, chmn., 1989-90; mem. Pa. Housing Fin. Agy., 1981-88, vice chmn., 1983-87; alt. del. Rep. Nat. Conv., 1980; elder The Presbyn. Ch. of Sewickley, 1986-92; past pres. Harvard Law Sch. Assn. W. Pa.; bd. advisors Geneva Coll., 1993-94, trustee, 1994-97; trustee Sewickley Pub. Libr., 1994—, vice chmn., 1997—; trustee World Learning, Inc., 1995—, vice chmn., 1998-2000, chmn., 2000—; dir. Allegheny County Libr. Assn., 1994-96; chair Czech Working Group, Presbyn. Ch. USA, 1995-2000; bd. visitors U. Ctr. Internat. Studies, U. Pitts., 1996—; bd. advisors The Ctr. for Bus., Religion, and Pub. Life, Pitts. Theol. Sem., 1997—; bd. dirs. World Affairs Coun. Pitts., 1998—, Am. Coun. Germany, 1998—. Capt. U.S. Army, 1968-71. Recipient Disting. Svc. award Allegheny County Libr. Assn., 2001. Fellow Am. Coll. Bankruptcy, Am. Bar Found.; mem. ABA (mem. bus. bankruptcy com., chmn. subcom. on bankruptcy coms., trust indentures and claims trading 1991-97). Bankruptcy, Contracts commercial, General corporate. Office: Kirkpatrick & Lockhart LLP Henry W Oliver Bldg 535 Smithfield St Pittsburgh PA 15222-2312 E-mail: dmurdoch@kl.com

MURDOCH, ROBERT WHITTEN, lawyer; b. Pitts., Mar. 21, 1937; s. Thomas and Julia (Whitten) M.; m. Eleanore L. Uram, Sept. 26, 1967; 1 child, Robert John. BA, U. Pitts., 1960; pvt. law study, 1963-67. Bar: Pa. 1967, U.S. Dist. Ct. (we. dist.) Pa. 1968, U.S. Ct. Appeals (3d cir.) 1978, U.S. Supreme Ct. 1978, U.S. Ct. Appeals (8th cir.) 1983, U.S. Ct. Appeals (11th cir.) 1986. Ptnr. Jones, Gregg, Creehan & Gerace, Pitts., 1967-85, Grogan, Graffam, McGinley & Lucchino, P.C., Pitts., 1985-98, Zimmer Kunz P.C., 1998—. Author: Pfeifer: The Supreme Court on The Longshoremen's and Harbor Workers Compensation Act and Inflation, 1983, 84. Nat. chmn. Tartan Day. 2d lt. U.S. Army, 1960-61. Fellow Soc. Antiquities Scotland; mem. ABA, Pa. Bar Assn., Allegheny County Bar Assn., Maritime Law Assn. U.S., Def. Rsch. Inst., Pa. Def. Inst., Acad. Trial Lawyers Allegheny County, Nat. Assn. R.R. Trial Counsel, Pa. Claims Assn. (assoc.), Pitts. Claims Assn. (assoc.), Pitts. Fire Loss Conf. (assoc.), Am. Coll. Legal Medicine, Avanti Owners' Assn., Internat., SAR, Descs. Colonial Clergy, Sons Union Vets. Civil War, Nat. Soc. Sons Colonial New Eng., Am. Soc. Law and Medicine, Hon. Order Blue Goose Internat., Clan Donald, Pitt Varsity Letter Club, 65 Roses Club (cystic fibrosis), Rivers Club, Pitt. Golden Panthers, Continental Soc. Sons of Indian Wars, St. Andrews Soc. Pitts., Plymouth Hereditary Soc., Caledonian Found., Phi Alpha Delta. Republican. Presbyterian. Avocations: genealogy, golf, basketball, tenor soloist. Admiralty, General civil litigation, Personal injury. Office: Zimmer Kunz PC 3300 USX Tower Pittsburgh PA 15219 E-mail: murdoch@zklaw.com

MURDOCK, CHARLES WILLIAM, lawyer, educator; b. Chgo., Feb. 10, 1935; s. Charles C. and Lucille Marie (Tracy) M.; m. Mary Margaret Hennessy, May 25, 1963; children: Kathleen, Michael, Kevin, Sean. BSChemE, Ill. Inst. Tech., 1956; JD cum laude, Loyola U., Chgo., 1963. Bar: Ill. 1963, Ind. 1971. Asst. prof. law DePaul U., 1968-69; assoc. prof. law U. Notre Dame, 1969-75; prof., dean Law Sch. Loyola U., Chgo., 1975-83, 86—; dep. atty. gen. State of Ill., 1983-86; of counsel Chadwell & Kayser, Ltd., 1986-89. Vis. prof. U. Calif., 1974; cons. Pay Bd., summer 1972, SEC, summer 1973; co-founder Loyola U. Family Bus. Program; arbitrator Chgo. Bd. Options Exch., Nat. Assn. Securities Dealers, N.Y. Stock Exch., Am. Arbitration Assn.; co-founder, mem. exec. com. Loyola Family Bus. Ctr., 1990—; bd. dirs. Plymouth Tube Co., 1993—. Author: Business Organizations, 2 vols., 1996; editor: Illinois Business Corporation Act Annotated, 2 vols., 1975; tech. editor The Business Lawyer, 1989-90. Chmn. St. Joseph County (Ind.) Air Pollution Control Bd., 1971; bd. dirs. Nat. Center for Law and the Handicapped, 1973-75, Minority Venture Capital Inc., 1973-75. Capt. USMCR. Mem. ABA, Ill. Bar Assn. (cert. of award for continuing legal edn.), Chgo. Bar Assn. (cert. of award for continuing legal edn., bd. mgrs. 1976-78), Ill. Inst. Continuing Legal Edn. (adv. com) Roman Catholic. General corporate, Securities. Home: 2126 Thornwood Ave Wilmette IL 60091-1452 Office: Loyola U Sch Law 1 E Pearson St Chicago IL 60611-2055 E-mail: cmurdoc@luc.edu

MUROFF, ELENA MARIE, lawyer; b. Waterbury, Conn., Mar. 14, 1957; d. John Andrew Muroff. AS in Bus. Adminstrn. summa cum laude, Teikyo Post Coll., Waterbury, 1979, BS in Mktg. in summa cum laude, 1981; JD, U. Bridgeport, 1986; postgrad., U. Conn. Bar: Conn., U.S. Dist. Ct. Conn. Legal intern Fl. Woodward Lewis, Yalesville, Conn., 1986-87; clk. New Haven Superior Ct., 1987-88; asst. appellate clk. Supreme and Appellate Ct., Hartford, Conn., 1988-89; asst. atty. gen. Office Atty. Gen., 1990-91; pvt. practice, pro bono Waterbury, 1989-90, 91—. Legal instr. Nat. Acad. Paralegal Studies, West Hartford, Conn., 1991; instr. living skills Greenshire Sch., Cheshire, Conn., 1988; care provider to mentally challenged Respite Resources, Wallingford, Conn., 1994—; co-facilitator group therapy Mental Health Assn., Wethersfield, Conn., 1995—; spkr. Rose Traurig scholars program Teikyo Post U., 1992, also for legal asst. program. Mem. Dem. Nat. Com.; U.S. del. Moscow Conf. Law and Bilateral Econ. Rels., 1990. Recipient letter of commendation Conn. Valley Hosp., 1990; scholar Teikyo Post Coll., 1980-81, Max Traurig scholar, 1981; Bank of Boston Marguerite McGraw scholar U. Bridgeport, 1983, Conn. grad. scholar, 1983, Sch. Law scholar, 1983-86. Mem. ATLA, ACLU, NOW, Conn. Bar Assn., Conn. Edn. and Legal Fund, Conn. Mental Health Assn., Conn. Assn. for Human Svcs., Campaign for Children, So. Poverty Law Ctr. Roman Catholic. Avocations: writing poetry, music and arts, avidly following politics. Government contracts and claims, Health, Landlord-tenant. Home and Office: 959 Meriden Rd Apt 4 Waterbury CT 06705-3143

MURPHY, ARTHUR JOHN, JR. lawyer; b. Aug. 13, 1950, s. Arthur John, Sr. and Joan Marie (von Albade) M.; m. Joanne Therese Blak, Dec. 18, 1976; children— Arthur John III, Matthew Newsom, Ryan. B.A., U. San Diego, 1972, J.D., 1975. Bar: Calif. 1975. Atty., SEC, Washington, 1975-78; assoc. Bronson, Bronson & McKinnon, San Francisco, 1979-82, ptnr., 1983— ; lectr.; arbitrator Nat. Assn. Securities Dealers, 1982—. Contbr. securities law articles to profl. jours. Recipient Franklin award for Outstanding Grad., U. San Diego, 1972. Mem. ABA, Calif. Bar Assn. (exec. com. bus. law sect. 1986-90, chmn. 1989-90), San Francisco Bar Assn. Roman Catholic. Club: Olympic, Bankers Club of San Francisco. General corporate, Securities. Home: 1116 Butterfield Rd San Anselmo CA 94960-1157 Office: Bronson Bronson & McKinnon 505 Montgomery St San Francisco CA 94111-2514

MURPHY, ARTHUR WILLIAM, lawyer, educator; b. Boston, Jan. 25, 1922; s. Arthur W. and Rose (Spillane) M.; m. Jane Marks, Dec. 21, 1948 (dec. Sept. 1951); 1 dau., Lois; m. Jean C. Marks, Sept. 30, 1954; children— Rachel, Paul. A.B. cum laude, Harvard, 1943; LL.B., Columbia, 1948. Bar: N.Y. State bar 1949. Asso. in law Columbia Sch. Law, N.Y.C., 1948-49; asso. dir. Legislative Drafting Research Fund, 1956, prof. law, 1963—; trial atty. U.S. Dept. Justice, 1950-52; asso. firm Hughes, Hubbard, Blair & Reed, N.Y.C., 1953-56, 57-58; partner firm Baer, Marks, Friedman & Berliner, 1959-63. Mem. safety and licensing panel AEC, 1962-73; mem. spl. commn. on weather modification NSF, 1964-66; mem. Presdl. Commn. on Catastrophic Nuclear Accidents, 1988-90 Author: Financial Protection against Atomic Hazards, 1957, (with others) Cases on Gratuitous Transfers, 1968, 3d edit., 1985, The Nuclear Power Controversy, 1976. Served with AUS, 1943-46. Decorated Purple Heart. Mem. ABA, Assn. of Bar of City of N.Y. (spl. com. on sci. and law) Office: Columbia Sch of Law 435 W 116th St New York NY 10027-7297

MURPHY, BRIAN CHARLES, lawyer; b. Albany, N.Y., Mar. 11, 1948; s. William Benno and Nan Catherine (Brennan) M.; 1 child, David Christopher. AB cum laude, Harvard U., 1970; JD, U. Va., 1973; postgrad. London Sch. Econs./Polit. Sci., U. London, 1975-76. Bar: Va. 1977, D.C. 1984, U.S. Supreme Ct. 1981. Atty. CSC, Washington, 1973-75; assoc. Barham, Radigan, Suiters & Brown, Arlington, Va., 1977; atty. U.S. OMB, Washington, 1980; atty., internat. trade adminstrn. U.S. Dept. Commerce, 1978-80, 81-87; legis. fellow Office of Senator Max Baucus, 1987; atty. Adminstrv. Conf. of U.S., 1987-92; sr. Fulbright lectr. U. Sofia, Bulgaria, 1992-98; cons. U.S. AID and UN, 1995; sr. democracy fellow U.S. AID, Nairobi, Kenya, 1996-97; country mgr. U.S. AID Trade and Investment Project, 1997; comml. law advisor U.S. AID Regional Mission for Ukraine, Moldova, Belarus, Kiev, 1999-2000. Lawyer; b. Albany, N.Y., Mar. 11, 1948; s. William Benno and Nan Catherine (Brennan) M.; 1 child, David Christopher. AB cum laude, Harvard U., 1970; JD, U. Va., 1973; postgrad., London Sch. Econs. and Polit. Sci., U. London, 1975-76. Bar: Va. 1977, U.S. Supreme Ct. 1981, D.C. 1985. Atty., CSC, Washington, 1973-75; assoc. Barham, Radigan, Suiters & Brown, Arlington, Va., 1977; atty. U.S. Office Mgmt. and Budget, Washington, 1980; atty. internat. trade adminstrn. U.S. Dept. Commerce, Washington, 1978-80, 1981-87; legis fellow, Office Sen. Max Baucus, 1987; atty. Adminstrv. Conf. of U.S., 1987-92; sr. Fulbright lectr. U. Sofia, Bulgaria, 1992-94; cons. USAID and UN, 1995;

sr. democracy fellow USAID for Kyrgyzhstan, Nairobi, Kenya, 1996-97; country mgr. USAID Trade and Investment Project, 1997; comml. law advisor USAID Regional Mission for Ukraine, Moldova, Belarus, Kiev, Ukraine, 1999—. Co-author: An Overview of U.S. Export Controls, 1989; contbr. articles to profl. publs. Mem. ABA (steering com., internat. trade com. adminstrv. law and internat. law sects.), Fed. Bar Assn. (editor jour. 1981-83, awards for outstanding and disting. svc. 1982-91, nat. coun. 1981-95, chmn. internat. trade and customs law commn. 1985-86, chmn. select com. on fed. adv. commn. act 1985-90, nat. mem. chmn. 1987-89, chmn. internat. law sect., co-chmn. dem. devel. initiative 1989-90, chmn. 1994-95, steering com. 1990—, pres. D.C. chpt. 1990-91, chairperson nat. conv. planning com. 1991, nat. pub. rels. com. 1992-95). Co-author: An Overview of U.S. Export Controls, 1989; contbr. articles to profl. publs. Rem. ABA (steering com., internat. trade com. adminstrv. law and internat. law sects.), Fed. Bar Assn. (editor jour. 1981-83, awards for outstanding and disting. svc. 1982-91, nat. coun. 1981-95, chmn. internat. trade and customs law com. 1985-86, chmn. select com. on fed. and adv. com. act 1985-90, nat. membership chmn. 1987-89, chmn. internat. law sect., cofounder dem. devel. initiative 1989-90, chmn. 1994-95, bd. dirs. 1990—, pres. D.C. chpt. 1990-91, chair nat. conv. planning com. 1991, nat. pub. rels. com. 1992-95). Home: 4601 N Park Ave Apt 1704 Chevy Chase MD 20815-4525 E-mail: briancmurphy@earthlink.net

MURPHY, C. WESTBROOK, lawyer; b. 1940; AB, Duke U.; LLB, Yale U. Bar: D.C., 1966. Gen. counsel Harry S. Truman Scholarship Found., Washington. Mem. ABA. Office: Harry S Truman Scholarship Found 712 Jackson Pl NW Washington DC 20006-4901 also: Pricewaterhouse Coopers 1301 K St NW Ste 800W Washington DC 20005-3317

MURPHY, DANIEL IGNATIUS, lawyer; b. Phila., Mar. 14, 1927; s. John Anthony Murphy and Irene Cooper Thorn; m. Jeanne B. Genetti, July 28, 1956 (div. Aug. 1978); children: Jewel A., Daniel I. Jr.; m. Barbara Ann Uncles, Jan. 1, 1979. BS in Econs., U. Pa., 1950; LLB, Yale U., 1953. Bar: Pa. 1954, U.S. Dist Ct. (ea. dist.) Pa. 1954, U.S. Ct. Appeals (3d cir.) 1954, U.S. Tax Ct. 1956, U.S. Supreme Ct. 1959. Assoc. Evans, Bayard & Frick, Phila., 1953-55; asst. city solicitor City of Phila., Pa., 1956-59; ptnr. Cavanaugh, Murphy & Kalodner, Phila., 1958-64, Shapiro, Stalberg, Cook, Murphy & Kalodner, Phila., 1964-66, Takiff, Bolger & Murphy, Phila., 1966-72, Waters, Gallagher, Collins & Masterson, Phila., 1972-80, Stradley, Ronon, Stevens & Young, Phila., 1980-92, ret., of counsel, 1993. Tchr. Am. Soc. CLUs, Villanova, Pa., 1956-57; mem. exec. com. Phila. Estate Planning Coun., 1958-60; lectr. Pa. Bar Inst., Harrisburg, 1974-92, Pa. Coll. Orphans Ct. Judges, Harrisburg, 1978, Pitts., 1991; apptd. spl. master for trial mgmt. of complex litigation Phila. County Ct. Common Pleas, 1994—; judge pro tem Comm. Ct., Phila. County Ct. Common Pleas, 2000—; arbitrator Nat. Assn. Securities Dealers, 2001. Editor: Phila. Bar Assn. Mag. The Shingle, 1958-67; contbr. chpts. to manuals and articles to profl. jours. Chmn. Phila. Chpt. Am. Cancer Soc., 1956-63; mem. Com. of 70, Phila., 1968—, chmn., 1972-74; trustee Hahnemann U., Phila., 1983-86. With USN, 1945-46. Fellow Pa. Bar Found. (life); mem. ABA, Pa. Bar Assn., Phila. Bar Assn. (vice-chmn. com. censors 1971), Nat. Assn. Securitites Dealers (mem. arbitration panel 2001, apptd. arbitrator 2001). Union League Phila., Soc. Colonial Wars, Phila. Country Club, Pa. Soc. S.R., Colonial Soc. of Pa. Democrat. Roman Catholic. Avocation: U.S. Civil War history. Office: 2600 One Commerce Sq Philadelphia PA 19103 E-mail: dmurphyesq@prodigy.net

MURPHY, DENNIS PATRICK, lawyer; b. Evanston, Ill., May 25, 1948; s. William F. and Virginia L. M.; m. Victoria T. Halford, Jan. 27, 1979; children: Benjamin P., Carl R., Katherine Monica. BA, U. N. Mex., 1970; JD, U. Denver, 1975. Bar: N. Mex. 1975, U.S. Dist. Ct. N. Mex. 1975. Asst. dist. atty. Office of Dist. Atty., Santa Fe, 1975-76; asst. atty. gen. N. Mex. Atty. Gen."s Office, 1976-78; ptnr. Montoya, Murphy, Garcia, 1978—. Bd. dirs., fund raiser Equal Access to Justice, Albuquerque, N. Mex., 1996. Mem. ATLA (N.Mex. state del. 1997-98), N. Mex. Trial Lawyers Assn. (bd. dirs. 1990—, vol. legis. lobbyist 1990—, pres.-elect), N. Mex. State Bar Assn. (lawyers assistance com. 1993—) Democrat. Roman Catholic. Avocation: skiing. Personal injury, Product liability. Home: 1803 Arroyo Chamiso Santa Fe NM 87505-5734 Office: Montoya Murphy & Garcia 303 Paseo De Peralta Santa Fe NM 87501-1860

MURPHY, DIANA E. federal judge; b. Faribault, Minn., Jan. 4, 1934; d. Albert W. and Adleyne (Heiker) Kuske; m. Joseph Murphy, July 24, 1958; children: Michael, John E. BA magna cum laude, U. Minn., 1954, JD magna cum laude, 1974; postgrad., Johannes Gutenberg U., Mainz, Germany, 1954-55, U. Minn., 1955-58; LLD, St Johns U., 2000. Bar: Minn. 1974, U.S. Supreme Ct. 1980. Assoc. Lindquist & Vennum, 1974-76; mcpl. judge Hennepin County, 1976-78, Minn. State dist. judge, 1978-80; judge U.S. Dist. Ct. for Minn., Mpls., 1980-94, chief judge, 1992-94; judge U.S. Ct. of Appeals (8th cir.), Minneapolis, 1994—. Chair U.S. Sentencing Commn., 1999—. Bd. editors: Minn. Law Rev., Georgetown U. Jour. on Cts., Health Scis. and the Law, 1989-92. Bd. dirs. Spring Hill conf. Ctr., 1978-84, Mpls. United Way, 1985—, treas., 1990-94, vice chair, 1996-97, chmn. bd. dirs., 1997-98; bd. dirs. Bush Found., 1982—, chmn. bd. dirs., 1986-91; bd. dirs. Amicus, 1976-80, also organizer, 1st chmn. adv. coun.; mem. Mpls. Charter Commn., 1973-76, chmn., 1974-76; bd. dirs. Ops. De Novo, 1971-76, chmn. bd. dirs., 1974-75; mem. Minn. Constl. Study Commn., chmn. bill of rights com., 1971-73; regent St. Johns U., 1978-87, 88-98, vice chmn. bd., 1985-87, chmn. bd. 1995-98, bd. overseers sch. theology, 1998-2001; mem. Minn. Bicentennial Commn., 1987-88; trustee Twin Cities Pub. TV, 1985-94, chmn. bd., 1990-92; trustee U. Minn. Found., 1990—, treas., 1992-98; bd. dirs. Sci. Mus. Minn., 1988-94, vice chmn., 1991-94; trustee U. St. Thomas, 1991—; dir. Nat. Assn. Pub. Interest Law Fellowships for Equal Justice, 1992-95; bd. dirs. Minn. Opera, 1998—. Fulbright scholar; recipient Amicus Founders' award, 1980, Outstanding Achievement award U. Minn., 1983, Outstanding Achievement award YWCA, 1981, Disting. Citizen award Alpha Gamma Delta, 1985, Devitt Disting. Svc. to Justice award, 2001. Fellow Am. Bar Found.; mem. ABA (mem. ethics and profl. responsibility judges adv. com. 1981-88, chmn. ethics and profl. responsibility judges adv. com. 1997-2000, standing com. on jud. selection, tenure and compensation 1991-94, mem. standing com. on fed. jud. improvements, 1994-97, Appelate Judges conf. exec. com. 1996-99), Minn. Bar Assn. (bd. govs. 1977-81), Hennepin County Bar Assn. (gov. coun. 1976-81), Am. Law Inst., Am. Judicature Soc. (bd. dirs. 1982-93, v.p. 1985-88, treas. 1988-89, chmn. bd. 1989-91), Nat. Assn. Governing Bds. Univs. Colls. (dir. 1998—), Nat. Assn. Women Judges (Leadership Judges Jud. Adminstrn. award 1998), Minn. Women Lawyers (Myra Bradwell award 1996), U. Minn. Alumni Assn. (bd. dirs. 1975-83, nat. pres. 1981-82), Fed. Judges Assn. (bd. dirs. 1982—, v.p. 1984-89, pres. 1989-91), Hist. Soc. for 8th Cir. (bd. dirs. 1988-91), Fed. Jud. Ctr. (bd. dirs. 1990-94, 8th cir. jud. coun. 1992-94, 97—, mem. U.S. jud. conf. com. on ct. adminstrn. and case mgmt. 1994-99, chair gender fairness implementation com. 1997-98, convener task force 1993), Order of Coif, Phi Beta Kappa. Office: 11 E US Courthouse 300 S 4th St Minneapolis MN 55415-1320

MURPHY, EARL FINBAR, legal educator; b. Indpls., Nov. 1, 1928; AB, Butler U., 1949, MA, 1954; JD, Ind. U., 1952; LLM, Yale U., 1955, JSD, 1959. Bar: Ind. 1952. Sole practice Indpls., 1952-54; asst. prof. SUNY-Binghamton, 1955-57; Rockefeller fellow U. Wis. Law Sch., Madison, 1957-58; asst. prof. Temple U., Phila., 1958-60, assoc. prof., 1960-65, prof. law, 1965-69; prof. Ohio State U., Columbus, 1969-81, C. William O'Neill prof. law and jud. adminstrn., 1981-2000, prof. emeritus, 2000—. Vis. prof. U. Ariz., 1980. Author: Water Purity, 1961; Governing Nature, 1967; Man and His Environment: Law, 1971; Nature, Bureaucracy and the Rules of Property, 1977; Energy and Environmental Balance, 1980; Quantitative Groundwater Law, 1991. Chmn. Ohio Environ. Bd. Rev., 1972-74. Mem. ABA, Ind. Bar Assn., Fed. Bar Assn., Am. Soc. Legal History, World Soc. Ekistics (pres. 1982-84). Democrat. Uniterian. Clubs: Masons. Home: 4475 Langport Rd Columbus OH 43220-4257 Office: Ohio State U Coll Law 1659 N High St Columbus OH 43210-1306 E-mail: Murphy.14@osu.edu

MURPHY, EWELL EDWARD, JR. lawyer; b. Washington, Feb. 21, 1928; s. Ewell Edward and Lou (Phillips) M.; m. Patricia Bredell Purnell, June 26, 1954 (dec. 1964); children: Michaela, Megan Patricia, Harlan Ewell. BA, U. Tex., 1946, LLB, 1948; DPhil, Oxford U., Eng., 1951. Bar: Tex. 1948. Assoc. Baker & Botts, Houston, 1954-63, ptnr., 1964-93, head internat. dept., 1972-89. Pres. Houston World Trade Assn., 1972-74; trustee Southwestern Legal Found., 1978—; chmn. Houston Com. on Fgn. Rels., 1984-85, Inst. Transnat. Arbitration, 1985-89, Internat. and Comparative Law Ctr., 1986-87; mem. J. William Fulbright Fgn. Scholarship Bd., 1991-96, vice chmn., 1992-93, chmn., 1993-95; vis. prof. U. Tex. Law Sch., 1993-97; Disting. lectr., U. Houston Law Ctr., 1996—. Contbr. articles to profl. jours. Served to lt. USAF, 1952-54. Recipient Carl H. Fulda award U. Tex. Internat. Law Jour., 1980; Rhodes scholar, 1948-51 Mem. ABA (chmn. sect. internat. law 1970-71), Houston Bar Assn. (chmn. internat. law com. 1963-64, 70-71), Houston C. of C. (chmn. internat. bus. com. 1964, 65), Philos. Soc. Tex., Internat. Law Inst. (bd. dirs. 1994—), Fulbright Assn. (bd. dirs. 1999—), Coun. on Fgn. Rels. General corporate, Private international. Home and Office: 17 W Oak Dr Houston TX 77056-2117

MURPHY, JOHN FRANCIS, law educator, consultant, lawyer; b. Portchester, N.Y., Apr. 25, 1937; s. Francis John and Emilie (Tourtellot) M.; children: Andrew, Robert. BA, Cornell U., 1959, LLB in Internat. Affairs, 1962. Bar: D.C. 1963, Kans. 1970, Pa. 1987. Afro-Asia Pub. Svc. fellow, India, 1962-63; assoc. Winthrop, Stimson, Putnam & Roberts, N.Y.C., 1963-64; atty. Office Legal Adv., Dept. State, Washington, 1964-67; assoc. Kirkland, Ellis, Hodson, Chaffetz & Masters, 1967-69; assoc. prof. law U. Kans., Lawrence, 1969-72, prof. law, 1972-84, assoc. dean Sch. Law, 1975-77; vis. prof. law Villanova (Pa.) U., 1983-84, prof. law, 1984—. Vis. prof. law Cornell U., Ithaca, N.Y., fall 1979, Georgetown U., summer 1982, San Diego U., summer Paris, 1986, 95, Mexico City, 1988, Lodon, 1989, La. State U. summer, Aix-en-Provence, 1990, Haifa (Israel) U., 1997; Charles H. Stockton Prof. Internat. Law, Naval War Coll., 1980-81. Author: Legal Aspects of International Terrorism: Summary Report of an International Conference, 1980, The United Nations and the Control of International Violence, 1982, Punishing International Terrorists, 1985, State Support of International Terrorism: Legal, Political and Economic Dimensions, 1989, (with Alan Swan) The Regulation of International Business and Economic Relations, 1991, Supplements, 1994, 95, 2d edit., 1999 (cert. of merit Am. Soc. Internat. Law 1992), (with James D. Dinnage) The Constitutional Law of the European Union, 1996, Supplement, 1999; contbr. articles, comments, book revs. to profl., popular jours.; editor (with Alona E. Evans), contbg. author: Legal Aspects of International Terrorism, 1978; bd. editors Cornell Law Quar., 1961, 62; mem. bd. editors Terrorism: An Internat. Jour., 1981-92, Terrorism and Polit. Violence, 1993—, The Internat. Lawyer, 1998—, Transnat. Publishers, 1999—. Mem. ABA, Am. Soc. Internat. Law, Internat. Law Assn. Episcopalian. Office: Villanova Law Sch Villanova PA 19085 E-mail: murphy@law.villanova.edu

MURPHY, JOHN THOMAS, lawyer; b. Pierre, S.D., July 20, 1932; s. Bernard J. and Gertrude (Loner) M.; m. Rose Marie Cogorno. LLB, U. S.D., 1957. Bar: S.D. 1957, Calif. 1962. Pvt. practice, Stockton, Calif., 1965-75, Modesto, 1975—; atty. office gen. counsel quartermaster gen. U.S. Army, 1957-58, asst. chief counsel, 1958-63, gen. counsel, 1963-65; assoc. Short, Short, Scott & Murphy (and predecessor firm), 1965-68; ptnr. Hulsey, Beus, Wilson, Scott & Murphy, Stockton, 1968-70. Bd. dirs. Delta-Stockton Humane Soc., 1970-75, Tuolumne River Preservation Trust; bd. govs. Calif. Trout Inc.; mem. Stanislaus River Task Force, Stanislaus County Water Coord. Com.; chmn. Southwestern Trial Bd. Mem. State Bar Calif., Assn. Trial Lawyers Am., Beta Theta Pi, Phi Delta Phi, Stockton Beagler's Club (sec., dir.), Am. Kennel Club (Beagle adv. com. 1984-86). Republican. Episcopalian. Office: 1124 11th St Modesto CA 95354-0826 E-mail: bigbad@inreach.com

MURPHY, JOSEPH ALBERT, JR. lawyer; b. Grosse Pointe, Mich., May 29, 1934; s. Joseph Albert and Isabel C. (Callahan) M.; m. Joanne Becker, June 24, 1961; children: Michael, Joseph III. BS, Georgetown U., 1956; JD, Detroit Coll. Law, Mich. State U., 1962. Bar: Mich. 1962, D.C. 1996. House counsel Blue Cross Mich., Detroit, 1964-69, gen. counsel, corp. sec., 1969-75; v.p., dep. gen. counsel Blue Cross & Blue Shield Mich., 1975-88; sr. assoc. gen. counsel Blue Cross and Blue Shield Assn., Washington, 1989—. Chmn. Health Care Network, Southfield, Mich., 1981-85; chmn. Blue Care Inc., Southfield, 1986-88. Mem. Allocations panel United Found., Detroit, 1985—; treas. Grosse Pointe Dem. Club, 1972-73; chmn. Health and People's Polit. Action Commn., Detroit, 1978-84. Served with U.S. Army, 1957-59. Mem. ABA, Mich. Bar Assn., Detroit Bar Assn., Nat. Health Lawyers Assn. (pres. 1981-82), Am. Corp. Counsel Assn., Am. Arbitrators Assn. (panel of arbitrators). Roman Catholic. Administrative and regulatory, General corporate, Health. Home: 2717 O St NW Washington DC 20007-3128

MURPHY, KATHLEEN MARY, former law firm executive; b. Bklyn., Dec. 16, 1945; d. Raymond Joseph and Catherine Elizabeth (Kearney) M. BA in Edn., Molloy Coll., 1971; MS in Edn., Bklyn. Coll., 1975. Ordained minister Ch. of the Loving Servant; cert. hypnotherapist; cert. elem. sch. tchr., N.Y. Elem. sch. tchr. various parochial schs., L.I., Bklyn., Queens, N.Y., 1969-80; from asst. prin. to prin. parochial sch. Queens, 1980-82; supr.-trainer Davis, Polk, Wardwell law firm, N.Y.C., 1982-88; mgr. Schulte Roth & Zabel, 1988-95; Reiki master (alternative healing profl.), 1996—. Trainer program for new employees, 1984; speaker edn. topics, Bklyn., Queens, 1979-81. Mem. NAFE, Reiki Alliance. Democrat. Roman Catholic. Avocations: psychic phenomenon, workings of mind, ancient histories, crossword puzzles, museums.

MURPHY, LEWIS CURTIS, lawyer, former mayor; b. N.Y.C., Nov. 2, 1933; s. Henry Waldo and Elizabeth Wilcox (Curtis) M.; m. Carol Carney, Mar. 10, 1957; children— Grey, Timothy, Elizabeth. BSBA, U. Ariz., 1955, LLB, 1961. Bar: Ariz. 1961. Pvt. practice, Tucson, 1961-66; trust officer So. Ariz. Bank & Trust Co., 1966-70; atty. City of Tucson, City of Tucson, 1970-71; mayor, 1971-87; ret., 1987. Mem. Schroeder & Murphy, Tucson, 1978-88; trustee U.S. Conf. Mayors, 1978-87, chmn. transp. com., 1984-87; pub. safety steering com. Nat. League Cities, 1973-87, transp. steering com., 1973-87; v.p. Ctrl. Ariz. Project Assn., 1978-87. Bd. dirs. Cmty. Food Bank, 1987-2000, United Way Greater Tucson, 1988-90. With USAF, 1955-58. Mem. Ariz. Bar Assn., Pima County Bar Assn., Ariz. Acad. Republican. Presbyterian.

MURPHY, MAX RAY, lawyer; b. July 18, 1934; s. Loren A. and Lois (Mink) M.; children: Michael Lee, Chad Woodrow. BA, DePauw U., 1956; JD, Yale U., 1959; postgrad., Mich. State U., 1960. Bar: Mich. 1960. Assoc. Glassen, Parr, Rhead & McLean, Lansing, Mich., 1960-67, Lokker, Boter & Dalman, Holland, 1967-69; ptnr. Dalman, Murphy, Bidol, & Bouwens, P.C., 1969-91, Cunningham Dalman, P.C., Holland, 1991—. Instr. Lansing Bus. U., 1963-67; asst. pros. atty. Ottawa County, Mich., 1967-69. Democratic candidate for Ingham County (Mich.) Pros. Atty., 1962, 1964. Mem. ABA, Ottawa County Bar Assn. (sec. 1970-71), Mich. Bar Assn. (mem. family law sect.). Family and matrimonial, General practice. Home: 3169 E Crystal Waters 3 Holland MI 49424-8091 Office: 321 Settlers Rd Holland MI 49423-3778 E-mail: mmurphy@sirus.com

MURPHY, MICHAEL R. federal judge; b. Denver, Aug. 6, 1947; s. Roland and Mary Cecilia (Maloney) M.; m. Maureen Elizabeth Donnelly, Aug. 22, 1970; children: Amy Christina, Michael Donnelly. BA in History, Creighton U., 1969; JD, U. Wyo., 1972. Bar: Wyo. 1972, U.S. Ct. Appeals (10th cir.) 1972, Utah 1973, U.S. Dist. Ct. Utah 1974, U.S. Dist. Ct. Wyo. 1976, U.S. Ct. Appeals (5th cir.) 1976, U.S. Tax Ct. 1980, U.S. Ct. Appeals (9th cir.) 1981, U.S. Ct. Appeals (fed. cir.) 1984. Law clk. to chief judge U.S. Ct. Appeals (10th cir.), Salt Lake City, 1972-73; with Jones, Waldo, Holbrook & McDonough, 1973-86; judge 3d Dist. Ct., 1986-95, pres. judge, 1990-95; judge U.S. Ct. Appeals (10th cir.), 1995—. Mem. adv. com. on rules of civil procedure Utah Supreme Ct., 1985-95, mem. bd. dist. ct. judges, 1989-90; mem. Utah State Sentencing commn., 1993-95, Utah Adv. Com. on child Support Guidelines, 1989-95, chair 1993-95; mem. Utah Child Sexual Abuse Task Force, 1989-93. Recipient Freedom of Info. award, Soc. Profl. Journalists, 1989, Utah Minority Bar Assn. award, 1995, alumni Achievement citation, Creighton U., 1997; named Judge of Yr., Utah State Bar, 1992. Fellow Am. Bar Found.; mem. ABA (editl. bd. Judges' Jour. 1997-99), Utah Bar Assn. (chmn. alternative dispute resolution com. 1985-88), Sutherland Inn of Ct. II (past pres.). Roman Catholic. Office: 5438 Federal Bldg 125 S State St Salt Lake City UT 84138-1102

MURPHY, RICHARD PATRICK, lawyer; b. Elizabeth, N.J. AB with distinction, Cornell U., 1976; JD cum laude, AM, U. Mich., 1980. Bar: D.C. 1980, U.S. Dist. Ct. (D.C.) 1981, U.S. Ct. Appeals (D.C. cir.) 1981, U.S. Supreme Ct. 1984, Calif. 1987, U.S. Dist. Ct. (so. dist.) Calif. 1987, U.S. Dist. Ct. (cen. dist.) Calif. 1992, Ga. 1993, U.S. Dist. Ct. (no. dist.) Ga. 1993, U.S. Ct. Appeals (11th cir.) 1993. Assoc. Bergson, Borkland, Margolis & Adler, Washington, 1980-82; atty. enforcement div. SEC, 1982-84, br. chief enforcement div., 1984-87; assoc. Gray, Cary, Ames & Frye, San Diego, 1987-92; sr. trial counsel SEC, Atlanta, 1993-99, asst. dist. adminstr., 1999—. Mem. ABA, D.C. Bar Assn., Calif. Bar Assn., Ga. Bar Assn. Office: SEC 3475 Lenox Rd NE Ste 1000 Atlanta GA 30326-1239

MURPHY, RICHARD VANDERBURGH, lawyer; b. Syracuse, N.Y., May 9, 1951; s. Robert Drown and Reta (Vanderburgh) M.; m. Patricia Lynn Eades, May 18, 1973; children: Alan Christopher, Ryan Patrick. AB, Dartmouth Coll., 1973; JD, U. Ky., 1976. Bar: Ky. 1976, U.S. Dist. Ct. (ea. dist.) Ky. 1977, U.S. Supreme Ct. 1980. Corp. counsel Lexington-Fayette Urban County Govt., Lexington, 1976-82; asst. county atty. Fayette County, 1982-84; assoc. H. Foster Pettit, 1982-83; ptnr. Pettit & Murphy, 1983-84; sr. atty., prin Wyatt, Tarrant & Combs, 1984-88; pvt. practice, 1988—. Cons. zoning ordinance update Lexington-Fayette Urban County Govt., Lexington, 1982-83. Author: Kentucky Land Use and Zoning Law, 1998. Elder, chmn. bd. South Elkhorn Christian Ch., Lexington, 1982—. Mem. Am. Planning Assn., ABA, Ky. Bar Assn., Order of Coif, Phi Beta Kappa. Democrat. Administrative and regulatory, Land use and zoning (including planning), Real property. Home: 3278 Pepperhill Rd Lexington KY 40502-3545 Office: 250 W Main St Ste 3010 Lexington KY 40507-1745

MURPHY, SEAN PATRICK, lawyer; b. Rochester, N.Y., Aug. 22, 1963; s. Thomas Edward and Mary Patricia (Brasted) M.; m. Susan Marie Barnes, June 10, 1989; children, Katherine Anne, Caroline Grace. BS of Fgn. Svc., Georgetown U., 1985, JD, 1989. Bar: N.Y. 1989, D.C. 1991, Fla. 1995, Maryland, 1998, U.S. Ct. Fed. Claims 1991, U.S. Ct. Appeals (fed. cir.) 1991, U.S. Supreme Ct. 1995, U.S. Ct. Appeals (9th cir.) 1994, U.S. Ct. Appeals (11th cir.) 1995, U.S. Dist. Ct. (so., mid., no. dists.) Fla. 1995, U.S. Dist. (so. dist.) N.Y. 1991, U.S. Dist. Ct. (D.C. dist.) 1997, U.S. Ct. Appeals (D.C. cir.) 1997, U.S. Ct. Appeals (4th cir.) 1999. Assoc. Dewey Ballantine, N.Y.C., 1989-91; fed. trial atty. U.S. Dept. Justice, Washington, 1991-95; sr. assoc. Annis Mitchell, Tampa, Fla., 1995-97; of counsel Muldoon, Murphy & Faucette LLP, Washington, 1997-2000, Patton Boggs, LLP, Washington, 2000—. Instr. trial preparedness courses Fla. Bar, Miami, Ft. Lauderdale and Tampa, 1995-97. Bd. dirs., dir. athletic adv. bd. Georgetown U., Washington, 1989-99; mem. bd. trustees, v.p. Serra Club of Washington, 1991-99, John Carroll Soc., Washington, 1991—; vol. trial atty. Archdiocesan Pro Bono Legal Network, 1992-99. Recipient Cardinal's medal Archdiocesan Pro Bono Legal Network, 1998. Mem. Am. Inns of Ct. (barrister William Glen Terrell 1995-97), Univ. Club Washington, Potomac Boat Club. Roman Catholic. General civil litigation, General corporate, Securities. Office: Patton Boggs LLP 2550 M St NW Washington DC 20037 E-mail: Smurphy@pattonboggs.com

MURPHY, TERENCE ROCHE, lawyer; b. Oct. 20, 1937; s. M. Leonard and Alice Lenore (Roche) M.; m. Suzanne Kathryn Duprè, Oct. 14, 1967 (div. Apr. 1980); children: Braden Mathias, Fiona Elizabeth Duprè; m. Patricia Ann Sherman, May 21, 1983. AB, Harvard Coll., 1959; JD with distinction, U. Mich., 1966. Bar: D.C. 1967, U.S. Supreme Ct. 1971. Trial atty. Dept. Justice, Washington, 1966-68; assoc. Wald, Harkrader & Ross, 1968-72, ptnr., 1972-83, McDermott, Will & Emery, Washington, 1983-84, Adams, Duque & Hazeltine, Washington, 1984-86; founding ptnr. Murphy Ellis Weber and predecessors, 1986—. Bd. dirs. Am. Assn. Exporters and Importers; founding chmn. Brit.-Am. Bus. Coun., 1989-90, legal counsel, 1993-96; officer, bd. dirs. Industry Coalition of Tech. Transfer; lectr. North and South Am., Europe and Mediterranean on internat. and bus. law and on strategic trade; chmn. and lectr. ann. Globalization of Export Controls Conf., London; bd. advisors The European Inst., 1993—; advisor on export policy, Ctr. for Strategic and Internat. Trade, 2000—, advisor on export regulation, U.S. Dept. Commerce, 2001—. Author, lectr. on internat. trade, antitrust and adminstrv. law.; co-editor: Coping With U.S. Export Controls, ann. edits., 1986, 87, 88; contbr. articles to European and Am. legal publs. Mem. com. visitors U. Mich. Law Sch., 1975—; trustee Lawyer's Com. for Civil Rights Under Law, 1975-89. Lt. USN, 1959-63. Decorated U.S. Navy Commendation, Cuban Missile Crisis, 1962, Hon. Officer, Order Brit. Empire, 1993; fellow Royal Soc. of Arts. Mem. ABA (coun. adminstrv. law sect. 1980-83, co-chmn. com. on internat. and comparative adminstrv. law 1994-97), Am. Law Inst., Internat. Bar Assn. (sec. antitrust and monopolies com. 1981-83), Am. Soc. Internat. law, Brit.-Am. Bus. Assn. (Washington, founding dir. 1987—, chmn. 1989-92, legal adv. 1992-95), Royal Inst. Internat. Affairs (London), Am. Coun. on Germany, Met. Club (Washington), Harvard Club (N.Y.C.), Miscowaubik Club (Calumet, Mich.). Administrative and regulatory, General corporate, Private international. Home: 4425 Boxwood Rd Bethesda MD 20816-1817 Office: Murphy Ellis Weber 818 Connecticut Ave NW Washington DC 20006-2702 E-mail: tmurphy@murphyellisweber.com

MURPHY, WILLIAM PATRICK, lawyer, editor, writer; b. Scranton, Pa., Feb. 17, 1952; s. William James and Mildred Mary (Ferguson) M. AB, U. Scranton, 1973; JD, U. Pa., 1976. Jud. law clk. U.S. Dist. Ct. (ea. dist.) Pa., U.S. Ct. Appeals (3rd cir.), Pa. Supreme Ct., Phila., Erie, 1976-79; from asst. to assoc. prof. law St. John's U., Queens, N.Y., 1979-81, 83; atty. Beasley, Casey, Colleran, Erbstein, Thistle, Kline & Murphy, Phila., 1982, 84-89; pvt. practice, 1989-94; legal editor Pa. Law Weekly, 1994-95, editor-in-chief, 1995-96; legal editor Pa. Dist. & County Reports, 1994-96; pvt. practice, 1996—. Instr. Temple U., Phila., 1987-88; mem. faculty continuing legal edn. Pa. Bar Inst., Harrisburg, 1989—. Author: White Dogs, 1996, columnist, 1999—. U. Pa. scholar, 1977. Mem. Pa. Bar Assn. Roman Catholic. Avocations: running, wolves. Office: Two Penn Ctr Plz Ste 200 Philadelphia PA 19102

MURRAY, DANIEL CHARLES, trial lawyer; b. Evanston, Ill., Jan. 21, 1949; s. John Joseph and Marjorie Ellen (Pequignot) M.; m. Martha Jane Gerity, Dec. 18, 1971; children: Michaela, Tyler, Brian. BA in Econs., Marquette U., 1971; JD, Loyola U., Chgo., 1976. Bar: Ill. 1976, U.S. Ct. Appeals (7th cir.) 1979, U.S. Dist. Ct. (no. dist.) Ill. 1980, U.S. Dist Ct. (ea.

dist.) Mich. 1992, U.S. Dist. Ct. (ea. dist.) Wis. 1994. Law clk. U.S. Ct. Appeals for 7th Cir., Chgo., 1976-78; asst. U.S. atty. Office U.S. Atty. U.S. Dept. Justice No. Dist., 1978-91; shareholder, chmn. pro bono program Johnson & Bell, Ltd., 1991—. Trial instr. U.S. Atty. Gen.'s Advocacy Inst., Washington, 1989; mem. Environ. Crimes Task Force, 1991. Active Chgo. Vol. Legal Svcs. Found., 1977—, Chgo. Legal Advocacy to Incarcerated Mothers, 1995—; participant Chgo. North-of-Howard Task Force. Recipient Disting. Svc. award Chgo. Vol. Legal Svcs. Found., 1983, 87, award for significant contbns. in drug law enforcement U.S. Drug Enforcement Adminstrn., 1988, Insp. Gen.'s nat. award GSA, 1989, Spl. Achievement award U.S. Dept. Justice, 1990. Mem. Fed. Bar Assn. (bd. dirs. Chgo. chpt.), 7th Fed. Cir. Bar Assn. Federal civil litigation, Criminal, Environmental. Office: Johnson & Bell Ltd Ste 4100 55 E Monroe St Chicago IL 60603-5896 E-mail: murrayd@jbltd.com

MURRAY, DANIEL RICHARD, lawyer; b. Mar. 23, 1946; s. Alfred W. and Gloria D. Murray. AB, U. Notre Dame, 1967; JD, Harvard U., 1970. Bar: Ill. 1970, U.S. Dist. Ct. (no. dist.) Ill. 1970, U.S. Ct. Appeals (7th cir.) 1971, U.S. Supreme Ct. 1974. Ptnr. Jenner & Block, Chgo., 1970—. Trustee Chgo. Mo. and Western Rlwy. Co., 1988-97; adj. prof. U. Notre Dame, 1997—. Co-author: Secured Transactions, 1978, Illinois Practice: Uniform Commercial Code with Illinois Code Comments, 1997. Bd. regents Big Shoulders Fund, Archdiocese of Chgo., Bernadin Ctr., Cath. Theol. Union. Mem. Am. Bankruptcy Inst., Am. Law Inst., Am. Coll. Comml. Fin. Lawyers (bd. regents), Transp. Lawyers Assn., Assn. Transp. Practitioners, Cath. Lawyers Guild (bd. dirs.), Law Club, Legal Club. Roman Catholic. Bankruptcy, Contracts commercial, Transportation. Home: 1307 N Sutton Pl Chicago IL 60610-2007 Office: Jenner & Block One IBM Plz Chicago IL 60611-3605 E-mail: dmurray@jenner.com

MURRAY, FLORENCE KERINS, retired state supreme court justice; b. Newport, R.I., Oct. 21, 1916; d. John X. and Florence (MacDonald) Kerins; m. Paul F. Murray, Oct. 21, 1943 (dec. June 2, 1995); 1 child, Paul F. AB, Syracuse U., 1938; LLB, Boston U., 1942; EdD, R.I. Coll. Edn., 1956; grad., Nat. Coll. State Trial Judges, 1966; LLD (hon.), Bryant Coll., 1956, U. R.I., 1963, Mt. St. Joseph Coll., 1972, Providence Coll., 1974, Roger Williams Coll., 1976, Salve Regina Coll., 1977, Johnson and Wales Coll., 1977, Suffolk U., 1981, So. New Eng. Law Sch., 1995; D (hon.), New England Inst. Tech., 1998. Bar: Mass. 1942, R.I. 1947, U.S. Dist. Ct. 1948, U.S. Tax Ct. 1948, U.S. Supreme Ct. 1948. Sole practice, Newport, 1947-52; mem. firm Murray & Murray, 1952-56; assoc. judge R.I. Superior Ct., 1956-78; presiding justice Superior Ct. R.I., 1978-79; assoc. justice (ret.-active) R.I. Supreme Ct., 1979—. Staff, faculty adv. Nat. Jud. Coll., Reno, Nev., 1971-72, dir., 1975-77, chmn., 1979-87, chair emeritus, 1990—; mem. com. Legal Edn. and Practice and Economy of New Eng., 1975—; former instr. Prudence Island Sch.; legal adv. R.I. Girl Scouts; sec. Commn. Jud. Tenure and Discipline, 1975-79; apptd. by Pres. Clinton to bd. dirs. State Justice Inst., 1994-99; participant, leader various legal seminars; presdl. appointment R.I. State Justice Inst. Mem. R.I. Senate, 1948-56; chmn. spl. legis. com.; mem. Newport Sch. Com., 1948-57, chmn., 1951-57; mem. Gov.'s Jud. Coun., 1950-60, White House Conf. Youth and Children, 1950, Ann. Essay Commn., 1952, Nat. Def. Adv. Com. on Women in Service, 1952-58, Gov.'s Adv. Com. Mental Health, 1954, R.I. Alcoholic Adv. Com., 1955-58, R.I. Com. Youth and Children, Gov.'s Adv. Com. on Revision Election Laws, Gov.'s Adv. Com. Social Welfare, Army Adv. Com. for 1st Army Area; mem. civil and polit. rights com. Pres.'s Commn. on Status of Women, 1960-63; mem. R.I. Com. Humanities, 1972—, chmn., 1972-77; mem. Family Ct. Study Com., R.I. com. Nat. Endowment Humanities; bd. dirs. Newport YMCA; sec. Bd. Physicians Service; bd. visitors Law Sch., Boston U.; bd. dirs. NCCJ; mem. edn. policy and devel. com. Roger Williams Jr. Coll.; trustee Syracuse U.; pres. Newport Girls Club, 1974-75, R.I. Supreme Ct. Hist. Soc., 1988—; chair Supreme Ct. Mandatory Continuing Legal Edn. Com., 1993—; apptd. bd. dirs. Touro Synague; apptd. R.I. Found. Served to lt. col. WAC, World War II. Decorated Legion of Merit; recipient Arents Alumni award Syracuse U., 1956, Carroll award R.I. Inst. Instn., 1956, Brotherhood award NCCJ, 1983, Herbert Harley award Am. Judicature Soc., 1988, Melvin Eggers Sr. Alumni award Syracuse U., 1992, Merit award R.I. Bar Assn., 1994, John Manson/Carl Robinson award, 1996, Longfellow Humanitarian award ARC, 1997; named Judge of Yr. Nat. Assn. Women Judges, 1984, Outstanding Woman, Bus. and Profl. Women, 1972, Citizen of Yr. R.I. Trial Lawyers Assn.; Newport courthouse renamed in her honor, 1990. Mem. ABA (chmn. credentials com. nat. conf. state trial judges 1971-73, chair judges adv. com. on standing com. on ethics and profl. responsibility 1991—, joint com. on jud. discipline of standing com. on profl. discipline 1991-94), R.I. Found. (bd. dirs. 1998—), AAUW (chmn. state edn. com. 1954-56), Am. Arbitration Assn., Nat. Trial Judges Conf. (state chmn. membership com., sec. exec. com.), New Eng. Trial Judges Conf. (com. chmn. 1967), Boston U. Alumni Coun., Am. Legion (judge adv. post 7, mem. nat. exec. com.), Bus. and Profl. Women's Club (past state v.p., past pres. Newport chpt., past pres. Nat. legis. com.), Auota Club (past gov. internat., past pres. Newport chpt.), Alpha Omega, Kappa Beta Pi.

MURRAY, FRED F. lawyer; b. Corpus Christi, Tex., Aug. 1, 1950; s. Marvin Frank and Suzanne Louise Murray. BA, Rice U., 1972; JD, U. Tex., 1974. Bar: Tex. 1975, U.S. Dist. Ct. (so. dist.) Tex. 1976, U.S. Ct. Claims 1976, U.S. Tax Ct. 1976, U.S. Ct. Appeals (5th, D.C. and fed. cirs.) 1976, U.S. Supreme Ct. 1978, U.S. Ct. Internat. Trade 1985, N.Y. 1987, D.C. 1987, U.S. Dist. Ct. (ea. dist.) Tex. 1987; CPA, Tex. Ptnr. Chamberlain, Hrdlicka, White, Williams & Martin, P.C., Houston, 1985-92; spl. counsel (legislation) U.S. Dept. Treasury, IRS, Washington, 1992-96; v.p. tax policy Nat. Fgn. Trade Coun., 1996—. Mem. Tax Law Adv. Commn., Tex. Bd. Legal Specialization, 1984-99, vice chmn., 1987-92; mem. Commn. Tax Law Examiners, 1984-99, vice chmn., 1987-92; adj. prof. U. Houston Law Ctr., 1984-92, U. Tex. Sch. Law, 1987; faculty lectr. Rice U. Jones Grad. Sch. Adminstrn., 1987-92; spkr. various assns. and univs.; mem. bd. advisors Houston Jour. Internat. Law, 1986-92, chmn., 1987-91. Author various pubis. Del. Bishop's Diocesan Pastoral Coun., 1979-80; chmn. parish coun. Sacred Heart Cathedral, Cath. Diocese Galveston-Houston, 1979-81, 89, mem. Red Mass steering com., 1986-92; mem. exec. com., bd. dirs., 1987-91, chmn. deferred giving com. Houston Symphony Soc., 1987-88, chmn. govt. and pub. affairs com., 1988-91; co-trustee Houston Symphony Soc. Endowment Fund, 1987-91; mem. fund coun. Rice U., 1987-96, exec. com. 1988-92, chmn. Major Gifts Com., 1988-92; gen. counsel, bd. dirs., com. on fin. and adminstrn. S.E. Tex. chpt. Nat. Multiple Sclerosis Soc.; mem. Red Mass com. Archdiocese Washington, 1993—; bd. dirs. John Carroll Soc., Archdiocese of Washington, 1996—, chmn. pilgrimage com. Knighted equestrian order Holy Sepulchre Jerusalem, 1998—. Fellow Am. Coll. Tax Counsel; mem. ABA (chmn. formation tax policy com. 1998-2001), FBA (mem. steering com. tax sect. 1995—, chmn. tax sect. 1998-99), AICPA, Am. Arbitration Assn. (panels comml. and internat. arbitrators 1980—), Internat. Bar Assn., Houston Bar Assn., State Bar of Tex. (various coms.), N.Y. State Bar Assn., D.C. Bar Assn., Tex. Soc. CPA, Internat. Tax Forum of Houston (sec. 1981-84, pres. 1984-92), Internat. Fiscal Assn., Am. Soc. Internat. Law, Am. Fgn. Law Assn., Am. Law Inst. (tax adv. group 1990—), Am. Tax Policy Inst. (bd. dirs.).

MURRAY, JAMES MICHAEL, librarian, law librarian, legal educator, lawyer; b. Seattle, Nov. 8, 1944; s. Clarence Nicholas and Della May (Snyder) M.; m. Linda Monthy Murray. MLaw Librarianship, U. Wash., 1978; JD, Gonzaga U., 1971. Bar: Wash. 1974, U.S. Dist. Ct. (we. dist.) Wash. 1975, U.S. Dist. Ct. (ea. dist.) Wash. 1985. Reference/reserve libr. U. Tex. Law Libr., Austin, 1978-81; assoc. law libr. Washington U. Law Libr., St. Louis, 1981-84; law libr., asst. prof. Gonzaga U. Sch. Law, Spokane, 1984-91; libr. East Bonner County Libr., 1991-97, U.S. Cts. Libr., Spokane, 1997—. Mem. state adv. bd. Nat. Reporter on Legal Ethics and Profl. Responsibility, 1982-91; cons. in field. Author: (with Reams and McDermott) American Legal Literature: Bibliography of Selected Legal Resources, 1985, (with Gasaway and Johnson) Law Library Administration During Fiscal Austerity, 1992; editor Tex. Bar Jour. (Books Appraisals Column), 1979-82; contbr. numerous articles and revs. to profl. jours., acknowledgements and bibliographies in field. Bd. dirs. ACLU, Spokane chpt., 1987-91, Wash. Vol. Lawyers for the Arts, 1976-78. Mem. ABA, Idaho Libr. Assn., Wash. State Bar Assn. (law sch. liaison com. 1986-88, civil rights com. 1996-97). Home: 921 W 29th Ave Spokane WA 99203-1318 Office: US Cts Libr 920 W Riverside Ave Ste 650 Spokane WA 99201-1008

MURRAY, JOHN DANIEL, lawyer; b. Cleve., Feb. 13, 1944; s. Clarence Daniel and Mary Anne (Bormann) M.; m. Pamela Mary Seese, Aug. 20, 1966 (div. Sept. 1978); children: Laura Jane, Joshua Daniel, Katherine Anne; m. Marilyn Nohren, June 15, 1979. BA, Marquette U., 1965, JD, 1968. Bar: Wis. 1968, Ill. 1968, U.S. Dist. Ct. (ea. and we. dist.) Wis. 1968, U.S. Supreme Ct. 1971, U.S. Ct. Appeals (7th cir.) 1979. Assoc. Law Offices of Elmo Koos, Peoria, Ill., 1968-70; ptnr. Coffey, Lerner & Murray, Milw., 1970-72, Coffey, Murray & Coffey, Milw., 1972-76, Murray & Burke, S.C., Milw., 1983-85; pvt. practice, 1976-83; shareholder Habush, Habush & Rottier, S.C., Appleton, Wis., 1985—. Adj. prof. law Marquette U., Milw., 1993—; lectr. Law Sch. U. Wis., Madison, 1976-80. Contbg. author: Wisconsin Trial Practice, 1999. Mem. ABA, ATLA, Nat. Bd. Trial Advocacy (cert.), Am. Bd. Trial Advocates, Am. Soc. Law and Medicine, Wis. State Bar (chmn. criminal law sect. 1977-78, tort law com. 1990-94, bd. dirs. litigation sect. 1995-2001, chmn. 1997-98), Wis. Acad. Trial Lawyers (bd. dirs. 1990-99), Woolsack Soc. Roman Catholic. Avocations: golf, travel. State civil litigation, Personal injury, Product liability. Home: 1867 E Shady Ln Neenah WI 54956-1177 Office: Habush Habush Davis Rottier PO Box 1915 Appleton WI 54912-1915

MURRAY, JOHN MICHAEL, lawyer; b. Birmingham, Ala., Aug. 20, 1946; s. Leon Benton and Zena (Griffith) M.; m. Dona Pounds, Aug. 24, 1968 (div. 1979); m. Nancy Simon, Apr. 11, 1986 (div. 2000). BS in Aviation Mgmt., Auburn U., 1968; JD, Memphis State U., 1972. Bar: Fla. 1973, U.S. Dist. Ct. (so. dist.) Fla. 1973, U.S. Dist. Ct. (mid. dist.) Fla. 1978, U.S. Dist. Ct. (no. dist.) Fla. 1983, U.S. Ct. Appeals (5th cir.) 1973, U.S. Ct. Appeals (11th cir.) 1981, U.S. Supreme Ct. 1976, U.S. Dist. Ct. (mid. dist.) Ala. 1999; bd. cert. trial lawyer. Airport planner R. Dixon Speas Assocs., Manhasset, N.Y., 1968-70; assoc., ptnr. Walton Lantaff Schroeder & Carson, Miami, Fla., 1973-81; ptnr. Thornton David & Murray, P.A., 1981-2000, Murray, Marin & Herman, P.A., Tampa, Fla., 2000—. Mem. Fla. Bar, Ala. State Bar. Aviation, Federal civil litigation, State civil litigation. Office: Murray Marin & Herman PA 101 E Kennedy Blvd Ste 1010 Tampa FL 33602 E-mail: jmurray@mmhlaw.com

MURRAY, KATHLEEN ANNE, lawyer; b. Los Angeles, Feb. 14, 1946; d. Francis Albert and Dorothy (Thompson) M.; 1 child, Anne Murray Ladd; m. Arthur J. Perkins Jr., June 29, 1991. BA, U. Mich., 1967; JD, Hastings Coll. of Law, 1973. Bar: Calif. 1973, U.S. Dist. Ct. (no. dist.) Calif. 1973, U.S. Ct. Appeals (9th cir.) 1973. Sr. staff atty Child Care Law Ctr., San Francisco, 1979-84, cons. child day care law and regulation, 1984-86; atty Epstein & Harris, 1985-86; gen. counsel Fisher Friedman Assocs., 1986-89; assoc. gen. counsel Calif. State Automobile Assn., 1989-98; sr. counsel Firemen's Fund Ins. Co., 1998—. Exec. dir., mem. editorial adv. bd. Parenting Mag., 1985—; chair Labor and Employment Law Com., Am. Corp. Coun. Assn. Editor: Child Care Center Legal Handbook; Tax Guide for California Child Care Providers; contbr. articles to profl. jours. Mem. adv. coun. Humanities West, Inc., 1986-96, North of Market Child Devel. Ctr., San Francisco, 1987-90; vestry Episcopal Ch. of St. Mary the Virgin, 1990-92; pres. Parents' Assn., Lick-Wilmerding High Sch., 1993-94; Personnel Practices Com. of Episcopal Diocese of Calif. Democrat. Episcopalian. E-mail: kmurray@ffic.com

MURRAY, MARY P. law clerk; b. Pitts., July 6, 1970; d. Paul Edward and Betty Stiney Murray. BS, Duquesne U., 1992, MBA, 1995, JD, 1996. Bar: Pa. 1997, Fla. 1997. Law clk. Goldberg & Kamin, Pitts., 1996; atty. Gobel & Beisler, 1996-98, Dodaro Kennedy Cambest, Pitts., 1996-98; jud. law clk. Beaver (Pa.) County, 1998-2000; of counsel Witherell & Kovacik, 2001; agy. counsel Commonwealth Land Title Ins. Co., Pitts., 2001—. Pvt. estate planning and adminstrn. practice. Auditor Moon Twp., Pa., 1998—; co-coach New Brighton (Pa.) Mock Trial Team, 1999—. Mem. Fin. Women Internat. (treas. 1999-2000), Women's Bus. Network (bd. mem. 1998-00), Women in Comml. Real Estate, Phi Sigma Epsilon, Phi Delta Phi (pres., treas.). Republican. Roman Catholic. Avocations: dancing, golf, cross-stitching. Home: 100 Parliament Dr Moon Township PA 15108-3245

MURRAY, MICHAEL KENT, lawyer; b. Missoula, Mont., Feb. 14, 1948; s. Paul R. and Virginia F. Murray; children: Britton M., Spencer J. BA, U. Calif., Santa Barbara, 1970; JD, U. Santa Clara, 1974. Bar: Wash. 1974, U.S. Ct. Claims 1975, U.S. Tax Ct. 1976, U.S. Dist. Ct. Wash. 1977, U.S. Ct. Appeals (fed. cir.) 1982. Trial atty. honor law grad. program U.S. Dept. Justice, Washington, 1974-76; atty. Foster Pepper & Riviera, Seattle, 1976-79, ptnr. Seattle and Bellevue, 1980-86, ptnr.-in-charge Bellevue, 1983-86; atty., pres. Michael K. Murray, P.S., Seattle, 1986—. Pres. N.W. Properties Devel. Corp., Seattle, 1986-92; of counsel Lasher Holzapfel Sperry & Ebberson, Seattle, 1992-2001; v.p. BELFOR USA Group, Inc., Seattle, 2001—. Articles editor Santa Clara Lawyer, U. Santa Clara Sch. Law, 1973-74. Trustee Pacific Northwest Ballet, Seattle, 1979-81; dir. Bellevue Downtown Assn., 1984-87. Mem. Wash. State Bar Assn., King County Bar Assn., Seattle Yacht Club, Seattle Tennis Club. Avocations: sailing, fly fishing, biking, computing. Construction, Land use and zoning (including planning), Real property. Home: 1570 9th Ave N Edmonds WA 98020-2627 Office: BELFOR USA Group Inc 3826 Woodland Park Ave N Seattle WA 98036 E-mail: mmurray@US.belfor.com

MURRAY, MICHAEL PATRICK, lawyer; b. Milw., Jan. 31, 1930; s. Michael James and Florence Mary M.; m. Allene Vereen, May 8, 1976; children: Bryan Patrick, Laura Renee. BA, Milton (Wis.) Coll., 1953; JD, Marquette U., 1958; LLM, John Marshall Law Sch., 1960; D of Juridicial Sci., George Washington U., Washington, D.C., 1973; M of Liberal Arts, Johns Hopkins U., 1996. Bar: Wis. 1958, Calif. 1966, U.S. Supreme Ct. 1967, U.S. Ct. Appeals (9th cir.) 1982, D.C. 1989, Va. 1989, U.S. Ct. Appeals (D.C. cir.) 1989, U.S. Ct. Appeals (4th cir.) 1990. Commd. 2d lt. USMC, 1953, advanced through grades to col., 1975, prosecutor and def. counsel, 1960-66, trial judge and SJA, 1966-69, dir. policy and research, 1969-72, dir. Law Ctr. Iwakuni, Japan, 1973-74, ret., 1978; trail atty. Anderson & Murphy, Milw., 1958-60; counsel to the chmn. Joint Chiefs of Staff, Washington, 1974-75; apellate judge USN Ct. of Rev., 1975-78; pvt. practice, San Diego, 1982-89; atty., counsel Clary, Lawrence, Lickstein & Moore, Falls Church, Va., 1989-91; ptnr. Michael Patrick Murray & Assocs., South Riding, 1991—; asst. gen. counsel NRA, Washington, 1992-95. Assoc. prof. law Pepperdine U., Malibu, Calif., 1978-80, Marquette U., Milw., 1980-81; adj. prof. law Western State U., San Diego, 1983-88, Nat. U. Coll. Law, 1988-89; pro bono vol. atty. for indigents, San Diego, 1982-89. Author: Quarter: the Warrior's Dilemma, 1967, (law study) Eichman and Major German War Criminal Trials, 1973, O'Ryans Law, 1992, Murder By Class, 1997, Law Is a Jealous Mistress, 1999, People Needing People, 2000. Mem. Calif. Bar Assn., Wis. Bar Assn., D.C. Bar Assn., Va. Bar Assn., Am. Legion, First and Third Marine Div. Assn., Marine Corps Assn., Marine Mustang Assn., Phi Delta Phi. Roman Catholic. Avocations: poetry, creative writing. General civil litigation, Constitutional, General corporate. Office: Michael Patrick Murray & Assocs 26223 Lands End Dr South Riding VA 20152 E-mail: michael.p.murray@att.net

MURRAY, PHILIP EDMUND, JR. lawyer; b. Floral Park, N.Y., Mar. 4, 1950; s. Philip Edmund and Anne Marie (Mackin) M.; m. Karen Anne McLeavey, Aug. 14, 1976; children: Erin Anne, Philip E. III. BS cum laude, Boston Coll., 1972, JD, 1975. Bar: Mass. 1975, U.S. Dist. Ct. Mass. 1976, U.S. Supreme Ct. 1992. Law clk. to presiding justices Mass. Superior Ct., Boston, 1975-76; sr. ptnr. Martin Magnuson McCarthy & Kenney, 1976—. Hearing officer Bd. of Bar Overseers of the Supreme Judicial Ct., Boston, 1990-96. Editor: Boston Coll. Law Rev., 1973-75; contbr. articles to profl. jours. Mem. Mass. Bar Assn., Mass. Bar Found.; mem. Am. Soc. Law and Medicine, Am. Coll. Legal Medicine. General civil litigation, Health, Personal injury. Office: Martin Magnuson McCarthy & Kenney 101 Merrimac St Ste 700 Boston MA 02114-4716

MURRAY, STEPHEN JAMES, lawyer; b. Phila., Jan. 27, 1943; s. Paul Martin and Hannah (Smith) M.; m. Linda Sanders, June 20, 1970; children: Gordon Joshua, Cara Sanders. AB cum laude, Brown U., 1963; LLB, Harvard U., 1966; LLM, George Washington U., 1967. Bar: N.Y. 1968, U.S. Ct. Appeals (2nd cir.) 1971, U.S. Ct. Appeals (fed. cir.) 1998, U.S. Dist. Ct. (so. and ea. dists.) N.Y. 1972, U.S. Ct. Claims 1974, U.S. Supreme Ct. 1975, Conn. 1988, U.S. Dist. Ct. Conn. 1988, U.S. Ct. Internat. Trade 1998. Spl. asst. SEC, Washington, 1966-67, Maritime Adminstrn., Washington, 1967-68; assoc. Hill, Betts & Nash, N.Y.C., 1970-76; transp. atty. Union Carbide Corp., 1976-78, sr. transp. atty., 1978-85, chief transp. counsel Danbury, Conn., 1985—2001, group counsel, 1986—2001, real estate counsel, 1992—2001, comml. counsel, 1993—2001, customs and internat. trade counsel, 1997—2001; of counsel Mahoney & Keane, New York City, 2001—. Spkr. in field. Contbr. articles to profl. jours. Lt. JAGC, USN, 1968-70. Mem. ABA, Conn. State Bar, U.S. Naval Inst., Navy League of U.S., Maritime Law Assn., U.S. Transp. Lawyers Assn., N.Y. State Bar Assn., Am. Corp. Counsel Assn. (co-chair real estate com. Westchester-So. Conn. chpt.), Conn. Maritime Assn., Harvard Club, Brown Club (co-pres.), Brown Faculty Club, Brown Alumni Schs. Commn. (chmn. Fairfield County), Brown Alumni Assn. (bd. govs.). Admiralty, Real property, Transportation. Home: 14 Pilgrim Ln Weston CT 06883-2412 Office: Union Carbide Corp Law Dept 39 Old Ridgebury Rd Danbury CT 06817-0001 E-mail: lsmurray@erols.com, murraysj@ucarb.com

MURRAY, VIRGINIA, lawyer; b. Harlow, Essex, Eng., Feb. 13, 1968; m. Nikolaos Melanitis, Jan. 4, 1997. BA, Cambridge (Eng.) U., 1989, MA, 1993. Bar: Eng. 1992, Wales 1992, Athens Ct. Appeal 1998. Barrister Chambers of David Farrer, London, 1992-96; assoc. IKRP Rokas & Ptnrs., Athens, 1997—. Contbg. author: Telcommunications Law in Europe, 1998. Consumer commercial, Communications, Insurance. Office: IKRP Rokas & Ptnrs 25 Boukourestiou St Athens 104 44 Greece E-mail: athens@rokas.com

MURRAY, WILLIAM MICHAEL, lawyer; b. Buffalo, Dec. 21, 1953; s. William Joseph and Mary Ann (Lichtenthal) M.; m. Suzanne M. Raynor; children: Colleen Elizabeth, William Michael Jr., Caitlin Anne, Matthew Francis Johnson. BA, U. Notre Dame, 1975; JD, U. Detroit, 1978. Bar: N.Y. 1978, U.S. Dist. Ct. (we. dist.) N.Y. 1980. Asst. county atty. Erie County, Buffalo, 1978-79; ptnr. Stamm & Murray, Williamsville, N.Y., 1979-96, Renaldo Myers & Palumbo, Williamsville, 1996-98; dep. atty. Town of Amherst, 1993-96; gen. counsel Town of Amherst Indsl. Devel. Agy., 1996—. Mem. Amherst (N.Y.) Rep. Com., 1980—; chmn. Amherst Zoning Bd. Appeals, 1986-93. Mem. N.Y. State Bar Assn., Erie County Bar Assn., Williamsville Bus. Assn. (bd. dirs., v.p. 1985-96), Rotary (pres. Williamsville 1989). Roman Catholic. General practice, Land use and zoning (including planning), Municipal (including bonds). Office: 130 John Muir Dr Amherst NY 14228-1148 E-mail: wmurray@amherstida.com

MURREN, PHILIP JOSEPH, lawyer; b. Hanover, Pa., Mar. 29, 1950; s. Joseph Edward and Jeune (Mathews) M.; m. Kathleen Mary Buckley, Oct. 28, 1978; children: Andrew, Patrick, David, Brian. BA, LaSalle U., 1972; JD, Villanova U., 1975. Bar: Pa. 1975, U.S. Dist. Ct. (ea. dist.) Pa. 1976, U.S. Dist. Ct. (mid. dist.) Pa. 1978, U.S. Supreme Ct. 1978, U.S. Ct. Appeals (3d cir.) 1977, (5th cir.) 1979, (D.C. cir.) 1980, (6th cir.) 1984, (9th cir.) 1984. Ptnr. Ball, Skelly, Murren & Connell, Harrisburg, Pa., 1975—; mem. Camp Hill Borough Coun., 1989—. Mem. allocations exec. com. Tri-County United Way, Harrisburg, 1983-89; mem. bd. edn. Diocese of Harrisburg. Mem. Pa. Bar Assn., Dauphin County Bar Assn. Republican. Roman Catholic. Constitutional, Legislative, Non-profit and tax-exempt organizations. Home: 206 Willow Ave Camp Hill PA 17011-3652 Office: Ball Skelly Murren & Connell PO Box 1108 Harrisburg PA 17108-1108

MURRIAN, ROBERT PHILLIP, judge, educator; b. Knoxville, Tenn., Apr. 1, 1945; s. Albert Kinzel and Mary Gilbert (Eppes) M.; m. Jerrilyn Sue Boone, Oct. 29, 1983; children: Kimberley Ann, Jennifer Rebecca, Albert Boone, Samuel Robert. BS, U.S. Naval Acad., 1967; JD, U. Tenn., 1974. Bar: Tenn. 1974, U.S. Dist. Ct. (ea. dist.) Tenn. 1975, U.S. Ct. Appeals (6th cir.) 1982. Law clk. to judge U.S. Dist. Ct. (ea. dist.) Tenn., 1974-76; assoc. Butler, Vines, Babb & Threadgill, Knoxville, 1976-78; magistrate, judge U.S. Dist. (ea. dist.) Tenn., 1978—. Adj. prof. U. Tenn. Coll. Law, 1990-93, 95-96. Lt. USN, 1967-71. Green scholar, 1973-74, Nat. Moot Ct. scholar, 1974. Fellow Tenn. Bar Found.; mem. ABA, Tenn. Bar Assn., Knoxville Bar Assn. (bd. govs. 1994), Order of Coif, Am. Inn of Ct. (master of the bench, pres. 1997-98), Phi Kappa Phi. Presbyterian. Office: US Dist Ct 800 Market St Knoxville TN 37902-2327

MURRIN, REGIS DOUBET, lawyer; b. Erie, Pa., June 2, 1930; s. John III and Gabrielle (Doubet) M.; m. Evelyn L. Alessio, Aug. 22, 1959; children: Catherine Shaw Murrin Hargenrader, Mary Murrin Smith, Elizabeth Murrin Talotta, Rebecca Fielding Lamanna. BA, U. Notre Dame, 1952; JD, Harvard U., 1959; LLM, Temple U., 1968. Bar: Pa. 1959, U.S. Supreme Ct. 1971. Assoc. Murrin & Murrin, Butler, Pa., 1959-62; atty. Housing & Home Fin. Agy., Phila., 1962-64; ptnr. Baskin & Sears, Pitts., 1964-84, Reed Smith Shaw & McClay, Pitts., 1985-95, of counsel, 1995-99, counsel, 1999—. Trustee Pitts. Oratory, 1976-97; chmn. Zoning Bd. Adjustment, City of Pitts., 1994—; bd. dirs. Ellis Sch., 1991-99. Served as lt. USNR, 1952-55, Korea, Vietnam. Mem. Allegheny County Bar Assn., Edwin Sorin Soc. Democrat. Roman Catholic. Land use and zoning (including planning), Real property, Condominium and cooperative law. Office: Reed Smith Shaw & McClay 435 6th Ave Ste 2 Pittsburgh PA 15219-1886

MURRY, HAROLD DAVID, JR. lawyer; b. Holdenville, Okla., June 30, 1943; s. Harold David Sr. and Willie Elizabeth (Dees) M.; m. Ann Moore Earnhardt, Nov. 1, 1975; children: Elizabeth Ann, Sarah Bryant. BA, Okla. U., 1965, JD, 1968. Bar: Okla. 1968, D.C. 1974. Asst. to v.p. U. Okla., Norman, 1968-71, legal counsel Research Inst., 1969-71; atty. U.S. Dept. Justice, Washington, 1971-74; spl. asst. U.S. Atty., 1972; assoc. Clifford & Warnke, 1974-78, ptnr., 1978-91, Howrey & Simon, Washington, 1991-98, Baker Botts LLP, Washington, 1998—. Mem. ABA, Okla. Bar Assn., D.C. Bar Assn., Fed. Bar Assn., Met. Club (Washington), Chevy Chase Club (Md.), Phi Alpha Delta. Democrat. Administrative and regulatory, Antitrust, Federal civil litigation. Home: 8931 Bel Air Pl Potomac MD 20854-1606 Office: Baker Botts LLP Ste 1300 1299 Pennsylvania Ave NW Washington DC 20004-2408

MUSGRAVE, R. KENTON, federal judge; b. 1927; Student, Ga. Inst. Tech., 1945-46, U. Fla., 1946-47; BA, U. Wash., 1948; JD with distinction, Emory U., 1953. Asst. gen. counsel Lockheed Internat., 1953-62; v.p., gen. counsel Mattel, Inc., 1963-71; mem. firm Musgrave, Welbourn and Fertman, 1972-75; asst. gen. counsel Pacific Enterprises, 1975-81; v.p., gen. counsel Vivitar Corp, 1981-85; v.p., dir. Santa Barbara Applied Rsch.,

1982-87; judge U.S. Ct. Internat. Trade, N.Y.C., 1987—. Trustee Morris Animal Found., The Dian Fossey Gorilla Fund, Dolphins of Sharks Bay (Australia); hon. trustee Pet Protection Soc.; mem. United Way, South Bay-Centinela Svc. Orgn., Save the Redwoods League; active LWV, Legal Aid, Palos Verdes Community Assn. Mem. ABA, Internat. Bar Assn., Pan Am. Bar Assn., State Bar Calif. (chmn. corp. law sect. 1965-66, del. 1966-67), L.A. County Bar Assn., State Bar Ga., Fng. Trade Assn. So. Calif. (bd. dirs.), Sierra Club. Office: US Ct Internat Trade 1 Federal Plz New York NY 10278-0001

MUSICK, ROBERT LAWRENCE, JR. lawyer; b. Richlands, Va., Oct. 3, 1947; s. Robert Lawrence and Virginia (Brooks) M.; m. Beth Pambianchi, 1996; children: Elizabeth, Robert. BA in History with honors, U. Richmond, 1969; JD, MA in Legal History, U. Va., 1972; LLM, Coll. William and Mary, 1986. Bar: Va. 1972, U.S. Ct. Appeals (4th cir.) 1974. Law clk. Supreme Ct. Va., Richmond, 1972-73; assoc. Williams, Mullen & Christian, 1973-78; ptnr. Williams, Mullen, Christian & Dobbins, 1978-99, Williams Mullen Clark & Dobb, Richmond, 1999—. Bd. govs. estates and property sect. Va. State Bar, 1977-80, chmn., 1980. Author: RIA Non Qualified Deferred Compensation, 1997, (with others) CCH Federal Tax Service, 1989; contbr. articles to profl. jours. Trustee U. Richmond, 1991-94; mem. Estate Planning Coun. Richmond, 1981—, U. Richmond Estate Planning Coun., 1984—; bd. dirs. Barksdale Theatre, 1994-98, Va. Bapt. Homes, Inc., 1994—. Lt. col. USAR. Mem. ABA, Va. Bar Assn., Richmond Bar Assn., So. Pension Conf., Va. Assn. Professions (pres. 1980-81), Commonwealth Club, Willow Oaks Country Club (dir. 1999—). Baptist. Avocations: tennis, golf, scuba. General corporate, Estate planning, Pension, profit-sharing, and employee benefits. Office: Williams Mullen Clark & Dobbins 2 James Center PO Box 1320 Richmond VA 23218-1320

MUSKIN, VICTOR PHILIP, lawyer; b. N.Y.C., Mar. 1, 1942; s. Jacob Cecil and Fanya (Solomonoff) M.; m. Odette Cheryl Spreier, June 10, 1979; children: Adam James, Liana Jeanne. BA, Oberlin Coll., 1963; JD, NYU, 1966. Bar: N.Y. 1969, U.S. Dist. Ct. (so. and ea. dists.) N.Y. 1972, U.S. Ct. Appeals (2d cir.) 1974, U.S. Supreme Ct. 1974, U.S. Ct. Appeals (9th and 10th cirs.) 1978, U.S. Ct. Appeals (3d cir.) 1987. Asst. corp. counsel divsn. gen. litigation City of N.Y., 1969-73; assoc. Wolf, Popper, Ross, Wolf & Jones, N.Y.C., 1973-74, Reavis and McGrath, N.Y.C., 1974-78; pvt. practice, 1979; ptnr. Gruen & Muskin, 1980-81, Gruen, Muskin & Thau, N.Y.C., 1981-89, Munves, Tanenhaus & Storch, N.Y.C., 1989-90, Solin & Breimdel, N.Y.C., 1991-92; pvt. practice, 1992—. Served with Peace Corps, 1966-68. Mem. N.Y.C. Bar Assn. (com. computer law 1982-84, com. internat. law 1996-99). Federal civil litigation, State civil litigation, Private international. Home: 529 E 84th St New York NY 10028-7330 Office: 445 Park Ave Fl 14 New York NY 10022-2606 E-mail: vp.muskin@verizon.net

MUSSER, SANDRA G. retired lawyer; b. Hollywood, Calif., July 23, 1944; d. Donald Godfrey Gumpertz and Gloria G. (Rosenblatt) King; m. Michael R.V. Whitman, Feb. 19, 1980. BA, UCLA, 1965; JD, Hastings Coll. of Law, 1970. Bar: Calif. 1971, U.S. Dist. Ct. (no. dist.) Calif. 1971, U.S. Ct. Appeals (9th cir.) 1971. Clk. 9th Cir. Ct. of Appeals, 1971-72; lawyer pvt. practice of family law, 1972-86; ptnr. Musser & Ryan, San Francisco, 1986-97; pvt. practice, 1997-98; ret., 1998. Judge pro tem San Francisco County Superior Ct., 1988-98; dealer antique Chinese rugs and textiles, 1996—. Contbr. articles to profl. jours. Mem. adv. coun. Textile Mus., Washington, 1996—. Fellow Acad. Matrimonial Lawyers; mem. ABA (chair litig. sect. domestic rels. and family law com. 1993-94), State Bar Calif. (state bar family law sect. 1977—, chair 1982-83, advisor 1983-84), Bar Assn. San Francisco. Family and matrimonial. Office: 361 Oak St San Francisco CA 94102-5615

MUSSMAN, WILLIAM EDWARD, III, lawyer; b. San Francisco, Jan. 31, 1951; s. William Edward and Janet John (Skittone) M.; m. Carol Lynne Johnson, Jan. 9, 1988; children: Katherine Ann, Laura Lynne, Elizabeth Ashley. BS cum laude, Stanford U., 1973; JD, U. Calif.-San Francisco, 1976. Bar: Calif. 1976, U.S. Dist. Ct. (cen. dist.) Calif. 1982, U.S. Dist. Ct. (ea. dist.) Calif. 1998, U.S. Supreme Ct. 1985, U.S. Ct. Appeals (9th cir.) 1987. Assoc. Lasky, Haas, Cohler & Munter, San Francisco, 1980-82, Pillsbury, Madison & Sutro, San Francisco, 1982-84, Carr & Mussman, San Francisco, 1984-91, ptnr., 1991-95, Carr, Mussman & Harvey, LLP, San Francisco, 1996-99, Mussman & Mussman, LLP, San Francisco and Modesto, Calif., 2000—. Contbr. articles to profl. jours. Vol., rep., Ch. Jesus Christ Latter Day Sts., Tokyo, 1977-78. Mem. Calif. State Bar Assn. (litigation sect., law practice mgmt. sect.), Stanislaus County Bar Asns., Stanford Alumni Assn. (life), Tau Beta Phi. Antitrust, Alternative dispute resolution, General civil litigation. Office: Mussman & Mussman LLP 1101 Sylvan Ave Ste C106 Modesto CA 95350-1687 also: 3 Embarcadero Ctr Ste 1060 San Francisco CA 94111-4056 E-mail: WMussman3@Mussmanlaw.com

MUSTAIN, DOUGLAS DEE, lawyer; b. Shreveport, La., Nov. 2, 1945; s. Reginald K. and Dorothy J. (Green) M.; m. Sharon L. Tegarden, Aug. 19, 1967; children: Kristi Kaye, Kari Dee, Kenton Douglas, Kyle Robert, Kirk Stephen, Kali Elizabeth. Student Knox Coll., 1963-64, Murray State U., 1964-66; BS, U. Ill., 1971; JD, U. Iowa, 1974. Bar: Iowa 1974, Ill. 1974; U.S. Dist. Ct. (cen. dist.) Ill. 1974, U.S. Ct. Appeals (7th cir.) 1980, U.S. Supreme Ct. 1986. Law clk. Shulman, Phelan, Tucker, Boyle & Mullin, Iowa City, 1972-74; assoc. Stuart, Neagle & West, Galesburg, Ill., 1974-76; ptnr. West, Neagle & Williamson, Galesburg, 1977-89, Mustain & Lindstrom, Galesburg, 1989—; instr. real estate law Carl Sandburg Coll., Galesburg, 1977-81. Chmn. Citizens Referendum Com., Galesburg, 1983, 1987-88; bd. dirs. YMCA, Galesburg, 1983—, Cottage Hosp. Care Corp., Galesburg, 1984—; trustee 1st Presbyn. Ch., Galesburg, 1984; commr. Galesburg Pub. Transp. Commn., 1985—; pres., founder Galesburg Pub. Sch. Found., 1987-94. Served to SP5 U.S. Army, 1966-69, Vietnam. Decorated Army Commendation with oak leaf cluster. Mem. Knox County Bar Assn. (pres. 1980-82), ABA (comml. litigation com. 1981—), Assn. Trial Lawyers Am., Ill. Trial Lawyers Assn. Republican. State civil litigation, General practice. Home: 1234 N Prairie St Galesburg IL 61401-1852 Office: Mustain Lindstrom & Henson 1865 N Henderson St Ste 11B Galesburg IL 61401-1377

MUSTO, JOSEPH JOHN, lawyer; b. Pittston, Pa., Nov. 22, 1943; s. James and Rose Musto; m. Fortunata Giudice, July 5, 1969; children: Laura, Joseph Robert. BA, King's Coll., Wilkes-Barre, Pa., 1965; JD, Dickinson Sch. Law, Carlisle, Pa., 1968. Bar: Pa. 1968, U.S. Ct. Appeals (3d cir.) 1968, U.S. Dist. Ct. (mid. dist.) Pa. 1971. Asst. dist. atty. City of Phila., 1968-69; assoc. Bedford, Waller, Griffith, Darling & Mitchell, Wilkes-Barre, 1969-73; ptnr. Griffith, Darling, Mitchell, Aponick & Musto, 1973-75; prin. Griffith, Aponick & Musto, 1975-90; ptnr. Rosenn, Jenkins & Greenwald, 1990-93; judge Ct. Common Pleas of Luzerne County, 1993-94; mem. Hourigan, Kluger, Spohrer & Quinn, Wilkes-Barre, Pa., 1994-97; prin. Musto & Saunders, PC, Plymouth, 1997—. Solicitor Yatesville (Pa.) Borough, 1973-80, Duryea (Pa.) Borough, 1975-80, Pittston Area Sch. Dist., 1973-93. Mem. Luzerne County Gov. Study Com., Wilkes-Barre, 1973-74; mem., chmn. No. Luzerne Health Adv. Coun., Wilkes-Barre, 1976-80; pres., mem. Health Sys. Agy. of N.E. Pa., Avoca, 1980-86; pres. Pa. Health Planning Assn., Harrisburg, 1985-86; mem. civil justice reform act adv. com. Fed. Dist. Ct. Pa. Ct., 1991-95. Mem. Fed. Bar Assn. (past pres. Ctrl. Pa. chpt.), Pa. Bar Assn., Wilkes-Barre Law and Libr. Assn. Democrat. Roman Catholic. Alternative dispute resolution, Health. Home: 7 Prospect Pl Pittston PA 18640-2627 Office: Musto & Saunders 117 W Main St Plymouth PA 18651-2926

MUTH, MICHAEL RAYMOND, lawyer; b. Chgo., Dec. 28, 1950; s. Michael Jacob Muth and Mary (Birch) LaSpesa. B in Gen. Studies, Ohio U., 1972; JD, U. N.C., 1975. Bar: Ky. 1975, Pa. 1976, U.S. Dist. Ct. (mid. dist.) Pa. 1979. Chief pub. defender Monroe County, Stroudsburg, Pa., 1978— ; sole practice, Stroudsburg, 1976-84; ptnr. Muth, Zulick & Worthington, Stroudsburg, 1984— . Treas., bd. dirs. Women's Resources, Inc., Stroudsburg, 1981-86; pres., bd. dirs. Monroe County Youth Employment Service, Inc., Stroudsburg, 1977-81, Twin-Boro Teenage Baseball League, Inc., East Stroudsburg, 1982-90; treas. Carbon-Monroe-Pike Drug and Alcohol Commn; speech coach East Stroudsburg State Coll., 1977-79; asst. prof. East Stroudsburg U., 1987—. Mem. Ky. Bar Assn., Pa. Bar Assn., Pub. Defender Assn. Pa. (pres. 1994-97), Omicron Delta Kappa. Democrat. Roman Catholic. Club: Aardvark Enterprises (pres. 1977—) (Stroudsburg). Civil rights, Criminal, Family and matrimonial. Home: 271 Prospect St East Stroudsburg PA 18301-2943 Office: Muth & Zulick 819 Ann St Stroudsburg PA 18360-1606

MWENDA, KENNETH KAOMA, legal consultant, advisor, educator; LLB, U. Zambia, 1990; Gr.Dip, LCCI, U.K, 1991; DMS, IoC, U.K, 1992; BCL, U. Oxford, U.K., 1994; MBA, U. Hull, U.K, 1995; DBA, Pacific Western U., L.A., 1996, PhD in Publs., 1999; PhD, U. Warwick, U.K., 2000. Cert. Bar, Zambia, 1991; cert. cumpolsory edn., devels. in comml. securities, intellectual property law. Worked in trust funds and co-financing dept. Vice-Presidency of World Bank, Washington, 1998-99, worked in poverty reduction, mgmt. and pub. sector reform unit, 1999; worked as counsel in legal dept. World Bank, 1999-2000, projects officer, 2000—. Vis. prof. U. Miskolc Sch. Law, Hungary, 1996; lectr. U. Zambia Law Sch., 1991-95, Warwick U. Law Sch., 1995-98; speaker and presenter in field. Author: Legal Aspects of Corporate Capital and Finance, 1999, Contemporary Issues In Corporate Finance and Investment Law, 2000,Banking Supervision and Systemic Bank Restructuring, 2000, Zambia's Stock Exchange and Privatization Programme, 2001, The Dynamics of Market Integration: African Stock Exchange's in the New Millennium, 2000. Tutor U. Zambia Law Sch., 1991-95. Staff Devel. fellow in law U. Zambia, 1991, U. Yale Law Faculty fellow, 1998; Rhodes scholar U. Zambia, 1992, U. Oxford, 1992-94, U. Hull, 1994-95. Fellow Royal Soc. Arts. of England, Inst. Commerce of England; mem. Internat. Bar Assn., Law Assn. of Zambia, Brit. Assn. Lawyers for Def. of Unborn. Office: The World Bank 1818 H St NW Washington DC 20433-0001 E-mail: kmwenda@yahoo.com, kmwenda@worldbank.org

MYCOCK, FREDERICK CHARLES, lawyer; b. Columbus, Ga., Oct. 3, 1943; s. Edwin S. and Elaine M.M. BSBA, Boston U., 1965, LLB, 1968. Bar: Mass. 1968, U.S. Dist. Ct. Mass. 1974, U.S. Supreme Ct. 1980. Assoc. Roderick E. Smith, Hyannis, Mass., 1968-71; asst. atty. gen. State of Mass., 1972-73; ptnr. Mycock, Kilroy, Green & Mycock, Hyannis, 1972-77, Mycock, Nwewll & Morse, Barnstable, Mass., 1977-86; atty. pvt. practice, 1987—. Mem. ABA, Assn. Trial Lawyers Assn., Nat. Assn. Criminal Defense Lawyers, Mass. Bar Assn., Mass. Acad. Trial Lawyers, Barnstable County Bar Assn. Republican. Methodist. Criminal, General practice. Home: Santuit Rd Cotuit MA 02635 Office: 3291 Main St Barnstable MA 02630-1105

MYERS, DANE JACOB, lawyer, podiatrist; b. Murray, Utah, June 20, 1948; s. Lorin LaVar Myers and Irma Lee (Bell) Willette; m. Mary Jo Jackson, June 22, 1970; children: Troy, Chad, Melissa, Apryll, Tristan, Remington. DPM, Pa. Coll. Podiatric Medicine, 1977; BA, U. Utah, 1983; JD, U. Ark., 1986. Bar: Ark. 1986. Pres. Tooele (Utah) Foot Clinic, 1977-83; owner N.W. Ark. Foot Clinic, Rogers, Ark., 1983—; pvt. practice law Fayetteville, 1986-97. Served to maj., med. svc. corps USAR, 1977-94. Mem. ABA, APHA, Am. Coll. Foot and Ankle Surgeons (assoc.), Am. Diabetes Assn., Ark. Bar Assn., Am. Soc. Law and Medicine, Am. Podiatric Med. Assn., Ark. Podiatric Med. Assn., Delta Theta Phi. Republican. Mem. LDS Ch. Avocations: golf, computers, history. Health. Home: 106 Woodcliff Rd Springdale AR 72764-3691 Office: NW Ark Foot Clinic 700 N 13th St Rogers AR 72756-3436 E-mail: danejmyers@hotmail.com

MYERS, DANIEL, lawyer; b. Celina, Ohio, Jan. 27, 1950; s. David M. and Ruth E. (Henderson) Myers; m. Terry L. Noel, Oct. 25, 1975 (div. Apr. 1982); m. Jill E. Snyder, July 21, 1988. BS, U. Tenn., 1972; JD, Ohio No. U., 1975. Bar: Ohio 1976, Pa. 1977. Assot. Myers & Myers, Celina, 1975-77, ptnr., 1978-96; sole practice Myers Law Office, Ligonier, Pa., 1996—. Pros. atty. Mercer County, Celina, 1980-92. Mem. Lions (bd. dirs. 1982-95), Elks (exalted knight 1976-77). Family and matrimonial, General practice, Probate. Office: PO Box 230 90 N Ash St Celina OH 45822-1702

MYERS, FRANKLIN, lawyer, oil service company executive; b. Pensacola, Fla., Nov. 2, 1952; s. T.F. Sr. and D. Bernice (Brewer) M.; children: Amanda C., Adam F., Anne Marie M. BS, Miss. State U., 1974; JD, U. Miss., 1977. Bar: Miss. 1977, Tex. 1978. Ptnr. Fulbright and Jaworski, Houston, 1978-88; sr. v.p., gen. counsel Baker Hughes Inc., 1988-95; sr. v.p. Cooper Cameron Corp., 1995—. Adj. prof. U. Tex. Sch. Law, 1990—; bd. dirs. Reunion Industries, Inc., Metals USA, Inc., Input Output, Inc., InPut Output Inc. Bd. dirs. Tex. Bus. Law Found. Fellow Houston Bar Found., Tex. Bar Assn., Miss. Bar Assn., Houston Bar Assn. Baptist. General corporate, Mergers and acquisitions, Securities. Office: Cooper Energy Svcs 10810 Northwest Fwy Houston TX 77092-7304

MYERS, HARDY, state attorney general, lawyer; b. Electric Mills, Miss., Oct. 25, 1939; m. Mary Ann Thalhofer, 1962; children: Hardy III, Christopher, Jonathan. AB with distinction, U. Miss., 1961; LLB, U. Oreg., 1964. Bar: Oreg., U.S. Ct. of Appeals (9th cir.), U.S. Dist. Ct. Law clerk U.S. Dist. Judge William G. East, 1964-65; pvt. practice Stoel Rives LLP, 1965-96; atty. gen. State of Oregon, 1997—. Mem. Oreg. Ho. of Reps., 1975-85, speaker of the ho., 1979-83. Pres. Portland City Planning Commn., 1973-74; chair Oreg. Jail Project, 1984-86, Citizens' Task Force on Mass Transit Policy, 1985-86, Oreg. Criminal Justice Coun., 1987-91, Portland Future Focus, 1990-91, Metro Charter com., 1991-92, task force on state employee benefits, 1994; co-chair gov. task force on state employee compensation, 1995. Office: Oreg Atty Gen Justice Dept 1162 Court St NE Salem OR 97310-1320

MYERS, J(OSEPH) MICHAEL, lawyer; b. Austin, Tex., Sept. 5, 1947; s. Joseph Marion and Constance Lorraine (Clarke) M.; children: Joseph Merritt, Jordan Robertson. B.A., U. Tex., 1970; J.D., St. Mary's U., San Antonio, 1974. Bar: Tex. 1974, U.S. Dist. Ct. (we. dist.) Tex. 1975, U.S. Dist. Ct. (so. dist.) Tex. 1976, U.S. Ct. Appeals (5th cir.) 1976, U.S. Supreme Ct. 1976. Briefing atty. to chief judge U.S. Dist. Ct. (we. dist.) Tex., San Antonio, 1974-75; ptnr. Groce, Locke & Hebdon, San Antonio, 1975— . Editor, contbr. St. Mary's U. Law Sch. Rev., 1974. Mem. ABA, Fed. Bar Assn. (speaker 1982-89), San Antonio Bar Assn. (Outstanding Service award 1980), Am. Judicature Soc., Tex. Assn. Def. Counsel, Internat. Assn. Def. Counsel, Phi Delta Phi (historian 1974-75). Episcopalian. Federal civil litigation, State civil litigation, Personal injury. Home: 11530 Vance Jackson Rd San Antonio TX 78230-1666 Office: Groce Locke Hebdon 2000 Frost Bank Tower San Antonio TX 78205

MYERS, KENNETH RAYMOND, lawyer; b. N.Y.C., Apr. 14, 1939; s. Cyril Burleigh and Dorothy (Podolyn) M.; m. Susan Kay Plotnick, Sept. 9, 1962; children: Lisa R., Jonathan S., Andrew C. SB, MIT, 1960; JD, Harvard U., 1963. Bar: Ill. 1963, Pa. 1968. Assoc. Ross, Hardies & O'Keefe, Chgo., 1963-68, Morgan, Lewis & Bockius, Phila., 1968-71, ptnr., 1972-2000; of counsel High, Swartz, Roberts & Seidel LLP, Norristown, Pa., 2000—. Mem. rules com. Environ. Hearing Bd., Harrisburg, Pa., 1984-89. Editor: Environmental Spill Reporting Handbook, 1992—; contbg. author: Environmental Law Practice Guide, 1992—; contbr. articles to profl. jours. Dir. Water Resources Assn. Del. River Basin, Valley Forge, Pa., 1975-2000, Albert Einstein Healthcare Network, 1997—, Germantown Hosp., 1998-99, Belmont Hosp., 1999-2001; pres. Am. Jewish Congress, Phila., 1996-99, mem. nat. commn., N.Y.C., 1984-99. Mem. ABA (rep. to U.S. Office Personnel Mgmt. 1975—), Pa. Bar Assn., Montgomery Bar Assn., Eta Kappa Nu. Administrative and regulatory, Environmental, Public utilities. Home: 7719 Sycamore Ln Elkins Park PA 19027-1025 E-mail: kmyers@highswartz.com

MYERS, RODMAN NATHANIEL, lawyer; b. Detroit, Oct. 27, 1920; s. Isaac Rodman and Fredericka (Hirschman) M.; m. Jeanette Polisei, Mar. 19, 1957 (dec. 1996); children: Jennifer Sue, Rodman Jay. BA, Wayne State U., 1941; LLB, U. Mich., 1943. Bar: Mich. 1943, U.S. Supreme Ct. 1962. Agt. IRS, Detroit, 1943; from assoc. to ptnr. Butzel, Keidan, Simon, Myers & Graham, 1943-90; of counsel Honigman Miller Schwartz and Cohn, 1991—. Bd. dirs. United Cmty. Svcs. of Met. Detroit, 1978-85, v.p., 1981-85, chmn. social svcs. divsn., 1982-85; bd. dirs. Children's Ctr. of Wayne County (Mich.), 1963-88, pres., 1969-72; mem. blue ribbon task force Mich. Dept. Edn., 1988-89; founding mem., trustee Detroit Sci. Ctr.; trustee Mich. chpt. Leukemia Soc. Am., founding pres., 1984-86, nat. trustee, 1984—; commr. Detroit Mcpl. Parking Authority, 1963-71; trustee Temple Beth El, Bloomfield Hills, Mich.; pres. Bloomfield Twp. Pub. Libr. Mem. ABA, State Bar Mich. (chmn. atty. discipline panel, past vice chmn. unauthorized practice of law com., past mem. character and fitness com.). General corporate. Home: 3833 Lakeland Ln Bloomfield Hills MI 48302-1328 Office: 2290 1st National Bldg Detroit MI 48226

MYERS, STEPHEN HAWLEY, lawyer; b. Washington, Mar. 28, 1953; s. Robert Holt and Antoinette (Hawley) M.; children: Stephen, Hampton, Brielle; m. Laura Lee Fuller, Dec. 1, 1989. BA in Polit. Sci. with honors, Union Coll., 1976; JD, Loyola U., 1979. Bar: D.C. 1979, La. 1979, U.S. Dist. Ct. D.C. 1980, U.S. Tax Ct. 1980, U.S. Ct. Claims 1980, U.S. Ct. Appeals (fed. and D.C. cirs.) 1980, U.S. Ct. Appeals (5th cir.) 1985, U.S. Dist. Ct. (we., mid. and ea. dists.) La. 1985, U.S. Supreme Ct. 1989. Atty. advisor to hon. judge Edward S. Smith U.S. Ct. Appeals (Fed. cir.), Washington, 1979-80; assoc. Duncan Allen & Mitchell, 1980-82; atty. advisor to Judge Jules G. Körner U.S. Tax Ct., 1982-84; assoc. Davidson Meaux Sonnier & McElligott, Lafayette, La., 1984-85; ptnr. Roy Forrest, Lopresto, DeCourt & Myers and predecessor firms, 1985-97; pvt. practice Stephen Hawley Myers, LLC, La., 1997—. Lectr. for continuing legal edn. seminars on corp., bus. and sales tax litigation. Vice chmn., bd. dirs. La. Coun. for Fiscal Reform, New Orleans, 1986-96; bd. dirs., treas. Acadiana Youth, Inc., Lafayette, 1986-94. Mem. ABA, Am. Platform Assn., Lafayette Bar Assn., La. Counsel Def. Attys., La. Trial Lawyer's Assn., Phi Delta Phi. Avocations: writing, photography, skeet shooting, sports clay shooting, hunting. General civil litigation, General corporate, State and local taxation. Home: 100 Old Settlement Rd Lafayette LA 70508-7030 Office: 600 Jefferson St Ste 401 Lafayette LA 70501-8919 also: 15 W Lenox St Chevy Chase MD 20815-4208

MYHAND, WANDA RESHEL, paralegal, legal assistant; b. Detroit, Aug. 15, 1963; d. Ralph and Geraldine (Leavell) M. Office mgr./adminstrv. asst. Gregory Terrell & Co., CPA, Detroit, 1987-90; legal sec. Ford Motor Co., 1990-91; office mgr. M.G. Christian Builders, Inc., 1991; paralegal, legal asst. Law Office of Karri Mitchell, 1991-98; legal sec., paralegal The KPM Group, Southfield, Mich., 1998—. Vol. UNCF Telethon Detroit, 1988. Mem. NAFE. Avocations: crossword puzzles, travel, theatre and concerts.

MYTELKA, ARNOLD KRIEGER, lawyer; b. Jersey City, July 24, 1937; s. Herman Donald and Jeannette (Krieger) M.; m. Rosalind Marcia Kaplan, Dec. 17, 1961; children: Andrew Charles, Daniel Sommer. AB, Princeton U., 1958; LLB cum laude, Harvard U., 1961; postgrad., London Sch. Econs., 1961-62. Bar: N.J. 1961, U.S. Dist. Ct. N.J. 1963, U.S. Supreme Ct. 1970, U.S. Ct. Appeals (3d cir.) 1978, U.S. Dist. Ct. (so. and ea. dist.) N.Y. 1983. Law sec. Chief Justice N.J. Supreme Ct., Newark, 1962-63; assoc. Clapp & Eisenberg, 1963-68, ptnr., 1968-94; prin. Kraemer, Burns, Mytelka, Lovell & Kulka, Springfield, N.J., 1994—. Lectr. Rutgers Law Sch., Newark, 1973; mem. Am. Law Inst., Phila., 1989—; mem. cons. group The Law Governing Lawyers, 1990-99; founding trustee Newark Legal Svcs. Project, 1965-68; trustee Edn. Law Ctr., 1974-75; chmn. dist. V ethics com. Supreme Ct. N.J., 1983-84, mem. 1981-84; trustee Legal Svcs. Found. Essex County, 1982—, pres., 1990-92; lectr. in land use law. Mem. editorial bd. N.J. Law Jour., 1991—; contbr. legal articles to profl. jours. Chmn. bd. trustees Ramapo Coll. N.J., 1979-80, mem. 1975-80; mediator chancery divsn. N.J. Superior Ct., 1990—, trustee, 1998-2000, spl. fiscal agt., 1997, spl. master, 1999, 2000. Frank Knox Meml. fellow Harvard U., London Sch. Econs. and Polit. Sci., 1961-62. Mem. ABA (mem. litigation sect.), N.J. State Bar Assn. (chmn. appellate practices study com. 1977-79, chmn. land use sect. 1984-85). Administrative and regulatory, General civil litigation, Land use and zoning (including planning). Home: 56 Hall Rd Chatham NJ 07928-1723 Office: Kraemer Burns Mytelka Lovell & Kulka 675 Morris Ave Springfield NJ 07081-1523 E-mail: amytelka@kraemerburns.com

NACE, BARRY JOHN, lawyer; b. York, Pa., Nov. 28, 1944; s. John Harrison and Mildred Louise (Orwig) N.; m. Andrea Marcia Giardini. Apr. 28, 1973; children: Christopher Thomas, Jonathan Barry, Matthew Andrew. BS, Dickinson Sch. of Law, 1965, JD, 1969, DL, 1994. Bar: Md. 1970, D.C. 1971, Pa. 1972, W.Va. 1997, U.S. Ct. Appeals (3d, 4th and D.C. cirs.), U.S. Supreme Ct. Ptnr. Davis & Nace, Washington, 1972-78, Paulson & Nace, Bethesda, Md., 1978-85, 98—; sr. ptnr. Paulson, Nace & Norwind, Washington, 1986-97. Fellow Roscoe Pound Found. (trustee); mem. Nat. Bd. Trial Advocacy in Civil Litigation (bd. govs. 2001—), D.C. Bar Assn., Montgomery County Bar Assn., Assn. Trial Lawyers Am. (gov. 1976-87, pres. 1993-94), Met. D.C. Trial Attys. (pres. 1977-78, 87-88, Atty. of Yr. 1976), Trial Lawyers for Pub. Justice, Internat. Acad. Trial Lawyers, Lambert Soc., Am. Inns of Ct., Am. Law Inst. Am. Bd. of Profl. Liability Attorneys. Avocations: golf, tennis, reading, racquetball. Federal civil litigation, State civil litigation, Personal injury. Home: 6208 Garnett Dr Bethesda MD 20815-6618 Office: Paulson & Nace 1814 N St NW Washington DC 20036-2404 E-mail: BJN@Lawtort.com

NACHMAN, MERTON ROLAND, JR. lawyer; b. Montgomery, Ala., Dec. 21, 1923; s. Merton Roland and Maxine (Mayer) N.; m. Martha Street, June 8, 1968; children: Nancy Nachman Yardley, Linda Nachman Connelly, Betsy Wild, Amy N. DeRoche, Karen Vann. AB cum laude, Harvard U., 1943, JD, 1948. Bar: Ala. 1949, U.S. Supreme Ct. 1953, U.S. Ct. Appeals (5th and 11th cirs.), U.S. Ct. Claims, U.S. Tax Ct. Asst. atty. gen. State of Ala., 1949-54; ptnr. Knabe & Nachman, Montgomery, 1954-59; adminstrv. asst. to Senator John Sparkman, Ala., 1956; ptnr. Steiner, Crum & Baker, Montgomery, 1959-86, counsel mem., 2000—; from ptnr. to coun. mem. Balch & Bingham, 1986-2000. Chmn. human rights com. Ala. Prison System, 1976-78. With USN, 1943-46. Recipient Merit award Ala. State Bar, 1974;, cert. of appreciation Supreme Ct. of Ala., 1974. Fellow Am. Coll. Trial Lawyers; mem. ABA (com. on fed. judiciary 1982-88, bd. govs. 1978-81), Ala. State Bar (pres. 1973-74), Am. Judicature Soc. (dir. 1976-80, Herbert Lincoln Harley award 1974), Am. Law Inst., Ala. Law Inst., Unity club (Montgomery), Am. Acad. Appellate Lawyers. Episcopalian. Administrative and regulatory, General civil litigation, Constitutional. Office: PO Box 668 8 Commerce St Ste 8 Montgomery AL 36101-0668

NACHTIGAL, PATRICIA, lawyer; b. 1946; BA, Montclair State U.; JD, Rutgers U.; LLM, NYU. Tax atty. Ingersoll-Rand Co., Woodcliff Lake, N.J., 1979-83, dir. taxes and legal, 1983-88, sec., mng. atty., 1988-91, v.p., gen. counsel, 1991-2000, sr. v.p., gen. counsel, 2000—. General corporate. Office: Ingersoll-Rand Co 200 Chestnut Ridge Rd Woodcliff Lake NJ 07677-7700

NACHWALTER, MICHAEL, lawyer; b. N.Y.C., Aug. 31, 1940; s. Samuel J. Nachwalter; m. Irene, Aug. 15, 1965; children: Helynn, Robert. BS, Bucknell U., 1962; MS, L.I. U., 1967; JD cum laude, U. Miami, 1967; LLM, Yale U., 1968. Bar: Fla. 1967, D.C. 1979, U.S. Dist. Ct. (so. dist.) Fla. 1967, U.S. Dist. Ct. (mid. dist.) Fla. 1982, U.S. Ct. Appeals (5th and 11th cirs.) 1967, U.S. Supreme Ct. 1975. Law clk. to judge U.S. Dist. Ct. (so. dist.) Fla.; shareholder Kelly, Black, Black & Kenny; now shareholder Kenny Nachwalter Seymour Critchlow & Spector, P.A., Miami. Lectr. Law Sch. U. Miami. Editor-in-chief U. Miami Law Rev., 1966-67. Fellow Am. Coll. Trial Lawyers; mem. ABA, FBA, Am. Bd. Trial Advs., Fla. Bar Assn. (bd. govs. 1982-90), Internat. Soc. Barristers (dir.), Dade County Bar Assn., Jud. Qualifications Commn. (vice chmn. 1995-2000), Iron Arrow, Soc. Wig and Robe, Omicron Delta Kappa, Phi Kappa Phi, Phi Delta Phi. Antitrust, Federal civil litigation, State civil litigation. Office: Kenny Nachwalter Seymour Arnold Critchlow & Spector PA 201 S Biscayne Blvd Ste 1100 Miami FL 33131-4327

NACOL, MAE, lawyer; b. Beaumont, Tex., June 15, 1944; d. William Samuel and Ethel (Bowman) N.; children: Shawn Alexander Nacol, Catherine Regina Nacol. BA, Rice U., 1965; postgrad., South Tex. Coll. Law, 1966. Bar: Tex. 1969, U.S. Dist. Ct. (so. dist.) Tex. 1969. Diamond buyer/appraiser Nacol's Jewelry, Houston, 1961—; pvt. practice law, 1969—; escrow officer Commonwealth Land Title Co. Author, editor ednl. materials on multiple sclerosis, 1981-85. Nat. dir. A.R.M.S. of Am. Ltd., Houston, 1984-85. Recipient Mayor's Recognition award City of Houston, 1972. Mem. Houston Bar Assn. (chmn. candidate com. 1970, membership com. 1971, chmn. lawyers referral com. 1972), Assn. Trial Lawyers Am., Tex. Trial Lawyers Assn., Am. Judicature Soc. (sustaining), Houston Fin. Coun. Women, Houston Trial Lawyers Assn. Presbyterian. Admiralty, General corporate, Personal injury. Office: 600 Jefferson St Ste 750 Houston TX 77002-7326 also: 8401 Westheimer Ste 104 Houston TX 77063

NADEAU, JOSEPH P. judge; AB, Dartmouth Coll.; LLB, Boston U., 1962. Pvt. practice trial atty., 1962—81; justice Durham Dist. Ct., 1968-81; judge N.H. Superior Ct., 1981-92, chief justice, 1992; assoc. justice N.H. Supreme Ct., 2000—. Mem. Jud. Br. Adminstrv. Coun., Supreme Ct. Jud.Ednl. Svcs. Com., Supreme Ct. Accreditation Commn.; pres. Am. Acad. Jud. Edn., 1990-92; participant ct. study program former Soviet Union, facutly jud. edn. program, Latvia, study programs in Russia, Georgia, Armenia; involved in jud. edn. seminars and legis. activities in Albania, Bulgaria, Kazakhstan, Poland. Mem. Gov.'s Commn. on Domestic Violence. Office: Supreme Ct Bldg One Noble Dr Concord NH 03301-6160*

NADEAU, ROBERT BERTRAND, JR. lawyer; b. Miami Beach, Fla., July 15, 1950; s. Robert B. and Ernestine Inez (Nicholson) N. BBA, U. Notre Dame, 1972; JD, U. Fla., 1975. Bar: Fla. 1975, U.S. Dist. Ct. (mid. dist.) Fla. 1976, U.S. Dist. Ct. (so. dist.) Fla. 1982, U.S. Ct. Appeals (11th cir.) 1982. Asst. to pres. The Fla. Bar, Tampa, Fla., 1975-76; ptnr. Akerman, Senterfitt & Eidson, P.A., Orlando, 1976—. Arbitrator Am. Arbitration Assn., Orlando, 1987—. Mem. ABA, The Fla. Bar (chmn. student edn. and admission to bar com., vice chmn. 9th cir. grievance com.), Notre Dame Club Greater Orlando (pres. 1979-80). Avocations: golf, running. Alternative dispute resolution, General civil litigation, Construction. Office: Akerman Senterfitt & Eidson PA 255 S Orange Ave Orlando FL 32801-3445

NADEAU, ROBERT MAURICE AUCLAIR, lawyer; b. Sanford, Maine, Feb. 8, 1955; s. Roland Maurice Nadeau and Nancy Lee (Leighton) Auclair; m. Kimberly J. Brennan, Oct. 11, 1982; children: Matteson Leigh, Ian Robert, Erin Roland. BA, Johns Hopkins U., 1977; JD, Widener U., 1980. Bar: Mass. 1981, U.S. Ct. Appeals (1st cir.) 1982, U.S. Ct. Mil. Appeals 1982, U.S. Dist. Ct. Mass. 1986, Maine 1992, N.H. 1994, U.S. Dist. Ct. Maine 1994, U.S. Dist. Ct. N.H. 1994. Asst. probation officer Mcpl. Ct., Wilmington, Del., 1978-80; with U.S. Army Judge Advocate Gen.'s Corps, 1981-85; spl. asst. U.S. atty. (Kans.), 1982-83; asst. town prosecutor Hampden, Mass., 1985-87, Wilbraham, 1985-87; city prosecutor Law Dept., Chicopee, 1988-90; pvt. practice Springfield, 1985-93; sr. assoc. Smith Elliott Smith and Garmey, P.A., Kennebunk, Maine, 1993-95; sr. ptnr. Nadeau & Assocs., P.A., Sanford and Wells, 1995—; judge York County Probate Court, 1997—. Dir. Kennebunk Health and Home Care Svcs., 1994. Trustee Seashore Trolley Mus., 1994-97; dir. York County chpt. ARC, 1998—. Capt. U.S. Army, 1980-85. Mem. Sanford Kiwanis Club, Wells Rotary Club. Democrat. Roman Catholic. Avocations: sports, running, music collecting, travel. General civil litigation, General practice, Personal injury. Office: Nadeau & Assocs PA 883 Main St Sanford ME 04073-3527 also: Nadeau & Assocs PA 1332 Post Rd Wells ME 04090-4561 E-mail: rnadeau3@maine.rr.com

NADLER, ANDREAS, lawyer; b. Cologne, Germany, Dec. 25, 1963; s. Norbert A. and Marianne C. Nadler. LLB, U. Bonn, Germany, 1990, Dr, 1995. Cert. specialist in labor law. Assoc. Busse & Miessen, Bonn, 1994-98, ptnr., 1999—. Mem. German Jurists Assn. (gen. sec. 1994—), German Lawyers Assn., European Labor Lawyers Assn. General civil litigation, Land use and zoning (including planning). Office: Busse & Miessen Oxfordstr 21 Bonn 53111 Germany Fax: 49 (0) 228 98391-40. E-mail: buero.nadler@busse-miessen.de

NAEGELE, JOSEPH LOYOLA, SR. lawyer; b. San Francisco, July 19, 1955; s. Charles Frederick and Rosemary Cecilia (Ledogar) N.; m. BeaLisa Elizabeth Sydlik, Feb. 21, 1981; children: Joseph Loyola Jr., Elizabeth Anne. BA, U. Calif., Davis, 1977; JD, U. Calif., San Francisco, 1981. Bar: Calif. 1982. Legal intern U.S. Congress, Washington, 1976; legal extern Calif. Ct. Appeals, San Francisco, 1980; law clk. U.S. Dist. Ct., San Francisco, 1981, Sacramento Dist. Atty.'s Office, Sacramento, 1982; tchr. St. Francis High Sch., Sacramento, 1982; atty. Law Offices of Jack Komar, San Jose, Calif., 1983-85; ptnr. Naegele & Naegele, San Jose, 1985—; prof. Lincoln Law Sch., San Jose, 1983-85. Mem. Santa Clara County Bar Assn., Calif. Trial Lawyers Assn., Santa Clara County Trial Lawyers Assn., St. Thomas Moore Soc., Barristers Club. Roman Catholic. Home: 949 Hilmar St Santa Clara CA 95050-5918 Office: 111 W Saint John St Ste 650 San Jose CA 95113-1120

NAFTALIS, GARY PHILIP, lawyer, educator; b. Newark, Nov. 23, 1941; s. Gilbert and Bertha Beatrice Naftalis; m. Donna Arditi, June 30, 1974; children: Benjamin, Joshua, Daniel, Sarah. AB, Rutgers U., 1963; AM, Brown U., 1965; LLB, Columbia U., 1967. Bar: N.Y. 1967, U.S. Dist. Ct. (so. dist.) N.Y. 1969, U.S. Ct. Appeals (2d cir.) 1968, U.S. Ct. Appeals (3d cir.) 1973, U.S. Ct. Appeals (D.C. cir.) 1993, U.S. Supreme Ct. 1974. Law clk. to judge U.S. Dist. Ct. So. Dist. N.Y., 1967-68; asst. U.S. atty. So. Dist. N.Y., 1968-74, asst. chief criminal divsn., 1972-74; spl. asst. U.S. atty. for V.I., 1972-73; spl. counsel U.S. Senate Subcom. on Long Term Care, 1975, N.Y. State Temp. Commn. on Living Costs and the Economy, 1975; ptnr. Orans, Elsen, Polstein & Naftalis, N.Y.C., 1974-81, Kramer, Levin, Naftalis & Frankel, N.Y.C., 1981—. Lectr. Law Sch. Columbia U., 1976-88; vis. lectr. Law Sch. Harvard U., 1979; mem. deptl. disciplinary com. Appellate div. 1st Dept., 1980-86. Author: (with Marvin E. Frankel) The Grand Jury: An Institution on Trial, 1977, Considerations in Representing Attorneys in Civil and Criminal Enforcement Proceedings, 1981, Sentencing: Helping Judges Do Their Jobs, 1986, SEC Actions Seeking to Bar Securities Professionals, 1995, SEC Cease and Desist Powers Limited, 1997, The Foreign Corrupt Practices Act, 1997, Prosecuting Lawyers Who Defend Clients in SEC Actions, 1998, Obtaining Reports from a Credit Bureau for Litigation May be a Crime, 1999; editor: White Collar Crimes, 1980. Trustee Boys Brotherhood Rep., 1978—, Blueberry Treatment Ctr., 1981-91, Joseph Haggerty Children's Fund, 1991—; bd. dirs. The Legal Aid Soc., 2000—. Fellow Am. Coll. Trial Lawyers; mem. ABA (white collar crime com. criminal justice sect. 1985—), Assn. of Bar of City of N.Y. (com. criminal cts. 1980-83, com. judiciary 1984-87, com. on criminal law 1987-90, 97—, coun. criminal justice 1985-88), Fed. Bar Coun. (com. cts. 2d cir. 1974-77), N.Y. Bar Assn. (com. state legis. 1974-76, exec. com. comml. and fed. litigation sect.), Internat. Bar Assn. (bus. crimes com. 1988—), N.Y. Coun. Def. Lawyers (bd. dirs. 2000—). Administrative and regulatory, Federal civil litigation, Criminal. Home: 1125 Park Ave Apt 7B New York NY 10128-1243 Office: Kramer Levin Naftalis & Frankel 919 3rd Ave New York NY 10022-3902

NAGEL, KAREN ANNETTE ELIZABETH, lawyer, editor; b. Chgo. BA in Sociology and Fgn. Langs., Northestern Ill. U., 1981; JD, John Marshall Law Sch., 1988. Bar: Ill. 1989. Legal intern Law Dept. City of Chgo., 1987-88; pvt. practice Chgo., 1989—. Polit., legal commentator radio, TV, Chgo., 1992—; spkr. in field; pres., bd. dirs. Ginco Enterprises, Park Ridge, Ill. Editor-in-chief Ill. Politics, 1991—; author, editor: 1992 Election Special Report, 1992; contbr. articles to profl. jours. Co-Recipient Peter Lisagor Journalism award. Mem. ABA, AAUW, Ill. State Bar Assn., Chgo. Bar Assn., Justinian Soc. Office: Ill Politics PO Box 136 Park Ridge IL 60068-0136

NAGEL, ROBERT FORDER, legal educator, lawyer; b. Dover, Del., Jan. 17, 1947; s. William George and Ethel Marion (Forder) N.; m. Prudence Elizabeth Brown, Sept. 5, 1970; children— David, Andrew, Rebecca, Sarah. BA, Swarthmore Coll., 1968; JD, Yale U., 1972. Bar: Pa. 1972, Colo. 1982, U.S. Ct. Appeals (3d cir.) 1974, U.S. Supreme Ct. 1983. Dep. atty. gen. Dept. Justice, Commonwealth of Pa., Harrisburg, 1972-75; assoc. prof. law U. Colo., Boulder, 1975-81, prof., 1981—; cons. Ind. Petroleum Assn. Am., Adv. Commn. on Intergovtl. Relations. Author: Constitutional Cultures: The Mentality and Consequences of Judicial Review, 1989, Judicial Power and American Power: Censoring Ourselves in An Anxious Age, 1994; contbr. articles to profl. publs. Home: 3140 3rd St Boulder CO 80304-2541 Office: U Colo Sch Law Campus PO Box 401 # U Boulder CO 80309-0401

NAGIN, STEPHEN ELIAS, lawyer, educator; b. Phila., Nov. 7, 1946; s. Harry S. and Dorothy R. (Pearlman) N.; m. Marjorie Riley, Sept. 4, 1983. BBA, U. Miami, 1969; JD, 1974. Bar: Fla. 1974, D.C. 1976, U.S. Supreme Ct. 1978. Asst. atty. gen. State of Fla., Miami, 1974-75; atty. FTC, 1975-80; spl. asst. U.S. Atty., Washington, 1980-81; ptnr. Nagin, Gallop & Figueredo, P.A., 1987—. Adj. prof. St. Thomas U. Sch. Law, 1984-94; instr. Nat. Inst. Trial Advocacy, 1992—. Mem. ABA (editor, trial lawyers sect. 1983-84, mem. spl. antitrust task force 1983—, chmn. editl. bd., Florida Bar Jour. 1982-83, chmn. antitrust com. 1996-98, chmn. intellectual property com. 2001—, chmn. antitrust and trade regulation cert. com. 2000—), Patent Lawyers Assn. South Fla. (sec., 2000), Coral Gables Bar Assn. (bd. dirs. 1983-87), Assn. Trial Lawyers Am., Am. Arbitration Assn., Nat. Health Lawyers Assn. Antitrust, Federal civil litigation, Intellectual property. Office: Nagin Gallop & Figueredo PA 3225 Aviation Ave Fl 3D Miami FL 33133-4741

NAGLE, ROBERT OWEN, lawyer; b. Watertown, S.D., Feb. 10, 1929; s. John Raymond and Kathleen Margaret (McQuillen) N.; m. Louise Emerson H'Doubler, Mar. 14, 1954; children— Robert Owen, Charles Francis, Margaret Louise. BS in Econs., U. Wis., 1951; LLB, U. Calif., 1957. Bar: Calif. 1957. Asso. firm Morrison, Foerster, Holloway, Clinton and Clark, San Francisco, 1957-62, ptnr., 1962-64; gen. atty. Spreckels Sugar div. Amstar Corp., San Francisco, 1964-66, v.p., 1966-68, exec. v.p., 1968-71, v.p. parent co., 1971-76; exec. v.p. Am. Sugar div. Amstar Corp., 1975-76; pres., chief exec. officer Calif. and Hawaiian Sugar Co., San Francisco, 1976-82, also dir.; ptnr. Brobeck, Phleger & Harrison, 1982-86; pvt. investor Piedmont, Calif., 1986—. Bd. dirs. Providence Hosp., Oakland, Calif. Mem. Law Rev. Bd. dirs. San Francisco Bay Area coun. Boy Scouts Am.; trustee U. Calif. Berkeley Found., Wis. Alumni Rsch. Found., Pacific Vascular Rsch. Found., San Francisco. Served to lt. j.g. USN, 1951-54, Korea. Decorated Bronze Star with V, Air medal. Mem. ABA, State Bar Calif., Bar Assn. San Francisco, Order of Coif. Clubs: Claremont Country, Pacific Union.

NAJJOUM, LINDA LEMMON, lawyer; b. Washington, June 15, 1946; d. Alexis William and Elizabeth Jane (Button) Lemmon. BS in Nursing, Ohio State U., 1970; MS in Nursing, Va. Commonwealth U., 1973; JD, U. S.C., 1981. Bar: S.C. 1981, Va. 1983. Law clk. S.C. Supreme Ct., Columbia, 1981-82; assoc. atty. Hunton & Williams, Richmond, Va., 1982-85, Fairfax, 1985-89, counsel, 1989—. Contbr. articles to Law Rev. Mem. ABA (litigation sect.), Va. Bar Assn., S.C. Bar Assn., Fairfax County Bar Assn., Va. Trial Lawyers Assn. Bankruptcy, Federal civil litigation, State civil litigation. Office: Hunton & Williams 1751 Pinnacle Dr Ste 1700 Mc Lean VA 22102-3836 E-mail: lnajjoum@hunton.com

NAKATA, GARY KENJI, lawyer; b. Okinawa, Japan, Nov. 13, 1964; came to the U.S., 1971; s. Hiroshi Nakata and Miwako Kin; m. Jo Ann Akiko Tengan, Aug. 22, 1998. BBA in Fin., U. Hawaii, 1988; JD with distinction, U. of the Pacific, 1995. Bar: Hawaii 1996, Calif. 1996, U.S. Dist. Ct. Hawaii, 1996; cert. mgmt. acct.; cert. fin. mgr.; cert. grad. Am. Banker's Assn. Nat. Sch. Regulatory Compliance. Credit analyst Bank of Hawaii, Honolulu, 1988-90, sr. credit analyst, 1990-92; law clk. Hawaii Atty. Gen. Tax Divsn., 1994; sr. assoc. Kobayashi, Sugita & Goda, 1995—. Mem. new product devel. adv. bd. Warren Gorham & Lamont, N.Y.C., 1997-98. Editor-in-chief: The Transnational Lawyer, 1994, 95. Pres., enlisted adv. coun. Hawaii Air Nat. Guard, Honolulu, 1986-92; mem. ex officio alumni coun., mem. membership com., mem. membership benefits subcom. U. Hawaii Alumni Assn., Honolulu, 1990-91; mem. fin. com. and bylaws subcom. Soc. Coll. Bus. Alumni and Friends, U. Hawaii Coll. Bus. Adminstrn. Alumni Affairs, Honolulu, 1990-91, founding mem., treas., 1990-91, mem. steering com. to form alumni orgn., 1997—, pres., 1998—; at-large rep., treas., legis. liaison Neighborhood Bd., Kaneohe, Hawaii, 1991-92. Mem. ABA (bus. law sect., comml. fin. svcs. com., consumer fin. svcs. com.), Hawaii State Bar Assn. (mem. real property and fin. svcs. sect. 1997—), Calif. State Bar Assn., Inst. Cert. Mgmt. Accts. (bd. dirs. 1998-2000, dir. mem. acquistion 1998-2000), Hawaii Fin. Regulatory Compliance Assn. (bd. dirs. 1997—, chairperson fair credit reporting act regulatory update com. 1998—), Hawaii Bus. Jaycees (charter mem. 1991—, charter pres. 1991-92, chmn. bd. 1992-93, R. Allen Watkins Outstanding Chpt. Pres. award 1992, Hampton Whetsell award 1992, Clarence Howard award 1992), Hawaii Jaycees (legal counsel 2000-2001). Banking, General corporate, Real property. Office: Kobayashi Sugita & Goda 999 Bishop St Ste 2600 Honolulu HI 96813-4430

NAKAYAMA, PAULA AIKO, state supreme court justice; b. Honolulu, Oct. 19, 1953; m. Charles W. Totto; children: Elizabeth Murakami, Alexander Totto. BS, U. Calif., Davis, 1975; JD, U. Calif., 1979. Bar: Hawaii 1979. Dep. pros. atty. City and County of Honolulu, 1979-82; ptnr. Shim, Tam & Kirimitsu, Honolulu, 1982-92; judge 1st Cir. Ct. State of Hawaii, Oahu, 1992-93; justice State of Hawaii Supreme Ct., Honolulu, 1993—. Mem. Am. Judicature Soc., Hawaii Bar Assn., Sons and Daughters of 442. Office: Hawaii Supreme Ct Ali'iolani Hale 417 S King St Honolulu HI 96813-2914*

NAKER, MARY LESLIE, legal firm executive; b. Elgin, Ill., July 6, 1954; d. Robert George and Marilyn Jane (Swain). BS in Edn., No. Ill. U., 1976, MS in Edn., 1978, postgrad., 1980, Coll. Fin. Planning, 1990. Cert. tchr., Ill., fin. paraplanner. Retail sales clk. Fin'n Feather Farm, Dundee, Ill., 1972-75; pvt. practice tchr. South Elgin, 1974-78; tchg. asst. Sch. Dist #13, Bloomingdale, 1976-78, substitute tchr.; office mgr. Tempo 21, Carol Stream, 1978-82, LaGrange, 1982-85; sales coord. K&R Delivery, Hinsdale, 1986-89; fin. planner coord. Elite Adv. Svcs., Inc., Schaumburg, 1989-90; adminstrv. coord. Export Transports, Inc., Elk Grove Village, 1990-98; adminstrn. mgr. SBS Worldwide Chgo. Inc., Bensenville, 1998-99; office adminstr. DiMonte & Lizak, Attys. at Law, Park Ridge, 2000—. Leader Girl Scouts U.S.A., 1972-77, camp counselor, 1972-79. Music Scholar PTA, U. Wis., 1967, PTA, U. Iowa, 1968-69. Mem. Nat. Geographic Soc., Smithsonian Assn. Lutheran. Avocations: ceramics, bowling, knitting, camping, sewing. Home: 2020 Clearwater Way Elgin IL 60123-2588 Office: DiMonte & Lizak 216 Higgins Rd Park Ridge IL 60068-5706

NANCE, ALLAN TAYLOR, retired lawyer; b. Dallas, Jan. 31, 1933; s. A.Q. and Lois Rebecca (Taylor) N. BA, So. Meth. U., 1954, LLB, 1957; LLM, NYU, 1978. Bar: Tex. 1957, N.Y. 1961. With Simpson Thacher & Bartlett, N.Y.C., 1960-65; asst. counsel J.P. Stevens & Co., Inc., 1965-70, sec., 1970-78, asst. gen. counsel, 1970-89; counsel J.P. Stevens & Co. Inc. and WestPoint-Pepperell Inc., 1989-93; asst. gen. counsel WestPoint Stevens Inc., N.Y.C., 1993-98, ret., 1998. With USNR, 1957-59. Woodrow Wilson fellow Columbia U., 1959-60. Mem. Phi Beta Kappa. General corporate, Mergers and acquisitions, Real property. Home: 201 E 66th St New York NY 10021-6451

NANCE, JOHN JOSEPH, lawyer, writer, air safety analyst, broadcaster, consultant; b. Dallas, July 5, 1946; s. Joseph Turner and Margrette (Grubbs) N.; m. Benita Ann Priest, July 26, 1968; children: Dawn Michelle, Bridgitte Cathleen, Christopher Sean. BA, So. Meth. U., 1968, JD, 1969; grad., USAF Undergrad. Pilot Tng., Williams AFB, Ariz., 1971. Bar: Tex. 1970, U.S. Ct. Appeals (fed. cir.) 1994. News reporter, broadcaster, newsman various papers and stas, Honolulu and Dallas, 1957-66; news anchorman Sta. WFAA-AM, Dallas, 1966-70; newsman including on camera Sta. WFAA-TV; pvt. practice, 1970—; news dir. Newscom Network, 1970; airline pilot Braniff Internat. Airways, 1975-82, Alaska Airlines, Inc., Seattle, 1985—; chmn., pres. Exec. Transport, Inc., Tacoma, 1979-85; chmn., CEO EMEX Corp., Kent, Wash., 1987—; mng. ptnr. Phoenix Ptnrs., Ltd., Tacoma, 1995—; project devel. assoc. Columbia Tristar TV, 1997—; with Nance & Carmichael, PLLC, Austin, Tex., 1997—. Spkr. Human Mgmt., 1984—, Teamwork and Comms. in the Med. Profession; airline safety, advocate Ind. Cons., earthquake preparedness spokesman Ind. Cons.; dir. steering com. Found. for Issues Resolution in Sci. Tech., Seattle, 1987-89; speaker Northwestern Transp. Ctr. Deregulation and Safety Conf., 1987; cons. NOVA Why Planes Crash, PBS, 1987, ABC World News Tonight Crash of US AIR 427, 1994; aviation analyst ABC-TV and radio, 1995—; aviation editor: ABC Good Morning Am., 1995—; broadcast analyst, 1986—; spkr. in field. Author: Splash of Colors, 1984, Blind Trust, 1986 (Wash. Gov.'s award 1987), On Shaky Ground, 1988, Final Approach, 1990, What Goes Up, 1991, Scorpion Strike, 1982, Operating Handbook USAF Air Carrier Safety and Inspection Office, 1991, Phoenix Rising, 1994, Pandora's Clock, 1995, Medusa's Child, 1997, The Last Hostage, 1998, Blackout, 2000, Headwind, 2001; contbr. to Transportation Deregulation in the U.S., 1988; appeared in Sheep on the Runway Tacoma Little Theater, 1975; tech. advisor, actor Pandora's Clock NBC mini-series, 1996; appeared in Medusa's Child, ABC Mini-series, 1997; prodr., writer, dir. USAF Video Prodns.: ANG Introduction to CRM, 1992, USAF SOC CRM Program, 1992, Test and Evaluation CRM, 1993, The Teamwork Connection, 1996. Pres. Fox Glen Homeowners Assn., Tacoma, 1974-77; cons. Congl. Office Tech. Assessment, Tacoma, 1987; witness air safety hearings U.S. Congress, Washington, 1986-88; bd. dirs. St. Charles Borromeo Sch., Tacoma, 1975-78, Nat. Patient Safety Found. of AMA, 1997—; mem. Mayor's Vets. Task Force, Tacoma, 1991; bd. advisors Jour. Air Law and Commerce So. Meth. Sch. Law, 1995—, exec. bd. Sch. of Law, 1998—; bd. advisors Pacific Northwest Writer's Conf., 1994—; adv. bd. supply and logistics mgmt. program Portland State U., 1997-98. Capt. USAFR, 1975-94; lt. col. Persian Gulf. Decorated Merit Svc. medal; named Airline Safety Man of Year Wash. State Div. of Aeronautics, 1987. Fellow Chartered Inst. Transport (Canberra, Australia); mem. ABA, SAG, Tex. Bar Assn., Author's Guild Am., Res. Officers Assn. (life), Aircraft Owners' and Pilots' Assn., Phi Alpha Delta, Delta Chi. Home and Office: John Nance Prodns 4512 87th Ave W Tacoma WA 98466-1920 Office: Phoenix Ptnrs Ltd PO Box 24465 Federal Way WA 98093-1465

NANDA, VED PRAKASH, law educator, university official; b. Gujranwala, India, Nov. 20, 1934; came to U.S., 1960; s. Jagan Nath and Attar (Kaur) N.; m. Katharine Kunz, Dec. 18, 1982; 1 child, Anjali. MA, Punjab U., 1952; LLB, U. Delhi, 1955, LLM, 1958, Northwestern U., 1962; postgrad., Yale U., 1962-65; LLD, Soka U., Tokyo, 1997, Bundelkhand U., Jhansi, India, 2000. Asst. prof. law U. Denver, 1965-68, assoc. prof., 1968-70, prof. law, dir. Internat. Legal Studies Program, 1970—, Thompson G. Marsh prof. law, 1987—, Evans Univ. prof., 1992—, asst. provost, 1993-94, vice provost, 1994—; sst. prof. law . Denver, 965-68, ssoc. prof., 968-70, rof. law, dir. Internat. Legal Studies Program, 970—, hompson G. Marsh prof. law, 987—, vans Univ. prof., 992—, sst. provost, 993-94, ice provost, 994—. Is. prof. Coll. Law, U. Iowa, Iowa City, 1974-75, Fla. State U., 1973, U. San Diego, 1979, U. Colo., 1992; disting. vis. prof. internat. law Chgo. Kent Coll. Law, 1981, Calif. We. Sch. Law, San Diego, 1983-84; disting. vis. scholar Sch. Law, U. Hawaii, Honolulu, 1986-87; cons. Solar Energy Rsch. Inst., 1978-81, Dept. Energy, 1980-81. Uthor: (with David Pansius) Litigation of International Disputes in U.S. Courts, 1987; editor: (with M. Cherif Bassiouni) A Treatise on International Criminal Law, 2 vols., 1973, Water Needs for the Future, 1977; (with George Shepherd) Human Rights and Third World Development, 1985; (with others) Global Human Rights, 1981, The Law of Transnational Business Transactions, 1981, World Climate Change, 1983, Breach and Adaption of International Contracts, 1992, World Debt and Human Conditions, 1993, Europe Community Law After 1992, 1993, International Environmental Law and Policy, 1995; (with William M. Evan) Nuclear Proliferation and the Legality of Nuclear Weapons, 1995, (with others) European Union Law After Maastricht, 1996, (with S.P. Sinha) Hindu Law and Legal Theory, 1996, (with D. Krieger) Nuclear Weapons and the World Court, 1998; editor, contbr.: Refugee Law and Policy, 1989; editl. bd. Jour. Am. Comparative Law, Indian Jour. Internat. Law, Transnational Pubs. O-chmn. Colo. Pub. Broadcasting Fedn., 1977-78; mem. Gov.'s Commn. on Pub. Telecommunications, 1980-82. Em. World Jurist Assn. (v.p. 1991—, pres. 1997—), World Assn. Law Profs. (pres. 1987-93), UN Assn. (v.p. Colo. divsn. 1973-76, pres. 1986-88, 93-96, nat. coun. UNA-USA 1990—, mem. governing bd. UNA-USA 1995—), World Fedn. UN Assns. (vice-chmn. 1995—), Am. Assn. Comparative Study Law (bd. dirs. 1980—), Am. Soc. Internat. Law (v.p. 1987-88, exec. coun. 1969-72, 81-84, bd. rev. and devel. 1988-91, hon. v.p. 1995—), Assn. Am. Law Schs., U.S. Inst. Human

Rights, Internat. Law Assn. (mem. exec. com. 1986—), Colo. Coun. Internat. Orgns. (pres. 1988-90), Assn. U.S. Mems. Internat. Inst. Space Law (bd. dirs., mem. exec. com. 1980-88), Internat. Acad. Comparative Law (assoc.), Order St. Ives (pres.), Rotary, Cactus Club. Office: U Denver Coll Law 1900 Olive St Denver CO 80220-1857 E-mail: vnanda@mail.law.du.edu

NANGLE, JOHN FRANCIS, federal judge; b. St. Louis, June 8, 1922; s. Sylvester Austin and Thelma (Bank) N.; m. Jane Adams, June 7, 1986; 1 child, John Francis Jr. AA, Harris Tchrs. Coll., 1941; BS, U. Mo., 1943; JD, Washington U., St. Louis, 1948. Bar: Mo. 1948. Pvt. practice law, Clayton, 1948-73; judge U.S. Dist. Ct., St. Louis, 1973—, chief judge, 1983-90, sr. judge, 1990—91, Ga., 1991—. Mem. 8th Cir. Jud. Coun.; mem. exec. com. Jud. Conf. U.S.; chmn. Jud. Panel on Multidist. Litigation, mem. working group on mass torts, mem. jud. resources working group. Mem. Mo. Rep. Com., 1958-73; mem. St. Louis County Rep. Cen. Com., 1958-73, chmn., 1960-61; pres. Mo. Assn. Reps., 1961, Reps. Vets. League, 1960; mem. Rep. Nat. Com., 1972-73; bd. dirs. Masonic Home Mo. With AUS, 1943-46. First Sgt. USAR, 1943—46. Named Mo. Republican of Year John Marshall Club, 1970, Mo. Republican of Year Mo. Assn. Reps., 1971; recipient Most Disting. Alumnus award Harris-Stowe Coll., Most Disting. Alumnus award Washington U. Sch. Law, 1986. Mem. ABA, Legion of Honor DeMolay, Mo. Bar Assn., St. Louis Bar Assn., St. Louis County Bar Assn.

NANTS, BRUCE ARLINGTON, lawyer; b. Orlando, Fla., Oct. 26, 1953; s. Jack Arlington and Louise (Hulme) N. BA, U. Fla., 1974, JD, 1977. Bar: Fla. 1977. Asst. state's atty. State Atty.'s Office, Orlando, 1977-78; pvt. practice, 1979—. Columnist The Law and You, 1979-80. Auctioneer pub. TV sta., 1979; campaign coord. cen. Fla. steering com. Bob Dole for Pres., 1988; bd. dirs. Cystic Fibrosis Found. Mem. Acad. Fla. Trial Lawyers, Am. Arbitration Assn., Fellowship Christian Athletes (past bd. dirs. Cen. Fla.), Tiger Bay Club Cen. Fla., Orlando Touchdown Club, Fla. Blue Key, Omicron Delta Kappa, Phi Beta Kappa, Phi Delta Theta. Democrat. Baptist. Avocations: tennis, golf, swimming, scuba diving. Home: 1112 Country Ln Orlando FL 32804-6934 Office: PO Box 547871 Orlando FL 32854-7871

NAPIERSKI, EUGENE EDWARD, lawyer; b. Albany, N.Y., Jan. 9, 1944; s. Eugene J. and Elizabeth (Doran) N.; children: Christine, Eugene, Michelle, Daniel. BA, Siena Coll., 1965; JD cum laude, Union U., 1968. Bar: N.Y. 1968, U.S. Dist. Ct. (fed. dist.) N.Y. 1968, U.S. Supreme Ct. 1975. Atty. Forsyth, Howe & O'Dwyer, Rochester, N.Y., 1968-69; staff atty. Rsch. Found. SUNY, Albany, 1969-70; assoc. Carter & Conboy, 1970-76; ptnr. Carter, Conboy, Case, Blackmore, Napierski & Maloney, 1976-2000, Napierski, VanDenburgh & Napierski, LLP, Alabny, 2000—. Mem. Am. Bd. Trial Advocates (past pres. upstate N.Y.), Am. Coll. Trial Lawyers, N.Y. State Bar Assn., Capitol Dist. Trial Lawyers Assn. (past pres.), Ft. Orange Club, Wolferts Roost Country Club. Avocations: reading, golf, travel. Personal injury, Product liability. Home: 11 Duth Hill Terr Voorheesville NY 12186 Office: Napierski VanDenburgh & Napierski LLP 296 Washington Ave Ext Albany NY 12203 E-mail: een@nvnlaw.com

NAPLETON, ROBERT JOSEPH, lawyer; b. Evergreen Park, Ill., Jan. 13, 1963; s. Francis Edward and Elizabeth (Raynor) N.; m. Clare Therese McEnery, June 6, 1992; children: Martin Joseph, Nora Elizabeth, Patricia Clare, Francis James. BBA, Loyola U., Chgo., 1985, JD, 1988. Bar: Ill. 1988, U.S. Dist. Ct. (no. dist.) Ill. 1989, U.S. Dist. Ct. (cen. dist.) Ill. 1995, U.S. Dist. Ct. (we. dist.) Wis. 1998, U.S. Supreme Ct. 1999. Law clk. to Chief Judge James E. Murphy Circuit Ct. of Cook County, Chgo., 1985-87; mem. staff State's Atty. Office of Cook County, Markham, Ill., 1987-88; assoc. Motherway & Glenn, Chgo., 1988-98; ptnr. Motherway, Glenn & Napleton, 1999—. Spkr., presenter in field. Treas. campaign Citizens to Elect James Brosnahan State Rep. for 36th Dist., Ill., 1996—. Fellow Roscoe Pound Found.; mem. ATLA (aviation law com.), Ill. Trial Lawyers Assn. (bd. advocates 1993-97, bd. mgrs. 1997—, med. negligence and product liability coms. 1994—, civil practice com. 1995—), Ill. State Bar Assn. (bd. govs. 1994-2000, tort law sect. coun. 1992-95), Southwest Bar Assn., Chgo. Bar Assn. (trial techniques com. 1991-92), Catholic Lawyers Guild, Brother Rice H.S. St. Thomas More Soc. Democrat. Roman Catholic. Avocations: golf, skiing, ice hockey, reading. Personal injury, Product liability, Professional liability. Home: 400 Sunset Ave La Grange IL 60525-6115 Office: Motherway Glenn & Napleton 100 W Monroe St Ste 200 Chicago IL 60603-1923

NAPOLITANO, JANET ANN, state attorney general; b. N.Y.C., Nov. 29, 1957; d. Leonard Michael and Jane Marie (Winer) N. BS summa cum laude, U. Santa Clara, Calif., 1979; JD, U. Va., 1983. Bar: Ariz. 1984, U.S. Dist. Ct. Ariz. 1984, Ct. Appeals (9th cir.) 1984, U.S. Ct. Appeals (10th cir.) 1988, U.S. Ct. Appeals (5th cir.), U.S. Ct. Appeals, U.S. Ct. Appeals (7th cir.), U.S. Ct. Appeals (8th Cir.). Law clk. to Hon. Mary Schroeder U.S Ct. Appeals (9th Cir.), 1983-84; assoc. Lewis & Roca, Phoenix, 1984-89, ptnr., 1989-93; U.S. atty. Dist. Ariz., 1993-97; atty. Lewis and Roca, 1997-98; atty. gen. State of Ariz., 1999—. Mem. Atty. Gen.'s Adv. Com., 1993—, chair, 1995-96; mem., chmn. victims rights subcom. Ariz. Criminal Justice Commn.; chmn. Ariz. High Intensity Drug Traficking Area; mem. Ariz. Peace Officer Stds. and Tng. Bd., Ariz. Pros. Attys.' Adv. Coun.; former mem. com. to study civil litigation abuse, cost and delay Ariz. Supreme Ct.; past pres. Ariz. Cmty. Legal Svcs. Corp.; former judge pro tem Ariz. Ct. Appeals. Contbr. articles to legal jours. 1st vice chmn. Ariz. Dem. Com., 1990-92; mem. Dem. Nat. Com., 1990-92; chmn. Ariz. del. Dem. Nat. Conv., 1992, co-chmn., 2000; chmn. Nucleus, 1989-91; mem. Ariz. Bd. Tech. Registration, 1989-92; Phoenix Design Standards Rev. Com., 1989-91; bd. dirs. Ariz. Cmty. Legal Svcs. Corp., 1987-92, Ariz. Fire Fighters and Emergency Paramedics Meml., Phoenix Children's Hosp., Actors' Lab Ariz., Inc., Ariz. Peace Officers Meml.; mem. Ariz. Women's Forum, Charter 100; bd. regents Santa Clara U., 1992—; hon. chmn. Camp Fire Boys and Girls, 1999. Recipient Leader of Distinction award Anti-Defamation League, Human Betterment award Roots and Wings, Golden Apple award West Valley NOW, award Nat. Network To End Domestic Violence, Woman of Distinction award Crohns and Colitis Disease Found., Women Making History award Nat. Mus. Women's History, Tribute to Women award YWCA; named Ariz. Dem. of Yr., 1989; scholar Truman Scholarship Found., 1977; Dillard fellow. Fellow Ariz. Bar Found.; mem. ABA, Am. Law Inst., Nat. Assn. Attys. Gen. (exec. com., tobacco bankruptcy working group, health care fraud group, co-chmn. civil rights com., stop underage smoking com., mem. exec. working group on prosecutorial rels.), Ariz. Bar Assn. (former mem. com. on minorities in law, past chmn. civil practice and procedure com.), Maricopa County Bar Assn. (past mem. long range planning com.), Am. Judicature Soc., Ariz. State Bar (chmn. civil practice and procedure com. 1991-92), Ariz. Women Lawyers Assn., Sandra Day O'Connor Inn of Ct. (barrister), Raven Soc., Phi Beta Kappa, Alpha Sigma Nu. Avocations: hiking, trekking, travel, reading, film. Office: 1275 W Washington St Phoenix AZ 85007-2926

NARAYAN, BEVERLY ELAINE, lawyer; b. Berkeley, Calif., June 19, 1961; d. Jagjiwan and Alexandra (Mataras) N.; m. James Dean Schmidt, Jan. 7, 1989; children: Sasha Karan, Kaiya Maria. Student, San Francisco State U., 1979-80; BA, U. Calif., Berkeley, 1983; JD, U. Calif., San Francisco, 1987. Bar: Calif. 1987, U.S. Dist. Ct. (no. dist.) Calif. 1987, U.S. Dist. Ct. (ctrl. dist.) Calif. 1988. Atty. Daniels Barratta & Fine, L.A., 1988-89, Kornblum Ferry & Frye, L.A., 1990-91, Clapp Moroney Bellagamba Davis & Vucinich, Menlo Park, Calif., 1991-93, pvt. practice, Burlingame, 1993—; mng. dir. KarmaTek, 1999—2000. Arbitrator Nat. Assn. Securities Dealers, San Francisco, 1987—, Pacific Exch., San Francisco, 1994—; mediator Peninsula Conflict Resolution Ctr., San Mateo, Calif., 1995—; appellate mediator First Dist. Ct. Appeals, 2000—; neutral San Mateo County Multi-Option ADR Project. Candidate Sch. Bd. San Mateo (Calif.) Unified Sch. Dist., 1993; mem. San Mateo County Task Force Violence Against Women. Recipient U. Calif. Hastings Coll. Law Achievement award, 1986; named Barrister of Yr., San Mateo County, 1996. Mem. ABA, San Mateo County Bar Assn. (co-chair women lawyers 1995, bd. dirs. 1994-96), South Asian Bar Assn., Nat. Women's Polit. Caucus (bd. dirs., diversity chair 1993-96), San Mateo County Barristers Club (bd. dirs. 1993-99, child watch chair 1995-99). Avocations: baking, cooking, reading, travel, motorcycles, family. Alternative dispute resolution, General civil litigation, Securities. Office: 1508 Howard Ave Burlingame CA 94010-5216

NARDI RIDDLE, CLARINE, association administrator, judge; b. Clinton, Ind., Apr. 23, 1949; d. Frank Jr. and Alice (Mattioda) Nardi; m. Mark Alan Riddle, Aug. 15, 1971; children: Carl Nardi, Julia Nardi. AB in Math with honors, Ind. U., 1971, JD, 1974; LHD (hon.), St. Joseph Coll., 1991. Bar: Ind. 1974, U.S. Dist. Ct. (so. dist.) Ind. 1974, Conn. 1979, Fed. Dist. Ct. Conn. 1980, U.S. Supreme Ct. 1980, U.S. Ct. Appeals (2d cir.) 1986, U.S. Ct. Appeals (D.C. cir.) 1994. Staff atty. Ind. Legis. Svc. Agy., Indpls., 1974-78, legal counsel, 1978-79; dep. corp. counsel City of New Haven, 1980-83; counsel to atty. gen. State of Conn., Hartford, 1983-86, dep. atty. gen., 1986-89, acting atty. gen., 1989, atty. gen., 1989-91, judge Superior Ct., 1991-93; sr. v.p., gen. counsel Nat. Multi-Housing Coun., Nat. Apartment Assn., 1995—. Asst. counsel state majority Conn. Gen. Assembly, Hartford, 1979, legal rsch. asst. to prof. Yale U., New Haven, 1979; legal counsel com. on law revision Indpls. State Bar Assn., 1979; mem. Chief Justice's Task Force on Gender Bias, Hartford, 1988-90; mem. ethics and values com. Ind. Sector, Washington, 1988-90; co-organizer Ind. Continuing Legal Edn. Forum Inst. Legal Drafting Legislature and Pvt. Practice; Internat. Women's Yr. panelist Credit Laws and Their Enforcement; mem. Atty. Gen.'s Blue Ribbon Commn., Chief Justice's Com. Study Pubs. Policy Conn. Law. Jour., Law Revision Commn. Adminstrv. Law Study, Chief Justice's Task Force Gender, Justice and Cts., Gov.'s Task Force Fed. Revenue Enhancements; mem. exec. com. Jud. Dept.; mem. panel arbitrators Am. Arbitration Assn., 1994; gen. counsel Nat. Multi Housing Coun.; lectr. in field. Author: (with F.R. Rembusch) Drafting Manual for the Indiana General Assembly, 1976; sr. editor Ind. U. Law Sch. Interdisciplinary Law Jour.; contbr. articles to profl. jours. Bd. visitors Ind. U., Bloomington, 1974-92; mem. Gov.'s Missing Children Com., Hartford, Conn. Child Support Guidelines Com., Gov.'s Task Force on Justice for Abused Children, Hartford, 1988-90; mem. Mayor's City of New Haven Task Force Reorganization Corp. Counsel's Office, Gov.'s Child Support Commn., Mayor of New Haven's Blue Ribbon Commn.; former bd. dirs. New Haven Neighborhood Music Sch.; bd. dirs., mem. youth adv. com. Gov.'s Partnership Prevent Substance Abuse Workforce-Drugs Don't Work. Recipient Women in Leadership Recognition award Hartford Region YWCA, 1986, Award of Merit, Women & Law Sect. Conn. Bar Assn., 1989, Fellowship award South End Ladies Dem. Club, 1989, Woman of Yr. award Greater Hartford Fedn. of Bus. & Profl. Women's Clubs, 1990, Conn. Original award Somers-Mabelle B. Avery Sch., 1990, Cert. of Recognition, Consortium Law-Related Edn., 1990, Citizen award Conn. Task Force Children's Constl. Rights, 1991, Ann. award Hartford Assn. Women Attys., 1993; named Conn. History Maker, U.S. Dept. Labor, Women's Bur. & Permanent Commn. Status Women, 1989, Impact Player, The Conn. Law Tribune, 1992; inductee Ind. U. Sch. Law Alumni Acad. Fellow, 1999. Mem. ABA, Conn. Bar Assn. (chair com. on gender bias, Citation of Merit women and law sect. 1989), Nat. Assn. Attys. Gen. (chair charitable trusts and solicitation 1988-90), New Haven Neighborhood Music Sch. (bd. dirs.), Am. Arbitration Assn. (arbitration panel 1994), Ind. Bar Assn., Conn. Bar Assn. (chair com. gender bias legal profession), Indpls. Bar Assn., Ind. Civil Liberties Union (bd. dirs., mem. exec. com., chair long range planning com., mem. women's rights project, membership v.p., Disting. Svc. award), Conn. Consortium Law and Citizenship Edn., Inc. (bd. dirs.), Conn. Judges Assn. (mem. legislation com.), Ind. U. Law Sch. Alumni Assn. (bd. dirs.), Enomene Hon. Soc., Pleiades Hon. Soc., Mortar Bd. (nat. fellow), Alpha Lambda Delta. Democrat. Presbyterian. Office: Nat Multi Housing Coun 1850 M St NW Ste 450 Washington DC 20036-5803

NARDONE, WILLIAM ANDREW, lawyer; b. Groton, Conn., June 16, 1954; s. Henry Joseph and Mary Frances (Herley) N.; m. Diane Ruth Hall, July 1, 1988; children: Madison Catherine, William Chase. BA, U. R.I., 1976; JD, Suffolk U., 1980. Bar: R.I. 1981, U.S. Dist. Ct. R.I. 1981, U.S. Supreme Ct. 1991. Assoc. Law Office of M.L. Lewiss, Westerly, R. I., 1980-83; ptnr. Orsinger & Nardone Law Offices, 1983—. Solicitor Westerly Sch. Dept., 1984-90, 94-96, 98—. Mem. com. Westerly YMCA, 1980, bd. dirs., 1991—, exec. com., 1994—; bd. dirs., pres. Westerly Adult Day Care Ctr., 1985-93; trustee Westerly Hosp., 1993—, sec., asst. treas., 1999—; trustee SNEPHO, 1994—. Mem. Nat. Coun. Sch. Attys., R.I. Bar Assn. (rep. Ho. of Dels. 1984-90), Nat. Assn. Legal Problems in Edn. Republican. Roman Catholic. Contracts commercial, Land use and zoning (including planning), Real property. Home: 38 Wicklow Rd Westerly RI 02891-3644 Office: Orsinger & Nardone 53 High St Westerly RI 02891-6001

NARKO, MEDARD MARTIN, lawyer; b. Chgo., Sept. 14, 1941; s. Casimer and Stephanie (Wasylik) N.; m. Mary Kathleen Hanrahan, June 8, 1963; children— Kevin, Sue. B.S., Loyola U., 1963; J.D., Northwestern U., 1966. Bar: Ill. 1966, U.S. Dist. Ct. (no. dist.) Ill. 1967, U.S. Ct. Appeals (7th cir.) 1970. Instr., John Marshall Law Sch., Chgo., 1970-71; prof. lawyers assistance program Roosevelt U., Chgo., 1975-81; ptnr. Narko & Sonenthal, Chgo., 1974-79, Medard Narko & Assocs., Oak Forest, Ill., 1979—; arbitrator Am. Arbitration Assn., Chgo.; hearing officer Ill. Pollution Control Bd., Evanston, Civil Service Commn., Evanston, Ill. Dept. Edn., State Univ. Civil Service System. City atty. City of Oak Forest, 1985—, prosecutor City of Oak Forest, 1976-85 ; atty. Oak Forest Park Dist., 1974—, Bridgeview Park Dist., Ill., 1976-80, Midlothian Park Dist., Ill., 1983—, Posen Pk. Dist., Ill., 1991—. Contbr. articles to profl. jours. Mem. Ill. Bar Assn., Chgo. Bar Assn., Ill. Trial Lawyers Assn., Assn. Trial Lawyers Am., Ill. Mcpl. League, Nat. Inst. Mcpl. Law Officers. Lodge: Rotary. General practice, Personal injury. Home: 5 Equestrian Way Lemont IL 60439-9786 Office: Medard M Narko and Assocs PC 15000 Cicero Ave Oak Forest IL 60452-1444

NARMONT, JOHN STEPHEN, lawyer; b. Auburn, Ill., June 24, 1942; s. Stephen and Luriel (Welle) N.; m. Sondra J. Nicholls, Feb. 12, 1978. BBA magna cum laude, U. Notre Dame, 1964; JD, U. Ill., Champaign, 1967. Bar: Ill. 1967, U.S. Dist. Ct. (so. dist.) Ill. 1967, U.S. Ct. Appeals (7th cir.) 1967, U.S. Supreme Ct. 1973, U.S. Tax Ct. 1978. Pvt. practice, Springfield, Ill. Founder, pres., owner Richland Ranch, Inc., Auburn; originator, pres. The Solid Gold Futurity, Ltd. Mem. Sangamon Valley Estate Planning Coun. Mem. ABA, Sangamon County Bar Assn., Ill. State Bar Assn., Assn. Trial Lawyer Am., Am. Agrl. Law Assn., Ill. Inst. for Continuing Legal Edn., Internat. Livestock Exposition (pres., founder). Bankruptcy, General civil litigation, Family and matrimonial. Office: 209 N Bruns Ln Springfield IL 62702-4612

NARODICK, KIT GORDON, lawyer, consultant; b. Nov. 29, 1937; s. Philip H. and Blanche G. (Gordon) N.; m. Sally Gould, APr., 1970; children: Lisa Ann, Philip H. BA, U. Wash., 1960; MBA, 1962; PhD, Columbia U., 1967; JD, U. Puget Sound, 1987. Prof. econs. NYU, 1967-73; dir. Boeing Comml. Airplane Co., Seattle, 1973-85; of counsel Bogle & Gates, 1988-98; ptnr. Lane, Powell, Spears, Lubersky LLP, 1998—. Vis. prof. Columbia U., N.Y.C., 1967-69. Bd. dirs. Seattle Repertory Theatre, 1978-85; chmn. Wash. State Com. on Tourism, Olympia, 1984; mem. Puget Sound Air Transp. Com., 1990-93; bd. trustees Mus. Flight. 1994—. Mem. ABA, Am. Mktg. Assn., Nat. Transp. Safety Bd. Bar Assn., Wash. State Bar Assn., King County Bar Assn., ISTAT, Lawyer-Pilots Bar Assn., Transp. Rsch. Forum, Transp. Rsch. Bd., European Soc. Market Rsch., Travel and tourism Rsch. Assn. (dir. 1979-83, pres., 1983-84), Pacific Area Travel Assn. (dir. 1980-84, chmn. 1984-85). Jewish. Clubs: Wash. Athletic, Rainier (Seattle) , Rainier Club, Columbia Tower, Bellevue Athletic. Aviation, Contracts commercial, General corporate. Home: 4513 54th Ave NE Seattle WA 98105-3834 Office: Lane Powell Spears Lubersky LLP 2 Union Square 1420 5th Ave Seattle WA 98101 E-mail: norodickk@lanepowell.com

NARSUTIS, JOHN KEITH, lawyer; b. Oak Park, Ill., Mar. 23, 1948; s. John and Ann Narsutis; m. Carol Lynn Voth, Aug. 26, 1972; 1 child, Ashley Lynn. B.A., Baylor U., 1970, J.D., 1972. Bar: Tex., U.S. Dist. Ct. (no. dist.) Tex., U.S. Dist. Ct. (ea. dist.) Tex. U.S. Ct. Appeals (5th cir.). Tchr. Waco Ind. Sch. Dist., Tex, 1972; asst. dist. atty. City of Denton, Tex., 1973-75, acting city atty., 1975; ptnr. firm Vick & Narsutis, Denton, 1976-82, Narsutis & Preston, Denton, 1983— ; dist. judge 158th Jud. Dist., Denton, 1982; judge 16th Jud. Dist. Ct., 1984— ; instr. Tex. Women's U., Denton, 1977; pres. Dentex Title Co., Denton, 1983— . Bd. dirs., exec. bd. Tex. Area 5 Health Systems Agy., 1977-78; bd. dirs. Lake Cities War on Drugs, Denton, 1978-80; mem. budget and admissions com. Denton United Way; vol. for legal services Denton Area Council on Alcoholism, Denton Community Band, also numerous chs.; vol., flag football coach Denton YMCA; chmn. legal div. Denton Handicap Awareness Week; mem. Denton County Juvenile Bd.; chmn. Denton County Com. for Pres. Ford, Denton County Rep. Com., Denton County Will Garwood Campaign; del. Denton County Rep. Conv. Mem. Denton Bar Assn. (sec.-treas.), Denton County Bar Assn., Christian Legal Soc., Tex. Bar Assn. Club: Denton Kiwanis (v.p. 1977, sec.-treas. 1978, pres. 1979-80). State civil litigation, General practice, Real property. Home: 3517 Granada Trl Denton TX 76205-8403 Office: PO Box 50271 1121 Dallas Dr Suite 3 Denton TX 76206

NASH, GORDON BERNARD, JR. lawyer; b. Evergreen, Ill., Feb. 24, 1944; s. Gordon Bernard and Lilyan (Grafft) N.; m. Roseanne Joan Burke, Aug. 24, 1968; children: Caroline, Brian, Terry, Maureen. BA, Notre Dame U., 1966; JD, Loyola U., Chgo., 1969. Bar: Ill., U.S. Dist. Ct. (no. dist.) Ill. Atty. Office U.S. Atty. No. Dist. Ill., Chgo., 1971-78; ptnr. Gardner, Carton & Douglas, 1978—. Chmn. Ill. Bd. Ethics, Springfield, 1980-85. Served to capt. U.S. Army, 1969-71. Recipient John Marshall award U.S. Dept. Justice, 1978, Spl. Commendation award, 1975, Disting. Achievement award Internat. Acad. Trial Lawyers, 1969. Mem. ABA, Ill. Bar Assn., Chgo. Bar Found. Local Chpt. (bd. dirs. 1983-85, 87-89), Fed. Bar Assn. (bd. govs. 1986-91), Chgo. Bar Assn. (bd. mgrs. 1983-85, pres. 1990-91), Constl. Rights Found. Com. (bd. dirs. 1993—, chmn., 1998-2001), Am. Coll. Trial Lawyers, Ctr. for Conflict Resolution (bd. 1992-2000, v.p. 1995-2000), Chgo. Inn of Ct. (pres. 1996-97), Olympia Fields Country Club. Democrat. Roman Catholic. Federal civil litigation, State civil litigation, Criminal. Home: 5101 Harvey Ave Western Springs IL 60558-2042 Office: Gardner Carton & Douglas Quaker Tower 321 N Clark St Ste 3400 Chicago IL 60610-4795 E-mail: gnash@gcd.com

NASH, PAUL LENOIR, lawyer; b. Poughkeepsie, N.Y., Jan. 29, 1931; s. George Matthew and Winifred (LeNoir) N.; m. Nancy Allyn Thouron, Dec. 30, 1961; children: Andrew Gray, Laurie LeNoir, Daphne Thouron. BA, Yale U., 1953; LLB, Harvard U., 1958. Bar: N.Y. 1959. Assoc. Dewey Ballantine, N.Y.C., 1958-66, ptnr., 1966—. Pres. bd. trustees Peck Sch., Morristown, N.J., 1978-82. Served to capt. USMC, 1953-55; Japan. Mem. Assn. of Bar of City of N.Y. Republican. General corporate, Mergers and acquisitions, Securities. Home: 4 Westminster Pl Morristown NJ 07960-5810 Office: Dewey Ballantine LLP 1301 Avenue Of The Americas New York NY 10019-6022 E-mail: pnash@deweyballantine.com, pnash65131@aol.com

NASKY, H(AROLD) GREGORY, lawyer; b. Titusville, Pa., June 9, 1942; s. Harold G. and Majella Marie (Beck) N.; m. Rosanne Guson, July 22, 1967. AB, St. Bonaventure U., 1964; JD, U. Notre Dame, 1967. Bar: Pa. 1967, Nev. 1972. Assoc. Eaton & Hill, Warren, Pa., 1967-68, Vargas, Bartlett & Dixon, Reno, 1972-73; ptnr. Vargas & Bartlett, Las Vegas, Nev., 1974-94, mng. ptnr., 1981-91; of counsel Kummer, Kaempfer, Bonner & Renshaw, 1994—; prin. Resort Devel. Cons., 1998—. Corp. sec. Showboat, Inc. (NYSE-SBO), Las Vegas, 1978-98, bd. dirs., 1983-98, exec. v.p., 1995-98; bd. dirs. U. Notre Dame Law Assn., 1990-2000; mem. adv. bd. U. Nev. Sch. Medicine.; chmn. 1990-93, bd. dirs. Author: Inter Alia Jour. of State Bar of Nevada, A Glimpse of China, 1986; Nev. contbg. author: Real Property, Probate & Trust Law Jour., Disposition of Rents, 1981. Legal advisor Nev. Dance Theatre, Las Vegas, 1977-94, bd. dirs. 1988-2000; legal com. Nev. Resort Assn., Las Vegas, gaming regulations com. 1990-93; bd. dirs. Boulder Dam coun. Boy Scouts Am., Las Vegas, 1986-96; del. People to People Citizen Ambassador Program, People's Republic China, 1985, New Zealand/Australia, 1987, Hungary, Czechoslovakia and Poland, 1990, Russia and Estonia, 1992. Served to capt. JAGC, U.S. Army, 1968-72, Vietnam. Decorated Bronze Star, 1970. Mem. ABA (bus. sect. task force conflicts interest com. 1993—), State Bar Nev. (chmn. fee dispute com. 1983-89, exec. com. mem. Gaming Law Sect. 1985-93), Am. Soc. Corp. Secs., Internat. Assn. Gaming Attys., Notre Dame Club Las Vegas (past pres. 1978-79), U. Nev. Las Vegas Found. (president's assocs. 1988-93, chmn.). Contracts commercial, General corporate, Securities. Office: Kummer Kaempfer Bonner & Renshaw 3800 Howard Hughes Pky Fl 7 Las Vegas NV 89109-0925 also: Resort Devel Cons PMB A14 9101 W Sahara Ave Ste 105 Las Vegas NV 89117

NASON, LEONARD YOSHIMOTO, lawyer, writer, publisher; b. N.Y.C., Feb. 17, 1954; s. Leonard Hastings and Mary Yukiko (Yoshimoto) N.; m. Linda Thayer, Sept. 26, 1981; children: Victoria, Kelsey, Jennifer. BA, Tufts U., 1975; JD, Northeastern U., Boston, 1979. Bar: Mass. 1979, U.S. Dist. Ct. 1979, U.S. Ct. Appeals (1st cir.) 1985. Assoc. Ricklefs & Uehlein, Natick, Mass., 1979-84; ptnr. Uehlein, Nason & Wall, 1985-95, Nason, Wall & Wall, P.C., Lexington, Mass., 1995—. Pres. Legal Info. Svcs., Inc., Lexington, 1986—; interviewer admissions Tuft U. Author: (handbook) Mass. Workers' Compensation, 1986, (statute book) Mass. Workers' Compensation, 1987; co-author: Massachusetts Practice Series, Vol. 29, 1989, 95; contbg. author: A Judicial Guide to Labor and Employment Law, 1990. Bd. dirs. Newton Community Service Ctr., 1981; coach soccer, basketball and softball, Little League. Mem. ABA, Mass. Bar Assn., Boston Bar Assn., Assn. Trial Lawyers Am. Avocations: tennis, sailing, softball, music. Personal injury, Workers' compensation. Office: Nason Wall & Wall PC 113 The Great Rd Bedford MA 01730 E-mail: Lyn@Legalinfosysinc.com, LNASON1750@aol.com

NASRI, WILLIAM ZAKI, legal educator, copyright consultant; b. Tanta, Gharbeya, Egypt, Apr. 19, 1925; came to U.S., 1964, naturalized, 1967; s. Zaki F. and Nadima (Hanna) N.; m. Eunice McConkey, June 14, 1960; children: Nadine Elizabeth, William Peter. BA, U. Alexandria, Egypt, 1953, LLB, 1957; PhD, U. Pitts., 1975. Pvt. practice law, Cairo, 1957-64; asst. prof. libr. and info. sci. and law U. Pitts., 1970-75, assoc. prof., 1976-95, prof. emeritus, 1996—, copyright cons., 1976—. Translator Dept. Justice, Pitts., 1973-74; copyright cons., Pitts., 1970—; speaker, lectr. nationwide, 1975—. Author: Crisis in Copyright, 1976, Legal Issues for Library and Information Managers, 1987; editor: (monograph series) Communication, Information, Technology and the Law, 1984, Legal Issues for Library and Information Managers, 1987; editor column Jour. Libr. Adminstrn., 1981-87; asst. editor Encyclopedia of Library and Information Science, 1968—. Pres. Brothers Brother Found., 1987-90; bd. dirs.

Collegiate YMCA, Pitts., 1978—; v.p. Greentree (Pa.) Pub. Libr., 1978—. Sr. Fulbright scholar to Morocco, 1988. Mem. Nat. Assn. Coll. and Univ. Attys., Assn. Libr. and Info. Sci. Edn., AAUP, Rotary (bd. dirs. Oakland 1980-89, pres. 1986-87), Masons. Republican. Home: 179 Parkedge Rd Pittsburgh PA 15220-2607 Office: U Pitts Sch of Info Sci 135 Bellefield Anx Pittsburgh PA 15260-6795

NASSAR, WILLIAM MICHAEL, lawyer; b. Methuen, Mass., June 5, 1958; s. William M. and Catherine M. Nassar; m. Ermelinda Amezcua, June 26, 1982; children: Brandon Michael, Elyse Renae. AAS, R.I. C.C., 1978; BSBA, U. Redlands, 1980; JD, Western State Coll. of Law, 1986. Legal adminstr. Bourns Inc., Riverside, Calif., 1988-90, dir. worldwide contracts adminstr., 1990-94, dir. worldwide contracts/legal counsel, 1994-97, sr. legal counsel, 1997-2000; v.p., gen. counsel Standard MEMS, Inc., Burlington, Mass., 1999—. Bd. dirs. Advanced Med. Inc., Riverside, Calif., Global Pathways Inc., Riverside; v.p. Bourns Employees Fed. Credit Union, bd. dirs. Adv. bd. Ronald McDonald House, Loma Linda, Calif., 1994-98. Roman Catholic. Avocations: sailing, boating, skiing, reading. Contracts commercial, General corporate, Intellectual property. Home: 13015 Burns Ln Redlands CA 92373-7415 Office: 673 S Waterman Ave San Bernardino CA 92408-2329

NAST, DIANNE MARTHA, lawyer; b. Mount Holly, N.J., Jan. 30, 1948; d. Henry Daniel and Anastasia (Lovenduski) N.; m. Joseph Francis Roda, Aug. 23, 1980; children: Michael, Daniel, Joseph, Joshua, Anastasia. BA, Pa. State U.; JD, Rutgers U., 1976. Bar: Pa. 1976, U.S. Dist. Ct. Pa. 1976, N.J. 1976, U.S. Dist. Ct. N.J. 1976, U.S. Ct. Appeals (3d, 5th, 6th, 7th, 8th and 11th cirs.) 1976, U.S. Supreme Ct. 1982, U.S. Dist. Ct. Ariz. 1985. Dir., v.p. Kohn, Nast & Graf, P.C., Phila., 1976-95, Roda & Nast, P.C., Lancaster, Pa., 1995—. Mem. lawyers adv. com. U.S. Ct. Appeals (3d cir.), 1982-84, chmn., 1983-84, mem. com. on revision jud. conf. conduct rules, 1982-84; mem. U.S. Ct. Appeals for the 3d Cir. Jud. Conf. Permanent Planning Com., 1983-90; bd. dirs. 3d Cir. Hist. Soc., 1993—; bd. dirs. Phila. Pub. Def., 1980-89; dir. U.S. Fed. Judicial Ctr. Found., 1991—, chair, 1996—; chmn. lawyers adv. com. U.S. Dist. Ct. (ea. dist.) Pa., 1982-90. Pres. Hist. Soc., 1988-91. Fellow ABA (coun. litigation sect. 1986-89, co-chmn. anti-trust com. litigation sect. 1984-86, div. dir. 1990-91, practical litigation editl. bd. 1989—, ho. of dels. 1992-94, mem. task force state justice initiatives, mem. task force state of justice system, 1993, mem. task force long range planning com. 1994), Am. Law Inst. (chair internat. professionalism com. 1991-94, civil justice task force 1993-95), Am. Arbitration Assn. (bd. dirs., mem. alt. dispute resolution and mass torts task force), Am. Judicature Soc., Pa. Bar Assn. (bd. of dels. 1983-95), N.J. Bar Assn., Pa. Trial Lawyers Assn., Phila. Bar Assn. (bd. govs. 1985-87, chmn., bicentennial com. 1986-87, chmn. bench bar conf. 1988-89), Lancaster Bar Assn. (co-chair civil litigation and rules com. trial law sect.), Rutgers Law Sch. Alumni Assn. Antitrust, Federal civil litigation, Product liability. Home: 1059 Sylvan Rd Lancaster PA 17601-1923 Office: Roda & Nast PC 801 Estelle Dr Lancaster PA 17601-2130

NATCHER, STEPHEN DARLINGTON, lawyer, business executive; b. San Francisco, Nov. 19, 1940; s. Stanlus Zoch and Robena Lenore Collie (Goldring) N.; m. Carolyn Anne Bowman, Aug. 23, 1969; children: Tanya Michelle, Stephanie Elizabeth. A.B. in Polit. Sci., Stanford U., 1962; J.D., U. Calif., San Francisco, 1965. Bar: Calif. 1966. Assoc. firm Pillsbury, Madison & Sutro, San Francisco, 1966-68; counsel Douglas Aircraft div. McDonnell Douglas Corp., Long Beach, Calif., 1968-70; v.p., sec. Security Pacific Nat. Bank, 1971-79; asst. gen. counsel Security Pacific Corp., 1979-80; v.p., sec., gen. counsel Lear Siegler, Inc., Santa Monica, Calif., 1980-87; v.p., gen. counsel Computer Sci. Corp., El Segundo, 1987-88; exec. v.p., gen. counsel, sec. CalFed Inc., 1989-90; sr. v.p. adminstrn., gen. counsel, sec. Wyle Electronics, Irvine, Calif., 1991-98; gen. counsel VEBA Electronics LLC, Santa Clara, 1998-2001. With USCG, 1965-71. Mem. St. Francis Yacht Club (San Francisco), The Pacific Club (Newport Beach). Republican. General corporate, General practice, Securities. E-mail: sdnatcher@earthlink.net

NATE, STEVEN SCOTT, prosecutor; b. Boise, Idaho, Feb. 7, 1969; s. Charles Reed and Jean Ann Nate. BA in Philosophy, BA in Polit. Sci., U. Idaho, 1992; JD, DePaul U., 1997. Bar: Ill. 1997. Asst. state's atty. Will County State's Atty., Joliet, Ill., 1998—. Mem. Ill. State Bar Assn. Home: 644 W Wrightwood # 114 Chicago IL 60614 Office: Will County State's Atty's Office 14 W Jefferson Joliet IL 60432

NATES, JEROME HARVEY, publisher, lawyer; b. N.Y.C., Sept. 19, 1945; s. Louis and Lillian (Berger) N.; m. Marilyn Arlene Weiss, June 6, 1971; children: Lori Jennifer, Scott Eric. BA, Hunter Coll., 1968; JD, Bklyn. Law Sch., 1972. Bar: N.Y. 1973. Assoc. atty. Natiss & Rogers, Long Island, N.Y., 1972-73; editorial dir. Matthew Bender & Co., N.Y.C., 1973-84; editor-in-chief Kluwer Law Book Pub., 1984-88; legal pub. cons., 1988-98; edtl. dir. Aspen Law & Bus., N.Y.C., 1998—. Co-author: Damages in Tort Actions, 1982; editor: Personal Injury Deskbook-1983, Personal Injury Deskbook-1984. Avocations: tennis, golf. Home: 19 Hummingbird Ct Marlboro NJ 07746-2510

NATHAN, ANDREW JONATHAN, lawyer, real estate developer; b. Honolulu, Mar. 20, 1957; s. Joel Joseph and Wendy Barbra (Bernstein) N.; m. Bonnie Lynn Raymond, Aug. 16, 1981 (div. Sept. 1987); m. Holly Lorraine Marshall, Feb. 17, 1990; children: Jake, Tyler. BA cum laude, Brandeis U., 1978; JD with distinction, Hofstra U., 1981. Assoc. Schulte Roth & Zabel, N.Y.C., 1981-87; counsel Tishman Speyer Properties, 1987, gen. counsel, 1990, gen. counsel, mng. dir., 1993-97, sr. mng. dir., co-head domestic acquisitions and devel., 1997-99, chief legal officer, 1999—. Articles editor Hofstra Law Rev., 1981. Mem. ABA, N.Y. State Bar Assn. General corporate, Private international, Real property. Office: Tishman Speyer Properties 520 Madison Ave New York NY 10022-4213

NATIONS, HOWARD LYNN, lawyer; b. Dalton, Ga., Jan. 9, 1938; s. Howard Lynn and Eva Earline (Armstrong) Lamb; m. Ella Lois Johnson, June 4, 1960 (div. Nov. 1976); children: Cynthia Lynn Nations Garcia, Angela Jean Gordon. BA, Florida State U., 1963; JD, Fla. State U., 1966. Bar: Tex. 1966; cert. trial atty. Tex. Bd. Legal Specialization. Assoc. Butler, Rice Cook & Knapp, Houston, 1966-71; pres. Nations & Cross, 1971—; v.p., dir., co-founder Ins. Corp. Am., 1972—; pres. Caplinger & Nations Galleries, 1973—, Nations Investment Corp., Houston, 1975—, NCM Trade Corp., Houston, 1975; v.p. Delher Am. Inc., 1975—; pres. Howard L. Nations, PC, 1971—, Trial Focus, Inc., 1995—. Founder Nations Found.; adj. prof. So. Tex. Coll. Law, Houston, 1967—; speaker in field. Author: Structuring Settlements, 1987; co-author: Texas Workers' Compensation, 1988, (with others) The Anatomy of a Personal Injury Lawsuit, 3rd rev. edit. 1991; editor: Maximizing Damages in Wrongful Death and Personal Injury Litigation, 1985; contbr. articles to profl. jours. Chmn., trustee Nat. Coll. Advocacy, Washington, 1985-92. With M.I. Corps, U.S. Army, 1957-60. Recipient Gene Cavin Excellence award State Bar Tex., 2000. Fellow Tex. Bar Found., Houston Bar Found. (life); mem. ATLA (exec. com. 1991-95), Nat. Bd. Trial Advocacy (diplomate civil trial advocacy), So. Trial Lawyers Assn. (pres. 1994-95), Tex. Trial Lawyers Assn. (pres. 1992-93). General civil litigation, Personal injury, Product liability. Office: The Sterling Mansion 4515 Yoakum Blvd Houston TX 77006-5821

NAUMAN, JOSEPH GEORGE, lawyer; b. Cleve., Jan. 1, 1928; s. George N. and Margaret M. (O'Dea) N.; m. Mary O'Donnell, July 28, 1951; children— George, Michael, Mary L., Nancy, Carolyn, Timothy, Patricia, William (dec.), Christine. B.S. in M.E., Notre Dame U., 1949; J.D, Georgetown U., 1953. Bar: Ohio 1953, U.S. Dist. Ct. (so. dist.) Ohio 1954. Patent examiner U.S. Patent Office, Washington, 1951-53; ptnr. Biebel, French & Nauman and predecessors, Dayton, Ohio, 1953— ; adj. prof. U. Dayton, Law Sch., 1972-82. Bd. dirs., pres. Dayton Opera Assn., 1973-77. Mem. ABA, Ohio Bar Assn., Ohio Bar Found., Am. Intellectual Property Assn., Engrs. Club Dayton (pres. 1979). Republican. Roman Catholic. Club: Dayton Racquet. Computer, Patent, Trademark and copyright. Home: PO Box 292470 Dayton OH 45429-0470 Office: Biebel French & Nauman 2500 Kettering Tower Dayton OH 45423-1004

NAVARRO, BRUCE CHARLES, lawyer; b. West Lafayette, Ind., Oct. 30, 1954; s. Joseph Anthony and Dorothy Gloria (Gnazzo) N.; children: Philip Joseph, Joanna Christina. BA, Duke U., 1976; JD, Ind. U., 1980. Bar: D.C. 1980. Asst. counsel U.S. Senate Labor Subcom., Washington, 1981-84; acting dep. undersec. for legis. affairs Dept. Labor, 1984-85; atty. advisor EEOC, 1985-86; dir. Office of Congl. Rels. Office of Pers. Mgmt., 1986-89; prin. dep. asst. atty. gen. for legis. U.S. Dept. of Justice, 1989-91; spl. asst. to gen. counsel U.S. Dept. HHS, 1991; expert cons. U.S. Dept. Def., 1992; counsel to the vice chmn. U.S. Consumer Product Safety Commn., Bethesda, Md., 1992-95; prin. Navarro Regulatory and Legis. Affairs, Washington, 1995—. Mem. Arlington County Republican Com. (Va.), 1983; bd. dirs. Prince William Cmty. Safe Kids Coalition, 1997-99. Mem. D.C. Bar Assn. Roman Catholic. Avocation: music, golf. Administrative and regulatory, Health, Legislative. Home: 6305 Lone Oak Dr Bethesda MD 20817-1745 Office: 1742 N St NW Washington DC 20036-2907

NAVATTA, ANNA PAULA, lawyer; b. Hackensack, N.J., Jan. 7, 1956; d. Jack Anthony and Natalie (Pretto) N. BA, Rutgers U., 1978, MA, 1979; JD, Seton Hall U., 1982. Bar: N.J. 1983, U.S. Dist. Ct. N.J. 1983, U.S. Ct. Appeals (3d cir.) 1986. Law clk. to presiding justice Superior Ct. N.J., Hackensack, 1982-83; staff atty. Bergen County Legal Svcs., 1983—. Instr. Am. Inst. Paralegal Studies, Mahwah, N.J., 1986-95; atty. Lyndhurst (N.J.) Planning Bd., 1987-89. Mem. ABA, Fed. Bar Assn., N.J. State Bar Assn., Bergen County Bar Assn., Emblem Club. Democrat. Roman Catholic. Administrative and regulatory, Land use and zoning (including planning), Landlord-tenant. Office: Bergen County Legal Svcs 61 Kansas St Hackensack NJ 07601-5351

NAVE, MICHELE GARRICK, lawyer; b. Lincoln, Nebr., Jan. 10, 1948; d. H. Michael and Elizabeth J. (Revale) Garrick; m. Robert L. Ragley, Dec. 24, 1967 (div.), m. Henry J. Nave, Oct. 9, 1999. BE, Lake Erie Coll., 1970; JD cum laude, Cleveland Marshall Coll., 1982. Bar: Ohio 1982, U.S. Dist. Ct. (no. dist.) Ohio 1983. Law clk. to presiding justice Ohio Appellate Ct. (8th cir.), Cleve., 1982-84; atty. Sherwin-Williams Co., 1984-87; asst. gen. counsel White Consol. Industries, Inc., 1987-95; sole practitioner, 1995—; of counsel Webster & Webster LLP. Chmn. bd. dirs. Light of Hearts Villa. Mem. ABA, Ohio Bar Assn., Cleve. Bar Assn. (trustee), Am. Arbitration Assn. (arbitrator, mediator). Avocations: reading, cross country and downhill skiing, hiking, biking. Contracts commercial, Computer, Mergers and acquisitions. Office: 3374 Rumson Rd Cleveland OH 44118-1355 E-mail: mgarricknave@att.net

NAYLOR, PAUL DONALD, lawyer; b. St. Bernard, Ohio, May 28, 1925; s. David Frederick and Erna Helen (Miller) N.; m. Geraldine L. Lacy, Jan. 20, 1945; children: Linda S., Paul Scott, Todd L. JD, U. Cin., 1948. Bar: Ohio 1948. Ptnr. Pulse & Naylor, Cin., 1949-65; pvt. practice, 1965—. Mem. Nat. Rep. Com. Lt. (j.g.) USN, 1943-46. Recipient Svc. to Mankind award Sertoma Internat. Mem. Cin. Bar Assn. (real property com. 1966-86), Ohio Bar Assn., Cin. Lawyers Club (pres. 1955), Order of the Coif. Real property. Office: 30 E Central Pky Ste 210 Cincinnati OH 45202-1118

NAZARYK, PAUL ALAN, lawyer, environmental consultant; b. Denver; s. Milton Paul and Margaret Ann Nazaryk; m. Jennifer Phillips, June 16, 1990; children: Krista Brooke, Carly Rebekah. BA, U. No. Colo., 1976; MA, Colo. State U., 1979; JD, U. Denver, 1986. Bar: Colo. 1987, Mont. 2000. Legis. intern Rep. James P. Johnson Ho. Reps., Washington, 1976; policy analyst U.S. Water Resources Coun., 1979, water policy specialist, 1979-81; environ. policy specialist, atty. Colo. Dept. Pub. Health and Environment, Denver, 1981-90; regulatory specialist ERM-Rocky Mountain Inc., Englewood, Colo., 1990-96; regulatory specialist, in-house atty. Harding Lawson Assocs., Denver, 1996-2000; regulatory specialist ERM-Rocky Mountain Inc., Greenwood Village, Colo., 2000—. Adj. faculty, U. Denver. Contbr. articles to profl. jours. Mem. Mont. Bar Assn. (natural resources and environ. law sect. 2000—), Colo. Bar Assn. (environ. law sect. 1987—), Denver C. of C. (environ. com. 1997-98). Democrat. Episcopalian. Avocations: western history, camping, cycling, skiing. Administrative and regulatory, Environmental, Natural resources. Office: ERM-Rocky Mountain cs 5950 S Willow Dr Cherry Hills Village CO 80111 E-mail: pnazaryk@ermrm.com

NEAGLE, CHRISTOPHER SCOTT, lawyer; b. Braintree, Mass., Mar. 21, 1952; s. Philip A. Neagle and Karin I. (Hauge) McConnell; m. Ruth Wyman Neagle, Oct. 11, 1981; children: Scott Wyman, Jeffrey Spiller. BA, Wesleyan U., Middletown, Conn., 1974; JD, Cornell U., 1977. Bar: Maine 1977, Mass. 1977, U.S. Dist. Ct. Maine 1977. Assoc. Verrill & Dana LLP, Portland, Maine, 1977-81, ptnr., 1982—. Instr. real estate law U. So. Maine, Portland, 1979-87; mem. Maine Legis. Trespass Commn., 1995. Mem. Maine Bar Assn. (chmn. real estate title standards com. 1984-94, chmn. real estate sect. 1995-96), Mass. Bar Assn. Congregationalist. Avocations: golf, hiking, soccer. Banking, Land use and zoning (including planning), Real property. Home: 568 Pleasant Valley Rd Cumberland Center ME 04021-9790 Office: Verrill & Dana PO Box 586 One Portland Sq Portland ME 04112 E-mail: cneagle@verrilldana.com

NEAL, CHARLES D., JR. lawyer; b. McAlester, Okla., Jan. 4, 1949; BSBA, Okla. State U., 1972; JD Okla. City U., 1975. Bar: Okla. 1975, U.S. Dist. Ct. Okla. (ea., we., no. dists.), U.S. Dist. Ct. Ark. (ea. and we. dists.), U.S. Ct. Appeals (10th, 8th and 5th cirs.), U.S. Supreme Ct. Ptnr. Steidley & Neal, McAlester, 1976—; mcpl. judge Kiowa, 1981—88, Krebs, 1981—. Fellow: Am. Bar Found., Okla. Bar Found. (trustee 1998—2001); mem.: ABA (ho. dels. 2000—01), Okla. Bar Assn. (pres. 2001—), Pittsburg county Bar Assn. (pres. 1980—81), Def. Rsch. Inst., Okla. Assn. Def. Counsel. Insurance. Office: Steidley & Neal 100 E Carl Albert Pkwy PO Box 1165 Mcalester OK 74502*

NEALON, WILLIAM JOSEPH, JR. federal judge; b. Scranton, Pa., July 31, 1923; s. William Joseph and Ann Cannon (McNally) N.; m. Jean Sullivan, Nov. 15, 1947; children: Ann, Robert, William, John, Jean, Patricia, Kathleen, Terrence, Thomas, Timothy. Student, U. Miami, Fla., 1942-43; B.S. in Econs, Villanova U., 1947; LL.B., Cath. U. Am., 1950; LL.D. (hon.), U. Scranton, 1975. Bar: Pa. 1951. With firm Kennedy, O'Brien & O'Brien (and predecessor), Scranton, 1951-60; mem. Lackawanna County Ct. Common Pleas, 1960-62; U.S. dist. judge Middle Dist. Pa., 1962—, chief judge, 1976-88, sr. judge, 1989—. Mem. com. on adminstrn. of criminal law Jud. Conf. U.S., 1979— ; lectr. bus. law and labor law U. Scranton, 1951-59; mem. jud. council 3d Cir. Ct. Appeals, 1984—; dist. judge rep. from 3d Cir. Jud. Conf. of U.S., 1987—. Mem. Scranton Registration Commn., 1953-55; hearing examiner Pa. Liquor Control Bd., 1955-59; campaign dir. Lackawanna County chpt. Nat. Found., 1961-63; mem. Scranton-Lackawanna Health and Welfare Authority, 1963—; assoc. bd. Marywood Coll., Scranton; pres. bd. dirs. Cath. Youth Center; pres. Father's Club Scranton Prep. Sch., 1966; chmn. bd. dirs. Mercy Hosp., 1991-95; chmn. bd. trustees U. Scranton; vice chmn. bd. trustees Lackawanna Jr. Coll., Scranton; bd. dirs. St. Joseph's Children's and Maternity Hosp., 1963-66, Lackawanna County unit Am. Cancer Soc., Lackawanna County Heart Assn., Lackawanna County chpt. Pa. Assn. Retarded Children, Scranton chpt. ARC, Lackawanna United Fund, Mercy Hosp., Scranton, 1975— ; trustee St. Michael's Sch. Boys, Hoban Heights; adv. com. Hosp. Service Assn. Northeastern Pa. Served to 1st lt. USMCR, 1942-45. Recipient Americanism award Amos Lodge B'nai B'rith, 1975; Cyrano award U. Scranton Grad. Sch., 1977; Disting. Service award Pa. Trial Lawyers Assn., 1979; named one of 50 Disting. Pennsylvanians Greater Phila. C. of C., 1980, Outstanding Fed. Trial Judge Assn. Trial Lawyers Am., 1983 Mem. Pa. Bar Assn., Lackawanna County Bar Assn. (Chief Justice Michael J. Eagen award 1987), Friendly Sons St. Patrick (pres. Lackawanna County 1963-64), Pi Sigma Alpha. Club: Scranton Country (Clarks Summit, Pa.) (bd. dirs.). Lodge: K.C. Office: US Courthouse PO Box 1146 Scranton PA 18501-1146

NEARING, VIVIENNE W. lawyer; b. N.Y.C. d. Abraham M. and Edith Eunice (Webster) N. BA, Queens Coll.; MA, JD, Columbia U. Bar: N.Y., D.C., U.S. Dist. Ct. (so. and ea. dists.) N.Y., U.S. Ct. Appeals (2d cir.), U.S. Claims Ct. Ptnr. Stroock & Stroock & Lavan, N.Y.C. Mem. editorial bd. Communications and the Law, 1978-82, adv. bd. 1982—; mem. editorial bd. U.S. Trademark Reporter, 1982-86, 91—. Bd. dirs. Light Opera of Manhattan, 1981-82, Lyric Opera N.Y., 1984-90, Concert Artists Guild, 1989-91. Mem. ABA, Fed. Bar Coun., N.Y. State Bar Assn., U.S. Trademark Assn., Copyright Soc. U.S.A., N.Y. Lawyers for Pub. Interest (bd. dirs. 1983-87), Am. Arbitration Assn., Commn. for Law and Social Justice, Carnegie Coun., Women's City Club. Federal civil litigation, Entertainment, Trademark and copyright. Office: Stroock Stroock & Lavan 7 Hanover Sq New York NY 10004-2616

NEBEKER, FRANK QUILL, federal judge; b. Salt Lake City, Apr. 23, 1930; s. J. Quill and Minnie (Holmgren) N.; m. Louana M. Visintainer, July 11, 1953; children: Caramaria, Melia, William Mark. Student, Weber Coll., 1948-50; B.S. in Polit. Sci, U. Utah, 1953; J.D., Am. U., 1955. Bar: D.C. 1956. Corr. sec. The White House, 1953-56; trial atty. Internal Security div. Justice Dept., Washington, 1956-58; asst. U.S. atty., 1958-69; assoc. judge D.C. Ct. Appeals, 1969-87, sr. judge, 2000—; dir. Office Govt. Ethics, 1987-89; chief judge U.S. Ct. of Vets. Appeals, 1989-2000. Cons. Nat. Commn. on Reform of Fed. Criminal Laws, 1967-68; adj. prof. Am. U. Washington Coll. Law, 1967-85. Mem. Am., D.C. Bar Assn., Am. Law Inst. Office: US Court Appeals 500 Indiana Ave Washington DC 20004

NEBLETT, STEWART LAWRENCE, lawyer; b. Houston, Dec. 8, 1948; s. Sterling A. and Esther G. (McLeroy) N.; m. Peggy L. Jacobson, Mar. 3, 1990. Student Southwestern U., 1967-68; B.B.A., U. Tex., 1970; J.D., South Tex. Coll. Law, 1975. Bar: Tex. 1976, U.S. Dist. Ct. (so. dist.) Tex. 1979, U.S. Ct. Appeals (5th cir.) 1979, U.S. Ct. Appeals (11th cir.) 1979, U.S. Supreme Ct. 1980. Sole practice, Houston, 1976-77; gen. counsel Fed. Intermediate Credit Bank, Austin, Tex., 1977-85; v.p., dep. gen. counsel Farm Credit Banks of Tex., Austin, 1985-92; with Strasburger & Price, L.L.P., 1992—. Mem. Coll. of State Bar Tex., State Bar Tex. (agrl. law com. 1984—). Republican. Presbyterian. General civil litigation, Contracts commercial. Home: 600 Crystal Creek Dr Austin TX 78746-4728 Office: 1700 One America Ctr 600 Congress Ave Austin TX 78701-3238

NECCO, ALEXANDER DAVID, lawyer, educator; b. Gary, Ind., Jan. 31, 1936; s. Alesandro Necco and Mary Millonovich; m. Caroline Chappel, Apr. 20, 1958 (dec. Mar. 1978); 1 child, Laurie Ann Necco Stansbury; m. Edna Joanne Painter, July 1, 1989. BA in Philosophy, U. Nev., 1958; JD, Oklahoma City U., 1965. Bar: Okla. 1965, U.S. Dist. Ct. (we. dist.) Okla. 1965, U.S. Ct. Appeals (10th cir.) 1987), U.S. Ct. Claims 1989, U.S. Ct. Vets. Appeals 1994. Assoc. Robert Jordan, Oklahoma City, 1965-66, Stuckey & Witcher, Oklahoma City, 1968-69; atty. Okla. Hwy. Dept., 1966, Oklahoma City Urban Renewal, 1966-67; ptnr. Stuckey & Necco, Oklahoma City, 1969-71, Necco & Dyer, Oklahoma City, 1978-82, Dyer, Necco & Byrd, Oklahoma City, 1982-88; pvt. practice, 1965—; ptnr. Necco & Byrd, 1988—. Adj. prof. Oklahoma City U. Sch. Bus., 1965—, Webster U., 1995—. Clubmaster Boy Scouts Am., Oklahoma City. With USMC, 1953-82, lt. col. Res. ret. Named Pro-bono Atty. of Month Okla. County. Mem. Assn. Trial Lawyers Assn., Okla. Trial Lawyers Assn., Marine Corps Res. Officers Assn. (pres. Oklahoma City 1984-85), Phi Delta Phi, Sigma Nu. Republican. Roman Catholic. Avocations: golf, swimming, tennis. General civil litigation, Family and matrimonial, Probate. Office: Necco & Byrd PC 5700 N Portland Ave Ste 121 Oklahoma City OK 73112-1662 E-mail: ADNecco@aol.com

NECHEMIAS, STEPHEN MURRAY, lawyer; b. St. Louis, July 27, 1944; s. Herbert Bernard and Toby Helen (Wax) N.; m. Marcia Rosenstein, June 19, 1966 (div. Dec. 1981); children: Daniel Jay, Scott Michael; m. Linda Adams, Aug. 20, 1983. BS, Ohio State U., 1966; JD, U. Cin., 1969. Bar: Ohio 1969. Ptnr. Taft, Stettinius & Hollister, Cin., 1969—. Adj. prof. law No. Ky. U., Chase Coll. Law. Tax comment author: Couse's Ohio Form Book, 6th edit., 1984. Mem. Ohio State Bar Assn. (chmn. taxation com.), Cin. Bar Assn. (chmn. taxation sect. 1985), Legal Aid Soc. Cin. (pres., trustee). Democrat. Jewish. Corporate taxation, Personal income taxation, State and local taxation. Home: 3122 Walworth Ave Cincinnati OH 45226-1047 Office: 1800 Star Bank Ctr 425 Walnut St Cincinnati OH 45202-3923

NECKERS, BRUCE WARREN, lawyer; b. Jamestown, N.Y., May 13, 1943; s. Carlyle and Doris (Van Lente) N.; m. Susan E. Sonnevelt, June 17, 1967; children: Matthew, Melissa, Allison. BA, Hope Coll., Holland, Mich., 1965; JD, Ohio State U., 1968. Bar: Mich. 1968, Ohio 1968, U.S. Dist. Ct. (we. dist.) Mich. 1968. Assoc., ptnr. Mohey, Goodrich & Titta, Grand Rapids, Mich., 1968-87; ptnr. Rhoades McKee Boer Goodrich & Titta, 1987—, chmn. exec. com., 1994—. Chmn. gen. program coun., mem. gen. synod exec. com., mem., officer Exec. Found., Ref. Ch. in Am. Fellow Mich. Bar Found.; mem. Fed. Bar Assn. (pres. Western Mich. chpt. 1980-81), State Bar Mich. (commr. 1995—, co-chair 21st century ct. reform com., pres. 2001-), Grand Rapids Bar Assn. (pres. 1991-92). Avocations: all sports, golf, skiing. General civil litigation, Personal injury, Product liability. Office: Rhoades McKee Boer Et Al 161 Ottawa Ave NW Ste 600 Grand Rapids MI 49503-2766*

NEELY, RICHARD, lawyer; b. Aug. 2, 1941; s. John Champ and Elinore (Forlani) N.; m. Carolyn Elaine Elmore, 1979; children: John Champ, Charles Whittaker. AB, Dartmouth Coll., 1964; LLB, Yale U., 1967. Bar: W.Va. 1967. Practiced in, Fairmont, W.Va., 1969-73; chmn. Marion County Bd. Pub. Health, 1971-72; mem. W.Va. Ho. of Dels., 1971-73; justice, chief justice W.Va. Supreme Ct. of Appeals, Charleston, 1973-95; ptnr. Neely & Hunter, 1995—. Chmn. bd. Kane & Keyser Co., Belington, W.Va., 1970-88. Author: How Courts Govern America, 1980, Why Courts Don't Work, 1983, The Divorce Decision, 1984, Judicial Jeopardy: When Business Collides with the Courts, 1986, The Product Liability Mess: How Business Can Be Rescued from State Court Politics, 1988, Take Back Your Neighborhood: A Case for Modern-Day Vigilantism, 1990, Tragedies of our Own Making: How Private Choices have Created Public Bankruptcy, 1994; contbr. articles to nat. mags. Mem. bd. advisors BNA Class Action Litigation Report. Capt. U.S. Army, 1967-69. Decorated Bronze Star,

Vietnam Honor medal 1st Class. Fellow: Internat. Acad. of Trial Lawyers; mem.: Am. Econ. Assn., W.Va. Bar Assn., Fourth Cir. Jud. Conf. (life)), Internat. Brotherhood Elec. Workers, VFW, Am. Legion, Moose, Phi Delta Phi, Phi Sigma Kappa. Episcopalian. Federal civil litigation, General civil litigation, State civil litigation. Office: Neely & Hunter 159 Summers St Charleston WV 25301-2134

NEELY, SALLY SCHULTZ, lawyer; b. L.A., Mar. 2, 1948; BA, Stanford U., 1970, JD, 1971. Bar: Ariz. 1972, Calif. 1977. Law clk. to judge U.S. Ct. appeals (9th cir.), Phoenix, 1971-72; assoc. Lewis and Roca, 1972-75; asst. prof. Law Sch. Harvard U., Cambridge, Mass., 1975-77; assoc. Shutan & Trost, P.C., L.A., 1977-79; ptnr. Sidley & Austin, 1980—. Mem. faculty Am. Law Inst.-ABA Chpt. 11 Bus. Reorgns., 1989-95, 97—, Banking and Comml. Lending Law, 1997-99, Nat. Conf. Bankruptcy Judges, 1988, 90, 95, 96, 97, 99, Fed. Jud. Ctr., 1989, 90, 94-95, Southeast Bankruptcy Law Inst., 2002, Workshop Bankruptcy and Bus. Reorganization NYU, 1992—; rep. 9th cir. jud. conf., 1989-91; mem. Nat. Bankruptcy Conf., 1993—. Chair Stanford U. Law Sch. Reunion Giving, 1996; bd. vis. Stanford U. Law Sch., 1990-92; atty. mem. editl. bd. Am. Bankruptcy Law Jour. Mem. ABA, Am. Coll. Bankruptcy, Calif. Bar Assn. Bankruptcy. Office: Sidley & Austin 555 W 5th St Ste 4000 Los Angeles CA 90013-3000 E-mail: sneely@sidley.com

NEFF, A. GUY, lawyer; b. Calcutta, India, Mar. 24, 1951; BA, Vanderbilt U., 1972; JD, U. Fla., 1975. Bar: Fla. 1975. Lawyer Holland & Knight, LLP, Orlando, Fla. Mem. ABA, Fla. Bar Assn., Phi Delta Phi (magister 1975). Immigration, naturalization, and customs, Private international, Real property. Office: Holland & Knight LLP 200 S Orange Ave Ste 2600 Orlando FL 32801-3453

NEFF, FRED LEONARD, lawyer; b. St. Paul, Nov. 1, 1948; s. Elliott Ira and Mollie (Poboisk) N.; m. Christa Ruth Powell, Sept. 10, 1989; 1 child, Lena. BS with high distinction, U. Minn., 1970; JD, William Mitchell Coll. Law, 1976. Bar: Minn. 1976, N.D. 1994, U.S. Dist. Ct. Minn. 1977, U.S. Ct. Appeals (8th cir.) 1985, U.S. Supreme Ct. 1985, Wis. 1986, U.S. Dist. Ct. (ea. and we. dists.) Wis. 1992. Tchr. Hopkins (Minn.) Pub. Schs., 1970-72; instr. U. Minn., Mpls., 1974-76; pvt. practice, 1976-79; asst. county atty. Sibley County, Gaylord, Minn., 1979-80; mng. atty. Hyatt Legal Svcs., St. Paul, 1981-83, regional ptnr., 1983-85, profl. devel. ptnr., 1985-86; pres. Neff Law Firm, PA, Mpls., 1986—; CEO Profl. Devel. Inst. Inc., Edina, Minn., 1994—, also bd. dirs. Instr. Inver Hills Coll., 1973-77; counsel Am. Tool Supply Co., St. Paul, 1976-78; cons. Nat. Detective Agy., Inc., St. Paul, 1980-83; CEO A Basic Legal Svc., Bloomington, 1990—; CEO, bd. dirs. Profl. Devel. Inst., Inc., Edina, Minn., 1994—; lectr., guest instr. U. Wis., River Falls, 1976-77; spl. instr. Hamline U., St. Paul, 1977; vis. lectr. Coll. St. Scholastica, Duluth, Minn., 1977; program. faculty, cons. Employment Law Seminar for Colo., Fla., La., Oreg., Employment and Labor Law Seminar for Ala., Alaska, Calif., Conn., Ind., N.C., Ohio, Va., N.C. Safety and Health at the Workplace, S.C. Labor Law, Ohio Safety at the Workplace; bd. dirs. Acceptance Ins. Holdings, Inc., Omaha; active Internat. Confederation Jurists, 1993; mem. faculty sem. Ariz. Safety at Workplace, Hawaii Employment & Labor, Miss. Employment & Labor Law, Del. Employment & Labor, Alaska Employment and Labor Law, Ga. Employment & Labor Law, N.J. Employment & Labor, Wash. Employment Law, Mass. Employment & Labor Law, 1995—, Ark. Employment and Labor Law, Mo. Employment and Labor Law, Iowa Employment and Labor Law, Utah Employment and Labor Law; pres. Martial Arts Bookstore Internat., Inc., 1998; pres. Endless Fist Soc., Inc., 1998. Author: Fred Neff's Self-Defense Library, 1976, Everybody's Self-Defense Book, 1978, Karate Is for Me, 1980, Running Is for Me, 1980, Lessons from the Samurai, 1986, Lessons from the Art of Kempo, 1986, Lessons from the Western Warriors, 1986, Lessons from the Fighting Commandos, 1990, Lessons from the Ancient Japanese Masters of Self-Defense, 1990, Lessons from the Eastern Warrors, 1990, Mysterious Persons of the Past, 1991, Great Mysteries of Crime, 1991; host TV series Great Puzzles In History; co-host TV series Great Unsolved Crimes, Minn.; asst. editor: Hennepic County Lawyer, 1992—. Advisor to bd. Sibley County Commrs., 1979-80; speaker civic groups, 1976-82; mem. Hennepin County Juvenile Justice Panel, 1980-82, Hennepin County (Minn.) Pub. Def. Conflict Panel, 1980-82, 86—, Hennepin County Bar Assn. Advice Panel Law Day, 1987, mem. dist. ethics com., 1990—; mem. Panel Union Privilege Legal Svcs. div. AFL-CIO, 1986—, Montgomery Wards Legal Svcs. Panel, 1986—, Edina Hist. Soc., Decathlon Athletic Club; charter mem. Commn. for the Battle of Normandy Mus.; founding sponsor Civil Justice Found., 1986—; mem. com. for publ. Hennepin County Lawyer, 1992; pres. Endless Fist Soc., Inc., 1998. Recipient Outstanding Tchr. award Inver Hills Coll. Student Body, 1973, St. Paul Citizen of Month award Citizens Group, 1975, Kempo Club award U. Minn., 1975, U. Minn. Student Appreciation award Kempo Club, 1978, Sibley County Atty. Commendation award, 1980, Good Neighbor award WCCO Radio, 1985, Lamp of Knowledge award Twin Cities Lawyers Guild, 1986, N.W. Cmty. TV Commendation award, 1989-91, Presdl. Merit medal Pres. George Bush, 1990, N.W. Cmty. TV award, 1991, HLS Leadership award, 1984, Mng. Attys. Guidance award, 1985, Creative Thinker award Regional Staff, 1986, HLS Justice award, 1986, Honors cert. for Authors, Childrens Reading Round Table of Chgo., 1988, Wisdom Soc. Wisdom award, 1998. Fellow Roscoe Pound Found., Nat. Dist. Attys. Assn.; mem. ABA, ATLA, Minn. Bar Assn. (com. on ethics 1994—, com. on alternative dispute resolution 1994—), Minn. Trial Lawyers Assn., Hennepin County Bar Assn. (dist. ethics com. 1990—), Wis. Bar Assn., Ramsey County Bar Assn., Am. Judicature Soc., Internat. Platform Assn., Am. Arbitration Assn. (panel of arbitrators 1992), Minn. Martial Arts Assn. (pres. 1974-78, Outstanding Instr. award 1973), Nippon Kobudo Rengokai (bd. dirs. North Ctrl. States 1972-76, regional dir. 1972-76), Endless Fist Soc. (pres. 1998), Internat. Confedn. Jurists, Edina C. of C., Southview Country Club, Masons, Kiwanis, Scottish Rite, Sigma Alpha Mu. Avocations: reading, Far Eastern and Oriental studies, civic activities, physical conditioning, gardening. General civil litigation, Criminal, Labor. Home: 4515 Andover Rd Minneapolis MN 55435-4031 Office: 5930 Brooklyn Blvd Ste 206 Brooklyn Center MN 55429-2518 also: 1711 County Road B W Ste 340N Roseville MN 55113-4077 also: Minn Ctr 7760 France Ave S Ste 720 Bloomington MN 55435-5921

NEFF, MARK EDWARD, lawyer; b. Evansville, Ind., Mar. 16, 1950; s. Edward Eugene and Esterlyne (Odom) N.; m. L. Ann Gentry, Jan. 8, 1972; children: Travis, Kristin. AB, Ind. U., 1972, JD, 1975. Bar: Ind. 1975, U.S. Dist. Ct. (so. dist.) Ind. 1975. Ptnr. Weyerbacher, Dewey, Neff, and Weyerbacher, Boonville, Ind., 1975-86; dep. pros. atty. Warrick County, Boonville, 1975-76, 79— . Bd. dirs. Boonville Little League Football, 1981. Mem. Ind. Bar Assn., Warrick County Bar Assn. (pres. 1981), Boonville Country Club (pres. 1981), Kiwanis (bd. dirs. 1981-82). Democrat. State civil litigation, General practice, Municipal (including bonds). Home: 5166 Jenner Rd Boonville IN 47601-8700 Office: PO Box 603 224 W Locust St Boonville IN 47601-3035

NEFF, MICHAEL ALAN, lawyer; b. Springfield, Ill., Sept. 4, 1940; s. Benjamin Ezra and Ann (Alpert) N.; m. Lin Laghi, Mar. 26, 1977; 1 son, Aaron Benjamin. Student, U. Ill., 1958-61; BA, U. Calif., Berkeley, 1963, postgrad., 1963-64; JD, Columbia U., 1967. Bar: N.Y. 1967, U.S. Dist. Ct. (so. and ea. dists.) N.Y. 1969, U.S. Ct. Appeals (2d cir.) 1988, U.S. Supreme Ct. 1988. Congl. intern U.S. Ho. of Reps., 1965; assoc. Sage, Gray, Todd & Sims, N.Y.C., 1967-74, Fellner & Rovins, N.Y.C., 1974-75; ptnr. Poier, Tulin, Clark & Neff, 1976-77; pvt. practice, 1977-83; pres. private practice, 1983—. Counsel St. Dominic's Home, 1971-74, Louise Wise Services, 1976-77, Edwin Gould Service for Children, 1969-79, 76— , Family Service of Westchester, Inc., 1977-87, The Children's Village, 1977-84, Brookwood Child Care, 1980— , Forestdale, 1988—, Fam. Support Systems Unlimited, 1990—, Educational Assistance Corp., 1990-95, Coalition for Hispanic Family Services, 1992-93, Soc. Children and Families, 1996—, Pius XII Youth and Family Services, 2000—, Child Developmen Support Corp, 2001—, Hale House Ctr., Inc., 2001—; teaching asst. U. Calif., 1963-64; instr. Social Welfare Policy and Law, Marymount Manhattan Coll., 1973; mem. Indigent Defendant's Legal Panel, Appellate Div., First Dept., 1974-84; participant N.Y. State Conf. on Children's Rights, 1974; asst. sec. Edwin Gould Services for Children, 1977—; cons. N.Y. Task Force on Permanency Planning For Children in Foster Care, 1985-90, N.Y. State Foster and Adoptive Parent Assn., Inc., 1988—, N.Y. Spaulding for Children, 1988-90, Ct. Appointed Spl. Advocates, 1988-91; instr. adoption law in N.Y., City Bar Ctr. for CLE, 2001—; mem. Adoption Adv. Com. N.Y. State Dept. Social Svcs., 1997-98; advisor Nat. Resource Ctr. for Foster Care and Permanency Planning, 2000—; trainer Inst. for Families and Children, 1992-95, New York City Adminstrn. for Children's services, 1996-97; facilitator Parenting Journey, 2000—; group leader Model Approach to Partnerships in Parenting, 2001—. Author: Freeing Foster Children for Adoption, A Child's Right to a Plan of Permanency, 1972, Permanent Neglect Proceedings, 1980, Adoption Proceedings, Basic Matrimonial Practice in New York, 1980, Foster Parenting Handbook, 1997 Adopting Foster Children: A Handbook for Foster Parents, 1999, Permanency Planning ASFA,Best Practices: A Handbook for Caseworkers, 2000; Contbr. articles to profl. jours. Mem. Protestant Bd. of Guardians, 2001—. Mem. ABA, Am. Acad. Adoption Attys., Assn. Bar City of N.Y. (mem. com. on children and law, family law sect.). State civil litigation, Family and matrimonial, General practice. Home: 5 W 86th St Apt 6B New York NY 10024-3664 Office: 36 W 44th St Ste 1212 New York NY 10036-8102 E-mail: manpc@aol.com

NEFF, OWEN CALVIN, lawyer; b. Hartville, Ohio, Sept. 4, 1918; s. Irving Roy and Pearl Belle (Swineheart) N.; m. Harriett Eshelman, June 10, 1950; children— Jane Penn Neff Stanton, Bruce Calvin, Gail Anne Neff Cost. B.A., Ohio Wesleyan U., 1940; J.D., U. Mich., 1948. Bar: Ohio. Ptnr. Snyder, Neff & Chamberlin, Cleve.; prof. Cleve. Marshall Law Sch., 1951-56, 66-70. Served with U.S. Army, 1941-46; PTO. Decorated Purple Heart, Bronze Star, Air Medal. Mem. ABA, Greater Cleve. Bar Assn., Ohio Bar Assn. (ho. of dels.). Republican. Lodge: Masons. General corporate, General practice, Probate. Office: Snyder Neff & Chamberlin Hanna Bldg 1422 Euclid Ave Cleveland OH 44115-1901

NEFF, ROBERT CLARK, SR. lawyer; b. St. Marys, Ohio, Feb. 11, 1921; s. Homer Armstrong and Irene (McCulloch) N.; m. Betty Baker, July 3, 1954 (dec.); children: Cynthia Lee Neff Schifer, Robert Clark Jr., Abigail Lynn (dec.); m. Helen Picking, July 24, 1975. BA, Coll. Wooster, 1943; postgrad., U. Mich., 1946-47; LLB, Ohio No. U., 1950. Bar: Ohio 1950, U.S. Dist. Ct. (no. dist.) Ohio, 1978. Pvt. practice, Bucyrus, Ohio, 1950—; ptnr. Neff Law Firm Ltd.; law dir. City of Bucyrus, 1962-95. Chmn. blood program Crawford County (Ohio) unit ARC, 1955-89; life mem. adv. bd. Salvation Army, 1962—; clk. of session 1st Presbyn. Ch., Bucyrus, 1958-96; bd. dirs. Bucyrus Area Cmty. Found., Crawford County Bd. Mental Retardation and Devel. Disabilities, 1977-82. With USNR, WWII; comdr. Res. ret. Recipient "Others" plaque for 30 yrs. adv. bd. svc. Salvation Army, Ohio No. U. Coll. Law Alumni award for cmty. svc., 1996; inducted Ohio Vets. Hall Fame, Columbus, 1996. Mem. Ohio Bar Assn., Crawford County Bar Assn., Naval Res. Assn., Ret. Officers Assn., Am. Legion, Bucyrus Area C. of C. (past bd. dirs., Outstanding Citizen award, 1973, Bucyrus Citizen of Yr. 1981), Kiwanis (life mem., past pres.), Masons. Republican. Estate planning, General practice, Probate. Home: 1085 Mary Ann Ln Bucyrus OH 44820-3145 Office: 840 S Sandusky Ave PO Box 406 Bucyrus OH 44820-0406 Fax: 419-562-1660. E-mail: nefflaw@cybrtown.com

NEFF, ROBERT MATTHEW, lawyer, financial services executive; b. Huntington, Ind., Mar. 26, 1955; s. Robert Eugene and Ann (Bash) N.; m. Lee Ann Loving, Aug. 23, 1980; children: Alexandra, Graydon, Philip. BA in English, DePauw U., 1977; JD, Ind. U., Indpls., 1980. Bar: Ind. 1980, U.S. Dist. Ct. (so. dist.) Ind. 1980, U.S. Supreme Ct., 1993. Assoc. Krieg, DeVault, Alexander & Capehart, Indpls., 1980-85, ptnr., 1986-88, Baker & Daniels, Indpls., 1988-92; of counsel, 1993-96; dept. to chmn. Fed. Housing Fin. Bd., Washington, 1992-93; pres., CEO Circle Investors, Inc., Indpls., 1993-97, also bd. dirs.; chmn., CEO Senex Fin. Corp., 1998—. Mem. faculty Grad. Sch. of Banking of South, 1988—90; chmn. Liberty Bankers Life Ins. Co., 1995—98, Am. Founders Life Ins. Co., Laurel Life Ins. Co., Aztek Life Assurance Co., 1996—97; bd. dirs. First Internet Bank of Ind. Exec. editor Ind. Law Rev., 1979-80. Participant Lacy Exec. Leadership Conf., Indpls., 1985-86; trustee DePauw U., 1977-80. Mem. Ind. Bar Assn. (chmn. corps. banking and bus. law sect. 1987-88), ABA (chmn. bus. law com. young lawyers div. 1988-90, mem. banking law com. 1990-92), James Whitcomb Riley Meml. Assn. (bd. govs. 1999—), DePauw Alumni Assn. (bd. dirs. 1982-88), Phi Kappa Psi, Phi Beta Kappa. Avocations: tae kwon do, golf. Banking, General corporate, Securities. Home: 7202 Merriam Rd Indianapolis IN 46240 Office: Senex Fin Corp 3500 DePauw Blvd # 3050 Indianapolis IN 46268 E-mail: neffrm@senexco.com

NEGOVAN, JULIE, lawyer; b. Binghamton, N.Y., Jan. 22, 1968; d. Keith Edward and Mary Hickling; m. Mark Edward Negovan, June 13, 1987; children: Daniel Austin, Andrea Nicole. AAS, Broome C.C., 1989; BS, SUNY, Binghamton, 1994; JD, Villanova Law Sch., 1997. Bar: N.Y. 1998, N.J. 1998, Pa. 1998, U.S. Dist. Ct. N.J. 1998. Law clk. Dechert, Price & Rhoades, Phila., 1997; assoc. Saul, Ewing, Remick & Saul, LLP, Princeton, N.J., 1997—. Mem. Phi Beta Kappa. Methodist. General civil litigation, Environmental. Home: 1511 Margaret Ct Jamison PA 18929 Office: Saul Ewing Rumick & Saul LLP Ste 202 214 Carnegie Ctr Princeton NJ 08540

NEGRON-GARCIA, ANTONIO S. territory supreme court justice; b. Rio Piedras, P.R., Dec. 31, 1940; s. Luis Negron-Fernandez and Rosa M. Garcia-Saldana; m. Gloria Villardefrancos-Vergara, May 26, 1962; 1 son, Antonio Rogelio. B.A., U. P.R., 1962, LL.B., 1964. Bar: P.R. bar 1964. Law aide and lawyer legal div. Water Resources Authority, 1962-64; judge Dist. Ct., 1964-69, Superior Ct., 1969-74; justice P.R. Supreme Ct., San Juan, 1974—; administrating judge, 1969-71; exec. officer Constl. Bd. for Revision Senatorial and Rep. Dists., 1971-72; mem. Jud. Conf., 1974; first exec. sec. Council for Reform of System of Justice in P.R., 1973-74. Chmn. Gov.'s Advisory Com. for Jud. Appointments, 1973-74; lectr. U. P.R. Law Sch., 1973-74 Mem. P.R. Bar Assn., Am. Judicature Soc. Roman Catholic. Office: Supreme Ct PR PO Box 2392 San Juan PR 00902-2392*

NEHRA, GERALD PETER, lawyer; b. Detroit, Mar. 25, 1940; s. Joseph P. and Jeanette M. (Bauer) N.; m. children: Teresa, Patricia; m. Peggy Jensen, Sept. 12, 1987. B.I.E., Gen. Motors Inst., Flint, Mich., 1962; JD, Detroit Coll. Law, 1970. Bar: Mich. 1970, N.Y. 1972, Colo. 1992, U.S. Dist. Ct. (ea. dist.) Mich. 1970, U.S. Dist. Ct. (so. dist.) N.Y. 1972, U.S. Dist. Ct. (no. dist.) N.Y. 1976, U.S. Ct. Appeals (6th cir.) 1978. Successively engr., supr., gen. supr. Gen. Motors Corp., 1958-67; mktg. rep. to regional counsel IBM Corp., 1967-79; v.p. gen. counsel Church & Dwight Co., Inc., 1979-82; dep. chief atty. Amway Corp., 1982-83; dep. gen. counsel, 1983-92; dir. legal div., 1989-91; sec., dir. corp. law, 1991-92; v.p. gen. cousnel Fuller Brush, Boulder, Colo., 1991-92; pvt. practice, 1992—. Adj. instr. Dale Carnegie Courses, 1983-91. Recipient Outstanding Contbn. award Am. Cancer Soc., 1976. Mem. ABA, Mich. Bar Assn., Colo. Bar Assn., N.Y. State Bar Assn. Antitrust, Contracts commercial, General corporate. Home and Office: 1710 Beach St Muskegon MI 49441-1008 E-mail: gnehra@home.com

NEIDICH, GEORGE ARTHUR, lawyer; b. N.Y.C., Feb. 22, 1950; s. Hyman and Rosalyn N.; m. Alene Wendrow, Jan. 10, 1982; 1 child, Hannah Lauren. BA, SUNY, Binghamton, 1971; JD magna cum laude, SUNY, Buffalo, 1974; MLT, Georgetown U., 1981. Bar: N.Y. 1975, D.C. 1979, Va. 1996, Conn. 1990. Assoc. Runfola & Birzon, Buffalo, 1973-75, Duke, Holzman, Yaeger & Radlin, Buffalo, 1975-77; gen. counsel subcom. on capital, investments and bus. opportunity, com. on small bus. U.S. Ho. of Reps., Washington, 1977-79, subcom. on gen. oversight, 1979-80; sr. legal advisor Task Force Product Liability and Accident Compensation Office of Gen. Counsel, Dept. Commerce, 1980-81; assoc. Steptoe & Johnson, 1981-86, of counsel, 1986-89; gen. counsel, sr. v.p. Preferred Health Care, Ltd., Wilton, Conn., 1989-93; COO Value Behavioral Health, Inc., Falls Church, Va., 1993-95; cons., counsellor at law, 1995—. Adj. prof. Georgetown U. Law Ctr., 1985-87. Author: Report on Product Liability, 1980; contbr. articles to profl. jours. General corporate, Health. Office: 9301 Morison Ln Great Falls VA 22066-4153 E-mail: gneidich@aol.com

NEIL, BENJAMIN ARTHUR, lawyer, educator; b. Chambersburg, Pa., Nov. 9, 1950; s. Donald Arthur Neil and Betty Elizabeth (Geedy) Chase; m. Janice Joyce Czosnowski, Aug. 11, 1973; children: Benjamin Arthur, Brian Andrew. BA, U. Balt., 1973, JD, 1978; MS, Morgan State U., Balt., 1975; continuing legal edn. courses Northwestern U., 1981, U.S. Atty Gens. Adv. Inst., Washington, 1981. Bar: Md. 1978, U.S. Dist. Ct. Md. 1979, D.C. 1988, U.S. Ct. Appeals (4th cir.) 1980, (5th cir.) 1983, (D.C.) 1988, (3d cir.) 1990, U.S. Supreme Ct. 1982. Pvt. practice Benjamin A. Neil & Assocs., Balt., 1978— ; pres. Ben Neil Realty Inc., Balt., 1984-92; assoc. prof. law Towson State U., Balt., 1979—; asst. state's atty. Carroll County, Westminster, Md., 1980-81; pres. Highland Title Co., Inc., Balt., 1985—, All-Metro Ins. Co., Inc., Balt., 1991, Canton Realty, Inc., Balt., 1998—; chmn. Balt. City Bd. Mcpl. and Zoning Appeals, 1995; v.p., gen. mgr. Balt. Bays Profl. Soccer Team; presenter George Washington U., 1991. Contbr. articles to law jours. Pres. parish council Our Lady of Fatima, Balt., 1978-80, 83-85, pres. sch. bd., 1994—; legal counsel Highlandtown Mchts. Assn., Balt., 1980-84; mem. Mayor's Police Adv. Commn., Balt., 1989; trustee Nat. Exchange Club Found. Prevention Child Abuse, 1989-90; chmn. bd. dirs. Balt. City Mcpl. and Zoning Appeals, 1996—. Recipient Gov.'s citation, Annapolis, Md., 1983, Mayor's cert. City of Balt., 1982, Gov.'s cert. Disting. Citizenship, Md., 1987. Mem. ABA, Assn. Trial Lawyers Am., Md. State Bar Assn., Balt. City Bar Assn. (legislation com. 1983—), Md. State's Attys. Assn. (faculty 1981—), Nat. Inst. Trial Advocacy (faculty 1984). Democrat. Roman Catholic. Clubs: Exchange of Highlandtown (v.p. 1984, pres. 1985-86, 88), Mason-Dixon Dist. Exchange Clubs (pres. 1989-90), St. Gerard's YMA (dir. 1980-81). Home: 324 Imla St Baltimore MD 21224-2807 Office: 3224 Eastern Ave Baltimore MD 21224-4012

NEILSEN, CHRISTINA J. lawyer; b. Vicenzia, Italy, Sept. 24, 1970; d. Dorothy E. Block; m. Randall W. Nielsen, Feb. 6, 1993; children: Breanna, Kaleb. AS in Legal Assistance Study, Drury Coll., 1991, BS in Psychology, BS in Criminal Justice, Drury Coll., 1993; JD, U. Mo., Kansas City, 1997. Bar: Mo. 1997, U.S. Dist. Ct. (we. dist.) Mo. 1997. Atty. Welch, Martin, Albano & Manners, Independence, Mo., 1997—. Mem. ABA, Mo. Bar Assn., Mo. Assn. of Trial Attys. (co-chair new lawyers sect. steering com. 1998), Assn. of Trial Lawyers of Am., Kansas City Met. Bar Assn., Ea. Jackson County Bar Assn., Assn. for Women Lawyers of Greater Kansas City. General civil litigation, Labor, Personal injury. Office: Welch Martin Albano & Manners 311 W Kansas Ave Independence MO 64068

NEIMAN, TANYA MARIE, legal association administrator; b. Pitts., June 28, 1949; d. Max and Helen (Lamaga) N. AB, Mills Coll., 1970; JD, U. Calif. Hastings Coll. of Law, San Francisco, 1974. Bar: Calif. 1975. Law assoc. Boalt Hall U. Calif., Berkeley, 1974-76; pub. defender State of Calif., San Francisco, 1976-81; assoc. gen. counsel, dir. vol. legal services Bar Assn. San Francisco, 1982—. Bd. dirs. Jack Berman Advocacy Ctr., Probono.net. Bd. dirs. United Way of Bay Area, 1998. Tanya Neiman Day proclaimed in her honor by Mayor of San Francisco, 1991; recipient Disting. Citizen award Harvard Club San Francisco, 1995, Kutak-Dodds prize Nat. Legal Aid and Defender Assn., 1996; honored by Nat. Lawyers Guild of San Francisco Bay Area, 2001. Mem. ABA (ABA Commn. on Homelessness 1993-96, standing com. on pro bono and pub. svcs. com., 1997—, spkr. 1985—, Harrison Tweed award 1985, 97), Calif. Bar Assn. (exec. com. 1984—, legal svcs. sect., chair steering com. State Bar Legal Corps, Loren Miller award), Golden Gate Bus. Assn. Found. (v.p. grant making 1985—), Nat. Conf. Women and Law (spkr. 1975—), Nat. Lawyers Guild. Office: The Bar Assn San Francisco 465 California St Ste 1100 San Francisco CA 94104-1804

NEITZKE, ERIC KARL, lawyer; b. Mobile, Ala., Dec. 10, 1955; s. Howard and Otti S. Neitzke; m. Kathryn Sloan; children: Kyle, Blake, Blaire. BA, U. Fla., 1979, JD, 1982. Bar: Fla. 1982, U.S. Dist. Ct. (mid. dist.) Fla. 1987. Asst. state atty. 7th Jud. Cir., State Atty., Daytona Beach, Fla., 1982; atty. Dunn, Smith & Withers, 1982-88, Monaco, Smith, Hood and Perkins, Daytona Beach, 1988—. Adj. faculty family law and criminal law Daytona C.C.; chmn. adv. com. Juvenile Detention Ctr. Contbr. articles to profl. jours. Mem. Fla. Acad. Trial Lawyers, Assn. Trial Lawyers Am., Volusia Bar Assn., Fla. Assn. Criminal Def. Lawyers, Phi Beta Kappa. Avocations: water sports, shooting, travel. Criminal, Family and matrimonial, Personal injury. Home: 19 Lost Creek Ln Ormond Beach FL 32174-4840 Office: Eric K Neitzke PA 444 Seabreeze Blvd Ste 900 Daytona Beach FL 32118-3953

NELON, ROBERT DALE, lawyer; b. Shawnee, Okla., Aug. 8, 1946; s. Cecil Eug and Neata Madelyn (Fox) N.; m. Freddie Anne Tippton, Aug. 2, 1975; children: Lindsay Anne, Gregory Tipton. BA, Northwestern U., 1968; JD, U. Okla., 1971. Bar: Okla. 1971, U.S. Dist. Ct. (we., no. and ea. dists) Okla. 1971, U.S. Ct. Appeals (10th cir.) 1971, (8th cir.) 1992, (ed cir.) 1993, U.S. Mil. Ct. Appeals 1972, U.S. Supreme Ct. 1989. Law clk. Okla. Atty. Gen., Oklahoma City, 1966-70; mem. Andrews, Davis, Legg, Bixler, Milsten & Price, 1971-95, Hall Estill Hardwick Gable Golden & Nelson, Oklahoma City, 1995—. Served to capt. USMCR, 1972=74. Mem. ABA, Okla. Bar Assn., Am. Judicature Soc. Democrat. Methodist. Antitrust, Federal civil litigation, Libel. Office: Hall Estill Hardwick Gable Golden & Nelson Bank One Center, Suite 2900 100 N Broadway Ave Oklahoma City OK 73102-8606 E-mail: bnelon@hallestill.com

NELSON, DAVID ALDRICH, federal judge; b. Watertown, N.Y., Aug. 14, 1932; s. Carlton Low and Irene Demetria (Aldrich) N.; m. Mary Dickson, Aug. 25, 1956; 3 children. AB, Hamilton Coll., 1954; postgrad., Cambridge U., Eng., 1954-55; LLB, Harvard U., 1958. Bar: Ohio 1958, N.Y. 1982. Atty.-advisor Office of the Gen. Counsel, Dept. of the Air Force, 1959-62; assoc. Squire, Sanders & Dempsey, Cleve., 1958-67, ptnr., 1967-69, 72-85; cir. judge U.S. Ct. Appeals (6th cir.), Cin., 1985-99, sr. cir. judge, 1999—. Gen. counsel U.S. Post Office Dept., Washington, 1969-71; sr. asst. postmaster gen., gen. counsel U.S. Postal Svc., Washington, 1971; mem. nat. coun. Coll. Law, Ohio State U., 1988-98. Trustee Hamilton Coll., 1984-88. Served to maj. USAFR, 1959-69. Fulbright scholar, 1954-55; recipient Benjamin Franklin award U.S. Post Office Dept., 1969. Fellow Am. Coll. Trial Lawyers; mem. Fed. Bar Assn., Ohio Bar Assn., Cin. Bar Assn., Emerson Lit. Soc., Ct. of Nisi Prius (sgt. emeritus), Phi Beta Kappa. Office: US Ct Appeals 6th Cir Potter Stewart US Ct House 5th and Walnut St Cincinnati OH 45202-3988

NELSON, DOROTHY WRIGHT (MRS. JAMES F. NELSON), federal judge; b. San Pedro, Calif., Sept. 30, 1928; d. Harry Earl and Lorna Amy Wright; m. James Frank Nelson, Dec. 27, 1950; children: Franklin Wright, Lorna Jean. B.A., UCLA, 1950, J.D., 1953; LL.M., U. So. Calif., 1956;

LLD honoris causa, U. San Diego, 1997, U. So. Calif., 1983, Georgetown U., 1988, Whittier U., 1989, U. Santa Clara, 1990; LLD (honoris causa), Whittier U., 1989. Bar: Calif. 1954. Research assoc. fellow U. So. Calif., 1953-56; instr., 1957; asst. prof., 1958-61; assoc. prof., 1961-67; prof., 1967; assoc. dean., 1965-67; dean., 1967-80; judge U.S. Ct. Appeals (9th cir.), 1979-95, sr. judge, 1995—. Cons. Project STAR, Law Enforcement Assistance Adminstrn.; mem. select com. on internal procedures of Calif. Supreme Ct., 1987—; co-chair Sino-Am. Seminar on Mediation and Arbitration, Beijing, 1992; dir. Dialogue on Transition to a Global Soc., Weinacht, Switzerland, 1992. Author: Judicial Adminstration and The Administration of Justice, 1973, (with Christopher Goelz and Meredith Watts) Federal Ninth Circuit Civil Appellate Practice, 1995; Contbr. articles to profl. jours. Co-chmn. Confronting Myths in Edn. for Pres. Nixon's White House Conf. on Children, Pres. Carter's Commn. for Pension Policy, 1974-80, Pres. Reagon's Madison Trust; bd. visitors U.S. Air Force Acad., 1978; bd. dirs. Council on Legal Edn. for Profl. Responsibility, 1971-80, Constnl. Right Found., Am. Nat. Inst. for Social Advancement, Pacific Oaks Coll., Childrens Sch. & Rsch. Ctr., 1996-98; adv. bd. Nat. Center for State Cts., 1971-73; adv. bd. World Law Inst., 1997—; chmn. bd. Western Justice Ctr., 1986—; mem. adv. com. Nat. Jud. Edn. Program to promote equality for woman and men in cts.; bd. advisors Tahirih Justice Inst., Washington, 1998—; chair 9th Cir. Standing Com. on Alternative Dispute Resolution, 1998—. Named Law Alumnus of Yr. UCLA, 1967, Times Woman of Yr., 1968, Disting. Jurist, Ind. U. Law, 1994; recipient Profl. Achievement award, 1969, AWARE Internat. award, 1970, U. Judaism Humanitarian award, 1973, Ernestine Stalhut Outstanding Woman Lawyer award, 1972, Pub. Svc. award Coro Found., 1978, Pax Orbis ex Jure medallion World Peace thru Law Ctr., 1975, Hollzer Human Rights award Jewish Fedn. Coun., L.A., 1988, Medal of Honor UCLA, 1993, Emil Gumpert Jud. ADR Recognition award L.A. County Bar Assn., 1996, Julia Morgan award YWCA Pasadena, 1997, Samuel E. Gates Litigation award Am. Coll. Trial Lawyers, 1999, D'Alemberte/Raven award ABA Dispute Resolution Sect., 2000, Bernard E. Witkin award State Bar Assn. Calif., 2000; Lustman fellow Yale U. 1977. Fellow Am. Bar Found., Davenport Coll., Yale U.; mem. Bar Calif. (bd. dirs. continuing edn. bar commn. 1967-74), Am. Judicature Soc. (dir., Justice award 1985), Assn. Am. Law Schs. (chmn. com. edn. in jud. adminstrn.), ABA (sect. on jud. adminstrn., chmn. com. on edn. in jud. adminstrn. 1973-89), Phi Beta Kappa, Order of Coif (nat. v.p. 1974-76), Jud. Conf. U.S. (com. to consider standards for admission to practice in fed. cts. 1976-79) Office: US Ct Appeals Cir 125 S Grand Ave Ste 303 Pasadena CA 91105-1621

NELSON, EDWARD SHEFFIELD, lawyer, former utility company executive; b. Keevil, Ark., Feb. 23, 1941; s. Robert Ford and Thelma Jo (Mayberry) N.; m. Mary Lynn McCastlain, Oct. 12, 1962; children: Cynthia, Lynn (dec.), Laura. BS, U. Cen. Ark., 1963; LLB, Ark. Law Sch., 1968; JD, U. Ark., 1969. Mgmt. trainee Ark. La. Gas Co., Little Rock, 1963-64, sales engr., 1964-67, sales coordinator, 1967-69, gen. sales mgr., 1969-71, v.p., gen. sales mgr., 1971-73, pres., dir., 1973-79, pres., chmn., chief exec. officer, 1979-85; ptnr., chmn. bd., chief exec. officer House, Wallace, Nelson & Jewel, Little Rock, 1985-86; pvt. practice law, 1986—; of counsel Jack, Lyon & Jones, P.A., 1991—. Bd. dirs. Fed. Res. Mem. N.G., 1957-63, Fellowship Bible Ch.; bd. dirs. U. Ark., Little Rock, vice chmn. bd. visitors, 1981; bd. dirs. Philander Smith Coll., 1981; chmn. Ark. Indsl. Devel. Commn., 1987, 88; past chmn. Little Rock br. Fed. Res. Bd. St. Louis; chmn. Econ. Expansion Study Commn., 1987—; bd. dirs. Ark. Ednl. TV Found., Ark. Game and Fish Commn. Found.; founder, 1st pres. Jr. Achievement Ark., 1987-88; Rep. nominee for Gov. of Ark., 1990, 94; co-state chmn. Ark. Reps., 1991-92, nat. committeeman Ark. GOP, 1993-2000; mem. Ark. Higher Edn. Coord. Bd., 1997-99; apptd. commr. Ark. Game and Fish Commn., 2000—. Named Ark.'s Outstanding Young Man Ark. J. C. of C., 1973; One of Am.'s Ten Outstanding Young Men U.S. Jr. C. of C., 1974; Citizen of Yr. Ark. chpt. March of Dimes, 1983; Humanitarian of Yr. NCCJ, 1983; Best Chief Exec. Officer in Natural Gas Industry Wall Street Transcript, 1983; recipient 1st Disting. Alumnus award U. Cen. Ark., 1987. Mem. Am., Ark., Pulaski County bar assns., Ark. C. of C. (dir.), Little Rock C. of C. (dir., pres. 1981), Sales and Mktg. Execs. Assn. (pres. 1975, Top Mgmt. award 1977), U. Ark. Law Sch. Alumni Assn. (pres. 1980), Sigma Tau Gamma (Ben T. Laney Leadership award for leadership and achievment 2000). Fellowship Bible Ch. General corporate, Finance. Office: 6th and Broadway 3400 TCBY Bldg Little Rock AR 72201

NELSON, FREDERICK DICKSON, lawyer; b. Cleve., Oct. 19, 1958; s. David Aldrich and Mary Ellen (Dickson) N. AB, Hamilton Coll., 1980; JD, Harvard U., 1983. Bar: Ohio 1984, D.C. 1985. Majority counsel subcom. on criminal law U.S. Senate Judiciary Com., Washington, 1983-85; spl. asst. to asst. atty. gen., Office of Legal Policy U.S. Dept. Justice, 1985-86, dep. asst. atty. gen., Office of Legal Policy, 1986-87; assoc. Taft, Stettinius & Hollister, Cin., 1988-89, of counsel, 1991-93; assoc. counsel to Pres. of U.S. The White House, Washington, 1989-90. Advisor to govts. of Ukraine and Russia, ABA Ctrl. and East European Law Initiative, 1992-93; adj. prof. constl. law Salmon P. Chase Coll. Law, U. No. Ky., 1994; chief of staff U.S. Rep. Steve Chabot, 1995-97; cons. Constnl. Commn. Albania, per Internat. Rep. Inst., 1998; pres. Civic Solutions, LLC, Cin., 1998—; co-creator, panelist Hotseat, Sta. WCPO-TV, (Cin. Channel 9), 2000—. Exec. editor Harvard Jour. of Law and Pub. Policy, 1982-83. Mem. Hamilton County Rep. Policy and Appts. Coms., 1999—; cons. Chabot for Congress Campaign, Cin., 1994, 98; mem. Ohio Bd. Uniform State Laws, Nat. Conf. Commrs. on Unifort State Laws, 2001—. Harry S. Truman Found. scholar, 1978-81. Mem. NATAS (Ohio Valley chpt.), Federalist Soc., Harvard Club. of Cin. (bd. dirs. 1989, 2001—), Phi Beta Kappa. Republican. Home: 2137 Sinton Ave Cincinnati OH 45206-2509 also: 1 W 4th St Ste 2201 Cincinnati OH 45202-3605

NELSON, JACK ODELL, JR. lawyer; b. Dallas, Oct. 8, 1947; s. Jack Odell and Rose Mary (Trepoy) N. BBA, Tex. Tech. U., 1969; JD, U. Tex., 1972. Bar: Tex. 1972, U.S. Dist. Ct. (no. dist.) Tex. 1973, U.S. Ct. Appeals (5th cir.) 1974, U.S. Supreme Ct. 1981. Assoc. Garner, Boulter, Jesko & Purdom and successor firms, Lubbock, Tex., 1972-76, 77-80, Gardere, Porter & DeHay, Dallas, 1976-77; ptnr. Nelson & Nelson, Lubbock, 1981—. Trustee Milam Children Tng. Ctr., 1988-93. Fellow Tex. Bar Found.; mem. Tex. Bar Assn. (dist. 16 grievance com.), Tex. Assn. Def. Counsel, Am. Bd. Trial Advocates, Internat. Assn. Def. Counsel, Lubbock County Bar Assn., Rotary, Lubbock Club, Sigma Chi, Phi Delta Phi. Mem. Disciples of Christ Ch. Banking, State civil litigation, Insurance. Office: Nelson & Nelson 1001 Main St Ste 601 Lubbock TX 79401-3306 E-mail: jonj@nelsonfirm.com

NELSON, JAMES C, state supreme court justice; b. Idaho; m. Chari Werner; 2 children. BBA, U. Idaho, 1966; JD cum laude, George Washington U., 1974. Fin. analyst SEC, Washington; pvt. practice Cut Bank; county atty. Glacier County; assoc. judge Mont. Supreme Ct., 1993—. Former mem. State Bd. Oil and Gas Conservation, also chmn.; former mem. State Gaming Adv. Counsel, Gov. Adv. Coun. on Corrections and Criminal Justice Policy; liaison to Commn. of Cts. of Ltd. Jurisdiction, mem. adv. com. Ct. Assessment Program. Served U.S. Army. Office: Justice Bldg Supreme Ct Mont 215 N Sanders St Rm 315 PO Box 203001 Helena MT 59620-3001*

NELSON, JOHN C. lawyer; b. Chgo., July 25, 1927; s. John E. and Astrid (Rutberg) N.; m. Barbara Otis, June 19,1955; children: Karen, Diana, John, James, Kristin. BS, Lawrence Coll., 1952; JD, NYU, 1955. Bar: N.Y. 1956. Assoc. Milbank, Tweed, Hadley & McCoy, N.Y.C., 1955-63, ptnr., 1963—. Mem. ABA, N.Y. State Bar Assn., Assn. Bar City N.Y. Episcopalian. Real property. Office: Milbank Tweed Hadley & McCloy 1 Chase Manhattan Plz Fl 47 New York NY 10005-1413

NELSON, KEITHE EUGENE, state court administrator, lawyer; b. Grand Forks, N.D. m. Shirley Jeanne Jordahl, June 10, 1955; children: Kirsti Lynn Nelson Hoerauf, Scott David, Kenen Edward, Karen Lee Nelson Strandquist. PhB, U. N.D., 1958, JD, 1959. Bar: N.D. 1959, U.S. Ct. Mil. Appeals 1967., U.S. Supreme Ct. 1967. With Armour & Co., Grand Forks, 1958-59; commd. 2d lt. USAF, 1958, advanced through grades to maj. gen., 1985, judge advocate N.D. and, Fed. Republic Germany and Eng., 1959-73, chief career mgmt., 1973-77; comdt. USAF JAG Sch., Montgomery, Ala., 1977-81; staff judge adv. Tactical Air Command USAF, Hampton, VA., 1981-82, SAC, Omaha, 1984-85; dir. USAF Judiciary, Washington, 1982-84; dep. JAG USAF, 1985, JAG, 1988-91, JAG, 1988, ret. JAG, 1991; dir. jud. planning Supreme Ct. N.D.; state ct. administr., 1992—. Chmn. editorial bd. USAF Law Rev., 1977-81. Decorated D.S.M., Legion of Merit with two oak leaf clusters. Mem. ABA. Lutheran. Avocations: skeet shooting, hunting, tennis, theater. Home: 800 Munich Dr Bismarck ND 58504-7050

NELSON, LEONARD JOHN, III, lawyer, educator; b. Spokane, Wash., July 31, 1949; s. Leonard John Jr. and Lois Marian (McCuaig) N.; m. Janice Helen Linebarger, Aug. 15, 1970; children: Leonard John IV, Mary Beth, Monica Teresa. Student, Whitman Coll., 1967-68; BA magna cum laude, U. Wash., 1970; JD cum laude, Gonzaga U., 1974; LLM, Yale U., 1984. Bar: Wash. 1974, Okla. 1979. Asst. prof. Gonzaga U. Law Sch., 1974; law clk. Wash. Supreme Ct., Olympia, 1975-76; ct. clk. Wash. Ct. Appeals, Spokane, 1976-78; from asst. to assoc. prof. O.W. Coburn Sch. Law, Tulsa, 1979-83; assoc. prof. Cumberland Sch. Law, Birmingham, Ala., 1984-87, prof., 1987—. Contbr. editor: The Death Decision, 1984; contbr. articles to law revs. Mem. instl. rev. bd. Samford U., 1986-2001. Mem. Fellowship Cath. Scholars, Phi Beta Kappa. Roman Catholic. Home: 1817 Parkside Cir Birmingham AL 35209-6960 Office: Cumberland Sch of Law 800 Lakeshore Dr Birmingham AL 35229-0001

NELSON, LUELLA ELINE, lawyer; b. Portland, Oreg., Apr. 11, 1952; d. Alben Wayne and Geneva Esther (Larsen) N. BS in Econs. and Polit. Sci., Macalester Coll., 1973; JD, Harvard U., 1976. Bar: Oreg. 1976, Calif. 1984. Counsel to bd. mem. NLRB, Washington, 1976-80, sr. counsel to bd. mem., 1980-81, field atty. Oakland, Calif., 1981-86; pvt. practice arbitrator, mediator, fact finder Oakland and Portland, Oreg., 1986—. Instr. Golden Gate U. Grad. Sch., 1987, 88, 90. Mem. Thomas Circle Singers, Washington, 1979-81, San Francisco Civic Chorale, 1982-97. Mem. ABA, State Bar Calif. (labor and employment law sect. chair 1991-92), Oreg. State Bar (labor and employment law sect., chair 1999-2000), Nat. Acad. of Arbitrators, Bar Assn. San Francisco (pro bono legalization project, labor and employment law sect.), Soc. Profls. in Dispute Resolution (bd. dirs. No. Calif. chpt., v.p.), Indsl. Rels. Rsch. Assn. (chmn.äelecä Oreg. chpt. 1998-99), Am. Arbitration Assn. Independent. Methodist. Avocations: singing, hiking, swimming, cross-country skiing, reading. Office: 4096 Piedmont Ave PMB 159 Oakland CA 94611

NELSON, MARGARET ROSE, lawyer, legal educator; b. St. George, Utah, May 27, 1952; d. V. Pershing and Hattie (Jones) N. B.A. magna cum laude, Brigham Young U., 1973, J.D., 1976. Bar: Utah 1977, U.S. Dist. Ct. Utah 1977, U.S. Ct. Appeals (10th cir.) 1977, U.S. Ct. Appeals D.C. 1979, U.S. Supreme Ct. 1980. Assoc. Aldrich & Nelson, Provo, Utah, 1977-80; dep. county atty. Utah County, Provo, 1977— ; instr. law and banking Utah Tech. Coll., Provo, 1978, Orem, 1981; law instr. Utah State Police Acad., Salt Lake City, 1981; trustee Utah Legal Services, Salt Lake City, 1983— ; charter mem., exec. com. Am. Inn of Ct. I, Provo and Salt Lake City, 1980-83; mem. Utah State ad hoc com. to revise juvenile ct. rules of practice and procedure, Salt Lake City, 1981-82; mem. adv. bd., Utah Legal Services, Provo, 1977-78, Utah State Permanent Community Impact Fund Bd., Salt Lake City, 1984— . Vice pres. bd. dirs. Utah Tech. Coll. Alumni and Friends, Orem, 1983— ; mem Utah State Disaster Relief Bd., Salt Lake City, 1984— , Bd. dirs. Mountainland Head Start, Provo, 1984— , joint liaison com. Utah State Bd. Edn./Utah Sch. Bds. Assn., 1983, joint liaison com. Utah State Bd. Edn./Utah State Bd. Regents, 1984— , Provo Sch. Dist. Vocat. Adv. Council, 1982— , Provo Freedom Festival Children's Parade Com., 1978; mem. Utah State Bd. Edn., Utah State Bd. Vocat. Edn., 1983— ; central com. Utah County Republican Party, 1982— ; del. Utah County Rep. Convs., 1982— , Utah State Rep. Convs., 1982— , alt. del. Nat. Rep. Conv., 1984— ; nominating com. Utah County LWV, 1983. Recipient Best Brief award 1st ann. Moot Ct. Competition Brigham Young U., 1975. Mem. ABA, Women Lawyers of Utah, Assn. Trial Lawyers Am., Utah Trial Lawyers Assn., Central Utah Bar Assn. (sec./treas. 1979), Nat. Dist. Attys. Assn., Utah Statewide Assn. Prosecutors, Am. Judicature Soc., Nat. Assn. State Bd. Edn., Provo C. of C. (v.p. bd. dirs. 1984— , chmn. legis. action com. 1983-84), Orem C. of C. (small bus. council 1983—), J. Reuben Clark Law Soc. (bd. advs. 1974), Phi Kappa Phi. Mormon. Club: Riverside Country (Provo). Home: 210 W 800 S Orem UT 84058-6223 Office: 2930 Vistapoint Rd Midlothian VA 23113-3925

NELSON, PAUL DOUGLAS, lawyer; b. Silverton, Oreg., Dec. 22, 1948; s. Robert Thorsen and Elene N.; m. Mary Linda Hilligoss, Feb. 28, 1981; children: Christopher R., Matthew D., Patrick D. BA cum laude, Lewis and Clark Coll., 1971; JD, U. Oreg., 1974. Bar: Calif. 1974, Oreg. 1975, U.S. Dist. (no., ea. and cen. dists.) 1975. Law clk. U.S. atty.'s office U.S. Dist. Ct. Oreg., Portland, 1973; assoc. Hoge, Fenton, Jones & Appel, San Jose, 1974-75; ptnr. Hancock, Rothert & Bunshoft, San Francisco and London, 1975—. Nat. Presbyn. scholar Lewis and Clark Coll., Portland, 1967, Oreg. Trial Lawyers scholar U. Oreg., 1973. Mem. ABA, San Francisco Bar Assn., San Francisco Lawyers Club, Am. Law Firm Assn., Assn. Ski Def. Attys., Internat. Amusement and Leisure Def. Assn., Assn. Internat. de Droit des Assurance, Lewis & Clark Coll. Alumni Assn. (bd. dirs.). Avocation: skiing. General civil litigation, Insurance, Personal injury. Office: Hancock Rothert & Bunshoft 4 Embarcadero Ctr San Francisco CA 94111-4106

NELSON, RICHARD ARTHUR, lawyer; b. Fosston, Minn., Apr. 8, 1947; BS in Math., U. Minn., 1969, JD, 1974. Bar: Minn. 1974, U.S. Ct. Appeals (D.C. cir.) 1975, U.S. Dist. Ct. Minn. 1975. Law clk. U.S. Ct. Appeals (D.C. cir.), Washington, 1974-75; ptnr. Faegre and Benson, Mpls., 1975—. Seminar lectr. in employee benefits and labor laws, 1983—. Note and articles editor Minn. Law Rev., 1973-74. Active Dem.-Farmer-Labor State Cen. Com., Minn., 1976—, del. dist. and local coms. and convs., 1970—, state exec. com., 1990—; student rep. bd. regents U. Minn., Mpls., 1973-74; mem. adv. coun. IRS Mid-States Key Dist. EP/EO, 1996-2000, IRS Ctrl. Mountains Region, 2001—; chair Mpls. Pension Coun., 1999-2000; mem. IRC Ctrl. Mountain TE/GE Adv. Coun., 2001—. Served with U.S. Army, 1970-72. Mem. ABA, Minn. Bar Assn. (chair employee benefits sect. 1997-98), Order of Coif, Tau Beta Pi. Lutheran. Immigration, naturalization, and customs, Labor, Pension, profit-sharing, and employee benefits. Office: Faegre and Benson 90 S 7th St Ste 2200 Minneapolis MN 55402-3901 E-mail: rnelson@faegre.com

NELSON, RICHARD PERRY, lawyer; b. Lincoln, Nebr., Sept. 1, 1940; s. Robert Anselm and Edyth Lavern (Perry) N.; m. Elizabeth Ann Wickersham, Jan. 27, 1968; children: Donald Robert, Catherine Elizabeth, Diane Evelyn. BA, U. Nebr., 1962, JD, 1964. Bar: Nebr. 1964, U.S. Dist. Ct. Nebr. 1964, U.S. Dist. Ct. D.C. 1970, U.S. Ct. Appeals (8th cir.) 1971, U.S. Supreme Ct. 1970, U.S. Ct. Appeals (D.C. cir.) 1976. Legal counsel U.S. Senate judiciary Com., Washington, 1967-68; legis. asst. to U.S. Senator R. L. Hruska, Washington, 1969; assoc. Nelson & Harding, Lincoln, 1970-71, ptnr., 1972-75; ptnr. Nelson, Morris & Holdeman, Lincoln, 1976-84, Peterson, Nelson, Johanns, Morris & Holdeman, Lincoln, 1985-90; ptnr. Nelson Morris & Titus, Lincoln, 1991-98; dir. Nebr. Health and Human Svcs. Regulation and Licensure, 1999—. Editor Nebr. Law Rev., 1963-64. Vice chmn. Nebr. Reps., Lincoln, 1971-72, legal counsel, 1986. Mem. ABA, Nebr. Bar Assn., Nat. Health Lawyers Assn., Order of Coif. Mem. Evang. Covenant Ch. Administrative and regulatory, General corporate, Health.

NELSON, ROBERT LOUIS, lawyer; b. Dover, N.H., Aug. 10, 1931; s. Albert Louis and Alice (Rogers) N.; m. Rita Jean Hutchins, June 11, 1955; children: Karen, Robin Andrea. BA, Bates Coll., Lewiston, Maine, 1956; LLB, Georgetown U., 1959. Bar: D.C. 1960. With U.S. Commn. Civil Rights, 1958-63, AID, 1963-66; program sec. U.S. Mission to Brazil, 1965-66; exec. dir. Lawyers Com. Civil Rights Under Law, 1966-70; dep. campaign mgr. Muskie for Pres., 1970-72; v.p. Perpetual Corp., Houston, 1972-74; sr. v.p., gen. counsel Washington Star, 1974-76; pres. broadcast div. Washington Star Communications, Inc., 1976-77; asst. sec. of army U.S. Dept. Def., 1977-79; spl. advisor to chief N.G. Bur., Dept. Def., 1980-85; pres., dir. Mid-Md. Communications Corp., 1981-85; ptnr. Verner, Liipfert, Bernhard, McPherson and Hand, 1979-87; gen. counsel Paralyzed Vets. Am., 1988-99, sr. counsel, 2000—. Vice chmn. D.C. Redevel. Land Agy., 1976-77; bd. dirs. Community Found. Greater Washington, 1977-78 ; bd. dirs. Friends of Nat. Zoo, 1975— , pres., 1982-84; bd. dirs. Downtown Progress, 1976-77, Fed. City Council, 1976-77, 83-87, Pennsylvania Ave. Devel. Corp., 1976-77. Served with AUS, 1953-54. Mem. ABA, D.C. Bar Assn., Army Navy Club (Washington). Democrat. Episcopalian. General corporate, Non-profit and tax-exempt organizations. Home: Robins Nest PO Box 52 Orrs Island ME 04066-0052 Office: 801 18th St NW Washington DC 20006-3517

NELSON, ROY HUGH, JR. lawyer, mediator, arbitrator; b. St. Paul, May 13, 1955; s. Roy H. and Helen S. Nelson; m. MaryJean G. Froehlich, Aug. 13, 1994; children: Benjamin, Calla. BS, U. Wis., Milw., 1979, MS, 1985; JD, U. Wis., 1988. Bar: Wis. 1988, U.S. Dist. Ct. (ea. and we. dists.) Wis. 1988, U.S. Dist. Ct. (ea. dist.) Mich. 1991, U.S. Ct. Appeals (7th cir.) 1988, U.S. Ct. Appeals (fed. cir.) 1996, U.S. Supreme Ct. 1999. Police officer City of Brookfield, Wis., 1978-88; assoc. Borgelt, Powell, Peterson & Frauen, Milw., 1988-92; shareholder, dir. Petrie & Stocking SC, 1992—; mediator, arbitrator, dir. Conflict Resolution Svcs., 1997—. Exec. dir. Conflict Mgmt. Edn. Project, 1999; chair adv. bd. Mediation Ministries, Sun Prairie, Wis., 1998—. Mem. Wis. Bar Assn., Milw. Bar Assn., Christian Legal Soc., Acad. Family Mediators, Bus. Network Internat., Wis. Intellectual Property Law Assn., Wis. Assn. Mediators. Lutheran. Alternative dispute resolution, General civil litigation, Intellectual property. Office: Petrie & Stocking SC 111 E Wisconsin Ave Ste 1500 Milwaukee WI 53202-4808 also: Conflict Resolution Svcs 756 N Milwaukee St Ste 310 Milwaukee WI 53202-3719 E-mail: rnelson@petriestocking.com

NELSON, SHARON L. lawyer; b. St. Joe, Mich., June 7, 1970; d. Harry Eugene and Marilyn Lee Orcutt; m. Thomas Victor Nelson, July 1, 1990. BA, Ea. Wash. U., 1994; JD, Whittier Law Sch., 1997. Bar: Nev. 1997, U.S. Dist. Ct. Nev. 1997. Ptnr. Carter, Nelson & Assocs., Las Vegas, Nev., 1997-98, Nersesian, Carter, Nelson, Bolton, Las Vegas, 1998—. Pres. Ea. Wash. chpt. Nat. Abortion Rights AL, Spokane, Wash., 1993-94. Mem. ABA, NOW, Nev. Young Lawyers Assn. Democrat. Federal civil litigation, Labor. Office: Nersesian Carter Et Al 333 S 3d St Ste A Las Vegas NV 89101

NELSON, STEVEN DWAYNE, lawyer; b. Austin, Minn. m. Vicky L. Staab, July 6, 1990. BA in English, SUNY, Buffalo, 1972; JD, U. Mont., 1978. Bar: Mont. 1978, U.S. Dist. Ct. Mont. 1978. Sole practice, Bozeman, Mont., 1978—; city prosecutor City of Bozeman, 1979-82; city atty. City of Ennis (Mont.), 1980-82; prof. U. Great Falls, Mont., 1990—, mediator, 1998—. Mem. ABA, Mont. State Bar Assn., Phi Delta Phi. Avocations: fishing, skiing, hiking. General civil litigation, Criminal, General practice. Home and Office: 4590 Maiden Rock Rd Bozeman MT 59715-7769 E-mail: Nelsonsvl@cs.com

NELSON, THOMAS G. federal judge; b. 1936; Student, Univ. Idaho, 1955-59, LLB, 1962. Ptnr. Parry, Robertson, and Daly, Twin Falls, Idaho, 1965-79, Nelson, Rosholt, Robertson, Tolman and Tucker, Twin Falls, from 1979; judge U.S. Ct. of Appeals (9th cir.), Boise, Idaho, 1990—. With Idaho Air N.G., 1962-65, USAR, 1965-68. Mem. ABA (ho. of dels. 1974, 87-89), Am. Bar Found., Am. Coll. Trial Lawyers, Idaho State Bar (pres., bd. commrs.), Idaho Assn. Def. Counsel, Am. Bd. Trial Advocates (pres. Idaho chpt.), Phi Alpha Delta, Idaho Law Found. Office: US Ct Appeals 9th Circuit 304 N Eighth St PO Box 1339 Boise ID 83701-1339*

NELSON, THOMAS HOWARD, lawyer; b. July 21, 1944; s. Harold Fletcher and Carrie ALice (Fogle) N.; m. Esther Pauline Hillila; children: Matthew Jacob, Maija Carrie. BA, U. Wash., 1966; JD, Valparaiso U., 1973; LLM, Yale U., 1974. Bar: Conn. 1974, Oreg. 1978, Wash. 1983, U.S. Ct. Appeals (D.C. 9th cirs.) 1984; U.S. Ct. Supreme Ct. 1985; U.S. Ct. Fed. Claims, 2000. Asst. prof. law U. Conn., West Hartford, 1974-77; vis. assoc. prof. law Valparaiso (Ind.) U., 1977-78; assoc. Rives, Bonyhadi & Smith, Portland, Oreg., 1978-82; ptnr. Stoel, Rives, Boley, Jones & Grey, 1982-96; escort, interpretor Farsi, U.S. Dept. State, Washington, 1970—. Contbr. articles to profl. jours. Chmn. bd. commrs. Redland Water Dist., Oregon City., 1980-83; trustee Atkinson Meml. Ch., Oregon City, 1980-84, moderator, 1991-92; commr. Clackamas County Fire Dist. Civil Svc., Oregon City, 1984—; bd. vis. Valparaiso U. Sch. Law, 1986-2001; Nat. Coun. Valparaiso U. Sch. Law, 2001—; planning com. Wichita State U. Pub. Utility Valuation Workshop, 1993—. With Peace Corps., Gonabad, Iran, 1966-70. Recipient Disting. Rsch. award Nat. Tax Assn.-Wichita State U. Mem. ABA, Fed. Energy Bar Assn. (mem. hydroelectric regulations com., rsch. and devel. com.), Multnomah County Bar Assn., Clark County Bar Assn. Republican. Muslim. Administrative and regulatory, FERC practice, State and local taxation. Home: 1505 Cherry Ln Lake Oswego OR 97034-6319 E-mail: thnelson@thnelson.com

NELSON, WALLACE JAY, patent attorney; b. Patrick County, Va., Aug. 1, 1926; s. Willie Everitt and Mollie Jane (Tudor) N.; m. Helen Nixon Blount Nelson, Oct. 27, 1951; children: Jane Elizabeth Shuart, Wallace J. Nelson Jr. BS, Va. Tech., Blacksburg, 1951; JD, The Am. U., Washington, 1960. Patent atty., U.S. Patent Office, Va. State Bar. Chem. lab. tech., analystical chemist Dept. U.S. Army, Radford, Va., 1951-55; patent examiner U.S. Patent Office, Washington, 1955-61; patent atty. Nat. Aeronautics and Space Adminstrn., Hampton, Va., 1961-86, pvt. practice, Hampton, 1986—. Inventor Slosh Alleviator, 1969. Mem. AF&AM #306 Masonic Lodge (past master), Scottish Rite of Freemasonry USA, Va. State bar. Methodist. Avocations: spectator sports, reading, golf, fishing. Home and Office: 34 Salt Pond Rd Hampton VA 23664-1736 E-mail: walheln@aol.com

NELSON, WALTER GERALD, retired insurance company executive; b. Peoria, Ill., Jan. 2, 1930; s. Walter Dennis and Hazel Marie (Tucker) Nelson; m. Mary Ann Olberding, Jan. 28, 1952 (dec. Nov. 1989); children: Ann Larkin, Michael, Susan Boor, Patrick, Thomas, Timothy, Molly Edwards; m. Mary Jo Sunderland, Apr. 06, 1991. Student, St. Benedict's Coll., Atchison, Kans., 1947-49, Bradley U., Peoria, Ill., 1949; JD, Creighton U., Omaha, 1952. Bar: Nebr 1952, Ill 1955. Practice in Peoria, 1955-56; with State Farm Life Ins. Co., Bloomington, Ill., 1956—, counsel, 1968—, v.p., 1970-96; adj. prof. Ill. State U., Bloomington, 1996—. Past dir Ill Life Ins Coun; past chmn legal sect Am Coun Life Ins; spkr in field. Contbr. articles to profl jours. Community bd dirs St Joseph Med Ctr, Bloomington, Ill., 1994. Mem.: ABA, Ill Bar Asn, Nebr Bar Asn, Asn Life Ins Counsel, Nat Orgn Life and Health Ins Guaranty Asns, Bloomington Country Club, KofC. Republican. Roman Catholic. E-mail: WGN1930@aol.com

NELSON, WILLIAM EUGENE, lawyer; b. Roland, Iowa, Sept. 23, 1927; s. Sam J. and Katherine A. (Coffey) N.; m. Sherlee M. Stanford, July 11, 1959; children: Anne, Kristin, William. BA, U. Iowa, 1950; JD, Drake U., 1957. Bar: Iowa 1957, D.C. 1965, Md. 1976. Trial atty. civil divsn. U.S. Dept. Justice, 1957-65, asst. chief tort sect., 1966-70, chief r.r. reorgn. unit, 1970-71; gen. counsel Cost of Living Coun. Phase I, 1971, chief econ. stblzn. sect., 1971-74; ptnr. Nelson and Nelson, LLP, Washington, Bethesda, Md., 1975—. Gen. counsel the Communicators, Inc., Myersville, Md. Assoc. editor Drake Law Rev., 1955-57. With USN, 1945-46. Recipient Atty. Gen.'s Disting. Svc. award, 1972. Mem. Order of Coif, Omicron Delta Kappa. General civil litigation, Estate planning, General practice. Home: 511 Colston Dr Falling Waters WV 25419 Office: Nelson & Nelson LLP 3 Bethesda Metro Ctr Ste 700 Bethesda MD 20814-6300 E-mail: sswen@aol.com

NELTNER, MICHAEL MARTIN, lawyer; b. Cin., July 31, 1959; s. Harold John and Joyce Ann Neltner; m. Barbara Ann Phair, July 9, 1988; children: Brandon August, Alexandra Nicole. BA, Mercy Coll., 1981; MA, Athenaeum of Ohio, 1987; JD, U. Cin., 1994. Bar: Ohio 1994, U.S. Dist. Ct. (so. dist.) Ohio 1995. Tchr. Elder H.S., Cin., 1985-91; ins. agt. Ky. Ctrl., 1987-91; mediator City of Cin., 1992-94; tchg. asst. Ohio Gov.'s Inst., Cin., 1992; legal extern to Chief Justice Thomas Moyer Ohio Supreme Ct., 1993; assoc. Eagen, Wykoff & Healy, LPA, Cin., 1994-99, Thompson Hine & Flory, Cin., 1999-2000, Freund, Freeze & Arnold, Cin., 2000—. Editor-in-chief Mercy Coll. Lit. Mag., 1980-81, U. Cin. Law Rev., 1993-94. Campaign coord. Rep. Orgn. Detroit, 1980. Recipient Merit scholarship Cin. Enquirer, 1977-81, Sage scholarship Mercy Coll., 1980, Am. Jurisprudence award Lawyers Coop. Publishing, 1994. Mem ABA, Ohio Bar Assn., Cin. Bar Assn. (mem. acad. medicine com. 1995—, chair Ct. Appeals com. 1998-2000). Estate planning, Insurance, Personal injury. Home: 3344 Milverton Ct Cincinnati OH 45248-2865 Office: Freund Freeze & Arnold LPA 105 E 4th St Cincinnati OH 45202-4006 E-mail: mneltner@ffalaw.com

NEMEROFF, MICHAEL ALAN, lawyer; b. Feb. 16, 1946; s. Bernard Gregor and Frances (Gotleib) N.; m. Sharon Lynn Leininger, Sept. 22, 1974; children: Theodore, Patrick, James. BA, U. Chgo., 1968; JD, Columbia U., 1971. Asst. counsel Subcom. on Juvenile Delinquency of Senate Jud. Com., Washington, 1971-73; assoc. Sidley & Austin, 1973-78, ptnr., 1978—. Treas. Friends of Jim Sasser, 1978-96, Andy Ireland Campaign Com., 1984-92. Administrative and regulatory, Government contracts and claims. Office: Sidley & Austin 1722 I St NW Fl 7 Washington DC 20006-3705

NEMETH, PATRICIA MARIE, lawyer; b. Flint, Mich., Sept. 18, 1959; d. Gyula Nemeth and Marie (Glaska) Adkins. BA, U. Mich., 1981; JD, Wayne State U., 1984, LLM, 1990. Bar: Ill. 1987, Mich. 1984, U.S. Ct. Appeals (6th cir.), U.S. Dist. Ct. (ea. dist.) Mich., U.S. Dist. Ct. (we. dist.) Mich. Teaching asst. Wayne State U., Detroit, 1982; intern. U.S. Dist. Ct. (ea. dist.) Mich., 1983; assoc. Bloom & Bloom, Birmingham, Mich., 1984-85, Stringari, Fritz, Kreger, Ahearn, Bennett & Hunsinger, Detroit, 1985-92; prin. Law Offices of Patricia Nemeth, P.C., 1992-97, Nemeth Burwell, P.C., Detroit, 1998—. Lectr. labor law seminar Inst. Continuing Legal Edn., 1990, Mich. Mcpl. Risk Mgmt. Assn., 1995; adj. prof. Walsh Coll., 1992-94; lectr. Health Care Assn. Mich., Joint Labor Mgmt. Coun., Am Soc. Employers. Guest appearance (TV) Straight Talk, 1994, 95; contbr. articles to profl. jours. Mem. adv. bd. Vista Maria, 2001—. Named one of Top 10 Best Places to Work in Southeastern Mich., Crain's/IKI. Mem. ABA (labor sect.), Mich. Bar Assn. (labor sect.), Ill. Bar Assn., Nat. Order Barristers, Nat. Assn. Women Bus. Owners (treas., exec. bd., bd. dirs.), Women Lawyers Assn. Mich., Detroit Bar Assn., Health Care Assn. of Mich., Small Bus. Assn. Mich. Roman Catholic. Avocations: sailing, golf, tennis, rollerblade. Civil rights, Labor. Office: 243 W Congress St Ste 1060 Detroit MI 48226-3214 E-mail: nemethburwell@michbar.org

NEMIR, DONALD PHILIP, lawyer; b. Oakland, Calif., Oct. 31, 1931; s. Philip F. and Mary (Shavor) N. AB, U. Calif., Berkeley, 1957, JD, 1960. Bar: Calif. 1961, U.S. Dist. Ct. (no. dist.) Calif. 1961, U.S. Ct. Appeals (9th cir.) 1961, U.S. Dist. Ct. (ctrl. dist.) Calif. 1975, U.S. Supreme Ct. 1980. Pvt. practice, San Francisco, 1961—. Pres. Law Offices of Donald Nemir, A Profl. Corp. Mem. Calif. State Bar Assn. General civil litigation, General corporate, Real property. Home: PO Box 1089 Mill Valley CA 94942-1089

NEMIROW, LAWRENCE H. lawyer; b. Bklyn., Dec. 4, 1948; s. Hyman W. Nemirow and Irma Carver; m. Sharz Dee Nemirow; children: Jennifer, Adam, Jaime. JD, Western State U., Fullerton, Calif., 1995; BBA, U. Detroit, 1978, MBA, 1980. V.p., ins. mgr. Ford Motor Co., Dearborn, Mich., 1973-80; dir. ins. and benefits John Morrell & Co., Northfield, Ill., 1980-84; dir. risk mgmt. Honda North Am., Torrance, Calif., 1985-88; prin., risk mgmt. Windes & McClaughry, Long Beach, 1988-89; risk mgmt. cons. The Nemirow Group, Los Alamitos, 1989-95; pvt. practice, 1995—. Amb. Cypress Chamber, Calif., 1988-98. Mem. ATLA, ABA, Orange County Bar Assn. Office: 5242 Katella Ave Ste 104 Los Alamitos CA 90720-2862 E-mail: nemirow@aol.com

NEMO, ANTHONY JAMES, lawyer; b. St. Paul, May 18, 1963; s. Joseph Marino Jr. and Dianne Marie (Wegner) N.; m. Mary Rose Mazzitello, July 17, 1987; children: Anne Marie, Katherine Mary, Anthony James Jr. BA in English Lit., U. St. Thomas, 1986; JD, William Mitchell Coll. Law, 1991. Bar: Minn. 1991, U.S. Dist. Ct. Minn., U.S. Dist. Ct. Ariz., U.S. Dist. Ct. (ea. dist.) Wis., U.S. Ct. Appeals (4th cir.), U.S. Supreme Ct. Account exec. div. info. svcs. TRW, Mpls., 1986-90; ptnr. Meshbesher & Spence, Ltd., St. Paul, 1990—. Assoc. editor William Mitchell Law Rev., 1988-90; author law rev. note. Recipient R. Ross Quaintance award, Douglas K. Amdahl-Mary O'Malley Lyons Trial Advocacy award. Mem. ABA, Minn. Trial Lawyers Assn., Assn. Trial Lawyers Am., Minn. State Bar Assn., Hennepin County Bar Assn., John P. Sheehy Legal History Soc. Roman Catholic. Criminal, Personal injury, Product liability. Home: 2125 Heath Ave N Oakdale MN 55128-5207 Office: Meshbesher & Spence Ltd 1616 Park Ave Minneapolis MN 55404

NEMON, NANCY SUSAN SCHECTMAN, lawyer; b. Providence, Jan. 20, 1943; d. Robert and Bessie (Greenberg) Schectman; m. Leonard I. Nemon, Oct. 24, 1971. A.B., Boston U., 1964; J.D., Harvard U., 1967. Bar: Mass. 1967, R.I. 1967, U.S. Dist. Ct. Mass. 1970, U.S. Ct. Appeals (2d cir.) 1987. Atty. John Hancock Mut. Life Ins. Co., Boston, 1967-72; dep. regional atty. HHS, Boston, 1972-86, dep. chief counsel, 1986-95, acting chief counsel, 1995-96, chief counsel, 1996—. Recipient Superior Service award HHS, 1982, Exceptional Service award HHS, 1987, Sec.'s Disting. Svc. award HHS, 1998. Mem. Mass. Bar Assn., R.I. Bar Assn., Boston Bar Assn., Harvard Law Sch. Assn., Phi Beta Kappa. Jewish. Office: HHS Office of Gen Counsel Jfk Federal Bldg Rm 2250 Boston MA 02203-0002

NEMSER, EARL HAROLD, lawyer; b. N.Y.C., Jan. 17, 1947; s. Harold Summers and Eleanor Patricia (Beckerman) N.; m. Randy Lynn Lehrer, June 17, 1974 (div.); children: Eliza Sarah, Maggie Lehrer. BA, NYU, 1967; JD magna cum laude, Boston U., 1970. Bar: N.Y. 1970, U.S. Supreme Ct. 1975, U.S. Claims Ct. 1979, U.S. Tax Ct. 1985. Law clk. hon. Collins J. Seitz chief judge U.S. Ct. Appeals 3rd Cir., 1970-71; ptnr. Cadwalader, Wickersham & Taft, N.Y.C., 1971-95, Swidler Berlin Shereff Friedman, LLP, N.Y.C., 1996—; pres. Park and 76th Street Co., Inc., 1998—. Vice chmn. Interactive Brokers Group, LLC, Greenwich, Conn., 1995—; dir. The Timber Hill, LLC, Greenwich, Caribbean Cellular Telephone Ltd., Tortola, BVI. Mem. ABA, Nat. Assn. Criminal Def. Lawyers, Assn. Bar City N.Y. State civil litigation, Contracts commercial, Securities. Office: Swidler Berlin Shereff Friedman LLP 405 Lexington Ave New York NY 10174-0002 E-mail: ehnemser@swidlaw.com

NEPPLE, JAMES ANTHONY, lawyer; b. Carroll, Iowa, Jan. 5, 1945; s. Herbert J. and Cecilia T. (Irlmeier) N.; m. Jeannine Ann Jennings, Sept. 9, 1967; children: Jeffrey B., Scott G., Carin J., Andrew J. BA, Creighton U., 1967; JD, U. Iowa, 1970; postgrad. in bus., Tex. Christian U., 1971; LLM in Taxation, NYU, 1982. Bar: Iowa 1970, U.S. Dist. Ct. (so. dist.) Iowa 1972, Ill. 1973, U.S. Dist. Ct. (cen. dist.) Ill. 1972, U.S. Dist. Ct.(no. dist.) Iowa 1975, U.S. Ct. Appeals (7th and 8th cirs.) 1975, U.S. Supreme Ct. 1975, U.S. Ct. Claims 1976, U.S. Tax Ct. 1976. Tax acct. Arthur Young & Co., Chgo., 1970; v.p., treas., bd. dirs. Stanley, Rehling, Lande & VanDerKamp, Muscatine, Iowa, 1972-92; pres. Nepple, VanDerKamp & Flynn, P.C., Rock Island, Ill., 1992-98; prin. Nepple Law Offices, P.L.C., 1999—. Scoutmaster Boy Scouts Am., Muscatine, 1982-85; trustee State Hist. Soc. Iowa, 1986-92, vice-chmn., 1991-92; bd. dirs. Iowa Hist. Found., 1988-95, pres., 1991-93. Capt. U.S. Army, 1971-72. Recipient Gov.'s Vol. award State of Iowa, 1988, 90, Jr. Achievement of the Quad Cities Bronze award, 1996, Silver award, 2000. Fellow ABA (tax sect. 1972—, chair agrl. tax com. 2001—), Am. Coll. Trust and Estate Counsel, Am. Bar Found., Iowa Bar Found.; mem. Ia (tax com. 1979-91, chmn. 1988-91), Fed. Bar Assn., Ill. Bar Assn. (mem. fed. tax. sect. coun. 1993-99, chair 1997-98), Muscatine Bar Assn. (pres. 1982-83), Scott County Bar Assn., Rock Island County Bar Assn., Iowa Assn. Bus. and Industry (tax. com. 1978—, chmn. 1986-88, leadership Iowa award 1985), Quad City Estate Planning Coun. (pres. 1987), Muscatine C. of C. (pres. 1985), Geneva Golf and Country Club (pres. 1990-91), Kiwanis (pres. Muscatine chpt. 1978), Elks. Republican. Roman Catholic. Estate planning, Pension, profit-sharing, and employee benefits, Taxation, general. Home: 2704 Mulberry Ave Muscatine IA 52761-2746 Fax: 563-264-6844. E-mail: jim@nepplelaw.com

NESBIT, PHYLLIS SCHNEIDER, judge; b. Newkirk, Okla., Sept. 21, 1919; d. Vernon Lee and Irma Mae (Biddle) Schneider; m. Peter Nicholas Nesbit, Sept. 14, 1939. BS in Chemistry, U. Ala., 1948, BS in Law, 1958, JD, 1969. Bar: Ala. 1958. Ptnr. Wilters, Brantley and Nesbit, Robertsdale, Ala., 1958-74; pvt. practice, 1974-76; dist. judge Baldwin County Juvenile Ct., 1977-88; supernumerary dist. judge and juvenile ct. judge Baldwin County, 1989—. Bd. dirs. Baldwin Youth Svcs.; bd. dirs., v.p. women's activities So. Ala. chpt. Nat. Safety Coun., 1978-83; chmn. quality assurance com. The Homestead Retirement Village, 1992-95. Mem. Nat. Assn. Women Lawyers, Nat. Assn. Women Judges, N.Am. Judges Assn., Ala. Dist. Judges Assn., Ala. Coun. Juvenile Judges, Am. Judicature Soc., Baldwin County Bar Assn., Baldwin Sr. Travelers (sec. 1994-98), Spanish Fort, Fairhope Bus. and Profl. Women's, Phi Alpha Delta. Democrat. Methodist.

NESBITT, CHARLES RUDOLPH, lawyer, energy consultant; b. Miami, Okla., Aug. 30, 1921; s. Charles Rudolph and Irma Louise (Wilhelmi) N.; m. Margot Dorothy Lord, June 6, 1948; children: Nancy Margot Nesbitt Nagle, Douglas Charles, Carolyn Jane Nesbitt Gresham. BA, U. Okla., 1942; JD, Yale U., 1947. Bar: Okla. 1947, U.S. Supreme Ct. 1957. Pvt. practice, Oklahoma City, 1948-62, 67-69, 75-91, 95—; atty. gen. Okla., 1963-67; mem. Okla. Corp. Commn., 1968-75, chmn., 1969-75; sec. of energy State of Okla., Oklahoma City, 1991-95; pvt. practice, 1995—. Okla. rep., v.p. Interstate Oil and Gas Compact. Bd, dirs., trustee endowment fund St. Gregory's Coll.; trustee Oklahoma City U.; pres. Hist. Preservation, Inc.; pres. bd. trustees Okla. Mus. Art; v.p., bd. dirs. Western History Collections Assocs., U. Okla. Librs.; mem. panel arbitrators Am. Arbitration Assn., NASD, NYSE; mem. Ecclesiastical Ct., Diocese Okla. With AUS, 1942-46. Mem. Am., Okla. bar assns., Oklahoma City C. of C., Phi Beta Kappa, Phi Delta Phi. Episcopalian. General civil litigation, Oil, gas, and mineral, General practice. Home: 1703 N Hudson Ave Oklahoma City OK 73103-3428 Office: 125 NW 6th St Oklahoma City OK 73102-6014

NESBITT, SEAN MILO, lawyer; b. Glasgow, United Kingdom, Feb. 25, 1966; BA with honors, Oxford U., England, 1987; Common Profl. Exam., Trent Polytechnic, Nottingham, 1988, Law Society Finals, 1989. Solicitor Slaughter and May, London, 1991-97; ptnr., solicitor Garretts, 1997—. Immigration, naturalization, and customs, Labor. Office: Garretts Solicitors 2 Arundel St WC2R 3GA London England Fax: 44 020 7466 6623. E-mail: sean.nesbitt@glegal.com

NESCI, VINCENT PETER, lawyer; b. New Rochelle, N.Y., Feb. 27, 1947; s. Vincent S. and Carmela (DeMasi) N.; m. Donna M. Dahlgren, July 21, 1968; children: Vincent P. Jr., Joseph E., Patricia A. BA, Sacred Heart U., 1969; JD, St. John's U., 1971. Bar: N.Y. 1972, U.S. Dist. Ct. (ea. dist.) N.Y. 1973, U.S. Dist. Ct. (so. dist.) N.Y. 1978), U.S. Supreme Ct. 1976. Assoc. Campbell, Hyman & Lang, New Rochelle, 1972-76; ptnr. Lang & Nesci, P.C., 1976-79; pvt. practice Yonkers, N.Y., 1980-93. Gen. counsel Liberty Lines, Yonkers, 1979-93; CEO Specialized Risk Mgmt., White Plains, N.Y., 1993—; mgr. ptnr. Nesci Keane Piekarski Keogh & Corrigan, White Plains, 1993—; cons. Summit Investment, Queensland, Australia, 1992—. Avocation: auto racing. State civil litigation, Personal injury, Transportation. Home: RR 2 Bedford NY 10506-9802 Office: 305 Old Tarrytown Rd White Plains NY 10603-2825 E-mail: vpn@aol.com

NESLAND, JAMES EDWARD, lawyer; b. Mobridge, S.D., Aug. 13, 1944; s. Virgil Robert and Thelma Loretta Nesland; m. Carol Ann Ide, Nov. 9, 1946; children: Matthew James, John Edward. BA, U. Denver, 1966; JD, George Washington U., 1970. Bar: N.Y. 1971, U.S. Dist. Ct. (so. dist.) N.Y. 1971, U.S. Ct. Appeals (2nd cir.) 1971, U.S. D.C. Colo. 1976, U.S. Ct. Appeals (10th cir.) 1976, Colo. 1977, U.S. Supreme Ct. 1988. Assoc. Donovan Leisure Newton & Irvine, N.Y.C., 1970-73; asst. U.S. atty. U.S. Atty.'s Office, 1973-76, Denver, 1977-78; assoc., ptnr. Ireland, Stapleton LLC, 1978-94; ptnr. Cooley Godward LLP, 1994—. Assoc. spl. coun. Pres. Jimmy Carter Warehouse Inv., 1979. Author: Federal Criminal Law, 1988. Mem. ABA, Colo. Bar Assn., Denver Bar Assn. General civil litigation, Criminal. Home: 14252 E Caley Ave Aurora CO 80016-1090 Office: Cooley Godward LLP 1200 17th St Ste 2100 Denver CO 80202-5821 E-mail: neslandje@cooley.com

NESS, ANDREW DAVID, lawyer; b. San Francisco, Oct. 29, 1952; s. Orville Arne and Muriel Ruth (Trendt) N.; m. Rita M. Kobylenski, May 25, 1980; children: Katherine, Austin, Emily. BS, Stanford U., 1974; JD, Harvard U., 1977. Bar: Calif. 1977, D.C. 1979, Va. 1986, U.S. Dist. Ct. (no. dist.) Calif. 1977, U.S. Dist. Ct. D.C. 1983, U.S. Dist. Ct. (ea. dist.) Va. 1988, U.S. Ct. Appeals (4th cir.) 1989. Law clk. U.S. Dist. Ct., San Francisco, 1977-78; assoc. Lewis, Mitchell & Moore, Vienna, 1979-82, ptnr., 1982-87, Morgan, Lewis & Bockius LLP, Washington, 1987-2000, Thelen Reid & Priest LLP, Washington, 2000—, mng. ptnr. D.C. office, 2001—. Instr. U. Md., College Park, 1987-90; mem. faculty constrn. exec. program Stanford (Calif.) U., 1984-87. Contbr. chpt. to books, articles to profl. jours. Mem. ABA (forum on constrn. industry, pub. contract law sect.). Avocations: hiking, bicycling. Construction, Government contracts and claims. Office: Thelen Reid & Priest LLP 701 Pennsylvania Ave NW Washington DC 20004-2608 E-mail: adness@thelenreid.com

NETEMEYER, MARGARET, lawyer; b. Breese, Ill., June 27, 1950; d. Alvin Gehart and Rita (Kues) N.; m. Leonard J. Cockerill, Mar. 5, 1983; children: Leslie Anne, Patrick Allen, Kasey, Alexander. BA, U. Ill., 1975, MA, 1976; JD, U. Tex., 1979; LLM in Taxation, NYU, 1982. Bar: Tex. 1979, U.S. Tax Ct. 1984; cert. estate planning Tex. Bd. Legal Specialization. Tax lawyer IRS, San Antonio, 1979-81; assoc. Cox & Smith, 1982-83, Plunkett, Gibson & Allen, San Antonio, 1983-96; sole practice, 1996—. Mem. San Antonio Estate Planners. Mem. Tex. Bar Assn., San Antonio Bar Assn. Probate, Estate planning, Estate taxation. Office: 929 Contour Dr San Antonio TX 78212-1763

NETTER, MIRIAM MACCOBY, lawyer; b. Nov. 30, 1935; d. Max and Dora Maccoby; m. Howard R. Netter, June 24, 1956 (dec. 1995); children: Mark, Beth Ann. BA, Brown U., 1956; JD cum laude, Union U., Albany, N.Y., 1972. Bar: N.Y. 1973, U.S. Dist. Ct. (no. dist.) N.Y. 1973, U.S. Ct. Appeals (2d cir.) 1990, U.S. Supreme Ct. 1984. Unemployment ins. claims examiner Dept. Labor State of N.Y., Rochester, 1956-59; tchr. Rush-Henrietta Sch., 1959-60; assoc. Harvey M. Lifset, Esquire, Albany, 1973, Pattison, Herzog, Sampson & Nichols, 1974-79; ptnr. Pattison, Sampson, Ginsberg & Griffin, P.C., Troy, N.Y., 1974-92; pvt. practice, 1992—. Mem. Com. on Character and Fitness 3d Jud. Dept. N.Y. State Supreme Ct., Albany, 1981— (gender fairness com., 1998—). Lead articles editor Albany Law Rev., 1971-72. Mem. exec. com. Legal Aid Soc. Northeastern N.Y., Albany, 1977-86, 1st c.p., 1982-84, pres. 1984-86; legal advisor, dir. Kidney Found. N.E. N.Y., Albany, 1983-97; founder Kate Stoneman Soc. at Albany Law Sch. Recipient Kate Stoneman award Albany Law Sch., 1996. Fellow ABA Found.; mem. N.Y. State Bar Assn (v.p. 3d judge dist. 1995-99, co-chaor copyright com, 1995-2000, intellectual property exec. comm. 1995—, chair membership com. 1986-89, Ho. of Dels. 1988-92, 93-99, 2000-01, nominating com. 1992-93, 98—, com. jud. selection 1988-95, women in law 1992-95) legal project cap. dist. Women's Bar, hon. dir. 1999—, Women's Bar Assn N.Y. (capital dist. chpt.), Albany County Bar Assn., Rensselaer County Bar Assn. (v.p. 1990-92, pres. 1993, exec. com. 1994—), Phi Kappa Phi. General corporate, Trademark and copyright. Home: 28 Devon Rd Delmar NY 12054-3534 Office: care MapInfo 1 Global Vw Troy NY 12180-8371 E-mail: mimi.netter@mapinfo.com

NETTLES, BERT SHEFFIELD, lawyer; b. Monroeville, Ala., May 6, 1936; s. George Lee and Blanche (Sheffield) N.; m. Elizabeth Duquet, Sept. 16, 1967; children: Jane, Mary Katherine, Susan, Anne. BS, U. Ala., Tuscaloosa, 1958, JD, 1960. Bar: Ala. 1960. Asst. atty. gen. State of Ala., Montgomery, 1961-62; ptnr. Johnston, Johnston & Nettles, Mobile, Ala., 1962-69, Nettles & Cox, Mobile, 1969-81, Nettles, Barker, Janecky & Copeland, Mobile, 1981-89, Spain, Gillon, Grooms, Blan & Nettles, Birmingham, Ala., 1989-94, London & Yancey, Birmingham, 1995—. Contbr. articles to profl. jours. Mem. Ala. Ho. of Reps., 1969-74; bd. dirs. U. South Ala. Med. Sci. Found., Mobile, 1982-89, U. So. Ala. Health Svcs. Found., 1985-89; chancellor Episcopal Diocese of Cen. Gulf Coast, Mobile, 1983-88; asst. chancellor Episcopal Diocese of Ala., 2000—. 2d lt. inf. U.S. Army, 1960-61. Recipient Exceptional Performance citation Def. Rsch. Inst. and ATLA, 1987. Mem. ABA (chmn. standing com. on legis. 1978), Ala. Bar Assn. (chmn. young lawyers divsn. 1966-67, chair task force on appellate restructuring 1988-91), Am. Right of Way Assn. (sr.), Ala. Def. Lawyers Assn. (pres. 1986-87), Ala. Supreme Ct. (com. on appellate rules 2001—, pattern jury instructions/civil, 1990—). Republican. Avocations: reading, children. General civil litigation, Insurance, Professional liability. Home: 1416 Windsor Cir Birmingham AL 35213-3434 Office: London & Yancey 2001 Park Pl Birmingham AL 35203-2735

NEUER, PHILIP DAVID, lawyer, real estate consultant; b. Bklyn., May 31, 1946; s. Murray and Adele (Jacobs) N.; m. Rena Donna Levine, July 30, 1972 (div. 1987); children: Jeremy Evan, Linzy Michelle, Sari Faith. BBA, CCNY, 1968; postgrad., Boston U., 1968-69; JD, Seton Hall U., 1976. Bar: N.J. 1976, U.S. Dist. Ct. N.J. 1977, U.S. Supreme Ct. 1980. Asst. town atty. Town of West Orange (N.J.), 1976-77; assoc. Margolis and Bergstein, Verona, N.J., 1979-80; ptnr. Slavitt and Slavitt, West Orange, 1980-81; assoc. Mandelbaum and Targan, 1981-83; ptnr. Margolis Neuer, Verona, 1984-91; of counsel Slavitt Simon & Neuer, Parsippany, 1991-2000; exec. v.p., gen. counsel Safer Textiles Group, Safer Devel. and Mgmt. Co., Newark, 1993—; of counsel Lum, Danzis, Drasco, Positan & Kleinberg, LLC, Roseland, N.J., 2000—. Mem. editl. bd. Internat. Jour. for Corp. Real Estate, 1998—. With USN, 1969-73. Mem. ABA, N.J. State Bar Assn., Essex County Bar Assn., Internat. Assn. Corp. Real Estate Execs. (pres., bd. dirs., gen. counsel N.J. chpt., designated internat. assoc., Mem. of Yr. 1993, N.J. Corp. Real Exec. of Yr. 1993, internat. bd. dirs.), Inst. Corporate Real Estate (bd. dirs., pres. 1998—), Internat. Real Estate Inst. (registered internat. mem.), Urban Land Inst., Mensa. Contracts commercial, Land use and zoning (including planning), Real property. Office: 1875 McCarter Hwy Newark NJ 07104-4211 E-mail: pdneuer@aol.com

NEUGARTEN, JERROLD LEE, lawyer; b. Chgo., May 18, 1948; s. Fritz and Bernice (Levin) N.; m. Rhea Kemble, Aug. 21, 1971 (div. Dec. 1978); m. Charlotte Gordon Carter, July 9, 1982; children: Rachel, Sarah, Carter. BA, New Coll., Sarasota, Fla., 1968; JD, Harvard U., 1972. Bar: N.Y. 1972, U.S. Dist. Ct. (so. and ea. dists.) 1972, U.S. Ct. Appeals (2d cir.) 1973, U.S. Supreme Ct. 1976. Dep. chief N.Y. County Narcotics Bur., N.Y.C., 1976-77; spl. asst. N.Y.C. Spl. Narcotics Prosecutor, N.Y.C., 1977-78; dep. chief appeals bur. N.Y. County Dist. Atty.'s Office, N.Y.C., 1978-80, sr. appellate counsel, 1980-81, dir. of tng., 1981-86, spl. asst. to dist. atty., 1983-86; coord. N.Y. State Law Enforcement Coun., 1982-86; spl. asst. to dir. Organized Crime Task Force State of N.Y., 1986—. Mem. N.Y. State Dist. Attys. Assn. (legis. sec. 1981-88). Democrat. Avocation: classical guitar.

NEUHAUS, JOSEPH EMANUEL, lawyer; b. Glen Ridge, N.J., Aug. 17, 1957; s. Gottfried and Helen (Bull) N.; m. Cynthia Ann Loomis. BA, Dartmouth Coll., 1979; JD, Columbia U., 1982. Bar: N.Y. 1986, D.C. 1986, U.S. Dist. Ct. (so. and ea. dists.) N.Y. 1987. Law clk. to sr. judge U.S. Ct. Appeals, Washington, 1982-83; law clk. to Hon. Lewis F. Powell, Jr. U.S. Supreme Ct., 1983-84; legal asst. Iran-U.S. Claims Tribunal, The Hague, Netherlands, 1984-85; assoc. Covington & Burling, Washington, 1986-87, Sullivan & Cromwell, N.Y.C., 1987-91, ptnr., 1992—. Co-author: Guide to the UNCITRAL Model Law on International Commercial Arbitration, 1989. Mem. Assn. Bar City N.Y. (com. sec. 1989-92). E-mila. General civil litigation, Private international. E-mail: neuhausj@sullcrom.com

NEUMAN, ERIC PATT, lawyer; b. Altoona, Pa., Mar. 22, 1948; s. Milton and Florence Louise (Patt) N. A.B. summa cum laude, Princeton U., 1971; J.D., Georgetown U., 1974. Bar: Ga. 1974, D.C. 1980, Md. 1983. Assoc. Powell, Goldstein, Frazer & Murphy, Atlanta, 1974-78, Hogan & Hartson, Washington, 1978-79; of counsel Lee F. Holdmann, Bethesda, Md., 1981-85; assoc. Berlin, Sequin, Karam & Ramos, C.P.A.s, Silver Spring, Md., 1985-86, Wilner & Scheiner, Washington, 1986-87, Law Offices of Eric P. neuman, 1989-95; dir. Internat. Coal Mktg. and Sales, Inc.; instr.

Montgomery Coll., 1981-83, Mt. Vernon Coll., 1982-83, Georgetown U., 1993—. Mem. ABA, Ga. State Bar Assn., D.C. Bar Assn., Montgomery County Bar Assn., Phi Beta Kappa. Jewish. Club: Bethesda Racquet and Health. Estate planning, Probate, Estate taxation. Office: Morton J Frome PA 109 N Adams St Rockville MD 20850-2234

NEUMAN, LINDA KINNEY, state supreme court justice; b. Chgo., June 18, 1948; d. Harold S. and Mary E. Kinney; m. Henry G. Neuman; children: Emily, Lindsey. BA, U. Colo., 1970, JD, 1973; LLM, U. Va., 1998. Ptnr. Betty, Neuman, McMahon, Hellstrom & Bittner, 1973-79; v.p., trust officer Bettendorf Bank & Trust Co., 1979-80; dist. ct. judge, 1982-86; supreme ct. justice State of Iowa, 1986—. Mem. adj. faculty U. Iowa Grad. Sch. of Social Work, 1981; part-time jud. magistrate Scott County, 1980-82; mem. Supreme Ct. continuing legal edn. commn.; chair Iowa Supreme Ct. commn. planning 21st Century; mem. bd. counselors Drake Law Sch., time on appeal adv. com. Nat. Ctr. State Cts. Trustee St. Ambrose U. Recipient Regents scholarship, U. Colo. award for disting. svc. Fellow ABA (chair appellate judges conf., mem. appellate standards com., JAD exec. coun.); mem. Am. Judicature Soc., Iowa Bar Assn., Iowa Judges Assn., Scott County Bar Assn., Nat. Assn. Woman Judges (bd. dirs.), Dillon Am. Inn of Ct., U.S. Assn. Constl. Law. E-mail: linda.k.neuman@jb.state.ia.us

NEUMANN, RITA NUNEZ, lawyer; b. New Brunswick, N.J., Apr. 23, 1944; d. Arno Otto and Florence (Alligier) N. BA in Math., Trenton State Coll., 1965; MS in Math., Stevens Inst. Tech., 1970; JD, Seton Hall U., 1976; LLM in Tax Law, U. San Diego, 1983. Bar: D.C. 1984, U.S. Tax Ct. 1984, N.Y. 1985, N.J. 1986, U.S. Supreme Ct. 1989, Mont. 1990, U.S. Ct. Appeals (9th cir.) 1991. Instr. math. Middlesex County Coll., Edison, N.J., 1971-74; tax cons. Evan Morris Esq. Offices, Woodland Hills, Calif., 1975-85; asst. to editor Jour. Taxation, N.Y.C., 1985-86; pvt. practice law New Brunswick, 1986-94, Las Cruces, N.Mex., 1994—; mcpl. prosecutor Manville, N.J., 1987. Adj. instr. bus. law and fin. L.A. C.C. Dist., 1976-82; adj. instr. law and bus. calculus Ventura (Calif.) C.C. Dist., 1977-82; adj. prof. bus. calculus Calif. State U., Northridge, 1981-83; adj. instr. internat. law Laverne U. and San Fernando Valley Coll. Law, 1983-85; disting. lectr. in law and mgmt. Troy State U., Holloman AFB/White Sands Missile Range. Author: Doing Business in North America, 1994, 95, 96; contbr. articles to profl. publs. Vol. to farm workers ctr., Moorpark, Calif., 1979; instr. community extension ctr. for women, Calif., 1980; vol. atty. for N.J. Vietnam Vets., 1986; organizer 10-kilometer run to benefit ill children, Manville, N.J., 1986; guest lectr. taxes Second Ann. Bus. Seminar for Vets. and Non-Vet. Am. Indians of N.W. U.S., Billings, Mont., 1988; candidate for freeholder, Middlesex County, 1988; active with numerous Am. Indian tribes thoughout the U.S. in bus. devel. and Indian rights. Fellow Nat. Sci. Found., 1968-71. Mem. Kappa Delta Phi. Avocation: 10-kilometer runs (recipient several medals). Labor. Office: 1850 N Solano Dr Las Cruces NM 88001-1851

NEUMANN, WILLIAM ALLEN, state supreme court justice; b. Minot, N.D., Feb. 11, 1944; s. Albert W. and Opal Olive (Whitlock) N.; m. Jaqueline Denise Buechler, Aug. 9, 1980; children: Andrew, Emily. BSBA, U. N.D., 1965; JD, Stanford U., 1968. Bar: N.D. 1969, U.S. Dist. Ct. N.D. 1969. Pvt. practice law, Williston, N.D., 1969-70, Bottineau, 1970-79; former judge N.D. Judicial Dist. Ct., N.E. Judicial Dist., Rugby and Bottineau, 1979-92; justice N.D. Supreme Ct., Bismarck, 1993—. Chmn. elect N.D. Jud. Conf., 1985-87, chmn. 1987-89. Mem. ABA, State Bar Assn. N.D., Am. Judicature Soc. (bd. dirs. 1998—). Lutheran. Office: ND Supreme Ct Jud Wing 1st Fl Dept 180 600 E Boulevard Ave Bismarck ND 58505-0530

NEUMARK, MICHAEL HARRY, lawyer; b. Cin., Oct. 28, 1945; s. Jacob H. and Bertha (Zubor) N.; m. Sue Daly, June 5, 1971; children: Julie Rebecca, John Adam. BS in Bus., Ind. U., 1967; JD, U. Cin., 1970. Bar: Ohio 1970, D.C. 1972. Atty. chief counsel's office IRS, Washington, 1970-74, acting br. chief, 1974-75, sr. atty. regional counsel's office, 1975-77; assoc. Paxton & Seasongood Legal Profl. Assn., 1977-80; ptnr. Thompson, Hine & Flory, 1980—, mem. mgmt. com., 1993—. Chmn. So. Ohio Tax Inst., 1987; mem. IRS and Bar Liaison Com., 1991-93; spkr. at profl. confs. Contbr. articles to profl. jours. Bd. dirs. 1987 World Figure Skating Chamionship, Cin., 1986-89; precinct exec. Hamilton County Rep. Orgn., 1980-86; vol. referee Hamilton County Juvenile Ct., 1980-86; trustee Cin. Contemporary Arts Ctr., St. Rita Sch. for Deaf, 1991-97, Legal Aid Soc. Cin., 1997—. Recipient Commendation Resolution Sycamore Twp., 1987. Mem. ABA (del. 1999—), Ohio State Bar Assn., Cin. Bar Assn. (pres. 1996-97, recognition award 1985, treas., bd. trustees 1988-91, trustee 1992—, chair tax sect., 1990-91), Leadership Cin., Ohio Met. Bar Assn. (pres. 1996-97), Kenwood Country Club, Indian Hill Club, Ohio Met. Bar (pres. 1996-97), Cin. Acad. of Leadership for Lawyers (founder, chair). Republican. Avocations: golf, travel. General corporate, Taxation, general. Office: Thompson Hine & Flory 312 Walnut St Ste 1400 Cincinnati OH 45202-4089

NEUMEIER, MATTHEW MICHAEL, lawyer, educator; b. Racine, Wis., Sept. 13, 1954; s. Frank Edward and Ruth Irene (Effenberger) N.; m. Annmarie Prine, Jan. 31, 1987; children: Ruthann Marie, Emilie Irene, Matthew Charles. B in Gen. Studies with distinction, U. Mich., 1981; JD magna cum laude, Harvard U., 1984. Bar: N.Y. 1987, Mich. 1988, Ill. 1991, U.S. Dist. Ct. (ea. dist.) Mich. 1988, U.S. Dist. Ct. (ea., no. dists. and trial bar) Ill. 1991, U.S. Ct. Appeals (7th cir.) 1992, U.S. Ct. Appeals (fed. cir.) 1998, U.S. Supreme Ct. 1991. Sec.-treas. Ind. Roofing & Siding Co., Escanaba, Mich., 1973-78; mng. ptnr. Ind. Roofing Co., Menominee, 1977-78; law clk. to presiding justice U.S. Ct. Appeals (9th cir.), San Diego, 1984-85; law clk. to chief justice Warren E. Burger U.S. Supreme Ct., Washington, 1985-86; spl. asst. to chmn. U.S. Constn. Bicentennial Commn., 1986; assoc. Cravath, Swaine & Moore, N.Y.C., 1986-88; spl. counsel Burnham & Ritchie, Ann Arbor, Mich., 1988; assoc. Schlussel, Lifton, Simon, Rands, Galvin & Jackier, P.C., 1988-90, Skadden, Arps, Slate, Meagher & Flom, Chgo., 1990-96; ptnr. Jenner & Block, 1996—. Adj. prof. computer law and high tech. litig. John Marshall Law Sch., Chgo., 1999—. Editor Harvard Law Rev., 1982-84. Pres., bd. dirs. Univ. Cellar Inc., Ann Arbor, 1979-81; bd. dirs. Econ. Devel. Corp., Menominee, 1978-79, Midwestern divsn. Am. Suicide Found., sec., 1992-97, Commonwealth Plaza Condominium Assn., dir., 1999—, pres., 2000—; mem. vestry Ch. of Our Savior, 1997-2000; bd. dirs. Chgo. Children's Mus., 1999—; chmn. Harvard Law Sch. 15 Yr. Reunion Gift Fund, 1999. Mem. ABA, State Bar Mich., Assn. of Bar of City of N.Y., Chgo. Bar Assn., Def. Rsch. Inst., The 410 Club, Econ. Club Chgo. Republican. Avocations: classic automobiles, piano, choir. General civil litigation, Consumer commercial, Product liability. Office: Jenner & Block Ste 4200 One IBM Plz Chicago IL 60611 E-mail: mneumeier@jenner.com

NEUMEIER, RICHARD L. lawyer; b. Boston, Nov. 22, 1946; s. Victor L. and Crystal Gladys (Mueller) N.; m. Mary Edna Malcolm, Mar. 15, 1975; children: Hannah Catherine, Edmund Malcolm, Thomas Richard. AB, AM, U. Chgo., 1968; JD, Columbia U., 1971. Bar: N.Y. 1972, U.S. Dist. Ct. (so. dist.) N.Y. 1972, Mass. 1973, U.S. Dist. Ct. Mass. 1973, U.S. Ct. Appeals (1st cir.) 1974, R.I. 1979, U.S. Supreme Ct. 1985. Assoc. Hart & Hume, N.Y.C., 1971-73; from assoc. to ptnr. Parker, Coulter, Daley & White, Boston, 1973-95; ptnr. McDonough, Hacking & Neumeier, LLP, 1995—. Mem. editl. bd. Def. Counsel Jour., 1989-92, editor, chmn. bd. editors, 1992—; mem. editl. bd. Boston Bar Jour., 1988-94; contbr. articles to profl. jours. Bd. dirs. Common Cause/Mass., Boston, 1980-91, 94-96, chmn., 1990-91; active Town Meeting, Lexington, Mass., 1989—. Fellow Am. Bar Found.; mem. ABA, Fed. Bar Assn. (pres. Mass. chpt. 1989-90), Am. Law Inst., Mass. Bar Assn., Boston Bar Assn. (chmn. ethics com. 1991-94, chmn. torts com. 1994-96), Internat. Assn. Def. Counsel (exec. com. 1992-97). Democrat. Civil rights, Insurance, Personal injury. Home: 2 Pitcairn Pl Lexington MA 02421-7134 Office: McDonough Hacking & Neumeier LLP 11 Beacon St Ste 1000 Boston MA 02108-3013 E-mail: rneumeier@mhnattys.com

NEUMEYER, DEBORA HEWITT, lawyer; b. La Grange, Ill., June 24, 1967; d. Thomas Edward and Jeraldine (Spurgeon) Hewitt; m. Gregory Wayne Neumeyer, Nov. 30, 1996; children: Katherine Marie, Matthew Thomas. BA, DePauw U., 1989; JD, Drake U., 1991. Bar: Iowa 1992, Minn. 1992. Jud. law clk. to Hon. Albert Habhab Iowa Ct. Appeals, Des Moines, 1992; asst. atty. gen. Iowa Atty. Gen., 1992-96, Cedar Rapids, 1996—. Bd. dirs. Jr. League, Cedar Rapids, 1999—. Mem. ABA, P.E.O. (treas. 1998-99), Iowa State Bar Assn., (young lawyers divsn., sec. 1998-99, pres.-elect 1999-2000, pres. 2000-2001), Linn County Bar Assn. Republican. Methodist. Home: 1685 Mackenzie Dr Cedar Rapids IA 52411-9503 Office: PO Box 11351 Cedar Rapids IA 52410-1351

NEUNER, GEORGE WILLIAM, lawyer; b. Buffalo, Oct. 3, 1943; s. George J. and Geraldine M. (O'Connor) N.; m. Kathleen M. Stoeckl, Aug. 28, 1965; children: George W., Kathleen E. BSChemE, SUNY, Buffalo, 1965; SM, MIT, 1966; JD, George Washington U., 1975. Bar: Va. 1975, N.Y. 1976, D.C. 1976, Mass. 1978, U.S. Dist. Ct. Mass. 1978, U.S. Ct. Appeals (Fed. cir.) 1982. From engr. to patent atty. Eastman Kodak Co., Rochester, N.Y., 1966-77; assoc. Dike Bronstein Roberts & Cushman, LLP, Boston, 1977-80, ptnr., 1980—, mng. ptnr., 1988—; ptnr. Edwards & Angell, LLP, 2000—. Arbitration panelist 4th Judicial Dept., Rochester, 1976-77. Grantee Sun Oil Co. MIT, 1966. Mem. ABA, Mass. Bar Assn., Am. Intellectual Property Lawyers Assn., Boston Patent Law Assn. (treas. 1985-86, v.p. 1986-87, pres. elect 1987-88, pres. 1988-89, U.S. Bar/Japanese Patent Office liason coun. 1990—, vice chair 1999-2000, chair 2001—), Assn. Patent Law Firms (sec. 1999, pres. 2000), Fed. Cir. Bar Assn., Tau Beta Pi, MIT Club (Rochester) (bd. dirs. 1976-77). Federal civil litigation, Patent, Trademark and copyright. Home: 8 Ravenscroft Rd Winchester MA 01890-3807 Office: Dike Bronstein Roberts & Cushman LLP IP Group Edwards & Angell 101 Federal St Boston MA 02110-1817 also: Edwards & Angell LLP 101 Federal St Boston MA 02110-1817 E-mail: gneuner@ealaw.com

NEUNER, ROBERT, lawyer; b. N.Y.C., Dec. 11, 1938; s. John G.R. and Helen C. (Shanley) N.; m. Claire A. Cavaliere, Jan. 27, 1961; children: Kristin Lynne, Karen Elizabeth, Robert Christopher, Christopher Michael. BEE, Manhattan Coll., 1960; LLB, Fordham U., 1965. Bar: U.S. Dist. Ct. (so. dist.) N.Y. 1967, U.S. Dist. Ct. (ea. dist.) N.Y. 1978, U.S. Ct. Customs and Patent Appeals 1979, U.S. Ct. Appeals (1st cir.) 1971, U.S. Ct. Appeals (2d cir.) 1975, U.S. Ct. Appeals (3d cir.) 1972, U.S. Supreme Ct. 1980, U.S. Ct. Appeals (D.C. cir.) 1982, U.S. Ct. Appeals (4th cir.) 1983, U.S. Ct. Appeals (7th cir.) 1984. Ptnr. Brumbaugh, Graves, Donohue & Raymond, N.Y.C., 1965—, Baker Botts L.L.P. Lectr. on patent litigation techniques and practice before U.S. Internat. Trade Commn., Practicing Law Inst., 1974—. Former columnist N.Y. Law Jour.; contbr. articles to profl. jours. Mem. bd. edn. Teaneck, N.J., 1969-72. Mem. Am. Intellectual Property Law Assn. (pres. 2001-02), Assn. Bar City N.Y. (com. on profl. and jud. ethics 1976-78, com. on fed. cts. 1982-85, com. on antitrust and trade regulation 1985—). Patent, Trademark and copyright, Banking. Office: Baker Botts LLP 30 Rockefeller Plz New York NY 10112-0002 E-mail: robert.neuner@bakerbotts.com

NEUSTADT, PAUL, lawyer; b. N.Y.C., July 6, 1931; s. Samuel and Etta (Gottlieb) N.; m. Zelda Miller, June 21, 1959; children: Beth, Mark. BA, NYU, 1952; JD, Harvard U., 1955; MA, Columbia U., 1956. Bar: N.Y. 1956. With The Title Guarantee Co., N.Y.C., 1959-71, v.p., until 1971; v.p., gen. counsel Security Title and Guaranty Co., 1971-92; counsel N.Y. Land Svcs., Inc., 1994—; chief counsel Metropolis Abstract Corp., Elmsford, N.Y. Adj. prof. real property law NYU, 1985—. Pres. Beacon Hill Estates Coop., Inc., Dobbs Ferry, N.Y., 1961-63, 71-73; pres. Greenburgh Hebrew Ctr., Dobbs Ferry, 1979—. Mem. N.Y. State Bar Assn., B'nai Brith (v.p. Henry Jones lodge 1982-84, pres. 1984-86). Democrat. Jewish. Consumer commercial, Insurance, Real property. Home: 15 Manor House Dr Dobbs Ferry NY 10522-2519 Office: Metropolis Abstract Corp 570 Taxter Rd Elmsford NY 10523 E-mail: production@metropolisabstract.com

NEUSTROM, PATRIK WILLIAM, lawyer; b. Kearney, Nebr., Dec. 15, 1951; s. Willys Edward and Geraldine (Slocum) N.; m. Debra Thornton, Aug. 3, 1974; children: Cassie, Emily, Nicholas. BA in English and History with honors, Kans. U., 1974; JD, Washburn U., 1976. Bar: Kans. 1977, U.S. Dist. Ct. Kans. 1977, U.S. Ct. Appeals (10th cir.) 1984. Assoc. Gilliland, Hayes & Goering, Hutchinson, Kans., 1976-78; ptnr. Achterberg & Neustrom, Salina, 1979—. Asst. county counsellor Saline County, Salina, 1981-88, county counsellor, 1989—. Bd. editors Washburn U. Law Rev., 1976-77. Chmn. Salina Arts & Humanities Commn., 1983-85; mem. adv. bd. Salina Bus. Improvement Dist., 1985-87; mem. Ctrl. Kans. Artists Coalition. Mem. ABA, Kans. Bar Assn. (litigation sect. exec. com. 1986-90), N.W. Kans. Bar Assn. (pres. 1982-83), Assn. Trial Lawyers Am., Kans. Trial Lawyers Assn. (bd. govs. 1991—, v.p. membership, chmn. bd. editors 1988), Salina C. of C., Salina Jaycees (pres. 1979), Salina Country Club, Rotary, Phi Alpha Theta, Phi Delta Phi, Sigma Nu. Presbyterian. Avocations: hunting, fly fishing, ranching, art. General practice, Personal injury, Workers' compensation. Office: Achterberg & Neustrom 118 S 7th St Salina KS 67401-2806 E-mail: patrik@midkan.net

NEVELOFF, JAY A. lawyer; b. Bklyn., Oct. 11, 1950; m. Arlene Sillman, Aug. 26, 1972; children: David, Kevin. BA, Bklyn. Coll., 1971; JD, NYU, 1974. Bar: N.Y. 1975, D.C. 1992, U.S. Dist. Ct. (so. and ea. dists.) N.Y. 1975, U.S. Ct. Appeals (2d cir.) 1975, U.S. Supreme Ct. 1982. Assoc. Marshall, Bratter, Greene, Allison & Tucker, N.Y.C., 1974-82, Rosenman, Colin, Freund, Lewis & Cohen, N.Y.C., 1982-83, ptnr., 1983-88, Kramer, Levin, Naftalis, Nessen, Kamin & Frankel, N.Y.C., 1988—. Editor N.Y. Real Property Service. Mem. planning bd. Briarcliff Manor, 1995—. Mem. ABA (vice chmn. com. partnerships, joint ventures and other investment vehicles 1988-95), Am. Law Inst., Am. Coll. Real Estate Attys., N.Y. State Bar Assn. (financing com.), Practising Law Inst. (lectr. 1988—, mem. adv. bd. 1991—), N.Y. County Lawyers Assn. (lectr. 1984—), Assn. of Bar of City of N.Y. (real property law com., lectr. 1984-88), Cmty. Assns. Inst. (lectr. 1986), Law Jours. Seminars (lectr. 1987—), Strategic Resources Inst. (lectr. 1994—), Internat. Health Network Soc. (vice chmn. 1995-2000), Inst. Internat. Rsch. (lectr. 1994—). Real property. Home: 134 Alder Dr Briarcliff Manor NY 10510-2218 Office: Kramer Levin Naftalis & Frankel LLP 919 3rd Ave New York NY 10022-3902 E-mail: jneveloff@kramerlevin.com

NEVES, KERRY LANE, lawyer; b. San Angelo, Tex., Dec. 19, 1950; s. Herman Walter and Geraldine (Ball) N.; m. Sharon Lynn Briggs, July 28, 1973; 1 child, Erin Lesli. BBA, U. Tex., 1975, JD, 1978. Bar: Tex. 1978, U.S. Dist. Ct. (so. and ea. dists.) Tex. 1979, U.S. Ct. Appeals (5th cir.) 1979, U.S. Dist. Ct. (we. dist.) 1980; cert. personal injury trial law, Tex. Bd. Legal Specialization, 1994. Ptnr. Mills, Shirley, Eckel & Bassett, Galveston, Tex., 1978-93, Neves & Crowther, Galveston, 1993—. Vice-chmn. Bldg. Stnds. Commn., Dickinson, Tex., 1991-98; mem. City Coun. Dickinson, Tex., 1998—. Sgt. USMC, 1969-72. Fellow Tex. Bar Found. (life); mem. ABA, State Bar Tex. (grievance com. 1989-92, disciplinary rules profl. conduct com. 1990-92, dir. dist. 5 1997-2000), Galveston County Bar Assn. (pres. 1989-90), U. Tex. Law Alumni Assn. (pres. 1991-92). Avocations: gardening, bicycling, wine, books. General civil litigation, Personal injury, Professional liability. Home: RR 2 Box 95 Dickinson TX 77539-9204 Office: Neves & Crowther 1802 Broadway St Ste 206 Galveston TX 77550-4953

NEVILLE, JAMES MORTON, retired lawyer, consumer products executive; b. Mpls., May 28, 1939; s. Philip and Maurene (Morton) N.; m. Judie Martha Proctor, Sept. 9, 1961; children: Stephen Warren, Martha Maurene Hereford. BA, U. Minn., JD magna cum laude, 1964. Bar: Minn. 1964, Mo. 1984. Assoc. Neville, Johnson & Thompson, Mpls., 1964-69, ptnr., 1969-70; assoc. counsel Gen. Mills, Inc., 1970-77, sr. assoc. counsel, 1977-83, corp. sec., 1976-83; v.p., sec., asst. gen. counsel Ralston Purina Co., St. Louis, 1983-84, v.p., gen. counsel, sec., 1984-96, v.p., gen. counsel, 1996-2000, v.p., sr. counsel, 2000-01; ret., 2001. Lectr. bus. law. U. Minn., 1967-71. Named Man of Yr., Edina Jaycees, 1967. Mem. ABA, Minn., Mo. Bar Assns., U.S. Supreme Ct. Bar Assn., Hennepin County Bar Assn., St. Louis Bar Assn., U. Minn. Law Sch. Alumni Assn., Old Warson Country Club, Ladue Racquet Club, Order of Coif, Phi Delta Phi, Psi Upsilon. Episcopalian. General corporate. Home: 9810 Log Cabin Ct Saint Louis MO 63124-1133 E-mail: jnev57@aol.com

NEVINS, ARTHUR GERARD, JR. lawyer; b. Bklyn., Dec. 23, 1948; s. Arthur Gerard Sr. and Gertrude Anna May (Schlueter) N.; m. Reine T. Hughes, June 26, 1982; m. Amanda Mitchell, May 16, 1989. BS, Cornell U., 1971; JD, Fordham U., 1974. Bar: N.Y. 1975, N.J. 1976. Assoc. Lester, Schwab, Katz & Dwer, N.Y.C., 1975-77, Law Offices of Peter De Blasio, N.Y.C., 1977-80, Law Offices of Robert Ginsberg, N.Y.C., 1980-82; pvt. practice, 1982—. Mem. ABA, N.Y. State Bar Assn., N.J. Bar Assn., N.Y. County Bar Assn., Hudson County Bar Assn., Phi Gamma Delta. Roman Catholic. Personal injury, Professional liability, Workers' compensation. Home: 41 Charlestown Rd Hampton NJ 08827-2781 Office: 138 Central Ave Jersey City NJ 07306-2119 also: 225 Broadway Ste 3111 New York NY 10007-3001

NEVOLA, ROGER, lawyer; b. N.Y.C., Apr. 30, 1947; m. Molly Cagle; children: Adrienne L., Jake F. Student, U. Notre Dame, 1964-66; BSME, Stanford U., 1968; JD, U. Tex., 1974. Bar: Tex. 1974. Assoc. Vinson & Elkins, Houston, 1974-79, Austin, 1979-81, ptnr., 1981-95; pvt. practice, 1995—. Fellow Tex. Bar Found. (life). Administrative and regulatory, Environmental, Real property. Home: 4304 Bennedict Ln Austin TX 78746-1940 Office: PO Box 2103 Austin TX 78768-2103 E-mail: roger@nevola.com

NEWACHECK, DAVID JOHN, lawyer, writer; b. San Francisco, Dec. 8, 1953; s. John Elmer and Estere Ruth Sybil (Nelson) N.; m. Dorothea Quandt, June 2, 1990. AB in English, U. Calif., Berkeley, 1976; JD, Pepperdine U., 1979; MBA, Calif. State U., Hayward, 1982; LLM in Tax, Golden Gate U., 1987. Bar: Calif. 1979, D.C. 1985, N.Y. 1987, U.S. Dist. Ct. (no. dist.) Calif. 1979, U.S. Ct. Appeals (9th cir.) 1979, U.S. Supreme Ct. 1984. Tax cons. Pannell, Kerr and Forster, San Francisco, 1982-83; lawyer, writer, editor Matthew Bender and Co., 1983—. Instr. taxation wills and trusts Oakland (Calif.) Coll. of Law, 1993—; lawyer, tax cons., fin. planner San Leandro, Calif., 1983—; bd. dirs. Aztec Custom Co., Orinda, Calif., 1983—; cons. software Collier Bankruptcy Filing Sys., 1984. Author/editor: (treatises) Ill. Tax Service, 1985, Ohio State Taxation, 1985, N.J. Tax Service, 1986, Pa. Tax Service, 1986, Calif. Closely Held Corps., 1987, Texas Tax Service, 1988; author: (software) Tax Source 1040 Tax Preparation, 1987, Texas Tax Service 1988, California Taxation, 1989, 2d edit., 1990, Bender's Federal Tax Service, 1989, Texas Litigation Guide, 1993, Family Law: Texas Practice & Procedure, 1993, Texas Transaction Guide, 1994, Ohio Corporation Law, 1994, Michigan Corporation Law, 1994, Massachusetts Corporation Law, 1994. Mem. youth com. Shepherd of the Valley Luth. Ch., Orinda, 1980-85, ch. coun., 1980-82; bd. dirs. Oakland Coll. Law, treas., CFO, 1997—. Mem. ABA, Internat. Platform Assn., State Bar Assn. Calif., Alameda County Bar Assn., U. Calif. Alumni Assn., U. Calif. Band Alumni Assn., Kiwanis Club San Leandro (bd. dirs. 1998—, v.p. 1999-2000, pres. elect 2000-01, pres. 2001—), Commonwealth Club (San Francisco chpt.), Mensa. Republican. Avocations: music, competitive running, sports. Home: 5141 Vannoy Ave Castro Valley CA 94546-2558 Office: 438 Estudillo Ave San Leandro CA 94577-4908 E-mail: dnewacheck@abanet.com

NEWBERN, WILLIAM DAVID, retired state supreme court justice; b. Oklahoma City, May 28, 1937; s. Charles Banks and Mary Frances (Harding) N.; m. Barbara Lee Rigsby, Aug. 19, 1961 (div. 1968); 1 child, Laura Harding; m. Carolyn Lewis, July 30, 1970; 1 child, Alistair Elizabeth. B.A., U. Ark., 1959, J.D., 1961; LL.M., George Washington U., 1963; M.A., Tufts U., 1967. Bar: Ark. 1961, U.S. Dist. Ct. (we. dist.) Ark. 1961, U.S. Supreme Ct. 1968, U.S. Ct. Appeals (8th cir.) 1983. Commd. 1st lt. advanced to maj. U.S. Army JAGC, 1961-70; Prof. law U. Ark., Fayetteville, 1970-84; adminstr. Ozark Folk Ctr., Mountain View, Ark., 1973; judge Ark. Ct. Appeals, Little Rock, 1979-80; assoc. justice Ark. Supreme Ct., 1985-99. Mem. faculty sr. appellate judges seminar NYU, 1987-91. Editor Ark. Law Rev., 1961; author: Arkansas Civil Practice and Procedure, 1985, 2d edit., 1993. Mem. Fayetteville Bd. Adjustment, 1972-79; bd. dirs. Decision Point, Inc., Springdale, Ark., 1980-85, Hot Springs Music Festival, 2000—; bd. dirs. Little Rock Wind Symphony, 1993-2001, pres. 1993-95. Fellow Ark. Bar Found.; mem. Ark. Bar Assn., Am. Judicature Soc. (bd. dirs. 1985-89), Inst. Jud. Adminstrn., Ark. IOLTA Found. (bd. dirs. 1985-87). Democrat. Avocation: string band-guitar, mandolin, banjo and brass quintet-tuba. E-mail: dnewbern@aristotle.net

NEWCOM, JENNINGS JAY, lawyer; b. St. Joseph, Mo., Oct. 18, 1941; s. Arden Henderson and Loyal Beatrice (Winans) N.; m. Cherry Ann Phelps, Apr. 4, 1964; children: Shandra Karine, J. Derek Arden. BA, Graceland U., Lamoni, Iowa, 1964; JD, Harvard U., 1968; LLD (hon.), Graceland U., 1999. Bar: Ill. 1968, Calif. 1973, Mo. 1979, Kans. 1981, Colo. 1999. Atty. McDermott, Will & Emery, Chgo., 1968-73; ptnr. Rifkind, Sterling & Lockwood, Beverly Hills, Calif., 1973-79, Shook, Hardy & Bacon L.L.P., Kansas City, Mo., 1979-99, Davis, Graham & Stubbs, LLP, Denver, 1999—; gen. counsel Putnam, Lovell Capital Ptnrs., Inc., L.A., 1999—; dir. Stein Roe Investment Counsel, Chicago. Chmn. bd. Graceland Coll. Trustee Hubbard Found., Linde Found. Mem. Denver Bar Assn., State Bar Assn. Calif. General corporate, Mergers and acquisitions, Securities. Office: Davis Graham & Stubbs LLP 1550 17th St Ste 500 Denver CO 80202-1500

NEWCOMER, CLARENCE CHARLES, federal judge; b. Mount Joy, Pa., Jan. 18, 1923; s. Clarence S. and Marion Clara (Charles) N.; m. Jane Moyer Martin, Oct. 2, 1948; children: Judy (Mrs. Kenneth N. Birkett Jr.), Nancy Jane Newcomer (Mrs. Edward H. Vick), Peggy Jo Pollack (dec.). A.B., Franklin and Marshall Coll., 1944; LL.B., Dickinson Sch. Law, 1948. Bar: Pa. 1950, U.S. Dist. Ct. Pa., U.S. Ct. Appeals (3rd cir.), U.S. Supreme Ct. Pvt. practice, Lancaster, 1950-52; spl. dep. atty. gen. Dept. Justice, Commonwealth of Pa., 1952-54; partner firm Rohrer, Honaman, Newcomer & Musser, Lancaster, 1957-60; with Office of Dist. Atty., 1960-64, 1st asst. dist. atty., 1964-68, dist. atty., 1968-72; partner Newcomer, Roda & Morgan, 1968-72; fed. dist. judge Eastern Dist. Pa., Phila., 1972-88, sr. judge, 1988—. Served to lt. (j.g.) USNR, 1943-46, PTO. Office: US Dist Ct 13614 US Courthouse 601 Market St Philadelphia PA 19106-1713

NEWHALL, DAVID GILLETTE, lawyer; b. Mpls., July 3, 1941; s. Norman Leslie and Deborah (Anson) N.; m. Carol Ann Ludington, Feb. 3, 1994; children: Sara Grace, Nathan David. B.A., Kenyon Coll., 1963; J.D., U. Minn., 1966. Bar: Minn. 1966, U.S. Ct. Appeals (8th cir.), U.S. Dist. Ct. Minn. 1967. Ptnr. Lindquist & Vennum, Mpls., 1966—; staff judge adv., col. Minn. Army N.G., 1970—; with Lindquist & Vennum, Mpls. Mem. Citizens League, Mpls., 1984-85. Mem. ABA, Assn. Trial Lawyers Am., Nat. Assn. R.R. Trial Counsel, Minn. Bar Assn. Lutheran. Clubs: Minikahda, Athletic (Mpls.). Federal civil litigation, Family and matrimonial, Military. Office: Lindquist & Vennum 4200 IDS Ctr 80 S 8th St Ste 4200 Minneapolis MN 55402-2274

NEWITT, JOHN GARWOOD, JR. lawyer; b. Charlotte, N.C., Apr. 9, 1941; s. John Garwood and Sarah Elizabeth (Stratford) N.; m. Catherine Elizabeth Hubbard, Aug. 28, 1965; children: Catherine Stratford, Elizabeth Blake. BA, Wake Forest U., 1963, JD, 1965; postgrad., U. Va., 1966-68. Bar: N.C. 1965, U.S. Ct. Mil. Appeals 1965, U.S. Dist. Ct. (we. dist.) N.C. 1968, U.S. Ct. Claims 1968, U.S. Tax. Ct. 1968, U.S. Ct. Appeals (4th cir.) 1984. Ptnr. Newitt & Newitt, Charlotte, 1968-73; sr. ptnr. Newitt & Bruny, 1973—. Lectr. The Judge Advocate Gen.'s Sch., 1965-68, United Way Vol. Leadership Devel. Program, 1986-93. Contbr. articles to profl. jours. Chmn. Bd. Zoning Adjustment, 1971-77; bd. dirs. Carolina Group Homes, 1992-95. Recipient awards ASCAP. Mem. N.C. Bar Assn., Mecklenburg County Bar Assn., N.C. Coll. Advocacy (cert. competency), Charlotte Econs. Club, Myers Park Country Club (past pres., bd. dirs.), Selwyn Men's Fellowship (past pres.), Good Fellows, Phi Delta Phi (past sec.). Republican. Presbyterian. Avocations: jogging, golf. General civil litigation, General corporate, Mergers and acquisitions. Home: 3216 Ferncliff Rd Charlotte NC 28211-3259 Office: Newitt & Bruny 417 East Blvd Ste 104 Charlotte NC 28203-5163 E-mail: johnnewitt@cs.com, newittbru@cs.com

NEWLIN, WILLIAM RANKIN, lawyer; b. Pitts., Dec. 1, 1940; s. Theodore F. Newlin and Elizabeth Crooks; m. Ann Kleinschmidt, Aug. 25, 1962; children: Steffler Ann, Shelley Kay, William Rankin II. AB, Princeton U., 1962; JD, U. Pitts., 1965; DBA (hon.), Robert Morris Coll., 1997. Bar: Pa. 1965. Assoc. Buchanan Ingersoll, Pitts., 1965-71, ptnr., 1971—, mng. dir., 1980—; mng. gen. ptnr. CEO Venture Fund, 1985—; chmn. bd. Kennametal Inc., Latrobe, Pa., 1996—. Bd. dirs. bd. Nat. City Bank Pa., Pitts., Parker/Hunter, Pitts., Black Box Corp., Pitts., Pitts. Regional Alliance. Editor in chief U. Pitts. Law Rev., 1963; contbr. articles to profl. jours. Chmn., Gov. Thornburgh's Corp. Adv. Com., 1980-82; bd. dirs. Mfr. Studies Bd. nat. Rsch. Coun., Washington, 1988-89, Pitts. High Tech. Coun., 1982—, Pa. Tech. Coun. Recipient Entrepreneur of Yr. award Ernst & Young, Inc. Mag./ Merrill Lynch, 1991. Fellow Am. Bar Found., Pa. Bar Found.; mem. ABA (corp. banking, bus. law sect.), Pa. Bar Assn. (mem. coun. corp. banking and bus. law sect. 1973-82, chmn. sect. 1979-81, Spl. Achievement award 1982), Allegheny County Bar Assn., Assn. of Bar of City of N.Y., Am. Law Inst., Pa. S.W. Assn. (trustee), Greater Pitts. C. of C. (bd. dirs.), Duquesne Club (dir. 1982-85), Rivers Club (bd. dirs. 1983—), Laurel Valley Golf Club, Allegheny Country Club (bd. dirs. 1988—). General corporate, Finance, Mergers and acquisitions. Office: Buchanan Ingersoll One Oxford Centre 301 Grant St Fl 20 Pittsburgh PA 15219-1410 E-mail: newlinwr@bipc.com

NEWMAN, CAROL L. lawyer; b. Yonkers, N.Y., Aug. 7, 1949; d. Richard J. and Pauline Frances (Stoll) N. AB/MA summa cum laude, Brown U., 1971; postgrad., Harvard U. Law Sch., 1972-73; JD cum laude, George Washington U., 1977. Bar: D.C. 1977, Calif. 1979. With antitrust divsn. U.S. Dept. Justice, Washington and L.A., 1977-80; assoc. Alschuler, Grossman & Pines, L.A., 1980-82, Costello & Walcher, L.A., 1982-85, Rosen, Wachtell & Gilbert, L.A., 1985-88, ptnr., 1988-90, Keck, Mahin & Cate, L.A., 1990-94; pvt. practice, 1994-2001. Adj. prof. Sch. Bus., Golden Gate U., spring 1982. Commr. L.A. Bd. Transp. Commrs., 1993—98, v.p., 1995—96; pres. Bd. Taxicab Commrs., 1999—2001; Cand. for State Atty. Gen., 1986; bd. dirs. Women's Progress Alliance, 1996—98. Mem. ABA, State Bar Calif., L.A. County Bar Assn., L.A. Lawyers for Human Rights (co. pres. 1991-92), Log Cabin (bd. dirs. 1992-97, pres. 1996-97), Calif. Women Lawyers (bd. dirs., bd. govs. 1991-94), Order of Coif, Phi Beta Kappa. Antitrust, Appellate, General civil litigation. E-mail: cnewman540@aol.com

NEWMAN, CHARLES A. lawyer; b. L.A., Mar. 18, 1949; s. Arthur and Gladys Newman; children: Anne R., Elyse S. BA magna cum laude, U. Calif., 1970; JD, Washington U., 1973. Bar: Mo. 1973, D.C. 1981, U.S. Dist. Ct. (ea. dist.) Mo. 1973, U.S. Dist. Ct. (ctrl. dist.) Ill., 1996, U.S. Ct. Appeals (3d, 5th, 7th and 10th cirs.) 1996, (8th cir.) 1975, (9th cir.) 1995, (11th cir.) 1994, U.S. Tax Ct. 1981, U.S. Claims Ct. 1981, U.S. Supreme Ct. 1976. From assoc. to ptnr. Thompson & Mitchell, St. Louis, 1973-96; ptnr. Thompson Coburn, 1996-97, Bryan Cave LLP, St. Louis, 1997—. Lectr. law Washington U., St. Louis, 1976-78. Bd. dirs. Hawthorn Found., 1997—; trustee Mo. Bar Found., 1990-96, mem. Mo. Bar Bd. Govs, 1980-84; bd. dirs. United Israel Appeal, N.Y.C., 1990-93, Coun. Jewish Fedns., N.Y.C., 1992-95, United Jewish Appeal Young Leadership Cabinet, N.Y.C., 1985-88, Ctr. for Study of Dispute Resolution, 1985-88, Legal Svcs. Ea. Mo., 1985-94, St. Louis Community Found., 1992—, vice-chmn. 1997-99, St. Louis chpt. Young Audiences 1993-95, Planned Parenthood St. Louis, 1986-89, Jewish Fedn., St. Louis, 1986-98, asst. treas., 1989-90, v.p. fin. planning, 1990-93, asst. sec., 1994—; v.p. Repertory Theatre, St. Louis, 1986-89, sr. v.p., 1990-91; pres. St. Louis Opportunity Clearinghouse, 1974-78. Recipient Lon O. Hocker Meml. Trial award Mo. Bar Found., 1984. Mem. Bar Assn. Met. St. Louis (Merit award 1976). Democrat. Avocations: golf, reading, music, sailing. Appellate, General civil litigation, Transportation. Office: Bryan Cave LLP One Metropolitan Square Saint Louis MO 63102-2750

NEWMAN, CHRISTOPHER JOHN, lawyer; b. Lancaster, Pa., Apr. 2, 1948; s. Covelle J. and Sarah (Easton) N.; m. Anna Marie Schiavone, Sept. 1, 1975; children: Alexa Juliet, Ashley Louisa, Elizabeth Christina, Emily Anne. BA, Denison U., 1970; JD, Case Western Res. U., 1973. Bar: Ohio 1973. Mem. Henderson Covington, Messenger, Newman Thomas, Youngstown, Ohio, 1973—; counsel Better Bus. Bur. Mahoning Valley, Inc., 1973—. General corporate, Family and matrimonial, Labor. Home: 2883 Autumnwood Trl Poland OH 44514-2858 Office: Henderson Covington Messenger Newman and Thomas 600 W Ick Bldg Youngstown OH 44503

NEWMAN, FREDRIC SAMUEL, lawyer, business executive; b. York, Pa., June 22, 1945; s. Nat. Howard and Josephine (Farkas) N.; m. Mary E. Kiley, May 19, 1973; children: Lydia Ann, Anne Marie, Pauline. AB cum laude, Harvard U., 1967; JD, Columbia U., 1970; cert. the exec. program, U. Va., 1984. Bar: N.Y. 1971, U.S. Dist. Ct. (so. and ea. dists.) N.Y. 1972, U.S. Ct. Appeals (2d cir.) 1974, U.S. Ct. Claims 1993. Assoc. White & Case, N.Y.C., 1970-80; asst. gen. counsel Philip Morris Cos., 1981-87; gen. counsel, v.p., sec. Philip Morris, Inc., 1987-90; chief exec. officer TeamTennis, Inc., 1991; prin. Law Office of Fredric S. Newman, N.Y.C., 1992-95; founding ptnr. Hoguet Newman & Regal, LLP, 1996—; pres., CEO, Pathe Comm. Corp., N.Y.C., 1993-97. Bd. dirs. Exel Ins. Co., Bermuda. Trustee Calhoun Sch., N.Y.C., 1985-88; bd. dirs. N.Y. Fire Safety Found., N.Y.C., 1985-88. Fellow Am. Bar Found. General civil litigation, General corporate, Product liability. Office: 10 E 40th St New York NY 10016-0200

NEWMAN, GEORGE HENRY, lawyer; b. Cheverly, Md., Dec. 16, 1949; s. Leon and Ruth (Patt) N.; m. Linda Joan Fahy; children: Joshua Michael, David Peter. BA, U. Pa., 1971; JD, Temple U., 1975. Bar: Penn. 1975, U.S. Dist. Ct. (ea. dist.), Penn. 1976, U.S. Ct. Appeals (3d cir.) 1985, U.S. Supreme Ct. 1985. Staff atty. Defender Assn. Phila., 1975-79; law clk. to judge Ct. of Common Pleas, Phila., 1979-82; ptnr. Ellis and Newman, P.C., 1982-86, Newman and McGlaughlin, P.C., Phila., 1986—. Mem. ABA, Internat. Assn. Young Lawyers, Nat. Assn. Criminal Def. Lawyers, Phila. Bar Assn. (chmn. criminal justice sect. 1987, bd. govs. 1987-88), Pa. Assn. Criminal Def. Lawyers (v.p. 1988-89). Democrat. Avocations: skiing, sailing, tennis, swimming. Criminal, Forfeiture. Office: Newman and McGlaughlin PC The Benjamin Franklin Ste 400 Philadelphia PA 19107

NEWMAN, JAMES MICHAEL, judge, lawyer; b. Bklyn., Apr. 3, 1946; s. Sheldon and Ethel (Silverman) N.; m. Lee Galen; children: Danielle Cari, Matthew Evan, Merrie Lee, Cindy Joy, Bradley Curtis. BA, Queens Coll., 1966; JD, NYU, 1969, LLM, 1975. Bar: N.Y. 1970, N.J. 1977; cert. matrimonial atty., N.J. Assoc. Kramer, Marx, Greenlee & Backus, N.Y.C., 1970-73, Forsyth, Decker, Murray & Broderick, N.Y.C., 1973-74; ptnr. Tommaney & Newman, 1975-82, Goldzweig, Reilly, Grossman & Newman, Marlboro, N.J., 1978-79, Canarick & Newman, Freehold, 1979-97, Newman, Scarola & Assocs., Freehold, 1998—; pub. defender Marlboro Twp. (N.J.), 1984-86; judge Marlboro Twp., 1986—, Englishtown Borough, 1990—, Farmingdale Borough, 1991—, Manalapan Township, 1993—, Borough Fair Haven, 1996—. Dep. mayor Marlboro Twp., 1975-79, dir. econ. devel., 1975-79, dir. commuter affairs, 1974; interim commr. Western Monmouth Utilities Authority, 1977; mem. Central N.J. Transp. Bd., 1974-76. Mem. N.J. Bar Assn., Monmouth County Bar Assn. (co-chairperson family law com. 1996-98, trustee 1999), Monmouth County Judges Assn. (pres. 1995), Am. Judges Assn., Masons. Jewish. Office: 64 W Main St Freehold NJ 07728-2142 E-mail: jnewman@monmouthlaw.com

NEWMAN, JOHN M., JR. lawyer; b. Youngstown, Ohio, Aug. 15, 1944; BA, Georgetown U., 1966; JD, Harvard U., 1969. BAr: Ill. 1970, Calif. 1972, Ohio 1976. Law clerk ctrl. dist. U.S. Dist. Ct., Calif., 1969-70, asst. U.S. Atty. ctrl. dist., 1970-75; ptnr. Jones, Day, Reavis & Pogue, Cleve. Fellow Am. Coll. Trial Lawyers; mem. Phi Beta Kappa. General civil litigation. Office: Jones Day Reavis & Pogue North Point 901 Lakeside Ave E Cleveland OH 44114-1190 E-mail: jmnewman@jonesday.com

NEWMAN, JON O. federal judge; b. N.Y.C., May 2, 1932; s. Harold W. Jr. and Estelle L. (Ormond) N.; m. Martha G. Silberman, June 19, 1953; children: Leigh, Scott, David. Grad., Hotchkiss Sch., 1949; AB magna cum laude, Princeton U., 1953; LLB, Yale U., 1956; LLD (hon.), U. Hartford, 1975, U. Bridgeport, 1980, Bklyn. Law Sch., 1995, N.Y. Law Sch., 1996. Bar: Conn. 1956, D.C. 1956. Law clk. to Hon. George T. Washington U.S. Ct. Appeals, 1956-57; sr. law clk. to chief justice Hon. Earl Warren, U.S. Supreme Ct., 1957-58; ptnr. Ritter, Satter & Newman, Hartford, Conn., 1958-60; counsel to majority Conn. Gen. Assembly, 1959; spl. counsel to gov. Conn., 1959-61; asst. to sec. HEW, 1961-62; adminstrv. asst. to U.S. senator, 1963-64; U.S. atty. Dist. of Conn., 1964-69; pvt. practice law, 1969-71; U.S. dist. judge Dist. of Conn., 1972-79; U.S. cir. judge 2d Cir. Ct. of Appeals, Hartford, 1979-93, chief judge, 1993-97, sr. judge, 1997—. Co-author: Politics: The American Way. With USAR, 1954-62. Recipient Learned Hand medal Fed. Bar Coun., 1987. Fellow Am. Bar Found.; mem. ABA, Am. Law Inst., Conn. Bar Assn., Am. Judicature Soc. Democrat. Office: US Ct Appeals 2d Cir 450 Main St Hartford CT 06103-3022*

NEWMAN, LAWRENCE WALKER, lawyer; b. Boston, July 1, 1935; s. Leon Bettoney and Hazel W. (Walker) N.; children: Timothy D., Isabel B., Thomas H. A.B., Harvard U., 1957, LL.B., 1960. Bar: D.C. 1961, N.Y. 1965. Atty. U.S. Dept. Justice, 1960-61, Spl. Study of Securities Markets and Office Spl. Counsel on Investment Co. Act Matters, U.S. SEC, 1961-64; asst. U.S. atty. So. Dist. N.Y., 1964-69; assoc. Baker & McKenzie, N.Y.C., 1969-71, ptnr., 1971—. Mem. internat. adv. coun. World Arbitration Inst., 1984-87; mem. adv. com. Asia Pacific Ctr. for Resolution of Internat. Trade Disputes, 1987—; mem. adv. bd. Inst. for Transnational Arbitration, 1988—; chmn. U.S. Iranian Claimants Com., 1982—; mem. adv. bd. World Arbitration and Mediation Report, 1993—; mem. bd. adv. to Corporate Counsel's Internat. Adviser, 1995—. Co-author: The Practice of Internat. Litigation, 1992, 93, 2nd edit. 1998, Litigating Internat. Commercial Disputes, 1996; columnist N.Y. Law Jour., 1982—; adv. bd. World Arbitration and Mediation Report; bd. advisors Corp. Counsel's Internat. Adviser; contbr. articles to profl. jours. and books on litigation and internat. arbitration; editor: Enforcement of Money Judgments, Attachment of Assets; chmn. editl. bd. Juris Pub., Inc.; co-editor: Revolutionary Days: The Iran Hostage Crisis and the Hague Claims Tribunal, A Look Back, 1999. Mem. ABA (internat. litigation com., internat. arbitration com.), Internat. Bar Assn. (com. dispute resolution, com. constrn. litigation), Inter-Am. Bar Assn., Fed. Bar Coun., Am. Fgn. Law Assn., Maritime Law Assn. U.S., Assn. Bar City N.Y. (com. on arbitration & alternative dispute resolution 1991-94), Am. Arbitration Assn. (corp. counsel com. 1987—, panel comml. arbitrators), U.S. Coun. Internat. Bus., Ct. Arbitration of Polish Chamber Fgn. Trade (panel of arbitrators), Brit. Col. Internat. Comml. Arbitration Ctr., Am. Law Inst., Bar Assn. City N.Y. (inaugural mem. com. on internat. dispute resolution). E-mail: lwn@ bakernet.com. Federal civil litigation, Contracts commercial, Private international. Office: Baker & McKenzie 805 3rd Ave New York NY 10022-7513

NEWMAN, MICHAEL RODNEY, lawyer; b. N.Y.C., Oct. 2, 1945; s. Morris and Helen Gloria (Hendler) N.; m. Cheryl Jeanne Anker, June 11, 1967; children: Hillary Abra, Nicole Brooke. Student NASA Inst. Space Physics, Columbia U., 1964; BA, U. Denver, 1967; JD, U. Chgo., 1970. Bar: Calif. 1971, U.S. Dist. Ct. (cen. dist.) Calif. 1972, U.S. Ct. Appeals (9th cir.) 1974, U.S. Dist. Ct. (no. dist.) Calif. 1975, U.S. Supreme Ct. 1978, U.S. Dist. Ct. (so. dist.) Calif. 1979, U.S. Tax Ct. 1979, U.S. Dist. Ct. (ea. dist.) Calif. 1983. Assoc. David Daar, 1971-76; ptnr. Daar & Newman, 1976-78, Miller & Daar, 1978-88, Miller, Daar & Newman, 1988-89, Daar & Newman, 1989—; judge pro-tem L.A. Mcpl. Ct., 1982—, L.A. Superior Ct., 1988—. Bd. dirs. German-Am. C. of C., bd. govs. U. Haifa, Israel, mem. fin. and phys. devel. com.; bd. dirs. Consulegis EEIG; founder, facilitator First, Second and Third Ann. German-Am. Strategic Partnership Conf.; lectr. Ea. Claims Conf., Ea. Life Claims Conf., Nat. Health Care Anti-Fraud Assn., AIA Conf. on Ins. Fraud, Consulegis A.G.M.'s Paris, 1997, Madrid, 1998, Dublin, 1999; bd. gov.'s U. Haifa, Israel (mem. finance and physical devel. com.). Mem. L.A. Citizens Organizing Com. for Olympic Summer Games, 1984, mem. govtl. liaison adv. commn., 1984; mem. So. Calif. Com. for Olympic Summer Games, 1984; cert. ofcl. Athletics Congress of U.S., co-chmn. legal com. S.P.A.-T.A.C., chief finish judge; trustee Massada lodge B'nai Brith. Recipient NYU Bronze medal in Physics, 1962, Maths. award USN Sci., 1963. Mem. ABA (multi-dist. litigation subcom., com. on class actions), L.A. County Bar Assn. (chmn. attys. errors and omissions prevention com., mem. cts. com. litigation sect., mem. internat. law com.), Conf. Ins. Counsel, So. Pacific Assn., TAC (bd. dirs., Disting. Svc. award 1988), Porter Valley Country Club, Breakfast Club. Federal civil litigation, State civil litigation, Insurance. Office: 865 S Figueroa St Ste 2300 Los Angeles CA 90017-2567

NEWMAN, PAULINE, federal judge; b. N.Y.C., N.Y., June 20, 1927; d. Maxwell Henry and Rosella N. BA, Vassar Coll., 1947; MA, Columbia U., 1948; PhD, Yale U., 1952; LLB, NYU, 1958. Bar: N.Y. 1958, U.S. Supreme Ct. 1972, U.S. Ct. Customs and Patent Appeals 1978, Pa. 1979, U.S. Ct. Appeals (3d cir.) 1981, U.S. Ct. Appeals (fed. cir.) 1982. Research chemist Am. Cyanamid Co., Bound Brook, N.J., 1951-54; mem. patent staff FMC Corp., N.Y.C., 1954-75, Phila., 1975-84, dir. dept. patent and licensing, 1969-84; judge U.S. Ct. Appeals (fed. cir.), Washington, 1984—; Disting. prof. George Mason Law Sch., 1995—. Bd. dir. Research Corp., 1982-84; program specialist Dept. Natural Scis. UNESCO, Paris, 1961-62; mem. State Dept. Adv. Com. on Internat. Indsl. Property, 1974-84; lectr. in field Contbr. articles to profl. jours. Bd. dirs. Med. Coll. Pa., 1975-84, Midgard Found., 1973-84; trustee Phila. Coll. Pharmacy and Sci., 1983-84. Mem. ABA (council sect. patent trademark and copyright 1983-84), Am. Patent Law Assn. (bd. dirs. 1981-84), U.S. Trademark Assn. (bd. dirs. 1975-79, v.p. 1978-79), Am. Chem. Soc. (bd. dirs. 1972-81), Am. Inst. Chemists (bd. dirs. 1960-66, 70-76), Pacific Indsl. Property Assn. (pres. 1979-80), Cosmos Club, Vassar Club, Yale Club. Office: US Ct Appeals Nat Cts Bldg 717 Madison Pl NWRm 904 Washington DC 20439-0002*

NEWMAN, SANDRA SCHULTZ, state supreme court justice; BS, Drexel U., 1959; MA, Temple U., 1969; JD, Villanova U., 1972; D (hon.), Gannon U., 1996, Widener U., 1996, Clarion U., 2000. Bar: Pa., U.S. Dist. Ct. (ea. dist.) Pa., U.S. Ct. Appeals (3d cir.), U.S. Supreme Ct. Asst. dist. atty. Montgomery County, Pa.; pvt. practice; judge Commonwealth Ct. of Pa., 1993-95; justice Supreme Ct. of Pa., 1995—. Past chair bd. consultors Villanova U. Law Sch.; mem. jud. coun. of the Supreme Ct. of Pa., liaison to the 3rd cir. task force on mgmt. of death penalty litigation, liaison to Pa. lawyers fund for client security bd., liaison to domestic rels. procedural rules com., liaison to Pa. Bar Inst.; jud. work group for HHS; mem. adv. com. Nat. Ctr. for State Cts., Am. Law Inst.; mem. Drexel U. Coll. Bus. and Adminstrn.; lectr. and spkr. in field. Author: Alimony, Child Support and Counsel Fees, 1988; contbr. articles to profl. jours. Recipient Phila. award for Super Achiever Pediatric Juvenile Colitis Found. Jefferson Med. Coll. and Hosp., 1979, award for Dedicated Leadership and Outstanding Contbns. to the Cmty. and Law Employment Police Chiefs Assn. of Southeastern Pa., Drexel 100 award, 1993, Medallion of Achievement award Villanova U., 1993, Susan B. Anthony award Women's Bar Assn. Western Pa., 1996, award Justinian Soc., 1996, award Tau Epsilon Law Soc., 1996, Legion of Honor Gold Medallion award Chapel of Four Chaplains, 1997; honored by Women of Greater Phila., 1996; named Disting. Daughter of Pa. Fellow Am. Bar Found., Pa. Bar Found.; mem. Am. Law Inst., Nat. Assn. Women Judges, Montgomery Bar Assn. Office: Supreme Ct Pa Ste 400 100 Four Falls Corporate Ctr West Conshohocken PA 19428-2950

NEWMAN, STEPHEN MICHAEL, lawyer; b. Buffalo, Jan. 12, 1945; s. Howard A. and Mildred (Ballow) N.; m. Gayle Mallon, May 24, 1969; children: Holly, Deborah. AB, Princeton U., 1966; JD, U. Mich., 1969. Bar: N.Y. 1969, Fla. 1976. Assoc. Hodgson, Russ, Andrews, Woods & Goodyear, Buffalo, 1969-73; ptnr. Hodgson Russ, LLP (formerly Hodgson, Russ, Andrews, Woods &, 1973—. Lectr. in field. Bd. dirs. Leukemia Soc., United Jewish Fedn. Buffalo Inc., Jewish Ctr. Greater Buffalo Inc., Temple Beth Zion; bd. dirs., chpt. chmn., exec. com. Am. Jewish Com., Buffalo chpt.; active Vol. Action Ctr. United Way of Buffalo and Erie County. Fellow Am. Coll. Trusts and Estates Coun.; mem. ABA (personal svc. corps. com. tax sect.), N.Y. State Bar Assn. (chair trusts and estates law sect. 2001), Princeton Club of Western N.Y. (sch. com.). Estate planning, Pension, profit-sharing, and employee benefits, Probate. Office: Hodgson Russ LLP 2000 1 M&T Plz Buffalo NY 14203 E-mail: snewman@hodgsonruss.com

NEWMAN, STUART, lawyer; b. Hackensack, N.J., June 7, 1947; s. Joseph and Rose (Wilenski) N.; m. Tina Gilson; children: Leslie, Dara, Mindy, Robert, Jessica. BA, SUNY, Cortland, 1971; JD cum laude, Albany Law Sch., 1974. Bar: N.Y. 1975, Ga. 1978. Assoc. Dewey, Ballantine, Bushby, Palmer & Wood, N.Y.C., 1974-76; from assoc. to ptnr. Jackson, Lewis, Schnitzler & Krupman, Atlanta, 1976—. Lectr. U. Ala., Tuscaloosa, 1980-84, Auburn U., 1986—. Dir. Ruth Mitchell Dance Co. of Atlanta, 1986-88; bd. trustees N.Y. Mil. Acad., 2000. Mem. ABA, Atlanta Bar Assn., Ga. Bar Assn., Lawyers Club Atlanta, Commerce Club, Shakerag Hounds, Inc., Midlands Fox Hounds, Inc. Labor. Office: Jackson Lewis Schnitzler & Krupman 1900 Marquis One Tower 245 Peachtree Center Ave NE Atlanta GA 30303-1222

NEWMAN, THEODORE ROOSEVELT, JR. judge; b. Birmingham, Ala., July 5, 1934; s. Theodore R. and Ruth L. (Oliver) N. A.B., Brown U., 1955, LL.D., 1980; J.D., Harvard U., 1958. Bar: D.C. 1958, Ala. 1959. Atty. civil rights div. Dept. Justice, Washington, 1961-62; practiced law in, 1962-70; assoc. judge D.C. Superior Ct., 1970-76; judge D.C. Ct. Appeals, 1976-91, chief judge, 1976-84, sr. judge, 1991—; bd. dirs. Nat. Center for State Cts., v.p., 1980-81, pres., 1981-82. Trustee Brown U. With USAF, 1958-61. Fellow Am. Bar Found.; mem. Nat. Bar Assn. (past pres. jud. coun., C. Francis Stradford award 1984, William H. Hastie award 1988). E-mail;. E-mail: tnewman@dcca.state.dc.us

NEWMAN, WILLIAM BERNARD, JR. consultant; b. Providence, Nov. 16, 1950; s. William Bernard and Virginia (Crosby) N.; m. Karen O'Connor, Jan. 11, 1951. BA, Ohio Wesleyan U., 1972; JD, George Mason U., Arlington, Va., 1977; postgrad., Harvard U., 1987. Bar: Va. 1977, D.C. 1978. Atty. com. energy Ho. of Reps., Washington, 1978-81; v.p., Washington counsel Consol. Rail Corp. Dept. Govt. Affairs, 1981-98; cons., 1999—. Bd. dirs. Nat. Coun. for Adoption, 1994-98. Mem. ABA, Va. Bar Assn., D.C. Bar Assn. Home: 1009 Priory Pl Mc Lean VA 22101-2134

NEWSOM, JAMES THOMAS, lawyer; b. Carrollton, Mo., Oct. 6, 1944; s. Thomas Edward and Hazel Love (Mitchell) N.; m. Sherry Elaine Retzloff, Aug. 9, 1986; stepchildren: Benjamin A. Bawden, Holly K. Bawden. AB, U. Mo., 1966, JD, 1968. Bar: Mo. 1968, U.S. Supreme Ct. 1971. Assoc. Shook, Hardy & Bacon, London and Kansas City, Mo., 1972, ptnr., 1976—. Mem. Mo. Law Rev., 1966-68. Lt. comdr. JAGC, USNR, 1968-72. Mem. ABA, Kansas City Met. Bar Assn., U. Mo. Law Sch. Law Soc., U. Mo. Jefferson Club, Order of Coif, Perry (Kans.) Yacht Club, Stone Horse Yacht Club (Harwich Port, Mass.). Avocations: skiing, sailing, car racing. General civil litigation, Product liability. Office: Shook Hardy & Bacon One Kansas City Pl 1200 Main St Ste 3100 Kansas City MO 64105-2139 E-mail: jnewsom@shb.com

NEWSOM, JAN LYNN REIMANN, lawyer; b. Madison, Wis., Feb. 28, 1947; d. Curtis Whitt and Doris Elizabeth (Jerde) Reimann; m. Neil Edward Newsom, Apr. 15, 1972; children— Kelly Ann, Loren Elizabeth. B.A., U. Tex., 1969, J.D., 1971. Bar: Tex., 1972, U.S. Dist. Ct. (no. dist.) Tex. 1982. Vice pres. legal Nat. Compliance Cons., Dallas, 1972; corp. atty. Blue Cross & Blue Shield of Tex., Dallas, 1972-87, v.p. legal dept., 1987-90, sr. v.p., gen counsel, 1990—. Bd. dirs., chmn. pub. edn. com. Dallas cen. unit, Am. Cancer Soc., 1978— ; mem. Innovators, Dallas Symphony Orch. League, 1983—, v.p., bd. dirs., 1990— sponsor 500, Inc. (arts support group), Dallas, 1980—; apptd. State of Tex. Interagy. Coun. on Autism and Pervasive Devel. Disorders, 1988—; bd. dirs. Dallas chpt. Autism Soc. Am., 1988—, pres., 1991-92; mem parents adv. com. spl. edn. Dallas Ind. Sch. Dist., 1990—. Recipient Outstanding Leadership award Am. Cancer Soc., 1977, Sword of Hope award, 1984. Mem. ABA, Dallas Bar Assn. (various coms. 1974—), State Bar of Tex., Nat. EEO Task Force, Blue Cross and Blue Shield Assn., Assn. for Retarded Citizens (edn. com.), Alpha Chi Omega. Republican. Methodist. General corporate, Health, Insurance. Home: 6040 Preston Haven Dr Dallas TX 75230-2967 Office: Blue Cross Blue Shield Tex Legal Div PO Box 655730 Dallas TX 75265-5730

NEWSOME, RANDALL JACKSON, judge; b. Dayton, Ohio, July 13, 1950; s. Harold I. and Sultana S. (Stony) N. BA summa cum laude, Boston U., 1972; JD, U. Cin., 1975. Bar: Ohio 1975, U.S. Dist. Ct. (so. dist.) Ohio 1977, U.S. Ct. Appeals (6th cir.) 1979, U.S. Supreme Ct. 1981. Law clk. to chief judge U.S. Dist. Ct. (so. dist.) Ohio, 1975-77; assoc. Dinsmore & Shohl, Cin., 1978-82; judge U.S. Bankruptcy Ct. (so. dist.) Ohio, 1982-88, U.S. Bankruptcy Ct. (no. dist.) Calif., Oakland, 1988—. Faculty mem. Fed.

Jud. Ctr., ALI-ABA, 1987—; mem. Nat. Conf. of Bankruptcy Judges, 1983—, mem. bd. govs., 1987-88, pres., 1998-99. Contbg. author: Chapter 11 Theory and Practice, 1994—, Collier on Bankruptcy, 1997—. Fellow Am. Coll. Bankruptcy; mem. Am. Law Inst., Phi Beta Kappa. Democrat. Office: US Bankruptcy Ct PO Box 2070 Oakland CA 94604-2070

NEWTON, ALEXANDER WORTHY, lawyer; b. Birmingham, Ala., June 19, 1930; s. Jeff H. and Annis Lillian (Kelly) N.; m. Sue Aldridge, Dec. 22, 1952; children: Lamar Aldridge Newton, Kelly McClure Newton Hammond, Jane Worthy Newton, Robins Jeffry Newton. B.S., U. Ala., 1952, J.D., 1957. Bar: Ala. 1957. Pvt. practice law, Birmingham; assoc. Hare, Wynn & Newell, 1957; ptnr. Hare, Wynn, Newell & Newton, 1961—. Del. U.S. Ct. Appeals (11th cir.) Jud. Conf., 1988, 89, 90, 91; mem. Jefferson County Jud. Nominating Com., 1983-89; mem. Birmingham Airport Authority, 1991—; founding dir. First Comm. Bank. Co-author: (with others) Federal Appellate Procedure, 11th Circuit, 1996. Vice chmn. Birmingham Racing Commn., 1984-87; v.p. U. Ala. Law Sch. Found., 1978-79, pres., 1980-82, exec. com., 1987—; mem. Leadership Ala. Class IV; trustee Ala. Trust Fund. Capt. inf. U.S. Army, 1952-54. Recipient Disting. Alumnus award Farrah Law Soc. U. Ala., 1982, Sam W. Piples Disting. Alumnus award 1982. Fellow Am. Coll. Trial Lawyers (state chmn. 1983-84, regents' nominatin com. 1984-85), Internat. Soc. Barristers (bd. dirs. 1974-75, sec.-treas. 1976-77, v.p. 1977-78, pres. 1979-80), Internat. Acad. Trial Lawyers (bd. dirs. 1998—); mem. ABA, ATLA, Am. Bar Found., Ala. State Bar (chmn. practices and procedures subsect. 1965, governance com. and pres.'s task force 1984-86, pres.'s com. 1987-88), Birmingham Bar Assn. (exec. com. 1967), Ala. Trial Lawyers Assn. (sec.-treas. 1958-65), Am. Judicature Soc., 11th Cir. His. Soc. (trustee 1988—), Sigma Chi. Democrat. Presbyterian. Clubs: Shoal Creek, Birmingham Country (Birmingham); Capital City (Atlanta); Garden of the God (Colorado Springs, Colo.); University Club (New York). Federal civil litigation, State civil litigation, Personal injury. Home: 2837 Canoe Brook Ln Birmingham AL 35243-5908 Office: Hare Wynn Newell & Newton 800 Massey Bldg 2025 3d Ave N Birmingham AL 35203-3330

NEWTON, NELL JESSUP, dean, law educator; b. St. Louis, Apr. 30, 1944; d. Robert Edward and Marcella (Boehm) Mier. BA, U. Calif., Berkeley, 1973; JD, U. Calif., Hastings, 1976. Bar: Calif., Washington, U.S. Ct. Appeals (9th crct.), U.S. Supreme Ct. Prof. Cath. U. Sch. Law, 1976-92; prof. Washington Coll. Law Am. U., Washington, 1992—98; dean U. Denver Law Sch., 1998—2000, U. Conn. Sch. Law, Hartford, 2000—. Lectr. Internat. Law Inst., Washington, 1984-89; prof. Pre-Law Summer Inst. for Native Am. Students, U. N.Mex. Law Sch., Albuquerque, 1990, 91, 93; panelist, speaker NEH, 1981; presenter S.W. Intertribal Ct. of Appeals, 1990; panelist Orgn. Am. Historians, 1991. Co-author: American Indian Law, 3d edit., 1991; contbr. articles to profl. jours. NEH fellow Harvard Law Sch., 1980. Mem. Assn. Am. Law Schs. (Native Am. rights sect., mem. exec. com. 1987—, chair 1987-88, oral argument newsletter editor 1987—, mem. women in legal edn. sect. 1987—, chair profl. devel. workshop com. 1992, sec. 1993), Balt.-Washington-Va. Women Law Tchrs. Group (planning com. Symposium on Scholarship I 1985, II 1986), Thurston Soc., Order of Coif. Office: U Conn Sch Law Hartranft 103 55 Elizabeth St Hartford CT 06105*

NEXSEN, JULIAN JACOBS, lawyer; b. Kingstree, S.C., Apr. 14, 1924; s. William Ivey and Barbara (Jacobs) N.; m. Mary Elizabeth McIntosh, Jan. 28, 1948; children: Louise Ivey (Mrs. Heyward Harles Bouknight, Jr.), Julian Jacobs Jr. Student, The Citadel, 1941-43; BS magna cum laude, U. S.C., 1948, JD magna cum laude, 1950. Bar: S.C. 1950, U.S. Supreme Ct. 1960. Partner firm Nexsen Pruet Jacobs & Pollard, Columbia, S.C., 1950—. Trustee Richland County Pub. Libr., chmn., 1976-77; trustee Providence Hosp., chmn., 1984-86; trustee Providence Found., Providence Ministries, Sisters of Charity of St. Augustine Health Sys.; past bd. dirs. Columbia Music Festival Assn., ARC Richland-Lexington Counties, Ctrl. Carolina Cmty. Found.; mem. U.S.C. Law Sch. partnership bd.; elder Presbyn. Ch., trustee Congaree Presbytery, 1967-87, Synod, S.C., 1969-74, mem. Trinity Presbytery Coun., 1991-95. Lt. inf. AUS, 1943-46, ETO, capt., 1950-51, Korea. Decorated Bronze Star with oak leaf cluster; named in Best Lawyers in Am., 1989-2000. Mem. ABA, S.C. Bar (treas., bd. govs. 1974-79, ho. of dels. 1980-92), Richland County Bar Assn. (pres. 1974-75, Disting. Svc. award 1987), Am. Bar Found., S.C. Bar Found. (pres. 1971-72), S.C. Law Inst. (coun., exec. com. 1986—), Am. Law Inst., Am. Coll. Trust and Estate Counsel (regent 1973-82), Am. Judicature Soc., Forest Lake Country Club, Palmetto Club, Kiwanis (bd. dirs. 1972-74, 77-79), Phi Beta Kappa. General corporate, Estate planning, Probate. Home: 2840 Sheffield Rd Columbia SC 29204-2332 Office: Nexsen Pruet Jacobs & Pollard Drawer 2426 1441 Main St Columbia SC 29202-2848 E-mail: jjn@npjp.com

NICHOL, GENE RAY, JR. university dean; b. Dallas, May 11, 1951; s. Gene R. and Dolores (Dumas) N.; m. Janet Castle, Aug. 20, 1973 (div. 1978); m. Glenn George, Nov. 25, 1984. BA in Philosophy, Okla. State U., 1973; JD, U. Texas, 1976. Bar: Alaska 1978. Assoc. Ely, Guess and Rudd, Anchorage, 1976-78; asst. prof. W.Va. U., Morgantown, 1978-80, assoc. prof., 1980-82; prof. law U. Fla., Gainesville, 1983-84; Cutler prof. law, dir. Inst. of Bill of Rights Law Coll. William and Mary, Williamsburg, W.Va., 1984-88; dean U. Colo. Law Sch., 1988-95; dean, Burton Craige prof. law U.N.C. Host Culture Wars, KBDI T.V., Denver, 1995-96. Author: (with M. Redish) Federal Courts; contbr. articles to profl. jours. Posten research grantee U. W.Va., 1980, 81, 82. Mem. Nat. Lawyers Guild (coms. 1978, vice chair Colo. reapportionment commn.), Am. Law Inst., ACLU (coms. 1978—), Am. Bar Found. Fellows, Order of Coif. Roman Catholic. Avocation: back packing. Office: U N C Chapel Hill Van Hecke-Wettach Hall CB No 3380 Hill Chapel Hill NC 27599-0001

NICHOLAS, FREDERICK M. lawyer; b. N.Y.C., May 30, 1920; s. Benjamin L. and Rose F. (Nechols) N.; m. Eleanore Berman, Sept. 2, 1951 (div. 1963); children: Deborah, Jan, Tony; m. Joan Fields, Jan. 2, 1983. AB, U. So. Calif., 1947; postgrad., U. Chgo., 1949-50; JD, U. So. Calif., 1952. Bar: Calif. 1952, U.S. Dist. Ct. Calif. 1952, U.S. Ct. Appeals (9th cir.) 1952. Assoc. Loeb & Loeb, L.A., 1952-56; ptnr. Swerdlow, Glikbarg & Nicholas, Beverly Hills, Calif., 1956-62; pvt. practice, 1962-80; pres., atty. Hapsmith Co., 1980—. Bd. dirs. Malibu Grand Prix, L.A., 1982-90; gen. counsel Beverly Hills Realty Bd., 1971-79; founder, pres. Pub. Counsel, L.A., 1970-73. Author: Setting Up a Shopping Center, 1960, Commercial Real Property Lease Practice, 1976. Chmn. Mus. Contemporary Art, L.A., 1987-93, chmn. com. Walt Disney Concert Hall, L.A., 1987-95; trustee Music Ctr. L.A. County, 1987-95, L.A. Philharm. Assn., 1987-95, Art Ctr. Pasadena, Calif., 2001—; chmn. Calif. Pub. Broadcasting Commn., Sacramento, 1972-78; pres. Maple Ctr., 1977-79; co-developer Ronald Reagan Bldg., Washington, 1998; adminstr. Estate of Sam Francis, 1996—; trustee Pitzer coll., 1992-95; hon. trustee Art Ctr. Coll. of Design, 2001—. Recipient Citizen of Yr. award Beverly Hills Bd. Realtors, 1978, Man of Yr. award Maple Ctr., 1980, Pub. Svc. award Coro Found., 1988, The Medici award L.A. C. of C., 1990, Founders award Pub. Counsel, 1990, Trustees award Calif. Inst. Arts, 1993, City of Angels award L.A. Ctrl. Bus. Assn.; named Outstanding Founder in Philanthropy, Nat. Philanthropy Day Com., 1990. Mem. Beverly Hills Bar Assn. (bd. govs. 1970-76, Disting. Svc. award 1974, 81, Exceptional Svc. award 1986), Beverly Hills C. of C. (Man of Yr. 1983). Real property. Home: 1001 Maybrook Dr Beverly Hills CA 90210-2715 Office: Hapsmith Co 5440 McConnell Ave Los Angeles CA 90066

NICHOLAS, WILLIAM RICHARD, lawyer; b. Pontiac, Mich., June 19, 1934; s. Reginald and Edna Irene (Bartlett) N.; m. Diana Lee Johnson, Aug. 20, 1960; children: Susan Lee, William Richard Jr. BS in Bus., U. Idaho, 1956; JD, U. Mich., 1962. Bar: 1963. Of counsel Latham & Watkins, Los Angeles, 1962-96. Contbr. numerous articles on taxation. Lt. (j.g.) USN, 1956-59. Mem. Calif. Bar Assn., Los Angeles County Bar Assn., Am. Coll. Tax Counsel. Home: 1808 Old Ranch Rd Los Angeles CA 90049-2207 Office: Latham & Watkins 633 W 5th St Ste 4000 Los Angeles CA 90071-2005

NICHOLLS, RICHARD H. lawyer; b. Toronto, Ont., Can., Oct. 27, 1938; s. Richard S. and Roberta T. Nicholls; m. Judy Carter, Apr. 15, 1963; children: Christopher T., Jamie C.; m. Anne Delaney, June 10, 1978. BA cum laude, Amherst Coll., 1960; LLB, Stamford U., 1963; LLM, NYU, 1964. Bar: Calif. 1964, N.Y. 1965, D.C. Assoc. Mudge Rose Guthrie, Alexander & Ferdon and predecessor, N.Y.C., 1964-70, ptnr., 1971-94; of counsel Orrick, Herrington & Sutcliffe, N.Y., 1995—. Mem. ABA, N.Y. State Bar Assn., Nat. Assn. Bond Lawyers, Stamford Yacht Club. Municipal (including bonds), Corporate taxation, Personal income taxation. Home: 159 Ocean Dr W Stamford CT 06902-8004 Office: Orrick Herrington & Sutcliffe 666 5th Ave Rm 203 New York NY 10103-1798

NICHOLS, F(REDERICK) HARRIS, lawyer; b. Chgo., Jan. 31, 1936; s. Frederick M. and Keturah (Rollinson) N.; div.; children: Rebecca K., Pamela R., Katurah I. BA cum laude, Williams Coll., 1958; LLB, Harvard U., 1961. Bar: N.Y. 1961. Assoc. Cohen Swados Wright Hanifin Bradford & Brett LLP, Buffalo, 1962-65, ptnr., 1965—. Chmn. youth svcs. com. neighborhood svcs. United Way of Erie County, 1998—; membership com., bd. dirs. Buffalo Fine Arts Acad.; chmn. bd. dirs. Child and Family Svcs. Buffalo, 1984-85, bd. dirs., chmn. com., 1983-85; mem. resource mgmt. com. United Way Buffalo and Erie County, 1998—. Fulbright scholar U. Hamburg, Fed. Republic of Germany, 1961-62. Mem. ABA, N.Y. Bar Assn., Erie County Bar Assn., Saturn Club. Republican. Episcopalian. Contracts commercial, General corporate, Securities. Office: Cohen Swados Wright Hanifin Bradford & Brett 70 Niagara St Ste 1 Buffalo NY 14202-3467 E-mail: fhn@cohen-swados.com

NICHOLS, HENRY ELIOT, lawyer, savings and loan executive; b. N.Y.C. m. Frances Griffin Morrison, Aug. 12, 1950 (dec. July 1978); children: Clyde Whitney, Diane Spencer; m. Mary ann Wall, May 31, 1987. BA, Yale U., 1946; JD, U. Va., 1948. Bar: D.C. 1950, U.S. Dist. Ct. 1950, U.S. Ct. Appeals 1952, U.S. Supreme Ct. 1969. Assoc. Frederick W. Berens, Washington, 1950-52; sole practice, 1952—. Real estate columnist Washington Star, 1966-81; pres., gen. counsel Hamilton Fed. Savs. & Loan Assn., 1971-74; vice chmn. bd. Columbia 1st Bank (formerly Columbia 1st Fed. Savs. & Loan Assn.), Washington, 1974-90, bd. dirs.; pres. Century Fin. Corp., 1971-90; regional v.p. Preview, Inc., 1972-78; bd. dirs., exec. com. Columbia Real Estate Title Ins. Co., Washington, 1968-78. Contbr. articles to profl. jours.; patentee med. inventions. Nat. adv. bd. Harker Prep. Sch., 1975-80; exec. com. Father Walter E. Schmitz Meml. Fund, Cath. U., 1982-83; bd. dirs. Vincent T. Lombardi Cancer Rsch. Ctr., 1979-84; del. Pres. Johnson's Conf. LAw and Poverty, 1967; vice chmn. Mayor's Ad Hoc Com. Housing Code Problems, Washington, 1968-71; mem. Commn. Landlord-Tenant Affairs Washington City Coun., 1970-71; vice chmn. Washington Area Realtors Coun., 1970; exec. com., dir. Downtown Progress, 1970; bd. dirs. Washington Mental Health Assn., 1973, Washington Med. Ctr., 1975. Capt. USAAF, 1942-46. Mem. Am. Land Devel. Assn., Nat. Assn. Real Estate Editors, Washington Bd. Realtors (pres. 1970, Realtor of Yr. 1970, Martin Isen award 1981), Greater Met. Washington Bs. Trade (bd. dirs. 1974-80), U.S. League Savs. Assns. (attys. com. 1971-80), Washington Savs. and Loan League, ABA, D.C. Bar Assn., Internat. Real Estate Fedn., Yale Club, Cosmos Club, Rolls Royce Club, Antique Auto Club, St. Elmo Club, Omega Tau Rho. Episcoppalian. Real property. Home: 1 Kittery Ct Bethesda MD 20817-2137 Office: 1112 16th St NW Washington DC 20036-4823

NICHOLSON, BRADLEY JAMES, lawyer, court staff; b. Montebello, Calif., Sept. 22, 1958; s. Thomas Edwin and Charlotte Elizabeth (Knight) N.; m. Anne Marie Dooley, Oct. 6, 1990. BA, Reed Coll., 1983; JD, U. Pa., 1990. Bar: Calif. 1990, Nev. 1998, Oreg. 2001. Atty. Wilson, Sonsini, Goodrich & Rosati, Palo Alto, Calif., 1990-91; law clk. to Hon. Morris S. Arnold U.S. Dist. Ct., Ft. Smith, Ark., 1991-92; atty. Coudert Bros., San Jose, Calif., 1992-94; law clerk to Hon. Morris S. Arnold U.S. Cir. Ct., Little Rock, 1994-96; atty. Brown & Bain, Palo Alto, Calif., 1997-98; staff atty. ctrl. legal staff Nev. Supreme Ct., Carson City, 1998-99, prin. staff atty., ctrl. legal staff, 1999-2000; appellate staff atty. Oreg. Supreme Ct., Salem, Oreg., 2000—. Contbr. articles to profl. jours. Mem. Federalist Soc.(vice chmn. publications Litigation practice group, 1997-98, pres. Little Rock lawyers chpt. 1995-96). Avocations: golf, fishing, music. Office: Oreg Supreme Ct 1163 State St Salem OR 97301-2563

NICHOLSON, MICHAEL, lawyer; b. Alexandroupolis, Greece, Nov. 26, 1936; m. Diana Long, June 21, 1964. BSCE, Northwestern U., 1961; MSCE, Columbia U., 1963; JD, St. John's U., 1970. Bar: N.Y. 1971, U.S. Dist. Ct. (ea. dist.) N.Y. 1979, U.S. Ct. Appeals (2d cir.) 1990. Counsel George A. Fuller Co., N.Y.C., 1970-72, Leonard Wegman Cons. Engrs., N.Y.C., 1972-73; sr. ptnr. Corner, Finn, Nicholson & Charles, Bklyn., 1978—. Contbr. articles to profl. jours. Bd. dirs. Bklyn. Nephrology Found., 1979, Pelham Bay Gen. Hosp., 1979. Mem. ABA, NSPE, Am. Arbitration Assn., N.Y. State Bar Assn., N.Y. State Soc. Profl. Engrs., Mcpl. Engrs. City N.Y. (award 1972). State civil litigation, Contracts commercial, Government contracts and claims. Office: 75 Livingston St 29th Fl Brooklyn NY 11201-5054

NICKEL, HENRY V. lawyer; b. Chgo., Aug. 8, 1943; AB, U. Va., 1965; JD, George Washington U., 1968. Bar: D.C. 1968. Mem. Hunton & Williams, Washington. Rsch. editor: George Washington Law Rev., 1967-68. Mem. Order of Coif. Administrative and regulatory, Appellate, Environmental. Office: Hunton & Williams 1900 K St NW Washington DC 20006-1110 E-mail: hnickel@hunton.com

NICKELL, CHRISTOPHER SHEA, lawyer; b. Paducah, Ky., Mar. 21, 1959; s. Carl Duane and Anna June (Starrett) N. BA, DePauw U., 1981; JD, U. Ky., 1984. Bar: Ky. 1984, U.S. Dist. Ct. (ea. dist.) Ky., 1985, U.S. Dist. Ct. (we. dist.) Ky. 1989. Assoc. Truman L. Dehner, Morehead, Ky., 1984-87; asst. commonwealth atty. 21st Jud. Dist. Ky., 1986-87; assoc. Boehl, Stopher, Graves & Deindoerfer, Paducah, 1989-91, Saladino Law Firm, Paducah, Ky., 1991-97, Nickell Law Firm, Paducah, 1997—. Vis. lectr. U. N.C., Chapel Hill, 1987-88; adj. prof. Murray State U., 1989-91. Trustee DePauw U., Greencastle, 1981-84; bd. dirs. N.E. Ky. Legal Svcs., Inc., Morehead, 1985-87, Western Ky. Easter Seal Soc., 1993-99. Named to Hon. Order Ky. Cols., 1981. Mem. ABA, Ky. Bar Assn. (Ky. Outstanding Young Lawyer award 1995), McCracken County Bar Assn., Ky. Acad. Trial Attys., Masons (32 deg.) Paducah Lions Club (bd. dirs., chmn. Easter Seals telethon, pres., vice dist. gov., dist. gov.), Elks, Delta Theta Phi. Democrat. General civil litigation, Personal injury, Workers' compensation. Office: Nickell Law Firm Old Courthouse Sta 634 Kentucky Ave Paducah KY 42003-1720 E-mail: nlf@ssi-net.net

NICKERSON, DON C. lawyer, former prosecutor; U.S. atty. U.S. Dist. Ct. (So. Dist.), Iowa, 1993—2001; assoc. gen. counsel Wellmark Blue Cross & Blue Shield , 2001—. Office: Wellmark Blue Cross & Blue Shield of Iowa 636 Grand Ave Des Moines IA 50309-2565*

NICOARA, ANDRA CHRISTINA, lawyer; b. Deva, Romania; naturalized, 1982; d. Vasile Marius and Dorina Lavinia Nicoara. Student, King's Coll. London, 1992; BS summa cum laude, Georgetown U., 1993; JD cum laude, Harvard U., 1997. Bar: N.Y. 1997. Program advisor Ptnrs. for Internat. Edn. and Tng., Washington, 1993-94; assoc. Coudert Bros., N.Y.C., 1997—. Editor: Attacks on Justice: Harassment and Persucution of Jduges and Lawyers, 1994, Harvard Human Rights Jour., 1996. Avocations: literature, foreign languages, piano. Alternative dispute resolution, Private international, Public international. Home: 243 West End Ave Apt 1404 New York NY 10023 Office: Coudert Bros 11134 Ave of Americas New York NY 10036

NICOLAIDES, MARY, lawyer; b. N.Y.C., June 7, 1927; d. George and Dorothy Nicolaides. BCE, CUNY, 1947; MBA with distinction, DePaul U., 1975, JD, 1981. Bar: Ill. 1982, U.S. Dist. Ct. (no. dist.) Ill. 1982, U.S. Patent Office 1983. Sr. design engr. cement subs. U.S. Steel Corp., N.Y.C., then Pitts., 1948-71; sole practice Chgo., 1982—. Mem. ABA. Republican. Greek Orthodox. Patent, Probate, Elder. Address: 233 E Erie St Apt 1804 Chicago IL 60611-2903

NICOLL, JOHN, lawyer, financial executive; b. Goshen, N.Y., Oct. 5, 1931; s. Alfred and Jessie (McLaughlin) N.; B.A., George Washington U., 1958; LL.B., Yale U., 1961; m. Rosalie Rizzo, Feb. 22, 1956; children— Stephanie, John Isaac, Alfred Augustus. Bar: N.Y. 1961, Pa. 1977, U.S. Supreme Ct. 1969. Sr. v.p., corp. sec., house counsel Empire Nat. Bank, Middletown, asst., assoc. 1969-72, administrv. asst., chief counsel Office of Comptroller of Currency, Washington, 1964-69; asst. gen. counsel, dep. gen. counsel to bd. govs. FRS, Washington, 1972-75; sr. v.p., gen. counsel, sec. Equimark Corp./Equibank, Pitts., 1975— . Served with USMC, 1951-55. Mem. ABA, Pa. Bar Assn., N.Y. State Bar Assn. Club: Duquesne, City (Pitts.). Contracts commercial, General corporate. Office: Equimark Corp Tw Oliver Pla Pittsburgh PA 15222 also: Colo Nat Bancshares Inc 950 7th St TA Denver CO 80202

NIEHOFF, LEONARD MARVIN, lawyer; b. St. Louis, Dec. 2, 1957; s. Leonard Marvin and May (Gordon) N.; m. Nancy Wright Blotner, July 31, 1981. BA with high distinction, U. Mich., 1981, JD, postgrad., U. Mich., 1984. Bar: Mich. 1984, U.S. Dist. Ct. (ea. dist.) Mich., 1985, U.S. Dist. Ct. (we. dist.) Mich. 1985, U.S. Ct. Appeals (6th cir.) 1985, U.S. Supreme Ct. 1988. Research asst. U. Mich. Law Sch., Ann Arbor, 1983; shareholder Butzel Long, Detroit, 1984—. Adj. prof. law U. Detroit Law Sch., 1988—, Wayne State U. Law Sch., 1989—. Editor U. Mich. Jour. Law Reform, 1983-84. Bd. advisors C.S. Mott Children's Hosp.; bd. dirs. Mich. Theatre Found. Named to 40 Under 40, Crain's Detroit Bus., 1996. Mem. ABA (forum com. on comms. law 1985—), Fed. Bar Assn. (exec. bd. 1995—), State Bar Mich. (chmn. constl. law com., mem. law and media com., bar jour. adv. bd.), Detroit Bar Assn., Washtenaw Bar Assn. (chmn. trial practice sect.), U. Musical Soc. (bd. dirs.), Mich. Theater Found. (bd. dirs.), CS Mott Children's Hosp. (bd. dirs.). Avocations: music, film, art. General civil litigation, Constitutional, Libel. Office: 350 S Main St Ste 300 Ann Arbor MI 48104-2131

NIEHOFF, PHILIP JOHN, lawyer; b. Beaver Dam, Wis., Dec. 31, 1959; s. John Henry and Muriel Jean (Moore) N. BBA with distinction, U. Wis., 1982, JD cum laude, 1985; LLM in Securities Regulation, Georgetown U., 1988. Bar: Wis. 1985, U.S. Dist. Ct. (we. dist.) Wis. 1985, Ill. 1991. Atty. SEC, Washington, 1985-90; assoc. Mayer, Brown & Platt, Chgo., 1990-95, ptnr., 1996—. Co-author: Current Law of Insider Trading, 1990, Public Offerings, securities law handbook, 1997; contbg. author: Securitization of Financial Assets, 1991. Fed. Bar Assn. scholar, 1988. Mem. ABA, State Bar Wis., State Bar Ill., Chgo. Bar Assn., Order of Coif, Golden Key Honor Soc., Beta Gamma Sigma, Phi Kappa Phi, Phi Eta Sigma. Republican. Lutheran. Avocations: fishing, computers, reading, travel. General corporate, Securities. Home: 2800 N Lake Shore Dr Apt 2416 Chicago IL 60657-6248 Office: Mayer Brown & Platt 190 S La Salle St Ste 3100 Chicago IL 60603-3441

NIEHUSS, JOHN MARVIN, lawyer; b. Ann Arbor, Mich., Mar. 7, 1937; s. Marvin Lemmon Niehuss and Lois Celicia Markham; m. Rosemary Juliette Neaher, June 30, 1973 (div. Mar. 1991); children: Juliette, John. BA, Amherst Coll., 1958; JD, U. Mich., 1962. Assoc. atty. Sullivan & Cromwell, N.Y.C., 1966-69; legal advisor Govt. of Zambia, Lusaka, 1969-71; loan officer, dir. World Bank, Washington, 1971-73, 90-91; dep. asst. sec. U.S. Treasury Dept., 1974-77, 89-90; v.p. Merrill Lynch, N.Y.C., 1977-89; gen. counsel Inter-Am. Devel. Bank, Washington, 1992-99, Export-Import Bank U.S., Washington, 1999-2001. Mem. adv. bd. Internat. Law Inst., Washington, 1977—. Mem. Coun. Fgn. Rels., Met. Club. Republican. Avocations: golf, hiking, fly fishing, whitewater rafting. Finance. Home: 3019 45th St NW Washington DC 20016-3523

NIELSEN, CHRISTIAN BAYARD, lawyer; b. San Jose, Calif., May 10, 1954; s. Bayard R. and June (Morgan) N.; m. Kathleen Dearden, Oct. 25, 1980; children: Bayard Douglas, Chandler Kathleen. BA, U. Pacific, Stockton, Calif., 1976; JD, Pepperdine U., 1979. Bar: Calif. 1979, U.S. Dist. Ct. (no. and ea. dists.) Calif. 1979. Sr. ptnr. Robinson & Wood, Inc., San Jose, Calif., 1979—. Arbitrator Fed. Panel and State Panel, 1982—; lectr. Calif. Continuing Edn. of the Bar, 1989—. Mem. ABA, Assn. Def. Counsel of No. Calif. (lectr. 1988—), Am. Bd. Trial Advocates (cert. civil trial advocate), Nat. Bd. Trial Advocacy, Def. Rsch. Inst., Internat. Assn. Ins. Counsel, Santa Clara County Bar Assn. Republican. Methodist. General civil litigation, Personal injury, Product liability. Office: Robinson & Wood Inc 227 N 1st St Fl 2 San Jose CA 95113-1000 E-mail: cbn@r-winc.com

NIELSEN, LYNN CAROL, lawyer, educational consultant; b. Perth Amboy, N.J., Jan. 11, 1950; d. Hans and Esther (Pucker) N.; m. Russell F. Baldwin, Nov. 22, 1980; 1 child, Blake Nielsen Baldwin. BS, Millersville U., 1972; MA, NYU, 1979; JD, Rutgers U., 1984. Bar: N.J. 1984; cert. tchr. handicapped, reading specialist, learning disability tchr. cons., elem. edn. supr. Instr. Woodbridge (N.J.) Twp. Bd. Edn., 1972-83; legal intern appellate sect. divsn. criminal justice Atty. Gen. State N.J., Trenton, 1983, dep. atty. gen. divsn. civil law, 1985; assoc. Kantor & Kusic, Keyport, N.J., 1984-86, Kantor & Linderoth, Keyport, 1986-92. Officer Fords (N.J.) Sch. # 14 PTO, 1974-75; elder First Presbyn. Ch. Avenel, N.J., 1985-88, Flemington (N.J.) Presbyn. Ch., 1997-99; bd. dirs. New Beginnings Nursery Sch., Woodbridge, 1989-90, Flemington Presbyn. Nursery Sch., 1991-93; elder Flemington Presbyn. Ch., 1997-99; bd. mem. Woodside Farms Homeowners Assn., 1996-99. Mem. ABA, N.J. Bar Assn., Monmouth County Bar Assn., Hunterdon County Bar Assn. Avocations: reading, skiing, sailing. Home and Office: 3 Buchannan Way Flemington NJ 08822-3205

NIEMEYER, PAUL VICTOR, federal judge; b. Princeton, N.J., Apr. 5, 1941; s. Gerhart and Lucie (Lenzner) N.; m. Susan Kinley, Aug. 24, 1963; children Jonathan K., Peter E., Christopher J. AB, Kenyon Coll., 1962; student, U. Munich, Federal Republic of Germany, 1962-63; JD, U. Notre Dame, 1966. Bars: Md. 1966, U.S. Dist. Ct. Md. 1967, U.S. Ct. Appeals (4th cir.) 1968, U.S. Supreme Ct. 1970, U.S. Dist Ct. (so. dist.) Tex. 1977, U.S. Ct. Appeals (5th cir.) 1978, U.S. Ct. Appeals (3d cir.) 1980. Assoc. Piper & Marbury, Balt., 1966-74, ptnr., 1974-88; U.S. dist. judge U.S. Dist. Ct. Md., 1988-90; fed. judge U.S. Ct. Appeals (4th cir.), 1990—. Lectr. advanced bus. law Johns Hopkins U., Balt., 1971-75; lectr. Md. Jud. Conf., Md. Ct. Clks. Assn.; sr. lecturing fellow in appellate advocacy Duke U. Sch. of Law, 1994—; mem. standing com. on rules of practice and procedure cts. appeals, 1973-88, atty. grievance com.-hearing panel,

1978-81, select com.-profl. conduct, 1983-85, adv. com. on Fed. Rules of Civil Procedure, 1993—, chmn., 1996-2000. Co-author: Maryland Rules Commentary, 1984, supplement, 1988, 2d edit., 1992; contbr. articles to profl. jours. Recipient Spl. Merit citation Am. Judicature Soc., 1987. Fellow Am. Coll. Trial Lawyers, Am. Bar Found., Md. Bar Found., Md. Bar Assn. (Disting. Svc. award litigation sect. 1981), Am. Law Inst.; mem. Wednesday Law Club, Lawyers' Round Table. Republican. Episcopalian. Office: US Cir Ct Md US Courthouse 101 W Lombard St Ste 910 Baltimore MD 21201-2611

NIESET, JAMES ROBERT, lawyer; b. Ann Arbor, Mich., Oct. 29, 1942; s. Robert Thomas and Mary Elizabeth (Young) N.; m. Mercedes Elizabeth Plauche, June 11, 1966; children— Susan Lane, James Robert, Jr., John Kearney, Amy Plauche. B.S. Tulane U., 1964, J.D, 1967. Bar: La., 1967, U.S. Dist. Ct. (ea. and we. dist.) La. 1967, U.S. Dist. Ct. (ea. dist.) Tex. 1975, U.S. Ct. Appeals (5th cir.) 1970, U.S. Supreme Ct. 1978. Assoc. Chaffe, McCall, Phillips, Toler & Sarpy, New Orleans, 1967-70; ptnr. Plauche, Smith & Nieset, Lake Charles, La., 1970— . Mem. Immaculate Conception Cathedral Parish Council, Lake Charles, 1982-84, pres., 1984. Bd. dirs. St. Louis High Sch., Lake Charles, 1981-89; bd. dirs. Tulane Law Sch., mem. deans coun., 1982—, pres. coun., 1992—; bd. dirs. Nat. Lake Charles Civic Symphony, 1992-96. Served to capt. USAF, 1967-70. Mem. ABA, La. State Bar Assn., S.W. La. Bar Assn. (treas. 1972, pres., 1992-93), S.W. La. Assn. Def. Counsel (v.p. 1982), Maritime Law Assn., Internatl. Assn. Ins. Counsel. Democrat. Roman Catholic. Admiralty, Insurance, Product liability. Home: 1505 Shell Beach Dr Lake Charles LA 70601-5657 Office: Plauche Smith & Nieset 1123 Pithon St Lake Charles LA 70601

NIGRO, RUSSELL M. state supreme court justice; b. Mar. 23, 1946; Assoc. justice Pa. Supreme Ct., Phila., 1996—. Office: Pa Supreme Ct 1818 Market St Ste 3730 Philadelphia PA 19103-3639

NIKAS, RICHARD JOHN, lawyer; b. Long Beach, Calif., Sept. 9, 1968; s. John Nikolas and Dorothy (Bernardo) N. BA in Internat. Rels., U. So. Calif., 1991, JD, 1995. Bar: Calif. Spl. projects coord. Vessel Assist Assn. Am., Newport Beach, Calif., 1989-94; lawyer Williams Woolley Cogswell Nakazawa & Russell, Long Beach, 1994—. Guest lectr. maritime law U. So. Calif., L.A., 1998—; chmn. USCG Working Group on Nat. Maritime Incident Reporting Sys., Washington, 1997—. Author: Benedict on Admiralty, 1998, Moore's Federal Practice, 1998, The Last Yankee, 1999, Recreational Boating Law, 2000, Admiralty Practice and Procedure, 2000. Head football coach Ocean View H.S., Long Beach, 1995; mentor Long Beach Unified Sch. Dist., 1997—; pitcher Greek Olympic Baseball Team, Atlantic City Surf Profl. Baseball Club; bd. govs. The Am. Mariner, Loyola U., 1999. Recipient Best Oralist award Spong Nat. Invitational Moot Ct., Williamsburg, Va., 1995, Meritorious Pub. Svc. medal USCG. Mem. Calif. State Bar Assn., Maritime Law Assn., Soc. of Naval Architects and Marine Engrs. (chmn. panel 0-38). Avocation: baseball. Admiralty, Federal civil litigation, Transportation. Address: 17652 Wrightwood Ln Huntington Beach CA 92649-4969

NILES, JOHN GILBERT, lawyer; b. Dallas, Oct. 5, 1943; s. Paul Dickerman and Nedra Mary (Arendts) N.; m. Marian Higginbotham, Nov. 21, 1970; children: Paul Breckenridge, Matthew Higginbotham. BA in History, Stanford U., 1965, LLB, U. Tex., 1968. Bar: Tex. 1968, Calif. 1969, U.S. Dist. Ct. (cen. dist.) Calif. 1973, U.S. Ct. Appeals (9th cir.) 1973, U.S. Dist. Ct. (so. dist.) Calif. 1977, U.S. Supreme Ct. 1979, U.S. Dist. Ct. (no. dist.) Calif. 1983. Assoc. O'Melveny & Myers, Los Angeles, 1973-77, ptnr., 1978-99; of counsel, 1999—. Judge pro tem mcpl. ct. L.A.; spkr., panel mem. Practicing Law Inst., Calif. C.E.B. Served to lt. comdr. USNR, 1968-72, Vietnam. Mem. ABA, Los Angeles County Bar Assn., Am. Judicature Soc. Clubs: Bel-Air Bay (Pacific Palisades, Calif.); Calif. (Los Angeles). Avocation: sailing. Federal civil litigation, State civil litigation, Insurance. Home: 1257 Villa Woods Dr Pacific Palisades CA 90272-3953 Office: O'Melveny & Myers 400 S Hope St Los Angeles CA 90071-2899

NILLES, JOHN MICHAEL, lawyer; b. Langdon, N.D., Aug. 20, 1930; s. John Joseph and Isabel Mary (O'Neil) N.; m. Barbara Ann Cook, June 22, 1957; children: Terese M., Daniel J., Marcia L., Thomas M., Margaret J. BA cum laude, St. Johns U., 1955; JD cum laude with distinction, U. N.D., 1958. Bar: N.D. 1958, U.S. Dist. Ct. N.D. 1958, U.S. Ct. Appeals (8th cir.) 1958, Minn. 1991. Shareholder, dir., pres. Nilles, Hansen and Davies, Ltd., Fargo, N.D., 1958-90, of counsel, 1990-95; exec. v.p., gen. counsel Met. Fin. Corp., Mpls., 1990-95, First Bank F.S.B., Mpls., 1995; ret., 1996. Pres., bd. dirs. Legal Aid Soc. N.D., Fargo, 1970-76, Red River Estate Planning Coun., 1980-87; vice-chmn. disciplinary bd. Supreme Ct. N.D., 1984-90. Bd. editors N.D. Law Rev., 1957-58. Mem. exec. bd. Red. River Valley coun. Boy Scouts Am., 1959-70; bd. regents U. Mary, Bismarck, N.D., 1967-77; pres., bd. dirs. Cath. Charities, Fargo, 1959-65, Southeast Mental Health Ctr., Fargo, 1972-80. Staff sgt. USAF, 1951-54. Fellow Am. Coll. Trust and Estate Counsel (state dir. 1979-90); mem. ABA, State Bar Assn. N.D., Minn. Bar Assn., Order of Coif. Republican. Roman Catholic. Avocations: tennis, downhill skiing, cross-country skiing, hunting, gun collecting. Banking, General corporate. Home: 10412 Fawns Way Eden Prairie MN 55347-5117

NIMETZ, MATTHEW, lawyer, investment company executive; b. Bklyn., June 17, 1939; s. Joseph L. and Elsie (Botwinik) N.; m. Gloria S. Lorch, June 24, 1975; children: Alexandra Elise, Lloyd. B.A., Williams Coll., 1960, LL.D. (hon.), 1979; B.A. (Rhodes scholar), Balliol Coll., Oxford (Eng.) U., 1962, M.A., 1966; LL.B., Harvard U., 1965. Bar: N.Y. 1966, D.C. 1968. Law clk. to Justice John M. Harlan, U.S. Supreme Ct., 1965-67; staff asst. to Pres. Johnson, 1967-69; asso. firm Simpson Thacher & Bartlett, N.Y.C., 1969-74, ptnr., 1974-77; counselor Dept. of State, Washington, 1977-80, acting coord. refugee affairs, 1979-80, under sec. of state for security assistance, sci. and tech., 1980; ptnr. firm Paul, Weiss, Rifkind, Wharton & Garrison, N.Y.C., 1981-2000; ptnr., mng. mem. Gen. Atlantic Ptnrs. LLC, Greenwich, Conn., 2000—. Commr. Port Authority N.Y. and N.J., 1975-77; dir. World Resources Inst., chmn., 1982-94; mem. N.Y. State Adv. Coun. on State Productivity, 1990-92; presdl. envoy Greece-Macedonian Negotiations, 1994-95, spl. rep. UN Sec. Gen., 1999—. Trustee William Coll., 1981-96; chmn. UN Devel. Corp., 1986-94; bd. dirs. Charles H. Revson Found., 1990-98, N.Y. State Nature Conservancy, 1997—; chmn. Carnegie Forum in U.S., Greece and Turkey, 1996-98; chmn. Ctr. for Democracy and Reconciliation in S.E. Europe, 1998—; dir. Inst. Pub. Adminstrn., 1999—; mem. internat. adv. com. Ctrl. European U., Budapest, Hungary, 1998—. Mem. Assn. of Bar of City of N.Y., Coun. on Fgn. Rels. Club: Harvard (N.Y.C.). General corporate, Private international, Securities. Office: Gen Atlantic Ptnrs LLC 3 Pickwick Plz Greenwich CT 06830-5538 E-mail: mnimetz@gapartners.com

NIMMONS, RALPH WILSON, JR. federal judge; b. Dallas, Sept. 14, 1938; s. Ralph Wilson and Dorothy (Tucker) N.; m. Doris Penelope Pickels, Jan. 30, 1960; children: Bradley, Paige, Bonnie. BA, U. Fla., 1960, JD, 1963. Bar: Fla. 1963, U.S. Dist. Ct. (mid. dist.) Fla. 1963, U.S. Ct. Appeals (5th cir.) 1969, U.S. Supreme Ct. 1970. Assoc. Ulmer, Murchison, Ashby & Ball, Jacksonville, Fla., 1963-65, ptnr., 1973-77; asst. pub. defender Pub. Defender's Office, 1965-69; first asst. state atty. State Atty.'s Office, 1969-71; chief asst. gene. counsel City of Jacksonville, 1971-73; judge 4th Jud. Cir. Ct., Jacksonville, 1977-83, First Dist. Ct. of Appeal Fla., Tallahassee, 1983-91, U.S. Dist. Ct. Mid. Dist. Fla., 1991—. Mem. faculty Fla. Jud. Coll., Tallahassee, 1985, 86; mem. Fla. Bar Grievance Com., 1973-76, vice chmn., 1975-76; mem. Fla. Conf. Cir. Judges, 1977-83, mem. exec. com., 1980-83; mem. Met. Criminal Justice Adv. Coun., 1977-79; mem. Fla. Gov.'s Task Force on Prison Overcrowding, 1983; mem. Trial Ct. Study Commn., 1987-88. Chmn. lay bd. Riverside Baptist Ch., Jacksonville, 1982; chmn. deacons First Bapt. Ch., Tallahassee, 1988—; trustee Jacksonville Wolfson Children's Hosp., 1973-83. Recipient Carroll award for Outstanding Mem. Judiciary Jacksonville Jr. C. of C., 1980, Disting. Svc. award Fla. Council on Crime and Delinquency, 1981; named Outstanding Judge in Duval County, Jacksonville Bar Assn. Young Lawyers Sect., 1981. Mem. Phi Alpha Delta (pres. chpt. 1962-63), Am. Inns of Ct. (master of bench), Delta Tau Delta (pres. chpt. 1959-60). Office: US Dist Ct US Courthouse 311 W Monroe St Jacksonville FL 32202-4242

NIPPERT, ALFRED KUNO, JR. lawyer; b. Asheville, N.C., Mar. 15, 1951; s. Alfred Kuno Sr. and Ecetra (Anderson) N. BS in Polit. Sci., U. Southwestern at Memphis, 1973; JD, U. Cin., 1976. Bar: Ohio 1976, Tenn. 1997, U.S. Dist. Ct. (so. dist.) Ohio 1976, U.S. Supreme Ct. 1986. Ptnr. Nippert and Nippert, Cin., 1976—. Cons. passenger and freight rail transp.; guest lectr. Am. U., Washington, Xavier U., Cin. Pre-publ. reviewer numerous articles. Bd. dirs. Cin-Hamilton County YMCA, 1978-86, Christ Hosp., Cin., 1977-85. Mem. ATLA, ABA, Cin. Bar Assn. (numerous coms.), Assn. Transp. Practitioners, Ohio Nat. Auctioneer Assn. Personal injury, Probate, Transportation. Office: 11 Village Sq Village of Glendale Cincinnati OH 45246

NIRO, CHERYL, lawyer; b. Feb. 19, 1950; d. Samuel James and Nancy (Canezaro) Ippolito; m. William Luciano Niro, July 01, 1979; children: Christopher William, Melissa Leigh. BS with highest honors, U. Ill., 1972; JD, No. Ill. U., 1980. Bar: Ill 1981, US Dist Ct (no dist) Ill 1981, cert.: negotiator, mediator, facilitator. Assoc. Pope Ballard Sheppard & Fowle, Chgo., 1980-81; ptnr. Partridge and Niro PC; now ptnr. Quinlan & Carroll, Chgo. Spec counsel to atty gen Office Ill Atty Gen; consult Ill Office Educ, 1975; conflict resolution program develop US Atty Gen; pres Assocs in Dispute Resolution Inc; exec dir Comt to Commerorate US Constituion in Ill, 1985—86; coord Forum on First Amendment, 1986; creator Bicentennial Law Sch Program; tchg asst program instrn lawyers mediation and negotiation worshops; guest lectr Harvard Univ; mem appt panel US Ct Appeals (7th cir). Chmn Task Force on Children; co-chair Ill Conclave on Legal Educ Ill State Scholar, 1968—72; bd dirs Univ Chicago Lying-In Hosp, 1982—. Named one of Ten Most Influential Women Lawyers in Ill, Am Lawyer Media, 2000. Mem.: ABA (comn multijurisdictional practice, standing comt bar servs, dispute resolution sect coun, house delegs), NEA, ATLA, Ill Trial Lawyers Asn, Ill Bar Asn (standing comt legal-related educ pub, mem assembly 1993, bd govs 1994—97, treas 1995—96, 2d vpres 1997—98, pres 1999—2000), Chicago Bar Asn, DuPage County Bar Asn, Mortar Bd, Phi Kappa Phi, Alpha Lambda Delta, Delta Gamma. Home: 633 N East Ave Oak Park IL 60302-1715 Office: Quinlan & Carroll 30 N Lasalle St Ste 2900 Chicago IL 60602-2590 Business E-Mail: cniro@qclaw.com

NITIKMAN, FRANKLIN W. lawyer; b. Davenport, Iowa, Oct. 26, 1940; s. David A. and Janette (Gordon) N.; m. Adrienne C. Drell, Nov. 28, 1972. BA, Northwestern U., 1963; LLB, Yale U., 1966. Bar: Ill. 1966, U.S. Dist. Ct. (no. dist.) Ill. 1967, U.S. Tax Ct. 1972, Fla. 1977, D.C. 1981. Assoc. McDermott, Will & Emery, Chgo., 1966-72, ptnr., 1973—. Co-author: Drafting Wills and Trust Agreements, 1990. Bd. dirs. Owen Coon Found., Glenview, Ill., 1985—, Jewish United Fund, Jewish Fedn. Met. Chgo., 1994—; bd. dirs. Spertus Inst. Jewish Studies, Chgo., 1991—, chmn. bd., 1999—. Fellow Am. Coll. Trust and Estate Coun., Am. Bar Found.; mem. Standard Club, Arts Club (Chgo.). Estate planning, Probate, Estate taxation. Home: 365 Lakeside Pl Highland Park IL 60035-5371 Office: McDermott Will & Emery 227 W Monroe St Ste 3100 Chicago IL 60606-5096 E-mail: fnitikman@mwe.com

NITTOLY, PAUL GERARD, lawyer; b. Bklyn., July 13, 1948; s. Edward Joseph and Philomena (Lorenzo) N.; m. Maryann Racioppi, May 31, 1970; children: Melissa Beth, Matthew Edward. AB, Rutgers U., 1970; JD, N.Y. Law Sch., 1973. Bar: N.J. 1973, U.S. Dist. Ct. N.J. 1973, U.S. Supreme Ct. 1979; cert. trial atty. civil and criminal law N.J. Supreme Ct. Asst. prosecutor, sr. trial atty. Essex County Prosecutor's Office, Newark, 1974-79; ptnr. Shanley & Fisher, P.C., Morristown, N.J., 1979-99, Drinker Biddle & Shanley LLP, Florham Park, 1999—. Moot trial ct. judge Seton Hall Law Sch., Newark, 1982—; lectr. symposium on perinatal malpractice Am. Coll. Ob-Gyn and Rutgers U. Med. Sch., Morristown, N.J., 1984; mem. practitioner's adv. group to U.S. Sentencing Commn., 1992—. Author: Readings in White Collar Crime, 1991; mem. editl. adv. bd. Corporate Criminal Liability Reporter; contbr. chpts. to books. Past pres., master C. Willard Heckel Am. Inn of Ct.; del. adv. Am. Bd. Trial Advs.; bd. trustees Pub. Interest Law Ctr. N.J., 1998—. Capt. U.S. Army, 1972. Mem. ABA, N.J. Bar Assn., Essex County Bar Assn. (pres. 1998-99), Morris County Bar Assn., Nat. Assn. Criminal Def. Lawyers, Assn. Criminal Def. Attys. N.J., Trial Attys. N.J. (v.p.), Assn. Fed. Bar State N.J. (trustee 2000—), Park Ave. Club (Morristown), Delta Upsilon. Roman Catholic. Criminal, Labor. Home: 275 Meetinghouse Ln Mountainside NJ 07092-1305 Office: Drinker Biddle & Shanley LLP 500 Campus Dr Fl 4 Florham Park NJ 07932-1047 E-mail: pnittoly@dbr.com

NITZE, WILLIAM ALBERT, government official, lawyer; b. N.Y.C., Sept. 27, 1942; s. Paul Henry and Phyllis (Pratt) N.; m. Ann Kendall Richards, June 5, 1971; children: Paul Kendall, Charles Richards. BA, Harvard U., 1964, JD, 1969; BA, Oxford U., 1966. Bar: N.Y. 1970, U.S. Supreme Ct. 1987. Assoc. Sullivan and Cromwell, N.Y.C., 1970-72; v.p. London Arts, Inc., 1972-73; counsel Mobil South, Inc., 1974-76; gen. counsel Mobil Oil Japan, Tokyo, 1976-80; asst. gen. counsel exploration and producing divsn. Mobil Oil Corp., N.Y.C., 1980-87; dep asst. sec. for environment, health and natural resources U.S. Dept. State, Washington, 1987-90; pres. Alliance to Save Energy, 1990-94; asst. adminstr. for internat. activities U.S. EPA, 1994-2001; pres. Gemstar Group, 2001—. Mem. adv. com. Sch. Advanced Internat. Studies, Washington, 1982-95, professorial lectr., 1993-94; vis. scholar Environ. Law Inst., Washington, 1990; dir. Charles A. Lindbergh Fund, Mpls., 1990-94, Nat. Symphony Orch. Assn., Washington, 1990—. Trustee Aspen Inst., Queenstown, Md., 1988—, Krasnow Inst., Fairfax, Va., 1996—; co-chmn. Climate Inst., Washington, 2001—. Mem. Assn. of Bar of City of N.Y., Coun. on Fgn. Rels., Met. Club, Links Club. Republican. Episcopalian. Avocations: running, piano, collecting art. Home: 1537 28th St NW Washington DC 20007-3059 Office: Gemstar Group 910 17th St NW Ste 1110 Washington DC 20006 E-mail: wanitze@aol.com

NIX, ROBERT ROYAL, II, lawyer; b. Detroit, Mar. 27, 1947; s. Robert R. and Betty Virginia (Karicofe) N.; m. Suzanne Martha Turner, July 11, 1970; children: Christian Michael, Heather Michele. BS, Ea. Mich. U., 1968; JD cum laude, Wayne State U., 1971. Bar: Mich. 1971, U.S. Dist. Ct. (ea. dist.) Mich. 1971, U.S. Ct. Appeals (6th cir.) 1976. Rsch. atty. Mich. Ct. Appeals, Lansing, 1971-72, law clk. to Hon. Charles L. Levin, 1971, law clk. to Hon. S. Jerome Bronson, 1972-73; ptnr. Kerr, Russell and Weber, 1973—. Lectr. in field. Contbr. articles to Michigan Real Property Law Review. Mem. Mich. Land Title Stds. Com., 1990—. Fellow Mich. State Bar Found.; mem. ABA (partnership com. real property, probate and trust law sect., mortgages and secured financing com. corp., banking and bus. law sect., forum constrn. industry sect.), State Bar Mich. (chmn. real property law sect. 1994-95, coun. vice-chmn. 1992-93, chmn. com. on mortgage related financing devices, 1984-87, mem. sect., 1973—, partnership com. 1982—), Oakland County Bar Assn., Detroit Bar Assn., Am. Coll. Real Estate Lawyers, Am. Coll. Mortgage Attys. Republican. Methodist. General civil litigation, Contracts commercial, Real property. Office: Kerr Russell and Weber Detroit Ctr Ste 2500 Detroit MI 48226 E-mail: rrn@krwplc.com

NIXON, CHARLES RICHARD, lawyer; b. Alice, Tex., Feb. 8, 1940; s. Edward J. and Maude B. (Walker) N.; m. Laura Belle King, Mar. 4, 1961; children: Allison Anne, Michael Stephen, Charles Jarrod. BBA, U. Tex., 1962, JD, 1965. Bar: Tex. 1965, Wyo. 1975, U.S. Dist. Ct. (so. dist.) Tex. 1968. Ptnr. Grose, Nixon & Erck, Alice, 1965-75; exec. v.p., gen. counsel Darenco, Inc., Casper, Wyo., 1975-81; assoc. gen. counsel J.W. Bateson Co., Inc., Dallas, 1981-82, v.p., gen. counsel, 1982-86, v.p. gen. counsel Centex Gen. Constrn. Cos., Dallas, 1986—, M.H. Golden Co., San Diego, Centex-Rodgers Constrn. Co., Nashville; gen. counsel Centex-Great Southwest Corp., Orlando and Tampa, Fla.; v.p., gen. counsel Centex-Rooney Constrn. Co., Ft. Lauderdale, Fla., Forcum-Lannom Assocs., Inc., Dyersburg, Tenn.; v.p., gen. counsel Centex Rooney Thermac, Inc., St. Croix, V.I.; of counsel Centex Bateson Construction Co., Dallas, Centex-Simpson Constrn. Co., Fairfax, Va. Editorial adv. bd. Construction Bus. Review. Gen. counsel Bush for Pres. campaign, Wyo., 1980. Mem. Dallas Bar Assn., Coastal Bend Bar Assn. (pres. 1968-69), State Bar Tex. (dist. grievance com.). Republican. Episcopalian. Construction, Government contracts and claims, Labor. Office: Centex Gen Constrn Cos 3333 Lee Pkwy Ste 1200 Dallas TX 75219-5111

NIXON, JOHN TRICE, judge; b. New Orleans, Jan. 9, 1933; s. H. C. and Anne (Trice) N.; children: Mignon Elizabeth, Anne Trice. A.B. cum laude, Harvard Coll., 1955; LL.B., Vanderbilt U., 1960. Bar: Ala. bar 1960, Tenn. bar 1972. Individual practice law, Anniston, Ala., 1960-62; city atty., 1962-64; trial atty. Civil Rights Div., Dept. Justice, Washington, 1964-69; staff atty., comptroller of Treasury State of Tenn., 1971-76; pvt. practice law Nashville, 1976-77; cir. judge, 1977-78; gen. sessions judge, 1978-80; judge U.S. Dist. Ct. (mid. dist.) Tenn., Nashville, 1980—, sr. judge, 1998—. Served with U.S. Army, 1958. Mem. Fly Club (Cambridge), Harvard-Radcliffe Club (Nashville). Democrat. Methodist. Office: US Dist Ct 745 US Courthouse Nashville TN 37203

NIXON, SCOTT SHERMAN, lawyer; b. Grosse Pointe, Mich., Feb. 7, 1959; s. Floyd Sherman and Marjorie Jane (Quermann) N.; m. Cathryn Lynn Starnes, Aug. 27, 1983; children: Jeffry Sherman, Kelsy Jane, James Robert. BABA, Mich. State U., 1981; JD, U. Denver, 1984. Bar: Colo. 1984, U.S. Dist. Ct. Colo. 1984, U.S. Ct. Appeals (10th cir.) 1984. Assoc. Pryor, Carney & Johnson, P.C., Englewood, Colo., 1984-89, shareholder, 1990-95; pres., shareholder Pryor, Johnson, Montoya, Carney & Karr, P.C., 1995—. Officer, bd. dirs. Luth. Brotherhood Br. 8856, Denver, 1993-99, Mark K. Ulmer Meml. Native Am. Scholarship Found., Denver, 1994—; officer, mem. coun. Bethan Luth Ch., Englewood, 1993-95. Mem. ABA, Colo. Bar Assn., Denver Bar Assn., Colo. Def. Lawyers Assn. Avocations: music performance, physical fitness, carpentry/construction. Personal injury, Product liability, Professional liability. Home: 6984 S Pontiac Ct Englewood CO 80112-1127 Office: Pryor Johnson Montoya Carney & Karr PC Ste 1313 6400 S Fiddlers Green Cir Englewood CO 80111-4939 E-mail: snixon@pjmck.com

NOACK, HAROLD QUINCY, JR. lawyer; b. San Francisco, May 1, 1931; m. Ann Crosby, Nov. 1952 (div. Sept. 1974); children: Stephen Tracy, Peter Quincy, Andrew Crosby; m. Susan K. Sherwood, Dec. 1975 (div. Jan. 1983); m. Penny Jo Orth, Apr. 2, 1988 (div. May 1989); m. Linda F. Killeen, Mar. 15, 1994 (div. May 1996). BA, U. Calif., Berkeley, 1953; LLB, U. Calif., San Francisco, 1959. Bar: Calif. 1960, Idaho 1969, U.S. Dist. Ct. Idaho 1969. Assoc. Fernoff & Wolfe, Oakland, Calif., 1959-64, Cooley, Crowley, Gaither, Godward, Castro & Huddleson, San Francisco, 1964-65; pvt. practice Oakland, 1965-66; ptnr. Oliphant, Hopper, Stribling & Noack, 1966-69; assoc. Eberle, Berlin, Kading & Turnbow, Boise, Idaho, 1969-70; pvt. practice, 1970-83, 85-88; assoc. Anthony Parks, 1970-75; ptnr. Noack & Korn, 1970-75, Noack & Hawley, Boise, 1983-85, Lyons & Noack, Boise, 1988-89; pvt. practice law, 1989—. Contbr. articles to profl. jours. Bd. dirs., pres. Idaho Planned Parenthood, Boise, 1970-72; bd. dirs. Idaho Heart Assn., Boise, 1975. 2d lt. U.S. Army, 1954-55. Mem. ABA, Calif. Bar Assn., Idaho Bar Assn. (fee grievance com. 1986—), Boise Bar Assn., Rotary (bd. dirs. Boise club 1980). Avocations: running, walking, fishing, cooking. Bankruptcy, General civil litigation, General practice. Home: PO Box 875 1915 N 24th St Boise ID 83702-0204 Office: 733 N 7th St Boise ID 83702-5500

NOBLE, LAWRENCE MARK, lawyer, association administrator; b. N.Y.C., Mar. 30, 1952; s. Hyman S. and Jeanette (Lapides) N.; m. Patricia Fay Bak, Mar. 28, 1981; children: Jonathan, David. BA, Syracuse U., 1973; JD, George Washington U., 1976; Program for Sr. Mgrs. in Govt., John F. Kennedy Sch. Govt., Boston, 1991. Bar: D.C. 1976, U.S. Dist. Ct. 1977, U.S. Ct. Appeals (D.C. cir.) 1977, U.S. Supreme Ct. 1980, U.S. Ct. Appeals (4th cir.) 1989, U.S. Ct. Appeals (5th cir.), 1992. Atty. Aviation Consumer Action Project, Washington, 1976-77; litigation atty. Fed. Election Commn., 1977-79, asst. gen. counsel for litigation, 1979-83, dep. gen. counsel, 1983-87, gen. counsel, 1987-2000; exec. dir., gen. counsel Ctr. Responsive Politics, 2001; adj. prof. law George Washington U. Law Sch., 1999—. Mem. ABA election law commn., 1988-93; mem. administrv. conf. U.S., Washington, 1987-96. Contbr. articles to profl. jours.; lectr., spkr. in field. Mem. Coun. on Govt. Ethics Laws (pres. 1997-98), D.C. Bar Assn. Avocations: computer graphics, photography, writing. Home: 9438 Sunnyfield Ct Potomac MD 20854-2090 Office: Ctr Responsive Politics 1101 14th ST NW Ste 1030 Washington DC 20005 E-mail: lnoble@crp.org

NOBUMOTO, KAREN S. prosecutor; BA, U. Hartford, 1973; JD Southwestern U., 1989. Dep. dist. atty. County of L.A. Mem.: State Bar Calif. (pres. 2001—), John M. Langston Bar Assn., Women Lawyers Assn. L.A., Black Women Lawyers L.A., Assn. Dep. Dist. Attys. Office: LA Dist Attys Office 210 N Figueroa St 15th Fl Los Angeles CA 90012*

NOCAS, ANDREW JAMES, lawyer; b. L.A., Feb. 2, 1941; s. John Richard and Muriel Phyliss (Harvey) N.; 1 child, Scott Andrew. BS, Stanford U., 1962, JD, 1964. Bar: Calif. 1965. Assoc. Thelen, Marrin, Johnson & Bridges, L.A., 1964-71, ptnr., 1972-91; pvt. practice, 1992-2000; with Office L.A. City Atty., 2000—. Del. Calif. Bar Conv., 1972-92. Served to capt. JAGC, USAR. Fellow Am. Bar Found.; mem. Los Angeles County Bar Assn. (chmn. sect. law office mgmt. 1980-82, chair errors and ommissions com. 1987-88, chair litigation sect. 1988-89), ABA (chmn. arbitration com. 1981), Am. Bd. Trial Advocates, Los Angeles County Bar Found. (trustee 1992-99). Office: Office LA City Aty 200 No Main St 18th Fl Los Angeles CA 90012 E-mail: anocas@atty.lacity.org

NODDINGS, SARAH ELLEN, lawyer; b. Matawan, N.J. d. William Clayton and Sarah Stephenson (Cox) Noddings; children: Christopher, Aaron. BA in Math., Rutgers U., New Brunswick, N.J., 1965, MSW, 1968; JD cum laude, Seton Hall U., Newark, 1975; postgrad., UCLA, 1979. Bar: Calif. 1976, Nev. 1976, N.J. 1975, U.S. Dist. Ct. (ctrl. dist.) Calif. 1976, U.S. Dist. Ct. N.J. 1975. Social worker Carteret (N.J.) Bd. Edn., 1970-75; law clk. Hon. Howard W. Babcock, 8th Jud. Dist. Ct., Las Vegas, Nev., 1975-76; assoc. O'Melveny & Myers, L.A., 1976-78; atty. Internat. Creative Mgmt., Beverly Hills, Calif., 1978-81, Russell & Glickman, Century City, 1981-83, Lorimar Prodns., Culver City and Burbank, 1983-87, v.p., 1987-93; atty. Warner Bros. TV, Burbank, 1993-2001, v.p., 1993-2001, sr. atty., 1999-2001. Dir. county youth program, rsch. analyst Sonoma County People for Econ. Opportunity, Santa Rosa, Calif., 1968-69; VISTA vol. Kings County Cmty. Action Orgn., Hanford, Calif., 1965-66; officer, PTA bd. Casimir Mid. Sch. and Arlington Elem. Sch.

Mem. Acad. TV Arts and Scis. (nat. awards com. 1994-96), L.A. Copyright Soc. (trustee 1990-91), Women in Film, L.A. County Bar Assn. (intellectual property sect.), Women Entertainment Lawyers, Media Dist. Intellectual Propr. Bar Assn. (bd. dirs. 1999-2001). Avocations: travel, tennis, skiing, bicycling, swimming. General corporate, Entertainment, Intellectual property.

NOE, JAMES ALVA, retired judge; b. Billings, Mont., May 25, 1932; s. James Alva Sr. and Laura Madlen (Parmenter) N.; m. Patricia Arlene Caudill, Aug. 4, 1956; children: Kendra Sue, Jeffrey James, Bradley John, Kirkwood Merle. BA in Polit. Sci., U. Wash., 1954, LLB, 1957; LittD hon., Christian Theol. Sem., 1986. Bar: Wash. 1958, U.S. Dist. Ct. (we. dist.) Wash. 1958, U.S. Ct. Appeals (9th cir.) 1959. Dep. prosecuting atty. King County, Seattle, 1958-61; trial lawyer Williams, Kastner & Gibbs, 1961-67; judge Seattle Mcpl. Ct., 1967-71, King County Superior Ct., 1971-96; ret., 1996. Moderator Christian Ch. (Disciples of Christ) in the U.S. and Can., 1977-79. Fellow Am. Bar Found. (life); mem. ABA (ho. of dels. 1976-78, 82-87, 91-96, bd. govs. 1991-94, chmn. jud. divsn. 1988-89, nat. conf. state trial judges 1981-82, sr. lawyers divsn. coun. 2001—), Wash. State Superior Ct. Judges Assn. (pres. 1984-85), Nat. Jud. Coll. (trustee 1988-91, 95-2001, chair 1999-2001). Home: 8250 SE 61st St Mercer Island WA 98040-4902

NOEL, NICHOLAS, III, lawyer; b. Pottstown, Pa., June 5, 1952; s. Nicholas Jr. and Elaine (Buckwalter) N.; m. Karen Bean Schomp, Oct. 28, 1978; children: Carol Elaine, Nicholas IV. BA magna cum laude, Lehigh U., 1974; JD, U. Detroit, 1977. Bar: Pa. 1977, U.S. Dist. Ct. (ea. dist.) Pa. 1979, U.S. Ct. Appeals (3rd cir.) 1980, U.S. Supreme Ct. 1986, U.S. Dist. Ct. (mid. dist.) Pa. 1989. Assoc. Hahalis Law Office, Bethlehem, Pa., 1977-84; assoc. Teel, Stettz, Shimer & DiGiacomo, Easton, 1984-87; ptnr. Teel, Stettz, PC, 1987-2000, sr. litigation ptnr., 1989-2000, v.p., 1998-2000, pres., 2000, Noel & Kovacs, P.C., Easton, 2000—. Adj. prof. Northampton County C.C., Bethlehem, 1990, 97, 2000; solicitor Chiefs of Police Assn. of Mid. Ea. Pa., 1977—, Palmer Twp. Zoning Hearing Bd. solicitor, Easton, 1989—; arbitrator Am. Arbitration Assn., 1986—; lectr. Pa. Bar Inst., 2001. Contbr. to several books. Trustee Palmer Twp. Moravian Ch., 1985-97, 99—, pres., 1986-92, sec. bldg. expansion com., 1998-2001; mem. Moravian Ch. No. Province Ch. and Soc. Com., 1990—, Palmer Moravian Day Sch. bd., 1991-94, 99-2000. Named Outstanding Young Man Am., 1974. Fellow Pa. Bar Found.; mem. ABA, Pa. Bar Assn. (civil rights chair 1989-92, vice-chmn. legal edn. com. 1992, profl. stds. com. 1983, ho. of dels. 1998-2001), Northampton County Bar Assn. (legal ethics and responsibility com. 1987-94, bd. govs. 1991-99, treas. 1995, v.p. 1996, pres.-elect 1997, pres. 1998, past pres. 1999), Clinton Budd Palmer Inn of Ct. (1995-2000), Pa. Ho. Dels. (1998—). Avocations: most athletic events, swimming, hiking. Civil rights, General civil litigation, Professional liability. Home: 2840 Green Pond Rd Easton PA 18045-2504 Office: 400 S Greenwood Ave Ste 300 Easton PA 18045-3776 E-mail: nn6552@aol.com

NOEL, RANDALL DEANE, lawyer; b. Memphis, Oct. 19, 1953; s. D.A. and Patricia G. Noel; m. Lissa Johns, May 28, 1977; children: Lauren Elizabeth, Randall Walker. BBA with honors, U. Miss., 1975, JD, 1978. Bar: Miss. 1978, U.S. Dist. Ct. (no. and so. dists.) Miss. 1978, Tenn. 1979, U.S. Dist. Ct. (we., mid. and ea. dists.) Tenn. 1979, U.S. Ct. Appeals (5th and 6th cirs.) 1984, U.S. Supreme Ct. 1986. Assoc. Armstrong/Allen, PLLC, Memphis, 1978-85, ptnr., 1985—, mgr. litig. practice group, 1990-94; mgmt. com. Armstrong, Allen, Prewitt, Gentry, Johnston & Holmes, 1994-97—. Fin. com. Memphis in May Internat. Festival, 1980-81; pres. Carnival Memphis, 1996; bd. dirs. Christ United Meth. Ch., Memphis, 1984-87, 89-91, chmn. bd. trustees, 1995; mem. Leadership Memphis, 1994-95. Fellow Am. Bar Found., Tenn. Bar Found.; mem. ABA (young lawyers divsn., fellow dir. 1988-90, editor The Affiliate newsletter 1987-88, dir. Affiliate Outreach project 1988—, vice-chmn. Award of Achievement com. 1986, ALI-ABA bd. 1992-97, litig. sect. com. chmn., mem. house of dels.), Am. Counsel Assn. (pres. 1997), Tenn. Bar Assn. (pres. young lawyers divsn. 1990, pres. litig. sect. 1988, bd. govs. 1989—, pres., 1999, Pres.'s Disting. Svc. award 1988-89), Memphis and Shelby Bar Assn. (mem. jud, recommendations, law week nominations and membership coms.), Miss. Bar Assn., Def. Rsch. Inst., Tenn. Def. Lawyers Assn., Am. Judicature Soc. (bd. dirs. 1992-96), Tenn. Legal Cmty. Found.(pres. 1999-2000). Federal civil litigation, State civil litigation, Consumer commercial. Home: 2938 Tishomingo Ln Memphis TN 38111-2627 Office: Armstrong Allen PLLC 80 Monroe Ave Ste 700 Memphis TN 38103-2467 E-mail: rnoel@armstrongallen.com

NOELKE, PAUL, lawyer; b. La Crosse, Wis., Feb. 10, 1915; s. Carl Bernard and Mary Amelia (O'Meara) N.; m. Mary Jo Kamps, May 4, 1943; children: Paul William, Mary Nesius, Ann Witt, Kate Helms. A.B. magna cum laude, Marquette U., 1936, J.D. cum laude, 1938; LL.M., U. Chgo., 1947; D.H.L. (hon.), Mt. Senario Coll., 1976. Bar: Wis. 1938, D.C. 1975, U.S. Dist. Ct. (ea. dist.) Wis. 1938, U.S. Supreme Ct. 1960. Assoc. firm Miller, Mack & Fairchild, 1938-40; asst. prof. law Marquette U., 1940-42; spl. agt. FBI, 1942-45; assoc. Quarles & Brady and predecessor firms, Milw., 1943-52, ptnr., 1952-85, of counsel, 1985—. Trustee emeritus Viterbo Coll., LaCrosse, Wis.; mem. adv. bd. Cardinal Stritch Coll., Milw.; past chmn. Pres.'s Coun. Marquette U.; past pres. Serra Internat., Chgo.; past chmn. Bd. Tax Rev., Village of Shorewood, Wis. Recipient Alumnus of Yr. award Marquette U., 1980; recipient Conf. award NCCJ, 1967 Mem. ABA, Wis. State Bar Assn., Milw. Bar Assn., Am. Judicature Soc., Order Holy Sepulchre, Alpha Sigma Nu Roman Catholic. Home: 2462 N Prospect Ave Milwaukee WI 53211-4451 Office: 411 E Wisconsin Ave Milwaukee WI 53202-4461

NOFER, GEORGE HANCOCK, lawyer; b. Phila., June 14, 1926; B.A., Haverford Coll., 1949; J.D., Yale U., 1952. Bar: Pa. 1953. Pvt. practice, Phila., 1953—; ret. ptnr. Schnader, Harrison, Segal & Lewis, 1961-91, sr. counsel, 1992—. Pres. bd. sch. dirs. Upper Moreland Twp., Pa., 1965-73; trustee Beaver Coll., Glenside, Pa., 1969-76; co-trustee and exec. dir. Oberkotter Found.; bd. dirs. Fox Chase Cancer Ctr., Phila., 1989-94; elder, trustee, deacon Abington (Pa.) Presbyn. Ch.; bd. dirs. Phila. Presbyn. Homes, Inc.; bd. dirs. A.G. Bell Assn. for Deaf, Washington, 1992-98. Fellow Am. Coll. Trust and Estate Counsel (regent 1975—, pres. 1983-84, chmn. Pa. 1973-78), Am. Law Inst., Am. Bar Found.; mem. ABA (standing com. on specialization 1980-86, chmn. 1983-86), Pa. Bar Assn., Phila. Bar Assn., Internat. Acad. Estate and Trust Law, Phi Beta Kappa, Phi Delta Phi Home: 108 Quail Ln Radnor PA 19087-2729 Office: Schnader Harrison Segal & Lewis 1600 Market St Ste 3600 Philadelphia PA 19103-7287 E-mail: gnofer@schnader.com, ghnofer@aol.com

NOGEE, JEFFREY LAURENCE, lawyer; b. Schenectady, N.Y., Oct. 31, 1952; s. Rodney and Shirley Ruth (Mannes) N.; m. Freda Carolyn Wartel, Aug. 31, 1980; children: Rori Caitlen, Amara Sonia, Jaden Gwynn. BA cum laude, Bucknell U., 1974; JD, Boston U., 1977. Bar: N.Y. 1978, U.S. Dist. Ct. (so. and ea. dists.) N.Y. 1978. Assoc. Hale Russell & Gray, N.Y.C., 1977-83; sr. atty. Ebasco Services Inc., 1984-88, dir. Countertrade unit, 1985-88; sr. ptnr. Fogh & Nogee Assocs., 1988; ptnr. Brauner, Baron, Rosenzweig, Bauman & Klein, N.Y.C., 1988-90; sr. ptnr. Nogee & Wartel, Westbury, N.Y., 1990—. Pvt. counsellor for internat. bus. firms, 1987—. Prin. bassoonist, bd. dirs. The Band of L.I., 1997—, sec., 1997-99, pres., 1999—; prin. bassoonist Rockway-Five Towns Symphony Orch., 1998-99, Lawrence Philharm., 2000—. Trustee Temple Emanu-el of East Meadow, 1995-99, v.p., 1996-97. Mem. ABA, Am. Arbitration Assn., Assn. of Bar of City of N.Y., Nassau County Bar Assn., Internat. Platform Assn., N.Y. New Media Assn., Phi Beta Kappa, Pi Sigma Alpha. Avocations: fencing, bassoon and saxophone music, racquet sports, hiking, bicycling. Computer, Entertainment, Nuclear power. Office: Ste 211 900 Merchants Concourse Westbury NY 11590-5114 E-mail: jnogee@nogeelaw.com

NOHRDEN, PATRICK THOMAS, lawyer; b. Santa Cruz, Calif., Mar. 7, 1956; s. Thomas Allen and Roberta Eugenia (Brydon) Nohrden; children: Steven, Laura, Maranda, Patricia. AS, SUNY, Albany, 1980; BA in English with great distinction, San Jose State U., 1984; JD, U. Akron, 1992. Bar: Nev. 1993, U.S. Dist. Ct. Nev. 1993. Regional dir. CareerPro, Inc., Roseville, Calif., 1984-91; cons. Patrick T. Nohrden & Assocs., Youngstown, Ohio, 1991-93; pvt. practice, Las Vegas, Nev., 1993—. Exec. dir. Geisa Project; bd. dirs. Profl. Resume Svc., Inc., Las Vegas, Las Vegas Diamondbacks, Inc., Clark County Pro Bono Project, Maui Land Devel. Co., Inc., World Internat. Intelligence Bur., Inc.; adj. prof. C.C. So. Nev. Sgt. U.S. Army, 1975-81. Recipient 2 Spirit of Pro Bono awards, Meritorious Svc. award. Mem. ATLA, ABA (family law sect.), Fed. Bar Assn., Nev. Trial Lawyers Assn., State Bar Nev. (family law and bankruptcy sects.), Clark County Bar Assn., Phi Kappa Phi. Republican. Roman Catholic. Bankruptcy, General civil litigation, Family and matrimonial. Office: 6312 W Cheyenne Ave Ste A Las Vegas NV 89108 E-mail: patrick@nohrden.com

NOLAN, DAVID CHARLES, lawyer, mediator; b. San Mateo, Calif., Oct. 12, 1940; s. Clarence Charles and Leona Henrietta (Lindeman) N.; m. Cynthia Ann James, Feb. 20, 1971; children: Matthew, John, Scott. AB, Stanford U., 1962; JD, U. Calif., Berkeley, 1965. Bar: Calif. 1966, U.S. Ct. Appeals (9th cir.) 1971, U.S. Ct. Appeals (D.C. cir.) 1975, U.S. Dist. Ct. (no. dist.) Calif. 1969, U.S. Dist. Ct. (D.C. cir.) 1970, U.S. Tax Ct., U.S. Supreme Ct. 1972. Ptnr. Graham & James, San Francisco, 1968-93; sole practitioner Walnut Creek, Calif., 1993—. Bd. dirs., officer Family Homes for Retarded, Belmont, Calif., 1978-81; founding dir. Orinda (Calif.) Baseball Assn., 1982-86; commr. Diablo Valley Baseball League, Martinez, Calif., 1983-90. Lt. comdr. USCG, 1965-68. Mem. ABA, Calif. Bar Assn., Contra Costa County Bar Assn., No. Calif. Mediation Assn., Assn. Transp. Practitioners, Commonwealth Club, Maritime Law Assn., Order of Coif. Admiralty, General corporate, Private international. Home: 12 E Altarinda Dr Orinda CA 94563-2406 Office: 1990 N California Blvd Walnut Creek CA 94596-3742 Fax: 925-937-5442

NOLAN, JOHN MICHAEL, lawyer; b. Conway, Ark., June 21, 1948; s. Paul Thomas and Peggy (Hime) N. BA, U. Tex., 1970, JD, 1973; LLM in Taxation, George Washington U., 1976. Bar: Tex. 1973, D.C. 1975, U.S. Ct. Mil. Appeals 1973, U.S. Ct. Appeals (D.C. cir.) 1975, U.S. Tax Ct. 1975, U.S. Supreme Ct. 1975. Chief counsel to chief judge U.S. Ct. Mil. Appeals, Washington, 1976-77; assoc. Winstead, McGuire, Sechrest & Minick PC, Dallas, 1977-81; shareholder Winstead Sechrest & Minick PC, 1981—. Editor in Chief The Advocate, 1973-76. Capt. JAGC, U.S. Army, 1973-76. Named one of Outstanding Young Men in Am., U.S. Jaycess, 1976. Mem. ABA (real property, probate and trust sect., real property com., partnerships, joint ventrues, and other investment vehicles), Tex. Bar Assn. (real property, probate and trust sect.), D.C. Bar Assn., Dallas Bar Assn. (real estate group), Tex. Coll. Real Estate Lawyers, Coll. State Bar Tex., Real Estate Coun., Salesmanship Club Dallas, Royal Oaks Country Club. Presbyterian. Bankruptcy, Real property, Taxation, general. Home: 6681 Crest Way Ct Dallas TX 75230-2868 Office: Winstead Sechrest & Minick 5400 Renaissance Tower 1201 Elm St Ste 5400 Dallas TX 75270-2199

NOLAN, TERRANCE JOSEPH, JR. lawyer; b. Bklyn., Mar. 29, 1950; s. Terrance Joseph Sr. and Antonia (Pontecorvo) N.; m. Irene M. Rush, Aug. 2, 1980; children: Maryjane Frances, David Anthony. BA, St. Francis Coll., Bklyn., 1971; JD, St. Johns U., Jamaica, N.Y., 1974; LLM, NYU, 1982. Bar: N.Y. 1975, U.S. Dist. Ct. (ea. and so. dists.) N.Y. 1975, U.S. Ct. Appeals (2d cir.) 1975, U.S. Supreme Ct. 1980. Atty. N.Y.C. Transit Authority, Bklyn., 1974-77; specialist labor rels. Pepsi-Cola Co., Purchase, N.Y., 1977-80; asst. gen. counsel, assoc. dir. labor rels. NYU, N.Y.C., 1980-89, assoc. gen. counsel, dep. dir. labor rels., 1989—. Mem. Am. Corp. Coun. Assn., N.Y. State Bar Assn., Indsl. Rels. Rsch. Assn., Nat. Assn. Coll. and Univ. Attys., Met. Arbitration Group. Administrative and regulatory, Education and schools, Labor. Home: 41 Russell St Lynbrook NY 11563-1135 Office: NYU 70 Washington Sq S New York NY 10012-1091 E-mail: terrance.nolan@nyu.edu

NOLEN, ROY LEMUEL, retired lawyer; b. Montgomery, Ala., Nov. 29, 1937; s. Roy Lemuel Jr. and Elizabeth (Larkin) N.; m. Evelyn McNeill Thomas, Aug. 28, 1965; 1 child, Rives Rutledge. BArch, Rice U., 1961; LLB, Harvard U., 1967. Bar: Tex. 1968, U.S. Ct. Appeals (5th cir.) 1969. Law clk. to sr. judge U.S. Ct. Appeals (5th cir.), 1967-68; assoc. Baker Botts LLP, Houston, 1968-75, ptnr., 1976-2000; co-head Corp. Dept., 1985-90; mem. exec. com., 1988-91; adminstrv. ptnr., 1997-2000; ret., 2000. Bd. dirs. Houston Ballet Found., 1980-92, Rice Design Alliance, 1995-96; exec. com. Contemporary Arts Mus., 1990-96, 97—; exec. com. Houston Symphony Soc., 1994-99, gen. counsel, 1994-98; bd. dirs. Menil Found. (Menil Collection), 1999—, sr. warden Christ Ch. Cathedral, 1991-92; chmn. Houston area devel. initiative Episcopal Diocese of Tex., 1997. 1st lt. USMC, 1961-64. Mem. State Bar of Tex., Coronado Club, Allegro, Paul Jones Dancing Club. Episcopalian. General corporate, Securities. Office: 3000 One Shell Plz 910 Louisiana St Ste 3000 Houston TX 77002-4995

NOLFI, EDWARD ANTHONY, lawyer; b. Warren, Ohio, Sept. 30, 1958; s. Eugene Vincent Sr. and Margaret Joyce (Futey) N.; m. Sheri Ann Loue, June 5, 1982. AB, Brown U., 1980; JD, U. Akron, 1983. Bar: Ohio 1983, N.Y. 1986, U.S. Dist. Ct. (no. dist.) Ohio 1987, U.S. Tax Ct. 1987, U.S. Ct. Appeals (6th cir. 1989), U.S. Supreme Ct. 1989. Juggler Miracle Sta., Warren, 1976; instr. Sch. One, Providence, 1980; tech. writer Doctors' Hosp., Massillon, Ohio, 1982; pvt. practice Warren, 1983-84; ptnr. Schubert, Sopkovich & Nolfi, 1984; assoc. editor Lawyers Coop. Pub. Co., Rochester, N.Y., 1985-87; pvt. practice Akron, Ohio, 1987—. Prof. Acad. Ct. Reporting, Akron, 1988-91; prof. Kent State U., 1993, Mt. Aloysius Coll., Cresson, Pa., 1996; sr. case law editor LexisNexis, Miamisburg, Ohio, 1999—, lead sr. case law editor. Author: The Master Juggler, 1980, Basic Legal Research, 1993, Basic Wills, Trusts, and Estates, 1995; articles editor Am. Law Reports, Fed., 1986-87; law columnist Village Views, 1987-88. Mem. ABA. Roman Catholic. Avocation: juggling. General practice. Home: 1101 E Archwood Ave Akron OH 44306-2857 E-mail: nolfi@netzero.net

NOLLAU, LEE GORDON, lawyer; b. Balt., Feb. 6, 1950; s. E. Wilson and Carolyn G. (Blass) N.; m. Carol A. Haughney, Aug. 12, 1978; children: Ann G., Catherine E., Margaret C. BA, Juniata Coll., 1972; MAS, Johns Hopkins U., 1975; JD, Dickinson Sch. Law, 1976. Bar: Pa. 1976, U.S. Dist. Ct. (mid. dist.) 1982, U.S. Dist. Ct. (we. dist.) 1988, U.S. Ct. Appeals (3d cir.) 1980, U.S. Supreme Ct. 1982. Instr. Juniata Coll., Huntingdon, Pa., 1976-78; asst. dist. atty. Centre County, Bellefonte, 1978-80, dist. atty., 1981; assoc. Litke, Lee, Martin, Grine & Green, 1981-83, Jubelirer & Assocs., State College, Pa., 1983-87; ptnr. Jubelirer, Nollau, Young & Blanarik, Inc., 1988-89, Jubelirer, Rayback, Nollau, Walsh, Young & Blanarik, Inc., State College, 1989-94, Nollau & Young, State Coll., Pa., 1994—. Mental health rev. officer Centre County, Bellefonte, 1982—; instr. Pa. State U. Smeal Coll. Bus. Adminstrn., 1995—; lectr., author Pa. Bar Inst., 1995—. Author: Trial Tactics: Ten Tips for Direct Examination. Mem. ABA, Pa. Bar Assn., Centre Co. Bar, Pa. Assn. Criminal Def. Lawyers. Presbyterian. General civil litigation, Criminal, Personal injury. Office: Nollau & Young 2153 E College Ave State College PA 16801-7204

NOLTE, HENRY R., JR. lawyer, former automobile company executive; b. N.Y.C., Mar. 3, 1924; s. Henry R. and Emily A. (Eisele) N.; m. Frances Messner, May 19, 1951; children: Gwynne Conn, Henry Reed III, Jennifer Stevens, Suzanne. BA, Duke U., 1947; LLB, U. Pa., 1949. Bar: N.Y. 1950, Mich. 1967. Assoc. Cravath, Swaine & Moore, N.Y.C., 1951-61; assoc. counsel Ford Motor Co., Dearborn, Mich., 1961, asst. gen. counsel, 1964-71, assoc. gen. counsel, 1971-74, v.p., gen. counsel, 1974-89, Philco-Ford Corp., Phila., 1961-64; v.p., gen. counsel, sec. Ford of Europe Inc., Warley, Essex, Eng., 1967-69; gen. counsel fin. and ins. subs. Ford Motor Co., 1974-89; sr. ptnr. Miller, Canfield, Paddock & Stone, Detroit, 1989-93, of counsel, 1993—. Dir. emeritus Charter One Fin., Inc. Formerly vice chmn. and trustee Cranbrook Ednl. Cmty.; mem. Internat. and Comparative Law Ctr. of Southwestern Legal Found.; bd. dirs. Detroit Symphony Orch.; trustee Beaumont Hosp. Lt. USNR, 1943-46, PTO. Mem. ABA (past chmn. corp. law depts.), Mich. Bar Assn., Assn. Bar City N.Y., Assn. Gen. Counsel, Orchard Lake Country Club, Bloomfield Hills Country Club, Everglades Club (Fla.), Gulfstream Golf Club (Fla.), Ocean Club (Fla.). Episcopalian. Office: Miller Canfield Paddock & Stone 840 W Long Lake Rd Troy MI 48098-6356

NOME, WILLIAM ANDREAS, lawyer; b. Springfield, Ohio, May 21, 1951; s. Reidar Andreas and Nancy Louisa (Smith) N.; m. Carolyn Ruth Johnson, Feb. 7, 1981. BA, Akron U., 1973; JD, Cleve. State U., 1976. Bar: Ohio 1976, U.S. Dist. Ct. (no. dist.) Ohio 1977, U.S. Ct. Appeals (6th cir.) 1985, U.S. Supreme Ct. 1987. Asst. prosecutor Portage County Prosecutor's Office, Ravenna, Ohio, 1977; pvt. practice, 1977-82; assoc. Arthur & Clegg, Kent, Ohio, 1982-85; ptnr. Arthur, Nome & Assocs., 1985-96, Arthur, Nome, Can, Szymanski & Clinard, Kent, Cuyahoga Falls, 1996-97, Arthur, Nome, Can & Szymanski, Kent, Cuyahoga Falls, 1997-98, Arthur, Nome and Szymanski, Kent, Kent, Cuyahoga Falls, 1998—. Legal advisor Portage Area Regional Transit Authority, Kent, 1986–. Chmn. Highland Home Health Care, Ravenna, 1980, Kent Bd. Bldg. Appeals, 1987, Portage County Mental Health Bd., 1988; trustee Kevin Coleman Mental Health Ctr., 1989-93, pres., 1991-93; pres. Force Investment Club, 1999—. Col. Ohio Mil. Res., 1986—. Recipient Cert. of Achievement, Emergency Mgmt. Inst., Fed. Emergency Mgmt. Agy., 1987, 93, 95. Mem. Ohio Bar Assn., Akron Bar Assn., Portage County Bar Assn. (sec.-treas. 1982-85, 98-2000, v.p. 2000-2001, pres. 2001—), Portage County Estate Planning Coun., Delta Theta Phi. Republican. Lutheran. Avocations: gardening, cooking, target shooting, reading. Bankruptcy, General practice, Probate. Office: Arthur Nome & Assocs 1325 S Water St Kent OH 44240-3851 E-mail: anslawyers@aol.com

NONNA, JOHN MICHAEL, lawyer; b. N.Y.C., July 8, 1948; s. Angelo and Josephine (Visconti) N.; m. Jean Wanda Cleary, June 9, 1973; children: Elizabeth, Caroline, Marianne, Timothy. AB, Princeton U., 1970; JD, NYU, 1975. Bar: N.Y. 1976, U.S. Dist. Ct. (so. dist.) N.Y. 1978, U.S. Ct. Appeals (2d cir.) 1978, U.S. Ct. Appeals (9th cir.) 1980, U.S. Ct. Appeals (5th cir.) 1997, U.S. Dist. Ct. Conn. 1988, U.S. Supreme Ct. 1998. Law asst. to Hon. D.L. Gabrielli N.Y. Ct. Appeals, Albany, 1975-77; assoc. Reid & Priest, N.Y.C., 1977-84; ptnr. Werner & Kennedy, 1984-99, LeBoeuf, Lamb, Greene & MacRae, 1999—. Contbr. articles to profl. jours. Dep. mayor, trustee Village of Pleasantville, N.Y., 1990-95, mayor, 1995—, acting justice, 1983-89. With USNR, 1970-75. U.S. Olympic Team, Munich, 1972, Moscow, 1980. Fellow Am. Bar Found. (life); mem. ABA (torts and ins. practice sect. com. chair 1986-87, 92-93), N.Y. State Bar Assn. (chair comml. and fed. litigation sect. 1998-99, co-editor in chief 2000), Assn. Bar City N.Y., N.Y. Fencers Club (pres. 1990-93). Avocations: fencing, running, piano. General civil litigation, Insurance. Office: LeBoeuf Lamb Greene & MacRae 125 W 55th St New York NY 10019-5369 E-mail: jnonna@llgm.com

NOONAN, CHARLES THOMAS, lawyer; b. Ashland, Ky., May 27, 1924; s. Arthur Kelly and Tina May (Beam) N.; m. Constance Charlotte Snelling, Nov. 10, 1945; children: Thomas, Susan, Karl, James, Todd. AB magna cum laude, Harvard Coll., 1945, JD, 1949. Bar: Pa., U.S. Supreme Ct. English and lit. tchr. Harwich (Mass.) H.S., 1945-46; pvt. practice Allentown, Pa., 1950-52; ptnr. Donecker & Noonan, 1952-89, Noonan and Prokup, Allentown, 1989—. Dir., legal counsel Mchts. Bank Allentown, 1974-91; assoc. Cedar Crest Coll., 1986, trustee, 1994, chmn. bd., 1997. Dir., treas., pres. East Pa. Union Sch. Dist., Emmaus, 1954-59; deacon Solomons Ch., Macungie, Pa., 1959-60; dir., pres. Allentown Jr. C. of C., 1950-60; chmn. Lehigh County Pub. Solicitations Bd., Allentown, 1955-57. Recipient Disting. Svc. award Allentown Jr. C. of C., 1958; named Col. Order of Ky. Cols., Louisville, 1966. Mem. ABA, Pa. Bar Assn., Lehigh County Bar Assn., Phi Beta Kappa. Republican. Avocations: skiing, tennis, water skiing, music, reading. Estate planning, Probate, Estate taxation. Home: 3817 Larkspur Dr Allentown PA 18103-9740 Office: Noonan and Prokup 526 W Walnut St Allentown PA 18101-2322

NOONAN, JAMES C. lawyer, mediator-arbitrator; b. Chgo., July 16, 1928; s. T. Clifford and Ethel (Jennett) N.; m. Carol Colbert, Nov. 24, 1954 (div. June 1975); children: James, Christopher, Mary, Anne, Catherine; m. Ardis Niemann, May 24, 1986. AB, U. Notre Dame, 1953, MA in Criminology, 1954; JD, William Mitchell Coll. Law, St. Paul, 1962. Bar: Minn. 1962, U.S. Dist. Ct. Minn. 1963, U.S. Ct. Appeals (8th cir.) 1971, U.S. Supreme Ct. 1969. Probation officer Ramsey County Juvenile Ct., St. Paul, 1954-57; supt. Woodview Detention Home, 1957-63; assoc. Firestone, Fink, Krawetz, Miley, O'Neill, 1963-67; ptnr. Firestone Fink, Krawetz, Miley, Maas and Noonan, 1967-70, Magistad & Noonan, St. Paul, 1971-75; owner James C. Noonan and Assocs., 1975—. Mem. adv. bd. Home of Good Shepherd, St. Paul, 1958-74; mem. citizen adv. bd. Detention and Corrections Authority, St. Paul, 1966-80. Mem. ABA, Minn. State Bar Assn., Ramsey County Bar Assn., St. Paul Amateur Radio Club, Am. Radio Relay League. Roman Catholic. Avocation: amateur radio (W90SN). Alternative dispute resolution, Estate planning, Probate. Home and Office: 339 Summit Ave Saint Paul MN 55102-2176 Fax: (651) 222-3340. E-mail: nnn.nnn@juno.com, W90SN@arrl.net

NOONAN, JOHN T., JR. federal judge, law educator; b. Boston, Oct. 24, 1926; s. John T. and Marie (Shea) N.; m. Mary Lee Bennett, Dec. 27, 1967; children: John Kenneth, Rebecca Lee, Susanna Bain. B.A., Harvard U., 1946, LL.B., 1954; student, Cambridge U., 1946-47; M.A., Cath. U. Am., 1949, Ph.D., 1951, LHD, 1980; LL.D., U. Santa Clara, 1974, U. Notre Dame, 1976, Loyola U. South, 1978; LHD, Holy Cross Coll., 1980; LL.D., St. Louis U., 1981, U. San Francisco, 1985; student, Holy Cross Coll., 1980, Cath. U. Am., 1980, Gonzaga U., 1986, U. San Francisco, 1986. Bar: Mass. 1954, U.S. Supreme Ct. 1971. Mem. spl. staff Nat. Security Council, 1954-55; pvt. practice Herrick & Smith, Boston, 1955-60; prof. law U. Notre Dame, 1961-66, U. Calif., Berkeley, 1967-86, chmn. religious studies, 1970-73, chmn. medieval studies, 1978-79; judge U.S. Ct. Appeals (9th cir.), San Francisco, 1985-96, sr. judge, 1996—. Oliver Wendell Holmes, Jr. lectr. Harvard U. Law Sch., 1972, Pope John XXIII lectr. Cath. U. Law Sch., 1973, Cardinal Bellarmine lectr. St. Louis U. Div. Sch., 1973, Ernest Messenger lectr. Cornell U., 1982, John Dewey Meml. lectr. U. Minn., 1986, Baum lectr. U. Ill., 1988, Strassberger lectr. U. Tex., 1989; chmn. bd. Games Rsch., Inc., 1961-76; overseer Harvard U., 1991—. Author: The Scholastic Analysis of Usury, 1957; Contraception: A History of Its Treatment by the Catholic Theologians and Canonists, 1965; Power to Dissolve, 1972; Persons and Masks of the Law, 1976; The Antelope, 1977; A Private Choice, 1979; Bribes, 1984, The Responsible Judge, 1993, Professional and Personal Responsibilities of the Lawyer, 1997, The Lustre of Our Country, 1998; editor: Natural Law Forum, 1961-70, Am. Jour. Jurisprudence, 1970, The Morality of Abortion, 1970 Chmn. Brookline Redevel. Authority, Mass., 1958-62; cons. Papal Commn. on Family, 1965-66, Ford Found., Indonesian Legal Program, 1968; NIH, 1973, NIH,

1974; expert Presdl. Commn. on Population and Am. Future, 1971; cons. U.S. Cath. Conf., 1979-86; sec., treas. Inst. for Research in Medieval Canon Law, 1970-88; pres. Thomas More-Jacques Maritain Inst., 1977— ; trustee Population Council, 1969-76, Phi Kappa Found., 1970-76, Grad. Theol. Union, 1970-73, U. San Francisco, 1971-75; mem. com. theol. edn. Yale U., 1972-77; exec. com. Cath. Commn. Intellectual and Cultural Affairs, 1972-75; bd. dirs. Ctr. for Human Values in the Health Scis., 1969-71, S.W. Intergroup Relations Council, 1970-72, Inst. for Study Ethical Issues, 1971-73 Recipient St. Thomas More award U. San Francisco, 1974, Christian Culture medal, 1975, Laetare medal U. Notre Dame, 1984, Campion medal Cath. Book Club, 1987; Guggenheim fellow, 1965-66, 79-80, Laetare medal U. Notre Dame, 1984, Campion medal, 1987, Alemany medal Western Dominican Province, 1988; Ctr. for advanced Studies in Behavioral Scis. fellow, 1973-74; Wilson Ctr. fellow, 1979-80. Fellow Am. Acad. Arts and Scis., Am. Soc. Legal Historians (hon.); mem. Am. Soc. Polit. and Legal Philosophy (v.p. 1964), Canon Law Soc. Am. (gov. 1970-72), Am. Law Inst., Phi Beta Kappa (senator United chpts. 1970-72, pres. Alpha of Calif. chpt. 1972-73) Office: US Ct Appeals 9th Cir PO Box 193939 San Francisco CA 94119-3939

NOONAN, WILLIAM DONALD, lawyer, physician; b. Kansas City, Mo., Oct. 18, 1955; s. Robert Owen and Patricia Ruth Noonan. AB, Princeton (N.J.) U., 1977; JD, U. Mo., Kansas City, 1980; postgrad., Tulane U., 1981-83; MD magna cum laude, Oreg. Health Scis. U., 1991. Bar: Mo. 1980, U.S. Ct. Appeals (5th cir.) 1982, U.S. Patent & Trademark Office 1982, U.S. Ct. Appeals (D.C. cir.) 1984, Oreg. 1985, U.S. Ct. Appeals (9th Cir.) 1985. Assoc. Shurgue, Mion, Zinn, Washington, 1983-84, Keaty & Keaty, New Orleans, 1984-85; ptnr. Klarquist, Sparkman, Portland, Oreg., 1985—; intern in internal medicine Portland Providence Med. Ctr., 1993-94; resident in ophthalomology Casey Eye Inst., Portland, 1994-95. Adj. prof. patent law Tulane U., New Orleans, 1984-85, U. Oreg., 1992-93. Casenotes editor U. Mo. Law Rev., 1979. Nat. Merit scholar. Mem. ABA, AMA (Leadership award 1994), Alpha Omega Alpha (pres. Oreg. chpt. 1990-91). Republican. Avocation: raising horses, mountain climbing, hiking. Patent. Office: Klarquist Sparkman 121 SW Salmon 1600 World Trade Ctr Portland OR 97201

NORA, WENDY ALISON, lawyer; b. New Haven, Feb. 14, 1951; d. James Jackson Nora and Barbara June (Fluhrer) P.; m. Jay Robert Vercauteren, Aug. 21, 1973 (div. Nov. 1981); children: Lucas Jay, Eric Robert. BA, U. Wis., 1971, JD, 1975. Bar: Wis. 1975, U.S. Dist. Ct. (we. dist.) Wis. 1975, Minn. 1985, U.S. Dist. Ct. Minn. 1985, U.S. Supreme Ct. 1986. Pvt. practice, Cross Plains, Wis., 1975-81, Madison, 1981-84, Mpls., 1986-90, Madison, Wis., 1991—; developer, incorporator, pres. Cmty. Investment Credit Corp., 1997—. Atty. State of Wis., 1977-81, asst. pub. defender, 1983-84. Fellow U. Minn. Mem. ABA (vice-chmn. adminstrv. law sect., criminal law and juvenile justice com. 1982—). General corporate, Finance, Estate taxation. Home: 6931 Old Sauk Rd Madison WI 53717-1122 Office: 6515 Grand Teton Plz Madison WI 53717-1048

NORBERG, CHARLES ROBERT, lawyer; b. Cleve., July 25, 1912; s. Rudolf Carl and Ida Edith (Roberts) N. B.S. in Adminstrv. Engring, Cornell U., 1934; M.A. in Internat. Econs, U. Pa., 1937; LL.B., Harvard U., 1939. Bar: Pa. bar 1940, U.S. Supreme Ct. bar 1946, D.C. bar 1947. Lab. research asst. Willard Storage Battery Co., Cleve., 1934-35; asso. firm Hepburn and Norris, Phila., 1939-42; with Office of Assn. Sec. State for Public Affairs, Dept. State, 1948-51; asst. dir. psychol. strategy bd. Exec. Office of the Pres., 1952-54; mem. staff U.S. Delegation to UN Gen. Assembly, Paris, 1951; adviser U.S. Delegation to UNESCO Gen. Conf., Montevideo, 1954; assoc. firm Morgan, Lewis and Bockius, Washington, 1955-56; individual practice law, 1956—; treas., gen. counsel Inter-Am. Comml. Arbitration Commn., 1968-83, dir. gen., 1983-95, hon. dir. gen., 1995—; hon. mem. Corte Brasileira de Arbitragem Comercial. Chief Spl. AID Mission to Ecuador, 1961; spl. Aid Mission to Uruguay, 1961; mem. U.S. delegation to Specialized Inter-Am. Conf. on pvt. internat. law, Panama, 1975 Chmn. Internat. Visitors Info. Service, Washington, 1965-69; chmn. Mayor's Com. on Internat. Visitors, 1971-78; chmn., pres. Bicentennial Commn. of D.C., Inc., 1975-81. Served with USAF, 1942-46. Recipient medal of honor Inter-Am. Comml. Arbitration Commn., 1996. Mem. Phila. Bar Assn., Pa. Bar Assn., Inter-Am. Bar Assn., Washington Fgn. Law Soc. (pres. 1959-63), Am. Soc. Internat. Law, Am. Law Inst., Am. Bar Assn. (chmn. internat. legal exchange program 1974-79), Bar Assn. of D.C. (chmn. internat. law com. 1977-79), Inter-Am. Bar Found. (founder, dir. 1957, pres. 1969-84, chmn. bd. 1984—), Diplomatic and Consular Officers Retired (Washington), Washington Inst. Fgn. Affairs, Academia Colombiana de Jurisprudencia, Inter-Am. Acad. Internat. and Comparative Law, Colegio de Abogados de Quito. Clubs: Met. (Washington); Dacor (Washington); Racquet (Phila.); Harvard (N.Y.C.). Private international, Public international. Home: 3104 N St NW Washington DC 20007-3413 Office: 1819 H St NW Washington DC 20006-3603

NORCOTT, FLEMMING L., JR. state supreme court justice; b. New Haven, Oct. 11, 1943; BA, Columbia U., 1965, JD, 1968. Bar: Conn. 1968. Peace corps vol. U. East Africa, Nairobi, Kenya; legal staff Bedford-Stuyvestant Restoration Corp.; asst. atty. gen. Office Atty. Gen., V.I.; judge Superior Ct., 1979-87, Appellate Ct., 1987-92; assoc. justice Conn. Supreme Ct., Hartford, 1992—. Hearing examiner Conn. Commn. Human Rights and Opportunities; co-founder, exec. dir. Ctr. Advocacy, Rsch. and Planning, Ind., New Haven; lectr. Yale U. Bd. govs. U. New Haven; bd. dirs. Dixwell Community House, Ea. Collegiate Football Ofcls. Assn., New Haven Football Ofcls. Assn., Long Wharf Theatre; assoc. fellow Calhoun Coll., Yale U.; bd. trustees Yale-New Haven Hosp. Mem. Omega Psi Phi Office: Conn Supreme Ct Drawer N Sta A Hartford CT 06106-1548*

NORDAUNE, ROSELYN JEAN, lawyer; b. Montevideo, Minn., May 26, 1955; d. Herbert Palmer and Myrtle (Risdahl) N. BA, Augsburg Coll., 1977; JD, U. Minn., 1980. Bar: Minn. 1980, U.S. Dist. Ct. Minn. 1980, U.S. Ct. Appeals (8th cir.) 1980, U.S. Tax Ct. 1981. Assoc. Rossini, Cochran et al, Mpls., 1980-83; ptnr. Nodland, Conn, Nordaune & Perlman, 1983-86, Nordaune & Friesen, Mpls., 1987—. Mem. Minn. State Bd. on Jud. Standards, 1999—. Bd. dirs. Sr. Cmty. Svcs., Mpls., 1984-86; mem. bd. regents Augsburg Coll., 1982-94, mem. Heritage Soc. bd., 1999—. Mem. ABA, Minn. Bar Assn., Hennepin County Bar Assn., Augsburg Coll. Alumni Assn. (pres. 1984-87). Democrat. Lutheran. E-mial. General corporate, Family and matrimonial, Probate. Home: 4901 Valley Forge Ln N Plymouth MN 55442-3024 Office: Nordaune & Friesen 1140 Interchange Twr Minneapolis MN 55426 E-mail: cats@scc.net, rox@nandf.net

NORDBERG, JOHN ALBERT, federal judge; b. Evanston, Ill., June 18, 1926; s. Carl Albert and Judith Ranghild (Carlson) N.; m. Jane Spaulding, June 18, 1947; children: Carol, Mary, Janet, John Student, Carleton Coll., 1943-44, 46-47; J.D., U. Mich., 1950. Bar: Ill. 1950, U.S. Dist. Ct. (no. dist.) Ill. 1957, U.S. Ct. Appeals (7th cir.) 1961. Assoc. Pope & Ballard, Chgo., 1950-57; ptnr. Pope, Ballard, Shepard & Fowle, 1957-76; judge Cir. Ct. of Cook County, Ill., 1976-82, U.S. Dist. Ct. (no. dist.) Ill., Chgo., 1982-95, sr. judge, 1995—. Editor-in-chief, bd. editors Chgo. Bar Record, 1966-74 Magistrate of Cir. Ct. and justice of peace Ill., 1957-65. Served with USN, 1944-46; PTO Mem. ABA, Chgo. Bar Assn., Am. Judicature Soc., Law Club Chgo., Legal Club Chgo., Union League Club of Chgo., Order of Coif. Office: US Dist Ct #1886 219 S Dearborn St Chicago IL 60604-1706

NORDEN, WILLIAM BENJAMIN, lawyer; b. Bklyn., May 15, 1945; s. Henry H. and Helen (Sinkman) N.; m. Susan A. Brenner, Aug. 18, 1968 (div. 1984); children: Melissa, Stacy; m. Marianne Goodman, Sept. 20, 1986; children: Hillary, Samantha. BS, Bklyn. Coll., 1967; JD, NYU, 1969. Bar: N.Y. 1970, U.S. Tax Ct. 1971, U.S. Dist. Cts. (so. and ea. dists.) N.Y. 1974, U.S. Ct. Appeals (2d cir.) 1974. Assoc. Wynn Blattmachr, Campbell & Milas, N.Y.C., 1969-76, Baer Marks & Upham, N.Y.C., 1976-78, ptnr., 1978—; sec., counsel F.W. Olin Found., Inc., N.Y.C., 1980—, bd. dirs., 1988—. Bd. dirs. Samuel & Rae Eckman Charitable Found. Inc., N.Y.C, 1983—; trustee N.Y.C. Fire Mus., 1987—. Mem. ABA, N.Y. State Bar Assn., Assn. Bar City of N.Y. Jewish. Estate planning, Probate, Estate taxation. Office: Baer Marks & Upham 805 3rd Ave New York NY 10022-7513

NORDENBERG, MARK ALAN, law educator, university official; b. Duluth, Minn., July 12, 1948; s. John Clemens and Shirley Mae (Tappen) N.; m. Nikki Patricia Pirillo, Dec. 26, 1970; children: Erin, Carl, Michael. BA, Thiel Coll., 1970; JD, U. Wis., 1973. Bar: Wis. 1973, Minn. 1974, U.S. Supreme Ct. 1976, Pa. 1985. Atty. Gray, Plant, Mooty & Anderson, Mpls., 1973-75; prof. law Capital U. Law Ctr., Columbus, Ohio, 1975-77, U. Pitts., 1977—, acting dean Sch. Law, 1985-87, dean Sch. Law, 1987-93, interim univ. sr. vice chancellor and provost, 1993-94, Univ. Disting. Svc. prof., 1994—, interim univ. chancellor, 1995-96, univ. chancellor, 1996—. Mem. U.S. Supreme Ct. Adv. Com. on Civil Rules, Washington, 1988-93, Pa. Supreme Ct. Civil Procedure Rules Com., Phila., 1986-92; mem. large and complex case panel Am. Arbitration Assn.; reporter civil justice adv. group U.S. Dist. Ct., Pitts., 1991-96; bd. dirs. Mellon Fin. Corp. Author: Modern Pennsylvania Civil Practice, 1985, 2d edit., 1995. Trustee Thiel Coll., Greenville, Pa., 1987-97; bd. dirs. Inst. for Shipboard Edn. Found., Pitts. Tech. Coun., Pitts. Regional Alliance, Pitts. Digital Greenhouse, Boy Scouts of Allegheny County, Urban League of Pitts., United Way of Allegheny County, World Affairs Coun. of Pitts., The Carnegie Mus., Pitts., Allegheny Conf. on Cmty. Devel., Pitts., Pitts. Coun. on Higher Edn. Named Vectors Pitts. Person of Yr. in Edn., 1996, Person of Yr., 1997. Fellow Am. Bar Found.; mem. ABA, AAUP, Pa. Bar Assn., Allegheny County Bar Assn., Acad. Trial Lawyers Allegheny County, Pa. Assn. Colls. and Univs. (chmn.), Pitts. Athletic Assn., Law Club Pitts., Univ. Club, Duquesne Club, Wildwood Golf Club, Pitts. Golf Club. Office: U Pitts Cathedral of Learning Pittsburgh PA 15221-3662

NORDLING, BERNARD ERICK, lawyer; b. Nekoma, Kans., June 14, 1921; s. Carl Ruben Ebben and Edith Elveda (Freeburg) N.; m. Barbara Ann Burkholder, Mar. 26, 1949. Student, George Washington U., 1941-43; AB, McPherson Coll., 1947; JD, U. Kans., 1949. Bar: Kans. 1949, U.S. Dist. Ct. Kans. 1949, U.S. Ct. Appeals (10th cir.) 1970. Pvt. practice, Hugoton, Kans., 1949—; ptnr. Kramer, Nordling & Nordling, 1950-99; mem. Kramer, Nordling & Nordling, LLC, 1999—; city atty. City of Hugoton, 1951-87; county atty. Stevens County, Kans., 1957-63. Kans. mem. legal com. Interstate Oil Compact Commn., 1969-93; mem. supply tech. adv. com. nat. gas survey FPC, 1975-77. Editor U. Kans. Law Rev., 1949. Mem. Hugoton Sch. Bds., 1954-68, pres. grade sch. bd., 1957-63; trustee McPherson Coll., 1971-81, mem. exec. com., 1975-81; mem. Kans. Energy Adv. Coun., 1975-78, mem. exec. com., 1976-78. With AUS, 1944-46. Recipient Citation of Merit, McPherson Coll., 1987, Disting. Alumnus award Kans. U. Law Sch., 1993, Lifetime Achievement award Hugoton Kans. Area C. of C., 1994, James Woods Green medallion Kans. U. Law Sch., 2001. Fellow Am. Bar Found. (Kans.); mem. ABA, Kans. Bar Assn., S.W. Kans. Bar Assn., Am. Judicature Soc., City Attys. Assn. Kans. (exec. com. 1975-83, pres. 1982-83), Nat. Assn. Royalty Owners (bd. govs. 1980-99), S.W. Kans. Royalty Owners Assn. (exec. sec. 1968-94, asst. exec. sec. 1994—), U. Kans. Law Soc. (bd. govs. 1984-87), Kans. U. Endowment Assn. (trustee 1989—), Kans. U. Alumni Assn. (bd. dirs. 1992-97, Fred Ellsworth medallion 1997, James Woods Green medallion, 2001), Order of Coif, Phi Alpha Delta. Oil, gas, and mineral, General practice, Probate. Address: 4404 Nicklaus Dr Lawrence KS 66047 E-mail: benordling@sunflower.com

NORDLINGER, STEPHANIE G. lawyer; b. L.A., 1940; BA, UCLA, 1961, MA, 1969, U. Calif., Berkeley, 1962; JD, Loyola U., 1975. Bar: Calif. 1975, U.S. Dist. Ct. (ctrl. dist.) Calif. 1976, U.S. Ct. Appeals (9th cir.) 1976, U.S. Supreme Ct. 1992. Pvt. practice, L.A., 1976-77, 89—; dep. pub. defender L.A. County, 1977-79; adj. prof. Calif. State U., Northridge, 1979; pvt. practice Santa Monica, Encino, Calif., 1979-83; assoc. Baltaxe, Rutkin & Levin, Beverly Hills, 1983-84; pvt. practice Marina del Rey, 1984-87; exec. dir. Westside Legal Svcs., Santa Monica, 1988. Mem. adv. com. U.S. Ct. Appeals (9th cir.), San Francisco, 1987-90; dir. Joseph Beggs Found., Redlands, Calif., 1992-95. Cons.: (book) CEB California Civil Writ Practice, 1987; editor User Friendly, 1997-98. Bd. dirs., L.A. chpt. pres. ACLU, 1973-74; pres. Westwood Dem. Club, L.A., 1993-95; mem. state ctrl. com. Calif. Dems., 1995-96. Mem. RAND Alumni Assn., L.A. Computer Soc. (pres. 1994, 2000-01, dir., editor), Sierra Club. Avocations: genealogy, gardening, travel. Appellate, General civil litigation, Probate. Office: PO Box 78757 Los Angeles CA 90016-0757 E-mail: snordlinge@aol.com

NORDQUIST, STEPHEN GLOS, lawyer; b. Mpls., May 13, 1936; s. Oscar Alvin Nordquist and Georgiana (Glos) Ruplin; m. Cynthia Alexandra Turner, Aug. 16, 1958 (div. Aug. 1967); children: Darcy Alden Sullivan, Timothy Turner; m. Regina Frances Stanton, Nov. 1, 1969 (div. May 1996); 1 child, Nicholas Alden; m. Sandra Schnitzer Stern, Sept. 2, 1999. BA cum laude, U. Minn., 1958, LL.B cum laude, 1961. Bar: Minn. 1961, N.Y. 1962. Assoc. Dewey, Ballantine, Bushby, Palmer & Wood, N.Y.C., 1961-69, ptnr., 1969-85; sr. v.p. W.P. Carey & Co., Inc., 1985-86, exec v.p., sec., 1986-87; ptnr. Cole & Deitz (now Winston & Strawn), 1988-89; of counsel Dreyer and Traub, 1990-91; mem. Nordquist & Stern PLLC, 1996—. Pres., bd. dirs. Carey Corp. Property, Inc., Carey-Longmont Inc., Carey-Longmont Real Property, Inc., N.Y.C., 1985-87, 520 East 86th Street, Inc. Commr. N.Y. Law Revision Commn., 1999—. Mem. Knickerbocker Club (house com.), World Trade Ctr. Club. Republican. Congregationalist. Home: 211 E 53d St Apt 7D New York NY 10022-4805 also: 10791 & 10817 Rognaldson Rd Brainerd MN 56401-8444 Office: 509 Madison Ave Ste 612 New York NY 10022-5501 E-mail: SGNLAW@aol.com

NORFOLK, WILLIAM RAY, lawyer; b. Huron, S.D., Mar. 15, 1941; s. James W. and Helen F. (Thompson) N.; m. Marilyn E. Meadors; children: Stephanie G., Allison T., Meredith H. BA, Miami U., Oxford, Ohio, 1963; student, U. London, 1963-64; LLB, Duke U., 1967. Bar: N.Y. 1968, U.S. Dist. Ct. (so. and ea. dists.) N.Y. 1969, U.S. Ct. Appeals (2d cir.) 1969, U.S. Ct. Appeals (9th cir.) 1977, U.S. Ct. Appeals (5th cir.) 1979, U.S. Ct. Appeals (3d and 11th cirs.) 1981, U.S. Dist. Ct. (ea. dist.) Mich. 1986, U.S. Ct. Appeals (6th and 8th cirs.) 1986, U.S. Ct. Appeals (Fed. cir.) 1990, U.S. Ct. Internat. Trade 1990, U.S. Dist. Ct. (we. dist.) Mich. 1992. Assoc. Sullivan & Cromwell, N.Y.C., 1967-74, ptnr., 1974—. Trustee N.Y. Meth. Hosp. Mem. ABA, N.Y. State Bar Assn. Antitrust, General civil litigation, Mergers and acquisitions. Office: Sullivan & Cromwell 125 Broad St Fl 28 New York NY 10004-2489

NORGLE, CHARLES RONALD, SR. federal judge; b. Mar. 3, 1937; BBA, Northwestern U., Evanston, Ill., 1964; JD, John Marshall Law Sch., Chgo., 1969. Asst. state's atty. DuPage County, Ill., 1969-71, dep. pub. defender, 1971-73, assoc. judge, 1973-77, 78-81, cir. judge, 1977-78, 81-84; judge U.S. Dist. Ct. (no. dist.) Ill., Chgo., 1984—. Mem. exec. com. No. Dist. Ill.; mem. 7th Cir. Jud. Coun., 7th Cir. Jud. Conf. planning com., subcom. grant requests Fed. Defender Orgn., Fed. Defender Svcs. Com.; adj. faculty Northwestern U. Sch. Law, John Marshall Law Sch., Chgo.; pres. Atticus Finch Inn Ct. Mem. ABA, Fed. Bar Assn., Fed. Circuit Bar Assn., Ill. Bar Assn., DuPage County (Ill.) Bar Assn., Nat. Attys. Assn., DuPage Assn. Women Attys., Chgo. Legal Club, Northwestern Club. Office: US Dist Ct 219 S Dearborn St Ste 2346 Chicago IL 60604-1802

NORMAN, ALBERT GEORGE, JR. lawyer; b. Birmingham, Ala., May 29, 1929; s. Albert G. and Ila Mae (Carroll) N.; m. Catherine Marshall DeShazo, Sept. 3, 1955; children: Catherine Marshall, Albert George III. BA, Auburn U., 1953; LLB, Emory U., 1958; MA, U. N.C., 1960. Bar: Ga. 1957. Assoc. Moise, Post & Gardner, Atlanta, 1958-60, ptnr., 1960-62, Hansell & Post, Atlanta, 1962-86, Long, Aldridge & Norman, Atlanta, 1986-2000. Dir. Atlanta Gas Light Co., 1976-2000. Served with USAF, 1946-49. Mem. ABA, Ga. Bar Assn., Atlanta Bar Assn., Lawyers Club Atlanta (pres. 1973-74), Am. Law Inst., Am. Judicature Soc. (dir. 1975-78), Old War Horse Lawyers Club, (pres. 1991-92), Cherokee Town and Country Club. Episcopalian. General civil litigation, Communications, Public utilities. E-mail: almarnorman@mingspring.com

NORRIS, ALAN EUGENE, federal judge; b. Columbus, Ohio, Aug. 15, 1935; s. J. Russell and Dorothy A. (Shrader) N.; m. Nancy Jean Myers, Apr. 15, 1962 (dec. Jan. 1986); children: Tom Edward Jackson, Tracy Elaine; m. Carol Lynn Spohn, Nov. 10, 1990. BA, Otterbein Coll., 1957, HLD (hon.), 1991; cert., U. Paris, 1956; LLB, NYU, 1960; LLM, U. Va., 1986; HLD, Capital U. Law Sch., 2001. Bar: Ohio 1960, U.S. Dist. Ct. (so. dist) Ohio 1962, U.S. Dist. Ct. (no. dist) Ohio 1964. Law clk. to judge Ohio Supreme Ct., Columbus, 1960-61; assoc. Vorys, Sater, Seymour & Pease, 1961-62; ptnr. Metz, Bailey, Norris & Spicer, Westerville, Ohio, 1962-80; judge Ohio Ct. Appeals (10th dist.), Columbus, 1981-86, U.S. Ct. Appeals (6th cir.), Columbus, 1986—. Contbr. articles to profl. jours. Mem. Ohio Ho. of Reps., Columbus, 1967-80. Named Outstanding Young Man, Westerville Jaycees, 1971; recipient Legislator of Yr. award Ohio Acad. Trial Lawyers, Columbus, 1972. Mem. Ohio Bar Assn., Columbus Bar Assn. Republican. Methodist. Lodge: Masons (master 1966-67). Office: US Ct Appeals 328 US Courthouse 85 Marconi Blvd Columbus OH 43215-2823

NORRIS, CYNTHIA ANN, lawyer; b. South Bend, Ind., Aug. 3, 1951. B.S., Ind. State U., 1973; J.D., South Tex. Coll. Law, 1977. Bar: Tex. 1977, La. 1979, U.S. Dist. Ct. (ea. dist.) La. 1979, Calif. 1984, U.S. Dist. Ct. (ea. dist.) Calif. 1984, U.S. Dist. Ct. (so. dist.) Tex. 1978, U.S. Ct. Appeals (5th cir.) 1979. Atty. Brill, Brooks, Gillis & Yount, Houston, 1977-78, L.R. Koerner, New Orleans, 1978-80, Gulf Oil Corp., New Orleans, 1980-83, Bakersfield, Calif., 1983-84, Chevron U.S.A., Inc. San Francisco, 1984—; vis. scholar John Westburg & Assocs., Tehran, Iran, 1976; Mem. ABA, Tex. Bar Assn., La. Bar Assn., Calif. Bar Assn. Republican. Oil, gas, and mineral, Environmental, Business. Office: Chevron Corp 575 Market St Rm 2738 San Francisco CA 94105-2856

NORRIS, GLENN L. lawyer; b. Clarinda, Iowa, Sept. 25, 1946; s. Harold E. and Darlene Louise (Crane) N.; m. Dale Bailey, Jan. 28, 1967 (div. June 1990); m. Tiffinny C. Sparks, Nov. 14, 1998; children: Christopher Steven, Catherine Beth, Glenn Leonard Jr., Janet Darlene. BA, Simpson Coll., 1968; JD, U. Iowa, 1971. Bar: Iowa 1971, So. Dist. Iowa 1971, U.S. Dist. Ct., no. dist., Iowa, 8th circuit, 1972, U.S. Supreme Ct., 1976. Law clerk U.S. Dist. Judge Hanson, Ft. Dodge, Iowa, 1971-73; assoc. Hawkins, Hedberg & Ward, Des Moines, 1973-78; ptnr. Hawkins & Norris, P.C., 1978—. Editor: Iowa Academy of Trial Lawyers Handbook, 3d edit., 1999. Mem. tech. com. Iowa Supreme Ct. Commn. for Planning for 21st Century, 1996-98, Iowa Supreme Ct. Budget Adv. Com., 1997—; dir. men's chorus Sacred Heart Knights of Columbus. Fellow Iowa Acad. Trial Lawyers; master C. Edwin Moore Am. Inn of Ct. (pres. 1998-2000); mem. Am. Bd. Trial Advs. (cert. civil trial advocate 2000—), Iowa State Bar Assn. (mem. fed. practice com. 1999—). Roman Catholic. General civil litigation. Home: 6205 Oakwood Hills Dr Johnston IA 50131-1962 Office: Hawkins & Norris PC 2501 Grand Ave Ste C Des Moines IA 50312-5311 E-mail: gnorrislaw@hotmail.com

NORRIS, ROBERT WHEELER, lawyer, military officer; b. Birmingham, Ala., May 22, 1932; s. Hubert Lee and Georgia Irene (Parker) N.; m. Martha Katherine Cummins, Feb. 19, 1955; children— Lisha Katherine Norris Utt, Nathan Robert B.A. in Bus. Adminstrn., U. Ala., 1954, LL.B., 1955; LL.M., George Washington U., 1979; postgrad., Air Command & Staff Coll., 1968, Nat. War Coll., 1975. Commd. 2d lt. USAF, advanced through grades to maj. gen., dep. judge advocate gen., 1983-85, judge advocate gen., 1985-88; gen. counsel Ala. Bar Assn., Montgomery, 1988-95; ptnr. London & Yancey, Birmingham, Ala., 1995—. Decorated D.S.M., Legion of Merit, Meritorious Svc. medal. Mem. ABA. Methodist Military, Personal injury, Ethics. Office: London & Yancey 2001 Park Pl Ste 400 Birmingham AL 35203-2787

NORSWORTHY, ELIZABETH KRASSOVSKY, lawyer; b. N.Y.C., Feb. 26, 1943; d. Leonid Alexander and Wilma (Hudgens) Krassovsky; m. John Randolph Norsworthy, June 24, 1961 (div. 1962), m. Nov. 26, 1977 (div. 1984); 1 child, Alexander. AB magna cum laude, CUNY, 1965; MA, U. N.C., 1966; JD, Stanford U., 1977. Bar: D.C. 1978, Mass. 1992, Vt. 1998, U.S. Ct. Appeals (D.C. cir.) 1979. Atty. applications, disclosure rev. and investment adviser regulation, divsn. investment mgmt. SEC, Washington, 1978-79, 80-82, atty. operating brs. and disclosure policy divsn. corp. fin., 1979-80, chief, spl. counsel office of regulatory policy divsn. investment mgmt., 1983-86; assoc. Kirkpatrick & Lockhart, 1986-90; ptnr. Sullivan & Worcester, Boston, 1990-92; pvt. practice Norfolk, Mass., 1992-95, Concord, Vt., 1996—. Pub. arbitrator, chairperson NASD; mediator, facilitator Cmty. Justice Ctr., St. Johnsbury. Bd. dirs. First Night, St. Johnsbury; chair investment com. North Congl. Ch., St. Johnsbury; mem. adv. bd. Natural Resources, Concord; mem. North Country Choris, Weels River. Mem. Vt. Bar Assn. (arbitration com., family law com.), N.Y. '40 Acts. Com., Am. Livestock Breek Conservancy, Jacob Sheep Breed Assn., Am. Farmland Trust, Vt. Grass Farmers, Vt. Coverts, Catamount Arts (St. Johnsbury), Athenaeum (St. Johnsbury), College Club (St. Johnsbury), Phi Beta Kappa, Phi Alpha Theta. Democrat. Mem. United Church of Christ. Avocations: farming, swimming, singing, environmental protection. Estate planning, Family and matrimonial, Juvenile. Office: Winterbrook Farm 1342 Woodward Rd Concord VT 05824-9620 Fax: 802-695-2516. E-mail: ekn@kingcon.com

NORTELL, BRUCE, lawyer; b. Nov. 19, 1946; s. Joseph and Dorothy Nortell; m. Joan Ott, Apr. 05, 1975; children: Adam, Daniel, Anthony. AB, Boston U., 1968; JD, U. Chgo., 1971. Bar: Ill. 1971, U.S. Dist. Ct. (no. dist.) Ill. 1971, U.S. Supreme Ct. 1979. Sole practice, Chgo., 1971—74; asst. dir. legal affairs AMA, 1974—81, counsel, sec. jud. coun., 1976—81; dir. tax and fin. planning Loyola U., 1981—88, North Ctrl. Coll., Naperville, 1988—. Contbr. articles to profl. jours., author two books novels. Mem.: ABA, Ill. Bar Assn. (Lincoln award 1975), Chgo. Bar Assn., Phi Beta Kappa. Home: 1124 Dickens Ln Naperville IL 60563-4301 Office: 30 N Brainard St Naperville IL 60540-4607

NORTH, JAMES LITTLE, attorney; b. Anniston, Ala., Oct. 10, 1936; s. John Pelham and Winnie (Little) N.; m. Lettie Lane Hurlbert, Sept. 5, 1959; 1 child, James Little, Jr. BS, U. Ala., 1958; JD, U. Va., 1964. Law clk. U.S. Supreme Ct., Washington, 1964-65; from assoc. to ptnr. Bradley, Arant, Rose & White, Birmingham, Ala., 1965-73; ptnr. North, Haskell, Slaughter & Young, 1973-85, James L. North & Assocs., Birmingham, 1985—. Bd. dirs., gen. counsel Adtran, Inc. Lt. U.S. Army, 1959-61. Recipient commendation medal U.S. Army, 1961. Fellow Am. Bar Found. (life), Internat. Soc. Barristers; mem. ABA (ho. dels. 1986-88), Ala. Law Inst.

(coun.), Ala. State Bar (pres. 1985-86, award of merit), Eleventh Cir. Hist. Soc. (trustee). Trustee Dem. Nat. Com.; chmn. fin. Clinton-Gore campaign, Ala., 1992, 96; bd. trustees Presbyn. Home for Children, Talladega, Ala.; bd. dirs. Pub. Affairs Rsch. Coun., Birmingham. Home: 4008 Lenox Rd Birmingham AL 35213 Office: 300 21st St N 700 Title Bld Birmingham AL 35203

NORTH, STEVEN EDWARD, lawyer, educator; b. Oct. 16, 1941; s. Irving J. and Barbara (Grubman) N.; m. Sue J. Buznitsky, Dec. 24, 1966; children: Jennifer, Samantha. BA, CCNY, 1963; JD, Bklyn. Law Sch., 1966; LLM, NYU, 1967. Bar: N.Y. 1967, U.S. Dist. Ct. (so. and ea. dists.) N.Y. 1970, U.S. Supreme Ct. 1971. Asst. dist. atty. homicide bur. N.Y. County Dist. Attys. Office, N.Y.C., 1967-71; spl. asst. atty. gen., bur. chief N.Y. State Atty. Gen.'s Office, 1972-75; pvt. practice 1975—. Mem. adv. com. Ann. Civil Litigation Inst., Practicing Law Inst., 1996; chmn. Assn. Bar Subcom. on Investigation into Imposition of Legis. Limits on Awards for Non-Econ. Damages, 1995; mediator U.S. Dist. Ct. (so. dist.) N.Y., 1994—, apptd. jud. screening program; mem. adv. coms. solo law practice Practicing Law Inst., 1991, adv. bd. tort litigation, 1989—; vis. faculty Sch. Law, NYU, faculty workshop Cardozo Sch. Law, judge appellate argument, alumni advisor; faculty advisor Trial of Breast Cancer Case, Law Jour. Seminars, 2000; lectr. in field. Author: Prevention and Detection of Fraud in Industry, 1973, Controlling the Deposition: Winning Your Case Before Trial, 1978, Deposition Strategy, Law and Forms, vol. 1 (Introduction and Law), vol. 5 (Medical Malpractice), vol. 8 (Personal Injury), 1981, (course handbooks) Trial Mechanics, Personal Injury Desbook, 1983, Trial Mechanics and Discovery, 1985, 86, Medical Malpractice Litigation, 1988, Managing the Multi-Million Dollar Case, 1990, Objectifying Brain Damage in Closed Head Injury, 1990, Fundamentals of Medical Malpractice Litigation, 1991, Damage Update, 1992, 93, 94, 95, 96, 97—, Proving & Defending Damages, 1993, Conducting & Defending Depositions, 1993; contbr. chpts. to books; editor: Cancer Litigation Bull., 1994—, Fear of Developing Cancer; contbg. editor: Law and Order mag.; med.-legal editor Perinatology, 1983; contbr. articles to legal jours.; commentator Eyewitness News, 1994, Court TV, 1994-98, Talk News TV, 1996. Mem. leadership coun. So. Poverty Law Ctr. Mem. ATLA, NCCJ (lawyers divsn., ann. dinner com.), NOW (benefits com.), U.S. Holocaust Mus. (charter mem.), Am. Bd. Trial Advs., Soc. Med. Jurisprudence, N.Y. State Bar Assn. (faculty), N.Y. State Trial Lawyers Assn. (bd. dirs. 1990—, faculty chmn. Depositions in Action 2000, North's Ninety-Nine Pointers on Advanced Deposition Practices 1999), Lotos Club, Nat. Eagle Scout Assn., State Trial Lawyers Assn. (bd. dirs. 1990—, seminar faculty chmn. 1993, faculty decisions program 1991—, Law Day dinner com.), N.Y. County Lawyers Assn. (exec. com. med. malpractice sect., exec. com. gen. tort law sect.), Assn. Bar of City of N.Y. (civil ct. com. 1980-83, legal and continuing edn. com. 1983—, legal referral svc. com., med. malpractice mediator 1994—, chmn. subcom. on imposition of legis. limits to awards for non-econ. damages), Vol. Lawyers for the Arts, Million Dollar Advs. Forum, Vol. Lawyers for the Arts, N.Y. County Supreme Ct. Com. Med. Malpractice Litigation, N.Y. Soc. Anesthesiologist (speaker), N.Y. State Bar Assn. State civil litigation, Personal injury. Home: 148 E 74th St New York NY 10021 Office: 148 E 74th St New York NY 10021-3542

NORTHERN, RICHARD, lawyer; b. Louisville, Dec. 17, 1948; s. James William and Mary Helen (Barry) N.; m. Mary Lou Grundy, Aug. 28, 1971; children: James Barry, Nancy Hope, Mary Grace. BA in English, U. Louisville, 1970, JD, 1976; MPA, Harvard U., 1977. Bar: Ky. 1976, U.S. Dist. Ct. (we. and ea. dists.) Ky. 1977. Staff writer Courier-Jour., Louisville, 1970-72; dir. planning devel. Jefferson County Govt., 1972-76; legis. dir. Office of U.S. Rep. Romano Mazzoli, Washington, 1977-78; spl. asst. U.S. Sec. of Interior, 1979-80; ptnr. Wyatt, Tarrant & Combs, Louisville, 1980—. Chmn. bd. dirs. Cath. Edn. Found., Inc., Louisville, 1998—. White House fellow, 1979, U.S.-Japan Leadership fellow Japan Soc., Inc., 1988. Democrat. Roman Catholic. Administrative and regulatory, General corporate, Private international. Office: Wyatt Tarrant & Combs 2800 Citizens Plz Louisville KY 40202-2898

NORTHROP, EDWARD SKOTTOWE, federal judge; b. Chevy Chase, Md., June 12, 1911; s. Claudian Bellinger and Eleanor Smythe (Grimke) N.; m. Barbara Middleton Burdette, Apr. 22, 1939; children: Edward M., St. Julien (Mrs. Kevin Butler), Peter. LLB, George Washington U., 1937. Bar: Md. 1937, D.C. 1937. Village mgr., Chevy Chase, Md., 1934-41; pvt. practice, Rockville, Washington, 1937-61; mem. Md. Senate, 1954-61, chmn. fin. com., joint com. taxation fiscal affairs, majority leader, 1959-61; judge U.S. Dist. Ct. Md., Balt., 1961-70; chief judge U.S. Dist. Ct. of Md., 1970-81, sr. judge, 1981—. Mem. Met. Chief Judges Conf., 1970-81; mem. Jud. Conf. Com. on Adminstrn. of Probation System, 1973-79, Adv. Corrections Council U.S., 1976— , Jud. Panel on Multidist. Litigation, 1979— ; judge U.S. Fgn. Intelligence Surveillance Ct. of Rev., 1985— Trustee Woodberry Forest Sch.; founder Washington Met. Area Coun. Govts. & Mass Transp. Agy. Served to comdr. USNR, 1941-45. Decorated Army commendation medal, Navy commendation medal; recipient Profl. Achievement award George Washington U., 1975, Disting. Citizen award State of Md., 1981, Spl. Merit citation Am. Judicature Soc., 1982. Mem. ABA, Md. Bar Assn. (Disting. Svc. award 1982), D.C. Bar Assn., Montgomery County Bar Assn., Barristers, Washington Ctr. Met. Studies. Democrat. Episcopalian. Club: Chevy Chase (Md.). Lodge: Rotary Office: US Dist Ct 101 W Lombard St Ste 8A Baltimore MD 21201-2903

NORTON, GALE ANN, secretary of the interior; b. Wichita, Mar. 11, 1954; d. Dale Bentsen and Anna Jacqueline (Lansdowne) N.; m. John Goethe Hughes, Mar. 26, 1990. BA, U. Denver, 1975, JD, 1978. Bar: Colo. 1978, U.S. Supreme Ct. 1981. Jud. clk. Colo. Ct. of Appeals, Denver, 1978-79; sr. atty. Mountain States Legal Found., 1979-83; nat. fellow Hoover Instn. Stanford (Calif.) U., 1983-84; asst. to dep. sec. USDA, Washington, 1984-85; assoc. solicitor U.S. Dept. of Interior, 1985-87; pvt. practice law Denver, 1987-90; atty. gen. State of Colo., 1991-99; atty. Brownstein, Hyatt & Farber, P.C., sr. counsel, 1999-2000; sec. U.S. Dept. Interior, Washington, 2001—. Lectr. U. Denver Law Sch., 1989; transp. law program dir. U. Denver, 1978-79. Contbr. chpts. to books, articles to profl. jours. Past chair Nat. Assn. Attys. Gen. Environ. Com.; co-chair Nat. Policy Forum Environ. Coun.; candidate for 1996 election to U.S. Senate; chair environ. commn. Rep. Nat. Lawyers Assn. Named Young Career Woman Bus. and Profl. Wome, 1981, Young Lawyer of Yr., 1991, Mary Lathrop Trailblazer award Colo. Women's Bar Assn., 1999. Mem. Federalist Soc., Colo. Women's Forum, Order of St. Ives. Republican. Methodist. Avocation: skiing. Office: Dept of the Interior Office of the Sec 1849 C St NW Washington DC 20240

NORTON, JOHN WILLIAM, lawyer, investment advisory firm executive; b. St. Paul, Sept. 30, 1941; s. John William Jr. and Dorothy (Sheridan) N.; m. Kathleen L. Smith, Aug. 19, 1967 (div.); children: Tiffany, Sean. BA in Bus. Adminstrn., Marquette U., 1964; JD, Stetson U., 1968. Bar: Fla. 1968, Minn. 1968. Atty. Minn. Mut. Life Ins. Co., St. Paul, 1968-73; asst. counsel IDS Life Ins. Co., Mpls., 1973; atty., adviser fin. SEC, Washington, 1973-78; sr. v.p., gen. counsel, sec. Fortis Financial Group, St. Paul, 1978-95; sr. v.p. gen. counsel life & investment products Fortis Benefits Ins. Co., 1988-95; sr. v.p., gen. counsel life & investment products Time Ins. Co. Mem. ABA, Minn. Bar Assn., Fla. Bar Assn. E-mail: mediator@ABANET.org; lawpractitioner@aol.com. General corporate, Pension, profit-sharing, and employee benefits, Securities. Home: 7778 Pinehurst Rd Woodbury MN 55125-2325

NORTON, RANDELL HUNT, lawyer; b. Newport, R.I., Nov. 21, 1948; s. Gerald Sanford and Mary Kent (Hewitt) N.; m. Linda Sue Baughan, Aug. 12, 1972; children: Jackson Hewitt, Thomas Baughan. BA, U. Va., 1970, JD, 1973. Bar: Va. 1973, D.C. 1974, Md. 1984, U.S. Ct. Appeals (D.C. cir.) 1974, U.S. Ct. Appeals (4th cir.) 1975. Law clk. D.C. Superior Ct., Washington, 1973-74; assoc. Macleay, Lynch, Bernhard & Gregg, Washington, 1974-80, ptnr., 1981; assoc. Thompson, Larson, McGrail, O'Donnell & Harding, Washington, 1981-83, ptnr., 1983— . Pres. Capitol Hill Babysitting Coop, Washington, 1983-84; sr. warden St. George's Episcopal Ch., Arlington, Va., 1981-83. Named Lawyer of the Yr., 1987. Mem. D.C. Def. Lawyers' Assn. (sec. 1984-85, v.p. 1987—), D.C. Bar (rules com.). Episcopalian. Federal civil litigation, State civil litigation, Personal injury. Office: Thompson Larson McGrail Et Al 805 15th St NW Ste 705 Washington DC 20005-2284 also: The Pentagon Manpower & Res Affairs Washington DC 20330-0001

NORTON, SALLY PAULINE, lawyer; b. Elkhart, Ind., Jan. 28, 1964; d. Ronald F. and Peggy Lucille Hale; m. Peter Thomas Norton, Aug. 28, 1993; children: Alexander, Aileen. BA, Ind. U., 1986, JD, 1989. Bar: Ind. 1991, U.S. Dist. Ct. (no. and so. dists.) Ind. 1991. Law clk. Kalamaros & Assocs., South Bend, Ind., 1990-91, assoc., 1991—. Mem. Ind. Bar Assn., St. Joseph County Bar Assn., Def. Trial Counsel Ind., Robert A. Grant Inn of Ct. Avocation: martial arts. Insurance, Personal injury, Workers' compensation. Home: 10628 N Pheasant Cove Dr Granger IN 46530-7576 Office: Kalamoros & Assocs 129 N Michigan St South Bend IN 46601-1603

NORTON-LARSON, MARY JEAN, lawyer, planned giving officer; b. Adrian, Minn., Feb. 18, 1955; d. Robert Eugene and Natalie Norma (Nelson) Norton; m. Richard Allan Larson, Apr. 2, 1977; children: Kathryn, Bennett, Jackson. BA, Bethel Coll., St. Paul, 1977; JD, Hamline U., St. Paul, 1981. Bar: Minn. 1981. Assoc., ptnr. Eastlund, Solstad & Hutchinson, Ltd., Mpls., 1982-95; sole practitioner Cambridge, Minn., 1995-97; planned giving officer Bethel Coll. and Sem., St. Paul, 1997—. Editor notes and comments Hamline Law Rev., 1980-81. Mem. Minn. Women Lawyers. Methodist. Avocations: travel, golf, reading, volleyball. Estate planning, Non-profit and tax-exempt organizations. Home: 32299 Jackson Rd NE Cambridge MN 55008-6879 Office: Bethel Coll and Sem 3900 Bethel Dr Saint Paul MN 55112-6902

NORVILLE, CRAIG HUBERT, lawyer; b. N.Y.C., June 10, 1944; s. Hubert G. and Harriett (Johnson) N.; m. Loretta Norville; 1 child, Margaret Amelia. AB, Harvard U., 1966; LLB, U. Va., 1969. Bar: N.Y. 1971, Pa. 1979, Tenn. 1985. Instr. law U. Mich., 1969-70; assoc. Cravath, Swaine & Moore, N.Y.C., 1970-76; sr. atty. Bethlehem (Pa.) Steel Corp., 1976-80; v.p., assoc. gen. counsel Holiday Corp. (name changed to The Promus Cos. Inc.), Memphis, 1980-84, v.p., gen. counsel, 1984-86, sr. v.p., gen. counsel, 1986-93, spl. counsel, 1993-99; of cousnel Jones Vargas, Las Vegas, 2000-01, ptnr., stockholder, 2001—. Gen. counsel Diocese of the West, Orthodox Ch. in Am., 2000—. Articles editor U. Va. Law Rev. Mem. Raven Soc., Hasty Pudding Inst. of 1770, Order of Coif, Harvard Varsity Club (Cambridge, Mass.). Avocations: golf, skiing, fishing. General corporate, Real property, Securities. Address: 5305 Rim View Ln Las Vegas NV 89130-3646 E-mail: chn@jonesvargas.com

NOSEK, FRANCIS JOHN, lawyer, diplomat; b. Evanston, Ill., Apr. 13, 1934; s. Francis J. and Loretto (Brannan) N.; m. Janet Child, Dec. 30, 1964; children: Francis J. III, Peter C. BA in Polit. Sci., U. Idaho, 1956, JD, 1960. Bar: Calif. 1961, U.S. Dist. Ct. (no. dist.) Calif. 1961, U.S. Ct. Appeals (9th cir.) 1961, Alaska 1962, U.S. Dist. Ct. Alaska 1962, D.C. 1978. Pvt. practice, Anchorage, 1960-67, 75—; assoc. Bell, Sanders & Tallman, 1961-62; sr. ptnr. Nosek, Bradberry, Wolf and Schlossberg, 1967-75; hon. consul Czech Republic. Adj. prof. U. Alaska, Mat-Su C.C., Anchorage, 1976-82; lectr. Anchorage C.C., 1979-83, SBA, 1975-97; editor State of Alaska Real Estate Commn., Anchorage, 1983; presenter in field; bd. of dirs. on real estate and bus. topics. Author: Alaska Mortgage Law, How to Buy and Sell a Business; contbr. articles to law jours. Chmn. Anchorage Parks and Recreation, 1968-83, IIHF World Jr. Championships, Anchorage, 1988; named hon. Consul for Czech Republic. Mem. Am. Coll. Real Estate Lawyers, Alaska Bar Assn. (chmn. real estate law 1978, mem. internat. law exec. com. 1991-95), Calif. Bar Assn. (real estate law coms.), D.C. Bar Assn. (internat. law com.), Anchorage Bar Assn. Avocations: mountain climbing, ice hockey, antique cars. Private international, Real property. Office: 310 K St Ste 601 Anchorage AK 99501-2041

NOTTINGHAM, EDWARD WILLIS, JR. federal judge; b. Denver, Jan. 9, 1948; s. Edward Willis and Willie Newton (Gullett) N.; m. Cheryl Ann Card, June 6, 1970 (div. Feb. 1981); children: Amelia Charlene, Edward Willis III; m. Janis Ellen Chapman, Aug. 18, 1984 (div. Dec. 1998); 1 child, Spencer Chapman. AB, Cornell U., 1969; JD, U. Colo., 1972. Bar: Colo. 1972, U.S. Dist. Ct. Colo. 1972, U.S. Ct. Appeals (10th cir.) 1973. Law clk. to presiding judge U.S. Dist. Ct. Colo., Denver, 1972-73; assoc. Sherman & Howard, 1973-76, 78-80, ptnr., 1980-87, Beckner & Nottingham, Grand Junction, Colo., 1987-89; asst. U.S. atty. U.S. Dept. Justice, Denver, 1976-78; U.S. dist. judge Dist. of Colo., 1989—. Mem. Jud. Conf. of the U.S. Com. on Automation and Tech., 1994-2000, chmn., 1997-2000. Bd. dirs. Beaver Creek Met. Dist., Avon, Colo., 1980-88, Justice Info. Ctr., Denver, 1985-87, 21st Jud. Dist. Victim Compensation Fund, Grand Junction, Colo., 1987-89. Mem. ABA, Colo. Bar Assn. (chmn. criminal law sect. 1983-85, chmn. ethics com. 1988-89), Order of Coif, Denver Athletic Club, Delta Sigma Rho, Tau Kappa Alpha. Episcopalian. Office: US Dist Ct 1929 Stout St Denver CO 80294-1929 E-mail: Edward_W._Nottingham@cod.uscourts.gov

NOVAK, JOSEPH ANTHONY, lawyer; b. Detroit; s. Thomas Paul and Mary Cecilia N. AA, Macomb C.C., Warren, Mich., 1984; BA, Oakland U., 1986; JD, Mich. State U., 1991; M Libr. and Info. Sci., Wayne State U., 1998. Intern Wayne County Pub. Defender's Office, Detroit, 1986; intern Office of Jud. Assistance 3d Jud. Ct. Mich., 1993, law clk. to Hon. Diane M. Hathaway, intern, 1996; law libr. St. Louis Correctional Facility, 2000—. Vol., Vol. Income Tax Assistance Program, Detroit, 1995—. Recipient Outstanding Vol. Volunteer Income Tax Assistance Program, 1995, 96, 98, 99, 2000, The Spirit of Am. Is In the Heart of Its Volunteers IRS, 1995, 96, 97, 99. Mem. Am. Assn. Law Librs., Spl. Librs. Assn., Acctg. Aid Soc. Democrat. Roman Catholic. Avocations: coin and stamp collecting, water skiing, walking. Home: 1820 S Crawford St Apt C3 Mount Pleasant MI 48858-6150

NOVAK, MARK, lawyer; b. Buffalo, Jan. 28, 1952; s. Eugene Francis and Joan (Tross) N.; m. Charlene Mary Ingoglia, Sept. 2, 1972; children: Jason Charles, Jennifer Rose. BA, U. Rochester, 1974; JD, Loyola U., Chgo., 1977. Bar: Ill. 1977, U.S. Dist. Ct. (no. dist.) Ill. 1977, U.S. Ct. Appeals (7th cir.) 1978. Assoc. Anesi, Ozmon & Lewin, Ltd., Chgo., 1977-83; ptnr. Anesi, Ozmon, Rodin, Novak & Kohen, Ltd., 1983—. Fundraiser Christmas is for Kids Charity, Chgo., 1992—. Mem. ATLA (product liability sect. 1985—), ABA, Ill. Trial Lawyers Assn., Trial Lawyers for Pub. Justice, Chgo. Bar Assn. (jud. evaluation com. 1995—). Avocations: painting, gardening, traveling. General civil litigation, Personal injury, Product liability. Home: 1212 N Lake Shore Dr Chicago IL 60610-2371 Office: Anesi Ozmon Rodin Novak & Kohen Ltd 161 N Clark St Fl 21 Chicago IL 60601-3206

NOVIKOFF, HAROLD STEPHEN, lawyer; b. N.Y.C., Apr. 5, 1951; s. Eugene Benjamin and Vivian (Hirsch) N.; m. Amy Pearl, Aug. 20, 1972; children: Sara Heather, Elyse Fana. AB, Cornell U., 1972; JD, Columbia U., 1975. Bar: N.Y. 1976, U.S. Dist. Ct. (so. dist.) N.Y. 1976. Ptnr. Wachtell, Lipton, Rosen & Katz, N.Y.C., 1975—. Mem. ABA, N.Y. State Bar Assn., Assn. Bar City N.Y. (bankruptcy and reorgn. com. 1995-99, chair 1999—), Nat. Bankruptcy Conf. Bankruptcy, Finance. Office: Wachtell Lipton Rosen Katz 51 W 52nd St Fl 29 New York NY 10019-6150 E-mail: hsnovikoff@wlrk.com

NOVINS, ALAN SLATER, lawyer; b. Rochester, N.H., Oct. 23, 1937; s. Murray H. and Celia D. (Raphael) N. AB, Harvard U., 1961; JD, Columbia U., 1964. Bar: N.H. 1964, D.C. 1970. Legis. counsel to U.S. Senator Thomas J. McIntyre, 1964-70; asst. counsel U.S. Senate Com. on Banking, Housing and Urban Affairs, Washington, 1971; ptnr. Lobel, Novins & Lamont, Washington, 1972—. Chmn. hearing com. 6 D.C. Bd. on Profl. Responsibility, 1982-88 . Mem. ABA, Fed. Bar Assn., N.H. Bar Assn., D.C. Bar Assn., D.C. Bar (chmn. com. on specialization 1975-76). Administrative and regulatory, Federal civil litigation. Office: 1275 K St NW Ste 770 Washington DC 20005-4006

NOVOTNY, F. DOUGLAS, lawyer; b. Mineola, N.Y., Mar. 10, 1952; s. Frank Joseph and Eleanor Evans (Rose) N.; m. Norma R. Federici, Sept. 7, 1991; children: Nicholas, Christina, Alexander. BA cum laude, SUNY, Albany, 1974; postgrad., NYU, Hofstra U., C.W. Post U.; JD cum laude, Albany Law Sch., 1979. Bar: N.Y. 1980, U.S. Dist. Ct. (no. dist.) N.Y. 1980. Confidential law asst. Appellate Divsn. 3d Dept., Albany, 1979-80; ptnr. DeGraff, Foy, Conway, Holt-Harris & Mealey, 1980-91; pvt. practice Saratoga, N.Y., 1991-93; mng. atty. Law Offices of F. Douglas Novotny, 1993—; staff counsel Am. Internat. Group, Inc., 1993—. Mem. Albany County Arbitration Panel, 1984-88. Editor Albany Law Rev., 1978-79; contbr. articles to profl. jours. Mem. ATLA, Justinian Soc., Assn. Trial Lawyers Am., Capital Dist. Trial Lawyers Assn. Presbyterian. Federal civil litigation, State civil litigation. Home: 27 Mallard Lndg S Waterford NY 12188-1037

NOWACKI, JAMES NELSON, lawyer; b. Columbus, Ohio, Sept. 12, 1947; s. Louis James and Betty Jane (Nelson) N.; m. Catherine Ann Holden, Aug. 1, 1970; children: Carrie, Anastasia, Emma. AB, Princeton U., 1969; JD, Yale U., 1973. Bar: Ill. 1973, N.Y. 1982, U.S. dist. Ct. (no. dist.) Ill. 1973, U.S. Ct. Appeals (7th cir.) 1978, U.S. Ct. Appeals (6th cir.) 1987, U.S. Supremem Ct. 1992. Assoc. Isham, Lincoln & Beale, Chgo., 1976-79; ptnr. Kirkland & Ellis, 1980—. Mem. Winnetka Sch. Bd. Dist. 36, Ill. 1983-91, bd. pres., 1989-91; mem. New Trier Sch. Bd., 1997-99, pres., 1997-98. Harlan Fiske Stone prize Yale U., 1972. Mem. ABA (forum com. on constrn. industry, litigation sect.), Mid-Am. Club, Skokie Country Club. Federal civil litigation, State civil litigation, Construction. Home: 708 Prospect Ave Winnetka IL 60093-2320 Office: Kirkland & Ellis 200 E Randolph St Fl 54 Chicago IL 60601-6636

NOWADZKY, ROGER ALAN, lawyer, lobbyist; b. Cedar Rapids, Iowa, Dec. 28, 1949; s. James Richard and Harriet Marie (Kacer) N.; m. Karen Louise Urban, June 3, 1972 (div.); m. Lynn E. Maaske, Dec. 17, 1988 (div.); children— Robert, Jill, Brooke. B.A. summa cum laude, St. Mary's Coll., Winona, Minn., 1972; J.D. with distinction, U. Iowa, 1976. Bar: Iowa 1976, U.S. Dist. Ct. (no. and so. dists.) Iowa 1976, U.S. Ct. Appeals (8th cir.) 1976, Supreme Ct., 1989. Acct. Quaker Oats Co., Cedar Rapids, Iowa, 1972; legal clk. bankruptcy div. U.S. Dist. Ct. (no. dist.) Iowa, Cedar Rapids, 1976; legal counsel for Iowa Legislature, Legis. Service Bur., Des Moines, 1976-83; legis. counsel League Iowa Municipalities, Des Moines, 1983-88, dep. dir., counsel, 1988-89, legis. policy com., 1989—; corp. counsel City of Des Moines, Iowa, 1989-96; with Nowadzky & Assocs., Des Moines; mem. state govt. issues and orgn. com. Assembly on the Legislature, Nat. Conf. State Legislatures, 1983; participant Iowa Key Decision Makers Correctional Policy Conf. of Nat. Council on Crime and Delinquency, Des Moines, 1982; mem. tort liability/ins. focus group Iowa Dept. Human Resources, 1986. Contbr. articles to various mags. and profl. jours. Bd. dirs. Tatterdemalion Prodns. Theatre Prodn. Workshop, Des Moines, 1983— . Mem. Nat. Inst. Mcpl. Law Officers (vice chair 1992-93, chair 1993—), Iowa Mcpl. Attys. Assn. (ex-officio bd. dirs. 1983-89, 1st v.p. 1991-92, pres. 1992—), Iowa State Bar Assn. (penal reform com. 1977m, chair open meetings and open records com. 1991-92, ethics com., legis. com. govtl. practice sect. 1991-92, profl. com. 1991-92), Iowa Coalition Against Sexual Assault (task force on sexual exploitation by helping profls. 1987—), Phi Delta Phi McLain Inn (vice magister 1975-76, cert. appreciation U. Iowa chpt. 1976), Pi Gamma Mu. Home: 3006 46th St Des Moines IA 50310-3530 Office: Nowadsky & Assocs 3006 46th St Des Moines IA 50310-3530

NOWAK, JOHN E. law educator; b. Chgo., Jan. 2, 1947; s. George Edward and Evelyn (Bucci) N.; m. Judith Johnson, June 1, 1968; children: John Edwin, Jeffrey Edward. AB, Marquette U., 1968; JD, U. Ill., 1971. Law clk. Supreme Ct. of Ill., Chgo., 1971-72; asst. prof. U. Ill., Urbana, 1972-75, assoc. prof., 1975-87, law prof., 1978—, grad. coll. faculty, 1982—, Baum Prof. Law, 1993—. Chmn. Constl. Law Sch. Sect.; faculty rep. Big Ten Intercollegiate Conf., Schaumburg, Ill., 1981-91; vis. prof. law U. Mich., Ann Arbor, 1985; Lee Disting. vis. prof. Coll. William and Mary, 1993. Co-author: Constitutional Law, 6th edit. 2000, Treatise on Constitutional Law, 1986, 3d edit., 1999, Story's Commentaries on the Constitution, 1987. Scholar-in-Residence, U. of Ariz., Tucson, 1985, 87. Mem. Assn. of Am. Law Schs. (chm. constl. law sect., accreditation com. 1980-88), Nat. Collegiate Athletic Assn. (mem. infractions com. 1987—), Am. Law Inst., Am. Bar Assn., Ill. Bar Assn., Order of the Coif (Triennial Book award com.). Roman Catholic. Home: 1701 Mayfair Rd Champaign IL 61821-5522 Office: U Ill Coll Law 504 E Pennsylvania Ave Champaign IL 61820-6909

NOWLIN, JAMES ROBERTSON, federal judge; b. San Antonio, Nov. 21, 1937; s. William Forney and Jeannette (Robertson) N. BA, Trinity U., 1959, MA, 1962; JD, U. Tex., Austin, 1963. Bar: Tex. 1963, Colo. 1993, U.S. Dist. Ct. D.C. 1966, U.S. Ct. Claims 1969, U.S. Supreme Ct. 1969, U.S. Dist. Ct. (we. dist.) Tex. 1971. Assoc. Kelso, Locke, & King, San Antonio, 1963-65; assoc. Kelso, Locke & Lepick, 1966-69; legal counsel U.S. Senate, Washington, 1965-66; propr. Law Offices James R. Nowlin, San Antonio, 1969-81; mem. Tex. Ho. of Reps., Austin, 1967-71, 73-81; judge U.S. Dist. Ct. for Western Dist. Tex., 1981-99, chief judge, 2000—. Instr. Am. govt. and history San Antonio Coll., 1964-65, 71-73. Capt. U.S. Army, 1959-60, USAR, 1960-68. Fellow State Bar Found (life); mem. San Antonio Bar Assn., Colo. Bar Assn. Republican. Presbyterian Avocations: pilot, skiing, hiking, jogging. Office: US Courthouse 200 W 8th St Austin TX 78701-2325

NOZISKA, CHARLES BRANT, lawyer; b. Oakland, Calif., Aug. 28, 1953; s. Charles Richard and Shirley Ann (Orme) N. BA, Colo. Coll., 1975; JD magna cum laude, U. San Diego, 1982. Bar: Calif. 1982, U.S. Dist. Ct. (so. dist.) Calif. 1982. Ptnr. Thorsnes, Bartolotta, McGuire & Padilla, San Diego, 1982—. Co-author: Landslide and Subsidence Liability, 1988. Mem. Assn. Trial Lawyers Am., Calif. Trial Lawyers Assn., San Diego Trial Lawyers Assn., San Diego County Bar Assn. Democrat. Avocations: ocean sports. General civil litigation, Insurance. Office: Thorsnes Bartolotta McGuire & Padilla 2550 5th Ave Ste 11 San Diego CA 92103-6612

NUGENT, LORI S. lawyer; b. Peoria, Ill., Apr. 24, 1962; d. Walter Leonard and Margery (Frost) Meyer; m. Shane Vincent Nugent, June 14, 1986; children: Justine Nicole, Cole Tyler. BA in Polit. Sci. cum laude, Knox Coll., 1984; JD, Northwestern U., Chgo., 1987. Bar: Ill. 1987, U.S. Dist. Ct. (no. dist.) Ill. 1988, U.S. Ct. Appeals (7th cir.) 1995. Assoc. Peterson & Ross, Chgo., 1987-94, Blatt, Hammesfahr & Eaton, Chgo., 1994, ptnr., 1994-2000, Cozen and O'Connor, Chgo., 2000—. Co-author: Punitive Damages: A Guide to the Insurability of Punitive Damages in the United States and Its Territories, 1988, Punitive Damages: A State-by-State Guide to Law and Practice, 1991, Japanese edit., 1995, Pocket Part, 2001; contbr. articles to law jours. Alternative dispute resolution, Insurance. Office: Cozen and OConner Ste 1500 222 S Riverside Plz Chicago IL 60606-6000 E-mail: lnugent@cozen.com

NULL, WILLIAM SETH, lawyer; b. N.Y.C., Apr. 15, 1954; s. Douglas P. Null and Barbara M. (Black) Schacker; m. Lauren E. Thaler, May 10, 1981; children: Danielle, Evan. BA, Hampshire Coll., 1977; JD, Yeshiva U., 1980. Bar: N.Y. 1981, U.S. Dist. Ct. (ea. and so. dists.) N.Y. 1981, U.S. Supreme Ct. 1987. With Null & Null, P.C., Garden City, N.Y., 1980-83, Kraver & Martin, N.Y.C., 1983-85, Cuddy & Feder LLP (now Cuddy & Feder & Worby LLP), White Plains, NY, 1985—. Dir. The Housing Partnership, Elmsford, NY, 1995—, White Plains Bridge of Friendship Found., 1994—, S.E. N.Y. chpt. (formerly Westchester County chpt.) Juvenile Diabetes Rsch. Found. Internat., 1998—, Gilda's Club Westchester, 2001—, The Briarcliff Manor Edn. Found., 2001—. Federal civil litigation, General civil litigation, State civil litigation. Office: Cuddy & Feder & Worby LLP 90 Maple Ave White Plains NY 10601-5105 E-mail: wnull@cfwlaw.com

NUNEZ, PETER K. lawyer. U.S. atty. so. Calif., San Diego. Office: Dept Treas Asst Sec Enforcement 1500 Pennsylvania Ave NW Washington DC 20220-0001

NUNNALLY, KNOX DILLON, lawyer; b. Haynesville, La., Jan. 26, 1943; s. Miles Dillon and Linnie Mat (Knox) N.; m. Kay Clyde Webb; 1 child, Kevin Knox. B.B.A., U. Tex., 1965, LL.B., 1968. Bar: Tex. 1968, U.S. Dist. Ct. (ea. dist.) Tex. 1970, U.S. Dist. Ct. (so. dist.) Tex. 1969, U.S. Dist. Ct. (we. dist.) Tex. 1976; U.S. Ct. Appeals (5th cir.) 1978. Diplomate Tex. Bd. Legal Specialization. Ptnr., Vinson & Elkins L.L.P., Houston, 1976— . Mem. ABA, Am. Coll. Trial Lawyers, Tex. Bar Assn., Houston Bar Assn. Federal civil litigation, State civil litigation, Personal injury. Home: 3421 Meadow Lake Ln Houston TX 77027-4106 Office: Vinson & Elkins LLP 1001 Fannin St Ste 2300 Houston TX 77002-6760

NUSSBAUM, HOWARD JAY, lawyer; b. N.Y.C., Dec. 17, 1951; s. Norman and Ruth (Rand) N.; children: Martin Garrett, Daniel Todd. BA, SUNY, Binghamton, 1972; JD, Boston Coll., 1976. Bar: Fla. 1977, U.S. Dist. Ct. (so. dist. trial and bankruptcy bar) Fla. 1977, U.S. Ct. Appeals (5th and 11th cirs.) 1981. Mng. atty. Legal Aid. Svc., Ft. Lauderdale, Fla., 1976-88; ptnr. Weinstein, Zimmerman & Nussbaum, P.A., Tamarac, 1988-92; pres. Howard J. Nussbaum, P.A., 1993—. Chmn. Legal Aid com. North Broward Bar Assn., Pompano Beach, Fla., 1986-87; cons. Police Acad. of Broward County, Ft. Lauderdale, 1985-87.; gen. counsel Gene Glick Mgmt. Corp. Author: Florida Landlord/Tenant Law and the Fair Housing Act, 1989. Gen. counsel Registered Apt. Mgrs. Assn. South Fla., 1993—, Wynmoor Cmty. Coun., 1993—, The Accutrack Safety Systems Corp., 1997—, Dominium Mgmt. Svcs, Inc., J&B N. Am. Movers, Inc. Regents scholar N.Y. State, 1968-72, Presdl. scholar Boston Coll. Law Sch., 1973-76. Mem. ABA (litigation sect.), ATLA, Acad. Fla. Trial Lawyers, Broward Bar Assn., Justice Lodge J.C.C. Avocations: softball, tennis, swimming. General civil litigation, Contracts commercial, General corporate. Office: 3029 NW 28th Ave Boca Raton FL 33434-6023

NUSSBAUM, PETER DAVID, lawyer; b. Bklyn., June 26, 1942; s. Alfred and Olga (Thome) N.; m. Aleta Spaulding Wallace. BS, Cornell U., 1963; LLB, Harvard U., 1963-66; postgrad., London Sch. Econs., 1967-68. Bar: N.Y. 1967, Calif. 1971, U.S. Dist. Ct. (ea. and so. dists.) N.Y. 1968, U.S. Dist. Ct. (no., ea. and ctrl. dists.) Calif. 1971, U.S. Ct. Appeals (2d, 3d, 6th, 9th and D.C. cirs.). Law clk. U.S. Ct. Appeals, N.Y.C., 1966-67; staff atty. Vera Inst. of Justice, 1968-69, Ctr. for Social Welfare Policy and Law, N.Y.C., 1969-70, Legal Aid Soc. Alameda County, Oakland, Calif., 1971-74; ptnr. Neyhart, Anderson, Nussbaum, Reilly and Freitas, San Francisco, 1974-90, Altshuler, Berzon, Nussbaum, Rubin & Demain, San Francisco, 1990—. Lectr. in field; practice procedure NLRA. Contbr. articles to profl. jours. Dir. Kensington Cmty. Svcs. Dist., 1976-81; mem. fin. com. for Rep. George Miller; pres. Kensington Dem. Club; chmn. Contra Costa Ctrl. Dem. Com. Recipient Borden Found. award, 1960; Fulbright scholar, 1967-68. Mem. ABA (mem. Com. Practice and Procedure before the NLRB), Calif. Bar Assn. (fed. cts. com.), San Francisco Barristers (co-chmn. labor law com.), Ninth Cir. Jud. Conf. (lawyer rep., chmn. No. Calif. del., exec. com.), Phi Eta Sigma, Phi Kappa Phi. Entertainment, Labor. E-mail: pnussbaum@altshulerberzon.com

NUTE, LESLIE F. lawyer; BA, Bates Coll., 1963; JD, U. Chgo., 1966. Bar: Ind. 1966, Mich. 1973, Pa. 1998. Sr. v.p., gen. counsel, sec. Bayer Corp., Pitts., 1991—. General corporate. Office: Bayer Corp 100 Bayer Rd Pittsburgh PA 15205-9741

NUZUM, ROBERT WESTON, lawyer; b. Evanston, Ill., Dec. 11, 1952; s. John Weston and Janet Marie (Talbot) N.; m. Julia Ann Abadie, Sept. 16, 1983. BS in Fin., La. State U., 1974, JD, 1977; LLM in Taxation, N.Y.U., 1978. Bar: La. 1977, D.C. 1979. Assoc. Office Chief Counsel, Washington, 1978-81, Jones, Walker, Waechter, Poitevent, Carrere & Denegre, New Orleans, 1981-85; ptnr. Jones, Walker, Waechter, Potevent, Carrere & Denegre, 1985-88, Deutsch, Kerrigan & Stiles, New Orleans, 1988-89, Phelps Dunbar, L.L.P. and predecessor firm, New Orleans, 1989—. Prof. law, state and local taxation Tulane U. Sch. Law, New Orleans, 1998—. Editor La. Law Rev., 1977; contbr. articles to profl. jours. Wallace scholar N.Y.U., 1978. Mem. La. Bar Assn. (program chmn. tax sect. 1992-93, sec.-treas. 1993-94, vice-chmn. 1994-95, chmn. 1995-96), Tulane Tax Inst. (planning com. 1993—, tax specialization adv. commn. 1997—), Order of Coif. Republican. Roman Catholic. Avocations: golf, reading, fishing. Corporate taxation, Taxation, general, State and local taxation. Office: Phelps Dunbar LLP 365 Canal St Ste 2100 New Orleans LA 70130-1133 E-mail: nuzumb@phelps.com

NWASIKE, NDI CHUKS, lawyer, consultant; b. Enugu, Nigeria, July 9, 1961; s. Edmund Onura and Maudline Odinchezo Nwasike; m. Oby Chinyere Ubahakwe, Apr. 6, 1971; children: Ijeoma, Uchechi, Ogonna. LLB (hon.), U. Nigeria, Nsukka, Enugu, 1985; BL, 1986. Mng. assoc. Joseph I. Obi. & Co., Ikoyi, Lagos, Nigeria, 1987-92; head chambers Chuks Nwasike & co., Victoria Island, Lagos, Nigeria, 1992—. Cons. Novantus Corp., Westlake Village, 2000-2001; rep. multinat. cos. from U.S. and Europe in negotiating, drafting and executing multi-million dollar contracts. Mem. Beta Sigma Nigeria (registrar 1990-93), Rotary Club, Lagos Country Club. Mem. Christian Ch. Avocations: tennis, swimming, travel. Computer, Construction, Taxation, general. Office: Chuks Nwasike and Co 7 Oyin Jolayemi St 70679 Victoria Island Nigeria Fax: 1-209-797-7212. E-mail: practitioners@law.com

NYCE, JOHN DANIEL, lawyer; b. York, Pa., Sept. 7, 1947; s. Harry Lincoln and Dorothy (Wagner) N.; m. Deborah Faith Nyce; children: Joshua David, Laura Kimberly. BA, SUNY, Buffalo, 1970; JD, U. Miami, 1973. Bar: Fla. 1973, U.S. District Ct. (so. dist.) Fla. 1973, U.S. Dist. Ct. (middle dist.), Fla. 1973, U.S. Ct. Appeals (5th and 11th cirs.) 1986, U.S. Supreme Ct. 1984. Assoc. Ralph P. Douglas, Pompano Bch., Fla., 1974, Coleman, Leonard & Morrison, Ft. Lauderdale, 1975-78; ptnr. Nyce and Smith, 1979; sole practice, 1980—. Co-founder, dir. Rutherford Inst. Author books in field; author: Proof of God's Existence in the Seven C's and Christian Handbook of lists, 1999. Bd dirs. Alliance for Responsible Growth, Inc.; mem. Social Register Ft. Lauderdale, Broward County Right to Life, Operation Rescue, South Fla., Christ's Ministry to the Homeless of Ft. Lauderdale, Fla., Legis. Adv. Coun. on Adoptions, Nat. Right to Life Com., Inc., exec. com. Broward County Rep. Party; bd. dirs. Shepherd Care Ministries, Inc.; co-founder Christian Adoption Svcs. of Shepherd Care Ministries, Inc; cert. trainer Evangelism Explosion III Internat., Inc.; legal counsel and evangelism trainer Coral Ridge Presbyn. Ch., Christ the Rock Cmty. Ch., First Bapt. Ch., West Hollywood Fla, U. Miami Broward Citizens bd., U. Miami; mem. Broward County Christian Lawyers Assn. (founder, past pres., bd. dirs.), Christian Legal Soc., Conservative Caucus of Broward County. Mem. Attys. Title Ins. Fund, Nat. Assn. Elder Law Attys., Nat. Acad. Elder Law Attys. (bd. dirs.), U.S. Tennis Ctr., SUNY Buffalo Alumni Assn., U. Miami Alumni Assn., Holiday Park Tennis Ctr., Palm Aire Golf Club, Sports Fitness Clin., U. Miami Hurricane Club. Republican. Presbyterian. Estate planning, Family and matrimonial, General practice. Office: PO Box 11071 Fort Lauderdale FL 33339-1071 E-mail: nyceguy57@aol.com

NYCUM, SUSAN HUBBELL, lawyer; BA, Ohio Wesleyan U., 1956; JD, Duquesne U., 1960; postgrad., Stanford U. Bar: Pa. 1962, U.S. Supreme Ct. 1967, Calif. 1974. Sole practice law, Pitts., 1962-65; designer, adminstr. legal rsch. sys. U. Pitts., Aspen Sys. Corp., 1965-68; mgr. ops. Computer Ctr., Carnegie Mellon U., 1968-69; dir. computer facility Computer Ctr., Stanford U., Calif., 1969-72, Stanford Law and Computer fellow, 1972-73; cons. in computers and law, 1973-74; sr. assoc. MacLeod, Fuller, Muir & Godwin, Los Altos, Los Angeles and London, 1974-75; ptnr. Chickering & Gregory, San Francisco, 1975-80; ptnr.-in-charge high tech. group Gaston Snow & Ely Bartlett, Boston, NYC, Phoenix, San Francisco, Calif., 1980-86; mng. ptnr. Palo Alto office Kadison, Pfaelzer, Woodard, Quinn & Rossi, Los Angeles, Washington, Newport Beach, Palo Alto, 1986-87; sr. ptnr., chmn. U.S. intellectual property/info. tech. practice group Baker & McKenzie, Palo Alto, 1987—, mem. U.S. leadership team, 1987-97, mem. Asia Pacific regional coun., 1995—. Trustee EDUCOM, 1978-81; mem. adv. com. for high tech. Ariz. State U. Law Sch., Santa Clara U. Law Sch., Stanford Law Sch., U. So. Calif. Law Ctr., law sch. Harvard U., U. Calif.; U.S. State Dept. del. OECD Conf. on Nat. Vulnerabilities, Spain, 1981; invited speaker Telecom, Geneva, 1983; lectr. N.Y. Law Jour., 1975—, Law & Bus., 1975—, Practicing Law Inst., 1975—; chmn. Office of Tech. Assessment Task Force on Nat. Info. Sys., 1979-80. Author:(with Bigelow) Your Computer and the Law, 1975, (with Bosworth) Legal Protection for Software, 1985, (with Collins and Gilbert) Women Leading, 1987; contbr. monographs, articles to profl. publs. Mem. Town of Portola Valley Open Space Acquisition Com., Calif., 1977; mem. Jr. League of Palo Alto, chmn. evening div., 1975-76 NSF and Dept. Justice grantee for studies on computer abuse, 1972— Fellow Assn. Computer Machinery (mem. at large of coun. 1976-80, nat. lectr. 1977—, chmn. standing com. on legal issues 1975—, mem. blue ribbon com. on rationalization of internat. propr. rights protection on info. processing devel. in the '90s 1990—), Coll. Law Practice Mgmt.; mem. ABA (chmn. sect. on sci. and tech. 1979-80), Internat. Bar Assn. (U.S. mem. computer com. of corps. sect.), Computer Law Assn. (v.p. 1983-85, pres. 1986—, bd. dirs. 1975—), Calif. State Bar Assn. (founder first chmn. econs. of law sect., vice chmn. law and computers com.), Nat. Conf. Lawyers and Scientists (rep. ABA), Strategic Forum on Intellectual Property Issues in Software of NAS, Internat. Coun. for Computer Comm. (gov. 1998). Contracts commercial, Computer, Trademark and copyright. Home: 35 Granada Ct Portola Valley CA 94028-7736 Office: Baker & McKenzie PO Box 60309 Palo Alto CA 94306-0309

NYDEGGER, RICK D. lawyer; b. Salt Lake City, Apr. 24, 1949; s. A. Don and Jean Virginia (Hansen) N.; m. Denise Winegar, Oct. 22, 1970; children: Dan L., Chad E., Kurt D., Brittney, Trent R. BSEE cum laude, Brigham Young U., 1974, JD cum laude, 1977. Bar: Utah 1977, U.S. Dist Ct. (ctrl. dist.) Utah 1977, U.S. Patent Office 1977, U.S. Ct. Appeals (5th and 10th cirs.) 1980, U.S. Supreme Ct. 1990, U.S. Ct. Appeals (fed. cir.) 1994. Assoc. Fox, Edwards, & Gardiner, 1977-81, shareholder, dir., 1981-84; founding shareholder, dir., officer Workman, Nydegger & Seeley, Salt Lake City, 1984—. Adj. prof. U. Utah Coll. Law, 1988-99, Brigham Young U. Coll. Law, 1998—. Contbr. articles to profl. jours. Bd. dirs. Nat. Inventors Hall of Fame, 2000—, bd. dirs. found., 1998—; trustee Am. Intellectual Property Law Assn. Found., 2001—. Fellow Am. Intellectual Property Law Assn. (founding mem., chmn. electronic computer law com. 1990-93, bd. dirs. 1993-96, editl. bd. quar. jour., vice-chmn. ad hoc com. PCT practice, 1994-98, nominations com. 1997, chmn. mid-winter Inst. 2000 planning com., 2d v.p. 2000-01, 1st v.p. 2001—); mem. ABA, Utah State Bar (chmn. patent, trademark, copyright sect. 1985-87), Fed. Cir. Bar Assn., U.S. Supreme Ct. Hist. Soc. (10th cir. rep. 1993-94, Utah rep. 1992-93), Nat. Coun. Intellectual Property Law Assn. (chmn. 2000-01). Intellectual property. Office: Workman Nydegger & Seeley 60 E South Temple Ste 1000 Salt Lake City UT 84111-1011

NYE, DANIEL ALAN, lawyer, consultant; b. Shelton, Wash., May 19, 1952; children: Ingrid Marie, Ellen. BA, U. Oreg., 1971-75; MA, U. Wash., 1977; spl. diploma in admiralty law and petroleum law, U. Oslo, 1979; JD, U. Oreg., 1980. Bar: Oreg. 1981, Wash. 1987. Law clk. U.S. Dist. Court Oreg., Portland, 1981-83; asst. prof. Scandinavian Inst. of Maritime Law, Oslo, 1983-85; lectr. Norwegian Shipping Acad., 1984-85; atty. Christiania Bank og Kreditkasse, 1985; assoc. Lindsay, Hart, Neil & Weigler, 1985-88; mng. ptnr. Ater, Wynne, Hewitt, Dodson & Skeritt, Seattle, 1988-91; ptnr. Riddell, Williams, Bullitt & Walkinshaw, 1991-97, Graham & James/Riddell Williams, Seattle, 1997—. Internat. Rotary Grad. fellow, 1978. Mem. Maritime Law Assn., Norwegian-Am. C. of C., Finnish Am. C. of C., Sons of Norway. Admiralty, Banking, Private international. Office: Graham & James/Riddell Williams Bullitt & Walkinshaw 1001 4th Ave Ste 4500 Seattle WA 98154-1192

NYE, W. MARCUS W. lawyer; b. N.Y.C., Aug. 3, 1945; s. Walter R. and Nora (McLaren) N.; m. Eva Johnson; children: Robbie, Stephanie, Philip, Jennifer. BA, Harvard U., 1967; JD, U. Idaho, 1974. Bar: Idaho 1974, U.S. Dist. Ct. Idaho 1974, U.S. Ct. Appeals (9th cir.) 1980; lic. pilot. Ptnr. Racine, Olson, Nye, Budge & Bailey, Pocatello, Idaho, 1974—. Vis. prof. law U. Idaho, Moscow, 1984; adj. prof. Coll. Engring. Idaho State U., 1993—; pres.-elect Idaho State U. Found., U. Idaho Coll. Law Found. Commr., Idaho State Centennial Found., 1985-90. Recipient Alumni Svc. award U. Idaho, 1988. Fellow ABA (bd. govs. 1997-2000), Am. Bar Found. (stat. chmn. 1992-95); mem. Am. Bd. Trial Advs. (nat. bd. dirs.), Am. Coll. Trial Lawyers, Idaho State Bar Assn. (pres. 1987-88), Idaho Def. Counsel Assn. (pres. 1982), 6th Dist. Bar Assn. (pres. 1982). Avocation: flying. General civil litigation, Product liability. Home: 173 S 15th Ave Pocatello ID 83201-4056 Office: Racine Olson Nye Budge & Bailey PO Box 1391 Pocatello ID 83204-1391

NYGAARD, RICHARD LOWELL, federal judge; b. 1940; BS cum laude, U. So. Calif., 1969; JD, U. Mich. Mem. Orton, Nygaard & Dunlevy, 1972-81; judge Ct. Common Pleas, 6th Dist. Pa., Erie, 1981-88, U.S. Ct. Appeals (3d cir.), Erie, Pa., 1988—. Councilman Erie County, 1977-81. With USNR, 1958-64. Mem. ABA, Pa. Bar Assn., Erie County Bar Assn. Office: US Courthouse 717 State St Ste 500 Erie PA 16501-1323*

NYS, JOHN NIKKI, lawyer; b. Duluth, Minn., May 3, 1948; s. Leslie Leo and Kathleen Cecilia (Beaudin) N.; m. Sandra Ann Stephenson, Aug. 20, 1977; 1 child, John Stephenson. BA, Dartmouth Coll., 1970; JD, Stanford U., 1973. Bar: Minn. 1973, U.S. Dist. Ct. Minn. 1973, U.S. Ct. Appeals (8th cir.) 1984, U.S. Dist. Ct. (we. dist.) Wis. 1985, Wis. 1986. Ptnr. Johnson, Killen, Thibodeau & Seiler, Duluth, 1973—. Pres., treas., bd. dirs. Duluth Regional Care Ctr., 1979-85; v.p., bd. dirs. Western Community Coun., 1980-86; cubmaster Lake Superior coun. Boy Scouts Am., 1987-90; mem. state cen. com. Dem. Farmer Labor Party, 1976-78; pres., bd. dirs. Morgan Park Smithville Community Club, 1978-85. Mem. ABA, Duluth Young Lawyers (pres. 1974-75), Minn. State Bar Assn. (chmn. lawyers referral com. 1986-88, bd. govs. 1990-98, pres. 1996-97), 11th Dist. Bar Assn. (pres. 1989-90). Lutheran. Banking, Bankruptcy, General corporate. Office: Johnson Killen Thibodeau & Seiler 811 Norwest Ctr Duluth MN 55808 E-mail: jnys@duluthlaw.com

OAKES, JAMES L. federal judge; b. Springfield, Ill., Feb. 21, 1924; m. Evelena S. Kenworthy, Dec. 29, 1973 (dec. Oct. 1997); 3 children; m. Mara A. Williams, Jan. 1, 1999. AB, Harvard Coll., 1945; LLB, Harvard U., 1947; LLD, New Eng. Coll., 1976, Suffolk U., 1980, Vt. Law Sch., 1995. Bar: Calif. 1949, Vt. 1950. Pvt. practice, Brattleboro, Vt.; spl. counsel Vt. Pub. Service Commn., 1959-60; counsel Vt. Statutory Revision Commn., 1957-60; mem. Vt. Senate, 1961-65; atty. gen. Vt., 1967-69; U.S. dist. judge, 1970-71; U.S. cir. judge 2d Cir. Ct. Appeals, Brattleboro, 1971—; chief judge 2d Circuit Ct. Appeals, 1989-92. Adj. faculty Duke U. Law Sch., 1985-96, Iowa U. Coll. Law, 1993-97. Office: US Ct Appeals PO Box 696 Brattleboro VT 05302-0696

OATES, CARL EVERETTE, lawyer, director; b. Harlingen, Tex., Apr. 8, 1931; s. Joseph William and Grace (Watson) O.; m. Eileen Noble Hudnall; children: Carl William, Gregory Carl Hudnall, Patricia O. Chase, Matthew Noble Hudnall. BS, U.S. Naval Acad., 1955; LLB, So. Meth. U., 1962. Bar: Tex. 1962, D.C. 1977, Nebr. 1985. Assoc. Akin, Gump, Strauss, Hauer & Feld, Dallas, 1962-64, ptnr., 1965-91. Asst. atty. gen. State of Texas, 1992-94, spl. coun., Tex. Dept. Banking, 1994-95, prin. Carl E. Oates, P.C. Chmn. bd. trustees S.W. Mus. Sci. and Tech., Dallas; v.p. S.W. Sci. Mus. Found., Dallas; bd. dirs. Kiwanis Wesley Dental Ctr., Inc., Dallas; pres. Wesley Dental Found., Dallas. Lt. USN, 1955-59. Mem. ABA, D.C. Bar Assn., Tex. Bar Assn., Dallas Bar Assn., Barristers, Northwood Club, Delta Theta Phi. Administrative and regulatory, General corporate, Real property. E-mail: coates00@aol.com

O'BARR, BOBBY GENE, SR. lawyer; b. Houston, May 5, 1932; s. Walter Morris and Maggie (Whitt) O'B.; children: Morris Clayton, William Clinton, Candace Jean, Bobby G.; m. Jennifer Ryals, Dec. 5, 1984; 1 child, Richard. BA, U. Miss., 1959, JD, 1958. Bar: Miss. 1958, U.S. Dist. Ct. (no. dist.) Miss. 1958, U.S. Dist. Ct. (so. dist.) Miss. 1966, U.S. Ct. Appeals (5th cir.) 1970, U.S. Supreme Ct. 1971. Pvt. practice, Houston, 1958-59; assoc. W.M. O'Barr, Jr., Okolona, Miss., 1959-60; adminstrv. judge Miss. Workmen's Compensation Commn., 1960-65; assoc. Cumbest, Cumbest, O'Barr and Shaddock, Pascagoula, Miss., 1965-68, Hurlbert & O'Barr, O'Barr, Hurlbert and O'Barr, Biloxi, 1968-80; pvt. practice, owner Bobby G. O'Barr, P.A., 1980—. Mem., pres. Biloxi Port Commn., 1975-90; mem. mgmt. coun. Gulf Mex. Fishery, 1979-82. With USAF, 1951-54. Mem. VFW, State Bar Found., Southeastern Admiralty Law Inst., Miss. Trial Lawyers Assn., Am. Legion, Masons, Shriners. Admiralty, Personal injury, Workers' compensation. Office: PO Box 541 Biloxi MS 39533-0541

OBER, RICHARD FRANCIS, JR. lawyer, banker; b. Balt., Dec. 12, 1943; s. Richard Francis and Caroline Fisher (Gary) O.; m. Carol Laycock Munger, Aug. 25, 1973; children: Julia Keyser, Margaret Delancey. AB cum laude, Princeton U., 1965; LLB, Yale U., 1968. Bar: Md. 1968, Pa. 1970, N.J. 1977. Law clk. to chief judge Md. Ct. Appeals, Annapolis, 1968; assoc. Ballard, Spahr, Andrews & Ingersoll, Phila., 1969-75; gen. counsel Summit Bancorp, Princeton, NJ, 1975—2001. Sec. Summit Bancorp, Princeton, 1978-2001, sr. v.p., 1982-88, exec. v.p., 1988-2001; bd. dirs. sec. Summit Credit Life Ins. Co., Summit Credit Corp.; sec. Summit Bank, Summit Leasing Co., Summit Venture Capital, Inc. Fire commr. South Brunswick (N.J.) Fire Dist. 3, 1981-85; Republican county committeeman, 1975—; v.p. Republican Assn. Princeton, 1995-96; trustee Princeton Day Sch., 1986-92, treas., 1988-92, vice-chmn., 1990-92; trustee Yale Law Sch. Assn. N.J.; first vice-chmn., dir N.J. Spl. Olympics. Mem. ABA, Bank Corp. Counsel Com. (chmn. 1979-80), N.J. Bar Assn. (gen. council 1982-85, 93-94, exec. com. banking law sect. 1979-94, sec. sect. 1980-81, vice-chmn. 1981-82, chmn. 1984-85), N.J. Corp. Counsel Assn. (exec. com. 1980-91, 2d v.p. 1982-85, pres. 1985-86, chmn. banking and fin. instns. com. 1984-85), Am. Bankers Assn. (exec. com. bank counsel unit 1990-95, vice-chmn. 1993-94, chmn. 1994-95), N.J. Bankers Assn. (chmn. bank lawyers com. 1993-94, chmn. legal and tax com. 1994-95), N.J. Bus. and Industry Assn. (legal affairs com.), Pa. Bankers Assn. (legal affairs com.), Phila. Bar Assn., Assn. Corp. Counsel Am., Princeton Bar Assn., Fin. Svcs. Roundtable, Lawyers Coun., Bedens Brook Club (Princeton). Episcopalian. Banking, General corporate, Securities.

OBER, RUSSELL JOHN, JR. lawyer; b. Pitts., June 26, 1948; s. Russell J. and Marion C. (Hampson) O.; children: Lauren Elizabeth, Russell John III; m. Sandi J. Antill. BA, U. Pitts., 1970, JD, 1973. Bar: Pa. 1973, U.S. Dist. Ct. (we. dist.) Pa. 1973, U.S. Tax Ct. 1982, U.S. Ct. Appeals (4th cir.) 1976, U.S. Ct. Appeals (3d cir.) 1979, U.S. Ct. Appeals (D.C. cir.) 1985, U.S. Ct. Appeals (2d cir.), 1990, U.S. Ct. Appeals (7th cir.) 1993, U.S. Supreme Ct. 1976, U.S. Ct. Appeals (6th cir.) 2000. Asst. dist. atty. Allegheny County, Pitts., 1973-75; ptnr. Wallace Chapas & Ober, 1975-80, Rose, Schmidt, Hasley & DiSalle, Pitts., 1980-92, Meyer, Unkovic & Scott, Pitts., 1992—. Bd. dirs. Parent and Child Guidance Ctr., Pitts., 1983-90, treas., 1985-86, pres., 1986-88; bd. mgmt. South Hills Area YMCA, 1989-91; mem. Mt. Lebanon Traffic Commn., 1976-81; bd. dirs. Whale's Tale Youth Family Counseling Ctr., 1990-95. Mem. ABA (discovery com. litigation sect. 1982-88, ho. of dels. young lawyers div. 1982-83), Pa. Bar Assn. (ho. of dels. 1983—), Allegheny County Bar Assn. (chmn. young lawyers sect. 1983, bd. govs. 1984, fin. com. 1984-88, mem. coun. civil litigation sect. 1991-93), Nat. Bd. Trial Advocacy (diplomate), Acad. Lawyers Allegheny County (fellow 1983—, bd. govs. 1988-90) U. Pitts. Law Alumni Assn. (bd. govs. 1984-89, v.p. 1985-87, pres. 1987-88), Rivers Club. Federal civil litigation, State civil litigation, Insurance. Office: Meyer Unkovic & Scott 1300 Oliver Bldg Pittsburgh PA 15222 E-mail: rjo@muslaw.com

OBERLY, KATHRYN ANNE, lawyer; b. Chgo., May 22, 1950; d. James Richard and Lucille Mary (Kraus) O.; m. Daniel Lee Goelzer, July 13, 1974 (div. Aug. 1987); 1 child, Michael W. Student, Vassar Coll., 1967-69; BA, U. Wis., 1971, JD, 1973. Bar: Wis. 1973, D.C. 1981, N.Y. 1995. Law clk. U.S. Ct. Appeals, Omaha, 1973-74; trial atty. U.S. Dept. Justice, Washington, 1974-77, spl. asst., 1977-81, spl. litigation counsel, 1981-82, asst. to Solicitor Gen., 1982-86; ptnr. Mayer, Brown & Platt, 1986-91; assoc. gen. counsel Ernst & Young LLP, 1991-94, vice-chair, gen. counsel N.Y.C., 1994—. Exec. com. CPR Ctr. for Dispute Resolution. Named one of 50 Most Influential Women Lawyers in Am., Nat. Law Jour., 1998. Mem. ABA, Am. Law Inst., Am. Acad. Appellate Lawyers, Wis. Bar Assn., D.C. Bar Assn. Democrat. Office: Ernst & Young LLP 787 7th Ave New York NY 10019-6085 E-mail: kathryn.oberly@ey.com

OBERMAN, MICHAEL STEWART, lawyer; b. Bklyn., May 21, 1947; s. Hyman Martin and Gertrude O.; m. Sharon Land, Oct. 8, 1975; 1 child, Abigail Land. AB, Columbia U., 1969; JD, Harvard U., 1972. Bar: N.Y. 1973, U.S. Dist. Ct. (so. and ea. dists.) N.Y. 1973, U.S. Ct. Appeals (2d cir.) 1973, U.S. Supreme Ct. 1976, Calif. 1981, U.S. Dist. Ct. (no. dist.) Calif.

1981, U.S. Ct. Appeals (9th cir.) 1981, U.S. Dist. Ct. (so. and cen. dists.) Calif. 1982, U.S. Ct. Appeals (5th cir.) 1989, D.C. 1992, U.S. Ct. Appeals (7th cir.) 1993. Law clk. to Hon. Milton Pollack, U.S. Dist. Ct. (so. dist.) N.Y., 1972-73; assoc. Kramer Levin Naftalis & Frankel LLP, N.Y.C., 1973-79, ptnr., 1980—. Contbr. articles to profl. jours. Recipient Nathan Burkan prize ASCAP, 1973. Mem. N.Y. State Bar Assn. (mem. ho. of dels. 1989-91, exec. com. comml. and fed. litigation sect.). General civil litigation, Intellectual property. Office: Kramer Levin Naftalis & Frankel LLP 919 3rd Ave New York NY 10022-3902

OBERMAN, STEVEN, lawyer; b. St. Louis, Sept. 21, 1955; s. Albert and Marian (Kleg) O.; m. Evelyn Ann Simpson, Aug. 28, 1977; children: Rachael Diane, Benjamin Scott. BA in Psychology, Auburn U., 1977; JD, U. Tenn., 1980. Bar: Tenn. 1980, Tenn. Supreme Ct. 1980, Tenn. Criminal Ct. Appeals 1980, U.S. Dist. Ct. (ea. dist.) Tenn. 1980, U.S. Ct. Appeals (4th cir.) 1981, U.S. Ct. Appeals (6th cir.) 1983, U.S. Supreme Ct. 1985. Law clk. Daniel, Duncan & Claiborne, Knoxville, Tenn., 1978-80; assoc. Daniel, Claiborne & Lewallen, 1980-82; ptnr. Daniel, Claiborne, Oberman & Buuck, 1983-85, Daniel & Oberman, Knoxville, 1986—. Pres., Project First Offender, Knoxville, 1983-86; bd. dirs. Fed. Defender Svcs. Eastern Tenn., Inc., v.p. 1994-97, pres. 1998-2000; guest instr. U. Tenn. 1988-90; guest lectr. U. Tenn. Law Sch., 1982-88; guest instr. U. Tenn. Grad. Sch. Criminal Justice Program, 1983, 84; guest speaker Ct. Clk's Meeting, Cambridge, Eng., 1984; guest instr. legal clinic , trial advocacy program U. Tenn., 1984—; adj. prof. U. Tenn. Law Sch., 1993— (Forrest W. Lacey award for outstanding faculty contbn. to U. Tenn. Coll. Law Moot Ct. Program, 1993-94; coach U. Tenn. Law Sch. Nat. Trial Team, 1991-96; spl. judge Criminal Divsn. Knox County Gen. Sessions Court; founding mem. Nat. Coll. for DUI Def.; speaker in field. Author: D.U.I.: The Crime and Consequences in Tennessee, 1991, 2d edit., 1997, supplemented annually; co-author: D.W.I. Means Defend With Ingenuity, 1987; contbr. legal articles on drunk driving to profl. jours. Bd. dirs. Knoxville Legal Aid Soc., Inc., 1986-88 (pres. 1990), Arnstein Jewish Community Ctr., 1987-91, pres. 1990; bd. dirs. Knoxville Racquet Club, 1991-93, pres. 1992-93. Col. Aide de Camp Tenn. Gov.'s Staff, 1983, Moot Ct. Bd. Spl. Svc. award, 1995-96. Mem. ATLA, Nat. Assn. Criminal Def. Lawyers (chair/co-chair DUI advocacy com. 1995—), Nat. Coll. DUI Def. (founding, bd. regents 1999—), Tenn. Assn. Criminal Def. Lawyers (bd. dirs. 1983-89), Knoxville Bar Assn. Jewish. Criminal, Personal injury. Office: Daniel & Oberman 550 W Main St Ste 950 Knoxville TN 37902-2536

OBERST, PAUL, retired law educator; b. Owensboro, Ky., Apr. 22, 1914; m. Elizabeth Durfee; children— Paul, James, George, Mary, John. A.B., U. Evansville, 1936; J.D., U. Ky., 1939; LL.M., U. Mich., 1941. Bar: Ky. 1938, Mo. 1942. Assoc. firm Ryland, Stinson, Mag & Thomson, Kansas City, Mo., 1941-42; asst. prof. law Coll. of Law, U. Ky., Lexington, 1946-47, prof., 1947-82; acting dean, 1966-67; emeritus prof. Coll. of Law, U. Ky., 1982—. Vis. prof. U. Chgo., 1954-55, Duke U., 1980; prof., dir. civil liberties program N.Y. U., 1959-61; mem. Nat. Commn. on Acad. Tenure, 1971-73 Contbr. articles to legal jours. Mem. Ky. Commn. on Corrections, 1961-65; mem. Ky. Commn. on Human Rights, 1962-66, 80-90, chmn., 1966-70, 73-76; trustee U. Ky., Lexington, 1963-69, 72-75; mem. Ky. state adv. com. U.S. Civil Rights Commn., 1979-92, chmn., 1982-86. Served to lt. USNR, 1942-46. Mem. Assn. Am. Law Schs. (exec. com. 1970-72), Am., Ky. bar assns., Am. Law Inst., Order of Coif, Phi Delta Phi. Home: 829 Sherwood Dr Lexington KY 40502-2919

OBERT, KEITH DAVID, lawyer; b. Talladega, Ala., Nov. 22, 1962; s. Sam R. and Alice M. Obert; m. Alaine Anderson, Aug. 3, 1991; 1 child, Baylor Anderson. BS in Acctg., U. Ala., 1984; JD, U. Miss., 1988. Bar: Miss. 1988, Tenn. 1988, Ala. 1989. Acct. Challenger Lighting Co. Inc., Olive Branch, Miss., 1984-85; atty. Wells, Moore, Simmons, Stubblefield and Neeld, Jackson, 1988-89, Copeland, Cook, Taylor & Bush, Jackson, 1989-97; shareholder Akers & Obert, P.A., Brandon, 1997—. Verger, lector, usher, accolyte Chapel of the Cross, Madison, Miss. Mem. ABA, Miss. Bar Assn. (dir. young lawyers divsn., chmn. nomination com., code adv. com., chmn. membership svcs. com. chmn. pub. rels. com., bus. law sect. co-editor newsletter, Outstanding Young Lawyer in Miss. 2001), Rankin County Bar Assn., Hinds County Bar Assn. (dir., co-chmn. golf tournament com., mem. bench/bar com., newsletter editl. bd.), Tenn. Bar Assn., Ala. State Bar, Bar Assn. of the Fifth Fed. Cir., Miss. Def. Lawyers Assn., Def. Rsch. and Trial Lawyers Assn., Miss. Claims Assn., Jackson Young Lawyers Assn. (pres., v.p., treas., dir., chmn. bench/bar com., chmn. social com., chmn. golf com.), U. Ala. "A" Club. Avocations: golfing, hunting, skiing. General civil litigation, Insurance, Product liability. Office: Akers & Obert PA 20 Eastgate Dr Ste D Brandon MS 39042-2329

OBERT, PAUL RICHARD, lawyer, manufacturing company executive; b. Pitts. s. Edgar F. and Elizabeth T. Obert. B.S., Georgetown U., 1950; J.D., U. Pitts., 1953. Bar: Pa. 1954, D.C. 1956, Ohio 1972, Ill. 1974, U.S. Supreme Ct. 1970. Sole practice, Pitts., 1954-60; asst. counsel H.K. Porter Co., Inc., 1960-62, sec., gen. counsel, 1962-71, Addressograph-Multigraph Corp., Cleve., 1972-74; v.p. law Marshall Field & Co., Chgo., 1974-82, sec., 1976-82; v.p., gen. counsel, sec. CF Industries, Inc., Long Grove, Ill., 1982—, also officer, dir. various subs. Served to lt. col. USAF. Mem. ABA (corp. gen. counsel com.), Pa. Bar Assn., Allegheny County Bar Assn., Ill. Bar Assn., Chgo. Bar Assn., Am. Soc. Corp. Secs., Am. Retail Fedn. (bd. dirs. 1977-80), Georgetown U. Alumni Assn. (bd. govs.), Pitts. Athletic Assn., Univ. Club (Chgo.), Delta Theta Phi. Administrative and regulatory, Contracts commercial, General corporate. Office: CF Industries Inc 1 Salem Lake Dr Long Grove IL 60047-8401

OBNINSKY, VICTOR PETER, lawyer; b. San Rafael, Calif., Oct. 12, 1944; s. Peter Victor and Anne Bartholdi (Donston) O.; m Clara Alice Bechtel, June 8, 1969; children: Mari, Warren. BA, Columbia U., 1966; JD, U. Calif., Hastings, 1969. Bar: Calif. 1970. Sole practice, Novato, Calif., 1970-2001, Tiburon, 2001—. Arbitrator Marin County Superior Ct., San Rafael, 1979—; superior ct. judge pro tem, 1979—; lectr. real estate and partnership law. Author: The Russians in Early California, 1966. Bd. dirs. Calif. Young Reps., 1968-69, Richardson Bay San. Dist., 1974-75, Marin County Legal Aid Soc., 1976-78; baseball coach Little League, Babe Ruth League, 1970-84; mem. nat. panel consumer arbitrators Better Bus. Bur., 1974-88; leader Boy Scouts Am., 1970-84; permanent sec. Phillips Acad. Class of 1962, 1987—; mem. Phillips Acad. Alumni Coun., 1991-95; bd. cmty. advisors Buck Ctr. for Rsch. on Aging, 1990-2001. Mem ABA, State Bar Calif., Marin County Bar Assn. (bd. dirs. 1985-91, treas. 1987-88, pres.-elect 1989, pres. 1990), Phi Delta Phi, Phi Gamma Delta. Republican. Russian Orthodox. General corporate, General practice, Probate. Office: 6 Mateo Drive Belvedere Tiburon CA 94920-1046

O'BRIEN, BRADFORD CARL, lawyer; b. Lafayette, Ind., Jan. 25, 1949; s. Hubbert L. and Jeane (Howard) O'B.; m. Judith Mayer, June 19, 1971. A.B., Princeton U., 1971; J.D., UCLA, 1974. Bar: Calif. 1974. Assoc. Ruffo, Ferrari & McNeil, San Jose, Calif., 1975-81; ptnr. Wilson, Sonsini, Goodrich & Rosati, Palo Alto, Calif., 1981— . Mem. ABA, Santa Clara County Bar Assn. Landlord-tenant, Real property. Home: 1655 Bay Laurel Dr Menlo Park CA 94025-5809 Office: Wilson Sonsini Goodrich & Rosati 650 Page Mill Rd Palo Alto CA 94304-1055

O'BRIEN, CHARLES H. lawyer, retired state supreme court chief justice; b. Orange, N.J., July 30, 1920; s. Herbert Rodgers and Agnes Sidman (Montanya) O'B.; m. Anna Belle Clement, Nov. 9, 1966; children: Merry Diane, Steven Shawn (dec.), Heather Lynn. LLB, Cumberland U., 1947. Rep. Tenn. Legislature, Memphis, 1963-65, senator, 1965-67; assoc. judge Tenn. Ct. Criminal Appeals, Crossville, 1970-87; assoc. justice Tenn. Supreme Ct., 1987-94, chief justice, 1994-95; ret., 1995; pvt. practice, Crossville, 1995—. Bd. dirs. Lake Tansi Village Property Owners Assn., 1984-89, chmn., 1989. With U.S. Army, 1938-45, ETO, 1950, UN Command, Tokyo. Decorated Bronze Star, Purple Heart with oak leaf cluster. Fellow Tenn. Bar Found.; mem. Tenn. Bar Assn., Cumberland County Bar Assn., Am. Legion, Lake Tansi Village Chowder and Marching Soc. (pres.). Democrat. Avocation: outdoor activities. Estate planning, Finance, Probate.

O'BRIEN, DANIEL ROBERT, lawyer; b. Peoria, Ill., May 7, 1951; s. William Patrick and Irene Cornelia O'Brien; m. Eileen Mary Kahn, Aug. 17, 1974; children: Colleen, Patrick, Bridget. BS, No. Ill. U., 1973; JD, Wash. U., St. Louis, 1976. Bar: U.S. Dist. Ct. (so. dist.) Ill. 1977. Ptnr. Smith Moos Schmitt & O'Brien, Peoria, 1976-82, Moos, Schmitt & O'Brien, Peoria, 1982—. Lectr. Peoria County Bar Assn., Ill. Continuing Legal Edn., Springfield. Dem. precinct committeeman Dem. Party, 1986. Named to Greater Peoria Sports Hall of Fame, 2000. Fellow Ill. Bar Found. (charter mem., Leading Ill. Atty. award), Beta Gamma Sigma. Avocations: coaching children's basketball. Personal injury, Workers' compensation. Office: Moos Schmitt & O'Brien 331 Fulton St Ste 740 Peoria IL 61602-1499

O'BRIEN, DARLENE ANNE, lawyer; b. Cleve., July 14, 1955; d. Joseph and Suzanne (Belica) Mason; m. Thomas C. O'Brien, Feb. 2, 1984; children: John Michael, Lauren Katherine. BA summa cum laude, U. Toledo, 1977; JD, U. Notre Dame, 1980. Bar: Ind. 1980, Mich. 1981. Law clk. to presiding justice U.S. Bankruptcy Ct. (no. dist.), Ind., 1980-81; assoc. Smith and Brooker P.C., Saginaw, Mich., 1981-84, O'Brien and O'Brien, Ann Arbor, 1984—. Commentator, panelist Inst. Continuing Legal Edn. Mem. ABA, Mich. Bar Assn., Women's Law Assn. Mich., Washtenaw County Bar Assn. State civil litigation, Criminal, Personal injury. Office: O'Brien & O'Brien 300 N 5th Ave Ste 150 Ann Arbor MI 48104-1499

O'BRIEN, DAVID A. lawyer; b. Sioux City, Iowa, Aug. 30, 1958; s. John T. and Doris K. (Reisch) O'B. BA, George Washington U., 1981; JD with distinction, U. Iowa, 1984. Bar: Iowa 1985, U.S. Dist. Ct. (no. dist.) Iowa 1985, Nebr. 1990, U.S. Dist. Ct. Nebr. 1990. Legis. asst. Nat. Transp. Safety Bd., Washington, 1978-81; assoc. O'Brien, Galvin & Kuehl, Sioux City, 1985-88; ptnr. O'Brien, Galvin Moeller & Neary, 1989-94; chair Wage Appeals Bd. & Bd. of Svc. Contract Appeals U.S. Dept. Labor, Washington, 1994-96, acting dir. Office Adminstrv. Appeals, 1995-96, chair adminstrv. review bd., 1996-98; atty. White & Johnson, P.C., Cedar Rapids, Iowa, 1998-2000; ptnr. Willey, O'Brien, Beyer & Hanrahan, PLC, 2000—. Dem. candidate for Congress, 6th dist. of Iowa, Sioux City, 1988; chmn. Woodbury County Dem. Party, Sioux City, 1992-94, chair Iowa campaign Clinton for Pres., Des Moines, 1992; bd. dirs. Mid-Step Svcs. Inc., Sioux City, 1986-91, Mo. River Hist. Devel., Sioux City, 1989-94. Mem. Nat. Assn. Trial Lawyers, Iowa Trial Lawyers Assn. (bd. govs. 1991-94). Roman Catholic. Avocations: sports, politics. Labor, Personal injury, Workers' compensation. Office: Willey O'Brien Beyer & Hanrahan 3519 Center Pointe Rd NE Cedar Rapids IA 52402 Home Fax: 319-378-1413

O'BRIEN, DONALD EUGENE, federal judge; b. Marcus, Iowa, Sept. 30, 1923; s. Michael John and Myrtle A. (Toomey) O'B.; m. Ruth Mahon, Apr. 15, 1950; children: Teresa, Brien, John, Shuivaun. LL.B., Creighton U., 1948. Bar: Iowa bar 1948, U.S. Supreme Ct. bar 1963. Asst. city atty., Sioux City, Iowa, 1949-53; county atty. Woodbury County, 1955-58; mcpl. judge Sioux City, 1959-60; U.S. atty. No. Iowa, 1961-67; pvt. practice law Sioux City, 1967-78; U.S. Dist. judge, 1978—; chief judge U.S. Dist. Ct. (no. dist.) Iowa, 1985-92, sr. judge, 1992—. Rep. 8th cir. dist. ct. judges to Jud. Conf. U.S., 1990-97. Served with USAAF, 1943-45. Decorated D.F.C., air medals. Mem. Woodbury County Bar Assn., Iowa State Bar Assn. Roman Catholic. E-mail: Dan_O'Brien@iand.uscourts.gov. Office: US Dist Ct PO Box 267 Sioux City IA 51102-0267 E-mail: Don_O'brian@iand.uscourts.gov

O'BRIEN, EVA FROMM, lawyer; b. Herne, Germany, May 6, 1956; came to U.S., 1959; d. Georg and Eva (Aust) F.; m. John J. O'Brien, Feb. 12, 2000. BS in Chem. Enging., Syracuse U., 1978; JD, U. Houston, 1985. Bar: Tex. 1985, U.S. Dist. Ct. (so. dist.) Tex. 1987, U.S. Ct. Appeals (5th cir.) 1997. Engr. Chrysler Corp., Deer Park, Mich., 1978-79; process engr. Mobay Chem. Co., Baytown, Tex., 1980, ETI Engrs. Inc., Houston, 1981-82; engr. Petromas Inc., 1982-83; sr. chem. engr. NUS Corp., 1983-84; briefing clk., assoc. Hill Parker Franklin Cardwell & Jones, 1985-86; assoc. Fulbright & Jaworski LLP, 1986-93, ptnr., 1994—. Author, editor: Texas Environmental Law Handbook, 1989, 5th edit., 2000, (book chpt.) Environmental Aspects of Real Estate Transactions, 2d edit., 1999. Mem. ABA (co-chair real estate and probate sect., underground storage tank and RCRA com. 1994-95), Houston Bar Assn. (co-chair legal line com. 1988-90; sec. environ. law sect. 1991, vice-chair 1992, chair 1993). Environmental, Personal injury, Toxic tort. Home: 19 Serenity Woods Pl Houston TX 77383 Office: Fulbright & Jaworski LLP 1301 Mckinney St Ste 5100 Houston TX 77010-3031

O'BRIEN, JAMES EDWARD, lawyer; b. Mpls., June 10, 1937; s. Thomas Edward and Virginia Ann (Balster) O'B.; m. Patricia Jo Ann Cole, Mar. 1, 1958; children: Daniel J., Martin J. BA, U. Alaska, 1962; JD, U. Minn., 1965. Bar: Minn. Assoc. Moss & Barnett, Mpls., 1965—, chmn., CEO. With USAF, 1957-62. Mem. Unilaw (chmn.), Fund for Legal Aid Soc. (bd. dirs.), Kiwanis Internat. (George Hixon fellow 1996), Kiwanis Mpls. (bd. dirs.). Avocations: fishing, boating. General corporate, Finance, Mergers and acquisitions.

O'BRIEN, JOHN GRAHAM, lawyer; b. N.Y.C., May 12, 1948; s. John Edward and Marian Helen (FitzGerald) O'B.; m. Phyllis Mary Eyth, Apr. 10, 1976; children: John Graham Jr., Jennifer A. BS cum laude, Mt. St. Mary's Coll., Emmitsburg, Md., 1970; JD, Am. U., 1973. Bar: N.J. 1974, D.C. 1974, N.Y. 1982, U.S. Supreme Ct. 1982. Law clk. to Hon. F.C. Kentz and J.H. Coleman, Superior Ct. of N.J., Elizabeth, N.J., 1973-74; assoc. Carpenter, Bennett & Morrissey, Newark, 1975-81; sr. counsel GAF Corp., Wayne, N.J., 1981-90; assoc. gen. counsel Keene Corp., N.Y.C., 1990-93, ISS Internat. Svc. Sys., N.Y.C., 1994-95; cons. GE, Fairfield, Conn., 1993-94; mng. ptnr. Atkins O'Brien Ekblom LLP, N.Y.C., 1995-2000; of counsel McGivney, Kluger & Gannon, 2000—01; gen. counsel Brickforce Staffing Inc., Edison, NJ, 2001—. Author: (monograph) Responding to Products Liability Claims, 1986, also supplements; contbg. author: Toxic Torts Practice Guide, 1992. Recipient Disting. Young Alumni award Mt. St. Mary's Coll., 1976. Mem. N.J. Bar Assn., D.C. Bar, Irish Bus. Orgn. N.Y., Echo Lke Country Club (assoc.), Coll. Mens Club. Roman Catholic. General civil litigation, Insurance, Personal injury. Office: Brick Force Staffing Inc 2 Ethel Rd Ste 204B Edison NJ 08818 E-mail: obriennj2@aol.com

O'BRIEN, WALTER JOSEPH, II, lawyer; b. Apr. 22, 1939; s. Walter Joseph O'Brien and Lorayne (Stouffer) Steele; children: Kelly A., Patrick W., Kathleen; m. Sharon Ann Curling, July 8, 1978; 1 child, John Joseph. BBA, U. Notre Dame; JD, Northwestern U. Bar: Ill., U.S. Dist. Ct. (no. dist.) Ill., U.S. Supreme Ct. Assoc. Nicholson, Nisen, Elliott & Meier, Chgo., 1966-70; pres. Capstan Co., 1970-73, Walter J. O'Brien II, Ltd., Oak Brook, Ill., 1973-78, O'Brien & Assocs., P.C., Oakbrook Terrace, 1978—. Chmn., bd. dirs. Atty. Title Guaranty Fund, Inc., Champaign, Ill., 1979—; arbitrator chairperson 18th Judicial Ct., DuPage County, Ill. Contbr. articles to legal jours. Commr. Oak Brook Plan Commn., 1980-85; mem. Oak Brook Zoning Bd. Appeals, 1985-87, Bd. Edn. Elem. Dist. # 53, Oak Brook, 1991-95; commr. Ill. and Mich. Canal, Nat. Heritage Corridor Commn.; v.p. Oak Brook Civic Assn., 1972; trustee St. Isaac Jogues Ch., Hinsdale, Ill., 1975-76. Capt. Q.M.C., U.S. Army, 1964-66. Fellow Ill. Bar Found.; mem. Ill. State Bar Assn. (mem. assembly), DuPage Bar Assn. (bd. dirs. 1987-88, elected Man of Yr. 1988), Am. Inn of Ct. (master DuPage chpt.), Butterfield Country Club (bd. dirs. 1982-88). Roman Catholic. General corporate, Probate, Real property. Office: O'Brien & Assocs PC Ste 501 1900 Spring Rd Oak Brook IL 60523

O'BRIEN, WILLIAM J., III, lawyer; BS, Holy Cross Coll., 1965; LLB, Yale U., 1969. Bar: N.Y. 1970, Mich. 1985. With Hughes Hubbard and Reed, N.Y.C. and Paris, 1969-75; asst. gen. counsel Chrysler Corp., Highland Park, 1983, assoc. gen. counsel, 1984, dep. gen. counsel, 1986; v.p., gen. counsel, sec. DaimlerChrysler AG, 1987, sr. v.p., gen. counsel, 1998—. Office: DaimlerChrysler AG CIMS 485-14-96 1000 Chrysler Dr Auburn Hills MI 48326-2766

O'BRIEN, WILLIAM JEROME, II, lawyer; b. Darby, Pa., Oct. 22, 1954; s. Richard James O'Brien and Margaret (McGill) Hahn. BA in Econ. and Polit. Sci., Merrimack Coll., 1976; JD, Del. Law Sch., 1981. Bar: Pa. 1982, U.S. Dist. Ct. (ea. dist.) Pa. 1983, U.S. Supreme Ct. 1986. Law clk. Commonwealth Ct. of Pa., Harrisburg, 1982-83; assoc. Philips, Curtin and DiGiacomo, Phila., 1983-86, O'Brien & Assocs. PC, Phila., 1986—. Bd. dirs. New Manayunk Corp., Phila. counselor, 1987-98. Bd. dirs. North Light Inc., 1986-94, sec., 1988-90, pres., 1990-92; bd. dirs. Manayunk Cmty. Ctr. for Arts, 1988-90, chmn. Chaminouix Mansion, 1989—, chmn., 1991—; spl. asst. to U.S. Senator H. John Heinz, 1976-78; Rep. candidate for Phila. City Coun., 1991, for Phila. City Contr., 1997; mem. Rep. State Com. Pa., 1998-2000. Mem. Phila. Bar Assn., Pa. Bar Assn., Del. Law Sch. Alumni Assn. (sec. 1985-87), Bus. Assn. Manayunk (bd. dirs. 1987-89), Union League, Racquet Club (mem. com. 1985-87). Roman Catholic. Avocations: squash, court tennis, scuba, golf. General corporate, General practice, Real property. Office: O'Brien & Assocs PC 4322 Main St Philadelphia PA 19127-1421

O'BRYON, MAUREEN, lawyer; b. Marshalltown, Iowa, Apr. 3, 1946; d. Robert Maurice and Ruth Ida (Bratzel) O'B.; m. John P. Rupp, 1968; children: Megan, Erin O'Bryon. BA magna cum laude, U. Iowa, 1968; JD, Georgetown U., 1975. Bar: D.C. 1975, U.S. Supreme Ct. Assoc. Donovan Leisure Newton & Irvine, Washington, 1975-84, ptnr., 1984-86, Hogan & Hartson, Washington, 1986—. Mem. exec. com., trustee Washington Lawyers Com. for Civil Rights and Urban Affairs, Washington, 1977—. Mem. ABA (litigation and antitrust sects.), Phi Beta Kappa, Chi Omega.

OBRZUT, TED, lawyer; b. Hatfield, Eng., May 26, 1949; came to U.S., 1956; naturalized, 1961; s. Stanley Jan Obrzut and Christel Maira (Achenbach) Obrzut Wenzel; m. Rochelle Marie Lindsey, Sept. 24, 1983. Student, Columbia U., 1967-69; BA, U. Calif., Santa Barbara, 1969-71; LLB, UCLA, 1974. Bar: Calif. 1974, N.Y. 1990. Assoc. O'Melveny an dMyers, L.A., 1974-82; ptnr. Lillick, McHose and Charles, 1982-87, Milbank Tweed Hadley & McCloy, L.A., 1987—. Mem. ABA (com. comml. fin. svcs.), Calif. State Bar Assn. (uniform comml. code com. 1980-83), Order of Coif, Phi Beta Kappa. Aviation, Contracts commercial, Finance. Office: Milbank Tweed Hadley & McCloy 601 S Figueroa St Los Angeles CA 90017-5704

OBUCHOWSKI, RAYMOND JOSEPH, lawyer; b. LaGrange, Ill., Oct. 2, 1955; s. Harry John and Betty Lou (Roux) O.; m. Marie Ann Fowler, May 28, 1983; children: Michael Jozef, Brian Matthew. BS, Western Ill. U., 1976; JD, Vt. Law Sch., 1980. Bar: Ill. 1980, Vt. 1982, U.S. Dist. Ct. Ill., U.S. Dist. Ct. Vt., 1983, U.S. Ct. Appeals (7th cir.) 1982; bd. cert. in bus. and consumer bankruptcy law Am. Bankruptcy Bd. of Cert. State's atty. investigator McDonough County Gen. State Atty.'s Office, Macomb, Ill., 1976-77; asst. atty. gen. revenue litigation Ill. Atty. Gen.'s Office, Springfield, 1981-82; law clk. to Hon. Charles J. Marro U.S. Bankruptcy Ct. Dist. of Vt., Rutland, 1982-83, estate administrator, 1983-84; assoc. Law Office of Jerome Meyers, Springfield, Vt., 1983, Law Office of Joseph C. Palimisano, Barre, 1984-86; pvt. practice S. Royalton, 1986—; ptnr. Mayer, Berk & Obuchowski, 1988-90; pvt. practice Bethel, Vt., 1990-91; ptnr. Obuchowski & Reis, 1992-96; pvt. practice Obuchowski Law Office, 1997—. Co-author: Vermont Collection Law, 1988, Basic Bankruptcy in Vermont, 1989, Sucessful Creditor's Strategies in Bankruptcy in Vermont, 1990, Foreclosure and Repossession in Vermont, 1991. Mem. Ill. Bar Assn., Vt. Bar Assn. (chmn. bankruptcy com. 1997-2000), Nat. Assn. Bankruptcy Trustees, Am. Bankruptcy Inst., Blue Key. Roman Catholic. Avocation: baseball. Bankruptcy, Consumer commercial. Home: PO Box 25 South Royalton VT 05068-0025 Office: PO Box 60 Bethel VT 05032-0060

O'CARROLL, ANITA LOUISE, lawyer; b. Jersey City, Nov. 19, 1953; d. Henry Patrick and Anita (Babikian) O'C. BA, Rutgers U., 1975; JD, N.Y. Law Sch., 1978. Bar: N.J. 1983, Pa. 1983, U.S. Dist. Ct. N.J. 1983, Tex. 1995. Legal asst. to Manhattan Dist. Atty., N.Y.C., 1977, to Bergen County Counsel, Hackensack, N.J., 1977; jud. clk. City of Hackensack, 1978-79; legal editor West Pub. Co., Mineola, N.Y., 1980-85; staff atty. Social Security Adminstrn. Office of Hearings and Appeals, Newark, 1985-86; staff atty. Aetna Life and Casualty Co., Parsippany, N.J., 1986-95; pvt. practice, Basking Ridge, 1995-97; sr. claims rep. IHDS of N.J., Ltd., 1997—. Author: (with others) The Guide to American Law, 1981; A Synthesis of N.Y. Case Law on the Bill of Particulars and Pretrial Discovery, 1977. Mem. N.J. State Bar Assn., Pa. Bar Assn., Tex. Bar Assn. Republican. Insurance, Pension, profit-sharing, and employee benefits, Workers' compensation. Home and Office: 373 Penns Way Basking Ridge NJ 07920-3034

OCHMANSKI, CHARLES JAMES, retired bar association executive; b. Augusta, Maine, Aug. 17, 1932; s. Frank and Michalina (Popowich) O.; m. Martha Lillian Masters, July 1, 1961; children: Lisa Ellen, Angela Joan. BS in Edn., U. Maine, 1960, MEd, 1963. Sales rep. L.G. Balfour Co., Rochester, n.Y., 1960-62; tchr. Bloomfield High Sch., Conn., 1963-68; asst. exec. dir. Maine Tchrs. Assn., Augusta, 1968-74; exec. dir. Vt. Edn. Assn., Montpelier, 1974-81; asst. exec. dir. Vt. Bar Assn., 1981-82, exec. dir., 1982-89; ret. Served with USAF, 1952-56. Mem. Vt. Soc. Assn. Execs. Am. Soc. Assn. Execs.

OCHS, ROBERT DUANE, lawyer; b. LaCrosse, Kans., June 16, 1942; s. Manuel and Marie Elizabeth (Koch) O.; m. Catherine Clemens Fockele, Dec. 18, 1971; children: Elizabeth Marie, Thomas Fockele. AB, Ft. Hays State U., 1965; JD, Washburn U., 1968. Bar: Kans. 1968, U.S. Dist. Ct. Kans. 1968, U.S. Ct. Appeals (10th cir.) 1968, U.S. Supreme Ct. 1973. Exec. dir. Kans. Constn. Revision Com., Topeka, 1968; rsch. atty. Kans. Sup. Ct., 1968; asst. pardon atty. Gov.'s Office, 1968-69, legal counsel to gov., 1969; sr. ptnr. Ochs and Kelley, P.a., 1995-90; gen. counsel Golf Course Supts. Assn., 1991-94; pres. Kans. Advocacy & Protective Svcs., Inc., 1995—. Author supplement: Kansas Practice Methods, 1977. Mem. Kans. Bar Assn. (profl. ethics and grievance com. 1982-87, Outstanding Svc. award 1987), Topeka Bar Assn. (chmn. profl. ethis and grievance com. 1981-87). Republican. Lutheran. Federal civil litigation, State civil litigation, Personal injury. Home: 1936 SW Arrowhead Rd Topeka KS 66604-3725 Office: Kans Advocacy & Prot Svcs Inc 3745 SW Wanamaker Topeka KS 66610

O'CONNELL, DANIEL JAMES, lawyer; b. Evergreen Park, Ill., Aug. 14, 1954; s. Edmund J. and Kathryn J. (Hanna) O'C.; m. Nancy L. Eichler, March 21, 1992; children: Kelly Jacklyn, Kirby Kathryn. BS, Millikin U., 1976; JD, IIT, 1980; postgrad., DePaul U., 1981, U. Mich., 2000, U. Ill., 1999—. Bar: Ill. 1980, U.S. Dist. Ct. (no. dist.) Ill. 1980, U.S. Dist. Ct. (ctrl. dist.) Ill. 2000, U.S. Dist. Ct. Ariz. 1989. Ins. regulatory counsel Kemper Group, Long Grove, Ill., 1980-81, environ. claims counsel, 1981-82; sr. home office claim counsel Zurich Ins. Cos., Schaumburg, 1982-83; assoc. Clausen, Miller, Gorman et al, Chgo., 1983-86; ptnr. environ. toxic tort litigation O'Connell & Moroney, P.C., 1986-90; ptnr. toxic tort litigation Burditt, Bowles & Radzius, 1990-91; ptnr. Daniel J. O'Connell & Assocs., P.C., Elgin, 1991—. James S. Kemper Found. scholar, 1972-76. Mem. ABA, APHA, Ill. Bar Assn., Kane County Bar Assn., Def. Rsch. Inst., N.Y. Acad. Scis., Environmental, Insurance, Product liability. Home: 177 Macintosh Ct Glen Ellyn IL 60137-6478 E-mail: doconn3@uic.edu

O'CONNELL, FRANCIS JOSEPH, retired lawyer, arbitrator; b. Ft. Edward, N.Y., Mar. 19, 1913; s. Daniel Patrick and Mary (Bowe) O'C.; m. Adelaide M. Nagro, Sept. 27, 1937; children: Chris, Mary Gaynor Lavonas. AB, Columbia U., 1934; JD, Fordham U., 1938; SJD summa cum laude, Bklyn. Law Sch., 1945. Bar: N.Y. 1938, U.S. Dist. Ct. (so. dist.) N.Y. 1942, U.S. Tax Ct. 1941. Counsel and asst. to chmn. exec. com. for labor law and litigation Allied Chem. Corp., N.Y.C., 1942-70; ptnr. Bill & O'Connell and predecessor, Garden City, N.Y., 1970-76; pvt. practice, 1976-85, Cutchogue, 1985—; now semi-ret. Arbitrator, fact-finder, mediator Fed. Mediation and Conciliation Svc., 1970—, N.Y. State Mediation Bd., Am. Arbitration Assn., N.Y. State, Nassau and Suffolk County pub. employment rels. bds., 1970—; adminstrv. law judge N.Y. State Dept. Health, 1979—; instr. labor law and labor rels. Cornell U.; U.S. del. ILO, Geneva, 1948, 59, 69, 72. Author: Labor Law and the First Line Supervisor, 1945, Restrictive Work Practices, 1967, National Emergency Strikes, 1968. Trustee Village of Garden City, 1948-50; mem. bd. edn. Diocese of Rockville Centre (N.Y.), 1972-80; pres. various civic orgns., 1942—. Mem. ABA (labor and internat. law sects.), N.Y. State Bar Assn. (labor com.), Bar Assn. Nassau County (labor and arbitration coms., former chmn. arbitration andlabor law coms.), Mfg. Chemists Assn. (chmn. indsl. rels. com.), U.S. C. of C. (indsl. rels. com.), Southold Indian Mus. (bd. dirs.). Republican. Roman Catholic. Labor, Pension, profit-sharing, and employee benefits. Office: PO Box 819 Cutchogue NY 11935-0819

O'CONNELL, JOHN F. lawyer, retired law educator; b. Mahanoy City, Pa., Jan. 4, 1919; s. Thomas Vincent O'Connell and Mary Elizabeth Cunningham; m. Rosemary Teresa O'Connell, Jan. 9, 1943 (dec. June 1990); children: Paul, Rosemarie, Dennis, Michael, Patricia, Kevin; m. Yvonne Louise O'Connell, Dec. 2, 1993. BA, La Salle Coll., 1940; JD, Western Reserve U., 1950; MA, U. Md., 1960; PhD, So. Calif. U., 1995. Commd. 2d lt. USAF, 1943, advanced through grades to col., ret., 1968; dean, law prof. Western State U. Coll. Law, Fullerton, Calif., 1975-87; law prof. Am. Coll. Law, Brea, 1987-89; dean So. Calif. Coll. Law, 1989-91, ret., 1991. Author: Remedies in a Nutshell, 1985. Decorated Legion of Merit, Bronze Star, Army Commendation medal, Air Force Commendation medal. Mem. Air Force Office Spl. Agts., Delta Theta Phi. Republican. Roman Catholic. Home: 8764 Captains Pl Las Vegas NV 89117-3516

O'CONNELL, JOHN JAMES, JR. lawyer; b. Winter Park, Fla., Nov. 13, 1957; s. John James and Margaret K. O'Connell; divorced; 1 child, Logan Christian. BA, U. Ariz., 1979; JD, Western State U., San Diego, 1982. Bar: Mont. 1985, Ga. 1992, U.S. Dist. Ct. (no. dist.) Ga. 1992, U.S. Ct. Appeals (11th cir.) 1992, U.S. Dist. Ct. (no. dist.) Calif. 1987, U.S. Dist. Ct. Ariz. 1991, U.S. Ct. Appeals (9th cir.) 1987, U.S. Tax Ct. 1988. Sole practitioner, Helena, Mont., Atlanta, 1985-94; sole practitioner, owner firm Atlanta, 1994-97; mng. ptnr. Smith, Furr, Schroeder & O'Connell, Decatur, Ga., 1997-98, Smith, Schroeder & O'Connell, Decatur, 1999—. Mem ABA, ATLA. Avocations: photography, golf, tennis. General civil litigation, Criminal, Personal injury. Office: Smith Schroeder & O'Connell 125 E Trinity Pl Ste 300 Decatur GA 30030-3360

O'CONNELL, JOSEPH FRANCIS, III, lawyer; b. Apr. 18, 1948; s. Joseph Francis Jr. and Suzanne (O'Brien) O'C. BSBA, Villanova U., 1970; MBA, JD, So. Meth. U., 1975; M of Strategic Studies, U.S. Army War Coll., 2001. Bar: Tex. 1975, Mass. 1975, U.S. Dist. Ct. Mass. 1976, D.C. 1978, U.S. Supreme Ct. 1979. Assoc. firm Epstein, Salloway & Kaplan, Boston, 1976-78; corp. counsel Thomas E. Sears, Inc., 1978-97; ptnr. O'Connell & O'Connell, 1997—. Col. JAGC, USAR, 1979—. Mem. ABA, Boston Bar Assn. Clubs: University (Boston), Army and Navy (Washington). General corporate, Insurance, Military. Office: O'Connell & O'Connell 31 Milk St Boston MA 02109-5104

O'CONNELL, LAWRENCE B. lawyer; b. Corpus Christi, Tex., July 18, 1947; s. Lawrence M. and Isabelle Susan (Strawbridge) O.; m. Carolyn Janet Rush, Sept.24, 1967; children: Suzanne Michelle, Elizabeth Danielle, Jason Lawrence. BA, Purdue U., 1970; JD, Ind. U., Indpls., 1975. Bar: Ind. 1975, U.S. Dist. Ct. (no. and so. dists.) Ind. 1975. Chief investigator Consumer Protection Div. Office of the Ind. Atty. Gen., Indpls., 1974-75; dep. atty. gen. Office of the Ind. Atty. Gen., 1975; assoc. Schultz, Ewan & Burns Law Firm, Lafayette, Ind., 1975-79; ptnr. Schultz, Ewan, Burns & O'Connell, 1979-82, Gothard, Poelstra & O'Connell, Lafayette, 1982-86, Profl. Assn. Gothard & O'Connell, Lafayette, 1987-93; pvt. practice, 1994—. Atty. Tippecanoe County, Lafayette, 1983-95. Edn. cons. Ind. U., 1973-75; treas. Ind. Young Rep. Fedn. 1976-77, chmn. 1977-79; Hoosier Assoc. Ind. Reps., 1980—. Recipient Sagamore of the Wabash citation, Gov. Otis R. Bowen, M.D., Ind. 1978, Gov. Robert D. Orr, Ind. 1980. Mem. ABA, Ind. Bar Assn., Tippecanoe County Bar Assn. (treas. 1976-77), Columbia Club (Indpls.), Ind. Soc. of Chgo., Ind. Mcpl. Lawyers Assn. (bd. dirs. 1989-95, pres. 1994-95). Government contracts and claims, Private international, Municipal (including bonds). Office: Lawrence B O'Connell Esq # 558 223 Main St Lafayette IN 47901-1261

O'CONNELL, MAURICE DANIEL, lawyer; b. Ticonderoga, N.Y., Nov. 9, 1929; s. Maurice Daniel and Leila (Geraghty) O'C.; m. Joan MacLure Landers, Aug. 2, 1952; children: Mark M., David L., Ann M., Leila K., Ellen A. Grad., Phillips Exeter Acad., 1946; AB, Williams Coll., 1950; LLB, Cornell U., 1956. Bar: Ohio 1956. Since practiced in, Toledo; assoc. Williams, Eversman & Black, 1956-60; ptnr. Robison, Curphey & O'Connell, 1961-95, of counsel, 1996—; spl. hearing officer in conscientious objector cases U.S. Dept. Justice, 1966-68. Mem. complaint rev. bd. Bd. Commrs. on Grievance and Discipline of Supreme Ct. Ohio, 1987. Mem. Ottawa Hills Bd. Edn., 1963-66, pres., 1967-69; former trustee Toledo Soc. for Handicapped; past trustee Woodlawn Cemetery; past trustee Toledo Hearing and Speech Center, Easter Seal Soc.; mem. alumni council Phillips Exeter Acad. Served to 1st lt. USMCR, 1950-53. Fellow Ohio State Bar Found.; mem. NW Ohio Alumni Assn. of Williams Coll. (past pres.), Ohio Bar Assn., Toledo Bar Assn. (chmn. grievance com. 1971-74), Kappa Alpha, Phi Delta Phi. Club: Toledo. General corporate, Labor. Home: 3922 W Bancroft St Toledo OH 43606-2533 Office: 9th Flr Four SeaGate Toledo OH 43604

O'CONNOR, CHARLES P. lawyer; b. Boston, Sept. 29, 1940; m. Mary Linda Hogan; children: Jennifer, Amy, Austin, Catherine. Bachelors degree, Holy Cross Coll., Worcester, Mass., 1963; LLB, Boston Coll., 1966. Bar: Mass. 1966, D.C. 1968, U.S. Supreme Ct. 1974. Atty., gen. counsel's office NLRB, Washington, 1966-67; assoc. Morgan, Lewis & Bockius, LLP, 1968-71; ptnr. Morgan, Lewis & Bockius, 1971—, chmn. labor and employment law sect., 1996-99, mng. ptnr. Washington office, 1995-97. Gen. counsel Major League Baseball Player Rels. Com., N.Y.C., 1989-94. Contbr. numerous articles on labor and employment law to law jours. Spl. counsel elections com. U.S. Ho. of Reps., Washington, 1968-69. Fellow Coll. Labor and Employment Lawyers; mem. ABA, D.C. Bar Assn., Met. Club Washington, Belle Haven Country Club, N.Y. Athletic Club, Cape Cod Nat. Golf Club. E-mail: co'connor@morganlewis.com. Entertainment, Labor. Home: 6121 Vernon Ter Alexandria VA 22307-1152 Office: Morgan Lewis & Bockius 1800 M St NW Ste 800 Washington DC 20036-5802

O'CONNOR, EDWARD GEARING, lawyer; b. Pitts., May 5, 1940; s. Timothy R. and Irene B. (Gearing) O'C.; m. Janet M. Showalter, June 17, 1972; children: Mark G., Susan M. BA, Duquesne U., 1962, JD, 1965. Bar: Pa. 1965, U.S. Dist. Ct. (we. dist.) Pa. 1965, U.S. Ct. Appeals (3d cir.) 1968, U.S. Supreme Ct. 1976. Assoc. Eckert, Seamans, Cherin & Mellott, Pitts., 1965-72, ptnr., 1973-99, sr. counsel, 2000—. Mem. adv. com. on appellate ct. rules Supreme Ct. Pa., 1986-92, mem. procedures rules com., 1998-01; bd. dirs., mem. audit com. Federated Investors, Inc. Editor Duquesne U. Law Rev., 1964-65. Chmn. Hampton (Pa.) Twp. Planning Commn., 1986-87; mem. Hampton (Pa.) Twp. Zoning Hearing Bd., 1997—; bd. dirs. Duquesne U.; trustee Noble J. Dick Edn. Fund, 1989—. Recipient Disting. Alumni award Duquesne U. Law Rev., 1985, Disting. Law Alumni award Duquesne U. Sch. Law, 1991, Disting. Svc. award Hampton Twp., 1991, McAnurlty Svc. award Duquesne U., 1992; named Century Club Disting. Alumni, Duquesne U., 1985. Fellow Am. Bar Found., Pa. Bar Found.; mem. Pa. Bar Assn. (ho. of dels. 1985-90), Acad. Trial Lawyers Allegheny County (bd. govs. 1986-89, 98—), Duquesne U. Alumni Assn. (pres. 1980-82, 88-90, bd. govs. 1982-90, bd. dirs. 1988-89), Duquesne Club, Pitts. Athletic Assn., Ally City Bar Found. Republican. Roman Catholic. Antitrust, Federal civil litigation, State civil litigation. Home: 4288 Green Glade Ct Allison Park PA 15101-1202 Office: Eckert Seamans Cherin & Mellott 600 Grant St Ste 44th Pittsburgh PA 15219-2702 E-mail: ego@escm.com

O'CONNOR, EDWARD VINCENT, JR. lawyer; b. Yokosuka, Japan, Nov. 9, 1952; s. Edward Vincent and Margaret (Robertson) O'C.; m. Kathy J. Hunt, May 23, 1992. BA, Duke U., 1975; JD, N.Y. Law Sch., 1981. Bar: Va. 1982, D.C. 1983. Assoc. Lewis, Kinsey, Dack & Good, Washington, 1982-87; ptnr. Lewis, Dack, Paradiso & Good, 1988-89, Lewis, Dack, Paradiso, O'Connor & Good, Washington, 1989-94, The Lewis Law Firm, 1994, Byrd, Mische, Bevis, Bowen, Joseph & O'Connor, Fairfax, Va., 1995—. Arbitrator D.C. Superior Ct.; neutral case evaluator and concilliator Fairfax County Cir. Ct.; lectr. Va. Trial Lawyers Assn., Arlington County Bar Assn. Bd. dirs., treas. Potomac Legal Aid Soc., 2001—. Named One of Best 50 Divorce Lawyers Washingtonian mag., 1995, 2000. Mem. Va. State Bar (lectr., spl. com. on access to legal svcs. 1994—. 5th dist. discipline com.), D.C. Bar, Fairfax County Bar Assn. (lectr., vice chair family law sect. 1995-96, continuing edn. com. 1988-95, chair 1995, mem. pub. svc. com. 1995, chair 1996-98, mem. cir. ct. com. 1994-96, 99-2001, judicial selection com., pro bono com., James Keith award for pub. svc. 1999), Legal Svcs. No. Va. (bd. dirs., chmn. pro bono com., sec.-treas. 1998-2002, pres. 2002-, pro bono award for outstanding svc. 1997). Entertainment, Family and matrimonial, Probate.

O'CONNOR, GAYLE MCCORMICK, law librarian; b. Rome, July 8, 1956; d. John Joseph and Barbara Jane (Molyneaux) McC. Head libr. Bolling, Walter & Gawthrop, Sacramento, 1987-88, Weintraub, Genshlea & Sproul, Sacramento, 1988-93, Brobeck, Phleger & Harrison, San Diego, 1993-96; legal cons., author, 1996—; owner Automated legal Solutions, Ft. Lauderdale, Fla., 1997—; legal industry mktg. specialist CourtLink, Seattle, 1998—; dir. mktg. ABC Legal Svcs., 1999—. Instr. law Lincoln U., Sacramento. Assoc. editor, rsch. advisor Alert Publs., Chgo.; contbr. articles to profl. jours. Mem. ABA (tech. show bd.), No. Calif. Assn. Law Librs., So. Calif. Assn. Law Librs., Am. Assn. Law Librs., Spl. Librs. Assn. (chair legal divsn. 1997-98). Avocations: bodybuilding, skiing. Office: 910 5th Ave Seattle WA 98101 E-mail: bodybuilder@cybersleuther.com, gayleo@abclegal.com

O'CONNOR, HEIDI ROBERTS, federal appellate lawyer; b. Pueblo, Colo., Oct. 1965; m. John O'Connor, Jan. 1988. BA, U. Colo., 1986; JD, U. Kans., 1992. Bar: Kans. 1993, Mo. 1994. Sole practitioner law, Kans., 1993—. Universita Italiana per Stranieri scholar, 1986, Elks and Regents scholar, 1986. Mem. ACLU, So. Poverty Law Ctr. Avocation: travel (26 nations). Office: PO Box 19942 Boulder CO 80308-2942

O'CONNOR, JOSEPH A., JR. lawyer; b. N.Y.C., Aug. 12, 1937; s. Joseph A. and Louise G. (Lucht) O'C.; children: Joseph A. III, Edward W. BA, Yale U., 1959; LLB, Columbia U., 1962. Bar: N.Y. 1963, U.S. Supreme Ct. 1968, Pa. 1973, Fla. 1978. Assoc. Davis, Polk & Wardwell, N.Y.C., 1963-72; ptnr. Morgan, Lewis & Bockius, Phila., 1972—. Mem. ABA, N.Y. State Bar Assn., Pa. Bar Assn., Fla. Bar Assn., Phila. Bar Assn., Assn. of Bar of City of N.Y. Roman Catholic. Club: Racquet (Phila.). Office: Morgan Lewis & Bockius LLP 1701 Market St Philadelphia PA 19103-2903

O'CONNOR, KARL WILLIAM (GOODYEAR JOHNSON), lawyer; b. Washington, Aug. 1, 1931; s. Hector and Lucile (Johnson) O'C.; m. Sylvia Gasbarri, Mar. 23, 1951 (dec.); m. Judith Ann Byers, July 22, 1972 (div. 1983); m. Eleanor Celler, Aug. 3, 1984 (div. 1986); m. Alma Hepner, Jan. 1, 1987 (div. 1996); children: Blair, Frances, Brian, Brendan; m. Allie O'Connor, Jul. 15, 2000. BA, U. Va., 1952, JD, 1958. Bar: Va. 1958, D.C. 1959, Am. Samoa 1976, Calif. 1977, Oreg. 1993. Law clk. U.S. Dist. Ct. Va., Abingdon, 1958-59; practice law Washington, 1959-61; trial atty. U.S. Dept. Justice, 1961-65; dep. dir. Men's Job Corps OEO, 1965-67; mem. civil rights div. Dept. of Justice, chief criminal sect., prin. dep. asst. atty. gen., 1967-75, spl. counsel for intelligence coordination, 1975; v.p., counsel Assn. of Motion Picture and Television Producers, Hollywood, Calif., 1975-76; assoc. justice Am. Samoa, 1976; chief justice, 1977-78; sr. trial atty. GSA Task Force, Dept. Justice, 1978-81; insp. gen. CSA, 1981-82; spl. counsel Merit Systems Protection Bd., Washington, 1983-86; U.S. atty. for Guam and the No. Marianas, 1986-89; ret.; pvt. practice Medford, Oreg., 1989—; Am. counsel O'Reilly Vernier Ltd., Hong Kong, 1992-93; ptnr. O'Connor & Vernier, Medford, Oreg., 1993-94; pvt. practice, 1994—. Served with USMC, 1952-55. Mem. Oreg. Bar Assn., D.C. Bar Assn., Va. Bar Assn., Calif. Bar Assn., Am. Samoa Bar Assn., Soc. Colonial Wars, Phi Alpha Delta, Sigma Nu. Federal civil litigation, Criminal, Labor. Home: Box 126 6743 Griffin Ln Jacksonville OR 97530 Office: 916 W 10th St Medford OR 97501-3018

O'CONNOR, KATHLEEN MARY, lawyer; b. Camden, Jan. 14, 1949; d. John A. and Marie V. (Flynn) O'C. BA, U. Fla., 1971, JD, 1981. Bar: Fla. 1981, U.S. Ct. Appeals (11th cir.) 1982, U.S. Supreme Ct. 1987. Atty. Walton, Lantaff, Schroeder & Carson, Miami, 1981-84, Thornton, Davis & Murray PA, Miami, 1984-98, Shook, Hardy & Bacon LLP, Miami, 2001—. Exec. editor U. Fla. Law Rev., 1981; contbr. articles to profl. jours. Legal advocate Miami Project to Cure Paralysis, 1992-97. Mem. ABA, Dade County Bar Assn. (vice-chair appellate cts. com. 1981), Def. Rsch. Inst., Fla. Def. Lawyers Assn. Appellate, Aviation, Insurance. Office: Shook Hardy & Bacon LLP Ste 2400 201 S Biscayne Blvd Miami FL 33131-4332 E-mail: koconnor@shb.com

O'CONNOR, MICHAEL E. lawyer; b. Syracuse, N.Y., Sept. 15, 1948; s. Leo T. and Geraldine (Hager) O'Connor; m. Margaret A. Soplop, June 03, 1972. AA, Auburn (N.Y.) C.C., 1968; BA, SUNY, Buffalo, 1970; JD, Syracuse U., 1974. Bar: N.Y. 1975, U.S. Supreme Ct. 1983. Assoc. Coulter, Fraser, Bolton, Bird & Ventre, Syracuse, 1975-80, ptnr., 1981-90, Hancock & Estabrook, 1990-94, DeLaney & O'Connor LLP, 1994—. Pres. Onondaga Title Assn., 1979, Ctrl. N.Y. Estate Planning Coun., 1981; adj. prof. law U. Syracuse; pres. Most Holy Rosary Home Sch. Assn., 1985—86, Aurora of CNY, Inc., 1988—90. Bd. dirs. Syracuse Symphony Orch. Assn., CNY Cmty. Found.; pres. Citizens Found., Inc., 1983—85. Fellow: Am. Coll. Trust and Estate Counsel (state chair); mem.: ABA, N.Y. State Bar Assn. (ho. of dels. 1982—85, exec. com. trusts and estates sect. 1984—91, chair elder law sect. 1999—2000), Onondaga County Bar Assn. (chmn. estate and surrogates ct. com. 1981—87, bd. dirs. 1984—86), Syracuse Lions Club (pres. 1984—85), Century Club, Club of Syracuse. Republican. Roman Catholic. Estate planning, Probate, Estate taxation. Home: 154 Robineau Rd Syracuse NY 13207-1644 Office: DeLaney & O'Connor LLP One Lincoln Ctr Syracuse NY 13202

O'CONNOR, OTIS LESLIE, lawyer, director; b. Charleston, W.Va., July 6, 1935; s. Robert Emmett and Julia Elizabeth (Aultz) O'C.; m. Elizabeth Frances Morris, Aug. 7, 1965; children: Otis Leslie, James M. AB, Princeton U., 1957; JD, Harvard U., 1963; MBA, W.Va. Coll. Grad. Studies, 1979. Bar: W.Va. 1963, U.S. Dist. (so. dist.) W.Va. 1963. Assoc. Steptoe & Johnson, Charleston, 1963-69, ptnr., 1969—. Mem. city council, Charleston, 1971-75; bd. dirs. Daymark, Inc., 1974-84, 94—, pres., 1981-82. Bd. dirs. Union Mission Ministries, Inc., 1986—; Rep. committeeman, 1970-75. Served with USN, 1957-60; served to comdr. JAGC, USNR, 1960-81. Mem. ABA, W.Va. Bar Assn., Kanawha County Bar Assn., Res. Officers Assn., Rotary Internat. Club (Charleston). Presbyterian. Banking, Probate, Real property. Home: 890 Chester Rd Charleston WV 25302-2817

O'CONNOR, ROBERT EDWARD, JR. lawyer; b. Omaha, June 1, 1950; s. Robert Edward Sr. and Agnes (Flynn) O'C.; m. Jean Patricia Mergens; children: Maureen, Kathleen. undergrad. degree, JD, Creighton U., 1974. Bar: Nebr. 1974, U.S. Dist. Ct. Nebr., U.S. Ct. Appeals (8th cir.). Sole practice, Omaha, 1974—. Mem. Nebr. State Bar Assn. (del. 1982-84, pres. 2001-), Nebr. Assn. Trial Attys. (del.), Assn. Trial Lawyers Am. (del.). Democrat. Roman Catholic. Avocation: sailing. State civil litigation, Appellate, Aviation. Office: 2433 S 130th Cir Omaha NE 68144-2528*

O'CONNOR, SANDRA DAY, United States supreme court justice; b. El Paso, Tex., Mar. 26, 1930; d. Harry A. and Ada Mae (Wilkey) Day; m. John Jay O'Connor, III, Dec. 1952; children: Scott, Brian, Jay. AB in Econs. with great distinction, Stanford U., 1950, LLB, 1952. Bar: Calif., Ariz. Dep. county atty., San Mateo, Calif., 1952-53; civilian atty. Q.M. Market Ctr., Frankfurt am Main, Fed. Republic Germany, 1954-57; pvt. practice Phoenix, 1958-65; asst. atty. gen. State of Ariz., 1965-69; state senator Ariz., 1969-75; chmn. com. on state, county and mcpl. affairs, 1972-73; majority leader, 1973-74; judge Maricopa County Superior Ct., 1975-79, Ariz. Ct. Appeals, 1979-81; assoc. justice U.S. Supreme Ct., 1981—. Referee juvenile ct. Maricopa County, 1962-64; chmn. vis. bd. Maricopa County Juvenile Detention Home, 1963-64; mem. Maricopa County Bd. Adjustments and Appeals, 1963-64, Anglo-Am. Legal Exchange, 1980, Maricopa County Superior Ct. Judges Tng. and Edn. Com., 1977-79, Maricopa Ct. Study Com.; chair com. to reorganize lower cts. Ariz. Supreme Ct., 1974-75; faculty Robert A. Taft Inst. Govt.; mem. Ariz. Criminal Code Commn., 1974-76; bd. visitors Ariz. State U. Law Sch., 1981; liaison com. on med. edn., 1981. Mem. bd. editors Stanford (Calif.) U. Law Rev. Mem. Ariz. Pers. Commn., 1968-69, Nat. Def. Adv. Com. on Women in Svcs., 1974-76; trustee Heard Mus., Phoenix, 1968-74, 76-81, pres., 1980-81; mem. adv. bd. Phoenix Salvation Army, 1975-81; trustee Stanford U., 1976-81, Phoenix County Day Sch.; mem. citizens adv. bd. Blood Svcs., 1975-77; nat. bd. dirs. Smithsonian Assocs., 1981—, Colonial Williamsburg Found., 1988-2000; exec. bd. Ctrl. Eastern European Law Initiative, 1990—; past Rep. dist. chmn.; bd. dirs. Phoenix Cmty. Coun., 1969-75, Jr. Achievement Ariz., 1975-79, Blue Cross/Blue Shield Ariz., 1975-79, Channel 8, 1975-79, Phoenix Hist. Soc., 1974-78, Maricopa County YMCA, 1978-81, Golden Gate Settlement; past Rep. dist. chmn., bd. dirs. Phoenix Cmty. Coun.; adv. bd., v.p. Nat. Conf. of Christians and Jews, Maricopa County, 1977-81; bd. dirs., sec. Ariz. Acad., 1969-75, Cathedral chpt. Washington Nat. Cathedral, 1991-99. Recipient Ann. award NCCJ, 1975, Disting. Achievement award Ariz. State U., 1980, Sara Lee Frontrunner award 1997; recipient ABA medal, 1997; named Woman of Yr., Phoenix Advt. Club, 1972; inducted, National Women's Hall of Fame, 1995. Mem. ABA (select law enforcement revision commn. vice chair 1979-80), Ariz. Bar Assn. (legal edn., pub. rels. com., lower ct. reorgn. com.), Calif. Bar Assn., Maricopa County Bar Assn. (referral svc. chair 1960-62), Soroptimist Club (Phoenix). Office: US Supreme Ct Supreme Ct Bldg 1 First St NE Washington DC 20543

O'CONNOR, WILLIAM MATTHEW, lawyer; b. Pensacola, Fla., Apr. 5, 1955; s. William Francis and Rosalind (Shea) O'C.; m. Mary Patricia Keepnews, Oct. 13, 1984; children: William Lawrence, Thomas Patrick, Robert Austin. BS in Psychology, Fordham U., 1977, JD, 1980. Bar: N.Y. 1981, N.J. 1987, U.S. Dist. Ct. N.J. 1987, U.S. Dist. Conn. 1988, U.S. Dist. Ct. (so., ea., no. and we. dists.) N.Y., 1981, U.S. Ct. Appeals (2nd cir.) 1983, U.S. Ct. Appeals (3d cir.) 1996. Intern N.Y. Atty. Gen., N.Y.C., 1978-79; legis. intern Am. Lung Assn., 1979; assoc. Keane & Butler, 1979-81, Keane & Beane, White Plains, N.Y., 1981-83, Cooperman, Levitt & Winikoff, P.C., N.Y.C., 1983-86; sr. assoc. Sullivan, Donovan, Hanrahan & Silliere, 1986-87; ptnr. O'Connor Reddy & Seeler, 1987-95, Harris Beach & Wilcox LLP, N.Y.C., 1995-2000, Buchanan Ingersoll PC, N.Y.C., 2000—. Author: Lobbying Guidebook Am. Lung Assn., 1979. Contbr. articles to profl. jours. Legis. com. pub. schs., White Plains, 1981-82; councilman Town of Pelham, N.Y., 1998—. Mem. ABA, Fed. Bar Coun., N.Y. State Bar Assn. (mem. comml. and fed. litigation sect., creditor's rights com. 1989—), Westchester Bar Assn. (editor in chief Jour. 1983-89, mem. labor law com. 1981—, com. on profl. ethics 1989—), Fordham ILJ Alumni Assn. (bd. dirs. 1984—), New Rochelle Bar Assn. Republican. Roman Catholic. Banking, Federal civil litigation, State civil litigation. Home: 684 Esplanade Pelham NY 10803-2403 Office: Buchanan Ingersoll PC 140 Broadway New York NY 10005 E-mail: oconnorwn@bipc.com

O'DEA, DENNIS MICHAEL, lawyer; b. Lowell, Mass., Nov. 1, 1946; s. James Lawrence and Carol Francis (Gibbons) O'D.; m. Mary Gail Frawley; children: Emily C., Dennis C., Daniel P., Mollie G., Igor Ibradzic. BA in Govt., U. Notre Dame, 1968; JD magna cum laude, U. Mich., 1972. Bar: Mass. 1972, D.C. 1980, Ill. 1981, N.Y. 1994. Assoc. Goodwin, Procter & Hoar, Boston, 1972-74, Fine & Ambrogne, Boston, 1974-77; assoc. prof. Syracuse U. Coll. Law, 1977-78; vis. assoc. prof. Nat. Law Ctr., George Washington U., 1978-80; ptnr. Keck Mahin & Cate, N.Y.C., 1980-96; pvt. practice, 1996-97; ptnr. Wolf, Block, Schorr and Solis-Cohen LLP, N.Y.C., 1997—. Co-dir. The Gilmore Inst., 1995—. Mem. Order of the Coif, Chgo. Lit. Club (pres. 1993). Presbyterian. Bankruptcy, State civil litigation, Contracts commercial. Home: 5 Opal Ct New City NY 10956-7021 Office: Wolf Block Schorr & Solis-Cohen 250 Park Ave Ste 1000 New York NY 10177-0001

ODELL, HERBERT, lawyer; b. Phila., Oct. 20, 1937; s. Samuel and Selma (Kramer) O.; m. Valerie Odell; children: Wesley, Jonathan, James, Sarah, Samuel. BS in Econs., U. Pa., 1959; LLB magna cum laude, U. Miami, 1962; LLM, Harvard U., 1963. Bar: Fla. 1963, Pa. 1968. Trial atty. tax div. U.S. Dept. Justice, Washington, 1963-65; assoc. Walton, Lantaff, Schroeder, Carson & Wahl, Miami, Fla., 1965-67; from assoc. to ptnr. Morgan, Lewis & Bockius, Phila., 1967-89; ptnr. Zapruder & Odell, 1989-98, Odell & Ptnrs., Phila., 1998-99, Miller & Chevalier (PA) LLC, Phila., 2000—. Adj. prof. U. Miami, Villanova U.; lectr. various tax insts. Contbr. articles to profl. jours. Ford fellow, 1962-63. Mem. ABA, Fla. Bar

Assn., Pa. Bar Assn., Phila. Bar Assn., Phi Kappa Phi, Omicron Delta Kappa, Beta Alpha Psi. Club: Harvard. vocations: sailing, running, tennis, scuba diving. Corporate taxation, Taxation, general, Personal income taxation. Office: Miller & Chevalier 401 E City Ave Ste 415 Bala Cynwyd PA 19004-1121 E-mail: hodell@milchev.com

O'DELL, JOAN ELIZABETH, lawyer, mediator, business executive, educator; b. East Dubuque, Ill., May 3, 1932; d. Peter Emerson and Olive (Bonnet) O'D.; children: Dominique R., Nicole L. BA cum laude, U. Miami, 1956, JD, 1958. Bar: Fla. 1958, U.S. Supreme Ct. 1972, D.C. 1974, Ill. 1978, Va. 1987; lic. real estate broker, Ill., Va. Trial atty. SEC, Washington, 1959-60; asst. state atty. Office State Atty., Miami, Fla., 1960-64; asst. county atty. Dade County Atty.'s Office, 1964-70; county atty. Palm Beach County Atty.'s Office, West Palm Beach, Fla., 1970-71; regional gen. counsel Region IV EPA, Atlanta, 1971-73, assoc. gen. counsel Washington, 1973-77; sr. counsel Nalco Chem. Co., Oakbrook, Ill., 1977-78; v.p., gen. counsel Angel Mining, Washington and Tenn., 1979-96; pres. S.W. Land Investments, Miami, 1979-88; v.p. Events U.S.A., Washington, 1990—. Bd. dirs. Tucson Women's Found., 1982-84, U. Ariz. Bus. and Profl. Women's Club, Tucson, 1981-85; bd. dirs. LWV, Tucson, 1981-85, pres., 1984-85; bd. dirs. LWV Ariz., 1984-85, chmn. nat. security study; bd. dirs. LWV, Palm Beach County, Fla., 1990-92; mem. Exec. Women's Coun., Tucson, 1982-85. Mem. Fla. Bar Assn., D.C. Bar Assn., Va. State Bar Assn., Ill. Bar Assn. Avocations: camping, hiking, skiing. Appellate, General corporate, Probate. E-mail: jeod@aol.com

ODELL, STUART IRWIN, lawyer; b. Phila., Jan. 1, 1940; s. P. Samuel and Selma Odell; m. Andrea L. Villegas; children: Stuart Irwin Jr., Benjamin Eaton, Manuela, Sebastian Patricio. BS in Econs., U. Pa., 1961; LLB cum laude, U. Miami, 1964; LLM in Tax, NYU, 1965. Bar: Fla. 1965, Pa. 1966, N.Y. 1982. Assoc. Morgan, Lewis & bockius, N.Y.C., 1966-70, ptnr., 1970-88, Dewey Ballantine, N.Y.C., 1988—. Lectr. law NYU, 1965-66, adj. prof. law, 1966-80; adj. lectr. Temple U. Law Sch., 1972. Assoc. editor U. Miami Law Rev., 1963-64. Recipient Harry J. Ruddick award NYU. Mem. ABA, N.Y. State Bar Assn., Fla. Bar Assn., Assn. of Bar of City of N.Y. Contracts commercial, Private international, Corporate taxation. Office: Dewey Ballantine 1 Underenue Of The Americas New York NY 10019-6022 also: Dewey Ballantine 1 Undershaft London EC3A 8LP England E-mail: sodell@Deweyballantine.com

ODGERS, RICHARD WILLIAM, lawyer; b. Detroit, Dec. 31, 1936; s. Richard Stanley and Elsie Maude (Trevarthen) O.; m. Gail C. Bassett, Aug. 29, 1959; children: Thomas R., Andrew B. AB, U. Mich., 1959, JD, 1961. Bar: Calif. 1962. Assoc. Pillsbury Winthrop, San Francisco, 1961-69, ptnr., 1969-87, 98-2000; exec. v.p., gen. counsel Pacific Telesis Group, 1987-98; ptnr. Pillsbury Winthrop, 2001—. Chmn., bd. dirs. Legal Aid Soc. San Francisco; dir. Legal Cmty. Against Violence; dir., sec./treas. Van Loben Sels Charitable Found. Served with USNR. Fellow Am. Bar Found., Am. Judicature Soc., Am. Coll. Trial Lawyers; mem. ABA, Am. Law Inst., Coll. Law Practice Mgmt. Administrative and regulatory, Antitrust, Public utilities. Office: Pillsbury Winthrop 50 Fremont St San Francisco CA 94105-2228 E-mail: rwodgers@pillsburywinthrop.com

ODIORNE, JAMES THOMAS, lawyer, accountant; b. Austin, Tex., Mar. 9, 1947; s. Thomas King and Mary Ann (McInnis) O.; m. Alice Bell Soulek, Apr. 26, 1980; children— James Michael, Raymond Andrew. B.B.A., U. Tex.-Austin, 1969; J.D., Baylor U., 1973. Bar: Tex. 1973; CPA, Tex. Atty., acct. Bastrop, Tex., 1974-83; atty. Tex. State Bd. Ins., Austin, 1983-85, statutory liquidator and receiver, 1985-89, sr. dep. com. of ins. Tex. State Bd. Ins., Austin, 1988— . Candidate for Sheriff Bastrop County, Tex., 1974, for County Judge Bastrop County, 1978; chmn. Bastrop County ARC, 1977. Mem. Bastrop County Bar Assn. (past sec.), Kiwanis. Democrat. Methodist. Home: RR 1 Box 408 Cedar Creek TX 78612-9758

O'DONNELL, DENISE ELLEN, lawyer; BS in Polit. Sci., Canisius Coll., 1968; MSW, SUNY, Buffalo, 1973, JD summa cum laude, 1982. Bar: NY 1983, US Dist Ct (we, no, ea and so dists) NY, US Ct Appeals (2d cir.) Law clerk Hon. M. Dolores Denman U.S. Ct. Appellate Divsn. 4th Dept., Buffalo, 1982-85; asst. U.S. atty. Western Dist. N.Y., 1985-90, appellate chief, 1990-93, 1st asst. U.S. atty., 1993-97, U.S. atty., 1997-2001; ptnr. Gen. Litigation Practice Group, Hodgson, Russ, LLP, 2001—. Part-time instr trial technique program SUNY, 1990—; lectr ethics, evidence & trial practice Office Legal Educ US Dept Justice, 1988—; lectr NITA seminar Western NY Trial Acad, 1994, 98; mem Atty Gen's Adv Comt, 1999—2001, vice-chair, 2000—01. Mem Vol Lawyers Prog, 1997—, bd dirs nat conf, 2000—; mem Women's Group, 1994—; bd dirs Dean's Coun U Buffalo Sch Social Work. Mem.: ABA, Bar Asn Erie County (dep treas 1992—93, treas 1993—94), Erie County Bar Found (co-chair pub serv div 1992—93), Women's Bar Asn State NY (founding mem Western NY chpt 1985), Nat Asn Former US Attys, Western NY Trial Lawyers Asn, NY State Bar Asn, West Side Rowing Club. Office: Hodgson Russ LLP One M&T Plz Ste 2000 Buffalo NY 14203-2931 E-mail: dodonnell@hodgsonruss.com

O'DONNELL, LAWRENCE, III, lawyer; b. Houston, Dec. 14, 1957; s. Lawrence Jr. and Annell (Haggart) O'D.; m. Dare Boswell, May 22, 1981; children: Linley, Lawrence IV. BS in Archtl. Engring., U. Tex., 1980; JD cum laude, U. Houston, 1983. Bar: Tex. 1983. Assoc. Wood, Campbell, Moody & Gibbs, Houston, 1983-84; ptnr. Campbell & Riggs, 1984-91; dep. gen. counsel Baker Hughes Inc., 1991-94; v.p., gen. counsel Baker Hughes Oilfield Ops., 1993-95; corp. sec. Baker Hughes Inc., 1991-96, v.p., gen. counsel, 1995-2000; sr. v.p., gen. counsel, sec. Waste Mgmt., Inc., 2000-01, exec. v.p., gen. counsel, corp. sec., 2001—. Bd. dirs., mem. exec. com. Spring Br. Edn. Found.; bd. dirs. Am. Arbitration Assn., U. Tex. Med. Br. Trustee Houston Police Activities League. Fellow Tex. Bar Found., Houston Bar Found.; mem. ABA, ASCE, Tex. State Bar (corp. law com. of bus. law sect.), Houston Bar Assn., Am. Corp. Counsel Assn., Am. Soc. Corp. Sec., Tex. Bus. Law Found., Houston Bar Assn., Tex. Gen. Counsel Forum (pres. Houston chpt. 2000-01), Order of Barons, Phi Delta Phi. Avocations: golf, sailing, skiing. Contracts commercial, General corporate, Mergers and acquisitions. Office: Waste Mgmt Inc 1001 Fannin St Ste 4000 Houston TX 77002-6711

O'DWYER, BRIAN, lawyer, educator; b. N.Y.C., Oct. 10, 1945; s. Paul and Kathleen (Rohan) O.; m. Marianna Page, Sept. 7, 1968; children: Brendan, Kathleen. AB, George Washington U., 1967, LLM, 1976; MA, Middlebury Coll., 1968; JD, Georgetown U., 1971. Bar: N.Y. 1972, U.S. Dist. Ct. (so., ea. and no. dists.) N.Y. 1973, U.S. Ct. Appeals (2d cir.) 1975, U.S. Supreme Ct. 1983. Atty. NLRB, Newark, 1972-73, N.Y. State Labor Bd., 1973-74; mng. ptnr. O'Dwyer & Bernstein, N.Y.C., 1974—. Commr. N.Y.C. Commn. on Human Rights, 1993-96; dir. Malcom King Coll., 1980-88; pres. Bohola Enterprises Inc.; mem. Pres. Commn. on White House Fellows, 1998—. Trustee Clara Miller Found., Mayo Found for the Handicapped; nat. vice-chmn. Irish Ams. for Clinton Gore; citizens adv. com. Quincenntial Commn.; chmn. Emerald Isle Immigrant Ctr. Mem. ABA, Nat. Assn. Coll. and Univ. Attys., Brehon Law Soc., Kappa Sigma (nat. pres.). Democrat. Roman Catholic. General civil litigation, Labor, Pension, profit-sharing, and employee benefits. Home: 350 Central Park W New York NY 10025-6547 Office: O'Dwyer & Bernstein 52 Duane St Fl 5 New York NY 10007-1250

ODZA, RANDALL M. lawyer; b. Schnectady, May 6, 1942; s. Mitchell and Grace (Mannes) O.; m. Rita Ginness, June 19, 1966; children: Kenneth, Keith. BS in Indsl. and Labor Rels., Cornell U., 1964, LLB, 1967. Bar: N.Y. 1967, U.S. Ct. Appeals (2d cir.) 1970, U.S. Dist. Ct. (so. and ea. dists.) N.Y. 1969, U.S. Dist. Ct. (we. dist.) N.Y. 1970, Fed. Dist. Ct. (we. dist.) N.Y. Assoc. Proskauer, Rose, Goetz & Mandelsohn, N.Y.C., 1967-69, Jaeckle, Fleischmann & Mugel, Buffalo, 1969-72, ptnr., 1972—. Trustee, legal counsel, past treas. Temple Beth Am. Recipient Honow award Western N.Y. Retail Mchts. Assn., 1980. Mem. ABA, Indsl. Rels. Rsch. Assn. Western N.Y., Erie County Bar Assn., N.Y. State Bar Assn. Labor. Office: Jaeckle Fleischmann & Mugel 12 Fountain Plz Rm 700 Buffalo NY 14202-2292

OECHLER, HENRY JOHN, JR. lawyer; b. Charlotte, N.C., Apr. 9, 1946; s. Henry J. and Convere Jones (McAden) O. AB, Princeton U., 1968; JD, Duke U., 1971. Bar: N.Y. 1972, U.S. Ct. Appeals (2d cir.) 1974, U.S. Ct. Appeals (D.C. cir.) 1975, U.S. Ct. Appeals (8th cir.) 1986, U.S. Ct. Appeals (9th cir.) 1995. Assoc. Chadbourne & Parke, N.Y.C., 1971-80, ptnr., 1980—. Avocations: studying airline schedules. General civil litigation, Labor, Transportation. Office: Chadbourne & Parke 30 Rockefeller Plz Fl 31 New York NY 10112-0129

OEHLER, RICHARD DALE, lawyer; b. Iowa City, Dec. 9, 1925; s. Harold Lawrence Oehler and Bernito Babb; m. Rosemary Heineman, July 11, 1952, (div.); m. Maria Luisa Holguin-Zea, June 11, 1962; children: Harold D., Richard L. BA in Med. Scis., U. Calif., Berkeley, 1951; JD, Loyola U., L.A., 1961. Bar: Calif. 1962, Fla. 1968. Sales rep. Abbott Labs., Pasadena, Calif., 1951-63; with claims dept. Allstate Ins., Tampa, 1963-70; pvt. practice, 1970—. Instr. Dale Carnegie Courses West Fla. Inst., Tampa, Scott Hitchcock & Assocs., Tampa, 1969—. Pres. U. South Fla. Parents Assn., Tampa, 1986-87. Mem. Fla. Bar Assn., Hillsborough County Bar Assn., Acad. of Fla. Trial Lawyers, Assn. of Trial Lawyers of Am., Masons (32d degree), Shriners, Phi Beta Kappa. Republican. Presbyterian. Avocations: jogging, road races, target shooting, fishing. Personal injury, Probate. Office: 200 N Pierce St Tampa FL 33602-5020 E-mail: doehler@mindspring.com

OETTING, ROGER H. lawyer; b. Ft. Wayne, Ind., Dec. 17, 1931; s. Martin W. and Valetta E. (Holman) O.; m. Marcia J. Highlands, Aug. 10, 1957; children: Richard H., Susan E., Catherine R. BBA, U. Mich., 1953, MBA, JD, U. Mich., 1956; LLM in Taxation, Georgetown U., 1958. Ptnr. Touche Ross & Co., Detroit, 1960-80, Warner Norcross & Judd LLP, Grand Rapids, Mich., 1980—. Adj. prof. taxation Grand Valley State U., 1984—. Past pres., dir. treas. Chamber Music Soc. Grand Rapids, 1980-89; past dir., treas. Opera Grand Rapids, 1980-87; dir. Porter Hills Presbyn. Village, 1989—, treas., 1990—. Fellow Am. Coll. Tax Lawyers; mem. State Bar Mich. (coun. fed. tax sect. 1991—), Grand Rapids Bar Assn. (chair fin. com. 1983—), Econ. Club (past treas., bd. dirs. 1982-91), Sugar Bush Assn. (dir., sec., treas. 1985—), Kent Country Club, Leland Yacht Club, Univ. Club (bd. dirs., treas.), Rotary (bd. dirs. 1989-93), Delta Kappa Epsilon. Corporate taxation, Taxation, general, Personal income taxation. Office: Warner Norcross & Judd LLP 900 Old Kent Bldg 111 Lyon St NW Grand Rapids MI 49503-2487

OETTINGER, JULIAN ALAN, lawyer, pharmacy company executive; BS, U. Ill., 1961; JD, Northwestern U., 1964. Bar: Ill. 1964. Atty. SEC, 1964-67, Walgreen Co., Deerfield, Ill., 1967-72, sr. atty., 1972-78, dir. law, 1978-89, v.p., gen. counsel, corp. sec., 1989-2000, sr. v.p., 2000—. General corporate, Real property, Securities. Office: Walgreen Co 200 Wilmot Rd Deerfield IL 60015-4616

OFFER, STUART JAY, lawyer; b. Seattle, June 2, 1943; m. Judith Spitzer, Aug. 29, 1970; children: Rebecca, Kathryn. BA, U. Wash., 1964; LLB, Columbia U., 1967. Bar: D.C. 1968, U.S. Tax Ct. 1968, Calif. 1972. Atty., advisor U.S. Tax Ct., Washington, 1967-68; assoc. Morrison & Foerster, LLP, San Francisco, 1972-76, ptnr., 1976—. Trustee Am. Tax Policy Inst. Served as capt. U.S. Army, 1968-72. Mem. ABA (chmn. taxation sect., corp. tax com. 1991-92, coun. dir. 1995-98, vice chair adminstrn. 1998-2000), Internat. Fiscal Assn., Am. Coll. Tax Counsel. Private international, Corporate taxation. Office: Morrison & Foerster LLP 425 Market St San Francisco CA 94105-2482 E-mail: soffer@mofo.com

OGDEN, DAVID WILLIAM, lawyer; b. Washington, Nov. 12, 1953; s. Horace Greeley and Elaine Celia (Condrell) O.; m. Wannett Smith, 1988; children: Jonathan Smith, Elaine Smith. BA summa cum laude, U. Pa., 1976; JD magna cum laude, Harvard U., 1981. Bar: D.C. 1983, Va. 1986, U.S. Dist. Ct. D.C. 1984, U.S. Dist. Ct. (ea. dist.) Va. 1988, U.S. Ct. Appeals (D.C. cir.) 1984, U.S. Ct. Appeals (4th cir.) 1986, U.S. Ct. Appeals (1st cir.) 1989, U.S. Ct. Appeals (10th cir.) 1991, U.S. Supreme Ct. 1987, U.S. Ct. Appeals (5th and 9th cirs.) 2000. Law clk. to presiding judge U.S. Dist. Ct. (so. dist.) N.Y., N.Y.C., 1981-82; law clk. to assoc. justice Harry A. Blackmun U.S. Supreme Ct., Washington, 1982-83; assoc. atty. Ennis, Friedman, Bersoff & Ewing, 1983-85; atty., ptnr. Ennis, Friedman & Bersoff, 1986-88, Jenner & Block, Washington, 1988-94; legal counsel, dep. gen. counsel U.S. DOD, 1994-95; assoc. dep. atty. gen. U.S. Dept. Justice, 1995-97, counselor to the atty. gen., 1997-98, chief of staff to atty. gen., 1998-99, acting asst. atty. gen. for civil divsn., 1999-2000, asst. atty. gen. for civil divsn., 2000-2001; ptnr. Wilmer, Cutler & Pickering, 2001—. Adj. prof. law Georgetown U. Law Ctr., 1992-95. Author: (with Jerald A. Jacobs) Legal Risk Management for Associations, 1995. Recipient Disting. Pub. Svc. medal Dept. Def., 1995, Atty. Gen.'s medallion, 1999, Edmund J. Randolph award in recognition of outstanding svc. to Dept. Justice, 2001. Mem. ABA, D.C. Bar Assn., Phi Beta Kappa. Democrat. Federal civil litigation, Constitutional, Appellate. Fax: 202 663-6363

OGDEN, HARRY PEOPLES, lawyer; b. Memphis, Jan. 30, 1949; s. Harry K. and Mary (Peoples) O.; m. Amy Inklebarger, Aug. 5, 1972; children: Emily Rebecca, Sarah Ruth, Stephen Robinson. BA, Rohdes Coll., 1971; JD, U. Tenn., 1975. Bar: Tenn. 1976, U.S. Dist. Ct. (we. dist.) Tenn. 1976, U.S Dist. Ct. (ea. dist.) Tenn. 1977, U.S. Dist. Ct. (mid. dist.) Tenn. 1987, U.S. Ct. Appeals (6th cir.) 1986, U.S. Supreme Ct. 1984. Tchr. English, Knoxville (Tenn.) City High Schs., 1971-73; law clk. to juedge, western sect. Tenn. Ct. Appeals, Memphis, 1975-76; sole practitioner Knoxville, 1977-79; mem., shareholder Egerton, McAfee, Armistead & Davis, P.C., 1980-88; shareholder Lewis, King, Krieg, Waldrop & Catron, P.C., 1990—. Spl. counsel Morton, Lewis, King & Krieg, Knoxville and Nashville, 1988-89; participant Tenn. Coll. Trial Advocacy, Knoxville, 1983; firm rep. Am. Law Firm Assn. Mem. alumni adv. coun. U. Tenn. Coll. Law, Knoxville, 1983-93; bd. dirs., officer Goodwill Industries, Knoxville, 1978—. Fellow Tenn. Bar Found.; mem. ATLA, ABA (litigation, torts and ins. practice sect.), Tenn. Bar Assn., Knoxville Bar Assn., Def. Rsch. Inst., Tenn. Def. Lawyers Assn., Tenn. Trial Lawyers Assn., Am. Inns of Ct. (master of the bench), LeConte Club (Knoxville). Presbyterian. Federal civil litigation, State civil litigation, Product liability. Home: 4704 Simona Dr Knoxville TN 37918-4534 Office: Lewis King et al One Centre Sq 5th Fl PO Box 2425 Knoxville TN 37901-2425 E-mail: hogden@lkkwc.com

OGDEN, JOHN HAMILTON, lawyer; b. Newport News, Va., Sept. 14, 1951; s. Donald Thomas and Bernice (Hamilton) O.; m. Mary Lynne Vogel, May 11, 1973; children: Amy Elizabeth, Christopher Michael, Andrew David. AB, Villanova U., 1973; JD, Fordham U., 1977. Bar: N.J. 1977, U.S. Dist. Ct. N.J. 1977, U.S. Ct. Internat. Trade 1990. Sr. buyer Consol. Edison of N.Y., N.Y.C., 1973-77; contract mgr. Jersey Cen. Power & Light, Morristown, N.J., 1977-80; atty. Foster Wheeler Corp., Livingston, 1980-83; gen. counsel Werner & Pfleiderer Corp., Ramsey, 1983—; corp. sec. Krupp, Werner & Pfleiderer Corp., 1989—; asst. sec., counsel Krupp USA Fin. Svcs. Inc., 1993-98; asst. sec. Krupp USA, Inc., 1998—. Recipient Profl. Lawyer of Yr. award N.J. Commn. on Professionalism in the Law, 1998. Mem. Am. Corp. Counsel Assn. (chair 1990-91, small law dept. subcom., chmn. small law dept. com. 1991-92, bd. dirs. 1991-98, sec. bd. dirs. 1994— chmn. edn. bd. com. 1992-94, exec. com. 1992-98, chair coun. nat. coms. 1994, sec. 1995, treas. 1996, vice chair 1997, founder and chair Leadership Devel. Inst. 1998—), N.J. Corp. Counsel Assn. (bd. dirs. 1992-96, v.p., sec. 1992-93, pres. 1994-95, past pres., editor, contbr. Small Law Department Practitioners Desk Manual, 1993), N.J. State Bar Found. (bd. trustees 1998—, pub. edn. com. 1995—). Contracts commercial, General corporate, Private international. Office: Werner & Pfleiderer Corp 663 E Crescent Ave Ramsey NJ 07446-1287

OGG, WILSON REID, lawyer, poet, retired judge, lyricist, curator, publisher, educator, philosopher, social scientist, parapsychologist; b. Alhambra, Calif., Feb. 26, 1928; s. James Brooks and Mary (Wilson) O. Student, Pasadena Jr. Coll., 1946; AB, U. Calif., Berkeley, 1949; JD, U. Calif., 1952; Cultural D in Philosophy of Law, World U. Roundtable, 1983. Bar: Calif. 1955. Assoc. trust dept. Wells Fargo Bank, San Francisco, 1954-55; pvt. practice Berkeley, 1955—. Adminstrv. law judge, 1974-93; real estate broker, cons., 1974—; curator-in-residence, Pinebrook, 1964—; owner Pinebrook Press, Berkeley, 1988—; rsch. atty., legal editor Dept. of Continuing Edn. of Bar U. Calif., 1958-63;instr. 25th Sta. Hosp., Taegu, Korea, 1954, Taegu English Lang. Inst., 1954; trustee World U., 1976-80; dir. admissions Internat. Soc. for Phil. Enquiry, 1981-84; dep. dir. gen. Internat. Biographical Ctr., England, 1986—; dep. gov. Am. Biographical Inst. Rsch. Assn., 1986—. Author: The Unified Theory; contbr. articles to profl. jours.; contbr. poems to mags. With AUS, 1952-54. Elected to Internat. Poetry Hall of Fame Nat. Libr. Poetry, 1997. Mem. VFW, AAAS, ABA, ASCAP, ACLU, Internat. Platform Assn., Internat. Soc. Unified Sci., Internat. Soc. Poets (life), Amnesty Internat., Internat. Soc. Individual Liberty, State Bar Calif., San Francisco Bar Assn., Am. Arbitration Assnl. (nat. panel arbitrators), Calif. Soc. Psychical Study (pres., chmn. bd. 1963-65), Intertel, Triple Nine Soc., Wisdom Soc., Inst. Noetic Scis., Men's Inner Circle of Achievement, Truman Libr. Inst. (hon.), Am. Legion, City Commons Club (Berkeley), Commonwealth Club of Calif., Town Hall Club Calif., Marines Meml. Club, Masons, Shriners, Elks. Unitarian. Constitutional, General practice, Probate. Home: Pinebrook 8 Bret Harte Way Berkeley CA 94708-1611 Office: 1104 Keith Ave Berkeley CA 94708-1607 also: 39231 Liberty St Fremont CA 94538-1501 Fax: 510-540-6052. E-mail: wilsonogg@home.com

O'GRADY, DENNIS JOSEPH, lawyer; b. Hoboken, N.J., Nov. 16, 1943; s. Joseph A. and Eileen (Broderick) O'Grady; m. Mary Anne Amoruso, Sept. 9, 1966 (div. Apr. 1984); 1 child, Kara Anne. AB, Seton Hall Coll., 1965; MA, U. So. Calif., 1969; JD, Rutgers U., 1973. Bar: N.J. 1973, U.S. Ct. Appeals (3d cir.) 1975, U.S. Dist. Ct. N.J. Ptnr. Riker, Danzig, Scherer, Hyland & Perretti, Newark, Trenton and Morristown, N.J., 1974—. Adj. asst. prof. of bus. law St. Peter's Coll., Jersey City, 1973—; adj. prof. law Rutgers U. Law Sch., 1997—. Mem. ABA (bus./bankruptcy sect.), N.J. State Bar Assn. (debtor/creditor sect.), Fed. Bar Assn., Am. Bankruptcy Inst. (health car subcom., bd. profl. cert.), Am. Bd. Cert. (faculty subcom.). Democrat. Roman Catholic. Banking, Bankruptcy, General civil litigation. Office: Riker Danzig Scherer Hyland & Perretti 1 Speedwell Ave Ste 2 Morristown NJ 07960-6823 E-mail: dogrady@riker.com

OH, MATTHEW INSOO, lawyer; b. Seoul, Republic of Korea, Aug. 5, 1938; s. Young Whan and Jeom-soon (Kim) Oh; m. Young Ok, May 24, 1973; children: John Z., Amy J. LLB, Seoul Nat. U., 1963, LLM, 1968, Columbia U., 1972; JD, William Mitchell Coll. Law, St. Paul, 1982. Bar: Minn. 1982, N.Y. 1988, D.C. 1989. Sr. planning researcher Ministry of Constrn., Seoul, 1968-71; planner Altamaha, Ga. Regional Planning Commn., 1972-74; sole practice St. Paul, 1982—. Mem. North Korea Human Rights Project, Mpls., 1985-87; chmn. State of Minn. Coun. on Asian-Pacific Rels., St. Paul, 1985-86; v.p. Minn. Asian Advocacy Coalition, St. Paul, 1983-85; bd. dirs. Urban Concern Workshop, Inc., St. Paul, 1985-86. Fulbright fellow Fulbright Commn., Seoul, 1971; recipient Yogi Berra award, Ramsey County Bar Assn. Mem. D.C. Bar Assn., Am. Immigration Lawyers Assn. Presbyterian. Immigration, naturalization, and customs, Private international. Home: 9 Woodhill Ln Saint Paul MN 55127-2140 Office: 1130 Minn World Trade Ctr 325 Cedar St Ste 812 Saint Paul MN 55101

OH, SEUNG JONG, lawyer, law educator; b. Seoul, Oct. 21, 1959; s. Dong Il Oh and Eun Sook Kim; m. Hae Won Yoon; children: Min Jeong, Min Seong. LLB, Seoul Nat. U., 1981; LLM, Columbia U., 1995. Judge Seoul Dist. Ct., 1987-99; judge, prof. Jud. Rsch. and Tng. Inst., Seoul, 1997-99; prof. law Syngkyunkwan U., 1999—; lawyer C.J. Internat. Law Offices, 1999—. Author: Patent Law, 1998, Copyright Law, 1999. With armed forces, 1981-82. Fellow Korea Intellectual Proptery Law Inst. Patent, Trademark and copyright. Office: CJ Internat Law Offices 51-5 Daedong BD Banpo 4 Seocho-gu 137-044 Seoul Republic of Korea Fax: 82-2-536-7455. E-mail: osj@cjintl.co.kr

O'HAIRE, MICHAEL, lawyer; b. Buffalo, Feb. 8, 1939; s. John and Beatrice C. A. (McCaffery) O'H; m. Shirley Smith, Feb. 1, 1958; children: Sean Michael, Meghan O'Haire Candler, Deirdre Kloski. Bar: Fla. 1963, U.S. Dist. Ct. (so. dist.) Fla. 1964, U.S. Tax Ct. 1969, U.S. Ct. Appeals (5th and 11th cirs.) 1964. Assoc. Smith, Heath & Smith, Vero Beach, Fla., 1963-67; ptnr. Smith, Heath, Smith & O'Haire, 1967-73; exec. v.p., mng. dir. John's Island Co., 1973-76; ptnr. Smith, O'Haire, Quinn & Smith, 1976-93, O'Haire, Quinn, Candler & O'Haire, Vero Beach, 1993—. Mem. Indian River County Real Property Coun., Indian River County Estate Planning Coun., Community Assn. Inst. Mem. ABA, Fla. Bar Assn., Indian River County Bar Assn. Democrat. Episcopalian. Avocation: sailing. State civil litigation, Probate, Real property. Home: PO Box 3674 Vero Beach FL 32964-3674 Office: O'Haire Quinn el al 3111 Cardinal Dr Vero Beach FL 32963-1920 E-mail: moh@oqc-law.com

O'HARA, MICHAEL JAMES, law educator, researcher; b. Feb. 4, 1953; s. Edward Richard and Eileen Mary (Friel) O.; m. Mary Catherine Cortese, June 1, 1981. BA in Sociology, U. Nebr., 1975; JD, 1978, MA in Econs., 1979, PhD in Econs., 1983. Bar: Nebr. 1978, U.S. Dist. Ct. Nebr. 1978. Rsch. asst. S.E. Nebr. Health Sys. Agy. Lincoln, 1979; legis. aide State of Nebr., 1979-81; instr. econs. U. Nebr., Omaha, 1981-82; asst. prof. law, 1982-88; assoc. prof. law, 1988-2001; prof., 2001—. Interim dir. Internat. Ctr. Telecommunications Mgmt. U. Nebr. at Omaha, 1991-92. Contbr. articles to profl. jours. Econs. advisor 2nd Congl. Dist. Campaign, Omaha, 1984; mem. Nebr. Power Rev. Bd., 1985-89; bd. dirs. Omaha Pub. Power Dist., 1990-94, sec. 1990-92, v. chair 1993; mem. State Ctrl. Com. Nebr. Dem. Com., 1990-96; mem. adv. group LR 455 (resolution to study how Nebr. will deregulate electric utilities), 1996-99; bd. dirs. Corcord Ctr., 1999—, v.p., 2001-. Mem. ABA (intellectual property law sect., sci. and tech. sect., task force on iniform distbn. practices act), Am. Econs. Assn., Nat. Assn. Forensic Econs., Am. Acad. Econ. Fin. Experts, Nat. Gov.'s Assn. (task force on electricity transmission), Omicron Delta Epsilon, Beta Gamma Sigma. Home: 8081 Dorcas St Omaha NE 68124-2240 Office: Univ Nebr at Omaha 60th And Dodge St Omaha NE 68182-0001 E-mail: mohara@unomaha.edu

O'HARA, PATRICIA A. dean, law educator; BA summa cum laude, Santa Clara U., 1971; JD summa cum laude, Notre Dame, 1974. Bar: Calif. 1974. Assoc. Brobeck, Phleger & Harrison, 1974—79, 1980—81; assoc. prof. law Notre Dame Law Sch., 1981, prof., 1990, v.p. student affairs, 1990—99, dean, law educator, 2001—. Contbr. chapters to books, articles to law jours. . Office: U Notre Dame 203 Law Sch PO Box R Notre Dame IN 46556 Office Fax: 219-631-8400. E-mail: Patricia.A.O'Hara.3@nd.edu*

O'HEARN, MICHAEL JOHN, lawyer; b. Akron, Ohio, Jan. 29, 1952; s. Leo Ambrose and Margaret Elizabeth (Clark) O'H. BA in Econs., UCLA, 1975; postgrad., U. San Diego, 1977; JD, San Fernando Valley Coll. Law, 1979; postgrad., Holy Apostles Sem., 1993-94. Bar: Calif. 1979, U.S. Dist. Ct. (ctrl. dist.) Calif. 1979. Document analyst Mellonics Info. Ctr., Litton Industries, Canoga Park, Calif., 1977-79; pvt. practice Encino, 1979-80; atty. VISTA/Grey Law Inc., L.A., 1980-81; assoc. Donald E. Chadwick & Assocs., Woodland Hills, Calif., 1981-84, Law Offices of Laurence Ring, Beverly Hills, 1984-85; atty., in-house counsel Coastal Ins. Co., Van Nuys, 1985-89; atty. Citrus Glen Apts., Ventura, 1989-92; pvt. practice Ventura County, 1992-2000; arbitrator, 1995—; propr., property mgr. Channel Islands Village Mgmt. Co., 1998-2000. Life mem. Rep. Nat. Com. Recipient Cert. of Appreciation, Agy. for Vol. Svc., 1981, San Fernando Valley Walk for Life, 1988, Cert. of Appreciation, Arbitrator for the Superior and Mcpl. Cts., Ventura County Jud. Dist., 1996. Mem. KC, Ventura County Bar Assn., Ventura County Trial Lawyers Assn., Secular Franciscan Order., Pioneer Total Abstinence Assn. of the Sacred Heart. Republican. Roman Catholic. Avocations: golf, yachting, fishing. Estate planning, Insurance, Personal injury. Home: 1941 Fisher Dr Apt B Oxnard CA 93035-3022 Office: 3650 Ketch Ave Oxnard CA 93035-3029 E-mail: mohearn_brightstar@yahoo.com

O'HERN, DANIEL JOSEPH, retired state supreme court justice; b. Red Bank, N.J., May 23, 1930; s. J. Henry and Eugenia A. (Sansone) O'H.; m. Barbara Ronan, Aug. 8, 1959; children: Daniel J., Eileen, James, John, Molly. AB, Fordham Coll., 1951; LLB, Harvard U., 1957. Bar: N.J. 1958. Clk. U.S. Supreme Ct., Washington, 1957-58; assoc. Abramoff, Apy & O'Hern, Red Bank, N.J., 1966-78; commr. N.J. Dept. Environ. Protection, 1978-79; counsel to Gov. N.J. Trenton; assoc. justice N.J. Supreme Ct., Trenton, 1981—2000; counsel Gibbons, Del Deo, Dolan, Griffinger & Vecchione, Newark, 2000—. Former mem. adv. com. profl. ethics N.J. Supreme Ct. Past trustee Legal Aid Soc. Monmouth County, (N.J.); mayor Borough of Red Bank, 1969-78, councilman, 1962-69. Served as lt. (j.g.) USNR, 1951-54. Fellow Am. Bar Found.; mem. ABA, N.J. Bar Assn., Monmouth County Bar Assn., Harvard Law Sch. Assn. N.J. (past pres.) Office: NJ Supreme Ct 151 Bodman Pl Red Bank NJ 07701-1070 also: NJ Supreme Ct PO Box 970 Trenton NJ 08625-0970 Office: Gibbons Del Deo Dolan et al One Riverfront Plaza Newark NJ 07102

OHLGREN, JOEL R. lawyer; b. Mpls., July 21, 1942; BA, UCLA, 1965, JD, 1968. Bar: Calif. 1969. Ptnr. Sheppard, Mullin, Richter & Hampton LLP, L.A. Fellow Am. Coll. Bankruptcy; mem. ABA, State Bar Calif., Los Angeles County Bar Assn. (past chmn. comml. law and bankruptcy sect.), Order of Coif. Bankruptcy, Consumer commercial. Office: Sheppard Mullin Richter & Hampton LLP 333 S Hope St Fl 48 Los Angeles CA 90071-1406

O'KEEFE, KEVIN MICHAEL, lawyer; b. Vincennes, Ind., Sept. 24, 1946; s. Roy Daniel and Mildred (Pawlak) O'K.; m. Margaret Yvonne Green, Sept. 25, 1971; children— Kathleen, Kelly. B.S. in Communications, U. Ill., 1969; J.D., Ill. Inst. Tech., 1973. Bar: Ill. 1973, Fla. 1974. Assoc. O'Keefe, Ashenden, Lyons & Ward, Chgo., 1973-76; ptnr., 1976—; bd. dirs. Healthcorp Affiliates, Naperville, Ill. Bd. dirs. Central DuPage Hosp., Winfield, Ill., 1981—, B.R. Ryall YMCA, Glen Ellyn, Ill., 1979-81. Mem. Inst. Property Taxation, Internat. Assn. Assessing Officers. Democrat. Roman Catholic. State and local taxation. Home: 45 E Bellevue Pl Chicago IL 60611-1133 Office: O'Keefe Ashenden Lyons & Ward 1 1st National Plaza Suite 5100 Chicago IL 60603

O'KEEFE, RAYMOND PETER, lawyer, educator; b. N.Y.C., Jan. 16, 1928; s. William Bernard and Catherine Irene (Smith) O'K.; m. Stephanie Ann Fitzpatrick, June 19, 1954; children: Raymond, William, Ann, Kevin, Mary, James, John. A.B. cum laude, St. Michael's Coll., 1950; J.D., Fordham U., 1953. Bar: N.Y. 1954, U.S. Dist. Ct. (so. dist.) N.Y. 1955, U.S. Ct. Claims 1960, U.S. Ct. Appeals (2d cir.) 1963, U.S. Supreme Ct. 1971, Fla. 1976. Assoc. Thayer & Gilbert, N.Y.C., 1953-55; prof. law Fordham U. Sch. Law, N.Y.C., 1955-63; sr. assoc. Carter, Ledyard & Milburn, N.Y.C., 1963-68; ptnr. Ide & Haigney, N.Y.C., 1968-74; sr. ptnr. McCarthy, Fingar, Donovan, Drazen & Smith, White Plains, N.Y., 1974—; adj. prof. law Pace U. Sch. Law, White Plains, 1979—, Fordham U. Sch. Law, 1983—; lectr. N.Y. Med. Coll., Valhalla, N.Y., 1979—; prof. law St. Thomas of Villanova Miami Sch. Law, 1984—; vis. prof. law Thomas M. Cooley Sch. Law, Lansing, 1991, Fordham U. Sch. Law, 1992; justice of Justice Ct. State of N.Y., 1978-81. Trustee Am. Irish Hist. Soc.; chmn. bd. Westchester Halfway House, 1974-78; bd. dirs. Westchester Youth Shelter, 1980. Served with USN, 1945-48. Recipient Alumni award St. Michael's Coll., 1961. Mem. ABA (commn. on youth, drugs and alcoholism 1984), N.Y. State Bar Assn. (chmn. spl. com. on lawyer alcoholism and drug abuse 1979—), Fla. Bar, Assn. Trial Lawyers Am., N.Y. State Trial Lawyers Assn., Assn. of Bar of City of N.Y. Clubs: Larchmont (N.Y.) Shore; Harbor View (N.Y.C.), Surf (Miami). General practice. Home: 802 Kure Village Way Kure Beach NC 28449-4900 Office: St Thomas Law Sch 16400 NE 32nd Ave Miami FL 33160

O'KELLEY, WILLIAM CLARK, federal judge; b. Atlanta, Jan. 2, 1930; s. Ezra Clark and Theo (Johnson) O'K.; m. Ernestine Allen, Mar. 28, 1953; children: Virginia Leigh O'Kelley Wood, William Clark Jr. AB, Emory U., 1951, LLB, 1953. Bar: Ga. 1952. Pvt. practice, Atlanta, 1957-59; asst. U.S. atty. No. Dist. Ga., 1959-61; partner O'Kelley, Hopkins & Van Gerpen, Atlanta, 1961-70; U.S. dist. judge No. Dist. Ga., 1970—, chief judge, 1988-94. Mem. com. on adminstrn. of criminal law Jud. Conf. U.S., 1979-82, exec. com., 1983-84, subcom. on jury trials in complex criminal cases, 1981-82, dist. judge rep. 11th cir., 1981-84, mem. adv. com. of fed. rules of criminal procedure, 1984-87; bd. dirs. Fed. Jud. Ctr., 1987-91, adv. com. history program, 1989-91, com. on orientation of newly appointed dist. judges, 1985-88; mem. Com. Jud. Resources, 1989-94; mem. Jud. Coun. 11th Cir., 1990-96, exec. com., 1990-96; mem. Fgn. Intelligence Surveillance Ct., 1980-87; mem. Alien Terrorist Removal Ct., 1996—; corp. sec., dir. Gwinnett Bank & Trust Co., Norcross, Ga., 1967-70. Mem. exec. com., gen. counsel Ga. Republican Com., 1968-70; mem. fin. com. Northwest Ga. Girl Scout Coun., 1958-70; trustee Emory U., 1991-97. Served as 1st lt. USAF, 1953-57; capt. USAFR. Mem. Fed. Bar Assn., Ga. State Bar, Atlanta Bar Assn., Dist. Judges Assn. 5th Cir. (sec.-treas. 1976-77, v.p. 1977-78, pres. 1978-80), Lawyers Club Atlanta, Kiwanis (past pres.), Atlanta Athletic Club, Sigma Chi (named Significant Sig 1983), Phi Delta Phi, Omicron Delta Kappa. Baptist. Home: 550 Ridgecrest Dr Norcross GA 30071-2158 Office: US Dist Ct 1942 US Courthouse 75 Spring St SW Atlanta GA 30303-3309

OKINAGA, CARRIE KIYONO, lawyer; b. Honolulu, Sept. 9, 1967; d. Lawrence Shoji and Carolyn (Hisako) O.; m. Scott Wai Hin Seu, Nov. 14, 1998. BA, Pomona Coll., 1989; JD, Stanford U., 1992. Bar: Calif., Hawaii, 1993; U.S. Dist. Ct. Hawaii, 1993. Ptnr. McCorriston, Miller Mukai MacKinnon LLP, Honolulu, 1992—. Asst. editor: (newsletter) The Affiliate, 1998. Mem. P.A.R.E.N.T.S., 1994-98. Pacific Century fellow, Honolulu, 1998-99. Mem. ABA (dist. rep. young lawyers divsn. 1996-98, vice-chair minorities in the profession com. 1997-99, liaison to sect. labor and employment law 1999-2000, asst editor The Affiliate 1998), Hawaii State Bar Assn. (bd. dirs. young lawyers divsn. 1995-99). Office: McCorriston Miller Mukai MacKinnon LLP Five Waterfront Plz 4th Fl 500 Ala Moana Blvd Honolulu HI 96813-4989 E-mail: okinaga@m4law.com

OKINAGA, LAWRENCE SHOJI, lawyer; b. Honolulu, July 7, 1941; s. Shohei and Hatsu (Kakimoto) O.; m. Carolyn Hisako Uesugi, Nov. 26, 1966; children: Carrie, Caryn, Laurie. BA, U. Hawaii, 1963; JD, Georgetown U., 1972. Bar: Hawaii 1972, U.S. Dist. Ct. Hawaii 1972, U.S. Ct. Appeals (9th cir.) 1976. Adminstrv. asst. to Congressman Spark Matsunaga, Honolulu, 1964, 65-69; law clk. to chief judge U.S. Dist. Ct. Hawaii, 1972-73; assoc. Carlsmith Ball, 1973-76, ptnr., 1976—. Mem. Gov.'s Citizens Adv. Com. Coastal Zone Mgmt., 1974-79; sec. Hawaii Bicentennial Corp., 1975-77, chmn., 1985-87, vice chmn., 1983-85; mem. Jud. Selection Commn., State of Hawaii, 1979-87, vice chmn., 1986; mem. consumer adv. coun. Fed. Res. Bd., 1984-86; chmn. State of Hawaii Jud. Conduct Commn., 1991-94; apptd. mem. Fed. Savings and Loan Adv. Council, Washington, 1988-89; mem. nat. adv. coun. U.S. Small Bus. Adminstrn., 1994-2000; mem. adv. coun. Fed. Res. Bank of San Francisco, 1995—. Bd. dirs. Moiliili Cmty. Ctr., Honolulu, 1965-68, 73-86, trustee 1993—; bd. visitors Georgetown U. Law Ctr., 1993—; trustee Kuakini Med. Ctr., 1984-88, 89-96. Capt. USAFR, 1964-72, 74-76. Mem. ABA (ho. of dels. 1991-94, standing com. on jud. selection tenure and compensation 1993-96, standing com. on jud. independence 1999—), Hawaii Bar Assn. (sec., bd. dirs. 1981), Am. Judicature Soc. (bd. dirs. 1986—, treas. 1995-97, pres. 1997-99), Georgetown U. Law Alumni Assn. (bd. dirs. 1986-91), Omicron Delta Kappa. Banking, General corporate, Real property. Office: Carlsmith Ball PO Box 656 Honolulu HI 96809-0656

OKUMA-SEPE, CHERYL, lawyer; b. Honolulu, Apr. 16, 1955; d. S. Raymond and Joanne M. Okuma; m. Donald M. Sepe. BA, U. Hawaii, 1977; JD, Calif. Western Sch. Law, 1980. Pvt. practice, Honolulu, 1980-1986; mgmt. analyst U.S. Army, West Germany, 1987-1989; dep. corporation counsel Dept. Corporation Counsel, Honolulu, 1989-1994; dep. dir. Dept. Wastewater Mgmt., 1994-1998, Dept. Environ. Services, Honolulu, 1998-1999; first dep. Dep. Corporation Counsel, 1999-2000; dir. Dept. Human Resources, 2001—. Mem. Hawaii United Okinawan Assn., Nat. Assn. Women in Constrn. (pres.), Am. Planners Assn., Hawaii Water Environment Assn., Hawaii Women's Lawyers Assn. Office: Dept Human Resources Ste 550 715 S King St Honolulu HI 96813 E-mail: cokumasepe@co.honolulu.hi.us

OLASOV, DAVID MICHAEL, lawyer; b. Charleston, S.C., July 7, 1945; s. Bernard Jason and Harriet Jean (Tigler) O.; m. Sharon Marie Spellman, Aug. 13, 1977; children: Jacob, Michael, Ian. AB, Columbia U., 1967; LLB, Yale U., 1970. Bar: N.Y. 1971. Assoc. Sullivan & Cromwell, N.Y.C., 1970-79; ptnr. Edwards & Angell, N.Y.C., 1980-93, ptnr. in charge N.Y. office, 1983-88; ptnr. Winick & Rich, N.Y.C., 1993—. Mem. ABA, Assn. of Bar of City of N.Y., N.Y. State Bar Assn. Federal civil litigation, State civil litigation, Private international. Office: 919 3rd Ave New York NY 10022-3902

OLDENBURG, RONALD TROY, lawyer; b. Eldora, Iowa, June 2, 1935; s. Lorenz Frank and Bess Louise (Lewis) O.; m. Vickie Yu; children: John, Keith, Mark. BA, U. N.C., 1957; postgrad., Brunnsvik Folkhogskola, Sorvik, Sweden, 1957-58; JD, U. Miss., 1961. Bar: Miss. 1961, Hawaii 1975. Mgr. Continental Travel Svc., Chapel Hill, N.C., 1956-57, Meridian Travel Svc., Raleigh, 1961, Linmark Internat. Devel., Seoul, 1972-74; fgn. atty. Li Chun Law Office, Taipei, Taiwan, 1965-67; pvt. practice, 1967-72, Honolulu, 1975—. Compiler: International Directory of Birth, Death, Marriage and Divorce Records, 1985; contbr. articles on immigration law to legal jours. Capt. JAGC, USAF, 1962-65. Mem. Am. Immigration Lawyers Assn. E-mail:. Immigration, naturalization, and customs. Office: 700 Bishop St Ste 2100 Honolulu HI 96813-3215 Also: 94-229 Waipahu Depot Rd Ste 204 Waipahu HI 96797

OLDFIELD, E. LAWRENCE, lawyer; b. Lake Forest, Ill., Dec. 21, 1944; s. W. Ernest and Evelyn Charlotte (Gyllenberg) O.; m. Kaaren Elaine Sabey, Aug. 24, 1974; 1 stepchild, Kimberly Jo; 1 child, Lauren Elizabeth. Student, L.I. U., 1961-62, Wheaton Coll., 1962-64, Near East Sch. Archeology, Jordan, 1964; BA in Polit. Sci., No. Ill. U., 1969; JD, DePaul U., 1973. Bar: Ill. 1973, U.S. Dist. Ct. (no. dist.) Ill. 1973, U.S. Ct. Appeals (7th cir.) 1974, U.S. Supreme Ct. 1979, U.S. Ct. Appeals (3d cir.) 1985, U.S. Ct. Appeals (10th cir.) 1986, U.S. Ct. Appeals (8th cir.) 1990. Fed. agt. Dept. HUD, 1969-70; assoc. Ruff & Grotefeld Ltd., Chgo., 1973-77; gen. counsel livestock dept. Hartford Fire Ins. Co., 1977-87; prin. E. Lawrence Oldfield & Assocs., Oak Brook, 1987-2000, Oldfield & Fox, P.C., Oak Brook, 2000—. Mediator, arbitrator U.S. Arbitration and Mediation, 1994-97, Resolute Systems, Inc., 1997—. Dir. Edgewater Cmty. Coun., 1973-74; precinct capt. 50th Ward Dems., 1974-77; trustee North Shore Bapt. Ch., 1974-77, chmn. constn. com., 1976-77; dir. Chgo. Bapt. Assn., 1974-77, treas., 1976-77; dir. Ctrl. Bapt. Children's Home, 1978-81, chmn. personel com., 1980-81, deacon, 1981-83, chmn. bd. deacons, 1983, First Presbyn. Ch. Glen Ellen, 1983-84; dir. Chgo. Bible Soc., 1980-84; v.p., 1983-84; trustee Village of Glen Ellyn, 1981-85; committeeman Milton Twp., DuPage County Reps., Wheaton, Ill., 1985-88; publicity chmn. Milton Twp. Reps., Wheaton, 1986-88; mem. Dist. 41 Sch. Bd., 1991-95; elder Christ Ch. of Oak Brook, 1993-2000; bd. govs. Execs. Breakfast Club of Oak Brook 1993—, 1st v.p., 1997-99, pres., 1999-2001. Served in U.S. Army, 1964-67. Mem. ABA, Ill. State Bar Assn., Chgo. Bar Assn., DuPage County Bar Assn., West Suburban Bar Assn., Ill. Trial Lawyers' Assn., Assn. Trial Lawyers Am., U.S. Golf Assn., Safari Club Internat., Wheaton Comty. Radio Amateurs, Am. Legion, VFW, Kiwanis, Moose, Masons, Shriners (mem. sec. 1998-2001), Jesters, Elks. Avocations: fishing, hunting, golf, amateur radio, chess. General civil litigation, General corporate, General practice. Home: 1050 Crescent Blvd Glen Ellyn IL 60137-4276 Office: Oldfield & Fox PC 2021 Midwest Rd Ste 201 Oak Brook IL 60523-1367 also: 30 N Lasalle St Ste 1524 Chicago IL 60602-2502 also: 1622 W Colonial Pkwy Palatine IL 60067-4795 E-mail: eloesq@oldfieldfox.com

OLDMAN, OLIVER, law educator; b. N.Y.C., July 19, 1920; s. Max and Rose (Meyers) O.; m. Barbara Lublin, May 2, 1943; children: Andrew, Margaret, Michele. Grad., Mercersburg Acad., 1938; S.B., Harvard, 1942, LL.B., 1953. Bar: N.Y. 1953, Mass. 1959. Jr. economist OPA, 1942; instr. econs. U. Buffalo, 1946-50; v.p. Lublin Constrn. Co., 1946-50; asso. firm Hodgson, Russ, Andrews, Woods & Goodyear, Buffalo, 1953-55; dir. tng. internat. tax program Law Sch. Harvard U., 1955-64, dir. internat. tax program Law Sch., 1964-89, prof. law, 1961-76, Learned Hand prof. law, 1976-93, dir. East Asian Legal Studies Law Sch., 1981-90, emeritus, 1993—. Cons. on taxation Govts. of Argentina, Bolivia, Chile, Colombia, Egypt, El Salvador, Ethiopia, Indonesia, Jamaica, Senegal, Venezuela, Mass., N.Y., N.H., N.Y.C., R.I. and, UN Secretariat; sr. advisor Lincoln Inst. of Land Policy, 1989—. Author: (with others) The Fiscal System of Venezuela, 1959, Financing Urban Development in Mexico City, 1967; Editor: (with R. Bird) Readings on Taxation in Developing Countries, 1964, rev. edit., 1967, 3d edit., 1975, 4th edit., 1990, (with P. Kelley) Readings on Income Tax Administration, 1973, (with F.P. Schoettle) State and Local Taxes and Finance, 1974, (with R.D. Pomp) State and Local Taxation, 3d edit., 2000, (with A. Schenk) Value Added Taxation, 2001. Served to 1st lt. AUS, 1943-46. Mem. ABA (com. on value added taxation 1990—, chmn. adv. bd. tax notes internat. 1989—), Nat. Tax Assn., Am. Econ. Assn., Pacific Cmty. Legal Rsch. Seminar (founder). Home: 33 Linnaean St # 4 Cambridge MA 02138-1511 Office: Harvard U Law Sch AR 332 Cambridge MA 02138

O'LEARY, DANIEL BRIAN, lawyer, educator; b. May 20, 1947; s. John Patrick and Cecilia Frances (May) O'Leary; m. Patricia Anne Adams, June 22, 1974. BA, U. Minn., 1972; JD, William Mitchell Coll. Law, 1976. Bar: Minn. 1976, U.S. Dist. Ct. Minn. 1977. Assoc. Mansur & Mansur, St. Paul, 1976—81; ptnr. Mansur O'Leary & Gabriel, P.S., 1981—96, Mansur & O'Leary, P.A., St. Paul, 1996—. Adj. prof. William Mitchell Coll. Law, St. Paul, 1981—90; mem. charter commn. West St. Paul, Minn., 1984—90, 2001—. Mem.: ABA, Assn. Trial Lawyers Am., Minn. Trial Lawyers Assn. (bd. govs. 1976—). Roman Catholic. State civil litigation, Personal injury, Workers' compensation. Home: 1660 Humboldt Ave Saint Paul MN 55118-3905

O'LEARY, DANIEL VINCENT, JR. lawyer; b. Bklyn., May 26, 1942; s. Daniel Vincent and Mary (Maxwell) O'L.; m. Marilyn Irene Gavigan, June 1, 1968; children: Daniel, Katherine, Molly, James. AB cum laude, Georgetown U., 1963; LLB, Yale U., 1966. Bar: Ill. 1967. Assoc. Wilson & Mc Ilvaine, Chgo., 1967-75, ptnr., 1975-1987, Peterson & Ross, Chgo., 1987-94, Schwartz & Freeman, Chgo., 1994-95; of counsel Mandell, Menkes & Surdyk, LLC. Pres., bd. dirs. Jim's Cayman Co., Ltd.; pres. TV and Radio Purchasing Group Inc.; asst. sec. L.M.C. Ins. Co. Bermuda, 1990—; pres. Wagering Ins. N.Am. Purchasing Group Inc., 1997—. Lt. comdr. USNR, ret. Mem. Kenilworth Sailing Club (commodore 1985-87). Roman Catholic. Avocations: fishing, scuba diving. Office: Mandel Menkes & Surdyk LLC Ste 300 333 W Wacker Dr Chicago IL 60606 E-mail: doleary@mms-law.net

O'LEARY, THOMAS MICHAEL, lawyer; b. N.Y.C., Aug. 16, 1948; s. James and Julia Ann (Connolly) O'L.; m. Luise Ann Williams, Jan. 13, 1978; 1 child, Richard Meridith. BA, CUNY, 1974; JD, Seattle U., 1977. Bar: Wash. 1977, U.S. Ct. Mil. Appeals 1978, U.S. Ct. Appeals (9th cir.), U.S. Supreme Ct. 1983. Dep. pros. atty. Pierce County, Tacoma, 1978; commd. 1st lt. U.S. Army, 1978, advanced through grades to capt., 1978; chief trial counsel Office of Staff Judge Adv., Ft. Polk, La., 1978-79, trial def. counsel, trial def. svc., 1979-81; chief legal advisor Office Insp. Gen., Heidelberg, Fed. Republic of Germany, 1981-82; sr. def. counsel Trial Def. Svc., Giessen, Fed. Republic of Germany, 1982-84; asst. chief adminstrv. law U.S. Army Armor Ctr., Ft. Knox, Ky., 1984-85, chief adminstrv. law, 1985, chief legal asst., 1985-86; ret. U.S. Army, 1996; sr. trial atty. Immigration and naturalization Svc., Phoenix, 1987; sector counsel, spl. asst. U.S. atty., U.S. Border Patrol, Tucson, 1987-90; enforcement counsel U.S. Immigration and Naturalization Svc., 1990-95, asst. dist. counsel Phoenix litigation, 1995-97. Apptd. U.S. Immigration Judge, U.S. Immigration Ct., Imperial, Calif., 1997-2000, apptd. sr. U.S. Immigration Judge, Tucson, 2000—. Decorated Purple Heart, Cross of Gallantry (Vietnam). Mem. Judge Advs Assn., Wash. State Bar Assn. E-mail: Thomas.O'Leary@usdoj.gov. Administrative and regulatory, Immigration, naturalization, and customs, Military. Home: 9080 E 25th St Tucson AZ 85710-8675 Office: US Immigration Ct 1705 E Hanna Rd Ste 366 Eloy AZ 85231-9612

OLEISKY, ROBERT EDWARD, lawyer; b. Mpls., Nov. 23, 1966; s. Allen L. and Marcia E. O. BA, U. Minn., 1989; JD, Hamline U., 1992. Bar: Minn. 1992. Atty. Oleisky & Oleisky P.A., Mpls., 1993—. Bd. dirs. Jewish Family & Children's Svcs., Mpls., 1998-99, vol., 1995-98. Mem. Minn. Assn. Criminal Defense Lawyersm Douglas Andahl Inn of Ct. Democrat. Avocations: basketball, softball, rollerblading, movies, volunteer work. Criminal, Juvenile. Office: Oleisky & Oleisky PA 250 2d Ave S #225 Minneapolis MN 55401

OLEJKO, MITCHELL J. lawyer; b. Jersey City, June 15, 1951; s. Frank Edward and Eugenia Joan Olejko; m. Jill Wolcott, Aug. 5, 1988. AB, Boston Coll., 1973; JD, Washington U., St. Louis, 1977. Bar: Wash. 1977, Oreg. 1992, Calif. 1998, U.S. Dist. Ct. (we. dist.) Wash. 1977, (ea. dist.) Wash. 1978, U.S. Dist. Ct. Oreg. 1992, U.S. Ct. Appeals (9th cir.) 1980, U.S. Dist. Ct. (no. dist.) Calif. 1999. Assoc. Davis, Wright, Todd, Riese & Jones, Seattle, 1977-82; ptnr. Davis, Wright & Jones, 1982-92; chief legal officer, sr. v.p. Legacy Health System, Portland, Oreg., 1992-98; ptnr. Morrison & Foerster, San Francisco, 1998—. Contbr. Ambulatory Care Management, 2d edit., 1991. Mem. Am. Acad. Hosp. Attys., Wash. State Soc. Hosp. Attys. (pres. 1991-92). General corporate, Health, Non-profit and tax-exempt organizations. Office: Morrison & Foerster 425 Market St San Francisco CA 94105-2482

OLENDER, JACK HARVEY, lawyer; b. McKeesport, Pa., Sept. 8, 1935; m. Lovell Olender. BA, U. Pitts., 1957, JD, 1960; LLM, George Washington U., 1961. Bar: D.C. 1961, U.S. Supreme Ct. 1965, Md. 1966, Pa. 1985; diplomate Am. Bd. Trial Advocates,Inner Cir. Advocates. Pvt. practice, Washington, 1961-79; prin. Jack H. Olender & Assocs., P.C., 1979—. Contbr. articles to profl. jours. Active World Peace through Law, Washington. Named to Hall of Fame Nat. Assn. Black Women Attys., 1987, D.C. Hall of Fame, 2000, Washington Bar Assn. Hall of Fame, 2000; recipient Presdl. award Nat. Bar Assn., 1996, Advocate for Justice award Nat. Bar Assn., 2000. Fellow Am. Coll. Trial Lawyers, Internat. Acad. Trial Lawyers and Inner Cir. Advs.; mem. ATLA, Nat. Bar Assn. (adv. for justice 2000), Am. Bd. Profl. Liability Attys. (bd. dirs.), Trial Lawyers Pub. Justice (bd. dirs.), Internat. Assn. Jewish Lawyers and Jurists (bd. dirs.), Bar Assn. of D.C. (pres. 1999-2000). Personal injury. Office: Jack H Olender & Assocs PC 888 17th St NW Fl 4 Washington DC 20006-3939

OLIAN, ROBERT MARTIN, lawyer; b. Cleve., June 14, 1953; s. Robert Meade and Doris Isa (Hessing) O.; m. Terri Ellen Ruther, Aug. 10, 1980; children: Andrew Zachary, Alix Michelle, Joshua Brett. AB, Harvard U., 1973, JD, M in Pub. Policy, 1977. Bar: Ill. 1977, U.S. Dist. Ct. (no. dist.) Ill. 1977, U.S. Ct. Appeals (7th cir.) 1983, U.S. Dist. Ct. (no dist. trial bar) Ill. 1992, U.S. Dist. Ct. (we. dist.) Mich. 1994. Assoc. Sidley & Austin, Chgo., 1977-84; ptnr. Sidley Austin Brown & Wood, 1985—. Editor: Illinois Environmental Law Handbook, 1988, 97. Panel atty. Chgo. Vol. Legal Svcs., Chgo., 1983—; mem. regional strategic planning/mktg. com. Alexian Bros. Ill., Inc., Elk Grove, 1985-88; trustee North Shore Congregation Israel, 1990—, sec., 1995-96, v.p., 1996—. Mem. ABA, Chgo. Bar Assn., Std. Club, Harvard Club (Chgo.). Jewish. Environmental. Home: 85 Oakmont Rd Highland Park IL 60035-4111 Office: Sidley Austin Brown & Wood Bank One Plaza 10 S Dearborn St #5200 Chicago IL 60603-2003 E-mail: rolian@sidley.com

OLIPHANT, CHARLES FREDERICK, III, lawyer; b. Chattanooga, Sept. 25, 1949; s. Charles Frederick and Jayne (Shutting) O.; m. Nancy Ann Stewart, May 15, 1976; children: James Andrew, Alexander Stewart. BA in Econs., U. N.C., 1971; JD, U. Mich., 1975. Bar: D.C. 1975. Assoc. Miller & Chevalier, Chartered, Washington, 1975-81, mem. firm, 1982—. Bd. adv. Jour. of Pension Planning and Compliance. Fellow Am. Coll. Employee Benefits Counsel; mem. ABA, Bar Assn. D.C. Episcopalian. Avocations: music, reading. Pension, profit-sharing, and employee benefits, Taxation, general. Office: Miller & Chevalier Chartered 655 15th St NW Ste 900 Washington DC 20005-5799

OLIVAS, ADOLF, lawyer, mayor; b. Hamilton, Ohio, Jan. 31, 1956; s. Henry and Eloina (Lopez) O.; children: Maria Christa, Alexa Lynne, Phillipa Gabrielle, Nicholas Henry. BA, U. Cin., 1978, JD, 1981. Bar: Ohio 1981, U.S. Dist. Ct. (so. dist.) Ohio 1981. Law clk U.S. Dist. Ct. Ea. Dist. Ky., Covington, 1981; assoc. Holbrock, Jonson, Bressler & Houser, Hamilton, Ohio, 1981-85; ptnr. Rogers & Olivas, 1985-88; mem. Holbrock & Jonson, 1989-91; ptnr. Holbrock, Jonson, Evans & Olivas, 1991-96; v.p., sec. Holbrock & Jonson Co. LPA, 1996-2000; owner Adolf Olivas LLC, 1999—. Active Hamilton City Coun., 1983—; vice-mayor City of Hamil-

ton, 1986-90, 94-97, mayor, 1990-94, 97-98, 2000—; co-chmn. Hamilton Schs. Chem. Abuse Prevention Program; bd. dirs. Open Door Food Pantry, Hamilton, 1982-85, Hamilton Com. Improvement Corp., 1986-88. Mem. ABA, Butler County Bar Assn., Cin. Bar Assn., Assn. Trial Lawyers Am., Ohio State Bar Coll., U.S. Jaycees. Roman Catholic. Avocations: racquetball, running, biking. State civil litigation, Criminal, Personal injury. Home: 130 W Fairway Dr Hamilton OH 45013-3527 Office: Adolf Olivas LLC 350 N 2d St Hamilton OH 45011 also: Office of Mayor Mcpl Bldg 345 High St Ste 700 Hamilton OH 45011

OLIVAS, DANIEL ANTHONY, lawyer; b. L.A., Apr. 8, 1959; s. Michael A. and Elizabeth M. (Velasco) O.; m. Susan L. Formaker, Oct. 19, 1986; 1 child, Benjamin Formaker-Olivas. BA in English Lit., Stanford U., 1981; JD with honors, UCLA, 1984. Bar: Calif. 1987, U.S. Dist. Ct. (cen. dist.) Calif. 1988, U.S. Ct. Appeals (9th cir.) 1988, U.S. Supreme Ct. 1995. Law clk., atty. Hunt & Cochran-Bond, L.A., 1984-88; atty. Heller, Ehrman, White & McAuliffe, 1988-90; dep. atty. gen. dept. of justice antitrust div. State of Calif., 1990-91, dep. atty. gen. dept. of justice land law sect., 1991—. State apptd. bd. dirs. Western Ctr. Law and Poverty, L.A., 1988-94; mem. Hispanic employees adv. com. Calif. Dept. Justice, 1990—. Contbr. articles to L.A. Daily Jour., and others; writer fiction and poetry. Recipient Atty. Gen.'s award for outstanding achievement in litigation, 1994; named one of Outstanding Young Men of Am., 1984. Mem. Mex.-Am. Bar Assn., Mex.-Am. Bar Found. (bd. dirs. 1993-94), L.A. County Bar Assn. (Jud. Appointments Com 1993-97), Stanford Chicano/Latino Alumni Assn. (pres.-elect 1992-93, pres. 1993-94). Democrat. Jewish. Administrative and regulatory, General civil litigation, Environmental. Office: State of Calif 300 S Spring St Ste 5212 Los Angeles CA 90013-1230 E-mail: olivasdan@aol.com

OLIVER, ANTHONY THOMAS, JR. lawyer; b. San Jose, Calif., July 19, 1929; s. Anthony Thomas and Josephine Gertrude (Bem) O.; m. Beverly J. Wirz, Jan. 27, 1952; children: Jeanne M. Hall, Marilyn M Guins, Cynthia M. Eschardies, Michelle M. Rogan.; m. Margaret E. Gurke, Mar. 31, 1984; 1 child, Christopher A. BS, U. Santa Clara, 1951; JD, 1953. Bar: Calif. 1954, U.S. Supreme Ct. 1979. Asst. counsel Bank Am. Legal Sept., L.A., 1953-57; assoc. Taylor & Barker, 1957-58, John F. O'Hara, L.A., 1958-63; sr. shareholder, chmn. emeritus labor dept. Parker, Milliken, Clark, O'Hara & Samuelian A Profl. Corp., 1963—. Mem. Town Hall Calif., 1981—; bd. visitors U. Santa Clara Coll. Law, 1982—. Served to lt. col. USAR. Recipient Edwin J. Owens Lawuer of Yr. award U. Santa Clara Coll. Law, 1976. Mem. ABA, (co-chmn. com. labor arbitration 1985-88), L.A. County Bar Assn. (chmn. labor law sect. 1985-86), Indsl. Rels. Rsch. Assn., Am. Arbitration Assn., Coll. of Labor & employment Lawyers, N.G. Assn. U.S., N.G. Assn. Calif., State Bar Calif., So. Calif. Indsl. Rels. Rsch. Assn., Orange County Indsl. Rels. Rsch. Assn. Roman Catholic. Club: Chancery (L.A.). Labor. Office: 333 S Hope St Fl 27 Los Angeles CA 90071-1406 E-mail: ato@pmcos.com

OLIVER, DALE HUGH, lawyer; b. Lansing, Mich., June 26, 1947; s. Alvin Earl and Jean Elizabeth (Stanton) O.; m. Mylbra Ann Chorney, Aug. 16, 1969; children: Nathan Corey, John Franklin. BA, Mich. State U., 1969; JD cum laude, Harvard U., 1972. Bar: D.C. 1973, U.S. Dist. Ct. (D.C. dist.) 1973, U.S. Ct. Appeals (D.C. cir.) 1976, U.S. Supreme Ct. 1980, U.S. Ct. Appeals (fed. cir.) 1983, U.S. Ct. Claims 1983, Calif. 1991. Assoc., ptnr. Jones, Day, Reavis & Pogue, Washington, 1975-79; ptnr. Crowell & Moring, Washington, 1979-84; ptnr. Gibson, Dunn & Crutcher, Washington, 1984-87; ptnr. Jones, Day, Reavis & Pogue, Washington, 1987-92; ptnr. Quinn Emanuel Urquhart & Oliver, L.A., 1992—. Editor jour. Pub. Contracts Law, 1980-86; contbr. articles to profl. jours. Spl. counsel 1980 Presdl. Inaugural Com., Washington, 1980; bd. dirs. L.A. coun. Boy Scouts Am., 1991—. Capt. USAF, 1973-75. Mem. ABA (com. chmn. pub. contract sect. 1979—), Nat. Contract Mgmt. Assn., Nat. Security Indsl. Assn., Harvard Law Sch. Assn., Mich. State U. Alumni Club of Washington (pres., dir. 1984-88). Federal civil litigation, Government contracts and claims, Private international. Home: 1414 Paseo La Cresta Palos Verdes Estates CA 90274-2073 Office: Quinn Emanuel Urquhart & Oliver & Hedges 865 S Figueroa St Fl 10 Los Angeles CA 90017-2543

OLIVER, JOHN PERCY, II, lawyer, consultant; b. Alexander City, Ala., Dec. 3, 1942; s. Samuel William and Sarah Pugh (Coker) D.; m. Melissa Vann, June 11, 1966. AB, Birmingham (Ala.) So. Coll., 1964; JD, U. Ala., 1967. Bar: Ala. 1967, U.S. Dist. Ct. (mid. dist.) Ala. 1969, U.S. Supreme Ct. 1971, U.S. Ct. Appeals (5th cir.) 1975, U.S. Ct. Appeals (11th cir.) 1981, U.S. Dist. Ct. (mid. dist.) Ga. 1989. Assoc. Samuel W. Oliver, Atty., Dadeville, Ala., 1967; prin. John P. Oliver II, Atty., 1967-71; ptnr. Oliver & Sims, Attys., 1972-83, Oliver, Sims & Jones, Attys., Dadeville, 1984-85, Oliver & Sims, Attys., Dadeville, 1985—. Dir. Bank of Dadeville. Mem. State Dem. Exec. Com., Tallapoosa County, Ala., 1986-94: judge Tallapoosa County Dist. Ct., Dadeville, 1973-76; mcpl. judge, Dadeville, 19765; spl. probate judge Tallapoosa County Probate Ct., Dadeville, 1987-88. Mem. Ala. State Bar Assn. (bd. bar commrs. 1992-98), Ala. Trial Lawyers Assn. (exec. com. 1975-77), Tallapoosa County Bar Assn. (pres. 1990). Baptist. Avocations: sailing, skiing. General civil litigation, Real property, Workers' compensation. Office: Oliver & Sims 129 W Columbus St Dadeville AL 36853-1308 E-mail: jpo2@mindspring.com

OLIVER, MILTON MCKINNON, lawyer, German translator, patent database searcher; b. Columbia, S.C., 1951; s. Caldwell Hardy and Eleanor (McKinnon) O.; m. Joan Nichols, July 12, 1981; children— John, James, Lindsay. B.A., Harvard U., 1972; J.D., Golden Gate U., 1975. Bar: Calif. 1975, Mass. 1975, Fla. 1978, D.C. 1983, N.Y. 1984, U.S. Supreme Ct. 1979, U.S. Ct. Appeals (fed. cir.) 1982. Assoc. Wolf, Greenfield & Sacks, P.C., Boston, 1977-83; assoc., then ptnr. Frishauf, Holtz, Goodman & Woodward, P.C., N.Y.C., 1983-94; of counsel Dike, Bronstein, Roberts & Cushman, 1994-97; ptnr. Ware, Fressola, Van Der Sluys & Adolphson, L.L.P., Monroe, Conn., 1997—. Mem. IEEE, Am., Conn., N.Y., Boston Patent Law Assns., Calif. State Bar, Computer Law Assn., Aircraft Owners and Pilots Assn. Episcopalian. Computer, Patent, Trademark and copyright. Home: 72 Green St Canton MA 02021-1020 Office: Ware Fressola Van Der Sluys & Adolphson LLP 755 Main St Monroe CT 06468-2830

OLIVER, SAMUEL WILLIAM, JR. lawyer; b. Birmingham, Ala., Apr. 18, 1935; s. Samuel William and Sarah Oliver; m. Anne Holman Marshall, Aug. 26, 1961; children: Sarah Bradley Oliver Crow, Samuel William III, Margaret Nelson Oliver Little. BS, U. Ala., 1959, JD, 1962. Bar: Ala. 1962, U.S. Dist. Ct. (no. dist.) Ala. 1963. Law clk. Supreme Ct. Ala., Montgomery, 1962-63, U.S. Dist. Ct. (no. dist.) Ala., Birmingham, 1963; assoc. Burr & Forman, 1964-65, ptnr., 1966—, also chmn. bus./corp. law sect., 1990-93. Dir. Metalplate Galvanizing Inc., Birmingham; mem. panel arbitrators commercial Am. Arbitration Assn., Atlanta, 1981-99. Chmn. bd. govs. The Relay House, Birmingham, 1985-89; mem. Leadership Birmingham, 1990; bd. dirs. Jr. Achievement Greater Birmingham, Inc., 1975—; mem. diocese coun. Episcopal Diocese Ala., Birmingham, 1981-85; chmn. bd. trustees Highlands Day Sch. Found., Inc., Birmingham, 1980-81; bd. dirs. Ala. Kidney Found., Birmingham, 1990-94, hon. mem., 1995—. With U.S. Army, 1956-58. Mem. ABA (bus. law sect. 1965—, negotiated acquisitions com. 1990—, task force on joint venture and asset purchase agreements 1994—, corp. counsel com. 1994—, sect. internat. law and practice), Internat. Bar Assn. (corp. law sect.), Southeastern Corp. Law Inst. (planning com. 1996—), Birmingham Bar Assn., Ala. Bar Assn., Summit Club (bd. govs., founding mem.), Monday Morning Quarterback Club, Rotary Club, Venture Club, Newcomen Soc. U.S. Episcopalian. Contracts commercial, General corporate, Mergers and acquisitions.

OLIVER, SOLOMON, JR. judge; b. Bessemer, Ala., July 20, 1947; s. Solomon Sr. and Willie Lee (Davis) O.; married; 2 children. BA, Coll. of Wooster, 1969; JD, NYU, 1972; MA, Case Western Res. U., 1974. Bar: Ohio 1973, U.S. Dist. Ct. (no. dist.) Ohio 1977, U.S. Ct. Appeals (6th cir.) 1977, U.S. Supreme Ct. 1980. Asst. prof. dept. polit. sci. Coll. of Wooster, Ohio, 1972-75; sr. law clk. to Hon. William H. Hastie U.S. Ct. Appeals (3d cir.), Phila., 1975-76; asst. U.S. atty. U.S. Atty.'s Office, Cleve., 1976-82, chief civil divsn., 1978-82; spl. asst. U.S. atty., chief appellate divsn. Dept. Justice, 1982, spl. asst. U.S. atty., 1982-85; prof. law Cleve. State U., 1982-94, assoc. dean faculty and adminstrn., 1991-94. Lectr. in law, trial practice Case Western Res. U., Cleve., 1979-82; vis. scholar Stanford U. Coll. Law, 1987; vis. prof. Comenius U., Bratislava, Czechoslovakia, 1991, Charles U., Prague, Czechoslovakia, 1991. Chair O.K. Hoover Scholarship com. Bapt. Ch., 1987-89; trustee Coll. of Wooster, Ohio, 1991-97, 2000—. Mem. ABA, Nat. Bar Assn. Office: US Dist Ct No Dist Ohio 300 US Courthouse 201 Superior Ave NE Cleveland OH 44114-1201 Fax: 216-522-7951

OLIVERI, PAUL FRANCIS, lawyer; b. Far Rockaway, N.Y., Feb. 27, 1954; s. Alphonse J. and Rita (Gregorace) O.; m. Debra Lynn Malkin, Aug. 7, 1977; 1 child, Jason Robert. BA, NYU, 1976; JD, St. John's U., Queens, N.Y., 1978. Bar: N.Y. 1979, U.S. Dist. Ct. (ea. and so. dists.) N.Y. 1980. Assoc. Fuchsberg & Fuchsberg, N.Y.C., 1979-83; ptnr. Oliveri & Schwartz, 1983—. Cons. atty. Alliance for Consumer Rights, N.Y.C., 1986—. Mem. N.Y. State Bar Assn., Am. Trial Lawyers Assn., N.Y. State Trial Lawyers Assn. (bd. dirs.). Avocations: music, numismatics. State civil litigation, Insurance, Personal injury. Office: Oliveri & Schwartz 30 Vesey St New York NY 10007-2914

OLIVIER, JASON THOMAS, lawyer; b. New Orleans; s. Gerald L. and Beverly Olivier; m. Chellie Olivier, 1991. BS in Elec. Engring. Tech., Nicholls State U., Thibodaux, La., 1985; JD, Loyola U., New Orleans, 1990. Bar: La. 1990, U.S. Dist. Ct. (ea., we., and mid. dists.) La. Dir. music Sta. KNSU-FM, Thibodaux, 1984-85; prodn. dir. Sta. WTIX, New Orleans, 1987, 89; owner, pres. Jason T. Olivier, A P.L.C., Metairie, La., 1990-96; ptnr. Deas and Olivier, 1992—. CEO, pres., gen. counsel Interstate Collection Bur., New Orleans, 1993-99; host Hidden Talent Theatre TV Variety Show, Sta. WCOX, 1987; instr. Loyola Law Sch. Computer Ctr., 1988; extern U.S. Ct. Appeals (4th cir.) La. Author poetry; composer songs; vocal arranger, performer album Menagerie; mus. rev. columnist Rockaraound Mag., 1987-88. Pres., chair bd. Northlake Performing Arts Soc. Mem. FBA, Am. Collectors Assn. Atty. Program (media rels. spokesperson, chmn. La. 1999), La. Bar Assn., Comm. Law Soc. (past v.p.), Federalist Soc., Comml. Law League Am., Tau Kappa Epsilon. Republican. Roman Catholic. Avocations: computers, web site programming, audio engineering, music. Office: PO Box 714 Mandeville LA 70470-0714

OLLINGER, W. JAMES, lawyer, director; b. Kittanning, Pa., Apr. 5, 1943; s. William James and Margaret Elizabeth (Reid) Ollinger; m. Susan Louise Gerspacher, Oct. 20, 1979; children: Mary Rebecca, David James. BA, Capital U., Columbus, Ohio, 1966; JD, Case Western Res. U., 1968. Bar: Ohio 1968, US Dist Ct (no dist) Ohio 1971. Ptnr. Baker & Hostetler, Cleve., 1968—. Bd dirs Parts Assocs Inc, Cleveland, Ohio. Mem Bentleyville Village Coun, Ohio, 1990—93; mayor Bentleyville, 1997—99. Mem.: Order of Coif, Phi Delta Phi. General corporate, Pension, profit-sharing, and employee benefits, Taxation, general. Office: Baker & Hostetler 3200 Nat City Ctr 1900 E 9th St Ste 3200 Cleveland OH 44114-3475 E-mail: jollinger@bakerlaw.com

OLMSTEAD, CLARENCE WALTER, JR. lawyer; b. Alexandria, Va., Jan. 24, 1943; s. Clarence Walter and Rhea Nancy (Donnelly) O.; m. Kathleen Frances Heenan, Sept. 7, 1973; children: Nicholas Heenan, Jonathan Heenan, Caitlin Heenan. AB, Stanford U., 1965; LLB, Columbia U., 1968. Bar: N.Y. 1970, U.S. Dist. Ct. (so. and ea. dists.) N.Y. 1970, U.S. Ct. Appeals (2d cir.) 1970, U.S. Supreme Ct. 1986. Law clk. to presiding judge U.S. Dist. Ct. (we. dist.) Wis., 1968-69; assoc. Shearman & Sterling, N.Y.C., 1969-76, ptnr., 1976—. Bd. dirs. West Side Montessori Sch., N.Y.C., 1983-89, pres., 1985-87; mem. sch. com. Cathedral Sch., N.Y.C., 1992-95; trustee North Country Sch. Camp Treetops, 1992-95. Mem. ABA, N.Y. State Bar Assn., Assn. Bar City of N.Y., Phi Beta Kappa. Contracts commercial, Finance, Private international. Home: 470 W End Ave New York NY 10024-4933 Office: 599 Lexington Ave New York NY 10022

O'LOUGHLIN, JOHN PATRICK, lawyer; b. Cape Girardeau, Mo., Nov. 21, 1950; s. Thomas King and Agnes (Schmuke) O'L. BA, Southeast Mo. State U., 1973; JD, U. Tulsa, 1976. Bar: Mo. 1977, U.S. Dist. Ct. (ea. dist.) Mo. 1977, U.S. Ct. Appeals (8th cir.) 1978. Asst. prosecutor Cape Girardeau County, Mo., 1977-79; ptnr. O'Loughlin, O'Loughlin & McManaman, Cape Girardeau, 1977—. Faculty Southeast Mo. State U., Cape Girardeau, 1977. Contbr. articles to profl. jours. Democratic committeeman, Cape Girardeau County, 1984; active United Way, Cape Girardeau, 1977-78. Mem. Cape Girardeau County Bar Assn., Mo. Bar Assn., ABA (vice chmn. bankruptcy law com. 1986-88), Bankruptcy Trustees Assn., Assn. Trial Lawyers Am., Cape Girardeau C. of C. (agr. com. 1980-82). Roman Catholic. Lodges: K.C., Elks. Bankruptcy, Contracts commercial, General corporate. Home: 920 W Adams Jackson MO 63755 Office: O'Loughlin O'Loughlin & McManaman 1736 N Kingshighway St Cape Girardeau MO 63701-2122

OLSCHWANG, ALAN PAUL, lawyer; b. Chgo., Jan. 30, 1942; s. Morton James and Ida (Ginsberg) O.; m. Barbara Claire Miller, Aug. 22, 1965; children: Elliot, Deborah, Jeffrey. BS, U. Ill., 1963, JD, 1966. Bar: Ill. 1966, N.Y. 1984, Calif. 1992. Law clk. Ill. Supreme Ct., Bloomington, 1966-67; assoc. Sidley & Austin and predecessor firms, Chgo., 1967-73; with Montgomery Ward & Co. Inc., 1973-81, assoc. gen. counsel, asst. sec., 1979-81; ptnr. Seki, Jarvis & Lynch, 1981-84, dir., mem. exec. com.; dir. Mitsubishi Electric & Electronics USA, Inc. and predecessors, N.Y.C., 1983-91, Cypress, Calif., 1991—. Mem. ABA, Am. Corp. Counsel Assn., Calif. Bar Assn., Ill. Bar Assn., Chgo. Bar Assn., N.Y. State Bar Assn., Bar Assn. of City of N.Y., Am. Arbitration Assn. (panel arbitrators). Contracts commercial, General corporate, Private international. Office: Mitsubishi Elec & Electronics USA Inc PO Box 6007 5665 Plaza Dr Cypress CA 90630-0007

OLSEN, HANS PETER, lawyer; b. Detroit, May 21, 1940; s. Hans Peter and Paula M. (Olsen) O.; m. Elizabeth Ann Gayton, Sept. 14, 1968; children: Hans Peter, Heidi Susanne, Stephanie Elizabeth BA, Mich. State U., 1962; JD, Georgetown U., 1965; LLM, NYU, 1966. Bar: Mich. 1967, Pa. 1969, R.I. 1974. Law clk. firm Monaghan, McCrone, Campbell & Crawmer, Detroit, 1964; law clk. U.S. Ct. of Claims, Fed. Appellate Ct., Washington, 1966-68; assoc. firm Pepper, Hamilton & Scheetz, Phila., 1968-72; ptnr. firm Hinckley, Allen, & Snyder, Providence and Boston, 1972—. Adv. planning com. U. R.I. Fed. Taxation Inst.; continuing legal edn. adv. bd., tax symposium adv. bd. Bryant Coll.; mem. Gov.'s State Task Force, R.I. Pub. Expenditure Coun.; cons. Bur. Nat. Affairs; liaison Bar Assn. and North Atlantic region IRS; tax adminstrs. adv. com. R.I.; lectr. tax insts. and other profl. groups N.Y., L.A., Phila., Boston, R.I.; advisor R.I. Econ. Policy com. Contbr. numerous articles on taxation to legal jours. Fellow Am. Bar Found.; mem. ABA (sect. taxation, exempt orgns. com., subcom. healthcare, corp.-shareholders rels. com., partnerships com.), R.I. Bar Assn. (sect. taxation, sec.-treas. 1977-80, liaison with CPAs, specialization com., mem. various coms.), Providence C. of C., R.I. C. of C. (chmn. com. on bus. taxes and public spending, mem., past chmn. legis. action council), Mich. State Bar, Pa. State Bar. Corporate taxation, Personal income taxation, State and local taxation. Home: 274 Olney St Providence RI 02906-2305 Office: 1500 Fleet Ctr Providence RI 02903 E-mail: holsen@haslaw.com, hpeterolsen@home.com

OLSEN, M. KENT, lawyer, educator; b. Denver, Mar. 10, 1948; s. Marvin and F. Winona (Wilker) O.; m. Shauna L. Casement; children: Kristofor Anders, Alexander Lee, Nikolaus Alrik, Amanda Elizabeth. BS, Colo. State U., 1970; JD, U. Denver, 1975. Bar: Colo., U.S. Dist. Ct. Colo. 1982, U.S. Tax Ct. Law clk. Denver Probate Ct., 1973-75; assoc. ptnr. Johnson & McLachlan, Lamar, Colo., 1975-80; assoc. Buchanan, Thomas and Johnson, Lakewood, 1981-82, William E. Myrick, P.C., Denver, 1982-83; referee Denver Probate Ct., 1983-89; ptnr. Haines & Olsen, P.C., 1989-95; pvt. practice, 1995—2001; ptnr. Olsen & Traeger, LLP, 2001—. Adv. bd. Denver Paralegal Inst., 1993—, Elder Law Inst., 1994—. Mem. Gov.'s Commn. on Life and the Law, Denver, 1991-2000; bd. dirs. Adult Care Mgmt., Inc., Denver, 1985-95; bd. dirs. Arc of Denver, Inc., 1990—, pres., 1995-97; bd. dirs. Colo. Guardianship Alliance, Denver, 1990-91; bd. dirs. Colo. Fund for People with Disabilities, 1994—, pres., 1994-2000. Recipient Outstanding Vol. Svc. award Adult Care Mgmt., 1990, Outstanding Svc. award The Arc of Denver, 1991, Vol. Svc. award Colo. Gerontol. Soc., 1997, Pres.'s award Arc of Denver, 1998. Mem. ABA, Colo. Bar Assn. (past chair probate sect.), Am. Assn. Home for Aging, Nat. Acad. Elder Law Attys., Denver Bar Assn. Episcopalian. Avocations: running, skiing, racquetball, art, hiking. Estate planning, Probate, Estate taxation. Home: 3030 S Roslyn St Denver CO 80231-4153 Office: 650 S Cherry St Ste 850 Denver CO 80246-1805 E-mail: mkolsen@earthlink.net

OLSON, CAROL DUANE, lawyer; b. Cambridge, Mass., Dec. 3, 1946; d. James Turner and Jeanne Hagan Duane; m. Robert Wyrick Olson, June 12, 1971; children: John Hagan, Mary Catherine Duane. BA, Newton Coll. of Sacred Heart, 1968; LLB, U. Va., 1971; LLM (Taxation), NYU, 1975. Bar: N.Y. 1972, Ohio 1990. Assoc. Mudge, Rose, Guthrie & Alexander, N.Y.C., 1971-74; atty. Union Carbide Corp., 1974-75; prof. Pace U. Law Sch., White Plains, N.Y., 1978-88; of counsel Keating, Muething & Klekamp, Cin., 1988-93; ptnr. Peck, Shaffer & Williams LLP, 1993—. Author: (book chpt.) State and Local Debt Financing. Pres. Great Rivers Girl Scout Coun., Cin., 1991—; bd. overseers Cin. Ballet, 1991—; v.p. Contemporary Arts Ctr., Cin., 1995—. Mem. Ohio State Bar Assn. (mem. exec. com. fed. taxation com. 1996—, com. mem. fed. taxation specialty bd. 1998—). Fax: 513-621-3813

OLSON, ROBERT HOWARD, lawyer; b. July 6, 1944; s. Robert Howard and Jacquiline (Wells) O.; m. Diane Carol Thorsen, Aug. 13, 1966; children: Jeffrey, Christopher. BA in Govt. summa cum laude, Ind. U., 1966; JD cum laude, Harvard U., 1969. Bar: Ohio 1969, Fla. 1980, Ariz. 1985, Calif. 2001, U.S. Supreme Ct. 1973. Assoc. Squire, Sanders & Dempsey, L.L.P., Cleve., 1969, 70-71, 76-81, ptnr., 1981—, Phoenix, 1985—; sr. law clk. U.S. Dist. Ct., No. Dist., Ind., 1969-70; chief civil rights divsn. Ohio Atty. Gen.'s Office, Columbus, 1971-73, chief consumer protection, 1973-75, chief counsel, 1975, 1st asst. (chief of staff), 1975-76. Instr. Ohio State U. Law Sch., Columbus, 1974; mem. Cen. Phoenix com. to advise city council and mayor, 1987-89; bd. dirs. Orpheum Theater Found., sec., 1989-90, pres., 1990-97, exec. com., 1997-99; bd. dirs. The Ariz. Ctr. for Law in the Pub. Interest, exec. com., 1990-94, 97-2001, treas. 1992-93, 97-2001, v.p., 1993-94; mem. Ariz. Ctr. for Disability Law, 1994-96, treas. 1994-95; mem. Valley Leadership Class XIV, Ariz. Town Hall, 1977, rsch. com., 1998—. Contbr. articles to profl. jours. Bd. dirs. 1st Unitarian Ch. Phoenix, 1987-89, 98-2001, v.p., 1987-89, 2000-2001, pres. 1998-99; bd. dirs. 1st Unitarian Ch. Found., 1987-93, pres., 1990-93. Named Arts Advocate of Yr. Bus. Vols. Arts/Phoenix, 1997. Mem. Ariz. State Bar Assn., Calif. Bar Assn., Phi Beta Kappa. Democrat. Contracts commercial, Health, Municipal (including bonds). Home: 5201 E Paradise Dr Scottsdale AZ 85254-4746 Office: Squire Sanders & Dempsey LLP 40 N Central Ave Ste 2700 Phoenix AZ 85004-4498

OLSON, ROBERT WYRICK, lawyer; b. Madison, Wis., Dec. 19, 1945; s. John Arthur and Mary Katherine (Wyrick) O.; m. Carol Jean Duane, June 12, 1971; children: John Hagan, Mary Catherine Duane. BA, Williams Coll., 1967; JD, U. Va., 1970. Assoc. Cravath, Swaine & Moore, N.Y.C., 1970-79; asst. gen. counsel Penn Cen. Corp., Cin., 1979-80, assoc. gen. counsel, 1980-82, v.p., dep. gen. counsel, 1982-87; sr. v.p., gen. counsel, sec. Am. Premier Underwriters, Inc. (formerly Penn Cen. Corp.), 1987-95, Chiquita Brands Internat., Inc., Cin., 1995—. Mem. ABA. General corporate, Mergers and acquisitions, Securities. Office: Chiquita Brands Internat 250 E 5th St Ste 25 Cincinnati OH 45202-4119 E-mail: bolson@chiquita.com

OLSON, RONALD LEROY, lawyer; b. Carroll, Iowa, July 9, 1941; s. Clyde L. and Delpha C. (Boyens) O.; m. Jane Tenhulzen, June 21, 1964; children— Kristin, Steven, Amy. B.S., Drake U., 1963; J.D., U. Mich., 1966; Diploma in Law, Oxford U., Eng., 1967. Bar: Wis. 1966, Calif. 1969, U.S. Dist. Ct. (cen. dist.) Calif. 1969, U.S. Dist. Ct. (so. dist.) Calif. 1973, U.S. Ct. Appeals (9th cir.) 1974, U.S. Ct. Appeals (10th cir.) 1980, U.S. Ct. Appeals (5th cir.) 1982, U.S. Supreme Ct. 1976, U.S. Dist. Ct. Alaska 1983. Atty. U.S. Dept. Justice, 1967; clk. to chief judge U.S. Ct. Appeals (D.C. cir.), Washington, 1967-68; ptnr. Munger, Tolles & Olson, Los Angeles, 1968— ; ; lawyer del. Ann. 9th Cir. Conf., 1984-89; lectr. in field. Mem. editorial bd. Alternatives, 1983— . Contbr. numerous articles to legal jours. Mem. adv. com. Los Angeles and Orange Counties chpt. Lawyers Alliance for Nuclear Arms Control; trustee Drake U., 1977— , Sequoia Nat. Park Natural History Assn., 1983— ; bd. dirs., pres. Fraternity of Friends of Music Ctr., 1978—; chmn. bd. fellows Claremont U. Ctr. and Grad. Sch., 1984— ; bd. dirs. Legal Aid Found. L.A., 1975-86, pres., 1984-85; bd. dirs. Salzburg Seminar; com. visitors U. Mich. Law Sch., 1986—, sec. L.A. Arts Festival, 1985—; mem. Skid Row Housing Trust of L.A., 1986—; mem. editorial bd. Alternatives, 1983-88. Burton scholar U. Mich.; Ford Found. fellow Oxford U., 1967. Fellow Am. Coll. Trial Lawyers, Am. Bar Found.; mem. ABA (litigation sect. council 1976—, chmn. 1981-82, chmn. spl. com. on dispute resolution 1976-86, litigation sect. Soviet Exchange Program com. 1983—, editorial bd. Human Rights publ. sect. ind. rights and responsiblities, 1986—, task force on tng. the advocate 1986—, standing com. fed. judiciary), Am. Judicature Soc., L.A. Bar Found. (bd. dirs. 1977—), Am. Arbitration Assn. (bd. dirs. 1983— , comml. panel 1983—), L.A. County Bar Assn., State Bar Calif. (bd. dirs. 1985—, v.p. 1986-87), Assn. Bus. Trial Lawyers (mem. adv. com. trial ct. improvement fund for Calif. jud. coun. 1988—), L.A. County Barristers (pres. 1976), 9th Cir. Jud. Conf. (exec. com. 1984-89), Chancery. Democrat. Episcopalian. Antitrust, Federal civil litigation, State civil litigation. Office: Munger Tolles & Olson 355 S Grand Ave Fl 35 Los Angeles CA 90071-1560

OLSON, THEODORE BEVRY, lawyer; b. Chgo., Sept. 11, 1940; 2 children. B.A., U. Pacific, 1962; LL.B., U. Calif.-Berkeley, 1965. Bar: Calif. 1965, D.C. 1982. Assoc., ptnr. Gibson, Dunn & Crutcher, Los Angeles, 1972-81, 84—; asst. atty. gen. Dept. Justice, Washington, 1981—84; ptnr. Gibson, Dunn & Crutcher, 1984—2001; U.S. solicitor gen. Dept. Justice, 2001—. Mem. Calif. Commn. on Uniform State Laws, 1972-74; del. Republican Nat. Conv., 1976, 80. Fellow Am. Acad. of Appellate Lawyers, Am. Coll. Trial Lawyers; mem. ABA, L.A. County Bar Assn. Office: Office Solicitor Gen 950 Pennsylvania Ave NW Washington DC 20530-0001*

OLSON, WILLIAM JEFFREY, lawyer; b. Paterson, N.J., Oct. 23, 1949; s. Walter Justus and Viola Patricia (Trautvetter) O.; m. Janet Elaine Bollen, May 22, 1976; children: Robert J., Joanne C. AB, Brown U., 1971; JD, U. Richmond, 1976. Bar: Va. 1976, D.C. 1976, U.S. Ct. Claims 1976, U.S. Ct. Appeals (4th, 6th, 10th, and D.C. cirs.) 1976, U.S. Supreme Ct. 1982. Assoc. Jackson & Campbell, Washington, 1976-79; ptnr. Gilman, Olson & Pangia, 1980-92; prin. William J. Olson PC, McLean, Va. and Washington, 1992—. Sec., treas. bd. dirs. Victims Assistance Legal Orgn., McLean, Va., 1979—; presdl. transition team leader Legal Svcs. Corp., Washington, 1980; chmn. and bd. dirs. nat. Legal Svcs. Corp., 1981-82; mem. Pres.'s Export Coun. Subcom. on Export Adminstrn., Washington, 1982-84; spl. counsel bd. govs. U.S. Postal Svc., Washington, 1984-86. Author: Tuition Tax Credits and Alternatives, 1978; co-author: Debating National Health Policy, 1977, Executive Orders and National Emergencies, 1999. Trustee Davis Meml. Goodwill Industries, Washington, 1980-86, 88-93; chmn. Fairfax County Rep. Com., Fairfax, Va., 1980-82; mem. Rep. State Ctrl. Com., Richmond, Va., 1982-86. Mem. Va. Bar Assn., Assn. Trial Lawyers Am., Va. Trial Lawyers Assn. Republican. Baptist. Avocation: gardening. Administrative and regulatory, Government contracts and claims, Nonprofit and tax-exempt organizations. Office: 8180 Greensboro Dr Ste 1070 Mc Lean VA 22102-3860 E-mail: wjo@mindspring.com

O'MALLEY, CARLON MARTIN, judge; b. Phila., Sept. 7, 1929; s. Carlon Martin and Lucy (Bol) O'M.; m. Mary Catherine Lyons, Aug. 17, 1957; children: Carlon Martin III, Kathleen B. O'Malley Aikman, Harry Tighe, John Todd, Cara M. O'Malley Colombo. BA, Pa. State U., 1951; LLB, Temple U., 1954. Bar: Pa. 1955, Fla. 1973, U.S. Supreme Ct. 1973. Practiced law, 1957-61; asst. U.S. atty. for Middle Dist. Pa., Dept. Justice, 1961-69, U.S. atty., 1979-82; ptnr. O'Malley & Teets, 1970-72, O'Malley, Jordan & Mullaney (and predecessor firms), 1976-79; pvt. practice Pa. and Fla., 1972-79, 82-87; judge Ct. Common Pleas of Lackawanna County (45th Judicial Dist.), 1987-97, sr. judge, 1998—. Dir. pub. safety City of Scranton, 1983-86; lectr. Lackawanna Jr. Coll., 1982-86. Editorial bd.: Temple Law Rev, 1952-53. Pres. Lackawanna County (Pa.) unit Am. Cancer Soc., 1966-67; bd. dirs. Pa. Cancer Soc., 1967-68, Lackawanna county chpt. ARC, 1967-69; mem. solicitation team, govtl. divsn. Lackawanna United Fund, 1963-68; chmn. profl. divsn. Greater Scranton (Pa.) YMCA Membership Drives; trustee Everhart Mus., Scranton, 1987—. Pilot USAF, 1955-57, Pa. N.G., 1957-59. Mem. Am. Judges Assn., Nat. Assn. Former U.S. Attys., Pa. Bar Assn., Lackawanna County Bar Assn., Fla. Bar Assn., Country Club of Scranton, Elks (pres. Pa. chpt. 1978-79, judiciary com. 1985-89, justice Grand Forum 1991, 1995-97, chief justice 1992-93, nat. pres. 1997-98), K.C., Phi Kappa (pres.), Delta Theta Phi (pres.). Democrat. Office: Judges Chambers Lackawanna County Courthouse Scranton PA 18503

O'MALLEY, KEVIN FRANCIS, lawyer, writer, educator; b. St. Louis, May 12, 1947; s. Peter Francis and Dorothy Margaret (Cradick) O'M.; m. Dena Hengen, Apr.2, 1971; children: Kevin Brendan, Ryan Michael. AB, St. Louis U., 1970, JD, 1973. Bar: Mo. 1973, U.S. Ct. Appeals D.C. 1974, U.S. Ct. Appeals (8th cir.) 1979, Ill. 1993. Trial lawyer U.S. Dept. Justice, Washington, 1973-74, Los Angeles, 1974-77, Phoenix, 1977-78, asst. U.S. atty. St. Louis, 1978-83. Adj. prof. law St. Louis U., 1979—; lectr. Ctrl. and Ea. European Law Initiative, Russian Fedn., 1996, Poland, 1999. Author: (with Devitt, Blackmar, O'Malley) Federal Jury Practice and Instruction, 1990, 92, (with O'Malley, Grenig & Lee), 1999, 2000, 01; contbr. articles to law books and jours. Community amb. Expt. in Internat. Living, Prague, Czechoslovakia, 1968; bd. dirs. St. Louis-Galway (Ireland) Sister Cities. Capt. U.S. Army, 1973. Recipient Atty. Gen.'s Disting. Service award U.S. Dept. Justice, 1977, John J. Dwyer Meml. Scholarship award, 1967-70. Fellow Am. Coll. Trial Lawyers; mem. ABA (chmn. govt. litigation counsel com. 1982-86, chmn. jud. com. 1986-87, chmn. com. on ind. and small firms, chmn. trial practice com. 1991-94, health care litigation 1994-98), Am. Law Inst., Met. Bar Assn. St. Louis (chmn. criminal law sect.), Nat. Inst. Trial Advocacy, Mo. Athletic Club. Roman Catholic. Office: 10 S Brentwood Blvd Ste 102 Saint Louis MO 63105-1694 E-mail: komalley@omalleylaw.com

OMAN, RALPH, lawyer; b. Huntington, N.Y., July 1, 1940; s. Henry Ferdinand and Annamarie (Retelsdorf) O.; m. Anne K. Henehan, Oct. 21, 1967; children: Tabitha Russell, Caroline Adams, Charlotte Ericsson. Diploma, Sorbonne U., Paris, 1961; BA, Hamilton Coll., 1962; LLD, Georgetown U., 1973. Bar: D.C. 1973, U.S. Dist. Ct. Md. 1973, U.S. Ct. Appeals (4th cir.) 1974, U.S. Supreme Ct. 1977. Law clk. to U.S. Dist. Ct. judge U.S. Dist. Ct. Md., Balt., 1973-74; trial atty U.S. Dept. Justice, Washington, 1974-75; chief minority counsel patents, trademarks and copyrights subcom. U.S. Senate, 1975-77; legis. dir. Senator Charles Mathias, 1977-78; minority counsel judiciary com. U.S. Senate, 1978-81, chief counsel, staff dir. criminal law subcom., 1981-82, chief counsel patents, copyrights and trademarks subcom., 1982-85; register of copyrights U.S. Copyright Office, 1985-94; counsel Dechert Price and Rhoads, 1996—. Adj. prof. copyright law George Washington U.; speaker in field. Contbr. numerous articles to profl. jours. Served to lt. USN, 1965-70, Vietnam. Mem. ABA (chair authors com.), Fed. Bar Assn. (past pres. Capitol Hill chpt.). Episcopalian. Home: 1110 E Capitol St NE Washington DC 20002-6225 Office: Dechert Price and Rhoads 1775 Eye St NW Ste 1100 Washington DC 20006-2424 E-mail: ralph.oman@dechert.com

O'MARA, JAMES WRIGHT, lawyer; b. McComb, Miss., Jan. 7, 1940; s. Junior and Mary Jane (Wright) O'M.; m. Jeanette Walter, June 28, 1963; children: James W. Jr., Angela J. BA, U. Miss., 1962, JD with distinction, 1967. Bar: Miss. 1967. Ptnr. Butler, Snow, O'Mara, Stevens & Cannada, Jackson, Miss., 1967-97, chmn., 1990-97; sr. ptnr. Phelps & Dunbar, 1997—. Vis. prof. Jackson Sch. Law, 1970-72. Editor-in-chief Miss. Law Jour., 1966-67. Pres. Jackson Prep. Sch., 1984-85, Woodland Hills Bapt. Acad., Jackson, 1973-84. Capt. U.S. Army, 1962-64. Fellow Miss. Bar Found.; mem. ABA, Miss. Bar Assn., Am. Bankruptcy Inst., Miss. Bankruptcy Conf. (pres. 1980-81). Baptist. Bankruptcy, General civil litigation, Contracts commercial. Home: 42 Eastbrooke St # I Jackson MS 39216-4714 Office: Phelps & Dunbar PO Box 23066 Jackson MS 39225-3066 E-mail: omaraj@phelps.com

O'MARA, WILLIAM MICHAEL, lawyer; b. Milw., May 8, 1938; s. Olivar Edward and Winifred Agnes (Morrisroe) O'M.; m. Maureen Teresa Lidster, Sept. 3, 1970; children: Timothy, Erin, Brian, David, Matthew, Catherine, Patrick, Bridget, Michael. BA in History, Loyola U., Los Angeles, 1960; JD, Hastings Coll. Law, 1967. Bar: Calif. 1968, Nev. 1968. Assoc. Belford & Anglim, 1968-69, ptnr., 1969-74; ptnr. firm W.M. O'Mara, Reno, 1974-82, O'Mara and Kosinski, 1983-87, O'Mara & Jacques, 1988—; tchr. Manogue High Sch., Chapman Coll., 1970-76. Candidate for U.S. Ho. of Reps., 1978. Served to capt., USNR, 1961— . Mem. ABA, Nev. Bar Assn., Calif. Bar Assn., Washoe Bar Assn., U.S. Navy League, Serra Internat. (past pres.), U.S. Naval Res. Assn., Air Force Assn. Republican. Roman Catholic. Federal civil litigation, State civil litigation, Contracts commercial.

O'MEARA, JOHN FRANCIS, lawyer; b. Chgo., Apr. 14, 1936; s. John J. and Mary (Joyce) O'M.; children: Marcia A. Hiehle, John A., Timothy D. BS, Loyola U., 1959; JD, Northwestern U., 1960. Bar: Ill. 1961, U.S. Dist. Ct. (no. dist.) Ill. 1964, U.S. Ct. Appeals (7th cir.) 1992. Assoc., ptnr. Lord, Bissell & Brook, Chgo., 1961-74; atty. pvt. practice, Chgo. and Park Ridge, Ill, 1975—. Instr. John Marshall Sch. Law, Chgo., 1966-71. Author: Tort Liability of Illinois Land Occupiers, 1968. Bd. dirs. St. Mary of Angels, 1987—; founder, officer Ind. Precinct Orgn., Chgo., 1969-71. With U.S. Army Res., 1960-66. Mem. Holy Name Soc. Roman Catholic. Office: 1737 N Wolcott Ave Chicago IL 60622-1350

O'MELILIA, DAVID E. prosecutor; Atty. Tulsa County Dist. Atty.'s Office, 1980—84; asst. U.S. atty. No. Dist. Okla. U.S. Dept. Justice, Tulsa, 1986—96, U.S. atty.; with Nichols, Wolfe, Stamper, Nally, Fallis and Robertson, 1996—99; ptnr. Lyons, Clark, Danielson and O'Melilia, Tulsa, 1999—2001. Office: 3460 US Courthouse 333 W 4th St Tulsa OK 74103-3809*

ONCKEN, HENRY KUCK, lawyer; b. Shiner, Tex., Sept. 17, 1938; s. William Otto and Stella Helen (Kuck) O.; m. Jacqueline Ann Mansker, Aug. 6, 1960; 1 child, Leah Ann. BBA, U. Houston, 1965, JD, 1966. Bar: Tex. 1966, U.S. Dist. Ct. (so. dist.) Tex. 1968. Ptnr. Mabry & Oncken, Houston, 1966-69; asst. dist. atty. Harris County, 1969-81; judge Texas Dist. Ct. (248th jud. dist.), 1981-82; assoc. Gardner, Wald & Evans, Houston, 1983-84; U.S. Atty. so. dist. Tex. U.S. Dept. Justice, 1985-90; with firm Butler, Ewalt & Hailey, 1990-91; atty. Oncken & Oncken, P.C., 1991—97; vis. judge Harris County Criminal Courts; sole practitioner, 1997—. Pres. Mcpl. Utility Dist., Houston, 1976-81. Served with USNG, 1956-63. Republican. Avocations: hunting, fishing, pistol shooting, automobiles. Home: 9303 Godstone Ln Spring TX 77379-6510

O'NEAL, MICHAEL RALPH, state legislator, lawyer; b. Kansas City, Mo., Jan. 16, 1951; s. Ralph D. and Margaret E. (McEuen) O'N.; children from a previous marriage: children: Haley Anne, Austin Michael; m. Cindy Wulfkuhle, Apr. 9, 1999. BA in English, U. Kans., 1973, JD, 1976. Bar: Kans. 1976, U.S. Dist. Ct. Kans. 1976, U.S. Ct. Appeals (10th cir.) 1979. Intern Legis. Counsel State of Kans., Topeka, 1975-76; assoc. Hodge, Reynolds, Smith, Peirce & Forker, Hutchinson, Kans., 1976-77; ptnr. Reynolds, Peirce, Forker, Suter, O'Neal & Myers, 1980-88; shareholder Gilliland & Hayes, P.A., 1988—, mng. ptnr., 2000—; mem. Kans. Ho. of Reps., 1984, chmn. jud. com., 1989-90, 93-94, 97—; pres. Gilliland & Hayes, P.C., 1999-2000; minority whip Kans. Ho. of Reps., 1991-92, majority whip, 1995-96, chmn. edn. com., 1995-96, mem. fiscal oversight com., 1997—, chair redistricting com., 2001—, mem. bus., commerce, labor com. Chmn. Ho. Reappointment Com., 2001, instr. Hutchinson C.C., 1977-88. Vice chmn. Rep. Ctrl. Com., Reno County, Kans., 1982-86; bd. dirs. Reno County Mental Health Assn., Hutchinson, 1984-89, YMCA, 1984-86, Crime Stoppers (ex-officio), Hutchinson; chmn. adv. bd. dirs. Wesley Towers Retirement Cmty., 1984-96; mem. Kans. Travel and Tourism Commn., 1990-94; mem. bd. govs. U. Kans. Law Sch., 1991—; mem. Kans. Sentencing Commn., 1997—. Recipient Leadership award Kans. C. of C. and Industry, 1985; named one of Outstanding Young Men Am., 1986. Mem. ABA, Nat. Conf. State Legislatures (criminal justice com.), Kans. Assn. Def. Counsel, Def. Rsch. Inst., Kans. Bar Assn. (prospective legis. com., Outstanding Svc. award), Hutchinson C. of C. (ex-officio bd. dirs., Leadership award 1984), Am. Coun. Young Polit. Leaders (del. to Atlantic conf. biennial assembly), Kans. Jud. Coun., Commn. on Uniform State Laws. Avocations: basketball, tennis, golf. Home: 8 Windemere Ct Hutchinson KS 67502-2020 Office: Gilliland & Hayes PA 2d Flr Box 2977 20 W 2nd Ave Hutchinson KS 67504-2977 E-mail: mroneal@southwind.net

O'NEAL, MICHAEL SCOTT, SR. lawyer; b. Jacksonville, Fla., Dec. 22, 1948; s. Jack Edwin and Lucille (Colvin) O'N.; m. Barbara Louise Hardie, Jan. 30, 1971 (div. Sept. 1974); 1 child, Jennifer Erin; m. Helen Margaret Joost, Mar. 18, 1985; children: Mary Helen, Angela Marie, Michael Scott O'Neal Jr. AA, Fla. Jr. Coll., 1975; BA in Econs. summa cum laude, U. No. Fla., 1977; JD cum laude, U. Fla., 1979. Bar: Fla. 1980, U.S. Dist. Ct. (mid. dist.) Fla. 1980, U.S. Dist. Ct. (no. dist.) Fla. 1981, U.S. Ct. Appeals (5th and 11th cirs.) 1981, U.S. Supreme Ct. 1986. Assoc. Howell, Liles, Braddock & Milton, Jacksonville, Fla., 1980-83; ptnr. Commander, Legler, Werber, Dawes, Sadler & Howell, 1983-91, Foley & Lardner, Jacksonville, 1991-93, Howell O'Neal & Johnson, Jacksonville, 1993-96, Howell & O'Neal, Jacksonville, 1996—. Pro bono atty. Legal Aid Soc., Jacksonville, 1980—; practicing atty. Lawyers Reference, Jacksonville, 1980—. Pres. Julington Landing Homeowners Assn., Jacksonville, 1980-83. Served to staff sgt. USAF, 1968-74. Mem. ABA, Jacksonville Bar Assn., Fed. Bar Assn., Assn. Trial Lawyers Am., Fla. Def. Lawyers Assn., Northeast Fla. Med. Malpractice Claims Coun. (pres. 1996), Jacksonville Assn. Def. Counsel (pres. 1999), Internat. Assn. Def. Counsel, Def. Rsch. Inst. Republican. Methodist. Clubs: University, San Jose Country (Jacksonville). Avocations: golf, music. Federal civil litigation, State civil litigation, Personal injury. Home: 1299 Norwich Rd Jacksonville FL 32207-7525 Office: Howell O'Neal 200 N Laura St Ste 1100 Jacksonville FL 32202-3500 E-mail: msoneal@hotmail.com

O'NEAL, MIKE ELKINS, university business executive, lawyer; b. Paris, Tex., Feb. 6, 1946; s. Foy Elkins O'Neal and Margie Louise (Thompson) Eagon; m. Nancy Lavender, Dec. 21, 1974; children— Michael David, Amanda Louise. Student Okla. Christian Coll., Heidelberg, Ger., 1966; B.A. summa cum laude, Harding U., 1968; J.D., Stanford U., 1974. Bar: Ark., Calif.; C.P.A. Staff auditor Ernst & Ernst, Dallas, 1968, Touche, Ross & Co., Memphis, 1971; staff tax acct. Coopers & Lybrand, Palo Alto, Calif., part time 1971-74; univ. counsel, asst. prof. bus. adminstrn., devel. spl. rep. Harding U., Searcy, Ark., 1974-76; sole practice law, part time 1974-76; legal counsel Pepperdine U., Malibu, Calif., 1976-78, v.p. fin. and legal counsel, 1978-81, v.p. fin., 1986— ; sole practice law, Malibu, part time 1976—. Bd. dirs. Calif. Christian Sch.; counsel African Christian Hosps. Found., San Diego Christian Found. Served to lt. USN, 1968-70. Decorated Bronze Star. Mem. ABA, Calif. State Bar Assn., Ark. Bar Assn., Am. Inst. C.P.A.s, Okla. Bd. Pub. Accountancy, Ark. Bd. Pub. Accountancy, Nat. Assn. Coll. and Univ. Bus. Officers, Nat. Assn. Coll. and Univ. Attys. Republican. Mem. Ch. of Christ. Office: Pepperdine U 24255 Pacific Coast Hwy Malibu CA 90265

O'NEIL, JOHN JOSEPH, lawyer; b. Detroit, July 20, 1943; s. John J. and Dora J. (Collins) O'N.; children: Meghan, Kathryn. BA, Trinity Coll., 1965; LLB, U. Va., 1968. Bar: N.Y. 1969, U.S. Ct. Appeals (2d cir.) 1969, Fla. 1979, D.C. 1982. Assoc. Jackson & Nash, N.Y.C., 1968-71, Paul, Weiss, Rifkind, Wharton & Garrison, N.Y.C., 1971-77, ptnr., 1977—. Fellow Am. Coll. Trusts and Estates Counsel; mem. ABA (com. on spl. problems of aged), N.Y. State Bar Assn. (com. on taxation, trusts and estates sect.), Assn. Bar City N.Y. (com. on trusts and estates), Pi Gamma Mu. Family and matrimonial, Probate. Office: Paul Weiss Rifkind Wharton & Garrison Ste 1225 1285 Avenue Of The Americas Fl 21 New York NY 10019-6028

O'NEIL, ROBERT MARCHANT, university administrator, law educator; b. Boston, Oct. 16, 1934; s. Walter George and Isabel Sophia (Marchant) O'N.; m. Karen Elizabeth Elson, June 18, 1967; children— Elizabeth, Peter, David, Benjamin AB, Harvard U., 1956, AM, 1957, LLB, 1961; LLD, Beloit Coll., 1985, Ind. U., 1987. Bar: Mass. 1962. Law clk. to Justice William J. Brennan Jr. U.S. Supreme Ct., 1962-63; acting assoc. prof. law U. Calif.-Berkeley, 1963-66, prof., 1966-67, 69-72; exec. asst. to pres., prof. law SUNY-Buffalo, 1967-69; provost, prof. law U. Cin., 1972-73, exec. v.p., prof. law, 1973-75; v.p., prof. law Ind. U., Bloomington, 1975-80; pres. U. Wis. System, 1980-85; prof. law U. Wis.-Madison, 1980-85, U. Va., Charlottesville, 1985—, pres., 1985-90; gen. counsel AAUP, 1970-72, 91-92. Author: Civil Liberties: Case Studies and the Law, 1965, Free Speech: Responsible Communication Under Law, 2d edit., 1972, The Price of Dependency: Civil Liberties in the Welfare State, 1970, No Heroes, No Villians, 1972, The Courts, Government and Higher Education, 1972, Discriminating Against Discrimination, 1976, Handbook of the Law of Public Employment, 1978, 2d rev. edit., 1993, Classrooms in the Crossfire, 1981, Free Speech in the College Community, 1997; co-author: A Guide to Debate, 1964, The Judiciary and Vietnam, 1972, Civil Liberties Today, 1974. Trustee Tchrs. Ins. and Annuity Assn.; bd. dirs. Commonwealth Fund, Fort James Corp., Sta. WVPT Pub. TV, Am. Law Inst., Media Inst. Home: 1839 Westview Rd Charlottesville VA 22903-1632 Office: Thomas Jefferson Ctr Protection Free Expression 400 Peter Jefferson Pl Charlottesville VA 22911-8691

O'NEIL, THOMAS FRANCIS, III, lawyer, business executive; b. Fairfield, Conn., Apr. 8, 1957; s. Thomas F. Jr. and Carmen A. (Therrien) O'N.; m. Nancy D., Aug. 14, 1982; children: Caley Elizabeth, Patrick McGee. AB magna cum laude, Dartmouth Coll., 1975-79; JD, Georgetown U., 1979-82. Bar: Md. 1982, U.S. Dist. Ct. Md. 1983, U.S. Ct. Appeals (4th cir.) 1983, D.C. 1992. Legis. asst. Congressman Stewart B. McKinney, Washington, 1980-82; law clk. Hon. Alexander Harvey II U.S. Dist. Ct. Md.; assoc. Venable, Baetjer & Howard, Balt., 1984-86; asst. U.S. atty. U.S. Dept. Justice, 1986-89; assoc. Hogan & Hartson, 1990-91, ptnr., 1992-95; chief litigation counsel MCI Comms. Corp., Washington, 1995-98; chief legal counsel, sr. v.p. MCI Worldcom, Inc., 1998-2000; sr. v.p., gen. counsel MCI, 2001—. Bd. govs. Ged. Bar Assn., Balt., 1992; Walters Art Museum, ex officio trustee, 1995-96, trustee, 1999—; chairperson William T. Walters Assocs., Georgetown U. Law Ctr. mem., bd. visitors, 1999—; mem. adv. bd. Marbury Inst., 2000—; trustee The Contemporary Mus., 2001—. Recipient Chief Postal Insps. Spl. award U.S. Postal Svc., Washington, 1988, Letter of Commendation award Bur. of Investigation, Washington, 1989, Spl. Achievement award U.S. Dept. Justice, 1989. Mem. Serjeants Inn Law Club. Republican. Roman Catholic. Federal civil litigation, Criminal, Health. Office: MCI Worldcom Inc 1133 19th St NW Washington DC 20036-3604

O'NEILL, ALBERT CLARENCE, JR. lawyer; b. Gainesville, Fla., Nov. 25, 1939; s. Albert Clarence and Sue Virginia (Henry) O'N.; m. Vanda Marie Nigels, Apr. 26, 1969; 1 child, Heather Marie. B.A. with high honors, U. Fla., 1962; LL.B. magna cum laude, Harvard U., 1965. Bar: Fla. bar 1965. Law clk. to judge U.S. Dist. Ct. (mid. dist.) Fla., Jacksonville, 1965-66; assoc. Fowler, White, Collins, Gillen, Humkey & Trenam, Tampa, Fla., 1966-69; ptnr. Trenam, Simmons, Kemker, Scharf & Barkin, 1970-77; mem. firm Trenam, Kemker, Scharf, Barkin, Frye, O'Neill & Mullis (P.A.), 1977—, also bd. dirs. Vis. lectr. law Stetson Law Sch., 1970-73; mem. adv. coun. IRS, 2001—. Exec. editor Harvard Law Rev., 1964-65; contbr. articles to profl. jours. Bd. dirs. Fla. Gulf Coast Symphony, Inc., 1975-86, U. Fla. Found., Inc., 1976-84, 97-2001, Fla. Orch., 1988—. Mem. ABA (chmn. tax sect. 1992-93), Am. Law Inst., Am. Coll. Tax Counsel, Fla. Bar (chmn. tax sect. 1975-76), Am. Bar Retirement Assn. (pres. 2000-01, bd. dirs.), Phi Beta Kappa. General corporate, Pension, profit-sharing, and employee benefits, Taxation, general. Office: Trenam Kemker Scharf Barkin Frye O'Neill & Mullis 101 E Kennedy Blvd Ste 2700 Tampa FL 33602-5150 E-mail: aconeill@trenam.com

O'NEILL, BRIAN BORU, lawyer; b. Hancock, Mich., June 7, 1947; s. Brian Boru and Jean Anette (Rimpela) O'N.; m. Ruth Bohan, Sept. 18, 1991; children: Dru Groves, Brian Boru, Maggie Byrne, Phelan Boru, Ariel Margaret. BS, U.S. Mil. Acad., 1969; JD magna cum laude, U. Mich., 1974; D in Pub. Svc. (hon.), Northland Coll., 1999. Bar: Mich. 1974, U.S. Dist. Ct. Minn. 1977, U.S. Ct. Mil. Appeals 1975, U.S. Ct. Appeals (6th cir.) 1975, U.S. Ct. Appeals (8th cir.) 1977, U.S. Ct. Appeals (Fed. cir.) 1983, U.S. Ct. Appeals (7th cir.) 1985, U.S. Ct. Appeals (10th cir.) 1986, U.S. Ct. Appeals (9th cir.) 1990, U.S. Ct. Claims 1981, U.S. Supreme Ct. 1981. Asst. to gen. counsel Dept. Army, Washington, 1974-77; assoc., ptnr. Faegre & Benson, Mpls., 1977—. Mem. com. vis. Mich. Law Sch., 1994—; counsel Defenders of Wildlife, Washington, 1977—, also bd. dirs; counsel Sierra Club, Audubon Soc. Served to capt. U.S. Army, 1969-77. Named Environmentalist of Yr. Sierra Club North Star, 1982, 96, 97, 98; recipient William Douglas award Sierra Club, 1985, Trial Lawyer of Yr. award Trial Lawyers for Pub. Justice, 1995. Fellow Am. Coll. Trial Lawyers, Order of the Coif; mem. Mpls. Golf, Mpls. Athletic. Federal civil litigation, State civil litigation, Environmental. Office: Faegre & Benson 2200 Wells Fargo Tower 90 S 7th St Ste 2200 Minneapolis MN 55402-3901 E-mail: boneill@faegre.com

O'NEILL, BRIAN DENNIS, lawyer; b. Phila., Feb. 21, 1946; s. Harry William and Margaret Elizabeth (Miller) O'N.; m. Bonnie Anne Ryan, Aug. 17, 1968; children: Aimee Kathleen, Catherine Margaret. BA, Fla. State U., 1968, JD, 1971. Bar: Fla. 1971, D.C. 1975, U.S. Ct. Appeals (D.C. cir.) 1978, U.S. Ct. Appeals (5th and 11th cirs.) 1981, U.S. Ct. Appeals (10th cir.) 1985. Trial atty. Fed. Power Commn., Washington, 1972-75; assoc. Farmer, Shibley, McGuinn & Flood, 1975-80; ptnr. LeBoeuf, Lamb, Greene & MacRae, 1980—. Lectr. in field. Editorial bd. Energy Law Jour., Washington, 1983-84; contbr. articles to profl. jours. Bd. dirs. Immaculata Coll., Rockville, Md., 1989-91; bd. advisors Acad. of the Holy Cross, Kensington, Md., 1994—; bd. visitors Fla. State U. Coll. of Law, 1994—. 2d lt. USAF, 1971-72. Mem. ABA, Fla. Bar Assn. (pub. utilities com. 1985-90), Fed. Energy Bar Assn. (chmn. coms. 1983-84), Congl. Country Club (Bethesda, Md.), Phi Alpha Delta. Democrat. Roman Catholic. Administrative and regulatory, FERC practice, Public utilities. Office: LeBoeuf Lamb Green & MacRae 1875 Connecticut Ave NW Washington DC 20009-5728

O'NEILL, HARRIET, state supreme court justice; Undergrad. degree with honors, Converse Coll.; JD, JD, U. S.C., 1982. Practice law, Houston; with Porter & Clements, Morris & Campbell; pvt. practice, 1982-92; judge 152d Dist. Ct., Houston, 1992; justice 14th Ct. Appeals, 1995, Tex. Supreme Ct., 1998—. Lectr. continuing edn. courses; adv. bd. CLE Inst., 1996; panelist Tex. Ctr. Advanced Jud. Studies., Austin, 1993. Contbr. articles to profl. publs. Mem. U. S.C. academic honors soc.; law sch. rep. ABA. Office: Supreme Ct PO Box 12248 Austin TX 78711-2248*

O'NEILL, PHILIP DANIEL, JR. lawyer, educator; b. Boston, Sept. 19, 1951; s. Philip Daniel Sr. and Alice Maureen (Driscoll) O'N.; m. Lisa G. Arrowood, June 25, 1983; children: Alexander Edwin, Sean Matthew, Madeleine Clarice. BA, Hamilton Coll., 1973; JD cum laude, Boston Coll., 1977. Bar: Mass. 1977, N.Y. 1985, R.I. 1988. Assoc. Hale and Dorr, Boston, 1977-83, ptnr., 1983-87, Edwards & Angell, Boston, 1987—. Adj. rsch. fellow John F. Kennedy Sch. Govt., Ctr. for Sci. and Internat. Affairs Harvard U., 1983-86; adj. prof. law Boston U., 1992, Boston Coll., 1988—; cons. Arms Control and Disarmament Agy. U.S. Dept. Def., 1983-84; guest lectr., commentator Boston Coll. Law Sch., Harvard U. Bus. Sch., Kennedy Sch. Govt., 1985, Boston U. Law Sch., 1990-91, Harvard Law Sch., 1994-95, 98; current pastor internat. and domestic comml. arbitrator Am. Arbiration Assn., Hong Kong Ctr. for Internat. Arbitration, N.Am. Free Trade Agreement, Internat. C. of C., London Ct. Internat. Arbitration, Stockholm Arb. Ctr., Euro-Arab C. of C., World Intellectual Property Orgn.; panelist in internat. and domestic legal programs. Contbr. chpts. to books and articles to profl. jours. Fellow Chartered Inst. Arbitrators (Eng.); mem. ABA, Internat. Law Assn. (chmn. am. br. arbitration com. 1985-89, rep. internat. arbitration com. 1989—), Boston Bar Assn. (chmn. internat. law sect. 1994-96, past chmn. internat. litigation and arbitration com.), Am. Soc. Internat. Law. General civil litigation, General corporate, Private international. Home: 11 Blackburnian Rd Lincoln MA 01773-4137 Office: Edwards & Angell 101 Federal St Fl 23 Boston MA 02110-1800

O'NEILL, PHOEBE JOAN, retired lawyer; b. Seattle, Sept. 5, 1934; d. Herald A. and Phoebe (Titus) O'N.; m. Edward Palfreyman, Sept. 20, 1981. BSE, Marylhurst Coll., 1959; MA, Seattle U., 1970; JD, Lewis & Clark U., 1975. Bar: Oreg. 1975, U.S. Dist. Ct. Oreg. 1975, Wash. 1987, U.S. Dist. Ct. Wash. 1987. Tchr. various schs., Portland and Oreg., 1957-70; dean of students Marylhurst (Oreg.) Coll., 1970-72; law clk. Multnomah County Cir. Ct., Portland, 1972-75, pro tem judge, 1986; law clk. U.S. Dist.

Ct. Oreg., 1975-76; from assoc. to ptnr. Black, Tremaine et al, 1976-84; ptnr. Dunn, Carney, Allen, Higgins & Tongue, 1984—; now ret. Mem. Oreg. State Bar, Multmonah County Bar Assn., Oreg. Assn. Def. Counsel, Def. Rsch. Inst., Wash. Assn. Def. Counsel, Wash. State Bar, Clark County Bar, Fed. Bar Assn. Avocations: hiking, climbing. Federal civil litigation, State civil litigation. Office: Dunn Carney Allen Higgins & Tongue 851 SW 6th Ave Ste 1500 Portland OR 97204-1357

O'NEILL, THOMAS NEWMAN, JR. federal judge; b. Hanover, Pa., July 6, 1928; s. Thomas Newman and Emma (Cornpropst) O'N.; m. Jeanne M. Corr., Feb. 4, 1961; children: Caroline Jeanne, Thomas Newman, III, Ellen Gitt. A.B. magna cum laude, Catholic U. Am., 1950; LL.B. magna cum laude, U. Pa., 1953; postgrad. (Fulbright grantee), London Sch. Econs., 1955-56. Bar: Pa. 1954, U.S. Supreme Ct. 1959. Law clk. to Judge Herbert F. Goodrich U.S. Ct. Appeals (3d cir.), 1953-54; to Justice Harold H. Burton U.S. Supreme Ct., 1954-55; assoc. Montgomery, McCracken, Walker & Rhoads, Phila., 1956-63, ptnr., 1963-83; judge U.S. Dist. Ct. (ea. dist.) Pa., 1983—; counsel 1st and 2d Pa. Legis. Reapportionment Commns., 1971, 81. Lectr. U. Pa. Law Sch., 1973 Articles editor: U. Pa. Law Rev, 1952-53. Former trustee Lawyers Com. for Civil Rights Under Law; former mem. Gov.'s Trial Ct. Nominating Commn. for Phila. County; former mem. bd. overseers U. Pa. Mus. Fellow Am. Coll. Trial Lawyers; mem. Am. Law Inst. (life), Phila. Bar Assn. (chancellor 1976), Pa. Bar Assn. (gov. 1978-81), U. Pa. Law Alumni Soc. (pres. 1976-77), Pa. Conf. County Bar Officers (pres. 1981-82), Am. Inn of Ct. (founding chmn. U. Pa.), Order of Coif (pres. U. Pa. chpt. 1971-73), Merion Cricket Club, Edgemere Club, Broadacres Trouting Assn., Phi Beta Kappa, Phi Eta Sigma. Office: US Dist Ct 4007 US Courthouse 601 Market St Philadelphia PA 19106-1713

O'NEILL, THOMAS NICHOLAS STEPHEN, lawyer; b. Detroit, Jan. 1, 1947; s. Thomas William and Julia Josephine (Pasdertz) O'N.; m. Devon Rae Calonge, Mar. 9, 1975; children: Thomas Guy, Nicholas Wren. BA, Creighton U., 1969; JD, U. Ill., 1972. Bar: Colo. 1973, U.S. Dist. Ct. Colo. 1973, Wash. 1979, U.S. Dist. Ct. (we. dist.) Wash. 1980, U.S. Ct. Appeals (9th cir.) 1981. Staff, supervisory atty. Colo. Rural Legal Services, Alamosa, La Junta, and Durango, 1972-78; staff atty. Evergreen Legal Services, Longview, Wash., 1978-84; assoc. firm Putka & Styve, 1984-95; ptnr. Crandall, Long & O'Neill, 1985—. Pres. bd. dirs. Community Alcoholism Ctr., Longview, 1982-90; bd. dirs. Longview Soccer Club, 1982-89. Mem. Wash. Bar Assn. Administrative and regulatory, State civil litigation, Pension, profit-sharing, and employee benefits. Home: 216 Isaacson Dr Kelso WA 98626-9262 Office: Crandall Long & O'Neill PO Box 336 Longview WA 98632

O'NEILL, TIMOTHY P. lawyer; b. Shotts, Scotland, Sept. 23, 1940; came to U.S., 1953; s. Thomas P. and Catherine (O'Connor) O'N.; m. Maria E. Karagianis, May 19, 1982; children: Katherine, Elizabeth. STB, Gregorian U., Rome, 1965; MA, Brandeis U., 1970; JD, Boston U., 1971. Bar: Mass. 1972, U.S. Dist. Ct. Mass. 1982, U.S. Ct. Appeals (1st cir.) 1982. Asst. dist. atty. Suffolk County, Mass., 1972-81; assoc. Driscoll and Gillespie, Lynn, 1981-83; ptnr. Murphy, DeMarco & O'Neill, Boston, 1983-93, Hanify & King, P.C., Boston, 1993—. Clin. supr. Sch. Law Harvard U., Cambridge, Mass., 1976-81; lectr. Mass. Continuing Legal Edn., 1988—. Chmn. fin. com. City of Boston, 1984-86. Recipient Disting. Prosecutor award Citizens for Decency Through Law, Phoenix, 1981. Mem. ABA, Internat. Assn. Defense Coun., Mass. Bar Assn., Inns Ct. Avocations: skiing, reading, classical music. Federal civil litigation, State civil litigation, Personal injury. Home: 145 Dudley Ln Milton MA 02186-4019 Office: Hanify & King PC One Federal St Boston MA 02110

ONYEMAECHI, PAULINE, lawyer; b. Lagos, Nigeria, Feb. 29, 1960; d. Boniface Onyiro and Veronica Lolo Onyewuche; m. Anozie Chikezie Onyemaechi, Dec. 18, 1981; children: Chinenye, Kelechi, Chioma, Anozie Jr. LLB, U. Benin, Nigeria, 1984; BL, Nigerian Law Sch., Lagos, 1985; M of Comparative Laws, U. Mich., 1988. Bar: Nigeria 1985, Pa. 1991, Md. 1993. Legal asst. Office of Pub. Defender, Balt., 1991-83, asst. pub. defender, 1993; staff atty. Legal Aid Bur., 1993—. W.W. Cook fellow U. Mich., 1987. Mem. ABA, Bar Assn. of Balt. City, Md. State Bar Assn. Home: 5810 Barnwood Pl Columbia MD 21044-2842 Office: Legal Aid Bur Inc 500 E Lexington St Baltimore MD 21202-3560

OPALA, MARIAN P(ETER), state supreme court justice; b. Lódz, Poland, Jan. 20, 1921; BSB in Econs., Oklahoma City U., 1957, JD, 1953, LLD (hon.), 1981; LLM, NYU, 1968; HHD, Okla. Christian U. Sci. & Arts, 1981. Bar: Okla. 1953, U.S. Supreme Ct. 1970. Asst. county atty., Oklahoma County, 1953-56; practiced law Oklahoma City, 1956-60, 65-67; referee Okla. Supreme Ct., 1960-65; prof. law Oklahoma City U. Sch. Law, 1965-69; asst. to presiding justice Supreme Ct. Okla., 1967-68; administrv. dir. Cts. Okla., 1968-77; presiding judge Okla. State Indsl. Ct., 1977-78; judge Workers Compensation Ct., 1978; justice Okla. Supreme Ct., 1978—, chief justice, 1991-92. Adj. prof. law Okla. City U., 1962—, U. Okla. Coll. Law, 1969—; prof. law U. Tulsa Law Sch., 1982—; mem. permanent faculty Am. Acad. Jud. Edn., 1970—; mem. NYU Inst. Jud. Adminstrn.; mem. faculty Nat. Jud. Coll., U. Nev., 1975—; chmn. Nat. Conf. State Ct. Adminstrs., 1976-77; mem. Nat. Conf. Commrs. on Uniform State Laws, 1982—. Co-author: Oklahoma Court Rules for Perfecting a Civil Appeal, 1969 Mem. Adminstrn. Conf. U.S., 1993-95. Recipient Herbert Harley award Am. Judicature Soc., 1977, Disting. Alumni award Oklahoma City U., 1979, Americanism medal Nat. Soc. DAR, 1984, ABA/Am. Law Inst. Harrison Tweed Spl. Merit award, 1987, Humanitarian award NCCJ, 1991, Jour. Record award, 1995, Constn. award Rogers State U., 1996, Jud. Excellence award Okla. Bar Assn., 1997, Leo H. Whinery Disting. Svc. award, 1999, Lifetime Achievement award Oklahoma City Univ. Sch. Law, 2000; inductee Okla. Hall of Fame, 2000. Mem. AbA (edn. com. appellate judges conf. 1984-93), Okla. Bar Assn. (Earl Sneed Continuing Legal Edn. award 1988, Jud. Excellence award 1997), Okla. County Bar Assn., Am. Soc. Legal History, Oklahoma City Title Lawyers Assn., Am. Judicature Soc. (bd. dirs. 1988-92), Am. Law Inst. (elected), Order of Coif, Phi Delta Phi (Oklahoma City Alumni award). Office: Okla Supreme Ct State Capitol Rm 238 Oklahoma City OK 73105

OPPENHEIM, JEFFREY ALAN, lawyer; b. N.Y.C., Dec. 27, 1949; s. Stephen A. and Annette B. Oppenheim; m. Ellen Wiener, May 28, 1978; 1 child, Kara Alison. B.A., Kenyon Coll., 1967-71; J.D., Boston Coll., 1975. Bar: N.Y. 1976, U.S. Dist. Ct. (so. dist.) N.Y. 1976, U.S. Dist. Ct. (ea. dist.) N.Y. 1976, U.S. Ct. Appeals (2nd cir.) 1983, U.S. Supreme Ct., 1983. Assoc. Whitman & Ransom, N.Y.C., 1975— ; instr. Cardozo Law Sch., N.Y.C., 1977. Author: Collier's Bankruptcy Practice Guide, 1982. Trustee Tougaloo Coll., 1980— . Mem. Assn. Bar N.Y.C. Antitrust, Bankruptcy, Federal civil litigation. Office: Whitman & Ransom Whitman Ransom 522 Fif New York NY 10036

OPPENHEIMER, JESSE HALFF, lawyer; b. San Antonio, Jan. 4, 1919; s. Jesse D. and Lillie (Halff) O.; m. Susan R. Rosenthal, July 31, 1946; children: David, Jean, Barbara. Student, U. Tex., 1935-37; BA with honors in Econs., U. Ariz., 1939; JD in Taxation cum laude, Harvard U., 1942, postgrad., 1946. Bar: Tex. 1946. Ptnr. firm Oppenheimer, Blend, Harrison and Tate, Inc., San Antonio, 1970—. Former instr. taxation St. Mary's Law Sch.; lectr. taxation; dir., organizer S.W. Tex. Nat. Bank. Editor Harvard Law Rev., 1942. Former mem. adv. coun. and UTSA Assocs., U. Tex.-San Antonio, v.p., 1977-78; bd. dirs., mem. exec. com. Symphony Soc. San Antonio, former pres., chmn. bd.; former trustee Robert B. Green Hosp., San Antonio, St. Mary's Hall girls sch.; former bd. dirs. Santa Rosa Children's Hosp., United Fund, Children's Svc. Bur., Bexar County Mental Health Assn.; former mem. planning com. U. Tex. Law Sch. Ann. Tax Inst.; former mem. steering com. Met. San Antonio Urban Coalition; former adv. bd. trustees Southwest Found. for Rsch. and Edn.; former mem. Adv. Hosp. Coun., State of Tex.; former mem. adv. bd. Coll.-Cmty. Creative Arts Ctr., Our Lady of the Lake Coll., San Antonio; former mem. Centro-21, San Antonio, 1975-77; mem. economy study group Adv. Coun. Elected Ofcls., Dem. Nat. Com., 1975-76; mem. chancellor's coun., Centennial Commn., U. Tex.; trustee, former pres. Marion Koogler McNay Art Mus., San Antonio; former mem. adv. bd. Ursuline Acad., San Antonio; mem. Kenwood Neighborwood Coun.; trustee The Woodrow Wilson Internat. Ctr. for Scholars, Washington, 1980-87. Served to lt. col. U.S. Army; World War II; ETO, PTO. Mem. ABA (former mem. taxation com.). Clubs: Argyle (organizing bd., bd. dirs.), San Antonio Country Club, Giraud. Estate planning, General practice, Real property. Office: Oppenheimer Blend Harrison and Tate Attys 711 Navarro St Fl 6 San Antonio TX 78205-1721 E-mail: jho@obht.com

OPPENHEIMER, RANDOLPH CARL, lawyer; b. N.Y.C., Feb. 5, 1954; s. Bennett and Sandra (Haber) O.; m. Cynthia Ellen Shatkin, June 19, 1976; children: Benjamin David, Adam Jeremy, Jacob Aaron, Jordan Michael, Daniel Corey. BA, U. Vt., 1976; JD, Case Western Res. U., 1979. Bar: N.Y. 1980, U.S. Dist. Ct. (we. dist.) N.Y. 1980, U.S. Dist. Ct. (no. dist.) N.y. 1995, U.S. Bankruptcy Ct. 1980, U.S. Ct. Appeals (2d cir.) 1981. Assoc. Kavinoky & Cook, Buffalo, 1979-84, ptnr., 1984—. Instr. legal research, writing and adv., Case Western Res. U., 1978-79. Assoc. editor Case Western Reserve Law Rev., 1977-79. Mem. ABA, N.Y. Bar Assn., Erie County Bar Assn. E-mail (office). Contracts commercial, General corporate, Labor. Home: 195 Greenaway Rd Buffalo NY 14226-4165 Office: Kavinoky & Cook 120 Delaware Ave Rm 600 Buffalo NY 14202-2793 E-mail: roppenheimer@kavinokycook.com

ORBERSON, WILLIAM BAXTER, lawyer, educator; b. Jeffersonville, Ind., Aug. 24, 1962; s. William B. and Nancy Lee Orberson; m. Lea Lynn Mater, May 18, 1984; children: Katherine, Madeline, Allyson. BA in Bus. Adminstrn. magna cum laude, Bellarmine Coll., 1983; JD cum laude, U. Louisville, 1986. Bar: Ky. 1986, U.S. Dist. Ct. (ea. dist.) Ky. 1987, U.S. Dist. Ct. (we. dist.) Ky. 1990. Ptnr. Phillips, Parker, Orberson and Moore P.L.C., Louisville, 1986—. Adj. prof. U. Louisville Sch. Law, 1994—. Bd. dirs. Chapel Creek Neighborhood Assn., New Albany, Ind., 1997, v.p., 1998. Mem. ABA, Am. Judicature Soc., Def. Rsch. Inst., Ky. Bar Assn., Louisville Bar Assn. (exec. com. litigation sect. 1994), St. Xavier Legal Soc., Ky. Def. Counsel, U. Louisville Sch. Law Alumni Assn. (class dir. 1994—). Republican. Roman Catholic. Avocations: golf, fishing. General civil litigation, Insurance, Personal injury. Office: Phillips Parker Orberson and Moore 716 W Main St Ste 300 Louisville KY 40202-2634 Fax: 502-587-1927

ORDOVER, ABRAHAM PHILIP, lawyer, mediator; b. Far Rockaway, N.Y., Jan. 18, 1937; s. Joseph and Bertha (Fromberg) O.; m. Carol M. Ordover, Mar. 23, 1961 (dec. 1999); children: Andrew Charles, Thomas Edward; m. Eleanor Musick, Feb. 24, 2001. BA magna cum laude, Syracuse U., 1958; JD, Yale U., 1961. Bar: N.Y. 1961, U.S. Dist. Ct. (so. and ea. dists.) N.Y., U.S. Ct. Appeals (2d cir.), U.S. Supreme Ct. Assoc. Cahill, Gordon & Reindel, N.Y.C., 1961-71; prof. law Hofstra U., Hempstead, N.Y., 1971-81; L.Q.C. Lamar prof. law Emory U., Atlanta, 1981-91; CEO Resolution Resources Corp., 1991—; mediator and arbitrator. Vis. prof. Cornell U., Ithaca, N.Y., 1977; vis. lectr. Tel Aviv U., 1989, Am. Law Inst.; team leader nat. program Nat. Inst. Trial Advocacy, Boulder, Colo., 1980, 82, 84, 86, 89, tchr. program Cambridge, Mass., 1979-84, 88, adv. program Gainesville, Fla., 1978-79, northeast regional dir., 1977-81; team leader SE regional program, 1983; team leader Atlanta Bar Trial Tech. Program, 1981-91; lectr. in field; sr. v.p. Resolute Sys. Inc., bd. dirs. Author: Argument to the Jury, 1982, Problems and Cases in Trial Advocacy, 1983, Advanced Materials in Trial Advocacy, 1988, Alternatives to Litigation, 1993, Cases and Materials in Evidence, 1993, Art of Negotiation, 1994; prodr. ednl. films; contbr. articles to profl. jours. Bd. dirs. Atlanta Legal Aid Soc., 1984-91, 7 Stages Theatre, 1991-96. Recipient Gumpert award Am. Coll. Trial Lawyers, 1984, 85, Jacobsen award Roscoe Pound Am. Trial Lawyer Found., 1986. Fellow Am. Coll. Civil Trial Mediators; mem. ABA, N.Y. State Bar Assn., Assn. Am. Law Schs. (chair litigation sect.), Atlanta Lawyers Club, Am. Law Inst., Am. Acad. of Civil Trial Mediators. Avocation: photography. Office: Resolution Resources Corp 303 Peachtree St Atlanta GA 30308-3201 E-mail: ordover@rrcatlanta.com

O'REILLY, DENIS, aluminum company executive, lawyer; b. Pointe Gatineau, Que., Can., Feb. 9, 1950; s. Florian D. and Marielle O'R.; B.A. with honors, Three Rivers U., 1969; LL.L., Montreal U., 1973; postgrad. Ecole des Hautes Etudes Commerciales, Montreal, 1976; m. Jocelyne Ryter, Aug. 16, 1980; children: Marianne, Patrick. Called to Que. bar, 1975; research worker Sec. of State, Ottawa, Ont., Can., 1971; analyst Datum Sedoj, Montreal, Que., Can., 1972; assoc. firm Lette & Assocs., Montreal, 1973-76; legal officer Aluminum Co. of Can., Ltd., Montreal, 1977-80; chief legal officer, sec. Alcan Smelters and Chems. Ltd., Montreal, 1981-82, also dir. adminstrn.; pres., gen. mgr. Vic Metal Corp., Victoriaville, Que., 1982—; pres., Vic West Steel, Oakville, Ont., 1986—. Mem. Bd. Trade (Que.), Quebec Bar Assn., Can. Bar Assn., Can. Constrn. Assn. (dir.). Office: 1296 So Svc Rd W Oakville ON Canada L6L 5M7

O'REILLY, JAMES THOMAS, lawyer, educator, author; b. N.Y.C., Nov. 15, 1947; s. Matthew Richard and Regina (Casey) O'R.; children: Jean, Ann. BA cum laude, Boston Coll., 1969; JD, U. Va., 1974. Bar: Va. 1974, Ohio 1974, U.S. Supreme Ct. 1979, U.S. Ct. Appeals (6th cir.) 1980. Atty. Procter & Gamble Co., Cin., 1974-76, counsel, 1976-79, sr. counsel for food, drug and product safety, 1979-85, corp. counsel, 1985-93, assoc. gen. counsel, 1993-98; adj. prof. in adminstrv. law U. Cin., 1980-97, vis. prof. law, 1998—. Cons. Adminstrv. Conf. U.S., 1981-82, 89-90, Congl. Office of Compliance, 1995-96; arbitrator State Employee Rels. Bd.; mem. Ohio Bishops Adv. Coun., Mayor's Infrastructure Commn., Cin. Environ. Adv. Coun. Author: Federal Information Disclosure, 1977, Food and Drug Administration Regulatory Manual, 1979, Unions' Rights to Company Information, 1980, Federal Regulation of the Chemical Industry, 1980, Administrative Rulemaking, 1983, Ohio Public Employee Collective Bargaining, 1984, Protecting Workplace Secrets, 1985, Emergency Response to Chemical Accidents, 1986, Product Defects and Hazards, 1987, Protecting Trade Secrets Under SARA, 1988, Toxic Torts Strategy Deskbook, 1989, Complying With Canada's New Labeling Law, 1989, Solid Waste Management, 1991, Ohio Products Liability Handbook, 1991, Toxic Torts Guide, 1991, ABA Product Liability Resource Manual, 1993, RCRA and Superfund Practice Guide, 1993, Clean Air Permits Manula, 1994, United States Environmental Liabilities, 1994, Elder Safety, 1995, Environmental and Workplace Safety for University and Hospital Managers, 1996, Indoor Environmental Health, 1997, Product Warnings, Defects & Hazards, 1999, Accident Prevention Manual, 2000; mem. editl. bd. Food and Drug Cosmetic Law Jour.; contbr. articles to profl. jours. Mem. Hamilton County Dem. Ctrl. Com. Served with U.S. Army, 1970-72. Mem. ABA (chmn. AD law sect.), FBA, Food and Drug Law Inst. (chair program com.), Leadership Cin. Democrat. Roman Catholic. Administrative and regulatory, Environmental. Office: 24 Jewett Dr Cincinnati OH 45215-2648

O'REILLY, TERENCE JOHN, lawyer; b. Farnborough, Eng., Apr. 12, 1945; came to U.S., 1960, naturalized, 1965; s. Arthur Francis and Doris Eileen (Burden) O'R.; m. Katharine Van Dyke Wallace, Sept. 26, 1970; children: Tobin Cooper, Matthew Wallace. BA, Loyola U., 1966; JD, U. Calif., Berkeley, 1969. Bar: Calif. 1970. Assoc. Voegelin, Barton, L.A., 1969-70, Walkup, Downing & Sterns, San Francisco, 1970-75; mem. Walkup, Shelby, Bastian, Melodia, Kelly & O'Reilly, 1975-87; prin. O'Reilly, Collins & Danko, San Mateo, Calif., 1987—. Lectr. Kennedy Law Sch., Moraga, Calif., 1975-76, Inner Cir. of Advocates, 1998—; bd. govs., Consumer Attys. of Calif., 1995—. V.p. No. Calif. Rugby Football, San Francisco, 1975-80, bd. dirs., 1975—; bd. dirs. U.S. Rugby Football Found.; trustee The Philip Brooks Sch., 1986-89, Coun. of Bancroft Libr., U. Calif. Mem. Am. Bd. Profl. Liability Lawyers (bd. dirs. 1989—), Boalt Hall Alumni (bd. dirs. 1982-85), Assn. San Francisco Trial Lawyers (bd. dirs. 1985—), Assn. San Mateo Trial Lawyers (dir. 1992—), Bohemian Club, Burlingame Country Club, Menlo Circus Club, Pacific Union Club. Roman Catholic. Personal injury, Product liability. Office: attn Debra Foster 1900 O'Farrell St Ste 360 San Mateo CA 94403 E-mail: toreilly@oreillylaw.com

O'REILLY, TIMOTHY PATRICK, lawyer; b. San Lorenzo, Calif., Sept. 12, 1945; s. Thomas Marvin and Florence Ann (Ohlman) O'R.; m. Susan Ann Marshall, July 18, 1969; children: T. Patrick Jr., Sean M., Colleen K. BS, Ohio State U., 1967; JD, NYU, 1971. Bar: Pa. 1971, U.S. Dist. Ct. (ea. dist.) Pa. 1971, U.S. Dist. Ct. (mid. dist.) Pa. 1972, U.S. Ct. Appeals (3d cir.) 1977, U.S. Supreme Ct. 1988. Ptnr. Morgan, Lewis & Bockius, Phila., 1978—. Editor: Developing Labor Law, 1989; contbr. articles to profl. jours. V.p. Chester Valley Bd. Govs., Malvern, Pa., 1980-85; bd. dirs. Notre Dame Acad. and Devon Preparatory Sch. Elected to Coll. of Labor and Employment Lawyers. Mem. ABA (chmn. com. on devel. of the law under the Nat. Labor Rels. Act., editor-in-chief The Developing Labor Law jour., mem. coun. labor and employment sect.), Pa. Bar Assn., Phila. Bar Assn., Ohio State U. Alumni Assn. Avocation: golf. Labor, Pension, profit-sharing, and employee benefits. Home: 1127 Cymry Dr Berwyn PA 19312-2056 Office: Morgan Lewis & Bockius 1701 Market St Philadelphia PA 19103-2903 E-mail: toreilly@morganlewis.com

ORLEANS, NEIL JEFFREY, lawyer; b. N.Y.C., June 7, 1948; s. Fred Allan and Shirley (Kovner) O.; m. Joan Elizabeth Painter, Aug. 10, 1974; children: David Anthony, Kimberly Ann. BA with high honors, U. Tex., Austin, 1969; JD with honors, U. Tex., 1971. Bar: Tex. 1972, U.S. Ct. Mil. Appeals 1972, U.S. Ct. Appeals (5th cir.) 1981, U.S. Dist. Ct. (no. dist.) Tex. 1978, U.S. Dist. Ct. (we. dist.) Tex. 1981, U.S. Dist. Ct. (ea. dist.) Tex. 1983. Assoc. Eldridge, Goggans, Dallas, 1976-78, Baldwin & Assocs., Dallas, 1978-79; ptnr. Wise, Stuhl, Andrea, Orleans and Morris, 1979-87, Goins, UnderKofler, Crawford & Langdon, Dallas, 1988—. Ruler elder North Park Presbyn. Ch., Dallas, 1980-82, 97-99. Capt. JAGC, USAF, 1972-76. Mem. ABA, Tex. Bar Assn., Dallas Bar Assn., Dallas Bankruptcy Bar Assn., Dallas Hist. Preservation Soc., Phi Beta Kappa. Republican. Alternative dispute resolution, Bankruptcy, General civil litigation. Office: Goins UnderKofler Crawford & Langdon 3300 Thanksgiving Tower Dallas TX 75201

ORMASA, JOHN, retired utility executive, lawyer; b. Richmond, Calif., May 30, 1925; s. Juan Hormaza and Maria Inocencia Olondo; m. Dorothy Helen Trumble, Feb. 17, 1952; children: Newton Lee, John Trumble, Nancy Jean Davies. BA, U. Calif.-Berkeley, 1948; JD, Harvard U., 1951. Bar: Calif. 1952, U.S. Supreme Ct. 1959. Assoc. Clifford C. Anglim, 1951-52; assoc. Richmond, Carlson, Collins, Gordon & Bold, 1952-56, ptnr., 1956-59; with So. Calif. Gas Co., L.A., 1959-66, gen. atty., 1963-65, v.p., gen. counsel, 1965-66; v.p., sys. gen. counsel Pacific Lighting Service Co., Los Angeles, 1966-72; v.p., gen. counsel Pacific Lighting Corp., Los Angeles, 1973-75, v.p., sec., gen. counsel, 1975. Acting city atty., El Cerrito, Calif., 1952. Served with U.S. Navy, 1943-46. Mem. ABA, Calif. State Bar Assn., Richmond (Calif.) Bar Assn. (pres. 1959), Kiwanis (v.p. 1959). Republican. Roman Catholic.

ORNITZ, RICHARD MARTIN, lawyer, business executive; b. Annapolis, Md., July 4, 1945; s. Martin Nathaniel and Beatrice Cynthia (Swick) O.; m. Margareth Adams, June 15, 1971 (div. Apr. 1977); m. Janet Alma Steen, Dec. 5, 1981; children— Alexandra, Zachary, Darren, Erik, Nicholas. B.S. in Metall. Engring., Cornell U., 1967; J.D., NYU, 1970; grad. sr. exec. program, MIT, 1985. Bar: N.Y. 1971, U.S. Dist. Ct. (ea. dist.) 1972, U.S. Supreme Ct. 1984. Assoc. Cravath, Swaine & Moore, N.Y.C., 1972-77; v.p., gen. counsel, sec. Degussa Corp., Teterboro, N.J. 1977-90, mem. mgmt. com., 1987-90; of counsel, Hughes, Hubbard & Reed, N.Y.C., 1985-92; dir. Degussa Corp. subs., 1980-92; ptnr. Stroock, Stroock & Lavan, 1991-95; ptnr., chmn., fin. Coudert Bros., 1996—; speaker Risk Ins. Mgmt. Soc., 1984, 85, 86, IBA, 1986, ACCA, 1986, European Co. Lawyers Assn., 1986; Swiss Co. Lawyers Assn., 1987; Norwegian Co. Lawyers Assn., 1988; mem. pvt. law adv. com. Office of Legal Adv. U.S. Dept. State, adv. bd. Nat. Inst. Preventive Maintenance, adv. bd. corp. counsel Am. Arbitration Assn. Assoc. editor Ann. Survey of Law, NYU, 1970. Fin. com. Conn. Spl. Olympics; bd. dirs. Old Greenwich Civic Assn. Served to 1st lt. U.S. Army, 1970-72. Mem. ABA (chmn. European law sect., human relations and labor law, 1987-90), N.Y. State Bar Assn., Internat. Bar Assn., Am. Corp. Counsel Assn. (chmn. of internat. sect. com., 1986-90) European Am. Gen. Counsels Group (chmn. 1986-87), N.J. Gen. Counsels Group, Cornell Soc. Engrs. Republican. Jewish. Clubs: Old Greenwich Republican (Conn.), Innis Arden, Rocky Point. General corporate, Insurance, Private international. Home: 18 Meadowbank Rd Old Greenwich CT 06870-2312 Office: Coudert Bros 1411 Avenue Of The Americas New York NY 10019-2512

O'ROURKE, JAMES LOUIS, lawyer; b. Bridgeport, Conn., July 5, 1958; s. James G. and Margaret Elizabeth (Fesco) O'R.; m. Margaret C. DiCicco, Sept. 18, 1994. BS, U. Bridgeport, 1984, JD, 1987. Bar: Conn. 1988, U.S. Dist. Ct. Conn. 1989, Mashantucket Pequot Tribal Bar 1995, Supreme Ct. of U.S., 1998. Pvt. practice, Stratford, Conn., 1987—. With USN, 1976-79. Mem. ABA, Assn. Am. Trial Lawyers Assn., Conn. Trial Lawyers Assn., Conn. Bar Assn., Greater Bridgeport Bar Assn. Roman Catholic. Avocations: boating, cycling, swimming, golf. General practice, Personal injury, Workers' compensation. Office: The Barnum Profl Bldg 1825 Barnum Ave Ste 201 Stratford CT 06614-5333

O'ROURKE, WILLIAM ANDREW, III, lawyer; b. Columbus, Ohio, Jan. 11, 1958; s. William A. Jr. and Jean (Solari) O'R.; m. Sandra Statum; children: Kevin, Melanie, Brian, Patrick. BA, Holy Cross Coll., 1980; JD, Suffolk U., 1983. Bar: Vt. 1984, U.S. Dist. Ct. Vt. 1985. Atty., shareholder Ryan, Smith & Carbine, Rutland, Vt., 1984—. Mem. Vt. Health Policy Coun., Montpelier, 1987, Mt. Saint Joseph Sch. Bd. Mem. ABA, ATLA., Def. Rsch. Inst., Christ the King Sch. Athletic Assn. Insurance, Personal injury, Workers' compensation. Home: 10 Hilltop Ter Rutland VT 05701-4612 Office: Ryan Smith & Carbine PO Box 310 Rutland VT 05702-0310 E-mail: wor@rsclaw.com

ORR, ROBERT F. state supreme court justice; b. Norfolk, Va., Oct. 11, 1946; AB, U. N.C., 1971, JD, 1975. Bar: N.C. 1975. Pvt. practice, Asheville, N.C., 1975-86; assoc. judge N.C. Ct. Appeals, 1986-94; assoc. justice N.C. Supreme Ct., Raleigh, 1994—. Mem. N.C. Beverage Control Commn., 1985-86; adj. prof. appellate advocacy N.C. Ctrl. U. Sch. Law, 1989—, adj. prof. N.C. State constl. law, 1998. Mem. Asheville-Revitalization Commn., 1977-81, Asheville-Buncombe Hist. Resources Commn., 1980-81; bd. trustees Hist. Preservation Found. N.C., 1982-85; mem. Nat. Park Sys. Adv. Bd., 1990-95, chmn., 1992-93; bd. visitors U. N.C.-Chapel Hill, 1996—; mem. NCBAs Appellate Rules Study com., 1999—, Gov.'s Crime Commn. With U.S. Army, 1968-71. Mem. N.C. State Bar, 28th Jud. Dist., N.C. Bar Assn. Republican. Office: PO Box 1841 Raleigh NC 27602-1841 also: 304 Justice Bldg 2 E Morgan St Raleigh NC 27601-1428*

ORRILL, R. RAY, JR. lawyer; b. Port Arthur, Tex., June 17, 1944; s. R. Ray and Jo Ella (LaCaze-Iles) O.; m. Gwendolyn Kay Dartez, Aug. 26, 1967; 1 child, R. Ray; m. Teresa Elizabeth Zeringue, Sept. 24, 1977. B.S., Lamar U., 1966; J.D., Loyola U., New Orleans, 1972. Bar: La. 1972, U.S. Dist. Ct. (ea. dist.) La. 1972, U.S. Ct. Appeals (5th cir.) 1977, U.S. Supreme Ct. 1981; diplomate Nat. Bd. Trial Advocacy. Grad. fellow La. State U. Med. Sch., 1966-69; asst. trial practice Loyola Law Sch., 1971; asst. Fred J. Gisevius, Jr., New Orleans, 1972-73; ptnr. Orrill & Hecker, New Orleans, 1975-79, Orrill & Avery, New Orleans, 1982-85; vice-chmn. bd. dirs. First Eastern Bank & Trust, New Orleans, 1983-98; ptnr. Orrill & Shearman, New Orleans, 1987— . Author videotape lectr. series: Federal and State Trial Procedure: A Comparison, Inst. Audio Video Ct. Reporting, Inc., 1974. Bd. dirs. Bd. Zoning Adjustments, City of New Orleans, 1987, Nat. Investigation Rev. Bd., New Orleans, 1987. Mem. Am. Trial Lawyers Assn., La. Bar Assn., La. Trial Lawyers Assn., New Orleans Acad. Trial Lawyers, La. Real Estate Lawyers Assn., Internat. Head injury Inst. (diplomate). Methodist. Federal civil litigation, State civil litigation, Personal injury. Office: 7240 Crowder Blvd Ste 300 New Orleans LA 70127-1979

ORSATTI, ERNEST BENJAMIN, lawyer; b. Pitts., Nov. 14, 1949; s. Ernest Ubaldo and Dorothy Minerva (Pfeiffer) O.; m. Ingrid Zalman, May 3, 1975; 1 child, Benjamin E. BA, Marquette U., 1971; JD, Duquesne U., 1974; postgrad., Army Command and Gen. Staff Coll., 1984. Bar: Pa. 1974, U.S. Dist. Ct. (we. dist.) Pa. 1974, U.S. Ct. Appeals (3d cir.) 1977, U.S. Supreme Ct. 1978, U.S. Ct. Appeals (6th cir.) 1992. Assoc. Jubelirer, Pass & Intrieri, Pitts., 1974-81, ptnr., 1981—. Contbg. editor: The Developing Labor Law, 3d edit., 1992. Bd. dirs. Am. Italian Cultural Inst., Pitts. Served to capt. U.S. Army, 1975, lt. col., USAR, ret. Mem. ABA, ACLU (legal com. 1996—), Am. Arbitration Assn., Pa. Bar Assn., Allegheny County Bar Assn. (profl. ethics com. 2000—), Am. Legion. Democrat. Roman Catholic. Labor, Military. Home: 9343 N Florence Rd Pittsburgh PA 15237-4815 Office: Jubelirer Pass & Intrieri 219 Fort Pitt Blvd Pittsburgh PA 15222-1576 E-mail: ebo@jpilaw.com, eborsatti@aol.com

ORSBON, RICHARD ANTHONY, lawyer; b. Sept. 23, 1947; s. Richard Chapman and Ruby Estelle (Wyatt) Orsbon; m. Susan Cowan Shivers, June 13, 1970; children: Sarah Hollingsworth, Wyatt Benjamin, David Allison. BA Distng. mil. grad. ROTC, Davidson Coll., 1969; JD, Vanderbilt U., 1972; hon. grad. Officers Basic Course, U.S. Army, 1972. Bar: N.C. 1972, U.S. Dist. Ct. (we. dist.) N.C. 1972, cert.: (specialist in probate and fiduciary law). Assoc. Kennedy, Covington, Lobdell & Hickman, Charlotte, NC, 1972—75, Parker, Poe et al, Charlotte, 1975—77, ptnr., 1978—. Lectr. on estate planning, probate; pres. ECO, Inc., Charlotte, 1982—. Editor (assoc., contbr.): (law rev.) Vanderbilt Law Rev., 1971—72. Mem. planning bd. Queens Coll. Estate Planning Day, 1978—, chmn., 1991; trustee Davidson Coll., 1990—91, Camp Tekoa, Hendersonville, NC; mem. YMCA basketball com.; bd. vis. Johnson C. Smith U., 1986—89; mem. Dem. state exec. com., 1980; chmn. adminstrv. bd. Myers Park United Meth. Ch., 1994—96; bd. dir. Charlotte United Way, 1983—; bd. dir. law explorer program Boy Scouts Am., Charlotte, NC, 1976—78. 1st lt. U.S. Army, 1972—73. Named Outstanding Vol., Charlotte Observer/United Way, 1984; scholar Patrick Wilson Merit, Vanderbilt U. Law Sch., 1969—72. Mem.: ABA (real property probate sect.), N.C. State Bar (cert. specialist estate planning and probate 1987), N.C. Bar Assn. (probate and fiduciary law sect., author, spkr. 1987—92), N.C. Bar Assn. Coll. of Advocacy, Charlotte Estate Planning Coun. (exec. com. 1992—, sec. 1994—, pres. 1996—97), Mecklenburg County Bar Assn. (law day com., vol. lawyers program, bd. dir., chmn. 1988—89, grievance com. 1987—88), Deans Assn. of Vanderbilt U. Law Sch. (bd. dir.), Davidson Coll. Alumni Assn. (bd. dir. 1983, class alumni sec. 1986—, pres.-elect 1989—90, pres. 1990—91, bd. dir. Wildcat Club 1989—, pres. 1993—98), Foxcroft Swim and Racquet Club (pres. 1986—87, bd. dir. 1985—88), Omicron Delta Kappa. Estate planning, Probate, Estate taxation. Home: 2819 Rothwood Dr Charlotte NC 28211-2623 Office: Parker Poe Thompson 2600 Charlotte Plz Charlotte NC 28244

ORTEGO, JIM, lawyer, legal educator; b. Lake Charles, La., Oct. 6, 1944; s. Yves and Lucille May (Dougay) O. JD, Tulane U., 1969; LLM, U. Toronto, 1973. Bar: La. 1969; bd. cert. family law specialist. Prof. law Dalhousie U., Halifax, N.S., Can., 1974-78; vis. fellow in law U. Chgo., 1978; prof. law Whittier Coll. Law, L.A., 1978-82. Cons. Law Reform Commn. of Can., Ottawa, 1975-78, Stats. Can., Ottawa, 1975-80, Law Enforcement Assistance Adminstrn., Washington, 1978-81; vis. prof. law La. State U. Law Ctr., 1980; mem. La. Family Law Adv. Commn.; mem. La. S. Ct. Task Force on Legal Svcs., mem. La. Supreme Ct. com. on prompt and affordable justice symposium. Co-author: Criminal Law, 1975, Selected Problems in Criminal Law, 1976; editor La. Family Law Newsletter. Mem. ABA (family law sect.), La. State Bar Assn. (chair family law sect., editor La. family law newsletter, Pro Bono award 1994), S.W. La. Bar Assn. Democrat. Family and matrimonial. Address: 1011 Lake Shore Dr Ste 402 Lake Charles LA 70601-9416 E-mail: joswlls@aol.com

ORTH, PAUL WILLIAM, retired lawyer; b. Balt., May 7, 1930; s. Paul W. and Naomi (Howard Bevard) O.; m. Isle Haertle, June 15, 1956; children: Ingrid, Ilse Christine. AB, Dartmouth Coll., 1951; JD, Harvard U., 1954. Bar: Mass. 1954, Conn. 1957, U.S. Dist. Ct. Conn. 1958, U.S. Ct. Appeals (2d cir.) 1960, U.S. Ct. Appeals (1st cir.) 1983, U.S. Supreme Ct. 1960. Assoc. Hoppin, Carey & Powell, Hartford, Conn., 1957-62, ptnr., 1962-86, Shipman & Goodwin, Hartford, 1987-2000, MacDermid, Reynods & Glissman P.C., Hartford, 2000—. Instr. Sch. Law U. Conn., 1959-81. Editor: Every Employee's Guide to the Law, 1993, 96. Chmn. Farmington Conservation Commn., 1982-83; mem. town com. Town of Farmington, 1973-81; dir. Conn. Opera Assn., 2000—. With AUS, 1954-56. Fellow Am. Bar Found., Conn. Bar Found.; mem. ABA, Hartford County Bar Assn. (pres. 1983-84), Conn. Bar Assn. (chmn. coms.). Democrat Alternative dispute resolution, General civil litigation, Labor. Office: MacDermid Reynold & Glissman PC 86 Farmington Ave Hartford CT 06105 E-mail: porth@mrglaw.com

ORTIQUE, REVIUS OLIVER, JR. city official, retired state supreme court justice; b. New Orleans, June 14, 1924; s. Revius Oliver and Lillie Edith (Long) O.; m. Miriam Marie Victorianne, Dec. 29, 1947; 1 child: Rhesa Marie (Mrs. Alden J. McDonald). AB, Dillard U., 1947; MA, Ind. U., 1949; JD, So. U., 1956; LLD (hon.), Campbell Coll., 1960; LHD (hon.), Ithaca Coll., 1971; LLD (hon.), Ind. U., 1983, Morris Brown Coll., 1992, Loyola U. South, 1993, Dillard U., 1996. Bar: La. 1956, U.S. Dist. Ct 1956, Eastern Dist. La 1956, U.S. Fifth Circuit Ct. of Appeals 1956, U.S. Supreme Ct 1964. Practiced in, New Orleans, 1956-78; judge Civil Dist. Ct. for Orleans Parish, 1978-92; assoc. justice La. Supreme Ct., 1993-94; chmn. New Orleans Aviation Bd., 1994—. Lectr. labor law Dillard U., 1950-52, U. West Indies, 1986; formerly assoc. gen. counsel Cmty. Improvement Agy.; former gen. counsel 8th Dist. A.M.E. Ch.; former mem. Fed. Hosp. Coun., 1966, Pres.'s Commn. on Campus Unrest, 1970, Bd. Legal Svcs. Corp., 1975-83; chief judge civil cts. Orleans Parish, 1986-87; spkr. in field; U.S. alt. rep. to 54th Gen. Assembly UN, 1999-2000. Contbr. articles to profl. jours. Former pres. Met. Area Com.; former mem. Bd. City Trusts, New Orleans Legal Assistance Corp. Bd., Ad Hoc Com. for Devel. of Ctrl. Bus. Dist. City of New Orleans; bd. dirs. Cmty. Rels. Coun., Am. Lung Assn.; trustee Antioch Coll. Law, New Orleans chpt. Operation PUSH, 1981-84; pres. Louis A. Martinet Soc., 1959; active World's Fair, New Orleans, 1984, Civil Rights Movement, 1960-79; bd. dirs., mem. exec. com. Nat. Sr. Citizens Law Ctr., L.A., 1970-76, Criminal Justice Coordinating Com., UN Assn. New Orleans, 1980—; former mem. exec. bd. Nat. Bar Found.; mem. exec. com. Econ. Devel. Coun. Greater New Orleans; past chmn. Health Edn. Authority of La.; trustee, mem. exec. com. Dillard U.; former mem. bd. mgmt. Flint Goodridge Hosp.; former mem. adv. bd. League Women Voters Greater New Orleans; former mem. men's adv. bd. YWCA; trustee AME Ch., former connectional trustee; former chancellor New Orleans Fedn. Chs.; bd. dirs. Nat. Legal Aid and Defender Assn.; trustee Civil Justice Found.; served on over 50 bds., commns. 1st lt. AUS, 1943-47, PTO. Recipient Arthur von Briesen medal Disting. Svcs. Disadvantaged Ams. NLADA, 1971, Weiss award NCCJ, 1975, Brotherhood award NCCJ, 1976, Nat. Black Achievement award, 1979, Poor People's Banner award, 1979, William H. Hastie award, 1983, Outstanding Citizen award Kiwanis of Pontchartrain, 1986, Civil Justice award, 1989, Daniel E. Byrd award NAACP, 1991, A.P. Tureaud Meml. medal La. State NAACP, 1993; Revius O. Ortique Jr. Law Libr. named in his honor, Lafayette, La., 1988; named Outstanding Young Man Nat. Urban League, 1958, Outstanding Person in La. Inst. Human Understanding, 1976, Citizen of Yr. Shreveport, 1993. Mem. ABA (del., Legal Svcs. program, Nat. adv. coun., 1964-71, jud. divsn., Thurgood Marshal award 2000), Nat. Bar Assn. (pres. 1965-66, exec. bd., Raymond Pace Alexander award, jud. coun. 1987, William Hastie award 1982, Gertrude E. Rush award 1991, Thurgood Marshall award 2000), La. State Bar Assn. (former mem. ho. of dels., Lifetime Achievement award 1986, WTC award for Exceptional Internat. Distinction, 2001), Nat. Legal Aid and Defender Assn. (past pres., mem. exec. bd.), La. District Judges Assn., Am. Judicature Soc. (bd. dirs. 1975-79), Civil Justice Found. (trustee 1989-93), Louis A. Martinet Legal Soc., World Peace Through Law (charter mem.), Blue Key Honor Soc., Phi Delta Kappa, Alpha Kappa Delta. Home: 10 Park Island Dr New Orleans LA 70122-1229 Office: New Orleans Aviation Bd PO Box 20007 New Orleans LA 70141-0007

ORTIZ, JAY RICHARD GENTRY, lawyer; b. Washington, Mar. 21, 1945; s. Charles and Catherine Gentry (Candlin) O.; m. Lois Wright Hatcher Greer, June 12, 1982. B.A., Yale U., 1967; postgrad. Stanford U. 1967-68; J.D., U. N.Mex., 1972. Bar: N.Mex. 1973, Mo. 1978, Tenn. 1982, Ga., 1991, U.S. Dist. Ct. N.Mex. 1973, U.S. Ct. Appeals (10th cir. 1973), U.S. Supreme Ct. 1977, U.S. Dist. Ct. (western dist.) Mo. 1978, U.S. Dist. Ct. (no. dist.) Ga. 1991, U.S. Ct. Appeals (8th cir.) 1978, U.S. Ct. Appeals (11th cir.) 1991. Assoc. Rodey, Dickason, Sloan, Akin & Robb, Albuquerque, 1972-75; ptnr. Knight, Sullivan, Villella, Skarsgard & Michael, Albuquerque, 1975-77; litigation atty. Monsanto Co., St. Louis, 1977-81; environ. atty. Eastman Kodak Co., Kingsport, Tenn., 1981-84; sr. atty. AT&T, Atlanta, 1984-91; gen. counsel AMS Group, Inc., 1991-96, 98—; ConsultaAmerica Internat., 1994-97, Vision Net, Inc., 1994—, Cross Constrn. Internat., Inc., 1996-97, Ophthalmic Solutions, LLC, 1996-97, Univest, Ltd., 1996-97; pres. VMS, Inc., 1994—. Precinct vice chmn. Dem. Party, Albuquerque, 1971-77. Served to lt. (j.g.), USN, 1969-70. Mem. ABA, Ga. Bar Assn., N.Mex. Bar Assn., Mo. Bar Assn., Tenn. Bar Assn., Order of Coif, Yale Club of Ga., English Speaking Union, Delta Theta Phi (tribune 1972-77). Episcopalian. Federal civil litigation, General corporate, Environmental. Home: 1000 Buckingham Cir NW Atlanta GA 30327-2704 Office: VMS Inc 1419 Windridge Dr Atlanta GA 30350-6401

ORTON, R. WILLIS, lawyer; b. St. George, Utah, Apr. 4, 1954; s. Rulon D. and Laprele (Gubler) O.; m. Deborah Ann Ash, Aug. 20, 1977; children: Jacob, Laurie, Rachel, Nathan, David. BS, Brigham Young U., 1977; JD, U. Utah, 1981. Bar: Utah, Pa., U.S. Dist. Ct. Utah 1981, U.S. Dist. Ct. (no. dist.) Calif. 1989, U.S. Dist. Ct. (we. dist.) Pa. 1991, U.S. Ct. Appeals (10th cir.) 1984, U.S. Ct. Appeals (3rd cir.) 1992. Assoc., shareholder Callister, Nebeker & McCullough, Salt Lake City, 1981-94; assoc. Parson, Davies, Kinghorn & Peters, 1995-96, Mackey, Price & Williams, Salt Lake City, 1996-98, Kirton & McConkie, Salt Lake City, 1998—. Mem. Bonneville Knife and Fork Club, Salt Lake City, 1994—. Named to Outstanding Young Men of Am., 1986., Mem. Rotary. Federal civil litigation, General civil litigation, State civil litigation. Office: Kirton & McConkie 60 E South Temple Salt Lake City UT 84111-1004

ORWOLL, GREGG S. K. lawyer; b. Austin, Minn., Mar. 23, 1926; s. Gilbert M. and Kleonora (Kleven) O.; m. Laverne M. Flentie, Sept. 15, 1951; children: Kimball G., Kent A., Vikki A., Tristen A., Erik G. BS, Northwestern U., 1950; JD, U. Minn., 1953. Bar: Minn. 1953, U.S. Supreme Ct. 1973. Assoc. Dorsey & Whitney, Mpls., 1953-59, ptnr., 1959-60; assoc. counsel Mayo Clinic, Rochester, Minn., 1960-63, gen. counsel, 1963-87, sr. legal counsel, 1987-91, sr. counsel, 1991-92. Gen. counsel, dir. Rochester Airport Co., 1962-84, v.p., 1981-84; gen. counsel Mayo Med. Svcs., Ltd., 1972-90; bd. dirs., sec. and gen. counsel Mayo Found. for Med. Edn. and Rsch., 1984-90; gen. counsel Mid-Am. Orthop. Assn., 1984—, Minn. Orthop. Soc., 1985-95; counsel Norwegian Am. Orthopaedic Soc., 1999—; asst. sec./sec. Mayo Found., Rochester, 1972-91; sec. Mayo Emeritus Staff, 1998-99, vice chair, 1999-2000, chair, 2000—; bd. dirs. Charter House, 1986-90; dir., officer Travelure Motel Corp., 1968-86; dir., v.p. Echo Too Ent., Inc.; dir., v.p. Oberhamer Inc., 1989-99; bd. dirs. Am. Decal and Mfg. Co., 1989-93, sec., 1992-93; adj. prof. William Mitchell Coll. Law, 1978-84. Contbr. articles and chpts. to legal and medico-legal publs.; mem. bd. editors HealthSpan, 1984-93; mem. editl. bd. Minn. Law Rev., 1952-53. Trustee Minn. Coun. on Founds., 1977-82, Mayo Found., 1982-86; trustee William Mitchell Coll. Law, 1982-88, 89-98, mem. exec. com. 1990-98; bd. visitors U. Minn. Law Sch., 1974-76, 85-91; mem. U. Minn. Regent Candidate Adv. Coun., 1988-99, Minn. State Compensation Coun., 1991-97. With USAF, 1944-45. Recipient Outstanding Svc. medal U.S. Govt., 1991. Mem. ABA, AMA (affiliate), Am. Corp. Counsel Assn., Minn. Soc. Hosp. Attys. (bd. dirs. 1981-86), Minn. State Bar Assn. (chmn. legal/med. com. 1977-81), Olmsted County Bar Assn. (v.p., pres. 1977-79), Rochester C. of C., U. Minn. Law Alumni Assn. (bd. dirs. 1973-76, 85-91), Rochester U. Club (pres. 1977), The Doctors Mayo Soc., Mid Am. Orthop. Assn. (hon.), Mayo Alumni Assn. (hon.), Phi Delta Phi, Phi Delta Theta. Republican. General corporate, Personal injury. Home: 2233 5th Ave NE Rochester MN 55906-4017 Office: Mayo Clinic 200 1st St SW Rochester MN 55905-0002

ORZEL, MICHAEL DALE, lawyer; b. Milw., Mar. 6, 1952; s. Stanley and Tela Mary (Kranski) O.; m. Patti Jayne McGilvray, June 25, 1977. BA, Marquette U., 1974, JD, 1977. Bar: Wis. 1977, U.S. Dist. Ct. (ea. and we. dists.) Wis. 1977. Assoc. Karius & Kay, Milw., 1977-79, Herman L Wiernick, S.C., Milw., 1979-81; pvt. practice Wauwatosa, Wis., 1981—. Mem. State Bar Wis., Milw. Bar Assn., Waukesha County Bar Assn. Roman Catholic. Criminal, Family and matrimonial, General practice. Home: 3040 S 145th St New Berlin WI 53151-1233 Office: 6525 W Bluemound Rd Milwaukee WI 53213-4073 E-mail: orzelaw@aol.com

OSAKWE, CHRISTOPHER, lawyer, educator; b. Lagos, Nigeria, May 8, 1942; came to U.S. 1970, naturalized 1979; s. Simon and Hannah (Morgan) O.; m. Maria Elena Amador, Aug. 19, 1982; 1 child, Rebecca E. LLB, Moscow State U., 1967, PhD, 1970; JSD, U. Ill., 1974. Bar: Moscow, 1967, Kazakhstan, 1997. Prof. sch. law Tulane U., New Orleans, 1972-81, 86-88; ptnr. firm Riddle and Brown, 1989—; Eason-Weinmann prof. comparative law, dir. Eason-Weinmann Ctr. for Comparative Law Tulane U., 1981-86. Vis. prof. U. Pa., 1978, U. Mich., 1981, Washington and Lee U., 1986; vis. fellow St. Anthony's Coll., Oxford U., Eng., 1980, Christ Ch. Coll., Oxford U., 1988-89, Lomonosov Moscow State U., 1999-2000; cons. U.S. Dept. Commerce, 1980-85. Author: The Participation of the Soviet Union in Universal International Organizations, 1972, The Foundations of Soviet Law, 1981, Joint Ventures with the Soviet Union: Law and Practice, 1990, Soviet Business Law, 2 vols., 1991, (with others) Comparative Legal Traditions in a Nutshell, 1982, Comparative Legal Traditions--Text, Materials and Cases, 1985, The Russian Civil Code Annotated: Translation and Commentary, 2000, Comparative Law in Diagrams: General and Special Parts, 2000; editor Am. Jour. Comparative Law, 1978-85. Carnegie doctoral fellow Hague Acad. Internat. Law, 1969; Russian rsch. fellow Harvard U., 1972; USSR sr. rsch. exch. fellow, 1982, rsch. fellow Kennan Inst. for Advanced Russian Studies, 1988. Mem. ABA, Am. Law Inst., Am. Soc. Internat. Law, Supreme Ct. Hist. Soc., Soc. de Legislation Comparée, Order of Coif. Republican. Roman Catholic Home: 339 Audubon Blvd New Orleans LA 70125-4124 Office: 201 S Charles Ave Ste 3100 New Orleans LA 70170 E-mail: osakwec@aol.com

OSBORN, DONALD ROBERT, lawyer; b. N.Y.C., Oct. 9, 1929; s. Robert W. and Ruth C. (Compton) O.; m. Marcia Lontz, June 4, 1955; children: David, Judith, Robert; m. Marie A. Johnson, Sept. 11, 1986. BA, Cornell U., 1951; LLB, Columbia U., 1957. Bar: N.Y. 1957, U.S. Tax Ct. 1958, U.S. Ct. Claims 1961, U.S. Ct. Appeals (2d cir.) 1974, U.S. Ct. Appeals (8th cir.) 1974, U.S. Dist. Ct. (so. and ea. dists.) N.Y. 1975, U.S. Supreme Ct. 1975. Assoc. Sullivan & Cromwell, N.Y.C., 1957-64, ptnr., 1964-96, sr. counsel, 1997—. Trustee Hamilton Coll., 1978-88, Mus. of Broadcasting, 1975-80; trustee, treas. Kirkland Coll., 1969-78; mem. coun. White Burkett Miller Ctr. Pub. Affairs, 1976-82; bd. dirs., pres. Stevens Kingsley Found., 1967—; sec., treas. Dunlevy Milbank Found., 1974—; bd. dirs. Spanel Found., 1978-88, CBS, Inc., 1975-80. Served with USN, 1951-54. Mem. ABA, N.Y. State Bar Assn., Assn. of Bar of City of N.Y., Am. Bar Found., Scarsdale Golf Club, India House, Regency Whist Club, Country Club of the Rockies. Presbyterian. Private international, Probate, Corporate taxation. Home: 1049 Park Ave New York NY 10028-1061 Office: Sullivan & Cromwell 125 Broad St Fl 32 New York NY 10004-2498

OSBORN, JOE ALLEN, lawyer; b. Friona, Tex., Mar. 1, 1932; s. Sloan H. and Ilene (McFarland) O.; m. Carolyn Culbert, July 5, 1955; children: William, Claire. BA, U. Tex., 1954, LLB, 1958. Bar: Tex. 1958. Asst. atty. gen. State of Tex., Austin, 1958-62; assoc. Wilson, Kendall, Koch & Randall, 1962-65, ptnr., 1966—. Served to 1st lt., U.S. Army, 1955-57. Presbyterian. General corporate, Probate, Real property. Home: 3612 Windsor Rd Austin TX 78703-1538 Office: Kendall and Osborn 515 Congress Ave Austin TX 78701-3504 Fax: 512-474-2461. E-mail: KFGO@SWBell.net

OSBORN, JOHN EDWARD, lawyer, pharmaceutical and biotechnology industry executive, former government official, writer; b. Davenport, Iowa, Sept. 4, 1957; s. Edward Richard and Patricia Anne (O'Donovan) O.; m. Deborah Lynn Powell, Aug. 11, 1984; children: Delaney Powell, Keeley Rush. Student, Coll. William and Mary, 1975-76; BA, U. Iowa, 1979; cert., Georgetown U., 1980; JD, U. Va., 1983; cert., Wadham Coll., Oxford U., 1987; M Internat. Pub. Policy, Johns Hopkins U., 1992; cert., Wharton Sch., U. Pa., 1994-95; postgrad., Princeton U., 1997-99. Bar: Mass. 1985, U.S. Supreme Ct. 2001. Law clk. to Hon. Albert V. Bryan U.S. Ct. Appeals (4th cir.), Alexandria, Va., 1983-84; assoc. Hale and Dorr, Boston, 1984-88, Dechert Price & Rhoads, Phila., 1988-89; spl. asst. to legal adviser U.S. Dept. State, Washington, 1989-92; sr. counsel DuPont Merck Pharm. Co., Wilmington, Del., 1992-94, assoc. gen. counsel, 1994-96, v.p., assoc. gen. counsel, asst. sec., 1996-97; v.p. legal affairs Cephalon, Inc., West Chester, Pa., 1997-98, sr. v.p., gen. counsel, sec., 1998—. Contbr. articles to profl. jours., newspapers and periodicals including N.Y. Times, Wall St. Jour., Wash. Post, Christian Sci. Monitor, Am. Jour. Internat. Law; articles editor: Va. Jour. Internat. Law, 1982-83. Bd. advisors U. Pa. Inst. Law and Econs., Phila., 1999—; mem. Friends of Child Devel. Ctr., Georgetown U. Med. Ctr., Washington, 1999—, Johns Hopkins U. Alumni Coun., Balt., 1997—, U. Va. Law Sch. Bus. Adv. Coun., Charlottesville, 1996—, U. Iowa Liberal Arts Dean's Adv. Bd., Iowa City, 1999—; trustee Tower Hill Sch., Wilmington, Del., 1997—, Del. Art Mus., 1999—, asst. sec., 2001—; mem. del. Rep. State Com., 1995—99; del. Rep. Nat. Conv., 1996; rsch. aide, speechwriter George Bush for Pres. Com., 1979—80, 1987—88; bd. dirs. Del. Ctr. for the Contemporary Arts, 1994—, v.p., 1997—99; bd. dirs. Am. Civil Liberties Found. Del., 1995—98, adv. bd., 1998—. Fellow, Eisenhower fellow, Ireland, 1998; grantee study grantee, Andrew W. Mellon Found., 1999. Mem. Am. Corp. Counsel Assn., Am. Soc. Corp. Secs., Atlantic Coun. of the U.S., Coun. Fgn. Rels., Greenville Country Club, Capitol Hill Club, Princeton Club N.Y., Fieldstone Golf Club, Mortar Bd., Phi Beta Kappa, Phi Delta Phi, Omicron Delta Kappa, Omicron Delta Epsilon. Republican. Roman Catholic. Contracts commercial, General corporate, Private international. Home: 5 Doe's Lane Way Ridge Greenville DE 19807-1548 Office: 145 Brandywine Pkwy West Chester PA 19380-4245 E-mail: josborn@cephalon.com

OSBORN, MALCOLM EVERETT, lawyer; b. Bangor, Maine, Apr. 29, 1928; s. Lester Everett and Helen (Clark) O.; m. Claire Anne Franks, Aug. 30, 1953; children: Beverly, Lester, Malcolm, Ernest. BA, U. Maine, 1952; postgrad., Harvard U., 1952-54; JD, Boston U., 1956, LLM, 1961. Bar: Maine 1956, Mass. 1956, U.S. Dist. Ct. Mass. 1961, U.S. Tax Ct. 1961, U.S. Claims Ct. 1961, N.C. 1965, U.S. Supreme Ct. 1979, U.S. Ct. Appeals (4th cir.) 1980, Va. 1991. Tax counsel State Mut. Life Assurance Co., Worcester, Mass., 1956-64; v.p., gen. tax counsel Integon Corp. and other group cos., Winston-Salem, N.C., 1964-81; ptnr. House, Blanco & Osborn, P.A., 1981-88; v.p., gen. counsel, dir. Settlers Life Ins. Co., Bristol, Va., 1984-89; prin. Malcolm E. Osborn, P.A., Winston-Salem, 1988—. Lectr. The Booke Seminars, Life Ins. Co., 1985-87; adj. prof. Wake Forest U. Sch. Law, Winston-Salem, 1974-82; Disting. guest lectr. Ga. State U., 1965; guest lectr. NYU Ann. Inst. Fed. Taxation, 1966, 68, 75, 80. Com. editor The Tax Lawyer, ABA, 1974-76; author numerous articles in field. Trustee N.C. Coun. Econ. Edn., 1968-76; bd. dirs. Christian Fellowship Home, 1972-80; co-founder Bereaved Parents Group Winston-Salem, 1978—. Mem. ABA (chmn. com. ins. cos. of taxation sect. 1980-82, chmn. subcom. on continuing legal edn. and publs. 1982-88), Am. Bus. Law Assn. (mem. com. fed. taxation 1968—, chmn. 1972-75), Assn. Life Ins. Counsel (com. on co. tax, tax sect. 1965—), N.C. Bar Assn. (com. taxation 1973—), Fed. Bar Assn. (taxation com. 1973—), Maine State Bar Assn., Va. State Bar Assn., Internat. Bar Assn. (com. on taxes of bus. law sect. 1973—), AAUP, Southeastern Acad. Legal Studies in Bus., Masons (Lincoln, Maine). Insurance, Corporate taxation, Personal income taxation. Office: PO Box 5192 Winston Salem NC 27113-5192

OSBORNE, FRANK R. lawyer, educator, lecturer; b. Cleve., Dec. 7, 1946; s. Thomas L. and Doris E. O.; m. Charlotte A. Caston, July 8, 1972; children: James, Thomas, Patricia, Janet, Karen, Kathleen, Linda, Jennifer. AB in Polit. Sci., John Carroll U., 1969; JD, Cleve. State U., 1973. Bar: Ohio 1973, U.S. Dist. Ct. (no. dist.) 1975, U.S. Supreme Ct. 1979, U.S. Ct. Appeals (6th cir.) 1979, U.S. Tax Ct. 1980, U.S. Ct. Appeals (7th cir.) 1982. Law clk. to Hon. John V. Corrigan Ohio Ct. Appeals (8th appellate dist.), Cleve., 1973-76; atty. Roudebush, Brown & Ulrich, LPA, 1976-86, Arter & Hadden, LLP, Cleve., 1986—. Adj. prof. law Ohio civil procedure Cleve. Marshall Coll. Law, Cleve. State U., 1994—; alternative dispute resolution neutral U.S. Dist. Ct. (no. dist.), Cleve., 1990—. Co-author: Civil Discovery Practice in Ohio, 1995. Mem. Ohio State Bar Assn., Cleve. Bar Assn. Appellate, General civil litigation, Contracts commercial. Home: 1278 Croyden Rd Lyndhurst OH 44124-1413 Office: Arter & Hadden LLP 1100 Huntington Bldg Cleveland OH 44115 Fax: 216-696-2645. E-mail: fosborne@arterhadden.com

OSBORNE, JOHN EDWARDS, lawyer; b. Tucson, Feb. 10, 1953; s. Earle Dean and Helen Edwards Osborne; m. Diana Kuhel, Apr. 10, 1976; children: Monica, Valerie. AB with honors, Stanford U., 1975; JD, U. Tex., 1981. Bar: Ariz. Supreme Ct. 1981, U.S. Dist. Ct. Ariz. 1981, U.S. Ct. Appeals (9th cir.) 1990, U.S. Supreme Ct. 1994, White Mountain Apache Tribal Ct. Assoc. Chandler, Tullar, Udall & Redhair, Tucson, 1981-85; mng. atty. Tucson br. personal injury dept. Jacoby & Meyers Law Offices,

1985-89; mng. ptnr. Goldberg & Osborne, 1989—. Referee adminstr. Am. Youth Soccer Orgn., Tucson, 1997—. Fellow Ariz. Bar Found.; mem. ATLA, ABA, Am. Bd. Trial Advs. (assoc. mem., Tucson chpt.), Ariz. Trial Lawyers Assn. (sustaining mem., bd. govs.), State Bar Ariz. (cert. specialist in personal injury and wrongful death, pub. rels. com. 1985-89, trial practice sect. 1988—), Pima County Bar Assn. (pro bono com. 1982-95, v.p. young lawyers divsn. 1987-88). Avocations: private pilot, scuba diving, skiing, hunting, soccer referee. Insurance, Personal injury, Product liability. Office: Goldberg & Osborne 33 N Stone Ave Ste 1850 Tucson AZ 85701-1426

OSBORNE, SOLOMON CURTIS, b. Miss., May 26, 1948; s. Cassie and Doris (McCool) O.; m. Deborah Osborne; children: Solomon, Kai, Shadwich, Alyah. BA in Polit. Sci., Tougalou Coll., 1970; JD, U. Ill., Champaign, 1973. Bar: Miss. 1975, U.S. Dist. Ct. (no. and so. dists.) Miss., U.S. Ct. Appeals (5th and 11th cirs.). Staff atty. No. Miss. Rural Legal Svcs., West Point, 1973-74, mng. atty. West Point and Greenwood, 1974-78, sr. atty., 1982—; exec. dir. S.W. Miss. Legal Svcs., McComb, 1978-82; CEO, Osborne Lawe Office and Legal Clinic, Greenwood, 1990—. Adj. prof. Tougaloo Coll., 1982; Mississippi Valley State U., Itta Bena, 2000; cons. in field. Recipient Cmty. Svcs. award Greenwood Voters League, 1978; named Atty. of Yr., No. Miss. Rural Legal Svcs., 1978. Mem. ABA, Nat. Conf. Black Lawyers (bd. dirs.) Magnolia Bar Assn., Alpha Phi Alpha. Baptist. Address: 216 Star St Greenwood MS 38930-7527

O'SCANNLAIN, DIARMUID FIONNTAIN, judge; b. N.Y.C., Mar. 28, 1937; s. Sean Leo and Moira (Hegarty) O'S.; m. Maura Nolan, Sept. 7, 1963; children: Sean, Jane, Brendan, Kevin, Megan, Christopher, Anne, Kate. BA, St. John's U., 1957; JD, Harvard U., 1963; LLM, U. Va., 1992. Bar: Oreg. 1965, N.Y. 1964. Tax atty. Standard Oil Co. (N.J.), N.Y.C., 1963-65; assoc. Davies, Biggs, Strayer, Stoel & Boley, Portland, Oreg., 1965-69; dep. atty. gen. Oreg., 1969-71; public utility commr. of Oreg., 1971-73; dir. Oreg. Dept. Environ. Quality, 1973-74; sr. ptnr. Ragen, Roberts, O'Scannlain, Robertson & Neill, Portland, 1978-86; judge, U.S. Ct. Appeals (9th cir.), San Francisco, 1986—, mem. exec. com., 1988-89, 1993-94, mem. Jud. Coun. 9th Cir., 1991-93; mem. U.S. Judicial Conf. Com. on Automation and Tech., 1990—; cons. Office of Pres.-Elect and mem. Dept. Energy Transition Team (Reagan transition), Washington, 1980-81; chmn. com. adminstrv. law Oreg. State Bar, 1980-81. Mem. council of legal advisers Rep. Nat. Com., 1981-83; mem. Rep. Nat. Com., 1983-86, chmn. Oreg. Rep. Party, 1983-86; del. Rep. Nat. Convs., 1976, 80, chmn. Oreg. del., 1984; Rep. nominee U.S. Ho. of Reps., First Congl. Dist., 1974; team leader Energy Task Force, Pres.'s Pvt. Sector Survey on Cost Control, 1982-83, trustee Jesuit High Sch.; mem. bd. visitors U. Oreg. Law Sch., 1988—; mem. citizens adv. bd. Providence Hosp., 1986-92. Maj. USAR, 1955-78. Mem. Fed. Bar Assn., ABA (sec. Apellate Judges Conf. 1989-90, exec. com. 1990—, chmn.-elect 1994—), Arlington Club, Multnomah Club. Roman Catholic. Office: US Ct Appeals 313 Pioneer Courthouse 555 SW Yamhill St Ste 104 Portland OR 97204-1321*

OSGOOD, ROBERT MANSFIELD, lawyer; b. Elmira, N.Y., Jan. 27, 1942; s. Roland Lorenzo and Isabelle (Mansfield) O.; m. Janice Deakin, 1992; children: Christopher, Elisabeth, Abigail, Antonia. BA, Syracuse U., 1963, JD, 1968; postgrad. diploma in EC law, Kings Coll., London, 1994. Bar: N.Y. 1968, U.S. Dist. Ct. (no. dist.) N.Y. 1969, U.S. Dist. Ct. (so. dist.) N.Y. 1970, U.S. Ct. Appeals (2d cir.) 1971, U.S. Dist. Ct. (ea. dist.) N.Y. 1974, U.S. Ct. Appeals (D.C. cir.) 1976, U.S. Supreme Ct. 1977. Ptnr. Sullivan & Cromwell, N.Y.C. and London, 1968—. Fellow Am. Coll. Trial Lawyers; mem. Am. Law Inst. Antitrust, Federal civil litigation, General corporate. Office: Sullivan & Cromwell 125 Broad St Fl 28 New York NY 10004-2489 also: 9A Ironmonger Ln London EC2V 8EY England E-mail: osgoodr@sullcrom.com

OSGOOD, RUSSELL KING, academic administrator; b. Fairborn, Ohio, Oct. 25, 1947; s. Richard Magee and Mary (Russell) O.; m. Paula Haley, June 6, 1970; children: Mary, Josiah, Micah, Iain. BA, Yale U., 1969, JD, 1974. Bar: Mass. 1974, U.S. Dist. Ct. Mass. 1976. Assoc. Hill & Barlow, Boston, 1974-78; assoc. prof. Boston U., 1978-80; prof. Cornell U., Ithaca, N.Y., 1980-88, dean law sch., 1988-98; pres. Grinnell (Iowa) Coll., 1998—. Lt. USNR, 1969-71. Mem. Mass. Hist. Soc., Stair Soc., Selden Soc. Office: Grinnell Coll 1121 Park St Grinnell IA 50112-1640 E-mail: osgood@grinnell.com

O'SHEA, PATRICK JOSEPH, lawyer, electrical engineer; b. Chgo., Apr. 10, 1950; s. John Raymond and Alta M. (Bauert) O'S.; m. Patricia Ann Dalaker, Aug. 11, 1980; children: Erin, Tarah, Brian, Maghan. BSEE, U. Ill., 1972; JD, John Marshall Law Sch., 1979. Bar: Ill. 1979, U.S. Dist. Ct. (no. dist.) Ill. 1979, U.S. Patent Office 1982. Elec. engr. elec. div. City of Chgo. Police Dept., 1976-79; elec. engr. Commonwealth Edison, Chgo., 1972-76; atty. Patricik Mazza & Assocs., 1979-80, Richard E. Alexander & Assocs., Chgo., 1980-81; sole pratice Chgo. and Lombard, Ill., 1981—; spl. asst. states atty. Du. Page County, 1988. Spl. appellate prosecutor, 1989. Elected Rep. committeeman, York Twp., Ill., 1982, chmn. rep. committeeman's orgn., 1996; mem. exec. com. York Twp. Rep. Committeeman's Orgn., vice-chmn., 1992, chmn., 1996; mem. exec. com. DuPage County Bd., 1989—, chmn. landfill com., 1989, 94, vice chmn. legis. com., 1994; commr. Forest Preserve, 1992; gen. counsel Ill. Rep. Party; gen. counsel Ill. Rep. Party. Mem. Ill. Bar Assn., DuPage Bar Assn., Chgo. Bar Assn., Lombard C. of C., Lombard Rotary. Roman Catholic. Avocations: politics, golf, chess. Federal civil litigation, Criminal, Personal injury. Home: 1051 S Fairview Ave Lombard IL 60148-4035 Office: 156 S Main St Lombard IL 60148-2628

OSHIMA, MICHAEL W. lawyer; b. Big Rapids, Mich., Apr. 4, 1957; s. Walter W. and Mitsue Oshima. AB, Brown U., 1979; MA, Harvard U., 1984; JD, NYU, 1987. Bar: N.Y. 1988, D.C. 1989. Sr. rsch. asst. Harvard U. John F. Kennedy Sch. Govt., Cambridge, Mass., 1981-84; assoc. Davis Polk & Wardwell, N.Y.C., 1987-90, Arnold & Porter, N.Y.C., 1990-96, ptnr., 1997—. Contbr. articles, reports to profl. publs. Mem. Am. Sociol. Assn., Law and Soc. Assn., N.Y. State Bar Assn., Assn. Bar City N.Y. Banking, Private international, Securities. Office: Arnold & Porter 399 Park Ave Fl 35 New York NY 10022-4690 E-mail: michael_oshima@aporter.com

OSIS, DAIGA GUNTRA, lawyer; b. Riga, Latvia, July 24, 1943; d. Voldemars and Sandra (Seja) Amatnieks; m. Aivars Osis, Dec. 2, 1967; 1 child, Andre. BA cum laude, CUNY, Bklyn., 1971; JD, U. (Bridgeport) Conn., 1980. Bar: Conn. 1980, U.S. Dist. Ct. Conn. 1981, U.S Ct. Appeals (2d cir.) 1982, U.S. Supreme Ct. 1984. Assoc. DePiano & Palmesi, Bridgeport, 1980-85; ptnr. Gans, Leo & Osis, 1985-88, Gans, Osis, Reynolds & Riccio, Bridgeport, 1989-90, Gans, Osis & Reynolds, Bridgeport, 1990-94; pvt. practice law, 1994—. Asst. prof. law U. Bridgeport, 1982-83. Research editor U. Bridgeport Law Review, 1979-80. Mem. Bd. Edn., Trumbull, Conn., 1982-84; bd. dirs. Conn. Inst. of Vocal Arts, Southport, Conn., 1984-87. Mem. Conn. Bar Assn., Conn. Trial Lawyers Assn. Democrat. Lutheran. State civil litigation, Family and matrimonial, Personal injury. Home: 175 Middlebrooks Ave Trumbull CT 06611-3016 Office: 325 Reef Rd Ste 212 Fairfield CT 06430-6537 E-mail: osisatty@aol.com

OSMAN, EDITH GABRIELLA, lawyer; b. N.Y.C., Mar. 18, 1949; d. Arthur Abraham and Judith (Goldman) Udem; children: Jacqueline, Daniel. BA in Spanish, SUNY, Stony Brook, 1970; JD cum laude, U. Miami, 1983. Bar: Fla. 1983, U.S. Dist. Ct. (so. dist.) Fla. 1984, U.S. Dist. Ct. (mid. dist.) Fla. 1988, U.S. Ct. Appeals (11th cir.) 1985, U.S. Supreme Ct. 1987, U.S. Ct. Mil. Appeals 1990. Assoc. Kimbrell & Hamann, PA, Miami, 1984-90, Dunn & Lodish, PA, Miami, 1990-93; pvt. practice, 1993-98; shareholder Carlton Fields, 1998—. Spkr. in field. Adv. com. for Implementation of the Victor Posner Judgement to Aid the Homeless, 1986-89. Recipient Breaking the Glass Ceiling award Ziff Mus., 2000, In the Company of Women award Dade County, 2000, Judge Mattie Belle Davis award, 2000; selected for photographic exhibit Florida Women of Achievement, 2000. Fellow Am. Bar Found.; mem. ABA (family law, Ho. of Dels. 1998—, standing com. on independence of judiciary 2000—), Fla. Bar Assn. (budget com. 1989-92, 97-98, voluntary bar liaison com. 1989-90, spl. com. on formation of All-Bar Conf. 1988-89, chair mid-yr. conv. 1989, long range planning com. 1988-90, bd. govs. 1991-98, spl. commn. on delivery of legal svcs. to the indigent 1990-92, bus. law cert. com. 1995-96, practice law mgmt. com. 1995-96, chair program evaluation com., 1993-94, exec. com. 1992-93, 96—, rules and bylaws com., 1993-94, vice-chair disciplinary rev. com. 1994-95, investment com. 1994-95, vice-chair rules com. 1994-95, All-Bar Conf. chair 1997, chair grievance mediation com. 1997-99, pres.-elect 1998-99, pres. 1999-2000, exec. coun. family law sect., vice-chair legis. 2001—, Outstanding Past Voluntary Bar Pres. award 1996, Rosemary Barkett award 1997, Fla. Women of Achievement award 2000, Breaking the Glass Ceiling award 2000, In the Company of Women award 2000, Mattie Belle Davis award 2000, Fla. Women of Achievement award 2000, Dade County Womens Park & Photo Gallery honoree 2000), Dade County Bar Assn. (fed. ct. rules com. 1985-86, chmn. program com. 1988-91, 96-97, exec. com. 1987-88), Fla. Assn. Women's Lawyers Assn. (Dade County chpt. bd. dirs. 1984-85, treas. 1985-86, v.p. 1986-87, pres. 1987-88), Fla. Assn. Women Lawyers (v.p. 1988-89, pres. 1989-90), Fla. Bar Found. (dir. 1998—), Nat. Conf. Women's Bar Assn. (dir. nat. conf. 1990-91), Fla. Acad. Trial Lawyers, Dade County Trial Lawyers Assn., Nat. Conf. Bar Pres., So. Conf. Bar Pres. General civil litigation, Contracts commercial, Family and matrimonial. Office: Carlton Fields PA 100 SE 2nd St Ste 4000 Miami FL 33131-2148 E-mail: eosma@carltonfields.com

OSSICK, JOHN JOSEPH, JR. lawyer; b. Charleston, W. Va., Dec. 20, 1951; s. John Joseph and Dorothy (Tezack) O. Student La. State U., 1969-71; BS, U. Ga., 1973, JD, 1976. Bar: Ga. 1976. Asst. dist. atty. Brunswick Jud. Cir., Ga., 1976-78; atty. City of Kingsland, 1981—, Camden County Bd. Edn., Kingsland, 1979—, Kingsland Downtown Devel. Auth., 1983—. Mem. ABA, Camden County Bar Assn., Brunswick Jud. Cir. Bar Assn., Ga. Trial Lawyers Assn., Assn. Trial Lawyers Am., Nat. Assn. Criminal Def. Lawyers, Ga. Assn. Criminal Def. Lawyers, Exch. Club, Beta Gamma Sigma, Phi Delta Phi. Republican. Roman Catholic. Federal civil litigation, General civil litigation, Criminal. Home: 1305 Downing St Saint Simons GA 31522-4212 Office: PO Box 1087 230 N Lee St Kingsland GA 31548-5830

O'STEEN, VAN, lawyer; b. Sweetwater, Tenn., Jan. 10, 1946; s. Bernard Van and Laura Emelyne (Robinson) O.; m. Deborah Ann Elias, May 18, 1974; children— Jonathan Van, Laura Ann. B.A., Calif. Western U., 1968; J.D. cum laude, Ariz. State U., 1972. Bar: Ariz. 1972, U.S. Dist. Ct. Ariz. 1972, U.S. Ct. Appeals (9th cir.) 1973, U.S. Supreme Ct. 1975. Staff atty. Maricopa Legal Aid Soc., Phoenix, 1972-74; atty. Bates & O'Steen, Legal Clinic, Phoenix, 1974-77; atty. O'Steen Legal Clinic, Phoenix, 1977-80; mng. ptnr. Van O'Steen and Ptnrs., Phoenix and Tucson, 1980—; pres. Van O'Steen Mktg. Group, Inc., Phoenix, 1985—. Author numerous self-help legal books. Founding dir. Ariz. Ctr. for Law in the Pub. Interest, 1974-80. Served with USNR, 1963-69. Mem. ABA (chmn. spl. com. delivery legal services 1982-85), Am. Legal Clinic Assn. (pres. 1979), Assn. Trial Lawyers Am. Democrat. Administrative and regulatory, Personal injury. Address: 3605 N 7th Ave Phoenix AZ 85013-3638

OSTEEN, WILLIAM L. federal judge; b. 1930; BA, Guilford Coll., 1953; LLB, U. N.C., 1956. With Law Office of W.H. McElwee, Jr., North Wilkesboro, N.C., 1956-58; pvt. practive Greensboro, 1958-59; with Booth & Osteen, 1959-69; U.S. atty. U.S. Attys. Office, 1969-74; ptnr. Osteen, Adams & Osteen, 1974-91; fed. judge U.S. Dist. Ct. (mid. dist.) N.C., 1991—. With USAR, 1958-51. Fellow Am. Coll. Trial Lawyers; mem. ABA, N.C. State Bar, N.C. Bar Assn. (mem. and chair subcom. N.C. sentencing comm.), U. N.C. Law Alumni Assn. Office: US Dist Ct PO Box 3485 Greensboro NC 27402-3485

OSTENDORF, LANCE STEPHEN, lawyer, investor, financial consultant and planner; b. New Orleans, Aug. 16, 1958; 1 child, Christine Marie Ostendorf. BBA summa cum laude, Loyola U., 1976, JD, 1980. Bar: La. 1980, U.S. Dist. Ct. (ea. dist.) La. 1981, U.S. Dist. Ct. La., U.S. Supreme Ct. 1980, U.S. Dist. Ct. (we. and mid. dists.) La. 1983. Ptnr. McGlinchey Stafford Lang, New Orleans, 1980-92, Campbell McCranie Sistrunk, Anzelmo & Hardy, New Orleans, 1992-2000; founder Law Firm of Ostendorf, Tate, Barnett & Wells PLC, New Orleans, L.A., and, Houston; owner RCO Internat. Inc. Treas., CFO La. State U. Med. Ctr. Found., New Orleans, 1992—; lectr. Lorman Ednl. Seminars; bd. dirs. La. State U. Med. Ctr. Found., New Orleans, tech. transfer com.; speaker and tchr. Lorman Ednl. Svcs., Inc. Author: Insurance Law; contbr. articles to profl. jours. Mem. ABA, Fed. Bar Assn., Internat. Bar Assn., La. Bar Assn., Metairie Bar Assn., Maritime Law Assn., Comite Maritime Internat., Assn. for Transp. Law, Trucking Industry Def. Assn., Logistics and Policy, Assn. Average Adjusters of U.S., Jefferson Bar Assn., New Orleans Bar Assn., La. Restaurant Assn., Am. Trial Lawyers Assn., La. Bar Assn., Jefferson Bar Assn., Fifth Cir. Bar Assn., Def. Rsch. Inst., La. Trial Lawyers Assn., Law Def. Lawyers Assn., Houston Mariners Club, Southeastern Adm. Law Inst., St. Thomas Moore Club, La. Notary Soc., Blue Key Honor Soc. Finance, Insurance, Private international. Home: 838 Gravier St New Orleans LA 70112-1408 Office: Ste 1460 650 Poydras St New Orleans LA 70130 Fax: 504-527-5111. E-mail: lanceostendorf@yahoo.com

OSTERBERG, EDWARD CHARLES, JR. lawyer; b. Honolulu, Jan. 1, 1942; s. Edward Charles and Emily Julia (Preston) O.; m. Susan Rhea Snider, Aug. 26, 1967; 1 child, Edward Charles III. BA, Northwestern U., 1963, JD cum laude, 1966; LLM in Taxation, So. Meth. U., 1972. Bar: Tex. 1966, Ill. 1966. Assoc. Vinson & Elkins, Houston, 1967-73, ptnr., 1974—. Reporter Internat. Fiscal Assn., Sydney, Australia, 1978, Barcelona, Spain, 1991. Contbr. articles to profl. publs. Mem. ABA (chmn. taxation com.), Houston Bar Assn. (chmn. taxation sect. 1987-91), Petroleum Club, Metro. Racquet Club. Methodist. Corporate taxation, Estate taxation, Taxation, general. Home: 11222 Wilding Ln Houston TX 77024-5308 Office: Vinson & Elkins LLP 1001 Fannin St Ste 3300 Houston TX 77002-6706 E-mail: oesterberg@velaw.com

OSTERGAARD, JONI HAMMERSLA, lawyer; b. Seattle, May 26, 1950; d. William Dudley and Carol Mae (Gillett) Hammersla; m. Gregory Lance Ostergaard, May 22, 1976 (div. 1985); 1 child, Bennett Gillett; m. William Howard Patton, Jan. 1, 1988; 1 child, Morgan Hollis; stepchildren: Colin W., Benjamin C. BS, U. Wash., 1972; MS, Purdue U., 1974; JD, U. Wash., 1980. Bar: Wash. 1980, U.S. Dist. Ct. (we. dist.) Wash. 1980, U.S. Ct. Appeals (9th cir.) 1981, U. S. Ct. Claims 1983. Clin. psychol. intern Yale Med. Sch., 1976-77; law clk. U.S. Ct. Appeals (9th cir.), Seattle, 1980-81; assoc. Roberts & Shefelman, 1982-86, ptnr., 1987, Foster Pepper & Shefelman, Seattle, 1988-92; sole practitioner, 1996—. Contbr. articles to profl. jours.; notes and comments editor Wash. Law Rev., 1979-80. Recipient Sophia and Wilbur Albright scholarship U. Wash. Law Sch., 1979-80, law sch. alumni scholarship U. Wash. Law Sch., 1978-79; fellow NIMH. Avocations: gardening, reading. Appellate, Municipal (including bonds), Public utilities. Fax: 206-725-8121. E-mail: jostergaard@worldnet.att.net

OSTERHOUT, RICHARD CADWALLADER, lawyer; b. Abington, Pa., Nov. 16, 1945; s. Robert Edward and Charlotte Leedom (Cadwallader) O.; m. Diane Renee Higgins, Sept. 15, 1982; children: Steven M., Schuyler C., Cody R. BA in History magna cum laude, Pa. State U., 1967; JD, Temple U., 1974. Bar: Pa. 1974, U.S. Dist. Ct. (ea. dist.) Pa. 1974, U.S. Ct. Appeals (3d cir.) 1984. Assoc. Wood & Floge, Bensalem, Pa., 1974-77; pvt. practice Trevose, 1978-85, Feasterville, 1985—. Solicitor Zoning Hearing Bd., Hulmeville, Pa., 1983—. Contbr. articles to publs. of various hist. socs. Mem. Langhorne Borough Planning Commn. (Pa.), 1974; candidate Rep. Nat. Conv., 1984. With U.S. Army, 1968-70. Mem. Pa. Bar Assn., Bucks County Bar Assn., Feasterville Business Assn. (treas. 1985, 86, v.p. 1987), Nat. Assn. Outlaw and Lawman History, Inc., Phi Beta Kappa. State civil litigation, Family and matrimonial, General practice. Home: 309 Hemlock Ave Bensalem PA 19020-7331 Office: Richard C Osterhout 1744 Bridgetown Pike Feasterville Trevose PA 19053-2362

OSTERMAN, MELVIN HOWARD, lawyer, writer; b. N.Y.C., Sept. 26, 1934; s. Melvin Howard and Selma Elsie (Lenz) O.; m. Norma Grace Meacham, May 29, 1982; children: Lawrence, Edith, Jeffrey, Laura, Andrew. AB, Cornell U., 1955, LLB with distinction, 1957. Bar: N.Y. 1957, U.S. Dist. Ct. (so. dist.) N.Y. 1957, U.S. Dist. Ct. (ea. dist.) N.Y. 1957, U.S. Dist. Ct. (no. dist.) N.Y. 1975, U.S. Ct. Appeals (2d cir.) 1958, U.S. Supreme Ct. 1974. Assoc. White & Case, N.Y.C., 1957-58, 59-62; law clk. to justice Charles D. Breitel N.Y. App. Div. 1st Dept., 1958-59; asst. counsel to Gov. Nelson A. Rockefeller Albany, N.Y., 1962-64; counsel for employee relations, 1968-72; assoc. Graubard Moskowitz McGoldrick Dannett & Horowitz, N.Y.C., 1964-65, mem., 1965-72; dir. employee relations State of N.Y., Albany, 1972-75; mem. Whiteman Osterman & Hanna, 1975—. Author: Productivity Bargaining in New York State, 1975, N.Y. Lawyers Deskbook (Labor Law); contbr. articles to legal publs.; mem. Cornell Law Rev., 1955-57, Labor Rels. in the Pub. Sector, 1999. Cons. on judiciary Temporary State Commn. on Constl. Conv., 1966; spl. cons. on legal services N.Y.C. Bd. Edn., 1967; mem. Temporary State Commn. on Eminent Domain and Real Property Tax Assessment Rev., 1974-75; mem. faculty Sch. Indsl. and Labor Relations, Cornell U., 1974-76, Empire State Coll., SUNY, 1976-77; cons. N.Y. State Sch. Bds. Assn., 1978-86; mem. faculty Grad. Sch. Pub. Affairs, SUNY, Albany, 1979-86, Siena Coll., 2000—; pres. Northeastern Living and Learning Center, 1981—. Mem. ABA, N.Y. State Bar Assn. (chmn. com. govt. employee labor relations 1979-82, 84—, mem. exec. com. labor law sect. 1979-82, 92—, mem. com. on arbitration 1982-84, editor Pub. Sector Labor and Employment Law 1988—), Assn. of Bar of City of N.Y., Albany County Bar Assn., Saratoga County Bar Assn. State civil litigation, Education and schools, Labor. Home: 32 Darnley Grn Delmar NY 12054-9707 Office: One Commerce Plaza Albany NY 12260 E-mail: mho@woh.com, melvinho@capital.net.com

OSTRACH, MICHAEL SHERWOOD, lawyer, business executive; b. Providence, Nov. 7, 1951; s. Morris Louis and Marion Molly Ostrach. AB magna cum laude, Brown U., 1973; JD, Stanford U., 1976. Bar: N.Y. 1977, Calif. 1977, U.S. Dist. Ct. (so. and ea. dists.) N.Y. 1977. Assoc. Debevoise & Plimpton, N.Y.C., 1976-78, Pillsbury, Madison & Sutro, San Francisco, 1978-81; v.p., gen. counsel Cetus Corp., Emeryville, Calif., 1981-86, sr. v.p. legal affairs and gen. counsel, 1986-88, sr. v.p. law and adminstrn., gen. counsel, 1988—. Bd. editors Stanford Law Rev., 1976. Mem. ABA, Phi Beta Kappa. General corporate, Health, Securities. Office: Cetus Corp 1400 53rd St Emeryville CA 94608-2919

OSTRAGER, BARRY ROBERT, lawyer; b. N.Y.C., July 14, 1947; m. Pamela Goodman, Apr. 8, 1972; children: Anne Elizabeth, Katie, Jane. BA, CCNY, 1968, MA, 1973; JD, NYU, 1972. Bar: N.Y. 1973, Calif. 1996. Sr. ptnr., trial lawyer Simpson Thacher & Bartlett, N.Y.C., 1973—. Co-author: Handbook on Insurance Coverage Disputes, 10th edit., 2000, Modern Reinsurance Law and Practice, 2d edit., 2000. Mem. Am. Law Inst., Assn. of Bar of City of N.Y. E-mail: b. Office: Simpson Thacher & Bartlett 26th Fl 425 Lexington Ave Fl 26 New York NY 10017-3903 E-mail: ostrager@stblaw.com

OSTROW, MICHAEL JAY, lawyer; b. Baldwin, N.Y., Apr. 25, 1934; s. Oscar I. and Ethel M. (Morganstern) O.; m. Judith L. Loewenthal, Aug. 25, 1957; children: Thomas L., Kenneth A., Nancy M. BA, Alfred U., 1955; JD, Cornell U., 1958. Bar: N.Y. 1958, U.S. Supreme Ct. 1964, U.S. Dist. Ct. (so. and ea. dists.) N.Y. 1970; diplomate Am. Coll. Family Trial Lawyers. Ptnr. Taylor & Ostrow, Mineola, N.Y., 1961-69, Taylor Atkins & Ostrow, Garden City, 1969-96, Ostrow and Taub, Garden City, 1996-2000. Bd. dirs., lectr Advanced Practice Inst. Hofstra Law Sch., Hempstead; lectr. Practicing Law Inst., N.Y.C. Mem. ABA, Acad. Matrimonial Lawyers (pres. N.Y. chpt. 1980-81, sec. nat. acad. 1988-90, nat. v.p. 1990-94, pres.-elect 1995-96, pres. 1996-97), Internat. Acad. Matrimonial Lawyers (bd. govs. 1990-92), Am. Coll. Family Trial Lawyers (diplomate), N.Y. State Bar Assn. (chmn. family law sect. 1976-78), Nassau County Bar Assn. (pres. 1984-85, chmn. judiciary com. 1992-93), Order of Coif, Zeta Beta Tau, Phi Delta Phi. Family and matrimonial. Home: 8 Randolph Dr Dix Hills NY 11746-8308 Office: Schlissel Ostrow Karabatos Poepplein and Taub PLLC 190 Willis Ave Mineola NY 11501 E-mail: MJODIX@aol.com

O'SULLIVAN, JUDITH ROBERTA, lawyer, author; b. Pitts., Jan. 6, 1942; d. Robert Howard and Mary Olive (O'Donnell) Gallick; m. James Paul O'Sullivan, Feb. 1, 1964; children: Kathryn, James. BA, Carlow Coll., 1963; MA, U. Md., 1969, PhD, 1976; JD, Georgetown U., 1996. Editor Am. Film Inst., Washington, 1974-77; assoc. program coord. Smithsonian Resident Assocs., 1977-78; dir. instl. devel. Nat. Archives, 1978-79; exec. dir. Md. State Humanities Coun., Balt., 1979-81, 82-84, Ctr. for the Book, Libr. of Congress, Washington, 1981-82; dep. asst. dir. Nat. Mus. Am. Art, 1984-87, acting asst. dir., 1987-89; pres., CEO The Mus. at Stony Brook, N.Y., 1989-92; exec. dir. Nat. Assn. Women Judges, Washington, 1993; clk. Office Legal Adviser U.S. Dept. State, 1994-96; trial atty. Atty. Gen.'s honors program U.S. Dept. Justice, 1996—; spl. asst. U.S. atty. Ea. Dist. Va., 1999-2001; asst. U.S. atty., Tucson, 2000. Assoc. Piper & Marbury, Balt., summer 1995; chair Smithsonian Women's Coun., Washington, 1988-89. Author: The Art of the Comic Strip, 1971 (Gen. Excellence award Printing Industry Am.); Workers and Allies, 1975; (with Alan Fern) The Complete Prints of Leonard Baskin, 1984, The Great American Comic Strip, 1991; editor Am. Film Inst. Catalogue: Feature Films, 1961-70, 1974-77; mem. editl. bd. Am. Film Inst., 1979—. Trustee Child Life Ctr., U. Md., College Pk., 1971-74; chair Smithsonian Women's Coun., 1988-89. Univ. fellow U. Md., 1967-70, Mus. fellow, 1970-71, Smithsonian fellow Nat. Collection Fine Arts, Washington, 1972-73. Mem. Assn. Assn. Art Mus. Dirs., Am. Assn. Mus., Mid-Atlantic Mus. Conf., AAUW, Md. Bar Assn. Avocations: mystery writing. E-mail: judith.r.o'sullivan@usdoj.gov. Home: # 606 7111 Woodmont Ave Chevy Chase MD 20815 Office: US Dept Justice Northern Criminal Enforcement Sect Tax Divsn Washington DC 22041

O'SULLIVAN, LYNDA TROUTMAN, lawyer; b. Oil City, Pa., Aug. 30, 1952; d. Perry John and Vivian Dorothy (Schreffler) Troutman; m. P. Kevin O'Sullivan, Dec. 15, 1979; children: John Perry, Michael Patrick. BA, Am. U., 1974; JD, Georgetown U., 1978, postgrad., 1982-83. Bar: D.C. 1978.

Ptnr. Perkins Coie, Washington, 1985-92, Fried, Frank, Harris, Shriver & Jacobson, Washington, 1993-97, Miller & Chevalier, Washington, 1997—. Former mem. adv. bd. Govt. Contract Costs, Pricing & Acctg. Report, 1997-99; mem. faculty govt. contracts program George Washington U., 1990-99; lectr. Contbr. articles to profl. jours. Fellow Am. Bar Found.; mem. ABA (chair truth in negotiations com. 1991-94, chair acctg., cost and pricing com. 1996-2000, coun. sect. pub. contract law 1993-95, co-chair fed. procurement divsn. 2000—). Federal civil litigation, Government contracts and claims. Office: Miller & Chevalier 655 15th St NW Ste 900 Washington DC 20005-5799 E-mail: losullivan@milchev.com

O'SULLIVAN, THOMAS J. lawyer; b. New Haven, Apr. 7, 1940; s. Thomas J. and Marjorie (Hession) O'S.; m. Anita Brady, Aug. 10, 1968; children: Kathleen, Margaret, Mary Tess, Anne Elizabeth. BA in History, Yale U., 1961; LLB, Harvard U., 1966. Bar: Conn. 1966, U.S. Dist. Ct. Conn. 1967, N.Y. 1967, U.S. Dist. Ct. (so. and ea. dists.) N.Y. 1967, U.S. Ct. Appeals (2d cir.) 1971, U.S. Supreme Ct. 1971, U.S. Dist. Ct. (no. dist.) N.Y. 1976. Assoc. White & Case, N.Y.C., 1966-74, ptnr., 1974—. 1st lt. U.S. Army, 1961-63. Mem. ABA, N.Y. State Bar Assn., Assn. of Bar of City of N.Y., Internat. Bar Assn. Clubs: Milbrook (Greenwich, Conn.); Yale (N.Y.C.). Federal civil litigation, State civil litigation, Private international. Home: 56 Hillside Rd Greenwich CT 06830-4835 Office: White & Case Bldg Ll 1155 Avenue of The Americas New York NY 10036-2787

OSWALD, BILLY ROBERTSON, lawyer; b. Columbia, S.C., Feb. 24, 1948; s. James Robertson and Berlie Ruth (Rast) O.; m. Brenda Gale McQuatters, Jan. 31, 1970. B.A. in Polit. Sci., U. S.C., 1971, J.D. 1974. Bar: S.C. 1974, U.S. Ct. Appeals (4th cir.) 1974, U.S. Dist. Ct. S.C. 1975. Pvt. practice, West Columbia, S.C., 1974-75, 88—; ptnr. Sheftman & Oswald, West Columbia, 1975-78, Oswald & Floyd, West Columbia, 1979-88. Mem. Lexington County Council, Lexington, S.C., 1979-82, chmn., 1982; mem. Central Midlands Regional Planning Council, 1982, S.C. State Employment and Tng. Council, 1979, Columbia Area Transp. Council, Lexington County Bd. Edn., 1989—; vice chmn. bd. Opportunities Industrialization Ctr. of Midlands, S.C., 1985-86, chmn., 1986—; state campaign dir., State of S.C., Gary Hart for Pres. of U.S., 1984. Served with USAR, 1969-74. Recipient cert. of appreciation Lexington Sch. Dist. 5, 1979, resolution of appreciation Lexington County Council, 1982. Mem. S.C. Trial Lawyers, Assn. Trial Lawyers Am., ABA, S.C. Bar Assn., Lexington and Richland County Bar Assn., N.Y. Trial Lawyers Assn., Assn. to Advance Ethical Hypnosis. Democrat. Mem. Ch. of Nazarene. Lodges: Woodmen of World, Optimists. Insurance, Personal injury, Workers' compensation. Home: 2124 Raven Trl West Columbia SC 29169-3748 Office: PO Box 4052 1031 Center St W Columbia SC 29169

OTERO, LETTICE MARGARITA, lawyer; b. May 7, 1952; JD, Ind. U., Bloomington, 1977; LLM, U. Calif., Berkeley, 1986. Bar: Ind. 1978, Calif. 1989. Sole practice, Gary, Ind., 1978-85; estate and gift tax atty. IRS, San Jose, Calif., 1988-93; chief legal counsel Ind. Dept. Revenue, Indpls., 1993—, inheritance tax adminstr., 1997—. Vol. Girl Scouts Am., Indpls., 1998—; chairwoman Hispanic caucus Ind. Dem. Party, Indpls., 1999; mem. adv. coun. Office of Women's Affairs Ind. U., 1996—; mem. Gov.'s Task Force on Election Integrity, 2001. Mem. Calif. Bar Assn. (mem. exec. com. 1992). Office: Ind Dept Revenue 100 N Senate Ave Rm N248 Indianapolis IN 46204-2217

OTIS, ROY JAMES, lawyer; m. Susan Wish, 1975; children: Lindsay, Ryan. BA, Stanford (Calif.) U., 1968; JD, Golden Gate U., 1980. Bar: Calif. 1980, U.S. Dist. Ct. (no. dist.) Calif. 1980; cert. specialist in workman's compensation. Ptnr. Gearheart & Otis, Pleasant Hill, 1996—. Coach childrens' teams MOL Flag Football, 1988-96, CYO Basketball, LMYA Baseball; trek leader Boy Scouts, Sierra Mountains, Calif., Philmont, N.Mex., 1996-98. Mem. Calif. Applications Atty. Assn. (pres. no. Calif. chpt., 1994-96, bd. govs. 1997—), Assn. of Trial Lawyers of Am. (workplace injury litigation group sect. 1996—). Democrat. Avocations: skiing, tennis, bicycle riding, fiction. Workers' compensation. Office: Gearheart & Otis 367 Civic Dr Ste 17 Pleasant Hill CA 94523-1935

O'TOOLE, AUSTIN MARTIN, lawyer; b. New Bedford, Mass., Oct. 5, 1935; s. John Brian, Jr. and Helen Veronica O'T.; children: Erin Ann, Austin Martin 2d. BBA, Coll. Holy Cross, 1957; JD, Georgetown U., 1963. Bar: N.Y. 1965, D.C. 1963, Tex. 1975. Law clk. to judge U.S. Ct. Appeals, Washington, 1962-63; assoc. White & Case, N.Y.C., 1963-74; sr. v.p., sr. counsel, sec. Coastal Corp., Houston, 1974—. Bd. dirs. A.A. White Dispute Resolution Inst. Bd. editors Georgetown Law Jour., 1962-63. Bd. dirs., pres. Houston Coun. on Alcohol and Drug Abuse Found., 1995—; com. mem. Compaq Houston Marathon. Officer USMCR, 1957-60. Mem. ABA, Am. Soc. Corp. Secs. (bd. dirs. 1982-85), State Bar of Tex., Houston Bar Assn. (past chmn. corp. counsel sect. 1979-80), Am. Arbitration Assn. (comml. com.). E-mail: austin.o'toole@coastalcorp.com. General corporate, Finance, Mergers and acquisitions. Home: 1400 Hermann Dr Unit 14-c Houston TX 77004-7137 Office: Coastal Corp 9 E Greenway Plz Houston TX 77046-0905

O'TOOLE, WILLIAM GEORGE, lawyer; b. Chgo., Oct. 25, 1934; s. George P. and Margaret (Battenhouse) O'T.; m. Gail M. McGregor, Aug. 13, 1960; children: Joyce M. Masterton, Paul G., Katherine A. Gorski. BS, U. Detroit, 1956; JD, DePaul U., 1961. Bar: Ill. 1961, U.S. Dist. Ct. (no. dist.) Ill. 1962. Assoc. Jaros, Tittle & O'Toole (and predecessor firm), Chgo., 1961-74, ptnr., 1974-90, pres., 1990—. Mem. ABA, Ill. Bar Assn., Ill. Mortgage Bankers Assn. (bd. dirs.), Chgo. Bar Assn., Southwest Bar Assn. (past pres.), Chgo. Athletic Assn., Abbey Springs Country Club, Ridge Country Club, Elks, K.C., Beta Alpha Psi. Roman Catholic. Banking, General civil litigation, Real property. Home: 10736 S Kolmar Ave Oak Lawn IL 60453-5349 Office: Jaros Tittle & O'Toole 20 N Clark St Ste 510 Chicago IL 60602-4188

OTOROWSKI, CHRISTOPHER LEE, lawyer; b. Teaneck, N.J., Nov. 20, 1953; s. Wladyslaw Jerzy and Betty Lee (Robbins) O.; m. Shawn Elizabeth McGovern, Aug. 4, 1978; children: Kirsten, Hilary. BSBA cum laude, U. Denver, 1974, MBA, JD, U. Denver, 1977. Bar: Wash. 1977, Colo. 1977, U.S. Dist Ct. (we. dist.) D.C. 1977, U.S. Dist. Ct. (we. dist.) Wash. 1978. Asst. atty. gen. Wash. State Atty. Gen., Spokane, 1978-79; atty. Bassett, Gemson & Morrison, Seattle, 1979-81; pvt. practice, 1981-88; atty. Sullivan, Golden & Otorowski, 1988-91, Morrow & Otorowski, Bainbridge Island, 1996—; pvt. practice Morrow and Otorowski, Wash., 1991-96. Contbr. articles to profl. jours. Bd. dirs. Bainbridge Edn. Support Team, Bainbridge Island, 1991-97. Mem. Fed. Bar Assn. We. Dist. Wash. (sec. 1979-82, trustee 1990-93), Wash. State Trial Lawyers Assn. (bd. govs. 1991-93), Assn. Trial Lawyers Am., Seattle Tennis Club, Seattle Yacht Club. Avocations: photography, sailing. General civil litigation, Personal injury. Office: 298 Winslow Way W Bainbridge Island WA 98110 E-mail: clo@medilaw.com

OTT, ANDREW EDUARD, lawyer; b. Vancouver, B.C., Can., Sept. 23, 1962; s. Eduard Karl and Elfriede Marie (Petryc) O. BA in English, Seattle U., 1986, JD, 1989; D (hon.), U. Graz, Austria, 1986. Bar: Wash. 1990, U.S. Dist. Ct. (we. dist.) Wash. 1992. Contract atty. Keller Rohrback, Seattle, Lieff Cabraser Heimann & Bernstein, San Francisco, Jamin, Ebell, Schmitt & Mason, Kodiak, Alaska, 1989—. Cons. OMNI Tech. Engring., Bothell, Wash., 1986-2000. Actor musicals and theater, 1992, 93, 95, 96, 98, 99, 2000; musician Cmty. Orch. and Jazz, 1990-2000. Trustee Kodiak Arts Coun. Mem. ABA, ATLA, Nat. Assn. Self-Employed. Avocations: snow skiing, soccer, bike riding, running, acting. General civil litigation, Environmental, General practice. Office: Jamin Ebell Schmitt & Mason 323 Carolyn Ave Kodiak AK 99615-6348 E-mail: Andrew@JESMKOD.com

OTT, WILLIAM GRIFFITH, law educator, writer; b. Wilmington, Del., Feb. 21, 1909; s. David Lewes and Greta Blauvelt (Griffith) O.; m. Joanna Seyffarth, Dec. 28, 1961; children— Michael, William Griffith Jr., Nancy, David. B.S. in Bus. Adminstrn., U. Del., 1932; LL.B., LaSalle Extension U. Chgo., 1946. Prof. law Goldey Beacom Coll., Wilmington, 1946— , v.p., dir. admissions, 1973-78, pres., 1978; advisor Nat. Assn. Legal Secs. (Del. chpt.); founder W. G. Ott Law Assn. Author: (with others) College Business Law, 6th edit., 1983; Business and the Law, 1979; (series) Business Law, 1980-85; and additional books. Mem. Del. Bus. Tchrs. Assn., Eastern Bus. Tchrs. Assn. (past bd. dirs.). Home: 508 Milltown Rd Wilmington DE 19808-2225 Office: Goldey Beacom Coll Limestone Rd Wilmington DE 19808

OTTEN, ARTHUR EDWARD, JR. lawyer, corporate executive; b. Buffalo, Oct. 11, 1930; s. Arthur Edward Sr. and Margaret (Ambrusko) O.; m. Mary Therese Torri, Oct. 1, 1960; children: Margaret, Michael, Maureen Staley, Suzanne Hoodecheck, Jennifer. BA, Hamilton Coll., 1952; JD, Yale U., 1955. Bar: N.Y. 1955, Colo. 1959. Assoc. Hodges, Silverstein, Hodges & Harrington, Denver, 1959-64; ptnr. Hodges, Kerwin, Otten & Weeks (predecessor firms), 1964-73, Davis, Graham & Stubbs, Denver, 1973-86; gen. counsel Colo. Nat. Bankshares, Inc., 1973-93; mem. Otten, Johnson, Robinson, Neff & Ragonetti, P.C., Denver, 1986—. Rec. sec. Colo. Nat. Bankshares, Inc., Denver, 1983-93; gen. counsel Regis U., Denver, 1994-99; mediator Denver Dist. Ct., 1997-99; com. bd. Centura Health, Denver, St. Anthony Hosps., Denver. Bd. dirs. Cath. Charities Archdiocese of Denver, 1998—. Lt. USN, 1955-59. Mem. ABA, Colo. Bar Assn., Denver Bar Assn., Am. Arbitration Assn. (panel arbitrators, large complex case panel, mediator panel), Nat. Assn. Securities Dealers (bd. arbitrators), Law club, Univ. Club, Denver Mile High Rotary (pres. 1992-93), Phi Delta Phi. Republican. Roman Catholic. Avocations: hiking, biking, church activities. Banking, General corporate, Education and schools. Home: 3774 S Niagara Way Denver CO 80237-1248 Office: Otten Johnson Robinson Neff & Ragonetti PC 950 17th St Ste 1600 Denver CO 80202-2828 E-mail: aeotten@ojrnr.com

OTTESEN, REALFF HENRY, lawyer; b. Davenport, Iowa, July 10, 1941; s. Henry Realff and Florence (Laffer) O.; m. Ann Steninger, June 9, 1963; children: Reid Thomas, Michael James. BA, U. Iowa, 1963, JD, 1965. Bar: Iowa 1965, U.S. Dist. Ct. (so. and no. dist.) Iowa 1965, U.S. Dist. Ct. (cen. dist.) Ill. 1969, U.S. Ct. Appeals (8th cir.) 1980. Mng. ptnr. Ottesen & Ottesen, Davenport, 1965-81; asst. county atty. Scott County, Davenport, 1967—; sr. and mng. ptnr. Ottesen, Hoffman & Priester, Davenport, 1981—. Chmn. adv. council Gov's. Hwy. Safety Office, Des Moines, 1983-87; co-chmn. Citizens against Adolescent Alcohol Abuse, Bettendorf, Iowa, 1983-85. Recipient District award of merit Boy Scouts Am., 1982. Mem. Scott County Bar Assn., Iowa State Bar Assn., ABA, Iowa County Atty's. Assn. (assoc. dir. 1982-83, Outstanding Atty. award 1990), Nat. Dist. Attys. Assn. (assoc. dir. 1986—), U.S. Jaycees (Named Outstanding Young Men of Am. 1973). Republican. Methodist. Bankruptcy, Consumer commercial, Criminal. Home: PO Box 651 Shell Rock IA 50670-0651

OTTINGER, RICHARD LAWRENCE, dean, law educator; b. N.Y.C., Jan. 27, 1929; s. Lawrence and Louise (Lowenstein) O.; children from previous marriage: Ronald, Randall, Lawrence, Jenny Louise; m. June Godfrey. BA, Cornell U., 1950; LLB, Harvard U., 1953. Assoc. Cleary, Gottlieb, Friendly & Hamilton, N.Y.C., 1955-56; ptnr. William J. Kridel, Law Firm, 1956-60; second staff mem., dir. programs Peace Corps, L.Am., 1961-64; mem. 89th-91st Congresses, 1965-71, 94th-98th Congresses, 1975-85; prof. Pace U. Sch. Law, White Plains, N.Y., 1985—, dean, 1994—. Bd. dirs. Environ. and Energy Study Inst., Washington, Am. Coun. for Energy-Efficient Economy, Washington. Author: Environmental Costs of Electricity, 1990. Contract mgr. Internat. Coop. Adminstrn., 1960-61; organizer Grassroots to Action, 1971-73. Office: Pace U Sch Law 78 N Broadway White Plains NY 10603-3710

OTTMAR, TIMOTHY JON, lawyer, municipal judge; b. Grand Forks, N.D., Oct. 19, 1954; s. Clinton Ray and Grace Bertha (Gackle) O.; m. Joanne Harriet Hager, June 3, 1978; children— Steven Timothy, Jeffrey Clinton. B.A. in Bus. Adminstrn. summa cum laude with honors, Jamestown Coll., 1976; J.D., U. N.D., 1979. Bar: N.D. 1979, U.S. Dist. Ct. N.D. 1979. Ptnr. Ottmar & Ottmar, Jamestown, N.D., 1979— ; asst. mcpl. judge City of Jamestown, 1980-82, mcpl. judge, 1982— ; asst. mcpl. judge City of Valley City, N.D., 1981— . Bd. dirs. United Way, Jamestown, 1979-81. Named to Outstanding Young Men Am., 1981. Mem. ABA, Stutsman County Bar Assn. (pres. 1983-84). Republican. Methodist. Lodges: Rotary (sec. local club 1982—), Elks. Home: 113 18th Ave NE Jamestown ND 58401-3934 Office: Ottmar & Ottmar PO Box 1397 400 2d Ave SW Jamestown ND 58402

OTTO, BYRON LEONARD, lawyer, state administrator; b. Battle Creek, Mich., Oct. 4, 1940; s. Henry John and Mildred Alice (Wagner) O. BBA, St. Edward's U., 1964, MBA, 1979; JD, U. Tex., 1968. Staff atty. State Welfare Dept., Austin, Tex., 1968-75; sole practice, 1975-77; assoc. James R. Sloan, 1978-79; adminstr. State Comptroller, 1980—; ret., 2000. Author articles and monographs. St. Edward's U. scholar, Austin, 1978. Mem. ABA, Tex. Bar. Democrat. Roman Catholic. Home: 7203 Sir Gawain Dr Austin TX 78745-5569

OTTO, HARRO, law educator; b. Sobbowitz/Danzig, Germany, Apr. 1, 1937; s. Bruno and Frida (Tischkowski) O.; m. Ute Heide Franz; children: Tania, Malte. 1st state exam. in law, U. Hamburg (Germany), 1960; final state exam in law, grad. acad. asst., , 1965; D honoris causa, U. Pécs (Hungary), 1986. Bar: jurist. Acad. asst. U. Giessen (Germany), 1965-69; lectr., 1969-70; atty. of professorship U. Hamburg, 1970-71; prof. criminal law, criminal trial law, philosophy of law U. Marburg (Germany), 1971-77, U. Bayreuth (Germany), 1977—; v.p., 1988-91. Author: Conflict of Duties and Illegality, 1964, The Structure of Protection of Property in Criminal Law, 1970, Elementary Course in Criminal Law, All the Elements of an Offense, 1998, Elementary Course in Criminal Law The General Instruction of Criminal Law, 2000. Home: Weserstr 5 95445 Bayreuth Bavaria Germany Office: University Universitätstr 30 95440 Bayreuth Bavaria Germany Fax: 0921/552898

OTTO, JAMES DANIEL, lawyer; b. Long Beach, Calif., June 9, 1949; s. Paul Daniel and Bethal Bertine (Hudspeth) O. BA summa cum laude, San Diego State U., 1971; JD, Northwestern U., 1974. Bar: Calif. 1974, U.S. Dist. Ct. (cen. dist.) Calif. 1974, U.S. Dist. Ct. (so. dist.) Calif. 1981, U.S. Ct. Appeals (9th cir.) 1983. Assoc. firm Cummins & White and predecessor firms, L.A., 1974-78, ptnr., 1978-80, sr. ptnr., 1980—, mng. ptnr., 1981-85, chairperson of mgmt. com., mng, ptnr. 1989-94; speaker Practicing Law Inst., 1987; moderator/panelist Lorman Bus. Ctr., L.A., 1994, 95. Contbr. articles to profl. jours. Active Big Bros. Am., L.A., 1975-79. Mem. ABA (panelist various seminars), Assn. So. Calif. Def. Counsel, Internat. Assn. Def. Counsel, L.A. County Bar Assn. (mem. superior cts., errors and omissions coms., mem. state cts. com., mem. jud. resources com.), Phi Kappa Phi, Pi Sigma Alpha, Alpha Mu Gamma, Jonathan Club (L.A.). General civil litigation, Environmental, Professional liability. Office: Cummins & White 2424 SE Bristol St Ste 300 Newport Beach CA 92660-0764

OUDERKIRK, MASON JAMES, lawyer; b. Des Moines, Feb. 1, 1953; s. Mason George and Florence Astor (Lowe) O.; m. Kari Aune Hormel, May 28, 1983; 1 child, Mason Christopher. BA, Drake U., 1975, JD, 1978. Bar: Iowa 1978, U.S. Dist. Ct. (so. dist.) Iowa 1978, U.S. Ct. Appeals (8th cir.); lic. real estate broker. Assoc. M.G. Ouderkirk Law Office, Indianola, Iowa, 1978-79; ptnr. Ouderkirk Law Firm, 1979-96; sr. mem. Ouderkirk, Ouderkirk & Dougherty, P.L.C., 1996-98; proprietor Ouderkirk Law Firm, Iowa, 1998—; pres. Avanti Realty Co. (formerly Landmark Real Estate, Ltd.), 1978—, Avanti Builders Co., Indianola, 1991—. Mem. Vol. Lawyers Project of Iowa, 1987-93. Mem. Indianola Police Retirement Bd., 1983-88; instr. Eric Heintz Black Belt Acad., 1988-93, Indianola Parks and Recreation Dept., 1988-93; mem. Nominating Commn., Warren County Assoc. Dist. Ct., 1999—. Mem. ABA, Iowa Bar Assn. (pub. rels. com. 1989-94, family law com. 1989-90), Warren County Bar Assn. (sec., treas. 1985-89, v.p. 1989-90, pres. 1990-92), 5th Jud. Dist. Bar Assn. (sec., treas. 1995), Assn. Trial Lawyers Am., Iowa Trial Lawyers Assn. Episcopalian. Avocations: fishing, hunting, gardening. Family and matrimonial, Personal injury, Probate. Home: 1231 Fulton St Lot 10 Indianola IA 50125-9083 Office: Ouderkirk Law Firm 108 S Howard St PO Box 156 Indianola IA 50125-0156 Fax: 515-961-0304. E-mail: ouderkirklaw@earthlink.net

OULTON, DONALD PAUL, lawyer; b. Kingston, N.Y., July 22, 1930; s. Francis Terrance and Anne Agnes (Carrol) O.; m. Carol Jane Burke; children— David P., Nancy, Sarah, Carol. A.A. in Edn., Boston U., 1955; B.S in Bus. Adminstrn., Boston U., 1958; J.D., Suffolk U., 1969. Bar: Mass. 1970, U.S. Dist. Ct. Mass. 1973, U.S. Supreme Ct. 1978, U.S. Ct. Appeals (1st cir.) 1980, U.S. Ct. Claims 1980, U.S. Tax Ct. 1980, U.S. Ct. Mil. Appeals 1981, U.S. Ct. Internat. Trade 1984, U.S. Ct. Appeals (fed. cir.) 1984. Contract negotiator Raytheon Corp., Bedford, Mass., 1959-65; chief negotiator claims Quincy Shipbldg. Div., Mass., 1965-72; assoc. div. counsel Quincy Shipbldg. 1970-72; asst. dist. atty. Middlesex County, Cambridge, Mass., 1972-75; contract negotiator Electronic Systems div. Office of Staff Judge Adv., U.S. Air Force, Hanscom AFB, Mass., 1974-76, chief atty. fgn. mil. sales, 1976-87 ; chief Internat Law Br., 1987— . trial counsel Natick, Mass., Part-time, 1970— ; real estate broker Mass. Realtors Assn., Boston, 1972— . Author: Inquests, 1973, Technology Transfer, 1983, Air Force Trivia, 1985, A Review of Executive Agreements From The Standpoint of Current Case Law, 1999, (with others) In Remembrance of Korea, 1987. Hearing officer Zoning Bd. Appeals, Natick, 1976; lectr. Western New Eng. Coll. Tchr. 9th grade, CCD, St. James Ch., Wellesley, Mass., 1976-83; bd. dirs., co-founder Shamrock Soc., Natick, Mass., 1976— ; bd. dirs., counsel Little League, Natick, 1972-75, Mass. Korean War Meml. Com., 1988—. Served with inf. U.S. Army, 1951-53, Korea. Named Outstanding Civilian Atty. of Yr., U.S. Air Force Systems Command, 1980; Outstanding Civilian Atty. of Yr., U.S. Air Force, Pentagon, 1980, Outstanding Civilian, Air Force Electronic Systems Div., 1983. Mem. Am. Soc. Internat. Law, Air Force Assn., Middlesex Bar Assn., Mass. Bar Assn., Fed. Bar Assn., Mass. Police Chiefs Assn. Democrat. Roman Catholic. Club: Officers. Home: 54 Macarthur Rd Natick MA 01760-2938 Office: Internat Sales Br Office Staff Judge Adv Contract Law Div Electronic S Hanscom AFB MA 01731

OUTERBRIDGE, CHERYL, lawyer; b. Monte Vista, Colo., July 11, 1943; d. George Herbert and Gladys Mae (Walker) Hazard; m. J. Robert Outerbridge, June 4, 1961 (div. 1984); 1 child, Grant Hazard; m. Carl F. Nagy, Nov. 16, 1985; B.A., U. Denver, 1968; J.D., U. Colo., 1975. Bar: Colo. 1975, U.S. Dist. Ct. Colo. 1975. Assoc., Gorsuch, Kirgis, Campbell, Walker & Grover, Denver, 1975-79; staff atty. Amax Inc., Golden, Colo., 1979-81; editor-in-chief American Law of Mining, 2d edit., Rocky Mountain Mineral Law Found., Boulder, Colo., 1981-85; sr. atty. AMAX Inc., Golden, Colo., 1985— . Contbr. articles to profl. jours. Mem. ABA, Order of Coif, Colo. Bar Assn., Denver Bar Assn., The Alliance of Profl. Women, Phi Beta Kappa. Mining and minerals. Office: AMAX Inc 1707 Cole Blvd Golden CO 80401-3210

OUTMAN, WILLIAM DELL, II, lawyer; b. St. Petersburg, Fla., Nov. 10, 1940; s. Boyd Johnson and Marion Lucetta (Banks) O.; m. Sally Rockwell June 29, 1963 (dec. Sept. 1998); children: William Dell III, Stephanie O. Kiker, Sarah O. Brophy. BS in Bus. Adminstrn., Wash. & Lee U., 1962; JD, Georgetown U., 1965, LLM in Taxation, 1968. Bar: D.C. 1966, N.Y. 1999. Assoc. atty. Baker & McKEnzie, Wash., 1965-70, ptnr., 1970-97, mng. ptnr. N.Y.C., 1997-2000, ptnr. Washington, 2000—. Staff sgt., U.S. Army, 1965-71. Mem. Customs and Internat. Trade Bar Assn. (v.p., bd. dirs. 1992—), Ct. Internat. Trade Adv. Com. (current chmn. 1990—), Congl. Country Club, Met. Club, Omicron Delta Kappa. Immigration, naturalization, and customs, Private international. Office: Baker & McKenzie 815 Connecticut Ave NW Ste 900 Washington DC 20006-4004 E-mail: william.d.outman@bakernet.com

OVERHOLSER, JOHN W. lawyer; b. Portland, Oreg., June 29, 1937; s. Wayne D. and Evaleth M. (Miller) O.; m. Carol T. Overholser, June 20, 1935; children: Vicki, Stacia, John, Jason. BA, U. Colo., 1959, LLB, 1962. Bar: Colo. 1962, U.S. Dist. Ct. Colo. 1962, U.S. Ct. Appeals (10th cir.) 1967. Assoc. Brooks and Miller, Montrose, Colo., 1962-64; sole practice, 1964-68; ptnr. Overholser & Slee, P.C., and predecessors, 1968—. Lay spkr., Montrose United Meth. Ch.; past chmn., Montrose County Rep. Ctrl. Com.; past mem., chmn., Regional Libr. Dist.; bd. dirs., Montrose Econ. Devel. Coun.; active cmty. activities. Mem. ABA, Colo. Bar Assn., 7th Jud. Bar Assn., Montrose C. of C. (bd. dirs.). State civil litigation, General practice, Real property. Office: 333 S Townsend St PO Box 729 Montrose CO 81402-0729 E-mail: johnoverholser@hotmail.com

OVERHOLT, HUGH ROBERT, lawyer, retired army officer; b. Beebe, Ark., Oct. 29, 1933; s. Harold R. and Cuma E. (Hall) O.; m. Laura Annell Arnold, May 5, 1961; children: Sharon, Scott. Student, Coll. of Ozarks, 1951-53; B.A., U. Ark., 1955, LL.B., 1957. Bar: Ark. 1957. Commd. 1st lt. U.S. Army, 1957, advanced through grades to maj. gen., 1981; chief Criminal Law Div., JAG Sch., Charlottesville, Va., 1971-73; chief personnel, plans and tng. Office of JAG, U.S. Army, Washington, 1973-75; staff judge adv. XVIII Airborne Corps, Ft. Bragg, N.C., 1976-78; spl. asst. for legal and selected policy matters Office of Dep. Asst., 1978-79; asst. judge adv. gen. for mil. law Office of JAG, Washington, 1979-81, asst. judge adv. gen., 1981-85, judge adv. gen., 1985-89; atty. Ward & Smith, New Bern, N.C., 1989—. Notes and comment editor Ark. Law Rev, 1956-57. Decorated Army Meritorious Service medal with oak leaf cluster, Army Commendation medal with 2 oak leaf clusters., Legion of Merit, Def. Meritorious Service medal, D.S.M. Mem. ABA, N.C. Bar Assn., Ark. Bar Assn., Assn. U.S. Army, Delta Theta Phi, Omicron Delta Kappa, Sigma Pi. Presbyterian. Office: Ward and Smith 1001 College Ct New Bern NC 28562-4972

OWEN, H. MARTYN, lawyer; b. Decatur, Ill., Oct. 23, 1929; s. Honore Martyn and Virginia (Hunt) O.; m. Candace Catlin Benjamin, June 21, 1952; children: Leslie W., Peter H., Douglas P. AB, Princeton U., 1951; LLB, Harvard U., 1954. Bar: Conn. 1954, U.S. Dist. Ct. Conn. 1962, U.S. Supreme Ct. 1963, U.S. Dist. Ct. Vt., 1965. Assoc. Shipman & Goodwin, Hartford, Conn., 1958-61, ptnr., 1961-94, of counsel, 1995-96. Lawyer; b. Decatur, Ill., Oct. 23, 1929; s. Honore Martyn and Virginia (Hunt) O.; m. Candace Catlin Benjamin, June 21, 1952; children— Leslie W., Peter H., Douglas P. A.B., Princeton U., 1951; LL.B., Harvard U., 1954. Bar: Conn.

1954. Assoc. Shipman & Goodwin, Hartford, Conn., 1958-61, ptnr., 1961-94, of counsel, 1995-96. Mem. Simsbury (Conn.) Zoning Bd. Appeals, 1961-67, Simsbury Zoning Commn., 1967-79; sec. Capitol Region Planning Agy., 1965-66; bd. dirs. Symphony Soc. Greater Hartford, 1967-73; trustee Renbrook Sch., West Hartford, Conn., 1963-72, treas., 1964-68, pres., 1968-72, hon. life trustee, 1972— ; trustee Simsbury Free Library, 1970-84; pres. Hartford Grammar Sch., 1987-98, trustee; corporator Hartford Hosp, 1984-96. Lt. USNR, 1954-57. Mem. ABA, Conn. Bar Assn., Hartford County Bar Assn., Am. Law Inst. Democrat. Episcopalian. Clubs: Princeton (N.Y.C.); Ivy (Princeton, N.J.). Mem. Simsbury (Conn.) Zoning Bd. Appeals, 1961-67, Simsbury Zoning Commn., 1967-79; sec. Capitol Region Planning Agy., 1965-66; bd. dirs. Symphony Soc. Greater Hartford, 1967-73; trustee Renbrook Sch., West Hartford, Conn., 1963-72, treas. 1964-68, pres., 1968-72, hon. life trustee, 1972—; trustee Simsbury Free Libr., 1970-84; pres. Hartford Grammar Sch., 1987-98, trustee; corporator Hartford Hosp., 1984-96; vestry St. Alban's Ch., Simsbury, 1988-94; warden, vestry St. Paul's Ch., Brunswick, Maine, 1999-2001. Lt. USNR, 1954-57. Mem. ABA, Conn. Bar Assn., Hartford County Bar Assn., Am. Law Inst., Princeton (N.Y.C.) Club, Ivy Club (Princeton, N.J.). Democrat. Episcopalian. Antitrust, General corporate, Municipal (including bonds). Home: 80 Matthew Dr Brunswick ME 04011-3275

OWEN, JOE SAM, lawyer; b. Gulfport, Miss., Dec. 31, 1948; s. Tofie and Amelia (Numnum) O., Sr.; m. Sandra Donohue, July 26, 1969; children—Ashley, Sam; m. 2d, Sherry Lynn Welch, Jan. 31, 1982; 1 child, Mitch. B.A. in History, U. Miss., 1970, J.D., 1972. Bar: Miss. 1972, U.S. Dist. Ct. (no. and so. dists.) Miss. 1972, U.S. Ct. Appeals (5th cir.) 1974, U.S. Ct. Claims 1978, U.S. Tax Ct. 1978, U.S. Supreme Ct. 1978. Sole practice, Gulfport, Miss., 1972-82; ptnr. Blackwell, Owen & Galloway, Gulfport, Miss., 1982-83, Owen, Galloway and Dickinson, Gulfport, 1983-84, Owen and Galloway, Gulfport, 1984— ; asst. dist. atty. Harrison, Hancock and Stone Counties, Miss., 1974-77; referee Harrison County Family Ct., Miss., 1971— . Mem. ABA, Miss. Bar Assn., Harrison County Bar Assn., Assn. Trial Lawyers Am., Miss. Trial Lawyers Assn., Am. Judicature Soc., Comml. Law League Am., Southeastern Bankruptcy Law Inst. Criminal, Personal injury, Product liability. Office: PO Box 673 Gulfport MS 39502-0673

OWEN, PRISCILLA RICHMAN, state supreme court justice; BA, Baylor U., JD, 1977. Bar: Tex. 1978, U.S. Ct. Appeals (4th, 5th, 8th and 11th cirs.). Former ptnr. Andrews & Kurth, L.L.P., Houston; justice Supreme Ct. Tex., Austin, 1995—. Liaison to Tex. Legal Svcs. for Poor Spl. Supreme Ct. Tex., Supreme Ct. Adv. Com. on Ct.-Annexed Mediations. Named Young Lawyer of Yr., Outstanding Young Alumna, Baylor U. Office: Supreme Ct Tex PO Box 12248 Austin TX 78711-2248*

OWEN, RICHARD, federal judge; b. N.Y.C., Dec. 11, 1922; s. Carl Maynard and Shirley (Barnes) O.; m. Lynn Rasmussen, June 6, 1960; children: Carl R., David R., Richard. AB, Dartmouth Coll., 1947; LLB, Harvard U., 1950; MusD (hon.), Manhattan Sch. Music, 1989. Bar: N.Y. 1950. Practiced in, N.Y.C., 1950-74; assoc. Willkie Owen Farr Gallagher & Walton, 1950-53, Willkie Farr Gallagher Walton & Fitzgibbon, 1958-60; pvt. practice, 1960-65; ptnr. Owen & Aarons, 1965-66, Owen & Turchin, 1966-74; asst. U.S. atty. So. Dist. N.Y., 1953-55; trial atty. antitrust div. U.S. Dept. Justice, 1955-58; U.S. dist. judge So. Dist. N.Y., 1974-89, sr. judge, 1989—. Asst. prof. N.Y. Law Sch., 1951-53; adj. prof. law Fordham U. Sch. Law, 1996—. Composer, librettist operas Dismissed with Prejudice, 1956, A Moment of War, 1958, A Fisherman Called Peter, 1965, Mary Dyer, 1976, The Death of the Virgin, 1980, Abigail Adams, 1987, Tom Sawyer, 1989, Sadie Thompson, 1997. Trustee Manhattan Sch. Music, N.Y.C.; founder, bd. dirs. Maine Opera Assn., 1975-85; pres., bd. dirs. N.Y. Lyric Opera Co. 1st lt. USAAC, 1942-45. Decorated D.F.C. with oak leaf cluster, Air medal with 3 oak leaf clusters. Mem. ASCAP, Century Assn., Chelsea Yacht Club. Republican. Mem. Soc. of Friends. Office: US Dist Ct US Courthouse Foley Sq New York NY 10007-1501

OWEN, ROBERT DEWIT, lawyer; b. St. Louis, Nov. 15, 1948; s. Kenneth Campbell Owen and Mary Elenor (Fish) Luebbers; m. Rebecca Roberts Baxter, June 4, 1977; children: Abigail Mary, James Roy, Charlotte Grace. BA, Northwestern U., 1970; JD cum laude, U. Pa., 1973. Assoc. Sullivan & Cromwell, N.Y.C., 1973-81; ptnr. Towne, Dolgin, Furlaud, Sawyier & Owen, 1981-83, Owen & Fennell, N.Y.C., 1983-87, Owen & Davis, N.Y.C., 1987—. Instr. Nat. Inst. Trial Advocacy, Boulder, Colo., 1988—; faculty mem. ABA Nat. Inst. 1992, 93. Bd. dirs. St. Christopher's-Jennie Clarkson Child Care Svcs., Dobbs Ferry, N.Y., 1991-97. Mem. Assn. Bar City N.Y., Fed. Bar Coun., Nat. Assn. Securities Dealers (bd. arbitrators 1985—), Nat. Futures Assn. (bd. arbitrators 1999—), Colonial Springs Club (pres. 1986-94), India House. Episcopalian. Avocations: boating, running. General civil litigation, Contracts commercial, Oil, gas, and mineral. Office: Owen & Davis 805 3rd Ave New York NY 10022-7513

OWENDOFF, STEPHEN PETER, lawyer; b. Morristown, N.J., Aug. 1, 1943; m.; 4 children. Student, Bowdoin Coll., 1966; BA, Kent State U., 1966; JD, Georgetown U., 1969. Bar: Ohio 1969. Assoc. Hahn Loeser & Parks and predecessor firms, Cleve., 1969-77; ptnr. Hahn Loeser & Parks (formerly Hahn, Loeser, Freedheim, Dean and Wellman), 1977—; mgmt. com. Hahn Loeser & Parks (formerly Hahn, Loeser, Freedheim Dean). Lectr. in field. Active Gesu Ch., University Heights, Ohio; mem. adv. bd. Learning About Bus., Inc.; past pres. Parmadale (Ohio) Adv. Bd.; bd. trustees, cmty. svcs. panel Fedn. Cath. Cmty. Svcs.; rep. United Way Assembly, Parmadale; bd. trustees LeBlond Housing Corp., Health Hill Hosp. Mem. Nat. Assn. Bond Lawyers, Nat. Assn. Coll. and Univ. Attys., Shaker Heights (Ohio) Country Club. Banking, General corporate, Real property. Office: Hahn Loeser & Parks 200 Public Square 3300 BP Tower Cleveland OH 44114-2301

OWENS, BETTY RUTH, lawyer; b. Texas City, Tex., Dec. 21, 1951; d. Marvin Lee Jr. and Ellen Frances (Nunnally) O.; m. Robert Foster Geary, Oct. 1, 1994. BS, La. State U., 1973, MA, 1975; JD, U. Tex., 1988. Bar: Tex., U.S. Dist. Ct. (so. dist.) Tex. 1989, U.S. Ct. Appeals (5th cir.) 1989, U.S. Dist. Ct. (we. dist.) Tex. 1999. Ptnr. Vinson & Elkins LLP, Houston, 1988—. Author: (with others) ABA Antitrust Law Developments, 4th edit., ABA Annual Review of Antitrust Law Developments, 1992-95; editor ABA Antitrust Summary Judgment Newsletter, 1996-98. Trustee St. Luke's United Meth. Ch., Houston, 1998, mem. adv. com. Senior's Place, 1994-98, personnel com. 1999—. Recipient U. Tex. Sch. Law Faculty Service Award, 2001. Mem. ABA (vice chair civil practice and procedure com., antitrust sect. 1993-98, v. chair books and treatises com. 2000-2001), Am. Law Inst., Tex. Bar Found., Houston Bar Found. Avocations: reading, cooking, travel. Antitrust, Appellate, General civil litigation. Office: Vinson & Elkins LLP 1001 Fannin St Ste 2300 Houston TX 77002-6760 E-mail: bowens@velaw.com

OWENS, ROBERT PATRICK, lawyer; b. Spokane, Wash., Feb. 17, 1954; s. Walter Patrick and Cecile (Phillippay) O.; m. Robin Miller, Aug. 12, 1978; children: Ryan Barry, Meghan Jane. BA, Wash. State U., 1976; JD, Gonzaga U., 1981; LLM in Admiralty Law, Tulane U., 1983. Bar: Wash. 1982, Alaska 1984, U.S. Dist. Ct. (ea. dist.) Wash. 1982, U.S. Dist. Ct. Alaska 1984, U.S. Ct. Appeals (5th cir.) 1983. Assoc. Groh, Eggers & Price, Anchorage, 1983-88; mng. atty. Taylor & Hintze, 1988-90; Anchorage office mgr. Copeland, Landye, Bennett and Wolf, 1990-99; prin. Law Offices of Robert P. Owens, PC, 2000—. V.p. bd. dirs. Hope Cmty. Resources, Inc., 1999-2001, pres., 2001—. Coord. supplies Insight Seminars, Anchorage, 1985-86. Mem. ABA (dist. 27 rep. young lawyers div. 1988-90), Alaska Bar Assn., Wash. State Bar Assn., Anchorage Bar Assn. (pres. 1991-92, v.p. 1990-91, pres. young lawyers sect. 1986-88), Alaska Fly Fishers, Phi Alpha Delta. Roman Catholic. Avocations: fishing, photography, skiing, softball. Admiralty, Contracts commercial, Environmental. Office: Law Offices Robert P Owens PC 310 K St Ste 200 Anchorage AK 99501 E-mail: rpowens@alaska.com

OWENS, RODNEY JOE, lawyer; b. Dallas, Mar. 7, 1950; s. Hubert L. and Billie Jo (Foust) O.; m. Sherry Lyn Bailey, June 10, 1972; 1 child, Jonathan Rockwell. BBA, So. Meth. U., 1972, JD, 1975. Bar: Tex. 1975, U.S. Dist. Ct. (no. dist.) Tex. 1975, U.S. Tax Ct. 1975, U.S. Ct. Appeals (5th cir.) 1975. Assoc. Durant & Mankoff, Dallas, 1975-78, ptnr., 1978-83, Meadows, Owens, Collier, Reed, Cousins & Blau, Dallas, 1983—. Contbr. articles to profl. jours. Baptist. Estate planning, Estate taxation, Taxation, general. Home: 6919 N Jan Mar Dr Dallas TX 75230-3111 Office: Meadows Owens Collier Reed 901 Main St Ste 3700 Dallas TX 75202-3725 E-mail: rowens@meadowsowens.com

OWENS, SUSAN, judge; b. Kinston, N.C., Aug. 19, 1949; BA, Duke U., 1971; JD, U. N.C., Chapel Hill, 1975. Bar: Oreg. 1975, Wash. 1976. Judge Dist. Ct., Western Clallam County, 1981—2001; justice Wash. State Supreme Ct., 2001—. Mem.: Dist. and Mcpl. Ct. Judges' Assn. (bd. dirs., sec.-treas., v.p., pres.-elect). Office: PO Box 40929 Olympia WA 98504-0929*

OWENS, WILBUR DAWSON, JR. federal judge; b. Albany, Ga., Feb. 1, 1930; s. Wilbur Dawson and Estelle (McKenzie) O.; m. Mary Elizabeth Glenn, June 21, 1958; children: Lindsey, Wilbur Dawson III, Estelle, John. Student, Emory U., 1947-48; JD, U. Ga., 1952. Bar: Ga. 1952. Mem. firm Smith, Gardner & Owens, Albany, 1954-55; v.p., trust officer Bank of Albany, 1955-59; sec.-treas. Southeastern Mortgage Co., Albany, 1959-65; asst. U.S. atty. Middle Dist. Ga., Macon, 1962-65; assoc., then ptnr. Bloch, Hall, Hawkins & Owens, 1965-72; judge U.S. Dist. Ct. for Mid. Dist. Ga., 1972—, now sr. U.S. dist. judge. Served to 1st lt., JAG USAF, 1952-54. Mem. State Bar Ga., Macon Bar Assn., Am. Judicature Soc., Phi Delta Theta, Phi Delta Phi. Republican. Presbyterian. Clubs: Rotarian, Idle Hour Golf and Country. Office: US Dist Ct PO Box 65 Macon GA 31202-0065

OWLES, PETER GARY, lawyer; b. Christchurch, New Zealand, Feb. 6, 1963; m. Michele Hollis; children: Samuel, Katie. LLB, Auckland U., 1984. Bar: barrister and solicitor High Ct. of New Zealand; solicitor Eng. and Wales. Lawyer Clifford Chance, London, 1991-94, Buddle Findlay, Auckland, New Zealand, 1987-91, ptnr. New Zealand, 1995—. Mem. Inter Pacific Bar Assn. (vice chair fin. instns. and tranactions 1999—). General corporate, Finance, Mergers and acquisitions. Office: Buddle Findlay, Tower One 51-53 Shortland St Auckland New Zealand E-mail: peter.owles@buddlefindlay.com

OWNBY, JERE FRANKLIN, III, lawyer; b. Chicago Heights, Ill., Oct. 1, 1956; s. Jere Franklin Jr. and Emogene (Stephens) O.; m. Melissa Cooley, Mar. 17, 1990. BA, U. Tenn., 1986, JD, 1991. Bar: Tenn. 1991. Assoc. Law Offices of Peter G. Angelos, Knoxville, Tenn., 1991-2000, The Neal Law Firm, Knoxville, 2000—. Mem. Order of Barristers, William B. Spong Invitational Moot Ct. Team. Mem. ABA, Assn. Trial Lawyers Am., Am. Inn of Ct., Tenn. Bar Assn., Knoxville Bar Assn., Tenn. Trial Lawyers Assn., Omicron Delta Epsilon, Pi Sigma Alpha. Democrat. Avocations: gardening, raising dogs, the life tng. program. Personal injury, Product liability, Workers' compensation. Home: 3902 Glenfield Dr Knoxville TN 37919-6698 Office: The Neal Law Firm 2108 Keller Bend Rd Knoxville TN 37922

OXFORD, HUBERT, III, lawyer; b. Beaumont, Tex., Sept. 25, 1938; s. Hubert Burton and Virginia Mary (Cunningham) O.; m. Cynthia Lynn Culp, Apr. 25, 1987; children: Mary Francelia, Hubert IV, Mary Cunningham, Virginia Barrett, Alaina Danielle, Adriana Victoria, Gabriella Elizabeth. BSME, Tex. A&M U., 1960; JD, U. Tex., 1963. Bar: Tex., 1963, U.S. Ct. Appeals (5th cir.), 1967, (11th cir.), Tex., U.S. Dist. Ct. (ea., so., no., we. dists.) Tex., U.S. Supreme Ct., 1975, U.S. Dist. Ct. (we. dist.) Okla., Mont., 1996, Wyo., 1996, Okla., 1996, DC 1998, Colo. 1998. Briefing atty. to U.S. dist. judge Eastern Dist. Tex., Beaumont, 1966; asst. dist. atty. Jefferson County, Tex., 1967; mng. ptnr. firm Beckenstein & Oxford, L.L.P., Beaumont, 1966; gen. counsel Jefferson County Nav. Dist., Lower Neches Valley Authority. Mem. Gov. Reorganization Commn. Tex. 70th Legislature, 1987-88, Tex. Oil Spill Commn.; U.S. Commr. Ea. Dist. Tex., 1968-70; mem. Tex. Bd. Registration for Profl. Engrs., 1994-2000. Assoc. editor Tex. Law Rev., 1962-63. Bd. dirs. Ducks Unltd., 1978-86, Gulf Coast Conservation Assn., 1978-86; sec. bd. regents Lamar U., 1978-84, gen. counsel, 1986; mem. Tex. Air Control Bd., 1984-90; chmn. Tex. Clean Air Study Com., 1989. Capt. JAGC, USAF, 1963-66. Fellow Tex. Bar Assn., Internat. Soc. Barristers, Am. Bar. Assn.; mem. ABA, ATLA, Southeastern Admiralty Law Inst., Internat. Assn. Def. Counsel, Tex. Assn. Def. Lawyers, Nat. Bd. Trial Advocacy, State Bar Tex. (chmn. CLE com. 1979-81, course dir. admiralty and maritime seminar 1991, 96, grievance com. Dist. 3A, dir. Dist. 3 1997-2000), Maritime Law Assn., Jefferson County Bar Assn. (pres. 1987-88, Outstanding Young Lawyer 1972), Def. Rsch. Inst., Beaumont C. of C. (dir. 1978-84), Phi Delta Theta, Tau Beta Pi, Phi Kappa Phi, Phi Delta Phi. Democrat. Roman Catholic. Admiralty, General civil litigation, Insurance. Home: 490 Yount Beaumont TX 77706-5328 Office: Benckenstein & Oxford LLP 3535 Calder Ave Ste 300 Beaumont TX 77706-5087 E-mail: hubertoxford@benoxford.com

OXMAN, DAVID CRAIG, lawyer; b. Summit, N.J., Mar. 10, 1941; s. Jacob H. and Kathryn (Grear) O.; m. Phyllis Statter; children— Elena, Lee A.B., Princeton U., 1962; LL.B., Yale U., 1969. Bar: N.Y. 1970, N.J. 1974, U.S. Dist. Ct. (so. and ea. dists.) N.Y. 1974, U.S. Ct. Appeals (2d cir.) 1974, U.S. Tax Ct. 1977, U.S. Supreme Ct. 1974. Assoc. Davis Polk & Wardwell, N.Y.C., 1970-76, ptnr., 1977-95, sr. counsel, 1995—. Served with USN, 1962-66 Fellow Am. Coll. Trust and Estate Counsel; mem. ABA, N.Y. State Bar Assn., Assn. of Bar of City of N.Y. Probate. Office: Davis Polk & Wardwell 450 Lexington Ave Fl 31 New York NY 10017-3982

OXMAN, STEPHEN ELIOT, lawyer; b. Denver, July 16, 1947; s. Irving Isadore and Marguerite Frances (Dinner) Oxman; m. Lynne Marie Caniff, Feb. 03, 1974 (div. 1986); children: Jennifer, Chad; m. Florianne Solin, Sept. 03, 2000. BA, U. Ariz.; JD, John Marshall Law Sch. Bar: Ill. 1974, U.S. Dist. Ct. Colo. 1974. V.p. Oxman & Oxman, P.C., Denver, 1974—. Mem. ABA, Colo. Trial Lawyers Assn., Denver Bar Assn. Democrat. Jewish. State civil litigation, Family and matrimonial, General practice. Home: 1027 Fillmore St Denver CO 80206-3331 Office: 210 Clayton St Ste 1 Denver CO 80206-4804

OXNER, G. DEWEY, lawyer; b. Greenville, S.C., Dec. 31, 1933; s. George Dewey and Frances (Ruckman) O.; m. Louise Earle, Sept. 16, 1960; children: Frances, Dewey, Earle. BA, Washington & Lee U., 1956; LLB, U. S.C., 1959. Bar: S.C. 1959, U.S. Dist. Ct. S.C. 1959, U.S. Ct. Appeals (4th cir.) 1959. From assoc. to mng. ptnr. Haynsworth, Marion, McKay & Guerard, Greenville, 1959-98, ptnr., 1998—. Fellow Am. Coll. Trial Lawyers, S.C. Def. Trial Attys. Assn. (pres. 1976), S.C. Bar Assn. (sec. 1997-98, treas. 1998—), Assn. (sec. 1997-98, treas. 1998-99, pres. elect, 1999—). Home: 10 Parkins Lake Rd Greenville SC 29607-3668 Office: Haynsworth Marion McKay & Guerard 75 Beattie Pl Greenville SC 29601-2130

OYADONGHA, KEREPAMO PETER, lawyer; b. Lagos Island, Lagos, Nigeria, Mar. 2, 1966; s. Joseph Toro and Ogolere (Ayemi) O.; m. Rachel Oiza Baiye, July 29, 2000. LLB, Rsust, Nigeria, Port Harcourt, 1990; BL, Nigeria Law Sch., Lagos, 1991. Cert. barrister-at-law. Assoc. O. Akinkugbe & Co., Lagos, Nigeria, 1992-2000, head of chambers Nigeria, 2001—. Legal adviser Nigerian Girl Guides Assn., Lagos, 1992—; counsel Lloyd's Register of Shipping, Nigeria, 1992—. V.p., sec. Fedn. Cath. Students, Port Harcourt, 1988; chmn. elections com. Jaycees, Port Harcourt, 1990. Mem. Nigerian Bar Assn., Inst. Maritime Law (assoc.). Avocations: music, reading, football, travelling. General practice, Probate, Real property. Home: 15 Ezekiel St Ikeja Lagos Nigeria Office: Obafunke Akinkugbe & Co 21 Igbosere Rd Lagos Nigeria Office Fax: 234-1-2630910. E-mail: obaakinc@hyperia.com

OYLER, GREGORY KENNETH, lawyer; b. Moses Lake, Wash., Sept. 16, 1953; s. Eugene Milton and Annetta Diane (Williams) O.; m. Evelyn Hartwell Wright, Oct. 18, 1986; 1 child, Elizabeth Atwood. AB, Princeton U., 1975; JD, Georgetown U., 1978; LLM, NYU, 1981. Bar: Pa. 1978, U.S. Tax Ct. 1978, U.S. Ct. Appeals (D.C. cir.) 1979, D.C. 1981, U.S. Supreme Ct. 1982, U.S. Ct. Fed. Claims 1983, U.S. Ct. Appeals (fed. cir.) 1987. Law clk. to judges U.S. Tax Ct., Washington, 1978-80; assoc. Hamel & Park, Washington, 1981-85; ptnr. Hopkins & Sutter, 1985-95, Scribner, Hall & Thompson, Washington, 1995—. Mem. adv. com. IRS Info. Reporting Program, 1993-94. Mem. ABA (tax sect., ins. and govt. submissions coms.), D.C. Bar Assn. (tax sect.), Fed. Bar Assn., Soc. Preservation Md. Antiquities (bd. dirs. 1991-97), Clark-Winchcole Found. (trustee 1999—). Corporate taxation, State and local taxation, Non-profit and tax-exempt organizations. Office: Scribner, Hall & Thompson 1875 Eye St NW Ste 1050 Washington DC 20006-5441

PAARZ, ROBERT EMIL, lawyer; b. Phila., Mar. 4, 1948; s. Walter F. and Ethel Kurtz) P.; m. Susan Ann Speed, June 22, 1968; children: Stacy, Keri, Kelli, Rebecca. B.S. cum laude, Ga. Tech. U., 1970; J.D. cum laude, Rutgers U.-Camden, 1974. Bar: N.J. 1974. Ptnr. Dimon Eleuteri & Paarz, Mt. Holly, N.J., 1974-79, Horn, Kaplan, et. al., Atlantic City, 1979—; city solicitor City of Absecon, N.J., 1984—. Elder Presbyterian Ch. at Absecon, 1983—; judicial commr. W. Jersey Presbytery, Haddonfield, 1984-89. Recipient Am. Jurisprudence award 1973, 74. Mem. ABA, N.J. Bar Assn., Atlantic County Bar Assn. State civil litigation, Personal injury. Office: Horn Kaplan 1300 Atlantic Ave Ste 500 Atlantic City NJ 08401-7278

PACE, STANLEY DAN, lawyer; b. Dayton, Ohio, Dec. 10, 1947; s. Stanley Carter and Elaine (Cutchall) P.; m. Judy Roehm, Sept. 8, 1973; children: Stanley Carter, Barbara Roehm. BA, Denison U., Granville, Ohio, 1970; JD, U. Toledo (Ohio), 1975. Bar: U.S. Dist. Ct. (so. dist.) Ohio 1975, U.S. Dist. Ct. (no. dist.) Ohio 1977, U.S. Ct. Appeals (6th cir.) 1975. Atty. ARMCO Steel Corp., Middletown, Ohio, 1975-77; assoc. Spieth, Bell, McCurdy & Newell, Cleve., 1977-82, dir., 1982—, co-mng. dir., 1987—. Bd. mem. Indsl. Rels. Rsch. Assn., Cleve., 1985. Bd. pres. Judson Retirement Community, Cleve., 1985; bd. mem. Arthritis Found. N.E. Ohio, Cleve., 1984, Western Res. Hist. Soc., 1998. Mem. ABA, Ohio Bar Assn., Greater Cleve. Bar Assn., The Country Club, Pepper Pike Club, Tavern Club, Rolling Rock Club. Labor. Office: Spieth Bell McCurdy & Newell 2000 Huntington Bldg Cleveland OH 44115

PACHIU, LAURENTIU VICTOR, lawyer; b. Bucharest, Romania, Oct. 6, 1969; s. Victor and Elena (Ganciu) P.; m. Simona Delia Urs, Apr. 26, 1993. LLM, Bucharest U., 1993; grad., Diplomatic Acad., Berlin, 1995. Intern. Koelner Bank, Cologne, Germany, 1992; asst. tchr. Bucharest U., 1993-94; pvt. practice law Bucharest, 1993—; diplomat Romanian Min. Fgn. Affairs, 1994-97. Sec. Nat. Liberal Party, Bucharest, 1990-93. Mem. Romanian Nat. Union Lawyers. Banking, Contracts commercial, Mergers and acquisitions. Home: No 33 B1 105A scB ap 46 Sos Iancului Bucharest 2 Romania Office: Hall Dickler Romania SRL Kiseleff Blvd No 11-13 71269 Bucharest 1 Romania E-mail: fx.ro;1pachiu@hotmail.com, laurentiu@hdr.ro

PACKARD, STEPHEN MICHAEL, lawyer; b. Hartford, Conn., Nov. 26, 1953; s. Charles David and Anne (Moriarty) P.; m. Eileen Mary Joyce, May 23, 1981; children: Stephen Michael Jr., Sheila Marie, James Charles, Brian Joseph. BS, Fairfield U., 1975; JD magna cum laude, N.Y. Law Sch., 1981. Bar: N.Y. 1981, U.S. Dist. Ct. (ea. and so. dists.) N.Y. 1981, U.S. Dist. Ct. Conn. 1983, Conn. 1984. Assoc. Mudge, Rose, Guthrie, Alexander & Ferdon, N.Y.C., 1981-83, Wiggin & Dana, New Haven, 1983-87; atty. Aetna Life & Casualty, Hartford, 1987-96; ptnr. Accenture, N.Y.C., 1996—. Adj. prof. law U. Bridgeport Law Sch., Conn., 1987. Bd. dirs. New Haven Literacy vols., 1985-87. Mem. Conn. Bar Assn., N.Y.C. Bar Assn., Fed. Bar Coun., Conn. Def. Lawyers Assn. Republican. Roman Catholic. General civil litigation, Insurance. Office: Accenture 1345 Avenue Of The Americas New York NY 10105-0302

PACKENHAM, RICHARD DANIEL, lawyer; b. Newton, Pa., June 23, 1953; s. John Richard and Mary Margaret (Maroney) P.; m. Susan Patricia Smillie, Aug. 20, 1983. BA, Harvard U., 1975; JD, Boston Coll., 1978; LLM in Taxation, Boston U., 1985. Bar: Mass. 1978, Conn. 1979, U.S. Dist. Ct. Mass. 1979, U.S. Dist. Ct. Conn. 1979, U.S. Ct. Appeals (1st cir.) 1981, U.S. Supreme Ct. 1985. Staff atty. Conn. Superior Ct., 1978-79; ptnr. McGrath & Kane, Boston, 1979-94, Packenham, Schmidt & Federico, Boston, 1994—. Mem. ABA, Mass. Bar Assn., Conn. Bar Assn., Boston Bar Assn., Mass CLE (faculty). Democrat. Roman Catholic. Club: Harvard (Boston). State civil litigation, Family and matrimonial. Home: 1062 North St Walpole MA 02081-2307 Office: Packenham Schmidt & Federico 4 Longfellow Pl Boston MA 02114-2838

PACKER, MARK BARRY, lawyer, financial consultant, foundation official; b. Phila., Sept. 18, 1944; s. Samuel and Eve (Devine) P.; m. Donna Elizabeth Ferguson (div. 1994); children: Daniel Joshua, Benjamin Dov, David Johannes; m. Helen Margaret (Jones) Klinedinst, July, 1995. AB magna cum laude, Harvard U., 1965, LLB, 1968. Bar: Wash. 1969, Mass. 1971. Assoc. Ziontz, Pirtle & Fulle, Seattle, 1968-70; pvt. practice Bellingham, Wash., 1972—. Bd. dirs., corp. sec. BMJ Holdings (formerly No. Sales Co., Inc.), 1977—; trustee No. Sales Profit Sharing Plan, 1977—; bd. dirs. Whatcom State Bank, 1995-98. Mem. Bellingham Planning and Devel. Commn., 1975-84, chmn., 1977-81, mem. shoreline subcom., 1976-82, capital improvements adv. com., 1999-01; mem. Bellingham Mcpl. Arts Commn., 1986-91, landmark rev. bd., 1987-91; chmn. Bellingham campaign United Jewish Appeal, 1979-90; bd. dirs. Whatcom Cmty. Coll. Found., 1989-92; trustee, chmn. program com. Bellingham Pub. Sch. Found., 1991-98, Heavy Culture classic lit. group, 1991—, Jewish studies group, 1993—; trustee Kenneth L. Kellar Found., 1995—; mng. trustee Bernard M. & Audrey Jaffe Found.; Torah reader; pres. Congregation Eytz Chaim, Bellingham, 1998-2000. Recipient Blood Donor award ARC, 1979, 8-Gallon Pin, 1988, Mayor's Arts award City of Bellingham, 1993. Mem. Wash. State Bar Assn. (sec. environ. and land use law, sec. bus. law, sec. real property, probate and trust, com. law examiners 1992-94). Contracts commercial, Estate planning, Real property. Office: PO Box 1151 Bellingham WA 98227-1151 E-mail: Packer@nas.com

PACKERT, G(AYLA) BETH, lawyer; b. Corpus Christi, Tex., Sept. 25, 1953; d. Gilbert Norris and Virginia Elizabeth (Pearce) P.; m. James Michael Hall, Jan. 1, 1974 (div. 1985); m. Richard Christopher Burke, July 18, 1987; children: Christopher Geoffrey Makepeace Burke Packert, Jeremy Eliot Marvell Packert Burke. BA, La. Tech. U., 1973; MA, U. Ark., 1976; postgrad., U. Ill., 1975-81, JD, 1985. Bar: Ill. 1985, U.S. Dist. Ct. (no. dist.) Ill. 1985, U.S. Ct. Appeals (7th cir.) 1987, Va. 1988, U.S. Dist.

Ct. (we. dist.) Va. 1989. Assoc. Jenner & Block, Chgo., 1985-88; law clk. U.S. Dist. Ct. Va. (we. dist.), Danville, 1988-89; asst. commonwealth atty. Commonwealth of Va., Lynchburg, Va., 1989-95; pvt. practice, 1995—. Notes and comments editor U. Ill. Law Rev., 1984-85. Mem. Phi Beta Kappa. General civil litigation, Criminal, Family and matrimonial. Home: 3900 Faculty Dr Lynchburg VA 24501-3110 Office: PO Box 529 Lynchburg VA 24505-0529

PADDISON, DAVID ROBERT, lawyer; b. Savannah, Ga., May 15, 1949; s. Richard Milton and Josephine Butler (Bowles) P.; m. Frances M. Phares (div. Mar. 1995); children: Hunt, Brian, Margery; m. Jane Ingrid Caddell, Mar. 30, 1996; 1 child, Ethan David. BSBA, La. State U., 1971; JD, Tulane U., 1976. Bar: La. 1976; U.S. Dist. Ct. (ea. dist.) 1976; U.S. Ct. Appeals (5th cir.) 1976; bd. cert. specialist in family law La. State Bar Assn., 1995. Asst. dist. atty. Dist. Atty.'s Office, Covington, La., 1983-86, New Orleans, 1978-83; pvt. practice Covington, 1986—. Advisor Contemporary Arts Ctr., New Orleans, 1978-79; clin. advisor Tulane U. Sch. Law, New Orleans, 1980-81; spl. cons. Dist. Atty.'s Office, New Orleans, 1981. Legal advisor Christ Episcopal Church (sch. planning com., lector, usher). Mem. Covington Bar Assn., La. Trial Lawyers Assn., ATLA. Republican. Episcopalian. Avocations: golf, sailing, snow skiing. Criminal, Family and matrimonial, Personal injury. Office: PO Box 1830 Covington LA 70434-1830

PADDOCK, MICHAEL BUCKLEY, lawyer; b. Odessa, Tex., Oct. 13, 1947; s. William B. and Elvira Paddock; children: Mary Katherine, Courtney Anne. BSBA, U. Ark., 1970, JD, 1973. Bar: Tex. 1973, U.S. Ct. Appeals (5th cir.) 1973, U.S. Dist. Ct. (no. dist.) Tex. 1973, U.S. Supreme Ct. 1973. Chief of misdemeanor criminal ct. Tarrant County Dist. Atty., Ft. Worth, 1973-76, chief spl. crime unit, 1973-76, chief criminal divsn., 1973-76; sole practitioner, 1976—. Mem. panel U.S. Steel Workers Arbitration Panel, Dallas, 1982. Trustee Trinity Valley Mental Health Mental Retardation, 1975-79. Mem. ATLA, State Bar Tex., Tex. Trial Lawyers Assn., Tarrant County Trial Lawyers and Family Bar, Tarrant County Bar Assn. (chmn. fee arbitration panel 1984-86). Family and matrimonial, General practice, Insurance. Office: 1300 Summit Ave Ste 400 Fort Worth TX 76102-4418

PADEN, LYMAN R. lawyer; b. Oklahoma City, Jan. 10, 1954; s. Lyman C. and Wyatt (Rushton) P. BA cum laude, Rice U., 1976, M in Acctg., 1977; JD, Stanford U., 1980. Bar: Tex. 1980. Assoc. Liddell, Sapp, Zivley & LaBoon, Houston, 1980-85; ptnr. Locke Liddell & Sapp LLP, 1986—. Articles editor Stanford Law Rev., 1979-80. Mem. ABA, Houston Bar Assn., Tex. Assn. Bank Counsel, Houston Club. Episcopalian. Avocation: gardening. Banking, Contracts commercial, General corporate. Home: 2015 Bolsover St Houston TX 77005-1615 Office: Locke Liddell & Sapp LLP 3400 Chase Houston TX 77002 E-mail: lpaden@lockeliddell.com

PADGETT, ANNE, lawyer; b. Walnut Creek, Calif., July 9, 1965; d. Robert Talfourd and Carolyn Lee Bibb Padgett; m. Stan D. Ver Nooy, Aug. 27, 1994. BS in Bus. Adminstrn., Calif. State U., Sacramento, 1988; JD, Lewis & Clark Coll., 1994. Bar: Oreg. 1994, Ark. 1996, Nev. 1998. Contract editor West Bar Rev., San Francisco, 1995-97; contract law clk. Oakland (Calif.) Naval Supply Ctr., 1997-98; assoc. Helm & Helm, Las Vegas, Nev., 1998-2000; staff atty. The Hartford Ins. Group, 2000—. Mem. ABA, Oreg. State Bar, Ark. Bar Assn., State Bar Nev., Clark County Bar Assn., Nev. Trial Lawyers Assn., Phi Delta Phi. Construction, Insurance, Personal injury. Office: Hanlon & Assocs Ste 320 Box 19 750 E Warm Springs Rd Las Vegas NV 89119

PADGETT, GREGORY LEE, lawyer; b. Greenfield, Ind., May 9, 1959; s. William Joseph and Anna Katherine (Hyre) P.; m. Ruth Anne Dorworth, June 5, 1982; children: Joshua David, William Joel. BA summa cum laude, DePauw U., 1981; JD, Northwestern U., 1984. Bar: Ill., U.S. Dist. Ct. (no. dist.) Ill. 1984, U.S. Ct. Appeals (7th cir.) 1986, Ind. 1988, U.S. Dist. Ct. (no. & so. dists.) Ind. 1988. Assoc. Kirkland & Ellis, Chgo., 1984-88, Baker & Daniels, Indpls., 1988-92; ptnr. Johnson, Lawhead, Buth & Pope, P.C., 1992-2000; of counsel Barnes & Thornburg, 2000—. Adj. prof. Butler U., 1989-90. Mem. Marion County Prosecutor's Rev. Task Force, Indpls., 1991; pres., bd. dirs. Theatre on the Square, Indpls., 1994-95; mem. coun. Hope Evang. Covenant Ch., 1992-96; bd. dirs. Meridian St. Found., 1994-96. Mem. Ind. State Bar Assn., Indpls. Bar Assn. (exec. com. alternative dispute resolution sect.), Christian Legal Soc., Phi Beta Kappa. Avocations: theatre arts, vocal music, hiking, writing. General civil litigation, Probate, Securities. Office: Barnes & Thornburg 11 S Meridian St Indianapolis IN 46204 E-mail: gpadgett@btlaw.com

PADILLA, JAMES EARL, lawyer; b. Miami, Fla., Dec. 28, 1953; s. Earl George and Patricia (Bauer) P. BA, Northwestern U., 1975; JD, Duke U., 1978. Bar: Ill. 1978, U.S. Ct. Appeals (5th and 7th cir.) 1978, U.S. Supreme Ct. 1981, Colo. 1982, U.S. Ct. Appeals (10th cir.) 1982, D.C. 1985, N.Y. 1989. Assoc. Mayer, Brown & Platt, Chgo. and Denver, 1978-84, ptnr. Denver, 1985-87, N.Y.C., 1988-96; private investor, 1996—. Contbg. author: Mineral Financing, 1982, Illinois Continuing Legal Education, 1993. Mem. ABA, Ill. Bar Assn., D.C. Bar Assn., Colo. Bar Assn., N.Y. State Bar Assn. Avocation: golf. Banking, Bankruptcy, Contracts commercial. Office: 1900 Summer St Unit 19 Stamford CT 06905-5024

PAEZ, RICHARD A. federal judge; b. 1947; BA, Brigham Young U., 1969; JD, U. Calif., Berkeley, 1972. Staff atty. Calif. Rural Legal Assistance, Delano, Calif., 1972-74, Western Ctr. on Law and Poverty, 1974-76; sr. counsel, dir. litigation, acting exec. dir. Legal Aid Found. of L.A., 1976-81; judge L.A. Mcpl. Ct., 1981-94, U.S. Dist. Ct. (ctrl. dist.) Calif., L.A., 1994-2000, U.S. Dist. Ct. (9th cir.), Pasadena, Calif., 2000—. Active Hollywood-Los Feliz Jewish Cmty. Ctr. Mem. Calif. State Bar Assn., L.A. County Bar Assn., Mex.-Am. Bar Assn. L.A. County, Calif. Jud. Coun. Office: US Ct Appeals Edward R Roybal Ctr & Fed Bldg 125 S Grand AveRm 204 Pasadena CA 91105-1652*

PAGE, ALAN CEDRIC, state supreme court justice; b. Canton, Ohio, Aug. 7, 1945; s. Howard F. and Georgianna (Umbles) P.; m. Diane Sims, June 5, 1973; children: Nina, Georgianna, Justin, Khamsin. BA, U. Notre Dame, 1967; JD, U. Minn., 1978; LLD, U. Notre Dame, 1993; LLD (hon.), St. John's U., 1994, Westfield State Coll., 1994, Luther Coll., 1995, U. New Haven, 1999. Bar: Minn. 1979, U.S. Dist. Ct. Minn. 1979, U.S. Supreme Ct. 1988. Profl. athlete Minn. Vikings, Mpls., 1967-78, Chgo. Bears, 1978-81; assoc. Lindquist & Vennum, Mpls., 1979-85; former atty. Minn. Atty. Gen.'s Office, 1985-92; assoc. justice Minn. Supreme Ct., St. Paul, 1993—. Cons. NFL Players Assn., Washington, 1979-84. Commentator Nat. Pub. Radio, 1982-83. Founder Page Edn. Found., 1988. Named NFL's Most Valuable Player, 1971, one of 10 Outstanding Young Men Am., U.S. Jaycees, 1981; named to NFL Hall of Fame, 1988, Coll. Football Hall of Fame, 1993. Mem. ABA, Minn. Bar Assn., Hennepin County Bar Assn., Minn. Minority Lawyers Assn., Minn. Assn. Black Lawyers. Avocations: running, biking. Office: 423 Minnesota Judicial Ctr 25 Constitution Ave Saint Paul MN 55155-1500

PAGE, CLEMSON NORTH, JR. lawyer; b. Bossier City, La., June 18, 1945; s. Clemson North and Nancy Jean (Strelinger) P.; m. Hollace Esleton Triller, Aug. 29, 1970 (div.); children: Janet North, Lindsay Coleman; m. Nikiya Itam, Oct. 9, 1993. AB in English Lit., Dartmouth Coll., 1967; JD, Villanova Law Sch., 1977. Bar: Pa. 1977, U.S. Dist. Ct. (ea. dist.) Pa. 1981. Reporter, editor Phila. Bulletin, 1969-74; from assoc. to ptnr. Bingaman, Hess, Coblentz & Bell, Reading, Pa., 1977-98; ptnr. Austin, Boland, Connor & Giorgi, 1998—. Solicitor Borough Zoning Hearing Bd., Wyomissing Hills, Pa. 1986—, St. Andrew's Soc. of Phila. Lt. comdr. USNR (ret.). Mem. Pa. Bar Assn., Berks County Bar Assn. (chmn. profl. edn. com. 1982, chmn. pub. relation com. 1986, bd. dirs. 1989—), Endlich Law Club. Republican. Episcopalian. Banking, Consumer commercial, General corporate. Home: 42 Wyomissing Hills Blvd Reading PA 19609-1777 Office: Austin Boland Connor & Giorgi 44 N 6th St PO Box 8521 Reading PA 19603-8521 E-mail: clempage@ptd.net

PAGE, GEORGE ALFRED, JR. lawyer; b. Evanston, Ill., June 30, 1932; AB, Princeton U., 1954; JD, Harvard U., 1959; LLM in Taxation, Boston U., 1964. Bar: Mass 1959. From assoc. to ptnr. Peabody & Arnold, Boston, 1959-79; sr. ptnr. Csaplar & Bok, 1979-90; pvt. practice, 1990—. Lectr grad tax program Boston Univ Sch Law, 1974—77; gen counsel to bd dirs and sr mgmt Woodside Mgmt Sys Inc, Boston, 1978—87. 1st lt USAR, 1954—56. Mem.: ABA (mem real property, probate and trust law sect), Boston Bar Asn (chmn state tax comt 1971—74, sect taxation 1974—75, fed tax comt 1980—82, sr sect 1994—96, mem trusts and estates law sect, mem estate planning comt), Boston Probate Forum, Boston and Essex County Estate Planning Couns. Estate planning, Probate, Taxation, general. Office: 50 Congress St Ste 350 Boston MA 02109-4008

PAGE, JACK RANDALL, lawyer; b. Waco, Tex., Aug. 1, 1956; s. Jack Bennett and Mary Elizabeth (Cobbs) P.; m. Shirley Jean Hull, Aug. 5, 1978; children: Anna Christine, Sara Elaine. BBA magna cum laude, Baylor U., 1977, JD, 1980. Bar: Tex. 1980, U.S. Tax Ct. 1985, U.S. Dist. Ct. (we. dist.) Tex. 1987, U.S. Ct. Appeals (5th cir.) 1989; cert. in tax law Tex. Bd. Legal Specialization; CPA, Tex. Acct. Allie B. Gates Jr., CPA, Waco, 1975-78; assoc. Pakis, Giotes, Page & Burleson, P.C., 1980-86, ptnr., 1986—. Chmn. exploring sales team Heart O' Tex. coun. Boy Scouts Am., 1983, dist. chmn., 1984-85, v.p., 1986-88, coun. commr., 1989-91, coun. pres., 1991-94, asst. coun. commr., 1994-95, v.p., 1995-96, mem. adv. coun. Longhorn Coun., 2000—; mem. adv. coun. dept. acctg. Baylor U., 1993—; co-chmn. Food for Families, 1995—. Recipient Dist. Award of Merit Heart O' Tex. coun. Boy Scouts Am., 1985, Silver Beaver award 1993, Commrs. Key, 1994. Fellow Tex. Bar Found.; mem. AICPA, Tex. Bar Assn., Coll. of State Bar of Tex., Waco-McLennan County Bar Assn., Tex. Soc. CPAs, Waco Estate Planning Coun. (pres. 1983), Rotary (Paul Harris fellow), Order of Demolay (chevalier 1975). Roman Catholic. Avocations: hiking, fly fishing, outdoor activities. General corporate, Estate planning, Taxation, general. Office: Pakis Giotes Page & Burleson PC 801 Washington Ave Ste 800 Waco TX 76701-1266

PAGE, JOHN MARSHALL, JR. lawyer; b. Little Rock, Mar. 27, 1935; s. John Marshall and Edith Luzenberg (McCay) P.; m. Elizabeth Duane Leach, Nov. 30, 1961; children: John Marshall III, Caroline McCay. BA, U. Tex., 1956; LLB, Tulane U., 1960. Bar: La. 1960, Tex. 1960, U.S. Dist. Ct. (ea. dist.) La. 1960, (mid. dist.) La. 1960, U.S. Ct. Appeals (5th cir.) 1970, U.S. Supreme Ct. 1971, U.S. Customs Ct. 1962. Assoc. Lemle, Kelleher, Kohlmeyer, Dennery, Hunley, Moss & Foilot (formerly McCloskey, Dennery, Page & Hennesy), New Orleans, 1960-63, ptnr., 1964—. Former mem. bd. New Orleans Ednl. TV Found., New Orleans Legal Assistance Corp. Served as lt. USN, 1956-59. Mem. ABA, La. Bar Assn. (bd. govs. 1977-79), New Orleans Bar Assn. (pres. 1983-84), State Bar Tex. Republican. Episcopalian. Clubs: New Orleans Lawn Tennis (pres. 1978-79), Stratford (treas. 1978—), Boston, Louisiana (New Orleans). General corporate, Probate, Real property. Home: 1415 Octavia St New Orleans LA 70115-4226 Office: Lemle Kelleher Kohlmeyer et al Pan-Am Life Ctr 21st Floor 601 Poydras St New Orleans LA 70130-6029

PAGLIERANI, RONALD JOSEPH, lawyer; b. Cambridge, Mass., Jan. 27, 1947; s. Joseph and Irene (Woronicz) P.; m. Patricia Ann Sullivan, June 14, 1969; children: Paul J., Stacy E., Claire L. BS in Physics, Boston Coll., 1967; MS in Physics, Northeastern U., 1975; JD, Suffolk U., 1979. Bar: Mass. 1979, U.S. Dist. Ct. Mass. 1980. Assoc. Kenway and Jenney, Boston, 1979-80; patent atty. The Foxboro (Mass.) Co., 1980-83, patent counsel, 1983-84, Prime Computer, Inc., Natick, Mass., 1984-89; sr. atty. Digital Equipment Corp., Maynard, 1989-90; gen. coun. Open Software Found., Inc., Camridge, 1990-94; gen. counsel The Registry, Inc., Newton, Mass., 1995; intellectual property counsel Wang Labs., Billerica, 1996—, Commerce TV Corp, Braintree, 2000—. Instr. patent law Suffolk U. Law Sch. 1988-95; instr. Boston U., 1996. Served to lt. USNR, 1968-71. Mem. Boston Patent Law Assn. (bd. govs. 1985-93, pres. 1992), Am. Intellectual Property Law Assn., Assn. Corp. Patent Counsel, KC. Roman Catholic. Avocations: music, exercise, reading, collecting antique cameras. Computer, Patent, Trademark and copyright. Home: 4 Acorn St Scituate MA 02066-3325 Office: Commerce TV Corp 325 Wood Rd Braintree MA 02184

PAGNI, ALBERT FRANK, lawyer; b. Reno, Jan. 28, 1935; s. Bruno and Daisy Rose (Recami) P.; m. Nancy Lynne Thomas, Aug. 12, 1961; children: Elisa, Michelle, Melissa, Michael. AB, U. Nev., 1961; JD, U. Calif.-Hastings Coll. Law, 1964. Bar: Nev. 1964. Assoc. Vargas, Dillon, Bartlett & Dixon, Reno, 1965-70; ptnr. Vargas & Bartlett and Jones Vargas, Reno, 1970—. Mem. adminstrv. council U. Nev., 1974-81; treas. U. Nev. Legis. Commn., 1973-74, pres., 1975; bd. dirs. Better Bus. Bur.; mem. Nev. Dist. Appeal Bd.; mem. hospice coun. St. Mary's Hosp. With U.S. Army, 1955-57. Recipient Outstanding Alumni award U. Nev., 1978. Fellow Am. Coll. Trial Lawyers (state chair), Nev. Law Found. (trustee, vice chair), Am. Inns Ct. (Master Bruce Thompson, Am. Bd. Trial Advs. (nat. bd.); mem. ABA, Washoe County Bar Assn., Nev. Trial Lawyers Assn., ATLA, Def. Research Inst., Assn. Def. Counsel Calif. and Nev. (no. state chmn. 1983-85), Am. Softball Found. (bd. dirs.), Am. Judicature Assn., State Bar Nev. (bd. govs. 1976-87, v.p. 1984-85, pres. elect 1985-86, pres. 1986-87), Order of Coif, Wolf Club, Elks. State civil litigation, Insurance, Personal injury. Office: 12th Fl 100 W Liberty St Fl 12 Reno NV 89501-1962

PAGTER, CARL RICHARD, lawyer; b. Balt., Feb. 13, 1934; s. Charles Ralph and Mina (Amelung) P.; m. Judith Elaine Cox, May 6, 1978; 1 child by previous marriage: Corbin Christopher. AA, Diablo Valley Coll., 1953; BA, San Jose State U., 1955; LLB, U. Calif., Berkeley, 1964. Bar:Calif. 1965, D.C. 1977, U.S. Supreme Ct. 1976. Law clk. Kaiser Industries Corp., Oakland, Calif., 1963-64, counsel, 1964-70, assoc. counsel Washington, 1970-73, counsel Oakland, Calif., 1973-75, dir. govt. affairs Washington, 1975-76; v.p., sec., gen. counsel Kaiser Cement Corp., Oakland, Calif., 1976-88, cons., gen. counsel San Ramon, 1988-98, cons., 1998—. Author: (with A. Dundes) Urban Folklore from the Paperwork Empire, 1975, More Urban Folklore from the Paperwork Empire, 1987, Never Try to Teach a Pig to Sing, 1991, Sometimes the Dragon Wins, 1996, Why Don't Sheep Shrink When It Rains, 2000. With USNR, 1957-61, to comdr., 1978. Mem. ABA, Calif. Bar, Am. Folklore Soc., Calif. Folklore Soc., Calif. Bluegrass Assn. (founder), Mariners Square Athletic Club, Univ. Club. Republican. Antitrust, General corporate, Product liability. Home and Office: 17 Julianne Ct Walnut Creek CA 94595-2610

PAINTER, MARK PHILIP, judge; b. Cin., Apr. 6, 1947; s. John Philip and Marjorie (West) P.; m. Sue Ann Painter. BA, U. Cin., 1970, JD, 1973. Bar: Ohio 1973, U.S. Dist. Ct. (so. dist.) Ohio 1973, U.S. Supreme Ct. 1980. Assoc. Smith & Schnacke (now part of Thompson Hine), 1973-78; pvt. practice Cin., 1978-82; judge Hamilton County Mcpl. Ct., 1982-95, Ohio 1st Dist. Ct. Appeals, Cin., 1995—. Adj. prof. law U. Cin., 1990—; lectr. in field. Co-author: Ohio DUI Law, 1988, 10th edit., 2001; mem. editl. bd. Criminal Law Jour. Ohio, 1989-92; contbr. articles to profl. jours. Bd. dirs. Citizens Sch. Com., Cin., 1974-76; trustee Freestore Foodbank, Cin., 1984-90, Mary Jo Brueggeman Meml. Found., Cin., 1981-92; bd. commrs. on grievances and discipline Ohio Supreme Ct., 1993-95; mem. Rep. Ctrl. Com., Cin., 1972-82. Recipient Superior Jud. Svc. award Ohio Supreme Ct., 1982, 84, 85. Mem. ABA, Ohio State Bar Assn., Cin. Bar Assn. (trustee 1988-90), Am. Judges Assn., Am. Judicature Soc., Am. Soc. Writers on Legal Subjects, Potter Stewart Inn of Ct. (master of bench emeritus), Bankers Club. Home: 2449 Fairview Ave Cincinnati OH 45219-1170 Office: Ct of Appeals William Howard Taft Law Ctr 230 E 9th St Cincinnati OH 45202-2174 E-mail: JuqPainter@aol.com

PAINTER, PAUL WAIN, JR. lawyer; b. Cleveland, Tenn., Aug. 10, 1945; s. Paul Wain and Juanita (Davis) P.; m. Judith Ann Babine, Aug. 28, 1971; 1 child, Paul Wain III. BS, Ga. Tech., 1968; JD, U. Ga., 1974. Bar: Ga. 1974, U.S. Dist. Ct. (so. dist.) Ga., U.S. Ct. Appeals (11th cir.). Assoc. Bouhan, Williams & Levy, Savannah, Ga., 1974-79; ptnr. Karsman, Brooks, Painter & Callaway, 1979-88, Ellis, Painter, Ratterree & Bart, Savannah, 1988—. Faculty mem. Nat. Inst. Trial Advocacy, Emory U. Sch. Law, 1982-90; mem. com. on lawyer qualifications and conduct U.S. Ct. Appeals for 11th Cir., 1995—; mem. ct. adv. com. U.S. Dist. Ct. (so. dist.) Ga., 1992-2000; mem. Gov.'s Adv. Com. on Tort Reform, Atlanta, 1986; mem. Ga. Bd. Bar Examiners, 1998—. Trustee Ga. Inst. Continuing Legal Edn., Athens, 1992-95; pres. Savannah Arthritis Found., 1982-83; bd. dirs. Ga. Arthritis Found., Atlanta, 1983; grad. Leadership Savannah, 1986-88. Lt. (j.g.) USN, 1968-71. Fellow Am. Coll. Trial Lawyers; mem. ABA, State Bar Ga. (chair trial sect. 1992-93), Def. Rsch. Inst. (Ga. state chmn. 1988-91), Savannah Bar Assn. (pres. 93), Ga. Def. Lawyers Assn. (pres. 1986-87), U. Ga. Law Sch. Alumni Assn. (dir. 1997-2000, treas. 2000—). Avocations: golf, reading history and fiction, hunting, fishing. Federal civil litigation, General civil litigation. Office: Ellis Painter Ratterree Bart PO Box 9946 Savannah GA 31412-0146 E-mail: ppainter@eprb-law.com

PAINTER, SAMUEL FRANKLIN, lawyer; b. Lynchburg, Va., Oct. 31, 1946; s. Simon Marcellus and Laura Francis (Lackey) P.; m. Brenda Irene Bogan, Dec. 23, 1972; children: Laura Marcella, Samuel Bogan. BA, U. Va., 1969; JD, Washington and Lee U., 1972. Bar: S.C. 1972, U.S. Dist. Ct. S.C. 1973, U.S. Ct. Appeals (4th cir.) 1974, U.S. Supreme Ct. 1982. Atty. Nexsen Pruet Jacobs and Pollard, Columbia, S.C., 1972—. Legal advisor S.C. Self-Insurers Assn., Columbia, 1976—. Author: S.C. Workers' Compensation Casebook, 1990, Workers' Compensation in South Carolina: What Employers Need to Know, 1993. Mem. S.C. Def. Trial Lawyers Assn. Insurance, Workers' compensation. Office: Nexsen Pruet Jacobs & Pollard PO Box 2426 Columbia SC 29202-2426

PAINTON, RUSSELL ELLIOTT, lawyer, mechanical engineer; b. Port Arthur, Tex., Dec. 5, 1940; s. Clifford Elliott and Edith Virginia (McCutcheon) P.; m. Elizabeth Ann Mullins, July 2, 1965 (div. Dec. 1977); 1 child, Todd Elliott; m. Mary Lynn Weber, May 9, 1981. BS in Mech. Engring., U. Tex.-Austin, 1963, JD, 1972. Bar: Tex. 1972; registered profl. engr., Tex. Engr. Gulf States Utilities, Beaumont, Tex., 1963-66, Tracor, Inc., Austin, 1966-70, corp. counsel, 1973-83, v.p., gen. counsel, 1983-98, corp. sec., 1991-98; atty. Brown, Maroney, Rose, Baker & Barber, 1972-73, Childs, Fortenbach, Beck & Guyton, Houston, 1973; corp. sec. Westmark Systems, Inc., Austin, 1990-91; sole practitioner, 1998—. Gen. counsel Paramount Theatre for Performing Arts, 1977-83, 2d vice chmn., 1978-80, 1st vice chmn., 1980-82, chmn. bd., 1982-84, retiring chmn., 1984-85; mem. Centex chpt. ARC; mem. adv. bd. Austin Sci. Acad., 1985-88, 93-95; mem. adv. coun. Austin Transp., 1985-88; bd. dirs. Tex. Industries for the Blind and Handicapped, 1988-95, vice chmn., 1990-91. Named Boss of Yr. Austin Legal Secs. Assn., 1981. Mem. ABA, Tex. Bar Assn. (treas. corp. counsel sect. 1982-83), Travis County Bar Assn., Nat. Chamber Litigation Ctr., Better Bus. Bur. (arbitrator 1983—), Am. Electronics Assn. (chmn. Austin coun. 1985-86), Austin Yacht Club (race comdr. 1968-69, treas. 1970-71, sec. 1972, 75, vice commodore 1980, commodore 1981, fleet comdr. 1986), Order Blue Gavel, Houston Yacht Club, Poueport Yacht Club, Delta Theta Phi. Republican. Episcopalian. Contracts commercial, General corporate, Securities. E-mail: sailor44@swbell.net

PAIST, MARK C. lawyer; b. Arlington, Va. AB in Econs., Stanford U., 1987; JD, U. Va., 1991. Bar: Calif. 1994, Md. 1995, D.C. 1996. Of counsel Morrison & Foerster, McLean, Va., 1991-2001. General corporate. Office: Morrison & Foerster 1750 Tysons' Blvd Ste 1550 Mc Lean VA 22102 Fax: 703-760-7900. E-mail: mpaist@mofo.com

PAJAK, DAVID JOSEPH, lawyer, consultant; b. Buffalo, June 19, 1956; s. William H. and Theresa A. (Granato) P.; m. Peggy J. Fisher, Aug. 1, 1981; children: Andrew J., Karl W. BA, State Coll. Buffalo, 1978; JD, U. Buffalo, 1982. Bar: N.Y. 1983, U.S. Dist. Ct. (we. dist.) N.Y., 1991. Social svcs. counsel Genesee County Dept. Social Svcs., Batavia, N.Y., 1984-93; pvt. practice Corfu, 1983—, Buffalo, N.Y., 1993—; town justice Town of Pembroke, N.Y., 1994—; with Genesee County Attys. Office, 2001—. Mem. legis. com. N.Y. Fed. on Child Abuse and Neglect, Albany, 1986-99, bd. dirs., 1987-89; cons. N.Y. Pub. Welfare Assn., Inc., Albany, 1987-92; pres. Social Svcs. Attys. Assn. N.Y. State, 1990-91; instr. Bill Adam's Martial Arts & Fitness Ctr., Buffalo, 1997-2000; cons. Cornell U. Family Life Devel. Ctr., 1993-97; instr. Klassic Karate Studios, Buffalo, 1988-97. Contbr. articles to profl. jours. Mem. N.Y. State Bar Assn., N.Y. State Magistrate's Assn., Erie County Bar Assn., Genesee County Bar Assn., Genesee County Magistrate's and Peace Officers Assn., Corfu Area Bus. Assn., Western Genesee County Bus. Assn. Republican. Avocations: karate, martial arts. State civil litigation, Family and matrimonial, Legislative. Home: 17 E Main St Corfu NY 14036-9665 Office: 170 Franklin St Ste 701 Buffalo NY 14202-2412 E-mail: dave@djpajak.com

PAKTER, WALTER JAY, legal scholar and educator, aviation lawyer; b. Aug. 1, 1943; married; 3 children. BA, CCNY, 1965; postgrad., U. Munich, 1970-73; PhD in History, Johns Hopkins U., 1974; LLM, U. Calif., Berkeley, 1991; DPhil in Law, Oxford (Eng.) U., 1989. Bar: (Calif.). Rsch. asst. Inst. bayerische and deutsch Rechtsgeschichte U. Munich, 1972-73; jr. instr. Johns Hopkins U., Balt., 1966-68, 69-70; scholar-in-residence Inst. Medieval Canon Law, U. Calif., Berkeley, 1974-77; assoc. prof. U. Montpellier (France) Faculty of Law, 1977-78; scholar-in-residence U. Calif. Sch. Law, Berkeley, 1978-2000; atty. Moore & Dimick, Castro Valley, Calif., 1996-98, Law Offices Walter J. Pakter, Berkeley, 1998—. Author: Medieval Canon Law and the Jews, 1988, (with Stefan A. Riesenfeld) Casebook on Comparative Law, 2001; contbr. articles to profl. jours. Gilman fellow, 1966-68, 69-70; NDEA fellow, 1968-69, Fulbright scholar, 1970-72. Home: 615 Woodmont Ave Berkeley CA 94708-1233

PALAHACH, MICHAEL, lawyer; b. N.Y.C., Jan. 30, 1948; s. Michael and Mary Palahach; m. Miriam Ann Boghos, May 10, 1980; children: Michael IV, Stephen. BS in Bus. Adminstrn., U. Fla., 1970, JD, 1973. Bar: Fla. 1973, U.S. Dist. Ct. (so. dist.) Fla. 1973, U.S. Ct. Appeals (5th cir.) 1973, U.S. Dist. Ct. (mid. dist.) Fla. 1979; cert. trial lawyer, Fla. Ptnr. High, Stack, Lazenby, Palahach & Goldsmith, Coral Gables, Fla., 1973— . Mem. Fla. Bar Assn., Dade County Bar Assn., Coral Gables Bar Assn., Fla. Acad. Trial Lawyers, Am. Acad. Trial Lawyers, Nat. Bd. Trial Adv. (cert. trial lawyer). Federal civil litigation, State civil litigation, Personal injury. Home: 6932 Sunrise Pl Miami FL 33133-7028 Office: High Stack Lazenby Palahach and Goldsmith 3929 Ponce De Leon Blvd Miami FL 33134-7323

PALAZZO, ROBERT PAUL, lawyer, accountant; b. L.A., Apr. 14, 1952; s. Joseph Francis and Mickey Palazzo. BA in Econs., UCLA, 1973; MBA, JD, U. So. Calif., 1976; postgrad., U. Oxford, 1979. CPA Calif., Nev., Colo.; Bar: Calif. 1976, U.S. Dist. Ct. (so. dist.) Calif. 1977, U.S. Tax Ct. 1977, U.S. Ct. Appeals (9th cir.) 1978, U.S. Supreme Ct. 1980. Assoc. Graham & James, L.A., 1976-78; ptnr. Rader, Cornwall, Kessler & Palazzo CPAs, 1978-81, Palazzo & Kessler, L.A., 1978-81; pvt. practice L.A., Darwin, Calif., 1981—. Judge pro tem L.A. Mcpl. Ct., 1982—; bd. dirs.

Cons. Am. Oil Co., Fin. Systems Internat. Inc., Adventures Prodns., Inc.; alumni advisor UCLA, 1977-81, mem. adv. and scholarship com., 1978-81; mem. profl. adv. com. West L.A. Coll., 1993-96; lectr. U. Oxford, 1979, U. So. Calif., 1986, Calif. Poly. Inst., Pomona, 1997; hist. cons. A&E Civil War Jour., Death Valley Memories (motion picture), A&E Biography, (history channel) Guns of Infamy; spkr. Calif. State U., Northridge, 1996, Death Valley 49ers Encampment, 1996, 5th Death Valley History Conf., 1999; hist. cons. A&E Biography, Medieval Conf. Plymouth State Coll. U. N.H., 1999, 2000; session chair Medieval and Renaissance Conf., Aris. State U., 2000, 2001; spkr. in field; archival cons. Haunted History, History Channel, hist. cons. Author: Darwin, California, 1996; contbg. editor: The Gun Report; prodr. (motion picture) L.A. Bounty, the 20 Mule Team of Death Valley, (History channel) Magnificent Failures, Haunted History, 20th Century Infamous Guns; contbr. articles to profl. jours.; featured Tales of the Gun, History Channel, 1998, 99, 2000. Founder Ohio History Flight Mus.; bd. dirs. Calif. Cancer Found., L.A., 1978-85, pres., 1979-80; bd. dirs. Friends of William S. Hart Park and Mus., 1990-93, v.p. Mus. Relations; chmn. dist. bd. dirs. Darwin Community Svcs., 1990-92. Mem. L.A. County Bar Assn. (arbitration com., fee dispute resolution program), Italian Am. Lawyers Assn. (bd. govs. 1980—, 1st v.p. 1984-88), Nat. Acad. Rec. Arts and Scis., Western Writers Assn., Century City Bar Assn. (vice-chmn. estate planning, trust and probate com. 1979-80), English Westerners' Soc., Nat. Italian Am. Bar Assn., Am. Numismatic Assn. (dist. rep. Carson City 1981-82, L.A. 1982-83), Medieval Acad. Am., English Westerners Soc., S.E. Ohio Oil and Gas Assn., Death Valley History Assn. (life, conf. spkr. 1992, 95, 99), Medieval Acad. Am. (conf. session chair 2001), Mensa, Wig and Pen Club (London), So. Calif. Autograph Soc. (v.p.), Omicron Delta Epsilon, Beta Alpha Psi (pres. 1972), Pi Gamma Mu, Phi Alpha Delta, Zeta Phi Eta. Entertainment, Corporate taxation, Personal income taxation. Office: 3002 Midvale Ave Ste 209 Los Angeles CA 90034-3418 also: 230 S Main St Darwin CA 93522

PALENBERG, HANS-PETER, lawyer; b. Düsseldorf, Germany, Dec. 8, 1955; Ptnr. Rechtsanwalte Clev & Pape , Germany. Mem. German Soc. for Inheritance Law, Tax Adv. Chamber. Estate planning, Taxation, general, Initial public offer. Office: Rechtsanwalte Clev & Pape Konigsallee 70 40212 Dusseldorf Germany E-mail: hans-peter.palenberg@clev-pape.de

PALERMO, ANTHONY ROBERT, lawyer; b. Rochester, N.Y., Sept. 30, 1929; s. Anthony C. and Mary (Palvino) P.; m. Mary Ann Coyne, Jan. 2, 1960; children: Mark Henry, Christopher Coyne, Peter Stuart, Elisabeth Megan McCarthy, Julie Coyne Lawther, Gregg Anthony. BA, U. Mich., 1951; JD, Georgetown U., 1956. Bar: D.C. 1956, N.Y. 1957, U.S. Supreme Ct. 1961. Trial atty. U.S. Dept. Justice, Washington, 1956-58, asst. atty. N.Y.C., 1958-60, asst. U.S. atty. in charge Rochester, N.Y., 1960-61; ptnr. Brennan, Centner, Palermo & Blauvelt, 1962-81, Harter, Secrest & Emery, Rochester, 1981-94, Hodgson, Russ, Andrews, Woods & Goodyear, LLP, Rochester, 1994-97, of counsel, 1998, Woods Oviatt Gilman LLP, Rochester, 1999—. Note editor Georgetown Law Jour., 1956. Bd. dirs. McQuaid Jesuit H.S., Rochester, 1978-84, St. Ann's Home for Aged, Rochester, 1974-2001; bd. dirs., sec. St. Ann's Found., Rochester, 1989-2001; trustee, charter chmn. Clients' Security Fund N.Y. (now Lawyer's Fund for Client Protection), 1981-90; chmn. Govs. Jud. Screening Com. 4th Jud. Dept., mem. statewide com., 1987-89; chair magistrate selection com. U.S. Dist. Ct. (we. dist.) N.Y., 1995, 98; mem. N.Y. Chief Judge's Commn. on Jud. Salaries, 1997—; mem. N.Y. Office Ct. Adminstrn. Commn. on Fiduciary Appointments, 2000—. Fellow Am. Bar Found., N.Y. State Bar Found. (bd. dirs. 1978-91), Am. Coll. Trial Lawyers; mem. ABA (ho. dels. 1980-98, state del. 1982-85, bd. govs. 1985-88, 1989-93, sec. 1990-93), N.Y. State Bar Assn. (pres. 1979-80, ho. dels. 1973-75, 77—), Monroe County Bar Assn. (pres. 1973), Oak Hill Country Club. Roman Catholic. Avocation: golf. General civil litigation, Estate planning, General practice. Home: 38 Huntington Meadow Rochester NY 14625-1813

PALERMO, NORMAN ANTHONY, lawyer; b. Whittier, Calif., Mar. 14, 1937; s. Anthony and Alice Lucille (Ingram) P.; m. Wynne Harrison Kieffer, Apr. 12, 1989; children by previous marriage: David I., Pamela B. BS in Geology, Tulane U., 1958; LLB, Georgetown U., 1966. Bar: Colo. 1966, U.S Dist. Ct. Colo. 1966, U.S. Ct. Appeals (10th cir.) 1966, U.S. Supreme Ct. 1971. Assoc., ptnr. Quigley Wilder & Palermo, Colorado Springs, Colo., 1966-75; v.p. Quigley & Palermo, P.C., 1975-85; pres. Norman A. Palermo, P.C., 1985—. Chmn. El Paso County Rep. Cen. Com., Colorado Springs, 1985-87; bd. dirs. Goodwill Industries, Colorado Springs, 1973—; mem. State Commn. on Jud. Performance, 1993-97; bd. dirs. Colorado Springs Symphony, 1981-87; bd. dirs. Centura Health Penrose-St. Francis Health Svcs. Cmty. Bd., 2000—, chmn., 2001—; co-chmn. SPRINGS 2000; mem. Colo. Commn. on Taxation, 2000—. Comdr. USNR, 1958-66. Mem. ABA, Colo. Bar Assn. (bd. govs. 1999—), El Paso County Bar Assn., Colorado Springs C. of C. (bd. dirs. 1980-83, 93-97, chmn. bd. dirs. 1993-95, chmn. Chamber Found. 1996-97), Colo. Commn. on Taxation. Republican. Avocations: golf, travel. General corporate, Estate planning, Real property. Home: 1835 Cantwell Grv Colorado Springs CO 80906-6911 Office: 102 E Pikes Peak Ave 5th Fl Colorado Springs CO 80903-1823 also: PO Box 1718 Colorado Springs CO 80901-1718 E-mail: norm@palermolaw.com

PALIZZI, ANTHONY N. lawyer, retail corporation executive; b. Wyandotte, Mich., Oct. 27, 1942; s. Vincenzo and Nunziata (Dagostini) P.; children: A. Michael, Nicholas A. PhB, Wayne State U., 1964, JD, 1966; LLM, Yale U., 1967. Bar: Mich. 1967. Prof. law Fla. State U., Tallahassee, 1967-69; prof. law Tex. Tech U., Lubbock, 1969-71; atty. Kmart Corp., Troy, Mich., 1971-74, asst. sec., 1974-77, asst. gen. counsel, 1977-85, v.p., assoc. gen. counsel, 1985-91, sr. v.p., gen. counsel, 1991-92, exec. v.p., gen. counsel, 1992—. Editor law rev. Wayne State U., 1964-66 Chmn. Brandon Police and Fire Bd., Mich., 1982-87. Mem. ABA, Am. Corp. Counsel Assn., Mich. State Bar Assn. Roman Catholic. General corporate.*

PALLMEYER, REBECCA RUTH, federal judge; b. Tokyo, Sept. 13, 1954; came to U.S., 1957; d. Paul Henry and Ruth (Schrieber) P.; m. Dan P. McAdams, Aug. 20, 1977; children: Ruth, Amanda. BA, Valparaiso (Ind.) U., 1976; JD, U. Chgo., 1979. Bar: Ill. 1980, U.S. Ct. Appeals (7th cir.) 1980, U.S. Ct. Appeals 11th and 5th cirs.) 1982. Jud. clk. Minn. Supreme Ct., St. Paul, 1979-80; assoc. Hopkins & Sutter, Chgo., 1980-85; judge administrv. law Ill. Human Rights Commn., 1985-91; magistrate judge U.S. Magistrate Ct., 1991-98; dist. judge U.S. Dist. Ct. for No. Dist. Ill., 1998—. Mem. jud. resources com. Jud. Conf. of U.S., 1994-2000. Bd. govs. Augustana Ctr., 1990-91. Mem. FBA (bd. mgrs. Chgo. chpt. 1995—), Womens Bar Assn. Ill. (bd. mgrs. 1995-98), Nat. Assn. Women Judges, Fed. Magistrate Judges Assn. (bd. dirs. 1994-97), Chgo. Bar Assn. (chair devel. law com. 1992-93, David C. Hilliard award 1990-91, Valparaiso U. Alumni Assn. (bd. dirs. 1992-94). Lutheran. Avocations: choral music, sewing, running. Office: US Dist Ct 219 S Dearborn St Ste 2178 Chicago IL 60604-1877

PALLOT, JOSEPH WEDELES, lawyer; b. Coral Gables, Fla., Dec. 23, 1959; s. Richard Allen Pallot and Rosalind Brown (Wedeles) Spak; m. Linda Fried, Oct. 12, 1956; children: Richard Allen, Maxwell Ross. BS, Jacksonville U., 1981; JD cum laude, U. Miami, Coral Gables, Fla., 1986. Bar: Fla. 1986. Comml. lending officer S.E. Bank, N.A., Miami, 1981-83; ptnr. Steel Hector & Davis, 1986-2000, Devine Goodman Pallot & Wells, P.A., Miami, 2000—. Bd. dirs. MOSAIC: Jewish Mus. Fla., Miami Beach, 1993—; dir. Fla. Grand Opera, 1996—, The Beacon Coun., 1997—, exec. com., 2001-. Avocations: golf, tennis. Contracts commercial, General corporate, Public utilities. E-mail: jpallot@devinegoodman.com

PALMA, NICHOLAS JAMES, lawyer; b. Newark, Oct. 28, 1953; s. James Thomas and Venice Maria (Dibenedetto) P.; m. Mary Jo Cugliari, Sept. 1, 1973; children: Nicholas J., Valerie Michele, James Michael. BS cum laude, William Paterson U., 1975; JD, Seton Hall U., 1979. Bar: N.J. 1979, U.S. Dist. Ct. N.J. 1979, U.S. Ct. Appeals (3d cir.) 1985, N.Y. 1986; cert. firearms expert, Hudson County, N.J. Investigator N.J. Pub. Defender's Office, Essex Region, Newark, 1974-75; investigator Hudson County Prosecutor's Office, Jersey City, 1975-79, asst. prosecutor, 1979-81; ptnr. A.J. Fusco, Jr., P.A., Passaic, N.J., 1981-90; sole practice, Clifton, N.J., 1990—. Recipient Commendation, Dade County Sheriff, Fla., 1976. Mem. Passaic County Bar Assn., N.J. State Bar Assn. Roman Catholic. State civil litigation, Criminal, Personal injury. Home: 221 Cedar St Cedar Grove NJ 07009-1615 Office: 1425 Broad St Clifton NJ 07013-4201

PALMER, ANN THERESE DARIN, lawyer; b. Detroit, Apr. 25, 1951; d. Americo and Theresa (Del Favero) Darin; m. Robert Towne Palmer, Nov. 9, 1974; children: Justin Darin, Christian Darin. BA, U. Notre Dame, 1973, MBA, 1975; JD, Loyola U., Chgo., 1978. Bar: Ill. 1978, U.S. Supreme Ct. 1981. Reporter Wall Street Jour., Detroit, 1974; freelancer Time Inc. Fin. Publs., Chgo., 1975-77; extern, Midwest regional solicitor U.S. Dept. Labor, 1976-78; tax atty. Esmark Inc., 1978; counsel Chgo. United, 1978-81; ind. contractor Legal Tax Rsch., 1981-89; fin. and legal news contbr. The Chgo. Tribune, 1991—, Bus. Week Chgo. Bur., 1991—, Automotive News, 1993-97, Crain's Chgo. Bus., 1994-2000. Mem. Woman's Athletic Club Chgo. Labor, Corporate taxation, Taxation, general. Home: 873 Forest Hill Rd Lake Forest IL 60045-3905

PALMER, DEBORAH JEAN, lawyer; b. Williston, N.D., Oct. 25, 1947; d. Everett Edwin and Doris Irene (Harberg) P.; m. Kenneth L. Rich, Mar. 29, 1980; children: Andrew, Stephanie. BA, Carleton Coll., 1969; JD cum laude, Northwestern U., 1973. Bar: Minn. 1973, U.S. Dist. Ct. Minn. 1973, U.S. Ct. Appeals (8th cir.) 1975, U.S. Supreme Ct. 1978, U.S. Ct. Appeals (11th cir.) 1999. Econ. analyst Harris Trust & Savs. Bank, Chgo., 1969-70; assoc. Robins, Kaplan, Miller & Ciresi LLP, Mpls., 1973-79, ptnr., 1979—. Trustee Carleton Coll., 1984-88; mem. bd. religious edn. Plymouth Congl. Ch., 1992-95; bd. dirs. Mpls. YWCA, 1996-99; mem. Dist. Minn. Civil Justice Reform Act Adv. Group, 1990-93; bd. dirs. RKM&C Found. Edn., Pub. Health & Social Justice, 1999—. Mem. ABA, Minn. Bar Assn., Minn. Women Lawyers Assn. (sec. 1976-78), Minn. Fed. Bar Assn. (chpt. bd. dirs. 1996-98), Hennepin County Bar Assn., Hennepin County Bar Found. (bd. dirs. 1978-81), Carleton Coll. Alumni Assn. (bd. dirs. 1978-82, sec. 1980-82), Women's Assn. of Minn. Orch. (bd. dirs. 1980-85, treas. 1981-83). Antitrust, Federal civil litigation, Securities. Home: 1787 Colfax Ave S Minneapolis MN 55403-3008 Office: Robins Kaplan Miller & Ciresi LLP 800 Lasalle Ave Ste 2800 Minneapolis MN 55402-2015 E-mail: djpalmer@rkmc.com

PALMER, DENNIS DALE, lawyer; b. Alliance, Nebr., Apr. 30, 1945; s. Vernon D. Palmer and Marie E. (Nelson) Fellers; m. Rebecca Ann Turner, Mar. 23, 1979; children: Lisa Marie, Jonathan Paul. BA, U. Mo., 1967, JD, 1970. Bar: Mo. 1970, U.S. Dist. Ct. (we. dist.) Mo. 1970, U.S. Ct. Appeals (8th and 10th cirs.) 1973, U.S. Supreme Ct. 1980. Staff atty. Legal Aid Soc. Western Mo., Kansas City, 1970-73; assoc. Shughart, Thomson & Kilroy, P.C., 1973-76, ptnr., bd. dirs., 1976—. Contbr. articles on franchise and employment law to legal jours. Bd. dirs., chmn. legal assts. adv. bd. Avila Coll., Kansas City, 1984-87. 2d lt. U.S. Army, 1970. Mem. ABA (litigation com. 1980, forum com. on franchising 1987), Mo. Bar Assn. (antitrust com. 1975—, civil practice com. 1975—), Kansas City Bar Assn. (chmn. franchise law com. 1987—), Univ. Club. Avocations: jogging, golf, tennis, outdoor activities, reading. Federal civil litigation, General civil litigation, Franchising. Home: 13100 Canterbury Rd Leawood KS 66209-1700 Office: Shughart Thomson & Kilroy 12 Wyandotte Plz 120 W 12th St Fl 17 Kansas City MO 64105-1902

PALMER, DOUGLAS S., JR. lawyer; b. Peoria, Ill., Mar. 15, 1945; AB cum laude, Yale U., 1966; JD cum laude, Harvard U., 1969. Bar: Wash. 1969. Mem. Foster Pepper & Shefelman PLLC, Seattle, 1975—. General corporate, Private international, Real property. Office: Foster Pepper & Shefelman PLLC 1111 3rd Ave Ste 3400 Seattle WA 98101-3299

PALMER, JOHN BERNARD, III, lawyer; b. Ft. Wayne, Ind., May 18, 1952; s. John Bernard and Dorothy Alma (Lauer) P. BA, Mich. State U., 1974; JD, U. Mich., 1977. Bar: Ill. 1977, U.S. Dist. Ct. (no. dist.) Ill. 1977, U.S. Tax Ct. 1979. Assoc. Mayer Brown & Platt, Chgo., 1977-80, Hopkins & Sutter, Chgo., 1980-83, ptnr., 1983-2001, Foley & Lardner, Chgo., 2001—. Adj. prof. Ill. Inst. Tech.- Kent Coll. of Law, Chgo., 1984—. Mem. ABA. Corporate taxation, State and local taxation. Office: Foley & Lardner Three First Nat Plaza Chicago IL 60602

PALMER, JUDITH GRACE, university administrator; b. Washington, Apr. 2, 1948; d. William Thomas and Laura Margaret (Routt) P. BA, Ind. U., 1970; JD cum laude, Ind. U., Indpls., 1973. Bar: Ind. 1974, U.S. Dist. Ct. (so. dist.) Ind. 1974. State budget analyst State of Ind., Indpls., 1969-76, exec. asst. to gov., 1976-81, state budget dir., 1981-85; spl. asst. to pres. Ind. U., 1985-86, v.p. for planning, 1986-91, v.p. for planning and fin. mgmt., 1991-94, v.p., CFO, 1994—. Bd. dirs. Ind. Fiscal Policy Inst., Washington Park Cemetery Assn., Kelley Exec. Ptnrs.; bd. dirs., treas. Advanced Rsch. and Tech. Inst. Bd. dirs., sec.-treas. Columbian Found., 1990-94, 2000—; bd. dirs. Columbia Club, 1989-98, pres. 1995; bd. dirs. Commn. for Downtown, 1984, mem. exec. bd., 1989-92, chmn. cmty. rels. com., 1989-93; mem. State Budget Commn., 1981-85. Named one of Outstanding Young Women in Am., 1978; recipient Sagamore of the Wabash award, 1977, 85, Citation of Merit, Ind. Bar Assn. of Young Lawyers, 1978, Appreciation award, 1980. Mem. ABA, Ind. Bar Assn., Indpls. Bar Assn. Roman Catholic. Office: Ind Univ Bryan Hall Rm 204 Bloomington IN 47405 E-mail: jgpalmer@indiana.edu

PALMER, LARRY ISAAC, lawyer, educator; b. 1944; AB, Harvard U., 1966; LLB, Yale U., 1969. Bar: Calif. 1970. Asst. prof. Rutgers U., Camden, N.J., 1970-73, assoc. prof., 1973-75, Cornell U., Ithaca, N.Y., 1975-79, prof. law, 1979—, vice provost, 1979-84, v.p. acad. programs, 1987-91, v.p. acad. program and campus affairs, 1991-94. Vis. fellow Cambridge U., 1984-85. Author: Law, Medicine, and Social Justice, 1989, Endings and Beginnings: Law, Medicine and Society in Assisted Life and Death, 2000. Mem. Am. Law Inst. Office: Cornell U Law Sch 120 Myron Taylor Hall Ithaca NY 14853-4901 E-mail: lip1@cornell.edu

PALMER, MICHAEL PAUL, lawyer, mediator, educator; b. San Francisco, Mar. 7, 1944; s. Coy Cornelius and Fay Janetta (Conley) P.; m. Gisela Schultz, Jan. 8, 1969; children: Eva Rebecca, Esther Marie. BA, McMurry Coll., Abilene, Tex., 1967; MA, Freie U., Berlin, 1971, PhD, 1976; JD, Georgetown U., 1980. Bar: Ill. 1980, Vt. 1987. Asst. prof. Freie U., Berlin, 1971-76; assoc. Jenner & Block, Chgo., 1980-87; pres. Palmer Legal Svcs., Middlebury, 1987—. Adj. prof. Kent U., Ill. Inst. Tech., Chgo., 1983, Middlebury Coll., 1995; pres. The Negotiation Ctr., Palmer Legal Svcs.; mem. Rule of Law Project, Karelia, Russia. Author: Das Problem der Technik, 1976, Problem Solving Negotiation: The Art of a Just Peace, 1999, The Respectful Workplace, 2001; contbr. articles to profl. jours. Active Amnesty Internat.; bd. dirs. Middlebury Union H.S. Hon. mention Ammy award Am. Lawyer, 1982. Mem. ACLU, Vt. Bar Assn., Soc. of Profls. in Dispute Resolution. Bankruptcy. Office: Palmer Legal Svcs PO Box 528 Middlebury VT 05753-0528

PALMER, PHILIP ISHAM, JR. lawyer; b. Dallas, June 25, 1929; s. Philip I. and Charlene (Bolen) P.; m. Eleanor Hutson, Mar. 7, 1951; children— Stephen Edward, Michael Bolen. B.B.A., So. Methodist U., 1952; LL.B., U. Tex., 1957. Bar: Tex. 1957, U.S. Dist. Ct. (no. dist.) Tex. 1957, U.S. Ct. Appeals (5th cir.) 1958, U.S. Supreme Ct. 1963, U.S. Dist. Ct. (we. dist.) Tex. 1968, U.S. Ct. Appeals (9th cir.) 1973, U.S. Ct. Appeals (10th cir.) 1974, U.S. Supreme Ct. 1974, U.S. Ct. Appeals (11th cir.) 1981, U.S. Dist. Ct. (ea. dist.) Tex. 1987. Since practiced in, Dallas; ptnr. Palmer & Palmer P.C. (and predecessor firms), 1957—. Chmn. bd. Carolina Mfg. Corp., 1973—, pres., 1969-73; chmn. bd. Commonwealth Nat. Bank, 1967-69; pres. Pennyrich Corp., 1969-72 Co-author: Texas Creditors Rights; Contbr. articles to profl. jours. Vice consul Republic Costa Rica, 1973— ; bd. dirs. Shepherd's Care, 1987—. Fellow Am. Coll. Bankruptcy; mem. Am. Bar Assn., Am. Judicature Soc., 5th Cir. Bar Assn. (atty. mem. 5th cir. jud. conf.), Dallas Bankruptcy Bar (chmn. bd. 1986—). Club: City. Bankruptcy, Federal civil litigation. Office: Palmer & Palmer PC 1201 Main St Ste 1510 Dallas TX 75202-3985

PALMER, RICHARD N. state supreme court justice; b. Hartford, Conn., May 27, 1950; BA, Trinity Coll., 1972; JD with high honors, U. Conn., 1977. Bar: Conn. 1977, U.S. Dist. Ct. Conn. 1978, D.C. 1980, U.S. Ct. Appeals (2nd cir.) 1981. Law clk. to Hon. Jon O. Newman U.S. Ct. Appeals (2nd cir.), 1977-78; assoc. Shipman & Goodwin, 1978-80; asst. U.S. atty. Office U.S. Atty. Conn., 1980-83, 87-90, U.S. atty. dist. Conn., 1991, chief state's atty. Conn., 1991-93; ptnr. Chatigny and Palmer, 1984-86; assoc. justice Conn. Supreme Ct., Hartford, 1993—. Mem. Phi Beta Kappa. Office: 231 Capitol Ave Hartford CT 06106-1548

PALMER, RICHARD WARE, lawyer; b. Boston, Oct. 20, 1919; s. George Ware and Ruth French (Judkins) P.; m. Nancy Fernald Shaw, July 8, 1950; children: Richard Ware Jr., John Wentworth, Anne Fernald. AB, Harvard U., 1942, JD, 1948. Bar: N.Y. 1950, Pa. 1959. Sec., dir. N.Am. Mfg. Co., Natick, Mass., 1946-48; assoc. Burlingham, Veeder, Clark & Hupper, Burlingham, Hupper & Kennedy, N.Y.C., 1949-57; ptnr. Rawle & Henderson, Phila., 1958-79, Palmer, Biezup & Henderson, Phila., 1979-95, of counsel, 1996—. Sec., bd. dirs. Underwater Technics, Inc., Camden, N.J., 1967-85; adv. on admiralty law to U.S. del. Inter-Govtl. Maritime Consultative Orgn., London, 1967; mem. U.S. Shipping Coordinating Com., mem. Washington legal sub com., 1967—; U.S. del. 30th-34th internat. confs. Titular mem. Comité Maritime Internat.; v.p., sec., bd. dirs. Phila. Belt Line R.R.; bd. dirs. Mather (Bermuda) Ltd. Editor: Maritime Law Reporter. Mem., permanent adv. bd. Tulane Admiralty Law Inst., Tulane U. Law Sch., New Orleans, 1975—; trustee Seamen's Ch. Inst., Phila., 1967—2001, pres., 1972—84; mem. exec. com. Harvard Law Sch. Assn., 1986—; bd. dirs. Havrford (Pa.) Civic Assn., 1972—85, pres., 1976—79; consul for Denmark State of Pa., 1980—91, consul emeritus, 1992—; bd. dirs. Woodlands Cemetary Co. of Phila., Woodlands Trust for Historic Preservation. Lt.comdr. USNR. Fellow World Acad. Art and Sci. (treas. 1988—); mem. ABA (former chmn. stdg. com. on admiralty and maritime law 1978-79), Internat. Bar Assn., N.Y.C. Bar Assn., Phila. Bar Assn., Am. Judicature Soc., Maritime Law Assn. (chmn. limitation liability com. 1977-83, 2d v.p. 1984-86, 1st v.p. 1986-88, pres. 1988-90, immediate past pres. 1990-92), Internat. Bar Assn., Assn. Average Adjusters USA and Gt. Britain, Port of Phila. Maritime Soc., Harvard Law Sch. Assn. of Phila. (exec. com. 1986—), Fgn. Consul assn. of Phila., Danish Order of Dannebrog, Merion Cricket Club, Phila. Club, Rittenhouse Club, India House, Geneal. Soc. Pa. (bd. dirs. 1997—), Harvard Club of N.Y.C. and Phila. (exec. com. 1983-86, 94-97). Republican. Episcopalian. Admiralty, Insurance, Private international. Home: 432 Montgomery Ave Haverford PA 19041-1527 Office: Palmer Biezup & Henderson Pub Ledger Bldg 620 Chestnut St Philadelphia PA 19106-3409

PALMER, ROBERT ALAN, lawyer, educator; b. Somerville, N.J., June 29, 1948; BA, U. Pitts., 1970; JD, George Washington U., 1976. Bar: Va. 1977. Dir. labor relations Nat. Assn. Mfrs., Washington, 1976-79; assoc. gen. counsel Nat. Restaurant Assn., 1979-85, gen. counsel, 1985-87; assoc. prof. Pa. State U., State College, 1987-88, Calif. State Poly. U., 1988-92, prof., 1992—. Mem. ABA, Va. State Bar Assn. Home: 557 Fairview Ave Arcadia CA 91007-6736 Office: 3801 W Temple Ave Pomona CA 91768-2557

PALMER, ROBERT JOSEPH, lawyer; b. Ft. Wayne, Ind., Oct. 23, 1954; s. Herman Joseph and Ruth E. (Hamilton) P.; m. Cynthia Jo Bender, Nov. 6, 1982. AB in Psychology, U. Notre Dame, 1977; JD, Valparaiso U., 1980. Bar: Ind. 1980, U.S. Dist. Ct. (so. dist.) Ind. 1980, U.S. Dist. Ct. (no. dist.) Ind. 1982, U.S. Ct. Appeals (7th cir.) 1985, U.S. Supreme Ct. 1986. Law clk. Ind. Ct. Appeals, Indpls., 1980-82; ptnr. May, Oberfell & Lorber, South Bend, Ind., 1982—. Asst. prof. law U. Notre Dame Sch. Law, 1992—. Note editor Valparaiso U. Law Rev., 1979-80. Mem. ABA, Ind. Bar Assn., St. Joseph County Bar Assn., 7th Cir. Bar Assn., South Bend-Mishawaka Area C. of C., Notre Dame Club of St. Joseph Valley. Roman Catholic. Appellate, State civil litigation, Insurance. Home: 17795 Fox Den Dr Granger IN 46530-8528 Office: May Oberfell & Lorber 300 N Michigan St Ste 230 South Bend IN 46601-1297

PALMER, ROBERT LESLIE, lawyer; b. Porterville, Calif., Apr. 10, 1957; s. Harrison Rowe and Margaret Elizabeth (Witty) P.; m. Huisuk Kim, Feb. 1, 1986; 1 child, Aaron Rowe. BA, Tulane U., 1979; JD, Georgetown U., 1982. Bar: D.C. 1982, U.S. Ct. Mil. Appeals 1985, Tex. 1987, Ala. 1987, U.S. Dist. Ct. (no. dist.) Ala. 1987, U.S. Ct. Appeals (11th cir.) 1987. Assoc. Lewis Martin Burnett & Dunkle, P.C., Birmingham, Ala., 1987-89, Lewis and Martin, Birmingham, 1989-90, Martin, Drummond and Woosley, Birmingham, 1990-91, bd. dirs., 1991-92, Martin, Drummond, Woosley and Palmer, Birmingham, 1992-95; atty. Environ. Litig. Group, P.C., Ala., 1995—. Ala. del. 6th Joint Conf. between Korea and S.E. U.S., Kyongju, Republic of Korea, 1991, 7th Joint Conf., Atlanta, 1992. Capt. JAGC, U.S. Army, 1983-87, USAR, 1987-91. Recipient commendation Republic of Korea Ministry of Justice, 1984. Mem. ATLA, Christian Legal Soc., Phi Beta Kappa, Omicron Delta Kappa. Independent. Baptist. Environmental, Personal injury, Toxic tort. Home: 1408 E Whirlaway Helena AL 35080-4102 Office: Environ Litig Group PC 3529 7th Ave S Birmingham AL 35222-3210

PALMER, ROBERT TOWNE, lawyer, banker; b. Chgo., May 25, 1947; s. Adrian Bernhardt and Gladys (Towne) P.; m. Ann Therese Darin, Nov. 9, 1974; children: Justin Darin, Christian Darin. BA, Colgate U., 1969; JD, U. Notre Dame, 1974. Bar: Ill. 1974, D.C. 1978, U.S. Supreme Ct. 1978. Law clk. to Hon. Walter V. Schaefer Ill. Supreme Ct., 1974-75; assoc. McDermott, Will & Emery, Chgo., 1975-81, ptnr., 1982-86, Chadwell & Kayser, Ltd., Chgo., 1987-88, Connelly, Mustes, Palmer & Schroeder, Chgo., 1988-89; of counsel Garfield & Merel Ltd., 1990-2000. Mem. adj. faculty Chgo. Kent Law Sch., 1975—77, Loyola U., 1976—78; mem. adv. com. Fed. Home Loan Mortgage Corp., 1988—89; dir. Ctrl. Fed. Savs. & Loan Assn. of Chgo., 1988—, chmn., 2000—, Chgo. Assn. Fin. Insts., 2001—; mem. Chgo. Ctr. Adv. Bd. Voyageur Outward Bound Sch., 1988—91; chmn. Lake Forest Cemetery Commn., 2001—. Contbr. articles to legal jours. and textbooks. Mem. Chgo. Crime Commn., 2001—. Mem. ABA, Ill. State Bar Assn. (Lincoln award 1983), Chgo. Bar Assn., Chgo. Club, Chicagoland Assn. Fin. Instns. (dir. 2001—), Dairymen's Country Club, Lambda Alpha. Federal civil litigation, State civil litigation, Insurance. Office: Central Fed Savs 1601 W Belmont Ave Chicago IL 60657-3044

PALMER, VENRICE ROMITO, lawyer, educator; b. Springfield, Mass., Jan. 11, 1952; s. Venrice Wellesley and Mildred Adlay (Foster) P. Higher diploma, U. Besançon, France, 1973; AB maxima cum laude, King's Coll., Wilkes-Barre, Pa., 1974; JD, Harvard U., 1977. Bar: N.Y. 1978, U.S. Dist.

Ct. (so. and ea. dists.) N.Y. 1979, Ill. 1986, Calif. 1997. Spl. asst. atty. gen. Office N.Y. Atty. Gen., N.Y.C., 1977-79; staff atty. SEC, 1979-82, br. chief, 1982-83, spl. trial counsel, 1983-85, acting asst. regional adminstr., 1984-85; sr. counsel Sears, Roebuck and Co., Hoffman Estates, Ill., 1985-97, Bank of Am., San Francisco, 1997-99; counsel McCutchen, Doyle, Brown & Enersen, LLP, 1999—. Guest lectr. St. John's U. Bus. Sch., N.Y.C., 1984; lectr. Practicing Law Inst., N.Y.C., 1995—, Glasser LegalWorks, Little Falls, N.J., 1997—, Am. Soc. Corp. Secs., 1997-99, Nat. Bus. Inst., Eau Claire, Wis., 2000—. Contbr. articles to various law publs. Recipient cert. of appreciation N.Y. State Bar Assn., 1978. Mem. ABA, Calif. State Bar Assn. (mem. fin. instns. com. 2000—). Avocations: opera, ballet, reading. General corporate, Finance, Securities. Home: 1200 Gough St Apt 7A San Francisco CA 94109-6616 Office: McCutchen Doyle Brown & Enersen LLP Three Embarcadero Ctr San Francisco CA 94111 E-mail: vpalmer@mdbe.com

PALMER, VERNON VALENTINE, law educator; b. New Orleans, Sept. 9, 1940; s. George Joseph and Juliette Marie (Wehrmann) P. B.A., Tulane U., 1962, LL.B., 1965; LL.M., Yale U., 1966; PhD, Pembroke Coll., Oxford U., 1985. Bar: La. 1965, U.S. Supreme Ct. 1981. Asst. prof. law Ind. Sch. Law, Indpls., 1966-70; lectr. law U. Botswana, Lesotho & Swaziland, Roma, Lesotho, 1967-69; prof. Tulane Law Sch., New Orleans, 1970—, Clarence Morrow research prof. law, 1980—, Thomas Pickles prof. law, 1989—; external examiner Nat. U. Lesotho, Roma, 1978-81. Dir. Tulane Paris Inst. European Legal Studies, European Legal Studies; reporter for revision of civil code La. Law Inst. 1979; vis. prof. Faculty Law, U. Strasbourg, 1988, The Sorbonne, U. Paris, 1986, 92, Universite des Antilles, Martinique, 1998, Universidad Ramon Llull, Barcelona, 1998, U. Trento, 1999—, U. Laussanne, 2000. Author: The Roman-Dutch and Lesotho Law of Delict, 1970, The Legal System of Lesotho, 1971, The Paths to Privity, 1992, The Civil Law of Lease in Louisiana, 1997, Louisiana: Microcosm of a Mixed Jurisdiction, 1999, Mixed Jurisdictions Worldwide: The Third Legal Family, 2001; contbr. numerous articles to profl. jours. Pres. French Quarter Residents Assn., 1973-75, Alliance for Good Govt., 1974-75; del. Nat. Democratic Conv., N.Y.C., 1976. Decorated chevalier L'ordre des Palmes Académiques. Mem. La. Law Inst. Democrat. Roman Catholic. Home: 3311 Coliseum St New Orleans LA 70115-2401 Office: 6329 Freret St New Orleans LA 70118-6231 E-mail: vpalmer@law.tulane.edu

PALMER, WILLIAM D. judge; b. Adrian, Mich., 1952; BS in Mgmt. cum laude, Rensselaer Poly. Inst., 1973; JD cum laude, Boston Coll., 1976. Bar: Fla. 1976; cert. civil mediator, family mediator, arbitrator, Fla. Assoc. Carlton, Fields, Ward, Emmanuel, Smith & Cutler, Orlando, Fla., 1976-82, ptnr., 1982-97, Palmer & Palmer, PA, Orlando, 1997-2000; dist. judge 5th dist. Fla. Ct. Appeal, Daytona Beach, 2000—. Lectr. in field. Editor-in-chief Boston Coll. Environ. Affairs Law Rev., 1975-76. Past bd. dirs. Fla. Hosp. Found., Life for Kids Adoption Agy.; past chmn. bd. dirs. Ctrl. Fla. Helpline; bd. dirs. Boys and Girls Club of Ctrl. Fla. Mem. ABA (mem. litigation sect., mem. antitrust sect., mem. dispute resolution com.), Fla. Bar (mem. litigation, appellate law and family law sects., chair Fla. Bar jour. com. 1993-95, vice chair amicus com. 1993-95, chair judicial nominating procedures com. 1992-94, mem. judicial adminstrn. selection and tenure com. 1995-98), Orange County Bar Assn. (chmn. various coms.). Office: 5th Dist Ct Appeal 300 S Beach St Daytona Beach FL 32114-5097 E-mail: palmerw@flcourts.org

PALMER, WILLIAM RALPH, retired lawyer; b. South Boston, Va., Jan. 30, 1950; m. Barbara Anne Link, Dec. 25, 1976; children: Alexis Grynell, William Ralph Jr. BA, Lincoln U., 1972; JD, Howard U., 1975. Bar: Va. 1979, U.S. Dist. Ct. (ea. dist.) Va. 1979, U.S. Ct. Appeals (4th cir.) 1979, U.S. Supreme Ct. 1985. Law clk. Bongiovanni & Collins, Denville, N.J., 1975-76; trust asst. Sovran Bank, Richmond, Va., 1977-78; sole practice, 1979-85; ptnr. Ealey, Palmer & Palmer, 1985-90; solo practice South Boston, 1990-2000. Legal counsel Anyabwile Angaza Fraternity, Inc., 1985-89, Concerned Black Men of Richmond, Va., Inc., 1987-88; mem. State Social Work Bd., 1988-89. Appointed escheator for the city of Richmond Gov. of Commonwealth of Va., 1986. Mem. Va. State Bar Assn., Old Dominion Bar Assn., Nat. Bar Assn. Methodist. Avocations: reading, running. Bankruptcy, State civil litigation, Personal injury. Home: 1201 Hunting Ridge Rd Raleigh NC 27615-7017

PALMETER, N. DAVID, lawyer; b. Elmira, N.Y., Jan. 29, 1938; s. Neal Henry and Elizabeth Jane (McHale) P.; m. Mary Lee Morken, 1964 (div. 1979); m. Mary Faith Tanney, Jan. 15, 1983; children: Stephen Michael, John David, Elizabeth Jane, James Martin. AB, Syracuse U., 1960; JD, U. Chgo., 1963. Bar: N.Y. 1963, D.C. 1969. Trial atty. U.S. Dept. Justice, Washington, 1966-68; assoc. Daniels & Houlihan, 1969-73, ptnr., 1973-75, Daniels, Houlihan & Palmeter, Washington, 1975-84, Mudge, Rose, Guthrie, Alexander & Ferdon, Washington, 1984-95, Graham & James, Washington, 1995-98, Powell, Goldstein, Frazer and Murphy, 1998—. Co-author: Dispute Settlement in the World Trade Organization, 1999; contbr. articles to profl. publs. Mem. ABA, Internat. Bar Assn. (chmn. internat. trade and customs law com. 1989-93, liaison to World Trade Orgn. 1993—), N.Y. State Bar Assn., D.C. Bar Assn., Washington Fgn. Law Soc. (pres. 1992-93), Am. Soc. Internat. Law, Can. Coun. on Internat. Law, Brit. Inst. Internat. and Comparative Law. Private international, Public international. Home: 2804 29th St NW Washington DC 20008-4112 E-mail: dpalmeter@pgfm.com

PALMIERI, JOHN ANTHONY, lawyer; b. Aliquippa, Pa., June 13, 1933; s. Samuel and Mary A. (Pontillo) P.; m. Dorothy T. Shall, May 27, 1961; children: Anne Marie, Mary Jo, John Michael. BA, Duquesne U., 1955; LLB, Georgetown U., 1957. Bar: Pa. 1958, U.S. Dist. Ct. (we. dist.) Pa. 1958. juvenile ct. legal officer Ct. Common Pleas of Beaver County, Beaver, Pa., 1967-69; asst. dist. atty. Ct. of Common Pleas of Beaver County, 1969-89; solicitor Center Area Sch. Dist., Center Twp., Pa., 1970—, Center Twp. Water Authority, 1968—. Author: Pennsylvania Law of Juvenile Delinquency and Deprivation, 1976, 91. Pres. Beaver County Heart Assn., 1981, 82; v.p. Beaver County Cancer and Heart Assn.; mem. hearing bd. Soliciton Ctr. Twp. Zoning, 1991. With U.S. Army, 1957-63. Mem. Assn. Trial Lawyers Am., Pa. Trial Lawyers Assn., ABA, Pa. Bar Assn., Beaver County Bar Assn. (chmn. continuing legal edn. com. 1972—), Pa. Assn. Probation, Parole and Corrections (assoc.). Democrat. Roman Catholic. Clubs: MPIC Band (Aliquippa, Pa.); Monaca Coronet Band. Lodges: Eagles, Sons of Italy, Elks, K. of C. Avocations: music, walking, swimming. Criminal, Personal injury, Probate. Home: 109 Cardiff Dr Aliquippa PA 15001-1659 Office: 1081 N Brodhead Rd Aliquippa PA 15001-1239

PALTER, JOHN THEODORE, lawyer; b. Berwyn, Ill., Feb. 20, 1960; s. Theodore John and Josephine Sophie P.; m. Kathleen Elizabeth Bagwell Palter, May 17, 1992; children: John Luke, Eliza Kathleen. BS in Fin., No. Ill., 1982; JD, Drake U., 1985. Bar: Tex. 1985, U.S. Dist. Ct. (no. and ea. dists.) Tex. 1989, U.S. Tax Ct. 1987; CPA, Tex. Staff atty. Coopers & Lybrand, Dallas, 1985-87; assoc. Geary, Stahl & Spencer, PC, 1987-91, Holmes Millard & Duncan, Dallas, 1991-93; shareholder McCue & Lee, PC, 1993-99, Novakou Davis, Dallas, 1999—. Pres. Holy Trinity Sch. Bd., Dallas, 1997—. Mem. Dallas Bar Assn., Assn. Attys. and CPA's. Roman Catholic. Avocation: marathon running. Federal civil litigation, State civil litigation, Contracts commercial. Home: 2712 Amherst Ave Dallas TX 75225-7901 Office: McCue & Lee PC 5430 Lbj hwy Ste 1050 Dallas TX 75240-2612

PANDOLFE, JOHN THOMAS, JR. lawyer; b. Neptune, N.J., Dec. 15, 1941; s. John T. and Jeannette R. (Pullen) P.; m. Linda Lee Fritzsche, July 12, 1969; children: Leslie, Matthew. AB, U. Miami, 1965; MS, Monmouth Coll., 1973; JD, U. Miami, 1975. Bar: Fla. 1976, N.J. 1976, U.S. Dist. Ct. N.J. 1976. Ptnr. Pandolfe, Shaw & Rubino, Spring Lake, N.J. Mem. ABA, Fla. Bar Assn., N.J. Bar Assn., Monmouth Bar Assn., Spring Lake Golf Club. General practice. Office: Pandolfe Shaw and Rubino 215 Morris Ave Spring Lake NJ 07762-1360

PANELLI, EDWARD ALEXANDER, retired state supreme court justice; b. Santa Clara, Calif., Nov. 23, 1931; s. Pilade and Natalina (Della Maggiora) P.; m. Lorna Christine Mondora, Oct. 27, 1956; children: Thomas E., Jeffrey J., Michael P. BA cum laude, Santa Clara U., 1953, JD cum laude, 1955, LLD (hon.), 1986, Southwestern U., L.A., 1988. Bar: Calif. 1955. Ptnr. Pasquinelli and Panelli, San Jose, Calif., 1955-72; judge Santa Clara County Superior Ct., 1972-83; assoc. justice 1st Dist. Ct. of Appeals, San Francisco, 1983-84; presiding justice 6th Dist. Ct. of Appeals, San Jose, 1984-85; assoc. justice Calif. Supreme Ct., San Francisco, 1985-94. Chief judicial officer JAMS/Endispute, 1995—; instr. Continuing Legal Edn., Santa Clara, 1976-78. Trustee West Valley Community Coll., 1963-72; trustee Santa Clara U., 1963—, chmn. bd. trustees, 1984—. Recipient Citation, Am. Com. Italian Migration, 1969, Community Legal Svcs. award, 1979, 84, Edwin J. Owens Lawyers of Yr. award Santa Clara Law Sch. Alumni, 1982, Merit award Republic of Italy, 1984, Gold medal in recognition of Italians who have honored Italy, Lucca, Italy, 1990, St Thomas More award, San Francisco, 1991, Filippo Mazzei Internat. award, Florence, Italy, 1992; Justice Edward A. Panelli Moot Courtroom named in his honor Santa Clara U., 1989. Mem. ABA, Nat. Italian Bar Assn. (inspiration award 1986), Calif. Trial Lawyers Assn. (Trial Judge of Yr. award Santa Clara County chpt. 1981), Calif. Judges Assn. (bd. dirs. 1982), Jud. Coun. Calif. (vice-chair 1989-93), Alpha Sigma Nu, Phi Alpha Delta Law Found. (hon. mem. Douglas Edmonds chpt.). Republican. Roman Catholic. Avocations: golf, jogging, sailing. Office: JAMS Endispute Inc 160 W Santa Clara St San Jose CA 95113-1701

PANICCIA, PATRICIA LYNN, journalist, writer, lawyer, educator; b. Glendale, Calif., Sept. 19, 1952; d. Valentino and Mary (Napoleon) P.; m. Jeffrey McDowell Mailes, Oct. 5, 1985; children: Alana Christine, Malia Noel. BA in Comm., U. Hawaii, 1977; JD, Pepperdine U., 1981. Bar: Hawaii 1981, Calif. 1982, U.S. Dist. Ct. Hawaii 1981. Extern law clk. hon. Samuel P. King U.S. Dist. Ct., Honolulu, 1980; reporter, anchor woman Sta. KEYT-TV, Santa Barbara, Calif., 1983-84; reporter Sta. KCOP-TV, L.A., 1984-88, CNN, L.A., 1989-93; corr. Cable News Network (CNN), 1989—. Adj. prof. comm. law Pepperdine Sch. Law, 1987, gender & the law, 1994—, adj. prof.; profl. surfer, 1977-81. Author: Worksmarts for Women: The Essential Sex Discrimination Survival Guide, 2000. Recipient Clarion award Women in Comm., Inc., 1988. Mem. ABA (chair of law and media com. young lawyers divsn. 1987-88, nat. conf. com. lawyers and reps. of media 1987-91), Calif. State Bar (mem. com. on fair trial and free press 1983-84, pub. affairs com. 1985-87), Hawaii Bar Assn., Phi Delta Phi (historian 1980-81). Office: PO Box 881 La Canada CA 91012-0881

PANICH, DANUTA BEMBENISTA, lawyer; b. East Chicago, Ind., Apr. 9, 1954; d. Fred and Ann Stephanie (Grabowski) B.; m. Nikola Panich, July 30, 1977; children: Jennifer Anne, Michael Alexei. AB, Ind. U., 1975, JD, 1978. Bar: Ill. 1978, U.S. Dist. Ct. (no. dist.) Ill. 1978, U.S. Dist. Ct. (ctrl. dist.) Ill. 1987, U.S. Ct. Appeals 1987, U.S. Dist. Ct. (no. dist.) Ind. 2001. Assoc. Mayer Brown & Platt, Chgo., 1978-86, ptnr., 1986—. Bd. dirs. Munster (Ind.) Med. Rsch. Found., 1990—. Mem. ABA, Ill. Bar Assn. Republican. Roman Catholic. General civil litigation, Labor. Office: Mayer Brown & Platt 190 S La Salle St Ste 3100 Chicago IL 60603-3441 E-mail: dpanich@mayerbrown.com

PANIOTO, RONALD ANGELO, judge; b. Dec. 18, 1935; s. Judith K. Panioto; 1 child, Ronald A. Jr. BBA, U. Cin., 1963; JD, No. Ky. U., 1967. Bar: Ohio 1967. Constable Ct. Common Pleas, Cin., 1958-63, 1963-67; adminstrv. asst. U.S. Congressman Donald Clancy, Cin. and Washington, 1967-68; asst. pros. atty. Hamilton County Prosecutor's Office, Cin., 1968-75; judge Hamilton County Mcpl. Ct., 1975-82, Hamilton County Ct. Common Pleas, Cin., 1982-83, adminstrv. judge, 1983—, judge domestic rels. divsn., 1982—. Mem. Ohio State Bar Assn., Order Sons of Italy, Lawyers' Club Cin., Queen City Club, United Italian Soc. Greater Cin. (pres.), DaVinci U. Club, So. OHio Dog and Game Protective Assn., Cin. Athletic Club, Met. Club, Order Sons of Italy (pres.). Republican. Roman Catholic. Avocation: golf. Office: Hamilton County Ct Domestic Rels 800 Broadway Rm 225 Cincinnati OH 45202

PANKOPF, ARTHUR, JR. lawyer; b. Malden, Mass., Feb. 1, 1931; BS in Marine Transp., Mass. Maritime Acad., 1951; BS in Fgn. Svc. and Internat. Transp., Georgetown U., 1957, JD, 1965. Bar: Md. 1965, D.C. 1966, U.S. Supreme Ct. 1977. Ea. area mgr. Trans Ocean Van Service of Consol. Freightway, 1958-61; with U.S. Maritime Adminstrn., 1961-65; assoc. firm Preston, Thorgrimson, Ellis & Holman, Washington, 1976-77; minority chief counsel Com. on Mcht. Marine & Fisheries U.S. Ho. of Reps., 1965-69; minority chief counsel, staff dir. Com. on Commerce, U.S. Senate, 1969-76; mng. dir. Fed. Maritime Commn., 1977-81; pvt. practice Washington, 1981-84; dir. legis. affairs Corp. Pub. Broadcasting, 1984-86, v.p., gen. counsel, sec., 1986-88; pvt. practice Washington, 1988-90, 96—; dir. fed. affairs Matson Navigation Co. Inc., 1990-95. Mem. Maritime Adminstrv. Bar Assn. (pres. 1995-96), Propeller Club Port of Washington (bd. govs. 1992—). Administrative and regulatory, Legislative, Transportation. Address: 7819 Hampden Ln Bethesda MD 20814-1108 E-mail: a.pankopf@worldnet.alt.net

PANNER, OWEN M. federal judge; b. 1924; Student, U. Okla., 1941-43, LL.B., 1949. Atty. Panner, Johnson, Marceau, Karnopp, Kennedy & Nash, 1950-80; judge, now sr. judge U.S. Dist. Ct. Oreg., Portland, 1980—, sr. judge, 1992—. Recipient Am. Bd. Trial Advocates Trial Lawyer of Yr., 1973. Mem. Am. Coll. Trial Lawyers, Am. Bd. Trial Advs., Order of Coif. Office: US Dist Ct 1000 SW 3rd Ave Ste 1207 Portland OR 97204-2942

PANNILL, WILLIAM PRESLEY, lawyer; b. Houston, Mar. 5, 1940; s. Fitzhugh H. and Mary Ellen (Goodrum) P.; m. Deborah Detering, May 9, 1966 (div. Nov. 1986); children: Shelley, Katherine, Elizabeth. BA, Rice U., 1962; MS, Columbia U., 1963; JD, U. Tex., 1970. Bar: Tex. 1970, U.S. Ct. Appeals (5th cir.) 1973, U.S. Ct. Appeals (D.C. cir.) 1974, U.S. Dist. Ct. (so. dist.) Tex. 1975, U.S. Supreme Ct. 1975, U.S. Ct. Appeals (10th cir.) 1980, U.S. Dist. Ct. (no. dist.) Tex. 1991. Assoc. Vinson, Elkins, Searls & Connally, 1970-71, Vinson, Elkins, Searls, Connally & Smith, 1972-75; staff asst. to sec. Treasury Treasury Dept., Washington, 1971-72; pvt. practice, Houston, 1975-76, 85-88, 2000—; ptnr. Pannill and Hooper, 1977-80, Pannill and Reynolds, Houston, 1982-85, Pannill, Moser, Mize & Hermann, Houston, 1988-90, Pannill & Moser, L.L.P., Houston, 1990-93, Pannill, Moser & Barnes, L.L.P., Houston, 1993-2000; atty. pvt. practice, 2000—. Assoc. editor Litigation Jour. sect. litigation, ABA, 1979-81, exec. editor, 1981-82, editor-in-chief, 1982-84, dir. publs., 1984-86, mem. coun., 1986-89; lectr. Southwestern Legal Found., 1980; chmn., Legal Found. Am., 1981-82, bd. dirs., 1983-97. Contbr. articles to profl. jours. Bd. dirs. Houston Grand Opera, 1989-92, mem. adv. bd., 1995-97; mem. adv. bd. Houston Symphony Soc., 1990-98. With USMCR, 1963-64. Mem. ABA, Tex. Bar Assn., Houston Bar Assn., Rice U. Alumni Assn. (bd. dirs. 1989-92). Episcopalian. Alternative dispute resolution, Appellate, General civil litigation. E-mail: wpannill@swbell.net

PANNIZZO, FRANK J. general counsel; BA, St. Johns U., 1959, JD, 1962; LLM, NYU, 1966. Bar: N.Y. 1962; cert. review appraiser. Asst. atty. gen. N.Y. State Dept. Law, N.Y.C., 1962-67; asst. counsel N.Y.C. Dept. Marine and Aviation, 1967-68; dep. gen. counsel N.Y.C. Econ. Devel. Adminstrn., N.Y.C., 1968-72; first dep. commr. N.Y.C. Dept. Ports and Terminals, 1972-79; gen. counsel N.Y.C. Energy Office, 1979-87, Bklyn. Borough Pre, 1987—. Mem. N.Y.C. Community Bd. 15, Bklyn., 1978-87. Mem. N.Y. State Bar Assn. (pub. utility law com.), Bklyn. Bar Assn. (chmn., mcpl. affairs com.), Nat. Assn. Review Appraisers. Office: Bklyn Borough Pres's Office 209 Joralemon St Brooklyn NY 11201-3749

PANZER, MITCHELL EMANUEL, lawyer; b. Phila., Aug. 2, 1917; s. Max and Cecelia P.; m. Edith Budin, Apr. 13, 1943; children: Marcy C. Pokotilow, Leslie S. Katz. AB with distinction and 1st honors, Temple U., 1937; JD magna cum laude, U. Pa., 1940; LLD honoris causa, Gratz Coll., 1972. Bar: Pa. 1942, U.S. Dist. Ct. (ea. dist.) Pa. 1948, U.S. Ct. Appeals (3d cir.) 1949, U.S. Supreme Ct. 1961. Gowen Meml. fellow U. Pa. Law Sch., 1940-41; law clk. Phila. Ct. Common Pleas, No. 7, 1941-42; assoc. Wolf, Block, Schorr and Solis-Cohen, Phila., 1946-54, ptnr., 1954-88, of counsel, 1988—; spl. adv. counsel Fed. Home Loan Mortgage Corp., Fed. Nat. Mortgage Assn., 1972-82; dir. emeritus, former counsel St. Edmond's Savs. and Loan Assn.; former dir. State Chartered Group, Pa. Bldg. and Loan Assn. Treas., Jewish Fedn. Greater Phila., 1981-82, v.p., 1982-86, trustee, 1963—, mem. exec. com., 1981-86, hon. life trustee, 1992—; trustee emeritus Pa. Land Title Inst., 1992—; bd. overseers Gratz Coll., 1958—, pres., 1962-68. Served to capt. USAF, 1942-46. Decorated Bronze Star medal; recipient Man of Year award Gratz Coll. Alumni Assn., 1964. Mem. Am. Coll. Real Estate Lawyers, ABA (chmn. spl. com. on residential real estate transactions 1972-73), Pa. Bar Assn. (mem. spl. com. on land titles), Phila. Bar Assn. (chmn. com. censors 1966, chmn. bd. govs. 1971, parliamentarian 1965-67, 71, chmn. charter and by-laws com. 1972), Jewish Publ. Soc. (trustee 1966-81, 85-88, v.p. 1972-75, sec. 1975-78), Order of Coif (pres. 1961-63, exec. com.). Jewish. Clubs: 21 Jewel Square (Phila.); Masons. Patentee in field. Business e-mail: mpanzer@wolfblock.com; Home e-mail: mepanzer@erols.com. Landlord-tenant, Real property. Home: 505 Oak Ter Merion Station PA 19066-1340 Office: Wolf Block Schorr & Solis-Cohen 22nd Fl Arch St Philadelphia PA 19103-2097

PAPADAKIS, MYRON PHILIP, lawyer, educator, retired pilot; b. N.Y.C., Dec. 11, 1940; s. Philip E. and Helen (Eastman) P.; m. Ann Hall, Sept. 1968; children: Wade, Nicholas. BS in Mech. Engring., U. Nebr., 1963; JD, South Tex. Coll. Law, 1974. Bar: Tex. 1975. Pilot, capt. Delta Airlines, Houston, 1970-2001; pvt. practice Papadakis et al. 1975-90; of counsel Slack & Davis, Austin, Tex., 1994—. Adj. prof. South Tex. Coll. Law, Houston, 1980-97; labor law negotiator, airline negotiator, 1996-98. Author: Civil Trial Practice Techniques of Winning Trial Attorneys, 2000; co-author: Best of Trial-Products Liability, 1991, Aviation Accident Reconstruction and Litigation, 1995; contbr. articles to profl. jours. Lt. USN, 1963-69. Fellow Internat. Soc. Air Safety Investigators (chmn. ethics com. 1986-92); mem. ATLA (past vice chmn. aviation sect.), State Bar Tex. (past chair aviation sect.), Million Dollar Advocates Forum. Avocations: flying, test flying, photography, fishing. Aviation, Product liability. Home: 5 Mayleaf Cv Austin TX 78738-1508 Fax: 512-261-9803. E-mail: papadak@aol.com

PAPE, DIETER, lawyer; b. Düsseldorf, Germany, Aug. 23, 1961; Ptnr. Rechtsanwalte Cleve & Pape, Dusseldorf, Germany. Mem. German Bar Assn. (study group of specialist lawyers in labor law). Consumer commercial, Franchising, Labor. Office: Rechtsanwalte Cleve & Pape Konigsallee 70 40212 Dusseldorf Germany E-mail: dieter.pape@clev-pape.de

PAPE, GLENN MICHAEL, lawyer; b. Aug. 20, 1954; s. Gilbert Thomas and Janine Elizabeth (Beheyt) P.; m. Nancy Ann Vaske, Apr. 7, 1979; children: Katherine Jo, Courtney Johanna. BA in Classics, U. Chgo., 1978, MBA, 1981; JD, DePaul U., 1979. Bar: Ill. 1979; CPA, CLU, CIMA. Cons. tax divsn. No. Trust Co., Chgo., 1980-81, fin. planner, 1981-82; fin. counselor Continental Ill. Nat. Bank, 1982-84; tax mgr. Arthur Andersen & Co., 1984-88; v.p., ptnr. Fin. Related Svcs., Ayco Co., L.P., Albany, N.Y., 1988-96; ptnr., nat. svc. leader broad market fin. planning svcs. Ernst & Young, Chgo., 1996—. Developer Money in Motion Fin. Edn. System; mem. bd. govs. Cert. Fin. Planning Standards, 2001—. Active Five Hosp. Homebound Elderly Program, Chgo., 1981; treas. Chamber Music Coun., Chgo., 1982. Mem. AICPA (accredited pers. fin. specialist), Nat. Spkrs. Assn. (cert. profl. spkr.). Estate planning, Pension, profit-sharing, and employee benefits, Personal income taxation. Home: 428 S Lincoln St Hinsdale IL 60521-4010 Office: Ernst & Young 233 S Wacker Dr Ste 1700 Chicago IL 60606-6429 E-mail: GlennPape@aol.com

PAPE, STUART M. lawyer; b. Paterson, N.J., Dec. 24, 1948; BA, U. Va., 1970, JD, 1973. Bar: Va. 1973, U.S. Ct. Appeals (6th cir.) 1975, U.S. Supreme Ct. 1976, D.C. 1980. Law clk. to Hon. Leonard Braman Superior Ct. D.C., 1973-74; exec. asst. to commr. FDA, 1979; mng. ptnr. Patton Boggs LLP and predecessors, Washington. Mem. ABA (com. food and drug law, sect. adminstrv. law 1973-92), Va. State Bar, D.C. Bar. Address: 2950 Chain Bridge Rd NW Washington DC 20016-3408 E-mail: spape@pattonboggs.com

PAPERNIK, JOEL IRA, lawyer; b. N.Y.C., May 4, 1944; s. Herman and Ida (Titefsky) Papernik; m. Barbara Ann Barker, July 28, 1972; children: Deborah, Ilana. BA, Yale U., 1965; JD cum laude, Columbia U., 1968. Bar: NY 1969. Assoc. Shea & Gould, N.Y.C., 1968-76, ptnr., 1976-91; ptnr., chmn. corp. and securities dept., mem. mgmt. com. Squadron, Ellenoff, Plesent & Sheinfeld, 1991-2000; ptnr., co-chair mergers and acquisitions practice group, mem. bus. fin. dept. Mintz, Levin, Cohn, Ferris, Glovsky and Popeo PC, 2000—. Lectr various panels. Author: (book) Risks of Private Foreign Investments in the U.S. With 11th Spec Forces USAR, 1967—73. Mem.: ABA (sect corp law, mem forum sports and entertainment law), NY Biotechnology Asn, NY State Bar Asn (lectr various panels, mem securities law comt), Asn Bar City NY (chmn, lectr, mem corp law comt, mem securities regulation comt 1992—95), NY Tri-Bar Opinion Comt, Yale Club. General corporate, Entertainment, Securities. Office: Mintz Levin Cohn Ferris Glovsky and Popeo PC 666 3rd Ave New York NY 10017-4011 E-mail: jpapernik@mintz.com

PAPPAS, DAVID CHRISTOPHER, lawyer; b. Kenosha, Wis., Mar. 18, 1936; s. theros and Marion Lucille (Piperas) P.; m. Laurie Jean LaCaskey, Nov. 26, 1956 (div. 1969); children: Christopher David, Andrea Lynn; m. Nancy Marie Pratt, June 11, 1983. BS, U. Wis., 1959, JD, 1961. Bar: Wis. 1961, U.S. Dist. Ct. (ea. and we. dists.) Wis. 1965, U.S. Supreme Ct. 1971; lic. master mariner. Asst. corp. counsel Racine County (Wis.), 1961; atty., advisor U.S. Dept. Labor, Washington, 1961-62; staff atty. U.S. Commn. Civil rights, 1962-63; asst. city atty. City of Madison (Wis.), 1963-65; atty. pvt. practice, Madison, 1965—. Chmn. Madison Mayor's Citizen Adv. Com., 1964-65; pres. Wis. Cup Assn., Madison, 1965; c0-chmn. 2d Congl. Dist. Humphrey for Pres., Madison, 1972. Recipient commendation for Supreme Ct. work Madison County Coun., 1965, commendation resolution City of Madison, 1965. Mem. Wis. Bar Assn., Dane County Bar Assn., Wis. Acad. Trial Lawyers, Am. Assn. Trial Lawyers, Lawyer-Pilot Bar Assn. (master mariner), Gt. Lakes Hist. Soc., Madison Club, South Shore Yacht Club (Milw.). General civil litigation, Family and matrimonial, General practice. Home and Office: 1787 Strawberry Rd Deerfield WI 53531-9779

PAPPAS, EDWARD HARVEY, lawyer; b. Midland, Mich., Nov. 24, 1947; s. Charles and Sydell (Sheinberg) P.; m. Laurie Weston, Aug. 6, 1972; children: Gregory Alan, Steven Michael. BBA, U. Mich., 1969, JD, 1973. Bar: Mich. 1973, U.S. Dist. Ct. (ea. dist.) Mich. 1973, U.S. Dist. Ct. (we. dist.) Mich. 1980, U.S. Ct. Appeals (6th cir.) 1983, U.S. Supreme Ct. 1983. Ptnr. firm Dickinson & Wright, P.L.L.C., Detroit and Bloomfield Hi, Mich., 1973—. Mediator Oakland County Cir. Ct., Pontiac, Mich., 1983—; hearing panelist Mich. Atty. Discipline Bd., Detroit, 1983—, chmn., 1987—; mem. bus. tort subcom. Mich. Supreme Ct. Com. Standard Jury Instructions, 1992-94; bd. commrs. State Bar Mich., 1999—. Trustee Oakland Community Coll., Mich., 1982-90, Oakland-Livingston Legal Aid, 1982-90, v.p., 1982-85, pres., 1985-87; trustee, adv. bd. Mich. Regional Anti-Defamation League of B'nai B'rith, Detroit, 1983-90; planning commr. Village of Franklin, Mich., 1987-91, chmn. 1989-91, councilman, 1991-92, chmn. charter com., 1993-94; chmn. State Bar Mich. Long Range Planning com.; pres.-elect Oakland County Bar Assn., 1996-97, pres., 1997-98, chmn. Jud. Selection Task Force, 1997; bd. dirs. Franklin Found., 1989-92; trustee The Oakland Medication Ctr., 1992-96. Master Oakland County Bar Assn. Inn of Ct.; fellow Mich. State Bar Found., Oakland Bar-Adams Pratt Found., ABA Found.; mem. ABA, Fed. Bar Assn., State Bar Mich. (co-chmn. nat. moot ct. competition com. 1974, 76, com. on legal aid, chmn. standing com. on atty. grievances 1989-92, comml. litigation com., civil procedure com. 1992-94, bd. commrs. 1999—), Oakland County Bar Assn. (vice-chmn. continuing legal edn. com., chmn. continuing legal edn. com. 1985-86, mediation com. 1989-90, chmn. mediation com. 1990-91, bd. dirs. 1990-98, chmn. select com. Oakland County cir. ct. settlement week 1991, chmn. strategic planning com. 1992-93, editor Laches monthly mag. 1986-88, co-chair task force to improve justice systems in Oakland County 1993—, pres.-elect, bd. dirs. 1996-97, pres. 1997-98), Am. Judicature Soc., Mich. Def. Trial Lawyers, Def. Rsch. and Trial Lawyers Assn. (com. practice and procedure), B'nai B'rith Barristers. Federal civil litigation, State civil litigation. Home: 32223 Scenic Ln Franklin MI 48025-1702 Office: Dickinson Wright Moon Van Dusen & Freeman 525 N Woodward Ave Bloomfield Hills MI 48304-2971

PAPPAS, GEORGE FRANK, lawyer; b. Washington, Oct. 5, 1950; s. Frank George and lora Marie (Stauber) P.; m. Susan Elizabeth Bradshaw, Apr. 25, 1980; children: Christine Bradshaw, Alexandra Stauber. BA, U. Md., 1972, JD, 1975. Bar: Md. 1976, D.c. 1991, u.S. Dist. Ct. Md. 1976, U.S. Dist. Ct. (d.C. cir.) 1986, U.S. Dist. Ct. (we. dist.) Tex. 1993, U.S. Ct. Appeals (4th cir.) 1976, U.S. Ct. Appeals (d.c. cir.) 1984, U.S. Ct. Appeals 9fed. cir.) 1991, U.S. Ct. Appeals (2d cir.) 1993, U.S. Ct. Appeals (6th and 7th cirs.) 1994, U.S. Supreme Ct. 1984, U.S. Ct. of Fed. Claims, 1995. Assoc. H. russell Smouse, Balt., 1976-81, Melnicove, Kaufman, Wiener & Smouse, Balt., 1981-83, prin., 1983-88; ptnr. Venable, Baetjer and howard, 1986—. Lectr. Wash. Coll. Law, Am. U., Washington, 1980-84; mem. moot ct. bd., 1974-75; Master of the Bench , Inn XIII, Am. Inns of Ct., 1989; mem. U.S. Dist. Ct. of Delaware Judges' Intellectual property Adv. Com., 1998—; mem. Dist. Judge Edn. Adv. Com. for the Fed. Jud. Ctr., 2001—. Founding editor-in-chief Internat. Trade law Jour., 1974-75. Mem. bd. vis. U. Md. Sch. of Law, 2000—. 1st lt. USAF, 1972-76. Mem. ABA, Internat. Assn. Def. Counsel, Md. Bar Assn. (chmn. internat. coml. law sect., 1980-81), Am. Intellectual Property Law Assn., U.S. Trademark Assn., Omicron Delta kappa, Phi Kappa Phi, Phi Beta Kappa, L'Hirondelle Club. Republican. Greek Orthodox. Federal civil litigation, State civil litigation, Intellectual property. Home: 9 Roland Ct Baltimore MD 21204-3550 Office: Venable Baetjer & Howard 2 Hopkins Plz Ste 2100 Baltimore MD 21201-2982 also: 1201 New York Ave NW Ste 1000 Washington DC 20005-6197

PAPPAS, HERCULES, lawyer, educator; b. Canton, Ohio; s. George Pappas and Linda Sandra Molina; children: Alexander, Dominique. BA, East Stroudsburg U., 1993; JD, Widener U., 1997. Bar: Pa., N.J., U.S. Dist. Ct. (ea. dist.) Pa., U.S. Dist. Ct. N.J. Atty. Blumstein, Block & Pease, Phila., Frederick L. Horn; ptnr. Pappas & Richardson, Marlton, N.J. Instr. paralegal studies Camden County Tech. Sch., Pennsauken, N.J. Mem. ATLA, ABA, Pa. Bar Assn., Phila. Bar Assn., Camden County Bar Assn. General civil litigation, General practice, Personal injury. Home: 40 Homewood Rd Wilmington DE 19803 Office: Pappas & Richardson LLC Greentree Commons Ste B 9002 Lincoln Dr W Marlton NJ 08053

PAPROCKI, THOMAS JOHN, lawyer, priest; b. Chgo., Aug. 5, 1952; s. John Henry and Veronica Mary (Bonat) P. BA, Loyola U., Chgo., 1974; student Spanish lang. study, Middlebury Coll., 1976, student Italian lang. study, 1987; M in Divinity, St. Mary of the Lake Sem., 1978; student Spanish lang. study, Instituto Cuannahuac, 1978; Licentiate in Sacred Theology, St. Mary of the Lake Sem., 1979; JD, DePaul U., 1981; JCD, Gregorian U., Rome, 1991; student Polish lang. study, Cath. U. Lublin, Poland, 1989, Jagiellonian U., Cracow, Poland, 2000. Bar: Ill. 1981, U.S. Dist. Ct. (no. dist.) Ill. 1981, U.S. Supreme Ct. 1994. Assoc. pastor St. Michael Ch., Chgo., 1978-83; pres. Chgo. Legal Clinic, 1981-87, 91—; exec. dir. South Chgo. Legal Clinic, 1981-85, bd. dirs., 1987—; adminstr. St. Joseph Ch., Chgo., 1983-86; vice-chancellor Archdiocese of Chgo., 1985-92, chancellor, 1992-2000; adj. faculty Loyola U. of Law, 1999—; pastor St. Constance Parish, 2001—. Senator Presbyteral senate Archdiocese of Chgo., 1985-87, mem. Presbyteral coun., 1992-2000, mem. Cardinal's cabinet, 1992-2000, sec. coll. consultors, 1992-2000; chmn. incardination com., 1991-2000, chmn. policy devel. com., 1998-2000, chmn. Fgn. Priests Initiative, 1998-2000; asst. to the Gen. Sec., Vatican Synod of Bishops, Spl. Assembly for Am., Rome, 1997, cardinal's del. to profl. rev. bd., 1991—, chmn. profl. conduct adminstrv. com., 1991—; bd. dirs. Cath. Conf. Ill., 1985-87. Editorial Adv. Bd. Chicago Catholic Newspaper, 1984-85; contbr. articles to profl. jours. Bd. dirs. United Neighborhood Orgn., Chgo., 1982-85, S.E. Community Youth Svc. Bd., Chgo., 1985, Ctr. for Neighborhood Tech., Chgo., 1986-87, Chgo. Area Found. for Legal Svcs., 1994—; active Chgo. Cmty. Trust Com. on Children, Youth and Families, 1991—, Ill. Family Violence Coordinating Coun., 1994—. Recipient Humanitarian award Polish Am. Congress, 1997, Alumni award for Outstanding Pub. Svc., DePaul Coll. of Law, 2001; named Man of Yr., Nat. Advs., 1999. Fellow Leadership Greater Chgo.; mem. Ill. Bar Assn., Chgo. Bar Assn. (bd. mgrs. 1999-2001, Maurice Weigle award 1985), Advs. Soc. (award of merit 1996), Cath. Lawyers Guild, Canon Law Soc. Am., Polish Am. Leadership Initiative (bd. dirs. 2001—), Polish Am. Assn. (bd. dirs. 1998—), The Chgo. Jr. Assn. Commerce and Industry (Ten Outstanding Young Citizens award 1986), Union League Club of Chgo., Pi Sigma Alpha, DePaul U. Alumni Assn. Avocations: hockey, running, reading. Immigration, naturalization, and customs, Non-profit and tax-exempt organizations. Home and Office: St Constance Parish 5843 W Strong St Chicago IL 60630-2098 E-mail: frthomaspaprocki@cs.com

PAQUIN, JEFFREY DEAN, lawyer; b. Milw., Dec. 7, 1960; s. James DeWayne and Helen Ann (Walter) P. BA, U. Wis., 1983; JD, U. Ky., 1986. Bar: Ga. 1986, U.S. Dist. Ct. (no. dist.) Ga. 1986, U.S. Ct. Appeals (11th cir.) 1986, U.S. Dist. Ct. (mid. dist.) Ga. 1987, D.C. 1989, U.S. Ct. Appeals (D.C. cir.) 1989, U.S. Supreme Ct. 1990. Assoc. Powell, Goldstein, Frazer & Murphy, Atlanta, 1986-94; chief litigation counsel United Parcel Svc., 1994-98; nat. practice leader ADR and litig. mgmt. Price Waterhouse, 1998; global practice leader Legal Mgmt. Svcs. Ernst & Young, LLP, 1998-2000; practice leader ADR and conflict mgmt. svcs. Kritzer & Levick, 2000-01; ptnr. Paquin, Victor & Sanchez, 2001—. V.p. Prodn. Values, Inc., Atlanta, 1987-88. Exec. editor U. Ky. Law Rev., 1985-86. Bd. dirs. Children's Motility Disorder Found., 1995-2000, Ctr. Corp. Counsel Innovation, 2000—. Mem. ABA, FBA, Soc. Profls. in Dispute Resolution, The Ombudsman Assn., Am. Corp. Counsel Assn. (bd. dirs. Ga. 1997-98), D.C. Bar Assn., Ga. Bar Assn., Atlanta Bar Assn. (v.p., dir. alternative dispute resolution sect.), Mortar Board, Phi Delta Phi, Sigma Epsilon Sigma, Psi Chi. Roman Catholic. Federal civil litigation, General civil litigation, State civil litigation. Home: 3620 Woodshire Chase Marietta GA 30066-8719 Office: Paquin Victor & Sanchez LLP 2221 Peachtree Rd Ste D-434 Atlanta GA 30339 E-mail: jpaquin@adrcns.com

PAQUIN, THOMAS CHRISTOPHER, lawyer; b. Quincy, Mass., Feb. 12, 1947; s. Henry Frederick and Rita Marie (St. Louis) P.; m. Jean Jacqueline O'Neill, Aug. 5, 1972; children: Martha, Edward. BS in Acctg., Bentley Coll., 1969; JD, U. Notre Dame, 1974. Bar: Mass. 1974, U.S. Dist. Ct. Mass. 1976. Tax atty. Coopers and Lybrand, Boston, 1974-76; assoc. Cargill, Masterman & Cahill, 1976, Wilson, Curran & Malkasian, Wellesley, Mass., 1976-77; ptnr. Bianchi and Paquin, Hyannis, 1977-98; shareholder, dir. Quirk and Chamberlain, P.C., Yarmouthport, 1998—. Bd. dirs., chmn. nominating com. Elder Svcs. Cape Cod and Islands, Inc., Dennis, Mass., 1986-91; bd. dirs., corporator Vis. Nurse Assn. Cape Cod Found., Inc., Dennis, 1988-97; pres. Life Svcs. Inc., 1991-95; bd. dirs. Woodside Cemetery Corp., 1998—, pres., 1999—. Mem. Bass River Golf Commn., Yarmouth, Mass., 1980-83, chmn., 1982-83; chmn. Yarmouth Golf Course Bldg. Com., 1985-89; mem. hearing com. bd. Bar Overseers of the Supreme Jud. Ct., 1989-95; bd. dirs. Project Coach, Inc., 1990-97; conciliator Barnstable Superior Ct., 1992—; trustee Cape Symphony Orch., 1999—. Fellow Mass. Bar Found.; mem. ABA, Mass. Bar Assn. (del. 1986-87, mem. com. on bicentennial U.S. Constn. 1986-88, fee arbitration bd. 1985-86, chmn. spkrs. and writers subcom. 1986-88), Barnstable County Bar Assn. (chmn. seminar com. 1979-83, mem. exec. com. 1981-84, v.p. 1984-86, pres. 1986-87), Estate Planning Coun. Cape Cod (exec. com. 1985-98, sec. 1991-93, pres.-elect 1993-95, pres. 1995-97), Mass. Conveyancers Assn., Mid-Cape Men's Club (v.p. 1992, pres. 1993), Cummaquid Golf Club. Estate planning, Probate, Real property. Office: Quirk and Chamberlain PC PO Box 40 Yarmouth Port MA 02675-0040

PARA, GERARD ALBERT, lawyer, real estate broker, consultant; b. Oak Park, Ill., June 27, 1953; s. Bruno Joseph and Bernice Agnes Para; m. Gayle Louise Keegan, Sept. 15, 1979; children; Eric, Teresa. BA with honor, De Paul U., 1973, JD, 1976. Bar: Ill. 1977, U.S. Dist. Ct. (no. dist.) Ill. 1977, U.S. Ct. Appeals (7th cir.) 1977, Fed. Trial Bar. 1984; lic. real estate broker, Ill., 1981. Jud. law clk. Ill Appellate Ct. (1st dist.), Chgo., 1977-78; divsnl. counsel Household Internat. Franchisor Divsns., Prospect Heights, Ill., 1978-85; v.p. Bannockburn (Ill.) Pk. Concepts, Inc., 1986-93; dir. real estate ops., asst. gen. counsel Ben Franklin Stores, Carol Stream, Ill., 1994-96; v.p., gen. counsel DiMucci Devel. Corp., Palatine, 1996-97; gen. counsel Urban Investment Trust Inc., Chgo., 1998-99; prin. Franchise ESQ.sm, Lincolnshire, Ill., 1999—; arbitrator 19th Jud. Cir., Lake County, 1999—, 18th Jud. Cir., DuPage County, 2000—, Cir. Ct. of Cook County, 2000—. Real estate broker, Long Grove, Ill., 1987—; franchise cons. Elliotts' Off Broadway Deli, Oak Brook, Ill., 1993—. Editor: Medical Malpractice, 1975, Trial Technique, 1975. Asst. coach Little League Buffalo Grove (Ill.) Recreation Assn., 1988-2000; asst. scoutmaster Boy Scouts Am., Long Grove, 1995—. Mem. ABA, Internat. Coun. Shopping Ctrs., Internat. Corp. Real Estate Execs. (bd. dirs. Chgo. chpt.), Chgo. Bar Assn., Internat. Franchise Assn., Coun. Franchise Suppliers. Roman Catholic. Avocations: lap swimming, boating, scuba diving, weightlifting. General corporate, Franchising, Real property. Office: Franchise ESQ sm 125 Shelter Rd #450 Lincolnshire IL 60069 E-mail: franchiseesq@aol.com

PARAN, MARK LLOYD, lawyer; b. Cleve., Feb. 1, 1953; s. Edward Walter and Margaret Gertrude (Ebert) P. AB in Sociology cum laude, Harvard U., 1977, JD, 1980. Bar: Ill. 1980, Mass. 1986, Tex. 1993. Assoc. Wilson & McIlvaine, Chgo., 1980-83, Lurie Sklar & Simon, Ltd., Chgo., 1983-85, Sullivan & Worcester, Boston, 1985-92; pvt. practice, 1992, Euless, Tex., 1992—. Mem. ABA, State Bar Tex. Avocations: tornado hunting, severe thunderstorms, photography. Finance, Real property, Securities. Home and Office: 1050 W Ash Ln Apt 1015 Euless TX 76039-2171 E-mail: tornado@home.net

PARDIECK, ROGER LEE, lawyer; b. Seymour, Ind., Mar. 1, 1937; s. Martin W. and Lorna (Wente) P.; m. Mary Ann Pardieck; children: Amy, Andrew, Melissa, Duncan. AB, Ind. U., 1959, LLB, 1963; student, Internat. Grad. Sch., Stockholm, 1960. Bar: Ind. 1963, U.S. Dist. Ct. (so. dist.) Ind. 1964, U.S. Ct. Appeals (7th cir.) 1965; diplomate Am. Bd. Trial Advocates. Tchg. asst. Ind. U., Bloomington, 1963-64; spl. prosecutor Jackson County, Ind., 1964-65; ptnr. Montgomery, Elsner and Pardieck, 1965-84; prin. Pardieck & Gill, PC, Seymour, Ind., 1985—. Faculty Nat. Inst. Trial Advocacy, Ind.; lectr. in field. Contbr. articles to profl. jours. Bd. dirs. Seymour Girls Club, 1968-72, Seymour C. of C., 1971-75; bd. dirs. Luth. Comty. Home, 1964-82, pres., 1970; trustee Immanuel Luth. Ch., 1977-80, bd. Immanuel Luth. Sch., 1980-83; adv. bd. Ind. U., Purdue U.-Indpls., 1981-83. Fellow Am. Coll. Trial Lawyers, Ind. Trial Lawyers Assn. (bd. dirs. 1969—, pres. 1975), Ind. Coll. Trial Lawyers, Roscoe Pound Found., Ind. Bar Assn.; mem. FBA, ATLA (bd. govs. 1985-88), Ind. State Bar Assn. (bd. govs. 1980-82), Inst. for Injury Reduction (bd. dirs. 1992-95), Nat. Bd. Trial Advocacy, Safety Attys. Fedn. (bd. dirs. 1993-95), Internat. Soc. Primerus Law Firms (bd. dirs. 1995—), Am. Bd. Trial Advocates, Trial Lawyers Pub. Justice (IN coord. 1991-)Am. Judicature Soc., Inner Cir. Advocates. Federal civil litigation, State civil litigation, Personal injury. Office: 100 N Chestnut St PO Box 608 Seymour IN 47274-0608 E-mail: pgv@pgvlaw.com, rlp@pardieckgilllaw.com

PARENT, LOUISE MARIE, lawyer; b. San Francisco, Aug. 28, 1950; d. Jules D. and Mary Louise (Bartholomew) P.; m. John P. Casaly, Jan. 5, 1980. AB, Smith Coll., 1972; JD, Georgetown U., 1975. Bar: N.Y. 1976, U.S. Dist. Ct. (so. dist.) N.Y. 1976. Assoc. Donovan Leisure, N.Y.C., 1975-77; various positions, then gen. counsel Am. Express Info. Svcs. Corp., 1977-92; dep. gen. counsel Am. Express Co., 1992-93, exec. v.p., gen. counsel, 1993—. Bd. dirs. A Better Chance Inc., Cooke Ctr. for Learning and Devel., YWCA N.Y., Nat. Ctr. State Cts.; mem. adv. bd. Studio in a Sch. Mem. ABA (com. depts. corp. law; mem. steering com. commerce and industry), N.Y.C. Bar Assn., N.Y. State Bar Assn., Coun. on Fgn. Rels. General corporate, Mergers and acquisitions, Securities. Home: 1170 5th Ave New York NY 10029-6527 Office: Am Express Co Am Express Tower World Fin Ctr New York NY 10285-0001

PARHAM, JAMES ROBERT, lawyer; b. East St. Louis, Ill., June 3, 1921; s. James Elbert and Edith Virginia (May) P.; m. Caroline Short, Nov. 4, 1950 (dec.); m. Elizabeth Joan Rinck, June 29, 1957; children: James R., Jr., Joseph R., J. Randolph. A.B., Princeton U., 1943; J.D. with honors, U. Ill., 1948. Bar: Ill. 1948, U.S. Dist. Ct. (so. dist.) Ill. 1948, U.S. Supreme Ct. 1968. Assoc., Pope & Driemeyer, East St. Louis, 1948-59, ptnr., Belleville, Ill., 1960-84, Thompson & Mitchell, 1985-95, Thompson Coburn, 1996—; mem. adv. coun. Ill. Inst. for Continuing Legal Edn., Springfield, Ill., 1965-74. Contbr. articles to profl. jours. Sec., YMCA of S.W. Ill., Belleville, 1979-84. Served with U.S. Air Corps, 1943, 45, USAFR, 1950—. Recipient Man of Yr. award Bicounty YMCA, Belleville, 1973; Disting. Service award Ill. Inst. Continuing Edn., 1974. Fellow Am. Bar Found., Ill. State Bar Found.; mem. Ill. State Bar Assn. (chmn. state tax sect. 1974), ABA, Met. St. Louis Bar Assn., Res. Officers Assn., Order of Coif, Phi Delta Phi. Republican. Methodist. Clubs: St. Clair Country (Belleville, v.p. 1955-56); Grey Oaks Country Club (Naples, Fla.). Lodge: Rotary (pres. East St. Louis club 1976-77). General practice, Labor, State and local taxation. Home: 7535 Claymont Ct Apt 3 Belleville IL 62223-2218 Office: Thompson Coburn PO Box 750 Belleville IL 62222-0750

PARISH, J. MICHAEL, lawyer, writer; b. Decatur, Ill., Nov. 9, 1943; s. John Mitchell and Gladys Margaret (Daulton) P.; m. Susan Lee Sgarlat, July 24, 1976 (div.); m. Ellen R. Harnett, Dec. 3, 1991; children: Margaret Ruth, William Walter. AB cum laude, Princeton U., 1965; LLB, Yale U., 1968. Assoc. LeBoeuf Lamb et al, N.Y.C., 1968-73, ptnr., 1974-89, Winthrop Stimson Putnam & Roberts, N.Y.C., 1989-95, Thelen, Reid & Priest, N.Y.C., N.Y.C., 1995—. Bd. dirs. Forum Funds, Portland, Maine, Core Trust. Contbr. stories and poetry to mags. Dir. PBS Am. Poetry Project, 1985-90; coord. Yale Law Sch. Clinton Election com.; class sec. Princeton Class of 1965. Univ. scholar Princeton U., 1965. Mem. Princeton Club N.Y. Avocation: creative writing. General corporate, Public utilities, Securities. Home: 100 Riverside Dr New York NY 10024-4822 Office: Thelen Reid & Priest 40 W 57th St Fl 28 New York NY 10019-4097

PARISI, FRANK NICHOLAS, lawyer; b. Sept. 13, 1932; s. James P. and Mary (Tomaso) P. m. Marilyn Campriello; children: Adam, Matthew, Gerard. Student, Union Coll., 1951-54; LLB, Albany U., 1957; JD, 1968. Bar: N.Y. 1957, U.S. Tax Ct. 1963. Sr. mem. Parisi & Parisi, Schnectady; asst. dist. atty., 1962-65; U.S. Govt. appeal agt., 1971; mem. adv. bd. Cmty. State Bank (now Key Bank N.Y.), 1977-83. Former bd. dirs. Schenectady County YCA, Tippecanoe br.; past pres., mem. parish council, trustee Our Lady of the Assumption Ch.; mem. Nat. Selective Service Appeal Bd., 1971-76, draft bd. mem. 1977-97; mem. panel arbitrators Am. Arbitration Assn. Mem. ANA, N.Y. Start Bar Assn., Schenectady County Bar Assn. Republican. Roman Catholic. Estate planning, Probate, Real property. Home: 2773 Maida Ln Schenectady NY 12306-1633 Office: 670 Franklin St Schenectady NY 12305-2011

PARK, WILLIAM ANTHONY (TONY), lawyer; b. Blackfoot, Idaho, June 4, 1934; s. William Clair and Thelma Edelweiss (Shear) P.; m. Elizabeth Taylor, Aug. 26, 1961 (div.); children: Susan E., W. Adam, Patricia A.; m. Gail Chaloupka, Aug. 6, 1983. AA, Boise Jr. Coll., 1954; BA, U. Idaho, 1958; JD, U. Idaho, 1963. Bar: Idaho 1963. Sole practice, Boise, Idaho, 1963-70, 82-83; atty. gen. State of Idaho, 1971-75; ptnr. Park & Meuleman, Boise, 1975-81, Park & Burkett, Boise, 1983-84, Martin, Chapman, Park & Burkett, Boise, 1984-90, Park, Costello & Burkett, Boise, 1990-93, Park, Redford, Thomas & Burkett, Boise, 1994-97, Park, Thomas, Burkett & Williams, Boise, 1997-99; of counsel Huntley, Park, Thomas, Burkett, Olsen & Williams, 1999—. Chmn. Idaho Bicentennial Commn., 1971—77; bd. dirs. ACLU, Idaho, 1976—2000, pres., 1997—99; chmn. Idaho State Dem. Party, 1998—99; bd. dirs. Radio Free Europe/Radio Liberty, Inc., , 1977—82, Am. Lung Assn., 1978—90, Am. Lung Assn. of Idaho/Nev., 1976—96, 1999—, pres., 1991—95. Served with U.S. Army, 1956—58. Recipient Disting. Svc. award. Alternative dispute resolution, General civil litigation, Personal injury. Home: 706 Warm Springs Ave Boise ID 83712-6420 Office: PO Box 2188 Boise ID 83701-2188 E-mail: gchaloupka@msn.com

PARK, WILLIAM WYNNEWOOD, law educator; b. Philadelphia, Pa., July 2, 1947; s. Oliver William and Christine (Lindes) P. BA, Yale U., 1969; JD, Columbia U., 1972; MA, Cambridge U., 1975. Bar: Mass. 1972, D.C. 1980. Law practice, Paris, 1972-79; prof. law Boston U., 1979—. Counsel Ropes & Gray, Boston; v.p. London Ct. Internat. Arbitration; dir. Boston U. Ctr. Banking Law Studies, 1990-93; vis. prof. U. Dijon, France, 1983-84, Inst. U. Hautes Etudes Internat., Geneva, 1983, U. Hong Kong, 1990; fellow Selwyn Coll., Cambridge, Eng., 1975-77; arbitrator Claims Resolution Tribunal for Dormant Accts., Switzerland. Author: International Chamber of Commerce Arbitration, 3d edit., 2000, International Forum Selection, 1995, International Commercial Arbitration, 1997, Annotated Guide to the 1998 ICC Arbitration Rules, 1998, Arbitration in Banking and Finance, 1998; contbr. articles and book revs. to profl. jours. Trustee Mass. Bible Soc.; mem. vestry King's Chapel, Boston. Fellow Chartered Inst. Arbitrators (Chartered Arbitrator U.K.). Home: 36 King St Cohasset MA 02025-1304 Office: Boston U Law Sch 765 Commonwealth Ave Boston MA 02215-1401 also: Ropes and Gray 1 International Pl Boston MA 02110-2602

PARKER, CHRISTOPHER WILLIAM, lawyer; b. Evanston, Ill., Oct. 26, 1947; s. Robert H. and Dorothy Boynton P.; m. Mary Ann P., Dec. 28, 1984. BA, Tufts U., 1969; JD, Northeastern U., 1976. Bar: Mass. 1977, U.S. Dist. Ct. Mass. 1977, U.S. Dist. Ct. (we. dist.) Tex. 1986, U.S. Ct. Appeals (1st cir.) 1988, U.S. Supreme Ct. 1988. Law clk. to judge U.S. Bankruptcy Ct. Mass. dist., Boston, 1976-77; assoc. Fletcher, Tilton & Whipple, Worcester, Mass., 1977-79; counsel U.S. Trustee, Boston, 1979-81; assoc. Craig and Macauley P.C., 1982-84, ptnr., 1984-87; counsel Hinckley, Allen, Snyder & Comen, 1987-88, ptnr., 1989-91, McDermott, Will & Emery, Boston, 1991—. Mem. ABA, Mass. Bar Assn., Am. Bankruptcy Inst. Boston Bar Assn., Comml. Law League. Club: Union Boat (Boston). Banking, Bankruptcy, Federal civil litigation. Home: 11 Tophet Rd Lynnfield MA 01940-1616 Office: McDermott Will & Emery 28 State St Boston MA 02109-1775 E-mail: cparker@mwe.com

PARKER, EMILY ANN, lawyer; b. Winnsboro, Tex., Aug. 17, 1949; d. Roy Denver and Helen Crowder Parker. BA summa cum laude, Stephen F. Austin Coll., 1970; JD cum laude, So. Meth. U., 1973. Bar: U.S. Tax Ct. 1976, U.S. Ct. Appeals (5th cir.) 1977, U.S. Supreme Ct. 1977, U.S. Ct. Claims 1978, U.S. Ct. Appeals (10th and fed. cirs.) 1984; cert. in tax law. Assoc. Thompson & Knight, Dallas, 1973-79, ptnr., 1979—. Bd. dirs. Child Care Dallas, 1978-83, Easter Seals of Greater Dallas, 1998—. Mem. ABA (natural resources com. chmn. 1991-92, court procedure com. tax sect.), Tex. Bar Assn. (chmn. natural resources com. 1982-84, coun. 1984-87, tax sect.), Dallas Bar Assn. (chmn. coun. tax sect. 1983), Am. Coll. Tax Counsel. Democrat. Avocations: golf, tennis, skiing. Environmental, Corporate taxation. Home: 2805 Milton Ave Dallas TX 75205-1522 Office: Thompson & Knight 1700 Pacific Ave Ste 3300 Dallas TX 75201-4693 E-mail: parkere@tklaw.com

PARKER, FRED I. federal judge; b. 1938; BA, U. Mass., 1962; LLB, Georgetown U., 1965. With Lyne, Woodworth & Everts, Boston, 1965-66, Office Atty. Gen., Montpelier, Vt., 1969-72, Langrock and Sperry, Middlebury, 1972-75; ptnr. Langrock, Sperry, Parker & Stahl, 1975-82, Langrock, Sperry, Parker & Wool, Middlebury, 1982-90; fed. judge U.S. Dist. Ct. (Vt. dist.), 1990-91, chief judge, 1991-94; fed. judge U.S. Ct. Appeals (2d cir.), 1994—. Mem. conduct bd. Vt. Supreme Ct., 1975-79, jud. conduct bd., 1982-88. Active Vt. Lawyers Project. Mem. Vt. Bar Assn. (chair spl. com. reform of judiciary 1988-89), Chittendon County Bar Assn. Office: US Dist Ct PO Box 392 11 Elmwood Ave Burlington VT 05402-0392 Also: US Dist CourtFederal Building PO Box 392 11 Elmwood Avenue Burlington VT 05402-0392*

PARKER, HAROLD ALLEN, lawyer, real estate executive; b. Denver, Sept. 14, 1924; s. Hyman and Sophia P.; m. Gertrud Parker; children: David, Rodney, Diana, Jesse, Jonathan. JD, Golden Gate U., 1971. Bar: Calif. 1972. Pvt. practice, San Francisco; gen. ptnr. Harold Parker Properties. Legal cons. San Francisco Craft and Folk Art Mus.; past mem. Bay Area Lawyers for the Arts; spkr. in field; prime developer Union St. Comml. Corridor, San Francisco, 1963—. Pub.: Wolfgang Paalen, His Art and His Writings, 1980, Richard Bowman, Forty Years of Abstract Painting, 1986. Chmn. Fine Arts Commn., Tiburon, Calif., 1976-78. Mem. Family Club (San Francisco). Avocations: music, art, tennis. Office: 1844 Union St San Francisco CA 94123-4308

PARKER, JAMES AUBREY, federal judge; b. Houston, Jan. 8, 1937; s. Lewis Almeron and Emily Helen (Stuessy) P.; m. Florence Fisher, Aug. 26, 1960; children: Roger Alan, Pamela Elizabeth. BA, Rice U., 1959; LLB, U. Tex., 1962. Bar: Tex. 1962, N.Mex. 1963. With Modrall, Sperling, Roehl, Harris & Sisk, Albuquerque, 1962-87; judge U.S. Dist. Ct. N.Mex., 1987—. Mem. Standing Commn. on Rules of Practice and Procedures of U.S. Cts., 1993-99, N.Mex. Commn. on Professionalism, 1986—; bd. visitors U. N.Mex. Law Sch., 1996—. Articles editor Tex. Law Rev., 1961-62. Mem. Fed. Judges Assn., Am. Judicature Soc., Am. Bd. Trial Advocates, N.Mex. Bar Assn. (Outstanding Judge award 1994), Albuquerque Bar Assn. (Outstanding Judge award 1993, 2000), Order of Coif, Chancellors, Phi Delta Phi. Avocations: ranching, fly fishing, running, skiing. Office: US Dist Ct 333 Lomas Blvd NW Ste 770 Albuquerque NM 87102-2277 Fax: 505 348-2225. E-mail: jparker@nmcourt.fed.us

PARKER, JAMES FRANCIS, lawyer, airline executive; b. San Antonio, Jan. 1, 1947; s. Raymond Francis and Libbie Olivia (Dusek) P.; m. Patricia Elaine Lorang, May 15, 1971; children: James, Jennifer. BA with hons., U. Tex., 1969, JD with hons., 1971. Bar: Tex., U.S. Dist. Ct. (ea., we., so. no. dists.) Tex., U.S. Ct. Appeals (5th and 11th cirs.), U.S. Supreme Ct. Law clk. to presiding judge U.S. Dist. Ct., Austin, Tex., 1972-76; asst. atty. gen. State of Tex., 1976-79; atty. Oppenheimer, Rosenberg, Kelleher & Wheatley, San Antonio, 1979-86; v.p., gen. counsel SW Airlines Co., Dallas, 1986—. Mem. ABA, Tex. Bar Assn. Democrat. Lutheran. Aviation, General corporate, General practice. Office: SW Airlines Co 2702 Love Field Dr Dallas TX 75235-1908

PARKER, JAMES LEE, lawyer; b. Pitts., Nov. 3, 1938; s. Wallace Mc. and Virginia (Crawford) P.; m. Susan Bruce, July 18, 1962; children— Lee, Heather. B.B.A., U. Pitts., 1963; J.D., Case-Western Res. U., 1967. Bar: Ohio 1967, Pa. 1967, U.S. Supreme Ct. 1972. Gen. counsel, v.p., sec. Matthews Internat. Corp., Pitts., 1967— , also dir.; trustee JHM Ednl. and Charitable Trust, Pitts., 1973— ; dir. Fox Chapel Land Trust, Pitts. Author: Pennsylvania Cemetery Law, 1976, 2d edit., 1984. Mem. Borough Environ. Council, Fox Chapel, Pa., 1979— ; mem. Fox Chapel Borough Council, 1983— . Mem. Allegheny County Bar Assn. Republican. Episcopalian. Club: Pitts. Field. General corporate. Office: Matthews Internat Corp 2 N Shore Ctr Pittsburgh PA 15212-5838

PARKER, JOHN FRANCIS, retired lawyer; b. L.A., Aug. 17, 1928; s. Ignatius Francis and Helen Mary P.; m. Mary Ann Kirkpatrick, Dec. 26, 1950; children: Kathleen Ann, John Patrick. BA cum laude, Loyola U., L.A., 1950; JD, UCLA, 1953; LLD, Southwestern U., 1975. Bar: Calif. 1953, U.S. Dist. Ct. (so. dist.) Calif. 1953, U.S. Ct. Mil. Appeals 1954, U.S. Supreme Ct. 1965, U.S. Ct. Appeals (9th cir.) 1982. Atty. Title Ins. & Trust Co., L.A., 1956-57, State Compensation Ins. Fund, L.A., 1957-58; assoc. Herlihy & Herlihy, L.A., San Bernardino, 1958-63; pvt. practice San Bernardino, Pomona, Calif., 1962-63; ptnr. Parker & Dally, 1964-77; pres. Parker & Dally PC, 1977-94; ret., 1994. Adj. prof. law Southwestern U., L.A., 1956-64, pres., chmn. bd. trustees, 1969-75, trustee, exec. com., 1956-97, trustee emeritus, 1997—; workers compensation judge, San Bernardino, 1994-97. 1st lt. JAG, U.S. Army, 1953-56. Mem. ABA (vice-chmn. workers compensation employers liability com.), Calif. Bar Assn. Republican. Roman Catholic. Insurance, Workers' compensation.

PARKER, JOHN HILL, lawyer; b. High Point, N.C., Feb. 1, 1944; s. George Edward and Tullia Virginia (Hill) P.; children from previous marriage: Alice Lindsey, Elizabeth Shelby (dec.); m. Lynette Becton Smith, July 7, 1977. BA, U. N.C., 1966; JD, U. Tenn., 1969. Bar: N.C. 1969, U.S. Dist. Ct. (ea dist.) N.C. 1970, U.S. Supreme Ct. 1975. Assoc. Sanford, Cannon, Adams & McCullough, Raleigh, N.C., 1969-73; pvt. practice, 1974-76; judge N.C. Dist. Ct., 1976-82; ptnr. Cheshire & Parker, 1982—. Instr. judges seminars Inst. Govt. Chapel Hill, N.C., 1977-82. Parlementarian Wake County Young Dems., 1971-73; mem. Raleigh Arts Commn., 1981-84, chmn. 1983. Fellow Am. Acad. Matrimonial Lawyers (ethics com. 1995-97, pres. N.C. chpt. 1999-2000); mem. ABA, N.C. Bar Assn. (editor family law sect. 1984-85, chmn. 1985-86, 96-97, continuing legal edn. for family law 1979—, chmn. 1985-87, 96-98, chmn. ethics com. 1989-90, chmn. gen. curriculum com. 1989-90), N.C. Acad. Trial Lawyers, Wake County Bar Assn. Episcopalian. Avocations: travel, backpacking, fishing, reading, music. State civil litigation, Family and matrimonial. Home: 1620 Park Dr Raleigh NC 27605-1609 Office: Cheshire & Parker PO Box 1029 133 Fayetteville St Mall Raleigh NC 27601-1356 E-mail: John.Parker@Cheshirepark.com

PARKER, JOHN VICTOR, federal judge; b. Baton Rouge, Oct. 14, 1928; m. Mary Elizabeth Fridge, Sept. 3, 1949; children: John Michael, Robert Fridge, Linda Anne. B.A., La. State U., 1949, J.D., 1952. Bar: La. 1952. Atty. Parker & Parker, Baton Rouge, 1954-66; asst. parish atty. City of Baton Rouge, Parish of East Baton Rouge, 1956-66; atty. Sanders, Downing, Kean & Cazedessus, Baton Rouge, 1966-79; chief judge U.S. Dist. Ct., Middle Dist. La., 1979—. Vis. lectr. law La. State U. Law Sch. Served with Judge Adv. Gen.'s Corps U.S. Army, 1952-54. Mem. ABA, Am. Judicature Soc., Am. Arbitration Assn., La. State Bar Assn. (past mem. bd. govs.), Baton Rouge Bar Assn. (past pres.), Order of Coif, Phi Delta Phi. Democrat. Club: Baton Rouge Country. Lodges: Masons (32 deg.); Kiwanis (past pres.). Office: Russell B Long Fed Bldg & Courthouse 777 Florida St Ste 355 Baton Rouge LA 70801-1717

PARKER, MICHELLE, lawyer; b. Buffalo, May 5, 1963; d. Michael Francis and Mary Dorothy (Brady) Wynne; m. Mark Daniel Parker, Aug. 11, 1990. B in English Lit., Canisius Coll., 1989; JD, U. Buffalo, 1993. Bar: N.Y. 1994. Tng. coord. Empire of Am. Realty Credit Corp., Buffalo, 1989-90; rsch. intern City Coun. Mem. Hon. Brian Higgins, summer 1991; law clk. N.Y. State Atty. Gens. Office, 1991-93; assoc. Altreuter & Habermehl, 1994-98, Feldman, Kieffer & Herman, Buffalo, 1998-2000, O'Shea Reynolds & Cummings, Buffalo, 2000—. N.Y. state rep. to exec. coun. Am. Bar Assn. Young Lawyers Divsn., Chgo., 1997-99. Founding mem. Ebenezer Literary Cir., 1999. Recipient Pathfinder award Niagara Frontier Industry Edn. Coun., Buffalo, 1998. Mem. Def. Trial Lawyers Western N.Y. (bd. dirs. 1999, sec. 2000—), Bar Assn. Erie County (chair young lawyers com. 1996-99, chair negligence law com. 2000—). Democrat. Roman Catholic. Avocations: golf, reading, fishing. General civil litigation, Insurance, Personal injury. Home: 6526A Hamilton Dr Derby NY 14047-9650 Office: O'Shea Reynolds & Cummings Main Seneca Bldg 237 Main St Ste 500 Buffalo NY 14203-2712 E-mail: mparker@osheareynolds.com

PARKER, RICHARD WILSON, lawyer, rail transporation executive; b. Cleve., June 14, 1943; s. Edgar Gael and Pauline (Wilson) P.; m. Helen Margaret Shober, Jan. 3, 1998; children from previous marriage: Brian Jeffrey, Lauren Michelle, Lisa Christine. BA in Econs. cum laude, U. Redlands, 1965; JD cum laude, Northwestern U., 1968. Bar: Ohio 1968, Va. 1974. Assoc. Arter & Hadden, Cleve., 1968-71; asst. gen. atty. Norfolk & Western Ry. Co., Cleve. and Roanoke, Va., 1971-74, asst. gen. solicitor Roanoke, 1974-78, gen. atty., 1978-84, Norfolk So. Corp., 1985-88, sr. gen. atty., 1988-93, asst. v.p. real estate, 1993-99, v.p. properties, 1999-2000, v.p. real estate, 2000—. Mem. ABA, Va. State Bar, Norfolk-Portsmouth Bar Assn. Presbyterian. Contracts commercial, Environmental, Real property. Office: 3 Commercial Pl Norfolk VA 23510-2108

PARKER, ROBERT ERNSER, lawyer; b. Howell, Mich., Dec. 9, 1938; s. Robert W. and Maxine (Ernser) P.; m. Dona Scott, June 27, 1969 (div. Oct. 1988); children; Robert S., Donald S. BS, Ea. Mich. U., 1967; JD, Oklahoma City U., 1973. Bar: Mich. 1973, U.S. Dist. Ct. (ea. dist.) Mich. 1973, U.S. Ct. Appeals (6th cir.) 1973, Ind. 1987, Wis. 1988. Magistrate 53d Jud. Dist. Ct., Howell, Mich., 1968-72; owner Parker Abstract and Title Co., 1969-78; ptnr. Parker & Parker, 1979—. Arbitrator Nat. Assn. Security Dealers, N.Y. Stock Exch., Nat. Futures Assn., 1983-97. Mayor City of Howell, 1975-76. Mem. Mich. Bar Assn. (com. trial cts. adminstrn. 1982-88), Rep. Assembly of State Bar, Livingston County Bar Assn. (pres. 1987), Rotary (pres. 1990), Masons, Phi Delt aPhi, Sigma Alpha Epsilon. Probate, State and Federal civil litigation. Home: 609 Curzon Ct Howell MI 48843 Office: Parker & Parker 704 E Grand River PO Box 888 Howell MI 48844-0888 E-mail: parkerp@ismi.net

PARKER, ROBERT M. federal judge; b. 1937; BBA, U. Tex., 1961, JD, 1964. Bar: Tex. 1964. Ptnr. Parish & Parker, Gilmer, Tex., 1964-65, Kenley & Boyland, Longview, 1965, Roberts, Smith & Parker, Longview, 1966-71, Rutledge & Parker, Ft. Worth, 1971-72, Nichols & Parker, Longview, 1972-79; judge U.S. Dist. Ct. (ea. dist.) Tex., 1979-94, chief judge, 1991-94; judge U.S. Ct. Appeals (5th Cir.), Tyler, Tex., 1994—. Mem. Tex. Bar Assn. Office: 221 W Ferguson St Ste 400 Tyler TX 75702-7200*

PARKER, ROBERT MARC, lawyer, insurance executive; b. N.Y.C., Apr. 3, 1952; s. Robert I. Parker and Doris Helen (Mintz) Taradash; m. Nancy M. Gaidish, Dec. 22, 1974; 1 child, Ashley Justis. BA, Lehigh U., 1973; JD, N.Y. Law Sch., 1981. Bar: N.Y. 1982, U.S. Dist. Ct. (ea. and so. dists.) N.Y. 1982. Account rep. Liberty Mutual Ins. Co., N.Y.C., 1974-80; account exec. Cooroon & Black of N.Y., 1980-81; ins. def. atty. Wilson, Elser, Edelman & Dicker, 1981-84; counsel, v.p. profl. liability The Home Ins. Co., 1984-87; sr. v.p. profl. liability ops., account mgmt. group leader Rollins Burdick Hunter Direct Group, Chgo., 1987—. Mem. N.Y. State Task Force on Lawyers Profl. Liability, 1985-87. Author: Manufacturer Liability for Kerosene Heaters: The Controversy Burns On, 1982. Exec. dir. Quakertown United Environmentally Safe Tomorrow, Quakertown, Pa., 1987—. Mem. ABA (com. profl. liability), Assn. Trial Lawyers Am. (membership com.), N.Y. Bar Assn. (mem. com. profl. responsibility, com. products liability), N.Y. County Lawyers Assn., Am. Mgmt. Assn. Avocations: swimming, water and snow skiing, scuba diving, tennis, photography. Insurance, Personal injury.

PARKER, ROSS GAIL, lawyer; b. Council Bluffs, Iowa, July 13, 1948; s. Gail Francis and Mildred Julia P.; m. Deborah Jo LeVan, May 5, 1984; children: Sarah LeVan, Alexander LeVan. BS, Iowa State U., 1970; JD, U. Pitts., 1974. Bar: U.S. Dist. Ct. (ea. dist.) Mich. 1975, U.S. Ct. Appeals (6th cir.) 1975. Law clk. to Hon. Michael Cavanagh Mich. Ct. Appeals, Lansing, 1974-75; atty. Fink and LaRene, Detroit, 1975-78; asst. U.S. atty. U.S. Attys. Office, U.S. Dist. Ct. (ea. dist.) Mich., 1978—, chief criminal divsn., 1981-89, chief asst. U.S. atty., 1989-94. Adj. prof. Detroit Coll. Law, 1980-82. Editor-in-chief U. Pitts. Law Rev., 1973-74. Coach Neighborhood Club, Grosse Pointe, Mich., 1998; mgr. SCH Hockey Assn., St. Clair Shores, Mich., 1998—. Recipient Dirs. award U.S. Dept. Justice, 1990. Mem. FBA (Leonard R. Gilman award 1997). Presbyterian. Avocations: reading, coaching, volunteering in church activities. Office: US Attys Office 211 W Fort St Detroit MI 48226-3202

PARKER, SARAH ELIZABETH, state supreme court justice; b. Charlotte, N.C., Aug. 23, 1942; d. Augustus and Zola Elizabeth (Smith) P. AB, U. N.C., 1964, JD, 1969; LHD (hon.), Queens Coll., 1998. Bar: N.C. 1969, U.S. Dist. Ct. (mid., ea. and we. dists.) N.C. Vol. U.S. Peace Corps, Ankara, Turkey, 1964-66; pvt. practice Charlotte, 1969-84; former judge N.C. Ct. Appeals, Raleigh; now assoc. justice N. C. Supreme Ct. Bd. visitors U. N.C., Chapel Hill, 1993-97; bd. dirs. YWCA, Charlotte, 1982-85; pres. Mecklenburg County Dem. Women, Charlotte, 1973. Recipient Disting. Woman of N.C. award, 1997, Woman of Achievement award Nat. Fedn. Women's Clubs, 1997. Mem. ABA, Inst. Jud. Adminstrn., N.C. Bar Assn. (v.p. 1987-88), Mecklenburg County Bar (sec.-treas. 1982-84), Wake County Bar Assn., N.C. Internat. Women's Forum, Women Attys. Assn. (Gwyneth David Pub. Svc. award 1986). Episcopalian. Office: NC Supreme Ct PO Box 1841 Raleigh NC 27602-1841

PARKER, WILLIAM JERRY, lawyer; b. Bowling Green, Ky., Sept. 11, 1931; s. Joseph B. Parker and Rubye Smith; m. Eva Jane Martin, Dec. 19, 1954; children: Jane Beth, William Jerry Jr., Jo Martin, Frederick Smith. BA, Western Ky. U., 1954; JD, Vanderbilt U., 1959. Bar: Ky. 1959, Tenn. 1959, U.S. Dist. Ct. (we. dist.) Ky. 1960, U.S. Ct. Appeals (6th cir.) 1979, U.S. Supreme Ct. 1965. Ptnr. Harlin & Parker, Bowling Green, 1959—. Served to capt. USAF, 1954-57. Mem. Ky. Bar Assn. (gov. 1969-82, pres. 1980). Democrat. Methodist. Lodges: Rotary (pres. 1969, gov. R.I. Dist. 1997-98), Elks. Federal civil litigation, State civil litigation, Probate. Home: 2120 Sycamore Dr Bowling Green KY 42104-3827 E-mail: Paarker@harlinparker.com

PARKER, WILMER, III, lawyer, educator; b. Ozark, Ala., Oct. 3, 1951; s. Wilmer and Anne Laura (Ragsdale) P.; m. Rebecca Joy Skillern, Aug. 25, 1984; children: R. Virginia, J. William; m. Beverly Laura Barnard, Dec. 23, 1972 (div. Dec. 1977). BS in Commerce, U. Ala., 1972, MBA, JD, U. Ala., 1975; LLM, Emory U., 1976. Bar: Ala. 1975, Ga. 1976, Fla. 1976, U.S. Dist. Ct. (no. dist.) Ga. 1976, U.S. Tax Ct. 1976, U.S. Ct. Appeals (11th cir.) 1986, U.S. Dist. Ct. (mid. dist.) Ga. 1997. Assoc. Nall, Miller & Cadenhead, Atlanta, 1975-78; trial atty. tax divsn. U.S. Dept. Justice, Washington, 1978-83; asst. U.S. atty. Organized Crime Drug Enforcement Task Force, Atlanta, 1983-97; ptnr. Kilpatrick Stockton LLP, 1997—. Lectr. trial advocacy Emory U. Law Sch., Atlanta, 1984—. Named Outstanding Trial Atty. Tax Divsn., U.S. Dept. Justice, Washington, 1979; recipient Spl. Commendation award U.S. Dept. Justice, 1985, 87, Superior Performance as Asst. U.S. Atty. Dirs. award, 1986, 94. Mem. ABA, Internat. Bar Assn., Atlanta Bar Assn., Lawyers Club Atlanta. Presbyterian. Office: Kilpatrick Stockton LLP 1100 W Peachtree St NW Ste 2800 Atlanta GA 30309-3609 E-mail: bparker@kilstock.com

PARKERSON, HARDY MARTELL, lawyer; b. Longview, Tex., Aug. 22, 1942; s. James Dee and Winifred Lenore (Robertson) P.; m. Janice Carol Johnson, Aug. 3, 1968; children: James Blaine, Stanley Andrew, Paul Hardy. BA, McNeese State U., Lake Charles, La.; JD, Tulane U., 1966. Bar: La. 1966, U.S. Supreme Ct. 1971. Assoc. Rogers, McHale & St. Romain, Lake Charles, 1967-69; pvt. practice, 1969—. Chmn. 7th Congl. Dist. Crime and Justice Task Force, La. Priorities for the Future, 1980; asst. prof. criminal justice La. State U., 1986. Bd. dirs. 1st Assembly of God Ch., Lake Charles, 1980—; bd. regents So. Christian U., Lake Charles, 1993—; mem. La. Dem. State Ctrl. Com., 1992-96, Calcasieu Parish Dem. Com., 1988—, past sec.-treas., exec. com.; former mem. Gulf Assistance Program, Lake Charles; 7th Congl. Dist. La. mem. Imports and Exports Trust Authority, Baton Rouge, 1984-88. Mem. Fed. Bar Assn. (chmn. fed. cts. com., sr. lawyers divsn.), Pi Kappa Phi Housing Corp. of Lake Charles (bd. dirs., sec.-treas. 1985—), Pi Kappa Phi. Democrat. Mem. Assembly of God Ch. Avocations: political activism, hosting television talk show. Federal civil litigation, State civil litigation, Toxic tort. Home: 127 Greenway St Lake Charles LA 70605-6821 Office: The Parkerson Law Firm 504 East College St Lake Charles LA 70605

PARKINSON, PAUL K. lawyer; b. Durango, Colo., Feb. 8, 1952; s. Philip Fulton and Ruth Eloise (Knight) P.; m. Amy Lee Dunham, May 17, 1975; children: Calista R., Karen S. BSE in Psychology, Truman State U., 1977; JD, U. Mo., Kansas City, 1979; LLM in Estate Planning, U. Miami, 1981. Bar: Mo. 1980, U.S. Dist. Ct. (we. dist.) Mo. 1980, U.S. Tax Ct. 1981, Kans. 1989. Assoc. Polsinelli, White, Vardeman & Shelton, Kansas City, Mo., 1981-83; pvt. practice, 1984-85; dir. Van Hooser, Olsen & Parkinson, P.C., 1986-89; pvt. practice Overland Park, Kans. and Kansas City, 1989-90; with Hess & Parkinson, Macon, Mo., 1990-2000; asst. pros. atty. Macon County, 1999-2000, assoc. circuit judge Mo., 2001—. Adj. prof. U. Mo., Kansas City, 1982-85. Pres., dir., program com. chmn. Mid-Am. Planned giving Coun., Kansas City, 1990. Mem. ABA (real property, probate and trust sect. 1980-94), Mo. Bar Assn. (lectr. 1983-90, probate and trust com. 1981—, hosp. law com., banking law com., pres. 41st jud. cir. 1992-94). Banking, General corporate, Estate planning. Office: 101 E Washington Bldg # 2 PO Box 491 Macon MO 63552 Fax: 660-385-3132. E-mail: Paul_Parkinson@osca.state.mo.us

PARKIN-SPEER, DIANE, English law educator; b. Salt Lake City, Feb. 19, 1941; d. Lorin David and Thora (Bauer) Parkin; m. Richard L. Speer, June 3, 1963; divorced. BA magna cum laude, Lewis & Clark Coll., 1963; MA, Bowling Green State U., 1965; PhD, U. Iowa, 1970. Grad. asst. U. Iowa, Iowa City, 1965-69; prof. English SW Tex. State U., San Marcos, 1969—; rschr. in history English law and rhetoric. Mem. Am. Soc. Legal History, Sixteenth Century Studies Conf., ACLU. Presbyterian. Contbr. articles on English law to profl. jours. Office: SW Tex State U San Marcos TX 78666

PARKS, ALBERT LAURISTON, lawyer; b. Providence, July 18, 1935; s. Albert Lauriston and Dorothy Isabel (Arnold) P.; m. Martha Ann Anderson, Jan. 12, 1961; children: Amy Woodward, George Webster, Reed Anderson. BA, Kent State U., 1958; JD, U. Chgo., 1961. Bar: R.I. 1962, U.S. Dist. Ct. R.I. 1963, U.S. Ct. Appeals (1st cir.) 1966, U.S. Supreme Ct. 1980. Assoc. Hanson, Curran, Parks & Whitman, Providence, 1961-65, ptnr., 1966-2000. Town solicitor, North Kingstown, R.I., 1978-80, 97—. Fellow Am. Coll. Trial Lawyers; mem. ABA, Maritime Law Assn., R.I. Bar Assn., Saunderstown Yacht Club. Republican. Episcopalian. State civil litigation, Labor, Municipal (including bonds). Home: 40 Hammond Hl Saunderstown RI 02874-3509 Office: 10 Coronado St Jamestown RI 02835 E-mail: alp@hcpw.com

PARKS, GEORGE BROOKS, land development consultant, university dean; b. Lebanon, Ky., Feb. 18, 1925; s. George W. and Eleanor B. (Brooks) P.; children— Paula, William. Student N.C. Central Coll., 1942-44; LL.B., Howard U., 1948; LL.M., George Washington U., 1949. Bar: U.S. Dist. Ct. D.C. 1948, U.S. Ct. Appeals 1949, Ky. 1951, U.S. Supreme Ct. 1952. Assoc. Coleman, Parks & Washington, Washington, 1948-60; sr. title officer Security Title Ins. Co., 1960-63; founder, pres. Mchts. Title Co., Los Angeles, 1963-69; dir. urban affairs Title Ins. & Trust Co., Los Angeles, 1969-70; exec. dir. Housing Opportunity Ctr., Los Angeles, 1970-73; asst. to councilman David Cunningham, Los Angeles, 1973-74; dep. county supr. Los Angeles County, 1974-76; asst. dean South Bay U. Sch., Carson, Calif., 1976-78, Glendale U. Sch. Law, Los Angeles, 1978— ; cons. Summa Corp., Los Angeles, 1978-84; pvt. practice cons., Los Angeles, 1978— . Appointed to Productivity Adv. com. City of Los Angeles by Mayor Tom Bradley, 1986. Recipient Cert. of Appreciation, City of Los Angeles, 1979, Outstanding Leadership award Lutheran Housing Corp., 1980; named Disting. Lectr., Nat. Soc. Real Estate Appraisers, 1981, Disting. Alumni, Howard U. Alumni Assn., 1982. Mem. ABA. Democrat. Lutheran. Home: 1149 S Alfred St Los Angeles CA 90035-2503 Office: George B Parks & Assocs 1122 S La Cienega Blvd Ste 104 Los Angeles CA 90035-2500

PARKS, GERALD THOMAS, JR. lawyer, business executive; b. Tacoma, Wash., Feb. 25, 1944; s. Gerald Thomas and Elizabeth (Bell) P.; m. Susan Simenstad, July 22, 1967; children: Julie, Christopher; m. Bonny Kay O'Connor, Jan. 15, 1979, children: Garrett, Adrienne. BA in Polit. Sci., U. Wash., 1966; JD, U. Oreg., 1969. Bar: Wash. 1969. Assoc. Graham & Dunn, 1972-77, ptnr., 1977-82; sole practice, 1982—; sec., treas. Holaday-Parks Fabricators, Inc., 1972-78, v.p., gen. mgr. (named changed to Holaday-Parks, Inc.), 1978-84; pres., CEO, 1984-98, chmn., CEO, 1998—. Trustee The Bush Sch., 1992-95. Served to lt. with USN, 1969-72. Mem. Wash. State Bar Assn., Sheet Metal and Air Conditioning Contractors of Western Wash., Inc. (pres. 1989-91), Sheet Metal and Air Conditioning Contractors Nat. Assn. (dir. 1989-92, pres. 1994-95), Seattle Yacht Club, Seattle Tennis Club. Office: PO Box 69208 4600 S 134th Pl Seattle WA 98168-3241

PARKS, JAMES WILLIAM, II, public facilities executive, lawyer; b. Wabash, Ind., July 30, 1956; s. James William and Joyce Arlene (Lillibridge) P.; m. Neil Ann Armstrong, Aug. 21, 1982; children: Elizabeth Joyce, Helen Frances, James William III. BS, Ball State U., 1978; JD, U. Miami, 1981. Bar: La. 1981, U.S. Dist. Ct. (ea. dist.) La. 1981, U.S. Ct. Appeals (5th and 11th cirs.) 1981. Fla. 1982, U.S. Dist. Ct. (mid. dist. La.) 1982.. Atty. Jones, Walker, Waechter, Poitevent, Carrere et al., New Orleans, 1981-83, Foley & Judell, New Orleans, 1983-88, McCollister & McCleary, pc, Baton Rouge, 1988-95; pres., CEO La. Pub. Facilities Authority, 1995—. Mem. AICPA, Nat. Assn. Bond Lawyers, La. State Bar Assn., Fla. Bar Assn., Assn. for Gifted and Talented Students, Baton Rouge (treas. 1994-96, pres.-elect 1996-97, pres. 1997-98), Soc. La. CPA (govt. acctg. and auditing com. 1994-95), Nat. Assn. Higher Edn. Facilities Authorities (bd. dirs. 1996—, v.p. 1997-99, pres. 1999—). Avocations: travel, computers. Home: 5966 Tennyson Dr Baton Rouge LA 70817-2933 Office: La Pub Facilities Authority 2237 S Acadian Thruway Ste 650 Baton Rouge LA 70808-2380 E-mail: jwp7@hotmail.com, parks@lpfa.com

PARKS, JANE DELOACH, retired law librarian, legal assistant; b. Atlanta, June 7, 1927; d. John Keller and Martha Lorena (Lee) deLoach; m. James Bennett Parks, Dec. 28, 1951 (dec. Sept. 1983); children: Carrie Anne Parks-Kirby, Susan Jane, Lora Beth Parks-Maury. BA magna cum laude, Vanderbilt U., 1949; postgrad., Emory U., 1950-51; tchr. cert., U. Chattanooga, 1954; postgrad., U. Tenn., Chattanooga, 1971-73. Med. rsch./writing dept. surgery Emory U., Atlanta, 1949-51; sec. to med. dir. Tenn. Tuberculosis Hosp., Chattanooga, 1951-53; tchr. Signal Mountain (Tenn.) Elem. Sch., 1954-55; tchr., dean jr. sch. Cleve. (Tenn.) Day Sch., 1963-70; law firm libr., legal asst. Stophel, Caldwell & Heggie, Chattanooga, 1972-85, Caldwell, Heggie & Helton, Chattanooga, 1985-93, Heiskell, Donelson, Bearman, Adams, Williams & Caldwell, Chattanooga, 1993-94, Baker, Donelson, Bearman & Caldwell, Chattanooga, 1994-99; ret., 1999. Tchr. various seminars on legal rsch. and writing, organizing one-person librs. and ch. librs., Chattanooga Legal Secs. Assn., Chattanooga-Hamilton County Bicentennial Libr. Editor (mag.) The Gadfly, 1947-49; editorial asst.: Studio Collotype, 1988 and to profl. jours., 1949—. Tchr. Chattanooga Area Literacy Movement, 1984-86; exec. coun. Friends of Chattanooga-Hamilton County Bicentennial Libr., 1989-94; del. Gov.'s Conf.-White House Conf. on Librs. and Info. Svcs., Nashville, 1990; libr. vol. Tenn. Aquarium. Environ. Learning Lab.; allocations com. United Way, 1994—, Signal Mountain Cmty. Guild, 1999—; dir. Lit. Dept., 2000—. Mem. Tenn. Paralegal Assn., Chattanooga Area Libr. Assn. (2d v.p. 1989-90, sec. 1992-93), Non-Atty. Profl. Assn. (chmn. 1989-93), Phi Beta Kappa, Mortar Bd. Republican. Methodist. Avocations: genealogy, reading, storytelling, needlework.

PARLER, WILLIAM CARLOS, lawyer; b. Cameron, S.C., Aug. 12, 1929; s. Marion Carlos and Anna (Keller) P.; m. Anne Hemenway, Aug. 13, 1955; children: William Carlos, Blair Hemenway, Bethanie Rene, Beatrice Carolyn. B.S., U.S. Naval Acad., 1951; LL.B. magna cum laude, U. S.C.-Columbia, 1958; LL.M., Harvard U., 1959. Bar: S.C. 1958, U.S. Dist. Ct. (ea. and we. dists.) S.C. 1958, U.S. Ct. Appeals (D.C. cir.) 1967, U.S. Supreme Ct. 1966. Atty., AEC, Germantown, Md., 1959-70; counsel to Congl. Joint Com. on Atomic Energy, Washington, 1971-72, 75-76; adminstrv. judge AEC, Washington, 1973-74; sr. atty. Nuclear Regulatory Commn., Bethesda, Md., 1977-81, legis. counsel, Washington, 1982, sr. atty., 1983—; group leader Spl. Inquiry Group on Three Mile Island Accident, Bethesda, 1979; gen. counsel Nuclear Regulatory Commn., 1986—; govt. mem. Adminstrv. Conf. U.S. Author, editor: Background TMI Accident, Vol. II, 1980; adviser: History of U.S. Atomic Energy. Contbr. articles to profl. jours. Active Naval Res. and def. related orgns., 1971—. With USN, capt. res. ret. Recipient Outstanding Performance award AEC, 1965, Outstanding Achievement award Nuclear Regulatory Commn., 1980, Presdl. Disting. and Meritorious Exec. Rank award, Disting. Svc. award NRC, 1992, Disting. Govt. Svc. award ABA, 1993. Mem. Naval Res. Assn. (Disting. svc. award), Wig and Robe Soc., Phi Beta Kappa. Office: Nuclear Regulatory Commn Gen Counsel 11555 Rockville Pike Rockville MD 20852-2738

PARR, CAROLYN MILLER, federal judge; b. Palatka, Fla., Apr. 17, 1937; d. Arthur Charles and Audrey Ellen (Dunklin) Miller; m. Jerry Studstill Parr, Oct. 12, 1959; children: Kimberly Parr Trapasso, Jennifer Parr Turek, Patricia Audrey Smith. BA, Stetson U., 1959; MA, Vanderbilt U., 1960; JD, Georgetown U., 1977; LLD (hon.), Stetson U., 1986. Bar: Md. 1977, U.S. Tax Ct. 1977, D.C. 1979, U.S. Supreme Ct. 1983. Gen. trial atty. IRS, Washington, 1977-81, sr. trial atty. office of chief counsel, 1982; spl. counsel to asst. atty. gen. tax divsn. U.S. Dept. Justice, 1982-85; judge U.S. Tax Ct., 1985-2000, sr. judge, 2001—. Nat. Def. fellow Vanderbilt U., 1959-60; fellow Georgetown U., 1975-76; recipient Spl. Achievement award U.S. Treasury, 1979. Mem. ABA, Md. Bar Assn., Nat. Assn. Women Judges, D.C. Bar Assn. Office: US Tax Ct 400 2nd St NW Washington DC 20217-0002

PARRIGIN, ELIZABETH ELLINGTON, lawyer; b. Colon, Panama, May 23, 1932; d. Jesse Cox and Elizabeth (Roark) Ellington; m. Perry G. Parrigin, Oct. 8, 1975. BA, Agnes Scott Coll., 1954; JD, U. Va., 1959. Bar: Tex. 1959, Mo. 1980. Atty., San Antonio, 1960-69; law libr. U. Mo., Columbia, 1969-77, rsch. assoc., 1977-82; atty. pvt. practice, 1982—. Elder, clk. of session First Presbyn. Ch., Columbia; mem. permanent jud. commn. Presbyn. Ch. U.S., 1977-83, mem. advisory com. on constitution, 1983-90. Mem. ABA, Mo. Bar Assn. (chmn. sub-com. revision of Mo. trust law 1988-92), Columbia Kiwanis Club (pres. 1997-98). Democrat. Presbyterian. Avocations: music, gardening, reading. Family and matrimonial, General practice, Probate. Home: 400 Conley Ave Columbia MO 65201-4219 Office: 224 N 8th St Columbia MO 65201-4844

PARRISH, DAVID WALKER, JR. legal publishing company executive; b. Bristol, Tenn., Feb. 8, 1923; BA, Emory & Henry Coll., 1948, LLD, 1978; BS, U.S. Merchant Marine Acad., 1950; LLB, U. Va., 1951. Pres. The Michie Co., Charlottesville, Va., 1969-89, vice chmn., 1989-96; pub. cons., 1996—. Home: 114 Falcon Dr Charlottesville VA 22901-2013 Office: 300 Preston Ave Ste 103 Charlottesville VA 22902-5044

PARROTT, NANCY SHARON, lawyer; b. Atoka, Okla., Jan. 11, 1944; d. Albert L. and Willie Jo (Parkhill) Furr. BA, Okla. U., 1967; MA, No. Tex. U., 1974; JD, Okla. City U., 1982. Bar: Okla. 1984, U.S. Supreme Ct. 1984. Ptnr. Chapman & Chapman, Oklahoma City, 1984-85; chief legal asst. marshal Okla. Supreme Ct., 1985—. Mem. Leadership Oklahoma, Leadership Oklahoma City; bd. dirs. Youth Leadership Exch., recruitment chmn., mentor. Mem. ABA, Okla. Bar Assn. (awards com., civil procedure com.), Okla. County Bar Assn. (bd. dirs., del., mem. cmty. svc. com., Law Day co-chair), Am. Judicature Soc. Office: Okla Supreme Ct State Capital Bldg 245 Oklahoma City OK 73105

PARRY, WILLIAM DEWITT, lawyer; b. Hartford, Conn., June 4, 1941; s. William Brown and Mary Elizabeth (Caton) p.; m. Andrea Hannah Lewis, June 30, 1973; children: Sara, Jessica. BA, U. Mass., 1963; JD, U. Pa., 1966. Bar: N.J. 1987, Pa. 1967, U.S. Dist. Ct. (ea. dist.) Pa. 1974, U.S. Ct. Appeals (3d cir.) 1980, U.S. Ct. Appeals (9th cir.) 1998, U.S. Supreme Ct. 1980. Assoc. Shapiro, Cook & Bressler, Phila., 1966-67; asst. dir. ABA joint com on continuing legal edn. Am. Law Inst., 1967-73; assoc. Lowenschuss Assocs., 1973-85; of counsel Weiss, Golden & Pierson, 1985-88; pvt. practice, 1988; ptnr. Rubin, Quinn, Moss & Patterson, 1989-93; pvt. practice, 1993—. Author: Understanding and Controlling Stuttering: A Comprehensive New Approach Based on the Valsalva Hypothesis, 1994, 2000; editor U. Pa. Law Rev., 1964-66, The Practical Lawyer, 1967-73. Founder Phila. area chpt. Nat. Stuttering Assn., 1996—, bd. dirs.; trustee Unitarian Soc. Germantown, Phila., 1983-86. Mem. ABA, ATLA, Pa. Bar Assn., Phila. Bar Assn., Pa. Trial Lawyers Assn. Democrat. Avocations: writing, lecturing. Federal civil litigation, State civil litigation, Personal injury. Home: 520 Baird Rd Merion Station PA 19066-1302 Office: 1608 Walnut St Ste 900 Philadelphia PA 19103-5451 E-mail: wdparry@aol.com

PARSONS, CHARLES ALLAN, JR. lawyer; b. Mpls., July 16, 1943; s. Charles Allan and Grace Adelaide (Covert) P.; m. JoAnne Ruth Russell, Oct. 16, 1965; children: Charles, Daniel, Nancy. BS, U. Minn., 1965, JD cum laude, 1972. Bar: Minn. 1972, U.S. Dist. Ct. Minn. 1972, U.S. Supreme Ct. 1995. Ptnr. Moss & Barnett, P.A., 1972—. Bd. dirs. Legal Advice Clinics Ltd., Mpls., 1975-93, Legal Aid Soc. Mpls., 1999—, first v.p., 2000—; bd. dirs. Mid-Minn. Legal Assistance, 2001—; chair steering com. S.E. Asian Legal Assistance Project, Mpls., 1988-93. Named Vol. Atty. of Yr., Legal Advice Clinics, Ltd., Mpls., 1990. Mem. ABA, Am. Coll. Real Estate Lawyers, Minn. State Bar Assn. (co-chair legis. com. real property sec. 1986—, coun. mem. 1986—, chair real property sect. 1993-94), Hennepin County Bar Assn. (chair real property sect. 1988-89). Roman Catholic. Avocations: reading, walking, biking, hiking. Finance, Real property. Office: Moss & Barnett PA 4800 Norwest Ctr 90 S 7th Minneapolis MN 55402-4119 E-mail: parsonsc@goldengate.net

PARSONS, RYMN JAMES, lawyer; b. Binghamton, N.Y., Sept. 23, 1955; s. James Edward and Dauna Dee (Robinson) P.; m. Mary Helen Pietro, Apr. 7, 1979; 1 child, Mary Katherine. AB, Eisenhower Coll., 1977; JD, Albany Law Sch., 1981; LLM, George Washington U., 1996. Bar: Conn. 1981, U.S. Dist. Ct. Conn. 1981, U.S. Ct. Mil. Appeals 1986, U.S. Supreme Ct. 1986. Assoc. Ells, Quinlan & Robinson, Canaan, Conn., 1981-83, Cramer & Anderson, New Milford, 1983-85; commd. lt. USN, 1985; advanced through grades to comdr. USNR, 1999; judge adv. naval legal svc. office USN, Newport, R.I., 1985-88; staff judge advocate Naval Surface Group Four, 1988-90; command judge advocate USS Dwight D. Eisenhower (CVN 69), 1990-92; mil. judge Navy-Marine Corp. Trial Judiciary, Norfolk, Va., 1992-95; staff judge advocate Submarine Group Two, 1996-99; asst. command counsel Navy Pub. Works Ctr., Norfolk, 1999—; exec. officer Naval Res. Trial Svc. Office East, 2000—. Contbr. articles to profl. jours. Counsel St. Andrew's Soc. Conn. Inc., 1984-85; scoutmaster Boy Scouts Am., Salisbury, Conn., 1985, Sea Exploring advisor, Newport, R.I., 1987-89; bd. dirs. Glenwood Homeowners Assn., Virginia Beach, Va., 1993-94; men's tennis coach U.S. C.G. Acad., 1997-99. Mem. ABA, Am. Judicature Soc. (bd. dirs. 1980-81), U.S. Naval Inst., Am. Judges Assn., U.S. Profl. Tennis Registry (profl. instr. 1999—), Nat. Inst. Trial Advocacy (instr. 1989—). Republican. Admiralty, Criminal, Military. Office: Navy Pub Works Ctr 9742 Maryland Ave Ste 211 Norfolk VA 23511-3015 E-mail: parsonsr@pwcnorva.navy.mil

PARTIN, C. FRED, lawyer; b. Cin., Apr. 9, 1945; s. Charles F. and Marian (Carroll) P.; m. Susan Fischer; children: Amy Beth, Kelly Blythe, Frederick Matthew. BA, U. Ky., 1968; JD, U. Louisville, 1971. Bar: U.S. Dist. Ct. (we. dist.) Ky. 1971, U.S. Dist. Ct. (ea. dist.) Ky. 1973, U.S. Ct. Appeals (6th cir.) 1971, U.S. Supreme Ct. 1976, U.S. Dist. Ct. (so. dist.) Ohio 1983, U.S. Dist. Ct. (mid. dist.) Calif. 1983, U.S. Ct. Appeals (9th cir.) 1984. Asst. U.S. atty. Western Dist Ky., Louisville, 1971-74, 1st asst. U.S. atty., 1975-81; ptnr. Wood, Pedley, Stansbury, Rice & Warner, 1974-75, Parker & Partin, Louisville, 1981-84. Recipient spl. award for outstanding achievement U.S. Aty. Gen., Washington, 1974. Republican. Roman Catholic. Federal civil litigation, Criminal. Home: 3223 Canterbury Ln Louisville KY 40207-3676 Office: 809 Ky Home Life Bldg 239 S 5th St Louisville KY 40202-3213 E-mail: scarymason@aol.com

PARTLETT, DAVID F. dean, law educator; b. 1947; LLB, Sydney U., 1970; LLM, Mich. U., 1972, 74; SJD, U. Va., 1980. Bar: New South Wales 1971, Australian Cap. Terr. 1978. Vis. asst. prof. U. Ala., 1972-73; legis. officer Australia Atty. Gen.'s Office, 1974—75; dir, rsch. Australian Law Reform Commn. , 1975—78; lectr. Australian Nat. U., 1978-80, sr. lectr., 1980-87, assoc. dean, 1982—85; vis. prof. Vanderbilt U., Nashville, 1987-88, prof. law, 1988-2000, acting dean, 1996-97; v.p., dean, prof. Sch. Law Washington & Lee U., Lexington, Va., 2000—. Sparkman Dist. vis. prof. Ala. U., 1986-87. Office: Washington & Lee U Sydney Lewis Hall Lexington VA 24450*

PARTLOW, JAMES JUSTICE, lawyer; b. Sanford, Fla., Apr. 3, 1970; s. Patrick Grieder Partlow and Deborah Justice Partridge; m. Chandra Denise Partlow, Sept. 27, 1997. BS in Criminology cum laude, Fla. State U., 1991; JD, Miss. Coll., 1994. Bar: Fla. 1994, U.S. Dist. Ct. (mid. dist.) Fla. 1996, U.S. Supreme Ct. 1998. Atty. Stenstrom, McIntosh, Colbert, Whigham & Simmons, P.A., Sanford, 1994—. City atty. Code Enforcement Bd., Sanford, 1997—, Nuisance Abatement Bd., Sanford, 1997—, Code Enforcement Bd., DeBary, Fla., 1997—. Coach baseball and flag football City of Sanford Dept. Recreation, 1998—. Mem. Fla. Bar Assn. (trial lawyer sect., family and matrimonial law sect.), Seminole County Bar Assn. (family law sect., trial lawyers sect., treas. 1998). Republican. Baptist. Avocations: whale watching, classic cars, scuba diving, travel. General civil litigation, Family and matrimonial. Home: 57 Lake Dr Debary FL 32713-2873 Office: 200 W 1st St Ste 22 Sanford FL 32771-1268

PARTNOY, RONALD ALLEN, lawyer; b. Norwalk, Conn., Dec. 23, 1933; s. Maurice and Ethel Marguerite (Roselle) P.; m. Diane Catherine Keenan, Sept. 18, 1965. B.A., Yale U., 1956; LL.B., Harvard U., 1961; LL.M., Boston U., 1965. Bar: Mass. 1962, Conn. 1966. Atty. Liberty Mut. Ins. Co., Boston, 1961-65; assoc. counsel Remington Arms Co., Bridgeport, Conn., 1965-70, gen. counsel, 1970-88, sec., 1983-93; sr. counsel E.I. du Pont de Nemours & Co., Wilmington, Del., 1985-95. Served with USN, 1956-58; to capt. USNR (ret.) Mem. ABA, Sporting Arms and Ammunition Mfrs. Inst. (chmn. legis. and legal affairs com. 1971-86), Am. Judicature Soc., U.S. Navy League (pres. Bridgeport coun. 1975-77, nat. dir., Conn. pres. 1977-80, v.p. Empire region 1980-85), Naval Res. Assn. (3d dist. pres., nat. exec. com. 1981-85, nat. v.p. 1997-99), Chancery Club, Harvard Club of Boston, Harvard Club of Phila., Yale Club of N.Y.C., Assn. of Yale Alumni (del. 1997-2000). Antitrust, Contracts commercial, General corporate. Home: 616 Bayard Rd Kennett Square PA 19348-2504

PARTOYAN, GARO ARAKEL, lawyer; b. Toledo, Dec. 6, 1936; s. Garo and Vartoohi (Yessayan) P.; children: Garo Linck, Elizabeth Margaret, Martin Joseph. BS in Chem. Engring., Northwestern U., 1959; JD, U. Mich., 1962; LLM, NYU, 1964. Bar: N.Y. 1963, U.S. Dist. Cts. (so. dist.) N.Y. 1964, U.S. Ct. Claims 1966, U.S. Ct. Appeals (2nd cir.) 1966, U.S. Dist. Ct. (ea. dist.) N.Y. 1968. Ptnr. Curtis, Morris & Safford, N.Y.C., 1962-76; gen. counsel mktg. and tech. Mars, Inc., McLean, Va., 1976-98; pres. Mgmt. of Intellectual Property, Inc., Sarasota, Fla., 1998—. Mem. Dobbs Ferry (N.Y.) Bd. Edn., 1972-76, pres., 1975-76; chmn. Fairfax Citizens Group, Fairfax County, Va., 1988-90. Mem. ABA, Am. Intellectual Property Law Assn., N.Y. Intellectual Property Law Assn., Internat. Trademark Assn. (pres. 1990-91, bd. dirs. 1983—), Intellectual Property Owners (bd. dirs. 1992-99). Avocations: sailing, curling. Private international, Patent, Trademark and copyright. Office: 4756 Sweetmeadow Cir Sarasota FL 34238 Fax: (941) 922-2410. E-mail: partoyanga@aol.com

PARTRIDGE, BRUCE JAMES, lawyer, educator, writer; b. Syracuse, N.Y., June 4, 1926; came to Can., 1969; s. Bert James and Lida Marion (Rice) P.; m. Mary Janice Smith, June 13, 1948 (dec. 1986); children: Heather Leigh, Eric James, Brian Lloyd, Bonnie Joyce; m. May S. Archer, May 28, 1988; stepchildren: Sheila Archer, Laurel Archer. AB cum laude, Oberlin Coll., Ohio, 1946; LLB, Blackstone Coll., Chgo., 1950, JD, 1952; LLB, U. B.C., 1974. Bar: B.C. 1976, N.W.T. 1980. Rsch. physicist Am. Gas Assn., Cleve., 1946-48; bus. mgr., purchasing agt., asst. treas. Rochester Inst. Tech., N.Y., 1953-58; bus. adminstr. Baldwin-Wallace Coll., Berea, Ohio, 1951-53; bus. mgr. Cazenovia (N.Y.) Coll., 1948-51; v.p. bus. and mgmt. U. Del., Newark, 1958-63; v.p. adminstrn. Johns Hopkins U., Balt., 1963-69; pres. U. Victoria, B.C., Can., 1969-72; assoc. Clark, Wilson & Co., Vancouver, Can., 1975-78; successively solicitor, mng. solicitor, gen. solicitor, v.p. law and gen. counsel, sec. Cominco Ltd., 1978-88; exec. dir. Baker & McKenzie, Hong Kong, 1988-90; v.p. Pacific Creations, Inc., 1990-92; faculty Camosun Coll., 1992-99. Author: Management in Canada: The Competitive Challenges, 2000; co-author: College and University Business Administration, 1968; chmn. editl. com. Purchasing for Higher Education, 1962; contbr. numerous articles to profl. jours. Chmn. commn. on adminstrv. affairs Am. Coun. on Edn., Washington, 1966-69; mem. Pres.'s Com. on Employment of Handicapped, Washington, 1967-69; mem. adv. coun. Ctr. for Resource Studies, Queen's U.; bd. dirs. L'Arche in the Americas; mem. adv. coun. Westwater Rsch. Ctr., U. B.C. Mem. Law Soc. B.C., Law Soc. of N.W. Ters., Assn. Can. Gen. Counsel, Fedn. Ins. and Corp. Counsel, Def. Rsch. Inst. (product liability com.), Am. Corp. Counsel Assn., Vancouver Club, Aberdeen Marina Club, Hong Kong Football Club. Unitarian. Office: Camosun Coll 4461 Interurban Rd Victoria BC Canada V8X 3X1 E-mail: brucepart@sprint.ca

PARTRIDGE, MARK VAN BUREN, lawyer, educator, writer; b. Rochester, Minn., Oct. 16, 1954; s. John V.B. and Constance (Brainerd) P.; m. Mary Roberta Moffitt, Apr. 30, 1983; children: Caitlin, Lindsay, Christopher. BA, U. Nebr., 1978; JD, Harvard U., 1981. Bar: Ill. 1981, U.S. Dist. Ct. (no. dist.) Ill. 1981, U.S. Dist. Ct. (ea. dist.) Mich. 1983, U.S. Ct. Appeals (fed. cir.) 1983, U.S. Ct. Appeals (4th cir.) 1986, U.S. Ct. Appeals (5th cir.) 1993, U.S. Ct. Appeals (3rd cir.) 1998. Assoc. Pattishall, McAuliffe, Newbury, Hilliard & Geraldson, Chgo., 1981-88, ptnr., 1988—. Adj. prof. John Marshall Law Sch., Chgo., 1987—; arbitrator Cook County Mandatory Arbitration Program, 1989—; v.p. Harvard Legal Aid Bur., 1980-81; mediator no. dist. Ill. Voluntary Mediation Program, 1997—; panelist World Intellectual Property Orgn., Domain Name Dispute Resolution Svc., 1999—. Contbr. articles to profl. jours.; mem. editl. bd. The Trademark Reporter, 1994-97; adv. bd. IP Litigator, 1995—. Vol. Chgo. Vol. Legal Svcs., 1983—. Mem. ABA (com. chmn. 1989-91, 94-99), Internat. Trademark Assn. (com. vice chmn. 1996), World Intellectual Property Orgn. (experts panel internet domain name process 1998-99), Am. Intellectual Property Law Assn. (com. chmn. 1989-91, 96-98, bd. dirs. 1998—), Intellectual Property Law Assn. Chgo. (com. chmn. 1993-96), Brand Names Ednl. Found. (moot ct. regional chmn. 1994-96, nat. vice-chmn. 1997-98, nat. chmn. 1998-99), Legal Club (v.p. 1998, pres. 1999), Lawyers Club Chgo. (pres. 2000, bd. dirs. 2000-01), Union League Club, Boy Scouts Am. Avocations: writing, genealogy, travel, internet. Federal civil litigation, Private international, Trademark and copyright. Office: Pattishall McAuliffe Newbury Hilliard & Geraldso 311 S Wacker Dr Ste 5000 Chicago IL 60606-6631 E-mail: mpartridge@pattishall.com

PARTRIDGE, WILLIAM FRANKLIN, JR. lawyer; b. Newberry, S.C., July 16, 1945; s. William F. and Clara (Eskridge) P.; m. Ilene S. Stewart, Aug. 16, 1969; children: Allison, William F. BA in History, The Citadel, 1967; JD, U. S.C., 1970. Bar: S.C. 1970, U.S. Ct. Claims 1971, U.S. Ct. Mil. Appeals 1971, U.S. Tax Ct. 1971, U.S. Supreme Ct. 1973, U.S. Dist. Ct. S.C. 1980. Instr. internat. law Chapman Coll., 1973-74; pub. issue com. S.C. Bar, 1982-83. Lt. Col. USAFR. Mem. Newberry Bar Assn. (pres. 1982-83), Palmetto Club, County of Newberry Club, Cotillion Club, Assn. Citadel Mens Club, Masons, Phi Delta Phi. Democrat. Methodist. Oil, gas, and mineral, Family and matrimonial. Home: 2029 Harrington St Newberry SC 29108-3055 Office: 1201 Boyce St Newberry SC 29108-2705

PARTRITZ, JOAN ELIZABETH, lawyer, educator; b. Chgo., July 16, 1931; d. Norman John and Florence May (Russell) P. AB, Ball State U., 1953; MA, Whittier Coll., 1963; JD, Loyola U., L.A., 1977. Bar: Calif. 1977, U.S. Dist. Ct. (cen. dist.) Calif. 1981, U.S. Ct. Appeals (9th cir.) 1984, U.S. Supreme Ct. 1985. Copy writer Nelson Advt. Service, L.A., 1953-53; speech, hearing therapist Port Hueneme Sch. Dist., Calif., 1953-54; math. tchr. Montebello Sch. Dist., Calif., 1954-77; comedy writer Foster Prodns., L.A., 1980-83; prof. Calif. State U., L.A., 1978—; assoc. Parker & Dally, Pomona, Calif., 1977—; dir., speaker Inservice Law Sems., Pomona, 1977—; cons. Foxtail Press, Inc., Whittier, Calif., 1978—. Author: California Modern Mathematics, 1960. Vol. ACLU, L.A., 1981—. NSF grantee, 1965, 66, 69; recipient Nat. Jurisprudence award, 1976. Mem. ABA (tort com. 1978-80, ins. com. 1978—, convention speaker 1989), Assn. Univ. Attys., Calif. Tchrs. Assn. (salary chmn. 1970-71, keynote speaker 1979), La Habra Art Assn. (first prize Water Color Show 1979, 87), AAUW, NOW (speakers bur. 1984—), Women's Political Caucus, Women Trial Lawyers Assn. Democrat. State civil litigation, Probate, Workers' compensation. Home: 10515 Portada Dr Whittier CA 90603-2430 Office: Parker & Dally 300 S Park Ave Fl 9 Pomona CA 91766-1501

PARZEN, STANLEY JULIUS, lawyer; b. N.Y.C., Feb. 6, 1952; BA, Earlham Coll., 1973; LLB cum laude, Harvard U., 1976. Bar: Ill. 1978, U.S. Dist. Ct. (no. dist.) Ill. 1978, U.S. Dist. Ct. (no. dist.) Calif. 1989, U.s. Dist. Ct. (we. dist.) Mich. 1995, U.S. Ct. Appeals (7th cir.) 1981, U.S. Ct. Appeals (8th cir.) 1983, U.S. Ct. Appeals (5th cir.) 1992, U.S. Ct. appeals (D.C. cir.) 1992, U.S. Ct. Appeals (2d cir.) 1990, U.S. Ct. Appeals (9th cir.) 1996. Law clk. to judge U.S. Ct. Appeals 4th cir., 1976-77; ptnr. Mayer, Brown & Platt, Chgo. Mem. Phi Beta Kappa. Office: Mayer Brown & Platt 190 S La Salle St Ste 3100 Chicago IL 60603-3441 E-mail: sparzen@mayerbrown.com

PASAHOW, LYNN H(AROLD), lawyer; b. Ft. Eutiss, Va., Mar. 13, 1947; s. Samuel and Cecelia (Newman) P.; m. Leslie Aileen Cobb, June 11, 1969; 1 child, Michael Alexander. AB, Stanford U., 1969; JD, U. Calif., Berkeley, 1972. Bar: Calif. 1972, U.S. Ct. Appeals (9th cir.) 1972, U.S. Dist. Ct. (no. dist.) Calif. 1973, U.S. Dist. Ct. (cen. dist.) Calif. 1974, U.S. Supreme Ct. 1976, U.S. Dist. Ct. (ea. dist.) Calif. 1977, U.S. Ct. Appeals (fed. cir.) 1990. Law clk. judge U.S. Dist. Ct. (no. dist.) Calif., San Francisco, 1972-73; assoc. McCutchen, Doyle, Brown & Enersen, Palo Alto, Calif., 1973-79, ptnr. San Francisco, 1979-2001, Fenwick & West LLP, 2001—. Attys. adv. panel Bay Area Biosci. Ctr., 1993—; mem. adv. bd. Berkeley Ctr. for Law and Tech., 1998—. Author: Pretrial and Settlement Conferences in Federal Court, 1983; co-author: Civil Discovery and Mandatory Disclosure: A Guide to Effective Practice, 1994; contbr. articles to profl. jours. Mem. ABA, Calif. Bar Assn. Democrat. Federal civil litigation, Patent, Trademark and copyright. Office: Fenwick & West LLP Two Palo Alto Sq Palo Alto CA 94306 E-mail: lpasahow@fenwick.com

PASAL, EMMANUEL PASTORES, lawyer, mining executive; b. Malaybalay, Bukidnon, Philippines, Oct. 8, 1971; s. Justiniano Limansag and Magdalena (Pastores) P.; m. Florence suico, June 3, 1997; 1 child, Gregory. BS in Devel. cum laude, Xavier U., 1992; LLB, U. Philippines, Metro Manila, 1998. Bar: Philippines, 1999. Reporter Glodstar daily, Cagayan de Oro, Misamis Oriental, Philippines, 1990-91, DXIF Radyo Bombo, Cagayan de Oro, 1991-92; corp. sec. Greenwater Mining Corp., Makati, Metro Manila, 1999—. Mem. Integrated Bar Philippines. General civil litigation, General corporate, Intellectual property. Office: Belo Gozon Parel Asuncion Makati Metro Manila 1227 The Philippines Fax: 812 0008. E-mail: bglaw@pworld.net.ph

PASCAL, ROBERT ALBERT, lawyer; b. Fort Lauderdale, Fla., Sept. 29, 1965; s. Albert and Maria Pascal. BA, Loyola U., 1987; JD, Nova Southeastern U., 1991. Bar: Fla. 1991. Pvt. practice, Fort Lauderdale, Fla., 1991—. Editor E-Mag., 1997, Ibl.com.. Vol. Broward Lawyers Care, Ft. Lauderdale, 1992-97, Lawyer for Arts, Ft. Lauderdale, 1993-98; v.p. Quantum Resource Mgmt. Internat., Ft. Lauderdale, 1992—. Avocations: cycling, swimming, travel, linguistics. Criminal, Immigration, naturalization, and customs, Private international. Home: 1506 SE 12th St Fort Lauderdale FL 33316-1410 Office: Pascal L Proff Offices 300 Ave of Arts Fort Lauderdale FL 33316

PASCARELLA, HENRY WILLIAM, lawyer; b. New Haven, Aug. 15, 1933; s. John Manlio and Mary (Iannotti) P.; m. Tessa Peruzzi, Jan. 28, 1967; children: Averardo, Leonora, Cassandra. BS in Econs., U. Pa., 1955; LLB, Yale U., 1958. Bar: Conn. 1958, U.S. Supreme Ct. 1963. Ptnr. Badger, Fisher, Cohen & Barnett and predecessors, Greenwich, Conn., 1959-73; sr. counsel to Taylor Cooper & Alcorn, 1978—. Pres., dir. The Timber Trails Corp. Sherman, Conn.; dir. Nine West Group, Inc., 1995-99. Author column, theater critic Greenwich Times, 1964-67. Dir. Planned Parenthood League of Conn., Greenwich coun. Boy Scouts Am., 1990-96. Served to lt. (j.g.) USCG, 1959. Me.m ABA, Greenwich Bar Assn. (pres. 1967), Conn. Bar Assn., Yale Club (N.Y.C.), Belle Haven Club (Greenwich). Environmental, Probate, Real property. Home: 675 Steamboat Rd Greenwich CT 06830-7140 E-mail: henry@pascarellalaw.com

PASCOE, DONALD MONTE, lawyer; b. Jan. 4, 1935; s. Donald Leslie and Marjorie Lucille (Powers) P.; m. Patricia Hill, Aug. 3, 1957; children: Sarah Lynn, Edward Llewellyn, William Arthur. AB, Dartmouth Coll., 1957; LLB, Stanford U., 1960. Bar: Colo. 1960, Calif. 1961. Assoc., then ptnr. and officer, also bd. dirs. Ireland, Stapleton, Pryor & Pascoe, P.C., Denver, 1960—. Exec. dir. Colo. Dept. of Natural Resources, Denver, 1980-83; bd. dirs. G.G. Shaw, Inc., Denver. Trustee Colo. Sch. of Mines, Golden, 1979-91; trustee Webb-Waring Lung Inst., Denver, 1985-91, pres., 1986-91; commr. Denver Water Bd., 1983-95, pres., 1986-89; mem. Moffat Tunnel Commn., 1996-98; trustee Inst. Internat. Edn., 1998-2001, mem. Rocky Mountain Regional Ctr., 1995—. Mem. ABA, Colo. Bar Assn., Calif. Bar Assn., Am. Judicature Soc., Law Club of Denver, Cactus Club, Rotary. Federal civil litigation, General corporate, Real property. Home: 744 Lafayette St Denver CO 80218-3503 Office: Ireland Stapleton Pryor & Pascoe PC 1675 Broadway Suite 2600 Denver CO 80202

PASI, ANGELA, lawyer; b. Messina, Sicily, Italy, May 25, 1963; JD, U. Messina, 1987. Assoc. Notary, Messina, 1988-92; ptnr. Studio Legale Arena, 1992—. Office: Studio Legale Arena Via Faranza 2 15 188 98123 Messina France Fax: 0039.090.719307

PASICH, KIRK ALAN, lawyer; b. La Jolla, Calif., May 26, 1955; s. Chris Nick and Iva Mae (Tormey) P.; m. Pamela Mary Woods, July 30, 1983; children: Christopher Thomas, Kelly Elizabeth, Connor Woods. BA in Polit. Sci., UCLA, 1977; JD, Loyola Law Sch., L.A., 1980. Bar: Calif. 1980, U.S. Dist. Ct. (no., so., ea. and cen. dists.) Calif. 1981, U.S. Ct. Appeals (9th cir.) 1982, U.S. Ct. Appeals (1st cir.) 1992. Assoc. Paul, Hastings, Janofsky & Walker, L.A., 1980-88, ptnr., 1988-89, Troop Steuber Pasich Reddick & Tobey, LLP, L.A., 1989-2000, Howrey Simon Arnold & White LLP, L.A., 2001—. Author: Casualty and Liability Insurance, 1990, 2000; co-author: Officers and Directors: Liabilities and Protections, 1996, 2000, The Year 2000 and Beyond: Liability and Insurance for Computer Code Problems, 2000; contbg. editor: West's California Litigation Forms: Civil Procedure Before Trial, 2000; entertainment law columnist, ins. law columnist L.A. and San Francisco Daily Jour., 1989—; contbr. articles to profl. jours. Active bd. dirs. Nat. Acad. Jazz, L.A., 1988-89, chmn. bd. dirs. Woody Herman Found., L.A., 1989-92, Constnl. Rights Found., 2000; active L.A. City Atty's. Task Force for Econ. Recovery, 1992-93. Named to Calif's. Legal Dream Team as 1 of state's top 25 litigators, Calif. Law Bus., 1992, as one of the nation's top 45 lawyers under age 45, The Am. Lawyer, 1995. Mem. ABA (mem. Task Force on Complex Insurance Coverage Litigation). General civil litigation, Entertainment, Insurance. Home: 10419 Lindbrook Dr Los Angeles CA 90024-3323 Office: Ste 2100 1925 Century Park E Los Angeles CA 90067 E-mail: pasichk@howrey.com

PASTORIZA, JULIO, lawyer; b. Havana, Cuba, Sept. 22, 1948; came to U.S., 1960; s. Julio S. and Emilia (Bardanca) P.; m. Gloria M. Alvarez-Pedroso, Jan. 5, 1974; 1 child, Gloria Cristina. AA, Miami Dade C.C., 1967; BA, U. Fla., 1969; JD, U. Miami, 1973. Bar: Fla. 1973, U.S. Tax Ct. 1974, U.S. Supreme Ct. 1977. Assoc. Miguel A. Suarez P.A., Miami, Fla., 1973-77; ptnr. Sulli, Pastoriza & Hill, 1977-82; shareholder Julio Pastoriza, P.A., Coral Gables, Fla., 1982-85; ptnr. LaCapra & Wiser, Miami, 1985-87; pvt. practice Coral Gables, 1987—. Agent Attys. Title Ins. Fund, Miami, 1979—; instr. Biscayne Coll., Miami, 1972-76. Spkr. pre-marital conf. St. Theresa Cath. Ch., Coral Gables, 1981-88, mem. adv. bd., 1987-89; mem. adv. bd. Our Lady of Lourdes Acad., Miami, 1991-95; counselor St. Robert Bellarmine Cath. Ch., 2000—. Democrat. Avocations: fishing, photography. Bankruptcy, Family and matrimonial, Real property. Home: 2601 San Domingo St Coral Gables FL 33134-5534 Office: 7101 SW 99 Ave Ste 109B Miami FL 33173-4661

PATE, MICHAEL LYNN, lawyer; b. Ft. Worth, July 9, 1951; s. J.B. and Mary Anna (Hable) P.; m. Barbara Ann Linch, May 28, 1977. AA, Schreiner Coll., 1971; BS, Tex. Wesleyan Coll., 1973; JD, U. Tex., 1975. Bar: Tex. 1976, D.C. 1983, U.S. Tax Ct. 1986, U.S. Supreme Ct. 1987. Adminstrv. asst. to Senator Sherman, counsel natural resources com. Tex. Senate, 1976-77; adminstrv. asst. to Lt. Gov. Bill Hobby, Austin, Tex., 1977-79; legis. asst. Senator Bentsen, Washington, 1979-81, legis. dir., 1981-86; ptnr., head Washington office Bracewell & Patterson, 1986—. Trustee Schreiner U. Mem. ABA, Tex. Bar Assn., D.C. Bar Assn. Democrat. Methodist. Avocations: basketball, tennis, golf. Legislative. Office: Bracewell & Patterson 2000 K St NW Ste 500 Washington DC 20006-1872 E-mail: mpate@bracepatt.com

PATE, STEPHEN PATRICK, lawyer; b. Beaumont, Tex., May 6, 1958; s. Gordon Ralph and Shirley Jean (Riley) P.; m. Jean Janssen; 1 child, Teddy. BA, Vanderbilt U., 1980, JD, 1983. Bar: Tex. 1984, U.S. Dist. Ct. (ea. dist.) Tex. 1984, U.S. Dist. Ct. (so. dist.) Tex. 1985. Law clk. to judge Joe J. Fisher U.S. Dist. Ct. Tex., Beaumont, 1983-84; ptnr. Fulbright & Jaworski, Houston. Contbr. articles to profl. jours. Fellow Houston Bar Found., Tex. Bar Found.; mem. ABA (vice chmn. property ins. com. tort and ins. practice sect. 1994—, chmn. 1999-2000), Fedn. Ins. and Corp. Counsel, Tex. Bar Assn., Tex. Young Lawyers Assn. (bd. dirs. 1992-94), Houston Young Lawyers Assn. (bd. dirs. 1990-92, sec. 1992-93, chmn. professionalism com., mem. sunset rev. com. 1990), Sons of the Republic Tex., SAR (sec. Paul Carrington chpt. 2001—), Soc. Colonial Wars, Manitoba Master Angler, Billfish Found. (Top Angler 1993), Knight of Momus, The Briar Club, Phi Beta Kappa. Republican. Roman Catholic. Avocations: hunting, fishing. General civil litigation, Insurance, Personal injury. Home: 2740 Arbuckle St Houston TX 77005-3932 Office: Fulbright & Jaworski 1301 Mckinney St Houston TX 77010-3031 E-mail: spate@fulbright.com

PATEL, APEXA, lawyer; b. India, July 26, 1970; came to U.S., 1971; d. Niranjan and Jashoda Patel. BA, George Washington U., 1993; MSA, Audrey Cohen Coll., 1994; JD, So. Ill. U., 1996. Assoc. atty. Ice Miller Donadio & Ryan, Indpls., 1997—. Mem. adv. bd. Spiritual Devel. Ctr., Forest Hills, N.Y., 1997—. General corporate, Private international, Public international. Office: Ice Miller Donadio & Ryan Box 82001 1 American Sq Indianapolis IN 46282

PATMAN, PHILIP FRANKLIN, lawyer; b. Atlanta, Nov. 1, 1937; s. Elmer Franklin and Helen Lee (Miller) P.; m. Katherine Sellers, July 1, 1967; children: Philip Franklin, Katherine Lee. BA, U. Tex., 1959, LLB, 1964; MA, Princeton U., 1962. Bar: Tex. 1964, U.S. Supreme Ct. 1970, U.S. Dist. Ct. (so. dist.) Tex. 1971, U.S. Dist. Ct. (we. dist.) Tex. 1975. Atty. office of legal adviser Dept. State, Washington, 1964-67; dep. dir. office internat. affairs HUD, 1967-69; pvt. practice Austin, Tex., 1969—. Contbr. articles to legal jours. Ofcl. rep. of Gov. Tex. to Interstate Oil Compact Commn., 1973-83, 87-91. Woodrow Wilson fellow, 1959. Fellow Tex. Bar Found. (life); mem. ABA, State Bar Tex., Tex. Ind. Prodrs. and Royalty Owners Assn., Tex. Oil and Gas Assn., Tex. Law Rev. Assn., Austin Club, Headliners Club, Westwood Country Club, Rotary, Phi Beta Kappa, Phi Delta Phi. Administrative and regulatory, Oil, gas, and mineral, Environmental. Office: Patman & Osborn 515 Congress Ave Ste 1704 Austin TX 78701-3503

PATRICK, CHARLES WILLIAM, JR. lawyer; b. Monroe, N.C., Oct. 9, 1954; s. Charles William and Louise (Nisbet) P.; m. Celeste Hunt, June 5, 1976; children: Laura Elizabeth, Charles William III. BA magna cum laude, Furman U., 1976; JD, U. S.C., 1979. Bar: S.C. 1979, U.S. Dist. Ct. S.C. 1981, U.S. Ct. Appeals (11th cir.) 1981, U.S. Ct. Appeals (10th cir.) 1983, U.S. Ct. Appeals (4th cir.) 1986. Law clk. to presiding judge 9th Cir. Ct. State of S.C., Charleston, 1979-80; assoc. Ness, Motley, Loadholt, Richardson and Poole and predecessor firm Blatt and Fales, 1980—, Motley, Loadholt, Richardson and Poole and predecessor firm Blatt and Fales, Charleston, 1980-84, ptnr., 1984—. Exec. editor S.C. Law Review, 1978; contbr. articles to profl. jours. Mem. ABA, Assn. Trial Lawyers Am., S.C. Assn. Trial Lawyers, Trial Lawyers for Pub. Justice, Phi Beta Kappa. Democrat. Presbyterian. Avocations: boating, skiing, jogging. General civil litigation, Personal injury, Product liability. Home: 38 Church St Charleston SC 29401-2742 Office: Ness Motley Loadholt Richardson & Poole 174 East Bay St PO Box 879 Charleston SC 29402-0879

PATRICK, DANE HERMAN, lawyer; b. San Antonio, Oct. 18, 1960; s. Kae Thomas and Joyce Lynn (von Scheele) P.; m. Kelly Marie Carlson, May 17, 1986. BA in Econs. with honors, U. Tex., 1983; JD, So. Meth. U., 1987. Assoc. Law Office of Earl Luna, Dallas, 1987-88, Veitch & Davis, San Antonio, 1988-91; pvt. practice, 1991—. Mem. ATLA, San Antonio Trial Lawyers Assn. (bd. dirs.), San Antonio United Shareholder Assn. (chmn. 1988-92). Democrat. Methodist. Avocations: weight lifting, hunting, martial arts. General civil litigation, Insurance, Personal injury. Office: 111 Soledad St Ste 300 San Antonio TX 78205-2298

PATRICK, H. HUNTER, judge; b. Gasville, Ark., Aug. 19, 1939; s. H. Hunter Sr. and Nelle Frances (Robinson) P.; m. Charlotte Anne Wilson, July 9, 1966; children: Michael Hunter, Colleen Annette. BA, U. Wyo., 1961, JD, 1966. Bar: Wyo. 1966, U.S. Dist. Ct. Wyo. 1966, Colo. 1967, U.S. Supreme Ct. 1975. Mcpl. judge City of Powell (Wyo.), 1967-68; sole practice law Powell, 1966-88; atty. City of Powell, 1969-88; justice of the peace County of Park, Wyo., 1971-88; bus. law instr. Northwest Community Coll., Powell, 1968-98; dist. judge State of Wyo. 5th Jud. Dist., 1988—. Mem. Wyo. Dist. Judges Conf., sec.-treas., 1993-94, vice chair, 1994-95, chair, 1995-96. Editor: Bench Book for Judges of Courts of Limited Jurisdiction in the State of Wyoming, 1980-90. Dir. cts. Wyo. Girls State, Powell, 1982-85, 89-99; elder, deacon, moderator of deacons Powell Presbyn. Ch., 1997; mem. Wyo. Commn. Jud. Conduct & Ethics, 1997—. Recipient Wyo. Crime Victims Compensation Commn. Judicial award, 1995. Fellow Am. Bar Found., Wyo. Jud. Adv. Coun.; mem. ABA (Wyo. state del. to ho. of dels. 1994-2001, Wyo. del. judicial adminstrn. divsn., exec. com. nat. conf. trial ct. judges representing Wyo., Colo., Kans., Nebr., N.Mex. 1996-2000, bd. govs. 2001—, Pub. Svc. award for ct.-sponsored Law Day programs 1990, 92), Wyo. Bar Assn. (Cmty. Svc. award 1999, Ann. Pub. Svc. award 1999), Colo. Bar Assn., Park County Bar Assn. (sec. 1969-70, pres. 1970-71), Wyo. Assn. Cts. Ltd. Jurisdiction (pres. 1973-80), Am. Judicature Soc. Avocations: photography, travel, fishing, reading, writing. Home: PO Box 941 Powell WY 82435-0941 Office: PO Box 1868 Cody WY 82414-1868 E-mail: hpatrick@parkco.wtp.net

PATRICK, JAMES DUVALL, JR. lawyer; b. Griffin, Ga., Dec. 28, 1947; s. James Duvall and Marion Wilson (Ragsdale) P.; m. Cynthia Hill, Jan. 19, 1991. BS in Indsl. Mgmt., Ga. Inst. Tech., 1970; JD, U. Ga., 1973. Bar: Ga. 1973, U.S. Dist. Ct. (mid. dist.) Ga. 1973, U.S. Dist. Ct. (so. dist.) Ga. 1983, U.S. Ct. Appeals (5th cir.) 1974, U.S. Ct. Appeals (11th cir.) 1981, U.S. Tax Ct. 1985, U.S. Supreme Ct. Assoc. Cartledge, Cartledge & Posey, Columbus, Ga., 1973-74; ptnr. Falkenstrom, Hawkins & Patrick, 1975, Falkenstrom & Patrick, Columbus, 1975-77; sole practice, 1977—. Instr. bus. law Chattahoochee Valley C.C., Phenix City, Ala., 1975-77; instr. paralegal course Columbus Coll., 1979, 84; del. U.S./China Joint Session on Trade, Investment, and Econ. Law, Beijing, 1987, Moscow Conf. on Law and Bilateral Econ. Rels., Moscow, 1990; U.S. del. U.S./Cuba Law Initiative, Havana, 2000. Mem. Hist. Columbus Found., Mayor's Commn. for the Handicapped, 1987-88; local organizer, worker Joe Frank Harris for Gov. Campaign, Columbus, 1982; bd. dirs. Columbus Symphony Orch., 1988-94. Mem. ATLA, ABA, Am. Judicature Soc., State Bar Ga., Ga. Trial Lawyers Assn., Columbus Lawyers Club, Columbus Kappa Alpha Alumni Assn. (sec.), Civitan (bd. dirs. 1975-77), Country Club of Columbus, Georgian Club (Atlanta), Buckhead Club, Chattahoochee River Club (local chpt.), Phi Delta Phi, Kappa Alpha. Methodist. State civil litigation, General practice, Personal injury. Office: PO Box 2745 Columbus GA 31902-2745

PATRICK, LYNN ALLEN, lawyer, corporate governance and land development; b. Stettler, Alta., Can., Dec. 7, 1935; s. Allen Russell and Florence Lorene (Lynn) P.; m. Roberta Colleen Hughes, May 9, 1959; children: Diane Elizabeth, Ross Gordon. BSc, U. Alta., Edmonton, Can., 1957, LLB, 1960. Bar: Alta. Ptnr. Cormie Kennedy, Edmonton, Alta., Can., 1961-83; sr. v.p., gen. counsel Mutual Fund Group, Can., 1983-88; pres. Stuart Olson Constrn., Inc., Can., 1989-92; v.p., corp. counsel, sec. The Churchill Corp., 1992-98. Dir. Sparta Water Corp., SNG Telecom, Inc., Red Oak Trail Corp. (now Innovative Sewage Systems Inc.); sec. mem. subdivsn. and devel. appeal bd. City of Edmonton; bd. dirs. Home Bank Techs., Inc. Past pres., trustee Minerva Found., Edmonton; adv. coun. mem. Minister of Edn., Alta.; gov. Banff Ctr. Mem. Can. Bar Assn., Edmonton Bar Assn., Law Soc. Alta., Real Estate Coun. Alta., Royal Glenora Club (Edmonton). Progressive. Home: 64 Quesnell Rd Edmonton AB Canada T5R 5N2 Office: 2500 10104 103rd Ave Edmonton AB Canada T5J 1V3 E-mail: lpatrick@telusplanet.net

PATRICK, MARTY, lawyer; b. N.Y.C., May 10, 1949; s. Harry and Evelyn (Beroza) P.; m. Yolande Andree, Feb. 26, 2000; 1 child, Jason. BS, L.I. U., 1971; cert., Inst. for Leadership Devel., Jerusalem, 1974; JD, Nova Southeastern U., 1981. Exec. dir. Zionist Orgn. Am., Miami Beach, Fla., 1975-78; pres. Enigma Enterprises, Inc., Miami, 1978-82; ptnr. Martin Howard Patrick, P.A., Miami Beach, 1982—. Pres. Patrick Law Ctr., Miami Beach, 1983-89; pres. First Fla. Title & Abstract Co., Boca Raton, Fla., 1983—; CEO Atlantic Coast Title Co., 1989—; founding ptnr. Patrick & Schwartz, P.A, Boca Raton, 2001—; CEO Laughing in the Dark Prodns., 1994—. Contbr. articles to profl. jours. Pres. United Orthodox Cmty. Coun. of So. Fla., Miami Beach, 2001—. Horovitz scholar, 1980. Mem. ABA, Ga. Bar Assn., Fla. Bar Assn., Mensa. Estate planning, Real property. E-mail: mpatrick@dirtlaw.com

PATRICK, WILLIAM BRADSHAW, lawyer; b. Indpls., Nov. 29, 1923; s. Fae William and Mary (Bradshaw) P.; m. Ursula Lantzsch, Dec. 28, 1956; children: William Bradshaw, Ursula, Nancy. AB, The Principia, 1947; LLB, Harvard U., 1950. Bar: Ind. Supreme ct. 1950, U.S. Dist. Ct. (so. dist.) Ind. 1950, U.S. Ct. Apls. (7th cir.) 1961. Ptnr., Patrick & Patrick, Indpls., 1950-53; pvt. practice, Indpls., 1953—; gen. counsel Met. Planning Commn. Marion County and Indpls., 1955-66; dep. proscecutor Marion County, Ind., 1960-62; past pres., dir. The Cemetery Co., operating Meml. Park Cemetery, Indpls.; sec., dir. Rogers Typesetting Co., Indpls., 1966-85. Pres. Indpls. Legal Aid Soc., 1963. Lt. (j.g.) USNR, 1942-46. Recipient DeMolay Legion of Honor. Mem. ABA, Ind. Bar Assn., Indpls. Bar Assn., Lawyers Assn. Indpls., Indpls. Estate Planning Coun., Am. Legion, SAR (sec. Ind. Soc. 1953-59), Svc. Club Indpls., U.S. Navy League, Mil. Order Loyal Legion (comdr. Ind. Soc. 1979), Mason (33d degree), Shriner. General corporate, Probate, Estate taxation. Address: 7 N Meridian St Indianapolis IN 46204-3002

PATRICOSKI, PAUL THOMAS, lawyer; b. Ft. Rucker, Ala., Mar. 24, 1955; s. Thomas S. and Marie L. (Andruscavage) P.; m. Stephanie M. Galiardi, Aug. 5, 1978; children: Adam Thomas, Matthew Philip, Amanda Katharine. BS in Biology, St. Vincent Coll., 1977; JD, U. Notre Dame, 1981. Bar: Ill. 1981, U.S. Dist. Ct. (no. dist.) Ill. 1982, U.S. Ct. Appeals (7th cir.) 1997. Assoc. Dreyer, Foote, Streit, Furgason & Slocum, P.A., Aurora, Ill., 1981-88, ptnr., 1988—. Mem. youth adv. commn. Aurora Twp., 1998—; mem. parish coun. Annunciation B.V.M. Ch., 1991—95; mem. edn. commn. Annunciation B.V.M. Sch., 1988—89, 1990—96, chmn. edn. commn., 1992—95, chmn. strategic planning com., 1995—97, mem. athletic com., 1997—2001, athletic dir., 1998—2001; pres. Annunciation B.V.M. Home and Sch. Assn., 1989; bd. dirs. Ill. divsn. South Kane unit Am. Cancer Soc., 1985—92, chmn., 1986—89, mem. pub. affairs com. Ill. divsn., 1994—2001. Recipient U. Notre Dame Award Alumni Club, 1988. Mem. ABA, Ill. State Bar Assn., Kane County Bar Assn. (pub. rels. com. 1986, mem. jud. evaluation com. 1995—), Notre Dame Alumni Club (bd. dirs. 1982—, pres. 1983, treas. 1989-95). Roman Catholic. Avocations: hunting, fishing, hockey. Bankruptcy, Consumer commercial, General practice. Home: 685 Audrey Ave Aurora IL 60505-1001 Office: Dreyer Foote Streit Furgason and Slocum 900 N Lake St Ste 1 Aurora IL 60506-2578 Fax: 630-897-1735

PATRIKIS, ERNEST T. lawyer, banker; b. Lynn, Mass., Dec. 1, 1943; s. Theodore A. and Ethel (Stasinopolous) P.; m. Emily Herrick Trueblood, Mar. 18, 1972. BA, U. Mass., 1965; JD, Cornell U., 1968. Bar: N.Y. 1969. Exec. v.p., gen. counsel Fed. Res. Bank N.Y., 1968-95 1st v.p., 1995—; dep. gen. counsel Fed. Open Market Com., 1988-95. Contbr. articles to legal jours. Fellow Fgn. Policy Assn., 1995—. Fellow Fgn. Policy Assn.; mem. Assn. of Bar of City of N.Y. (banking law com. 1982-84, 90—, futures regulation com. 1986-89); N.Y. State Bar Assn. (chmn. com. internat. banking, securities and fin. transaction 1987-91, banking law com. 1986—, vice chmn. internat. practice sect. 1991—), ABA (subcom. on gen. banking matters 1986), Coun. on Fgn. Rels., Joint Year 2000 Coun. (chmn.). Banking, Contracts commercial, Private international. Home: 20 E 9th St New York NY 10003-5944 Office: Fed Reserve Bank NY 33 Liberty St New York NY 10045-0001

PATT, HERBERT JACOB, lawyer; b. Chgo., Feb. 12, 1935; s. Abraham and Esther Blanch (Kuchinsky) P.; m. Yvonne Phyllis Shavell, Oct. 9, 1958 (dec. Mar. 1986); children: Aldon Wayne, Bradley Earl, Colette Emile; m. Lynn Cheryl Feingold, December 26, 1993. BA, Northwestern U., 1956, JD, 1958; Diploma, Indsl. Coll., Johannesburg, South Africa. Bar: Ill. 1959, U.S. Dist. Ct. (no. dist.) Ill. 1959, U.S. Supreme Ct. 1977, Calif. 1986, U.S. Dist. Ct. (ctrl. and so. dists.) Calif. 1987, U.S. Ct. Appeals (9th cir.) 1987. Assoc. Andres & Andres, Santa Ana, Calif. Pres. Jewish Nat. Fund Orange Co., Santa Ana, 1994-95, chmn., 1996-98, nat. bd. dirs., N.Y., 1994-98; pres. Temple Judea, Laguna Hills, Calif., 1992-93. General civil litigation, Personal injury, Probate. Office: Andres & Andres 2041 N Main St Santa Ana CA 92706 E-mail: pattlaw@aol.com

PATTEN, THOMAS LOUIS, lawyer; b. St. Joseph, Mo., Oct. 3, 1945; m. Sherry V. Patten; children: Elizabeth, Caroline, Brooke. BS, U. Mo., 1967, JD, 1969. Bar: Mo. 1969, D.C. 1972, U.S. Dist. Ct. D.C. 1972, U.S. Claims Ct. 1972, U.S. Ct. Appeals (fed. cir.) 1972, U.S. Supreme Ct. 1972, U.S. Ct. Appeals (9th cir.) 1974, U.S. Ct. Appeals (4th cir.) 1981, Va. 1983, U.S. Dist. Ct. (ea. and we. dists.) Va. 1983. Ptnr Latham & Watkins, Washington. Fellow Am. Coll. Trial Lawyers. Federal civil litigation, Criminal, Government contracts and claims. Office: Latham & Watkins 555 Eleventh St NW Washington DC 20004-2585

PATTERSON, BURTON HARVEY, lawyer; b. Ft. Smith, Ark., Aug. 11, 1935; s. Frank Willard and Pauline (Gilliland) P.; m. Robert Kay Taylor, July 15, 1962 (div. 1975); children: Patricia, Paula, Pamela; m. Virginia Lee Avery, Sept. 1, 1977. AB, Okla. Baptist U., 1956; JD, Northwestern U., 1959; MRE, Southwestern Bapt. Sem., 1962. Bar: Tex. 1959, Ohio 1967, U.S. Supreme Ct. 1969. Mem. faculty Tex. Christian U., Ft. Worth, 1959-67, Cleve. State Law Sch., 1967-68; office gen. counsel El Paso Natural Gas Co., Tex., 1968-72; ptnr. Patterson, Sargent & Glanville, El Paso, 1972— ; lectr. on estate planning, taxation. Trustee Lighthouse for Blind, El Paso, 1975-78, Downtown Rescue Mission, El Paso, 1979— ; bd. dirs. El Paso Symphony, 1977—, Hospice El Paso, 1985—. Republican. Baptist. Club: Kiwanis (trustee El Paso club 1971-72). Estate planning, Probate, Corporate taxation. Office: Patterson Sargent & Glanville 7300 Viscount Blvd # 102 El Paso TX 79925-4837

PATTERSON, CHARLES ERNEST, lawyer; b. Rockford, Ill., Jan. 4, 1941; s. Alvin Maurice and Helen Mae (Mitchell) P. A.B. cum laude, U. Kans., 1963; J.D. with distinction U. Mich., 1966. Bar: Mo. 1966, U.S. Dist. Ct. (we. dist.) Mo. 1966, U.S. Ct. Mil. Appeals 1968, U.S. Supreme Ct. 1969, U.S. Ct. Appeals (8th cir.) 1971, Calif. 1985, U.S. Dist. Ct. (cen., no. dists.) Calif. 1985. Assoc. Watson, Ess, Marshall & Enggas, Kansas City, Mo., 1966-74, ptnr., 1974-85; ptnr. Lillick, McHose & Charles, Los Angeles; chmn. exec. com. 1987—; now ptnr. Pillsbury Madison & Sutro, L.A.; chmn. various coms. Def. Research Inst., 1978—; bd. govs. Legal Aid of Western Mo., 1978-80; mem. bench/bar com. Western div. Mo. Ct. Appeals, 1983—, 16th Jud. Cir. Ct. Mo., 1983—; mem. fed. practice com. U.S. Dist. Ct. (we. dist.) Mo. 1983— . Contbr. articles to profl. jours. Bd. dirs. Boys Clubs Greater Kansas City, Inc., 1974-78, Dismas House Kansas City, 1978-84, Mo. Assn. for Ex-Offenders, 1976-79, YMCA, 1976-79; v.p. Heart of Am. Rugby Football Union, Kansas City, 1976-78; pres. Pre Trial Diversion Services, Inc., Kansas City, 1976-78, Kansas City Vietnam Vets. Meml. Fund, 1984—; mem. bd. Kansas City Arts Council, 1984, Mo. Boys Town, Kansas City, 1983-84. Served to capt. USMC, 1966-69; Vietnam. Decorated Bronze Star medal with Combat V, Vietnamese Cross of Gallantry with Palm, Vietnamese Medal of Honor. Mem. ABA (ho. of dels. 1984—), Mo. Bar (bd. govs. 1978-84, pres. 1983-84, Award of Merit 1984, Jud. Conf. award 1984), Kansas City Bar Assn., Lawyers Assn. Kansas City, Western Mo. Def. Lawyers Assn. (pres. 1981-82), Mo. Orgn. Def. Lawyers (bd. dirs. 1984-85), Internat. Assn. Ins. Counsel. Clubs: Kansas City, Carriage (Kansas City, Mo.). Federal civil litigation, State civil litigation. Office: Pillsbury Madison & Sutro 725 S Figueroa St Ste 1200 Los Angeles CA 90017-5443

PATTERSON, CHRISTOPHER NIDA, lawyer; b. Washington Courthouse, Ohio, Apr. 17, 1960; s. Donis Dean and JoAnne (Nida) O.; m. Vicky Patterson; children: Travis, Kirsten. BA, Clemson U., 1982; JD, Nova U., 1985. Bar: Fla. 1985, U.S. Dist. Ct. (mid. dist.) Fla. 1985, U.S. Ct. Mil. Rev. 1986, U.S. Ct. Mil. Appeals 1987, U.S. Dist. Ct. (ea. dist.) Va. 1987, U.S. Supreme Ct. 1990, U.S. Ct. Appeals (11th cir.) 1992, U.S. Dist. Ct. (no. dist.) Fla. 1992, U.S. Dist. Ct. (so. dist.) Tex. 1995; cert. criminal trial lawyer Fla. Bar. and Nat. Bd. Trial Advocacy. Pros. Fla. State Attys. Office, Orlando, Fla., 1985; spl. asst. U.S. Atty. U.S. Dist. Ct. (ea. dist.) Va., 1987-90; ptnr. Patterson & Hauversburk, Panama City, Fla., 1992—. Adj. prof. law Gulf Coast Coll.; mem. Fla. Supreme Ct. Mediators Qualifications Bd.; family law mediator, dependency law mediator Fla. Supreme Ct., mem. mediators qualifications bd. Author: Queen's Pawn, 1996, Treasure Trove, 1997; contbr. Nat. DAR Mag., Fla. Defender mag. Chancellor St. Thomas Episcopal Ch. Capt. JAGC, U.S. Army, 1986-92, Desert Storm. Recipient Guardian ad litem commendation Fla. Supreme Ct., 1999. Mem. ABA, ATLA, FBA, SAR, NACDL (life), Am. Coll. Barristers, Fla. Assn. Criminal Def. Lawyers, Acad. Fla. Trial Lawyers, Assn. Fed. Def. Attys., Fla. Acad. Profl. Mediators, Fla. Bar Spkrs. Bur. (criminal law sect., mil. law standing com., del. 11th cir. jud. conf. 1999, Pro Bono Svc. award, nominee Jefferson award for pub. svc. 1999), Bay County Bar Assn., The Ret. Officers' Assn., Christian Legal Soc., Am. Legion, Fellowship of Christian Athletes, Nat. Triathlon Fedn., Soc. Colonial Wars, Mil. Order Fgn. Wars. Episcopalian. Avocations: athletics, triathlons. Office: PO Box 1368 1021 Grace Ave Panama City FL 32401-2420

PATTERSON, DENNIS MICHAEL, lawyer, educator; b. N.Y.C., Sept. 29, 1955; s. Patrick Joseph and Mary Theresa (Philbin) P.; m. Barbara Jean Zehler, June 30, 1978; children: Sarah Elspeth, Graham Philip. BA in Philosophy, SUNY, Buffalo, 1976, MA in Philosophy, 1978, PhD in Philosophy, JD, SUNY, 1980. Bar: Maine 1981, N.Y. 1981, U.S. Dist. Ct. Maine 1981, U.S. Supreme Ct. 1984. Law clk. to presiding justice Supreme Ct. Maine, Portland, 1980-81; assoc. Preti, Flaherty & Beliveau, 1981-82; lectr. philosophy U. So. Maine, 1983-84; prof. law U. Maine, 1985-87; ptnr. Loyd, Bumgardner, Field & Patterson, Brunswick, Maine, 1983-87;

asst. prof. Sch. of Law Western New Eng. Coll., Springfield, Mass., 1987-90; prof. Sch. of Law Rutgers U., Camden, N.J., 1990—. Contbr. articles to profl. jours. Mem. ABA, Am. Philos. Assn., Maine State Bar Assn., Phi Beta Kappa. Republican. Home: 40 Regan Ln Kirkwood Voorhees NJ 08043-4146 Office: Rutgers Sch Law 217 N Fifth St Camden NJ 08102

PATTERSON, DONALD ROSS, lawyer, educator; b. Sept. 9, 1939; s. Sam Ashley and Marguerite (Robinson) P.; m. Peggy Ann Schulte, May 1, 1965; children: D. Ross, Jerome Ashley, Gretchen Anne. BS, Tex. Tech U., 1961; JD, U. Tex., 1964; LLM, So. Meth. U., 1972. Bar: Tex. 1964, U.S. Ct. Claims 1970, U.S. Ct. Customs and Patent Appeals 1970, U.S. Ct. Mil. Appeals 1970, U.S. Supreme Ct. 1970, U.S. Dist. Ct. (ea. dist.) Tex. 1982, U.S. Ct. Appeals (5th cir.) 1991, U.S. Ct. Appeals (D.C. cir.) 1994; bd. cert. in immigration and naturalization law, Tex. Commd. lt. (j.g.) USN, 1964, advanced through grades to lt. comdr., 1969; asst. officer in charge Naval Petroleum Res., Bakersfield, Calif., 1970-72; staff judge adv. Kenitra, Morocco, 1972-76; officer in charge Naval Legal Svcs. Office, Whidbey Island, Wash., 1976-79; head mil. Justice divsn., Subic Bay, The Philippines, 1979-81; ret. USN, 1982; pvt. practice Tyler, Tex., 1982—. Former instr. U. Md., Chapman Coll., U. LaVerne, Tyler Jr. Coll., Jarvis Christian Coll., U. Tex., Tyler. Mem. East Tex. Estate Planning Coun. Mem. Coll. of State Bar of Tex., Tex. Bar Assn., Smith County Bar Assn., Am. Immigration Lawyers Assn., Masons, Rotary (past pres.), Shriners, Toastmasters (past pres.), Phi Delta Phi. Republican. Baptist. Bankruptcy, Consumer commercial, Immigration, naturalization, and customs. Home: 703 Wellington St Tyler TX 75703-4666 Office: 777 S Broadway Ave Ste 106 Tyler TX 75701-1648 E-mail: oneworld2gether@cs.com

PATTERSON, ELIZA, lawyer; b. Princeton, N.J., May 12, 1950; d. Gardner and Evelyn P. Student, U. Madrid, Spain, 1971; BA summa cum laude, U. Mich., 1972; JD, Harvard U., 1975. Assoc. Morgan, Lewis & Bockus, Phila., 1975-1978, Daniels, Houlihan & Palmeter, Washington, 1978; atty. advisor Foreign Agrl. Svc. U.S. Dept. Agr., 1978-1982; internat. affairs fellow Coun. on Foreign Relations and Resident Scholar at the GATT, Geneva, Switzerland, 1983-1985; sr. assoc. Internat. Trade Govt. Rsch. Corporation, Washington, 1985-1987; atty. advisor Office of Chairman U.S. Internat. Trade Commn., 1987-1988; dep. dir. Office Exec. and Internat. Liaison U.S. Internat. Trade Commn., 1988-1992; wash. rep. internat. trade The Port Authority of N.Y. and N.J., 1992—. Cons., Internat. Law Inst., 1998—, Overseas Devel. Coun., 1997-1998, OAS, 1995, pres., Consumers for World Trade Ednl. Fund, 1996-1997, adj. prof. internat. trade and trade policy, U. MD. Coll. Grad. Sch. and Mgmt. Tech., 1995, internat. bus. transactions and internat. trade, Wash. Coll. Law Am. U., 1991-1992, analyst internat. econ. law and policy, Oxford Analytical Ltd., Oxford, 1990—, wash. corr. internat. econ. law and policy, EuroBusiness, London, 1988-1992, non-resident fellow, Resources for the Future, 1988. Contbr. articles to profl. jours. Home: 1514 Swann St NW Washington DC 20009-3942 E-mail: epatters@panynj.gov

PATTERSON, JOHN DE LA ROCHE, JR. lawyer; b. Schenectady, N.Y., July 8, 1941; s. John de la Roche Sr. and Jane C. (Clay) P.; m. Michele F. Demarest, Nov. 28, 1987; children: Daniel C., Sara R., Amy C. BA, Johns Hopkins U., 1963; LLB, Harvard U., 1966. Bar: Mass. 1968. Vol. Peace Corps, Chad, 1966-67; assoc. Foley, Hoag & Eliot, Boston, 1967-73, ptnr., 1974—, exec. com., 1989-97. Chmn. Kodaly Ctr. Am. Inc., Newton, Mass., 1977-87. Mem. ABA, Boston Bar Assn. Democrat. Avocations: sailing, tennis, travel, reading. General corporate, Intellectual property, Mergers and acquisitions. Office: Foley Hoag & Eliot 1 Post Office Sq Ste 1700 Boston MA 02109-2175 E-mail: jpatters@fhe.com

PATTERSON, MICHAEL P. former prosecutor; BA, Tulane U.; JD, U. Fla., 1973. Bar: Fla. 1974. Pvt. practice, 1974-81; asst. state atty. First Jud. Cir. Ct., Fla., 1981-91; U.S. atty. U.S. Dist. Ct. (no. dist), 1993—2001. Com. mem. U.S. Atty. Gen. Adv. Com. of U.S. Attys., 1995—.*

PATTERSON, P(ICKENS) ANDREW, lawyer; b. Cotton Plant, Ark., Aug. 1, 1944; s. Pickens Andrew and Willie Mae (Miller) P.; m. Gloria Neltine Peebles, Nov. 25, 1967; children— Pickens Andrew, Staci Elizabeth. B.A., Fisk U., 1965; J.D., Harvard U., 1968. Bar: Ga. 1969, N.C. 1978, U.S. Dist. Ct. (no. dist.) Ga. 1969, U.S. Dist. Ct. (mid. dist.) N.C. 1978, U.S. Ct. Appeals (11th cir.) 1983. Vice pres. Urban East Housing Consl. Atlanta, 1968-69; mng. atty. Atlanta Legal Aid, 1968-70; sr. ptnr. Patterson, Parks, Jackson & Howell, Atlanta, 1970-77; atty. adviser HUD, Greensboro, N.C., 1977-81; exec. v.p. Arrington, Patterson & Thomas, P.C., Atlanta, 1982— ; dir. Gladden Devel. Corp., Atlanta; Davis-Hudson Assoocs., Inc., Atlanta, Creance Internat., Inc., Atlanta; Pres. Atlanta Legal Aid Soc., 1976, Central Carolina Legal Services, Greensboro, 1980; Co-author pamphlet. Mem. Atlanta Charter Study Commn., 1972; bd. dirs. Louisville Presbyn. Theol. Sem., 1983— . Recipient Key to City Atlanta, 1972, plaque awards Atlanta Legal Aid Soc., 1977, Central Carolina Legal Services, 1981, Cert. of Spl. Achievement, Office of Gen. Counsel, HUD, 1980. Mem. Nat. Bar Assn., State Bar Ga., N.C. Bar Assn., Atlanta Bar Assn., Gate City Bar Assn., Alpha Phi Alpha. Democrat. Presbyterian. Construction, Landlord-tenant, Real property. Home: 3905 Somerled Trl Atlanta GA 30349-2035 Office: Suite 2000 Equitable Bldg 100 Peachtree St NE Atlanta GA 30043

PATTERSON, ROBERT PORTER, JR. federal judge; b. N.Y.C., July 11, 1923; s. Robert Porter and Margaret (Winchester) P.; m. Bevin C. Daly, Sept. 15, 1956; children: Anne, Robert, Margaret, Paul, Katherine. AB, Harvard U., 1947; LLB, Columbia U., 1950. Bar: N.Y. 1951, D.C. 1966. Law clk. Donovan, Leisure, Newton & Lumbard, N.Y.C., 1950-51; asst. counsel N.Y. State Crime Commn. Waterfront Investigation, 1952-53; asst. U.S. atty. Chief of Narcotics Prosecutions and Investigations, 1953-56; asst. counsel Senate Banking and Currency Com., 1954; assoc. Patterson, Belknap, Webb & Tyler, N.Y.C., 1956-60, ptnr., 1960-88; judge U.S. Dist. Ct. (so. dist.) N.Y., 1988—. Counsel to minority select com. pursuant to house resolution no. 1, Washington, 1967; mem. Senator's Jud. Screening Panel, 1974-88, Gov.'s Jud. Screening Panel, 1975-82, Gov.'s Sentencing Com., 1978-79. Contbr. articles to profl. jours. Chmn. Wm. T. Grant Found., 1974-94, Prisoners' Legal Services N.Y., 1976-88; dir. Legal Aid Soc., 1961-88, pres., 1967-71; chmn. Nat. Citizens for Eisenhower, 1959-60, Scranton for Pres., N.Y. State, 1964; bd. mgrs. Havens Relief Fund Soc., 1994—, Millbrook Sch., 1966-78, Vera Inst. Justice, 1981-99, New Sch. for Social Rsch., 1986-94, George C. Marshall Found., 1987-93; mem. exec. com. Lawyers Com. for Civil Rights Under Law, 1968-88; mem. Goldman Panel for Attica Disturbance, 1972, Temporary Commn. on State Ct. System, 1971-73, Rockefeller U. Council, 1986-88, exec. com. N.Y. Vietnam Vets. Meml. Commn., 1982-85, Mayor's Police Adv. Com., 1985-87. Served to capt. USAAF, 1942-46. Decorated D.F.C. with cluster, Air medal with clusters. Mem. ABA (ho. of dels. 1976-80), N.Y. State Bar Assn. (pres. 1978-79), Assn. Bar City N.Y. (v.p. 1974-75), N.Y. County Lawyers Assn., Am. Law Inst., Am. Judicature Soc. (bd. dirs. 1979). Republican. Episcopalian. Home: Fair Oaks Farm 1657 Route 9D Cold Spring NY 10516-3543 Office: US Dist Ct So Dist NY US Court House 500 Pearl St New York NY 10007-1316

PATTERSON, ROBERT SHEPHERD, lawyer; b. Odessa, Tex., May 18, 1953; s. Robert Charles and Ouida Inez (Shepherd) P.; m. Ann Gayley Atkinson; 2 children. BA in Physics, Rice U., 1975; JD, Vanderbilt U., 1978. Bar: Tenn. 1978, U.S. Dist. Ct. (mid. sect.) Tenn. 1978, U.S. Ct. Appeals (6th cir.) 1979; cert. as civil trial specialist, Tenn. Supreme Ct. Assoc. atty. Boult, Cummings, Conners & Berry, Nashville, 1978-83, ptnr., atty., 1984—, adminstrv. ptnr., 1997-99, mng. dir., 2000—. Bd. dirs. Outlook Nashville, 1985-91; chmn. McNeilly Ctr. for Children, 1992-93, The Caduceus Soc. Bapt. Hosp., Young Exec. Coun. Dominion Bank of Mid. Tenn.; chmn., bd. mem. Kids on the Block, 1992—; bd. mem., exec. com. Vanderbilt Children's Hosp., 2001—; legal counsel Nashville C. of C. Mem. ABA, Tenn. Bar Assn., Nashville Bar Assn., C. of C., Cumberland Club, Belle Meade Country (Nashville), Chaine des Rotisseur. Methodist. Avocations: sports, snow and water skiing, reading. Federal civil litigation, State civil litigation, Consumer commercial. Office: Boult Cummings Conners & Berry 414 Union St PO Box 198062 Nashville TN 37219-8062 E-mail: bpatterson@boultcummings.com

PATTISHALL, BEVERLY WYCKLIFFE, lawyer; b. Atlanta, May 23, 1916; s. Leon Jackson and Margaret Simkins (Woodfin) P.; children by previous marriage: Margaret Ann Arthur, Leslie Hansen, Beverly Wyckliffe, Paige Terhune Pattishall Watt, Woodfin Underwood; m. Dorothy Daniels Mashek, June 24, 1977; 1 stepchild, Lyssa Mashek Piette. BS, Northwestern U., 1938; JD, U. Va., 1941. Bar: Ill. 1941, D.C. 1971. Pvt. practice law, Chgo., 1946—; ptnr. Pattishall, McAuliffe, Newbury, Hilliard & Geraldson and predecessor firms. Dir. Juvenile Protective Assn. Chgo., 1946-79, pres., 1961-63, hon. dir., 1979— ; dir. Vol. Interagy. Assn., 1975-78, sec., 1977-78; U.S. del. Diplomatic Confs. on Internat. Trademark Registration Treaty, Geneva, Vienna, 1970-73, Diplomatic Conf. on Revision of Paris Conv., Nairobi, 1981; mem. U.S. del. Geneva Conf. on Indsl. Property and Consumer Protection, 1978; adj. prof. trademark, trade identity and unfair trade practices law Northwestern U. Sch. Law, Chgo. Author: (with David C. Hilliard and Joseph Nye Welch II) Trademarks, Trade Identity and Unfair Trade Practices, 1974, Unfair Competition and Unfair Trade Practices, 1985, Trademarks, 1987, Trademarks and Unfair Competition, 1994, 3d edit., 1998; contbr. articles to profl. jours. Bd. dirs. Constl. Rights Found. Chgo., 1996-98. Lt. comdr. USNR, WWII, ETO, PTO, ATO, ret. comdr USNR. Fellow Am. Coll. Trial Lawyers (bd. regents 1979-83); mem. ABA (chmn. sect. patent, trademark copyright law 1963-64), Internat. Patent and Trademark Assn. (pres. 1955-57, exec. com. 1955—), Assn. Internat. Pour La Protection Propriete Indsl. (mem. of honor), Ill. Bar Assn., Chgo. Bar Assn., D.C. Bar Assn., Chgo. Bar Found. (dir. 1977-83), U.S. Trademark Assn. (dir. 1963-65), Legal Club, Law Club (pres. 1982-83), Econ. Club, Chikaming Country Club, Univ. Club, Mid-Am. Club, U. Va. Lile Law Soc. (sr. counselor), Selden Soc. (London, Ill. rep.). Federal civil litigation, State civil litigation, Trademark and copyright. Office: Pattishall McAuliffe Newbury Hilliard & Geraldson 311 S Wacker Dr Ste 5000 Chicago IL 60606-6631

PATTON, DAVID ALAN, lawyer; b. Oakland, Calif., Nov. 14, 1960; s. Douglas Kieth and Joan Erlene P.; m. Renee Theresa, Nov. 21, 1987 (div. Dec. 1996); children: Thomas, Joseph. BA, U. Calif., Berkeley, 1983; JD, Santa Clara U., 1987. Bar: Calif. 1988. Atty. Collins & Schlothauer, San Jose, 1988-93; ptnr. Lonich & Patton, 1993—. Judge pro tem Santa Clara Superior Ct., San Jose, 1996—, arbitrator, 1994—. General civil litigation, Insurance. Office: Lonich & Patton 111 W Saint John St Ste 600 San Jose CA 95113-1105 E-mail: dpatton@lonichandpatton.com

PATTON, FRANCES ANNE, lawyer; b. Jan. 14, 1917; d. Peter Mathew and Frances Helen (Lovrencic) Basar; m. Earl Richard Patton, Apr. 20, 1945 (div. Oct. 1963); 1 child John Michael. LLB, Columbus U. (now Cath. U. Am.), 1940, LLM, 1941. Bar: D.C. 1940, U.S. Dist. Ct. D.C. 1940, U.S. Ct. Appeals (D.C. cir.) 1940, U.S. Supreme Ct. 1944. With U.S. Dept. Interior, Washington, 1938—95; spl. asst. to dir. Office Hearings and Appeals, Arlington, Va., 1970—82, spl. counsel to dir., 1982—95; pvt. practice DC, 1996—. Recipient Superior Performance award, Dept. Interior, 1966, Meritorious Performance award, 1968, Spl. Achievement award, 1980. Roman Catholic. Home: 3725 Macomb St NW Apt 112 Washington DC 20016-3841

PATTON, JAMES LEELAND, JR. lawyer; b. Wilmington, Del., Sept. 28, 1956; s. James L. Patton and Eleanor Phillips Crawford Brown; m. Kathleen Long Patton, May 29, 1981; children: Kathryn Stuart, Diana Lantz. BA in Philosophy, Davidson (N.C.) Coll., 1979; JD, Dickinson Sch. Law, Carlisle, Pa., 1983. Bar: Del. 1983, U.S. Dist. Ct. Del. 1983, U.S. Ct. Appeals (3rd cir.) 1988, U.S. Supreme Ct. 1991. Ptnr., chair Bankruptcy Dept. Young Conaway Stargatt & Taylor, Wilmington, 1983—. Trustee Pvt. Panel Bankruptcy Trustees, 1985-88. Contbr. (ref. ency.): Fletcher Corporate Bankruptcy, Reorganization and Dissolution, 1992. Mem. ABA, Del. State Bar Assn. (bankruptcy law subcom. chmn. 1986—). Avocation: photography, sailing. Bankruptcy, Contracts commercial, General corporate. Office: Young Conaway Stargatt & Taylor PO Box 391 11th & Market Wilmington DE 19899

PATTON, JAMES RICHARD, JR. lawyer; b. Durham, N.C., Oct. 27, 1928; s. James Ralph and Bertha (Moye) P.; m. Mary Margot Maughan, Dec. 29, 1950; children: James Macon, Lindsay Fairfield. AB cum laude, U. N.C., 1948; postgrad., Yale U., 1948; JD, Harvard U., 1951. Bar: D.C. bar 1951, U.S. Supreme Ct. 1963. Attache of Embassy; spl. asst. to Am. ambassador to, Indochina, 1952-54; with Office Nat. Estimates, Washington, 1954-55; atty. Covington & Burling, 1956-61; founding ptnr., chmn. exec. com. Patton Boggs, LLP, 1962—. Lectr. internat. law Cornell Law Sch., 1963-64, U.S. Army Command and Gen. Staff Coll., 1967-68; Mem. Nat. Security Forum, U.S. Air War Coll., 1965, Nat. Strategy Seminar, U.S. Army War Coll., 1967-70, Global Strategy Discussions, U.S. Naval War Coll., 1968, Def. Orientation Conf., 1972; mem. Com. of 100 on Fed. City, Washington; mem. adv. council on nat. security and internat. affairs Nat. Republican Com., 1977-81; bd. dirs. Security Nat. Bank (Wash.), Signet, N.A., Madeira Sch., Greenway, Va., 1975-81, Lawyers Com. for Civil Rights Under Law, Washington, Legal Aid Soc. Washington; mem. Industry Policy Adv. Com. for Trade Policy Matters, 1984-87; mem. visiting com. Ackland Art Mus. U. N.C., 1987—, Nat. Coun. Anderson Ranch Arts Ctr., 1987—. Adv. coun. mem. Johns Hopkins U. Sch. Advanced Internat. Studies, 1989-92; nat. bd. dirs. Aspen Mus., 1987-90; nat. coun. mem. Whitney Mus., 1992—; bd. dirs., exec. com. Nat. Mus. Natural History, Smithsonian, 1992—; bd. dirs. Smithsonian Nat. Bd., 1999—; trustee Aspen Music Festival and Sch., 1993—. Fellow U.N.C. Wilson Library, 1996—. Mem. ABA (past com. chmn.), Inter-Am. Bar Assn. (past del.), Internat. Law Assn. (past com. chmn.), Am. Soc. Internat. Law (treas., exec. coun.), Washington Inst. Fgn. Affairs, Nat. Gallery (collectors com. 1988-91), Gerrard Soc., Met. Club (Washington), Phi Beta Kappa, Alpha Epsilon Delta. General corporate, Private international, Public international.

PATURIS, E(MMANUEL) MICHAEL, lawyer; b. Akron, Ohio; s. Michael George and Sophia (Manos) P.; m. Mary Ann Toompas, Febr. 28, 1965. BS, U. N.C., 1954, JD with Honors, 1959, student, 1959-60. Bar: N.C. 1959, D.C. 1969, Va. 1973; CPA. Acct., Charlotte and Wilmington, N.C., 1960-63; assoc. Poyner, Geraghty, Hartsfield & Townsend, Raleigh, 1963-64; atty. advisor Chief Counsel's Office, Washington, 1964-66, sr. trial atty. Richmond, Va., 1966-69; ptnr. Reasoner, Davis & Vinson, Washington, 1969-78; sole practice Alexandria, 1978—. Acctg. instr. U. N.C., Chapel Hill, 1959-60; acctg., econs. lectr. N.C. State U., Raleigh, 1963-64; business law lectr. George Mason U., Fairfax County, Va., 1978-79. Mem. bd. editors U. N.C. Law Rev. With U.S. Army, 1954-56. Recipient U. N.C. Law Sch. Block award, 1959. Mem. Phi Beta Kappa., Beta Gamma Sigma. General corporate, Corporate taxation, Estate taxation. Home: 6326 Stoneham Ln Mc Lean VA 22101-2345 Office: Law Offices of E Michael Paturis 431 N Lee St Alexandria VA 22314-2301

PATZKE, JOHN CHARLES, lawyer; b. Mar. 23, 1954; s. Clifford C. and Valerie S. (Duenow) Patzke; m. Mary T. Silver, Oct. 02, 1982. BA magna cum laude, Marquette U., 1976; JD, U. Wis., 1979. Bar: Wis. 1979, U.S. Dist. Ct. (ea. dist.) Wis. 1979, U.S. Dist. Ct. (ea. dist.) Tex. 1982, U.S. Dist. Ct. (we. dist.) Wis. 1984, U.S. Dist. Ct. (no. dist.) Calif. 1988, U.S. Ct. Appeals (7th cir.) 1980, U.S. Ct. Appeals (9th cir.) 1993, U.S. Ct. Appeals (11th cir.) 1996. Law clk. Melli, Shiels, Walker & Pease, Madison, Wis., 1977, Wis. Employment Rels. Commn., 1978, NLRB, Milw., 1979; from assoc. to ptnr. Brigden & Petajan, 1979—. Author: (mag.) Milw. Lawyer, 1985, (non-fiction) Communications and the Law, 1986; author, author, author: Bus. Age Mag., 1986, author: Women in Bus. Mag., 1987; mem. adv. bd. editors: jour. Med-West Labor and Employment Law Jours., 1983—90. Mem.: ABA (subcom. chmn.), Soc. Resource Mgmt., Human Resource Mgmt. Assn. Southeastern Wis. (com. chmn.), Alpha Sigma Nu, Pi Sigma Alpha. Lutheran. Labor. Home: 8143 W Winston Way Franklin WI 53132-9296 Office: Brigden & Petajan 600 E Mason St Milwaukee WI 53202-3870

PAUL, DENNIS EDWARD, lawyer; b. Lakewood, Ohio, Sept. 6, 1949; s. Edward and Louise Marie Paul; m. Cheryl Lynn Burnett, Aug. 21, 1976; children— Jennifer Ruth, Molly Anna. B.S. in Journalism, Ohio U., 1971; J.D., Ohio No. U., 1975. Bar: Ohio 1975, U.S. Dist. Ct. (no. dist.) Ohio 1977, U.S. Dist. Ct. (so. dist.) Mich. 1981. Asst. county prosecutor Medina County Prosecutor's Office, Medina, Ohio, 1976; city prosecutor Medina City Prosecutor's Office, 1977; assoc. Gilbert & Parish, Medina, 1978-80; ptnr. Gilbert, Parish & Paul, Medina, 1980; sole practice, Medina, 1981-83; ptnr. Palecek, McIlvaine, Foreman & Paul, Wadsworth, Ohio, 1983— . Chmn. Medina City CSC, 1984— ; atty. Medina County Bd. Realtors, 1980. Mem. Ohio Acad. Trial Lawyers, Medina County Bar Assn. (pres. 1984-85), Assn. Trial Lawyers Am., Ohio Bar Assn. Roman Catholic. Criminal, Family and matrimonial, Personal injury. Office: Palecek McIlvaine Foreman & Paul 210 Bank Wadsworth OH 44281

PAUL, EVE W. lawyer; b. N.Y.C., June 16, 1930; d. Leo I. and Tamara (Sogolow) Weinschenker; m. Robert D. Paul, Apr. 9, 1952; children: Jeremy Ralph, Sarah Elizabeth. BA, Cornell U., 1950; JD, Columbia U., 1952. Bar: N.Y. 1952, Conn. 1960, U.S. Ct. Appeals (2nd cir.) 1975, U.S. Supreme Ct. 1977. Assoc. Botein, Hays, Sklar & Herzberg, N.Y.C., 1952-54; pvt. practice Stamford, Conn., 1960-70; staff atty. Legal Aid Soc., N.Y.C., 1970-71; assoc. Greenbaum, Wolff & Ernst, 1972-78; v.p. legal affairs Planned Parenthood Fedn. Am., 1979—, v.p., gen. counsel, 1991—. Bd. dirs. Ctr. for Gender Equality, Inc. Contbr. articles to profl. jours. Trustee Cornell U., Ithaca, N.Y., 1979-84; mem. Stamford Planning Bd., Conn., 1967-70; bd. dirs. Stamford League Women Voters, 1960-62, Ctr. for Gender Equality, 1995—. Harlan Fiske Stone scholar Columbia Law Sch., 1952. Mem. ABA, Conn. Bar Assn., Assn. of Bar of City of N.Y., Stamford/Norwalk Regional Bar Assn., U.S. Trademark Assn. (chair dictionary listings com. 1988-90), Phi Beta Kappa, Phi Kappa Phi. Health, Intellectual property, Non-profit and tax-exempt organizations. Office: Planned Parenthood Fedn 810 7th Ave New York NY 10019-5818 E-mail: eve.paul@ppfa.org

PAUL, HERBERT MORTON, lawyer, accountant, taxation educator; b. N.Y.C. s. Julius and Gussie Paul; m. Judith Paul; children: Leslie Beth, Andrea Lynn. BBA, Baruch Coll.; MBA, LLM, NYU; JD, Harvard U. Ptnr. Touche Ross & Co., N.Y.C., assoc. dir.-tax, dir. fin counseling; mng. ptnr. Herbert Paul, P.C., N.Y.C., 1983—. Prof. taxation, trustee NYU. Author: Ordinary and Necessary Expenses; editor: Taxation of Banks; adv. tax editor The Practical Acct.; mem. adv. bd. Financial and Estate Planning, Tax Shelter Insider, Financial Planning Strategist, Tax Shelter Litigation Report; bd. dirs. Partnership Strategist, The Business Strategist; cons. Profl. Practice Mgmt. Mag.; mem. panel The Hot Line; advisor The Partnership Letter, The Wealth Formula; cons. The Insider's Report for Physicians; mem. tax bd. Business Profit Digest; cons. editor physician's Tax Advisor; bd. fin. cons. Tax Strategies for Physicians; tax and bus. advisor Prentice Hall; contbg. editor. Jour. of Accountancy; mem. editl. bd. Family Bus. Advisor. Trustee NYU, mem. bd. overseers Grad. Sch. Bus.; mem. com. on trusts and estates Rockefeller U.; trustee Alvin Alley Am. Dance Theatre, Assoc. Y's of N.Y.; mem. accts. divsn. Fedn. Philanthropies; mem. adv. bd. Family Bus. Advisor; pres. coun. NYU. Mem. NYU Alumni Assn. (pres., bd. dirs.). Mem. ABA, Inst. Fed. Taxation (adv. com. chmn.), Internat. Inst. on Tax and Bus. Planning (adv. bd.), Assn. Bar City N.Y., NYU Tax Soc. (pres.), Bur. Nat. Affairs-Tax Mgmt. (adv. com. on exec. compensation), Am. Inst. CPAs (com. on corp. taxation), Tax Study Group, N.Y. County Lawyers Assn., N.Y. State Soc. CPAs Dir. (chmn. tax div. com. on fed. taxation, gen. tax com., furtherance com., com. on rels. with IRS, bd. dirs.), Nat. Assn. Accts., Assn. of Bar of City of N.Y., Accts. Club of Am., Pension Club, Nat. Assn. Estate Planners (bd. dirs.), N.Y. Estate Planning Coun. (bd. dirs.), N.Y. C. of C. (tax com.), Grad. Sch. Bus. of NYU Alumni Assn. (pres.), NYU Alumni Assn. (pres.). Clubs: Wall St., City Athletic (N.Y.C.), Inwood Country. Estate planning, Corporate taxation, Personal income taxation. Office: Herbert Paul PC 370 Lexington Ave Rm 1001 New York NY 10017-6503

PAUL, JAMES WILLIAM, lawyer; b. Davenport, Iowa, May 3, 1945; s. Walter Henry and Margaret Helene (Hillers) P.; m. Sandra Kay Schmid, June 15, 1968; children: James William, Joseph Hillers. BA, Valparaiso U., 1967; JD, U. Chgo., 1970. Bar: N.Y. 1971, U.S. Ct. Appeals (2d cir.) 1971, U.S. Dist. Ct. (so. and ea. dists.) N.Y. 1972, U.S. Supreme Ct. 1977, U.S. Ct. Appeals (6th cir.) 1981, Ind. 1982, U.S. Dist. Ct. (no. dist.) Ind. 1982, U.S. Claims Ct. 1989, U.S. Dist. Ct. (ea. dist.) Mich. 1989, U.S. Ct. Appeals (fed. cir.) 1991. Assoc. Rogers & Wells, N.Y.C., 1970-78, ptnr., 1978—. Dir., officer Musica Sacra, Inc., 1972-81 Bd. dirs. Turtle Bay Music Sch., Am. Lutheran Publicity Bur. Recipient Disting. Alumnus award Valparaiso U., 1994. Mem. ABA (antitrust sect. ins. com.), Assn. Bar City N.Y. (com. on legal and jud. ethics, com. on civil ct.), Fed. Bar Council. Democrat. Antitrust, General civil litigation, Labor. Home: 360 E 72nd St Apt A-710 New York NY 10021-4755 also: 5 Curtis Dr Sherman CT 06784-1220 Office: Rogers & Wells 200 Park Ave Ste 5200 New York NY 10166-0005

PAUL, JEREMY RALPH, law educator; b. N.Y.C., July 22, 1956; s. Robert D. and Eve (Weinschenker) P.; m. Laurel Ann Leff, Aug. 29, 1981. AB, Princeton U., 1978; JD, Harvard U., 1981. Bar: N.Y.C. 1982. Law clk. to presiding judge U.S. Ct. Appeals (2d cir.), N.Y.C., 1982-83; instr. U. Miami, Coral Gables, Fla., 1981-82, asst. prof. law, 1983-87, assoc. prof. law, 1987-92; assoc. dean for acad. affairs, prof. law U. Conn., Hartford, 1992—. Asst. to the pres. Travelers Group, 1993-94; vis. prof. law Boston Coll. Law Sch., 1997-98. Democrat. Office: U Conn Sch Law 65 Elizabeth St Hartford CT 06105-2290 E-mail: jepaul@law.uconn.edu

PAUL, RICHARD WRIGHT, lawyer; b. Washington, May 23, 1953; s. Robert Henry Jr. and Betty (Carey) P.; m. Paula Ann Coolsaet, July 25, 1981; children: Richard Haven, Timothy Carey, Brian Davis. AB magna cum laude, Dartmouth Coll., 1975; JD, Boston Coll., 1978. Bar: Mich. 1978, U.S. Dist. Ct. (ea. dist.) Mich. 1978, U.S. Ct. Appeals (6th cir.) 1982, U.S. Supreme Ct. 1989, U.S. Dist. Ct. (we. dist.) Mich. 1991. Assoc. Dickinson, Wright, Moon, Van Dusen & Freeman, Detroit, 1978-85, ptnr., 1985—. Mediator Wayne County Cir. Ct., Oakland County Dist. Ct. Co-author, Barbarians At The Gate: Daubert Two Years Later, 1995; contbr. articles to profl. publs. Trustee Bloomfield Village Assn., Birmingham, Mich., 2001—; bd. dirs. Little League, Birmingham, 2000—. Mem. ABA, State Bar of Mich. (treas. litig. sect. 1998-99, sec. litig. sect. 1999-2000, chmn. elect litig. sect. 2000-01), Def. Rsch. Inst., Detroit Bar Assn., Mich. Def. Trial Counsel, Dartmouth Lawyers Assn., Oakland County Bar Assn., Assn. Def. Trial Counsel, Alumni Coun. Dartmouth Coll., Dartmouth Detroit Club (pres. 1980—). Avocations: tennis, cycling. General civil litigation, Product liability, Professional liability. E-mail: rpaul@dickinson-wright.com

PAUL, ROBERT, lawyer; b. N.Y.C., Nov. 22, 1931; s. Gregory and Sonia (Rijock) P.; m. Christa Holz, Apr. 6, 1975; 1 child, Gina. BA, NYU, 1953; JD, Columbia U., 1958. Bar: Fla. 1958, N.Y. 1959. From assoc. to ptnr. Paul Landy Beiley & Harper, P.A., Miami, 1964-94; ptnr. Sacher Zelman Van Sant Paul Beiley Hartman & Waldman, P.A., 1964-94; counsel Republic Nat. Bank, 1967-95; chmn. internat. affiliation of law firms TerraLex, 1990—. Past pres. Fla. Philharm., Inc., 1978-79; trustee U. Miami. Mem. ABA, N.Y. Bar Assn., Fla. Bar Assn., Fla. Zool. Soc. (past pres.), French-Am. C. of C. of Miami (pres. 1986-87). Banking, General corporate, Private international. Home: 700 Alhambra Cir Coral Gables FL 33134-4808 E-mail: rpaul@terralex.com

PAUL, ROBERT CAREY, lawyer; b. Washington, May 7, 1950; s. Robert Henry and Betty Jane (Carey) P. AB, Dartmouth Coll., 1972; JD, Georgetown U., 1978. Assoc. Milbank, Tweed, Hadley & McCloy, N.Y.C., 1978-85; ptnr. Dechert Price & Rhoads, 1986-89, Kelley Drye & Warren, Brussels, 1989-93; counsel Rockefeller & Co., Inc., N.Y.C., 1995—. Finance, Private international, Real property. Home: 310 E 46th St Apt 19E New York NY 10017-3029 Office: Rockefeller & Co Inc 30 Rockefeller Plz 56th Fl New York NY 10112-0256 E-mail: rpaul@rockco.com

PAUL, STEPHEN HOWARD, lawyer; b. Indpls., June 28, 1947; s. Alfred and Sophia (Nahmias) P.; m. Deborah Lynn Dorman, Jan. 22, 1969; children: Gabriel, Jonathan. AB, Ind. U., 1969, JD, 1972. Bar: Ind. 1972, U.S. Dist. Ct. (so. dist.) Ind. 1972. Assoc. Baker & Daniels, Indpls., 1972-78, ptnr., 1979—. Editor in chief Ind. U. Law Jour., 1971. Pres. Belle Meade Neighborhood Assn., Indpls., 1974-78; v.p., counsel Brentwood Neighborhood Assn., Carmel, Ind., 1985-88, pres., 1988-91. Mem. ABA (state and local tax com. 1985—, sports and entertainment law com.), Am. Property Tax Counsel (founding mem.), Ind. State Bar Assn., Order of Coif. General corporate, Municipal (including bonds), State and local taxation. Office: Baker & Daniels 300 N Meridian St Ste 2700 Indianapolis IN 46204-1782

PAUL, THOMAS FRANK, lawyer; b. Aberdeen, Wash., Sept. 23, 1925; s. Thomas and Loretta (Ounstead) P.; m. Dolores Marion Zaugg, Apr. 1, 1950; chilren: Pamela, Peggy, Thomas Frank. BS in Psychology, Wash. State U., 1951; JD, U. Wash., 1957. Bar: Wash. 1958, U.S. Dist. Ct. (no. and so. dists.) Wash. 1958, U.S. Ct. Appeals (9th cir.) 1958, U.S. Supreme Ct. 1970. Ptnr., shareholder, dir. LeGros, Buchanan & Paul, Seattle, 1958—. Lectr. on admiralty and maritime law. Mem. ABA (chmn. com. on admiralty and maritime litigation 1982-86), Wash. State Bar Assn., Maritime Law Assn. U.S.A. (com. on nav. and C.G. matters 1981-82, com. on U.S. Mcht. Marine program 1981-82, com. on practice and procedure 1982-86, com. on limitation of liability 1982-86, com. on maritime legislation 1982—, nom. com. 1998-99), bd. Adv. U. San Fransisco Law Journ. Republican. Admiralty, General civil litigation, Product liability. Home: 1323 Willard Ave W Seattle WA 98119-3460 Office: LeGros Buchanan & Paul 701 5th Ave Ste 2500 Seattle WA 98104-7051 E-mail: tpaul@legros.com

PAUL, WILLIAM GEORGE, lawyer; b. Pauls Valley, Okla., Nov. 25, 1930; s. Homer and Helen (Lafferty) P.; m. Barbara Elaine Brite, Sept. 27, 1963; children: George Lynn, Alison Elise, Laura Elaine, William Stephen. B.A., U. Okla., 1952, LL.B., 1956. Bar: Okla. bar 1956. Pvt. practice law, Norman, 1956; ptnr. Oklahoma City, 1957-84; with Crowe & Dunlevy, 1962-84, 96—; sr. v.p., gen. counsel Phillips Petroleum Co., Bartlesville, Okla., 1984-95; ptnr. Crowe & Dunlevy, Oklahoma City, 1996—. Assoc. prof. law Oklahoma City U., 1964-68; adv. bd. Martindale Hubbell, 1990—. Author: (with Earl Sneed) Vernon's Oklahoma Practice, 1965. Bd. dirs. Nat. Ctr. for State Cts., 1993-99, Am. Bar Endowment, 1986—. 1st lt. USMCR, 1952-54. Named Outstanding Young Man Oklahoma City, 1965, Outstanding Young Oklahoman, 1966 Fellow Am. Bar Found. (chmn. 1991), Am. Coll. Trial Lawyers; mem. ABA (bd. govs. 1995—, pres. 1999), Okla. Bar Assn. (pres. 1976), Oklahoma County Bar Assn. (past pres.), Nat. Conf. Bar Pres. (pres. 1986), U. Okla. Alumni Assn. (pres. 1973), Order of Coif, Phi Beta Kappa, Phi Delta Phi, Delta Sigma Rho. Democrat. Presbyterian. Federal civil litigation, State civil litigation, General corporate. Home: 13017 Burnt Oak Rd Oklahoma City OK 73120-8919 Office: Crowe & Dunlevy Mid-Am Tower 20 N Broadway Ave Ste 1800 Oklahoma City OK 73102-8273

PAUL, WILLIAM MCCANN, lawyer; b. Cambridge, Mass., Feb. 9, 1951; s. Kenneth William and Mary Jean (Lamson) P.; m. Janet Anne Forest, Feb. 25, 1984; children: Emily L'Engle, Andrew Angwin, Elizabeth Seton. Student, U. Freiburg, Fed. Republic of Germany, 1971-72; BA, Johns Hopkins U., 1973; JD, U. Mich., 1977. Bar: D.C. 1978, U.S. Dist. Ct. D.C. 1978, U.S. Ct. Claims 1984, U.S. Ct. Appeals (4th cir.) 1980, U.S. Ct. Appeals (fed. cir.) 1983, U.S. Tax Ct. 1990. Law clk. to judge U.S. Ct. Appeals (5th cir.), Austin, Tex., 1977-78; assoc. Covington & Burling, Washington, 1978-87, ptnr., 1987-88, 89—; dep. tax legis. counsel U.S. Treasury Dept., 1988-89. Mem. ABA (asst. sec. tax sect. 1995-97, sec. 1997-99, coun. mem. 1999—), D.C. Bar Assn., Am. Law Inst., Am. Coll. Tax Counsel, Order of Coif. Presbyterian. Corporate taxation, Personal income taxation. Home: 5604 Chevy Chase Pkwy NW Washington DC 20015-2520 Office: Covington & Burling PO Box 7566 1201 Pennsylvania Ave NW Washington DC 20004-2401 E-mail: wpaul@cov.com

PAULE, DONALD WAYNE, lawyer; b. St. Louis, Jan. 9, 1943; s. William Arthur and Selma (Clithero) P.; m. Maureen Ridgeway, Apr. 16, 1966 (div. 1979); children: Thomas, Stephanie, Daniel; m. Mary Joan Breslin, Sept. 5, 1980. BS in Engring., Washington U., St. Louis, 1964, JD, 1966, LLM in Taxation, 1978. Bar: Mo. 1967, U.S. Dist. Ct. (ea. dist.) Mo. 1968, U.S. Tax Ct. 1970, U.S. Ct. Appeals (8th cir.) 1984, U.S. Supreme Ct. 1985. Assoc. Tremayne, Lay, Carr, Bauer & Paule, Clayton, Mo., 1967-72, ptnr. 1973-75; pvt. practice law, Clayton, 1975-78; ptnr. Paule, Beach & Kaveney Inc., Clayton, 1979-81; ptnr. Love, Lacks & Paule P.C., Clayton, 1981-92, mng. ptnr., 1989-90, 91-92, prin., mng. dir., pres., 1993—, pres. Paule, Camazine & Blumenthal, P.C., Clayton, 1994—; adj. asst. prof. bus. law and taxation Washington U., 1970—. Chmn. St. Louis County Civil Svc. Commn., Clayton, 1975-83; mem. St. Louis Area Bd. AMC Cancer Rsch. Ctr., 1987-93, pres. 1987-89; bd. dirs. Coll. Sch. 1981-85, 89-95, pres., 1993; bd. dirs. West County YMCA, 1973-80, chmn. 1978-80, Vis. Nurse Assn., St. Louis, 1974-82, 89—, pres. 1979-81, 1993-97, Home Health Care Found., Vis. Nurse Assn. Found., St. Louis, 1984-87, 1995—. Mem. ABA, Mo. Bar Assn. (pub. info. com. 1975-83), St. Louis County Bar Assn. (Roy F. Essen Meml. award 1972, pres. 1975-76), Am. Arbitration Assn. (mem. panel 1980—), Lawyers Assn. St. Louis, Washington U. Law Alumni Assn. (pres. 1983-84), St. Louis Club. E-mail: dpaule@pcblawfirm.com. General corporate, Estate planning, Probate. Home: 255 Lindeman Rd Saint Louis MO 63122-3541

PAUPP, TERRENCE EDWARD, research associate, educator; b. Joliet, Ill., Aug. 10, 1952; s. Edward Theodore and Mary Alice (Combs) P. BA in Social Scis., San Diego State U., 1974; ThM, Luth. Sch. Theology, 1978; JD, U. San Diego, 1990. Instr. philosophy San Diego City Coll., 1983-86, Southwestern Coll., Chula Vista, Calif., 1980-83; law clerk Sch. Law U. San Diego, 1987-88; law clerk Office of Atty. Gen., San Diego, 1988-89; rsch. assoc. Frank & Milchen, 1989, Dougherty & Hildre, San Diego, 1990-95; sr. rsch.-assoc. Inst. for Ctrl. and Ea. European Studies, San Diego State U., 1996-98; sr. policy analyst Nuc. Age Peace Found., Santa Barbara, Calif., 2001—. Cons. Cmty. Reinvestment Act, San Diego, 1993-95; sr. rsch. assoc. Inst. Ctrl. and Ea. European Studies San Diego State U., 1994-95; adj. faculty in criminal justice and polit. sci. Nat. U.; cons., contbr. Inst. for Policy Studies, Washington, Interhemispheric Resource Ctr., N.Mex., The Ctr. of Concer, Washington, Global Exch., San Francisco. Author: Achieveing Inclusionary Governance: Advancing Peace and Development in First and Third World Nations, 2000;contbr. articles to law jours. Appointed National Chancellor of the USA Internat. Assn. of Educators for World Peace, 2001; cons. Neighborhood House 5th Ave., 1994—95, PBS Frontline documentary The Nicotine Wars, 1994, Bethel Baptist Ch., 1994—95. Mem. ATLA, N.Y. Acad. Scis. Democrat. Lutheran. Avocation: tennis. E-mail: tpaupp@aol.com

PAVALON, EUGENE IRVING, lawyer; b. Chgo., Jan. 5, 1933; m. Lois M. Frenzel, Jan. 15, 1961; children: Betsy, Bruce, Lynn. BSL, Northwestern U., 1954, JD, 1956. Bar: Ill. 1956. Sr. ptnr. Pavalon, Gifford, Laatsch & Marino, Chgo., 1970—. Mem. com. on discovery rules Ill. Supreme Ct., 1981—; lectr., mem. faculty various law schs.; bd. dirs. ATLA Mut. Ins. Co. Author: Human Rights and Health Care Law, 1980, Your Medical Rights, 1990; contbr. articles to profl. jours., chpts. in books. Former mem. state bd. dirs. Ind. Voters Ill. bd. overseers Inst. Civil Justice, Rand Corp., 1993-99; mem. vis. com. Northwestern U. Law Sch., 1990-96. Capt. USAF, 1956-59. Fellow Am. Coll. Trial Lawyers, Internat. Soc. Barristers, Internat. Acad. Trial Lawyers, Roscoe Pound Found. (life, pres. 1988-90); mem. ABA, Chgo. Bar Assn. (bd. mgrs. 1978-79), Ill. Bar Assn., Ill. Trial Lawyers Assn. (pres. 1980-81), Trial Lawyers for Pub. Justice (founding mem., v.p. 1991-92, pres.-elect 1992-93, pres. 1993-94), Assn. Trial Lawyers Am. (parliamentarian 1983-84, sec. 1984-85, v.p. 1985-86, pres.-elect 1986-87, pres. 1987-88), Am. Bd. Profl. Liability Attys. (diplomate), Am. Bd. Trial Advocates, Inner Circle of Advocates, Chgo. Athletic Assn., Std. Club. Federal civil litigation, State civil litigation, Personal injury. Home: 1540 N Lake Shore Dr Chicago IL 60610-6684 Office: Pavalon Gifford et al 2 N La Salle St Chicago IL 60602-3702 E-mail: pavalon@pglmlaw.com

PAVELA, D. JEAN, lawyer, law association administrator; b. Lawrence, Kans., Jan. 26, 1938; d. Harlan W. and Frances May (McLean) Miller; m. Todd Harold Pavela, Sr., June 2, 1958 (dec. Oct. 1967); children: Linda Kirsten Gentile, Todd Harold. BA, Midland Luth. Coll., Fremont, Nebr., 1960; MS, Purdue U., 1962; JD, John Marshall Law Sch., Chgo., 1981. Bar: Ill. 1981, U.S. Dist. Ct. (no. dist.) Ill. 1981, U.S. Ct. Appeals (7th cir.) 1982. Research asst. Chgo. Urban League, 1963-64; exec. dir. Commn. on Human Relations, Kansas City, Kans., 1967-72, dir. Maywood, Ill., 1972-82; sole practice, 1982-84; dir. lawyer referral service Chgo. Bar Assn., 1984—. Bd. dirs. Project Equality of Ill., Chgo., 1982-87, Augustana Coll., Rock Island, Ill., 1982-90, Delaney Theater Co., Oak Park, Ill., 1985-86; mem. adv. bd. Near West Suburban Housing Ctr., Westchester, Ill., 1982-88; mem. council St. John's Luth. Ch., Maywood, Ill., 1977-84, 86-96, synod council Met. Chgo. Synod Evang. Luth. Ch. in Am., 1987-93, Emmanuel Luth. Ch., Maywood, Ill., 1998—. Recipient Alumni Achievement award Midland Luth. Coll., Fremont, 1982. Mem. ABA, Ill. State Bar Assn., Chgo. Bar Assn., Cook County Legal Assistance Found. (bd. dirs. 1972-74, 82-86, chmn. personnel com. 1984-85), Maywood C. of C. (bd. dirs. 1983-86), Delta Theta Phi. Avocations: reading, listening to music, sewing, travel. Home: 2027 S 11th Ave Maywood IL 60153-3113 Office: Chgo Bar Assn Lawyer Referral Service 321 S Plymouth Ct Chicago IL 60604-3912

PAVELA, GARY MICHAEL, legal educator, administrator; b. Albuquerque, June 25, 1946; s. Harold Jack and Mae (Dennison) P.; m. Margaret Ann Potts, Apr. 17, 1982; 1 son, Gregory Michael. B.A., Lawrence Coll., 1968; M.A., Conn. Wesleyan U., 1970, M.A., 1970; J.D., U. Ill.-Champaign, 1973. Bar: N.Y. 1976. Law clk. U.S. Ct. Appeals, 10th cir., Oklahoma City, 1973-74; asst. dean Colgate U., 1974-76; asst. counsel State of N.Y., Albany, 1976-78; dir. jud. programs U. Md.-College Park, 1978— ; cons. Fed. Jud. Ctr., Washington, 1979. Mem. editorial bd. Jour. College and University Law, 1984— ; contbr. articles to law revs.; co-author: Administering College and University Housing, 1983; author Dismissal of Students with Mental Disorders, 1984. Magistrate, N.Y. Cts., Hamilton, 1975-76. U. Wis. Ctr. for Behavioral Sci. and Law fellow, 1974. Mem. Phi Beta Kappa. Democrat. Unitarian. Home: 5906 Westchester Park Dr College Park MD 20740-2802 Office: Judicial Programs U Md 2108 A North Adminstrn Bldg College Park MD 20783

PAVIA, GEORGE M. lawyer; b. Genoa, Italy, Feb. 14, 1928; s. Enrico L. and Nelly (Welisch) P.; m. Ellen Salomon, June 15, 1952; children—Andrew, Alison; m. 2d, Antonia Pearse, Dec. 2, 1976; children— Julian, Philippa. B.A., Columbia U., 1948, LL.B., 1951; postgrad. U. Genoa, 1954-55. Bar: N.Y. 1951, U.S. Supreme Ct. 1956, U.S. Dist. Ct. (so. and ea. dists.) N.Y. 1956. Assoc., Fink & Pavia, N.Y.C., 1955-65; sr. ptnr. Pavia & Harcourt, N.Y.C., 1965— . Served to capt. JAGC, U.S. Army, 1951-54. Mem. ABA, Internat. Law Soc., Consular Law Soc. General corporate, Private international. Home: 18 E 73rd St New York NY 10021-4130 Office: 600 Madison Ave New York NY 10022-1615

PAWLIK, JAMES DAVID, lawyer, historian; b. Cleve., May 26, 1958; s. Eugene Joseph and Eleanor Therese Marie (Gorzelanczyk) P. BA cum laude, Ohio State U., 1980, MA, 1991; JD cum laude, Harvard U., 1983. Bar: Calif. 1984, U.S. Dist. Ct. (no. dist.) Calif. 1984, U.S. Ct. Appeals (9th cir.), 1985, U.S. Dist. Ct. (ctrl. and ea. dists.), Calif. 1986, Ohio 1990, U.S. Ct. Appeals (6th cir.) 1994, U.S. Dist. Ct. (no. and so. dists.) Ohio 2001. Intern Dept. Def., Washington, 1980; assoc. Chandler, Wood, Harrington & Maffly, San Francisco, 1983-87, ptnr., 1988-89; teaching assoc. Ohio State U., 1990-91; pvt. practice Law Offices of James D. Pawlik, Cleve., 1991-93; ind. contractor Gallagher, Sharp, Fulton & Norman, 1992-93; jud. law clk. to Hon. Robert J. Krupansky U.S. Ct. Appeals (6th cir.), 1993—. Instr. dept. history Cuyahoga C.C., Parma, Ohio, 1993—; instr. dept. polit. sci. Lourdes Coll., Sylvania, Ohio, 1993; co-founder, co-owner The Vicar Sauce Co. Ltd., 2000—. Mem. staff Harvard Internat. Law Jour., 1981-83. Campaign mgr. for city coun. candidate, Westerville, Ohio, 1977; bd. trustees Midpark H.S. Alumni Assn., 1999—, vice chair, 2000—. William Green Meml. scholar 1979, Kosciuszko scholar 1989-91; Ohio State U. fellow, 1989-90; named Midpark H.S. Acad. Hall of Fame, 1997. Mem. AAUP, State Bar Ohio, Fed. Bar Assn., Mensa, Ohio State U. Alumni Assn., Harvard Alumni Assn., Ohio State U. Undergrad. Student Govt. Alumni Assn., Phi Beta Kappa, Phi Kappa Phi, Phi Alpha Theta. E-mail: jdpesq546@msn.com

PAYMENT, KENNETH ARNOLD, lawyer; b. Rochester, N.Y., Aug. 6, 1941; s. Arnold F. and Eleanor J. (Kinsey) P.; m. Jane A. Conrad, Aug. 16, 1996; children: Simone, Elise, Ryan. BS, Union Coll., Schenectady, 1963; LLB, Cornell U., 1966. Bar: N.Y. 1966, U.S. Dist. Ct. (we. dist.) N.Y. 1967, U.S. Ct. Appeals (2d cir.) 1968, U.S. Supreme Ct. 1989. Assoc. Wiser, Shaw, Freeman, Van Graafeiland, Harter & Secrest, Rochester, 1966-75, ptnr. Harter, Secrest & Emery, 1975—; instr. Rochester Inst. Tech., 1969, U. Rochester, 1970, Cornell U. Law Sch., Ithaca, N.Y., spring 1971-72. Mem. ABA, N.Y. State Bar Assn. (chmn. constrn. and suretyship div. 1978), Monroe County Bar Assn. (trustee), Rochester C. of C., Best Lawyers in Am. (bus. litigation 1989—), Cornell Club (N.Y.C.). Presbyterian. Antitrust, Federal civil litigation, State civil litigation. Home: 268 Harmon Rd Churchville NY 14428-9518 Office: Harter Secrest & Emery 700 Midtown Tower Rochester NY 14604-2006

PAYNE, LUCY ANN SALSBURY, law librarian, educator, lawyer; b. Utica, N.Y., July 5, 1952; d. James Henry and Dorothy Eileen (Seavy) Salsbury; m. Albert E. Payne, June 2, 1973 (div. 1983); 1 child, Joni Eileen. MusB, Andrews U., 1974; MA, Loma Linda (Calif.) U., 1979; JD, U. Notre Dame, Ind., 1988; MLS, U. Mich., 1990. Bar: Ind. 1988, Mich. 1988, U.S. Dist. Ct. (no. and so. dists.) Ind. 1988, U.S. Ct. Appeals (7th cir.) 1992. Rsch. specialist Kresge Libr. Law Sch. U. Notre Dame, 1988-90, asst. libr., 1990-91, assoc. libr., 1991-96, librarian, 1996—. Vis. prof. Notre Dame London Law Programme, 2001. Contbr. articles to profl. jours. Recipient Rev. Paul J. Foik award, 2001. Mem. ABA, Am. Assn. Law Librs., Mich. Bar Assn., Ind. Bar Assn., Ohio Regional Assn. Law Librs., Mich. Assn. Law Librs., St. Joseph County Bar Assn. Adventist. Office: U Notre Dame Law Sch Kresge Law Libr Notre Dame IN 46556

PAYNE, MARGARET ANNE, lawyer; b. Aug. 10, 1947; d. John Hilliard and Margaret Mary (Naughton) P. Student, Trinity Coll., Washington, 1965-66; BA magna cum laude, U. Cin., 1969; JD, Harvard U., 1972; LLM in Taxation, NYU, 1976. Bar: N.Y. 1975, U.S. Dist. Ct. (so. dist.) N.Y. 1975, Calif. 1979, U.S. Dist. Ct. (so. dist.) Calif. 1979. Assoc. Mudge, Rose, Guthrie, and Alexander, N.Y.C., 1972-75, Davis, Polk and Wardwell, N.Y.C., 1976-78, Seltzer, Caplan, Wilkins and McMahon, San Diego, 1978-79, Higgs, Fletcher and Mack, San Diego, 1980-82, ptnr., 1983-90, of counsel, 1991—. Adj. prof. grad. tax program U. San Diego Sch. Law, 1979-89, Calif. Western Sch. Law, San Diego, 1980-82; judge pro tem Mcpl. Ct., San Diego Jud. Dist., 1983, 92. Bd. dirs. Artist Chamber Ensemble, Inc., 1983-86, Libr. Assn. La Jolla, Calif., 1983-86, San Diego County Crimestoppers, Inc., 1993-95, San Diego Crime Commn., 1994-95, St. Augustine's H.S., 1994-95, San Diego Hist. Soc., 1993-95. Mem. ABA, Calif. State Bar Assn., San Diego County Bar Assn., Mortar Bd., Guidon Soc., Charter 100, Phi Beta Kappa. Estate planning, Probate, Estate taxation. Office: Higgs Fletcher & Mack 401 W A St Ste 2600 San Diego CA 92101-7913

PAYNE, MARY LIBBY, retired judge; b. Gulfport, Miss., Mar. 27, 1932; d. Reece O. and Emily Augusta (Cook) Bickerstaff; m. Bobby R. Payne; children: Reece Allen, Glenn Russell. Student, Miss. U. for Women, 1950-52; BA in Polit. Sci. with distinction, U. Miss., 1954, LLB, 1955. Bar: Miss. 1955. Ptnr. Bickerstaff & Bickerstaff, Gulfport, 1955-56; sec. Guaranty Title Co., Jackson, Miss., 1957; assoc. Henley, Jones, & Henley, 1958-61; freelance rschr. Pearl, 1961-63; solo practitioner Brandon, 1963-68; exec. dir. Miss. Judiciary Commn., Jackson, 1968-70; chief drafting & rsch. Miss. Ho. Reps., 1970-72; asst. atty. gen. State Atty. Gen. Office, 1972-75; founding dean, assoc. prof. Sch. Law Miss. Coll., 1975-78, prof., 1978-94; judge Miss. Ct. Appeals, 1995—2001; ret., 2001. Mem. bd. disting. alumnae Miss. U. Women, 1988—2000. Contbr. articles to profl. jours. Founder, bd. dirs. Christian Conciliation Svc., Jackson, 1983-93; bd. dirs. Exchange Club's Child Abuse Prevention Ctr. of Jackson, 1999—; counsel Christian Action Com. Rankin Bapt. Assn., Pearl, 1968-92; advisor Covenant Ministerial Fellowship, 1995—. Named Miss. Coll. Lawyer of Yr., Miss. Coll. Sch. Law Alumni Assn., 1998, Outstanding Woman Lawyer, Miss. Women Lawyers Assn., 1999, Susie Blue Buchanan award, Women in Profession Com. of Miss. Bar, 2000; recipient Book of Golden Deeds award, Pearl Exch. Club, 1989, Excellence medallion, Miss. U. Women, 1990, Woman of Yr. award, Miss. Assn. Women Higher Edn., 1989, Power of One award, Miss. Govs. Conf., 1996. Fellow Am. Bar Found.; mem. Miss. Bar Found., Christian Legal Soc. (nat. bd. dirs. 1992-2001, Skeeter Ellis Svc. to Law Students award 1999), Margaret Brent League. Baptist. Avocations: public speaking, travel, needlepoint, sewing, reading.

PAYNE, ROY STEVEN, judge; b. New Orleans, Aug. 30, 1952; s. Fred J. and Dorothy Julia (Peck) P.; m. Laureen Fuller, Sept. 8, 1973; children: Julie Elizabeth, Kelly Kathryn, Alex Steven, Michael Lawrence. BA with distinction, U. Va., 1974; JD, La. State U., 1977; LLM, Harvard U., 1980. Bar: La. 1977, U.S. Dist. Ct. (we. dist.) La. 1980, U.S. Ct. Appeals (5th cir.) 1980, U.S. Supreme Ct. 1983. Law clk. to judge U.S. Dist. Ct., Shreveport, La., 1977-79; assoc. Blanchard, Walker, O'Quin & Roberts, 1980-83, ptnr., 1984-87; U.S. Magistrate judge We. Dist. La., 1987—. Instr. New Eng. Sch. Law, Boston, 1979-80. Contbr. articles to profl. jours. Chmn. Northwest La. Legal Svcs. Assn., Shreveport, 1984-85. Mem. 5th Cir. Bar Assn., 5th Cir. Jud. Coun. (magistrate judges com. 1992—), La. State Bar Assn. (editorial bd. Forum jour., 1983-87, legal aid com.), Fed. Magistrate Judges Assn., Shreveport Bar Assn., La. Assn. Def. Counsel (bd. dirs. 1987), Harry V. Booth Am. Inn of Ct. (pres. elect 1994-95, pres. 1996-98), Order of Coif, Rotary, Phi Kappa Phi, Phi Delta Phi. Republican. Methodist. E-mail: Roy. Home: 12494 Harts Island Rd Shreveport LA 71115-8505 Office: US Courthouse 300 Fannin St Ste 4300 Shreveport LA 71101-3122 E-mail: Payne@lawd.uscourts.gov

PAYTON, JOHN, lawyer; BA, Pomona Coll.; JD, Harvard U. Corp. counsel D.C., 1991—94; ptnr. Wilmer, Cutler & Pickering. Mem.: D.C. Bar (pres. 2001—). Contracts commercial, Civil rights, Libel. Office: Wilmer Cutler & Pickering 2445 M St NW Washington DC 20037*

PEAR, CHARLES E., JR. lawyer; b. Macon, Ga., June 18, 1950; s. Charles Edward and Barbara Jane P.; m. Linda Sue King; children: Jennifer Sue, Charles Edward III, Stephanie Sue. BA, U. Hawaii, 1972 with honors; JD, U. Calif., Berkeley, 1975. Bar: Hawaii 1976, Fla. 1977, Colo. 1994, U.S. Ct. of Appeals (9th cir.). Assoc. Rush, Moore, Craven, Sutton, Morry & Beh, Honolulu, 1976-77, of counsel, 1987-90; assoc., ptnr. Carlsmith & Dwyer, 1977-82; ptnr. Burke, Sakai, McPheeters, Bordner & Gilardy, 1983-87; vis. prof. law and computers U. British Columbia, 1990-93; of counsel Holland & Hart, Denver, 1993-96; counsel, ptnr. McCorriston, Miller, Mukai, MacKinnon, Honolulu, 1996—. Mem. Hawaii Real Estate Commn. com. on condominium and resort real estate legis., 1978-79; spl. counsel to consumer protection com. Hawaii State Ho. of Reps., 1981-82; chair real property and fin. svcs. sect. Hawaii State Bar Assn., ABA. Editor-in-Chief Hawaii Conveyance Manual II, 1987; editor Hawaii Commercial Real Estate Manual, 1988; bd. editors Hawaii Inst. of Continuing Legal Edn.; co-author: Nat. Assn. of Real Estate Licensing Law Officials and Nat. Timesharing Coun. Model Timesharing Act, 1981-82; contbg. author: Winning With Computers, 1992, Hawaii Real Estate Manual, 1997; lectr. in field, 1981—. Mem. ABA (document assembly interest group, expert sys. interest group, hypermedia interest group). Computer, Finance, Real property.

PEARCE, HARRY JONATHAN, lawyer; b. Bismarck, N.D., Aug. 20, 1942; s. William R. and Jean Katherine (Murray) P.; m. Katherine B. Bruk, June 19, 1967; children: Shannon Pearce Baker, Susan J., Harry M. BS, USAF Acad., Colorado Springs, Colo., 1964; JD, Northwestern U., 1967; Degree in Engring. (hon.), Rose-Hulman Inst. Tech., 1997; LLD (hon.), Northwestern U., 1998. Bar: N.D. 1967, Mich. 1986. Mcpl. judge City of Bismarck, 1970-76, U.S. magistrate, 1970-76, police commr., 1976-80; sr. ptnr. Pearce & Durick, Bismarck, 1970-85; assoc. gen. counsel GM, Detroit, 1985-87, v.p., gen. counsel, 1987-92, exec. v.p., gen. counsel, 1992-94, exec. v.p., 1994-95, vice chmn., 1996—. Bd. dirs. GM Corp., Hughes Electronics Corp., GM Acceptance Corp., Delphi Automotive Sys. Corp., Alliance of Automobile Mfrs. of Marriott Internat. Inc., Econ. Strategy Inst., Theodore Roosevelt Medora Found., MDU Resources Group, Inc., Nat. Def. U. Found., Detroit Investment Fund. Mem. law bd. Sch. Law, Northwestern U.; mem. bd. visitors U.S. Air Force Acad.; chmn. Product Liability Adv. Coun. Found.; founding mem. minority counsel demonstration program Commn. on Opportunities for Minorities in the Profession, ABA; chmn. The Sabre Soc., USAF Acad.; trustee Howard U., U.S. Coun. for Internat. Bus., New Detroit, Inc.; mem. The Mentor's Group Forum for U.S.-European Union Legal-Econ. Affairs, The Conf. Bd., Network of Employers for Traffic Safety's Leadership Coun., Pres.'s Coun. on Sustainable Devel., World Bus. Coun. for Sustainable Devel., World Economic Forum Coun. Innovative Leaders in Globalization. Capt. USAF,

1964-70. Named Michiganian of Yr., The Detroit News, 1997; Hardy scholar Northwestern U., Chgo., 1964-67, recipient Alumni Merit award, 1991. Fellow Am. Coll. Trial Lawyers, Internat. Soc. Barristers; mem. Am. Law Inst. Avocations: amateur radio, woodworking, sailing. General corporate. Office: GM Corp 300 Renaissance Ctr PO Box 100 Detroit MI 48265-1000

PEARCE, JOHN Y. lawyer; b. New Orleans, Mar. 26, 1948; s. John Young II and Marina (Harris) P.; m. Marjorie Pamela Doyle, May 22, 1971 (div.); children: Andrea Elizabeth, Roger Wellington. BA, La. State U., 1973, JD, 1976. Bar: La. 1977, U.S. Dist. Ct. (ea., mid. and we. dists.) La., U.S. Ct. Claims, U.S. Ct. Appeals (5th and 11th cirs.). Assoc. Doyle, Smith & Doyle, New Orleans, 1977-79, ptnr., 1979-80, mng. ptnr., 1980-84; ptnr. Montgomery, Barnett, Brown, Read, Hammond & Mintz, 1984—. Sgt. U.S. Army, 1969-71. Mem. ABA (ho. dels. 1998-2000), La. Bar Assn. (chmn. mineral law coun. 1994-95), New Orleans Bar Assn. (exec. com., pres. 1997-98). Republican. Episcopalian. General civil litigation, Oil, gas, and mineral, Environmental. Office: Montgomery Barnett Brown Read Hammond & Mintz 1100 Poydras St New Orleans LA 70163-1101

PEARLMAN, MICHAEL ALLEN, lawyer; b. Phila., Sept. 22, 1946; s. William and Mary (Stark) P.; m. Ann Gerald, June 1, 1969; children: Benjamin, Amy. BA, Duke U., 1968, JD, 1970. Bar: N.C. 1970, D.C. 1971, U.S. Dist. Ct. (mid. dist.) N.C. 1973, N.Y. 1982, Ct. Internat. Trade 1982. Atty. FTC, Washington, 1970-73; assoc. gen. counsel, asst. sec. Fieldcrest Mills, Inc., Eden, N.C., 1973-81; counsel GE, Syracuse, N.Y., 1981-85; corp. counsel Eastman Kodak Co., Rochester, 1985-96, internat. counsel, 1997-98, dir. legal affairs L.Am. region, 1998-2001; v.p., gen. counsel PictureVision, Inc., 2001—. Pres. ctrl. and western N.Y. chpt. Am. Corp. Counsel Assn., 1992-93. Pres. Rockingham County Arts Coun., N.C., 1979-80. Mem. Duke Law Sch. Alumni Assn. (bd. dirs. 1994-97). General corporate, Private international, Mergers and acquisitions. Home: 864 Station St Herndon VA 20170 Office: Eastman Kodak Co 520 Herndon Pky Herndon VA 20170 E-mail: michael.pearlman@picturevision.com

PEARLMAN, PETER STEVEN, lawyer; b. Orange, N.J., June 11, 1946; s. Jack Kitchener and Tiela Josephine (Fine) P.; m. Joan Perlmutter, June 19, 1969; children: Heather, Christopher, Megan. BA, U. Ill., 1967; JD, Seton Hall U., 1970. Bar: N.J. 1970, U.S. Dist. Ct. N.J. 1970, U.S. Tax Ct. 1973, U.S. Supreme Ct. 1974, U.S. Ct. Appeals (2d cir.) 1981, U.S. Ct. Appeals (3d cir.) 1983, U.S. Ct. Appeals (7th cir.) 1985, U.S. Ct. Appeals (D.C. cir.) 1998, U.S. Ct. Appeals (4th cir.) 1999, U.S. Ct. Claims 2000; cert. civil trial atty., 1982. Assoc. Cohn & Lifland, Esquires, Saddle Brook, N.J., 1970-72; ptnr. Cohn, Lifland, Pearlman, Herrmann & Knopf, 1972—. Lectr. Nat. Inst. Trial Advocacy, Hempstead, N.Y., 1988—; active trial advocacy program Widener Law Sch.; adj. faculty mem. trial advocacy program Hofstra Law Sch.; master C. Willard Heckel Inn of Ct.; guest lectr. appellate advocacy Roger Williams Law Sch., 1995—; mem. panel arbitrators Am. Arbitration Assn.; lectr. for Inst. Continuing Legal Edn. for State of N.J. Mem. ABA, ATLA, N.J. Bar Assn. Federal civil litigation, State civil litigation, General corporate. Home: 9 Harvey Dr Short Hills NJ 07078-1122 Office: Cohn Lifland Pearlman Herrmann & Knopf 1 Park 80 Plz W Ste 4 Saddle Brook NJ 07663-5808 E-mail: psp@njlawfirm.com

PEARLMAN, SAMUEL SEGEL, lawyer, educator; b. Pitts., May 28, 1942; s. Merle Maurice and Bernice Florence (Segel) P.; m. Cathy Schwartz, Aug. 16, 1964; children: Linda P. Kraner, Caren E. AB, U. Pa., 1963, LLB magna cum laude, 1966. Bar: Pa. 1966, Ohio 1967, U.S. Ct. Appeals (3d cir.) 1967. Law clk. U.S. Dist. Ct. for Ea. Dist. Pa., Phila., 1966-67; assoc. Burke, Haber & Berick, Cleve., 1967-72, prin., 1973-86, Berick, Pearlman & Mills, Cleve., 1986-99; ptnr. Squire, Sanders & Dempsey L.L.P., 2000—. Lectr. law Case Western Res. U. Sch. Law, 1978-82; mem. registration com. Ohio Div. Securities, 1979-89; adv. dir. Midland Title Security, Inc.; trustee Realty ReFund Trust, N.Y. Stock Exch., 1990-98. Author: Cases, Forms and Materials for Modern Real Estate Transactions, 1978, 82. Mem. ABA, Ohio Bar Assn., Greater Cleve. Bar Assn. (chmn. securities law sect. 1985-86), Order of Coif. Republican. Jewish. General corporate, Finance, Real property. Office: Squire Sanders & Dempsey 4900 Key Tower 127 Public Sq Ste 4900 Cleveland OH 44114-1304 E-mail: spearlman@ssd.com

PEARMAN, ROBERT CHARLES, lawyer; b. N.Y.C., Apr. 2, 1953; s. Robert C. and Audrey Joyce (Ketchens) P. BS in Econs. cum laude, U. Pa., 1974; JD, Yale U., 1977. Assoc. Kadison, Pfaelzer, Woodard, Quinn & Rossi, L.A., 1977-81; pvt. practice, 1981-84; ptnr. Robinson & Pearman, 1984—. Foreclosure commr. HUD, 1995; spkr., cons. in field. Mem. editl. bd. L.A. Lawyer 1989-93, editor ann. real estate issue, 1989-93; contbr. articles to profl. jours. Chmn. Polit. Action Com. Assn. of Minority Real Estate Developers, L.A., 1983; mem. L.A. County Assessment Appeals Bd., 1991-94, Transp. Commn. City of Oceanside (Calif.); mem. neighborhood planning bd. L.A. City 8th Coun. Dist., 1993-98; former bd. dirs. Homeowners Helping the Homeless, Opportunities Industrialization Ctr., L.A., Crenshaw Neighborhood Devel. Corp.; dir. L.A. Neighborhood Initiative/Leimert, 1994—, Nat. Housing Law Project, 1995—. Mem. Nat. Bus. League, Am. Pub. Transit Assn., Bldg. Industry Assn. (home builders coun.), Assn. Corp. Real Estate Execs., State Bar Calif. (mem. exec. com. real property law sect., vice-chmn. exec. com. ethnic minority rels., exec. com. real property law sect. 1991-95, exec. com. pub. law sect. 2000—), Los Angeles County Bar Assn. (real property, bus. and corps., comml. law and bankruptcy sects.), Mensa, Phi Delta Phi. Roman Catholic. General corporate, Real property, Transportation. Home: 2351 Short Hill Dr Oceanside CA 92056-3610 Office: Robinson & Pearman 700 S Flower St Ste 1100 Los Angeles CA 90017-4113 E-mail: rpllp@tcorp.net

PEARSALL, JOHN WESLEY, lawyer; b. Richmond, Va., Aug. 21, 1914; BS, Randolph-Macon Coll., 1935; LLB, U. Richmond, 1941. Bar: Va. 1940. Assoc. McGuire, Riely & Eggleston, Richmond, 1941-50; ptnr. McGuire, Eggleston, Bocock & Woods, 1950-53; gen. counsel Va.-Carolina Chem. Corp., 1953-56; sole practice, 1956-60; ptnr. McCaul, Grigsby & Pearsall, 1960-86, Pearsall & Pearsall, 1986—; gen. counsel, dir. Estes Express Lines, 1972—. Chpt. chmn. ARC, Chesterfield County, Va., 1944-49, campaign chmn., 1949, campaign chmn. Richmond, Henrico, and Chesterfield, Va., 1950, nat. vice chmn. fund dr., 1956, nat. gov., 1953-55; mem. budget com. Richmond Area Community Chest, 1946-47, mem. exec. com., 1947-55, trustee, 1946-50, campaign chmn., 1951, pres., 1955, United Giver's Fund, 1970; v.p. Children's Aid Soc., Richmond, 1950-55, trustee, 1948-55; active Boy Scouts Am., 1953-56; mem. exec. com. Randolph-Macon Coll., 1958-76, chmn. long range plan com., 1960-76, trustee, 1955-76, mem. alumni bd., 1994-99; mem. Chesterfield County Welfare Bd., 1951-55; trustee Sheltering Arms Hosp., Richmond, 1949-80; dir. Jr. Achievement, 1975-81; vestryman St. Stephens Ch., 1967-70, ch. bearer, 1986-87; mem. exec. com. Hist. Richmond Found. (1965-70), Falls of James adv. bd., 1979—, Chesterfield Hist. Soc., 1985-95. Served to lt. j.g. USNR, 1944-46. Mem. ABA, Va. Bar Assn., Richmond Bar Assn., Chesterfield County Bar Assn. (pres. 1963-64), Am. Judicature Soc., Va. State Bar Council (chmn. judicial ethics com. 1970-71), Am. Archaeol. Soc. (local chpt., pres. 1976), Phi Beta Kappa (pres. Richmond area chpt. 1976-77), Jr. C. of C. (Disting. Svc. award 1948, state pres. 1948-49), Omicron Delta Kappa, Lambda Chi Alpha. State civil litigation, General corporate, General practice. Home: 7701 Riverside Dr Richmond VA 23225-1036 Office: Ellen Glasgow House 1 W Main St Richmond VA 23220-5623

PEARSON, CHARLES THOMAS, JR. lawyer, director; b. Fayetteville, Ark., Oct. 14, 1929; s. Charles Thomas and Doris (Pinkerton) P.; m. Wyma Lee Hampton, Sept. 9, 1988; children: Linda Sue, John Paddock. B.S., U. Ark., 1953, J.D., 1954; postgrad., U.S. Naval Postgrad. Sch., 1959; A.M., Boston U., 1963. Bar: Ark. bar 1954. Practice in, Fayetteville, 1963—. Dir. officer N.W. Comms., Inc., Dixieland Devel., Inc., Jonlin Investments, Inc., World Wide Travel Svc., Inc., Okliania Farms, Inc., N.W. Arl. Land & Devel., Inc., Garden Plaza Inns, Inc. Word Data, Inc., M.P.C. Farms, Inc., Fayetteville Enterprises, Inc., NWA Devel.Co., Delta Comm., Inc.; past. dir., organizer N.W. Nat. Bank. Adviser Explorer Scouts, 1968— ; past pres. Washington County Draft Bd.; past pres. bd. Salvation Army. Served to comdr. Judge Adv. Gen. Corps USNR, 1955-63. Mem. ABA, Ark. Bar Assn., Washington County Bar Assn., Judge Advs. Assn., N.W. Ark. Ret. Officers Assn. (past pres.), Methodist Men (past pres), U. Ark. Alumni Assn. (past dir.), Sigma Chi (past pres. N.W. Ark. alumni, past chmn. house corp.), Alpha Kappa Psi, Phi Eta Sigma, Delta Theta Phi. Republican. Methodist. Clubs: Mason (32 deg., K.T., Shriner), Moose, Elk, Lion, Metropolitan. General practice, Personal injury, Real property. Office: 9 N College Ave Fayetteville AR 72701-5301 E-mail: tpesq1101@aol.com

PEARSON, DAVID BROOKSBANK, lawyer, educator; b. Springfield, Mo., Mar. 6, 1935; s. Otis Brackingham and Mary Helen (Brooksbank) P.; m. Betty Jean Sloan, Feb. 5, 1955; children— Marlon Kim, Julie Michele Logan. Student Los Angeles City Coll., 1958-59, U.C.L.A., 1982-84, USC, 1980; LL.B., LaSalle Sch. Law, 1967. Bar: Calif. 1967, U.S. Dist. Ct. Calif. 1967, U.S. Supreme Ct. 1971, U.S. Ct. Appeals (9th cir.) Calif. 1973; cert. in criminal law Calif. Bd. Legal Specialization. Dep. sheriff Los Angeles County Sheriff, 1960-62; Dist. Atty.'s investigator Los Angeles County Dist. Atty., 1962-67; dep. dist. atty., 1967-69, 1969-93; sole practice, Los Angeles, 1969; prof. criminal law Glendale Sch. Law, 1972-75, USC Law Center, 1981, Beverly Sch. Law, 1976, USC Sch. Pub. Adminstrn., 1984; adj. prof. Pepperdine Law Sch., Malibu, Calif., 1977-84; asst. prof. clin. law USC Sch. Psychiatry and Law, 1976- 78; instr. Cerritos Coll. Norwalk, Calif., 1972-75; lectr. Nat. Coll. Dist. Attys., Houston, 1975-84; Calif. Inst. for Trial Advocacy Skills, Los Angeles, 1979-80; Calif. Continuing Edn. of the Bar, 1979-84, Rossi-Field Center for Clinical Hypnotherapy, 1983; faculty mem. Los Angeles Coll. Trial Advocacy, 1979-84; tech. adv. Columbia Pictures TV, 1978; legal advisor Atty. Coun. Altanta, 1993-. Editor, author booklet Law Enforcement Legal Bulletin, 1980. Inventor parlor game 1979. Adv. bd. mem. El Camino Coll., Torrance, Calif., 1976-84; active mem. Nat. Conf. Christians and Jews criminal justice com., Los Angeles, 1983-84, Crime, Violence and Vandalism on Campus Com., Los Angeles, 1976-84. Served as pfc. USMCR, 1953-57. Named Heavy Weight Boxing Champion Sr. Olympics, 1977-79; Recipient Western States Police Pistol Combat Champion Team award Nat. Rifle Assn., 1965; Outstanding Contribution to Youth award Constl. Rights Found., 1975-77; Disting. Faculty award Nat. Coll. Dist. Attys., 1982. Mem. Calif. Dist. Attys. Assn., Assn. Dep. Dist. Attys., ABA, South Bay Policetraining Assn., Southeast Policetraining Assn., Northeast Police Training Assn. Home: 3139 S Las Marias Ave Hacienda Heights CA 91745-6219

PEARSON, HENRY CLYDE, judge; b. Ocoonita Lee County, Va., Mar. 12, 1925; s. Henry James and Nancy Elizabeth (Seals) P.; m. Jean Calton, July 26, 1956; children: Elizabeth, Frances, Timothy Clyde. Student, Union Coll., 1947-49; LLB, U. Richmond, 1952. Bar: Va. 1952, U.S. Ct. Appeals (4th cir.) 1957, U.S. Supreme Ct. 1958. Sole practice, Jonesville, Va., 1952-56; asst. U.S. atty. Western Dist. Va., Roanoke, 1956-61; ptnr. Hopkins, Pearson & Engleby, 1956-61; judge U.S. Bankruptcy Ct. Western Dist. Va., 1970-98; ret., 1998. Participant Va. Continuing Edn. Seminars; mem. adv. com. fed. rules bankruptcy procedure; mem. Va. Ho. of Reps., 1954-56, Va. Senate, 1968-70; Republican nominee Gov. of Va., 1961. Editl. bd. Am. Survey Bankruptcy Law, 1979. Served with USN, 1943-46, PTO. Mem. Va. State Bar, ABA, Va. Trial Lawyers Assn., Assn. Trial Lawyers Am., Am. Judicature Soc., Am. Judges Assn., Fed. Bar Assn., Delta Theta Phi, Tribune Jefferson Senate, Am. Legion, VFW, Masons, Shriners. Methodist. Office: 1910 Mcvitty Rd Salem VA 24153-7406

PEARSON, JOHN EDWARD, lawyer; b. Jamaica, N.Y., Aug. 20, 1946; s. Stanley Charles and Rose Margaret (Manning) P.; m. Laura Marie Johannes, Dec. 28, 1968; children: Laura Rose, Jack. BA, Manhattan Coll., 1968; JD, St. John's U., 1972. Bar: N.Y. 1973, Fla. 1981, U.S. Dist. Ct. (so. dist.) N.Y. 1977, U.S. Dist. Ct. (so. dist.) Fla. 1982, U.S. Ct. Appeals (11th cir.) 1982, U.S. Ct. Appeals (5th cir.) 1982. Assoc. Sage, Gray, Todd & Sims, N.Y.C., 1972-78, ptnr., 1979, Miami, Fla., 1980-87, Hughes, Hubbard & Reed, Miami, 1987-91, 94-98, counsel, 1998—, ptnr. N.Y.C., 1992-93. Author jour. article (Best Article award 1971). With USMCR, 1968-69. Mem. ABA, Fla. Bar Assn., N.Y. State Bar Assn., Assn. Bar City N.Y., Dade County Bar Assn., N.Y. County Lawyers Assn., Greater Miami C. of C. (trustee). Republican. Roman Catholic. Avocations: sailing, running. Finance, Real property. Home: 161 Island Dr Key Biscayne FL 33149-2409 Office: Hughes Hubbard & Reed 201 S Biscayne Blvd Ste 2500 Miami FL 33131-4305 E-mail: jep8436@aol.com

PEARSON, JOHN YEARDLEY, JR. lawyer; b. Norfolk, Va., July 23, 1942; BA, Washington & Lee U., 1964; JD, U. Va., 1971. Bar: Va. 1971. Atty. Willcox & Savage P.C., Norfolk, Va. Bd. editors: Va. Law Rev., 1969-71. Fellow Am. Coll. Trial Lawyers; mem. ABA (mem. litigation, tort and ins. practice sects.), Va. Assn. Def. Attys., Order of Coif. General civil litigation, Product liability, Professional liability. Office: Willcox & Savage PC 1800 Bank of America Ctr Norfolk VA 23510-2197

PEARSON, PAUL DAVID, lawyer, mediator; b. Boston, Jan. 22, 1940; s. Bernard J. and Ruth (Bayla) Horblit; m. Carol A. Munschauer; children: David Todd, Lisa Kari, Grant M. BA, Bucknell U., 1961; LLB, U. Pa., 1964. Bar: Mass. 1966, N.Y. 1987. Staff atty., tech. assoc. lab. cmty. psychiatry dept. psychiatry Med. Sch. Harvard U., Boston, 1966-68; assoc. Snyder Tepper & Berlin, 1968-71; ptnr., 1971-77; ptnr., chmn. family law dept. Hill & Barlow, 1977-87; ptnr. chmn. family law dept. Hodgson, Russ, Andrews, Woods and Goodyear, Buffalo, 1987-96; of counsel Sullivan Oliverio & Gioia, 1996—. Lectr. Mass. Con. Legal Edn., New Eng. Law Inst., dept. psychiatry SUNY, Scho. of Med., Buffalo, 1989—; instr. law and mental health Boston Psychoanalytic Soc. and Inst., 1975-87; lectr. in law, mental health, alternative dispute resolution. Contbr. articles to profl. jours. Founding mem. Alliance for Dispute Resolution, 1996; bd. dirs. Jewish Cmty. Ctr. Greater Buffalo, 1991-96, Am. Jewish Com. Buffalo, 1991—, pres., 1995-97, nat. bd. govs., 1997—; bd. dirs. Arts Coun. Buffalo and Erie County, 1992-99; legal coord. Parent Edn. And Custody Effectiveness program N.Y. 8th jud. dist.; pres., trustee, legal counsel Wayland (Mass.) Townhouse; trustee Family Counseling Svc. (region West); mem., chmn., clk. Wayland Zoning Bd. Appeals, 1970-80; v.p., counsel Arts Wayland Found., 1982-87; vis. fellow Woodrow Wilson Found., 1985-87, Mass. Gov.'s Spl. Commn. on Divorce, 1985-87. Capt. Mil. Police Corps USAR. Fellow Am. Acad. Matrimonial Lawyers (pres., bd. mgrs. Mass); mem. Mass. Bar Assn. (chmn. family law sect.), Assn. Conflict Resolution (advanced practitioner), N.Y. State Coun. on Divorce Mediation, Assn. Family and Conciliation Cts., Boston Bar Assn. (family law com., legis. chmn.), N.Y. Bar Assn. (family law com., ADR com.), Erie County Bar Assn. (chmn. alternative dispute resolution com. 1992-96, family law com.). Alternative dispute resolution, Family and matrimonial, Probate. Home: 605 Lebrun Rd Amherst NY 14226-4232 Office: 600 Main Place Tower Buffalo NY 14202-3706 Fax: 716-854-5299. E-mail: sulliolaw@aol.com

PECCARELLI, ANTHONY MARANDO, lawyer; b. Newark, Apr. 12, 1928; s. Adolph and Mary (Marano) P.; m. Mary Dearborn Hutchison, Dec. 23, 1953; children: Andrew Louis, David Anthony, Laura Elizabeth. BS, Beloit Coll., 1953; JD, John Marshall Law Sch., 1959; M in Jud. Studies, U. Nev., 1990. Bar: Ill. 1961, U.S. Dist. Ct. (no. dist.) Ill., U.S. Supreme Ct. Supr. real estate and claims Gulf Oil Corp., Chgo., 1956-61; asst. state's atty. DuPage County, Wheaton, Ill., 1961-65; first asst. state's atty. DuPage County State's Atty., 1965-69; mem.-del. Ill. Constnl. Conv., Springfield, 1969-70; exec. dir. Ill. State's Atty. Assn., Elgin, 1970-71; ptnr. Barclay, Damisch & Sinson, Chgo., 1971-79; assoc. cir. judge 18th Jud. Cir. Ct., Wheaton, 1979-82, cir. judge, 1982-93, chief judge, 1989-93, presiding judge domestic rels. divsn., 1982-83, presiding judge law divsn., 1987-89, chief judge, 1989-93; justice 2nd dist. Ill. Appellate Ct., 1993-94; state's atty. DuPage County, Ill., 1995-96; assoc., of counsel Ottosen Trevarthen Britz Kelly & Cooper, Ltd., 1996—. Exec. Conflict Resolution Ltd.; chair Ill. Jud. Conf. Ill. Supreme Ct., Springfield, 1987-89. Contbr. articles to profl. jours. Bd. dirs., treas. DuPage Coun. for Child Devel.; bd. dirs. Ctrl. DuPage Pastoral Counseling Ctr.; chair Wheaton Com. for Jud. Reform, 1962; trustee Midwestern U., 1993—, vice chmn., bd. trustees 1997-99. Cpl. USMC, 1946-48. Mem. DuPage County Bar Assn. (pres. 1972-73), DuPage County Legal Assistance Fedn. (pres. 1973-74), DuPage County Lawyer Referral Svc. (pres. 1972). Alternative dispute resolution, Appellate, State civil litigation.

PECHACEK, FRANK WARREN, JR. lawyer; b. Winona, Minn., May 1, 1944; s. Frank Warren and Gladys (Bjoraker) P.; m. Beth E. Horn, June 4, 1966; children: Jill Ellan, Holly Jo, Frank Warren III. Student Iowa State U., 1963-64; BA with honors, U. No. Iowa, 1966; JD with honors, U. Iowa, 1969. Bar: Iowa 1969, Nebr. 1983, U.S. Dist. Ct. (so. dist.) Iowa 1969, U.S. Dist. Ct. (no. dist.) Iowa 1970, U.S. Ct. Appeals (8th cir.) 1970, U.S. Ct. Claims 1980, U.S. Tax Ct. 1982. Assoc. Smith, Peterson, Beckman & Willson, Council Bluffs, Iowa, 1969-72, ptnr., 1973— ; lectr. Iowa State U., Ames, 1973—; bd. dirs. Nebr. Venture Group, 1989—; mem. Iowa Supreme Ct. Commn. on Continuing Legal Edn., Des Moines, 1975-82. Contbr. articles to profl. jour. Chmn. Garner Twp. Republican Party, Council Bluffs, 1978-88; co-founder, bd. dirs. Pottawattamie County Taxpayers Assn., Council Bluffs, 1979— , pres. 1979-80; bd. dirs. St. John's Luth. Ch., Council Bluffs, 1979-83; co-founder, bd. dirs., pres. Southwest Iowa Ednl. Found., Inc., Council Bluffs, 1984—, pres. 1986—. Mem. Internat. Assn. Assessing Officers, ABA, Nat. Assn. Rev. Appraisers and Mortgage Underwriters (sr. mem., cert. rev. appraiser, cert.), Nat. Assn. Real Estate Appraisers, Nebr. Bar Assn., Iowa Bar Assn. Club: Kiwanis (bd. dirs. 1977-83) (Council Bluffs). Banking, General corporate, Estate planning. Home: 17 Vista Ln Council Bluffs IA 51503-9482 Office: Smith Peterson Beckman & Willson PO Box 249 Council Bluffs IA 51502-0249

PECK, KENNETH E. lawyer; b. Carson City, Nev., June 20, 1950; s. Donald Leon and Thelma Louise (Robinson) P.; m. Katherine Louise Weeks, Oct. 20, 1973; children: Jason Z., Jennifer D., Joy H., Jessica K. BA in Polit. Sci. cum laude, U. Colo., 1971; MA in Pub. Adminstrn., U. Va., 1975; JD, Georgetown U., 1979. Bar: Colo. 1979, U.S. Dist. Ct. Colo. 1979, U.S. Ct. Appeals (10th cir.) 1980, U.S. Supreme Ct. 1983. Rsch. analyst Va. Hwy. Rsch. Coun., Charlottesville, 1972-73; budget and mgmt. analyst Prince Georges County Schs., Upper Marlboro, Md., 1974-76; chief legis. asst. U.S. Rep. Paul Trible, Washington, 1977-79; atty. Holland & Hart, Denver, 1979-83, Hopper & Kanouff, Denver, 1983-85, Phelps, Singer & Dunn, Denver, 1985-90, Law Firm of Kenneth E. Peck, Denver, 1990-98, Bushell & Peck, L.L.C., Denver, 1999—. Mem. nat., regional and state adv. councils SBA, 1981-86; mem. bd. appeals U.S. Dept. Edn., Washington, 1982-84; profl. lobbyist Colo. Legis., Denver, 1983-84; nat. commr. of econ. policy 1986 White House Conf. on Small Bus. Asst. campaign mgr. Jim Tate for Congress, Fairfax, Va., 1976; bd. dirs. Jefferson County Srs.' Resource Ctr., Wheatridge, Colo., 1982-88; pres. Arvada Rep. Club, Colo., 1982; mem. bd. mgrs. Northwest YMCA, Arvada, 1982-88. William McIntyre fellow U. Va., 1971-72; law fellow Georgetown U. Law Ctr., 1976-77. Mem. ABA (litigation sect., various coms.), Colo. Bar Assn. (various coms.), Colo. Assn. Comml. Industry (chmn. small bus. legis. com. 1983-85), Denver Bar Assn. (various coms.). Republican. Mem. Ch. of Christ. Avocations: golf, hiking, coaching youth sports. General civil litigation, Personal injury, Real property. Home: 10935 W 68th Ave Arvada CO 80004-2744

PECK, LEONARD WARREN, JR. lawyer; b. El Paso, Tex., June 3, 1948; s. Leonard Warren and Perry Elizabeth (Lewis) P.; m. Johanna Lee Blaschke, July 23, 1976; 1 child, Margaret Elizabeth. AB, Harvard U., 1970; JD, U. Tex., 1973. Bar: Tex. 1973, U.S. Dist. Ct. (no. dist.) Tex. 1984, U.S. Dist. Ct. (so. dist.) Tex. 1980, U.S. Dist. Ct. (ea. dist.) Tex. 1980, U.S. Dist. Ct. (we. dist.) Tex. 1980, U.S. Ct. Appeals (5th cir.) 1981, U.S. Ct. Appeals (11th cir.) 1981, U.S. Supreme Ct. 1980. Analyst Tex. Gov.'s Office, Austin, 1974-75; cons. Atty. Gen. Tex. Office, Austin, 1976-80, asst. atty. gen., 1981; dir. research and devel. Tex. Dept. Corrections, Huntsville, 1981-82, legal counsel, 1982— ; trustee Tri-County MHMR Svcs., 1985—. Home: 489 Elkins Lk Huntsville TX 77340-7312 Office: Tex Dept Criminal Justice PO Box 99 Huntsville TX 77342-0099

PECK, MIRA P. lawyer; b. Minsk, USSR, Mar. 31, 1946; d. Wolf and Zofia (Wlaznik) Paszko; m. David O. Peck, May 15, 1971; children: Lena Ruth, Benjamin Jay. BEChemE, Melbourne U. Tech., Australia, 1972; MS in Indsl. Adminstrn., Union Coll., 1976; JD, Rutgers U., 1984. Bar: N.J. 1984, U.S. Dist. Ct. N.J. 1984. Tchr. sci. Victoria Edn. Dept., 1971-72; process engr. GAF Corp., Rensselaer, N.Y., 1974-77; design engr. BASF Corp., Parsippany, N.J., 1977-80, product mgr., 1980-86, mgr. corp. strategic planning, 1986-92, v.p. tech. purchasing Mount Olive, 1993-2000; pvt. law practice Denville, 1984—. Mem., counsel Protect Wildlife Water and Woods, Denville, 1987—; mem. Mus. Modern Art, N.Y.C. Mem. ABA, NOW, N.J. Bar Assn., Am Inst. Chem. Engrs., Am. Humanist Assn., Amnesty Internat., Simon Wiesenthal Ctr., So. Poverty Law Ctr. Democrat. Avocations: art, reading, music, hiking, bicycling. General corporate, Environmental, Real property.

PECK, ROBERT STEPHEN, lawyer, educator; b. Bklyn., Dec. 11, 1953; s. Irwin and Edith Rose (Welt) P.; m. Terre Garcia; 1 child, Zachary Madison. BA in Polit. Sci., George Washington U., 1975; JD, Cleve.-Marshall Law Sch., 1978; postgrad., NYU, 1978; LLM, Yale U., 1990. Bar: N.Y. 1979, U.S. Dist. Ct. (so. and ea. dists.) N.Y. 1979, D.C. 1989. Congl. aide U.S. Ho. of Reps., Washington, 1972-74; divsn. dir. Automated Correspondence, 1974-75; law clk. to presiding justice Cleve. Mcpl. Ct., 1976; editor Matthew Bender & Co., N.Y.C., 1977-78; legal dir. Pub. Edn. Assn., 1978-82; staff dir. ABA, Chgo., 1982-87, Washington, 1987-89; jud. fellow U.S. Supreme Ct., 1990-91; legis. counsel ACLU, 1991-95; adj. prof. Am. U., Washington, 1991—, George Washington U., Washington, 2000—; dir. legal affairs Assn. Trial Lawyers Am., 1995-98, sr. dir. legal affairs, 1998—; pres. Ctr. for Constl. Litigation, 2001—. Legal advisor Freedom to Read Found., Chgo., 1986—, exec. com. bd. trustees, 1987-90, 93-97, pres., 1988-90, v.p., trustee, 1993-97; bd. dirs. Nat. Constl. Ctr., 1990-93; lectr. on constl. law, legal ethics. Author: We the People, 1987, The Bill of Rights and the Politics of Interpretation, 1991, Libraries, the First Amendment and Cyberspace, 1999; co-author: Speaking and Writing Truth, 1985; editor: Understanding the Law, 1983, Blessings of Liberty, 1986, To Govern A Changing Society, 1990; contbr. numerous articles on constl. law to law revs. Mem. N.Y. State Edn. Adv. Bd., Albany, N.Y., 1979-81; bd. dirs. Nat. Com. on Pub. Edn. and Religious Liberty, 1995-97, Ams. for Religious Liberty, 1995-2000, Citizens for Constitution, 1997—; nat. chair Lawyers for Librs., 1996—; chair legal adv. com. Nat. Ctr. for Sci. Edn., 1996-2000; mem. first amendment adv. coun. Media Inst.,

1996—. NEH grantee 1983, 85. Mem.: ABA (chmn. pub. election law com. 1983—85, chmn. pub. election law com. 1987—90, vice chmn. access to justice com. 1997—98, chmn. 1998—99, program chmn. consumer and personal rights litigation com. 1997—2000, chmn. first amendment com. 1999—, chmn. appellate adv. com. 2001—). Democrat. Jewish. Avocations: tennis, music, travel. Office: Ctr for Constl Litigation 1050 31st St NW Washington DC 20007-4499 E-mail: robert.peck@atlahq.org

PECKERMAN, BRUCE MARTIN, lawyer; b. Milw., Sept. 28, 1949; s. Joseph and Doris (Kassel) P.; m. Jeanette Chrustowski. BA, U. Wis., 1971; JD, Washington U., St. Louis, 1973. Bar: Wis. 1974, U.S. Dist. Ct. (we. dist.) Wis. 1974, U.S. Ct. Appeals (7th cir.) 1977. Sole practice, Milw., 1985—. Recipient young leadership award Milw. Jewish Fedn. Mem. ABA, Wis. Bar Assn. (past chmn. family law sect.), Milw. Bar Assn. (bench/bar com. 1987-88), Am. Acad. Matrimonial Lawyers (past pres.). Family and matrimonial. Office: 920 E Mason St Milwaukee WI 53202-4015 E-mail: bruce_pec@execpc.com

PECKHAM, EUGENE ELIOT, suurogate judge, lawyer, educator; b. Stamford, Conn., Aug. 11, 1940; s. Joseph E. and Margaret (Nabors) P.; m. Judith Alice Chamberlain, Dec. 19, 1964; children: Margaret, Joseph, Elizabeth. BA with honors, Wesleyan U., Middletown, Conn., 1962; JD, Harvard U., 1965. Bar: N.Y. 1965, Fla. 1981, U.S. Tax Ct. 1974, U.S. Ct. Appeals (2d cir.) 1975, U.S. Dist. Ct. (no. dist.) N.Y. 1965. Assoc. Hinman, Howard & Kattell, Binghamton, N.Y., 1965-72, ptnr., 1972-2000; surrogate judge Broome County, 2001—. Instr. Broome C.C., Binghamton, 1968-69, Am. Coll. Life Underwriters, Bryn Mawr, Pa., 1969-70, Am. Coll. Property and Casualty Underwriters, Bryn Mawr, 1970-71; adj. lectr. SUNY, Binghamton, 1972-77, adj. asst. prof., 1977-81, adj. assoc. prof., 1981-87, adj. prof. acctg., 1987—; vis. lectr. Cornell U., Ithaca, N.Y., 1978, adj. prof., 1984. Author: Warren's Heaton Surrogate's Courts, Federal and New York Estate Taxes, vol., revised, 1988, 89, Bender's Federal Tax Service " Income Taxation of Estates & Trusts", 1989; contbr. articles to profl. jours. Peace Corps vol. tchr. Santa Maria U., Arequipa, Peru, 1966-67, treas. Joint Legis. Adv. Com. on Estates, Powers and Trusts Law and The Surrogates Ct. Procedure Act, 1990—; pres. Binghamton Girls Club, N.Y., 1974-76, bd. dirs., 1970-77; chmn. bd. Binghamton Boys and Girls Club, 1977, trustee, 1987-2000, chmn. bd. trustees, 1996-2000; bd. dirs. A. Lindsay and Olive B. O'Connor Found., 1982—, Dr. G. Clifford and Florence B. Decker Found., 1984—; sec.-treas. Greater Broome Cmty. Found., 1996—; mem. trust fund. com. Broome County United Way, N.Y., 1979-94; pres. SUNY Found., Binghamton, 1977-79, bd. dirs., 1975-82; bd. dirs. Estate Planning Coun. So. Tier, 1983-87, treas., 1983, sec., 1984, v.p., 1985, pres., 1986; bd. dirs. Samaritan Counselling Ctr. So. Tier, Inc., 1982-87, v.p., 1986, pres., 1987; co-chmn. sta. WSKG-TV auction, 1983; treas. Roberson Ctr. Arts & Scis., 1980, bd. dirs., 1977-80, 87-95; bd. dirs. Twin Tier Home Health, Inc., 1990-97, v.p., 1991-93, pres., 1993-95; chmn. Broome County Cmty. Ambassador Project, 1970-71; mem. Broome Bd. Ethics, 1985-89, chair, 1999-2000; mem. Broome County Arena Bd., 1987-89; deacon 1st Presbyn. Ch., Binghamton, 1971-74, moderator, 1974, elder, 1975-78, 87-90, trustee, 1980-83, 92-95; exec. comn. Broome County Rep. Com., 1980-83, 96-2000, co-chmn. fin. com., 1982-83, vice chmn., 1996-2000; pres. Broome County Young Rep. Club, 1969-70. Recipient SUNY-Binghamton Alumni Recognition award, 1984. Fellow Am. Coll. Trust & Estate Coun.; mem. N.Y. State Bar Assn. (exec. com. trusts & estates sect. 1980-84, 86-92, treas. 1986, sec. 1987, chmn. elect 1988, chmn. 1989, tax sect. 1972-2000, chmn. spl. commn. on alt. sources funding legal svcs. 1976-78, action unit 6 1984-86, ethics com. 1979-82, bd. editors N.Y. State Bar Jour. 1998—, v.p. 1999—, ho. dels. 1990-94, 95—), Fedn. Bar Assns. 6th Jud. Dist. (pres. 1984-85), Broome County Bar Assn. (chmn. prepaid legal ins. com. 1976-80, ethics com. 1981-87, chmn. jud. rating com. 1988-90). Estate planning, Probate, Taxation, general. Home: 12 Campbell Rd Binghamton NY 13905-4304 Office: Broome County Surrogate Ct PO Box 1766 Binghamton NY 13902-1766

PEDEN, ROBERT F., JR. retired lawyer; b. Ft. Worth, July 26, 1911; s. Robert F. and Laura (Phillips) P.; LLB, Cumberland U., 1933; m. Virginia LeTulle, May 25, 1939. Bar: Tex. 1934; practice law, Bay City, 1934-91; ret. 1991; city atty., Bay City, 1935-38, 65-79; county atty. Matagorda County, Tex., 1939-46, 50-54. Bd. dirs. Bay City Library Assn., 1969-88; pres. men. of ch. South Tex. Presbytery, 1959. Mem. ABA, Am. Judicature Soc., State Bar Tex., Matagorda County Bar Assn. (pres. 1961-62, v.p. 1967-69), Lambda Chi Alpha. Presbyterian (clk. session 1969-71, elder 1969—). Rotarian (v.p. 1968-69, pres. 1969-70). Club: Knife and Fork (dir. 1968-69, pres. 1970-71). Home: PO Box 1245 Bay City TX 77404-1245

PEDLEY, LAWRENCE LINDSAY, lawyer; b. Hopkinsville, Ky., May 27, 1932; s. Gracean McGoodwin and Elizabeth Lindsay Pedley; m. Ellen Mack, Oct. 9, 1957 (div. 1981); children: Lawrence Lindsay Jr., David M., Joan Elizabeth; m. Jill Plick, 1981 (div. 1991); 1 child, Jill Katharine; m. Wanda Polk, Feb. 3, 1995. BA, The Citadel, S.C., 1955; JD, Yale U., 1959. Bar: Ky. 1959, Fla. 1980, U.S. Dist. Ct. Ky. 1959, U.S. Ct. Appeals (6th cir.), 1975, U.S. Supreme Ct. 1981. Prin. atty. Ky. Dept. of Hwys., Frankfort, 1960; v.p. Nat. Industries, Louisville, 1964-66; gen. counsel, v.p., dir. Life Ins. Co. Ky., 1966-69; ptnr. Goldberg & Pedley, 1970-80, Pedley, Zielke, Gordinier & Pence, Louisville, 1980—. Ptnr. Hardin Properties Group, Louisville, Pedley Ptnrs., Louisville; owner Exec. Express, Louisville, 1969-80. Capt. JAGC, 1967. Mem. ABA, Ky. Bar Assn., Fla. Bar Assn., Filson Club, Harmony Landing Country Club, Pendennis Club. Clubs: Harmony Landing, Pendennis (Louisville), Filson. General corporate, Oil, gas, and mineral, Securities. Office: Pedley Zielke Gordinier & Pence 455 S 4th St Ste 1150 Louisville KY 40202-2512

PEDRI, CHARLES RAYMOND, lawyer; b. Hazleton, Pa., Sept. 1, 1951; s. Charles John and Barbara Theresa (Tait) P.; m. Sharon Jones, May 19, 1973; children: Melissa, C. David. BA, Pa. State U., 1973; JD, Temple U., 1976. Bar: 1976, U.S. Dist. Ct. (mid. dist.) Pa. 1980; cert. civil trial adv. Mem. Laputka, Bayless, Ecker & Cohn, P.C., Hazleton, 1976-88, ptnr. Laputka & Pedri, Hazleton, 1988—; instr. Pa. State U., Hazleton, 1978—. Pres. Meals on Wheels, Hazleton, 1985; solicitor Hazleton Planning Commn., 1986—. Mem. ABA, Pa. Trial Lawyers Assn., Pa. Bar Assn., Luzerne County Bar Assn., Phi Beta Kappa, Phi Kappa Phi, Mountain City Lions Club (pres. 1980). Republican. Roman Catholic. Federal civil litigation, State civil litigation, Personal injury. Home: 1418 Terrace Blvd Hazleton PA 18201-7524 Office: Laputka & Pedri 903 Northeastern Bldg 8 W Broad St Hazleton PA 18201-6412

PEEBLES, E(MORY) B(USH), III, lawyer; b. Hattiesburg, Miss., May 3, 1943; s. E.B. Jr. and Lee (Baldwin) P.; m. Celeste H. Hodges; children: E.B. IV, Catharine Celeste, Thomas Hill. BA, Vanderbilt U., 1965; JD, U. Ala., 1967. Bar: Ala. 1967, U.S. Dist. Ct. (so. dist.) Ala., U.S. Ct. Appeals (5th and 11th cirs.), U.S. Supreme Ct. Assoc. Armbrecht, Jackson, DeMouy, Mobile, Ala., 1967-72, ptnr., 1972—. Bd. dirs. South Ala. area bd. Am. South Bank. Mem. Ala. Securities Commn., 1989-93; chmn. sports com. Mobile Area C. of C., 1988-90; bd. dirs. Am.'s Jr. Miss Orgn., Mobile, 1983-90; active Mobile area coun. Boy Scouts Am., 1979—; mem. Sr. Bowl Com., Mobile, 1978—; chmn. trustees Maritime Mus. of Mobile. Mem. ABA (chmn. fin. svcs. com., tort and ins. practice sect. 1989-90, comml. fin. svcs. com. bus. law sect. 1984—), Ala. Bar Assn., Maritime Law Assn. U.S., Southea. Admiralty Law Inst., Internat. Bar Assn., Am. Soc. Internat. Law, Inter-Am. Bar Assn., Ala. Law Inst. (mem. governing coun. 1975—, corp. law com., letters of credit com.), Mobile Touchdown Club (pres. 1987-88), Mobile Area C. of C. (bd. dirs. 2000—). Contracts commercial, General corporate, Finance. Office: 1300 Riverview Plz Mobile AL 36602

PEET, CHARLES D, JR. lawyer; b. N.Y.C., Sept. 3, 1935; s. Charles D and Margaret Louise (Sherman) P.; children: Alisa, Amanda. BA, Yale U., 1957; JD, Harvard U., 1960. Bar: N.Y. 1962. Assoc. Milbank, Tweed, Hadley & McCloy, N.Y.C., 1960-68, ptnr., 1969-98; of counsel Freshfields Bruckhaus Deringer LLP (and predecessor firm), 1998—. Mem. Assn. Bar N.Y.C. Banking, Private international. Office: Freshfields Bruckhaus Deringer LLP 520 Madison Ave Fl 34 New York NY 10022-4213 E-mail: charles.peet@freshfields.com

PEET, RICHARD CLAYTON, lawyer, consultant; b. N.Y.C., Aug. 24, 1928; s. Charles Francis and Florence L. (Isaacs) P.; m. Barbara Jean McClure, Mar. 17, 1956 (div. July, 1988); children: Victoria Clementine, Alexandra Constance, Elizabeth Erica, Clarissa Barbara. JD, Tulane U., 1953. Bar: La. 1955, D.C. 1955. Law clk. Melvin M. Belli, San Francisco, 1954; with The Calif. Co., Standard Oil of Calif., 1955; atty. appellate sect. Lands div. Dept. Justice, Washington, 1956; asst. to dep. gen. counsel Dept. Commerce, 1957; legis. asst. Republican policy com. U.S. Senate, 1958; legis. asst. U.S. Senate minority leader William F. Knowland, 1958; asso. counsel House Judiciary Com., 1959-62; asso. minority counsel House Pub. Works Com., 1969-74; pres. Citizens for Hwy. Safety, 1978-84; practiced in Washington, 1962-68; prin. Richard Clayton Peet & Assos., 1972—; ptnr. Anderson, Pendleton, McMahon, Peet & Donovan, 1977-80, Anderson, Peet & Co., 1980-84. Pres., mng. dir. Lincoln Rsch. Ctr., 1965-72; v.p. Oil East Corp., 1978-83. Author: Goals for a Constructive Opposition, 1966; contbg. editor: Congressional Digest, 1960-61, Jour. Def. and Diplomacy, 1983-86, Senate Rep. Week, 1991; (weekly radio show) Across the Aisle, 1992; composer: song Stand Up For America, 1971 (George Washington medal Freedom's Found. 1971), A Monologue With God, 1996, Remembrance House. Chmn. bd. Workshop Library on World Humor; Rep. candidate Pres. of U.S., 1999-2000. With U.S. Army, 1946-47, with USAFR, 1950-55. Nominated for Rockefeller Public Svcs. Awd. Mem. Phi Delta Phi, Pi Kappa Alpha. Achievements include conceiving Highway Safety Act of 1973 with Cong. Wm. Harsha, OH, establishing road safety improvement programs, created (with congress) Natl. Bicentennial Highway Safety Year to promote, organized and chaired (with Pres. Ford) White House Conf. on Highway Safety, 1976, Rep. candidate for U.S. Pres., 1999-2000. Appellate, Constitutional, Legislative. Home: Remembrance House Inc Ste 186-184 4200 Wisconsin Ave NW Washington DC 20016 E-mail: Dick079@aol.com

PEGRAM, JOHN BRAXTON, lawyer; b. Yeadon, Pa., June 29, 1938; s. William Bement and Marjorie (Rainey) P.; m. Patricia Jane Narbeth; Aug. 21, 1965; children: Catherine, Stephen. AB in Physics, Columbia U., 1960; LLB, NYU, 1965. Bar: N.Y. 1965, U.S. Dist. Ct. Del. 1994, U.S. Dist. Ct. (ea. and so. dists.) N.Y. 1994, U.S. Supreme Ct. 1971. Engr. Fairchild Camera and Instrument Corp., Clifton, N.J., 1960-66; assoc. Hoxie Faithfull and Hapgood, LLP, N.Y.C., 1966-71; ptnr. Davis Hoxie Faithfull and Hapgood, 1972-95; prin. Fish & Richardson P.C., 1995—. Mem. intellectual property litig. adv. com. U.S. Dist. Ct. for the Dist. Del., 1994-96; mem. neutral evaluation and mediation panels U.S. Dist. Ct. for the Eastern Dist. of N.Y., 1994-97; mem. mediation panel U.S. Dist. Ct. for the So. Dist. N.Y., 1994-97. Editor The Trademark Reporter jour., 1984-86, mem. editorial adv. bd., 1986—; contbr. articles to profl. jours. Fellow Am. Bar Found. (life); mem. IEEE, ABA (chmn. antitrust law sect. com. on patents, trademarks and know how 1986-89, mem. legal econs. sect., bus. law sect., chmn. intellectual property law divsn. IV 1995-96), Am. Phys. Soc. (life), Fed. Bar Coun., Fed. Cir. Bar Assn., N.Y. State Bar Assn., Assn. of Bar of City of N.Y., Am. Intellectual Property Law Assn. (chmn. fed. practice and procedure com. 1974-76, chmn. unauthorized practice com. 1977-79, chmn. trade secrets com. 1992-94, mem. Japan practice com. 1992—, mem. editl. bd. Quar. Jour., 1994-95, chmn. fed. litig. com. 1995-97, chmn. internat. com. 1998-2000, bd. dirs. 2000—), N.Y. Intellectual Property Law Assn. (sec. 1981-84, dir. 1984-86, pres. 1989-90), U .S. Bar/Japan Patent Office Liaison Coun. (del. 1990—), Am. Judicature Soc., Internat. Intellectual Property Soc., Internat. Patent and Trademark Assn. (U.S. group AIPPI), Internat. Trademark Assn. (bd. dirs. 1985-87, fin. com. 1987-95, pub. com. 1997-98). Intellectual property, Patent, Trademark and copyright. Office: Fish & Richardson PC 45 Rockefeller Plz Fl 28 New York NY 10111-2889

PEIRCE, FREDERICK FAIRBANKS, lawyer; b. Torrington, Conn., Jan. 28, 1953; s. Everett L. and Frederica (Fairbanks) P.; m. Sandra Marie MacMillan, Dec. 16, 1989. BS with high honors, Colo. State U., 1975; JD, U. Colo., 1979. Bar: Colo. 1979, U.S. Dist. Ct. Colo. 1979. Assoc. Bratton & Zimmerman, Gunnison, Colo., 1979-80; staff atty. Holland & Hart, Aspen, 1980-82; assoc. Austin, McGrath & Jordan, 1982-84, Austin & Jordan, Aspen, 1984-87; ptnr. Austin, Jordan, Young & Peirce, 1987-89, Austin & Peirce, Aspen, 1989-92, Austin, Peirce & Smith, P.C., Aspen, 1992—. Bd. dirs. Aspen Nordic Coun. Inc., 1985-88, Aspen Velo Club Inc., 1986-88, Aspen Cycling Club, Inc., 1988-93, Kids First, 1997—, pres., 2000—; bd. dirs. Aspen Ctr. for Environ. Studies, 1991-97, v.p., 1992-94, pres., 1994-97; bd. dirs. Pitkin County Pks. Assn., Inc., 1990-98, v.p., 1991-92, pres., 1992-95; mem. Aspen Valley Land Trust, 1990-98, v.p., 1991-92, pres., 1992-95; mem. bd. edn. Aspen Sch. Dist., 1997—. NSF grantee, 1975. Mem. Colo. Bar Assn. (bd. govs. 1989-93, exec. coun. 1993-95, v.p. 1995-96, ethics com., 1995-97), Pitkin County Bar Assn. (v.p. 1985-86, pres. 1986-88, bd. govs. rep. 1989-93), Phi Kappa Phi. Avocations: skiing, hiking, fly fishing, cycling, flying. General corporate, Landlord-tenant, Real property. Office: Austin Peirce & Smith PC Ste 205 600 E Hopkins Ave Aspen CO 81611-2933 E-mail: fpeirce@aps-pc.com, feircto@rof.net

PEITHMANN, WILLIAM A. lawyer; married; 3 children. BA, DePauw U. and Loretto Heights Coll., 1975; JD, U. Ill. and U. Denver Coll. Of Law, 1978. Bar: Colo., 1978, Ill., 1979, Calif., 1980. Formerly with internat. law dept. Getty Oil Co., L.A.; atty. The Peithmann Law Office, Farmer City, Ill., 1985—. Elected to Am. Coll. of Trust and Estate Counsel, 1994; lectr. on various tax and estate planning insts. Contbg. chapter author: Illinois Estate Adminstration (IICLE-1993 and 1995, supp. wholly revised, 1999); contbg. author to legal publs. Named Leading Ill. Atty., 1996. Mem.: ABA (vice chair 1994—98, real property, probate & trust law sect., B-1 generation skipping transfers com.), Ill. Bar Assn. (trusts & estates section council 1988—2001, chair 1994—95, Bd. Gov. 1995—2001), Ill. Bar Found. (dir. 1997—98, dir. 2001—, Life Fellow and Stalwart Fellow), Colo. Bar Assn. (trust and estate section). Estate planning, Real property, Estate taxation. Office: PO Box 228 111 South Main St Farmer City IL 61842

PELLECCHIA, JOHN MICHAEL, lawyer; b. Orange, N.J., Dec. 6, 1958; BA, Lafayette Coll., 1980; JD cum laude, Tulane U., 1983. Bar: N.J. 1983, U.S. Dist. Ct. N.J. 1983, U.S. Supreme Ct. 1994. Assoc. Pitney, Hardin, Kipp & Szuch, Morristown, N.J., 1983-86; asst. counsel to gov. Thomas H. Kean State of N.J., Trenton, 1986-88; ptnr. Riker, Danzig, Scherer, Hyland & Perretti, LLP, Morristown and Trenton, 1988—. Mem. mgmt. com. Riker, Danzig, Scherer, Hyland & Perretti LLP, Morristown and Trenton, 1995-98; jud. extern to fed. dist. ct. judge, U.S. Dist. Ct., New Orleans, 1982-83; sr. fellow Tulane Law Sch., 1982-83, mem. N.J. Supreme Ct. Com. on Tax Ct., 1993-96, 2000-2002; mem. bus. and fin. svcs. task force of Gov. Whitman's Econ. Master Plan Commn., 1994. Trustee, v.p. Leukemia Soc. Am. North Jersey chpt., 1991—; trustee N.J. Shakespeare Festival, 1996—. Vol. of Yr., Leukemia Soc. Am. North Jersey chpt., 1994. Administrative and regulatory, General civil litigation, Legislative. Office: Riker Danzig Scherer Hyland & Perretti LLP 50 W State St Ste 1010 Trenton NJ 08608-1220

PELLETT, JON MICHAEL, lawyer; b. Orlando, Fla., Nov. 16, 1961; s. Milton Francis and Jean Ellen (Avery) P.; m. Karen Walker, July 21, 1984 (div. Sept. 1990). BS in Biology, U. Ctrl. Fla., Orlando, 1984, BS in Stats., 1985; JD, Fla. State U., 1993. Bar: Fla. 1995, U.S. Dist. Ct. (mid. dist.) Fla. 1996. Legal trainee Dept. Bus. and Profl. Regulation, Tallahassee, 1993-95; staff atty. Agy. for Health Care Adminstrn., 1995-96; assoc. Freeman, Hunter & Malloy, Tampa, Fla., 1996-2000, Barr, Murman, Tonelli et al, Tampa, 2000—. Vol. guardian ad litem Guardian ad Litem Program, Tallahassee, 1991-95. Bd. dirs. Friends of Arboretum, Orlando, 1998—. Mem. ABA, ATLA, Hillsborough County Bar Assn. Avocations: racquetball, beach volleyball. Administrative and regulatory, Appellate, Health. Office: Barr Murman Tonelli Et Al 201 E Kennedy Blvd Ste 1750 Tampa FL 33602-5829

PELLOW, DAVID MATTHEW, lawyer, law educator; b. Batavia, N.Y., Oct. 5, 1950; s. Louis Matthew and M. Beverly (Sizing) P.; m. Barbara Terry Walzer, Aug. 24, 1975; children— Matthew Aaron, Jonathan Adam. B.S. in Bus. Adminstrn., Boston Coll., 1972; J.D., U. Mich., 1975. Bar: N.Y. 1976, U.S. Dist. Ct. (no. dist.) N.Y. 1976, U.S. Ct. Appeals (3d cir.) 1980, U.S. Supreme Ct. 1981, U.S. Dist. Ct. (we. dist.) N.Y. 1985. Ptnr. Bond, Schoeneck & King, Syracuse, N.Y.; adj. asst. prof. labor law LeMoyne Coll., Syracuse, N.Y., 1981—; bd. dirs. Legal Services Central N.Y. Inc., Syracuse, 1978-81. Active N.Y. State Human Rights Arbitration Adv. Com., 1990—. Contbr. articles to profl. jours. Mem. ABA (labor and employment law sect.), N.Y. State Bar Assn., Indsl. Relations Research Assn. (v.p. central N.Y. chpt. 1981-82). Office: Bond Schoeneck & King 1 Lincoln Ctr Fl 18 Syracuse NY 13202-1324

PELOFSKY, JOEL, lawyer; b. Kansas City, Mo., June 23, 1937; s. Louis J. and Naomi (Hecht) P.; m. Brenda L. Greenblatt, June 19, 1960; children: Mark, Lisa, Carl. AB, Harvard U., 1959; LLB, 1962. Bar: Mo. 1962, U.S. Dist. Ct. (we. dist.) Mo. 1962, U.S. Ct. Appeals (8th cir.) 1968, U.S. Ct. Appeals (10th cir.) 1970. Law clk. to judge U.S. Dist. Ct. (we. dist.) Mo., 1962-63; mem. Miniace & Pelofsky, Kansas City, Mo., 1965-80; asst. pros. atty. Jackson County (Mo.), 1967-71; mem. Kans. City (Mo.) City Council, 1971-79; judge U.S. Bankruptcy Ct., Western Dist. Mo., Kansas City, 1980-85; ptnr. Shughart, Thomson & Kilroy P.C., Kansas City, 1986-95; apptd. U.S. trustee Ark., Mo., Nebr., 1995—; intermittent lectr. in law U. Mo.; mem. Region I, Law Enforcement Assistance Adminstrn. Bd. dirs. Greater Kansas City Mental Health Found.; mem. adv. bd. Urban League, Kansas City, Mo., chmn. human resource devel. com. Mo. Mcpl. League; bd. dirs., mem. exec. com. Truman Med. Ctr., Kansas City, Mo., pres. bd. 1988-90, chmn. bd., 1990-92. Served to lt. U.S. Army, 1963-65. Mem. ABA, Mo. Bar, Kansas City Bar Assn., Comml. Law League, Am. Coll. Bankruptcy. Banking, Bankruptcy, Contracts commercial. Office: US Trustee 400 E 9th St Ste 3440 Kansas City MO 64106-2625

PELSTER, WILLIAM CHARLES, lawyer; b. St. Louis, May 11, 1942; s. William R. and Marie C. (Graefe) P.; m. Terry C. Cuthbertson, Aug. 9, 1969. BA, Oberlin Coll., 1964; JD, U. Mich., 1967. Bar: Mo. 1967, N.Y. 1968, U.S. Dist. Ct. (so. dist.) N.Y. 1968, U.S. Ct. Appeals (2d cir.) 1968, U.S. Supreme Ct. 1972. Law clk. to judge Lenord P. Moore U.S. Ct. Appeals (2d cir.), N.Y.C., 1967-68; assoc. Donovan, Leisure, Newton & Irvine, 1968-75; ptnr. Skadden, Arps, Slate, Meagher & Flom, LLP, 1976—. Trustee Cancer Care Inc., N.Y.C., 1975—. Mem. ABA, Assn. of Bar of City of N.Y. Antitrust. Office: Skadden Arps Slate Meagher & Flom LLP 4 Times Sq Fl 24 New York NY 10036-6595 E-mail: wpelster@skadden.com

PELTON, RUSSELL GILBERT, lawyer; b. Monticello, N.Y., July 23, 1914; s. William and May (Morgan) P.; m. Marion Gosart, Dec. 14, 1940; children: William, Marjorie, Marilyn Pelton Barringer. BS, Syracuse U., 1935; JD, George Washington U., 1944. Bar: D.C. 1944, N.Y. 1947, U.S. Supreme Ct. 1948, U.S. Dist. Ct. N.Y. 1947; U.S. Dist. Ct. (fed. dist.). Ptnr. Darby & Darby, N.Y.C., 1945-56; sr. v.p. N.Am. Philips Corp., 1956-75; exec. v.p. U.S. Philips Corp., 1968-75; of counsel Rogers, Hoge & Hills, 1976-78; ptnr. Spellman, Joel & Pelton, White Plains, N.Y., 1979-81, Eslinger & Pelton, N.Y.C., 1983-85. Officer, dir. Tech. Container Corp., N.Y.C., 1977-95; former dir. Ferroscube Corp., Savgerties, N.Y., Polyseal Corp., N.Y.C.; lectr. Practising Law Inst., 1953-69; arbitrator, mediator Am. Arbitration Assn., 1985—. Patentee in field. V.p. Siwanoy coun. Boy Scouts Am., 1948-53; v.p. Rye Neck Bd. Edn., Mamaroneck, N.Y., 1952-62; mem. Zoning Bd. Appeals, 1966-70; town justice, 1970-85; trustee Syracuse U., 1967-73. Served with Signal Corps, U.S. Army, 1941-45. Mem. ABA, Am. Patent Law Assn. (past chmn. antitrust com.), N.Y. State Bar Assn. (ethics com., Iola com.), N.Y. Patent Law Assn. (past bd. govs.), State Magistrates Assn., County Magistrates Assn. (treas., v.p., pres.), Westchester County Bar Assn. (dir., chmn. ethics com., alternative dispute resolution com.), Assn. Bar City N.Y. (patent com.), IEEE, Am. Radio Relay League, Aircraft Owners and Pilots Assn., Wings Club, Cloud Club, Winged Foot Golf Club, Waccabuc Country Club, Masons, Elks. Federal civil litigation, Patent, Trademark and copyright. Home: 3 Oxford Rd Larchmont NY 10538-1428

PELTON, RUSSELL MEREDITH, JR. lawyer; b. Chgo., May 14, 1938; BA, DePauw U., 1960; JD, U. Chgo., 1963. Bar: Ill. 1963, U.S. Supreme Ct. 1979. Assoc. Peterson, Ross, Schloerb & Seidel, Chgo., 1966-72, ptnr., 1972-90, Oppenheimer, Wolff & Donnelly, Chgo., 1990-2000, Chgo. mng. ptnr., 1992-95, 98-2000; ptnr. Ross & Hardies, 2000—. Co-founder, gen. counsel Chgo. Opportunities Industrialization Ctr., 1969-83; gen. counsel Delta Dental Plan Ill., 1979-96; bd. dirs. First United Life Ins. Co., 1979-82; gen. counsel Am. Assn. Neurol. Surgeons, 1981—. Pres. Wilmette Jaycees, 1970; chmn. Wilmette Sch. Bd. Caucus, 1970-71; Wilmette Dist. 39 Bd. Edn., 1972-80; bd. dirs. Wilmette United Way, 1980-86, campaign chmn., 1983-85, pres., 1985-86; Wilmette Zoning Bd. Appeals, 1989-2000, chmn., 1990-2000. Served to capt. USAF, 1963-66. Mem. Chgo. Bar Assn., Ill. Bar Assn., ABA, Soc. Trial Lawyers. Labor, General civil litigation, Health. Office: Ross & Hardies 150 N Michigan Ave Ste 2500 Chicago IL 60601-7567 E-mail: russell.pelton@rosshardies.com

PELTONEN, JOHN ERNEST, lawyer; b. Dec. 25, 1942; s. Ernest and Anna Frances (McCarthy) P.; m. Katherine Frances Zak, July 29, 1967; children: John Ernest, Laura Katherine Ann, Brian Joseph. BA, Dartmouth Coll., 1964; JD, Boston Coll., 1967; MA, U. Ark., 1972. Bar: N.H. 1967, U.S Dist. Ct. N.H. 1967, U.S. Ct. Appeals (1st cir.) 1975, U.S. Supreme Ct. 1980. Assoc. Nixon, Christy & Tessler, Manchester, 1972-74; ptnr. Nixon, Christy, Tessier & Peltonen, 1974-76; sole practice, 1977; ptnr. Stark & Peltonen, 1978-92, Sheehaw, Phinney, Bass & Green, 1992—. Incorporator, Catholic Med. Ctr., Manchester, 1978— ; mem. N.H. Bd. Claims, 1982— ; incorporator, bd. dirs. N.H. Lions Sight and Hearing Found., 1978-81. Served to capt, USAF, 1967-72. Mem. ABA, N.H. Bar Assn., Am. Trial Lawyers Assn., N.H. Trial Lawyers Assn., Pi Sigma Alpha. Democrat. Roman Catholic. Lodge: Lions (Goffstown) (pres. 1978-79). Environmental, Insurance, Personal injury. Home: 6 Lesnyk Rd Goffstown NH 03045 Office: Sheehaw Phinney Bass & Green 1000 Elm St Manchester NH 03105

PELTZ, ROBERT DWIGHT, lawyer; b. Apr. 25, 1951; s. Charles Peltz and Ethel Ann (Grower) P.; m. Sharyn E. Marks, Dec. 19, 1976; children: Jeremy Michael Marks-Peltz, David Jordan Marks-Peltz. AB, Duke U., 1973; JD, U. Miami, 1976. Bar: Fla. 1976, U.S. Dist. Ct. (so. dist.) Fla. 1977, U.S. Dist. Ct. (mid. dist.) Fla. 1988, D.C. Ct. Appeals 1977, U.S. Supreme Ct. 1992. Ptnr. Rossman, Baumberger & Peltz, PA, Miami, Fla., 1974-90, Canning, Murray and Peltz, PA, 1990-98, McIntosh, Sawran, Peltz & Cartaya, PA, Miami, 1998—. Editor: U. Miami Law Rev., 1975-76. Mem. Acad. Fla. Trial Lawyers (amicus curiae com. 1981-90, Coll.

Diplomates 1983—, continuing legal edn. lectr. 1982—, legis. adv. counsel 1985-90), Dade County Trial Lawyers Assn. (pres. 1988—, pres.-elect 1987, treas. 1986, sec. 1985, bd. dirs. 1982-84, editor legal update periodical 1981-86), Soc. Wig and Robe, Am. Bd. Trial Advs. (charter), So. Regional Trial Lawyers Assn. (charter), Maritime Law Assn. (proctor), S.E. Admiralty Law Inst. (port dir.), Civil Trial Lawyers (cert.), Fla. Bar and Nat. Bd. Trial Advs., Phi Kappa Phi. Democrat. Jewish. Admiralty, Personal injury, General civil litigation. Home: 10220 SW 141st St Miami FL 33176-7006 Office: McIntish Sawran Peltz & Cartaya PA 19 W Flagler St Ste 920 Miami FL 33130-4407 E-mail: rpeltz@mspcesq.com

PELUSO, DANA C.M. lawyer; b. Reddlands, Calif., Oct. 30, 1970; d. Dennis John and Marjorie Sue Makielski; m. Joseph R., June 6, 1998. BS in Fin., Va. Tech., Blacksburg, 1992; JD cum laude, U. Richmond, 1997. Bar: Va. 1997, U.S. Dist. Ct. (ea. dist.) Va. 1997, U.S. Bankruptcy Ct. Va., 1998. Mgmt. trainee First Va. Bank, Falls Church, Va., 1992; mortgage broker Home First Mortgage Corp., Fairfax, 1992-94; assoc. Williams, Mullen, Christian and Dobbins, Richmond, 1997—. Vol. Ctrl. Va. Legal Aid, Richmond, 1997-98. Recipient award acad. excellence in contracts Corpus Juris Secundum, 1994. Mem. Va. Bar Assn., Richmond Bar Assn., Va. Trial Lawyers Assn., Metro-Richmond Women's Bar Assn. (jud. candidate develop com. 1997-98). Federal civil litigation, General civil litigation, State civil litigation. Office: Williams Mullen Christ Dobbins 2 James Ctr 1021 E Cary St Richmond VA 23219

PEÑA, AARON, JR. lawyer; b. Austin, Tex., June 8, 1959; s. Lionel Aron and Sylvia (Alamia) P.; m. Monica Solis, Mar. 29, 1991; children: Adrienne, Aaron, John, Alyssa, Anthony. BA in Liberal Arts, U. Tex., 1984; JD, Tex. So. U., 1987. Bar: Tex. 1988. Legis. asst. Tex. Legislature, Austin; mem. staff Tex. Dem. Party, Tex. U.S. Senator Bob Krueger, Austin; tchr. Austin Ind. Sch. Dist.; ptnr. Peñna, McDonald, Prestia & Ornelas, Edinburg, Tex., 1988-90, Aaron Peña & Assocs., Edinburg, 1990—. Author, spkr. published rec.: Million Dollar Arguments, 1997. Mem. ABA, ATLA, State Bar Tex., Nat. Employment Lawyers Assn. Roman Catholic. Avocations: travel, golf. Civil rights, State civil litigation, Personal injury. Home: 2709 Lakeshore Dr Edinburg TX 78539-7713 Office: Aaron Peña & Assocs 1110 S Closner Blvd Edinburg TX 78539-5662

PENA, GUILLERMO ENRIQUE, lawyer; b. Miami Beach, Fla., Aug. 16, 1963; s. Gustavo A. and Rosa Amelia (LeRiverend) P.; m. Jacqueline Torre, Sept. 11, 1993; children: Austin Jake, Allison Lee. BBA, Austin Peay State U., Clarksville, Tenn., 1988; JD, Fla. State U., 1991. Bar: Fla. 1991, U.S. Dist. Ct. (no. and so. dists.) Fla. 1991, U.S. Ct. Appeals (11th cir.) 1991, U.S. Supreme Ct. 1996; cert. in criminal trial law Criminal Trial Law Found., Middle Dist. of Fla., 1998, Dist. of Utah, 1999, Western Dist. of Tex., 1998. Assoc. Boehm, Brown, Rigdon & Seacrest, P.A., Tallahassee, 1990-92, Raia & Preira, Miami Beach, Fla., 1992-95, Jeffrey S. Weiner, P.A., Miami, 1995-96; pvt. practice, 1996—. Guest judge U. Miami Sch. Law-Moot Ct. Camp, 1996-99. Sgt. U.S. Army, 1984-86, ETO. Young pres. Mt. Sinai Hosp., Miami Beach, Fla. Recipient Recognition award Legal Svcs. Greater Miami, 1996, Pro Bono Svc. award Dade County Bar Assn., Miami, 1995, Young Pres. Mt. Sinai Hosp., 1999. Mem. ABA (criminal justice sect.), Cuban Am. Bar Assn. (Pro Bono Project 1996), Nat. Assn. Criminal Def. Lawyers, Am. Judicature Soc., Am. Inns of Ct. (barrister), Fla. Assn. Criminal Def. Lawyers, Fla. Bar (cert. as specialist in criminal law), Young Pres. Club. Criminal. Office: 1101 Brickell Ave Ste 1801 Miami FL 33131-2407 E-mail: gepena@yahoo.com

PENA, RICHARD, lawyer; b. San Antonio, Feb. 13, 1948; s. Merced and Rebecca (Trejo) P.; m. Carolyn Sarah Malley, May 25, 1979; 1 stepchild, Jason Charles Schubert. BA, U. Tex., 1970, JD, 1976. Bar: Tex. 1976, Colo. 1986. Pvt. practice, Austin, Tex., 1976—. Instr. bus. law St. Edwards U., Austin, 1983, Austin C.C., 1981-82; broker Tex. Real Estate Commn., 1980—; sports editor Austin Light, 1982. Bd. dirs. Ctr. for Battered Women, Austin, 1979-82, Austin Assn. Retarded Citizens, 1980-82; chmn. Austin Travis County Mental Health/Mental Retardation Pub. Responsibility Com., 1979-84; chmn. pvt. facilities monitoring com. Austin Assn. Retarded Citizens, 1981; bd. dirs. Boys Club of Austin, 1987-88; chair Homeless Task Force Austin, 1999—. Named to Outstanding Young Men. of Am., 1982. Fellow Tex. Bar Found. (sustaining life; trustee 1994, sec., treas. 1994, vice-chmn. 1995, chmn. 1996); mem. ABA (ho. dels., nominating com. 1998—, credentials com. 2001), Am. Bar Found. (bd. dirs. 2000, immigration bono com. 2000—), Nat. Conf. Bar Pres. (exec. com. 2001—), State Bar Tex. (bd. dirs. Dist. 9 1991—, exec. com. 1992—, chmn. minority representation com. 1991-92, chair James Watson Inn 1997-98, pres. 1998-99, chmn. profl. devel. com. 1991-92, policy manual com. 1993, fed. jud. appts. com. 1984-86, opportunities for minorities in the profession com. 1990-91, mem. advt. rev. com., pres.-elect 1997, pres. 1998-99), Travis County Bar Assn. (trustee lawyer referral svc. 1984-85, bd. dirs. 1986-88, sec. 1988, pres. 1990-91, chmn. jud. screening com. 1987, chmn. 1988-89, ins. com. 1988, 89, chmn. law day banquet com. 1988-89, lawyer referrel svc. com. 1983-84, trustee 1984-86, membership com. 1989), Capitol Area Mex. Am. Lawyers (pres. 1985, Outstanding Hispanic Lawyer Austin 1989), Legal Aid Soc. Ctrl. Tex. (bd. dirs. 1984), Austin Young Lawyers Assn., Tex. Trial Lawyers Assn., Austin C. of C. (Leadership Austin 1985-86). Democrat. Personal injury, Workers' compensation. Home: 107 Top O The Lake Dr Austin TX 78734-5234 Office: 2028 E Ben White #220 Austin TX 78741

PENCE, STEPHEN BEVILLE, prosecutor; MBA, Ea. Ky. U.; JD, U. Ky. Assoc. Taustine and Post, 1987—88, Borowitz and Goldsmith, 1988—90; served in U.S. Attys. Office we. dist. Ky., 1990—95; ptnr. Sheffer and Hoffman, 1995—96; U.S. atty. we. dist. Ky. Office: 510 W Broadway Louisville KY 40202 Office Fax: 502-582-5067*

PENDYGRAFT, GEORGE WILLIAM, lawyer; b. Jeffersonville, Ind., Nov. 3, 1946; s. George Benjamin and Norma Jean (Hall) P.; m. Melissa Ann Pendygraft, 1977 (div. Sept. 1990); children: Alexandrea Jean, Ryan Samuelson; m. Jacqueline Sue Samuelson, Jan. 15, 1991. AB in Chemistry, Franklin Coll., 1968; PhD in Phys. Organic Chemistry, U. Ky., 1972; JD, Columbia U., 1975. Bar: N.Y. 1976, Ind. 1976, U.S. Patent and Trademark Office 1976, U.S. Dist. Ct. (ea. and so. dists.) N.Y. 1980, U.S. Ct. Appeals (D.C. cir.) 1980. Lectr. in chemistry U. Ky., Lexington, 1968-70; assoc. Watson, Leavenworth, Kelton & Taggart, N.Y.C., 1975-76; ptnr. Baker and Daniels, Indpls., 1976-88, Pendygraft, Plews & Shadley, Indpls., 1988-90; prin., pres. George W. Pendygraft, P.C., 1990—. Contbr. articles to profl. jours. Bd. trustees Franklin Coll., 1982-86, nat. chmn. ann. fund, 1981. NDEA fellow, NSF fellow; Franklin Coll. scholar. Environmental, Patent. Office: 1000 Waterway Blvd Indianapolis IN 46202-2155 also: 10414 Muir Ln Fishers IN 46038

PENICK, MICHAEL PRESTON, lawyer; b. Covington, Ky., Aug. 9, 1947; s. James Preston and Edith Marie (Smith) P.; m. Christina Sue Lund, June 9, 1979. BA, Union Coll., 1970; cert. highest proficiency Def. Lang. Inst., 1971; JD, U. Louisville, 1976. Bar: Ky. 1976, U.S. Dist. Ct. (we. dist.) Ky. 1976, U.S. Ct. Appeals (6th cir.) 1980, U.S. Supreme Ct. 1980, Tex. 1988, U.S. Dist. Ct. (no. dist.) Tex. 1988. Ptnr. Boehl, Stopher, Graves & Deindoerfer, Paducah, Ky., 1978-88; chmn. med. negligence Windle Turley, P.C., Dallas, 1988—. Author: Beginning Bridge Complete, 1983, Expert Witnesses, vol 49, 1988, Beginning Bridge Quizzes, 1989; contbr. articles to legal jours. With U.S. Army, 1970-73, ETO. Recipient Life Master Cert. Am. Contract Bridge League, 1976 . Mem. ABA (products liability com. 1982—), Ky. Bar Assn. (ho. of dels. 1981, 84—), Def. Rsch. Inst. (products liability com. 1979-88), Tex. Bar Assn., Ky. Def. Counsel, Young Lawyers Assn. (pres. 1977). Methodist. Federal civil litigation, Personal injury. Home: 4423 Hollow Oak Dr Dallas TX 75287-6850 Office: Windle Turley PC 1000 Univ Tower 6440 N Central Expy Dallas TX 75206-4123

PENNAMPED, BRUCE MICHAEL, lawyer; b. Kearney, Nebr., July 16, 1948; s. Matthew Paul and Betty Fern (Harper) P.; mm. Victoria A. Crull, May 13, 1972 (div. Dec. 1980); 1 child, Katheryn A.; m. Melissa J. Barth, July 22, 1985. BS in Mgmt., Ind. U., 1970, JD, 1972. Bar: Ind. 1972, U.S. Dist. Ct. (no. and so. dists.) Ind. 1972, U.S. Ct. Appeals (7th cir.) 1978. Assoc. Rocap Rocap Reese & Young, Indpls., 1972-76; pvt. practice, 1976-78, 88-91; ptnr. Forbes & Pennamped, 1978-88, Lowe Gray Steele & Hoffman, Indpls., 1991-96, Lowe Gray Steele & Darko, Indpls., 1996—. Chair and panelist Ind. Continuing Legal Edn. Forum; mem. Ind. Child Custody and Support Adv. Commn. Contbr. articles to profl. jours. Majority atty. Ind. Ho. of Reps., Indpls. Cpl. USMCR, 1967-69. Fellow Am. Acad. Matrimonial Lawyers. Family and matrimonial. Home: 9662 Decatur Dr Indianapolis IN 46256-9654 Office: Lowe Gray Steele & Darko 4600 Bank One Tower Indianapolis IN 46204-5146

PENNELL, STEPHEN RICHARD, lawyer; b. Cheyenne, Wyo., Apr. 7, 1952; s. Richard Loren and Glenna Dean (Maple) P.; m. Diana Sue Dirlam, Mar. 9, 1974; children: James Richard, Lauren Michelle. AB summa cum laude, Ind. U., 1973, JD magna cum laude, 1976. Bar: Ind. 1976, U.S. Dist. Ct. (no. and so. dists.) Ind. 1976, U.S. Ct. Appeals (7th cir.) 1978. Assoc. Stuart & Branigin, Lafayette, Ind., 1976—. Editor Ind. U. Law Jour., 1976. Pres. Wesley Found., West Lafayette, Ind., 1980-86, 99-2001. Served to capt. USAR, 1976-84. Mem. ABA, Ind. Bar Assn. (bd. dirs.), Def. Trial Counsel of Ind. (sec. 2001), Def. Rsch. Inst. (Ind. state rep. 1998-2000), Phi Beta Kappa, Order of Coif. Republican. Methodist. Federal civil litigation, General civil litigation, Product liability. Home: 3111 Decatur St West Lafayette IN 47906-1135 Office: Stuart & Branigin PO Box 1010 Lafayette IN 47902-1010 E-mail: ssp@stuartlaw.com

PENNELL, WILLIAM BROOKE, lawyer; b. Mineral Ridge, Ohio, Oct. 28, 1935; s. George Albert and Katherine Nancy (McMeen) P. AB, Harvard U., 1957; LLB cum laude, U. Pa., 1961; m. Peggy Polsky, June 17, 1958; children: Katherine, Thomas Brooke. Bar: N.Y. 1963, U.S. Dist. Ct. (so. dist.) N.Y. 1964, U.S. Dist. Ct. (ea. dist.) N.Y. 1964, U.S. Ct. Appeals (2d cir.) 1966, U.S. Ct. Claims 1966, U.S. Tax Ct. 1967, U.S. Supreme Ct. 1967. Clk. U.S. Dist. Ct., (so. dist.) N.Y., N.Y.C., 1961-62; assoc. Shearman & Sterling, N.Y.C., 1962-71, ptnr., 1971-91. Recent case editor U. Pa. Law Rev., 1960-61. Bd. govs. Bklyn. Heights Assn., 1964-74, pres., 1969-71; chmn. bd. Willoughby House Settlement, 1972-95. Served with U.S. Army, 1957. Fellow Salzburg Seminar Am. Studies, 1965. Mem. Rembrandt Club. Federal civil litigation, State civil litigation, Private international. Office: PO Box 249 Canaan NY 12029-0249

PENNINGTON, AL, lawyer; b. Birmingham, Ala., Jan. 31, 1949; s. Vader Richards and Johnnie Fae (Hill) P.; m. Andrea Pearson, Aug. 3, 1974; children: Katherine Sigrid, Anna Caroline. BS, U. Ala., 1971, JD, 1974. Bar: Ala. 1974, U.S. Dist. Ct. (so. dist.) Ala. 1976, U.S. Supreme Ct. 1978, U.S. Ct. Appeals (11th cir.) 1983. Trust adminstr. 1st Nat. Bank of Birmingham, 1974; asst. dist. atty. Jefferson County, Birmingham, 1974-76; ptnr. Pennington & Pennington, Mobile, Ala., 1976-80, Pennington, McCleave & Patterson, 1982-88; chief asst. dist. atty. Mobile County, 1981; sole practice, Mobile, 1988—; cons. on jail overcrowding Mobile County Commn.-Mobile County Sheriff, 1983—. Com. chmn. Mobile County Wildlife and Conservation Assn., 1976—; mem. Mobile United Way, 1977—; bd. dirs. Hist. Mobile Preservation Soc., 1981; bd. dirs. Old Dauphinway Assn., Mobile, pres., 1985-86; pres. E. Church St. Devel. Assn., Mobile, 1979-81; elected mem. Mobile County Dem. Exec. Com., Ala. Dem. Exec. Com., Ala. Dem. Exec. Bd. Named Outstanding Young Man in Am., U.S. Jaycees, 1980; recipient Community Service award Mobile United, 1980. Mem. ABA, Ala. Bar Assn. (chmn. criminal law sect. 1988), Assn. Trial Lawyers Am., Nat. Assn. Criminal Def. Lawyers, Ala. Assn. Criminal Def. Lawyers (regional v.p. 1988-89). Democrat. Roman Catholic. Criminal, Libel, Personal injury. Home: 25 S Julia St Mobile AL 36604-2127 Office: 113 S Dearborn St Mobile AL 36602-1705

PENTELOVITCH, WILLIAM ZANE, lawyer; b. Mpls., Sept. 6, 1949; s. Norman Oscar and Esther (Misel) Pentelovitch; m. Barbara Susan Ziman, Aug. 21, 1971 (dec. Oct. 1994); m. Vivian Gail Fischer, June 14, 1998; children: Norman Henry, Tovah Elana, Noah Ziman, Ari Benjamin Fischer. BA summa cum laude, U. Minn., 1971; JD, U. Chgo., 1974. Ptnr. Maslon, Edelman, Borman & Brand, Mpls., 1974—. Federal civil litigation, State civil litigation, Construction. Home: 6 Park Ln Minneapolis MN 55416-4340 Office: Maslon Edelman Borman et al 3300 Wells Fargo Ctr Minneapolis MN 55402 E-mail: bill.pentelovich@maslon.com

PENZA, JOSEPH FULVIO, JR. lawyer; b. Providence, Sept. 23, 1947; s. Joseph Fulvio Sr. and Ann M. (Barbieri) P. BBA, U. R.I., 1969; JD, Boston U., 1972, LLM in Taxation, 1975. Bar: R.I. 1972, U.S. Dist. Ct. R.I. 1972, U.S. Ct. Appeals (1st cir.) 1975, U.S. Supreme Ct. 1980. Sole practice, Providence, 1972-82; ptnr. Olenn & Penza, 1982—. Fellow Am. Coll. Trial Attys.; mem. R.I. Bar Assn. (chmn. bench/bar com. 1985-87), R.I. Trial Lawyers Assn. (v.p. 1986, bd. govs. 1984-89), Am. Bd. Trial Advocates (advocate, mem. ethics adv. panel 1995-2000, chmn., 1999-2000), Nat. Amateur Softball Assn. (mem. coun.), R.I. Amateur Softball Assn. (pres. 1980-95). Avocations: softball, golf. Federal civil litigation, General practice, Personal injury. Office: Olenn & Penza 530 Greenwich Ave Warwick RI 02886-1824 E-mail: JFP@Olenn-Penza.com

PEPE, LOUIS ROBERT, lawyer, educator; b. Derby, Conn., Mar. 7, 1943; s. Louis F. and Mildred R. (Vollaro) P.; m. Carole Anita Roman, June 8, 1969; children: Marissa Lee, Christopher Justin, Alexander Drew. B in Mgmt. Engring., Rensselaer Poly. Inst., 1964, MS, 1967; JD with distinction, Cornell U., 1970. Bar: Conn. 1970, U.S. Dist. Ct. Conn. 1970, U.S. Ct. Appeals (2d cir.) 1971, U.S. Supreme Ct. 1975, U.S. Ct. Claims 1978. Assoc. Alcorn, Bakewell & Smith, Hartford, Conn., 1970-75, ptnr., 1975-82; sr. ptnr. Pepe & Hazard, 1983—. Adj. assoc. prof. Hartford Grad. Ctr., 1972-87; dir. BayBank Conn., 1987-93; Adv. coun. Cornell Law Sch., 1990—. Mem. New Hartford Housing Authority, 1971-72, New Hartford Planning Zoning Commn., 1973-84, chmn., 1980-84, New Hartford Inland Wetlands Commn., 1975-78; mem. adv. coun. Cornell Law Sch., 1990—; dir. Capitol Area Found. Equal Justice, 1993—, pres., 1999-2001. 1st lt. U.S. Army, 1964-66. Decorated Army Commendation medal. Fellow Am. Bar Found., Am. Coll. Constl. Lawyers; mem. ABA, Am. Coll. Trial Lawyers, Am. Bd. Trial Advocates, Conn. Bar Assn. (chmn. constrn. law sect. 1989-92, chmn. standing com. on professionalism), Conn. Trial Lawyers Assn., Hartford County Bar Assn., Phi Kappa Phi. E-mail; (office). Federal civil litigation, State civil litigation, Construction. Home: 3 Metacom Dr Simsbury CT 06070-1851 Office: Pepe & Hazard Goodwin Sq Hartford CT 06103-4300 E-mail: lpepe@pepehazard.com

PEPE, STEVEN DOUGLAS, federal magistrate judge; b. Indpls., Jan. 29, 1943; s. Wilfrid Julius and Roselda (Gehring) P.; m. Janet L. Pepe. BA cum laude, U. Notre Dame, 1965; JD magna cum laude, U. Mich., 1968; postgrad., London Sch. Econs. and Polit. Sci., 1970-72; LLM, Harvard U., 1974. Bar: Ind. 1968, U.S. Dist. Ct. Ind. 1968, D.C. 1969, U.S. Dist. Ct. D.C. 1969, mass. 1973, Mich. 1974, U.S. Dist. Ct. (ea. dist.) Mich., 1983. Law clk. Hon. Harold Leventhal U.S. Cir. Ct. Appeals, Washington, 1968-69; staff atty. Neighborhood Legal Svcs. Program, 1969-70; cons. Office of Svcs. to Aging, Lansing, Mich., 1976-77, Administrn. Aging, Dept. Health and Human Svcs., 1976-78; U.S. magistrate judge Eastern Dist., Ann Arbor, Mich., 1983—. Mem. Biregional Older Am. Advocacy Assistance Resource and Support Ctr., 1979-81; cons., bd. dirs. Ctr. Social Gerontology (1988-93); clin. prof. law, dir. Mich. Clin. Law Program, U. Mich. Law Sch., 1974-83; adj. prof. law Detroit Mercy Sch. Law, 1985; lectr. U. Mich. Law Sch., 1985-97. Editor Mich. Law Rev.; contbr. articles to profl. jours. Recipient Reginald Heber Smith Cmty. Lawyer fellowship, 1969-70; Mich.-Ford Internat. Studies fellow, 1970-72, Harvard Law Sch. Clin. Teaching fellow, 1972-73. Mem. State Bar Mich., State Bar Ind., Fed. Bar Assn., Washtenaw County Bar Assn., Am. Inn Court XI, U. Detroit Mercy, Pi Sigma Alpha, Order of Coif. Office: US District Court PO Box 7150 Ann Arbor MI 48107-7150 E-mail: Steven_Pepe@ck6.uscourts.gov

PEPER, CHRISTIAN BAIRD, lawyer; b. St. Louis, Dec. 5, 1910; s. Clarence F. and Christine (Baird) P.; m. Ethel C. Kingsland, June 5, 1935 (dec. Sept. 1995); children: Catherine K. Peper Larson, Anne Peper Perkins, Christian B.; m. Barbara C. Pleiter, Jan. 25, 1996. AB cum laude, Harvard U., 1932; LLB, Washington U., 1935; LLM, Yale U., 1937. Bar: Mo. 1934. Pvt. practiced, St. Louis; of counsel Blackwell Sanders Peper Martin LLP. Lectr. various subjects Washington U. Law Sch., St. Louis, 1943-61; ptnr. A.G. Edwards & Sons, 1945-67; pres. St. Charles Gas Corp., 1953-72; bd. dirs. El Dorado Paper Bag Mfg. Co., Inc. Editor: An Historian's Conscience: The Correspondence of Arnold J. Toynbee and Columba Cary-Elwes, 1986. Mem. vis. com. Harvard Div. Sch., 1964-70; counsel St. Louis Art Mus. Sterling fellow Yale U., 1937. Mem. ABA, Mo. Bar Assn., St. Louis Bar Assn., Noonday Club, Harvard Club, East India Club (London), Order of Coif, Phi Delta Phi. Roman Catholic. Home: 1454 S Mason Rd Saint Louis MO 63131-1211 Office: Blackwell Sanders Peper Martin LLP 720 Olive St Saint Louis MO 63101-2338 E-mail: cpeper@ospmlaw.com

PEPPER, ALLAN MICHAEL, lawyer; b. Bklyn., July 5, 1943; s. Julius and Jeanette (Lasovsky) P.; m. Barbara Benjamin, Aug. 30, 1964; children— Leslie Anne, Joshua Benjamin, Adam Richard, Robert Benjamin B.A. summa cum laude, Brandeis U., 1964; LL.B. magna cum laude, Harvard U., 1967. Bar: N.Y. 1968, U.S. Dist. Ct. (so. and ea. dists.) N.Y. 1968, U.S. Ct. Appeals (2d cir.) 1968, U.S. Supreme Ct. 1988. Law clk. U.S. Ct. Appeals for 2d Circuit, N.Y.C., 1967-68; assoc. Kaye, Scholer, Fierman, Hays & Handler LLP, 1968-74, ptnr., 1975—. Lectr. in field. Mem. exec. com., assoc. nat. chmn. Brandeis U. Alumni Fund, 1979-82, nat. chmn., 1982-85, chmn. 25th Reunion gift com., 1989, devel. com., trustee, 1982-85, pres., councillor, 1980—, mem. 35th Reunion gift com., 1999; trustee Brandeis U., 1985-95, sec., 1992-93, budget and fin. com., 1988-95, chmn. com. strategic plan, 1990-91, acad. affairs com., 1985-92, student life and phys. facilities com., 1985-89, vice chmn. ad hoc by-laws com., 1988-89, long range planning com., 1989-91, chmn. audit com., 1991-95, exec. com., 1990-91, mem. 35th Reunion gift com., 1999; bd. dirs. Styles Brook Homeowners Assn., 1990—, exec. com., 1994—; nominating com. Edgemont Sch. Bd., 1992-93; trustee Edgemont Sch. Found., 1994—; mem. 30th reunion gift com. Harvard Law sch., 1996-97, class agt., 1998—. Recipient Henry Jones-Golda Meier Bnai Brith Youth Services award, 1986, L.I. Press Valedictory medal, 1960; Felix Frankfurter scholar Harvard U. Law Sch., 1964-65; Louis D. Brandeis hon. scholar Brandeis U., 1964 Mem. ABA, Assn. of Bar of City of N.Y. (mem. law firm mgmt. com. 1987-91, litigation com, 1998—), N.Y. State Bar Assn. (comml. and fed. lit. sect., vice chmn. com. on discovery 1993-97), Brandeis U. Alumni Assn. (exec. com. 1982-87, alumni giving strategic planning com., 1992, Alumni Svc. award 1988), Phi Beta Kappa (L.I. Alumni award 1960). Democrat. Jewish. Lodge: B'nai B'rith (pres. Henry Jones Lodge 1982-84, mem. Westchester-Putnam council 1982-85, bd. govs. dist. 1, 1985-86) Antitrust, Federal civil litigation, State civil litigation. Office: Kaye Scholer Fierman Hays & Handler LLP 425 Park Ave New York NY 10022-3506 E-mail: apepper@kayescholer.com

PEPYNE, EDWARD WALTER, lawyer, psychologist, former educator; b. Springfield, Mass., Dec. 27, 1925; s. Walter Henry and Frances A. (Carroll) P.; m. Carol Jean Dutcher, Aug. 2, 1958; children— Deborah, Edward, Jr., Susan, Byron, Shari, Randy, David, Allison, Jennifer B.A., Am. Internat. Coll., 1948; M.S., U. Mass., 1951, Ed.D., 1968; postgrad., NYU, 1952-55; prof. diploma, U. Conn., 1964; J.D., Western New Eng. Coll., 1978. Bar: Mass. 1978, U.S. Supreme Ct. 1981. Prin., tchr. Gilbertville Grammar Sch., Hardwick, Mass., 1948-49; sch. counselor West Springfield High Sch., 1949-53; instr. NYU, 1953-54; supt. schs. New Shoreham, R.I., 1954-56; asst. prof. edn. Mich. State U., 1956-58; sch. psychologist, guidance dir. Pub. Sch. System, East Long, Mass., 1958-62; lectr. Westfield State Coll., 1961-65; dir. pupil services Chicopee Pub. Sch., 1965-68; assoc. prof. counselor edn. U. Hartford, West Hartford, Mass., 1968-71, prof., 1971-85, dir. Inst. Coll. Counselors Minority and Low Income Students, 1971-72, dir. Div. Human Services, 1972-77; cons. Aetna Life & Casualty Co., Hartford, 1962-75; hearing officer Conn. State Bd. Edn., 1980-99; exec. dir. Sinapi Assocs., 1959-78; pvt. practice, Ashfield, Mass., 1978—. Co-author: Better Driving, 1958; assoc. editor: Highway Safety and Driver Education, 1954; chmn. editorial com.: Man and the Motor Car, 5th edit., 1954; contbr. numerous articles to profl. jours. Chief Welfare Svcs. Civil Def., Levittown, N.Y., 1953-54; chmn. Ashfield Planning Bd., Mass., 1979-83; moderator Town of Ashfield, 1980-81, town counsel, Charlemont, Mass., 1983-84; mem. jud. nominating coun. Western Regional Com., 1993-99; mem. Mohawk Regional Sch. Com., 1999-2000. Mem. ABA, APA, Mass. Bar Assn., Mass. Acad. Trial Attys., Am. Pers. and Guidance Assn., New Eng. Pers. and Guidance Assn. (bd. dirs.), New Eng. Ednl. Rsch. Orgn. (pres. 1971), Am. Assn. Sch. Adminstrs., Am. Ednl. Rsch. Assn., Mt. Tom Amateur Radio Assn., Franklin County Amateur Radio Club, Elks, Kiwanis (pres. 1988-89, lt. gov. div. 12, 1991-92), Masons (master 1994-96), Shriners, Phi Delta Kappa. Administrative and regulatory, State civil litigation, Education and schools. Home: PO Box 31 134 Ashfield Mountain Rd Ashfield MA 01330-9505 Office: PO Box 345 134 Ashfield Mountain Rd Ashfield MA 01330-9505 Home: 3808 Airport Rd Coventry VT 05855 E-mail: pepyne@shaysnet.com

PERANTEAU, MARY ELIZABETH, lawyer; b. San Diego, Oct. 22, 1965; d. George Herbert and Mary Frances (Frechette) P. BS, Beloit Coll., 1989; JD, U. Wis., 1996. Bar: Wis. 1996, U.S. Dist. Ct. (we. dist.) Wis. 1996, U.S. Dist. Ct. (ea. dist.) Wis. 1997. Assoc. Halling & ayo, S.C., Milw., 1997—. Mem. Milw. Bar Assn. General practice, Securities. Office: Halling & Cayo SC 839 N Jefferson St Ste 200 Milwaukee WI 53202

PERERA, LAWRENCE THACHER, lawyer; b. Boston, June 23, 1935; s. Guido R. and Faith (Phillips) P.; m. Elizabeth A. Wentworth, July 5, 1961; children: Alice V. Perera Lucey, Caroline F. Perera Barry, Lucy E., Lawrence Thacher. B.A., Harvard U., 1957, LL.B., 1961. Bar: Mass. 1961, U.S. Supreme Ct. 1973. Clk. Judge R. Ammi Cutter, Mass. Supreme Jud. Ct., Boston, 1961-62; assoc. Palmer & Dodge, 1962-69, ptnr., 1969-74; judge Middlesex County Probate Ct., East Cambridge, Mass., 1974-79; ptnr. Hemenway & Barnes, Boston, 1979—. Mem. faculty and nat. coun. Hon. Nat. Jud. Coll., Reno, prof./pres. Mass. Continuing Legal Edn., Inc., 1988-90. Chmn. Boston Fin. Commn., 1969-71; overseer Brigham and Women's Hosp., Boston, Boston Lyric Opera; chmn. bd. overseers Boston Opera Assn.; chmn. Back Bay Archtl. Commn., 1966-72; trustee emeritus Sta. WGBH Ednl. Found., Boston Athenaeum, Wang Ctr. Performing Arts; trustee Social Law Libr., Boston. Fellow Am. Acad. Matrimonial Lawyers, Am. Coll. Trust and Estate Counsel; mem. ABA, Am. Bar Found., Am. Law Inst., Mass. Bar Assn., Mass. Bar Found., Boston Bar Assn.. Family and matrimonial, General practice, Probate. Home: 18 Marlborough St Boston MA 02116-2101 Office: 60 State St Boston MA 02109-1800

PEREZ, LUIS ALBERTO, lawyer; b. Havana, Cuba, Dec. 22, 1956; came to U.S., 1961; s. Alberto and Estela (Hernandez) P. BBA cum laude, Loyola U., New Orleans, 1978, JD, 1981. Car: La. 1981, U.S. Dist. Ct. (ea. and mid. dists.) La. 1981, U.S. Ct. Appeals (5th and 11th cirs.) 1981, U.S. Dist. Ct. (we. dist.) La. 1983, D.C. 1989, U.S. Dist. Ct. (D.C. cir.) 1989, U.S. Ct. Appeals D.C. 1989, U.S. Supreme Ct. 1989, Tex. 1994, U.S. Ct. Internat. Trade 1999. Of counsel Shook, Hardy & Bacon, LLP, Miami, 2000—. Chmn. internat. practice team Adams & Reese. Mem. ABA, La. Bar Assn., Fed. Bar Assn., Interamerican Bar Assn., D.C. Bar Assn., State Bar Tex., Hispanic Lawyers Assn. La. (pres. 1988-94), Beta Gamma Sigma. Avocations: scuba diving, cycling, volleyball. Federal civil litigation, Contracts commercial, General corporate. Office: Shook Hardy & Bacon LLP Ste 2400/Miami Ctr 201 S Biscayne Blvd Miami FL 33131-4332 E-mail: lperez@shb.com

PERISHO, RUSSELL L. lawyer; b. Oregon, Ill., May 23, 1953; s. George D. and Margaret E. (Wehking) P.; m. Caroline H. Archer, June 13, 1981; 1 child, Alysha Christine. B.A., U. Ill., 1974; J.D., Harvard U., 1978. Bar: Wash. 1978. Staff asst. Congressman Robert H. Michel, Washington, 1972-74; clk. Lord Bissell & Brook, Chgo., 1976; assoc. Perkins Coie Stone Olsen & Williams, Seattle, 1978-84, ptnr., 1984— . Vol., Lake City Legal Clinic, Seattle, 1982— . Mem. ABA, Wash. Bar Assn., Seattle-King County Bar Assn. Office: Perkins Coie 1201 3rd Ave Fl 40 Seattle WA 98101-3029

PERKIEL, MITCHEL H. lawyer; b. N.Y.C., Oct. 26, 1949; s. Frank and Ella Perkiel; m. Lois E. Perkiel, June 24, 1984; children: Joshua L., Alexa Kim, Griffin. BA, SUNY, Stony Brook, 1971; JD, New York Law Sch., 1974. Bar: N.Y. 1975, U.S. Dist. Ct. (so. and ea. dists.) N.Y. 1975, U.S. Ct. Appeals (2d cir.) 1975, Conn. 1988, Utah 1999. Law clk. to presiding justice N.Y. County Civil Ct., 1975; assoc. Levin & Weintraub & Crames, N.Y.C., 1975-80, ptnr., 1980-90, Kaye, Scholer, Fierman, Hayes & Handler, N.Y.C., 1990—. Notes and comments editor New York Law Rev., 1973-74. With USAR, 1969-73. Mem. ABA, Assn. of Bar of City of N.Y., Am. Bankruptcy Inst., Turnaround Mgmt. Assn. (dir.). Bankruptcy. Office: Kaye Scholer Fierman Hayes & Handler LLP 425 Park Ave New York NY 10022-3506

PERKINS, DOSITE HUGH, JR. retired lawyer; b. Shreveport, La., Jan. 8, 1930; s. Dosite Hugh and Cora Lee (Henry) P.; m. Dolores Bates, Apr. 27, 1956; children— Dosite John, Dolores Ann, Desmond Lee. J.D., Tulane U., 1953. Bar: La. 1953, U.S. Ct. Appeals (5th cir.) 1981, U.S. Dist. Ct. (we. dist.) La. 1953. Asst. city atty. City of Shreveport, 1953-57; asst. U.S. Atty. Dept. Justice, Shreveport, 1957-87. Republican. Episcopalian.

PERKINS, ROGER ALLAN, lawyer; b. Port Chester, N.Y., Mar. 4, 1943; s. Francis Newton and Winifred Marcella (Smith) P.; m. Katherine Louise Howard, Nov. 10, 1984; children: Marshall, Morgan, Matthew, Justin, Ashley. BA, Pa. State U., 1965; postgrad., U. Ill., 1965-66; JD with honors, George Washington U., 1969. Bar: Md. 1969, Mass. 1975. Trial atty. Nationwide Ins. Co., Annapolis, Md., 1969-72; assoc. Arnold, Beauchemin & Huber, PA, Balt., 1973; from assoc. to ptnr. Goodman & Bloom, PA, Annapolis, 1973-76; ptnr. Luff and Perkins, 1976-78; pvt. practice Annapolis, 1978—. Temp. adminstrv. hearing officer Anne Arundel County, 1984-99; asst. city atty., Annapolis, 1980-82; atty. Bd. Appeals of City of Annapolis, 1986—; mem. Appellate Jud. Nominating Commn., 1995—. Editl. adv. bd. Daily Record, 1996-97. Mem. Gov.'s Task Force on Family Law, 1991-94; adv. coun. on family legal need of low income persons MLSC, 1991; coach youth sports. Fellow Am. Acad. Matrimonial Lawyers, Am. Bar Found., Md. Bar Found. (bd. dirs. 1992-95); mem. ABA (ho. dels. 1991-93, 94-96, standing com. on solo and small firm practitioners 1993-97, chair 1996-97), Md. State Bar Assn. (pres. 1992-93, treas. 1988-91, bd. govs. 1985-87, chair spl. com. on lawyer profl. responsibility 1994-95, family and juvenile law sect. coun. 1983-89, chair 1987-88), Anne Arundel County Bar Assn. (pres. 1984-85). Republican. Methodist. State civil litigation, Family and matrimonial. Home: 503 Bay Hills Dr Arnold MD 21012-2001 Office: The Courtyards 133 Defense Hwy Ste 202 Annapolis MD 21401-8907 E-mail: roger@perkinslaw.com

PERKINS, ROSWELL BURCHARD, lawyer; b. Boston, May 21, 1926; AB cum laude, Harvard U., 1945, LLB cum laude, 1949; LLD (hons.), Bates Coll., 1988. Bar: Mass. 1949, N.Y. 1949. Assoc. Debevoise, Plimpton & McLean, N.Y.C., 1949-53; ptnr. Debevoise & Plimpton and predecessor firm, 1957-96; of counsel, head rep. office Debevoise & Plimpton LLC, Moscow, 1997-01. Asst. sec. U.S. Dept. Health, Edn. and Welfare, 1954-56; counsel to Gov. Nelson A. Rockefeller State of N.Y., 1959; asst. counsel spl. subcom. Senate Commerce Com. to investigate organized crime in interstate commerce, 1950; chmn. N.Y.C. Mayor's Task Force on Transp. Reorgn., 1966; mem. Pres.'s Adv. Panel on Pers. Interchange, 1968, chmn. adv. com. Medicare Adminstrn. Contracting, Subcontracting HEW, 1973-74; dir. Fiduciary Trust Co., N.Y., 1963—; trustee Bowery Savs. Bank, 1975-82; mem. legal com. to bd. dirs. N.Y. Stock Exch., 1995— Editor Harvard Law Rev., 1948-49. Mem. N.Y. Lawyers Com. Civil Rights, 1970-73; mem. nat. exec. com., 1973—, co-chmn. 1973-75; mem. adv. coun. Woodrow Wilson Sch. Pub. and Internat. Affairs, Princeton U., 1967-69; bd. dirs. The Commonwealth Fund, 1974-97, Sch. Am. Ballet, 1974-85, chmn bd. 1976-80; dir., sec. N.Y. Urban Coalition, 1967-74; trustee Pomfret Sch., 1961-76; The Brearly Sch., 1969-75; dir. Salzburg Seminar Am. Studies, 1970-80; mem. overseers vis. com. Kennedy Sch. Govt., Harvard U., 1971-77, Harvard and Radcliffe Colls., 1958-64, 1971-77. Recipient Spl. Merit citation Am. Judicature Soc., 1989, Harvard Law Sch. Assn. award, 1994. Mem. ABA (commn. on law and economy, 1975-79, mem. house of dels. 1980-93), N.Y. State Bar Assn., Assn. of the Bar of the City of N.Y. (chmn. spl. com. on fed. conflict of interest laws 1958-60). Harvard Alumni Assn. (pres. 1970-71), Am. Law Inst. (mem. coun. 1969, pres. 1980-93, chmn. coun. 1993—), Am. Arbitration Assn. (bd. dirs. 1966-71). General corporate, Private international, Mergers and acquisitions. Home: 1120 5th Ave New York NY 10128-0144 Office: Debevoise & Plimpton 919 3rd Ave 46th Fl New York NY 10022-6225 E-mail: rbperkins@debevoise.com

PERKINS SENN, KARON ELAINE, lawyer; b. Lexington, Ky., Nov. 9, 1959; d. John Robert and Sharon Lynn (Cook) Perkins; m. F. Anthony Senn. BA, Purdue U., 1980; cert. of proficiency, Pushkin Inst. Russian Lang., Moscow, 1980; JD, Ind. U., 1983. Bar: Ind. 1984, U.S. Dist. Ct. (so. dist.) Ind. 1984, U.S. Dist. Ct. (no. dist.) Ind. 1990. Internt. mktg. specialist Ind. Dept. Commerce, Indpls., 1980-81; law clk. Mendelson, Kennedy, Miller, Muller & Hall, 1981-83; assoc. Jewell, Crump & Angermeier, Columbus, Ind., 1983-86; ptnr. Dalmbert, Marshall & Perkins, 1986-92; pvt. practice Ind., 1992—. Asst. city atty. City of Columbus, 1985-95; town atty. Town of Hope (Ind.), 1987-89; course coord. law for non lawyers Ind. U.-Purdue U., Columbus, 1985-95; course coord. inst. law Sr. Citizen Ctr., Columbus, 1990; author, speaker continuing legal edn. seminar, 1988, 89, 90, 91, 92, 94, 96; bd. dirs., sec. Bartholomew Area Legal Aid, 1984-96. Mem. Leadership Bartholomew County, Columbus, 1986; bd. dirs. Salvation Army, Columbus, 1986-92, Columbus Dance Workshop; chmn. Bartholomew County Young Reps., 1986-88, 2d dist. Young Reps., 1987-91; treas. Columbus Task Force on Poor Relief, 1985-90. Recipient Outstanding Female Young Rep., Ind. Young Rep. Fedn., 1987, cert. of appreciation Ind. Tsk Force on Poor Relief, 1987; faculty alumni fellow Ind. U., 1983. Mem. ABA (del. young lawyers div. 1986-87), Ind. Bar Assn. (council, bd. dirs. young lawyers sect., sec.-treas., chair), Bartholomew Bar Assn. (sec., sec.-treas. 1984-90), Ind. Assn. Trial Lawyers, Columbus Jayshees (v.p. 1986, Outstanding New Mem. award 1985), Columbus Jaycees (bd. dirs. 1987), Zonta Club (parliamentarian Columbus 1986-88), Kiwanis. Baptist. Avocations: hiking, reading, sports. General civil litigation, Criminal, Labor. Home: 15830 E Lake Shore Dr N Hope IN 47246-9783 Office: Ste 2C 415 Washington St Columbus IN 47201-6757

PERKO, KENNETH ALBERT, JR. lawyer, real estate executive, mathematics researcher; b. Iron Mountain, Mich., Feb. 9, 1943; s. Kenneth Albert and Alice Ellen (Hamad) P.; m. Susan Jane Roodenburg, Oct. 5, 1968; children: Kathryn Ann, Kenneth Albert. AB in Math. with honors magna cum laude, Princeton U., 1964; JD, Harvard U., 1967. Bar: Ohio, N.Y.; cert. real estate broker, N.Y. Assoc. Milbank, Tweed, Hadley & McCloy, N.Y.C., 1967-79; asst. sec. The Rockefeller Group, 1979-96, 98—; counsel Radio City Music Hall, 1985-96, Tishman Speyer Properties, 1996-97. Lectr. Cambridge U., 1979, U. Paris, 1979; asst. sec. RCPI Trust, Rockefeller Ctr. Properties, Inc., The Rockefeller Ctr. Tower Condominium, 1996-97; reviewer Math. Revs., 1980—. Contbr. aricles to profl. jours. Trustee Princeton Libr., N.Y.C., 1968—, Rockette Alumnae Found., 1992—. Grantee NSF, Blacksburg, Va., 1982. Mem. Assn. Bar of the City N.Y. (com. profl. and judicial ethics 1994-97, com. profl. discipline 1997—). Democrat. Roman Catholic. General civil litigation, General corporate, Insurance. Home: 325 Old Army Rd Scarsdale NY 10583-2643

PERLIS, MICHAEL FREDRICK, lawyer; b. N.Y.C., June 3, 1947; s. Leo and Betty F. (Gantz) P.; children: Amy Hannah, David Matthew; m. Angela M. Rinaldi, Dec. 23, 1988. BS in Fgn. Svc. , Georgetown U., 1968, JD, 1971. Bar: D.C. 1971, N.Y. 1993, U.S. Dist. Ct. D.C. 1971, U.S. Ct. Appeals 1971, D.C. Ct. Appeals 1971, Calif. 1980, U.S. Dist. Ct. (no. dist.) Calif. 1980, U.S Dist. Ct. (cen. dist.) Calif. 1985, U.S. Ct. Appeals (9th cir.) 1980, U.S. Supreme Ct., 1980, N.Y. 1993. Law clerk D.C. Ct. Appeals, Washington, 1971-72; asst. corp. counsel D.C., Washington, 1972-74; counsel U.S. SEC, div. enforcement, Washington, 1974-75, br. chief, 1975-77, asst. dir., 1977-80; ptnr. Pettit & Martin, San Francisco, 1980-89, Stroock & Stroock & Lavan, L.A., 1989—; adj. prof. Cath. U. Am., 1979-80. Mem. ABA (co-chmn. subcom. securities and commodities litigation 1982-83), D.C. Bar Assn., Calif. State Bar Assn. Federal civil litigation. Office: Stroock & Stroock & Lavan 2029 Century Park E Ste 1800 Los Angeles CA 90067-3086

PERLMAN, BURTON, judge; b. Dec. 17, 1924; s. Phillip and Minnie Perlman; m. Alice Weihl, May 20, 1956; children: Elizabeth, Sarah, Nancy, Daniel. BE, Yale U., 1945, ME, 1947; LLB, U. Mich., 1952. Bar: Ohio 1959, N.Y. 1953, Conn. 1952, U.S. Dist. Ct. (so. and ea. dists.) N.Y. 1954, U.S. Dist. Ct. (so. dist.) Ohio 1959, U.S. Ct. Appeals (2d cir.) 1953, U.S. Ct. Appeals (6th cir.) 1959. Assoc. Armand Lackenbach, N.Y.C., NY, 1952—58; pvt. practice Cin., 1958—61; assoc. Paxton and Seasongood, 1961—67; ptnr. Schmidt, Effton, Josselson and Weber, 1968—71; U.S. magistrate U.S. Dist. Ct. (so. dist.) Ohio, 1971—76, U.S. bankruptcy judge, 1976—. Chief bankruptcy judge so. dist. Ohio, 1986—93; adj. prof. U. Cin. Law Sch., 1976—. Served with U.S. Army, 1944—46. Mem.: ABA, Fed. Bar Assn., Am. Judicature Soc., Cin. Bar Assn. Office: US Bankruptcy Ct Atrium 2 8th Fl 221 E 4th St Cincinnati OH 45202-4124

PERLMAN, JERALD LEE, lawyer; b. Baton Rouge, Feb. 25, 1947; s. Ralph Robert and Carol Mayer (Herzberg) P.; m. Francine Evonne McKelvey, May 8, 1984; children: Louise, Lee, Kevin. BA, Washington & Lee U., 1969; JD, La. State U., 1972. Bar: La. 1972, Tex. 1994, U.S. Dist. Ct. (we. dist.) La. 1972, U.S. Dist. Ct. (ea. and we. dists.) Ark. 1991, U.S. Ct. Appeals (5th cir.) 1977, U.S. Supreme Ct. 1990. Assoc. Blanchard, Walker, O'Quin & Roberts, Shreveport, La., 1972-76, ptnr., 1976-83, Walker, Tooke, Perlman & Lyons, Shreveport, 1983-94; regional office chief litigation divsn. La. Dept. Justice, 1994—. Assoc. editor La. State U. Law Rev., 1971-72. Bd. dirs. Broadmoor Southside YMCA, Shreveport, 1984-88, vice chmn., 1986, chmn., 1987; bd. dirs. Shreveport Met. YMCA, 1987; bd. dirs. NW La. chpt. ACLU, 1987-93. Capt. USAR, 1972. Named to La. State U. Law Ctr. Hall of Fame. Mem. La. Bar Assn. (com. on uniform court rules 1998—), Shreveport Bar Assn., La. Assn. Def. Counsel (bd. dirs. 1979-81), Fedn. Ins. and Corp. Counsel, Order of Coif, Phi Beta Kappa, Omicron Delta Kappa. Democrat. Jewish. Avocations: tennis, reading. Office: La Dept Justice Litigation Divsn 330 Marshall St Ste 777 Shreveport LA 71101-3016

PERLMAN, RICHARD BRIAN, lawyer; b. N.Y.C., Aug. 19, 1951; s. William H. and Beryl N. (Cohen) P.; m. Virginia Merrill, Aug. 1, 1976; 1 child, Jason Eric. BA, Franklin and Marshall Coll., 1973; JD, Temple U., 1976. Bar: Pa. 1976, U.S. Dist. Ct. (ea. dist.) Pa. 1977, U.S. Supreme Ct. 1982, Fla. 1999; cert. family mediator Fla. Supreme Ct., 1996. Assoc. Law Offices of Peter N. Harrison, Doylestown, Pa., 1976-77, Zion & Klein, Bryn Mawr, 1977-78; founder, owner The Law Ctr., Norristown, 1978-96, West Chester, 1982-96. Pres. Mothers Against Drunk Driving, Chester and Delaware Counties, Pa., 1987-89, 90-92; bd. dirs. Big Bros./Big Sisters, Montgomery County, Pa., 1979-85. Avocations: music, boating, golf. Alternative dispute resolution, Bankruptcy, Family and matrimonial. E-mail: rbpesqlbk@aol.com

PERLMUTH, WILLIAM ALAN, lawyer; b. N.Y.C., Nov. 21, 1929; s. Charles and Roe (Schneider) P.; m. Loretta Kaufman, Mar. 14, 1951; children: Carolyn, Diane. AB, Wilkes Coll., 1951; LLB, Columbia U., 1953. Bar: N.Y. 1954. Assoc. Cravath, Swaine & Moore, N.Y.C., 1955-61; ptnr. Stroock & Stroock & Lavan, 1962—. Dir. Sentry Tech. Corp., Hauppage, N.Y. Editor Columbia U. Law Rev., 1952-53. Trustee Aeroflex Found., N.Y.C., 1965—, City Ctr. 55th St. Theater Found., 1995—, Harkness Founds. for Dance, N.Y.C., 1976—, Sch. Am. Ballet, 1997—, Wilkes U., Wilkes-Barre, Pa., 1980—, Weininger Found., 1985—, Mount Sinai-NYU Health Sys., 1995—; trustee Hosp. for Joint Diseases Orthopaedic Inst., N.Y.C., 1980—, chmn. bd. trustees, 1994—. Mem. N.Y. State Bar Assn., Assn. of Bar of City of N.Y. Jewish. General corporate, Mergers and acquisitions, Securities. Home: 880 5th Ave New York NY 10021-4951 Office: Stroock & Stroock & Lavan 180 Maiden Ln Fl 34 New York NY 10038-4937

PERLOFF, JEAN MARCOSSON, lawyer; b. Lakewood, Ohio, June 25, 1942; d. John Solomon and Marcella Catherine (Borngen) Marcosson; m. Lawrence Storch, Stpe. 8, 1991. BA magna cum laude, Lake Erie Coll., 1965; MA in Italian, UCLA, 1967; JD magna cum laude, Ventura Coll. Law, 1976. Bar: Calif. 1976, U.S. Dist. Ct. (cen. dist.) Calif. 1978. Assoc. in Italian U. Calif.-Santa Barbara, 1967-70; law clk., paralegal Ventura County Pub. Defender's Office, Ventura, Calif., 1975; sole practice, 1976-79; co-prin. Clabaugh & Perloff, A Profl. Corp., 1979-82; sr. jud. atty. to presiding justice 6th divsn. 2d Dist. Ct. Appeals, L.A., 1982-97; comml. property mgr. Santa Barbara, Calif., 1997—. Instr. Ventura Coll. Law, 1976-79. Pres., bd. dirs. Santa Barbara Zool. Gardens, 1987-88; bd. dirs. Montecito Found., 1999—; trustee Lake Erie Coll., 1993—; mem. 19th Agrl. Dist. Bd., 2001—. Named Woman of Yr., 18th Senatorial dist. and 35th Assembly dist. Calif. Legislature, 1993; recipient Disting. Alumnae award Lake Erie Coll., 1996. Mem. Calif. Bar Assn. (appellate ct. com. 1993-95), Fiesta City Club, Kappa Alpha Sigma. Democrat. Avocations: tennis, jogging, biking, reading, music. Home: 1384 Plaza Pacifica Santa Barbara CA 93108-2877

PERLSTEIN, WILLIAM JAMES, lawyer; b. N.Y.C., Feb. 7, 1950; s. Justin Sol and Jane (Goldberg) P.; m. Teresa Catherine Lotito, Dec. 20, 1970; children: David, Jonathan. Student, London Sch. Econs., 1969-70; BA summa cum laude, Union Coll., 1971; JD, Yale U., 1974. Bar: Conn. 1974, D.C. 1976, U.S. Dist. Ct. D.C. 1977, U.S. Ct. Appeals (D.C. cir.) 1978, U.S. Supreme Ct. 1993, N.Y. 2000. Law clk. to judge Marvin Frankel U.S. Dist. Ct., N.Y.C., 1974-75; assoc. Wilmer, Cutler & Pickering, Washington, 1975-82, ptnr., 1982—, mem. mgmt. com., 1995—, chmn., 1998—. Mng. editor Yale Law Jour., 1973-74; contbg. author The Workout Game, 1987. Dir. Neighborhood Legal Svcs. program. Mem.: ABA (bus. bankruptcy com 1983—, v.chmn. executory contracts subcom. of bus. bankruptcy com. 1988—90, bankruptcy cts. subcom. 1990—97, chmn. legislation subcom. 1997—), Am. Bankruptcy Inst. (chmn. legis. com. 1986—89, bd. dirs. 1989—93, bd. dirs. 1997—), Am. Law Inst. (gen. counsel), Am. Coll. Bankruptcy, Am. Bar Found., Phi Beta Kappa. Jewish. Bankruptcy, Legislative. E-mail: wperlstein@wilmer.com

PERMUT, SCOTT RICHARD, lawyer; b. N.Y.C., Apr. 23, 1954; arrived in Israel, 1980; BA magna cum laude, Queens Coll., N.Y.C., 1977; JD, St. Johns Law Sch., 1980. Ptnr. Goldsobel & Permut, Haifa, Israel, 1980—. With Israeli Def. Forces, 1986. Intellectual property, Probate, Real property. Office: 5 Hantke St Haifa Israel Fax: 972.4.8253663. E-mail: srp@permlaw.com

PERNITZ, SCOTT GREGORY, lawyer; b. Jan. 28, 1953; s. William John and June Mary (Shaw) Pernitz; m. Constance Denise Sheffer, Aug. 04, 1979; children: Justin William, Julia Dawn, Jeffrey Scott. BA cum laude in Polit. Sci., U. Wis., Madison, 1975, JD cum laude , 1979. Bar: Wis. 1979, U.S. dist. Ct. (we. dist.) Wis. 1979, U.S. Dist. Ct. (ea. dist.) Wis. 1986, U.S. Ct. Appeals (7th cir.) 1979, U.S. Supreme Ct. 1986, cert.: Nat. Bd. Trial Advocacy (civil trial specialist). Assoc. Winner, McCallum, Hendee & Wixson, Madison, Wis., 1980—82; ptnr. Winner, McCallum, Wixson & Pernitz, 1983—89, Winner Wixson & Pernitz, Madison, 1990—. Mem.: Wis. Acad. Trial Lawyers, ATLA, Def. Rsch. Inst., Civil Trial Counsel of Wis., Wis. Bar Assn., Dane County Bar Assn., Nat. Tae Kwon Do Assn. State civil litigation, Insurance, Personal injury. Home: 8019 Shag Bark Cir Cross Plains WI 53528-9307 Office: Winner Wixson & Pernitz 22 E Mifflin St Ste 702 Madison WI 53703-4242

PERON, SABRINA, lawyer; b. Milan, Italy, Dec. 16, 1964; d. Giancarlo Peron and Rosaria Previtera Degree in law, Milan U., 1991. Bar: Milan 1995. Asst. Studio Valli-Donvito, Milan, 1991-94; assoc. Studio Prof. AVV. Granelli, 1995-97, Franzosi Dal Negro Avvocati Associati, Milan, 1997-99; ptnr. Studio Legale Avvocati Associati, 2000—. Asst. lectr. Pavia U., 1994-96, Milan U., 1997—; lectr. Istituto Formazione Giornalismo, 1998-99; spkr. in field. Contbr. articles to profl. jours. Avocations: philosophy, journalism. Communications, Entertainment, Libel. Office: Studio Legale Avvocati Assn Via U Foscolo 4 20121 Milan Italy Fax: 0039/02/866935. E-mail: stleaa@tiscalinet.it

PERONI, ROBERT JOSEPH, law educator, lawyer; b. 1953; BSC, DePaul U., 1973; JD, Northwestern U., 1976; LLM in Taxation, NYU, 1980. Bar: Ill. 1976, U.S. Dist. Ct. (no. dist.) Ill. 1976, U.S. Ct. Appeals 7th cir.) 1977, Calif. 1979, U.S. Dist. Ct. (no. dist.) Calif. 1979, U.S. Ct. Appeals (9th and D.C. cirs.) 1979, U.S. Tax Ct. 1979, U.S. Ct. Claims 1979. Assoc. Jenner & Block, Chgo., 1976-78; with Orrick, Herrington & Sutcliffe, San Francisco, 1978-79; instr. taxation NYU Sch. Law, N.Y.C., 1980-81; asst. prof. law Tulane U., New Orleans, 1981-84, assoc. prof., 1984-89; prof.-in-residence Office of Chief Counsel IRS, Washington, 1985-86; prof. law George Washington U., 1999—. Vis. assoc. prof. law NYU, 1989; vis. prof. law UCLA, 1995, U. Tex., 1998, U. Pa., 2001; Robert Kramer res. prof. law, 1992—. Articles editor Jour. Criminal Law and Criminology, 1975-76, grad. editor, 1979-80; co-mng. editor Tax Law Rev., 1980-81. Recipient Felix Frankfurter Disting. Tchg. award Tulane U. Sch. Law, 1984. Mem. ABA, Calif. Bar Assn., Order of Coif. Office: George Washington U Law Sch Washington DC 20052-0001

PERRETT, ROSS GRAHAM, lawyer; b. Ipswich, Australia, Nov. 2, 1957; s. Graham F. and Glenice A. P.; m. Jennifer Anne Dunning, Dec. 20, 1980; children: Sarah, Elise Jonathon. B of Law, Queensland U., Brisbane, Australia, 1981, B of Commerce, 1979. Clk. Clayton Utz, Brisbane, Australia, 1979-80, solicitor Australia, 1981-84, ptnr. Australia, 1984-98, mng. ptnr. Australia, 1998—. Mem. Queensland Law Soc., Valley Cricket Club (life), Royal Queensland Golf Club, Brisbane Club. Administrative and regulatory, General civil litigation, Alternative dispute resolution. Office: Clayton Utz 215 ADelaide St Brisbane QLD 4000 Australia Fax: 61 073292 7950. E-mail: rperrett@claytonutz.com

PERRIN, MICHAEL WARREN, lawyer; b. Cameron, Tex., Nov. 10, 1946; s. Frank W. and Mary Ann (Green) P.; m. Melinda Elizabeth Hill, Aug. 9, 1969; children: Elizabeth, Carter, Hunter. BS, U. Tex., Austin, 1969, JD, 1971. Bar: Tex. 1972, U.S. Dist. Ct. (no., ea., we. and so. dists.) Tex., U.S. Ct. Appeals (5th and 11th cirs.), U.S. Supreme Ct. Assoc. Vinson & Elkins, Houston, 1972-73; assoc. Fisher, Roch & Gallagher, 1973-76; ptnr. Fisher, Gallagher, Perrin & Lewis, 1976-91; sole practice, 1991-96; ptnr. King & Spalding, 1996—. Fellow Am. Coll. Trial Lawyers, Internat. Acad. Trial Lawyers, Internat. Soc. Barristers; mem. Am. Bd. Trial Advocates, Am. Bar Found., Houston Young Lawyers Assn. (sec. 1974-75), Tex. Young Lawyers Assn. (dir. 1976-78, chmn. bd. 1978-79), Houston Trial Lawyers Assn. (pres. 1987-88), Tex. Trial Lawyers Assn. (pres. 1989-90), Tex. Bar Found. (Houston chpt.), U. Tex. Devel. bd. Methodist. General civil litigation, Personal injury.

PERRIS, TERRENCE GEORGE, lawyer; b. L.A., Oct. 18, 1947; s. Theodore John Grivas and Penny (Sfakianos) Perris. BA magna cum laude, U. Toledo, 1969; JD summa cum laude, U. Mich., 1972. Bar: Ohio 1972, U.S. Tax Ct. 1982, U.S. Ct. Claims 1983, U.S. Supreme Ct. 1983. Law clk. to judge U.S. Ct. Appeals (2d cir.), N.Y.C., 1972-73; law clk. to Justice Potter Stewart U.S. Supreme Ct., Washington, 1973-74; assoc. Squire, Sanders & Dempsey LLP, Cleve., 1974-80; ptnr. Squire, Sanders & Dempsey, 1980—. V.p., trustee SS&D Found., Cleve., 1984—; nat. coord. Taxation Practice Area, 1987—, mgmt. com., 1996—; chmn. Cleve. Tax Inst., 1993; vis. prof. law U. Mich., 1996; adj. prof. law Case Western Res. U., 2001; lectr. in field. Vis. com. U. Mich. Law Sch., 1986—. Capt. U.S. Army, 1974. Mem. ABA, Ohio Bar Assn., Cleve. Bar Assn. (subchpt. C of internal revenue code task force), Supreme Ct. Hist. Soc., Tax Club Cleve., Order of Coif, Union Club of Cleve., U. Mich. Club of Cleve., The Club of Cleve., Pres.'s Club (Ann Arbor, Mich.), Phi Kappa Phi. Republican. Eastern Orthodox. Avocation: landscape gardening. Constitutional, Corporate taxation, Personal income taxation. Office: Squire Sanders & Dempsey LLP 4900 Key Tower 127 Public Sq Cleveland OH 44114-1216 E-mail: tperris@ssd.com

PERRITT, HENRY HARDY, JR. law educator; b. Little Rock, Dec. 30, 1944; s. Henry Hardy and Margaret Frances (Floyd) P. SB in Engring., MIT, 1966, SM in Mgmt., 1970; JD, Georgetown U., 1975. Bar: Va. 1976, Pa. 1977, D.C. 1981, Md. 1995, Ill. 1998, U.S. Supreme Ct. 1981, U.S. Ct. Appeals (3d cir.) 1979, U.S. Ct. Appeals (2d cir.) 1979, U.S. Ct. Appeals (6th cir.) 1983. Sr. sales planner Lockheed Corp., Marietta, Ga., 1968-71; exec. sec. Cost of Living Coun., Washington, 1972-75; legis. analyst U.S. Dept. Commerce, 1971-72; mem. staff White House, Washington, 1975; dep. undersec. U.S. Dept. Labor, 1975-76; gen. counsel labor Conrail, Phila., 1976-81; prof. law Villanova U., 1981-99, dir. Villanova Ctr. for Info. Law and Policy, 1992-99, dir. Project Bosnia, 1996-99; dean Kent Coll. of Law, Chgo., 1999—. Cons. atty. Morgan, Lewis & Bockius, Washington, 1981-90, Conrail, 1981-90; Apptd. vice chmn. Coal Commn., U.S. Sec. of Labor, 1990; mem. computer sci. and telecom. bd. Nat. Rsch. Coun. Author: Employee Dismissal Law and Practice, 1984, 4th edit., 1997, Labor Injunctions, 1986, How to Practice Law with Computers, 1988, Employee Benefits Claims Law and Practice, 1989, Workplace Torts

Rights and Liabilities, 1990, Americans with Disabilities Act Handbook, 1990, 3d edit., 1998, Trade Secrets: A Practitioner's Guide, 1994, Law and The Information Superhighway, 1996, 2d edit., 2001; contbr. articles to profl. jours. Mem. ABA (chmn. com. on r.r. and airline labor law 1983-86, chmn. com. on regulatory initiatives and info. tech., adminstrv. law sect., co-vice chmn. dispute resolution com., adminstrv. law sect. 1987-90, sec. labor and employment sect. 2000—), Assn. Am. Law Schs. (chmn. sect. on law and computers 1991), Coun. on Fgn. Rels., Econ. Club. Democrat. Office: Office of Dean Kent Coll of Law Chicago IL 60600 E-mail: hperritt@kentlaw.edu

PERRY, BLAIR LANE, lawyer; b. Oct. 2, 1929; s. Elwyn Lionel and Ruth Hubbard (Kelley) Perry; m. Margaret James, July 04, 1959; children: Jennifer E., Andrew B.; m. Theodora Pearson, Mar. 29, 1998. BA, Williams Coll., 1951; LLB, Harvard U., 1957. Bar: Mass. 1957, U.S. Dist. Ct. Mass. 1958, U.S. Dist. Ct. (no. dist.) Tex 1978, U.S. Ct. Appeals (1st cir.) 1958, U.S. Supreme Ct. 1971. Assoc. Hale and Dorr, Boston, 1957—63, jr. ptnr., 1963—68, sr. ptnr., 1968—90; of counsel Fish & Richardson, 1991—. Contbr. articles to profl. jours. With USMC, 1951—53. Mem.: ABA, Mass. Bar Assn., Boston Patent Law Assn. Antitrust, General civil litigation, Intellectual property. Home: 340 Baytree Dr Melbourne FL 32940-2105 Office: Fish & Richardson 225 Franklin St Fl 32 Boston MA 02110-2809

PERRY, BRIAN DREW, SR. lawyer, career officer; b. New Orleans, Feb. 3, 1955; s. Donald Roy and Helen Magaret P.; m. Karla Leigh, Mar. 17, 1984; children: Ashleigh, Brain-Drew, Morgan, Max, Emmaline, Kevin. BS, Our Lady of Holy Cross, 1985; JD, Loyola U., 1989. Bar: La. Asst. city atty. City of New Orleans, 1989-91; adv. Saudi Arabian Oil Co., Dhahran, Saudi Arabia, 1991-98; pvt. practice New Orleans, 1998—. Bd. govs. Saudi Aramco Employees Assn., Dhahran, Saudi Arabia, 1984-88. Pub.: New Orleans Legis. Digest, 1990; author: Algiers Point, 1999. Mem. Saudi Aramco Sch. Bd., New Orleans, 1995-98. Lt. Col. U.S. Army, 1973—. Mem. La. State Bar Assn. Catholic. General civil litigation, General practice, Private international. Home: 38 Park Timbers New Orleans LA 70131 Office: Law Office Brian D Perry Sr 4041 Tulane Ave New Orleans LA 70119-6849 Fax: (504) 361-9333. E-mail: Brian.d.Perry@u.s.army.mil

PERRY, DAVID, lawyer, insurance executive, real estate consultant; b. Phila., Nov. 13, 1940; s. Harry J. and Alice M. (Heller) P.; B.A. in English Lit., Carleton Coll., 1962; LL.B., U. Pa., 1965, M.A. in Econs., 1972, Ph.D. in Econs., 1974; m. Sherryl Frances Rosenbaum, June 24, 1962. Bar: Pa. 1965. Law clk. firm Freedman, Borowsky and Lorry, Phila., 1964-65; atty. HUD, Phila., 1965-67; sole practice law, Phila., 1967-72; sr. fin. and planning analyst INA Corp., Phila., 1972-74; exec. asst. to pres. Certain-Teed Products Corp., Valley Forge, Pa., 1974; dir. capital budgeting INA Corp., Phila., 1974-75, asst. treas., 1975-78, v.p., 1979-82, pres. Phila. Investment Corp. subs. INA Corp., 1980-82; partner, real estate cons. Ironwood Assocs., 1982-83; ptnr. law firm Perry, Goldstein, Fialkowski and Perry, 1983— . Brookings Inst. research fellow, 1968-69. Mem. Phila. Bar Assn., Am. Econ. Assn. Club: Union League of Phila. Home: 431 Boxwood Rd Bryn Mawr PA 19010-1254 Office: Ironwood Assocs Two Mellon Bank Ctr 2 Mellon Bank Ctr Fl 2400 Philadelphia PA 19102-2365

PERRY, EDWARD NEEDHAM, lawyer; b. Cambridge, Mass., Oct. 16, 1946; s. Arthur and Marjorie (Bemis) P.; m. Cynthia Wilson Wood, May 31, 1980. BA, Williams Coll., 1968; JD, Vanderbilt U., 1975. Bar: Mass. 1975, U.S. Supreme Ct. 1980, U.S. Ct. Appeals (9th cir.) 1981, (1st cir.) 1984, (2d cir.) 1984, U.S. Dist. Ct. Mass. 1983. Assoc. cons. Charles Evans & Assocs., Boston, 1971; litigation atty. U.S. Dept. Labor, Washington, 1975-82; ptnr. Perkins, Mecsas, Smith, Arata & Howard, Boston, 1982-87, Woodman, Eaton & Perry, P.C., 1988—. Trustee Northfield Mt. Hermon Sch. (Mass.), 1975-80, 83-86, 88—, Trinitarian Congl. Ch., Concord, Mass, 1970—; mem. Town Libr. Com., Concord, Mass., 1986—; bd. dirs. Concord-Carlisle Community Chest, 1988—. Lt. (j.g.) USN, 1968-70. Recipient Meritorious Achievement awards U.S Dept. Labor, 1979, 80, Spl. Achievement award, 1981, award Am. Trial Lawyers Assn., 1975. Mem. ABA, Mass. Bar Assn., Alumni Pres.'s Coun. Ind. Secondary Schs. (v.p. 1987—, bd. dirs.), Northfield Mt. Hermon Sch. Alumni Assn. (pres. 1983-86). Republican. Federal civil litigation, State civil litigation, Labor. Home: 21 Thoreau St Concord MA 01742-2410 Office: Woodman Eaton & Perry PC 801 Main St Ste 14 Concord MA 01742-3366

PERRY, EDWIN CHARLES, lawyer; b. Lincoln, Nebr., Sept. 29, 1931; s. Arthur Edwin and Charlotte C. (Peterson) P.; m. Joan Mary Hanson, June 5, 1954; children: Mary Mills, Judy Phipps, James Perry, Greg Perry, Jack Perry, Pricilla Hoffel Finger. BS, U. Nebr., 1953, JD, 1955. Bar: Nebr. 1955; U.S. Dist. Ct. Nebr., 1955; U.S. Ct. Appeals Nebr., 1968. Of counsel Perry, Guthery, Haase & Gessford, P.C., Lincoln, 1957—. Chmn. Lincoln Lancaster County Planning Com., Madonna Rehab. Hosp. Fellow Am. Bar Found., Nebr. Bar Found.; mem. Nebr. State Bar Assn. (chair ho. dels. 1987-88, pres. 1991-92), Nebr. Coun. Sch. Attys. (pres. 1978-79), Lincoln Bar Assn. (pres. 1982-83). Republican. Roman Catholic. Banking, Education and schools, Estate planning. Office: Perry Guthery Haase & Gessford PC 223 S 13th St Ste 1400 Lincoln NE 68508-2005

PERRY, JOHN F. lawyer; b. Pitts., July 12, 1950; s. Paul G. and Virginia (Patterson) P.; m. Marianne Duffy, Feb. 16, 1980. BA, U. Pa., 1972; JD, Dickinson Sch. Law, 1976. Bar: Pa. 1976, U.S. Dist. Ct. (we. dist.) Pa. 1976, U.S. Ct. Appeals (3d cir.) 1977, U.S. Supreme Ct. 1984. Ptnr. Springer Bush & Perry P.C., Pitts., 1976—. Mem. Fed. Bar Assn. (pres. western Pa. chpt., sec. fed. litigation sect., editor Side Bar newsletter), Pa. Bar Assn., Corpus Juris Soc., Oakmont Country Club. Republican. Presbyterian. Federal civil litigation, Health, Insurance. Home: 204 Highland Ter Pittsburgh PA 15215-1716 Office: Springer Bush & Perry PC 15th Fl 2 Gateway Ctr Pittsburgh PA 15222 E-mail: joepa@springerlaw.com

PERRY, JOHN RICHARD, JR. lawyer, mediator; b. Los Angeles, June 2, 1946; s. John Richard Perry and Betty Jane (Davis) Bouquet; m. Linda Mershon; children— Jennifer Lorraine, Garth James, Joseph Dee, Anthony Dee. Midshipman U.S. Naval Acad., 1966-68; B.A., U. Ariz., 1971; J.D., 1975. Bar: Ariz. 1975, U.S. Dist. Ct. Ariz. 1976, U.S. Ct. Appeals (9th cir.) 1977. Law clk. Ariz. Ct. Appeals, Tucson, 1975-76; sole practice, Tucson, 1976-78; assoc., then ptnr. Favour & Quail P.A., Prescott, Ariz., 1978-80; assoc. George M. Ireland, P.C., Prescott, 1980-83; sole practice, Prescott, 1983-84, 87-88; mng. ptnr. Perry & Hammond, Prescott, 1984-87, John R. Perry, Jr. & Assocs., Prescott, 1988—; mediator Yavapai County Conciliation Ct., Prescott, 1983— . Co-author: Ariz. Appellate Handbook, 1980. Mem. Dominican Laity, Cath. Ch. Served with USN, 1963-68. Mem. ABA, Assn. Trial Lawyers Am., Ariz. Trial Lawyers Assn., Soc. of Profls. in Dispute Resolution. Republican. Lodge: Rotary (past pres. Prescott Sun Up chpt. 1983). General civil litigation, Contracts commercial, Probate. Home: 4619 Quincy St Saint Louis MO 63116-1052 Office: Law Firm John R Perry Jr & Assocs 143 N Mccormick St Ste 202 Prescott AZ 86301-2726

PERRY, JON ROBERT, lawyer; b. Kane, Pa., May 14, 1965; s. James Felix and Judith Rose (Zelina) P.; m. Joni Lee Detrick, Aug. 10, 1991; children: Alex Joseph, Trevor James. BA summa cum laude, Pa. State U., 1987; JD magna cum laude, Duquesne U., 1991. Bar: Pa. 1991, U.S. Dist. Ct. (we. dist.) Pa. 1991, U.S. Ct. Apppeals (3d, 6th, 7th and fed. cirs.). Assoc. Reed Smith Shaw & McClay, Pitts., 1990-94; ptnr. Betts & Perry, 1994-97, Meyers Rosen Louik & Perry, Pitts., 1998—. Bd. dirs. Flying Pig Theatre, Pitts., J's Place, Inc., Kane, RBCI, Inc., Cranberry, Pa., CDS, Inc., Pitts. Exec. editor Duquesne Law Rev., 1991. Vol. mentor/spkr. elem. and high schs., Pitts., 1992—. Mem. ATLA, Pa. Trial Lawyers Assn., Pa. Bar Assn., Allegheny County Bar Assn., Allegheny County Acad. Trial Lawyers, Phi Beta Kappa. General civil litigation, Personal injury, Product liability. Office: Meyers Rosen Louik and Perry 437 Grant St Pittsburgh PA 15219-6002

PERRY, RONALD, lawyer; b. Pitts., Feb. 20, 1952; s. Joseph E. and Margaret (Majhan) P.; m. Deborah Lauer, July 19, 1975; children: Meredith Lyn, Erin Michelle. BA in Polit. Sci., Ind. U., Pa., 1974; JD, Western New Eng. U., 1978; LLM in Taxation, Temple U., 1982. Bar: Pa. 1978, U.S. Dist. Ct. (mid. dist.) Pa. 1979, U.S. Tax Ct. 1980, U.S. Supreme Ct. 1984. Pvt. practice, York, Pa., 1978-82; ptnr. Carn, Vaughn & Perry, 1982-85, Countess, Gilbert, Andrews, York, 1985—. Asst. dist. atty., York County, 1982-85. Pres. Self-Help Counseling, York, 1978-84; bd. dirs. West York (Pa.) Sch. Dist., 1983-85, York County Jr. Achievement, 1998—, dir. White Rose Invitational track and Field Meet, 1998—; solicitor West York Zoning Bd., 1987-88; chmn. Manchester Twp. Planning Commn., 1992-98; pres. York County Literacy Coun., 1992-98; bd. dirs. Jr. Achievement York County. Mem. ABA, Pa. Bar Assn., York County Estate Planning Coun. (bd. dirs. 1986-91), Rotary Club. Avocation: music. Contracts commercial, Corporate taxation, Taxation, general. Office: Countess Gilbert Andrews 29 N Duke St York PA 17401-1204

PERSCHBACHER, REX ROBERT, dean, law educator; b. Chgo., Aug. 31, 1946; s. Robert Ray and Nancy Ellen (Beach) P.; children: Julie Ann, Nancy Beatrice. AB in Philosophy, Stanford U., 1968; JD, U. Calif., Berkeley, 1972. Bar: Calif. 1972, U.S. Dist. Ct. (no. dist.) Calif. 1973, U.S. Dist. Ct. (so. dist.) Calif. 1979, U.S. Ct. Appeals (9th cir.) 1980, U.S. Dist. ct. (ea. dist.) Calif. 1985. Law clk. to judge U.S. Dist. Ct. (no. dist.) Calif., San Francisco, 1973-74; asst. prof. law U. Tex., Austin, 1974-75; assoc. Heller, Ehrman, White & McAuliffe, San Francisco, 1975-78; asst. prof. law U. San Diego, 1978-79, assoc. prof. law, 1980-81; mem. faculty Inst. on Internat. and Comparative Law, London, 1984—; acting prof. law U. Calif., Davis, 1981-85, prof., 1988—, assoc. dean, 1993-98, dean Law Sch., 1998—. Dir. clin. edn. Univ. Calif., Davis, 1981-93, acad. senate, law sch. rep., 1989-91; vis. prof. law Univ. Santa Clara (Calif.), summer 1986. Co-author: California Civil Procedure and Practice, 1996, California Legal Ethics, 2nd edit., 1997, Problems in Legal Ethics, 4th edit., 1997, Cases and Materials on Civil Procedure, 3d edit., 1998; contbr. articles to legal jours. Bd. dirs. Legal Svcs. of No. Calif., 1990-96. Mem. ABA, Calif. Bar Assn., Am. Assn. Law Schs., Inn of Ct. Democrat. Avocations: travel. Office: U Calif Sch Law King Hall Davis CA 95616*

PERSONS, JOHN WADE, lawyer; b. Fitchburg, Mass., Dec. 6, 1953; s. Roger W. and Vivian A. (Boudreau) P.; m. Marjorie L. Smith, July 18, 1980; children: Katherine A., Elizabeth W. BA in History magna cum laude, U. Conn., 1975, MA, 1977; JD, Albany Law Sch., 1980. Bar: N.Y. 1981, U.S. Dist. Ct. (no. dist.) N.Y. 1981, U.S. Dist. Ct. (ea. dist.) N.Y. 1985. From law clk. to assoc. Cade & Saunders, Albany, N.Y., 1978-84; legal researcher, writing instr. Albany Law Sch., 1979-80; assoc. Glynn and Mercep, Stony Brook, N.Y., 1984-86; ptnr. Glynn, Mercep and Persons, 1987-91; assoc. Faruolo, Caputi, Weintraub & Neary, Huntington, N.Y., 1991-96, Grey & Grey, L.L.P., Farmingdale, 1996—. Law guardian Albany County Family Ct., 1984. Mem. N.Y. State Bar Assn. (ins. sect., negligence and compensation law sect.), Suffolk County Bar Assn. (ins., negligence and compensation-plantiff's coun.), Killington Sch. for Instrs., Stony Brook Yacht Club. Democrat. Episcopalian. Club: Stony Brook Yacht. Federal civil litigation, State civil litigation, Personal injury. Home: 53 Cedar St Stony Brook NY 11790-1732 Office: Grey & Grey LLP 360 Main St Farmingdale NY 11735-3592 E-mail: jow6@aol.com

PERSYN, MARY GERALDINE, law librarian, law educator; b. Elizabeth, N.J., Feb. 25, 1945; d. Henry Anthony and Geraldine (Sumption) P. AB, Creighton U., 1967; MLS, U. Oreg., 1969; JD, Notre Dame U., 1982. Bar: Ind. 1982, U.S. Dist. Ct. (no. and so. dists.) Ind. 1982, U.S. Supreme Ct. 1995. Social scis. libr. Miami U., Oxford, Ohio, 1969-78; staff law libr. Notre Dame (Ind.) Law Sch., 1982-84; dir. law libr. Valparaiso (Ind.) U., 1984-87, law libr., assoc. prof. law, 1987—. Editor Journal of Legislation, 1981-82; mng. editor Third World Legal Studies, 1986—. V.p. Ind. Coop. Libr. Svcs. Auth., 1997-98, pres., 1998-99. Mem. ABA, Ind. State Bar Assn., Am. Assn. Law Librs. Ohio Regional Assn. Law Librs. (pres. 1990-91), Ind. State Quilt Guild (pres. 1996-2000). Roman Catholic. Home: 1308 Tuckahoe Park Dr Valparaiso IN 46383-4032 Office: Valparaiso U Law Libr Sch Law Valparaiso IN 46383 E-mail: mary.persyn@valpo.edu

PESHKIN, SAMUEL DAVID, lawyer; b. Des Moines, Oct. 6, 1925; s. Louis and Mary (Grund) P.; m. Shirley R. Isenberg, Aug. 17, 1947; children: Lawrence Allen, Linda Ann. BA, State U. Iowa, 1948, JD, 1951. Bar: Iowa 1951. Ptnr. Bridges & Peshkin, Des Moines, 1953-66, Peshkin & Robinson, Des Moines, 1966-82. Mem. Iowa Bd. Law Examiners, 1970—. Bd. dirs. State U. Iowa Found., 1957—, Old Gold Devel. Fund, 1956—, Sch. Religion U. Iowa, 1966—. Fellow Am. Bar Found., Internat. Soc. Barristers; mem. ABA (chmn. standing com. membership 1959— , ho. of dels. 1968— , bd. govs. 1973—), Iowa Bar Assn. (bd. govs. 1958— , pres. jr. bar sect. 1958-59, award of merit 1974), Inter-Am. Bar Assn., Internat. Bar Assn., Am. Judicature Soc., State U. Iowa Alumni Assn. (dir., pres. 1957) General corporate, Private international, Corporate taxation. Home: 6445 E Winchcomb Dr Scottsdale AZ 85254-3356

PESKIN, STEPHAN HASKEL, lawyer; b. N.Y.C., Oct. 31, 1943; s. Michael and Ruth (Berger) P.; m. Victoria Bond, Jan. 27, 1974. BA, NYU, 1965; JD, Bklyn. Coll., 1968. Bar: N.Y. 1968, U.S. Supreme Ct. 1972, U.S. Dist. Ct. D.C. 1974, Pa. 1979. Assoc. Rothblatt & Rothblatt, N.Y.C., 1968-70; ptnr. Rothblatt, Rothblatt, Seijas & Peskin, 1970-79, Tolmage, Peskin, Harris & Falick, N.Y.C., 1979—. Pres. N.Y. State Trial Lawyers Ins. Co., 1986-88; sr. faculty mem. Nat. Coll. Trial Advocacy, 1978—. Author: Settlement for Top Dollar, 1988; contbr. articles to law jours. Comdg. officer N.Y.C. Aux. Police, Central Park Precinct, 1978-90. Mem. ABA, N.Y. County Lawyers Assn., N.Y. Trial Lawyers Assn. (bd. dirs. 1980—, treas. 1982-86, v.p. 1986-88, pres. 1993-94), N.Y. Bar Assn., Assn. Trial Lawyers Am. (bd. govs. 1984—, chmn. tort sect. 1988—). Federal civil litigation, Criminal, Personal injury. Home: 256 W 10th St New York NY 10014-6520 Office: Tolmage Peskin Harris & Falick 20 Vesey St New York NY 10007-2913

PESSANHA, TOMAS VASCONCELOS, lawyer; b. Lisbon, Portugal, Apr. 22, 1972; s. Joao Vasconcelos Pessanha and Maria Cabral Moraes; m. Margarida Pinto Leite, July 4, 1998; 1 child, Margarida. Degree, U. Lisbon Law Sch., Portugal, 1995; postgrad., U. Coimbra, Portugal, 1997-98. Trainee Jose Maria Calherios & Assocs., Lisbon, Portugal, 1995-97, assoc. Portugal, 1997-2000, PMBGR, Lisbon, Portugal, 2000—. Author: Legal Implications of the Millenium Bug, 1999. Mem. Ctr. internat. Legal Studies (hon.). , Computer, General corporate, Mergers and acquisitions. Home: Rua Manuel Almeida Vasconcelos 26-2E 2775-713 Lisbon Portugal Office: PMBGR Conselheiro Fernando 19-18 1070-072 Lisbon Portugal E-mail: tpessanha@pmbgr.pt

PETER, BERNARD GEORGE, lawyer; b. Balt., July 28, 1944; S. Bernard George and Ella (Galvin) P.; m. Ellen Cherobina Carosselli; children: Kyle, Jared. AB, Coll. Holy Cross, 1966; JD, U. Md., 1969. Bar: Md. 1969, Ill. 1974. Lawyer, asst. sec. C.F. Industries, Inc., Long Grille, Ill., 1974-78; assoc. gen. counsel Joslyn Corp., Chgo., 1978-80; asst. gen. counsel Marshall Field & Co., 1980-84; atty., asst. cons. William M. Mercer Inc., 1984-89; atty., cons. Alexander & Alexander Cons. Group, 1989-94, Watson Wyatt and Co., Chgo., 1994—. Bd. dirs. John T. Galvin, Inc., Balt., treas., 2000. Contbr. articles to profl. jours. Usher St. Mary's Ch., Lake Forest, 1983—; recruiter high sch. athletes. Mem. Chog. Bar Assn. (vice-chmn. corp. law depts., com. mem. sect. coun. corp. law 1988-90, mem. corp. law com. 1994—), John Purole Club. Avocations: Purdue U. sports, swimming, tennis. General corporate, Labor, Pension, profit-sharing, and employee benefits. Home: 622 Timber Ln Lake Forest IL 60045 Office: Watson Wyatt Co 303 W Madison St Chicago IL 60606-3309

PETER, PHILLIPS SMITH, lawyer; b. Washington, Jan. 24, 1932; s. Edward Compston and Anita Phillips (Smith) P.; m. Jania Jayne Hutchins, Apr. 8, 1961; children: Phillips Smith Peter Jr., Jania Jayne Hutchins Stone. BA, U. Va., 1954, JD, 1959. Bar: Calif. 1959. Assoc. McCutchen, Doyle, Brown, Enerson, San Francisco, 1959-63; with GE (and subs.), various locations, 1963-94, v.p. corp. bus. devel., 1973-76, v.p., 1976-79, v.p. corp. govtl. rels., 1980-94; counsel, head govt. rels. dept. Reed Smith Shaw & McClay, 1994—. Chmn. bd. govs. Bryce Harlow Found., 1990-92, bd. dirs. Mem. editl. bd. Va. Law Rev., 1957-59. Trustee Howard U., 1981-89; bd. dirs., exec. com. Nat. Bank of Washington, 1981-86; v.p. Fed. City Coun., Washington, 1979-85; bd. dirs. Carlton, 1987-90, 95-98, pres., 1995-96; bd. dirs. Tudor Place Found., 1999—, v.p., 2001—. With transp. corps U.S. Army, 1954-56. Mem. Calif. Bar Assn., Order of Coif, Wee Burn Club, Ea. Yacht Club, Farmington Country Club, Ponte Vedra Club, Lago Mar Club, Landmark Club, Congl. Country Club, Georgetown Club, Chevy Chase Club, Pisces Club, F Street Club, Fairfax Club, Carlton Club (bd. dirs. 1990-98), Coral Beach and Tennis Club, Johns Island Club, The Windsor Club, Omicron Delta Kappa. Episcopalian. Home: 10805 Tara Rd Potomac MD 20854-1341 also: Johns Island 1000 Beach Rd & 690 Ocean Vero Beach FL 32963-3429 E-mail: ppeter@reedsmith.com

PETERS, ELLEN ASH, judge, trial referee, retired state supreme court justice; b. Berlin, Mar. 21, 1930; came to U.S., 1939, naturalized, 1947; d. Ernest Edward and Hildegard (Simon) Ash; m. Phillip I. Blumberg; children: David Bryan Peters, James Douglas Peters, Julie Peters Haden. BA with honors, Swarthmore Coll., 1951, LLD (hon.), 1983; LLB cum laude, Yale U., 1954, MA (hon.), 1964, LLD (hon.), 1985, U. Hartford, 1983, Georgetown U., 1984; LLD (hon.), Yale U., 1985, Conn. Coll., 1985, N.Y. Law Sch., 1985; HLD (hon.), St. Joseph Coll., 1986; LLD (hon.), Colgate U., 1986, Trinity Coll., 1987, Bates Coll., 1987, Wesleyan U., 1987, DePaul U., 1988; HLD (hon.), Albertus Magnus Coll., 1990; LLD (hon.), U. Conn., 1992; LLD, U. Rochester, 1994, Detroit U. Mercer Sch. Law, 2001. Bar: Conn. 1957. Law clk. to judge U.S. Circuit Ct., 1954-55; assoc. in law U. Calif., Berkeley, 1955-56; prof. law Yale U., New Haven, 1956-78, adj. prof. law, 1978-84; assoc. justice Conn. Supreme Ct., Hartford, 1978-84, chief justice, 1984-96; judge trial referee Superior Ct., 2000—. Author: Commercial Transactions: Cases, Texts, and Problems, 1971, Negotiable Instruments Primer, 1974; contbr. articles to profl. jours. Bd. mgrs. Swarthmore Coll., 1970-81; trustee Yale-New Haven Hosp., 1981-85, Yale Corp., 1986-92; mem. conf. Chief Justices, 1984—, pres., 1994; hon. chmn. U.S. Constl. Bicentennial Com., 1986-91; mem. Conn. Permanent Commn. on Status of Women, 1973-74, Conn. Bd. Pardons, 1978-80, Conn. Law Revision Commn., 1978-84; bd. dirs. Nat. Ctr. State Cts., 1992-96, chmn., 1994, Hartford Found., 1997—. Recipient Ella Grasso award, 1982, Jud. award Conn. Trial Lawyers Assn., 1982, citation of merit Yale Law Sch., 1983, Pioneer Woman award Hartford Coll. for Women, 1988, Disting. Svc. award U. Conn. Law Sch. Alumni Assn., 1993, Raymond E. Baldwin Pub. Svc. award Quinnipiac Coll. Law Sch., 1995, Disting. Svc. award Conn. Law Tribune, 1996, Nat. Ctr. State Cts., 1996; named Laura A. Johnson Woman of Yr. Hartford Coll., 1996. Mem. ABA, Conn. Bar Assn. (Jud. award 1992, Spl. award 1996), Am. Law Inst. (coun.), Am. Acad. Arts and Scis., Am. Philos. Soc. Office: Superior Ct 95 Washington St Hartford CT 06106-4431 Fax: 860-548-2887

PETERS, FREDERICK WHITTEN, lawyer; b. Omaha, Aug. 20, 1946; s. Jordan Holt and Elizabeth (O'Bryant) P.; children: Mary Irvin, Elizabeth Holt, Margaret Etheridge. BA magna cum laude, Harvard U., 1968; MS with distinction, London Sch. Econs., 1973; JD magna cum laude, Harvard U., 1976. Bar: D.C. 1978, U.S. Dist. Ct. D.C. 1978, U.S. Dist. Ct. Md., 1994, U.S. Ct. Appeals (3d and D.C. cirs.) 1979, U.S. Ct. Claims 1981, U.S. Ct. Appeals (11th cir.) 1986, U.S. Ct. Mil. Appeals 1993. Law clk. to Hon. J. Skelly Wright U.S. Ct. Appeals (D.C. cir.), Washington, 1976-77; law clk. to justice William J. Brennan U.S. Supreme Ct., 1977-78; assoc. Williams & Connolly, 1978-84, ptnr., 1984-95, 2001—; prin. dep. gen. counsel Dept. of Defense, 1995-97, undersec., acting sec. USAF, 1997-99, sec. USAF, 1999-2001; ptnr. Williams & Connolly LLP, Washington, 2001—. Mem. legal ethics com. D.C. Bar, 1988-94, chmn. rules rev. com., 1991-96; rules com. U.S. Ct. Mil. Appeals, 1993-95. Pres. Harvard Law Rev., 1975-76. Bd. dirs. Cleveland Park Hist. Soc., Washington, 1986-91, 2001—, Washington Area Lawyers for the Arts, 1987-93, Air Force Enlisted Found., 2001—; mem. adv. com. on streamlining procurement laws DOD, 1991-93, adv. com. on future of US aerospace industry. Lt. USNR, 1969-72. Fellow Am. Bar Found.; mem. ABA. Democrat. Episcopalian. Avocations: sailing, tennis, computer science. Federal civil litigation, Computer, Criminal. Home: 3250 Highland Pl NW Washington DC 20008-3231 Office: Williams & Connolly 725 12th St NW Washington DC 20005 E-mail: secaf19@aol.com, wpeters@wc.com

PETERS, LEE IRA, JR. public defender; b. Jamestown, N.Y., Dec. 17, 1946; s. Lee Ira and Carrie Irene (Roberson) P.; m. Mabel Luisa Thompson, June 21, 1969; children: Tammy M., Lee III, Ryan J. BA in Criminology, Fla. State U., 1971; JD, U. Fla., 1984. Bar: Fla. 1984, U.S. Dist Ct. (mid. dist.) Fla. 1989. Sr. intern Pub. Defender State of Fla., Gainesville, Fla., 1983; spl. asst. U.S. Atty No. Dist. Fla., Tallahassee, 1987-89; asst. states atty. 3d cir. State's Atty. Office, Live Oak, Fla., 1984-89; asst. pub. defender, felony divsn. chief 3rd cir. Pub. Defender's Office, 1989—. Spl. agt. crim. investigation Bur. ATF- U.S. Treas., Anniston, Ala., Boise, Idaho, 1971-77, resident agt.-in-charge Portland, Oreg., 1977-81; assoc. counsel (pro bono) Nat. Assn. Treas. Agts., 1993—. With USN, 1965-67, Vietnam, U.S. Army Res., 1981-95. Recipient Disting Svc. award Fla. Coun. Crime & Delinquency, Chpt. XV, 1989; Meritorious Svc. Sec. Army U.S., 1997. Mem. ACLU, Fla. Assn. Criminal Def. Lawyers, Fla. Bar Assn. (3d cir. grievance com. 1993-96), Acad. Fla. Trial Lawyers, 3d Cir. Bar Assn., Am. Legion (fin. officer post 107, Live Oak), McAlpin Comty. Club (pres. 1990-96), Rotary Club, Elks, Phi Alpha Delta. Avocation: cattle and Arabian horse raising. Office: Third Cir Pub Defender 106 Ohio Ave S Live Oak FL 32060-3212 E-mail: pd3liveoak@hotmail.com

PETERS, R. JONATHAN, lawyer, manufacturing company executive; b. Janesville, Wis., Jan. 6, 1927; m. Ingrid H. Varvayn, 1953; 1 dau., Christina. BS in Chemistry, U. Ill., 1951; JD, Northwestern U., 1954. Bar: Ill. 1954. Chief patent counsel Englehard Industries, 1972-82, Kimberly-Clark Corp., Neenah, Wis., 1982-85; gen. counsel Lanxide Corp., Newark, 1985-87; pvt. practice Chgo., 1985—. Served with CIC, U.S. Army, 1955-57. Patentee in field. Mem. ABA, Am. Intellectual Property Law Assn., Lic. Execs. Soc., Assn. Corp. Patent Counsel, North Shore Golf (Menasha, Wis.), Masons, Scottish Rite, Shriners. Patent, Trademark and copyright.

PETERS, ROBERT TIMOTHY, judge; b. Memphis, Dec. 28, 1946; s. Rhulin Earl and Bertie Nichols (Moore) P.; m. Ruth Audrey Allen, Dec. 11, 1973; children: Lindsay Elizabeth, Christopher Andrew. AA, St. Petersburg Jr. Coll., 1969; BA, U. Fla., 1971, JD, 1973. Bar: Fla. 1973, U.S. Dist. Ct. (mid. dist.) Fla. 1977, U.S. Ct. Appeals (5th cir.) 1981; cert. real estate lawyer. Ptnr. Goza, Hall & Peters P.A., Clearwater, Fla., 1973-84; sole

practice, 1984-95; apptd. cir. judge Fla., 1995—. Gov. Fla.'s appointee Condominium Study Commsn., Clearwater, 1990-91. Columnist Clearwater Sun newspaper, 1985—. 1st Lt. U.S. Army, 1966-68, Vietnam. Decorated Silver Star, Purple Heart, Bronze Star with oak leaf cluster. Mem. Fla. Bar (condominium and planned devel. com.), Clearwater Bar Assn. Avocations: reading, exercise. Office: Pinellas County Courthouse 315 Court St Clearwater FL 33756-5165 Address: PO Box 6316 Clearwater FL 33758-6316

PETERSEN, BENTON LAURITZ, paralegal; b. Salt Lake City, Jan. 1, 1942; s. Lauritz George and Arleane (Curtis) P.; m. Sharon Donnette Higgins, Sept. 20, 1974 (div. Aug. 9, 1989); children: Grant Lauritz, Tashya Eileen, Nicholas Robert, Katrina Arleane. AA, Weber State Coll., 1966, BA, BA, Weber State Coll., 1968; M of Liberal Studies, U. Okla., 1980; diploma, Nat. Radio Inst. Paralegal Sch., 1991; JD, Monticello U., 1999. Registered paralegal. Announcer/news dir. KWHO Radio, Salt Lake City, 1968-70, KDXU Radio, St. George, Utah, 1970-73, KSOP Radio, Salt Lake City, 1973-76; case worker/counselor Salvation Army, Midland, Tex., 1976-84; announcer/news dir. KBRS Radio, Springdale, Ark., 1984-86; case worker/counselor Office of Human Concern, Rogers, 1986-88; announcer KAZM Radio, Sedona, Ariz., 1988-91; paralegal Benton L. Petersen, Manti, Utah, 1991—. Cons. Sanpete County Srs., Manti, 1992—. Award judge Manti City Beautification, 1992-96; treas. Manti Destiny Com., 1993-98; tourism com. Sanpete County Econ. Devel., Ephraim, Utah, 1993-96. Served with U.S. Army N.G., 1959-66. Mem. Nat. Assn. Attys. in Fact (pres.). Mem. LDS Ch. Avocation: reading. Home: 470 E 120 N Manti UT 84642-1164 E-mail: bpfreedom@hotmail.com

PETERSEN, CATHERINE HOLLAND, lawyer; b. Norman, Okla., Apr. 24, 1951; d. John Hays and Helen Ann (Turner) Holland; m. James Frederick Petersen, June 26, 1973 (div.); children: T. Kyle, Lindsay Diane. BA, Hastings Coll., 1973; JD, Okla. U., 1976. Bar: Okla. 1976, U.s. Dist. Ct. (we. dist.) Okla. 1978. Legal intern, police legal advisor City of Norman, 1974-76; sole practice Norman, 1976-81; ptnr. Williams Petersen & Denny, 1981-82; pres. Petersen Assocs., Inc., 1982—. Adj. prof. Oklahoma City U. Coll. Law, 1982, U. Okla. Law Ctr., 1987; instr. continuing legal edn. U. Okla. Law Ctr., Norman, 1977, 79, 81, 83, 84, 86, 89-95; instr. Okla. Bar Assn., ABA, Am. Acad. Matrimonial Lawyers. Bd. dirs. United way, Norman, 1978-84, pres., 1981; bd. dirs. Women's Resource Ctr., Norman, 1975-77, 82-84; mem. Jr. League, Norman, 1980-83, Norman Hosp. Ayx., 1982-84; trustee 1st Presbyn. Ch., 1986-87. Named to Outstanding Okla. Women of 1980s, Women's Polit. Caucus, 1980, Outstanding Young Women of Am., 1981, 83. Fellow Am. Acad. Matrimonial Lawyers (pres. Okla. chpt. 1990-91, bd. govs. 1991-95); mem. ABA (family law sect.), Cleveland County Bar Assn., Okla. Bar Assn. (chmn. family law sect. 1987-88), Phi Delta Phi. Republican. Family and matrimonial. Home: 4716 Sundance Ct Norman OK 73072-3900 Office: PO Box 1243 314 E Comanche St Norman OK 73069-6009

PETERSEN, MARK ALLEN, lawyer; b. Burnsville, Minn., Apr. 28, 1972; s. Gunner and M. Diane Petersen; m. Karen Diane Viplock, May 27, 1995. BA, Gustavus Adolphus Coll., 1994; JD, U. Minn., 1997. Bar: Minn. 1997, U.S. Dist. Ct. Minn. 1998. Staff atty. Kaplan Strangis & Kaplan, Mpls., 1997-98; assoc. Maun & Simon, 1998—. Dir. Danish Am. Fellowship, Mpls., 1997—; founder, dir. Gustavus Lawyers Guild, Mpls., 1995—; chair Asylum Law Project, Mpls., 1995-97. Mem. Hennepin City Bar Assn. (treas. and sec. corp., bus. and franchise sect. 1998—). Democrat. Lutheran. Avocations: golf, softball. General corporate, Securities. Office: Maun & Simon 2000 Midwest Plaza Bldg W 801 Nicollet Mall Minneapolis MN 55402-2500

PETERSON, DONALD GEORGE, lawyer; b. Oak Park, Ill., May 20, 1940; s. Otto S. and Catherine E. Peterson. BA, Miami U., Oxford, Ohio, 1962; JD, Northwestern U., 1965. Bar: Ill. 1966, U.S. Dist. Ct. (no. dist.) Ill. 1966, U.S. Ct. Appeals (7th cir.) 1982, U.S. Supreme Ct. 1984. Assoc., Garbutt & Jacobson, Chgo., 1967-72; ptnr. Schaffenegger, Watson & Peterson, Ltd., Chgo., 1972— ; speaker, instr. Ill. State Bar, Ill. Inst. Continuing Legal Edn., ABA, Am. Law Inst., Chgo. Bar, Ill. Trial Lawyers Assn., Casualty Adjusters Assn., Nat. Inst. Mcpl. Law Officers. Bd. dirs. United Way, Clarendon Hills, Ill., 1980-81; legal advisor Community Caucus, Clarendon Hills, 1981. Recipient Hodes Local Govt. award Northwestern U., 1965. Mem. Ill. Bar Assn. (chmn. civil practice council 1983-84, assoc. editor Ill. Bar Jour. 1987—, editor newsletter 1980-85, assembly del. 1985-88, sec. publs. com. 1986-87, mem. fin. com., bar elections supervision com., chmn. assembly spl. com. to propose a program manditory cont. legal edn. 1987, bd. govs. 1988—), Chgo. Bar Assn. (chmn. judiciary com. 1986-88, mem. fed. civil procedure com., civil practice com.), Def. Rsch. Inst. (constrn. law com.), Ill. Assn. Def. Trial Counsel (legis. com., continuing legal edn. com.), Appellate Lawyers Assn., Soc. Trial Lawyers. Ill., Trial Lawyers Club Chgo., East Bank Club. Federal civil litigation, State civil litigation, Insurance. Office: Schaffenegger Watson & Peterson Ltd One East Wacker Dr Ste 3504 Chicago IL 60601-1802

PETERSON, EDWIN J. retired supreme court justice, law educator; b. Gilmanton, Wis., Mar. 30, 1930; s. Edwin A. and Leora Grace (Kitelinger) P.; m. Anna Chadwick, Feb. 7, 1971; children: Patricia, Andrew, Sherry. B.S., U. Oreg., 1951, LL.B., 1957. Bar: Oreg. 1957. Assoc. firm Tooze, Kerr, Peterson, Marshall & Shenker, Portland, 1957-61, mem. firm, 1961-79; assoc. justice Supreme Ct. Oreg., Salem, 1979-83, 91-93, chief justice, 1983-91; ret., 1993; disting. jurist-in-residence, adj. instr. Willamette Coll. of Law, Salem, Oreg., 1994—. Chmn. Supreme Ct. Task Force on Racial Issues, 1992-94; mem. standing com. on fed. rules of practice and procedure, 1987-93; bd. dirs. Conf. Chief Justices, 1985-87, 88-91. Chmn. Portland Citizens Sch. Com., 1968-70; vice chmn. Young Republican Fedn. Orgn., 1951; bd. visitors U. Oreg. Law Sch., 1978-83, 87-93, chmn. bd. visitors, 1981-83; pres. Understanding Racism Found., 1999—. Served to 1st lt. USAF, 1952-54. Mem. Oreg. State Bar (bd. examiners 1963-66, gov. 1973-76, vice chmn. profl. liability fund 1977-78), Multnomah County Bar Assn. (pres. 1972-73), Phi Alpha Delta, Lambda Chi Alpha. Episcopalian. Home: 3365 Sunridge Dr S Salem OR 97302-5950 Office: Willamette Univ Coll Law 245 Winter St SE Salem OR 97301-3916 E-mail: epeterso@willamette.edu

PETERSON, FRANKLIN DELANO, lawyer; b. Braham, Minn., Nov. 11, 1932; s. John Erick and Myrtle M. (Anderson) P.; m. Beverly Ann Crabb, Aug. 2, 1958; children: Heidi, Durward, Heather. Student, Augsburg Coll., 1950-51; BA, St. Cloud State Coll., 1955; LLB, William Mitchell Coll. Law, 1961. Bar: Minn. 1961. Field claims adjuster Farmers Mut. Ins. Co., St. Paul, 1955-57; asst. dist. claims mgr. Minn. Farmers Ins. Group, Mpls., 1957-62; sole practice Kenyon, Minn., 1963—. Atty. City of Kenyon, 1964-82; v.p. Kenyon Devel. Corp., bd. dirs.; sec. Tri-Valley Constrn. Co., Kenyon, bd. dirs. Chmn. Goldwater for Pres. campaign, Village of Kenyon Reps., 1964, Goodhue County LeVander for Gov., 1966, Goodhue County Reps, 1969-70; sec. Goodhue Selective Service Bd., 1968—; pres. Mineral Springs Chem. Dependency Ctr., 1974-85; mem. Kenyon Pub. Sch. Bd. Edn., 1976-82, treas. 1980-82, Kenyon Booster Club (charter), v.p. 1983; mgr. mgr. Kenyon Legion Baseball, 1979—; bd. dirs. Kenyon Roseview Apts., 1967—, pres. 1985—. Served with USAF, 1950-52. Mem. ABA, Minn. Bar Assn. (jud. dist. del., pres. 1st dist. 1979-80), Goodhue County Bar Assn., Minn. Assn. Plaintiffs Attys., Nat. Assn. Claimants Counsel, Sons of Norway (pres. Kenyon lodge 1969), Kenyon Comml. Club, Kenyon Country Club (pres. Osman Shrine Clowns 1993), Masons, Shriners, Lions (pres. Kenyon chpt.), royal Order Jesters, Ct. of St. Paul and Shriner Clowns. Lutheran. Estate planning, General practice, Probate. Home: RR Box B Kenyon MN 55946 Office: 634 2nd St Kenyon MN 55946-1334

PETERSON, H. DALE, lawyer; b. Amherst, Wis., Jan. 4, 1951; s. Harold C. and Eva I. (Hansen) P.; m. Julie A. Goplin, Jan. 1, 1995; children: Matt, David, Alex, Ellen. BS with honors, U. Wis., Stevens Point, 1973; JD cum laude, U. Wis., 1978. Bar: U.S. Dist. Ct. (we. dist.) Wis., U.S. Ct. Appeals (7th cir.) Wis. Rsch. analyst U.S. Dept. Justice, Washington, 1973-75; ptnr. Stroud, Willink & Howard, LLC, Madison, Wis., 1978—. Dir. Wis. Farm Bur. Svc. Bd., Inc., Madison, 1994—. Co-author: Contract Law in Wisconsin, 1995. Mem. Dane County Bar Assn. (dir./treas. 1987-91). General civil litigation, Contracts commercial, General corporate. Office: Stroud Willink & Howard LLC PO Box 2236 Madison WI 53701-2236

PETERSON, HOWARD COOPER, lawyer, accountant; b. Decatur, Ill., Dec. 12, 1939; s. Howard and Lorraine (Cooper) P. BEE, Ill., 1963; MEE, San Diego Sate Coll., 1967; MBA, Columbia U., 1969; JD, Calif. Western Sch. Law, 1983; LLM in Taxation, NYU, 1985. Bar: Calif.; CFP; CPA, Tex.; registered profl. engr., Calif.; cert. neuro-linguistic profl. Elec. engr. Convair divsn. Gen. Dynamics Corp., San Diego, 1963-67, sr. electronics engr., 1967-68; v.p., dirl Equity Programs Corp., 1973-83; gen. ptrn. Costumes Characters & Classics Co., 1979-86; pres., dir. Coastal Properties Trust, 1979-89, Juno Securities, Inc., 1983-96, 1974—, Juno Fin. Svcs., Inc., 1999—, Scripps Mortgage Corp., 1987-90, Juno Transport Inc., 1988-89. CFO, dir. Imperial Screens of San Diego, 1977-96, Heritage Transp. Mgmt. Inc., 1989-91, A.S.A.P. Ins. Svcs. Inc., 1983-85. Mem. ABA, Interam. Bar Assn., Nat. Soc. Pub. Accts., Internat. Assn. Fin. Planning, Assn. Enrolled Agts., Am. Assn. Atty.-CPAs. Estate planning, Real property, Taxation, general.

PETERSON, JAN ERIC, lawyer; b. Seattle, Apr. 28, 1944; s. Theodore Dare and Dorothy Elizabeth (Spofford) P.; children: Nels Andrew, Anne Elizabeth; m. Marguerite Victoria Caggiano, Mar. 31, 1984. AB in History, Stanford U., 1966; JD, U. Wash., 1969. Bar: Wash. 1969, U.S. Dist. Ct. (we. and ea. dists.) Wash. 1970, U.S. Ct. Appeals (9th cir.) 1970. Gen. counsel ACLU, Seattle, 1969-71; assoc. Daniel F. Sullivan, 1972-73; sr. ptnr. Peterson, Young, Putra, Fletcher, Zeder, Massong & Knopp, 1973—. Drafter (state statute) Tap Water Regulation Act, 1983. Fellow Am. Coll. Trial Lawyers; mem. ABA (editor assoc. 1976-78), Damages Attys. Round Table (founding, pres. 1997-98), ATLA (del. 1985-86), Wash. State Trial Lawyers Assn. (bd. 1973-85, pres. 1982-83, Trial Lawyer of Yr. 1999), Wash. State Bar Assn. (jud. selection 1985-87, bd. govs. 1992-95, pres. elect. 1999—), Am. Bd. Trial Adv. (diplomate, pres. Wash. chpt. 1990), ACLU, Bd. Legal Found. Wash. Democrat. Avocations: piano, baseball, basketball, golf. Personal injury, Product liability, Professional liability. Office: Peterson Young Putra Fletcher Zeder Massong & Knopp 1501 4th Ave Ste 2800 Seattle WA 98101-1609 E-mail: janeric@pypfirm.com

PETERSON, LINDA ELLEN, lawyer; b. Kearny, N.J., Feb. 8, 1960; d. Walter Raymond and JoAnn Evelyn Peterson; m. Domenic James Valentine, Oct. 2, 1988 (div. Apr. 1991); m. Nicholas Joseph Mango, Aug. 17, 1996; 1 child, Jessica Lynn Valentine. BA with honors, Rutgers U., 1983; JD, Pace U., 1987. Bar: N.J. 1987. Law clk. to Hon. Bruce A. Gaeta, Hackensack, N.J., 1987-88; asst. county counsel Bergen County Counsel, 1988-91; asst. dep. pub. defenders Passaic County Pub. Defenders, Paterson, N.J., 1991-93, Bergen County Pub. Defenders, Hackensack, 1993—. Vol. St. Catherine's Parish, Ringwood, N.J.1995—. Ranking scholar Pace U., 1986. Mem. Nat. Assn. Criminal Def. Lawyers, N.J. State Bar. Methodist. Avocations: dance, yoga, antiques, gardening, moutain biking. Office: Office Pub Defender 60 State St Ste 4 Hackensack NJ 07601-5469

PETERSON, OSLER LEOPOLD, lawyer; b. Mpls., Oct. 19, 1946; s. Osler Luther and Delores (Kealy) P.; m. Sandra Ann Freeto, Jan. 2, 1971 (div. Dec. 1983); m. Deborah Jean Bero, July 30, 1989. BA, Brown U., 1969; JD cum laude, Suffolk U., 1976. Bar: Mass. 1976, U.S. Dist. Ct. Mass. 1976. Pvt. practice, Newton, Mass., 1976-84; ptnr. Freeto, Peterson & Scoll, 1984—. Bd. mem. Riverside Cmty. Care (formerly Neww Ctr., Inc.), 1976-96, clk., 1978-84, pres., 1984-89; bd. mem. Lasell Coll. (formerly Lasell Jr. Coll.), 1983-97, 98—, clk., 1984-91; bd. mem. Lasell Village, Inc., 1990-2000, chmn., 1992-2000; bd. mem. Medfield Zoning Bd. Appeals, 1993-2000; selectman Town of Medfield, 2000—. Mem. ABA, ATLA, Mass. Bar Assn., Mass. Conveyancers Assn., Mass. Acad. Trial Attys. General civil litigation, Personal injury, Real property. Home: 10 Copperwood Rd Medfield MA 02052-1034 Office: Freeto Peterson & Scoll 580 Washington St Newton MA 02458-1416 also: Medfield Profl Bldgs 5 N Meadows Rd Ste 27 Medfield MA 02052-2317 E-mail: opeterson@juno.com

PETERSON, PAUL AMES, lawyer, educator; b. Los Angeles, Feb. 17, 1928; s. Ames and Norma (Brown) P.; m. Cynthia Peterson, June 21, 1953 (div.); children: Daniel C., Andrew G., Matthew A., James F.; m. Barbara J. Henderson, Sept. 12, 1976. BS in Econs., U. Calif., Berkeley, 1953, JD, 1956. Bar: Calif. 1956, U.S. Ct. Appeals (9th cir.) 1956, U.S. Supreme Ct. 1964. Assoc. Law Offices of George W. Phillips, Castro Valley, Calif., 1956-57; ptnr. Peterson & Price, San Diego, 1958—. Assoc. prof. Calif. Western Coll. Law, San Diego, 1960-63, U. San Diego Law Sch., 1958-60; assoc. prof. U. Calif., San Diego, 1984-87, chmn., bd. overseers, 1994—, chmn., 2000—; bd. trustees U. Calif. Found., San Diego, 1988—; bd. dirs. Childrens Advocacy Inst.; mem. State of Calif. San Diego Regional Govt. Efficiency Commn., 2001—. Contbr. articles to profl jours. Bd. dirs. San Diego Stadium Authority, 1964-72, San Diego County Water Authority, 1984-90, San Diego Conv. Ctr. Corp., 1985-90, San Diego Regional Govt. Efficiency Commn., 2001—. Served as tech. sgt. U.S. Army, 1946-48, Korea. Fellow Am. Judicature Soc.; mem. State Bar of Calif., Phi Beta Kappa, Order of Coif. Democrat. Avocation: hiking. Administrative and regulatory, Environmental, Real property. Home: 7020 Neptune Pl La Jolla CA 92037-5328 Office: Peterson & Price 7979 Ivanhoe Ave Ste 520 La Jolla CA 92037-4513 E-mail: lspycia@price-entities.com

PETERSON, RANDALL THEODORE, law educator and librarian; b. Sioux City, Iowa, Aug. 27, 1944; s. Theodore Melvin and Ileann Grace (Wendrich) P.; m. Judith Ashcroft, Aug. 24, 1967; children— Kristin, Randall, Heidi, Travis, Robert, Quinn. Student Dixie Coll., 1962-63; BS, Brigham Young U., 1968, MLS, 1974; JD, U. Utah, 1972. Asst. law librarian Brigham Young U., Provo, Utah, 1972-74, assoc. law librarian, 1974-77; asst. prof. law , dir. libr. svcs. John Marshall Law Sch., Chgo., 1977-86, assoc. prof., , 1986—, dir. libr. svcs., 1986-90. Mem. ABA, Am. Soc. Info. Sci. Mormon. Office: John Marshall Law Sch 315 S Plymouth Ct Chicago IL 60604-3968

PETERSON, RICHARD WILLIAM, judge, lawyer; b. Council Bluffs, Iowa, Sept. 29, 1925; s. Henry K. and Laura May (Robinson) P.; m. Patricia Mae Fox, Aug. 14, 1949; children: Katherine Ilene Peterson Sherbondy, Jon Eric, Timothy Richard. BA, U. Iowa, 1949, JD with distinction, 1951; postgrad., U. Nebr.-Omaha, 1972-80, 86. Bar: Iowa 1951, U.S. Dist. Ct. (so. dist.) Iowa 1951, U.S. Supreme Ct. 1991, U.S. Ct. Appeals (8th cir.) 1997. Pvt. practice law, Council Bluffs, 1951—; U.S. commr. U.S. Dist. Ct. (so. dist.) Iowa, 1958-70. Part-time U.S. magistrate judge U.S. Dist. Ct. (so. dist.) Iowa, 1970-99; mem. nat. faculty Fed. Jud. Ctr., Washington, 1972-82; emeritus trustee Children's Square, U.S.A.; verifying ofcl. Internat. Prisoner Transfer Treaties, Mexico City, 1977, La Paz, Bolivia, 1980, 81, Lima, Peru, 1981. Author: The Court Moves West: A Study of the United States Supreme Court Decision of Appeals from the United States Circuit and District Court of Iowa, 1846-1882, 1988, West of the Nishnabotna: The Experiences of Forty Years of a Part-Time Judicial Officer as United States Commissioner, Magistrate and Magistrate Judge, 1958-1998, 1998; co-author: (with George Mills) No One is Above the Law: The Story of Southern Iowa's Federal Court, 1994; contbr. articles to legal publs. Bd. dirs. Pottawattamie County (Iowa) chpt. ARC, state fund chmn., 1957-58; state chmn. Radio Free Europe, 1960-61; dist. chmn. Trailblazer dist. Boy Scouts Am., 1952-55; mem. exec. coun. Mid-Am. Coun., 1976—. With inf. U.S. Army, 1943-46. Decorated Purple Heart, Bronze Star; named Outstanding Young Man Council Bluffs C. of C., 1959 Fellow Am. Bar Found. (life); mem. ABA, Am. Judicature Soc., Iowa Bar Assn. (chmn. com. fed. practice 1978-80, probate and trust coun. and sect. 1997—), Pottawattamie County Bar Assn. (pres. 1979-80), Fed. Bar Assn., Inter-Am. Bar Assn., Supreme Ct. Hist. Soc., Fed. Magistrate Judges Assn. (pres. 1978-79), Iowa Conf. Bar Assn. (pres. 1985-87), Hist. Soc. of U.S. Cts. Eighth Jud. Cir. (pres. 1989-99), Kiwanis (pres. Council Bluffs club 1957), Masons, Phi Delta Phi, Delta Sigma Rho, Omicron Delta Kappa. Republican. Lutheran. Home: 1007 Arbor Ridge Cir Council Bluffs IA 51503-5000 Office: PO Box 248 25 Main Pl Ste 200 Council Bluffs IA 51503-0790

PETERSON, RONALD ROGER, lawyer; b. Chgo., July 27, 1948; married; children: Elizabeth G., Ronald W. AB, Ripon, 1970; JD, U. Chgo., 1973. Bar: Ill. 1974, U.S. Dist. Ct. (no. dist.) Ill. 1974, U.S. Ct. Appeals (7th cir.) 1974, U.S. Dist. Ct. (ea. dist.) Wis. 1975, U.S. Dist. Ct. (no. dist.) Ind. 1978, U.S. Dist. Ct. (cen. dist.) Ill. 1980, U.S. Dist. Ct. (we. dist.) Mich. 1999, U.S. Ct. Appeals (8th cir.) 1984, U.S. Ct. Appeals (6th cir.) 1990, U.S. Ct. Appeals (9th cir.) 1996. Ptnr. Jenner & Block, Chgo., 1974—; commd. 2d lt. U.S. Army, 1968, advanced through grades to 1st lt., 1973, ret., 1978, with mil. intelligence, 1968-78. Mem. ABA, Chgo. Bar Assn., Internat. Soc. Insolvency Practitioners, Comml. Law League, Am. Bankruptcy Inst., Am. Coll. Bankruptcy Lawyers. Avocation: skiing. Bankruptcy, Contracts commercial, State and local taxation. Office: Jenner & Block 1 E Ibm Plz Fl 4000 Chicago IL 60611-7603 E-mail: rpeterson@jenner.com

PETERSON, WILLIAM ALLEN, lawyer; b. Marshall, Mo., Oct. 1, 1934; s. R.O. and Marjorie E. (Mallot) P.; m. Mary Kay Moore, July 26, 1958; children: Laura, Clayton, Mary M., Sarah. BS, Drury Coll., Springfield, Mo., 1958; JD, Washington U., 1963. Bar: Mo. 1963, U.S. Dist. Ct. (ea. dist.) Mo. 1964, U.S. Dist. Ct. (we. dist.) Mo. 1965, U.S. Supreme Ct. 1967. Assoc. Riddle, O'Herin & Newberry, Malden, Mo., 1963-65; asst. atty. gen. State of Mo., Jefferson City, 1965-70; legislator Mo. Ho. Reps., 1970-74; pvt. practice Marshall, 1974—. Atty. City of Marshall, 1976-78, City of Slater, Mo., 1988-89; judge mcpl. divsn. State Cir. Ct., Marshall, 1979-80, 2000—, Slater, 1990-94; pros. atty. County of Saline, Marshall, 1979-80, 84-88. With USN, 1954-56. Mem. ABA, Mo. Bar Assn., Assn. Trial Lawyers Am., Am. Legion, VFW. Methodist. General civil litigation, Probate, Workers' compensation. Home: 503 E Eastwood St Marshall MO 65340-1535 Office: 54 W Arrow St PO Box 9 Marshall MO 65340-0009

PETERSON, WILLIAM GEORGE, lawyer; b. Minn., Sept. 30, 1944; s. Henry Gaufin and Grace Marie (Reker) P.; m. Ann Ophoven; children: Emily Marie, Elizabeth Ann. B.A., U. Minn., 1966, J.D., U. Pitts., 1969. Bar: Minn. 1969, U.S. Dist. Ct. Minn. 1970, U.S. Ct. Appeals (8th cir.) 1976, U.S. Supreme Ct. 1976, Wis. 1983. Spl. asst. atty. gen. State of Minn., St. Paul, 1969-78; sole practice, Bloomington, Minn., 1978-80; ptnr. Peterson & Lange, Bloomington, 1980-81; owner Peterson & Assocs., Bloomington, 1981—; instr. hotel and restaurant law Normandale Community Coll., Bloomington, 1981-87; referee Hennepin County Conciliation Ct., Mpls., 1982—; arbitrator ins. claims Am. Arbitration Assn., 1988—. Contbr. articles to profl. jours. Bd. dirs. Viking Council Boy Scouts Am., 1981-84, Minn. Valley YMCA; chmn. Hennepin County Ind. Republicans, Mpls., 1984-90; mem. Minn. Legislature, 1978-82, Bloomington City Merit Bd., 1983—. Recipient Silver Beaver award Boy Scouts Am., 1981; Legis. Excellence award Minn. Legis. Evaluation Assembly, 1981. Mem. ABA, Minn. State Bar Assn., Minn. Trial Lawyers Assn., Assn. Trial lawyers Am. Roman Catholic. Club: Toastmasters. Lodges: Rotary, K.C. State civil litigation, Criminal, Personal injury. Home: 4103 Overlook Cir Minneapolis MN 55437-3540 Office: Peterson and Assocs Ltd 8400 Lyndale Ave S Minneapolis MN 55420-2273

PETH, HOWARD ALLEN, lawyer, educator; b. Calif., Apr. 20, 1955; s. Howard Allen and Diane Marie (Munyan) P.; m. Gloria Gene Stockton, Aug. 9, 1992; children: Andrew Howard, Rachel Gloria. BA, U. Calif., San Diego, 1980; MD, U. Santiago, 1984; JD, U. Mo., 1991. Bar: Calif. 1993, U.S. Ct. Appeals (9th cir.) 1993, U.S. Ct. Claims, U.S. Ct. Appeals (fed. cir.) 1993, U.S. Dist. Ct. (so. dist.) Calif. 1993, U.S. Supreme Ct. 1997; diplomate Am. Bd. Internal Medicine, Am. Bd. Emergency Medicine; lic. physician, Calif., Mo., Wis. Asst. prof. U. Mo. Sch. Medicine, Columbia, 1997—. Fellow Am. Coll. Legal Medicine; mem. AMA, ABA (health law sect.), ACP, Am. Coll. Emergency Physicians. Republican. Episcopalian. Office: U Mo Hosp and Clinic One Hospital Dr Columbia MO 65212 Business E-Mail: perthh@health.missouri.edu

PETILLON, LEE RITCHEY, lawyer; b. Gary, Ind., May 6, 1929; s. Charles Ernest and Blanche Lurene (Mackay) P.; m. Mary Anne Keeton, Feb. 20, 1960; children: Andrew G., Joseph R. BBA, U. Minn., 1952; LLB, U. Calif., Berkeley, 1959. Bar: Calif. 1960, U.S. Dist. Ct. (so. dist.) Calif. 1960. V.p. Creative Investment Capital, Inc., L.A., 1969-70; corp. counsel Harvest Industries, 1970-71; v.p., gen. counsel, dir. Tech. Svcs. Corp., Santa Monica, Calif., 1971-78; ptnr. Petillon & Davidoff, L.A., 1978-92, Gipson Hoffman & Pancione, 1992-93; pvt. practice Torrance, Calif., 1993-94; ptnr. Petillon & Hansen, 1994—. Co-author: R&D Partnerships, 2d edit., 1985, Representing Start-Up Companies, 1992, 7th edit., 2000, Chapter 9, California Transaction Forms, 1996. Chmn. Neighborhood Justice Ctr. Com., 1983-85, Middle Income Co., 1983085; active Calif. Senate Commn. on Corp. Governance, State Bar Calif. Task Force on Alternative Dispute Resolution, 1984-85; chmn. South Bay Sci. Found., Inc.; vice-chmn. Calif. Capital Access Forum, Inc.; dir., legal counsel ACE-Net.org, Inc. Recipient Cert. of Appreciation L.A. City Demonstration Agy., 1975, United Indian Devel. Assn., 1981, City of L.A. for Outstanding Vol. Svcs., 1984, Outstanding Vol. award Torrance C. of C., 2000, Small Bus. Adv. of Yr. award Calif. C. of C., 2001; named Small Bus. Adv. of Yr. Calif. C. of C., 2001. Mem. ABA, Calif. State Bar Assn. (pres., Pro Bono Svcs. award 1983), L.A. County Bar Found. (bd. dirs. 1986-89), L.A. County Bar Assn. (chmn. law tech. sect., alt. dispute resolution sect. 1992-94, trustee 1984-85, Griffin Bell Vol. Svc. award 1993). Avocations: backpacking, reading, music, painting. General corporate, Securities. Home: 1636 Via Machado Palos Verdes Estates CA 90274-1930 Office: Petillon & Hansen 21515 Hawthorne Blvd Ste 1260 Torrance CA 90503-6503 E-mail: lpetillon@corplawp-h.com

PETITO, CHRISTOPHER SALVATORE, lawyer; b. Trenton, N.J., Nov. 7, 1955; s. Robert A. and Bebe C. (Chianese) P. BA cum laude, Yale U., 1977, JD, 1981. Bar: N.Y. 1982, D.C. 1995, U.S. Dist. Ct. (so. dist.) N.Y. 1984, U.S. Ct. Appeals (6th cir.) 1986. Assoc. Rosenman & Colin, N.Y.C, 1981-88; br. chief U.S. Securities Exch. Commn.-N.Y. Regional Office, 1989-90, atty., 1988-89, asst. reg. dir., 1991-94, sr. counsel, 1990-91. Asst. counsel Gov.'s Judicial Screening Com. 1st Dept., N.Y.C., 1985. Mem. ABA. Democrat. Roman Catholic. General corporate, Finance. Office: Jordan Burt LLP Ste 700E 1025 Thomas Jefferson St NW Washington DC 20007-5214 E-mail: csp@wde.jordenusa.com

PETRASICH, JOHN MORIS, lawyer; b. Long Beach, Calif., Oct. 13, 1945; s. Louis A. and Margaret A. (Moris) P.; children from previous marriage: Jason, Jacquelyn; m. Mary T. Nevin, Aug. 22, 1997. BA, U. So. Calif., 1967, JD, 1970. Bar: Calif. 1971, U.S. Dist. Ct. (cen. dist.) 1971, U.S. Ct. Appeals (9th cir.) 1973, U.S. Dist. Ct. (no. dist.) Calif. 1974, U.S. Ct. Appeals (ea. dist.) Calif. 1976. Assoc. Fulop, Rolson, Burns & McKittrick, Beverly Hills and Newport Beach, Calif., 1971-74, ptnr., 1975-82; ptnr., head litigation McKittrick, Jackson, DeMarco & Peckenpaugh, Newport Beach, 1983-93; shareholder, head litigation Jackson, DeMarco & Peckenpaugh, 1993—; also bd. dirs. McKittrick, Jackson, DeMarco & Peckenpaugh. Mem. editorial staff U. So. Calif. Law Rev., 1969-70. Mem. ABA, Beverly Hills Bar Assn., L.A. Bar Assn., Assn. Trial Lawyers Am., Orange County Bar Assn., Lawyers Club L.A., Order of Coif. General civil litigation, Insurance, Real property. Office: Jackson DeMarco Peckenpaugh PO Box 19704 Irvine CA 92623-9704 E-mail: jpetrasich@jdplaw.com

PETRIE, BRUCE INGLIS, lawyer; b. Washington, Nov. 8, 1926; s. Robert Inglis and Marion (Douglas) P.; m. Beverly Ann Stevens, Nov. 3, 1950 (dec. Oct. 1993); children: Laurie Ann Roche, Bruce Inglis, Karen Elizabeth Medsger. BBA, U. Cin., 1948, JD, 1950. Bar: Ohio 1950, U.S. Dist. Ct. (so. dist.) Ohio 1951, U.S. Ct. Appeals (6th cir.) 1960, U.S. Supreme Ct. Assoc. Kunkel & Kunkel, Cin., 1950-51, Graydon, Head & Ritchey, 1951-57, ptnr., 1957—. Exec. prodr. (sch. video) Classical Quest, 2000; contbr. articles to legal jours. Mem. bd. Charter Com. Greater Cin., 1952—; pres. Charter Rsch. Inst., 2000; mem. bd. edn. Indian Hill Exempted Village Sch. Dist., 1965-67, pres., 1967; mem. adv. bd. William A. Mitchell Ctr., 1969-86; mem. Green Areas adv. com. Village of Indian Hill, Ohio, 1969-80, chmn., 1976-80; mem. Ohio Ethics Com., 1974-75; co-founder Sta. WGUC-FM; mem. WGUC-FM Cmty. Bd., 1974—, chmn., 1974-76; bd. dirs. Murray Seasongood Good Govt. Fund, 1975—, pres., 1989—; bd. dirs. Nat. Civic League, Cin. Vol. Lawyers for Poor Found., Linton Music Series, Amernet Chamber Music Soc.; founder parents as tchrs. Metro Housing Authority Commn., 1991—; elder, trustee, deacon Knox Presbyn. Ch.; a prin. advocate merit selection judges, Ohio; trustee, mem. bd., Seven Hills Neighborhood Houses, Inst. for Learning in Retirement; mem. bd. Hamilton County Good Govt. League; organizer Late Great Lakes Book Distbn. project. Recipient Pres.'s award U. Cin., 1976, Disting. Alumnus award, 1995. Fellow Am. Bar Found.; mem. ABA, Ohio Bar Assn., Cin. Bar Assn. (pres. 1981, Trustee's award 2000), Am. Judicature Soc. (Herbert Lincoln Harley award 1973, dir.), Nat. Civic League (Disting. Citizen award 1985, coun. 1984—), Am. Law Inst., Ohio State Bar Assn. Found. (Outstanding Rsch. in Law and Govt. award 1986, Charles P. Taft Civic Gumption award 1988, Ohio Bar medal 1988), Cincinnatus Assn., Order of Coif, Lit. Club, Univ. Club, Cin. Club. Avocations: tennis, squash, woodworking, writing, horticulture, music. General corporate, Estate planning, Real property. Home: 2787 Walsh Rd Cincinnati OH 45208-3428 Office: Graydon Head & Ritchey 1900 Fifth 3d Ctr 511 Walnut St Ste 1900 Cincinnati OH 45202-3157

PETRIE, GREGORY STEVEN, lawyer; b. Seattle, Feb. 25, 1951; s. George C. and Pauline P.; m. Margaret Fuhrman, Oct. 6, 1979; children: Kathryn Jean, Thomas George. AB in Polit. Sci and Econs., UCLA, 1973; JD, Boston U., 1976. Bar: Wash. 1976, U.S. Dist. Ct. (we. dist.) Wash. 1976. Adminstr. Action/Peace Corps, Washington, 1973, Fed. Power Commn., Washington, 1974; assoc. Oles Morrison et al, Seattle, 1976-80; ptnr. Schwabe Williamson Ferguson & Burdell, 1981-94; mng. shareholder Krutch Lindell Bingham Jones & Petrie, 1994—. Mem. Seattle-King County Bar Assn., Profl. Liability Architects and Engrs., Wash. Athletic Club. Avocations: woodworking, skiing. Construction, Health, Pension, profit-sharing, and employee benefits. Office: Krutch Lindell Bingham Jones & Petrie 1201 3rd Ave Ste 3100 Seattle WA 98101-3079 E-mail: gsp@nwlink.com

PETRILA, JOHN PHILIP, health law educator; b. Terre Haute, Ind., June 25, 1951; s. John Joseph and Patricia Ann (McCrisaken) P.; m. Amelia Ann Thompson, Oct. 18, 1953; 1 child, Patrick John. BA, St. Joseph's Coll., Renssalaer, Ind., 1973; JD, U. Va., 1976, LLM, 1977. Bar: Va. 1976. Fellow in mental health law U. Va. Law Sch., Charlottesville, 1976-78; asst. atty. gen. State of Mo., Jefferson City, 1978-79; dir. forensic svcs. Mo. Mental Hygiene Dept., 1979-81; dep. counsel N.Y. Office Mental Health, Albany, 1981-87, counsel, dep. commr., 1987-92; chmn. dept. mental health law and policy Fla. Mental Health Inst./ U. South Fla., Tampa, 1992—. Mem. mental health planning coun. State of Fla., 1993-95, mem. steering com. on managed behavioral health care, 1996; mem. Fla. Gov.'s Task Force on Medicaid Reform, 1996; interim dir. Statewide Pub. Guardianship Office, 2000—. Co-author: Psychological Evaluations for the Courts: A Handbook for Mental Health Professionals and Attorneys, 1987, 2d edit., 1997, Law and Mental Health Professionals: Florida, 1996, Mental Health Services: A Public Health Perspective, 1996; contbr. articles to profl. jours. Mem. Keel Club Hillsborough County United Way, Tampa, 1993—. Recipient Cmty. Svc. award Sch. Social Work U. South Fla., 1995, Saleem Shah award for contbn. to forensic mental health, 1999. Avocations: biking, sailing. Office: U South Fla 13301 Bruce B Downs Blvd Tampa FL 33612-3807

PETRILLI, MICHELLE LESLIE, lawyer; b. Bridgeport, Conn., Sept. 3, 1953; d. Russell Moreton and Patricia Aldona (Yasonis) Cory; m. Jeffrey S. Welch, May 24, 1978 (div.); 1 child, Stephanie Cory. BA in Biol. Sci., U. Del., 1976; JD, Del. Law Sch., Widener U., 1979. Bar: Del. 1979, Pa. 1980. Law clk. Schmittinger & Rodriguez, P.A., Wilmington, Del., 1977-79; jud. clk. Del. Ct. Chancery, Wilmington, 1980-81; assoc. legal counsel Bank of Del. and Bank of Del. Corp., Wilmington, 1981-84, gen. counsel, V.P., 1984—; mem. exec. com. bd. dirs. Industry Coun. for Tangible Assets, Washington, 1983-86; state rep. Conf. of State Bank Suprs., 1986—. Elected bd. dirs. New Castle County Econ. Devel. Corp., chmn. affordable housing com.; apptd. chair Gov.'s Pub. Safety Coun. Mem. ABA, Del. Bar Assn., Fin. Women Internat., Del. Valley Corp. Counsel Assn. (bd. dirs. 1986-89), Lawyers Forum, Del. Bankers Assn. (govt. affairs com.), Del. State C. of C. (elected dir. 1989). Republican. Roman Catholic. Home: 2618 Tonbridge Dr Wilmington DE 19810-1217 Office: Bank of Del 222 Delaware Ave Wilmington DE 19801-1621

PETRIN, HELEN FITE, lawyer, consultant, mediator; b. Bklyn., June 22, 1940; d. Clyde David and Connie Marie Keaton; m. Michael Richard Petrin, June 29, 1963; children: Jennifer Lee, Michael James, Daniel John. BS, Rider Coll. (now Rider U.), 1962, MA, 1980; postgrad., Glassboro (N.J.) Coll. (now Rowan U.), 1981; JD, Widener U., 1987. Bar: Pa. 1989, N.J. 1990, U.S. Dist. N.J. 1990. Tchr. bus. edn. Pennsville (N.J.) Meml. High Sch., 1962-66; asst. prof. Salem Community Coll., Carney's Point, N.J., 1977-81; asst. prof. Brandywine Coll. Widener U., Wilmington, Del., 1981-87, asst. prof., adminstr., dir. paralegal program, 1987-88; dir. continuing legal edn. Widener U. Sch. Law, Brandywine, 1987-88; pvt. practice computer cons. Del., Pa., N.J., Del., Pa., N.J., 1988—; pvt. practice law Salem, N.J., 1989—; prosecutor Pilesgrove Township, 1990-91; dep. surrogate Salem County, 1991-2000. Word processing cons. New Castle County (Del.) Pers. Dept., 1983; mem. dist. I ethics com. N.J. Supreme Ct., 1993-96; instr. N.J. Inst. for CLE, 1995—; adv. com. on minority concerns Superior Ct. N.J. Vicinage 15, 1995—; judge mock trial N.J. State Bar, 1994—; mem. women's advocacy panel Salem C.C., 1998—. Pres. bd. Salem County YMCA, 1983, bd. dirs., 1980-98; dir. mediator Salem County YMCA Mediation Svcs., 1995-2001; vol. atty. Phila. Vols. for Indigent Program, 1990-95, Camden Legal Svcs., Inc. for Salem County, 1990-2001; bd. dirs. United Way Salem County, 1991-97, treas., 1994-95; bd. dirs. United Ways of Pa. & N.J., 1994-97; mem. Hope III com. (Home Ownership and Opportunity for People Everywhere), Salem, N.J., 1992—; vol. atty. Salem County N.J. Office Aging Sr. Law Day, 1991—, vol. dir. Guardianship Monitoring Program, 1993-2001; bd. dirs. Stand Up for Salem, Inc., 1991—, sec.-treas., 1997—; bd. dirs. Salem Main St. Program, 2000—. Mem. ABA (chmn. young lawyers econs. com. 1990-93, vice chmn. mktg. legal svcs. com. gen. practice sect. 1993-98), N.J. State Bar Assn. (exec. com. young lawyers divsn. 1990-93, trustee 1998—, pro bono com. 1998-2000), Pa. Bar Assn., Phila. Bar Assn. (probate adv. panel 1992-94), Salem County Bar Assn. (treas. 1991-92, sec. 1992-93, v.p., pres.-elect 1993-94, pres. 1994-95, dir. of Salem County, N.J. YMCA Family Ct. Mediation program 1995-2001), Delta Pi Epsilon (sec. bd. dirs. 1980-82). Avocations: swimming, music, walking, reading. Civil rights, General practice, Probate. Home: 99 Marlton Rd Woodstown NJ 08098-2722 Office: 51 Market St Salem NJ 08079-1909

PETRO, JAMES MICHAEL, lawyer, politician; b. Cleve., Oct. 25, 1948; s. William John and Lila Helen (Janca) P.; m. Nancy Ellen Bero, Dec. 16, 1972; children: John Bero, Corbin Marie. BA, Denison U., 1970; JD, Case Western Res., 1973. Bar: Ohio 1973, U.S. Dist. Ct. (no. dist.) Ohio 1974, U.S. Ct. Appeals (6th cir.) 1981. Spl. asst. U.S. senator W.B. Saxbe, Cleve., 1972-73; asst. pros. atty. Franklin County, Ohio, 1973-74; asst. dir. law City of Cleve., 1974; ptnr. Petro & Troia, Cleve., 1974-84; dir. govt. affairs Standard Oil Co., 1984-86; ptnr. Petro, Rademaker, Matty & McClelland, 1986-93, Buckingham, Doolittle & Burroughs, Cleve., 1993-95. Mem. city coun. Rocky River, Ohio, 1977-79, dir. law, 1980; mem. Ohio Ho. of Reps., Columbus, 1981-84, 86-90; commr. Cuyahoga County, Ohio, 1991-95; Auditor of State of Ohio, 1995—. Mem. ABA, Ohio State Bar Assn., Cleve. Bar Assn. Republican. Methodist. Home: 1933 Lake Shore Dr Columbus OH 43204-4963 Office: 88 E Broad St Columbus OH 43215-3506 E-mail: petro@auditor.state.oh.us

PETROS, RAYMOND LOUIS, JR. lawyer; b. Pueblo, Colo., Sept. 19, 1950; BS, Colo. Coll., 1972; JD, U. Colo., 1975. Bar: Colo. 1975. Jud. clk. to Justice Paul V. Hodges Colo. Supreme Ct., Denver, 1975-77; assoc. Bermingham, White, Burke & Ipsen, 1977-78; from assoc. to ptnr. Hall & Evans, 1978-81; ptnr. Kirkland & Ellis, 1981-86; mem. Holme, Roberts & Owen, 1986-96, Petros & White, LLC, 1996—. Contbr. articles to profl. jours. Bd. dirs. Rocky Mountain Poison Control Found., Denver, 1988-94. Land use and zoning (including planning), Real property. Office: Petros & White LLC 730 Seventeenth St Ste 820 Denver CO 80202-3518

PETRUCELLI, JAMES MICHAEL, judge; b. Fresno, Calif., Dec. 28, 1949; s. Gene Vincent and Josephine Marie (Frediani) P.; m. Toby Laura Petrucelli; 1 child, Vincent Michael. BS, Fresno State Coll., 1972; JD, San Joaquin Coll., 1989. Bar: Calif. 1989, U.S. Dist. Ct. (ea. dist.) Calif. 1989, U.S. Dist. Ct. (no. dist.) Calif. 1990, U.S. Ct. Appeals (9th cir.) 1990, U.S. Supreme Ct., 1993. Dep. sheriff Fresno County Sheriff's Dept., 1974-89; pvt. practice Fresno, 1989-98; judge Fresno County Superior Ct., 1999—. Del. State Bar Conf. of Dels., Fresno, 1990-98; State Bar Law Practice Mgmt. Sect., 1994-98, dir. Commn. For Adv. Calif. Paralegal Specialation Inc., 1995-2000. Pres. San Joaquin Coll. Law Alumni Assn., Fresno, 1990-96; mem. exec. com. San Joaquin Coll. Law, 1990-91, 20th anniversary com., 1990-91; trustee Kerman (Calif.) Unified Sch. Dist., 1982-88; bd. dirs. North Cen. Fire Protection Dist., Kerman, 1990-98. Mem. ABA, Am. Trial Lawyers Assn., Consumer Attorney of Calif., Calif. Bar Assn., Fresno County Bar Assn., Inns of Ct. Office: Fresno Co Courthouse 1100 Van Ness Ave Fresno CA 93724-0001 E-mail: JPetrucelli@Fresno.CA.gov

PETRUSH, JOHN JOSEPH, lawyer; b. Rochester, Pa., Oct. 15, 1942; s. Joseph Anthony and Helen Rosemarie (Klucarich) P.; children: John Joseph, Joshua Laurence. AB cum laude, Princeton U., 1964; LLB, Stanford U., 1967. Bar: Calif. 1967, Pa. 1970. Assoc. Bernard Petrie, San Francisco, 1967-68; law clk. to judge Common Pleas Ct. Beaver County, Pa., 1969; assoc. Buchanan, Ingersoll, Rodewald, Kyle & Buerger, Pitts., 1970-75; pvt. practice Beaver, Pa., 1976—. Mem. Beaver Town Coun., 1973-88; bd. dirs. Beaver County unit Am. Cancer Soc., 1976-90, United Way of Beaver County, 1986-92; trustee Beaver Area Sch. Dist. Edn. Found. With USMCR, 1961-63. Mem. ABA, ATLA, Pa. Bar Assn., Pa. Trial Lawyers Assn. (bd. govs. western chpt. 1984-90), Allegheny County Bar Assn., Beaver County Bar Assn. (treas. 1987—). Republican. State civil litigation, Personal injury, Workers' compensation. Home: 331 Wilson Ave Beaver PA 15009-2323 Office: 348 College Ave Beaver PA 15009-2209 E-mail: john.j.petrush@verizon.net

PETTIBONE, PETER JOHN, lawyer; b. Schenectady, N.Y., Dec. 11, 1939; s. George Howard and Caryl Grey (Ketchum) P.; m. Jean Kellogg, Apr. 23, 1966; children: Stephen, Victoria. AB summa cum laude, Princeton U., 1961; JD, Harvard U., 1964; LLM, NYU, 1971. Bar: Pa. 1965, D.C. 1965, N.Y. 1968, U.S. Supreme Ct. 1974, Russia (fgn. legal cons.) 1995. Lectr. Heidelberg (Fed. Republic Germany) U., 1965-67; assoc. Cravath, Swaine & Moore, N.Y.C., 1967-74, Lord Day & Lord, Barrett Smith, N.Y.C., 1974-76, ptnr. N.Y.C. and Washington, 1976-94, Patterson, Belknap, Webb & Tyler LLP, N.Y.C. and Moscow, 1994-99, Hogan & Hartson LLP, N.Y.C. and Moscow, 2000—. Pres. 1158 Fifth Ave. Corp., N.Y.C., 1991-94; pres. North Ferry Co., Shelter Island, N.Y., 1987-90; bd. dirs., vice-chmn. N.Y. State Facilities Devel. Corp., N.Y.C., 1983-89. Editor USSR Legal Materials, 1990-92. Trustee, treas. Hosp. Chaplaincy Inc., N.Y.C., 1980-86, Civitas, N.Y.C., 1984-92; mem. Coun. Fgn. Rels., 1993—; trustee Union Chapel, Shelter Island, N.Y., 1990—, CEC Internat. Ptnrs., 1996—; bd. dirs., vice chmn. Geonomics Inst., Middlebury, Vt., 1991-98; mem. vestry Ch. of Heavenly Rest, N.Y.C., 1987-93; mem. Nat. Adv. Coun. Harriman Inst. Columbia U., 1996—; mem. Russia com. Episcopal Diocese of N.Y. Capt. U.S. Army, 1965-67, Heidelberg, Germany. Mem. ABA, Assn. Bar City N.Y. (chmn. com. on CIS affairs 1991-94), U.S.-USSR Trade and Econ. Coun. Inc. (U.S. co-chmn. legal com. 1980-92), U.S.-Russia Bus. Coun. (bd. dirs.), Soc. of Cin., Anglers Club N.Y.C., N.Y. Yacht Club, Shelter Island Yacht Club, Amateur Ski Club N.Y. (pres. 1980-82), Canterbury Choral Soc. (pres. 1983-84), Phi Beta Kappa. Episcopalian. General corporate, Private international, Securities. Home: 1158 5th Ave New York NY 10029-6917 also: 10 Wesley Ave Shelter Island Heights NY 11965 Office: Hogan & Hartson LLP 885 3rd Ave New York NY 10022-7519

PETTIETTE, ALISON YVONNE, lawyer; b. Brockton, Mass., Aug. 16, 1952. Student Sorbonne, Paris, 1971-72; BA, Sophie Newcomb Coll., 1972; MA, Rice U., 1974; JD, Bates Coll., 1978. Bar: Tex. 1979, U.S. Dist. Ct. (so. dist.) Tex. 1980, U.S. Ct. Appeals (5th cir.) 1981. Ptnr. Harvill & Hardy, Houston, 1979-83; pvt. practice, Houston, 1983-84; assoc. O'Quinn & Hagans, Houston, 1984-86, Jones & Granger, Houston, 1986-88; pvt. practice, Houston, 1988—. Editor Houston Law Rev. U. Houston, 1976-78. Exercise instr. YWCA, Houston, 1976-81, U. St. Thomas, Houston. NDEA fellow Rice U., Houston, 1972-74; Woodrow Wilson scholar, Tulane U., New Orleans, 1972. Mem. ABA, Assn. Trial Lawyers Am., Tex. Trial Lawyers Assn., Houston Trial Lawyers Assn., Phi Delta Phi, Phi Beta Kappa. Federal civil litigation, Personal injury, Product liability. Home: PO Box 980847 Houston TX 77098-0847

PETTIT, ROGER LEE, lawyer; b. Winfield, Kans., Dec. 14, 1946; s. Ned Marsten and Roberta (Maxine) P.; m. Rebecca Ann Noltner, Oct. 28, 1968 (div. Sept. 1987); 1 child, Tristan Roger. BA, Washburn U., 1968; JD, Marquette U., 1974. Bar: Wis. 1974, U.S. Dist. Ct. (ea. and we. dists.) Wis. 1974, U. S. Ct. Appeals (7th cir.) 1977; cert. civil trial specialist. Sole practice, Milw., 1974-75; ptnr. Richman & Pettit, 1974; assoc. Hausmann, McNally & Hupy, 1975-81, Styler & Kostich, Milw., 1981-85; ptnr. Petrie & Socking S.C., 1985—. Recipient Outstanding Service award Milw. Young Layers Assn./Legal Action Wis., 1984. Mem. Assn. Trial Lawyers Am., Wis. Bar Assn., Wis. Acad. Trial Lawyers, South Shore Yacht Club (vice commodore 1984—), U.S. Power Squadron (sec., law officer 1983—). Avocation: sailing. General civil litigation, Labor, Personal injury. Office: Petrie & Stocking SC 111 E Wisconsin Ave Ste 1500 Milwaukee WI 53202-4808 E-mail: rpettit@petriestocking.com

PETTUS, E. LAMAR, lawyer; b. 1945; m. Donna C.; children: Evan Lamar, Carrie Anne, Samuel Chase. BSME, U. Ark., 1968, JD with honors, 1973. Bar: U.S. Dist. Ct. 1974 Ark., U.S. Ct. Appeals (8th cir.) 1974, Ark. Supreme Ct. 1974, U.S. Supreme Ct. 1979. Canton works plant engr. trainee Internat. Harvester, 1971; assoc. Pearson & Woodruff Law Firm, 1973; pvt. practice Pettus Law Firm, Fayetteville, Ark., 1974—. City atty. Farmington, 1981; mem. com. bar examiners Ark. Supreme Ct., 1986, chmn., 1988-89. Bus. mgr. Ark. Law Rev.; participant: televised "Ask Your Lawyer Program", 1981-83. Fin. chair Ctrl. United Meth. Ch., 1994-96, chair adminstrv. bd., 1997-2000; mem. Fayette Sch. Bd., 1991-97; active Assn. Voluntary Lawyers for Elderly, 1990—, Washington County Rep. Party. Comdr. USN, 1968-71, Vietnam, res. 1971-86. Recipient Navy Achievement medal, Navy Commendation medal. Mem. ABA, Ark. Bar Assn (pres. 1993-94, various positions and coms.), Ark. Trial Lawyers Assn., Washington County Bar Assn. (pres. 1989-90, v.p. 1989-90, sec.-treas. 1978-79), Fayetteville C. of C. (legis. com. 1994—), Rotary Internat. (various coms.). Consumer commercial, General corporate, Real property. Office: PO Box 1665 151 W Dickson St Fayetteville AR 72702 E-mail: lpettus@pettuslaw.com

PETTYJOHN, SHIRLEY ELLIS, lawyer, real estate executive; b. Liberty, Ky., Aug. 16, 1935; d. Wesley Barker and Ada Lou (Bryant) Ellis; m. Flem D. Pettyjohn, Sept. 24, 1955; children: Deena Renee, Ellisa Denise. BS in Commerce, U. Louisville, 1974, JD, 1977. Bar: Ky. 1978, Ind. 1988; lic. real estate broker, Ky., Ind.; cert. mediator. Pres. Universal Devel. Corp., Ky. and Fla., 1984—, Pettyjohn Inc., Ky. and Ind., 1967—, Ind. Mediation Svcs., Inc., 1990—, Ky. Mediation Svcs., Inc., 1991—; v.p. Continental Investments Corp., 1986—; sr. ptnr. Pettyjohn & Assocs., Attys., 1987—. Editor Law-Hers Jour. Vice chmn. Louisville and Jefferson County Planning Commn., 1971-75; mem. Gov.'s Conf. on Edn., 1977, jud. nominee, 1981, Met. Louisville Women's Polit. Caucus, Bluegrass State Skills Corp., 1992-96, Ky. Opera Assn. Guild; elected mem. Ky. State Dem. Exec. Com., 1988-92; del. Nat. Dem. Conv. and Dem. Nat. Platform Com., 1988; bd. dirs. Ky. Dem. Hdqs., Inc., 1988-92, Pegasus Rising, Inc.; chmn. Okolona Libr. Task Force; mem. Clinton-Gore Nat. Steering Com., 1995; hon. mem. Gore 2000 Presdl. Campaign Com. Recipient Mayor's Cert. Recognition, 1974, Mayor's Fleur de lis award, 1969-73, Excellence in Writing award Arts Club Louisville, 1986, 87, 93, 99; inducted into Casey County Alumni Hall of Fame, 1997. Mem. ABA, NAFE, Nat. Assn. Adminstrv. Law Judges, Ky. Bar Assn., Louisville Bar Assn., Women Lawyers Assn. of Jefferson County, Am. Judicature Soc., Clark County Bar Assn., Ind. Bar Assn., Ind. Assn. Mediators, Am. Inst. Planners, Women's C. of C. of Ky. (past bd. dirs., chmn. legis. com.), Am. Legion (aux.), Fraternal Order Police Assn. (award 1982), Louisville Legal Secs. (past pres., editor Law-Hers Jour.), Coun. of Women Pres. (past pres., Woman of Achievement award 1974), Louisville Visual Arts Assn. (past bd. dirs.), Louisville Ballet Guild (chair audience devel. 1989-91), Fern Creek Woman's Club, Ky. Fedn. Women's Clubs, Gen. Fedn. Women's Clubs, Dem. Leadership Coun., Casey County Alumni Assn. (pres. 1998-2000), Poplar Level Area Bus. Assn., Jefferson County Dem. Women's Club (past v.p.), Nat. Fedn. Dem. Women's Clubs, Spirit of 46th Club, Mose Green Club, North End Club, 12th Ward Club, S. End Club, 3rd Ward Club, Highland Pk. Club, Grass Roots Club, Harry S. Truman Club, Beargrass Club, Arts Club of Louisville (past pres.), Sigma Delta Kappa (life), Chi Thi Theta, Century 2000 Democrat Club. Administrative and regulatory, General practice, Probate. Home: 6924 Norlynn Dr Louisville KY 40228-1471 Office: 4500 Poplar Level Rd Louisville KY 40213-2124

PETZOLD, JOHN PAUL, judge; b. 1938; BA, U. Maine, 1961; LLB, Washington & Lee U., 1962. Bar: Ohio 1962, Va. 1962. Pvt. practice law, Ohio, 1962-91; asst. atty. gen. State of Ohio, 1964-71; law dir. City of Miamisburg, Ohio, 1979-91; judge Montgomery County Common Pleas Ct., Dayton, 1991—. Bd. tax appeals City of Kettering, Ohio, 1971-91. Mem. ABA, Ohio State Bar Assn. (bd. govs., former chairperson young lawyers sect., chairperson pub. rels. com., vice chairperson lawyers assistance com., eminent domain com., banking, comml., and bankruptcy law com., pres. 1998-99), Dayton Bar Assn. (pres. 1989-90), Common Pleas Judge Assn. (mem. bd. commrs. on grievances and discipline 1995-97). Avocations: golf, swimming, writing, teaching, reading, genealogy. Office: Montgomery County Common Pleas Ct 41 N Perry St Dayton OH 45402-1431

PEW, JOHN GLENN, JR. lawyer; b. Dallas, Apr. 18, 1932; s. John Glenn Sr. and Roberta (Haughton) P. BA, U. Tex., 1954, LLB, 1955. Bar: Tex. 1955, U.S. Dist. Ct. (no. dist.) Tex. 1959, U.S. Supreme Ct. 1959, U.S. Ct. Appeals (5th cir.) 1961, U.S. Ct. Appeals (10th cir.) 1982. Ptnr. Jackson & Walker, LLP, Dallas, 1964—. With USNR, 1955-58. Mem. Order of Coif, Phi Beta Kappa. Republican. Presbyterian. Federal civil litigation, State civil litigation. Office: Jackson Walker LLP 901 Main St Ste 6000 Dallas TX 75202-3797 E-mail: jpew@jw.com

PEYTON, GORDON PICKETT, lawyer; b. Washington, Jan. 22, 1941; s. Gordon Pickett and Mary Campbell (Grasty) P.; m. Marjorie G. Parish, June 9, 1962 (div.); children: Janet Porter, William Parish; m. Jean Nye Groseclose, Oct. 20, 1979. BA cum laude, U. of the South, 1962; JD, Duke U., 1965. Bar: Va. 1965, U.S. dist. Ct. (ea. dist.) Va. 1966, U.S. Ct. Appeals (4th cir.) 1975, U.S. Ct. Mil. Appeals 1980. Asst. city atty., Alexandria, Va., 1966-69; pvt. practice, 1966-99; ptnr. Redmon, Peyton & Braswell, LLP, 2000—. Asst. commr. accounts Alexandria Cir. Ct., 1978—, commr. accounts, 2001—; trustee U. of the South, 1972-76, Ch. Schs. in Diocese of Va., 1974-84; sr. warden Immanuel Ch.-on-the-Hill, 1990-91. 1st lt. USAF Res. ret. Fellow Am. Bar Found.; mem. ABA, 4th Cir. Jud. Conf., Va. Bar Assn., Va. State Bar (chmn. 8th dist. grievance com. 1988-90, chmn. disciplinary bd. 1996-97), Va. Trial Lawyers Assn., Alexandria Bar Assn. (pres. 1982-83, Am. Judicature Soc., Va. Conf. Commrs. of Accts., Alexandria C. of C. (v.p., dir. 1974-77). Episcopalian. Bankruptcy, Probate. Office: Redmon Peyton & Braswell 510 King St Ste 301 Alexandria VA 22314-3132

PFAFF, ROBERT JAMES, lawyer; b. Pitts., Jan. 12, 1943; s. William Michael and Elizabeth (Ludwig) P.; m. Carol Pillich, June 18, 1977. BS in Edn., Slippery Rock U., 1965; JD, Duquesne U., 1973. Bar: Pa. 1973, U.S. Dist. Ct. (we. dist.) Pa. 1973, U.S. Supreme Ct. 1980. Tchr. secondary schs., Norwin and Jeanette, Pa., 1965-66; suit group supr. Liberty Mut. Ins. Co., Pitts., 1966-70; assoc. Egler, McGregor & Reinstadtler, 1973-76; ptnr. Leopold, Eberhardt & Pfaff, Altoona, Pa., 1976-80; sr. ptnr. Meyer, Darragh, Buckler, Bebenek & Eck, Pitts., 1980-84, Pfaff, McIntyre, Dugas, Hartye & Schmitt, Hollidaysburg, Pa., 1984—. Bd. dirs. Blair County Legal Services, Altoona. Mem. ABA, Internat. Assn. Def. Counsel, Def. Rsch. Inst., Pa. Bar Assn., Blair County Bar Assn., Allegheny County Bar Assn., Pa. Assn. Mut. Ins. Cos. (claims com.), Pa. Def. Inst., Altoona Area Claims Assn. Republican. Roman Catholic. Avocations: golf, music, licensed pilot. General civil litigation, State civil litigation, Insurance. Home: 405 Kingsberry Cir Pittsburgh PA 15234-1065 Office: Pfaff McIntyre Dugas Hartye & Schmitt PO Box 533 Hollidaysburg PA 16648-0533 E-mail: rjmpfaff@aol.com

PFAFFENROTH, PETER ALBERT, lawyer; b. Mineola, N.Y., Mar. 29, 1941; s. Albert and Genevieve Astrid (Anderson) P.; m. Sara Ann Beekey, June 26, 1966; children: Elizabeth Cartwright, Peter Cyrus, Catherine Genevieve. BS in Engring., dipl. in European Civilization, Princeton U.,

1963; JD, U. Mich., 1966; LLM in Taxation, NYU, 1972, LLM in Corp., 1976, LLM in Internat. Law, 1998. Bar: N.J. 1966, U.S. Dist. Ct. (N.J. dist.) 1966. With Daimler-Benz, Stuttgart, Fed. Republic Germany, 1961, B.P. Benzin & Petroleum, Hamburg, Fed. Republic Germany, 1962, Office of Internat. Affairs, U.S. Treasury Dept., Washington, 1963, Office of Export Control, U.S. Commerce Dept., Washington, 1964, Commrs. Office, U.S. Patent Office, Washington, 1965; atty. McCarter & English, Newark, 1966-68, Kentz & Gilson, Esqs., Summit, N.J., 1968-69; corp. counsel Tex. Plastics, Maine Sugar Industries, Robbinsville, 1969-70; atty. c/o Lewis Stein, Esq., Netcong, 1970-71; pvt. practice Chester, 1971—. Avocations: antiques, foreign languages, travel, wine. Family and matrimonial, Real property, Taxation, general. Home: Route 24 At Twin Brooks Trail Chester NJ 07930

PFALTZ, HUGO MENZEL, JR. lawyer; b. Newark, Sept. 23, 1931; s. Hugo M. and Mary E. (Horr) P.; m. Marilyn M. Muir, Sept. 29, 1956; children— Elizabeth W., William M., Robert L. BA, Hamilton Coll., 1953; JD, Harvard U., 1960; LLM, NYU, 1965. Bar: N.J. 1960, U.S. Dist. Ct. N.J. 1960, U.S. Supreme Ct. 1977. Assoc. McCarter & English, Newark, 1960-61, Bourne & Noll, Summit, N.J., 1961-74; sole practice, Summit, 1974-82; ptnr. Pfaltz & Woller, 1983— ; dir. Elizabethtown Corp.; mem. Battleship N.J. Commn., 1985—, N.J. Law Revision Commn., 1986—. Assoc. editor N.J. Law Jour., 1966—, editor, 1984-86. Chmn. Summit Rep. City Com., 1966, mem. N.J. Constl. Conv., 1966; mem. N.J. Assembly, 1968-72. Served to lt. USNR, 1953-62. Mem. ABA, N.J. Bar Assn., Union County Bar Assn., Summit Bar Assn., Univ. Club (N.Y.C.), Univ. Club (Washington), Baltusrol Club (Springfield, N.J.); Beacon Hill Club (Summit, N.J.). Banking, Probate, Estate taxation. Home: 118 Prospect St Summit NJ 07901-2472 Office: 382 Springfield Ave Summit NJ 07901-2707

PFANNKUCHE, CHRISTOPHER EDWARD KOENIG, lawyer; b. Chgo., May 1, 1955; s. Edward Louis and Barbara (Koenig) P. BA in Polit. Sci., Loyola U., Chgo., 1977, BS in Edn., 1978, JD, 1980. Bar: Ill. 1980, U.S. Dist. Ct. (no. dist.) Ill. 1980, U.S. Ct. Claims 1984, U.S. Ct. Internat. Trade 1984, U.S. Tax Ct. 1983, U.S. Ct. Mil. Appeals 1983, U.S. Ct. Appeals (7th cir.) 1983, U.S. Ct. Appeals (D.C. cir.) 1984, U.S. Supreme Ct. 1983. Asst. states atty. State's Atty.'s Office, Cook County, Skokie, Ill., 1981—, Macon County, Decatur, Ill., 1981. Author: Traffic Trial Procedure Handbook, 1981. Mem. ABA, Ill. Bar Assn., Chgo. Bar Assn., Decatur Bar Assn., N.W. Suburban Bar Assn. (membership chmn. 1982-83, law day chmn. 1982-86, bd. govs. 1985—), Nat. Dist. Attys. Assn., Assn. Trial Lawyers Am., Am. Judicature Soc., Ill. Trial Lawyers Assn., Phi Alpha Delta. Roman Catholic. Avocations: pilot, scuba diving. Home: 7220 W Greenleaf Ave Chicago IL 60631-1013 Office: States Attys Office Cook County 5600 Old Orchard Rd Skokie IL 60077-1051

PFATTEICHER, LINDA E. lawyer; b. Phila., Sept. 29, 1971; d. Philip Henry and Lois Virginia (Sharpless) P. BA, Simmons Coll., 1992; JD, New Eng. Sch. of Law, 1995; LLM, Georgetown U., 1996. Bar: Mass. 1995, Calif. 1997. Mgr. KPMG, L.A., 1996—. Mem. ABA, L.A. County Bar Assn. Office: KPMG Ste 200 1901 Avenue of the Stars Los Angeles CA 90067-4611

PFEFFER, DAVID H. lawyer; b. N.Y.C., Mar. 15, 1935; B. Chem. Engring., CCNY, 1956; J.D., NYU, 1961, LL.M. in Trade Regulation, 1967. Bar: N.Y. 1961. With patent dept. U.S. Rubber Co., Wayne, N.J., 1957-61; assoc. Watson, Leavenworth, Kelton & Taggart, N.Y.C., 1961-63, Morgan & Finnegan, LLP, N.Y.C., 1963-70, ptnr., 1971—. Village prosecutor Roslyn Harbor, N.Y., 1976-78, village justice, 1979—; panel of arbitrators Am. Arbitration Assn. Mem. ABA (litigation sect.), N.Y. State Bar Assn., Assn. Bar City N.Y., Nassau County Bar Assn. (coms. on patent and trademarks, fed. practice), Am. Intellectual Property Law Assn. (com. alt. dispute resolution), N.Y. Intellectual Property Law Assn. (com. on alt. dispute resolution), N.Y. State Magistrates Assn., Nassau County Magistrates Assn., Order of Coif. Antitrust, Patent, Trademark and copyright. Office: Morgan & Finnegan LLP 345 Park Ave Fl 22 New York NY 10154-0053 E-mail: dpfeffer@morganfinnegan.com

PFEIFER, PAUL E. state supreme court justice; b. Bucyrus, Ohio, Oct. 15, 1942; m. Julia Pfeifer; 3 children. BA, Ohio State U., 1963, JD, 1966. Asst. atty. gen. State of Ohio, 1967-70; mem. Ohio Ho. of Reps., 1971-72; asst. prosecuting atty. Crawford County, 1973-76; mem. Ohio Senate, 1976-92, minority floor leader, 1983-84, asst. pres. pro-tempore, 1985-86; ptnr. Cory, Brown & Pfeifer, 1973-92; justice Ohio Supreme Ct., 1992—. Chmn. jud. com. Ohio Senate, 10 yrs. Mem. Grace United Meth. Ch., Bucyrus. Mem. Bucyrus Rotary Club. Office: Supreme Court of Ohio 30 E Broad St Fl 3 Columbus OH 43266-0419*

PFEIFFER, MARGARET KOLODNY, lawyer; b. Elkin, N.C., Oct. 7, 1944; d. Isadore Harold and Mary Elizabeth (Brody) K.; m. Carl Frederick Pfeiffer II, Sept. 2, 1968. BA, Duke U., 1967; JD, Rutgers U., 1974. Bar: N.J. 1974, N.Y. 1976, D.C. 1981, U.S. Supreme Ct. 1979. Law clk. to Hon. F.L. Van Dusen U.S. Ct. Appeals 3d cir., Phila., 1974-75; assoc. Sullivan & Cromwell, N.Y.C. and Washington, 1975-82, ptnr., 1982—. Contbr. articles to profl. jours. Trustee Am. Found. for Blind, Nat. Law Ctr. on Homelessness and Poverty; mem. bd. visitors Trinity Coll. Mem. ABA, Internat. Bar Assn., D.C. Bar Assn., N.Y. State Bar Assn., Assn. of Bar of City of N.Y. Avocations: hiking, reading, music. Antitrust, Federal civil litigation, Intellectual property. Office: Sullivan & Cromwell 1701 Pennsylvania Ave NW Washington DC 20006-5866

PFEIFFER, PHILIP J. lawyer; b. Houston, Aug. 16, 1947; BS, Sam Houston State U., 1969; JD, So. Meth. U., 1972. Bar: Tex. 1972. Mem. Fulbright & Jaworski L.L.P., San Antonio. Mem. ABA, State Bar Tex., San Antonio Bar Assn., Order of Coif, Phi Alpha Delta. Labor, Alternative dispute resolution. Office: Fulbright & Jaworski 300 Convent St Ste 2200 San Antonio TX 78205-3792 E-mail: ppfeiffer@fulbright.com

PFEUFFER, ROBERT TUG, lawyer, mediator, arbitrator; b. New Braunfels, Tex., May 15, 1937; s. Tug Somers and Laura Mildred Pfeuffer; m. Jean Louise Hillje, Mar. 24, 1959; children: Michael Somers, David Gregory, Susan Gode. BA, Tex. A&M U., 1959; JD, U. Tex., 1962. Bar: Tex., U.S. Dist. Ct. (we. dist.) Tex., U.S. Supreme Ct. Asst. staff judge advocate USAF, Dover AFB, 1962-65; assoc. Bartram, Reagan & Burrus, New Braunfels, Tex., 1965-70; ptnr. Bartram, Reagan Burrus & Pfeuffer Attys., 1970-73; state dist. judge 207th Dist. Ct. Tex., 1973-95; sr. dist. judge Tex. State Jud., 1995—; mediator, arbitrator Brazle & Pfeuffer Attys., 1995—. Pres. Comal County Fair Assn., New Braunfels, 1977. Cpt. USAF. Fellow Tex. Bar Found. (life); mem. Comal County Bar Assn. (pres. 1972), Lions (pres. New Braunfels club 1973). Democrat. Methodist. Alternative dispute resolution, Probate, Real property. Home: 3735 River Rd New Braunfels TX 78132-3123 Office: Brazle & Pfeuffer Attys 170 E San Antonio St New Braunfels TX 78130-4534 Fax: 830 629-2161. E-mail: jpfeuffer@aol.com

PFIFFNER, FRANK ALBERT, lawyer; b. Waukon, Iowa, July 21, 1948; s. Albert Gustave and Wilma (Hirth) P.; m. Mary Michaeline Victor, May 31, 1969; children: Christopher, Amanda, Rebecca. BA magna cum laude, Loras Coll., 1970; MA, JD, U. Iowa, 1974. Bar: Iowa 1974, Alaska 1975, U.S. Dist. Ct. Alaska 1975, U.S. Ct. Appeals (9th cir.) 1975, U.S. Supreme Ct. 1990, U.S. Ct. Appeals (fed. cir.) 1994, U.S. Ct. Fed. Claims 1994, U.S. Ct. Internat. Trade 1994. Mem. Hughes, Thorsness, Powell, Huddleston & Bauman LLC, Anchorage, 1974—. Served with U.S. Army, 1970-72. Mem. ABA, Iowa State Bar Assn., Alaska Bar Assn., Am. Arbitration Assn. (nat. panel arbitrators). Roman Catholic. Federal civil litigation, State civil litigation, Construction. Home: 8111 Evans Cir Anchorage AK 99507-3203 Office: Hughes Thorsness Powell Huddleston & Bauman LLC 550 W 7th Ave Ste 1100 Anchorage AK 99501-3563

PFLAUMER, KATRINA C. lawyer; BA in English Lit. cum laude, Smith Coll.; MA in Tchg. English, Columbia U.; JD, NYU. Tchr. English and Am. Lit. Westtown Sch., Pa., 1970-72; staff atty. Seattle King County Defender Assn., 1975-77, Fed. Pub. Defender's Office, Seattle, 1977-80; pvt. practice, 1980-93; U.S. atty. Dept. Justice (we. dist.) Washington, 1993-01. Pro tem judge King County Superior Ct.; adj. prof. U. Puget Sound Sch. Law; guest lectr. U. Washington, Hastings, Cardozo, Nat. Inst. Trial Advocacy programs; lawyer rep. 9th Cir. Jud. Conf.; named to Atty. Gen. Adv. Com., 1994-95. Mem. Fire Brigade Emergency Response Team. Mem. FBA (pres. we. dist. Washington 1991, chair implementation of gender task force report com.), Nat. Assn. Criminal Def. Lawyers (mem. nominating com.), U.S. Sentencing Commn. (practitioners adv. group), Am. Civil Liberties Union (mem. legal com.), Seattle-King County Bar Assn. (mem. jud. conf. com.), Washington Assn. Criminal Def. Lawyers (pres. 1988-89), State Bench Bar (mem. press com.), Phi Beta Kappa. Office: US Dept Justice 601 Union St Ste 5100 Seattle WA 98101*

PHAIR, JOSEPH BASCHON, lawyer; b. N.Y.C., Apr. 29, 1947; s. James Francis and Mary Elizabeth (Baschon) P.; m. Bonnie Jean Hobbs, Sept. 04, 1971; children: Kelly I., Joseph B., Sean P. BA, U. San Francisco, 1970, JD, 1973. Bar: Calif., U.S. Dist. Ct. (no. dist.) Calif., U.S. Ct. Appeals (9th cir.). Assoc. Berry, Davis & McInerney, Oakland, Calif., 1974-76, Bronson, Bronson & McKinnon, San Francisco, 1976-79; staff atty. Varian Assocs., Inc., Palo Alto, Calif., 1979-83, corp. counsel, 1983-86, sr. corp. counsel, 1986-87, assoc. gen. counsel, 1987-90, v.p., gen. counsel, 1990-91, v.p., gen. counsel, sec., 1991-99; v.p. adminstrn., gen. counsel, sec. Varian Med. Sys., Inc., 1999—. Mem. devel. bd. St. Vincent de Paul Devel. Coun., San Francisco, 1992—. Mem. Bay Area Gen. Counsel, Silicon Valley Assn. Gen. Counsel, The Olympic Culb. Roman Catholic. General corporate, Mergers and acquisitions, Securities. Office: Varian Med Sys Inc M S V 250 3100 Hansen Way Palo Alto CA 94304-1030

PHELAN, ROBIN ERIC, lawyer; b. Steubenville, Ohio, Dec. 28, 1945; s. Edward John and Dorothy (Borkowski) P.; m. JoAnn Keach, June 27, 1970 (dec. May 1994); children: Travis McCoy, Tiffany Marie, Trevor Monroe; m. Melinda Jo Rickets, May 27, 1995; 1 child, Taezja Monet. BSBA, Ohio State U., 1967, JD, 1970. Bar: Tex. 1971, U.S. Ct. Appeals (5th cir.) 1981, U.S. Ct. Appeals (11th cir.) 1981, U.S. Ct. Appeals (6th cir.) 1986, U.S. Ct. Appeals (10th cir.) 1988, U.S. Supreme Ct. Ptnr. Haynes and Boone, Dallas, 1970—. Co-author: Bankruptcy Practice and Strategy, 1987, Cowans Bankruptcy Law and Practice, 1987, Annual Survey of Bankruptcy Law, 1988, Bankruptcy Litigation Manual; contbr. articles to profl. jours. Mem. ABA (chmn. bankruptcy litigation subcom. 1990-95, chmn. unconventional bankruptcy issues), Internat. Bar Assn., Internat. Insolvency Inst., Am. Bankruptcy Inst. (dir., past pres.), Am. Coll. Bankruptcy, State Bar Tex. (chmn. bankruptcy law com. sect. bus. law 1989-91), Dallas Bar Assn. Roman Catholic. Avocation: athletics. Bankruptcy. Home: 4214 Woodfin St Dallas TX 75220-6416 E-mail: phelanr@haynesboone.com

PHELPS, KATHY BAZOIAN, lawyer; JD, UCLA, 1991. With Danning, Gill, Diamond & Kollitz LLP, L.A. Office: Danning Gill Diamond and Kollitz LLP 2029 Century Park E Fl 3D Los Angeles CA 90067-2901

PHELPS, ROBERT FREDERICK, JR. lawyer; b. Evanston, Ill., Aug. 20, 1956; s. Robert F. and Hanna (Kulej) P.; m. Joan Ann Brisky, Oct. 6, 1984; children: Jennifer Katherine, William Robert. BA, Trinity Coll., Hartford, Conn., 1978; JD cum laude, U. Mich., 1981; LLM, NYU, 1987. Bar: Conn. 1981, U.S. Tax Ct. 1987. Atty. Cummings & Lockwood, Stamford, Conn., 1981-87; atty. Day, Berry & Howard, 1987-91; v.p. J.P. Morgan, N.Y.C., 1991—. Cons. Conn. Safe Deposit Assn., 1983-87; mem. Fairfield County Estate Planning Coun., 1987-98; mem. Conn. Tax and Estate Planning Coun., 1990-92, Dallas Estate Planning Coun., Estate Planning Coun. North Tex., 1998—. Contbr. articles to profl. jours. Bd. dirs. Greenwich Coun. on Youth and Drugs, Inc., 1985-89; elder Noroton Presbyn. Ch., Darien, Conn., 1990-93; mem. Rep. Town Meeting, Darien, 1992-95; res. elder Highland Park Presbyn. Ch., 1998—; mem. adv. bd. So. Meth. U. Cox Sch. Bus., 2000—; mem. fin. com. George Bush Presdl. Libr. Found. Mem. ABA (real property and probate sect., tax sect., lectr. tax sect. fall meeting 2000), Conn. Bar Assn. (estates sect., tax and real property sects.), Middlesex Club, Northwood Country Club, Phi Beta Kappa. Republican. Avocation: tennis. E-mail: phelps. Estate planning, Probate, Estate taxation. Home: 3816 Greenbrier Dr Dallas TX 75225-5217 Office: JP Morgan Texas 300 Crescent Ct Ste 400 Dallas TX 75201-7847 E-mail: robert@jpmorgan.com

PHILION, NORMAN JOSEPH, III, lawyer; b. Colchester, Vt., Jan. 2, 1946; s. Norman Joseph and Concetta Ann (D'Orazio) P.; m. Diane Marcia Yeager, May 9, 1974. A.B., Ind. U., 1972; J.D., Duke U., 1975. Bar: D.C. 1976, U.S. Dist. Ct. D.C., U.S. Ct. Appeals (D.C. cir.). Mem. firm Thompson, Hine & Flory, Washington, 1975— . Served with USAF, 1965-69. Mem. Assn. Transp. Practitioners (chmn. D.C. chpt. 1985-86), Am. Hist. Assn., Inst. Early Am. History and Culture, Orgn. Am. Historians, Phi Beta Kappa. Administrative and regulatory, Federal civil litigation, Public utilities. Office: Thompson Hine & Flory 1920 N St NW Ste 700 Washington DC 20036-1600

PHILIPSBORN, JOHN TIMOTHY, lawyer, writer; b. Paris, Oct. 19, 1949; s. John David and Helen (Worth) P. AB, Bowdoin Coll., 1971; MEd, Antioch Coll., 1975; JD, U. Calif., Davis, 1978. Bar: Calif. 1978, U.S. Dist. Ct. (no. and ea. dists.) Calif. 1978, U.S. Ct. Appeals (9th cir.) 1985, U.S. Supreme Ct. 1985; cert-specialist in criminal law State of Calif. VISTA vol. Office of Gov. State of Mont., Helena, 1972-73; cons. U.S. Govt., Denver, 1974; lectr. Antioch New Eng. Grad. Sch., Keene, N.H., 1973-75, U. N.H., Durham, 1973-75; ptnr. Philipsborn & Cohn, San Jose, Calif., 1978-80; atty., supr. Defenders Inc., San Diego, 1980-83; assoc. Garry, Dreyfus & McTernan, San Francisco, 1983-87; pvt. practice, San Diego and San Francisco, 1987—. Cons. Nicaraguan ct. evaluation projects, 1987-88, UN Internat. Tribunal, 1995—; coord. Internat. Conf. Adversarial Sys., Lisbon, Portugal, 1990; mem. adj. faculty New Coll. Law, San Francisco, 1991—; legal asst. project refugee camps S.E. Asia, 1992—, legal edn. projects, Cambodia, 1995—, Pakistan, 2001; cons. on continuing edn. of bar, 1995—. Bd. editors Champion, Forum; contbr. articles to profl. jours., chpts. to book. Founder trial program San Francisco Schs., 1986; bd. dirs. Calif. Indian Legal Svcs., 1990-96. Fulbright scholar, Portugal, 1989, Pakistan, 2001—. Mem. Nat. Assn. Criminal Def. Lawyers (assoc., co-chmn. death penalty impact litigation group 1989, co-chmn. govtl. misconduct com. 1990-92, vice chmn. task force on emerging democracies 1990-91), Calif. State Bar (evaluation panel criminal law specialists 1986—, com. on continuing edn. of bar 1991-94, criminal law subcom. state bd. legal specialists 1995-96), Calif. Attys. for Criminal Justice (bd. govs. 1989-94, assoc. editor jour. 1987—, chmn. Amicus Curiae com. 1992—, co-chmn. govtl. misconduct com. 1989-92), World Affairs Coun. Criminal, Public international. Office: 507 Polk St Ste 250 Civic Ctr Bldg San Francisco CA 94102-3375

PHILLIPS, ALMARIN, economics educator, consultant; b. Port Jervis, N.Y., Mar. 13, 1925; s. Wendell Edgar and Hazel (Billett) P.; m. Dorothy Kathryn Burns, June 14, 1947 (div. 1976); children: Almarin Paul, Frederick Peter, Thomas Rock, David John, Elizabeth Linett, Charles Samuel; m. Carole Cherry Greenberg, Dec. 19, 1976. B.S., U. Pa., 1948, M.A., 1949; Ph.D., Harvard, 1953. Instr. econs. U. Pa., 1948-50, 51-53, asst. prof. econs., 1953-56, prof. econs. and law, 1963-91; Hower prof. pub. policy U. Pa, 1983-91; chmn. dept. econs. U. Pa., 1968-71, 72-73, assoc. dean Wharton Sch., 1973-74, dean Sch. Pub. and Urban Policy, 1974-77, chair faculty senate, 1990-91. Teaching fellow Harvard, 1950-51; assoc. prof. U. Va, 1956-61, prof., 1961-63; vis. prof. U. Hawaii, summer 1968, U. Warwick, London Grad. Sch. Bus. Studies, 1972, Ohio State U., McGill U., 1978, Calif. Inst. Tech, Northwestern U., 1980, Ariz. Coll. Law, 1987, Inst. Europeén d'Adminstrn. des Affairs (INSEAD), France, spring 1990; co-dir. Pres.'s Commn. Fin. Structure and Regulation, 1970-71; mem. Nat. Commn. Electronic Fund Transfers, 1976-77; chmn. bd. Econsult Corp., 1990-96. Author: (with R.W. Cabell) Problems in Basic Operations Research Methods for Management, 1961, Market Structure, Organization and Performance, 1962, Technology and Market Structure: A Study of the Aircraft Industry, 1971, (with P. Phillips and T.R. Phillips) Biz Jets: Technology and Market Structure in the Corporate Jet Aircraft Industry, 1994; Editor: Perspectives on Antitrust Policy, 1965, (with O.E. Williamson) Prices: Issues in Theory, Practice and Policy, 1968, Promoting Competition in Regulated Markets, 1975 ; editor Jour. Indsl. Econs., 1974-90; Contbr. articles to tech. lit. Served with AUS, 1943-45. Decorated Purple Heart, Bronze Star. Fellow Am. Statis. Assn., AAAS; mem. Am. Econ. Assn., Econometic Soc., European Econ. Assn., Internat. Telecommunications Soc. (bd. dirs. 1990—). Home: 1115 Remington Rd Wynnewood PA 19096-4021

PHILLIPS, ANTHONY FRANCIS, lawyer; b. Hartford, Conn., May 18, 1937; s. Frank and Lena Phillips; m. Rosemary Karran McGowan, Jan. 28, 1967; children: Karran, Antonia, Justin. BA, U. Conn., 1959; JD, Cornell U., 1962. Bar: N.Y. 1964, U.S. Dist. Ct. (so. dist., ea. dist.) N.Y. 1965, (ctrl. dist.) Calif. 1980, U.S. Tax Ct. 1981, U.S. Ct. Appeals (2nd cir.) 1967, (3d cir.) 1985, (4th cir.) 1983, (5th cir.) 1972, (7th cir.) 1987, (9th cir.) 1983, (10th cir.) 1983, U.S. Supreme Ct. 1971. Assoc. Willkie, Farr & Gallagher, N.Y.C., 1963-69, ptnr., 1969—. Mem. adv. com. Cornell U. Law Sch., 1994—. Fellow Am. Bar Found.; mem. ABA, N.Y. State Bar Assn., N.Y. County Bar Assn. (bd. dirs. 1989-95), Assn. of Bar of City of N.Y. Federal civil litigation, State civil litigation. Home: 3 Elm Rock Rd Bronxville NY 10708-4202 Office: Willkie Farr & Gallagher 787 7th Ave Lbby 2 New York NY 10019-6018 E-mail: aphillips@willkie.com

PHILLIPS, BARNET, IV, lawyer; b. New York, N.Y., July 5, 1948; s. Barnet III and Isabelle (Auriema) P.; m. Sharon Walsted Packey, Jan. 2, 1981; children: Victoria Ilonka, Caroline Walsted. BA, Yale U., 1970; JD, Fordham U., 1973; LLM, NYU, 1977. Bar: N.Y. 1974. Assoc. Hughes Hubbard & Reed, N.Y.C., 1973-76, Skadden, Arps, Slate, Meagher & Flom, N.Y.C., 1977-81, ptnr., 1981—. Adj. assoc. prof. Fordham U., N.Y.C., 1987-88; articles editor The Tax Lawyer, 1989-91. Co-author: Structuring Corporate Acquisition - Tax Aspects. Bd. dirs Student/Sponsor Partnership, N.Y.C., 1990-95; bd. cons. Portsmouth (R.I.) Abbey Sch., 1991-96, chmn., 97—. Republican. Avocations: skiing, opera, triathlons. Corporate taxation, Taxation, general, Personal income taxation. Home: 6 Hycliff Rd Greenwich CT 06831-3223 Office: Skadden Arps Slate Meagher & Flom Four Times Square 42nd Flr New York NY 10036-6522 E-mail: bphillip@skadden.com

PHILLIPS, DOROTHY KAY, lawyer; b. Nov. 2, 1945; d. Benjamin L. and Sadye (Levinsky) Phillips; children: Bethann P., David M. Schaffzin. BS inEnglish Lit. magna cum laude, U. Pa., 1964; MA in Family Life & Marriage Counseling, NYU, 1975; JD, Villanova U., 1978. Bar: Pa,=. 1978, N.J. 1978, U.S. Dist. Ct. (ea. dist.) Pa. 1978, U.S. Dist. Ct. N.J., 1978, U.S. Ct. Appeals (3d cir.), 1984, U.S. Supreme Ct. 1984. Tchr. Haddon (N.J.) Twp. H.S., Haddon Heights H.S., 1964-70; lectr., counselor Marriage Coun. of Phila., U. Pa., Hahnemann Med. Schs., Phila., 1970-75; atty. Adler, Barish, Daniels, Levin & Creskoff, 1978-79, Astor, Weiss & Newman, Phila., 1979-80; ptnr. Romisher & Phillips. P.C., 1981-86; prin. Lawq Office of Dorothy K. Phillips, 1986—. Faculty Sch., of Law Temple U.; guest spkr. on domestic rels. issues on radio and TV shows; featured in newspaper and mag. articles; bd. mem. Anti-Defamation League of B'nai B'rith, Nat. Mus. Jewish History; mem. friend's circle, Athenaeum, Phila., shareholder. Contbr. articles to profl. jours. Mem. ABA, ATLA (membership com. 1990-91, co-chair 1989-90), Pa. Trial Lawyers Assn. (chair membership com. family sect. 1989-90, presenter ann. update civil litigators-family law, author procedures practice of family law Phila. County Family Law Litigation Sect. County practiced database 1991) Pa. Bar Assn. (continuing legal edn. com. 1990-92, faculty, lectr. Pa. Bar Inst. Continuing Legal Edn. 1990, panel mem. summer meeting 1991), N.J. Bar Assn., Phila. Bar Assn. (chmn. early settlement program 1983-84, mem. custody rules drafting com. for Supreme Ct. Pa., spl. events spkr. on pensions, counsel fees, critten fee agreements 1989-91, co-chair and moderator of panel mandatory continuing legal edn. 1994), Nat. Bus. Inst. (lectr. for mandatory continuing legal edn. 1997—), Phila. Trial Lawyers Assn., Montgomery County Bar Assn., Lawyers Club. Appellate, State civil litigation, Family and matrimonial. Address: 121 S Broad St Ste 21 Philadelphia PA 19107-4534 E-mail: dkphillips@dkphillips.com

PHILLIPS, ELLIOTT HUNTER, lawyer; b. Birmingham, Mich., Feb. 14, 1919; s. Frank Elliott and Gertrude (Zacharias) P.; m. Gail Carolyn Isbey, Apr. 22, 1950; children— Elliott Hunter, Alexandra. A.B. cum laude, Harvard U., 1940, J.D., 1947. Bar: Mich. 1948. Since practiced in, Detroit; ptnr. Hill Lewis (formerly Hill, Lewis, Adams, Goodrich & Tait), 1953-89, of counsel, 1989-96, Clark Hill, 1996—. Chmn. bd. dirs. Detroit & Can. Tunnel Corp.; pres., dir. Detroit and Windsor Subway Co.; mem. Mich. Bd. Accountancy, 1965-73. Contbr. to legal and accounting jours. Chmn. bd. dirs. Southeastern Mich. chpt. ARC; pres., trustee McGregor Fund; trustee Boys Republic, Detroit Inst. for Children, United Way Southeastern Mich., Univ. Liggett Sch.; mem. nat. maj. gifts com. Harvard U., Harvard Pres.'s Assocs., 1974—; Pres.'s Coun., 1990, mem. overseers com. to visit Law Sch., overseers com. univ. resouces, Mich. chmn. Harvard Coll. Fund; trustee, pres. Ch. Youth Svc.; mem. Detroit Area coun. Boy Scouts Am. Lt. comdr. USNR, 1946. Recipient Spitzley award Detroit Inst. for Children, 1986, Harvard Alumni Assn. Disting. Svc. award, 1991. Fellow Mich. State Bar Found. (life), Am. Bar Found. (life); mem. ABA, State Bar Mich., Detroit Bar Assn., Lincoln's Inn Soc., Soc. Colonial Wars in Mich. (gov. 1999—) and Fla., Country Club Detroit, Detroit Club (pres. 1988-89), Yondotega Club, Grosse Pointe Club, Harvard Ea. Mich. Club (pres. 1955-56, Disting. Alumnus award 1992), Harvard Club N.Y.C., John's Island Club. Episcopalian (vestryman, sr. warden). General corporate, Non-profit and tax-exempt organizations, Pension, profit-sharing, and employee benefits. Home: 193 Ridge Rd Grosse Pointe MI 48236-3554 E-mail: elliottphillips@earthlink.net

PHILLIPS, ELVIN WILLIS, lawyer; b. Tampa, Fla., Feb. 27, 1949; s. Claude Everett and Elizabeth (Willis) P.; m. Sharon Gayle Alexander, June 20, 1970; children: Natasha Hope, Tanya Joy, Trey Alexander. BA, U. Fla., 1971; MA, Western Carolina U., 1974, EdS, 1975; JD, Stetson U., 1980. Bar: Fla. 1980, U.S. Dist. Ct. (mid. dist.) Fla. 1981, U.S. Dist. Ct. (so. dist.) Fla. 1982, U.S. Ct. Appeals (11th cir.) 1988. Tchr. Monroe County Schs., Key West, Fla., 1970-73; asst. prin. Habersham County Schs., Clarksville, Ga., 1973-77; assoc. Dixon, Lawson & Brown, Tampa, Fla., 1980-81, Yado, Keel, Nelson et al, Tampa, 1981; ptnr. Lawson, McWhirter, Grandoff & Reeves, 1981-88, Williams, Parker, Harrison, Dietz & Getzen, Sarasota, 1988—. Leadership Devel. Program fellow Southern Regional Coun.,

Atlanta, 1975. Mem. ABA (forum com. constrn. industry 1989-96), Assn. Legal Adminstrs., Fla. Bar (chmn. 1991-92, vice chmn. 1990-91, mem. benefits com.), Sarasota County Bar Assn., Phi Kappa Phi, Phi Alpha Delta, Phi Delta Kappa. Democrat. Baptist. Alternative dispute resolution, Construction, Government contracts and claims. Home: 3310 Del Prado Ct Tampa FL 33614-2721 Office: Williams Parker Harrison Dietz & Getzen 200 S Orange Ave Sarasota FL 34236-6802 E-mail: ephillips@williamsparker.com

PHILLIPS, GARY STEPHEN, lawyer; b. Far Rockaway, N.Y., June 26, 1957; s. Lawrence and Ilene (Kaufman) P.; m. Debbie J. Kanner, Mar. 27, 1983; children: Joshua Charles, Allison Ilyse. BA with high honors, U. Fla., 1978, JD with honors, 1981. Bar: Fla. 1982, U.S. Dist. Ct. (so. dist.) Fla. 1982, U.S. Ct. Appeals (11th cir.) 1982, U.S. Supreme Ct. 1986. With Sparber, Shevin, Shapo & Heilbronner, Miami, Fla., 1981-87; pvt. practice law, 1987-90; with Buchanan Ingersoll P.C., 1990-95, Phillips, Eisinger, Koss, Rothstein & Rosenfeldt, P.A., Hollywood, Fla., 1996—. Contbr. editor U. Fla. Law Rev., 1980-81. Mem. ABA, Am. Judicature Soc., Fla. Bar Assn. (litigation, real property, probate and trust law sects.), Dade County Bar Assn., North Dade Bar Assn. (treas. 1992), B'nai Brith, Phi Beta Kappa, Omicron Delta Epsilon, Omicron Delta Kappa. Democrat. Jewish. Federal civil litigation, State civil litigation, Personal injury. Office: 4000 Hollywood Blvd Ste 265 Hollywood FL 33021-6782

PHILLIPS, JAMES HAROLD, lawyer; b. Bowie, Tex., Dec. 18, 1934; s. Frank Carroll and Mabel Lorraine (James) P.; m. Jean Keir Woodruff, Oct. 2, 1959; children— Susan, John (dec.), Sara, Jamie. B.S.E.E., Rose-Hulman Inst. Tech.-Terre Haute, Ind., 1960; J.D., George Washington U., 1967. Bar: Ariz. 1968, U.S. Dist. Ct. Ariz. 1968, U.S. Patent Office 1968, U.S. Supreme Ct. 1972, U.S. Ct. Customs & Patent Appeals 1974, Tex. 1980, U.S. Ct. Appeals (fed. cir.) 1982. Atty., Gen. Electric, 1967-68; ptnr. Drummond, Cahill & Phillips, Phoenix, 1968-73; asst. patent counsel NCR Corp., Dayton, Ohio, 1973-76; sr. profl. atty. Sun Co. Inc., Dallas, 1976-84; ptnr. Cates & Phillips, Phoenix, 1984-88; sr. patent atty. Honeywell Bull Inc., Phoenix, 1988—; dir., v.p. Environ. Geotechnics Inc., Dallas, 1982-84; cons. Sun Co. Inc., Dallas, Atlantic-Richfield Co., Plano, Tex., 1984-88. Contbr. articles to profl. jours. Charter mem. Phoenix Symphony Council; pres. AMICA-Tex. chpt. Served with USN, 1952-55. Mem. Am. Intellectual Property Law Assn., Am. Arbitration Assn. (arbitrator), Licensing Exec. Soc., Ariz. Bar Assn. (chmn. patent, trademark and copyright sect. 1985-86), Tex. Bar Assn. Republican. Methodist. Patent, Trademark and copyright. Home: 410 E Braeburn Dr Phoenix AZ 85022-3624 Office: Honeywell Bull Inc 13430 N Black Canyon Hwy Phoenix AZ 85029-1361

PHILLIPS, JOHN BOMAR, lawyer; b. Murfreesboro, Tenn., Jan. 28, 1947; s. John Bomar Sr. and Betty Blanche (Primm) P.; m. Ellen Elizabeth Ellis, Aug. 9, 1969; children: John Bomar III, Anna Carroll, Ellis Elizabeth. BS, David Lipscomb Coll., 1969; JD, U. Tenn., 1974. Bar: Tenn. 1974, U.S. Dist. Ct. (ea. dist.) Tenn. 1975, U.S. Ct. Appeals (6th cir.) 1980. Assoc. Stophel, Caldwell & Heggie, Chattanooga, 1974-79; ptnr. Caldwell, Heggie & Helton, 1979-91, Miller & Martin, Chattanooga, 1991—. Author: Tennessee Employment Law, 1989, 3d edit., 2000, Employment Law Desk Book for Tennessee Employers, 1989; editor: The Tennessee Employment Law Letter, 1986—; host Danger Zones Video Tng. Series for Suprs., 1998—; mem. nat. moot ct. team U. Tenn. Law Rev. Pres. Chattanooga State coll. Found., 1992-94, Boys Club of Chattanooga, 1983-84; sec. Tenn. Aquarium, 1989—; chmn. Chattanooga Conv. and Visitors Bur., 1996-97; bd. dirs. Vol. Comty. Sch., Chattanooga, 1980-85, Coun. for Alcohol and Drug Abuse, Chattanooga, 1981-83, Creative Discovery Mus., 1994-99, Girls Prep. Sch., 1997—, Allied Arts of Gtr. Chattahooga, 1997—; mem. Hamilton County Juvenile Ct. Commn., 1995-99. Fellow Tenn. Bar Found., Chattanooga Bar Found.; mem. ABA (labor law sect.), Tenn. Bar Assn. (chair labor law sect. 1992-93, Justice Joseph W. Henry award 1986-87), Chattanooga Bar Assn. (bd. govs. 1978-79), Chattanooga C. of C. (bd. dirs. 1998-2001), Order of Coif, Fairyland Country Club (Lookout Mountain, Tenn.), Walden Club (bd. govs. 1992-95), Mountain City Club, Kiwanis (pres. Chattanooga 1986-87). Episcopal. Avocations, reading, writing. Labor, Libel. Home: 1107 E Brow Rd Lookout Mountain TN 37350-1015 Office: Miller & Martin 832 Georgia Ave Ste 1000 Chattanooga TN 37402-2289 E-mail: jphillips@millermartin.com

PHILLIPS, JOHN C. lawyer; b. S.I., N.Y., June 6, 1948; s. John D. G. and Eleanor (Stier) P.; m. Karen Francis McKenna, June 5, 1971; children: James, Thomas, Robert. AB in Govt., Cornell U., 1970; MA in Polit. Sci., Rutgers U., 1972, JD, 1975. Bar: N.J. 1975, U.S. Dist. Ct. N.J. 1975, N.Y. 1982, U.S. Supreme Ct. 1985, U.S. Ct. Appeals (3d cir.) 1985, Fla. 1988. Assoc. Carpenter, Bennett & Morrisey, Newark, 1975-79, Buttermore, Mullen & Jeremiah, Westfield, N.J., 1979-80; mng. ptnr. Buttermore, Mullen, Jeremiah & Phillips, 1981-85, 87-2001; with DeVos, Phillips & Co. PC, 1986-87; of counsel Price, Meese, Shulman & D'Arminio, 2001—. Trustee, dir. Animal Care Fund Inc., East Smithfield, Pa., 1983-98. Author: (with others) New Jersey Transactins, Zoning and Planning, 1993. Dir., coach Police Athletic League, Berkeley Heights, N.J., 1967-99; mem. Kappa Alpha Literary Soc., 1967—, trustee Kappa Alpha Assn., 1974-90, v.p. Kappa Alpha Assn. Found., 1978-87, vice-chmn., 1983, chmn., 1984; dir. Youth Soccer Club, Berkeley Heights, 1983-94; mem. Berkeley Heights Twp. Com., 1985-87, dep. mayor, 1986, 87; Twp. atty., Berkeley Heights, 1989, 91, 94—; planning bd. atty. Twp. Warren, 1987—; mem. N.J. Hotel and Multiple Dwelling Safety Bd., 1988—, vice chmn., 1998—; mem. Rep. Mcpl. Com., 1985-2000, vice chmn., 1990-92, 98-2000, mem. dist. XII ethics com., 1993-97, dist. XII fee arbitration com., 1998—. Recipient award for Assistance and Dedication to youth, Police Athletic League, Berkeley Heights, 1975, Dedicated Svc. award Berkeley Heights Twp. Com., 1983. Mem.: ABA, N.J. State Bar Assn., Union County Bar Assn., Fedn. of Planning Ofcls., Inst. of Mcpl. Attys., Urban Land Inst., Canoe Brook Country Club, Jaycees (sec. New Providence-Berkeley Heights chpt. 1982, Jaycee of Yr. 1982). Republican. Methodist. State civil litigation, Land use and zoning (including planning), Personal injury. Home: 56 Emerson Ln Berkeley Heights NJ 07922-2414 Office: Price Meese Shulman & D'Arminio 50 Tice Blvd Woodcliff Lake NJ 07677 E-mail: jphillips@pricemeese.com

PHILLIPS, J(OHN) TAYLOR, judge; b. Greenville, S.C., Aug. 20, 1921; s. Walter Dixon and Mattie Sue (Taylor) P.; m. Mary Elizabeth Parrish, Dec. 18, 1954; children: John Allen, Susan, Linda-Lea, Julia. AA, Glenville State Coll., 1952; JD, Mercer U., 1955; LLD, Asbury Coll., 1992. Bar: Ga. 1954, U.S. Supreme Ct. 1969. Mem. Ho. of Reps. State of Ga., Atlanta, 1959-62, Senate, 1962-64. With USMC, 1942-51. Methodist. Home: 1735 Winston Dr Macon GA 31206-3241 Office: State Ct Bibb County PO Box 6242 Macon GA 31208

PHILLIPS, JOSEPH BRANTLEY, JR. lawyer; b. Greenville, S.C., Dec. 5, 1931; BS in Bus. Adminstrn., U. S.C., 1954, JD, 1955. Bar: S.C. 1955. Assoc. Leatherwood, Walker, Todd & Mann, Greenville, 1958-63, ptnr., 1963—. Chmn. bd. deacons Presbyterian Ch., 1970-71, pres. Men of Ch., 1968-69, chmn. Christian Service Ctr., 1972-73; bd. dirs. Greenville Urban Ministry, 1978. Mem. ABA, S.C. Bar Assn., Greenville Bar Assn., Greenville Young Lawyers Club (pres. 1961-62), Lawyers Pilots Bar Assn., Kiwanis (pres. 1973). Clubs: Greenville Country (pres. 1977). Antitrust, Aviation, General corporate. Home: 207 Butler Springs Rd Greenville SC 29615-2261 Office: PO Box 87 Greenville SC 29602-0087 E-mail: jbphillipsjr@aol.com

PHILLIPS, KAREN BORLAUG, economist, railroad industry executive; b. Long Beach, Calif., Oct. 1, 1956; d. Paul Vincent and Wilma (Tish) Borlaug. Student, Cath. U. P.R., 1973-74; BA, BS, U. N.D., 1977; postgrad., George Washington U., 1978-80. Rsch. asst. rsch. and spl. programs adminstrn. U.S. Dept. Transp., Washington, 1977-78, economist, office of sec., 1978-82; profl. staff mem. (majority) Com. Commerce Sci., Transp. U.S. Senate, 1982-85, tax economist (majority) com. on fin., 1985-87, chief economist (majority) senate com. on fin., 1987-88; commr. Interstate Commerce Commn., 1988-94; v.p. legis. Assn. Am. Railroads, 1994-95, sr. v.p. policy, legis. and comm., 1995-98; pres. Policy & Advocacy Assocs., Alexandria, Va., 1998-2000; v.p. U.S. govt. affairs Can. Nat. Rlwy. Co., 2000—. Contbg. author studies, publs. in field. Recipient award for Meritorious Achievement, Sec. Transp., 1980, Spl. Achievement awards, 1978, 80, Outstanding Performance awards, 1978, 80, 81. Mem. Am. Econ. Assn., Women's Transp. Seminar (Woman of Yr. award 1994), Transp. Rsch. Forum, Assn. Transp. Law, Logistics and Policy, Tax Coalition, Blue Key, Phi Beta Kappa, Omicron Delta Epsilon. Republican. Lutheran. Office: Can Nat Rlwy Co Ste 500 601 Pennsylvania Ave NW Washington DC 20004 E-mail: karen.phillips@cn.ca

PHILLIPS, LARRY EDWARD, lawyer; b. Pitts., July 5, 1942; s. Jack F. and Jean H. (Houghtelin) P.; m. Karla Ann Hennings, June 5, 1976; 1 son, Andrew H.; 1 stepson, John W. Dean IV. BA, Hamilton Coll., 1964; JD, U. Mich., 1967. Bar: Pa. 1967, U.S. Dist. Ct. (we. dist.) Pa. 1967, U.S. Tax Ct. 1969. Assoc. Buchanan, Ingersoll, Rodewald, Kyle & Buerger, P.C., Pitts., 1967-73, mem., 1973—. Mem. ABA (sect. taxation, com. on corp. tax and sect. real property, probate and trust law), Am. Coll. Tax Counsel, Pa. Bar Assn., Tax Mgmt. Inc. (adv. bd.), Pitts. Tax Club, Allegheny County Bar Assn., Duquesne Club. Republican. Presbyterian. Corporate taxation, Estate taxation, Personal income taxation. Office: Buchanan Ingersoll PC One Oxford Ctr 301 Grant St Fl 20 Pittsburgh PA 15219-1410 E-mail: phillipsle@bipc.com

PHILLIPS, LEO HAROLD, JR. lawyer; b. Jan. 10, 1945; s. Leo Harold and Martha C. (Oberg) P.; m. Patricia Margaret Halcomb, Sept. 3, 1983. BA summa cum laude, Hillsdale Coll., 1967; MA, U. Mich., 1968, JD cum laude, 1973; LLM magna cum laude, Free U. of Brussels, 1974. Bar: Mich. 1974, N.Y. 1975, U.S. Supreme Ct. 1977, D.C. 1979. Fgn. lectr. Pusan Nat. U., Korea, 1969-70; assoc. Alexander & Green, N.Y.C., 1974-77; counsel Overseas Pvt. Investment Corp., Washington, 1977-80, sr. counsel, 1980-82, asst. gen. counsel, 1982-85, Manor Care, Inc., Gaithersburg, Md., 1985-91, asst. sec., 1988-99, assoc. gen. counsel, 1991-99, v.p., 1996-99. Vol. Peace Corps, Pusan, 1968-71; mem. program for sr. mgrs. in govt. Harvard U., Cambridge, Mass., 1982. Contbr. articles to legal jours. Chmn. legal affairs com. Essex Condominium Assn., Washington, 1979-81; mem. fin. com., cmty. leadership bd. Miami City Ballet, 2001—; deacon Chevy Chase Presbyn. Ch., Washington, 1984-87, moderator, 1985-87, supt. ch. sch., elder, trustee, 1987-90, pres., 1988-90, mem. nominating com., 1995-96. Recipient Alumni Achievement award Hillsdale Coll., 1980; Meritorious Honor award Overseas Pvt. Investment Corp., 1981, Superior Achievement award, 1984. Mem. ABA (internat. fin. transactions com., vice-chmn. com. internat. ins. Law), Am. Soc. Internat. Law (Jessup Internat. Law moot ct. judge semi-final rounds 1978-83, chair corp. counsel com. 1993-97), Internat. Law Assn. (Am. br.; com. sec. 1982), D.C. Bar, N.Y. State Bar Assn., Royal Asiatic Soc. (Korea br.), State Bar Mich., Washington Fgn. Law Soc. (sec.-treas. 1980-81, bd. dirs., program coord. 1981-82, v.p. 1982-83, pres.-elect 1983-84, pres. 1984-85, chmn. nominating com. 1986, 88), Washignton Internat. Trade Assn. (bd. dirs. 1984-87), Assn. Bar City N.Y., Hillsdale Coll. Alumni Assn. (co-chmn. Washington area 1977-90), Univ. Club (N.Y.C.). Contracts commercial, General corporate, Private international. Home: 4740 Connecticut Ave NW Apt 702 Washington DC 20008-5632

PHILLIPS, PAMELA KIM, lawyer; b. San Diego, Feb. 23, 1958; d. John Gerald and Nancy Kimiko (Tabuchi) Phillips; m. R. Richard Zanghetti, Sept. 16, 1989. BA cum laude, The Am. U., 1978; JD, Georgetown U., 1982. Bar: N.Y. 1983, U.S. Dist. Ct. (so. dist.) N.Y. 1983, Fla. 1994, U.S. Dist. Ct. (mid. dist.) Fla. 1994. Assoc. Curtis, Mallet-Prevost, Colt & Mosle, N.Y.C., 1982-84, LeBoeuf, Lamb, Greene & MacRae, N.Y.C., 1984-90, ptnr., 1991—. Mng. editor The Tax Lawyer, Georgetown U. Law Sch., Washington, 1980-81. Mem. coun. The Fresh Air Fund, 1991-94, Youth Leadership Jacksonville, 1999—; bd. dirs. Jacksonville Zool. Soc., Inc., 1996—, sec., 1997—; pres. First Coast Venture Capital Group, Inc., 1996-98. Am. Univ. scholar, Washington, 1976-78. Mem. ABA, Bar Assn. City N.Y. (sec. young lawyers com. 1987-89, chmn. 1989-91, second century com. 1990-93, banking law com. 1991-94), Jacksonville Bar Assn., River Club. Democrat. Roman Catholic. Avocations: tennis, travel. General corporate, Finance, Mergers and acquisitions. Home: 109 Carriage Lamp Way Ponte Vedra Beach FL 32082-1903 Office: LeBoeuf Lamb Greene & MacRae 125 W 55th St New York NY 10019-5369 also: 50 N Laura St Ste 2800 Jacksonville FL 32202-3656 E-mail: pamela.phillips@LLgm.com

PHILLIPS, PATRICIA DOMINIS, lawyer; b. Los Angeles, July 21, 1934; d. Anthony P. and Louise (Brown) Dominis; m. John T. Phillips, Jan. 1, 1964; children: Toni, Lisa, Paul, Samantha, John. BA in Psychology, U. Calif., Santa Barbara, 1956; JD, Loyola U., Los Angeles, 1967. Bar: Calif. 1968, U.S. Supreme Ct., U.S. Dist. Ct. (cen. dist.) Calif., U.S. Dist. Ct. (so. dist.) Calif. Law Clk. Los Angeles County Superior Ct., Los Angeles, 1968; assoc. Beardsley, Hufstedler, Los Angeles, 1969-72; ptnr. Hufstedler, Miller, Carlson & Beardsley, and predecessor firm Beardsley, Hufstedler & Kemble, Los Angeles, 1972—; lectr. continuing edn. of the bar Rutter Group. Contbr. articles to profl. jours. Mem. bd. councillors U. So. Calif., Los Angeles, 1983—; mem. bd. visitors Loyola U. Law Sch., 1985—. Mem. ABA, Am. Acad. Matrimonial Lawyers, State Bar Calif., Los Angeles County Bar Assn. (pres. 1984-85, bd. govs. 1986—). Club: Chancery. State civil litigation, Family and matrimonial. Office: Hufstedler Miller Carlson & Beardsley 700 S Flower St Ste 1600 Los Angeles CA 90017

PHILLIPS, RICHARD LEE, lawyer; b. Fresno, Calif., Apr. 3, 1948; s. Floyd Gilbert and Emma Beatrice (Rivas) P.; m. Joan Elizabeth Hadley, Sept. 19, 1990; children: Lisa Marie, Laurel Jane, Andrew Clement, Taryn Siobhan. BA in Polit. Sci., U. Ill., Urbana, 1970; JD, U. Puget Sound, 1975. Dep. pros. atty. office of King County Prosecutor, Seattle, 1975-77; assoc. Hutchins, Plumb & Wheeler, Tacoma, 1977-79, Moriarty and Mikkelborg, Seattle, 1979-83, ptnr., 1984-85, Mikkelborg, Broz, Wells & Fryer, Seattle, 1985-2000. Editor notes and comments U. Puget Sound Law Rev. Mem. ABA (litigation sect. bus. com.), Computer Law Assn., Maritime Law Assn. of U.S., Nat. Assn. Criminal Def. Lawyers, U. Ill. Alumni Assn., U. Puget Sound Alumni Assn. Democrat. Avocations: baseball, guitar, photography, science and space technology, woodworking. Federal civil litigation, Computer, Intellectual property. Office: 16088 85th NE Redmond WA E-mail: mail@RichardLPhillips.com

PHILLIPS, ROBERT JOHN, lawyer; b. Bournemouth, Hampshire, Eng., May 15, 1947; s. Geoffrey Charles and Betty Eileen P.; m. Eleanor Jean Jack, Dec. 12, 1974; children: Nichola, Hannah, James. Bar: solicitor Eng. and Wales, Hong Kong; barrister, solicitor Victoria, Australia. Ptnr. CMS Cameron McKenna, London, 1977—, McKenna & Co., London, 1979-83, 88-97; Hong Kong, 1983-88. Mem. Major Projects Assn. Public utilities. Office: CMS Cameron McKenna Mitre House 160 Aldersgate EC1A 4DD London England Fax: 02073672000. E-mail: rjp@cmlk.com

PHILLIPS, RONALD FRANK, retired academic administrator; b. Houston, Nov. 25, 1934; s. Franklin Jackson and Maudie Ethel (Merrill) P.; m. Jamie Jo Bottoms, Apr. 5, 1957 (dec. Sept. 1996); children: Barbara Celeste Phillips Oliveira, Joel Jackson, Phil Edward. BS, Abilene Christian U., 1955; JD, U. Tex., 1965. Bar: Tex. 1965, Calif. 1972. Bldg. contractor Phillips Homes, Abilene, Tex., 1955-56; br. mgr. Phillips Weatherstripping Co., Midland and Austin, 1957-65; corp. staff atty. McWood Corp., Abilene, 1965-67; sole practice law, 1967-70; mem. adj. faculty Abilene Christian U., 1967-70; prof. law Pepperdine U., Malibu, Calif., 1970—, dean Sch. Law, 1970-97, dean emeritus, 1997—, vice chancellor, 1995—. Deacon North A and Tenn. Ch. of Christ, Midland, 1959-62; deacon Highland Ch. of Christ, Abilene, 1965-70; elder Malibu Ch. of Christ, 1978-95; mgr., coach Little League Baseball, Abilene, Huntington Beach and Malibu, 1968-78, 90-95; coach Youth Soccer, Huntington Beach, Westlake Village and Malibu, 1972-80, 85-86, 91. Recipient Alumni citation Abilene Christian U., 1974 Fellow Am. Bar Found. (life); mem. ABA, State Bar Tex., State Bar Calif., Christian Legal Soc., L.A. Bar Assn., Assn. Am. Law Schs. (chmn. sect. on adminstrn. law schs. 1982, com. on cts. 1985-87), Am. Law Inst., Nat. Conf. Commrs. on Uniform State Laws. Republican. Office: Pepperdine U 24255 Pacific Coast Hwy Malibu CA 90263-0002 E-mail: rphillip@pepperdine.edu, ronald.phillips@pepperdine.edu

PHILLIPS, THOMAS ROYAL, state supreme court chief justice; b. Dallas, Oct. 23, 1949; s. George S. and Marguerite (Andrews) P.; m. Lyn Bracewell, June 26, 1982; 1 son, Daniel Austin Phillips; 1 stepson, Thomas R. Kirkham. BA, Baylor U., 1971; JD, Harvard U., 1974; LLD (hon.), Tex. Tech. U., 1997; DHL (hon.), St. Edwards U., 1998. Bar: Tex. 1974; cert. in civil trial law Tex. Bd. Legal Specialization. Briefing atty. Supreme Ct. Tex., Austin, 1974-75; assoc. Baker & Botts, Houston, 1975-81; judge 280th Dist. Ct., 1981-88; chief justice Supreme Ct. Tex., Austin, 1988—. Mem. com. on fed.-state rels. Jud. Conf. U.S., 1990-96; chair Tex. Jud. Dists. Bd., 1988—; mem. State Judges Mass Tort Litig. Com., 1991-96; bd. dirs. Elmo B. Hunter Citizens Ctr. for Jud. Selection, 1992-94, Southwestern Legal Found.; mem. Nat. Conf. Chief Justices, 1988—, pres., 1997-98; adv. dir. Rev. of Litig., U. Tex. Law Sch., 1990—; chair Nat. Mass Tort Conf. Planning Com., 1993-94. Bd. advisors Ctr. for Pub. Policy Dispute Resolution, U. Tex. Law Sch., 1993—; mem. planning com. South Tex. Coll. of Law Ctr. for Creative Legal Solutions, 1993—. Recipient Outstanding Young Lawyer award Houston Young Lawyers Assn., 1986, award of excellence in govt. Tex. C. of C., 1992; named Appellate Judge of Yr., Tex. Assn. Civil Trial and Appellate Specialists, 1992-93, Disting. Alumnus, Baylor U., 1998. Mem. ABA (task force lawyers polit. contbns. 1997-98), Am. Law Inst. (advisor Fed. Jud. Code Project 1996—), Nat. Ctr. for State Ctrs. (chair, bd. dirs. 1997-98), State Bar Tex. (chmn. pattern jury charges IV com. 1985-87, vice chmn. adminstrn. justice com. 1986-87), Am. Judicature Soc. (bd. dirs. 1989-95, 99—, exec. bd. 1995-96), Tex. Philol. Soc., Houston Philol. Soc., Houston Bar Assn., Travis County Bar Assn. Republican. Episcopalian. Office: Tex Supreme Ct PO Box 12248 Austin TX 78711-2248 E-mail: cj@tomphillips.com

PHILLIPS, TRAVIS R. lawyer; b. Longview, Tex., Feb. 20, 1948; s. Lowell T. and Alice (Tucker) P.; m. Barbara Shepherd, June 30, 1973 (div. Mar. 1981); m. Mary Diane Bialaszewski, Sept. 10, 1983. B.B.A., Stephen F. Austin State U., 1970; J.D., U. Tex.-Austin, 1972. Bar: Tex. 1972, U.S. Dist. Ct. (we. dist.) Tex. 1974, U.S. Dist. Ct. (so. dist.) Tex. 1981, U.S. Ct. Appeals (5th cir.) 1974. Juvenile pub. defender County of Travis, Austin, 1972-73; ptnr. Phillips & Dorsett, Austin, 1973-76, Phillips, Neals & Woods, Austin, 1976—; gen. counsel Tex. Rental Assn., 1973-81; pres. Tramco Mortgage Co., Austin, 1983—. Mayor City of Rollingwood, Tex., 1986-88. Author: (manual) Texas Mechanics Lien Laws, 1976. Mem. Travis County Bar Assn. Democrat. Lodges: Masons, Shriners. State civil litigation, Contracts commercial, Real property. Office: Phillips Neal & Woods 1303 San Antonio St Austin TX 78701-1636

PHILLIPS, W. ALAN, entertainment lawyer, educator; b. Mobile, Ala., Aug. 26, 1963; s. Billy Ray and Clara Joanne (Andrews) P.; m. Molly Melissa Stocks, Nov. 3, 1984; children: Abigail Alston, James Andrew. MusB, James Madison U., 1985; JD, U. Richmond, 1994. Bar: Tenn., 1994, U.S. Dist. Ct. (mid. dist.) Tenn., 1995. Mktg. mgr. Silver Bells Music, Nashville, 1986; field rep. ASCAP, Richmond, Va., 1986-88; regional sales mgr. Independence Comm., 1988-91; law clerk Press, Jones & Waechter, 1992-93, Jack, Lyon & Jones, P.A., Nashville, 1993, assoc., 1995-2000; atty. OrNda Health Corp., 1994-95; sr. assoc. McCutchen, Doyle, Brown & Enersen, Palo Alto, 2000—. Adj. prof. copyright Middle Tenn. State U., Murfreesboro, 1996-99, Belmont U., Nashville, 1997-98. Assoc. editor: U. Richmond Law Rev., 1992-94; contbr. articles to profl. jours. Mem. ABA (chmn. arts, entertainment and sports law com. young lawyers divsn. 1997-98), Nashville Bar Assn. (chmn. entertainment and sports law com. 2000, chmn. intellectual property com. 1997-98), Country Music Assn., Copyright Soc. of South, Internat. Entertainment Buyers Assn. (gen. coun. 1998-2000), Friends Against Mus. Exploitation Artists (gen. counsel 1998-2000). Baptist. Avocation: computers. Federal civil litigation, Entertainment, Trademark and copyright. Office: McCutchen Doyle Brown & Enersen 3150 Porter Dr Palo Alto CA 94304-1212 Fax: 950-849-4800

PHILLIPS, WALTER RAY, lawyer, educator; b. Democrat, N.C., Mar. 19, 1932; s. Walter Yancey and Bonnie (Wilson) P.; m. Patricia Ann Jones, Aug. 28, 1954; children: Bonnie Ann, Rebecca Lee. A.B., U. N.C., 1954; LL.B., Emory U., 1957, LL.M., 1962, J.D., 1970; postgrad., Yale U., 1965-66. Bar: Ga. 1957, Fla. 1958, Tex. 1969, Mo. 2001, U.S. Supreme Ct. 1962. With firm Jones, Adams, Paine & Foster, West Palm Beach, Fla., 1957-58; law clk. to chief judge U.S. Dist. Ct., Atlanta, 1958-59; with firm Powell, Goldstein, Frazer & Murphy, 1959-60; bankruptcy judge U.S. Cts., 1960-64; prof. law U. N.D., 1964-65; teaching fellow Yale U., 1965-66; prof. law Fla. State U., 1966-68, Tex. Tech. U., Lubbock, 1968-71; Disting. vis. prof. law Baylor U., 1971; atty. Commn. on Bankruptcy Laws of U.S., Washington, 1971-72; dep. dir., adminstrv. officer, 1972-73; prof. Sch. Law, U. Ga., 1973-2000, assoc. dean, 1975-83, acting dean, 1976, Joseph Henry Lumpkin prof., 1977-94, also dir. univ's self. study, 1978, Herman E. Talmadge prof., 1994-2000. Chapman disting. vis. prof. law U. Okla., 1985-86; vis. prof. law U. Okla., 1990, U. Mo., Columbia, 1993, 94, 2001—; reporter Gov.'s Legislation for Ga., 1973; v.p., dir. Killearn Estates, Inc.; mem. Conf. on Consumer Fin. Law; prof. London Law Consortium, 1999. Author: Florida Law and Practice, 1960, Encyclopedia of Georgia Law, 1962, Seminar for Newly Appointed Referees in Bankruptcy, 1964, Damages: Cases and Materials, 1967, (with James William Moore) Debtors' and Creditors' Rights, Cases and Material, 1966, 5th edit., 1979, The Law of Debtor Relief, 1969, 2d edit., 1972, supplement, 1975, (with James William Moore) Rule 6, Moore's Federal Practice, 1969, Adjustment of Debts for Individuals, 1979, 2d edit., 1981, supplement, 1982, 84, 85, Liquidation Under the Bankruptcy Code, 3d edit., 1988, supplement, 1989, 90, 91, 92, 93, 94, Cases and Materials on Corporate Reorganization, 1983, 3d edit., 1986, 4th edit., 1988, 5th edit., 1990, 7th edit., 1996, 8th edit., 1998, Family Farmer and Adjustment of Individual Debts, 1987, supplement, 1988, 89, 90, 91, 92, 93, 94, A Primer of Chapters 12 and 13 of the Bankruptcy Code, 1995. Bd. dirs. Lubbock Day Nurseries, 1969, pres., 1970-71. Served with USAF, 1950. Mem. ATLA, ABA (consumer bankruptcy com. 1973—, chmn. 1986-90), Fed. Bar Assn., Fla. Bar Assn., Tex. Bar Assn., Western Circuit Bar Assn., Ga. Bar Assn. (vice chmn. publs. com. 1977-89, com. on profl. responsibility 1983—), Mo. Bar Assn., Am. Judicature Soc., Phi Alpha Delta (chief tribune) Baptist. Home: 3800 Wakefield Dr Columbia MO 65203-5630 E-mail: wrppjp033209321@aol.com

PHILLIPS, WILLIAM RUSSELL, SR. lawyer; b. N.Y.C., June 4, 1948; s. Samuel Russell and Annie Laura (Galloway) P.; m. Dorothy Elizabeth Lowery, Apr. 10, 1976; 1 child, William Russell Jr. BS, Washington & Lee U., 1970; JD, Georgetown U., 1974. Bar: Va. 1975, Ga. 1977, U.S. Dist. Ct. (no. dist.) Ga. 1977, U.S. Ct. Appeals (11th cir.) 1979. Law clk., atty. advisor EPA, Washington, 1973-75, asst. regional counsel region IV Atlanta, 1976-85, assoc. regional counsel region IV, 1986-90; sr. assoc. Thompson, Mann & Hutson, 1990-91; of counsel Peterson, Dillard, Young, Asselin & Powell, 1992-97; chief dep. atty. gen. State of Ga., 1997—, sr. asst. atty. gen., 1998—. Editor: Environmental Desk Manual, 1992, 94. Apptd. by gov. to Legis. Wetlands Study Com., 1992; cubmaster Cub Scouts Am., Lilburn, Ga., 1989-92; pres. Wyndemere Neighborhood Assn., Stone Mountain, Ga., 1990-94; v.p. Meth. Men's Fellowship, Glenn Meml. United Meth. Ch., 1989, pres., 1990. 1st lt. U.S. Army, 1972. Mem. Ga. Bar Assn. (sec. environ. law sect. 1985, vice chmn. 1986, chmn. 1987), Va. Bar Assn., Lawyers Club Atlanta. Avocations: golf, tennis, church service. Office: Ga Dept Law 40 Capital Sq Atlanta GA 30334

PHIPPS, BENJAMIN KIMBALL, II, lawyer; b. Boston, Jan. 16, 1933; s. Benjamin Kimball and Bertha Elizabeth (Forsyth) P.; m. Phyllis Jarrett Anderson, Jan. 10, 1962; children: Lisa Jarrett, Christina Caroline. BS in Commerce, U. Va., 1955, LLB, 1958. Bar: Fla. 1964, U.S. Dist. Ct. (no. dist.) Fla., U.S. Claims Ct., U.S. Ct. Appeals (5th and 11th cirs.), U.S. Tax Ct. Editor Mcpl. Code Corp., Tallahassee, 1964-65; pvt. practice, 1965—. Counsel tax com. Fla. Ho. of Reps., 1966-72, counsel to speaker, 1973-74, mem. adv. com. fin. & tax com., 1983-84; mem. Legis. Task Force Taxpayers' Bill Rights, 1989-91; cons. in field. Contbr. articles to profl. jours.; columnist Tallahassee Democrat. Chmn. Hist. Tallahassee Preservation Bd., 1970-91; trustee Maclay Sch.; mem. adv. coun., Sta. WFSU-TV, chmn., 1970-92; mem. Fla. Mus. History, 1990—, v.p., 1997-99, gen. counsel, 2000—; mem. Tallahassee Trust for Hist. Preservation, 1997—, treas., 1998—. Served to capt., U.S. Army, 1958-64. Listed in Am.'s Leading Lawyers. Mem. ABA (tax sect. state and local tax com.), Tallahassee Bar Assn., Fla. Bar (treas., vice chmn., chmn. tax sect. 1985-86, editl. bd. Fla. Bar News, chmn. 1975-76), Gov.'s Club, Univ. Ctr. Club, Cosmos Club, Exchange Club, Tiger Bay Club (dir.), Fla. Econ. Club, St. Andrews Soc. (pres. 1978-79), Sigma Alpha Epsilon, Phi Alpha Delta, Pi Delta Epsilon. Republican. Episcopalian. Taxation, general, State and local taxation. Office: PO Box 1351 Tallahassee FL 32302-1351

PHOENIX, G. KEITH, lawyer; b. Centralia, Ill., Aug. 13, 1946. BA in Liberal Arts, So. Ill. U., 1968; JD, St. Louis U., 1973. Bar: Mo. 1974, Ill. 1974, U.S. Dist. Ct. (ea. dist.) Mo. 1974, U.S. Dist. Ct. (so. dist.) Ill. 1975, U.S. Ct. Appeals (7th and 8th cirs.) 1982. Assoc. firm Coburn, Croft & Shepherd & Putzell, St. Louis, 1974-79; ptnr., pres. firm Sandberg, Phoenix & von Gontard, St. Louis, 1979—; legal cons. to Am. Acad. Pediatrics. Contbr. articles on med./legal topics to profl. jours. Served to 1st lt. U.S. Army, 1968-71, Vietnam. Decorated Bronze Star with cluster, Air medal with cluster, Vietnam medal. Mem. Ill. Bar Assn., Mo. Bar Assn., St. Louis Bar Assn., Lawyer's Assn. (past pres.), Am. Bd. Trial Advocacy (past pres.) State civil litigation, Personal injury. Office: Sandberg Phoenix & von Gontard 1 City Ctr Ste 1500 Saint Louis MO 63101-1880

PIAZZA, ROSANNA JOY, paralegal; b. Lincoln, Nebr., Sept. 10, 1950; d. Augustine Joseph Piazza and Mary Lou Pease; m. Pennell Spencer, Sept. 20, 1972 (div. Dec. 1979); children: Madeleine, Adrian, Aurora, Angelica, Marissa, Raquel. BA in Psychology, BA in Sociology, U. Calif., 1987, postgrad., 1987-89. Legal asst. Legal Aid, Pacoima, Van Nuys, Calif., 1980-81, Tomas Castelo, Santa Barbara, 1982-84; counselor Battered Women's Network, Calif., 1984-89; pres. The Venus Found., Livingston, Mont., 1993; legal asst. Lyman H. Bennett III, Bozeman, 1996—. Poet Mont. Poets, Bozeman, 1989—. Author: (Liberté) (poetry) The Magical Mystical Miracle, 1977, Gods in Exile, Zonderzonde, 1999, The Littlest Buddha, 1999, The Littlest Page of Lancelot de Lac, 1999. Senate candidate dist. 14 Natural Law Party, Bozeman, 1998; mem. disaster emergency team ARC, Fiver Rivers chpt., 1999—; sec. mission for life Pro Life Orgn., 1998. Mem. AAUW (natual law party), Bus. Women's Assn., Mont. Assn. of Paralegals, Mont. Paralegal Assn., Nat. Assn. of Legal Secs., Mont. State Bar Assn. (paralegal sect.). Avocations: writer, poetry, songwriting, folk guitar and mandolin. Home: PO Box 141 Bozeman MT 59771-0141 Office: Lyman H Bennett III PO Box 1168 Bozeman MT 59771-1168

PICCO, STEVEN JOSEPH, lawyer; b. N.Y.C., Sept. 9, 1948; s. Carl and Constance (Speers) P.; m. Ada T. Ryan, July 15, 1972; children: Christopher, Timothy, Kaitlin. BS, Rider Coll., Lawrenceville, N.J., 1970; JD, Seton Hall U., 1975. Bar: N.J. 1975, U.S. Dist. Ct. N.J. 1975, U.S. Ct. Appeals (3d cir.) 1975. Data processing programmer-sys. engring. N.J. Dept. Labor and Industry, Trenton, 1970-75; project specialist N.J. Dept. Environ. Protection, 1975-76, dir. regulatory and govtl. affairs, 1976-78, acting dep. commr., 1979-80, asst. commr., 1979-81, N.J. Dept. Energy, Newark, 1978-79; ptnr. Greenstone & Sokol, Trenton, 1981-87, Picco Mack Herbert Kennedy Jaffe & Yoskin, Trenton, 1988-97, Reed Smith LLP, Princeton, N.J., 1997—. Chmn. bd. dirs. Northeast-Midwest Inst., Robert Wood Johnson Health Care Corp. at Hamilton; treas. N.J. Orgn. for a Better State; mem. N.J. Seed. Mem. Am. Credit Assn. (pres. 2001—). Avocations: golf, reading, community volunteer work. Administrative and regulatory, Environmental. Office: Reed Smith Shaw & McClay LLP Princeton Forrestal Village 136 Main St Ste 250 Princeton NJ 08540-5789 E-mail: spicco@reedsmith.com

PICKARD, JOHN ALLAN, lawyer; b. White Plains, N.Y., Sept. 4, 1940; s. Victor and Rhoda (Walinshinsky) P. BA, The Am. U., 1963; JD, Washington Coll. Law, 1966. Bar: N.Y. 1987, Oreg. 1969, U.S. Ct. Appeals (9th cir.) 1970, U.S. Ct. Appeals (2d cir.) 1988, U.S. Dist. Ct. Oreg. Dep. dist. atty., 1970; criminal appeals atty., 1967-71; tax law specialist IRS, Washington, 1966-67; dep. dist. atty. Clackamas County, Oregon City, Oreg.; pvt. practice fed. appeals, 1972—; with Arnold, Fortac & Porter, 1964-65. Advisor Mental Health Law Project, N.Y.C., 1984—, ACCESS Inc. Homeless. Appt. to Lawyers Conf. on Appellate Cts. ABA. Fellow Roscoe Pound Found.; mem. ABA (litigation sect., sole practice and adminstrv. law sects., jud. adminstrv. sec., health law forum, legal edn. and bar admissions, pub. law sect.), Am. Trial Lawyers Assn., Am. Mus. Natural History, Criminal Law Soc., Am. Jud. Soc., Democratic Nat. Com., Nat. Assn. Defense Lawyers, ASPCA. Democrat. Avocation: politics. Federal civil litigation, Constitutional, Criminal. Home: 90 Bryant Ave Apt 3B White Plains NY 10605-1952 Office: PO Box 1907 White Plains NY 10602-1907

PICKARD, TERRY ROY, lawyer; b. Syracuse, N.Y., May 25, 1945; s. Roy Allen and Frances A. (Bridgette) P.; children: Matthew Terry, Stuart William. BA, Ohio Wesleyan U., 1967; JD, Boston U., 1970. Bar: Mass. 1970, N.Y. 1971, Fla. 1974, U.S. Dist. Ct. (no. dist.) N.Y. 1978, U.S. Supreme Ct. 1979, U.S. Ct. Mil. Appeals, 1984, U.S. Tax Ct. 1991. Atty. office of gen. counsel Fed. Home Loan Bank Bd., Washington, 1974-76; ptnr. firm Byrne, Costello & Pickard, P.C., Syracuse, 1976—; bankruptcy trustee U.S. Bankruptcy Ct. No. Dist. N.Y., 1988. Mem. Onondaga County Legislature, 1979—; N.Y. chpt. atty. Am. Subcontractors Assn., 1995—; lectr. N.Y. State Inst. Health and Human Svcs., 1983—; faculty N.Y. Assn. Homes and Svcs. for the Aging, 1983—. Mem. F-M Chem. People Task Force, Inc., 1984-90; bd. dirs. Co-op. Extension Assn. Onondaga County, 1980-82, Central N.Y. Health Systems Agy., 1983-85; mem. Seguin Adv. Bd., 1981-85, Stop DWI Adv. Bd., 1982-83; mem. adv. bd. Emergency Med. Svcs., Syracuse, 1982-87; bd. dirs. Greater Syracuse Bus. Devel. Corp., 1990—, Syracuse Symphony Orch., 1990—, Community Health Info. and Planning Svc., Inc., 1987—, Fayetteville Sr. Ctr., Inc., 1986—. Served to lt. JAGC, USN, 1971-74. Mem. Onondaga County Bar Assn., N.Y. State Bar Assn., Am. Arbitration Assn. (panel of arbitrators). Bankruptcy, Environmental, Real property.

PICKERING, JOHN HAROLD, lawyer; b. Harrisburg, Ill., Feb. 27, 1916; s. John Leslie and Virginia Lee (Morris) P.; m. Elsa Victoria Mueller, Aug. 23, 1941 (dec. Nov., 1988); children: Leslie Ann, Victoria Lee; m. Helen Patton Wright, Feb. 3, 1990. AB, U. Mich., 1938, JD, 1940, LLD, 1996, D.C. Sch. Law, 1995. Bar: N.Y. 1941, D.C. 1947. Practiced in N.Y.C., 1941; practiced in Washington, 1946—; assoc. Cravath, de Gersdorff, Swaine & Wood, 1941; law clk. to Justice Murphy, Supreme Ct. U.S., 1941-43; assoc. Wilmer & Broun, 1946-48, ptnr., 1949-62, Wilmer, Cutler & Pickering, 1962-79, Wilmer & Pickering, 1979-81, Wilmer, Cutler & Pickering, 1981-88, sr. counsel, 1989—. Vis. lectr. U. Va. Law Sch., 1958; mem. com. visitors U. Mich. Law Sch., 1962-68, chmn. devel. com., 1973-81; mem. com. on adminstrn. of justice U.S. Ct. Appeals (D.C. cir.), 1966-72, chmn. adv. com. on procedures, 1976-82, chmn. mediation project, 1988—; bd. govs. D.C. Bar, 1975-78, pres., 1979-80; dir. Nat. Ctr. for State Cts., 1987-93. Lt. comdr. USNR, 1943-46. Recipient Outstanding Achievement award U. Mich., 1978, Disting. Svc. award Nat. Ctr. for State Cts., 1985, 50 Yr. award from Fellows Am. Bar Found., 1993, Paul C. Reardon award Nat. Ctr. for State Cts., 1994, Pro Bono award NAACP Legal Def. Fund, 1990, Am. Bar Assn. medal, 1999, Justice William J. Brennan Jr. award, D.C. Bar, 1998, Justice Potter Stewart award, Coun. for Court Excellence, 1999, numerous other awards. Mem. ABA (state del. 1984-93, chmn. commn. on legal problems of elderly 1985-93, sr. advisor 1993-95, chmn. 1995-96, commr. emeritus 1996—, chmn. sr. lawyers divsn. 1996-97), D.C. Bar Assn. (Lawyer of the Yr. 1996), Am. Law Inst., Barristers Washington, Lawyers Club, Met. Club, Chevy Chase Club, Wianno Club, Order of Coif, Phi Beta Kappa, Phi Kappa Phi. Democrat. Mem. United Ch. Christ. Home: 8100 Connecticut Ave Chevy Chase MD 20815 Office: Wilmer Cutler & Pickering 2445 M St NW Ste 8 Washington DC 20037-1435 E-mail: jpickering@wilmer.com

PICKLE, GEORGE EDWARD, lawyer; b. New Orleans, Nov. 22, 1950; s. George E. Sr. and Virginia (Crowe) P.; m. Karen Lyle, Sept. 18, 1976; children: George E. III, Lauren M. Student, Rhodes Coll., 1968-70; BA, Millsaps Coll., 1972; JD, Georgetown U., 1975. Bar: Miss. 1975, U.S. Ct. Claims 1979, U.S. Tax Ct. 1979, U.S. Ct. Mil. Appeals 1976, U.S. Ct. Appeals (D.C. cir.) 1979, U.S. Supreme Ct. 1979, U.S. Dist. Ct. (so. dist.) Miss. 1980, U.S. Ct. Appeals (5th cir.) 1980, La. 1982, U.S. Dist. Ct. (ea. dist.) La. 1982, U.S. Dist. Ct. (mid. dist.) La. 1985, Tex. 1986., U.S. Dist. Ct. (so. dist.) Tex. 1986, U.S. Dist. Ct. (we. dist.) La. 1988. Law clk.to presiding justice U.S. Ct. Appeals (5th cir.), Askerman, Miss., 1975-76; assoc. Upshaw & Ladner, Jackson, 1980-82, Barham & Churchill, New Orleans, 1982-85; sr. atty. litigation, energy, environ., admiralty and products Shell Oil Co., Houston, 1985-96, assoc. general counsel, 1997—. Contbr. law rev., 1975; co-author, editor: Syllabus on Environmental Law, 1986. Bd. dirs. Tex. Civil Justice League, 1996—, Product Liability Advisory Coun., 1997—, chair operating Com. Civil Justice Reform Group, 1994—, Lawyers for Civil Justice Class Action Task Force, 2001-; sr. warden Episcopal Ch. of the Good Shepherd, Kingwood, Tex., 1991, dir. capital fund corp., 1988, lay eucharistic min., 1986-99; del. Tex. Senatorial and State Rep. convs., 1988-92; mem. exec. and vacancy coms. Rep. Party Harris County, 1990-96, chmn. precinct, 1990-96; mem. Georgetown U. Barristers Coun. , 1973-75; referee N.W. Aquatic League, 1990-97; pres. Bear Br. Swim Team, 1991-93. Lt. cmdr. (head environ. litigation) USNR, 1976-79. Southwestern Scholar Rhodes Coll., Memphis, 1968. Mem. ABA (vice chmn. young lawyers div. com. on environ. law, exec. editor Am. Criminal Law Rev. 1973-75, award for Profl. Merit 1976), Def. Rsch. Inst., Miss. Bar Assn. (elections com. 1982), La. Bar Assn., Tex. Bar Assn., Internat. Assn. Defence Coun. (vice chmn., sec. corp coun. 1991—), Alpha Tau Omega, Phi Alpha Theta, Omicron Delta Kappa, Pi Kappa Delta. Republican. Avocations: golf, water skiing. Admiralty, Federal civil litigation, Environmental. Home: 3507 Tree Ln Humble TX 77339-2639 E-mail: edpickle@shell.com

PICKLE, JERRY RICHARD, lawyer; b. Paris, Feb. 2, 1947; s. Joseph Rambert and Martha Marie (Biggers) P.; m. Helen Leigh Russell, May 3, 1975; children: Jonathan Russell, Stephen Richard (dec.), Sarah Elizabeth. BA in History, U. Houston, 1969, JD, 1971. Bar: Tex. 1972, U.S. Dist. Ct. (no. dist.) Tex. 1974, U.S. Dist. Ct. (we. dist.) Tex. 1989. Mem. Luna, Ballard & Pickle, Garland, Tex., 1972-74; assoc. Hightower & Alexander, Dallas, 1974-76, Cuba & Johnson, Temple, Tex., 1976-77; sr. corp. counsel Scott & White Clinic, 1977—. Asst. prof. Tex. A&M U. Coll. of Medicine, Temple, 1986—. Contbr. articles to profl. jours. V.p. The Caring House, Temple, 1989, Tex. divsn. Am. Cancer Soc., Temple, 1976-77; adv. bd. R.R. & Pioneer Mus., Temple, 1982-84; hist. preservation bd. City of Temple, 1979-90; chmn. Bell County Hist. Commn., 1980-82; bd. dirs. Bell County Mus., 1992-96, Temple Coord. Child Care Coun., 1991-93, Sr. Citizens Activites Ctr., Temple, 1993-94, pres., 1994-95; bd. dirs. Temple Cultural Activities Ctr., 1992-98, 2001—, pres., 1994-95; chair Heart o'Tex. Coun., Chisholm Trail Dist., Boy Scouts Am., 1987-88. Mem.: ABA, State Bar Tex. (health law sect. councilman 1980—84, health law sect. councilman 1985—87, chmn. 1983—84), Tex. Young Lawyers Assn., Tex. Bar Found., State Bar Coll., Bell-Lampasas-Mills Counties Bar Assn. (bd. dirs. 1985—90, pres. 1988—89), Bell-Lampasas-Mills Counties Young Lawyers Assn. (pres. 1980—81), Am. Health Lawyers Assn. (chair tchg. hosp. and acad. med. ctrs. 1997—99), Coun. Med. Group Practice Attys. (chair 2001—), Temple C. of C. (bd. dirs. 1983—85, bd. dirs. 1988—90), Rotary (chpt. dir. 1981—85, chpt. dir. 1986—87), Jaycees (chpt. dir. 1977—78). Democrat. Episcopalian. Avocations: reading, golf, music. General corporate, Health, Insurance. Office: Scott & White Clinic 2401 S 31st St Temple TX 76508-0001 Fax: 254-724-4501. E-mail: jpickle@swmail.sw.org

PICKLE, ROBERT DOUGLAS, lawyer, footwear industry executive; b. Knoxville, Tenn., May 22, 1937; s. Robert Lee and Beatrice Jewel (Douglas) P.; m. Rosemary Elaine Noser, May 9, 1964. AA summa cum laude, Schreiner Mil. Coll., Kerrville, Tex., 1957; BSBA magna cum laude, U. Tenn., 1959, JD, 1961; honor grad. seminar, Nat. Def. U., 1979; hon. grad., U.S. Army JAG Sch., U.S. Army Logistics Mgmt. Sch.; grad., U.S. Army Inf. Sch., Army Command-Gen. Staff Coll. Bar: Tenn. 1961, Mo. 1964, U.S. Ct. Mil. Appeals 1962, U.S. Supreme Ct. 1970. Atty. Brown Shoe Co., Inc., St. Louis, 1963-69, asst. sec., atty., 1969-74, sec., gen. counsel, 1974-85; v.p., gen. counsel, corp. sec. Brown Shoe Co., Inc. (formerly Brown Group, Inc.), 1985—. Indiv. mobilization augmentee, asst. army judge adv. gen. civil law The Pentagon, Washington, 1984-89. Provisional judge Municipal Ct., Clayton, Mo., summer 1972; chmn. Clayton Region attys. sect., profl. div. United Fund Greater St. Louis Campaign, 1972-73, team capt., 1974-78; chmn. City of Clayton Parks and Recreation Commn., 1985-87; liaison admissions officer, regional and state coordinator U.S. Mil. Acad., 1980—. Col. JAGC, U.S. Army, 1961-63. Decorated Meritorious Svc. medal; 1st U. Tenn. Law Coll. John W Green law scholar; recipient Cold War Recognition cert. Sec. Def. Fellow Harry S. Truman Meml. Library; mem. ABA, Tenn. Bar Assn., Mo. Bar Assn., St. Louis County Bar Assn., Bar Assn. Met. St. Louis, St. Louis Bar Found. (bd. dirs. 1979-81), Am. Corp. Counsel Assn., Am. Soc. Corp. Secs. (treas. St. Louis regional group 1976-77, sec. 1977-78, v.p. 1978-79, pres., mem. Quarter-Century Club 1979-80), U. Tenn. Gen. Alumni Assn. (pres., bd. dirs. St. Louis chpt. 1974-76, 80-84, bd. govs. 1982-89), U.S. Trademark Assn. (bd. dirs. 1978-82), Tenn. Soc. St. Louis (bd. dirs. 1980-88, treas., sec., v.p. 1984-87, pres. 1987-88), Smithsonian Nat. Assocs., World Affairs Coun. St. Louis, Inc., Am. Legion, University Club (v.p., sec. St. Louis chpt. 1976-81, bd. dirs. 1976-81), Stadium Club, West Point Soc. St. Louis (hon. mem., bd. dirs. 1992—), Conf. Bd. (coun. chief legal officers), Fontbonne Coll. Pres.'s Assocs. (O'Hara and Tower Socs), St. Louis U. Billiken Club, St. Louis U. DuBourg Soc. (hon. v.p.). Republican. Presbyterian. Avocations: reading, spectator sports. Antitrust, General corporate, Securities. Home: 214 Topton Way Saint Louis MO 63105-3638 Office: Brown Shoe Co Inc 8300 Maryland Ave Saint Louis MO 63105-3645 E-mail: rpickle@brownshoe.com

PIEDMONT, RICHARD STUART, lawyer; b. Niskayuna, N.Y., Mar. 28, 1948; s. Henry Stuart and Lucille (Gagnon) P.; m. Marcia J. Quick, Apr. 11, 1981; children: Denise Nicole Rochette, Michael Norman Rochette, Alexandria Q. BA, U. Notre Dame, 1971. Bar: N.Y. 1977, U.S. Dist. Ct. (no. dist.) N.Y. 1977. Pres. Phoenix Abstract Corp., Albany, N.Y., 1979-84, v.p., 1984-89; ptnr. Piedmont & Rutnik, 1980-85, Devine, Piedmont & Rutnik, Albany, 1985-89; 58482 Phoenix Abstract Corp., N.Y., 1979-84; pvt. practice Piedmont Law Firm, 1990-95; ptnr. Harris Beach & Wilcox LLP, Albany, 1995-2000, Harris Beach, LLP (formerly Harris Beach & Wilcox LLP), Albany, 2000—. Founding bd. dirs. Make-a-Wish Found. of Northeastern N.Y.; former trustee Empire State Aerosci. Mus.; mem. parish coun. St. John the Evangelist Ch. Mem. N.Y. State Bar Assn., N.Y. State Land Title Assn., Ea. N.Y. Land Surveyors Assn., Schenectady County Bar Assn., Albany County Bar Assn., Aircraft Owners and Pilots Assn., Notre Dame Club Northeastern N.Y. (bd. dirs.). Democrat. Roman Catholic. Administrative and regulatory, Probate, Real property. Home: 1016 N Country Club Dr Niskayuna NY 12309-5405 Office: 20 Corporate Woods Blvd Albany NY 12211-2396 E-mail: rpiedmont@harrisbeach.com

PIEPER, DAROLD D. lawyer; b. Vallejo, Calif., Dec. 30, 1944; s. Walter A. H. and Vera Mae (Ellis) P.; m. Barbara Gillis, Dec. 20, 1969; 1 child, Christopher Radcliffe. AB, UCLA, 1967; JD, USC, 1970. Bar: Calif. 1971. Ops. rsch. analyst Naval Weapons Ctr., China Lake, Calif., 1966-69; assoc. Richards, Watson & Gershon, L.A., 1970-76, ptnr., 1976—; gen. counsel Foothill Transit, 2000—; spl. counsel L.A. Unified Sch. Dist., 2000—. Spl. counsel L.A. County Transp. Commn., 1984-93, L.A. County Met. Transp. Authority, 1993-94; commr. L.A. County Delinquency and Crime Commn., 1983-94, pres., 1987-94; chmn. L.A. County Delinquency Prevention Planning Coun., 1987-90. Contbr. articles to profl. jours. Peace officer Pasadena (Calif.) Police Res. Unit, 1972-87, dep. comdr., 1979-81, comdr., 1982-84; chmn. pub. safety commn. City of La Canada Flintridge, Calif., 1977-82, commr. 1977-88; bd. dirs. La Canada Flintridge Coordinating Council, 1975-82, pres. 1977-78; exec. dir. Cityhood Action Com., 1975-76; chmn. Youth Opportunities United, Inc., 1990-96, vice-chmn. 1988-89, bd. dirs. 1988-96; mem. L.A. County Justice Systems Adv. Group, 1987-92; trustee Lanterman Hist. Mus. Found., 1989-94, Calif. City Mgmt. Found., 1992—. Recipient commendation for Community Service, L.A. County Bd. Suprs., 1978, Commendation for Svc. to Youth, 1996. Mem. La Canada Flintridge C. of C. and Cmty. Assn. (pres. 1981, bd. dirs. 1976-83), Navy League U.S., Peace Officers Assn., L.A. County, UCLA Alumni Assn. (life), L.A. County Bar Assn., Calif. Bar Assn., ABA, U. So. Calif. Law Alumni Assn. Construction, Government contracts and claims, Transportation. Office: Richards Watson & Gershon 333 S Hope St Fl 38 Los Angeles CA 90071-1406

PIERCE, DONALD FAY, lawyer; b. Bexley, Miss., Aug. 28, 1930; s. Percy O. and Lavada S. (Stringfellow) P.; m. Norma Faye Scribner, June 5, 1954; children: Kathryn Pierce Peake, D. F. Jr., John S., Jeff G. BS, U. Ala., 1956, JD, 1958. Bar: Ala. 1958, U.S. Ct. Appeals (5th cir.) 1958, U.S. Dist. Ct. (no., mid. and so. dists.) Ala. 1958, U.S. Ct. Appeals (11th cir.) 1982. Law clk. to presiding judge U.S. Dist. Ct. (so. dist.) Ala., 1958-59; ptnr. Hand, Arendall, Bedsole, Greaves & Johnston, Mobile, Ala., 1964-91, Pierce, Carr, Alford, Ledyard & Latta, P.C., Mobile, 1991—. Trustee, UMS Prep. Sch., 1980-87; mem. Products Liability Adv. Coun., 1990—; bd. overseers The Vanderbilt Cancer Ctr., 1994—. 1st lt. U.S. Army, 1951-53. Mem. Ala. Def. Lawyers Assn. (past pres.), Fedn. Ins. and Corp. Counsel, Am. Acad. Hosp. Attys., Internat. Assn. Def. Counsel, Def. Counsel Trial Acad. (bd. dirs. 1983-84), Def. Research Inst. (pres. 1987, chmn. 1988). Baptist. Contbr. articles to profl. jours. Federal civil litigation, Environmental, Health. Home: 4452 Winnie Way Mobile AL 36608-2221 Office: Pierce Ledyard Latta & Wasden P C Colonial Bank Ctr 41 N Beltline Hwy Ste 400 Mobile AL 36608-1291

PIERCE, JOHN GERALD (JERRY PIERCE), lawyer; b. Winter Haven, Fla., Jan. 12, 1937; s. Francis E. and Margaret (Butler) P.; m. Kathleen E., Dec. 1, 1989; children: Kathleen M. Cooke, Nancy A., John Gerald Jr., Michael J. B in Chem. Engring., U. Fla., 1959, JD with honors, 1965. Bar: Fla. 1966, U.S. Dist. Ct. (mid. dist.) Fla. 1966, U.S. Ct. Appeals (11th cir.). Assoc. Anderson & Rush, Dean & Lowndes, Orlando, Fla., 1966-68, Arnold, Matheny & Eagen, Orlando, 1968-70; ptnr. Pierce, Lewis & Dolan, 1970-74; sole practice, 1974—. Served to 1st lt. U.S. Army, 1959-62. Mem. ABA, Fla. Bar Assn., Orange County Bar Assn. Republican. Roman Catholic. Avocations: golf, boating, skiing. General corporate, Real property, Securities. Home: 605 Fox Valley Dr Longwood FL 32779-2417 Office: 800 N Ferncreek Ave Orlando FL 32803-4127 E-mail: jerryaty@aol.com, jerry@johnpierce.com

PIERCE, LAWRENCE WARREN, retired federal judge; b. Phila., Dec. 31, 1924; s. Harold Ernest and Leora (Bellinger) P.; m. Wilma Taylor (dec.); m. Cynthia Straker, July 8, 1979; children: Warren Wood, Michael Lawrence, Mark Taylor. BS, St. Joseph's U., Phila., 1948, DHL, 1967; JD, Fordham U., 1951, LLD, 1982, Fairfield U., 1972, Hamilton Coll., 1987, St. John's U., 1990. Bar: N.Y. State 1951, U.S. Supreme Ct. 1968. Civil law practice, N.Y.C., 1951-61; asst. dist. atty. Kings County, N.Y., 1954-61; dep. police commr. N.Y.C., 1961-63; dir. N.Y. State Div. for Youth, Albany, 1963-66; chmn. N.Y. State Narcotic Addiction Control Commn., 1966-70; vis. prof. criminal justice SUNY, Albany, 1970-71; U.S. dist. judge So. dist. N.Y., 1971-81; judge U.S. Fgn. Intelligence Surveillance Ct., 1979-81; apptd. U.S. cir. judge for 2d Cir., 1981-89; sr. U.S. cir. judge for 2d Cir., 1990-95; ret., 1995. Dir. Cambodian ct. tng. project Internat. Human Rights Law Group, 1995. Past bd. dirs. CARE, Fordham U., Havens Fund. Soc., Lincoln Hall for Boys, S-R N.Y. Chpt., Cath. Interracial Coun., Inst. Jud. Adminstrn., Am. Law Inst.; bd. dirs. St. Joseph's U., Phila., Practising Law Inst. Mem. ABA (site evaluation com., sec. legal edn. 1996-98, alt. observer U.S. Mission to UN 1988-90), Coun. Fgn. Rels. Home: PO Box 2234 Sag Harbor NY 11963-0111

PIERCE, MORTON ALLEN, lawyer; b. Liberec, Czechoslovakia, June 25, 1948; m. Nancy Washor, Dec. 14, 1975; children: Matthew J., Nicholas L. BA, Yale Coll., 1970; JD, U. Pa., 1974; postgrad., Oxford U., 1974-75. Bar: N.Y. 1975. Assoc. Reid & Priest, N.Y.C., 1975-83, ptnr., 1983-86, Dewey Ballantine, N.Y.C., 1986—. Mem. mgmt. com. 1988—, chmn. corp. dept., 1999—, chmn., mergers and acquisitions group, 1990—, mem. exec. com., 2001—. Contbr. articles to profl. jours. Mem. ABA (chmn. subcom. on internat. securities matters 1985-91, adv. com. to fed. regulation of securities com. 1991—, task force on rev. of the fed. securities law 1991—), Assn. of the Bar of the City of N.Y. (securities law com. 1988-91, chmn. subcom. on securities and exch. commn. enforcement matters 1990-91); Internat. Bar Assn. (com. on securities transactions). Private international, Mergers and acquisitions, Securities. Home: 188 E 76th St New York NY 10021-2826 Office: Dewey Ballantine LLP 1301 Ave Of The Americas New York NY 10019-6022

PIERCE, RICKLIN RAY, lawyer; b. Waukegan, Ill., Sept. 16, 1953; s. Forest Ellsworth and Mildred Colleen (Cole) P. BBA in Acctg., Washburn U., 1975; BA in Econs., 1978, JD, 1978. Bar: Kans. 1978, U.S. Dist. Ct. Kans. 1978, U.S. Ct. Appeals (10th cir.) 1981, U.S. Supreme Ct. 1986.

Assoc. Law Firm of C. C. Whittaker, Jr., Eureka, Kans., 1978-79; trust officer Smith County State Bank & Trust Co., Smith Center, Kans., 1979-80; staff atty. Northwest Kans. Legal Aid Soc., Goodland, 1980-81; assoc. Jochems, Sargent & Blaes, Wichita, Kans., 1981-82, Garden City, Kans., 1982-83; pvt. practice, Garden City, 1983-88; atty. County of Finney, 1988-93; pvt. practice, Garden City, 1993—. Pres., chmn. bd. dirs. Volunteers, Inc. of Finney County. Mem. Western Kans. Coun. Estate Planning & Giving. Mem. ABA, Assn. Trial Lawyers Am., Kans. Bar Assn., Southwest Kans. Bar Assn., Kans. Trial Lawyer Assn., Finney County Bar Assn. (treas.). Republican. Methodist. State civil litigation, General corporate, Criminal. Home: 2015 Campus Dr Garden City KS 67846-3706 Office: 206 W Pine St Garden City KS 67846-5347

PIERCE, WILLIAM JAMES, law educator; b. Flint, Mich., Dec. 4, 1921; s. Francis Scott and Ellen (Pelton) P.; m. Betty Kathren Wise, Nov. 20, 1954; children— Darrell William, Margery Marie, Constance Ellen, Kathren Elizabeth. A.B. in Econs, U. Mich., 1947, J.D., 1949. Faculty U. Mich., 1953-89; emeritus prof. U. MIch., 1989—; prof. law, dir. Legis. Rsch. Ctr. U. Mich., 1958-89, asso. dean, 1971-79. Exec. sec. Mich. Law Revision Commn., 1966-69; chmn. Citizens Adv. Com. Juvenile Ct., 1964-66; pres. Nat. Conf. Commrs. Uniform State Laws, 1966-69, exec. dir., 1969-92, emeritus exec. dir., 1992—. Author: (with Estep, Stason) Atomic Energy and the Law, 1957, (with Lamb, White) Apportionment and Representative Institutions, 1963, (with Read, MacDonald, Fordham) Materials on Legislation, 1973. Mem. Pres.'s Consumer Adv. Coun., 1967-69, Mich. Gov.'s Commn. on Mental Health Laws, 1969-72; mem. exec. com. Inst. Continuing Legal Edn., 1964-89. With AUS, 1943-45. Decorated Bronze Star medal. Mem. Am. Law Inst., Am. Bar Assn. (ho. of dels. 1966-69), State Bar Mich. Home: 1505 Roxbury Rd Ann Arbor MI 48104-4047 Office: U Mich Law Sch Ann Arbor MI 48109-1215

PIERLUISI, PEDRO R. lawyer; b. San Juan, P.R., Apr. 26, 1959; s. Jorge A. and Doris (Urrutia) P.; children: Anthony, Michael, Jacqueline, Rafael. BA, Tulane U., 1981; JD, George Washington U., 1984. Bar: D.C. 1984, U.S. Dist. Ct. D.C. 1985, U.S. Ct. Appeals (D.C. cir.) 1985, P.R. 1990, U.S. Supreme Ct. 1990, U.S. Dist. Ct. P.R., 1990, U.S. Ct. Appeals (1st cir.), 1993. Assoc. Verner, Liipfert, Bernhard, McPherson & Hand, Washington, 1984-85, Cole, Corette & Abrutyn, Washington, 1985-90; ptnr. Pierluisi Pierluisi & Mayol-Bianchi, San Juan, 1990-93; atty. gen. Govt. of P.R., 1993-96; ptnr. O'Neill & Borges, San Juan, 1997—. Mem. ABA (ho. of dels. 1995-96, standing com. on substance abuse 1995-98, coordinating com. on gun violence, 1998—, state membership chair, 2000—), Nat. Assn. Attys. Gen. (chair eastern region 1996), George Washington U. Internat. Law Soc. (pres. 1982-83), Phi Alpha Delta (hon., Munoz chpt.), N.Y. Stock Exch. (arbitrator), Nat. Assn. Securities Dealers, (arbitrator) 1998—, Am. Arbitration Assn. (arbitrator). Avocation: jogging. Administrative and regulatory, General civil litigation, General corporate. Office: O'Neill & Borges 250 Ave Munoz Rivera Am Internat Plz San Juan PR 00918-1808

PIERNO, ANTHONY ROBERT, lawyer; b. Uniontown, Pa., Apr. 28, 1932; s. Anthony M. and Mary Jane (Saporita) P.; m. Beverly Jean Kohn, June 20, 1954; children: Kathryn Ann Pierno, Robert Lawrence Pierno, Linda Jean Pierno, Diane Marie Leonard. BA with highest honors, Whittier Coll., 1954; JD, Stanford U., 1959; LLD (hon.), Whittier Coll., 2000. Bar: Calif. 1960, D.C. 1979, Tex. 1994. Assoc. Adams, Duque & Hazeltine, L.A.; ptnr. Pointdexter & Barger; chief dep. commr. State of Calif., 1967-69, commr. of corps., 1969-71; ptnr. Wyman, Bautzer, Rothman & Kuchel, Beverly Hills, Calif.; sr. ptnr. Memel, Jacobs, Pierno & Gersh, L.A., 1976-86; ptnr. Pillsbury, Madison & Sutro, 1986-89; sr. v.p., gen. counsel MAXXAM, Inc., L.A. and Houston, 1989-97. Author: Corporate Disaggregation, 1982; editor Stanford U. Law Rev. Trustee Whittier Coll., 1977-2000, chmn. bd. trustees, 1994-2000, chmn. presdl. selection com., 1989-90; chmn. Marymount Coll., Palos Verdes, Calif., 1989-92, trustee, 1976-93; past mem. Los Angeles County Children's Svcs. Commn. With U.S. Army, 1954-56. Recipient Emcalian award Marymount Palos Verdes Coll., 1983. Mem. ABA, Los Angeles County Bar Assn., State Bar Calif. (chmn. com. on corps. 1971-75, advisor to com. on corps. 1975-76, mem. exec. com. bus. law sect. 1976-80, chmn. spl. com. on franchise law), Calif. Club (L.A.). Republican. Roman Catholic. Administrative and regulatory, Alternative dispute resolution, General corporate. Office: 418 Malaga Ln Palos Verdes Estates CA 90274 also: 74361 Highway 111 Ste 1 Palm Desert CA 92260-4125

PIERSOL, LAWRENCE L. federal judge; b. Vermillion, S.D., Oct. 21, 1940; s. Ralph Nelson and Mildred Alice (Millette) P.; m. Catherine Anne Vogt, June 30, 1962; children: Leah C., William M., Elizabeth J. BA, U. S.D., 1962, JD summa cum laude, 1965. Bar: S.D. 1965, U.S. Ct. Mil. Appeals, 1965, U.S. Dist. Ct. S.D. 1968, U.S. Supreme Ct. 1972, U.S. Dist. Ct. Wyo. 1980, U.S. Dist. Ct. Nebr. 1986, U.S. Dist. Ct. Mont. 1988. Ptnr. Davenport, Evans, Hurwitz & Smith, Sioux Falls, S.D., 1968-93; judge U.S. Dist. Ct., 1993—; chief judge Dist. of S.D., 1999—. Mem. budget com. chair, economy sub com., Jud. Conf. U.S.; chmn. tribal ct. com. 8th Cir. Jud. Coun.; editor-in-chief Law Review. Majority leader S.D. Ho. of Reps., Pierre, 1973-74, minority whip, 1971-72; del. Dem. Nat. Conv., 1972, 76, 80; S.D. mem. del. select commn. Dem. Nat. Com., 1971-75. Mem. ABA, State Bar S.D., Fed. Judges Assn. (bd. dirs., v.p.). Roman Catholic. Avocations: reading, running, painting, mountaineering. Office: US Dist Ct 400 S Phillips Ave Sioux Falls SD 57104-6824

PIERSON, W. DEVIER, lawyer; b. Pawhuska, Okla., Aug. 12, 1931; s. Welcome D. and Frances (Ratliff) P.; m. Shirley Frost, Feb. 1, 1957; children: Jeffrey, Elizabeth, Stephen. AB, U. Okla., 1953, LLB, 1957. Bar: Okla. 1957, U.S. Dist. Ct. Okla. 1957, U.S. Supreme Ct. 1966, U.S. Ct. Appels D.C. 1969, U.S. Ct. Appeals (5th cir.) 1972, U.S. Ct. Appeals (10th cir.) 1975, U.S. Ct. Appeals (2d cir.) 1996. Assoc. Duval & Head, Oklahoma City, 1957-59; sole practice, 1959-65; chief counsel Joint Com. on Orgn. of Congress, 1965-67; assoc. spl. counsel to Pres. and Counselor White House Office, 1967-68; spl. counsel to Pres. of U.S., 1968-69; ptnr. Pierson Semmes and Bemis and predecessor firms, Washington, 1969-2000; spl. counsel Verner, Liipfert, Bernhard, McPherson and Hand Chartered, 2000—. Trustee U. Okla. Found., 1996—; chmn. bd. visitors U. Okla. Coll. of Law; mem. bd. visitors U. Okla. Internat. Programs Ctr.; dir. Atlantic Coun. of U.S., 1995—. Served to 1st lt. U.S. Army, 1953-54. Recipient Outstanding Alumnus award U. Okla., 1995. Mem. ABA, D.C. Bar Assn., Fed. Bar Assn., Okla. Bar Assn., Met. Club (Washington). Alternative dispute resolution, Appellate, General civil litigation. Home: 5326 Chamberlin Ave Chevy Chase MD 20815-6661 Office: Verner, Liipfert, Bernhard, McPherson and Hand, Chartered 901 15th St NW Ste 700 Washington DC 20005

PIERSON, WILLIAM GEORGE, lawyer; b. Pontiac, Mich., Oct. 13, 1951; s. Robert D. and Elizabeth C. (Brode) P.; m. Mary K. Grossa, Sept. 25, 1986; children: Megan Ewing, Robert John. BBA, Cen. Mich. U., 1973; JD, Detroit Coll. Law, 1980. Bar: Mich. 1980, U.S. Dist. Ct. (ea. dist.) Mich. 1982, U.S. Supreme Ct. 1985. Sr. assoc. Kohl, Secrest, Wardle, Lynch, Clark & Hampton, Farmington Hills, Mich., 1980-89, Schwartz & Jalkanen, Southfield, 1989-90; sole practice Howell, 1991-99; counsel Oakland County Corp., Pontiac, 1999—. Mem. ABA, Mich. Bar Assn. (negligence sect., elected to rep. assembly 1999—), Oakland County Bar Assn (dist. ct. com. 1983-84, cir. ct. com. 1984-85, negligence com. 1987—, med.-legal com. 1989—), Livingston County Bar Assn. Avocations: golf, skiing, boating, camping. State civil litigation, Insurance, Personal injury. Home: 2153 Ridge Rd White Lake MI 48383-1742 Office: Oakland County Dept Corp Counsel 1200 N Telegraph Rd Dept 419 Pontiac MI 48341-0419 E-mail: piersonw@co.oakland.mi.us, megrob1@msn.com

PIETRZAK, ALFRED ROBERT, lawyer; b. Glen Cove, N.Y., June 26, 1949; s. Alfred S. and Wanda M. (Wapniarski) P.; m. Sharon Esther Chizek, July 9, 1978; children: Eric A., Daniel J. BA, Fordham U., 1971; JD, Columbia U., 1974. Bar: N.Y. 1975, U.S. Dist. Ct. (so., ea., we. and no. dists.) N.Y. 1975, U.S. Dist. Ct. (no. dist.) Calif. 1983, U.S. Ct. Appeals (2d. cir.) 1975, U.S. Ct. Appeals (9th cir.) 1983, U.S. Ct. Appeals (11th cir.) 1985, U.S. Supreme Ct. 1985. Assoc. Brown & Wood (formerly Brown, Wood, Ivey, Mitchell & Petty), N.Y.C., 1974-82, ptnr., 1983—; also head litigation practice group. Mem. fin. products adv. com. Commodity Futures Trading Commn.; mem. CLE faculty Fordham U. Sch. Law.; mem. litig. adv. com. Bond Market Assn.; bd. advisors Rev. of Securities and Commodities Regulation; bd. editors Futures Internat. Law Letter; adv. bd. Fordham Internat. Law Jour. Contbr. articles to legal jours. Mem. ABA, Assn. Bar City N.Y. (securities regulation com., chmn. futures regulation com., retail fin. svcs. com.), Am. Law Inst. (lectr.), Securities Industry Assn., Futures Industry Assn. Democrat. Roman Catholic. Federal civil litigation, State civil litigation, Securities.

PIGMAN, JACK RICHARD, lawyer; b. Fostoria, Ohio, June 5, 1944; s. Jack R. and A. Ada (McDevitt) P.; m. Judy Lynn Price, June 19, 1968 (div. 1983); m. Carolyn Ruth Parker, May 31, 1986; children: Shaeney E. Pigman Craig, J. Ryan Pigman, Adam Parker. BA, U. Notre Dame, 1966; JD cum laude, Ohio State U., 1969. Bar: Ohio 1969, U.S. Ct. Mil. Appeals 1970. Law clk. Ohio Supreme Ct., Columbus, 1969-70; assoc. Wright, Harlor, Morris & Arnold, 1970, 74-76; ptnr. Porter, Wright, Morris & Arthur and predecessor firms, 1977—. Speaker in field. Trustee Dublin Arts Coun., 2001—, Ctr. for New Directions, 1990-96, treas., 1996; trustee United Cerebral Palsy of Columbus and Franklin County, 1976-82, pres., 1980. Capt. JAG U.S. Army, 1970-74. Mem. Ohio State Bar Assn., Columbus Bar Assn. (chmn. bankruptcy com. 1982-84), Columbus Met. Club (trustee 1980-87, pres. 1985-86). Republican. Avocations: tennis, skiing, reading, cooking, photography. Bankruptcy, Contracts commercial, Finance. Office: Porter Wright Morris & Arthur 41 S High St Ste 2800 Columbus OH 43215-6194

PIKCUNAS, CHARLES RICHARD, lawyer; b. Chgo., Sept. 18, 1952; s. Charles J. and Frances B. (Chaikowsky) P.; m. Anne Elizabeth Meehan, Dec. 31, 1973 (div. July 1978); m. Susan Frances Strohm, July 22, 1978. B.A. with honors, John Carroll U., 1973; J.D. cum laude, Chgo.-Kent Coll. Law, 1976. Bar: Ill. 1977, U.S. Dist. Ct. (no. dist.) Ill. 1977, Mich. 1982, U.S. Dist. Ct. (we. dist.) Mich. 1982, U.S. Ct. Appeals (6th cir.) 1988. Gen. ptnr. Pikcunas, Bawolek & Rompala, Chgo., 1977-81, Law Offices Charles R. Pikcunas, Lincolnwood, Ill., 1981-82; treas. Stanley, Davidoff & Gray, P.C., Kalamazoo, 1982-91; pvt. practice, 1991—; arbitrator U.S. Dist. Ct. (we. dist.) Mich., 1985—. Cultural Arts com. John Carroll U., Ohio, chmn. 1973. Mem. Ill. Bar Assn. (council on workmen's compensation law 1978-80), Mich. Bar Assn., Kalamazoo County Bar Assn. (co-chmn. unauthorized practice com. 1983-84), Comml. Law League Am., Kalamazoo County Bar Assn. (audit com. chmn. 1987-88), Phi Delta Phi. Republican. Roman Catholic. Bankruptcy, Contracts commercial, Real property. Office: PO Box 19187 Kalamazoo MI 49019-0187

PIKE, ROBERT WILLIAM, insurance company executive, lawyer; b. Lorain, Ohio, July 25, 1941; s. Edward and Catherine (Stack) P.; m. Linda L. Feitz, Dec. 26, 1964; children: Catherine, Robert, Richard. BA, Bowling Green State U., 1963; JD, U. Toledo, 1966. Bar: Ohio 1966, Ill. 1973. Ptnr. Cubbon & Rice Law Firm, Toledo, 1968-72; asst. counsel Allstate Ins. Co., Northbrook, Ill., 1972-74, assoc. counsel, 1974-76, asst. sec., asst. gen. counsel, 1976-77, asst. v.p., asst. gen. counsel, 1977-78, v.p., asst. gen. counsel, 1978-86, sr. v.p., sec., gen. counsel, bd. dirs., 1987-99, exec. v.p., 1999—. Bd. dirs. Allstate subs. Bd. dirs., exec. com. Assn. Calif. Ins. Cos., Nat. Assn. Ind. Insurers; mem. bd. overseers Inst. for Civil Justice. Served to capt. inf. U.S. Army, 1966-68. Mem. ABA, Ill. Bar Assn., Ohio Bar Assn., Ivanhoe (Ill.) Club. Roman Catholic. Home: 46 Fox Trl Lincolnshire IL 60069-4012 Office: Allstate Ins Co 2775 Sanders Rd Ste F8 Northbrook IL 60062-6127

PILCHER, JAMES BROWNIE, lawyer; b. Shreveport, La., May 19, 1929; s. James Reece and Martha Mae (Brown) P.; m. Lorene Pilcher; children: Lydia, Martha, Bradley. BA, La. State U., 1952; JD summa cum laude, John Marshall Law Sch., 1955; postgrad., Emory U., 1957. Bar: Ga. 1955. Legal aide to Spkr. of Ho. of Reps., Ga., 1961-64; assoc. city atty. City of Atlanta, 1964-69; pvt. practice law Atlanta, 1969—. Exec. committeeman Dem. Exec. Com. of Fulton County, Ga., 1974-86; bd. dirs. Whitehead Boys Club, 1961-89; trustee Ga. Inst. Continuing Legal Edn., 1988-89. Fellow Lawyers Found. Ga., 1996—. Mem. ABA, State Bar Ga. (chmn. 1988-89, gen. practice and trial sect., chmn. criminal law sect. 1986-87), Ga. Assn. Criminal Def. Lawyers (pres. 1980-82), Ga. Trial Lawyers Assn. (life), Ga. Claimants Attys. Assn. (pres. 1983-84), NACDL (bd. dirs. 1980-85), Ga. Inst. Trial Advocacy (bd. dirs. 1986-89), South Fulton Bar Assn. (pres. 1987-88), Am. Bankruptcy Inst., Nat. Assn. Consumer Bankruptcy Attys., Trial Lawyers for Pub. Justice, Atlanta Consumer Bankruptcy Attys. Group (pres. 2001—), Kiwanis (Peachtree, Atlanta pres. 1983-84, gov. Ga. dist. 1992-93), Sierra Club of Am. (life). Presbyterian. Criminal, Personal injury. Home: 1195 W Wesley Rd NW Atlanta GA 30327-1407 Office: One Northside 75 Atlanta GA 30318-7715 E-mail: pilcher@mediaone.net

PILIERO, ROBERT DONALD, lawyer; b. N.Y.C., Oct. 6, 1948; s. Joseph Robert and Madelyn (Colantuoni) P.; m. Gloria Fusillo, Apr. 18, 1981. BS in Econs., U. Pa., 1970; JD, Georgetown U., 1974. Bar: N.Y. 1975, D.C. 1983, N.J. 1984, U.S. Dist. Ct. (so. dist.) N.Y. 1975, U.S. Dist. Ct. (ea. dist.) N.Y. 1975, U.S. Dist. Ct. N.J. 1984, U.S. Ct. Internat. Trade 1981, U.S. Ct. Appeals (2d cir.) 1975, U.S. Ct. Appeals (fed. cir.) 1982, U.S. Ct. Appeals (D.C. cir.) 1983. Acct., Haskins & Sells, N.Y.C., 1970-71; assoc. Curtis, Mallet-Prevost, Colt & Mosle, N.Y.C., 1974-78; assoc. Marks, Murase & White (formerly Wender, Murase & White), N.Y.C., 1978-80, ptnr., 1980-87, ptnr. Pilerso and Goldstein, N.Y.C., 1988—. Mem. ABA, Assn. Bar City N.Y., Bar Assn. D.C., N.J. Bar Assn., Fed. Bar Council. Antitrust, Federal civil litigation, Private international. Office: Piliero & Goldstein 380 Lexington Ave New York NY 10168-0002

PILLAI, K. G. JAN, law educator, lawyer; b. Quilon, India, Jan. 23, 1936; came to U.S., 1966, naturalized, 1975; s. Raman and Janaky (Amma) P.; m. Sarada J., May 16, 1966; children: Jay J., Jan. BA, U. Kerala, India, 1957, LLB, 1959, LLM, 1965; LLM, Yale U., 1967, JSD, 1969. Bar: D.C. 1975, U.S. Dist. Ct. D.C. 1975, U.S. Ct. Appeals (D.C. cir.) 1975, U.S. Dist. Ct. (ea. dist.) Pa. 1982, U.S. Supreme Ct. 1982. Mgr. Indian affairs Overseas Nat. Airways, N.Y.C., 1970-71; exec. dir. Aviation Consumer Project, Washington, 1971-73; assoc. prof. law Temple U., Phila., 1973-75, prof., 1975-86, 87—; dir. office regulatory analysis Fed. Energy Regulatory Commn., 1986-87; mem. consumer adv. com. CAB, Washington, 1970-72; chmn. Temple U. Law Sch. Dean Search Com.. Author: The Air Net, 1969; contbr. articles to legal publs. Nat. chmn. Asian and Pacific Am. Civil Rights Alliance, Washington, 1987-90, Dole for Pres. com., Washington, 1987-88. Mem. ABA (chmn. adjudication com. adminstrv. law sect. 1991-94), Nat. Assn. Ams. of Asian Indian Descent (nat. chmn. 1980-85), Asian Indian C. of C. (nat. chmn. 1983-85). Republican. Office: Sch Law Temple U 1719 N Broad St Philadelphia PA 19122-6002

PILLANS, CHARLES PALMER, III, lawyer; b. Orlando, Fla., Feb. 22, 1940; s. Charles Palmer Jr. and Helen (Scarborough) P.; m. Judith Hart, July 6, 1963; children: Charles Palmer IV, Helen Hart. BA, U. Fla., 1962, JD, 1966. Bar: Fla. 1967, U.S. Dist. Ct. (mid. dist.) Fla. 1967, U.S. Ct. Appeals (2d cir.) 1968, U.S. Supreme Ct. 1971, U.S. Ct. Appeals (3d cir.) 1976, U.S. Ct. Appeals (5th and 11th cirs.) 1981. Assoc. Bedell, Bedell, Dittmar, Smith & Zehmer, Jacksonville, Fla., 1966-70; asst. state atty. 4th jud. cir., 1970-72; asst. gen. counsel City of Jacksonville, 1972; ptnr. Bedell, Dittmar, DeVault Pillans & Coxe, P.A., Jacksonville, 1972—. Mem. Fla. Bd. Bar Examiners, Tallahassee, 1979-84, chmn., 1983-84, Jud. Nominating Commn., 1988-92, chmn., 1990-91, 1st Dist. Ct. Appeal, Tallahassee, 1988-92, chmn., 1990-91, Supreme Ct. com. on standard jury instructions in civil cases, 1998—. Master Chester Bedell Inn of Ct.; fellow Am. Coll. Trial Lawyers, ABA; mem. Am. Bar Found., Fla. Bar Assn. (chmn. profl. ethics com. 1998—, chmn. 1998-99). Methodist. Federal civil litigation, State civil litigation, Criminal. Home: 10 Buckthorne Dr Amelia Island FL 32034-6518 Office: Bedell Dittmar DeVault Pillans & Coxe PA Bedell Bldg 101 E Adams St Jacksonville FL 32202-3303 E-mail: cpillans@bedellfirm.com

PILLION, MICHAEL LEITH, lawyer; b. Sept. 4, 1957; BS, Pa. State U., 1979; JD, Villanova U., 1985. Bar: Pa. 1985, N.J. 1986. Ptnr. Morgan, Lewis & Bockius LLP, Phila. General corporate, Intellectual property, Landlord-tenant. Office: Morgan Lewis & Bockius LLP 1701 Market St Philadelphia PA 19103-2903

PIMENTEL, JULIO GUMERESINDO, lawyer, accountant; b. Chgo., Aug. 11, 1961; s. Julio Caesar and Jeannie Irene (Jakovac) P.; m. Margaret Mary O'Donnell, July 5, 1987 (div. Jan. 1995); children: Ashley Adel, Benjamin Maximillion. BS in Commerce, DePaul U., 1983, M of Accountancy, 1984; JD, John Marshall Law Sch., 1991. Bar: Ill. 1992; CPA, Ill.; cert. internal auditor. Deli clk. Jewel Food Stores, Chgo., 1978-84; field auditor Harris Bank, 1984-85; asset-based lending field auditor Chase Comml. Corp., 1985-86; acct. Allstate Ins., Northbrook, Ill., 1986-87; revenue agt. IRS, Chgo., 1987-91, estate tax atty., 1991—; pvt. practice, acct., 1992—. Ill. State scholar, 1979. Mem. ATLA, Inst. Internal Auditors, Chgo. Bar Assn., IRS Bowling League (Most Polite award 1994-95), Freemen. Avocations: weightlifting, martial arts, gun collecting, old cars, archery. Estate planning, Family and matrimonial, Personal injury. Home and Office: PO Box A3761 Chicago IL 60690-3761

PINCZOWER, KENNETH EPHRAIM, lawyer; b. N.Y.C., Aug. 24, 1964; s. Joachim and Dinah Pinczower; m. Julie Rieder; children: Devorah, David C., Chana. BA, Queens Coll., 1985; postgrad., Rabbinical Sem. of Am., N.Y.C., 1983-86; JD, Benjamin N. Cardozo Sch. Law, 1989. Bar: N.Y. 1990, N.J. 1990, D.C. 1991, Fla. 1993, U.S. Dist. Ct. (so. and ea. dist.) N.Y. 1990, U.S. Dist. Ct. N.J. 1990. Auditor Seidman & Seidman/B.D.O., N.Y.C., 1986-87; summer assoc. U.S. Attys. Office, So. Dist. N.Y., 1988; Alexander jud. fellow U.S. Dist. Judge, So. Dist. N.Y., 1987-88; asst. corp. counsel N.Y.C. Law Dept., 1989-95; atty. Barron, McDonald, Carroll & Cohen, N.Y.C., 1995—. Editor Cardozo Arts & Entertainment Law Jour., 1988-89. Vol. instr. Jewish Edn. Program, N.Y.C., 1983-86; instr. Aish Ha Torah, 1994-98; chmn. Torah Chesed Fund, Yeshiva U., 1995—; Talmud assoc. Artscroll Mesorah Heritage Found., 1993—; com. mem. Nat. Conf. Synagogue Youth, 1991—. Avocations: Talmudic law, tennis, basketball. Home: 3950 Blackstone Ave Bronx NY 10471-3703 Office: Barron McDonald et al 1 Whitehall St New York NY 10004-2109 E-mail: pinczok@nationwide.com

PINGREE, BRUCE DOUGLAS, lawyer; b. Salt Lake City, June 6, 1947; s. Howard W. and Lois (Ivie) P.; m. Lorraine Bertelli, Oct. 11, 1981; children: Christian James, Matthew David, Alexandra Elizabeth, Meredith Gillian, Lauren Ashley, Geoffrey Nicholas. BA in Philosophy, U. Utah, 1970, JD, 1973. Bar: Ariz. 1973, Tex. 1990. Ptnr. Snell & Wilmer, Phoenix, 1973-89; shareholder Johnson & Gibbs, Dallas, 1989-93; ptnr. Gardere & Wynne, 1993-95, Baker Botts, L.L.P., Dallas, 1995—. Lectr. in field of taxation. Contbr. articles to profl. jours. Served to capt. USAR. Fellow Am. Coll. Employee Benefit Counsel, Inc. (charter); mem. ABA (tax sect., past chair employee benefits com., past vice chair, past chmn. various subcoms., 1993-94, chair joint com. on employee benefits 1994-95), Tex. State Bar Assn. (chair, tax sect. benefits and compensation com. 2000), Dallas Bar Assn. (sec. employee benefits sect. 2001—), S.W. Benefits Conf., Nat. Assn. Stock Plan Profls., Order of Coif. Episcopalian. Pension, profit-sharing, and employee benefits, Corporate taxation, Personal income taxation. Home: 4065 Bryn Mawr Dr Dallas TX 75225-7032 Office: Baker & Botts LLP 2001 Ross Ave Ste 600 Dallas TX 75201-2900

PINKAS, ROBERT PAUL, lawyer, venture capitalist; b. Cleve., Nov. 11, 1953; s. Ludvik and Esther (Safir) P.; m. Jane Elliott, July 14, 1979; children: Robert Paul Jr., Caroline L., Benjamin A., Elizabeth S., Katherine E. BA, Harvard U., 1975, MA cum laude, 1976; JD, U. Pa., 1978. Bar: N.Y. 1979. Corp. atty. Simpson Thacher & Bartlett, N.Y.C., 1978-80; sr. assoc. McKinsey & Co., Cleve., 1980-82; gen. ptnr. Brantley Ptnrs., 1981-87, Brantley Venture Ptnrs., Cleve., 1987—. Bd. dirs. Quad Systems Corp., Horsham, Pa., Brantley Capital Corp., Cleve., Waterlink, Inc., Canton, Pediatric Svcs. Am., Inc., Atlanta; chmn. bd. Gliatech, Inc., Cleve. Mem. Harvard Schs. and Scholarship Com., Cambridge, Mass., 1982—, Hotchkiss Sch. Regional Admissions Com., Lakeville, Conn., 1982—; mem. steering com. Hotchkiss Sch.; mem. centennial com. Hathaway Brown, Shaker Heights, Ohio, 1990—; mem. Univ. Technology, Inc., Cleve., 1990—. Mem. Nat. Venture Capital Assn., N.Y. State Bar Assn., Ohio Venture Assn., Harvard Club of Cleve. (trustee 1982—), Union Club of Cleve., Power Ten. Avocations: running, reading, golf. Contracts commercial, General corporate, Finance. Office: Brantley Partners 20600 Chagrin Blvd Ste 1150 Cleveland OH 44122-5342 E-mail: rpinkas@brantleypartners.com

PINKERTON, ALBERT DUANE, II, lawyer; b. Portland, Oreg., Aug. 28, 1942; s. Albert Duane and Barbara Jean Pinkerton; 1 child, Albert Duane III. BA, Willamette U., 1964, JD, 1966. Bar: Oreg. 1966, U.S. Dist. Ct. Oreg. 1966, U.S. Ct. Appeals (9th cir.) 1966, Alaska 1985, Calif. 1986, U.S. Dist. Ct. Calif. 1987. Gen. practice, Springfield, Oreg., 1966-69, Burns, 1969-86, Concord, Calif., 1986-88; assoc. Sellar Hazard McNeely Alm & Manning, Walnut Creek, 1988—. Mem. Oreg. State Bar (com. Uniform Jury Instrns. sec. 1972-73, 82-83, chmn. 1973-74, 83-84; com. Procedure and Practice sec. 1985-86, chmn. 1986-87), Am. Judicature Soc., Masons (master 1980-81), Grand Lodge of Oreg. (dist. dep. 1983-86). State civil litigation, General practice, Insurance. Home: PO Box 21347 Concord CA 94521-0347 Office: 1111 Civic Dr Ste 300 Walnut Creek CA 94596-3894 E-mail: dpinkerton@sellarlaw.com

PINNEY, SIDNEY DILLINGHAM, JR. lawyer; b. Hartford, Conn., Nov. 17, 1924; s. Sydney Dillingham and Louisa (Griswold) Wells P.; m. Judith Munch, Sept. 30, 1990; children from previous marriage: William Griswold, David Rees. Student, Amherst Coll., 1941-43, Brown U., 1943; also, M.I.T., 1943-44; BA cum laude, Amherst Coll., 1947; LLB, Harvard U., 1950. Bar: Conn. 1950. Pvt. practice, Hartford, 1950; assoc. Shepherd, Murtha and Merritt, 1950-53; ptnr. Murtha, Cullina, Richter & Pinney (1967) (name changed to Murtha Cullina LLP 2000), 1953-92; of counsel Shepherd, Murtha and Merritt (name changed to Murtha Cullina LLP 2000), 1993—. Lectr. on estate planning. Contbr. to: Estate Planning mag. Bd. dirs. Greater Hartford Area TB and Respiratory Diseases Health Soc., 1956-69, pres., 1966-67; mem. Wethersfield (Conn.) Town Coun., 1958-62; trustee Hartford Conservatory Music, 1967-71, 75-81; trustee, pres. Historic Wethersfield Found., 1961-81; bd. dirs. Hartford Hosp., 1971-80, adv. bd., 1980—; mem. adv. com. Jefferson House, 1978-82; mem. Mortensen

Libr. Bd. of Visitors U. Hartford, 1984—; corporator Hartford Pub. Libr., 1969—, Renbrook Sch., West Hartford, Conn., 1970-75. 1st lt. USAF, 1943-46. Fellow Am. Coll. Trust and Estate Counsel; mem. ABA, Nat. Acad. Elder Law Attys., Conn. Bar Assn. (com. elder law sect.), Hartford County Bar Assn. Republican. Congregationalist. Office: City Place 185 Asylum St Hartford CT 06103-3408

PINNISI, MICHAEL DONATO, lawyer, educator; b. Buffalo, Oct. 12, 1960; s. Frank Joseph and Dolores Ann Pinnisi; children: Kerry Lynn, Rose. AB cum laude, Cornell U., 1982, JD, 1985. Bar: N.Y. 1986, U.S. Dist. Ct. (so. dist.) N.Y. 1987, U.S. Dist. Ct. (no. dist.) N.Y. 1991, U.S. Dist. Ct. (we. dist.) N.Y. 1993, U.S. Ct. Appeals (2d. cir.) 1988, U.S. Ct. Appeals (fed. cir.) 1998. Trial atty. honor program U.S. Dept. of Justice, Washington, 1985-87; assoc. atty. Shearman & Sterling, N.Y.C., 1987-88; asst. U.S. atty. U.S. Attys., So. Dist. N.Y., 1988-91; assoc. atty. Cleary, Gottlieb, Steen & Hamilton, Washington, 1991-92; prin. atty. Pinnisi, Wagner et al, Ithaca, N.Y., 1992-97, Brown, Pinnisi and Michaels, Ithaca, 1997-2000; gen. counsel Kionix Inc., 1999—. Adj. prof. law Cornell Law Sch., Ithaca, 1992-2000; cert. arbitrator U.S. Dist. Ct. No. Dist. N.Y., 1993-2000; spkr. in field. Dir. Ithaca Cmty. Childcare, 1993-94, F.I.R.S.T., Phila., 1996-97. Mem. ABA, N.Y. State Bar Assn., Tompkins County Bar Assn., Phi Delta Phi. Appellate, General civil litigation, Intellectual property. Office: Kionix Inc 36 Thornwood Dr Ithaca NY 14850 E-mail: mpinnisi@kionix.com

PINOVER, EUGENE ALFRED, lawyer; b. N.Y.C., Jan. 8, 1948; s. Maurice Alfred and Harriet (Ortner) P.; m. Diana Elzey, Feb. 14, 1974; children: Julia, Benjamin, Hannah. BA cum laude, Dartmouth Coll., 1969; JD cum laude, NYU, 1973. Bar: N.Y. 1974, U.S. Dist. Ct. (so. and ea. dists.) N.Y. 1974. Ptnr. Willkie Farr & Gallagher, N.Y.C. Real property. Office: Willkie Farr & Gallagher 787 7th Ave Lbby 2 New York NY 10019-6099 E-mail: epinover@willkie.com

PINSON, JERRY D. lawyer; b. Harrison, Ark., Sept. 7, 1942; s. Robert L. and Cleta (Keeter) P.; m. Jane Ellis, Sept. 11, 1964; 1 child, Christopher Clifton. BA, U. Ark., 1964, JD, 1967. Bar: Ark. 1967, U.S. Ct. Appeals (8th cir.) 1967, U.S. Supreme Ct. 1967, U.S. Dist. Ct. (ea. and we. dists.) Ark. 1968. Dep. atty. gen. State of Ark., Little Rock, 1967-70; ptnr. Pinson & Reeves, Harrison, 1973-88; sole practice, 1970-73, 88—. Mem. Ark. Supreme Ct. com. on the unauthorized practice of law in Ark., 1979-91, chmn. 1990-91; spl. justice Ark. Supreme Ct., 1991, 94; active state bd. law examiners, 1997—. Pres. United Way Boone County, Harrison, 1974. Mem. ABA, Assn. Trial Lawyers Am., Ark. Bar Assn., Boone County Bar Assn., Harrison C. of C. (sec. bd. dirs. 1977). Lodge: Rotary (bd. dirs. 1975, v.p. 1976, pres. 1977). State civil litigation, General practice, Personal injury. Office: Atty at Law PO Box 1111 Harrison AR 72602-1111

PIPER, JAMES WALTER, lawyer; b. Mpls., Apr. 28, 1950; s. Mansell Garrett and Maxine (Sorenson) P.; m. Jane Marie Quentan, May 27, 1995. BBA, Baylor U., 1971; JD, U. Tex., 1974. Bar: Tex. 1974, U.S. Dist. Ct. (we. dist.) Tex. 1976, U.S. Ct. Appeals (5th cir.) 1978, U.S. Supreme Ct. 1980; bd. cert. in family law. Atty. Legal Aid Soc. Ctrl. Tex., Austin, 1974-76, mng. atty., 1976-84; ptnr. Piper & Powers, L.L.P., 1984—. Mem. faculty Tex. Coll. Trial Advocacy, Houston, 1980. Founding mem. Family PAC, Austin, 1998. Mem. Travis County Bar Assn. (sec.-treas. family law sect. 1989-90), Coll. of State Bar of Tex., Tex. Acad. Family Law Specialists, Travis County Family Law Advocates. Avocations: reading, hiking, boating, music. Family and matrimonial. Office: Piper & Powers LLP 2206 Lake Austin Blvd Austin TX 78703-4548

PIPKIN, MARVIN GRADY, lawyer; b. San Angelo, Tex., Nov. 15, 1949; s. Raymond Grady and Lillie Marie (Smith) P.; m. Dru Cheatham, July 24, 1971; children: Lacey Elizabeth, Matthew Todd. BBA, U. Tex., 1971, JD, 1974. Bar: Tex. 1974, U.S. Dist. Ct. (we. dist.) Tex. 1979, U.S. Ct. Appeals (5th cir.) 1983. Assoc. Green & Kaufman, San Antonio, 1974-79, ptnr., 1979-82, Kendrick & Pipkin, San Antonio, 1982-93, Drought & Pipkin L.L.P., San Antonio, 1993-98, Pipkin, Oliver & Bradley, LLP, San Antonio, 1998—. Mem. coms. on ethics and admissions Tex. Supreme Ct., admissions com.; adv. dir. Trinity Nat. Bank, San Antonio, 1983; bd. dirs. Allied Am. Bank, San Antonio, First Interstate Bank, San Antonio. Bd. dirs. Monte Vista Hist. Assn., San Antonio, 1975-78. Fellow Tex. Bar Found., San Antonio Bar Found.; mem. ABA, Tex. Assn. Def. Counsel, Tex. Bar Assn., San Antonio Bar Assn. Republican. Methodist. Avocations: sports, outdoor activities. General civil litigation, General corporate, Real property. Home: 2 Dorchester Pl San Antonio TX 78209-2203 Office: Pipkin Oliver & Bradley LLP 1020 NE 600 P 410 #810 San Antonio TX 78209 E-mail: mpipkin@texas.net

PIRCHER, LEO JOSEPH, lawyer, director; b. Berkeley, Calif., Jan. 4, 1933; s. Leo Charles and Christine (Moore) P.; m. Phyllis McConnell, Aug. 04, 1956 (div. Apr. 1981); children: Christopher, David, Eric; m. Nina Silverman, June 14, 1987. BS, U. Calif., Berkeley, 1954, JD, 1957. Bar: Calif. 1958, (N.Y.) 1985, cert.: Calif. Bd. Legal Specialization (cert. specialist taxation law). Assoc. Lawler, Felix & Hall, L.A., 1957-62, ptnr., 1962-65, sr. ptnr., 1965-83, Pircher, Nichols & Meeks, L.A., 1983—. Adj. prof. Loyola U. Law Sch., L.A., 1959—61; corp. sec. Am. Metal Bearing Co., Gardena, Calif., 1975—; dir. Valco Internat., Inc., Orange, Calif.; spkr. various law schs. and bar assns. edn. programs. Author (with others): (novels) Definition and Utility of Leases, 1968. Chmn. pub. fin. and taxation sect. Calif. Town Hall, L.A., 1970—71. Mem.: ABA, Calif. State Bar, N.Y. State Bar, Nat. Assn. Real Estate Investment Trusts Inc. (cert. specialist taxation law), L.A. County Bar Assn. (exec. com. comml. law sect.), Regency (L.A.). Republican. General corporate, Real property, Corporate taxation. Office: Pircher Nichols & Meeks Ste 1700 1925 Century Park E Los Angeles CA 90067-6022 E-mail: lpircher@pircher.com

PIROK, EDWARD WARREN, lawyer, consultant; b. Chgo., June 2, 1947; s. Edward Warren and Elinor Jean Pirok; m. Christine Merk, Jan. 23, 1973; children: Edward, Christopher, Jennifer, Elizabeth. BS, Ill. Inst. Tech., 1970; JD, Loyola U., 1973. Bar: N.Y. 1988, Ill. 1973, U.S. Supreme Ct., U.S. Ct. Appeals (2d and 7th cirs.) U.S. Dist. Ct. (so. and ea. dists.) N.Y., U.S. Dist. Ct. (no. dist.) Ill. Trial atty. Burlington No., Inc., Chgo., 1975-77; asst. gen. counsel Regional Transp. Authority, 1977-82; gen. counsel Metra, The N.E. Ill. R.R. Corp., 1982-87; trial atty. Metro-North Commuter R.R., N.Y.C., 1987-89; of counsel Peltz & Walker, 1990-93; ptnr. Frank & Assocs., Ltd., Chgo., 1999. 1st lt. Ill. Army N.G. Mem. ATLA, Ill. Trial Lawyers Assn. Roman Catholic. Avocations: golf, tennis. Environmental, Personal injury, Transportation. Home: 5 Ashbury Ln Barrington Hills IL 60010 Office: Frank & Assocs Ltd 734 N Wells St Chicago IL 60610

PIRTLE, H(AROLD) EDWARD, lawyer; b. Detroit, Apr. 6, 1948; s. Edward Bensen Pirtle and Lorraine Virginia (La Pointe) Schwartz; m. Maxine Mary Stencel, June 10, 1971 (div. May 1981); children: Kimberly, Jeffrey, Michelle; m. Betsy Yvonne Mark, Sept. 1, 1984. AS, Macomb County Cmty. Coll., Warren, Mich., 1977; B in applied sci., Siena Heights Coll., 1983; JD, U. Toldeo, 1990. Bar: Mich. 1990, U.S. Dist. Ct. (ea. dist.) Mich. 1990, U.S. Ct. Appeals (6th cir.) 1997. Assoc. Beaman & Beaman, Jackson, Mich., 1990-91; pvt. practice, H. Edward Pirtle, Atty. at Law, Detroit, 1991-96; assoc. Calligaro & Meyering, PC, Taylor, Mich., 1996-97; mng. mem. H. Edward Pirtle, PLC, Detroit, 1997—. With U.S. Navy, 1967-72. Mem. ABA, Macomb County Bar Assn., Met. Detroit Bar Assn., Am. Mensa (gen. rep. 1984-85, legal counsel Mensa Edn. and Rsch. Found., trustee, found. sec.). Avocations: computers, financial markets. Bankruptcy, Contracts commercial, Criminal. Office: 1805 Ford Bldg 615 Griswold Detroit MI 48226-3989 E-mail: epirtle@aol.com, legaldetroit@aol.com

PISANO, VINCENT JAMES, lawyer; b. Englewood, N.J., Sept. 12, 1953; s. Vincent Paul and Georgette (Cernek) P.; m. Lissa Roth, May 4, 1996; children: Catherine Callahan Steele, Elisabeth Lynden Steele. BA, Vassar Coll., 1975; JD, St. Johns U., 1978. Bar: N.Y. 1979. With Skadden, Arps, Slate, Meagher and Flom, N.Y.C., 1978—; ptnr. Skadden, Arps, Slate and Meagher, 1986—. Bd. dirs. Make a Wish Found. Met. N.Y., 1988-90. Mem. N.Y. Bar Assn., N.Y.C. Bar Assn., Vassar Coll. Alumni Assn. E-mial. General corporate, Mergers and acquisitions, Securities. Office: Skadden Arps Slate Meagher & Flom 4 Times Sq 31st Fl New York NY 10036-6595 E-mail: vpisano@skadden.com

PISTILLI, MARK STEPHEN, lawyer, author; b. Adelaide, Australia, May 8, 1969; s. Romolo and Maria Concetta Pistilli; m. Lidia Beatrice Manuele, Sept. 10, 1994; children: Emily, Jessie. BEcons, U. Adelaide, 1990, LLB with hons., 1991; Grad. Diploma in Legal Practice, U. South Australia, 1992; Grad. Diploma in Applied Fin./Investment, Securities Inst. Australia, 1995. Bar: High Ct. of Australia 1995, Fed. Ct. of Australia 1995, Supreme Ct. South Australia, 1992, Supreme Ct. NSW, 1997, Supreme Ct. QLD. Atty. Finlaysons, Adelaide, 1993-97, Atanaskovic Hartnell, Sydney, Australia, 1998-99, mng. ptnr. Australia, 1999—. Bd. dirs. FMC Software, Montreal, Pistol Corp.; lectr. Securities Inst. Australia, 1996-97. Author: Corporations Law and Practice, 1998, 99, 2000, also articles. State dir. Abbeyfield Soc., Adelaide, 1995-97. Mem. Securities Inst. Australia (assoc., lectr. 1995—), Australian Mining and Petroleum Law Inst. (bd. dirs.). Mem. Liberal Party. Roman Catholic. Avocations: film making, reading, thoroughbred racing, opera, boating. General corporate, Mergers and acquisitions, Natural resources. Office: Atanaskovic Hartnell 75-85 Elizabeth St Sydney NSW 2000 Australia Fax: 612 9777 8777. E-mail: msp@ah.com.au

PITCHER, GRIFFITH FONTAINE, lawyer; b. Balt., Nov. 1, 1937; s. William Henry and Virginia Griffith (Stein) P.; m. Sandra E. Barnett, Dec. 16, 1994; children; Virginia T. Pitcher Ballinger, L. Brooke Pitcher Fick, William T.B., Margaret W. Pitcher Saylors. BA, Johns Hopkins U., 1960; JD, U. Va., 1963. Bar: Ala. 1963, Fla. 1971, Ga. 1996. Assoc. Bradley, Arant, Rose & White, Birmingham, Ala., 1963-71; mem. Van den Berg, Gay & Burke, Orlando, Fla., 1971-76, Mahoney, Hadlow & Adams, Jacksonville, 1976-82; ptnr. Squire, Sanders & Dempsey, Miami, 1982-93; of counsel Mershon, Sawyer, Johnston, Dunwoody & Cole, 1994-95, Chamberlain, Hrdlicka, White, Williams & Martin, Atlanta, 1996—. Contbr. articles to profl. jours. Vice chmn. Winter Park (Fla.) Planning & Zoning Bd., 1974-75. With Army N.G., 1961-64. Fellow Am. Coll. Bond Counsel (founding fellow, treas./dir.); mem. ABA, Nat. Assn. Bond Lawyers, Fla. Bar Assn., Ga. State Bar, Ala. State Bar Assn., Order of Coif, Delta Phi. Republican. Municipal (including bonds).

PITEGOFF, THOMAS MICHAEL, lawyer; b. N.Y.C., Aug. 12, 1949; s. Joseph and Libbie (Shapiro) P. BA, Sarah Lawrence Coll., 1971; postgrad. U. Heidelberg, Germany, 1971-72; Maitrise, Sorbonne, U. Paris, 1973; JD, Syracuse U., 1976. Bar: N.Y. 1977. counsel Hunton & Williams, N.Y.C., 1986-89; panelist numerous confs. and seminars. Contbr. articles to profl. jours. Westchester regional coord. Export Legal Assistance Network, 1995—; bd. govs. World Trade Coun. Westchester, 1995—. Mem. ABA (gov. com. forum on franchising 1993-96, former chair franchising subcom. bus. sect. small bus. com., editor Franchise Law Jour. 1990-93, co-chair internat. subcom. bus. sect. cyberspace law com. 1998—), Internat. Bar Assn., N.Y. State Bar Assn., Assn. of Bar of City of N.Y. (mem. computer law com. 1988-91), Computer Law Assn. Computer, Franchising, Private international. Office: Halket & Pitegoff LLP The Gateway Bldg 11th Fl 1 N Lexington Ave White Plains NY 10601-1712

PITMAN, ROBERT L. prosecutor; JD, U. Tex., 1988. Atty. advisor Executive Office for US Atty., Office of Legal Council, Washington, DC, 1996; cheif Austin Div., Western Dist. , Tex.; asst US atty.; US atty. Western Dist., Tex. Recipient commendations from Exec. Office for US Atty, Fed. Bureau of Investigation, US Dept. of State, US Drug Enforcement Adminstrn., US Secret Service. Office: US Attorney 601 NW Loop 410 Ste 600 San Antonio TX 78216-5597 Fax: 210-384-7105*

PITT, GEORGE, lawyer, investment banker; b. Chgo., July 21, 1938; s. Cornelius George and Anastasia (Geocaris) P.; m. Barbara Lynn Goodrich, Dec. 21, 1963 (div. Apr. 1990); children: Elizabeth Nanette, Margaret Leigh; m. Pamela Ann Pittsford, May 19, 1990. BA, Northwestern U., 1960, JD, 1963; hon. grad., U.S. Army Intelligence Sch., Ft. Holabird, Md., 1964; Leading Strategic Change course, U. Va., 1999. Bar: Ill. 1963. Assoc. Chapman and Cutler, Chgo., 1963-67; ptnr. Borge and Pitt, and predecessor, 1968-87, Katten Muchin & Zavis, Chgo., 1987-97; sr. mng. dir. Banc One Capital Markets, Inc. (formerly First Chgo. Capital Markets, Inc.), 1998-2000; mng. dir. UBS PaineWebber Inc., Chgo., 2000—. Conf. chmn. Bond Buyer's 3d Ann. Midwest Pub. Fin. Conf., 1994; conf. co-chmn. Bond Buyer's 8th Ann. Midwest Pub. Fin. Conf., 1999. Notes and comments editor Northwestern U. Law Rev., 1962-63. 1st lt. AUS, 1964. Fellow Am. Coll. of Bond Counsel; mem. Ill. State Bar Assn., Univ. Club, Chgo., Michigan City Yacht Club, Ind. Soc. of Chgo., Eta Sigma Phi, Phi Delta Phi, Phi Gamma Delta. Municipal (including bonds). Home: 600 N McClurg Ct Chicago IL 60611-3044 Office: UBS PaineWebber Inc 181 W Madison St 42d Fl Chicago IL 60602-4510 E-mail: gpitt@ubspainewebber.com

PITTMAN, EDWIN LLOYD, state supreme court chief justice; b. Hattiesburg, Miss., Jan. 2, 1935; s. Lloyd H. and Pauline P.; m. Virginia Lund, 1996; children: Melanie, Win, Jennifer. BS, U. So. Miss.; JD, U. Miss., 1960. Bar: Miss. Practiced law until, 1964; mem. Miss. Senate, 1964-72; treas. State of Miss., Jackson, 1976-80, sec. of state, 1980-84, atty. gen., 1984-88; justice Supreme Ct. Miss., 1990—; chief justice Miss. Supreme Ct. , Miss., 2000—. Trustee William Carey Coll. 2nd lt., Inf. U.S. Army. Mem. U. Miss. Alumni Assn., U. So. Miss. Alumni Assn., Miss. Jaycees (past state dir.), ABA, South Central Miss. Bar Assn. Democrat. Baptist. Clubs: Lions, Masons. Office: Miss Supreme Ct Gartin Justice Bldg Jackson MS 39205-0117*

PITTMAN, VIRGIL, federal judge; b. Enterprise, Ala., Mar. 28, 1916; s. Walter Oscar and Annie Lee (Logan) P.; m. Floy Lasseter, 1944 (dec.) 2000; children— Karen Pittman Gordy, Walter Lee. B.S., U. Ala., 1939, LL.B., 1940. Bar: Ala. bar 1940. Spl. agt. FBI, 1940-44; practice law Gadsden, Ala., 1946-51; judge Ala. Circuit Ct., Circuit 16, 1951-66; U.S. dist. judge Middle and So. Dist. Ala., 1966-71; chief judge U.S. Dist. Ct. for Ala. So. Dist., 1971-81, sr. judge, 1981—; periodically sits as judge U.S. Ct. Appeals 11th Cir., 1981—96. Lectr. bus. law, econs. and polit. sci. U. Ala. Center, Gadsden, 1948-66 Author: Circuit Court Proceedings in Acquisition of a Tract of Right of Way, 1959, A Judge Looks at Right of Way Condemnation Proceedings, 1960, Technical Pitfalls in Right of Way Proceedings, 1961. Mem. Ala. Bd. Edn., 1951; bd. trustees, life trustee Samford U, 1975-. Lt. (j.g.) USN, 1944-46, USS Wharton, Pacific Supply Corp. Mem. Ala. State Bar, Etowah County Bar Assn. (pres. 1949), Baptist Oaks (bd. dirs. lower income housing), Omicron Delta Kappa. Democrat. Baptist. Office: US Dist Ct PO Box 465 Mobile AL 36601-0465

PITTNER, NICHOLAS ANDREW, lawyer; b. Ottoville, Ohio, Mar. 14, 1942; s. Andrew Martin and Catheryn (Boehmer) P.; m. Susan Eleanore Hess, June 19, 1965; children: Christina Marie, David Andrew, Victoria Susan. BA, Ohio State U., 1964; JD, Capital U., Columbus, Ohio, 1970; LLD (hon.), Capital U., 2001. Bar: Ohio 1970, U.S. Dist. Ct. (no. dist.) Ohio 1973, U.S. Dist. Ct. (so. dist.) Ohio 1971, U.S. Ct. Appeals (6th cir.) 1973. Computer sys. analyst Anchor-Hocking Glass, Lancaster, Ohio, 1964-66, Reiland Page & Assocs., Columbus, 1966-67; courtroom bailiff Franklin County Mcpl. Ct., 1967-68; adminstrv. asst. Ohio Sec. State, 1968-71; assoc. Means, Bichimer, Burkholder & Baker, 1971-86, Bricker & Eckler, Columbus, 1986—. Presenter in field; cons. Baker's Ohio Sch. Law, 1982-86, Planning, Promoting and Passing School Tax Issues (booklet), 1983. Contbr. articles to profl. jours. Bd. dirs. Ohio Theatre for Youth, Columbus, 1984-95, Upper Arlington Civic Assn., Ohio, 1985-87. Mem. ABA, Ohio State Bar Assn. (sch. law com. program chmn. 1986, chmn. sch. law com. 1991-93), Ohio Coun. Sch. Bd. Attys. (chmn. 1984), Nat. Coun. Sch. Attys. (cp. law sch. annual fund chmn. 1993, alumni bd. 1992-93), Columbus Bar Assn., Columbus Amateur Radio Assn. (pres. 1980). Republican. Roman Catholic. Avocations: amateur radio, personal computing. Education and schools, Finance. Home: 5103 Goodson Rd West Jefferson OH 43162-9609 Office: Bricker & Eckler 100 S 3rd St Columbus OH 43215-4291 E-mail: npittner@bricker.com

PITTONI, LUKE M. lawyer; b. Rockville, N.Y., May 14, 1945; s. Mario and Grace (Henjes) P.; m. Mary Jo Rocque, July 8, 1972; children: Elizabeth, Katherine, Ellen. BA in Econs., Holy Cross Coll., 1967; JD, Fordham U., 1971. Bar: N.Y. 1972, U.S. Ct. Appeals (2d. cir.) 1975, U.S. Dist. Ct. (so. and ea. dists.) N.Y. 1975, U.S. Supreme Ct. 1976, U.S. Dist. Ct. Conn. 1977, Conn. 1986. Assoc. Martin, Clearwater & Bell, N.Y.C., 1972-75; trial atty. Anthony L. Schiavetti, 1975-78; assoc. Alexander & Green, 1978-79; ptnr. Heidell, Pittoni, Murphy & Bach, P.C., 1979—. Mem. faculty Practicing Law Inst., Law Journal Press; lectr. in field. Mem. ABA, Conn. Bar Assn., N.Y. State Bar Assn., Am. Acad. Hosp. Attys., Am. Bd. Profl. Liability Attys., Am. Bd. Trial Advocates, Am. Soc. Law and Medicine, N.Y. State Med. Def. Lawyers Assn., DRI, IADC. Personal injury. Home: 283 Quarry Rd Stamford CT 06903-5011 Office: Heidell Pittoni Murphy & Bach 99 Park Ave Fl 7 New York NY 10016-1506 E-mail: pittoni@hpmb.com

PITTS, GARY BENJAMIN, lawyer; b. Tupelo, Miss., Aug. 23, 1952; s. Dextar Derward Pitts and Eva Margaret (Holcomb) Bush; m. Nicole Palmer; children: Andrew Ross, Caitlan Taylor, Austin Palmer. Student, U. Miss., Oxford, 1970-71, Coll. Charleston (S.C.), 1971-73; BA, McGill U., Montreal, Que., Can., 1973-74; JD, Tulane U., New Orleans, 1979. Bar: Tex. 1979, U.S. Ct. Appeals (5th cir.) 1980, U.S. Supreme Ct. 1983. Assoc. Julian & Seele, Houston, 1979-84, Ogletree, Pitts & Collard, Houston, 1984-85; ptnr. Pitts & Collard LLP, Houston and Dallas, 1985-96; owner Pitts & Assocs., Houston, 1996—. Organizer, legal counsel for Neighborhood Watch Coalition. Capt. USNG, 1975-87. Mem. ATLA, Maritime Law Assn. (Proctor in Admiralty 1980—). Admiralty, Personal injury, Workers' compensation. Office: Pitts & Assocs 8866 Gulf Fwy Ste 117 Houston TX 77017-6528

PLAEGER, FREDERICK JOSEPH, II, lawyer; b. New Orleans, Sept. 10, 1953; s. Edgar Leonard and Bernice Virginia (Schiwetz) P.; m. Kathleen Helen Dickson, Nov. 19, 1977; children: Douglas A., Catherine E. BS, La. State U., 1976, JD, 1977. Bar: La. 1978, Tex. 1999, U.S. Dist. Ct. (ea. dist.) La. 1978, U.S. Ct. Appeals (5th cir.) 1981, U.S. Supreme Ct. 1989. Law clk. U.S. Dist. Ct. (ea. dist.) La., New Orleans, 1977-79; assoc. Milling, Benson, Woodward, Hillyer, Pierson & Miller, 1979-85, ptnr., 1985-89; v.p., gen. counsel, corp. sec. La. Land and Exploration Co., 1989-97; v.p., gen. counsel Burlington Resources Inc., Houston, 1997—. Bd. dirs. New Orleans Speech and Hearing Ctr., 1985-91, pres., 1988-90; bd. dirs. Children's Oncology Svcs. La. (Ronald McDonald House of New Orleans), 1987-90; selected mem. Met. Area Com. Leadership Forum, 1986; bd. dirs. Soc. Environ. Edn., La. Nature and Sci. Ctr., 1992-94; bd. dirs. New Orleans City Park Assn., 1996-97; bd. trustees Houston Ballet, 2001—, adv. cd. Internat. Oil and Gas Educational Ctr., 2001-. Recipient Service to Mankind award Sertoma, 1989. Mem. ABA, La. Bar Assn., Am. Corp. Counsel Assn. (bd. dirs. New Orleans chpt. 1995-98), Am. Petroleum Inst. (mem. gen. commn. law), Southwestern Legal Found. (mem. adv. bd. 2001—), Univ. Club, Lakeside Country Club. Republican. Avocations: golf, hunting, fishing. General corporate, Oil, gas, and mineral, General practice. Home: 5105 Longmont Dr Houston TX 77056-2417 Office: Burlington Resources Inc 5051 Westheimer Rd Ste 1400 Houston TX 77056-5686

PLAGER, S. JAY, federal judge; b. Long Branch, N.J., May 16, 1931; s. A.L. and Clara L. Plager; children: Anna Katherine, David Alan, Daniel Tyler. A.B., U. N.C., 1952; J.D., U. Fla., 1958; LL.M., Columbia U., 1961. Bar: Fla. 1958, Ill. 1964. Asst. prof. law U. Fla., 1958-62, assoc. prof., 1962-64; assoc. prof. law U. Ill., Champaign-Urbana, 1964-65, prof., 1965-77; dir. Office Environ. and Planning Studies, 1972-74, 75-77; dean, prof. law Ind. U. Sch. Law, Bloomington, 1977-84, prof. law, 1984-90; counselor to undersec. U.S. Dept. Health and Human Svcs., 1986-87; assoc. dir. Office of Mgmt. and Budget Office of Mgmt. and Budget, 1987-88; adminstr. info. and regulatory affairs Exec. Office of the Pres., 1988-89; cir. judge U.S. Ct. Appeals (fed. cir.), 1989—. Vis. research prof. law U. Wis., 1967-68; vis. scholar Stanford U., 1984-85 Author: (with others) Water Law and Administration, 1968, Social Justice Through Law-New Approaches in the Law of Property, 1970, (with others) Florida Water Law, 1980. Chmn. Gainesville (Fla.) Planning Commn., 1962-63; mem. Urbana Plan Commn., 1966-70; mem. nat. air pollution manpower devel. adv. com., 1971-75; cons. Ill. Inst. for Environ. Quality, U.S. EPA; chmn. Ill. Task Force on Noise, 1972-76; vice chmn. Nat. Commn. on Jud. Discipline and Removal, 1991-93. With USN, 1952-55. Office: US Ct Appeals for Fed Cir The National Courts Bldg 717 Madison Pl NW Washington DC 20439-0002

PLAINE, LLOYD LEVA, lawyer; b. Washington, Nov. 3, 1947; d. Marx (deceased) and Shirley P. Leva; m. James W. Hill. BA, U. Pa., 1969; postgrad., Harvard U.; JD, Georgetown U., 1975. Bar: D.C. 1975. Legis. asst. to U.S. Rep. Sidney Yates, 1971-72; with Sutherland, Asbill & Brennan, Washington, 1975-82, ptnr., 1982—. Fellow Am. Bar Found., Am. Coll. Trust and Estate Counsel (past regent), Am. Coll. Tax Counsel; mem. ABA (past chmn. real property, probate and trust law sect.). Estate planning, Probate, Estate taxation. Office: Sutherland Asbill & Brennan 1275 Pennsylvania Ave NW Ste 1 Washington DC 20004-2415

PLAKAS, LEONIDAS EVANGELOS, lawyer; b. Akron, Ohio, July 18, 1951; s. Evangelos Leonidas and Catherine (Chibis) P.; m. Mary Ann J. Deuri, Sept. 17, 1978; children: Alexander Evangelos, Alyssa Catherine, Katherine Nicole. BSBA cum laude, U. Akron, 1973, JD, 1976. Bar: Ohio 1976, U.S. Dist. Ct. (no. dist.) Ohio 1982, U.S. Ct. Appeals (6th cir.) 1984; cert. civil trial advocate. Mng. ptnr. Tzangas, Plakas & Mannos, Canton, Ohio, 1976—. Spl. counsel Ohio Atty. Gen. Contbg. author U. Akron Law Rev., 1976, Products Liability Cases and Commentary, 1987. Trustee Greek Orthodox Ch. the Annunciation, Akron, 1973-76, 80-82, U. Akron Sch. Law Alumni. Named Outstanding Alumnus, U. Akron Sch. Law, 2001. Mem. Stark County Acad. Trial Lawyers (trustee, sec., treas. 1982-87, pres. 1987-89, bd. dirs. 1989—), Ohio Acad. Trial Lawyers (state bd. trustees 1988-96), Am. Trial Lawyers Acad. State civil litigation, General corporate, Personal injury. Office: Tzangas Plakas & Mannos 110 Central Plz S Ste 454 Canton OH 44702-1455 E-mail: lawlion@raex.com

PLANEY, ANNETTE LORRAINE, lawyer, law firm advertising consultant; b. Wilkes-Barre, Pa., Mar. 17, 1963; d. William Bernard and Lorraine Helen Planey. BS in Edn., U. North Tex., 1985; JD, Tex. Wesleyan U., Ft. Worth, 1994. Bar: Tex. 1995. Legal placement cons. Capstone Legal Staffing, Washington, 1993-94; assoc. atty. Quilling, Selander, Commiskey & Lownds, P.C., Dallas, 1995-97; law firm advt. coms. Am. Lawyer Media, 1991-93, 97—. Mem. ABA, Dallas Bar Assn., Legal Mktg. Assn., Dallas Young Lawyers Assn. Roman Catholic. Avocations: skiing, model horse collecting, travel. Home: 2334A Connecticut Ln Dallas TX 75214-4107 Office: Am Lawyer Media 900 Jackson St Ste 500 Dallas TX 75202-4457

PLANKENSTEINER, MARCO, lawyer, researcher; b. Bolzano, Italy, Mar. 29, 1974; s. Mario Angelo P. and Mitzi Baldessari; life ptnr. Virginie Rue. D, Cath. U., Milan, 1998; LLM, PhD, U. Paris II, 1999. Bar: Ct. Milan 1998. Lawyer Studio Santa Maria, Milan, 1998—. Rschr. U. Paris II, 1999—. Avocation: international history. Banking, Public international, Taxation, general. Home: Via Fago 56/A 39100 Bolzano Italy Office: Studio Santa Maria L go Toscanini 1 20121 Milan Italy Fax: 00390277197260. E-mail: m_planke@hotmail.com, mp@santalex.com

PLATT, HAROLD KIRBY, lawyer; b. Southampton, N.Y., Nov. 7, 1942; s. William Bangs and Edith (Guldi) P.; m. Joan Pritchard, June 20, 1970; 1 child, Timothy Ross. BS in Fgn. Svc., Georgetown U., 1964; JD, Fordham U., 1971. Bar: N.Y. 1972, U.S. Dist. Ct. (ea. dist.) N.Y. 1988, U.S. Supreme Ct. 1976. Sole practice, Southampton, 1972-77; ptnr. Platt & Platt, 1977-80, Platt, Platt & Platt, Southampton, 1980-2000; sole practice, 2001—. Articles editor Fordham Law Rev., N.Y.C., 1970-71. Bd. dirs., sec. Southampton Hosp. Assn., 1979-85. Served with Mil. Police, U.S. Army, 1965-67. Mem. ABA, Suffolk County Bar Assn. (fee disputes com. 1974-82, chmn. 1981-82, mem. real property law com. 1975-78, mem. law office econ. com. 1981-82, mem. taxation com. 1984-85, 92-93), N.Y. State Bar Assn. General practice, Probate, Real property. Home: 9 Dovas Path Southampton NY 11968-2830 Office: 99 Sanford Pl Southampton NY 11968-3338 E-mail: HPlatt@Plattlaw.com

PLATT, LESLIE A. lawyer; b. Bronx, N.Y., Aug. 7, 1944; s. Harold and Ann (Bienstock) P.; m. Marcia Ellin Berman, Aug., 1969; 1 son, Bill Lawrence. BA, George Washington U., 1966; JD, NYU, 1969. Bar: N.Y. 1970, U.S. Dist. Ct. D.C. 1972. Atty. advisor Office Gen. Counsel HUD, Washington, 1971-72, legis. atty., 1972-75, asst. gen. counsel for legis. svcs., 1975-78, assoc. gen. counsel for legis., 1978-80; dep. gen. counsel-legal counsel HEW (HHS 1980) Office Gen. Counsel, 1980-81, legal counsel and staff dir. White House Agent Orange group, 1980-81; pvt. practice, 1982-91; exec. asst. to dir. NIH, 1991-92; exec. v.p., COO, gen. counsel The Inst. for Genomic Rsch., Gaithersburg, Md., 1992-95; sr. v.p. strategic devel., gen. counsel Am. Type Culture Collection, Manassas, Va., 1996-98; prin., litig. adv. svcs., assurance and adv. bus. practice Ernst & Young LLP, McLean, 1999—. Pres, dir. Found. for Genetic Medicine, Inc., 1997—. Patentee in field. Chmn. cmty. adv. bd. Fairfax Hosp. Assn. Cameron Glen Facility; chair steering com. Reston/Herndon Bus.-H.S. partnership. Recipient Disting. Svc. award HUD, 1978. Mem. ABA, Fed. Bar Assn., Am. Jud. Soc., Fed. Sr. Exec. Svc. (charter), Internat. Bar Assn. Administrative and regulatory, Health, Legislative. Home: 11901 Triple Crown Rd Reston VA 20191-3015

PLATT, RUTHERFORD HAYES, lawyer, educator, geographer, consultant; b. N.Y.C., Nov. 1, 1940; s. Rutherford and Jean (Noyes) P.; children: Anne, Stephen. BA, Yale U., 1962; JD, U. Chgo., 1967, PhD, 1971. Bar: Ill. 1968. Staff atty. Open Lands Project, Chgo., 1968-72; prof. law U. Mass., Amherst, 1972—. Cons. U.S. Water Resources Council, Washington, 1979-81, U.S. Army C.E., Washington, 1977-79; mem. 8 Nat. Rsch. Coun. coms., 1979—. Author: Land Use and Society, 1996, Disasters and Democracy, 1999; contbr. articles to profl. jours. Mem. Assn. Am. Geographers, Faculty Club (Mass.), Cosmos Club (Washington). Home: 78 Hillcrest Dr Florence MA 01062-1362 Office: U Mass Amherst MA 01003

PLATT, STEVEN IRVING, lawyer, judge; b. Woodstock, Va., Jan. 1, 1947; s. Nathan and Adele (Lober) P.; m. Patricia Lynn Hartlove, Sept. 29, 1973; children: Jason Benjamin, Sarah Edan. BA, U. Va., 1969; JD, Am. U., 1973; cert. of completion, Nat. Jud. Coll., 1980, Nat. Coll. of Probate Judges, 1983. Bar: Md. 1976, U.S. Dist. Ct. Md., 1976. Ptnr. Stern, Platt & Risner, Oxon Hill, Md., 1976-79; judge Orphans Ct., Prince Georges County, 1978-85; ptnr. Platt & Risner, Clinton, 1980-86; chief judge Orphans Ct., Prince Georges County, 1985-86; assoc. judge Dist. Ct. Md., Upper Marlboro, 1986-88, adminstrv. judge Prince Georges County, 1988-90; assoc. judge Cir. Ct., Md., 1990—. Instr. Paralegal Inst. U. Md.; chmn. Jud. Adminstrn. Com., Md. Jud. Conf., 1989-90. Bd. dirs. United Way, Prince Georges, 1980; bd. mgrs. YMCA, Prince Georges, 1980; chmn. Labor Law Revision Task Force, Prince Georges, 1981—; chmn. bd. trustees Henson Valley Montessori Sch., Temple Hills, Md., 1985-86. With Md. NG, 1970-76; v.p. Md. Bus. and Tech. Case Mgmt. Task Force. Mem. ABA, Md. Bar Assn., Prince Georges Bar Assn. (bd. dirs. 1978-85, treas. 1985-86, sec. 1986-87), Am. Trial Lawyers Assn., Nat. Coll. Probate Judges (state rep. 1985-86), Md. State Bar Assn. (bd. govs., sect. coun. jud. adminstrn.), Prince Georges County Bar Assn. (pres. 1988—), Delta Theta Phi. Jewish. Home: 8607 Grey Fox Trl Upper Marlboro MD 20772-9618 Office: Cir Ct Judges Chambers 2D Fl Courthouse Upper Marlboro MD 20772

PLATT, THOMAS COLLIER, JR. federal judge; b. N.Y.C., N.Y., May 29, 1925; s. Thomas Collier and Louise Platt; m. Ann Byrd Symington, June 25, 1948; children: Ann Byrd, Charles Collier, Thomas Collier, III, Elizabeth Louise. B.A., Yale U., 1947, LL.B., 1950. Bar: N.Y. 1950. Assoc. Root, Ballantine, Harlan, Bushby & Palmer, N.Y.C., 1950-53; asst. U.S. atty. Bklyn., 1953-56; assoc. Bleakley, Platt, Schmidt, Hart & Fritz, N.Y.C., 1956-60, ptnr., 1960-74; judge U.S. Dist. Ct. (ea. dist.) N.Y., Uniondale, 1974—, chief judge Bklyn., 1988-95. Former dir. Phoenix Mut. Life Ins. Co., RAC Corp., McIntyre Aviation, Inc.; atty. Village of Laurel Hollow, N.Y., 1958-74; acting police justice Village of Lloyd Harbor, N.Y., 1958-63 Alt. del. Republican Nat. Conv., 1964, 68, 72; del. N.Y. State Rep. Conv., 1966; trustee Brooks Sch., North Andover, Mass., 1968-82, pres., 1970-74. Served with USN, 1943-46 Mem. Fed. Judges Assn. (sec., bd. dirs. 1982-91). Episcopalian. Clubs: Phelps Assn. (New Haven) (bd. govs. 1960-98); Cold Spring Harbor Beach (N.Y.) (bd. mgrs. 1964-70); Yale of N.Y.C. Office: US Dist Ct 1044 Federal Plaza Central Islip NY 11722-4442

PLATT, WILLIAM HENRY, judge; b. Allentown, Pa., Jan. 25, 1940; s. Henry and Genevieve (McElroy) P.; m. Maureen Hart, Nov. 29, 1969; children: Meredith H., William H., James H. AB, Dickinson Coll., 1961; JD, U. Pa., 1964. Bar: Pa. 1967, U.S. Supreme Ct. 1971. Ptnr. Yarus and Platt, Allentown, 1967-77; asst. pub. defender Lehigh County (Pa.), 1972-75, chief pub. defender, 1975-76, dist. atty., 1976-91; ptnr. Eckert, Seamans, Cherin & Mellott, 1991-95; city solicitor City of Allentown, 1994-95; judge Ct. Common Pleas of Lehigh County, Allentown, 1996—. Mem. criminal procedural rules com. Supreme Ct. Pa., 1982-92, chmn., 1986-92. Mem. Gov.'s Trial Ct. Nominating Commn. Lehigh County, 1984-87; mem. Pa. Commn. on Crime and Delinquency Victim Services Adv. Com., 1983-91. Served with M.P., U.S. Army, 1964-66. Mem.: ABA, Pa. Bar Assn., Lehigh County Bar Assn., Nat. Assn. Dist. Attys. (state dir. 1982—84), Pa. Assn. Dist. Attys. (exec. com. 1980—86, pres. 1983—84, chmn. 1986—87, tng. inst. mem. 1986—91), Pa. Bar Inst. (life; bd. dirs. 1989—2000, exec. com. 1994—2000, pres. 1997—98), Pa. Conf. of State Trial Judges (edn. com. 1997—), Pa. Bar Inst. (hon.)). Office: Lehigh County Courthouse 455 W Hamilton St Allentown PA 18101-1614

PLATTNER, RICHARD SERBER, lawyer; b. N.Y.C., Aug. 10, 1952; s. Milton and Sallee Sarah (Serber) P.; m. Susan M. Madden, June 4, 1976 (div. June 1979); m. Susan K. Morris, Mar. 30, 1983; children: Samuel Morris, Katherine Elise. BA cum laude, Mich. State U., 1973; JD, Ariz. State U., 1977. Bar: Ariz. 1977, U.S. Dist. Ct. Ariz. 1977, U.S. Ct. Appeals (9th cir.) 1987; cert. specialist personal injury and wrongful death. Assoc. Wolfe & Harris, Pa., 1977-79, Monbleau, Vermeire & Turley, Phoenix, 1979-81, Phillips & Lyon, Phoenix, 1981; sole practice Phoenix, 1982-91; ptnr. Plattner Verderame, P.C., 1991—. Posse comdr. Maricopa County Sheriff Adj. Posse, 1986—; judge pro tem Maricopa County Superior Ct., 1986—, Ariz. Ct. Appeals, 1993—. Editor: Trial Judges of Maricopa County, 1985; co-editor Jury Verdict Research newsletter, 1982-83. Mem. ATLA (sustaining mem.), Am. Bd. Trial Advs. (assoc. 1997—), Ariz. Trial Lawyers Assn. (sustaining mem., editor Ariz. Appellate Highlights, 1985—, bd. dirs., 1987—, pres. 1991), Ariz. Bar Assn. (mem. civil practice and procedure com. 1988-99, civil jury instrn. com. 1991), Maricopa County Bar Assn., Phoenix Trial Lawyers Assn. (bd. dirs. 1983-95, pres. 1986-87), Ariz. Bus. and Profl. Assn. (pres. 1984-86). Insurance, Personal injury, Product liability. Office: PO Box 36570 Phoenix AZ 85067-6570 E-mail: rplattner@plattner-verderame.com

PLAX, KAREN ANN, lawyer; b. St. Louis, June 29, 1946; d. George J. and Evelyn G. Zell; m. Stephen E. Plax, Dec. 19, 1968; 1 child, Jonathan. BA magna cum laude, U. Mo., St. Louis, 1969; JD with distinction, U. Mo., Kansas City, 1976. Bar: Mo. 1976, U.S. Supreme Ct. 1980. Atty. Thayer, Gum & Wickert, Grandview, Mo., 1976-84, Plax & Cochet, Kansas City, 1984-87; pvt. practice, 1987—. Past chair divsn. 3, region IV Mo. Supreme Ct. Com. to review ethical conduct of attys., 1997-98. Author: Missouri Bar Practical Skills, 1998; asst. editor: Racial Integration in the Inner Suburb, 1970; contbr. articles to profl. jours. Recipient Pub. Svc. award U. Mo. Kansas City Law Found., 1998, Woman of Yr. award Assn. Women Lawyers of Greater Kansas City, 1999. Fellow: Am. Acad. Matrimonial Lawyers (pres. Mo. chpt. 1999—2001); mem.: ABA (family law sect. 1976—), Kansas City Met. Bar Assn., Mo. Bar Family Law (legis. chair 1997—98, v.p. 1999—2000, Spl. Commendation for Legis. Role in Family Law 1998). Family and matrimonial. Office: Ste 300 1310 Carondelet Dr Kansas City MO 64114-4803 E-mail: kaplax@swbell.net

PLAYER, MACK ALLEN, legal educator; b. Springfield, Mo., Aug. 24, 1941; s. Guy Allen and Pauline Ann (Mack) P.; m. Lois Ann Cook, June 4, 1964 (div. Aug. 1981); children— Evan Mack, Allen Cook; m. Jeanne Lois Milligan, Mar. 27, 1982. A.B. in Polit. Sci., Drury Coll., 1963; J.D., U. Mo., 1965; LL.M., George Washington U., 1972. Bar: Mo. 1965, U.S. Dist. Ct. (we. dist.) Mo. 1965, U.S. Ct. Appeals (8th cir.) 1966, U.S. Ct. Appeals (4th cir.) 1971, U.S. Ct. Appeals (5th cir.) 1971, U.S. Ct. Appeals (11th Cir.) 1984, U.S. Supreme Ct. 1972, Ga. 1975, U.S. Dist. Ct. (mid. dist.) Ga. 1984. Prof. law U. Ga., Athens, 1967-70, 72-78, 80— , Bd. Regents prof., 1983— ; atty. U.S. Dept. Labor, Washington, 1970-72; vis. prof. U. Hawaii, Honolulu, 1978-79, 81, 82; cons. Ga. Inst. Govt., Athens, 1975-80; spl. master Ga. Office Fair Employee Practices, Atlanta, 1984— . Author teaching casebook: Employment Discrimination Law, 1980, 2d edit., 1984; author handbook: Employment Discrimination in a Nutshell, 1976, 2d edit., 1980; contbr. numerous articles to legal jours. NEH fellow, summer 1981. Mem. Law Sch. Assn. Profs. U. Ga. Office: U Ga Sch Law Athens GA 30602

PLEASANT, JAMES SCOTT, lawyer; b. Anniston, Ala., July 14, 1943; s. James C. and Barbara (Scott) P.; m. Susan M. Pleasant, May 17, 1966; children: Deborah Kaye, Carol Ann, Julie Ruth. BS, Oreg. State U., 1965; JD summa cum laude, Williamette U., 1972. Bar: Tex. 1972, U.S. Dist. Ct. (no. dist.) Tex. 1973, U.S. Ct. Appeals (5th cir.) 1975, U.S. Supreme Ct. 1977. Ptnr. Gardere Wynne Sewell, LLP, Dallas, 1972—. Mem. Smithsonian Assn., Washington, 1985—, Dallas Mus. of Art, 1987—. Capt. U.S. Army, 1966-69, Vietnam. Mem. ABA (partnership law sect. 1969—), Tex. Bar Assn. (partnership law sect. 1989—), Vietnam Pilots Assn., Dustoff Assn. General corporate, Real property, Securities. Office: Gardere Wynne Sewell LLP 1601 Elm St Ste 3000 Dallas TX 75201-4761 E-mail: pleja@gardere.com

PLEICONES, COSTA M. judge; b. Greenville, SC, Feb. 29, 1944; BA in English, Wofford Coll., 1965; JD, U. SC, 1968. Pub. defender Richland County, SC; pvt. practice law; resident cir. ct. judge 5th Judicial Cir., 1991—2000; assoc. justice SC Supreme Ct., 2000. With JAG U.S. Army, 1968—73, with USAR, 1973—99. Office: SC Supreme Ct 1231 Gervais St Columbia SC 29211 also: PO Box 11330 Columbia SC 29211*

PLESKO, JEFFREY MICHAEL, lawyer; b. Streator, Ill., May 17, 1948; s. Manley and Gladys G. (Berta) P.; m. Megan Kathleen Miller, Oct 5, 1984; children: Megan Carter, Peter Michael. BA, U. Ill., 1970; JD, So. Ill. U., 1977. Bar: Ill. 1977, U.S. Dist. Ct. (so. dist.) Ill. 1977, U.S. Ct. Appeals (7th cir.) 1986, U.S. Supreme Ct. 1994. Asst. defender Ill. Office of State Appelate Defender, Mt. Vernon, 1977-80; mng. atty. Ill. Guardianship and Advocacy Commn., Carbondale, Ill., 1980-98, dir. Anna, 1998—. Presenter Chgo. Bar Assn., 1986, Am. Bar Assn., 1990; guest lectr. So. Ill. U. Sch. Law, Rehab. Inst., Behavior Analysis & Treatment Grad. Program, DePaul U. Sch. Law, Gov.'s Conf. on Aging and Human Svcs., Ctr. Comprehensive Svcs., Nat. Assn. Rights Protection & Advocacy, Behavior Analysis Soc. Ill., Ill. Assn. Rehab., So. Ill. Regional Family Law Pro Bono Project. Author: LAS Mental Health Decisions Outline. Mem. Mental Health Treatment & Evaluation Task Force, Dept. Pub. Health Alzheimer's Adv. Com., Gov.'s Task Force on Alzheimer's Disease, Dept. Human Svcs. So. Network Adv. Coun., Am. Disabilities Act Grievance Panel, Disability Rights Adv. Coun., Gov.'s Planning Coun. Devel. Disabilities. Served with U.S. Army, 1970-72, Germany. Recipient U.S. Law Week award Bur. Nat. Affairs, Inc., 1977, Alumni Achievement award So. Ill. Univ. Sch. Law, 2001. Mem. Ill. Bar Assn., So. Ill. U. Alumni Assn., Am. Motorcyclist Assn., Nat. Guardianship Assn., Ill. Guardianship Assn., Nat. Assn. Rights Protection & Advocacy, Jensen Healey Preservation Soc., Nat. Resources Def. Coun., Nature Conservancy. State civil litigation, Health, Probate. Office: Ill Guardianship and Advocacy Commn No 7 Cottage Dr Anna IL 62906 E-mail: jplesko@gac.il.state.us

PLESS, LAURANCE DAVIDSON, lawyer; b. Jacksonville, Fla., Dec. 22, 1952; s. James William Pless III and Anne (Dodson) Martin; m. Dana Halberg, June 20, 1980; children: Anna Amesbury, William Davidson, Deane Ahlgren. AB cum laude with distinction, Duke U., 1975; JD, U. N.C., Chapel Hill, 1980. Assoc. Neely & Player, P.C., Atlanta, 1980-86, ptnr., 1986-92, Welch, Spell, Reemsnyder, Pless & Davis, P.C., Atlanta, 1992—. Contbr. articles to profl. jours.; mem. staff N.C. Law Rev. Vol. Saturday Vol. Lawyer's Found., Atlanta, 1980-92; mem. bd. visitors U. N.C., Chapel Hill, 2001—; bd. dirs. Christian Coun. Met. Atlanta, 2000—. Mem. ABA, Lawyer's Club of Atlanta, Atlanta Bar Assn., Capital City Club, Lake Rabun Assn. Democrat. Episcopalian. Avocations: hiking, tennis, coaching kid's sports, canoeing. General corporate, General practice, Mergers and acquisitions. Home: 25 Palisades Rd NE Atlanta GA 30309-1530 E-mail: ldp@welchspell.com

PLETZ, THOMAS GREGORY, lawyer; b. Toledo, Oct. 3, 1943; s. Francis G. and Virginia (Connell) P.; m. Carol Elizabeth Connolly, June 27, 1969; children: Anne M., John F. BA, U. Notre Dame, 1965; JD, U. Toledo, 1971. Bar: Ohio 1971, U.S. Ct. Appeals (6th cir.) 1978, U.S. Supreme Ct. 1985. Ct. bailiff Lucas County Common Pleas Ct., Toledo, 1967-71; jud. clk. U.S. Dist. Ct. (no. dist.) Ohio, 1971-72; assoc. Shumaker, Loop & Kendrick, 1972-76, litigation ptnr., 1976—. Acting judge Sylvania (Ohio) Mcpl. Ct., 1990—; mem. Ohio Bar Bd. Examiners, 1993—, chmn., 1996-99. Active Toledo Parish Coun., 1987-2001; chmn., trustee Kiroff Trial Adv. Com., Toledo, 1982-91. With USNR, 1965-92; ret. CDR. Recipient Toledo Jr. Bar award, 1995. Mem. ABA, Ohio State Bar Assn., Toledo Bar Assn. (trustee 1981-93), Diocesan Attys. Bar Assn., 6th Cir. Jud. Conf. (life), Nat. Conf. Bar Examiners Com. Roman Catholic. General civil litigation, Education and schools, Libel. Office: Shumaker Loop & Kendrick 1000 Jackson St Toledo OH 43624-1573 E-mail: tpletz@slk-law.com

PLEVAN, KENNETH A. lawyer; b. Havre De Grace, Md., 1944; BA cum laude, Harvard U., 1966, JD cum laude, 1969. Bar: N.Y. 1970. Mem. Skadden, Arps, Slate, Meagher & Flom, LLC, N.Y.C. General civil litigation, Intellectual property, Trademark and copyright. Office: Skadden Arps Slate Meagher & Flom 4 Times Sq Fl 24 New York NY 10036-6595 E-mail: kplevan@aol.com

PLEVY, ARTHUR L. lawyer; b. N.Y.C., May 26, 1936; s. Louis and Sarah Plevy; children: Scott Eric, Robert Todd. Student, Bklyn. Coll., 1953-57; BEE, CCNY, 1959; LLB, JD, Bklyn. Law Sch., 1967. Bar: N.Y. 1965, N.J. 1970, Ct. Customs and Patent Appeals 1970, U.S. Supreme Ct. 1970. Design engr. IT&T Labs., Nutley, N.J., 1959-60; project engr. Westrex, N.Y.C., 1960-62; sr. mem. tech. staff RCA, 1962-65; patent counsel RCA Rsch. Ctr., Princeton, N.J., 1965-70; pvt. practice patent law Edison, 1970-98; sr. ptnr. Plevy & Assocs., 1991—. Cons. electronic firms; pres. New Ventures, Edison, N.J., 1970—; arbitrator Am. Arbitration Assn. Contbr. numerous articles on electronics, patent and trademark law to profl. jours.; patentee in field of electronics. Mem. ABA, IEEE, CCPA, N.J. Patent Law Scch., Fed. Bar Assn., N.Y. Bar Assn., N.J. Bar Assn., Masons. Patent, Trademark and copyright. Home: 77 Colfax Rd Skillman NJ 08558-2310 Office: Buchanan Ingersoll 650 College Rd E Princeton NJ 08540-6603 E-mail: plevyal@bipc.com

PLOSCOWE, STEPHEN ALLEN, lawyer; b. N.Y.C., Jan. 30, 1941; s. Samuel Stuart and Molly Florence (Slutsky) P.; m. Wendie Sue Malkin, Sept. 5, 1964; children— Jon, Lauren. B.S., Cornell U., 1962, LL.B., 1965. Bar: N.J. 1965, U.S. Dist. Ct. N.J. 1965, U.S. Ct. Appeals (3d cir.) 1979. Assoc. Cole, Berman & Belsky (and predecessor firm) Paterson, N.J. also Rochelle Park, N.J. 1965-69, ptnr., 1970-78; ptnr. Grotta, Glassman & Hoffman, Newark also Roseland, N.Y., 1979— ; borough atty. North Caldwell, N.J., 1973-79. Mem. Passaic County Bar Assn., Bergen County Bar Assn., N.J. State Bar Assn., Indsl. Relations Research Assn., ABA. Republican. Jewish. Club: Green Brook Country. Labor. Home: 76 Brookside Ter Caldwell NJ 07006-4413 Office: Grotta Glassman & Hoffman PA 75 Livingston Ave Ste 13 Roseland NJ 07068-3701 E-mail: ploscowes@gghlaw.com

PLOTKIN, LOREN H. lawyer; b. Bklyn., Feb. 8, 1943; s. Arthur and Betty Ann (Strugatz); m. Carol Baxter, Aug. 25, 1990; children: Lily, Kate. BA, Harpur Coll., SUNY, Binghamton, 1963; JD, St. John's U., N.Y.C., 1966. Bar: N.Y. 1966, U.S. Dist. Ct. (so. and ea. dists.) N.Y. 1972, U.S. Tax Ct. 1976. Law asst. appellate divsn., first dept. N.Y. State Supreme Ct.; ptnr. Lans Feinberg & Cohen, N.Y.C., 1969-81; mem. Levine & Thall, P.C., 1981-84, Levine Thall and Plotkin, N.Y.C., 1984-96, Levine Thall, Plotkin & Menin, L.L.P., N.Y.C., 1996-99, Levine, Plotkin & Menin, L.L.P., N.Y.C., 2000—. Lectr. on entertainment law. Notes and comments editor St. John's U. Law Rev., 1965-66. Entertainment, General practice, Real property. Home: 34 Lawrence Ln Palisades NY 10964-1604 Office: Levine Plotkin & Menin LLP 1740 Broadway Fl 22 New York NY 10019-4315

PLOTNICK, PAUL WILLIAM, lawyer; b. Chgo., Mar. 16, 1947; s. Sam and Mary P.; m. Eleanor Levy, Jan. 18, 1970; 1 child, Sarah Jennie. BA, So. Ill. U., 1969; JD, DePaul U., 1974. Bar: Ill. 1974., U.S. Dist. Ct. (no. dist.) Ill. 1974, U.S. Ct. Appeals (7th cir.) 1974, U.S. Tax Ct. 1975, U.S. Supreme Ct. 1977. Tchr. Chgo. Pub. Schs., 1969-74; pvt. practice Chgo., 1974-75; pres. Paul W. Plotnick, Ltd., Skokie, Ill., 1979—; asst. pub. defender Cook County Pub. Defender's Office, Chgo., 1975-79. Felony asst. Cook County Pub. Defender's Office, Evanston, Ill., 1976-79. Contbr. articles, poem to profl. publs. Pres. Budlong Woods Civic Group, Chgo., 1982-83; candidate for judge Circuit Ct. Cook County, 1998-2000. Staff sgt. U.S. Army, 1969. Named Man of the Yr. Midwest Fedn. Men's Clubs, 1995; recipient Disting. Svc. award Chgo. Vol. Legal Svcs., 1995. Mem. ABA, ATLA, Ill. State Bar Assn., Chgo. Bar Assn., N.W. Suburban Bar Assn., N. Suburban Bar Assn., Kiwanis (pres. Skokie Valley chpt. 1989-90, Disting. Sec. award 1987, Disting. Pres. award 1991, Lay Person of the Yr. I.I. Dist. divsn. 7), Beth Hillel Men's Club (pres. 1991-93), Decalogue Soc., Phi Kappa Phi (DePaul U. chpt. Disting. Alumnus). State civil litigation, Criminal, Real property. Office: Paul W Plotnick Ltd 9933 Lawler Ave Ste 312 Skokie IL 60077-3706

PLOTTEL, ROLAND, lawyer; b. N.Y.C., Oct. 1, 1934; s. Charles and Frances (Banner) P.; m. Jeanine Parisier, June 3, 1956; children— Claudia, Michael, Philip. B.A., Columbia U., 1955, LL.B., 1958, M.S. in E.E., 1964. Bar: N.Y. 1958, U.S. Patent Office 1962, U.S. Ct. Appeals 1964, U.S. Supreme Ct. 1964. House counsel Radiotronix Communications Labs., N.Y.C., 1958-61; patent atty. Bendix Corp., Teterboro, N.J., 1961-64; internat. patent atty. Western Electric Co., N.Y.C., 1964-70; sole practice, N.Y.C., 1970—; of counsel Frishauf, Holtz, Goodman & Woodward, N.Y.C.; lectr. patent law Practising Law Inst.; arbitrator Civil Ct., 1964—. Harlan Fiske Stone fellow. Mem. ABA, N.Y. County Lawyers Assn., Am. Intellectual Property Law Assn., N.Y. Patent Trademark and Copyright Law Assn., IEEE, Internat. Soc. Hybrid Microelectronics, Am. Arbitration Assn. Club: City N.Y. Intellectual property, Patent, Trademark and copyright. Home: 50 E 77th St New York NY 10021-1842 Office: 45 Rockefeller Plz New York NY 10111-0100

PLUCIENNIK, THOMAS CASIMIR, lawyer, former assistant county prosecutor; b. Irvington, N.J., Apr. 8, 1947; s. Casimir Stanley and Helen Victoria (Sienicki) P.; m. Maria Anne Soriano, June 16, 1974. BS in Acctg., Seton Hall U., 1969, JD, 1983; MA in Criminal Justice, CUNY, 1976. Bar: N.J. 1983, U.S. Ct. Mil. Appeals 1986, U.S. Dist. Ct. N.J. 1983, D.C. 1994, U.S. Supreme Ct. 1995, N.Y. 1996, U.S. Ct. Appeals (3rd cir.), U.S. Dist. Ct. (so., ea., fed. dists.) N.Y. 1998; cert. criminal trial atty., mil. trial atty.; lic. pvt. investigator. Mng. ptnr. Joe Bell's Tavern & Restaurant, Newark, 1979; police officer City of Newark, 1972-79; criminal investigator Essex County Prosecutor, Newark, 1980-84, asst. prosecutor, 1984-88; sr. asst. prosecutor Warren County, N.J., 1988-89; atty. Voorhees & Acciavatti Esq., Morristown, 1989-94; defense atty. Picillo Caruso, 1994-96; assoc. Netchert, Dineen & Hillman, 1996-97; litigator Francis J. Dooley, 1998-99; pvt. practice, 1999—. Cert. instr. N.J. State Police Tng. Commn., Trenton, 1984; asst. dir. instruction Officers Candidate Sch. N.J. Mil. Acad., Sea Girt. Committeeman South Orange Republican Club, N.J., 1978-83; treas., founder Tuxedo Park Neighborhood Assn., South Orange, 1977; fin. sec. J. T. Kosciusko Assn., Irvington, N.J., 1979. Served to 1st lt. U.S. Army, 1969-71, maj. (ret.) JAGC, 1985-90. Recipient Class C. Commendations, Newark Police Dept., 1973, 74, 75, Command Citations, 1973, 74, 75, 77, 78. Master: Worrall F. Mountain Inn of Ct., Masons; mem.: ATLA, ABA, Trial Attys. N.J., N.J. State Bar Assn., N.J. Def. Assn., Morris County Bar Assn., N.Y. State Bar Assn., Washington D.C. Bar Assn., Officers Club (pres. Sea Girt, N.J. 1979—81), Picatinny Officers Club, South Orange Lions Club (charter), Polish Univ. Club, Am. Legion, Congdon-Overlook Lodge #163, Ret. Officers Assn. Republican. Roman Catholic. General civil litigation, Criminal, Insurance. Home: 11 Laurel Ln Morris Plains NJ 07950-3216

PLUECKELMANN, KATJA, lawyer; b. Hagen, Westfalia, Germany, May 5, 1971; d. Udo Friedrich and Sigrid P. 1st state exam, U. Osrabrück, Germany, 1994, LLD, 2000; 2nd state exam, U. Düsseldorf, Germany, 1997. Assoc. Dr. Roggen, Düsseldorf, 1997-98, Kaufmann & Madsen, Cologne, Germany, 1998-99, Heunking Kuehn Lueer Wojtek, Düsseldorf, 2000—. Avocations: sailing, tennis, skiing. General corporate, Mergers and acquisitions, Securities. Office: Heuking Kuehn Lueer Wojtek Cecilienallee 5 40474 Düsseldorf Germany Fax: 49 (0) 211-60055050. E-mail: k.plueckelmann@heuking.de

PLUIMER, EDWARD J. lawyer; b. Rapid City, S.D., 1949; BA cum laude, U. S.D., 1971; JD cum laude, NYU, 1974. Bar: Minn. 1975. Law clk. to Hon. Robert A. Ainsworth, Jr. U.S. Ct. Appeals (5th cir.), 1974-75; ptnr. Dorsey & Whitney, Mpls., 1975—. Mem. Minn. Supreme Ct. ADR Task Force, 1988-92. Editor N.Y. U. Law Rev. Mem. Order of the Coif. General civil litigation, Franchising, Securities. Office: Dorsey & Whitney LLP 220 S 6th St Ste 2200 Minneapolis MN 55402-1498 E-mail: pluimer.ed@dorseylaw.com

PODBOY, ALVIN MICHAEL, JR. law library director, lawyer; b. Cleve., Feb. 10, 1947; s. Alvin Michael and Josephine Esther (Nagode) P.; m. Mary Ann Gloria Esposito, Aug. 21, 1971; children: Allison Marie, Melissa Ann. AB cum laude, Ohio U., 1969; JD, Case Western Res. U., 1972, MLS, 1977. Bar: Ohio 1972, U.S. Dist. Ct. (no. dist.) Ohio 1973, U.S. Supreme Ct. 1992. Assoc. Joseph T. Svete Co. LPA, Chardon, Ohio, 1972-76; dir. pub. svcs. Case Western Res. Sch. Law Libr., Cleve., 1974-77, assoc. law libr., 1977-78; libr. Baker & Hostetler, LLP, 1978-88, dir. librs., 1988—. Instr. Notre Dame Coll. of Ohio, Cleve., 1991—, Am. Inst. Paralegal Studies, Cleve., 1991-96. Mem. editl. adv. bd. Law Tech. News, 1999—. Bd. overseers Case Western Res. U., 1981-87, mem. vis. com. sch. libr. sci., 1980-86, mem. Westlaw adv. bd., 1987-92, bd. govs. law sch. alumni assn., 1992-95, West's Legal Directory Ohio Adv. Panel, 1990-91; mem. adv. com. West's Info. Innovators Inst., 1995-97; chmn. Case Western Res. Libr. Sch. Alumni Fund, 1979-80; Rep. precinct committeeman Cuyahoga County, Cleve., 1981-95, mem. exec. com., 1984-87. 1st lt. USAF, 1972. Mem.: ABA, Am. Assn. Law Librs. (cert., chmn. pvt. law librs. spl. interest sect. 1994—95, mem. exec. bd. 2001—), Ohio State Bar Assn. (chmn. librs. com. 1989—91, pres. 1985), Case Western Res. U. Libr. Sch. Alumni Assn., Arnold Air Soc., Ohio Regional Assn. Law Librs., Cleve. Bar Assn. (pres. 1981), KC, Pi Gamma Mu, Phi Alpha Theta. Roman Catholic. Avocation: alpine skiing. Home: 417 East Parkway Blvd Aurora OH 44202 Office: Baker & Hostetler LLP 3200 National City Ctr Cleveland OH 44114-3485 E-mail: apodboy@bakerlaw.com

PODGOR, ELLEN SUE, law educator; b. Bklyn., Jan. 30, 1952; d. Benjamin and Yetta (Shilensky) Podgor. BS magna cum laude, Syracuse U., 1973; JD, Ind. U., Indpls., 1976; MBA, U. Chgo., 1987; LLM, Temple U., 1989. Bar: Ind. 1976, N.Y. 1984, Pa. 1987. Dep. prosecutor Lake County Prosecutor's Office, Crown Point, Ind., 1976-78; ptnr. Nicholls & Podgor, 1978-87; instr. Temple U. Sch. Law, 1987-89; assoc. prof. law St. Thomas U., Miami, Fla., 1989-91, Ga. State U., Atlanta, 1991—. Vis. scholar Yale Law Sch., fall 1998; vis. prof. U. Ga., fall 2000. Author: (with Israel) White Collar Crime in a Nutshell, (with Israel and Borman) White Collar Crime: Law and Practice, (with Wise) International Criminal Law: Cases and Materials; assoc. editor Ind. Law Rev., 1975-76; contbr. articles to legal jours; mem. adv. bd. BNA Criminal Practice Manual. Del. Ind. Dem. Conv., 1982. Mem. ABA, NACDL, Am. Law Inst., Ind. Bar Assn. Democrat. Jewish. Office: Ga State U Coll Law PO Box 4037 Atlanta GA 30302-4037

PODHURST, AARON SAMUEL, lawyer; b. N.Y.C., Apr. 29, 1936; s. Louis and rae (Pomerantz) P.; m. Dorothy Ellen Podhurst, Sept. 7, 1958; children: Karen Beth Dern, Laura Koffsky, Julie Weinberg. BBA, U. Mich., 1957; JD, Columbia U., 1960. Bar: Fla., 1961, N.Y., 1961. Assoc. Nichols, Gaither, Miami, Fla., 1962-67; founding ptnr. Podhurst, Orseck, Josefsberg, Eaton, Meadow, Olin & Perwin, P.A., 1967—. Vice pres. Miami Coalition for Safe Cmty., 1994—; mem. Orange Bowl Com., Miami, 1996—. Recipient Nat. Medallion award NCCJ, 1994; Harlan Fiske Stone scholar, 1960. Mem. ABA (aviation com.), Internat. Acad. Trial Lawyers (pres. 1990), Acad. Fla. Trial Lawyers (pres. 1978, aviation com.), Am. Coll. Trial Lawyers, Assn. Trial Lawyers Am. (bd. govs., aviation com.), Internat. Soc. Barristers, Inner Cir. of Advocates. Aviation, Consumer commercial, Personal injury. Office: Podhurst Orseck Josefsberg Eaton Meadow Olin & Perwin PA 25 W Flagler St Miami FL 33130-1712

POFF, RICHARD HARDING, state supreme court justice; b. Radford, Va., Oct. 19, 1923; s. Beecher David and Irene Louise (Nunley) P.; m. Jo Ann R. Topper, June 24, 1945 (dec. Jan. 1978); children: Rebecca, Thomas, Richard Harding; m. Jean Murphy, Oct. 26, 1980. Student, Roanoke Coll., 1941-43; LL.B., U. Va., 1948, LL.D., 1969. Bar: Va. 1947. Partner law firm Dalton, Poff, Turk & Stone, Radford, 1949-70; mem. 83d-92d congresses, 6th Dist. Va.; justice Supreme Ct. Va., 1972-89, sr. justice, 1989—. Vice chmn. Nat. Commn. on Reform Fed. Crime Laws; chmn. Republican Task Force on Crime; sec. Rep. Conf., House Rep. Leadership. Named Va.'s Outstanding Young Man of Year Jr. C. of C., 1954; recipient Nat. Collegiate Athletic Assn. award, 1966, Roanoke Coll. medal, 1967, Distinguished Virginian award Va. Dist. Exchange Clubs, 1970, Presdl. certificate of appreciation for legislative contbn., 1971, legislative citation Assn. Fed. Investigators, 1969, Thomas Jefferson Pub. Sesquicentennial award U. Va., 1969, Japanese Am. Citizens League award, 1972, Carrio Professionalism award Va. State Bar Assn. Criminal Law Sect., 1998; named to Hall of Fame, Am. Legion Boys State, 1985; fellow Va. Law Found., 1997. Mem. Bar Assn., VFW, Am. Legion, Pi Kappa Phi, Sigma Nu Phi. Clubs: Mason, Moose, Lion. Office: Va Supreme Ct 100 N 9th St Richmond VA 23219-2335

POGREBIN, BERTRAND B. lawyer; b. Bklyn., Apr. 10, 1934; s. Abraham and Esther Pogrebin; m. Letty Cottin; children: Abigail, Robin, David. AB, Rutgers U., 1955; LLB, Harvard U., 1958. Bar: N.Y. 1959, U.S. Dist. Ct. (ea. and so. dists.) N.Y. 1963, U.S. Ct. Appeals (2d cir.) 1965, U.S. Ct. Appeals (4th cir.) 1965, U.S. Ct. Appeals (6th cir.) 1970, U.S. Ct. Appeals (9th cir.) 1987, U.S. Supreme Ct. 1991. Pres. Rains & Pogrebin, P.C., N.Y.C., 1959—. Adj. prof. law NYU, 1975-90, Hofstra Law Sch., 1980-82, 86-91, 97-98; vis. lectr. Yale Law Sch., 1983. Co-author: Labor Relations: The Basic Process, Law and Practice, 1988, 2d edit., 1999. Mem. Am. Jewish Congress; v.p., bd. dirs. Appleseed Found. Mem. ABA, N.Y.C. Bar Assn., Nassau County Bar Assn., Suffolk County Bar Assn., Indsl. Rels. Rsch. Assn. Education and schools, Labor, Pension, profit-sharing, and employee benefits. Home: 33 W 67th St New York NY 10023-6224 Office: 210 Old Country Rd Mineola NY 11501-4218 also: 375 Park Ave New York NY 10152-0002 E-mail: BPogrebin@Rainslaw.com

POGSON, STEPHEN WALTER, lawyer; b. N.Y.C., May 11, 1937; s. Percy Walter and Catherine (Hawbaker) P.; m. Linda Hammond, Aug. 20, 1966; children: Clyde Hammond, Catherine Anne. BA, U. Ariz., 1958, LLB, 1961. Bar: Ariz. 1961, U.S. Ct. Appeals (9th cir.) 1968, U.S. Supreme Ct. 1970. Assoc. Evans, Kitchel & Jenckes, Phoenix, 1962-67, ptnr., 1967-90; adminstrv. law judge Indrl. Commn. Ariz., 1990—, vice chief ALJ, 1997—. Served with U.S. Army, 1961-62. Mem. ABA. Democrat. Presbyterian. Office: 800 W Washington St Ste 400 Phoenix AZ 85007-2934

POGUE, L(LOYD) WELCH, lawyer; b. Grant, Iowa, Oct. 21, 1899; s. Leander Welch and Myrtle Viola (Casey) P.; m. Mary Ellen Edgerton, Sept. 8, 1926; children: Richard Welch, William Lloyd, John Marshall. AB, U. Nebr., 1924; JD, U. Mich., 1926; SJD, Harvard U., 1927. Bar: Mass., N.Y., D.C., Ohio, U.S. Supreme Ct. Assoc. Ropes, Gray, Boyden and Perkins, 1927-33; ptnr. affiliated firm Searle, James and Crawford, N.Y.C., 1933-38; asst. gen. counsel CAB, 1938-39, gen. counsel, through 1941, chmn. bd., 1942-46; mem., mng. ptnr. Pogue & Neal, Washington, 1946-67; Washington mng. ptnr. Jones, Day, Reavis & Pogue, 1967-79, ret., 1981. Lindbergh Meml. lectr. Nat. Air and Space Mus., Smithsonian Inst., 1991; presenter essay 50th Ann. Internat. Civil Aviation Orgn., Montreal, 1994; Wright Bros. Meml. lectr.; spkr. and lectr. in field. Author: International Civil Air Transport—Transition Following WW II, 1979, Pogue/Pollock/Polk Genealogy as Mirrored in History, 1990 (1st pl. in Anna Ford Family history book contest 1991, Nat. Genealogical Soc. award for excellence genealogy and family history 1992, William H. and Benjamin Harrison Book award Coun. Ohio Genealogists 1992, Outstanding Achievement award County and Regional History category Ohio Assn. Hist. Socs. and Mus. 1992, 1st pl. award Iowa Washington County Geneal. Soc. 1994, cert. commendation Am. Assn. State and Local History 1994, 1st place award Lake Havasu Geneal. Soc. 1996), Airline Deregulation, Before and After: What Next? (Lindbergh Meml. lectr. 1991), The International Civil Aviation Conference, and Its Sequel, The Anglo-American Bermuda Air Transport Agreement, 1946, 94; The Wright Brothers Memorial Lecture (Annually given) NASA Langley Research Center, 1999; contbr. articles to profl. publs. Mem. U.S. dels.: Chgo. Internat. Civil Aviation Conf., 1944; vice chmn. Bermuda United Kingdom-U.S. Conf., 1946; vice chmn. Provisional Internat. Civil Aviation Orgn. Assembly, 1946; active Internat. Civil Aviation Orgn. Assembly, 1947. With AUS, 1918. Recipient Elder Statesman of Aviation award Nat. Aeronautic Assn., Golden Eagle award Soc. Sr. Aerospace Execs., 1st annual recipient of L. Welch Pogue award for Aviation Achievement, McGraw-Hill Orgn.'s Aviation Week Group, 1994; fellow Am. Helicopter Soc., Benjamin Franklin fellow Royal Soc. Arts. Fellow Royal Aero. Soc.; mem. AIAA (hon.), Soc. of Sr. Aerospace Execs. (hon. mem.), Merit Certificate of 60 years of continuous membership. Helicopter Assn. Internat. (hon. mem.), Am. Air Mus. in Britain (founding mem.), Can. Aeronautics and Space Inst., Nat. Aeronautic Assn. (pres. 1947), Nat. Air and Space Soc. (founder), Nat. Geneal. Soc., Soc. Sr. Aerospace Execs., New Eng. Hist. Geneal. Soc. (life, former trustee), Ohio Geneal. Soc. (life), Md. Geneal. Soc. (life), Md. Hist. Soc. (life), Provincial Families of Md., First Families of Ohio, Met. Club, Univ. Club, Wings Club (hon., N.Y.C.), Bohemian Club (San Francisco), Cosmos Club, Masons, Order of the First World War (charter), Aero Club of Washington (hon. mem.), Am. Legion (cert. of 80 years continuous membership, Life Membership, 2002). Aviation, General corporate, Finance. Home: 5204 Kenwood Ave Chevy Chase MD 20815-6604 Office: Jones Day Reavis & Pogue 51 Louisiana Ave NW Washington DC 20001-2113

POGUE, RICHARD WELCH, lawyer; b. Cambridge, Mass., Apr. 26, 1928; s. Lloyd Welch and Mary Ellen (Edgarton) P.; m. Patricia Ruth Raney, July 10, 1954; children: Mark, Tracy, David. B.A., Cornell U., 1950; J.D., Mich. Law Sch., 1953. Bar: Mich. 1953, Ohio 1957, U.S. Dist. Ct. (no. dist.) Ohio 1960, U.S. Ct. Appeals (6th cir.) 1972, U.S. Ct. Appeals (D.C. and 9th cirs.) 1979. Assoc. Jones, Day, Reavis & Pogue, Cleve., 1957-60, ptnr., 1961—, mng. ptnr., 1984-92, sr. ptnr., 1993-94; sr. advisor Dix & Eaton, 1994—. Vis. prof. Mich. Law Sch., 1993-95; bd. dirs. Derlan Industries, Toronto, Continental Airlines, Inc., Houston, OHM Corp., Findlay, Ohio, M.A. Hanna Co., Cleve., Redland PLC, Reigate, Eng., Rotek Inc., Aurora, Ohio, Key Corp., Cleve, TRW Inc., Cleve. Chmn. Cleve. Found., 1985-89, Greater Cleve. Roundtable, 1986-89, Greater Cleve. Growth Assn., 1991-93, Univ. Hosps., 1994—, trustee 1975—, Cleve. Ballet, 1983-85, United Negro Coll. Fund., Cleve., 1979. Mem. Adminstrv. Conf. U.S., 1974-80; vice chmn. Cleve. Tomorrow, 1988-93, 50 Club Cleve., 1988-89; United Way Cleve., 1989; trustee Case Western Res. U.; active Coun. Fgn. Rels., 1989—, Am./EC Assn. Bus. Adv. Coun., 1988-93; trustee Rock and Roll Hall of Fame and Mus., 1986—; co-chmn. 1996 Cleve. Bicentennial Commn., interim chmn. Cleve. Inst. Music, 1994. Army, 1954-57. Recipient Outstanding Alumnus award U. Mich. Club, Cleve., 1983, Torch of Liberty award Anti-Defamation League, 1989, Leadership Cleve. Vol. of Yr. award, 1990, 1st Econ. Devel. Workshop award Nat. Coun. on Urban Econ. Devel., 1992, Humanitarian award Nat. Conf. Christians and Jews, 1992. Mem. ABA (chmn. antitrust sect. 1983-84), Ohio State Bar Assn. (chmn. antitrust sect. 1969-73). Clubs: Bohemian (San Francisco), Soc., Union (Cleve.), Metropolitan (Washington), Links (N.Y.C.). Republican. Mem. United Ch. of Christ. Antitrust.

POHL, MICHAEL A. lawyer; b. Cleve., Oct. 25, 1942; s. Irwin P. and Ruth B. (Bishko) P.; m. Ellen Durchslag, Dec. 12, 1970 (div. 1982); children: Matthew E., Andrew F. BA, Amherst Coll., 1965; JD, Case Western Res. U., 1968. Bar: Ohio 1968, Fla. 1972, U.S. Supreme Ct. 1974. Atty. NLRB, 1971-72; asst. state's atty. for Dade County State of Fla., Miami, 1973-74; asst. dir. of law City of Cleve., 1979-83; instr. employment discrimination law and Title VII Cleve. State U., 1982-83; litigation mgr. Leader Nat. Ins. Co., 1985-90, Ins. Inst. Am., 1990—; Mazanec, Raskin & Ryder Co., L.P.A., Cleve., 1991-95; Ulmer & Berne, 1995-96; Reid, Berry & Stanard, 1997-98; asst. v.p. Aon Risk Services, 1998-2000; Henderson, Franklin, Starnes & Holt, P.A., Ft. Myers, Fla., 2000—. Mem. Ohio State Bar Assn., The Fla. Bar., Defense Research Inst. Avocations: opera, golf. General civil litigation, Insurance, Personal injury. Home: Gulf Harbour 14971 Rivers Edge Ct #204 Fort Myers FL 33908 Office: Henderson Franklin Starnes & Holt PA PO Box 280 Fort Myers FL 33902-0280 Fax: 941-334-4100

POHL, PAUL MICHAEL, lawyer; b. Erie, Pa., July 17, 1948; s. Joseph Paul and Mary (Strenio) P.; m. Kaya Lynn Gavriloff, Aug. 13, 1970; children: Thomas Michael, Mary Elizabeth, Michael David. AB, Princeton U., 1970; JD, U. Pitts., 1975. Bar: Pa. 1975, Ohio 1976, U.S. Dist. Ct. (we. dist.) Pa. 1975, U.S. Dist. Ct. (no. dist.) Ohio 1976, U.S. Ct. Appeals (5th cir.) 1980, U.S. Ct. Appeals (11th cir.) 1983, U.S. Ct. Appeals (1st, 3d and 6th cir.) 1993, U.S. Ct. Appeals (D.C. cir.) 1995. Reporter Erie Daily Times, 1970-71; law clk. to presiding justice Pa. Supreme Ct., 1975-76; assoc. Jones, Day, Reavis & Pogue, Cleve., 1976-82, ptnr., 1982—, ptnr.-in-charge Pitts., 1989—. Guest mem. faculty Sch. Law, Hofstra U., Hempstead, N.Y., 1982, 84; mem. trial advocacy program Sch. Law, Emory U., Atlanta, 1983—; bd. dirs. JURA Corp., Erie, Lord Corp., Cary, N.C.; mem. CLE bd. Supreme Ct. of Pa. Co-author: Conflicts of Interest—A Trial Lawyers Guide, 1984. Bd. dirs. Franciscan U., Steubenville, Ohio, 1991—, vice chmn., 1994—; bd. dirs. Gannon U., Erie; chmn. bd. dirs. Seton Hill Coll., Greensburg, Pa., 1997—; mem. supervisory bd. Found. Maria Thron, Gaming, Austria, 1996—. With USMC, 1971-72. Named one of Cleve.'s 78 Most Interesting People, Cleve. mag., 1978. Mem. Cleve. Bar Assn. (mem. com. task force on violent crime 1983). Roman Catholic. Antitrust, Federal civil litigation, State civil litigation. Office: Jones Day Reavis & Pogue 500 Grant St Pittsburgh PA 15219-2502 also: Jones Day Reavis & Pogue 901 Lakeside Ave E Cleveland OH 44114-1116

POINTER, SAM CLYDE, JR. retired federal judge, lawyer; b. Birmingham, Ala., Nov. 15, 1934; s. Sam Clyde and Elizabeth Inzer (Brown) P.; m. Paula Purse, Oct. 18, 1958; children: Minge, Sam Clyde III. A.B., Vanderbilt U., 1955; J.D., U. Ala., 1957; LL.M., NYU, 1958. Bar: Ala. 1957. Ptnr. Brown, Pointer & Pointer, 1958-70; judge U.S. Dist. Ct. (no. dist.) Ala., Birmingham, 1970-2000, chief judge, 1982-99; judge Temp. Emergency Ct. Appeals, 1980-87; mem. Jud. Panel Multi-dist. Litigation, 1980-87; ptnr. Lightfoot, Franklin & White, 2000—. Mem. Jud. Conf. U.S., 1987-90; mem. Jud. Coun. 11th Cir., 1987-90, mem. standing com. on rules, 1988-90, chmn. adv. com. on civil rules, 1990-93. Bd. editors: Manual for Complex Litigation, 1979-91. Mem. ABA, Ala. Bar Asn., Birmingham Bar Assn., Am. Law Inst., Am. Judicature Soc., Farrah Order of Jurisprudence, Phi Beta Kappa. Episcopalian. Office: Lightfoot Franklin & White The Clark Bldg 400 N 20th St Birmingham AL 35203 E-mail: spointer@lfwlaw.com

POKA LAENUI, See BURGESS, HAYDEN FERN

POKEMPNER, JOSEPH KRES, lawyer; b. Monessen, Pa., June 11, 1936; s. Leonard and Ethel Lee (Kres) P.; m. Judith Montague Stephens, Aug. 23, 1970; children: Elizabeth, Jennifer, Amy. AB, Johns Hopkins U., 1957; LLB, U. Md., 1962. Bar: Md. 1962. Law clk. to judge Supreme Bench Balt., 1960-62; field atty. 5th region NLRB, 1962-64; pvt. practice labor law Balt., 1964—; ptnr. Wolf, Pokempner & Hillman, 1972-86, Whiteford, Taylor & Preston, Balt., 1986—. Contbr. articles to legal jours. Capt. AUS, 1969-74. Mem. ABA, Fed. Bar Assn. (pres. Balt. chpt. 1979-80), Md. Bar Assn., Balt. Bar Assn. (pres. 1984-85), Serjeant's Inn Law Club. Jewish. E-mial. Labor. Home: 1500 Willow Ave Baltimore MD 21204-3611 E-mail: jpokempner@wtplaw.com

POLAK, CAROL SCHRIER, lawyer; BA, Brandeis U., 1967; MSW, SUNY, Buffalo, 1969; JD, Temple U., 1977. Bar: D.C. 1978, Va. 1983. Assoc. planner Comty. Coun. Atlanta, 1969-72, project coord., 1972-73; exec. dir. Coun. for Children, 1973-74, Support Ctr. for Child Advocacy, Phila., 1977-83; legal cons. ABA, Washington, 1983-84; assoc. Sharon Lieblich, Alexandria, Va., 1984-88; ptnr. Bean, Kinney & Korman, Arlington, 1988—. Mem. faculty Va. State Bar Professionalism Course, 1999-2001; bd. dirs. No. Va. Legal Svcs., Arlington, 1991-97, Mental Health Assn. Va., Fairfax, 1989-92; bd. govs. Va. State Bar Family Law Soc., 1990-94. Fellow Am. Acad. Matrimonial Lawyers (sec.-treas. 1999-2001, v.p. 2001—); mem. Fairax Bar Assn. (pres. 1997-98). Family and matrimonial. Office: Bean Kinney & Korman 2000 14th St N Ste 100 Arlington VA 22201-2552

POLAK, WERNER L. lawyer; b. Bremen, Germany, May 19, 1936; came to U.S., 1946, naturalized, 1955; s. Ludwig and Hilde (Schultz) P.; m. Evelyn F. Ruhmann, June 21, 1959; children— Douglas H., Deborah L. BA, Columbia U., 1960, LLB, 1963. Bar: N.Y. 1963. Assoc., Shearman & Sterling, N.Y.C., 1963-72, ptnr., 1972— . Served with U.S. Army, 1954-56. Mem. Trustee Practicing Law Inst. Federal civil litigation, General civil litigation, State civil litigation. Office: Shearman & Sterling 599 Lexington Ave New York NY 10022-6069

POLANSKY, LARRY PAUL, court administrator, consultant; b. Blkyn., July 24, 1932; s. Harry and Ida (Gershgom) P.; m. Eunice Kathryn Neun; children: Steven, Harriet, Bruce. BS in Acctg., Temple U., 1958, JD, 1973. Bar: Pa. 1973, U.S. Dist. Ct. (ea. dist.) Pa. 1973, U.S. Ct. Appeals (3d cir.) 1973, D.C. 1978, U.S. Supreme Ct. 1980. Acct., systems analyst City of Phila., 1956-63; data processing mgr. Jefferson Med. Coll. and Hosp., Phila., 1963-65; systems engr. IBM Corp., 1965-67; dep. ct. adminstr. Common Pleas Cts. of Phila., 1967-76; dep. state ct. adminstr. Pa. Supreme Ct., Phila., 1976-78; exec. officer D.C. Cts., Washington, 1979-90. Presdl. appt. to bd. dirs. State Justice Inst., 1985-89; bd. dirs. Search Group, Inc. Author: A Primer for the Technologically Challenged Judge, 1995; contbr. articles to profl. jours. Served as cpl. U.S. Army, 1951-53, Korea. Fellow Inst. for Ct. Mgmt., Denver, 1984; recipient Reardon award Nat. Ctr. for State Cts., 1982, Disting. Svc. award Nat. Ctr. for State Cts., 1986, Justice Tom C. Clark award Nat. Conf. of Metro. Cts., 1991, award of merit Nat. Assn. Ct. Mgmt., 1996. Mem. ABA (jud. adminstrn. divsn., chmn. tech. com. 1991-93, 95, exec. com. lawyers conf. 1985-98, chmn. 1991-92, JAD coun. 1994-97), Conf. State Ct. Adminstrn. (bd. dirs. 1980-86, pres. 1984-85). Republican. Jewish. Avocations: tennis, skiing, computers, golf. Home and Office: PO Box 752 Lake Harmony PA 18624-0752 E-mail: polanskyl@aol.com

POLASZEK, CHRISTOPHER STEPHEN, lawyer; b. Denville, N.J., May 9, 1970; s. Leon and Danuta Lydia Polaszek. BS cum laude, Fla. State U., 1992, MBA, JD cum laude, 1997. Bar: Fla. 1997, U.S. Dist. Ct. (mid. dist.) Fla. 1997, U.S. Ct. Appeals (11th cir.) 1997. Atty. Fowler, White, Gillen, Boggs, Villareal & Banker, Tampa, Fla., 1997—. Vol. Habitat for Humanity, Tallahassee, Fla., 1994, Met. Ministries Adopt a Family, Tampa, Fla., 1997; com. mem. Suncoast Children's Dream Fund, St. Petersburg, Fla., 1998-99. Mem. ABA, Fla. Def. Lawyer's Assn., Fla. Bar Assn. (workers'compensation sect. 1997—), Cath. Lawyer's Guild, Hillsborough County Bar Assn. Roman Catholic. Avocations: fitness, fishing, golf, traveling. Appellate, Workers' compensation. Office: Fowler White Gillen Boggs Villareal & Banker Ste 1700 501 E Kennedy Tampa FL 33602

POLIAKOFF, GARY A. lawyer, educator; b. Greenville, S.C, Nov. 25, 1944; s. Herman and Dorothy (Ravitz) P.; m. Sherri D. Dublin, June 24, 1967; children: Ryan, Keith. BS, U. S.C., 1966; JD, U. Miami, 1969. Bar: Fla. 1969, D.C. 1971, Colo. 1999. Founding prin., sr. ptnr., pres. Becker & Poliakoff, P.A., Hollywood, Miami, Naples, Sarasota, West Palm Beach, Clearwater, Tampa, Ft. Myers, Boca Raton, St Petersburg, Orlando, Ft. Walton Beach, Fla., Prague and Beijing, 1973—. Adj. prof. condominium law and practice Nova Southeastern U.; panelist Nat. Confs. Community Assns.; testified before coms. of the U.S. Senate on Condominiums; lectr. ann. condominium seminars Fla. Bar; participant Fla. Law Revision Council; cons. to State Legis. and the White House in drafting Condominium and Coop. Abuse Relief Act, 1980; mem. condominium study commn. State of Fla., 1990; chmn. State of Fla. Advisory Coun. on Condominiums, 1992, 93.; atty. Town of Southwest Ranches. Author: The Law of Condominium Operations, 1988; co-author: Florida Condominium Law and Practice, 1982, The Florida Bar Continuing Legal Education, 1982; contbr. articles to legal jours. Mem. pres.'s adv. group U. S.C., U.S.C. Ednl. Found., 1999—. Recipient Judge Learned Hand award Am. Jewish Com. for devel. of co-ownership housing law, 1999. Mem. Fla. Bar (co-chmn. legis. sub-com. condominium and coop. law), Coll. Cmty. Assn. Lawyers (bd. govs.), Scribes. Real property.

POLICY, VINCENT MARK, lawyer; b. Warren, Ohio, Mar. 29, 1948; s. Vincent James and Anna Marie (Berardi) P.; m. Katherine Anne Veazey; children: Nicholas, Katherine Nicole. BA, U. Md., 1970; JD, Georgetown U., 1973. Bar: N.Y. 1974, D.C. 1975, U.S. Supreme Ct. 1977. Assoc. Cahill Gordon & Reindel, Washington and N.Y.C., 1973-78, Hogan & Hartson, Washington, 1978-85; prin. Pohoryles & Greenstein PC, 1985-89, Greenstein, Delorme & Luchs, P.C., Washington, 1989—. Author: Speedy Trial, A Constitutional Right in Search of Definition, 1973. Mem. D.C. Bar Assn. (chmn. rental housing com. 1985-88), D.C. Assn. Realtors (speaker 1984—), Apt. and Office Bldg. Assn. (lectr. 1985—), Greater Washington Bd. Trade (subcom. on initiatives, econ. growth com.), D.C. Builders Assn. (legis. affairs com.), Phi Beta Kappa, Omicron Delta Kappa. Democrat. Roman Catholic. Lodge: KC. Avocation: sailing. Banking, State civil litigation, Real property. Office: Greenstein DeLorme & Luchs 1620 L St NW Ste 900 Washington DC 20036-5613

POLIN, ALAN JAY, lawyer; b. N.Y.C., Sept. 5, 1953; s. Mortin and Eleanor (Clarke) P.; m. Sharon Lynn Hirschfeld, Oct. 10, 1976; children: Jay Michael, Meryl Beth. Student, Cornell U., 1971-74; BA cum laude, Seton Hall U., 1978; JD, Nova U., 1981. Bar: Fla. 1981, N.Y. 1990; lic. athlete agt., Fla. Assoc. Berryhill, Avery, Williams & Jordan, Esq., Ft. Lauderdale, Fla., 1981-82, Greenspoon & Marder, P.A., Miami, 1982-83; pvt. practice Ft. Lauderdale, 1983-86; ptnr. Mousaw, Vigdor, Reeves & Hess, 1986-90; pvt. practice Coral Springs, Fla., 1990—. Adj. faculty mem.

Nova U; mem. grievance com. Fla. Bar, 1989-92, vice chair, 1990-91, chair, 1991-92. Chmn. Broward County Crct. Ct. Handbook, 1988; contbr. chpt. to Bridge the Gap Attorney's Handbook, 1987. Dir. Temple Beth Am., Margate, Fla., 1991-93; mem. Anti-Defamation League, Fla. Regional Bd., 1994—; mem. exec. com. Broward County Dem., 1989-96; vice mayor City of Coral Springs, 1994-96, commr., 1991—; mem. bd. dirs. Fla. Regional Bd. of Anti-Defamation League, 1994—, Children's Cardiac Rsch. Found., Inc., 1996—, The Irving Fryer Found., Inc., 1995-96, Am. Heart Assn., 1997—; mem. bd. dirs. Junior Achievement South Fla., 2001-. Recipient Am. Jurisprudence award Nova U. Law Ctr., 1981, Disting. Pub. Svc. award, Anti-Defamation League, 2000. Mem. Fla. Bar Assn. (bd. govs. young lawyers divsn. 1987-89), Broward County Bar Assn. (exec. com. young lawyers sect. 1986-87), North Broward Assn. Realtors, Inc. (affiliate, std. contract forms com. 1989-95, atty./realtor rels. com. 1989-91), Kiwanis (Key Club advisor 1990-91). Contracts commercial, Estate planning, Real property. Office: 3300 University Dr Ste 601 Coral Springs FL 33065-4132 E-mail: alanpolin@polinlaw.com

POLITZ, HENRY ANTHONY, federal judge; b. Napoleonville, La., May 9, 1932; s. Anthony and Virginia (Russo) P.; m. Jane Marie Simoneaux, Apr. 29, 1952; children: Nyle, Bennett, Mark, Angela, Scott, Jane, Michael, Henry, Alisa, John, Nina. BA, La. State U., 1958, JD, 1959. Bar: La. 1959. Assoc., then ptnr. firm Booth, Lockard, Jack, Pleasant & LeSage, Shreveport, 1959-79; judge U.S. Ct. Appeals (5th cir.), 1979-99, chief judge, 1992-99, sr. cir. judge, 1999—. Vis. prof. La. State U. Law Center; bd. dirs. Am. Prepaid Legal Services Inst., 1975— ; mem. La. Judiciary Commn., 1978-79; mem. U.S. Jud. Conf., 1992-99, exec. com., 1996-99. Mem. editl. bd. La. State U. Law Rev., 1958-59. Mem. Shreveport Airport Authority, 1973-79, chmn., 1977; bd. dirs. Rutherford House, Shreveport, 1975— , pres., 1978; pres. Caddo Parish Bd. Election Suprs., 1975-79; mem. Electoral Coll., 1976. Served with USAF, 1951-55. Named Outstanding Young Lawyer in La., 1971, Outstanding Alumnus La. State U. Law Sch., 1991; inducted in La. State U. Hall of Distinction, 1992. Mem. Am. Bar Assn., Am. Judicature Soc., Internat. Soc. Barristers, La. Bar Assn., La. Trial Lawyers Assn., Shreveport Bar Assn., Justinian Soc., K.C., Omicron Delta Kappa. Democrat. Roman Catholic. Office: US Ct Appeals 300 Fannin St Ste 5226 Shreveport LA 71101-3120 E-mail: henry_politz@ca5.uscourts.gov

POLITZ, NYLE ANTHONY, lawyer; b. Lake Charles, La., May 7, 1953; s. Henry Anthony and Jane Marie (Simoneaux) P.; m. Catherine Bordelon, May 28, 1977; children: Brandon, Jared, Caroline. Student, La. State U., Shreveport, 1971-72, U. Guadalajara, 1972, La. State U., 1972-74, JD, 1977. Bar: La. 1978, U.S. Dist. Ct. (ea., mid. and we. dists.) La. 1978, U.S. Ct. Appeals (5th cir.) 1979. Assoc. Booth, Lockard, Jack, Pleasant & LeSage, Shreveport, La., 1978-79; ptnr. Booth, Lockard, Politz, LeSage & D'Anna, L.L.C., 1979-96; assoc. Pendley Law Firm, Plaquemine, La., 1996-98; ptnr. Jones, Odom, Davis & Politz, LLP, Shreveport, 1998—. Lectr. La. State U., Shreveport. Resolutions com. La. Dem. Party, 1980; bd. dirs. Liberty Bank & Trust, Greenwood, La., 1980-86. Mem. ABA, ATLA, La. State Bar Assn. (ho. of dels. 1986-98), La. Trial Lawyers Assn. (bd. govs. 1983-94), Shreveport Bar Assn. (exec. com. 1983-85, 93-94, bd. dirs. pro bono project, chmn. 1993-94), N.W. La. Trial Lawyers Assn. (treas. 1987-90), KC. Democrat. Roman Catholic. Avocations: whitetail deer and wild turkey hunting, golf. General civil litigation, Personal injury, Toxic tort. Office: Jones Odom et al PO Box 1320 Shreveport LA 71164-1320 E-mail: nyle.politz@jodplaw.com

POLK, LEE THOMAS, lawyer; b. Chgo., Feb. 25, 1945; s. Lee Anthony and Mary Josephine (Lane) P.; m. Susan Luzader, Mar. 21, 1975; children: Adam, Angela. AB, Coe Coll., 1967; JD, U. Chgo., 1970. Bar: Ill. 1970, U.S. Dist. Ct. (no. dist.) Ill. 1970, U.S. Ct. Mil. Appeals 1972, U.S. Dist. Ct. (ea. dist.) Mich. 1983, U.S. Claims Ct. 1983, U.S. Ct. Appeals (7th cir.) 1984, U.S. Ct. Appeals (6th cir.) 1987, U.S. Tax Ct. 1987, U.S. Ct. Appeals (3rd cir.) 1989, U.S. Dist. Ct. (ea. dist.) Wis. 1998. Assoc. firm Vedder, Price, Kaufman & Kammholz, Chgo., 1970-72, 75-77, ptnr., 1977-86, Murphy, Smith & Polk, 1986-98, Ogletree, Deakins, Murphy, Smith & Polk, 1999—. Author: ERISA Practice & Litigation, 1993, updated annually; contbr. articles on employee benefits and health law to profl. jours. Served to capt. JAGC, U.S. Army, 1972-75. Fellow Am. Coll. Employee Benefits Counsel (charter); mem. ABA (sects. on real property, trust and probate, chair ESOP com. tax and bus.), Am. Soc. Writers on Legal Subjects, Ill. Bar Assn., Chgo. Bar Assn. (chmn. employee benefits com. 1987-88), Midwest Pension Conf. (chmn. Chgo. chpt. 1986), Am. Health Lawyers Assn., Phi Beta Kappa, Phi Kappa Phi, Union League Club. Roman Catholic. General corporate, Health, Pension, profit-sharing, and employee benefits. Home: 820 Sheridan Rd Evanston IL 60202-2513 Office: Ogletree Deakins Murphy Smith & Polk 2 1st Nat Plz Fl 25 Chicago IL 60603 E-mail: lee.polk@odnss.com

POLLACK, JANE SUSAN, lawyer; BS, U. Pa.; JD, Rutgers U., 1976; LLM, NYU, 1983. Bar: N.J. 1976, U.S. Dist. Ct. N.J. 1976, N.Y. 1982. Assoc. McCarter & English, Newark, 1976-82; labor counsel CBS, Inc., N.Y.C., 1982-84, broadcast counsel, 1984-87; assoc. gen. counsel Athlone Industries, Inc., Parsippany, N.J., 1987-93; v.p., sec., gen. counsel Forstmann & Co., N.Y.C., 1993-95, BMW of N.Am., Inc., 1995—. Assoc. trustee U. Pa.; mem. editorial bd. N.J. Lawyer. Mem. ABA, N.J. Bar Assn., Am. Corp. Counsel Assn., Assn. of Bar of City of N.Y.), Trustees Coun. Penn Women, Phi Beta Kappa. Republican. General corporate, Entertainment, Labor. Home: 280 Millburn Ave Millburn NJ 07041-1704 Office: BMW of NAm Inc 300 Chestnut Ridge Rd Woodcliff Lake NJ 07677-7731

POLLACK, JESSICA GLASS, lawyer; b. Bridgeport, Conn., June 29, 1964; d. MacEllis Kopel and Judith Wilson Glass; m. Russel Leon Pollack, Apr. 19, 1964; children: Nathaniel Bruce, Jason Henry. BA, Barnard Coll., 1986; JD, U. Chgo., 1990. Assoc. Shearman & Sterling, London, N.Y.C., 1990-94, White & Case, Budapest, N.Y.C., 1994-96; corp. counsel securities and fin. Colgate-Palmolive Co., N.Y.C., 1996—. Office: Colgate-Palmolive Co 300 Park Ave Fl 8 New York NY 10022-7499

POLLACK, MICHAEL, lawyer; b. N.Y.C., July 14, 1946; s. Irving and Bertha (Horowitz) P.; m. Barbara Linda Shore, Aug. 23, 1970; children: Matthew, Ilana. BEng, Cooper Union, 1967; MS, U. Pa., 1970; JD, Temple U., 1974. Bar: Pa. 1974, U.S. Dist. Ct. (ea. dist.) Pa. 1974. Rsch. scientist Pa. Rsch. Assocs., Phila., 1968-69; engr. GE Co., Valley Forge, Pa., 1969-70, Burroughs Corp., Great Valley, 1970-71; assoc. Blank, Rome, Comisky & McCauley, Phila., 1974-82, ptnr., 1982—. Ptnr. and mem. mgmt. com. dept. real estate Blank, Rome, Comisky & McCauley, 1997—; lectr., course planner Pa. Bar Inst., Phila. Mem. ABA, Pa. Bar Assn., Phila. Bar Assn., Internat. Assn. Attys. and Execs. in Corp. Real Estate, Eta Kappa Nu, Tau Beta Pi. Republican. Avocations: music, tennis. Real property. Office: Blank Rome Comisky & McCauley 1 Logan Sq Fl 3 Philadelphia PA 19103-6998 E-mail: pollack@blankrome.com

POLLACK, MILTON, federal judge; b. N.Y.C., Sept. 29, 1906; s. Julius and Betty (Schwartz) P.; m. Lillian Klein, Dec. 18, 1932 (dec. July 1967); children: Stephanie Pollack Miller, Daniel A.; m. Moselle Baum Erlich, Oct. 24, 1971. A.B., Columbia U., 1927, J.D., 1929. Bar: N.Y. 1930. Assoc. Gilman & Unger, N.Y.C., 1929-38; ptnr. Unger & Pollack, 1938-44; propr. Milton Pollack, 1945-67; dist. judge U.S. Dist. Ct. (so. dist.) N.Y., 1967—, sr. status, 1983. Mem. com. on ct. adminstrn. Jud. Conf., 1968-87, mem. Jud. Panel on Multi-dist. Litigation, 1983-95. Mem. Prospect Park So. Assn., Bklyn., pres., 1948-50, counsel, 1950-60, bd. dirs., 1945-60; mem. local SSS, 1952-60; chmn. lawyers div. Fedn. Jewish Philanthropies, 1957-61, vice chmn., 1954-57; chmn. lawyers div. Am. Jewish Com., 1964-66, bd. dirs., from 1967; hon. dir. Beth Isreal Hosp.; trustee Temple Emanu-El, from 1977, v.p., from 1978. Decorated chevalier Legion of Honor (France); recipient Learned Hand award Am. Jewish Com., 1967, Proskauer medal lawyers divsn. Fedn. Jewish Philanthropies, 1968, Disting. Svc. medal N.Y. County Lawyers Assn., 1991, Fordham-Stein Prize award, 1994, Devitt award Disting. Svc. to Justice, 1995. Mem. ABA, N.Y. State Bar Assn., Assn. of Bar of City of N.Y., Columbia Law Sch. Alumni Assn. (pres. 1970-72), Harmonie Club (past bd. trustees). Office: US Dist Ct US Courthouse Foley Sq New York NY 10007-1501

POLLAK, JAY MITCHELL, lawyer; b. Chgo., Apr. 5, 1937; s. Bertram L. and Florence (Molner) P.; m. Patricia Pollak, May 11, 1963; children: Mitchell Emery, John Andrew. BS, Miami U., Oxford, Ohio, 1959; JD, Northwestern U., 1962. Bar: Ill. 1962, U.S. Dist. Ct. (no. dist.) Ill. 1971, U.S. Ct. Appeals (7th cir.) 1982, U.S. Supreme Ct. 1982. V.p. Pollak & Hoffman LTD, Northbrook, Ill., 1963—. Atty. Counsel to Northbrook (Ill.) Hist. Soc.; prosecutor Village of Northbrook; mem. Page Ctr. for Entrepreneurship at Miami U. Pres. Northbrook Hockey League, 1986-88; mem. bus. adv. coun. Miami U., mem. adv. bd. Mem. ABA (anti-trust law sect.), Ill. Bar Assn., Chgo. Bar Assn., Forum Com. on Franchising, Atty. Gen.'s Ill. Franchise Adv. Bd. General corporate, Probate, Real property. Home: 846 Dundee Rd Northbrook IL 60062-2705 Office: Pollak and Hoffman Ltd 1200 Shermer Rd Ste 301 Northbrook IL 60062-4563 E-mail: jomi37@aol.com

POLLAK, LOUIS HEILPRIN, judge, educator; b. N.Y.C., Dec. 7, 1922; s. Walter and Marion (Heilprin) P.; m. Katherine Weiss, July 25, 1952; children: Nancy, Elizabeth, Susan, Sarah, Deborah. A.B., Harvard, 1943; LL.B., Yale, 1948. Bar: N.Y. bar 1949, Conn. bar 1956, Pa. bar 1976. Law clk. to Justice Rutledge U.S. Supreme Ct., 1948-49; with Paul, Weiss, Rifkind, Wharton & Garrison, N.Y.C., 1949-51; spl. asst. to Amb. Philip C. Jessup State Dept., 1951-53; asst. counsel Amalgmated Clothing Workers Am., 1954-55; mem. faculty Yale Law Sch., 1955-74, dean, 1965-70; Greenfield prof. U. Pa., 1974-78, dean Law Sch., 1975-78, lectr., 1980—; judge U.S. Dist Ct. (ea. dist.) Pa., Phila., 1978—, now sr. judge. Vis. lectr. Howard U. Sch. Law, 1953; vis. prof. U. Mich. Law Sch., 1961, Columbia Law Sch., 1962 Author: The Constitution and the Supreme Court: A Documentary History, 1966. Mem. New Haven Bd. Edn., 1962-68; chmn. Conn. adv. com. U.S. Civil Rights Commn., 1962-63; mem. bd. NAACP Legal Def. Fund, 1960-78, v.p., 1971-78. Served with AUS, 1943-46. Mem. ABA (chmn. sec. individual rights 1970-71), Fed. Bar Assn., Phila. Bar Assn., Assn. Bar City N.Y., Am. Acad. Arts and Scis., Am. Philos. Soc., Am. Acad. Polit. and Social Sci. (bd. dirs. 2001—), Am. Law Inst. (coun. 1978—). Office: US Dist Ct 16613 US Courthouse 601 Market St Philadelphia PA 19106-1713

POLLAN, STEPHEN MICHAEL, lawyer, personal finance expert, speaker, author; b. N.Y.C., May 19, 1929; m. Corinne Steller; children: Michael, Lori, Tracy, Dana. LLB, Bklyn. Law Sch., 1951; BBS, L.I. U., 1985. Bar: N.Y. 1951. Asst. prof. Marymount Coll., 1960-70; pres. Royal Bus. Funds AMEX, 1970-76; sr. real estate cons. Nat. Westminster Bank, 1976-78; asst. prof. fin. C.W. Post Coll., L.I. U. Sch. Bus., 1994-96; prin. Stephen M. Pollan, P.C., N.Y.C., 1980—. Mem. President's Commn. on Small Bus.; personal fin. commentator Nightly Bus. Report, CNBC; personal fin. expert Oprah, Good Morning Am., Today, CNN, CBS Evening News. Co-author: Die Broke, Live Rich, The Total Negotiator, 1994, Lifescripts, 1996, also 13 other personal bus. books; contbr. numerous articles to nat. bus. publs.; contbg. op-ed writer N.Y. Times; contbg. editor Money, Worth; former columnist Working Women. Pres. Gay Head Cmty. Coun., 1975; vice chmn. UN Com. for UN Day, 1971-72. Mem. Nat. Assn. Small Bus. Investment Cos. (regional pres. 1975, bd. govs.). Contracts commercial, Estate planning, Real property. Home: 1095 Park Ave New York NY 10128-1154 also: Warshaw Burstein Cohen Schlesinger & Kuh 555 5th Ave New York NY 10017-2416 Office: 555 5th Ave Fl 11 New York NY 10017-2416

POLLARD, DENNIS BERNARD, lawyer, educator; b. Phila., May 12, 1968; BS in Psychology, Pa. State U., 1990; JD, Ohio State U., 1993; postgrad., U. Mich., 1996. Bar: Ohio 1993, U.S. Dist. Ct. (no. dist.) Ohio 1994, U.S. Ct. Appeals (6th cir.) 1994. Staff atty. The Legal Aid Soc. Cleve., 1993-95; atty. student affairs, student life Pa. State U., 1995-96; acad. adminstrv. intern U. Mich. Law Sch., Ann Arbor, 1996-97; asst. dean student affairs U. Tenn. Coll. Law, Knoxville, 1997-98; program dir. tenants' rights unit Tenants' Action Group of Phila., 1998-99, dir. devel., legis. affairs and spl. projects, 1999-2000, dir. devel. & quality assurance, 2000-01. Mem. ABA, Ohio State Bar Assn., Phila. Bar Assn. (assoc.), Assn. Fundraising Profls., Phi Delta Phi. Avocation: biking. Home: 2057 W York St Philadelphia PA 19132-3715

POLLARD, FRANK EDWARD, retired lawyer; b. Framingham, Mass., Oct. 26, 1932; s. Frank E. and Marjorie G. (Bayer) P.; m. Joyce A. Angell, June 4, 1955; children: Gary R., Jeffrey F., Donald B., Edward D., Laurie J. AB, Northeastern U., 1954; JD, Boston U., 1956. Bar: Conn. 1956, Mass. 1956, Fla. 1959, U.S. Dist. Ct. Mass., U.S. Supreme Ct. 1969. Ptnr., atty. Lee & Pollard, Westfield, Mass., 1958-80; pvt. practice, 1980-96; pres. Pollard & Pollard P.C., 1997-2000, ret., 2000. Pres. Westfield 2000 Redevel. Corp., 1978, counsel, 1980-2000; atty. City of Westfield, 1970-71; parlimentarian Mass. Jr. C. of C., 1964; pres. Boys Club Greater Westfield, Inc., 1972-73. Recipient Distinguished Svc. award U.S. Jaycees, Westfield, 1966. Mem. Westfield C. of C. (pres. 1975, counsel 1975-2000), Westfield Boys and Girls Club (pres. 1972-73, Man and Boy award 1973), Kiwanis (life mem., lt. gov. 1977-78, Westfield pres. 1967-68). Avocations: golf, photography, carpentry. Estate planning, Probate, Real property. Home: 419 Southwick Rd Apt 10C Westfield MA 01085-4764

POLLARD, OVERTON PRICE, state agency executive, lawyer; b. Ashland, Va., Mar. 26, 1933; s. James Madison and Annie Elizabeth (Hutchinson) P.; m. Anne Aloysia Meyer, Oct. 1, 1960; children: Mary O., Price, John, Anne, Charles, Andrew, David AB in Econs., Washington and Lee U., 1954, JD, 1957. Bar: Va. Claims supr. Travelers Ins. Co., Richmond, Va., 1964-67; asst. atty. gen. State of Va., 1967, 70-72; spl. asst. Va. Supreme Ct., 1968-70; exec. dir. Pub. Defender Commn., 1972—; ptnr. Pollard & Boice and predecessor firms, 1972-87. Bd. govs. Va. Criminal Law Sect., Richmond, 1970-72, 91-93; chmn. prepaid legal svcs. com. Va. State Bar, Richmond, 1982-85, chair sr. lawyers sect., 1999; pres. Met. Legal Aid, Richmond, 1978 Del. to State Dem. Cong., Richmond, 1985; mem. Va. Commn. on Family Violence Prevention, 1995; bd. dirs. Henrico Cmty. Housing Corp., 1999. With USN, 1957-59. Recipient Svc. award, Criminal Law Bd. of Govs. for Pub. Defender Study, 1971, Outstanding Svc. award, Pub. Defender Commn., 1998. Mem. ABA, Va. Bar Assn. (chmn. criminal law sect. 1991-93), Richmond Bar Assn., Nat. Legal Aid and Defender Assn. (Reginald Heber Smith award 1991), Va. Bar Assn. (Pro Bono Publico award 1995). Democrat. Baptist. Avocation: fishing. Home: 7726 Sweetbriar Rd Richmond VA 23229-6622 Office: Pub Defender Commn 701 E Franklin St Ste 1416 Richmond VA 23219-2510 E-mail: opollard@pdcmail.state.va.us

POLLARD, WILLIAM ALBERT, lawyer; b. Nashville, July 7, 1946; s. Thomas Brown and Hilda Alexine (Jolly) P.; divorced; children: William A. Jr., Thomas Barnes. B.S., U. S.C., 1968, J.D., 1974. Bar: S.C. 1974, U.S. Dist. Ct. S.C. 1974, U.S. Ct. Appeals (4th cir.) 1974, U.S. Tax Ct. 1977. Assoc. Nexsen, Pruet, Jacobs & Pollard, Columbia, S.C., 1974-78, ptnr., 1978—, chmn. 1993—. Mem. adv. bd. Midlands Tech. Coll., Columbia, 1978-84, Bank of Am.; endowment chmn., exec. coun. Indian Rivers Coun. Boy Scouts Am., 1986—, United Way of the Midlands, 1983, 84; chmn. Cystic Fibrosis Fund, 1998, Am. Heart Assn. Heart Walk, 1999; bd. mem. Richland Sch. Dist. One Found., A.C. Moore Edn. Found., Windsor Edn. Found.; clin. prof. S.C. Sch. Medicine. Served to lt. USN, 1968-71. Mem. Am. Soc. Hosp. Attys., Am. Soc. Law and Medicine, Nat. Health Lawyers Assn., S.C. Hosp. Assn., S.C. Soc. Hosp. Attys. (bd. govs. 1985—, pres. 1988-94), ABA (forum com. on health law), S.C. Bar Assn. (med., legal affairs com. 1986-88 comm. on hosps. and health law, 1988—, chmn. 1992-93), Columbia C. of C. (health care task force). Methodist. Clubs: Capitol City, Sertoma (pres. 1981-82) (Columbia). Administrative and regulatory, Health. Home: 321 Trentwood Dr Columbia SC 29223-8417 Office: Nexsen Pruet Jacobs & Pollard PO Box 2426 Columbia SC 29202-2426

POLLET, SUSAN L. lawyer; b. Manhasset, N.Y., Dec. 17, 1954; d. Myron J. and Barbara Audrey (Kananack) Feldman; m. Richard Pollet, June 30, 1985; children: Katharine Ann, Eve Whitney. BS in Consumer Econ. and Pub. Policy, Cornell U., 1976; JD, Emory U., 1979. Bar: Ga. 1979, N.Y. 1980; trained legal facilitator for P.E.A.C.E. program. Legal asst. ICC Industries, Inc., N.Y.C., 1979; lawyer Dwyer, Peltz & Walker, 1980-82, Acito & Klein P.C., N.Y.C., 1982-84; supervising atty. litigation Long Island Lighting Co., Hicksville, N.Y., 1984-86; part-time county atty. Westchester County Family Ct., Putnam County Dept. of Social Svcs., 1994-97; sr. ct. atty. Westchester County Family Ct., N.Y., 1997—. Adj. prof. Mercy Coll., N.Y., 1991-97; pvt. practice, 1988-97; law guardian for children, 1988-97. Contbr. articles to profl. jours. Bd. dirs. Chappaqua Children's Workshop, 1991-92, Pleasantville Children's Ctr., 1988-89; amb. Cornell Alumni Admissions, 1991—; bd. dirs. Westchester Children's Assn., 2000—; mem. nominating com. Temple Bethel, 1999-2001; mem. parent com. Horace Greeley H.S., 2000—. Mem. Westchester Women's Bar Assn. (v.p. 1993-95, pres. 1995-97), Westchester Co. Bar Assn. (family ct. com. 1991-92), Women's Bar Assn. of the State of N.Y. (state dir. 1997-2001, co-chair legis. com. 1999-2001, v.p. 2001—), 9th Jud. Dist. Task Force. Avocations: reading, art, hiking, writing. Home: 67 Ludlow Dr Chappaqua NY 10514-1222 E-mail: richsue67@aol.com

POLLEY, TERRY LEE, lawyer; b. Long Beach, Calif., June 2, 1947; s. Frederick F. and Geraldine E. (Davis) P.; m. Patricia Yamanoha, Aug. 4, 1973; children: Todd, Matthew. AB, UCLA, 1970; JD, Coll. William and Mary, 1973. Bar: Calif. 1973, U.S. Tax Ct. 1974, U.S. Supreme Ct. 1987. Assoc. Loeb & Loeb, L.A., 1973-78; ptnr. Ajalat, Polley & Ayoob, 1978—. Lectr. taxation law U. So.Calif., 1978-94. Author (with Charles R. Ajalat) California's Water's Edge Legislation, 1987; contbr. articles to profl. jours, legal jours.; editorial bd. William and Mary Law Rev. Chmn. bd. dirs. Greater Long Beach Christian Schs., 1988-92, sec., 1994-99; elder Grace Brethren Ch., Long Beach, 1988—. Mem. ABA (state and local tax com. 1973-92), Calif. Bar Assn. (chmn. taxation sect. 1990-91, exec. com. 1987-92, state and local tax com. 1975—, taxation sect., recipient V. Judson Klein award 1993), L.A. County Bar Assn. (exec. com. 1980-87, chmn. exec. com. 1985-86, taxation sect.), Nat. Assn. State Bar Tax Sects. (exec. com. 1990—, chmn. 1995-96, treas. 1998—). Republican. State and local taxation. Office: Ajalat Polley & Ayoob 643 S Olive St Ste 200 Los Angeles CA 90014-1651

POLLIHAN, THOMAS HENRY, lawyer; b. St. Louis, Nov. 15, 1949; s. C.H. and Patricia Ann (O'Brien) P.; m. Donna M. Bickhaus, Aug. 25, 1973; 1 child, Emily Christine. BA in Sociology, Quincy U., 1972; JD, U. Notre Dame, 1975; Exec. Masters in Internat. Bus., St. Louis U., 1992. Bar: Mo. 1975, Ill. 1976. Jud. law clk. to judge Mo. Ct. of Appeals, St. Louis, 1975-76; from assoc. to ptnr. Greenfield, Davidson, Mandelstamm & Voorhees, 1976-82; asst. gen. counsel Kellwood Co., 1982-89, gen. counsel, sec., 1989-93, v.p., sec., gen. counsel, 1993—. Trustee Quincy (Ill.) U., 1987-93, 97—, pres. alumni bd., 1986-87; pres. S.W. Neighborhood Improvement Assn., St. Louis, 1984, Quincy (Ill.) U. Found., 1993-94, 97—; dir., sec. New Piasa Chautauqua, Ill., 1996-97. Named Quincy U. Alumnus of Yr., 1997. Mem. Bar Assn. Met. St. Louis. Roman Catholic. Avocations: soccer, cycling. Contracts commercial, General corporate, Real property. Home: 415 Spring Ave Saint Louis MO 63119-2634 Office: Kellwood Co 600 Kellwood Pkwy Ste 300 Chesterfield MO 63017-5897 E-mail: tom_pollihan@kellwood.com

POLLINGER, WILLIAM JOSHUA, lawyer; b. Passaic, N.J., Dec. 14, 1944; s. Irving R. and Ethel (Groudan) P.; m. Helen Rizzo, May 30, 1977; children: Samantha, Zachary. BA, Rutgers U., 1966; JD, Am. U., 1969. Bar: N.J. 1969, U.S. Dist. Ct. N.J. 1969, N.Y. 1981, U.S. Supreme Ct. 1982, U.S. Ct. Appeals (3d cir.) 1986; cert. Civil Trial Atty. N.J. Supreme Ct., 1983; masters level cert. U.S.A. Track and Field Ofcl. Assoc. Krieger & Klein, Passaic, 1969-75; ptnr. Delorenzo & Pollinger, Hackensack, N.J., 1975-84; pres. William J. Pollinger, P.A., 1984-88, Pollinger, Fearns & Kemezis, P.A., 1988-90, Pollinger & Fearns, P.A., Hackensack, 1990-92, William J. Pollinger P.A., Hackensack, N.J., 1992—. Mem. Bergen County Ethics Com., N.J., 1984-88; lectr. ins. N.J.-ICLE, master Robert L. Clifford Am. Inn of Court. Arbitrator Better Bus. Bur. of Bergen and Rockland Counties, Paramus, N.J., 1983-89, Am. Arbitration Assn., 1983—. Assoc. of Yr. award Builders Assn. No. N.J., Paramus, 1981. Master Justice Robert L. Clifford Am. Inn of Ct.; mem. N.J. State Bar Assn. (ins. law com.), Passaic County Bar Assn., Bergen County Bar Assn., Assn. Trial Lawyers Am., Trial Attys. N.J., Am. Arbitration Assn., Def. Research Inst., Phi Delta Phi. Lodge: Masons (past master). Avocation: track and field officiating. State civil litigation, Insurance, Personal injury. Office: 302 Union St Hackensack NJ 07601-4303

POLLOCK, BRUCE GERALD, lawyer; b. Providence, Feb. 18, 1947; s. Reuben and Stella (Reitman) P.; m. Sheri Barbara Tepper, Dec. 21, 1969; children: Dawn, Meah. BA, U. R.I., 1968; JD, Suffolk U., 1974. Bar: R.I. 1974, U.S. Supreme Ct. 1978, U.S. Dist. Ct. R.I. 1980. Law clk. R.I. Superior Ct., Providence, 1974, adminstrv. asst. to chief justice, 1975; asst. pub. defender R.I. Dept. Pub. Defender, 1975-80; pvt. practice Warwick and West Warwick, R.I., 1980—. Adj. instr. So. N.E. Law Sch., New Bedford, Mass., 1990. Dist. chmn. Narragansett Coun. Shawomet Dist. Boy Scouts Am., 1996-98. Fellow R.I. Bar Found. (bd. dirs. 1990-2000; v.p. 2000—); mem. ABA, Nat. Conf. Bar Pres., New Eng. Bar Assn. (del. 1991-93), R.I. Bar Assn. (pres. 1992-93, award of merit 1995). Democrat. Avocations: golf, skiing, stained glass craftsman, bicycling, Tai Chi. Criminal, General practice, Personal injury. Office: 45 Providence St West Warwick RI 02893-3714 E-mail: brucepollock@juno.com, bgpollock@yahoo.com

POLLOCK, JOHN PHLEGER, lawyer; b. Sacramento, Apr. 28, 1920; s. George Gordon and Irma (Phleger) P.; m. Juanita Irene Gossman, Oct. 26, 1945; children: Linda Pollock Harrison, Madeline Pollock Chiotti, John, Gordon. A.B., Stanford U., 1942; J.D., Harvard U., 1948. Bar: Calif. 1949, U.S. Supreme Ct. 1954. Ptnr. Musick, Peeler & Garrett, L.A., 1953-60, Pollock, Williams & Berwanger, L.A., 1960-80, Rodi, Pollock, Pettker, Galbraith & Cahill, L.A., 1980-89, of counsel, 1989—. Contbr. articles to profl. publs. Active Boy Scouts Am.; trustee Pitzer Coll., Claremont, Calif., 1968-76, Pacific Legal Found., 1981-91, Fletcher Jones Found., 1969—, Good Hope Med. Found., 1980—. Fellow Am. Coll. Trial Lawyers; mem. ABA, Los Angeles County Bar Assn. (trustee 1964-66). Home: 30602 Paseo Del Valle Laguna Niguel CA 92677-2317 Office: 444 S Flower St Ste 1700 Los Angeles CA 90071-2918 E-mail: Phleger1@msn.com

POLLOCK, STACY JANE, lawyer; b. Palmerton, Pa., Dec. 24, 1969; d. Charles Paul Pollock and Marianne (Kovatch) Althouse. BA, Allentown Coll. St. Francis, Center Valley, Pa., 1991; postgrad., U. De Las Americas, Puebla, Mex., 1991; JD with honors, George Wash. U., 1994. Bar: Pa. 1995, D.C. 1996, U.S. Ct. Appeals (11th cir.) 1996. Assoc. Arnold & Porter,

Washington, 1994-95, 96—; jud. clk. U.S. Ct. Appeals, 11th Cir., Montgomery, Ala., 1995-96. Bd. dirs. Palisade Gardens Condominiums, Arlington, Va., 1998-99. Democrat. Roman Catholic. Federal civil litigation, General civil litigation, Product liability. Office: Arnold and Porter 555 12th St NW Washington DC 20004-1206

POLLOCK, STEWART GLASSON, lawyer, former state supreme court justice; b. East Orange, N.J., Dec. 21, 1932; BA, Hamilton Coll., 1954, LLD (hon.), 1995; LLB, NYU, 1957; LLM, U. Va., 1988. Bar: N.J. 1958. Asst. U.S. atty., Newark, 1958-60; ptnr. Schenck, Price, Smith & King, Morristown, N.J., 1960-74, 76-78; commr. N.J. Dept. Pub. Utilities; counsel to gov. State of N.J., Trenton, 1978-79; assoc. justice N.J. Supreme Ct., Morristown, 1979-99; of counsel Riker Danzig Hyland & Perretti, 1999—. Mem. N.J. Commn. on Investigation, 1976-78; chmn. coordinating coun. on life-sustaining med. treatment decision making Nat. Ctr. for State Cts., 1994-96; bd. dirs. NYU Law Ctr. Found., Inst. of Jud. Adminstrn., N.J. Conv. Found. Assoc. editor N.J. Law Jour.; contbr. articles to legal jours. Trustee Coll. Medicine and Dentistry, N.J., 1976. Mem. ABA (chmn. appellate judges conf. 1991-92), N.J. Bar Assn. (trustee 1973-78), Am. Judicature Soc. (dir. 1984-88), Morris County Bar Assn. (pres. 1973). Alternative dispute resolution, Appellate, General civil litigation. Office: Riker Danzig Scherer Hyland & Perretti One Speedwell Ave Morristown NJ 07962-0900

POLOZOLA, FRANK JOSEPH, federal judge; b. Baton Rouge, Jan. 15, 1942; s. Steve A. Sr. and Caroline C. (Lucito) P.; m. Linda Kay White, June 9, 1962; children: Gregory Dean, Sheri Elizabeth, Gordon Damian. Student bus. adminstrn., La. State U., 1959-62, JD, 1965. Bar: La. 1965. Law clk. to U.S. Dist. Ct. Judge E. Gordon West, 1965-66; assoc. Seale, Smith & Phelps, Baton Rouge, 1966-68, ptnr., 1968-73; part-time magistrate U.S. Dist. Ct. (mid. dist.) La., 1972-73, magistrate, 1973-80, judge, 1980—, chief judge, 1998—. Adj. prof. Law Ctr., La. State U., 1977-95. Bd. dirs. Cath. High Sch. Mem. La. Bar Assn., Baton Rouge Bar Assn., Fed. Judges Assn., 5th Cir. Dist. Judges Assn., La. State U. L Club, KC, Wex Malone Inns of Ct., Omicron Delta Kappa. Roman Catholic. Office: US Dist Ct Russell B Long Fed Bldg & US Courthouse 777 Florida St Ste 313 Baton Rouge LA 70801-1717

POMERANTZ, JERALD MICHAEL, lawyer; b. Springfield, Mass., July 9, 1954; s. Lawrence Louis Pomerantz and Dolores (Barez) Chaudoir. BA in Econs. cum laude, Brandeis U., 1976; JD, Vanderbilt U., 1979; student, Am. Inst. Banking, 1983-99. Atty., McAllen, Tex., 1979-80, Weslaco, 1980-85; gen. counsel, sec. Tex. Valley Bancshares, Inc., 1985-87; atty. for Hidalgo County Rural Fire Prevention Dist., Tex., 1982-88; atty. SBA, Harlingen, 1987; pvt. practice Weslaco, 1987-89; adv. dir. South Tex. Fed. Credit Union, 1995-98. Atty. Elsa (Tex.) Housing Authority, Weslaco (Tex.) Housing Authority, 1997—. Mem. Weslaco Charter Review Com., 1981-82,; drafted S.B. 139 (amending Tex. bus. and commerce code sect. 9.402(g)) regular session Tex. Legislature), 1989, S.B. 140, 1989, enacted as H.B. 2005 (amending Tex. Credit Code sect. 1.06) regular session Tex. Legislature, 1993. Recipient continuing edn. award Banking Law Inst., 1992. Mem.: Tex. Assn. Bank Counsel (bd. dirs. 1990—95, bd. dirs. 1997—2000, v.p. 2001—02), State Bar Tex., Conf. on Consumer Fin. Law, Coll. State Bar Tex. (bd.dirs. 1990—95), Hidalgo County Bar Assn. (law libr. com. 1999—), Rio Grande Valley Bankruptcy Bar Assn. (v.p. 2000—01). Banking, Consumer commercial, Real property. Home and Office: PO Box 10 Weslaco TX 78599-0010 E-mail: jmp@justice.com

POMERANZ, MORTON, lawyer, educator; b. Bklyn., Jan. 11, 1922; s. Jacob S. and Mildred M. (Gover) P.; m. Janet Putnam Morrison, Dec. 18, 1960 (div. 1980); children: John Putnam, Matthew David, Harold Robert; m. Judith Ann Davis, Sept. 2, 1984. AB, Columbia U., 1943, JD, 1945. Bar: N.Y. 1948, U.S. Dist. Ct. D.C. 1955. Vice consul U.S. Fgn. Svc., La Paz, Bolivia, 1945-48; legal cons. U.S. Dept. Commerce, Washington, 1949-59; internat. activities asst. U.S. Dept. Interior, 1960-65; various positions and acting gen. counsel U.S. Trade Rep., 1965-80; of counsel Gage, Tucker & Von Baur, 1980-86, Gage & Tucker, Washington, 1986-92, Faegre and Benson, Washington, 1993—95. Adj. prof. Antioch Ctr. Legal Svcs., Washington, 1983-84; panelist dispute resolutions Can.-U.S. Free Trade Agreement, 1989—. Contbr. articles to profl. jours. Mem. adv. bd. on social studies, Arlington (Va. Sch. Bd., 1978-80. Mem. ABA (chmn. L.Am. law com. 1958-61), Am. Soc. Internat. Law. Home: 1300 Crystal Dr # 1409 Arlington VA 22202-3234

POMERENE, TONI GRAVEN, lawyer; b. Tacoma, Aug. 5, 1950; BA, Webster U., 1971; JD, Hamline U., 1978. Bar: Minn. 1978, U.S. Dist. Ct. Minn. 1978, Ga. 1997. Ptnr. Wilson & Pomerene, Mpls., 1978-89; shareholder Conflict Mgmt. Svcs., 1989—. Vis. prof. Hamline U., St. Paul, Minn., 1993-94, U. Ga., Athens, 1996—; spl. asst. Anoka (Minn.) County Atty., 1992-94; settlement conf. referee Hennepin County, 1987-94, sub. referee family ct., 1986-94, arbitrator dist. ct., 1986-94. Mem. ABA, ATLA, Am. Arbitration Assn., Hennepin County Bar Assn. (bd. govs. family law sect., 1986-89, chmn. 1986), Minn. Trial Lawyer s Assn. General civil litigation, Government contracts and claims, Land use and zoning (including planning). E-mail: pomerene@arches.uga.edu

POMEROY, HARLAN, lawyer; b. Cleve., May 7, 1923; s. Lawrence Alson and Frances (Macdonald) P.; m. Barbara Lesser, Aug. 24, 1962; children: Robert Charles, Caroline Macdonald, Harlan III BS, Yale U., 1945; JD, Harvard U., 1948. Bar: Conn. 1949, U.S. Supreme Ct. 1954, U.S. Ct. Appeals (fed. cir.) 1954, Ohio 1958, U.S. Dist. Ct. (no. dist.) Ohio 1958, U.S. Claims Ct. 1958, U.S. Ct. Appeals (6th cir.) 1958, U.S. Tax Ct. 1958, D.C. 1975, Md. 1981, U.S. Dist. Ct. (D.C. dist.) 1984, U.S. Ct. Internat. Trade 1984, U.S. Ct. Appeals (D.C. cir.) 1986; cert. county ct. mediator, Fla. Atty. trial sect. tax div. Dept. Justice, Washington, 1952-58; assoc. Baker & Hostetler, Cleve., 1958-62, ptnr., 1962-75, Washington, 1975-92. Gen. chmn. Cleve. Tax Inst., 1971; fgn. legal advisor to Romanian Securities Mkts., 1997, Macedonia, 1998, UN Interim Adminstrn. Mission in Kosovo, 2000-2001; arbitrator Nat. Assn. Securities Dealers, 1992—, N.Y. Stock Exch., 1995—, Sarasota Better Bus. Coun., 1997—; arbitrator Multistate Tax Commn., 1996—, mem. neutral roster IRS mediation program; lectr. on tax and comml. law. Author: (monographs) The Privatization Process in Bulgaria; Bulgarian Government Structure and Operation-An Overview; contbr. articles to profl. jours. Treas. Shaker Heights (Ohio) Dem. Club, 1960-62; trustee, mem. exec. com. 1st Unitarian Ch. Cleve., 1965-68; trustee River Road Unitarian Ch., Bethesda, Md., 1988-90; gen. counsel, former asst. treas. John Glenn Presdl. Com., 1983-87; participant Vol. Lawyers Project, Legal Counsel for Elderly, Washington, 1983-92; vol. Guardian Ad Litem Program, Sarasota, Fla., 1990-92, GED-H.S. Equivalency Program, Sarasota, 1990-92; participant Guardianship Monitoring program 12th Jud. Cir., Fla., 1996-97; vol. exec. fgn. legal advisor Internat. Exec. Svc. Corps. with Privatization Ministry, Prague, Czech Republic, 1994-95; mem. spl. mission to Bulgarian Ministry of Fin., U.S. Dept. Treasury, 1995. Mem. ABA (resident liaison Bulgaria for Ctrl. and East European Law Initiative 1992-93), Am. Arbitration Assn. (arbitrator 1992-2000), D.C. Bar Assn., The Field Club (Sarasota, Fla.), Yale Club of the Suncoast, Ivy League Club of Sarasota. Private international, Public international, Taxation, general. Home: 7336 Villa D Este Dr Sarasota FL 34238-5648 Office: Baker & Hostetler 1050 Connecticut Ave NW Ste 11 Washington DC 20036-5351 also: 3200 National City Ctr Cleveland OH 44414-3485

POMPA, RENATA, lawyer; b. N.Y.C., Sept. 8, 1961; BA, Columbia U., 1983; JD, St. John's U., 1986. Bar: N.Y. 1987. Assoc. atty. employee benefits Shea & Gould, N.Y.C., 1989-94; assoc. atty. employee benefits, exec. compensation and corp. securities Thacher, Proffitt & Wood, 1994—. Mem. Nat. Assn. Stock Plan Profls., Am. Compensation Assn., Assn. Bar City N.Y. Labor, Pension, profit-sharing, and employee benefits, Securities. Home: 350 W 57th St Apt 10G New York NY 10019-3762 Office: Thacher Proffitt & Wood Two World Trade Ctr New York NY 10048

PONDER, LESTER MCCONNICO, lawyer, educator; b. Walnut Ridge, Ark., Dec. 10, 1912; s. Harry Lee and Clyde (Gant) P.; m. Sallie Mowry Clover, Nov. 7, 1942; children— Melinda, Constance; m. Phyllis Gretchen Harting, Oct. 14, 1978 B.S. summa cum laude in Commerce, Northwestern U., 1934; J.D. with honors, George Washington U., 1938. Bar: Ark. 1937, Ind. 1948. Atty. Ark. Dept. Revenue, Little Rock, 1939-41; atty. IRS, Chgo. and Indpls., 1941-51; ptnr. Barnes & Thornburg and predecessor Barnes, Hickam, Pantzer & Boyd, Indpls., 1952—. Adj. prof. Sch. Law, Ind. U., Bloomington, 1951-54, Sch. Law, Ind. U., Indpls., 1954-63; lectr. polit. sci. Ind. U., Indpls., 1982-85. Author: United States Tax Court Practice & Procedure, 1976 Bd. dirs., vice chmn., chmn. Ind. chpt. The Nature Conservancy, 1981-89; mem. adv. coun. Ind. Dept. Natural Resources, 1986—; past bd. mem. Sigma Chi Found. Served with USN, 1942. Fellow Am. Bar Found., Ind. State Bar Found., Ind. Bar Found., Am. Coll. Tax Counsel; mem. ABA (coun., taxation sect. 1970-73, chair sr. lawyers div. 1993-94, adv. coun. Commr. Internal Revenue 1964—), Ind. State Bar Assn., Indpls. Bar Assn., Assn. of Seventh Fed. Cir. Republican. Presbyterian. Club: Meridian Hills Country (Indpls.). Lodge: Rotary (past bd. dirs.) Corporate taxation, Estate taxation, Personal income taxation. Office: Barnes & Thornburg Merchants Bank Bldg Ste 1313 Indianapolis IN 46204-3506

PONITZ, JOHN ALLAN, lawyer; b. Battle Creek, Mich., Sept. 7, 1949; m. Nancy J. Roberts, Aug. 14, 1971; children: Amy, Matthew, Julie. BA, Albion Coll., 1971; JD, Wayne State U., 1974. Bar: Mich. 1974, U.S. Dist. Ct. (ea. dist.) Mich. 1975, (we. dist.) Mich. 1986, U.S. Ct. Appeals (6th cir.) Mich. 1981, U.S. Supreme Ct. 1992. Assoc. McMachan & Kaichen, Birmingham, Mich., 1973-75; atty. Grand Trunk Western R.R., Detroit, 1975-80, sr. trial atty., 1980-89; gen. counsel, 1990-95; ptnr. Hopkins & Sutter, Detroit, 1995-2000, Maxwell, Ponitz & Sclawy, Troy, Mich., 2000—. V.p. Beverly Hills (Mich.) Jaycees, 1981. Served to capt. USAR, 1974-82. Mem. Mich. Bar Assn., Nat. Assn. R.R. Trial Counsel, Oakland County Bar Assn. Lutheran. Avocation: golf. Federal civil litigation, General corporate, Personal injury. Office: Maxwell Ponitz & Sclawy City Ctr Bldg 888 W Big Beaver Ste 1470 Troy MI 48084-4738 E-mail: japonitz@pbmaxwell.com

PONOROFF, LAWRENCE, law educator, legal consultant; b. Chgo., Sept. 10, 1953; s. Charles Melvin and Jean Eileen (Kramer) P.; m. Monica J. Moses, July 25, 1981; children: Christopher J., Devon E., Laura J., Scott C. AB, Loyola U., Chgo., 1975; JD, Stanford U., 1978. Bar: Colo. 1978, Ohio 1988, U.S. Dist. Ct. Colo., U.S. Dist. Ct. (no. dist.) Ohio, U.S. Ct. Appeals (10th cir.). Assoc. Holme Roberts & Owen, Denver, 1978-84, ptnr., 1984-86; asst. prof. law U. Toledo, 1986-88, assoc. prof. coll. of law, 1988-90, prof. law, assoc. dean academic affairs, 1990-92, prof., 1990-95, Tulane U. Sch. Law, New Orleans, 1995-00, Mitchell Franklin prof., 2000—, vice dean, 1998-2001, dean, 2001—. Vis. prof. Wayne State U. Law Sch., 1993, U. Mich. Law Sch., 1997, lectr. fed. juc. ctr.; cons. long range planning subcom. of com. on adminstrn. of bankruptcy system Jud. Conf. of the U.S.; dir. Am. Bd. Certification, 2000—; bd. adv. editors Am. Bankruptcy Inst. Law Rev., 2000—; bd. dirs. Am. Bs. Certification. Co-author: (with S.E. Snyder) Commerical Bankruptcy Litigation, 1989, (with J. Dolan) Basic Concepts in Commercial Law, 1998, (with Epstein and Markell) Making and Doing Deals: An Introduction to Contract and Related Laws, 2001. Mem. ABA, Am. Bar Ist., Am. Law Inst., La. State Bar Assn. (bd. govs.). Home: 6025 Pitt St New Orleans LA 70118-6010 Office: Tulane Law Sch Coll Law 6329 Freret St New Orleans LA 70118-6231 E-mail: lponoroff@law.tulane.edu

PONSOLDT, JAMES FARMER, law educator; b. Jersey City, June 14, 1946; s. Raymond Samuel and Margaret Elizabeth (Farmer) P.; m. Susan Elizabeth Teason, Sept. 5, 1968; children— Katherine, James. A.B., Cornell U., 1968; J.D., Harvard U., 1972. Bar: S.C. 1974, U.S. Dist. Ct. S.C. 1974, U.S. Ct. Appeals (4th cir.) 1975, U.S. Ct. Appeals (7th cir.) 1976, U.S. Ct. Appeals (9th cir.) 1977, U.S. Supreme Ct. 1977, U.S. Ct. Appeals (11th cir.) 1981, U.S. Ct. Appeals (D.C. cir.) 1975. Editorial asst. Atlantic Monthly, Boston, 1968; assoc. firm Paul, Weiss, Rifkind, Wharton & Garrison, N.Y.C., 1972-73; law clk. U.S. Ct. Appeals, 1973-74; sr. trial atty. U.S. Dept. Justice, Washington, 1975-78; vis. prof. law Tulane U., 1982; assoc. prof. law U. Ga. Law Sch., 1978-86, prof., 1986—, Joseph Henry Lumpkin prof. law, 1997—; lectr. internat. competition law U.U.B., Brussels, Belgium, 1986; vis. prof. U. Lyon, France, 1998; witness U.S. Ho. Monopolies Subcom., Washington, 1980-85, Ga. Atty. Gen.'s Office, 1979-80; witness cons. U.S. Senate Judiciary Com., 1983-84. Contbr. articles to profl. jours., editorials to N.Y. Times, Wall St. Jour. Cons., Concerned Water Users of Clarke County, 1983-84; tutor Clarke County Sch. System, 1979-80. Served with USNR, 1969-71. NDEA fellow, 1970-71. Mem. S.C. Bar Assn. Club: Harvard. Home: 305 Great Oak Dr Athens GA 30605-4506 Office: U Ga Law Sch Herty Dr Athens GA 30602

PONSOR, MICHAEL ADRIAN, federal judge; b. Chgo., Aug. 13, 1946; s. Frederick Ward and Helen Yvonne (Richardson) P.; chidren from previous marriage, Anne, Joseph; 1 stepchild, Christian Walker; m. Nancy L. Coiner, June 30, 1996. BA magna cum laude, Harvard Coll., 1969; BA second class honors, Oxford U., 1971, MA, 1979; JD, Yale U., 1975. Bar: Mass., U.S. Dist. Ct. Mass., U.S. Ct. Appeals (1st cir.), U.S. Supreme Ct. Tchr. Kenya Inst. Adminstrn., Nairobi, 1967-68; law clk. U.S. Dist. Ct., Boston, 1975-76; assoc. Homans, Hamilton, Dahmen & Lamson, 1976-78; ptnr. Brown, Hart & Ponsor, Amherst, Mass., 1978-83; U.S. magistrate judge U.S. Dist. Ct., Springfield, 1984-94, U.S. dist. judge, 1994—. Adj. prof. Western N.E. Coll. Sch. Law, Springfield, 1988—, Yale Law Sch., New Haven, 1989-91; presenter in field. Rhodes scholar Oxford U., 1969. Mem. Mass. Bar Assn., Hampshire County Bar Assn., Boston Bar Assn. Office: US Dist Ct Rm 539 1550 Main St Springfield MA 01103-1422

PONTAROLO, MICHAEL JOSEPH, lawyer; b. Walla Walla, Wash., Sept. 1, 1947; s. Albert and Alice Mary (Fazzari) P.; m. Elizabeth Louise Onley, July 18, 1970; children: Christie, Amy, Nick, Angela. BA, Gonzaga U., 1969, JD, 1973. Bar: Wash. 1973, U.S. Dist. Ct. (ea. dist.) Wash. 1974. Assoc. Mullin & Etter, Spokane, Wash., 1973-74, William Iunker, Spokane, 1974-75, Delay, Curran & Boling, Spokane, 1975-77; prin. Delay, Curran, Thompson & Pontarolo, P.S., 1977-97, Delay, Curran, Thompson, Pontarolo & Walker, Spokane, 1997—. Mem. Spokane County Med. Legal Com., 1987-88, 91; chmn. liaison com. Superior Ct., 1987-88, 94-97, chair, 1994-95, mem. arbitration bd., 1987—; mem. Bench Bar Com., 1987-88; bd. govs., nom. com., superior ct. judge adv. com. to Gov. Locke, Wa.; adj. prof. Gonzaga U. Sch. Law, 1987—, bd. advisors, 2000—. Bd. dirs. Community Ctrs. Found., Spokane, 1986-89; active Spokane C.C. Legal Secretary Adv. Com.; mem. adv. bd. Spokane C.C., 1992—. Recipient Cert. of Recognition, Superior Ct. Clk., Spokane, 1986. Mem. ATLA, ABA, Wash. State Bar Assn. (interprofl. com. 1987-90, character and fitness com. 1991-94, com. chair 1993-94, spl. dist. counsel 1984—, mem. jud. recommendation com. 1994-98, co-chair jud. recommendation com. 1996—, chair judicial recommendation com. 1997-98, consumer protection com. 2000-01, spl. disciplinary counsel 2001, rules of profl. conduct com. 2000-01), Wash. State Trial Lawyers Assn. (v.p. east 1979-80, Cert. Appreciation 1982, 90, 92, Leadership award 1984, CLE program chmn. 1984, mem. awards com. 1995-99, chair 1995-96), Spokane County Bar Assn. (v.p., sec.-treas. 1986-89, pres. 1989-90, trustee 1984-86, membership com. chair 1992-93), Alpha Sigma Nu. Insurance, Personal injury, Workers' compensation. Office: Delay Curran Thompson Pontarolo & Walker PS 601 W Main Ave Ste 1212 Spokane WA 99201-0684 E-mail: dctpw@msn.com

PONTIKES, REBECCA GEORGE, lawyer; b. Evanston, Ill., Aug. 4, 1972; d. George Constantine and Harriet (George) P. BA, Tufts U., 1994; JD, U. Mich., 1997. Bar: Mass. 1997. Atty. Law Office Ara H. Margoshian II, Watertown, Mass., 1997-98, Law Office Judith E. Smith, Cambridge, 1998—. Mem. Women's Bar Assn., Mass. Bar Assn., Boston Bar Assn., Nat. Orgn. Women. Democrat. Avocations: theater, reading, synchronized swimming, aerobics, history. General civil litigation, Family and matrimonial, Personal injury. Office: Law Office Judith E Smith 701 Concord Ave Ste 2 Cambridge MA 02138

POOLER, ROSEMARY S. federal judge; b. 1938; BA, Brooklyn Coll., 1959; MA, Univ. of Conn., 1961; JD, Univ. of Mich. Law Sch., 1965. With Crystal, Manes & Rifken, Syracuse, 1966-69, Michaels and Michaels, Syracuse, 1969-72; asst. corp. counsel Dir. of Consumer Affairs Unit, 1972-73; common counsel City of Syracuse N.Y. Public Interest Rsch. Group, 1974-75; chmn., exec. dir. Consumer Protection Bd., 1975-80; commr. N.Y. State Public Services Commn., 1981-86; staff dir. N.Y. State Assembly, Com. on Corps., Authorities and Commns., 1987-94; judge Supreme Ct., 5th Judicial Dist., 1991-94; district judge U.S. Dist. Ct. (no. dist.) N.Y., Syracuse, 1994-98; cir. judge U.S. Ct. Appeals, 2nd circuit, 1998—. Vis. prof. of law Syracuse Univ. Coll. of Law, 1987-88; v.p. legal affairs Atlantic States Legal Found., 1989-90. Mem. Onondaga County Bar Assn., N.Y. State Bar Assn., Women's Bar Assn. of the State of N.Y., Assn. of Supreme Ct. Justices of the State of N.Y. Office: Federal Bldg PO Box 7395 100 S Clinton St Syracuse NY 13261-6100*

POOLEY, JAMES, lawyer, author; b. Dayton, Ohio, Oct. 4, 1948; s. Howard Carl and Daisy Frances (Lindsley) P.; children by previous marriage: Jefferson Douglas, Christopher James; m. Laura-Jean Anderson, Oct. 13, 1984; 1 child, Catherine Lindsley. BA, Lafayette Coll., 1970; JD, Columbia U., 1973. Bar: Calif. 1973, U.S. Dist. Ct. (no. dist.) Calif. 1973, U.S. Ct. Appeals (9th cir.) 1974, U.S. Supreme Ct. 1977, U.S. Dist. Ct. (ctrl. dist.) Calif. 1978. Assoc. Wilson, Mosher & Sonsini, Palo Alto, Calif., 1973-78; ptnr. Mosher Pooley & Sullivan, 1978-88, Graham and James, 1988-93, Fish & Richardson, Menlo Park, 1993-98, Gray Cary Ware & Freidenrich LLLP, Palo Alto, 1998—. Arbitrator, spl. master U.S. Dist. Ct. (no. dist.) Calif., Santa Clara Superior Ct., San Jose, 1979—; lectr. Practicing Law Inst., N.Y.C., 1983, 85-86, 88, 95, 97, 98, 99, Santa Clara U. Sch. Law, 1985-87, 98, U. Calif., Boalt Hall Sch. Law, 1997—. Author: Trade Secrets, 1982, Protecting Technology, 1983, Trying the High Technology Case, 1984, Trade Secrets: A Guide to Protecting Proprietary Business Information, 1989, Trade Secrets, 1997; co-author: Millennium Intelligence, 2000; editor, co-author: Californial Trade Secrets Law, 1996; contbr. articles to profl. jours.; editor-in-chief Trade Secret Law Reporter, 1984-85; bd. advisors Santa Clara Computer and High Tech. Law Jour., 1984—. Bd. advisors Berkeley Ctr. for Law and Tech., 1997—; chmn. Nat. Trade Secret Law Inst., 1994; pres. Am. Friends of the Acad. of St. Martin in the Fields, 1998—. Mem. Am. Intellectual Property Lawyers Assn. (chmn. trade secrets com. 1996-98), Am. Electronics Assn. (chmn. lawyers' com. 1981-82), Internat. Bar Assn., Union Internationale des Avocats. Federal civil litigation, State civil litigation, Patent. Address: Gray Cary Ware & Freiendrich 3340 Hillview Ave Palo Alto CA 94304-1203

POPE, ANDREW JACKSON, JR. (JACK POPE), retired judge; b. Abilene, Tex., Apr. 18, 1913; s. Andrew Jackson and Ruth Adelia (Taylor) P.; m. Allene Esther Nichols, June 11, 1938; children: Andrew Jackson III, Walter Allen. BA, Abilene Christian U., 1934, LLD (hon.), 1980; LLB, U. Tex., 1937; LLD (hon.), Pepperdine U., 1981, St. Mary's U., San Antonio, 1982, Okla. Christian U., 1983. Bar: Tex. 1937. Practice law Corpus Christi, Corpus Christi, 1937-46; judge 94th Dist. Ct., 1946-50; justice Ct. Civil Appeals, San Antonio, 1950-65, Supreme Ct. of Tex., Austin, 1965-82, chief justice, 1982-85. Author: John Berry & His Children, 1988; chmn. bd. editors Appellate Procedure in Tex., 1974; author numerous articles in law revs. and profl. jours. Pres. Met. YMCA, San Antonio, 1956-57; chmn. Tex. State Law Libr. Bd., 1973-80; trustee Abilene Christian U., 1954—. Seaman USNR, 1944-46. Recipient Silver Beaver award Alamo council Boy Scouts Am., 1961, Distinguished Eagle award, 1983; Rosewood Gavel award, 1962, St. Thomas More award, St. Mary's U., San Antonio, 1982; Outstanding Alumnus award Abilene Christian U., 1965; Greenhill Jud. award Mcpl. Judges Assn., 1980; Houston Bar Found. citation, 1985; San Antonio Bar Found. award, 1985; Disting. Jurist award Jefferson County Bar, 1985; Outstanding Alumnus award U. Tex. Law Alumni Assn., 1988; George Washington Honor medal Freedom Found., 1988; Disting. Lawyer award Travis County, 1992. Fellow Tex. Bar Found. (Law Rev. award 1979, 80, 81); mem. ABA, State Bar Tex. (pres. jud. sect. 1962, Outstanding Alumnus U. Tex. Sch. of Law 1994, Outstanding Fifty Years Lawyer award 1994), Tex. Bar Found., Order of Coif, Nueces County Bar Assn. (pres. 1946), Travis County Bar Assn., Bexar County Bar Assn., Tex. Philos. Soc., Austin Knife and Fork (pres. 1980), Am. Judicature Soc., Tex. State Hist. Assn., Tex. Supreme Ct. Hist. Soc. (v.p.), Sons of Republic of Tex., Statesmanship award State Bar Tex., 1998, Christian Chronicle Coun. (chmn.), Masons, K.P. (grand chancellor 1946), Alpha Chi, Phi Delta Phi, Pi Sigma Alpha. Mem. Ch. of Christ. Home: 2803 Stratford Dr Austin TX 78746-4626

POPE, DAVID BRUCE, lawyer; b. Nov. 15, 1945; s. Thomas Bass and Nathalie Jane (Estill) P.; m. Martha McEvoy, Aug. 26, 1967. BA, Tex. Tech. U., 1968; JD, U. Houston, 1971. Bar: Tex. 1971, U.S. Ct. Appeals (5th cir.) 1973, U.S. Ct. Appeals (11th cir.) 1981, U.S. Ct. Appeals (10th cir.) 1990, U.S. Supreme Ct. 1975, Colo. 1990. Briefing atty. 1st Ct. Civil Appeals, Houston, 1971-72; assoc. Lynch, Chappel, Allday & Aldridge, Midland, Tex., 1972-76; atty. Texaco, Inc., Houston, 1976-80, Midland, Tex., 1980-82, chief atty., 1982-84, sr. atty., 1985, Denver, 1989-2000, sr. counsel Houston, 2000—. Administrative and regulatory, Oil, gas, and mineral, Environmental. Office: Texaco Inc 1111 Bagby St PO Box 4596 Houston TX 77210-4596 E-mail: popedb@texaco.com

POPE, FRED WALLACE, JR. lawyer; b. Sanford, Fla., Feb. 9, 1941; s. Fred Wallace and Dorothy (Marshall) P.; m. Jane Laird Miller, Dec. 27, 1962 (div. Oct. 1986); children: Catherine W., Gregory W.; m. Christine R. Fredrick, Jan. 4, 1991. BA in Polit. Sci., U. Fla., 1962, JD with honors, 1969; AM in Internat. Rels., Boston U., 1965. Bar: Fla. 1970, U.S. Dist. Ct. (so., mid. and no. dists.) Fla., U.S. Supreme Ct. 1975, U.S. Ct. Appeals (11th cir.) 1983. Rsch. aide 2d Dist. Ct. Appeal, Lakeland, Fla., 1970; assoc. Trenam, Simmons, Kemker, Scharf & Barkin, Tampa, 1970-74; ptnr. Johnson, Blakely, Pope, Bokor, Ruppel & Burns, P.A., Clearwater, 1974—. Dir. Citizens Bank Clearwater, 1986-98, First Nat. Bank of Fla., 1998-01. Trustee The Fla. Orch., Tampa, 1984—, chmn. bd. trustees, 1991-93; bd. dirs. Pinellas County Arts Coun., Clearwater, 1988-93. Capt. U.S. Army, 1962-67. Mem. ABA (coun. mem. sect. litigation 1983-86, editor, chief Litigation 1979-80), The Fla. Bar (gov. 1982-86), Clearwater Bar Assn. (pres. 1980-81). General civil litigation. Office: Johnson Blakely Pope Bokor Ruppel & Burns PA 911 Chestnut St Clearwater FL 33756-5643 E-mail: wallyp@jbpfirm.com

POPE, JOHN WILLIAM, judge, law educator; b. San Francisco, Mar. 12, 1947; s. William W. and Florence E. (Kline) P.; m. Linda M. Marsh, Oct. 23, 1970 (div. Dec. 1996); children: Justin, Ana, Lauren. BA, U. N.Mex., 1969, JD, 1973. Bar: N.Mex. 1973, U.S. Dist. Ct. N.Mex. 1973,

U.S. Ct. Appeals (10th cir.) 1976. Law clk. N.Mex. Ct. of Appeals, Santa Fe, 1973; assoc. Chavez & Cowper, Belen, N.Mex., 1974; ptnr. Cowper, Bailey & Pope, 1974-75; pvt. practice law, 1976-80; ptnr. Pope, Apodaca & Conroy, 1980-85; dir. litigation City of Albuquerque, 1985-87; judge State of N.Mex., Albuquerque, 1987-92, Dist. Ct. (13th jud. dist.), N.Mex., 1992—. Instr. U. N.Mex., Albuquerque, 1983—, prof. law , 1990—; lectr. in field. Mem. state cen. com. Dem. Party, N.Mex., 1971-85; state chair Common Cause N.Mex., 1980-83; pres. Valencia County Hist. Soc., Belen, 1981-83; active Supreme Ct. Jury (UJI civil instructions com., state bar hist. com., bench and bar com.). Recipient Outstanding Jud. Svc. award N.Mex. State Bar, 1996; named City of Belen Citizen of Yr. 1995, Excellence in Tchg. award 1998. Mem. Valencia County Bar, Albuquerque Bar Assn. Avocations: swimming, golf, photography, historical research. Home: 400 Godfrey Ave Belen NM 87002-6313 Office: Valencia County Courthouse PO Box 1089 Los Lunas NM 87031-1089

POPE, MARK ANDREW, lawyer, university administrator; b. Munster, Ind., May 22, 1952; s. Thomas A. and Eleanor E. (Miklos) P.; m. Julia Risk Pope, June 15, 1974; children: Brent Andrew, Bradley James. BA, Purdue U., 1974; JD cum laude, Ind. U., 1977. Bar: Ind. 1977, U.S. Dist. Ct. (so. dist.) Ind. 1977, U.S. Ct. Appeals (7th cir.) 1984. Assoc. Johnson & Weaver, Indpls., 1977-79, Rocap, Rocap, Reese & Young, Indpls., 1980-82, Dutton & Overman, Indpls., 1982-88, ptnr., 1988-89; asst. gen. counsel Lincoln Nat. Corp., Fort Wayne, Ind., 1989-91, sr. counsel, 1991-95, v.p. govt. rels., 1995-2001; dir. athletics Ind. U.-Purdue U., Ft. Wayne, 2001—. Bd. dirs. Ft. Wayne Bicentennial Coun.; pres., bd. dirs. ARCH, Inc., 1994-97. Bd. editors, devel. editor Ind. U. Law Rev., 1976-77 Mem. pres.'s coun. Purdue U., 1977—; applied eoncs. cons. Jr. Achievement, 1989-95; bd. dirs. Jr. Achievement of No. Ind., 1992-94; grad. Leadership, Fort Wayne, 1992; mem. parish coun. St. Elizabeth Ann Seton Ch., 1993-96, pres. 1993-95; bd. edn. mem. Bishop Luers H.S., 2000—; adv. coun. Ind. U. Bus. Sch., Purdue U., Fort Wayne, Ind., 2000—. Named Disting. Hoosier, Gov. of Ind., 1974. Fellow Ind. Bar Found., Indpls. Bar Found. (disting.); mem. ABA (dist. rep. young lawyers divsn. 1981-83, dir. 1983-84, liaison coord. 1985-86, 87-88, exec. coun. 1981-88, cabinet 1982-88, gen. practice sect. coun. mem. 1986—, membership chmn. 1987-89, chmn. career and family com. 1990-92, dir. 1991-93), Indpls. Bar Assn. (v.p. 1983, chmn. young lawyers divsn. 1981), 500 Festival Assocs. (vice-chmn. of 500 festival parade 1985-89), Orchard Ridge Country Club (bd. dirs. 1995—, sec. 1996-97, pres. 1999-2001). Avocations: tennis, golf, running. Education and schools, General civil litigation, Contracts commercial. Office: Ind U-Purdue U at Fort Wayne Gates Sports Ctr 2101 E Coliseum Blvd Fort Wayne IN 46805-1499 E-mail: popem@ipfw.edu

POPE, MICHAEL ARTHUR, lawyer; b. Chgo., June 27, 1944; s. Arthur Wellington and Phyllis Anne (O'Connor) P.; m. Christine Collins, Nov. 19, 1966; children: Jennifer, Amy, Katherine. BS, Loyola U., Chgo., 1966; JD cum laude, Northwestern U., 1969. Bar: Ill. 1969, N.Y. 1985, U.S. Dist. Ct. (no. dist.) Ill. 1969, U.S. Ct. Appeals (7th cir.) 1970, U.S. Supreme Ct. 1980. Tchg. asst. U. Ill. Coll. Law, Champaign, 1969-70; assoc. Isham, Lincoln & Beale, Chgo., 1970-76; prin. Phelan, Pope & John, Ltd., 1976-90, prin., 1990-95; capital ptnr. McDermott, Will & Emery, 1995—. Adj. prof. law Chgo.-Kent Law Sch. Ill. Inst. Tech., 1982-85; bd. trustees Nat. Jud. Coll., 1997—. Mem. ABA, Ill. Bar Assn., Chgo. Bar Assn., Am. Bd. Profl. Liability Attys. (pres. 1985-87), Am. Law Inst. 7th Cir. Bar Assn., Internat. Assn. Def. Counsel (pres. 1993-94), Internat. Soc. Barristers, Am. Coll. Trial Lawyers, Internat. Acad. Trial Lawyers, Am. Law Inst., The Chgo. Club, Skokie Country Club (Glencoe Ill.), East Bank Club (Chgo.). General civil litigation, Environmental, Insurance. Office: McDermott Will & Emery 227 W Monroe St Ste 3100 Chicago IL 60606-5096 E-mail: mpope@mwe.com

POPE, PATRICK HARRIS, lawyer, business executive; b. Dunn, N.C., Aug. 27, 1944; s. Claude Efton and Rochelle Olive (Jackson) P.; m. Mary Norfleet Tilghman, Aug. 21, 1965; children: Patrick Tilghman, Wiley Jackson. Caroline Denning. BS in Bus. Adminstrn., U. N.C., 1966, J with honors, 1969. BAr: N.C. 1969, U.S. Dist. Ct. (ea. dist.) N.C. 1969. Ptnr. Doffermyre & Pope, Dunn, 1969-72; sr. ptnr. Pope & Tart and predecessor firms, 1972—. Bd. dirs. Centura Banks, Inc., Master Developers, Inc. Rsch. editor N.C. Law Rev., 1969; contbr. articles to profl. jours. Bd. dir. Gen. William C. Lee Meml. Commn., Inc., Dunn, 1983—; trustee Betsy Johnson Meml. Hosp., Inc., Dunn, 1977-82, 96—, vice chmn., 1983-84, 99—, chmn., 1984. Mem. N.C. Bar Assn., N.C. State Bar, Hartnett County Bar Assn. (pres. 1974-75), 11th Jud. Dist. Bar Assn. (pres. 1974-75, v.p. 1973-74), N.C. Acad. Trial Lawyers, Order of Coif, Masons. Republican. Presbyterian. State civil litigation, General practice, Personal injury. Home: 208 W Pearsall St Dunn NC 28334-5236 Office: Pope & Tart 403 W Broad St Dunn NC 28334-4807

POPE, ROBERT DEAN, lawyer; b. Memphis, Mar. 10, 1945; s. Ben Duncan and Phyllis (Drenner) P.; m. Elizabeth Dante Cohen, June 26, 1971; 1 child, Justin Nicholas Nathanson. AB, Princeton U., 1967; Diploma in Hist. Studies, Cambridge U., 1971; JD, Yale U., 1972, PhD, 1976. Bar: Va. 1974, D.C. 1980. Assoc. Hunton & Williams, Richmond, Va., 1974-80, ptnr., 1980—. Mem. steering com. Bond Attys. Workshop, 1994—98; lectr. in law U. Va. Law Sch., 2000—; advisor, com. on govtl. debt and fiscal policy Govt. Fin. Officers Assn., 1993—99. Author: Disclosure Rules of Counsel in State and Local Government Securities Offerings, 2d edit., 1994, Making Good Disclosure: The Role and Responsibilities of State and Local Officials Under the Federal Security Laws , 2001. Mem. adv. com. Va. Sec. of Health and Human Svcs. on Continuing Care Legislation, 1992-94; mem. Anthony Commn. on Pub. Fin.; adv. coun. dept. history Princeton U., 1987-91; mem. Mcpl. Securities Rulemaking Bd., 1996-99, vice chmn. 1998-99. Mem.: NCCJ (bd. dirs. Richmond), Nat. Assn. Bond Lawyers (treas. 1984—85, sec. 1985—86, pres. 1987—88, bd. dirs. 1982—89, Bernard P. Friel medal for contbns. to pub.fin. 1994), Am. Acad. Hosp. Attys., Am. Coll. Bond Counsel, Va. Bar Assn. (chmn. legal problems of elderly 1982—88), Yale Law Sch. Assn. (exec. com. 1985—88), Bond Club Va. (bd. dirs. 1990—98, v.p. 1993—94, pres. 1994—95), Phi Beta Kappa. Republican. Episcopalian. Avocations: history, golf, music, book reviews. Health, Municipal (including bonds), Securities. Home: 8707 Ruggles Rd Richmond VA 23229-7918 Office: Hunton & Williams 951 E Byrd Richmond VA 23219-4074 E-mail: dpope@hunton.com

POPE, WILLIAM L. lawyer, judge; b. Brownsville, Tex., Nov. 5, 1960; s. William E. and Maria Antonieta P.; m. Sandra Solis, May 16, 1992; children: Ana Lauren, William E.H. AA, Tex. Southmost Coll., 1980; postgrad., U. Tex., 1980-81, Tex. Christian U., 1982, Tex. Coll. Osteo. Medicine, 1982-83; JD, Baylor U., 1986; MD (hon.), Cosmopolitan U. & Rsch. Inst., Vina del Mar, Chile, 1998. Bar: Tex. 1986, U.S. Dist. Ct. (so. dist.) Tex. 1988, U.S. Supreme Ct. 1990. Assoc. Adams & Graham, Harlingen, Tex., 1986-91, ptnr., 1991—; mcpl. ct. judge City of La Feria, 1987—. Bd. trustees Episcopal Day Sch., Brownsville, Tex., 1999-2000. Mem. Tex. State Bar Assn. Mem. Ch. of Christ. General civil litigation, Health, Professional liability. Office: Adams & Graham L L P PO Box 1429 Harlingen TX 78551-1429 E-mail: Pope@adamsgraham.com

POPPLER, DORIS SWORDS, lawyer; b. Billings, Mont., Nov. 10, 1924; d. Lloyd William and Edna (Mowre) Swords; m. Louis E. Poppler, June 11, 1949; children: Louis William, Kristine, Mark J., Blaine, Claire, Arminda. Student, U. Minn., 1942-44; JD, Mont. State U., 1948. Bar: Mont. 1948, U.S. Dist. Ct. Mont. 1948, U.S. Ct. Appeals (9th cir.) 1990. Pvt. practice law, Billings, 1948-49; sec., treas. Wonderpark Corp., 1959-62; atty. Yellowstone County Attys. Office, 1972-75; ptnr. Poppler and Barz, 1972-79, Davidson, Veeder, Baugh, Broeder and Poppler, Billings, 1979-84, Davidson and Poppler, P.C., Billings, 1984-90; U.S. atty. Dist. of Mont., 1990-93; field rep. Nat. Indian Gaming Commn., Washington, 1993-2000. Pres. Jr. League, 1964-65; bd. dirs., pres. Yellowstone County Metre Bd., 1982; trustee Rocky Mt. Coll., 1984-90, mem. nat. adv. bd., 1993—; mem. Mont. Human Rights Commn., 1988-90; bd. dirs. Miss Mont. Pageant, 1995—. Recipient Mont. Salute to Women award, Mont. Woman of Achievent award, 1975, Disting. Svc. award Rocky Mt. Coll., 1990, 1st ann. U. Montana Law Sch. Disting. Female Alumna award, 1996. Mem. AAUW, Mont. Bar Assn., Nat. Assn. Former U.S. Attys., Nat. Rep. Lawyers Assn., Internat. Women's Forum, Yellowstone County Bar Assn. (pres. 1990), Alpha Chi Omega. Republican.

PORFILIO, JOHN CARBONE, federal judge; b. Denver, Oct. 14, 1934; s. Edward Alphonso Porfilio and Caroline (Carbone) Moore; m. Joan West, Aug. 1, 1959 (div. 1983); children: Edward Miles, Joseph Arthur, Jeanne Kathrine; m. Theresa Louise Berger, Dec. 28, 1983; 1 stepchild, Katrina Ann Smith Student, Stanford U., 1952-54; BA, U. Denver, 1956, LLB, 1959, LLD (hon.), 2000. Bar: Colo. 1959, U.S. Supreme Ct. 1965. Asst. atty. gen. State of Colo., Denver, 1962-68, dep. atty. gen., 1968-72, atty. gen., 1972-74; U.S. bankruptcy judge Dist. of Colo., 1975-82; judge U.S. Dist. Ct. Colo., 1982-85, U.S. Ct. Appeals (10th cir.), Denver, 1985—. Instr. Colo. Law Enforcement Acad., Denver, 1965-70, State Patrol Acad., Denver, 1968-70; guest lectr. U. Denver Coll. Law, 1978 Committeeman Arapahoe County Republican Com., Aurora, Colo., 1968; mgr. Dunbar for Atty. Gen., Denver, 1970 Mem. ABA. Roman Catholic Office: US Ct Appeals Byron White US Courthouse 1823 Stout St Denver CO 80257-1823

PORITZ, DEBORAH T. state supreme court chief justice, former attorney general; Atty. gen. State of N.J., 1994-96; chief justice Supreme Ct. N.J., Trenton, 1996—. Office: Supreme Ct NJ Hughes Justice Complex PO Box 23 Trenton NJ 08625-0023*

PORTEOUS, G. THOMAS, JR. judge; b. 1946; BA, La. State U., 1968, JD, 1971. Spl. counsel, atty. gen., 1971-73; asst. dist. atty. Dist. Atty. Office Parrish of Jefferson, 1973-75; ptnr. Edward, Porteous & Amato, Grenta, La., 1973-74, Edwards, Porteous & Lee, Grenta, 1974-76, Porteous, Lee & Mustakas, 1976-80, Porteous & Mustakas, Metairie, La., 1980-84; city atty. City of Harahan, La., 1982-84; dist. ct. judge divsn. A State of La., 1984-94; dist. judge U.S. Dist. Ct. (ea. dist.), La., 1994—. Mem. ABA, Fed. Bar Assn., La. State Bar Assn., 4th and 5th Cir. Judges Assn., Jefferson Bar Assn., Am. Judges Assn., La. Dist. Atty. Assn. Office: US Dist Ct E Dist 500 Camp St Rm C-206 New Orleans LA 70130-3313

PORTER, J. RIDGELY, III, lawyer; b. Va., Apr. 28, 1948; s. John R and Mary Manning (Barclay) P.; m. DeLane Williams, 1978; 1 child, Eleanor M. BA, U. Va., 1970; JD, Washington & Lee U., 1973. Law clerk to U.S. judge, 1973-74; ptnr. Carr & Porter, 1974—; pres. Va. Internat. Terminals, 1985-92; chmn. bd. Chesapeake Gen. Hosp., 1986-96; owner Cattle Farms. Mem.: ABA, Va. Bar Assn., Met. Club (D.C.). Episcopalian. Federal civil litigation, General corporate, Public international. Office: 355 Crawford Pkwy Portsmouth VA 23704

PORTER, JAMES HARRY, JR. lawyer; b. Balt., Jan. 16, 1956; s. James Harry and Ruth (Parks) P. B.A., Salisbury State Coll., 1977; J.D., U. Balt., 1980. Bar: Md. 1982, U.S. Dist. Ct. Md. 1982, U.S. Bankruptcy Ct. Md. 1982. Law clk., baliff Dist. Ct. Md. for Howard County, Ellicott City, 1980; law clk. Cir. Ct. for Carroll County, Md., 1980-81; assoc. Henry P. Walters, P.A., Pocomoke, Md., 1982— ; legal adviser Legal Intern Program for Worcester County, 1983— ; instr. Wor-Wic Tech. Community Coll., Salisbury, 1983— . Mem. ABA, Assn. Trial Lawyers Am., Md. Bar Assn., (com. on ethics 1984-85), Worcester County Bar Assn., Md. Trial Lawyers Assn., U. Balt. Alumni Assn. (v.p. Eastern Shore chpt. 1984, pres. 1985-87), Pocomoke City Jaycees. Democrat. Methodist. Lodge: Rotary (bd. dirs., sec. 1986-87). State civil litigation, Criminal, General practice. Home: 147 Pine St Princess Anne MD 21853 Office: Henry P Walters PA 111 Vine St Pocomoke City MD 21851-1034

PORTER, JAMES KENNETH, retired judge; b. Newport, Tenn., Apr. 6, 1934; s. John Calhoun and Bessie Betis (Crouch) P.; m. Evelyn Janet Rhodes, Sept. 17, 1955; children: Jane Caroline, James Kenneth Jr. BS, U. Tenn., 1955, JD, 1957. Bar: Tenn. 1957, U.S. Dist. Ct. (ea. dist.) Tenn. 1958, U.S. Ct. Appeals (6th cir.) 1971. Ptnr. Porter, Porter & Dunn, Porter & Porter, Newport, 1957-74; state rep. Tenn. Gen. Assembly, Nashville, 1961-65, minority fl. leader, 1963-65; county atty. Cocke County, Tenn., 1961-63, commr. County Election Commn., 1966-72, chmn., 1968-70; mem. Tenn. Senate, Nashville, 1972-74; state cir. judge 4th Jud. Cir., Newport, 1974-93; ret., 1993; state presiding judge 4th Jud. Cir., Newport, 1984-86, 88-90, 1992-93; judgeship nominee U.S. Dist. Ct. (ea. dist.), Tenn., 1986; Tenn. Ct. Appeals nominee, 1990. Del. S.E. Law Rev. Conf., Durham, N.C., 1957, Nat. Conf. State Legislator Leaders, Boston, 1963; discussion leader Nat. Jud. Coll., Reno, 1981, faculty adviser, 1982; mem. Gov.'s Correction Overcrowding Commn., Nashville, 1985-86. Contbr. articles to U. Tenn. Law Rev., 1956-57, editor in chief, 1957. Active Farm Bur., 1962-82; mem. adv. coun., trustee Walters State Community Coll., Morristown, Tenn., 1975-86. Mem. ABA (Tenn. jud. del. 1984), Tenn. Jud. Conf. (v.p. 1980-81), Tenn. Trial Judges Assn. (bd. dirs. 1976-86, pres. 1982-85), Tenn. Bar Assn. (spl. trial counsel 1973-76), Cocke County Bar Assn., Smoky Mountain Country Club (bd. dirs. 1964-67, v.p. 1966-67), Order of Coif, Sigma Alpha Epsilon (Highest Effort Law award 1986), Phi Delta Phi. Republican. Baptist. Avocations: golf, gardening, guitar. Home: 306 North St Newport TN 37821-2413 Office: 106 S Mims Ave Newport TN 37821-3125 E-mail: porterk@planetc.com

PORTER, JAMES MORRIS, retired judge; b. Cleve., Sept. 14, 1931; s. Emmett Thomas and Mary (Connell) P.; m. Helen Marie Adams, May 31, 1952; children: James E., Thomas W., William M., Daniel J. A.B., John Carroll U., 1953; J.D., U. Mich., 1957. Bar: Ohio 1957. Assoc. firm M.B. & H.H. Johnson, Cleve., 1957-62, McAfee, Hanning, Newcomer, Hazlett & Wheeler, Cleve., 1962-67; ptnr. firm Squire, Sanders & Dempsey, 1967-92; judge Ohio Ct. Appeals, 8th Dist., 1993-2000, Cuyahoga County Common Pleas Ct., Cleve., 2001. 1st lt. U.S. Army, 1953-55. Fellow Am. Coll. Trial Lawyers; mem. The Country Club (Cleve.). Republican. Roman Catholic.

PORTER, LEON EUGENE, JR. lawyer; b. Winston-Salem, N.C., Sept. 22, 1953; s. Leon E. and Ruby H. (Dodson) P.; m. Mary THompson, June 18, 1977; children: William Markland, Meredith Dodson, Matthew Garrett, Michael Lee. BA in Econs. with honors, U. N.C., 1975; JD cum laude, Wake Forest U., 1978. Bar: N.C. 1978, U.S. Dist. Ct. (we., mid. and ea. dists.) N.C., U.S. Ct. Appeals (4th cir.). Law clk. to presiding magistrate U.S. Dist. Ct., Winston-Salem, 1978-79, law clk. to presiding judge, 1979-81; assoc. Petree Stockton, 1981-87, ptnr., 1988-91; chief cons. personal products Sara Lee Corp., 1991-97; ptnr. Kilpatrick Stockton, LLP, 1997—. Deacon First Presbyn. Ch., Winston-Salem, 1986-88. 90—, pers. com., 1988—. Mem. ABA (forum com. health law, litigation sect., Young Lawyers Div. litigation and health law com. 1988, exec. com. 1988), N.C. Bar Assn. (co-chmn. young lawyers div. com. on lawyers for the arts 1968-88, dist. dir. 1988-89), Forsyth County Bar Assn., Winston-Salem C. of C. (profl. task force), N.C. Soc. Health Care Attys. Democrat. Avocation: swimming. Federal civil litigation, State civil litigation, Health. Home: 1001 Fairhope Ct Winston Salem NC 27104-1213 Office: Kilpatrick Stockton LLP 1001 W 4th St Winston Salem NC 27101-2400 Fax: (336) 607-7500. E-mail: lporter@kilpatrickstockton.com

PORTER, MICHAEL PELL, lawyer; b. Indpls., Mar. 31, 1940; s. Harold Troxel and Mildred Maxine (Pell) P.; m. Alliene Laura Jenkins, Sept. 23, 1967 (div.); 1 child, Genevieve Natalie Porter Eason; m. Janet Kay Smith Hayes, Feb. 13, 1983 (div.). Student, DePauw U., 1957-58; BA, Tulane U., 1961, LLB, 1963. Bar: La. 1963, U.S. Ct. Mil. Appeals 1964, N.Y. 1969, Hawaii 1971. Clk. U.S. Ct. Appeals (5th cir.), New Orleans, 1963; assoc. Sullivan & Cromwell, N.Y.C., 1968-71, Cades Schutte Fleming & Wright, Honolulu, 1971-74, ptnr., 1975-94; mem. faculty Addis Ababa (Ethiopia) U. Sch. Law, 1995-99; sr. regulatory advisor Egyptian Capital Market Authority, Cairo, 1999—. Legal advisor St. Matthews Anglican Ch. Addis Ababa, 1995-99; cons. Rep. of Yemen, 1997; mem. deans coun. Law Sch. Tulane U., 1981-88; dep. vice chancellor Episcopal Diocese Hawaii, 1980-88, chancellor, 1988-94; chancellor Episcopal Ch., Micronesia, 1988-95. Author: Hawaii Corporation Law & Practice, 1989; Hawaii reporter State Limited Partnership Laws, 1992-94. Bd. dirs. Jr. Achievement Hawaii, Inc., 1974-84, Inst. Human Svcs., Inc., 1980-88; donor Michael P. Porter Dean's Scholastic Award, U. Hawaii Law Sch., 1977—. With JAGC, U.S. Army, 1963-66, Vietnam. Fulbright scholar, 1997-99; Tulane U. fellow, 1981; lectorship named in his honor, Addis Abba, 1994-97; established Michael P. Porter Prizes on Ethnic Harmony and Religious Tolerance in a Dem. Soc. at Addis Ababa, 1995. Mem. ABA, Hawaii State Bar Assn. Republican. General corporate, Securities. E-mail: mporter@capmkt.com

PORTER, ROBERT CARL, JR. lawyer; b. Cin., Sept. 21, 1927; s. Robert Carl and Lavinia (Otte) P.; m. Joanne Patterson, July 5, 1952; children: Robert Carl III, David M., John E. BA with distinction, U. Mich., 1949; JD, Harvard U., 1952. Bar: Ohio 1952, U.S. Dist. Ct. (so. dist.) Ohio 1954, U.S. Ct. Appeals (6th cir.) 1954, U.S. Ct. Mil. Appeals 1956, U.S. Tax Ct. 1980, U.S. Supreme Ct. 1956. Ptnr. Porter & Porter, Cin., 1953-54; sole practice, 1954-63; sr. ptnr. Porter & McKinney, 1963-88, Porter & Porter, Cin., 1989—. Dir. and officer numerous cos. Served with JAGC, USAF, 1952-53. Mem. ABA, Ohio State Bar Assn., Cin. Bar Assn., Cin. Country Club, Univ. Club, U. Mich. Club, Harvard Law Sch. Assn., Masons, Scottish Rite, Shriners, Phi Beta Kappa. Presbyterian. General corporate, Probate, Taxation, general. Home: 2365 Bedford Ave Cincinnati OH 45208-2656 Office: Porter & Porter 2100 4th and Vine Tower Cincinnati OH 45202

PORTER, THOMAS WILLIAM, III, lawyer; b. Dallas, Aug. 23, 1941; s. Thomas William and Ruth Mae (Campbell) P.; m. Sally Ann Shell, May 10, 1963 (div. July 1983); children: Elizabeth Elisse, Laura Christina; m. Patty Ann Sanders, Nov. 2, 1985. BBA in Fin., So. Meth. U., 1963; LLB, Duke U., 1966. Bar: Tex. 1966, U.S. Dist. Ct. (no. dist.) Tex. 1967, U.S. Dist. Ct. (so. dist.) Tex. 1975, U.S. Dist. Ct. (we. dist.) Tex. 1977, U.S. Ct. Appeals (5th cir.) 1977. Assoc. Jackson & Walker, Dallas, 1966-72; ptnr. Bracewell & Patterson, Houston, 1972-74, Foreman & Dyess, Houston, 1974-81; sr. ptnr. Porter & Hedges LLP, 1981—. Lectr. securities and corp. law State Bar Tex. Continuing Legal Edn. Program, 1977—; bd. visitors Duke U. Law Sch., 1985-92. Fellow Tex. Bar Found.; mem. ABA (fed. regulation of securities com. 1979—, com. on law firms 1981—), State Bar Tex. Assn. (coun. mem. sect. corp. baning and bus. law 1984-86, securities and investment banking com. 1976—), Houston Bar Assn., Assn. for Corp. Growth (bd. dirs. 1981-83), Lakeside Country Club, Lochinvar Golf Club, Coronado Club, Phi Delta Phi. Republican. Methodist. General corporate, Private international, Securities. Office: Porter & Hedges LLP 35th Fl Nations Bank Center 700 Louisiana St Houston TX 77002-2700

PORTER, VERNA LOUISE, lawyer; b. May 31, 1941; BA, Calif. State U., 1963; JD, Southwestern U., 1977. Bar: Calif. 1977, U.S. Dist. Ct. (ctrl. dist.) Calif. 1978, U.S. Ct. Appeals (9th cir.) 1978. Ptnr. Eisler & Porter, L.A., 1978-79, mng. ptnr., 1979-86; pvt. practice, 1986—. Judge pro-tempore L.A. Mcpl. Ct., 1983—, L.A. Superior Ct., 1989—, Beverly HIlls Mcpl. Ct., 1992—; mem. subcom. landlord tenant law, State Calif., panelist conv.; mem. real property law sect. Calif. State Bar, 1983; mem. client rels. panel, vol. L.A. County Bar Dispute Resolution; ct. appointed arbitrator civil cases, fee arbitrator L.A. Superior Ct.; mem. Better Bus. Bur. Abitrator Automobile Lemon Laws, 2000—. Editl. asst., contbr. Apt. Bus. Outlook, Real Property News, Apt. Age. Mem. adv. coun. Freddie Mac Vendor, 1995—; mem. World Affairs Coun. Mem. ABA, L.A. County Bar Assn. (client-rels. vol. dispute resolution fee arbitration 1981—; arbitrator lemon law claims), L.A. Trial Lawyers Assn., Wilshire Bar Assn. Women Lawyers' Assn., Landlord Trial Lawyers Assn. (founding, pres.), Da Camera Soc. Republican. Consumer commercial, Landlord-tenant, Real property. Office: 2500 Wilshire Blvd Ste 1226 Los Angeles CA 90057-4365

PORTMAN, GLENN ARTHUR, lawyer; b. Cleve., Dec. 26, 1949; s. Alvin B. and Lenore (Marsh) P.; m. Katherine Seaborn, Aug. 3, 1974 (div. 1984); m. Susan Newell, Jan. 3, 1987. BA in History, Case Western Res. U., 1968; JD, So. Meth. U., 1975. Bar: Tex. 1975, U.S. Dist. Ct. (no. dist.) Tex. 1975, U.S. Dist. Ct. (so. dist.) Tex. 1983, U.S. Dist. Ct. (we. and ea. dists.) Tex. 1988. Assoc. Johnson, Bromberg & Leeds, Dallas, 1975-80, ptnr., 1980-92, Arter, Hadden, Johnson & Bromberg, Dallas, 1992-95, Arter & Hadden LLP, Dallas, 1996—. Chmn. bd. dirs. Physicians Regional Hosp., 1994-96; mem. exec. bd. So. Meth. U. Sch. Law, 1994—; lectr. bankruptcy topics South Tex. Coll. Law, State Bar Tex.; mem. vis. com. Coll. Arts and Scis., Case Western Res. U., 1999—. Asst. editor-in-chief Southwestern Law Jour., 1974-75; contbr. articles to profl. jours. Firm rep. United Way Met. Dallas, 1982-92; treas. Lake Highlands Square Homeowners Assn., 1990-93. Mem. ABA, Am. Bankruptcy Inst., State Bar Tex. Assn., Dallas Bar Assn., So. Meth. U. Law Alumni Assn. (council bd. dirs., v.p. 1980-86, chmn. admissions com., chmn. class agt. program 1986-89, chmn. fund raising 1989-91), 500 Club Inc., Assemblage Club. Republican. Methodist. Bankruptcy, Contracts commercial, Real property. Home: 9503 Winding Ridge Dr Dallas TX 75238-1451 Office: Arter & Hadden LLP 1717 Main St Ste 4100 Dallas TX 75201-7389 E-mail: g.portman@att.net, gportman@anterhadden.com

PORTNOY, JEFFREY STEVEN, lawyer; b. Bklyn., July 5, 1947; s. Bernard and Edna (Fure) P.; m. Sandi Edelstein, Mar. 29, 1970; 1 child, Carrie Paige. AB in Polit. Sci. cum laude, Syracuse U., 1969; JD, Duke U., 1972. Bar: Hawaii 1972, U.S. Dist. Ct. Hawaii 1972, U.S. Ct. Appeals (9th cir.) 1973, U.S. Supreme Ct. 1978. U.S. Dist Ct. No. Mariana Islands 1984. With Cades Schutte, Fleming and Wright, Honolulu, 1972-78, ptnr. 1979—; adj. prof. media law dept. journalism U. Hawaii, Honolulu, 1986-92; chairperson adv. com U.S. Dist. Ct., 1991—. Pres., bd. dirs. Manoa Valley Theatre, Honolulu, 1980—; mem. Honolulu Community Media Coun., 1983—; chmn. Honolulu Neighborhood Commn., 1984-88; mem. panel of arbitrators Am. Arbitration Assn., 1984—; del. Hawaii Jud. Conf., 1985-87; mem. Hawaii Bicentennial Commn. Recipient Freedom of Press award Sigma Delta Chi, 1984. Mem. ABA (forum com. communication, media and law com. 1985-86, chmn. We The People orgn.), Hawaii State Bar Assn. (dir. 1990-93), Hawaii Def. Lawyers Assn. (pres. 1991-95, lawyer del. 9th cir. jud. conf. 1989-91), Def. Rsch. Inst. (HSBA del. to ABA House Dels. 1994—, state chairperson, Amb. award 1988, Exceptional Performance award 1991, 92). Jewish. State civil litigation, Insurance, Libel. Home: 5111 Palaole Pl Honolulu HI 96821-1530 Office: Cades Schutte Fleming & Wright PO Box 939 Honolulu HI 96808-0939

PORTNOY, SARA S. lawyer; b. N.Y.C., Jan. 11, 1926; d. Marcus and Gussie (Raphael) Spiro; m. Alexander Portnoy, Dec. 13, 1959 (dec. 1976); children: William, Lawrence. BA, Radcliffe Coll., 1946; LLB, Columbia U., 1949. Bar: N.Y. 1949, U.S. Dist. Ct. (so. dist.) N.Y. 1952, U.S. Dist. Ct. (eas. dist.) N.Y. 1975, U.S. Ct. Appeals (2d cir.) 1975, U.S. Supreme Ct. 1975. Assoc. Seligsberg, Friedman & Berliner, N.Y.C., 1949-51; atty. AT&T, 1951-61; vol. atty. Legal Aid Soc. of Westchester, N.Y., 1966-74;

assoc. Proskauer Rose Goetz & Mendelsohn, N.Y.C., 1974-78, ptnr., 1978-94; ret., 1994. Mem. Commn. on Human Rights, White Plains, N.Y., 1973-78; mem. bd. visitors Columbia Law Sch., 1996—; bd. dirs. Legal Aid Soc. of Westchester County, N.Y., 1975-83, Columbia Law Sch. Assn., 1990-94, Mosholu Montifiore Cmty. Ctr., 1998—; mem. Pres.'s Coun. Yaddo; dir. Muscular Dystrophy Assn., 2000—. Mem. Assn. Bar City of N.Y. (chair com. legal support staff 1994, mem. Com. on Homeless, Sr. Lawyer's Com. and Pub. Svc. Network), South Fork Country Club (dir. 1997—), The Children's Storefront (dir. 1998—). Civil rights, Labor, Pension, profit-sharing, and employee benefits.

POSCOVER, MAURY B. lawyer; b. St. Louis, Jan. 13, 1944; s. Edward and Ann (Chapnick) P.; m. Lorraine Wexler, Aug. 14, 1966; children: Michael, Daniel, Joanna. BA, Lehigh U., 1966; JD, Washington U., 1969. Bar: Mo. 1969. Assoc. Husch & Eppenberger LLC, St. Louis, 1969-75, ptnr., mem., 1975—. Lectr. Washington U., St. Louis, 1972-79. Editor-in-chief: The Business Lawyer, 1995-96; contbr. articles to profl. jours. Bd. dirs. Childhaven, St. Louis, 1978-92, pres. 1986; pres. Jewish Community Rels. Coun., 1990-92. Mem.: ABA (bd. govs. 1999—, chmn. comml. fin. svcs. com. bus. law sect. coun., chair bus. law sect. 1997—98, editor-in-chief jour., mem. exec. com. bd. govs. 2001—, chair ops. and comms. com. 2001—), Bar Assn. Met. St. Louis (pres. 1983—84), Mo. Bar Assn. (bd. govs. 1979—81), Am. Judicature Soc. (dir. 1981—87), Am.-Israel C. of C. (pres. 1999—), Wash. U. Alumni Law Assn. (pres. 1980—81), Mo. Athletic Club. Jewish. Banking, Contracts commercial, General corporate. Office: Husch & Eppenberger LLC 100 N Broadway Ste 1300 Saint Louis MO 63102-2706 E-mail: maury.poscover@husch.com

POSEY, JANETTE ROBISON, lawyer; b. Gentry, Mo., Mar. 5, 1939; d. John Otto and Daphne Elainee (Ross)_ Robison; m Walter Daniel Posey, July 6, 1958; children: Sheree Lanae Posey Tyner, Jennifer, Renee. AA, Fullerton (Calif.) C.C., 1967; BA, Calif. State U., Fullerton, 1970, MA, 1971; JD, Western State U., Fullerton, 1976. Bar: Calif. 1976, U.S. Dist. Ct. (so. and ctrl. dists.) Calif. 1977, U.S. Ct. Appeals (9th cir.) 1977, U.S. Supreme Ct. 1977; life C.C. tchr. credential, Calif. Pvt. practice, Anaheim, Calif., 1977—; pvt. practice, owner Posey and Posey, Tustin, 1977—. Co-founder Orange County Women's Law Ctr., Fullerton, 1973-76; adj. prof. law Am. Coll. Law, Brea, Calif., 1991-93, Western State U. Coll. Law, 1993-96. 2d v.p. Villa Park (Calif.) Women's League, 1988-89, 3d v.p., 1989-90; educator smile project VISTA, Yorba Linda, Calif., 1972. Mem. State Bar Calif., Orange County Bar Assn., Orange County Women Lawyers Assn. (bd. dirs. 1977-78), L.A. Bar Assn. Presbyterian. Avocations: writing, ballroom dancing, swimming, traveling. Personal injury, Probate. Office: 17671 Irvine Blvd Ste 208 Tustin CA 92780-3129

POSNER, DAVID S. lawyer; b. Pitts., Dec. 27, 1945; s. Mortimer B. and Lillian P.; m. Marilyn Hope Ackerman, Aug. 14, 1966; children: Morton J., Jennifer L. BS, Carnegie Mellon U., 1969; JD, U. Pitts., 1972. Bar: Pa. 1972, U.S. Supreme Ct. 1981. Ct. adminstr. Washington County, Pa., 1972-76, asst. dist. atty., 1976-79; ptnr. Goldfarb & Posner, Washington, 1979-97, Goldfarb, Posner, Beck, DeHaven & Drewitz, Washington, 1997—. Pres. Pa. Council of Trial Ct. Adminstrs., 1972-76; solicitor Clk. of Cts., Washington, 1983—. Mem. sect. 85 YMCA, Washington, 1980-85; bd. dirs. United Way, Washington, 1979-85; pres. Beth Israel Congregation, 1992-94. With USAR, 1966-72. Mem. ABA, Pa. Bar Assn. (ho. of dels. 1995-97), Washington County Bar Assn. (treas. 1982-83, pres. 1995), B'nai B'rith (past pres.). Banking, Probate, Real property. Home: 149 S Wade Ave Washington PA 15301-4926 Office: Goldfarb Posner Beck DeHaven & Drewitz 26 S Main St Ste 200 Washington PA 15301-6812 E-mail: dsp@gpbdd.com

POSNER, ERNEST GARY, lawyer; b. Nashville, July 2, 1937; s. Alvin Joseph and Bertha (Halpern) P.; m. Gretel Roberta Tishler, Dec. 22, 1963; children: Suzanne Lyn, Deborah Ariel. BChE, Vanderbilt U., 1959; postgrad., Suffolk U., 1963-64; JD, Am. U., 1967. Bar: Va. 1967, Pa. 1968, U.S. Dist. Ct. (ea. dist.) Pa. 1969, U.S. Patent Office 1970, U.S. Supreme Ct. 1975. Advanced through grades to capt., 1967; commd. U.S. Navy, 1959, ret., 1981; staff Interagy. Com. Oceanography, Washington, 1967-68; patent lawyer Atlantic Richfield Co., Phila., 1968-72; v.p., gen. counsel, corp. sec. PQ Corp., Valley Forge, 1972—. Commr., vice chmn. Govt. Study Commn., Upper Merion, Pa., 1975-76. Mem. ABA, Soap & Detergent Assn. (legal com. 1974—), Am. Intellectual Property Law Assn., Internat. Bus. Forum (spkr.), Lic. Exec. Soc. (trustee 1993-2000, v.p. 1997-2000), Am. Corp. Counsel Assn., Masons, B'nai B'rith (sec. 1974-76, chpt. founder). General corporate, Private international, Patent. Office: PQ Corp Swedesford Rd PO Box 840 Valley Forge PA 19482-0840 E-mail: paernie@aol.com, ernest.posner@pqcorp.com

POSNER, LOUIS JOSEPH, lawyer, accountant; b. N.Y.C., May 29, 1956; s. Alex Pozner and Hilda G. (Gottlieb) Weinberg; m. Betty F. Osin, June 21, 1986; 1 child, Daniel. BS in Acctg., Drexel U., 1979; MS in Taxation, Pace U., 1985; JD, N.Y. Law Sch., 1989. Bar: N.Y. 1990, N.J. 1990, U.S. Dist. Ct. (so. and ea. dists.) N.Y., 1990, D.C. 1991, U.S. Ct. Appeals (2d cir.) 1993, U.S. Supreme Ct. 1994. Auditor Arthur Andersen & Co., CPAs, Phila., 1979-81; tax sr. Kenneth Leventhal & Co., CPAs, N.Y.C., 1981-82; tax mgr. Mann Judd Landau, CPAs, 1983-86; tax dir. Integrated Resources, Inc., 1986-89; pvt. practice, 1989—. Spkr. in field. Producer, dir. TV show Your Legal Rights. Founder, nat. chmn., Voter March, 2000—. Mem.: ABA, AICPA, Assn. Bar. City of N.Y., N.Y. State Soc. CPA's (tax. com. 1985—90, mem. faculty N.Y.C. chpt. Found. for Acctg. Edn. 1989—90), N.Y. State Bar Assn. (trusts and estates sect.), N.Y. County Lawyers Assn. (trusts and estates sect.), Assn. Atty CPA's, Mensa (coord. spl. interest group N.Y.C. chpt. 1978—99). Bankruptcy, Estate planning, Taxation, general. Home: 160 E 48th St Apt 12T New York NY 10017-1225 Office: PO Box 731 Grand Canyon Sta New York NY 10163-1225 E-mail: lawline@nyc.rr.com

POSNER, MARTIN LOUIS, lawyer; b. N.Y.C., June 8, 1948; s. Carl and Evelyn Rachel P.; m. Jane Yvonne Kaplowitz, June 7, 1970. BA in Biology, CCNY, 1970, MA in Environ. Edn., 1975; JD, Pace U., 1984, LLM in Environ. Law, 1993. Bar: N.Y. 1985, U.S. Dist. Ct. (ea. and so. dists.) N.Y. 1991, U.S. Dist. Ct. (we. and no. dists.) N.Y., 1998. Tchr. N.Y. Pub. Sch. Sys., N.Y.C., 1970-84; assoc. Law Offices of Henry Greenburg, White Plains, N.Y., 1984-85; ptnr. Posner, Posner & Assocs. PC, 1985—. Commr. Patterson (N.Y.) Environ. Conservation Commn., 1989-93; mem. Putnam County Environ. Mgmt. Coun., Carmel, N.Y., 1990-93; councilman Town of Patterson, 1996—. Mem. ABA, N.Y. State Bar Assn., White Plains Bar Assn., Westchester Bar Assn. Bankruptcy, Environmental, Real property. Office: Posner Posner & Assocs PC 399 Knollwood Rd White Plains NY 10603-1931 E-mail: relawyer@aol.com

POSNER, RICHARD ALLEN, federal judge; b. N.Y.C., Jan. 11, 1939; s. Max and Blanche Posner; m. Charlene Ruth Horn, Aug. 13, 1962; children: Kenneth A., Eric A. AB, Yale U., 1959, LLD (hon.), 1996; LLB, Harvard U., 1962; LLD (hon.), Syracuse U., 1986, Duquesne U., 1987, Georgetown U., 1992, U. Pa., 1997; D honoris causa, U. Ghent, 1995. Bar: N.Y. 1963, U.S. Supreme Ct. 1966. Law clk. Justice William J. Brennan Jr. U.S. Supreme Ct., Washington, 1962-63; asst. to commr. FTC, 1963-65; asst. to solicitor gen. U.S. Dept. Justice, 1965-67; gen. counsel Pres.'s Task Force on Communications Policy, 1967-68; assoc. prof. Stanford U. Law Sch., Calif., 1968-69; prof. U. Chgo. Law Sch., 1969-78, Lee and Brena Freeman prof., 1978-81, sr. lectr., 1981—; circuit judge U.S. Ct. Appeals (7th cir.), Chgo., 1981—, chief judge, 1993-2000. Research assoc. Nat. Bur. Econ. Research, Cambridge, Mass., 1971-81; pres. Lexecon Inc., Chgo., 1977-81 Author: Antitrust Law: An Economic Perspective, 1976, Economic Analysis of Law, 5th edit., 1998, The Economics of Justice, 1981, (with William M. Landes) The Economic Structure of Tort Law, 1987, The Problems of Jurisprudence, 1990, Cardozo: A Study in Reputation, 1990, Sex and Reason, 1992, The Essential Holmes, 1992, (with Tomas J. Philipson) Private Choices and Public Health: The AIDS Epidemic in an Economic Perspective, 1993, Overcoming Law, 1995, Aging and Old Age, 1995, The Federal Courts: Challenge and Reform, 1996, Law and Legal Theory in England and America, 1996, The Federal Courts: Challenge and Reform, 1997, Law and Literature, revised and enlarged edit., 1998, The Problematics of Moral and Legal Theory, 1999, An Affair of State: An Investigation, Impeachment, and Trial of President Clinton, 1999, Frontiers of Legal Theory, 2001, Breaking the Deadlock: The 2000 Election, The Constitution, and the Courts, 2001; pres. Harvard Law Rev., 1961-62; editor Jour. Legal Studies, 1972-81, Am. Law and Econs. Review, 1999—. Fellow AAAS, Am. Law Inst., Brit. Acad.; mem. Am. Econ. Assn., Am. Law and econ. Assn. (pres. 1995-96), Century Assn. Office: US Ct Appeals 7th Cir 219 S Dearborn St Chicago IL 60604-1702

POST, ALAN RICHARD, lawyer; b. Milw., Feb. 6, 1948; s. John Wesley and Catherine Frances (Eviston) P.; children: Andrew, Lisa, Dana Michael. BBA, U. Wis., 1970, JD, 1972. Bar: Md. 1973, D.C. 1975, Nebr. 1976, U.S. Supreme Ct. 1980, Ill. 1983, Kans. 1992. Atty. ICC, Washington, 1972-76; asst. gen. atty. Union Pacific R.R. Co., Omaha, Nebr., 1976-78; asst. gen. solicitor BNRR Co., St. Paul, 1978-83; atty. Ill. Bell Telephone Co., Chgo., 1983-86; assoc. Sorling, Northrup, Hanna, Cullen and Cochran, Ltd, Springfield, Ill., 1986-90; atty. Kans. Gas & Electric Co., Wichita, 1990-92; pvt. practice,Wichita, 1992—. Past pres. Deaf and Hard of Hearing Svcs., Wichita, 1990-96; mem. Kans. Com. Deaf and Hard of Hearing, 1992-93. Administrative and regulatory, Antitrust, Public utilities. Home: 3031 Dahlia Dr West Carrollton OH 45449-2905 Office: Lexis Nexis Customer Svc 9443 Spring Dr Pike Washington Township OH 45458

POST, PETER DAVID, lawyer; b. Reading, Pa., Jan. 2, 1947; s. Carl B. and Frances (Gaughan) P.; children: Michael, Elizabeth. BS, Pa. State U., 1968; JD, Harvard U., 1971. Bar: Pa. 1971, La. 1974. Assoc. Reed, Smith, Shaw & McClay, Pitts., 1975-81, ptnr., 1982—, dept. head, 1992—2000. Commr. Upper St. Clair (Pa.) Twp., 1989-93. Lt. USN, 1971-75. Avocations: golf, skiing. Labor. Office: Reed Smith Shaw & McClay 435 6th Ave Pittsburgh PA 15219-1886 E-mail: ppost@reedsmith.com

POSTER, MICHAEL SOLLOD, lawyer; b. N.Y.C., Nov. 7, 1971; s. Paul Michael and Sandra Sollod P.; m. Kendra Lynn Schwartz, Nov. 29, 1997. BA magna cum laude, U. Mass., 1993; JD, NYU, 1997. Bar: N.Y. 1998. Assoc. Rosenman & Colin LLP, N.Y.C., 1997—. Avocations: judo, film, music. General corporate, Entertainment, Mergers and acquisitions. Office: Rosenman & Colin LLP 575 Madison Ave New York NY 10022 Fax: 212 940-8776

POSTOL, LAWRENCE PHILIP, lawyer; b. Bridgeport, Conn., Oct. 18, 1951; s. Sidney Samuel and Eunice Ruth (Schine) P.; m. Ellen Margaret Russell, Mar. 22, 1975; children: Raymond Russell, Stephan Russell, Carolyn Russell. BS, Cornell U., 1973, JD, 1976. Bar: Conn. 1976, D.C. 1977, U.S. Dist. Ct. D.C. 1977, U.S. Ct. Appeals (D.C. cir.) 1977, U.S. Supreme Ct. 1980, Va. 1982, U.S. Ct. Appeals (4th cir.) 1982, U.S. Dist. Ct. (ea. dist.) Va. 1985, U.S. Dist. Ct. Md. 1989, U.S. Dist. Ct. Conn. 1990. Assoc. Arent, Fox, Kintner & Plotkin, Washington, 1976-80, Seyfarth, Shaw, Washington, 1980-83, ptnr., 1985—; assoc. Jones, Day, Reavis and Pogue, 1983-85. Lectr. Loyola U., New Orleans, 1983—, U. Cin., 1987-93; bd. advisers The Environ. Counselor Jour.; spl. counsel Greater Washington Bd. Trade, 1991-93. Author: Legal Guide to Handling Toxic Substances in the Workplace, 1990, Americans with Disabilities Act - A Compliance Manual for Employers, 1993. Jewish. Avocation: sports. Federal civil litigation, Health, Labor. Home: 6340 Chowning Pl Mc Lean VA 22101-4129 Office: Seyfarth Shaw 815 Connecticut Ave NW Washington DC 20006-4004 Fax: 202-828-5393. E-mail: postol@dc.seyfarth.com

POSTON, ANITA OWINGS, lawyer; b. Sylacauga, Ala., Sept. 24, 1949; d. John T. and Margaret Owings; m. Charles E. Poston, June 9, 1973; children: Charles E. Jr., John W., Margaret Elizabeth. BA, U. Md., 1971; JD, Coll. William & Mary, 1974. Bar: Va. 1974. Atty. Vandeventer Black LLP, Norfolk, Va., 1974—. Substitute judge Norfolk (Va.) Gen. Dist. Cts., 1982-90; mem. Bar Examiners Bd. Mem. State Bd. for Community Colls., Richmond, 1985-90, chmn. 1988-89; mem. Norfolk Sch. Bd., 1990—, chmn., 1997—; bd. dirs. WHRO Pub. Broadcasting, Tidewater Scholarship Found., Learning Bridge Acad., Govs. Sch. for the Arts Found. Mem. ABA (law fellows), Va. Bar Assn. (exec. com., pres. 2000), Norfolk-Portsmouth Bar Assn. (pres. 1998-99), Va. Law Fellows, Am. Inn of Ct. General corporate, Estate planning, Health. Office: Vandeventer Black LLP 500 World Trade Ctr Norfolk VA 23510-1679 Fax: 757-446-8670. E-mail: aposton@vanblk.com

POSTON, BEVERLY PASCHAL, lawyer; b. Birmingham, Ala., Aug. 21, 1955; d. Arthur Buel and Nellie Jo (Weaver) P.; m. Richard F. Poston, Aug., 1992. BA with honor, U. North Ala., 1976; JD, Birmingham Sch. Law, 1982. Bar: Ala. 1982, U.S. Dist. Ct. (no. dist.) Ala. 1982, U.S. Ct. Appeals (11th cir.) 1983. Assoc. St. John & St. John, Cullman, Ala., 1982-84; pvt. practice, 1984-85, 92-96; ptnr. Paschal & Collins, 1986-92. Pres. Cullman County Hist. Soc., 1986-87, bd. dirs., 1996—. Named one of Outstanding Young Women Am., 1984; recipient Citiation of Honor, Young Career Women Program, 1989. Mem. ABA, ATLA, Ala. Trial Lawyers Assn., Cullman County Bar Assn. (sec. tres. 1997-98, v.p. 1998-99, pres. 1999-2000), Pilot Club Internat. (Sweetheart award Cullman 1985), Cullman Bus. and Profl. Women's Assn. (young careerist award), Cullman Home Builder Assn. Avocations: horseback riding, rodeos, farming, writing. State civil litigation, Criminal, Family and matrimonial. Home: 1797 County Road 972 Cullman AL 35057-5861 Office: 200 1st Ave SE Cullman AL 35055-3402

POSTON, REBEKAH JANE, lawyer; b. Wabash, Ind., Apr. 20, 1948; d. Bob E. and April (Ogle) P. BS, U. Miami, 1970, JD, 1974. Bar: Fla. 1974, Ohio 1977, U.S. Dist. Ct. (so. and mid. dists.) Fla., U.S. Ct. Appeals (11th cir.). Asst. U.S. atty. U.S. Atty.'s Office, Miami, Fla., 1974-76; spl. atty. organized crime and racketeering sect. Strike Force, Cleve., 1976-78; ptnr. Fine, Jacobson, Schwartz, Nash & Block, Miami, 1978-94, Steel Hector & Davis, Miami, 1994—. Adj. prof. U. Miami Law Sch., Coral Gables, 1986; mem. U.S. sentencing guidelines com. So. Dist. of Fla., Miami, 1987-88. Mem. Fla. Bar Assn., Nat. Assn. Criminal Def. Attys., Nat. Directory Criminal Lawyers, Am. Immigration Lawyers Assn., Dade County Bar Assn. Democrat. Lutheran. Avocations: power boat racing, swimming. Criminal, Immigration, naturalization, and customs, Private international. Home: 1541 Brickell Ave Apt 3706 Miami FL 33129-1229 Office: 200 SE 2nd St Miami FL 33131 E-mail: RJP@steelhector.com

POTASH, VELLA ROSENTHAL, lawyer, educator; b. Balt., Oct. 3, 1937; d. Joseph and Rona (Glasner) Rosenthal; m. Michael Donald Potash, June 20, 1957 (div. Aug., 1982); children: James Bennet, John Lawrence. BA in Edn., Goucher Coll., 1959; JD, U. Balt., 1974. Bar: Md. 1975, Pa. 1975, Family Mediation Fla., 1992. Tchr. Balt. Sch. System, 1959-62; pub. rels. dir. Citizens Planning & Housing Assn., Balt., 1968-69; asst. pub. defender Pub. Defender's Office, 1975-78; lawyer pvt. practice, 1978-82, Guardian Ad Litem Program Family Law Sect., Broward County, Fla., 1987—; family mediator pvt. practice, 1992—. Pres., lectr. The Changing Am. Family. Rev. bd. Palm Beach County Foster Care, 1999—. Mem. NOW (bd. dirs., chair women's ctr. Boca Raton), Md. Bar, Pa. Bar, Broward County Bar Assn. (assoc.), So. Fla. Goucher Alumnae Assn. (pres.), Broward County Mediation Assn. (bd. dirs.). Avocations: bus. investment, golf, reading. Home: 2900 N Palm Aire Dr Apt 301 Pompano Beach FL 33069-3445

POTENZA, JOSEPH MICHAEL, lawyer; b. Stamford, Conn., June 27, 1947; s. Michael Joseph Sr. and Rose Elizabeth (Coppola) P.; m. Karen Louise Yankee, Jan. 28, 1978; children: Wendy Lynn, Chiara Micol. BSEE cum laude, Rochester Inst. Tech., 1970; JD, Georgetown U., 1975. Bar: Va. 1975, D.C. 1976, U.S. Dist. Ct. D.C., U.S. Ct. Appeals (fed. cir.), U.S. Ct. Appeals (6th cir.), U.S. Supreme Ct. Patent examiner U.S. Patent and Trademark Office, Arlington, Va., 1970-74, law clk. bd. appeals, 1974-75, law clk. to presiding judge 6th cir. U.S. Ct. Appeals, 1975-76; assoc. Banner, Birch, McKie & Beckett, Washington, 1976-80, ptnr., 1980—. Adj. prof. Georgetown U. Law Ctr., Washington, 1985—; faculty Nat. Inst. Trial Advocacy--Patent Inst., 1996—. Editor (monographs) Sorting Out Ownership Rights in Intellectual Property, 1980, Recent Developments in Licensing, 1981. Bd. dirs. Found. for a Creative Am., 1991—. Recipient Patent and Trademark Office Superior Performance award Dept. Commerce, 1973-75. Fellow Am. Bar Found.; mem. ABA (young lawyers divsn. exec. coun. 1979—, chmn. legis. action com. 1980—, chmn. patent trademark and copyright com. 1977—, house of dels. 1984-86, sci. and tech. sect., coun. mem. 1985—, membership chmn. 1985—, budget co-chmn. 1987—, budget officer 1988—, vice chmn. 1991—, chmn.-elect 1992-93, chmn. 1993, chmn. standing com. on pub. oversight, 1996—, fed. practice and procedure com. intellectual property law sect. 1995-96, spring CLE program 1997-98, chmn. summer CLE 1999, 2001, chair fed. practice and procedure com. div. chmn., div. VI IP law sec. 1995-97, sec. sec. 2001—), IEEE, AAAS (nat. conf. lawyers and scientists), Am. Intellectual Property Law Assn. (chmn. unfair competition com. 1980-81), D.C. Bar Assn. (sec. patent, trademark, copyright sect.), Va. Bar Assn., Wash. Patent Lawyers Club (pres. 1988-89), Am. Inns of Ct. (founding mem. and exec. com. Giles S. Rich 1991—, v.p. 1997, pres. 1998-99), Phi Sigma Kappa, Alpha Sigma (pres. 1979-80), Tau Beta Pi. State civil litigation, Patent, Trademark and copyright. Home: 1238 Gilman Ct Herndon VA 20170-2418 Office: Banner & Witcoff 1001 G St NW Ste 1100 Washington DC 20001-4545

POTTER, ERNEST LUTHER, lawyer; b. Anniston, Ala., Apr. 30, 1940; s. Ernest Luther and Dorothy (Stamps) P.; m. Gwyn Johnston, June 28, 1958; children: Bradley S., Lauren D. A.B., U. Ala., 1961, LL.B., 1963, LL.M., 1979. Bar: Ala. 1963, U.S. Dist. Ct. (no. dist.) Ala. 1964, U.S. Ct. Appeals (5th cir.) 1965, U.S. Supreme Ct. 1972, U.S. Ct. Appeals (11th cir.) 1982. Assoc. Burnham & Klinefelter, Anniston, Ala., 1963-64, Bell, Richardson, Cleary, McLain & Tucker, Huntsville, 1964-66, ptnr., 1967-70, Butler & Potter, Huntsville, 1971-82; pvt. practice, 1983—. Bd. dirs. VMIC, Inc.; mem. faculty Inst. Bus. Law and Polit. Sci., U. Ala.-Huntsville, 1965-67. Contbg. author: Marital Law, 1976, 2d edit. 1985. V.p. No. Ala. Kidney Found., 1976-77; treas. Madison County Dem. Exec. Com., 1974-78; bd. dirs. United Way Madison County, 1982-87, Girls Inc., Huntsville, 1988-94, pres., 1991. Mem. Ala. Law Inst., ABA, Ala. Bar Assn., Madison County Bar Assn., Madison County Am. Inn of Ct. (pres. 1999), Phi Beta Kappa, Order of Coif. Episcopalian Estate planning, Family and matrimonial, General practice. Home: 1284 Becket Dr SE Huntsville AL 35801-1670 Office: 200 Clinton Ave W Huntsville AL 35801-4918

POTTER, FRED LEON, lawyer, insurance company executive, consultant; b. Kansas City, Kans., Dec. 15, 1948; s. Donald Warren and Olive Lucile (Ater) P.; m. Mertie Lorraine Scribner, June 13, 1970; children: Mark, Amy, Joy. BA, Harvard U., 1970, MBA, 1972; JD, U. Mich., 1975. Bar: N.H. 1975, U.S. Dist. Ct. N.H. 1975. Atty. Sulloway, Hollis & Soden, Concord, N.H., 1975-80, 96—; pres., gen. counsel Christian Mut. Life Ins. Co., 1980-96. Ptnr., mgmt. cons. Potter-Brock Assn., Tucson, 1969-82; trustee Gordon-Conwell Theol. Seminar, South Hamilton, Mass., 1983—; bd. dirs. N.H. Savs. Bank Corp., Concord, 1987-90. Clk. Concord Union Sch. Dist., 1978-84; deacon 1st Bapt. Ch., Concord, 1978-85; elder Grace Bible Fellowship, 1993—; coach Concord Little League, 1985-87, 90-93. Mem. ABA, N.H. Bar Assn. (treas. 1980-84, v.p. 1984-85, pres. 1986-87, Pres. Disting. Service award 1983), Merrimack County Bar Assn. (sec. 1976-80), Christian Legal Soc., Computer Law Assn., Order of Coif. Evangelical. General corporate, Insurance, Mergers and acquisitions. Home: 4 Pond Place Ln Concord NH 03301-3033 Office: Sulloway-Hollis PLLC 9 Capitol St Concord NH 03302-1256 E-mail: FPotter@sulloway.com

POTTER, JOHN WILLIAM, federal judge; b. Toledo, Oct. 25, 1918; s. Charles and Mary Elizabeth (Baker) P.; m. Phyllis May Bihn, Apr. 14, 1944; children: John William, Carolyn Diane, Kathryn Susan. PhB cum laude, U. Toledo, 1940; JD, U. Mich., 1946. Bar: Ohio 1947. Assoc. Zachman, Boxell, Schroeder & Torbet, Toledo, 1946-51; ptnr. Boxell, Bebout, Torbet & Potter, 1951-69; mayor City of Toledo, 1961-67; asst. atty. gen. State of Ohio, 1968-69; judge 6th Dist. Ct. Appeals, 1969-82, U.S. Dist. Ct., Toledo, 1982—, sr. judge, 1992—. Presenter in field. Sr. editor U. Mich. Law Rev., 1946. Pres. Ohio Mcpl. League, 1965; past assoc. pub. mem. Toledo Labor Mgmt. Commn.; past pres., bd. dirs. Commn. on Rels. with Toledo (Spain); past bd. dirs. Cummings Sch. Toledo Opera Assn., Conlon Ctr.; past trustee Epworth United Meth. Ch.; hon. chmn. Toledo Festival Arts, 1980. Capt. F.A., U.S. Army, 1942-46. Decorated Bronze Star; recipient Leadership award Toledo Bldg. Congress, 1965, Merit award Toledo Bd. Realtors, 1967, Resolution of Recognition award Ohio Ho. of Reps., 1982, Outstanding Alumnus award U. Toledo, 1966, conf. rm. named in his honor, U.S. Courthouse, Toledo, 1998; named to Field Arty. Officer Candidate Sch. Hall of Fame, 1999. Fellow Am. Bar Found., Am. Judicature Soc., 6th Jud. Cir. Dist. Judges Assn., Fed. Judges Assn.; mem. ABA, Ohio Bar Assn. (Found. Outstanding Rsch. award 1995), Toledo Bar Assn. (exec. com. 1962-64, award 1992), Lucas County Bar Assn., U. Toledo Alumni Assn. (past pres.), Toledo Zool. Soc. (past bd. dirs.), Old Newsboys Club, Toledo Club, Kiwanis (past pres.), Phi Kappa Phi. Home: 2418 Middlesex Dr Toledo OH 43606-3114 Office: US Dist Ct 307 US Courthouse 1716 Spielbusch Ave Toledo OH 43624-1363

POTTER, ROBERT DANIEL, federal judge; b. Wilmington, N.C., Apr. 4, 1923; s. Elisha Lindsey and Emma Louise (McLean) P.; m. Mary Catherine Neilson, Feb. 13, 1954; children: Robert Daniel, Mary Louise, Catherine Ann. AB in Chemistry, Duke U., 1947, LLB, 1950; LLD (hon.), Sacred Heart Coll., Belmont, N.C., 1982. Bar: N.C. 1951. Pvt. practice law, Charlotte, N.C., 1951-81; dist. judge U.S. Dist. Ct. (we. dist.) N.C., 1981-2000; chief judge, 1984-91; now sr. judge U.S. Dist. Ct. (we. dist.) N.C. Commr. Mecklenburg County, Charlotte, 1966-68. Served as 2d lt. U.S. Army, 1944-47, ETO Mem. N.C. Bar Assn. Republican. Roman Catholic. Club: Charlotte City Office: US Courthouse 250 Federal Bldg 401 W Trade St Charlotte NC 28202-1619

POTTER, TANYA JEAN, lawyer; b. Washington, Oct. 30, 1956; d. John Francis and Tanya Agnes (Kristof) P.; m. Howard Bruce Adler; 1 child, Alexandra Potter Adler. BA, Georgetown U., 1978, JD, 1981. Bar: D.C. 1982, U.S. Ct. Appeals (D.C. cir.), U.S. Ct. Appeals (fed. cir.), U.S. Dist. Ct. (D.C. dist.), U.S. Ct. Internat. Trade. Assoc. Ragan and Mason, Washington, 1981-88; atty.-adviser Office of Chief Counsel for Import Adminstrn., U.S. Dept. Commerce, 1989-92. Mediator D.C. Superior Ct., 1982-84. Author: Practicing Before the Federal Maritime Commission, 1986, supplement, 1988, Preferentiality Under the Proposed Commerce Department Regulations, 1990, Oil Refining in U.S. Foreign-Trade Zones,

1990. Rep. Avenel Homeowners Adv. Coun., 1994-97; dir. Avenel Bd. Dirs., 1997, 98, 99-2001. Recipient Cmty. Svc. Recognition award ARC, Washington, 1986. Mem. ABA, Bar Assn. of D.C. (exec. coun. ad law sect. 1985-89). Avocations: sports, travel, visiting museums and art galleries. Administrative and regulatory, Private international.

POTTER, TREVOR ALEXANDER MCCLURG, lawyer; b. Chgo., Oct. 24, 1955; s. Charles Steele and Barbara (McClurg) P. AB, Harvard Coll., 1978; JD, U. Va., 1982. Bar: Ill. 1983, D.C. 1988, U.S. Supreme Ct. 1997. Counsel office of legal policy U.S. Dept. Justice, Washington, 1982-84; asst. gen. counsel FCC, 1984-85; atty. Wiley, Rein & Fielding, 1985-88, ptnr., 1988-91,96-2001; commr. Fed. Election Commn., 1991—, vice chmn., 1993, chmn., 1994-95; ptnr. Caplin & Drysdale, 2001—. Merrill lectr. Sch. Law U. Va., 1996-97. Republican. Episcopalian. Fellow Brookings Instn. (sr.); mem. ABA (chmn. com. on election law, adminstrv. law sect. 1993-95, 99—, mem. standing com. on election law 2000—). Office: Caplin & Drysdale One Thomas Cir NW Washington DC 20005 E-mail: tp.@capdale.com

POTTER-HILL, LYNNE ANN, lawyer; b. Pasadena, Calif., Sept. 20, 1955. d. Robert Earl and Vivian Ann (Cox) P.; m. Gregory S. Hill, Apr. 14, 1985; children: Brianna Elizabeth, Kathryn Ann, Kimberly Joanne. BA, San Diego State U., 1976; MA, U. Denver, 1978; JD, Nat. U., 1984. Bar: Calif. 1984, U.S. Dist. Ct. (so. and cen. dists.) Calif. 1987, Librarian, Ripey Car Mus., Denver, 1978; catalog librarian Western State Coll. Law, San Diego, 1978-79; law librarian Nat. U. Sch. Law, San Diego, 1979-84, San Diego City Atty., 1984-85; rsch. atty., 1985-86; assoc. Alford & MacLeod, 1986-87, Chapin, Fleming & Whet, 1987-91, assoc. Patterson & Assocs., 1991—; instr. legal rsch. Mem. ALA, Am. Assn. of Law Librs., So. Calif. Assn. of Law Librs., Calif. Bar Assn., San Diego County Bar Assn., San Diego Def. Lawyers Assn. Office: 3131 Camino Del Rio N Ste 1550 San Diego CA 92108-5743

POTTS, DENNIS WALKER, lawyer; b. Santa Monica, Calif., Dec. 17, 1945; s. James Longworth and Donna (Neely) P.; m. Chung Wan; children: Brandon Earl Woodward, Trevor Shipley. BA, U. Calif., Santa Barbara, 1967; JD, U. Calif., San Francisco, 1970. Bar: Hawaii 1971, Calif. 1971, U.S. Dist. Ct. Hawaii 1971, U.S. Ct. Appeals (9th cir.) 1973, U.S. Supreme Ct. 1978, U.S. Dist. Ct. (cen. dist.) Calif. 1983. Assoc. Chuck Mau, Honolulu, 1971-74; sole practice, 1974—. Mem. litigation com. ACLU Hawaii, 1977-82; former mem. Hawaii Acad. Plaintiff's Attys. Recipient cert. Coll. of Advocacy, Hastings Coll. Law, U. Calif., San Francisco-Sch. Law Loyola U., San Francisco, 1973. Mem. ATLA (sustaining), Consumer Lawyers Hawaii, Honolulu Club. Federal civil litigation, State civil litigation, Personal injury. Office: 2755 Pacific Tower 1001 Bishop St Honolulu HI 96813-3429

POTUZNIK, CHARLES LADDY, lawyer; b. Chgo., Feb. 11, 1947; s. Charles William and Laverne Frances (Zdenek) P.; m. Mary Margaret Quady, Jan. 2, 1988; children: Kylie Brommell, Kathryn Mary. BA with high honors, U. Ill., 1969; JD cum laude, Harvard U., 1973. Bar: Minn. 1973. Assoc. Dorsey & Whitney LLP, Mpls., 1973-78, ptnr., 1979—. Co-head Broker-Dealer and Investment Markets Regulation Practice Group. Mem. Minn. State Bar Assn. (chmn. state securities law subcom. 1987-2000), Hennepin County Bar Assn., Minn. Securities Adv. Com., Phi Beta Kappa. Mem. Evang. Free Ch. Avocations: hunting, fishing, camping, canoeing, foreign travel. Finance, Securities. Office: Dorsey & Whitney LLP Pillsbury Ctr S 220 S 6th St Ste 2200 Minneapolis MN 55402-1498 E-mail: potuznik.charles@dorseylaw.com

POULAIN DE SAINT-PERE, AUDE, lawyer; b. Paris, Sept. 29, 1958; s. Philippe Poulain de Saint-Pere and Nicole Baigneres. Degree in law, DAAD, Dusseldorf, 1987; degree in legal rsch. and writing, Stetson U., 1988; MBA, INSEAD, Fontainebleau, France, 1989. Assoc. Funck-Brentano & Gewelbe, Paris, 1984-85, Doise & Coutard & Gewelbe, Paris, 1985-86, Bignon & Lebray, Paris, 1990; corp. lawyer Union Laitiere Normande, Neuilly Sur Seine, France, 1991, Ernst & Young, Paris, 1992; pvt. practice, 1993—. Contbr. articles to profl. jours. Mem. DAAD Alumni Assn., INSEAD Alumni Assn. General corporate, Private international, Labor. Office: Soc D'Avocats Poulain St Pe 7 Rue Saint-Lazare 75009 Paris France Fax: 00331-53200031. E-mail: STPERE@aol.com

POULAKIDAS, MICHAEL JOHN, lawyer; b. Wilmington, Del., Sept. 13, 1972; s. John E. and Betty Ann P. BA, North Ctrl. Coll., 1994; JD, Thomas M. Cooley, 1998. Bar: Ill. 1998, U.S. Dist. Ct. (no. dist.) Ill. 1998. Pres. Law Office of Michael Poulakidas, Aurora, Ill., 1998—. Mem. ABA, Kane County Bar Assn., Ill. State Bar Assn. Greek Orthodox. General practice, Personal injury. Office: 346 N Lake St Aurora IL 60506

POULSON, JEFFREY LEE, lawyer; b. Storm Lake, Iowa, Dec. 22, 1951; s. Burton L. and Gretchen (Jorgenson) P.; m. Janice Benton, May 24, 1975; children— William, Whitney. B.A. with honors, U. Wyo., 1974; J.D., Drake U., 1976. Bar: Iowa 1977, Neb. 1990, U.S. Dist. Ct. (no. dist.) Iowa, 1977, U.S. Dist. Ct. (so. dist.) Iowa 1982, Ct. of Appeals (8th cir. ct.) Neb. 1986. Assoc. Corbett Anderson Corbett & Daniels, Sioux City, Iowa, 1977-82; ptnr. Corbett, Anderson, Corbett, Paulson, Flom & Vellinga, Sioux City, Iowa, 1982—. Mem. ABA, Iowa Bar Assn., Sioux City Bar Assn. Bankruptcy, State civil litigation, General practice. Home: 5500 West St Sioux City IA 51108-9531 Office: Corbett Anderson Corbett Flom & Vellinga PO Box 3527 Sioux City IA 51102-3527

POUND, JOHN BENNETT, lawyer; b. Champaign, Ill., Nov. 17, 1946; s. William R. and Louise Catherine (Kelly) P.; m. Mary Ann Hanson, June 19, 1971; children: Meghan Elizabeth, Matthew Fitzgerald. BA, U. N.Mex., 1968; JD, Boston Coll., 1971. Bar: N. Mex. 1971, U.S. Dist. Ct. N. Mex. 1971, U.S. Ct. Appeals (10th cir.) 1972, U.S. Supreme Ct., 1993. Law clk. to Hon. Oliver Seth, U.S. Ct. Appeals, 10th Cir., Santa Fe, 1971-72. Asst. counsel Supreme Ct. Disciplinary Bd., 1977-83, dist. rev. officer, 1984—; mem. Supreme Ct. Com. on Jud. Performance Evaluation, 1983-85; bd. dirs. Archdiocese Santa Fe Cath. Social Svcs., 1995—. Contbr. articles to profl. jours. Pres. bd. dirs. N.Mex. Ind. Coll. Fund, Santa Fe; chmn. N.Mex. Dem. Leadership Coun., 1991—; bd. dirs. Santa Fe Boys Club, 1989-92; rules com. N.Mex. Dem. Party, 1982—; v.p. Los Alamos Nat. Lab. Comm. Coun., 1985-90; fin. chmn. N.Mex. Clinton for Pres. campaign, 1992; co-chmn. Clinton-Gore Re-election Campaign, N.Mex., 1996, 2000 Fellow Am. Bar Found., Am. Coll. Trial Lawyers, N.Mex. Bar Found.; mem. ABA, Am. Bd. Trial Advocates, N.Mex. Bar Assn. (health law sect. 1987—), Santa Fe County Bar Assn. Democrat. Roman Catholic. Avocations: history, foreign language, literature, swimming, baseball. General civil litigation, General corporate, Health. Office: Herrera Long Pound Komer PA PO Box 5098 2200 Brothers Rd Santa Fe NM 87505-6903 E-mail: HLPLaw@aol.com

POVICH, DAVID, lawyer; b. Washington, June 8, 1935; s. Shirley Lewis and Ethyl (Friedman) P.; m. Constance Enid Tobriner, June 14, 1959; children: Douglas, Johanna, Judith, Andrew. BA, Yale U., 1958; LLB, Columbia U., 1962. Bar: D.C. 1962, U.S. Ct. Appeals (4th cir.) 1980, U.S. Tax Ct. 1981, U.S. Ct. Appeals (5th and 11th cirs.) 1984, U.S. Dist. Ct. Md., U.S. Ct. Appeals (3d cir.) 1997. Law clk. to assoc. judge D.C. Ct. Appeals, Washington, 1962-63; ptnr. Williams & Connolly, 1963—, exec. com., 1986-87. Bd. dirs., officer Lisner Home for Aged. Mem. ABA, D.C. Bar Assn., Bar Assn. D.C., Barristers (exec. com. 1992-93). Federal civil litigation, Criminal, Personal injury. Office: Williams & Connolly 725 12th St NW Washington DC 20005-5901 E-mail: dpovich@wc.com

POWDERLY, WILLIAM H., III, lawyer; b. Pitts., Feb. 23, 1930; BS, Georgetown U., 1953; LLB, U. Pitts., 1956. Bar: Pa. 1956. Ptnr. Metz Schermer & Lewis, LLC, Pitts. Office: Metz Schermer & Lewis LLC Ste 187 11 Stanwix St Pittsburgh PA 15222-1312

POWELL, DOUGLAS RICHARD, lawyer; b. Staton Island, N.Y., Dec. 20, 1953; s. Percy Lloyd and Ruth Martha (Raisch) P.; m. Elizabeth Hammond, Dec. 31, 1977; children: Guyton David, Catherine Hammond. BA, Susquehanna U., 1975; JD, Wake Forest U., 1980. Bar: N.C. 1980, Ga. 1980, U.S. Dist. Ct. (ea. dist.) N.C. 1980, U.S. Dist. Ct. (no. dist.) Ga. 1985, U.S. Ct. Appeals (11th cir.) 1986. Assoc. LeRoy, Wells, Shaw, Hornthal & Riley, Elizabeth, N.C., 1980-81; atty. Fortson and White, Atlanta, 1985-88; of counsel McGee and Oxford, 1988-96, Hinton & Powell, Atlanta, 1996—. Served to lt. JAGC, USNR, 1981-85. Mem. ABA, Ga. Bar Assn., Atlanta Bar Assn., N.C. Bar Assn. Democrat. Presbyterian. Avocation: tennis. Federal civil litigation, State civil litigation, Personal injury. Office: Hinton & Powell 2800 Tower Pl 3340 Peachtree Rd NE Atlanta GA 30326-1000 E-mail: hptriallaw@aol.com

POWELL, DURWOOD ROYCE, lawyer; b. Raleigh, N.C., Nov. 21, 1951; s. Albert Royce and Powell; m. Leej Ida Copperfield, Mar. 1, 1980. BS, U. N.C., 1974, JD, 1979; LLM in Taxation, Emory U., 1985. Bar: N.C. 1979, U.S. Dist. Ct. (ea., mid. and we. dists.) N.C. 1981, U.S. Tax Ct. 1981, U.S. Ct. Appeals (4th cir.) 1984, U.S. Ct. Claims 1984, U.S. Supreme Ct. 1984, D.C. 1988, U.S. Ct. Appeals (D.C. cir.) 1988, N.Y. 1989. Mgmt. analyst GAO, Norfolk, Va., 1974-76; tax staff Arthur Andersen & Co., Washington, 1979-80; assoc. Biggs, Meadows, Etheridge & Johnson, Rocky Mount, N.C., 1980-82, Biggs Law Firm, Rocky Mount, 1982-83; ptnr. Maupin, Taylor, Ellis & Adams, Raleigh, N.C., 1985—, also bd. dirs., 1985—. Adj. prof. corp. taxation Grad. Sch. Bus., U. N.C., Chapel Hill, 1989-92; faculty Duke U. Tax and Estate Planning Conf., 1991; mem. negotiation project Harvard U., Cambridge, Mass., 1992. Contbr. articles to profl. jours. Tax reform com. Duke U., Washington, 1988. Mem. ABA (tax, corp., banking and securities sects.), N.C. Bar Assn. (tax and corp. sects.), Phi Beta Kappa, Phi Eta Sigma. Mergers and acquisitions, Securities, Corporate taxation. Home: 7616 Wingfoot Dr Raleigh NC 27615-5485 Office: Maupin Taylor Ellis & Adams 3200 Beech Leaf Ct Ste 500 Raleigh NC 27604-1064

POWELL, KATHLEEN LYNCH, lawyer, real estate executive; b. N.Y.C., Dec. 30, 1949; d. Daniel Francis and Mary Margaret (Flynn) L.; m. P. Douglas Powell. BA in Math. cum laude, Coll. of Mt. St. Vincent, 1970; postgrad., U. Pa., 1976-77; JD cum laude, U. Md., 1977; LL.M. in Taxation, NYU, 1991. Bar: Pa. 1977, N.J. 1978, N.Y. 1984, D.C. 1985, Conn. 1995, U.S. Ct. Appeals (3d cir.) 1980, U.S. Supreme Ct. 1981. Research analyst, claims rep. Social Security Adminstrn., Balt., 1973-76; assoc. Drinker, Biddle & Reath, Phila., 1977-84, ptnr., 1984-86; v.p., gen. counsel M. Alfieri Co., Inc., Edison, N.J., 1987-89; v.p., counsel Berwind Property Group, Phila., 1992—. Instr. Inst. for Paralegal Tng., Phila. 1984—. Vol. atty. Support Ctr. for Child Advocates, Phila., 1979-86, Queen Village Neighbors Assn., Phila., 1984-86; pres. Soc. Hill Towers Buyers Assn., Phila., 1979-80; bd. dirs. Soc. Hill Civic Assn., 1980. Mem. ABA, Pa. Bar Assn., Phila. Bar Assn. (chair zoning and land use com. 1985-86), Conn. Bar Assn.

POWELL, KENNETH EDWARD, investment banker; b. Danville, Va., Oct. 5, 1952; s. Terry Edward and C. Anne (Wooten) P.; m. Cicely Grandin Moorman, Jan. 3, 1976; children: Tanner, Priscilla. Student, Hampden-Sydney Coll., 1971-73; BA in Polit. Sci., U. Colo., 1975; JD, U. Richmond, 1978; LLM in Taxation, Coll. of William and Mary, 1982. Bar: Va. 1978, U.S. Dist. Ct. (ea. dist.) Va. 1979, U.S. Tax Ct. 1980. Ptnr. Maloney, Yeatts & Barr, Richmond, Va., 1978-87; ptnr., owner Hazel & Thomas, P.C., 1987-94, mem. bus./tax team, internat. bus. team; v.p. Legg Mason, Va., 1994—. Vice chmn. Sci. Mus. Va., Richmond, 1984-91; chmn. Va. Police Found., Inc., 1987; bd. dirs. State Edn. Assistance Authority, 1991—; mem. adv. bd. Va. Opera, 1991—; candidate U.S. Congress, Va., 1986. Recipient Disting. Svc. award Fraternal Order of Police, 1986; named Outstanding Young Man of the Yr., Jaycees, 1981, Outstanding Young Alumni, U. Colo., 1982. Mem. ABA, Va. Bar Assn. (chmn. profl. responsibility com. 1989-92, chmn. com. on legal edn. and admission to the Bar 1991—), Richmond Bar Assn., Richmond C. of C. (bd. dirs. 1988), Va. Econ. Developers Assn. (gen. counsel), Va. Econ. Bridge Initiative. Episcopal. Office: Legg Mason Wood Walker Inc 2234 Monument Ave Richmond VA 23220

POWELL, WILLIAM DON, lawyer; b. Kansas City, Mo., June 7, 1943; s. Earl Ezra and Isabel Francis (Church) P.; m. Dorothy Q. Allemann, June 10, 1967; children— Wesley Brent, Kerri Lynn. B.A., Central Meth. Coll., 1965; postgrad. U. Mo.-Kansas City, 1965-66; J.D., Washburn U., 1969. Bar: Mo. 1970, U.S. Dist. Ct. (we. dist.) Mo. 1970. Assoc., Daniel, Clampett, Ellis, Ritterhouse and Dalton, Springfield, Mo., 1970-75; ptnr. Daniel, Clampett, Ritterhouse, Lilley, Dalton, Powell & Cunningham, Springfield, 1976— . Bd. dirs. Codac Inc., 1973-78, pres., 1975; bd. dirs. Regional Girls Shelter Inc., 1974-80 , sec., 1978 ; bd. dirs., pres. Children's Hearing Sch. S.W. Mo. Inc., 1978; bd. dirs. Ozark br., Nat. Multiple Sclerosis Soc., 1981-87 ; Pres. bd. trustees First Unitarian-Universalist Ch. Springfield, 1984-86 . Mem. Def. Research Inst., Mo. Orgn. Def. Lawyers (bd. dirs. 1984—), ABA, Mo. Bar Assn., Greene County Bar Assn. (sec. 1987). Office: PO Box 10306gs Springfield MO 65808

POWELL-SMITH, MARC EDGAR RAOUL, lawyer; b. Levallois-Perret, France, June 13, 1970; s. David Edward and Teresa (Bonvecchiato) P.-S.; m. Sabine Louvet, Apr. 8, 2000. Diploma in Anglo-Am. Bus. Law, Maitrise in Bus. Law, U. Paris, 1992; DESS in Internat. Comml. Law, U. Paris X, 1993; LLM in Corp. Law, Widener U., Wilmington, Del., 1994; DESS in Litigation Law, U. Rouen, France, 1996. Bar: France 1996. Assoc. Lette Lette & Ptnrs., Paris, 1997-99, Jobard Chemla & Assocs., Paris, 1999-2001; ptnr. Lachkar & Powell-Smith, 2001—. With French Air Force, 1994-95. Mem. Franco-Brit. Lawyer's Soc., Franco-Brit. C. of C. and Industry, Chambre de Commerce Italienne pour la France, Chambre de commerce Franco-Arabe. Avocations: travel, tennis, open water diving, fencing, languages. Home: 57 bis ave Motte-Picquet Paris 75015 France Office: 148 avenue de Wagram Paris 75017 France Fax: 1-56-79-01-55

POWER, JOHN BRUCE, lawyer; b. Glendale, Calif., Nov. 11, 1936; m. Sandra Garfield, Apr. 27, 1998; children by previous marriage: Grant, Mark, Boyd. AB magna cum laude, Occidental Coll., 1958; JD, NYU, 1961; postdoctoral, Columbia U., 1972. Bar: Calif. 1962. Assoc. O'Melveny & Myers, L.A., 1961-70, ptnr., 1970-97, resident ptnr. Paris, 1973-75; Sheffelman disting. lectr. Sch. Law, U. Wash., Seattle, 1997. Mem. Social Svcs. Commn. City of L.A., 1993, pres., 1993; pres. circle, exec. com. Occidental Coll., 1979-82, 91-94, chair, 1993-94. Contbr. articles to jours. Bd. dirs. Met. L.A. YMCA, 1988—, treas., 1998—; mem. bd. mgrs. Stuart Ketchum Downtown YMCA, 1985-92, pres., 1989-90; mem. Los Angeles County Rep. Ctrl. Com., 1962-63; trustee Occidental Coll., 1992—, vice-chmn., 1998-2001, chmn., 2001—. Root Tilden scholar. Fellow Am. Coll. Comml. Fin. Lawyers (bd. regents 1999—); mem. ABA (comml. fin. svcs. com., com. 3d party legal opinions, UCC com., bus. law sect.), Am. Bar Found. (life), Calif. Bar Assn. (chmn. partnerships and unincorporated assns. com. 1982-83, chmn. uniform commn. code com. 1984-85, exec. com. 1987-91, chmn. bus. law sect. 1990-91, chmn. coun. sect. chairs 1992-93, liaison to state bar commn. on future of legal profession and state bar 1993-95), L.A. County Bar Assn. (exec. com. comml. law and bankruptcy sect. 1970-73, 86-89), Internat. Bar Assn., Fin. Lawyers Conf. (bd. govs. 1982—, pres. 1984-85), Exec. Svc. Corps (sec. 1985-2000, vice-chmn. 2000—, dir. 1994—), Occidental Coll. Alumni Assn. (pres. 1967-68), Phi Beta Kappa (councilor So. Calif. 1982—, pres. 1990-92). General corporate, Private international, Securities. Office: O Melveny & Myers 400 S Hope St Los Angeles CA 90071-2899

POWER, JOSEPH ALOYSIUS, JR. lawyer; b. Oct. 15, 1952; s. Joseph Aloysius and Mary Ellen (Cavenaugh) Power; m. Susan Vohs, Apr. 26, 1980; children: Joseph Aloysius III, Michael Anthony, Ryan Patrick, James Ian. BA, U. Notre Dame, 1974; JD, Loyola U., Chgo., Ill., 1977. Bar: Ill. 1977, U.S. Dist. Ct. (no. dist.) Ill. 1977, U.S. Ct. Appeals (7th cir.) 1994, U.S. Supreme Ct. 1992. Assoc. John D. Hayes & Assocs., Chgo., 1977—84; ptnr. Hayes & Power, 1984—91, Power, Rogers & Lavin, Chgo., 1991—93, Power, Rogers & Smith, Chgo., 1993—. Chmn. bd. dirs. Assn. of Trial Lawyers Assurance a mutual risk retention group, 1988—2000; author, lectr. Ill. Inst. Contg. Legal Edn., Springfield, Ill., 1983—89; bd. mgrs. Trial Lawyers for Pub. Justice, 1994—, v.p., 1996—97, pres.-elect, 1997—98, pres., 1998—99. Bd. dir. Ill. Pub. Action, Chgo., 1987—93. Fellow: Am. Coll. Trial Lawyers, Internat. Acad. Trial Lawyers; mem.: ABA, Chgo. Bar Assn. (chmn. young lawyers sect. fed. trial bar advocacy program No. dist. Il 1984), Ill. Trial Lawyers Assn. (author, lectr. 1984—, bd. mgrs. 1984—, chmn. membership com. 1985—87, chmn. legis. com. 1987—89, 3d v.p. 1989—90, 2d v.p. 1990—91, pres. elect 1991—92, pres. 1992—93), Ill. Bar Assn., ATLA, U.S. Sen. Judiciary Com. (chmn.'s adv. coun. 1994, Ill. Supreme Ct. rules com. 1995—, chmn. 1996—2001), Chgo. Athletic Assn. Democrat. Roman Catholic. Personal injury. Home: 344 W Wellington Ave Chicago IL 60657-5637 Office: Power Rogers & Smith 35 W Wacker Dr Ste 3700 Chicago IL 60601-1642

POWERS, ALBERT THEODORE, lawyer, administrator; b. Norfolk, Nebr., Feb. 11, 1953; s. Albert Theodore and Maxine Loretta (Kohlhof) P.; m. Victoria Mae Schulte, June 8, 1974; children: Albert Theodore III, Elizabeth Victoria, Katherine Alexandria. BA, U. Denver, 1974; JD, U. Pa., 1977; LLM, NYU, 1979. Bar: Colo. 1978, N.Y. 1982, Calif. 1983, Hong Kong 1996. Law clk. to Judge Robert H. McWilliams U.S. Ct. Appeals, 10th Cir., Denver, 1977-78; assoc. atty. Davis, Graham & Stubbs, 1979-81, Simpson, Thacher & Bartlett, N.Y.C., 1981-83, Heller, Ehrman, White & McAuliffe, Hong Kong, 1983-86, mng. ptnr., 1986-87, Gibson, Dunn & Crutcher, Hong Kong, 1987-94, Shearman & Sterling, Hong Kong, 1994-95; sr. resident ptnr. Fulbright & Jaworski LLP, 1996—. Author: Federal Income Taxation of Corporations, 1983; contbr. articles to profl. jours. Mem. ABA, Internat. Bar Assn., Internat. Fiscal Assn., Hong Kong Club, Shek-O Country Club, Ladies' Recreation Club, China Club, Rolls Royce Enthusiasts Club, Bentley Drivers Club, Chaine des Rotisseurs. Avocations: classic cars, wine, sports, music. Home: 10-B Grenville House 1 Magazine Gap Rd Hong Kong Hong Kong Office: Fulbright & Jaworski LLP 1901 Hong Kong Club Bldg Hong Kong Hong Kong

POWERS, EDWARD HERBERT, lawyer; b. Jersey City, N.J., June 21, 1942; s. Samuel and Ruth (Handman) P.; m. Phyllis Elinor Alpern, May 29, 1966; children: Alexander, Jill, Annette. BA, U. Mich., 1964, JD, 1967. Bar: Mich. 1968, U.S. Dist. Ct. (ea. dist.) Mich. 1968, U.S. Ct. Appeals (6th cir.) 1989, U.S. Supreme Ct. 1990. Owner, mem. Pelavin, Powers & Behm PC., Flint, Mich., 1968—; instr. Mott Adult Edn., Flint, 1970-74 Chmn. region XI U. Mich. Law Sch. Fund, 1980-81; v.p. Flint Jewish Fedn., 1978-82; chmn. Flint United Jewish Appeal, 1978; v.p. Congregation Beth Israel, 1979-82. Mem. Assn. Trial Lawyers Am., Mich. Trial Lawyers Assn., State Bar Mich., ABA (forum on constrn. industry), Genesee County Bar Assn., Am. Mensa Soc., Univ. Club (Flint). Contracts commercial, General practice, Real property. Home: 1071 Briarcliffe Dr Flint MI 48532-2102 Office: 300 Phoenix Bldg 801 S Saginaw St Flint MI 48502

POWERS, ELIZABETH WHITMEL, lawyer; b. Charleston, S.C., Dec. 16, 1949; d. Francis Persse and Jane Coleman Cotten (Wham) P.; m. John Campbell Henry, June 11, 1994 (dec. Jan. 1997); m. Henry C. B. Lindh, June 16, 2000. AB, Mt. Holyoke Coll., 1971; JD, U. S.C., 1978. Bar: S.C. 1978, N.Y. 1979. Law clk. to justice S.C. Cir. Ct., Columbia; assoc. Reid & Priest, N.Y.C., 1978-86, ptnr., 1986-97; of counsel LeBoeuf, Lamb, Greene & MacRae, 1997—. Exec. editor S.C. Law Rev., Columbia, 1977-78. Bd. dirs. The Seamen's Ch. Inst., 1996—, sec., 1999—; vol. N.Y. Jr. League, N.Y.C., 1983—; bd. trustees Ch. Club, 1991-94, 97-2001, v.p. 1992-94. Mem. ABA, S.C. Bar Assn., Nat. Soc. Colonial Dames of Am. (parliamentarian 1994-2000), Nat. Soc. Colonial Dames in State of N.Y. (pres. 1992-95), Gunston Hall (regent 2001-). Avocations: bridge, tennis. General corporate, Public utilities, Securities.

POWERS, JOHN KIERAN, lawyer; b. Schenectady, Aug. 2, 1947; s. Paul Joseph and Anne Marie (Leahy) P.; children: Erin Kelly, Megan Kerry. BS, U. Notre Dame, 1969; JD, Union U., 1972. Bar: N.Y. 1973, U.S. Dist. Ct. (no. dist.) N.Y. 1973, U.S. Dist. Ct. (so., ea. and we. dists.) N.Y. 1982, U.S. Ct. Appeals (2d cir.) 1984, U.S. Supreme Ct. 1985, U.S. Dist. Ct. Vt. 1988. Assoc. Medwin and McMahon, Albany, 1973-77; pvt. practice law, 1973-80; pres. John K. Powers, P.C., 1980-87; ptnr. Powers and Santola, 1987—. Contbr. articles to profl. publs. Trustee N.Y. State Lawyers Polit. Action Com., 1983-88, treas., 1989-93, chair, 1993—; trustee ATLA Polit. Action Com., 1995-98. Fellow Roscoe Pound Found. Mem. ABA (sustaining vice-chair, legis. subcom., automobile law com., trial and ins. practice sect., state leader com. on state legis. sect.), Nat. Coll. Adv. (co-founder), ATLA (life, state del. 1990, bd. govs. 1990—, exec. com. 1995—), Am. Bd. Trial Advocates (advocate), N.Y. State Bar Assn. (sustaining, lectr., exec. com. and chmn. legis. com. trial lawyers sect.), N.Y. State Trial Lawyers Assn. (sustaining, bd. dirs. 1983-88, chmn. key person legis. com., chmn. pubs. com., chmn. atty. referral com., exec. com. 1986—, treas. 1988-89, v.p. 1989-91, 1st v.p. 1990-91, pres.-elect 1991-92, pres. 1992-93, award of merit 1990, 94, award of excellence 1991, Pres. award 1995, 96, 98, 99, 2000, dist. svc. award 1997), N.Y. Trial Lawyers Inst. (lectr. and program chmn. 1981—, treas. 1988-89, pres. 1992-93), (life) N.Y. State Head Injury Assn. (co-counsel 1983-85, bd. dirs. 1992-93, 1st v.p. 1993—), Capitol Dist. Trial Lawyers Assn. (bd. dirs. 1979-81, v.p. 1983-85, pres. 1985-86), Pa. Trial Lawyers Assn., Alban County Bar Assn. (lectr.), Chief Judge's Com. to Improve Availability of Legal Svcs., Chief Judge's Pro-Bono Monitoring Com., Civil Justice Found. (guest lectr. Law Sch. NYU, Albany Law Sch., U. Syracuse Law Sch., Albany Med. Coll.), Trial Lawyers for Pub. Justice, Lions (pres. Scotia, N.Y. chpt. 1979-80). Democrat. Roman Catholic. Federal civil litigation, State civil litigation, Personal injury. Home and Office: 39 N Pearl St Albany NY 12207-2785

POWERS, MARK GREGORY, consultant, lawyer; b. Galveston, Tex., Aug. 14, 1948; s. Robert Kenneth and Ann Joan (Brugliera) P.; m. Kim M. Walker, Aug. 21, 1971; children: Jason Robert, Erin Alison. BBA in Acctg., Georgetown U., 1970; MBA, Gonzaga U., 1972, JD, 1974; CLU, Am. Coll., Bryn Mawr, Pa., 1975, Chartered Fin. Cons., 1982. Bar: Wash. 1974. Prin. Profl. Services Group, Spokane, Wash., 1970-82; sr. v.p. Nat. Assocs., Inc., Spokane, 1982-92, pres., 1992—. Pres. Spokane Indoor Soccer Ctr., 1986-93. Mem. Wash. State Bar Assn., Nat. Assn. Life Underwiters, Am. Soc. CLU's (pres. 1980-81), United Investors and Mgrs. (pres. 1993), Powers Candy & Nut Co. (sec., treas. 1993-97). Home: 25315 N Orchard Bluff Rd Chattaroy WA 99003-9540 Office: National Assocs Spokane Inc 600 W Riverside Ave Spokane WA 99201-0602

POWERS, NOYES THOMPSON, lawyer; b. Apr. 29, 1929; BA magnum cum laude, Duke U., 1951; LLB cum laude, Harvard U., 1954. Asst. to Under Sec. of Labor, 1961; dep. solicitor labor, 1962-63; exec. asst. to Sec. of Labor, 1964-65; exec. dir. EEOC, 1965; ptnr. Steptoe & Johnson, Washington, Phoenix, 1966-94; sr. labor counsel Motorola, Inc., Phoenix, 1993-99. Mem. ABA (chair pub. utility, comm. and transp. sect. 1994-95). Office: Motorola Inc Corp Law Dept 3102 N 56th St Phoenix AZ 85018-6697

POWERS, RICHARD EDWARD, JR. lawyer; b. Evanston, Ill., July 20, 1952; s. Richard Edward and Helen Lufen Powers; m. Diane Wojda, Aug. 12, 1978. BS, Gonzaga U., 1974; JD, U. Notre Dame, 1977. Ptnr. Butler & Binion LLP, Washington, 1977-99, Dorsey & Whitney LLP, Washington, 1999—. Mem. ABA, Tex. Bar Assn., D.C. Bar, Energy Bar Assn. Home: 5233 Elliott Rd Bethesda MD 20816-2910 Office: Dorsey & Whitney 1001 Penn Ave NW Ste 300S Washington DC 20004-2505

POWERS, WILLIAM CHARLES, JR. dean, law educator; b. 1946; AB, U. Calif., Berkeley, 1967; JD, Harvard U., 1973. Bar: Wash. 1974, Tex. 1980. Law clk. to Hon. E. A. Wright U.S. Ct. Appeals (9th cir.), Seattle, 1973-74; asst. prof. Wash. U. , 1974-77; assoc. prof. Wash. U., 1977-78; prof. law U. Tex., Austin, 1978—, assoc. dean acad. affairs, 1984—87, 1994—95, univ. disting. prof. and Hines H. Baker and Thelma Kelly Baker chair in law, 1997—, John Jeffers Rsch. Chair in law, 2000—, dean Sch. Law, 2000—. Office: U Tex Sch Law 727 E Dean Keeton St Austin TX 78705-3224*

POYDASHEFF, ROBERT STEPHEN, lawyer; b. N.Y.C., Feb. 13, 1930; s. Stephen Alexander Poydasheff and Pauline M. Miller; m. Anastasia Catherine Latto, Aug. 29, 1954; children: Catherine Alexandra, Robert Stephen Jr. BA in Polit. Sci., The Citadel, 1954; JD, Tulane U., 1957; MA, Boston U., 1966; diploma, Command and Gen. Staff Coll., 1969, Army War Coll., 1976. Bar: S.C. 1958, Ga. 1979, U.S. Supreme Ct. 1964, U.S. Ct. Mil. Appeals, U.S. Ct. Mil. Rev., U.S. Dist. Ct. (fed. dist.) S.C., U.S. Dist. Ct. (fed. and mid. dists.) Ga. Commd. 2d lt. U.S. Army, 1955, advanced through grades to col., 1975, ret., 1979; sr. v.p. SunTrust Bank of West Ga., Columbus, 1979-95; pvt. practice, 1995—. Instr. bus. law Am. U. Ext. Divsn., Ft. Benning, 1961-63; adj. prof. internat. law, Am. govt., and bus. law U. Md. Ext. Divsn., Berlin, 1964-67, Vietnam, 1967-68; adj. prof. Troy State U., Ft. Benning, Ga., 1976—; cons., exec. v.p. ATI-Allied Tech. Internat. Inc., Columbus, 1995—; past legal advisor to Sec. of Army and Sec. of Def. on mil. dependent schs. and labor rels. Contbr. commentaries, papers, and analyses to profl. jours. City councilor City of Columbus, 1996—; bd. dirs. Springer Opera House Assn., 1998—; trustee Ga. Coun. of Humanities, exec. com., 1998—; past mem. Bd. Edn., Ft. Benning Schs., 1976-79, chmn. pers. actions com., 1976-79; trustee Drs. Hosp., Columbia; bd. dirs. Columbus United Way; past pres. Chattahoochee coun. Boy Scouts Am., Columbus; past pres. Chattahoochee Valley, Assn. of U.S. Army, Anne Elizabeth Shepherd Home, Columbus Symphony; chmn. bd. dirs. Leadership Morality Inst.; chair Civilian Mil. Coun. Decorated Legion of Merit with 2 oak leaf clusters, Bronze Star; recipient Order of St. George, Episcopal Ch., 1997, Infantry Order of St. Maurice. Fellow Leadership Morality Inst. (chair of bd.); mem. Columbus Bar Assn., C. of C. (mil. affairs com.), Kiwanis, Masons (32 deg.), Phi Delta Phi, Pi Sigma Alpha. Republican. Episcopalian. Avocations: jogging, reading, gymnastics. Home: 6349 Mountainview Dr Columbus GA 31904-2213 Office: 3575 Macon Rd Ste 12 Columbus GA 31907-8229 E-mail: alliedtech@mindspring.com

PRAGER, SUSAN WESTERBERG, law educator, provost; b. Sacramento, Dec. 14, 1942; d. Percy Foster Westerberg and Aileen M. (McKinley) P.; m. James Martin Prager, Dec. 14, 1973; children: McKinley Ann, Case Mahone. AB, Stanford U., 1964, MA, 1967; JD, UCLA, 1971. Bar: N.C. 1971, Calif. 1972. Atty. Powe, Porter & Alphin, Durham, N.C., 1971-72; acting prof. law UCLA, 1972-77, prof. Sch. Law, 1977—, Arjay and Frances Fearing Miller prof. of law, 1992-99, assoc. dean Sch. Law, 1979-82, dean, 1982-98; provost Dartmouth Coll., Hanover, N.H., 1999—. Bd. dirs. Pacific Mut. Life Holding Co., Newport Beach, Calif. Editor-in-chief, UCLA Law Rev., 1970-71. Trustee Stanford U., 1976-80, 87-97. Mem. ABA (council of sect. on legal edn. and admissions to the bar 1983-85), Assn. Am. Law Schs. (pres. 1986), Order of Coif. Address: Dartmouth College Office of the Provost 6004 Parkhurst Hall Rm 204 Hanover NH 03755-3529

PRATHER, JOHN GIDEON, JR. lawyer; b. Lexington, Ky., Sept. 10, 1946; s. John Gideon Sr. and Marie Jeanette (Moore) P.; m. Hilma Elizabeth Skonberg, Aug. 4, 1973; children: John Hunt, Anna Russell. BS in Acctg., U. Ky., 1968, JD, 1970. Bar: Ky. 1971, U.S. Dist. Ct. (ea. dist.) Ky. 1978, U.S. Dist. Ct. (we. dist.) Ky. 1984, U.S. Ct. Appeals (6th cir.) 1988, U.S. Supreme Ct. 1988. Ptnr., prin. Law Offices John G. Prather, Somerset, Ky., 1972—. Bd. dirs. Lawyers Mutual Ins. Co. Ky., 1989—, treas., 1995—. Bd. dirs. United Way, 1978—; mem. state cen. com. Ky. Young. Dems., Frankfort, 1972. Served to 1st lt. USAF, 1971-72, JAG, 1972. Fellow U. Ky., 1998—. Mem. ABA (house dels.), ATLA, Am. Bd. Trial Advs., Am. Coll. Trial Lawyers, Am. Bd. Trial Attys., Ky. Bar Assn. (ho. of dels. 1984-85, bd. govs. 1985-91, v.p. 1991-92, pres.-elect 1992-93, pres. 1993-94, lectr.), Coun. Sch. Bd. Attys. (state pres., bd. dirs. 1986—, lectr.), Ky. Def. Coun. (bd. dirs. 1987-91), Pulaski County Indsl. Found. (bd. dirs. 1982-95), Phi Delta Phi. Mem. Christian Ch. Avocations: boating, flying. E-mial. General practice, Personal injury, Probate. Home: 510 N Main St Somerset KY 42501-1434 Office: PO Box 616 Somerset KY 42502-0616 E-mail: pratherlaw@msn.com

PRATHER, JOHN GIDEON, lawyer; b. Somerset, Ky., Dec. 12, 1919; s. James Frederick and Josephine Linnwood (Collier) P.; m. Marie Jeanette Moore, Oct. 1945; children: John G., Jerome Moore. B.A., U. Ky., 1940, J.D., 1947. Bar: Ky. 1947, U.S. Dist. Ct. (ea. dist.) Ky. 1950. Pros. atty. Somerset, Ky., 1950-63; commonwealth atty. 28th Jud. Dist., 1963-64; sole practice, Somerset; sr. ptnr. Law Offices of John G. Prather, Somerset; dir. First & Farmers Bank, Somerset. Served to lt. USN, 1942-46; Mem. Pulaski County Bar Assn., Ky. Bar Assn. (ethics com., com. on fees), ABA (probate sect.), Def. Research Inst. Democrat. Mem. Christian Ch. (Disciples of Christ). Clubs: Kiwanis (Somerset), Shriners, Odd Fellows, Masons. General practice, Probate, Estate taxation. Office: PO Box 616 Somerset KY 42502-0616

PRATHER, LENORE LOVING, former state supreme court chief justice; b. West Point, Miss., Sept. 17, 1931; d. Byron Herald and Hattie Hearn (Morris) Loving; m. Robert Brooks Prather, May 30, 1957; children: Pamela, Valerie Jo, Malinda Wayne. B.S., Miss. Univ. Women, 1953; JD, U. Miss., 1955. Bar: Miss. 1955. Practice with B. H. Loving, West Point, 1955-60; sole practice, 1960-62, 65-71; assoc. practice, 1962-65; mcpl. judge City of West Point, 1965-71; chancery ct. judge 14th dist. State of Miss., Columbus, 1971-82, supreme ct. justice Jackson, 1982-92, presiding justice, 1993-97, chief justice, 1998-2001; interim pres. Miss. U. for Women, Columbus, Miss., 2001—. V.p. Conf. Local Bar Assn., 1956-58; sec. Clay County Bar Assn., 1956-71 1st woman in Miss. to become chancery judge, 1971, and supreme ct. justice, 1982, and chief justice, 1998-2001. Mem. ABA, Miss. State Bar Assn., Miss. Conf. Judges, DAR, Rotary, Pilot Club, Jr. Aux. Columbus Club. Episcopalian. Office: Miss U for Women 1100 College St Columbus MS 39701 Fax: 662-328-7119

PRATHER, ROBERT CHARLES, SR. lawyer; b. Kansas City, Mo., Feb. 16, 1945; s. Charles William and Shirley Anne P.; m. Lana Jo Ball, Jan. 25, 1969; children: Robert Charles Jr., Lisa Michelle. BSc in Comm., U. Tex., 1967, JD, 1970; postgrad., U. Tasmania, Australia, 1968. Bar: Tex. 1971, U.S. Dist. Ct. (no. dist.) Tex. 1978, U.S. Ct. Appeals (5th and 11th cirs.) 1981, U.S. Supreme Ct. 1978. Staff atty., com. clk. Senator W.T. Moore State Affairs Com. Tex. State Senate, Austin, 1971; asst. dist. atty. Dallas, 1971-74; asst. atty. U.S. Dist. Ct. No. Dist. Tex., Dalls, 1974-80; econ. crime enforcement specialist U.S. Dept. Justice, Dallas, 1980-81; assoc. trial atty. Turner, Rodgers, Sailers, Jordan & Calloway, 1981-83; ptnr., trial atty. Jordan, Dunlap, Prather & Harris LLP, 1983—. Author: (with others) A Document Numbering System, 1981, Texas ADR Practice Guide West, 1995. Gen. counsel, bd. dirs. Childrens Cancer Fund Dallas, Inc., 1982-91; soccer coach YMCA, North Dallas C. of C., 1979-84. Recipient Spl. Achievement award U.S. Dept. Justice, Washington, 1976; Rotary Found. fellow, 1968. Mem. ABA, Dallas Bar Assn., Argyle Club (pres. Dallas), Park City Club (bd. dirs.), Rotary (parliamentarian, bd. dirs.), Phi Alpha Delta. Baptist. Federal civil litigation, State civil litigation, Contracts commercial. Office: Jordan Dunlap Prather & Harris LLP 8111 Preston Rd Ste 400 Dallas TX 75225-6373 E-mail: prather@jdplegal.com

PRATHER, WILLIAM C., III, lawyer, writer; b. Toledo, Feb. 20, 1921; s. Hollie Cartmill and Effie Fern (Deppen) P. BA, U. Ill., 1942, JD, 1947. Bar: Ill. 1947, U.S. Supreme Ct. 1978. Co-pres. student govt. U. Ill., 1942, asst. dean, 1942-43; atty. First Nat. Bank Chgo., 1947-51; asst. gen. counsel U.S. Savs. and Loan League, Chgo., 1951-59; gen. counsel U.S. League of Savs. Instns., 1959-82, gen. counsel emeritus, 1982—; sole practice Cumberland County, Ill., 1981—. Sem. lectr. in law, banking. Editor: The Legal Bulletin, 1951-81, The Federal Guide, 1954-81; author: Savings Accounts, 8th edit., 1981; contbr. articles to publs. Lt. U.S. Armed Forces, 1943-45. Decorated Bronze Star. Mem. ABA, FBA, Internat. Bar Assn., Ill. Bar Assn., Chgo. Bar Assn., Union Internat. des Avocats, Nat. Lawyers Club Washington, Cosmos Club, Univ. Club Chgo., Kiwanis, Mattoon Golf and Country Club, Exeter and County Club (Eng.), Club de Bonmont Melisande (France), Tennis Club de Beaulieu (France), Soc. Colonial Wars, Phi Delta Phi, Phi Gamma Delta, Phi Eta Sigma, Phi Alpha Chi. Banking, Contracts commercial, General corporate. Home: Applewood Farm PO Box 157 Toledo IL 62468-0157 Office: 142 Courthouse Sq Toledo IL 62468 also: L'Orangeraie 42 Av General Leclerc Villefranche-sur-Mer 06230 France

PRATT, GEORGE CHENEY, law educator, retired federal judge; b. Corning, N.Y., May 22, 1928; s. George Wollage and Muriel (Cheney) P.; m. Carol June Hoffman, Aug. 16, 1952; children: George W., Lise M., Marcia Pratt Burke, William T. BA, Yale U., 1950, JD, 1953. Bar: N.Y. 1953, U.S. Supreme Ct. 1964, U.S. Ct. Appeals 1974. Law clk. to Charles W. Froessel (Judge of N.Y. Ct. Appeals), 1953-55; assoc. then ptnr. Sprague & Stern, Mineola, N.Y., 1956-60; ptnr. Andromidas, Pratt & Pitcher, 1960-65, Pratt, Caemmerer & Cleary, Mineola, 1965-75; partner Farrell, Fritz, Pratt, Caemmerer & Cleary, 1975-76; judge U.S. Dist. Ct. (Eastern Dist. of N.Y.), 1976-82, U.S. Circuit Ct. Appeals for 2d circuit (Uniondale), N.Y., 1982-93; sr. circ. judge U.S. Cir. of Appeals for 2d Cir., 1993-95; counsel Parnon & Pratt L.L.P., N.Y.C., 1995-2000, Farrell Fritz PC, 2001—. Prof. Touro Law Sch., Huntington, N.Y., 1993—. Mem. ABA, N.Y. State Bar Assn., Nassau County Bar Assn., Soc. Am. Law Tchrs. Mem. United Ch. of Christ. Office: Touro Law Ctr 300 Nassau Rd Huntington NY 11743-4342 E-mail: gpratt@farrellfritz.com

PRATT, HAROLD IRVING, lawyer; b. N.Y.C., Apr. 13, 1937; s. H. Irving and Ellen (Hallowell) P.; m. Frances Gillmore, July 2, 1960; children: Frances H., Harold I. Jr., Charles Q.A. BA cum laude, Harvard U., 1959, LLB, 1963. Bar: Mass. 1963. Assoc. Goodwin, Procter & Hoar, Boston, 1963-68; sole practice, Boston, 1968-77; ptnr. law firm, pvt. trustee Nichols & Pratt, Boston, 1977—; ptnr. law firm Pratt & Bator, Boston, 1993—. Chmn. budget com. Cambridge Republican City Com., 1966-68; dir. Cambridge Civic Assn., 1966-70. Mem. ABA, Boston Bar Assn., Mass. Bar Assn., Union Club (gov. 1980-86, pres. 1994-96, sec. 1996—), Harvard Club, Country Club. Episcopalian. Estate planning, Probate, Estate taxation. Home: 1010 Memorial Dr Apt 9A Cambridge MA 02138-4855 Office: Nichols & Pratt 50 Congress St Ste 832 Boston MA 02109-4017

PRATT, JOHN EDWARD, law educator; b. Key West, Fla., June 29, 1945; s. Lloyd Edward and Marilyn June (Havercamp) P.; m. Sharon Louise Brown, Aug. 31, 1968; 1 child, Randolph Winfield. BA, So. Meth. U., 1967, JD, 1974. Bar: Tex. 1974, U.S. Dist. Ct. (no. dist.) Tex. 1975. Ptnr. Schuerenberg, Grimes & Pratt, Mesquite, Tex., 1974-77; asst. city atty. City of Dallas, 1978-80; mem. faculty Cedar Valley Coll., Lancaster, Tex., 1981—. Pres. Friends of Mesquite Pub. Libr., Tex., 1975-77; del. Dem. State Conv., Houston, 1988, 98; pres. Ponderosa Estates Homeowners Assn., 1986-96. Served to lt. USNR, 1967-71. Mem. State Bar Tex., Acad. Legal Studies in Bus., Tex. Jr. Coll. Tchrs. Assn., Cedar Valley Coll. Faculty Assn. (pres. 1983-85, 93-95, 97-99), ACLU, Mensa Internat., NAACP. Democrat. Home: 1001 Villa Siete Mesquite TX 75181-1237 Office: Cedar Valley Coll 3030 N Dallas Ave Lancaster TX 75134-3705

PRATT, KEVIN BURTON, lawyer; b. Mpls., Oct. 26, 1949; s. Wendall Ballou Pratt and Beth Turney (Meyer) Pratt Moerke; m. Pamela Lane Sampson, Oct. 26, 1983. BA, U. Tex., 1970, JD, 1975. Bar: Tex. 1975, Colo. 1979, U.S. Dist. Ct. (we. dist.) Tex. 1978, U.S. Dist. Ct. Colo. 1979, U.S. Ct. Appeals (10th cir.) 1984. Trial atty. Dept. Justice, Dallas, 1975-78; asst. atty. gen. Tex. Atty. Gen.'s Office, Austin, 1978-79; dep. dist. atty. 18th Jud. Dist. Colo., Littleton, 1979-80; ptnr. Fairfield & Woods, P.C., Denver, 1980—. Author: (with Ernest Drapela) 30 Bike Rides in Lane County, 1972, 30 Bike Rides in Austin, Texas, 1973; contbr. articles to profl. jours. Mem. ABA (antitrust law sect., litigation sect., environ. law sect.), Tex. Bar Assn., Colo. Bar Assn. (water law sect.), Denver C. of C., Colo. Water Congress, City Club Denver, Rotary. Antitrust, State civil litigation, Environmental. Office: Fairfield & Woods PC 1700 Lincoln St Ste 2400 Denver CO 80203-4524

PRATTE, GEOFFREY LYNN, lawyer, arbitrator; b. Bonne Terre, Mo., Sept. 14, 1940; s. Charles John and Ruth Jane (Thornton) P.; m. Gretchen Ann Westendorf, Mar. 15, 1969; children: Stephen Charles, Geoffrey Marc, Nicole Elizabeth, Gregory Lynn, Robert Wendell. BA in Philosophy, Kilroe Coll., 1963; MA in French, St. Louis U., 1967; JD, Wash. U., 1974. Bar: Mo. 1974, U.S. Dist. Ct. (ea. dist.) Mo. Tchr. Divine Heart Sem., Donaldson, Ind., 1963-65; analyst CIA, McLean, Va., 1967-71; assoc. Roberts & Roberts, Farmington, Mo., 1974-87; pvt. practice, 1987—; asst. pros. atty. St. Francis County, 1987-93; city pros. atty. Bonne Terre, 1988—. Labor arbitrator Fed. Mediation and Conciliation Svc., Washington, 1988—. Bd. dirs. Terre du Lac Property Owners Assn., 1976-87. Mem. Order of the Coif, KC. Roman Catholic. Avocations: jogging, gardening. Office: 205 E Liberty St Farmington MO 63640-3129

PRATTER, GENE E. K. lawyer; b. Feb. 25, 1949; d. Eugene Anthony and Laurel Marilyn (Dauer) Kreyche; m. Robert Lawrence Pratter, Oct. 21, 1978; children: Virginia Paige, Matthew Robert. BA, Stanford U., 1971; JD, U. Pa., 1975. Bar: Pa. 1975, U.S. Dist. Ct. (ea. dist.) Pa. 1975, U.S. Ct. Appeals (3d cir.) 1981. Assoc. Duane, Morris & Heckscher, Phila., 1975—83, ptnr., 1983—. Judge pro tem Phila. Ct. Common Pleas, 1994—; bd. overseers U. Pa. Law Sch., Phila., 1994—; lectr. Ctr. on Professionalism. Contbr. articles to profl. jours. Fund raiser U. Pa. Law Sch. Mem.: ABA (litigation sect. chmn. com. on ethics and professionalism 1995—), Def. Rsch. Inst., Pa. Bar Assn., Phila. Bar Assn., Stanford U. Alumni Club (fund raiser, officer 1976—83). Republican. Roman Catholic. Construction, Insurance, Professional liability. Office: Duane Morris & Heckscher LLP Ste 4200 One Liberty Pl Philadelphia PA 19103

PRAVEL, BERNARR ROE, lawyer; b. Feb. 10, 1924; BSChemE, Rice U., 1947; JD, George Washington U., 1951. Bar: D.C. 1951, Tex. 1951, U.S. Supreme Ct. 1951. Ptnr. Pravel, Hewitt, Kimball and Krieger, Houston, 1970-99; sr. counsel Akin, Gump, 1999—. Patent editor George Washington U. Law Rev., 1950. Precinct chmn. Houston Rep. Com., 1972-74. Served to lt. (j.g.) USNR. Fellow Am. Bar Found., Tex. Bar Found.; mem. ABA (chair intellectual property sect. 1991-92), Tex. Bar Assn. (chmn. patent, trademark sect. 1968-69, bd. dirs. 1976-79, Outstanding Contbn. 1982), Nat. Coun. Patent Law (chmn. 1970-71), Am. Intellectual Property Law Assn. (pres. 1983-84), Houston Intellectual Property Law Assn. (pres. 1983-84, Outstanding Svc. award 1986), Order of Coif, Kiwanis, Tau Beta Pi. Intellectual property, Patent, Trademark and copyright. Home: 10806 Oak Hollow St Houston TX 77024-3017 Office: Akin Gump South Tower 1900 Pennzoil Pl Houston TX 77002 E-mail: bpravel@wt.inet, bpravel@akingump.com

PREATE, ROBERT ANTHONY, lawyer; b. Scranton, Pa., July 7, 1944; s. Ernest D. and Anne R. (Smith) P.; m. Jane L. Vitzakovitch, May 22, 1981; children— Michael, Jacquelyn, Allison. B.S., U. Scranton, 1966; J.D., U. N.D., 1969. Bar: Pa. 1969, U.S. Ct. Common Pleas 1969, U.S. Dist. Ct. (mid. dist.) Pa. 1969. Sr. ptnr. Levy & Preate, Scranton, 1973—; dir. Leatherneck Mag., 1972-73. Author: Feasibility Study of a Mine Water Heat Pump Concept-Legal and Environmental Issues and Impacts on System Characteristics, 1980. Bd. dirs. Red Cross of Northeast Pa., Scranton, 1976— , Boy Scouts Am., Scranton, 1976-78; Broadway Theater of Northeast Pa., Scranton, 1979— , Econ. Devel. Council Northeastern Pa., Pittston, 1983. Served to capt. USMC, 1969-73. Recipient Am. Jurisprudence prize for Excellence in Legal Research. Mem. ABA, Pa. Bar Assn., Lackawanna County Bar Assn., Greater Scranton C. of C., VFW, Am. Legion, Phi Delta Phi. Republican. Roman Catholic. Club: Scranton. Contracts commercial, Environmental, Pension, profit-sharing, and employee benefits. Office: Levy & Preate 507 Linden St Scranton PA 18503-1608

PREGERSON, HARRY, federal judge; b. L.A., Oct. 13, 1923; s. Abraham and Bessie (Rubin) P.; m. Bernardine Seyma Chapkis, June 28, 1947; children: Dean Douglas, Kathryn Ann. B.A., UCLA, 1947; LL.B., U. Calif.-Berkeley, 1950. Bar: Calif. 1951. Pvt. practice, Los Angeles, 1951-52; Assoc. Morris D. Coppersmith, 1952; ptnr. Pregerson & Costley, Van Nuys, 1953-65; judge Los Angeles Mcpl. Ct., 1965-66, Los Angeles Superior Ct., 1966-67, U.S. Dist. Ct. Central Dist. Calif., 1967-79, U.S. Ct. Appeals for 9th Circuit, Woodland Hills, 1979—. Faculty mem., seminar for newly appointed distr. Judges Fed. Jud. Center, Washington, 1970-72; mem. faculty Am. Soc. Pub. Adminstrn., Inst. for Ct. Mgmt., Denver, 1973—; panelist Fed. Bar Assn., L.A. chpt., 1989, Calif. Continuing Edn. of Bar, 9th Ann. Fed. Practice Inst., San Francisco, 1986, Internat. Acad. Trial Lawyers, L.A., 1983; lect. seminars for newly-appointed Fed. judges, 1970-71. Author over 450 published legal opinions. Mem. Community Rels. Com., Jewish Fedn. Coun., 1984—, Temple Judea, Encino, 1955—; bd. dirs. Marine Corps Res. Toys for Tots Program, 1965—, Greater Los Angeles Partnership for the Homeless, 1988—; bd. trustees Devil Pups Inc., 1988—; adv. bd. Internat. Orphans Inc., 1966—, Jewish Big Brothers Assn., 1970—, Salvation Army, Los Angeles Met. area, 1988—; worked with U.S. Govt. Gen. Svcs. to establish the Bell Shelter for the homeless, the Child Day Care Ctr., the Food Partnership and Westwood Transitional Village, 1988. 1st lt. USMCR, 1944-46. Decorated Purple Heart, Medal of Valor Apache Tribe, 1989; recipient Promotion of Justice Civic award, City of San Fernando, 1965, award San Fernando Valley Jewish Fedn. Coun., 1966, Profl. Achievement award Los Angeles Athletic Club, 1980, Profl. Achievement award UCLA Alumni Assn., 1985, Louis D. Brandeis award Am. Friends of Hebrew U., 1987, award of merit Inner City Law Ctr., 1987, Appreciation award Navajo Nation and USMC for Toys for Tots program, 1987, Humanitarian award Los Angeles Fed. Exec. Bd., 1987-88, Grateful Acknowledgement award Bet Tzedek Legal Svcs., 1988, Commendation award Bd. Suprs. Los Angeles County, 1988, Others award Salvation Army, 1988, numerous others. Mem. ABA (vice-chmn., com. on fed. rules of criminal procedure and evidence sect. of criminal 1972—, panelist Advocacy Inst., Phoenix, 1988), L.A. County Bar Assn., San Fernando Valley Bar Assn. (program chmn. 1964-65), State Bar Calif., Marines Corps Res. Officers Assn. (pres. San Fernando Valley 1966—), DAV (Birmingham chpt.), Am. Legion (Van Nuys Post), Office: US Ct Appeals 9th Cir 21800 Oxnard St Ste 1140 Woodland Hills CA 91367-7919*

PREM, F. HERBERT, JR. lawyer; b. N.Y.C., Jan. 14, 1932; s. F. Herbert and Sybil Gertrude (Nichols) P.; m. Patricia Ryan, Nov. 18, 1978; children from previous marriage: Julia Nichols, F. Herbert III AB, Yale U., 1953; JD, Harvard U., 1959. Bar: N.Y. 1960. Assoc. Whitman & Ransom, N.Y.C., 1959-66, ptnr., 1967-93, co-chmn. exec. com., 1988-92, chmn., 1993, Whitman Breed Abbott & Morgan LLP, N.Y.C., 1993-99, of counsel, 2000; vol. atty. The Legal Aid Soc., 2000—. Bd. dirs. Fuji Photo Film U.S.A., Inc., Fuji Med. Sys. U.S.A., Inc., Noritake Co., Inc., Seiko Instruments America, Inc., The HealthCare Chaplaincy, Inc. Bd. dirs. Bagaduce Music Lending Libr., Inc., 1988-95, pres., 1989-93; bd. dirs. Cmty. Action for Legal Svc. Inc., 1967-70, treas., Legal Aid Soc. N.Y.C., 1967-70. Lt. (j.g.) USNR, 1953-56. Mem. ABA, Assn. of Bar of City of N.Y. (sec. 1967-69), N.Y. State Bar Assn., Am. Law Inst. (life), Yale Club. Episcopalian. General corporate, Private international, Education and schools.

PRENTISS, RICHARD DANIEL, lawyer; b. Xenia, Ohio, Feb. 16, 1947; s. Vernon and Florence May (Madden) P.; m. Debra Ann Gaietto, July 17, 1982; 1 child, Alexandra Madden. Sc.B. cum laude, Brown U., 1969; J.D., Harvard U., 1973. Bar: R.I. 1975, U.S. Dist. Ct. R.I. 1975, U.S. Ct. Appeals (D.C. cir.) 1975, U.S. Ct. Appeals (3d cir.) 1977, U.S. Supreme Ct. 1978, U.S. Ct. Appeals (1st cir.) 1982. Spl. asst. atty. gen. Dept. Atty. Gen., Providence, 1975-78; chief legal counsel Dept. Environ. Mgmt., Providence, 1978-80; assoc. Decof & Grimm, Providence, 1980— ; mem. bd. fed. examiners U.S. Dist. Ct. for R.I., 1984— . Bd. dirs. Mus. Yachting, Newport, R.I., 1980— ; waterfront commr. City of Newport, R.I., 1984— . Mem. R.I. Bar Assn., Assn. Trial Lawyers Am., Sigma Xi, Tau Beta Pi. Democrat. Federal civil litigation, State civil litigation, Public utilities. Home: 6 Greenough Pl Newport RI 02840-2713 Office: R Daniel & Assoc 321 S Main St # 200 Providence RI 02903-7108

PRENTKE, RICHARD OTTESEN, lawyer; b. Cleve., Sept. 8, 1945; s. Herbert E. and Melva B. (Horbury) P.; m. Susan Ottesen, June 9, 1974; children: Catherine, Elizabeth. BSE, Princeton U., 1967; JD, Harvard U., 1974. Assoc. Perkins Coie, Seattle, 1974-80, ptnr., 1981—, CFO, 1989-94. Author: School Construction Law Deskbook, 1989, rev. 2d edit. 1998; contbr. articles to profl. jours. Pres., trustee Seattle County Day Sch., 1990-95; trustee Pocock Rowing Found., 1996—. With USN, 1967-70. Fellow Leadership Tomorrow, Seattle, 1985-86. Mem. ABA, Wash. State Bar Assn. (mem. jud. screening com. 1985-91, chmn. 1987-91), Seattle-King County Bar Assn. (chmn. jud. task force 1990-93), Am. Arbitration Assn. (arbitrator 1988—), Princeton U. Rowing Assn. (pres. 1993—, trustee 1976—), Rainier Club, Princeton Club Wash. (trustee 1986—, pres. 1990-92), Seattle Tennis Club. Avocations: art, carpentry, travel, rowing, sports. Computer, Construction. Office: Perkins Coie 1201 3rd Ave Fl 40 Seattle WA 98101-3029

PRESANT, SANFORD CALVIN, lawyer, educator, writer; b. Buffalo, Nov. 15, 1952; s. Allen and Reeta Presant; children: Jarrett, Danny, Lauren. BA, Cornell U., 1973; JD cum laude, SUNY, Buffalo, 1976; LLM in Taxation, Georgetown U., NYU, 1981. Bar: N.Y. 1977, D.C. 1977, U.S. Tax Ct. 1977, U.S. Ct. Claims 1978, Calif. 1992, U.S. Supreme Ct. 1982. Staff atty. SEC Options Task Force, Washington, 1976-78; assoc. Barrett Smith Schapiro, N.Y.C., 1978-80, Trubin Sillcocks, N.Y.C., 1980-81; ptnr. Carro, Spanbock, Fass, Geller, Kaster, 1981-86, Finley, Kumble, Wagner, Heine, Underberg, Manley, Myerson & Casey, N.Y.C., 1987, Kaye, Scholer, Fierman, Hays & Handler, N.Y.C., 1987-95, Battle Fowler LLP, L.A., 1995-2000, Ernst & Young, L.A., 2000—; nat. dir. real estate tax strategies, opportunity funds Ernst & Young LLP, 2000—. Adj. assoc. prof. real estate NYU, 1984—; frequest lectr. in tax law; regular TV appearances on Nightly Business Report, Pub. Broadcasting System, 1986-88; co-chmn. NYU Conf. Fed. Taxation of Real Estate Transactions, 1987, PLI Advanced Tax Planning for Real Estate, 1987, PLI Real Estate Tax Forum, 1999—; conf. chmn. various confs. in field. Author: (with others) Tax Aspects of Real Investments, 1999, Understanding Estate Partnership Tax Allocations, 1987, Realty Joint Ventures, 1980-86, Tax Sheltered Investments Handbook-Special Update on Tax Reform Act of 1984, Real Estate Syndication Handbook, 1986, Real Estate Syndication Tax Handbook, 1987, The Tax Reform Act of 1986, 1987, The Final Partnership Nonrecourse Debt Allocation Regulations, 1987, Taxation of Real Estate Investments, 1987, Understanding Partnership Tax Allocations, 1987, Tax Aspects of Environmental (Superfund) Settlements, 1994, The Proposed Publicly Traded Partnership Regulations, 1995, others. Kripke Securities Law fellow NYU, 1976. Mem. ABA (nat. chmn. audit subcom. of tax sect. partnership com. 1984-86, partnership tax allocation subcom. chmn. 1986-90, nat. chmn. partnership com. 1992-94, chmn. task force publicly traded partnerships 1995—, others), N.Y. State Bar Assn. (tax sect. partnership com. 1980—), Assn. of Bar of City of N.Y. Republican. Jewish. Securities, Corporate taxation, Personal income taxation. Office: Ernst & Young LLP Ste 1800 2049 Century Park E Los Angeles CA 90067-3119 Fax: 310-284-7970. E-mail: sanford.presant@ey.com

PRESKA, LORETTA A. federal judge; b. 1949; BA, Coll. of St. Rose, 1970; JD, Fordham U., 1973; LLM, NYU, 1978; LHD (hon.), Coll. of St. Rose, 1995. Assoc. Cahill, Gordon & Reindel, N.Y.C., 1973-82; ptnr. Hertzog, Calamari & Gleason, 1982-92; fed. judge U.S. Dist. Ct. (so. dist.) N.Y., 1992—. Mem. N.Y. State Bar Assn., N.Y. County Lawyers Assn., Fed. Bar Coun., Fordham Law Alumni Assn. (v.p.). Office: US Courthouse 500 Pearl St Rm 1320 New York NY 10007-1316

PRESSER, STEPHEN BRUCE, lawyer, educator; b. Chattanooga, Aug. 10, 1946; s. Sidney and Estelle (Shapiro) P.; m. Carole Smith, June 18, 1968 (div. 1987); children: David Carter, Elisabeth Catherine; m. ArLynn Leiber, Dec. 13, 1987; children: Joseph Leiber, Eastman Leiber. A.B., Harvard U., 1968, J.D., 1971. Bar: Mass. 1971, D.C. 1972. Law clk. to Judge Malcolm Richard Wilkey U.S. Ct. Appeals (D.C. cir.), 1971-72; assoc. Wilmer, Cutler & Pickering, Washington, 1972-74; asst. prof. law Rutgers U., Camden, N.J., 1974-76; vis. assoc. prof. U. Va., 1976-77; prof. Northwestern U., Chgo., 1977—, class 1940 rsch. prof., 1992-93, Raoul Berger prof. legal history, 1992—, assoc. dean acad. affairs Sch. Law, 1982-85. Prof. bus. law Kellogg Grad. Sch. Mgmt., Northwestern U., Chgo., 1992—. Author: (with Jamil S. Zainaldin) Law and Jurisprudence in American History, 1980, 4th edit., 2000, Studies in the History of the United States Courts of the Third Circuit, 1983, The Original Misunderstanding: The English, The Americans and the Dialectic of Federalist Jurisprudence, 1991, Piercing the Corporate Veil, 1991, revised ann., (with Ralph Ferrara and Meridith Brown) Takeovers: A Strategist's Manual, 2d edit., 1993, Recapturing the Constitution, 1994, (with Douglas W. Kmiec) The American Constitutional Order: History, Cases, and Philosophy, 1998; assoc. articles editor Guide to American Law, 1985. Trustee Village of Winnetka, Ill., 2000—; mem. acad. adv. bd. Washington Legal Found. Recipient summer stipend NEH, 1975; Fulbright Sr. scholar Univ. Coll., London Sch. Econs. and Polit. Sci., 1983-84, Inst. Advanced Legal Studies, 1996; Adams fellow Inst. U.S. Studies, London, 1996; assoc. rsch. fellow Inst. U.S. Studies, 1999—. Mem. Am. Soc. Legal History (bd. dirs. 1979-82), Am. Law Inst., Univ. Club Chgo. (bd. dirs. 1997-99, sec., 1999), Legal Club Chgo., Reform Club (London), Arts Club Chgo. Office: Northwestern U Law Sch 357 E Chicago Ave Chicago IL 60611-3069 E-mail: s-presser@law.northwestern.edu

PRESSLEY, FRED G., JR. lawyer; b. N.Y.C., June 19, 1953; s. Fred G. Sr. and Frances (Sanders) P.; m. Cynthia Denise Hill, Sept. 5, 1981. BA cum laude, Union Coll., 1975; JD, Northwestern U., 1978. Bar: Ohio 1978, U.S. Dist. Ct. (so. dist.) Ohio 1979, U.S. Dist. Ct. (no. dist.) Ohio 1985, U.S. Dist. Ct. (ea. dist.) Wis. 1980, U.S. Ct. Appeals (6th cir.). Assoc. Porter, Wright, Morris & Arthur, Columbus, Ohio, 1978-85, ptnr., 1985—. Bd. dirs. Columbus Area Leadership Program, 1981-84, Franklin County Bd. Mental Retardation and Devel. Disabilities, Columbus, 1989-97, Union Coll., Schenectady, N.Y., 1992—. Recipient Civic Achievement award Ohio Ho. of Reps., 1988. Mem. ABA. Avocations: jogging, golf, basketball, military history. Civil rights, Labor. Office: Porter Wright Morris & Arthur 41 S High St Ste 2800 Columbus OH 43215-6194

PRESTON, CAROLINE MARY, lawyer; b. London, Apr. 12, 1955; d. Robert Edmund and Barbara ALice Orr; m. John Peter Preston, June 6, 1981; children: Eliza, Arthur. BA (hon.) in History, Polit. Sci., Dublin, Ireland, 1977; Solicitor, Law Soc. of Ireland, 1980. Qualified solicitor. Solicitor A&L Goodbody, Dublin, Ireland, 1980-86, ptnr. Ireland, 1986—, head of litigation Ireland, 1997—. Personal solicitor Atty. Gen. of Ireland, 1994—97. Dir. St. Patrick's Hosp., Dublin, 1993—, Cancer Soc. Ireland, 1990-95. Mem. IWF Ireland. Avocations: fox hunting, fishing, travel. General civil litigation, Product liability, Professional liability. Home: Swainstown Kilmessan 25256 Ireland Office: A&L Goodbody 1 North Wall Dublin 1 Ireland E-mail: cpreston@algoodbody.ie

PRESTON, CHARLES GEORGE, lawyer; b. Nov. 11, 1940; s. Charles William and Gudveig Nicoline (Hoem) P.; m. Hilde Delphine van Stappen, Mar. 12, 1970; children: Charles William, Stephanie Delphine, Christina Nicoline. BA, U. Wash., 1963, MPA, 1968; JD, Columbia U., 1971. Bar: Wash. 1971, D.C. 1981, U.S. Dist. Ct. D.C. 1981, U.S. Dist. Ct. (we. dist.) Wash. 1971, U.S. Ct. Appeals (9th cir.) 1972, U.S. Ct. Appeals (4th cir.) 1979, U.s. Ct. Appeals (5th and D.C. cirs.) 1978, U.S. Ct. Appeals (2d cir.) 1980, U.S. Ct. Appeals (11th cir.) 1981, U.S. Supreme Ct. 1977, U.S. Ct. Claims 1982, U.S. Ct. Appeals (1st cir.) 1984, U.S. Ct. Appeals (3d, 6th and 7th cirs.) 1987, Va. 1987, U.S. Dist. Ct. (ea. dist.) Va. 1989, U.S. Dist. Ct. (we. dist.) Wash. 1971, U.S. Dist. Ct. (no. dist.) Calif. 1981, U.S. Bankruptcy Ct. Va. 1990. Assoc. Jones, Grey, Bayley & Olson, Seattle, 1971-72; atty., asst. counsel for litigation Officer of Solicitor U.S. Dept. Labor, 1972-76, Washington, 1976-81; atty. Air Line Pilots Assn., 1981-82; mng. ptnr. MacNabb, Preston & Waxman, 1981-86, Preston & Preston, Great Falls, Va., 1986-95, Charles G. Preston, P.C., 1995—. Pres. Preston Group, Inc. 1989-98; lectr. seminars. Mem. Wash. State Bar, D.C. Bar Assn., Va. Bar Assn., Tng. Law Inst. (pres. 1985-95), Gt. Falls Bus. and Profl. Assn. (pres. 1990), The Serbian Crown, Va. (pres. 1989-99). State civil litigation, General corporate, Real property. Office: Charles G Preston PC 774C Walker Rd Great Falls VA 22066-2639 E-mail: prestonlaw@aol.com

PRESTON, CHARLES MICHAEL, lawyer; b. Balt., Oct. 11, 1945; s. Carlton Edward and Jeannette Thorn (Baker) P.; m. Carol Ann Armacost, June 21, 1969 (div. Dec. 1978). BA, Western Md. Coll., 1967; JD, U. Balt., 1970. Bar: Md. 1970, U.S. Dist. Ct. Md. 1972, U.S. Supreme Ct. 1974, U.S. Dist. Ct. (trial bar) 1984. Law clk. to Hon. E.O. Weant, Jr., Westminster, Md., 1970-71; assoc. Hoffman & Hoffman, 1972-75; ptnr. Hoffman, Hoffman & Preston, 1976-77, Hoffman, Stoner & Preston, Westminster, 1978-79; ptnr., v.p. Stoner, Preston & Boswell Chartered, 1980—. Rev. bd., panel mem. Atty. Grievance Commn., Annapolis, Md., 1978-95; mem. Md. Ct. Appeals Commn. on alternate dispute resolution, 1998-2000, adv. bd., Md. Mediation and Conflict Resolution Office, 2001-. Contbr. articles to profl. jours. Mem. Carroll County Gen. Hosp., Westminster, 1983—; trustee Raymond I. Richardson Found., Middleburg, Md., 1979-93; bd. dirs. Carroll County Agrl. Ctr., Westminster, 1975—; dir. N.W. dist. ARC, Balt., 1987-95; trustee Balt. Opera Co., 1998-2001. With U.S. Army, 1970-71. Fellow Md. Bar Found., Am. Bar Found.; mem. ABA (del. ho. of dels.), Md. State Bar Assn. (treas. 1991-96, bd. govs. 1985-86, 91-2000, pres.-elect 1997, pres. 98), Carroll County Bar Assn. (pres. 1985), Pro Bono Resource Ctr. Md. (bd. dirs. 1997-2000), Elks. Presbyterian. Avocations: snow skiing, ice skating, woodworking, music, travel. Appellate, General civil litigation, Land use and zoning (including planning). Office: Stoner Preston & Boswell PO Box 389 188 E Main St Westminster MD 21157-5017

PRESTON, JAMES YOUNG, lawyer; b. Atlanta, Sept. 21, 1937; s. James William and Mary Lou (Young) P.; m. Elizabeth Buxton Gregory, June 13, 1959; children: Elizabeth P. Carr, Mary Lane P. Lennon, James Brenton Preston. BA in English, U. N.C., 1958, JD with high honors, 1961. Bar: N.C. 1961. Assoc. to ptnr. Parker, Poe, Adams & Bernstein L.L.P. and predecessors, Charlotte, N.C., 1961—. Pres. Charlotte Area Fund, 1968, Cmty. Sch. of Arts, 1976-78; pres. Arts and Sci. Coun. Charlotte/Mecklenburg, Inc., 1986-87, chair The Nat. Conf. for Cmty. and Justice, Charlotte, 1996-99, Wildacres Leadership Initiative, 1994—; vice chair N.C. Dance Theatre, 1995-97. Mem. ABA (ho. dels. 1988-92, 95-97), N.C. State Bar (pres. 1987-88), Am. Law Inst., Nat. Conf. Bar Presidents (exec. coun. 1989-92), Phi Beta Kappa, Phi Eta Sigma. Democrat. Episcopalian. Avocations: travel, tennis, profl. and civic activities. General corporate, Estate planning, Taxation, general. Office: Parker Poe Adams Bernstein LLP 3000 Three First Union Ctr 401 S Tryon St Ste 3000 Charlotte NC 28202 E-mail: jimpreston@parkinpoe.com

PRESTON, JEROME, JR. lawyer; b. Staten Island, N.Y., Nov. 15, 1922; s. Jerome and Iva (Stone) P.; m. Dorothy Greeno McCann, Oct. 3, 1953; children: Richard M., Douglas J., David G. A.B., Harvard U., 1947; LL.B., Yale U., 1950. Bar: Mass. 1951. Ptnr. Foley, Hoag & Eliot, Boston, 1956—. Trustee Eaton-Vance Income Fund of Boston, Inc., 1976-95. Trustee Univ. Hosp., 1956-96, overseer, 1996—; bd. dirs. Cambridge Sch. of Weston, 1973-78, pres., 1975-77; mem. Wellesley (Mass.) Planning Bd., 1962-70, chmn., 1966-68. Served to 1st lt. Signal Corps AUS, 1943-46. Mem. ABA, Mass. Bar Assn., Boston Bar Assn., Am. Law Inst., Handel and Haydn Soc. (pres. 1988, gov. 1988-92), Tavern Club. Democrat. Probate, Estate taxation, State and local taxation. Home: 62 Foster St Cambridge MA 02138-4817 Office: Foley Hoag & Eliot 1 Post Office Sq Ste 1900 Boston MA 02109-2175

PRESTON, STEPHEN W. lawyer; BA summa cum laude, Yale U., 1979; diploma., Trinity Coll., U. Dublin, 1980; JD magna cum laude, Harvard U., 1983. Bar: D.C. Law clk. to Hon. Phyllis A. Kravitch U.S. Ct. Appeals (11th cir.), 1983-84; vis. fellow Ctr. for Law in Pub. Interest, Washington, 1984-85; ptnr. Wilmer, Cutler & Pickering, 1986-93; dep. gen. counsel, prin. dep. gen. counsel, acting gen. counsel Dept. of Defense, 1993-95; dep. asst. atty. gen. Dept. of Justice, 1995-98; gen. counsel Dept. of Navy, 1998-2000; ptnr. Wilmer, Cutler & Pickering, Washington, 2001—. Recipient Disting. Pub. Svc. medal Dept. of Def., 1995, 2000, Dept. of Navy, 2000. Office: Wilmer Cutler & Pickering 2445 M St NW Washington DC 20037-1420 E-mail: spreston@wilmer.com

PRESTRIDGE, PAMELA ADAIR, lawyer; b. Delhi, La., Dec. 25, 1945; d. Gerald Wallace Prestridge and Louis Baugh and Peggy Adair (Arender) Martin. BA, La. Poly. U., 1967; M in Edn., La. State u., 1968, JD, 1973. Bar: U.S. Dist. Ct. (mid. dist.) La. 1975, U.S. Dist. Ct. (so. dist.) Tex. 1982, U.S. Ct. Appeals (5th cir.) 1982, U.S. Supreme Ct. 1990. Law clk. to presiding justice La. State Dist. Ct., Baton Rouge, 1973-75; ptnr. Breazeale, Sachse & Wilson, 1975-82, Hirsch & Westheimer P.C., Houston, 1982-92; pvt. practive, 1992—. Counselor Big Bros./Big Sisters, Baton Rouge, 1968-70; legal cons., bd. dirs. Lupus Found. Am., Houston, 1984-93; bd. dirs. Quota Club, Baton Rouge, 1979-82, Speech and Hearing Found., Baton Rouge, 1981-82, The Actors Workshop, Houston, 1988-93, Tex. Satsang Soc., 2000—; active Tex. Accts. and Attys. for the Arts. Recipient Pres.'s award Lupus Found. Am., 1991, cert. of appreciation Assn. Atty. Mediators, 1992, Outstanding Profl. Woman of Houston award Fedn. Profl. Women, 1984. Mem. ABA, La. Bar Assn., Tex. Bar Assn., Houston Bar Assn., Houston Bar Found., Assn. Atty. Mediators (bd. dirs. 1994-96, Citation for Outstanding Mems. 1993), Profl. Atty.-Mediators Coop. (v.p. 1994, bd. dirs. 1994-96, pres. 1995), Phi Alpha Delta. Eckankar. Avocations: acting, ultralite flying. Alternative dispute resolution, Bankruptcy, General civil litigation. Home: 1701 Hermann Dr Unit 407 Houston TX 77004-7345 Office: 3300 Phoenix Tower PO Box 130987 Houston TX 77219-0987

PRESTWOOD, ALVIN TENNYSON, lawyer; b. Roeton, Ala., June 18, 1929; s. Garrett Felix and Jimmie (Payne) P.; m. Sue Burleson Lee, Nov. 27, 1974; children: Ann Celeste Prestwood Peeples, Alison Bennett, Cynthia Joyce Lee Koplos, William Alvin Lee, Garret Courtney. BS, U. Ala., 1951, LLB, 1956, JD, 1970. Bar: Ala. 1956, U.S. Ct. Appeals (6th and 11th cirs.) 1981, U.S. Supreme Ct. 1972. Law clk. Supreme Ct. Ala., 1956-57; asst. atty. gen. Ala., 1957-59; commr. Ala. Dept. Pensions and Security, 1959-63; pvt. practice Montgomery, Ala., 1963-65, 77-82; ptnr. Volz, Capouano, Wampold, Prestwood & Sansone, 1965-77, Prestwood & Rosser, 1982-85, Capouano, Wampold, Prestwood & Sansone, 1986-94, Volz, Prestwood & Hanan, Montgomery, 1995—. Chmn. Gov.'s Com. on White House Conf. on Aging, 1961; mem. adv. com. Dept. Health, Edn. and Welfare, 1962; sec. Nat. Coun. State Pub. Welfare Adminstrs., 1962 Mem. editl. bd. Ala. Law Rev., 1955-56; contbr. articles to profl. jours. Pres. Morningview Sch. P.T.A., 1970; chmn. Am. Nursing Home Assn. Legal Com., 1972; bd. dirs. Montgomery Bapt. Hosp., 1958-65; chmn. bd. mgmt. East Montgomery YMCA, 1969; chmn. deacons Cloverdale Bapt. Ch., 1994-95, 98. 1st lt., inf. AUS, 1951-53. Decorated Combat Inf. Badge.; recipient Sigma Delta Kappa Scholastic Achievement award U. Ala. Sch. Law, 1956, Law Day Moot Ct. award U. Ala. Sch. Law, 1956 Mem. ABA (chmn. com. on jud. performance and conduct 1996, chmn. Judiciary's Image Evaluation Task Force 1996-2000), Ala. Bar Assn. (chmn. adminstrv. law sect. 1972, 78, 83, 97), Montgomery County Bar Assn. (chmn. exec. com. 1971), Farrah Order Jurisprudence, Eleventh Cir. Jud. Conf., Am. Judicature Soc., Kappa Sigma. Administrative and regulatory, Civil rights, Federal civil litigation. Home: 1431 Magnolia Curv Montgomery AL 36106-2043 Office: Volz Prestwood & Hanan 350 Adams Ave Montgomery AL 36104-4204 E-mail: attys@bellsouth.net

PRETL, MICHAEL ALBERT, lawyer; b. Balt., Oct. 20, 1942; s. Stephen Anthony and Mildred Alice (Sramek) P.; children: Patricia, Julia, Katherine. BA, Cath. U. Am., 1964; JD, Georgetown U., 1969. Bar: Md. 1969, D.C. 1969, U.S. Dist. Ct. Md. 1970. Assoc. Smith, Somerville & Case, Balt., 1969-75, ptnr., 1976-81, Pretl & Schultheis PA, Balt., 1982-86, Pretl & Erwin PA, Balt., 1986-95; counsel Ashcraft & Gerel, 1996-98; gen. counsel Am. Urological Assn., 1998—. Bd. dirs. Balt. Neighborhoods, Inc., 1979-84; trustee Kidney Found. Md., 1985-95, pres., 1988-90; pres. Marylanders Against Handgun Abuse, 1993-96. Democrat. Roman Catholic. Health, Personal injury, Product liability. Office: Am Urological Assn Inc 1120 N Charles St Baltimore MD 21201-5506 Fax: 410-468-1835. E-mail: mpretl@auanet.org

PREWITT, DAVID EDWARD, lawyer; b. Phila., Oct. 13, 1939; s. Richard Hickman and Jean (Simpkins) P.; m. Joan Rosella Taylor, June 16, 1939; children: Mary-Alice Graham, Katherine Estill, Elizabeth Bowen. AB, Dartmouth Coll., 1961; JD, Duke U., 1968. Bar: Ky. 1968, Fla. 1970, Pa. 1971, U.S. Dist. Ct. (ea.dist.) Pa. 1971, U.S. Ct. Appeals (3d cir.) 1971; cert. civil trial adv. Nat. Bd. Trial Advocacy. Trial atty. U.S. Dept. Justice, Washington, 1968-69; assoc. Mahoney, Hadlow, Chambers & Adams, Jacksonville, Fla., 1969-70, White & Williams, Phila., 1971-76, ptnr., 1976-79, Prewitt & Oplinger, Phila., 1979-80; pres. David E. Prewitt Assocs., 1980-88; ptnr. Korn, Kline & Kutner, 1988-91; pres. David E. Prewitt Assocs., 1991-95; ptnr. Miller, Dunham & Doering, 1995-99; of counsel Bennett, Bricklin & Saltzburg, 1999—. Judge pro tem Phila. Ct. Common Pleas, 1995—; mediator U.S. Dist. Ct. Ea. Dist., Pa., 1990—. Contbr. articles to profl. jours. Mem. Com. of Seventy, 1977—. Col. USAR, 1961-93. Decorated Air medal, Vietnam Service medal, Meritorious Svc. medal. Mem. ATLA, ABA, Fla. Bar Assn., Pa. Bar Assn. (past chmn. aero. and space law com.), Phila. Bar Assn. (past chmn. aviation law com., past chmn. mil. affairs com.), Lawyer-Pilots Bar Assn., Phila. Assn. Def. Counsel (exec. com. 1996—), Mil. Order World Wars, Mil. Order Fgn. Wars, Pa. Soc. Sons of Revolution, Merion Cricket Club (Haverford, Pa.). Democrat. Episcopalian. Aviation, Federal civil litigation, Personal injury. Office: 1601 Market St 16th Fl Philadelphia PA 19103 E-mail: davidprewitt@hotmail.com, prewitt@bbs-law.com

PREWOZNIK, JEROME FRANK, lawyer; b. Detroit, July 15, 1934; s. Frank Joseph and Loretta Ann (Parzych) P.; m. Marilyn Ruth Johnson, 1970; 1 child, Frank Joseph II. AB cum laude, U. Detroit, 1955; JD with distinction, U. Mich., 1958. Bar: Calif. 1959. Pvt. practice, Calif., 1960-91. Served in U.S. Army, 1958-60. Mem. ABA, State Bar Calif. Republican. Home: 431 Georgina Ave Santa Monica CA 90402-1909

PRIBANIC, VICTOR HUNTER, lawyer; b. McKeesport, Pa., Apr. 7, 1954; s. John Edward and Marlene Cecilia (Hunter) P. BA, Bowling Green State U., 1976; JD, Duquesne U., 1979. Bar: Pa. 1979, U.S. Dist. Ct. (we. dist.) Pa. 1979, U.S. Ct. Appeals (3d cir.) 1979, U.S. Supreme Ct. 1989, U.S. Ct. Claims 1990. Asst. dist. atty. Office of Dist. Atty., Pitts., 1980-82; law clk. to presiding justice Pa. Ct. Common Pleas, 1982-85; pvt. practice Pitts. and McKeesport, 1982—; pres. Pribanic & Pribanic, P.C., 1987—. Mem.: ATLA, Nat. Assn. Criminal Def. Lawyers, Pa. Trial Lawyers Assn., Acad. Trial Lawyers Allegheny County, Roscoe Pound Found., Million Dollar Adv. Forum. Democrat. Roman Catholic. State civil litigation, Criminal, Personal injury. Home: 100 Victoria Dr Mc Keesport PA 15131-1224 Office: 1735 Lincoln Way White Oak PA 15131-1715 Address: 513 Court Pl Pittsburgh PA 15219-2002

PRICE, CHARLES STEVEN, lawyer; b. Inglewood, Calif., June 10, 1955; s. Frank Dean Price and Ann (Rounds) Bolling; m. Sandra Helen Laney, Feb. 26, 1983; children: Katherine Laney, Courtney Ann, Diana Emily. BA, U. Calif., Santa Barbara, 1976; JD, U. Chgo., 1979. Bar: Ariz. 1980, U.S. Dist. Ct. Ariz. 1980, U.S. Ct. Appeals (9th cir.) 1982. Assoc. Brown & Bain P.A., Phoenix, 1979-85, ptnr., 1985-96, Allen & Price P.L.C., Phoenix, 1996-2000, Allen, Price & Padden, Phoenix, 2000—. Antitrust, Health, Securities. Office: Allen Price & Padden PLC 3131 E Camelback Rd Ste 110 Phoenix AZ 85016-4597 E-mail: price@aplaw.com

PRICE, DONALD DOUGLAS, lawyer; b. Maryville, Mo., July 30, 1943; s. Donald LeRoy and Julia Catherine (Aley) P.; m. Jane Davis, Nov. 4, 1967; children— Andrew Douglas, Eric Montgomery. B.S. in Chem. Engring., U. Mo., 1965; J.D. with honors, George Washington U., 1968. Bar: D.C. 1968, U.S. Ct. Appeals (D.C. cir.) 1969, Calif. 1970, U.S. Supreme Ct. 1973, U.S. Ct. Appeals (Fed. cir.) 1975. Examiner U.S. Patent and Trademark Office, Washington, 1965-66; patent agt., assoc. Bacon & Thomas, Washington, 1966-69; asst. patent counsel N.Am. Rockwell, Canoga Park, Calif., 1969-71; assoc., then ptnr. Fleit, Jacobson, Cohn, Price, Holman & Stern, Washington, 1971— . Mem. ABA, Am. Intellectual Property Law Assn., Fedn. Internationale des Conseils en Propriete Industrielle, Assn. Internationale pour la Protection de la Propriete Industrielle, Licensing Execs. Soc., Washington Golf and Country Club. Patent, Trademark and copyright. Home: 1134 Randolph Rd Mc Lean VA 22101-2929 Office: Fleit Jacobson Cohn Price 400 7th St NW Ste 600 Washington DC 20004-2218

PRICE, GRIFFITH BALEY, JR. lawyer; b. Lawrence, Kans., Aug. 15, 1942; s. Griffith Baley and Cora Lee (Beers) P.; m. Maria Helena Martin, June 29, 1968 (div.); children: Andrew Griffith, Alexandra Helena; m. Nancy Culver Rhodes, Aug. 17, 1997; 1 child, Carolyn Rhodes. AB (cum laude), Harvard U., 1964; LLB, NYU, 1967. Bar: N.Y. 1967, D.C. 1991, U.S. Ct. Appeals (6th cir.) 1975, U.S. Ct. Appeals (2nd cir.) 1978, U.S. Ct. Appeals (3d, 5th and 11th cirs.) 1981, U.S. Ct. Appeals (fed. cir.) 1984, U.S. Supreme Ct. 2001. Assoc. Dewey, Ballantine, Bushby, Palmer & Wood, N.Y.C., 1967-75; ptnr. Milgrim Thomajan & Lee, 1976-86; of counsel, ptnr. Finnegan, Henderson, Farabow, Garrett & Dunner, LLP, Washington, 1987—. Adj. prof., lectr. George Washington U. Law Ctr., Washington, 1989—93; mem., chair pub. adv. com. U.S. Patent and Trademark Office, 1999—2001; lectr. in field. Author: (with others, treatise) Milgrim on Trade Secrets, 1986; contbr. articles to publs. Root-Tilden scholar NYU Law Sch., 1964-67. Mem. ABA (intellectual property sect., com. chmn.), Internat. Trademark Assn. (bd. dirs., com. chmn.), Am. Intellectual Property Law Assn. (bd. dirs., com. chmn.), Licensing Execs. Soc., N.Y. Athletic Club, Harvard Club (Washington), Nat. Press Club, Cosmos Club. Presbyterian. Federal civil litigation, Intellectual property, Trademark and copyright. Office: Finnegan Henderson Farabow Garrett & Dunner LLP 1300 I St NW Ste 700 Washington DC 20005-3314 E-mail: gbprice@finnegan.com

PRICE, JAMES TUCKER, lawyer; b. Springfield, Mo., June 22, 1955; s. Billy L. and Jeanne Adele Price; m. Francine Beth Warkow, June 8, 1980; children: Rachel Leah, Ashley Elizabeth. BJ, U. Mo., 1977; JD, Harvard U., 1980. Bar: Mo. 1980. Assoc. firm Spencer Fane Britt & Browne, Kansas City, 1980-86; ptnr. Spencer Fane Britt & Browne LLP, 1987—, chair environ. practice group, 1994—, mem. exec. com., 1997—. Mem. Brownfields Commn., Kansas City, 1999—; mem. steering com. Kansas City Bi-State Brownfields Initiative, 1997—. Contbr. to monographs, other legal publs. Mem. ABA (coun. sect. environ, energy and resources 1992-95, vice chmn. solid and hazardous waste com. 1985-90, chmn. 1990-92, chmn. brownfields task force 1995-97, vice chmn. environ. transactions and brownfield com. 1998-2000), Mo. Bar Assn., Kansas City Met. Bar Assn. (chmn. environ. law com. 1985-86), Greater Kansas City C. of C. (co-chair Brownfields Working Group, 1996-98, chmn. energy and environ. com. 1987-89). Federal civil litigation, State civil litigation, Environmental. Office: Spencer Fane Britt & Browne LLP 1000 Walnut St Ste 1400 Kansas City MO 64106-2140 E-mail: jprice@spencerfane.com

PRICE, JOHN ALEY, lawyer; b. Maryville, Mo., Oct. 7, 1947; s. Donald Leroy and Julia Catherine (Aley) P.; m. Deborah Diadra Gunter, Aug. 12, 1995; children: Theodore John, Joseph Andrew. BS, N.W. Mo. State U., 1969; JD, U. Kans., 1972. Bar: Kans. 1972, U.S. Dist. Ct. Kans. 1972, U.S. Ct. Appeals (10th cir.) 1972, Tex. 1984, U.S. Ct. Appeals (5th cir.) 1984, U.S. Supreme Ct. 1987; cert. civil trial law Tex. Bd. Legal Specialization. Law clk. U.S. Dist. Ct. Kans., Wichita, 1972-74; from assoc. to ptnr. Weeks, Thomas and Lysaught, Kansas City, Kans., 1974-82; ptnr. Winstead, Sechrest & Minick, Dallas, 1982-96, litigation sect. coord., 1990-92, intellectual property sect. litigation coord., 1993-95; gen. counsel Travelhost Inc., 1996—, Club Co., Inc., 1999-2001. Pres. Umansys, Inc., Dallas, 2000—; spl. prosecutor Leavenworth County Office Dist. Atty., 1970-71, Sedgwick County Offce Dist. Atty., Wichita, Kans., 1971-72. Author: Our

Boundless Self (A Call to Awake), 1992, A Gathering of Light: Eternal Wisdom for a Time of Transformation, 1993; co-author: Soular Reunion: Journey to the Beloved, 1998; editor (mag.) Academic Analyst, 1968-69; assoc. editor U. Kans. Law Rev., 1971-72, Dallas Bus. Jour.; contbr. articles to profl. jours. Co-dir. Douglas County Legal Aid Soc., Lawrence, Kans., 1971-72; co-pres. Northwood Hills PTA, Dallas, 1984, Westwood Jr. H.S. PTA, 1989-90; founder New Frontiers Found., 1993; co-founder Wings of Spirit Found., 1994, dir., v.p. 1994—. Mem. ABA, Kans. Bar Assn. (mem. task force for penal reform; Pres.'s Outstanding Svc. award 1981), Tex. Bar Assn., Pro Bono Coll., State Bar Tex., World Bus. Acad., Inst. Noetic Scis., UN Assn. (human rights com. Dallas chpt. 1991-93, bd. dirs. 1991-93), Campaign for the Earth (chpt. coord. Global Report 1991-92, coord. govt. and polit. area 1991-92), Blue Key, Order of Coif, Phi Delta Phi, Sigma Tau Gamma (v.p. 1968-69). Mem. Unity Ch. Antitrust, Federal civil litigation, Trademark and copyright. Office: Travelhost Inc 10701 N Stemmons Fwy Dallas TX 75220-2419 E-mail: japrice@travelhost.com

PRICE, JOHN RICHARD, lawyer, law educator; b. Indpls., Nov. 28, 1934; s. Carl Lee and Agnes I. P.; m. Suzanne A. Leslie, June 22, 1963; children: John D., Steven V. B.A. with high honors, U. Fla., 1958; LL.B. with honors, NYU, 1961. Bar: Calif. 1962, Wash. 1977, U.S. Ct. Appeals (9th cir.), U.S. Dist. Ct. (we. dist.) Wash. Assoc. McCutchen, Doyle, Brown & Enersen, San Francisco, 1961-69; prof. law U. Wash., Seattle, 1969-97, dean, 1982-88; of counsel Perkins Coie, 1976—. Author: Contemporary Estate Planning, 1983, Price on Contemporary Estate Planning, 1992, 2d edit., 2000, Conflicts, Confidentiality and Other Ethical Issues, 2000. Served with U.S. Army, 1953-55 Root-Tilden fellow NYU Sch. Law, 1958-61 Fellow Am. Coll. Trust and Estate Counsel (former regent); mem. ABA, Am. Law Inst., Internat. Acad. of Estate and Trust Law, Order of Coif, Phi Beta Kappa. Congregationalist Home: 3794 NE 97th St Seattle WA 98115-2564 Office: 1201 3rd Ave Ste 4800 Seattle WA 98101-3029 E-mail: pricj@perkinscole.com

PRICE, JOSEPH MICHAEL, lawyer; b. St. Paul, Dec. 2, 1947; s. Leon and Rose (Kaufman) P.; m. Louise Rebecca Braunstein, Dec. 19, 1971; children: Lisa, Lauri, Julie. BA, U. Minn., 1969, JD, 1972. Bar: Minn. 1972, U.S. Dist. Ct. Minn. 1974. Ptnr. Faegre & Benson, Mpls., 1972—. Mem. Minn. Bar Assn., Hennepin County Bar Assn. General civil litigation, Insurance, Product liability. Home: 4407 Country Club Rd Minneapolis MN 55424-1148 Office: Faegre & Benson 2200 Wells Fargo Ctr 90 S 7th St Ste 2200 Minneapolis MN 55402-3901 E-mail: jprice@faegre.com

PRICE, PAUL L. lawyer; b. Chgo., Apr. 21, 1945; s. Walter S. and Lillian (Czerepkowski) L.; m. Dianne L. Olech, June 3, 1967; children: Kristen, Kathryn. BBA, Loyola U., Chgo., 1967; JD with honors, Ill. Inst. Tech., 1971. Bar: Ill. 1971, U.S. Dist. Ct. (no. dist.) Ill., U.S. Ct. Appeals (7th cir.). Tax acct. Arthur Anderson & Co., Chgo., 1970-71; assoc. Doyle & Tarpey, 1971-75, Gordon & Assocs., Chgo., 1975-76; from assoc. to ptnr. Pretzel & Stouffer, Chartered, 1976-96; ptnr. Price, Tunney, Reiter & Bruton, 1996—. With USMC, 1969-70. Fellow Am. Coll. Trial Lawyers; mem. ABA, Ill. Bar Assn., Soc. Trial Lawyers, Ill. Assn. Def. Trial Counsel (pres. 1990-91), Fedn. Ins. and Corp. Counsel (pres.1999-2000), Def. Rsch. Inst. (bd. dirs. 1999-2001), Lawyers for Civil Justice (bd. dirs. 1999-2001), Assn. Def. Trial Attys., Ill. Inst. Tech.-Chgo. Kent Coll. Law Alumni Assn. (pres. 1989-90). Roman Catholic. General civil litigation, Product liability, Professional liability. Office: Price Tunney Reiter & Bruton 200 N Lasalle St Ste 3050 Chicago IL 60601-1014

PRICE, ROBERT, lawyer, media executive, investment banker; b. N.Y.C., Aug. 27, 1932; s. Solomon and Frances (Berger) P.; m. Margery Beth Wiener, Dec. 18, 1955 (div.); children: Eileen Marcia, Steven. AB, NYU, 1953; LLD, Columbia U., 1958. Bar: N.Y. 1958, U.S. Dist. Ct. 1958, U.S. Ct. Appeals 1958, U.S. Supreme Ct 1958, ICC 1958, FCC 1958, IRS 1958. With R.H. Macy & Co., Inc., 1955-58; practiced in N.Y.C., 1958—; law clk. to judge U.S. Dist. Ct. (so. dist.) N.Y., 1958-59; asst. U.S. atty. So. Dist. N.Y., 1959-60; ptnr. Kupferman & Price, 1960-65; dep. mayor N.Y.C., 1965-66; exec. v.p., dir. Dreyfus Corp., 1966-69; v.p., investment officer Dreyfus Fund, until 1969; gen. ptnr. Lazard, Freres & Co., 1972-82; pres. N.Y. Law Jour., Nat. Law Jour.; pres., treas., dir. Price Comm. Corp., 1979—; chmn., pres., dir. PriCellular Corp., 1988-95; pres., dir. TLM Corp., 1989—. Mem. adv. com. Bankers Trust Co. N.Y.; dir. Holly Sugar Corp., Lane Bryant, Inc., Graphic Scanning Corp.; chmn. N.Y.C. Port Authority Negotiating Com. for World Trade Ctr., 1965-66; spl. counsel N.Y. State Joint Legis. Com. on Ct. Reorgn.; asst. counsel N.Y. State Joint Legis. Com. on N.Y. Banking Laws; mem. The N.Y. State Mcpl. Assistance Corp., 1996-2000; commr. N.Y. State Commn. of Investigations, N.Y.C., 2000—. Contbr. articles to profl. publs. Trustee CUNY, 1996-98; chmn. govt. and civil svc. divsn. United Jewish Appeal Greater N.Y., 1966; co-chmn. met. N.Y. blood drive ARC, 1966; campaign mgr. John V. Lindsay, Campaigns for Congressman, N.Y.C., 1958, 64, for Nelson A. Rockefeller Oreg. Rep. presdl. primary campaign, 1964, Lindsay campaign for mayor, N.Y.C., 1965; del. N.Y. Rep. State Conv., 1962, 66; del. Rep. Nat. Conv., 1988, 92, 96; lectr. Rep. Nat. Com., 1966; bd. dirs. Am. Friends Hebrew U.; past trustee Columbia U. Sch. Pharm. Scis. With U.S. Army, 1953-55. Recipient Yeshiva U. Heritage award, Pub. Svc. award Queens Catholic War Vets. Mem. ABA, FCC Bar Assn., Assn. Bar City N.Y., N.Y. State Dist. Attys. Assn., Coun. Fgn. Rels., Columbia Law Sch. Alumni Assn. (dir.), Scribes, Tau Kappa Alpha. General corporate, Trademark and copyright. Home: 25 E 86th St New York NY 10028-0553 Office: Price Communications Corp 45 Rockefeller Plz Ste 3200 New York NY 10111-0100 Fax: (212) 344-6868

PRICE, ROBERT DEMILLE, lawyer; b. N.Y.C., Oct. 11, 1915; s. Willard DeMille Price and Eugenia Reeve; m. Newell Potter, Aug. 15, 1940 (div. May 1946); 1 child, Jonathan; m. Ruth Bentley, July 5, 1946; children: Katharine, Susannah, Rebecca. AB in Econs. with honors, Cornell U., 1936; JD, Harvard U., 1940; MBA, Clark U., 1973. Bar: Mass. 1940, U.S. Dist. Ct. Mass. 1941, U.S. Ct. Appeals (1st cir.) 1976, U.S. Tax Ct. 1977, U.S. Supreme Ct. 1978. Assoc. Ropes & Gray, Boston, 1940-43, 1946-50; ptnr. Vaughan, Esty, Crotty & Mason, Worcester, Mass., 1950-53, Sibley, Blair & Mountain, Worcester, 1953-70, Corbin, Sarapas, Madaus & Arakelian, Worcester, 1970-73, Price & Madaus, Worcester, 1973-87; pres. Robert D. Price, PC, Holden, Mass., 1987—. Dir. Appian Way Pizza, Ltd., Worcester, 1951-61, Food Specialties, Inc., Worcester, 1951-61, James Monroe Wire and Cable Co., S. Lancaster, Mass., 1973—; mem. Fin. Com., Holden, 1989-95, conservation com., 1999—. Moderator (TV series) Am. Bar Assn. Jr. Bar Assn., 1947-50. Bd. dirs., treas. Friends Gale Free Librs. Inc., Holden, 1988—; mem. adv. bd. Met. Dist. Commn., 1990-96; pres. Humanist Chaplaincy at Harvard, 1995—; bd. dirs. Humanist Assn. Mass., 1979—, Am. Humanist Assn., 1991-94; trustee AHA Humanist Found., 1999—. Lt. USNR, 1943-51. Mem. Mass. Bar Assn., Worcester County Bar Assn., Worcester Club (dir. 1953-56), Boston Athenaeum (propr. 1949—). Avocations: museum and art show, photography, alpine climbing, sailing. General corporate, Estate planning, Estate taxation. Office: 2 Malden St Holden MA 01520-1827

PRICE, ROBERT STANLEY, lawyer; b. Phila., Jan. 21, 1937; s. Benjamin and Estelle B. (Muchnick) P.; m. Emilie W. Kirschbaum, June 27, 1965 (dec. Mar. 1998); children: Louise P. Kelly, Marianna R. BA, Kenyon Coll., 1958; LLB, Yale U., 1961. Bar: Pa. 1963, U.S. Dist. Ct. (ea. dist.) Pa. 1963, U.S. Ct. Appeals (3d cir.) 1963, N.Y. 1993. Assoc. Dechert, Price & Rhoads, Phila., 1961-63; asst tax atty. Smith, Kline & French, 1963-67; tax atty. Pa. Ctrl. Transp. Co., 1967-70; tax counsel IU Internat., 1970-72; ptnr. Townsend, Elliott & Munson, 1972-76, Pepper, Hamilton & Scheetz, Phila., 1977-86, Saul, Ewing, Remick & Saul, Phila., 1986-93; spl. cons. Saul, Ewing, Remick & Saul (now Saul Ewing LLP), 1994—. Ind. tax cons. Fischbein-Badillo-Wagner-Harding, N.Y.C., 1998—. Author: ABCs of Industrial Development Bonds, 1981, 5th edit., 1990; contbr. articles to legal jours. Served with U.S. Army, 1961-62. Mem. ABA (tax exempt fin. com.), Pa. Bar, Phila. Bar Assn., N.Y. Bar, Racquet Club Phila. (v.p. 1987-88), Alpha Delta Phi (pres. 1975-78). Office: Saul Ewing LLP 3800 Centre Sq W Philadelphia PA 19102 E-mail: rprice@saul.com

PRICE, RUSSELL EUGENE, lawyer; b. Kenton, Ohio, Dec. 18, 1931; s. Russell Cessna and Hilda E. (Kimmel) P.; m. Margaret Gaynell Atkins, Aug. 20, 1955; children: John Russell, Mary Jo, Brenda. BBA, U. Mich., 1953; JD, Wayne State U., 1958. Bar: Mich. 1958, U.S. dist. ct. (ea. dist.) Mich. 1958. Labor relations supr. Chevrolet Gear & Axle div. Gen. Motors Corp., Detroit, 1959-61; labor atty. NLRB, Detroit, 1961-64, Gerber Products Co., Fremont, Mich., 1964-69; assoc. Landman, Latimer, Clink & Robb, Fremont, 1969-71, ptnr., 1971-88; pvt. practice Russell E. Price, P.C., Fremont, 1988— ; city atty. City of White Cloud (Mich.), 1978-89. Trustee Fremont Pub. Schs., 1969-79, bd. attys., 1981-89. Served to 1st lt. U.S. Army, 1953-55. Mem. ABA, Mich. Bar Assn., 27th Jud. Cir. Bar Assn., Newaygo-Oceana County Bar Assn. Republican. Episcopalian. Club: Ramshorn Country. Lodge: Rotary (Fremont pres. 1976). Labor, Probate, Real property. Home: 503 Lewis Ln Fremont MI 49412-1368 Office: 8 E Main St Fremont MI 49412-1244

PRICE, STEPHEN CONWELL, lawyer; b. Hornell, N.Y., July 17, 1949; s. Ralph Conwell and Berta Lee (Davis) P.; children: Margaret Davis, Mary Darden, John Tyler, Diana Allison, Thomas Garrett. BA in History, Va. Mil. Inst., 1971; JD, U. Va., 1974; LLM, U. Cambridge, Eng., 1977. Bar: Va. 1974, U.S. Dist. Ct. (ea. dist.) Va. 1974, U.S. Ct. Appeals (4th cir.) 1976, U.S. Supreme Ct. 1977. Assoc. McCandlish, Lillard, Church & Best, Fairfax, Va., 1974-76; pvt. practice Leesburg, 1977-82; ptnr. Price & Zimmerman, 1982-88; prin. McCandlish & Lillard PC, 1998—. Substitute judge Gen. Dist. Ct., 20th Dist. Va., 1982-91; escheator for Loudoun County, Va., 1983-94. Chmn. Loudoun County Dem. Com., 1981; sec., bd. dirs. Oatlands of the Nat. Trust, Leesburg, 1981—; pres., bd. dirs. Am. Friends Cambridge U., 1983-2000; dedication chmn. George C. Marshall Meml., Leesburg, 1980; chmn. colonial bd. George Washington U., 1996-98; pres. George C. Marshall Internat. Ctr. at Dodona Manor, 2000—. Capt. U.S. Army, 1973. Mem. Va. Bar Assn., Selden Soc., Sons of Confederate Vets., Univ. Club, Unitd Oxford and Cambridge Club, Hawks Club (Cambridge), Colonnade Club (Charlottesville), Kappa Alpha. Democrat. Episcopalian. General civil litigation, Condemnation, Contracts commercial. Home: PO Box 374 Leesburg VA 20178 Office: McCandlish & Lillard PC 305 Harrison St SE Leesburg VA 20175-3729 E-mail: sprice@mccandlaw.com

PRICE, WILLIAM RAY, JR. state supreme court judge; b. Fairfield, Iowa, Jan. 30, 1952; s. William Ray and Evelyn Jean (Darnell) P.; m. Susan Marie Trainor, Jan. 4, 1975; children: Emily Margret, William Joseph Dodds. BA with distinction, U. Iowa, 1974; postgrad., Yale U., 1974-75; JD cum laude, Washington and Lee U., 1978. Bar: Mo. 1978, U.S. Dist. Ct. (we. dist.) Mo. 1978, U.S. Ct. Claims 1978, U.S. Ct. Appeals (8th cir.) 1985. Assoc. Lathrop & Norquist, Kansas City, Mo., 1978-84, ptnr., 1984-92, chmn. bus. litigation sect., 1987-88, 90-92, exec. com., 1989-92; judge Supreme Ct. Mo., Jefferson City, 1992—, chief justice, 1999—. G.L.V. Zumwalt monitoring com. U.S. Dist. Ct. (we. dist.) Mo., Kansas City. Pres. Kansas City Bd. Police Commrs.; mem. Together Ctr. & Family Devel. Ctr., Kansas City; chmn. merit selection com. U.S. marshal Western Dist. of Mo., Kansas City; bd. dirs. Truman Med. Ctr., Kansas City. Rockefeller fellow, 1974-75; Burks scholar Washington & Lee U., 1976. Mem. Christian Ch. Office: Supreme Ct Mo PO Box 150 207 W High St Jefferson City MO 65102-0150*

PRICHARD, VINCENT MARVIN, lawyer; b. Kirksville, Mo., July 16, 1946; s. George William and Mary Elizabeth (Love) P. BS, U. Colo., 1969; JD, U. Denver, 1974. Bar: Colo. 1975, U.S. Dist. Ct. Colo. 1975. Atty. Bur. Hearings and Appeals Social Security Adminstrn., Denver, 1975-79; asst. regional counsel Dept. Energy, Lakewood, Colo., 1979-82; atty. Fed. Legal Info. Through Electronics, Denver, 1982-93; info. tech. profl. U. Colo. Health Scis. Ctr., 1994-99; info. tech. mgr. Colo. Water Conservation Bd., 2000—. With U.S. Army, 1969-71. Mem. Colo. Bar Assn., 1st Jud. Dist. Bar Assn. Home: 30191 Peggy Ln Evergreen CO 80439-7227 Office: Colo Water Conservation Bd 1313 Sherman St Ste 721 Denver CO 80203

PRIEST, ANDREW DAVID, lawyer; b. Hitchin, Eng., Mar. 21, 1965; s. David Barry and Ann Patricia Priest; m. Marlene Zwickler, Sept. 18, 1999. LLB, U. Birmingham, Eng., 1987. Cert. solicitor, Eng., Wales, 1990, Scotland, 1997. Assoc. ptnr. Andersen Legal, Glasgow, 1997—. Computer, Intellectual property, Trademark and copyright. Office: Andersen Legal 191 West George St Glasgow G2 2LB Scotland Office Fax: 0141-304-6155. E-mail: andrew.priest@dundas-wilson.com

PRIEST, GEORGE L. law educator; b. 1947; BA, Yale U., 1969; JD, U. Chgo., 1973. Assoc. prof. U. Puget Sound, Tacoma, 1973-75; law and econ. fellow U. Chgo., 1975-77; prof. U. Buffalo, 1977-80, UCLA, 1980-81, Yale U., New Haven, 1981—. Dir. program in civil liability; John M. Olin prof. law and econs., 1986—. Mem. Pres.' Com. on Privatization, 1987-88. Office: PO Box 208215 New Haven CT 06520-8215

PRIMEAUX, LAWRENCE, lawyer; b. Abbeville, La., Sept. 23, 1949; s. Walter Joseph and Natalie (Ardoin) P.; m. Lisa Meierhoefer, Aug. 14, 1971; children— Aimee Marr, Paul Ledet, Mark David. Student U. S.W. La., 1967-69; B.A., U. Miss., 1971, J.D., 1973. Bar: Miss. 1973, Tenn. 1974, U.S. Dist. Ct. (no. dist.) Miss. 1974, U.S. Dist. Ct. (so. dist.) Miss. 1978. Assoc. E. H. Coles, P.C., Memphis, 1973-75; asst. appeals officer U.S. Civil Service Commn., Atlanta, 1975-78; sr. staff atty. E. Miss. Legal Services, Meridian, 1978-81; ptnr. Goldman, Dreyfus & Primeaux, Meridian, Miss., 1981— ; chmn. State Bd. Trustees of Eleemosynary Instns., Jackson, Miss., 1984-88. Pres. Mental Health Assn. in Lauderdale County, Meridian, 1984. Fellow Miss. Bar Found.; mem. Assn. Trial Lawyers Am., Miss. Bar Assn., Miss. Trial Lawyers Assn., Lauderdale County Young Lawyers (pres. 1984). Lodge: Rotary. Family and matrimonial, General practice, Personal injury. Home: 3640 24th Ave Meridian MS 39305-3833 Office: Goldman,Dreyfus,Primeaux & Doherty,PA PO Box 1625 Meridian MS 39302-1625

PRINCE, DAVID CANNON, lawyer; b. Hawkinsville, Ga., July 4, 1950; s. Carl Willis and Carobel (Cannon) P.; m. Mary MacIntyre, June 30, 1973. BA in Econs., Clemson U., 1972; JD, St. John's U., Jamaica, N.Y., 1980. Bar: N.Y. 1981, Ga. 1982, U.S. Dist. Ct. (no. dist.) Ga. 1982. Atty. enforcement SEC, Atlanta, 1981-86; regional counsel Shearson Lehman Bros. Inc., 1986-92; gen. counsel Robinson-Humphrey Co., Inc., 1992—. Capt. USAF, 1972-78. Mem. ABA (co-chairperson young lawyers div. 1986-88). Democrat. Avocations: sailing, running. Administrative and regulatory, Federal civil litigation, Securities. Home: 1824 Lenox Rd NE Atlanta GA 30306-3031 Office: 3333 Peachtree Rd NE Atlanta GA 30326-1070

PRINCE, KENNETH STEPHEN, lawyer; b. Newton, Mass., Jan. 28, 1950; s. Samuel and Edna L. Prince; m. Patricia Denning, Jan. 15, 1977 (dec. Nov. 1985); 1 child, Kenneth Stephen Jr.; m. Jane M. McCabe, Sept. 5, 1987; 1 child, Allison Pamela. BA, U. Pa., 1972; JD, Boston Coll., 1975. Bar: N.Y. 1976, Mass. 1975, U.S. Dist. Ct. (so. and ea. dists.) N.Y. 1978. Assoc. Shearman & Sterling, N.Y.C., 1975-83, ptnr., 1984—, antitrust group practice leader, 1992—. Mem. N.Y. Law Inst. (exec. com. 1984-96), Order of Coif. Antitrust, Mergers and acquisitions. Home: 15 Dellwood Rd Darien CT 06820-2915 E-mail: kprince@shearman.com

PRINCE, WILLIAM TALIAFERRO, retired federal judge; b. Norfolk, Va., Oct. 3, 1929; s. James Edward and Helen Marie (Taliaferro) P.; m. Anne Carroll Hannegan, Apr. 12, 1958; children: Sarah Carroll Prince Pishko, Emily Taliaferro, William Taliaferro, John Hannegan, Anne Martineau Thompson, Robert Harrison. Student, Coll. William and Mary, Norfolk, 1947-48, 49-50; AB, Williamsburg, 1955, BCL, 1957, MLT, 1959. Bar: Va. 1957. Lectr. acctg. Coll. William and Mary, 1955-57; lectr. law Marshall-Wythe Sch. Law, 1957-59; assoc. Williams, Kelly & Greer, Norfolk, 1959-63, ptnr., 1963-90; U.S. magistrate judge Eastern Dist. of Va., 1990-2000; ret., 2000. Pres. Am. Inn of Ct. XXVII, 1987-89. Bd. editors: The Virginia Lawyer, A Basic Practice Handbook, 1966. Bd. dirs. Madonna Home, Inc., 1978-93, Soc. Alumni of Coll. William and Mary, 1985-88. Fellow Am. Coll. Trial Lawyers, Am. Bar Found., Va. Law found. (bd. dirs. 1976-90); mem. ABA (ho. of dels. 1984-90), Am. Judicature Soc. (bd. dirs. 1984-88), Va. State Bar (coun. 1973-77, exec. com. 1975-80, pres. 1978-79). Roman Catholic. Home: 1227 Graydon Ave Norfolk VA 23507-1006 Office: Walter E Hoffman US Courthouse 600 Granby St Ste 341 Norfolk VA 23510-1915

PRINSLOO, JOJANNES CHRISTIAAN, lawyer; b. Pitchefstroom, South Africa, Mar. 19, 1971; s. Johannes Christiaan and Judith Uys P.; m. Mirinda Grobler, Oct. 23, 1999. LLB, Rand Afrikaanse U., Johannesburg, South Africa, 1997. Legal advisor Pearless Security, Johannesburg, South Africa, 1997; atty. De Vries Attys., Inc., South Africa, 1997—. Mem. Law Soc. Transvaal. General civil litigation, Insurance, Personal injury. Office: De Bries Attys Inc Commissioner St Johannesburg 2000 South Africa Fax: 0911 331 7035. E-mail: cprinsloo@devries.co.za

PRINZ, KRISTIE DAWN, lawyer; b. Columbus, Ga., July 26, 1973; d. Stephen Charles and Helen Ann (Dunlap) P. BA in Spanish and Polit. Sci. summa cum laude, Furman U., 1995; JD, Vanderbilt U., 1998. Bar: Ga. 1998. Summer assoc. Rose Immigration Law Firm, Nashville, 1996; rsch. asst. Vanderbilt U., 1996-97; summer assoc. Bruce, Weathers, Corley, Dughman & Lyle, 1997; assoc. Mozley, Finlayson & Loggins, LLP, Atlanta, 1998, Schnader Harrison Segal & Lewis LLP, Atlanta, 1999-2000, Pennie & Edmonds LLP, Palo Alto, Calif., 2000—. Mem. adv. bd. Knoxville Jour., 1990-91. Vol. tchr. English Classes for Refugees, Knoxville, Tenn, 1993; mem. Collegiate Ednl. Svc. Corps. Furman U., Greenville, S.C., 1991-95; mem. Therrell High Sch. com. Atlanta Coun. Younger Lawyers, 1999. Mem. ABA, Atlanta Bar Assn. (mem. programs and spl. events, cmty. outreach coms. police 1999), Sr. Order Furman U., Phi Sigma Alpha, Sigma Delta Pi (Hispanic hon.), Phi Sigma Iota (fgn. lang. hon.), Kappa Alpha Theta (Elizabeth Staley Leadership award 1995), Phi Beta Kappa. Avocations: running, watching Spanish language movies and programs. Contracts commercial, General corporate, Intellectual property. Office: 3300 Hillview Ave Palo Alto CA 94304

PRITCHARD, LLEWELYN G. lawyer; b. N.Y.C., Aug. 13, 1937; s. Llewelyn and Anne Mary (Streib) P.; m. Joan Ashby, June 20, 1959; children: David Ashby, Jennifer Pritchard Vick, Andrew Harrison, William Llewellyn. AB with honors, Drew U., 1958; LLB, Duke U., 1961. Ptnr. Helsell & Fetterman, Seattle. Trustee, corp. counsel Allied Arts Found.; pres. Allied Arts Seattle, 1974-76; trustee Meth. Ednl. Found., 1970-85, pres., 1991-92; life trustee Patrons of Pacific N.W. Civil, Cultural and Charitable Orgns., 1969—, pres., 1972-73; bd. dirs. Planned Parenthood of Seattle/King County, 1972-78; trustee Seattle Symphony Orch., 1979-83, chmn. bd., 1980-82, hon. trustee; trustee U. Puget Sound., 1972-99, mem. exec. com., chmn. bd. visitors to Law Sch., 1984-88; trustee Mus. of Glass, 2000—; chancellor Pacific N.W. Ann. conf. United Meth. Ch., 1969—. Fellow Am. Bar Found. (life, state chmn. 1988-98); mem. ABA (bd. govs. 1986-89, chmn. program com. 1988-89, exec. com. 1988-89, Ho. of Dels. 1979—, nat. dir. young lawyers divsn. 1971, chmn. sect. of individual rights and responsibilities 1975-76, exec. coun. family law sect. 1992-98, chair standing com. on legal aid and indigent defendants 1973-75, chair legal needs study 1995-98, chair adv. com. to pro bono immigration project 1995—), Wash. State Bar Assn. (bd. govs. King County 1972-75), King County Bar Assn. (chair young lawyers sect. 1970). Avocations: reading, art collector. Family and matrimonial, General practice. Home: 5229 140th Ave NE Bellevue WA 98005-1024 Office: Helsell & Fetterman 1500 Puget Sound Plz Seattle WA 98101 E-mail: lpritchard@helsell.com

PRITCHARD, WILLIAM WINTHER, lawyer, drilling company executive; b. Bartlesville, Okla., Mar. 20, 1951; s. James Edward and Agnes Kathryn (Winther) P.; m. Susan Jane Parsons, Aug. 12, 1972; children—Jane, Kathryn, Robert. BA with honors, U. Kans., 1973; JD, U. Tulsa, 1976. Bar: Okla. 1976. With Parker Drilling Co., Tulsa, 1976—, v.p., gen. counsel, 1984—. Mem. ABA, Okla. Bar Assn., So. Hills Country Club (Tulsa). Republican. Presbyterian. General corporate, Oil, gas, and mineral, Labor. Office: Parker Drilling Co 8 E 3rd St Tulsa OK 74103-3637

PRITIKIN, JAMES B. lawyer, employee benefits consultant; b. Chgo., Feb. 18, 1939; s. Stan and Anne (Schwartz) P.; m. Barbara Cheryl Demovsky, Apr. 20, 1968 (dec. 1988); children: Gregory, David, Randi; m. Mary Szatkowski, July 7, 1990; 1 child, Peyton. BS, U. Ill., 1961; JD, DePaul U., 1965. Bar: Ill. 1965, U.S. Dist. Ct. (no. dist.) Ill. 1965, U.S. Supreme Ct. 1985; cert. matrimonial arbitrator. Pvt. practice, Chgo., 1965-68, 1984—; ptnr. Sudak, Grubman, Pritikin, Rosenthal & Feldman, 1969-80, Pritikin & Sohn, Chgo., 1980-84, Nadler, Pritikin & Mirabelli, Chgo., 1997—. Pres. Prepaid Benefits Plans Inc., Chgo., 1978—; exec. dir. The Ctr. for Divorce Mediation Ltd. Fellow Internat. Acad. Matrimonial Lawyers, Am. Acad. Matrimonial Lawyers (pres.-elect); mem. ABA, Am. Acad. Matrimonial Lawyers (pres. Ill. chpt.), Ill. Bar Assn., Chgo. Bar Assn. (cir. ct. Cook County liaison com.), Chgo. Pub. Schs. Alumni Assn. (v.p. 1984—). Family and matrimonial. Office: 1 Prudential Plz 130 E Randolph Dr Chicago IL 60601-6207

PRITSKER, KEITH WAYNE, lawyer; b. L.A., June 4, 1952; s. Bentley Donald and Virginia June (Graff) P.; m. Ellen Isabel Hacker, Aug. 26, 1990; children: Laura, Lindsay, Kelsey. BA, U. Calif., Santa Barbara, 1974; MA in Econs., U. So. Calif., 1978; JD, Southwestern U., 1977. Bar: Calif. 1979, U.S. Dist. Ct. (cen. dist.) Ill. 1979. Dep. city atty. City Atty.'s Office, L.A., 1979-2000. Columnist Santa Clarita Sun, 1998—. Pres. The Arts Cmty. Assn., Stevenson Ranch, Calif., 1992-98; v.p. Stevenson Ranch Town Coun, 1994, pres., 1998—. Recipient Outstanding Citizen award Stevenson Ranch Town Coun., 1994, A-V Rating, Martindale-Hubbell, 1996. Mem. Calif. Bar Assn., Los Angeles County Bar Assn. (chmn. environ. law 1989-90). Avocations: philosophy, hiking. Office: Office of City Atty 200 N Main St Ste 1800 Los Angeles CA 90012-4131

PRIVETT, CARYL PENNEY, lawyer; b. Birmingham, Ala., Jan. 7, 1948; d. William Kinnaird Privett and Katherine Speake (Binford) Ennis. BA, Vanderbilt U., 1970; JD, NYU, 1973. Bar: Ala. 1973, U.S. Dist. Ct. (so. dist.) Ala. 1973, U.S. Dist. Ct. (no. dist.) Ala. 1974, U.S. Ct. Appeals (5th cir.) 1974, U.S. Ct. Appeals (11th cir.) 1981. Assoc. Crawford & Blacksher, Mobile, Ala., 1973-74, Adams, Baker & Clemon, Birmingham, 1974-76;

asst. U.S. atty. no. dist. Ala. U.S. Atty.'s Office, U.S. Dept. Justice, 1976-92, 93-94, first asst. U.S. atty., 1992-93, U.S. atty., 1995-97, chief asst., 1997-98; pvt. practice Ala., 1998—; city prosecutor City of Mountain Brook, 1998—. Adj. prof. Cumberland Sch. Law, Samford U., 1998—. Bd. dirs. Legal Aid Soc., Birmingham, 1986-88, pres., 1988; sec., founder Lawyers for Choice, Ala., 1989-92; bd. dirs. Planned Parenthood Ala., Birmingham, 1998—, v.p.1; chair domestic violence com. City of Birmingham, 1989-91; suaining mem. Jr. League Birmingham; active Downtown Dem. Club, Birmingham, Photography Guild, Birmingham Mus. Art. Recipient Cert. in Color Photography U. Ala., Birmingham, 1989, Commr.'s Spl. citation Food and Drug Adminstrn.; named one of Outstanding Young Women Am., 1977, 78. Mem. ABA, Fed. Bar Assn. (pres. Birmingham chpt. 1979), Birmingham Bar Assn. (mem. exec. com. 1996-98), Ala. Bar Assn. (chmn. com. women in the profession 1997-99, chair women's sect. 1999-2001), Birmingham Bar Found. (pres. 2001), Ala. Acad. Atty. Mediators (v.p. 2001), Ala. Dispute Resolution Found., Administrative Dir., Ala. Law Inst., Women's Fund, Women's Network, Summit Club, Altamont Alumni Assn., Leadership Birmingham, Ala. Solution. Presbyterian. Avocation: photography. Home: 30 Norman Dr Birmingham AL 35213-4310 Office: 300 Union Hill Ste 220 Birmingham AL 35209 E-mail: carylprivett@mindspring.com

PRO, PHILIP MARTIN, judge; b. Richmond, Calif., Dec. 12, 1946; s. Leo Martin and Mildred Louise (Beck) P.; m. Dori Sue Hallas, Nov. 13, 1982; 1 child, Brenda Kay. BA, San Francisco State U., 1968; JD, Golden Gate U., 1972. Bar: Calif. 1972, Nev. 1973, U.S. Ct. Appeals (9th cir.) 1973, U.S. Dist. Ct. Nev. 1973, U.S. Supreme Ct. 1976. Pub. defender, Las Vegas, 1973-75; asst. U.S. atty. Dist. Nev., 1975-78; dep. atty. gen. State of Nev., Carson City, 1979-80; U.S. magistrate U.S. Dist. Ct. Nev., Las Vegas, 1980-87, U.S. dist. judge, 1987—. Instr. Atty. Gen.'s Advocacy Inst., Nat. Inst. Trial Advocacy, 1992; chmn. com. adminstrn. of magistrate judge system Jud. Conf. U.S., 1993—. Bd. dirs. NCCJ, Las Vegas, 1982—, mem. program com. and issues in justice com. Mem. ABA, Fed. Judges Assn. (bd. dirs. 1992—, v.p. 1997-2001), Nev. State Bar Assn., Calif. State Bar Assn., Nev. Judges Assn. (instr.), Assn. Trial Lawyers Am., Nev. Am. Inn Ct. (pres. 1989-91), Ninth Cir. Jury (instructions com.), Nat. Conf. U.S. Magistrates (sec.). Republican. Episcopalian. Office: US Dist Ct 7015 Fed Bldg 300 Las Vegas Blvd S Ste 4650 Las Vegas NV 89101-5883

PROBSTEIN, JON MICHAEL, lawyer; b. N.Y.C., June 24, 1953; s. Albert and Lila (Levin) P. BA in Psychology, Syracuse U., 1973; JD, St. John's U., 1976. Bar: N.Y. 1977, U.S. Dist. Ct. (so. dist. and ea. dists.) N.Y. 1982, U.S. Ct. Appeals (2d cir.) 1983. Assoc. Marchi, Jaffe, Cohen, Crystal & Mintz, N.Y.C., 1977-78, Berman & Zivyak, N.Y.C., 1979-80, Graubard, Moskovitz McGoldrick Dannett & Horowitz, N.Y.C., 1981-82; ptnr. Probstein & Napolitano, N.Y.C., 1982-88, Probstein & Weiner, 1988—; instr. legal rsch. and writing Benjamin Cardozo Sch. Law Yeshiva U., N.Y.C., 1976-77. Playwright Radio Roast, 1987; music mgr. That's Mgmt., N.Y.C., 1987—; producer, dir. actor Avner Prodns., N.Y.C., 1985—; editor St. John's Law Rev. Mem. ABA, Assn. Trial Lawyers Am., Assn. of Bar of City of N.Y., N.Y. State Bar Assn. State civil litigation, General corporate, Entertainment. Address: Ste 1100 488 Madison Ave New York NY 10022

PROBUS, MICHAEL MAURICE, JR. lawyer; b. Louisville, Jan. 26, 1963; s. Michael Maurice and Jerilyn Ann (Burks) P.; m. Luz Marie Probus, May 22, 1985; children: Michael Julian, Lauren Michael. BA, U. Dallas, 1985; JD, U. Tex., 1988. Bar: Tex. 1988, U.S. Dist. Ct. (we. dist.) Tex. 1990, U.S. Ct. Appeals (5th cir.) 1993. Jud. law clk. to chief judge U.S. Dist. Ct. Tex., Houston, 1988-90; assoc. Law Offices of Michael A. Wash, Austin, Tex., 1990-97; pvt. practice, 1997—. Pro bono atty. Vol. Legal Svcs., Austin, 1994—. Mem. Travis County Bar Assn. (mem. CLE com. 1993—). Democrat. Roman Catholic. Personal injury, Product liability, Professional liability. Office: Law Office M Probus 100 Congress Ave Ste 1550 Austin TX 78701 E-mail: mprobusjr@msn.com

PROCHNOW, HERBERT VICTOR, JR. lawyer; b. Evanston, Ill., May 26, 1931; s. Herbert V. and Laura (Stinson) P.; m. Lucia Boyden, Aug. 6, 1966; children: Thomas Herbert, Laura. A.B., Harvard U., 1953, J.D., 1956; A.M., U. Chgo., 1958. Bar: Ill. 1957, U.S. Dist. Ct. (no. dist.) Ill. 1961. With 1st Nat. Bank Chgo., 1958-91, atty., 1961-70, sr. atty., 1971-73, counsel, 1973-91, adminstrv. asst. to chmn. bd., 1978-81; pvt. practice, 1991—. Author: (with Herbert V. Prochnow) A Treasury of Humorous Quotations, 1969, The Changing World of Banking, 1974, The Public Speaker's Treasure Chest, 1986, The Toastmaster's Treasure Chest, 1988; also articles in legal publs. Mem.: ABA, Ill. Bar Assn., Chgo. Bar Assn. (chmn. com. internat. law 1970—71), Am. Soc. Internat. Law, Harvard Club (N.Y.C.), Lawyers Club (Chgo.), Chgo. Club, Univ. Club (Chgo.), Onwentsia, Econ. Club, Phi Beta Kappa. Banking, Private international. Home: 949 Woodbine Pl Lake Forest IL 60045-2275 Office: 155 N Michigan Ave Chicago IL 60601-7511

PROCOPIO, JOSEPH GUYDON, lawyer; b. Paterson, N.J., May 1, 1940; s. Joseph A. and V. Genevieve (Kievitt) P.; m. Joanne Julia Roccato, June 30, 1962 (div. Aug. 1980); children: Jennifer Tehani Tyler, Joseph Christian; m. Frances Mary Hansen Schmieder, Apr. 16, 1988 (div. Oct. 1998); stepchildren: Timothy James Schmieder, Julie Ann Schmieder. BS, U.S. Naval Acad., 1962; MS in Ops. Rsch., Naval Postgrad. Sch., 1971; JD, Cath. U. Am., 1979; LLM, George Washington U., 1987. Bar: Va. Commd. ensign USN, 1962, served to comdr., 1978, ret., 1983; gen. counsel, sec. Presearch, Inc., Fairfax, Va., 1983-85; dir. bus. devel., then v.p. corp. communications ERC Internat., 1985-90; pres., CEO Advanced Engring. Group, Inc., 1990-92; chmn., CEO JP Fin. Group Ltd., 1992—; exec. USPS. Prin. The Poretz Group, 1996-98, Viking Profl. Seminars; bd. dirs. Solomon Group; prin. The Millenium Group, Ltd. (formerly Ashley-Boden-Keenan, Inc.); v.p. Valuation Techs., LLC, 1999-01; corp. comm. cons., 1999-01; substitute tchr. Douglas County. Chmn. Pub. Works & Utilities Commn., Castle Rock, Colo.; v.p., judge advocate Navy League U.S., Denver Coun.; election judge Douglas Co., vestry Christ's Ch., Castle Rock. Decorated Bronze Star, Meritorious Svc. medal, 3 Joint Svc. Commendation medal, Nat. Def. medal (Cambodia), Navy Achievement medal, Combat Action ribbon. Mem. Internat. Inst. Strategic Studies, Va. Bar Assn., The Atlantic Coun., George Washington U. Law Alumni Assn., U.S. Naval Acad. Alumni Assn., U.S. Naval Acad. Class of 1962 Assn. (bd. dirs. 1978-80, 87—, spl. asst. to pres. 1984-87), U.S. Naval Acad. Alumni Colo. (bd. dirs.), Nat. Eagle Scout Assn. Avocations: reading, history (legal, military, naval, economic), golf. General corporate, Finance, Private international. Home: 237 Cherry St Castle Rock CO 80104-3206 E-mail: JoePro@aol.com

PROCTOR, DAVID RAY, lawyer; b. Nashville, Apr. 18, 1956; s. Raymond Douglas and Margaret Florence (Coffey) P.; m. Robbin Lynn Fuqua, May 12, 1984 (div.); children: Rachael Lynne, Benjamin David. AA in Polit. Sci., Cumberland Jr. Coll., 1976; BA in Polit. Sci., Vanderbilt U., 1978; JD, Cumberland Sch. Law, 1981; LLM in Taxation, U. Fla., 1983. Bar: Ala. 1981, Tenn. 1983, U.S. Tax Ct. 1983. Law clk. to presiding justice Ala. Supreme Ct., Montgomery, 1981-82; assoc. Thrailkill & Goodman, Nashville, 1983-84; v.p. taxes Alfa Mut. Ins. Co., Montgomery, 1984—. Contbg. editor Cumberland Law Rev., 1980-81; contbr. articles to profl. jours. Tchr. Rsch. Bd., Birmingham, Ala., 1980; active Montgomery Area United Way, 1985—; mem. stewardship com. Montgomery Bapt. Assn., 1995-96; treas. Taylor Rd. Bapt. Ch., 1994-95, asst. treas., 1996, treas., 1997-98; mem. adv. bd. Montgomery Therapeutic Recreation Ctr., 2000—, v.p. 2001. Mem. ABA, Nat. Assn. Ind. Insurers (exec. tax com. 2000—), Nat. Assn. Mut. Ins. Cos. (tax com. 1988—, chmn. 1997-99, exec. tax com. 2000—), Ala. Bar Assn., Tenn. Bar Assn., Sunrise Exch. Club Montgomery (treas. 1989-91), Phi Alpha Delta, Pi Sigma Alpha. Baptist. Avocations: running, music, sports, charities. Corporate taxation, Personal income taxation, State and local taxation. Home: 317 Arrowhead Dr Montgomery AL 36117-4142 Office: Alfa Mut Ins Co 2108 E South Blvd Montgomery AL 36116-2015

PROCTOR, GEORGE EDWIN, JR. lawyer; b. Oklahoma City, Jan. 11, 1951; s. George Edwin and Naomi Francis (Boyington) P.; m. Nancy Dumoff, Jan. 6, 1978. BA, Okla. State U., 1973; JD, Oklahoma City U., 1976; LLM, U. Mo.-Kansas City, 1981. Bar: Okla. 1977, Mo. 1978, U.S. Dist. Ct. (we. dist.) Okla. 1977, U.S. Ct. Appeals (10th cir.) 1977, U.S. Dist. Ct. (we. dist.) Mo. 1978, U.S. Supreme Ct. 1981. Legis. asst. Okla. Senate, Oklahoma City, 1975; research atty. and analyst Midwest Research Inst., Kansas City, Mo., 1976-77; assoc. Paxton, Farrington & Block, Independence, Mo., 1977-78; asst. pros. atty. Jackson County Prosecutor's Office, Kansas City, 1978-81; assoc. Polsinelli, White & Vardeman, Kansas City, 1981-85, Heavner, Jarrett & Kimball, P.C., 1985—. Bd. dirs. Com. for County Progress, 1979—, Citizens Assn., Kansas City, 1983—. Mem. Okla. Bar Assn., Mo. Bar Assn., Assn. Trial Lawyers Am. Democrat. Methodist. Federal civil litigation, State civil litigation, Environmental. Office: Heavner Jarrett & Kimball PC 900 Bryant Bldg 1102 Grand Blvd Ste 1100 Kansas City MO 64106-2313 Address: 618 Westwoods Dr Liberty MO 64068-1184

PROCTOR, KENNETH DONALD, lawyer; b. Balt., Apr. 28, 1944; s. Kenneth Chauncey and Sarah Elizabeth (Kent) P.; m. Judith Danner Harris, Aug. 2, 1969; children: Kenneth Scott, Kent Harris, Janet Cameron BS, Lehigh U., 1966; JD, U. Md., 1969. Bar: Md. 1969, U.S. Dist. Ct. Md. 1970, U.S. Supreme Ct. 1974, U.S. Ct. Appeals (4th cir.) 1980. Law clk. to judge Md. Ct. Appeals, 1969-70; assoc. Miles & Stockbridge, Balt., 1970-73, 74-76, ptnr., 1976-81, Towson, 1981-96; asst. atty. gen. State of Md., Balt., 1973-74. Trustee Gilman Sch., Balt., 1982-85. Mem. ABA, Md. Bar Assn., Baltimore County Bar Assn. Democrat. Episcopalian. General civil litigation, State and local taxation. Office: K Donald Proctor PA 102 W Pennsylvania Ave Ste 505 Towson MD 21204-4542 E-mail: kdproctor@proctorlaw.com

PROFUSEK, ROBERT ALAN, lawyer; b. Cleve., Jan. 14, 1950; s. George John and Geraldine (Hobl) P.; m. Linda Gail Schmidt, May 7, 1972; children: Robert Charles, Kathryn Anne. B.A., Cornell U., 1972; J.D., NYU, 1975. Bar: Ohio 1975, Tex. 1981, N.Y. 1994. Assoc. Jones, Day, Reavis & Pogue, Cleve., 1975-81, Dallas, 1981-82, ptnr., 1982—, N.Y., 1993. bd. dir. Maybelline, Inc. Contbr. articles to profl. jours. Mem. ABA, N.Y. Bar Assn., Assn. Bar City of N.Y., Tex. Bar Assn., Greenwich Country Club. Republican. Episcopalian. General corporate, Securities. Home: 541 North St Greenwich CT 06830-3424 Office: Jones Day Reavis & Pogue 32nd Flr 599 Lexington Ave Fl 32 New York NY 10022-6070

PROM, STEPHEN GEORGE, lawyer; b. Jacksonville, Fla., July 8, 1954; s. George W. and Bonnie M. (Porter) P.; divorced; children: Ashley Brooke, Aaron Jacob, Adam Glenn; m. Charlotte Rutter. AA in Polit. Sci. with high honors, Fla. Jr. Coll., 1974; BA in Polit. Sci. with high honors, U. Fla., 1977, JD with honors, 1979. Bar: Fla. 1980, U.S. Dist. Ct. (mid. dist.) Fla. 1980, U.S. Dist. Ct. (no. dist.) Fla. 1981, U.S. Tax Ct. 1982, U.S. Ct. Appeals (11th cir.) 1985, U.S. Supreme Ct. 1985. Assoc. Rogers, Towers, Bailey, Jones & Gay, Jacksonville, 1979-83, Foley & Lardner, Jacksonville, 1983-86; ptnr. Christian & Prom, 1986-87, Prom, Korn & Zehmer, P.A., Jacksonville, 1987-95, Brant, Moore, MacDonald & Wells, P.A., 1995-2001, Akerman, Senterfitt & Eldson, P.A., 2001—. Sr. mgmt. editor U. Fla. Law Rev., 1978-79. Mem. Leadership Jacksonville, 1984, Jacksonville Cmty. Coun. Inc., 1985-86; bd. dirs. Mental Health Resource Ctr., Jacksonville, 1984-87, Mental Health Resource Foun., Jacksonville, 1985-87, Mental Health Found., Inc., 1987-89, mem. cmty. bd., 1989-91; bd. dirs. Youth Crisis Ctr., Jacksonville, 1984-86, Young Profls. Bd. Multiple Sclerosis Soc., 1988-89; bd. dirs. The Team, Inc., 1992-94; vol. Jacksonville, Inc., 1993-96, Jacksonville Found., Inc., 1993-96, Positively Jacksonville!, Inc., 1993-95. Mem. ABA (tax, health law sects.), Fla. Bar Assn. (tax, health law bd., bd. govs. young lawyers sect. 1983-87), Jacksonville Bar Assn. (chmn. health law sect.), Am. Acad. Healthcare Attys., Am. Hosp. Assn., Nat. Health Lawyers Assn., Fla. Acad. Healthcare Attys. (bd. dirs. 1994-97), Jacksonville Sailing Found., Inc. (bd. dirs. 1997—), N.E. Fla. Sailboat Rating Assn., Inc. (bd. dirs. 1997-98, chair 1998), Epping Forest Yacht Club (bd. govs., rear commodore sail), Ponte Vedra Club, North Fla. Cruising Club, Phi Beta Kappa, Phi Theta Kappa, Phi Kappa Phi. Republican. Baptist. Avocations: sailing, surfing, weightlifting, tennis, jogging. Contracts commercial, Health. Office: Akerman Senterfitt & Eldson PA 50 N Laura St Jacksonville FL 32202 E-mail: sprom@akerman.com

PROMISLO, DANIEL, lawyer; b. Bryn Mawr, Pa., Nov. 15, 1932; s. Charles and Pearl (Backman) P.; m. Estelle Carasso, June 10, 1961; children: Mark, Jacqueline, Steven. BSBA, Drexel U., 1955; JD magna cum laude, U. Pa., 1966. Bar: Pa. 1966. Pres., owner Hist. Souvenir Co., Phila., 1957—; assoc. Wolf, Block, Schorr & Solis-Cohen, 1966-70, ptnr., 1977-94, exec. com., 1987-89, of counsel, 1994—, mng. dir., 1997-2001; founder, pres. dir. Inst. for Paralegal Tng., 1970-75, cons., 1975-77. Editor: Corporate Law, 1970, Real Estate Law, 1971, Estates and Trusts, 1971, Civil Litigation, 1972, Employee Benefit Plans, 1973, Criminal Law, 1974; contbr. articles to profl. jours. Bd. dirs. Phila. Drama Guild, 1977-95, chmn., 1982-86; bd. dirs. Phila. Israel Econ. Devel. Program, 1983-88, Inst. for Arts in Edn., 1990-93, WHYY, Inc., 1994—, vice-chmn., 1995-96, chmn., 1996-97; bd. dirs. U.S. Physicians, Inc., 1995-98; trustee Resource Asset Investment Trust (now RAIT), 1997—. Mem. Order of Coif, Drexel U. 100, Blue Key, Phi Kappa Phi. Democrat. Jewish. Avocations: movies, basketball, tennis. General corporate, Mergers and acquisitions, Securities. Office: Wolf Block Schorr & Solis-Cohen 1650 Arch St Fl 22 Philadelphia PA 19103-2097 E-mail: dpromislo@wolfblock.com

PRO-RISQUEZ, JUAN C. lawyer; b. Madrid, Feb. 25, 1967; arrived in Venezuela, 1970; s. Francisco Pro and Marisol Risquez; 1 child, Alvard. Law degree magna cum laude, U. Ctrl. Venezuela, Caracas, 1990; MLS, So. Meth. U., 1994. Assoc. Baker & M. Kenzie, Caracas, 1990-98; ptnr. Steel Hector & Davies, 1998-99; ptrn. Macleod-Dixon, 1999—. Prof. U. Ctrl. Venezuela, 1995—. Author: Comments on the Organic Labor Law, 1997. Recipient Excellence award Fundayacucaw, 1990. Mem. Bar Assn. Caracas. Avocations: reading. Oil, gas, and mineral, Labor, Transportation. Office: Macleod Dixon Piso 5 Calle Orinoco Torre Uno Las Mercenes Venezuela Fax: 58-2-9932611. E-mail: proj@macleoddixon.com.ve

PROSPERI, LOUIS ANTHONY, lawyer; b. Altoona, Pa., Jan. 12, 1954; s. Louis Alfred and Ann Francis (DiDimenico) P.; m. Susan Lynn Irwin, Sept. 14, 1985. BS in Bus. Adminstrn. summa cum laude, Georgetown U., 1975; JD cum laude, Harvard U., 1978. Bar: Pa. 1978, U.S. Dist. Ct. (we. dist.) Pa. 1978, U.S. Ct. Appeals (Fed. cir.) 1985, U.S. Ct. Fed. Claims, 1985, U.S. Tax Ct. 1979. From assoc. to ptnr. Reed, Smith, Shaw & McClay, Pitts., 1978-94; pvt. practice Law Office Louis A. Prosperi, 1994—. Mem. Allegheny County Bar Assn., Pitts. Tax Club. Republican. Roman Catholic. Club: Longue Vue (Verona, Pa.). Avocations: golf, tennis, paddle tennis, cross-country skiing. Corporate taxation, Personal income taxation, State and local taxation. Home: 3036 Grassmere Ave Pittsburgh PA 15216-1862 Office: Law Office of Louis A Prosperi Grant Bldg 310 Grant St Ste 3601 Pittsburgh PA 15219-2305 E-mail: laprosperi@acba.org

PROSSER, DAVID THOMAS, JR. state supreme court justice, former state representative; b. Chgo., Dec. 24, 1942; s. David Thomas Sr. and Elizabeth Averell (Patterson) P. BA, DePauw U., 1965; JD, U. Wis., 1968. Bar: Wis. 1968. Lectr. Ind. U., Indpls., 1968-69; advisor U.S. Dept. Justice, Washington, 1969-72; adminstrv. asst. to U.S. Rep. Harold V. Froehlich, 1973-74; pvt. practice, 1975, Appleton, Wis., 1976; dist. atty. Outagamie County, 1977-78; state rep. State of Wis., Madison, 1979-96; commr. Tax Appeals Commn., 1997-98; justice Supreme Ct. Wis., 1998—. Commr. Nat. Conf. Commrs. on Uniform State Laws, 1982-96; mem. Wis. Sesquecentennial Commn., Madison, 1993-99; minority leader Wis. Assembly, 1989-94, speaker, 1995-96.. Mem. Wis. Bar Assn., Dane Bar Assn., Milw. Bar Assn., Outagamie Bar Assn. Presbyterian. Avocation: art collector of American prints. Home: 2904 N Meade St Appleton WI 54911-1561 Office: Supreme Ct Wis PO Box 1688 Madison WI 53701-1688 E-mail: david.prosser@courts.state.wi.us

PROVINE, JOHN C. retired lawyer; b. Asheville, N.C., May 15, 1938; s. Robert Calhoun and Harriet Josephine (Thoms) P.; m. Martha Ann Monson, Aug. 26, 1966 (div. Jan. 1975); m. Nancy Frances Lunsford, Apr. 17, 1976 (div. Mar. 1996); children: Robert, Frances, Harriet. AB, Harvard U., 1960; JD, U. Mich., 1966; MBA, NYU, 1972, LLM in Taxation, 1975. Bar: N.Y., Tenn., U.S. Dist. Ct. (so. and ea. dists.) N.Y., U.S. Ct. Appeals (2nd and 6th cirs.), U.S. Dist. Ct. (mid. dist.) Tenn., U.S. Supreme Ct. From assoc. to ptnr. White & Case, N.Y.C., 1966-74, ptnr., 1974-81, 92-94, Jakarta and Ankara, 1982-91; counsel Dearborn & Ewing, Nashville, 1982-94; ret., 1994. Lt. USN, 1960-63. Mem. ABA, N.Y. Bar Assn., Tenn. Bar Assn., Assn. of Bar of City of N.Y. Avocations: bluegrass music, rural activities. Contracts commercial, General corporate, Private international. Home and Office: 6630 Manley Ln Brentwood TN 37027-3401 E-mail: jprovine@compuserve.com

PROVORNY, FREDERICK ALAN, lawyer, educator; b. Bklyn., Sept. 7, 1946; s. Daniel and Anna (Wurm) P.; m. Nancy Ileene Wilkins, Nov. 21, 1971; children: Michelle C., Cheryl A., Lisa T., Robert D. BS summa cum laude, NYU, 1966; JD magna cum laude, Columbia U., 1969. Bar: N.Y. 1970, U.S. Supreme Ct. 1973, D.C. 1975, Mo. 1977, Md. 1987, Calif. 1989; CPA, Md., Mo. Law clk. to Judge Harold R. Medina U.S. Ct. Appeals (2d cir.), N.Y.C., 1969-70; asst. prof. law Syracuse (N.Y.) U., 1970-72; assoc. Debevoise, Plimpton, Lyons & Gates, N.Y.C., 1972-75, Cole & Groner P.C., Washington, 1975-76; with Monsanto Co., St. Louis, 1976-86, asst. co. counsel, 1978-86; pvt. practice Washington, 1986-89; ptnr. Provorny & Jacoby, 1989-91; counsel Shaw, Pittman, Potts & Trowbridge, 1991-93; ptnr. Tydings & Rosenberg, Balt., 1993-94; pvt. practice, 1994-95, Washington, 1995-98; Harold R. Tyler prof. of law and tech., dir. Sci. and Tech. Law Ctr., Albany (N.Y.) Law Sch., 1998—. Lect. Bklyn Law Sch., 1973-74; adj. prof. U. Balt. Sch. of Law, 1996-98; pres. Sci. and Tech. Assocs., Inc., 1986-91. Contbr. articles to profl. jours. Trustee Christian Woman's Benevolent Assn. Youth Home, 1979-83. Mem. ABA, Am. Law Inst., Am. Arbitration Assn. (panel comml. abitrators), Philo-Mt. Sinai Lodge 968, Masons, Beta Gamma Sigma. Jewish. Administrative and regulatory, General corporate, Environmental. Home: 11803 Kemp Mill Rd Silver Spring MD 20902-1511 Office: Albany Law School 80 New Scotland Ave Albany NY 12208-3494

PRUDEN, JAMES NORFLEET, III, lawyer; b. Edenton, N.C., Sept. 1, 1948; s. James Norfleet II and Helen (Goodwin) P.; m. Cynthia Haines Gridley, Aug. 7, 1971; children: Matthew Gridley, Haines Goodwin. AB, U. N.C., 1970; JD, U. Va., 1973. Assoc. Kennedy Covington Lobdell & Hickman, Charlotte, N.C., 1973-78, ptnr., 1979—. Author manuscripts for continuing legal edn. programs, 1979—. Mem. county selection com. John Motley Morehead Found., Chapel Hill, N.C., 1990-92; vestryman Christ Episcopal Ch. Recipient John Motley Morehead award, 1966-70. Mem. ABA, N.C. Bar Assn. (chmn. bus. law sect. 1991-92, pres.-elect 2001-), Charlotte Country Club. Democrat. Avocations: photography, coaching little league. Home: 1139 Queens Rd Charlotte NC 28207-1849 Office: Kennedy Covington Lobdell Bank of Am Corp Ctr 100 N Tryon St 42d Fl Charlotte NC 28202-4006*

PRUESSNER, DAVID MORGAN, lawyer; b. Corpus Christi, Tex., May 13, 1955; s. Harold Trebus and Alma (Morgan) P.; m. Becky McKinney, May 21, 1977; children: Jennifer, Daniel, Heather. BA cum laude, Baylor U., 1977, JD cum laude, 1980. Bar: Tex. 1980, U.S. Dist. Ct. (no. dist.) Tex. 1980, U.S. Ct. Appeals (5th cir.) 1986, U.S. Supreme Ct. 1989. Atty. Coke & Coke, Dallas, 1980-83, Shank, Irwin & Conant, Dallas, 1983-90, Pettit & Martin, Dallas, 1990-92, Fletcher & Springer, Dallas, 1992-99; pvt. practice Law Office of David Pruessner, 1999—. Instr. legal assts. program So. Meth. U., Dallas, 1989-91. Mem. editl. bd. Baylor Law Rev., 1980. Avocations: world religions, history, chess. Appellate, General civil litigation, Insurance. Office: Law Offices of David M Pruessner Ste 600 10100 N Central Expy Dallas TX 75231-4156 Fax: 214-378-7401. E-mail: david@prulaw.com

PRUSAK, MAXIMILIAN MICHAEL, lawyer; b. Granite City, Ill., Mar. 22, 1943; s. Max Emil and Catherine Theresa (Jakich) P.; m. Carolyn Irene Pinkel, July 2, 1966; children: Scott Michael, Stephanie K. BS in Math., U. Ill., 1965, JD, 1968. Bar: Ill. 1968, U.S. Dist. Ct. (so. dist.) Ill. 1973. Staff atty. Atty.'s Title Guaranty Fund, Champaign, Ill., 1968-69; ptnr. Goldsworthy, Fifield & Prusak, Peoria, 1973-80, Nicol, Newell, Prusak & Winne, Peoria, 1980-83, Prusak & Winne, Peoria, Ill., 1983-88, Prusak, Winne & Wombacher, Peoria, 1988-93, Prusak & Winne, Ltd., Peoria, 1993—. Contbr. articles to profl. publs. Bd. dirs. Human Svc. Ctr., Peoria, 1970's, Friendship House, Peoria, 1980, Southside Mission, Peoria, 1988-89; pres. adminstrv. bd. 1st United Meth. Ch., Peoria, 1990—. Capt. USAF, 1969-73. Mem. Ill. State Bar Assn. (chmn. law office cons. sect. coun. 1997-98) , PeoriaCounty Bar Assn. (bd. dirs. 1982, 94, 98, 99, v.p. 1999, pres. 2000), Union League Club Chgo., Ill. Valley Yacht Club. Avocations: computers, sailing, reading. General civil litigation, Insurance, Personal injury. Home: 5821 N Mar Vista Dr Peoria IL 61614-3850 Office: Prusak & Winne Ltd 704 Jefferson Bldg 331 Fulton St Peoria IL 61602-1499 E-mail: prusakwinne@ameritech.net, mprusak@cityscape.net

PRUTZMAN, LEWIS DONALD, lawyer; b. Phila., Nov. 1, 1951; s. L. Donald and Caroline (Butler) P.; m. Deborah Sorace, May 24, 1975 (div. 1998); children: Sarah, Stephen; m. Elizabeth Clement, July 7, 1998. AB, Harvard Coll., 1973; JD, NYU, 1976. Bar: Pa. 1976, N.Y. 1977, U.S. Dist. Ct. (so. and ea. dists.) N.Y. 1977, U.S. Dist. Ct. (ea. dist.) Pa. 1977, U.S. Ct. Appeals (9th cir.) 1979, U.S. Supreme Ct. 1980, U.S. Ct. Appeals (2d cir.) 1983. Law clk. to judge U.S. Dist. Ct., Phila., 1976-77; assoc. Cravath, Swaine & Moore, N.Y.C., 1977-84; ptnr. Stecher Jaglom & Prutzman, 1984-2000, Tannenbaum Helpern Syracuse & Hirsch Tritt LLP, 2000—. Dir., v.p. Respect for Law Alliance, Inc. Mem.: ABA, N.Y. State Bar Assn. (co-chair intellectual property subcom. of internat. law and practice s). Antitrust, Federal civil litigation, State civil litigation. Office: 900 3rd Ave New York NY 10022-4728 E-mail: prutzman@tanhelp.com

PRUZANSKY, JOSHUA MURDOCK, lawyer; b. N.Y.C., Mar. 16, 1940; s. Louis and Rose (Murdock) P.; m. Susan R. Bernstein, Aug. 31, 1980; 1 child, Dina Gabrielle. BA, Columbia Coll., 1960, JD, 1965. Bar: N.Y., 1965, U.S. Dist. Ct. (ea. and so. dists.) N.Y., 1968, U.S. Supreme Ct., 1980. Ptnr. Scheinberg, DePetris & Pruzansky, Riverhead, N.Y., 1965-85, Greshin, Ziegler & Pruzansky, Smithtown, 1985-2000, Pruzansky & Besunder, LLP, Islandia, 2001—. Mem. exec. coun. N.Y. State Conf. Bar Leaders, 1984—, chmn., 1988-89; mem. grievance com. Appellate Divsn. 10th Judicial Dist., 1992-96; mem. adv. bd. Ticor Title Guarantee Co., 1992-2001; mem. L.I. adv. bd. HSBC Bank, 1995—; dir. N.Y. State Com. for Modern Cts., 1998—; mem. adv. task force N.Y. Dept. State Corps.,

1998—. Mem. bd. visitors Columbia Law Sch., 1998—; chair bd. visitors Touro Law Sch., 1998—; dir., sec. L.I. Mus., 1998—. Fellow ABA Found., N.Y. State Bar Found. (bd. dirs. 1994—); mem. ABA (ho. of dels. 1997—, probate and real property sect., standing com. on solo and small firm practitioners 1998-2000, N.Y. state del. Caucus of State Bar Assns.), N.Y. State Bar Assn. (ho. dels. 1982—, pres. 1997-98, exec. com. 1992-99, spl. com. women and law 1986-91, task force om small firms 1991-92, spl. com. on MDP 1999-2000, nominating com. 1999-2000, chair 2000-01, trusts and estates sect., gen. practice, elder law sects.), Suffolk County Bar Assn. (bd. dirs. 1979-89, pres. 1985-86), N.Y. County Lawyers Assn., Nassau County Bar Assn. General corporate, Probate, Real property. Office: Pruzanksy & Besunder LLP One Suffolk Sq Ste 315 Islandia NY 11749 E-mail: pruzansk@villagenet.com

PRYOR, MARK LUNSFORD, state attorney general; b. Fayetteville, Ark. m. Jill Pryor; children: Adams, Porter BA in History, U. Ark., 1985, JD, 1988. Pvt. practice Wright, Lindsey & Jennings, Little Rock, 1988-97; mem. Ark. Ho. of Reps., 1990, chmn. Freshman Caucus, mem. judiciary com., com. on aging and legis. affairs; atty. gen. State of Ark., 1999—. Office: Office of Attorney General 200 Tower Bldg Little Rock AR 72201

PRYOR, SHEPHERD GREEN, III, lawyer; b. Fitzgerald, Ga., June 27, 1919; s. Shepherd Green Jr. and Jeffie (Persons) P.; m. Lenora Louise Standifer, May 17, 1941 (dec.); m. Ellen Wilder, July 13, 1984; children from previous marriage: Sandra Pryor Clarkson, Shepherd Green IV, Robert Stephen, Patty Pryor Smith (dec.), Alan Persons, Susan Lenora. BSAE, Ga. Inst. Tech., 1947; JD, Woodrow Wilson Coll. Law, Atlanta, 1974. Bar: Ga. 1974, U.S. Dist. Ct. (no. dist.) Ga. 1974, U.S. Ct. Appeals (5th cir.) 1974, U.S. Ct. Appeals (11th cir.) 1982, U.S. Supreme Ct. 1977; registered profl. engr., Ga. Comml. pilot engr. Hartford Accident and Indemnity Co., 1947-56; nuclear engr. Lockheed Ga. Co., 1956-64, research and tech. rep., 1964-76; real estate salesman Cole Realty Co. and Valient Properties, 1955-74; sole practice law Atlanta, 1974—. Past pres. Loring Heights Civic Assn.; past mem. Sandy Springs Civic Assn. Devonwood Br.; former trustee Masonic Children's Home of Ga.; bd. advisors Reinhardt Coll.; mem. North Springs Homeowners Assn.; chmn. Bd. Equalization Fulton County, Ga. Capt. U.S. Army, 1942-45, USAFR, 1942-55. Mem. Ga. Bar Assn., Ga. Trial Lawyers Assn., Mensa, Intertel, Soc. Automotive Engrs., Assn. Old Crows, The Old Guard of the Gate City Guard (past commandant), Masons, Shriners, Sigma Delta Kappa, Pi Kappa Phi, Kappa Kappa Psi. Republican. Methodist. General corporate, General practice, Real property. Address: 135 W Spalding Dr NE Atlanta GA 30328-1912

PRYOR, WILLIAM HOLCOMBE, JR. state attorney general; b. Mobile, Ala., Apr. 26, 1962; s. William Holcombe Sr. and Laura Louise (Bowles) P.; m. Kristan Camille Wilson, Aug. 15, 1987; children: Caroline Elizabeth, Victoria Camille. BA in Legal Studies with honors, U. of La. (now N.E. La. U.), Monroe, 1984; JD with honors, Tulane U., 1987. Law clk. U.S. Ct. Appeals (5th cir.), Judge John Minor Wisdom, New Orleans, 1987-88; assoc. Cabaniss, Johnston, Gardner, Dumas & O'Neil, Birmingham, Ala., 1988-91, Walston, Stabler, Wells, Anderson & Bains, Birmingham, 1991-95; dep. atty. gen. State of Ala., Montgomery, 1995-97, atty. gen., 1997—. Adj. prof. Samford U. Cumberland Sch. Law, Birmingham, 1989-94. Bd. student editors Tulane Law Rev., 1985-86, editor-in-chief 1986-87, bd. advisory editors, 1995—. La. nat. com. Young Rep. Nat. Fedn., 1984-86; mem. Ala. Rep. Exec. Com., 1994-95. Order of Coif, Phi Kappa Phi, Omicron Delta Kappa. Roman Catholic. Office: Office Atty Gen 11 S Union St Montgomery AL 36130-2103 E-mail: billpryor@ago.state.al.us

PUCCINELLI, ANDREW JAMES, lawyer; b. Elko, Nev., July 21, 1935; BA cum laude, U. of the Pacific, 1975, JD, 1978. Bar: Nev. 1978. Ptnr. Puccinelli & Puccinelli, Elko, Nev., 1978—. Bus. law adj. prof. No. Nev. C.C., 1982-93; legal advisor Nev. Home Health Svcs., 1980-88. Bd. dirs. Nev. Legal Svcs., 1986-93. Mem. ATLA, Nev. Trial Lawyers Assn., Nev. State Bar Assn. (bd. govs. 1993-2000, v.p. 1996-97, pres.-elect 1997-98, pres. 1998-99, No. Nev. disciplinary bd. 1988-93, CLE com. 1981-85), Elko County Bar Assn. (pres. 1985-86), Phi Delta Phi. Office: Puccinelli & Puccinelli 700 Idaho St Elko NV 89801-3824

PUCKETT, ELIZABETH ANN, law librarian, law educator; b. Evansville, Ind., Nov. 10, 1943; d. Buell Charles and Lula Ruth (Gray) P.; m. Joel E. Hendricks, June 1, 1964 (div. June 1973); 1 child, Andrew Charles; m. Thomas A. Wilson, July 19, 1985. BS in Edn., Eastern Ill. U., 1964; JD, MS in L.S., U. Ill., 1977. Bar: Kans. 1978, Ill. 1979. Acquisitions/reader services librarian U. Kans. Law Library, Lawrence, 1978-79; asst. reader services librarian So. Ill. U. Law Library, Carbondale, 1979-81, reader services librarian, 1981-83; assoc. dir. Northwestern U. Law Library, Chgo., 1983-86, co-acting dir., 1986-87; dir./assoc. prof. South Tex. Coll. Law Library, Houston, 1987-89; dir./prof. South Tex. Coll. Law Libr., 1990-94, U. Ga. Law Libr., Athens, 1994—. Co-author: Evaluation of System-Provided Library Services to State Correctional Centers in Illinois, 1983; co-editor Uniform Commercial Code: Confidential Drafts, 1993. Mem. ABA, Am. Assn. Law Librs. (mem. exec. bd. 1993-96). Avocations: reading, antiques. Office: U Georgia Law Libr Athens GA 30602-6018 E-mail: apuckett@arches.uga.edu

PUCKETT, TONY GREG, lawyer; b. Oklahoma City, Mar. 28, 1961; s. Tony Gene and Sandra Claire P.; m. Jennifer Ann Tubb, Aug. 8, 1987. BA, Colo. Coll., 1983; JD with distinction, U. Okla., 1988. Bar: U.S. Supreme Ct., 10th Cir. Ct. Appeals, 8th Cir. Ct. Appeals, U.S. Dist. Ct. Okla. (we. dist.), U.S. Dist. Ct. Okla. (no. dist.), U.S. Dist. Ct. Okla. (ea. dist.), U.S. Dist. Ct. Tex (No. Tex. dist.). Law clk. Lytle Soule & Curlee, Oklahoma City, 1986-88, assoc., 1988-92, shareholder, 1993-97, McAfee & Taft, Oklahoma City, 1998—. Author: Supreme Court Broadens Liability for Harassment, 1998, Supreme Court Dicples Same-Sex Sexual Harassment Issue, 1998; contbg. author: Age Discrimination in the Workplace: A Primer for Human Resources Professionals, 1999. Trustee McAfee & Taft Found., Oklahoma City, 1998-99. Mem. ABA (labor and employment law sect.), Okla. Bar Assn. (labor and employment sect., chmn. 1997-98), Okla. County Bar Assn., Okla. Assn. Muncipal Attys., Soc. for Human Resources. Republican. Presbyterian. Avocations: soccer coaching and playing, kids. Labor. Office: McAfee & Taft 211 N Robinson Ave Ste S1000 Oklahoma City OK 73102-7103 E-mail: tony.puckett@mcafeetaft.com

PUGH, WILLIAM WHITMELL HILL, III, lawyer; b. Baton Rouge, June 25, 1954; s. George Willard and Jean (Hemphill) P.; m. Beth Smith, Mar. 12, 1983; children: Brendan Kelly, Bryan Clayton, Katharine Elaine. BA, U. Va., 1976; JD, La. State U., 1979. Bar: La. 1979, U.S. Supreme Ct. 1986, U.S. Ct. Appeals (5th and 11th cirs.) 1983. Law clk. to presiding justice U.S. Ct. Appeals (5th cir.), New Orleans, 1979-80. Editor-in-chief La. Law Rev., 1978-79. Mem. Maritime Law Assn., La. Assn. Def. Counsel, La. State Bar Assn., Coun. of La. State Law Inst. (young lawyers rep. 1988-91, mem. 1992—). Admiralty, General civil litigation, Contracts commercial. Office: Liskow & Lewis One Shell Sq 50th Fl New Orleans LA 70139-5001

PUGLIESE, ROBERT FRANCIS, lawyer, business executive; b. Jan. 15, 1933; BS, U. Scranton, 1954; LLB, Georgetown U., 1957, LLM, 1959; grad. advanced mgmt. program, Harvard U., 1976. Bar: D.C. 1957, U.S. Dist. Ct. 1957, U.S. Ct. Claims 1958, U.S. Tax Ct. 1957, U.S. Ct. Appeals 1957. Assoc. Hedrick & Lane, Washington, 1957-60; tax counsel Westinghouse Electric Corp., Pitts., 1961-70, gen. tax counsel, 1970-75, v.p., gen. tax counsel, 1975-76, v.p., gen. counsel, sec., 1976-86, sr. v.p., 1987, exec. v.p., 1988-92; spl. counsel Eckert, Seamans, Cherin & Mellott, 1993—. Bd. dirs. IT Group. Mem. Assn. Gen. Counsel. General corporate. Office: Eckert Seamans Cherin & Mellott 600 Grant St Ste 45 Pittsburgh PA 15219-2703

PUGSLEY, ROBERT ADRIAN, law educator; b. Mineola, N.Y., Dec. 27, 1946; s. Irvin Harold and Mary Catherine (Brusselars) P. BA, SUNY-Stony Brook, 1968; JD, NYU, 1975, LLM in Criminal Justice, 1977. Instr. sociology New Sch. Social Rsch., N.Y.C., 1969-71; coord. Peace Edn. programs The Christophers, 1971-78; assoc. prof. law Southwestern U., L.A., 1978-81, prof., 1981—, Paul E. Treusch prof. law, 2000-01. Adj. asst. prof. criminology and criminal justice Southampton Coll.-Long Island U., 1975-76; acting dep. dir. Criminal Law Edn. and Rsch. Ctr., NYU, 1983-86; bd. advisors Ctr. Legal Edn. CCNY-CUNY, 1978, Sta. KPFK-FM, 1985-86; founder, coord. The Wednesday Evening Soc., L.A., 1979-86; vis. prof. Jacob D. Fuchsberg Law Ctr. Touro Coll., L.I., N.Y., summers, 1988, 89; lectr. in criminal law and procedure Legal Edn. Conf. Ctr., L.A., 1982-96; prof., dir. Comparative Criminal Law and Procedure Program U. B.C., Vancouver, summers, 1994, 98, 99, 2000, 01; chair pub. interest law com. Southwestern U., 1990-2001; lectr. legal profl. responsibility West Bar Rev. Faculty, Calif., 1996-98; legal analyst/commentator for print and electronic media, 1992—. Creative advisor Christopher Closeup (nationally syndicated pub. svc. TV program), 1975-83; host Earth Alert, Cable TV, 1983-87; prodr., moderator (pub. affairs discussion program) Inside L.A., Sta. KPFK-FM, 1979-86, Open Jour. program, Sta. KPFK-FM, 1991-94; contbr. articles to legal jours. Founding mem. Southwestern U. Pub. Interest Law com., 1992—; mem. L.A. County Bar Assn. Adv. Com. on Alcohol & Drug Abuse, 1991-95, co-chair, 1993-95; mem. exec. com. non-govtl. orgns. UN Office Pub. Info., 1977; mem. issues task force L.A. Conservancy, 1980-81, seminar for law tchrs. NEH UCLA, 1979; co-convenor So. Calif. Coalition Against Death Penalty, 1981-83, convener, 1983-84; mem. death penalty com. Lawyer's Support Group, Amnesty Internat., U.S.A.; founding mem. Ch.-State Coun., L.A., 1984-88; bd. dirs. Equal Rights Sentencing Found., 1983-85, Earth Alert, Inc., 1984-87; mem. adv. bd. First Amendment Info. Resources Ctr., Grad. Sch. Libr. and Info. Scis., UCLA, 1990—; mem. coun. Friends UCLA Libr., 1993—, pres., 1996—; mem. adv. bd. Children Requiring a Caring Kommunity, 1998—. Robert Marshall fellow Criminal Law Edn. and Rsch. Ctr., NYU Sch. Law, 1976-78. Mem. Am. Legal Studies Assn., Am. Soc. Polit. and Legal Philosophy, Assn. Am. Law Schs., Inst. Soc. Ethics and Life Scis., Soc. Am. Law Tchrs., Internat. Platform Assn., Internat. Soc. Reform of Criminal Law, The Scribes. Roman Catholic. Office: Southwestern U Sch Law 675 S Westmoreland Ave Los Angeles CA 90005-3905 E-mail: rpugsley@swlaw.edu

PUJADAS, THOMAS EDWARD, lawyer; b. Havana, Cuba, Sept. 20, 1953; s. Guillermo Manuel and Yolanda Ezperanza (de Moya) P.; m. Jeanne Ruth Thigpen, Oct. 28, 1978; children: Kristin Joy, Kari Ann. Student, Emory U., 1971-72; BS, Fla. State U., 1975; JD, U. Fla., 1978. Bar: Fla. 1978, Ga. 1981, U.S. Dist. Ct. (mid. dist.) Ga. 1981, U.S. Dist. Ct. (mid. dist.) Fla. 1981, U.S. Ct. Appeals (5th and 11th cirs.) 1981. Asst. state atty. 4th Jud. Cir. Fla., Jacksonville, 1978-81; ptnr. Walters & Pujadas P.C., Ocilla, Ga., 1981—. Atty. Wilcox County, Ga., 1984—. Mem. Fla. Bar Assn., Ga. Bar Assn., Tifton Jud. Cir. Bar Assn. Democrat. Roman Catholic. Avocations: sailing, fishing, hunting, carpentry, scuba diving. State civil litigation, Contracts commercial, General practice. Office: Walters & Jujadas PC Cherry St Ocilla GA 31774-1504

PULEO, FRANK CHARLES, lawyer; b. Montclair, N.J., Nov. 25, 1945; s. Frank and Kathren (Despenzerie) P.; m. Alice Kathren Leek, June 1, 1968; children— Frank C., Richard James. B.S.E., Princeton U., 1967; J.D., N.Y.U., 1970. Bar: N.Y., 1971. Ptnr., Milbank, Tweed, Hadley & McCloy, N.Y.C., 1970— . Mem. ABA (mem. com. on fed. regulation securities), N.Y. State Bar Assn. Banking, Contracts commercial, General corporate. Office: Milbank Tweed Hadley & McCloy 1 Chase Manhattan Plz Fl 47 New York NY 10005-1413

PULLEY, LEWIS CARL, lawyer; b. Oklahoma City, Aug. 19, 1954; s. Harriet Ruth (Meyers) P.; foster sons: Tuan Le, Chien Hoang. Student, Oxford U., England, 1974; BA with high honors, U. Okla., 1976; JD, Am. U., 1979. Bar: Pa. 1981, U.S. Ct. Mil. Appeals 1982, U.S. Ct. Appeals (D.C. cir.) 1985, U.S. Supreme Ct. 1985, D.C. 1987. Commd. 1st lt. USAF, 1982, advanced through grades to capt., 1982, judge advocate, 1982-88; atty. Def. Logistics Agy., Alexandria, Va., 1988-90; atty. EEO staff mass media bur. FCC, 1990-97, supr. atty. EEO staff mass media bur., 1997—, acting chief EEO staff Nasa Media Bar, 2001—. Contbr. over 500 articles to 11 newspapers and mags. (recipient Investigative Reporting award, Okla. City Gridiron Found., 1975, Media award for Econ. Understanding, Dartmouth Bus. Sch., 1980). Vol. Nat. Pub. Radio, Washington, 1989-90, Connections, 1990-98, White House, 1993-94; mem. Ams. for Med. Progress Ednl. Found. Ewing Found. fellow, 1975. Mem. Pa. Bar Assn., D.C. Bar Assn. Democrat. Jewish. Avocations: travel, collecting polit. paraphernalia. Office: FCC Mass Media Bur EEO Staff 445 12th St SW Washington DC 20554-0001

PULVERMACHER, LOUIS CECIL, lawyer; b. N.Y.C., May 10, 1928; s. Joseph and Lucille Lottie (Meyer) P.; m. Jo Kuchai, May 17, 1974; children: Lewis, Andrew, Stanley, Robin. Grad., Horace Mann Sch., 1945; AB, Franklin and Marshall Coll., 1948; JD, U. Pa., 1951. Bar: N.Y. 1955. Ptnr. Port & Pulvermacher, N.Y.C., 1956-68; sole practice Louis C. Pulvermacher P.C., 1968—. Mem. pro bono panel U.S. Dist. Ct. (so. and ea. dists.) N.Y. Served with USNR, 1951-54, sch. bd. Millbrook Ctrl. Sch. Dist., 1995-98. Mem. ABA (co-chmn. econs. law), Found. Fed. Bar coun. (v.p. 1978-90, chmn. bd. 1990-92), Fed. Bar. Coun. (chmn. bd. dirs. 1983-88), Dutchess County Bar Assn. (exec. com. 1995-98). Jewish. Federal civil litigation, State civil litigation, General practice. Address: 2214 Harbour Court Dr Longboat Key FL 34228-4174 E-mail: PulverLo@mohaawk.net

PUMPHREY, GERALD ROBERT, lawyer; b. Flushing, N.Y., May 31, 1947; s. Fred Paul and Anne (Afferman) P.; m. Joann DeLillo, Oct. 6, 1968; children: Gerald, Christopher, Elena. BBA, St. John's U., 1969, MBA, 1974; JD, Nova U., 1978. Bar: Fla. 1978. Assoc. Walden & Walden, Dania, Fla., 1978; v.p. legal svcs. Golden Bear, Inc., North Palm Beach, Jack Nicklaus & Assocs., Air Bear, Inc., also bd. dirs.; v.p., sec. Triple P., Inc., 1978-83; pvt. practice, 1983—. Bd. advdisor Benjamin Sch. Found. Athletics Assn., 1980-83; coord. Benjamin Sch. Found., Inc.; mem. golf com. St. Clare's Sch.; pres. Home and Sch. Assn., 1983-84; bd. dirs. Deaf Svc. Ctr. Palm Beach County Inc., 1988-89. Mem. ABA, Palm Beach County Bar Assn., North Palm Beach County Bar Assn. (pres. 1991-92), Palm Beach Gardens C. of C. (counsel 1983-87), Kiwanis (charter mem., bd. dirs. Palm Beach Gardens 1983-87), No. Palm Beaches C. of C. (counsel 1987—), Rotary North Palm Beach (bd. dirs. 1998—, pres. 2001—), Phi Alpha Delta. E-mail: pumph. General civil litigation, General practice, Real property. Office: Ste 300 11000 Prosperity Farms Rd Palm Beach Gardens FL 33410-3462 Fax: 561-626-4824. E-mail: gr@bellsouth.net

PUNDT, RICHARD ARTHUR, lawyer; b. Iowa City, Iowa, Apr. 18, 1944; s. Arthur Herman and Johanna Celeste (Pasterik) P.; B.A., State U. Iowa, 1966; J.D., Drake U., 1969; m. Joyce Kay Schoenfelder, Dec. 1, 1968; children— Vincent Arthur, Jennifer Johanna, Heather Ann. Temporary claims dep. Iowa Employment Security Commn., 1968-69; admitted to Iowa bar, 1969; staff atty. Polk County Legal Aid, Office Econ. Opportunity, 1969; spl. agt. FBI, 1969-71; prin. Richard A. Pundt Law Office; dir. Cedar Rapids Profl. Football Corp., 1972-73, pres., 1972-73. Exec. dir. Iowans for Rockefeller, 1968; exec. dir. Polk County Republican Com. 1968-69; mem. Linn County Rep. Central Com., 1972-78; chmn. Linn County Rep. party, 1977-78; asst. prosecuting atty. Linn County, 1972-76. Mem. Am., Iowa, Linn County bar assns., Metro Athletic Assn. (dir. 1976—). Roman Catholic. Club: Sertoma. Home: 3851 Hickory Ridge Ln SE Cedar Rapids IA 52403-3765 Office: 330 1st St SE Cedar Rapids IA 52401-1702

PURCELL, BILL, mayor; b. Phila., Oct. 25, 1953; s. William Paxson Jr. and Mary (Hamilton) P.; m. Deborah Lee Miller, Aug. 9, 1986; 1 child, Jesse Miller. AB, Hamilton Coll., 1976; JD, Vanderbilt U., 1979. Bar: Tenn. 1979, U.S. Ct. Appeals (6th cir.) 1985, U.S. Supreme Ct. 1986. Staff atty. West Tenn. Legal Svcs., Jackson, Tenn., 1979-81; asst. pub. defender Metro Pub. Defender, Nashville, 1981-84, sr. asst. pub. defender, 1984-85; assoc. Lionel R. Barrett, P.C., 1985-86; ptnr. Farmer, Berry & Purcell, 1986-90; mem. Tenn. Ho. of Reps., 1986-96, also majority leader, 1990-96; dir. child and family policy ctr. Vanderbilt Inst. for Pub. Policy Studies, Vanderbilt U., 1996-99; mayor Met. Govt. of Nashville and Davidson county, 1999—. Hon. select com. on children and youth Tenn. Gen. Assembly, 1989—96; exec. dir. Vanderbilt Legal Aid Soc., 1978—79; chmn. NCSL Assembly of State Issues, 1995; chmn. policy makers' program adv. bd. Danforth Found.; mem. adv. bd. U.S. Conf. of Mayors, 2001—. Mem. bd. advs., exec. com. U.S. Conf. Mayors, 2001—; exec. com. 6th Dist. Dems., Nashville, 1986—88; mem. Tenn. State Gen. Assembly, 1986—96, majority leader, 1990—96; chmn. human svcs. com. Nat. Conf. State Legislatures, Washington, 1993; mem. exec. com. Dem. Nat. Com. , 1994—97; chmn. Dem. Legislative Campaign Com., 1994—96. Toll fellow Coun. State Govts., 1988; named Legislator of Yr. Dist. Attys.' Gen. Conf. 1989, Tenn. Conservation League, 1991. Mem. ABA, Tenn. Bar Assn., Nashville Bar Assn. Methodist.

PURNELL, OLIVER JAMES, III, judge; b. Richmond, Va., Jan. 18, 1949; s. Oliver James Jr. and Margaret Helen (Hodges) P.; m. Cheryl Naomi Williams, June 30, 1973; children: Oliver James IV, Amy Susan. AA, U. Hartford, 1969; AB, Middlebury Coll., 1972; MSLS, Case Western Res. U., 1976; JD, Western New England Sch. Law, 1982. Bar: Conn. 1982, U.S. Dist. Ct. Conn. 1982. Dir., pharmacy libr. U. Conn. Sch. Pharmacy, Storrs, Conn., 1977-81; assoc. Lavitt, Hutchinson & Kaplan, Vernon, 1981-84, DuBeau & Ryan, Vernon, 1984-87, Howard, Kohn Sprague & Fitzgerald, Hartford, 1987-89; pvt. practice Vernon, 1989-92; reference libr. U. Conn. Sch. Law, Hartford, 1992-98; regional info. mgr. Lexis-Nexis, Vernon, 1998-99; judge Ellington Dist. Probate Ct., 1999—. Contbr. articles to profl. jours. Scoutmaster Boy Scouts of Am., Rockville, Conn., 1990—; trustee Rockville (Conn.) Pub. Libr.; corporator Ea. Conn. Health Network; mem. U. Hartford Alumni Coun. Recipient Eagle Scout award Boy Scouts of Am., 1964. Mem. Am. Assn. Law Libraries, So. New England Law Libr. Assn. (pres. 1998-99), Conn. Bar Assn. (pres. coun. of bar 1995-96), Tolland County Bar Assn. (pres. 1995-96), Nat. Coll. Probate Judges, Masonic Lodge, A.F. & A.M. (master Fayette Lodge 1970). Avocations: skiing, camping, hiking, church organist. Office: 6 Forestview Dr Vernon Rockville CT 06066-4807 E-mail: jpurnell3@att.net

PURSLEY, RICKY ANTHONY, communications analyst; b. Wareham, Mass., July 11, 1954; s. Gene Everett and Evelyn May (Silveira) P.; m. Susan Elizabeth Scott, Nov. 27, 1982 (div.); children: Carinda Elizabeth, Julia Rayner, Rianna Susan. BA in Polit. Sci., Boston U., 1976; postgrad., Southwestern U., 1976-78. Notary public, D.C., 1991—. Law librarian Graham & James, Los Angeles, 1977-79; legal copy editor Arnold & Porter, Washington, 1980-85; rsch. libr., info. svcs. mgr. Fisher Wayland Cooper Leader & Zaragoza LLP, 1985-2000, law libr., 1985-97, accounts mgr., 1990; comms. analyst Shaw Pittman Potts & Trowbridge, 2000—. Jury commr. Circuit Ct. of Arlington County and City of Falls Church, Va., 1993. Bd. deacons Little Falls Presbyn. Ch., Arlington, Va., 1995-97, elder, mem. session, 1998—, clk. session, 1998—; mem. Nottingham Elem. Sch. PTA Capital Improvement Plan adv. com., 1995—, legis. coord., 1996—; mem. Arlington, Va. Pub. Schs. Vocat., Career and Adult Edn. adv. com., 1996—, adv. coun. on Sch. Facilities and Capital Programs, 1996—. Named one of Outstanding Young Men in Am. U.S. Jaycees, 1978. Mem. Am. Assn. Law Librs., Law Librs.' Soc. Washington, Am. Soc. Notaries. Democrat. Presbyterian. Avocations: music, writing, carpentry. Home: 2704 N Sycamore St Arlington VA 22207-1132 Office: 2300 N St NW Washington DC 20037-1128

PURTELL, LAWRENCE ROBERT, lawyer; b. Quincy, Mass., May 2, 1947; s. Lawrence Joseph and Louise Maria (Loria) P.; m. Cheryl Lynn Tymon, Aug. 3, 1968; children: Lisa Ann, Susan Elizabeth. AB, Villanova U., 1969; JD, Columbia U., 1972. Bar: N.Y. 1973, N.J. 1978, Conn. 1988. Assoc. White & Case, N.Y.C., 1972-73; judge advocate USMC, Washington, 1973-76; assoc. White & Case, N.Y.C., 1977-79; corp. counsel Great Atlantic & Pacific Tea Co., Montvale, N.J., 1979-81; asst. gen. counsel United Techs. Corp., Hartford, Conn., 1981-84, assoc. gen. counsel, 1984-92, sec., gen. counsel, 1989-92; v.p., gen. counsel and sec. Carrier Corp., 1992-93; sr. v.p., gen. counsel and corp. sec. Mc Dermott Internat., New Orleans, 1993-96; sr. v.p., gen. counsel Koch Industries, Wichita, Kans., 1996-97; exec. v.p., gen. counsel Alcoa, Pitts., 1997—. Capt. USMC, 1973-76. Roman Catholic. Avocations: running. Finance, Mergers and acquisitions, Securities. Home: 637 Shoreline Dr Naples FL 34119 Office: Alcoa 390 Park Ave New York NY 10022 also: 401 E 60th St Apt 3K New York NY 10022

PURVIS, JOHN ANDERSON, lawyer, educator; b. Aug. 31, 1942; s. Virgil J. and Emma Lou (Anderson) P.; m. Charlotte Johnson, Apr. 3, 1976; 1 child, Whitney; children by previous marriage: Jennifer, Matt. BA cum laude, Harvard U., 1965; JD, U. Colo., 1968. Bar: Colo. 1968, U.S. Dist. Ct. Colo. 1968, U.S. Ct. Appeals (10th cir.) 1978. Dep. dist. atty., Boulder, Colo., 1968-69; asst. dir., dir. legal aid U. Colo. Sch. Law, 1969; assoc. Williams, Taussig & Trine, Boulder, 1969; head Boulder office Colo. Pub. Defender Sys., 1970-72; assoc., ptnr. Hutchinson, Black, Hill, Buchanan & Cook, Boulder, 1972-85; ptnr. Purvis, Gray, Schuetze and Gordon, 1985-98, Purvis, Gray & Gordon, LLP, 1999—. Acting Colo. State Pub. Defender, 1978; adj. prof. law U. Colo., 1981, 84-88, 94, others; lectr. in field; chmn. Colo. Pub. Defender Commn., 1979-89; mem. nominating commn. Colo. Supreme Ct., 1984-90; mem. com. on conduct U.S. Dist. Ct., 1991-97, chmn., 1996-97; chmn. Boulder County Criminal Justice Com., 1975-81. Recipient Ames award Harvard U., 1964, Outstanding Young Lawyer award Colo. Bar Assn., 1978, Dist. Achievement award U. Colo. Law Sch. Alumni Assn., 1997. Mem. Internat. Soc. Barristers, Internat. Acad. Trial Lawyers, Am. Bd. Trial Advocates, Am. Coll. of Trial Lawyers (state chmn. 1998-2000), Colo. Bar Assn. (chair litigation sect. 1994-95), Boulder County Bar Assn., Colo. Trial Lawyers Assn., Am. Trial Lawyers Assn., Trial Lawyers for Pub. Justice, Colo. Bar Found., Am. Bar Found., Supreme Ct. Hist. Soc. (state chmn. 1998—), Faculty of Fed. Advocates (bd. dirs. 1999—). Democrat. Federal civil litigation, State civil litigation, Personal injury. Address: 1050 Walnut St Ste 501 Boulder CO 80302-5144

PURVIS, RANDALL W. B. lawyer; b. Summit, N.J., Mar. 2, 1957; s. Merton B. and Marjory L. (Baker) P.; m. Robin Head Intemann Purvis; children: Zachary, Timothy, Andrew. BS, Ohio State U., 1979; JD, Georgetown U., 1982. Bar: Colo. 1983, U.S. Dist. Ct. Colo. 1983, U.S. Ct. Appeals (10th cir.) 1983. Pvt. practice, Colorado Springs, Colo., 1983—. Bd. dirs. Nova Resources Corp., Dallas, 1985-88. Councilman Colorado Springs City Coun., 1987-99, re-elected 1991, 95; mem. steering com. Nat. League of Cities, Washington; elder 1st Presbyn. Ch., Colorado Springs,

1987-91; bd. trustees Meml. Hosp. Colorado Springs, 1991-99. Mem. Colo. Bar Assn., El Paso County Bar Assn. (com. chmn. 1986), Colorado Springs C. of C. (com. chmn. 1986), Colorado Springs Bridge Club, Phi Beta Kappa. Republican. Avocations: bridge, woodworking. General civil litigation, Probate, Real property. Office: 13 S Tejon Ste 302 Colorado Springs CO 80903-1520

PUSATERI, JAMES ANTHONY, judge; b. Kansas City, Mo., May 20, 1938; s. James A. and Madeline (LaSalle) P.; m. Jacqueline D. Ashburne, Sept. 1, 1962; children: James A., Mark C., Danielle L. BA, U. Kans., 1960, LLB, 1963. Bar: Kans. 1963, U.S. Dist. Ct. Kans. 1963, U.S. Ct. Appeals (10th cir.) 1964. Assoc. Payne, Jones, Chartered, Olathe, Kans., 1963-65, James Cashin, Prairie Village, 1965-69; asst. U.S. atty. Dept. Justice, Kansas City, 1969-76; judge U.S. Bankruptcy Ct. Dist. Kans., Topeka, 1976—. Judge; b. Kansas City, Mo., May 20, 1938; s. James A. and Madeline (LaSalle) P.; m. Jacqueline D. Ashburne, Sept. 1, 1962; children— James A., Mark C., Danielle L. B.A., U. Kans., 1960, LL.B., 1963. Bar: Kans. 1963, U.S. Dist. Ct. Kans. 1963, U.S. Ct. Appeals (10th cir.) 1964. Assoc. Payne, Jones, Chartered, Olathe, Kans., 1963-65; assoc. James Cashin, Prairie Village, Kans., 1965-69; asst. U.S. atty. Dept. Justice, Kansas City, Kans., 1969-76; judge U.S. Bankruptcy Ct. Dist. Kans., Topeka, 1976—; mem. Kans. Bar Assn., Topeka Bar Assn., Nat. Conf. Bankruptcy Judges, Am. Bankruptcy Inst. Active Prairie Village City Coun., 1967-69. Mem. Kans. Bar Assn., Topeka Bar Assn., Nat. Conf. Bankruptcy Judges, Am. Bankruptcy Inst.

PUSATERI, LAWRENCE XAVIER, lawyer; b. Oak Park, Ill., May 25, 1931; s. Lawrence E. and Josephine (Romano) P.; m. Eve M. Graf, July 9, 1956; children: Joanne, Lawrence F., Paul L., Mary Ann, Eva. JD summa cum laude, DePaul U., 1953. Bar: Ill. 1953. Asst. state's atty. Cook County, 1957-59; ptnr. Newton, Wilhelm, Pusateri & Naborowski, Chgo., 1959-77; justice Ill. Appellate Ct., 1977-78; ptnr. Peterson, Ross, Scloerb & Seidel, 1978-95; of counsel Peterson & Ross, 1996—. Pres. Conf. Consumer Fin. Law, 1984-92, chmn. gov. com., 1993-99; mem. Ill. Supreme Ct. Com. on Pattern Jury Instrns., 1981-96; mem. adv. bd. Ctr. for Analysis of Alt. and Dispute Resolution, 1999—; mem. U.S. Senate Jud. Nominations Commn. State Ill., 1993, 95; exec. dir. State of Ill. Jud. Inquiry Bd., 1995-96; panel chmn. Cook County mandatory arbitration, 1990—, judicate Am. Arbitration; mem. Merit Selection Panel for U.S. Magistrate; lectr. law DePaul U., Chgo., 1962, Columbia U., N.Y.C., 1965, Marquette U., Milw., 1962-82, Northwestern U. Law Sch., Def. Counsel Inst., 1969-70; apptd. by U.S. Senator Paul Simon to Merit Screening Com. Fed. Judges, U.S. Atty. and U.S. Marshal, 1993, others; mem. task force indigent appellate def. Cook County Jud. Adv. Coun., 1992-95; mem. Ill. Gen. Assembly, 1964-68. Contbr. articles to profl. jours. Chmn. Ill. Crime Investigating Commn., 1967-68, chmn. Ill. Parole and Pardon Bd., 1969-70; bd. dirs. Ill. Law Enforcement Commn., 1970-72; chmn. Com. on Correctional Facilities and Services; exec. v.p. and gen. counsel Ill. Fin. Svcs. Assn., 1980-95; chmn. law forum Am. Fin. Svcs. Assn., 1975-76; mem. spl. commn. on adminstrn. of justice in Cook County, Ill. (Greylord Com.) 1984-90, bd. dirs. Chgo. Crime Commn., 1986-91; mem. Ill. Supreme Ct. Spl. Commn. on the Adminstrn. of Justice, Ill. Supreme Ct. Appointment, 1991. Served to capt. JAGC, AUS, 1955-58. Named One of Ten Outstanding Young Men in Chgo., Chgo. Jr. Assn. Commerce and Industry, 1960, 65; recipient Outstanding Legislator award Ill. Gen. Assembly, 1966. Mem. ABA (com. consumer fin. svcs. 1975-99, ho. dels. 1981-90, judicial adminstrn. divsn. 1980-95, mem. exec. com. lawyer's conf. 1994-95, mem. bench and bar rels. com. 1994-96, mem. adv. com. to Ill. State Del., Jud. Adminstrn. Divsn. in Recognition of Leadership in Improvement of Adminstrn. of Justice award 1993), Ill. State Bar Assn. (pres. 1975-76, com. on fed. jud. and related appointments; Abraham Lincoln Legal Writing award 1959, mem. adv. com., state del., 1994-99, bd. dirs.), Chgo. Bar Assn. (bd. mgrs. 1965-66), Fred B. Snite Found. (sec., counsel 1976-90), Gertrude and Walter Swanson Found. (sole trustee 1995—), Mid-Am. Club Chgo. Republican. Roman Catholic. Finance.

PUSHINSKY, JON, lawyer; b. N.Y.C., May 30, 1954; s. Paul and Harriet (Rosenberg) P.; m. M. Jean Clickner, July 31, 1982; children: Matthew Clickner-Pushinsky, Jeremy Clickner-Pushinsky. BA, MA, U. Pa., 1976; JD, U. Pitts., 1979. Bar: Pa. 1979, U.S. Dist. Ct. (we. dist.) Pa. 1979, U.S. Ct. Appeals (3rd cir.) 1980, U.S. Supreme Ct. 1988. Staff counsel W.Va. Legal Svcs. Plan, Wheeling, 1979-80; pvt. practice Pitts., 1980—. Dem. candidate Superior Ct. Pa., 1993, 95; solicitor Cmty. Human Svcs. Corp., Pitts., 1992—; consulting lawyer ARC-Allegheny, Pitts., 1981—. Recipient Civil Libertarian award ACLU of Pa., 1994, Cmty. Citation of Merit Allegheny County Mental Health/Mental Retardation Bd., 1992, Cert. Appreciation Pitts. Commn. on Human Rels., 1992. Mem. Pa. Trial Lawyers Assn., Allegheny County Bar Assn. (appellate practice com., civil rights com.). Democrat. Avocations: reading, hiking, movies. Civil rights, Constitutional, General practice. Office: 429 4th Ave Pittsburgh PA 15219-1500

PUSTILNIK, DAVID DANIEL, lawyer; b. N.Y.C., Mar. 10, 1931; s. Philip and Belle (Gerberholtz) P.; m. Helen Jean Todd, Aug. 15, 1959; children: Palma Elyse, Leslie Royce, Bradley Todd. BS, NYU, 1952, JD, 1958, LLM, 1959; postgrad., Air War Coll., 1976. Bar: N.Y. 1959, U.S. Supreme Ct. 1962, Conn. 1964. Legis. tax atty. legis. and regulations div. Office Chief Counsel, IRS, Washington, 1959-63; atty. Travelers Ins. Co., Hartford, Conn., 1963-68, assoc. counsel, 1968-73, counsel, 1973-75, assoc. gen. counsel, 1975-87, dep. gen. counsel, 1987-93. Mem. adv. coun. Hartford Inst. on Ins. Taxation, 1978-93, vice chmn., 1991-92, chmn., 1992-93. Grad. editor NYU Tax Law Rev., 1958-59. Trustee Hartford Coll. for Women, 1985-91; life sponsor Am. Tax Policy Inst.; dir. Congregation Beth Yam, 1996-99. Served to col. USAFR. Kenneson fellow NYU, 1958-59. Fellow Am. Coll. Tax Counsel; mem. ABA (chmn. ins. cos. com. 1976-78), Am. Coun. Life Ins. (chmn. co. tax com. 1982-84), Am. Ins. Assn. (chmn. tax com. 1979-81), Assn. Life Ins. Counsel (chmn. tax sect. 1991-93), Twentieth Century Club, Sea Pines Country Club (co-chair social com. 1997-99). Pension, profit-sharing, and employee benefits, Corporate taxation.

PUTMAN, LINDA MURRAY, lawyer; b. Greenwich, Conn., June 22, 1953; d. Francis Joseph and Clare Marie (Fassinger) P. AB, Brown U., 1975; JD, U. Conn., 1978. Bar: Conn. 1979, Pa. 1981, U.S. Dist. Ct. (we. dist.) Pa. 1983, U.S. Ct. Appeals (3d cir.) 1983. Assoc. Law Offices of Lawrence E. Larson, Greenwich, 1978-80; law clk. to presiding justice Lawrence County Ct. Common Pleas, New Castle, Pa., 1980-83; assoc. Law Office of Lawrence E. Larson, Greenwich, 1983-86; cons. GTE Consumer Communications Products Corp., Stamford, Conn., 1986-88; assoc. counsel Simmons Communications, 1989-95; corp. atty. Brink's Inc., Darien, 1995-98, consulting Atty., 1998—. Mem. Women in Mgmt., Westchester-Fairfield Corp. Counsel Assn. Avocations: endurance and competitive trail riding, running. Contracts commercial, General corporate, Intellectual property. Home and Office: 36 Ridgeview Ave Greenwich CT 06830-4749

PUTMAN, MICHAEL (JAMES PUTMAN), lawyer; b. San Antonio, May 12, 1948; s. Harold David and Elizaeth Finley (Henderson) P.; m. Kris J. Bird. BBA, S.W. Tex. State U., 1969; JD, St. Mary's U., 1972. Bar: Tex. 1972, U.S. Dist. Ct. (we. dist.) Tex. 1980, U.S. Ct. Appeals (5th and 11th cirs.) 1981; cert. personal injury trial law specialist Tex. Bd. Legal Specialization. Ptnr. Putman & Putman (Inc. 1981), San Antonio, 1972-81, officer, dir., 1981—. Mem. ATLA, State Bar Tex., Nat. Employment Lawyers Assn., Tex. Trial Lawyers Assn. (assoc. dir. 1995, dir. 1996-99, dir. emeritus 1999), Tex. Employment Lawyers Assn. (founding mem. 1998—), San Antonio Trial Lawyers Assn. (dir., officer 1975—, Am. Bd. Trial Advocates. Labor, Personal injury, Product liability. Office: 310 S Saint Marys St Fl 27 San Antonio TX 78205-3113

PUTTER, DAVID SETH, lawyer; b. N.Y.C., Mar. 11, 1944; s. Norton Seth and Ruth Crystal P.; m. Lee Dow, Apr. 26, 1987. Student, U. Granada, Spain, 1964; BA in Biology, Beloit Coll., Spain, 1965; JD, Syracuse U., 1968. Bar: Vt. 1970, N.Y. 1971, U.S. Dist. Ct. Vt. 1970, U.S. Ct. Appeals (2d cir.) 1975, U.S. Ct. Claims 1998. Atty. Putter & Carrington, Arlington, Vt., 1970-73; Bennington County pub. defender State of Vt., Bennington, 1973-76, law clk. to Superior Ct. judges Burlington, 1976-78, asst. atty. gen. Montpelier, 1979-81; with Putter & Unger, 1981-88; assoc. Saxer, Anderson, Wolinsky & Sunshine, 1988-2000; ptnr. Putter and Edson, LLP, 2001—. Contbr. articles to profl. jours. Acting Superior Ct. judge, 1997—; chair legal panel ACLU Vt., 1988—; sponsored advisor on assembly, free press, free speech USIA, Lusaka, Zambia, Kampala, Uganda, 1996. Recipient Jonathan Chase award ACLU Vt., 1991, 97. Avocations: hiking, camping, theater, travel, music (folk and rock). Appellate, General civil litigation, Constitutional. Home: 6 Towne St Montpelier VT 05602-4231 Office: Putter and Edson LLP 15 E State St Montpelier VT 05602-3010

PYFER, JOHN FREDERICK, JR. lawyer; b. Lancaster, Pa., July 25, 1946; s. John Frederick and Myrtle Ann (Greiner) P.; m. Carol Trice, Nov. 25, 1970; children: John Frederick III, Carol Lee. Grad. cum laude, Peddie Sch., 1965; BA in Polit. Sci. and Econs., Haverford Coll., 1969; JD, Vanderbilt U., 1972. Bar: Pa. 1972, U.S. Dist. Ct. (ea. dist.) Pa. 1973, U.S. Tax Ct. 1975, U.S. Supreme Ct. 1975, U.S. Dist. Ct. (mid. dist.) Pa. 1984, U.S. Ct. Appeals (3d cir.) 1986. Law clk. to presiding justice Ct. Common Pleas, Lancaster, Pa., 1972-74; assoc. Xakellis, Perezous & Mongiovi, 1972-76; founding ptnr. Allison & Pyfer, 1976-85; pres. Pyfer & Assocs., 1986-88, Pyfer & Reese, Lancaster, 1988—. Prof. para-legal tng. Pa. State Ext. Svc., 1989-93; fed. ct. mediator, 1992—. Contbr. articles to law revs., law treatises. Pres. Lancaster-Lebanon Coun., Boy Scouts Am., 1989—93, coun. commr., 1987—89, mem. nat. com., 1996—, exec. bd. N.E. region, 1998—, area pres., 2000—01; bd. dirs. World of Scouting Mus. Fellow Am. Bd. Criminal Lawyers, Lancaster Heritage Ctr. (sec. 2001—); mem. ABA (First prize Howard C. Schwab Nat. Essay Contest in Writing 1972), ATLA, SAR, Nat. Assn. Criminal Def. Lawyers, Pa. Trial Lawyers Assn., Pa. Criminal Def. Lawyers Assn., Am. Arbitration Assn., Pa. Bar Assn., Lancaster Bar Assn., Inns Ct. (founder, pres. W. Hensel Brown 1993-94), Christian Lawyers Soc., Train Collector Assn. (divsn. pres. 1984), Am. Orchid Soc. (affiliate pres. 1998), Lions Club (pres. 1980-82, 2000-01) (Willow Street, Pa.), Masons (Lancaster). Republican. United Ch. of Christ (elder, pres. 1989, 95). Criminal, Family and matrimonial, General practice. Home: 1100 Little Brook Rd Lancaster PA 17603-6116 Office: Pyfer & Reese 128 N Lime St Lancaster PA 17602-2951 E-mail: pyfer@redrose.net, law@pyferreese.com

PYLE, HOWARD, lawyer, consultant; b. Richmond, Va., Feb. 1, 1940; s. Wilfrid and Anne Woolston (Roller) P.; children: Elizabeth Roller, Howard. AB, Princeton U., 1962; JD, U. Va., 1967. Bar: Va. 1967, D.C. 1969. Career trainee CIA, Washington, 1967-69; adminstrv. asst. to Congressman Odin Langen, U.S. Ho. of Reps., 1969-70, to Congressman Hastings Keith, 1971; asst. to sec. Dept. Interior, 1971-73; Washington rep. Std. Oil Co. Ind., 1973-77; mgr. fed. pub. affairs R.J. Reynolds Industries, Inc., Winston-Salem, N.C., 1977-80; dir. fed. rels. Houston Industries, Washington, 1980-99; pres. HPYLE Cons., Alexandria, Va., 1999—. Bd. govs., pres. Episcopal Sr. Ministries, 1986-96; bd. dirs., pres. Friendship Terrace, 1986-96; chair commn. com. Princeton Club, Washington, D.C., chair D.C. area ann. giving. Capt. USNR, 1962-89, ret. Mem. ABA, FBA, NRA, SAR, D.C. Bar, Va. Bar, Fed. Energy Bar Assn., Naval Res. Assn., Res. Officers Assn., Internet Soc., Va. Country Club, Princeton Club of Washington (chmn. comms. com., mem. coun. 1998—), Delta Theta Phi. Republican. Episcopalian. Home: 125 N Lee St Alexandria VA 22314-3260 also: PO Box 19645 Alexandria VA 22320-0645 Office: HPYLE Cons Po Box 19645 Alexandria VA 22320-0645 E-mail: hpyle@alumni.Princeton.EDU, howard@hpyle.net

PYLE, SUSAN H. legal association official; b. Thibodaux, La., Nov. 28, 1955; BA in Comm., Nicholls State U., Thibodaux, 1977. News reporter, writer Stas. KTIB and KHOM, Thobodaux, 1975-77; news reporter, anchor Sta. KLFY-TV, Lafayette, La., 1977-81; pub. rels. account exec. Weill & East Advt. & Pub. Rels., Baton Rouge, 1984-88; pub. rels. asst. Our Lady of Lake Regional Med. Ctr., 1994-95; coord. comm. La. Trial Lawyers Assn., 1996—. Editor La. Advs., 1996—. Mem. Baton Rouge Press Club. Home: La Trial Lawyers Assn 442 Europe St Baton Rouge LA 70802

PYLMAN, NORMAN HERBERT, II, lawyer; b. Grand Rapids, Mich., June 6, 1952; s. Norman Herbert and Yvonne Coral (Moelker) P.; m. Janet Lee VandenToorn, Sept. 9, 1977; children— Bradley David, Daniel Jonathan. BA, Calvin Coll., 1974; JD with honors, U. Detroit, 1977. Bar: Mich. 1977, U.S. Dist. Ct. (we. dist.) Mich. 1977. Assoc. Cholette, Perkins & Buchanan, Grand Rapids, 1977-82, ptnr., 1982-85, ptnr. Gruel, Mills, Nims & Pylman, Grand Rapids, 1985—. Bd. dirs. Honey Creek Christian Homes, Lowell, Mich., 1978— . Mem. Grand Rapids Bar Assn., Mich. Bar Assn. (civil procedure com.), ABA. Republican. Christian Reformed. Federal civil litigation, State civil litigation, Personal injury. Home: 1666 Tammarron Ave SE Grand Rapids MI 49546-9658 Office: Gruel Mills Nims & Pylman 50 Monroe Ave NW Ste 700 Grand Rapids MI 49503-2643

PYM, BRUCE MICHAEL, lawyer; b. Alameda, Calif., Sept. 29, 1942; s. Leonard A. and Willamay (Strandberg) P. B.B.A., U. Wash., 1964, J.D., 1967. Bar: Wash. 1967, U.S. Dist. Ct. (we. dist.) Wash. 1968, U.S. Ct. Appeals (9th cir.) 1968, U.S. Tax Ct. 1969, U.S. Supreme Ct. 1971. Law clk. Wash. State Supreme Ct., Olympia, 1967-68; assoc. Graham & Dunn, Seattle, 1968-73, shareholder, 1973-92; ptnr. Heller, Ehrman, White & McAuliffe, Seattle, 1992—; mng. ptnr. Northwest Offices, 1994-99. Bd. dirs. United Way of King County, 1986-92, chmn., 1990. Mem. ABA, Wash. State Bar Assn., King County Bar Assn. (pres. 1984-85). General corporate, Mergers and acquisitions, Securities. Office: Heller Ehrman White & McAuliffe 701 5th Ave Ste 6100 Seattle WA 98104-7098

QI, QING MICHAEL, lawyer; b. Shanghai, Apr. 4, 1968; s. Pei Yu Qi and Qi Lan Yang. BA in Law, Fudan U., Shanghai, 1990, cert. grad in capital markets, 1992; LLM, NYU, 1996. Bar: N.Y., Peoples Republic of China. Asst. dir. Shanghai Arts & Crafts Import & Export Corp., 1990-92; mem. law coun. Coudert Bros., Shanghai, 1992-95; assoc. Paul Weiss et. al., N.Y.C., 1996-97, Milbank, Tweed et. al., N.Y.C., 1997-99; ptnr. Fangda Ptnrs., Shanghai, 1996—. Guest spkr. Coun. Fgn. Rels., N.Y.C. 1997; adj. tchg. asst. NYU Law Sch., 1996; cons. Shanghai Zhang Jiang Hi-Tech. Zone, 2000. Editor-in-chief Law Rev., Fudan U. Law Sch., 1987-89; contbr. articles to profl. jours.; spkr. in field. Bd. dirs. Coudert scholarship appraisal com. Fudan U. Law Sch., Shanghai, 1995; contbr. Hope Project of China, 1999-2000, N.Y. Legal Aid Program, 1995-99. Hauser scholar NYU Law Sch., 1996, scholar Fudan U. Law Sch., 1987-90. Mem. Chinese Lawyers Assn., N.Y. State Bar Assn., Overseas Chinese Students Soc., numerous specialty law assns. in China. Avocations: painting, reading, travel, marathons, Chinese cuisine and tea serving. General corporate, Mergers and acquisitions, Corporate finance. Home: Ste 1604 Mao Ming Mansion 29 Yong Jia Rd Shanghai 200020 China Office: 19/F HSBC Bldg 101 Yin cheng E Rd Pu Dong New Area Shanghai 200120 China Fax: 8621 6841 2255/0099. E-mail: mqi@fangdalaw.com

QIAN, JIN, law librarian; b. Shanghai, China; came to the U.S., 1987; s. Bingchun and Shiyi Qian. BA, Shanghai Tchrs. U., ;, 1981; MA, Fordham U., 1988; MLS, St. John's U., 1990. Libr. trainee N.Y. Pub. Libr., N.Y.C., 1988; reference asst. N.Y. Hist. Soc., 1989-90; asst. libr. Wilson, Elser et al., 1990-92, head libr., 1992—. Presdl. scholar Fordham U., 1987. Mem. Law Libr. Assn. Greater N.Y., Am. Assn. Law Librs., Spl. Librs. Assn., ALA. Home: PO Box 811 New York NY 10163-0811 Office: Wilson Elser & Moskowitz 150 E 42nd St New York NY 10017-5612 E-mail: 1ianj@wemed.com

QUACKENBUSH, JUSTIN LOWE, federal judge; b. Spokane, Wash., Oct. 3, 1929; s. Carl Clifford and Marian Huldah (Lowe) Q.; m. Marie McAtee; children: Karl Justin, Kathleen Marie, Robert Craig. Student, U. Ill., 1947-49; BA, U. Idaho, 1951; LLB, Gonzaga U., Spokane, 1957. Bar: Wash. 1957. Dep. pros. atty., Spokane County, 1957-59; ptnr. Quackenbush, Dean, Bailey & Henderson, Spokane, 1959-80; dist. judge U.S. Dist. Ct. (ea. dist.) Wash., 1980—, now sr. judge. Part-time instr. Gonzaga U. Law Sch., 1960-67 Chmn. Spokane County Planning Commn., 1969-73. Served with USN, 1951-54. Mem. Wash. Bar Assn., Spokane County Bar Assn. (trustee 1976-78), Internat. Footprint Assn. (nat. pres. 1967), Shriners. Episcopalian. Office: US Dist Ct PO Box 1432 Spokane WA 99210-1432

QUADE, VICTORIA CATHERINE, editor, writer, playwright, producer; b. Chgo., Aug. 15, 1953; d. Victor and Virginia (Uryasz) Q.; m. Charles J. White III, Feb. 15, 1986 (div. Aug. 1996); children: Michael, David, Catherine. BS in Journalism, No. Ill. U., 1974. Staff reporter news divsn. The News-Tribune, LaSalle, Ill., 1975-77; staff writer news divsn. The News-Sun, Waukegan, 1977-81; staff writer ABA Jour., Chgo., 1981-85; mng. editor ABA Press, 1985-90, editor, 1990-2000, sr. editor, 1994-2000. Author: (poetry) Rain and Other Poems, 1976, Laughing Eyes, 1979, Two Under the Covers, 1981, (biography) I Remember Bob Collins, 2000; playwright Late Nite Catechism, 1993, (with Maripat Donovan) Room for Advancement, 1994, Mr. Nanny, 1997, (musical) Lost in Wonderland, 1998, (musical) Here Come the Famous Brothers, 2001; prodr. Late Nite Catechism, Mr. Nanny and Here Come the Famous Brothers; contbr. to numerous anthologies and publs.; contbd. to: 20th Century Chicago: 100 Years, 100 Voices (contbd. the year 1953). Recipient numerous awards from Soc. Nat. Assn. Publs., AP, UPI. Mem. Am. Soc. Bus. Press Editors (award), Chgo. Newspaper Guild (award), Am. Soc. Assn. Execs. (Gold Circle award 1989, 90). Avocations: traveling, photography.

QUADRI, FAZLE RAB, lawyer, government official; b. Dacca, Pakistan, Aug. 5, 1948; came to U.S., 1967; s. Gholam Moula and Jehan (Ara) Q.; children: Ryan F., Tania M. AA, Western Wyo. Coll., 1969; BA, Calif. State U., 1972; JD, Western State U., 1978; postgrad. cert. in criminal advocacy, U. Calif., San Francisco, 1988. Bar: Calif. 1981. Sr. adminstrv. analyst San Bernardino County, Calif., 1978-82, acting legis. adv., 1982, sr. legis. analyst, 1982-90, county legis. analyst, 1990-93, acting pub. defender, 1984; dist. counsel Mojave Desert Air Quality Mgmt. Dist., Victorville, 1993—; dist. counsel Antelope Valley Air Pollution Control Dist., 1997—. Local gov. rep. State Hazardous Waste Mgmt. Council, Sacramento, Calif., 1982-84; chmn.'s rep. County Projects Selection Coms., San Bernardino, 1983-91; county rep. South Coast Air Quality Mgmt. Dist., El Monte, Calif., 1983-87. Advisor Mcpl. Adv. Couns., San Bernardino, 1984-87; mem. Law Libr. Bd. Trustees, 1984-85, 93-95. Mem. ABA, Calif. Bar Assn. (mem. exec. com. pub. law section 2000—), Calif. State U. Alumni Assn. (bd. dirs. 1985-86), Masons, Shriners. Republican. Islamic. Avocations: personal computers, reading, music, karate, water sports. Home: 535 E Mariposa Dr Redlands CA 92373-7351 Office: Mojave Desert AQMD 14306 Park Ave Victorville CA 92392-2310 E-mail: quadri@mdaqmd.ca.gov

QUALE, ANDREW CHRISTOPHER, JR. lawyer; b. Boston, July 7, 1942; s. Andrew Christopher and Luella (Meland) Q.; m. Sally Sterling Ellis, Oct. 15, 1977; children: Andrew, Addison. BA magna cum laude, Harvard U., 1963, LLB cum laude, 1966; postgrad., Cambridge (Eng.) U., 1966-67. Bar: Mass. 1967, N.Y. 1971. Fellow Internat. Legal Ctr., Bogota, Colombia, 1967-68; cons. Republic of Colombia, 1968-69; assoc. Cleary, Gottlieb, Steen and Hamilton, N.Y.C., 1969-75; ptnr. Coudert Brothers, 1975-82, Sidley Austin Brown & Wood, N.Y.C., 1982—. Adj. prof. Sch. of Law U. Va., Charlottesville, 1976—88; cons. privatizations World Bank, UN, Harvard Inst. Internat. Devel., 1982—; bd. dirs. Bottell Stoeckel Assocs., Norfolk. Contbr. to profl. publs. Pres. Bronxville (N.Y.) Sch. Bd., 1991-93; founder, bd. dirs. Bronxville Sch. Found., 1991-95, 96—; bd. dirs. Coun. The Ams.; co-chair The Little Forum, Bronxville. Mem. ABA, Assn. Bar City N.Y. (chmn. Inter-Am. affairs com. 1982-85), N.Y. State Bar Assn., Colombian-Am. Assn. (v.p., bd. dirs.), Botelle-Steckel Assocs. (bd. dirs. Norfolk), The Little Forum (co-chair Bronxville), Bronxville Field Club, Norfolk (Conn.) Country Club, Doolittle Lake Co. (Norfolk, bd. dirs.). Banking, Private international, Mergers and acquisitions. Office: Sidley & Austin 875 3rd Ave Fl 14 New York NY 10022-6293

QUALLS, ALVIE EDWARD, II, lawyer; b. Huntington, W. Va., Dec. 3, 1960; s. Alvie Edward and Marion Inez (Clay) Q. BA, Marshall U., 1984, MA, 1986; JD, U. Tulsa, 1992. Bar: W. Va. 1992, U.S. Dist. Ct. (so. dist.) W. Va. 1992. Legal asst. Rood and Mills, Legal Corp., Huntington, W. Va., 1982-84; law clerk W. Va. Supreme Ct. of Appeals, 1992-94; attorney W. Va. Pub. Defender Office, 1994—. Vol. U. Tulsa Coll. Law; mem. City of Huntington Forces 2000 com., 1984, Covall County Democratic Party. Kevin Russell Bowen scholar Marshall U. Student Govt., Huntington, 1982. Mem. U. Tulsa Coll. Law Regional Alumni Bd., Cabell County Democratic Women's Club, Cabell County Bar Assn., Phi Alpha Delta, Pi Sigma Alpha, Pi Alpha Theta. Mem. Ch. of God. Avocations: working out, reading, travel, sports. Office: Mundy and Adkins 422 9th St Huntington WV 25701-1485

QUANDT, JOSEPH EDWARD, lawyer, educator; b. Port Huron, Mich., May 21, 1963; s. Herbert Raymond and Mary Katherine (West) Q.; m. Christine Ann Reilly, Aug. 21, 1993. BA, Oakland U., 1990; JD, Thomas M. Cooley Law Sch., Lansing, Mich., 1993. Bar: Mich. 1994, U.S. Dist. Ct. (ea. and we. dists.) Mich. 1994. Exec. dir. Lord & Taylor, Sterling Heights, Mich., 1985-90; compliance and enforcement specialist Mich. Dept. Environ. Quality, Lansing, 1990-93, adv. bd., 1997—; assoc. Stowe, Draling & Boyd, Traverse City, Mich., 1993-94, Smith & Johnson, Traverse City, 1994-98; ptnr. Menmuir, Zimmerman, Kuhn, Taylor and Quandt, 1998—. Lectr., commentator Inst. CLE, Ann Arbor, Mich., 1994—; adj. prof. Thomas M. Cooley Law Sch., 1997—; co-chair environ. law sect. State Bar Mich. Contbr. articles to profl. jours. Bd. dirs. Involved Citizens Enterprises, Traverse City, 1995—. Mem. Nat. Honor Soc. for Polit. Scientists, Ancient Order Hibernians, Pi Sigma Alpha. Republican. Roman Catholic. Avocations: ice hockey, golf, fly fishing. Environmental, Natural resources, Real property. Office: Menmuir Zimmerman Kuhn et al 122 W State St Traverse City MI 49684-2404

QUARLES, WILLIAM DANIEL, judge; b. Balt., Jan. 16, 1948; s. William Daniel and Mabel (West) Q.; m. Deborah Ann Grant, Oct. 7, 1969 (div. Aug. 1976); 1 child, Eloise; m. Mary Ann Pirog, Nov. 18, 2000. BS, U. Md., 1976; JD, Cath. U., 1979. Bar: D.C. 1979, Md. 1991. Law clk. to presiding judge U.S. Dist. Ct. Md., Balt., 1979-81; assoc. Finley Kumble, Washington, 1981-82; asst. U.S. atty. U.S. Dept. Justice, Balt., 1982-86; assoc., then ptnr. Venable, Baetjer, Howard & Civiletti, Washington, 1986-96, head litigation group, 1993-94; apptd. assoc. judge Cir. Ct. for Balt. City, 1996. Permanent mem. U.S. 4th Cir. Jud. Conf., Richmond, Va., 1986—; mem. D.C. Law Revision Commn., 1989-91; nominated to U.S. Dist. Ct., Dist. Md., 1992; mem. Md. Gov.'s Commn. on Volunteerism

Svc., 1994-95, 96—. Author: Summary Adjudication: Dispositive Motions and Summary Trials, 1991. Coord. Presdl. Regional Task Force on Organized Crime and Drug Law Enforcement, 1984-85; lector St. Michael Roman Cath. Ch. Home: 1 E Chase St Baltimore MD 21202-2526 Office: Circuit Court Bar for Baltimore City 111 N Calvert St Ste 324 Baltimore MD 21202-1910

QUAY, THOMAS EMERY, lawyer; b. Cleve., Apr. 3, 1934; s. Harold Emery and Esther Ann (Thomas) Q.; divorced; children: Martha Wyndham, Glynis Cobb, Eliza Emery; m. Winnifred B. Cutler, May 13, 1989. A.B. in Humanities magna cum laude (Univ. scholar), Princeton U., 1956; LLB (Univ. scholar), U. Pa., 1963. Bar: Pa. 1964. Assoc. Pepper, Hamilton & Scheetz, Phila., 1963-65; with William H. Rorer, Inc., Ft. Washington, Pa., 1965—, sec., counsel, 1974-79, v.p., gen. counsel, sec., 1979-88; v.p. legal planning and adminstrn. Rorer Group, 1988-90; counsel Reed Smith Shaw and McClay, Phila., 1991-93; v.p., gen. counsel Athena Inst., Chester Springs, Pa., 1993—. Bd. dirs. Main Line YMCA, Ardmore, Pa., 1971-73, chmn. bd., 1972-73; editor 10th Reunion Book Princeton Class of 1956, 1966, 25th Reunion Book, 1981—, class sec., 1966-71, class v.p., 1971-81, pres., 1981-86. Lt. (j.g.) USNR, 1957-60. Recipient Svc. Commendation Main Line YMCA, 1973. Mem. ABA, Pa. Bar Assn., Phila. Bar Assn., Pharm. Mfrs. Assn. (chmn. law sect. 1983), Pa. Biotech. Assn. (chmn. legis. com., mem. exec. com. 1991-93), Phila. Drug Exch. (chmn. legis. com. 1975-78), Cannon Club of Princeton U., Sharswood Law Club of U. Pa., Princeton Club of Phila. Democrat. Presbyterian. Antitrust, General corporate, Intellectual property. Office: 601 Swedesford Rd Ste 201 Malvern PA 19355-1573

QUAYLE, MARILYN TUCKER, lawyer, wife of former vice president of United States; b. 1949; d. Warren and Mary Alice Tucker; m. J. Danforth Quayle, Nov. 18, 1972; children: Tucker, Benjamin, Corinne. BA in Polit. Sci., Purdue U., 1971; JD, Ind. U., 1974. Pvt. practice atty., Huntington, Ind., 1974-77; ptnr. Krieg, DeVault, Alexander & Capehart, Indpls., 1993-2001; pres. BTC Inc., Phoenix, 2001—. Author: (with Nancy T. Northcott) Embrace the Serpent, 1992, The Campaign, 1996. General corporate, Health, Public international.

QUEEN, BARRY LLOYD, lawyer, real estate executive; b. Springfield, Mass., Feb. 7, 1942; s. Sidney E. and Dinah Queen; B.S., St. Lawrence U., 1963; LL.B., Western New England Coll., 1969; m. Norine M. Cohen, June 22, 1963; children— Heidi, Dara. Real Estate analyst Mass. Mut. Life Co., Springfield, 1964-69; mortgage officer Schostak Bros., Detroit, 1969-71; v.p. Citizens Mortgage Corp., Detroit, 1971-75; v.p. Rainbow Devel., also Bella Vista Devel., Buffalo, 1975-77; pres. Mut. Investment Group, Boston, 1977-84; v.p. Mut. Bank, Boston, 1977-84; gen. ptnr. Mabell Assocs., Boston, 1978— ; mem. firm Warner & Stackpole, 1984—; pres. Univ. Fin. Services Corp., 1985-88, pres. First Am. Service Corp., 1988—; lectr. in field. Mem. ABA, Nat. Assn. Mut. Banks, Mass. Bar Assn. Home: 958 Salem End Rd Framingham MA 01702-5534 Office: 50 Redfield St Boston MA 02122-3630

QUIAT, MARSHALL, lawyer; b. Denver, Mar. 10, 1922; s. Ira Louis and Esther Quiat; m. Ruth Laura Saunders, Nov. 26, 1950 (dec. Nov. 1995); 1 child, Matthew Philip; m. Jane Cooley, May 1, 1996. BA, U. Colo., 1947, JD, 1948. Bar: Colo. 1949, U.S. Dist. Ct. Colo. 1949, U.S. Ct. Appeals (10th cir.) 1968. Pvt. practice, Denver, 1949—. Judge Gilpin County (Colo.) Ct., 1956, 1st Jud. Dist. Ct., Golden, Colo., 1959; mem. com. on jud. reform Colo. Legis. Commn., 1958. Mem. Colo. Ho. of Reps., Denver, 1949-51; bd. dirs. Luth. Med. Ctr., Denver, 1961-87. 1st lt. F.A., U.S. Army, 1941-46, MTO, ETO. Mem. Am. Radio Relay League (nat. bd. dirs. 1986-99, honorary v.p. 1999—), Pi Gamma Mu, Delta Sigma Rho, Phi Alpha Delta. Avocations: amateur radio, skiing, mathematics, history. State civil litigation, Communications, Family and matrimonial. Home: 714 Pontiac St Denver CO 80220-5540 Office: PO Box 200878 Denver CO 80220-0878 E-mail: quiat@qwest.net

QUICK, ALBERT THOMAS, law educator; b. Battle Creek, Mich., June 28, 1939; s. Robert and Vera Quick; m. Brenda Jones; children: Lori, Traci, Becki, Breton, Regan, Leigh. BA, U. Ariz., 1962; MA, Cen. Mich. U., 1964; JD, Wayne State U., 1967; LLM, Tulane U., 1974. Bar: Mich. 1968. Asst. prosecutor Calhoun County, Marshall, Mich., 1968-69; assoc. Hatch & Hatch, 1969-70; asst. prof. U. Maine, Augusta, 1970-73; prof. law U. Louisville, 1974-87, spl. asst. to univ. provost, 1983-87; dean, prof. law Ohio No. U., Ada, 1987-95; prof. law, dean U. Toledo, Ohio, 1995-99, dean and prof. emeritus, 1999—. Co-author: Update Federal Rules of Criminal Procedure; contbr. articles to profl. jours. Trustee Traverse Dist. Libr. Recipient Medallion of Justice Nat. Bar Assn., 1995. Mem. ABA, ACLU, Mich. State Bar Assn., Willis Soc., Ohio State Bar Assn., Phi Kappa Phi, Coif. Episcopalian. Avocations: golf, art, reading. Office: 542 5th St Traverse City MI 49684-2408 E-mail: atquick@aol.com

QUIDD, DAVID ANDREW, paralegal; b. Chicago Heights, Ill., Sept. 8, 1954; s. John Richard and Mary (Wingate) Q. BA in Polit. Sci., U. New Orleans, 1976; postgrad., La. State U., 1976-79; paralegal cert., U. New Orleans, 1990. Coord. vols. Carter/Mondale Re-election Commn., New Orleans, 1980; paralegal Kitchen & Montagnet, 1981-84, Herman, Herman, Katz & Cotlar, New Orleans, 1985-92; freelance paralegal Metairie, La., 1992—. Pres. Alliance for Good Govt., Jefferson Parish, La., 1982, Young Dems. La., 1975-77; mem. Jefferson Parish Dem. Exec. Com., 1983-87, 89-96, chmn., 1990-93, treas., 1994, vice chmn., 1995; mem. Dem. State Ctrl. Com., 1996—; chmn. Jefferson Dem. Alliance, 1997—. Mem. Nat. Fedn. Paralegal Assns. (primary rep. 1995-97, 2001—, secondary rep. 1998-2000), New Orleans Paralegal Assn. (treas. 1991-94), Gretna Hist. Soc. (parliamentarian 1998—). Roman Catholic. Avocation: jogging. Home: 1141 Papworth Ave Metairie LA 70005-2338

QUIGLEY, JOHN BERNARD, law educator; b. St. Louis, Oct. 1, 1940; s. John Bernard and Ruth Rosina (Schieber) Q. BA, Harvard U., 1962, MA, LLB, 1966. Bar: Ohio 1973, Mass. 1967, U.S. Dist. Ct. (so. dist.) Ohio 1976, U.S. Ct. Appeals (6th cir.) 1986, U.S. Supreme Ct. 1989. Research assoc. Harvard U. Law Sch., Cambridge, Mass., 1967-69; prof. law Ohio State U., Columbus, 1969—. Author: Basic Laws on the Structure of the Soviet State, 1969, The Soviet Foreign Trade Monopoly, 1974, Palestine and Israel: A Challenge to Justice, 1990, The Ruses for War: American Interventionism since World War II, 1992, Flight into the Maelstrom: Soviet Immigration to Israel and Middle East Peace, 1997, Genocide in Cambodia, 2000. Mem. Nat. Lawyers Guild (v.p. 1977-79), Am. Soc. Internat. Law, AAUP. Avocations: tennis, speed skating, violin. Office: Ohio State U Coll of Law Coll of Law 55 W 12th Ave Columbus OH 43210-1338

QUIGLEY, LEONARD VINCENT, lawyer; b. Kansas City, Mo., June 21, 1933; s. Joseph Vincent and Rosemary (Cannon) Q.; m. Lynn Mathis Pfohl, May 23, 1964; children: Leonard Matthew, Cannon Louise, Daniel Pfohl, Megan Mathis. A.B., Coll. Holy Cross, 1953; LL.B. magna cum laude, Harvard U., 1959; LL.M. in Internat. Law, NYU, 1962. Bar: N.Y. 1960. Assoc. Cravath, Swaine & Moore, N.Y.C., 1959-67; ptnr. Paul, Weiss, Rifkind, Wharton & Garrison, 1968—; gen. counsel Archaeol. Inst. Am., Boston. Served to lt. USN, 1953-56. Mem. ABA, Can. Bar Assn., N.Y. State Bar, Coun. Fgn. Rels., Assn. Bar City N.Y., Harvard Club (N.Y.C.), West Side Tennis Club (Forest Hills, N.Y.). General corporate, Oil, gas, and mineral, Private international. E-mail: lquigley@paulweiss.com

QUIGLEY, THOMAS J. lawyer; b. Mt. Carmel, Pa., July 22, 1923; s. James S. and Helen C. (Laughlin) Q.; m. Joan R. Reifke, Aug. 11, 1956; children: Thomas J., Jr., Joan E., James S. AB, Bucknell U., 1947; LLB, Yale U., 1950. Bar: Ohio, U.S. Dist. Ct. Ohio, U.S. Ct. Appeals (6th and D.C. cirs.). With Squire, Sanders & Dempsey, 1950— , adminstr. labor dept., 1971-80, mng. ptnr., Washington, 1980-85; nat. vice chmn., 1985-86; nat. chmn., 1986-90. Past pres., dir. exec. com. Nat. Symphony Orch., nat. trustee Musical Arts Assn. Cleve.; bd. dirs. Call for Action, Belgian Am. C. of C. 1st lt. USAAF, 1942-45. Decorated D.F.C., Air medal with oak leaf cluster, Belgium's Order of the Crown. Mem. ABA, Ohio Bar Assn., D.C. Bar Assn., Cleve. Bar Assn., Fed. City Coun., Yale Law Sch. Alumni. Assn. Roman Catholic. Clubs: Yale (N.Y.C.), Edgartown Yacht (Mass.), Chevy Chase, Metropolitan (Wash.). Labor. Office: Squire Sanders & Dempsey PO Box 407 1201 Pennsylvania Ave NW Washington DC 20004-2491 also: Key Tower Bldg Cleveland OH 44114

QUILLEN, CECIL DYER, JR. lawyer, consultant; b. Kingsport, Tenn., Jan. 21, 1937; s. Cecil D. and Mary Louise (Carter) Q.; m. Vicey Ann Childress, Apr. 1, 1961; children: Cecil D. III, Ann C. BS, Va. Poly. Inst., 1958; LLB, U. Va., 1962. Bar: Va. 1962, N.Y. 1963, Tenn. 1974. Atty. patent dept. Eastman Kodak Co., Rochester, N.Y., 1962-65; atty. patent sect. Tenn. Eastman Co. (divsn. Eastman Kodak), Kingsport, 1965-69, mgr. patent sect., 1969-72, mgr. licensing, 1972-74, sec. and asst. chief counsel, 1974-76, v.p., chief counsel, 1983-85; dir. patent litigation Eastman Kodak, 1976-82, dir. antitrust litigation, 1978-82, v.p., assoc. gen. counsel, 1986, sr. v.p., gen. counsel, dir., 1986-92; sr. adv. Putnam, Hayes, Bartlett and Hagler Bailly, Washington, 1992-99; sr. advisor Cornerstone Rsch., 2000—. Mem. ABA, Va. State Bar, Am. Intellectual Property Law Assn., Va. Poly. Inst. Com. of 100, Assn. Gen. Counsel. Antitrust, General civil litigation, Intellectual property. E-mail: cquillen@cornerstone.com

QUILLEN, CECIL DYER, III, lawyer; b. Rochester, N.Y., Aug. 15, 1963; s. Cecil Dyer, Jr. and Vicey Ann (Childress) Q.; m. Mary Stuart Humes, Oct. 20, 1990; children: Caroline, James C.D. AB magna cum laude, Harvard U., 1985; JD, U. Va., 1988. Bar: N.Y. 1989, D.C. 1991, U.S. Ct. Appeals (4th cir.) 1989. Law clk., Sr. Cir. Judge U.S. Ct. Appeals (4th cir.), Richmond, Va., 1988-89; assoc. Sullivan & Cromwell, N.Y.C., 1989-95, Linklaters, N.Y.C., 1995-96, ptnr., 1996—, ptnr. London office, 2000—. Spkr. various profl. confs. Notes editor Va. Law Rev., 1987-88. Mem. ABA, N.Y. State Bar Assn., Assn. Bar City of N.Y., Raven Soc., Order of Coif, Phi Beta Kappa. Banking, Private international, Securities. Office: Linklaters One Silk St London EC2Y 8HQ England

QUINA, MARION ALBERT, JR. lawyer; b. Mobile, Ala., Apr. 18, 1949; s. Marion Albert Sr. and Tallulah (Dunlap) Q.; children: Marion Albert III, Elliott Richardson; m. Jamie Mayhall Curtis, May 2, 1998. BS, U. Ala., 1971; JD, Samford U., 1974. Bar: Ala. 1974, U.S. Dist. Ct. (so. dist.) Ala. 1975, U.S. Ct. Appeals (5th cir.) 1977, U.S. Ct. Appeals (11th cir.) 1981. Assoc. Lyons, Pipes & Cook, Mobile, 1974-77, ptnr., 1978-87; shareholder Lyons, Pipes & Cook, P.C., 1988—. Past mem., bd. dirs. Mobile Touchdown Club, Presch. for the Sensory Impaired; mem. United Way, 1989—; mem. adv. bd. Cumberland Sch. of Law, Birmingham; sec., treas., vice chmn., chmn. Southeastern Admiralty Law Inst., Athens, Ga., 1996—. 1st lt. U.S. Army. Mem. ABA, Ala. Bar Assn., Mobile Bar Assn. (chmn. admiralty and maritime law com.), Maritime Law Assn. U.S. (assoc.), Ala. Wildlife Fedn. (past dir.), Mobile Area C. of C. (past vice chmn., gen. counsel), Kiwanis (past dir.), Mobile County Wildlife Assn., Mobile Propeller Club, Mobile Area C. of C. Diplomat Club, among others. Avocations: hunting, fishing. Admiralty, Contracts commercial, General corporate. Office: Lyons Pipes & Cook PC 2 N Royal St Mobile AL 36602-3896

QUINCE, PEGGY A. state supreme court justice; b. Norfolk, Va., Jan. 3, 1948; m. Fred L. Buckine; children: Peggy LaVerne, Laura LaVerne. BS in Zoology, Howard U., 1970; JD, Cath. U. of Am., 1975. Hearing officer Rental Accomodations Office, Washington; pvt. practice Norfolk, 1977-78, Bradenton, Fla., 1978-80; asst. atty. gen. criminal divsn. Atty. Gen.'s Office, 1980; apptd. 2d Dist. Ct. of Appeals, 1994-98; state supreme ct. justice Fla. Supreme Ct., 1998—. Lectr. in field. Asst. Sunday sch. tchr., mem. #3 usher bd. New Hope Missionary Bapt. Ch.; active Jack and Jill of Am., Inc., Urban League, NAACP, Tampa Orgn. for Black Affairs. Recipient award Cath.'s Neighborhood Legal Svcs. Clinic. Mem. Nat. Bar Assn., Fla. Bar, Va. State Bar, George Edgecomb Bar Assn., Hillsborough County Bar Assn., Fla. Assn. Women Lawyers, Hillsborough Assn. Women Lawyers, Tampa Bay Inn of Ct., Alpha Kappa Alpha. Office: 500 S Duval St Tallahassee FL 32399-6556 E-mail: supremecourt@mail.flcourts.org*

QUINLAN, GUY CHRISTIAN, lawyer; b. Cambridge, Mass., Oct. 28, 1939; s. Guy Thomas and Yvonne (Carver) Q.; m. Mary-Ella Holst, Apr. 18, 1987. AB, Harvard Coll., 1960; JD, Harvard U., 1963. Bar: N.Y. 1964, U.S. Dist. Ct. (so. and ea. dists.) N.Y. 1965, U.S. Ct. Appeals (2d cir.) 1967, U.S. Supreme Ct. 1969, U.S. Ct. Appeals (8th cir.) 1973, (10th cir.) 1977, (4th cir.) 1993, (11th cir.) 1995, U.S. Tax Ct. 1977. Assoc. Clifford, Chance, Rogers & Wells, N.Y.C., 1963-70, ptnr., 1970-80, of counsel, 1991—. Past pres. Unitarian Universalist Svc. Com., Yorkville Common Pantry; Unitarian Universalist Dist. of Met. N.Y.; mem. adv. council on ministerial studies Harvard U. Div. Sch.; chair nuclear disarmament task force All Souls Unitarian Ch. Mem.: ABA, N.Y. State Bar Assn., Fed. Bar Coun., Am. Assn. Internat. Commn. Jurists, Amnesty Internat. Legal Network, Lawyers Com. on Nuclear Policy, Harvard Club. Democrat. Antitrust, Environmental, Insurance. Office: Clifford Chance Rogers & Wells 200 Park Ave Fl 8E New York NY 10166-0899

QUINLAN, WILLIAM JOSEPH, JR. lawyer; b. Chgo., Nov. 4, 1939; s. William Joseph and Catherine E. (Bowman) Q.; m. Susan L. Collins, June 16, 1962; children— Kathleen, Michael, Julie, Jennifer. A.B. cum laude, Loyola, U., Chgo., 1961, J.D. cum laude, 1966. Bar: Ill. 1966, U.S. Dist. Ct. (no. dist.) Ill. 1966, U.S. Tax Ct. 1968, U.S. Ct. Appeals (7th cir.) 1972. Assoc. Wilson & McIlvaine, Chgo., 1966-73; ptnr. McDermott, Will & Emery, Chgo., 1973-78, sr. ptnr., 1978— ; dir. Wickman Machine Tools, Elk Grove Village, Ill., 1978-81, Eiger Machinery, Inc., Bensenville, Ill., 1981— . Contbr. articles to profl. publs. Mem. St. Athanasius Bd. Edn., Evanston, Ill., 1976, pres., 1978. Mem. ABA (com. on fed. regulation of securities), Chgo. Bar Assn. (chmn. subcom. on securities law), Ill. Bar Assn., Blue Key, Phi Alpha Delta. Roman Catholic. Clubs: Union League, Wilmette Harbor Assn. General corporate, Municipal (including bonds), Securities. Office: McDermott Will & Emery 227 W Monroe St Ste 3100 Chicago IL 60606-5096

QUINN, ANDREW PETER, JR. lawyer, insurance executive retired; b. Providence, Oct. 22, 1923; s. Andrew Peter and Margaret (Canning) Q.; m. Sara G. Bullard, May 30, 1952; 1 child, Emily H. AB, Brown U., 1945; LLB, Yale U., 1950. Bar: R.I. 1949, Mass. 1960, U.S. Tax Ct. 1960, U.S. Supreme Ct. 1986. Pvt. practice, Providence, 1950-59, Springfield, Mass., 1959-88; ptnr. Letts & Quinn, 1950-59; with Mass. Mut. Life Ins. Co., 1959-88, exec. v.p., gen. counsel, 1971-88; of counsel Day, Berry & Howard, Hartford, Conn. and Boston, 1988-99; retired, 1999. Pres., trustee MML Series Investment Fund, 1971-88; bd. dirs. Sargasso Mut. Ins. Co., Ltd., 1986-95, pres., 1986-89, chmn. bd. dirs., 1989-93. Trustee, MacDuffie Sch., 1974-87, chmn. bd., 1978-85; trustee Baystate Med., Springfield, 1977-80. Lt. (j.g.) USNR, 1944-46. Mem. ABA (co-chmn. nat. conf. lawyers and life ins. cos. 1973), Assn. Life Ins. Counsel (pres. 1983-84), Am. Coun. Life Ins. (chmn. legal sect. 1971), Life Ins. Assn. Mass. (chmn. exec. com. 1975-77), Brown U. Alumni Assn. (bd. dirs. 1969-72), N.Y. Yacht club, Longmeadow Country Club, Dunes Club, Hillsboro Club, Conn. Valley Brown U. (past pres.). General corporate, Insurance. Home: 306 Ellington Rd Longmeadow MA 01106-1559

QUINN, CHARLES NORMAN, lawyer; b. Abington, Pa., Nov. 5, 1943; s. Charles Ransom and Lela Josephine (Cooper) Q.; m. Mary Bernadette Bradley, Oct. 4, 1975 (div. Oct. 1976); m. Vicki Lou Erickson, Nov. 11, 1978; stepchildren: Scott L., Kymbra Lynn Kaznay. BSME, Purdue U., 1965; ME, Pa. State U., 1970; JD, Villanova (Pa.) U., 1973. Bar: U.S. Dist. Ct. (ea. dist) Pa. 1974, U.S. Ct. Appeals (fed. cir.) 1984. Systems engr. GE Co., King of Prussia, Pa., 1965-70; atty. Paul and Paul, Phila., 1973-75, Penwalt Corp., Phila., 1976-80, A.R. Miller, P.C., Phila., 1981-85; ptnr. Miller & Quinn, 1986-91; atty., of counsel Dann Dorfman Herrell & Skill, 1992-2000; ptnr. Saul Ewing LLP and predecessor, 2000—. Contbr. articles to profl. jours. Mem. ABA, Phila. Patent Law Assn. (treas. 1980-83, gov. 1987-89), Phila. Intellectual Property Law Assn., Am. Intellectual Property Law Assn., Phila. Bar Assn. Avocations: golf, classical music, personal computers. Patent, Trademark and copyright. Home: 419 Bowen Dr Exton PA 19341 Office: Saul Ewing LLP 15th and Market Sts Philadelphia PA 19102 E-mail: cquinn@saul.com

QUINN, FRANCIS XAVIER, arbitrator, mediator, author, lecturer; b. Dunmore, Pa., June 9, 1932; s. Frank T. and Alice B. (Maher) Q.; m. Marlene Stoker Quinn; children: Kimberly, Catherine, Cameron, Lindsay, Megan, Savannah, Jackson Blair. BA, Fordham U., 1956, MA, 1958; STB, Woodstock Coll., 1964; MS in Indsl. Rels., Loyola U., Chgo., 1966; PhD in Indsl. Rels., Calif. Western U., 1966. Assoc. dir. Inst. Indsl. Rels. St. Joseph's Coll., Phila., 1966-68; Manpower fellow Temple U., 1969-74, asst. to dean Sch. Bus. Adminstrn., 1972-78. Arbitrator Fed. Mediation and Conciliation Svc., Nat. Mediation Bd., Am. Arbitration Assn., Nat. Assn. Railroad Referees, Dem. Nat. Steering Com.; ; apptd. to Rail Emergency Bd., 1975, to Fgn. Service Grievance Bd., 1976, 78, 80. Author: The Ethical Aftermath of Automation, 1963, Ethics and Advertising, 1965, Population Ethics, 1968, The Evolving Role of Women in the World of Work, 1969, Developing Community Responsibility, 1970; editor: The Ethical Aftermath Series; contbr. articles to profl. jours. Chmn. Hall of Fame com. Internat. Police Assn., 1990—, Tulsa City-County Mayor's Task Force to Combat Homelessness, 1991-92; mem. exec. bd. Tulsa Met. Ministries, 1990-92, Labor-Religion Coun. Okla., 1990—. Named Tchr. of Yr. Freedom Found., 1959; recipient Human Rels. award City of Phila.; inducted into Hall of Fame, Internat. Police Assn., 2000. Mem. Nat. Acad. Arbitrators (v.p. 1999-2001), Indsl. Rels. Rsch. Assn., Assn. for Social Econs., Soc. for Dispute Resolution, Am. Arbitration Assn. (arbitrator), Nat. Assn. Railroad Refs. (pres. 2000-01, arbitrator), Internat. Soc. Labor Law and Social Security, Internat. Ombudsman Inst. Democrat. Home: 4213 Blackhaw Ave Fort Worth TX 76109-1618 E-mail: FXQ@prodigy.com

QUINN, LINDA CATHERINE, lawyer; b. Rockville Centre, N.Y., 1948; BA, Mt. Holyoke Coll., 1969; JD, Georgetown U., 1972. Bar: N.Y. 1973. Law clk. Hon. J. Joseph Smith U.S. Ct. Appeals (2d cir.), 1972-73; assoc. Sullivan & Cromwell, 1973-80; atty. fellow SEC, 1980-82, assoc. dir. divsn. corp. fin., 1982-84, exec. asst. to chmn., 1984-86, dir. corp. fin. divsn., 1986-96; ptnr. Shearman & Sterling, N.Y.C., 1996—. Named one of 50 Top Women Lawyers Nat. Law Jour., 1998. Mem. ABA. Banking, General corporate, Securities. Office: Shearman & Sterling 599 Lexington Ave Fl 16 New York NY 10022-6069 E-mail: lquinn@shearman.com

QUINN, R. JOSEPH, former judge; m. Carole Quinn. BA, St. John's U.; JD, Hamline U. Minn. State rep., 1983-90; judge Minn. Supreme Ct., 1991-99; ret., 1999. Office: Anoka County Court 325 E Main St Anoka MN 55303-2483

QUINN, YVONNE SUSAN, lawyer; b. Spring Valley, Ill., May 13, 1951; d. Robert Leslie and Shirley Eilene (Morse) Q.; m. Ronald S. Rolfe, Sept. 1, 1979. BA, U. Ill., 1973; JD, U. Mich., 1976, MA in Econs., 1977. Bar: N.Y. 1978, U.S. Dist. Ct. (ea. and so. dists.) N.Y. 1978, U.S. Ct. Appeals (3d, 5th, 9th, 10th and D.C. cirs.) 1982, U.S. Ct. Appeals (2d cir.) 1992, U.S. Ct. Appeals (4th cir.) 1994, U.S. Supreme Ct. 1982. Assoc. Cravath, Swaine & Moore, N.Y.C., 1977-80, Sullivan & Cromwell, N.Y.C., 1980-84, ptnr., 1984—. Mem. ABA, Assn. of Bar of City of N.Y., India House Club. Antitrust, Federal civil litigation, State civil litigation. Office: Sullivan & Cromwell 125 Broad St New York NY 10004-2489

QUINT, ARNOLD HARRIS, lawyer; b. Boston, Jan. 3, 1942; s. Milton and Esther (Kirshen) Q.; m. Susan Arenson, July 23, 1967; children: Edward, Michael. AB, Haverford (Pa.) Coll., 1963; LLB, Yale U., 1966. Bar: D.C. 1967. Supervisory atty. Power Commn., Washington, 1967-70; assoc. Hunton & Williams, 1970-74, ptnr., 1974—. Mem. ABA, Energy Bar Assn. (com. chmn. 1979-83, bd. dirs. 1989-92). Administrative and regulatory, FERC practice. Office: Hunton & Williams 1900 K St NW Washington DC 20006-1110 E-mail: aquint@hunton.com

QUINTIERE, GARY GANDOLFO, lawyer; b. Passaic, N.J., Nov. 26, 1944; s. Benjamin and Sadie (Riotto) Q.; m. Judy Rosenthal, Aug. 16, 1966; children: Karen, Geoffrey. AB in Govt., Lafayette Coll., 1966; JD, George Washington U., 1969. Bar: Va. 1969, D.C. 1970. Law clk. to Judge Philip Nichols, Jr. U.S. Ct. Appeals (Fed. cir.), Washington, 1969-70; from assoc. to ptnr. Miller & Chevalier, 1970-85; ptnr. Morgan, Lewis & Bockius, 1985—. Mem. ABA, D.C. Bar Assn., Va. Bar Assn., Am. Coll. Employee Benefits Counsel. Avocations: tennis, skiing, golf. Pension, profit-sharing, and employee benefits. Home: 14 Mercy Ct Potomac MD 20854-4540 Office: Morgan Lewis & Bockius 1800 M St NW Washington DC 20036-5802

QUIRANTES, ALBERT M. lawyer; b. Cuba, Jan. 25, 1963; came to U.S., 1966; s. Alberto adn Haydee (Mendez) Q. B in Bus., U. Miami, Fla., 1984; JD, U. Fla., 1987. Bar: Fla. 1988, U.S. Dist. Ct. (so. dist.) Fla. 1990, U.S. Dist. Ct. (mid. dist.) Fla. 1990, U.S. Ct. Appeals (11th cir.) 1990, U.S. Supreme Ct. 1991, U.S. Dist. Ct. Ariz. 1991. Pub. defender Ct. 8th cir., Gainsville, Fla., 1988-89; pvt. practice Miami, Fla., 1989—; sr. ptnr. Ticket Law Ctr., P.A., Miami, Fla., 1990—. Mem. Fla. Traffic Ct. Rules Com., Tallahassee, 1991—. Mem. Fla. Assn. Criminal Def. Attys., Dade Bar (cts. com. 1992—, criminal cts. com. 1992—), Latin C. of C., Jaycees. Administrative and regulatory, Criminal, Health. Home and Office: 1800 NW 7th St Miami FL 33125-3504 E-mail: lawyer@ticketlawyer.com

QUIROZ, LOURDES GABRIELA, lawyer; b. Mexico City, Mex., Feb. 11, 1969; d. Florencio Quiroz and Lourdes Luna; m. Victor Manuel Martinez, May 8, 1999. Law degree, 1993; M, Escurla Libre de Derecho, Mex., 1999. Asst. Notary Pub. 161, Mex., 1991-94; atty. Notary Pub. 102, Mex., 1993-94; legal dir. Tycoon Enterprises, Mex., 1994-95; assoc. Gaxiola, Robina & Assocs., Mex., 1995—. Avocations: antique collecting, travel. Contracts commercial, General corporate, Intellectual property. Office: Gaxiola Robina & Assocs Bosque de Ciruelos 140-505 Mexico 11700 Mexico

QUIST, GORDON JAY, federal judge; b. Grand Rapids, Mich., Nov. 12, 1937; s. George J. and Ida F. (Hoekstra) Q.; m. Jane Capito, Mar. 10, 1962; children: Scot D., George J., Susan E., Martha J., Peter K. BA, Mich. State U., 1959; JD with honors, George Washington U., 1962. Bar: D.C. 1962, Ill. 1964, U.S. Dist. Ct. (no. dist.) Ill. 1964, U.S. Supreme Ct. 1965, Mich. 1967, U.S. Dist. Ct. (we. dist.) Mich. 1967, U.S. Ct. Appeals (6th cir.)

1967. Assoc. Hollabaugh & Jacobs, Washington, 1962-64, Sonnenschein, Levinson, Carlin, Nath & Rosenthal, Chgo., 1964-66, Miller, Johnson, Snell & Cummiskey, Grand Rapids, 1967-72, ptnr., 1972-92, mng. ptnr., 1986-92; judge U.S. Dist. Ct. (we. dist.) Mich., 1992—. Bd. dirs. Wedgewood Acres-Ch. Youth Home, 1968-74, Mary Free Bed Hosp., 1979-88, Christian Ref. Publs., 1968-78, 82-88, Opera Grand Rapids, 1986-92, Mary Free Bed Brace Shop, 1988-92, Better Bus. Bur., 1972-80, Calvin Theol. Sem., 1992-93; bd. dirs. Indian Trails Camp, 1970-78, 82-88, pres., 1978, 88. Recipient Disting. Alumnus award George Washington U. Law Sch. Mem. Am. Indicature Soc., Mich. State Bar Found., Univ. Club Grand Rapids, Order of Coif, Am. Inns Ct. Avocations: reading, travel. Office: 482 Ford Fed Courthouse 110 Michigan St NW Grand Rapids MI 49503-2313

RAAB, IRA JERRY, lawyer, judge; b. N.Y.C., June 20, 1935; s. Benjamin and Fannie (Kirschner) R.; m. Regina Schneider, June 4, 1957 (div. 1978); children: Michael, Shelley; m. Katie Rachel McKeever, June 30, 1979 (div. 1991); children: Julie, Jennifer, Joseph; m. Gloria Silverman, Nov. 7, 1996; children: Jill, Todd, John. BBA, CCNY, 1955; JD, Bklyn. Law Sch., 1957; MPA, NYU, 1959, postgrad., 1961; MS in Pub. Adminstrn., L.I. U., 1961; MBA, Adelphi U., 1990. Bar: N.Y. 1958, U.S. Dist. Ct. (so. and ea. dists.) N.Y. 1960, U.S. Supreme Ct. 1967, U.S. Tax Ct. 1976, U.S. Ct. Appeals (2d cir.) 1977. Pvt. practice, Woodmere, N.Y., 1958-96; agt. Westchester County Soc. Prevention of Cruelty to Children, White Plains, 1958; counsel Dept. Correction City of N.Y., 1959, trial commr. Dept. Correction, 1976, asst. corp. counsel Tort divsn., 1963-70; staff counsel SBA, N.Y.C., 1961-63; counsel Investigation Com. on Willowbrook State Sch., Boro Hall, S.I., N.Y., 1970; gen. counsel Richmond County Soc. Prevention of Cruelty to Children, Boro Hall, 1970-81; pro bono counsel N.Y.C. Patrolmen's Benevolent Assn., 1974-81; rep. to UN Internat. Criminal Ct. , 1977-78; arbitrator Small Claims Ct. Day Cts., N.Y.C., 1970-96; arbitrator L.I. Better Bus. Bur., 1976-93, Nassau County Dist. Ct., 1978-93, arbitrator Small Claims Ct., 1978-96; spl. master N.Y. County Supreme Ct., 1977-96; judge N.Y.C. Parking Violations Bur., 1991-93. Small claims arbitrator N.Y.C. Civil Ct., 1970-96; arbitrator U.S. Dist. Ct. (ea. dist.) N.Y., 1986-96; lectr. comty. and ednl. orgns.; instr. paralegal course Lawrence Sch. Dist., N.Y., 1982-84; law prof. Briarcliff Coll., Bethpage, N.Y., 1997. Chmn. Businessmen's Luncheon Club, Wall St. Synagogue, 1968-79; exec. sec. Cmty. Mediation Ctr., Suffolk County, 1978-80, exec. v.p., 1980-81; vice chmn. Woodmere Inc., Com., 1980-81; mem. adv. bd. Nassau Expressway Com., 1979-80; bd. dirs. Woodmere Mchts. Assn., 1979-80, v.p., 1979-83, chmn., 1984-93; candidate for dist. ct. judge Nassau County, 1987, 88, 89, 91, 93, 94, 2000; candidate for supreme ct. justice Nassau and Suffolk Counties, 1995, 98; elected judge Nassau County Dist. Ct., 1997-99; candidate for county ct., Nassau County, 1997; elected presiding judge dist. ct., 1999-2000; sec. Congregation Aish Kodesh, Woodmere, 1992—; elected justice Nassau County Supreme Ct., 2000. Recipient Consumer Protection award FTC, 1974, 76, 79, Recognition award Pres. Ronald Reagan, 1986, Man of Yr. award L.I. Coun. of Chambers, 1987, N.Y. State Ct. Reporters Assn., 1999. Mem. ABA (chmn. cts. and comty. com. 1988-93, exec. com. jud. adminstrn. divsn. lawyers conf. 1989-95), Am. Judges Assn. (rep. to UN 2000—, bd. govs. 1973-78, 82-88, 89-96, 97—, nat. treas. 1978-82, chmn. civil ct. ops. com. 1975-76, chmn. ednl. film com. 1974-77, editl. bd. Ct. Rev. mag. 1975-79, 82-86, chmn. spkrs. bur. com. 1976-77, chmn. legis. com. 1983-95, chmn. resolutions com. 1995-98, 2000—, chmn. jud. concerns com. 1997-99, historian 1988—, William H. Burnett award 1983), Am. Judges Found. (pres. 1977-79, chmn. bd. trustees 1979-83, treas. 1974-75, 76-77, trustee 1983-97, 2000—), Assn. Arbitrators of Civil Ct. City of N.Y. (past pres.), N.Y. State Bar Assn. (sec. dist., city, town and villages cts. com.), Nassau County Bar Assn. (criminal cts. com., matrimonial and family ct. com., ct. com., ethics com., Supreme Ct. com.), Profl. Group Legal Svc. Assn. (past pres.), Internat. Assn. Jewish Lawyers and Jurists (com. to draft Internat. Bill of Rights to Privacy 1982, coun. 1981-95, bd. govs. 1984-95), adv. bd. comty. dispute ctr. 1979-81), K.P. (past chancellor comdr.). Democrat. State civil litigation, General practice, Personal injury. Home: 375 Westwood Rd Woodmere NY 11598-1624 Office: Supreme Court 100 Supreme Ct Dr Mineola NY 11501 Fax: 516-571-2555. E-mail: iraab@courts.state.ny.us

RAAB, SHELDON, lawyer, Bklyn. Nov. 30, 1937; s. Morris and Eva (Shereshevsky) R.; m. Judith Deutsch, Dec. 15, 1963; children: Michael Kenneth, Elisabeth Louise, Andrew John. AB, Columbia U., 1958; LLB cum laude, Harvard U., 1961. Bar: N.Y. 1961, U.S. Ct. Appeals (2d cir.) 1963, U.S. Dist. Ct. (so. and ea. dists.) 1967. Dep. asst. atty. gen. State of N.Y., 1961-63, asst. atty gen., 1963-64; assoc. Fried, Frank, Harris, Shriver & Jacobson and predecessor firm, N.Y.C., 1964-69, ptnr., 1970-81, inc. ptnr., 1981—. Mem. exec. com. lawyers' div. United Jewish Appeal, 1982—. Mem. ABA, Am. Law Inst., N.Y. State Bar Assn. (trial lawyers sect. 1968—), Assn. of Bar of City of N.Y. (adminstrv. law com. 1968-71, spl. com. electric power and environment 1971-73, chmn. energy com. 1974-79, fed. cts. com. 1981-84, state superior cts. juris. com. 1985-88). Democrat. Appellate, General civil litigation, Securities. Office: Fried Frank Harris Shriver & Jacobson 1 New York Plz Fl 22 New York NY 10004-1980

RAAS, DANIEL ALAN, lawyer; b. Portland, Oreg., July 6, 1947; s. Alan Charles and Mitzi (Cooper) R.; m. Deborah Ann Becker, Aug. 5, 1973; children: Amanda Beth, Adam Louis. BA, Reed Coll., 1969; JD, NYU, 1972. Bar: Wash. 1973, Calif. 1973, U.S. Dist. Ct. (we. dist.) Wash. 1973, U.S. Ct. Appeals (9th cir.) 1975, U.S. Supreme Ct. 1977, U.S. Tax Ct. 1983, U.S. Ct. Claims 1984. Atty. Seattle Legal Svcs, VISTA, 1972-73; reservation atty. Quinault Indian Nation, Taholah, Wash., 1973-76, Lummi Indian Nation, Bellingham, 1976-97, spl. counsel, 1997—; mem. Raas, Johnsen & Stuen, P.S., 1982—. Cons. Falmouth Inst., Fairfax, Va., 1992-2000, Nat. Am. Ind. Ct. Judges Assn., McLean, Va., 1976-80. Rules chmn. Whatcom County Dem. Conv., Bellingham, 1988, 92, 94, 96; bd. dirs. Congregation Beth Israel, Bellingham, 1985-2000, pres., 1990-92; mem. adv. com. legal asst. program Bellingham Vocat. Tech. Inst., 1985-91; trustee Whatcom County Law Libr., 1978—; pres. Vol. Lawyer Program, 1990-93, bd. dirs., 1988-94; pres. Cliffside Cmty. Assn., 1978-80, bd. dirs., 1977-89; bd. dirs. Friends Maritime Heritage Ctr., 1983-86, Samish Camp Fire Coun., 1988-94, pres. 1991-94, v.p., 1989-91, regional v.p. Union Am. Hebrew Congregations, 1986-93, nat. trustee, 1995—, exec. com., 1995-99, sec. Pacific N.W. region, 1993-95, pres., 1995-99. John Ben Snow scholar, NYU, 1969-70, Root-Tilden scholar, NYU, 1970-72. Mem. Wash. State Bar Assn. (trustee Ind. law sect. 1989-95, Pro Bono award 1991), Whatcom County Bar Assn. (v.p. 1981, pres. 1982, Pro Bono award 1991), Grays Harbor Bar Assn. (v.p. 1976). General civil litigation, Consumer commercial, Native American. Home: 1929 Lake Crest Dr Bellingham WA 98226-4510 Office: Raas Johnsen & Stuen PS 1503 E St Bellingham WA 98225-3007

RABB, BRUCE, lawyer; b. Cambridge, Mass., Oct. 4, 1941; s. Maxwell M. and Ruth (Cryden) R.; m. Harriet Rachel Schaffer, Jan. 4, 1970; children: Alexander Charles, Katherine Anne. AB, Harvard U., 1962; Cert. d'Etudes Politiques, Institut d'Etudes Politiques, Paris, 1963; LLB, Columbia U., 1966. Bar: N.Y. 1966. Law clk. to judge U.S. Ct. Appeals (5th cir.), 1966-67; assoc. Stroock & Stroock & Lavan, N.Y.C., 1967-68, 71-75, ptnr., 1976-91, Kramer, Levin, Naftalis & Frankel, N.Y.C., 1991—. Staff asst. to Pres. U.S., 1969-70; vice-chmn. Lawyers Com. Human Rights, 1977-95, nat. coun., 1996—; bd. dirs. Chiquita Italia, SpA; supr. bd. dirs. Agora-Gazeta, sp.zo.o., 1993-98, Agora-Druk, sp.zo.o., 1995-98; pub. mem. Adminstrv. Conf. U.S., 1982-86, 89-92, spl. counsel, 1986-88. Sec. Lehrman Inst., 1978-88; bd. dirs. Citizens Union of N.Y., 1981-87, 88-94, 95—, Am. Friends of Alliance Israelite Universelle, 1987—, Human Rights Watch, 1987—, Welfare Law Ctr., 1997—; mem. Human Rights Watch/Ams., 1982—, Human Rights Watch/Helsinki, 1985-97, Fund for Free Expression, 1987-97, Human Rights Watch/Middle East and No. Africa, 1989—, vice chmn., 1990—; mem. internat. adv. com. Internat. Parliamentary Group for Human Rights in the Soviet Union, 1984-88, Prin. of the Coun. for Excellence in Govt., 1990—; adv. coun. Doctors of the World USA, 1996—, FilmAid Internat., 2000—. Mem. ABA (adv. panel Internat. Human Rights Trial Observer project), Am. Law Inst., Assn. of Bar of City of N.Y. (fed. legis., internat. law chair 1992-95, internat. human rights, civil rights, legal edn. and admission to bar, internat. trade coms., coun. on fgn. affairs), Harvard Club N.Y.C., Met. Club of Washington. General corporate, Finance, Private international. Office: Kramer Levin et al 919 3rd Ave New York NY 10022-3902

RABB, HARRIET SCHAFFER, government official, lawyer, educator; b. Houston, Sept. 12, 1941; d. Samuel S. and Helen G. Schaffer; m. Bruce Rabb, Jan. 4, 1970; children: Alexander, Katherine. BA in Govt., Barnard Coll., 1963; JD, Columbia U., 1966. Bar: N.Y. 1966, U.S. Supreme Ct. 1969, D.C. 1970. Instr. seminar on constl. litigation Rutgers Law Sch., 1966-67; staff atty. Center for Constl. Rights, 1966-69; spl. counsel to commr. consumer affairs N.Y.C. Dept. Consumer Affairs, 1969-70; sr. staff atty. Stern Community Law Firm, Washington, 1970-71; asst. dean urban affairs Law Sch., Columbia U., N.Y.C., 1971-84, prof. law, dir. clin. edn., 1984-99, George M. Jaffen prof. law and social responsibility, 1991-99, vice dean, 1992-93; gen. counsel Dept. Health and Human Svcs., Washington, 1993—. Mem. faculty employment and tng. policy Harvard Summer Inst., Cambridge, Mass., 1975-79 Author: (with Agid, Cooper and Rubin) Fair Employment Litigation Manual, 1975, (with Cooper and Rubin) Fair Employment Litigation, 1975. Bd. dirs. Ford Found., 1977-89, N.Y. Civil Liberties Union, 1972-83, Lawyers Com. for Civil Rights Under Law, 1978-86, Legal Def. Fund NAACP, 1978-93, Mex. Am. Legal Def. and Edn. Fund, 1986-90, Legal Aid Soc., 1990-93; mem. exec. com. Human Rights Watch, 1991-93; trustee Trinity Episcopal Sch. Corp., 1991-93. Office: Dept Health and Human Svcs 200 Independence Ave SW Rm 722A Washington DC 20201-0004

RABBITT, DANIEL THOMAS, JR. lawyer; b. St. Louis, Sept. 19, 1940; s. Daniel Thomas and Charlotte Ann (Carpenter) R.; m. Susan Lee Scherger, July 26, 1969. BA in Commerce, St. Louis U., 1962, JD cum laude, 1964. Bar: Mo. 1964, U.S. Supreme Ct. 1970. Assoc. Moser, Marsalek, Carpenter, Cleary, Jaeckel, Keaney & Brown and predecessor, St. Louis, 1964-68; ptnr. Moser, Marsalek, Carpenter, Cleary, Jaeckel, Keaney & Brown, 1969-81, Brown, James & Rabbitt, P.C., St. Louis, 1981-91, Rabbitt, Pitzer & Snodgrass, P.C., St. Louis, 1991—. Recipient Lon Hocker Meml. Trial Atty. award Mo. Bar Found., 1975. Fellow: Am. Coll. Trial Lawyers; mem.: ABA (chmn. young lawyers sect. 1973—74, product liability adv. coun.), Mo. Bar Assn., Internat. Assn. Def. Counsel (product liability adv. coun.), Bar Assn. Met. St. Louis, Mo. Athletic Club (gov. 1978—81, v.p. 1980—81). Federal civil litigation, State civil litigation, Product liability. Office: 800 Market St Ste 2300 Saint Louis MO 63101-2506 E-mail: rabbitt@rabbitt.law.com

RABECS, ROBERT NICHOLAS, lawyer; b. Scranton, Pa., Mar. 19, 1964; s. Nicholas and Anne Marie (Stull) R. BA summa cum laude, U. Scranton, 1986; JD cum laude, Georgetown U., 1990. Bar: Pa. 1990, D.C. 1992. Assoc. Reed Smith Shaw & McClay, Washington, 1990-94, Hogan & Hartson, Washington, 1994—. Columnist Managed Healthcare News, Belle Meade, N.J., 1994-98. Fulbright scholar, 1986-87; NEH undergrad. fellow, 1985. Mem. ABA, Am. Health Lawyers Assn., Pa. Bar Assn. (health law com.), D.C. Bar Assn. (health law sect.), Alpha Sigma Nu. Roman Catholic. Health. Home: 3401 38th St NW Apt 914 Washington DC 20016-3045 Office: Hogan & Hartson 555 13th St NW Washington DC 20004-1161 E-mail: rnrabecs@hhlaw.com

RABIN, JACK, lawyer; b. Aug. 19, 1930; s. Leo and Bertha Rabin; m. Roberta Edith Libson, Oct. 25, 1953; children: Keith Warren, Michael Jay, Adam Douglas. Student, Bklyn. Coll., 1948-50; LLB, Bklyn. Law Sch., 1953. Bar: N.Y. 1957, U.S. Tax Ct. 1960, U.S. Ct. Claims 1964, U.S. Supreme Ct. 1964, U.S. Ct. Appeals (2d cir.) 1968. Ptnr. Hoffberg, Rabin & Engler and predecessor firms, N.Y.C., 1968-82, Javits, Hinckley, Rabin & Engler, N.Y.C., 1982-84, Phillips, Nizer, Benjamin, Krim & Ballon, N.Y.C., 1984-94, counsel, 1994—. Arbitrator gen. comml. and constrn. panel Am. Arbitration Assn., 1968—; instr. Real Estate Inst., NYU, 1976-78; ct. apptd. mediator U.S. Dist. Ct. (so. dist.), N.Y., 1994—, N.Y. Supreme Ct., N.Y. County, 1999. Assoc. editor Bklyn. Law Rev., 1952, editor-in-chief, 1953, also author law rev. note. 1st lt. JAGC, U.S. Army, 1954-57, col. res., ret., 1983. Mem. N.Y. State Bar Assn., Res. Officers Assn. U.S. (pres. Rockland County chpt. 1967-68), B'nai B'rith (pres. New City, N.Y. 1965-66). Jewish. State civil litigation, General corporate, Real property. Home: Box 233 Goshen CT 06756-0233 Office: 10 W 66th St Ste 8G New York NY 10023 E-mail: sutleg@earthlink.net

RABINOVITZ, JOEL, lawyer, educator; b. 1939. A.B., Cornell U., 1960; LL.B., Harvard U., 1963. Bar: N.Y. 1963, Calif. 1981. Asst. prof. U. Fla., Gainesville, 1966-68; vis. assoc. prof. UCLA, 1968-69, acting prof., 1969-72, prof., 1972-79; vis. prof., NYU, 1976; dep. Internat. Tax Counsel, Dept. Treasury, 1980-81; ptnr. with Irell & Manella, L.A., 1981—. E-mail: jrabinovitz@irell.com. Office: Irell & Manella 1800 Avenue Of The Stars Los Angeles CA 90067-4212

RABINOWITZ, DANIEL LAWRENCE, lawyer; b. N.Y.C., Sept. 23, 1950; s. Bernard and Ann Hoch (Kubie) R.; m. Ann F. Thomas, Aug. 18, 1974. AB, Harvard U., 1972; JD, Yale U., 1975. Bar: N.Y. 1976, N.J. 1979, U.S. Supreme Ct., U.S. Ct. Appeals (2d and 3d cirs.), U.S. Dist. Ct. N.J., U.S. Dist. Ct. (so. and ea. dists.) N.Y., U.S. Tax Ct. Law clk. to Judge Herbert J. Stern, U.S. Dist. Ct. N.J., Newark, 1975-77; assoc. Nickerson, Kramer, Lowenstein, Nessen, Kamin & Soll, N.Y.C., 1977-78; asst. U.S. atty. Dist. of N.J., Newark, 1978-81; ptnr. McCarter & English, Newark, 1981—; vis. lectr. Yale Law Sch., 1985-86, 1988—. Mem. N.J. Bar Assn., Assn. Bar City of N.Y., Assn. Fed. Bar of N.J., Essex County Bar Assn., Hudson County Bar Assn. Clubs: Harvard of N.J. (exec. com., schs. com. 1981—); Essex (Newark); Harvard (N.Y.C.). Environmental. Office: 599 Lexington Ave New York NY 10022-6030

RABKIN, PEGGY ANN, retired lawyer; b. Buffalo, Apr. 13, 1945; d. Anthony J. and Margaret G. (Catuzzi) Marano; m. Samuel S. Rabkin, June 29, 1969. BA, SUNY, Buffalo, 1967, MEd, 1970, MA, 1972, JD, PhD, 1975. Tchr. Buffalo Pub. Schs., 1967-69; grad. teaching asst. SUNY, Buffalo, 1969-72; case analyst U.S. Equal Employment Opportunity Com., 1974; dir. affirmative action U. Louisville, 1975-78, adj. prof. of law, 1976-77; atty. office for civil rights HEW, N.Y.C., 1978; sr. atty. for labor and employment Am. Home Products Corp., 1978-86, sr. atty., 1986—. Author: Fathers to Daughters, 1980; editor: Buffalo Law Rev., 1974-75; contbr. articles to profl. jours. Commr. Louisville & Jefferson Co. Human Relations Com., Louisville, 1977-78. Recipient Christopher Baldy fellow, SUNY at Buffalo Law Sch., 1974-75, Regents Coll. Scholarship N.Y. State Bd. of Regents, 1963-67. Mem. ABA, Assn. of Bar of City of N.Y., Am. Corp. Counsel Assn., Soc. of Human Resources Mgmt., U.S. C. of C. (labor com. 1991—). Avocations: skiing, reading, cooking, and nutrition. Civil rights, Labor.

RABY, KENNETH ALAN, lawyer, retired army officer; b. Dec. 29, 1935; s. Carl George and Helen Josette (Milne) R.; m. Shirley Rae Nelson, June 2, 1957; children: Randolph Carlton, Shelly Ann. BA, U. S.D., 1957, JD, 1960; grad. with honors, Command and Gen. Staff Coll., 1975, U.S. Army War Coll., 1981. Bar: S.D. 1960, Ga. 1988, Supreme Ct. Ga., Supreme Ct. S.D., Ga. Ct. Appeals, U.S. Supreme Ct. Commd. 2d lt. U.S. Army, 1957, advanced through grades to col. JAGC, 1979, ret., 1987; dep. staff judge adv. Am. Divsn., Chu Lai, Vietnam, 1968-69; chief legal team U.S. Army Inf. Sch., Ft. Benning, Ga., 1969-71; team chief, acting divsn. chief adminstrv. law divsn. Office JAG, Dept. Army, 1971-74; staff judge adv. Hdqs. 24th Inf. Divsn., Ft. Stewart, Ga., 1974-79; staff judge adv. U.S. Army Armor Ctr., Ft. Knox, Ky., 1979; chief criminal law divsn. Office of JAG, Washington, 1981-84; sr. judge Army Ct. Mil. Rev., Falls Church, Va., 1984-87; staff atty. Ga. Ct. Appeals, 1987—; chief mil. def. counsel U.S. vs. Calley (My Lai Massacre) U.S. Army, 1969—71. Former chmn., mem. Joint Service Com. on Mil. Justice, 1981-84; mem. Mil. Justice Act of 1983 Adv. Commn., 1984-87; army liaison to criminal law sect. ABA, 1981-84. Decorated Legion of Merit, Bronze Star with oak leaf cluster, Meritorious Svc. medal with 2 oak leaf clusters, Joint Svc. Commendation medal, Air medal, Army Commendation medal with oak leaf cluster, Army Achievement medal. Mem. FBA (chmn. law enforcement liaison com. 1986-87), Assn. U.S. Army, Ga. Bar Assn., Order Ea. Star (worthy grand patron, grand chpt. Ga. 1999-2000), Masons, Shriners, Scottish Rite (32d degree, KCCH), Delta Theta Phi, Theta Xi. Home: 575 Spender Trce Atlanta GA 30350-5017 Office: Staff Atty Ga Ct Appeals Jud Bldg Rm 336 Capitol Sq Atlanta GA 30334-9003 E-mail: alan.raby@juno.com

RACHIE, CYRUS, retired lawyer; b. Willmar, Minn., Sept. 5, 1908; s. Elias and Amanda (Lien) R.; m. Helen Evelyn Duncanson, Nov. 25, 1936; children: John Burton Rachie, Janice Carolyn MacKinnon, Elisabeth Dorthea Becker. Student, U. Minn., 1927-28; JD, George Washington U., 1932, William Mitchell Coll. Law, 1934. Bar: Minn. 1934, U.S. Supreme Ct. Atty. Minn. Hwy. Dept., 1934-43; spl. asst. atty. gen. Minn., 1946-50; counsel Luth. Brotherhood (fraternal life ins. co.), 1950-61; pvt. practice law Mpls., 1961-62; v.p., counsel Gamble-Skogmo, Inc., 1962-64; v.p., gen. counsel Aid Assn. Lutherans, Appleton, Wis., 1964-70, sr. v.p., gen. counsel, 1970-73; with Rachie & Rachie, 1973-83; pvt. practice Minn., 1983—2001; part-time spl. master Minn. 4th Jud. Dist., 1977; ret., 2001. One of eleven com. mems. planning 1957 Luth. World Fedn. in Mpls. Councillor Nat. Luth. Coun., 1959-66, sec., 1962-64, mem. exec. com., 1965-66; United Luth. Ch. in Am. del. to 4th Assembly Luth. World Fedn., Helsinki, 1963; past pres. Luth. Welfare Soc. Minn.; past chmn. Mpls. Mayor's Coun. on Human Rels.; chmn. finance United Fund drive, 1967-68; past mem. bd. dirs. Mpls. YMCA; trustee emeritus William Mitchell Coll. Law Augsburg Coll. With USNR, 1943-46. Recipient Disting. Alumnus award William Mitchell Coll. Law, 1987. Mem. ABA Minn. Bar Assn., Am. Legion, Minn. Fraternal Congress (past pres.) Lutheran. Club: Rotarian. Probate. Home: 7500 York Ave S Apt 101 Minneapolis MN 55435-4736

RACHLIN, ALAN SANDERS, lawyer; b. N.Y.C., Mar. 14, 1942; s. Irving Louis and Blanche (Klein) R.; m. Gail S. Kaufman, June 11, 1972 (dec. Apr. 1987); m. Charlotte D. Moslander, Aug. 15, 1992. BA, CCNY, 1965; MPA, CUNY, 1971; JD, N.Y. Law Sch., 1975. Bar: N.Y. 1976, U.S. Dist. Ct. (so. and ea. dists.) 1976, U.S. Supreme Ct. 1983. Atty. N.Y. State Dept. Ins., N.Y.C., 1976-79, sr. atty., 1979-81, assoc. atty., 1981-87, supervising atty., 1987-96, prin. atty., 1996—. With U.S. Army, 1966-67. Mem. ABA, Assn. Bar City N.Y., N.Y. State Bar Assn., N.Y. County Lawyers Assn., Med. Jurisprudence. Democrat. Jewish. Avocations: science fiction, mysteries. Office: NY State Ins Dept 25 Beaver St New York NY 10004-2310 E-mail: arachlin@ins.state.ny.us

RADDING, ANDREW, lawyer, educator; b. N.Y.C., Nov. 30, 1944; m. Bonnie A. Levinson, Oct. 7, 1972; children: Judith Lynne, Joshua David. BBA, CCNY-Baruch Sch., 1965; JD, Boston U., 1968. Bar: N.Y. 1968, Md. 1977, D.C. 1977, U.S. Supreme Ct. Grad. fellow Northwestern U. Sch. Law, 1968-69; asst. counsel U.S. Ho. of Reps. Select Com. on Crime, 1969-72; asst. U.S. atty. for Dist. Md., 1972-77; ptnr. Francomano, Radding & Mannes, Balt., 1977-80, Burke, Gerber, Wilen, Francomano & Radding, Balt., 1980-85, Blades & Rosenfeld P.A., Balt., 1985-97, Adelberg, Rudow, Dorf and Hendler LLC, Balt., 1997—. Mem. adj. faculty clin. practice skills, criminal law, fed. criminal practice U. Balt. Sch. Law, 1980—; mem. trial experience com. U.S. Dist. ct., 1986-88; apptd. by gov. State Adminstrv. Bd. of Election Laws, 1995-96; instr. professionalism course Md. State Bar Assn., 1999—. Bd. dirs. Copper Hill Condominium, 1979-82, pres., 1981-82; subcom. Md. Republican Conv., 1981; sen. C.M. Mathias Jud. Selection com., 1986, chmn. U.S. Dist. Ct. Bicentennial Program, 1989-90; mem. Mayor's Domestic Violence Coord. com., 2001—. Mem. ABA, Md. Bar Assn., Balt. City Bar Assn. (jud. selection com. 1990-92, 94—, chmn. 1996-97, exec. coun. 1998-99, 2000—, co-chmn. membership com. 1999-2000), Fed. Bar Assn. (Balt. chpt. pres. 1986-87), U.S. Atty. Alumni Assn. Md. (pres. 1978—), Md. Inst. Continuing Profl. Edn. for Lawyers (bd. govs. 1987-92, inquiry panel atty. grievance com. 1991—), U.S. Arbitration and Mediation (mediator and arbitrator), Nat. Arbitration Forum (arbitrator). Jewish. Federal civil litigation, State civil litigation, Criminal. Office: Adelberg Rudow et al LLC 2 Hopkins Plz Baltimore MD 21201-2930 E-mail: aradding@adelbergrudow.com

RADER, RALPH TERRANCE, lawyer; b. Clarksburg, W.Va., Dec. 5, 1947; s. Ralph Coolidge and Jeanne (Cover) R.; m. Rebecca Jo Vorderman, Mar. 22, 1969; children: Melissa Michelle, Allison Suzanne. BSME, Va. Poly. Inst., 1970; JD, Am. U., 1974. Bar: Va. 1975, U.S. Ct. Customs and Patent Appeals, 1977, U.S. Dist. Ct. (ea. dist.) Mich. 1978, Mich. 1979, U.S. Ct. Appeals (6th cir.) 1979, U.S. Dist. Ct. (we. dist.) Mich. 1981, U.S. Ct. Appeals (fed. cir.) 1983. Supervisory patent examiner U.S. Patent Office, Washington, 1970-77; patent atty., ptnr. Cullen, Sloman, Cantor, Grauer, Scott & Rutherford, Detroit, 1977-88; ptnr. Dykema, Gossett, 1989-96, Rader, Fishman & Grauer, Bloomfield Hills, Mich., 1996—. Contbr. articles to profl. jours. Mem. adminstrv. bd. 1st United Meth. Ch., Birmingham, Mich., 1980—. With U.S. Army, 1970-76. Mem. ABA, Am. Patent Law Assn., Mich. Patent Law Assn., Mich. Bar (governing coun. patent, trademark and copyright law sect. 1981-84), Engring. Soc. Detroit, Masons, Tau Beta Pi, Pi Tau Sigma, Phi Kappa Phi. Methodist. Federal civil litigation, Patent, Trademark and copyright. Home: 4713 Riverchase Dr Troy MI 48098-4186 Office: Rader Fishman & Grauer 39533 Woodward Ave Ste 140 Bloomfield Hills MI 48304-5098 E-mail: rtr@raderfishman.com

RADER, RANDALL RAY, federal judge; b. 1949; BA magna cum laude, 1974; JD with honors, George Washington U., 1978. Bar: D.C., U.S. Ct. Appeals (fed. cir.) 1990, U.S. Claims Ct., U.S. Supreme Ct. Legis. asst. to Congresswoman Virginia Smith U.S. Ho. of Reps., 1975-78; mem. staff Ways and Means Com. U.S. Ho. Reps., 1978-81; chief counsel subcom. on Constn. U.S. Senate Judiciary Com., chief counsel, staff dir. subcom. on patents, copyrights and trademarks, 1981-87; counsel to Senator Orrin Hatch, 1981-87; judge U.S. Ct. Claims, Washington, 1988-90, U.S. Ct. Appeals (fed. cir.), Washington, 1990—. Lectr. patent law U. Va. Sch. Law; lectr. trial advocacy, lectr. George Washington U. Nat. Law Ctr., Washington; lectr. comparative patent law Georgetown U. Law Ctr., Washington. Co-author: Patent Law, 1997; co-editor: Criminal Justice Reform, 1983; contbr. articles to profl. jours. Mem. FBA. Office: US Ct Appeals Fed Cir 717 Madison Pl NW Ste 913 Washington DC 20439-0002

RADIN, SAM, lawyer, estate planner; b. N.Y.C., Aug. 1, 1951; s. Clarence and Marjorie (Rembar) R.; m. Pamela Anderson, Sept. 13, 1981; children: Clarence Anderson, Elizabeth Rebecca. BA, Columbia U., 1973; JD, Boston U., 1976. Bar: N.J. 1976, U.S. Dist. Ct. N.J. 1976, N.Y. 1978, U.S. Dist. Ct. (so. dist.) N.Y. 1978, U.S. Ct. Appeals (D.C. cir.) 1978, U.S. Supreme Ct. 1980. Assoc. Burns, Van Kirk, N.Y.C., 1976-79, Lovejoy Wasson successor to Burns, Van Kirk, N.Y.C., 1979-80; pvt. practice,

1980-84; v.p., gen. counsel Nat. Madison Group, Inc., 1984-99, pres., 1999—. Contbg. author: Executive Compensation Answer Book, 1998; contbg. author, editor: Estate and Retirement Planning Answer Book, 1999; also articles. Bd. dirs. Student Athletes Inc., N.Y.C., 1992-98, Westchester Conservatory Music, White Plains, N.Y., 1995-97; trustee Payomet Performing Arts Charitable Trust, 1999—, Nat. Lighthouse Ctr. and Mus., 2000—, pres., 2001—. Recipient Nathan Burkan Meml. prize ASCAP, 1975. Mem. ABA (subcom. on life ins. tax sect. 1996—), N.Y. State Bar Assn., Assn. Bar City N.Y., Assn. Advanced Life Underwriting, Comm. on Estate Taxation. Avocations: salt water fly fishing, collecting books, skiing, running. Estate planning, Estate taxation. Home: 71 Greenacres Ave Scarsdale NY 10583-1442 Office: Nat Madison Group Inc 261 Madison Ave New York NY 10016-2401 E-mail: sradin@nationalmadison.com

RADLO, EDWARD JOHN, lawyer, mathematician; b. Pawtucket, R.I., Mar. 7, 1946; s. Edward Zygmund and Sue Mary (Borek) R.; m. Patricia Jackson, Feb. 22, 1989; children: Heather Sue, Graeme Michael, Connor Anderew. BS, MIT, 1967; JD, Harvard U., 1972. Bar: Calif. 1972, U.S. Dist. Ct. (no. dist.) Calif. 1972, R.I. 1973, U.S. Patent Office 1973, Can. Patent Office 1974. Staff dir. Atty. Gen.'s Adv. Commn. on Juvenile Code Revision, Boston, 1970-72; law clk. R.I. Supreme Ct., 1972-73; patent atty. Honeywell Info. Systems, Waltham, Mass., 1973-74, Varian Assocs., Palo Alto, Calif., 1974-78, Ford Aerospace Corp., Palo Alto, Calif., 1978-83, patent counsel, 1983-90; ptnr. Fenwick & West, LLP, Palo Alto, Calif., 1991—; lectr. law U. Calif., San Jose State U., U. Santa Clara, 1975-78; organizer So. Peninsula Emergency Comms. Sys., 1979— . Mem., Lawyers' Alliance for Nuclear Arms Control, 1982-83, Environ. Def. Fund., 1979— . With USPHS, 1967-69. Mem. Silicon Valley Intellectual Property Law Assn., San Francisco Intellectual Property Law Assn., ABA, Calif. Bar (intellectual property sect.), No. Calif. Contest Club (pres. 1984-85), Assn. Radio Amateurs of So. New England Inc. (sec. 1962-63), Sigma Xi. Intellectual property, Private international, Patent. Home: 28040 Elena Rd Los Altos Hills CA 94022-2454 Office: Fenwick & West LLP 2 Palo Alto Sq Palo Alto CA 94306-2105

RADLOFF, STUART JAY, lawyer; b. St. Louis, Sept. 6, 1949; s. David A. and Marian (Silverstein) R.,; m. Barbara Jean Brodkin, Aug. 7, 1974; children: Jessica Dale, Laura Susan. BA in History, U. Ill., 1972; JD, Washington U., St. Louis, 1975. Bar: Mo. 1975, U.S. Dist. Ct. (ea. dist.) Mo. 1975, U.S. Ct. Appeals (8th cir.) 1978, U.S. Supreme Ct. 1979. Assoc. Friedman & Fredericks, St. Louis, 1975-79; ptnr. Friedman, Fredericks & Radloff, 1979-80; sole practice, 1980-81, 86-90; ptnr. Radloff & Riske, 1990—. Mem. Campbell & Radloff, P.C., St. Louis, 1981-84, Newman, Goldfarb, Freyman & Stevens, P.C., St. Louis, 1984-86; of counsel Rosenblum, Goldenhersh, Silverstein & Zafft P.C., 1986—; bankruptcy trustee U.S. Bankruptcy Ct., Eastern Dist. Mo., St. Louis, 1979—. Co-author and lectr. Mo. Bar CLE-Bankruptcy Series; asst. articles editor Urban Law Ann., 1974-75; contbr. Missouri Lawyer's Guide, 1984. Served with U.S. Army, 1971. Edmund J. James scholar U. Ill., Champaign, 1969. Mem. ABA, Mo. Bar, Assn. Trustees in Bankruptcy (treas. Ea. dist. Mo. 1981—), Bar Assn. Met. St. Louis, B'nai B'rith, Phi Beta Kappa, Phi Kappa Phi, Phi Alpha Theta, Phi Delta Phi. Bankruptcy, State civil litigation, General practice. Home: 518 Glenfield Ridge Ct Chesterfield MO 63017-2782

RADMER, MICHAEL JOHN, lawyer, educator; b. Wisconsin Rapids, Wis., Apr. 28, 1945; s. Donald Richard and Thelma Loretta (Donahue) R.; children from previous marriage: Christina Nicole, Ryan Michael; m. Laurie J. Anshus, Dec. 22, 1983; 1 child, Michael John B.S., Northwestern U., Evanston, Ill., 1967; J.D., Harvard U., 1970. Bar: Minn. 1970. Assoc. Dorsey & Whitney, Mpls., 1970-75, ptnr., 1976—. Lectr. law Hamline U. Law Sch., St. Paul, 1981-84; gen. counsel, rep., sec. 163 federally registered investment cos., Mpls. and St. Paul, 1977—. Contbr. articles to legal jours. Active legal work Hennepin County Legal Advice Clinic, Mpls., 1971—. Mem. ABA, Minn. Bar Assn., Hennepin County Bar Assn. Club: Mpls. Athletic. General corporate, Securities. Home: 4329 E Lake Harriet Pky Minneapolis MN 55409-1725 Office: Dorsey & Whitney 50 South 6th St Ste 1500 Minneapolis MN 55402

RADNOR, ALAN T. lawyer; b. Cleve., Mar. 10, 1946; s. Robert Clark and Rose (Chester) R.; m. Carol Sue Hirsch, June 22, 1969; children: Melanie, Joshua, Joanna. BA, Kenyon Coll., 1967; MS in Anatomy, Ohio State U., 1969, JD, 1972. Bar: Ohio 1972. Ptnr. Vorys, Sater, Seymour & Pease, Columbus, Ohio, 1972—. Adj. prof. law Ohio State U., Columbus, 1979-99. Contbr. articles to profl. jours. Bd. dirs., trustee Congregation Tifereth Israel, Columbus, 1975—, pres., 1985-87; trustee Columbus Mus. Art, 1995-98. Named Boss or Yr., Columbus Assn. Legal Secs., 1983. Fellow Am. Coll. Trial Lawyers; mem. ABA, Ohio State Bar Assn., Columbus Bar Assn., Def. Rsch. Inst., Internat. Assn. Def. Counsel. Avocations: reading, sculpture. Personal injury, Product liability. Home: 400 S Columbia Ave Columbus OH 43209-1629 Office: Vorys Sater Seymour & Pease 52 E Gay St PO Box 1008 Columbus OH 43216-1008

RADO, PETER THOMAS, lawyer; b. Berlin, Germany, Nov. 12, 1928; came to U.S., 1931; naturalized, 1937; s. Sandor and Emmy (Chrisler) R.; m. Jacqueline Danenberg, Sept. 11, 1977. AB, HArvard U., 1949, LLB, 1952, LLM, 1953. Bar: N.Y. 1952. Assoc. Ide, Haigney & Rado, N.Y.C., 1956-61, ptnr., 1961—. With U.S. Army, 1953-55. Mem. ABA, N.Y. State Bar Assn., Assn. of Bar of City of N.Y., Internat. Bar Assn., Harvard Club (N.Y.C.). General corporate, Probate, Corporate taxation. Home: 176 E 71st St New York NY 10021-5159 Office: Ide Haigney & Rado PO Box 2339 New York NY 10021-0056 E-mail: radopandj@aol.com

RADON, JENIK RICHARD, lawyer; b. Berlin, Jan. 14, 1946; came to U.S., 1951, naturalized, 1956; s. Louis and Irmgard (Hinz) R.; m. Heidi B. Duerbeck, June 10, 1971 (dec. Sept. 1999); 1 child, Kaara H.D. BA, Columbia Coll., 1967; MCP, U. Calif., Berkeley, 1971; JD, Stanford U., Berkeley, 1971. Bar: Calif. 1972, N.Y. 1975, U.S. Ct. Appeals (2d cir.) 1975, U.S. Dist. Ct. (so. dist.) N.Y. 1975. Atty. Radon & Ishizumi, N.Y.C., Berlin and Tokyo, 1981—; counsel Walter, Conston, Alexander & Green, N.Y.C., 1991—, ptnr., 2000. Lectr. Polish Acad. Scis., 1980, Tokyo Arbitration Assn., 1983, Japan External Trade Orgn., 1983, 86, Japan Mgmt. Assn., 1983, 90, Japan Inst. Internat. Bus. Law, 1983-84, Va. Ctr. World Trade, 1985, UN Indsl. Devel. Orgn., Warsaw, 1987, Wichita World Trade Coun., 1987, Inst. Nat. Economy of Poland, 1987, Hungarian Econ. Roundtable, 1987, Tallinn, 1988, USSR Com. on Sci. and Tech., 1988, USSR Fgn. Trade Ministry, 1988, Tallinn Tech. Inst., 1988, Tartu State U., 1988, U. Ottawa, 1988-89, Palm Beach World Trade Coun., 1988, Fla. Atlantic U., 1988, Bus. Assn. Latin Am. Studies, 1989—, Assn. France-Poland, 1989, Russian and East European Studies Inst. Stanford U., 1989, Ukrainian Profl. Assn. N.Y. and N.J., 1989, Columbia U. Harriman Inst., 1989, Inst. East-West Security Studies, 1989, Friedrich-Schiller U. Jena, East Germany, 1990, East European Inst. Free U. Berlin, numerous others; bd. dirs. Gland Pharma Ltd., India, 1996—, HTM Sport, Estonia, 1993—; pub. Baltic Rev., 1993—, City Paper (Baltic), 1993—; mem. exec. com. Vetter Group, Germany; adj. mem. faculty/lectr. Stanford Sch. of Law, 2000—, Stanford Bus. Sch., 2000-01. Editor-in-chief Stanford Jour. Internat. Studies, 1970-71; contbr. The International Acquisitions Handbook, 1987, Negotiating and Financing Joint Ventures Abroad, 1989, How to Form and Manage Successful Strategic Alliances, 1990, Risks Management in International Business, 1991, Comrade Goes Private, 1992, Investing in Reform, 1991, Fordham Internat. Law Jour., 1996, various jours. in U.S., Germany, Canada. Active Am. Coun. on Germany, N.Y.C., 1978—; vice-chmn. U.S.-Polish Econ. Coun., 1989-93; mem. exec. com. Afghanistan Relief Com., N.Y.C., 1980-95; bd. dirs. Columbia Coll. Alumni Assn., 1988-92, nat. coun., 1996-98, Freedom Medicine, 1987-94, chmn., 1989-94; trustee Direct Relief Internat., Santa Barbara, Calif., 1987-89; founder and dir. Eesti and Eurasian Fellowship of Columbia U., 1990—; profl. Harriman Inst., 1993—; advisor Estonian Ministry of Economy, Reform and Justice, 1991-95; adv. Prime Min. of Crimea, Ukraine, 1994-95; advisor to Parliament Republic of Georgia, 1996-98, to Pres. of Georgia, 1999—; advisor Min. of Fin. of Georgia, 1998—, Georgian Internat. Oil Corp., 1998—; chmn. Estonian-Am. C. of C., 1990-93, Deutsche Stiftung fuer internationale rechtliche Zusammenarbeit, Estonia Commn., Beirat, 1992-94. Recipient Order of Honor award Republic of Georgia, 2000. Mem. ABA, Asia-Pacific Lawyers Assn., German-Am. Law Assn. Roman Catholic. Banking, General corporate, Private international. Office: Radon & Ishizumi 269 W 71st St New York NY 10023-3701

RADWAY, ROBERT J. lawyer, consultant, educator; b. Lansing, Mich., June 8, 1940; s. David Radway and Sophie C. (Zidell) R.; m. Barbara L. Bernstein, June 18, 1967 (div. June 1975); children: Rachel, Theodore. BBA, U. Mich., 1961, MBA, 1962; postgrad., Hague Acad. Internat. Law, The Netherlands, 1966; JD, U. Calif., Hastings, 1969. Bar: Mass. 1970, Ohio 1973, N.Y. 1978, U.S. Dist. Ct. Mass. 1970, U.S. Ct. Appeals (1st cir.) 1970. Various jr. mgmt. positions Gen. Dynamics Corp. and IBM Corp., San Diego, 1962-65; various mgmt. positions GTE Corp., Calif., 1967-69, internat. contract adminstr. Mass., 1969-70; atty. New Eng. Tel., Boston, 1970-72; counsel-internat. Arthur G. McKee & Co., Cleve., 1972-76; counsel and dir. tech. programs Coun. of Americas, N.Y.C., 1976-78; pvt. practice, 1978-82; ptnr. Radway & Dalto, 1983-85, Radway & Assocs., N.Y.C., 1986-92. Cons. UN Centre on Transnat. Corps., UN Indsl. Devel. Orgn., UN Devel. Programme, Ctr. for Latin Am., U. Wis., Milw.; adj. prof. NYU, 1983—; vis. adj. prof., lectr. Europe and Asia, 1988-93; lectr. in field. Co-editor: Reference Manual on Doing Business in Latin America, 1979; mem. editl. bd. Multinat. Corp. Law, Vol. 1-Mexico and Central America, 1981; contbr. articles to profl. jours. Pres. Tenants Assn., 1984-85. Mem. ABA (sects. internatl. and bus./corp. law), Inter-Am. Bar Assn. (council 1984—, chmn. organizing host com. 1988, exec. com. 1995—), Assn. of Bar of City of N.Y., Am. Fgn. Law Assn. (bd. dirs. 1985-96), Dickinson Soc. Internat. Law (founder, pres. 1966-67), Greater Cleve. Internat. Lawyers Group (founder, pres. 1973-76), Licensing Execs. Soc., U. Mich. Alumni Club of N.Y. (bd. dirs. 1977—, pres. 1988), Hastings Coll. Law Alumni Club N.Y. and New England (founder, bd. dirs. 1979—), Princeton Club of N.Y. Republican. Jewish. Avocations: sailing, tennis, golf, biking. Contracts commercial, General corporate, Private international. Home and Office: 250 E 73rd St New York NY 10021-4307 E-mail: rjrvector@acninc.net

RAE, MATTHEW SANDERSON, JR. lawyer; b. Pitts., Sept. 12, 1922; s. Matthew Sanderson and Olive (Waite) R.; m. Janet Hettman, May 2, 1953; children: Mary-Anna, Margaret Rae Mallory, Janet S. Rae Dupree. AB, Duke, 1946, LLB, 1947; postgrad., Stanford U., 1951. Bar: Md. 1948, Calif. 1951. Asst. to dean Duke Sch. Law, Durham, N.C., 1947-48; assoc. Karl F. Steinmann, Balt., 1948-49, Guthrie, Darling & Shattuck, L.A., 1953-54; nat. field rep. Phi Alpha Delta Law Frat., 1949-51; research atty. Calif. Supreme Ct., San Francisco, 1951-52; ptnr. Darling, Hall & Rae (and predecessor firms), L.A., 1955—. Mem. Calif. Commn. Uniform State Laws, 1985—, chmn., 1993-94; chmn. drafting com. for revision Uniform Prin. and Income Act of Nat. Conf., 1991-97, Probate and Mental Health Task Force, Jud. Coun. Calif., 1996-2000. Vice pres. L.A. County Rep. Assembly, 1959-64; mem. L.A. County Rep. Ctrl. Com., 1960-64, 77-90, 2000—, exec. com., 1977-90; vice chmn. 17th Congl. Dist., 1960-62, 28th Congl. Dist., 1962-64; chmn. 46th Assy. Dist., 1962-64, 27th Senatorial Dist., 1977-85, 29th Senatorial Dist., 1985-90, sec. 53d Assembly Dist., 2000-; mem. Calif. Rep. State Ctrl. Com., 1966—, exec. com., 1966-67; pres. Calif. Rep. League, 1966-67; trustee Rep. Assocs., 1979-94, pres., 1983-85, chmn. bd. dirs., 1985-87. 2d lt. USAAF, WWII. Fellow Am. Coll. Trust and Estate Counsel; academician Internat. Acad. Estate and Trust Law (exec. coun. 1974-78); mem. ABA, L.A. County Bar Assn. (chmn. probate and trust law com. 1964-66, chmn. legis. com. 1980-86, chmn. program com. 1981-82, chmn. membership retention com. 1982-83, trustee 1983-85, dir. Bar Found., 1987-93, Arthur K. Marshall award probate and trust law sect. 1984, Shattuck-Price Meml. award 1990), South Bay Bar Assn., State Bar of Calif. (chmn. state bar jour. com. 1970-71, probate com. 1974-75; exec. com. estate planning trust and probate law sect. 1977-83, chmn. legis. com. 1977-89; co-chmn. 1991-92; probate law cons. group Calif. Bd. Legal Specialization 1977-88; chmn. conf. dels. resolutions com. 1987, exec. com. conf. dels. 1987-90), Lawyers Club L.A. (bd. govs. 1981-87, 1st v.p. 1982-83), Am. Legion (comdr. Allied post 1969-70), Legion Lex (bd. dirs. 1964-99, pres. 1969-71), Air Force Assn., Aircraft Owners and Pilots Assn., Town Hall (gov. 1970-78, pres. 1975), World Affairs Coun., Internat. Platform Assn., Breakfast Club (law, pres. 1989-90), Commonwealth Club, Chancery Club (pres. 1996-97), Rotary, Phi Beta Kappa (councilor Alpha Assn. 1983—, pres. 1996), Omicron Delta Kappa, Phi Alpha Delta (supreme justice 1972-74, elected to Disting. Svc. chpt. 1978), Sigma Nu. Presbyterian. Estate planning, Probate, Estate taxation. Home: 600 John St Manhattan Beach CA 90266-5837 Office: Darling Hall & Rae LLP 520 S Grand Ave Fl 7 Los Angeles CA 90071-2645

RAEDER, MYRNA SHARON, lawyer, educator; b. N.Y.C., Feb. 4, 1947; d. Samuel and Estelle (Auslander) R.; m. Terry Oliver Kelly, July 13, 1975; children: Thomas Oliver, Michael Lawrence. BA, Hunter Coll., 1968; JD, NYU, 1971; LLM, Georgetown U., 1975. Bar: N.Y. 1972, D.C. 1972, Calif. 1972. Spl. asst. U.S. atty. U.S. Atty's Office, Washington, 1972-73; asst. prof. U. San Fransisco Sch. Law, 1973-75; assoc. O'Melveny & Myers, L.A., 1975-79; assoc. prof. Southwestern U. Sch. Law., 1979-82, prof., 1983—, Irwin R. Buchalter prof. law, 1990; mem. faculty Nat. Judicial Coll., 1993—. Prettyman fellow Georgetown Law Ctr., Washington, 1971-73. Author: Federal Pretrial Practice, 3d edit., 2000; co-author: Evidence, State and Federal Rules in a Nutshell, 3d edit., 1997, Evidence, Cases, Materials and Problems, 2d edit., 1998. Fellow Am. Bar Found.; mem. ABA (trial evidence com. litigation sect. 1980—, criminal justice sect. 1994-97, vice-chair planning 1997-98, chair elect 1997-98, chair 1998-99, mem. mag. bd., 2000—, adv. to nat. conf. commrs. uniform state laws drafting com. uniform rules of evidence 1996-1999), Assn. Am. Law Schs. (chair women in legal edn. sect. 1982, com. on sects. 1984-87, chair elect evidence sect. 1996, chair 1997), Nat. Assn. Women Lawyers (bd. dirs. 1991-98, pres.-elect 1993, pres. 1994-96), Women Lawyers Assn. L.A. (bd. dirs., coord. mothers support group 1987-96), Order of Coif, Phi Beta Kappa. Office: Southwestern U Sch Law 675 S Westmoreland Ave Los Angeles CA 90005-3905

RAFEEDIE, EDWARD, senior federal judge; b. Orange, N.J., Jan. 6, 1929; s. Fred and Nabeeha (Hishmeh) R.; m. Ruth Alice Horton, Oct. 8, 1961; children: Fredrick Alexander, Jennifer Ann. BS in Law, U. So. Calif., 1957, JD, 1959; LLD (hon.), Pepperdine U., 1978. Bar: Calif. 1960. Pvt. practice, Santa Monica, Calif., 1960-69; mcpl. ct. judge Santa Monica Jud. Dist., 1969-71; judge Superior Ct. State of Calif., L.A., 1971-82; dist. judge U.S. Dist. Court (cen. dist.) Calif., 1982-96, sr. judge, 1996—. With U.S. Army, 1950-52, Korea. Office: US Dist Ct 312 N Spring St Ste 244P Los Angeles CA 90012-4704

RAFFALOW, JANET TERRY, law librarian; b. Burbank, Calif., Oct. 11, 1947; d. Melvin and Honey (Sobel) Whitney; m. Richard Elliott Raffalow, June 9, 1984; 1 child, Melissa Rose. BA, UCLA, 1968, MLS, 1969, cert. in pub. adminstrn., 1980. Cert. community coll. tchr., Calif. Young adult libr. L.A. Pub. Libr., 1969-70; libr. Calif. Atty. Gen.'s Libr., L.A., 1970-78; supervising libr. Calif. Atty. Gen.'s Library, Los Angeles, 1978—. Vol. Pub. TV-KCET, Los Angeles, 1973—; vice chmn. Los Angeles Jr. C. of C., 1979-81; vol. citizens commn. Los Angeles Olympic Organizing Com., 1982-84; mem. City of Hope. Recipient Atty. Gen.'s award for excellence, 1991. Mem. L.A. Law Librs. Assn. (long-range planning com.), Am. Assn. Law Librs. (cert.), So. Calif. Assn. Law Librs., UCLA Libr. Sch. Alumni Assn., Sunshines of Cedars Sinai (v.p. 1971-73). Democrat. Jewish. Avocations: tennis, photography, travel. Office: Calif Atty Gen's Libr 300 S Spring St 7th Flr Los Angeles CA 90013 E-mail: raffaloj@hdcdojnet.state.calif

RAFFERTY, JAMES GERARD, lawyer; b. Boston, July 9, 1951; s. James John and Helen Christine (Kennedy) R.; m. Rhonda Beth Friedman, May 17, 1981; children: Jessica Faith, Evan Louis Quinn. BA, Brown U., 1974; MA, Princeton U., 1980; JD, Georgetown U., 1984. Bar: Md. 1985, D.C. 1985, U.S. Tax Ct. 1988, U.S. Ct. Appeals (4th cir.) 1989, U.S. Ct. Appeals (3d cir.) 1992. Assoc. Piper & Marbury, Washington, 1984-91, Pepper, Hamilton & Scheetz, Washington, 1991-92; founding ptnr. Harkins Cunningham, 1992—. Contbr. articles to legal jours. Brown U. Club of Boston scholar, 1969-70. Mem. ABA (chmn. com. on affiliated and related corps. tax sect. 1994-95). Roman Catholic. Avocation: golf. General corporate, Mergers and acquisitions, Corporate taxation. Office: Harkins Cunningham 801 Pennsylvania Ave NW Ste 600 Washington DC 20004-2664 E-mail: jrafferty@harkinscunningham.com

RAFFERTY, WILLIAM BERNARD, lawyer; b. Balt., May 15, 1912; s. John Patrick and Dorothy Amalye (Hartje) R.; m. Elizabeth Catherine Henkel, Dec. 26, 1938; children: Patricia Carol Buchan, Susan Elizabeth Magri, Dorothy Lee Schultz. AB with honors, U. Md., 1934, LLB with honors, 1936. Bar: Md. 1936, U.S. Supreme Ct. 1942. Ptnr. Miles & Stockbridge (and predecessor firms), Balt., 1936-41, ptnr., 1941-92, of counsel, 1992-94, ret., 1994; bd. dirs. Fidelity Fed. Savs. and Loan Assn., Henkel-Harris Co. Inc., Rolling Road Realty Co., Balt., 1975—; lectr. pub. utility law U. Balt. Law Sch., 1951-56. Pres., Roland Park Civic League, 1954-57. Fellow Md. Bar Found.; mem. Wednesday Law Club (pres. 1953), Merchants. Democrat. Presbyterian. Banking, Contracts commercial, Public utilities. Office: Miles & Stockbridge 10 Light St Ste 1100 Baltimore MD 21202-1487

RAFFIN, MARIE-HÉLÈNE J. lawyer; b. Paris, France, Jan. 23, 1963; d. Jacques and Françoise Raffin. 1st cert., Cambridge U., Paris, 1980; diploma in Econs., Spanish C. of C., Paris, 1981, Brit. C. of C., 1983; BA with honors, U. Paris II, 1984, LLM, 1985, degree in Tax Law, 1986; degree in Advanced Business, Ecole Supérieure des Scis. Econs. Commerciales, Paris, 1984; degree in Acctg., D.E.S.C.F., 1985. Bar: France. Asst. to mem. Nat. Assembly, Paris, 1986-87; from assoc. to ptnr. Arthur Andersen, 1987—. Prof. in Tax U. Paris, 1995—; cons. Assn. Française des Entreprises Privées, 1996—, Nat. Fedn. French Entrepreneurs, 1997—. Author: La révolution fiscale à refaire, 1986, La Fiscalité des fusions et des apports partiels d'actifs, 1994, 2d edit., 2001; contbr. articles to profl. jours. Mem. Hauts-de-Seine Bar Assn. Avocations: classical music, theater, philosophy. Mergers and acquisitions, Corporate taxation, Taxation, general. Office: Arthur Andersen Internat(Andersen legal) 41 rue Ybry 92576 Neuilly sur Seine Cedex France Office Fax: 33155611515

RAGAN, CHARLES OLIVER, JR. lawyer; b. Knoxville, Tenn., Dec. 23, 1935; s. Charles Oliver and Jeanette (Butler) R.; m. Pauline Iona Kimsey, Apr. 19, 1958. BSBA, U. Tenn., 1958, JD, 1963. Bar: Tenn. 1964, U.S. Dist. Ct. (ea. dist.) Tenn. 1965; cert. consumer bankruptcy specialist. Staff atty. State of Tenn., Chattanooga, 1964-69; atty. Bean & Phillips, 1969-73; sr. ptnr. Ragan & Schulman, 1973-75, Ragan & Littleton, Chattanooga, 1975-80, Ragan & Wulforst, Chattanooga, 1980-84; pvt. practice, 1984—. Tenn. commnr. Nat. Conf. Commrs. on Uniform State Laws, 1976-80. Campaign treas. for Dem. candidates. Democrat. Methodist. Bankruptcy, Consumer commercial. Home: 185 Woodcliff Cir Signal Mountain TN 37377-3142 Office: 707 Georgia Ave Ste 300 Chattanooga TN 37402-2047

RAGAN, CHARLES RANSOM, lawyer; b. N.Y.C., Aug. 13, 1947; s. Charles Alexander Jr. and Josephine Forbes (Parker) R.; m. Barbara Thiel McMahon, Aug. 30, 1969; children: Alexandra Watson, Madeline McCue. AB, Princeton U., 1969; JD, Fordham U., 1974. Bar: N.Y. 1975, U.S. Ct. Appeals (3d cir.) 1975, Calif. 1976, U.S. Ct. Appeals (9th cir.) 1976, U.S. Dist. Ct. (no. dist.) Calif. 1976, U.S. Supreme Ct. 1981, U.S. Dist. Ct. (so. dist.) N.Y. 1982, U.S. Ct. Appeals (2d cir.) 1984. Law clk. to Hon. R.J. Aldisert U.S. Ct. Appeals (3rd cir.), 1974-76; assoc. Pillsbury, Madison & Sutro, San Francisco, 1976-81, ptnr., 1982-97, Palo Alto, 1997-2000, Pillsbury Winthrop, Palo Alto, 2001—. Mem. exec. com. 9th Cir. Judicial Conf., 1987-91; mem. Civil Justice Reform Act Adv. Group, No. Dist. Calif., 1995-99. Contbr. articles to profl. jours. Mem. San Francisco Bar Assn. (chair feds. cts. 1982-89). Avocations: biking, swimming, spectator sports. Federal civil litigation, Private international. Office: Pillsbury Winthrop LLP 50 Fremont St San Francisco CA 94105

RAGATZ, THOMAS GEORGE, lawyer; b. Madison, Wis., Feb. 18, 1934; s. Wilmer Leroy and Rosanna (Kindschi) R.; m. Karen Christensen, Dec. 19, 1965; children: Thomas Rolf, William Leslie, Erik Douglas. BBA, U. Wis., 1957, LLB, 1961. Bar: Wis. 1961, U.S. Dist. Ct. (ea. and we. dists.) Wis. 1961, U.S. Tax Ct. 1963, U.S. Ct. Appeals (7th cir.) 1965, U.S. Supreme Ct. 1968; CPA, Wis. Staff acct. Peat, Marwick, Mitchell & Co., Mpls., 1958; instr. Sch. Bus., U. Wis., Madison, 1958-60; formerly lectr. in acctg. and law Sch. U. Wis.; law clk. Wis. Supreme Ct., 1961-62; assoc. Boardman Suhr Curry & Field, Madison, 1962-64, ptnr., 1965-78, Foley & Lardner, Madison, 1978—, mng. ptnr., 1984-93, chmn. budget com., 1994-99. Dir. Sub-Zero Freezer Co., Inc., Mortenson, Matzell & Meldrem, Inc., Norman Bassett Found., Wis. Sports Found., United Way Found., Courtier Found.; dir., past pres. Wis. Sports Devel. Corp.; lectr. seminars on tax subjects. Editor in chief Wis. Law Rev., 1960-61; chmn. Nat. Conf. Law Revs., 1960-61; author: The Ragatz History, 1989; contbr. articles to profl. jours. Formerly dir. United Way, Meth. Hosp. Found; mem. U. Wis. Found., United Way of Dane County; former moderator 1st Congl. Ch.; past pres. First Congl. Ch. Found.; chmn. site selection com. U. Wis. Hosp.; bd. regents U. Wis., panel provision of legal svcs.; bd. dirs. Met. YMCA, Madison, 1983—90, YMCA Found., Norman Bassett Found., Courtier Found.; pres. Bus. & Edn. Partnership, 1983—89, also bd. dirs. Fellow Am. Bar Found.; mem. ABA, Seventh Cir. Bar Assn., Wis. Bar Found., State Bar Wis. (sec. 1969-70, bd. govs. 1971-75, chmn. fin. com. 1975-80, chmn. tax sect., chmn. spl. com. on econs., chmn. svcs. for lawyers com.), Dane County Bar Assn. (pres. 1978-79, chmn. jud. qualification com., sec.), Am. Judicature Soc., Wis. Inst. CPAs, Madison Club (pres. 1980-81), Madison Club House Corp. (pres. 1999—, bd. dirs.), Order of Coif, Bascom Hill Soc., Beta Gamma Sigma, Sigma Chi, Order of Constantine. Republican. General civil litigation, General corporate, Corporate taxation. Home: 3334 Lake Mendota Dr Madison WI 53705-1469 Office: Foley & Lardner PO Box 1497 Madison WI 53701-1497 also: Foley & Lardner 1st Wisconsin Ctr 777 E Wisconsin Ave Ste 3800 Milwaukee WI 53202-5302

RAGGI, REENA, federal judge; b. Jersey City, May 11, 1951; BA, Wellesley Coll., 1973; JD, Harvard U., 1976. Bar: N.Y. 1977. U.S. atty. Dept. Justice, Bklyn., 1986; ptnr. Windels, Marx, Davies & Ives, N.Y.C., 1987; judge U.S. Dist. Ct. (ea. dist.) N.Y., Bklyn., 1987—. Office: US Courthouse 225 Cadman Plz E Brooklyn NY 11201-1818

RAGLAND, ROBERT ALLEN, lawyer; b. Bartlesville, Okla., Apr. 18, 1954; s. Thomas Martin and Joan Ethel (Murphy) R. BA, U. Md., 1976; JD, George Mason Sch. of Law, 1980. Dir. regulatory reform and govt. orgn. Nat. Assn. Mfrs., Washington, 1979-82, asst. v.p. taxation, 1983-86; mgr. congl. rels. The Clorox Co., Oakland, Calif., 1982-83; dir. tax rsch. U.S. C. of C., Washington, 1988-93. Chief tax counsel, mng. dir. Nat. Chamber Found., Washington, 1989-93; v.p. Trust First Union Nat. Bank, 1995—, officer, 1995—. Author: Transportation Reform, 1980, Employee Stock Ownership Plans, 1989, Taxation of Foreign Source Income, Distributional Impact of Excise Taxes, 1990; editor Taxation of Intercorporate Profits, 1990, Jour. Regulation and Social Costs, 1992—, Jour. Regulation, 1992-93. Active Boy Scouts Am., Washington, 1967—, bd. dirs. nat. capital area coun.; dep. dir. duPont for Pres., 1987-88; v.p. Nat. Chamber Found. U.S. C. of C., 1989-93, dir., Liz Lerman Dance Exchange, 1993-2001, dir. Our House, Inc., 1988-2000. Republican. Roman Catholic. Home: 4100 Cathedral Ave NW Washington DC 20016-3584

RAHM, DAVID ALAN, lawyer; b. Passaic, N.J., Apr. 18, 1941; s. Hans Emil and Alicia Katherine (Onuf) R.; m. Susan Eileen Berkman, Nov. 23, 1972; children: Katherine Berkman, William David. AB, Princeton U., 1962; JD, Yale U., 1965. Bar: N.Y. 1966, D.C. 1986. Assoc. Paul, Weiss, Rifkind & Wharton, N.Y.C., 1965-66, 1968-69; asst. counsel N.Y. State Urban Devel. Corp., 1969-72, assoc. counsel, 1972-75; counsel real estate div. Internat. Paper Co., 1975-80; ptnr. Stroock & Stroock & Lavan, 1980-83, sr. ptnr., 1984—. Mem. legis. com. Real Estate Bd. N.Y., 1988—92; lectr. Old Dominion Coll., Norfold, Va., 1967—68, NYU, 1986—; mem. editl. bd. Comml. Leasing Law and Strategy, 1988—95; mem. N.Y.C. bd. advisors Commonwealth Land Title Ins. Co., 1996—2000. Contbr. articles to profl. jours. Fund raiser corp. com. N.Y. Philharm., N.Y.C., 1980-84; trustee Manhattan Sch. Music, 1989—, treas., 1991-94, chmn., 1994—; bd. dir. New Dramatists, Inc., 2001—. Mem. ABA (comml. leasing com. 1987-88, 94—, pub./pvt. devel. com. 1989—, real property sect.), Assn. of Bar of City of N.Y. (housing and urban devel. com. 1977-80, 81-84, real property com. 1989-92), Princeton Club. Democrat. Presbyterian. Avocations: music, reading, travel. Landlord-tenant, Real property. Office: Stroock Stroock & Lavan 180 Maiden Ln Fl 17 New York NY 10038-4937

RAHM, SUSAN BERKMAN, lawyer; b. Pitts., June 25, 1943; d. Allen Hugh and Selma (Wiener) Berkman; m. David Alan Rahm, Nov. 23, 1972; children: Katherine, William. BA with honors, Wellesley Coll., 1965; postgrad., Harvard U., 1966-68; JD, NYU, 1973. Bar: N.Y. 1974, D.C. 1988. Assoc. Marshall, Bratter, Greene, Allison & Tucker, N.Y.C., 1973-81, ptnr., 1981-82, Kaye Scholer, LLP, N.Y.C., 1982—; chair real estate dept. Kaye, Scholer, Fierman, Hays & Handler, LLP, 1993-98, chair internat. practice group, 1999—. N.Y. adv. bd., Chgo. Title Ins. Co., 1995. Editor: New York Real Property Service, 1987. Bd. dirs. Girls Inc., 1989-93; mem. aux. bd. Mt. Sinai Hosp., N.Y.C., 1976-78. Recipient cert. of outstanding svc. D.C. Redevel. Land Agy., 1969, She Knows Where She's Going award Girls' Clubs of Am., 1987, Woman of Yr. award CREW.NY, 1999. Mem. ABA, Assn. Bar City N.Y., N.Y. Bar Assn. (real property law com., co-chmn. real-estate devel. . 1987-91), Am. Coll. Real Estate Lawyers, Comml. Real Estate Women N.Y. (bd. dirs. 1988-94, v.p. 1988-91, pres. 1991-93). Real property. Office: Kaye Scholer Fierman Hays & Handler LLP 425 Park Ave New York NY 10022-3506

RAIKES, CHARLES FITZGERALD, retired lawyer; b. Mpls., Oct. 6, 1930; s. Arthur FitzGerald and Margaret (Hawthorne) R.; m. Antonia Raikes, Dec. 20, 1969; children: Jennifer Catherine, Victoria Samantha. B.A., Washington U., 1952; M.A., Harvard U., 1955, LL.B., 1958. Bar: N.Y. State 1959. Assoc. White & Case, N.Y.C., 1958-69; assoc. gen. counsel Dun & Bradstreet, Inc., 1969-72, v.p., gen. counsel, 1972-73, The Dun & Bradstreet Corp., N.Y.C., 1973-76, sr. v.p., gen. counsel, 1976-94, of counsel, 1994-95; ret., 1995. Cons. Bd. Govs. Fed. Reserve System, 1958-95. Served with U.S. Army, 1952-54. Woodrow Wilson fellow, 1952 Mem. Assn. Bar City of N.Y., Harvard Club, Phi Beta Kappa. General corporate. Home: 26 Crooked Trl Norwalk CT 06853-1106

RAILTON, WILLIAM SCOTT, lawyer; b. Newark, July 30, 1935; s. William Scott and Carolyn Elizabeth (Guiberson) R.; m. Karen Elizabeth Walsh, Mar. 31, 1979; 1 son, William August; children by previous marriage: William Scott, Anne Greenwood. BSEE, U. Wash., 1962; JD with honors, George Washington U., 1965. Bar: D.C. 1966, Md. 1966, Va. 1993, U.S. Patent Office 1966. Assoc., then ptnr. Kemon, Palmer & Estabrook, Washington, 1966-70; sr. trial atty. Dept. Labor, 1970-71, asst. counsel for trial litigation, 1971-72; chief counsel U.S. Occupational Safety and Health Rev. Commn., 1972-77, acting gen. counsel, 1975-77; ptnr. Reed Smith LLP, Pitts., 1977—. Lectr. George Washington U. Law Sch., 1977-79, seminar chmn. Occupational Safety and Health Act, Govt. Inst., 1979-96; lectr. Practicing Law Inst., 1976-79. Author: (legal handbooks) The Examination System and the Backlog, 1965, The OSHA General Duty Clause, 1977, The OSHA Health Standards, 1977; OSHA Compliance Handbook, 1992; contbg. author: Occupational Safety and Health Law, 1988, 93. Regional chmn. Montgomery County (Md.) Republican party, 1968-70; pres. Montgomery Sq. Citizens Assn., 1970-71; bd. dirs., pres. Foxvale Farms Homeowners Assn., 1979-82; pres. Orchards on the Potomac Homeowners Assn., 1990-92; dir. Great Falls Hist. Soc., 1991-94; scoutmaster Troop 55 Boy Scouts Am., 1993-98. With USMC, 1953-58. Recipient Meritorious Achievement medal Dept. Labor, 1972, Outstanding Service award OSHA Rev. Commn., 1977, elected fell. Coll. Labor and Employment Lawyers, 1998. Fellow Coll. Labor and Employment Lawyers; mem. ABA (mgmt. co-chmn. occupational safety and health law com. 1995-98), Md. Bar Assn., Va. Bar Assn., Bar Assn. D.C. (vice chmn. young lawyers sect. 1971), Order of Coif, Sigma Phi Epsilon, Phi Delta Phi. Federal civil litigation, Labor, Patent. Home: 10102 Walker Lake Dr Great Falls VA 22066-3502 also: East Tower 1301 K St NW # 1100 Washington DC 20005-3317 E-mail: srailton@reedsmith.com

RAIMI, BURTON LOUIS, lawyer; b. Detroit, May 5, 1938; s. Irving and Rae (Abel) R.; m. Judith Morse, Mar. 31, 1963 (div. Mar. 1985); children: Diane L., and Matthew D. BA, Brandeis U., 1960; JD with honors, U. Mich., 1963; LLM, George Washington U., 1964. Bar: Mich. 1963, D.C. 1964, Fla. 1991; U.S. Supreme Ct., U.S. Ct. Appeals (4th, 7th, 8th, 9th, 10th, 11th and D.C. cirs.). Atty. appelate ct. sect. NLRB, Washington, 1964-69; assoc. Morgan, Lewis & Bockius, 1969-71; dep. gen. counsel FDIC, 1971-78; ptnr. Rosenman and Colin, 1978-86, Dechert Price & Rhoads, Washington, 1986-93; shareholder McCaffrey & Raimi, P.A., Naples and Sarasota, Fla., 1994—. Speaker various insts. Mem. ABA (past chmn. bank receiverships subcom. of banking com.), D.C. Bar Assn. (past chmn. banking law com., com. on interest on lawyers trust accounts), Fla. Bar (fin. instns., securities coms.). Avocations: sailing, travel, golf, fishing. Banking, General corporate, Securities. Home: 4452 Staghorn Ln Sarasota FL 34238-5626 Office: McCaffrey & Raimi PA 1800 2nd St Ste 753 Sarasota FL 34236-5900 Fax: 941-957-0449. E-mail: burt@moneylaw.com

RAIMO, BERNARD (BERNIE RAIMO), lawyer; b. Kansas City, Mo., May 29, 1944; m. Sharon Marie Brady, Aug. 23, 1974; children: Sarah Elizabeth, Peter Bernard. BA, U. Notre Dame, 1965; MA, U. Mich., 1967; JD with honors, George Washington U., 1972. Bar: D.C. Staff asst. to Sen. Stuart Symington, Mo., 1968-72; asst. corp. counsel D.C., Washington, 1972-76; legis. analyst Am. Petroleum Inst., 1976-78; counsel Permanent Select Com. Intelligence U.S. Ho. Reps., Washington, 1978-91, chief counsel Ho. Com. Standards of Official Conduct, 1991-95; minority counsel Ho. Com. Standards of Official Conduct, 1995-97; counsel to Dem. leader U.S. Ho. of Reps., 1997—. Office: Office of the Dem Leader H-204 The Capitol Washington DC 20515-0001 E-mail: bernard.raimo@mail.house.gov

RAINES, JIM NEAL, lawyer; b. Memphis, Sept. 11, 1943; s. J.E. and Amelia C. Raines; m. Julia Walters, Sept. 1, 1979; 1 dau., Lee Pierceson. BBA, Memphis State U., 1965, JD, 1968. Bar: Tenn. 1968, U.S. Dist. Ct. (we. dist.) Tenn. 1968, U.S. Ct. Appeals (6th cir.) 1970, U.S. Ct. Appeals (5th cir.) 1975, U.S. Supreme Ct. 1974. Trial atty. antitrust divsn. U.S. Dept. Justice, Washington, 1968-70; asst. U.S. atty. We. Dist. Tenn., Memphis, 1970-74; ptnr. Burch, Porter & Johnson, 1975-76, Glankler, Brown, Gilliland, Chase, Robinson, Raines, Memphis, 1976—. Served with USMC, 1960-64. Mem. ABA, Memphis Bar Assn., Shelby County Bar Assn., Univ. Club. Antitrust, Federal civil litigation, Criminal. Office: Glankler Brown, PLLC 1 Commerce Sq Ste 1700 Memphis TN 38103

RAINES, RICHARD CLIFTON, lawyer; b. Phila., Aug. 20, 1946; s. Arnold and Barbara Harriet R.; m. Patricia Marie O'Brien, June 22, 1968; children: Heather Lee, Zachary Ryan. AB, U. Calif.-Santa Barbara, 1968; JD, Hastings Coll. Law, 1974. Bar: Calif. 1974, U.S. Dist. Ct. (no. dist.) Calif. 1974, (ea. dist.) Calif., 1987, U.S. Dist. Ct. (so. dist.) Calif. 1989, U.S. Ct. Appeals (9th cir.) 1974. Ptnr. Hoberg, Finger, Brown, Cox & Molligan, San Francisco, 1974-88; trial atty. Thiessen, Gagen & McCoy, Danville, Calif., 1988-90; ptnr. Gagen, McCoy, McMahon & Armstrong, Danville, 1990—; judge pro tem. San Francisco Mcpl. Ct., 1980—; arbitrator San Francisco Superior Ct., 1979—, Contra Costa (Calif.) Superior Ct., 1989—; lectr. Calif. Continuing Edn. of Bar, 1985, 86, 90, 92; dir. Contra Costa Legal Svcs. Found., 1989—. Author: California Continuing Education of the Bar Action Guide, 1986, rev. edit., 1992; contbr. articles to legal jours. Bd. dirs. Woodlands Homeowners Assn., Walnut Creek, Calif., 1982-86; trustee Centra Costa County Legal Svcs. Found., 1990—. Served with AUS, 1969-71. Mem. State Bar Calif. (mem state bar ct. 1984—, mem. exec. com. litigation sect. 1984-86, conv. del. County of Contra Costa chpt., 1989—, co-chair 1992, 93), Conf. Dels., Lawyers' Club San Francisco (del. 1977-86). Democrat. General civil litigation, Product liability, Real property. Office: Gagen McCoy McMahon & Armstrong 279 Front St Danville CA 94526-3401

RAINEY, WILLIAM JOEL, lawyer; b. Flint, Mich., Oct. 11, 1946; s. Ralph Jefferson and Elsie Matilda (Erickson) R.; m. Cynthia Hetsko, June 15, 1968; children: Joel Michael, Allison Elizabeth. AB, Harvard U., 1968; JD, U. Mich., 1971. Bar: N.Y. 1973, Wash. 1977, Ariz. 1987, Mass. 1992, Kans. 1997, U.S. Dist. Ct. (so. and ea. dists.) N.Y. 1973, U.S. Ct. Appeals (2nd cir.) N.Y. 1973, U.S. Dist. Ct. (we. dist.) Wash. 1977, U.S. Supreme Ct. 1976, U.S. Ct. Appeals (9th cir.) Wash. 1978, U.S. Dist. Ct. Ariz. 1987, U.S. Dist. Ct. Mass. 1992. Assoc. atty. Curtis, Mallet-Prevost, Colt & Mosle, N.Y.C., 1971-76; atty., asst. corp. sec. Weyerhaeuser Co., Tacoma, 1976-85; v.p., corp. sec., gen. counsel Southwest Forest Industries Inc., Phoenix, 1985-87; sr. v.p., corp. sec., gen. counsel Valley Nat. Corp. and Valley Nat. Bank, 1987-91; v.p., gen. counsel Cabot Corp., Boston, 1991-93; exec. v.p., gen. coun., corp. sec. Fourth Fin. Corp., Wichita, Kans., 1994-96; sr. v.p., gen. counsel, corp. sec. Payless ShoeSource, Inc., Topeka, 1996—. Editor U. Mich. Jour. Law Reform, 1970-71 Bd. dirs. Big Bros./Big Sisters, 1994-96. Maj. USAR, 1970-91. Mem. ABA (chmn. task force 1984-91), Wash. State Bar Assn., State Bar of Ariz., Assn. Bank Holding Cos. (steering com. 1989-91, chmn. lawyers com. 1990-91), Harvard Club of Phoenix (bd. dirs. 1989-91). Avocations: backpacking, running, fishing, bicycling. General corporate, Pension, profit-sharing, and employee benefits, Securities. Home: 901 Deer Run Dr Lawrence KS 66049-4731 Office: Payless ShoeSource Inc PO Box 1189 Topeka KS 66601-1189

RAINONE, MICHAEL CARMINE, lawyer; b. Phila., Mar. 4, 1918; m. Ledena Tonioni, Apr. 10, 1944; children: Sebastian, Francine. LLB, U. Pa., 1941. Bar: Pa. 1944, U.S. Dist. Ct. Pa. 1944, U.S. Supreme Ct. 1956. Del. 3d cir. Jud. Conf., 1984-95. Bd. dirs. C.C., Phila. 1970-85; past pres. Nationalities Svc. Ctr., hon. bd. dirs.; commr. Fellowship Commn., 1973-82; internat. pres. Orphans of Italy, Inc., 2975-83; bd. dirs., mem. govt. rels. com. Mental Health Assn. Southeastern Pa., 1979-91; pres. Columbus Civic Assn. Pa., Inc., 1984-91; chmn. Lawyers' Biog. Com. Hist. Soc., U.S. Dist. Ct.; trustee Balch Inst. for Ethnic Studies, 1989-92; regional v.p. Nat. Italian-Am. Found.; pres. Seaview Harbor Civic Assn., 1990-95, pres. emeritus, 1996—; apptd. judge Final Law Sch. Trial Advocacy Program for the Northeast, 1996; counsel, v.p. Piccola Opera Com., Phila., 1997—; pres. Grad. Club, bd. dirs., 2000; task force chmn. Mazzei Nat. Constn. Ctr., 2001. Recipient Disting. Svc. award Nationalities Svc. Ctr., 1975, Man of Yr. award Columbus Civic Assn., 1969, Legion of Honor, Chapel of Four Chaplains, 1979, Bronze Medallion award, 1982, commendation Pa. Senate, 1982, Villanova Law Sch. Appreciation award 1993, Syracuse U. Achievement award 1994, Hon. Lifetime award KC, 1997; Resolution of Praise, pres. City Coun. of Phila., 1999. Mem. ABA (chmn. U.S. Surpeme Ct. admissions com. 2001), ATLA (Supervising Judge Advocacy award Phila. region 2000, supr. judge law sch. trial advocacy competition, 2000, Phila. chpt. emeritus chmn. of Justice Michael A. Musmanno award 2000), Internat. Acad. Law and Sci., Justinian Soc. (bd. govs. 1980-83, sr. lawyer award 2000), Pa. Bar Assn., Pa. Trial Lawyers Assn. (bd. govs. 1982-84), N.Y. Trial Lawyers Assn. (assoc.), Phila. Bar Assn. (bd. dirs. 1980-83, asst. sec. 1983, 84, chmn. emeritus Beccaria award, 1993—), Lawyers Club Phila. (pres. 1982-84, chmn. Centennial Celebration 2001), Phila. Trial Lawyers Assn. (pres. 1982-83, Disting. Svc. award 2000), Nat. Italian-Am. Bar Assn. (bd. govs. 1985-90, historian 1987-90, pres. 1991-93, bd. chmn. 1993-95), Am. Arbitration Assn. (arbitrator 1950—), Sons of Italy (Man of Yr. award 1995). General civil litigation, Contracts commercial, Estate planning. Home: 2401 Pennsylvania Ave Philadelphia PA 19130-3010 Office: 1530 Chestnut St Fl 4 Philadelphia PA 19102-2739

RAINS, M. NEAL, lawyer; b. Burlington, Iowa, July 26, 1943; s. Merritt and Lucille (Lepper) R.; m. Jean Baldwin, July 26, 1980 (div. 1995); children: Robert Baldwin, Kathleen Kellogg. B.A. in Polit. Sci. with honors, U. Iowa, 1965; J.D., Northwestern U., 1968. Bar: Ohio 1968. Assoc. Arter & Hadden, Cleve., 1968-76, ptnr., 1976—, mem. exec. com., 1981-90, mem. mgmt. com., 1987-90, mng. ptnr., 1990-92; master bencher Inns of Ct., 1990—. Lectr. on profl. topics, including alternative dispute resolution, distbn. law, litigation practice and procedure, and antitrust. Contbr. articles to profl. jours. Former trustee Legal Aid Soc. Cleve.; trustee Cleve. Play House, mem. adv. coun., 1988—; trustee Citizens League Greater Cleve., Cleve. Art Assn. With U.S. Army, 1968-70 Fellow Am. Bar Found.; mem. ABA, Ohio Bar Assn., Bar Assn. Greater Cleve. (chmn. young lawyers sect. 1975-76, recipient cert. merit 1975), Def. Rsch. Inst., Internat. Assn. Def. Counsel, Ohio Assn. Civil Trial Attys., Cleve. Bar Found. (trustee 1999—), Harold H. Burton Am. Inn Ct. (pres. 1999—), Union Club, Cleve. Skating Club, City Club, Print Club (trustee 2001—), Rowfant Club, Phi Beta Kappa, Omicron Delta Kappa, Phi Delta Phi. Antitrust, General civil litigation. Home: 18400 Shelburne Rd Shaker Heights OH 44118 Office: Arter & Hadden 1100 Huntington Bldg Cleveland OH 44115 E-mail: nrains@arterhadden.com

RAINVILLE, CHRISTINA, lawyer; b. N.Y.C., Feb. 7, 1962; d. Dewey and Nancy Rainville; m. Peter S. Greenberg, May 1994; children: Jeremy, Catharine. BS, Northwestern U., 1984, JD, 1988. Atty. Schnader Harrison Segal & Lewis, Phila., 1988—. Mem. ABA (pro bono publico award 1999), Nat. Assn. Criminal Def. Lawyers. Presbyn. Civil rights, Federal civil litigation, Criminal. Office: Schnader Harrison et al 1600 Market St Ste 3600 Philadelphia PA 19103-7287 E-mail: trainville@schnader.com

RAINWATER, TONYA B. judge; b. Granite City, Ill., Apr. 13, 1956; d. Markus Vernell and Shirley (Pohl) Baccus; m. Giles Dean Rainwater, Oct. 29, 1983; children: Sabrina B., Kali B., Blake B. BS, Fla. State U., 1976; JD, U. Fla., 1978; MBA, Fla. Inst. Tech., 1988. Bar: Fla. 1979. Asst. state atty. Office State Atty., Titusville, Fla., 1979-80; prin. Tonya L. Baccus, P.A., Indian Harbour Beach, 1981-86; county ct. judge Brevard County, Melbourne, 1987-91; cir. ct. judge 18th Jud. Cir., 1991—. Adj. prof. Fla. Inst. Tech., Melbourne, 1985-86. Pres. Explorer Elem. PTA, Melbourne, 1998-99, v.p., 1999-2000; mem. WestShore Jr./Sr. High Sch. Improvement Coun., Melbourne, 1999-2000. Mem. Inns. of Ct. (dir. 1999—), Civilian-Mil. Coun. Office: 2825 Judge Fran Jamieson Way Viera FL 32940-8006

RAISLER, KENNETH MARK, lawyer; b. New Rochelle, N.Y., May 15, 1951; s. Herbert A. and Norma (Glaubach) R.; m. Sara Ann Kelsey, June 11, 1978; children: Caroline Elisabeth, Katharine Kelsey, David Mark. BSBA, Yale Coll., 1973; JD, NYU, 1976. Bar: N.Y. 1977, D.C. 1977, U.S. Dist. Ct. (so. dist.) N.Y. 1977, U.S. Dist. Ct. D.C. 1977, U.S. Ct. Appeals (2d cir.) 1977, U.S. Ct. Appeals (D.C. cir.) 1977, U.S. Ct. Appeals (7th cir.) 1982, U.S. Ct. Appeals (10th cir.) 1983, U.S. Supreme Ct. 1985. Law clk. U.S. Dist. Ct. (so. dist.) N.Y., N.Y.C., 1976-77; asst. U.S. atty., Washington, 1977-82; dep. gen. counsel Commodity Futures Trading Commn., Washington, 1982-83, gen. counsel, 1983-87; ptnr. Rogers & Wells, N.Y.C., 1987-92, Sullivan & Cromwell, N.Y.C., 1992—. Mem. Assn. of Bar of City of N.Y. (chair futures regulation com. 1988-91). Office: Sullivan & Cromwell 125 Broad St Fl 28 New York NY 10004-2489

RAJAN, ANANDHI, lawyer; b. Mayavaram, India, Nov. 5, 1966; d. G. Soundara and Vathala S. Rajan; m. Srinivas Alugupalli, Apr. 5, 1997 (dec. Oct. 1998). BS, Emory U., 1988; JD, Ga. State U., 1992. Bar: Ga. 1992. Jud. clk., Atlanta, 1992-94; assoc. Long, Weinberg, Ansley and Wheeler, 1994-99, Swift, Currie, McGhee & Hiers, Atlanta, 1999—. Mem. ABA, Def. Rsch. Inst., Ga. State Bar Assn., Atlanta Bar Assn., Ins. Profls. of Atlanta. Hindu. Avocations: reading, travel. Office: Swift Currie MdGhee & Hiers 1355 Peachtree St NE Ste 300 Atlanta GA 30309-3238

RAJTAR, STEVEN ALLEN, lawyer; b. Cleve., Aug. 16, 1951; s. Steve and Rose (Golembiewski) R.; m. Gayle Prince, June 15, 1974; children—Jason Paul, Kelly Rose. B.A. in Anthropology, U. Central Fla., Orlando, 1973, B.S. in Math., 1973; J.D., U. Fla., 1976, LL.M., 1977. Bar: Fla. 1976, Tenn. 1977, U.S. Dist. Ct. (no. dist.) Fla. 1977, U.S. Tax Ct. 1977, U.S. Dist. Ct. (ea. dist.) Tenn. 1978, U.S. Dist. Ct. (middle dist.) Fla. 1980. Assoc. Clayton, Duncan, Johnston, Quincey, Ireland & Felder, Gainesville, Fla., 1976-77, Gearhiser & Peters, Chattanooga, 1977-79; assoc. Matthias & Matthias, Orlando, 1979-84, ptnr., 1985-85; sole practice law, 1985—. Contbr. articles to Tenn. Bar Jour. Mem. Fla. Bar, Orange County Bar Assn., U. Central Fla. Alumni Assn. (dir. 1979-82, 83-85). Unitarian. General corporate, Real property, Corporate taxation. Home: 1614 Bimini Dr Orlando FL 32806-1512 Office: 155 Sabal Palm Dr Longwood FL 32779-2558

RAK, LORRAINE KAREN, lawyer; b. Trenton, N.J., Jan. 8, 1959; d. Charles Walter and Lottie Mary (Debiec) R. BA in Polit. Sci., Seton Hall U., South Orange, N.J., 1981; JD, Cornell U., 1984. Bar: N.J. 1986, N.Y. 1986, U.S. Dist. Ct. N.J. 1986, U.S. Dist. Ct. (so. and ea. dists.) N.Y. 1988, U.S. Dist. Ct. (no. dist.) N.Y. 1991, U.S. Ct. Appeals (4th cir.) 1989, U.S. Ct. Appeals (2d cir.) 1990, U.S. Ct. Appeals (3d cir.) 1991. Assoc. Shearman & Sterling, N.Y.C., 1984-91, Robinson, St. John & Wayne, N.Y.C., 1992-93; dep. atty. gen. State of N.J., Newark, 1993—. Active Lawyers' Com. for Human Rights, N.Y.C. Mem. ABA, ACLU, LWV, Cornell Law Assn., Amnesty Internat., Polish Arts Club Trenton. Democrat. Roman Catholic. Federal civil litigation, State civil litigation, Consumer commercial. Office: State of NJ Divsn Law Consumer Affairs Pros Sect 124 Halsey St 5th Fl Newark NJ 07101 E-mail: raklor@law.dol.lps.state.nj.us

RAKER, IRMA STEINBERG, judge; b. Bklyn. m. Samuel K. Raker, Apr. 3, 1960; children: Mark, Stefanie, Leslie. BA, Syracuse U., 1959; cert. of attendance (hon.), Hague (The Netherlands) Acad. Internat. Law, 1959; JD, Am. U., 1972. Bar: Md. 1973, D.C. 1974, U.S. Dist. Ct. Md. 1977, U.S. Ct. Appeals (4th cir.) 1977. Asst. state's atty. State's Atty.'s Office of Montgomery County, Md., 1973-79; ptnr. Sachs, Greenebaum & Tayler, Washington, 1979-80; judge Dist. Ct. Md., Rockville, 1980-82, Cir. Ct. for Montgomery County, Md., 1982-94, Ct. of Appeals of Md., 1994—. Adj. prof. Washington Coll. Law, Am. U., 1980—; faculty seminar leader child abuse course Nat. Coll. Dist. Attys. at U. Mass., 1977; mem. faculty Md. Jud. Inst., Nat. Criminal Def. Inst., 1980, 81, 82; instr. litigation program Georgetown Law Ctr.-Nat. Inst. Trial Advocacy; mem. legis. com. Md. Jud. Conf., mem. exec. com., 1985-89, mem. commn. to study bail bond and surety industry in Md.; mem. spl. com. to revise article 27 on crimes and punishment State of Md., 1991—; mem. inquiry com. atty. Grievance Commn. Md., 1978-81; chairperson jud. compensation com. Md. Jud. Conf., 1997—. Past editor Am. U. Law Rev. Treas., v.p. West Bradley Citizens Assn., 1964-68; mem. adv. com. to county exec. on child abuse Montgomery County, 1976-77, mem. adv. com. to county exec. on battered spouses, 1977-78, mem. adv. com. on environ. protection, 1980; mem. citizens adv. bd. Montgomery County Crisis Ctr., 1980. Recipient Robert C. Heeney award Md. State Bar Assn., 1993, Dorothy Beatty Meml. award Women's Law Ctr., 1994, Rita Davidson award Women's Bar Md., 1995, Margaret Brent Trailblazers award ABA Commn. on Women in the Profession/Women's Bar Assn. Md., 1995, Elizabeth Dole Woman of Achievement award ARC, 1998, Leadership in Law award The Daily Record, 2001, Nat. Assn. Social Workers' Pub. Citizen of Yr. award, 2001, others; named of Md.'s Top 100 Women Warfield's Bus. Record, 1997, 99, 2001. Fellow Md. Bar Found.; mem. ABA (chairperson criminal justice stds. com. 1995-96, mem. coun. criminal law sect. 1997—, del. nat. conf. state trial judges, active various coms.), Md. State Bar Assn. (chairperson coun. criminal law and practice sect., mem. bd. govs. 1981, 82, 85, 86, 90, mem. coun. litigation sect., active coms., chairperson com. to draft pattern jury instrns. in civil and criminal cases 1980—), Nat. Assn. Women Judges, Internat. Acad. Trial Judges, Am. Law Inst., Montgomery County Bar Assn. (chairperson criminal law sect. 1978-79, mem. exec. com. 1979-80, active other coms., Outstanding Jurist award 2000), Montgomery County Bar Leaders, Women's Bar Assn. Md., Women's Bar Assn. D.C., Hadassah Women's Orgn. (life), Pioneer Women Na'amat (hon. life, Celebration of Women award 1985), Pi Sigma Alpha. Avocations: photography, tennis, needlework. Office: Ct of Appeals of Md 50 Maryland Ave Rockville MD 20850-2320

RALEY, JOHN W., JR. lawyer; b. May 23, 1932; s. John Wesley and Helen Thames; children: John Wesley III, Robert Thames. AB, Okla. Baptist U., 1954; JD, U. Okla., 1959. Bar: Okla. 1959, U.S. Supreme Ct. 1973, U.S. Ct. Appeals (10th cir.), 1962, U.S. Dist. Ct. (we. dist.) 1961, U.S. Dist. Ct. (no. dist.) 1988, U.S. Dist. Ct. (ea. dist.) 1989 Okla. Asst. U.S. atty. We. Dist. Okla. U.S. Dept. Justice, 1961-69; ptnr. Northcutt, Raley, Clark and Gardner, Ponca City, Okla., 1969-90; U.S. atty. Ea. Dist. Okla. U.S. Dept. Justice, 1990-97; of counsel Northcutt, Clark, Gardner & Hron, Ponca City, 1997-01; municipal ct. judge, 2001—. Mayor of Ponca City, Okla., 1980-83. Capt. USNR, 1950-84, ret. Recipient George Washington

Honor medal Freedoms Found. at Valley Forge, 1971, Spl. Initiative award U.S. Dept. Justice, 1994, Outstanding Alumni Achievement award Okla. Bapt. U., 1981, Outstanding Citizen award Ponca City, 1984. Fellow Am. Coll. Trial Lawyers; mem. ABA, Am. Bd. Trial Advs., Okla. Bar Assn. (mem. bd. govs.), Kay County Bar Assn. (pres. 1980), Am. Legion, Mason, Reserve Officers Assn., Naval Reserve Assn., VFW. Republican. So. Baptist. Office: 400 E Central Ave Ste 401 Ponca City OK 74601-5428 Address: PO Box 1412 Ponca City OK 74602-1412

RALLO, DOUGLAS, lawyer; b. Orange, N.J., Nov. 22, 1953; s. Vito and Mary (Spiduro) Rallo. BA, Montclair (N.J.) State Coll., 1975; cert., Inst. Internat. and Comparative Law, 1977; JD, John Marshall Law Sch., 1978. Bar: Ill 1979, US Dist Ct (no dist) Ill 1979, US Ct Appeals (7th cir) 1979, US Dist Ct (ea dist) Wis 1995, Wis 1998, US Dist Ct (we dist) Wis 2001. Corp. lawyer Bendix Corp., N.Y.C., 1979-81; assoc. David T. Rallo & Assocs., Ltd., Chgo., 1981-83, Horwitz & Assocs., Ltd., Chgo., 1983-84, Semmelman & Bertucci Ltd., Lake Forest, Ill., 1984-98; pvt. practice Law Offices of Douglas Rallo, P.C., Libertyville, 1998—. Research asst A Functional Analysis of the Criminal Code Reform Act of 1978 for US Congress; panel atty Ill State Appellate Defender's Office, 1980; profiled in Newsweek mag, 1989, Chicago Tribune, 1989; tchr adult legal educ programs Libertyville High Sch, Ill., 1988—90, Mundelein High Sch, Ill., 1989; Notable cases include: Sherrod vs. Berry, 629F. Supp. 159 (1985) and 589F Supp. 433 (1984). Contbr. articles to profl jours. Vpres Lake County chpt NW Ill MADD, 1989—91; comnr Libertyville Youth Comn, 1990—94; bd dirs Civic Ctr Found, Libertyville. Mem.: Ill State Bar Asn (lectr hedonic damages, civil practice procedure, sem expert witnesses 1989), Ill Trail Lawyers Asn, State Bar Wis, Lake County Bar Asn, Libertyville CofC, Mundelein CofC, Vernon Hills CofC, Pi Sigma Alpha. Avocations: water sports, swimming, softball. Personal injury, Product liability, Workers' compensation. Office: Law Offices Douglas Rallo P C 611 S Milwaukee Ave Libertyville IL 60048-3256

RALSTON, JAMES ALLEN, lawyer; b. Cin., Oct. 24, 1946; s. Edward John and Gladys Mae (Herrmann) Overman R.; m. Karen Lee Kilgore, Dec. 29, 1969; children— Matthew Allen, Emily Anne. B.A., U. Va., 1968; J.D., U. Cin., 1973. Bar: Ohio 1973, U.S. Dist. Ct. (so. dist.) Ohio 1973. Assoc. Frost & Jacobs, Cin., 1973-79; atty. Eagle-Pitcher Industries, Inc., Cin., 1979-82, asst. sec., 1982— , gen. counsel, 1982— , v.p., 1984— . Served with U.S. Army, 1969-71. Contracts commercial, General corporate, Personal injury. Office: Eagle-Picher Industries Inc 250 E 5th St Ste 500 Cincinnati OH 45202-4154

RAMBE, LARS JOACHIM, lawyer; b. Täby, Sweden, Sept. 19, 1968; s. Swen and Birgitta Rambe; m. Anna Ingrid Karlsson. LLM, Uppsala (Sweden) U., 1994. Assoc. legal counsel Pharmacia AB, Uppsala, Sweden, 1994-95; internat. legal counsel Pharmacia & Upjohn, 1995-96, Amersham Pharmacia Biotech, Uppsala, 1996-99; mng. ptnr. Rambe Legal, Stockholm, 1999—. Sec. Voxi AB, Stockholm, 1999—. Author: The Use of Change of and Control Clauses, 1994. General corporate, Intellectual property, Mergers and acquisitions. Home: Kungsholms Strand 171 Stockholm SE-11248 Sweden Office: Rambe Legal Stagneliusvagen 31 Stockholm SE-11259 Sweden Fax: 4686508835. E-mail: lawyers@rambe.com

RAMBO, SYLVIA H. federal judge; b. Royersford, Pa., Apr. 17, 1936; d. Granville A. and Hilda E. (Leonhardt) R.; m. George F. Douglas, Jr., Aug. 1, 1970. BA, Dickinson Coll., 1958; JD, Dickinson Sch Law, 1962; LLD (hon.), Wilson Coll., 1980, Dickinson Sch. Law, 1993, Dickinson Coll., 1994, Shippensburg U., 1996, Widener U., 1999. Bar: Pa. 1962. Atty. trust dept. Bank of Del., Wilmington, 1962-63; pvt. practice Carlisle, 1963-76; from public defender to chief public defender Cumberland County, Pa., 1974-76; judge Ct. Common Pleas, Cumberland County, 1976-78, U.S. Dist. Ct. (mid. dist.) Pa., Harrisburg, 1979-92, chief judge, 1992-99; federal judge U.S. Dist. Ct., Harrisburg, 2000—. Asst. prof., adj. prof. Dickinson Sch. Law, 1974-76. Bd. govs. Dickinson Sch. Law., Pa. State U., 2000—. Mem. Nat. Assn. Women Judges, Phi Alpha Delta. Democrat. Presbyterian. Office: US Dist Ct Federal Bldg PO Box 868 Harrisburg PA 17108-0868

RAMEY, DENNY L. bar association executive director; b. Portsmouth, Ohio, Feb. 22, 1947; s. Howard Leroy and Norma Wylodine (Richards) R.; m. Jeannine Gayle Dunmyer, Sept. 24, 1971 (div. Nov. 1991); children: Elizabeth Michelle, Brian Michael. BBA, Ohio U., 1970; MBA, Capital U., 1976. Cert. assn. exec. Adminstrv. mgr. Transit Warehouse div. Elston Richards Storage Co., Columbus, Ohio, 1970-73; mgr. continuing profl. edn. Ohio Soc. CPA's, 1973-79; exec. dir. Engrs. Found. of Ohio, 1979-80; asst. exec. Ohio State Bar Assn., 1980-86, exec. dir., sec., treas., 1986—. Treas., exec. com., bd. dirs. Ohio Bar Liability Ins. Co., Columbus, 1986—; treas. Ohio State Bar Found., 1986—; treas. Ohio Legal Ctr. Ins., Columbus, 1988-91; sec. Ohio Printing Co., Ltd., 1991; v.p. Osbanet, Inc., 1993—; chmn. Lawriter LLC, 2000—; bd. dirs. OSBA.com, LLC. Mem. Nat. Assn. Bar Execs. (chmn. various coms.), Am. Soc. Assn. Execs., Ohio Soc. Assn. Execs., Scioto Country Club, Brookside Golf & Country Club, The Player's Club. Methodist. Avocations: tennis, golf, sports, music, wine appreciation. Office: Ohio State Bar Assn 1700 Lake Shore Dr PO Box 16562 Columbus OH 43216-6562 E-mail: dramey@ohiobar.org

RAMIL, MARIO R. state supreme court justice; b. Quezon City, The Philippines, June 21, 1946; came to U.S., 1956; s. Quintin A. and Fausta M. (Reyes) R.; m. Judy E. Wong, Nov. 6, 1971; children: Jonathan, Bradley. BA in Polit. Sci., Calif. State U., Hayward, 1972; JD, U. Calif., San Francisco, 1975. Bar: Calif. 1976, Hawaii 1976, U.S. Dist. Ct. Hawaii, U.S. Dist. Ct. (no. dist.) Calif., U.S. Ct. Appeals (9th cir.). Law clk. San Francisco Neighborhood Legal Aid Found., 1973-75; legal counsel Sandigan-Newcomers Svcs., Inc., San Francisco, 1975-76; dep. atty. gen. Dept. Labor and Indsl. Rels., 1976-79; dep. atty. gen. cen. adminstrn. U. Hawaii, 1979-80; staff atty. house majority atty.'s office Hawaii Ho. of Reps., 1980; pvt. practice, 1980-82; dep. atty. gen. adminstrv. div. State of Hawaii, 1982-84, ins. commr., 1984-86; dir. Hawaii State Dept. Labor and Indsl. Rels., Honolulu, 1986-91; of counsel Lyons, Brandt, Cook and Hiramatsu, 1991-93; assoc. justice Hawaii Supreme Ct., Honolulu, 1993—. Bd. dirs. Hawaii Youth-At-Risk, 1989; co-chair state conv. Dem. Party State of Hawaii, 1984; mem. Adv. Coun. on Housing and Constrn., State of Hawaii, 1981; pres., bd. dirs. Hawaii Non-Profit Housing Corp.; exec. sec., chmn. adminstrv. budget com. Oahu Filipino Community Coun.; bd. dirs, legal advisor Oahu Filipino Jaycees, 1978-81. Office: Ali'iolani Hale Hawaii Supreme Ct 417 S Kinga St Honolulu HI 96813-2902*

RAMIREZ, ANTHONY BENJAMIN, lawyer; b. Frizell, Kans., Jan. 17, 1937; s. Jesus Ruiz Ramirez and Francisca Lopez; m. Jeanette Marilyn Lee, Sept. 19, 1964; children: Christopher Benjamin, Andrew Anthony. BA, St. Benedict's Coll., Atchison, Kans., 1959; JD, St. Louis U., 1967. Bar: Mo. 1967, U.S. Dist. Ct. (ea. dist.) Mo. 1968. Legal staff probate divsn. St. Louis City Cir. Ct., 1967-72; atty. various law offices St. Louis, St. Louis, 1972-81; ptnr. Coleman, Ross, Goetz, Robert & Ramirez, 1981-86; pvt. practice St. Louis, 1986—. Legal advisor Mexican Consulate in St. Louis, 1979—; adj. prof. law Webster U., St. Louis, 1988-93. Editor (newsletter) DeNuevo, 1978-80; co-host Latin Rhythms radio program KDHX FM, 1992-93. Bd. dirs. Confluence St. Louis, 1990-96, ARC, Bi-State chpt. St. Louis, 1990-94, Springboard to Learning, 1996-2000; mem. Coro Fellows Program, 1994-95; facilitator Hispanic Leaders Group Greater St. Louis, 1985-93, sec., 1993-95, chmn., 1995—; Mo. del. White House Conf. on Small Bus., 1986; mem. SBA St. Louis Dist. Adv. Coun., 1985-93; mem. Fordyce Two Leadership Summit, 1990; commr. Mo. Commn. on Human Rights, 1983-87; charter mem. Gov.'s Coun. on Hispanic Affairs, 1980. Staff sgt. U.S. Army, 1959-60, 61-64. Named Mo. Minority Advocate of Yr. U.S. SBA, St. Louis, 1984; recipient Pres. award Hispanic C. of C., St. Louis, 1986, St. Louis Cmty. award of merit KPLR-TV, St. Louis, 1989, MICAH award St. Louis chpt. Am. Jewish Com., 2001. Mem. ABA, Nat. Assn. Criminal Def. Attys., Mo. Bar Assn., Bar Assn. Metro St. Louis, Law Alumni Assn. St. Louis U. Sch. Law (v.p. 1984-88), Hispanic C. of C. Met. St. Louis (co-founder, pres. 1982-85, chmn. bd. 1983-88). Republican. Roman Catholic. General civil litigation, Criminal, Personal injury. Office: 1221 Locust St Ste 503 Saint Louis MO 63103-2380

RAMIREZ, FRANK TENORIO, lawyer; b. Fresno, Calif., July 16, 1952; s. Ramon and Connie Ramirez; m. Teresa Gonzales, Apr. 15, 1978; children: Irene, Isabel, Francesca. BS, Calif. State U., Fresno, 1974; JD, U. Calif., Berkeley, 1977. Bar: Calif. 1978, U.S. Dist. Ct. (ea. dist.) Calif. 1978, U.S. Dist. Ct. (so. dist.) Calif. 1983, U.S. Ct. Appeals (9th cir.), 1984. Staff atty. Calif. Rural Legal Assistance, Inc., Madera, 1977-81, regional counsel Fresno, 1982-84, trustee San Francisco, 1986-98; pub. defender Fresno County Pub. Defender's Office, Fresno, 1982; ptnr. Hernandez & Ramirez, 1984—. Trustee Fresno County Law Libr., 1998. Mem. Fresno County Bar Assn., Madera County Bar Assn. (pres. 1996), La Raza Lawyers Assn. (pres. San Joaquin Valley chpt. 1983). Democrat. Roman Catholic. State civil litigation, Criminal, Personal injury. Office: Hernandez & Ramirez 6103 N 1st St Ste 102 Fresno CA 93710-5406

RAMO, ROBERTA COOPER, lawyer; b. Denver, Aug. 8, 1942; d. David D. and Martha L. (Rosenblum) Cooper; m. Barry W. Ramo, June 17, 1964. BA magna cum laude, U. Colo., 1964; JD, U. Chgo., 1967; LLD, U. Mo., 1995, U. Denver, 1995; LHD (hon.), U. Colo., 1995; JD (hon.), Golden Gate U., 1996, U. S.C., 2001. Bar: N.Mex. 1967, Tex. 1971. With NC. Fund, Durham, 1967-68; nat. tchg. fellow Shaw U., Raleigh, N.C., 1968-70; mem. Sawtelle, Goode, Davidson & Troilo, San Antonio, 1970-72, Rodey, Dickason, Sloan, Akin & Robb, Albuquerque, 1972-74; sole practice law, 1974-77; dir., shareholder Poole, Kelly & Ramo, 1977-93; shareholder Modrall, Sperling, Roehl, Harris & Sisk, 1993—. Lectr. in field., bd. dirs. Merrill Lynch Asset Mgmt. Cluster D. Funds, Ednl. Credit Mgmt. Corp. Co-author: New Mexico Estate Administration System, 1980; editor: How to Create a System for the Law Office, 1975; contbg. editor: Tex. Probate Sys., 1974; contbr. articles to profl. jours., chpts. to books. Bd. dirs., past pres. N.Mex. Symphony Orch., 1977-86; bd. dirs. Albuquerque Cmty . Found., N.Mex. First, 1987-90; bd. regents U. N.Mex., 1989-94, pres., 1991-93, chmn. presdl. search com., 1990; mem. steering com. World Conf. Domestic Violence, 1996-99; mem. Am. Law Inst. Coun., 1997—, exec. com., 2000—; mem. Martindale-Hubbell Legal Adv. Bd., 1996-2000; chmn. bd. Cooper's Inc., 1999—; founding bd. mem. Think N.Mex., 1998—; mem. Civitas Initiative, 1997—. Recipient Disting. Pub. Svc. award Gov. of N.Mex., 1993. Fellow Am. Bar Found.; mem. ABA (pres. 1995, bd. govs. 1994-97, chmn. London 2000 com. 1997—, Asia Law Initiatives Coun. 1999—, others), Albuquerque Bar Assn. (bd. dirs., pres. 1980-81), N.Mex. Bar Assn. (Outstanding Contbn. award 1981, 84), Am. Bar Retirement Assn. (bd. dirs. 1990-94), Am. Judicature Soc. (bd. dirs. 1988-91), Law Inst. Coun., Am. Arbitration Assn. (bd. dirs. 1997—, bd. trustees Global Ctr. Dispute Resolution Rsch. 1999—), Greater Albuquerque C. of C. (bd. dirs., exec. com. 1987-91). Pension, profit-sharing, and employee benefits, Probate, Real property. Address: Modrall Sperling Roehl Harris & Sisk PO Box 2168 Albuquerque NM 87103-2168

RAMOS, CARLOS E. law educator; b. Caguas, P.R., Oct. 20, 1952; s. Francisco E. and Olga (Gonzalez) R.; m. Lesbia Hernandez, July 30, 1988; children: Carlos Francisco, Isabel Maria, Macarena Eugenia. BA, U. P.R., 1974, JD, 1978; diploma, U. Stockholm, 1975; LLM, U. Calif., Berkeley, 1987. Bar: P.R. 1978, U.S. Dist. Ct. P.R. 1978, U.S. Ct. Appeals (1st cir.) 1979. Staff atty. P.R. Legal Svcs., San Juan, P.R., 1978-79; asst. prof. law InterAm. U. P.R., 1979-86, assoc. prof., 1986-93, dean, 1993-2000, prof. law, 1993—; exec. dir. Santurce Law Firm, San Jose, 1983-86. Co-author: Derecho Constitucional de Puerto Rico y los Estados Unidos, 1990, Teoria y Practica de la Litigacion en Puerto Rico. Mem. ABA, ATLA, Am. Judicature Soc., P.R. Bar Assn. Office: InterAm U PR Sch Law PO Box 70351 San Juan PR 00936-8351 E-mail: ceramos@inter.edu

RAMSAY, LOUIS LAFAYETTE, JR. lawyer, banker; b. Fordyce, Ark., Oct. 11, 1918; s. Louis Lafayette and Carmile (Jones) R.; m. Joy Bond, Oct. 3, 1945; children: Joy Blankenship, Richard Louis. JD, U. Ark., 1947; LLD (hon.), U. Ark., Fayetteville, 1988, U. Ark., Pine Bluff, 1992. Bar: Ark. 1947, U.S. Dist. Ct. Ark. 1947, U.S. Ct. Appeals (8th cir.) 1948, U.S. Supreme Ct. 1952. Of counsel Ramsay, Bridgforth, Harrelson & Starling and predecessor firm Ramsay, Cox, Lile, Bridgforth, Gilbert, Harrelson & Starling, Pine Bluff, Ark., 1948—; pres. Simmons First Nat. Bank, 1970-78, CEO, chmn. bd. dirs., 1978-83. Chmn. exec. com., bd. dirs. Blue Cross-Blue Shield of Ark., Usable Life Ins. Co.; chmn. exec. com. Simmons First Nat. Corp. Mem. bd. Econ. Devel. Alliance of Jefferson County; mem. ofcl. bd. First United Meth. Ch. With USAF, 1942-45, maj. Res., 1945-49. Recipient Disting. Alumnus award U. Ark., 1982, Outstanding Lawyer award Ark. Bar Assn./Ark. Bar Found., 1966, 87. Mem. ABA (mem. spl. com. on presdl. inability and vice presdl. vacancy 1966), Ark. Bar Assn. (pres. 1963-64), Ark. Bar Found. (pres. 1960-61, Joint Bar Assn.,-Bar Found. Outstanding Lawyer award 1966, Lawyer Citizen award 1987), Ark. Bankers Assn. (pres. 1980-81), Pine Bluff C. of C. (pres. 1968), Rotary (pres. Pine Bluff 1954-55). Methodist. General corporate, Probate. Office: Ramsay Bridgforth Harrelson & Starling 11th Fl Simmons 1st Nat Bldg 501 S Main St Pine Bluff AR 71601-4327 E-mail: firm@ramsaylaw.com

RAMSEY, HENRY, JR. university official, lawyer, retired judge; b. Florence, S.C., Jan. 22, 1934; s. Henry Ramsey and Mary Ann Brunson; reared by Charles Arthur and Nellie Tillman; m. Evelyn Yvonne Lewis, June 11, 1961 (div. Sept. 1967); children: Charles, Githaiga, Robert, Ismail; m. Eleanor Mason Ramsey, Sept. 7, 1969; children: Yetunde, Abeni. Student, Howard U.; BA, U. Calif., Riverside, 1960; LLB, U. Calif., 1963; student Inst. Edn. Mgmt., Harvard U., 1992; LLD (hon.), William Mitchell Coll. Law, 1996. Bar: Calif., 1964, U.S. Supreme Ct., 1967. Dep. dist. atty. Contra Costa County, Calif., 1964-65; pvt. practice Ramsey & Rosenthal, Richmond, 1965-71; prof. law U. Calif., Berkeley, 1971-80; judge Superior Court County of Alameda State Calif., Oakland, 1980-90; dean Sch. Law, Howard U., Washington, 1990-96, v.p. for legal affairs, acting gen. counsel, 1994-95, ret. Vis. prof. law U. Tex., Austin, 1977, U. Colo., Boulder, 1977-78, Am. Indian Law Ctr., U. N.Mex., 1980; mem., pres. Coun. Legal Edn., Opportunity, Washington, 1987-93; chair Law Sch. Admission Coun.-Bar Passage Rate Study Group, 1990-93; mem. Fellows of Am. Bar Found. Adv. Rsch. Com., 1995—; mem. Coun. for Ct. Excellence, D.C. Jury Project, 1996-97; panelist Washington, D.C. region Ctr. for Pub. Resources, Institute for Dispute Resolution. Mem. City Coun. Berkeley, 1973-77, Criminal Justice Planning Bd., County of Alameda, 1973-76; trustee City of Berkeley Libr., 1973-74, Fibreboard Asbestos Compensation Trust, 1994—; bd. dirs. Redevel. Agy., Berkeley, 1971-73; dir. Rosenberg Found., San Francisco, 1999—. With USAF, 1951-55. Recipient Jefferson Jurist award Calif. Assoc. Black Lawyers, 1986, Disting. Alumnus award U. Calif., 1987, Disting. Svc. award Wiley Manuel Law Found., 1987. Mem. ABA (mem. sect. legal edn. and admissions to bar 1982—, chair 1991-92, mem. standards rev. com. 1992-95), Nat. bar Assn., Nat. Ctr. State Cts. (mem. commn. trial ct. performance stds. 1987-95, Dist. Svc. award 1990), Am. Law Inst., Am. Judicature Soc., Calif. Judges Assn., Cosmos Club, Fed. City Club, Alpha Phi Alpha. Democrat. Avocations: cooking, reading, gardening, travel.

RAMSEY, JOHN ARTHUR, lawyer; b. Apr. 1, 1942; s. Wilbert Lewis and Lillian (Anderson) R.; m. Nikki Ann Ramsey, Feb. 9, 1943; children: John William, Bret Anderson, Heather Nicole. AB, San Diego State U., 1965; JD, Calif. Western Sch. Law, 1969. Bar: Colo. 1969, Tex. 1978. Assoc. Henry, Cockrell, Quinn & Creighton, 1969-72; atty. Texaco Inc., 1972-80; asst. to pres. Texaco U.S.A., 1980-81, asst. to divsn. v.p., 1981-82, divsn. atty. Denver, 1982-88; ptnr. Holland & Hart, 1989—. Editor-in-chief: Calif. Western Law Rev., 1969. Bd. dirs. Selective Svc., Englewood, Colo., 1972-76; chmn. coun. Bethany Luth. Ch., Englewood, 1976; mem. exec. bd. Denver Area coun. Boy Scouts Am., 1999—. Mem. ABA (vice-chmn. oil, natural gas exploration and prodn. com. sect. natural resource law 1983-88, chmn. 1989—, coun. sect. natural resources, energy and environ. law 1993). Republican. Natural resources, Litigation, UST. Office: Holland & Hart 8390 E Crescent Pkwy Ste 400 Greenwood Vlg CO 80111-2822

RAMSEY, NATALIE D. lawyer; b. Greenville, Tenn., Dec. 6, 1959; d. William Trent and Nancy Elizabeth (Maupin) R. BS, U. Del., 1981; JD, Villanova U., 1984. Bar: Pa. 1984, U.S. Dist. Ct. (ea. dist.) Pa. 1985, U.S. Ct. Appeals (3rd cir. and 11th cirs.) 1989. Assoc. atty. Frederick L. Reigle, Esq. and Assocs., Reading, Pa., 1984-85, Montgomery, McCracken, Walker & Rhoads, LLP, Phila., 1985-93; ptnr. Montgomery, McCracken, Walker & Rhoads, 1993—. Sec. East. Dist. of Pa. Bankruptcy Conf., 2000—; dir. Consumer Bankruptcy Advocacy Project. Co-author various articles on bankruptcy. Vol. Habitat for Humanity. Mem. Comml. Law League, Turnaround Mgmt. Assn. Presbyterian. Avocations: travel, reading. Bankruptcy, Federal civil litigation. Office: Montgomery McCracken Walker & Rhoads LLP 123 S Broad St Fl 24 Philadelphia PA 19109-1099 E-mail: nramsey@mmwr.com

RAMSEY, ROBERT SCOTT, JR. lawyer; b. New Orleans, May 13, 1949; s. Robert S. and June Eve (thaller) R.; m. Tammy Gaudet, Jan. 20, 1995; 1 child, Marc Christian. BA, Nicholls State U., 1973; JD, Loyola U., 1974. Pvt. practice, Morgan City, La. Legal counsel Nicholls Alumni Assn., Thibodeaux, La., 1983-85. Mem. ABA, ATLA, La. Trial Lawyers Assn., La. Bar Assn., St. Mary Parish Bar Assn., East St. Mary Parish C. of C. (bd. dirs. 1980), Theta Psi, KC. Democrat. Roman Catholic. Admiralty, Personal injury, Workers' compensation. Home: 1915 Highway 182 E Morgan City LA 70380-5415 Office: Law Office of R Scott Ramsey Jr 1915 Highway 182 E Morgan City LA 70380-5415

RANA, HARMINDERPAL SINGH, lawyer; b. Bombay, July 4, 1968; came to U.S., 1970; s. Baljit Singh and Devinder (Kaur) R.; m. Aasjot Kaur Sidhu, Mar. 8, 1998. BS in Fgn. Svc., cert. in Asian studies, Georgetown U., 1990; JD, honors cert. in internat. law, Rutgers U., Camden, N.J., 1994. Bar: N.J. 1994, U.S. Dist. Ct. N.J. 1994, N.Y. 1995, U.S. Dist. Ct. (so. and ea. dists.) N.Y. 1995. Pvt. practice, Warren, N.J., 1994—. Assoc. staff analyst N.Y.C. Dept. Mental Health, Bklyn., 1995-97, borough coord., Bklyn. and S.I., 1997; pool atty. family law litigation N.J. Office Pub. Defender, Middlesex and Somerset counties, 1995. Mem. traffic safety com. Warren Twp. (N.J.) Coun., 1997-2000. NYU Trustees scholar, 1986, N.Y. State Regents scholar, 1986. Mem. ABA, Assn. Bar City N.Y. (health law com. 1997-2000). Sikh. Avocations: literature, philosophy, world affairs, athletic cross training, public service. Contracts commercial, General practice, Immigration, naturalization, and customs. Office: 3 Krausche Rd Warren NJ 07059 E-mail: rajranaesq@aol.com

RAND, ANTHONY EDEN, lawyer; b. Garner, N.C., Sept. 1, 1939; s. Walter and Geneva R., Jr.; m. Karen Skarda; children: Ripley E., Craven M. AB, U. N.C., 1961, LLB, 1964; LLB (hon.), U. N.C., Fayetteville, N.C., 2000. Ptnr. Mitchiner, Andrews, Rand, Raleigh, N.C., 1965-68, Rose, Thorp, Rand & Ray, Fayetteville, 1968-81, Rose, Rand, Winfrey & Gregory, Fayetteville, 1982-89, Rand, Finch & Gregory, Fayetteville, 1989-93; mem. from 24th dist. N.C. Senate, 1995—, chmn. rules and operations, 1995—, majority leader, 2001—. Sec., legal counsel Lithotripters, Inc., 1989-96; cons., Prime Med. Svcs., 1996—. Mem. N.C. State Dem. Exec. Com., 1975-77; chmn. exec. com. Cumberland County Dem. party (N.C.), 1977-81; bd. visitors U. N.C.-Chapel Hill, Meth. Coll.; bd. dirs., mem. exec. com. Pub. Sch. Forum; bd. dirs. Fayetteville Area Sentencing, 1985; mem. adv. bd. Mus. Cape Fear, 1989—; mem. nat. adv. panel Child Care Action Com., 1989—; pres. Med-Tech Investments, 1989—. Mem. ABA, ATLA (state commiteeman 1968-72), N.C. Bar Assn., Am. Judicature Assn., Govtl. and Legis. Affairs C. of C., Alpha Tau Omega, Delta Theta Phi. Episcopalian. Office: 2008 Litho Pl Fayetteville NC 28304-2518 E-mail: randla@ncleg.net

RAND, DEBORAH, lawyer; b. Wasington, Sept. 16, 1944; d. Harry I. and Anna T. R. BA, Carleton Coll., 1964; MAT, Harvard U., 1966; JD, Rutgers U., 1974. Bar: N.Y. 1975, U.S. Ct. Appeals (2d cir.) 1975, U.S. Dist. Ct. (so. dist.) N.Y. 1977, U.S. Dist. Ct. (ea. dist.) N.Y. 1995. Tchr. social studies N.Y. h.s., 1966-71; staff atty. EEOC, Washington, 1974-76; sr. atty. MFY Legal Svcs., N.Y.C., 1976-81; project dir. West Side Single Rm. Occupancy Law Project, 1981-85; staff Rutgers Urban Legal Clinic, 1985-86; coord. cmty. housing project Bklyn. Legal Svcs., 1986-87; dep. chief office of Corp. Counsel, N.Y.C., 1987—. Office: Office Corp Counsel NYC Law Dept 100 Church St New York NY 10007-2601

RANDALL, KENNETH C. dean, law educator; JD, Hofstra U., 1981; Master's, Yale U., 1982, Columbia U., 1985, Doctorate, 1988. Practice law Simpson Thacher & Bartlett, N.Y.C., 1982-84; with faculty U. Ala. Sch. Law, Tuscaloosa, 1985—, vice dean, 1989-93, dean, 1993—. Author book on international law; contbr. articles to law jours. and revs. W. Bayard Cutting Jr. fellow of internat. law Columbia U. Sch. Law, 1984-85. Office: U Ala Law Sch PO Box 870382 Tuscaloosa AL 35487-0001

RANDELS, ED L. lawyer; b. Albuquerque, Nov. 17, 1953; s. James L. and Betty J. (Ridgeway) R.; m. Kathryn J. Eddleman, July 11, 1975; children: Nancy L, Joshua L. BA, Mid-Am. Nazarene Coll., Olathe, Kans., 1975; JD, U. Kans., 1982. Bar: Kans. 1982, U.S. Dist. Ct. Kans. 1982, U.S. Ct. Appeals (10th cir.) 1994. Asst. county atty. Montgomery County, Indpendence, Kans., 1982-85, Miami County, Paola, 1985-86; asst. city atty. City of Wichita, 1986-92; asst. county counselor Sedgwick County, Wichita, 1992—. Law day dir. Miami County Bar Assn., Paola, Kans., 1985-86. Contbr. articles to profl. jours. Mem. ABA, Kans. Bar Assn., Wichita Bar Assn. (chair law in edn. com. 1999-2000, mem. mcpl. practice com.), Christian Legal Soc. (pres. Wichita chpt. 1998-99, 2000-01). Republican. Nazarene. Office: Sedgwick County Counselor 525 N Main St Ste 359 Wichita KS 67203-3731 E-mail: erandels@sedgwick.gov

RANDOLPH, A(RTHUR) RAYMOND, federal judge; b. Riverside, N.J., Nov. 1, 1943; m. Eileen J. O'Connor, May 18, 1984; children: John Trevor, Cynthia Lee. BS, Drexel U., 1966; JD summa cum laude, U. Pa., 1969. Bar: Calif. 1970, D.C. 1973, U.S. Supreme Ct. 1973. Law clk. to hon. judge Henry J. Friendly U.S. Ct. Appeals, 2d Cir., N.Y.C., 1969-70; asst. to solicitor gen. U.S. Dept. Justice, Washington, 1970-73, dep. solicitor gen., 1975-77; ptnr. Sharp, Randolph & Green, 1977-83, Randolph & Truitt, Washington, 1983-87, Pepper, Hamilton & Scheetz, Washington, 1987-90; judge U.S. Ct. Appeals (D.C. cir.), 1990—. Spl. asst. atty. gen. State of Mont., 1983-90, State of N.Mex., 1985-90, State of Utah, 1986-90; mem. adv. panel Fed. Cts. Study Com., 1989-90; spl. counsel Com. on Stds. of Ofcl. Conduct, U.S. Ho. of Reps., 1979-80; adj. prof. law Georgetown U. Law Ctr., 1974-78; exec. sec. Atty. Gen.'s Com. on Reform of Fed. Jud. System, 1975-77; mem. com. on Fed. Rules of Evidence U.S. Justice Dept., 1972; chmn. Com. on Govtl. Structures, McLean, Va., 1973-74; adj. prof.

law sch. George Mason U., 1992, disting. prof., 1998—; mem. com. codes conduct Jud. Conf. U.S., 1993-98, chmn., 1995-98. Recipient Spl. Achievement award U.S. Dept. Justice, 1971. Mem. Am. Law Inst., Calif. Bar Assn., D.C. Bar Assn., Order of Coif. Office: US Ct Appeals 333 Constitution Ave NW Washington DC 20001-2866

RANDOLPH, CHRISTOPHER CRAVEN, lawyer; b. Washington, May 26, 1956; s. William Barksdale and Elizabeth Page (Craven) R.; m. Linda Bubernak Dressler, June 6, 1982; children: Alexander Dressler, Brian Donovan. BA summa cum laude, U. Va., 1978; JD cum laude, Harvard U., 1982. Bar: D.C. 1983, N.Y. 1983. Assoc. Debevoise & Plimpton, N.Y.C., 1982-86, Washington, 1987-92; atty. advisor Agy. for Internat. Devel., 1992-95; investor, entrepreneur Vienna, 1995—. Editor Harvard Law Rev., 1980-82; contbr. articles to profl. jours. Mem. ABA, D.C. Bar Assn., Phi Beta Kappa. Republican. Episcopalian. Avocations: travel, reading, sports. General corporate, Government contracts and claims, Securities. Home and Office: 2619 Five Oaks Rd Vienna VA 22181-5436 E-mail: ccrandolph@aol.com

RANDOLPH, ROBERT MCGEHEE, lawyer; b. San Antonio, June 15, 1936; s. Nowlin and Marjorie (McGehee) R.; children: Jeanette, Anne, Nowlin. BA, Tex. Christian U., Ft. Worth, 1957; LLB, U. Tex., 1961. Bar: Tex. 1961, U.S. Dist. Ct. (no. dist.) Tex. 1963, U.S. Supreme Ct. 1972, U.S. Ct. Appeals (5th cir.) 1981. Of counsel Law, Snakard & Gambill, Ft. Worth, 1963—. 1st lt. U.S. Army. Fulbright scholar, 1957-58. Fellow Tex. Bar Found.; mem. Tex. Assn. Def. Counsel, Ft. Worth-Tarrant County Bar Assn., Ft. Worth Club, Alpha Chi. Federal civil litigation, General civil litigation, State civil litigation. Office: Law Snakard & Gambill 500 Throckmorton St Ste 3200 Fort Worth TX 76102-3859

RANKIN, CLYDE EVAN, III, lawyer; b. Phila., July 3, 1950; s. Clyde Evan, Jr. and Mary E. (Peluso) R.; m. Camille Cozzone, Aug. 24, 1997; A.B., Princeton U., 1972; J.D., Columbia U., 1975; postgrad. Hague Acad. Internat. Law, 1975. Bar: N.Y., N.J., D.C., U.S. Supreme Ct. Law clk. to judge U.S. Dist. Ct. So. Dist. N.Y., 1975-77; assoc. Debevoise, Plimpton, Lyons & Gates, N.Y.C., 1977-79; assoc. Coudert Bros., N.Y.C., 1979-83, ptnr., 1984—. Trustee The Rensselaerville (N.Y.) Inst., 1989—, Coun. on Fgn. Rels., 1996—. Stone scholar, 1974. Mem. ABA, Assn. of Bar of City of N.Y., N.Y. State Bar Assn., D.C. Bar Assn., N.J. Bar Assn. Roman Catholic. Club: Amateur Comedy (N.Y.C.). Contbr. article to legal jour. E-mail: rankinc@coudert.com. General corporate, Private international. Office: Coudert Bros 1114 Ave of Americas New York NY 10036-7703

RANKIN, GENE RAYMOND, lawyer; b. Madison, Wis., Sept. 29, 1940; s. Eugene Carleton and Mildred Florence (Blomster) R.; m. Katherine E. Hundt, Aug. 25, 1979; 1 child, Abigail Hundt. BS, U. Wis., 1966, MS in Planning, 1973, JD, 1980. Bar: Wis. 1980, U.S. Dist. Ct. (we. dist.) Wis. 1980, U.S. Ct. Appeals (7th cir.) 1992. Systems analyst U. Wis. Primate Research Ctr., Madison, 1967-72; planner Dane County Regional Planning Commn., 1973-79; pres. Mendota Rsch., 1978—; with Risser and Risser, Madison, 1980-89; dir. land regulation and records dept. Dane County, 1984-89; pvt. practice Wis., 1989—; dir. bd. examiners Wis. Supreme Ct., 1994—. Planning cons., Madison, 1973-77; guest lectr. land use, ethics and admiralty law Law Sch. U. Wis., 1982, 86, 93, 94, 95, 96, guest lectr. land econs. Planning Sch., 1973-81; guest lectr. various legal subjects U. Wis. Ext., 1988—. Author: Historic Preservation Law in Wisconsin, 1982; The First Bite at the Apple: State Supreme Court Takings Jurisprudence Antedating First English, 1990; (with others) Boundary Law in Wisconsin, 1991; contbr. articles to profl. jours. Bd. dirs. Madison Trust for Hist. Preservation, 1984-87, Madison Zoning Bd. of Appeals, 1986-94, Dane County Humane Soc., 1988-90, Dane County Housing Devel. Corp., 1975-79; spl. counsel City of Fitchburg, 1983-84, Nat. Trust for Hist. Preservation, 1989-90, City of Shullsburg, 1990-98; gen. counsel Cat Fanciers' Assn. Midwestern Region, 1990-95, Hist. Madison, Inc., 1981—, Wis. Lead Region Hist. Trust, Inc., 1992—; mem. legis. coun. Spl. Com. on Condo. Issues, Madison, 1984-85; commr. and vice-chmn. Dane County Housing Authority, 1979-84; chmn. Wis. Chamber Orch. Bd., 1979-81; state chmn. McCarthy 1976 campaign, Madison, 1974-76. With USCGR, 1958-60. Fellow Nat. Endowment for the Arts and Humanities, 1972; Olympic finalist for Internat. 470 yachting competition, 1976. Mem. Am. Planning Assn., Urban Land Inst., Urban and Regional Info. Sys. Assn., Wis. Bar Assn. (bd. dirs., treas., founder environ. law sect.), Dane County Bar Assn., Coun. Bar Admission Adminstrs., U. Wis. Hoofers Sailing Club (vice commodore 1972), Meml. Union Club, U.S. Yacht Racing Union, Downtown Madison Rotary, Ixion. Avocations: sailing, racquet sports, music, skating, motorcycling. Environmental, Land use and zoning (including planning), Real property. Home: 2818 Ridge Rd Madison WI 53705-5224 Office: 715 Tenney Bldg 110 E Main St Madison WI 53703-3395

RANKIN, JAMES WINTON, lawyer; b. Norfolk, Va., Sept. 9, 1943; s. Winton Blair and Edith (Griffin) R.; m. Donna Lee Carpenter, June 25, 1966 (dec.); children— Thomas James, William Joseph, Elizabeth Jeanne; m. JoAnne Katherine Murray, Feb. 11, 1978. A.B. magna cum laude, Oberlin Coll., 1965; J.D. cum laude, U. Chgo., 1968. Bar: Ill. 1968, U.S. Dist. Ct. (no. dist.) Ill. 1969, U.S. Ct. Appeals (7th cir.) 1971, U.S. Ct. Appeals (5th cir.) 1979, U.S. Supreme Ct. 1975, Calif. 1986. Law clk. U.S. Dist. Ct. (no. dist.) Ill., 1968-69; assoc. Kirkland & Ellis, Chgo., 1969-73, ptnr., 1973—. Mem. ABA, Order of Coif, Mid-Am. Club, Univ. Club, Mich. Shores Club, Kenilworth Club, Ephriam Yacht Club. Presbyterian. Antitrust, Federal civil litigation, Health. Home: 633 Kenilworth Ave Kenilworth IL 60043-1070 Office: Kirkland & Ellis 200 E Randolph St Fl 54 Chicago IL 60601-6636

RAPAPORT, MARK SAMUEL, lawyer; b. N.Y.C., July 31, 1947; s. Joseph and Sadie (Schwartz) R.; m. Jennifer Munnell, Nov. 22, 1971. B.A. cum laude, U. Wis., 1968, J.D. cum laude, 1973. Bar: Wis. 1973, N.Y. 1974, Calif. 1981. Assoc. Dewey, Ballantine, Bushby, Palmer & Wood, N.Y.C., 1973-80; assoc. Hahn and Cazier, Los Angeles, 1980-82, ptnr. 1982— . Mem. donor fin. planning com. Greater Los Angeles affiliate Heart Fund, 1981— ; mem. devel. com. The Dance Gallery, 1984—. Mem. State Bar Calif. (vice chmn. trust adminstrn. subcom. 1982— , probate com. 1985—), ABA (investments by fiduciaries com. 1979—), N.Y. State Bar Assn., State Bar of Wis. Note and comment editor Wis. Law Rev., 1972-73. Office: Morgan Lewis & Bockius 300 S Grand Ave Ste 2200 Los Angeles CA 90071-3132

RAPER, WILLIAM CRANFORD, lawyer; b. Asheville, N.C., Aug. 17, 1946; s. James Sidney and Kathryn (Cranford) R.; m. Patricia Dotson, Sept. 28, 1974; children: Kimber-leigh, Heather, James. AB, U. N.C., 1968; JD, Vanderbilt U., 1972. Bar: N.C. 1972, U.S. Ct. Appeals (4th cir.) 1972, U.S. Supreme Ct. 1977, U.S. Ct. Appeals (fed. cir.) 1985. Law clk. to Senator Sam Ervin Jr., Washington, 1970; law clk. to presiding justice U.S. Ct. Appeals (4th cir.), Richmond, Va., 1972-73; ptnr. Womble, Carlyle, Sandridge & Rice, Winston-Salem, N.C., 1974—. Fellow Am. College Trial Lawyers; mem. ABA, N.C. Bar Assn., N.C. Assn. of Def. Attys. (charter). Federal civil litigation, State civil litigation, Personal injury. Office: Womble Carlyle Sandridge & Rice 3300 One First Union Ctr 301 S College St Ste 3300 Charlotte NC 28202-6025 E-mail: braper@wcsr.com

RAPINET, CRISPIN WILLIAM, lawyer; b. London, Feb. 18, 1964; s. Michael William and Christina Mary R.; m. Ruth Margaret Ingledow, May 3, 1998; children: Francesca Hero, Juliette Eloise. BA with honors, Corpus Christi Coll., Cambridge, Eng., 1987; Law Soc. Finals, Coll. Law, London, 1988. Bar: solicitor Eng., Wales, 1990, Hong Kong, 1998. Articled clk., solicitor Lovell White Durrant, London, 1990-98; ptnr., 1998, Hong Kong, 1998-2000, Lovells, 2000—. Mem. Soc. Practitioners of Insolvency/R3, Insolvency Interest Group. Bankruptcy, General civil litigation, Private international. Office: Lovells 23rd Fl Cheung Kong Ctr 2 Queens Rd Ctrl Hong Kong China Fax: (852) 2219-0222. E-mail: crispin.rapinet@lovells.com

RAPKIN, STEPHANIE GAYLE, lawyer, educator; b. Milw., Oct. 17, 1956; d. Sheldon Rapkin and Rae R. (McClean) R. BS, U. Wis., Milw., 1979; JD, Calif. Western, 1982; LLM in Taxation, DePaul U., 1990. Bar: Wis. 1982. Atty. Crossot & Rapkin, Mequon, Wis., 1987—. Adj. prof. U. Wis., Milw., 1989—. Contbr. articles to profl. jours. Bd. dirs. Future Milw., 1994-96. Mem. Wis. Bar (bd. dirs. 1998—). Office: 11514 N Port Washington Rd Mequon WI 53092-3457 Fax: 262-241-5045. E-mail: srapkin@juno.com

RAPOPORT, BERNARD ROBERT, lawyer; b. N.Y.C., Jan. 18, 1919; s. Max and Rose (Gerard) R.; m. Robyrta Wechter, May 31, 1959; 1 son: Michael. AB, Cornell U., 1939, JD, 1941. Bar: N.Y. 1941, Fed. Ct. (so. dist.) 1946. Assoc. firm Proskauer, Rose, Goetz, Mendelsohn, N.Y.C., 1941-50; gen. counsel M. Lowenstein Corp., N.Y.C., 1950-86, bd. dirs., 1961-86, treas., 1975-86, sec., 1970-86; dir., treas., sec. Leon Lowenstein Found. Served to capt. Signal Corps, U.S. Army, 1942-45. Mem. ABA, Assn. of Bar of City of N.Y. General corporate. Address: 910 5th Ave New York NY 10021-4155

RAPOPORT, DAVID E. lawyer; b. Chgo., May 27, 1956; s. Morris H. and Ruth (Teckteil) R.; m. Andrea Gail Albun; children: Alyson Faith, Steven Andrew. BS in Fin., No. Ill. U., 1978; JD with high honors, Ill. Inst. Tech., 1981; cert. trial work, Lawyers Postgrad. Inst., Chgo., 1984; cert. civil trial specialist, Nat. Bd. Trial Adv., 1991. Bar: Ill. 1981, Wis. 1995, U.S. Dist. Ct. (no. dist.) Ill. 1981, U.S. Dist. Ct. (trial bar) Ill. 1993, U.S. Dist. Ct. (so. and ctrl. dists.), U.S. Ct. Appeals (7th cir.) 1981, U.S. Ct. Appeals (7th cir.) 1981, U.S. Ct. Appeals (4th cir.) 1996. Assoc. Katz, Friedman, Schur & Eagle, Chgo., 1981-90, of counsel, 1990—; ptnr. Baizer & Rapoport, of counsel Highland Park, Ill., 1990-95; founder, pres. Rapoport Law Offices, P.C. (formerly Rapoport & Kupets P.C.), 1995—. Instr. legal writing Ill. Inst. Tech.-Kent Coll. Law, Chgo., 1981, guest lectr., 1985—; instr. Ill. Inst. CLE, 1995—; arbitrator Cir. Ct. Cook County, Ill., Million Dollar Advs. Forum, 1995—; state coord., lead trial counsel, mem. plaintiff's steering com. In Air Disaster at Charlotte Douglas Airport, 1994; mem. lead counsel com. In Air Disaster at Morrisville, N.C., 1994; lead trial counsel, In The Air Disaster at Sioux Gateway Airport, 1989. Bd. dirs. Congregation Beth Judea, Long Grove, Ill. Fellow Roscoe Pound Found.; mem. ABA, ATLA (sustaining mem.), Ill. Bar Assn., Ill. Trial Lawyers Assn., Chgo. Bar Assn., Ill. Inst. for CLE, Trial Lawyers for Pub. Justice, Trial Lawyers for Pub. Justice, Trial Lawyers for Civil Justice, Lake County Bar Assn. Aviation, Personal injury, Product liability. Office: Rapoport & Kupets Law Offices 77 W Washington St Fl 20 Chicago IL 60602-2801 also: O'Hare Internat Ctr 20 N Clark Ste 3500 Chicago IL 60602

RAPOPORT, NANCY B. dean, law educator; b. Bryan, Tex., June 29, 1960; m. Jeffrey D. Van Niel, Oct. 13, 1996. BA in legal studies, honors psychology summa cum laude, Rice U., 1982; JD, Stanford Law Sch., 1985. Bar: Calif. 1987, U.S. Dist. Cts. (no., ea., ctrl., and so. dists.) Calif. 1987, Ohio 1993, Nebr. 1999, U.S. Ct. Appeals (ninth cir.) 1987. Jud. clerk Hon. Joseph T. Sneed, United States Ct. Appeals for Ninth Cir. , San Francisco, 1985—86; assoc. bus.dept. of bankruptcy and workouts group Morrison & Foerster, 1986—91; asst. prof. Ohio State U. Coll. Law, Columbus, Ohio, 1991—95, tenured assoc. prof., 1995—98, assoc. dean student affairs, 1996—98, prof., 1998; dean, prof. law U. Nebr. Coll. Law , Lincoln, 1998—2000, U. Houston Law Ctr., 2000—. Invited spkr., panelist, and presenter in field; mem. Robert Wood Johnson Found. Partnership Initiative, Policy and Enforcement Workgroup , 1998—2000; mem. , chancellor spl. budget adv. com., 1999; chair UNL search com. Dean Coll. Arch., 1999—2000, Dean Coll. Arts & Scis., 2000. Note editor (rev.) Stanford Law; author: (with co-author Jeffrey D. Van Niel) "Retail Choice" Is Coming: Have you Hugged Your Utility Lawyer Today? , 2001;contbr. articles to profl. jours. and revs. ; (mem. editl. bd.) Calif. Bankruptcy Jour., 1995—, State Bar Tex., Bar Jour. Editl. Bd. Com., 2001—04. Bd. trustees Law Sch. Admissions Coun., 2001—; bd. dirs. Friends of Girl Scouting Adv. Bd., 2001—; bd. dirs. Pro Bono Rsch. Group, 2000—, St. Elizabeth Found., 1999—2000; bd. dirs. ADL Southwest Regional Bd., 2001—. Named Legal Pioneer for Women in Law (firts womna to seve as dean of Nebr. Law Sch.), Nebr. State Bar Assn., 2000, Outstanding Prof. of Yr., Ohio State U. Coll. Law., 1997; named to Louis Nemzer meml. lectr., 1998; fellow 1998 Fellowship, Am. Bankruptcy Law Jour. Mem.: ABA (task force on law student debt 2001—), Am. Law Inst., Houston Bar Assn., Houston Bar Found. (selection com. Best Article award 2000—), Nebr. State Bar Assn. (bankruptcy sect. 1998—2000, exec.com., bankruptcy sect. 1999—2000, access to profession com. 1999—2001), Nat. Assn. Coll. and U. Attys., Nebr. Continuing Legal Edn. (long-range planning com. 1998—2000), Bar Assn. San Francisco, Am. Bankruptcy Inst. (law sch. com. 1994—), Ohio State Bar Assn. (legal edn. com. 1997—98), Assn. Am. Law Sch.'s Profl. Develop. Com., A.A. White Inn of Ct. (exec. com. 2000—). Avocations: tae kwon do, ballroom dancing, Latin dancing, black and white photography, music. Office: U Houston Law Ctr 100 Law Ctr Houston TX 77204-6060 Business E-Mail: nrapoport@uh.edu*

RAPP, ELAINE, paralegal; b. Englewood, N.J., Feb. 4, 1950; d. Otto Adam and Jean Dorothy (Lohman) Krumbach; m. Chris Philip Rapp, Oct. 13, 1973; children: Keith, Brian, Erica. BA, Ohio Wesleyan U., 1972; cert., Rivier Coll., Nashua, N.H., 1995. Intern N.H. State Senate Rsch., Concord, 1994, clerical asst., 1995, 96, paralegal, rsch. asst., 1997—. Chair N.H. Home Edn. Adv Coun., Concord, 1990—. Editor newsletter N.H. Homeschool News, 1983-86. Co-founder, chair N.H. Home Educators Assn., 1983-88; presenter at media and coll. workshops in New Eng. Recipient N.H. Homemaker award Eagle Forum, 1987. Mem. Lambda Epsilon Chi. Avocation: piano. Office: NH Senate Rsch 33 N State St Concord NH 03301-6305

RAPP, GERALD DUANE, lawyer, manufacturing company executive; b. Berwyn, Nebr., July 19, 1933; s. Kenneth P. and Mildred (Price) R.; children: Gerald Duane Jr., Gregory T., Amy Frances Wanzek. B.S., U. Mo., 1955; J.D., U. Mich., 1958. Bar: Ohio bar 1959. Practice in, Dayton, 1960—; ptnr. Smith & Schnacke, 1963-70; asst. gen. counsel Mead Corp., Dayton, 1970, v.p. human resources and legal affairs, 1973, v.p., corp. sec., 1975, v.p., gen. counsel, corp. sec., 1976, v.p., gen. counsel, 1979, sr. v.p., gen. counsel, 1981-91, counsel to bd. dirs., 1991-92; of counsel Bieser, Greer & Landis, 1992—. Pres. R-J Holding Co., Weber Canyon Ranch, Inc. Sr. editor U. Mich. Law Rev., 1957-58. Past chmn. Oakwood Youth Commn.; past v.p., bd. dirs. Big Bros. Greater Dayton; mem. pres.'s visitors com. U. Mich. Law Sch.; past trustee Urbana Coll.; past pres., trustee Ohio Ctr. Leadership Studies, Robert K. Greenleaf Ctr., Indpls.; past pres. bd. trustees Dayton and Montgomery County Pub. Libr.; past. mem. bd. visitors Law Schs. of Dayton. 1st lt. U.S. Army, 1958-60. Mem. ABA, Ohio Bar Assn., Dayton Bar Assn., Moraine Country Club, Dayton Racquet Club, Dayton Lawyers Club, Met. Club Washington, Phi Kappa Psi, Phi Delta Phi, Beta Gamma Sigma. Presbyterian. Office: 108 Green St Dayton OH 45402-2835 Fax: 937-224-0403

RAPP, JAMES ANTHONY, lawyer, author; b. Williamson, W.Va., Feb. 25, 1949; s. Roy Thomas and Lucille (Middendorf) R.; m. Martha Brune, Dec. 28, 1972; children: Rebecca, Elizabeth Marie, Amy Christine. BS in Comm., U. Ill., Urbana, 1971; JD, Washington U., 1974. Bar: Ill. 1974, Mo. 1975, U.S. Dist. Ct. (so. dist.) Ill. 1975, U.S. Ct. Appeals (7th cir.) 1976, U.S. Ct. Appeals (8th cir.) 1976, U.S. Tax Ct. 1976, U.S. Supreme Ct. 1979, U.S. Dist. Ct. (cen. dist.) Ill. 1980. Prin. Hutmacher & Rapp PC and predecessors, Quincy, Ill., 1974—. Asst. corp. counsel City of Quincy, 1976-85; cons. Ill. Corps. Legal System, 1984. Author: Education Law, 1984, Victims Rights: Law and Litigation, 1988; co-author: Illinois Public Community College Act: Tenure Policies and Procedures, 1980, School Crime and Violence: Victims Rights, 1986, Illinois Domestic Relations Legal System, 1983; contbr. chpts. to books, articles to profl. jours. Bd. dirs. United Way Adams County, Inc., Quincy, 1975-81, pres., 1981-82; bd. dirs. Quincy Symphony Orch. Assn., 1976-79, pres., 1979-82. Mem. ABA, Ill. State Bar Assn., Mo. Bar Assn., Adams County Bar Assn., Chgo. Bar Assn. General corporate, General practice. Home: 1223 Scotia Trl Quincy IL 62301-6287 Office: Hutmacher & Rapp PC 428 N 6th St Quincy IL 62301-2502

RAPP, STEPHEN JOHN, international procecutor; b. Waterloo, Iowa, Jan. 26, 1949; s. Spurgeon John and Beverly (Leckington) R.; m. Donna J.E. Maier, 1981; children: Alexander, Stephanie. AB cum laude, Harvard U., 1970; JD with honors, Drake U., 1973. Bar: Iowa 1974, U.S. Dist. Ct. (no. and so. dists.) Iowa 1978, U.S. Ct. Appeals (8th cir.) 1979, U.S. Supreme Ct. 1979. Rsch. asst. Office of U.S. Senator Birch Bayh, Ind., 1970; community program asst. HUD, Chgo., 1971; mem. Iowa Ho. Reps., 1972-74, 79-83, Coun. to Majority Caucus, Iowa Ho. Reps., 1975; staff dir., counsel subcom. on juvenile delinquency U.S. Senate, Washington, 1977-78; ptnr. Rapp & Gilliam, Waterloo, 1979-83; pvt. practice, 1983-93; U.S. atty. U.S. Dist. Ct. (no. dist.) Iowa, 1993—2001; sr. prosecuting atty. United Nations Internat. Crime Tribunal for Rwanda, 2001—. Del., mem. com. Dem. Nat. Conv., 1976, 80, 84, 88, 92; mem. Dem. Nat. Adv. Com. on Econ., 1982-84, chmn. Black Hawk Dem. Com., 1986-91; mem. Iowa Dem. Com., 1990-93, chair 2d C.D. Dem. Com., 1991-93. Mem. ABA, Iowa Bar Assn., Order of Coif. Methodist. Home: 219 Highland Blvd Waterloo IA 50703-4229 Office: K-708, UN-ITR PO Box 6016 Arusha Tanzania E-mail: rapp@un.org

RAPPAPORT, CHARLES OWEN, lawyer; b. N.Y.C., May 15, 1950; s. Edward and Edith (Novick) R.; m. Valerie B. Ackerman, Oct. 11, 1987; children: Emily Randle, Sarah Elisabeth. BA, Columbia U., 1970; JD, NYU, 1975. Bar: N.Y. 1976. Assoc. Simpson, Thacher & Bartlett, N.Y.C., 1975-82, ptnr., 1982—. Office e-mail: c. Corporate taxation. Home: 26 N Moore St Apt 4W New York NY 10013-2436 Office: Simpson Thacher & Bartlett 425 Lexington Ave 14th Fl New York NY 10017-3954 E-mail: rappaport@stblaw.com

RAPPAPORT, LINDA ELLEN, lawyer; b. Freeport, N.Y., Jan. 12, 1952; d. William Jay and Marcia Ann (Wiland) R.; m. Leonard Chazen, June 1, 1980; 1 child, Matthew Ross. BA, Wesleyan U., Middletown, Conn., 1974; JD, NYU, 1977. Bar: N.Y. 1977. Law clk. Chief Judge James S. Holden U.S. Dist. Ct. Vt., Rutland, 1978; assoc. Shearman & Sterling, N.Y.C., 1979-85, ptnr., 1986-2000, mem. policy com., 1995—. Bd. dirs. N.Y. Women's Found., N.Y.C., 1995-2001, AIESEC Internat., N.Y.C., 1994-2000. Mem. Bar Assn. of City of N.Y. (employee benefits com. 1986—, employment law com. 1986—). Office: Shearman & Sterling 599 Lexington Ave Fl 13 New York NY 10022-6069 E-mail: lrappaport@shearman.com

RAPPAPORT, STUART RAMON, lawyer; b. Detroit, Apr. 13, 1935; s. Reuben and Zella (Golechen) R.; m. Anne M. Plotnick; children: Douglas, Erica Rappaport Witt. BA in History, U. Mich., 1956; JD, Harvard U., 1959. Bar: Calif. 1962. Trial lawyer, chief trials, bur. chief, chief. asst. pub. defender L.A. County Pub. Defender's Office, L.A., 1962-87; pub. defender Santa Clara County, San Jose, Calif., 1987-95; pvt. practice, 1995—. Mem. standing adv. com. on criminal law Jud. Coun. Calif., San Francisco, 1993—; mem. discipline evaluation com. State Bar of Calif. Contbr. articles to profl. jours. Recipient Lifetime Achievement award Calif. Attys. for Criminal Justice. Mem. Calif. Pub. Defenders Assn. (pres. 1982-83, Lifetime Achievement award), L.A. County Pub. Defenders Assn. (pres.). Democrat. Jewish. Address: 1415 Arch St Berkeley CA 94708 E-mail: sturap@mcn

RAS, ROBERT A. lawyer; b. River Forest, Ill., Oct. 5, 1946; s. Anthony S. and Bernice Ras; 1 child, Kristen. A.B., Georgetown U., 1967, J.D., 1976; M.B.A., U. Chgo., 1973. Bar: D.C. 1976, Ill. 1977, N.Y. 1982. Vice pres. Am. Nat. Bank, Chgo., 1970-75; atty. office of chmn. Arthur Young & Co., N.Y.C. and Chgo., 1976-85; gen. ptnr. Midwest Real Estate Ptnrs., 1983—; dir. tax services, Deloitte, Haskins & Sells, Oak Brook, Ill., 1985-88; atty., mng. dir. The Pvt. Bank & Trust Co. Banking, Securities, Estate taxation. Office: The Private Bank & Trust Co 1603 16th St Oak Brook IL 60523-8860

RASH, ALAN VANCE, lawyer; b. Fallbrook, Calif., Dec. 10, 1931; s. Glenn John and Clara Beatrice (Chambers) R.; m. Joy Ann Shinaut, May 21, 1956; children: Stephen, Richard, Paul. BA, Tex. Western Coll., 1953; JD, U. Tex., 1960. Bar: Tex. 1960, U.S. Dist. Ct. (we. dist.) Tex. 1968, U.S. Ct. Appeals (5th cir.) 1970, U.S. Supreme Ct. 1975. Ptnr. Diamond, Rash, Leslie, Smith & Samamiego, P.C., El Paso, Tex., 1968-92; shareholder Diamond Rash Gordon & Jackson, P.C., El Paso, 1992—; Pres. Sun Bowl Assn., 1977; chmn. El Paso County Republican Com., 1963-65, 69-71; Presdl. elector State of Tex., 1972, 92; chmn. bd. dirs. Tex. Guaranteed Student Loan Corp. With U.S. Army, 1953-55. Fellow Tex. Bar Found. Methodist. Lodges: Kiwanis (pres. El Paso 1966-67), Masons. Finance, Real property. Home: 531 Regency Dr # El El Paso TX 79912-4208 Office: Diamond Rash Gordon & Jackson PC 300 E Main Dr Fl 7 El Paso TX 79901-1372

RASHKIND, PAUL MICHAEL, lawyer; b. Jamaica, N.Y., May 21, 1950; s. Murray and Norma (Dorfman) Weinstein; m. Robin Shane, Dec. 20, 1975; children: Adam Charles, Noah Hamilton, Jennifer Elizabeth. AA, Miami-Dade Jr. Coll., 1970; BBA, U. Miami, Coral Gables, Fla., 1972, JD, 1975. Bar: Fla. 1975, D.C. 1981, N.Y. 1981, U.S. Dist. Ct. (so. dist.) Fla. 1975, U.S. Ct. Appeals (5th cir.) 1976, U.S. Supreme Ct. 1978, U.S. Dist. Ct. (mid. dist.) Fla. 1979, U.S. Ct. Appeals (2d and 11th cirs.) 1981, U.S. Ct. Appeals (4th and 6th cirs.) 1986, U.S. Dist. Ct. (no. dist.) Fla. 1987, U.S. Dist. Ct. (no. dist.) Calif. 1989; diplomate Nat. Bd. Trial Advocacy-Criminal Law (bd. examiners), bd. cert. Criminal Trial Law, Fla. Bar. Asst. state atty. Dade County State Attys. Office, Miami, Fla., 1975-78, chief asst. state atty. in charge of appeals, 1977-78; atty. Sams, Gerstein & Ward, P.A., 1978-83; ptnr. Bailey, Gerstein, Rashkind & Dresnick, 1983-92, supr. asst. Fed. Defender Chief of Appeals, 1992—. Spl. master Ct. Appointment, Miami, 1982-83; arbitrator Dade County Jail Inmates Grievance Program, Miami, 1981-92; mem. Fla. Bar Unauthorized Practice of Law Com. C, 11th Jud. Cir., Miami, 1980-84, Fed. Ct. Practice Com., 1992—; mem. So. Dist. Fla. Fed. Ct. Rules Com., 1996—. Contbr. articles on ethics and criminal law to profl. jours. Pres., bd. dirs. Lindgren Homeowners Assn., Miami, 1981-86. Fellow Am. Bd. Criminal Lawyers (bd. govs. 1980-86); mem. ABA (ethics com. criminal justice sect. 1979-92, vice chmn. 1985-87, chmn. 1987-89, ethics advisor to chair 1992-97, criminal justice sect. coun. 1998—), Fla. Bar Assn. (commn. on lawyer professionalism 1988-89, criminal law cert. com. 1989-94, standing com. on professionalism 1989-94), N.Y. Bar Assn., D.C. Bar Assn., Dade County Bar Assn., Assn. Trial Lawyers Am., Acad. Fla. Trial Lawyers (chmn. criminal law sect. 1985-86, diplomate 1986—), Nat. Assn. Criminal Def.

Lawyers, Soc. Bar and Gavel, Iron Arrow, Hon. Order Ky. Cois, Omicron Delta Kappa, Delta Sigma Rho-Tau Kappa Alpha, Pi Sigma Alpha, Phi Rho Pi, Delta Theta Phi. Democrat. Jewish. Appellate, Constitutional, Criminal. Office: Fed Pub Defender's Office SD FL 150 W Flagler St Ste 1500 Miami FL 33130-1555 E-mail: paul@rashkind.wm

RASKIN, DANIEL ELLIS, lawyer; b. Savannah, May 10, 1949; s. Sidney L. and Anita (Liptan) R.; m. Susan Marks, Apr. 17, 1982. B.A., Tulane U., 1971; J.D., Emory U., 1974. Bar: Ga. 1975. Regional counsel Nature Conservancy, Washington, 1974-77; ptnr. Raskin & Debele, Savannah, 1977-80; assoc. Lefkoff Pike Fox & Sims, Atlanta, 1980-81; regional ptnr. Hyatt Legal Services, Atlanta, 1981-86; ptnr. Raskin & Nagel, Atlanta, 1986—. Democrat. Jewish. Bankruptcy, Family and matrimonial, Real property. Office: Raskin & Nagel 325 Hammond Dr NE Atlanta GA 30328-5032

RASMUS, JOHN CHARLES, trade association executive, lawyer; b. Rochester, N.Y., Dec. 27, 1941; s. Harold Charles and Myrtle Leota (Dybevik) R.; m. Elaine Green Reeves, Mar. 19, 1982; children: Kristin, Stuart, Karin. AB, Cornell U., 1963; JD, U. Va., 1966. Bar: Va. 1970, U.S. Supreme Ct. 1974. Spl. agt. Def. Dept., Washington, 1966-70; v.p., adminstrv. officer, legis. rsch. counsel U.S. League Savs. Instns., 1970-83; asst. to exec. v.p. Nat. Assn. Fed. Credit Unions, 1983-84; sr. fed. adminstrv. counsel, mgr. regulatory & trust affairs Am. Bankers Assn., 1985—. Mem. ABA, FBA (disting. svc. award 1980, 82, past chmn. long range planning com., past chmn. coun. fin. instns. and economy), Univ. Club, Exchequer Club, Masons. Home: 303 Kentucky Ave Alexandria VA 22305-1739 Office: Am Bankers Assn 1120 Connecticut Ave NW Washington DC 20036 E-mail: jrasmus@aba.com

RASMUSSEN, DOUGLAS JOHN, lawyer; b. Mt. Clemens, Mich., Jan. 18, 1941; s. Kenneth Edward and Laura Jean (Fletcher) R.; m. Andrea Marie Smart, Aug. 22, 1964; children: Mark Douglas, Michael Andrew. BBA, U. Mich., 1962, MBA, JD, 1965. Bar: Mich. 1965, U.S. Dist. Ct. (ea. dist.) Mich. 1965, U.S. Tax Ct. 1973, U.S. Ct. Appeals (6th cir.) 1973. Assoc., Detroit, 1965-73; mem., 1973—; CEO, 1994-2000. Trustee Community Found. for S.E. Mich., Holley Found., bd. dirs. S.E. chpt. ARC, Detroit, 1987—, chmn., 1994-96; bd. dirs. YMCA of Metro Detroit, chmn., 1992-93; unit chmn. United Way, Detroit, 1987-92; bd. dirs. Detroit Symphony Orch., 1999—, Friends of Detroit Pub. Libr., 2000—, pres., 2001-. Recipient Outstanding Vol. award Mich. Chpt. Nat. Assn. Fund Raising Execs., 1988, Fundraiser Yr. award Nat. ARC, 1997, Stanley S. Kresge award Rotary Club. Fellow Am. Coll. Trust and Estate Counsel (regent 1987-93); mem. ABA, State Bar Mich., Internat. Acad. Estate and Trust Law, Fin. and Estate Planning Coun. Detroit (pres. 1986-87), Detroit Athletic Club (bd. dirs. 1992, pres. 1997), Econ. Club Detroit (bd. dirs. 1999—). Republican. Presbyterian. Avocations: music, photography, Nordic skiing, golf. Estate planning, Probate, Taxation, general. Home: 466 Lakeland St Grosse Pointe MI 48230-1655 Office: Clark Hill PLC 500 Woodward Ave Ste 3500 Detroit MI 48226-3435 E-mail: drasmussen@clarkhill.com

RASMUSSEN, FREDERICK TATUM, lawyer; b. Madison, Wis., Feb. 21, 1943; s. Aaron Frederick and Besse Carol (Tatum) R.; children: Wendy, Frderick, Lauren. BA, UCLA, 1965; JD, U. Wis., 1974. Bar: Wash. 1974, U.S. Dist. Ct. (ea. and we. dists.) Wash. 1974. Ptnr. Stokes Lawrence, Seattle. Lt. comdr. USCG, 1966-69. Mem. ABA, Wash. State Bar Assn., Seattle-King County Bar Assn., Order of Coif. Alternative dispute resolution, Labor. Office: Stokes Lawrence 800 5th Ave Ste 4000 Seattle WA 98104-3179

RASMUSSEN, GARRET GARRETSON, lawyer; b. Bronxville, N.Y., Nov. 14, 1949; s. Harold Forbes and Sara Wilson (Jackson) R.; m. Jean Reynolds Middendorf, Apr. 17, 1976; children— William Middendorf, Lisa G. Daniel R., Robert R. A.B., Dartmouth Coll., 1971; J.D., Harvard U., 1974. Bar: Mass. 1974, D.C. 1977, U.S. Supreme Ct. 1982, U.S. Ct. Appeals (2d, 3d, 4th, 5th and 6th cirs.). Assoc. Hill & Barlow, Boston, 1974-76; trial atty FTC, Washington, 1976-77; assoc. Patton, Boggs & Blow, Washington, 1977-81, ptnr., 1982— ; dir. Lithuanian Inst. Georgetown, Netherlands-Am. Amity Trust, Washington, 1980-86. Vestryman Christ Ch. Georgetown, Washington, 1983-86, sr. warden, 1991-94. Served to lt. (j.g.) USN, 1975. Republican. Episcopalian. Clubs: Metropolitan (Washington), Chevy Chase, Harvard (N.Y.), Potomac Boat. Administrative and regulatory, Antitrust, Federal civil litigation. Home: 3321 Q St NW Washington DC 20007-2717 Office: Patton Boggs & Blow 2550 M St NW Washington DC 20037-1301

RASMUSSEN, RICHARD ROBERT, lawyer; b. Chgo., July 5, 1946; s. Robert Kersten Rasmussen and Marisa Bruna Batistoni; children: Kathryn, William. BS, U. Oreg., 1970, JD, 1973. Bar: Oreg. 1973. Atty. U.S. Bancorp, Portland, Oreg., 1973-83, 95-00, v.p. law divsn., 1983-87, mgr. law divsn, 1983-95, sr. v.p., 1987-95, mgr. corp. sec. divsn., 1990-94; exec. v.p., gen. counsel, sec. West Coast Bancorp, Lake Oswego, 2000—. Mem. editl. bd. Oreg. Bus. Law Digest, 1979-81, Oreg. Debtor/Creditor newsletter, 1980-84; contbr. articles to profl. jours. Chmn. mgmt. com. YMCA of Columbia-Willamette, Portland, 1978-79; bd. dirs. Camp Fire, 1988-89, v.p., 1990-91; bd. dirs. Portland Repertory Theatre, 1994-96. Mem. ABA, Oreg. State Bar Assn. (chmn. corp. counsel com. 1979-81, debtor/creditor sect. 1982-83; sec. com. on sects. 1982-83), Multnomah County Bar Assn., Am. Bankers Assn. (bank counsel com. 1996-99), Founders Club (Portland), Beta Gamma Sigma. Club: Founder's (Portland). Avocations: mountaineering, white-water rafting, tennis, basketball. Banking, General corporate, Finance. Office: West Coast Bancorp 5335 Meadows Rd Ste 201 Lake Oswego OR 97035

RASMUSSON, THOMAS ELMO, lawyer; b. Lansing, Mich., Dec. 5, 1941; s. William and Mary Jane Rasmusson; m. Alice Wolo, Oct. 1, 1989; children: David, Jane. BA, Mich. State U., 1963; JD, U. Mich., 1966; MA, Fletcher Sch., 1988. Bar: Mich. 1967, U.S. Ct. Appeals (6th cir.) 1982, U.S. Supreme Ct. 1982. Law clk. to presiding justice Mich. Supreme Ct., Lansing, 1966-68; asst. prosecutor Ingham Prosecutor's Office, 1968-72, criminal divsn. chief, 1972-75; spl. prosecutor Ingham County, 1975-76; pvt. practice, 1975—. Fulbright prof. U.S. Info. Svc., Washington, 1986-88; cons. U.S. AID, Monrovia, Liberia, 1989-90; contractor U.S. Dept. of State, Monrovia, 1987-90; adj. prof. Cooley Law Sch., Lansing, 1991-97; rsch. assoc. program on negotiation Harvard U., Cambridge, 1987-88; mem. Ct. Rule Com., Lansing, 1979-81. Editor: Jurisprudence and System Science, 1986, Interactive Systems, 1988, (series) Liberian Law Reports, 1988-90; contbr. articles to profl. jours. Chair fin. Ingham Rep. Party, Lansing, 1994-98, mem. exec. com., 1994—; mem. 8th Congl. Com., Lansing, 1997—. Recipient Outstanding Svc. award U.S. Edn. Found., 1987; grantee U.S. Edn. Found., 1987. Mem. AAAS, State Bar Mich. Republican. Methodist. Avocations: physics, history of science. Federal civil litigation, State civil litigation, Criminal. Home: 3715 Delta River Dr Lansing MI 48906-3476 Office: Rasmusson and Assoc 501 S Capitol Ave Ste 305 Lansing MI 48933-2331

RATH, FRANCIS STEVEN, lawyer; b. N.Y.C., Oct. 10, 1955; s. Steven and Elizabeth (Chorin) R.; m. Denise Stephania Thompson, Aug. 2, 1980. BA cum laude, Wesleyan U., Middletown, Conn., 1977; JD cum laude, Georgetown U., 1980; postgrad., Harvard U., 1999-2000. Bar: D.C. 1980, U.S. Dist. Ct. D.C. 1981, U.S. Ct. Appeals (D.C. cir.), 1981, U.S. Supreme Ct. 1987, Va. 1988. Atty., advisor Comptr. of the Currency, Washington, 1980-84; assoc. Verner, Liipfert, Bernhard, McPherson & Hand, 1984-85; founding mem. Wolf, Arnold & Monroig (merged with Burnham, Connolly, Oesterly & Henry), 1986-88; pvt. practice Great Falls, Va., 1989—. Internat. cons. Fried, Frank, Harris, Shriver and Jacobson, 1991-95; counsel Seward & Kissel, Washington, 1995-98; of counsel, Squire Sanders & Dempsey, Washington, 1998—. Editor: Law and Policy in Internat. Bus., 1979-80; contbg. author Business Ventures in Eastern Europe and Russia; contbr. articles to profl. jours. Trustee Dunn Loring (Va.) Vol. Fire Dept., 1986. Mem. ABA, D.C. Bar Assn., Va. Bar Assn., Bar of U.S. Supreme Ct., U.S. Combined Tng. Assn. (legal com. 1989-91, 96-99, safety com. 1990-91, 96-99, bd. govs. 1995-98). General corporate, Private international, Public international. Home and Office: 1051 Kelso Rd Great Falls VA 22066-2032 E-mail: frath@fsrpc.com

RATH, HOWARD GRANT, JR. lawyer; b. L.A., Sept. 2, 1931; s. Howard Grant and Helen (Cowell) R.; m. Peyton McComb, Sept. 13, 1958 (dec. Apr. 1984); children: Parthenia Peyton, Francis Cowell; m. Dorothy Moser, Aug. 29, 1986. BS, U. Calif., 1953; JD, U. So. Calif., 1958. Bar: Calif. 1959, U.S. Dist. Ct. (cen. dist.) Calif., 1959, U.S. Ct. Claims 1974, U.S. Tax Ct. 1960. Assoc. O'Melveny & Myers, L.A., 1959-66; tax counsel, dir. tax adminstrn., asst. treas. Northrop Corp. L.A., 1966-74; sr. tax ptnr. Macdonald, Halsted & Laybourne, L.A., 1974-86, Hill & Weiss, L.A., 1986-90; ptnr. Lewis, D'Amato, Brisbois & Bisgaard, L.A., 1990—; dir. Rath Packing Co., Waterloo, Iowa, 1966-81. 1st lt. U.S. Army, 1953-55. Mem. State Bar Calif., L.A. County Bar Assn., L.A. Yacht Club, Valley Hunt Club (pres. 1981-82), Order of Coif, Phi Beta Kappa. Republican. Episcopalian. E-mail: rath@ldbb.com. Corporate taxation, Estate taxation, Personal income taxation. Office: Lewis D'Amato Brisbois & Bisgaard 221 N Figueroa St Ste 1200 Los Angeles CA 90012-2646

RATHKE, STEPHEN CARL, lawyer; b. Rockford, Ill., Apr. 28, 1946; s. Gerhard C. and Genevieve (Brentner) R.; m. Susan E. Bertram, Dec. 12, 1948; children— Sarah, Justin. B.A., Valparaiso U., 1968, J.D., 1971. Bar: Minn. 1971, U.S. Dist. Ct. Minn. 1973. Law clk. Minn. Supreme Ct., St. Paul, 1971-72; asst. city atty. City of St. Paul, 1972; counsel Minn. Senate, St. Paul, 1972-74; ptnr. Borden, Steinbauer, Rathke & Krueger, Brainerd, Minn., 1974-91; county atty. Crow Wing County, Brainerd, 1975-91; chmn. Sentencing Guidelines Commn., St. Paul, 1978-91. Mem. County Attys. Assn. Lutheran. Lodges: Rotary. General civil litigation, Criminal, Professional liability. Home: 1384 W Minnehaha Pkwy Minneapolis MN 55409-2220 Office: Lommen Nelson 1800 IDS Ctr 80 S 8th St Minneapolis MN 55402-2100

RATHKOPF, DAREN ANTHONY, lawyer; b. Lynbrook, N.Y., May 12, 1933; s. Arden Herman and Florence Marie (Gortikov) R.; m. Mira Torgersen, Mar. 30, 1963; children: Ann, Erika. BA, Columbia U., 1955, LLB, 1958. Bar: N.Y. 1958, U.S. Dist. Ct. (ea., so. dists.) N.Y. 1962. Assoc. Mendes & Mount, N.Y.C., 1961-62, Rathkopf & Rathkopf, N.Y.C., 1962-66, ptnr. Glen Cove, N.Y., 1966-81, Payne, Wood & Littlejohn, Glen Cove and Melville, 1982-98, of counsel Melville, Bridgehampton, Locust Vly, N.Y., 1999-2001, Farrell Fritz, P.C., Uniondale, Melville, N.Y., Bridghampton, Locust Valley, 2001—. Author: (with others) The Law of Zoning and Planning, 4th edit., 1977. Mem. N.Y. State Bar Assn., Nassau County Bar Assn. Land use and zoning (including planning). Home: 149 Turkey Ln Cold Spring Harbor NY 11724-1712 Office: Farrell Fritz PC 290 Broadhollow Rd Melville NY 11747-4818 E-mail: drathkopf@aol.com

RATNER, DAVID LOUIS, retired law educator; b. London, Sept. 2, 1931; AB magna cum laude, Harvard U., 1952, LLB magna cum laude, 1955. Bar: N.Y. 1955. Assoc. Sullivan & Cromwell, N.Y.C., 1955-64; assoc. prof. Cornell Law Sch., Ithaca, N.Y., 1964-68, prof., 1968-82; prof. law U. San Francisco Law Sch., 1982-99, dean, 1982-89, prof. emeritus, 1999—. Exec. asst. to chmn. SEC, Washington, 1966-68; chief counsel Securities Industry Study, Senate Banking Com., Washington, 1971-73; vis. prof. Stanford (Calif.) U., 1974, Ariz. State U., Tempe, 1974, U. San Francisco, 1980, Georgetown U., Washington, 1989-90, U. Calif., Hastings, San Francisco, 1992; mem. Larkspur (Calif.) Planning Commn., 1992—. Author: Securities Regulation; Cases and Materials, 5th edit., 1998, Securities Regulation in a Nutshell, 6th edit., 1998, Institutional Investors: Teaching Materials, 1978. Fulbright scholar Monash U., Australia, 1981. Mem. Cosmos Club (Washington), Harvard Club of San Francisco (pres. 1999-2000), Phi Beta Kappa. Home and Office: 84 Polhemus Way Larkspur CA 94939-1928 E-mail: dlratner@aol.com

RATNER, GERALD, lawyer; b. Chgo., Dec. 17, 1913; s. Peter I. and Sarah (Soreson) R.; m. Eunice Payton, June 18, 1948. PhB, U. Chgo., 1935, JD cum laude, 1937. Bar: Ill. 1937. Since practiced in, Chgo.; sr. ptnr. Gould & Ratner and predecessor firm, 1949—. Officer Henry Crown & Co., CC Industries, Inc., Material Svc. Corp., Freeman United Coal Mining Co., Mineral and Land Resources Corp.; lectr., writer on real estate law. Capt. AUS, 1942-46. Gerald Ratner Athletics Ctr. named in his honor, U. Chgo. Mem. ABA, Ill. Bar Assn., Chgo. Bar Assn., Order of Coif, U. Chgo. Pres. Coun. and Endowment Assn., Phi Beta Kappa. Home: 180 E Pearson St Apt 6205 Chicago IL 60611-2191 Office: 222 N La Salle St Ste 800 Chicago IL 60601-1086

RATNER, MICHAEL D. lawyer; b. June 13, 1943; s. Harry and Anne (Spott) Ratner. BA, Brandeis U., 1966; JD magna cum laude, Columbia U., 1971. Bar: N.Y. 1971, U.S. Supreme Ct. 1983. Law clk. U.S. Dist. Ct. (so. dist.), N.Y.C., 1971-72; prof. NYU Law Sch., 1973-74; atty. Ctr. for Constl. Rights, 1978-85, legal dir., 1985-90. Adj. prof. Yale Law Sch., New Haven, Conn., 1990-95; spl. counsel for human rights Govt. of Haiti, 1996; lectr. Columbia Law Sch., 1999-2001, Yale Law Sch., 2000. Author: International Human Rights Litigation in U.S. Cours, 1997, Che Guevara and the FBI, 1997, The Pinochet Papers, 2000; contbr. articles to profl. jours. Named Trial Lawyer of Yr., Trial Lawyers for the Pub. Interest; Skelly Wright fellow Yale Law Sch., 2000. Mem. Nat. Lawyers Guild (pres. 1982-83). Office: Ctr Constitutional Rights 666 Broadway New York NY 10012-2317 E-mail: mratner@igc.org

RATNER, PAYNE HARRY, JR. lawyer; b. Parsons, Kans., Aug. 31, 1924; s. Payne Harry and Cliffe (Dodd) R.; m. Adelaide Bryant Schutz, June 30, 1950 (div. 1970); children: Payne Harry, Charlotte, Carl; m. Barbara H. Urquhart, July 3, 1970. BSBA, U. Kans., 1947, JD, 1950. Bar: Kans. 1950. Ptnr. Ratner, Mattox, Ratner, Brimer & Elam, P.A. and predecessor firms, Wichita, Kans., 1950—; mem. Kans. Ho. of Reps., 1966-73. Mem. editorial bd. Kans. Law Rev., 1949-50. Contbr. articles to publs. Served with USNR, 1942-46. Fellow Internat. Acad. Trial Lawyers, Am. Coll. Trial Lawyers; mem. Wichita Bar Assn. (chmn. com. on bench and bar 1969-70, 73-74, med. legal, 1971-72, 74-76), Kans. Bar Assn. (chmn. litigation sect. 1977-78, aviation sect. 1978-79), ABA (exec. coun. jr. bar conf. 1954-58, chmn. rules and procedure com., ins. negligence and compensation law sect. 1973-75, mem. coun. 1974-78), Lawyer-Pilots Bar Assn. (bd. dirs. 1968-72), Am. Bd. Trial Advocates, Wichita Area C. of C. (bd. dirs.), Wichita Country Club, Masons, Beta Theta Pi, Phi Delta Phi, Scribes. Republican. Episcopalian. Federal civil litigation, State civil litigation, Personal injury. Address: PO Box 306 Wichita KS 67201-0306

RATTI, RICARDO ALLEN, lawyer; b. Humacao, P.R., Sept. 3, 1922; s. Augustus Peter and Gertrude Alice (Allen) R.; m. Ruth Anne Holland, Aug. 15, 1947; children— Carolyn, Christine, Steven, Julia; m. Jean E. Royer, May 26, 1991. B.S. in Marine Engring., USCG Acad., 1944; J.D., George Washington U., 1956. Bar: U.S. Ct. Appeals (D.C. cir.) 1956. Chief counsel U.S. Coast Guard, Washington, 1973-76; dep. asst. chief counsel FAA, Washington, 1976-78; chief counsel subcom. on Mcht. Marine, U.S. Ho. of Reps., Washington, 1978-85. Served to rear adm. USCG, 1972-76. Decorated Legion of Merit; recipient John Ordronaux prize George Washington Law Sch., 1954, John B. Larner medal, 1956. Mem. Fed. Bar Assn., Ret. Officers Assn., Nat. Assn. Uniformed Services (dir. 1981-84). Republican.

RATTO, EUGENE JOSEPH, lawyer, commercial arbitrator and mediator; b. Boston, Dec. 7, 1926; s. John Baptista and Theodora Anna (Cuneo) R.; m. Patricia Ann Parks, Sept. 26, 1959; children— Eugene Jr., Elizabeth, Jane, Mary Ellen. Student Boston Coll., 1947-48; LL.B., Boston Coll. Law, 1951. Bar: Mass. 1951, N.H. 1952, U.S. Dist. Ct. Mass. 1954, ICC 1954. Law clk. to judge U.S. Dist. Ct., Concord, N.H., 1951-53; gen. atty. Boston & Maine R.R., Boston, 1954-60; atty. John Hancock Mut. Life Ins. Co., Boston, 1960-61, asst. counsel, 1961-66, assoc. counsel, 1966-70, sr. assoc. counsel, 1970-80, counsel, 1980-84, v.p., 1984-87. Pres. parish council, chmn. religious edn. St. Margaret Mary Roman Catholic Parish, Westwood, Mass., 1977; mem. parish council St. Ignatius Parish, Chestnut Hill, Mass., 1983, mem. adminstrn. and fin. council, 1984. Served with USNR, 1944-46, Atlantic, Pacific. Mem. ABA (probate, trust and real estate sect.), Assn. Life Ins. Counsel, Am. Land Title Assn. (assoc. 1966-88), Life Ins. Real Estate Counsel Group (chmn. 1982), NE Real Estate Life Ins. Group (chmn. 1975), Boston World Affairs Coun., Longwood Cricket Club (sec. 1975-79, pres. 1979-80) (Chestnut Hill, Mass.). Home: 1970 Commonwealth Ave Apt 68 Brighton MA 02135-5822 Office: 1970 Commonwealth Ave Brighton MA 02135-5817

RAU, LEE ARTHUR, lawyer; b. Mpls., July 22, 1940; s. Arthur W. and Selma A. (Lund) R.; m. Janice R. Childress, June 27, 1964; children: Brendan D., Patrick C., Brian T. BSB, U. Minn., 1962; JD, UCLA, 1965. Bar: Calif. 1966, D.C. 1972, Va. 1986, U.S. Dist. Ct. D.C. 1973, U.S. Dist. Ct. (ea. dist.) Va. 1988, U.S. Ct. Mil. Appeals 1966, U.S. Ct. Appeals (D.C. cir.) 1972, U.S. Ct. Appeals (3d cir.) 1975, U.S. Ct. Appeals (6th cir.) 1980, U.S. Ct. Appeals (4th cir.) 1988, U.S. Supreme Ct. 1971. Trial atty. evaluation sect. antitrust div. U.S. Dept. Justice, Washington, 1965-66, appellate sect., 1970-72; assoc. Reed Smith Shaw & McClay, 1972-74, ptnr., 1975—. Former mem. constl. and adminstrv. law adv. com. Nat. Chamber Litigation Ctr. Inc.; sec., bd. dirs. Old Dominion Land Co., Inc. Contbr. articles to profl. jours. Sec. bd. dris. Reston Found., 1982-93; bd. dirs. Reston Interfaith Inc., 1973-89, pres, 1984-88; bd. dirs. Greater Reston Arts Ctr., 1988-96, pres., 1989-91, sec., 1991-95; mem. Washington Dulles Task Force, 1982-91; mem. exec. com. and ops. com. Fairfax-Falls Ch. United Way, mem. regional coun., 1988-92. Capt. JAGC, U.S. Army, 1966-70. Named Restonian of Yr., 1990; decorated Commendation with oak leaf cluster; recipient Best of Reston award. Mem. ABA (antitrust, adminstrv. law, corp. banking and bus., sci. and tech. sects.), D.C. Bar Assn. (past chmn. energy study group), Calif. Bar Assn., U.S. C. of C. (antitrust policy com.). Democrat. Lutheran Administrative and regulatory, Antitrust, General corporate. Home: 11654 Mediterranean Ct Reston VA 20190-3401 Office: Reed Smith Shaw & McClay Ste 1100 East Tower 1301 K St NW Washington DC 20005-3317

RAUBICHECK, CHARLES JOSEPH, lawyer; b. N.Y.C., Oct. 9, 1946; s. Walter Alan and Catherine Gertrude (Fordrung) R.; A.B., Georgetown U., 1968; J.D., Georgetown U., 1971; m. Ann S. Macdonald, Feb. 18, 1978. Admitted to D.C. bar, 1971, N.Y. State bar, 1976; atty. Office Gen. Counsel FDA, Washington, 1971-75; ptnr. Frommer Lawrence & Haug LLP, N.Y.C., 2000—; adj. prof. N.Y.U. Sch. Law, N.Y.C., 1976—; elder Lafayette Ave. Presbyn. Ch., Bklyn., 2000—; trustee Riverside Ch., N.Y.C., 1993-94. Mem. ABA, N.Y. State Bar Assn. (chair food, drug, cosmetic law sect. 1986-88, 98-2000, vice-chair 1996—), Assn. Bar City N.Y., Union League Club (N.Y.C.).

RAUH, THEO, lawyer, solititor; b. Erkelenz, Germany, Dec. 21, 1961; With Rechtsanwalte Clev & Pape , Dusseldorf, Germany. Mem. Internat. Bar Assn., German-British Jurists Assn. Antitrust, Real property, Trademark and copyright. Office: Rechtsanwalte Clev & Pape Konigsallee 70 40212 Dusseldorf Germany E-mail: theo.rauh@clev-pape.de

RAUL, ALAN CHARLES, lawyer; b. Bronx, N.Y., Sept. 9, 1954; s. Eugene and Eduarda (Müller-Mañas) R.; m. Mary Tinsley, Jan. 30, 1988; children: Caroline Tinsley, William Eduardo Tinsley, Alexander Tinsley. AB magna cum laude, Harvard U., 1975, MPA, 1977; JD, Yale U., 1980. Bar: N.Y. 1982, D.C. 1982, U.S. Ct. Appeals (D.C. cir.) 1982, U.S. Supreme Ct. 1988. Law clk. to judge U.S. Ct. Appeals (D.C. cir.), Washington, 1980-81; assoc. Debevoise & Plimpton, N.Y.C., 1981-86; White House assoc. counsel Pres. Reagan, Washington, 1986-88; gen. counsel Office Mgmt. and Budget, 1988-89, USDA, Washington, 1989-93; prin. Beveridge & Diamond P.C., 1993-97; ptnr. Sidley Austin Brown & Wood, 1997—. Cons. Reagan-Bush campaign, N.Y.C., 1984; mem. implementation task force Internet Corp. for Assigned Names and Numbers, 2000—. Author: (book) Privacy and the Digital State, 2001. Co-chairperson, co-founder Lawyers Have Heart; chmn. bd. USDA Grad. Sch., 1991-93; bd. dirs. Am. Heart Assn., Nations Capital Affiliate, 1993-97; treas., dir. Citizens Assn. Georgetown, 1993-97; mem. Nat. Policy Forum's Environ. Policy Coun. Recipient Disting. Achievement award Am. Heart Assn., 1991, Vol. of Yr. award, 1993, Lifetime Achievement award, 1999. Mem. ABA (coun. sect. internat. law and practice 1992-98, chmn. com. on nat. security and internat. law 1990-92, standing com. on election law 1995-99, sect. internat. law and practice govt. affairs officer 1996-98), Assn. of Bar of City of N.Y. (chmn. subcom. on Gen. Am. issues 1985, mem. com. on inter-Am. affairs 1983), Federalist Soc. (mem. nat. practitioners adv. coun., chair environ. and property rights practice group 1996-99), FDA Reform Group, Coun. on Fgn. Rels. Administrative and regulatory, Environmental, Private international. Office: Sidley Austin Brown & Wood 1501 K St NW Washington DC 20005 E-mail: araul@sidley.com

RAUNER, VINCENT JOSEPH, lawyer, electronics company executive, retired; b. Kalamazoo, Mich., Apr. 4, 1927. BSE, U. Mich., 1950, JD, 1953. Bar: Ill. 1953. Ptnr. Mueller, Aichele and Rauner, Chgo., 1953-70; dir. patent dept. Motorola, Inc., Franklin Park, Ill., 1970-73, v.p., Schaumburg, Ill., 1973-88, sr. v.p. patents, trademarks and licensing, 1988-92, ret. 1992; cons. Motorola Inc., 1992-93. General corporate, Patent, Trademark and copyright. Home: 399 W Fullerton Pkwy # 10W Chicago IL 60614-2810

RAVESON, LOUIS SHEPPARD, lawyer, educator; b. Passaic, N.J., Dec. 14, 1951; s. Irwin Harold and Lorelei Rose (Levine) R. BA, Antioch Coll., 1972; JD, Rutgers U., 1976. Bar: N.J. 1976, U.S. Dist. Ct. N.J. 1976, U.S. Ct. Appeals (3d cir.) 1976, N.Y. 1977, U.S. Supreme Ct. 1988. Law clk. U.S. Ct. Appeals (3d cir.), Phila., 1976-77; staff atty. Essex-Newark Legal Svcs., Newark, 1977-79, Rutgers Urban Legal Clinic, Newark, 1979-81, co-dir., 1982-89, dir., 1989—. Asst. prof. law Rutgers U. Law Sch., Newark, 1982-85, assoc. prof., 1985-89, prof. 1990—; chmn. bd. trustees Essex-Newark Legal Svcs., Newark, 1982; bd. dirs. Nat. Equal Justice Found., 1984—, Urban Legal Clinic. Mem. Soc. Am. Law Tchrs., N.J. Bar Assn., N.J. Supreme Ct. Com. (civil litigation and complimentary dispute resolution). Jewish. Office: Rutgers U Law Sch 123 Washington St Newark NJ 07102-3105

RAVNAAS, ERNST, lawer; b. Kritiansand, Norway, Apr. 18, 1955; s. Nils and Nelly (Synnöve) R.; m. Grethe Karlsen, July 1, 1978; children: Niels Ruben, Alexander, Stephen, Waar Helene. Grad. in Law, U. Bergen (Norway), 1978; B of Commerce, Coll. Bus. Adminstrn. and Econs., Bergen, 1980. Assoc. prof. Coll. Bus. Adminstrn. and Econs. B.I., Oslo, 1983-89; assoc. Bugge, Arentz-Hansen & Rasmussen, 1990; ptnr., 1991—.

Chmn. Itera ASA, Oslo, Blom ASA, Oslo; bd. dirs. FoincoInvest AS, Oslo. Author: Tax Planning for Business, 1987, Tax Economy, 1988, Tax Reform, 1992; editor: Taxation of Energy Business, 1998. Mem. Wimbledon Football Club (dir. 1999). Mergers and acquisitions, Corporate taxation, Taxation, general. Home: Skonnerten 7 1394 Nesbru Norway Office: Bugge Arentz-Hansen & Rasmu Stranden 7 1524 Vika Oslo Norway Fax: 47-22830795. E-mail: erad@ba-hr.no

RAWLES, EDWARD HUGH, lawyer; b. Chgo., May 7, 1945; s. Fred Wilson and Nancy (Hughes) R.; m. Margaret Mary O'Donoghue, Oct. 20, 1979; children: Lee Kathryn, Jacklyn Ann. BA, U. Ill., 1967; JD summa cum laude, Ill. Inst. Tech., 1970. Bar: Ill., 1970, Colo. 1984, U.S. Dist. Ct. (cen. dist.) Ill. 1970, U.S. Ct. Appeals (7th cir.) 1983, U.S. Supreme Ct. 1973. Assoc. Reno, O'Byrne & Kepley, Champaign, Ill., 1970-73, ptnr., 1973-84; pres. Rawles, O'Byrne, Stanko & Kepley P.C., Champaign, 1984-98, pres., 1990-97; mem. student legal svc. adv. bd. U. Ill., Urbana, 1982—; hearing officer Ill. Fair Employment Practice Commn., Springfield, 1972-74; mem. rules com. U.S. Dist. Ct. for Ctrl. Dist. Ill., 1994—. Diplomate Nat. Bd. Trial Advocacy. Fellow Ill. State Bar Found., 1984. Mem. Ill. Bar Assn., Bar Assn. 7th Fed. Cir., Rules Com. U.S. Dist. Court (ctrl. dist. Ill.), Assn. Trial Lawyers Am., Ill. Trial Lawyers Assn., Colo. Trial Lawyers Assn., Kent Soc. Honor Men, Phi Delta Theta. Roman Catholic. Federal civil litigation, State civil litigation, Personal injury. Home: 6 Alice Dr White Heath IL 61884-9747 Office: Rawles O'Byrne Stanko & Kepley PC 501 W Church St Champaign IL 61820-3412

RAWLINSON, JOHNNIE BLAKENEY, judge; b. Dec. 16, 1952; BS in Psychology summa cum laude, NC A&T State U., 1974; JD, U. of Pacific, 1979. From dep. dist. atty. to asst. dist. atty. Clark County Dist. Atty.'s Office, 1980—98; judge U.S. Dist. Ct. Nev., 1998—2000, U.S. Ct. Appeals (9th cir.), 2000—. Office: 333 LAs Vegas Blvd S Rm 7072 Las Vegas NV 89101*

RAWLINSON, MARK STOBART, lawyer; b. Eccles, Manchester, Eng., May 3, 1957; MA, Cambridge (Eng.) U., 1980. Trainee Freshfields Bruckhans Deringer, London, 1982-84; assoc., 1984-90; ptnr., 1990—. Mergers and acquisitions. Office: Freshfields Bruckhans Derin 65 Fleet St EC4Y 1HS London England

RAWLS, FRANK MACKLIN, lawyer; b. Suffolk, Va., Aug. 24, 1952; s. John Lewis and Mary Helen (Macklin) R.; m. Sally Hallum Blanchard, June 26, 1976; children: Matthew Christopher, John Stephen, Michael Andrew. BA in History cum laude, Hampden Sydney Coll., 1974; JD, U. Va., 1977. Bar: Va. 1977, U.S. Dist. Ct. (ea. dist.) Va. 1977, U.S. Ct. Appeals (4th cir.) 1977. Assoc. Rawls, Habel & Rawls, Suffolk, 1977-78, ptnr., 1978-91, Ferguson & Rawls, Suffolk, 1991-96, Ferguson, Rawls, MacDonald, Overton & Grissom PC, Suffolk, 1996-98, Ferguson, Rawls, MacDonald & Overton PC, Suffolk, 1999—. Sec., bd. dirs. Suffolk Title Ltd., 1986-95; bd. dirs Old Dominion Investors Trust, Inc. 1994—, Secure Title, Inc., 1996—. Deacon Westminster Reformed Presbyn. Ch., Suffolk, 1979-83, elder, clk. of session, 1984-91, 94-99; chmn. bd. dirs. Suffolk Crime Line, 1982-90, Suffolk Cheer Fund, 1982—, Covenant Christian Schs., Suffolk, 1982-84; bd. dirs. Norfolk Christian Schs., 1990—, v.p., 1998-99, pres., 1999—; pres. Parent Tchr. Fellowship, 1995-97, vice-chmn. steering com. for capital campaign, 1996-98, v.p., 1997-98; adv. bd. dirs. Salvation Army, Suffolk, 1977-95, chmn., 1989-90; chmn. Suffolk Com. on Affordable Housing, 1989-90; bd. dirs. Suffolk YMCA, 1988-90, Suffolk Youth Athletic Assn., 1999-2000. Mem. ATLA, Suffolk Bar Assn. (past pres.), Va. State Bar, Va. Bar Assn., Christian Legal Soc., Va. Trial Lawyers Assn., Suffolk Bar Assn. General corporate, General practice, Personal injury. E-mail: frawls@frmolaw.com

RAWLS, JOHN D. lawyer; b. Jacksonville, Fla., Sept. 16, 1943; s. Hugh Miller Sr. and Katherine (Dickenson) R. BA, Williams Coll., 1965; JD, Fla. State U., Tallahassee, 1974. Bar: Fla. 1975, La. 1986, U.S. Dist. Ct. (mid. dist.) Fla. 1975, U.S. Dist. Ct. (ea. dist.) La. 1986, U.S. Dist. Ct. (no. dist.) Fla. 1989, U.S. Dist. Ct. (we. dist.) La. 1996, U.S. Ct. Appeals (5th cir.) 1986. Assoc. Foerster & Hodge, Jacksonville Beach, Fla., 1975-78; ptnr. Thames, Rawls & Skinner, Jacksonville, 1978-80; pvt. practice, 1980-85; pres. At Your Svc. Supply Co., New Orleans, 1985-86; assoc. Oestreicher, Whalen & Hackett, 1986-87; pvt. practice, 1987—. Charter mem. Fla. Commn. on Ethics, Tallahassee, 1974-75. Mem. Fla. State U. Law Rev., 1973-74. Bd. dirs. Celebration '86, New Orleans, 1985-86; vol. NO/AIDS Task Force, New Orleans, 1986—; bd. dirs. La. Lesbian and Gay Polit. Action Caucus, New Orleans, 1987-89, Nat. Lesbian and Gay Law Assn., Washington, 1992-94, Supreme Ct. of La. Hist. Soc., New Orleans, 1992-96; founder, sec., bd. dirs. La. Electorate of Gays and Lesbians, New Orleans, 1993-96; chair La. Gov.'s Commn. on HIV and AIDS, Baton Rouge, 1994-95; unofcl. advisor on Gay and AIDS issues Gov. of La., Baton Rouge, 1992-96. Capt. U.S. Army, 1968-72, Vietnam. Nat. Merit scholar, 1961; Forum for Equality ACCLAIM award Outstanding Polit. Activist, 1999, Champion for Equality award La. Lesbian and Gay Polit. Action Caucus, 2000. Fellow: La. Bar Found.; mem.: New Orleans Bar Assn., La. Landmarks Soc., Inc. (trustee 2001—). Democrat. Episcopalian. Avocation: reading. Civil rights, Personal injury. Office: 400 Magazine St Ste 100 New Orleans LA 70130-2439

RAWSON, MARJORIE JEAN, lawyer; b. Okolona, Miss., Dec. 5, 1939; d. E.P. and Marjorie J. R. BS, U. Miss., 1961; MS, Ind. U., 1969); JD, John Marshall Law Sch., 1977. Bar: Ind. 1977, U.S. Dist. Ct. (no. dist.) Ind. 1977, U.S. Ct. Appeals (7th cir.) 1983, U.S. Supreme Ct. 1983, Fla. 1988, U.S. Dist. Ct. (mid. dist.) Fla. 1991, U.S. Ct. Mil. Appeals, 1995. Tchr. Munster (Ind.) High Sch., 1966-77; atty. pvt. practice, Munster, 1977-90; deputy prosecutor Lake County Juvenile Ct., Gary, Ind., 1978-90; pvt. practice Naples, Fla., 1991—. Adj. prof. Ind. U., Gary, 1984-87, Purdue U., Hammond, Ind., 1988-90, John Marhsall Law Sch., Chgo., 1984-87, U. South Fla., Ft. Myers, 1992-97; compliance specialist Collier County Pub. Schs., Naples, 1997-99. Author: A Manual of Special Education Law for Educators and Parents, 2000; editor: Handbook for Legal Assistants, 1987. Past pres. Women's Polit. Caucus, Naples, 1995-97, Women's Rep. Club, Naples, 1992-94; mem. adv. bd. Naples Alliance Children, 1997—. Mem. AAUW, LWV, Collier County Bar Assn. (bd. dirs. 1996-99), Naples C. of C. (bd. dirs. 1997—), Zonta Club. Republican. Avocations: jogging, swimming, music. Education and schools, Family and matrimonial. Office: 400 5th Ave S Ste 300 Naples FL 34102-6556

RAY, DAVID LEWIN, lawyer, accountant; b. L.A., June 17, 1929; s. Herbert and Beatrice (Lewin) R.; m. Arlene Opas, July 15, 1951; children: Stephan, Robyn. BS, UCLA, 1954; JD, U. LaVerne, 1970. Bar: U.S. Dist. Ct. (so., no. and cen. dists.) Calif.; CPA, Calif. Ptnr., acct. Ray & Ray, Los Angeles, 1957-71, Zigmond, Ray & Co., Beverly Hills, Calif., 1971-73; ptnr. Ray, Rolston & Ress, 1970-80, Ray & Murray, Beverly Hills, 1973-80, Saltzburg, Ray & Bergman, Los Angeles, 1980—. Contbr. articles to profl. jours. Served with U.S. Army, 1951-53. Mem. AICPA, Calif. Soc. CPAs, Am. Assn. Attys.-CPAs, Beverly Hills Bar Assn., L.A. County Bar Assn. (past chair exec. com. of provisional and postjudgement remedies sect.), State Organization of Calif. Receivers Forum, Los Angeles chapter (founding chair), L.A. Trial Lawyers Assn., Am. Arbitration Assn., Brentwood Contry Club, Masons. Avocations: sailing, golfing, deep sea diving, photography, skiing. Bankruptcy, State civil litigation, Receivership. Office: Saltzburg Ray & Bergman LLP 12121 Wilshire Blvd # 600 Los Angeles CA 90025

RAY, FRANK ALLEN, lawyer; b. Lafayette, Ind., Jan. 30, 1949; s. Dale Allen and Merry Ann (Fleming) R.; m. Carol Ann Olmutz, Oct. 1, 1982; children: Erica Fleming, Robert Allen. BA, Ohio State U., 1970, JD, 1973. Bar: Ohio 1973, U.S. Dist. Ct. (so. dist.) Ohio 1975, U.S. Supreme Ct. 1976, U.S. Tax Ct. 1977, U.S. Ct. Appeals (6th cir.) 1977, U.S. Dist. Ct. (no. dist.) Ohio 1980, Pa. 1983, U.S. Dist. Ct. (ea. dist.) Mich. 1983, U.S. Ct. Appeals (1st cir.) 1986; cert. civil trial adv. Nat. Bd. Trial Advocacy. Asst. pros. atty. Franklin County, Ohio, 1973-75, chief civil counsel, 1976-78; dir. econ. crime project Nat. Dist. Attys. Assn., Washington, 1975-76; assoc. Brownfield, Kosydar, Bowen, Bally & Sturtz, Columbus, Ohio, 1978, Michael F. Colley Co., L.P.A., Columbus, 1979-83; pres. Frank A. Ray Co., L.P.A., 1983-93, 2000—, Ray & Todaro Co., LPA, Columbus, 1993-94, Ray, Todaro & Alton Co., L.P.A., Columbus, 1994-96, Ray, Todaro, Alton & Kirstein Co., L.P.A., Columbus, 1996, Columbus, Ray, Alton & Kirstein Co., L.P.A., 1996-98; sr. ptnr. Ray & Alton, L.L.P., 1998-2000. Mem. seminar faculty Nat. Coll. Dist. Attys., Houston, 1975-77; mem. nat. conf. faculty Fed. Jud. Ctr., Washington, 1976-77; bd. editors Man. for Complex Litigation, Fed. Jud. Ctr., 1999—; bd. mem. bar examiners Ohio Supreme Ct., 1992-95, Rules Adv. Com., 1995-99. Editor: Economic Crime Digest, 1975-76; co-author: Personal Injury Litigation Practice in Ohio, 1988, 91. Mem. fin. com. Franklin County Rep. Orgn., Columbus, 1979-84; trustee Ohio State U. Coll. Humanities Alumni Soc., 1991-93, Nat. Coun. Ohio State U. Coll. Law Alumni Assn., 1998—; mem. Legal Aid Soc. of Columbus Capital Campaign Fund Cabinet, 1998. Capt. inf. U.S. Army, 1976. Named to Ten Outstanding Young Citizens of Columbus, Columbus Jaycees, 1976; recipient Nat. award of Distinctive Svc., Nat. Dist. Attys. Assn., 1977. Fellow Am. Coll. Trial Lawyers, Internat. Soc. Barristers, Columbus Bar Found., Roscoe Pound Found., Ohio Acad. Trial Lawyers, Ohio State Bar Found.; mem. ABA, Am. Bd. Trial Advocates (treas. Ohio chpt. 2001—), Columbus Bar Assn. (pres. 2001—, Profl. award 1997), Million Dollar Advs. Forum, Ohio State Bar Assn. (com. negligence law 1990-97), Assn. Trial Lawyers Am. (state del. 1990-92), Ohio Acad. Trial Lawyers (pres. 1989-90, Pres.' award 1986), Franklin County Trial Lawyers Assn. (pres. 1987-88, Pres.'s award 1990), Inns of Ct. (pres. Judge Robert M. Duncan chpt. 1993-94). Presbyterian. General civil litigation, Personal injury, Product liability. Home: 2030 Tremont Rd Columbus OH 43221-4330 Office: 175 S 3rd St Ste 350 Columbus OH 43215-5188 E-mail: far@raylaw.com

RAY, GILBERT T. lawyer; b. Mansfield, Ohio, Sept. 18, 1944; s. Robert Lee Ray and Renatha (Goldie) Washington; m. Valerie J. Reynolds, June 14, 1969; children: Tanika, Tarlin. BA, Ashland Coll., 1966; MBA, U. Toledo, 1968; JD, Howard U., 1972. Assoc. O'Melveny & Myers, L.A., 1972-79, ptnr., 1980-2000, ret. ptnr., 2000—. Bd. dirs. Host Marriott Svcs. Corp., Sierra Monolithins, Inc., Automobile Club of So. Calif., Haynes Found., Watson, Wyatt & Co. Mem. The Calif. Club, L.A. Country Club. Democrat. Office: O'Melveny & Myers 400 S Hope St Los Angeles CA 90071-2899

RAY, HUGH MASSEY, JR. lawyer; b. Vicksburg, Miss., Feb. 1, 1943; s. Hugh Massey and Lollie Landon (Powell) R.; m. Florence Hargrove, Sept. 3, 1966; children: Hugh, Hallie BA, Vanderbilt U., 1965, JD, 1967. Bar: Tex. 1967, U.S. Dist. Ct. (so. dist.) Tex. 1967, U.S. Dist.Ct. (we. dist.) La. 1979, U.S. Dist. Ct. (we. dist.) Tex. 1979, U.S. Dist Ct. (no. dist.) Tex. 1980, U.S. Ct. Appeals 1st, 5th, 9th, 11th cirs.) 1982, U.S. Dist. Ct. (no. dist.) Calif. 1989, N.Y. 1992; cert. Tex. Bd. Legal Specialization. Asst. U.S. atty. So. Dist. Tex., 1967-68; assoc. Andrews & Kurth, Houston, 1968-77, ptnr., 1977—. Lectr. Ctrl. and Ea. European Law Initiative, Vilnius, Lithuania, 1996. Co-author: Bankruptcy Investing, 1992, Creditor's Rights, vol. 1 & 2, 1998; contbr. articles to profl. jours. Mem. ABA (chmn. real property practice com. 1975-77, chmn. continuing legal edn. com. young lawyers divsn. 1976-78, vice-chmn. 1979, chmn. oil and gas subcom. bus. bankruptcy com. 1985-89, chmn. executory contracts subcom. 1989-93, chmn. bus. bankruptcy com. 1993-96, chmn. com. on trust indentures and indenture trustees 1995-97, mem. standing com. on jud. selection, tenure and compensation 1996-97, coun. mem. bus. law sect. 1997-2001, chmn. ad hoc com. on bankruptcy ct. structure 1996-2001, chair energy bus. com. 2001—), Houston Bar Assn., Tex. Bar Assn. (chmn. bankruptcy com. 1985-88), Am. Law Inst., Houston Country Club, Tex. Club, Houston Club. Episcopalian. Bankruptcy, Federal civil litigation, State civil litigation. Home: 5785 Indian Cir Houston TX 77057-1302 Office: Andrews & Kurth 600 Travis St Ste 4200 Houston TX 77002-2910

RAY, MARY LOUISE RYAN, lawyer; b. Houston, Dec. 8, 1954; d. Cornelius O'Brien and Mary Anne (Kelley) R.; m. Marshall Ransome Ray, Jan. 30, 1982; children: Siobhan Elisabeth Kelley, Johanna Frances Morris, Jonathan Jordan Willson. BA with honors, U. Tex., 1976; JD, St. Mary's Univ., San Antonio, Tex., 1980. Bar: Tex. 1980, U.S. Dist. Ct. (so. dist.) Tex. 1981, U.S. Ct. Appeals (5th cir.) 1993, U.S. Supreme Ct. 1994. Assoc. Kelley & Ryan, Houston, 1980-82, R.W. Armstrong, Brownsville, Tex., 1982-83; ptnr. Armstrong & Ray, 1983-87; shareholder Ransome and Ray, P.C., 1987—. Bd. dirs. Brownsville Soc. for Crippled Children, 1984-95, pres., 1992-93; bd. dirs. Valley Zool. Soc., 1990—, sec., 2000-01; bd. dirs. United Way of Southern Cameron County, 1989-95, pres., 1994; bd. dirs. Crippled Children's Found., Brownsville, 1989—; bd. dirs. Episcopal Day Sch. Found., 1995—, pres., 1995—. Fellow Tex. Bar Found.; mem. Tex. Bar Assn., Cameron County Bar Assn. (bd. dirs. 1990-99, pres. 1998), Tex. Assn. Bank Counsel, Brownsville C. of C. (bd. dirs. 1998-99). Episcopalian. General civil litigation, General corporate, Probate. Office: Ransome & Ray PC 550 E Levee St Brownsville TX 78520-5343

RAY, RONALD DUDLEY, lawyer; b. Hazard, Ky., Oct. 30, 1942; BA in Psychology and English, Centre Coll., 1964; JD magna cum laude, U. Louisville, 1971. Assoc. Greenebaum, Doll & McDonald, 1971-75, ptnr., 1975-84, 85-86, Ray & Morris, Louisville, 1986-89; mng. ptnr. Ronald Ray Attys., 1990—; dep. asst. sec. def. Pentagon, Washington, 1984-85. Adj. prof. law U. Louisville Sch. Law, 1972-80; commr. Presdl. Commn. on Assigment of Women in Mil., 1992. Author: Military Necessity & Homosexuality, 1993; sr. legal editor: Personnel Policy Manual, Bank Supervisory Policies, The Bank Employee Handbook, 1985-86; mil. historian. State fin. chmn. Nat. Fin. Com. for George Bush for Pres.; chmn. Vietnam Vets. Leadership Program in Ky., 1982-85, Ky. Vietnam Vets. Meml. Fund, 1985-91; trustee Marine Corps Command and Staff Found., 1985-92; mem. exec. com. State Cen. Com., Ky. Rep. Party, 1986-90; mem. Am. Battle Monuments Commn., 1990-94; chmn. Vets. for Bush in Ky., 2000; mem. Nat. Com. Vets. for Bush, 2000; spokesman Coalition of Am. Vets., 1998—, chmn., 1999—. With USMC, 1964-69; col. USMCR (ret.). Decorated Silver Star medal with gold star, Bronze Star medal, Purple Heart, Vietnamese Cross of Gallantry, Vietnamese Honor Medal; recipient Nat. Eagle award Nat. Guard Assn., 1985. Mem. Naval Inst. (life), Marine Corps Res. Officers' Assn. General civil litigation, Legislative, Military. Home: Halls Hill Farm 3317 Halls Hill Rd Crestwood KY 40014-9523 E-mail: euniceray@aol.com

RAY, STEPHEN ALAN, academic administrator, lawyer; b. Oklahoma City, Aug. 26, 1956; s. Thompson Eugene and Dorothea Hodges. BA summa cum laude, St. Thomas Sem., 1978; PhD, Harvard U., 1986; JD, U. Calif., Hastings, 1990. Bar: Calif. 1990, Mass. 1994. Assoc. Richards, Watson & Gershon, L.A., 1990-93; lectr. theology Boston Coll., Chestnut Hill, Mass., 1993-95; staff counsel Houghton Mifflin Co., Boston, 1995-96; asst. dean acad. affairs Harvard Law Sch., Cambridge, 1998—, dir. acad. affairs, 1996-98. Vis. lectr. religion Harvard Divinity Sch., spring 1995; adv. bd. Harvard Native Am. Program, 1999—. Author: The Modern Soul, 1987. Vol. AIDS action com., Boston, 1994-96; atty. vol. AIDS Project L.A., 1991-93; Native Am. Adv. Com. on Repatriation, Peabody Mus., 1999—. Mem. ABA, Cherokee Nation Okla. Office: Harvard Law Sch Griswold Hall 207 Cambridge MA 02138 E-mail: aray@law.harvard.edu

RAYLESBERG, ALAN IRA, lawyer; b. N.Y.C., Dec. 6, 1950; s. Daniel David and Sally Doris (Mantell) R.; m. Caren Thea Coven, Nov. 20, 1983; children: Lisa Maris, Jason Todd. BA, NYU, 1972; JD cum laude, Boston U., 1975. Bar: N.Y. 1976, U.S. Dist. Ct. (so. dist.) N.Y. 1976, U.S. Dist. Ct. (ea. dist.) N.Y. 1978, U.S. Tax Ct. 1981, U.S. Ct. Appeals (2d and 5th cirs.) 1982, U.S. Ct. Appeals (1st cir.) 1986, U.S. Ct. Appeals (9th cir.) 1996. Assoc. Orans, Elsen & Polstein, N.Y.C., 1975-77, Guggenheimer & Untermyer, N.Y.C., 1977-83, ptnr., 1983-85, Rosenman & Colin, N.Y.C., 1985—, co-chmn. litigation dept., 1998-99, chmn. litigation dept., 1999—. Adj. instr. N.Y. Law Sch., 1980-83; instr. Nat. Inst. of Trial Advocacy; mem. adv. group comml. divsn., mem. mediation panel N.Y. State Supreme Ct.; mem. arbitration panel U.S. Dist. Ct. (ea. dist.) N.Y.; judge Nat. Moot Ct. Competition, 1980—. Bd. dirs. Fund for Modern Cts., 1994—. Mem. ABA, Fed. Bar Coun., Assn. Bar City N.Y., N.Y. County Lawyers Assn. (bd. dirs. 1995-98, 99—, fed. ct. com. 1988—, appellate ct. com. 1990—, co-chmn. appellate ct. com. 1992-93, chair appellate ct. com. 1993-96), N.Y. County Lawyers Assn. Found. (bd. dirs. 1998—), N.Y. State Bar Assn. (ho. delegates 1996-2000), Securities Industry Assn. (legal and compliance divsn) N.Y. Coun. Def. Lawyers, Town Club of Newcastle (mem. exec. com. 1987-91). Democrat. Jewish. Federal civil litigation, State civil litigation, Criminal. Office: Rosenman & Colin 575 Madison Ave Fl 16 New York NY 10022-2585 E-mail: airaylesberg@rosenman.com, araylesberg@compuserve.com

RAYMOND, DAVID WALKER, lawyer; b. Chelsea, Mass., Aug. 23, 1945; s. John Walker and Jane (Beck) R.; m. Sandra Sue Broadwater, Aug. 12, 1967 (div.); m. Margaret Byrd Payne, May 25, 1974; children: Pamela Payne, Russell Wyatt. BA, Gettysburg Coll., 1967; JD, Temple U., 1970. Bar: Pa. 1970, D.C. 1971, Ill. 1975, U.S. Dist. Ct. (no. dist.) Ill. 1981, U.S. Supreme Ct. 1974. Govtl. affairs atty. Sears, Roebuck and Co., Washington, 1970-74, atty. Sears Hdqrs. law dept. Chgo., 1974-80, asst. gen. counsel advt., trademarks and customs, 1981-84, asst. gen. counsel adminstrn., 1984-86, mgr. planning and analysis corp. planning dept., 1986-89, sr. corp. counsel pub. policy corp. law dept., 1989-90; assoc. gen. counsel litigation and adminstrn. law dept. Sears Mdse. Group, 1990-92, dep. gen. counsel, 1992-93, v.p., gen. counsel, 1993-95; v.p. law Sears Roebuck and Co., 1996; of counsel Winston & Strawn, Washington, 1996-2001; v.p., gen. counsel C-NAV Systems, Inc., McLean, Va., 2001—. Mem. staff Temple Law Quar., 1968-69, editor, 1969-70. Trustee No. Ill. U., 1996-98; mem. bd. visitors Christopher Newport U., 1999—; mem. bd. fellows Gettysburg Coll., 1999—. Mem. ABA, Nat. Assn. Coll. and Univ. Attys., Assn. Governing Bds., Phi Alpha Delta. Presbyterian. Administrative and regulatory, General corporate, Legislative. Office: C-NAV Systems Inc 8260 Greensboro Dr Ste 155 Mc Lean VA 22102

RAYNOLDS, WILLIAM F., II, lawyer; b. San Antonio, Feb. 7, 1948; s. William F. and Doris Raynolds; m. Kathryn Raynolds, July 11, 1987; children: Lisa Chipman, Mike Chipman, Casey Raynolds. BS, U. Tulsa, 1973, JD, 1976. Atty. Hood & Raynolds, Tulsa, 1987—. Adj. prof. legal assistant program U. Tulsa, 1993—, adj. prof. coll. law, 1995—. Editor Okla. Family Law Jour., 1995. Fellow Am. Acad. Matrimonial Lawyers; mem. ABA (family law sect.), Tulsa County Bar Assn. (family law sect., pres. 1993-97), Okla. Bar Assn. (family law sect.). Roman Catholic. Family and matrimonial. Office: Hood & Raynolds 1914 S Boston Ave Tulsa OK 74119-5222 E-mail: hood_raynalds@compuserve.com

RAYNOVICH, GEORGE, JR. lawyer; b. Pitts., Dec. 30, 1931; s. George Sr. and Zora (Mamula) R.; m. Mary Ann Senay, July 11, 1953; children: George III, Andrew. BS, U. Pitts., 1957; JD, Duquesne U., 1961. Bar: Pa. 1962, U.S. Dist. Ct. (we. dist.) Pa. 1962, U.S. Patent and Trademark Office 1962, U.S. Supreme Ct. 1966, U.S. Ct. Appeals (fed. cir.) 1986. Patent agt. Consolidation Coal Co., Library, Pa., 1959-62; ptnr. Stone & Raynovich, Pitts., 1962-75; atty. Wheeling-Pitts. Steel Corp., 1975-77, gen. counsel, sec., 1978-85, v.p., 1980-85; sr. atty. Buchanan Ingersol P.C., 1986-88, 89-96; ptnr. Price & Raynovich, 1988-89; of counsel Gorr Moser Dell and Loughney, 1997-2000, Paul A. Beck and Assocs., Pitts., 2001—. Councilman Borough of Baldwin, Allegheny County, Pa., 1972-75, govt. study commr., 1973. 1st lt. USAF, 1952-56. Mem. Allegheny County Bar Assn., Pitts. Intellectual Property Law Assn., Acad. Trial Lawyers Allegheny County. Democrat. Mem. Serbian Orthodox Ch. Federal civil litigation, Patent, Real property. Home: 335 Jean Dr Pittsburgh PA 15236-2511 Office: Paul A Beck & Assocs 1575 McFarland Rd Ste 100 Pittsburgh PA 15216-1808

RAZZANO, FRANK CHARLES, lawyer; b. Bklyn., Feb. 25, 1948; s. Pasquale Anthony and Agnes Mary (Borgia) R.; m. Stephanie Anne Lucas, Jan. 10, 1970; children: Joseph, Francis, Catherine. BA, St. Louis U., 1969; JD, Georgetown U., 1972. Bar: N.Y. 1973, U.S. Dist. Ct. (so. dist.) N.Y. 1973, U.S. Dist. Ct. (es. dist.) N.Y. 1973, N.J. 1976, D.C. 1981, Va. 1984, U.S. Dist. Ct. N.J. 1976, U.S. Dist. Ct. Md. 1977, U.S. Dist. Ct. (no. dist.) Calif. 1981, U.S. Dist. Ct. D.C. 1982, U.S. Dist. Ct. (ea. dist.) Va. 1989, U.S. Dist. Ct. (we. dist.) Va. 1990, U.S. Ct. Appeals (2d cir.) 1973, U.S. Ct. Appeals (3d cir.) 1975, U.S. Ct. Appeals (D.C. and 5th cirs.) 1983, U.S. Ct. Appeals (4th cir.) 1984, U.S. Ct. Appeals (6th cir.) 1990, U.S. Ct. Appeals (8th and 9th cirs.) 2000, U.S. Supreme Ct. 1976. Assoc. Shea & Gould, N.Y.C., 1972-75; asst. U.S. atty. Dist. of N.J., Newark, 1975-78; asst. chief trial atty. SEC, Washington, 1978-82; ptnr. Shea & Gould, 1982-94, mng. ptnr., 1991-92; ptnr. Camhy Karlinsky Stein Razzano & Rubin, 1994-96, Dickstein, Shapiro, Morin & Oshinsky, Washington, 1996—. Lectr. in field; adv. bd. Securities Litigation Reform Act Reporter, Securities Regulation Law Jour.; adj. prof. law U. Md. Sch. Law. Civil law editor Rico Law Reporter; mem. adv. bd. Corp. Confidentiality and Disclosure Letter; hon. adv. com. Jour. Internat. Law and Practice, Detroit Coll. Law; contbr. articles to legal jours. Scoutmaster Vienna coun. Boy Scouts Am., 1984. Recipient spl. achievement award Justice Dept., 1977, spl. commendation, 1978, Outstanding Achievement award Detroit Coll. of Law, 1993. Mem. ABA (chmn. criminal law com., sect. bus. law 1996—), Va. Bar, D.C. Bar (chmn. litigation sect. 1987-89, vice-chmn. com. sects. 1988-89), Assn. Securities & Exch. Commn. Alumni (pres. 1993-95), Phi Beta Kappa, Eta Sigma Phi. Roman Catholic. Federal civil litigation, State civil litigation, Securities. Home: 1713 Paisley Blue Ct Vienna VA 22182-2326

RAZZANO, PASQUALE ANGELO, lawyer; b. Bklyn., Apr. 3, 1943; s. Pasquale Anthony and Agnes Mary (Borgia) R.; m. Maryann Walker, Jan. 29, 1966; children: Elizabeth, Pasquale, Susan, ChristyAnn. BSCE, Poly. Inst. Bklyn., 1964; student law, NYU, 1964-66; JD, Georgetown U., 1969. Bar: Va. 1969, N.Y. 1970, U.S. Ct. Appeals (2d, 3d, 7th, 9th and fed. cirs.), U.S. Supreme Ct., U.S. Dist. Ct. (so., ea. and western dists.) N.Y., U.S. Dist. Ct. (we. dist.) Tex., U.S. Dist. Ct. Hawaii, U.S. Dist. Ct. Conn. Examiner U.S. Patent Office, 1966-69; assoc. Curtis, Morris & Safford, P.C., 1969-71, ptnr., 1971-91, Fitzpatrick, Cella, Harper & Scinto, 1991—. Guest lectr. U.S. Trademark Assn., Am. Intellectual Property Law Assn., Practicing Law Inst., NYU Law Ctr., ABA, N.Y. Intellectual Property Law Assn. Mem. bd. editors Licensing Jour., 1986—; mem. bd. editors Trademark Reporter, 1987—, book rev. editor, 1989-91, pub. articles editor, 1991-94, domestic articles editor, 1992-93, 95, editor-in-chief 1996—. Rep. committeeman Rockland County. Recipient Robert Ridgeway award, 1964. Mem. ABA (guest lectr.), Fed. Bar Assn. (chmn. patent law com. 1999—), N.Y. Intellectual Property Law Assn. (bd. dirs. 1985—, sec. 1988-91, pres. 1994-95), Licensing Exec. Soc. (chmn. N.Y. chpt.

1996-99), Internat. Trademark Assn. (bd. dirs. 1996-99), Am. Intellectual Property Law Assn., N.Y. Bar Assn., N.Y. Coun. Bar Leaders (exec. coun. 1993-94), Va. Bar Assn., Italian Am. Bar Assn., Bar Assn. City N.Y., Columban Laws Assn., N.Y. Athletic Club, Minute Man Yacht Club, Shorehaven Golf Club. Republican. Roman Catholic. Federal civil litigation, Patent, Trademark and copyright. Address: 21 Covlee Dr Westport CT 06880-6407 also: 14 Deerwood Trl Lake Placid NY 12946-1834

RE, EDWARD DOMENIC, law educator, retired federal judge; b. Santa Marina, Italy, Oct. 14, 1920; s. Anthony and Marina (Maetta) R.; m. Margaret A. Corcoran, June 3, 1950; children: Mary Ann, Anthony John, Marina, Edward, Victor, Margaret, Matthew, Joseph, Mary Elizabeth, Mary Joan, Mary Ellen, Nancy Madeleine. BS cum laude, St. John's U., 1941, LLB summa cum laude, 1943, LLD (hon.), 1968; JSD, NYU, 1950; DPed (hon.), Aquila, Italy, 1960; LL.D. (hon.), St. Mary's Coll., Notre Dame, Ind., 1968, Maryville Coll., St. Louis, 1969, N.Y. Law Sch., 1976, Bklyn. Coll., CUNY, 1978, Nova U., 1980, Roger Williams Coll., 1982, Dickinson Sch. Law, Carlisle, Pa., 1983, Seton Hall U., 1984, Stetson U., 1990, William Mitchell Coll. Law, 1992, St. Francis Coll., Bklyn., 1993; L.H.D. (hon.), DePaul U., 1980, Coll. S.I., CUNY, 1981, Pace U., 1985, Am. U. of Rome, 1995; D.C.S. (hon.), U. Verona, Italy, 1987; J.D. (hon.), U. Bologna, Italy, 1988, U. Urbino, 1994. Bar: N.Y. 1943. Appointed faculty St. John's U., N.Y., 1947, prof. law, 1951-69, adj. prof. law, 1969-80, Disting. prof., from 1980; vis. prof. Georgetown U. Sch. Law, 1962-67; adj. prof. law N.Y. Law Sch., 1972-82, Martin disting. vis. prof., 1982-90; spl. hearing officer U.S. Dept. Justice, 1956-61; chmn. Fgn. Claims Settlement Commn. of U.S., 1961-68; asst. sec. ednl. and cultural affairs U.S. Dept. State, 1968-69; judge U.S. Customs Ct. (now U.S. Ct. Internat. Trade), N.Y.C., 1969-91, chief judge, 1977-91, chief judge emeritus, 1991—. Mem. Jud. Conf. U.S., 1986-91, adv. com. on appellate rules, 1976-88, com. on internat. jud. rels., 1994-97; chmn. adv. com. on experimentation in the law Fed. Jud. Ctr., 1978-81; mem. bd. higher edn. City of N.Y., 1958-69, emeritus, 1969—; Jackson lectr. Nat. Coll. State Trial Judges, U. Nev., 1970. Author: Foreign Confiscations in Anglo-American Law, 1951, (with Lester D. Orfield) Cases and Materials on International Law, rev. edit., 1965, Selected Essays on Equity, 1955, Brief Writing and Oral Argument, 6th edit., 1987, (with Joseph R. Re) 8th edit., 1999, (with Zechariah Chafee Jr.) Cases and Materials on Equity, 1967, Cases and Materials on Equitable Remedies, 1975; (with Joseph R. Re) Law Students' Manual on Legal Writing and Oral Argument, 1991; chpt., freedom in internat. soc. Concept of Freedom (editor Rev. Carl W. Grindel), 1955; Cases and Materials on Remedies, 1982, (with Joseph R. Re) 5th edit., 2000; contbr. articles to legal jours. Served with USAAF, 1943-47; col. JAGD, ret. Decorated Grand Cross Order of Merit Italy; recipient Am. Bill of Rights citation; Morgenstern Found. Interfaith award; USAF commendation medal; Distinguished service award Bklyn. Jr. C. of C., 1956 Mem. ABA (ho. of dels. 1976-78, chmn. sect. internat. and comparative law 1965-67), Am. Fgn. Law Assn. (pres. 1971-73), Am. Law Inst., Fed. Bar Coun. (pres. 1973-74), Am. Soc. Comparative Law (pres. 1969-91), Am. Justinian Soc. Jurists (pres. 1974-76), Internat. Assn. Jurists: Italy-USA (pres. 1991—), Internat. Assn. Judges (prin. rep. to UN 1993-2000), Scribes Am. Soc. Writers on Legal Subjects (pres. 1978). Home: 305 B 147th St Neponsit NY 11694 Office: 305 B 147th St Neponsit NY 11694

REA, JOHN MARTIN, lawyer, state official; b. San Francisco, Dec. 4, 1944; s. John Joseph and Madeline (Weldon) R.; m. Patricia Pearson, Nov. 29, 1969; children: Christopher, Alexander. AB with honors, Georgetown U., 1966; JD cum laude, NYU, 1969, LLM cum laude, 1971. Bar: N.Y. 1970, Calif. 1970, U.S. Dist. Ct. (so. dist.) N.Y. 1970, JU.S. Dist. Ct. (no. dist.) Calif. 1973, U.S. Dist. Ct. (ctrl. dist.) Calif. 1974, U.S. Dist. Ct. (ea. dist.) Calif. 1978, U.S. Ct. Appeals (9th cir.) 1975. Atty. VISTA, N.Y.C., 1969-71; sr. trial atty. EEOC, San Francisco, 1973-82; chief counsel Calif. Dept. Indsl. Rels., 1982—. Cons. on affirmative action Fed. Govt. Can., Ottawa, 1979-80; arbitrator state and fed. cts., San Francisco, 1979— ; lectr. pub. interest legal advocacy orgns., Los Angeles and San Francisco, 1979—. Bd. dirs. Hastings Law Sch. Child Care Ctr., San Francisco, 1979-82. Mem. Calif. Bar, San Francisco Bar (labor law sect.). Home: 1537 Edith St Berkeley CA 94703-1123 Office: Office Chief Counsel Dept Indsl Relations 525 Golden Gate Ave San Francisco CA 94102 E-mail: Jrea@hq.dir.ca.gov

READE, KATHLEEN MARGARET, paralegal, author; b. Ft. Worth, Sept. 6, 1947; d. Ralph S. and Margaret Catherine (Stark) R.; 1 child, Kathryn Michelle Carter. BA in English and Polit. Sci., Tex. Christian U., 1978; student, El Centro Coll.; postgrad., Tex. Christian U., Tex. Tech. Asst. land and legal dept. Am. Quasar Petroleum, Ft. Worth, 1971-74; paralegal and office mgr. Law Offices of George Sims, 1974-81; asst. Criminal Cts. #2 and #3 Tarrant County Dist. Atty., 1981; ind. paralegal, 1982-84; paralegal Law Offices of Brent Burford, 1982-85; sr. paralegal/litigation Law Offices of Windle Turley, Dallas, 1985-90; major case supr. The Dent Law Firm, Ft. Worth, 1990-96, Whitaker, Chalk, Swindle & Sawyer, LLP, Ft. Worth, 1996—. Cons./instr. paralegal program, U. Tex., Arlington, 1996—; active Tex. Christian U. Writer's Continuous Workshop. Author: Plaintiff's Personal Injury Handbook, 1995; contbg. author: Legal Assistant's Letter Book, 1995; editl. com. Tex. Paralegal Jour.; contbr. articles to profl. jours. Recipient scholarship Tex. Christian U., Ft. Worth. Mem. AAUW, Am. Assn. Paralegal Edn., Assn. Trial Lawyers, State Bar of Tex. (Legal Asst. Divsn.), Nat. Assn. Legal Assts., Nat. Paralegal Assn., Ft. Worth Paralegal Assn., Freelance Writers' Network, Austin Writer's League, Okla. Writers' Fedn., Text and Acad. Authors. Home: PO Box 101641 4336 Whitfield Avenue Fort Worth TX 76185-1641 E-mail: kmrparal@aol.com

REAGAN, GARY DON, state legislator, lawyer; b. Amarillo, Tex., Aug. 23, 1941; s. Hester and Lois Irene (Marcum) R.; m. Nedra Ann Nash, Sept. 12, 1964; children: Marc Kristi, Kari, Brent. BA, Stanford U., 1963, JD, 1965. Bar: N.Mex. 1965, U.S. Dist. Ct. N.Mex. 1965, U.S. Supreme Ct. 1986. Assoc. Smith & Ransom, Albuquerque, 1965-67; ptnr. Smith, Ransom, Deaton & Reagan, 1967-68, Williams, Johnson, Houston, Reagan & Porter, Hobbs, 1968-77, Williams, Johnson, Reagan, Porter & Love, Hobbs, 1977-82; pvt. practice pvt. practice, 1982—; city atty. City of Hobbs, 1978-80, 97—, City of Eunice, N.Mex., 1980—; mem. N.Mex. State Senate, 1993-96. Instr. N.Mex. Jr. Coll. and Coll. of S.W., Hobbs, 1978-84; N.Mex. commr. Nat. Conf. Commrs. Uniform State Laws, 1993-96; adv. mem. N.Mex. Constl. Revision Commn., 1993-95. Mayor City of Hobbs, 1972-73, 76-77, city commr., 1970-78; pres., dir. Jr. Achievement of Hobbs, 1974-85; pres., trustee Landsun Homes, Inc., Carlsbad, N.Mex., 1972-84; trustee Lydia Patterson Inst., El Paso, Tex., 1972-84, N.Mex. Conf. United Meth. Ch., 1988—, Coll. S.W. Hobbs, 1989-2001; chmn. County Dem. Com., 1983-85. Mem. ABA, State Bar N.Mex. (coms. 1989-96, v.p. 1992-93, pres. 1994-95), Lea County Bar Assn. (pres. 1976-77), Hobbs C. of C. (pres. 1989-90), Rotary (pres. Hobbs 1985-86), Hobbs Tennis Club (pres. 1974-75). Home: 200 E Eagle Dr Hobbs NM 88240-5323 Office: 1819 N Turner Ste G Hobbs NM 88240-3834 E-mail: lglregan@nm.net

REAGAN, HARRY EDWIN, III, lawyer; b. Wichita, Kans., Sept. 9, 1940; s. Harry E. II and Mary Elizabeth (O'Steen) R.; m. Marvene R. Rogers, June 17, 1965; children: Kathleen, Leigh, Mairen. BS, U. Pa., 1962, JD, 1965. Bar: Pa. 1965, U.S. Dist. Ct. (ea. dist.) Pa. 1965, U.S. Ct. Appeals (3d cir.) 1965. From assoc. to ptnr. Morgan, Lewis & Bockius, Phila., 1965-98. Chmn. Northhampton Twp. Planning Commn., Bucks County, Pa., 1974-79; mem. Warwick Twp. Planning Commn., 1980-95, chmn., 1994; supr. Warwick Twp., 1996-98; chmn. San Miguel County (Colo.) Open Space Commn., 1998—, chmn., 2001—, Town of Telluride Open Space Commn., 1999—. Mem. ABA (labor sect.), Pa. Bar Assn. (labor sect.), Phila. Bar Assn. (labor sect.), Indsl. Rels. Assn. (pres. Phila. chpt. 1990-91). Republican. Presbyterian. Avocations: coaching rugby, skiing, raising horses, bicycling. Labor, Pension, profit-sharing, and employee benefits. Home and Office: 12350 McKenzie Springs Rd Placerville CO 81430

REAL, FRANK JOSEPH, JR. lawyer, accountant; b. Phila., Nov. 23, 1952; s. Frank J. and Kathleen L. (Fleming) R.; m. Monica M. Driscoll, Sept. 12, 1980; children: Monica, Joseph, Timothy. BA, U. Notre Dame, 1974; JD, Temple U., 1977; LLM, Georgetown U., 1984. Bar: Pa. 1977, D.C. 1978, N.J. 1977; CPA, Md., Fla. Atty. U.S. Rlwy. Assn., Phila., 1977-79, IRS, Washington, 1979-84; sr. tax mgr. Ernst & Young, Orlando and Ga., 1984-91; assoc. gen. counsel Conrail Inc., Phila., 1992—. Mem. adv. bd. acctg. dept. Widener U., Chester, Pa., 1993-96; mem. adv. bd. Exec. Masters of Bus. Adminstrn., St. Joseph's U., Phila., 1996—. Mem. editl. adv. bd. Tax Mgmt. Inc., Bur. Nat. Affairs, Inc., Washington, 1991-94. Assoc. dir. Fla. Citrus Bowl, Orlando, 1986-89. Mem. AICPA, Phila. Bar Assn., Tax Execs. Inst. Phila. (dir. 1995—, ISR adminstrv. affairs com. 1995—). Avocations: reading, running, fishing, baseball. General corporate, Corporate taxation. Home: 4501 Cedar Ln Drexel Hill PA 19026-4015 Office: Conrail 2001 Market St # 16A Philadelphia PA 19103-7044

REAM, DAVIDSON, law publications administrator, writer; b. Ossining, N.Y., May 2, 1937; s. Joseph H. and Anita (Biggs) R.; m. Judith Krampitz, Oct. 1, 1966; children: Michael E., Caitlin D. BA, Yale U., 1961; JD, U. Va., 1964; LLM, U. Calif., Berkeley, 1971. Bar: D.C. 1972. Spl. asst. Supreme Ct. of Pakistan, 1964-65; law program developer The Asia Found., San Francisco and Sri Lanka, 1966-69; rsch. atty. Continuing Edn. of the Bar, Berkeley, 1970-75; publ. dir. ABA, Chgo., 1975-78; publ. mgr. Callaghan & Co., Wilmette, Ill., 1978-83; publs. dir. Def. Rsch. Inst., Chgo., 1984—. Editor: Condemnation Practice in California, 1973, Landslide and Subsidence Liability, 1974, Attorney's Guide to Professional Responsibility, 1978, Products Liability Pretrial Notebook, 1989, Products Liability Defenses, 1992, Products Liability Defenses, 2001; editor For The Defense, 1984—. Pres. Ridgeville Assn., Evanston, Ill., 1977-81, Mental Health Assn., Evanston, 1992-95; alderman City of Evanston, 1983-87; bd. dirs. Dem. Party Evanston, 1978-90, First Night Evanston, 1995—. Mem. ABA, D.C. Bar Assn. Avocations: hiking, camping, travel, community affairs. Office: Def Rsch Inst 150 N Michigan Ave Chicago IL 60601-7553 E-mail: dream@dri.org

REAMS, BERNARD DINSMORE, JR. lawyer, educator; b. Lynchburg, Va., Aug. 17, 1943; s. Bernard Dinsmore and Martha Eloise (Hickman) R.; m. Rosemarie Bridget Boyle, Oct. 26, 1968 (dec. Oct. 1996); children: Andrew Dennet, Adriane Bevin. BA, Lynchburg Coll., 1965; MS, Drexel U., 1966; JD, U. Kans., 1972; PhD, St. Louis U., 1983. Bar: Kans. 1973, Mo. 1986, N.Y. 1996. Instr., asst. librarian Rutgers U., 1966-69; asst. prof. law, librarian U. Kans., Lawrence, 1969-74; mem. faculty law sch. Washington U., St. Louis, 1974-95, prof. law, 1976-95, prof. tech. mgmt., 1990-95, librarian, 1974-76, acting dean univ. libraries, 1987-88; prof. law, assoc. dean, dir. Law Libr. St. John's U. Sch. Law, Jamaica, N.Y., 1995-97, assoc. dean acad. affairs, 1997-98; prof., dir. law libr. St. Mary's U., San Antonio, 2000—, prof. law, 2000—. Vis. fellow Max-Planck Inst., Hamburg, 1995, 97, 98, 2001; vis. prof. law Seton Hall U., 1998-2000. Author: Author: Law For The Businessman, 1974, Reader in Law Librarianship, 1976, Federal Price and Wage Control Programs 1917-1979: Legis. Histories and Laws, 1980; author, author: Education of the Handicapped: Laws, Legislative Histories, and Administrative Documents, 1982 actor: Internal Revenue Acts of the United States: The Revenue Act of 1954 with Legislative Histories and Congressional Documents, 1983; author: Congress and the Courts: A Legislative History 1978-1984, 1984, University-Industry Research Partnerships: The Major Issues in Research and Development Agreements, 1986, Deficit Control and the Gramm-Rudman-Hollings Act, 1986, The Semiconductor Chip and the Law: A Legislative History of the Semiconductor Chip Protection Act of 1984, 1986, American International Law Cases, 2d series, 1986, Technology Transfer Law: The Export Administration Acts of the U.S., 1987, Insider Trading and the Law: A Legislative History of the Insider Trading Sanctions Act, 1989, Insider Trading and Securities Fraud, 1989, The Health Care Quality Improvement Act of 1989: A Legislative History of P.L. No. 99-660, 1990, The National Organ Transplant Act of 1984: A Legislative History of P.L. No. 98-507, 1990, A Legislative History of Individuals with Disabilities Education Act, 1994, Federal Legislative Histories: An Annotated Bibliography and Index to Officially Published Sources, 1994, Electronic Contracting Law, 1996, Health Care Reform, 1994, The American Experience: Clinton and Congress, 1997, The Omnibus Anti-Crime Act, 1997, The Law of E-SIGN: A Legislative History of the Electronic Signature in Global and National Commerce Act, 2001; co-author: Segregation and the Fourteenth Amendment in the States, 1975, Historic Preservation Law: An Annotated Bibliography, 1976, Congress and the Courts: A Legislative History 1787-1977, 1978, Federal Consumer Protection Laws, Rules and Regulations, 1979, A Guide and Analytical Index to the Internal Revenue Acts of the U.S., 1909-1950, 1979, The Numerical Lists and Schedule of Volumes of the U.S. Congressional Serial Set: 73d Congress through the 96th Congress, 1984, Human Experimentation: Federal Laws, Legislative Histories, Regulations and Related Documents, 1985, American Legal Literature: A Guide to Selected Legal Resources, 1985. Bd. trustees Quincy Found. for Med. Rsch. Charitable Trust, San Francisco. Fellow Am. Bar Foun.; recipient Thornton award for excellence Lynchburg Coll., 1986, Joseph L. Andrews Bibliog. award, 1995; named to Hon. Order Ky. Cols., 1992. Mem. ABA, Am. Law Inst., ALA, Am. Soc. Law and Medicine, Nat. Health Lawyers Assn., Am. Assn. Higher Edn., Spl. Librs. Assn., Internat. Assn. Law Libr. Coll. and Univ. Attys., Order of Coif, Phi Beta Kappa, Sigma Xi, Beta Phi Mu, Phi Delta Phi, Phi Delta Epsilon, Kappa Delta Pi, Pi Lambda Theta. Office: St Marys U Sch Law One Camino Santa Maria San Antonio TX 78228 E-mail: reamsb@law.stmarytx.edu

REARDON, FRANK EMOND, lawyer; b. Providence, May 22, 1953; s. J. Clarke and Dorothy (Emond) R.; m. Deborah Walsh, Sept. 30, 1978; children: Kathleen Elizabeth, Brendan Francis, William James, Sean Patrick. BA, Holy Cross Coll., Worcester, Mass., 1975; JD, Suffolk U., 1978; MS, Harvard U., 1981. Bar: Mass. 1978, R.I. 1978, U.S. Dist. Ct. Mass. 1980, U.S. Dist. Ct. R.I. 1980, U.S. Supreme Ct. 1986. Counsel Nat. Assn. Govtl. Employment and Internat. Brotherhood Police Officers, Cranston, R.I., 1978-81; asst. gen. counsel Brigham and Women's Hosp., Boston, 1981-84; litigation counsel Risk Mgmt. Found. Harvard Med. Instns., Cambridge, Mass., 1984-87; ptnr. Hassan and Reardon, Boston, 1987—. Chmn. bd. dirs. St. Monica's Nursing Home, 1984-89, Med. Area Fed. Credit Union, 1984-89; clk., trustee Deaconess Glover Hosp., Needham, Mass.; ethics com. Boston Children's Hosp., 1993-96. Contbr. articles to profl. jours. Chmn. fin. com. Town of Needham, Mass.; mem. pres.'s council Coll. Holy Cross, 1985—. Beuilacqua scholar, 1978. Mem. ABA, Mass. Bar Assn. (chmn. health law sect. 1987—), Assn. Trial Lawyers Am., Am. Soc. Law and Medicine (cmty. rep. children's hosp. ethics com.). Democrat. Roman Catholic. Avocations: tennis, sailing, golf, writing. General civil litigation, Health, Labor. Home: 44 Sargent St Needham MA 02492-3434 Office: Hassan & Reardon 535 Boylston St Boston MA 02116-3720

REARDON, MICHAEL EDWARD, lawyer; b. Independence, Mo., Apr. 15, 1948; s. Neil Willison and Marjorie (Winters) R.; m. Gloria Kay Nelson, Jan. 31, 1970; children— Darin Thomas, Laura Michelle. B.A. magna cum laude, William Jewell Coll., 1970; J.D. with distinction, U. Mo.-Kansas City, 1973, LL.M. in Criminal Law, 1978. Bar: Mo. 1973, U.S. Dist. Ct. (we. dist.) Mo. 1974, U.S. Supreme Ct. 1978. Assoc. Morris, Larson, King, Stamper-Bold, Kansas City, Mo., 1973-74, M. Randall Vanet, North Kansas City, Mo., 1974-75; ptnr. Duncan, Russell & Reardon, Kansas City, 1975-82, Michael E. Reardon & Assocs., Kansas City, 1982-86; Clay County Pros. Atty., Liberty, Mo., 1987-98; pvt. practice, 1999—. Bd. dirs. Clay County Sheltered Facilities, 1982-84; chmn. Clay County Dem. Com., Kansas City, 1982-84; treas. Mo. 6th Congl. Dist. Dem. Com., 1982-86; bd. dirs. Clay County Investigative Squad, Liberty, 1987-98. Mem. Mo. Bar Assn., Mo. Assn. Trial Attys., Clay County Bar Assn., Kansas City Bar Assn., ATLA, Gladstone C. of C. Criminal. Office: Clay County Courthouse 5716 N Broadway St Kansas City MO 64118-3962

REASONER, BARRETT HODGES, lawyer; b. Houston, Apr. 16, 1964; s. Harry Max and Macey (Hodges) R.; m. Susan Hardig; children: Matthew Joseph, Caroline Macey, William Harry, Olivia Lucille. BA cum laude, Duke U., 1986; Grad. Dipl., London Sch. Econs., 1987; JD with honors, U. Tex., 1990. Bar: Tex. 1990, U.S. Dist. Ct. (so., we., and no. dists.) Tex. 1993, U.S. Ct. Appeals (5th cir.) 1993, U.S. Supreme Ct. 1997. Asst. dist. atty. Harris County Dist. Atty.'s Office, Houston, 1990-92; ptnr. Gibbs & Bruns, L.L.P., 1992—. Fellow Tex. Bar Found., Houston Bar Found.; mem. Am. Judicature Soc. (bd. dirs. 1994-99, exec. com. 1997-99), State Bar Tex. (jud. rels. com. 1998—), Houston Bar Assn. (bd. dirs. 2000—), Houston Young Lawyers Assn. (pub. schs. and pub. edn. com. 1994-99, chmn. pub. schs. and pub. edn. com. 1997-99, outstanding com. chair 1999), Order of Barristers. Episcopalian. General civil litigation. Office: Gibbs & Bruns LLP 1100 Louisiana St Ste 5300 Houston TX 77002-5215 E-mail: breasoner@gibbs-bruns.com

REASONER, HARRY MAX, lawyer; b. San Marcos, Tex., July 15, 1939; s. Harry Edward and Joyce Majorie (Barrett) R.; m. Elizabeth Macey Hodges, Apr. 15, 1963; children: Barrett Hodges, Elizabeth Macey Reasoner Stokes. BA in Philosophy summa cum laude, Rice U., 1960; JD with highest honors, U. Tex., 1962; postgrad., U. London, 1962-63. Bar: Tex., D.C., N.Y. Law clk. U.S. Ct. Appeals (2d cir.), 1963-64; assoc. Vinson & Elkins, Houston, 1964-69, ptnr., 1970—, mng.ptnr., 1992—. Vis. prof. U. Tex. Sch. Law, 1971, Rice U., 1976, U. Houston Sch. Law, 1977; chair adv. group U.S. Dist Ct. (so. dist.) Tex.; mem. adv. com. Supreme Ct. Tex. Author: (with Charles Alan Wright) Procedure: The Handmaid of Justice, 1965. Trustee U. Tex. Law Sch. Found., Southwestern Legal Found., Rice U., Baylor Coll. Medicine; chair Tex. Higher Edn. Coordinating Bd., 1991; bd. dirs. Houston Music Hall Found. Bd., 1996—; mem. Houston Annenberg Challenge Child Centered Schs. Initiative Bd., 1997—. Rotary Found. fellow 1962-63; named Disting. Alumnus, U. Tex., 1997, U. Tex. Sch. Law, 1998. Fellow Am. Coll. Trial Lawyers, Internat. Acad. Trial Lawyers, Internat. Soc. Barristers, ABA Found., Tex. Bar Found.; mem. ABA (chmn. antitrust sect. 1989-90), Houston Bar Assn., Assn. Bar City N.Y., Am. Law Inst., Houston Com. Fgn. Rels., Houston Philos. Soc., Philos. Soc. Tex., Am. Bd. Trial Advocates, Century Assn. N.Y.C., Houston Country Club, Eldorado Country Club (Calif.), Castle Pines Golf Club (Colo.), Cosmos Club (D.C.), Galveston Artillery Club, Chancellors, Barristers, Phi Beta Kappa, Phi Delta Phi. Antitrust, Federal civil litigation, State civil litigation. Office: Vinson & Elkins 2800 First City Tower 1001 Fannin St Houston TX 77002-6760

REASONER, STEPHEN M. federal judge; b. 1944; BA in Econs., U. Ark., 1966, JD, 1969. Mem. firm Barret, Wheatley, Smith & Deacon, Jonesboro, Ark., 1969-88; from judge to chief judge U.S. Dist. Ct. (ea. dist.) Ark., Little Rock, 1991-98, dist. judge. Bd. dirs. U. Ark. Law Rev.; mem. judicial coun. 8th cir., 1990-93. Trustee Craighead-Jonesboro Pub. Libr., 1972—, chmn. 1984-88; bd. dirs. Jonesboro C. of C., 1981-84, Ark. IOLTA, 1987—, Abilities Unltd., 1974-81; mem. St. Marks Episcopal Ch. Vestry, 1976-79, sr. warden, 1979. With USAR, 1969-73. Mem. ABA, Am. Counsel Assn., Am. Judicature Soc., Ark. Bar Assn. (exec. com., ho. of dels. 1984-87), Craighead County Bar Assn. (pres. 1983-84). Avocation: flying. Office: Courthouse 600 W Capitol Ave Ste 560 Little Rock AR 72201-3327

REATH, GEORGE, JR. lawyer, mediator, arbitrator; b. Phila., Mar. 14, 1939; s. George and Isabel Duer (West) R.; children from a previous marriage: Eric (dec. 1995), Amanda; m. Ann B. Rowland, 1990. BA, Williams Coll., 1961; LLB, Harvard U., 1964. Bar: Pa. 1965, U.S. Dist. Ct. (ea. dist.) Pa. 1966, U.S. Ct. Appeals (3d cir.) 1996. Assoc. Dechert Price & Rhoads, Phila., 1964-70, Brussels, 1971-74; atty. Pennwalt Corp., Phila., 1974-78, mgr. legal dept., asst. sec., 1978-87, sr. v.p.-law, sec., 1987-89; sr. v.p., gen. counsel, sec. Elf Atochem N.Am., Inc. (formerly Pennwalt Corp.), 1990-92; sr. v.p., gen counsel, sec. Legal Triage Svcs., Inc., 1993-98; sr. v.p., gen. counsel, sec. Triage Mediation Svcs., Inc., 1999—. Bd. dirs. Internat. Bus. Forum, Inc., 1978-91; arbitrator Am. Arbitration Assn. Trustee Children's Hosp., Phila., 1974—, sec., 1980-81, vice chmn., 1984-97; bd. mgrs. Phila. City Inst. Libr., 1974—, treas., 1981-88, pres., 1989-99; bd. dirs. Phila. Festival Theatre for New Plays, 1983-94, Ctrl. Phila. Devel. Corp., 1987-93; bd. dirs. Bach Festival Phila., 1990-98, v.p., 1992-93; bd. dirs. Crime Commn. Delaware Valley, 1st vice chmn., 1992-94, chmn., 1994-96; exec. com., 1996—; bd. coun. mem. Episcopal Cmty. Svcs. 1999—, treas., 2000—. Mem.: ABA, Am. Arbitration Assn., Pa. Bar Assn., Phila. Bar Assn., Am. Corp. Counsel Assn., Assn. for Conflict Resolution, Penllyn Club, Penn Club, Winter Harbor Yacht Club, Phi Beta Kappa. Alternative dispute resolution, Contracts commercial. Personal E-mail: greath@mindspring.com; Business E-Mail: gr@triagemediation.com

REATH, HENRY (THOMPSON), lawyer; b. Phila., Dec. 11, 1919; m. Elinor Williams; 5 children. AB, Princeton U., 1942; LLB, U. Pa., 1948. Bar: Pa. 1949. Assoc. Duane, Morris & Heckscher, Phila., 1948-52, ptnr., 1952—; mem. state disciplinary bd. Supreme Ct. Pa., 1974-79; sec. Phila. Jud. Council, 1968-78; co-chair Com. to Support the Gov.'s Jud. Appts., 1987, Gov. Casey's Commn. on Jud. Reform, 1987—, Com. on Financing Cts., 1987—; mem. Gov.'s Jud. Reform Commn., 1987—. Trustee Pa. Sch. for the Deaf, 1953-77, pres. bd., 1965-77; bd. dirs. Greater Phila. Movement, 1971-84, Urban Affairs Partnership, 1984—; trustee Ind. Ednl. Services, 1978-87. Recipient Learned Hand award Am. Jewish Com., 1985. Fellow Am. Bar Found.; mem. ABA, Am. Judicature Soc. (bd. dirs. 1972-77, Herbert Harley award 1982), Pa. Bar Assn. (ho. of dels., jud. adminstrn. com., chmn. subcom. on supreme ct. 1983), Phila. Bar Found. (trustee 1981), Phila. Bar Assn. (chmn. bd. govs. 1970-71, Fidelity Bank award 1974). Office: Duane Morris & Heckscher 1 Benjamin Franklin Pkwy Fl 1500 Philadelphia PA 19102-1512

REAVLEY, THOMAS MORROW, federal judge; b. Quitman, Tex., June 21, 1921; s. Thomas Mark and Mattie (Morrow) R.; m. Florence Montgomery Wilson, July 24, 1943; children— Thomas Wilson, Marian, Paul Stuart, Margaret. B.A., U. Tex., 1942; J.D., Harvard, 1948; LL.D., Austin Coll., 1974, Southwestern U., 1977, Tex. Wesleyan, 1982; LL.M., U. Va., 1983; LLD, Pepperdine U., 1993. Bar: Tex. 1948. Asst. dist. atty., Dallas, 1948-49; mem. firm Bell & Reavley, Nacogdoches, Tex., 1949-51; county atty., 1951; with Collins, Garrison, Renfro & Zeleskey, 1951-52; mem. firm Fisher, Tonahill & Reavley, Jasper, Tex., 1952-55; sec. state Tex., 1955-57; mem. firm Powell, Rauhut, McGinnis & Reavley, Austin, Tex., 1957-64; dist. judge, 1964-68; justice Supreme Ct., Tex., 1968-77; counsel Scott & Douglass, 1977-79; judge U.S. Ct. Appeals (5th cir.), Austin, 1979-90, now sr. judge TX, 1990—. Lectr. Baylor U. Law Sch., 1976-94; adj. prof. U. Tex. Law Sch., 1958-59, 78-79, 88-95. Chancellor S.W. Tex. conf. United Meth. Ch., 1972-93, chancellor emeritus, 1993—. Lt. USNR, 1943-45. Club: Mason (33 deg.). Office: US Ct Appeals Homer Thornberry Judicial Bldg 903 San Jacinto Blvd Ste 434 Austin TX 78701-2450 E-mail: tmr@ca5.uscourts.gov

REBACK, JOYCE ELLEN, lawyer; b. Phila., July 11, 1948; d. William and Sue (Goldstein) R.; m. Itzhak Brook, Aug. 2, 1981; children: Jonathan Zev, Sara Jennie. BA magna cum laude, Brown U., 1970; JD with honors, George Washington U., 1976. Bar: D.C. 1976, U.S. Dist. Ct. D.C. 1976, U.S. Ct. Appeals (D.C. cir.) 1976, U.S. Ct. Appeals (3d cir.) 1983, U.S. Ct. Appeals (Fed. cir.) 1985. Assoc. Fulbright & Jaworski, Washington, 1976-84, ptnr., 1984-87; legal cons. IMF, 1987—. Contbr. articles to profl. jours. Mem. ABA, D.C. Bar Assn., Phi Beta Kappa. Jewish. Office: Internat Monetary Fund 700 19th St NW Washington DC 20431-0001

REBANE, JOHN T. lawyer; b. Bamberg, Germany, Oct. 29, 1946; s. Henn and Anna (Inna) R.; m. Linda Kay Morgan, Sept. 22, 1972; children: Alexis Morgan, Morgan James. BA, U. Minn., 1970, JD, 1973. Bar: Minn. 1973. Atty. Land O'Lakes, Inc., Arden Hills, Minn., 1973-80, assoc. gen. counsel, 1983, v.p., gen. counsel, 1984—. Sec. Land O' Lakes Farmland Feed LLC; sec., dir. Land O' Lakes Internat. Devel. Corp. Mem. ABA, Minn. Bar Assn., Hennepin County Bar Assn., Nat. Coun. Farm Coop. (gen.coun. com. chmn.). Contracts commercial, General corporate, Mergers and acquisitions. Office: Land O'Lakes Inc PO Box 64101 Saint Paul MN 55164-0101 E-mail: jreba@landolakes.com

REBAZA, ALBERTO, lawyer; b. Lima, Peru, Sept. 14, 1965; s. Alberto and Gloria Rebaza; m. Patricia Mendoza, Nov. 15, 1991; 1 child, Micaela. BA summa cum laude, U. Catolica, Lima, 1991, degree in Law summa cum laude, 1992; LLM, U. Va., 1995. Prin. rschr. Liberty and Democracy Inst., Lima, 1990-93; ptnr. Yori & Bustamente, 1994-95, Rodrigo, Elias & Medrano, Lima, 1996—. Prof. econ. law analysis U. Catolica, Lima, 1994-95, prof. corp. law, 1996—; supervising com. Wiese Investment Fund, Lima, 2000—; cons. in fgn. trade regulations Govt. Honduras. Contbr. articles to profl. jours. Advisor Inst. de Arte Contemporáneo, Lima, 1999-2000. Fulbright fellow, Washington, 1995. Mem. ABA, Internat. Bar Assn., Soc. Sol and Armon$_g$a, Club Nacional. Avocations: running, triathlons, music, painting, reading. Antitrust, Finance, Mergers and acquisitions. Office: Rodrigo Elias & Medrano Av San Felipe 758 Lima 11 Peru Office Fax: (511) 463-7300; (511) 261-8807. E-mail: arebaza@estudiorodrigo.com

REBER, DAVID JAMES, lawyer; b. Las Vegas, Nev., Mar. 1, 1944; s. James Rice and Helen Ruth (Cusick) R.; m. Jacqueline Yee, Aug. 31, 1968; children: Emily, Brad, Cecily. BA, Occidental Coll., L.A., 1965; JD, Harvard U., 1968. Bar: Calif. 1969, Hawaii 1975, U.S. Dist. Ct. Hawaii, U.S. Ct. Appeals (9th cir.), U.S. Supreme Ct. Asst. prof. law U. Iowa, Iowa City, 1968-70; assoc. Sheppard Mullin Richter & Hampton, L.A., 1970-75, Goodsill Anderson Quinn & Stifel, Honolulu, 1975-76, ptnr., 1976—. Dir. Oahu Econ. Devel. Bd., Honolulu, Hawaii Appleseed Pub. Interest Law Ctr., Honolulu, Legal Aid Soc.; dir., pres. Legal A.d Soc. Hawaii. Mem. ABA (bus., antitrust and pub. utilities sects.), Hawaii Bar Assn. Avocations: golf, tennis, softball, travel. General corporate, Mergers and acquisitions, Securities. Office: Goodsill Anderson Et Al 1099 Alakea St Ste 1800 Honolulu HI 96813-4511 E-mail: dreber@goodsill.com

RECABO, JAIME MIGUEL, lawyer; b. Manila, Philippines, Oct. 6, 1950; came to U.S., 1969; s. Matthew M. and Luisa (De Leon) R.; children: James M., Danielle M.; m. Maureen Susan Ward, Dec. 1980; children: Matthew J., Maura E., Joseph A., Olivia M. BA, Fordham U., 1973, JD, 1988; MBA in Fin., St. John's U., 1977. Bar: N.Y. 1989, N.J. 1989, Conn. 1989. Bus. office mgr. Eger Nursing Home Inc., S.I., N.Y., 1974-77; sr. acct. Kingsbrook Jewish Med. Ctr., Bklyn., 1977-78; asst. compt. Jewish Home & Hosp. for the Aged, Bronx, N.Y., 1978-79; dir. fiscal svcs. Frances Schervier Home & Hosp., 1979-86; exec. v.p. finance & legal affairs Franciscan Health System N.Y., 1986-89; mgmt. cons., health and immigration atty. N.Y.C., 1989—; co-founder, exec. v.p., legal counsel Profl. Healthcare Assocs., Bronxville, N.Y., 1994—. Bd. dirs. Frances Schervier Home and Hosp., Bronx, 1987-90, Bklyn. United Meth. Ch. Home, 1991-94, Hudson Valley Med. Ctr. Found., Peekskill, N.Y., 1998—, Frances Schervier Housing Devel. Fund, 2000—; vice-chmn. NYAHSA Contrs. Com., N.Y.C., 1985-86, N.Y. Archdiocese Contrs. Coun., N.Y.C., 1980-83. Mem. ABA, Am. Immigration Lawyers Assn., N.J. Bar Assn., N.Y. Bar Assn., Conn. Bar Assn., Healthcare Fin. Mgmt. Assn., Nat. Health Lawyers Assn., Filipino Am. Lawyers Assn. Roman Catholic. Health, Immigration, naturalization, and customs. Office: 34 Palmer Ave Bronxville NY 10708-3404 E-mail: JRecaboLaw@msn.com

RECILE, GEORGE B. lawyer; b. New Orleans, Feb. 14, 1954; s. Sam J. Recile and Annie Mary Ciolino; m. Kathryn Nicole Morgan, July 1, 1995; children: Ashley, Bryan. BA, Tulane U., 1975; JD, Loyola U., 1978. Bar: La. 1978, U.S. Dist. Ct. (ea. dist.) La. 1979, U.S. Ct. Appeals (5th cir.) 1979, U.S. Dist. Ct. (we. and mid. dists.) 1989. Staff atty. La. State Atty. Gen., New Orleans, 1978-80; assoc. Tucker & Schonekas, 1980-82, Law Offices Charles McHale, New Orleans, 1982-83; atty. Recile & Gould, Metairie, La., 1983-87, George B. Recile & Assocs., New Orleans, 1987-95; ptnr. Chehardy, Sherman, Ellis, Breslin & Murray, Metairie, 1995—. Past mem. New Orleans Alcoholic Beverage Control Bd., La. State Bd. Pvt. Investigators. Mem. Am. Trial Lawyers Assn., La. Trial Lawyers Assn. (bd. govs.), Acad. New Orleans Trial Lawyers, La. State Bar Assn. (ho. of dels., 24th jud. dist.). Republican. Roman Catholic. General civil litigation, Personal injury. Office: Chehardy Sherman Ellis Breslin& Murray 1 Galleria Blvd Ste 1100 Metairie LA 70001-2033

RECORD, WARREN ARTHUR, lawyer; b. Baton Rouge, June 30, 1971; s. Warren A. and Sandi K. R.; Tammy K. Fisher, Jan. 7, 1995; 1 child, Jacob. BA, Rhodes Coll., 1993; JD, Miss. Coll., 1996. Bar: Miss. 1996. Legal asstance atty. USN, Gulfport, Miss., 1997-98, sr. def. counsel, 1998-99, legal advisor Washington, 1999—. Avocations: golf, boating, coaching youth sports. Home: 4015 Hirst Dr Annandale VA 22003 Office: Navy-Marine Corps AppoVak Rev Activity 901 M St SE Bldg 11 Washington DC 20374-5047

RECTOR, JOHN MICHAEL, association executive, lawyer; b. Seattle, Aug. 15, 1943; s. Michael Robert and Bernice Jane (Allison) R.; m. Mary Kaaren Sueta Jolly, Feb. 8, 1977 (div. 1994); m. Carmen De Ortiz Nouri, 1994; children: Christian Phillip, Ciera Rose, Zachary Ryan. BA, U. Calif., Berkeley, 1966; JD, U. Calif., Hastings, 1969; PharmD (hon.), Ark. State Bd. Pharmacy, 1991. Bar: Calif. 1970, U.S. Supreme Ct. 1974. Trial atty. civil rights div. Dept. Justice, 1969-71; dep. chief counsel judiciary com. U.S. Senate, 1971-73, counsel to Sen. Birch Bayh, 1971-77, chief counsel, staff dir., 1973-77; confirmed by U.S. Senate as assoc. adminstr. to Law Enforcement Assistance Adminstn. and adminstr. of Office Juvenile Justice Dept. Justice, 1977-79; spl. counsel to U.S. Atty. Gen., 1979-80; dir. govt. affairs Nat. Assn. Retail Druggists, Washington, 1980-85, sr. v.p. govt. affairs, gen. counsel, 1986—. Chmn. adv. bd. Nat. Juvenile Law Center, 1973-77; mem. Hew panel Drug Use and Criminal Behavior, 1974-77; mem. cons. panel Nat. Commn. Protection Human Subjects of Biomed. and Behavioral Research, 1975-76; mem. bd. Nat. Inst. Corrections, 1977-79; chmn. U.S. Interdepartmental Council Juvenile Justice, 1977-79; mem. bd. com. civil rights and liberties Am. Democratic Action, 1976-80, Pres.'s Com. Mental Health-Justice Group, 1978; com. youth citizenship ABA, 1978-84; mem. Pharm. Industry Adv. Com.; exec. dir., treas. polit. action com. Nat. Pharmacists Assn., 1981—; exec. dir. Retail Druggist Legal Legis. Def. Fund, 1985—, founder, chmn. Washington Pharmacy Industry Forum; mem. numerous fed. narcotic and crime panels and coms.; owner Second Genesis, an antique and furniture restoration co. Mem. editorial bd. Managed Care Law; contbr. articles to profl. jours. Exec. com. small bus. and fin. couns. Dem. Nat. Com., 1988-92; dir. Dem. Leadership Coun.'s Network, 1989-92, bd. advisers, 1992-94, Clinton-Gore Washington Bus. adv. com.; bd. dirs. Small Bus. Legis. Coun., 1987—, sec., 1999, treas., 2000, chmn. elect 2001; bd. dirs. Nat. Bus. Coalition for Fair Competition, 1984—. Perry E. Towne scholar, 1966-67; mem. U.S. Atty. Gen.'s Honors Program, 1968-71; recipient Children's Express Juvenile Justice award, 1981. Mem. Calif. Bar Assn., Nat. Health Lawyers Assn., Am. Soc. Assn. Execs. (govt. affirs sect.), Washington Coun. Lawyers, Assn. of Former Senior Senate Aides, Vinifera Wine Growers Assn. Va. (life), Health R Us, Am. League of Lobbyists, Theta Chi. Democrat. Avocation: collecting antique furniture, books and documents. Office: Nat Assn Retail Druggists 205 Daingerfield Rd Alexandria VA 22314-2885

REDDEN, JAMES ANTHONY, federal judge; b. Springfield, Mass., Mar. 13, 1929; s. James A. and Alma (Cheek) R.; m. Joan Ida Johnson, July 13, 1950; children: James A., William F. Student, Boston U., 1951; LL.B., Boston Coll., 1954. Bar: Mass., 1954, Oreg., 1955. Pvt. practice, Mass., 1954-55; title examiner Title & Trust Ins. Co., Oreg., 1955; claims adjuster Allstate Ins. Co., 1956; mem. firm Collins, Redden, Ferris & Velure, Medford, Oreg., 1957-73; treas. State of Oreg., 1973-77; atty. gen., 1977-80; U.S. dist. judge, now sr. judge U.S. Dist. Ct. Oreg., Portland, 1980—. Chmn. Oreg. Pub. Employee Relations Bd.; mem. Oreg. Ho. of Reps., 1963-69, minority leader, 1967-69. With AUS, 1946-48. Mem. ABA, Mass. Bar Assn., Oreg. State Bar. Office: US Dist Ct 1527 US Courthouse 1000 SW 3d Ave Portland OR 97204-2902

REDDEN, LAWRENCE DREW, lawyer; b. Tallassee, Ala., Dec. 16, 1922; s. A. Drew and Berta (Baker) R.; m. Christine U. Cunningham, Dec. 20, 1943. A.B., U. Ala., 1943, LL.B., 1949. Bar: Ala. bar 1949. Since practiced in, Birmingham; asst. U.S. atty. No. Dist. Ala., 1949-52; partner firm Rogers, Howard, Redden & Mills, 1952-79, Redden, Mills & Clark, 1979—; Civilian aide for Ala. to sec. army, 1965-69. Mem. Ala. Democratic Exec. Com., 1966-74 Editor-in-chief: Ala. Law Rev, 1948. Trustee Ala. Law Sch. Found.; adv. council Cumberland Law Sch. Served with AUS, 1943-46; maj. gen. Res. ret. Decorated D.S.M.; recipient Outstanding Civilian Service medal Dept. Army, 1970 Fellow Am. Coll. Trial Lawyers, Internat. Soc. Barristers; mem. ABA, Am. Judicature Soc., Ala. Bar Assn. (pres. 1972-73), Birmingham Bar Assn. (past pres.), Ala. Law Inst. (mem. coun.), U. Ala. Law Sch. Alumni Assn. (past pres.), Phi Beta Kappa, Alpha Tau Omega, Omicron Delta Kappa. Baptist. General civil litigation, Criminal, Family and matrimonial. Home: 2513 Beaumont Cir Birmingham AL 35216-1301 E-mail: ldr@rmclaw.com

REDDIEN, CHARLES HENRY, II, lawyer, corporate executive, consultant; b. San Diego, Aug. 27, 1944; s. Charles Henry and Betty Jane (McCormick) R.; m. Paula Gayle, June 16, 1974; 1 child, Tyler Charles. BSEE, U. Colo., Boulder, 1966; MSEE, U. So. Calif., 1968; JD, Loyola U., L.A., 1972. Bar: Calif. 1972, Colo. 1981, U.S. Dist. Ct. 1981. Mgr. Hughes Aircraft Co., 1966-81; pvt. practice, 1972—. Pres., broker R&D Realty Ltd., 1978-91; mem. spl. staff, co-dir. tax advantage group OTC Net Inc., 1981-82; pres., chmn. Heritage Group Inc., investment banking holding co., 1982-84, Plans and Assistance Inc., mgmt. cons., 1982-83, Orchard Group Ltd., investment banking holding co., 1982-84, J.W. Gant & Assocs., Inc., investment bankers, 1983-84; mng. ptnr., CEO J.W. Gant & Assocs., Ltd., 1984-85; chmn. bd. Kalamath Group Ltd., 1985-87, Heritage group Ltd. Investment Bankers, 1985-87; dir. Virtusonics Corp., 1985-92; v.p., dir. Heritage Fin. Planners Inc., 1982-83; pres., chmn. PDN Inc., 1987-89; pub., exec. v.p., dir. World News Digest Inc., 1987-90, LeisureNet Entertainment, Inc., 1989-90; chief exec. officer, Somerset Group Ltd., 1988-93, Inland Pacific Corp., 1989-91, World Info. Network, Inc., 1990-92, pres., CEO, chmn., Europa Cruises Corp., 1992-94; CEO, chmn. Casino World Inc., 1993-97, Miss. Gaming Corp., 1993-97; pres., chmn., CEO Chart Group Ltd., 1997—, SkyData Corp., 2000—; pres., Miss. Corrections, L.L.C. Contbr. articles to profl. jours. Pres. Diamondhead Business and Profl. Assn.; commr. Diamondhead Fire Dist. Recipient tchg. internship award, 1954. Mem. AIAA, IEEE (chmn. U. Colo. chpt. 1965), Calif. Bar Assn., Nat. Assn. Securities Dealers, Phi Alpha Delta, Tau Beta Pi, Eta Kappa Nu. General corporate. Office: PO Box 6133 Diamondhead MS 39525-6002 E-mail: chartgroup@aol.com

REDFEARN, PAUL L., III, lawyer; b. Camp Cook, Calif., Oct. 1, 1951; s. Paul Leslie Jr. and Alice Ruby Redfearn; children: Ashley, Lauren; m. Denise Jean Davis, July 24, 1993. BS, S.W. Mo. State U., 1973; JD, Oklahoma City U., 1976. Bar: Mo. 1977, U.S. Dist. Ct. (we. and ea. dists.) Mo., U.S. Dist. Ct. Kans., U.S. Dist. Ct. N.D., U.S. Dist. Ct. Mont., U.S. Ct. Appeal (8th ant 11th cirs.); bd. cert. civil trial advocate. Assoc. Sheridan, Sanders & Simpson, P.C., 1977-79, William H. Pickett, P.C., 1979-84; ptnr. The Redfearn Law Firm, P.C., Kansas City, Mo., 1984—. Bd. dirs. Lawyers Encouraging Acad. Performance; lectr. and presenter in field. Contbr. chpts. to books. Bd. govs. S.W. Mo. State U., 1998—. Mem. ABA, ATLA, Mo. Bar Assn., Mo. Assn. Trial Attys. (bd. govs. 1986-94, exec. com. 1990—, pres. 1992), Am. Bd. Trial Advocates (charter, pres. chpt. 1996-97), Trial Lawyers for Pub. Justice, Kansas City Met. Bar Assn., East Jackson County Bar Assn. Democrat. Avocation: tennis. State civil litigation, Personal injury, Product liability. Office: The Redfearn Law Firm PC 1125 Grand Blvd Ste 814 Kansas City MO 64106-2518 E-mail: predfearn@aol.com

REDFIELD, SARAH ERLICK, law educator; b. Oct. 18, 1948; d. Hyman and Rose Etta (Albling) Erlick. BA, Mt. Holyoke Coll., 1970; JD, Northeastern U., 1974; LLM, Harvard U., 1983. Bar: Maine 1974, U.S. Dist. Ct. Maine 1974. Asst. atty. gen. Maine Atty. Gen.'s Office, Augusta, 1974-80; prof. Franklin Pierce Law Ctr., Concord, N.H., 1983—. Cons., Concrd, 1982— ; adj. prof. Vt. Law Sch., So. Royalton, 1984— ; faculty assoc. U. Maine, Orono, 1976— , U. N.H., Durham, 1985—; dir. Edn. Law Inst., Concord, N.H., 1992—. Author: Vanishing Farmland: A Legal Solution for the States, 1984, Thinking Like A Lawyer, 2001. Pub. mem. Fin. Authority of Maine, Augustam, 1983-85. Mem. ABA, Maine Bar Assn., Am. Argl. Law Assn. (fin. publs. com.), edn. Law Assn. Home: 40 Riverwood Dr York ME 03909-5231 E-mail: sredfield@fplc.edu

REDING, JOHN ANTHONY, lawyer; b. Orange, Calif., May 26, 1944; AB, U. Calif., Berkeley, 1966, JD, 1969. Bar: Calif. 1970, U.S. Dist. Ct. (no., ctrl., ea. and so. dists.) Calif., U.S. Claims Ct., U.S. Supreme Ct. Formerly mem. Crosby, Heafey, Roach & May P.C., Oakland, Calif.; now ptnr. Paul, Hastings, Janofsky & Walker, LLP, San Francisco, nat. chmn. litigation dept. Mem. ABA (sects. on litigation, intellectual property, and natural resources, energy and eviron. law, coms. on bus. torts, internat. law, trial practice and torts and insurance), Am. Intellectual Property Law Assn., State Bar Calif. (sect. on litigation), Bar Assn. San Francisco, Assn. Bus. Trial Lawyers. General civil litigation, Environmental, Intellectual property. Office: Paul Hastings Janofsky & Walker LLP 345 California St San Francisco CA 94104-2606 E-mail: jackreding@paulhastings.com

REDLICH, MARC, lawyer; b. N.Y.C., Nov. 25, 1946; s. Louis and Mollie R.; m. Janis Redlich, Jan. 16, 1982; children: Alison, Suzanne, Rachel. BA, Queens Coll., 1967; JD, Harvard U., 1971. Bar: Mass. 1971, U.S. Dist. Ct. 1971, U.S. Ct. Appeals (1st cir.) 1974, U.S. Ct. Appeals (5th cir.) 1984. Assoc. Rubin & Rudman, Boston, 1971-75; mem., sr. dir. Widett, Slater & Goldman, 1975-84; prin. Law Offices of Marc Redlich, 1984—. Seminar chmn. Mass. Continuing Legal Edn., Inc., 1996. Mem. Mass. Bar Assn. (governing coun. civil litigation sect., participant/panelist chpt. 93A in the bus. context seminar 1996), Cambridge Bar Assn., Nat. Assn. Coll. and Univ. Attys., Harvard Sq. Bus. Assn. (bd. dirs. 1989-92, 93-94), Friends of Switzerland Inc. (bd. dirs. 1984—, assoc. pres. 1991-93, pres. 1993—), German Am. Bus. Club of Boston (exec. com. 1997-2001), Harvard Club Boston (co-chair music com. 1997-98, chair 1998—), Am. Council on Germany (Boston Chpt. Coord., 2001—) , Phi Beta Kappa. General civil litigation, General corporate, General practice. Office: Three Center Plz Boston MA 02108

REDLICH, NORMAN, lawyer, educator; b. N.Y.C., Nov. 12, 1925; s. Milton and Pauline (Durst) R.; m. Evelyn Jane Grobow, June 3, 1951; children: Margaret Bonny-Claire, Carrie Ann, Edward Grobow. AB, Williams Coll., 1947, LLD (hon.), 1976; LLB, Yale U., 1950; LLM, NYU, 1955; LLD (hon.), John Marshall Law Sch., 1990. Bar: N.Y. 1951. Practiced in, N.Y.C., 1951-59; assoc. prof. law NYU, 1960-62, prof. law, 1962-74, assoc. dean Sch. Law, 1974-75, dean Sch. Law, 1975-88, dean emeritus, 1992—, Judge Edward Weinfeld prof. law, 1982—; counsel Wachtell, Lipton, Rosen & Katz, N.Y.C., 1988—. Editor-in-chief Tax Law Rev., 1960-66; mem. adv. com. Inst. Fed. Taxation, 1963-68; exec. asst. corp. counsel, N.Y.C., 1966-68, 1st asst. corp. counsel, 1970-72, corp. counsel, 1972-74; asst. counsel Pres. Commn. on Assassination Pres. Kennedy, 1963-64; mem. com. on admissions and grievances U.S. 2d Circuit Ct. Appeals, 1978—, chmn., 1978-87. Author: Professional Responsibility: A Problem Approach, 1976, Constitutional Law, Cases and Materials, 1983, rev. edit., 1996, Understanding Constitutional Law, 1995, rev. edit., 1999; contbr. articles in field. Chmn. commn. on law and social action Am. Jewish Congress, 1978—, chmn. governing coun., 1996; mem. Borough Pres.'s Planning Bd. Number 2, 1959-70, counsel N.Y. Com. to Abolish Capital Punishment, 1958-77; mem. N.Y.C. Bd. Edn., 1969; mem. bd. overseers Jewish Theol. Sem., 1973—; trustee Law Ctr. Found. of NYU, 1975—, Freedom House, 1976-86, Vt. Law Sch., 1977-99, Practicing Law Inst., 1980-99; trustee Lawyers Com. for Civil Rights Under Law, 1976—, co-chmn., 1979-81; bd. dirs. Legal Aid Soc., 1983-88, NAACP Legal Def. Fund, 1985—, Greenwich House, 1987—. Decorated Combat Infantryman's Badge. Mem. ABA (coun. legal edn. and admissions to bar 1981—, vice chmn. 1987-88, chmn. 1989-90, equal opportunities in legal profession 1986-92, ho. of dels. 1991—), Assn. of Bar of City of N.Y. (exec. com. 1975-79, professionalism com. 1988-92), com. on capital punishment 1998—). Office: 51 W 52nd St Fl 30 New York NY 10019-6119

REDMAN, CLARENCE OWEN, lawyer; b. Joliet, Ill., Nov. 23, 1942; s. Harold F. and Edith L. (Read) R.; m. Barbara Ann Pawlan, Jan. 26, 1964 (div.); children: Scott, Steven; m. 2d, Carla J. Rozycki, Sept. 24, 1983. BS, U. Ill., 1964, JD, 1966, MA, 1967. Bar: Ill. 1966, U.S. Dist. Ct. (ea. dist.) Ill. 1970, U.S. Ct. Appeals (7th cir.) 1973, U.S. Ct. Appeals (4th cir.) 1982, U.S. Supreme Ct. 1975. Assoc. Keck, Mahin & Cate, Chgo., 1969-73, ptnr., corp. ptnr., 1973—, CEO, 1986-97; of counsel Lord, Bissell & Brook, 1997—. Spl. asst. atty. gen. Ill., 1975-8; bd. dirs. AMCOL Internat. Corp. Mem. bd. visitors U. Ill. Coll. of Law, 1991-95. Capt. U.S. Army, 1967-69. Decorated Bronze Star. Mem. Ill. State Bar Assn. (chmn. young lawyers sect. 1977-78, del. assembly 1978-81, 84-87), Seventh Cir. Bar Assn. Federal civil litigation, General corporate, Labor. Office: Lord Bissell & Brook 115 S Lasalle St Ste 3200 Chicago IL 60603-3902

REDMOND, DAVID DUDLEY, lawyer; b. Hartford, Conn., May 12, 1944; s. Robert LaVere and Dorothy Iva (Mylchreest) R.; m. Eugenia Blount Scott, Aug. 24, 1986; children: R. Scott, Sarah D. BA, Washington and Lee U., 1966, LLB, 1969. Bar: Va. 1970, U.S. Dist. Ct. (ea. dist.) Va. 1972, U.S. Ct. Appeals (4th cir.) 1972. Ptnr. Christisn & Barton LLP, Richmond, Va., 1972—. Edtl. bd. Washington and Lee U. Law Rev., 1968-69. Served to capt. U.S. Army, 1970-71. Decorated Bronze Star. Mem. Va. State Bar, Va. Bar Assn., Richmond Bar Assn. (exec. com. 1980), Washington and Lee U. Alumni Assn. (pres. Richmond chpt. 1980-82, bd. dirs. 1997-99), Omicron Delta Kappa. General corporate, Land use and zoning (including planning), Real property. Office: Mutual Bldg Ste 1200 Richmond VA 23219 E-mail: dredmond@cblaw.com

REDMOND, EDWARD CROSBY, lawyer; b. Fond du lac, Wis., Apr. 24, 1921; s. Frank and Mae Estelle (Crosby) R.; m. Kathleen T. Colbert, July 8, 1951; children: John C., Maureen T., Eileen C., Mary Kate. Student, Marquette U., 1939-40; BBA, U. Wis., 1947; JD, Cleve. State U., 1956. Bar: Ohio, 1957, U.S. Dist. Ct. (no. dist.) Ohio 1960, U.S. Supreme Ct. 1971. Ins. claim adjustor Gen. Adjustment Bur., Cleve., 1947-59; asst. pros. atty. Lake County, 1959-61; ptnr. Redmond and Walker, Painesville, Ohio, 1961—. Spl. counsel to atty. gen. State of Ohio, 1961-68; lectr. criminal law Lakeland C.C., 1968. Treas., Lake County Republican Com.; v.p. Painesville Bd. Edn., 1972. Recipient Outstanding Svc. award Elks Club, 1969, Meritorious Svc. award Fraternal Order Police, 1982, Cath. Svc. Bur., 1987. Fellow Ohio State Bar Found. (hon. life; pres. 1989); mem. Ohio State Bar Assn. (exec. com. 1980-83, coun. of dels. 1977-80, chmn. planning subcom. 1982-83), Lake County Bar Assn. (pres. 1974), Am. Judicature Soc., Ohio Continuing Legal Edn. Inst. (chmn. bd. trustees 1993), Lake County Bar Found. (trustee), Painesville C. of C. (bd. dirs., Outstanding Citizen of Yr. award 2001), Lake County Blue Coats (trustee), Exch. Club (pres. 1971), Gyro Club of Painesville (pres. 1974), Serra Club Lake County (pres. 1984), Elks (exalted ruler 1962). Roman Catholic. Family and matrimonial, General practice, Probate. Office: 174 N Saint Clair St Painesville OH 44077-4058

REDMOND, LAWRENCE CRAIG, lawyer; b. Chgo., Mar. 17, 1943; s. Lawrence Craig and Marie Alberta (Campbell) R.; m. Bess Peoples, Mar. 16, 1967 (div. Sept. 1980); children: Masai, Maya; m. Luanne Marie Bethke, May 23, 1986; children: Geneva Marie, Sarai Bernice, Darcy Milita, Abina Grace, Leni Louise. BA, U. Ill., Chgo., 1973; JD, John Marshall Law Sch., 1983. Pvt. practice, Chgo., 1986—; panel atty. Capital Litigation divsn. State Appellate Defender, 1992—; computer cons., 1986—. Author numerous poems. Mayoral nominee Harold Washington Party, Chgo., 1995, Cook County state's atty. nominee, 1996, 49th Ward Com., 1996; Ill. gubernatorial cand. Reform Party, 1997; elected chmn. Reform Party of Ill., 1999. With USAF, 1960-64. Avocations: creative writing, African drums, martial arts, photography. General civil litigation, Criminal, Election.

REDMOND, ROBERT, lawyer, educator; b. Astoria, N.Y., June 18, 1934; s. George and Virginia (Greene) R.; m. Georgine Marie Richardson, May 21, 1966; children: Kelly Anne, Kimberly Marie, Christopher Robert. BA, Queens Coll., 1955; MPA, CUNY, 1962; JD, Georgetown U., 1970. Bar: D.C. 1971, Va. 1974, U.S. Supreme Ct. 1974. Commd. 2d lt. USAF, 1955, advanced through grades to lt. col., 1972, ret., 1978; served as spl. investigations officer Korea, Vietnam, W. Germany; adj. prof., acad. dir. mil. dist. Washington Resident Ctr. Park U., Parkville, Mo., 1977—; pvt. practice Falls Church, Va., 1980—. Precinct capt. Fairfax County Rep. Party, Va., 1981-87; pres. PTO, Falls Church, 1984-86; bd. dirs. Chaconas Home Owners Assn., 1984—, Social Ctr. Psychiat. Rehab., 1987-93. Mem. ATLA, Va. Trial Lawyers Assn., Fairfax Bar Assn., Assn. Former Air Force Office Spl. Investigations Agts. (chpt. pres. 1984-86, nat. membership com. 1986—), Comml. Law League, Delta Theta Phi, K.C. (4th deg.). Roman Catholic. Consumer commercial, General practice, Personal injury. Home: 7802 Antiopi St Annandale VA 22003-1405 Office: Ste 900-N 7799 Leesburg Pike Falls Church VA 22043-2413 Address: PO Box 2103 Falls Church VA 22042-0103 E-mail: collectlaw@aol.com

REDPATH, JOHN S(LONEKER), JR. lawyer, cable television company executive; BA, Princeton U., 1966; JD, U. Mich., 1973; LLM, NYU, 1978. Bar: U.S. Dist. Ct. (so. dist.) N.Y. 1975. Assoc. Dewey, Ballantine, Bushby, Palmer & Wood, N.Y.C., 1974-78; assoc. counsel film programming Home Box Office, Inc., 1978-79, chief counsel programming, 1979-80, asst. gen.

counsel, 1980-81, v.p., gen. counsel, 1981-83, sr. v.p., gen. counsel, 1983-94, exec. v.p., gen. counsel, 1994—. Lt. USNR, 1966-69. Mem. ABA, N.Y. State Bar Assn., Assn. Bar City N.Y. Communications. Office: HBO Inc 1100 Avenue Of The Americas New York NY 10036-6740

REED, D. GARY, lawyer; b. Covington, Ky., June 4, 1949; m. Mary Elizabeth Goetz, May 20, 1972; children: Mark, Stacey. BA, Xavier U., 1971; JD, Catholic U. Am., 1974. Bar: Ohio 1974, Ky. 1975, U.S. Ct. Appeals (6th cir.) 1975, U.S. Dist. Ct. (so. dist.) Ohio 1974, U.S. Dist. Ct. (ea. dist.) Ky. 1977, U.S. Dist. Ct. (we. dist.) Ky. 1980. Law clk. to judge U.S. Dist. Ct. (so. dist.) Ohio, Cin., 1974-75; assoc. Dinsmore & Shohl, 1976-82, ptnr., 1982-90; dir. legal svcs. Choice Care Health Plans, Inc., 1991-96; asst. gen. coun., 1996-97; ins. counsel Humana, Inc., Louisville, 1998—. Asst. sec. Choice Care Found., 1996-97. Contbg. author: Woodside, Drug Product Liability, vol. 3, 1987. Asst. sec. The Choice Care Found., 1996-97. Mem. ABA, Ky. Bar Assn., Ohio Bar Assn., Nat. Health Lawyers Assn., No. Ky. C. of C. (Leadership award 1988), Greater Cin. Coun. for Epilepsy (bd. dirs. 1990-97), Leadership No. Ky. Alumni Assn. General corporate, Health, Insurance. Office: Humana Inc Insurance Cons-Law Dept 500 W Main St Ste 300 Louisville KY 40202-4268 E-mail: dgaryreed@aol.com, greed@humana.com

REED, EDWARD CORNELIUS, JR. federal judge; b. Mason, Nev., July 8, 1924; s. Edward Cornelius Sr. and Evelyn (Walker) R.; m. Sally Torrance, June 14, 1952; children: Edward T., William W., John A., Mary E. BA, U. Nev., 1949; JD, Harvard U., 1952. Bar: Nev. 1952, U.S Dist Ct. Nev. 1957, U.S. Supreme Ct. 1974. Atty. Arthur Andersen & Co., 1952-53; spl. dep. atty. gen. State of Nev., 1967-79; judge U.S. Dist. Ct. Nev., Reno, 1979—, chief judge, now sr. judge. Former vol. atty. Girl Scouts Am., Sierra Nevada Council, U. Nev., Nev. Agrl. Found., Nev. State Sch. Adminstrs. Assn., Nev. Congress of Parents and Teachers; mem. Washoe County Sch. Bd., 1956-72, pres. 1959, 63, 69; chmn. Gov.'s Sch. Survey Com., 1958-61; mem. Washoe County Bd. Tax Equalization, 1957-58, Washoe County Annexation Commn., 1968-72, Washoe County Personnel Com., 1973-77, chmn. 1973; mem. citizens adv. com. Washoe County Sch. Bond Issue, 1977-78, Sun Valley, Nev., Swimming Pool Com., 1978, Washoe County Blue Ribbon Task Force Com. on Growth, Nev. PTA (life); chmn. profl. div. United Way, 1978; bd. dirs. Reno Siver Sox, 1962-65. Served as staff sgt. U.S. Army, 1943-46, ETO, PTO. Mem. ABA (jud. adminstrn. sect.), Nev. State Bar Assn. (adminstrv. com. dist. 5, 1967-79, lien law com. 1965-78, chmn. 1965-72, probate law com. 1963-66, tax law com. 1962-65), Am. Judicature Soc. Democrat. Baptist. Named in his honor Edward C. Reed H.S., Sparks, Nev., 1972. Office: US Dist Ct 400 S Virginia St Ste 606 Reno NV 89501-2182

REED, GLEN ALFRED, lawyer; b. Memphis, Sept. 24, 1951; s. Thomas Henry and Evelyn Merle (Roddy) R.; m. Edith Jean Renick, June 17, 1972; children: Adam Christopher, Alec Banjamin. BA, U. Tenn., 1972; JD, Yale U., 1976. Bar: Ga. 1976. Project dir. Tenn. Rsch. Coordinating Unit, Knoxville, 1972-73; assoc. Alston Miller & Gaines, Atlanta, 1976-77, Bordurant Miller Hishon & Stephenson, Atlanta, 1978-81, ptnr., 1981-85, King & Spalding, Atlanta, 1985—. Author: Practical Hospital Law, 1979. Legal adv. Ga. Gov.'s Commn. in Healthcare, 1994; gen. coun. Assn. Retarded Citizens, Atlanta, 1979—, bd. dirs., 1986—, pres., 1992-96; mem. adv. bd. CARE Atlanta, 1992—, chmn., 1994-99; v.p. Ga. Network for People with Devel. Disabilities, 1991-92; bd. dirs. Ctrl. Health Ctr., 1989-95; bd. dirs. Vis. Nurse Health Sys., 1992—, chmn., 1996-99; dean's coun. Sch. Pub. Health Emory U., Atlanta, 1998—, Ga. Partnership for Caring, 1999—, MedShare Internat., vice chmn., 1999—; with Ga. Comm. Support and Solutions, 2000—. Mem. ABA, Ga. Bar Assn., Am. Acad. Hosp. Attys. (bd. dirs. 1991-97, pres. elect 1997), Ga. Acad. Hosp. Attys. (pres. 1981-92), Am. Health Lawyers Assn. (bd. dirs. 1997-2000, pres. 1998-99), Phi Beta Kappa. Methodist. Administrative and regulatory, General corporate, Health. Office: King & Spalding 191 Peachtree St NE Ste 40 Atlanta GA 30303-1740 E-mail: gareed@kslaw.com

REED, JOHN SQUIRES, II, lawyer; b. Lexington, Ky., Mar. 20, 1949; s. John Squires and Mary Alexander (O'Hara) R.; m. Nancy Claire Battles, Dec. 29, 1973; children: Alexandra Simmons, John Squires III. AB in Polit. Sci., U. Ky., 1971; JD, U. Va., 1974. Bar: Ky. 1974, U.S. Dist. Ct. (we. dist.) Ky. 1975, U.S. Ct. Appeals (6th cir.) 1975, U.S. Dist. Ct. (ea. dist.) Ky. 1979, U.S. Supreme Ct. 1980, U.S. Ct. Appeals (fed. cir.) 1985. Assoc. Greenbaum Doll & McDonald, Louisville, 1974-79, ptnr., 1979-87, Hirn, Doheny, Reed & Harper, Louisville, 1987-96, Reed Weitkamp Schell & Vice PLLC, Louisville, 1996—. Mem. Leadership Louisville, 1982, treas., mem. exec. com. Leadership Louisville Alumni Assn., 1984, pres., 1985; bd. dirs. Econs. Am. in Ky., 1985—, Nat. Assn. Cmty. Leadership, 1986-91, treas., 1987-88, v.p., 1988-89, pres., 1989-90, Leadership Louisville Found., Inc., 1986-92, Greater Louisville Econ. Devel. Partnership, 1987-97; chair Leadership USA, Inc., 1997, Louisville Collegiate Sch., 1996—. 1st lt. U.S. Army, 1974. Mem. ABA (antitrust, intellectual property, litig. sects.), Ky. Bar Assn., Louisville Bar Assn. (bd. dirs. 1985-86, treas. 1988, sec. 1989, v.p. 1990, pres. 1992), Louisville Boat Club, Valhalla Golf Club, Phi Beta Kappa. Democrat. Presbyterian. Antitrust, Federal civil litigation, Patent. Office: Reed Weitkamp Schell & Vice PLLC 2400 Citizens Plz Louisville KY 40202 E-mail: jreedrwsv@aol.com, jreed@rwslaw.com

REED, JOHN WESLEY, lawyer, educator; b. Independence, Mo., Dec. 11, 1918; s. Novus H. and Lilian (Houchens) R.; m. Imogene Fay Vonada, Oct. 5, 1946 (div. 1958); m. Dorothy Elaine Floyd, Mar. 5, 1961; children: Alison A., John M. (dec.), Mary V., Randolph F., Suzanne M. AB, William Jewell Coll., 1939, LLD, 1995; LLB, Cornell U., 1942; LLM, Columbia U., 1949, JSD, 1957. Bar: Mo. 1942, Mich. 1953. Assoc. Stinson, Mag, Thomson, McEvers & Fizzell, Kansas City, Mo., 1942-46; assoc. prof. law U. Okla., 1946-49; assoc. prof. U. Mich., 1949-53, prof., 1953-64, 68-85, Thomas M. Cooley prof., 1985-87, Thomas M. Cooley prof. emeritus, 1987—; dean, prof. U. Colo., 1964-68, Wayne State U., Detroit, 1987-92, prof. emeritus, 1992—. Vis. prof. NYU, 1949, U. Chgo., 1960, Yale U., 1963-64, Harvard U., 1982, U. San Diego, 1993; dir. Inst. Continuing Legal Edn., 1968-73; reporter Mich. Rules of Evidence Com., 1975-78, 83-84; mem. faculty Salzburg Sem., 1962, chmn., 1964. Author: (with W.W. Blume) Pleading and Joinder, 1952; (with others) Introduction to Law and Equity, 1953, Advocacy Course Handbook series, 1963-81; editor in chief Cornell Law Quar., 1941-42; contbr. articles to profl. jours. Pres. bd. mgrs. of mins. and missionaries benefit bd. Am. Bapt. Chs. U.S.A., 1967-74, 82-85, 88-94; mem. com. visitors JAG Sch., 1971-76; trustee Kalamazoo Coll., 1954-64, 68-70. Recipient Harrison Tweed award Assn. Continuing Legal Edn. Adminstrs., 1983, Samuel E. Gates award Am. Coll. Trial Lawyers, 1985, Roberts P. Hudson award State Bar Mich., 1989. Fellow Internat. Soc. Barristers (editor jour. 1980—); mem. ABA (mem. coun. litigation sect.), Assn. Am. Law Schs. (mem. exec. com. 1965-67), Am. Acad. Jud. Edn. (v.p. 1978-80), Colo. Bar Assn. (mem. bd. govs. 1964-68), Mich. Supreme Ct. Hist. Soc. (bd. dirs. 1991—), Sci. Club Mich., Order of Coif. Office: U Mich Sch Law Ann Arbor MI 48109-1215 E-mail: reedj@umich.edu

REED, JOHN WILSON, lawyer; b. Manchester, Eng., May 31, 1945; came to U.S., 1954; s. Firmin P. and Isabel (Woollam) R.; m. Leslee King, Dec. 27, 1969; children— Ashley King, Cameron King. B.A., Yale U., 1966; J.D., Harvard U., 1969. Bar: La. 1970, U.S. Dist. Ct. (ea. dist.) La. 1970, U.S. Ct. Apls. (5th cir.) 1970, U.S. Ct. Appeals (11th cir.) 1970, N.Y., 1980, U.S. Dist. Ct. (so. dist.) Ala., 1982. Vista vol. New Orleans Legal Assistance Corp., 1969-70, staff atty., 1970-72; sole practice, New Orleans, 1972-78; ptnr. Glass & Reed, New Orleans, 1978— ; gen. counsel ACLU of La., New Orleans, 1974-78; mem. faculty New Orleans Bar Rev., 1979— , Nat. Inst. Trial Advocacy, Boulder, Colo., 1984, 89, 97. Mem. Nat. Assn. Criminal Def. Lawyers, Am. Trial Lawyers Assn., La. Trial Lawyers Assn., La. Assn. Criminal Def. Lawyers (v.p. 1985—). Democrat. Criminal. Office: Glass & Reed 530 Natchez St New Orleans LA 70130-2700

REED, KEITH ALLEN, lawyer; b. Anamosa, Iowa, Mar. 5, 1939; s. John Ivan and Florence Lorine (Larson) R.; m. Beth Illana Kesterson, June 22, 1963; children: Melissa Beth, Matthew Keith. BBA, U. Iowa, 1960, JD, 1963. Bar: Ill. 1963, Iowa 1963. Ptnr. Seyfarth, Shaw, Fairweather & Geraldson, Chgo., 1963—. Co-author: Labor Arbitration in Healthcare, 1981; co-editor: Chicagoland Employment Law Manual, 1994, Employment and Discrimination, 1996, Federal Employment Law and Regulations, 1989-99; co-contbr. articles to Am. Hosp. Assn. publs., 1986-89. Trustee Meth. Hosp. Chgo., 1985—, Trinity Ch. North Shore, Wilmette, Ill., 1983—; mem. ad hoc labor adv. com. Am. Hosp. Assn., Chgo., 1980—; bd. dirs. Lyric Opera Chgo. Ctr. for Am. Artists, pres., 1983-86. Mem. ABA (dir. health law forum 1979-82), Chgo. Bar Assn. (labor and employment law com. 1978—), Union League Club Chgo. (bd. dirs. 1985-88), Sunset Ridge Country Club (Northbrook, Ill.). Republican. Methodist. Avocations: music, community theater, tennis, golf. Health, Labor. Office: Seyfarth Shaw Fairweather & Geraldson 55 E Monroe St Ste 4200 Chicago IL 60603-5863

REED, LOWELL A., JR. federal judge; b. Westchester, Pa., 1930; s. Lowell A. Sr. and Catherine Elizabeth R.; m. Diane Benson; four children. BBA, U. Wis., 1952; JD, Temple U., 1958. Bar: Pa. 1959, U.S. Dist. Ct. (ea. dist.) Pa. 1961, U.S. Ct. Appeals (3d cir.) 1962, U.S. Supreme Ct. 1970. Corp. trial counsel PMA Group, Phila., 1958-63; assoc. Rawle & Henderson, 1963-65, gen. ptnr., 1966-88; judge U.S. Dist Ct., 1988-99; sr. judge U.S. Dist. Ct., 1999—. Lectr. law Temple U., 1965-81, faculty Acad. Advocacy, 1988—, Pa. Bar Inst., 1972—. Contbr. articles to profl. jours. Elder Abington (Pa.) Presbyn. Ch.; past. mem. Pa. Senate Select Com. Med. Malpractice; past pres., bd. dirs. Rydal Meadowbrook Civic Assn.; bd. dirs. Abington Sch. Bd., 1971, World Affairs Coun. Phila., 1983-88; trustee Abington Health Care Corp., 1983-88, 90-93. Lt. comdr. USNR, 1952-57. Recipient Alumni Achievement award Temple U. 1988, Cert. of Honor, 2001. Mem. ABA, Phila. Bar Assn. (chmn. medico legal com. 1975, constl. bicentennial com. 1986-87, commn. on jud. selection and retention 1983-87), Temple Am. Inn of Ct. (pres. 1990-93, master of bench 1990—), Am. Judicature Soc., Temple U. Law Alumni Assn. (exec. com. 1987-90, 99—), Hist. Soc. U.S. Supreme Ct., Hist. Soc. U.S. Dist. Ct. Ea. Dist. Pa. Republican. Office: US Dist Ct 11614 US Courthouse Independence Mall W Philadelphia PA 19106

REED, ROBERT PHILLIP, lawyer; b. Springfield, Ill., June 14, 1952; s. Robert Edward and Rita Ann (Kane) R.; m. Janice Leigh Kloppenburg, Oct. 8, 1976; children: Kevin Michael, Matthew Carl, Jennifer Leigh, Rebecca Ann. AB, St. Louis U., 1974; JD, U. Ill., 1977. Bar: Ill. 1977, U.S. Dist. Ct. (ctrl. dist.) Ill. 1979, U.S.Ct. Appeals (7th cir.) 1983, U.S. Dist. Ct. (so. dist.) Ill. 1992, Colo. 1993. Intern Ill. Legislature, Springfield, 1977-78; assoc. Traynor & Hendricks, 1979-80; ptnr. Traynor, Hendricks & Reed, 1981-88; pvt. practice, 1988—. Pub. defender Sangamon County, Ill., Springfield, 1979-81; hearing examiner Ill. State Bd. Elections, Springfield, 1981-88; spl. asst. atty. gen. State of Ill., Springfield, 1983—; instr. Lincoln Land Community Coll., Springfield, 1988. Trustee Springfield Pk. Dist., 1985-89. Mem.: Nat. Assn. Securities Dealers, Inc (arbitrator 1996—), Ill. State Bar Assn., Colo. Bar Assn., Attys Title Guaranty Fund, Inc., Phi Beta Kappa. Roman Catholic. Family and matrimonial, Probate, Real property. Office: 1129 S 7th St Springfield IL 62703-2418

REED, T. MICHAEL, lawyer; b. Upland, Calif., Aug. 13, 1945; s. Michael E. adn Virginia F. (Moore) R.; children: Marty E., Michael E. BA, U. Calif., Riverside, 1967, MA, 1970; JD, U. San Diego, 1975. Bar: Calif. 1975, U.S. Dist. Ct. (so. and cen. dists.), Calif. 1975. Ptnr. Eckhardt, Reed & Reed, San Diego, 1975-79, Casey, Gerry, Casey, Westbrook & Reed, San Diego, 1979—. Lectr. CEB, 1984—. Named San Diego Trial Lawyer of Yr., 1985, 92. Mem. Assn. Trial Lawyers Am. (mem. faculty Nat. Coll. Advocacy 1984), Calif. Trial Lawyers Assn. (lectr. continuing edn. of bar 1982-84), San Diego Trial Lawyers Assn. (Outstanding Trial Lawyer 1983, 89, 91, 92, 93), We. Trial Lawyers Assn., TIPS (pres. 1984 San Diego). Democrat. Personal injury. Office: Casey Gerry Reed & Schenk 110 Laurel St San Diego CA 92101-1419

REED, W. FRANKLIN, lawyer; b. Louisville, Dec. 30, 1946; s. William Ferguson and Stella Elizabeth (Richardson) R.; m. Sharon Ann Coss, June 16, 1973; children: Jonathan Franklin, William Brian, Carrie Ann. BA, Williams Coll., 1968; JD, Columbia U., 1971. Bar: N.Y. 1972, U.S. Dist. Ct. (so. dist.) N.Y. 1975, U.S. Ct. Appeals (2d cir.) 1975, Pa. 1982, U.S. Dist. Ct. (we. dist.) 1983. Assoc. Milbank, Tweed, Hadley & McCloy, N.Y.C., 1971-82, Reed Smith Shaw & McClay, Pitts., 1982-83; ptnr. Reed, Smith, Shaw & McClay, 1984—. With Instnl. Devel. Com., The Pitts. Cultural Trust. Mem. ABA, Pa. Bar Assn., Allegheny Bar Assn., Carnegie 100, Williams Coll. Alumni Soc. W. Pa. (sec. 1983—), Rivers Club (Pitts.), St. Clair Country Club (Upper St. Clair, Pa.), Duquesne Club (Pitts.), Phi Beta Kappa. Democrat. Presbyterian. Avocations: fishing, golf. General corporate, Public utilities, Real property. Home: 525 Miranda Dr Pittsburgh PA 15241-2039 Office: Reed Smith LLP 435 6th Ave Pittsburgh PA 15219-1886 E-mail: wreed@reedsmith.com

REEDER, F. ROBERT, lawyer; b. Brigham City, Utah, Jan. 23, 1943; s. Frank O. and Helen H. (Heninger) R.; m. Joannie Anderson, May 4, 1974; children: David, Kristina, Adam. JD, U. Utah, 1967. Bar: Utah 1967, U.S. Ct. Appeals (1oth cir.) 1967, U.S. Ct. Appeals (D.C. and 5th cirs.) 1979, U.S. Ct. Mil. Appeals 1968, U.S. Supreme Ct. 1972. Shareholder Parsons, Behle & Latimer, Salt Lake City, 1968—. Bd. dirs. Holy Cross Found., 1981-90, chmn., 1987-90; bd. dirs. Holy Cross Hosp., 1990-93, treas., 1986-87, vice chmn., 1987-93; bd. dirs. Holy Cross Health Svcs. Utah, 1993-94, treas., 1993-94; bd. dirs. Sale Lake Regional Med. Ctr., 1995—, vice chmn., 1995-2000, chmn., 2000—; trustee Univ. Hosp. Found.; hon. col. Sale Lake City Police, Salt Lake County Sheriff. Served with USAF, 1967-73. Mem. ABA, Utah State Bar, Salt Lake County Bar (ethics adv. com. 1989-94), Cottonwood Country Club (bd. dirs. 1978-82, 83-86, pres. 1981-82), Rotary. General civil litigation, Contracts commercial, Public utilities. Office: Parsons Behle & Latimer PO Box 45898 Salt Lake City UT 84145-0898

REEDER, JAMES ARTHUR, lawyer; b. Baton Rouge, June 29, 1933; s. James Brown and Grace (Britt) R.; m. Mary Leone Guthrie, Dec. 30, 1958; children: Mary Virginia, James Jr., Elizabeth Colby. BA, Washington and Lee U., Lexington, Va., 1955; LLB, U. Tex., 1960; JD, La. State U., 1961. Ptnr. Booth, Lockard, Jack et al, Shreveport, La., 1961-72; pres. and mgng. ptnr. Shreveport Broadcasting Co., 1972-86; CEO, mng. gen. ptnr. Radio USA Limited, Houston, 1986-89; pres. SW subsidiaries Sun Group, Inc., 1990-92; atty. Patton & Boggs, LLP, Washington, 1991-94; ptnr. Patton, Boggs LLP, 1994—. Dir. ABC Radio Sta. Affiliates adv. bd., N.Y.C., 1978-84. Dir. Boys Country, Houston, 1986-90; pres. Holiday in Dixie, Shreveport, 1968; chmn. Ambassadors Club, Shreveport, 1979. 1st Lt. U.S. Army, 1955-57. Named La. Outstanding Young Man, La. Jaycees, 1969. Mem. ABA (bd. dirs. young lawyers sect. 1967-68, Gavel awards com. 1980), La. Bar Assn. (pres. young lawyers sect. 1966, La. Outstanding Young Lawyer award 1968), D.C. Bar Assn., Tex. Bar Assn., Nat. Assn. Broadcasters, Houston Country Club, Allegro Club (Houston). Roman Catholic. Legislative.

REEDER, ROBERT HARRY, retired lawyer; b. Topeka, Dec. 3, 1930; s. William Harry and Florence Mae (Cochran) R. AB Washburn U., 1952, JD, 1960. Bar: U.S. Dist. Ct. Kans. 1960, Kans. 1960, U.S. Supreme Ct. 1968. Rsch. asst. Kans. Legis. Council Rsch. Dept., Topeka, 1955-60; asst. counsel Traffic Inst., Northwestern U., Evanston, Ill., 1960-67, gen. counsel, 1967-92; exec. dir. Nat. Com. on Uniform Traffic Laws and Ordinances, Evanston, 1982-90. Co-author: Vehicle Traffic Law, 1974; The Evidence Handbook, 1980. Author: Interpretation of Implied Consent by the Courts, 1972. Served with U.S. Army, 1952-54. Mem. Com. Alcohol and Other Drugs (chmn. 1973-75). Republican. Methodist.

REEG, KURTIS BRADFORD, lawyer; b. St. Louis, Sept. 1, 1954; s. Jay Flory and Mary Louise (Braun) R.; m. Cynthia Diane Wable, June 25, 1994. BA cum laude, DePauw U., 1976; JD, St. Louis U., 1979. Bar: U.S. Dist. Ct. (ea. dist.) Mo. 1979, U.S. Dist. Ct. (so. dist.) Ill. 1981, U.S. Ct. Appeals (8th cir.) 1984, U.S. Ct. Appeals (7th cir.) 1986, U.S. Dist. Ct. Ariz. 1994, U.S. Ct. Appeals (2d cir.) 1994, U.S. Supreme Ct. 1994. Law clk. to presiding justice Ill. Appellate Ct. (5th dist.), Granite City, 1979-80; assoc. Coburn, Croft & Putzell, St. Louis, Mo. and Belleville, Ill., 1980-86, ptnr., 1986-91; ptnr., chmn. tort and ins. group, co-chmn. litigation dept. Gallop, Johnson & Neuman, L.C., St. Louis, 1991-98, mem. mgmt. com., 1991-98, mng. ptnr. Belleville, 1997-98; ptnr. Sonnenschein Nath & Rosenthal, St. Louis, 1998-2000, Kohn, Shands, Elbert, Gianoulakis & Giljum, LLP, St. Louis, 2001—. Nat. chmn. Products Liability Group; chmn. St. Louis Tort and Ins. Grp., instr. legal rsch. and writing St. Louis U., 1979-80. Mem. Police, Fire Commns., City of Town and Country, Mo., 1987-89; Rep. committeeman 24th ward, St. Louis, 1980. Mem. ABA, Ill. State Bar Assn., Mo. Bar Assn., Bar Assn. of Met. St. Louis, Internat. Assn. Def. Counsel, Ill. Assn. Def. Trial Counsel, Fedn. ins. and Corp. Counsel, Def. Rsch. Inst., Midwest Environ. Claims Assn., Phi Alpha Delta, Pi Sigma Alpha. Republican. Avocations: hunting, fishing, golf, astronomy. Insurance, Product liability, Toxic tort. Address: One First Plaza Ste 2410 Saint Louis MO 63101 also: 12720 Willowyck Dr Saint Louis MO 63146-3726 Office: Kohn Shands Elbert Gianoulakis & Giljum LLP Ste 2410 One Firstar Plaza Saint Louis MO 63101 Fax: (314) 206-5205. E-mail: kreeg@ksegg.com

REESE, THOMAS FRANK, lawyer; b. Feb. 21, 1953; s. William David and Elsa Edith (Bluhm) R.; m. Laurie Ann Evans, Jan. 10, 1976. BA, U. Wyo., 1975; JD, 1981. Bar: Colo. 1982, Wyo. 1981, U.S. Dist. Ct. Wyo. 1981, U.S. Dist. Ct. Colo. 1982. Tchr. Natrona County, Casper, Wyo., 1976-78; mem. Sherman & Howard, Denver, 1981-82, Brown & Drew, Casper, Wyo., 1983—. Wyo. editor Law Rev., 1980-81. Chmn. allocations and admissions com. Natrona County United Way, 1986, bd, dirs., 1984-87, chmn. allocations and admissions com., 1986-88, campaign chmn., 1987, v.p., 1988; pres. United Fund of Natrona County Found., 1987. L.W. Maxfield scholar, 1979-80; Bugas Law scholar, 1980. Mem. Wyo. Bar Assn., ABA, Phi Kappa Phi. Presbyterian. Construction, Oil, gas, and mineral, Environmental. Home: 3520 Valley Rd Casper WY 82604-4906 Office: Brown Drew Massey LLP 159 W Wolcott Ste 200 Casper WY 82601-2486 E-mail: tfr@browndrew.com

REEVES, GENE, judge; b. Meridian, Miss., Feb. 27, 1930; s. Clarence Eugene and May (Philyaw) R.; m. Brenda Wages, Sept. 26, 1980. JD, John Marshall U., 1964; cert. judge spl. ct. jurisdiction; postgrad., U. Nev., 1995. Bar: Ga. 1964, U.S. Ct. Appeals (11th cir.) 1965, U.S. Supreme Ct. 1969. Ptnr. Craig & Reeves, Lawrenceville, Ga., 1964-71; sole practice, 1971-85; prin. Reeves Law Firm, 1985-94; judge City Ct., Lawrenceville, 1969-70, Magistrate Ct. of Gwinnett County, Ga., 1994—. Sgt. USAF, 1951-54. Mem. ABA, ATLA, GTLA, Am. Jud. Soc., Gwinnett County Bar Assn. (pres. 1970-72), Criminal Def. Lawyers Assn., Atlanta Bar Assn. Baptist. E0-mail: greenWmindspring.com;. Home: 221 Pineview Dr Lawrenceville GA 30045-6035 Office: 75 Langley Dr Lawrenceville GA 30045-6935 E-mail: gwinmag4@mindspring.com

REGAL, EVAN CHARLES, lawyer; b. Port Jefferson, N.Y., Feb. 27, 1948; s. Evan C. and Agnes (Holly) R.; m. Mary E. Murphy, Oct. 11, 1975; children: Thomas E., Christopher A., Ellen M. A.B., Syracuse U., 1970; J.D., Albany Law Sch., Union U., 1974; grad. N.Y. State Bankers Assn. Estate Adminstrn. Sch., 1975, N.Y. State Bankers Assn. Trust Adminstrn. Sch., 1976; student Northwestern U. Nat. Grad. Trust Sch., 1978-79. Bar: N.Y. 1975, U.S. Dist. Ct. (no. dist.) N.Y. 1975, U.S. Tax Ct. 1981. Trust officer State Bank of Albany, N.Y., 1974-80; assoc. Tate Bishko & Regal, and predecessor firm, Albany, 1980-84, ptnr., 1984-87; prin. Hinman Straub Pigors & Manning, P.C., 1987—. Mem. bd. editors Adminstration of N.Y. Estates. Mem. N.Y. State Bar Assn. (com. on continuing legal edn. of trusts and estates sect. 1982-93, exec. com. trusts & estates sect. 1988-92, com. surrogate's ct. trusts and estates sect. 1993—), Albany County Bar Assn., Estate Planning Council N.E. N.Y. Roman Catholic. Lodge: Rotary (Albany) (bd. dirs.). Estate planning, Probate, Estate taxation. Home: 8 Longwood Dr Delmar NY 12054-3706 Office: Hinman Straub Pigors & Manning PC 121 State St Albany NY 12207-1693

REGALADO, ELOISA, lawyer; b. Pinar Del Rio, Cuba, Sept. 9, 1952; came to U.S., 1968; d. Osvaldo Nicanor and Eloisa F. (Tosca) R.; m. William Michael Hess, Oct. 4, 1975; children: Amaris Michelle Hess, Arianna Elizabeth Hess. AB magna cum laude, Rutgers U., 1975, JD, 1978. Bar: Pa. 1978, N.J. 1978, U.S. Dist. Ct. N.J. 1978, D.C. 1981, U.S. Claims Ct., 1987. Atty. advisor Naval Air Systems Command, Washington, 1978-80; asst. to gen. counsel Office Gen. Counsel Dept. Navy, 1980-82; assoc. counsel Naval Supply Systems Command, 1982-88, dep. counsel, 1988-90; sr. atty. AT&T, Silver Spring, Md., 1990-93; chief regional counsel AT&T Caribnean & Latin Am., Coral Gables, Fla., 1993-98; vice pres. Internat. Traffic Management & Operations AT&T, Caribbean and Latin American, 1998-2000; vice pres. Concert Communication USA, 2000—. Chmn. internat. acquisition com. Defense Acquisition Regulatory Council, Washington, 1984-88 Recipient Navy Superior Service Medal, 1990. Mem. ABA, Phi Beta Kappa. Avocations: reading, running, traveling. Office: Concert 2333 Ponce De Leon Blvd Coral Gables FL 33134-5422

REGAN, PAUL MICHAEL, lawyer; b. Detroit, May 8, 1953; s. Timothy J. and Adele (Anthony) R. BA, Duke U., 1975; JD, Cath. U., 1979. Bar: N.Y. 1983. Clearance officer, counsel Ticor Title Guarantee Co., Syracuse, N.Y., 1980-84; assoc. Van Epps & Shulman, 1984-87, Shulman Law Firm, Syracuse, 1987-91; ptnr. Shulman Curtin Grundner & Regan, P.C., 1992—. Speaker Nat. Bus. Inst., 1991, N.Y. State Bar Seminars, 1990-94, 99. Vestry Christ Ch., Malius, N.Y., 1991-96; bd. dirs. Cazenovia (N.Y.) Childrens House, 1990-94; counsel Save Our Cmty., Inc., Cazenovia, 1989-93. Mem. N.Y. State Bar Assn., Onondaga County Bar Assn. (chmn. real estate contract com. 1990-96, com. on title standards 1990-96, spkr. 1998). Environmental, Real property. Office: Shulman Curtin Grundner & Regan PC 250 S Clinton St Ste 502 Syracuse NY 13202-1262 E-mail: pregan@scgrslaw.com

REGAN, SUSAN GINSBERG, lawyer; b. N.Y.C., Oct. 20, 1947; d. Irwin Arthur and Sylvia (Rosen) Ginsberg; m. Neil A. Goldberg, Jan. 24, 1975 (div. May 1987); children: Jane Goldberg, Rafael Goldberg; m. Edward Van Buren Regan, Oct. 12, 1991. BA, U. Mich., 1969; JD, SUNY, Buffalo, 1974. Bar: N.Y. 1975. Asst. county atty. Erie County, Buffalo, 1975-78; ptnr. Magavern, Magavern & Grimm LLP, 1982-98; assoc. gen. counsel Vis. Nurse Svc. N.Y., N.Y.C., 1998—. Mem., chair establishment com.

N.Y. State Pub. Health Coun., 1996—; clin. asst. prof. SUNY Sch. Medicine and Biomed. Scis., Buffalo, 1997—. Mem. Nat. Health Lawyers Assn., N.Y. State Bar Assn. (health law com., com. on profl. ethics, N.Y.C., 1984-87). Avocation: skiing. Health, Non-profit and tax-exempt organizations. Office: Vis Nurse Svc NY 107 E 70th St New York NY 10021-5006 E-mail: sregan@maili.vnsny.org

REGENBOGEN, ADAM, judge; b. Steyer, Austria, June 12, 1947; s. William and Pauline (Feuerstein) R.; m. Paula Ruth Rothenberg, June 27, 1970 (div. Oct. 1992); children: Stacy, Candice; m. Helen Busuttil Drwal, Apr. 20, 1996; 1 stepchild, Jason A. Drwal. BA, Temple U., 1969; MSW, U. Pa., 1972; JD, Temple U., 1980. Bar: N.Y. 1983. Social worker VA, Coatesville, Pa., 1974-78, supr. Northport, N.Y., 1978-80, quality assurance dir., 1980-87; dir. quality assurance N.Y. State Office Mental Health, Willard, 1987-91; conciliator, acting judge N.Y. State Workers Compensation Bd., Binghamton, 1992-98; judge Binghamton, Norwich, Oneonta, Norwich, 1998—; pvt. practice N.Y., 1983-98; conciliator, acting judge Workers Compensation Bd., 1992-98, judge, 1998—. Organizer/incorporator Ithaca (N.Y.) Reform Temple, 1992; organizer Parents Without Partners, Ithaca, 1992. Recipient Pro Bono Svc. award Suffolk County Bar Assn., 1986. Mem. Tompkins County Bar Assn. Home: 14 Grant St Port Dickinson Binghamton NY 13901 Office: Workers Compensation Bd 44 Hawley St Binghamton NY 13901-4434 E-mail: adam.regenbogen@wcb.state.ny.us

REGENSTREIF, HERBERT, lawyer; b. N.Y.C., May 13, 1935; s. Max and Jeannette (Hacker) R.; m. Patricia Friedman, Dec. 20, 1967 (div. July 1968); m. Charlotte Lois Levy, Dec. 11, 1980; 1 child, Cara Rachael. BA, Hobart Coll., 1957; JD, N.Y. Law Sch., 1960; MS, Pratt Inst., 1985. Bar: N.Y. 1961, Ky. 1985, U.S. Dist. Ct. (ea. and so. dists.) N.Y. 1962, U.S. Dist. Ct. (ea. dist.) Ky. 1998, U.S. Tax Ct. 1967, U.S. Ct. Appeals (2d cir.) 1962, U.S. Supreme Ct. 1967. Ptnr. Fried & Regenstreif, P.C., Mineola, N.Y., 1963—; reservist atty. Fed. Emergency Mgmt. Agy., 1998-99. Cons. in field; arbitrator Dist. Ct., Nassau County, N.Y., 1989—, N.Y.C. Civil Ct., 1984-86; sec.-treas. Sta. WAHY-FM, Inc., 1998-2000. Contbr. articles to profl. jours. County committeeman Dem. Com., Queens County, N.Y., 1978-79. Mem. Bar Assn. Nassau County, Ky. Bar Assn., Phi Delta Phi, Beta Phi Mu, Hobart Club of N.Y. (gov. 1968-69). General practice, Religion.

REGNIER, JAMES, state supreme court justice; b. Aurora, Ill. m. Linda Regnier; 3 children. BS, Marquette U., 1966; JD, U. Ill., 1973. Judicial Fellow ACTL, Internat. Soc. Barristers; completed atty. mediator tng., Atty.-Mediator Tng. Inst., Dallas, 1993. Lawyer pvt. practice, Rochelle, Ill., 1973-78; co-founder, ptnr. Regnier, Lewis and Boland, Great Falls, Mont., 1979-91; lawyer pvt. practice, Missoula, 1991-97; justice Mont. Supreme Ct., Helena, 1997—. Appt. Mont. Supreme Ct. Commn. on Civil Jury Instrn.; appt. lawyer-rep. to 9th Cir. Judicial Confs., 1987, 88, 89, chair Mont. lawyer delegation, 1989; lectr. U. Mont. Sch. Law, numerous continuing legal edn. seminars. Contbr. Mont. Pattern Jury Instrns. for Civil Cases, 1985. Co-founder Mont. chpt. Am. Bd. Trial Advocates, 1989—, pres. Officer USN, Vietnam. Office: Montana Supreme Ct Justice Bldg 215 N Sanders St Helena MT 59601-4522 also: PO Box 203001 Helena MT 59620-3001*

REHBOCK, RICHARD ALEXANDER, lawyer; b. New Haven, Sept. 12, 1946; s. Morton J. and Evelyn (Norris) R.; m. Nanette DiFalco, June 5, 1997; 1 stepchild: Gregory. BA, Fairleigh Dickinson U., 1968; JD, St. John's U., 1973. Bar: N.Y. 1974, U.S. Dist. Ct. (ea. and so. dists.) N.Y. 1974, U.S. Ct. Appeals (2d cir.) 1977, U.S. Ct. Appeals (3d cir.) 1996, U.S. Supreme Ct. 1978, U.S. Dist. Ct. (we. dist.) N.Y. 1983, Fla. 1987. Atty. criminal divsn. Legal Aid Soc., N.Y.C., 1973-77; staff atty. U.S. Dist. Ct. N.Y. Legal Aid Soc., Bklyn., 1977-79; ptnr. Rehbock, Fishman & Kudisch, Kew Gardens, N.Y., 1979-83; pvt. practice law N.Y.C., 1983—. Staff sgt. U.S. Army, 1969-70, Vietnam. Fellow Am. Bd. Criminal Lawyers; mem. Criminal Ct. Bar Assn. (bd. dirs. Queens County chpt.), Am. Trial Lawyers Assn., Nat. Assn. Criminal Def. Attys. (vice chmn legis. com.), Nat. Assn. Trial Attys., Fed. Bar Coun., N.Y. State Bar Assn., Queens Bar Assn., N.Y. County Lawyers Assn., N.Y. State Assn. Criminal Def. Attys. (chair fed. legis com.), Fla. Bar Assn. Federal civil litigation, Contracts commercial, Criminal. Home and Office: 1 Maple Run Dr Jericho NY 11753-2827 E-mail: rrehbock@msn.com

REHM, JOHN BARTRAM, lawyer; b. Paris, Nov. 23, 1930; s. George and Mary (Torr) R.; m. Diana Mary Aed, Dec. 19, 1959; children: David Bartram, Jennifer Aed. AB, Harvard U., 1952; LLB, Columbia U., 1955; M.T.S., Wesley Sem., 1990. Bar: N.Y. 1955, D.C. 1969, U.S. Dist. Ct. D.C. 1971, U.S. Ct. Internat. Trade 1980, U.S. Supreme Ct. 1988. Assoc. Willkie, Owen, Farr, Gallagher & Walton, N.Y.C., 1955-56; atty.-advisor U.S. Dept. State, Washington, 1956-62, asst. legal advisor for econ. affairs, 1962-63; gen. counsel Office of Spl. Trade Rep., 1963-69; ptnr. Busby, Rivkin, Sherman, Levy & Rehm, 1969-77, Busby, Rehm and Leonard, Washington, 1977-87, Dorsey & Whitney, Washington, 1988-2000. Democrat. Episcopalian. Administrative and regulatory, Private international, Legislative. Home: 5005 Worthington Dr Bethesda MD 20816-2748 Office: Dorsey & Whitney 1001 Pennsylvania Ave NW Washington DC 20004-2505

REHNQUIST, WILLIAM HUBBS, United States supreme court chief justice; b. Milw., Oct. 1, 1924; s. William Benjamin and Margery (Peck) R.; m. Natalie Cornell, Aug. 29, 1953; children: James, Janet, Nancy. BA, MA, Stanford U., 1948; MA, Harvard U., 1949; LLB, Stanford U., 1952. Bar: Ariz. Law clk. to former justice Robert H. Jackson, U.S. Supreme Ct., 1952-53; with Evans, Kitchel & Jenckes, Phoenix, 1953-55; mem. Ragan & Rehnquist, 1956-57; ptnr. Cunningham, Carson & Messenger, 1957-60, Powers & Rehnquist, Phoenix, 1960-69; asst. atty.-gen. office of legal counsel Dept. of Justice, Washington, 1969-71; assoc. justice U.S. Supreme Ct., 1971-1986, chief justice, 1986—. Mem. Nat. Conf. Commrs. Uniform State Laws, 1963-69 Author: The Supreme Court: How It Was, How It Is, 1987, Grand Inquests: The Historic Impeachments of Justice Samuel Chase and President Andrew Johnson, 1992, All the Laws But One, 1999; contbr. articles to law jours., nat. mags. Served with USAAF, 1943-46, NATOUSA. Mem. Fed., Am. Maricopa (Ariz.) County bar assns., State Bar Ariz., Nat. Conf. Lawyers and Realtors, Phi Beta Kappa, Order of Coif, Phi Delta Phi. Lutheran. Office: Supreme Ct US 1 1st St NE Washington DC 20543-0001

REIBSTEIN, RICHARD JAY, lawyer; b. Phila., Mar. 12, 1951; s. Albert Simon and Alma (Wilf) R.; m. Susan Barbara Fisch, May 18, 1975. BA with distinction, U. Rochester, 1973; JD with honors, George Washington U., 1976. Bar: Pa. 1976, N.Y. 1979, N.J. 1979, U.S. Dist. Ct. (so. and ea. dists.) N.Y. 1979, N.J. 1979, U.S. Ct. Appeals (3d cir.) 1980, U.S. Ct. Appeals (2d cir.) 1982, U.S. Supreme Ct. 1983. Staff atty. Dept. Labor, Washington, 1976; counsel NLRB, 1976-78; assoc. Seham, Klein & Zelman (formerly Surrey, Karasik, Morse & Seham), N.Y.C., 1978-81, Epstein Becker & Green, P.C., N.Y.C., 1981-86, ptnr., 1986-92, McDermott, Will & Emery, N.Y.C., 1992-99, Wolf, Block, Schorr and Solis-Cohen, N.Y.C., 1999—. Co-author: Negligent Hiring, Fraud, Defamation, and Other Emerging Areas of Employer Liability, 1988, Employer's Guide to Workplace Torts, 1992; contbr. articles to profl. jours. Mem. ABA (devl. of law undr NLRA com., sect. labor and employment law 1976—), N.Y.State Bar Assn. Democrat. Federal civil litigation, State civil litigation, Labor. Office: Wolf Block Schorr and Solis-Cohen 250 Park Ave Ste 1000 New York NY 10177-0001 E-mail: rreibstein@wolfblock.com

REICH, ABRAHAM CHARLES, lawyer; b. Waterbury, Conn., Apr. 17, 1949; s. Samuel and Esther (Gurvitz) R.; m. Sherri Engelman, Aug. 15, 1971; children: Spencer, Alexander. BA, U. Conn., 1971; JD, Temple U., 1974. Bar: Pa. 1974, U.S. Supreme Ct. 1979. Assoc. Fox, Rothschild, O'Brien & Frankel, Phila., 1974-81, ptnr., 1981—, mng. ptnr., 2001—. Chair lawyers adv. com. Third Cir. Ct. Appeals, 1998. Fellow Am. Coll. Trial Lawyers; mem. ABA (ho. of dels. 1997-2000), Phila. Bar Assn. (chair profl. responsibility com. 1983-84, chair bench-bar com. 1985, chair profl. guidance com. 1987-88, bd. govs. 1987-89, chair bd. govs. 1989, chancellor 1995, del ABA 1996-2000). Antitrust, Federal civil litigation, Securities. Home: 2224 Mount Vernon St Philadelphia PA 19130-3115 Office: Fox Rothschild O'Brien Frankel 2000 Market St Ste 10 Philadelphia PA 19103-3231 E-mail: areich@frof.com

REICH, ALLAN J. lawyer; b. Chgo., July 9, 1948; s. H. Robert and Sonya (Minsky) R.; m. Lynne Susan Roth, May 23, 1971; children: Allison, Marissa, Scott. BA, Cornell U., 1970; JD cum laude, U. Mich., 1973. Bar: Ill. 1973, U.S. Dist. Ct. (no. dist.) Ill. 1973. Ptnr. McDermott, Will & Emery, Chgo., 1973-93; vice chmn. D'Ancona & Pflaum LLC, 1993—. Trustee Oakmark Family of Mutual Funds, 1994—. V.p., mem. exec. com. Coun. for Jewish Elderly, 1989—97; mem. men's coun. Mus. Contemporary Art, Chgo., 1988—89; mem. Chgo. exec. bd. Am. Jewish Com., 1989—, nat. bd. govs.; mem. met. Chgo. bd. Am. Heart Assn.; bd. dirs. Young Men's Jewish Coun., Chgo., 1974—84, Coun. for Jewish Elderly, 1986—97. Mem.: ABA, Chgo. Bar Assn., Standard Club (Chgo.), Northmoor Country Club (Highland Park, Ill.), Econ. Club Chgo., Execs. Club Chgo. General corporate, Finance, Securities. Home: 936 Skokie Ridge Dr Glencoe IL 60022-1434 Office: D'Ancona & Pflaum LLC 111 E Wacker Dr Chicago IL 60601-3713 E-mail: areich@dancona.com

REICH, EDWARD STUART, lawyer; b. N.Y.C., June 28, 1936; s. Herman and Frances R.; m. Arlene Albin, Aug. 11, 1974; children: Dawne, Heidi, Evan. BA, Cornell U., 1957; LLB, Bklyn. Law Sch., 1960, JD, 1967. Bar: N.Y. 1960, Fla. 1961, U.S. Dist. Ct. (ea. dist.) N.Y. 1961, U.S. Dist. Ct. (so. dist.) N.Y. 1962, U.S. Ct. Appeals (2d cir.) 1967, U.S. Supreme Ct. 1966. Pres. Reich and Reich PC, Bklyn., 1960—. Mem. State of N.Y. Grievance Commn., 2d and 11th jud. dists., Bklyn., 1982-90. Nat. chmn. MIT Parent Fund, 1997-98; bd. dirs. Jewish Nat. Fund, 1985-91, v.p., 1986-91; bd. govs. Rockwood Park Civic Assn., 1968-73; bd. dirs. Bklyn. Soc. Prevention Cruelty to Children, 1985—; adv. bd. Police Athletic League, 1985—. Fellow Am. Bar Found. (life), N.Y. State Bar Found. (life); mem. ABA (Ho. of dels. 1991-92), N.Y. State Trial Lawyers Assn. (parliamentarian emeritus, bd. dirs., chmn. nominating com. 1978-91), Bklyn. Bar Assn. (trustee, chmn. Supreme Ct. com. 1980-91, chmn. judiciary com. 1985—, treas. 1987-88, 2d v.p. 1988-89, 1st v.p. 1989-90, pres.-elect 1990-91, pres. 1991-92), N.Y. State Bar Assn. (exec. com. 1989—, ho. of dels. 1990-94, 96—, sec. ins., negl. and comp. law sect. 1993-94, vice-chmn. 1994-95, sec. chmn. torts, ins. and compensation law 1995-96, v.p. 1999—), Am. Trial Lawyers Assn., N.Y. State Conf. Bar Leaders (exec. com. 1991-95, chmn. 1994-95), Bklyn. Law Sch. Alumni Assn. (bd. dirs. 1990—), Dutchess Golf and Country Club, Masons (master 1968, trustee 1977-79). Federal civil litigation, State civil litigation, Personal injury. Home: 155 W 68th St New York NY 10023-5808 Office: Reich & Reich PC 26 Court St Ste 606 Brooklyn NY 11242-1106

REICH, LARRY SAM, lawyer; b. Bklyn., Sept. 24, 1946; s. Sidney and Regina (Brown) R.; m. Patricia S. Neustein, Aug. 18, 1968; children: Ilysa Jill, Shari Beth. BA, Hofstra U., 1969; JD, Bklyn. Law Sch., 1973. Bar: N.Y. 1974, U.S. Dist. Ct. (so. and ea. dists.) N.Y. 1974, U.S. Ct. Appeals (2d cir.) 1974, U.S. Supreme Ct. 1980. Assoc. S. Edward Orenstein PC, N.Y.C., 1973-78; ptnr. Herzfeld & Rubin PC, 1978-98, Blank Rome Tenzer Greenblatt, LLP, N.Y.C., 1999—. Arbitrator U.S. Dist. Ct. for Ea. Dist. N.Y., Bklyn., 1986—. Mem. ABA, N.Y. State Bar Assn. (chmn. com. on supreme cts. 1986-89, chmn. com. on jud. adminstrn. 1989-92, com. jud. adminstrn. 1989-94), N.Y. County Bar Assn., Nassau County Bar Assn., Assn. Trial Lawyers Am., N.Y. State Trial Lawyers Assn. Avocations: running, rowing, biking, reading. Federal civil litigation, State civil litigation. Office: Blank Rome Tenzer Greenblatt LLP The Chrysler Bldg New York NY 10174

REICH, LAURENCE, lawyer; b. Jersey City, Jan. 22, 1931; s. Victor and Miriam (Gross) R.; m. Doris Rita Diamond, Oct. 21, 1965. BA, U. Chgo., 1951, JD, 1953. Bar: N.J. 1954, N.Y. 1982, U.S. Dist. Ct. N.J. 1954, U.S. ct. appeals (3rd cir.) 1958, U.S. Supreme Ct. 1963, U.S. Tax Ct. 1971, U.S. Dist. Ct. (so. dist.) N.Y. 1982, U.S. Ct. Appeals (2nd cir.) 1987. Mem. firm Carpenter, Bennett & MOrrissey, Newark, 1957-63, ptnr., 1963-69, sr. ptnr., 1969—. Mem. Bur. Nat. Affairs Tax Adv. bd., 1972—; lectr. NYU Inst. Fed. Taxation, Tulane Tax Inst., Ark. Tax Inst., Fairleigh Dickinson U. Tax Inst., Seton Hall Tax Inst., N.J. Inst. Continuing Legal Edn., Internat. Bus. Conf., Mid-Atlantic Estate Planing Conf. Author: N.J. Corporation Law and Practice; contbr. articles to profl. jours. With U.S. Army, 1955-57. Fellow Am. Coll. Tax Counsel, Am. Bar Found.; mem. ABA (com. chmn. sect. taxation 1972-74, 85-86, mem. coun. 1991-94), N.J. Bar Assn. (chmn. taxation sect. 1975-76), Assn. Fed. Bar State N.J. (v.p. 1982-94, bd. trustees 1994-99), Essex County Bar Assn. General corporate, Pension, profit-sharing, and employee benefits, Corporate taxation. Office: 3 Gateway Ctr Newark NJ 07102-4079 E-mail: lr@carpben.com

REICH, WILLIAM ZEEV, lawyer; b. Tel Aviv, Oct. 5, 1947; came to U.S., 1958; s. Louis and Helen (Skura) R.; children: Eric, Justin, Zabrina, Aviva. BA, Queens Coll., CUNY, 1969; JD, SUNY, Buffalo, 1974. Bar: N.Y. 1974, U.S. Supreme Ct. 1980. Assoc. Serotte, Reich & Harasym, Buffalo, 1974-76; ptnr. Serotte, Reich, & Seipp, 1976—. Mem. ABA, N.Y. State Bar Assn., Erie County Bar Assn., Am. Immigration Lawyers Assn. (treas. Upstate chpt. 1982—, overseas practice com. 1984—, nat. liaison com. 1997). Immigration, naturalization, and customs. Home: 467 N Forest Rd Buffalo NY 14221-5036 Office: Serotte Reich & Seipp 300 Delaware Ave Ste 4 Buffalo NY 14202-1807

REICHE, FRANK PERLEY, lawyer, former federal commissioner; b. Hartford, Conn., May 8, 1929; s. Karl Augustus and LaFetra (Perley) R.; m. Janet Taylor, Sept. 26, 1953; children: Cynthia Reiche Schumacker, Dean S. AB, Williams Coll., 1951; LLB, Columbia U., 1959; MA, George Washington U., 1959; LLM in Taxation, NYU, 1966. Bar: N.J. 1960, D.C. 1981. Assoc. Stryker, Tams & Dill, Newark, 1959-61, Smith, Stratton, Wise & Heher, Princeton, N.J., 1962-64, ptnr., 1964-79; commr. Fed. Election Commn., Washington, 1979-85, chmn., 1982; ptnr. Katzenbach, Gildea & Rudner, Lawrenceville, N.J., 1986-93; pvt. practice law Princeton, 1993-97; of counsel Schragger, Lavine & Nagy, West Trenton, 1997-2000, Archer & Greiner, Princeton, 2001—. Trustee Westminster Choir Coll., Princeton, 1974-86, Ctr. Theol. Inquiry, Princeton, 1991-97, Wells Coll., Aurora, N.Y., 1994—; mem. planned giving com. Williams Coll., Williamstown, Mass., 1973-87, nat. chmn. planned giving, 1983-87. Lt. USN, 1952-56. Mem. ABA, D.C. Bar Assn., N.J. Bar Assn., Am. Coll. Trust and Estate Counsel (N.J. state chair 1995-2000, bd. regents 2001—). Republican. Presbyterian. Clubs: Washington Golf and Country, Capitol Hill. Estate planning, Probate, Estate taxation.

REICHEL, AARON ISRAEL, lawyer, rabbi, editor; b. N.Y.C., Jan. 30, 1950; s. Oscar Asher and Josephine Hannah (Goldstein) R. BA, Yeshiva U., 1971, MA, 1974; JD, Fordham U., 1976. Bar: N.J. 1977, N.Y. 1978; ordained rabbi, 1975. Atty. editor Securities Regulation Prentice-Hall, Englewood Cliffs, N.J., 1977-78, editor, founder govt. disclosure service Paramus, 1978-82, atty. editor fed. taxation, 1982-89; tech. editor Warren, Gorham & Lamont, Practical Acct., N.Y.C., 1989-90; assoc. Firm A. Edward Major, 1990-91, Firm Allen L. Rothenberg, N.Y.C., 1991-93; pvt. practice, 1993—. Author: The Maverick Rabbi, 1984, 2d edit. 1986, Back to the Past for Inspiration for the Future—West Side Institutional Synagogue Jubilee 1937-87, 1987; co-author (manual) Style and Usage, 1984; contbr. The 1986 Jewish Directory and Almanac, 1986, The 1987-88 Jewish Almanac, 1988; contbg. editor Complete Guide to the Tax Reform Act of 1986, Prentice-Hall's Explanation of the Tax Reform Act of 1986, 1986, Prentice Hall's Complete Guide to the Tax Law of 1987, 1988, Prentice Hall's Explanation of the Technical & Miscellaneous Revenue Act of 1988, 1988, Guide to Equal Employment Practices, 1997; contbr. articles to profl. jours. Bd. dirs. Union Orthodox Jewish Congregations Am., N.Y.C., 1973-74, Harry and Jane Fischel Found., N.Y.C., 1977—, West Side Instl. Synagogue, 1987-98, Amalgamated Dwellings, Inc., 1992-96; nat. pres. YAVNEH, N.Y.C., 1973-74; mem. youth commn. Am. Jewish Congress, N.Y.C., 1973-76. Mem. ABA, N.Y. State Bar Assn. (various coms.), N.Y. County Lawyers Assn. (various coms.), Am. Soc. Access Profls. (founder, 1st chmn. N.Y. chpt.), Nat. Jewish Commn. on Law and Pub. Affairs (family law com.), Yeshiva U. Alumni Assn. (exec. com. 1971-87, editor-in-chief Bull. 1974-78). Avocations: writing, baseball, tennis, compiling proverbs. Civil rights, General practice, Personal injury. Home: 83-28 Abingdon Rd Kew Gardens NY 11415-1714

REICHERT, BRENT LARRY, lawyer; b. Crookston, Minn., Dec. 17, 1956; s. Garfield G. and Juanne C. Reichert; m. Sandra Lee Smith, Apr. 25, 1987; children: Blake L., Brian L. BA summa cum laude, Concordia Coll., 1979; JD, U. Minn., 1982. Bar: Minn. 1982, U.S. Dist. Ct. Minn. 1982, U.S. Ct. Appeals (8th cir.) 1983, U.S. Tax Ct. 1983, Tex. Supreme Ct. 1990, U.S. Dist. Ct. (no. dist.) Tex. 1990, U.S. Dist. Ct. (we. dist.) Mich. 1998. Legal writing instr. U. Minn. Law Sch., Mpls., 1980-81, appellate advocacy instr., 1981-82; assoc. Robins, Kaplan, Miller & Ciresi L.L.P., 1982-89, ptnr., 1989—. Presenter in field. Chmn. music and worship com. Normandale Luth. Ch., 1998-99. Mem. ATLA, ABA (torts and ins. practice sect.), Minn. State Bar Assn., Minn. Trial Lawyers Assn., Tex. State Bar Assn., Hennepin County Bar Assn., Dallas County Bar Assn., Internat. Assn. Arson Investigators. Avocations: music, tennis, hunting, fishing, coaching youth sports teams. General civil litigation, Insurance, Product liability. Home: 6416 Glacier Pl Edina MN 55436-1808 Office: Robins Kaplan Miller & Ciresi LLP 2800 LaSalle Plaza 800 Lasalle Ave Ste 2800 Minneapolis MN 55402-2015

REICHMAN, DAWN LESLIE, lawyer, educator, deputy sheriff; b. Portsmouth, Va., Feb. 15, 1951; d. Stanley J. and Ernestine Enid (Kaiserman) Greif; m. James Richard Smith, Apr. 27, 1975 (div. July 1978); m. Victor I. Reichman, Nov. 24, 1979 (div. Jan. 2000); children: Mark Heath, Margo Ilene, Shelley Renee. BA, U. Calif., L.A., 1972; cert. dep. sheriff, Sheriff Acad., 1974; JD, Whittier Coll., 1988. Bar: Calif. 1988, U.S. Dist. Ct. (ea. and cen. dists.) Calif. 1988. Dep. sheriff L.A. County Sheriff's Dept., 1973-81; substitute tchr. Palmdale (Calif.) Sch. Dist., 1988-90; pvt. practice law Palmdale, 1988—; alt. def. counsel, 1990-91. Vol. arbitrator L.A. Superior and Mcpl. Cts., 1995-2000; vol. mediator L.A. Superior Ct., 1997-2000, vol. judge pro tem, 1998-2000. Spokesperson Ana Verde Homeowners Assn., Palmdale, 1989-95; assoc. Alpha Charter Guild of Antelope Valley Hosp.; bd. dirs. Palmdale Cmty. Assn., 1992; mem. prins. adv. com. Highland H.S., 1994-95, mock trial coach, 1997—; bd. dir. Families Caring for Families, 1995-98; v.p., bd. dirs. Desert Haven Enterprises, 1996-97; mem. strategic planning task force Antelope Valley Hosp. Med. Ctr., 1996; mem. Career Prep Coun. Law and Govt. Adv. Com., 1994-98; pres. Primary Source Profl. Referral Bd., 1995-96; mem. gala com. Antelope Valley Hosp. Gift Found., 1995. Mem. High Desert Criminal Def. Bar Assn. (v.p. 1993, former sec.), Antelope Valley Bar Citizens Law Sch. (chmn. 1991-97), Encouraging Potential in Children (co-chmn. 1991), Phi Alpha Delta. Avocations: reading, crosswords, cryptograms. General civil litigation, Criminal, Family and matrimonial. Office: 520 E Palmdale Blvd # C Palmdale CA 93550-4603

REICIN, ERIC DAVID, lawyer; b. Chgo. s. Ronald Ian and Alyta Reicin; m. Jodi Reicin, 1994. Student, Regent Coll., England, 1990; AB in Econs. and Polit. Sci., U. Mich., 1991; JD cum laude, U. Ill., 1994. Bar: Ill. 1994, U.S. Dist. Ct. (no. dist.) Ill. 1994, D.C. 1995, U.S. Dist. Ct. D.C. 1995, U.S. Ct. Appeals (D.C. cir.) 1995, U.S. Ct. Appeals (4th cir.) 1997, U.S. Supreme Ct. 1998. Intern U.S. Senator Robert W. Kasten, Washington, 1989; intern Office of Policy Devel. White House, 1990; intern U.S. Congressman Carl Pursell, 1991; law clk. State's Atty.-Champaign County, 1994; assoc. Laner Muchin Dombrow Becker Levin and Tominberg, Chgo., 1994-95, Birch Horton Bittner and Cherot, Washington, 1995-99; asst. gen. counsel Sallie Mae, Inc., Reston, Va., 1999-2000, assoc. gen. counsel, 2001—. Chpt. editor: Employment Discrimination Law, 3d edit., 1999, 2000. Harno scholar, 1993-94, Congrl. scholar, 1986; Pub. Interest Law Found. fellow. Mem. ABA (exec. lt. gov. 1993-94, EEO com. nat. co-chmn. regional liaison program 1997-98, nat. co-chmn. govt. liaison program 1998-2001, nat. co-chmn. ABA/EEOC joint tng. partnership 1997—,nat. chmn. EEO com., corp. coun. 2001—), D.C. Bar Assn. (litigation, labor and employment sect.), Met. Washington Employment Lawyers Assn. (sec., bd. dirs. 1997-99), Washington Met. Area Corp. Counsel Assn. (labor and employment com. chair 1999—), Mortar Bd., Pi Sigma Alpha, Omicron Delta Epsilon, Sigma Iota Rho, Alpha Epsilon Pi (Arnold B. Hoffman award 1990). Republican. Administrative and regulatory, General corporate, Labor. Office: Sallie Mae Inc 11600 Sallie Mae Dr Reston VA 20193-0001

REICIN, RONALD IAN, lawyer; b. Chgo., Dec. 11, 1942; s. Frank Edward and Abranita (Rome) R.; m. Alyta Friedland, May 23, 1965; children: Eric, Kael. BBA, U. Mich., 1964, MBA, JD cum laude, U. Mich., 1967. Bar: Ill. 1967, U.S. Tax Ct. 1967; CPA, Ill. Mem. staff Price Waterhouse & Co., Chgo., 1966; ptnr. Jenner & Block, 1967—. Bd. dirs. Nat. Kidney Found., Ill., 1978—, v.p., 1992-95, pres., 1995-98; bd. dirs. Ruth Page Found., 1985—, v.p., 1990—; bd. dirs. Scoliosis Assn. Chgo., 1981-90, Kohl Children's Mus., 1991-95, River North Chgo. Dance Co., 1999—. Mem.: ABA, Chgo. Bar Assn., Chgo. Mortgage Attys. Assn., Exec., Lawyers (Chgo.), Phi Kappa Phi, Beta Gamma Sigma, Beta Alpha Psi. General corporate, General practice, Real property. Office: Jenner & Block LLC 1 E Ibm Plz Fl 38 Chicago IL 60611-3586 E-mail: rreicin@jenner.com

REID, EDWARD SNOVER, III, lawyer; b. Detroit, Mar. 24, 1930; s. Edward S. Jr. and Margaret (Overington) R.; m. Carroll Grylls, Dec. 30, 1953; children: Carroll Reid Highet, Richard Gerveys, Jane Reid McTique, Margaret Reid Boyer. B.A., Yale U., 1951; LL.B. magna cum laude (Sheldon fellow), Harvard U., 1956. Bar: Mich. 1957, N.Y. 1958, D.C. 1982, Gaikokuho jimu-bengoshi, Tokyo 1991-96. Asso. Davis, Polk & Wardwell, N.Y.C., 1957-64, partner, 1964-95, sr. counsel, 1996—; dir. Gen. Mills, Inc., 1974-89. Mem. N.Y.C. Bd. Higher Edn., 1971-73; trustee Bklyn. Inst. Arts and Scis., 1966-93, chmn., 1974-79; trustee Bklyn. Mus., 1973-93, 94—; bd. dirs. Bklyn. Bot. Garden Corp., 1977-92, 96—, Bargemusic Ltd., 1990-93. Lt. USMCR, 1951-53. Mem. ABA, N.Y. State Bar Assn., Assn. of Bar of City of N.Y., Am. Law Inst., Internat. Bar Assn., Heights Casino Club, Rembrandt Club, Century Assn. Club, Yale Club, L.I. Wyandanch Club, Quoque Beach Club, Shinnecock Yacht Club, Quoque Field Club. General corporate, Mergers and acquisitions, Securities. Home: PO Box 39 Quogue NY 11959-0039 Office: Davis Polk & Wardwell 450 Lexington Ave New York NY 10017-3982 E-mail: ereid@dpw.com

REID, INEZ SMITH, lawyer, educator; b. New Orleans, Apr. 7, 1937; d. Sidney Randall Dickerson and Beatrice Virginia (Bundy) Smith. BA, Tufts U., 1959; LLB, Yale U., 1962; MA, UCLA, 1963; PhD, Columbia U., 1968. Bar: Calif. 1963, N.Y. 1972, D.C. 1980. Assoc. prof. Barnard Coll. Columbia U., N.Y.C., 1972-76; gen. counsel youth divsn. State of N.Y.,

1976-77; dep. gen. counsel HEW, Washington, 1977-79; inspector gen. EPA, 1979-81; chief legis. and opinions, dep. corp. counsel Office of Corp. Counsel, 1981-83; corp. counsel D.C., 1983-85; counsel Laxalt, Washington, Perito & Dubuc, Washington, 1986-90, ptnr., 1990-91; counsel Graham & James, 1991-93, Lewis, White & Clay, P.C., 1994-95; assoc. judge D.C. Ct. Appeals, 1995—. William J. Maier, Jr. vis. prof. law W.Va. U. Coll. Law, Morgantown, 1985-86. Contbr. articles to profl. jours. and publs. Bd. dirs. Homeland Ministries Bd. United Ch. of Christ, N.Y.C., 1978-83, vice chmn., 1981-83; chmn. bd. govs. Antioch Law Sch., Washington, 1979-81; chmn. bd. trustees Antioch U., Yellow Springs, Ohio, 1981-82; trustee Tufts U., Medford, Mass., 1988-98, trustee emeritus, 1999—; trustee Lancaster (Pa.) Sem., 1988—; bd. govs. D.C. Sch. Law, 1990-96, chmn., 1991-95. Recipient Emily Gregory award Barnard Coll., 1976, Arthur Morgan award Antioch U., 1982, Service award United Ch. of Christ, 1983, Disting. Service (Profl. Life) award Tufts U. Alumni Assn., 1988. General civil litigation, Constitutional, General corporate. Office: DC Ct Appeals 500 Indiana Ave NW Fl 6 Washington DC 20001-2138

REID, JAMES EDWARD, lawyer; b. Balt., Aug. 8, 1951; s. Edward Kessinger and Jane Kathryn (Fraver) R.; m. Linda Susan Peterson, Sept. 14, 1979; children: Edward Kessinger, Griffin Arthur, Andrew James. BA, Utica Coll. of Syracuse U., 1973, JD, 1976. Bar: N.Y. 1978, U.S. Ct. Mil. Appeals 1979, U.S. Dist. Ct. (no. dist.) N.Y. 1980, U.S. Ct. Appeals (2d cir.) 1979, U.S. Supreme Ct. 1983, U.S. Dist. Ct. (we. dist.) N.Y. 1988. Assoc. firm Davoli & McMahon, Syracuse, N.Y., 1979-82; ptnr. Greene & Reid, LLP, Syracuse, 1982—; instr. civil practice and litigation paralegal program Syracuse U., 1984-87; adj. prof. advanced trial practice Syracuse U., 1987—. Author: Service of Process Desk Reference Manual, 1984, Legal Implications of Fire Apparatus Color Selection-Its Impact on Liability Consideration, 1987, Jury Instructions in the Civil Law Suit , 1987, Handling the Plaintiff's Personal Injury Case, 1989, Uninsured MVAIC and Underinsured Claims and Problems under New York Law: What They Are and How to Avoid Them, 1992, Personal Injury Chapter: General Practice, 1998. Life mem. bd. visitors Syracuse U. Coll. Law. Maj. USMC, 1972-86. Mem. Onondaga County Bar Assn. (chmn. legis. com. 1983—, bd. dirs. 1985-87), N.Y. State Bar Assn. (chmn.-elect gen. practice sect. 1989, ho. of dels. 1990-92), Upstate Trial Lawyers Assn. (pres. 1988-90, 1997—, N.Y. State Trial Lawyers Assn. (bd. dirs. 1987-88, 1997—, asst. dist. atty. Wayne County, N.Y. 1992—), Order of Barristers, Phi Delta Phi. Republican. Roman Catholic. E-mail: jereid@greenereid.com. State civil litigation, Insurance, Personal injury. Home: 123 Grant St Newark NY 14513-1738 also: 330 East Ave Newark NY 14513-1743

REID, JOAN EVANGELINE, lawyer, stockbroker; b. Mich., Apr. 22, 1932; d. August W. and Evangeline R. (Brozeau) Rogers; m. Belmont M. Reid. AA in Bus., San Jose State U., 1951; JD, McGeorge Sch. Law, 1989. Bar: Nev.; lic. realtor, life, disability and annuity ins. Officer, dir. Lifetime Fin. Planning Corp., San Jose, Calif., 1967-77, Lifetime Realty Corp., San Jose, 1967-77; co-founder, officer, dir. Belmont Reid & Co., Inc., 1960-77; officer, corp. counsel, dir. JOBEL Fin. Inc., Carson City, Nev., 1980—. Past sec., treas. Nev. Fedn. Rep. Women; charter pres. Santa Clara Valley Rep. Women Federated; past v.p. Carson City Rep. Women's Club. Paul Harris fellow Rotary. Mem. First Jud. Dist. Bar Assn., State Bar Nev., No. Nev. Women Lawyers Assn., Carson City C. of C. General corporate, Estate planning, Probate.

REID, NELSON MARLIN, lawyer; b. Kettering, Ohio, July 24, 1972; s. M. David and Marilyn J. Reid; m. Anne Witty, Oct. 24, 1998. BA in Econs., Dartmouth Coll., 1994; JD, Duke U., 1997. Bar: Ohio 1997, U.S. Dist. Ct. (so. and no. dists.) Ohio 1998, U.S. Ct. Appeals (6th cir.) 1999. Assoc. Bricker & Eckler LLP, Columbus, Ohio, 1997—. General civil litigation, Federal civil litigation. Office: Bricker & Eckler LLP 100 S 3d St Columbus OH 43215

REID, RUST ENDICOTT, lawyer; b. N.Y.C., Dec. 31, 1931; s. Thorburn and Mary (Newhall) R.; m. Jeanne Inge, Aug. 5, 1955; children: Dorothy, Elizabeth, Margaret, Mary. BA, U. Va., 1954, LLB, 1960. Bar: Tex. 1960, Va. 1960. Bd. cert. in estate planning, probate. Assoc. Thompson & Knight, Dallas, 1960-65, ptnr., 1965—; lectr. SW Grad. Sch. Banking, Dallas, 1978-88; adj. prof. So. Meth. U., Dallas, 1980-86. Contbg. author: Texas Estate Administration, 1975. Trustee Child Care, Dallas, 1968-72, pres. 1970-72, Hockaday Sch., Dallas, 1972-82 (chmn. 1976-78), Texas coun. Girl Scouts U.S., 1982-83; trustee Vis. Nurse Assn., Dallas, 1984—, treas. 1986-89, v.p. 1989-91, pres., 1991-93; pres. Dallas Estate Planning Coun., 1988-89; trustee Dallas Children's Advocacy Center (v.p. 1993—). Lt. (j.g.) USNR, 1954-57. Fellow Am. Trust and Estate Counsel; mem. Tex. Bar Found. Presbyterian. Estate planning, Probate, Personal income taxation. Home: 7010 Tokalon Dr Dallas TX 75214-3830 Office: Thompson & Knight 1700 Pacific 3300 First City Ctr Dallas TX 75201

REID, WILLIAM OWEN, lawyer; b. Melbourne, Victoria, Australia, Feb. 22, 1963; LLB, U. Adelaide, Australia, 1985; GDLP, U. South Australia, 1986. Bar: South Australia 1986 South Wales 1991, Victoria 1998. Lawyer various firms, Adelaide, Australia, 1985-91, Blake Dawson Waldron, Sydney, Australia, 1991-97, ptnr. Melbourne, Australia, 1998—. Mem. trade practices com. Law Coun. Australia, 1996—. Antitrust, Intellectual property. Office: Blake Dawson Waldron 101 Collins St 3000 Melbourne Victoria Australia E-mail: bill.reid@bdw.com.au

REIDENBERG, JOEL R. law educator; AB in Govt., Dartmouth, 1983; JD, Columbia U., 1986; Diplôme d'études approfondies dr.int.eco., U. Paris-Sorbonne, 1987. Bar: N.Y. 1986, D.C. 1988. Friedmann fellow PROMETHEE, Paris, 1986-87; assoc. Debevoise & Plimpton, Washington, 1987-90; prof. law, dir. grad. program Fordham U. Sch. Law, N.Y.C., 1990—. Cons. FTC, Washington, 1997-99; expert advisor European Commn., Luxembourg, 1993-96, Brussels, 1997-98. Co-author: Data Privacy Law, 1996, Online Services and Data Protection and Privacy: Regulatory Responses, 1998; contbr. articles to profl. jours. Mem. Assn. Am. Law Schs. (chair sect. law and computers 1997, chair sect. defamation and privacy 1998). Fax: 212-636-6899

REIFF, JEFFREY MARC, lawyer; b. Phila., Jan. 24, 1955; s. Morton William and Phyliss (Rubin) R.; m. Dominiqus F. Edrei, June 3, 1979; children— Justin Alexander, Collin Michael. B.S., B.A. magna cum laude in Mktg. Fin., Am. U., 1976; J.D., Temple U., 1976. Bar: Pa. 1979, U.S. Dist. Ct. Pa. 1975, N.Y. 1985. Ptnr. Sablosky, Wertheimer & Reiff, Phila., 1979-82, Mozenter, Durst & Reiff, Phila., 1982-85; prin., founder Reiff, Haaz and Assocs. and predecessor firms, Phila., 1985— . Mem. young leadership bd. Fedn. Jewish Agys., Phila., 1982— ; bd. dirs. Golden Slipper Charities, Phila., 1979— , Solomon Schecker Schs., Phila., 1984. Mem. Phila. Bar Assn. (com. chmn. 1984—), Pa. Bar Assn. (com. chmn., mem. lawyers reference com. young lawyers div. 1980—), Am. Trial Lawyers Assn., Pa. Trial Lawyers Assn., Phila. Trial Lawyers Assn. Clubs: Locust, Golden Slipper (bd. dirs. 1980—), Abington Country (Phila.). Criminal, Entertainment, Personal injury. Office: Jeffrey M Reiff & Assocs 1429 Walnut St Fl 12 Philadelphia PA 19102-3204

REILLY, CHARLES JAMES, lawyer, educator, accountant; b. Pawtucket, R.I., Oct. 10, 1950; s. Thomas Joseph and Florence Marie (McKenna) R.; m. Barbara Bouffard, Aug. 7, 1971; children: Kristen, Elizabeth. BSBA, Providence Coll., 1972; JD, Suffolk U., 1979. Bar: R.I. 1979, U.S. Dist. Ct. R.I. 1979, U.S. Ct. Appeals (1st cir.) 1979, U.S. Supreme Ct. 1984, U.S. Ct. Claims, 1985; CPA, R.I. Agt. IRS, Providence, 1972-75; appellate conferee U.S. Dept. Treasury, Boston, 1976-81; ptnr. Arcaro & Reilly, Providence, 1981-91, Reilly Law Assocs., Providence, 1991—. Assoc. prof. Grad. MST program Bryant Coll., Smithfield, R.I., 1983—. Mem. AICPA, R.I. Soc. CPAs, ABA, R.I. Bar Assn. (chair tax sect. 1996-2000). Democrat. Roman Catholic. Club: R.I. Country. Avocation: golf. Corporate taxation, Personal income taxation, State and local taxation. Office: Reilly Law Assocs 1040 Turks Head Bldg Providence RI 02903 E-mail: reillylaw1@aol.com

REILLY, CONOR DESMOND, lawyer; b. Kansas City, Mo., Feb. 12, 1952; s. Desmond M. and Patricia (Carton) R.; m. Margaret M. Cannella, June 8, 1975; children: Katherine C., Michael C. BS, MIT, 1972; JD cum laude, Harvard U., 1975. Bar: N.Y. 1976, U.S. Dist. Ct. (ea. and so. dists.) N.Y. 1976, U.S. Ct. Appeals (2d. cir.) 1977, U.S. Dist. Ct. (D.C. cir.) 1979, U.S. Dist. Ct. (no. dist.) Calif. 1981, U.S. Dist. Ct. (cen. dist.) Calif. 1982. Law clk. to judge U.S. Dist. Ct. (ea. dist.), Bklyn., 1975-76; assoc. Cravath, Swaine & Moore, N.Y.C., 1976-77, Coudert Bros., N.Y.C., 1977-83, LeBoeuf, Lamb, Leiby & MacRae, N.Y.C., 1983-84, ptnr., 1985-88, Gibson, Dunn & Crutcher, N.Y.C., 1988—. Vice-chmn Memorex-Telex N.V., 1988-90; chmn. bd. dirs. Acorn Products Inc., 1996-99. Editor Harvard U. Law Rev., 1973-74. Hearing officer N.Y.C. Bd. Edn., 1977-79; elected mem. Millburn Twp. Bd. Edn., 1987-92. Mem. ABA, Am. Arbitration Assn. (arbitrator). Democrat. Avocation: tennis. Bankruptcy, General corporate, Insurance. Home: 62 Joanna Way Short Hills NJ 07078-3241 Office: Gibson Dunn & Crutcher 200 Park Ave Fl 47 New York NY 10166-0193

REILLY, EDWARD FRANCIS, JR. former state senator, federal agency administrator; b. Leavenworth, Kans., Mar. 24, 1937; s. Edward F. and Marian C. (Sullivan) R. BA, U. Kans., 1961. V.p. Reilly & Sons, Inc., Leavenworth, 1967-92; pres. Yllier Lake Estates, Inc., Easton, Kans., 1965-89; mem. Kans. Ho. of Reps., 1963-64, Kans. State Senate, 1964-92, asst. majority leader, 1977-80, vice-chmn. govtl. orgn., chmn. ins. subcom., chmn. fed. and state affairs com. Chmn. U.S. Parole Commn. Mem. Nat. Commn. on Accreditation of Law Enforcement Agys.; chmn. U.S. Parole Commn. Dept. of Justice, Md., 1992—; former commr. ex officio U.S. Sentencing Commn., Washington; del. to Rep. Nat. Conv., Miami Beach, Fla., 1968; chmn. Leavenworth County Radio Free Europe Fund, 1972; bd. dirs. St. John's Hosp., Leavenworth, 1970-79, sec.; bd. dirs. Leavenworth Assn. for Handicapped, 1968-69, ARC, Leavenworth chpt., Kans. Blue Cross/Blue Shield, 1969-72; apptd. by Pres. Reagan Nat. Hwy. Safety Adv. Com.; active Trinity Nat. Leadership Roundtable, Cath. Campaign Am., Kans. Adv. Bd. Juvenile Offenders, Nat. Com. Cmty. Corrections. Recipient Cmty. Leaders of Am., 1971, 85, 86, Hallpac Pub. Svc. award, 1988, Am. Police Hall of Fame award, 1990, Good Samaritan award Order of Michael the Arch Angel Police Legion, 1990, Commendation award mayor and city commn. of Leavenworth, Kans., 1990, Carnegie Hero Fund Commn. award and medallion, 1991, Silver Angel award Kans. Cath. Conf., 1992; named Outstanding Young Men Am., 1965-76. Mem. Nat. Inst. Corrections (adv. bd.), Am. Paroling Authorities Internat., Am. Correctional Assn., Am. Probation and Paroling Assn., Leavenworth C. of C. (hon. dir. 1970-73), No. Assn. Chiefs Police, Assn. U.S. Army (Henry Leavenworth award 1960), Kansas City (Kans.) C. of C., Leavenworth Hist. Soc. (dir. 1968-73), John Carroll Soc., Native Sons of Kansas City, Ancient Order of Hibernians, U.S. Supreme Ct. Hist. Soc., Kiwanis (dir. 1969-70, Connelly award 1991, Legion of Honor award 1996), K.C., Elks, Eagles, Order of Malta, Equestrian Order Holy Sepulchre Jerusalem. Republican. Roman Catholic.

REILLY, JOHN ALBERT, lawyer; b. N.Y.C., Dec. 8, 1919; s. John T. and Elizabeth (Pione) R.; m. Mary Veronica Kelly, July 10, 1971; m. Marjorie Jessie Snell, June 28, 1946. BS, CCNY, 1940; JD, Harvard U., 1947. Bar: Mass. 1947, N.Y. 1949, Conn. 1977. Patent counsel Kendall Co., Boston, 1947-48; assoc. Kenyon & Kenyon, N.Y.C., 1949-55; ptnr. Kenyon, & Kenyon Reilly Carr & Chapin, 1955-79; mem. firm Curtis, Morris & Safford, P.C., 1979—. Chmn. bd. CCNY Fund. 1st lt. C.E., AUS, 1944-46, ETO. Mem. ABA, N.Y. State Bar Assn., N.Y. Patent Law Assn. (pres. 1979), Am. Patent Law Assn., CCNY Alumni Assn., Harvard U. Law Sch. Assn. Club: Harvard (N.Y.C.). Federal civil litigation, Patent, Trademark and copyright. Office: 745 Fifth Ave 10th Fl New York NY 10151

REILLY, JOHN B. lawyer; b. Bangor, Maine, Sept. 12, 1947; s. Louis J. and Evelyn I. (Lindsay) R.; children: Carolyn, Bridget. BA, U. R.I., 1970; JD cum laude, Suffolk U., 1976. Bar: R.I. 1976, Mass. 1985, U.S. Dist. Ct. R.I. 1976, U.S. Dist. Ct. Mass. 1985, U.S. Dist. Ct. Conn. 1995, U.S. Claims Ct. 1980, U.S. Ct. Appeals (1st and 2d cirs.) 1984, U.S. Ct. Appeals (3d cir.) 1985, U.S. Supreme Ct. 1983; cert. fraud examiner. Sole practice, Providence, 1976-81, Warwick, R.I., 1981-83; sr. ptnr. John Reilly & Assocs. and predecessor firms, 1984-89, Reilly & Nikolyszyn, LLP, Warwick, 2000—. Mem. Gov.'s Automobile Ins. Task Force, 1992-93. Mem. ABA, R.I. Bar Assn., Def. Rsch. Inst., R.I. Assn. Auth Theft and Arson Investigators (sec. 1995-96, pres. 1997—), Trucking Ind. Def. Assn., Pi Sigma Alpha, Phi Kappa Psi. General civil litigation, Environmental, Insurance. Home: 80 Paterson Ave Warwick RI 02886-9110 Office: Reilly & Nikolyszyn LLP 300 Centerville Rd Warwick RI 02886-0200 E-mail: jrasoc@gis.net

REILLY, THOMAS F. state attorney general; b. Springfield, Mass. m. Ruth Reilly; 3 children. BA, Am. Internat. Coll., 1964; JD, Boston Coll., 1970. Atty. Civil Rights divsn. Atty. Gen.'s Office; dist. atty. Middlesex County Dist. Atty. Office, 1991-99; atty. gen. State of Mass., Springfield, 1999—. Founder The Cmty. Based Justice Program. Office: One Ashburton Pl Boston MA 02108-1698 also: 436 Dwight St Springfield MA 01103 also: One Exchange Place Worcester MA 01608

REIMER, BILL MONROE, lawyer; b. Kerrville, Tex., Dec. 20, 1947; s. Rudolf Robert and Billie Dove (Coots) R.; m. June Lynn Kovar, Dec. 27, 1969; children— Kristi Lynn, Kendra Lea, Lauren Rae. BBA, SW Tex. State U., 1970; JD, Tex. Tech. U., 1974. Bar: Tex. 1974, U.S. Dist. Ct. (we. dist.) Tex. 1976. Assoc. Bartram, Reagan, Burrus, New Braunfels, Tex., 1974-76; asst. county atty. Comal County, Tex., 1977-79, county atty., 1980-88, dist. atty., 1989-96; lectr. bus. law Tex. Luth. Coll., Seguin, 1977; ct. arbitrator U.S. Dist. Ct. (we. dist.) Tex. Founder, bd. dirs. Teen Connection, New Braunfels, 1980— ; cons., bd. dirs. New Braunfels, Christian Acad., 1983-84; founder Comal County Child Fatality Rev. Team; founder, bd. dirs. Comal County Child Advocacy Assn. Maj. JAGC, Tex. Army NG. Mem. Tex. Bar Assn., Comal County Bar Assn., Tex. County and Dist. Attys. Assn., Nat. Dist. Attys. Assn., South Ctrl. Bar Assn., Lions (charter mem., pres. 1982-83). Democrat. Home: 805 Encino Dr New Braunfels TX 78130-6648

REIMER, LISA J. lawyer; b. Neptune, N.J., July 2, 1970; d. Howard Sheldon and Nancy Unker; m. Eric Scott Reimer, Aug. 10, 1996. BSBA, Washington U., St. Louis, 1992; JD, U. Pa., 1997. Bar: N.Y., N.J., Conn. Assoc. Tenzer Greenblatt LLP, N.Y.C., 1997—. General civil litigation. Home: 200 East 72nd St Apt 12N New York NY 10021 Office: Tenzer Greenblatt LLP 405 Lexington Ave New York NY 10174

REINER, JOHN PAUL, lawyer; b. N.Y.C., Sept. 17, 1931; s. Charles Anthony and Jane Cecelia (Walsh) R.; m. Mary Elisabeth Wells, July 27, 1961; children: Mary Elisabeth, Clark Biddle. BS, Fordham U., 1954; MS, Columbia U., 1955, JD, 1960. Bar: N.Y. 1960, U.S. Ct. Appeals (2d cir.) 1961, U.S. Dist. Ct. (so. and ea. dists.) N.Y. 1961. Law clk. U.S. Dist. Ct. (so. dist.) N.Y., 1960-61; asst. U.S. atty. So. Dist. N.Y., 1961-63; assoc. Townley & Updike, N.Y.C., 1964-70, ptnr., 1971-95, White and Case, 1995—. Bd. dirs. Malta Human Svcs. Found., Thai Support Found.; mem. del. of Holy See to UN; pres. Am. Assn. of Sovereign Mil. Order of Malta. Lt. U.S. Army, 1955—57. Decorated Knight of Malta; Knight Comdr. Order of St. Sylvester, by Pope John Paul II, 1983. Mem. Union League Club. Republican. Federal civil litigation, State civil litigation, Trademark and copyright. Home: 3 E 77th St New York NY 10021-1710 Office: White & Case 1155 6th Ave New York NY 10036-2711

REINGLASS, MICHELLE ANNETTE, lawyer; b. L.A., Dec. 9, 1954; d. Darwin and Shirley (Steiner) R. Student, U. Calif., Irvine, 1972-75; BSL, Western State U., 1977, JD, 1978. Bar: Calif. 1979, U.S. Dist. Ct. (ctrl. dist.) Calif. 1979, U.S. Ct. Appeals (9th cir.) 1981, U.S. Dist. Ct. (so. dist.) Calif. 1989. Pvt. practice employee litig., Laguna Hills, Calif., 1979—. Instr. Calif. Continuing Edn. of Bar, 1990—, Western State Coll., 1991, Rutter Group, 1994—; chmn. magistrate selection com. U.S. Dist. Ct. (ctrl. dist.) Calif., L.A., 1991, 93, 94, 95, mem. commn., 1997; lectr. in field. Contbr. articles to profl. jours. Pres. Child or Parental Emergency Svcs., Santa Ana, Calif., 1982-92; bd. dirs. Pub. Law Ctr., Santa Ana, Coalition for Justice; mem. exec. com. CHOC Follies. Recipient Jurisprudence award Anti-Defamation League, 1997; named to Hall of Fame, Western State U., 1993; named one of Best Lawyers, bestlawyers.com, 2001. Mem. State Bar Calif., Orange County Bar Assn. (del. to state conv. 1980-94, bd. dirs. 1983-94, chmn. bus. litigation sect. 1989, sec. 1990, treas. 1991, pres.-elect 1992, pres. 1993), Orange County Trial Lawyers Assn. (bd. dirs. 1987-89, Bus. Trial Lawyer of Yr. award 1995), Orange County Women Lawyers (Lawyer of Yr. award 1996), Vols. in Parole (chmn. adv. com. 1990-91), Peter Elliot Inns Ct. (master), Am. Bd. of Trial Advocates. Avocations: distance running, skiing. Federal civil litigation, State civil litigation, Labor. Office: 23161 Mill Creek Dr Ste 170 Laguna Hills CA 92653-1650

REINHARD, PHILIP G. federal judge; b. LaSalle, Ill., Jan. 12, 1941; s. Godfrey and Ruth R.; married Virginia Reinhard; children: Bruce, Brian, David, Philip. BA, U. Ill., Champaign, 1962, JD, 1964. Asst. state atty. Winnebago County, 1964-67; atty. Hyer, Gill & Brown, 1967-68; state atty. Winnebago County, 1968-76; judge 17th Jud. Cir., 1976-80, Appellate Ct., 1980-92, U.S. Dist. Ct. (no. dist.) Ill., 1992—. Mem. security, space and facilities com. U.S. Jud. Conf. Mem. Am. Acad. Jud. Edn., Winnebago County Bar Assn. Office: US Courthouse 211 S Court St Rockford IL 61101-1219

REINHARDT, BENJAMIN MAX, lawyer, arbitrator, mediator; b. N.Y.C., Dec. 29, 1917; s. Meyer and Miriam (Fischer) R.; children: Dennis, Dixie, Sara, Shawn; m. Rosa Reinhardt. BA, Harvard U., 1940; JD magna cum laude, Southwestern U., L.A., 1956. Bar: Calif. 1956, U.S. Supreme Ct. 1960. Pvt. practice, Van Nuys, Calif., 1957-87, Palm Desert, 1987—. Chief legal counsel Northridge (Calif.) Hosp. Found., 1965-75; atty. Calif. Psychol. Assn., San Francisco, 1965-70; tchr. law Los Angeles County Bd. Edn., L.A., 1965-73; instr. law U. So. Calif., L.A., 1963-69, Coll. of Desert, Palm Desert, Calif., 1992-94; arbitrator Superior Ct. Calif., Palm Springs, 1994—; atty. Sr. T.V., Indian Wells, Calif., 1992—. Mem. Palm Desert Police Adv. Com., 1993-98; mem. adv. bd. Ret. Sr. Vol. Program, Palm Desert, 1994-96; instr. law Elderhostel, Indian Wells, Calif., 1993-98. Capt. U.S. Army, 1941-46. Mem. State Bar Calif., Desert Bar Assn. Republican. Avocations: golf, reading. State civil litigation, General practice, Probate. Office: Palm Desert Greens 38-101 Story Creek Dr Palm Desert CA 92260-8617 Fax: 760-346-0936. E-mail: reino81@earthlink.net

REINHARDT, STEPHEN ROY, federal judge; b. N.Y.C., Mar. 27, 1931; s. Gottfried and Silvia (Hanlon) R.; children: Mark, Justin, Dana. B.A. cum laude, Pomona Coll., 1951; LL.B., Yale, 1954. Bar: Calif. 1958. Law clk. to U.S. Dist. Judge Luther W. Youngdahl, Washington, 1956-57; atty. O'Melveny & Myers, L.A., 1957-59; partner Fogel Julber Reinhardt Rothschild & Feldman (L.C.), 1959-80; judge U.S. Ct. Appeals (9th cir.), 1980—. Mem. exec. com. Dem. Nat. Com., 1969-72, nat. Dem. committeeman for Calif., 1976-80; pres. L.A. Recreation an dParks Commn., 1974-75; mem. Coliseum Commn., 1974-75; mem. L.A. Police Commn., 1974-78, pres., 1978-80; sec., mem. exec. com. L.A. Olympic Organizing com., 1980-84; bd. dirs. Amateur Athletic Found. of L.A., 1984-92; adj. prof. Loyola Law Sch., L.A., 1988-90. Served to 1st lt. USAF, 1954-56. Mem. ABA (labor law coun. 1975-77).*

REINHART, RICHARD PAUL, lawyer; b. Cleve., Sept. 1, 1954; s. Richard A. and Carole F. (Kaspar) R.; m. Debra Rae Hitchcock, June 20, 1976; children: Geoffrey, Richelle Marie. BA with honors, Rollins Coll., 1976; JD with distinction, Emory U., 1979. Bar: Ga. 1979, Fla. 1980. Ptnr. Morris, Manning & Martin, Atlanta, 1979-89; officer McMillen Reinhart and Voght, P.A., Orlando, Fla., 1989—, also bd. dirs. Mem. ABA, ATLA, Fla. Bar Assn., Ga. Bar Assn., Orange County Bar Assn., Acad. Fla. Trial Lawyers, Order of Coif, Omicron Delta Kappa. Federal civil litigation, State civil litigation. Office: McMillen Reinhart and Voght PA 111 N Orange Ave Ste 1450 Orlando FL 32801-4641 E-mail: reinhart@floridamalpractice.com

REINHART, ROBERT ROUNTREE, JR. lawyer; b. Chgo., Oct. 21, 1947; s. Robert Rountree and Ruth (Duncan) R.; m. Elizabeth Aileen Plews, July 26, 1969; children: Andrea Jean, Jessica Elizabeth, Rebecca Jill. BA, Northwestern U., 1968; JD, U. Mich., 1971. Bar: Ill. 1971, Mich. 1972, Minn. 1973, U.S. Supreme Ct. 1976. Law clk. to judge U.S. Dist. Ct. (we. dist.) Mich., Grand Rapids, 1971-73; assoc. Oppenheimer Wolff & Donnelly, Mpls., 1973-77, ptnr., 1978-96, chair labor and employment bus. group, 1985-92; ptnr. Dorsey & Whitney, 1996—, co-chmn. labor and employment practice group, 2000—. Co-chmn. Upper Midwest Employment Law Inst., Mpls., 1984—; gen. counsel Minn. Empoyment Law Coun., 1990—. Mem. ABA (labor and employment, civil litigation sects.), Minn. Bar Assn. General civil litigation, Labor. Office: Dorsey & Whitney 1400 Pillsbury Ctr S 220 S 6th St Ste 2200 Minneapolis MN 55402-1498 E-mail: reinhart.robert@dorseylaw.com

REINIGER, DOUGLAS HAIGH, lawyer; b. Mt. Kisco, N.Y., Nov. 8, 1948; s. Haigh McDiarmid and Virginia (Munson) R.; m. Margaret Vrablic, Aug. 31, 1968 (div. Jan. 1983); 1 child, Brian Christopher; m. Anne Fanning, Aug. 5, 1984. BA, Iona Coll., 1970; MSW, Fordham U., 1974, JD, 1980. Bar: N.Y. 1981, Wyo. 1996, U.S. Dist. Ct. (so. dist.) N.Y. 1982, U.S. Dist. Ct. (ea. dist.) N.Y., 1991, U.S. Cir. Ct. Appeals (2d cir.) 1997, U.S. Supreme Ct 1986. Psychiat. aide St. Vincent's Psychiat. Hosp., Harrison, N.Y., 1968-69; child care worker Cardinal McCloskey Home for Children, White Plains, 1969-71, social worker, 1971-75, dir. legal affairs, 1975-81; sole practice N.Y.C., 1981-83; ptnr. Rosin & Reiniger, 1983—; assoc. prof. Sch. Social Work Columbia U., 1991-99, coord. law minor program, Sch. Social Work, 1994-99. Lectr. appellate divsn. N.Y. Supreme Ct., N.Y.C., 1985, 99, Fedn. Protestant Welfare, N.Y.C., 1987-91, Ct. Apptd. Spl. Advs., N.Y.C., 1987-94, Practicing Law Inst., N.Y.C., 1988, 99, 2000, 01. Mem. ABA (family law sect., com. on adoption, com. on custody 1992—), N.Y. State Bar Assn. (lectr. 1988, 99, family law sect., com. on family ct., com. on adoption), Assn. Bar City N.Y. (lectr. 1995, 99, com. on family law and family ct. 1985-88, com. on juvenile justice 1989-91, com. on children and the law 1993-97), Am. Acad. Adoption Attys. (lectr. 1995-96, 2000-01, chmn. adoption agy. com. 1998-2001, trustee 2000—), N.Y. State Foster and Adoptive Parents Assn. (bd. dirs. 1992—, lectr. 1992-2001), New York County Lawyers Assn. (lectr. 1994-2001). Roman Catholic. Family and matrimonial, Juvenile. Office: Rosin & Reiniger 630 3rd Ave New York NY 10017-6705 E-mail: dreiniger@aol.com

REINKE, STEFAN MICHAEL, lawyer; b. Concord, Calif., May 7, 1958; s. Albert Richard and Patricia Eleanor (Stefan) R.; m. Lisa Elaine Williams, June 7, 1997. AA, Bakersfield Coll., 1978; AB, U. So. Calif., 1981; JD, U. Calif., Davis, 1984. Bar: Hawaii 1984, U.S. Dist. Ct. Hawaii 1984, U.S. Ct. Appeals (9th and Fed. cirs.) 1985. Assoc. Carlsmith, Wichman, Case, Mukai & Ichiki, Honolulu, 1984-86; dir. Lyons, Brandt, Cook & Hiramatsu, 1986—. Lectr. Windward C.C., 1995-98; lawyer rep. 9th Cir. Jud. Conf., 1995; lawyer rep. Jud. Conf. for the U.S. Dist. Ct. Hawaii, 1996-98. Bd. dirs. Hawaii Ctrs. for Ind. Living, Honolulu, 1985-91, Prevent Child Abuse Hawaii, 1995—, v.p., 1999-2000, pres., 2000-2001; ofcl. U.S. Cycling Fedn. Mem. ABA, FBA (pres. Hawaii chpt. 1994-96, 98-99), Hawaii Bar Assn. (mem. jud. adminstrn. com.), Am. Arbitration Assn. (arbitrator and mediator), Def. Rsch. Inst., Hawaii State Cycling Assn. (bd. dirs. 1998—), Phi Beta Kappa, Phi Alpha Delta. General civil litigation, Insurance, Labor. Office: Lyons Brandt Cook & Hiramatsu 841 Bishop St Ste 1800 Honolulu HI 96813-3992 E-mail: sreinke@usa.net

REINKE, WILLIAM JOHN, lawyer; b. South Bend, Ind., Aug. 7, 1930; s. William August and Eva Marie (Hein) R.; m. Sue Carol Colvin, 1951 (div. 1988); children: Sally Sue Taelman, William A., Andrew J.; m. Elizabeth Beck Lockwood, 1991. AB cum laude, Wabash Coll., 1952; JD, U. Chgo., 1955. Bar: Ind. 1955. Assoc. Barnes & Thornburg and predecessors, South Bend, Ind., 1957-61, ptnr., 1961-96, of counsel, 1996—; former chmn. compensation com.; former mem. mgmt. com. Trustee Stanley Clark Sch., 1969-80, pres., 1977-80; mem. adv. bd. Salvation Army, 1973—, pres., 1990-92; bd. dirs. NABE Mich. chpt., 1990-94, pres. 1993-94, Isaac Walton League, 1970-81, United Way, 1979-81; pres. South Bend Round Table, 1963-65; trustee First Meth. Ch., 1976-70. Served with U.S. Army, 1955-57. Recipient Outstanding Local Pres. award Ind. Jaycees, 1960-61, Boss of Yr. award, 1979, South Bend Outstanding Young Man award, 1961. Mem. ABA, Ind. State Bar Assn., St. Joseph County Bar Assn., Ind. Bar Found. (patron fellow), Am. Judicature Soc., Ind. Soc. Chgo., Summit Club (past gov., founders com.), Rotary (bd. dirs. 1970-73, 94-97). General civil litigation, Contracts commercial, Construction. Home: 51795 Waterton Square Cir Granger IN 46530-8317 Office: Barnes & Thornburg 1st Source Bank Ctr 100 N Michigan St Ste 600 South Bend IN 46601-1632

REINSTEIN, JOEL, lawyer; b. N.Y.C., July 23, 1946; s. Louis and Ruth Shukovsky; children: Lesli, Louis, Mindy. BSE, U. Pa., 1968; JD cum laude, U. Fla., 1971; LLM in Taxation, NYU, 1974. Bar: Fla. 1971, U.S. Tax Ct. 1973, U.S. Dist. Ct. (so. dist.) Fla. 1976. Atty., office of chief counsel IRS, 1971-74; ptnr. Capp, Reinstein, Kopelowitz and Atlas, P.A., Ft. Lauderdale, Fla., 1975-85; dir., ptnr. Greenberg, Traurig, Hoffman, Lipoff, Rosen & Quentel, P.A., 1985-92; gen. counsel Internat. Magnetic Imaging, Inc., Boca Raton, Fla., 1992-94; prin. Law Offices of Joel Reinstein, 1993—. Lectr. Advanced Pension Planning, Am. Soc. C.L.U.s; lectr. in field. Mem. editl. bd. U. Fla. Law Rev. 1970-71; contbr. articles to profl. jours. Mem. Fla. Bar Assn. (tax sect.), ABA (tax sect.), Order of Coif, Phi Kappa Phi, Phi Delta Pi. General corporate, Estate planning, Corporate taxation. Office: The Plaza 5355 Town Center Rd Ste 801 Boca Raton FL 33486-1069

REINSTEIN, PAUL MICHAEL, lawyer; b. N.Y.C., Jan. 19, 1952; s. Joseph and Edith (Ambaras) R.; m. Gila Ann Moldoff, Apr. 16, 1978; children: Meira, Rachel, Aryeh, Joseph. BA, Yeshiva Coll., 1973; JD, Yale U., 1976. Bar: N.Y. 1977. Assoc. Fried Frank Harris Shriver & Jacobson, N.Y.C., 1976-83, ptnr., 1983—. Mem. ABA, N.Y. State Bar Assn. General corporate, Securities. Home: 282 Maple St West Hempstead NY 11552-3206 Office: Fried Frank Harris et al 1 New York Plz Fl 22 New York NY 10004-1980

REINTHALER, RICHARD WALTER, lawyer; b. N.Y.C., Feb. 27, 1949; s. Walter F. and Maureen C. (Tully) R.; m. Mary E. Maloney, Aug. 8, 1970; children: Brian, Scott, Amy. BA in Govt. magna cum laude, U. Notre Dame, 1970, JD summa cum laude, 1973. Bar: N.Y. 1974, U.S. Dist. Ct. (so. and ea. dists.) N.Y. 1974, U.S. Ct. Appeals (2d cir.) 1974, U.S. Ct. Appeals (9th cir.) 1976, U.S. Ct. Appeals (5th cir.) 1978, U.S. Ct. Appeals (11th cir.) 1981, U.S. Supreme Ct. 1977. Assoc. White & Case, N.Y.C., 1973-81, ptnr., 1981-95, Dewey Ballantine LLP, N.Y.C., 1995—. Mem. adv. group U.S. Dist. Ct. (ea. dist.) N.Y., 1992—, chairperson subgroup on ethics, 1993—. Contbr. articles to profl. jours. Served to 1st lt. U.S. Army, 1974. Fellow Am. Bar Found.; mem. ABA (2d cir. chmn. discovery com. 1982-87, program coord. 1986, ann. meeting litigation sect., vice chmn. com. on fed. procedure 1988-89, co-chmn. com. on profl. responsibility 1989-92, vice chmn. securities litigation com. 1993-94, vice chair Hong Kong meeting 1995, co-chair energy litigation com. 1996-97, co-chair antitrust litigation com. 1997-2000, mem. Ethics 2000 task force 1999-2000), N.Y. State Bar Assn., Assn. of Bar of City of N.Y. (mem. com. to enhance diversity in the profession 1990-95, mem. Orison S. Marden Meml. Lectrs. com. 1994-2000, chair 1997-2000, spl. com. on mergers, acquisitions and corp. control contests 1995—), Scarsdale Golf Club (Hartsdale, N.Y., bd. govs. 1994—), Capital Hill Club (Washington). Republican. Roman Catholic. Avocations: golf, tennis. Antitrust, Federal civil litigation, Securities. Office: Dewey Ballantine LLP 1301 Avenue Of The Americas New York NY 10019-6022

REISING, RICHARD P. lawyer; BA, Stanford U.; JD, U. Mo. Bar: Ill. 1970. Asst. gen. counsel, sec. Archer-Daniels-Midland Co., Decatur, Ill., v.p., sec., gen. counsel, 1991-97, sr. v.p., 1997—. General corporate. Office: Archer-Daniels-Midland Co 4666 E Faries Pky Decatur IL 62526-5666

REISS, JEROME, lawyer; b. Bklyn., Dec. 7, 1924; s. William and Eva (Marenstein) R.; m. Naomi Betty Plutzik, June 15, 1947; children: Robert Scott, Harlan Morgan, Andrea Ellen, SAmantha Glynis. BA, Bklyn. Coll., 1948; JD, Harvard U., 1951. Bar: N.Y. 1951, U.S. Dist. Ct. (so. dist.) N.Y. 1954, U.S. Ct. Claims 1960, U.S. Dist. Ct. (ea. dist.) N.Y. 1964, D.C. 1967, U.S. Dist. Ct. (we. dist.) N.Y. 1979, U.S. Supreme Ct. 1989. Staff atty. corp. counsel City of N.Y., 1954-58; assoc. Max E. Greenberg, 1958-67; sr. ptnr. Max E. Greenberg, Trayman, Cantor, Reiss & Blasky, 1967-80, Max E. Greenberg, Cantor & Reiss, N.Y.C., 1980-88, Thelen, Marrin, Johnson & Bridges, N.Y.C., 1989-97, Thelen, Reid & Priest, 1997-2000. Lectr. constrn. law Practicing Law Inst., Gen. Svcs. Adminstrn., Engring. News Record, Medger Evers C.C., Am. Arbitrators Assn., Prof. Edn. Sys.; arbitrator Small Claims Ct. , 1960—88; bd. advisors Fed. Pub., Inc.; chmn. bd. AMT-Pacific , 2000—. Contbr. numerous articles to profl. jours., chapters to books. Gen. counsel Artist Fellowship Inc. Cpl. USAAF, 1943-46. Fellow: Am. Coll. Constrn. Lawyers (founding); mem.: ABA, Am. Arbitrators Assn., Mcpl. Assist. Corp. of City of N.Y. (bd. dirs.), Jacob K. Javits Conv. Ctr. Oper. Corp. (bd. dirs.), Internat. Bar Assn., Am. Judges Assn. Federal civil litigation, Construction, Government contracts and claims.

REISS, JOHN BARLOW, lawyer; b. London, Aug. 29, 1939; came to U.S., 1963; s. James Martin and Margaret Joan (Ping) R.; m. Mary Jean Maudsley, Aug. 6, 1967 (div. 1978); m. Kathleen Strouse, Aug. 2, 1979; 1 child, Juliette Blanche. BA with honors, Exeter U., Devon, Eng., 1961; AM, Washington U., St. Louis, 1966, PhD, 1971; JD, Temple U., 1977. Bar: Pa. 1977, N.J. 1977, U.S. Dist. Ct. N.J. 1977, D.C. 1980, U.S. Supreme Ct. 1981, U.S. Dist. Ct. D.C. 1982. Economist Commonwealth Econ. Com., London, 1962-63; asst. prof. Allegheny Coll., Meadville, Pa., 1967-71; assoc. prof. Stockton State Coll., Pomona, N.J., 1971-75; asst. health commr. State of N.J., Trenton, 1975-79; dir. office of health regulation U.S. Dept. HHS, Washington, 1979-81; assoc. Baker & Hostetler, 1981-82, Dechert Price & Rhoads, Phila., 1982-86, ptnr., 1986-93, asst. chair health law group, 1984-91, chmn. health law group, 1991-93; ptnr. Saul Ewing LLP, 1993—, chmn. health law dept., 1995—. Mem. editl. bd. Topics in Hosp. Law, 1985-86, Hosp. Legal Forms Manual, 1985—, Jour. Health Care Tech., 1984-86; contbr. Hosp. Contracts Manual, 1983—; contbr. articles to profl. jours., chpts. to books. Bd. dirs. Gateway Sch. Little Children, Phila., 1986-99; bd. dirs. ECRI, Plymouth Meeting, Pa., 1994—, chmn. bd., 2001—; mem. bd. vestry All Saints Ch., Wynnewood, Pa., 1993, 96-2001. Pub. Health Svc. fellow, 1979-81, English Speaking Union fellow, 1963-66, Econ. Devel. Adminstr. fellow Washington U., 1966-67. Mem. Nat. Health Lawyers Assn., Phila. Bar Assn., Brit. Am. C. of C. of Greater Phila. (bd. dirs. 1991), Union League of Phila., Univ. Barge Club, Brit. Officers Club of Phila. Avocations: gardening, house restoring, reading, sculling. Administrative and regulatory, General corporate, Health. Home: 415 Wister Rd Wynnewood PA 19096-1808 Office: Saul Ewing LLP 3800 Centre Sq W Philadelphia PA 19102 E-mail: jreiss@saul.com

REITER, GLENN MITCHELL, lawyer; b. N.Y.C., Feb. 1, 1951; s. Bernard Leon and Helene (Edson) R.; m. Marilyn Beckhorn, Sept. 5, 1976; children: Benjamin, Diana, Julie. BA, Yale U., 1973, JD, 1976. Bar: N.J. 1976, Pa. 1977, D.C. 1978, N.Y. 1979. Law clk. to judge U.S. Ct. Appeals, Phila., 1976-77; assoc. Schnader, Harrison, Segal & Lewis, 1977-78, Simpson Thacher & Bartlett, N.Y.C., 1978-84, ptnr., 1984—, resident ptnr. London, 1986-90. Mem. Phi Beta Kappa. Banking, General corporate, Securities.

REITER, JOSEPH HENRY, lawyer, retired judge; b. Phila., Mar. 21, 1929; s. Nicholas and Barbara (Hellmann) R.; m. Beverlee A. Bearman, Nov. 8, 1993. AB, Temple U., 1950, LLB, 1953. Bar: D.C. 1953, Pa. 1954. Atty. advisor U.S. Army, 1955-61; asst. U.S. atty. Ea. Dist. Pa., 1961-63, asst. U.S. atty. in charge of civil div., 1963-69; chief organized crime and racketeering strike force Western N.Y. State, U.S. Dept. Justice, 1969-70, sr. trial atty. tax div. 1970-72, regional dir. office of drug abuse law enforcement, 1972-73; dep. atty. gen., dir. Drug Law Enforcement Office of Pa., 1973-77; ptnr. Stassen, Kostos and Mason, Phila. 1978-85, Kostos Reiter & Lamer, 1985-89; judge Armed Svcs. Bd. of Contract Appeals, Falls Church, Va., 1989-95; of counsel Kostos & Lamer, Phila., 1995—; mem. adv. com. Joint State Commn. on Procurement; lectr. in field. Contbr. articles to profl. jours. Mem. Citizens Crime Commn. Pa. With U.S. Army, 1953-55. Recipient Meritorious Svc. award U.S. Atty. Gen. Clark, 1967, Spl. Commendation Asst. U.S. Atty. Gen. Tax Div., 1969, Outstanding Performance award U.S. Atty. Gen. Richardson, 1973. Mem. ABA, Fed. Bar Assn., D.C. Bar Assn., Pa. Bar Assn., Phila. Bar Assn., Am. Legion, Vesper Club, Downtown Club. Office: Kostos & Lamer 1608 Walnut St Ste 1300 Philadelphia PA 19103-5407

REITH, DANIEL I. retired lawyer; b. Sacramento, Feb. 28, 1939; s. Mervin Henry and Nancy Elizabeth (Needham) R.; m. Susan Dorothea Totsu, June 16, 1971. AB cum laude, Dartmouth Coll., 1961; LLB, U. Calif., Berkeley, 1964. Bar: Calif. 1965; cert. specialist family law, 1980. Assoc. Thompson & Hubbard, Monterey, Calif., 1965-69; pvt. practice, 1969-71, 95-01; sr. ptnr. Reith, Bebermeyer & Wieben, 1971-95. Referee Calif. State Bar Ct., 1973-89; instr. Calif. Continuing Edn. of Bar, 1977. Assoc. editor: Calif. Law Rev., 1963-64; contbr. articles to profl. jours. Pres. Monterey County Legal Aid Soc., Calif., 1974; chmn. Monterey Nat. Rugby Tournament, 1971-73. Mem. Monterey County Bar Assn. (pres. 1975), Assn. Calif. Cert. Family Law Specialists, Order of Coif. Democrat. State civil litigation, Family and matrimonial, Probate.

RELKIN, ELLEN, lawyer; b. Bronx, N.Y., Aug. 27, 1959; d. Joseph and Marjorie Relkin; m. Alan Rojer, June 20, 1981; children: Rebecca, Isaac, Aurora. BA in History cum laude, Cornell U., 1980; JD, Rutgers U., 1984. Bar: N.J. 1985, U.S. Dist. Ct. (so., ea. no. and we. dists.) N.Y. 1985, D.C. 1986, U.S. Ct. Appeals (3d cir.) 1986. Law clk. to Hon. Sylvia B. Pressler appellate divsn. N.J. Superior Ct., 1984-85; assoc. Porzio, Bromberg, Newman & Baumeister, N.Y.C., 1985-88, Baumeister & Samuels, PC, N.Y.C., 1988-92, Weitz & Luxenberg, PC, N.Y.C., 1997—; of counsel Karl Asch, P.A., Clark, N.J., 1992-93, Sybil Shainwald, PC, N.Y.C., 1993-96. Bd. advisors BNA Toxics Law Reporter, Washington, 1990—, BNA Products Liability Law Reporter, Washington, 1995—; trustee Nat. Pre-Suit Mediation Program, Washington, 1997-98. Contbr. articles to profl. jours. Troop leader Girl Scouts U.S., Maplewood, N.J., 1993-98. Mem. ABA (vice chair com. on toxic torts and environ. law 1991-97), ATLA (1st vice chair sect. toxic, environ. and pharm. torts 1999), N.Y. Bar Assn. (co-chair toxic tort com. environ. law sect. 1990-94, 98). Environmental, Personal injury, Product liability. Office: Weitz & Luxenberg PC 180 Maiden Ln Fl 17 New York NY 10038-4937

REMAR, ROBERT BOYLE, lawyer; b. Boston, Nov. 19, 1948; s. Samuel Roy and Elizabeth Mary (Boyle) R.; m. Victoria A. Greenhood, Nov. 11, 1979; children: Daniel A.G., William B.G. BA, U. Mass., 1970; JD, Boston Coll., 1974. Bar: Ga. 1974, Mass. 1975, U.S. Ct. Appeals (5th cir.) 1978, U.S. Ct. Appeals (11th cir.) 1981, U.S. Ct. Appeals (2d cir.) 1995, U.S. Supreme Ct. 1981. Staff atty. Ga. Legal Svcs. Program, Savannah, 1974-76, Western Mass. Legal Svcs., Greenfield, 1976-77; sr. staff atty. Ga. Legal Svcs. Program, Atlanta, 1977-82; ptnr. Remar & Graettinger, 1983-95, Kirwan, Parks, Chesin & Remar PC, Atlanta, 1993-96, Rogers & Hardin, Atlanta, 1996—. Bd. dirs., exec. com. ACLU, N.Y.C., pres. Ga. chpt., 1985-87, gen. counsel, 1980-83; hearing officer Ga. Pub. Svc. Commn., Atlanta, 1985-98; adj. prof. Ga. State U., Atlanta, 1984-98, spl. asst. atty. gen., 1990-2000; bd. experts Lawyers Alert, Boston, 1985-94. Mem. Ga. Energy Regulatory Reform Commn., Gov. of Ga., 1980-82, Ga. Consumer Adv. Bd., 1981-82; pres. Ga. Consumer Ctr. Inc., 1988-91; bd. dirs., exec. com. Ga. Resource Ctr.; v.p. Ga Ctr. Law Pub. Inst., 1991-94. Mem. ABA (chmn. individual rights access to civil justice com. 1988-99), Ga. Bar Assn. (chmn. individual rights sect. 1981-83, co-chmn. consumer rights and remedies com. 1979-83, chmn. death penalty re. com. 1993—, mem. legis. adv. com. 1994-97, mem. indigent def. com. 2000—), Atlanta Bar Assn., Lawyers Club Atlanta, Lamar Inn of Ct. (master of the bench). Democrat. Avocations: golf, gardening. Administrative and regulatory, Federal civil litigation, Labor. Home: 1714 Meadowdale Ave NE Atlanta GA 30306-3114 Office: Rogers & Hardin Internat Tower Peachtree Ctr 229 Peachtree St NE Ste 2700 Atlanta GA 30303-1638 E-mail: RBR@RH-LAW.COM

REMBOLT, JAMES EARL, b. Nov. 13, 1943; s. Earl Lester and Dorothy Elouise (Mehring) Rembolt; m. Marilyn Sue Schmadeke, July 16, 1972; children: Tami Anne, Michelle Sue. BBA, U. Nebr., 1965; MA in Bus. Orgn. and Mgmt., 1967, JD with distinction, 1972. Bar: Nebr. 1972, U.S. Sist. Ct. Nebr. 1972, U.S. Tax Ct. 1978, U.S. Ct. Claims 1978. Pres. Nebr. Cts. Bd., 1972; pilot Nebr. Air Nat. Guard, Lincoln, 1969-74; lecr. legal writing U. Nebr. Coll. Law, 1973-74; ptnr. Rembolt, Ludtke & Berger, LLP, Lincoln, 1972—. Chmn. bd. trustees YWCA, Lincoln, 1982-83; bd. elders Eastridge Presbyterian Ch., Lincoln, 1979-82; mem. Lincoln/Lancaster Sr. Ctrs. Found., Ic., bd. dirs. 1988-90; bd. dirs. Madonna Found., Inc. 1989-91; trustee, dir. U. Nebr. Found., U. Nebr.-Lincoln Com. of Visitors, Nebr. Continuing Legal Edn., Inc. (past dir., pres.) Fellow: ABA, Am. Coll. Probate Counsel, Nebr. State Bar Found. (pres.-elect 2002, exec. coun., ho. of del.); mem.: Lincoln Bar Assn., Nebr. Bar Assn., Am. Jud. Soc., Lincoln Probate Discussion Group (charter mem., past pres.), Lincoln Estate Planning Coun. (past pres.), U. Nebr. Lincoln Coll. Bua. Adminstrn. Alumni Assn. General corporate, Estate planning, Probate. Office: Rembolt Ludtke & Berger LLP 1201 Lincoln Mall Ste 102 Lincoln NE 68508-2839 E-mail: jrembolt@remlud.com

REMINGER, RICHARD THOMAS, lawyer, artist; b. Cleve., Apr. 3, 1931; s. Edwin Carl and Theresa Henrietta (Bookmyer) R.; m. Billie Carmen Greer, June 26, 1954; children: Susan Greer, Patricia Allison, Richard Thomas. AB, Case-Western Res. U., 1953; JD, Cleve. State U., 1957. Bar: Ohio 1957, Pa. 1978, U.S. Supreme Ct. 1961. Pers. and safety dir. Motor Express, Inc., Cleve., 1954-58; mng. ptnr. Reminger & Reminger Co., L.P.A., 1958-90. Mem. nat. claims couns. adv. bd. Comml. Union Assurance Co., 1980-90; lectr. transp. law Fenn Coll., 1960-62; lectr. bus. law Case Western Res. U., 1962-64; lectr. products liability U. Wirtschaft at Schloss Gracht, Erfstadt-Liblar, Germany, 1990-91, Bar Assn. City of Hamburg, Germany, 1990; mem. faculty Nat. Inst. for Trial Advocacy, 1992. Mem. joint com. Cleve. Acad. Medicine-Greater Cleve. Bar Assn.; trustee Cleve. Zool. Soc., mem. exec. com., 1984-89, v.p., 1987-89; trustee Andrew Sch., 1984-96; Meridia Huron Hosp., Cleve., 1978-96, Cleve. Sch. for Blind, 1987-88, Cerebral Palsy Assn., 1984-87; trustee Intracoastal Health Sys., Palm Beach, Fla., 1992-2000. With AC, USNR, 1950-58. Mem. ABA (com. on law and medicine, profl. responsibility com. 1977-90), FBA, ATLA, Fedn. Ins. and Corp. Counsel, Internat. Bar Assn., Ohio Bar Assn. (coun. dels. 1987-90, internat. law com. 1990-91), Pa. Bar Assn., Cleve. Bar Assn. (chmn. med.-legal com. 1978-79, prof. liability com. 1977-90), Transp. Lawyers Assn., Cleve. Assn. Civil Trial Attys., Am. Soc. Hosp. Attys., Soc. Ohio Hosp. Attys., Ohio Assn. Civil Trial Attys., Am. Judicature Soc., Def. Rsch. Inst., Maritime Law Assn. U.S., Am. Coll. Law and Medicine, 8th Jud. Bar Assn. (life Ohio dist.), Internat. Ins. Law Soc., Palm Beach County Bar Assn., Cleve.-Marshall Law Alumni Assn. (hon. trustee 1980-), Oil Painters Am., Soc. Four Arts, Internat. Soc. Marine Painters (profl. mem., v.p.), Mayfield Country Club (pres. 1980-82), Union Club, Hermit Club (pres. 1973-75), Lost Tree Club (bd. govs. 1991-94), Everglades Club (Fla.), Kirtland Country Club (Cleve.), Rolling Rock Club (Pa.), Cleve. Marshall Law Alumni Assn. (hon. trustee 1980—), Salmagundi Club (N.Y.C.), Case Res. Athletic Club (life). Federal civil litigation, State civil litigation, Personal injury. E-mail: monhegan1@aol.com

RENBAUM, BARRY JEFFREY, lawyer; b. Balt., Feb. 26, 1948; s. David and Leah (Cohen) R.; m. Carol Barbash, June 22, 1980. BS magna cum laude, Rider U., 1970; postgrad., NYU, 1973; JD, Georgetown U., 1973. Bar: Md. 1973, U.S. Dist. Ct. (Md.), 1998. Jud. clk. to Hon. John C. Eldridge, Md. Ct. Appeals, 1974-75; asst. pub. defender State of Md., 1975-79; exec. v.p., gen. counsel Custom Savs. Bank, Tmple Fin. Co., Balt., 1980-91; pvt. practice Glyndon, Md., 1991—. Mem. ATLA, Md. Bar Assn., Alpha Epsilon Zeta. Civil rights, Education and schools, Non-profit and tax-exempt organizations. Office: Brydonwood Glyndon MD 21071-0326 E-mail: brydonwoods@earthlink.com

RENDELL, MARJORIE O. federal judge; m. Edward G. Rendell. BA, U. Pa., 1969; postgrad., Georgetown U., 1970-71; JD, Villanova U., 1973; LLD (hon.), Phila. Coll. Textile and Sci., 1992. Ptnr. Duane, Morris & Heckscher, Phila., 1972-93; judge U.S. Dist. Ct. (ea. dist.) Pa., 1994-97, U.S. Ct. Appeals (3d cir.), Phila., 1997—. Asst. to dir. annual giving Dept. Devel., U. Pa., 1973-78; mem. adv. bd. Chestnut Hill Nat. Bank/East Falls Adv. Bd.; mem. alternative dispute resolution com. mediation divsn. Ea. Dist. Pa. Bankruptcy Conf. Active Acad. Vocal Arts, Market St. East Improvement Assn., Pa.'s Campaign for Choice, Phila. Friends Outward Bound; vice chair Ave. of Arts, Inc.; vice chair bd. trustees Vis. Nurse Assn. Greater Phila. Mem. ABA, Am. Bankruptcy Inst., Pa. Bar Assn., Phila. Bar Assn. (bd. dirs. young lawyers sect. 1973-78), Phila. Bar Found. (bd. dirs.), Forum Exec. Women, Internat. Women's Forum, Phi Beta Kappa. Office: US Courthouse 601 Market St Rm 21613 Philadelphia PA 19106-1715*

RENFREW, CHARLES BYRON, lawyer; b. Detroit, Oct. 31, 1928; s. Charles Warren and Louise (McGuire) R.; m. Susan Wheelock, June 28, 1952 (div. June 1984); children: Taylor Allison Ingham, Charles Robin, Todd Wheelock, James Bartlett; m. Barbara Jones Orser, Oct. 6, 1984; 5 stepchildren. AB, Princeton U., 1952; JD, U. Mich., 1956. Bar: Calif. 1956. Assoc. Pillsbury, Madison & Sutro, San Francisco, 1956-65, ptnr., 1965-72, 81-82; U.S. dist. judge No. Dist. Calif., 1972-80; dep. atty. gen. U.S. Washington, 1980-81; instr. U. Calif. Boalt Hall Sch. Law, 1977-80; v.p. law Chevron Corp. (formerly Standard Oil Co. Calif.), San Francisco, 1983-93, also bd. dirs.; ptnr. LeBoeuf, Lamb, Greene & McRae, 1994-97; pvt. practice, 1998—. Mem. exec. com. 9th Cir. Jud. Conf., 1976-78, congl. liaison com. 9th Cir. Jud. Council, 1976-79, spl. com. to propose standards for admission to practice in fed. cts. U.S. Jud. Conf., 1976-79; chmn. spl. com. to study problems of discovery Fed. Jud. Ctr., 1978-79; mem. council on role of cts. U.S. Dept. Justice, 1978-83; mem. jud. panel Ctr. for Pub. Resources, 1981—; head U.S. del. to 6th UN Congress on Prevention of Crime and Treatment of Offenders, 1980; co-chmn. San Francisco Lawyers Com. for Urban Affairs, 1971-72, mem., 1983—; bd. dirs. Internat. Hospitality Ctr., 1961-74, pres., 1967-70; mem. adv. bd. Internat. Comparative Law Ctr., Southwestern Legal Found., 1983-93; trustee World Affairs Council No. Calif., 1984-87, 94—, Nat. Jud. Coll., 1985-91, Grace Cathedral, 1986-89. Contbr. articles to profl. jours. Bd. fellow Claremont U., 1986-94; bd. dirs. San Francisco Symphony Found., 1964-80, pres., 1971-72; bd. dirs. Coun. Civic Unity, 1962-73, pres., 1971-72; bd. dirs. Opportunity Through Ownership, 1969-72, Marin County Day Sch., 1972-74, No. Calif. Svc. League, 1975-76, Am. Petroleum Inst., 1984—, Nat. Crime Prevention Coun., 1982—; alumni trustee Princeton U., 1976-80; mem. vis. com. u. chgo. Law Sch., 1977-79, u.Mich. Law Sch., 1977-81; bd. visitors J. Reuben Clark Law Sch., Brigham Young U., 1981-83, Stanford Law Sch., 1983-86; trustee Town Sch. for Boys, 1972-80,pres. 1975-80; gov. San Fransciso Symphony Assn., 1974—; mem. nat. adv. bd. Ctr. for Nat. Policy, 1982—; bd. dirs. Nat. Coun. Crime and Deliquency, 1981-82,NAACP Legal Def. and Edn. Fund, 1982—; parish chancellor St. Luke's Episcopal Ch., 1968-71, sr. warden, 1974-76; mem. exec. coun. San Francisco Deanery, 1969-70; mem. diocesan coun. Episcopal Diocese of Calif., 1970; chmn. Diocesan Conv., 1977, 78, 79. Served with USN, 1946-48, 1st lt. U.S. Army, 1952-53. Fellow Am. Bar Found.; mem. ABA (coun. mem. sect. antitrust law 19778-82, vice c hmn. sect. antitrust law 1982-83), San Francisco Bar Assn. (past bd. dirs.), Assn. Gen. Counsel, State Bar Calif., Am. Judicature Soc., Am. Coll. Trial Lawyers (pres. 1995-96), Am. Law Inst., Coun. Fgn. Rels., Order of Coif, Phi Beta Kappa, Phi Delta Phi. Federal civil litigation, General corporate. Office: 710 Sansome St San Francisco CA 94111-1704

RENFRO, WILLIAM LEONARD, futurist, lawyer, inventor, entrepreneur; b. West Palm Beach, Fla., Sept. 9, 1945; s. Ernest Leonard and Oine Warren (McAdams) R. BS in Physics, Rensselaer Poly. Inst., 1967, MS in Nuclear Engring., 1972; postgrad., Yale U., 1967-68; JD, U. Conn., 1972. Bar: Conn. 1973. Physicist Compustion Engring., Windsor Locks, Conn., 1968-69; pvt. practice law, Hartford, 1973-74; sr. rsch. assoc. The Futures Group, Glastonbury, 1973-76; analyst futures rsch. Congl. Rsch. Svc., U.S. Congress, Washington, 1976-80; pres. Policy Analysis Co., Inc., 1980—. Vis. fellow Ark. Inst.; guest lectr. Georgetown U., Brookings Inst., Nat. War Coll.; adj. prof. George Washington U., Indsl. Coll. Armed Forces Nat. Def. U.; mem. nat. foresight network U.S. Congress. Author: (with others) The Futures Research Handbook, 1997, Anticipatory Democracy, 1978, The Public Affairs Handbook, 1983, The Legislative Role of Corporations, 1982, Applying Methods and Techniques of Futures Research, 1983, Future Research and the Straegic Planning Process, 1985, Non-Extrapolative Forecasting in Business, 1988, Futures Research Methodology: The UN Millennium Project, 1999; author: Issue Management in Stratetic Planning, 1993, Vision-2020, 1999; editor Futures Rsch. Quar. World Futures Soc.; issues mgmt. editor the Futurist, 1982—, Tech.

Analysis and Strategic Mgmt. Mem. long range planning com. United Way; trustee World Tech. Found. Mem. AAAS, ABA, Pub. Rels. Soc. Am., Issues Mgmt. Assn. (bd. dirs. 1981—, v.p. 1986-88, pres. 1988-96), World Futures Soc., Internat. Pub. Rels. Assn., Conn. Bar Assn., Hartford County Bar Assn., English Speaking Union (trustee), Clan Hamilton Soc., St. Andrews Soc. Episcopalian.

RENNER, CURTIS SHOTWELL, lawyer; b. Paris, France, June 24, 1958; Grad., Phillips Acad., Andover, Mass., 1981; BA, Wesleyan U., Middletown, Conn., 1981; JD cum laude, Harvard U., 1988. Bar: Mass. 1988, D.C. 1995. Assoc. Crowell & Moring, Washington, 1988-95; founding ptnr. Watson & Renner, 1995—. Contbr. articles to profl. jours. Mem. ABA, ATLA, D.C. Bar Assn., Phi Beta Kappa. General civil litigation, Product liability, Toxic tort. Office: Watson & Renner 2000 M St NW Ste 330 Washington DC 20036-3366

RENNER, RICHARD RANDOLPH, lawyer; b. Ann Arbor, Mich., July 24, 1958; s. Daniel S. and Carol R.; m. Laura R. Yeomans, Aug. 21, 1982. SB, MIT, 1978; JD, NYU, 1981. Bar: Ohio 1981, U.S. Dist. Ct. (no. and so. dists.) Ohio 1981, U.S. Supreme Ct. 1987, U.S. Ct. Appeals (5th and 6th cirs.) 1989. Staff atty. S.E. Ohio Legal Svcs., Zanesville, 1981-82, New Philadelphia, Ohio, 1987-95; ptnr. Tate & Renner, Dover, 1995—. Pres. Hispanic Ministries of Tuscarawas County, 1997—2001. Mem. UAW, AFL-CIO, ACLU, Nat. Orgn. Legal Svcs. Workers (regional v.p. 1990-95), Nat. Lawyers Guild, Tuscarawas County Bar Assn. (treas. 1997), Religious Soc. Friends. Home: 131 Park Ave NW New Philadelphia OH 44663-1817 Office: Tate & Renner 505 N Wooster PO Box 8 Dover OH 44622-0008 E-mail: rrenner@igc.org

RENNER, ROBERT GEORGE, federal judge; b. Nevis, Minn., Apr. 2, 1923; s. Henry J. and Beatrice M. (Fuller) R.; m. Catherine L. Clark, Nov. 12, 1949; children: Robert, Anne, Richard, David. BA, St. John's U., Collegeville, Minn., 1947; JD, Georgetown U., 1949. Bar: Minn. 1949. Pvt. practice, Walker, 1949-69; U.S. atty. Dist. of Minn., 1969-77, U.S. magistrate, 1977-80, U.S. dist. judge, 1980-92, assumed sr. status, 1992—. Mem. Minn. Ho. of Reps., 1957-69. Served with AUS, 1943-46. Mem. FBA. Roman Catholic. Office: US Dist Ct 748 US Courthouse 316 Robert St N Saint Paul MN 55101-1495

RENO, JANET, former attorney general; b. Miami, Fla., July 21, 1938; d. Henry and Jane (Wood) R. A.B. in Chemistry, Cornell U., 1960; LL.B., Harvard U., 1963. Bar: Fla. 1963. Assoc. Brigham & Brigham, 1963-67; ptnr. Lewis & Reno, 1967-71; staff dir. judiciary com. Fla. Ho. of Reps., Tallahassee, 1971-72; cons. Fla. Senate Criminal Justice Com. for Revision Fla.'s Criminal Code, spring 1973; adminstrv. asst. state atty. 11th Jud. Circuit Fla., Miami, 1973-76, state atty., 1978-93; ptnr. Steel Hector and Davis, 1976-78; U.S. atty. gen. Dept. Justice, Washington, 1993-2001. Mem. jud. nominating commn. 11th Jud. Circuit Fla., 1976-78; chmn. Fla. Gov.'s Council for Prosecution Organized Crime, 1979-80. Recipient Women First award YWCA, 1993. National Women's Hall of Fame, 2000. Mem. ABA (Inst. Jud. Adminstrn. Juvenile Justice Standards Commn. 1973-76), Am. Law Inst., Am. Judicature Soc. (Herbert Harley award 1981), Dade County Bar Assn., Fla. Pros. Atty.'s Assn. (pres. 1984-86). Democrat*

RENO, OTTIE WAYNE, former judge; b. Pike County, Ohio, Apr. 7, 1929; s. Eli Enos and Arbannah Belle (Jones) R.; m. Janet Gay McCann, May 22, 1947; children: Ottie Wayne II, Jennifer Lynn, Lorna Victoria. A in Bus. Adminstrn., Franklin U., 1949; LLB, Franklin Law Sch., 1953; JD, Capital U., 1966; grad. Coll. Juvenile Justice, U. Nev., 1973. Bar: Ohio 1953. Practiced in Pike County; recorder Pike County, 1957-73, common pleas judge probate and juvenile divsn., 1973-79. Author: Story of Horseshoes, 1963, Pitching Championship Horseshoes, 1971, 2d rev. edit., 1975, The American Directory of Horseshoe Pitching, 1983, Ohio vs. Smith, Murder, 1990, Reno and Apsaalooka Survive Custer, 1996. Mem. Camp Creek precinct Dem. Ctrl. Com., 1956-72, 83-90, 99—; sec. Pike County Ctrl. Com., 1960-70, 83-87; chmn. Pike County Dem. Exec. Com., 1971-72, 88-90, 97—; del. Dem. Nat. Conv., 1972, 96; mem. Ohio Dem. Ctrl. Com., 1969-70; Dem. candidate 6th Ohio dist. U.S. Ho. of Reps., 1966, 88th Dist. Ohio Ho. of Reps., 1992; pres. Scioto Valley Local Sch. Dist., 1962-66; mem. adv. bd. Ohio Youth Svcs., 1972-74; mem. internat. sports exch., U.S. and Republic South Africa, 1972, 80, 82. Recipient Disting. Svc. award Ohio Youth Commn., 1974, 6 Outstanding Jud. Svc. awards Ohio Supreme Ct.; 16 times Ala. horseshoe pitching champion; named to Nat. Horseshoe Pitchers Hall of Fame, 1978. Mem. Ohio Bar Assn., Pike County Bar Assn. (pres. 1964), Nat. Coun. Juvenile Ct. Judges, Am. Legion. Mem. Ch. of Christ in Christian Union. Home: 148 Reno Rd Lucasville OH 45648-9580

RENWICK, EDWARD S. lawyer; b. L.A., May 10, 1934; AB, Stanford U., 1956, LLB, 1958. Bar: Calif. 1959, U.S. Dist. Ct. (cen. dist.) Calif. 1959, U.S. Ct. Appeals (9th cir.) 1963, U.S. Dist. Ct. (so. dist.) Calif. 1973, U.S. Dist. Ct. (no. dist.) Calif. 1977, U.S. Dist. Ct. (ea. dist.) Calif. 1981, U.S. Supreme Ct. 1985. Ptnr. Hanna and Morton LLP, L.A. Mem., bd. vis. Stanford Law Sch., 1967-69; mem. environ. and natural resources adv. bd. Stanford Law Sch. Bd. dirs. Calif. Supreme Ct. Hist. Soc. Fellow Am. Coll. Trial Lawyers, Am. Bar Found.; mem. ABA (mem. sect. on litigation, antitrust law, bus. law, chmn. sect. of nat. resources, energy and environ. law 1987-88, mem. at large coord. group energy law 1989-92, sect. rep. coord. group energy law 1995-97, Calif. del. legal com., interstate oil compact com.), Calif. Arboretum Assn. (trustee 1986-92), L.A. County Bar Assn. (chmn. natural resources law sect. 1974-75), The State Bar of Calif., Chancery Club (pres. 1992-93), Phi Delta Phi. Office: Hanna and Morton LLP 444 S Flower St Ste 2050 Los Angeles CA 90071-2922 E-mail: erenwick@hanmor.com

REPPER, GEORGE ROBERT, lawyer; b. Topeka, Dec. 22, 1954; s. George Vincent Jr. and Maria Magdalena (Bullert) R.; m. Helen Linda Zeichner, Aug. 23, 1981; children: Brian Lawrence, Kevin Michael, Michelle Suzanne. BS, SUNY, Albany, 1977; JD, Albany Law Sch., 1981. Bar: N.Y. 1982, D.C. 1982, U.S. Patent and Trademark Office 1984, U.S. Ct. Appeals (fed. cir.) 1989. V.p. Rothwell, Figg, Ernst & Manbeck, Washington, also bd. dirs. Contbr. articles to profl. jours. including Patent World. Mem. ABA (patents, trademarks and copyrights sect.), D.C. Bar Assn. (patents, trademarks and copyrights sect.), Am. Intellectual Property Law Assn., Internat. Intellectual Property Assn., Internat. Fedn. Indsl. Property Attys., Intellectual Property Owners, Internat. Trademark Assn. Republican. Mergers and acquisitions, Patent, Trademark and copyright. Office: Rothwell Figg Ernst & Manbeck 555 13th St NW Ste 701E Washington DC 20004-1109

REPPY, WILLIAM ARNEILL, JR. law educator; b. Oxnard, Calif., Mar. 14, 1941; s. William Arneill and Margot Louise Reppy; m. Susan Westerberg, Sept. 30, 1967 (div. 1973); m. Juliann Tenney, Nov. 28, 1975. B.A. with great distinction, Stanford U., 1963, J.D. with great distinction, 1966. Bar: Calif. 1966, N.C. 1971, U.S. Supreme Ct. 1971. Law clk. to Justice William Douglas, U.S. Supreme Ct., Washington, 1967-68; assoc. Tuttle & Taylor, Los Angeles, 1968-71; prof. law Duke U., Durham, N.C. 1971— ; cons. Calif. Law Revision Com., Palo Alto, 1979-83; mem. Condominium Statutes Commn., Raleigh, N.C., 1980— . Author: Community Property in California, 1980; Community Property-Gilbert Law Summaries, 1983; co-author: Community Property in U.S., 2d edit., 1982, Texas Matrimonial Property Law, 1983. Mem. editorial bd. Community Property Jour., 1973— . Recipient Nathan Abbot award Stanford U., 1966. Mem. Am. Law Inst., Order of Coif, Phi Beta Kappa. Republican. Office: Duke Univ Sch Law Durham NC 27706

RESKE, STEVEN DAVID, lawyer, writer; b. Mpls., May 31, 1962; s. Albert Edgar Reske and Florence Mae Altland. BA with distinction, St. Olaf Coll., Northfield, Minn., 1985; JD cum laude, Boston U., 1988. Bar: Ill. 1988, Minn. 1989, D.C. 1998, U.S. Dist. Ct. Minn. 1991, U.S. Ct. Appeals (5th cir.) 1989, (7th and 8th cir.) 1992, (D.C. circuit) 1998, U.S. Supreme Ct. 1993. Intern U.S. Senator Durenberger, Washington, 1981-82, Citizens for Ednl. Freedom, Washington, 1981-82, Abbott-Northwestern Hosp., Mpls., 1984, U.S. Dist. Ct. Judge Magnuson, St. Paul, 1986; summer assoc. Faegre & Benson, Mpls., 1987; assoc. Sidley & Austin, Chgo., 1988; law clk. to Hon. Judge Politz U.S. Ct. Appeals 5th cir., Shreveport, La., 1988-89; pvt. practice, 1989—; writer, 1989—. Contbr. CD Rev., 1993-95, JAZZIZ, 1996—, Skyway News, 1997—, City Pages, 2000—; contbr. articles to profl. jours.; mem. Am. Jour. Law and Medicine, 1986-87, editor, 1987-88; legal editor-at-large Law and Politics, 1998—; columnist Twin Cities Revue, 1998—. Recipient Minn. Super Lawyer award, 1998, Am. Jurisprudence award, 1988; Edward F. Hennessey scholar, 1988, G. Joseph Tauro scholar, 1986. Mem. ABA (antitrust divsn.), Minn. State Bar Assn., Hennepin County Bar Assn., Am. Econ. Assn., Am. Philos. Assn. Antitrust, Federal civil litigation, Constitutional. Office: 3422 Douglas Dr N Crystal MN 55422-2414 E-mail: stevenresk@aol.com

RESNICK, ALICE ROBIE, state supreme court justice; b. Erie, Pa., Aug. 21, 1939; d. Adam Joseph and Alice Suzanne (Spizarny) Robie; m. Melvin L. Resnick, Mar. 20, 1970 PhB, Siena Heights Coll., 1961; JD, U. Detroit, 1964. Bar: Ohio 1964, Mich. 1965, U.S. Supreme Ct. 1970. Asst. county prosecutor Lucas County Prosecutor's Office, Toledo, 1964-75, trial atty., 1965-75; judge Toledo Mcpl. Ct., 1976-83, 6th Dist. Ct. Appeals, State of Ohio, Toledo, 1983-88; instr. U. Toledo, 1968-69; justice Ohio Supreme Ct., 1989—. Co-chairperson Ohio State Gender Fairness Task Force. Trustee Siena Heights Coll., Adrian, Mich., 1982— ; organizer Crime Stopper Inc., Toledo, 1981— ; mem. Mayor's Drug Coun.; bd. dirs. Guest House Inc. Mem. ABA, Toledo Bar Assn., Lucas County Bar Assn., Nat. Assn. Women Judges, Am. Judicature Soc., Toledo Women's Bar Assn., Ohio State Women's Bar Assn. (organizer), Toledo Mus. Art, Internat. Inst. Toledo. Roman Catholic Home: 2407 Edgehill Rd Toledo OH 43615-2321 Office: Supreme Ct Office 30 E Broad St Fl 3 Columbus OH 43266-0001*

RESNICK, JEFFREY LANCE, federal magistrate judge; b. Bklyn., Mar. 5, 1943; s. Bernard and Selma (Monheit) R.; m. Margery O'Connor, May 27, 1990. BA, U. Conn., 1964; LLB, U. Conn., West Hartford, 1967. Bar: Conn. 1967, N.Y. 1968, U.S. V.I. 1968, D.C. 1979, U.S. Ct. Appeals (3d cir.) 1979. Assoc. Office of J.D. Marsh, Christiansted, St. Croix, V.I., 1967-69; asst. atty. gen. Dept. Law, 1969-73; ptnr. James & Resnick, 1973-89; magistrate judge U.S. Dist. Ct. V.I., 1989—. Active V.I. Bridge Team, 1971—. Jewish. Avocations: writing poetry and palindromes. Office: US District Court 3013 East Golden Rock Christiansted VI 00820-4256

RESNICK, STEPHANIE, lawyer; b. N.Y.C., Nov. 12, 1959; d. Diane Gross. AB, Kenyon Coll., 1981; JD, Villanova U., 1984. Bar: Pa. 1984, N.J. 1984, U.S. Dist Ct. (ea. dist.) Pa. 1984, U.S. Dist Ct. N.J. 1984, N.Y. 1990, U.S. Ct. Appeals (3d cir.) 1993, U.S. Dist. Ct. (so. dist.) N.Y. 1996, U.S. Dist. Ct. (ea. dist.) N.Y. 2001, U.S. Supreme Ct. 1998. Assoc. Cozen and O'Connor, Phila., 1984-87, Fox, Rothschild, O'Brien & Frankel, Phila., 1987-92, ptnr., 1992—. Mem. Vols. for Indigent Program, Phila., 1987-92. Mem. ABA, Pa. Bar Assn. (disciplinary bd. and study com. 1989-91, prof. liability com. 1991-92, commr. on Women in the Profession, 1997-99), Phila. Bar Assn. (profl. responsibility com. 1992-2000, profl. guidance com. 1992-96, investigative divsn. Commn. on Jud. Selection and Retention 1988-94, women's rights com. 1993—, co-chair 1995-96, Women in the Profession com. 1993—, Comm. on Jud. Selection and Retention 1995-2001, vice-chair 1996, chair 1997, fed. cts. com. 2000—), N.J. Bar Assn., N.Y. Bar Assn., Womens Way (bd. dirs., co-chair campaign 1998-2000vice-chair 2000-01). Federal civil litigation, General civil litigation, Insurance. Home: 233 S 6th St Apt 2306 Philadelphia PA 19106-3756 Office: Fox Rothschild O'Brien & Frankel 2000 Market St Ste 10 Philadelphia PA 19103-3231

RESNICOW, NORMAN JAKOB, lawyer; b. N.Y.C., July 23, 1947; s. Herbert and Melly (Engelberg) R.; m. Barbara Jane Roses, June 14, 1970; children: Daniel Ilan, Joel Ethan. BA summa cum laude, Yale U., 1969, JD, 1972. Bar: N.Y. 1973, U.S. Dist. Ct. (so. and ea. dists.) N.Y. 1973. Assoc. Baker & McKenzie, N.Y.C., 1972-79, ptnr., 1979-98, Piper, Marbury Rudnick & Wolff, N.Y.C., 1998-2000, Fox Horan & Camerini, N.Y.C., 2000—. Term mem. Council Fgn. Relations, N.Y.C., 1976-81; exec. com., v.p., treas., bd. dirs. Hebrew Immigrant Aid Soc., N.Y.C., 1981—; mem. nat. young leadership cabinet United Jewish Appeal, N.Y.C., 1978-83. Recipient Young Leadership award United Jewish Appeal-Fedn. Jewish Philanthrophies, 1978. Mem. ABA (corp. bus. and banking law, internat. law sects.), Assn. of Bar of City of N.Y. (internat. trade com. 1987-89, com. nuclear law and tech. 1992-98), N.Y. State Bar Assn. (internat. law com. 1985-87, internat. employement law com. 1997—), Phi Beta Kappa. Democrat. Avocation: internat. polit. relations. Contracts commercial, Private international, Mergers and acquisitions. Home: 4701 Iselin Ave Bronx NY 10471-3323 Office: Fox Horan & Camerini LLP 825 Third Ave New York NY 10022 E-mail: njresnicow@foxlex.com

RESOR, STANLEY ROGERS, lawyer; b. N.Y.C., Dec. 5, 1917; s. Stanley Burnet and Helen (Lansdowne) R.; m. Jane Lawler Pillsbury, Apr. 4, 1942 (dec.); children: Stanley R., Charles P., John L., Edmund L., William B., Thomas S., James P.; m. Louise Mead Walker, May 1, 1999. BA, Yale U., 1939, LLB, 1946. Bar: N.Y. 1947. Assoc., then ptnr. firm Debevoise & Plimpton, N.Y.C., 1946-65, 71-73, 79-87, of counsel, 1988-90; undersec. Dept. Army, 1965, sec., 1965-71, ambassador negotiations for Mut. and Balanced Force Reductions in Central Europe, 1973-78; undersec. for policy Dept. Def., 1978-79. Fellow Yale Corp., 1979-86. Served to maj. AUS, 1942-45. Decorated Silver Star, Bronze Star, Purple Heart; recipient George C. Marshall award Assn. U.S. Army, 1974, Sylvanus Thayer award Assn. Graduates of U.S. Mil. Acad., 1984. Mem. ABA, Assn. of Bar of City of N.Y. (chmn. com. internat. arms control and security affairs 1983-86), Atlantic Coun. (bd. dirs.), Arms Control Assn. (chmn. bd.), UN Assn. U.S.A. (nat. coun.), Coun. Fgn. Rels., Lawyers Alliance for World Security (bd. dirs.), Internat. Inst. Strategic Studies. Republican. Episcopalian. Home: 809 Weed St New Canaan CT 06840-4023 Office: # 724 2801 New Mexico Ave NW Apt 724 Washington DC 20007-3934 Home Fax: (203) 966-3965; Office Fax: (202) 337-2306

RESSLER, PARKE E(DWARD), lawyer, accountant; b. Lancaster, Pa., Aug. 21, 1916; s. Parke H. and Sadie (Weiser) R.; m. Margaret B. Tucker, June 3, 1944; children: Nancy Parke, Margaret Anne. BS, U. Pa., 1947; BBA, Baylor U., 1947, LLB, 1952, JD, 1969; MBA, U. Houston, 1949. Bar: Tex. 1952. Agt. Internal Revenue Svc., 1947-50; part time instr. Baylor U., 1950-65; law practice Waco, 1952—; assoc. firm Edwin P. Horner. Mem. AICPA, ABA, Tex. Soc. CPA, Tex. Bar Assn., McLennan County Bar Assn., Am. Assn. Atty.-CPAs, Ridgewood Country Club, Hedonia Club, Ridgewood Yacht Club, Baylor Bear Club, Rotary, Phi Alpha Delta, Delta Sigma Pi. Mem. Christian Ch. Estate planning, Corporate taxation, Personal income taxation. Home and Office: 2209 Arroyo Rd Waco TX 76710-1626

RETTBERG, CHARLES CLAYLAND, JR. lawyer; b. Balt., Oct. 3, 1930; s. Charles Clayland and Drucilla Bell (Brown) R.; m. Elizabeth Margaret Koessler, June 9, 1956; children— Susan Victoria, Valerie Ann, Charles. A.B., U. Md., 1952, LL.B., 1955. Bar: Md. 1955, Ohio 1969, U.S. Supreme Ct. 1975. Atty. B&O R.R., Balt., 1955-58, asst. gen. atty., 1958-64, asst. gen. solicitor, 1964-68; gen. atty. Chessie System, Cleve., 1968-72, gen. comml. counsel, 1972-79, gen. solicitor, 1980-86; gen. counsel CSX Transp., Balt., 1986—; pres. Rail Transp. Inst., Washington, 1973. Editor-in-chief Md. Law Rev., 1955. Mem. ABA, ICC Practitioners Assn., Eastern R.R. Soc. (chmn. commerce law com. 1978-82), Order of Coif, Delta Theta Phi, Pi Sigma Alpha. Republican. Lutheran. Antitrust, Public utilities. Office: CSX Transp 100 N Charles St Baltimore MD 21201-3805

REUBEN, LAWRENCE MARK, lawyer; b. Akron, Ohio, Apr. 5, 1948; s. Albert G. and Sara I. (Rifkin) R. Student, London Sch. Econs., 1969; BS, Ind. U., 1970; JD, Ind. U., Indpls., 1973. Bar: Ind. 1973, U.S. Dist. Ct. (so. dist.) Ind. 1973, U.S. Dist. Ct. (no. dist.) Ind. 1975, U.S. Ct. Appeals (7th cir.) 1975, U.S. Supreme Ct. 1976, U.S. Ct. Appeals (9th cir.) 1978, U.S. Ct. Appeals (D.C. cir.) 1994, U.S. Ct. Appeals (fed. cir.) 1999. Ptnr. Atlas, Hyatt & Reuben, Indpls., 1976-87, Atlas & Reuben, Indpls., 1987-90; chief counsel Ind. Dept. Ins., 1990-91; gen. counsel Ind. Dept. Transp., 1991-93; chief deputy Ind. Atty. Gen., Indpls., 1993-94; gen. counsel State Lottery Commn. Ind., 1994-97; pvt. practice, 1997—. V.p. Ind. Civil Liberties Union, 1975-84; sec., bd. dirs. Indpls. Humane Soc., 1974-85; fellow Indpls. C. of C.-Lacey Leadership Program, 1982; sec., v.p., bd. dirs. Julian Ctr., Inc., 1983-89; mem. ch.-state commn. Nat. Jewish Community Relations Adv. Council, N.Y.C., 1982-89; bd. dirs. Indpls. Consumer Credit Counseling Bur., 1983-89; pres. Bur. Jewish Edn., 1984-86; parliamentarian Ind. State Dem. Party, 1985-86; mem. Indpls. Police Community Relations Rev. Com., 1983. Recipient Robert Risk award Ind. Civil Liberties Union, 1981, David M. Cook Meml. award Indpls. Jewish Community Rels. Coun., 1982; L.L. Goodman Leadership award, Jewish Fed. Indpls., 1989. Mem. ABA, Fed. Bar Assn., Ind. Bar Assn., Indpls. Bar Assn. Democrat. Jewish. E-mial. Federal civil litigation, General practice, Labor. Office: Jefferson Plaza 1 Virginia Ave Ste 600 Indianapolis IN 46204-3671 E-mail: Lmreubenlaw@yahoo.com

REUFELS, MARTIN J. lawyer; b. Jan. 17, 1968; m. Delia Gonzalez. Dr.iur., U. Heidelberg, Germany. Rechtsanwalt Heuking Kuhn Luer Wojtek, Cologne, Germany, 1996—. Author: Europaische Subventionkontrolle, 1997. Private international, Labor, Product liability. Office: Heuking Kuhn Luer Wojtek Magnusstr 13 D-50672 Koln Germany Fax: 492-221-20521. E-mail: m.reufels@heuking.de

REUM, JAMES MICHAEL, lawyer; b. Oak Park, Ill., Nov. 1, 1946; s. Walter John and Lucy (Bellegay) R. BA cum laude, Harvard U., 1968, JD cum laude, 1972. Bar: N.Y. 1973, D.C. 1974, U.S. Dist. Ct. (so. dist.) N.Y. 1974, Ill. 1979, U.S. Dist. Ct. (no. dist.) Ill. 1982. Assoc. Davis Polk & Wardwell, N.Y.C., 1973-78; assoc. Minority Counsel Com. on Judiciary U.S. Ho. of Reps., Washington, 1974; ptnr. Hopkins & Sutter, Chgo., 1979-93, Winston & Strawn, Chgo., 1994—. Midwest advance rep. Nat. Reagan Bush Com., 1980; nominee commr. Securities and Exchange Comm., Pres. Bush, 1992; mem. G.W. Bush fin. com, 2000. Served to SP4 USAR, 1969-75. Recipient Harvard U. Honorary Nat. Scholarship, 1964-72. Mem. Monte Carlo Country Club (Monaco), Univ. Club (N.Y.C.). Republican. Finance, Mergers and acquisitions, Securities. Home: 12 E Scott St Chicago IL 60610-2320 Office: Winston & Strawn 35 W Wacker Dr Ste 4200 Chicago IL 60601-1695 E-mail: jreum@winston.com

REUTER, JAMES WILLIAM, lawyer; b. Bemidji, Minn., Sept. 30, 1948; s. John Renee and Monica (Dugas) R.; m. Patricia Carol Creelman, Mar. 30, 1968; children: Kristine, Suzanne, Natalee. BA, St. John's U., 1970; JD, William Mitchell Coll. Law, 1974. Bar: Minn. 1974, U.S. Dist. Minn. 1975, U.S. Ct. Appeals (8th cir.) 1985; cert. civil trial specialist. Editor West Pub. Co., St. Paul, 1970-73; assoc. Terpstra & Merrill, Mpls., 1974-77; ptnr. Barna, Guzy, Merrill, Hynes & Giancola, Ltd., 1977-89, Lindquist & Vennum, Mpls., 1989—. Recipient Cert. award Nat. Inst. Trial Advocacy, 1978. Mem. ABA (torts and ins. practice, and civil litigation sects.), ATLA, Minn. Bar Assn. (civil litigation and computer sects.), Hennepin County Bar Assn. (ins. com.), Anoka County Bar Assn. (pres. 1981-82). Avocations: skiing, golf, camping, reading. Federal civil litigation, State civil litigation, Insurance. Office: Lindquist & Vennum 4200 IDS Ctr 80 S 8th St Ste 4200 Minneapolis MN 55402-2274

REUTER, MICHAEL F.M. law educator; b. Simmern, Germany, Sept. 15, 1954; s. Heinrich and Gertrud R. Degree in law & econs., U. Bonn, Germany; PhD, U. Muenster, Germany; LLM, U. B.C. With Deutsche Bank, Dusseldorf, Germany, 1973-75, U. Muenster, Germany; prof. U. Cologne, Germany, 1991-98; lectr. U. Essen, Germany, 1996-2000. Chmn. Hattinger Studienkreis Wirtschaftsfragen, Germany. Mem. ABA, IFA, IBA. Office: Reiter & Ptnr Lotharstr 94 57057 Duisburg Germany Fax: 0049-203-370065. E-mail: reuterpart@aol.com

REUTIMAN, ROBERT WILLIAM, JR. lawyer; b. Mpls., June 4, 1944; s. Robert William and Elsbeth Bertha (Doering) R.; m. Virginia Lee Traxler, June 25, 1983; children: Robert James, Joseph Lee. BA magna cum laude, U. Minn., 1966, JD, 1969. Bar: Minn. 1969, U.S. Ct. Mil. Appeals 1969, U.S. Dist. Ct. Minn. 1973, U.S. Ct. Appeals (8th cir.) 1976, U.S. Tax. Ct. 1979. Mem. Armstrong, Phleger, Reutiman & Vinokour, Ltd., Wayzata, Minn., 1973-76; ptnr. Phleger & Reutiman, 1976-81; pvt. practice, 1981—. Chmn. Spring Pk. Planning Commn., 1978. Capt. U.S. Army, 1969-73. Decorated Army Commendation medal. Mem. ABA, Minn. Bar Assn., Hennepin County Bar Assn., Am. Arbitration Assn. (panel of arbitrators), Phi Beta Kappa. Lutheran. Avocations: fishing, rose growing. General civil litigation, Consumer commercial, Family and matrimonial. Home: 11610 3rd Ave N Plymouth MN 55441-5919 Office: 305 Rice St E Wayzata MN 55391-1615

REVELEY, WALTER TAYLOR, III, dean; b. Churchville, Va., Jan. 6, 1943; s. Walter Taylor and Marie (Eason) R.; m. Helen Bond, Dec. 18, 1971; children: Walter Taylor, George Everett Bond, Nelson Martin Eason, Helen Lanier. AB, Princeton U., 1965; JD, U. Va., 1968. Bar: Va. 1970, D.C. 1976. Asst. prof. law U. Ala., 1968-69; law clk. to Justice Brennan U.S. Supreme Ct., Washington, 1969-70; fellow Woodrow Wilson Internat. Ctr. for Scholars, 1972-73; internat. affairs fellow Coun. on Fgn. Rels., N.Y.C., 1972-73; assoc. Hunton & Williams, Richmond, Va., 1970-76, ptnr., 1976-98, mng. ptnr., 1982-91, cons., 1998—; dean William and Mary Law Sch., 1998—. Lectr. Coll. William and Mary Law Sch., 1978-80; cons. in field. Author: War Powers of the President and Congress: Who Holds the Arrows and Olive Branch, 1981; mem. editl. bd. Va. Law Rev., 1966-68; contbr. articles to profl. jours. Trustee Princeton U., 1986-90, 91-2001, Presbyn. Ch. (U.S.A.) Found., 1991-97, Va. Hist. Soc., 1991-96, Union Theol. Sem., 1992-2000, Andrew W. Mellon Found., 1994—, JSTOR, 1995—, Va. Mus. Fine Arts, 1995—, pres. 1996-99, St. Christopher's Sch., 1996—, Carnegie Endowment for Internat. Peace, 1999—; bd. dirs. Fan Dist. Assn., Richmond, Inc., 1976-80, pres., 1979-80; bd. dirs. Richmond Symphony, 1980-92, pres., 1988-90, pres. symphony coun., 1994-99; bd. dirs. Presbyn. Outlook Found. and Book Svc., 1985—, pres., 1992-95; bd. dirs. Va. Mus. Found., 1990-99; elder Grace Covenant Presbyn. Ch.; bd. dirs. New Covenant Trust Co., 1997-99. Mem. ABA, Va. Bar Assn., D.C. Bar Assn., Am. Bar Found., Va. Bar Found., Princeton

Assn. Va. (bd. dirs. 1981—, pres. 1983-85), Va. State Bar (edn. Lawyers sect. bd. govs. 1992—, chmn. 1992-95), Raven Soc., Phi Beta Kappa, Omicron Delta Kappa. Home: 2314 Monument Ave Richmond VA 23220-2604 Office: William and Mary Law Sch PO Box 8795 Williamsburg VA 23187-8795 E-mail: Taylor@wm.edu

REVELOS, CONSTANTINE NICHOLAS, law educator, writer; b. Middletown, Ohio, Mar. 1, 1938; s. Nicholas George and Efrosine (Aredas) R. AB, Bowdoin Coll., 1961; JD, Duke U., 1965; LLM, U. Calif., Berkeley, 1971. Bar: Ohio 1965, Mich. 1975, U.S. dist. Ct. (so. dist.) Ohio 1967, U.S. Ct. Appeals (6th cir.) 1967, U.S. Supreme Ct. 1968. With sales-svc. dept. Armco Steel Corp., Middletown, 1961-62; asst. prof. law No. Ky. State U., Cin., 1965-67, assoc. prof., dean, 1968-70; prof. law Detroit Coll. Law, East Lansing, Mich., 1971—. Dir. King scholars program, 1996—; arbiter N.Y. Stock Exchange, 1981—, Am. Arbitration Assn; Ctrl. & Eastern European Law Initiative specialist and lectr. Faculty of Law, Babes/Bolyai U., Cluj, Romania, 1994-95; lectr., faculty of law, Vytautus Magnus Univ. Kaunas, Lithuania, 2000; dir. Blues Beer Co., 1996—. Author: Michigan Business Organizations, 1985. Pres. Sts. Constantine & Helen Greek Orthodox Ch., Middletown, 1967-70; trustee, Annunciation Cathedral, Detroit, 1982-91. Mem. ABA, Ohio Bar Asns., Mich. Bar Assn., Am. Judicature Soc., Am. Arbitration Assn. (arbitrator), N.Y. Stock Exch. (arbitrator), Order Ahepa. Home: 1575 Mojave Ct Okemos MI 48864-3442 Office: Mich State U-DCL 353 Law College Bldg East Lansing MI 48824-1300 E-mail: revelos@law.msu.edu

REVERCOMB, HORACE AUSTIN, III, judge; b. Richmond, Va., Sept. 22, 1948; s. Horace Austin Jr. and Mary Virginia (Kelley) R.; m. Annie S. Anthony, July 10, 1976; children: Brian Austin, Suzanne Melanie. BA, Pembroke State U., 1971; JD, George Mason U., 1977. Bar: Va. 1978. Pvt. practice law, King George, Va., 1978-82; ptnr. Revercomb & Revercomb, 1982-90; judge Gen. Dist. Cts. of 15th Jud. Dist. Va., 1990-99, Cir. Cts. 15th Jud. Cir. Va., 1999—. Mem. Va. Bar Assn. Methodist. Avocation: music. Home: PO Box 216 King George VA 22485-0216

REVOILE, CHARLES PATRICK, lawyer; b. Jan. 15, 1934; s. Charles Patrick and Olga Lydia (Zecca) R.; m. Sally Cole Gates, Nov. 8, 1963. BA, U. Md., 1957, LLB, 1960. Bar: Md. 1962, U.S. Dist. Ct. Md. 1962, U.S. Supreme Ct. 1970, U.S. Ct. Claims 1976, U.S. Ct. Appeals (fed. cir.) 1982. Legis. counsel Nat. Canners Assn., Washington, 1960-64; asst. counsel Deco Electronics Inc., 1964-67; divsn. counsel Westinghouse Electric, Leesburg, Va., 1967-71; v.p., gen. counsel Stanwick Corp., Arlington, 1971-85; sr. v.p., gen. counsel, sec. CACI Internat. Inc., 1985-92, bd. dirs., 1992—, chmn. compensation com., 1995—, exec. com., 1999—. Mem. regional adv. coun. NASD, 1989-92; lectr., panelist, advisor. Active in Md. Ednl. Found., College Park, 1974-98; assoc. Nat. Symphony Orch., Washington, 1972-93, Smithsonian Instn., 1980-93, M Club Found., 1985-98; lawyer, lobbyist various non-profit orgns., Washington, 1984-98; mem. exec. com. ann. bus. campaign Gallaudet U., 1989-91; chmn. various coms. Kemper Open Championships, 1980-86; exec. com. 1995 USGA Sr. Open, 1997 USGA Open Championships; gen. counsel, mem. exec. com. 1995, 96, 97 Kemper Open Championship. Mem. Md. Bar Assn., Washington Corp. Counsels Assn., Am. Corp. Counsels Assn., Nat. Assn. Corp. Dirs., USGA, Mid. Atlantic Golf Assn. (exec. com. 1989-99, v.p., pres. 1998), Roger Howell Soc. U. Md. Sch. Law (charter), Congl. Country Club (com. chmn. 1966-92, bd. govs. 1987-93, Bethesda, Md.), Avondale Golf Club (Pymble, Australia), Ocean Forest Golf Club (Sea Island, Ga.), Sea Island Club (founder). General corporate, Government contracts and claims, Private international. Home: PO Box 31223 Sea Island GA 31561-1223

REW, LAWRENCE BOYD, lawyer; b. Eugene, Oreg., June 22, 1936; BA, Whitman Coll., 1958; JD, Willamette U., 1961. Bar: Oreg. 1961. Ptnr. Corey, Byler, Rew, Lorenzen & Hojem, LLP, Pendleton, Oreg., 1965—. Fellow Am. Bar Found.; mem. ABA, Oreg. State Bar Assn. (pres. 2000, Pub. Svc. award 1991, bd. bar examiners 1975-79, bd. govs. 1996-2000). Estate planning, Probate, General practice. Office: Corey Byler Rew Lorenzen & Hojem LLP PO Box 218 222 SE Dorion Ave Pendleton OR 97801-2553

REYNOLDS, CHRISTOPHER JOHN, lawyer; b. Mpls., Aug. 1, 1947; s. Jack Elton and Virginia Mary (Foley) R.; m. Margaret Ann Weekes, June 21, 1969; 1 child, Rowan Foley. BA, U. Santa Clara, 1969; JD, Am. U., 1972. Bar: D.C. 1973, Md. 1992, U.S. Dist. Ct. D.C. 1974, U.S. Ct. Appeals (D.C. cir.) 1974, U.S. Supreme Ct. 1977. Atty., advisor Rev. Bd. FCC, Washington, 1972-74; assoc. Dempsey & Koplovitz, 1974-78, ptnr., 1978-88, Peper, Martin, Jensen, Maichel & Hetlage, Washington, St. Louis, others, 1988-92; atty. Law Offices to Christopher J. Reynolds, Prince Frederick, Md., 1992-94; shareholder Reynolds and Manning, P.A., 1995—. Mem. Calvert County Econ. Devel. Commn., 1994—, chmn., 1997-2000; bd. dirs. Calvert County Christmas in April, 1995-97; mem. core svc. agy. adv. bd. Calvert County Health Dept., 1996—; mem. av. bd. Entrepreneur and Leadership Ctr., Coll. So. Md., 2000—. Mem. ABA, AHA (Calvert County bd. dirs. 1994-97), Fed. Comms. Bar Assn., Md. Bar Assn., D.C. Bar Assn., Calvert County Bar Assn. (bd. dirs. 1995-96, pres. 2001—), Calvert County C. of C. (pres. 2000—), So. Md. Econ. Devel. Assn. (bd. dirs. 1999—), Barristers Club, John Carroll Soc. (Washington). Democrat. Roman Catholic. Communications, General corporate, Real property. Office: Reynolds & Manning PA PO Box 2809 260 Merrimac Ct Prince Frederick MD 20678-4110 E-mail: creynolds@olg.com

REYNOLDS, DENNIS DEAN, lawyer, educator; b. Port Angeles, Wash., July 11, 1947; s. William M. and Mary M. (Jackese) R.; m. Tedi C. Johnson; children— Deron D., Todd C., Jennifer R. B.A. in Govt., St. Martin's Coll., Lacey, Wash., 1969; J.D., U. Wash., 1972. Bar: Wash. 1972, U.S. Dist. Ct. (ea. dist.) Wash. 1975, (we. dist.) Wash. 1977, U.S. Ct. Appeals (9th cir.) 1978, U.S. Supreme Ct. 1983. Asst. atty. gen. State of Wash., Olympia, 1972-84; ptnr. Pressentin & Reynolds, Seattle, 1984-87, Mitchell, Lang & Smith, Portland and Seattle, 1988—; prof. law St. Martin's Coll., 1972— ; speaker Am. Indian Law Conf., 1984, Mcpl. Lawyers Conf., 1983, Environ. Lawyers Conf., 1983, 85. Contbg. editor Wash. Law Rev., 1972. Mem. Environ. Law Sect., St. Martin's Coll. Alumni Assn. (bd. dirs. 1975-78), Pi Kappa Delta. Democrat. Roman Catholic. Administrative and regulatory, Environmental, Indian. Home: 2340 62nd Ave NW Olympia WA 98502-3416

REYNOLDS, JOHN W. federal judge; b. Green Bay, Wis., Apr. 4, 1921; s. John W. and Madge (Flatley) R.; m. Patricia Ann Brody, May 26, 1947 (dec. Dec. 1967); children: Kate M. Reynolds Lindquist, Molly A., James B.; m. Jane Conway, July 31, 1971; children: Jacob F., Thomas J., Frances P., John W. III. PhB, U. Wis., 1946, LLB, 1949. Bar: Wis. 1949. Since practiced in Green Bay; dist. dir. price stblzn., 1951-53; U.S. commr., 1953-58; atty. gen. of Wis., 1958-62; gov. State of Wis., 1963-65; U.S. dist. judge Ea. Dist. Wis., Milwa., 1965-71, chief judge, 1971-86, sr. judge, 1986—. Served with U.S. Army, 1942-46. Mem. State Bar Wis., Am. Law Inst., Fed. Judges Assn., Former Govs. Assn. Office: US Dist Ct 296 US Courthouse 517 E Wisconsin Ave Milwaukee WI 53202-4500

REYNOLDS, MARK FLOYD, II, lawyer, management and labor consultant; b. Phila., Apr. 14, 1943; s. Marcus Reuben and Eleanor (Carter) R.; m. Pauline B. Douglass, Sept. 17, 1965; children— Meredith Lynn, Douglass Scott. B.A., Lincoln U., Pa., 1970; J.D., U. Balt., 1975. Bar: Pa. 1975, U.S. Dist. Ct. (ea. dist.) Pa. 1975, U.S. Supreme Ct. 1980, N.C. 1984, U.S. Dist. Ct. (ea. dist.) N.C. 1985, U.S. Ct. Mil. Appeals 1985, U.S. Ct. Appeals (4th cir.) 1986. Atty., Bethelehem Steel Corp., Pa., 1976-84; ptnr. Robert Sheahan & Assocs., High Point, N.C., 1985— ; dir. Ready Supply Corp., Johnstown, Pa., 1982— . Vice pres. Penns Woods council Boy Scouts Am., 1981-84; chmn. United Way Greater Johnstown, 1981-84; trustee Slatington Presbyterian Ch., Pa., 1976-81. Served with AUS, 1962-65. Mem. Pa. Bar Assn. (council labor law 1984), ABA (labor law sect. com. on OSHA), N.C. Bar Assn., Lehigh County Bar Assn., Guilford County Bar Assn., Alpha Phi Omega. Republican. Lodge: Masons. Federal civil litigation, State civil litigation, Labor. Home: 572 Pauls Airport Rd Thomasville NC 27360-0740

REYNOLDS, WILLIAM CARL, law editor; b. Lebanon, Ind., Sept. 10, 1942; s. Herbert Carl and Elma Merle (Gatewood) R.; m. Patsy Darlene Smith, Aug. 30, 1964; children— Bradley William, Shari Teresa. A.B., Ind. U., 1965, J.D., 1968. Bar: Ind. 1968, U.S. Dist. Ct. (so. dist.) Ind. 1968. Tax acct. Arthur Andersen & Co., Indpls., 1968-69; assoc. atty. Steers, Klee, Jay & Sullivan, Indpls., 1969-70; law editor Bobbs-Merrill Co., Indpls., 1970-76; law editor Allen Smith Co., Indpls., 1976-85, dir., 1981-85; tax analyst Ind. Dept. Revenue, 1986—. Office: Ind Dept Revenue State Office Bldg Rm 216 Indianapolis IN 46204-2728

RHEINSTEIN, PETER HOWARD, health care company executive, consultant, physician, lawyer; b. Cleve., Sept. 7, 1943; s. Franz Joseph Rheinstein and Hede Henrietta (Neheimer) Rheinstein Lerner; m. Miriam Ruth Weissman, Feb. 22, 1969; 1 child, Jason Edward BA with high honors, Mich. State U., 1963, MS, 1964; MD, Johns Hopkins U., 1967; JD, U. Md., 1973. Bar: Md. 1973, D.C. 1980, U.S. Supreme Ct. 2000; diplomate Am. Bd. Family Practice; cert. added qualifications in geriatric medicine. Intern USPHS Hosp., San Francisco, 1967-68, resident in internal medicine Balt., 1968-70; instr. internal medicine U. Md., 1970-73; med. dir. extended care facilities CHC Corp., 1972-74; dir. drug advt. and labeling divsn. FDA, Rockville, Md., 1974-82, acting dep. dir. Office Drugs, 1982-83, acting dir. Office Drugs, 1983-84, dir. Office Drug Standards, 1984-90, dir. medicine staff Office Health Affairs, 1990-99; sr. v.p. for med. and clin. affairs Cell Works, Inc., Balt., 1999—. Chmn. Com. on Advanced Sci. Edn., 1978-86, Rsch. in Human Subjects Com., 1990-92; adj. prof. forensic medicine George Washington U., 1974-76; WHO cons. on drug regulation Nat. Inst. for Control Pharm. and Biol. Products, China, 1981-90; advisor on essential drugs WHO, 1985-90; FDA del. to U.S. Pharmacopeial Conv., 1985-90, coord. com. for assessment and transfer of tech. NIH, 1990-99, mem. health care fin. adminstrn. tech. adv. com., 1990-98, Nat. Adv. Coun. on Healthcare Policy, Rsch. and Evaluation, 1990-99, Healthy People 2000/2010 Steering Com., 1990-99, CDC and Prevention Task Force on Cmty. Preventive Svcs., 1996-99, Nat. Task Force on Industry/Provider CME Collaboration, 1992—; cons. in legal medicine and regulatory affairs, 1999—. Co-author: (with others) Human Organ Transplantation, 1987; spl. editorial advisor Good Housekeeping Guide to Medicine and Drugs, 1977-80; mem. editorial bd. Legal Aspects Med. Practice, 1981-89, Drug Info. Jour., 1982-86, 91-95; contbr. articles to profl. jours. Recipient Commendable Svc. award FDA, 1981, Group award of merit, 1983, 88, Group Commendable Svc. award 1989, 92, 93, 95, 99, Commr.'s Spl. citation, 1993. Fellow Am. Coll. Legal Medicine (bd. govs. 1983-93, treas., chmn. fin. com. 1985-88, 90-91, chmn. publs. com. 1988-93, jud. coun. 1993-95; Pres.'s awards 1985, 86, 89-91, 93), Am. Acad. Family Physicians; mem. Am. Acad. Pharm. Phys. (bd. trustees 1999—, v.p. AMA rels. 1999—), AMA (life), ABA, Drug Info. Assn. (bd. dirs. 1982-90, pres. 1984-85, 88-89, v.p. 1986-87, chmn. ann. meeting 1991, 94, steering com. Ams. 1991—, Outstanding Svc. award 1990), Fed. Bar Assn. (chmn. food and drug com. 1976-79, Disting Svc. award 1977), Med. and Chirurgical Faculty Md., Balt. City Med. Soc., Johns Hopkins Med. and Surg. Assn., APHA, Md. Bar Assn., Math. Assn. Am., Soc. Indsl. and Applied Math., Mensa (life), U. Md. Alumni Assn. (life), Fed. Exec. Inst. Alumni Assn. (life), Johns Hopkins U. Alumni Assn., Mich. State U. Alumni Assn. (life), Mich. State U. Honors Coll. Alumni Assn. (bd. dirs. 1998—, pres. 2000—), Chartwell Golf and Country Club, Annapolis Yacht Club, Johns Hopkins Club, Delta Theta Phi (life). Avocations: boating, electronics, physical fitness, real estate investments. Home: 621 Holly Ridge Rd Severna Park MD 21146-3520 Office: Cell Works Inc 6200 Seaforth St Baltimore MD 21224-6506 E-mail: phr@jhu.edu, peter@cell-works.com

RHIND, JAMES THOMAS, lawyer; b. Chgo., July 21, 1922; s. John Gray and Eleanor (Bradley) R.; m. Laura Haney Campbell, Apr. 19, 1958; children: Anne Constance, James Campbell, David Scott. Student, Hamilton Coll., 1940-42; A.B. cum laude, Ohio State U., 1944; LL.B. cum laude, Harvard U., 1950. Bar: Ill. bar 1950. Japanese translator U.S. War Dept., Tokyo, Japan, 1946-47; congl. liaison Fgn. Operations Adminstrn., Washington, 1954; atty. Bell, Boyd & Lloyd, Chgo., 1950-53, 55—, ptnr., 1958-92, of counsel, 1993—. Bd. dirs. Kewaunee Scientific Corp., Statesville, N.C. Commr. Gen. Assembly United Presbyn. Ch., 1963; life trustee Ravinia Festival Assn., Hamilton Coll., Clinton, N.Y., U. Chgo.; Northwestern Univ. Assocs.; chmn. Cook County Young Republican Orgn., 1957; Ill. Young Rep. nat. committeeman, 1957-58; v.p., mem. bd. govs. United Rep. Fund Ill., 1965-84; pres. Ill. Childrens Home and Aid Soc., 1971-73, life trustee; bd. dirs. E.J. Dalton Youth Center, 1966- 69; governing mem. Chgo. Symphony Orch., Chgo.; mem. Ill. Arts Council, 1971-75; mem. exec. com. div. Met. Mission and Ch. Extension Bd., Chgo. Presbytery, 1966-68; trustee Presbyn. Home, W. Clement and Jessie V. Stone Found., U. Chgo. Hosps. Served with M.I. AUS, 1943-46. Mem. ABA, Ill. Bar Assn., Chgo. Bar Assn. (bd. mgrs. 1967-69), Fed. Bar Assns., Chgo. Council on Fgn. Relations, Japan Am. Soc. Chgo., Lawyers Club Chgo., Phi Beta Kappa, Sigma Phi. Clubs: Chicago, Glen View (Ill.), Commercial (Chgo.), Mid-Day Club (Chgo.), Economic (Chgo.). General corporate, Securities. Home: 830 Normandy Ln Glenview IL 60025-3210 Office: Bell Boyd & Lloyd 3 First National Pla 70 W Madison St Ste 3200 Chicago IL 60602-4244 E-mail: jrhind@bellboyd.com

RHOADES, JOHN SKYLSTEAD, SR. federal judge; b. 1925; m. Carmel Rhoades; children: Mark, John, Matthew, Peter, Christopher. AB, Stanford U., 1948; JD, U. Calif., San Francisco, 1951. Prosecuting atty. City of San Diego, 1955-56, dep. city atty., 1956-57; pvt. practice San Diego, 1957-60; ptnr. Rhoades, Hollywood & Neil, 1960-85; judge U.S. Dist. Ct. (so. dist.) Calif., 1985—. With USN, 1943-46. Office: US Dist Ct 940 Front St San Diego CA 92101-8994

RHOADS, NANCY GLENN, lawyer; b. Washington, Oct. 15, 1957; d. Donald L. and Gerry R. R.; m. Robert A. Koons, June 23, 1984. BA, Gettysburg Coll., 1980; JD, Temple U., 1983. Bar: Pa., U.S. Dist. Ct. (ea. dist.) Pa. 1983. Rsch. asst. Prof. Mikochick, Phila., 1982-83; law clk. Phila. Ct. of Common Pleas, 1983-85; assoc. Post and Schell P.C., Phila., 1985-90, Sheller, Ludwig and Badey, Phila., 1990—. Co-author: Aging and the Aged: Problems, Opportunities, Challenges, 1980. Vol. Spl. Olympics. Mem. ATLA, Phila. Bar Assn. (med. legal com.), Phi Beta Kappa, Phi Alpha Theta, Pi Delta Epsilon, Eta Sigma Phi. Avocations: classical piano, horticulture, swimming. Personal injury. Home: 401 Audubon Ave Wayne PA 19087-4006 Office: Sheller Ludwig and Badey 1528 Walnut St Philadelphia PA 19102-3604

RHODE, DEBORAH LYNN, law educator; b. Jan. 29, 1952; BA, Yale U., 1974, JD, 1977. Bar: D.C. 1977, Calif. 1981. Law clk. to judge U.S. Ct. Appeals (2d cir.), N.Y.C., 1977-78; law clk. to Hon. Justice Thurgood Marshall U.S. Supreme Ct., D.C., 1978-79; asst. prof. law Stanford (Calif.) U., 1979-82, assoc. prof., 1982-85, prof., 1985—; dir. Inst. for Rsch. on Women and Gender, 1986-90, Keck Ctr. of Legal Ethics and The Legal Profession, 1994—; sr. counsel jud. com. Ho. of Reps., Washington, 1998. Trustee Yale U., 1983-89; pres. Assn. Am. Law Schs., 1998; Ernest W. McFarland prof. Stanford Law Sch., 1997—; sr. counsel com. on the jud. U.S. Ho. of Reps., 1998. Author: Justice and Gender, 1989, (with Geoffrey Hazard) the Legal Profession: Responsibility and Regulation, 3d edit., 1993, (with Annette Lawson) The Politics of Pregnancy: Adolescent Sexuality and Public Policy, 1993, (with David Luban) Legal Ethics, 2001, (with Barbara Allen Babcock, Ann E. Freedman, Susan Deller Ross, Wendy Webster Williams, Rhonda Copelon, and Nadine H. Taub) Sex Discrimination and the Law, 1997, Speaking of Sex, 1997, Professional Responsibility: Ethics by the Pervasive Method, 1998, In the Interests of Justice, 2000; editor: Theoretical Perspectives on Sexual Difference, 1990, Ethics in Practice, 2000; contbr. articles to profl. jours. Mem. ABA (chair commn. on women and the profession 2000—). Office: Stanford U Law Sch Crown Quadrangle Stanford CA 94305

RHODES, ALICE GRAHAM, lawyer; b. Phila., June 15, 1941; d. Peter Graham III and Fannie Isadora (Bennett) Graham; m. Charles Milton Rhodes, Oct. 14, 1971 (div. Apr. 21, 1997); children: Helen, Carla, Shauna. BS, East Stroudsburg U. Pa., 1962; MS, U. Pa., 1966, LLB, 1969, JD, 1970. Bar: N.Y. 1970, U.S. Dist. Ct. (so. and ea. dists.) N.Y. 1971, U.S. Ct. Appeals (2d cir.) 1971, Ky. 1983, U.S. Dist. Ct. (ea. dist.) Ky. 1985. Staff atty. Harlem Assertion Rights, Mobilization for Youth Office Econ. Opportunity, N.Y.C., 1969-70, coord. Cmty. Action Legal Svcs., 1970-72; assoc. dir. in charge of civil representation HUD Model Cities Cmty. Law Offices, 1972-73; resource assoc. Commn. on Edn. & Employment of Women, N.C. Dept. Adminstrn., Raleigh, 1975-76; mgr. policies and procedures Div. for Youth, N.C. Dept. Human Resources, 1976; in-house counsel Ashland (Ky.), Inc. (formerly Ashland Oil, Inc.), 1980-82; corp. atty. core group Ashland, Inc., 1985-87, 88-91; corp. atty. Ashland City Commn. Human Rights, 1993-99; bd. regents Ea. Ky. U., 1994-2001; mem. exec. bd., chmn. internal affairs com., academic affairs, 1997-98; asst. county atty. family ct. Jefferson County, Louisville, 1999-2000; pub. mem. Fgn. Svc., 1995—; cons. Pub. Mems. Fgn. Svc., 1995—; atty., affirmative employment program, fed. sector programs Office of Fed. Ops., EEOC, 2001—. Mem. U.S. EEOC, on-site rev. program, 2001—; appellate judge decision writing atty. appeals; mem. Property Valuation Appeals Commn., 1994; cons. pub. mem. selection and performance stds. review bd. Fgn. Svc., U.S. Dept. State, 1995, Fgn. Agrl. Svc. USDA, 1997; prison program planner, cons. N.Y. City Dept. Corrections, 1971; lectr. N.Y.C. Correction Acad., Riker's, 1971; lectr. juvenile justice N.C. Law Enforcement Acad., Salemburg, 1976. Mem. usher bd. New Hope Bapt. Ch., Ashland, 1980-94; bd. dirs. YWCA Ashland, 1983-84, Ashland Heritage Pk. Commn., 1983-85; bd. dirs., budget com. United Way, Greenup County, Ashland, 1988-92; driver Meals on Wheels, Ashland, 1983-91; vol. Am. Heart Assn., 1982-91; bd. dirs. Our Lady of Bellefonte Hosp. Found. (Franciscan Sisters of the Poor), 1996-99, Ky. Coun. of Trustees, Ky. Health System, 1996-99, Carter G. Woodson Found. 1997-97, Study Afro-Am. Life and History; mem. adv. com. task force post secondary edn. Gov. of Ky.; bd. dirs. exec. com. Boyd County Dem. Women, 1996—; mem. presdl. search com. Ea. Ky. U., 1997-98; participant Ky. Gov.'s Conf. on Postsecondady Edn., 1999. Recipient Cmty. Svc. award Queens Community Corp., N.Y.C., 1972, Ashland C.C., 1986, Cmty. Svc. award NAACP, Ky.; NSF fellow, 1964, 65, ; faculty friends of Pa. scholar U. Pa., 1966-69, Reginald Heber Smith postgrad. fellow cmty. law, 1969-71; named to Hon. Order of Ky. Cols., 1989. Fellow Ky. Bar Found.; mem. AAUW (bd. dirs. Phila. chpt. 1963-65), Nat. Bar Assn., N.Y. Bar, Ky. Bar Assn. (mem. edn. law, corp. house counselw, anworkers compensation law sects.), Boyd County Bar Assn., Ky. Assn. Black Pub. Adminstrs., Nat. Forum Black Pub. Adminstrs., Ky. Blacks in Higher Edn., Pilot Club (exec. bd. Ashland 1983), Links, Inc., Paramount Women's Assn., Penn Club (charter mem. N.Y. chpt.), Aux. Our Lady of Bellefonte Hosp., Pub. Mems. Assn. of Fgn. Svc., Assn. Gov. Bds. Colls. and Univs., Greenup County Bar Assn., Jefferson Club, Bellefonte Country Club. Democrat. Avocations: interior decorating, sports, dancing, gourmet cooking, gardening. Home: 5300 Columbia Pike # 101 Arlington VA 22204-3118 Office: US EEOC Office Fed Ops 1801 L St NW Washington DC 20013

RHODES, THOMAS WILLARD, lawyer; b. Lynchburg, Va., Mar. 9, 1946; s. Howard W. and Ruth R.; m. Ann Bloodworth, May 31, 1975; children: Mildred Claiborne, Andrew. AB, Davidson (N.C.) Coll., 1968; JD, U. Va., 1971. Bar: Ga. 1971. Assoc. Smith, Gambrell & Russell and predecessor firms, Atlanta, 1971-76, ptnr., 1976—. Dir., pres. Atlanta Vol. Lawyers Found., 1984-89, Fed. Defender Program, Atlanta, 1989-94. Contbr. articles to profl. jours. Capt. USAR, 1971-72. Recipient Heiner award, Atlanta Vol. Lawyers Found., 1989. Fellow Am. Law Inst.; mem. Ga. Bar Assn. (past chmn. antitrust law sect.), ABA. Antitrust, Bankruptcy, General civil litigation. Office: Smith Gambrell & Russell Promenade II 1230 Peachtree St NE Ste 3100 Atlanta GA 30309-3592

RHYNE, SIDNEY WHITE, lawyer; b. Charlotte, N.C., Apr. 2, 1931; s. Sidney White and Ruth (Dry) R.; m. Rosemarie Kennedy, July 11, 1959; children: Patricia Ruth, Kendall Sidney, Randall Sylvanus. AB, Roanoke Coll., 1952; LLB, U. Pa., 1955; LLM, Georgetown U., 1961. Bar: Pa. 1955, D.C. 1957, U.S. Supreme Ct. 1959, Md. 1987. Assoc. Rhyne, Mullin, Connor and Rhyne, Washington, 1957-60; mem. Mullin, Rhyne, Emmons and Topel, 1961-97; individual practice law, 1997—. Lectr. law ctr. Georgetown U., Washington, 1964-70. Pres. Legal Aid Soc. of D.C., 1976-78, trustee, 1968-80, pres. coun., 1991—; trustee Luth. Theol. Sem. at Phila., 1988-93, pres. coun., 1993—. With U.S. Army, 1955-57. Prettyman fellow Georgetown U., 1960-61. Fellow Am. Bar Found. (life); mem. ABA (mem. house delegates 1972-73, 75, 76-78, 98-2001), Bar Assn. D.C. (bd. dirs. 1969-73, 92-94, 98-2002, trustee Found., v.p. 1990-91, presdl. award 2000-2001), Fed. Comm. Bar Assn. (mem. exec. com. 1988-96, treas. 1991-92, Disting. Svc. award 1992, pres. 1994-95). Republican. Lutheran. Communications, Probate. Office: 3250 Arcadia Pl NW Washington DC 20015-2330 E-mail: swrhyne@abanet.org

RHYNEDANCE, HAROLD DEXTER, JR. lawyer, consultant; b. New Haven, Feb. 13, 1922; s. Harold Dexter and Gladys (Evans) R.; m. Barbara Ann Hall (dec.); 1 child, Harold Dexter III; m. Ruth Cosline Hakanson. BA, Cornell U., 1943, JD, 1949; grad., U.S. Army Command and Gen. Staff Coll., 1961, U.S. Army War Coll., 1970. Bar: N.Y. 1949, D.C. 1956, U.S. Tax Ct. 1950, U.S. Ct. Mil. Appeals 1954, U.S. Supreme Ct. 1954, U.S. Ct. Appeals (D.C. cir.) 1956, (2d cir.) 1963, (3rd cir.) 1965, (4th cir.) 1973, (5th cir.) 1968, (7th cir.) 1973, (9th cir.) 1964, U.S. Temporary Emergency Ct. Appeals 1975, U.S. Dist. Ct. D.C. 1956, U.S. Dist. Ct. (so. and ea. dist.) N.Y. 1963. Pvt. practice, Buffalo, Eggertsville, N.Y., 1949-50; examiner/gen. atty. ICC, Washington, 1950-51; atty.-advisor Subversive Activities Control Bd., 1951-52; trial atty., spl. asst. to atty. gen., asst. U.S. atty. U.S. Dept. Justice, 1953-62; sr. trial atty., asst. gen. counsel, gen. counsel FTC, 1962-73; counsel Howrey & Simon, 1973-76; mng. atty., asst. gen. counsel, corp. counsel Washington Gas Light Co., 1977-87; counsel Conner & Wetterhahn, 1987-90; cons. Fairview, N.C., 1990—. Exec. sec. adv. coun. on rules of practice and procedures FTC; mem. Jud. Conf. (D.C. Cir.), 1967—; chmn. legal and regulatory subcom. Solar Energy Com., Am. Gas Assn., Washington, 1978-84; lectr. George Washington U. Law Ctr., 1974; faculty moderator Def. Strategy Seminar Nat. War Coll., 1973; participant spl. programs Indsl. Coll. of Armed Forces, 1962, 69, Armed Forces Staff Coll., 1964. V.p. bd. dirs. Peninsula Symphony Assn., Palos Verdes Peninsula, Calif., 1989-94; bd. dirs. Help-The-Homeless-Help-Themselves, Inc., Palos Verdes Peninsula, 1991-93. 1st lt. U.S. Army, 1943-46, PTO; col. AUS, 1982—. Mem. ABA, Fed. Bar Assn., D.C. Bar Assn., Bar Assn. of D.C., Washington Met. Area Corp. Counsel Assn. (bd. dirs. 1981-84), Cornell Lawyers Club D.C. (pres. 1959-61), The Selden Soc. (London), Biltmore Forest Country Club (Asheville, N.C.), Montreat (N.C.) Scottish Soc., Ret. Officers Assn., Res. Officers Assn. (life), Mil. Order Carabao, U.S. Army War Coll. Alumni

Assn. (life), Leadership Asheville Forum, Downtown Club Asheville (pres., bd. dirs. 1998—), Cornell Alumni Assn., Am. Legion (life), Sigma Chi, Phi Delta Phi. Republican. Episcopalian. Administrative and regulatory, Antitrust, Federal civil litigation. Home and Office: Eagles View 286 Sugar Hollow Rd Fairview NC 28730-9559

RICCI, BARNABA, lawyer; b. Milan, Jan. 11, 1950; s. Carlo Alberto Ricci and Anna Elisabetta Belloni Filippi; m. Laura Coppi, Jan. 11, 1950; chilldren: Maria Sofia, Maria Valeria, Carlo Alberto. JD, U. Milan, 1977. Bar: Milan 1982. Assoc. Redenti LLP, Milan, 1974-78, sr. assoc., 1978-80, ptnr., 1980-82; shareholder Ricci, 1982-90, Graham & James, Milan, 1990-98, Haarmann, Hemmelrath & Ptnrs., Milan, 1998—. Lectr. U. Milan, 1996—. Author: Italian Jurisdiction, 1978. Mem. Internat. Bar Assn., Circolo Unione. Contracts commercial, General corporate, Mergers and acquisitions. Office: Haarmann Hemmelrath & Ptnr C So Venezia 16 20121 Milan Lombardy Italy Fax: 39.02.77.194.133. E-mail: barnaba_ricci@hhp.de

RICCIO, FRANK JOSEPH, lawyer, educator; b. Somerville, Mass. BS, Boston Coll., 1973; JD, Suffolk U., 1985; D of Dental Medicine, Boston Coll., 1986. Bar: Mass. 1985, U.S. Dist. Ct. Mass. 1986, U.S. Ct. Appeals (1st cir.) 1986. Dentist, Lowell, Mass., 1977-83, Metheun, 1983-84; assoc. Sugarman & Sugarman, Boston, 1985-87; pvt. practice Braintree, Mass., 1987. Clin. instr. oral medicine Harvard U., Boston, 1995—. Dental extern USPHS, 1976. Mem. Am. Assn. Trial Attys., Nat. Bd. Trial Attys. (cert. civil trial specialist), Mass. Bar Assn., Mass. Acad. Trial Attys., Million Dollar Advocates Forum. Personal injury. Office: Law Offices of Frank J Riccio PC 25 Braintree Hill Park Ste 208 Braintree MA 02184-8702 E-mail: fjriccio@socialaw.com

RICE, CHARLES MARCUS, II, lawyer; b. June 20, 1946; s. Jay Goldman and Bonna (Lafferty) Rice; m. Marian Clifford Jones, June 16, 1979; children: Charles Marcus III, Rebecca Wells. AB magna cum laude, Princeton U., 1968; MPub. Policy, U. Mich., 1973, JD cum laude, 1974. Bar: N.Y. 1975, Mo. 1978. Mem. adv. coun. Sch. Forestry, U. Mo., Columbia, Mo., 1982—92; pres. Rice Money Mgrs., Inc., 1992—. Sec. Anglican Inst., St. Louis, 1984—87. Computer, Artificial intelligence. Home: 8510 Colonial Ln Saint Louis MO 63124-2007 Office: Rice Money Managers Inc 7777 Bonhomme Ave Ste 1400 Saint Louis MO 63105

RICE, DONALD SANDS, lawyer, entreprenuer; b. Bronxville, N.Y., Mar. 25, 1940; s. Anton Henry and Lydia Phipps (Sands) R.; m. Edgenie Higgins, Aug. 27, 1966; children: Alice Higgins, Edgenie Reynolds. AB magna cum laude, Harvard U., 1961, LLB/JD cum laude, 1964; LLM in Taxation, NYU, 1965. Bar: N.Y. 1964, U.S. Ct. Claims 1965, U.S. Supreme Ct. 1981. Law clk. to judge U.S. Ct. Claims, 1965-67; assoc. Barrett, Smith, Schapiro & Simon, N.Y.C., 1967-71; ptnr. Barrett, Smith, Schapiro, Simon & Armstrong, 1971-86; vice chmn. bd. The Bowery Savs. Bank, 1986-88; ptnr. Chadbourne & Parke, 1988-96; mng. dir. and prin. Ravitch Rice & Co. LLC, 1996—; ptnr. Rice & Ravitch LLP, 1996—. Bd. dirs. B-Line, LLC, CertCo, Inc., JAF Communications/Luxury Finder.com., LLC; lectr. Nat. Assn. Real Estate Investment Trusts, Bank Adminstrs. Inst., Bank Tax Inst., 1971-86; chmn., bd. dirs. Corp. of Yaddo, 1986—; co-chmn. Soviet-Am. Banking Law Working Group, 1991-96; v.p., treas., bd. dirs. Soviet Bus. and Comml. Law Edn. Found., 1991-96; vol. lectr. Fin. Svcs. Vol. Corps Mongolian Bank Tng. Program, 1993, Georgetown Internat. Law Inst., NYU Sch. Continuing Edn., Russian Trade Fair-U.S. Dept. Commerce, 1994; mem. nat. com. Am. fgn. policy study group dels. to China, Taiwan, 1996, 2000, Roundtable on U.S.-China Policy and Cross-Strait Rels., 1996—; mem. real estate adv. bd. to N.Y. State Comptr., 1987-93; bd. advisors Am.-Russian Investment Forum, 1999—. Bd. dirs. African Med. Rsch. Found., 1978—; trustee Marimed Found., 1984-97, Chapin Sch., 1980-91, v.p., 1989-91; trustee The Hackley Sch., 1974-81, St. Philip's Episcopal Ch., Mattapoisett, Mass., 1987—, Nat. Com. Am. Fgn. Policy, 1994—, sr. v.p. 1996—. Mem. ABA, Coun. Fgn. Rels., N.Y. State Bar Assn., Assn. of the Bar of the City of N.Y., Century Assn., Harvard Club N.Y., N.Y. Yacht Club, River Club N.Y. General practice, Mergers and acquisitions, Corporate taxation. Home: 1120 Fifth Ave New York NY 10128-0144 Office: Ravitch Rice & Co LLC 610 5th Ave Rm 420 New York NY 10020-2403 E-mail: ravricellc@aol.com

RICE, GEORGE LAWRENCE, III (LARRY RICE), lawyer; b. Jackson, Tenn., Sept. 24, 1951; s. George Lawrence Jr. and Judith W. (Pierce) R.; m. Joy Gaia, Sept. 14, 1974; children: George Lawrence IV (Nick), Amy Colleen. Student, Oxford U., 1972-73; BA with honors, Rhodes Coll., 1974; JD, U. Memphis, 1976, Nat. Coll. Advocacy, ATLA, 1978. Bar: Tenn. 1977, U.S. Supreme Ct. 1980; cert. family law trial advocate Nat. Bd. Trial Advocacy, family law specialist, Tenn. Assoc. Rice, Rice, Smith, Admundsen & Jewell LLPC, 1976-81, ptnr., 1981—, acting sr. ptnr., 1995. Cert. family law trial advocate NBTA and Family Law Specialist by Tenn. Author: Divorce Practice in Tenn., 1987, 2d edit., 1987, Family Law, 1988, Winning for Your Client, 1988, Divorce Practice A to Z, 1989, Divorce Lawyer's Handbook, 1989, (video) Divorce: What You Need to Know When it Happens to You, 1990, Rice's Divorce Practice Manual, 1990, Child Custody in Tennessee, 1992, Divorce Trial, Tribulations, Tactics and Triumphs, 1993, The Complete Guide to Divorce Practice, 1993, 2d edit., 1998, Divorce Practice Made Easier, 1993, Divorce Practice, 1994, Visual Persuasion, AIDS 1996 Clients, Prenuptial Agreements, 1996, The Ethical Effective Lawyer: Divorce and Personal Injury, 1996, In Pursuit of the Perfect Personal Injury Practice, 1997, Wiley Family Law Update, Discovery Supplement, 1997, Tennessee Evidence Workshop Handbook, 1997, Hot Topics in Family Law, 1997, Child Custody and Visitation in Tennessee, 1998, Larry Rice on Divorce: How to Run an Efficient and Effective Divorce Practice and Improve Client Satisfaction, 1998, Client Communications, 1998, Post Nuptial Agreement A Proposal for Consideration, 1998, Larry Rice of Divorce, 1998; mem. bd. editors Matrimonial Strategist, 1995-99, Hunt, Hide Shoot--a Guide to Paintball, 1996; contbr. articles to profl. jours. Founding chmn. Student Legal Assistance Program, 1975; active Supreme Ct. Child Support Guidelines Commn., 1989, Family Law Revision Commn., 1990—91, 1998—; mem. Timberwolves Paintball Team, 1988—2000; exec. com. Rhodes Coll. Red and Black Soc., 1999—, chmn., 2001—; treas. Rocky Mountain Elk Found., Memphis, 2001. Named one of Best Lawyers in Am., 1993, 94; recipient Excellence in Edn. award PESI, 1997; Outstanding intern supr. Rhodes Coll., Mentor award, 1997-98, award Amicus Curi Family Laws Sect. Wilson-Wilson, 1997-98. Mem. ABA (conv. lectr. 1993, 94, 98, 99, 01), ATLA, Tenn. Bar Assn. (chmn., co-founder family law sect. 1987-88), Memphis Bar Assn. (founding chmn. family law sect.), Tenn. Trial Lawyers Assn. (chair-legal asst. adv. com. 1997-98). Family and matrimonial, Personal injury. Office: Rice Rice Smith et al 275 Jefferson Memphis TN 38103-2251 E-mail: home@ricelaw.com, lrice@ricelaw.com

RICE, GUY GARNER, lawyer; b. Kansas City, Mo., Mar. 25, 1932; s. Guy William and Elizabeth (Smith) R.; m. Marcia Louise Clines, Dec. 15, 1978; children by previous marriage— Dierk B., Brenda L., Reid R., Sandra L., Student Beloit Coll., 1949-51; A.B., U. Mo., Columbia, 1953; J.D., U. Mo.-Kansas City, 1964. Bar: Mo. 1964, U.S. Dist. Ct. (we. dist.) Mo. 1965. Asst. pros. atty. Jackson County, Mo., 1965, Asst. county counselor, Jackson County, Mo., 1970-71; ptnr. Phillips, Rice & McElligott, Independence, 1968-74; sole practice, Independence, 1978-82; ptnr. Rice & Mouse, Independence, 1983-85, sole practice, 1985—; gen. counsel Med. Info. Service, Inc., 1976-80, Sugar Creek Nat. Bank, 1971-80. Served to 1st lt. U.S. Army, 1953-56. Named Outstanding Young Man, Jaycees, 1958-59; recipient Spoke award Jaycees, 1959. Mem. Estate Planning Assn. Greater Kansas City (pres. 1966-67), Independence Bar Assn. (sec. 1965-66), Eastern Jackson County Bar Assn., Independence C. of C. General corporate. Office: Suite 5 3640 S Noland Rd Ste 5 Independence MO 64055-6504

RICE, HUGH THOMPSON, JR. tax lawyer; b. Charleston, S.C., Aug. 4, 1957; s. Hugh Thompson and Katherine Louise (Miller) R.; m. Wrenzie Lee Calhoun, Aug. 7, 1982; children: Hugh Thompson III, Jacob Calhoun, James Lucas. BS in Acctg., U. S.C., 1979, MS, JD, U. S.C., 1982. Bar: S.C. 1982; CPA, S.C.; cert. tax specialist. Sr. tax cons. Deloitte Haskins & Sells, Charlotte, N.C., 1982-84; ptnr. Van Osdell, Lester, Howe & Rice, P.A., Myrtle Beach, S.C., 1984-97, Rice & MacDonald, 1997—. Adj. prof. acctg. U. S.C., Myrtle Beach, 1985-86. Vol. Bros. and Sisters Community Action, Columbia, S.C., 1978-82; mem. Probate Adv. Bd. Horry County, 1989—; mem. vestry Episcopalian Ch., 1989-92, treas. capital bldg. fund, 1989-92, fin. chmn., 1990-92; bd. dirs. YMCA, Myrtle Beach Haven, 1989—, pres. 1994—. Recipient Outstanding Svc. award Brothers and Sisters Community Action, 1980, 81. Mem. S.C. Bar Assn. (cert. specialist in taxation and estate planning), S.C. Assn. CPAs, Sertoma (Gem award 1987, Centurion award 1988, sec. 1988-89, pres. 1989-90, chmn. bd. dirs. 1990-91). Republican. Home: 3802 N Ocean Blvd Myrtle Beach SC 29577-2760 Office: Rice & MacDonald 950 48th Ave N Myrtle Beach SC 29577-5427

RICE, JIM, judge; b. Ramore Air Force Base, Ont., Canada, Nov. 15, 1957; , parents Am. citizens; BA in Polit. Sci., Mont. State U., 1979; JD U. Mont., 1982. Pub. defender Lewis and Clark County; ptnr. Jackson & Rice, Helena, Mont., 1985—2001; assoc. justice Mont. Supreme Ct., 2001—. Mem. Mont. Ho. Reps., 1989—95, ho. majority whip, 1993. Office: Justice Bldg 215 N Sanders St PO Box 203001 Helena MT 59620*

RICE, JOHN EDWARD, lawyer; b. Bridgeport, Nebr., Mar. 11, 1927; s. Charles R. and Lyla V. (French) R.; m. Ann M. Yanick, May 9, 1953; children— Mary C., John Michael, Theresa, Joan, Jane, Charles. J.D., Creighton U., 1951. Bar: Nebr. 1951. City atty. City of Bellevue, Nebr., 1955— ; ptnr. Rice & Adams, Bellevue, 1951— . Served to sgt. U.S. Army, 1944-46; PTO. Democrat. Roman Catholic. Real property. Home: 702 Kayleen Dr Bellevue NE 68005-2350 Office: Rice & Adams 1246 Golden Gate Dr Papillion NE 68046-2838

RICE, JULIAN CASAVANT, lawyer; b. Miami, Fla., Dec. 31, 1923; s. Sylvan J. and Maybelle (Casavant) R.; m. Dorothy Mae Haynes, Feb. 14, 1958; children— Scott B., Craig M. (dec.), Julianne C., Linda D., Janette M. Student, U. San Francisco, 1941-43; JD cum laude, Gonzaga U., 1950. Bar: Wash. 1950, Alaska 1959, U.S. Tax Ct. 1988. Pvt. practice law, Spokane, 1950-56, Fairbanks, Alaska, 1959—; prin. Law Office Julian C. Rice (and predecessor firms), 1959, Salcha, Alaska, 1999. Founder, gen. counsel Mt. McKinley Mut. Savs. Bank, Fairbanks, 1965-99, chmn. bd., 1979-80; v.p., bd. dirs., gen. counsel Skimmers, Inc., Anchorage, 1966-67; gen. counsel Alaska Carriers Assn., Anchorage, 1960-71, Alaska Transp. Conf., 1960-67. Mayor City of Fairbanks, 1970-72. Served to maj. USNG and USAR, 1943-58. Decorated Bronze Star, Combat Infantryman's Badge. Fellow Am. Bar Found. (life); mem. ABA, Wash. State Bar Assn. (50-Yr. mem. award 2000), Alaska Bar Assn., Transp. Lawyers Assn., Alternative Dispute Resolution Com., Am. Arbitration Assn. (mem. trasp. panel), Spokane Exchange Club (pres. 1956). E-moial. Estate planning, Family and matrimonial, Transportation. Home and Office: 2990 Joaquin Miller Rd Oakland CA 94602 Fax: 510-482-5609. E-mail: salcha@earthlink.net

RICE, LACY I., JR. lawyer; b. Martinsburg, W.Va., Dec. 29, 1931; s. Lacy Isaac and Anna (Thorn) R.; m. Linda Watkins, Mar. 2, 1957; children: Anne W., Lacy I. III, William T. BA, Princeton U., 1953; LLB, U. Va., 1956. Bar: W.Va. 1956, U.S. Dist. Ct. (no. Dist.) W.Va. 1956, U.S. Cir. Ct. Appeals (3d and 4th cirs.) 1968. Ptnr. Lacy I. Rice Sr. law firm & Rice, Hannis & Rice & successors, Martinsburg, 1956-89; sr. ptnr. Bowles, Rice, McDavid, Graff & Love, 1989—. Pres. Old Nat. Bank of Martinsburg, 1978, chmn. bd.; chmn., CEO One Valley Bank-East N.A.; vice chmn. One Valley Bancorp, Inc. Mem. W.Va. Bar Assn. (pres. 1984-85). Home: 600 N Tennessee Ave Martinsburg WV 25401-9281 Office: PO Drawer 1419 105 W Burke St Martinsburg WV 25401-3301

RICE, NANCY E. state supreme court justice; b. Denver, June 2, 1950; 1 child. BA cum laude, Tufts U., 1972; JD, U. Utah, 1975. Law clerk U.S. Dist. Ct. of Colo., 1975-76, dep. state pub. defender, appellate divn., 1976-77; asst. U.S. atty. Dist. of Colo., 1977-87; dep. chief civil divn. U.S. Attorney's Office, 1985-88; judge Denver Dist. Ct., 1988-98; apptd. judge Colo. Supreme Ct., 1998—. Contbr. articles to profl. jours. Mem. Denver Bar Assn., Colo. Bar Assn. (bd. govs. 1990-92, exec. coun., 1991-92), Women's Bar Assn., Rhone-Brackett Inn of Ct. (master 1993-97), Women Judges Assn. (co-chair nat. conf. 1990). Office: Colo Supreme Ct Colo State Jud Bldg 2 E 14th Ave Fl 4 Denver CO 80203-2115

RICE, PAUL JACKSON, lawyer, educator; b. East St. Louis, Ill., July 15, 1938; s. Ray Jackson and Mary Margaret (Campbell) R.; m. Carole Jeanne Valentine, June 6, 1959; children: Rebecca Jeanne Ross, Melissa Ann Hansen, Paul Jackson Jr. BA, U. Mo., 1960, JD, 1962; LLM, Northwestern U., 1970; student, Command and Gen. Staff Coll., 1974-75, Army War Coll., 1982-83. Bar: Mo. 1962, Ill. 1969, U.S. Dist. Ct. (no. dist.) Ill. 1970, U.S. Supreme Ct. 1972, U.S. Ct. Appeals (D.C. cir.) 1991, D.C. 1993, U.S. Dist. Ct. (D.C.) 2000. Commd. 1st lt. U.S. Army, 1962, advanced through grades to col., 1980; asst. judge advocate 4th Armored Div., Goeppingen, Fed. Republc Germany, 1966-69; dep. staff judge advocate 1st Cavalry Div., Republic Vietnam, 1970-71; inst., prof. The Judge Adv. Gen. Sch., Charlottesville, Va., 1971-74, commdt., dean, 1985-88; br. chief Gen. Law Br., Pentagon, 1975-78; chief adminstrv. law div. Office Judge Adv. Gen., Pentagon, Washington, 1978-79; staff judge adv. 1st Inf. Div., Ft. Riley, Kans., 1979-82, V Corps U.S. Army, Frankfurt, Fed. Republic Germany, 1983-85, USACAC, Ft. Leavenworth, Kans., 1989-90; faculty Indsl. Coll. Armed Forces, 1988-89; chief counsel Nat. Hwy. Traffic Safety Adminstrn., Washington, 1990-93; ptnr. Arent Fox Kintner Plotkin & Kahn, 1993—. Contbr. articles to profl. jours. Granted Legal Svc. award State of Hessen, Weisbaden, Fed. Republic Germany, 1985, Cert. Merit U. Mo. Alumni Assn., 1987. Mem. ABA, Mo. Bar Assn., Ctr. For Law and Nat. Security, U. Va. Sch. Law (1985-89), Lion Tamers, Phi Delta Phi. Methodist. Avocations: writing, reading, sports. Administrative and regulatory, Product liability, Transportation. Home: 7835 Vervain Ct Springfield VA 22152-3107 Office: Arent Fox Kintner Plotkin & Kahn 150 Connecticut Ave NW Washington DC 20036-5339

RICE, WALTER HERBERT, federal judge; b. Pitts., May 27, 1937; s. Harry D. and Elizabeth L. (Braemer) R.; m. Bonnie Rice; children: Michael, Hilary, Harry, Courtney Elizabeth. BA, Northwestern U., 1958; JD, MBA, Columbia U., 1962; LLD (hon.), U. Dayton, 1991; DHL (hon.), Wright State U., 2000. Bar: Ohio 1963. Asst. county prosecutor, Montgomery County, Ohio, 1964-66; assoc. Gallon & Miller, Dayton, 1966-69; 1st asst. Montgomery County Prosecutor's Office, 1969; judge Dayton Mcpl. Ct., 1970-71, Montgomery County Ct. Common Pleas, 1971-80, U.S. Dist. Ct. (so. dist.) Ohio, 1980-95, chief judge, 1996—. Adj. prof. U. Dayton Law Sch., 1976— , bd. visitors, 1976— ; chmn. Montgomery County Supervisory Council on Crime and Deliquency, 1972-74; vice chmn. bd. dirs. Pretrial Release, Inc., 1975-79 Author papers in field. Pres. Dayton Area Coun. on Alcoholism and Drug Abuse, 1971-73; chmn. bd. trustees Stillwater Health Ctr., Dayton, 1976-79, Family Svc. Assn. Dayton, 1978-80; chmn. RTA in 2000 Com., 2003 Com. Designed To Bring Nat. Park to Dayton To Honor Wright Bros. and Birth of Aviation; chmn. Martin Luther King Jr. Meml. Com., Dayton Aviation Heritage Commn.; trustee Montgomery County Vol. Lawyers Project, Miami Valley Cultural Alliance, Barbara Jordan Com. Racial Justice; co-chmn., Dayton Dialogue on Race Rels.; former bd. mem. Sinclair C.C., U.S. Air & Trade Show. Recipient Excellent Jud. Service award Ohio Supreme Ct., 1976, 77, Outstanding Jud. Service award, 1973, 74, 76, Man of Yr. award Disting. Service Awards Council, Dayton, 1977, Outstanding Jurist in Ohio award Ohio Acad. Trial Lawyers, 1986, Pub. Ofcl. of Yr. award Ohio region of Nat. Assn. Social Workers, 1992, Humanitarian award NCCJ, 1993, City Mgr.'s Cmty. Svc. award City of Dayton, 1994, Paul Laurence Dunbar Humanitarian award, 1996, Pres.' award NAACP, 1996, greater Dayton Peace Bridge (civil rights) Hall of Fame. Mem. Dayton Bar Assn., Carl D. Kessler Inn of Ct. (founder, former chmn.).

RICE, WINSTON EDWARD, lawyer; b. Shreveport, La., Feb. 22, 1946; s. Winston Churchill and Margaret (Coughlin) R.; m. Barbara Reily Gay, Apr. 16, 1977; 1 child, Andrew Hynes; children by previous marriage: Winston Hobson, Christian MacTaggart. Student, Centenary Coll. La., 1967; JD, La. State U., 1971. Bar: La. 1971, Colo. 1990, Tex. 1992. Cons. geologist, Gulfport, Miss., 1968-70; ptnr. Phelps, Dunbar, New Orleans, 1971-88; sr. ptnr. Rice, Fowler, Houston, Miami, Fla., London and Bogota, 1988-2000; gen. mgr. Winston Edw. Rice LLC, Covington, La., 2000—. Instr. law La. State U., Baton Rouge, 1970-71. Assoc. editor La. Law Rev., 1970-71. Mem. La. Bar Assn., Colo. State Bar Assn., Tex. State Bar, New Orleans Bar Assn., Canadian Transp. Lawyers Assn., New Orleans Assn. Def. Counsel, La. Assn. Def. Counsel, Fedn. Ins. and Corporate Counsel, Com. Maritime Internat. (titulary mem.), Maritime Law Assn. U.S. (chmn. subcom. on offshore exploration and devel. 1985-88, vice chmn. com. internat. law of the sea 1988-91, chmn. 1991-95, mem. sec. 1998—), Assn. Average Adjusters U.S., Assn. Average Adjusters (U.K.), Soc. Ins. Trainers and Educators, Ctr. Transp. Law and Policy, Trucking Ind. Defense Assn., Mariners Club (treas. 1974-75, 78-79, sec. 1975-76, v.p. 1976-77, pres. 1977-78), Boston Club, Stratford Club, Coral Beach and Tennis Club, Order of Coif, Phi Delta Phi, Phi Kappa Phi, Kappa Alpha. Republican. Episcopalian. Admiralty, Insurance, Private international. Office: 328 N Columbia St Covington LA 70433-2918

RICH, BEN ARTHUR, lawyer, educator; b. Springfield, Ill., Mar. 27, 1947; s. Ben Morris and Betty Lorraine (Ingalls) R.; m. Caroline Rose Castle, Oct. 4, 1984 (div. Nov. 1988); m. Kathleen Mills, Aug. 17, 1991. Student, U. St. Andrews, Scotland, 1967-68; BA, DePauw U., 1969; JD, Washington U., 1973; PhD, U. Colo., 1995. Bar: Ill. 1973, N.C. 1975, Colo. 1984. Rsch. assoc. U. Ill. Coll. Law, Urbana, 1973-74; staff atty. Nat. Assn. Attys. Gen., Raleigh, N.C., 1974-76; prin. Hollowell, Silverstein, Rich & Brady, 1976-80; dep. commr. N.C. Indsl. Commn., 1980-81; counsel N.C. Meml. Hosp., Chapel Hill, 1981-84; assoc. univ. counsel U. Colo. Health Scis. Ctr., Denver, 1984-86; gen. counsel U. Colo., Boulder, 1986-89, spl. counsel to the regents, 1989-90; asst. clin. prof. U. Colo. Sch. Medicine, 1992-94; asst. prof. U. Colo. Health Scis. Ctr., 1995-99, asst. dir. program in healthcare ethics, humanities and law, 1995-99; assoc. prof. bioethics program U. Calif.-Davis Med. Ctr., Sacramento, 2000—. Asst. prof. attendent U. Colo. Sch. Medicine, 1986-91, adj. instr. Sch. Law, 1988-95, adj. prof., 1996—; vis. assoc. prof., 1990-91; lectr. U. Denver Coll. Law; vis. prof. U. Calif. Davis Sch. Law. Contbr. articles to jours., chpts. to books. Mem. Am. Coll. Legal Medicine (assoc.-in-law 1987), Am. Philos. Assn., Am. Soc. Bioethics and Humanities, Am. Soc. Law, Medicine and Ethics (health law tchrs. sect.), Toastmasters Internat. (pres. Raleigh chpt. 1978). Unitarian. Avocations: sailing, jogging, tennis. Home: 4905 Ridgeline Ln Fair Oaks CA 95628-6585 Office: U Calif Davis Med Ctr Bioethics Program 4150 V St Ste 2400 Sacramento CA 95817

RICH, JOHN TOWNSEND, lawyer; b. Lansing, Mich., Mar. 10, 1943; s. Townsend and Jean (Trembley) R.; m. Charlotte Pia Mahon, Nov. 25, 1978; children: Anna-Sophie, Lucia Danforth. BA, Harvard U., 1965, postgrad., 1965-66; LLB, Yale U., 1969; postgrad., U. Coll., Oxford, Eng., 1969-70. Bar: N.Y. 1970, D.C. 1972. Law clk. to Hon. David L. Bazelon U.S. Ct.Appeals D.C. Cir., 1970-71; law clk. to Hon. Harry A. Blackmun U.S. Supreme Ct., Washington, 1971-72; assoc. Shea & Gardner, 1972-76, ptnr., 1976—. Adj. prof. Georgetown U. Law Ctr., 1972-75; spl. master U.S. Dist. Ct. for No. Dist. Tex., 1985-88. Administrative and regulatory, Antitrust, Federal civil litigation. Home: 6309 Kenhowe Dr Bethesda MD 20817-5419 Office: Shea & Gardner Ste 800 1800 Massachusetts Ave NW Washington DC 20036-1872 E-mail: jrich@sheagardner.com

RICH, MICHAEL JOSEPH, lawyer; b. N.Y.C., June 19, 1945; s. Jessee and Phyllis (Sternfeld) R.; m. Linda Christine Kubis, July 19, 1969; children: David lawrence, Lisa Diane. BA, Gettysburg Coll., 1967; JD, Am. U., 1972. Bar: Del. 1973, U.S. Dist. Ct. Del. 1973, U.S. Supreme Ct., 1976, Pa., 1981. Law clk. Del. Supreme Ct., Georgetown, 1972-73; assoc. Tunnell & Raysor, 1973-76; ptnr. Dunlap, Holland & Rich, P.A., 1976-80; gen. counsel Pearlette Fashions, Inc., Lebanon, Pa., 1981-83; assoc. Morris, Nichols, Arsht & Tunnell, Georgetown, 1983-86; ptnr., 1987-91, Twilley, Street, Rich Braverman & Hindman, P.A., Dover, Del., 1991-95; state solicitor, 1995-2001; dep. atty. gen., 2001—. Mem. Bd. Bar Examiners, Del., 1986-97, chmn., 1996-97;minority counsel Del. Ho. of Reps., Dover, 1977-79; mem. Del. Gov's Magistrate Commn., 1980, 83-86; sec. Del. Gov's. Jud. Nominating Commn., 1986-89. Bd. dirs. People's Place II, Inc., Milford, Del., 1973-77; pres. Bi-COunty United Way, Inc., Milford, 1977-78; mem. Partnership Greater Milford Commn., 1987-89, Friends Milford Library. Served to 1st lt. U.S. Army, 1967-69, Vietnam. Dean's fellow Am. U., 1971-72. Mem. ABA, Am. Judicature Soc., Del. Bar Assn. (pres. 1990-91), Sussex County Bar Assn. (pres. 1987-89). Republican. E-mail: mrich@deins.state.de.us

RICH, ROBERT STEPHEN, lawyer; b. N.Y.C., Apr. 30, 1938; s. Maurice H. and Natalie (Priess) R.; m. Myra N. Lakoff, May 31, 1964; children: David, Rebecca, Sarah. AB, Cornell U., 1959; JD, Yale U., 1963. Bar: N.Y. 1964, Colo. 1973, U.S. Tax Ct. 1966, U.S. Supreme Ct. 1967, U.S. Ct. Claims 1968, U.S. Dist. Ct. (so. dist.) N.Y. 1965, U.S. Dist. Ct. (ea. dist.) N.Y. 1965, U.S. Dist. Ct. Colo. 1980, U.S. Ct. Appeals (10th cir.) 1978; conseil juridique, Paris, 1968. Assoc. Shearman & Sterling, N.Y.C., Paris, London, 1963-72; ptnr. Davis, Graham & Stubbs, Denver, 1973—. Adj. faculty U. Denver Law Sch., 1977—; mem. adv. bd. U. Denver Ann. Tax Inst., 1985—, global bus. and culture divsn., U. Denver, 1992—, Denver World Affairs Coun., 1993—, Coll. Arts & Scis., U. Colo., Denver, 2000—; mem. Colo. Internat. Trade Coun., 1985—; mem. Rocky Mt. Dist. Export Coun., U.S. Dept. Commerce, 1993—; tax adv. com. U.S. Senator Hank Brown; bd. dirs. Clos du Val Wine Co. Ltd., Danskin Cattle Co., Ouray Ranch, Areti Wines, Ltd., Taltarni Vineyards, Christy Sports, others. Author treatises on internat. taxation; contbr. articles to profl. jours. Bd. dirs. Alliance Francaise, 1977—, Denver Internat. Film Festival, 1978-79, Copper Valley Assn.; actor, musician N.Y. Shakespeare Festival, 1960; sponosr Am. Tax Policy Inst., 1991—; trustee, sec. Denver Art Mus., 1982—; mem. adv. bd. Denver World Affairs Coun., 1993—; pres. So. Boulder Park Ecol. Assn., 1999—; dir. Anschutz Family Found.; mem. adv. bd. Coll. Arts and Sci., U. Colo., Denver, 2000—. Capt. U.S, Army, 1959-60; pres. & dir. Ouray Ranch, Colo., 2001-. Fellow Am. Coll. Tax. Coun. (bd. regents 10th cir. 1992—), Soc. Fellows Aspen Inst.; mem. ABA, Internat. Bar Assn., Colo. Bar Assn., N.Y. State Bar Assn., Assn. Bar City of N.Y., Asia-Pacific Lawyers Assn., Union Internat. des Avocats, Internat. Fiscal Assn. (pres. Rocky Mt. br. 1992—, U.S. regional v.p. 1988—), Japan-Am. Soc. Colo. (bd. dirs. 1989—, pres. 1991-93), Confrerie des

Chavaliers du Tastevin, Rocky Mt. Wine and Food Soc., Meadowood Club, Denver Club, Mile High Club, Cactus Club Denver, Yale Club, Denver Tennis Club. Private international, Corporate taxation, Taxation, general. Office: Cherry Creek Sta PO Box 61429 Denver CO 80206-8429 also: Antelope Co 555 17th St Ste 2400 Denver CO 80202-3941 E-mail: robertrich@aya.yale.edu

RICHARDS, DAVID ALAN, lawyer; b. Dayton, Ohio, Sept. 21, 1945; s. Charles Vernon and Betty Ann (Macher) R.; m. Marianne Catherine Del Monaco, June 26, 1971; children: Christopher, Courtney. BA summa cum laude, Yale U., 1967, JD, 1972; MA, Cambridge (Eng.) U., 1969. Bar: N.Y. 1973. Assoc. Paul, Weiss, Rifkind, Wharton 7 Garrison, N.Y.C., 1972-77, Coudert Bros., N.Y.C., 1977-80, ptnr., 1981-82; ptnr., head real estate group Sidley & Austin, 1983-2000; sr. counsel McCarter & English, 2001—. Gov. Anglo-Am. Real Property Inst. U.S./U.K., 1983-88, chair, 1993; mem. Chgo. Title N.Y. Realty Adv. Bd., 1992—. Contbr. articles to profl. jours. Trustee Scarsdale Pub. Libr., 1984-89, pres., 1988-89; co-chair N.Y. Lawyers for Clinton/Gore, 1996. Fellow Am. Bar Found.; mem. ABA (real property, probate and trust sect., coun. 1982-88, chair 1991-92), Am. Coll. Real Estate Lawyers (gov. 1987-93), Assn. of Bar of City of N.Y. (real property com. 1978-80, 84-87), Kipling Soc. (N.Am. rep.), Shenorock Shore Club (Rye, N.Y.), The Grolier Club (N.Y.C.), Yale Club (N.Y.C.). Democrat. Real property. Home: 18 Forest Ln Scarsdale NY 10583-6464 Office: McCarter & English 300 Park Ave Fl 18 New York NY 10022 E-mail: darichards21@aol.com, drichards@mccarter.com

RICHARDS, GARY R. lawyer; b. London, Nov. 19, 1955; s. John and Joan (Hodson) R.; m. Jan Welch, 1989; children: Fabia, Toby. BA, Cambridge U., 1977; LLB, 1978, MA (hon.), 1980. Bar: solicitor. Trainee, solicitor McKenna & Co., London, 1978-82; solicitor Rowe & Maw, 1982-85, Linklaters & Paines, London, 1985-92; sr. mgr. Price Waterhouse, 1992-94; tax ptnr., 1994-98, Barlow Lyde & Gilbert, London, 1998—. Co-author: Planning for Stamp Duty Reserve Tax, 1987; editor: Brit. Tax Rev., 1999—; contbr. chpt. to book. Mem. Chartered Inst. Taxation (assoc.). Office: Barlow Lyde & Gilbert Beaufort Ho 15 St Botolph St London EC3A 7NJ England E-mail: griehards@blg.co.uk

RICHARDS, GERALD THOMAS, lawyer, consultant, educator; b. Monrovia, Calif., Mar. 17, 1933; s. Louis Jacquelyn Richards and Inez Vivian (Richardson) Hall; children: Patricia M. Richards Grauf, Laura J., Dag Hammarskjold; m. Mary Lou Richards, Dec. 27, 1986. BS magna cum laude, Lafayette Coll., 1957; MS, Purdue U., 1963; JD, Golden Gate U., 1976. Bar: Calif. 1976, U.S. Dist. Ct. (no. dist.) Calif. 1977, U.S. Patent Office 1981, U.S. Ct. Appeals (9th cir.) 1984, U.S. Supreme Ct. 1984. Computational physicist Lawrence Livermore (Calif.) Nat. Lab., 1967-73, planning staff lawyer, 1979, mgr. tch. transfer office, 1980-83, asst. lab. counsel, 1984-93; sole practice Livermore, Calif., 1976-78, Oceanside, 1994-97; emeritus atty. pro bono participant Calif. State Bar, 1998—; staff atty. Contra Costa Sr. Legal Svcs., Concord, 1998—. Constrn. law instr. Contrs. State License Schs., Van Nuys, Calif., 1998; mem. exec. com., policy advisor Fed. Lab. Consortium for Tech. Transfer, 1980-88; panelist, del. White House Conf. on Productivity, Washington, 1983; del. Nat. Conf. on Tech. and Aging, Wingspread, Wis., 1981. Commr. Housing Authority, City of Livermore, 1977, vice chairperson, 1978, chairperson, 1979; pres. Housing Choices, Inc., Livermore, 1980-84; bd. dirs. Valley Vol. Ctr., Pleasanton, Calif., 1983, pres., 1984-86; mem. staff Calif. Boys' State Am. Legion, 1996—. Served to maj. U.S. Army, 1959-67. Recipient Engring. award GE, 1956. Mem. ABA, Calif. State Bar (conv. alt. del. 1990-92, del. 2000—), Alameda County Bar Assn., Contra Costa County Bar Assn., Ea. Alameda County Bar Assn. (sec. 1978, bd. dirs. 1991-92, chair lawyers referral com. 1992-93), Santa Barbara County Bar Assn., San Diego County Bar Assn., Bar Assn. No. San Diego County, San Francisco Bar Assn., Phi Beta Kappa, Tau Beta Pi, Sigma Pi Sigma. Contracts commercial, General practice, Probate. Home: 2505 Whitetail Dr Antioch CA 94509-7744 E-mail: hesiodsplace@yahoo.com

RICHARDS, JANET LEACH, lawyer, educator; b. Somerville, Tenn., Jan. 19, 1948; d. Wilmer Homer and Loraine Lottie (Robertson) Leach; m. William Michael Richards, Mar. 6, 1976; children— Jamie, Robert. B.S., Memphis State U., 1969, J.D., 1976. Bar: Tenn. 1976, U.S. Dist. Ct. (we. dist.) Tenn. 1976. Stewardess, methods analyst Delta Airlines, Atlanta, 1969-74; assoc. J.B. Cobb & Assocs., Memphis, 1976-78; asst. prof., asst. dean students affairs Memphis State Law Sch., 1978-1980, assoc. prof., 1981— , assoc. dean, 1986— . Recipient Sam A. Myar, Jr. Meml. award for Outstanding Young Lawyer in Memphis. Mem. Memphis and Shelby County Bar Assn. (pres. Young Lawyers' 1981, bd. dirs. 1980-81, 83-84), Memphis State Law Alumni Assn. Home: 2972 Cane Creek Dr Germantown TN 38138-7204 Office: Memphis State U Sch Law Memphis TN 38152

RICHARDS, MARTA ALISON, lawyer; b. Mar. 15, 1952; d. Howard Jay and Mary Dean (Nix) Richards; m. Richard Peter Massony, June 16, 1979 (div. Apr. 1988); 1 child, Richard Peter Massony Jr. Student, Vassar Coll., 1969-70; AB cum laude, Princeton U., 1973; JD, George Washington U., 1976. Bar: La. 1976, U.S. Dist. Ct. (ea. dist.) La. 1976, U.S. Ct. Appeals (5th cir.) 1981, U.S. Supreme Ct. 1988, U.S. Dist. Ct. (mid. dist.) La. 1991. Assoc. Phelps, Dunbar, Marks, Claverie & Sims, New Orleans, 1976-77; assoc. counsel Hibernia Nat. Bank, 1978; assoc. Singer, Hutner, Levine, Seeman & Stuart, 1978-80, Jones, Walker, Waechter, Poltevent, Carrere & Denegre, New Orleans, 1980-84; ptnr. Mmahat, Duffy & Richards, 1984, Montgomery, Barnett, Brown, Read, Hammond & Mintz, 1984-86, Montgomery, Richards & Ballin, 1986-89, Gelpi, Sullivan, Carroll and Laborde, 1989; gen. counsel Maison Blanche Inc., Baton Rouge, 1990-92, La. State Bond Commn., 1992-97; pvt. practice, cons., 1998—. Lectr. paralegal inst. U. New Orleans, 1984-89, adj. prof., 1989. Contbr. articles to legal jours. Treas. alumni coun. Princeton U., 1979-81. Mem. ABA, La. State Bar Assn., New Orleans Bar Assn., Baton Rouge Bar Assn., Nat. Assn. Bond Lawyers, Princeton Alumni Assn. New Orleans (pres. 1982-86). Episcopalian. Contracts commercial, General corporate, Municipal (including bonds). Home and Office: 4075 S Ramsey Dr Baton Rouge LA 70808-1653

RICHARDS, PAUL A. retired lawyer; b. Oakland, Calif., May 27, 1927; s. Donnell C. and Theresa (Pasquale) R.; m. Ann Morgans, May 20, 1948 (dec. 1984); 1 child: Paul M.; m. Elise Hall, Dec. 6, 1996. Practiced law, Reno, from 1953; settlement judge settle conf. program Supreme Ct. State of Nev., 1998-2000, ret., 2000. General civil litigation, General corporate, Environmental.

RICHARDS, ROBERT BYAM, lawyer, insurance company executive; b. Glen Ridge, N.J., Jan. 18, 1942; s. Kenneth Watson and Helen Leola (Wile) R.; divorced; children— Jennifer Lynn, Robert Thomson. BSBA, Lehigh U., 1963; JD, Duquesne U., 1973. Bar: Pa. 1973, U.S. Dist. Ct. (we. dist.) Pa. 1973, U.S. Supreme Ct. 1987. Exec. trainee Mfrs. Hanover Trust Co., N.Y.C., 1963-66; real estate staff asst. PPG Industries, Inc., Pitts., 1966-72; assoc. Goldman & Unatin P.A., Pitts., 1972-74; asst. title officer Commonwealth Land Title Ins. Co., Pitts., 1974-77, v.p., 1977—, assoc. counsel, 1977-83, counsel, 1983—; regional staff, 1985—, cons. mineral titles U.S. Steel Corp., Pitts., 1981; cons. real estate condemnation and mineral titles to dir. dept. aviation Allegheny County, 1981— ; cons. real estate ins. litigation Rose, Schmidt, Dixon & Hasley, Pitts., 1981— ; panelist Law 4 You, Sta. WTAE-TV, 1984-85; Law 2 You, Sta. KDKA-TV 1986; instr. in field Elder, trustee Southminster Presbyterian Ch., Mount Lebanon, Pa., 1980-84. Mem. Allegheny County Bar Assn. (council mem. real estate sec. 1979-81, asst. sec., sec. 1982-83, vice chmn. 1984, chmn. 1985, chmn. nominating com. 1986; mem. bankruptcy and comml. law sect. 1983—; mem. spl. fee determination com., 1986—). Republican. Contracts commercial, Probate, Real property. Office: Commonwealth Land Title Ins Co Frick Bldg Mezzanine Level 437 Grant St Pittsburgh PA 15219-6002

RICHARDS, THOMAS H. lawyer, arbitrator; b. Exeter, N.H., May 29, 1942; s. Frank F. and Ella (Higgins) R.; m. Barbara M. Blackmer, Mar. 23, 1975; children: Daniel, Matthew. BA cum laude, U. N.H., 1964; JD, NYU, 1967. Bar: N.H. 1967, U.S. Dist. Ct. N.H., U.S. Ct. Appeals (1st cir., D.C. cir.) 1987. Assoc. to v.p. Sheehan Phinney Bass & Green, Manchester, N.H., 1967-68, 70-99, ret., 1999, of counsel. Mem. N.H. Jud. Coun., Concord, 1988-90; mem. long range planning com. N.H. Supreme Ct., 1989-90, mem. profl. conduct com., 1989-90. Capt. 25th inf. divsn., U.S. Army, 1968-69. Root-Tilden fellow. Fellow Am. Bar Found., Am. Coll. Trial Lawyers, Internat. Soc. Barristers, N.H. Bar Found. (chmn. 1991-92); mem. Manchester Bar Assn. (bd. govs. 1975-80), New Eng. Bar Assn. (bd. govs. 1989-92), N.H. Bar Assn. (bd. govs. 1985-87, pres. 1989-90), Nat. Conf. Bar Pres., Phi Beta Kappa. Avocations: carpentry, collecting and restoring antique tools. Federal civil litigation, Environmental, Product liability. Home: 164 Browns Hill Rd Sunapee NH 03782 Office: Sheehan Phinney Bass & Green 1000 Elm St Manchester NH 03101-1801

RICHARDSON, ARTHUR WILHELM, lawyer; b. Glendale, Calif., Apr. 3, 1963; s. Douglas Fielding and Leni (Tempelaar-Lietz) R.; m. Noriko Satake, Nov. 14, 1998. AB, Occidental Coll., 1985; student, London Sch. Econs., 1983; JD, Harvard U., 1988. Bar: Calif. 1989. Assoc. Morgan, Lewis and Bockius, L.A., 1988-90; staff lawyer U.S. SEC, 1990-92, br. chief, 1992-96, sr. counsel, 1996—2001. Mem. ABA, Calif. Bar Assn., L.A. County Bar Assn., Harvard/Radcliffe Club So. Calif., Town Hall Calif., L.A. World Affairs Coun., Sierra Club, Phi Beta Kappa. Presbyterian. Home: 2328 Mallard Ln #6 Beavercreek OH 45431

RICHARDSON, BETTY H. lawyer, former prosecutor; b. Oct. 3, 1953; BA, U. Idaho, 1976; JD, Hastings Coll. Law, 1982. Staff aid U.S. Senator Frank Church, 1976-77; teaching asst. Hastings Coll. Law, 1980-82, tchg. asst., 1980-82; legal rsch. asst. criminal divsn. San Francisco Superior Ct., 1982-84; jud. law clk. Chamber of Idaho Supreme Ct. Justice Robert C. Huntley Jr., 1984-86; atty. U.S. Dept. Justice, Boise, Idaho, 1993-2001, Richardson & O'Leary, Eagle, 2001—. Instr. Boise State U., 1987, 89; mem. U.S. Atty. Gen.'s Adv. Com. subcoms. on environ., civil rights and native Am. issues, others; mem. hon. adv. bd. for Crime Victims Amendment in Idaho, 1994; mem. Dist. of Idaho Judges and Lawyer Reps. com., gender fairness com., Civil Justice Reform Act com. and criminal adv. com. Mem. Idaho Indsl. Commn., 1991-93, chmn., 1993; mem. adv. bd. Family and Workplace Consortium; mem. Assistance League of Boise. Recipient Harold E. Hughes Exceptional Svc. award Nat. Rural Inst. on Alcohol and Drug Abuse, 1999; Tony Patino fellow Hastings Coll. Law, 1982. Mem. Idaho Bar Assn. (governing coun. govt. and pub. sectors lawyers sect., Pro Bono Svc. award 1988—), Idaho Pros. Attys. Assn., Assistance league of Boise, YMCA. Office: Richardson & O'Leary 99 E State St Eagle ID 83616 also: 5796 N Dalspring Boise ID 83713

RICHARDSON, CAMPBELL, retired lawyer; b. Woodland, Calif., June 18, 1930; s. George Arthur and Mary (Hall) R.; m. Patricia Packwood, Sept. 3, 1957 (dec. Oct. 1971); children: Catherine, Sarah, Thomas; m. Carol Tamblyn, June 1975 (div. Dec. 1977); m. Susan J. Lienhart, May 3, 1980; 1 child, Laura. AB, Dartmouth Coll., 1952; JD, NYU, 1955. Bar: Oreg. 1955, U.S. Dist. Ct. Oreg. 1957. Ptnr. Stoel Rives LLP, Portland, 1964-2000; ret., 2000—. Co-author: Contemporary Trust and Will Forms for Oregon Attorneys and for Idaho Attorneys; contbr. articles to profl. jours. Mem. Portland/Metro Govt. Boundary Commn., 1976; mem. Oreg. Adv. Com. to U.S. Commn. on Civil Rights, 1976-84; bd. dirs. Ctr. for Urban Edn., Portland, 1980-84, Dorchester Conf., Inc., 1982, Oreg. Zoo Found., 1993—; chmn. planned giving com. St. Vincent Med. Found., 1988-98; mem. planned giving coun. Oreg. Health Scis. Found., 1994—; trustee Met. Family Svc. Found., 1990-98; bd. dirs. Elders in Action, Portland, 2000—. Served with U.S. Army, 1955-57. Mem. ABA, Oreg. Bar Assn., Multnomah County Bar Assn., Estate Planning Coun. Portland (pres. 1978), Am. Coll. Trust and Estate Counsel, City Club, Multnomah Athletic Club (Portland). Republican. Estate planning, Probate, Estate taxation. Home: 1500 SW 5th Ave Unit 1701 Portland OR 97201-5430 Office: Stoel Rives LLP 900 SW 5th Ave Ste 2300 Portland OR 97204-1229 E-mail: crichardson@stoel.com

RICHARDSON, DANIEL RALPH, lawyer; b. Pasadena, Calif., Jan. 18, 1945; s. Ralph Claude and Rosemary Clare (Lowery) R.; m. Virginia Ann Lorton, Sept. 4, 1965; children: Brian Daniel, Neil Ryan. BS, Colo. State U., 1969; MBA, St. Mary's Coll. of Calif., 1977; JD, JFK U., 1992. Bar: Calif. Systems engr. Electronic Data Systems, San Francisco, 1972-73; programmer/analyst Wells Fargo Bank, 1973-74; systems analyst Crown-Zellerbach Corp., 1974; programming mgr. Calif. Dental Svc., 1974-75, Fairchild Camera and Inst., Mountain View, Calif., 1975-77; sr. systems analyst Bechtel Corp., San Francisco, 1977; pres. Richardson Software Cons., Inc., 1977-99; pvt. practice, 1993—. Instr. data processing Diablo Valley Coll., Concord, Calif., 1979-80. Author: (book) System Development Life Cycle, 1976, (computer software) The Richardson Automated Agent, 1985. Asst. scoutmaster Boy Scouts Am., Clayton, Calif., 1983-91; soccer coach Am. Youth Soccer League, Clayton, 1978-83. 1st lt. USAF, 1966-72. Mem. ABA, State Bar Calif., Computer Law Assn. Avocations: travel, reading, writing. General civil litigation, Computer, Intellectual property. Office: 870 Market St Ste 400 San Francisco CA 94102-3010

RICHARDSON, DAVID ALEXANDER, lawyer; b. Hong Kong, Sept. 15, 1954; LLB, U. Hong Kong, 1977, Postgrad. Cert. of Laws, 1978; LLB, U. B.C., 1982. Bar: Hong Kong, B.C. Solicitor Fraser & Beatty, Vancouver, B.C., Can., 1984-85; trainee solicitor, solicitor Wilkinson & Grist, Hong Kong, 1985-88; solicitor Victor Chu & Co., 1988-91, ptnr., 1991-2001, Bird & Bird, Hong Kong, 2001—. General corporate, Securities. Office: Ste 602-4 6th Fl Asia Pacif Finance Twr Citibank Plaza 3 Garden Road Hong Kong

RICHARDSON, DENNIS MICHAEL, lawyer, educator; b. L.A., July 30, 1949; s. Ralph Lee and Eva Catherine (McGuire) R.; 1 child from previous marriage, Scott Randol; m. Catherine Jean Coyl, July 27, 1973; children: Jennifer Eve, Valerie Jean, Rachel Catherine, Nicole Marie, Mary Rose, Marie Christina, Laura Michelle, Alyssa Rose. BA, Brigham Young U., 1976, JD, 1979. Bar: Oreg. 1979. Owner Dennis Richardson & Assocs., P.C., Central Point, Oreg., 1979—; pvt. practice law, 1979—; CEO IMPEX U.S. Corp., 1999—. Guest lectr. in field. Contbr. articles to profl. jours. Bd. dirs. Oreg. Lung Assn., 1980, Shakespearean Festival, Ashland, 1981, Jackson County Legal Services, 1982; chmn. GOP Oreg. 2d. Congl. Dist., 1996-2000, treas. GOP Oreg. Exec. Com., 1999—; councilman Ctrl. Point City, 2001—. Served as helicopter pilot U.S. Army, 1969-71, Vietnam. Decorated Vietnamese Cross Gallantry. Republican. Personal injury, Product liability. Office: Dennis Richardson & Assocs PC 55 S 5th St Central Point OR 97502-2474 E-mail: dennis@law.com

RICHARDSON, JOHN CARROLL, lawyer, tax legislative consultant; b. Mobile, Ala., May 3, 1932; s. Robert Felder and Louise (Simmons) R.; m. Cicely Tomlinson, July 27, 1961; children: Nancy Louise, Robert Felder III, Leslie. BA, Tulane U., 1954; LLB cum laude, Harvard U., 1960. Bar: Colo. 1960, N.Y. 1965, D.C. 1972. Assoc. Holland & Hart, Denver, 1960-64; legal v.p. Hoover Worldwide Corp., N.Y.C., 1964-69; v.p., gen. counsel Continental Investment Corp., Boston, 1969; dep. tax legis. counsel U.S. Dept. Treasury, Washington, 1970-71, tax legis. counsel, 1972-73; ptnr. Brown, Wood, Ivey, Mitchell & Petty, N.Y.C., 1973-79, LeBoeuf, Lamb, Leiby & MacRae, N.Y.C., 1979-88, Morgan, Lewis & Bockius, N.Y.C., 1988-93; ret., 1993. Tax legis. cons., Orford, N.H., 1993—; adj. prof. Law Sch. Fordham U., 1990-94. Served to lt. comdr. USN, 1954-57 Mem. ABA (chmn. com. adminstrv. practice tax sect. 1984-86), N.Y. State Bar Assn. (exec. com. tax sect. 1975-84), D.C. Bar Assn., Am. Coll. Tax Counsel, N.Y. Athletic Club, Royal Automobile Club.

RICHARDSON, ROBERT ALLEN, retired lawyer, educator; b. Cleve., Feb. 15, 1939; s. Allen B. and Margaret C. (Thomas) R.; m. Carolyn Eck Richardson, Dec. 9, 1968. BA, Ohio Wesleyan U., 1961; LLB, Harvard U., 1964. Bar: Ohio 1964, Hawaii 1990. Ptnr. Caffee, Halter & Griswold, Cleve., 1968-89; counsel Mancini, Rowland & Welch (formerly Case & Lynch), Maui, Hawaii, 1990—; lectr., affirmative action officer, atty., exec. com. Maui (Hawaii) C.C., 1989—. Chmn. gov. fin. dept., chmn. cmty. svc. com., mem. oper. com. Caffee, Halter & Griswold; past lectr. Sch. Law Cleve. State U.; counsel Maui C. of C., Kahului, 1994-98. Pres. trustee Big Bros., Big Sisters of Maui, 1990-94; v.p., trustee, pres. Ka Hole A Ke Ole Homeless Resource Ctr., 1990—; trustee Maui Acad. Performing Arts, 1990-97, Maul Counseling Svc., 1990-96, Kapalua Music Festival, Friends of Children Advocate Ctr., Legal Aid Soc. Hawaii, pres., 1998-88; v.p., trustee, chmn. devel. com. Cleve. Playhouse, 1984-89; trustee, mem. exec. com., program chmn. Cleve. Coun. World Affairs, 1970-89; past model UN chmn. Cleve. Com. on Fgn. Rels.; trustee, mem. exec. com., budget chmn. Neighborhood Ctrs. Assn., 1980-89; trustee Maui Symphony, 1995-98, v.p., 1999—. Recipient T.S. Shinn award, 2000. Mem. Rotary Club of Maui, Maui Country Club, Roufant Club (adv.), Cleve. Skating Club. Home: 106 Poohina Rd Kula HI 96790-9724 Office: Mancini Rowland & Welch 33 Lono Ave Kahului HI 96732-1633

RICHIE, BOYD LYNN, lawyer; b. Breckenridge, Tex., July 11, 1945; s. Bradie Eugene adn Billie June (Robinson) R.; m. Betty Zoe Furr, May 28, 1966; children: Christophber Robin, Tracy Lynn. BA in Polit. Sci. and History, Midwestern State U., 1967; JD, Tex. Tech. U., 1970. Bar: Tex. 1970, U.S. Dist. Ct. (no. dist.) Tex. 1975. Trial atty. Fed. Power Commn., Washington, 1970-71; assoc. John Bradshaw, Graham, Tex., 1971-72; sole practice, 1972-77; dist. atty. 90th Jud. Dist., 1977-80; asst. dist. atty. Wichita County, Wichita Falls, Tex., 1980-81; ptnr. Neal, Neal, Richie & Hill, Graham, 1981—; atty. Young County, Tex., 1996—. Co-op, Inc, Bluegrove, Tex., 1979-83, Ft. Belknap Electric Coop., Inc., Olney, Tex., 1984—. Mem. State Bar Tex., Young County Bar Assn. (pres. 1972-73). Democrat. Episcopalian. Criminal, Family and matrimonial. Home: 1307 Roanoake Dr Graham TX 76450-4037 Office: Young County Courthouse Rm 102 PO Box 390 Graham TX 76450-0390 E-mail: ycatty@wf.net, brichie@wf.net

RICHMAN, GERALD F. lawyer; b. Bklyn., Apr. 30, 1941; s. Albert A. and Lee (Soifer) R.; m. Gwen Caldwell, Jan. 25, 1981; children: Tiffany Lynn, Ashlee Alaina. B.Bldg. Constrn. with honors, U. Fla., 1962, J.D., 1964. Bar: Fla. 1965, D.C. 1967, U.S. Dist. Ct. (no., mid., so. dists.) Fla., U.S. Ct. Appeals (5th, 11th and D.C. cirs.), U.S. Supreme Ct. Pres. Richman, Greer, Weil, Brumbaugh, Mirabito & Christensen, P.A., Miami, Fla., 1969—; mem. Article V Rev. Commn., Fla. Supreme Ct., 1983-84, mem. jud. coun., 1985-87. Vice chmn. Fla. Condominium Commn., 1972-73, chmn., Fla. Commn. on Human Rels., 1998, Fla. Commn. on Merit Selection and Retention, 1989-90; chmn. legal div. United Way of Dade County, 1976-77; mem. coun. U. Fla. Law Ctr.; dir. Fla. Bar Found.; Dem. nominee 18th congl. dist. U.S. Ho. of Reps., 1989; mem. Palm Beach County Econ. Coun.; mem. Criminal Justice Commn., Palm Beach County, 2001—. Capt. U.S. Army, 1966-69, Korea. Recipient Presdl. Svc. Badge, Pres. US., 1968. Fellow Am. Coll. Trial Lawyers, Am. Bar Found., Internat. Soc. Barristers (bd. govs.); mem. ATLA, FBA, ABA (litigation, anti-trust and corp., banking and bus. law sects., ho. of dels. 1985-89, 92-98, commn. responsiblity client devel. 2000—), Fla. Bar Found. (bd. dirs. 1984-90), Fla. Acad. Trial Lawyers, Fla. Bar (bd. govs. 1980-85, pres. 1984-85), Dade County Bar Assn. (pres. 1976-77, chmn. jud. trust fund com. 1973-76, 77-80, 5 merit awards), Am. Judicature Soc. (bd. dirs. 1986-90), Phi Alpha Delta (Outsdanding Alumnus award U. Fla. chpt. 1985). Democrat. Jewish. E-mail: grichman@aol.com. Antitrust, Federal civil litigation, State civil litigation. Home: 19 St George Pl Palm Beach Gardens FL 33418-4024 Office: Richman Greer Weil Et Al 201 S Biscayne Blve 10th Fl Miami FL 33131 also: One Clearlake Ctr Ste 1504 250 Australian Ave S West Palm Beach FL 33401-5016

RICHMAN, JOEL ESER, lawyer, mediator, arbitrator; b. Brockton, Mass., Feb. 17, 1947; s. Nathan and Ruth Miriam (Bick) R.; m. Elaine R. Thompson, Aug. 21, 1987; children: Shawn Jonah, Jesse Ray, Eva Rose. BA in Psychology, Grinnell Coll., 1969; JD, Boston U., 1975. Bar: Mass. 1975, U.S. Dist. Ct. Mass. 1977, U.S. Supreme Ct. 1980, U.S. Ct. Appeals (1st cir.) 1982, Hawaii 1985, U.S. Dist. Ct. Hawaii 1987. Law clk. Richman & Perenyi, Brockton, Mass., 1973-75, atty., 1975-77; pvt. practice pvt. practice, Provincetown, 1977-82, Paia, Hawaii, 1985—. Arbitrator Am. Arbitration Assn., Paia, 1992—, mediator, 1994—. Pres. Jewish Congregation Maui (Hawaii), 1989-97, bd. dirs., 1984-89; bd. dirs. Pacific Primate Ctr., 1991, pres., 1994. Mem. Haiku Cmty. Assn. (dir. 1998, pres. 2000-), Kalama Band Boosters (pres. 2001-). Avocations: windsurfing, youth soccer, T'ai Chi. Contracts commercial, Construction, Real property. Office: PO Box 791539 Paia HI 96779-0046 E-mail: jer@haikulaw.com

RICHMAN, STEPHEN CHARLES, lawyer; b. Nov. 13, 1943; s. Abraham and Sylvia (Weissman) Richman; m. Dinah Ellenberg, Aug. 25, 1968; children: Alex, Marni. BS in Bus. Adminstrn., SUNY, Buffalo, 1965; JD, George Washington U., 1968. Bar: D.C. 1968, Pa. 1972, N.Y. 1983. Field atty. NLRB, 1969—72; assoc. Wilderman, Markowitz & Kirschner, 1972—73; assoc. then ptnr. Markowitz & Kirschner, 1973—79; ptnr. Markowitz & Richman, Phila., 1979—. Lectr. Temple U. Sch. Law; former instr. Pa. State U. Mem.: ABA, Pa. Bar Assn. (chmn. labor and employment law sect.), Phila. Bar Assn. Labor.

RICHMAN, STEPHEN I. lawyer; b. Washington, Pa., Mar. 26, 1933; m. Audrey May Gefsky. BS, Northwestern U., 1954; JD, U. Pa., 1957. Bar: Pa. 1958, U.S. Dist. Ct. (we. dist.) Pa. With McCune Greenlee & Richman, 1960-63, Greenlee Richman Derrico & Posa, 1963-84, ptnr. Richman, Smith Law Firm, P.A., Washington, 1985—; bd. dirs. Three Rivers Bank; lectr. U. South Fla. Sch. Medicine, Mine Safe Internat. Chamber of Mines of Western Australia, W.Va. U. Med. Ctr. Grand Rounds, Am. Coll. Chest Physicians, Pa. Thoracic Soc., Am. Thoracic Soc., The Energy Bur., Coll. of Am. Pathologists, Allegheny County Health Dept., APHA, Internat. Assn. Ind. Accident Bds. and Commns., Indsl. Health Found., Nat. Coun. Self-Insurers Assn., Am. Iron and Steel Inst., Can. Thoracic Soc., I.L.O./N.I.O.S.H., Univs. Associated for Rsch. and Edn. in Pathology, Am. Ceramics Soc., Nat. Sand Assn.; mem. adv. com. U.S. Dist. Ct. Western Dist. Pa., 1994—; lectr. in field. Author: Meaning of Impairment and Disability, Chest, 1980, Legal Aspects for the Pathologist, in Pathology of Occupational and Environmental Lung Disease, 1988, A Review of the Medical and Legal Definitions of Related Impairment and Disability, Report to the Department of Labor and the Congress, 1986, Medicolegal Aspects of Asbestos for Pathologists, Arch. Pathology and Laboratory Medicine, 1983, Legal Aspects of Occupational and Environmental Disease, Human Pathology, 1993, Impairment and Disability in Pneunoconiosis, State of the Art Reviews in Occupational Medicine-The Mining Industry, 1993, other publs. and articles; author House Bills 2103 and 885 co-author Act 44 and 57 amending Pa. Workmen's Compensation Act. Mem. legal com. Indsl. Health Found., Pitts.; bd. dirs. Pitts. Opera Soc., 1994—, Pitts. Jewish Fedn., 1994-97; dir. Jewish Family and Children's

Svc., Pitts., 1995—. Mem. ABA (former vice chair workers compensation and employers liability law com., toxic and hazardous substance and environ. law com., lectr.), ATLA, Pa. Bar Assn. (former mem. coun. of worker's compensation sect., lectr., contbg. author bar assn. quarterly 1992, 93), Pa. Chamber Bus. and Industry (workers' compensation com., chmn. subcom. on legis. drafting, lectr.). Personal injury, Toxic tort, Workers' compensation. Home: 820 E Beau St Washington PA 15301-2906 Office: Washington Trust Bldg Ste 200 Washington PA 15301

RICHMOND, ALICE ELENOR, lawyer; b. N.Y.C. d. Louis A. and Estelle (Muraskin) R.; m. David L. Rosenbloom, July 26, 1981; 1 child, Elizabeth Lara. BA magna cum laude, Cornell U., 1968; JD, Harvard U., 1972, OPM, 2001; DLH (hon.), North Adams State U., 1987. Bar: Mass. 1973, U.S. Dist. Ct. Mass. 1975, U.S. Ct. Appeals (1st cir.) 1982, U.S. Supreme Ct. 1985. Law clk. to justices Superior Ct., Boston, 1972-73; asst. dist. atty. Office of Dist. Atty., 1973-76; spl. asst. atty. gen. Office of Atty. Gen., 1975-77; asst. prof. New Eng. Sch. of Law, 1976-78; assoc. Lappin, Rosen, 1978-81; ptnr. Hemenway & Barnes, 1982-92, Deutsch, Williams, Boston, 1993-95, Richmond, Pauly & Ault, Boston, 1996—. Asst. team leader, faculty Trial Advocacy Course, 1978—82; examiner Mass. Bd. Bar Examiners, Boston, 1983—; trustee Mass. Continuing Legal Edn., Inc., Boston, 1985—96, Boston, 1998—; treas. Nat. Conf. Bar Examiners, 1995—, sec.; v.p., bd. dirs. Am. Bar Ins., Inc., 1996—. Author (2 chpts.) Rape Crisis Intervention Handbook, 1976; contbr. articles to profl. jours. Bd. of overseers Handel & Haydn Soc., Boston, 1985-94, mem. bd. govs. Handel & Haydn Soc., 1994—, v.p., 1996—; mem. Pres. Adv. Com. on the Arts, 1995-99; mem. Boston 2000 Millenium Commn., 1997-98; sec., dir. Boston 2000, Inc., 1998-2001; mem., pres. Coun. of Cornell Women, Cornell U. Coun.; trustee Red Auerbach Youth Found., Fund for Justice and Edn.; mem. adv. bd. Cen. and Ea. European Law Initiative. Named one of Outstanding Young Leaders Boston Jaycees, 1982; Sloan Found. Urban fellow, N.Y.C., 1969 Fellow Am. Coll. Trial Lawyers; mem. ABA (ho. of dels. 1980—, vice chmn. com. on rules and calendar 1986-88), Am. Law Inst., Mass. Bar Assn. (pres. 1986-87), Mass. Bar Found. (pres. 1988-91), NOW, Legal Def. and Edn. Fund (trustee 1995—, sec. 1998—), Latin Am. Legal Initiatives Coun., Internat. Judicial Acad., Harvard Club, Boston Club. General civil litigation, Insurance, Personal injury. Office: Richmond Pauly & Ault One Beacon St Boston MA 02108

RICHMOND, DAVID WALKER, lawyer; b. Silver Hill, W.Va., Apr. 20, 1914; s. David Walker and Louise (Finlaw) R.; m. Gladys Evelyn Mallard, Dec. 19, 1936; children: David Walker, Nancy L. LL.B., George Washington U., 1937. Bar: D.C. 1936, Ill. 1946, Md. 1950. Partner firm Miller & Chevalier, Washington. Lectr. fed. taxation. Contbr. to profl. jours. Served from ensign to lt. comdr. USNR, 1942-46. Decorated Bronze Star; recipient Disting. Alumni Achievement award George Washington U., 1976 Fellow Am. Bar Found., Am. Coll. Tax Counsel; mem. ABA (chmn. taxation sect. 1955-57, ho. of dels. 1958-60), Am. Law Inst., Lawyers' Club of Washington, Union League (Chgo.), Masons. Republican. Methodist. Legislative, Corporate taxation. Home: 7979 S Tamiami Trl Apt 359 Sarasota FL 34231-6819 Office: 655 15th St NW Washington DC 20005-5701

RICHMOND, HAROLD NICHOLAS, lawyer; b. Elizabeth, N.J., Apr. 5, 1935; s. Benjamin I. and Eleanor (Turbowitz) R.; m. Elaine Zemel, June 16, 1957 (div. Nov. 1972); children: Bonnie J. Ross, Michele Weinfeld; m. Marilyn A. Wenrich, Aug. 26, 1973; children: Eric L., Kacy L. BA, Tulane U., 1957; LLB, NYU, 1961, LLM in Taxation, 1965. Estate tax examiner IRS, Newark, 1963-65; tax mgr. Puder & Puder/Touche Ross & Co., CPAs, 1965-73; ptnr. Sodowick Richmond & Crecca, 1973-84; prin. Harold N. Richmond, West Orange, N.J., 1984-86; ptnr. Wallerstein Hauptman & Richmond, 1986-91, Hauptman & Richmond, West Orange, 1992—. With U.S. Army, 1959-60. Mem. ABA (tax sect. closely held bus. com., real property and probate sect.), N.J. Bar Assn. (tax, real property and probate sects.), Essex County Bar Assn. (chmn. tax com. 1989, real property and probate sect.). Avocations: running, tennis. Estate planning, Corporate taxation, Taxation, general. Office: Hauptman & Richmond 100 Executive Dr Ste 330 West Orange NJ 07052-3309

RICHMOND, JAMES GLIDDEN, lawyer; b. Sacramento, Feb. 20, 1944; s. James Gibbs and Martha Ellen (Glidden) R.; m. Lois Marie Bennett, Oct. 22, 1988; 1 child, Mark R. BS in Mgmt., Ind. U., 1966, postgrad., 1966-69, JD, 1969. Bar: Ind. 1969, Ill. 1991, U.S. Dist. Ct. (no. dist.) Ind. 1971, U.S. Dist. Ct. (so. dist.) Ind., 1969, U.S. Ct. Appeals (7th cir.) 1975, U.S. Tax Ct. 1980. Spl. agent FBI, 1970-74; spl. agent Criminal Investigation Divsn. IRS, 1974-76; asst. U.S. atty. no. dist. U.S. Atty. Office, Ind., 1976-80; assoc. Galvin, Stalmack & Kirschner, Hammond, 1980-81; pvt. practice Highland, 1981-83; ptnr. Goodman, Ball & Van Bokkelen, 1983-85; U.S. atty. no. dist. State of Ind., Hammond, 1985-91; spl. counsel to dep. atty. gen. of the U.S. U.S. Dept. Justice, Washington, 1990-91; mng. ptnr. Ungaretti and Harris, Chgo., 1991-92, ptnr., 1995—; exec. v.p., gen. counsel Nat. Health Labs., 1992-95. Practitioner in residence Ind. U. Sch. Law, Bloomington, 1989. Minority counsel senate republicans October Surprise Hearings, 1992. Fellow Am. Coll. Trial Lawyers. Republican. Avocation: fishing. Office: Ungaretti & Harris 3500 Three First National Plz Chicago IL 60602-4283

RICHMOND, MICHAEL LLOYD, lawyer, educator; b. Jersey City, May 18, 1945; s. Abraham and Sarah Belle (Bernstein) R.; children: Henry Samuel, Amy Joann; m. Fran Leslie Tetunic. AB, Hamilton Coll., 1967; JD, Duke U., 1971; MLS, U. N.C., 1974. Bar: Ohio, 1971, U.S. Ct. Appeals (4th cir.) 1975, Fla. 1983. Assoc. Marshman, Snyder & Seeley, Cleve., 1971-72; asst. prof. law Capital U., Columbus, Ohio, 1972-73; assoc. prof. N.C. Cen. U., Durham, 1974-76; asst. law libr. Tarlton Law Libr., Austin, Tex., 1976-78; prof. Nova Law Ctr., Fort Lauderdale, Fla., 1978—. Author: Problems and Instructor's Manual To Accompany Fundamentals of Legal Research, 1981; editor: Comparative Negligence and Contribution in Florida, 1989; editor-in-chief Trial Adv. Quarterly, 1981-95; contbr. articles to profl. publs. Dir. Ramat Shalom Synagogue. Mem. ABA, Fla. Bar Assn. (vice chair com. on technology), Broward County Bar Assn. Democrat. Jewish. Office: Nova Law Ctr 3305 College Ave Davie FL 33314-7721

RICHMOND, ROBERT LAWRENCE, lawyer; b. St. Petersburg, Fla., Sept. 30, 1943; s. Chester A. and Barbara (O'Connell) R.; children: Kristen, Meghan, Alyson; m. Carol Richmond. AB, Georgetown U., 1965; JD, U. Oreg., 1970. Bar: Oreg. 1970, Alaska 1970, U.S. Dist. Ct. Alaska 1970, U.S. Ct. Appeals (9th cir.) 1971. Ptnr. Richmond, Willoughby & Willard, Anchorage, 1975-81; sr. ptnr. Richmond & Quinn, 1981—. Past pres. Alaska chpt. Am. Bd. Trial Advs., Alaska chpt. Def. Coun. Alaska; bd. visitors U. Oreg. Law Sch. Bd. dirs. Alaska Treatment Ctr., Anchorage, Girl's Club Alaska, Anchorage. Served to capt., U.S. Army, 1965-67. Speak Up winner Alaska Jaycees, 1971. Mem. ABA, Alaska Bar Assn., Oreg. Bar Assn., U.S. Maritime Law Assn. (practor in admiralty), IADC, FICC. Republican. Roman Catholic. Admiralty, Federal civil litigation, State civil litigation. Address: 360 K St Ste 200 Anchorage AK 99501-2038 E-mail: brichmond@richmondquinn.com

RICHTER, DAVID JEROME, lawyer; b. Fond du Lac, Wis., Oct. 1, 1940; s. Gerald George and Olive Marie (Schneider) R.; children— Angelica Maria, Anna Maria, Paul David, Andrea Maria. B.S. in Mech. Engring., U. Wis., 1962; M.B.A., U. Ill., 1967, J.D., 1970. Bar: Ohio 1970, Ill. 1974, U.S. Patent Office 1972, U.S. Ct. Customs and Patent Appeals 1973, U.S. Ct. Appeals (6th cir.) 1973. Engr. Twin Disc Clutch Co., Racine, Wis., 1962-63; patent atty. The Proctor & Gamble Co., Cin., 1970-74; corp. counsel, patent counsel Roper Corp., Kankakee, Ill., 1974— , asst. sec., 1974— . Patentee in field. Arbitrator City of Kankakee Police and Firemen Negotiation, 1975. Recipient scholarship Giddings & Lewis Machine Tool Co., Fond du Lac, Wis., 1958. Mem. ABA, Ill. Bar Assn., Kankakee County Bar Assn., Kankakee C. of C. (com. chmn. 1979-84), Theta Tau. Republican. Roman Catholic. Lodges: Elks (officer 1982—), KC. General corporate, Patent, Trademark and copyright. Home: 1188 S 6th Ave Kankakee IL 60901-4840 Office: Snap-On Tools Corp 2801 80th St Kenosha WI 53143-5699

RICHTER, DONALD PAUL, lawyer; b. New Britain, Conn., Feb. 15, 1924; s. Paul John and Helen (Racoske) R.; m. Jane Frances Gumpright, Aug. 10, 1946; children: Christopher Dean, Cynthia Louise. A.B., Bates Coll., 1947; LL.B., Yale U., 1950. Bar: N.Y. 1951, Conn. 1953. Assoc. Winthrop, Stimson, Putnam & Roberts, N.Y.C., 1950-52; ptnr. Murtha, Cullina, Richter and Pinney, Hartford, Conn., 1954-94; counsel Murtha Cullina LLP, 1994—. Trustee Bates Coll., 1962-94, Manchester (Conn.) Meml. Hosp., 1963-94, Hartford Sem., 1973-85; trustee Suffield Acad., 1974—, pres., 1982-89; bd. dirs. Met. YMCA Greater Hartford, 1970-94, pres., 1976-81, trustee, 1994—; mem. nat. coun. YMCA, 1978-82; bd. dirs. Church Homes, 1967-81; trustee, v.p., Silver Bay Assn., 1971-96. With USNR, 1943-46. Fellow Am. Coll. Trust and Estate Counsel; mem. ABA, Conn. Bar Assn., Univ. Club, Hartford Club, 20th Century Club, Rotary (Paul Harris fellow 1996), Phi Beta Kappa, Delta Sigma Rho. Congregationalist. General corporate, Estate planning. Home: 140 Boulder Rd Manchester CT 06040-4508 Office: Murtha Cullina LLP City Place I 185 Asylum St & 29th St Hartford CT 06103-3469

RICHTER, TOBIN MARAIS, lawyer; b. Washington, Dec. 31, 1944; s. Vivian Craig and Leora Chapelle (Aultman) R.; m. Elizabeth Mills Dunlop, July 11, 1970; children: Ian, Lauren. B in City Planning, U. Va., 1967, JD, 1973. Bar: Ill. 1973, U.S. Dist. Ct. (no. dist.) Ill. 1973, U.S. Ct. Fed. Claims, 1976, U.S. Ct. Appeals (7th cir.) 1977, U.S. Supreme Ct. 1979, U.S. Dist. Ct. (ea. dist.) Wis. 1987. Assoc. Ross & Hardies, Chgo., 1973-80, ptnr., 1981-84, Spindell, Kemp & Kimball, Chgo., 1984-89; pvt. practice, 1989—. Adj. instr. U. Wis., Osh Kosh, 1976; ct. apptd. arbitrator Cir. Ct. Cook County, 1991—; chancellor Seabury-Western Theol. Sem., 1998-2001. Co-author: Federal Land Use Regulation, 1977; contbr. articles to profl. jours. Legal counsel 44th Ward Community Zoning Bd., Chgo., 1980; v.p., Aux. Bd. Chgo. Architecture Found., 1983; pres., bd. dirs. Landmarks Preservation Council Ill., Chgo., 1986; v.p., bd. dirs. Counseling Ctr. of Lakeview, 1997—. 1st lt. U.S. Army, 1968-70, Vietnam. Mem. ABA, Chgo. Bar Assn., Soc. Am. Mil. Engrs. (v.p. 1980, 84, 86), Econ. Club (Chgo.). Avocations: tennis, pottery, genealogy. Federal civil litigation, State civil litigation, Real property. Office: 53 W Jackson Blvd Ste 560 Chicago IL 60604-3667 E-mail: tmrichter@corecomm.net

RICKERT, BRIAN PATRICK, lawyer; b. Mankato, Minn., Dec. 10, 1972; s. Marvin LeRoy and Maria Annette Rickert. BBA in Fin., U. Iowa, 1995; JD with honors, Drake U., 1998. Bar: Mo. 1998, U.S. Dist. Ct. (we. dist.) Mo. 1998. Assoc. Dysart, Taylor, Lay, Cotter & McMonigle, Kansas City, Mo., 1998—. Mem. staff Drake Law Rev., 1996-98. Vol. Rep. Party, Kansas City, 1998, Big Bros./Big Sisters, Kansas City, 1998. Mem. ABA, Kansas City Met. Bar Assn. Lutheran. Avocations: golf, volleyball, outdoor activities. General civil litigation, General corporate, Insurance. Office: Dysart Taylor Lay Cotter & McMinigle PC 4420 Madison Kansas City MO 64111

RIDDICK, WINSTON WADE, SR. lawyer; b. Crowley, La., Feb. 11, 1941; s. Hebert Hobson and Elizabeth (Wade) R.; m. Patricia Ann Turner, Dec. 25, 1961;1 child, Winston Wade. BA, U. Southwestern La., 1962; MA, U. N.C., 1963; PhD, Columbia U., 1965; JD, La. State U., 1973. Bar: La. 1974, U.S. Dist. Ct. (so., mid. and we. dists.) La., U.S. Ct. Appeals (5th cir.), U.S. Supreme Court. Asst. prof. gov., dir. Inst. Gov. Research, La. State U., Baton Rouge, 1966-67; dir. La. Higher Edn. Facilities Commn., 1967-72; exec. asst. state supt. La. Dept. Edn., 1972-73; law ptnr. Riddick & Riddick, 1973—; asst. commnr., gen. counsel La. Dept. Agr., 1981-82. Cons. Riddick & Assoc., Baton Rouge, 1973—; part-time law faculty mem. So. Univ. Law Ctr., Baton Rouge, 1974-95; assoc. prof., 1995-99, prof. law, 1999—, exec. asst. atty. gen. State of La., 1987-91. Spl. asst. to Gov. John J. McKeithen on Nat. Ctr. for Edn. in Politics Fellowship, 1966-67; state campaign mgr. Gillis W. Long for Gov., Baton Rouge, 1971; mem. East Baton Rouge Parish Dem. Exec. Com., 1981-84. Mem. La. Trial Lawyers Assn. (bd. govs. 1978-80), real estate investor and property mgr., 1975—. Presbyterian. Constitutional, Health, Insurance. Office: Riddick & Riddick 1563 Oakley Dr Baton Rouge LA 70806-8622 E-mail: wriddick@sus.edu

RIDDLE, CHARLES ADDISON, III, state legislator, lawyer; b. Marksville, La., June 8, 1955; s. Charles Addison Jr. and Alma Rita (Gremillion) R.; m. Margaret Susan Noone, Mar. 24, 1978; children: Charles Addison IV, John H., Michael J. BA, La. State U., 1976, JD, 1980. Bar: La. 1980, U.S. Dist. Ct. (mid. and we. dists.) La. 1983, U.S. Ct. Appeals (5th cir.) 1988, U.S. Supreme Ct. 1991, U.S. Ct. Vets. Appeals 1994. Assoc. Riddle & Bennett, Marksville, 1980; pvt. practice, 1981—; mem. La. Ho. of Reps., Baton Rouge, 1992—; reelected La. House of Reps., 1995-99, 1999—. Elected La. State Dem. Cen. com., Avoyelles Parish, 1983-87, Parish Exec. Demo. Com. 1987-91. Mem. Avoyelles Bar Assn. (pres. 1987-88), Bunkie Rotary (bd. dirs.), Marksville Lions, Marksville C. of C. (pres. 1988-92). Office: PO Box 608 208 E Mark St Marksville LA 71351-2416 E-mail: criddle777@aol.com

RIDDLE, MICHAEL LEE, lawyer; b. Oct. 7, 1946; s. Joy Lee and Francis Irene (Brandes) R.; m. Suzan Ellen Shaw, May 25, 1969 (div.); m. Carol Jackson, Aug. 13, 1977; 1 child, Robert Andrew. BA, Tex. Tech U., 1969, JD with honors, 1972. Bar: Tex. 1972, U.S. Dist. Ct. (no. dist.) Tex. 1972, U.S. Ct. Appeals (5th cir.) Tex. 1972. Assoc. Geary Brice Barron & Stahl, Dallas, 1972-75; ptnr. Baker Glast Riddle Tuttle & Elliott, 1975-80; ptnr., mng. ptnr. Middleburg, Riddle & Gianna, 1980—; chmn., CEO MRG Document Techs., 2000—. Bd. dirs. Dallas Opera. Bd. dirs. U.S.A. Film Festival, pres., 1984-86, North Tex. Pub. Broadcasting, 1992-97; chmn., bd. dirs. Provident Bancorp Tex., 1987-90. Mem. ABA, Tex. Bar Assn., Dallas Bar Assn., Coll. of State Bar of Tex., Lakewood Country Club, Crescent Club. Democrat. Lutheran. Banking, Real property. Office: 717 N Harwood Ste 2400 Dallas TX 75201 E-mail: mriddle@midrid.com

RIDDLE, VERYL LEE, lawyer; b. Campbell, Mo., Dec. 6, 1921; s. Elvis Lloyd and Etter Whitehead (Wood) R.; m. Mary J. Riggs, Jan. 15, 1941 (div. 1967); children— Kay, Jo, Janet, Veryl Lee, Jr.; m. Janet Lewis, Nov. 24, 1985. Student, Southeast Mo. U., 1939-41; student, U. Buffalo, 1942, 45-46; J.D., Washington U., St. Louis, 1948. Bar: Mo. 1948, U.S. Dist. Ct. (ea. and we. dists.) Mo. 1949, U.S. Ct. Appeals (8th cir.) 1949, U.S. Supreme Ct. 1969, U.S. Ct. Appeals (7th cir.) 1970, U.S. Ct. Appeals (5th cir.) 1974, U.S. Ct. Appeals (3d cir.) 1975. Agt. U.S. Dept. Justice, N.Y., Ohio, Tex., Mex., 1942-43; U.S. atty. Eastern Dist. Mo. Dept. Justice, St. Louis, 1967-69; ptnr. Riddle, Baker & O'Herin, Malden, Mo., 1948-67; sr. ptnr. Bryan Cave, St. Louis, 1969—. Pros. atty. Dunklin County, Mo., 1950-53; chmn. merit selection panel for U.S. Magistrate, St. Louis, 1983-84 Del., Nat. Democratic Conv., Chgo., 1956, Los Angeles, 1960. With U.S. Army, 1943-45, European Theatre, Military Intelligence. Recipient Disting. Alumni award Washington U. Sch. Law, 1993. Fellow Am. Coll. Trial Lawyers, Internat. Acad. Trial Lawyers; mem. Acad. Mo. Squires. Baptist. Clubs: Bellerive Country, Noonday, Round Table (St. Louis). Office: Bryan Cave 211 N Broadway Saint Louis MO 63102-2733

RIDEOUT, DAVID EDWARD, lawyer; b. Pitts., Nov. 4, 1937; s. Theodore R. and Barbara (Brooks) R.; m. Janice Everett, Aug. 24, 1963; children— Jennifer, Katherine, Marianne. B.S., Cornell U., 1959; LL.B., Columbia U., 1965. Bar: Mass. 1965. Research asst. Columbia U. Sch. Law, 1964-65; law clk. Mass. Supreme Jud. Ct., Boston, 1965-66; assoc. Palmer & Dodge, Boston, 1966-71, ptnr., 1972— ; lectr. law Boston U. Sch. Law, 1981— ; chmn. Mass. Legal Assistance Corp., Boston, 1983-85. Mem. Hamilton-Wenham Regional Sch. Com., 1973-75; trustee Wenham Pub. Library, 1973— , chmn., 1974-81; bd. dirs. Northshore Unitarian Universalist Ch., 1976-80, chmn., 1978-79; mem. Wenham Town Govt. Study Com., 1977— . Served to lt. USCGR, 1959-62. Mem. Boston Bar Assn. (mem. governing bd. 1977-81, chmn. sect. on delivery of legal services 1978-81, long range planning com. 1979—). General corporate, Real property. Home: 417 Ryerson Hill Rd South Paris ME 04281-6209 Office: Palmer & Dodge 1 Beacon St Ste 22 Boston MA 02108-3190

RIDER, BRIAN CLAYTON, lawyer; b. San Antonio, Oct. 8, 1948; s. Ralph W. and Emmie Rider; m. Patsy Anne Ruppert, Dec. 27, 1970; children: Christopher, David, James, Andrew. BA, Rice U., 1969; JD, U. Tex., 1972. Bar: Tex. 1972. Assoc. then ptnr. Dow, Cogburn & Friedman, Houston, 1972-83; ptnr. Brown, McCarroll & Oaks Hartline, Austin, Tex., 1983-96. Adj. prof. law U. Tex., 1997—. Contbr. articles to profl. jours.; lectr. in field. Mem. Am. Coll. Real Estate Lawyers, Travis County Bar Assn. (bd. dirs. 1986-88, chmn. Travis County real estate sect. 1986-88), State Bar of Tex. (coun. real estate and probate sect. 1992-96), Tex. Coll. Real Estate Lawyers (chair 1999—). Environmental, Finance, Real property. Home: 2906 Hatley Dr Austin TX 78746-4613 Office: 1300 S Mopac Austin TX 78746 E-mail: brider@ccsi.com, brider@lumbermensinv.com

RIDER, JAMES LINCOLN, lawyer; b. Newburgh, N.Y., Feb. 11, 1942; s. Meyer J. Rider and Marion (Weinberg) Levin; m. Eleanor Yazbeck, Nov. 5, 1977; children: Jordan E., Michael J. BA, Lafayette Coll., Easton, Pa., 1963; JD, Fordham U., 1966. Bar: N.Y. 1966, D.C. 1971, U.S. Ct. Appeals (D.C. cir.) 1971, U.S. Dist. Ct. D.C. 1971, Va. 1972, U.S. Dist. Ct. (ea. dist.) Va. 1972, U.S. Ct. Appeals (4th cir.) 1972, U.S. Dist. Ct. Md. 1973, U.S. Supreme Ct. 1975, U.S. Ct. Appeals (8th cir.) 1976. Ptnr. Margolius, Mallios, Davis, Rider & Tomar, Washington, 1971—. Capt. U.S. Army, 1967-71. Decorated Disting. Svc. medal. Fellow Am. Acad. Matrimonial Lawyers; mem. D.C. Bar, Va. Bar Assn., Assn. Trial Lawyers Am. State civil litigation, Family and matrimonial, Alternative dispute resolution. Office: Margolius Mallios Davis Rider & Tomar 1828 L St NW Ste 500 Washington DC 20036-5127

RIEGER, MITCHELL SHERIDAN, lawyer; b. Chgo., Sept. 5, 1922; s. Louis and Evelyn (Sampson) R.; m. Rena White Abelmann, May 17, 1949 (div. 1957); 1 child, Karen Gross Cooper; m. Nancy Horner, May 30, 1961 (div. 1972); stepchildren: Jill Levi, Linda Hanan, Susan Perlstein, James Geoffrey Felsenthal; m. Pearl Handelsman, June 10, 1973; stepchildren: Steven Newman, Mary Ann Malarkey, Nancy Halbeck. AB, Northwestern U., 1944; JD, Harvard U., 1949. Bar: Ill. 1950, U.S. Dist. Ct. (no. dist.) Ill. 1950, U.S. Supreme Ct. 1953, U.S. Ct. Mil. Appeals 1953, U.S. Ct. Appeals (7th cir.) 1954. Legal asst. Rieger & Rieger, Chgo., 1949-50, assoc., 1950-54; asst. U.S. atty. No. Dist Ill., 1954-60, 1st asst., 1958-60; assoc. gen. counsel SEC, Washington, 1960-61; ptnr. Schiff Hardin & Waite, Chgo., 1961—, sr. counsel, 1998—. Instr. John Marshall Law Sch. Chgo., 1952-54. Contbr. articles to profl. jours. Active Chgo. Crime Commn., bd. dirs., 1998—; pres. Park View Home for Aged, 1969-71; Rep. precinct committeeman, Highland Park, Ill., 1964-68; bd. dirs. Spertus Mus. Judaica, 1987-91, vis. com., 1991—. Served to lt. (j.g.) USNR, 1943-46, PTO. Fellow Am. Coll. Trial Lawyers; mem. ABA, FBA (pres. Chgo. chpt. 1959-60, nat. v.p 1960-61), Chgo. Bar Assn., Ill. Bar Assn., Am. Judicature Soc., 7th Circuit Bar Assn., Standard Club, Law Club Chgo., Vail Racquet Club, Phi Beta Kappa. Jewish. Avocations: photography, skiing, sailing. Professional liability. Home: 4950 S Chicago Beach Dr Chicago IL 60615-3207 Office: Schiff Hardin & Waite 6600 Sears Tower Chicago IL 60606 E-mail: mrieger@schiffhardin.com, msheridanr@aol.com

RIEGERT, ROBERT ADOLF, law educator, consultant; b. Cin., Apr. 21, 1923; s. Adolf and Hulda (Basler) R.; m. Roswitha Victoria Bigalke, Oct. 28, 1966; children: Christine Rose, Douglas Louis. BS, U. Cin., 1948; LLB cum laude, Harvard U., 1953; Doctoris Juris Utriusque magna cum laude, U. Heidelberg, Germany, 1966; postgrad., U. Mich., Harvard U., Yale U., MIT. Bar: D.C. 1953, Cts. Allied High Commn. Germany 1954. Mem. Harvard Legal Aid Bur., 1952-53; sole practice Heidelberg, 1954-63; vis. assoc. prof. So. Meth. U. Law Sch., Dallas, 1967-71; prof. law Cumberland Law Sch., Samford U., Birmingham, Ala., 1971-97, prof. emeritus, 1997—; dir. Cumberland Summer Law Program, Heidelberg, 1981-94. Disting. vis. prof. Salmon P. Chase Coll. Law, 1983-84. Author: (With Robert Braucher) Introduction to Commercial Transactions, 1977, Documents of Title, 1978; contbr. articles to profl. jours. Served to 1st lt. USAAF, 1943-46 Grantee Dana Fund for Internat. and Comparative Law, 1979; grantee Am. Bar Found., 1966-67; German Acad. Exchange, 1953-55, mem. Harvard Legal Aid Bur., Salmon P. Chase Coll. law scholar, 1950; Pres.'s scholar U. Cin., 1941 Mem. ABA (com. on new payment systems), Internat. Acad. Comml. and Consumer Law, Am. Law Inst., Ala. Law Inst. (coun.), Assn. Am. Law Schs. (sect. internat. legal exchs., subcom. on com. laws), German Comparative Law Assn., Acad. Soc. German Supreme Cts., Army-Navy Club (Washington). Office: Samford U Cumberland Law Sch Birmingham AL 35229-0001

RIEKE, FORREST NEILL, lawyer; b. Portland, Oreg., May 26, 1942; s. Forrest Eugene and Mary Neill (Whitelaw) R.; m. Madonna Bernardi, Apr. 2, 1966; children: Mary Jane, Forrest Ermelindo. AB in Polit. Sci., Stanford U., 1968; JD, Willamette U., 1971. Bar: Oreg. 1971, U.S. Dist. Ct. Oreg. 1974, U.S. Ct. Appeals (9th cir.) 1975, U.S. Supreme Ct. 1977. Sr. dep. dist. atty. Multnomah County, Portland, 1971-76; ptnr. Rieke & Savage P.C., 1977—. Instr. Oreg. State Police Acad., Ft. Rilea, 1979—. Contbr. editor Williamette U. Law Rev., 1971. Pres., bd. dirs. Council Great City Schs., Washington, 1985-93; trustee Emanuel Hosp. Found., 1987-93; bd. dirs. Portland Pub. Schs., 1978-93. Mem. ABA, Oreg. Bar Assn. (indigent accused def. com., chmn. law related edn. com. 1985, bd. dirs. criminal law sect. 1979-84, mem. pub. info. com. 1987-90, ho. dels. 1995-98), Nat. Criminal Def. Lawyers Assn., Multnomah County Bar Assn., Oreg. Criminal Def. Lawyers Assn., Multnomah Athletic, Rotary. Presbyterian. Avocations: skiing, reading, coaching youth sports. General civil litigation, Criminal, Personal injury. Home: 820 SW 2nd Ave Apt 6 Portland OR 97204-3086 Office: Rieke & Savage PC 140 SW Yamhill St Portland OR 97204-3007 E-mail: joe@rieke_savage.com

RIEKE, PAUL VICTOR, lawyer; b. Seattle, Apr. 1, 1949; s. Luvern Victor and Anna Jane (Bierstedt) R.; m. Judy Vivian Farr, Jan. 24, 1974; children: anna Katharina, Peter Johann. BA, Oberlin Coll., 1971; postgrad., U. Wash., 1971, Shoreline C.C., 1972-73; JD, Case Western Res. U., 1976. Bar: Wash, 1976, U.S. Dist. Ct. (we. dist.) Wash. 1976, U.S. Tax Ct. 1978. Assoc. Hatch & Leslie, Seattle, 1976-82, ptnr., 1982-91, Foster, Pepper & Shefelman, PLLC, 1991—. Exec. notes editor Case Western Res. U. Law Rev., 1975-76. Mem. exec. bd. dist. coun. N. Pacific dist. Am. Luth Ch., Seattle, 1978-83, coun. pres., 1983, Am. Luth. Ch. pub. bd., 1984-87; v.p. Northwest Wash. Synod of Evangelical Luth. Ch. Am., Seattle, 1988-90, mem. Synod Coun., 1990-92, del. ELCA Nat. Assembly, 1991, ELCA Northwest Synod Regional Rep., 1992-96, region one coun. pres., 1994-96. Mem. ABA, Wash. State Bar Assn., Seattle-King County Bar Assn., Order of Coif. Democrat. Lodge: Seattle Downtown Central Lions. General corporate, Probate, Real property. Home: 321 NE 161st St Shoreline WA 98155-5741 Office: Foster Pepper & Shefelman PLLC 34th Fl 1111 3rd Ave Seattle WA 98101 E-mail: RiekP@Foster.com

RIES, WILLIAM CAMPBELL, lawyer; b. Pitts., Apr. 8, 1948; s. F. William and Dorothy (Campbell) R.; m. Mallory Burns, Oct. 26, 1968; children: William Sheehan, Sean David. AB, Cath. U. Am., 1970; JD, Duquesne U., 1974; cert. Grad. Sch. Indsl. Adminstrn., Carnegie Mellon U., 1980. Bar: Pa. 1974, U.S. Dist. Ct. (we. dist.) Pa. 1974, U.S. Supreme Ct. 1979. Atty., then mng. counsel trust and investment svc. Mellon Bank, N.A., Pitts., 1974-90; ptnr. Dickie, McCamey and Chilcote, 1990-98; mem. Sweeney, Metz, Fox, McGrann & Schermer, LLC, 1998-2001; shareholder Tucker Arensberg, 2001—. Mem. adv. com. decedents' estates and trust law Pa. Joint State Govt. Commn., 1981—; adj. prof. Duquesne U., 1984—. Author: The Regulation of Investment Management and Fiduciary Services West, 1997. Pres. McCandless Twp. Civic Assn., Pitts., 1981—, McCandless Town Coun., chair pub. safety com., vice chair fin com.; sec. McCandless Indsl. Devel. Auth.; liaison McCandless zoning hearing bd. Fellow Am. Bar Found.; mem. ABA (chmn. fiduciary svcs. subcom.), Pa. Bar Assn., Allegheny County Bar Assn., Pitts. Estate Planning Coun., Am. Bankers Assn. (co-chmn. nat. conf. lawyers and corp. fiduciaries, chmn. trust counsel com.), Pa. Bankers Assn. (trust com., trust legis. com.), Rivers Club, Treesdale Golf and Country Club. Republican. Avocations: golf, sailing, cross-country skiing, fitness. Banking, Pension, profit-sharing, and employee benefits, Securities. Home: 9602 Fawn Ln Allison Park PA 15101-1737 E-mail: wries@tuckerlaw.com

RIESS, GEORGE FEBIGER, lawyer, educator; b. New Orleans, Oct. 22, 1943; s. Frank and Jane (Kelleher) R.; m. June 22, 1968 (div. June 1976); 1 child, Katherine Cody; m. Maida Magee, Aug. 23, 1980; children: Frank Henry, Carson Magee, Maida Jean. BA, Tulane U., 1965; JD, La. State U., 1969. Bar: La. 1969, Mich. 1972, U.S. Dist. Ct. (ea., we. and mid. dists.) La. 1970. Mng. ptnr. Johnson & Riess Law Firm, New Orleans, 1970-76; ptnr. Monroe & Lemann Law Firm, 1976-96, Polack, Rosenberg, Endom & Riess, L.L.P., New Orleans, 1996—. Bd. dirs. Plaquemines Oil and Devel. Corp., New Orleans; adj. prof. law Tulane U. Law Sch., New Orleans, 1987-94. Sec. of vestry St. Martin Episcopal Ch., Metairie, La., 1992—. Recipient Ford Found. grant, 1969. Fellow La. State Bar Found.; mem. ABA, Am. Judicature Soc., Fed. Bar Assn., La. Assn. Def. Counsel, La. State Bar Assn., New Orleans Assn. Def. Counsel, So. Yacht Club, New Orleans Lawn Tennis Club. Admiralty, Personal injury, Product liability. Office: Polack Rosenberg Edom & Riess LLP 938 Lafayette St Ste 100 New Orleans LA 70113-1067

RIFFER, JEFFREY KENT, lawyer, educator; b. Gary, Ind., Sept. 8, 1953; s. Howard and Jeanne (Fischer) R.; m. Catherine Anne Conway, Oct. 22, 1985. BS, Ind. U., 1975, JD, 1978. Bar: Ind. 1978, Calif. 1979, U.S. Ct. Appeals (7th cir.) 1979, U.S. Ct. Appeals (9th cir.) 1981. From assoc. to ptnr. Kadison, Pfaelzer, Woodard, Quinn & Rossi, Los Angeles, 1979-87; ptnr. Jeffer, Mangels, Butler& Marmaro, 1987—. Adj. prof. Pepperdine U., Malibu, Calif., 1981-91. Author: Sports and Recreational Injuries, 1985, (jour.) An Overview of Sex Discrimination in Amateur Athletics, 1983. Mem. ABA, Los Angeles County Bar Assn., Order of Coif, Beta Gamma Sigma, Beta Alpha Psi. Jewish. Federal civil litigation, State civil litigation, Libel. Office: Jeffer Mangels Butler & Marmaro 10th Flr 2121 Ave Of Stars Fl 10 Los Angeles CA 90067-5010

RIFFKIN, MITCHELL SANFORD, lawyer; b. Providence, Dec. 30, 1944; s. Ira and Rose (Kirshenbaum) R. BA, U. R.I., 1966; JD, Boston U., 1969. Bar: R.I. 1969, U.S. Dist. Ct. R.I. 1970, U.S. Ct. Appeals (1st cir.) 1980. Pros. atty. City of Warwick, R.I., 1971-72, mcpl. judge, 1980-93; magistrate bail commr. Kent County, R.I., 1973-99. Chmn. Fed. Block Grant Allocation Subcom., Warwick, 1976-99; chmn. Group Home Placement for Mentally Retarded, Warwick, 1976-93; chmn. Mayor's Fin. Adv. Commn., Warwick, 1985-93. Named One of Outstanding Young Men of Yr., U.S. Jaycees, 1976. Fellow Pi Sigma Alpha (past pres.); mem. ABA (arbitrator), R.I. Bar Assn. (ho. of dels., chmn. ethics com. 1982-86), R.I. Audubon Soc., U.S. Power Squadron. Democrat. Jewish. Lodges: B'nai B'rith (bd. govs. 1978), Masons. Home: 259 Merrymount Dr Warwick RI 02888-5524 Office: 631 Jefferson Blvd Warwick RI 02886-1318

RIFKIND, ROBERT S(INGER), lawyer; b. N.Y.C., Aug. 31, 1936; s. Simon H. and Adele (Singer) R.; m. Arleen Brenner, Dec. 24, 1961; children: Amy, Nina. BA, Yale U., 1958; JD, Harvard U., 1961; LHD (hon.), Jewish Theol. Sem. Am., 1998. Bar: N.Y. 1961, U.S. Supreme Ct. 1965. Asst. to solicitor gen. Dept. Justice, 1965-68; assoc. firm Cravath, Swaine & Moore, N.Y.C., 1962-65, 68-70, ptnr., 1971—. Trustee Dalton Sch., N.Y.C., 1975-83, hon. trustee, 1983—, pres., 1977-79; trustee Brandeis U., 1998—, The Loomis Inst., 1987-95, Citizens Budget Commn.; bd. dirs. Charles H. Revson Found., 1991—, chmn., 1997—; bd. dirs. Jewish Theol. Sem. Am., 1983—, Leo Baeck Inst., 1999—, Benjamin N. Cardozo Sch. Law, 1984-89; pres. Am. Jewish Com., 1994-98; chmn., adminstr. coun., Jacob Blaustein Inst. Advancement of Human Rights. Fellow Am. Coll. Trial Lawyers, Am. Bar Found.; mem. ABA, Coun. Fgn. Rels., Am. Law Inst., Assn. of Bar of City of N.Y., Phi Beta Kappa. Democrat. Antitrust, Federal civil litigation, State civil litigation. Office: Cravath Swaine & Moore Worldwide Pla 825 8th Ave Fl 38 New York NY 10019-7475

RIGBY, KENNETH, lawyer; b. Shreveport, La., Oct. 20, 1925; s. Samuel and Mary Elizabeth (Fearnhead) R.; m. Jacqueline Carol Brandon, June 8, 1951; children: Brenda, Wayne, Glen. BS magna cum laude, La. State U., 1950, JD, 1951. Bar: La. 1951, U.S. Ct. Appeals (5th cir.) 1966, U.S. Supreme Ct. 1971, U.S. Tax Ct. 1981, U.S. Ct. Appeals (11th cir.) 1982. Ptnr. Love, Rigby, Dehan & McDaniel, 1951—. Adj. prof. of law LSU Law Ctr., 1990—; mem. Marriage-Persons Com. La. Law Inst., 1981—, mem. coun., 1988—; mem. La. Supreme Ct. Jud. Coun., 1999—. Contbr. articles to profl. jours. Sec. mandatory CLE com. La. Supreme Ct., 1987-95. With USAF, 1943-46. Fellow Am. Acad. Matrimonial Lawyers, Am. Coll. Trial Lawyers; mem. ABA, La. State Bar Assn. (chmn. com. on CLE 1974-75, chmn. family law sect. 1981-82, bd. govs. 1986-88), Shreveport Bar Assn. (pres. 1973-74). Family and matrimonial, Personal injury, Probate. Office: Transcontinental Tower 330 Marshall St Ste 1400 Shreveport LA 71101-3018 E-mail: charli@prysm.net

RIGG, JOHN BROWNLEE, JR. lawyer; b. Lincoln, Nebr., May 31, 1947; s. John B. and Shirley A. (Tomlinson) R.; children: John III, Eaton James, Michael Torian; BA, George Washington U., 1969; JD, U. Denver, 1973. Staff, U.S. Senator Gordon Allott of Colo., Washington and Denver, 1967-73; adminstr. City of Idaho Springs (Colo.), 1973-75; regional rep. Motor Vehicle Mfrs. Assn., Denver, 1975-80; govt. affairs rep., Amoco Corp., Denver, 1980—. Legislative. Office: Amoco Corp PO Box 800 Denver CO 80201-0800

RIGGS, ARTHUR JORDY, retired lawyer; b. Nyack, N.Y., Apr. 3, 1916; s. Oscar H. and Adele (Jordy) R.; m. Virginia Holloway, Oct. 15, 1942 (dec.); children: Arthur James (dec.), Emily Adele Riggs Freeman, Keith Holloway, George Bennett; m. Priscilla McCormack, Jan. 16, 1993. AB, Princeton U., 1937; LLB, Harvard U., 1940. Bar: Mass. 1940, Tex. 1943; cert. specialist in labor law. Assoc. Warner, Stackpole, Stetson & Bradlee, Boston, 1940-41; staff mem. Solicitors Office U.S. Dept. Labor, Washington, Dallas, 1941-42; mem. Johnson, Bromberg, Leeds & Riggs, Dallas, 1949-81; of counsel Geary & Spencer, 1981-91. Mem. ABA, State Bar Tex., Phi Beta Kappa. Avocations: Maya archeology, history, photography. Home and Office: 2110 Antibes Dr Carrollton TX 75006-4326 E-mail: ariggs9@home.com

RIGGS, R. WILLIAM, state supreme court judge; Grad., Portland State U., 1961; JD, U. Oreg., 1968. Atty. Willner Bennett & Leonard, 1968-78; judge circuit ct. 4th Jud. Dist., 1978-88; judge Oreg. Ct. of Appeals, 1988-98, Oreg. Supreme Ct., 1998—. Active mem. Cmty. Law Poject; founder Integra Corp. Capt. USNR. Office: Supreme Ct Bldg 1163 State St Salem OR 97310-0260 E-mail: r.william.riggs@ojd.state.or.us

RIGOLOSI, ELAINE LA MONICA, lawyer, educator, consultant; b. Astoria, N.Y., Oct. 12, 1944; d. Richard Anthony La Monica and Caroline La Monica; m. Robert Salvatore Rigolosi, June 15, 1997. BS, Columbia Union Coll., Takoma Park, Md., 1964; MN, U. Fla., 1967; EdD, U. Mass., 1975; JD, Benjamin N. Cardozo Sch. Law, N.Y.C., 1993. Bar: N.J. 1994, N.Y. 1994, D.C. 1995; RN, N.Y. Chair dept. nursing edn. Tchrs. Coll., Columbia U., N.Y.C., 1988-91, prof. nursing edn., 1982-96, acting chair dept. nursing edn., 1994-96, prof. dept. orgn. and leadership, 1996—, dir. Inst. Rsch. in Nursing, 1981—; health care mgmt. cons. in pvt. practice, 1974—. Bd. dirs. Hooper Holmes, Inc., Basking Ridge, N.J., 1989—; cons. Delaware Valley Transplant Program, Phila., 1998, U. Tenn. Coll. Pharmacy, Memphis, 1995-98. Author: The Nursing Process: A Humanistic Approach, 1979 (Am. Jour. Nursing Book of Yr. 1979), Management in Health Care, 1994. Dept. HHS grantee, 1977-80, 80-83. Fellow Am. Acad. Nursing; mem. ABA, Assn. Bar City N.Y. (com. on health law 1994-97), Am. Health Lawyers Assn., Am. Assn. Nurse Attys., Am. Coll. Legal Medicine, Sigma Theta Tau. Avocations: tennis, skiing, needlepoint, interior design. Home: 158 Summit Dr Paramus NJ 07652-1312 Office: Tchrs Coll Columbia U 525 W 120th St New York NY 10027-6625

RIGOR, BRADLEY GLENN, lawyer; b. Cheyenne Wells, Colo., Aug. 9, 1955; s. Glenn E. and Lelia (Teed) R.; m. Twyla G. Helweg, Sept. 4, 1983; children: Camille, Brent, Tiffany, Lauren. BS in Mktg., Ft. Hays State U., 1977; JD, Washburn U., 1980. Bar: Kans. 1980, U.S. Dist. Kans., 1980, U.S. Tax Ct. 1981, U.S. Ct. Appeals (10th cir.) 1982, U.S. Supreme Ct. 1986, Colo. 1990, Tex. 1991, U.S. Dist. Ct. Colo. 1991, Mo. 1993, Fla. 1998; cert. trust and fin. advisor Inst. Cert. Bankers; cert. fin. planner. Ptnr. Zuspann & Rigor, Goodland, Kans., 1980-82; city atty., 1981-82; asst. county atty. Wallace County, Sharon Springs, Kans., 1982-84, county atty., 1984; city atty., 1983-84; judge Mcpl. Ct., Goodland, 1988-93; ptnr. Fairbanks, Rigor & Irvin, P.A., 1982-93; v.p., mgr. personal trusts Merc. Bank, St. Joseph, Mo., 1993-96; sr. v.p., mgr., personal trust adminstr. SunTrust Bank, Naples, Fla., 1996-98; ptnr. Bond Schoeneck & King P.A., 1998—. Mem. Estate Planning Coun., Naples. Mem. Kans. Bar Assn., Tex. Bar Assn., Mo. Bar Assn., Colo. Bar Assn., Fla. Bar Assn., Collier County Bar Assn. (trust and estates sect.). Republican. Baptist. Estate planning. Office: Bond Schoeneck & King PA 4001 Tamiami Trl N Ste 404 Naples FL 34103-3555 E-mail: rigorb@bsk.com

RIGSBY, LINDA FLORY, lawyer; b. Topeka, Dec. 16, 1946; d. Alden E. and Lolita M. Flory; m. Michael L. Rigsby, Aug. 14, 1963; children: Michael L. Jr., Elisabeth A. MusB, Va. Commonwealth U., 1969; JD, U. Richmond, 1981. Bar: Va. 1981, D.C. 1988. Assoc. McGuire, Woods, Battle & Boothe, Richmond, Va., 1981-85; dep. gen. counsel and corp. sec. Crestar Fin. Corp., 1985-99, gen. counsel, 1999-2000; mng. atty. Sun Trust Banks Inc., 2000—. Recipient Disting. Svc. award U. Richmond, 1987; named Vol. of Yr. U. Richmond, 1986, Woman of Achievement, Met. Richmond Women's Bar, 1995. Mem. Va. Bar Assn. (exec. com. 1993-96), Richmond Bar Assn. (bd. dirs. 1992-95), Va. Bankers Assn. (chair legal affairs 1992-95), U. Richmond Estate Planning Coun. (chmn. 1990-92). Roman Catholic. Avocations: music, gardening. Home: 163 W Square Pl Richmond VA 23233-6157 Office: SunTrust Bank 919 E Main St Richmond VA 23219-4625

RIGTRUP, KENNETH, state judge, arbitrator, mediator; b. Burley, Idaho, Mar. 13, 1936; s. Robert Peter and Bessie Viola (Price) R.; m. Susanne Joan Remund, May 15, 1964; children: Mark Robert, Michael James, Scott Kenneth, Melissa Ann, Jennifer Marie. BS in Acctg., U. Utah, 1960, JD, 1962. Bar: Utah 1962; U.S. Dist. Ct. Utah, 1962. Clk. Utah Supreme Ct., Salt Lake City, 1962; ptnr. Rigtrup & Hadley, 1962-68; pvt. practice, 1968-72; admin. law judge Indsl. Commn., 1972-77; mem. Pub. Svc. Commn., 1977-80; judge 3d Dist. Ct., 1980-97; active sr. judge Utah Cts., 1997—. Chmn. Bd. Sr. Judges, 1998-99; mem. adv. com. on rules of juvenile procedure Utah Supreme Ct., Salt Lake City, 1993-95. Copy and rsch. editor Utah Law Rev., 1961-62. Chmn. Utah White House Conf. on Handicapped Individuals, Salt Lake City, 1976-77; mem. Utah Gov.'s Com. on Employment of Handicapped, 1976-80, vice chmn. and acting chmn. 1977-80; mem. citizens evaluation and selection com. to rev. pvt. non-profit orgn. applications for urban mass transit authority grants, 1975-77, dir., vice chair. Utah Assistive Tech. Found., 1991—. Recipient Disting. Svc. award Utah Rehab. Counseling Assn., Salt Lake City, 1976-77; Nat. Citation award Nat. Rehab. counseling Assn., 1977; Maurice Warshaw Golden Key award, Utah Gov.'s Com. on Employment of Handicapped, 1975. Mem. ABA, ATLA, Utah Bar Assn. (exec. com. family sect. 1980-90, lawyers helping lawyers com., alt. dispute resolution com.), Nat. Ass. Regulatory Utility Commns. (water com. 1977-78, gas com. 1978-80), Am. Judicature Soc., Utah Coun. on Conflicts Resolution. Republican. Mem. LDS Ch. Home: 1961 Millbrook Rd Salt Lake City UT 84106-3853 Office: Arbitration/Mediation Svcs 3098 Highland Dr Ste 399 Salt Lake City UT 84106-6004

RIHERD, JOHN ARTHUR, lawyer; b. Belle Plaine, Iowa, Sept. 1, 1946; s. William Arthur and Julia Elizabeth Riherd; m. Mary Blanche Thielen, July 5, 1969; children: Elizabeth, Teresa. BA, U. Iowa, 1968, JD, 1974; MA, Gonzaga U., 1992. Bar: Wash. 1974, Iowa 1974, U.S. Dist. Ct. (ea. dist.) Wash. 1974, U.S. Ct. Appeals (9th cir.) 1980, U.S. Dist. Ct. (we. dist.) Wash. 1981. Ptnr. Woods & Riherd, Spokane, Wash., 1974-83, Richter-Wimberley, Spokane, 1983-88, Workland, Witherspoon, Riherd & Brajcich, Spokane, 1988-94; sr. v.p., gen. counsel Med. Svc. Corp. Ea. Wash., 1994-95; ptnr. Perkins Coie, Spokane, 1995-96, Riherd & Sherman P.S., Spokane, 1996—. Adj. prof. Whitworth Coll., Spokane, 1988-90; permanent deacon Cath. Diocese of Spokane. Bd. dirs. Salvation Army, 1976—, chmn., 1996-98; bd. dirs. Mead Sch. Dist., Spokane, 1986-95, pres., 1992-94; bd. dirs. Mayor's Leadership Prayer Breakfast, Spokane, 1986-90, Hospice of Spokane, 1984-87, 91-94, mem. bishop's fin. coun. Cath. Diocese of Spokane, 1993-99, chmn. 1997-98; pres. Spokane County Sch. Dirs. Assn., 1991-92; bd. dirs. Providence Svcs. Ea. Wash., 1999-2000, Wash. State Cath. Conf., 2000—. Mem. ABA, Wash. Bar Assn. (mem. coun. pub. procurement and constrn. law sect. 1986-89, sec.-treas. gen. practice sect. 1989-92), Am. Health Lawyers Assn. (ADR panel mem. 1999—), Am. Arbitration Assn. (panel mem. 1988—), North Spokane Exch. Club (pres. 1981), Spokane Country Club, Washingtonn Athletic Club. Estate planning, Health, Insurance. Home: 1309 W Crestwood Ct Spokane WA 99218-2918 Office: Riherd & Sherman PS 1212 N Washington St Ste 210 Spokane WA 99201-2401 E-mail: jriherd@riherdsherman.com

RIIKOLA, MICHAEL EDWARD, lawyer; b. Phoenix, July 5, 1951; s. Merlin Jacob and Kathleen Mary (Hanrahan) R. BA, U. Ariz., 1975, JD, 1978. Bar: Ariz. 1978, U.S. Dist. Ct. Ariz. 1979., U.S. Ct. Appeals (9th cir.) 1979. Law clk. to presiding justice Ariz. Supreme Ct., Phoenix, 1978-79; assoc. to ptnr. Shimmel, Hill, Bishop and Gruender, P.C., 1979-85, ptnr., 1985-86; pvt. practice Phoenix, 1986—. Cooperating atty. Christic Inst., Washington, 1986—. Contbr. articles to profl. jours. Spl. counsel Com. To Elect John J. Rhodes Gov., Ariz., 1988; issues dir. campaign com. Grant Woods for Ariz. Atty. Gen., 1990; issues dir. exploratory com. Bill Mundell for Congress, 1992. Mem. Trial Lawyers Pub. Justice, Phi Alpha Delta. Democrat. Roman Catholic. Participant Men's Sr. Baseball League World Series, 1991, 92. Constitutional, Legislative, Personal injury. Office: 3030 N Central Ave Ste 1000 Phoenix AZ 85012-2707

RIKLEEN, LAUREN STILLER, lawyer; b. Winthrop, Mass., Apr. 29, 1953; d. Joseph Stiller and Elaine Lillian (Brodie) Stiller; m. Sander A. Rikleen, May 25, 1975. Student, Clark U., 1971-73; BA, magna cum laude, Brandeis U., 1975; JD, Boston Coll., 1979. Bar: Mass. 1979, U.S. Dist. Ct. Mass. 1980, U.S. Ct. Appeals (1st cir.) 1980, U.S. Supreme Ct. 1985. Asst. dir. Flaschner Jud. Inst., Boston, 1979-81; atty. region one EPA, Boston, 1981-84; asst. v.p. for negotiations Clean Sites, Inc., Alexandria, Va., 1984-87; asst. atty. gen. Mass. Dept. of the Atty. Gen., 1987-88; chair environ. practice group Bowditch & Dewey, Worcester and Framingham, Mass., 1988—; lectr., author environ. law. Bd. dirs. Environ. League Mass.; mem. pres's. coun. Clark U., 1989—; pres. Metrowest Harvest; bd. dirs. Women's Independence Network; trustee Metrowest Health Systems, Inc.; Recipient Comm. and Leadership award Toastmaster Internat., 1993; named Woman of Yr. Middlesex News. Mem. ABA (natural resources com.), Boston Bar Assn. (mem. environ. sect., chair 1993-95, sec. 1995), Metrowest C. of C. (chair 1994-95). Office: Bowditch & Dewey PO Box 9320 Framingham MA 01701-9320

RIKON, MICHAEL, lawyer; b. Bklyn., Feb. 2, 1945; s. Charles and Ruth (Shapiro) R.; m. Leslie Sharon Rein, Feb. 11, 1968; children: Carrie Rachel, Joshua Howard. BS, N.Y. Inst. Tech., 1966; JD, Bklyn. Law Sch., 1969; LLM, NYU, 1974. Bar: N.Y. 1970, U.S. Dist. Ct. (so. and ea. dists.) N.Y. 1971, U.S. Ct. Appeals (2d cir.) 1972, U.S. Supreme Ct. 1973, U.S. Ct. Appeals (5th and 11th cirs.) 1981. Asst. corp. counsel City of N.Y., 1969-73; law clk. N.Y. State Ct. Claims, 1973-80; ptnr. Rudick and rikon, P.C., N.Y.C., 1980-88; pvt. practice, 1988-94; ptnr. Goldstein, Goldstein and Rikon, P.C., 1994—. Contbr. articles to profl. jours. Pres. Village Greens Residents Assn., 1978-79; chmn. bd. Arden Heights Jewish Ctr., Staten Island, N.Y., 1976-77; pres. North Shore Repub. Club., 1977; mem. cmty. bd. Staten Island Borough Pres., 1977. Fellow Am. Bar Found.; mem. ABA (chair com. Condemnation) ATLA, TLPJ Found., N.Y. State Bar Assn. (spl. com. of condemnation law), Suffolk County Bar Assn., N.Y. County lawyers Assn. (chair Condemnation com.), Assn. Bar of City of N.Y. (condemnation com.), Mt. Vernon Bar Assn. Republican. Jewish. Avocations: collecting stamps, photography, collecting miniature soldiers. State civil litigation, Condemnation, Real property. Home: 133 Avondale Rd Ridgewood NJ 07450-1301 Office: 80 Pine St New York NY 10005-1702

RILEY, ARCH WILSON, JR. lawyer; b. Wheeling, W.Va., Jan. 15, 1957; s. Arch W. Sr. and Mary List (Paull) R.; m. Sally Ann Goodspeed, Aug. 9, 1980; children: Ann Jerome, Sarah Paull. BA in French and Econs., Tufts U., 1979; JD, W.Va. U., 1982. Bar: W.Va. 1982, U.S. Dist. Ct. (no. and so. dists.) W.Va. 1982. Assoc. Riley & Yahn, Wheeling, 1982, Riley & Broadwater, Wheeling, 1982-83; ptnr. Riley & Riley, L.C., 1983-92, Bailey, Riley, Buch & Harman, L.C., Wheeling, 1993—. Bd. dirs. Wheeling Health Right, Inc.; mem. nat. coun. W.Va. U. Coll. Law. Pres. Upper Ohio Valley Crisis Hotline Inc., Wheeling, 1987-88; chmn. Human Rights Commn., Wheeling, 1985; committeeman Ohio County Dem. Execs., Wheeling, 1984-88; mem. Planning Commn., City of Wheeling, 2001—; bd. dirs., pres. Northwood Health Sys., Inc., Wheeling, 1988-89; bd. dirs. Ohio Valley ARC, Wheeling, 1988; del. 1988 Dem. Nat. Conv. Mem. Am. Bankruptcy Inst., Am. Health Lawyers Assn., W.Va. State Bar (bankruptcy law com., mental health law com.), W.Va. Bar Assn., Ohio County Bar Assn. (sec. 1983-84), Wheeling Country Club. Presbyterian. Bankruptcy, Health, Real property. Office: Bailey Riley Buch & Harman PO Box 631 Wheeling WV 26003-0081 E-mail: arileyjr@brbhlaw.com

RILEY, BENJAMIN KNEELAND, lawyer; b. Pompton Plains, N.J., June 3, 1957; s. Christopher Sibley and Katharine Louise (Piper) R.; m. Janet Welch McCormick, Sept. 15, 1984; children: Keith McCormick, Jamin McCormick. AB, Dartmouth Coll., 1979; JD, U. Calif., Berkeley, 1983. Bar: Calif. 1983, U.S. Dist. Ct. (no. dist.) Calif. 1983, U.S. Ct. Appeals (9th cir.) 1983, U.S. Dist. Ct. (ea. dist.) Calif. 1985, U.S. Dist. Ct. (cen. dist.) Calif. 1987. Assoc. McCutchen, Doyle, Brown & Enerson, San Francisco, 1983-84; ptnr. Cooley Godward LLP, 1984—. Lectr. Boalt Hall Sch. Law, 1989; mem. San Francisco Legal Svcs. Clinic, 1983—; mem. adv. bd. Berkeley Ctr. for Law and Tech., 1998—. Assoc. editor Calif. Law Rev. Spl. asst. dist. atty., San Francisco, 1988; chair, commr. Orinda Pks. & Recreation Commn., 1992-97; mem. City Orinda Task Force, Heart of Orinda Commn., Gateway and Cmty. Ctr. Renovation, 1990-97; bd. dirs. Children's Garden, 1987-92; v.p., mem. Orinda Assn., chmn. Orinda's 4th of July celebration, planning com. Orinda Union Sch. Dist., 1998. Mem.: ABA, Calif. Bar Assn., San Francisco Bar Assn., Assn. Bus. Trial Lawyers (bd. govs. No. Calif. chpt. 2001—, editor: Assn. Bus. Trial Lawyers No. Calif. Report). Democrat. General civil litigation, Intellectual property, Real property. Office: Cooley Godward 1 Maritime Plz Fl 20 San Francisco CA 94111-3510 E-mail: briley@cooley.com

RILEY, JAMES KEVIN, lawyer; b. Nyack, N.Y., July 21, 1945; s. Charles A. and Mary Lenihan R.; m. Joan Leavy Riley, Oct. 4, 1969; children: Carolyn, Tara, Sean. AB, Fordham Coll., 1967; JD, Rutgers U., 1970. Bar: N.Y. 1971, N.J. 1983, U.S. Supreme Ct. 1984; cert. fin. planner., estate planner. Asst. dist. atty. Rockland County, New City, N.Y., 1973-74; ptnr. Amend & Amend, N.Y.C., 1974-78, O'Connell Riley & Conway , Pearl River, NY, 1978—. Pub., pres. 1099 Express Software, 1099 Express Ltd., Pearl River, 1987-97; adj. prof. estate planning Pace Univ., White Plains, N.Y.; atty. Town of Orangetown. Bd. dirs. United Way of Rockland County, N.Y., 1974-80, Rockland Family Shelter for Victims of Domestic Violence, 1981-85, literacy vols. Rockland County, 1989—; chmn. bd. dirs. New Hope Manor, Barryville, N.Y., 1985-88. Mem. ABA, Am. Soc. Hosp. Attys., Nat. Coun. Sch. Dist. Attys., N.Y. State Bar Assn. (ho. of dels. 1988-92), Rockland County Bar Assn. (bd. dirs. 1986—, pres. 1997-98), Internat. Platform Assn., Rotary Club of Pearl River (pres. 1999—). Democrat. Roman Catholic. Education and schools, Estate planning, Municipal (including bonds). Home: 145 Franklin Ave Pearl River NY 10965-2510 Office: O'Connell Riley & Conway 144 E Central Ave Pearl River NY 10965 also: 103 Chestnut Ridge Rd Montvale NJ 07645

RILEY, KIRK HOLDEN, lawyer; b. San Diego, Sept. 5, 1950; s. Richard Ross and Jerrine Rhae (Dennis) R.; m. Cheryl Ann Wilde, Aug. 5, 1972; children: Brooke, Kevin, Matthew, Rebecca, Conor, Erin. BA, U.S. Internat. U., San Diego, 1972; JD, Calif. Western Sch. Law, San Diego, 1975; LLM, Boston U., 1978. Bar: Calif. 1975; cert. legal taxation specialist. Assoc. Brian D. Monaghan, San Diego, 1976; tax cons. Touche Ross & Co., San Francisco, 1979-80, mgr. tax dept., San Diego, 1980, 82-83, supr. tax dept., Washington, 1980-81; assoc., mem. Branton & Wilson, A.P.C., San Diego, 1983-88; self employed, 1988—; instr. U. Calif., San Diego, 1983. Co-author: Taxation of Real Property Transfers, CEB Supplement. Mem. ABA, San Diego County Bar Assn., Greater San Diego Sports Assn. Hall of Champions. Republican. Mormon. Real property, Corporate taxation, Personal income taxation. Home: 4909 Olde Grove Ln La Mesa CA 91941-5772 Office: 350 W Ash St Ste 600 San Diego CA 92101-3423

RILEY, MICHAEL HYLAN, lawyer; b. Ardmore, Okla., Oct. 26, 1951; s. Paul Emerson and Anne (Hylan) R. AB cum laude, Harvard U., 1973; JD, Northea. U., 1978. Bar: Mass. 1978, U.S. Dist. Ct. Mass. 1980, U.S. Ct. Appeals (1st cir.) 1980. Assoc. White, Inker, Aronson, Boston, 1979-83, Chaplin & Milstein, Boston, 1984-86, Goldstein & Manello, Boston,

1986-91; ptnr. Goldstein & Manello, P.C., 1992-95; of counsel King & Navins, P.C., Wellesley, Mass., 1995—. Lectr. Met. Coll. Boston U., 1986-92. Author: Estate Administration, 1985, 2nd edit., 1993. Mem. ABA, Boston Bar Assn. Democrat. Avocations: books, music, food, wine, backpacking. Estate planning, Probate, Estate taxation. Home: 83 Grove Hill Ave Newton MA 02460-2336 Office: King & Navins PC 20 William St Wellesley MA 02481-4103 E-mail: rileymh@sprynet.com

RILEY, SCOTT C. lawyer; b. Bklyn., Oct. 5, 1959; s. William A. and Kathleen (Howe) R.; m. Kathleen D. O'Connor, Oct. 6, 1984; children: Matthew, Brendan. BA, Seton Hall U., South Orange, N.J., 1981; JD, Seton Hall U., Newark, 1984. Bar: N.J. 1985, U.S. Dist. Ct. N.J. 1985. Assoc. Dwyer, Connell & Lisbona, Montclair, N.J., 1985-87; assoc. gen. counsel, v.p. Consolidated Ins. Group, Wilmington, Del., 1987-91; counsel Cigna Ins. Group, Phila., 1991-94; assoc. gen. counsel KWELM Cos., N.Y.C., 1994-98, head U.S. legal ops., 1998—; head U.S. ops. KMSIS Ltd., 1998—. Mem. ABA (com. on environ. ins. coverage), Fedn. of Ins. and Corp. Counsel, Excess and Surplus Lines Claims Assn., N.J. State Bar Assn., Profl. Liability Underwriting Soc. Environmental, Insurance, Toxic tort. Office: KWELM Companies 599 Lexington Ave New York NY 10022-6030

RILEY, STEWART PATRICK, lawyer; b. Spokane, Wash., July 18, 1944; s. Philip Edmund Riley and Theo Elizabeth (VonderHellen) Brubaker; m. Laurie Anne Gallup, May 16, 1970; children: Jessica, Peter. BA, U. Wash., 1966, JD, 1969. Bar: Wash. 1969, U.S. Ct. Appeals (9th cir.) 1972, U.S. Dist. Ct. (we. dist.) Wash. 1972, U.S. Dist. St. (ea. dist.) Wash. 1984, U.S. Supreme Ct. 1978. Sr. dep. pros. atty. King County Pros. Atty. Office, Seattle, 1973-76; ptnr. Paul, Johnson, Paul & Riley, 1976-82, Johnson & Riley, Seattle, 1983-93; pvt. practice, 1993—. Author: Legal Implictions of Sea Use Program, 1970. Trustee Source Child Ctr., 1989-93. Named Outstanding Lawyer, King County Superior Ct., 1974. Mem. Nat. Assn. Criminal Def. Attys., Wash. State Bar Assn., Wash. State Trial Lawyers Assn., Seattle-King County Bar Assn. (chmn. criminal law sect.), Wash. Athletic Club, Seattle Tennis Club, Phi Delta Theta. Republican. Criminal. Home: 1721 39th Ave Seattle WA 98122-3507 Office: 800 5th Ave Ste 4000 Seattle WA 98104-3180 E-mail: stewriley@yahoo.com

RILEY, TOM JOSEPH, lawyer; b. Cedar Rapids, Iowa, Jan. 9, 1929; s. Joseph Wendell and Edna (Kyle) R.; m. Nancy Evans, Jan. 21, 1952; children: Pamela Chang, Peter, Lisa Thirnbeck, Martha Brown, Sara Riley, Heather Mescher. BA, U. Iowa, 1950, JD, 1952. Bar: Iowa 1952, U.S. Dist. Ct. (no. dist.) Iowa 1952, U.S. Ct. Appeals (8th cir.) 1960, U.S. Supreme Ct. 1966. Assoc. Simmons, Perrine, Allbright & Ellwood, Cedar Rapids, 1952-60, ptnr., 1960-80; pres. Tom Riley Law Firm, P.C., 1980—. Adj. prof. trial advocacy Coll. Law, U. Iowa, Iowa City, 1979. Author: Proving Punitive Damages, 1981, The Price of a Life, 1986, Trial Handbook for Iowa Lawyers (Civil), 1997, Iowa Practice: Civil Litigation Handbook, 2000-01. Mem. Iowa Ho. of Reps., 1960-64, Iowa Senate, 1965-74. First lt. USAF, 1952-54. Named Outstanding Freshman Legislator, Des Moines Press and Radio Club, 1961. Fellow Iowa Acad. Trial Lawyers (bd. govs. 1982-91); mem. Iowa Trial Lawyers Assn. (bd. govs. 2000 —), Cedar Rapids Country Club, U. Athletic Club, Iowa City, Des Moines Club, Masons. Republican. Presbyterian. Avocations: tennis, sailing, downhill skiing. General civil litigation, Personal injury. Home: 5300 Lakeside Rd Rural Route Marion IA 52302 Office: 4040 1st Ave NE Cedar Rapids IA 52402-3143

RILEY, WILLIAM JAY, lawyer; b. Lincoln, Nebr., Mar. 11, 1947; s. Don Paul and Marian Frances (Munn) R.; m. Norma Jean Mason, Dec. 27, 1965; children: Brian, Kevin, Erin. BA, U. Nebr., 1969, JD with distinction, 1972. Bar: Nebr. 1972, U.S. Dist. Ct. Nebr. 1972, U.S. Ct. Appeals (8th cir.) 1974; cert. civil trial specialist Nat. Bd. Trial Advocacy. Law clk. U.S. Ct. Appeals (8th cir.), Omaha, 1972-73; assoc. Fitzgerald, Schorr Law Firm, P.C., LLO, 1973-79; shareholder Fitzgerald, Schorr Law Firm, 1979—2001; US Circuit Judge 8th Circuit Ct. Appeals , 2001—. Adj. prof. trial practice Creighton U. Coll. Law, Omaha, 1991—; chmn. fed. practice com. Fed. Ct., 1992-94. Scoutmaster Boy Scouts Am., Omaha, 1979-89, scout membership chair Mid Am. Coun., 1995-98. Recipient Silver Beaver award Boy Scouts Am., 1991. Fellow Am. Coll. Trial Lawyers (chair state com. 1997-99), Nebr. State Bar Found.; mem. Am. Bd. Trial Advs. (Nebr. chpt. pres. 2000, Best Lawyers in Am. 2001), Nebr. State Bar Assn. (chmn. ethics com. 1996-98, ho. of dels. 1998—), Omaha Bar Assn. (treas. 1997-98, pres. 2000-01, Best Lawyers in Omaha 2001), Robert M. Spire Inns of Ct. (master 1994—, counselor 1997-98), Order of Coif, Phi Beta Kappa. Republican. Methodist. Avocations: reading, hiking, cycling. Federal civil litigation, General civil litigation, State civil litigation. Office: Roman L Hruska US Courthouse 111 S 18th Plaza Ste 4179 Omaha NE 68102 E-mail: wriley@fitzlaw.com

RILL, JAMES FRANKLIN, lawyer; b. Evanston, Ill., Mar. 4, 1933; s. John Columbus and Frances Eleanor (Hill) R.; m. Mary Elizabeth Laws, June 14, 1957; children: James Franklin, Roderick M. AB cum laude, Dartmouth Coll., 1954; LLB, Harvard, 1959. Bar: D.C. bar 1959. Legis. asst. Congressman James P. S. Devereux, Washington, 1952; pvt. practice, 1959-89; assoc. Steadman, Collier & Shannon, 1959-63; ptnr. Collier, Shannon & Rill, 1963-69, Collier, Shannon, Rill & Scott, 1969-89; asst. atty. gen., antitrust div. U.S. Dept. Justice, Washington, 1989-92; ptnr. Collier, Shannon, Rill & Scott, 1992-2000; co-chair internat. competition policy adv. com. U.S. Dept. Justice, 1997-2000; ptnr. Howrey Simon Arnold & White, Washington, 2000—. Pub. mem. Adminstrv. Conf. of U.S., 1992-94; coun. prin. Coun. for Excellence in Govt.; mem., advisor panel Office of Tech. Assessment of Multinat. Firms and U.S. Tech. Base. Contbr. articles to profl. jours. Trustee emeritus Bullis Sch., Potomac, Md. Served to 1st lt. arty. AUS, 1954-56. Fellow: Am. Bar Found.; mem.: ABA (antitrust law sect., past chmn.), DC Bar Assn., Met. Club, Loudoun Valley Club, Phi Delta Theta. Home: 7305 Masters Dr Potomac MD 20854-3850 Office: Howrey Simon Arnold & White, LLP Rm 621 1299 Pennsylvania Ave NW Washington DC 20004-2402

RINER, JAMES WILLIAM, lawyer; b. Jefferson City, Mo., Dec. 25, 1936; s. John Woodrow and Virginia Loraine (Jackson) R.; m. Carolyn Ruth Hicke, May 14 1976; children: Alicia Gayle, Angela Gayle, Amity Gayle. BA, U. Mo., 1957, LLB, 1960. Bar: Mo. 1960, U.S. Dist. Ct. (we. dist.) Mo. 1982, U.S. Ct. Appeals (8th cir.) 1989. Asst. atty. gen. Atty. Gen's. Office Mo., Jefferson City, 1960; commd. 1st lt. U.S. Air Force, 1960, advanced through grades to lt. col., 1974, retired, 1981; ptnr. Inglish & Monaco, P.C., Jefferson City, 1985-91, Hendricks, Riner & Smith, P.C., Jefferson City, 1991-96, Riner & Turnbull, P.C., 1996-98, Riner, Turnbull & Walker, P.C., Jefferson City, 1998-99, Riner & Walker PC, Jefferson City, 1999—. City pros. Jefferson City, 1983-91; city atty. California, Mo., 1985-87. Contbr. author: Mo. Ins. Practice Manual, 1995, 4th edit., 2000. Decorated Bronze Star, Meritorious Svc. Medal. Mem. Am. Trial Lawyers Assn., Mo. Bar Assn. Democrat. General civil litigation, Personal injury, Labor. Home: 1205 Moreau Dr Jefferson City MO 65101-3522 Office: Riner & Walker PC 1731 E Elm St Jefferson City MO 65101 E-mail: jriner@riner-walker.com

RINES, ROBERT HARVEY, lawyer, inventor, educator, composer; b. Boston, Aug. 30, 1922; s. David and Lucy (Sandberg) R.; m. Carol Williamson, Dec. 29, 1972 (dec. 1993); 1 son, Justice Christopher; children by previous marriage: Robert Louis, Suzi Kay Ann; m. Joanne Hayes, June 2, 1996; 1 stepchild, Laura Ellen Hayes. BS in Physics, MIT, 1942; JD, Georgetown U., 1947; PhD, Nat. Chiao Tung U., 1972; DJ, New Eng. Coll. Law, 1974; DSc, Notre Dame Coll., 1994. Bar: Mass. 1947, D.C. 1947, N.H. 1974, Va. 1983, U.S. Supreme Ct., FCC, Tax Ct., U.S. and Can. patent offices; Registered profl. engr., Mass. Asst. examiner U.S. Patent Office, 1946; partner Rines & Rines, Boston, 1947—; pres., founder, chmn. emeritus Franklin Pierce Law Center, 1973-97. Bd. dirs. Megapulse, Inc., Astro Dynamics, Inc., Nat. Inventors Hall of Fame Found., Lord Corp., pres. Jura Corp., 1997—, New England Fish Farming Enterprises-D.E. Salmon Inc., 1983-99, Acad. Applied Sci.-Project Orbis Bangladesh and Singapore Opthamology Programs, Sportsmans Handbook, Beltronics Inc., Seagull Technology, Inc., Albavision Ltd., Promotion of Am. Chinese Tech., Knox Mt. Licensors Inc., Ctr. Broadcasting Corp. of N.H.; Gordon McKay lectr. patent law Harvard, 1956-58; lectr. inventions and innovation Mass. Inst. Tech., 1962—; Mem. commerce tech. adv. bd. Dept. Commerce, 1963-67, mem. nat. inventors council, 1963-67, 81—; mem. N.H. Gov.'s Crime Study Com., 1976-78. Author: A Study of Current World-Wide Sources of Electronic and Other Invention and Innovation; Computer Jurisprudence: Create or Perish--The Case for Patents and Inventions; patentee in field of radar and sonar, fish farming and plant nutrients; composer of music for onn and off broadway prodns. including, Drums Under the Windows, Different, Long Voyage Home, Whoman Portrait, Blasts and Bravas (H.L. Menken), Hizzoner the Mayor (Emmy winning tv prodn.), 1-800-Save Me (Jack Betts), and Lincoln Ctr. Bailer of Rines, Life at MIT suite. Campaign chmn. United Fund, Belmont Mass., 1960; mem. adv. bd. Harvard-Mass. Inst. Tech. Biomed. Engring. Center, 1976-80; bd. dirs. Allor Found. 2d lt. to capt. AUS, 1942-46, Brevet Col., 1994, U.S. Army Signal Corps. Silver Order of Mercury (inducted Wall of Fame, Ft. Gordon, GA, 1994). Named to Nat. Inventors Hall of Fame, 1994; recipient Inventions Citation Pres. Carter and U.S. Dept. Commerce, 1980, N.H. High Tech. Entrepreneur award, 1989, Beyond Peace award, 1989, Bangladesh (N.Am.) Disting. Svc. award, 1990, 96; recipient Robert H. Rines Bldg. dedication at Franklin Pierce Law Ctr., 1993; MIT Distance Learning Ctr. Bldg. dedication, 1997. Fellow Internat. Soc. Cryptozoology; mem. IEEE (sr.), AAAS, ABA, Acad. Applied Sci. (pres., Medal of Honor 1989), Am. Patent Law Assn., Sci. Rsch. Soc. Am., Aircraft Owners and Pilots Assn., Nat. Acad. Engring. (patent com. 1969-80, cons. to exec. officer 1979-80), Explorers Club, Harvard Club, Torquay Co. Theatrical Prodns., Chemists Club, MIT Faculty Club, Nat. Lawyers Club, Capitol Hill Club, Highland Club, Commonwealth Club, Sigma Xi. Unitarian. Intellectual property, Patent, Trademark and copyright. Home: 13 Spaulding St Concord NH 03301-2571

RING, RENEE ETHELINE, lawyer; b. Frankfurt, Germany, May 29, 1950; arrived in U.S., 1950; d. Vincent Martin and Etheline Bergetta (Schoolmeesters) R.; m. Paul J. Zofnass, June 24, 1982; Jessica Renee, Rebecca Anne. BA, Catholic U. Am., 1972; JD, U. Va., 1976. Bar: N.Y. 1977. Assoc. Whitman & Ransom, N.Y.C., 1976-83, Carro, Spanbock, Fass, Geller, Kaster & Cuiffo, N.Y.C., 1983-86, ptnr., 1986, Finley Kumble Wagner et. al., N.Y.C., 1987; of counsel Kaye, Scholer, Fierman, Hays & Handler, 1988; ptnr. Kaye, Scholer, Fierman, Hays & Handler, LLP, 1989-97, Hunton & Williams, N.Y.C., 1997—. Mem. exec. com. Lawyers for Clinton, Washington, 1991-92; team capt. Clinton Transition Team, Washington, 1992-93; mem. Nat. Lawyers Coun. Dem. Nat. Com., 1993-98; trustee The Clinton Legal Expense Trust, 1998—; mem. Alumni Coun. U. Va. Sch. of Law, 1997—, 2d v.p., 2000-2001, 1st v.p., 2001—; trustee The Spence Sch, 2001—. Mem. ABA, N.Y. Women's Bar Assn. Democrat. Roman Catholic. Banking, General corporate, Securities. Office: Hunton & Williams 200 Park Ave Rm 4400 New York NY 10166-0091 E-mail: rring@hunton.com

RING, RONALD HERMAN, lawyer; b. Flint, Mich., Nov. 30, 1938; s. Herman and Lydia (Miller) R.; m. Joan Kay Whitener, Aug. 5, 1966. AB, U. Mich., 1961, LLB, 1964. Bar: Mich. 1964, U.S. Dist. Ct. (ea. dist.) Mich. 1966. Assoc. Beagle, Benton & Hicks, Flint, 1964-69; ptnr. Beagle & Ring, 1970-80, Beagle, Ring & Beagle, Flint, 1980-85, Ring, Beagle & Busch, Flint, 1985-93, Ronald H. Ring, P.C., Flint, 1993-95; pvt. practice, 1991—. Mem. meml. com. Crossroads Village, Flint, 1981; pres. Family Service Agy., Genesee County, Mich., 1986. Mem. ABA, Assn. Trial Lawyers Am., Mich. Bar Assn. (delivery of legal service com. 1986, med. malpractice panel 1986), Genesee County Bar Assn. (pres. 1980-81, bd. dirs. 1979-82, cir. ct. mediation panel 1986). Club: Ostego Ski (Gaylord, Mich.). Avocations: skiing, sailing. State civil litigation, General practice, Personal injury. Office: 7993 Bussa Ln Rapid City MI 49676-9203 E-mail: ronhring@cs.com

RINGEL, DEAN, lawyer; b. N.Y.C., Dec. 12, 1947; m. Ronnie Sussman, Aug. 24, 1969; children: Marion, Alicia. BA, Columbia Coll., 1967; JD, Yale U., 1971. Bar: N.Y. 1972, U.S. Ct. Appeals (6th cir.) 1972, U.S. Ct. Appeals (2d and D.C. cirs.) 1974, U.S. Supreme Ct. 1976, U.S. Ct. Appeals (10th cir.) 1982, U.S. Ct. Appeals (11th cir.) 1997, U.S. Ct. Appeals (9th cir.) 2000. Law clk. to Judge Anthony J. Celebrezze U.S. Ct. Appeals (6th cir.), 1971-72; assoc. Cahill Gordon & Reindel, N.Y.C., 1972-79; ptnr. Cahill, Gordon & Reindel, 1979—. Mem. ABA (vice chmn. com. on freedom of speech and press 1978-79), Assn. Bar City N.Y. (commn. com., fed. litig., antitrust and trade regulation), N.Y. State Bar (chmn. antitrust litig. com., sect. comml. and fed. litigation 1994-96, co-chmn. fed. judiciary com. 1997—, media law com.), Pub. Edn. Assn. (trustee, sec. 1997-2000, trustee CEI-PEA 2000—). Antitrust, Federal civil litigation, Libel. Office: Cahill Gordon & Reindel 80 Pine St 17th Fl New York NY 10005-1790

RINGER, DARRELL WAYNE (DAN), lawyer; b. Elizabeth, N.J., Apr. 14, 1948; s. Darrell Wayne and Elva (Brown) R.; m. Rebecca Ruth Bonner, Feb. 23, 1979; children: Daniel Benjamin, Darren Wayne. BS in Physics, W.Va. U., 1971; MBA, U. N.D., 1975; JD, W.Va. U., 1978. Bar: W.Va. 1978, U.S. Dist. Ct. (no. and so. dists.) W.Va. 1978. Assoc. Jones, Williams, West & Jones, Clarksburg, W.Va., 1978-80, Moreland & Ringer, Morgantown, 1980-83, Reeder, Shuman, Ringer & Wiley, Morgantown, 1983-91, Ringer Law Offices, Morgantown, 1991—. 1st asst. prosecutor Monongalia County, W.Va., 1985-87; host W.Va. Pub. TV, PBS Pub. Affairs Programming, 1991—. Bd. dirs. Monongalia County (W.Va.) Mental Health Assn., Morgantown, 1981-83; mem. W.Va. U. Animal Care and Use Com., 1985—. Capt. USAF, 1971-75. Named W.Va. Bar Found. Lawyer Citizen of Yr., 1996. Mem. ABA (named Sole Practitioner of Yr., 2000), ATLA, W.Va. State Bar (pres. 1999-2000), Monongalia County Bar Assn. (sec. 1980-92, pres. 2001), W.Va. Trial Lawyers Assn. (bd. govs. 1982-91, Pres.'s award 2001). Democrat. Avocation: amateur radio. General corporate, Criminal, Personal injury. Home: 18 W Front St Morgantown WV 26501-4507 Office: 68 Donley St Morgantown WV 26501-5907

RINGKAMP, STEPHEN H. lawyer, educator; b. St. Louis, Nov. 14, 1949; s. Aloysius G. and Melba Ann (Finke) Ringkamp; m. Patricia Sue Fuse, July 05, 1971; children: Christa, Angela, Laura, Stephen M., Kara. BSEE, St. Louis U., 1971, JD cum laude, 1974. Bar: Mo. 1974, U.S. Dist. Ct. (ea. dist.) Mo. 1974, U.S. Ct. Appeals (8th cir.) 1974, U.S. Supreme Ct. 1990. Law clk. 22d Jud. Cir. Mo., St. Louis, 1974-75; mng. prin. The Hullverson Law Firm, 1976—. Chmn., mem. com. on civil instrns. Mo. Supreme Ct., 1981— ; adj. prof. law St. Louis U., 1983— ; mem. faculty Mo. Jud. Coll., 1993-2001; lectr. legal seminars. Contbr. articles to legal jours. Recipient Trial Lawyer award Mo. Bar Found. 1983, Smithson award for Excellence, 1996. Mem. ABA, ATLA, Mo. Bar Assn. (vice chmn. civil practice com. 1983-84), Mo. Assn. Trial Attys. (pres. 1991), Bar Assn. Met. St. Louis, Lawyers Assn. St. Louis. General civil litigation, Personal injury, Product liability. Office: The Hullverson Law Firm 1010 Market St Ste 1550 Saint Louis MO 63101-2091 E-mail: sringkamp@hullverson.com

RINGLE, BRETT ADELBERT, lawyer, petroleum company executive; b. Berkeley, Calif., Mar. 17, 1951; s. Forrest A. and Elizabeth V. (Darnall) R.; m. Sue Kinslow, May 26, 1973. BA, U. Tex., 1973, JD, 1976. Bar: Tex. 1976, U.S. Dist. Ct. (no. dist.) Tex. 1976, U.S. Supreme Ct. 1980, U.S. Ct. Appeals (5th cir.) 1984. Ptnr. Shank, Irwin & Conant, Dallas, 1976-86, Jones, Day, Reavis & Pogue, Dallas, 1986-96; v.p. Hunt Petroleum Corp., 1996—. Adj. prof. law So. Meth. U., Dallas, 1983. Author: (with J.W. Moore and H.I. Bendix) Moore's Federal Practice, 2d edit., Vol. 12, 1980, Vol. 13, 1981, (with J.W. Moore) Vol. 1A, 1982, Vol. 1A Part 2, 1989. Mem. Dallas Bar Assn. Federal civil litigation, State civil litigation, General practice. Home: 3514 Gillon Ave Dallas TX 75205-3220 Office: Hunt Petroleum Corp 5000 Thanksgiving Tower 1601 Elm St Dallas TX 75201 E-mail: bar@huntpetroleum.com

RINGLER, JEROME LAWRENCE, lawyer; b. Detroit, Dec. 26, 1948; BA, Mich. State U., 1970; JD, U. San Francisco, 1974. Bar: Calif. 1974, U.S. Ct. Appeals (9th cir.) 1974, U.S. Dist. Ct. (no. dist.) Calif. 1974, U.S. Dist. Ct. (ctrl. dist.) Calif. 1975, U.S. Dist. Ct. (so. dist.) Calif. 1981. Assoc. Parker, Stansbury et al, L.A., 1974-76, Fogel, Feldman, Ostrov, Ringler & Klevens, Santa Monica, Calif., 1976-80, ptnr., 1980—. Arbitrator L.A. Superior Ct. Arbitration Program, 1980-85. Named Verdictum Juris Trial Lawyer of Yr., 1996. Mem. ATLA, ABA, State Bar Calif., L.A. County Bar Assn. (litigation sect., exec. com. 1994—), L.A. Trial Lawyers Assn. (bd. govs. 1981—, treas. 1988, sec. 1989, v.p. 1990, pres.-elect 1991, pres. 1992, Trial Lawyer of the Yr. 1987), Calif. Trial Lawyers Assn., Am. Bd. Trial Advs. (assoc. 1988, adv. 1991), Inns of Ct. (master). Avocations: skiing, tennis. General civil litigation, Personal injury, Product liability. Office: Fogel Feldman Ostrov Ringler & Klevens 1620 26th St # 100S Santa Monica CA 90404-4013

RINGLER, KIM D. lawyer; b. Cleve., May 31, 1954; d. Albert and Norma (Miller) R.; 2 children. AB, Oberlin Coll., 1976; JD, Georgetown U., 1979. Bar: N.Y. 1980, N.J. 1981, U.S. Dist. Ct. (so. and ea. dists.) N.Y. 1980, U.S. Dist. Ct. N.J. 1981, U.S. Ct. Appeals (3d cir.) 1983. Asst. dist. atty. Kings County Dist. Atty's Office, Bklyn., 1979-80; spl. trial coun., dept. disciplinary com. Supreme Ct. N.Y., N.Y.C., 1980-82, 85-87; assoc. Stillman Friedman & Shaw, 1982-85; of counsel Horowitz & Jacobs, Hackensack, N.J., 1987-91; pvt. practice, 1991—. Pres. Bergen County Women Lawyers; chair fee arbitration com. N.J. Supreme Ct., mem. ethics com., 1995-99. Dep. mayor Village of Ridgewood, N.J., 1999—; bd. dirs. Ridgewood Libr., Alternatives to Domestic Violence, Hackensack; liaison Ridgewood C. of C.; pres. Friends of Music, Ridgewood; pres. Federated Home and Sch. Assn.; dir. Jean Robertson Scholarship Found. Mem. Assn. Profl. Responsible Lawyers, Bergen County Bar Assn., Assn. Bar City N.Y. Avocation: singing. Office: 401 Hackensack Ave Continental Plz 1 FL 6 Hackensack NJ 07601 E-mail: dirkesq@aol.com

RINGO, ROBERT GRIBBLE, lawyer; b. Spokane, Wash., Aug. 18, 1924; s. Floyd V. and Claire (Williams) R.; previous m. Kathryn Reese, May 24, 1953; children: Molly, Robert, Charles, Julie Ann, Mary Ellen; m. Jane Crider, Mar. 21, 1993. BS, U. Oreg., 1949; LLB, N.W. Coll. Law, Portland, Oreg., 1951. Bar: Oreg. 1951, U.S. Ct. Mil Appeals 1969, U.S. Supreme Ct. 1970, U.S. Ct. Appeals (9th Cir.) 1969. Dep. dist. atty. Benton Co., Corvallis, Oreg., 1951-53; ptnr. Ringo & Walton, 1953-85, Ringo, Stuber, Ensor & Hadlock P.C., Corvallis, 1986—. Bd. dirs. Good Samaritan Hosp., Corvallis, 1988—. Lt. col. USAFR, 1972. Mem. ABA, Benton County Bar Assn. (pres. 1964-65), Oreg. Bar Assn. (bd. govs. 1980-83, sec. 1982-83), ATLA (bd. govs. 1982-90), Oreg. Trial Lawyers Assn. (pres. (1979-80), Am. Bd. Trial Advs. (diplomat, nat. exec. com. 1982), State of Oreg. Profl. Responsibility Bd, State of Oregon Jud. Fitness Commn., Oregon Law Found. (Pres. 1994). Democrat. Episcopalian. General civil litigation, Personal injury, Product liability. Office: Ringo Stuber Ensor & Hadlock PC PO Box 1108 Corvallis OR 97339-1108

RINKER, ANDREW, JR. lawyer; b. New Orleans, Jan. 6, 1957; s. Andrew and Frances Marion (Fitzpatrick) R. BS, La. State U., 1978, MBA, 1981; JD, Tulane U., 1982. Bar: La. 1982, U.S. Ct. Appeals (5th cir.) 1982, U.S. Dist. Ct. (ea. and we. dists.) La., U.S. Supreme Ct. 1986, solicitor Supreme Ct. England and Wales, 1997. Ptnr. Chaffe, McCall, Phillips, Toler & Sarpy, New Orleans, 1982—. Editor in chief Tulane Law Rev., New Orleans, 1981-82. Contbr. articles to profl. jours. Mem. Bur. Govtl. Rsch., devel. com. Greater New Orleans Found.; founding mem., bd. dirs. Young Leadership Coun.; chmn. Greater New Orleans Ednl. TV Found. (Sta. WYES-TV); trustee and vice-chmn. La. Mus. Found., trustee La. Chldn's. Mus., Maison Hospitaliere; bd. advisors/editors Tulane Law Rev. Mem. ABA, La. State Bar Assn., Southwestern Legal Found., New Orleans Bar Assn., La. State Law Inst., Mortar Bd., Phi Kappa Phi, Beta Gamma Sigma, Omicron Delta Kappa, Phi Eta Sigma, Phi Alpha Delta, Delta Kappa Epsilon. Republican. Roman Catholic. Clubs: So. Yacht, Bachelor's (New Orleans). Avocations: sailing, tennis, hunting, fishing, skiing. General corporate, Finance, Probate. Home: 531 Saint Ann St New Orleans LA 70116-3318 Office: Chaffe McCall Phillips et al 2300 Energy Centre 1100 Poydras St Ste 2300 New Orleans LA 70163-2300 E-mail: Andrewrin@aol.com

RINSKY, JOEL CHARLES, lawyer; b. Bklyn., Jan. 29, 1938; s. Irving C. and Elsie (Millman) R.; m. Judith L. Lynn, Jan. 26, 1963; children: Heidi M., Heather S., Jason W. BS, Rutgers U., 1961, LLB, 1962, JD, 1968. Bar: N.J. 1963, U.S. Dist. Ct. N.J. 1963, U.S. Supreme Ct. 1967, U.S. Ct. Appeals (3d cir.) 1986; cert. civil trial atty., N.J. Pvt. practice, Livingston, N.J., 1964-97; sr. ptnr. Rinsky & Marley L.L.C., 1997-98; of counsel Gonzalez and Weichert P.C., 1999—. Committeeman Millburn-Short Hills (N.J.) Dem. Com., 1982-97, vice chmn., 1983-87; trustee Student Loan Fund, Millburn, 1983-91. Fellow Am. Acad. Matrimonial Lawyers; mem. N.J. Bar Assn., Essex County Bar Assn. (exec. com. sect. family law). Jewish. Avocations: tennis, chess, golf, piano. Family and matrimonial, Personal injury, Real property. Home: 87 Sullivan Dr West Orange NJ 07052-2262 Office: 127 E Mount Pleasant Ave Livingston NJ 07039-3005 E-mail: Rinsky3@aol.com

RINTAMAKI, JOHN M. automotive executive; BBA, U. Mich., 1964, JD, 1967. Bar: Mich. 1968, Pa. 1973. Sr. atty. internat. Ford Motor Co., 1978-84, assoc. counsel corp. and financings, 1984-86, asst. sec., assoc. counsel, 1986-92, sec., asst. gen. counsel, 1993-98, v.p., gen. counsel, sec., 1999-00, chief staff, 2000—. Office: Ford Motor Co One American Rd Dearborn MI 48126-1899

RINTELMAN, DONALD BRIAN, lawyer; b. Madison, Wis., May 25, 1955; s. Donald Carl Rintelman and Eugenie Elizabeth Kroll; m. Ann Marie Gall, Aug. 2, 1980; children: Katherine Ann, Brian James. BA, U. Wis., 1976; JD, U. Mich., 1980. Bar: Wis. 1980, U.S. Dist. Ct. (ea. dist.) Wis. 1980, U.S. Dist. Ct. (we. dist.) Wis. 1984. Assoc. Whyte & Hirschboeck, S.C., Milw., 1980-86, shareholder, 1986—; mng. dir. Whyte Hirschboeck Dudek, S.C., 1994—. Chmn. comml. practice group Am. Law Firm Assn. Internat., L.A., 1998—. Bd. dirs. Ozaukee County United Way Allocations, Mequon, Wis., 1986-88; treas. Cedarburg (Wis.) Cmty. Scholarship Fund, 1991-93; coun. pres. Advent Luth. Ch., Cedarburg, 1996-97. Fellow Am. Coll. Investment Counsel; mem. ABA, Wis. Bar Assn., Milw. Bar Assn. Republican. Avocations: travel, golf, enjoying children's soccer, swimming. Contracts commercial, General corporate, Mergers and acquisitions. Home: N108W7365 Balfour St Cedarburg WI 53012-3248 Office: Whyte Hirschboeck Dudek SC 111 E Wisconsin Ave Ste 2100 Milwaukee WI 53202-4861

RIORDAN, DEBORAH TRUBY, lawyer; b. Georgetown, S.C., May 29, 1968; d. David Charles and Vickie (Turner) Truby; m. Gary Ray Riordan, Aug. 26, 1995; children: Katherine Spencer, Neely McAdams. BA, U. Ark., 1990; JD, Vanderbilt U., 1993. Bar: Ark. 1993, U.S. Dist. Ct. (ea. and we. dists.) Ark. 1993. Law clk. various law firms, Little Rock, 1991-92; assoc. Shults & Ray LLP, 1993-99; dir. Hill, Gilstrap, Perkins & Trotter, 1999—. Staff writer Interaction mag., 1997-98; co-editor League mag., 2000-01. Vol. Ctrl. Ark. Legal Svcs., Little Rock, 1993-97, St. Vincents Hosp. Aux.; vol. coord. Ark. Arts Ctr., Little Rock, 1993-95; tng. com., sec., yearbook editor Jr. League, Little Rock, 1996—; chair, pastor parish rev. com. Trinity United Methodist Ch., Little Rock, 1998—. Mem. ABA, Arkansas County Bar Assn., Pulaski County Bar Assn. Avocations: tennis, walking, reading, Arkansas Razorbacks football, spending time with daughters. Contracts commercial, Communications, Real property. Home: 8 Auriel Dr Little Rock AR 72223-9111 Office: Hill Gilstrap Perkins & Trotter 1 Information Way Ste 200 Little Rock AR 72202-2290

RIPPLE, KENNETH FRANCIS, federal judge; b. Pitts., May 19, 1943; s. Raymond John and Rita (Holden) R.; m. Mary Andrea DeWeese, July 27, 1968; children: Gregory, Raymond, Christopher. AB, Fordham U., 1965; JD, U. Va., 1968; LLM, George Washington U., 1972, LLD (hon.), 1992. Bar: Va. 1968, N.Y. 1969, U.S. Supreme Ct. 1972, D.C. 1976, Ind. 1984, U.S. Ct. Appeals (7th cir.), U.S. Ct. Mil. Appeals, U.S. Dist. Ct. (no. dist.) Ind. Atty. IBM Corp., Armonk, N.Y., 1968; legal officer U.S. Supreme Ct., Washington, 1972-73, spl. asst. to chief justice Warren E. Burger, 1973-77; prof. law U. Notre Dame, 1977—; judge U.S. Ct. Appeals (7th cir.), South Bend, 1985—. Reporter Appellate Rules Com., Washington, 1978-85; commn. on mil. justice U.S. Dept. Def., Washington, 1984-85; cons. Supreme Ct. Ala., 1983, Calif. Bd. Bar Examiners, 1981; cons. Anglo-Am. Jud. Exch., 1977, mem., 1980; adv. com. Bill of Rights to Bicentennial Constn. Commn., 1989; mem. adv. com. on appellate rules Jud. Conf. U.S., 1985-90, chmn., 1990-93; chmn. adv. com. on appellate judge edn. Fed. Jud. Ctr., 1996—. Author: Constitutional Litigation, 1984. Served with JAGC, USN, 1968-72. Mem. ABA, Am. Law Inst., Phi Beta Kappa. Office: US Ct of Appeals 208 US Courthouse 204 S Main St South Bend IN 46601-2122 also: Fed Bldg 219 S Dearborn St Ste 2660 Chicago IL 60604-1803

RISI, JOSEPH JOHN, lawyer; b. N.Y.C., Oct. 4, 1956; m. Karen Ann Janusz; children: Joseph, Christopher, Kathryn. BA in Govt., St. John's U., 1978; JD, Widener U., 1982. Bar: N.Y. 1983, U.S. Ct. Mil. Appeals 1986, U.S. Tax Ct. 1988, U.S. Supreme Ct. 1994. Prin. law asst. N.Y. State Ct. System, Kew Gardens, 1983-88; mng. atty. Risi & Santospirito, L.I. City, N.Y., 1988-96, Risi & Assocs., L.I. City, 1996—. Arbitrator Civil Ct. N.Y.C., 1988—; mem. adv. bd. Chgo. Title Ins. Co., Mineola, N.Y., 1990—. Mem. adv. bd. Aviation Adv. Bd., Queens County, N.Y., 1990—, Caring & Sharing, Queens County, 1995—. Mem. N.Y. State Bar Assn., Queens County Bar Assn. (chmn. law & legis. 1997—), L.I. City Lawyers Assn. (past pres., grievance com. 1994—). General civil litigation, Contracts commercial, Estate planning. Office: Risi & Assocs 23-19 31st St Long Island City NY 11105

RISIK, PHILIP MAURICE, lawyer; b. N.Y.C., Jan. 8, 1914; s. Isidor Morton and Celia (Merken) R.; m. Natalie Wynn, Nov. 5, 1948; children: David, Stephen, Elizabeth. BS, NYU, 1932, JD, 1936. Bar: N.Y. 1937, U.S. Dist. Ct. (so. dist.) N.Y. 1940, U.S. Dist. Ct. (D.C. dist.) 1970, Md. 1975, U.S. Ct. Claims 1975, U.S. Ct. Appeals (D.C. cir.) 1975, U.S. Ct. Appeals (8th cir.) 1979, U.S Supreme Ct. 1979, U.S. Dist. Ct. Md. 1982, U.S. Ct. Appeals (4th and 5th cirs.) 1986, U.S. Ct. Appeals (fed. cir.) 1987. Pvt. practice, N.Y.C., 1937-41, 46-49; counsel N.Y. QM Procurement Agy., N.Y.C., 1949-51; procurement specialist Office Sec. Def., Washington, 1953-62; adminstrv. judge Armed Svcs. Bd. Contract Appeals, Washington, 1962-74; of counsel Wachtel Ross & Matzkin, Chevy Chase, Md., 1974-88; pvt. practice, 1988-90, ret., 1990; lectr. So. Meth. U. Law Sch., other law schs. and univs.; former mem. adv. bd. Fed. Contract Reports., Bur. Nat. Affairs; umpire emeritus U.S. Tennis Assn., BCA Judges Assn. (former pres. and gen. counsel). Contbr. articles to George Washington U. Law Rev., Fed. Bar Jour. Area v.p. Montgomery County PTAs, Rockville, Md., 1969; trustee sch. dist., Kemp Mill, Md., 1967. Col. U.S. Army, 1941-46, 51-53; ETO. Decorated Bronze Star; recipient Conspicuous Service Cross, State of N.Y., 1947, Meritorious Civilian Svc. medal Sec. Def., 1974. Mem. ABA (coun. pub. contract law sect. 1969), Am. Arbitration Assn. (nat. panel arbitrators), Masons (sr. steward 1949). Jewish. Home: 9412 Eagle Ridge Dr Bethesda MD 20817-3915

RISSETTO, HARRY A. lawyer; b. Dec. 1, 1943; AB, Fairfield U., 1965; JD, Georgetown U., 1968. Bar: N.Y. 1969, D.C. 1970. Law clk. to Hon. John J. Sirica U.S. Dist. Ct. D.C., 1968-69; law clk. to Chief Justice Warren E. Burger U.S. Supreme Ct., 1969-70; ptnr. Morgan, Lewis & Bockius, Washington. Adj. prof. law Georgetown U. Law Ctr., 1986-89. Mem. ABA (co-chmn. railway labor act com. sect. of labor and employment law 1987-89). Office: Morgan Lewis & Bockius 1800 M St NW Washington DC 20036-5802

RISTAU, KENNETH EUGENE, JR. lawyer; b. Knoxville, Tenn., Feb. 14, 1939; s. Kenneth E. and Frances (Besch) R.; m. Mary Emily George, Nov. 27, 1967 (div. Apr. 1985); children: Heidi, Mary Robin, Kenny, Michael, Robert; m. Emily Pettis, Mar. 31, 1990; 1 child, James Patrick. BA, Colgate U., 1961; JD, NYU, 1964. Bar: U.S. Ct. Appeals (9th cir.) 1968, U.S. Ct. Appeals (D.C. cir.) 1974, U.S. Supreme Ct. 1974, U.S. Dist. Ct., Southern Dist. of Calif., 1993. Assoc. Gibson, Dunn & Crutcher, L.A., 1964-69, ptnr. Irvine, Calif., 1969-2000, adv. ptnr., 2000—. Fellow Coll. Labor and Employment Lawyers (charter); mem. Employers Group (adv. bd.), Orange County Indsl. Rels. Rsch. Assn. (pres. 1992-93), Big Canyon Country Club, Rancho Las Palmas Country Club, Orange County Health Club, Santa Fe Hunt Club. Administrative and regulatory, Labor. Office: Gibson Dunn & Crutcher LLP Jamboree Ctr 4 Park Plz Irvine CA 92614-8557

RISTAU, MARK MOODY, lawyer, petroleum consultant; b. Warren, Pa., Mar. 21, 1944; s. Harold J. and Eleanor K. (Moody) R. BA, Pa. Mil. Coll., 1966; BA, Widner Coll., 1966; JD, Case Western Res. U., 1969. Bar: Pa. 1970, D.C. 1972, U.S. Supreme Ct. 1973, N.Y. 1982. Pvt. practice, Warren, 1970-85, Warren and Vancouver, B.C., Can., 1976-85, Jamestown, N.Y., 1982-85, sr. ptnr. Ristau & McKeirnan, Warren, 1986—; sr. dir. Pa. Allied Oil Producers, 1972-78, atty. for Pa. Field Producers, 1981-85; ptnr. SAR Devel., 1984-91, Slagle Almendinger & Ristau, 1983-89; dir. Try-M Fin. Co., 1978-81; counsel United Refining Co., Pennbank, Enchanced Oil Recovery, Consol. Services, 1982-84; chmn. bd. Comml. Service Corp., U.S. interim trustee, 1979-88, bankruptcy trustee, 1988-98; CEO, Silicon Electro-physics Corp., Inc., 1988-91, Phoenix Materials Corp., Inc., 1988-91; chmn. bd. dirs. Warren Industries, Inc., 1991-94; bd. dirs. Petrex, Inc., A & A Metal Fabricating; U.S. counsel Brazilian Promotions, Inc. of Brazilian Govt., 1981-85; v.p. Daytona Apts., Inc., Daytona Beach, Fla.; sec. Daytona Devel. League. Mem. Warren County Bd. Pub. Assistance, 1970-71, chmn., 1971-72; mem. Broward County (Fla.) Devel. League, 1981-83; mem. Fla. Profl. Recruitment Assn., 1980-83. Recipient Tate Meml. award, 1981; Sambas award, 1981. Mem. Assn. Trial Lawyers Am., Am. Arbitration Assn., Warren County Bar Assn. (past pres.). Clubs: Eagles (hon. life); Ipanema (Brazil); Conewango (Warren). Contbr. articles on law to profl. jours.; case reporter Legal Intelligencer, 1972-79. Banking, Bankruptcy, Contracts commercial. Home and Office: 203 W 3d Ave Warren PA 16365-2331

RITCH, JAMES EARLE, JR. lawyer; b. Charlotte, N.C., Apr. 27, 1931; s. James Earle and Nena Fay (Williams) R.; m. Maria de Lourdes Grande-Ampudia, Apr. 27, 1963; children— James, Alejandro, Lourdes. B.A., Duke U., 1953; LL.B., Yale U., 1956; Licenciate in Law, Nat. U. Mex., 1964. Bar: D.C. 1958, N.C. 1958, Tex. 1959, Republic of Mex. 1965. Assoc. firm Baker & Botts, Houston, 1958-59; assoc., then ptnr. firm Santamarina & Steta, Mexico City, 1959-75; ptnr. firm Ritch, Heather y Mueller, Mexico City, 1975— . Contbr. articles to legal publs. Angier B. Duke scholar, 1949-53; Fulbright scholar, Santiago, Chile, 1956; Rotary Found. fellow, Lima, Peru, 1957. Mem. ABA, Ilustre y Nacional Colegio de Abogados, Am. C. of C. of Mex. (dir. 1978-79), Academia Mexicana de Derecho Internacional Privado, Am. Soc. Internat. Law. Club: University (Mexico). Banking, Contracts commercial, Private international. Home: Fresnos 28 Lomas Palo Alto Mexico City 05110 Mexico Office: Ritch Heather & Mueller Amberes 5 PH Mexico City 06600 Mexico

RITCHEY, PATRICK WILLIAM, lawyer; b. Pitts., July 9, 1949; s. Joseph Frank and Patricia Ann (Giovengo) R. BA, Haverford Coll., 1971; JD, Yale U., 1974. Bar: U.S. Dist. Ct. (we. dist.) Pa. 1974, U.S. Ct. Appeals (3d. cir.) 1976, U.S. Supreme Ct. 1980, U.S. Ct. Appeals (4th cir.) 1981, U.S. Ct. Appeals (6th cir.) 1982, U.S. Dist. Ct. (ea. dist.) Wis. 1987, U.S. Ct. Appeals (7th cir.) 1991, U.S. Ct. Appeals (D.C. cir.) 1993, U.S. Ct. Appeals (8th cir.) 1993. Assoc. Reed Smith Shaw & McClay, Pitts., 1974-82, ptnr., 1982—. Mem. Pitts. Personnel Assn., Pitts., 1982—, U.S. Dist. Ct. Rules Task Force, Pitts., 1988. Bd. dirs. Pitts. Opera. Mem. ABA (labor law sect.), Allegheny County Bar Assn. (labor law and fed. ct. sects.), Harvard-Yale-Princeton Club, Duquesne Club. Labor. Office: Reed Smith LLP James H Reed Bldg 435 6th Ave Ste 2 Pittsburgh PA 15219-1886

RITCHIE, ALBERT, lawyer; b. Charlottesville, Va., Sept. 29, 1939; s. John and Sarah Dunlop (Wallace) R.; m. Jennie Wayland, Apr. 29, 1967; children: John, Mary. BA, Yale U., 1961; LLB, U. Va., 1964. Bar: Ill. 1964. Assoc. Sidley & Austin, Chgo., 1964-71, ptnr., 1972-99, ret., 1999. Bd. dirs. Erie Neighborhood House, Chgo., 1978-88; bd. dirs. United Charities of Chgo., 1979-90; trustee U. Va. Law Sch. Found., 1997-99. Capt. U.S. Army, 1965-67. Mem. ABA, Am. Coll. Real Estate Lawyers, Chgo. Legal Aid Soc., Legal Club Chgo. (pres. 1986-87), U. Va. Law Sch. Alumni Assn. (v.p. 1989-93, pres. 1993-95), LaSalle Club, Indian Hill Club. Episcopalian. Landlord-tenant, Real property. Home: 436 Boxwood Sq Knoxville TN 37919-6627 E-mail: arssi@ntown.com

RITCHIE, ALEXANDER BUCHAN, lawyer; b. Detroit, Apr. 19, 1923; s. Alexander Stevenson and Margaret (May) R.; m. Sheila Spellacy, June 1998; 1 child, Barbara Ritchie Drolshagen. BA, Wayne State U., 1947, JD, 1949. Bar: Mich. 1949. Pvt. practice, Detroit, 1949-52, 84—; asst. gen. counsel, asst. v.p. Maccabees Mutual Life Ins. Co., 1952-65, v.p., sec., gen. counsel Southfield, Mich., 1977-84; sec., house counsel Wayne Nat. Life Ins. Co., Detroit, 1966-67; ptnr. Fenton, Nederlander, Dodge & Ritchie, 1967-77. Spl. asst. atty. gen. State Mich., 1974-77. Bd. mem. Detroit Bd. Edn., 1971-77, Detroit Ctrl. Bd. Edn., 1971-73; bd. Police Commrs., Detroit, 1974-77; bd. dirs. Doctor's Hosp., Detroit, 1974-89. With U.S. Army, 1943-46. Recipient Key to the City of Detroit, Mayor Coleman Young, 1977. Mem. Mich. State Bar Assn. Avocations: reading, golf, theatre, gourmet. Home: 29255 Laurel Woods Dr Apt 201 Southfield MI 48034-4647

RITCHIE, DOUGLAS V. lawyer; b. Las Vegas, Nev., Dec. 20, 1967; s. Verl D. and Rose Ann Ritchie; m. Marleen Stratton, May 2, 1992; 1 child, Bethany. BSBA, Brigham Young U., 1993; JD, U. Utah, 1997. Bar: Utah 1997, Nev. 1998. Sr. loan officer Am. Pioneer Fin., Orem, Utah, 1992-94; clerk U.S. Securities and Exch. Commn., Salt Lake City, 1996; hearing officer Employeers Unity, 1997-98; asst. counsel Equinox Internat. Corp., Las Vegas, 1998—. Contracts commercial, General corporate, Securities. Office: Equinox Internat Corp 10190 Covington Cross Dr Las Vegas NV 89134

RITCHIE, STAFFORD DUFF, II, lawyer; b. Buffalo, June 13, 1948; s. Stafford Duff Ritchie and A. Elizabeth Smith Cavage; m. Rebecca P. Thompson, June 27, 1975; children: Stafford D. III, Thompson C., Glynis A. Student, Rensselaer Poly. Inst., Troy, N.Y., 1966-68; BS in Econs., U. Pa., 1970, JD, 1974. Bar: N.Y. 1975. Atty., advisor, asst. gen. counsel, spl. asst. gen. counsel Adminstrv. Office of U.S. Cts., Washington, 1974-82, assoc. gen. counsel, to 1982; gen. counsel Cavages, Inc., Buffalo, 1982-94; pvt. practice, 1994—. Counsel Coms. of Jud. Conf. of U.S., Jud. Conf. Com., Jud. Conf. of 9th Cir. of U.S.; spl. counsel for major procurement Supreme Ct. of U.S. Trustee Calasanctius Sch., Buffalo, 1990-92; dir. Suicide Prevention and Crisis Svc. Inc., Buffalo, 1997—, sec., 2000—. Sgt. USMCR, 1970-76. Mem. ABA, ATLA, N.Y. State Bar Assn., N.Y. State Trial Lawyers Assn. Avocation: computers. Contracts commercial, General practice, Real property. Office: 438 Main St Ste 200 Buffalo NY 14202-3207 E-mail: sdfr2@att.net

RITER, BRUCE DOUGLAS, lawyer; b. Harvey, Ill., Dec. 20, 1949; s. Russell and Kathryn Nina (Boller) R.; m. Gudrun Weinheimer, May 12, 1978; children: Christina Marianna, Andreas Karl. BEE, So. Ill. U., 1972; JD, Northwestern U., 1975. Bar: U.S. Patent and Trademark Office 1974, Md. 1975, U.S. Ct. Appeals (D.C. cir.) 1977, Va. 1979, U.S. Supreme Ct. 1980, Calif. 1987. Assoc. Beall & Jeffery, Bethesda, Md., 1975-78, Schwartz, Jeffery, Schwaab, Mack, Blumenthal & Koch, P.C., Alexandria, Va., 1979, ptnr., 1980; patent counsel Schlumberger Drilling and Prodn. Services N.Am., Sugarland, Tex., 1980-82, Schlumberger Wireline Atlantic, Clamart, France, 1982-85, Schlumberger Computer Aided Systems, Sunnyvale, Calif., 1985-88; of counsel Ware & Freidenrich, P.C., Palo Alto, 1988; pvt. practice Los Altos, 1988—. Stipendary, patent, copyright and competition law Max Planck Inst., Munich, 1978. Recipient stipend Max Planck Inst. Mem. ABA (patent, trademark and copyright com.), IEEE, Am. Intellectual Property Law Assn. Club: Commonwealth (San Francisco). Avocations: skiing, aviation, languages. Office: 101 1st St PMB 208 Los Altos CA 94022-2750 E-mail: briter@mindspring.com

RITT, ROGER MERRILL, lawyer; b. N.Y.C., Mar. 26, 1950; m. Mimi Santini, Aug. 25, 1974; children: Evan Samuel, David Martin. BA, U. Pa., 1972; JD, Boston U., 1975, LLM, 1976. Bar: Mass. 1977, Pa. 1975, U.S. Tax Ct. Sr. ptnr. Hale and Dorr, Boston, 1984—. Adj. prof. grad. tax program Boston U., 1979-92; panelist Am. Law Inst., Mass. Continuing Legal Edn., World Trade Inst., NYU Inst. on Fed. Taxation; mem. exec. com. Fed. Tax Inst. New Eng. Treas. Found. for Tax Edn. Mem. ABA (tax sect.), Boston Bar Assn. Corporate taxation, Taxation, general, Personal income taxation. Office: Hale and Dorr 60 State St Boston MA 02109-1816

RITTENBERRY, KELLY CULHANE, lawyer; b. Rockville Centre, N.Y., May 29, 1969; d. William and Eileen Patricia Culhane; m. Bryan Alex Rittenberry, July 8, 1995. BA, U. Okla., 1991; postgrad., So. Meth. U., 1993-94; JD, Marquette U., 1994. Bar: Tex. 1994, Wis. 1994, U.S. Dist. Ct. (no. dist.) Tex. 1994, U.S. Dist. Ct. (ea. dist.) Wis. 1994. Law clk. Gibson, Dunn & Crutcher, Dallas, summer 1992; summer assoc. Arter, Hadden, Johnson & Bromberg, 1993-94, assoc., 1994-95; counsel Akin, Gump, Strauss, Hauer & Feld, 1995—. Pro bono lawyer Martin Luther King Ctr., Dallas, 1997-98, Housing Crisis Ctr., Dallas, 1997-98, Legal Svcs. North Tex., Dallas. Mem. FBA (bd. mem. 1994—), State Bar Tex. (Coll.), Dallas Bar Assn. (judiciary com. 1996-98, media rels. com. 1996-98, entertainment com. 1996-98). Republican. Roman Catholic. Avocations: travel, skiing, reading, outdoor activities. General civil litigation, Franchising, Insurance. Office: Akin Gump Strauss Hauer & Feld LLP 816 Congress Ave Ste 1900 Austin TX 78701-2478

RITTER, ANN, lawyer; b. Gainesville, Fla. d. Herbert David and Mary Ellen Kimmel; m. H.N. Ritter III, Apr. 28, 1985; 1 child, Kristy Ann. BS, Fla. State U., 1980; JD, U. Tenn., 1982. Bar: S.C. 1983. Assoc. Gilreath & Rowland, Knoxville, 1982-83, Law Office D.A. Speights, Hampten, S.C., 1983-84, Ness Motley Loadholt Richardson Poole and predecessor, Charleston, 1984-92, ptnr., 1992—. General civil litigation, Product liability. Home: 140 Hibben St Mount Pleasant SC 29464-4309 Office: 28 Bridgeside Mount Pleasant SC 29464

RITTER, ANN L. lawyer; b. N.Y.C., May 20, 1933; d. Joseph and Grace (Goodman) R. BA, Hunter Coll., 1954; JD, N.Y. Law Sch., 1970; postgrad. Law Sch., NYU, 1971-72. Bar: N.Y. 1971, U.S. Ct. Appeals (2d cir.) 1975, U.S. Supreme Ct. 1975. Writer, 1954-70; editor, 1955-66; tchr., 1966-70; atty. Am. Soc. Composers, Authors and Pubs., N.Y.C., 1971-72, Greater N.Y. Ins. Co., N.Y.C., 1973-74; sr. ptnr. Brenhouse & Ritter, 1974-78; sole practice, 1978—. Editor N.Y. Immigration News, 1975-76. Mem. ABA, Am. Immigration Lawyers Assn. (treas. 1983-84, sec. 1984-85, vice-chair 1985-86, chair 1986-87, chair program com. 1989-90, chair spkrs. bur. 1989-90, chair media liaison 1989-90), N.Y. State Bar Assn., N.Y. County Lawyers Assn., Assn. Trial Lawyers Am., N.Y. State Trial Lawyers Assn., N.Y.C. Bar Assn., Watergate East Assn. (v.p., asst. treas. 1990—). Democrat. Jewish. Family and matrimonial, Immigration, naturalization, and customs, Personal injury. Home: 47 E 87th St New York NY 10128-1005 Office: 420 Madison Ave Rm 1200 New York NY 10017-1171

RITTER, JEFFREY BLAKE, lawyer, consultant; b. Iowa City, Sept. 13, 1954; s. Charles Clifford and Patricia Ann (Wise) R.; children: Jordan, Chelsea. BA, MA, Ohio State U., 1976; JD, Duke U., 1979. Bar: Ky. 1979, D.C. 1980, Ohio 1983. Assoc. Barnett & Alagia, Louisville, 1979-82, Schwartz, Kelm, Warren & Rubenstein, Columbus, Ohio, 1982-90; of counsel Vorys, Sater, Seymour & Pease, 1991-94; U.S. legal adviser for facilitation UN Working Party, Geneva, 1990-96; dir. ECLIPS, Columbus, 1994-98, Document Authentication Sys., Inc., Balt., 1998-99; counsel Kirkpatrick & Lockhart, Washington, 1999-2000, ptnr., 2000—. Chair Adv. Group on Internat. Trade, Columbus, 1990. Mem. ABA (chair sect. of bus. law com. on cyberspace law, 1995-98, reporter, subcom. on scope of uniform comml. code 1990-91). Democrat. Avocations: cycling, jazz, poetry. Computer, General corporate, Private international. Office: 1800 Massachusetts Ave NW Washington DC 20036-1806 E-mail: jritter@kl.com-office

RITTER, ROBERT FORCIER, lawyer; b. St. Louis, Apr. 7, 1943; s. Tom Marshall and Jane Elizabeth (Forcier) R.; m. Karen Gray, Dec. 28, 1966; children: Allison Gray Campione, Laura Thompson Capstick, Elisabeth Forcier Schoenecker. BA, U. Kans., 1965; JD, St. Louis U., 1968. Bar: Mo. 1968, U.S. Dist. Ct. (ea. and we. dists.) Mo. 1968. U.S. Ct. Mil. Appeals 1972, U.S. Supreme Ct. 1972, U.S. Ct. Appeals (8th cir.) 1980, U.S. Dist. Ct. (so. dist.) Ill. 1982. Assoc. Gray & Sommers, St. Louis, 1968-71; ptnr. Gray Ritter & Graham, P.C., 1974—; chmn., pres. Gray & Ritter, 1983—. Bd. dirs. United Mo. Bank St. Louis, Marine Bank and Trust Co.; adv. com. 22d cir. Supreme Ct., 1985-92; mem. Supreme Ct. com. civil jury instrns., 1988—, U.S. Dist. Ct. adv. com., 1993-95; lectr. Contbr. articles to profl. jours. Bd. dirs. Cystic Fibrosis Found., Gateway chpt., pres., 1991. Capt. USAR, 1968-74. Recipient Law Week award Bur. Nat. Affairs, 1968, award of merit Nat. Conf. Met. Cts., 1995. Fellow Internat. Soc. Barristers (bd. govs. 1994—), Am. Coll. Trial Lawyers, Internat. Acad. Trial Lawyers; mem. ABA, Am. Judicature Soc., Assn. Trial Lawyers Am., Am. Bd. Trial Advocates (advocate), Bar Assn. Met. St. Louis (chmn. trial sect. 1978-79, exec. com. 1980-82, award merit 1976, award achievement 1982, chmn. bench bar conf. 1983), Mo. Bar Assn. (coun. practice and procedure com. 1972—, coun. tort law com. 1982—, bd. govs. 1984-91, fin. com. 1984-91), Mo. Bar Found. (outstanding trial lawyer award 1978), Lawyers Assn. St. Louis (exec. com. 1976-81, pres. 1977-78), Mo. Assn. Trial Attys. (bd. govs. 1984—), Noonday Club, Old Warson Country Club, Bellerive Country Club, John's Island Club (bd. dirs. 1998—), Racquet Club (bd. govs. 1988-93, pres. 1991-92), Red Stick Golf Club (founding mem.), Roaring Fork Club (founding mem.), Windsor Club. Presbyterian. State civil litigation, Personal injury, Product liability. Office: Gray Ritter & Graham PC 701 Market St Fl 8 Saint Louis MO 63101-1850 E-mail: rritter@grgpc.com

RITTER, ROBERT THORNTON, lawyer; b. N.Y.C., Nov. 4, 1956; s. Robert J. and Barbara W. (Foust) R.; m. Rebecca L. Grubbs, July 25, 1981; children: Sarah, Luke, Robert R. BA, Duke U., 1979; JD, Washington U., 1984. Bar: Mo., 1984, U.S. Dist. Ct. (ea. dist.) Mo., 1985. Assoc. William Brown, Atty. at Law, Bridgeton, Mo., 1984-85, Kopsky & Vouga, Chesterfield, 1986; pvt. practice Clayton, 1987-89; ptnr. Ritter & Gusdorf, 1990-96; mem. Ritter & Gusdorf L.C., 1997—. Treas. Campaign Election of State Rep. Steve Moore, 1988; coach Little League Baseball; head coach Christian H.S. Baseball. Mem. Mo. Bar Assn., Bar Assn. Met. St. Louis, St. Louis Assn. Christian Attys. (bd. dirs. 1994—). Republican. Avocation: tennis. Family and matrimonial, Personal injury, Real property. Office: Ritter & Gusdorf LC 225 S Meramec Ave Ste 1220 Clayton MO 63105-3511

RITZ, STEPHEN MARK, financial advisor, lawyer; b. Midland, Mich., Aug. 23, 1962; s. Alvin H. and Patricia M. (Padway) R. BA, Northwestern U., 1985; JD, Ind. U., 1989. Bar: Ill. 1990, U.S. Dist. Ct. (no. dist.) Ill. 1990, Ind. 1996. Atty. Chapman & Cutler, Chgo., 1990-93; pres., CEO S.M. Ritz and Co., Inc., Indpls., 1994-97; CEO Newport Pension Mgmt. LLC, 1997—. Dir. Indsl. Logistics, Inc., Indpls., 1994-96. Mem. ABA, Inst. CFPs, Registry CFPs, Internat. Assn. Fin. Planners. Office: Newport Pension Mgmt 9465 Counselors Row Ste 108 Indianapolis IN 46240-3816

RIVERA, JOSE DE JESUS, lawyer; b. Zacatecas, Mex., 1950; m. Nina Rivera; 5 children. BA, No. Ariz. U.; JD, Ariz. State U. Atty. civil rights divsn. Dept. of Justice, 1976-77; asst. U.S. atty. Dist. Ariz., 1977-81; with Langerman, Beam, Lewis and Marks, 1981-84; ptnr. Rivera, Scales and Kizer, 1984-98; atty. City of El Mirage, U.S. Dept. Justice, Ariz., 1998-2001; with Haralson, Miller, Pitt & McAnally PLC, Phoenix, 2001—. Vice-chair adv. com. civil rights Atty. Gen. Ariz. dist., 1998-2001, adv. com. native Am. issues, domestic terrorism subcom., 1998-2001, chair subcom. no Mem. com. Los Abogados; bd. dirs. Inst. for Cmty. Initiatives, 1996-98; coach Little League. With N.G. Mem. Ariz. State Bar. (bd. govs. 1995-98, bd. officer, sec. treas. 1996, 2d v.p. 1997-98, exec. dir. search com. 1996-97, chair appointments com. 1997-98), Hispanic Bar Assn., Los Abogados Bar Assn. (bd. dirs. 1981-83). Democrat. Avocation: reading. General civil litigation, Private international, Personal injury. Office: Haralson Miller Pitt & McAnally PLC 3003 N Central Ave Ste 1400 Phoenix AZ 85012 E-mail: jrivera@hmpmlaw.com

RIVERA, OSCAR R. lawyer, corporate executive; b. Havana, Cuba, Dec. 8, 1956; s. Alcibiades R. and Marian (Fernandez) R.; children: Peter, Taylor. BBA, U. Miami, 1978; JD, Georgetown U., 1981. Bar: Fla. 1981, U.S. Dist. Ct. (so. dist.) Fla. 1982, U.S. Tax Ct. 1982. Assoc. Corrigan, Zelman & Bander P.A., Miami, Fla., 1981-83; ptnr. Siegfried, Rivera, Lerner De La Torre & Sobel P.A., 1984—. Adj. prof. law U. Miami, 1987—. Asst. mgr. campaign to elect Michael O'Donovan, Miami, 1976;

mem. youth adv. bd., Miami, 1975-78, youth planning council Dade County, Miami, 1975-78. Mem. ABA, Cuban Am. Bar Assn., Internat. Coun. Shopping Ctrs. (pres. Fla. polit. action com., v.p. Fla. govtl. affairs com., state dir. Fla.), Little Havana Kiwanis, Orange Key, Omicron Delta Kappa, Phi Kappa Phi. Avocations: photography, skiing. General corporate, Landlord-tenant, Real property.

RIVERA, RHONDA RAE, lawyer, labor arbitrator; b. Phila., Mar. 9, 1938; d. Preston Robert and Katherine Lowe (MacSorley) Rieley; 1 child, Robert Preston. BA cum laude, Douglass Coll., 1959; MPA, Syracuse U., 1960; JD magna cum laude, Wayne State U., 1967; cert. in urban econs., MIT, 1972. Bar: Mich. 1968, Ohio 1976, Ariz. 1995, U.S. Dist. Ct. (so. dist.) Hio 1977, Ariz. 1995. Asst. prof. law Ohio State U. Law Sch., Columbus, 1976-78, assoc. prof. law, 1978-81, prof. law, 1982-95, prof. emeritus, 1995, assoc. dean, 1982-86, dir. 2d Yr. Legal Writing Program, 1983-87. Vis. prof. law, U. Ariz., 1995-99; adj. prof. law, U. N.Mex, 2001-. Author: (with D.J. Whaley) Problems and Materials on Sales, 1983; contbr. articles and revs. to legal and bus. jours. Mem. fin. com. LWV, 1971-74; lay reader St. Stephen's Episcopal Ch., Collumbus, 1976-95, mem. Ctrl. Ohio Diocesan Coun., 1980-81, chancery judge So. diocese Ohio, 1982-90; active Boy Scouts Am., 1976-80, Columbus Com. for Battered Women, 1979-80; pres. Stonewall Union, Columbus, 1983-84, bd. dirs. and clk., 1981-88; founder Integrity Ctrl. Ohio, 1983; bd. dirs,. Ohio Women Ind., 1980-82, treas., 1981-82; bd. dirs., Franklin County Legal Aid Soc., Columbus, 1983-85. Recipient Susan B. Anthony award Woman Law Students Assn. U. Mich., 1976, Evelyn Hooker Rsch. award Gay Acad. Union, 1984, Dir.'s award Ohio Dept. Health for AIDS work, 1988, Woman of Achievement award YWCA, 1989. Mem. ABA (mem. adv. bd. sect. individual rights and responsibilities 1979-80), ACLU, NOW (Legal Achievement award Legal Def. and Edn. fund 1986, Uppity Woman of Yr. Ann Arbor chpt. 1975), AAUP, Am. Assn. Law Schs. (chmn. women in legal edn. sect. 1979-80, mem. sect. exec. com. 1980-82, chmn. gay and lesbian legal issues sect. 1982-83), Soc. Am. Law Tchrs. (mem. exec. com. of bd. govs. 1979-81, mem. bd. govs. 1978-95, pres. 1984-86), Nat. Lawyers Guild, Nat. Gay Task Force, Ohio Human Rights Bar Assn. (founder 1988, pres. 1989-91, bd. trustees 1991-95). Home and Office: 10218 Prescott Ct NW Albuquerque NM 87114-4519 E-mail: riveramorris@earthlink.net

RIVERA, WALTER, lawyer; b. N.Y.C., Jan. 18, 1955; s. Marcelino and Ana Maria (Reyes) R. BA, Columbia U., 1976; JD, U. Pa., 1979. Bar: N.Y. 1980. Law clk. to cen. legal research staff N.Y. State Ct. Appeals, Albany, 1979-81; asst. atty. gen. State of N.Y., N.Y.C., 1981-85; sole practice, 1985-88; shareholder Rivera & Muniz, P.C., 1988-93, Law Offices of Walter Rivera P.C., 1994-97; ptnr. Rivera, Hunter, Colon & Dobshinsky, LLP, N.Y.C., 1998—. Chmn. Third World Lawyers Caucus, N.Y. State Atty. Gen.'s Office, N.Y.C., 1984; arbitrator City Ct. N.Y.C., 1985. Mem. ABA, Puerto Rican Bar Assn., Nat. Hispanic Bar Assn., N.Y. State Bar Assn., Assn. Bar City N.Y. (past chmn. com. on small law firm mgmt.), Sch. of Visual Arts (bd. dirs.). Avocations: camping, travel. Federal civil litigation, General civil litigation, State civil litigation. Home: 2 Nob Hill Dr Elmsford NY 10523-2415 Office: Rivera Hunter Colon & Dohshinsky LLP 61 Broadway Rm 1030 New York NY 10006-2701 E-mail: wrivera@rhedlaw.com

RIVERS, KENNETH JAY, retired judicial administrator, consultant; b. N.Y.C., Feb. 13, 1938; s. Alexander Maximillian and Albertina Ray (Gay) R.; m. Leah B. Files, Sept. 21, 1957 (div.); children: Londa Denise, Nancy Laura, Terrie Ruth, Kenneth J. Jr. AAS in Criminal Justice, BS in Criminal Justice, St. Francis Coll., 1978; MPA, L.I. Univ., 1981. Correction officer N.Y.C. Dept. Correction, 1965-69; ct. officer N.Y. State Unified Ct. System, N.Y.C., 1969-71, asst. ct. clk., 1971-73, sr. ct. clk., 1973-85, assoc. ct. clk., 1985-88, prin. ct. clk., 1988-90, dep. chief clk., 1991-93; ret., 1993. Tng. instr. N.Y. State Unified Ct. System, N.Y.C., 1985—, pers. assessor, 1985—; lectr. John Jay Coll. NYU, N.Y.C., 1987. Author: Juvenile Crime Survey, 1982, New York State Jury Selection, 1984. Bd. dirs. Parkway Consumers Med. Coun., Bklyn., 1983—, Cen. Bklyn. Tenant's Rights, 1988—. Recipient Leadership award Tribune Soc., N.Y. State Cts., 1987, Svc. award, 1988, Cert. of Merit award Fedn. Afro-Am. Civil Svc. Orgns., 1987. Mem. ASPA, Internat. Pers. Mgmt. Assn., Acad. Polit. Sci., Conf. Minority Pub. Adminstrs., Masons. Democrat. Methodist. Avocation: jazz musician. E-mail: kchiefclerk@aol.com

RIVET, DIANA WITTMER, lawyer, developer; b. Auburn, N.Y., Apr. 28, 1931; d. George Wittmer and Anne (Jenkins) Wittmer Hauswirth; m. Paul Henry Rivet, Oct. 24, 1952; children: Gail, Robin, Leslie, Heather, Clayton, Eric. BA, Keuka Coll., 1951; JD, Bklyn. Law Sch., 1956. Bar: N.Y. 1956, U.S. Dist. Ct. (ea. and so. dists.) N.Y. 1975; cert. NOFA, 2001. Sole practice, Orangeburg, N.Y., 1957-2000; farmer Danny's Backyard Organic Farm, 2000—. County atty. Rockland County (N.Y.), 1974-77; asst. to legis. chmn. Rockland County, 1978-79; counsel, adminstr. Indsl. Devel. Agy., Rockland County, 1980-91, Rockland Econ. Devel. Corp., 1981-90; counsel, exec. dir. Pvt. IndustryCoun. Rockland county, 1980-90; pres., CEO Environ. Mgmt. Ltd., Orangeburg, 1980-98; mem. air mgmt. adv. com. N.Y. State Dept. Environ. Conservation 1984-92, Orangetown Planning Bd., 1993-2000, master plan com., 2000—. Pres. Rockland County coun. Girl Scouts U.S., 1981-84; chmn. Rockland County United Way, 1996-97, mem. campaign com., 1983-84, 88-89, 93, sec., 1997-99, bd. dirs., 1988-94, 95—; mem. Leadership Rockland, 1991-94. Recipient Cmty. Svc. award Keuka Coll., 1965, Disting. Svc. award Town of Orangetown, 1970, Disting. Svc. award Rockland County, 1989, Econ. Devel. award Rockland Econ. Devel. Corp., 1990; named Businessperson of Yr. Jour. News, Rockland County, 1982. Mem. ABA, N.Y. State Bar Assn. (mcpl. law sect. exec. com. 1976-83, environ. law sect. exec. com. 1974-86), Rockland County Bar Assn. (chair environ. law com. 1994-96), Rockland Bus. Assn. (bd. dirs. 1981-97, small bus. adv. com. 1998, gov. affairs com. 1998—), Rockland Computer Users' Group (bd. dirs. 1998-99). Democrat. Mem. Religious Soc. of Friends. Environmental, Municipal (including bonds), Real property. Home: 1 Lester Dr Orangeburg NY 10962-2316 E-mail: danny@ucs.net

RIVIERA, DANIEL JOHN, lawyer; b. N.Y.C., May 28, 1927; s. Charles Adrian and Ruth Blanche (Sinclair) R.; BA cum laude, Syracuse U., 1950; LLB, Georgetown U., 1953; children: Daniel C., Sara J., Jeffrey, Gloria, Spencer. Bar: Wash. 1953, Idaho 1981. Practiced in Seattle, 1953-96; mem. firm Foster, Pepper & Riviera, Seattle, 1953-96, ptnr., 1968-96. Instr. bus. law U. Wash., 1957-59, Journalism law Seattle U., 1965-67, 75-77; mem. Statute Law Com., 1963-72; mem. Bench, Bar, Press Com., 1964-72. Mem. Mercer Island City Council, 1961-68; bd. visitors J. Reuben Clark Law Sch., Brigham Young U., Provo, Utah, 1978-80. Served with AUS, 1946-47. Mem. ABA (vice-chmn. projects com. jr. bar conf. 1959-60), Wash. State Bar Assn. (mem. subcom. of local adminstrv. com. 1967-70), Seattle-King County Bar Assn. (labor law com. 1967—), Bellevue (Wash.) Athletic Club, Harbor Club (Seattle). Federal civil litigation, Family and matrimonial, Labor. Office: 1111 3rd Ave Seattle WA 98101-3292 Address: PO Box 6839 Ketchum ID 83340-6839

RIVKIN, JOHN LAWRENCE, lawyer; b. Hewlett, N.Y., Dec. 16, 1955; s. Leonard Lambert and Lenore Diana R.; m. Nancy Jean Sandarg, July 26, 1987; children: Erika, Diana, Michael. BA summa cum laude, Union Coll., 1978; JD, U. Va., 1981. Bar: N.Y. 1982, U.S. Dist. Ct. (ea. and so. dists.) N.Y. 1982, Fla. 1983, D.C. 1985, U.S. Claims Ct. 1985, U.S. Ct. Appeals (3rd, 5th, 11th cirs.) 1992, U.S. Supreme Ct. 1983. Sr. ptnr. Rivkin, Radler & Kremer, Uniondale, N.Y., 1981—. Disting. lectr. law, mem. nat. litig. panel U. Va. Sch. Law; lectr. law Practising Law Inst., N.Y., 1986; mem. adv. coun. Touro Law Sch., Huntington, N.Y.; mem. coun. overseers L.I. U., Old Brookville, N.Y.; spkr. in field. Contbr. articles to profl. jours. Nott scholar Union Coll., 1978. Mem. N.Y. State Trial Lawyers Assn., Fedn. Ins. Corp. Counsel, Def. Rsch. Inst., Huntington Yacht Club, Alpha Delta Phi. Avocation: yachting. E-mail: www.rivkinradler.com. Federal civil litigation, Environmental, Insurance. Office: Rivkin Radler & Kremer Eab Plz Uniondale NY 11556-0001 Fax: 516-357-3333

RIVLIN, LEWIS ALLEN, lawyer, entrepreneur; b. N.Y.C., Oct. 15, 1929; s. Benjamin and Lena (Levy) R.; m. Alice Mitchell Rivlin, June 28, 1955 (div. Sept. 1977); children: Catherine Amy, Allan Mitchell, Douglas Gray; m. Dianne M. Farrington, Oct. 7, 1977; children: Benjamin, Leigh. BA, Swarthmore Coll., 1951; JD, Harvard Law Sch., 1957. Bar: D.C. 1957, U.S. Ct. Appeals (D.C. cir.) 1957, U.S. Supreme Ct. 1960. From ensign to commdr. U.S. Naval Reserve, 1951-71; atty. patent sect., civil divsn. U.S. Dept. Justice, Washington, 1957-59, sr. trial atty. gen. litigation sect., antitrust divsn., 1959-64; advanceman Hubert H. Humphrey For V.P. Campaign, 1964; ptnr. O'Connor, Green, Thomas, Walters & Kelly, Washington, 1965-68; del. coord. Hubert H. Humphrey For Pres. Campaign, 1968; Humphrey-Muskie campaign coord. Pa. Dem. Nat. Com., Harrisburg, Pa., 1968; founding ptnr. Peabody, Rivlin, Lambert & Meyers, Washington, 1969-81; chmn. & CEO New Venture Capital Corp., Rockville, Md., 1981—; founding ptnr. Rivlin, Velarde & Taylor, LLP, Washington, 1995-98. Chmn. bd. dirs., CEO Tribal Funding Devel. and Mgmt. Corp., Rockville, Md., 1984—; pres. Gen. Internat. Fin. Corp., Rockville, 1985—; dir., exec. v.p., gen. counsel Hainan Zhonge Refinery, People's Rep. China, 1996— Co-author: (book) Report of the D.C. Circuit Judicial Conference Committee on ABA Standards for the Administration of Criminal Justice, 1973. Mem. ABA, Fed. Comms. Bar Assn., Fed. Bar Assn. Avocations: tennis, classical music, travel, sailing. Administrative and regulatory, Antitrust, Legislative. E-mail: laresq@aol.com, rivlinlaw@aol.com

RIZOWY, CARLOS GUILLERMO, lawyer, educator, political analyst; b. Sarandi Grande, Uruguay, Mar. 5, 1949; came to U.S., 1973, naturalized, 1981; s. Gerszon and Eva (Visnia) R.; m. Charlotte Gordon, Mar. 14, 1976; children: Brian Isaac, Yael Deborah, Michal Evie. BA, Hebrew U., Jerusalem, 1971; MA, U. Chgo., 1975, PhD, 1981; JD, Chgo. Kent Coll. Law, Ill. Inst. Tech., 1983. Bar: Ill. 1983, U.S. Dist. Ct. (no. dist.) Ill. 1983, U.S. Ct. Appeals (7th cir.) 1983. Asst. prof. polit. sci. Roosevelt U., Chgo., 1982-89, chmn. dept. polit. sci., 1983-86, dir. internat. studies program, 1986-89; mng. ptnr. Ray, Rizowy & Fleischer, 1983-90; ptnr. corp. law dept. Gottlieb and Schwartz, 1990-92; ptnr. Levenfeld, Eisenberg, Janger, Glassberg, Samotny & Halper, 1993-94; of counsel Sonnenschein, Nath & Rosenthal, 1994—. Dir. Midwest Am. Friends of Hebrew U., 1997—; hon. consul of Uruguay, Chgo., 1994—; adj. assoc. prof. Spertus Coll. Judaica, Chgo., 1984—; weekly polit. analyst on Middle East, internat. law and fgn. policy, resource specialist Sta. WBEZ Pub. Radio and BBC Latin Am.; mem. panel of arbitrators of Mediation and Arbitration Ctr., Internat. Arbitration Ct. for Mercosur Bolsa de Comercio, Uruguay, 1999—. Author: Avoiding Premises Liability Suits by Improving Security, 1991, Middle East Security: Five Areas to Watch, 1997. V.p., resource specialist to exec. com. Orgn. Children of Holocaust Survivors, Chgo., 1982; pres. Assn. Children Holocaust Survivors, 1986-91; pres. bd. dirs. Soviet Jewry Legal Advocacy Ctr., 1986-88; rsch. com. Nat. Strategy Forum, bd. dirs. UN Assn. U.S., 1985-89; mem. cmty. rels. com. Jewish Fedn. Met. Chgo., 1983-84; mem. adv. bd., chmn. internat. affairs commn. Am. Jewish Congress, Chgo., 1983-85, chmn. subcom. for Israel, 1986-88; mem. Nat. Spkrs. Bur. United Jewish Appeal, Nat. Spkrs. Bur. Devel. Corp. for Israel; mem. adv. bd. Chgo. Action for Soviet Jewry, 1983-85; bd. dirs. Am. Friends of Hebrew U., Chgo., 1984-86, Florence Heller Jewish Cmty. Ctr., 1986-88, Soviet Jewry Legal Advocacy Ctr., 1986-88; mem. human rights com. Anti-Defamation League, 1986, bd. dirs., 1989—; bd. dirs. Bd. Jewish Edn., 1989-91, Hispanic Coalition for Jobs, 1991-94; chmn. univ. educators divsn. Jewish United Fund, 1988-90; mem. consular corp. adv. bd. Internat. Vis. Ctr. Chgo., 1995—, com. fgn. affairs Chgo. Coun. Fgn. Rels., 1994—. Scholar Hebrew U., 1967-72, U. Chgo., 1972-78, Hillman Found., 1978, Peter Volid Found., 1980; recipient Globalist award Heritage Internat. Trade Assn., 1997. Mem. ATLA, ABA (chmn. bus. com. 1993-95), Assn. Ibero-Am. Consuls of Chgo., Ill. State Bar Assn., Chgo. Bar Assn. (internat. trade com.), Latin Am. Bar Assn., Nat. Hispanic Bar Assn., Am. Immigration Lawyers Assn., Am. Polit. Sci. Assn., Am. Judicature Soc., Exec. Club Chgo., Internat. Platform Assn., Wexner Heritage Found., Am. Forum, Latin Am. C. of C. (bd. dirs. 1991—, gen. counsel 1992—), Anshe Emet Congregation, Masons. Private international, Public international, Mergers and acquisitions. Office: Sonnenschein Nath & Rosenthal 8000 Sears Tower Chicago IL 60606

RIZZO, JAMES GERARD, lawyer; b. Hartford, Conn., Nov. 6, 1962; s. Thomas Dignan and Jean Kathryn (Foley) R.; m. Patricia Marie Conrad, Oct. 5, 1996; children: Madeleine Patrice, Abigail Rose. AB, Georgetown U., 1984; JD, Fordham U., 1990. Bar: Conn. 1990, N.Y. 1991, U.S. Dist. Ct. (ea. and so. dists.) N.Y. 1991, D.C. 1996, U.S. Supreme Ct. 1998. Assoc. Bower & Gardner, N.Y.C., 1990-93, Mudge, Rose, Guthrie, Alexander & Ferdon, N.Y.C., 1993-94, O'Melveny & Myers LLP, N.Y.C., 1994-97; ptnr. Carr Goodson Warner, Washington, 1997-2000, McDermott, Will & Emery, Washington, 2000—. Hon. usher St. Patrick's Cathedral, N.Y.C., 1984—; v.p. St. Joseph's Parish Coun., Bronxville, N.Y., 1988-90. Mem. Bar Assn. D.C., Soc. of the Friendly Sons of St. Patrick, John Carroll Soc., Lowes Island Club, Sea Island Club. Republican. Roman Catholic. General civil litigation, Environmental, Product liability. Office: McDermott Will & Emery 600 13th St NW Washington DC 20005

RIZZO, RONALD STEPHEN, lawyer; b. Kenosha, Wis., July 15, 1941; s. Frank Emmanuel and Rosalie (Lo Cicero); children: Ronald Stephen Jr., Michael Robert. BA, St. Norbert Coll., 1963; JD, Georgetown U., 1965, LLM in Taxation, 1966. Bar: Wis. 1965, Calif. 1967, Ill. 1999. Assoc. Kindel & Anderson, L.A., 1966-71, ptnr., 1971-86, Jones, Day, Reavis & Pogue, L.A., 1986-93, Chgo., 1993—. Bd. dirs. Guy LoCicero & Son Inc., Kenosha, Wis. Contbg. editor ERISA Litigation Reporter, 1994-99; mem. internat. adv. editl. bd. Jour. Pensions Mgmt. and Mktg. Schulte zur Hausen fellow Inst. Internat. and Fgn. Trade Law, Georgetown U., 1966. Fellow Am. Coll. Tax Counsel, Am. Coll. Employee Benefits Counsel (charter); mem. ABA (chmn. com. on employee benefits sect. on taxation 1988-89, vice chair com. on govt. submissions 1995-99), Los Angeles County Bar Assn. (chmn. com. on employee benefits sect. on taxation 1977-79, exec. com. 1977-78, 90-92), State Bar Calif. (co-chmn. com. on employee benefits sect. on taxation 1980), West Pension Conf. (steering com. L.A. chpt. 1980-83). Avocations: reading, golf, travel. Pension, profit-sharing, and employee benefits, Corporate taxation. Home: # 19C 1040 N Lake Shore Dr Chicago IL 60611-6164 Office: Jones Day Reavis & Pogue 77 W Wacker Ste 3500 Chicago IL 60601-1692 E-mail: rsrizzo@jonesday.com

ROACH, JON GILBERT, lawyer; b. Knoxville, Tenn., June 17, 1944; s. Walter Davis and Lena Rose (Chapman) R.; m. Mintha Marie Evans, Oct. 22, 1977; children: Jon G., II, Evan Graham. BS, U. Tenn., 1967, JD, 1969. Bar: Tenn. 1970, D.C. 1981, U.S. Ct. Appeals (6th cir.). Assoc. Stone & Bozeman, Knoxville, 1971-83; city atty., dir. of law City of Knoxville, 1976-83; ptnr. Peck, Shaffer & Williams, Knoxville, 1983-90, Watson, Hollow & Reeves, PLC, Knoxville, 1990—. City atty. City of Plainview, 1999—, City of Maynardville, 2000—; faculty Knoxville Bus. Coll., 1973-74; mem. Tenn. Commn. on Continuing Legal Edn. and Specialization of Tenn. Supreme Ct., 1995-2000. Mem. bd., Bapt. Health Sys. Found. Mem. ABA, Tenn. Bar Assn. (mem. ho. of dels.), Knoxville Bar Assn., D.C. Bar Assn., Kiwanis (East Knoxville). Democrat. Baptist. General civil litigation, Municipal (including bonds), Probate. Home: 1701 River Shores Dr Knoxville TN 37914-6023 Office: Watson Hollow & Reeves PLC PO Box 131 1700 Tennessee Ave Knoxville TN 37921-2639

ROACH, ROBERT MICHAEL, JR. lawyer; b. Bronxville, N.Y., May 27, 1955; s. Robert M. and Mary Dee R.; m. Elizabeth Preston Roach, Sept. 22, 2000. BA, Georgetown U., 1977; JD, U. Tex., 1981. Bar: Tex. 1981, U.S. Dist. Ct. (so. dist.) Tex. 1982, U.S. Ct. Appeals (5th cir.) 1982, U.S. Dist. Ct. (we. dist.) Tex. 1984, U.S. Supreme Ct. 1986, U.S. Dist. Ct. (ea. dist.) 1986, U.S. Dist. Ct. (no. dist.) Tex. 1988. Assoc. Vinson & Elkins, Houston, 1981-83, Ryan & Marshall, Houston, 1983, Mayor, Day & Caldwell, Houston, 1983-88; ptnr. Mayor, Day, Caldwell & Keeton, 1989-93; founding ptnr. Cook, Roach & Lawless, L.L.P. (former name Cook & Roach LLP), 1993—; dir. appellate advocacy U. Houston Law Ctr., 1994—. Adj. prof. law U. Houston, 1990; lectr. continuing legal edn. U. Houston Law Ctr., 1989—; lectr. continuing legal edn. State Bar Tex., U. Tex., South Tex. Coll. Law, So. Meth. U., ABA; rschr., editor U.S. Senate Com. on Nutrition, 1975, 76, 77; rschr. U.S Supreme Ct., Washington, 1977; mem. Tex. Law Rev., 1979-81. Editor Def. Counsel Jour., 1990-93. Active U.S. Supreme Ct. Hist. Soc. Mem. Internat. Assn. Def. Counsel, Fedn. Ins. and Corp. Counsel, Def. Rsch. Inst. (grievance com.), Tex. Assn. Def. Counsel, State Bar Tex. (appellate sect. coun. officer 1989—), Houston Bar Assn. (officer, appellate sect.), Houston Club, Houston Met. Racquet Club, Houston Ctr. Club. Avocations: music, travel, oenology, tennis. General civil litigation, Personal injury, Product liability. Office: Cook & Roach LLP Texaco Heritage Plz 1111 Bagby St Ste 2650 Houston TX 77002-2543

ROAN, FORREST CALVIN, JR. lawyer; b. Waco, Tex., Dec. 18, 1944; s. Forrest Calvin and Lucille Elizabeth (McKinney) R.; m. Vickie Joan Howard, Feb. 15, 1969 (div. Dec. 1983); children: Amy Katherine, Jennifer Louise; m. Leslie D. Hampton Roan, Jan. 2, 1999. BBA, U. Tex., Austin, 1973, JD, 1976. Bar: Tex. 1976, U.S. Dist. Ct. (we. dist.) Tex. 1977, U.S. Dist. Ct. (so. dist.) Tex. 1998, U.S. Ct. Appeals (5th cir.) 1977, U.S. Supreme Ct. 1979, U.S. Ct. Appeals (11th cir.) 1981, U.S. Ct. Appeals (fed. cir.) 1998, U.S. Ct. Internat. Trade, 1998. Prin. Roan & Assocs., Austin, 1969-71; counsel, com. dir. Tex. Ho. of Reps., 1972-75; assoc. Heath, Davis & McCalla, Austin, 1975-78; prin. Roan & Gullahorn, P.C., 1978-85, Roan & Autrey (formerly Roan & Simpson), P.C., 1986-99; sr. ptnr. Cantey, Hanger, Roan & Autrey, 1999—. Bd. dirs. Lawyers Credit Union, chmn., 1982-83; bd. dirs. pub. law sect. State Bar Tex., 1980-84; dir. Am. Bankers Gen. Agy.; mem. chancellor's coun. U. Tex. With Tex. Army N.G., 1966-74. Fellow Tex. Bar Found.; mem. ABA, Tex. Assn. Def. Counsel, Tex. Assn. Bank Counsel, Def. Rsch. Inst., Travis County Bar Assn., Tex.-Mexico Bar Assn., Knights of the Symphony (vice chancellor 1997—), Tex. Lyceum Assn. (v.p., bd. dirs. 1980-87), Austin C. of C., Austin Club, Headliners Club, Masons, Shriners (Parsons Masonic master 1976-77). Methodist. Administrative and regulatory, General corporate, Insurance. Office: Cantey Hanger Roan & Autrey 200 Wells Fargo Bank Tower 400 W 15th St Austin TX 78701-1600 E-mail: froan@canteyhanger.com

ROBB, JOHN DONALD, JR. lawyer; b. N.Y.C., Jan. 11, 1924; s. John D. and Harriett (Block) R.; m. Peggy Hight, Feb. 8, 1946; children: John D., Celeste Robb Nicholson, Ellen, Bradford, George G., David. Student, Yale U., N.Mex.; BSL, U. Minn., 1948, LLB, 1949. Bar: N.Mex. 1950, U.S. Dist. Ct. N.Mex. 1950, U.S. Ct. Appeals (10th cir.) 1955, U.S. Supreme Ct. 1961. Pvt. practice, Albuquerque, 1950-51; assoc. Rodey, Dickason, Sloan, Akin & Robb PA, 1951-56, ptnr., 1956-65, sr. dir., 1965-97, of counsel, 1997—. Nat. adv. com. legal svcs. program OEO, 1966-73. Contbr. articles to profl. jours. Pres. Albuquerque Legal Aid Soc., 1957, bd. dirs., 1960-74; bd. dirs. Navajo Legal Svcs., 1967-68, United Cmty. Fund, 1962-64; chmn. Albuquerque Christian Legal Aid and Referral Svc., 1982; pres. Albuquerque Cmty. Coun., 1958-60, Family Consultation Svc. Albuquerque, 1955-57; chmn. bd. Drug Addicts Recovery Enterprises, 1974-79. Named Outstanding Man of Yr., Albuquerque Jr. C. of C., 1956; recipient Disting. Svc. award Albuquerque United Cmty. Fund, 1960, Hatton W. Sumners award Southwestern Legal Found., 1971. Fellow Am. Bar Found.; mem. ABA (nat. chmn. standing com. on legal aid and indigent defendants 1966-73), Nat. Legal Aid and Defendants Assn. (v.p. 1966-72), Albuquerque Bar Assn. (chmn. legal aid com. 1962-65), N.Mex. Bar Assn. (chmn. legal aid com.), Internat. Legal Aid Assn., Christian Legal Soc. (bd. dirs. 1982—), Albuquerque Christian Lawyers Assn. (chmn. 1979-85), Am. Judicature Soc., Am. Bd. Trial Advs. General civil litigation, General corporate. Home: 7200 Rio Grande Blvd NW Albuquerque NM 87107-6428 Office: Rodey Dickason Sloan Akin & Robb PA PO Box 1888 Albuquerque NM 87103-1888 also: 201 3rd St NW Ste 2200 Albuquerque NM 87102-3380 E-mail: jdrobb@rodey.com

ROBBINS, NORMAN NELSON, lawyer; b. Detroit, Sept. 27, 1919; s. Charles and Eva (Gold) R.; m. Pamela Anne Eldred, April 22, 1946; children: Susan, Aimee. LLB, JD, Wayne State U., 1943. Bar: Mich. 1943. Pvt. practice, Birmingham, Mich., 1943—. Chmn. Mich. Bd. for Marriage Counselors, 1971-75; lectr. Inst. Continuing Legal Edn. Editor Mich. Family Law Jour., 1974—; mem. editorial bd. Am. Jour. Family Law; co-editor: Michigan Family Law, 2 vols., 1988; contbr. 600 articles to legal publs. Chmn. Wayne County unit Am. Cancer Soc., Detroit, 1971-76, Mich. Dept. Vets. Trust Fund, 1977-8. Capt. USMCR, 1943-46, PTO. Recipient Gov.'s award State of Mich., Cert. of Appreciation, Gov. of Mich., Cert. of Recognition, Detroit Common Coun. award Mich. Assn. Marriage Counselors, Lifetime Achievement award Mich. Family Law Sect. Mem. ABA (mem. family law coun. 1993-95, sr. editor ABA Family Adv. 1991—), Mich. Bar Assn. (chmn. family law sect. 1974-75), Oakland County Bar Assn., Am. Acad. Matrimonial Lawyers (pres. Mich. chpt. 1982), Am. Legion (judge adv. Mich. dept. 1968-69, comdr. Detroit chpt. 1970-71). Family and matrimonial. Home: 5543 Tadworth Pl West Bloomfield MI 48322-4016

ROBBINS, SARA ELLEN, law librarian, educator, lawyer; b. Balt., Mar. 3, 1952; d. Malcolm Lee and Norma Robbins. BA, U. Cin., 1974; MLS, Pratt Inst., 1977; JD, Ohio State U., 1985. Bar: Ohio 1985. Cataloger Bklyn. Law Sch. Libr., 1977-79, assoc. libr., 1984-85, acting dir., 1985-86, dir., 1986—. Head tech. svcs. Cardozo Law Sch. Libr., N.Y.C., 1979-81; rsch. editorial asst. Law Sch. Libr., Yale U., New Haven, 1982-83. Author: Surrogate Parenting: Annotated Review of the Literature, 1984, Baby M Case: The Complete Trial Transcripts, 1988, Law: A Treasury of Art and Literature, 1990; (with others) Library Automation: A Systems and Software Sampler, 1985. Recipient Am. Jurisprudence award Lawyer's Coop. Pub. Co., 1984. Mem. ABA, Ohio Bar Assn., Am. Assn. Law Librs., Law Libr. Assn. Greater N.Y. Office: Bklyn Law Sch 250 Joralemon St Brooklyn NY 11201-3700

ROBBINS, STEPHEN J. M. lawyer; b. Seattle, Apr. 13, 1942; s. Robert Mads and Aneita Elberta (West) R.; m. Nina Winifred Tanner, Aug. 11, 1967; children: Sarah E.T., Alicia S.T. AB, UCLA, 1964; JD, Yale U., 1971. Bar: D.C. 1973, U.S. Dist. Ct. D.C. 1973, U.S. Ct. Appeals (D.C. cir.) 1973, U.S. Ct. Appeals (3d cir.) 1973, U.S. Dist. Ct. (ea. and no. dists.) Calif. 1982, U.S. Dist. Ct. (cen. dist.) Calif. 1983, Supreme Ct. of Republic of Palau, 1994. Pres. U.S. Nat. Student Assn., Washington, 1964-65; dir. scheduling McGovern for Pres., 1971-72; assoc. Steptoe & Johnson, 1972-75; chief counsel spl. inquiry on food prices, com. on nutrition and human needs U.S. Senate, 1975; v.p., gen. counsel Straight Arrow Pubs., San Francisco, 1975-77; dep. dist. atty. City and County of San Francisco, 1977-78; regional counsel U.S. SBA, San Francisco, 1978-80; spl. counsel

Warner-Amex Cable Communications, Sacramento, 1981-82; ptnr. McDonough, Holland and Allen, 1982-84; v.p. Straight Arrow Pubs., N.Y.C., 1984-86; gen. legal counsel Govt. State of Koror, Rep. of Palau, Western Caroline Islands, 1994-95; pvt. practice law, 1986—. Adj. prof. govt. Calif. State U., Sacramento, 1999—. Staff sgt. U.S. Army, 1966-68. Mem. ABA (sect. urban, state and local govt. sect. real property, probate and trust law, sect. natural resources energy, environ. law, forum com. on affordable housing and cmty. devel.), D.C. Bar, State Bar of Calif., Urban Land Inst., Am. Hist. Assn., Supreme Ct. Hist. Soc., Acad. Polit. Sci., Chamber Music Soc. of Sacramento, Oreg. Shakespeare Festival, Shaw Island Hist. Soc. Democrat. Unitarian. Avocations: theatre, art, hiking. Environmental, Land use and zoning (including planning), Real property. Office: 2150 3rd Ave Sacramento CA 95818-3102

ROBERSON, BRUCE HEERDT, lawyer; b. Wilmington, Del., Mar. 7, 1941; s. A. L. and Virginia Amelia (Heerdt) R.; m. Mary E. Abrams; children: Cheryl Anne, David B., Douglas M. BS cum laude, Washington and Lee U., 1963; JD, U. Va., 1966. Bar: Va. 1966, Del. 1966, Fla. 1969. Assoc. Morris, Nichols, Arsht & Tunnell, Wilmington, 1966-67; assoc. Holland & Knight, Tampa, Fla., 1969-74; ptnr. Holland & Knight LLP, 1975—. Contbg. editor Pratt's Banking and Lending Institution Forms, 1992—. Capt. U.S. Army, 1967-69 Decorated Bronze Star. Fellow Am. Bar Found. (life), Fla. Bar Found.(life); mem. ABA (bus. law sect. com. on consumer fin. svcs. 1976—, banking law com. 1980—, savs. instns. com. 1989-96), Am. Judicature Soc., Fla. Bar Assn. (corp. banking and bus. law sect. exec. coun. 1978-86, chmn. banking law com. 1982-84), Del. Bar Assn., Va. Bar Assn., Hillsborough County Bar Assn., Univ. Club, Tampa Yacht and Country Club, Lambda Chi Alpha. Republican. Methodist. Banking, Consumer commercial, General corporate. Office: Holland & Knight LLP PO Box 1288 Tampa FL 33601-1288 E-mail: broberso@hklaw.com

ROBERSON, CLIFFORD EUGENE, law educator, lawyer; b. Iola, Tex., Feb. 24, 1937; s. Burrel Allen and Sue (Crouch) R.; children— Clif, Marshall, Kenneth, Dwayne; m. Mariam Daniels, Nov. 21, 1981. B.A., U. Mo., 1961; J.D., Am. U., 1967; LL.M., George Washington U., 1976; Ph.D., U.S. Internat. U., 1974. Bar: Tex. 1967, U.S. Tax Ct. 1969, U.S. Supreme Ct. 1970, Calif. 1978, U.S. Dist. Ct. (we. dist.) Tex. 1984. Prof. St. Edward's U., Austin, Tex., 1979-83; dir. Nat. Dist. Attys. Coll., Houston, 1983-84; prof. Calif. State U.-Fresno, 1984— , dir. Justice Ctr., 1984— . Author: Legal Guide for Pilots, 1972; Law of Employment, 1985. Contbr. articles on criminal justice to profl. jours. Served to maj. USMC, 1961-79. Mem. Nat. Assn. Dist. Attys., ABA, Tex. Bar Assn. Home: 1927 Richmond Ave Houston TX 77098-3401 Office: Calif State U Fresno CA 93740

ROBERSON, LINDA, lawyer; b. Omaha, July 15, 1947; d. Harlan Oliver and Elizabeth Aileen (Good) R.; m. Gary M. Young, Aug. 20, 1970; children: Elizabeth, Katherine, Christopher. BA, Oberlin Coll., 1969; MS, U. Wis., 1970, JD, 1974. Bar: Wis. 1974, U.S. Dist. Ct. (we. dist.) Wis. 1974. Legis. atty. Wis. Legis. Reference Bur., Madison, 1974-76, sr. legis. atty., 1976-78; assoc. Rikkers, Koritzinsky & Rikkers, 1978-79; ptnr. Koritzinsky, Neider, Langer & Roberson, 1979-85, Stolper, Koritzinsky, Brewster & Neider, Madison, 1985-93, Balisle & Roberson, Madison, 1993—. Adj. faculty U. Wis. Law Sch., Madison, 1978—. Co-author: Real Women, Real Lives, 1981, Wisconsin's Marital Property Reform Act, 1984, Understanding Wisconsin's Marital Property Law, 1985, A Guide to Property Classification Under Wisconsin's Marital Property Act, 1986, Workbook for Wisconsin Estate Planners, 2d edit., 1993, 3rd edit., 1997, 4th edit., 1999, Look Before You Leap, 1996, Family Estate Planning in Wis., 1992, rev. edit. 1996, The Marital Property Classification Handbook, 1999. Fellow Am. Acad. Matrimonial Lawyers (pres. Wisc. chap. 2001), Am. Bar Found.; mem. ABA, Wis. Bar Assn., Dane County Bar Assn., Legal Assn. Women, Nat. Assn. Elder Law Attys., Internat. Soc. Family Law. Estate planning, Family and matrimonial, Probate. Office: Balisle and Roberson PO Box 870 Madison WI 53701-0870 E-mail: lr@mail.b-rlaw.com

ROBERTS, BRIAN MICHAEL, lawyer; b. Cin., May 28, 1957; s. Shearl Joseph and Mary Ruth (Christian) R.; m. Carol Denise Zimmerman, July 28, 1979; children: Nicholas Brian, Mary Katelin, Kevin Matthew. BS in Bus., Miami U., Oxford, Ohio, 1979; JD, U. Dayton, 1982. Bar: Ohio 1982, U.S. Dist. Ct. (so. dist.) Ohio 1983, U.S. Ct. Appeals (6th cir.) 1984, U.S. Supreme Ct. 1988. Ptnr. Jablinski, Folino, Roberts & Martin Co. LPA, Dayton, 1982—. Organizer, scheduler legal presentations to engaged couples Family Life Office, Archdiocese of Cin., Dayton, 1982-92. Mem. Ohio State Bar Assn., Ohio Acad. Trial Lawyers, Dayton Bar Assn., Miami Valley Trial Lawyers Assn., Assn. Trial Lawyers Am. Republican. Roman Catholic. State civil litigation, Estate planning, Probate. Home: 3830 Gardenview Pl Dayton OH 45429-4517 Office: Jablinski Folino Roberts & Martin Co LPA PO Box 1266 Dayton OH 45402-9766 E-mail: huffman@megsinet.net

ROBERTS, BURTON BENNETT, lawyer, retired judge; b. N.Y.C., July 25, 1922; s. Alfred S. and Cecelia (Schanfein) R.; m. Gerhild Ukryn. B.A., NYU, 1943, LL.M., 1953; LL.B., Cornell U., 1949. Bar: N.Y. 1949. Asst. dist. atty., New York County, 1949-66; chief asst. dist. atty. Bronx County, Bronx, N.Y., 1966-68, acting dist. atty., 1968-69, dist. atty., 1969-72; justice Supreme Ct. State N.Y., 1973-98, adminstrv. judge criminal br. Bronx County 12th Jud. Dist., 1984-98, adminstrv. judge civil br. Bronx County 12th Dist., 1988-98; ret., 1998; counsel Fischbein, Badillo, Wagner & Hording, 1999—. Pres. Bronx div. Hebrew Home for Aged, 1967-72. With U.S. Army, 1943-45. Decorated Purple Heart, Bronze Star with oak leaf cluster. Mem. Assn. Bar City N.Y., Am. Bar Assn., N.Y. Bar Assn., Bronx County Bar Assn., N.Y. State Dist. Attys. Assn. (pres. 1971-72) Jewish (exec. bd. temple). Home: 215 E 68th St Apt 19A New York NY 10021-5727 Office: Fischbein Badillo et al 909 3rd Ave New York NY 10022-4731 E-mail: broberts@fbwhlaw.com

ROBERTS, CHARLES BREN, lawyer; b. Washington, Oct. 28, 1949; s. Ray Oliver and Ruth B. (Barlow) R.; children: Elisha Ruthanne, Jacquelyn Celene. BS, Wright State U., 1974; JD, U. Dayton, 1978; postgrad., Ohio State U., 1980, Harvard Law Sch., 1984. Bar: Ohio 1978, D.C. 1983, Va. 1986, U.S. Supreme Ct. 1987, U.S. Dist. Ct. (ea. dist.) Va., 1988, U.S. Ct. Appeals (4th cir.) 1990. Legal intern U.S. Atty's Office, Dayton, Ohio, 1977-78; law clk. Ohio Supreme Ct., Columbus, 1978-80; congl. intern U.S. Gen. Acctg. Office, Washington, summer 1977, atty. advisor, 1980-86; sr. ptnr. Roberts & Weiss, Woodbridge, Va., 1986—. With USN, 1971-77. Recipient Disting. Svc. award Washington Songwriter's Assn., 1986, Acad. scholarship U. Dayton Law Sch., 1977, 78. Mem. ABA, Va. Trial Lawyers Assn., Fairfax County Bar Assn., Prince William County Bar Assn., Woodbridge C. of C. Avocations: racquetball, running. General civil litigation, Family and matrimonial, Personal injury. Office: Roberts and Weiss 12620 Lake Ridge Dr Woodbridge VA 22192-2335 E-mail: crobertsjd@aol.com

ROBERTS, DAVID AMBROSE, lawyer; b. Pascagoula, Miss., Apr. 27, 1962; s. James Elmer and Edna Louise (Scott) R.; m. Elizabeth Anne Knecht, June 29, 1990. BA, U. Miss., 1985, JD, 1988. Bar: Miss. 1988, U.S. Dist. Ct. (no. dist.) Miss. 1988, U.S. Ct. Appeals (5th cir.) 1991, U.S. Dist. Ct. (so. dist.) Miss. 1991, U.S. Supreme Ct. 1996. Asst. dist. atty. Office of Dist. Atty., State of Miss., Pascagoula, 1988-90; ptnr. Gordon, Myers, Frazier & Roberts, 1991-94; pvt. practice, 1994—. Recipient Am. Jurisprudence award, 1988; named to Outstanding Young Men in Am. Mem. ATLA, Miss. Bar Assn., Jackson County Bar Assn., 5th Cir. Bar Assn., Nat. Assn. Criminal Def. Lawyers, Miss. Trial Lawyers Assn., Elks. Consumer commercial, Criminal, General practice. Office: PO Box 2009 Pascagoula MS 39569-2009 E-mail: droberts@datasync.com

ROBERTS, DELMAR LEE, editor; b. Raleigh, N.C., Apr. 9, 1933; s. James Delmer and Nellie Brockelbank (Tyson) R. BS in Textile Mgmt., N.C. State U., 1956; MA in Journalism, U. S.C., 1974. Product devel. engr. U.S. Rubber Co. (Uniroyal), Winnsboro, S.C., 1959-64; process improvement engr. Allied Chem. Co., Irmo, 1965-67; assoc. editor S.C. History Illustrated Mag., Columbia, 1970; editor-in-chief, editl. v.p. Sandlapper-The Mag. of S.C., 1968-74; mng. editor, art dir. Legal Econs. mag. of the ABA, Chgo., 1975-89, Law Practice Mgmt. mag. of the ABA, Chgo., 1990-2000, editor emeritus, 2000—. Editor: The Best of Legal Economics, 1979; freelance editor and/or designer of over 35 books. Active World Affairs Coun. Columbia, 1997—; 1st v.p. English-Speaking Union, 1996-97, pres. 1997—. With U.S. Army, 1956-58. Hon. fellow Coll. of Law Practice Mgmt., Golden, Colo., 1995—. Mem. Soc. Profl. Journalists, Capital City Club (Columbia), Phi Kappa Tau, Kappa Tau Alpha. Avocations: European travel, Turkish carpet/Kilim collecting, antique collecting.

ROBERTS, EDWARD THOMAS, lawyer; b. Washington, Oct. 3, 1949; s. Richard Brooke Titus and Irena Zuzanna (Eiger) R.; m. Theresa Yvonne Binczyk, Nov. 26, 1977; children: Emily Brooke, Jonathan Chambers. AB, Princeton U., 1971; JD, George Washington U., 1974. Bar: Md. 1974, D.C. 1975, U.S. Ct. Appeals (D.C. cir.) 1976, U.S. Ct. Appeals (4th cir.) 1986, U.S. Dist. Ct. D.C. 1982, U.S. Dist. Ct. Md. 1982, U.S. Supreme Ct. 1982. Asst. states atty. Prince Georges County States Attys. Office, Upper Marlboro, Md., 1975; asst. atty. U.S. Attys. Office, Washington, 1975-86; asst. atty. organized crime & drug enforcement task force U.S. Attys Office, Balt., 1986-94; chief narcotics divsn., sr. trial atty. terrorism and violent crime sect., criminal divsn. U.S. Dept. Justice, Washington, 1994-97, counsel to asst. atty. gen. criminal divsn., 1997—. Mem. Md. Bar Assn., D.C. Bar Assn., Columbia Country Club. Democrat. Episcopalian. Office: US Dept Justice Criminal Divsn Rm 2621 10th & Constitution Ave NW Washington DC 20850 E-mail: tom.roberts@usdoj.gov

ROBERTS, GEORGE PRESTON, JR. (RUSTY ROBERTS), lawyer; b. St. Louis, June 23, 1947; s. George P. and Eleanor Roberts; m. Barbara A. Smith, June 30, 1973; children: Christopher Dent, Craig Dane, Carrie Diana. BA, U. Tulsa, 1969, JD with honors, 1975. Assoc. Fleming, O'Bryan & Fleming, Ft. Lauderdale, Fla., 1976-81, mng. ptnr. West Palm Beach, 1981-86; sr. ptnr. Roberts & Reynolds, 1986—. Served with USAF, 1969-73. Mem. Def. Rsch. Inst., Fla. Mcpl. Attys. Assn. Presbyterian. Civil rights, General civil litigation, Personal injury. Office: 470 Columbia Dr Ste 101C West Palm Beach FL 33409 E-mail: rroberts@robertsreynolds.com

ROBERTS, J. WENDELL, federal judge; b. Somerset, Ky., May 1, 1943; s. Earl C. and Dorothy (Whitaker) R.; children: Stephen A., Shannon L. BA, Ea. Ky. U., 1964; JD, U. Ky., 1966. Bar: Ky. 1966, U.S. Dist. Ct. (we. dist.) Ky. 1978, U.S. Ct. Appeals (6th cir.) 1983. Atty. Ky. Dept. Revenue, Frankfort, 1966; law clk. Ky. Supreme Ct., 1966-67; atty. Charles A. Williams & Assoc., Paducah, Ky., 1967, Westberry & Roberts, Marion, 1968-87; city atty. City of Marion, 1968-84; judge U.S. Bankruptcy Ct. Western Dist. Ky., Louisville, 1987—, chief judge, 1988-95. Vice chmn. Pennyrile Area Devel. Dist., Hopkinsville, Ky., 1968-72; vol. Habitat for Humanity and Ctr. for the Arts, Louisville. Mem. Ky. Bar Assn., Louisville Bar Assn., Nat. Conf. Bankruptcy Judges (bd. govs. 1991-94), Mcpl. Attys. Assn. Ky. (pres. 1983). Methodist. Avocations: volunteer work. Office: US Bankruptcy Ct US Courthouse 601 W Broadway Ste 528 Louisville KY 40202-2238

ROBERTS, JAMES DONZIL, lawyer; b. St. Louis, Apr. 4, 1957; s. Donzil D. and Barbara V. Malona; m. Deena W. Waldman, June 17, 2000; children: James D. Jr., Jessica E., Colton D. Student, Calif. State U., Northridge, 1976-79, Calif. State U., Dominguez Hills, 1981; JD, U. LaVerne, 1985. Bar: Calif. 1985, U.S. Dist. Ct. (ctrl. dist.) Calif. 1986. Staff and supr. atty. Bollington Stilz & Bloeser, Woodland Hills, Calif., 1985-90; mng. atty. Bollington, Roberts, Hunkins and McDonald, Long Beach, 1990—. Judge pro tem Long beach Mcpl. Ct., Long Beach, 1992—; lectr. extension program UCLA, 1994—. Trustee U. LaVerne San Fernando Valley Coll. Law, Encino, 1984-85; active West L.A. County Coun., Boy Scouts Am., West Hills, Calif., 1995. Mem.: Assn. Calif. House Counsel (founding mem., past pres.), L.A. County Bar Assn., Long Beach Bar Assn., Assn. So. Calif. Def. Counsel, Long Beach Barristers Assn., Am. Inn Ct. (Long Beach, barrister). Avocations: baseball/softball, bowling, golf. General civil litigation, Insurance, Personal injury. Office: Bollington Roberts Hunkins and McDonald 3780 Kilroy Airport Way Ste 540 Long Beach CA 90806-6803

ROBERTS, JAMES LAMAR, JR. retired state supreme court justice; b. June 8, 1945; m. Rose D. Roberts. BA, Millsaps Coll., 1967; MBA, Miss. State U., 1968; JD, U. Miss., 1971; grad., Nat. Jud. Coll., 1988. Pvt. practice, Pontotoc County, Miss., 1971-84; chancellor 1st Chancery Ct. Dist., 1988-92; assoc. justice Miss. Supreme Ct., Jackson, 1992-99; prof. criminal justice U. So. Miss., 1999—. Prosecuting atty. Pontotoc County, 1972-84; speaker in field. Commr. pub. safety State of Miss., 1984-88; mem. Northeast Mental Health-Mental Retardation Commn., 1972-88; chmn. task force hearings Gov.'s Alliance Against Drugs, 1986-87; Sunday sch. leader, ch. officer Pontotoc United Meth. Ch.; candidate for Gov. of Miss., 1999—. Recipient Herman C. Galzier award Miss chpt. Am. Soc. Pub. Adminstrn., 1985. Mem. ABA (jud. divsn.), Miss. Bar Assn., 1st Jud. Dist. Bar Assn., Pontotoc County Bar Assn., Miss. Conf. of Judges, Nat. Coun. Juvenile and Family Ct. Judges, Nat. Coll. Probate Judges, Millsaps Coll. Alumni Assn., Miss. State U. Alumni Assn., U. Miss. Alumni Assn., Rotary Club, Omicron Delta Kappa, Delta Theta Phi, Alpha Kappa Psi, Kappa Sigma, Pi Alpha Alpha (hon.). Office: c/o Supreme Ct Clerks Office PO Box 249 Jackson MS 39205-0249

ROBERTS, JEAN REED, lawyer; b. Washington, Dec. 19, 1939; d. Paul Allen and Esther (Kishter) Reed; m. Thomas Gene Roberts, Nov. 26, 1958; children: Amy, Rebecca, Nathanial. AB in Journalism, U. N.C., 1966; JD, Ariz. State U., 1973. Bar: Ariz. 1974. Pvt. practice Jean Reed Roberts P.C., Scottsdale, Ariz., 1975—. Judge pro tem Superior Ct., Maricopa County, Ariz., 1979-92; judge pro tem Ariz. Ct. Appeals, 1995-99; chmn., adv. endowment bd. City of Scottsdale, Ariz., 1994-98; past pres. Charter 100 of Phoenix. Recipient Dorothy Wiley award YWCA Maricopa County, 1999. Mem. Ariz. Bar Assn., Ariz. Women's Town Hall, Scottsdale Bar Assn. Democrat. Jewish. Estate planning, Probate, Elder. Office: 8669 E San Alberto Dr Ste 101 Scottsdale AZ 85258-4309 E-mail: jean.roberts@azbar.org

ROBERTS, JOHN DERHAM, lawyer; b. Orlando, Fla., Nov. 1, 1942; s. Junius P. and Mary E. Roberts; m. Malinda K. Swineford, June 11, 1965; 1 child, Kimberlyn Amanda. Cert., Richmond (Va.) Bus. Coll., 1960; BS, Hampden-Sydney (Va.) Coll., 1964; LLB, Washington & Lee U., 1968. Bar: Va. 1968, Fla. 1969, U.S. Supreme Ct. 1969, U.S. Ct. Customs and Patent Appeals 1970, U.S. Tax Ct. 1970, U.S. Ct. Appeals (5th cir.) 1970, U.S. Ct. Appeals (9th cir.) 1974, U.S. Supreme Ct. 1969. Law clk. U.S. Dist. Ct., Jacksonville, Fla., 1968-69; assoc. Phillips, Kendrick, Gearhart & Aylor, Arlington, Va., 1969-70; asst. U.S. Atty. mid. dist. Fla. U.S. Dept. Justice, Jacksonville, 1970-74, Dist. of Alaska, Anchorage, 1974-77, U.S. magistrate judge, 1977—. Bd. dirs. Teen Challenge Alaska, Anchorage, 1984-93; chmn. Eagle Scout Rev. Bd., 1993—; bd. dirs. Alaska Youth for Christ, 1993-96; govs.'s Prayer Breakfast Com., 1994—, vice-chair, 1998—. Recipient Citizenship award DAR, Anchorage, 1984, plaque, U.S. Navy, Citizen Day, Adak, Alaska, 1980. Mem. ABA, Nat. Conf. Spl. Ct. Judges (exec. bd. 1985-92), 9th Cir. Conf. Magistrates (exec. bd. 1982-85, chmn. 1984-85), Alaska Bar Assn., Anchorage Bar Assn., Chi Phi, Psi Chi, Phi Alpha Delta. Republican. Office: US Magistrate Judge 222 W 7th Ave Unit 46 Anchorage AK 99513-7504

ROBERTS, JOHN M. law educator, former prosecutor; 2 children. Student, Tenn. Technol. U., Cookeville, 1954-57; degree, U. Tenn., Knoxville, 1960. Atty. TVA, 1960-62, Livingston, Tenn., 1962-77; gen. sessions judge, probate and juvenile judge Overton County, 1969-74; assoc. prof. criminal justice Tenn. Technol. U., 1974-85; dist. atty. gen. 13th judicial dist. State of Tenn., 1977-90, asst. atty. gen., co-dir. enforcement divsn., 1990-92; dep. dir. Dist. Attys. Gen. Conf., 1990-92; U.S. atty. State Tenn. (mid. dist.), 1993-98; assoc. prof. law Cumberland U., Lebanon, Tenn., 1998—. Mem. Tenn. Bar Assn., Overton County, City of Livingston C. of C. (exec. dir.). Office: 222 E Main St Livingston TN 38570-1904*

ROBERTS, MANLEY WOOLFOLK, lawyer; b. Durham, N.C., Feb. 26, 1958; s. John Manley and Eleanor Woolfolk Roberts; m. Jennifer Darrow Watson, May 8, 1993; children: Montana Watson, Manley Howell. AB, U. N.C., 1980; JD, Yale U., 1983. Bar: Ga. 1984, U.S. Ct. Appeals (D.C. dist.) 1985, U.S. Ct. Internat. Trade 1985, N.C. 1993, U.S. Dist. Ct. (we. dist.) N.C. 1993. Jud. clk. to Hon. Irving Goldberg U.S. Ct. Appeals (5th cir.), Dallas, 1983-84; assoc. Williams & Connolly, Washington, 1984-92; ptnr. Smith Helms Mulliss & Moore LLP, Charlotte, N.C., 1992—. Editor Yale Law Jour., 1982-83. Scholar Morehead Found., 1976-80; Grad. scholar Chi Psi Fraternity, 1980. Mem. ABA, N.C. Bar Assn. Banking, Contracts commercial, General corporate, Private international. Office: Smith Helms Mulliss and Moore 201 N Tryon St Charlotte NC 28202

ROBERTS, MARK SCOTT, lawyer; b. Fullerton, Calif., Dec. 31, 1951; s. Emil Seidel and Theda (Wymer) R.; m. Sheri Lyn Smith, Sept. 23, 1977; children: Matthew Scott, Meredith Lyn, Benjamin Price. BA in Theater, Pepperdine U., 1975; JD, Western State U., 1978; cert. civil trial advocacy program, U. Calif., San Francisco, 1985; cert. program of instrn. for lawyers, Harvard U., 1990. Bar: Calif. 1980, U.S. Dist. Ct. (cen. dist.) Calif. 1980, U.S. Supreme Ct. 1989, U.S. Ct. Mil. Appeals 1989, U.S. Tax Ct. 1990. Concert mgr. Universal Studios, Hollywood, Calif., 1973-74; tchr. Anaheim (Calif.) Union Sch Dist., 1979-80; prin. Mark Roberts & Assocs., Fullerton, Calif., 1980—. Instr. bus. law Biola U., La Mirada, Calif., 1980-84; judge pro tem Orange County Superior Ct., Santa Ana, 1989—; adj. prof. wills and trusts Trinity Law Sch., Santa Ana, 2000—. Co-author: Legacy-Plan, Protect and Preserve Your Estate, 1996, Generations Planning Your Legacy, 1999. Mem. Calif. State Bar Assn., Orange County Bar Assn. (charter), Nat. Network Estate Planning Attys. Avocations: snow and water skiing. Estate planning, Probate. Office: Mark Roberts & Assocs 1440 N Harbor Blvd Ste 900 Fullerton CA 92835-4122

ROBERTS, NORMAN LESLIE, lawyer; b. Yakima, Wash., Jan. 17, 1935; s. Leslie Clement Roberts and Marie (Dietzen) Delger; m. Dorita Gale Rushton, June 6, 1959; children— Theresa, Monica, Deborah. LL.B., Gonzaga U., 1959. Bar: Wash. 1959, U.S. Supreme Ct. 1965, Calif. 1969. Counsel guidance and control systems Litton Industries, Woodland Hills, Calif., 1968-73, v.p. group counsel, Beverly Hills, Calif., 1973-78, staff v.p., asst. gen. counsel, 1978-86, staff v.p., assoc. gen. counsel, 1986-88, corp. v.p. 1988-90, corp. sr. v.p., gen. counsel, 1990—, chmn. bd. dirs. Litton Saudi Arabia Ltd., 1982—; dir. Litton Employee Fed. Credit Union, 1971—; editorial advisor pub. contracts report Bur. Nat. Affairs, 1979—. Served to maj. U.S. Army, 1959-68. Mem. ABA (council mem. pub. contract law sect. 1984-87, sect. sec. 1987-88, vice chmn., 1988-89, sect. chmn. 1990-91, chmn. internat. procurement com. 1982-84), Warner Ctr. Club (L.A.), Tower Club (Oxnard, Calif.), Pacific Corinthian Yacht Club (Oxnard). General corporate, Government contracts and claims, Private international. Home: Woodland # 22449 Woodland Hills CA 91367 Office: Litton Industries Inc 360 N Crescent Dr Beverly Hills CA 90210-4802

ROBERTS, PATRICIA SUSAN, lawyer; b. Hammond, Ind., Sept. 1, 1953; d. Wayne Thomas and Lois (Schurgers) R.; m. James Stanley Kowalik, July 27, 1985. BA, Ind. U., 1975, JD, 1978. Bar: U.S. Dist. Ct. (so. dist.) Ind. 1978, U.S. Supreme Ct. 1987. Rep. State Farm Ins. Co., Indpls., 1978-79; atty. United Farm Bur. Mut. Ins. Co., 1979-85; sr. corp. counsel Farm Family Ins. Cos., 1985—. Mem. ABA (corp. counsel com. 1988). General corporate, Insurance, Pension, profit-sharing, and employee benefits. Home: 2018 E 106th St Carmel IN 46032-4008 Office: United Farm Family Ins Co 225 S East St Indianapolis IN 46202-4058 E-mail: proberts@farmbureau.com

ROBERTS, RANDAL WILLIAM, lawyer; b. June 30, 1951; s. Warren Read and Ruth Allene (hall) Roberts; m. Pegie Lynn McIntosh, Dec. 20, 1970; children: Nathaniel, Jonathan, Rebecca. BA magna cum laude, U. Colo., 1973, JD, 1976. Bar: N.Mex. 1976, U.S. Dist. Ct. N.Mex. 1976, U.S. Ct. Appeals (10th cir.) 1976, U.S. Supreme Ct. 1976. Assoc. Atwood & Malone, Roswell, N.Mex., 1976—80; ptnr. Farlow, Simone & Roberts, Albuquerque, 1980—90; shareholder Simone, Roberts & Weiss, PA, 1990—. Mem.: ABA, DRI, ABOTA, N.Mex. Bar Assn., N.Mex. Defense Lawyers, Order of Coif, Phi Beta Kappa, Omicron Delta Kappa. Federal civil litigation, State civil litigation, Insurance. Home: 905 Tramway Ln NE Albuquerque NM 87122-1309 Office: Simone Roberts & Weiss 8102 Menard NE Albuquerque NM 87110

ROBERTS, ROBERT, III, lawyer; b. Shreveport, La., July 22, 1930; s. Robert and Mary Hodges (Marshall) R.; m. Susan F. Forrester, Mar. 16, 1974; children: Robert (dec.), Marshall, Francis T. Kalmbach Jr., Ellen K. Tizian, Lewis K.F. Kalmbach, Samuel A. Kalmbach. BA, La. State U., 1951, JD, 1953. Bar: La. 1953, U.S. Dist. Ct. (we. dist.) La. 1958, U.S. Ct. Appeals (5th cir.) 1966, U.S. Supreme Ct. 1975. Assoc., then ptnr. and shareholder Blanchard, Walker, O'Quin & Roberts and predecessor, Shreveport, 1955-99, of counsel, 1999—. Former pres. Family Coun. and Children's Svcs.; former mem. Peabody study com. Caddo Parish Schs.; former chmn. legal div. United Way. 1st lt JAGC, U.S. Army, 1953-55. Mem. ABA, La. State Bar Assn. (former chmn. mineral law sect., former mem. ho. dels., former mem. bd. govs.), La. State Law Inst. (sr. officer, law reform agy. coun. 1962—, mineral code adv. com., civil code lease adv. com.), Soc. Bartolus, Shreveport Bar Assn. (pres. 1981), Shreveport Club. General corporate, Oil, gas, and mineral. Office: Blanchard Walker O'Quin & Roberts PO Box 1126 Shreveport LA 71163-1126

ROBERTS, THOMAS ALBA, lawyer; b. Ft. Wayne, Ind., Sept. 7, 1946; s. Jack and Elizabeth (Wallace) R.; m. Mary Alice Buckley, Aug. 11, 1973; children: Kaitrin M., John A., Kara B. BA, Georgetown U., 1969, JD, 1972. Bar: N.Y. 1973, U.S. Dist. Ct. (so. dist.) N.Y. 1973, U.S. Ct. Appeals (2d cir.) 1973, Tex. 1976, U.S. Supreme Ct. 1977, U.S. Dist. Ct. (so. dist.) Tex. 1978, U.S. Ct. Appeals (5th and 11th cirs.) 1982. Assoc. Winthrop, Stimson, Putnam & Roberts, N.Y.C., 1972-76; ptnr. Moore & Peterson, Dallas, 1976-89; mng. ptnr. Moore and Peterson, 1980-88; ptnr. Johnson & Gibbs, 1989-92; sr. ptnr. Weil, Gotshal & Manges, Dallas, N.Y.C., 1992—. Chmn. Internat. Corp. Practice Group, 1997—, mem. mgmt. com. 1997—; adj. prof. law So. Meth. U., Dallas, 1977-78. Lectr. in field. Mem. fin. com. St. Rita Ch., Dallas, 1983-88, Our Lady of Lake Ch., Rockwall, Tex.,

1987—; mem. Ch. of the Resurrection; bd. dirs. Make-A-Wish Found. Metro N.Y., 1998—. Mem. ABA, Tex. Bar Assn., Dallas Bar Assn., Assn. of Bar of City of N.Y. Roman Catholic. Avocations: skiing, golf, literature. General corporate, Mergers and acquisitions, Securities. Home: 133 Grandview Ave Rye NY 10580-2030 E-mail: thomas.roberts@weil.com

ROBERTS, THOMAS RAYMOND, lawyer; b. Mt. Vernon, N.Y., July 2, 1947; s. Alvin Vernon and Norma May (Raymond) R.; m. Mary Joan Wolfe, June 9, 1979; children: Douglas Joshua, Rebecca Jean. AB magna cum laude, Harvard U., 1969, JD cum laude, 1973. Bar: Calif. 1973, N.Y. 1978, U.S. Dist. Ct. (no. dist.) Calif. 1973, U.S. Dist. Ct. (ea. and so. dists.) N.Y. 1986. Assoc. Chickering & Gregory, San Francisco, 1973-75; staff counsel Trust for Pub. Land, 1975-76; v.p. Bookwrights, Inc., Scarsdale, N.Y., 1976-78; assoc. firm Miller, Montgomery, Sogi, Brady & Taft, N.Y.C., 1978-79; assoc. Beldock Levine & Hoffman LLP, 1980-84, ptnr., 1985—. Trustee Rochester (N.Y.) Zen Ctr., 1979-87, 90-2000. Democrat. Buddhist. Contracts commercial, General corporate, Entertainment. Home: 6 Cecilia Ln Pleasantville NY 10570-1502 Office: Beldock Levine & Hoffman LLP 99 Park Ave Rm 1600 New York NY 10016-1508 E-mail: troberts@blhny.com

ROBERTS, VIRGIL PATRICK, lawyer, business executive; b. Ventura, Calif., Jan. 4, 1947; s. Julius and Emma D. (Haley) R.; m. Brenda Cecilia Banks, Nov. 10, 1979; children: Gisele Simone, Hayley Tasha. AA, Ventura Coll., 1966; BA, UCLA, 1968; JD, Harvard U., 1972. Bar: Calif. 1972. Assoc. Pacht, Ross, Warne Bernhardt & Sears, L.A., 1972-76; ptnr. Manning, Reynolds & Roberts, 1976-79, Manning & Roberts, 1980-81; mng. ptnr. Bobbitt & Roberts, 1995—; exec. v.p., gen. counsel Solar Records, L.A., 1981—; pres. Dick Griffey Prodns., 1982—, Solar Records, 1988—; judge pro tem L.A., Beverly Hills Mcpl. Cts., 1975—. Past bd. dirs. L.A. Black Leadership Coalition, L.A. Mus. African Am. Art, Beverly Hills Bar Assn., L.A. Legal Aid Found.; bd. dirs. Coro Found., 1984-90, L.A. Ednl. Alliance for Restructuring Now, Cmty. Build; bd. dirs. Calif. Cmty. Found., 1991—, chmn. bd., 1999—; past pres. Beverly Hills Bar Scholarship Found.; commr. Calif. Commn. for Tchr. Credentialing, 1980-83; chmn. L.A. Ednl. Partnership, 1989—, v.p. 1983-89; vice-chmn. Nat. Pub. Edn. Fund Network; chmn. bd. dirs. L.A. Annenberg Metropolitan Project; trustee, Comm. Econ. Devel., 1991—. Recipient NAACP Legal Def. Fund Equal Justice award, 1988. Mem. Recording Industry Assn. Am., Black Entertainment and Sports Lawyers (treas., bd. dirs. 1982—). Lead atty. for NAACP in Crawford vs. Bd. Edn. desegregation case, L.A., 1979-80. Entertainment. Address: 4820 Vista De Oro Ave Los Angeles CA 90043-1611 Office: Bobbitt & Roberts 1620 26th St Ste 150 Santa Monica CA 90404-4067

ROBERTSON, EDWIN DAVID, lawyer; b. Roanoke, Va., July 5, 1946; s. Edwin Traylor and Norma Burns (Bowles) R.; m. Anne Littelle Ferratt, Sept. 7, 1968, 1 child, Thomas Therit. BA with honors, U. Va., 1968, LLB, 1971. Bar: N.Y. 1972, U.S. Ct. Appeals (2d cir.) 1972, U.S. Dist. Ct. (ea. and so. dists.) N.Y. 1973, U.S. Supreme Ct. 1975, U.S. Dist. Ct. (ea. dist.) Mich. 1986. Assoc. Cadwalader, Wickersham & Taft, N.Y.C., 1972-80, ptnr., 1980—. Bd. dirs. Early Music Found. N.Y.C., 1983-99, chmn., 1993-99; bd. dirs. Oratorio Soc. of N.Y.C., 1988—, sec., 1991—. 1st lt. USAF, 1971-72. Echols scholar. Mem. ABA, Fed. Bar Coun., N.Y. County Lawyers Assn. (chmn. bankruptcy com. 1983-87, chmn. fin. com., bd. dirs. 1985-88, 95-99, 2000—, investment com. 1992—, exec. com. 1996—, treas. 2001—), N.Y. State Bar Assn. (ho. of dels. 2001—), Assn. Bar City N.Y., Soc. Colonial Wars, Down Town Assn., Jefferson Soc., Echols Scholar, Order of Coif, Phi Beta Kappa, Phi Kappa Psi. Republican. Episcopalian. Federal civil litigation, Libel, Securities. Home: 315 E 72nd St New York NY 10021-4625 Office: Cadwalader Wickersham & Taft 100 Maiden Ln New York NY 10038-4818 E-mail: darob@cwt.com

ROBERTSON, EWAN, lawyer; b. Kirkcaldy, Scotland, Jan. 9, 1969; m. Kate Robertson. LLB with honors, U. Dundee, 1987, diploma with distinction, 1992. Sr. assoc. Dundas & Wilson CS, Edinburgh, 2000—. Mem. Law Soc. of Scotland, Law Soc. of Eng. and Wales. Avocations: contemporary music, travel, soccer, other sports. Office: Dundas & Wilson CS Saltire Ct 20 Castle Terr Edinburgh EH1 2EN Scotland Office Fax: 44-0-131-200-7663. E-mail: ewan.robertson@dundas-wilson.com

ROBERTSON, HUGH DUFF, lawyer; b. Grosse Pointe, Mich., Mar. 14, 1957; s. Hugh Robertson and Louise (Grey) Bollinger; m. Mercedes Dano, May 3, 1997. BBA in Fin., U. Wis., Whitewater, 1978; JD, Whittier Coll., 1982. Bar: Calif. 1983, U.S. Tax Ct. 1984. Pres., CEO, A. Morgan Maree Jr. & Assocs., Inc., L.A., 1979—. Mem. ABA (forum com. on entertainment 1982—), State Calif., L.A. County Bar Assn., Beverly Hills Bar Assn., Acad. TV Arts and Scis., Am. Film Inst., Phi Alpha Delta. Republican. Episcopalian. Avocations: sports, swimming. Entertainment, Finance, Real property. Office: A Morgan Maree Jr & Assocs 1125 Gayley Ave Los Angeles CA 90024-3403

ROBERTSON, JAMES, judge; b. Cleve., May 18, 1938; s. Frederick Irving and Doris Mary (Byars) R.; m. Berit Selma Persson, Sept. 19, 1959; children: Stephen Irving, Catherine Anne, Peter Arvid. AB, Princeton U., 1959; LLB, George Washington U., 1965. Bar: D.C. 1966, U.S. Supreme Ct. 1969. Assoc. Wilmer, Cutler & Pickering, Washington, 1965-69, ptnr., 1973-94; U.S. dist. judge D.C., 1994—; chief counsel Lawyers Com. for Civil Rights Under Law, Jackson, Miss., 1969-70, dir. Washington, 1970-72, co-chmn., 1985-87. Co-chmn. D.C. Lawyers Com. for Civil Rights Under Law, Washington, 1982-84; mem. com. on grievances U.S. Dist. Ct., 1988-92, vice chmn., 1989-92; bd. dirs. South Africa Legal Svcs. and Edn. Project, Inc., 1987-01, pres., 1989-94; bd. dirs. D.C. Prisoners Legal Svcs., Inc., 1992-94. Editor in chief George Washington Law Rev., 1964-65. Lt. USN, 1959-64. Fellow Am. Coll. Trial Lawyers, Am. Bar Found.; mem. ABA, D.C. Bar (bd. govs. 1986-93, pres.-elect 1990-92, pres. 1991-92), Am. Law Inst. Home: 3318 N St NW Washington DC 20007-2807 Office: US Courthouse Rm 6315 333 Constitution Ave NW Washington DC 20001-2854

ROBERTSON, JOSEPH DAVID, lawyer; b. Pitts., Dec. 24, 1944; s. Sinon Joseph and Marie Catherine (Nold) R.; m. Susan Louise Lyon, Apr. 10, 1968; children— Brian, Mark. Student Coll. Steubenville, 1962, U. Md., 1968-69; B.A., Willamette U., 1971, J.D. cum laude, 1974. Bar: Oreg. 1974, U.S. Dist. Ct. Oreg. 1974, U.S. Ct. Appeals (9th cir.) 1976. Shareholder Garrett, Seideman, Hemann, Robertson & De Muniz, P.C., Salem, Oreg., 1974— ; mem. Oreg. State Bd. Bar Examiners, Portland, 1983-86; adj. prof. law for trial practice Willamette U. Coll. Law, 1976-78. Contbr. articles to profl. publs. Mem., chmn. Faye Wright local Adv. Com., Salem, 1978-83; mem. Judson local sch. adv. com., Salem, 1984-85; cubmaster Willamette Council Boy Scouts Am., 1979-85, mem. troop com., 1983-85; mem. workers' compensation com. Associated Oreg. Industries, Salem, 1982— ; coach Salem Parks & Recreation soccer program, 1979-85; coach Judson Little League, Salem, 1981; mem. disciplinary rev. com. Faye Wright Sch., Salem, 1982. Served with USMC, 1963-67. Recipient Advocacy award Internat. Acad. Trial Lawyers, 1974. Mem. ABA, Workers' Compensation Def. Lawyers Assn., Am. Soc. Law and Medicine, Marion County Bar Assn., Oreg. State Bar Assn. (bd. govs. 1988—; mem. exec. com. litigation sect. 1983-84, bd. govs. 1988—), Oreg. Trial Lawyers Assn. (bd. govs. 1976-78), Oreg. Assn. Def. Counsel. Republican. Club: Salem Tennis and Swim. State civil litigation, Insurance, Workers' compensation. Office: Garrett Hemann et al Box 749 1011 Commercial St NE Salem OR 97301-1049

ROBERTSON, MARK ALLEN, lawyer; b. San Antonio, May 6, 1963; s. David Hearne and Margie Louise (McCleskey) R. BA, So. Meth. U., 1985; JD, Columbia U., 1989. Ptnr. Fulbright & Jaworski, L.L.P., Houston, 1989-2001, N.Y.C., 2001—. Editor: 2000 Antitrust Discovery Handbook, 1994-2000; prodr. play Glass Bottom Cadillac, 1995. Bd. dirs. Houston Black Tie Dinner, Inc., 1997—; class fundraising chair So. Meth. U., Dallas, 1995—; mem. adminstrv. bd. St. Paul's United Meth. Ch., Houston, 1991-97. Mem. ABA, Tex. Bar Assn., Houston Bar Assn. (chair antitrust and trade regulation sect. 1998-99), Pi Kappa Alpha (regional pres. 1997—, Advisor of Yr. Internat. Chpt. 1995). Avocations: travel, singing, golf. Office: Fulbright & Jaworski LLP 666 Fifth Ave New York NY 10103-3198

ROBEY, DANIEL LANCE, lawyer; b. Washington, Feb. 17, 1949; s. Herbert Daniel and Marjorie Irene (Spargo) R.; m. Jacqueline Rene Jackson, June 1, 1979; children: Brian Lance, Kevin Daniel. BA, Lebanon Valley Coll., 1972; JD, George Mason U., 1975. Bar: U.S. Dist. Ct. (ea. dist.) Va. 1976, Va. 1976, U.S. Ct. Appeals (4th cir.) 1977. Sole practice, Falls Church, Va., 1976-79; ptnr. Matthews & Robey Ltd., Falls Church, 1979—; atty. Falls Church Crime Solvers, 1981—; ad hoc faculty George Mason High Sch., Falls Church. Mem. Falls Church Sch. Bd. Bus. Industry Edn. Council; bd. dirs. Dublin Meth. Ch., Falls Church. Served to capt. U.S. Army. Mem. Assn. Trial Lawyers Am., Va. Trial Lawyers Assn., Fairfax Bar Assn. Republican. Methodist. Lodge: Lions. Federal civil litigation, State civil litigation, Personal injury. Office: Matthews & Robey Ltd 108 E Broad St Falls Church VA 22046-4501

ROBIN, THEODORE TYDINGS, JR. lawyer, engineer, consultant; b. New Orleans, Aug. 29, 1939; s. Theodore Tydings and Hazel (Corbin) R.; m. Helen Jones, June 8, 1963; children: Corbin, Curry, Ted, Phil. BME, Ga. Inst. Tech., 1961, MS in N.E., 1963, PhD, 1967; LLB, Blackstone Sch. Law, 1979. Bar: Calif. 1980, U.S. Patent and Trademark Office 1982; registered profl. engr., Ala., Calif. Rsch. engr. Oak Ridge (Tenn.) Nat. Lab., 1967; asst. prof. radiology and physics Emory U., Atlanta, 1968-69; project engr. Atomic Internat. divsn. N.Am. Rockwell, Canoga park, Calif., 1970-72; engr. mgmt. engring. divsn. So. Co. Svcs., Birmingham, Ala., 1972-83, mgr. nuclear support and quality assurance, 1989-90, mgr. quality assurance and resources, 1991-92; mgr. Hatch Design Configuration, 1993-94; program mgr. pooled inventory mgmt. program So. Electric Internat., Birmingham, 1984-88, bd. dirs. polit. action com., 1985-87; dir. nuclear stds., radiation safety officer, sr. patent counsel, prin. nuclear engring Theragenics Corp., Atlanta, 1996—. Mem. ABA, ASME (mem. nuclear quality assurance subcom. on stds. coordinating and radioactive waste 1991-99), Am. Assn. Physicists Medicine (legal info./risk mgmt. subcom. 2000—, mem. TG No6 Dose Equivalence in Br. Therapy 2001—), Am. Nuclear Soc. (chmn. Birmingham sect. 1987-88, nuclear power plant stds. com. 1989-94), Ga. Tech. Alumni Assn. (trustee 1997-00), Rotary (pres. Shades Valley club 1987-88, chmn. dist. 6860 internat. youth exch. com. 1989-90, dist. gov. 6860 1994-95, tech. task force zone 30 coord 2000-01), Sigma Xi. Achievements include research on power plant performance and reliability and effect of coal quality, space radiation effects on human cells, radiation safety, med. physics, boiling heat transfer, nuclear reactor safety, multi-utility contracting, reliability economics, benchmarking and total quality management; patent law. Nuclear power, Environmental, Patent. Home and Office: 4524 Pine Mountain Rd Birmingham AL 35213-1828 E-mail: robinty@mindspring.com

ROBINER, DONALD MAXWELL, federal official, lawyer; b. Detroit, Feb. 4, 1935; s. Max and Lucia (Chassman) Robiner; m. Phyllis F Goodman; children: Brian Roberts, Marc Roberts; children: Steven Ralph, Lawrence Alan. BA, U. Mich., 1957; postgrad., Wayne State U., 1957-58; JD, Case Western Res. U., 1961. Bar: Ohio 1961, US Supreme Ct 1964, US Ct Appeals (6th cir) 1965. Assoc. Metzenbaum, Gaines, Schwartz, Krupansky, Finley & Stern, Cleve., 1961-67; ptnr. Metzenbaum, Gaines, Krupansky, Finley & Stern, 1967-72; v.p. Metzenbaum, Gaines, Finley & Stern Co., L.P.A., 1972-77, Gaines, Stern, Schwarzwald & Robiner Co., Cleve., 1977-81; exec. v.p., sec. Schwarzwald, Robiner & Rock Co. LPA, 1981-90; prin. Buckingham, Doolittle & Burroughs Co, LPA, 1991-94; U.S. Trustee Ohio and Mich. region 9 U.S. Dept. of Justice, 1994—. Vpres, secy Richard L Bowen & Assocs Inc, Cleveland, Ohio, 1969—94; acting judge Shaker Heights Munic Ct, 1973; mem bd bar examiners State of Ohio, Columbus, 1974—79; life mem 6th Cir Jud Conf; mediator alt dispute resolution panel US Dist Ct (no dist) Ohio, 1993—94. Secy Friends of Beachwood Libr Inc, Ohio, 1981—88, 1981—96. Recipient Cert Appreciation, Ohio Supreme Ct, 1974—79, Appreciation Award, Am Soc Appraisers, 1975. Mem.: Am Bankruptcy Inst, Comml Law League Am, Am Arbit Asn (Serv Award 1975), Ohio Coun Sch Bd Attys (mem exec com 1990—94), Jud Conf 8th Appellate Dist Ohio (life)), Cleveland Bar Asn, KofP. Home: 3094 Richmond Rd Beachwood OH 44122-3247 Office: US Dept Justice Office of US Trustee BP Tower 200 Public Sq Ste 20-3300 Cleveland OH 44114-2397 Fax: 216-522-4988. E-mail: DonRobiner@law.com

ROBINSON, ADELBERT CARL, lawyer, judge; b. Shawnee, Okla., Dec. 13, 1926; s. William H. and Mayme (Forston) R.; m. Paula Kay Settles, Apr. 16, 1988; children from previous marriage: William, James, Schuyler, Donald, David, Nancy, Lauri. Student, Okla. Bapt. U., 1944-47; JD, Okla. U., 1950. Bar: Okla. 1950. Pvt. practice, Muskogee, Okla., 1956-97; with legal dept. Phillips Petroleum Co., 1950-51; adjuster U.S. Fidelity & Guaranty Co., 1951-54, atty., adjuster-in-charge, 1954-56; ptnr. Fite & Robinson, 1956-62, Fite, Robinson & Summers, 1963-70, Robinson & Summers, 1970-72, Robinson, Summers & Locke, 1972-76, Robinson, Locke & Gage, 1976-80, Robinson, Locke, Gage & Fite, 1980-83, Robinson, Locke, Gage, Fite & Williams, Muskogee, 1983-95, Robinson, Gage, Fite & Williams, Muskogee, 1995-97. Police judge, City of Muskogee, 1963-64, mcpl. judge, 1964-70; prin. justice Temp. Divsn. 36 Okla. Ct. Appeals, 1981-84, spl. dist. judge, 1997—; pres., dir. Wall St. Bldg. Corp., 1969-78, Three Forks Devel. Corp., 1968-77, Rolo Leasing Inc., 1971-97, Suroya II Inc., 1977—; sec. Muskogee Tom's Inc., Blue Ridge Corp., Harborcliff Corp.; adv. dir. First Nat. Bank & Trust Co. of Muskogee, 1978-96; mng. ptnr. RLG Ritz, 1980-97; ptnr. First City Real Estate Partnership, 1985-94; del. to U.S./China Jt. Session on Trade, Investment and Econ. Law, Beijing, 1987. Chmn. Muskogee County (Okla.) Law Day, 1963, Muskogee Area Redevel. Authority, 1963, Muskogee County chpt. Am. Cancer Soc., 1956; pres., bd. dirs. United Way of Muskogee Inc., 1980-88, v.p., 1982, pres., 1983; bd. dirs. Muskogee Cmty. Concert Assn., Muskogee Tourist Info. Bur., 1964-68; bd. dirs., gen. counsel United Cerebral Palsy Eastern Okla., 1964-68; trustee Connors Devel. Found., Connors Coll., 1981-99, chmn., 1987-89; active Muskogee Housing Authority, 1992-95. With inf. AUS, 1945-46. Mem. ABA, Okla. Bar Assn. (chmn. uniform laws com. 1970-72, chmn. profl. coop. com. 1965-69, past regional chmn. grievance com.), Muskogee County Bar Assn. (pres. 1971, mem. exec. coun. 1971-74), Okla. Assn. Def. Counsel (dir.), Okla. Assn. Mcpl. Judges (dir.), Muskogee c. of C., Delta Theta Phi., Rotary (pres. 1971-72). Methodist. Banking, Estate planning, Real property. Home: 2408 Saint Andrews Ct Muskogee OK 74403-1657 Office: Muskogee County Courthouse PO Box 1350 Muskogee OK 74402-1350

ROBINSON, BARBARA PAUL, lawyer; b. Oct. 19, 1941; d. Leo and Pauline G. Paul; m. Charles Raskob Robinson, June 11, 1965; children: Charles Paul, Torrance Webster. AB magna cum laude, Bryn Mawr Coll., 1962; LLB, Yale U., 1965. Bar: N.Y. 1966, U.S. Dist. Ct. (so. and ea. dists.) N.Y. 1975, U.S. Tax Ct. 1972, U.S. Ct. Appeals (2d cir.) 1974. Assoc. Debevoise & Plimpton (formerly Debevoise, Plimpton, Lyons & Gates), N.Y.C., 1966-75, ptnr., 1976—. Mem. adv. bd., lectr. Practicing Law Inst.; arbitrator Am. Arbitration Assn., 1987—, bd. dirs.; dir. Sch. Choice Scholarships Found., 1997—. Bd. editors Chase Jour., 1997—; contbr. articles to profl. jours. Mem. adv. coun., bd. visitors CUNY Law Sch., Queens, 1984-90; trustee Trinity Sch., 1982-86, pres., 1986-88; bd. dirs. Found. for Child Devel., 1989-2000, chmn., 1991-2000; mem. Coun. on Fgn. Rels.; bd. dirs. Catalyst, 1993—, Am. Judicature Soc., Fund Modern Cts., 1990—, Wave Hill, 1994—, Garden Conservancy, 1996—; trustee Lawyers Com. for Civil Rights Under Law, 1997—, The William Nelson Cromwell Found., 1993—; bd. dirs. Irish Legal Rsch. Found. Inc., 1996—, Citizens Union Found. Inc., 1996—; bd. trustees Bryn Mawr Coll., 2000—. Recipient Laura Parsons Pratt award, 1996. Fellow Am. Coll. Trust and Estate Counsel, Am. Bar Found., N.Y. Bar Found.; mem. ABA (mem. commn. on women in profession 1999—), N.Y. State Bar Assn. (vice chmn. com. on trust adminstrn., trusts and estates law sect. 1977-81, ho. of dels. 1984-87, 90-92, mem. com. ann. award 1993-94), Assn. of Bar of City of N.Y. (chmn. com. on trusts, estates and surrogates cts. 1981-84, judiciary com. 1981-84, coun. on jud. adminstrn. 1982-84, chair nominating com. 1984-85, 99—, mem. exec. com. 1986-91, chair 1989-90, v.p. 1990-91, pres. 1994-96, chair com. on honors 1993-94, mem. com. on long-range planning 1991-94, co-chair coun. on childen 1997-99), Assn. of Bar of City of N.Y. Fund Inc. (bd. dirs., pres.), Women's Forum, Yale Coun., Yale Law Sch. Assn. N.Y. (mem. devel. bd., exec. com. 1981-85, pres. 1988-93), Order of the Coif, Yale Club, Washington Club. Estate planning, Probate, Estate taxation. Office: Debevoise & Plimpton 919 Third Ave New York NY 10022 E-mail: bprobinson@debevoise.com

ROBINSON, BERNARD LEO, retired lawyer; b. Kalamazoo, Feb. 13, 1924; s. Louis Harvey and Sue Mary (Starr) R.; m. Betsy Nadell, May 30, 1947; children: Robert Bruce, Patricia Anne, Jean Carol. BS, U. Ill., 1947, MS, 1958; JD, U. N.Mex., 1973. Bar: N.Mex. 1973, U.S. Supreme Ct. 1976. Rsch. engr. Assn. Am. Railroads, 1947-49; instr. arch. Rensselaer Poly. Inst., 1949-51; commd. 2d lt. U.S. Army, 1945, advanced through grades to lt. col., 1965, ret., 1968; engr. Nuclear Def. Rsch. Corp., Albuquerque, 1968-71; lawyer, 1973-85, Silver City, N.Mex., 1985-89, Green Valley, Ariz., 1989-90, Sierra Vista, 1990-91; pres. Robinson Fin. Svcs., Tucson, 1993-95. Dist. commr. Boy Scouts Am., 1960-62. Decorated Air medal. Mem. ASCE, ABA, Ret. Officers Assn., DAV, Assn. U.S. Army, VFW. Banking, General corporate. Home: 11821 N Pyramid Point Dr Tucson AZ 85737-3726

ROBINSON, DAVID HOWARD, lawyer; b. Hampton, Va., Nov. 24, 1948; s. Bernard Harris and Phyllis (Canter) R.; m. Nina Jane Briscoe, Aug. 20, 1979. BA, Calif. State U., Northridge, 1970; JD, Cabrillo Pacific U., 1975. Bar: Calif. 1977, U.S. Dist. Ct. (so. dist.) Calif. 1977, U.S. Ct. Claims, 1979, U.S. Supreme Ct. 1980. Adminstr. Cabrillo Pacific U. Coll. Law, 1977; assoc. Gerald D. Egan, San Bernardino, Calif., 1977-78, Duke & Gerstel, San Diego, 1978-80, Rand, Day & Ziman, San Diego, 1980-81; pvt. practice, 1981-88; ptnr. Robinson and Rubin, 1988-95; dep. atty. gen. State of Calif., 1995—. Mem. Foothills Bar Assn. (bd. dirs., past treas.). Office: 110 West A St San Diego CA 92101-3711

ROBINSON, DOROTHY K. lawyer; b. New Haven, Feb. 18, 1951; children: Julia Robinson Bouwsma, Alexandra Toby Bouwsma. BA in Econs. with honors, Swarthmore Coll., 1972; JD, U. Calif., Berkeley, 1975; MA (hon.), Yale U., 1987. Bar: Calif. 1975, N.Y. 1976, Conn. 1981, U.S. Ct. Appeals (2d cir.) 1975, U.S. Dist. Ct. (so. dist.) N.Y. 1981. Assoc. Hughes Hubbard & Reed, N.Y.C., 1975-78; asst. gen. counsel Yale U., New Haven, 1978-79, assoc. gen. counsel, 1979-84, dep. gen. counsel, 1984-86, gen. counesl, 1986-95, dir. fed. rels., 1986-88, acting sec., 1993, v.p., gen. counsel, 1995—. Mem. Calif. Law Rev., 1973-75. Trustee Hopkins Grammar Day Prospect Hill Sch., New Haven, 1983-88, sec., 1986-88; trustee Wenner-Gren Found. Anthrop. Rsch., 1991—; bd. dirs. Cold Spring Sch., New Haven, 1990-95; mem. adv. bd. Conn. Mental Health Ctr., New Haven, 1979-89; bd. dirs. Nat. Assn. Ind. Coll. and Univs., 1995-98; mem. alumni coun. Swarthmore Coll., 1999—. Fellow Ezra Stiles Coll. Yale U., Am. Bar Found.; mem. ABA, Nat. Assn. Coll. and Univ. Attys. (bd. dirs. 1987-90), Conn. Bar Assn., Calif. Bar Assn., Assn. Bar City N.Y., Phi Beta Kappa. General corporate, Education and schools. Office: Yale U Office of Gen Counsel PO Box 208255 New Haven CT 06520-8255

ROBINSON, E. GLENN, lawyer; b. Charleston, W.Va., Jan. 1, 1924; s. Elmer George and Eva Elena (Rexrode) R.; m. Emma Lou Legg, Dec. 23, 1947; children: Richard G., Martha L., William E., Ann K. BSc, Ohio State U.; 1948; LLB, W.Va. U., 1950. Bar: W.Va. 1950, U.S. Ct. Appeals (4th cir.) 1953, U.S. Ct. Appeals (3d cir.) 1980, U.S. Supreme Ct. 1982. Ptnr. Shannon & Robinson, Charleston, 1950-52, Love, Wise, Robinson & Woodroe, Charleston, 1952-83, Robinson & McElwee, Charleston, 1983-91, of counsel, 1991—; pres. W.Va. State Bar, 1972-73. Served with AUS, 1942-45. Fellow Am. Bar Found.; mem. ABA, W.Va. Bar Assn. (pres. 1982-83), Kanawha County Bar Assn. (pres. 1968-69), Am. Coll. Trial Lawyers, Am. Bd. Trial Advs. Republican. Club: Rotary. Federal civil litigation, General civil litigation, State civil litigation. Home: 507 Superior Ave Charleston WV 25303-2024 Office: 600 United Ctr Charleston WV 25301-2135

ROBINSON, EDWARD T., III, lawyer; b. Glen Cove, N.Y., May 23, 1932; s. Edward Jr. and Helen (Rahilly) R.; m. Lynn Simmons; children: Edward IV, Wendy, Christopher, Jeffrey, Lesley, Michael. AB, Holy Cross Coll., 1954; JD, Georgetown U., 1960. Bar: N.Y. 1961, U.S. Ct. Appeals (2d cir.) 1966. Counsel Royal-Globe Ins. Co., Mineola, N.Y., 1960-64; pvt. practice, Oyster Bay, 1964-70, 91-2000; ptnr. Robinson & Cincotta, 1970-85, Robinson & Lynch, Oyster Bay, 1985-91; counsel Cammarata & Cronin LLP, 2000—. Mem. adv. bd. Chgo. Title Ins. Co., N.Y.C., 1982-2000, Fleet Bank, 1989-95, United Cerebral Palsy, 1980—; mem. Nassau County Commn. on Govt. Revision, 1993—; mem. County Exec. Blue Ribbon Panel on Criminal Justice; mem. exec. coun. N.Y. State Conf. Bar Leaders, 1986-90; counsel Oyster Bay-East Norwich Ctrl. Sch. Dist., 1966-2000; mem. N.Y. State grievance com. 10th Jud. Dist., 1995—. Mem. Nassau County Traffic and Parking Violations Bur.; pres. Holy Cross Coll. Club, L.I., 1989-90; trustee Nassau County coun. Boy Scouts Am.; chmn. Forget-Me-Not Ball, United Cerebral Palsy. Recipient Community Svc. award Nassau County coun. Boy Scouts Am.; named Man of Yr. United Cerebral Palsy, Nassau County, 1979. Mem. N.Y. State Bar Assn. (del., v.p. 1992-95, mem. ho. of dels. 1995—), Nassau County Bar Assn. (pres. 1986-87), Oyster Bay C. of C. (pres. 1976-79), Meadowbrook Golf Club, Country Club La Romana (Dominican Republic). Republican. Roman Catholic. Avocations: golf, tennis, jazz music. State civil litigation, Probate, Real property. Home: 60 Calvin Ave Syosset NY 11791-2106 Office: 34 Audrey Ave Unit 3 Oyster Bay NY 11771-1595

ROBINSON, HARLO LYLE, lawyer; b. Shelley, Idaho, Mar. 10, 1925; s. Clarence and Vilate (Hainey) R.; m. Janet Allen Alderson, Dec. 28, 1969; children— Thomas Allen, Harlo Todd. B.S., U. Utah, 1949; J.D., U. Calif.-Berkeley, 1952. Bar: Calif. 1953, Hawaii 1970. Gen. counsel Dillingham Corp., Honolulu, 1968-76; assoc. Ikazaki, Lo, Youth & Nakano, 1976-77; of legal counsel Bob Pomery Cons., Tehran, Iran, 1977-79, Saudi Arabia Parsons, Yanbu, Saudi Arabia, 1979— . Assoc. editor Calif. Law Rev., 1951-52. Adv. bd. Southwestern Legal Found., Dallas, 1971-82. Republican. Mem. Christian Ch. Home: 696 Kalanipuu St Honolulu HI 96825-2421

ROBINSON, IRWIN JAY, lawyer; b. Bay City, Mich., Oct. 8, 1928; s. Robert R. and Anne (Kaplan) R.; m. Janet Binder, July 7, 1957; children: Elizabeth Binder Schubiner, Jonathan Meyer, Eve Kimberly Wiener. AB, U. Mich., 1950; JD, Columbia U., 1953. Bar: N.Y. 1956. Assoc. Breed Abbott & Morgan, N.Y.C., 1955-58; asst. to ptnrs. Dreyfus & Co., 1958-59; assoc. Greenbaum Wolff & Ernst, 1959-65, ptnr., 1966-76; sr.

ptnr. Rosenman & Colin, N.Y.C., 1976-90; of counsel Pryor, Cashman, Sherman & Flynn, 1990-92; sr. ptnr. Phillips, Nizer, Benjamin, Krim & Ballon, N.Y.C., 1992-99; pvt. practice, 1999—. Treas. Saarsteel, Inc., Whitestone, N.Y., 1970—. Bd. dirs. Henry St. Settlement, N.Y.C., 1960-85, Jewish Cmty. Ctr. Assn. N.Am., N.Y.C., 1967-94, mem. adv. bd., 1998—; bd. dirs. Heart Rsch. Found., 1989-94, pres., 1991-93. Mem. ABA, N.Y. State Bar Assn., Assn. Bar City of N.Y., Internat. Bar Assn., Thai-Am. C. of C. (founder, bd. dirs. 1992-95, pres. 1992-95), Vietnam-Am. C. of C. (founder, bd. dirs. 1992-95, pres. 1992-95), Philippine-Am. C. of C. (bd. dirs. 1960-98), Sunningdale Country Club, The Desert Mountain Club. Jewish. Banking, General corporate, Real property. Home: 4622 Grosvenor Ave Riverdale NY 10471-3305 Office: care Kramer Levin Naftalis & Frankel 919 3d Ave 40th Fl New York NY 10022-3902 E-mail: ijrjbr@aol.com

ROBINSON, JAMES KENNETH, federal official; b. Grand Rapids, Mich., Nov. 27, 1943; s. Kenneth and Marguerite (Anderson) R.; m. Marietta Sebree; children: Steven James, Renee Elizabeth. BA with honors, Mich. State U., 1965; JD magna cum laude, Wayne State U., 1968. Bar: Mich. 1968, U.S. Dist. Ct. (ea. and we. dists) Mich. 1969, U.S. Ct. Appeals (6th cir.) 1969, U.S. Supreme Ct. 1977. Law clk. to judge U.S. Ct. Appeals (6th cir.), 1968-69; assoc. Miller, Canfield, Paddock & Stone, Detroit, 1969-71; from assoc. to ptnr. Honigman Miller Schwartz and Cohn, 1972-77, ptnr., 1981-93, chmn. litigation dept.; U.S. atty. Ea. Dist. Mich., 1977-80; adj. prof. Wayne State U. Law Sch., Detroit, 1973-84, dean, prof., 1993-98, prof., 2001—; asst. atty. gen. criminal divsn. U.S. Dept. Justice, Washington, 1998-2001. Adj. prof. Detroit Coll. Law, 1970-73; mem. evidence test drafting com.-multistate bar exam Nat. Conf. Bar Examiners, 1975—; mem. adv. com. on evidence rules Jud. Conf. U.S., 1993-98; chmn. com. on rules of evidence Mich. Supreme Ct., 1975-78; lectr. Mich. Jud. Inst., 1977-98, Mich. Inst. CLE. Author: (with others) Introducing Evidence-A Practical Guide for Michigan Lawyers, 1988, Scope of Discovery, 1986, Michigan Court Rules Practice-Evidence, 1996, Courtroom Handbook on Michigan Evidence, 1997; contbg. author Emerging Problems Under the Federal Rules of Evidence, 3d edit., 1998; contbr. articles to profl. jours.; editor in chief Wayne Law Rev., 1967-68. Chmn. Gov.'s Commn. on Future Higher Edn. in Mich., 1983-84; pres. State Bar of Mich., 1990-91, commr. 1980-81, 83-91. Recipient Disting. Alumni award Wayne State U. Law Sch., 1979, 1986. Fellow Am. Bar Found., Mich. Bar Found., Am. Coll. Trial Lawyers, Internat. Soc. Barristers, Am. Acad. of Appellate Lawyers; mem. ABA (litigation and criminal justice sects., lectr.), Fed. Bar Assn. (dir. 1975-81), Nat. Assn. Former U.S. Attys. (pres. 1984-85), Am. Law Inst., 6th Cir. Jud. Conf., Wayne U. Law Alumni Assn. (pres. 1975-76), Detroit Athletic Club. Office: US Dept Justice Asst Atty Gen Criminal Divs 10th & Constitution NW Washington DC 20530-0001

ROBINSON, JOHN VICTOR, lawyer; b. Harare, Zimbabwe, July 9, 1958; s. Denis Antony Beck and Elizabeth Jill R. BA, Rhodes U., Grahamstown, South Africa, 1983; MA, Oxford (Eng.) U., 1985; JD, U. Richmond (Va.), 1986. Bar: Va. Assoc. atty. Hunton & Williams, Richmond, Va., 1986-89, McSweeney, Burtch & Crump, Richmond, 1989-93, Cantor, Arkema & Edmonds, P.C., Richmond, 1993-97; pvt. practice, 1997—. Past mem. regional com. Nat. Trial Competition, Richmond; apptd. adminstrv. hearing officer Va. Supreme Ct.; adj. asst. prof. Law U. Richmond Sch. Law. Rhodes scholar Oxford U., 1983-85. Mem. ABA, Va. Bar Assn., Bar Assn. City of Richmond. General civil litigation, General corporate, Intellectual property. Office: 7102 Three Cropt Road Richmond VA 23226-3615

ROBINSON, JOHN WILLIAM, IV, lawyer; b. Atlanta, Apr. 29, 1950; s. J. William III and Elizabeth (Smith) R.; m. Ellen Showalter, Dec. 28, 1976; children: William, Anna. BA with honors, Washington & Lee U., 1972; JD, U. Ga., 1975. Bar: Fla., Ga., U.S. Dist. Ct. (no., so. and mid. dists.) Fla., U.S. Ct. Mil. Appeals, U.S. Ct. Appeals (5th and 11th cirs.), U.S. Supreme Ct.; cert. labor & employment law, civil trial and bus. litigation lawyer, Fla., Nat. Bd. Trial Advocacy. Trial atty. Nat. Labor Rels. Bd., New Orleans, 1975-76; trial def. counsel 8th infantry U.S. Army, Mainz, Germany, 1977-78, trial counsel 8th infantry Germany, 1979; law clerk, commr. Ct. Mil. Review, Washington, 1980; atty. Fowler, White, Gillen, Boggs, Villareal & Banker, P.A., Tampa, Fla., 1980—, head labor and employment law dept., 1993—, dir., 1998—, sec./treas, ops. com., 2001—. Mem. faculty U. Md., 1977-79; arbitrator U.S. Dist. Ct. (mid. dist.) Fla. Editor-in-chief: Employment & Labor Relations Law, 1991-95; editor: Developing Labor Law, 1982—, Model Jury Instructions for Employment Litigation, 1994—; editor: Employment Litigation Handbook, 1998. Chmn. Tampa Bay Internat. Trade Coun., 1990-91, Rough Riders Dist. Boy Scouts Am., 1990; legal counsel Drug Free Workplace Task Force, 1999-00, Greater Tampa C. of C., 1996, gen. counsel, 1999—. Capt. U.S. Army, 1976-80. Named one of Best Lawyers in Am. for labor and employment law. Mem. ABA (divsn. dir. 1996-2000, chmn. employment and labor rels. com. 1993-96, litigation sect., mem. coun. 2000—), Fla. Bar Assn. (chmn. labor and employment law sect. 1992-93), Wash. & Lee U. Bd. (pres. nat. alumni bd. 1990-91, trustee 1995—), Rotary (pres. Tampa Bay chpt.), Am. Inn of Ct. (pres., dir. and barrister). Avocations: tennis, history. General civil litigation, Labor, Pension, profit-sharing, and employee benefits. Office: Fowler White Gillen Boggs Villareal & Banker PA 501 E Kennedy Blvd Tampa FL 33602-5237

ROBINSON, KENNETH PATRICK, lawyer, electronics company executive; b. Hackensack, N.J., Dec. 12, 1933; s. William Casper and Margaret Agnes (McGuire) r.; m. Catherine Esther Lund, Aug. 26, 1961; children: James, Susan. BS in Elec. Engring., Rutgers U., 1955; JD, NYU, 1962. Bar: N.Y. 1962, U.S. Ct. Appeals (fed. cir.) 1990. With Hazeltine Corp., Greenlawn, N.Y., 1955-88, patent counsel, 1966-69, gen. counsel, 1969-88, sec., 1971-88; v.p. Hazeltine Rsch. Inc., Chgo., 1966-88; of counsel Brumbaugh, Graves, Donohue & Raymond, N.Y.C., 1989-92; prin. Kenneth P. Robinson, Huntington, N.Y., 1992—. Dir. Hazeltine Ltd., London, 1973-80; dir. Imlac Corp., Needham, Mass., 1978-83. Served to 1st lt. USAF, 1955-57. Mem. ABA, IEEE, Am. Intellectual Law Assn., Licensing Execs. Soc. Roman Catholic. Patent, Trademark and copyright, Technology. Home: 137 Darrow Ln Greenlawn NY 11740-2923 Office: 474 New York Ave Huntington NY 11743-3542

ROBINSON, MARVIN STUART, lawyer; b. Newark, June 9, 1933; s. Irwin and Eva (Harkavy) R.; m. Rona Kessner, June 24, 1956; children: Janet Robinson Adelsberg, Susan Robinson Briggs, Amy. BA, Cornell U., 1955, JD with distinction, 1957; LLM, NYU, 1963. Bar: N.Y. 1957, U.S. Dist. Ct. (so. and ea. dists.) N.Y. 1959, U.S. Ct. Appeals (2d and 5th cirs.) 1960, U.S. Supreme Ct. 1972. Assoc. Gallop, Climenko & Gould, N.Y.C., 1958-59; assoc. Tannenbaum Dubin & Robinson, 1959-64, ptnr., 1964—. Chmn. Council of Greenburgh Civic Assns., N.Y.; v.p., trustee Woodlawn Community Temple, Greenburgh; mem. planning bd., Democratic dist. leader Town of Greenburgh; active various civic orgns. Served to lt. U.S. Army, 1955-62. Mem. ABA, Cornell Law Assn., Westchester County Bar Assn., N.Y. State Bar Assn., N.Y. County Lawyers, N.Y.C. Bar Assn. Jewish. General corporate, Pension, profit-sharing, and employee benefits. Office: Tannenbaum Dubin & Robinson 20th Fl 1140 Avenue Of The Americas fl 20 New York NY 10036-5802

ROBINSON, MARY LOU, federal judge; b. Dodge City, Kans., Aug. 25, 1926; d. Gerald J. and Frances Strueber; m. A.J. Robinson, Aug. 28, 1949; children: Rebecca Aynn Gruhlkey, Diana Ceil, Matthew Douglas. B.A., U. Tex., 1948, LL.B., 1950. Bar: Tex. 1949. Ptnr. Robinson & Robinson, Amarillo, 1950-55; judge County Ct. at Law, Potter County, Tex., 1955-59, (108th Dist. Ct.), Amarillo, 1961-73; assoc. justice Ct. of Civil Appeals for 7th Supreme Jud. Dist. of Tex., 1973-77, chief justice, 1977-79; U.S. dist. judge No. Dist. Tex., Amarillo, 1979—. Named Woman of Year Tex. Fedn. Bus. and Profl. Women, 1973. Mem. Nat. Assn. Women Lawyers, ABA, Tex. Bar Assn., Amarillo Bar Assn., Delta Kappa Gamma. Presbyterian. Office: US Dist Ct Rm 226 205 E 5th Ave # F13248 Amarillo TX 79101-1559

ROBINSON, NEIL CIBLEY, JR. lawyer; b. Columbia, S.C., Oct. 25, 1942; s. Neil C. and Ernestine (Carns) R.; m. Judith Ann Hunter, Sept. 4, 1971 (div. Nov. 1979); 1 child, Hunter Leigh; m. Vicki Elizabeth Kornahrens, Mar. 2, 1985; children: Neil C. III, Taylor Elizabeth. BS in Indsl. Mgmt., Clemson U., 1966; JD, U. S.C., 1973. Bar: S.C. 1974, U.S. Ct. Appeals (4th cir.) 1974, U.S. Dist. Ct. S.C. 1976. Asst. to dean U. S.C. Law Sch., Columbia, 1973-74; law clk. to Hon. Charles E. Jr. Simons Jr. U.S. Dist. Ct. S.C., Aiken, 1974-76; assoc. Grimball & Cabaniss, Charleston, S.C., 1976-78; ptnr. Grimball, Cabaniss, Vaughan & Robinson, 1978-84; ptnr., pres. Robinson, Wall & Hastie, P.A., 1984-91; ptnr., exec. com. Nexsen, Pruet, Jacobs, Pollard & Robinson, 1991—. Permanent mem. 4th Cir. Jud. Conf., 1982—; pres. Coastal Properties Inst., Charleston, 1981—. Bd. dirs. Southeastern Wildlife Exposition, Charleston, 1987—, pres. 1994-99, Charleston Maritime Festival, 1993-99, pres. 1994-98, Parklands Found. of Charleston County; pres. S.C. Tourism Coun., Columbia, 1991-99; co-founder, chmn. Charleston Planning Project Pub. Edn., 1996—; bd. dirs. Charleston Edn. Found., Clemson U. Humanities Found., Charleston Edn. Network, chmn. bd. dirs., 2000—; edn. adv. bd. Coll. of Charleston; adv. bd. for design, Clemson U. Cpl. USMCR, 1960-66. Recipient Order of Palmetto, Gov. David Beasley, S.C., 1996. Mem. ABA, Urban Land Inst. (recreational devel. coun.), S.C. Bar Assn., Fed. Bar Assn., S.C. Def. Trial Lawyers Assn., Hibernian Soc. (mgmt. com. 1984—, sec. 1998-2000, chmn. 2000—), Kiawah Club, Haig Point Club, Country Club of Charleston, Phi Delta Phi. Presbyterian. Avocations: golf, hunting. Environmental, Land use and zoning (including planning), Real property. Home: PO Box 121 Charleston SC 29402-0121 Office: Nexsen Pruet Jacobs Pollard & Robinson 200 Meeting St Ste 301 Charleston SC 29401-3156 E-mail: nrobinson@npjp.com

ROBINSON, PAUL HARPER, lawyer, educator; b. Waterbury, Conn., Nov. 12, 1948; s. Edward Raymond and Ann (Harper) R.; m. Jane Grall, June 23, 1984; children by previous marriage— Samuel, Amanda. B.S., Rensselaer Poly. Inst., 1970; J.D., UCLA, 1973; LL.M., Harvard U., 1974; diploma in legal studies Cambridge U., Eng., 1976. Bar: Mass. 1974. Faculty fellow Nat. Ctr. for State Courts, Washington, 1973; fed. prosecutor U.S. Atty.'s Office, Alexandria, Va., 1976; legis. counsel U.S. Senate Jud. Com., Washington, 1977; prof. law Rutgers U. Sch. Law, Camden, N.J., 1977— , leave of absence, 1985— ; commnr. U.S. Sentencing Commn., Washington, 1985—; adj. prof. law, Georgetown U. Law Ctr., Washington, 1985— ; dir. R.I. Criminal Code Revision Project, 1982— . Author: Criminal Law Defenses, 1984. Contbr. numerous articles to profl. jours. Mem. ABA (chmn. criminal justice sect. com. on state legislation). Home: 230 S Cooper River Dr Collingswood NJ 08108-1100 Office: State U NJ Sch Law 5th & Penn Sts Camden NJ 08102

ROBINSON, ROBIN WICKS, lawyer; b. Roanoke Rapids, N.C., June 5, 1961; d. Wallace Wayne and Rozelle Royall Wicks; m. James Hendry Robinson, Jr., Nov. 7, 1992; children: James Hendry Robinson III, Wallace Katherine McLean Robinson. BA in Politics (hon.), Converse Coll., Spartanburg, S.C., 1982; JD, U. N.C., Chapel Hill, 1985. Bar: N.C. 1986; 5th Jud. Dist. 1986, U.S. Dist. Ct. (ea. dist.) 1987; U.S. Dist. Ct. (we. dist.) 1997, 5th Jud. Dist. Arbitrator 1993, Superior Ct. Cert. Mediator, N.C., Dispute Resolution Commn, 1996; family fin. cert. mediator N.C. Dispute Resolution Commn., 1999. Assoc. atty. Ryals, Jackson & Mills, Wilmington, N.C., 1986-90; ptnr. Pennington & Wicks, 1990-93; pres, profl. corp. Ryals, Robinson & Saffo P.C., 1993—. Ethics com. N.C. State Bar, Raleigh, N.C., 1990-93; exec. com. New Hanover County Bar Assn., Wilmington, 1994-97. Bd. mem. Cape Fear Mus. Assocs., Inc., Wilmington, N.C., 1991-2000, v.p. 1994-97, pres. 1997-2000; bd. mem., counsel Wilmington Symphony Orchestra, Inc., Wilmington, N.C., 1991-99; commn. mem. USS N.C. Battleship Commn., Wilmington, N.C., 1989-93; mem. Bd. Deacons First Presbyn. Ch., Wilmington, N.C., 1996-99, Chancel Choir, 1988—. Recipient Women of Achievement New Hanover Commn. for Women, Wilmington, N.C., 1997, Trustee Merit Scholarship Converse Coll., Spartanburg, S.C., 1978-82; named Mortar Bd. Converse Coll., Spartanburg, S.C., 1981—, Crescent Converse Coll., Spartanburg, S.C., 1979-80, Pro bono publico award Legal Svcs. of the Lower Cape Fear, 1997. Mem. Am. Bar Assn., N.C. Bar Assn., N.C. Acad. Trial Lawyers, New Hanover County Bar Assn., Phi Delta Phi, Phi Sigma Iota, Pi Gamma Mu. Republican. Presbyterian. Avocations: travel, piano, choral, swimming, tennis, sailing. Home: 1940 Hawthorne Rd Wilmington NC 28403-5329 Office: Ryals Robinson & Saffo PC 701 Market St Wilmington NC 28401-4646 E-mail: rrspc@bellsouth.net

ROBINSON, SANDRA ANN, lawyer; b. Hackensack, N.J.; d. John Henry and Martha Carrington (Toliver) R. BA, Howard U., 1969; JD, 1972. Bar: Pa. 1979, U.S. Dist. Ct. N.J. 1981, N.J. 1981, U.S. Supreme Ct. 1983, U.S. Ct. Appeals (3d cir.) 1987. Legal intern Ctr. Clin. Legal Studies, Washington, 1970-72; clk. to presiding justice Superior Ct. N.J., Passaic County, 1972-73; litigational appeals atty. Essex-Newark Legal Services Corp., Newark, 1973-78, assoc. exec. dir., 1979-84, acting exec. dir., 1984-85, exec. dir., 1985—; county adjuster County of Bergen, Hackensack, 1985; planning bd. atty. City of Hackensack, 1982-84. Legal rep. Mary McLeod Bethune Scholarship Fund, Hackensack, 1978— ; active Hackensack Mcpl. Com., 1975— , Rent Stabilization Bd., Hackensack, 1973-77, Urban League Bergen County Inc., 1980— ; sec. Hackensack Citizens Adv. Com., 1972— ; bd. govs., exec. com. Hackensack Med. Ctr., 1984— ; v.p. N.J. Assn. Correction, Trenton, 1978—; bd. dirs. Bergen County Family Svcs., 1986—, YWCA; mem. Bergen County Bd. Ethics, 1988—. Named Woman of Yr., Hackensack Day Care Ctr. 1983, one of Outstanding Young Women Am., 1981. Mem. ABA, Am. Judicature Soc., Bergen County Bar Assn., Bergen County Women Lawyers, Fed. Bar Assn., N.J. Inst. Mcpl. Attys., N.J. State Bar Assn., Pa. Bar Assn., Nat. Bus and Profl. Women's Assn. (Nat. Sojourner Truth Meritorious Svc. award 1984), Assn. Trial Lawyers Am., Howard U. Alumni Assn. (Bergen County sec., region II rep. 1972—, Disting. Daughter 1982), Bergen County Links Inc. (parliamentarian 1983—), Zonta, Kappa Beta Pi. Bankruptcy, Family and matrimonial, General practice. Home: 680 Summit Ave Hackensack NJ 07601-1605

ROBINSON, STEPHANIE, tax lawyer; b. L.A., Sept. 21, 1969; d. William Courtney Jr. and Suzanne Stevens (Trask) Robinson; m. Seth Alexander Rosenthal, Nov. 8, 1997. BA, U. N.C., 1991; JD, Harvard U., 1994. Bar: Ga. 1995, D.C. 1996. Law clk. to chief judge U.S. Dist. Ct. (ea. dist.) La., 1994-95; assoc. King & Spalding, Washington, 1995—99; atty. advisor Office Tax Policy U.S. Dept. Treasury, 2000—. Tutor, tutoring leader D.C. Works, Washington, 1995-98. Corporate taxation. Home: 5427 32d St NW Washington DC 20015 Office: US Dept Treasury 1500 Pennsylvania Ave NW Washington DC 20220

ROBINSON, THEODORE CURTIS, JR. lawyer; b. Chgo., Jan. 22, 1916; s. Theodore Curtis and Edna Alice (Willard) R.; m. Marynel Werner, Dec. 28, 1940; children: Theodore Curtis III, Peter S. BA, Western Res. U., 1938, LLB, 1940. Bar: Ohio 1940, U.S. Dist. Ct. (no. dist.) Ohio 1946, U.S. Ct. Appeals (8th cir.) 1948, U.S. Dist. Ct. (we. dist.) Wis. 1950, U.S. Dist. Ct. (we. dist.) N.Y. 1950, U.S. Ct. Appeals (6th cir.) 1950, Ill. 1957, U.S. Dist. Ct. (no. dist.) Ill. 1957, U.S. Ct. Appeals (7th cir.) 1964, U.S. Supreme Ct. 1972. Assoc. Davis & Young, Cleve., 1940; law clk. no. dist. ea. divsn. U.S. Dist. Ct., 1940-42; assoc. Leckie, McCreary, et al, 1945-52; ptnr. McCreary, Hinslea & Ray, 1953-57, McCreary, Hinslea, Ray & Robinson, Chgo., 1957-90; counsel Ray, Robinson, Hannin & Carle, 1990-91, Ray, Robinson, Carle, Davies & Snyder, Chgo., 1991-98, ret., 1998. Mem. exec. com. Maritime Law Assn. of U.S., N.Y.C., 1981-83; pres. Propellor Club of U.S., Chgo., 1966-67; sec., treas. Internat. Shipmasters Assn., Chgo., 1958-91. Contbr. articles to profl. law reviews. Lt. USCG, 1943-45. Fellow Am. Coll. Trial Lawyers; mem. ABA, Chgo. Bar Assn. (com. chmn. 1973), Internat. Assn. Def. Counsel, Order of Coif, Traffic Club Chgo. (dir. 1986, 87), Whitehall Club (N.Y.), Nat. Eagle Scout Assn. Republican. Avocations: gardening, golf, reading. E-mail: mwrtcr@aol.com

ROBINSON, THOMAS ADAIR, law educator, consultant; b. San Diego, July 24, 1943; s. Thomas Austin Robinson and Judith (Oswald) Olmsted; m. Diane Elaine Whitaker, Dec. 24, 1972 (div. 1982); 1 child, Sita Chantal Whitaker-Robinson; m. Christine Anderson, Mar. 17, 1984; children: Thomas Christopher, Christina Adair. B.S. in Elec. Engring., U. Idaho, 1966; J.D., UCLA, 1969; B.Litt., Oxford U. Eng., 1975. Bar: Calif. 1973, U.S. Supreme Ct. 1981, Fla. 1982. Assoc. Latham & Watkins, Los Angeles, 1973-77; prof. law sch. U. Ark., Fayetteville, 1977-81, sch. law U. Miami, Coral Gables, Fla., 1982—; dir. grad. programs in taxation, estate planning and property devel. U. Miami, 1992-95; mem. exec. council tax sect. Fla. Bar, 1983— ; prof. U. N.C. Law Sch., summer 1981; lectr. basic fed. taxes NPI, Denver, Seattle. Pres. Hertford Coll. Middle Common Room, Oxford, 1972-73. Grantee Am. Bar Found., 1968; recipient Ann. award Math. Assn. Am., Spain, 1961. Mem. ABA, Calif. Bar, Fla. Bar (tax sect.), Phi Delta Phi. Republican. Clubs: Rotary (treas. Coral Gables 1984-85). Office: Sch Law Univ Miami PO Box 248087 Miami FL 33124-8087

ROBINSON, THOMAS HART, lawyer, educator; b. Richmond, Va., Feb. 3, 1948; s. Carey Hart and Rose (Strauss) R. B.S. in Econs., Va. Commonwealth U., 1970, postgrad., 1978; J.D., Coll. William and Mary, 1973. Bar: Va. 1973, U.S. Dist. Ct. 1974. Clk., Richmond Legal Aid, 1972-73; asst. prof. Va. Commonwealth U., 1973-78; ptnr. Deal Felts & Robinson, Richmond, 1976-86; Felts, Robinson and Duval, 1986— ; guest lectr. various univs., 1973— ; dir. Va. Ski Inc., Richmond; gen. counsel Lowrey Organ Ctr., Inc., Fairmont, W. Va., 1977-83; gen. counsel, L & M Tile, 1986—. Author: Handbook for Name Changes, 1972; contbr. articles to profl. jours. Del., Democratic Com., Henrico County, Va., 1980; chmn. Credit Consumers Counsil, Richmond, 1981; spl. commr. Henrico County Ctr. Ct., 1982; mem. spl. com. Supreme Ct. of Va. for Edn. of Newly Appointed Cir. Ct. Judges, 1986-88; apptd. Henrico Area Mental Health Cmty. Svcs. Bd., 1995—. Recipient B.E. Major award R.P.I. of Richmond; Man of Yr. award Va. Ski Inc. Mem. Va. State Bar (mem. pres.'s council), Henrico Bar Assn. (pres. 1982-83), Richmond Criminal Bar Assn., Am. Trial Lawyers Assn., Soc. Am. Magicians, Phi Delta Phi (v.p.). Criminal, General practice, Personal injury. Office: 4799 S Laburnum Ave Richmond VA 23231-2711

ROBINSON, TIMOTHY STEPHEN, lawyer; b. Kilgore, Tex., Dec. 31, 1958; s. Eddie Max and Mitter Cleo Robinson; m. Anisa Jane Laurence, May 20, 1978; children: Aaron Caleb, Alexandra Grace. BA in Econs., Austin Coll., Sherman, Tex., 1984; JD, Baylor U., 1987. Bar: Tex. 1987, Okla. 1997; cert. in personal injury Tex. Bd. Legal Specialization. Atty., litigation assocs. Ramey & Flock, Tyler, Tex., 1987-88, Fulbright & Jaworski, Dallas, 1988-91; ptnr. Robinson Carmody, 1991-94, Robinson & Schwab, Plano, Tex., 1994—. Mem. ATLA, Tex. Bar Assn., Okla. Bar Assn. Personal injury. Office: Robinson & Schwab LLP 101 E Park Blvd Ste 769 Plano TX 75074-8820

ROBINSON, VIANEI LOPEZ, lawyer; b. Houston, Mar. 6, 1969; d. David Tiburcio and Romelia Gloria (Guerra) Lopez; m. Noel Keith Robinson, Jr., Apr. 16, 1994. AB in Psychology cum laude, Princeton U., 1988; JD, U. Tex., 1991. Bar: Tex. 1991; mediator's cert. Assoc. Bracewell & Patterson LLP, Houston, 1991-94, Wagstaff Law Firm, Abilene, Tex., 1994-97; owner Robinson Law Firm, 1997—. Contbr. articles to profl. jours., chpts. to School Law in Texas, A Practical Guide, 1996, Texas Employment Law, 1998; weekly wine columnist (with Keith Robinson), Abilene Reporter News. Bd. dirs. Noah Project Women's Shelter, Paramount Theatre; bd. dirs. Ctr. for Contemporary Arts, pres., 2000, sec., 2001; mem. adv. bd., Day Nursery of Abeline. Presdl. scholar, Nat. Merit scholar, Nat. Hispanic scholar, 1985, Vinson & Elkins scholar U. Tex. Sch. Law, Austin, 1988-91. Fellow Tex. Bar Found.; mem. ABA (v.p. labor and employment law com.), State Bar Tex. (coun. mem. sect. of labor and employment law, various coms.), Coll. of the State Bar of Tex. (bd. dirs. 2000-01), Tex. Young Lawyers Assn. (bd. dirs. 1994-97), Abilene Bar Assn., Abilene Young Lawyers Assn., Big Country Soc. for Human Resource Mgmt. (pres. 1999). Avocations: theater and dance, fine art, food and wine. Education and schools, Health, Labor. Home: 2410 Wyndham Ct Abilene TX 79606-4370 Office: Robinson Law Firm First Nat Bank Tower 400 Pine St Ste 1070 Abilene TX 79601-5173 Fax: 915-677-6044. E-mail: vlr@robinsonlawfirm.com

ROBINSON, WILKES COLEMAN, retired federal judge; b. Anniston, Ala., Sept. 30, 1925; s. Walter Wade and Catherine Elizabeth (Coleman) R.; m. Julia Von Poellnitz Rowan, June 24, 1955; children: Randolph C., Peyton H., Thomas Wilkes Coleman. AB, U. Ala., 1948; JD, U. Va., 1951. Bar: Ala. 1951, Va. 1962, Mo. 1966, Kans. 1983. Assoc. Bibb & Hemphill, Anniston, Ala., 1951-54; city recorder City of Anniston, 1953-55; judge Juvenile and Domestic Relations Ct. of Calhoun County, Ala., 1954-56; atty. legal dept. GM&O R.R., Mobile, 1956-58; commerce counsel, asst. gen. atty. Seaboard Air Line R.R., Richmond, Va., 1958-66; chief commerce counsel Monsanto Co., St. Louis, 1966-70; gen. counsel, v.p. Marion Labs., Inc., Kansas City, Mo., 1970-79; pres. Gulf and Gt. Plains Legal Found., 1980-85, also bd. dirs.; atty. Howard, Needles, Tammen & Bergendoff, 1985-86, also bd. dirs.; v.p. S.R. Fin. Group, Inc., Overland Park, Kans., 1986-87; judge U.S. Ct. Fed. Claims, Washington, 1987-97, sr. judge, 1997—. Bd. govs. Kansas City Philharmonic Orch., 1975-77. Served with USNR, 1943-44. Mem. Indian Bayou Golf Club, Scottish Rite, Phi Beta Kappa (past treas. Kansas City, Mo. chpt.), Phi Eta Sigma, Phi Alpha Theta, Kappa Alpha. Episcopalian. Home: 12 Weekewachee Cir Destin FL 32541-4426 Office: US Ct Fed Claims US Cts Bldg 717 Madison Pl NW Washington DC 20439-0002

ROBINSON, WILLIE EDWARD, law educator, consultant; b. Harrisburg, Pa., Feb. 22, 1952; s. Hazel and Mamie (Mingo) R.; m. Brenda Twyner, Sept. 20, 1980; children— Bryant Francis, Alexandra Rosemary. BA, Yale U., 1974; JD, U. Va., 1977. Bar: Ga. 1977, U.S. Dist. Ct. (no. dist.) Ga. 1978, U.S. Ct. Appeals (5th cir.) 1978, U.S. Ct. Appeals (11th cir.) 1982, U.S. Supreme Ct. 1983. Assoc. Powell, Goldstein et al, Atlanta, 1977-80, Parks, Jackson, et al, Atlanta, 1980-81; adj. prof. law Woodrow Wilson U., Atlanta, 1980-81; asst. prof. law Emory U., Atlanta, 1981-87; vis. asst. prof. sch. law U. Va., Charlottesville, 1984-85; of counsel Sumner & Hewes, Atlanta, 1983-87, Rogers & Hardin, Atlanta, 1987-88; v.p. CharLee Homes Inc., Atlanta, 1980— ; pres. Select Sports Profls., Inc., 1987—; ptnr. Robinson & Gilner, 1989—; spl. advisor Nat. Bar Assn., Washington, 1984— . Contbr. articles to profl. jours. Chmn. Joint Com. to Study Standard of Need AFDC Payments, Atlanta, 1984; v.p. Residential Care Facilities for Elderly of Fulton County, Atlanta, 1983. Mem. Gate City Bar Assn. (sec. 1979, pres.-elect 1988, pres. 1989), Atlanta Bar Assn., Nat. Bar Assn., Order of Coif., Handlers Ltd. Club (Atlanta), Atlanta City Club. Methodist. Office: Ste 9-300 7000 Peachtree Dunwoody Rd NE 9-300 Atlanta GA 30328-6701

ROBINSON, ZELIG, lawyer; b. Balt., July 7, 1934; s. Morton Matthew and Mary (Ackerman) R.; m. Karen Ann Bergstrom (div. Oct. 1987); children: John, Christopher, Kristin; m. Linda Portner Strangmann, Dec. 23, 1987. BA, Johns Hopkins U., 1954; LLB, Harvard U., 1957. Bar: Md.

1958. Legis. analyst Md. House of Dels., Annapolis, 1958; tech. asst. IRS, Washington, 1958-60; pvt. practice Balt., 1960-62; assoc. gen. counsel commerce com. U.S. Ho. of Reps., Washington, 1962-64; assoc. Weinberg & Green, Balt., 1964-66; special legal cons. commerce com. U.S. Ho. of Reps., Washington, 1966-68; pvt. practice Balt., 1966-72; mem. Gordon, Feinblatt, Rothman, Hoffberger & Hollander, LLC, 1972—. Bd. dirs. Durapak Mfg. Co., Balt., Vac Pac, Inc., Balt., Universal Die Casting Co., Inc., Saline, Mich.; chmn. Balt. City Minimum Wage Commn., 1974-82, Md. Pub. Broadcasting, 1991-95; mem. Gov's. Commn. to revise Md. Code, Annapolis, 1968-89. Contbr. articles to profl. jours. Bd. dirs., v.p./sec. Gov.'s Mansion Found., Annapolis, Md.; v.p. bd. dirs. Md. Cmtys. and Citizens Fund, Chestertown, Md.; sec. bd. dirs. William Donald Schaefer Civic Fund; bd. dirs. Md. Arts Pl., Balt., Balt. Coalition of Homeowners, 1989—; mem. Found. for Md. Pub. Broadcasting; bd. dirs., pres. Celebration 2000, Inc., 1998—; founder, bd. dirs. Baltimore Efficiency and Econ. Found., 1999—. With U.S. Army, 1958. Mem. ABA, Md. State Bar Assn. (laws com., internat. law com.). Democrat. General corporate, Private international, Mergers and acquisitions. Office: Gordon Feinblatt Rothman Hoffberger & Hollander LLC 233 E Redwood St Baltimore MD 21202-3332

ROBISON, CHARLES BENNETT, legal consultant; b. Lewistown, Ill., Jan. 6, 1913; s. Marvin Thomas and Minnie Dell (White) Robison; m. Katherine Louise Parkins, Sept. 23, 1939 (dec. Dec. 1996); children: Kenneth P, Peter C, Dianne R Marcell, Alice R Berntson. AB cum laude, Knox Coll., 1934; JD, Northwestern U., 1937. Bar: Ill 1937. Assoc. Meyers & Matthias and predecessors, Chgo., 1938-73; v.p., gen. counsel Protection Mut. Ins. Co., Park Ridge, Ill., 1973-78; cons., counsel Meyers & Matthias, Matthias & Matthias, Chgo., 1978-83; legal cons. Luth. Brotherhood, Mpls., 1983-2000, Nat. Fraternal Congress Am., Naperville, Ill., 1983-2000; ret., 2000. Mem adv bd NW suburban coun Boy Scouts Am, 1959—84. Recipient Silver Beaver, Boy Scouts Am, 1959. Mem.: ABA, Fedn Ins and Corp Counsel (past pres), Fedn Ins and Corp Counsel Found (pres 1975—93), Asn Fraternal Benefit Counsel, Ill State Bar Asn, Lions (pres Des Plains 1983—84, Melvin Jones Fellow Award 1998). Republican. Congregationalist. Home: 1639 Campbell Ave Des Plaines IL 60016-6636

ROBISON, KENT RICHARD, lawyer; b. Reno, May 22, 1947; s. Burle and Helen Jean (Martin-Szymanski) R.; m. Tonya Robison; 2 children. BA, U. Nev.-Reno, 1969; JD, U. San Francisco, 1972. Bar: Nev. 1972, U.S. Dist. Ct. Nev. 1973, U.S. Ct. Claims 1973, U.S. Ct. Appeals (9th cir.) 1976, U.S. Supreme Ct. 1977, U.S. Tax Ct. 1982. Law clk. Carson City Dist. Atty.'s Office, 1971; dep. pub. defender Washoe County, Reno, 1972-75; ptnr. Johnson Belaustegui & Robison, 1975-79, Johnson, Belaustegui, Robison & Adams, Reno, 1979-81, Robison, Lyle, Belaustegui & Robb, Reno, 1981-88, Robison, Belaustegui, Robb & Sharp, Reno, 1988-99, Robison, Belaustegui, Sharp & Low, Reno, 1999—. Lectr. West Nev. Community Coll., Reno Police Acad., Calif. Legal Secs., U. Nev., Reno Bus. Coll., assns., socs., others; mem. com. on ct. costs and speedy trials Nev. Supreme Ct.; mem. Nev. State Commn. on Sentencing Felony Offenders, Exec. Com. to Establish Appellate Ct., Commn. to Implement Cameras in the Courtroom, Com. on Rules of Civil Procedure, Ad Hoc Com. for Improved Tech. in Nev. Fed. Courtrooms; mem. No. Nev. Legal-Med. Screening Panel, 1981-85; Washoe County Juvenile Master pro tem, 1975-77; ex-officio mem. ethics com., jury instrn. com. Ne v. State Bar. Contbr. articles to law jours. Mem. ABA, Nev. State Bar Assn. (bd. dirs., bd. govs.), Washoe County Bar Assn., Nev. Trial Lawyers Assn. (past pres., bd. govs.), Nat. Assn. Criminal Def. Lawyers, Assn. Trial Lawyers Am., Am. Bd. Criminal Lawyers. Republican. Construction, Criminal, Personal injury. Office: Robison Belaustegui Sharp & Low Robison Lyle Belaustegui & Robb 71 Washington St Reno NV 89503

ROBISON, WILLIAM ROBERT, lawyer; b. Memphis, May 5, 1947; s. Andrew Cliffe and Elfrieda (Barnes) R. AB, Boston U., 1970; JD, Northeastern U., 1974. Bar: Mass. 1974, D.C. 1975, U.S. Dist. Ct. Mass. 1975, U.S. Ct. Appeals (1st cir.) 1975, U.S. Dist. Ct. Conn. 1977, U.S. Supreme Ct. 1977, Calif. 1978, U.S. Dist. Ct. (cen. dist.) Calif. 1979, U.S. Ct. Appeals (9th cir,) 1979. Assoc. Meyers, Goldstein, et al, Boston, 1975-76, Cooley, Shrair, et al, Springfield, Mass., 1976-78, Hertzberg, et al, Los Angeles, 1978-79, Marcus & Lewi, Santa Monica, Calif., 1980-81; pvt. practice, 1981—. Lectr. Northeastern U., Boston, 1975-76; judge pro-tem., Mcpl. Ct., Los Angeles, 1984—, Los Angeles Superior Ct., 1987—. Co-author: Commercial Transactions, 1976. Bd. dirs. Boston Legal Asst. Project, 1972-75, Action for Boston Community Devel., Inc., 1971-75. Mem. ABA, Los Angeles County Bar Assn., Santa Monica Bar Assn. (Cert. of Appreciation 1987). Democrat. Unitarian. State civil litigation, Construction, Real property. Home and Office: 2546 Amherst Ave Los Angeles CA 90064-2712 E-mail: billrobison@prodigy.net

ROBOL, RICHARD THOMAS, lawyer; b. Norfolk, Va., Feb. 8, 1952; s. Harry James and Lucy Henley (Johnson) R. BA, U. Va., 1974; JD, Harvard U., 1978. Bar: Va. 1979, Ohio 1996, U.S. Dist. Ct. (ea. dist.) Va. 1979, U.S. Ct. Appeals (4th cir.) 1979, U.S. Dist. Ct. (we. dist.) Va. 1981, U.S. Supreme Ct. 1982, D.C. 1991, U.S. Ct. Appeals (4th, 6th and 9th cirs.) 1995. Law clk. to presiding justice U.S. Dist. Ct. (ea. dist.) Va., 1978-79; ptnr. Seawell, Dalton, Hughes & Timms, Norfolk, 1979-87, Hunton and Williams, Norfolk, 1987-92; exec. v.p., gen. counsel Columbus Am. Discovery Group, Inc., 1992—. Adj. prof. U. Dayton Law Sch.; asst. prof. mil. sci. Capital U.; pro bono counsel Nat. Commn. for Prevention Child Abuse, Norfolk, 1983, Tidewater Profl. Assn. on Child Abuse, 1983, Parents United Va., 1981-82, Sexual Abuse Help Line, 1983-86; mem. Boyd-Graves Conf. on Civil Procedure in Va., 1981-87. Contbr. articles to law revs.; contbg. editor: International Law for General Practitioners, 1981. Bd. dirs. Va. Opera Assn. Guild, Norfolk, 1983-87, Tidewater br. NCCJ, 1991-92; deacon Ctrl. Bapt. Ch., Norfolk, 1980-83. Capt. USAR, 1992—. Fulbright scholar, 1974. Mem. Va. State Bar Assn. (bd. dirs. internat. law sect. 1984-87, chmn. 1982-83), Va. Young Lawyers Assn. (cir. rep. 1984-88), Va. Assn. Def. Attys., Maritime Law Assn., Norfolk-Portsmouth Bar assn. (chmn. speakers bur. 1987-88), Assn. Def. Trial Attys. (chmn. Va. 1987), Def. Rsch. Inst., 1982-88. Avocations: camping, rowing, scuba diving. Admiralty, Federal civil litigation, Private international. Home: 60 Kenyon Brook Dr Worthington OH 43085-3629 Office: Columbus Am Discovery Group 433 W 6th Ave Columbus OH 43201-3136 E-mail: rrobol@ralaw.com

ROBRENO, EDUARDO C. federal judge; b. 1945; BA, Westfield State Coll., 1967; MA, U. Mass., 1969; JD, Rutgers U., 1978. With antitrust divsn. U.S. Dept Justice, Phila., 1978-81; ptnr. Meltzer & Schiffrin, 1981-86, Fox, Rothschild, O'Brien & Frankel, Phila., 1987-92; judge U.S. Dist. Ct. for Ea. Dist. Pa., 1992—. Mem. Jud. Conf. Com. on Bankruptcy Rules. Fellow Am. Law Inst. Office: US Courthouse Rm 3810 Philadelphia PA 19106

ROCCOGRANDI, ANTHONY JOSEPH, lawyer; b. N.Y.C., Apr. 2, 1935; s. Joseph Anthony and Mary (Cannella) R.; m. Paulette Bolinskey, Apr. 25, 1973; children: Jacqueline Marie, John Michael. BS, CCNY, 1956; JD, NYU, 1965. Bar: N.Y. 1968, D.C. 1969, U.S. Dist. Ct. (so. dist.) N.Y. 1969, U.S. Dist. Ct. D.C. 1969, U.S. Ct. Appeals (D.C. cir.) 1969, U.S. Supreme Ct. 1988. Atty., Bur. Drug Abuse Control, Washington, 1965-67; asst. chief counsel Bur. Narcotics and Dangerous Drugs, Dept. Justice, Washington, 1968-71; spl. asst. U.S. atty. Dept. Justice, Washington, 1969; gen. counsel Nat. Commn. on Marihuana and Drug Abuse, Washington, 1971-73; assoc., ptnr. Chayet & Sonnenreich, Washington, 1974-81; ptnr. Sonnenreich & Roccograndi, Washington, 1982—; cons. Med. Device Cons., Inc., Attleboro, Mass., 1981—; dir. Genetic Rsch. Labs., Inc. Author: The 1970 Federal Drug Act, 1973; also articles. Mem. Brent Soc., N.Y. State Bar Assn., D.C. Bar Assn., Fed. Bar Assn., ABA. Administrative and regulatory, General corporate, Health. Home: 201 Longview Dr Alexandria VA 22314-4832 Office: Sonnenreich & Roccograndi 2600 Virginia Ave NW Ste 301 Washington DC 20037-1924

ROCHE, JOHN J. lawyer, consultant; BS, Manhattan Coll., 1957; LLB, Harvard U., 1963. Assoc., then ptnr. Shearman & Sterling, 1963-89; exec. v.p. Citicorp/Citibank, N.A., N.Y.C., 1989-98; co-gen. counsel Citigroup, 1998-2000; ret., 2000. Office: Citigroup 909 3rd Ave Fl 28 New York NY 10043-0001

ROCHELLE, DUDLEY CECILE, lawyer; b. Franklinton, La., Sept. 10, 1950; s. James Cecil and Mildred Grace (Stennis) R. BA in Polit. Sci., La. State U., 1972; JD, Yale U., 1975. Bar: Ga. 1976, U.S. Dist. Ct. (no. dist.) Ga. 1976, U.S. Ct. Appeals (5th cir.) 1976, U.S. Tax Ct., U.S. Ct. Appeals (11th cir.) 1997; cert. arbitrator and mediator. Vista atty. Atlanta Legal Aid Soc., 1975-76; law clk. to Hon. Joel J. Fryer Fulton County Superior Ct., Atlanta, 1976-77; trial atty. U.S. Dept. Labor, 1977-82; assoc. Hendrick Spanos & Phillips PC, 1982-88, shareholder (ptnr.), 1988-94, Spanos & Rochelle, P.C., Atlanta, 1994-97; shareholder Littler Mendelson, P.C., 1997—. Bd. dirs. Ga. Pub. Policy Found., 1996—, Midtown Alliance, Atlanta, 1982-92; mem. adv. bd. Coverdell Leadership Inst., Atlanta, 1996—. Mem. State Bar Ga. (mem. labor sect.), Atlanta Bar Assn. (mem. labor/employment sect., chairperson alt. dispute resolution com. 1986-92, mem. bench and bar com. 1986-87), Christian Legal Soc., Federalist Soc., Yale Club Ga. (bd. dirs. 1982-86), So. Inst. Bus. and Profl. Ethics (chair faith and work com.). Republican. Avocations: outdoor activity, scuba diving, music. Alternative dispute resolution, Federal civil litigation, Labor. Home: 2745 Brook Grove Ct Atlanta GA 30339-5329 Office: Littler Mendelson PC 3348 Peachtree Rd NE Ste 1100 Atlanta GA 30326-1447 E-mail: DRochelle@littler.com

ROCHEZ, NICHOLAS DUTFIELD, lawyer; b. Crotdom, England, Apr. 13, 1954; s. Paul Dutfield and Joyce McRae R.; m. Hazel Mary Jemkinson, Dec. 28, 1984; children: Charlotte, Harry, Guy, Freddie. BA in Law, Middlesex, England, 1976; MA in Bus. Law, London, 1980. Solicitor Davies Arnold Cooper, 1980-84, ptbr., 1984-99, mng. ptnr., 1988-93; ptnr. LeBoeuf, Lamb, Greene & McRae, London, 2000—. Dir. Semple Tignot Roches, London, Domestic & Gen. Group. Mem. Law Soc. England & Wales. Alternative dispute resolution, Insurance, Professional liability. Home: Crockerhill House Crockerhill PO18 0LH England Office: LeBoeuf Lamb Greene & McRae 1 Minster Ct Mincing Ln London EC3R 7AA England Fax: 0207 459 5099. E-mail: nrochez@llgn.com

ROCHKIND, LOUIS PHILIPP, lawyer; b. Miami, Fla., June 25, 1948; s. Reuben and Sarah R.; m. Rosalind H. Rochkind, July 4, 1971. BA in Psychology cum laude, U. Mich., 1970, JD cum laude, 1974. Bar: Mich. 1974, U.S. Dist. Ct. (ea. dist.) Mich. 1974. Ptnr. Jaffe, Raitt, Heuer & Weiss, Detroit, 1974—. Adj. prof. law Wayne St. U. Law Sch.; lectr. various profl. assns. and orgns. Assoc. editor U. Mich. Law Rev.; contbr. articles to profl. jours. publs. Mem. Am. Coll. Bankruptcy Lawyers, Detroit Bar Assn. (local rules in bankruptcy subcom. creditor-debtor law sect. 1980—), Phi Kappa Phi. Bankruptcy, Consumer commercial, Contracts commercial. Office: Jaffe Raitt Heuer & Weiss One Woodward Ave Ste 2400 Detroit MI 48226 E-mail: larrol@jafferaitt.com

ROCHLIN, PAUL R. lawyer; b. Balt., Dec. 14, 1934; s. Jack Ellis and Sara (Levin) R.; m. Lois David, Oct. 25, 1962 (div. 1969); children— Greg, Jennifer; m. Joyce Tretick, July 12, 1973; children: Keith Sopher, Maura Sopher. LLB, U. Balt., 1958. Bar: Md. 1959, U.S. Dist. Ct. Md. 1959. Assoc. firm Milton Talkin, Balt., 1959-61; assoc. firm Rochlin & Settleman, Balt., 1961-63, ptnr., 1963-78, pres., sr. ptnr. Rochlin & Settleman, P.A., Balt., 1978— . Bd. dirs. Balt. Jewish Council, 1979. Mem. Assn. Trial Lawyers Am., Md. State Bar Assn., Balt. City Bar Assn., Md. Trial Lawyers Assn. (bd. dirs. 1988—). Jewish. Clubs: The Suburban, The Center. State civil litigation, Personal injury, Workers' compensation.

ROCK, HAROLD L. lawyer; b. Sioux City, Iowa, Mar. 13, 1932; s. Harold L. and Helen J. (Gormally) R.; m. Marilyn Beth Clark Rock, Dec. 28, 1954; children: Michael, Susan, John, Patrick, Michele, Thomas. BS, Creighton U., 1954, JD, 1959. Bar: Nebr., N.Y., Minn., Mont., Wyo. Law clk. to judge U.S. Ct. Appeals 8th Circuit, Omaha, 1959-60, Fitzgerald Hamer Brown & Leahy, Omaha, 1960-65; ptnr. Kutak Rock, 1965—. Chmn. Nebr. Bd. Bar Examiners, 1989-96; bd. dirs. Mid City Bank, Omaha. Bd. dirs. Douglas County Hist. Soc., 1992—, Nat. Equal Justice Libr., 1995—, Nebr. Humanities Coun., 1996—. Served to 1st lt. U.S. Army, 1954-56. Recipient Alumni Achievement award Creighton U., 1995. Mem. ABA (ho. of dels. 1970-96, bd. govs. 1992-95), Nebr. Bar Assn. (ho. of dels., bd. dirs. 1985—, pres. 1988, Nebr. Bar found. bd. dirs., 1982—), Omaha Bar Assn. (pres. 1972-73), Omaha Legal Aid Soc. (pres. 1969-72), Nebr. State Bd. Pub. Accts. (bd. dirs. 1981-85). Roman Catholic. Constitutional, General corporate, Securities. Office: Kutak Rock The Omaha Bldg 1650 Farnam St Ste A Omaha NE 68102-2186

ROCKEFELLER, SHIRLEY E. court clerk; b. Sayre, Pa., May 24, 1938; d. Clayton A. and Eva M. Baldwin Wilbur; m. Richard L. Rockefeller, Sept. 27, 1937; 1 child, Randy L. Student, Ridley's Sec. Sch., 1956-57. Legal sec. A.S. Moscrip, Esq., Towanda, Pa., 1961-64; clk. Register and Recorder's Office Bradford County, 1965-75; register, recorder and clk. of orphan's ct. Bradford County Courthouse, 1976—. Hospitality chmn. Rep. Women, Towanda, 1996-99, scrapbook chmn., 1998—. Mem. DAR (regent), Order of Ea. Star (sec. 1965-99), Tuscarora Hist. Soc., Pa. Register of Wills Assn. (exec. bd. 1998-99). Republican. Mem. United Ch. of Christ. Avocations: crocheting, cooking, traveling, fishing. Home: RR 2 Box 425 Rome PA 18837-9568 Office: Bradford County Courthouse 301 Main St Towanda PA 18848-1824

ROCKETT, D. JOE, lawyer, director; b. Cushing, Okla., May 3, 1942; s. Gordon Richard and Hazel Peggy (Rigsby) R.; m. Mary Montgomery, Aug. 31, 1963; children: David Montgomery, Ann Morley. BA, U. Okla., 1964, JD, 1967. Bar: Okla. 1967, U.S. Dist. Ct. (we. dist.) Okla. 1968. Assoc. Kerr, Davis, Irvine & Burbage, Oklahoma City, 1967-69, Andrews Davis Legg Bixler Milsten & Price, Oklahoma City, 1969-73, mem., 1973—, also bd. dirs., pres., 1986-90, 96-00. Securities law advisor Oil Investment Inst., Washington, 1984-87. Bd. dirs. Myriad Gardens Conservatory, Oklahoma City, 1987—, chmn., 1991-92. Mem. ABA (fed. regulation of securities and partnership coms. of bus. law sect. 1984), Okla. Bar Assn. (securities liaison com. 1983, chmn. bus. assocs. sect. 1985, securities adminstr.'s select com. 1986—). Avocations: sailing, fishing, skiing. General corporate, Mergers and acquisitions, Securities. Office: Andrews Davis Legg Bixler Milsten & Price 500 W Main St Ste 500 Oklahoma City OK 73102-2275 E-mail: djrockett@andrewsdavis.com

ROCKLEN, KATHY HELLENBRAND, lawyer, banker; b. N.Y.C., June 30, 1951; BA, Barnard Coll., 1973; JD magna cum laude, New England Sch. Law, 1977. Bar: N.Y. 1978, U.S. Dist. Ct. (so. and ea. dists.) N.Y. 1982, U.S. Dist. Ct. (no. dist.) Calif. 1985. Interpretive counsel N.Y. Stock Exchange, N.Y.C.; 1st v.p. E.F. Hutton & Co. Inc.; v.p., gen. counsel and sec. S.G Warburg (U.S.A.) Inc.; mem. Proskauer Rose LLP, N.Y.C. Mem. exec. com. lawyers divsn. Am. Friends Hebrew U. Mem. N.Y. State Bar Assn., N.Y. Women's Bar Assn., Assn. Bar City N.Y. (v.p., chmn. exec. com., chmn. drugs and law com., chmn. fed. legis. com., securities law com., sec. 2d century com., sex and law com., young lawyers'com., corp. law com.). Banking, General corporate, Securities. Office: Proskauer Rose LLP 1585 Broadway New York NY 10036 E-mail: krocklen@proskauer.com

ROCKOWITZ, NOAH EZRA, lawyer; b. N.Y.C., Apr. 11, 1949; s. Murray and Anna Rae (Cohen) R.; m. Julie Rachel Levitan, Dec. 24, 1978; children: Shira Aviva, Leora Civia, Dahlia Yaffa. BA, Queens Coll., 1969; JD, Fordham U., 1973. Bar: N.Y. 1974, U.S. Dist. Ct. (so and ea. dists.) N.Y. 1974, U.S. Ct. Appeals (2d cir.) 1974. Tchr., chmn. social studies dept. Intermediate Sch. 74, Queens, N.Y., 1969-73; atty. Cahill Gordon & Reindel, N.Y.C., 1973-78; corp. sec., asst. gen. counsel Belco Petroleum Corp., 1978-85; v.p., gen. counsel Hudson Gen. Corp., Great Neck, N.Y., 1985-98, sr. v.p., 1998—. Trustee, exec. com., chmn. bd. edn. The Solomon Schechter Sch. Westchester; trustee Beth El Synagogue of New Rochelle; Westchester adv. com. Bd. Jewish Edn. Greater N.Y. Mem. ABA, Am. Soc. Corp. Secs., N.Y. State Bar Assn., Assn. of Bar of City of N.Y., Am. Corp. Counsel Assn., Phi Beta Kappa. Contracts commercial, General corporate, Securities. Office: Hudson Gen Corp 111 Great Neck Rd PO Box 355 Great Neck NY 11022-0355

ROCKWELL, WILLIAM HEARNE, lawyer; b. Taunton, Mass., Oct. 28, 1919; s. Julius and Alice (Hearne) R.; grad. Philips Acad.; AB, U. Mich., 1941, MA, 1947; LLB, Columbia, 1950; m. Elizabeth Virginia Goode, Feb. 3, 1948; children: Enid Rockwell, Karen Rockwell, William Goode Rockwell (dec.). Bar: N.Y. 1950. Assoc. Donovan, Leisure, Newton & Irvine, 1950-51; asst. sec. The Valve Mfrs. Assn., 1951-55; sec. Am. Carpet Inst., Inc., 1956-66, sec., treas., 1966-68; sec., gen. counsel Am. Nat. Standards Inst., N.Y.C., 1969—, v.p., 1984—; gen. counsel Contemporary Dance, Inc., 1962—, Rondo Dance Theatre, Inc., 1970—, Montserrat Found., 1972—, Turns and Caicos Found., 1985—, Product Liability Prevention Conf., 1974—. Mem. bd. ethics Town of Pound Ridge, N.Y.; pres. Heritage Hills Soc., Ltd.; bd. dirs. Heritage Hills Soc., Ltd. Maj. Transp. Corps, AUS, 1941-46. Mem. ABA (anti-trust com.), Assn. Bar City N.Y., Am. Soc. Assn. Execs. (legal com.), N.Y. Soc. Assn. Execs., Nat. Safety Council, Nat. Panel Arbitrators, Am. Arbitration Assn., Columbia Law Sch. Alumni Assn. (dir.), Pound Ridge Land Conservancy, Heritage Hills Soc., Ltd. (bd. dirs.). Clubs: Belham River Valley Country; Montserrat Yacht; Pound Ridge Tennis; New York Athletic; University (Washington), Heritage Hills Golf. Office: 1430 Broadway New York NY 10018-3308

ROCKWOOD, LINDA LEE, lawyer; b. Cedar Rapids, Iowa, July 25, 1950; d. Robert Walter and Dorothy Jean (Rehberg) Sorensen; children: Holly Lynn, Christian Douglas. BA, U. Denver, 1972; JD, U. Tex., 1984. Bar: Colo. 1984, U.S. Dist. Ct. Colo., U.S. Ct. Appeals (10th cir.). Econ. and consumer research analyst May Dept. Stores, St. Louis, 1973-75; asst. dir. Ctr. for Study Am. Bus., Washington U., 1975-77; mgr. Mid-Columbia Symphony, Richland, Wash., 1978-79; assoc. Holland & Hart, Denver, 1984-88; shareholder, dir. Parcel, Mauro & Spaanstra, 1988-98, pres., 1996-98; ptnr. Faegre & Benson, 1998—. Author: New Mines From Old Environmental Considerations in Remining and Reprocessing of Waste Materials, 1991, The Alcan Decisions: Causation Through the Back Door, 1993, RCRA Demystified: The Professional's Guide to Hazardous Waste Law, 1996, Citizen Suits: Public Interest or Private Advocacy, 2000, Institutional Controls: Brownfields Superweapon or Ultimate Trojan Horse?, 2000. Bd. dirs. Colo. Hazardous Waste Mgmt. Soc., 1986, 89-91, pres., 1987-88; mem. Mayor's Convention Ctr. Task Force, 1997-99, Ctrl. Platte Valley Devel. Coun., 1999—. Mem. ABA (vice chmn. environ. values com. adminstrv. law sect. 1986-91, hard minerals com. natural resources law sect. 1987-90), Colo. Bar Assn. (exec. coun. environ. law sect. 1987-90), Environ. Law Inst., Rocky Mountain Mineral Law Found., Order of Coif, Phi Beta Kappa. Administrative and regulatory, Environmental. Office: Faegre & Benson LLP 2500 Republic Plaza 370 17th St Denver CO 80202-5665 E-mail: lrockwoo@faegre.com

RODEFER, JEFFREY ROBERT, lawyer, prosecutor; b. Santa Fe, Mar. 29, 1963; s. Robert Jacob and Joanne D. (Thomas) R. BS, U. Nev., 1985; JD, cert. dispute resolution, Willamette U., 1988. Bar: Calif. 1990, Nev. 1990, U.S. Dist. Ct. Nev. 1990, U.S. Dist. Ct. (ea. dist.) Calif. 1990, U.S. Ct. Appeals (9th cir.) 1990, Colo. 1991, Oreg. 1997, U.S. Supreme Ct. 1997; cert. arbitrator, Nev. Legal intern Willamette U. Legal Aid Clinic, Salem, Oreg., 1987-88; legal rschr. transp. divsn. Nev. Atty. Gen. Office, Carson City, 1989-90, dep. atty. gen. taxation divsn., 1990-93, dep. atty. gen. gaming divsn., 1993-99, sr. dep. atty. gen. gaming divsn., 1999-2001, asst. chief dep. atty. gen. gaming divsn., 2001—. Author: Nevada Property Tax Manual, 1993, Nevada Gaming Law Index, 1999; contbr. articles to Nev. Lawyer. Contbg. mem. U. Nev. Coll. Bus. Adminstrn. and Athletic Dept., Reno, 1992, Willamette U. Coll. Law, Ann. Law Fund, Salem, 1992; active Nat. Parks and Recreation Assn., Washington, 1991; mem. First Christian Ch. Mem. Internat. Assn. Gaming Attys., U. Nev. Coll. Bus. Alumni Assn., Am. Inns of Ct. (Bruce R. Thompson chpt.), State Bar Nev. (functional equivalency com. 1993—, chmn. gaming law sect. 2000—), Phi Delta Phi. Republican. Office: Nev Atty Gen Office 555 E Washington Ave Ste 3900 Las Vegas NV 89101-1068 Fax: 702-486-2377. E-mail: jrrodefe@ag.state.nv.us

RODEMEYER, MICHAEL LEONARD, JR. lawyer; b. Balt., May 25, 1950; s. Michael Leonard and Claire Isabel (Gunther) R.; m. Dorrit Carolyn Green, June 7, 1975; children: Justin, Christoffer. AB, Princeton U., 1972; JD, Harvard U., 1975. Bar: Md. 1977, D.C. 1980, U.S. Ct. Appeals (10th cir.) 1980. Atty. Fed. Trade Commn., Washington, 1976-81, atty. advisor, 1981-84; counsel Subcom. on Natural Resources, Agr. Rsch. & Environ., 1984-88; staff dir., counsel U.S. Ho. of Reps., 1988-90, house com. on sci., chief dem. counsel, 1990-98; asst. dir. for environment White House Office of Sci. and Tech. Policy, 1998-99, dem. legis. dir., 1999-2000; exec. dir. Pew Initiative on Food and Biotech., 2000—. Democrat. Avocations: computing, bicycling. Home: 6000 Harvard Ave Glen Echo MD 20812-1114 Office: Pew Initiative on Food and Biotech 1331 H St NW Ste 900 Washington DC 20005 E-mail: m_rodemeyer@pewagbiotech.org

RODENBURG, CLIFTON GLENN, lawyer; b. Jamestown, N.D., Apr. 5, 1949; s. Clarence and Dorothy Irene (Peterman) R.; m. Donna Michele Stockman, Mar. 1, 1980. BS, N.D. State U., 1971; JD, U. N.D., 1974; M.L.I.R., Mich. State U., 1976. Bar: N.D. 1974, U.S. Dist. Ct. N.D. 1974, U.S. Ct. Appeals (8th cir.) 1974, Minn. 1980, U.S. Supreme Ct. 1980, S.D. 1983, Nebr. 1984, U.S. Dist. Ct. Minn. 1984, U.S. Dist. Ct. Nebr. 1984, Wis. 1985, U.S. Dist. Ct. Wis. 1985, Mont. 1986, U.S. Dist. Ct. Mont. 1986, bd. cert. Creditors' Rights Law, Am. Bd. Cert. Ptnr. Johnson, Rodenburg & Lauinger, Fargo, N.D., 1976—; pres., gen. counsel Rodenburg Group, Inc., 1980—. Contbg. editor: The Developing Labor Law, 1976-80; drafter N.D. garnishment statutes, 1982. Mem. Acad. Comml. and Bankruptcy Law Specialists. Consumer commercial, Contracts commercial, Labor.

RODGERS, FREDERIC BARKER, judge; b. Albany, N.Y., Sept. 29, 1940; s. Prentice Johnson and Jane (Weed) R.; m. Valerie McNaughton, Oct. 8, 1988; 1 child: Gabriel Moore. AB, Amherst Coll., 1963; JD, Union U., 1966. Bar: N.Y. 1966, U.S. Ct. Mil. Appeals 1968, Colo. 1972, U.S. Supreme Ct. 1974, U.S. Ct. Appeals (10th cir.) 1981, U.S. Ct. Appeals (fed. cir.) 2001. Chief dep. dist. atty., Denver, 1972-73; commr. Denver Juvenile Ct., 1973-79; mem. Mulligan Reeves Teasley & Joyce, P.C., Denver, 1979-80; pres. Frederic B. Rodgers, P.C., Breckenridge, Colo., 1980-89; ptnr. McNaughton & Rodgers, Central City, 1989-91; county ct. judge

Gilpin County Combined Cts., 1987—. Presiding mcpl. judge cities of Breckenridge, Blue River, Black Hawk, Central City, Edgewater, Empire, Idaho Springs, Silver Plume and Westminster, Colo., 1978-96; chmn. com. on mcpl. ct. rules of procedure Colo. Supreme Ct., 1984-96; mem. gen faculty Nat. Jud. Coll. U. Nev., Reno, 1990—, elected to faculty coun., 1993-99 (chair 1999). Author: (with Dilweg, Fretz, Murphy and Wicker) Modern Judicial Ethics, 1992; contbr. articles to profl. jours. Mem. Colo. Commn. on Children, 1982-85, Colo. Youth Devel. Coun., 1989-98, Colo. Family Peace Task Force, 1994-96. Served with JAGC, U.S. Army, 1967-72; to maj. USAR, 1972-88. Decorated Bronze Star with oak leaf cluster, Air medal. Recipient Outstanding County Judge award Colo. 17th Judicial Dist. Victim Adv. Coalition, 1991; Spl. Community Svc. award Colo. Am. Legion, 1979. Fellow Am. Bar Found., Colo. Bar. Found. (life); mem. ABA (jud. div. exec. coun. 1989-2000, vice-chair 1996-97, chair-elect 1997, chair 1998-99, mem. Ho. of Dels. 1993—, jud. divsn. del. to ABA nominating com. 2000—, bd. govs. Dist. 11 2001—), Colo. Bar Assn. (bd. govs. 1986-88, 90-92, 93-99), Continental Divide Bar Assn., Denver Bar Assn. (bd. trustees 1979-82), First Jud. dist. Bar Assn. (trustee 2000—), Nat. Conf. Spl. Ct. Judges (chmn. 1989-90), Colo. County Judges Assn. (pres. 1995-96), Colo. Mcpl. Judges Assn. (pres. 1986-87), Colo. Trial Judges Coun. (v.p. 1994-95, sec. 1996-97), Denver Law Club (pres. 1981-82), Colo. Women's Bar Assn., Am. Judicature Soc., Nat. Coun. Juvenile and Family Ct. Judges, Federalist Soc. for Law and Pub. Policy Studies, Judge Advs. Assn., Univ. Club (Denver), Arlberg Club (Winter Park), Marines Meml. Club (San Francisco), Rotary (charter pres. Peak to Peak 2000—, Paul Harris fellow 1996). Episcopalian. Office: Gilpin County Justice Ctr Central City CO 80427-0398 E-mail: frederic.rodgers@judicial.state.co.us

RODGERS, JOHN HUNTER, lawyer; b. Lubbock, Tex., Jan. 18, 1944; s. James O'Donnell Rodgers and Dorothy (Ulin) Carpenter; m. Anne C. Smith, Nov. 29, 1969; children; Anne Elizabeth, Catherine Hunter. BA, Tex. A&M, 1966; JD, U. Tex., 1969. Bar: Tex. 1969, U.S. Supreme Ct. 1973. Atty. The Southland Corp., Dallas, 1973-79, gen. counsel, 1979-91, sec., 1987-95, sr. v.p., chief adminstrv. officer, 1991-93, exec. v.p., chief adminstrv. officer, 1993-95; pres. Clairemead Corp., 1996-2000; sr. v.p., gen. counsel, sec. Am. Pad & Paper Co., 1998-2000, pres., 2000—. Mem. visual arts com. Tex. A&M U., 1985-94, bd. dirs. student fund enrichment bd., 1986-94; mem. exec. com. Jr. Achievement Dallas, 1988-93; mem. Dallas Citizens Coun., 1992-95; bd. dirs. Boys and Girls Clubs of Greater Dallas, 1998—; nat. chair Tulane U. Parents Coun., 1997-98; trustee Goals for Dallas, 1991-92; nat. bd. dirs. Boys and Girls Clubs Am., 1993-98; mem. mktg. com. Dallas Mus. Art, 1994-97. Capt. JAGC, U.S. Army, 1969-73, Vietnam. Mem. ABA, Tex. Bar Assn. (coun. mem. corp. counsel sect. 1988), Dallas Bar Assn., Southwestern Legal Found. (adv. bd. Internat. and Comparative Law Ctr., rsch. fellow 1986-94), Nat. Assn. Convenience Stores (bd. dirs. 1993-95). Roman Catholic. Contracts commercial, General corporate, Mergers and acquisitions. Office: 17304 Preston Rd Ste 700 Dallas TX 75252

RODGERS, RICARDO JUAN (RICK RODGERS), lawyer; b. Ardmore, Okla., Sept. 25, 1934; s. John Bush and Gladys Louise (James) R.; 1 child, Michelle Xan. B.B.A., U. Okla., 1963, J.D., 1965. Bar: Okla. 1965, U.S. Dist. Ct. (we. dist.) Okla. 1965, U.S. Supreme Ct. 1974. Asst. county atty. Stephens County Duncan, Okla., 1965-66; ptnr. Bennett & Rodgers, Duncan, 1966-74; sr. ptnr., pres. Rodgers & Link, P.C., Duncan, 1974— . Chmn. Duncan United Fund, 1969; trustee Okla. Christian Coll., 1968. Served with USN, 1955-57. Recipient Leadership award Sooner council Girl Scouts U.S., 1979, Disting. Service award Jaycees, 1969. Fellow Okla. Bar Found. (bd. dirs. 1978-83); mem. Okla. Bar Corp. Ins. Co. (trustee), Okla. Bar Assn. (bd. govs. 1977-79), Okla. Trial Lawyers Assn. (bd. dirs., v.p. 1986, pres.-elect 1989), ABA, Okla. U. Law Sch. Alumni Assn. (bd. dirs. 1973). Mem. Ch. of Christ. Lodge: Elks. Federal civil litigation, State civil litigation, Personal injury. Home: 2206 Carolin Dr Duncan OK 73533-3204

RODGERS, RICHARD M. management consultant, lawyer; b. Bklyn., Aug. 29, 1941; s. Lincoln and Dorothy (Zimmerman) R.; m. Sharan Raye Kaufman, Nov. 16, 1969; children: Jennifer Lynn, Suzanne Bari. BA, Adelphi U., 1963; MS, MBA in Indsl. Mgmt., Poly Inst. N.Y., 1973; JD, Bklyn. Law Sch., 1979. Bar: N.Y. 1980, Fla. 1980, U.S. Dist. Ct. (so. and ea. dists.) N.Y. 1980, U.S. Tax Ct. 1981, Pa. 1987, U.S. Dist. Ct. (ea. dist.) Pa. 1988, U.S. Supreme Ct. 1992. Mgr. N.Y. Tel., N.Y.C., 1967-71; v.p., dir. ops. ITT Comm. Sys., Hartford, Conn., 1971-74; supervising sys. analyst N.Y. State Office of Ct. Adminstrn., N.Y.C., 1974-80; dir. contracts adminstrn. Alta Tech., Inc., Stamford, Conn., 1981-84; cons. The Rodgers Group, Valley Stream, N.Y., 1984—. Prof. bus. adminstrn. Adelphia U., Garden City, N.Y., 1985—. 1st lt. U.S. Army, 1963-66. N.Y. State Bd. Regents scholar, 1979. Mem. ABA, N.Y. State Bar Assn., Fla. Bar Assn., Pa. Bar Assn., Montgomery County Bar Assn., Masons, Shriners. Republican. Jewish. Office: 210 Wooded Ln Ambler PA 19002-2429

RODMAN, LAWRENCE BERNARD, lawyer; b. N.Y.C., Oct. 4, 1949; s. Leroy E. and Toby (Chertcoff) R.; m. Linda Frank, June 25, 1978; children: Tara A., Max E. AB, Princeton U., 1970; JD, Harvard U., 1973. Bar: N.Y. 1974, U.S. Dist. Ct. (so. and ea. dists.) N.Y. 1974, U.S. Ct. Appeals (2d cir.) 1974. Law clk. U.S. Dist. Ct., So. Dist. N.Y., N.Y.C., 1973-74; assoc. Cleary, Gottlieb, Steen & Hamilton, N.Y.C., 1974-78; ptnr. law firm Rodman & Rodman, N.Y.C., 1978-89, Teitelbaum, Hiller, Rodman, Paden & Hibsher, P.C., 1990—. Trustee Brookdale Hosp. Med. Ctr., Bklyn., 1982-86, Associated YM-YWHA of Greater N.Y., 1986—. Mem. ABA, Assn. Bar City N.Y. Republican. Jewish. Club: Harvard. General corporate, Real property. Home: 1175 Park Ave New York NY 10128-1211 Office: Teitelbaum Hiller Rodman Paden & Hibsher PC 260 Madison Ave New York NY 10016-2401

RODOVICH, ANDREW PAUL, magistrate; b. Hammond, Ind., Feb. 24, 1948; s. Andrew H. and Julia (Makar) R.; m. Gail Linda Patrick, May 27, 1972; children: Caroline Anja, Mary Katherine, James Patrick. BA, Valparaiso (Ind.) U., 1970, JD, 1973. Bar: Ind. Ptnr. Hand, Muenich & Rodovich, Hammond, 1973-78; chief dep. prosecutor Lake County Prosecutor's Office, Crown Point, Ind., 1979-82; U.S. magistrate U.S. Dist. Ct., Hammond, 1982—. Referee Hammond City Ct., 1978; adj. prof. Valparaiso Law Sch., 1985—. Fellow Ind. Bar Found.; mem. Nat. Coun. U.S. Magistrates, Delta Theta Phi. Republican. Avocations: sports. Home: 7207 Baring Pky Hammond IN 46324-2218 Office: US Dist Ct 136 Federal Bldg Hammond IN 46320-1529

RODOWSKY, LAWRENCE FRANCIS, retired state judge; b. Balt., Nov. 10, 1930; s. Lawrence Anthony and Frances (Gardner) R.; m. Colby Fossett, Aug. 7, 1954; children: Laura Rodowsky Ramos, Alice Rodowsky-Seegers, Emily Rodowsky Savopoulos, Sarah Jones Rodowsky, Gregory, Katherine Rodowsky O'Connor. AB, Loyola Coll., Balt., 1952; LLB, U. Md., 1956. Bar: Md. 1956. Ct. crier, law clk. U.S. Dist. Ct. Md., 1954-56; asst. atty. gen. State of Md., 1960-61; assoc., ptnr. firm Frank, Bernstein, Conaway & Goldman, Balt., 1956-79; judge Ct. Appeals Md., Annapolis, 1980-2000, rules com., 1969-80. Lectr., asst. instr. U. Md. Law Sch., 1958-68, 87-91; reporter jud. dept. Md. Constl. Conv. Commn., 1966-67. Chmn. Gov. Md. Commn. Racing Reform, 1979. Fellow Am. Coll. Trial Lawyers; mem. Md. Bar Assn., Balt. Bar Assn. Roman Catholic. Home: 4306 Norwood Rd Baltimore MD 21218-1118 Office: 620 CM Mitchell Jr Courthse 100 N Calvert St Baltimore MD 21202 E-mail: Lawrence.Rodowsky@courts.state.md.us

RODRIGUEZ, ANNABELLE, state attorney general; BA, JD, U. P.R. From asst. solicitor gen. to solicitor gen. P.R. Dept. Justice; ptnr. Martino, Odell & Calabria, Hato Rey, PR, 1993—96; judge U.S. Dist Ct. (P.R. dist.), 1996; atty. gen. Commonwealth of P.R., 2001—. Office: Atty Gen PO Box 9020192 San Juan PR 00902*

RODRIGUEZ, ANTONIO JOSE, lawyer; b. New Orleans, Dec. 7, 1944; s. Anthony Joseph and Josephine Olga (Cox) R.; m. Virginia Anne Soignet, Aug. 23, 1969; children: Henry Jacob, Stephen Anthony. BS, U.S. Naval Acad., 1966; JD cum laude, Loyola U. of the South, New Orleans, 1973. Bar: La. 1973, U.S. Dist. Ct. (ea. dist.) La. 1973, U.S. Ct. Appeals (5th cir.) 1973, U.S. Dist. Ct. (mid. dist.) La. 1975, U.S. Dist. Ct. (we. dist.) La. 1977, U.S. Ct. Appeals (11th cir.) 1981, U.S. Supreme Ct. 1987, U.S. Dist. Ct. (so. dist.) Miss. 1991, U.S. Ct. Appeals (4th cir.) 1991, U.S. Ct. Appeals (1st cir.) 1997, U.S. Ct. Internat. Trade, 1991. Assoc. Phelps, Dunbar, Marks, Claverie & Sims, New Orleans, 1973-77; ptnr. Phelps Dunbar, 1977-92, Fowler Rodriguez Kingsmill Flint, Gray & Chalos, LLP, New Orleans, 1992—. Prof. law Tulane U., New Orleans, 1981—; mem. nat. rules of the road adv. coun. U.S. Dept. Transp., Washington, 1987-90, chmn. nat. navigation safety adv. coun., 1990-94, mem., 2000—; spkr. on admiralty and environ. Co-author: Admiralty-Limitation of Liability, 1981—, Admiralty-Law of Collision, 1990—; author: (chpt.) Benedict on Admiralty, 1995—; assoc. editor Loyola Law Rev., 1971-73; contbr. articles to profl. maritime and environ. jours. Bd. dirs. Greater New Orleans Coun. Navy League, 1988—, Propeller Club of New Orleans, 1997—. Lt. USN, 1966-70; capt. USNR, 1970-95. Decorated Navy Commendation medal; recipient Disting. Pub. Svc. award U.S. Dept. Transp., 1993. Fellow La. Bar Found.; mem. ABA, La. State Bar Assn., La. State Law Inst., Maritime Law Assn. U.S. (proctor 1975—), New Orleans Bar Assn., Southeastern Admiralty Law Inst., Assn. Average Adjusters U.S., Assn. Average Adjusters U.K., Naval Res. Assn. (chpt. pres. 1982-84), U.S. Naval Acad. Alumni Assn. (chpt. pres. 1981-83), Bienville club, Phi Alpha Delta, Alpha Sigma Nu. Republican. Roman Catholic. Admiralty, General civil litigation, Environmental. Home: 4029 Mouton St Metairie LA 70002-1303 Office: Fowler Rodriguez Kingsmill Flint Gray & Chalos LLP 201 Saint Charles Ave Fl 36 New Orleans LA 70170-1000

RODRIGUEZ, MARINA, lawyer, former judge; b. Cartagena, Colombia, Dec. 10, 1946; d. Molses Rodriguez and Mariana Madrid; m. Jose Carrasoosa Bachelor, Liceo Soledad Acosta, Cartagena, Colomia, 1956; D in Law and Polit. Sci., U. Cartagena, 1972; M in Jud. Assessory of Enterprises, Ctrl. U. of Caracas, 1980. Clk. of penal tribunal, Cartagena, Colombia, 1969-72; civil judge of first instance Colombia, 1972-78; chief fgn. dept. Carrasosa & Asociados, Caracas, 1980-96, pres., 1996—. Mem. Inter Am. Assn. of Indsl. Property, Asociacion Colombiana de la Propiedad Indsl. Avocations: art, history, music. Office: Carrascosa & Asociados Esquina Jesuitaas Torre Bandagro Pent Ho PO Box 154 Caracas 1010-A Venezuela Fax: (582) 8612671. E-mail: ext@carrascosa.com

RODRIGUEZ, VIVIAN N. lawyer, accountant; b. Riverdale, N.Y., Dec. 16, 1969; d. Felix and Maria Rodriguez. AA in Bus., Miami Dade C.C., Miami, Fla., 1989; B of Acctg., Fla. Internat. U., Miami, 1991, M of Acctg., 1992; JD, U. Miami, 1995, LLM in Taxation, 2001. Bar: Fla.; CPA, Fla. Acct. Norman A. Eliot & Co., Miami, 1991-96; atty., acct. Managed Recovery Svcs. Corp., 1996-97; sole practitioner, 1997—. Mem. ABA, AICPA, ATLA, Am. Assn. Atty.-CPAs, Fla. Assn. Atty.-CPAs, Fla. Inst. CPAs, Dade County Bar Assn., Fla. Bar. Republican. Roman Catholic. Avocation: science fiction. Estate planning, Probate, Taxation, general.

RODRIGUEZ-DIAZ, JUAN E. lawyer; b. Ponce, P.R., Dec. 27, 1941; s. Juan and Auristela (Diaz-Alvarado) Rodriguez de Jesus; m. Sonia de Hostos-Anca, Aug. 10, 1966; children: Juan Eugenio, Jorge Eduardo, Ingrid Marie Rodriguez. BA, Yale U., 1963; LLB, Harvard U., 1966; LLM in Taxation, NYU, 1969. Bar: N.Y. 1968, P.R. 1970. Assoc. Baker & McKenzie, N.Y.C., 1966-68, McConnell, Valdes, San Juan, P.R.; undersec. Dept. Treasury P.R., 1971-73; mem. Sweeting, Pons, Gonzalez & Rodriguez, 1973-81; pvt. practice San Juan, 1981-94, Totti & Rodriguez-Diaz, 1994—. Bd. dirs. Ochoa Indsl. Sales Corp., Ensco Caribe, Inc., Industrias Vassallo, Inc. Bd. govs. Aqueduct and Sewer Authority P.R., 1979-84; mem. adv. com. collective bargaining negotiation of P.R. elec. Power Authority to Gov. P.R., 1977-78; bd. govs. P.R. coun. Boy Scouts Am., mem. transition com., 1984-85; mem. adminstrv. coun. Ballajá. Mem. N.Y. State Bar Assn., P.R. Bar Assn., AFDA Club, Berwind Country Club, Palmas de Mar Country Club. Contracts commercial, General corporate, Taxation, general. Office: Suite 1200 416 Ave Ponce De Leon Hato Rey San Juan PR 00918-3418 E-mail: JERD@TRDLAW.com

ROE, CHARLES BARNETT, lawyer; b. Tacoma, June 25, 1932; s. Charles Brown and Gladys Luvena (Harding) R.; m. Marilyn Marie Quam, July 31, 1954; children: Sharon Lynn De Groot, Jeannine Carole Roe Dellwo. AB, U. Puget Sound, 1953; postgrad. U. Calif., Berkeley, 1957-58; JD, U. Wash., 1960. Bar: Wash. 1960, U.S. Dist. Ct. (ea. and we. dists.) 1960, U.S. Ct. Appeals (9th cir.) 1963, U.S. Supreme Ct. 1963, U.S. Ct. Appeals (D.C. cir.) 1964. Asst. atty. gen. depts. natural resources, conservation, water resources and pollution control commn., State of Wash., Olympia, 1960-70, asst. dir. dept. water resources, 1967-69, sr. asst. atty. gen., 1970-90; of counsel Perkins Coie, Olympia, 1991—; chief counsel dept. ecology and nuclear waste, 1970-85, Nuclear Waste Bd., 1983-90; counsel natural resources com. Wash. Ho. of Reps., Olympia, 1970; adj. prof. Gonzaga U. Sch. Law, Spokane, 1973-76, U. Puget Sound Law Sch., 1985-90; contractor Nat. Water Commn., Washington, 1970-71. Rep., Western States Water Coun., Salt Lake City, 1970-90; sec. Olympia Audubon Soc., 1962-63; chmn. bd. mgrs. United Chs., Olympia, 1967-68. Served to 1st USAF, 1954-57. Mem. ABA (chmn. water resources com. natural resources sect. 1981-83), Wash. State Bar (chmn. environ. law sect. 1971-72), Washington Cts. Hist. Soc. (bd. dirs. 1998—), Mason, Rotary, Kappa Sigma, Phi Delta Phi. Mem. United Ch. of Christ. Home: 2400 Wedgewood Dr SE Olympia WA 98501-3841 Office: Perkins Coie 1110 Capitol Way S Ste 405 Olympia WA 98501-2251

ROE, MARK J. law educator; b. N.Y.C., Aug. 8, 1951; m. Helen Hsu, Aug. 12, 1974; children: Andrea Hsu, Jessica Hsu. BA, Columbia U., 1972; JD, Harvard U., 1975. Bar: N.Y. 1976. Atty. Fed. Res. Bank, N.Y.C., 1975-77; assoc. Cahill Gordon & Reindel, 1977-80; prof. Rutgers U. Law Sch., Newark, 1980-86, U. Pa. Law Sch., 1986-88, Columbia U. Law Sch., N.Y.C., 1988-2001, Harvard Law Sch., Cambridge, Mass., 2001—. Author: Strong Managers, Weak Owners: The Political Roots of American Corporate Finance, 1994, Corporate Reorganization and Bankruptcy, 2000. Office: Harvard Law Sch 435 W 116th St Cambridge MA 02138 E-mail: mroe@law.harvard.edu

ROE, ROGER ROLLAND, JR. lawyer; b. Mpls., Dec. 31, 1947; s. Roger Rolland Roe Jr.; m. Paula Speltz, 1974; children: Elena, Madeline. BA, Grinnell Coll., 1970; JD, U. Minn., 1973. Bar: Minn. 1973, U.S. Dist. Ct. Minn. 1974, U.S. Ct. Appeals (8th cir.) 1977, U.S. Supreme Ct. 1978, Wis. 1988, U.S. Dist. Ct. Nebr. 1995, U.S. Dist. Ct. (ea. and we. dists.) Wis. Law clk. to Hon. Judge Amdahl Hennepin County Dist. Ct., Mpls., 1973-74; from assoc. to ptnr. Rider, Bennett, Egan & Arundel, 1974-91; mng. ptnr. Yaeger, Jungbauer, Barczak, Roe & Vucinovich, PLC, 1992-2000; ptnr. Best & Flanagan LLP, 2000—. Mem. nat. panel arbitrators Am. Arbitration Assn.; judge trial practice class and moot ct. competitions law sch. U. Minn.; guest lectr. Minn. Continuing Legal Edn. courses. Fellow Internat. Soc. Barristers; mem. ATLA (guest lectr.), Am. Bd. Trial Advs. (diplomat, Minn. chpt. pres. 1996-97), Minn. Trial Lawyers Assn., Million Dollar Round Table, Mich. Trial Lawyers Assn. Avocations: golfing, downhill skiing. General civil litigation, Personal injury, Product liability. Office: Best & Flanagan LLP 601 2d Ave S # 4000 Minneapolis MN 55402

ROEDDER, WILLIAM CHAPMAN, JR. lawyer; b. St. Louis, June 21, 1946; s. William Chapman and Dorothy (Reifeiss) R.; m. Gwendolyn Arnold, Sept. 13, 1968; children: William Chapman, Barcley Shane. BS, U. Ala., 1968; JD cum laude, Cumberland U., 1972. Bar: Ala. Law clk. to chief justice Ala. Supreme Ct., Montgomery, 1972; ptnr. McDowell Knight Roedder & Sledge, L.L.C., Mobile, Ala., 1997—. Comments editor Cumberland-Samford Law Rev.; contbr. articles to legal publs. Mem. ABA (vice chair com. trial tactics, torts and ins. practice 1995-96), Ala. State Bar Assn., Mobile County Bar Assn. (past sec., past chmn. ethics com. 1988-90, grievance com. 1994-96), Fed. Ins. and Corp. Counsel (chmn. products liability sect. 1990-93, regional v.p. 1994-96, bd. dirs. 1993-2000, exec. com. 1997—, sec.-treas. 1999-2000, pres.-elect 2000-2001), Ala. Def. Lawyers Assn., Curia Honoris, Order of Barristers, Def. Rsch. Inst., Phi Alpha Delta (pres. 1971-72). E-mial. Aviation, General civil litigation, Contracts commercial. Home: 211 Levert Ave Mobile AL 36607-3219 Office: McDowell Knight Roedder & Sledge LLC PO Box 350 Mobile AL 36601-0350 E-mail: broedder@mcdowellknight.com

ROESER, RONALD O. lawyer, consultant; b. Berwyn, Ill., May 6, 1950; s. John O. and Mary Jean (Marsden) R.; m. Susan Marie Gill, July 22, 1972; children: Michelle Marie, Michael Franklin. BA, So. Ill. U., 1972; JD, DePaul U., 1975. Bar: Ill. 1975, U.S. Dist. Ct. (no. dist.) Ill. 1975, U.S.Tax. Ct. 1975, U.S. Ct. Appeals (7th cir.) 1975. Assoc. Imming & Faber, Elgin, Ill., 1975-77; ptnr. Imming, Faber & Roeser, 1977-81, Imming & Roeser, Elgin, 1981-83, Roeser & Vucha, Elgin, 1983-84, Roeser, Vucha & Carbary, Elgin, 1984—. Mem. Fed. Trial Bar, Ill. Bar Assn., Kane County Bar Assn., Chgo. Bar Assn., Ill. Trial Lawyers Assn., Dundee Jaycees (treas., bd. dirs. 1975—, Outstanding Merit awards 1976, 78, 81), Lions. Republican. Roman Catholic. Avocations: history, reading, contact sports. General civil litigation, Contracts commercial. Home: 34w921 Duchesne Dr Dundee IL 60118-3101 Office: Roeser & Vucha 920 Davis Rd Elgin IL 60123-1390

ROESLER, JOHN BRUCE, lawyer, consultant; b. Portland, Oreg., Oct. 9, 1943; s. Bruce Emil and Charlotte Amanda (Naess) R.; m. Kathryne Elise Nilsen, Aug. 14, 1965; children: Paul, Mark, Nico. BA, U. Kans., 1966, JD, 1971. Bar: Mo. 1971, N.Mex. 1979, Colo. 1998, U.S. Dist. Ct. (we. dist.) Mo. 1971, U.S. Dist. Ct. N.Mex. 1979, U.S. Dist. Ct. Colo. 1998. U.S. Ct. Appeals (10th cir.) 1979, U.S. Ct. Appeals (5th cir.) 1988, U.S. Ct. Appeals (4th cir.) 1992, U.S. Supreme Ct. 1987. Assoc. The Gage Firm, Kansas City, Mo., 1971-74; civil rights advocate State of N.Mex. Human Rights, Santa Fe, 1977-78; law clk. Hon. Edwin L. Felter N.Mex. Supreme Ct., 1978-79; asst. dist. atty. Taos (N.Mex.) Dist. Atty.'s Office, 1979-80; asst. spl. pros. Santa Fe Dist. Atty.'s Office, 1980-82; pvt. practice Santa Fe, 1982-97; of counsel Roth, Van Amberg, Gross, Rogers & Ortiz, 1991-94; spl. asst. atty. gen. Colo. Atty. Gen's Office, 1997-99; assoc. Jones & Keller, Denver, 1999-2000; pvt. prac., 2000—. Instr. John Marshall Law Sch., Chgo., summer 1974; spkr. edn., law and civil rights issues, 2000, U. Miami Law Sch., 1991, U. Miami Sch. Medicine, 1991. Author: (books) How To Find the Best Lawyers, In Harm's Way: Is Your Child Safe in School; mem. law rev. U. Kans. Sch. Law, 1970-71; contbr. articles to profl. jours. and treatise. Mem. Colo. Bar Assn., Denver Bar Assn., Colo. Trial Lawyers Assn. Democrat. Roman Catholic. Avocation: downhill skiing, hiking, gardening. Civil rights, Federal civil litigation, Education and schools. Home: 2571 S Sherman St Denver CO 80210-5725

ROESSLER, P. DEE, lawyer, former judge, educator; b. McKinney, Tex., Nov. 4, 1941; d. W.D. and Eunice Marie (Medcalf) Powell; m. George L. Roessler, Jr., Nov. 16, 1963 (div. Dec. 1977); children: Laura Diane, Trey. Student, Austin Coll., 1960-61, 62-64, Wayland Bapt. Coll., 1961-62; BA, U. West Fla., 1968; postgrad., East Tex. State U., 1975, U. Tex.-Dallas, 1977; JD, So. Meth. U., 1982. Bar: Tex. 1982, U.S. Dist. Ct. (ea. dist.) Tex. 1983, U.S. Dist. Ct. (no. dist.) Tex. 1983, U.S. Supreme Ct. 2000. Tchr. Van Alstyne Ind. Sch. Dist., Tex., 1968-69; social worker Dept. Social Svcs., Fayetteville, N.C., 1971-73, Dept. Human Svcs., Sherman and McKinney, 1973-79, 81; assoc. atty. Abernathy & Roeder, McKinney, 1982-85, Ronald W. Uselton, Sherman, 1985-86; prof., program coord. for real estate Collin County C.C., McKinney, 1986-87, prof. criminal justice, 1986-91, legal asst., 1986-99; asst. county atty. Grayson County, Tex., 1999-2000; solo practice, 2000—. Mcpl. judge City of Mckinney Mcpl. Ct., 1986-89; mem. Tex. State Bar Com. on Legal Assts., 1990-94, Tex. State Bar Com. on Child Abuse & Neglect, 1996—. Mem. Collin County Shelter for Battered Women, 1984-86, chmn., 1984-85; v.p. Collin County Child Welfare Bd., 1986, pres., 1987-88, 96-97, treas., 1989, mem., 1985-89, 94-98; Rep. jud. candidate Collin County, 1986; chmn. bd. Tri County Consortium Mental Health Mental Retardation, 1984-85; mem. Tex. Area 5 Health System Agy., 1979, Collin County Mental Health Adv. Bd., 1978-79; trustee Willow Park Hosp., HCA, 1987-88; chair Collin County Criminal Justice Sub-com., 1987-88; mem. Collin County Pub. Responsibility Com., 1991-96, chair, 1994-95; bd. dirs. Ct. Apptd. Spl. Advocates, 1991-95. Mem. Collin County Bar Assn., Plano Bar Assn. Baptist. Avocations: gardening, reading, writing, traveling. Criminal, Family and matrimonial, Probate. Home: 5 Shadybrook Cir Melissa TX 75454-8912 Office: 117 S Tennessee Mc Kinney TX 75069

ROETHE, JAMES NORTON, lawyer; b. Milw., Jan. 27, 1942; s. Arthur Frantz and Bess Irma (Norton) R.; m. Nita May Dorris, July 15, 1967; children: Melissa Dorris, Sarah Rebacca. BBA, U. Wis., Madison, 1964, JD, 1967. Bar: Wis. 1967, Calif. 1968, U.S. Dist. Ct. (we. dist.) Wis. 1967, U.S. Dist. Ct. (no. dist.) Calif. 1972, U.S. Ct. Claims 1975, U.S. Ct. Appeals (9th cir.) 1980, U.S. Dist. Ct. (ea. dist.) Calif. 1982, U.S. Dist. Ct. (ctrl. dist.) Calif. 1986). U.S. Ct. Appeals (4th cir.) 1988, U.S. Ct. Appeals (2d cir.) 1989. Assoc. Pillsbury, Madison & Sutro, San Francisco, 1971-77, ptnr., 1978-92; sr. v.p., dir. litigation Bank of Am., 1992-96, exec. v.p., gen. counsel, 1996-98, dep. gen. counsel, 1998-99; ptnr. Pillsbury Winthrop LLP, 2000—. Staff atty. Commn. on CIA Activities within U.S., Washington, 1975. Editor: Africa, 1967; editor-in-chief Wis. Law Rev., 1966-67. Bd. dirs. Orinda (Calif.) Assn., 1984-85, pres., 1986; mem. City of Orinda Planning Commn., 1988-94, chmn., 1990, 93; bd. dirs. Calif. Shakespeare Festival, 1993—, pres., 2001; bd. visitors U. Wis. Law Sch., 1994-99. Served to lt. USNR, 1967-71. Fellow Am. Bar Found.; mem. ABA, Wis. Bar Assn., Calif. Bar Assn., Bar Assn. San Francisco, Wis. Law Alumni Assn. (bd. dirs. 2000—), Orinda Country Club, Order of Coif, Phi Kappa Phi. office e-mail: roethe. Federal civil litigation, General civil litigation, Public utilities. Home: 36 Fallen Leaf Ter Orinda CA 94563-1209 E-mail: jimroethe@aol.com, jn@pillsburywinthrop.com*

ROETTGER, NORMAN CHARLES, JR. federal judge; b. Lucasville, Ohio, Nov. 3, 1930; s. Norman Charles and Emma Eleanora R.; children: Virginia, Peggy. BA, Ohio State U., 1952; LLB magna cum laude, Washington and Lee U., 1958. Bar: Ohio 1958, Fla. 1958. Assoc. Frost & Jacobs, Cin., 1958-59; assoc. firm Fleming, O'Bryan & Fleming, Ft. Lauderdale, Fla., 1959-63, ptnr., 1963-69, 71-72; dep. gen. counsel HUD, Washington, 1969-71; judge U.S. Dist. Ct. (so. dist.) Fla., Ft. Lauderdale, 1972-97, sr. judge, 1997—. Lt. (j.g.) USN, 1952-55; to capt. Res. 1972. Mem. ABA, Fed. Bar Assn., Fla. Bar Assn., Broward County Bar Assn., Am. Judicature Soc., Order of Coif, Masons, Ridge Yacht Club, Masons, Omicron Delta Kappa, Kappa Delta Rho. Presbyterian. Office: US Dist Ct 299 E Broward Blvd Ste 205F Fort Lauderdale FL 33301-1902

ROFF, ALAN LEE, lawyer, consultant; b. Winfield, Kans., July 2, 1936; s. Roy Darlis and Mildred Marie (Goodaile) R.; m. Sonyia Ruth Anderson, Feb. 8, 1954; 1 child, Cynthia Lee Roff Edwards; m. Molly Gek Neo Tan, July 21, 1980. BA with honors and distinction, U. Kans., 1964, JD with distinction, 1966. Bar: Okla. 1967. Staff atty. Phillips Petroleum Co., Bartlesville, Okla., 1966-75, sr. atty., 1976-85, sr. counsel, 1986-94; cons. in Asia, 1995—. Mem. editl. bd. Kans. Law Rev., 1965-66. Precinct com. man Rep. Party, Lawrence, Kans., 1963-64; assoc. justice Kans. U. Chancery Club; mem. Kans. U. Young Reps. Elizabeth Reeder scholar U. Kans., 1965-66, Eldon Wallingford award, 1964-66. Mem. ABA, Okla. Bar Assn., Washington County Bar Assn., Phoenix Club (Bartlesville) (bd. dirs. 1985-86, gen. counsel 1986-91), Order of the Coif, Masons, Hon. Order Ky. Cols., Phi Alpha Delta, Pi Sigma Alpha. Mem. First Christian Ch. Avocation: travel. Contracts commercial, General corporate, Private international. Home and Office: 2247 Mountain Dr Bartlesville OK 74003-6954

ROGERS, ARTHUR HAMILTON, III, lawyer; b. Florence, S.C., Apr. 19, 1945; s. Arthur Hamilton Jr. and Suzanne (Wilson) R.; m. Karen Lyn Hess, June 22, 1968; children: Sarah Elizabeth, Thomas Hess. BA, Rice U., 1967; JD, Harvard U., 1970. Bar: Tex. 1970. Assoc. Fulbright & Jaworski LLP, Houston, 1970-74; participating assoc. Fulbright & Jaworski L.L.P., 1974-77; ptnr. Fulbright & Jaworski, L.L.P., 1977—; gen. counsel Lifemark Corp., 1981-82. Sec. Mosher, Inc., Houston, 1984-97. Bd. dirs. Alley Theatre, Houston, 1990—, v.p. fin., 2001—, mem. exec. com., 2001—; bd. dirs. Autry House, 1994-97; mem. exec. com. Rice U. Fund Coun., Houston, 1993-99, vice chmn., 1996-97, chmn., 1997-98. Mem. ABA, State Bar Tex., Assn. of Rice Alumni (treas. 1995-97), Petroleum Club of Houston, The Forest Club. Episcopalian. General corporate, Health, Securities. Home: 5309 Bordley Dr Houston TX 77056-2323 Office: Fulbright & Jaworski LLP 1301 Mckinney St Fl 51 Houston TX 77010-3031 E-mail: arogers@fulbright.com

ROGERS, CHARLES MYERS, lawyer; b. Monticello, Utah, Nov. 21, 1947; s. Milton David and Wanda (Myers) R.; m. Jean Evelyn Rankin, Dec. 12, 1970 (div. June, 1983); m. Christine Theresa Sill, Apr. 14, 1984; children: Christopher Thales, Fiona Eleanor. BA in Philosophy, U. Mo., Kansas City, 1973, JD, 1976. Bar: Mo. 1976, U.S. Dist. Ct. (we. dist.) Mo. 1976, U.S. Supreme Ct. 1994, U.S. Ct. Appeals (8th cir.) 1997, U.S. Ct. Appeals (9th cir.) 1999, U.S. Dist. Ct. Kans. 1999. From asst. pub. defender to 1st asst. pub. defender Jackson County Pub. Defender's Office, Kansas City, Mo., 1976-89; regional defender Mo. State Pub. Defender Sys., 1989-94; staff atty. Mo. Capital Punishment Resource Ctr., 1994-95; shareholder Wyrsch Hobbs Mirakian & Lee, 1995—. Sole practice law, Kansas City, 1982-86. Served in U.S. Army, 1968-70. Mem. ABA, Nat. Assn. Criminal Def. Lawyers, Mo. Bar Assn., Mo. Assn. Criminal Def. Lawyers (bd. dirs. 1988—, 1st. v.p. 1999-00), Kans. City Metro Bar Assn. (co-chair criminal law com.). Democrat. Avocations: cycling, oenology. Criminal. Home: 7434 Madison Ave Kansas City MO 64114-1506 Office: Wyrsch Hobbs et al 1101 Walnut St Ste 1300 Kansas City MO 64106-2180 E-mail: acquit@sprintmail.com

ROGERS, DAVID JOHN, lawyer; b. Lawrence, Mass., Aug. 13, 1960; s. James Martin and Eleanor Elizabeth (Jones) R. BA, Coll. William and Mary, 1982; JD, U. Pitts., 1988. Bar: N.H. 1988, Mass. 1989. Contract adminstr. Sanders Assocs., Inc., Nashua, N.H., 1983-85; assoc. Devine, Millimet, Stahl & Branch, Manchester, 1988-89; ptnr. Carpenito & Rogers, PA, Salem, 1989-90; asst. corp. counsel City of Nashua, 1991; pvt. practice Londonderry, N.H., 1991-98; atty. Landmark Title, Inc., Manchester, 1998-2000. Mem. Worker's Compensation Appeals Bd., State of N.H., 1993—. Active Salem Youth Com., 1989-95; fin. com. West Congl. Ch., Haverhill, Mass., 1990-95. U. scholar U. Pitts., 1988. Mem. Mass. Bar Assn., N.H. Bar Assn., Young Lawyers Com. Republican. Avocations: golf, running, reading, community theater. Estate planning, General practice, Workers' compensation. Home: 20 Cindy Dr Hooksett NH 03106-2003 Office: 1244 Hooksett Rd Ste 7 Hooksett NH 03106

ROGERS, ERNEST MABRY, lawyer; b. Demopolis, Ala., Sept. 22, 1947; s. James B. and Ernestine B. (Brewer) R.; m. Jeanne Edwards, Dec. 15, 1979; children: Gilbert B., Katherine B., Mary C. BA, Yale U., 1969; JD, Harvard U., 1974. Bar: Ala. 1974, U.S. Dist. Ct. (no. dist.) Ala. 1975, U.S. Ct. Appeals (5th cir.) 1976, U.S. Ct. Appeals (11th cir.) 1981, U.S. Supreme Ct. 1981, U.S. Ct. Claims 1983, U.S. Ct. Appeals (6th cir.) 1987. Law clk. to judge U.S. Dist. Ct. (no. dist.) Ala., 1974-75; ptnr. Bradley, Arant, Rose & White, Birmingham, Ala., 1981—. Contbr. articles to profl. jours. Fellow Am. Coll. Constrn. Lawyers, Kiwanis. Episcopalian. Federal civil litigation, State civil litigation, Construction. Office: Bradley Arant Rose & White 1400 Park Place Tower 2001 Park Pl Ste 1400 Birmingham AL 35203-2736 E-mail: emr@barw.com

ROGERS, GARTH WINFIELD, lawyer; b. Fort Collins, Colo., Nov. 4, 1938; s. Harlan Winfield and Helen Marie (Orr) R.; m. Joanne Kathleen Rapp, June 16, 1962; children: Todd Winfield, Christopher Jay, Gregory Lynn, Clay Charles. BS, U. Colo., 1958, LLB, 1962. Bar: Colo. 1962; U.S. Dist. Ct. Colo. 1962. Law clk. to presiding justice U.S. Dist. Ct., Denver, 1962-63; assoc. Allen, Stover & Mitchell, Ft. Collins, 1963-68; ptnr. Allen, Rogers & Vahrenwald, 1968-97; ret., 1997. Articles editor Rocky Mountain Law Rev., 1961-62. Past bd. dirs. Salvation Army, Ft. Collins, Ft. Collins C. of C., United Way of Ft. Collins, Trinity Luth. Ch., Ft. Collins, others; bd. dirs. Poudre Sch. Dist. Bd. Edn. Mem. ABA, Colo. Bar Assn., Larimer County Bar Assn. Avocations: Nicaragua projects, participative sports, amateur writing, reading. Banking, Real property. Office: 215 W Oak St Ste 202 Fort Collins CO 80521-2734

ROGERS, HON PAULLETTO, researcher, writer; b. Washington, Aug. 22, 1961; s. Paulleto Rogers I and Dorothy L.R. Rogers; children: Alexis R. Roycia July, Ambre L. Majasticaa, Ericka J. Student, Wayne County C.C.; cert. computer ops., Mother Waddles Sch. Cert. paralegal; notary pub. Pres. C.C.OA, L.A., 1983; gen. operator CBOU, 1983—; regent agent Security MGN, 1984; collector Nat. Credit Corp., L.A., 1985; craftman Vinyl Indsl. Products, Chgo., 1986; field insp. Mortgage Svcs. Assoc., Inc., 1995; sales cons. Swepo, 1996; legal tech. Probone Legal Svcs., 1997; directorate Prousa Internat. Projects 2001, 1998. Substaining member Rep. Platform Commn., 1986; substaining sponsor Ronald Reagan Presdl. Found., Libr., and Ctr. Pub. Affairs, Ventura County, Calif., 1988; sponsor Statue of Liberty Ellis Island Centennial Commn., 1985, Ronald Reagan Congressional-Vicotry Fund, 1987; advisorate Senate Adv. Coun., 1997; co-founder Justice Inst.; vol. Mother Waddles-Petr. Mission Support; del. at large Del. Adv. Coun.; legal adv. Alexis, Ambre, Dorthy-Lewis, Paul, Paulleto, Rogers, Sutton, Profl. Corp., 2001. Creator, founder The Collectionals Survey. At-large-del. Rep. Presdl. Task Force, 1992—, lobbyist, 1994—; activist U.S. Def. Com., 1985; lobbyist Prousa Legal Corpsusa, 1999; del. Wayne County Clk. Office; Mich. state advisor Rep. Senatorial Com.; mem. Jaycees, 1981, GOPAC, congl. VIP, 1984; GOP Victory Fund sponsor NRCC, 1984; supporter KIDSFIRST YESMI, 2000; assoc. mem. Ch. Tae Adv., 2000—. Decorated Rogers Coat of Arms, Medieval Knight, Chevron, 2000; recipient Cert. Recognition, NRCC, 1990, Cert. Appreciation, Presdl. Commn. A.A., 1990, Presdl. award Rep. Presdl. Legion of Merit. Mem. Oahspe (assoc.), World Peace Tonite/Freedom Inst. (assoc.), 2nd Ch. of Tae. Avocations: copyrights, activism, lobbying, community investing. Home: PO Box 27473 Detroit MI 48227-0473 Office: Paulleto Rogers & Assocs Inc PO Box 27473/PR2 13426 Strathmoor Sta/Sta Hy Detroit MI 48224-0473

ROGERS, JAMES DEVITT, judge; b. Mpls., May 5, 1929; s. Harold Neil and Dorothy (Devitt) R.; m. Leanna Morrison, Oct. 19, 1968. AB, Dartmouth Coll., 1951; JD, U. Minn., 1954. Bar: Minn. 1954, U.S. Supreme Ct. 1983. Assoc. Johnson & Sands, Mpls., 1956-60; sole practice, 1960-62; judge Mpls. Municipal and Dist. Ct., 1959-91. Mem. faculty Nat. Judicial Coll. Bd. dirs. Mpls. chpt. Am. Red Cross, chmn. service to mil. families and vets. com.; bd. dirs. Minn. Safety Council, St. Paul, 1988-91. Served to sgt. U.S. Army, 1954-56. Mem. ABA (chmn. nat. conf. spl. ct. judge, spl. com. housing and urban devel. law, traffic ct. program com., chmn. criminal justice sect., jud. adminstrn. div.), Nat. Jud. Coll. (bd. dirs.), Nat. Christmas Tree Grower's Assn. (pres. 1976-78), Mpls. Athletic Club. Congregational. Office: 14110 Prince Pl Minnetonka MN 55345-3027

ROGERS, JUDITH W. federal judge; b. 1939; AB cum laude, Radcliffe Coll., 1961; LLB, Harvard U., 1964; LLM, U. Va., 1988; LLD (hon.), D.C. Sch. Law, 1992. Bar: D.C. 1965. Law clk. Juvenile Ct. D.C., 1964-65; asst. U.S. atty. D.C., 1965-68; trial atty. San Francisco Neighborhood Legal Assistance Found., 1968-69; atty. assoc. atty. gen.'s office U.S. Dept. Justice, 1969-71, atty. criminal divsn., 1969-71; gen. counsel Congl. Commn. on Organization of D.C. Govt., 1971-72; coordinator legis. program Office of Dep. Mayor D.C., 1972-74, spl. asst. to mayor for legis., 1974-79, corp. counsel, 1979-83; assoc. judge D.C. Ct. Appeals, 1983-88, chief judge, 1988-94; cir. judge U.S. Ct. Appeals-D.C. Cir., 1994—. Mem. D.C. Law Revision Commn., 1979-83; mem. grievance com. U.S. Dist. Ct. D.C., 1982-83; mem. exec. com. Conf. Chief Justices, 1993-94. Bd. dirs. Wider Opportunities for Women, 1972-74; mem. vis. com. Harvard U. Sch. Law, 1984-90; trustee Radcliffe Coll., 1982-88. Recipient citation for work on D.C. Self-Govt. Act, 1973, Disting. Pub. Svc. award D.C. Govt., 1983, award Nat. Bar Assn., 1989; named Woman Lawyer of Yr., Women's Bar Assn. D.C., 1990. Fellow ABA; mem. D.C. Bar, Nat. Assn. Women Judges, Conf. Chief Justices (bd. dirs. 1988-94), Am. Law Inst., Phi Beta Kappa. Office: US Ct Appeals 333 Constitution Ave NWRm 5800 Washington DC 20001-2866*

ROGERS, LAURENCE STEVEN, lawyer; b. N.Y.C., Jan. 19, 1950; s. Henry and Frances (Kanarek) R.; m. Iris S. Rosen, July 2, 1977; children: Matthew Benjamin, Heather Aimee. BSEE with distinction, Cornell U., 1972; JD, NYU, 1975. Bar: N.Y. 1976, U.S. Dist. Ct. (ea. and so. dists.) N.Y. 1976, U.S. Ct. Appeals (Fed. cir.) 1983, U.S. Supreme Ct. 1999, U.S. Patent and Trademark Office. Ptnr. Fish & Neave, N.Y.C., 1986—. Mem. ABA, N.Y.C. Bar Assn., N.Y. Patent, Trademark and Copyright Law Assn., Fed. Cir. Bar Assn., Phi Kappa Phi, Eta Kappa Nu, Tau Beta Pi. Federal civil litigation, Patent, Trademark and copyright. Home: 15 Aspen Rd Scarsdale NY 10583-7346 Office: Fish & Neave 1251 Avenue Of The Americas Fl 50 New York NY 10020-1105

ROGERS, NANCY HARDIN, dean, law educator; b. Lansing, Mich., Sept. 18, 1948; d. Clifford Morris and Martha (Wood) Hardin; m. Douglas Langston Rogers, Jan. 30, 1970; children: Lynne, Jill, Kim. BA with highest distinction, U. Kans., 1969; JD, Yale U., 1972. Bar: D.C. 1975, Ohio 1972, U.S. Ct. Appeals (6th cir.) 1973, U.S. Dist. Ct. (no. dist.) Ohio 1974, U.S. Dist. Ct. (so. dist.) Ohio 1975. Law clk. U.S. Dist. Judge Thomas D. Lambros, Cleve., 1972-74; staff atty. Cleve. Legal Aid Soc., 1974-75; vis. asst. prof. Coll. of Law Ohio State U., Columbus, 1975-76, asst. prof., 1976-78, 83-89, assoc. prof., 1989-92, prof., assoc. dean acad. affairs, 1992-97, prof., 1992—, Joseph S. Platt, Porter, Wright, Morris & Arthur prof. law, 1995—2001, vice provost acad. adminstrn., 1999—2001, dean, Michael E. Moritz chair in alternative dispute resolution Michael E. Moritz Coll. Law, 2001—. Adj. prof. Ohio State U., Columbus, 1982-83; adj. prof. Ohio State Coll., 1981-83; vis. prof. law Harvard Law Sch., 2000. Author (with Frank E.A. Sander and Stephen B. Goldberg): (Book) Dispute Resolution: Negotiation, Mediation and Other Processes), 1992, 3d edit., 1999; author: (book with Craig A. McEwen) Mediation: Law, Policy, Practice, 2nd edit., 1994, (book with Frank E. Sander and Stephen B. Goldberg) Teacher's Manual to Dispute Resolution, 3d edit., 1999;contbr. articles and book chpts. ; mem. (adv. bd.) World Arbitration and Mediation Report , 1991—, Alternatives, 1992—, co-chair (editl. bd. with Frank E.A. Sander) Dispute Resolution mag., 1994—; author, author: Supplement to Mediation: Law, Policy, Practice, 2d. edit. , 1995, Supplement to Mediation: Law, Policy, Practice, 2d edit., 1997. Bd. dirs. Assn. for Developmentally Disabled, Columbus, 1980-85. Named Outstanding Prof., Ohio State U. Coll. Law Alumni Assn., 1996; recipient Book prize, Ctr. Pub. Resources for A Student's Guide to Mediation and the Law, 1987, Ctr. Pub. Resources for Mediation: Law, Policy, Practice, 1989, Peacemaker of Yr. award, Comty. Mediation Svcs. Ctrl. Ohio, 1990, Disting. Svc. Recognition, Soc. Profls. in Dispute Resolution, 1990, Whitney North Seymour sr. medal, Am. Arbitration Assn., 1990, Svc. Recognition award, Legal Aid Soc. Columbus, 1996, Ritter award, Ohio State Bar Found for outstanding contbns. to adminstrn. of justice, 1998; grantee Exxon Edn. Found., 1986, William and Flora Hewlett Found., 1990, Ohio State U. Interdisciplinary Seed, 1990, Ohio State U. Symposium, 1992, William and Flora Hewlett Found., 1992—96, Nat. Sci. Found., 1993—95, State Justice Instn., 1994, Fund for Improvement Post-Secondary Edn., U. Mo., 1996—97, William and Flora Hewlett Found., 1997—. Mem. ABA (chair, standing com. dispute resolution 1988-91), Phi Beta Kappa. Office: Ohio State U Coll Law 55 W 12th Ave Columbus OH 43210-1306 Business E-Mail: rogers.23@osu.edu*

ROGERS, RICHARD DEAN, federal judge; b. Oberlin, Kans., Dec. 29, 1921; s. William Clark and Evelyn May (Christian) R.; m. Helen Elizabeth Stewart, June 6, 1947; children— Letitia Ann, Cappi Christian, Richard Kurt. B.S., Kans. State U., 1943; J.D., Kans. U., 1947. Bar: Kans. 1947. Ptnr. firm Springer and Rogers (Attys.), Manhattan, Kans., 1947-58; instr. bus. law Kans. State U., 1948-52; partner firm Rogers, Stites & Hill, Manhattan, 1959-75; gen. counsel Kans. Farm Bur. & Service Cos., 1960-75; judge U.S. Dist. Ct., Topeka, 1975—. City commr., Manhattan, 1950-52, 60-64, mayor, 1952, 64, county atty., Riley County, Kans., 1954-58, state rep., 1964-68, state senator, 1968-75; pres. Kans. Senate, 1975. Served with USAAF, 1943-45. Decorated Air medal, Dfc. Mem. Kans., Am. bar assns., Beta Theta Pi. Republican. Presbyterian. Club: Masons. Office: US Dist Ct 444 SE Quincy St Topeka KS 66683

ROGERS, RICHARD MICHAEL, judge; b. Lorain, Ohio, Dec. 8, 1944; s. Paul M. and Lillie (Morris) R.; m. Sophia Lydia Wagner, Dec. 23, 1967; children: L. Danielle, David K., Marisa D., Matthew D. BA, Ohio No. U., 1966, JD, 1972. Bar: Ohio 1972, U.S. Dist. Ct. (no. dist.) Ohio 1973. Assoc. Martin, Hall & Rogers, Marion, Ohio, 1972-76; ptnr. Rogers & Rogers, 1976-81; asst. law dir., police prosecutor City of Marion, 1973-74; pub. defender, 1975; asst. county prosecutor Marion County, 1976-81; village solicitor La Rue, Ohio, 1976-81; judge Marion Mcpl. Ct., 1982-88, Common Pleas Ct., 1989—; mem. traffic rules rev. commn. Ohio Supreme Ct., 1989—. Judge dist. competition Nat. Bicentennial Competition on Constitution and Bill of Rights, 1988, judge state competition, 1988—, judge nat. competition, 1989, 93, 95; instr. faculty Ohio Jud. Coll. Mem. Marion Active 20/40 Svc. Club, 1973-84, treas., 1976-80, bd. dirs., 1976-84, pres., 1980-81; chmn. bd. dirs., pres., co-founder Marion Area Driver Re-edn. Project, 1974-81; pres. Big Bros./Big Sisters Marion County, 1986-87, bd. dirs., 1984-88; mem. sch. bd. St. Mary's Elem. Sch., 1985-88, v.p., 1986, bd. dirs. Marion Cath. High Sch. Endowment Fund, 1986—, v.p., 1991—; mem. Marion Cath. Jr./Sr. High Sch. Bd., 1988-94, pres., 1990-91; mem. fellow in criminal justice steering com. Marion campus Ohio State U., 1996—; mem. paralegal adv. com. Marion Tech. Coll., 1994-96; trustee Ohio State Bar Found., 1997-99. With U.S. Army, 1968-69. Mem. Ohio State Bar Assn. (modern cts. com. 1982-85, jud. adminstrn. and legal reform com. 1982-93, legis. subcom. of jud. adminstrn. and legal reform com. 1989-93, coun. dels. 1991-93, bd. govs. 1996-99, chmn. govt. affairs com. 1998-99, vice-chair criminal justice com. 2001—), Marion County Bar Assn. (pres. 1985-86), Ohio Jud. Conf. (gen. adminstrn. 1984-85, vice chair family matters video com. 1991—, chmn. subcom. legal matters video, civil law and procedure com. 1991-95, editl. bd. Ohio Jury Instrn. 1995—), Ohio Bar Coll., Marion County Law Libr. Assn. (trustee 1982—, pres. 1991-93), Ohio Common Pleas Judges Assn., Delta Theta Phi, Sigma Pi. Republican. Methodist. Avocations: golf, scuba diving. Home: 310 Edgefield Blvd Marion OH 43302-5802 Office: Common Pleas Ct Marion County Courthouse 100 N Main St Marion OH 43302-3089

ROGERS, THEODORE OTTO, JR. lawyer; b. West Chester, Pa., Nov. 17, 1953; s. Theodore Otto and Gladys (Bond) R.; m. Hope Tyler Scott, Nov. 7, 1981; children: Helen Elliot, Theodore Scott, Robert Montgomery Bond. AB magna cum laude, Harvard U., 1976, JD cum laude, 1979. Bar: N.Y. 1980, U.S Ct. Appeals (2nd cir.) 1984, U.S. Dist. Ct. (so. and ea. dists.) N.Y. 1980, D.C. 1981, U.S. Ct. Claims, 1982, U.S. Supreme Ct. 1983, U.S. Ct. Appeals (6th and 10th cirs.) 1983, U.S. Ct. Appeals (1st cir.) 1984, U.S. Ct. Appeals (fed. cir.) 1986. From assoc. to ptnr. Sullivan & Cromwell, N.Y.C., 1979—. Co-author: (books) Employment Litigation in New York, 1996, Employment Law DeskBook for Human Resources Professionals, 2001. Mem. U.S. Presdl. Transition Team, 1980. Mem. N.Y. State Bar Assn. (co-chair individual rights and responsibilities com. labor and employment law sect.), Assn. of Bar of City of N.Y. (labor and employment law). Republican. General civil litigation, Labor, Probate. Home: 535 E 86th St New York NY 10028-7533 Office: Sullivan & Cromwell 125 Broad St Fl 28 New York NY 10004-2489 E-mail: rogerst@sullcrom.com

ROGERS, THOMAS SYDNEY, communications executive; b. New Rochelle, N.Y., Aug. 19, 1954; s. Sydney Michael Rogers Jr. and Alice Steinhardt; m. Sylvia Texon, Oct. 9, 1983; children: Robert, Jessica, Jason. BA, Wesleyan U., 1975; JD, Columbia U., 1979. Bar: N.Y. 1980, U.S. Dist. Ct. (so. and ea. dists.) N.Y. 1980, U.S. Ct. Appeals (D.C. cir.) 1981. Legis. aide to Congressman Richard Ottinger U.S. Ho. Reps., Washington, 1975-76, sr. counsel subcom. telecommunications, 1981-86; assoc. Lord, Day & Lord, N.Y.C., 1979-81; v.p. policy planning and bus. devel. Nat. Broadcasting Co., Inc., 1987-88; pres. NBC Cable, 1988-89, NBC Cable & Bus. Devel., 1989-99; exec. v.p. NBC, N.Y.C., 1992-99; vice chmn. NBC Internet, 1999; chmn., CEO Primedia, Inc., 1999—. Pres., CEO internat. coun. Nat. Acad. TV Arts and Scis., 1994-97, chmn., 1998-99; lectr. in field. Named one of Outstanding Young Men in Am., 1985. Mem. N.Y. State Bar Assn., Internat. Radio and TV Soc. Office: Primedia Inc 745 5th Ave Fl 23D New York NY 10151-0099

ROGERS, WILLIAM JOHN, lawyer; b. Phila., Aug. 17, 1950; s. William John and Jean Marie (Dolan) R.; m. Mary K. Neff, July 29, 1978; children: Colin, Brian, Kevin. Diploma, Fairfield U., 1972; JD, Northwestern U., Chgo., 1975. Assoc. Wildman, Harrold, Allen & Dixon, Chgo., 1975-81, ptnr., 1981-90, Bollinger, Ruberry & Garvey, Chgo., 1991—. Article editor: Jour. of Criminal Law and Criminology, Northwestern U., 1973-75. Fellow Am. Coll. Trial Lawyers, Am. Bd. Trial Advs., Soc. Trial Lawyers/Ill. E-mila. Construction, Personal injury, Product liability. Home: 2229 Beechwood Ave Wilmette IL 60091-1507 Office: Bollinger Ruberry & Garvey 500 W Madison St Chicago IL 60661-2511 E-mail: billrogers@brg-law.com

ROGOVIN, LAWRENCE H. lawyer; b. N.Y.C., June 10, 1932; s. Abraham and Laura R.; m. Saundra Schwartz, Aug. 11, 1957; children: Jane Lina, Wendy Renee, Evan Lewis. BS in Econ., U. Pa., 1953; LLB cum laude, NYU, 1956. Bar: N.Y. 1956, Fla. 1971. Dep. asst. atty. gen. State of N.Y., 1956-57, asst. atty. gen., 1960-61; assoc. Fields, Zimmerman, Klopper, Skodnick & Segall, Queens, N.Y., 1961-62, Squadron, Gartenberg, Ellenoff & Plesent and predecessors, N.Y.C., 1962-67, ptnr., 1967-72; pvt. practice Miami, Fla., 1972-74, 83-97; ptnr. Squadron, Ellenoff, Plesent & Lehrer, N.Y.C., 1974-75; assoc. Cohen, Angel & Feinberg, North Miami, Fla., 1975-78; ptnr. Cohen, Angel & Rogovin, 1978-82, Cohen, Rogovin, Reed & Ivans, Miami, 1982-83; v.p., gen. counsel Rare, Inc., 1998—. 1st lt. JAGC, USAFR, 1957-60. Recipient Founders Day award NYU, 1956. Mem. ABA, Fla. Bar Assn., Fed. Bar Assn. General practice, Real property. Fax: 305-932-9583. E-mail: lrogovin@bellsouth.net, lrgovin@rareusa.com

ROHDE, BRUCE C. food company executive, lawyer; b. Sidney, Nebr., Dec. 17, 1948; BS, BA, Creighton U., 1971, JD cum laude, 1973. Bar: Nebr. 1974, U.S. Dist. Ct. Nebr. 1974, U.S. Tax Ct. 1975, U.S. Ct. Appeals (8th cir.) 1976, U.S. Ct. Appeals (5th cir.) 1979, U.S. Supreme Ct. 1980, U.S. Claims Ct. 1981, U.S. Ct. Appeals (D.C. cir.) 1982. Lawyer McGrath, North, Mullin & Kratz, Omaha, to 1996; pres., CEO Conagra Inc., 1996—. Mem. ABA (corp., banking and bus law sect., taxation sect., antitrust law sect., litigation sect.), Assn. Trial Lawyers Am., Nebr. Assn. Trial Lawyers, Nebr. State Bar Assn., Nebr. Soc. CPAs, Omaha Bar Assn., Beta Gamma Sigma, Beta Alpha Psi. Address: ConAgra Inc 1 ConAgra Dr Ste 302 Omaha NE 68102

ROHLFING, FREDERICK WILLIAM, lawyer, political consultant, retired judge; b. Honolulu, Nov. 2, 1928; s. Romayne Raymond and Kathryn (Coe) R.; m. Joan Halford, July 15, 1952 (div. Sept. 1982); children: Frederick W., Karl A., Brad (dec.); m. Patricia Ann Santos, Aug. 23, 1983. BA, Yale U., 1950; JD, George Washington U., 1955. Bar: Hawaii 1955, Am. Samoa 1978. Assoc. Moore, Torkildson & Rice, Honolulu, 1955-60; ptnr. Rohlfing, Nakamura & Low, 1963-68, Hughes, Steiner & Rohlfing, Honolulu, 1968-71, Rohlfing, Smith & Coates, Honolulu, 1981-84; sole practice, 1960-63, 71-81, Maui County, 1988—; dep. corp. counsel County of Maui, Wailuku, Hawaii, 1984-87, corp. counsel, 1987-88; land and legal counsel Maui Open Space Trust, 1992-97, also bd. dirs. Polit. cons., 1996, 98; magistrate judge U.S. Dist. Ct. Hawaii, 1991-96. Active Hawaii Ho. Reps., 1959-65, 80-84, Hawaii State Senate, 1966-75; U.S. alt. rep. So. Pacific Commn., Noumea, New Caledonia, 1975-77, 1982-84; Maui adv. coun. State Reappointment Commn., 2001; hon. chmn. Maui coms. George W. Bush for Pres. Capt. USNR, 1951-87. Mem. Hawaii Bar Assn., Maui Country Club, Naval Intelligence Profls. Avocations: ocean swimming, golf. Administrative and regulatory, Land use and zoning (including planning), Legislative. Home and Office: RR 1 Box 398 Kekaulike Ave Kula HI 96790

ROHM, BENITA JILL, lawyer; b. Altoona, Pa., Aug. 28, 1953; d. Clayton Benson and Betty Jean (Shaffer) R. BS, Carnegie-Mellon U., 1975, MS, 1976; JD, Seton Hall U., 1979. Bar: N.J. 1979, Mich. 1998, U.S. Ct. Appeals (3d cir.) 1979, U.S. Patent and Trademark Office, 1977. Patent atty. legal staff Bell Telephone Labs., Murray Hill, N.J., 1975-79; litigation atty. Hopgood, Calimafde, Kalil, Blaustein & Judlowe, N.Y.C., 1979-81; sole practice, 1981-84; ptnr. Rohm & Monsanto PLC, Detroit, 1984—. Tutor patent bar rev. course Practising Law Inst. Mem. editl. adv. bd. Obtaining Patents (by Thomas A. Turano, 1997. Mem. ABA, Am. Intellectual Property Law Assn., Licensing Execs. Soc. Avocation: music. Patent, Trademark and copyright. Office: 660 Woodward Ave Ste 1525 Detroit MI 48226-3518 E-mail: bjrohm@aol.com

ROHNER, RALPH JOHN, lawyer, educator, university dean; b. East Orange, N.J., Aug. 10, 1938; A.B., Cath. U. Am., 1960, J.D., 1963. Bar: Md. 1964. Teaching fellow Stanford (Calif.) U., 1963-64; atty. pub. health div. HEW, 1964-65; prof. law Cath. U. Am. Sch. Law, Washington, 1965—, acting dean, 1968-69, assoc. dean, 1969-71, dean, 1987-95; staff counsel consumer affairs subcom. U.S. Senate Banking Com., 1975-76; cons. Fed. Res. Bd., 1976-83, chmn. consumer adv. council, 1981; cons.

FDIC, 1978-80; spl. counsel Consumer Bankers Assn., 1984—. Cons. U.S. Regulatory Coun., 1979-80. Co-author: Consumer Law: Cases and Materials, 1979, 2d edit., 1991; co-author, editor The Law of Truth in Lending, 1984 Bd. dirs. Migrant Legal Action Program, Inc., Washington, Automobile Owners Action Coun., Washington, Credit Rsch. Ctr., Georgetown U., Am. Fin. Svcs. Assn. Edn. Found. Conf. on Consumer Fin. Law. Mem. ABA, Am. Law Inst., Coll. of Consumer Fin. Svcs. Lawyers. Home: 10909 Forestgate Pl Glenn Dale MD 20769-2047 Office: Cath U Sch Law 620 Michigan Ave NE Washington DC 20064-0001 E-mail: rohner@law.edu

ROHR, RICHARD DAVID, lawyer; b. Toledo, Aug. 31, 1926; s. Lewis Walter and Marie Janet (Pilliod) R.; m. Ann Casey, Aug. 25, 1951; children: Martha, Elizabeth, Matthew, Sarah, Margaret, Thomas. BA magna cum laude, Harvard U., 1950; JD, U. Mich., 1953. Bar: Mich. 1954, U.S. Dist. Ct. (so. dist.) Mich. 1954, U.S. Ct. Appeals (6th cir.) 1960, U.S. Supreme Ct. 1961. Assoc. Bodman, Longley & Dahling, L.L.P., Detroit, 1954-58, ptnr., 1958-75, mng. ptnr., 1975-2000. Adj. prof. U. Mich., Ann Arbor, 1976-82. With U.S. Army, 1945-46. Mem. ABA, Detroit Bar Assn., Mich. Bar Assn., Renaissance Club, Detroit Athletic Club, Order of Coif, Phi Beta Kappa. Roman Catholic. Banking, General corporate, Finance. Home: 441 Rivard Blvd Grosse Pointe MI 48230-1627 Office: Bodman Longley Dahling LLP 100 Renaissance Ctr Ste 34 Detroit MI 48243-1001

ROHRER, DEAN COUGILL, lawyer; b. Indpls., Jan. 25, 1940; s. William Jay and Frances (Cougill) R.; m. Christina Marie Scheele, Dec. 20, 1969; children— Jonathan William, Mary Kirstin, Jay Andrew. Student U. Edinburgh (Scotland), 1960-61, U. South Australia, 1964; A.B., Union Coll., 1962; LL.B., U. Va., 1966. Bar: N.Y. 1966, U.S. Dist. Ct. (so. dist.) N.Y. 1969, U.S. Ct. Appeals (2d cir.) 1968, Conn. 1974, U.S. Dist. Ct. (ea. dist.) N.Y. 1975, U.S. Dist. Ct. Conn. 1975. Assoc. Winthrop, Stimson, Putnam & Roberts, N.Y.C., 1966-68, Simpson Thacher & Bartlett, N.Y.C., 1969-71; asst. U.S. atty. U.S. Atty.'s Office, N.Y.C., 1971-73; sr. atty. GTE Corp., Stamford, Conn., 1973-76, asst. gen. counsel, 1976-84, v.p., assoc. gen. counsel telephone operating group, 1984-89, v.p. assoc. gen. counsel, 1989—. Trustee Pound Ridge Land Conservancy, N.Y., 1986—; coach Bedford Youth Soccer Club, N.Y., 1982-86; pres. Pound Ridge Elem. Sch. Assn., N.Y., 1983-84; mem. council on ministries Pound Ridge Community Ch., 1984. Mem. ABA, N.Y. State Bar Assn., Conn. Bar Assn., Westchester Fairfield Corp. Counsel Assn., Stamford Darien Bar Assn. Clubs: Royal Ocean Racing (London), Storm Trysail, Larchmont Yacht. Federal civil litigation, General corporate, Public utilities. Home: Woodland Rd Pound Ridge NY 10576 Office: GTE Corp One Stamford Forum Stamford CT 06904

ROHRMAN, DOUGLASS FREDERICK, lawyer; b. Chgo., Aug. 10, 1941; s. Frederick Alvin and Velma Elizabeth (Bridwell) R.; m. Susan Vitullo; children: Kathryn Anne, Elizabeth Clelia, Alessandra Claire. AB, Duke U., 1963; JD, Northwestern U., 1966. Bar: Ill. 1966. Legal coord. Nat. Communicable Disease Ctr., Atlanta, 1966-68; assoc. Keck, Mahin & Cate, Chgo., 1968-73, ptnr., 1973-97, Lord, Bissell and Brook, Chgo., 1997—. Exec. v.p., dir. Kerogen Oil Co., 1967—; chmn. bd. visitors Nicholas Sch. of Environment Duke U., 1993—. Co-author: Commercial Liability Risk Management and Insurance, 2 vols., 1978, 86, Lenders Guide to Environmental Law: Risk and Liability, 1993; contbr. articles on law to profl. jours. Vice chmn., commr. Ill. Food and Drug Commn., 1970-72. Lt. USPHS, 1966-68. Mem.: ABA, Chgo. Bar Assn. (chmn. com. food & drug law 1972—73), 7th Cir. Bar Assn., Environ. Law Inst., Am. Soc. Law and Medicine, Selden Soc., James B. Diske Soc., Am. Numismatic Soc. (life; chmn. adv. com.), Am. Numismatic Assn., Duke U. Alumni Assn., William Preston Few Assn. (mem. pres. coun.), Legal Club, Mich. Shores Club, Wagmore Club. Democrat. Epsicopalian. Contracts commercial, Environmental, Product liability. Home: 520 Brier St Kenilworth IL 60043-1064 Office: Lord Bissell & Brook 115 S La Salle St Ste 3200 Chicago IL 60603-3902

ROLAND, JOHN WANNER, lawyer; b. Reading, Pa., Aug. 4, 1950; s. John Harry and Mary Ann (Wanner) R.; m. Janis Richards, June 10, 1972; children: Katherine, Rebecca, Andrew J. AB, Princeton U., 1972; JD, Villanova U., Pa., 1976; LLM, Temple U., Phila., 1980. Bar: Pa. 1976, U.S. Dist. Ct. (ea. dist.) Pa. 1976, U.S. Ct. Appeals (3d cir.) 1982. Assoc. Balmer Mogel Speidel & Roland, Reading, 1976-81; ptnr. Mogel, Speidel & Roland, Reading, 1981-85; ptnr. Roland and Schlegel, 1985—, mng. ptnr.; mem. lawyers adv. com. U.S. Dist. Ct. (ea. dist.) Pa., 1984-90; mem. Berks County Capital Campaign Rev. Bd., 1992-94; mem. alumni schs. com. Princeton U., Reading; mem. adv. com. Ctr. for Mental Health, Reading; v.p. Greater Reading Conf. of Chs. Served to capt. Army N.G., 1972-78. Mem. ABA, Pa. Bar Assn., Berks County Bar Assn., Berks County C. of C. (chmn., bd. dirs. 1991-92, exec. com. 1986—). Berkshire Country Club. Republican. Presbyterian. General civil litigation, General corporate, Labor. Home: 2901 Cotswold Rd Sinking Spring PA 19608-9690 Office: Roland & Schlegel 627 N 4th St PO Box 902 Reading PA 19603-0902

ROLAND, RAYMOND WILLIAM, lawyer, mediator, arbitrator; b. Ocala, Fla., Jan. 3, 1947; s. Raymond W. and Hazel (Dunn) R.; m. Jane Allen, Dec. 28, 1968; children: John Allen, Jason William. BA, Fla. State U., 1969, JD, 1972. Bar: Fla. 1972, U.S. Dist. Ct. (no. dist.) Fla. 1973, U.S. Dist. Ct. (mid. dist.) Fla. 1985, U.S. Ct. Appeals (5th cir.) 1974, U.S. Ct. Appeals (11th cir.) 1983, U.S. Supreme Ct. 1985; cert. cir. ct. mediator. Assoc. Keen, O'Kelley & Spitz, Tallahassee, 1972-74, ptnr., 1974-77; ptnr., v.p. McConnaughhay, Roland, Maida & Cherr, P.A., 1978-97; owner, mediator Roland Mediation Svcs. Diplomate mem. Fla. Acad. of Profl. Mediators, Inc. Bd. dirs. So. Scholarship Found., Tallahassee, 1985-89, 98-99, v.p. 1989; bd. visitors Bapt. Coll. Fla. Mem. Internat. Assn. Def. Coun., Def. Rsch. Inst., Fla. Bar, Tallahassee Bar Assn. (treas. 1979), Kiwanis (life, lt. gov. 1984- 85), Capital City Kiwanis Club (Kiwanian of Yr. 1978, pres. 1979), Fla. Kiwanis Found. (life fellow). Republican. Baptist. Avocations: reading, hiking, camping, golf. General practice, Insurance, Personal injury. Home: 1179 Ox Bottom Rd Tallahassee FL 32312-3519

ROLFE, ROBERT MARTIN, lawyer; b. Richmond, Va., May 16, 1951; s. Norman and Bertha (Cohen) R.; m. Catherine Dennis Stone, July 14, 1973; children: P. Alexander, Asher B., Joel A., Zachary A. BA, U. Va., 1973, JD, 1976. Bar: Va. 1976, N.Y. 1985, U.S. Dist. Ct. (ea. and we. dists.) Va. 1976, U.S. Ct. Appeals (4th cir.) 1976, U.S. Ct. Appeals (2d cir.) 1979, U.S. Dist. Ct. (ea. dist.) Mich. 1985, U.S. Ct. Appeals (D.C. cir.) 1985, U.S. Dist. Ct. (so. and ea. dists.) N.Y. 1985, U.S. Ct. Appeals (7th cir.) 1995, U.S. Ct. Fed. Claims, 1997, U.S. Supreme Ct. 1979. Assoc. Hunton & Williams, Richmond, 1976-83, ptnr., 1983—, co-head litigation, intellectual property and antitrust team, mem. exec. com., 1998—. Contbr. articles to profl. jours. Trustee Jewish Family Supporting Found.; bd. dirs. Jewish Family Svcs., Richmond, pres., 1993-95; bd. mgrs., 2d v.p. Congregation Beth Ahabah, 1995-97, 1st v.p., 1997-99. Fellow Am. Bar Found.; mem. ABA (litig. sect.), Va. Bar Assn., Va. State Bar, Richmond Bar Assn., Am. Arbitration Assn. (comml. arbitrators panel), Order of Coif (Alumni award for acad. excellence U. Va. 1976). Federal civil litigation, Nuclear power, Professional liability. Home: 18 Greenway Ln Richmond VA 23226-1630 Office: Hunton & Williams Riverfront Plz East Tower PO Box 1535 Richmond VA 23218-1535 also: 200 Park Ave New York NY 10166-0005

ROLFE, RONALD STUART, lawyer; b. N.Y.C., Sept. 5, 1945; s. Nat and Florence I. (Roth) R.; 1 child, Andrew. AB, Harvard U., 1966; JD, Columbia U., 1969. Bar: N.Y. 1969, U.S. Ct. Appeals (2d cir.) 1970, U.S. Dist. Ct. (so. and ea. dists.) N.Y. 1971, U.S. Supreme Ct. 1973, U.S. Ct. Appeals (9th cir.) 1977, U.S. Dist. Ct. (no. dist.) Calif. 1982, U.S. Ct. Appeals (6th and 5th cirs.) 1982, U.S. Ct. Appeals (9th cir.) 1983, U.S. Dist. Ct. (ea. dist.) Ky. 1984, U.S. Ct. Appeals (7th and 10th cirs.) 1989, U.S. Ct. Appeals (fed. cir.) 1991, U.S. Ct. Appeals (3rd cir.) 1992, U.S. Ct. Appeals (4th cir.) 1999. Law clk. to judge U.S. Dist. Ct. (so. dist.) N.Y., 1969-70; assoc. Cravath, Swaine & Moore, 1970-77, ptnr., 1977—. Sec. bd. trustees Allen-Stevenson Sch., 1981-91, pres., 1992—; trustee Lawrenceville Sch., 1987—, v.p., 2001—; trustee Prep for Prep. Kent and Stone scholar, 1969; mem. bd. visitors Columbia Law Sch. Fellow Am. Bar Found.; mem. ABA, N.Y. State Bar Assn., Assn. of the Bar of the City of N.Y., Fed. Bar Coun. (trustee 1989-94), Am. Law Inst., Union Club, Univ. Club, Stanwich Club (Greenwich, Conn.), Turf and Field Club (N.Y.C.), Royal Automobile Club (London). Antitrust, General civil litigation, Securities. Office: Cravath Swaine & Moore Worldwide Plz 825 8th Ave 40th Fl New York NY 10019-7475 E-mail: rrolfe@cravath.com

ROLICH, FRANK ALVIN, insurance company executive, lawyer; b. Hudson, Wyo., Apr. 3, 1926; s. Frank Joseph and Mary Frances (Tekavec) R.; m. Margaret Geraldine Evans, Dec. 29, 1951; children— Zannifer Gail, Zinna Rae, Reef Kirby. B.A., U. Wyo., 1951, J.D., 1953. Bar: Wyo. 1953, U.S. Dist. Ct. Wyo. 1956. Claim rep. State Farm Ins. Co., Rock Springs, Wyo., 1953— , office adminstr., 1971— . Served with U.S. Army, 1944-46. Democrat. Roman Catholic. Lodge: Lions (pres. 1967-68). Insurance, Personal injury. Home: 712 B St Rock Springs WY 82901-6217 Office: State Farm Ins Co PO Box 2106 Rock Springs WY 82902-2106

ROLIN, CHRISTOPHER E(RNEST), lawyer; b. Santa Monica, Calif., Feb. 15, 1940; s. Carl A. and Kate (Northcote) R.; m. Debbie Best, April, 1994; children: Whitney, Brett. BA, U. Calif.-Berkeley, 1961; JD, U. So. Calif., 1965. Bar: Calif. 1966. Assoc. Meserve, Mumper & Hughes, L.A., 1966-71, ptnr., 1972; ptnr. Haight, Dickson, Brown & Bonesteel, Santa Monica, Clif., 1974-88; ptnr. Rodi Pollock, L.A., 1990-96, Newkirk, Newkirk & Rolin, 1996—. Bd. dirs. Legion Lex, 1991—, sec., 1995, v.p., 1996, pres. 1997-98. Mem. So. Calif. Def. Counsel (bd. dirs. 1981-85), Am. Bd. Trial Advs. (bd. dirs. 1994), L.A. County Bar Assn. (bd. dirs. and vice chmn. law mgmt. sect. 1994, chmn. 1995-96), Am. Arbitration Assn. (arbitrator 1977-95), Lawyers Profl. Liability Assn., Cowboy Lawyers. Republican. Club: Optimists (pres. 1989). Real property. Home: 1520 Beverly Glen Dr #503 Los Angeles CA 90024 Office: # 460 11620 Wilshire Blvd Ste 460 Los Angeles CA 90025-1779

ROLL, DAVID LEE, lawyer; b. Pontiac, Mich., May 1, 1940; s. Everett Edgar and Garnette (Houts) R.; m. Nancy E. Spindle, Aug. 17, 1963; children: Richard, Molly. BA cum laude, Amherst Coll., 1962; JD, U. Mich., 1964. Bar: Mich. 1965, U.S. Dist. Ct. (ea. dist.) Mich. 1965, U.S. Ct. Appeals (6th cir.) 1969, D.C. 1974, U.S. Dist. Ct. D.C. 1975, U.S. Supreme Ct. 1975, U.S. Ct. Appeals (4th cir.) 1976, U.S. Ct. Appeals (D.C. cir.) 1983, U.S. Ct. Appeals (3rd and 11th cirs.) 1985, U.S. Ct. Appeals (9th cir.) 1992, U.S. Ct. Appeals (fed. cir.) 1993. Assoc. Hill, Lewis, Detroit, 1965-70, ptnr., 1970-72; asst. dir. gen. litigation Bur. of Competition Fed. Trade Commn., Washington, 1972-75; ptnr. Steptoe & Johnson, 1975-93, chmn., 1993-98. V.p. bus. devel., bd. dirs. eLawForum, 2000—. Mem. ABA (chair Robinson Patman Act com., antitrust sect. 1984-86, Clayton Act com., antitrust sect. 1986-88, Energy Litigation com., litigation sect. 1992-93, mem. task force on indsl. competitiveness 1987, coun., antitrust sect. 1988-91, author, editor antitrust sect.), Lex Mundi (bd. dirs., chair competition com.). Administrative and regulatory, Antitrust, Federal civil litigation. Office: 1330 Connecticut Ave NW Washington DC 20036-1704 E-mail: droll@steptoe.com

ROLL, JOHN MCCARTHY, judge; b. Pitts., Feb. 8, 1947; s. Paul Herbert and Esther Marie (McCarthy) R.; m. Maureen O'Connor, Jan. 24, 1970; children: Robert McCarthy, Patrick Michael, Christopher John. BA, U. Ariz., 1969, JD, 1972; LLM, U. Va., 1990. Bar: Ariz. 1972, U.S. Dist. Ct. Ariz. 1974, U.S. Ct. Appeals (9th cir.) 1980, U.S. Supreme Ct. 1977. Asst. pros. atty. City of Tucson, 1973; dep. county atty. Pima County (Ariz.), 1973-80; asst. U.S. Atty. U.S. Attys. Office, Tucson, 1980-87; judge Ariz. Ct. Appeals, 1987-91, U.S. Dist. Ct. Ariz., 1991—. Mem. criminal justice mental health standards project ABA, 1980-83, mem. com. model jury instrns. 9th circuit, 1994—, chair, 1998—, mem. panel workshop criminal law CEELI program, Moscow, 1997; mem. U.S. Jud. Conf. Adv. Com. Criminal Rules, 1997—. Contbr. Merit Selection: the Arizona Experience, Ariz. State Law Jour., 1991, The Rules Have Changed: Amendments ot the Rules of Civil procedure, Defense Law Jour., 1994, Ninth Cir. Judges' Benchbook on Pretrial Proceedings, 1998, 2000. Coach Frontier Baseball Little League, Tucson, 1979-84; mem. parish coun. Sts. Peter and Paul Roman Cath. Ch., Tucson, 1983-91, chmn., 1986-91; mem. Roman Cath. Dioceses Tucson Sch. Bd., 1986-90. Recipient Disting. Faculty award Nat. Coll. Dist. Attys., U. Houston, 1979, Outstanding Alumnus award U. Ariz. Coll. Law, 1992. Mem. Fed. Judges Assn., KC (adv. coun. 1991). Republican. Office: US Dist Ct 405 W Congress Tucson AZ 85701

ROLLA, MARIO F. lawyer, business consultant; b. N.Y.C., Dec. 15, 1930; s. Peter L. and Irma (Testa) Rolla; children: Peter, Adrienne. BBA., Pace U., 1952; LLB, St. John's U., 1959. Bar: N.Y. 1959, Mo. 1970. With Morningstar Paisley, Inc., N.Y.C., 1959-65; sole practice law, N.Y.C., 1965-70; ptnr. Ronayne Hackeling & Rolla, N.Y.C., 1970— ; dir. Global Steel Products Corp., Deer Park, N.Y., Gem Industries Inc., Gardner, Mass. General corporate, Corporate taxation, Estate taxation. Office: 95 Marcus Blvd Deer Park NY 11729-4501

ROLLS, JOHN MARLAND, JR. lawyer, law educator; b. San Francisco, Nov. 18, 1937; s. Jack M. and Margaret Rita (Tracy) R.; m. Dorothy K. Higa, Oct. 2, 1976; children: Dana Kimiko, Jennifer Mariko. BA, Stanford U., 1959, LLB, 1962. Bar: Hawaii 1965, U.S. Dist. Ct. Hawaii 1965, U.S. Ct. Appeals (9th cir.) 1967, U.S. Supreme Ct. 1970. Asst. prof. dept. social scis. U.S. Mil. Acad., West Point, N.Y., 1962-65; assoc. Ashford & Wriston, Honolulu, 1965-68, ptnr. 1970-91; pvt. practice Honolulu, 1992—; instr. Grad. Realtors Inst., Hawaii Assn. Realtors, Honolulu, 1976-84; adj. prof. U. Hawaii Sch. Law, Honolulu, 1980-84; mem. adv. com. to commr. fin. instns., State of Hawaii, 1985-87. Author real estate fin. manual Loan Commitments and Agreements, 1990; co-editor: Hawaii Conveyance Manual, 1979, 3d edit., 1987, 4th edit., 1992; contbr. articles to profl. jours. Served to maj. U.S. Army, 1962-65, 68-69, Vietnam, col. Res., ret. Decorated Bronze Star. Mem. ABA, Hawaii Bar Assn. (bd. dirs. real property and fin. services sect. 1983—, vice-chmn. 1986, chmn. 1987). Republican. Episcopalian. Banking, Consumer commercial, Real property. Office: 810 Richards St Honolulu HI 96813-4728

ROMAN, RONALD PETER, lawyer; b. N.Y.C., Apr. 8, 1945; s. Charles Philip and Dorothy C. (Raphael) R.; m. Deborah Lynn, Dec. 21, 1969; children: Lindsay Rachel, Ryan Alan. BS in Bus., Pa. State U., 1968; MBA, Pace U., 1973; JD, Fordham U., 1976. Bar: N.J. 1976, U.S. Dist. Ct. N.J. 1976, U.S. Tax Ct. 1978, U.S. Ct. Appeals (3d cir.) 1979, Fla. 1980, U.S. Dist. Ct. (so. dist.) Fla. 1980, U.S. Supreme Ct. 1980, U.S. Ct. Appeals (11th cir.) 1981, N.Y 1985. Assoc., Eichler & Forgosh, Irvington, N.J., 1976-78; gen. counsel Flower World of Am., West Deptford, N.J., 1979; staff counsel Arthur Murray Internat., Coral Gables, Fla., 1979-80; gen. counsel, v.p. Wuv's Internat. Inc., Ft. Lauderdale, Fla., 1980; sr. ptnr. Ronald Peter Roman, P.A., Miami, Fla., 1980-86; pres. Franchise Resources Inc., Miami, 1981-87; lectr. in field. Co-author: (manual) Franchise Law: A Primer, 1982; Fla. Franchise Law and Practice, 1985, 2nd rev. edit., 1993. Contbr. articles to profl. jours. Mem. ABA, Internat. Franchise Assn., Am. Arbitration Assn. (arbitrator 1989-94), Fla. Bar Assn. General corporate, Franchising, Trademark and copyright. Office: Semet Lickstein Morgenstern Berger Friend Brooke & Gordon 201 Alhambra Cir Miami FL 33134-5107

ROMANO, J. ERIC, lawyer; b. Houston, Feb. 7, 1972; s. John Fletcher and Nancy Lee Romano; m. Rebecca Paige Badger, May 30, 1998. BS, Fla. State U., 1993; JD, Stetson U., 1997. Bar: Fla. 1997. Asst. state atty. Palm Beach County State Atty.'s Office, West Palm Beach, Fla., 1997—. Vol. evaluator Palm Beach County Youth Ct., West Palm Beach, 1998; vol. tchr. Law Related Edn. Program, Forest Hill H.S., 1998. Mem. ABA, ATLA. Democrat. Roman Catholic. Home: 2049 Normandy Cir West Palm Beach FL 33409 Office: State Atty's Office 401 N Dixie Hwy West Palm Beach FL 33401

ROMNEY, RICHARD BRUCE, lawyer; b. Kingston, Jamaica, Dec. 29, 1942; came to U.S., 1945, naturalized, 1956; s. Frank Oswald and Mary Ellen (Burton) R.; m. Beverly Cochran, Spet. 11, 1965 (dec. 1984); children: Richard Bruce, Jr., Stephanie Cochran; m. Lynthia H. Walker, Aug. 14, 1988; children: Alisa Dawn, Kristen Elizabeth. BA, U. Pa., 1964; JD, U. Va., 1972. Bar: N.Y. 1973, U.S. Ct. Appeals (2d cir.) 1975; registered foreign lawyer, Law Soc. Eng. and Wales. Assoc. Dewey, Ballantine, Bushby Palmer & Wood, N.Y.C., 1972-80, ptnr., 1981—. Mem. editl. bd. U. Va. Law Rev., 1970-72. Lt. USN, 1964-68. Mem. ABA, N.Y. State Bar Assn., Assn. Bar City N.Y., Order of Coif. Independent. General corporate, Mergers and acquisitions, Securities. Home: 35 Deerfield Rd Chappaqua NY 10514-1604 Office: Dewey Ballantine LLP 1301 Avenue Of The Americas New York NY 10019-6022 E-mail: rromney@deweyballantine.com

RONDEAU, CHARLES REINHARDT, lawyer; b. Jefferson, La., Oct. 14, 1966; s. Clement Robert and Irmtraut Juliana Rondeau. BA, Columbia U., 1988; JD, Southwestern U., L.A., 1992; diploma in Advanced Internat. Legal Stud, McGeorge Sch. Law, 1993. Bar: Calif. 1993, N.Y., N.J., U.S. Dist. Ct. N.J., U.S. Dist. Ct. (so. and ea. dists.) N.Y., U.S. Dist. Ct. (cent. dist.) Calif., U.S. Ct. Appeals (3rd and 9th cirs.), U.S. Tax Ct. 1994. Visiting jurist Cabinet Berlioz et Cie, Paris, 1992-93; assoc. Stanley A. Teitler, P.C., N.Y.C., 1993-95; ptnr. Rondeau & Homampour, Beverly Hills, Calif., 1995—. Judge Pro Tem, Los Angeles County Mcpl. Ct., 1999—. Rsch. editor: Southwestern U. Law Rev., 1989-92. Mem. ABA, L.A. County Bar Assn., Beverly Hills Bar Assn. Avocations: jazz, show jumping, skiing, sailing. General civil litigation, Entertainment, Private international. Office: Rondeau & Homampour PLC 8383 Wilshire Blvd Ste 830 Beverly Hills CA 90211-2407

RONDEPIERRE, EDMOND FRANCOIS, insurance executive; b. N.Y.C., Jan. 15, 1930; s. Jules Gilbert and Margaret Murray (Moore) R.; m. M. Anne Lerch, July 5, 1952; children: Aimee S., Stephen C., Peter E., Anne W. BS, U.S. Mcht. Marine Acad., 1952; JD, Temple U., 1959. Bar: D.C. 1959, Conn. 1988, U.S. Supreme Ct. 1992. Third mate Nat. Bulk Carriers, 1952-53; field rep. Ins. Co. N.Am., Phila., 1955-59, br. mgr., 1959-61, asst. sec. underwriting, 1965-67, asst. gen. counsel, 1967-70, sr. v.p., gen. counsel, 1970-76; v.p., dep. chief legal affairs INA Corp., 1976-77; v.p., gen. counsel Gen. Reins. Corp., Stamford, Conn., 1977-79, sr. v.p., corp. sec., gen. counsel, 1979-94, sr. v.p., 1994-95; pres., dir. ARIAS-US, 1994-99, dir. emeritus, 1999—. Bd. dirs. Arias-US. Lt. USN, 1953-55. Mem. ABA, Conn. Bar Assn., D.C. Bar Assn., Inter-Am. Bar Assn., Soc. CPCU, Internat. Assn. Def. Counsel (past bd. dirs.), AIDA Reins. and Ins. Arbitration Soc. (dir., pres.), Stamford Yacht Club. Roman Catholic.

RONDON, EDANIA CECILIA, lawyer; b. Santiago, Cuba, Oct. 22, 1960; came to U.S., 1965; d. Edalio Marcelino and Ylia Nayda (Jacas) R.; m. Antonio Omar Maldonado, Sept. 5, 1987. BA, Syracuse U., 1982; JD, Boston U., 1985. Bar: N.J. 1985, U.S. Ct. Appeals (3d cir.) 1985. Assoc. Thomas A. Declemente, P.C., Union City, N.J., 1985-88; pub. defender City of Union City, 1985—; assoc. ins. def. James D. Butler, P.A., Jersey City, 1988-93; assoc. Edania C. Rondon, P.A., Union City, 1993—. Mem. ABA, Hudson County Bar Assn. Democrat. Roman Catholic. Home: 630 Slocum Ave Ridgefield NJ 07657-1837 Office: Edania C Rondon PA 3700 Bergenline Ave Ste 201 Union City NJ 07087-4847

RONEY, JOHN HARVEY, lawyer, consultant; b. L.A., June 12, 1932; s. Harvey and Mildred Puckett (Cargill) R.; m. Joan Ruth Allen, Dec. 27, 1954; children: Pam Roney Peterson, J. Harvey, Karen Louise Hanke, Cynthia Allen Harmon. Student, Pomona Coll., 1950-51; BA, Occidental Coll., 1954; LLB, UCLA, 1959. Bar: Calif. 1960, D.C. 1976. Assoc. O'Melveny & Myers, L.A., 1959-67, ptnr., 1967-94, of counsel, 1994—; gen. counsel Pa. Co., 1970-78, Baldwin United Corp., 1983-84; dir. Coldwell Banker & Co., 1969-81, Brentwood Savs. & Loan Assn., 1968-80. Spl. advisor Rehab. of Mut. Benefit Life Ins. Co., 1991-94; cons., advisor to Rehab. of Confederation Life Ins. Co., 1994-95; mem. policy adv. bd. Calif. Ins. Commn., 1991-95. Served to 1st lt. USMCR, 1954-56. Mem. ABA, Calif. Bar Assn. (ins. law com. 1991-95, chmn. 1993-94), L.A. County Bar Assn., D.C. Bar Assn., N.Y. Coun. Fgn. Rels., Pacific Coun. on Internat. Policy, Conf. Ins. Counsel, Calif. Club, Sky Club (N.Y.), Gainey Ranch Golf Club (Scottsdale), L.A. Country Club. Republican. Home: The Strand Hermosa Beach CA 90254 Office: 400 S Hope St Ste 1665 Los Angeles CA 90071-2801 E-mail: jroney@omm.com

RONEY, PAUL H(ITCH), federal judge; b. Olney, Ill., Sept. 5, 1921; m. Sarah E. Eustis; children: Susan M., Paul Hitch Jr., Timothy Eustis. Student, St. Petersburg Jr. Coll., 1938-40; BS in Econs, U. Pa., 1942; LLB, Harvard U., 1948; LLD, Stetson U., 1977; LLM, U. Va., 1984. Bar: N.Y. 1949, Fla. 1950. Assoc. Root, Ballantine, Harlan, Bushby & Palmer, N.Y.C., 1948-50; ptnr. Mann, Harrison, Roney, Mann & Masterson (and predecessors), St. Petersburg, Fla., 1950-57; pvt. practice, 1957-63; ptnr. Roney & Beach, St. Petersburg, 1963-69, Roney, Ulmer, Woodworth & Jacobs, St. Petersburg, 1969-70; judge U.S. Ct. Appeals (5th cir.), 1970-81, U.S. Ct. Appeals (11th cir.), St. Petersburg, 1981-86, chief judge, 1986-89, sr. cir. judge, 1989—. Adv. com. on adminstrv. law judges U.S. CSC, 1976-77; pres. judge U.S. Fgn. Intelligence Surveillance Ct. of Rev., 1994-2001. With U.S. Army, 1942-46. Fellow Am. Bar Found.; mem. ABA (chmn. legal adv. com. Fair Trial-Free Press 1973-76, mem. task force on cts. and public 1973-76, jud. adminstrn. div., chmn. appellate judges conf. 1978-79, mem. Gavel Awards com. 1980-83), Am. Judicature Soc. (dir. 1972-76), Am. Law Inst., Fla. Bar, St. Peterburg Bar Assn. (pres. 1964-65), Nat. Jud. Coll. (faculty 1974-75), Jud. Conf. U.S. (subcom. on jud. improvements 1978-84, exec com. 1986-89, com. to review circuit coun. conduct and disability orders 1991-93). Office: US Ct Appeals Barnett Tower One Progress Plz 200 Central Ave Saint Petersburg FL 33701-3326 Fax: 727-893-3851

ROOKS, JOHN NEWTON, lawyer; b. Evanston, Ill., Jan. 7, 1948; s. R. Newton and Ruth Dunlop (Darling) R.; m. Mary Preston Noell, Sept. 15, 1973; children: John Newton, Thomas N. BA, DePauw U., 1970; JD, Washington U., 1973. Bar: Ill. 1973, U.S. Dist. Ct. (no. dist.) Ill. 1973. Corp. atty. No. Trust Co., Chgo., 1973-76; ptnr. Hynds, Rooks, Yoknka Mattingly & Bzdill, Morris, 1976—. Chmn. bd. dirs. ARC, Morris, 1980-82, adv. com., 1996-97; adminstrv. coun. 1st United Meth. Ch., Morris, 1985-86; trustee, 1982-84; citizens adv. com. Morris Cmty. H.S., 1984-87; bd. dirs. Morris Elem. Sch. Dist. 54, 1987-91, 95; v.p., bd. dirs. Morris Downtown Devel. Partnership, Inc., 1996—. Mem. ABA, Ill. Bar Assn., Chgo. Bar Assn., Grundy County Bar Assn. (pres. 1983-84), Grundy County C. of C. (chmn. bd. 1982). Republican. Methodist. General corporate, General practice, Probate. Home: 102 Briar Ln Morris IL 60450-1611 Office: Hynds Rooks Yohnka Mattingly & Bzdill PO Box 685 Morris IL 60450-0685 E-mail: rooksjn@uti.com

ROONEY, GEORGE WILLARD, lawyer; b. Appleton, Wis., Nov. 16, 1915; s. Francis John and Margaret Ellen (O'Connell) R.; m. Doris I. Maxon, Sept. 20, 1941; children: Catherine Ann, Thomas Dudley, George Willard. BS, U. Wis., 1938; JD, Ohio State U., 1948. Bar: Ohio 1949, U.S. Supreme Ct. 1956, U.S. Ct. Appeals 1956. Assoc. Wise, Roetzel, Maxon, Kelly & Andress, Akron, Ohio, 1949-54; ptnr. Roetzel & Andress, and predecessor, Akron, 1954—; dir. Duracote Corp. Nat. bd. govs. ARC, 1972-78; trustee, mem. exec. bd. Summit County chpt. ARC, 1968, 1975—; v.p. Akron coun. Boy Scouts Am., 1975—; pres. Akron Automobile Assn., 1980-83, trustee, 1983—; chmn. bd. Akron Gen. Med. Ctr., 1981-86, trustee, mem. exec. com., 1986—; trustee Mobile Meals Found., Bluecoats, Inc. Maj. USAAF, 1942-46. Decorated D.F.C. with 2 oak leaf clusters, Air medal with 3 oak leaf clusters; recipient Disting. Community Svc. award Akron Labor Coun.; Disting. Svc. award Summit County chpt. ARC, 1978. Mem. ABA, Ohio Bar Assn. Akron Bar Assn. Am. Judicature Soc., Rotary (past pres.), Portage Country Club (past pres.), Cascade Club (past chmn., bd. govs.), KC. Republican. Roman Catholic. Avocations: golf, travel, gardening. General corporate, Labor. Home: 2863 Walnut Ridge Rd Akron OH 44333-2262 Office: Roetzel & Andress 222 S Main St Akron OH 44308-1533

ROONEY, JOHN PHILIP, law educator; b. Evanston, Ill., May 1, 1932; s. John McCaffery and Bernadette Marie (O'Brien) R.; m. Jean Marie Kliss, Feb. 16, 1974 (div. Oct. 1988); 1 child, Caitlin Mairin. BA, U. Ill, 1953; JD, Harvard U., 1958. Bar: Ill. 1958, Calif. 1961, Mich. 1975, U.S. Tax Ct. 1973. Assoc. lawyer Chapman & Cutler, Chgo., 1958-60, Wilson, Morton, San Mateo, Calif., 1961-63; pvt. practice San Francisco, 1963-74; prof. law Cooley Law Sch., Lansing, Mich., 1975—. Author: Selected Cases (Property), 1985; contbr. articles to profl. jours. Pres. San Francisco coun. Dem. Clubs, 1970. 1st lt. U.S. Army, 1953-55. Recipient Beattie Teaching award Cooley Law Sch. Grads., 1979, 90, 92. Fellow Mich. Bar Found.; mem. ABA (real estate fed. tax problems com., title ins. com.), Mich. Bar Title Stds. Com., Ingham County Bar Assn., Univ. Club. Democrat. Unitarian. Office: Cooley Law Sch 300 S Capitol Ave Lansing MI 48933-1586 E-mail: rooneyj@cooley.edu

ROONEY, MATTHEW A. lawyer; b. Jersey City, May 19, 1949; s. Charles John and Eileen (Dunphy) R.; m. Jean M. Alletag, June 20, 1973 (div. Dec. 1979); 1 child, Jessica Margaret; m. Diane S. Kaplan, July 6, 1981; children: Kathryn Olivia, S. Benjamin. AB magna cum laude, Georgetown U., 1971; JD with honors, U. Chgo., 1974. Bar: Ill. 1975, U.S. Dist. Ct. (no. dist.) Ill. 1975, U.S. Ct. Appeals (7th cir.). 1990. Law clk. to cir. judge U.S. Ct. Appeals (7th cir.), Chgo., 1974-75; assoc. Mayer, Brown & Platt, 1975-80, ptnr., 1981—. Assoc. editor U. Chgo. Law Rev., 1973. Fellow Am. Coll. Trial Lawyers; mem. ABA, 7th Cir. Bar Assn., Order of Coif, Phi Beta Kappa. Democrat. Roman Catholic. Avocations: jogging, golfing. Federal civil litigation, Communications, Nuclear power. Home: 2718 Sheridan Rd Evanston IL 60201-1754 Office: Mayer Brown & Platt 190 S La Salle St Ste 3100 Chicago IL 60603-3441 E-mail: mrooney@mayerbrown.com

ROONEY, PAUL C., JR. lawyer, retired; b. Winnetka, Ill., Oct. 23, 1943; s. Paul C. and Mary K. (Brennan) R.; m. Maria Elena Del Canto, Sept. 6, 1980. BA, Harvard U., 1963, LLB, 1966. Bar: Mass. 1968, N.Y. 1972, Fla. 1980, Tex. 1980, U.S. Dist. Ct. (ea. and so. dists.) N.Y., U.S. Ct. Appeals (2d cir.). Ptnr. White & Case, N.Y.C., 1983-98, ret., 1998. Served to lt. USNR, 1966-69. Mem. N.Y. State Bar Assn., Univ. Club (N.Y.C.), Mashomack Preserve (N.Y.), Sharon Country Club (Conn.). Finance, Corporate taxation, Taxation, general. Home: 417 Park Ave New York NY 10022-4401 also: 11 Lilac Ln Sharon CT 06069-2302 Office: White & Case Bldg Ll 1155 Avenue Of The Americas New York NY 10036-2787

ROOSEVELT, JAMES, JR. health plan executive, lawyer; b. L.A., Nov. 9, 1945; s. James and Romelle (Schneider) R.; m. Ann M. Conlon, June 15, 1968; children: Kathy, Tracy, Maura. AB, Harvard U., 1968, JD, 1971. Bar. Mass. 1971, D.C. 1973, U.S. Ct. Appeals (D.C. cir.) 1973, U.S. Ct. Appeals (1st cir.) 1976, U.S. Supreme Ct. 1975. Assoc. Winthrop, Stimson, Putnam & Roberts, N.Y.C., 1971, Herrick & Smith, Boston, 1975-80, ptnr., 1981-86, Nutter, McClennen & Fish, Boston, 1986-88, Choate, Hall & Stewart, Boston, 1988-98; assoc. commr. for retirement policy Social Security Adminstrn., Washington, 1998-99; sr. v.p., gen. counsel Tufts Health Plan, Waltham, Mass., 1999—. Mem. Dem. Nat. Com., Washington, 1980—, Dem. State Com., Boston, 1980—; trustee Emmanuel Coll., Boston, 1982-92, 95—; trustee Care Group, Inc., Boston, 1996-00, Mt. Auburn Hosp., Cambridge, Mass., 1984-2000, chmn., 1988-92, chmn. bd. overseers, 2000—. Lt. JAGC, USN, 1972-75. Mem. ABA, Boston Bar Assn., Mass. Bar Assn., Am. Health Lawyers Assn. (chmn. Mass. chpt. 1982-85, dir. 1996—), Am. Hosp. Assn. (trustee 1999-00), Mass. Hosp. Assn. (trustee 1987-99, chmn. 1996-97), Harvard Club. Roman Catholic. Avocation: public policy. Office: Tufts Health Plan 333 Wyman St Waltham MA 02451-1282 E-mail: james_roosevelt@tufts-health.com

ROOT, GERALD EDWARD, legal administration; b. Gridley, Calif., May 5, 1948; s. Loris Leo Root and Mary Helen (Wheeler) Murrell; m. Tricia Ann Caywood, Feb. 13, 1982 (widowed); children: Jason Alexander, Melinda Ann. AA in Bus., Yuba C.C., Marysville, Calif., 1968; BA in Psychology, Calif. State U., Sonoma, 1974; MA in Social Sci., Calif. State U., Chico, 1977; EdD, U. San Francisco, 2001. Gen. mgr. Do-It Leisure Therapeutic Recreation, Chico, 1977-79; CETA projects coord. City of Chico, 1980-81; exec. dir. Voluntary Action Ctr., Inc., South Lake Tahoe, Calif., 1981-83; devel. dir. Work Tng. Ctr., Inc., Chico, 1983-92; exec. dir. North Valley Rehab. Found., 1986-92; dir. planning and operational support Superior Ct. of Calif., County of Sacramento, 1992—. Project mgr. Juvenile Detention Alternatives Initiative, 1992-98, Feather River Industries Vocat. Tng., 1991, Creative Learning Ctr. Constrn., 1988-89, Correctional Options-Drug Ct., 1994, Violence Prevention Resource Ctr., 1995-96, Communities That Care-Juvenile Delinquency Prevention Initiative, 1995, Securing the Health and Safety of Urban Children Initiative, 1995-97, Joint Cabinets Youth Work Group/Child Welfare League Am., 1996-97, Task Force on Fairness-The Juvenile Justice Initiative, 1994-97, SacraMentor, Inc., CA Wellness Found., 1994-95, Violent Injury Prevention Coalition/Calif. Dept. Health and Human Svcs., 1995—, Domestic Violence Coord. Coun., Sacramento County, 1995-98, Family Violence Summit, 1997, Ptnrs. in Protection Conf. 1997 Child Abuse Prevention Coun., The Drug Store, Calif. Nat. Guard drug demand reduction program, 1996-97, disporportionate minority confinement rsch. com. Criminal Justice Cabinet, 1997-99, Court Cmty.-Focused Strategic Plan, 1998-2000, Sunrise Recreation and Park Dist. 10 Yr. Master Plan, 1999-2000; steering com. Multicultural Family Violence Prevention Conf., 1997-2000; presenter in field. Bd. dirs. Cmty. Action Agy., Butte County, Calif., 1990-92, ARC, Butte County, 1989-90, Sunrise Recreation and Park Dist., 1996-2001; adv. bd. Butte C.C. Dist., 1987-92, Cmty. Svcs. Planning Coun., 1994-96; blue ribbon task force for strategic plan Calif. Found. for Parks and Recreation, 2000. Grantee Annie E. Casey Found., USDA, U.S. Dept. Justice, Robert Wood Johnson Found., Calif. Office Criminal Justice Planning, U.S. Dept. Labor, Office Juvenile Justice and Delinquency Prevention, Sacramento Criminal Justice Cabinet, Calif. Wellness Found., Calif. Endowment; recipient Ralph N. Kleps award Calif. Judicial Coun., 2000. Office: Supr Ct Calif County of Sacramento 720 9th St Sacramento CA 95814-1302 E-mail: gerald.root@saccourt.com

ROOX, KRISTOF, lawyer, educator; b. Maaseik, Belgium, Aug. 21, 1971; m. Astrid van Daele, Nov. 25, 1975. LicJur, Free U. Brussels, 1994; M in Intellectual Property Law, U. London, 1996. Bar: Brussels 1994. Atty. Crowell & Moring, Brussels, 1996—; asst. prof. conflicts of law U. Ghent, Belgium, 1998—. Contbr. articles to profl. jours. Office: Crowell & Moring 27 Ave des Arts Brussels B-1040 Belgium Fax: 32 0 2 230 6399. E-mail: kroox@crowell.com

ROPER, HARRY JOSEPH, lawyer; b. Bridgeport, Conn., Apr. 15, 1940; BEE, Rensselaer Poly. Inst., 1962; LLB, NYU, 1966. Assoc. Neuman, Williams, Anderson & Olson, Chgo., 1966-70, ptnr., 1970-90, Roper & Quigg, Chgo., 1990—. Federal civil litigation, Patent, Trademark and copyright. Home: 611 W Fullerton Pky Chicago IL 60614-2613 Office: Roper & Quigg 200 S Michigan Ave Chicago IL 60604-2402

ROPSKI, GARY MELCHIOR, lawyer; b. Erie, Pa., Apr. 19, 1952; s. Joseph Albert and Irene Stefania (Mszanowski) R.; m. Barbara Mary Schleck, May 15, 1982. BS in Physics, Carnegie-Mellon U., 1972; JD cum laude, Northwestern U. Sch. Law, 1976. Bar: Ill. 1976, U.S. Patent and Trademark Office 1976, U.S. Dist. Ct. (no. dist.) Ill. 1976, U.S. Ct. Appeals (7th cir.) 1977, U.S. Dist. Ct. (ea. dist.) Wis. 1977, U.S. Ct. Appeals (3d cir.) 1981, Pa. 1982, U.S. Ct. Claims 1982, U.S. Ct. Appeals (fed. cir.) 1982, U.S. Supreme Ct. 1982, U.S. Dist. Ct. (ea. dist.) Mich. 1984, U.S. Dist. Ct. (no. dist.) Calif. 1986. Assoc. Brinks Hofer Gilson & Lione, Chgo., 1976-81, shareholder, 1981—. Adj. prof. patents and copyrights Northwestern U. Sch. Law, Chgo., 1982-97. Contbr. numerous articles to profl. jours. Mem. ABA, Internat. Bar Assn., Internat. Trademark Assn., Am. Intellectual Property Law Assn., Ill. Bar Assn., Intellectual Property Law Assn. Chgo., Chgo. Bar Assn., Univ. Club, Chgo. Yacht Club. Roman Catholic. Intellectual property, Patent, Trademark and copyright. Office: Brinks Hofer Gilson & Lione Ste 3600 455 N Cityfront Plaza Dr Chicago IL 60611-5599 E-mail: gropski@brinkshofer.com

ROSBE, JUDITH WESTLUND, lawyer; b. Berwyn, Ill., July 3, 1941; d. Paul August and Donna (Roseberry) Westlund; m. Robert Lee Rosbe, Jr., Aug. 8, 1964; children: Kristina Westlund, Heather Westlund. BA, Northwestern U., 1963, MAT, 1964; JD, New Eng. Sch. Law, 1977. Bar: Mass. 1977. Assoc. Ropes & Gray, Boston, 1977-82; counsel Stop & Shop Cos., Inc., Boston, 1983-86; v.p., Eastern regional counsel Cabot, Cabot & Forbes, Boston, 1986—. Editor-in-chief New Eng. Law Rev., 1976-77. Bd. dirs., pres. Career and Voluntary Adv. Svc., Boston, 1983-85; dir. Vis. Nurse Assn., Marion, Mass., 1983-84; trustee Tobey Hosp., Wareham, Mass., 1983—; dir. United Way of Mass. Bay, 1972-82; bd. dirs., trustee Marion Hist. Soc., 1986—; bd. dirs. Sippican Lands Trust, 1987—. Mem. ABA, Mass. Bar Assn., Boston Pvt. Industry (sec., clk. 1988—). Real property. Office: Cabot Cabot & Forbes 60 State St Boston MA 02109-1800

ROSE, ALBERT SCHOENBURG, lawyer, educator; b. Nov. 9, 1945; s. Albert Schoenburg Sr. and Karleen (Klein) R.; children: Claudia, Micah Daniel. BSBA, U. Ala., 1967; JD, Washington U., St. Louis, 1970; LLM in Taxation, George Washington U., 1974. Bar: Mo. 1970, U.S. Dist. Ct. (ea. dist.) Mo. 1970, U.S. Tax Ct. 1970, U.S. Ct. Mil. Appeals 1970, U.S. Supreme Ct. 1970. Chmn. entrepreneurial and personal svcs. dept. Blackwell Sanders Peper Martin LLP, St. Louis, 1988-2001; assoc. Lewis Rice & Fingersh, 2001—. Adj. prof. law Washington U., 1979-98, Fontbonne Coll., 1993-96. Co-author: Missouri Taxation Law and Practice, 1986, supplement, 1989. Capt. U.S. Army, 1970-74, Korea. Mem. planning com., Mid-Am. Tax Conf.; mem. Tax Lawyers Club (pres.). General corporate, Estate planning, Corporate taxation. Office: Lewis Rice & Fingersh 500 North Broadway Ste 2000 Saint Louis MO 63102 E-mail: arose@lewisrice.com

ROSE, CHARLES ALEXANDER, lawyer; b. Louisville, June 14, 1932; s. Hector Edward and Mary (Shepard) R.; m. Moncie Watson; children: Marc, Craig, Lorna, Gordon, Alex, Sara. BA, U. Louisville, 1954, JD, 1960. Bar: Ky. 1960, U.S. Ct. Appeals (6th cir.) 1970, Ind. 1978, U.S. Supreme Ct. 1978. Pvt. practice, Louisville, 1960-63; assoc. Jones, Ewen & McKenzie, 1963-65; ptnr. Curtis & Rose, 1965-81, Weber & Rose, Louisville, 1981—. Organist Scottish Rite Temple, Louisville. Lt. USAF, 1954-56. Mem. ABA, Ky. Bar Assn., Ind. Bar Assn., Louisville Bar Assn., Am. Soc. Hosp. Attys., Am. Bd. Trial Advocates, Brandeis Soc., Fedn. Ins. Counsel, River Road Country Club, Pendennis Club (Louisville), Jefferson Club. Republican. Episcopalian. Personal injury. Office: 400 W Market St Ste 2700 Louisville KY 40202-3358

ROSE, DAVID L. lawyer; b. Ft. Monmouth, N.J., Feb. 18, 1955; s. Llewellyn Paterson and Bebe (Faulk) R.; m. Laura Marie Jarvis, Sept. 3, 1989; children: Allison Michelle, Jessica Morgan, Ashley Elizabeth. BA in Comm., U. Colo., 1980; JD, Ariz. State U., 1991. Bar: Ariz. 1991, U.S. Dist. Ct. Ariz. 1991, U.S. Ct. Appeals (9th cir.) 1993, U.S. Supreme Ct. 1997. Law clk. Bonn & Anderson, Phoenix, 1988-91, Maricopa County Superior Ct., Phoenix, 1990-91; lawyer Anderson, Brody, Levinson, Weiser & Horwitz, 1991-92, Brandes, Lane & Joffe, Phoenix, 1992-93; pvt. practice, 1993—; lawyer Rose & Hildebrand, P.C., 1997—. Editor: Missive, 1992. Bd. dirs. Maricopa County Family Support Adv. Com., Phoenix; adv. coun. Washington Sch. Dist., Phoenix; mem. Ariz. State Legis., Domestic Rels. Reform Com., Phoenix. Mem. Maricopa County Bar Assn. (adv. family law com.), ABA (adv. family law sect.), Nat. Congress for Men (pres.), Father's for Equal Rights of Colo. (pres.). Avocations: aviation, computer systems. General civil litigation, Criminal, Family and matrimonial. Office: 1440 E Washington St Phoenix AZ 85034-1109

ROSE, DONALD MCGREGOR, retired lawyer; b. Cin., Feb. 6, 1933; s. John Kreimer and Helen (Morris) R.; m. Constance Ruth Lanner, Nov. 29, 1958; children: Barbara Rose Mead, Ann Rose Weston. AB in Econs., U. Cin., 1955; JD, Harvard U., 1958. Bar: Ohio 1958, U.S. Supreme Ct. 1962. Asst. legal officer USNR, Subic Bay, The Philippines, 1959-62, with Office of JAG The Pentagon, Va., 1962-63; assoc. Frost & Jacobs, LLP, Cin., 1963-70, ptnr., 1970-93, sr. ptnr., 1993-97, ret. ptnr., 1997. Co-chmn. 6th Cir. Appellate Practice Inst., Cin., 1983, 90, mem. 6th Cir. adv. com., 1990-98, chmn. subcom. on rules, 1990-94, chmn., 1994-96. Trustee Friends of Cin. Pks., Inc., 1980-89, 93-98, pres. 1980-86; trustee Am. Music Scholarship Assn., Cin., 1985-88; pres. Social Health Assn. Greater Cin. Area Inc., 1969-72; co-chmn. Harvard Law Sch. Fund for So. Ohio, Cin., 1985-87; pres. Meth. Union, Cin., 1983-85; chmn. trustees Hyde Pk. Cmty. United Meth. Ch., Cin., 1974-76, chmn. coun. on ministries, 1979-81, chmn. adminstrv. bd., 1982-84, chmn. mem. canvass, 1985, chmn. staff parish rels. com., 1988-90, chmn. commn. missions, 1993-95; trustee Meth. Theol. Sch. Ohio, vice chmn. devel. com., 1990-94, sec. 1992-94, chmn. devel. com., 1994-98, vice chmn., 1998, chmn., 1999—; loaned exec. United Way, Cin., 1999. Lt. USNR, 1959-63. Mem. Cin. Bar Assn., Cin. Citizens Police Assn., On Air Reader, Cin. Assn. for Blind, Univ. Club (Cin.), Cin. Country Club. Republican. Avocations: sailing, golf. General civil litigation. Home: 8 Walsh Ln Cincinnati OH 45208-3435 also: 11 Blackstone Rd Boothbay Harbor ME 04538-1943 E-mail: dmrose@fbtlaw.com

ROSE, EDITH SPRUNG, retired lawyer; b. N.Y.C., Jan. 7, 1924; d. David L. and Anna (Storch) Sprung; m. David J. Rose, Feb. 15, 1948; children: Elizabeth Rose Stanton, Lawrence, Michael. BA, Barnard Coll., 1944; LLB, Columbia U., 1946. Bar: N.Y. 1947, N.J. 1973. Adminstr. Practising Law Inst., N.Y.C., 1947-48; ptnr. Smith, Lambert, Hicks & Miller, Princeton, N.J., 1974-88; counsel to Drinker, Biddle & Reath, 1988-91; ret., 19991. Mem. ABA, N.Y. Bar Assn., N.J. Bar Assn., Princeton Bar Assn., Womens Law Caucus of Mercer County, Princeton Club (N.Y.C.). Estate planning, General practice. Home: 201 Lambert Dr Princeton NJ 08540-2308

ROSE, I. NELSON, law educator; b. Los Angeles, May 23, 1950; s. Bernard and Helen Mae (Nelson) R. B.A., UCLA, 1973; J.D., Harvard U., 1979. Bar: Hawaii 1979, Calif. 1980, U.S. Dist. Ct. Hawaii 1979, U.S. Ct. Appeals (9th cir.) 1980, U.S. Supreme Ct. 1991. Pvt. practice, Honolulu, 1979-82; asst. prof. law Whittier Coll., Los Angeles, 1982-85, assoc. prof. 1985-89, tenured prof. law, 1989—; cons. legal gaming; vis. scholar Inst. for Study of Gambling and Comml. Gaming, U. Nev., Reno. Author: Gambling and the Law, 1986, Blackjack and the Law, 1998 (with Robert A. Loeb); also articles in profl. jours. Founder, counsel Hawaii Lions Eye Bank, Honolulu, 1979-82; founder, v.p., counsel Calif. Council on Compulsive Gambling. Mem. ABA, Calif. State Bar Assn., Hawaii Bar Assn., Internat. Assn. Gaming Attys. Democrat. Jewish. E-mail: rose@gamblingandthelaw.com. Home: 17031 Encino Hills Dr Encino CA 91436-4009 Office: Whittier Law Sch 3333 Harbor Blvd Costa Mesa CA 92626-1501

ROSE, JOEL ALAN, legal consultant; b. Bklyn., Dec. 26, 1936; s. Edward Isadore and Adele R.; m. Isadora Fenig, Apr. 12, 1964; children: Susan, Terri. BS in Econs., NYU, 1958; MBA, Wharton Grad. Sch., U. Pa., 1960. Asst. purchasing agt. Maidenform Inc., N.Y.C., 1960-62; personnel dir. E.J. Korvette Inc., 1962-66; mgmt. cons. Daniel J. Cantor & Co. Inc., Phila., 1966—, sr. v.p., 1987—; mgmt. cons. to legal profession. Coord. Ann. Conf. on Law Firm Mgmt. and Econs. Author: Managing the Law Office; mem. adv. bd. Law Office Economics and Management, 1987; contbg. columnist N.Y. Law Jour., 1984—, Nat. Law Jour. Extra, 1996—, Phila. Legal Intelligencer, 1995—, L.A. Daily Times, 1999—, Legal Times of Washington, 1998—, N.J. Law Jour., 2000-, The Barrister, 1995-; also articles to profl. jours.; bd. editors Acctg. for Law Firms; editl. adv. bd. Corp. Counsel's Guide to Law Dept. Mgmt. With U.S. Army, 1960, Res., 1960-66. Fellow Coll. of Law Practice Mgmt.; mem. ABA (chmn. acquisition and mergers com., practice mgmt. sect., large law firm interest group), Inst. Mgmt. Cons., Am. Arbitration Assn. (nat. panel), Adminstrv. Mgmt. Soc. (past chpt. pres.), Am. Mgmt. Assn., Assn. Legal Adminstrs. Office: Joel A Rose & Assoc Inc PO Box 162 Cherry Hill NJ 08003-0162

ROSE, KIM MATTHEW, lawyer, educator; b. Gallipolis, Ohio, Mar. 21, 1956; s. Dave and Lois Ann R.; m. Pamela Carol Sims, Aug. 11, 1990. Student, USMA, 1974-76; BBA, Ohio U., 1977; JD, Capital U. Law, 1981; MBA, Ashland Coll., 1988. Bar: Ohio 1981, U.S. Dist. Ct. (so. dist.) Ohio 1981, U.S. Ct. Appeals (6th cir.) 1987, U.S. Supreme Ct. 1988. Asst. prosecutor Knox County Prosecutor, Mt. Vernon, Ohio, 1982-90; with Critchfield, Critchfield & Johnston, 1982—. Adj. prof. Mt. Vernon Nazarene Coll., 1982—. Mem. Met. Housing Authority, Knox County, 1990—; mem. adv. bd. Salvation Army, Mt. Vernon, 1991—; mem. Boys Village Corp. Bd., Smithville, Ohio, 1991—; mem. Knox Cmty. Hosp. Bd., Mt. Vernon, Ohio, 2000. Maj. USAR, 1974-95. Mem. Ohio State Bar Assn. (mem. substance abuse lawyer's assistance com.), Knox County Bar Assn. (past pres.), Mt. Vernon Nazarene Coll. Found. (rec. sec. bd. 1995—), Mt. Vernon-Knox County C. of C., Masons. Avocations: flying, skiing, fishing, golfing, biking. General corporate, General practice, Probate. Home: 1413 Greenbrier Dr Mount Vernon OH 43050-9101 Office: Critchfield Critchfield & Johnston 10 S Gay St Mount Vernon OH 43050-3546 E-mail: rose@axom.com, kimr@ccj.com

ROSE, NORMAN, retired lawyer, retired accountant; b. N.Y.C., July 7, 1923; s. Edward J. and Frances (Ludwig) R.; div.; children: Ellen, Michael; m. Judith Rose; stepchildren: Dwight, Audrey, Jason. BBA, CCNY, 1947; JD, N.Y. Law Sch., 1953. Bar: N.Y. 1954, U.S. Dist. Ct. (ea. dist.) N.Y. 1956, U.S. Tax Ct. 1956, U.S. Dist. Ct. (so. dist.) N.Y. 1960, U.S. Supreme Ct. 1961, U.S. Ct. Appeals (2d cir.) 1967, Fla. 1979. Pvt. practice, N.Y.C., 1954-69, Ft. Lauderdale, Fla., 1979-91; ptnr. Dean, Falanga & Rose, Carle Pl., N.Y., 1979-81. Referee Small Claims Ct., N.Y.C., 1959-69; arbitrator Accident Claims Tribunal, Am. Arbitration Assn., 1960-65; C.P.A., N.Y.C., 1951-57; lectr. in field. Author law note Liability of Golfer to Person Struck by Ball, 1959 (Hon. Mention 1960). Pres. Nassau South Shore Little League, Lawrence, N.Y., 1966-68; treas. 5 Towns Dem. Club, Woodmere, N.Y., 1966-67; chmn. United Fund, Village of Lawrence, 1967. Capt. USAF, 1943-45, ETO. Decorated DFC, Air medal with 5 oak leaf clusters, Silver Star, Purple Heart. Mem. ATLA (sustaining), Acad. Fla. Trial Lawyers (sustaining), N.Y. State Assn. Plaintiffs Trial Lawyers, N.Y. State Bar Assn., Fla. Bar, Nassau County Bar Assn. (chmn. med-legal com. 1975-77), Lawyer/Pilots Bar Assn., Pompano Beach Power Squadron (safety officer), Masons, Shriners. State civil litigation, Insurance, Personal injury. Home: #2111 3200 Port Royale Dr N Apt 2111 Fort Lauderdale FL 33308-7808 E-mail: normierose@aol.com

ROSE, RICHARD LOOMIS, lawyer; b. Long Branch, N.J., Oct. 21, 1936; s. Charles Frederick Perrott and Jane Mary (Crotta) R.; m. Marian Frances Irons, Apr. 1, 1960; children: Linda, Cynthia, Bonnie. BA, Cornell U., 1958; JD, Washington and Lee U., 1963. Bar: N.Y. 1963, Conn. 1965, U.S. Dist. Ct. (so. dist.) N.Y. 1964, U.S. Dist. Ct. Conn. 1965, U.S. Ct. Appeals (2d cir.) 1965, U.S. Supreme Ct. 1970. Assoc. Cummings & Lockwood, Stamford, Conn., 1965-71, ptnr., 1971-91, Kleban & Samor, P.C., Southport, 1991-93; of counsel Whitman Breed Abbott & Morgan, Greenwich, Conn., 1993-95; prin. Roberts, Rose & Bates, P.C., Stamford, 1995—. Bd. dirs. and sec. Index Corp.; mem. adv. com. Conn. Banking Commr. on Conn. Securities Laws, 1982—; dir. Conn. World Trade Assn. Editor: Washington and Lee Law Rev. Chmn. Fgn. Trade Zone Com. to Mayor of City of Bridgeport, Conn., 1988-90; mem. fgn. trade awareness com. S.W. Area Industry and Commerce Assn., Task Force, 1987-88; bd. dirs. German Sch. of Conn., Inc., 1992—. 1st lt. U.S. Army, 1958-60, Korea. Mem. ABA, Conn. Bar Assn. (exec. com. corp. sect.), Internat. Bar Assn., New Canaan Country Club, Campfire Club Am. (bd. govs.), Phi Delta Phi, Omicron Delta Kappa, Phi Delta Theta. Republican. Banking, Contracts commercial, Public international. Office: Roberts Rose & Bates PC PO Box 15630 1055 Washington Blvd Stamford CT 06901-2216

ROSE, ROBERT E(DGAR), state supreme court chief justice; b. Orange, N.J., Oct. 7, 1939; B.A., Juniata Coll., Huntingdon, Pa., 1961; LL.B., NYU, 1964. Bar: Nev. 1965. Dist. atty. Washoe County, 1971-75; lt. gov. State of Nev., 1975-79; judge Nev. Dist. Ct., 8th Jud. Dist., Las Vegas, 1986-88; justice Nev. Supreme Ct., Carson City, 1989—, chief justice, 1993-94, 1999-2000. Office: Nev Supreme Ct Capitol Complex 201 S Carson St Carson City NV 89701-4702

ROSE, ROBERT GORDON, lawyer; b. Newark, June 25, 1943; s. Harry and Ann Shirley (Gordon) R.; m. Ellen Nadley Berkowitz, July 2, 1966; children: Lisa Pauline, Michael Allan. BA, SUNY, Buffalo, 1965; MA, Columbia U., 1969; JD, Seton Hall U., 1974. Bar: N.J. 1974, U.S. Dist. Ct. N.J. 1974, U.S. Ct. Appeals (3rd cir.) 1974, U.S. Ct. Appeals (2nd cir.) 1975. Law clk. to Hon. John J. Gibbons U.S. Ct. Appeals (3rd cir.), Newark, 1974-75; assoc. Pitney, Hardin, Kipp & Szuch, Morristown, N.J., 1975-80, ptnr., 1980—. Mem. com. on unauthorized practice of law Supreme Ct. N.J., 1989—, apptd. com. chair, 2000. Contbr. articles to profl. jours. Recipient Disting. Grad. award Seton Hall U. Law Sch., 2000. Mem.

ABA, N.J. Bar Assn., Morris County Bar Assn. (trustee 1989-90). Avocations: travel, philately. General civil litigation, Construction, Environmental. Office: Pitney Hardin Kipp & Szuch Park Ave at Morris County PO Box 1945 Morristown NJ 07962-1945 E-mail: rrose@phks.com

ROSE, TERRY WILLIAM, lawyer; b. Kenosha, Wis., Nov. 22, 1942; s. William S. and Kathryn J. (Williams) R.; children: Christopher, Juliet Sheridan. BS, Northwestern U., 1964; JD, U. Wis.-Madison, 1967. Bar: Wis. 1967, U.S. Dist. Ct. (ea. dist.) Wis. 1967, U.S. Dist. Ct. (we. dist.) Wis. 1970, U.S. Ct. Appeals (7th cir.) 1967, U.S. Supreme Ct. 1975. Law clk. to presiding justice U.S. Ct. Appeals (7th cir.), Chgo., 1967-68; ptnr. Cotton, Rose & Rose, Kenosha, 1968-78, Rose & Rose, Kenosha, 1979—; vice chmn. 1st dist. profl. responsibility com. Wis. Supreme Ct., 1979-83; mem. Kenosha County Bd. Suprs., 1986—. V.p. Kenosha Pub. Mus., 1968-70; trustee, pres. Kenosha Symphony Assn., 1972-78; mem. com. Dept. Social Svcs. & Comprehensive Mental Health Bd., Kenosha, Kenosha County Health Planning Com., 1981-82; mem. facilities utilization com. Kenosha Unified Sch. Dist., 1983; chmn. Wis. Civil Liberties Union, 1971, Racine-Kenosha chpt. ACLU; chmn. Kenosha County Democratic Party, 1979-80, 1st Congl. Dist. Dem. Party Wis., 1980-82; former pres. Planned Parenthood Kenosha; pres. Christian Youth Ctr., 1982-85; mem. vestry St. Matthew's Episcopal Ch., 1984-93, sr. warden 1993-96; supr. Kenosha County Bd., 1986—; pres. United Way of Kenosha County, 1996-97; chmn. Kenosha Airport Commn., 1995. Mem. Northwestern U. Alumni Club Racine/Kenosha (past pres.), Northwestern U. John Evans Club, Kenosha County Bar Assn. (sec. 1969-71, pres. elect 1984-85, pres. 1985-86), State Bar Wis. Lodge: Masons (32d deg.; jr. deacon 1984-85). Federal civil litigation, State civil litigation, Criminal. Office: Rose & Rose 5529 6th Ave Kenosha WI 53140-3709

ROSE-ACKERMAN, SUSAN, law and political economy educator; b. Mineola, N.Y., Apr. 23, 1942; d. R. William and Rosalie (Gould) Rose; m. Bruce A. Ackerman, May 29, 1967; children: Sybil, John BA, Wellesley Coll., 1964; PhD, Yale U., 1970. Asst. prof. U. Pa., Phila, 1970-74; lectr. Yale U., New Haven, 1974-75, asst. prof., 1975-78, assoc. prof., 1978-82; prof. law and polit. economy Columbia U., N.Y.C., 1982-87; Ely prof. of law and polit. econ. Yale U., New Haven, 1987-92, co-dir. Ctr. Law, Econ. and Pub. Policy, 1988—, Luce prof. jurisprudence law and polit. sci., 1992—. Panelist Am. studies program Am. Coun. Learned Socs., 1987-90; review panelist, faculty Fulbright Commn., 1993-96; vis. rsch. fellow World Bank, 1995-96. Author: (with Ackerman, Sawyer and Henderson) Uncertain Search for Environmental Quality, 1974 (Henderson prize 1982); Corruption: A Study in Political Economy, 1978; (with E. James) The Nonprofit Enterprise in Market Economies, 1986; editor: The Economics of Nonprofit Institutions, 1986; (with J. Coffee and L. Lowenstein) Knights, Raiders, and Targets: The Impact of the Hostile Takeover, 1988, Rethinking the Progressive Agenda: The Reform of the American Regulatory State, 1992, Controlling Environmental Policy: The Limits of Public Law in Germany and the United States, 1995, Corruption and Government: Causes, Consequences and Reform, 1999; contbr. articles to profl. jours.; bd. editors: Jour. Law, Econs. and Orgn., 1984—, Internat. Rev. Law and Econs., 1986—, Jour. Policy Analysis and Mgmt., 1989—, Polit. Sci. Quar., 1988—. Guggenheim fellow 1991-92, Fulbright fellow, Free U. Berlin, 1991-92. Mem. Am. Law and Econs. Assn. (bd. dirs. 1993-96), Am. Econ. Assn. (mem. exec. com. 1990-93), Am. Polit. Sci. Assn., Assn. Am. Law Schs., Assn. Pub. Policy and Mgmt. (policy coun. 1984-88, treas. 1998-2000). Democrat Office: Yale U Law Sch PO Box 208215 New Haven CT 06520-8215

ROSELLI, RICHARD JOSEPH, lawyer; b. Chgo., Mar. 2, 1954; s. H. Joseph and Dolores Roselli; m. Lisa McNelis; children: Nicholas Joseph, Christiana Elise, Alexandra Grace, Michaela Luciana, Anthony Santino. BA, Tulane U., 1976, JD, 1980. Bar: Fla. 1981, U.S. Dist. Ct. (so. dist.) Fla. 1981, U.S. Ct. Appeals (5th and 11th cirs.); bd. cert. civil trial lawyer. Assoc. Krupnick & Campbell, Ft. Lauderdale, Fla., 1981-84; ptnr. Krupnick, Campbell, Malone, Roselli, 1984-91, Krupnick Campbell Malone Roselli Buser Slama & Hancock P.A., Ft. Lauderdale, 1999—; mng. ptnr. Krupnick Campbell Malone Roselli Buser Slama Hancock McNelis Liberman & McKee P.A., 1999—. Trustee Fla. Dem. Party, 1992-95. Mem. ATLA (pres.' coun. 1996-97), Am. Bd. Trial Advocates, Am. Soc. Law and Medicine, So. Trial Lawyers Assn. (founder), Acad. Fla. Trial Lawyers (bd. dirs. 1987—, exec. com. 1990-97, sec. 1993, treas. 1994, pres. elect. 1995, pres. 1996, chmn. Fla. lawyers action group-PAC 1996, Golden Eagle award, 1989, 1996, 98, Silver Eagle award, 1990, Crystal Eagle award 1995), Broward County Trial Lawyers (bd. dirs.), Trial Lawyers for Pub. Justice, Lawyer Pilots Bar Assn., St. Jude Catholic Ch. Personal injury, Product liability. Office: 700 SE 3rd Ave Fort Lauderdale FL 33316-1154

ROSEMAN, CHARLES SANFORD, lawyer; b. Jersey City, Feb. 26, 1945; s. Leon and Edith (Neidorf) R.; children: Rochelle Lynn, Loren Scott. BA, Calif. State U., 1968; JD, U. San Deigo, 1971. Bar: Calif. 1972, U.S. Dist. Ct. (so. dist.) Calif. 1972, U.S. Dist. Ct. (cen. dist.) Calif. 1975, U.S. Supreme Ct. 1980, U.S. Claim Ct. 1990. Assoc. Greer, Popko, Nickoloff & Miller, San Diego, 1972-73; ptnr. Roseman & Roseman, 1973-78, Roseman & Small, San Diego, 1978-82, Frank, Roseman, Freedus & Mann, San Diego, 1982-86, Roseman and Mann, 1986-92; pvt. practice San Diego, 1992—; judge pro tem San Diego County Superior Ct., 1975—; also arbitrator, mediator, 1977—. Bd. dirs. Glenn Aire Cmty. Devel. Assn., San Diego, 1972-73, Big Bros. San Diego County, 1973-81; bd. dirs. San Diego County Anti-Defamation League, 1985—; chmn. exec. com. 1984-85, assoc. nat. commr., 1995—; bd. dirs. San Diego County Legal Aid Soc., 1988-89, Tifereth Israel Synagogue, pres. 1982-84. Mem. ABA, Assn. Trial Lawyers Am., Consumer Attys. of Calif. (Recognition of Experience award 1985), Calif. Bar Assn., Am. Arbitration Assn. (arbitrator, panel 1985—), San Diego Bar Assn., Consumer Attys. of San Diego (bd. dirs. 1982-84), U. San Diego Sch. Law Alumni Assn. (bd. dirs. 1972-73), B'nai B'rith (pres. 1978). Democrat. State civil litigation, Insurance, Personal injury. Office: Law Offices Charles S Roseman & Assocs 170 Laurel St San Diego CA 92101-1419 E-mail: csrl@flash.net

ROSEN, GERALD ELLIS, federal judge; b. Chandler, Ariz., Oct. 26, 1951; s. Stanley Rosen and Marjorie (Sherman) Cahn; m. Laurie DeMond; 1 child, Jacob DeMond. BA, Kalamazoo Coll., 1973; JD, George Washington U., 1979. Researchist Swedish Inst., Stockholm, 1973; legis. asst. U.S. Senator Robert P. Griffin, Washington, 1974-79; law clk. Seyfarth, Shaw, Fairweather & Gerardson, Wash., 1979; from assoc. to sr. ptnr. Miller, Canfield, Paddock and Stone, Detroit, 1979-90; judge U.S. Dist Ct (ea. dist.) Mich., 1990—. Mem. Jud. Evaluation Com. (co-chmn. 1983-88), Detroit; adj. prof. law Wayne State U., 1992—, U. Detroit Law Sch., 1994—; mem. U.S. Jud. Conf. Com. on Criminal Law; lectr. CLE confs., others. Co-author: Federal Civil Trials and Evidence, 1999, West's Michigan Civil Trials and Evidence, 2001; sr. editor: West's Michigan Practice Guide Series; contbr. articles to profl. jours. Rep. candidate for U.S. Congress, Mich., 1982; chmn. 17th Congl. Dist. Rep. Com., 1983-85; mem. Mich. Criminal Justice Commn., 1985-87; mem. Birmingham Athletic Club; bd. visitors George Washington U. Law Sch., 2000—; bd. dirs. Focus Hope, 2000—. Fellow Kalamazoo Coll. (sr. 1972); recipient Career Achievement award Rolex/Intercollegiate Tennis Assn. Mem. Fed. Judges Assn. (bd. dirs.). Jewish. Office: US Courthouse 231 W Lafayette Blvd Rm 802 Detroit MI 48226-2707

ROSEN, JON HOWARD, lawyer; b. Bklyn., May 20, 1943; s. Eli and Vera (Horowitz) R.; children from previous marriage, Jason Marc, Hope Terry. BA, Hobart Coll., 1965; JD, St. John's U., 1968; postgrad., CCNY, 1969-71. Bar: N.Y. 1969, Calif. 1975, Wash. 1977. Atty. FAA, N.Y.C., 1968-71; regional atty., contract adminstr. Air Line Pilots Assn., N.Y.C., Chgo., L.A., San Francisco, 1971-77; pvt. practice Seattle, 1977-80; ptnr. Frank and Rosen, 1981-98, Frank Rosen Freed Roberts LLP, Seattle, 1999—. Instr. labor studies Shoreline C.C., 1978-90. Trustee Temple DeHirsch Sinai, 1991-98, v.p., 1998-00, pres.-elect 2000-01, pres., 2001—; chair 4th N. and Ward Pk. Steering Com. Fellow Coll. Labor and Employment Lawyers; mem. ABA (union co-chmn. com. on employee rights and responsibilities 1992-96, union co-chmn. regional programs sub com. 1998-2000, union co-chmn. nat. programs sub com. 2000—, co-regional EEOC liaison), King County Bar Assn. (past chmn. aviation and space law sect., past chmn. Pacific Coast Labor and Employment Law Conf., past chmn. labor law sect.), Nat. Employment Lawyers Assn. (founding state chair, state steering com. 1990-95), Wash. State Trial Lawyers Assn. (past chair employment law com.). Administrative and regulatory, Civil rights, Labor. Office: Frank Rosen Freed Roberts LLP 705 2nd Ave Ste 1200 Seattle WA 98104-1729 E-mail: jhr@frankandrosen.com

ROSEN, MARTIN JAY, lawyer; b. N.Y.C., Nov. 15, 1942; s. Herman S. and Ida (Ginsberg) R.; m. Bonnie C., Dec. 24, 1964; children: Scott F., Brian M. BA, Hobart Coll., 1964; LLB, NYU, 1967. Bar: N.Y. 1967, U.S. Supreme Ct. 1976. Law asst. Appellate Divsn. First Dept., N.Y.C., 1967-68; assoc. Battle, Fowler, Stokes & Kheel, 1968-69; confdl. law sec. to justice Supreme Ct. Westchester County, N.Y., 1969-71; sole practice White Plains, 1975—. Lectr. in field. Past editor Domestic Law Rev.; contbr. articles to legal jours. Fellow Am. Acad. Matrimonial Lawyers; mem. ABA, N.Y. State Bar Assn., Westchester County Bar Assn. (past chmn. family law sect.), Rockland County Bar Assn., White Plains Bar Assn. Family and matrimonial. Office: 175 Main St Suite 415 White Plains NY 10601

ROSEN, MARVIN SHELBY, lawyer; b. Detroit, Aug. 8, 1947; s. Joseph P. and Rachel K. (Kaplan) R.; m. Sandra Mira Levy, Nov. 22, 1970; children: Joseph H., Bradley J. BA, Columbia U., 1970, JD, MBA, 1973; B in Hebrew Lit., Jewish Theol. Sem., N.Y.C., 1970. Bar: Mich. 1974, Fla. 1984. Assoc. Honigman Miller Schwartz and Cohn, Detroit, 1974-78, ptnr., 1978-84, mng. ptnr. Fla., 1984-97; shareholder Ruden, McClosky, Smith, Schuster & Russell, P.A., 1997—. Contbr. articles to profl. jours. Mem. bd. overseers List Coll., N.Y.C.; v.p. Pres. Country Club, 1995-99, Jewish Fedn. Palm Beach County, 1992-99; pres. Jewish Cmty. Day Sch., 1987-88; founding chmn. Commn. for Jewish Edn., 1990-93; pres. Temple Emanu-El, Palm Beach, 2000—. Named one of Best Lawyers in Am., 1989—. Mem. Mich. State Bar (chmn. com. on mortgages, land contracts and related security devices real property sect. 1982-84), Detroit Bar Assn. (chmn. real property sect. 1982-83). Finance, Real property. Office: Ruden McClosky Smith Schuster & Russell PA 222 Lakeview Ave Ste 800 West Palm Beach FL 33401-6148 Fax: 561-832-3036. E-mail: msr@ruden.com

ROSEN, MATTHEW A. lawyer; b. Phila., 1952; BA, Swarthmore Coll., 1973; JD cum laude, Boston U., 1976; LLM, NYU, 1979. Bar: Pa. 1976, N.Y. 1979. Sr. ptnr. Skadden, Arps, Slate, Meagher & Flom LLP, N.Y.C. Corporate taxation, Taxation, general, Personal income taxation. Office: Skadden Arps Slate Meagher & Flom LLP 4 Times Sq Fl 24 New York NY 10036-6595

ROSEN, MICHAEL JAMES, lawyer; b. Miami, Fla., Oct. 25, 1949; s. E. David and Muriel G. (Gerstein) R.; children: Jason, Lauren. BA, U. South Fla., 1971; JD, U. Miami, 1974. Bar: Fla. 1974, U.S. Dist. Ct. (so. dist.) Fla. 1974, U.S. Ct. Appeals (5th cir.) 1975, U.S. Ct. Appeals (6th cir.) 1979, U.S. Dist. Ct. (mid. dist.) Fla. 1980, U.S. Ct. Appeals (11th cir.) 1981, U.S. Ct. Appeals (2d cir.) 1983, U.S. Tax Ct., U.S. Supreme Ct. 1979. Asst. fed. pub. defender Fed. Pub. Defender, Miami, 1974-76; ptnr. Rosen & Rosen PA, 1976-87; pvt. practice, 1987—. Adj. prof. RICO fed. criminal law U. Miami Sch. Law; counselor Peter T. Fay Am. Inn. Ct., St. Thomas Sch. Law. Mem. ABA, FBA (chmn. criminal discovery com. 1983), ACLU, Nat. Assn. Criminal Def. Lawyers. Federal civil litigation, Criminal. Office: Michael J Rosen PA 2400 S Dixie Hwy Ste 105 Miami FL 33133-3141 E-mail: mjrpalaw@aol.com

ROSEN, RICHARD DAVID, lawyer; b. Pitts., June 24, 1940; s. Benjamin H. and Bertha B. (Broff) R.; m. Ellaine H. Heller, June 23, 1963; children: Deborah H. Fidel, Jaime M. Cohen. BA, Yale U., 1962; JD, Harvard U., 1965. Bar: Pa. 1966, Fla. 1979. Mgr. Bachrach, Sanderbeck & Co., Pitts., 1965-70; mng. ptnr. Grant Thornton, 1970-76; chmn. tax dept. Baskin & Sears, 1977-78; pres. Gas Transmission, Inc., 1979—; dir., shareholder Cohen & Grigsby, 1989—. Bd. dirs., pres R & R Oil Corp., Pitts.; bd. dirs., sec. Comml. Data Svcs., Sim Computer Leasing Corp., Pitts., Direct Mail Svc., Inc. Contbr. articles to profl. jours. Chmn. investment com.; trustee Jewish Healthcare Found., 1995—, chmn., 2001— Fellow Am. Coll. Trust and Estate Counsel; mem. ABA, Pa. Bar Assn. (mem. estate planning com. 1996—, chmn. 1998-2000), United Jewish Fedn. Greater Pitts. (chmn. profl. adv. com. 1997—), Green Oaks Country Club (dir. 1997—). Avocations: golf, tennis. Home: 1198 Beechwood Ct Pittsburgh PA 15206-4522 Office: Cohen & Grigsby PC 11 Stanwix St 15 Fl Pittsburgh PA 15222-1312 E-mail: rrosen@cohenlaw.com

ROSEN, RICHARD LEWIS, lawyer, real estate developer; b. N.Y.C., Mar. 6, 1943; s. Morris and Lorraine (Levy) R.; m. Doris Ellen Bloom, Aug. 28, 1983. BA, Cornell U., 1965; JD, N.Y. Law Sch., 1968; cert., NYU Real Estate Inst., 1980. Bar: N.Y. 1968, U.S. Dist. Ct. (so. and ea. dists.) N.Y. 1972; lic. real estate broker. Pvt. practice, N.Y.C., 1971-73; ptnr. Rosen, Wise, Felzen & Salomon, 1973-79, Rosen & Felzen, N.Y.C., 1979-84, Rosen, Rudd, Kera, Graubard & Hollender, N.Y.C., 1985-88, Bell, Kalnick, Klee and Green, N.Y.C., 1989-90; shareholder Rosen, Einbinder & Dunn, P.C., 1990—. Contbg. author: Francising 101, The Complete Guide to Evaluating, Buying and Growing Your Franchise Business. Named Ea. States Lightweight Weightlifting Champion, 1968; N.Y. State Regents scholar. Mem. ABA (mem. Forum Com. on Franchising), Am. Assn. Franchises and Dealers (former chmn. legal steering com., chmn. fair franchising stds. com., chmn. alternate dispute resolution com., bd. dirs.), Franchise Lawyers Assn., Am. Franchise Assn., N.Y. State Bar Assn. (founding mem. franchise law com., chmn. mission statement com. of franchise law com.), Nat. Franchise Mediation Program (mem. steering com.), Assn. Bar City N.Y. (panel mem. com. on franchising, panel mem. com. on corp. law), Red Key Hon. Soc., Cornell U., Sphinx Head Hon. Soc., Cornell U., Spiked Shoe Soc., Cornell U., Ea. Intercollegiate Athletic Assn. (named Lightweight Football All Ea. Selection 1963, 64). Avocations: tennis, skiing, physical fitness, guitar, reading. General corporate, Franchising, Real property. Home: 1 Old Jericho Tpke Jericho NY 11753-1205 also: Lamb Ave Quogue NY 11959 Office: Rosen Einbinder & Dunn PC 641 Lexington Ave New York NY 10022-4503 E-mail: RLR@redlawfirm.com

ROSEN, SIDNEY MARVIN, lawyer; b. Detroit, June 27, 1939; s. Fred A. and Gertrude (Cole) R.; children: Jordan, Aviva. BS, U. Ariz., 1961, JD, 1964. Bar: Ariz. 1964, U.S. Dist. Ct. Ariz. 1964, Calif. 1965, U.S. Dist. Ct. (so. dist.) Calif. 1965, U.S. Supreme Ct. 1971. Asst. atty. gen. State of Ariz., Phoenix, 1964-66, spl. asst. atty. gen., 1968-69; assoc. Kirkwood, Kaplan, Russin & Vechi, Bangkok and Saigon, Vietnam, 1967-68; ptnr. Rosen, Chemal, Ocampo and Fontes, Phoenix, 1970—. Co-founder, law instr. Ariz. Bar Rev. Course, 1965-73; prof. internat. law Am. Grad. Sch. of Internat. Mgmt., Phoenix, 1975-76; former gen. counsel Nat. Speakers Assn., 1973-85. Candidate Dem. nomination for atty. gen. State of Ariz., 1974, U.S. Congress, 1976; mem. Ariz.-Mex. Gov.'s Commn., 1974—, counsel commerce and industry sect., 1974—; chmn. campaign Bonds for Israel, Ariz., 1980-85; founding chmn., exec. bd. Internat. Found. for Anticancer Drug Discovery, 1996—. Baird scholar, University scholar; recipient Speaker Preview Auditions First Pl. award Internat. Platform Assn., 1969-70, Silver Bowl award, 1969-70. Mem. Ariz. Bar Assn. (internat. relations com.), Calif. Bar Assn., Maricopa County Bar Assn., World Assn. Lawyers, Nat. Speakers Assn. (founder, former gen. counsel 1973-85), World Affairs Council, Hospitality Internat. (host), FIABCI (law instr. Internat. Real Estate Fedn. 1985-90, gen. counsel Ariz. chpt. 1985—), Ariz. World Trade Assn. (former bd. dirs.), Jaycees (treas. Ariz. chpt. 1969-70, ambassador to Philippine Islands 1969-70), Pan Am. Club of Ariz. (past pres.), Traveler's Century Club, Valley Forward Assn. (bd. dirs.), Phi Alpha Delta (pres. 1963-64). Democrat. Jewish. Lodge: Kiwanis. Avocations: stamp collecting, photography, world traveling, camping, scuba diving. General corporate, Estate planning, Private international. Home: 2233 N Alvarado Rd Phoenix AZ 85004-1415 Office: Rosen Chemal Ocampo & Fontes 4323 N 12th St Ste 104 Phoenix AZ 85014-4506 Fax: (602) 263-9297. E-mail: baliinaz@aol.com

ROSEN, STEVEN, lawyer; b. N.Y.C., June 13, 1950; s. Louis Harold and Gladys (Berkowitz) R.; m. Linda Ellen Kert, Aug. 14, 1971; children— Lee Jacob, Joshua Daniel. B.A., U. Md., 1971; J.D., Georgetown U., 1974. Bar: Md. 1974, D.C. 1978, U.S. Dist. Ct. Md. 1975, U.S. Supreme Ct. 1978. Mem. DePaul, Willoner & Kenkel, P.A., College Park, Md., 1974-79, Willoner, Calabrese & Rosen, P.A., College Park, Md., 1980— . Mem. Md. State Bar Assn., Prince George's County Bar Assn. State civil litigation, Family and matrimonial, Personal injury. Home: 10100 Colebrook Ave Potomac MD 20854-1810 Office: Willoner Calabrese & Rosen PA 4603 Calvert Rd College Park MD 20740-3421

ROSEN, WILLIAM WARREN, lawyer; b. New Orleans, July 22, 1936; s. Warren Leucht and Erma (Stich) R.; m. Eddy Kahn, Nov. 26, 1965; children: Elizabeth K., Victoria A. BA, Tulane U., 1958, JD, 1964. Bar: La. 1964, U.S. Dist. Ct. (ea. dist.) La. 1965, U.S. Ct. Appeals (5th cir.) 1965, U.S. Supreme Ct. 1984, U.S. Dist. Ct. (mid. dist.) La. 1985, Colo. 1989. Assoc. Dodge & Friend, New Orleans, 1965-68, Law Office of J.R. Martzell, New Orleans, 1968-70; pvt. practice, 1970-79, 89-90; ptnr. Lucas & Rosen (and predecessor firms), 1979-87, Herman, Herman, Katz & Cotlar, New Orleans, 1987-88, Rosen and Samuel, New Orleans, 1990-95; of counsel Rittenberg & Samuel, 1996-99; founder & dir. Litigation Consultation Svcs., 1996-99; ptnr. Rosen & Lundeen, L.L.P., 1999—. Adj. prof. trial advocacy Law Sch. Tulane U., 1988—, mem. adv. com. paralegal studies program, 1977-86, instr. bus. orgns., 1978, instr. legal interviewing, 1980-81; mem. adv. com. Paralegal Inst. U. New Orleans, 1990—, instr. legal interviewing and investigations, 1986-87; lectr. legal and paralegal fields; lectr. real and demonstrative evidence Nat. Edn. Network, 1993; lectr. new judges seminar La. Jud. Coll., 2000, 01. Author: (with others) Trial Techniques publ. La. Trial Lawyers Assn., 1981; columnist Briefly Speaking publ. New Orleans Bar Assn., 1993-2000. Mem. budget and planning com. Jewish Welfare Fedn., 1970-73; mem. adv. coun. on drug edn. La. Dept. Edn., 1973; mem. profl. adv. com. Jewish Endowment Found., 1982—; mem. exec. com. U.S. Olympic Com., La., 1982-84; bd. dirs. Planned Parenthood La., 1994-2001; pres. Dad's Club, Isidore Newman Sch., 1984-85, Uptown Flood Assn., 1982-85; bd. dirs. Jewish Children's Home Svc., 1973-76, Met. Crime Commn. New Orleans, 1976-82; spl. agt. Office Spl. Investigations USAF, 1958-61. Fellow, Inst. of Politics. Loyola U. Mem. ABA, ATLA (keyperson com. 1986-89, vice chmn. paralegal com. 1986-89, mem. family law adv. com. 1989-90, sec. family law sect. 1990-91, lectr. legal edn. 1979, 81, 83, 86, 88); mem. La. Bar Assn. (vice chmn. pub. rels. com. 1970-73, 88-89, past chmn. state youth drug abuse edn. program, vol. lawyers for arts 1986-96, chmn. sr. counsel com. 1995-96), Am. Arbitration Assn., Nat. Fedn. Paralegal Assn. (adv. coun. 1989-1998), Assn. Atty. Mediators (pres. La. chpt. 1995), Nat. Choice in Dying (legal adv. com. 1992-96), Nat. Edn. Network (lectr. legal edn. 1993), New Orleans Bar Assn. (CLE com. 1990-91, chmn. 1991-92, mem. alternative dispute resolution com. 1996-2000, panel moderator 1997), Inn of Ct. (master 1992—), Rotary Club New Orleans (bd. dirs. 1996-98, chmn. legal com. 1996—). Avocation: photography (included in Louisiana Photographers publ. Contemporary Arts Ctr. 1988). Federal civil litigation, State civil litigation, General practice. Office: Rosen & Lundeen LLP 210 Baronne St Ste 704 New Orleans LA 70112-4132 Fax: 504-523-3370. E-mail: lcsno@aol.com

ROSENBAUM, JAMES MICHAEL, judge; b. Ft. Snelling, Minn., Oct. 12, 1944; s. Sam H. and Ilene D. (Bernstein) R.; m. Marilyn Brown, July 30, 1972; children: Alexandra, Victoria and Catherine (twins). BA, U. Minn., 1966. Bar: Minn. 1969, Ill. 1970, U.S. Supreme Ct. 1979. VISTA staff atty. Leadership Coun. for Met. Open Cmtys., Chgo., 1969-72; assoc. Katz, Taube, Lange & Frommelt, Mpls., 1972-77; ptnr. Rosenbaum & Rosenbaum, 1977-79, Gainsley, Squier & Korsh, Mpls., 1979-81; U.S. dist. atty. U.S. Dept. Justice, 1981-85; judge U.S. Dist. Ct., Minn., 1985—, chief judge, 2001—. 8th cir. rep. Jud. Conf. U.S., 1997—; mem. Jud. Conf. U.S. Author: (booklet) Guide to Practice Civil Rights Housing, 1972; co-author: U.S. Courts Design Guide, 1991-96; contbr. articles to profl. jours. Campaign chmn. People for Boschwitz, Minn., 1978, bd. vis. U. Minn. Law Sch. (pres. 1996-97). Mem. FBA (bd. dirs., pres. 1992-93, 8th cir. rep. Jud. Conf. of U.S. 1997—, exec. com. 1999—). Republican. Jewish. Office: US Courthouse 300 S 4th St Minneapolis MN 55415-1320

ROSENBAUM, MARK DALE, lawyer; b. Cin., May 9, 1948; s. David A. and Evelyn (Finkelman) R. BA, U. Mich., 1970; JD, Harvard U., 1974. Bar: Calif., U.S. Dist. Ct. (cen. dist.) Calif., U.S. Ct. Appeals (9th cir.), U.S. Ct. Mil. Appeals, U.S. Supreme Ct. Legal dir. ACLU, L.A., 1974—. Adj. prof. U. Mich., UCLA. Democrat. Civil rights, Criminal. Home: 885 W Kensington Rd Los Angeles CA 90026-4365 Office: 1616 Beverly Blvd Los Angeles CA 90026-5711 E-mail: mrosenbaum@aclu-sc.org

ROSENBAUM, MARTIN MICHAEL, retired insurance company executive, lawyer; b. Aug. 8, 1923; came to U.S., 1939, naturalized, 1944; s. emil Elias and Pauline (Latte) R.; m. Hanna Lore Serog, July 6, 1952; children: Thomas F., Evelyn J. BS in Bus. Adminstrn., Boston U., 1948; JD, N.Y.U., 1952, LLM in Taxation, 1956. Bar: N.Y. 1953, U.S. Supreme Ct. 1968. With Chubb & Son Inc., 1948-88, tax cons., 1988—; with Chubb Corp., N.Y.C., 1967-88, v.p. tax dir., sr. tax counsel, 1972-88; v.p. taxes subs., sr. v.p. Chubb & Son Inc., 1968-88, Fed. Ins. Co., N.Y.C., 1968-88, Vigilant Ins. Co., N.Y.C., 1979-88, Pacific Indemnity Co., N.Y.C., 1979-88; retired, 1998. Former dir. Gan-Anglo Am. Ins. Co., 1981-88, ret. 1998; past bd. dirs., pres. subs. DHC Corp. 1982-88; lectr. in taxation field. With AUS, 1943-46; ETO. Mem. ABA (past chmn. fgn. ins. subcom., past chmn. Non-Life Ins. Subcom.), Am. Ins. Assn. (past chmn. tax com.), Soc. Ins. Accts. (past chmn. tax com.). Jewish. Home and Office: Apt 205 724 12th St Wilmette IL 60091-2637

ROSENBAUM, RICHARD MERRILL, lawyer; b. Oswego, N.Y., Apr. 8, 1931; s. Jack M. and Shirley (Gover) R.; m. Judith Kanthor, June 1, 1958; children: Amy, Jill, Matthew, Julie. BA, Hobart Coll., 1952; JD, Cornell U., 1955. Bar: N.Y. 1956. Ptnr. Rosenbaum, Agnello, Agnello & Levine, Rochester, N.Y., 1955-70; justice Supreme Ct. N.Y. State, 1970-73; ptnr. Nixon, Hargrave, Devans & Doyle, Rochester, 1977-84, 88-98; counsel to chmn. of bd., dir. govt. rels. and pub. affairs. Integated Resources, Inc., 1984-88, also bd. dirs. Dir. Integrated Resources, Inc.; past mem. econ. adv. bd. U.S. Dept. Commerce; bd. dirs., sec. Jonathan Inst.; mem. mediation arbitration panel JAMS/Endispute, 1997, Am. Arbitration Assn., 1998, Empire Mediation, 1998; jud hearing officer, 1997; chmn. N.Y. State Unemployment Ins. Bd., 1998—. Contbr. writings in fields of politics and public affairs, legal opinions to publs., 1984-88. Trustee Hobart Coll., 1971-89; nat. committeeman N.Y. State Rep. Nat. Com., 1977—, rules rev. com., subcom. chmn. conv. procedures, 1977— ; del.-at-large Rep. Nat. Conv., 1980, 84, 88, congl. dist. del., 1968, chmn. N.Y. State del., 1976; chmn. Monroe County Rep. Com., 1968-70, N.Y. Rep. State Com.,

1973-77, Northeastern Rep. State Chairmen's Assn., 1973-76, Nat. Rep. State Chairmen's Assn., 1975-77; justice of peace Town of Penfield (N.Y.), 1962-66; mem. and asst. majority leader Monroe County Legislature, 1966-68; former mem. coun. SUNY, Brockport; dep. counsel U.S. Senate Majority, 1988; apptd. by Pres. Ronald Reagan, U.S. Holocaust Meml. Coun., reapptd. by Pres. George Bush; apptd. by U.S. Senate to Bd. of Fed. Jud. Ctr. Found., 1989—; bd. dirs. Cardozo Sch. Law Yeshiva U.; bd. dirs. Rochester Mus. & Sci. Ctr., 1978—, gen. chmn. devel. fund drive, 1977—; trustee Rochester Area Colls., 1979— ; mem. coun. of governing bds. of Ind. Colls. of State of N.Y., 1979— ; apptd. mem. N.Y. Mental Hygiene Council, 1973-77, Nat. Citizens Adv. Com. on Environ. Quality, 1977; past bd. dirs. Jewish Home for Aged, Rochester, bd. dirs. Rochester Philharmonic Orchestra; exec. com. Cornell Law Sch; Rep. candidate for nomination for N.Y. state gov., 1994. Recipient Congl. Medal Honor Ellis Island, 1992, Hobart Coll. Alumni citation. Mem. ABA, N.Y. State Bar Assn. Jewish. Clubs: Royal Order of Jesters, Masons, Shriners. General corporate, Legislative. Home: 19 Denonville Rdg Rochester NY 14625-1611 Office: NYS Unemployment Ins Appeal Bd 36 W Main St Ste 789 Rochester NY 14614-1704

ROSENBERG, DANIEL P. lawyer; b. London, May 8, 1962; s. Leonard Jack and Susanna (Sternfeld) R.; m. Helena Rudie, Aug. 11, 1985; children: David, Liana. BA in Law, U. Cambridge, 1984, LLM, 1986. Bar: High Ct. England and Wales. Articled clk. Slaughter & May, London, 1985-87; asst. solicitor Berwin Leighton, 1987-92, ptnr., 1992-2001, Taylor Johnson Garrett, London, 2001—. Co-author, gen. editor: Practical Commercial Precedents, 1991; co-author: Tolley's Financial Management Handbook, 1996, Commercial Transaction Checklists, 1997. Adv. bd. London Symphony Orch., 1997—; trustee The Young Musicians Fund, London, 1999—. Mem. ABA, Law Soc. England and Wales (company law com. 1998—), Confedn. Brit. Industry (corp. law panel 1999—), London First Ctr. (N.Am. adv. task force 1998—) Avocations: music, theatre, cycling, family. General corporate, Private international, Mergers and acquisitions. Office: Taylor Joynson Garrett Carmelite 50 Victoria Embk London EC4Y ODX England Office Fax: 44-207-300-7100. E-mail: drosenberg@tjg.co.uk

ROSENBERG, DAVID, lawyer; b. N.Y.C., May 6, 1946; s. Marvin and Helene (Feller) R.; m. Bernice Leber, June 25, 1989. BA, U. Chgo., 1968; JD, N.Y.U., 1971. Bar: N.Y. 1972, U.S. Dist. Ct. (so. dist.) N.Y. 1975, U.S. Dist. Ct. (ea. dist.) N.Y. 1975, U.S. Supreme Ct. 1980, U.S. Ct. Appeals (2nd. cir.) 1981. Atty. N.Y.C. Housing & devel. Adminstrn., 1971-72; law clk. N.Y. Supreme Ct., 1972-80; assoc., ptnr. Feldesman & D'Atri, N.Y.C., 1980-81; assoc. Summit Rovins & Feldesman, N.Y.C., 1981-82, ptnr., 1983-89, Marcus Borg Rosenberg & Diamond, 1989—; mem. Com. Character & Fitness 1st Jud. Dept., N.Y.C., 1984—; asst. counsel N.Y. Com. Jud. Nomination, 1982-89; mem. Adv. Council N.Y.C. Civil Ct., 1982—, chmn. 1986—. Mem. N.Y. Bar Assn. (real property law sect. exec. com. 1979—, landlord & tenant com. chmn. 1977-88), ABA (real property litigation, corp. sects. 1971—), N.Y.C. Bar Assn. (civil ct. com. 1981-84, judiciary com. 1985-88, chair common state cts. superior jurisdiction 1989-93). Federal civil litigation, General corporate, Real property. Home: 20 W 86th St New York NY 10024-3604 Office: Marcus Borg Rosenberg & Diamond LLP 488 Madison Ave New York NY 10022-5702

ROSENBERG, GARY MARC, lawyer; b. N.Y.C., June 4, 1950; s. David and Edna (Goldberg) R.; m. I. Denise Estes, July 3, 1971; children: Dena Elyse, Janna Beth, Adam Ilan. BA, Queens Coll., 1971; JD, Bklyn. Law Sch., 1974. Bar: N.Y. 1975, U.S. Dist. Ct. (so. dist.) N.Y. 1976, U.S. Supreme Ct. 1985. Pres. Rosenberg & Estis, P.C., N.Y.C., 1976—. State civil litigation, Landlord-tenant, Real property. Office: Rosenberg & Estis PC 733 3rd Ave New York NY 10017-3204

ROSENBERG, GERALD ALAN, lawyer; b. N.Y.C., Aug. 5, 1944; s. Irwin H. and Doris (Lowinger) R.; m. Rosalind Navin, Aug. 13, 1971; children: Clifford D., Nicholas D. BA cum laude, Yale U., 1966; JD, Harvard U., 1969. Bar: N.Y .1970, U.S. Dist. Ct. (so. dist.) N.Y. 1971, U.S. Ct. Appeals (2d cir.) 1974, U.S. Dist. Ct. (we. dist.) N.Y. 1977, U.S. Dist. Ct. (cen. dist.) Calif. 1978, U.S. Supreme Ct. 1979, U.S. Dist. Ct. (ea. dist.) N.Y. 1981, U.S. Tax Ct. 1984. Atty. Legal Aid Soc. San Mateo/VISTA, Redwood, Calif., 1969-70; asst. atty. U.S. Dept. Justice, N.Y.C., 1971-75; assoc. Rosenman & Colin, 1975-77, ptnr., 1978—, mem. mgmt. com., 1991—94. Arbitrator U.S. Dist. Ct. (ea. dist.) N.Y.; mem. faculty Ctr. Internat. Legal Studies, Salzburg, Austria, 1999—. Bd. dirs. Non Profit Coord. Com. Inc., N.Y.C., 1983—, N.Y. Lawyers for the Pub. Interest Inc., 1988—; bd. dirs. The Parks Coun., 1988—, pres., 1991-95. Mem. Yale U. Alumni Assn. (del. at large 1986-89), Yale Club (N.Y.C.). Federal civil litigation, State civil litigation, Real property. Office: Rosenman & Colin 575 Madison Ave Fl 22 New York NY 10022-2585 E-mail: garosenberg@rosenman.com

ROSENBERG, H. JAMES, lawyer; b. Chgo., June 8, 1945; s. Jay I. and Florence (Padnos) R.; m. Candy Lewis, Dec. 23, 1967; children— Tracey, Robyn. B.A., Northwestern U., 1966, J.D., 1969. Bar: Ill. 1969, U.S. Dist. Ct. (ea. dist.) Ill. 1969, U.S. Ct. Appeals (7th cir.) 1970, Calif. 1987. Assoc. Henehan, Donovan & Isaacson, Chgo., 1969-70, Weinberg & Weinberg, Chgo., 1970-72, Mover & Harhen, Chgo., 1972-74; ptnr. Mover, Harhen & Rosenberg, Chgo., 1975— ; dir. B'nai B'rith Credit Union, Chgo., 1980-81. Contbr. articles to legal jours. Mem. Schaumburg Village Plans Commn., Ill., 1971-75; bd. dirs. Schaumburg United Party, 1971-75; pres. Sheffield Towne Homeowner's Assn., Schaumburg, 1973-74; sec. Moriah Congregation, Deerfield, Ill., 1977-78. Recipient cert. of appreciation Village of Schaumburg, 1975. Mem. Ill. Bar Assn., Chgo. Bar Assn. (sec. mcpl. law com. 1986-87, vice chmn. mcpl. law com. 1987-88), Comml. Law League Am., Am. Motorcycle Assn. Club: Harley Owners Group. Bankruptcy, Consumer commercial, General practice. Office: Mover Harhen & Rosenberg 120 W Madison St Chicago IL 60602-4103

ROSENBERG, MARK LOUIS, lawyer; b. Lexington, Ky., Sept. 21, 1947; s. Edward George and Shirley Lee (Berkin) R.; m. Betty Adler, May 16, 1982; stepchildren: Aaron, Sarah Claxton; children: Eli, Daniel. BA, U. Mich., 1969; JD, harvard U., 1973; LLM in Taxation, Georgetown U., 1985. Bar: D.C. 1973, Md. 1991, U.S. Dist. Ct. D.C. 1973, U.S. Ct. Appeals (D.C. cir.) 1973. Asst. to v.p. George Washington U., 1973-75; counsel U.S. Ho. of Reps., Washington, 1975-77; sr. atty. FTC, 1977-85; ptnr. Gordon, Feinblatt et al, 1989-91; prin. Law Offices of Mark L. Rosenberg, 1991—; of counsel The Jacobovitz Law Firm, 1994-97. Mem. Fed. Bar Assn. (dep. sect. coord., Disting. Svc. award 1982, 83, 87). Democrat. Jewish. Real property, Taxation. Home: 6101 Shady Oak Ln Bethesda MD 20817-6027 Office: Law Offices of Mark L Rosenberg 6917 Arlington Rd Ste 301 Bethesda MD 20814-5211

ROSENBERG, MICHAEL, lawyer; b. N.Y.C., Oct. 13, 1937; s. Walter and Eva (Bernstein) Rosenberg; m. Jacqueline Raymonde Combe, Apr. 29, 1966; children: Andrew James, Suzanne Jennifer. AB in Econs. with honors, Ind. U., 1959; LLB, Columbia U., 1962. Bar: NY 1963, US Ct Appeals (2d cir) 1975, US Dist Ct (ea dist so div) Mich 1989. From. dep. asst. atty. gen. to asst. atty. gen. N.Y. State Dept. Law, N.Y.C., 1963-66; assoc. Hellerstein, Rosier & Rembar, 1966-73; assoc. gen. counsel Gen. Instrument Corp., 1973-78; from assoc. gen. counsel to dep. gen. counsel U.S. Filter Corp., 1978-82; v.p., gen. counsel, sec. Alfa-Laval Inc., Ft. Lee, N.J., 1982-88; counsel Becker Ross Stone De Stefano & Klein, N.Y.C., 1988-89; ptnr. Rosenberg & Rich, White Plains, N.Y., 1989-95, Quinn, Marantis & Rosenberg, LLP, White Plains, 1995-97, Marantis, Rosenberg & van Nes, LLP, White Plains, 1997-2001; atty. Law Offices of Michael Rosenberg, 2001—. Mem Zoning Bd Appeals Town of North Castle, NY, 1995—. Mem.: ABA, NY State Bar Asn, West Chester Bar Asn. Contracts commercial, Real property, Estate planning. Office: Law Offices of Michael Rosenberg 120 Bloomingdale Rd White Plains NY 10605

ROSENBERG, PETER DAVID, lawyer, educator; b. N.Y.C., Aug. 2, 1942; s. Frederick and Martha (Grossman) R. BA, NYU, 1962; B in Chem. Engring., 1963; JD, N.Y. Law Sch., 1968; LLM, George Washington U., 1971. Bar: N.Y. 1970, U.S. Ct. Appeals (2nd cir.) 1970, U.S. Dist. Ct. (no. and we. dists.) N.Y. 1979, U.S. Ct. Appeals (D.C. cir.) 1982, U.S. Ct. Internat. Trade, 1982, U.S. Ct. Mil. Appeals 1982, U.S. Ct. Appeals (fed. cir.) 1983; registered U.S. Patent and Trademark Office, Canadian Patent Office. Primary examiner U.S. Patent and Trademark Office, Washington, 1968-95; of counsel Harris Beach LLP, Syracuse, N.Y., 1995—. Adj. prof. law Syracuse U. Coll. Law. Recipient Silver Medal award U.S. Dept. Commerce, 1981. Author: Patent Law Fundamentals, 1975, 2nd edit., 1980, rev., 2001, Patent Law Basics, 1992, rev., 2001; asst. editor: Jour. Patent and Trademark Office Soc., 1968-95; contbr. articles to profl. jours. Mem. ABA (antiturst and intellectual property sects.). Home: PO Box 788 4916 Rte 11 Pierrepont Manor NY 13674

ROSENBERG, PRISCILLA ELLIOTT, lawyer; b. Rochester, NY, Feb. 17, 1952; d. Clarence Roy and Mary M. (Mascle) Elliott; m. Alan Mark Rosenberg, May 7, 1983; children: Anne Marian, Tracy Jean, Kate Rebecca. Student, U. Rochester, 1973, Rochester Inst. Tech., 1973-74; BA, SUNY, Stony Brook, 1975; JD, Bklyn. Law Sch., 1978. Bar: N.Y. 1979, U.S. Dist. Ct. (ea. and so. dists.) N.Y. 1979, Fla. 1995. Assoc. Shearman & Sterling, N.Y.C., 1978-84; asst. counsel Siemens Corp., 1985-86, assoc. counsel, 1986-91, counsel, 1991; assoc. counsel Armco Inc., Parsippany, N.J., 1991-94; environ. counsel Harris Corp., Melbourne, Fla., 1994-99; ptnr. Rosenberg & Rosenberg, Attys. at Law, L.L.C., 1999—. Contbr. articles to profl. jours. Mem. ABA, N.Y. State Bar Assn., Fla. Bar Assn. Jewish. General corporate, Environmental, Mergers and acquisitions. Home: 4172 Sparrow Hawk Rd Melbourne FL 32934-8526 Office: Rosenberg & Rosenberg 600 E Strawbridge Ave Melbourne FL 32901

ROSENBERG, RUTH HELEN BORSUK, lawyer; b. Plainfield, N.J., Feb. 23, 1935; d. Irwin and Pauline (Rudich) Borsuk; children— Joshua Cohen, Sarah, Rebecca, Daniel, Miriam, Tziporah, Isaac A.B., Douglass Coll., 1956; J.D., U. Pa., 1963. Bar: Pa. 1964, N.Y. 1967, D.C. 1986, Md. 1987, Va. 1994, Mass. 1995, U.S. Ct. Appeals (3d cir.) 1969, U.S. Supreme Ct. 1969, U.S. Ct. Appeals (4th cir.) 1994. Law clk. Ct. Common Pleas, Phila., 1963-64; assoc. Blank, Rudenko, Klaus & Rome, 1964-67; atty. Office Corp. Counsel, City of Rochester, 1967-68; assoc. Nixon, Hargrave, Devans & Doyle, Washington, 1968-74, ptnr., 1975-99, Nixon Peabody LLP, Washington, 1999—. Vice chairperson character and fitness com. Appellate divsn. 4th dept. 7th Jud. Dist. N.Y. Supreme Ct., 1976-80, mem. grievance com., 1981-84. Bd. dirs. Soc. Prevention Cruelty to Children, 1976-77, N.Y. Civil Liberties Union, 1972-85, v.p. 1976-85; bd. dirs. Jewish Home and Infirmary, 1978-83, pres., 1980-83; v.p. Jewish Fedn. Rochester, 1983, Yachad, Inc., Jewish Cmty. Housing Devel. Corp., 1990-94; bd. dirs. Jewish Cmty. Coun., Greater Washington, 1989-93, Leadership Washington, 1990-91, Libr. Theatre, 1994-97, Op. Understanding, D.C., 1994-95. Mem. ABA, D.C. Bar Assn., Md. Bar Assn., Va. Bar Assn., Phi Beta Kappa. Land use and zoning (including planning), Real property. Office: Nixon Peabody LLP 401 9th St NW Ste 900 Washington DC 20004-2128 E-mail: rrosenberg@nixonpeabody.com

ROSENBLATT, ALBERT MARTIN, state appeals court judge; b. N.Y.C., Jan. 17, 1936; s. Isaac and Fannie (Dachs) R.; m. Julia Carlson, Aug. 23, 1970; 1 child, Elizabeth. BA, U. Pa., 1957; LLB (JD), Harvard U., 1960. Bar: N.Y. 1961.. Dist. atty. Dutchess County, N.Y., 1969-75, county judge, 1976-81; justice N.Y. State Supreme Ct., 1982-89, justice, appellate divsn., 1989-98; justice N.Y. Ct. Appeals, 1999—. Instr. judge N.Y. State, 1987-89; vis. prof. Vaar Coll., 1993; moderator N.Y. State Fair Trial Free Press Conf., 2000, 2001; creator Dutchess County 1st consumer protection bur., 1973; instr. newly elected state supreme ct. judges and county judges; asst. dist. attys., 1974, 75; instr. law tng. N.Y. State Police Acad., 1997; lectr. Nat. Dist. Attys. Assn., 1968-74; mem. vis. faculty trial advocacy workshop Harvard Law Sch., 1998, 99. Mem. bd. editors N.Y. State Bar Jour., 1992—; contbr. articles on law to profl. jours. and popular mags. Bd. dirs. United Way Cmty. Chest, 1970; bd. dirs. Bardavon 1869 Opera House, Dutchess County Hist. Soc.; mem. adv. bd. Jewish Cmty. Ctr., 1987—. With USAR, 1960-66. Mem. N.Y. State Bar Assn. (named Outstanding Prosecutor 1974, Outstanding Jud. Svcs. award 1994), N.Y. State Dist. Attys. Assn. (pres. 1974, Frank S. Hogan award 1987, Jud. Svcs. award 1994), Profl. Ski Instrs. Am. (cert. 1984—), Baker St. Irregulars Club (former assoc. editor Baker St. Jour.). Republican. Jewish. Home: 300 Freedom Rd Pleasant Valley NY 12569-5431 Office: 10 Market St Poughkeepsie NY 12601-3228

ROSENBLOOM, LAWRENCE ANDREW, lawyer; b. Manhasset, N.Y., Mar. 3, 1969; s. Arthur Herbert Rosenbloom and Iris Lee Gair; m. Melissa Anne Katz, Aug. 11, 1996; 1 child, Gabrielle Brianna. Carmagna cum laude, U. Rochester, 1991; JD magna cum laude, Yeshiva U., 1997. Bar: N.Y. 1998. Campaign coord. Steve Orlins for Congress Com., Hicksville, N.Y., 1991-92; account exec. The Hudson Stone Group, N.Y.C., 1993-94; summer assoc. Squadron, Ellenoff, Plesant & Sheinfield, 1996; assoc. Battle Fowler LLP, 1997-2000, Paul, Hastings, Janofsky & Walker LLP, N.Y.C., 2000—. Mem. Juvenile Diabetes Found., 1990—, Intrepid Mus. Soc., 1994—. Mem. ABA, N.Y. County Lawyers Assn. Avocations: politics, basketball, football, music, food and wine. General corporate, Finance, Securities. Office: Paul Hastings Janofsky Walker LLP 75 E 55th St New York NY 10022

ROSENBLOOM, NORMA FRISCH, lawyer; b. N.Y.C., Dec. 2, 1925; d. Jacob Frisch and Anna (Fox) Frisch Schwartz; m. Philip Rosenbloom, Oct. 31, 1946; children: David, James, Eric. BA, New Sch. Social Rsch., 1951; JD, Rutgers U., Newark, 1979. Bar: N.J. 1979, N.Y. 1980. Mem. faculty, head dept. music Ranney Sch., Tinton Falls, N.J., 1962-74; chief law clk. Monmouth County (N.J.) Prosecutor's Office, 1979-80; assoc. Karasic & Karasic, P.C., Oakhurst, N.J., 1980-82; ptnr. Abrams, Gatta, Rosen & Rosenbloom, Ocean Twp., 1982-90, Abrams, Gatta, Rosen, Rosenbloom & Sevrin, P.C., 1990-92; of counsel Abrams, Gatta, Falvo & Sevrin, P.A., 1992-99, Abrams Gatta Falvo LLP; legal adv. Epiphany House Inc., Asbury Park, N.J., 1999—. Asst. county counsel Monmouth County, 1987-88; mem. N.J. Supreme Ct. Family Part Practice Com., 1997-98. Sec., mem. exec. bd. Temple Beth Miriam, Elberon, N.J., 1969-74; mcpl. leader Monmouth Beach (N.J.) Dem. Com., 1973—; del. Dem. Nat. Conv., 1976; freeholder rep. to Monmouth County Cmty. Action Program, poverty program, 1975-76; bd. dirs. Cen. Jersey Regional Health Planning Bd., 1973-75; trustee search com. Brookdale C.c., Lincroft, N.J., 1984-85; trustee Planned Parenthood Monmouth County, 1981-88. Recipient award for cmty. involvement Asbury Park-Neptune Youth Coun., 1970. Fellow Am. Acad. Matrimonial Lawyers; mem. ABA, N.J. Women Lawyers Assn. (pres. 1994-95), N.J. State Bar Assn. (dispute resolution sec., trustee women in the profession sect.), Women Lawyers Monmouth County. Democrat. Jewish. Avocation: classical pianist. Family and matrimonial. Home: Channel Club Towers Monmouth Beach NJ 07750 Office: Epiphany House 300 4th Ave Asbury Park NJ 07712-6006

ROSENBLUM, EDWARD G. lawyer; b. Union City, N.J., Aug. 2, 1944; s. Milton and Frances (Nardi) R.; m. Charis Ann Schlatter, Dec. 1, 1971; children: Deborah, Michelle. BA, Rutgers U., 1966, JD, 1969. Bar: N.J. 1969. Ptnr. Rosenblum & Rosenblum, P.A., Jersey City, 1971-79, Secaucus, N.J., 1979-93, Rosenblum Wolf & Lloyd, P.A., Secaucus, 1994—, Teaneck, 1998—. Lectr. in field. Author: N.J. Lawyer, 1980, N.J. Municipalities, 1987. Active Table to Table, Englewood, N.J. Mem. N.J. State Bar Assn. (vice chmn. tax ct. rules com. taxation sect. 1984—, chmn. real property tax com. 1984—, vice chmn. taxation sect. 1987—, chmn.-elect 1987, chmn. 1988-89, Supreme Ct. com. on tax ct. 1982-92). Condemnation, State and local taxation. Office: 300 Frank Burr Blvd Teaneck NJ 07666

ROSENBLUM, SCOTT S. lawyer; b. N.Y.C., Oct. 4, 1949; s. Harold Lewis and Greta Blossom (Lesher) R.; m. Barbara Anne Campbell, Oct. 29, 1977; children: Harold, Emma, Casey. AB summa cum laude, Dartmouth Coll., 1971; JD, U. Pa., 1974. Bar. U.S. Dist. Ct. (so. dist.) N.Y. 1975. From assoc. to ptnr. Stroock & Stroock & Lavan, N.Y.C., 1974-91; ptnr. Kramer, Levin, Naftalis & Frankel, 1991—, mng. ptnr., 1994-2000. Mem. N.Y. bd. govs., vice chmn. Mid. East Quarterly, Phila., 1994—; bd. dirs. Dovenmuehle Mortgage, Inc., Schaumburg, Ill, Greg Manning Auctions, Inc., West Caldwell, N.J., Temco Svc. Industries, Inc., N.Y.C., I.T. Internat. Theatres Ltd., Herzlia, Israel, Investec Ernst & Co., N.Y.C. Co-author: Public Limited Partnerships and Roll-Ups, Securities Law Techniques, The Practitioner's Guide to Transactions and Litigation, 1995. Trustee Village of Saltaire, N.Y., 1993—. Mem. ABA (high tech. com. 1983-84), Assn. Bar City N.Y. (corps. com. 1991-94), Phi Beta Kappa. Avocation: sailing. General corporate, Mergers and acquisitions, Securities. Home: 19 Wildwood Cir Larchmont NY 10538-3426 Office: Kramer Levin Naftalis & Frankel 919 3rd Ave New York NY 10022-3902 E-mail: srosenblum@kramerlevin.com

ROSENBLUT, ALVARO, lawyer; b. Santiago, Chile, Sept. 25, 1973; s. Arnoldo and Lucia (Gorodinsky) R. Trainee Harasic & Co., Santiago, 1994-95, Judicial Assistance Corp., Santiago, 1997; assoc. Albagli, Zaliasnik & Co., 1998—; asst. prof. U. Santiago, 1999—. Mem. Chilean Bar. Bankruptcy, Contracts commercial, General corporate. Office: Albagli Zaliasnik & Cia Miraflores 130 25th Fl Santiago Chile E-mail: arosenblut@az.cl

ROSENFELD, MARTIN JEROME, management consultant to law firms, educator; b. Flint, Mich., Oct. 3, 1944; s. Israel Edward and Lillian Edith (Natchez) R.; m. Marcy Tucker Colman; 1 child, Joshua; stepchildren: Jessica Colman, Zachary Colman. BA, Mich. State U., 1968, MHA, 1978; MBA with high honors, Ind. No. U., 1979. Adminstr. Care Corp., Grand Rapids, Mich., 1969-70, Chandler Convalescent Ctr., Detroit, 1970-71, Grand Community Hosp., Detroit, 1971-73; exec. v.p., chief exec. officer Msgr. Clement Kern Hosp. Spl. Surgery, Warren, 1973-84; pres. M.J. Rosenfeld Assocs., 1984-85; COO Dickenson, Wright, Moon, Van Dusen & Freeman, 1985-88; chmn. Rosenfeld Assocs., 1989-91; pres. Sanford Rose Assocs., Detroit, 1991-97; acting COO New Ctr. Hosp., 1995-96; pres., CEO, chmn. Rosenfeld & Co., Inc., 1998-99; CEO, chmn. Brookside Consulting Group, LLC, Farmington, Mich., 1999-2001; prin. Rosenfeld, LLC, Farmington Hills, 2001—; instr. U. Phoenix, 2001—. Instr. Marygrove Coll., 1975-80; assoc. prof. Mercy Coll., Detroit, 1978-80; mem. faculty Inst. on Continuing Legal Edn., Ann Arbor, Mich., Inst. Law Firm Mgmt., Ann Arbor; instr. Legal Tech '87, Chgo. Author papers in field. Mem. editl. bd. The Human-Size Hosp.; mem. panel of experts The Health Care News. V.p. Detroit chpt. Jewish Nat. Fund, 1978—; pres. Cranbrook Village Homeowners Assn., 1977; chmn. Community Hosps. of Southeastern Mich., 1981-84; mem. tech. work group Comprehensive Health Planning Coun. of Southeastern Mich., 1981-84; mem. fin. mgmt. com., mem. hosp. affairs bd. Greater Detroit Area Hosp. Coun., 1981-84; bd. dirs., com. chmn. Detroit Symphony Orch., 1984-90; bd. dirs., mem. fund raising com. Detroit Met. Orch., 1984-87. Mem. ABA, Assn. Legal Adminstrs., Am. Assn. Health Care Cons., Royal Soc. Health, Am. Podiatry Assn. (com. hosps. 1981-84), Warren C. of C. (com. chmn. 1975), Nat. Assn. Legal Search Cons., Nat. Assn. Pers. Svcs., Mich. Assn. Pers. Svcs., Sanford Rose Assocs. Dirs. Assn. (pres. 1993-95, treas. 1995-97). Office: Rosenfled, LLC 3278 Middlebelt Road Suite A Farmington Hills MI 48334-1770 E-mail: mjr@rosenfeldllc.com

ROSENFELD, STEVEN B. lawyer; b. N.Y.C., Apr. 12, 1943; s. Eugene David and Laura (Sipin) R.; m. Naomi Eve Winkler, Aug. 21, 1965; children: Kathryn Anne, Elizabeth Jane. BA, Columbia Coll., 1964; LLB, Columbia U., 1967. Bar: N.Y. 1967, D.C. 1984, U.S. Dist. Ct. (so. dist.) N.Y. 1969, U.S. Dist. Ct. (ea. dist.) N.Y. 1970, U.S. Ct. Appeals (2d cir.) 1971, U.S. Ct. Appeals (3d cir.) 1974, U.S. Ct. Appeals (Fed. cir.) 1978, D.C. 1979, U.S. Supreme Ct. 1979, U.S. Ct. Appeals (5th cir.) 1982, U.S. Ct. Appeals (6th and D.C. cirs.) 1984, U.S. Ct. Appeals (4th and 9th cirs.) 1987, U.S. Ct. Appeals (1st cir.) 1989, U.S. Ct. Appeals (10th cir.) 1991. Law clk. to Hon. Charles M. Metzner U.S. Dist. Ct. (so. dist.) N.Y., 1967-68; assoc. Rosenman & Colin, N.Y.C., 1968-71; dep. gen. counsel N.Y. State Commn. on Attica, N.Y.C., Batavia, N.Y., 1971-72; assoc. Paul, Weiss, Rifkind, Wharton & Garrison, N.Y.C., 1972-75, ptnr., 1976—. Lectr. Columbia U. Sch. Law, 1995—. Contbr. articles to profl. jours. Bd. dirs. N.Y. Assn. New Ams., N.Y.C., 1973-95; trustee Dalton Sch., N.Y.C., 1988-94; trustee Putney Sch. Putney, Vt., 1995-2001, N.Y. Theatre Workshop, 1996—. Mem. N.Y. State Bar Assn. (ho. of dels. 1996-98), Assn. Bar City N.Y. (exec. com. 1992-96, v.p. 1998-99, past mem. various coms.), Legal Aid Soc. (pres. 1989-91, bd. dirs., exec. com. 1978-95). Democrat. Jewish. Avocations: opera and chamber music, theatre, tennis. E-mail: srosenfeld.paulweiss.com. Federal civil litigation, State civil litigation, Trademark and copyright. Office: Paul Weiss Rifkind Et Al 1285 Ave of Americas New York NY 10019-6028

ROSENHAUER, JAMES JOSEPH, lawyer; b. Chgo., May 25, 1942; s. Norbert E. and Eleanor E. (Berg) R.; m. Vivian M. Garcia, June 11, 1966; 1 child, Christine. AB, Cath. U. Am., 1966; JD, Yale U., 1967. Bar: D.C. 1968. Assoc. Hogan & Hartson, Washington, 1967-74, ptnr., 1975—. Mem. ABA, Bar Assn. D.C., D.C. Bar, Internat. Bar Asssn., Interam. Bar Assn. Banking, General corporate, Private international. Office: Hogan & Hartson Columbia Square 555 13th St NW Washington DC 20004-1161

ROSENHOUSE, MICHAEL ALLAN, lawyer, editorial consultant; b. Chgo., Nov. 8, 1946; s. Seymour Samuel and Jeanne Mozette (Rosenthal) R. BA, Yale U., 1968; JD, U. Chgo., 1974. Bar: Ill. 1974, N.Y. 1982. Atty. in pvt. practice, Rochester, N.Y. Mng. editor: Am. Jurisprudence, 2d edit., 1991—93, mng. editor: Am. Law Reports (Fed.), 1991—93; editor: (newsletter) Bank Employment Law Report , 1998—99; author: Employment Law (Syracuse Law Rev.), 1998; columnist: The Daily Record, 2001—. Mem.: Monroe County Bar Assn. (co-chair Disability Labor and Employment Law Commn. 1998—99), N.Y. State Bar Assn., U. Chgo. Law Sch. Alumni Assn. (bd. dirs. 1977—80), U. Chgo. Club of Rochester (bd. dirs. 1999—2001), Yale Alumni Assn. (schs. com. 1997—). Avocation: squash, tennis, golf. Appellate, Labor. Office: 36 Wind Mill Rd Pittsford NY 14534-3135 E-mail: mike@rosenhouse.com

ROSENN, HAROLD, lawyer; b. Plains, Pa., Nov. 4, 1917; s. Joseph and Jennie (Wohl) R.; m. Sallyanne Frank, Sept. 19, 1948; 1 child, Frank Scott. BA, U. Mich., 1939, JD, 1941; LLD, Coll. Misericordia, 1991. Bar: Pa. 1942, U.S. Supreme Ct. 1957. Ptnr. Rosenn & Rosenn, Wilkes Barre, Pa., 1948-54, Rosenn, Jenkins & Greenwald, Wilkes Barre, 1954-87, of counsel, 1988—. Mem. Pa. State Bd. Law Examiners, 1983-93, Pa. Gov.'s Justice Commn., 1968-73, Pa. Crime Commn., 1968-73, Fed. Jud. Nominating Com., Pa., 1977-79, Appellate Ct. Nominating Com., Pa., 1979-81; asst. dist. atty. Luzerne County, Pa., 1952-54. Chmn. ARC, Wilkes-Barre, 1958-60, life mem. bd.; pres. Pa. Coun. on Crime and Delinquency, Harrisburg, 1969-71; bd. dirs. Coll. Misericordia, Dallas, Pa., 1976-86, emeritus, 1986—, Hoyt Libr., Kingston, Pa., 1971-78, Nat. Coun. on Crime

and Delinquency, N.Y.C., 1969-71; chmn. United Way Campaign of Wyoming Valley, 1975, chmn. of bd., 78-80; pres. Temple Israel of Wilkes Barre, 1972-74, chmn. bd. 1974-84, life mem. bd.; comdr. post 395 Am. Legion, Kingston, 1948; bd. dirs. Keystone State Games, 1982—, Jewish Fedn. Bd. of Greater Wilks-Barre, 1994—, St. Vincent de Paul Soup Kitchen, 1987-2000. Capt. USAAF, 1942-45, ETO. Decorated medal with 6 bronze stars, European combatant cross French Govt.; named Golden Key Vol. of Yr., United Way of Pa., 1989; recipient Erasmus medal, Dutch Govt., Disting. Svc. award in Trusteeship, Assn. Governing Bds., Univs. and Colls., 1990, Disting. Cmty. Svc. award, Greater Wilkes-Barre Soc. Fellows Anti-Defamation League, 1991, Clara Barton honor award, Wyoming Valley chpt. ARC, 1992, Lifetime Achievement award, United Way of Wyoming VAlley, 1992, Outstanding Vol. Fundraiser award, Greater Pocono chpt. Nat. Soc. of Fundraising Execs., 1995, honoree, Wyoming Valley Interfaith Coun., 1986, Ethics Inst. N.E. Pa., 2001, inductee, Jr. Achievement Hall of Fame for N.E. Pa., 1997. Mem. ABA, Pa. Bar Assn., Am. Judicature Soc., The Pa. Soc., B'nai B'rith (pres. Wilkes Barre 1952-53, Cmty. Svc. award 1976), U. Mich. Club N.E. Pa. (pres. 1946-76), Westmoreland Club (Wilkes-Barre), Huntsville Golf Club (Lehman, Pa.). Republican. Jewish. General corporate, Family and matrimonial, General practice. E-mail: hr@rjglaw.com

ROSENN, KEITH SAMUEL, lawyer, educator; b. Wilkes-Barre, Pa., Dec. 9, 1938; s. Max and Tillie R. (Hershkowitz) R.; m. Nan Raker, June 21, 1960; 1 child, Eva; m. Silvia R. Rudge, Mar. 21, 1968; children: Jonathan, Marcia AB, Amherst Coll., 1960; LLB, Yale U., 1963. Bar: Pa. 1964, U.S. Ct. Appeals (3rd cir.) 1979, Fla. 1981, U.S. Ct. Appeals (11th cir.) 1982. Law clk. to Judge Smith U.S. Ct. Appeals (2nd cir.), 1963-64; asst. prof. law Ohio State U. Coll. Law, 1965-68, assoc. prof., 1968-70, prof., 1970-79; project assoc. Ford Found., Rio de Janeiro, 1966-68; assoc. Escritorio Augusto Nobre, 1979-80; prof. law U. Miami, Fla., 1979—; project coord. Olin Fellowship Program Law and Econs. Ctr., U. Miami, 1980-81, assoc. dean Law Sch., 1982-83, chmn. fgn. grad. law program, 1985—. Cons. Hudson Inst., 1977, U.S. State Dept., 1981-82, World Bank, 1988-90; Fulbright lectr. Argentina, 1987, 88. Author: (with Karst) Law and Development in Latin America, 1975; Law and Inflation, 1982, Foreign Investment in Brazil, 1991; co-editor: A Panorama of Brazilian Law, 1992, Corruption and Political Reform in Brazil, 1999; advisor InterAm. Law Rev.; contbr. articles to law jours. Recipient Order of Democracy award Congress of Republic of Colombia, 1987, Lawyer of the Ams. award, 1989, Inter-Am. Jurisprudence prize, 1998, Order of Congress award Republic of Colombia, 2000; grantee Social Sci. Rsch. Coun., 1970, Dana Found., 1982. Mem. ABA, Am. Law Inst., Inter-Am. Bar Assn., Fla. Bar, Am. Soc. Comparative Law (bd. dirs.). Jewish Office: U Miami Law Sch PO Box 248087 Coral Gables FL 33124-8087

ROSENN, MAX, federal judge; b. Plains, Pa., Feb. 4, 1910; s. Joseph and Jennie (Wohl) R.; m. Tillie R. Hershkowitz, Mar. 18, 1934; children: Keith S., Daniel Wohl. BA, Cornell U., 1929; LLB, U. Pa., 1932. Bar: Pa. 1932, U.S. Supreme Ct. 1955, Cts. of Philippines 1946. Gen. practice, Wilkes-Barre, Pa., 1932-70; dir. Franklin Fed. Savs. & Loan, 1937-70, Wyoming Nat. Bank, Wilkes-Barre, 1958-70; spl. counsel Pa. Dept. Justice, 1939; asst. dist. atty. Luzerne County, 1942-44; also solicitor various mcpl. boroughs, ptnr. firm Rosenn & Rosenn, 1947-54, Rosenn, Jenkins & Greenwald, Wilkes-Barre, 1954-70; sec. pub. welfare Pa., 1966-67; judge U.S. Ct. Appeals (3d cir.), 1970-81, sr. judge, 1981—. Former mem. criminal procedure rules com. Supreme Ct. Pa., 1958-85; mem. Pa. Commn. to Revise Pub. Employee Laws, 1968-69; Pa. chmn. com. children and youth White House Conf., 1968-70. Contbr. articles to legal publs. Mem. Pa. Bd. Pub. Welfare, 1963-66; chmn. Pa. Gov.'s Hosp. Study Commn., Pa. Gov.'s Coun. for Human Svcs., 1966-67; mem. exec. bd. Commonwealth of Pa., 1966-67; chmn. Commn. Met. Govt., 1957-58; pres. Property Owners Assn. Luzerne County, 1955-57; chmn. Pa. Human Rels. Commn., 1969-70, Legis. Task Force Structure for Human Svcs., 1970; alt. del. Rep. Nat. Conv., 1964; pres. Wyoming Valley Jewish Com., 1941-42; life trustee Wilkes-Barre Jewish Community Ctr.; chmn. Flood Recovery Task Force, 1972. Max Rosenn U.S. Courthouse dedicated, 1996. Fellow Am. Coll. Trial Lawyers, Internat. Acad. Trial Lawyers; mem. ABA, Pa. Bar Assn., Luzerne County Bar Assn., Am. Law Inst., Am. Soc. Law and Medicine (charter mem., former assoc. editor jour.), Am. Judicature Soc., B'nai B'rith (pres. dist. grand lodge 1947-48, life bd. govs., former chmn. bd. dirs. Anti-Defamation League Pa., W.Va. and Del. 1955-58, nat. commr. 1964—), Westmoreland Club, Masons (33d degree), Alpha Epsilon Pi. Jewish. Office: US Ct Appeals Max Rosenn US CthseRm 235 197 S Main St Wilkes Barre PA 18701-1500*

ROSENSAFT, LESTER JAY, management consultant, lawyer, business executive; b. Leominster, Mass., Jan. 11, 1958; s. Melvin and Beatrice (Golombek) R.; m. Elisabeth Amanda Lahti, July 29, 1992, 1 child, Mia Elisabeth. BS in Econs., Wharton Sch., U. Pa., 1978; JD, MBA, Case Western Res. U., 1981; LLM in Corp. Law, NYU, 1983. Bar: Ohio 1981, U.S. Dist. Ct. (no. dist.) Ohio 1982, U.S. Dist. Ct. (all dists.) N.Y. 1982, Mass. 1992. Practice corp. and comml. law, Ohio, 1981—. Reorgn. law fed. cts. Ohio, N.Y., 1982—; mem. firm. Hall, Rosensafi & Yen, Cleve. and Singapore, 1961-90; with Cons. to Mgmt., Inc., Clve., N.Y.C., Boston, Hong Kong, 1977—, v.p., 1977-80, pres., CEO, 1980-83, chmn., 1983-85; pres., CEO Eljay Devel. Corp., 1985-86; chmn., CEO Logistix Ltd., 1987-90; ptnr. Sanctuary Assocs., Boston, 1988-89; exec. v.p., CFO The Union Meat Co., East Hartford, Conn., 1989-90, also bd. dirs.; pres. Golub Enterprises II, Inc., 1989-90; also bd. dirs.; COO The CCC Fin. Orgn., Cleve., 1992-95, also bd. dirs.; pres., CEO, bd. dirs. ASA Investment Commn., Inc., N.Y.C., 1995—; pres., CEO ASA Adminstrn., Inc., Chgo., Greensboro, N.C., 1999—, also mem. bd. dirs; bd. dirs. ASA Acquisition Corp., 1998—, fin. and strategic planning com.; mem. ASA Mgmt. and Exec. Com., 1995—, ASA Investment Com., 1996-98; chmn. Chatham Fin., Cleve., N.Y.C., 1995-96; vice chmn. bd. dirs. Paramount Sys. Design Group, Inc., N.Y.C., 1982-89, v.p. corp. devel.; bd. dirs. Ameritech Corp., N.Y.C., 1983-85; v.p., CFO, bd. dirs. Chipurnoi Inc., L.I. City, N.Y.; v.p., CFO Kannerton Industries, N.Y.C., London, 1983-85; vice chmn., gen. counsel, bd. dirs. GIOIA Couture, Inc., Akron, Ohio, 1984-86; dir. Honeybee Robotics Ltd., Taiwan and N.Y.C., Pelletier Brothers, Inc., 1986-88, Advanced Radiator Techs., Inc., Fitchburg, Mass., 1987-88. Co-author: Industrial Development Survey for City of Leominster, 1978; contbr. articles to profl. jours. Ednl. cons., advisor indsl. devel. and strategic urbanism; cons. federally funded biomed. rsch. projects; active Combined Jewish Philanthropies; participant 40th Anniversary II Pres.'s Mission, 1987; chmn. Region V Outreach Mission, 1988; vice chmn. Regional Campaign Leadership Nission, 1991; mem. Russian Resettlement Com., 1988-91, Major Gifts Gala Com., 1989; assoc. alumni trustee U. Pa., 1991-95; active U. Penn. Seondary Com. Ctrl. Mass., U. Penn. Bd. Govs., Cleve., 1992-95; exec. adv. coun. Keene State Coll., 1984-88. Recipient APEX Grand award 1999, ESMA best of show award, 1999, numerous ACE awards, silver and gold Quill awards, 1996-99. Mem. ABA, Assn. Crop. Growth Turnaround Mgmt. Assn., Greater Cleve. Bar Assn., Ohio State Bar Assn., Assn. Bar City N.Y., Bankruptcy Lawers Bar Assn., N.Y.C. Reorgn. Roundtable, Internat. Soc. Strategic Planning Cons., Soc. Profl. Mgmt. Cons., Inst. Mgmt. Cons. (cert.), Coun. Cons. Orgns., Coll. Firm Prins., North Ctrl. Mass. C. of C. (dinsl. devel. com. 1984-86), Phi Alpha Delta (vice justice), Boca Pointe Golf and Racquet Club. Address: 9 Whispering Ivy Way Mendham NJ 07945-1241 Office: 146 W 57th St New York NY 10019

ROSENSAFT, MENACHEM ZWI, lawyer, author, foundation executive, community activist; b. Bergen-Belsen, Germany, May 1, 1948; came to U.S., 1958, naturalized, 1962; s. Josef and Hadassah (Bimko) R.; m. Jean Bloch, Jan. 13, 1974; 1 child, Joana Deborah. BA, MA, Johns Hopkins U., 1971; MA, Columbia U., 1975, JD, 1979. Bar: N.Y. 1980. Adj. lectr. dept. Jewish studies CCNY, 1972-74, professorial fellow, 1974-75; rsch. fellow Am. Law Inst., 1977-78; law clk. to judge U.S. Dist. Ct. (so. dist.) N.Y., N.Y.C., 1979-81; assoc. Proskauer, Rose, Goetz & Mendelsohn, 1981-82, Kaye, Scholer, Fierman, Hays & Handler, N.Y.C., 1982-89; v.p., sr. assoc. counsel Chase Manhattan Bank, 1989-93; spl. counsel Hahn & Hessen, 1994-95; sr. internat. counsel Ronald S. Lauder Found., 1995-97; exec. v.p. Jewish Renaissance Found., Inc., 1996-2000; ptnr. Ross & Hardies, 2000—. Author: Moshe Sharett, Statesman of Israel, 1966, Fragments, Past and Future (poetry), 1968, Not Backward to Belligerency, 1969; editor: Bergen Belsen Youth mag., 1965, Life Reborn, Jewish Displaced Persons 1945-1951, 2001; book rev. editor Columbia Jour. Transnat. Law, 1978-79; co-editor (with Yehuda Bauer) Antisemitism: Threat to Western Civilization, 1988; contbg. editor: Reform Judaism, 1993—; contbr. to various publs. including N.Y. Times, Washington Post, Newsweek, N.Y. Post, L.A. Times, N.Y. Daily News, Phila. Inquirer, Miami Herald, Internat. Herald Tribune, Jerusalem Post, Liberation, Paris, Davar, Tel Aviv, El Diario, Santiago de Chile, Columbia Human Rights Law Rev., Jewish Social Studies, Leo Baeck Inst. Year Book XXI, Columbia Jour. Environ. Law, (with Michael I. Saltzman) Tax Planning Internat. Rev., Fellowship, Reform Judaism, United Synagogue Rev., Forward, Midstream, N.Y. Jewish Week, Jewish Telegraphic Agy. Bull.; dir., editor-in-chief Holocaust Survivors' Memoirs Project of World Jewish Congress, 2000—. Chmn. Internat. Network Children Jewish Holocaust Survivors, 1981-84, founding chmn., 1984—; nat. pres. Labor Zionist Alliance, 1988-91; chmn. commn. human rights World Jewish Congress, 1986-91, chmn. exec. com. Am. sect., 1986-90; mem. Gen. Coun. World Zionist Orgn., 1987-92; mem. U.S. Holocaust Meml. Coun., 1994-2000, chmn. content com., 1994-2000, chmn. collections and acquisitions com., 1996-2000, chmn. task force on procedures for com. on conscience, 1996, mem. exec. com., 1996—, chmn. governance com., 2001—; mem. N.Y.C. Holocaust Meml. Commn., 1982-96, chmn. collections com., 1987-89; bd. dirs., exec. com. Nat. Com. for Labor Israel, 1988-91, 95-2001; mem. Am. Zionist Tribunal, 1988-90, chmn., 1990; sec. Am. Zionist Fedn., 1990-93; bd. dirs. Am. Jewish Joint Distbn. Com., 1988-91, Mercaz, 1991-97; mem. nat. adv. bd. United Synagogue Conservative Judaism, 1995—, also chmn. United Synagogue delegation to Nat. Jewish Cmty. Rels. Adv. Coun., 1994-97; mem. exec. com. Nat. Jewish Cmty. Rels. Adv. Coun., 1994-97; mem. N.Y. County Dem. Com., 1981-85; organizer, leader demonstration against Pres. Reagan's visit to Bitburg Cemetery and Bergen-Belsen concentration camp, 1985; del. meeting on recognition of Israel between five Am. Jews and leaders of Palestine Liberation Orgn., Stockholm, 1988; sec. Park Ave. Synagogue, 1998—, trustee, 1994—, chmn. Sherr Inst. Adult Jewish Studies, 1993—. Recipient Abraham Joshua Heschel Peace award, 1989, Parker Sch. recognition of achievement with honors in internat. and fgn. law, 1979, 400th Anniversary medal City of Warsaw, 1999, commendation Jewish Heritage Week, Comptroller of N.Y.C., 1999; Harlan Fiske Stone scholar, 1977-79. Mem. ABA, Phi Beta Kappa. Federal civil litigation, Private international, Securities. Home: 179 E 70th St New York NY 10021-5109 Office: Ross & Hardies 65 E 55th St New York NY 10022-3219 E-mail: menachem.rosensaft@rosshardies.com

ROSENTHAL, ALAN, lawyer; b. Newark, N.J., Apr. 19, 1948; s. Robert Rosenthal; children: Keith Michael Rosenthal, Greg Jason Rosenthal. BA, Syracuse U., 1970, JD, 1974. Bar: N.Y. 1975, U.S. Dist. Ct. (no. and we. dists.) N.Y. 1975. Lawyer Rosenthal & Drimer, N.Y. Mem. N.Y. State Bar Assn., Nat. Lawyers Guild, Onondaga County Bar Assn., Nat. Legal Aid and Defender Assn., Assn. Trial Lawyers Am., N.Y. State Trial Lawyers Assn. Civil rights, Criminal, Personal injury. Home: 340 Kensington Pl Syracuse NY 13210-3310 Office: 472 S Salina St Ste 602 Syracuse NY 13202-2480

ROSENTHAL, EDWARD SCOTT, lawyer; b. Oct. 27, 1950; s. Robert and Blanche Ruth Rosenthal; m. Pamela C. Comfort, May 09, 1992; children: Amy Dawn, Lindsey Jean, Samantha Robyn. BA, Amherst Coll., 1973; JD, Georgetown U., 1976. Bar: Va. 1976, U.S. Dist Ct. (ea. dist.) Va. 1976, U.S. Dist. Ct. D.C. 1977, U.S. Ct. Appeals (4th and D.C. cirs.) 1977. Sole practice, Alexandria, Va., 1976—77; ptnr. Rich Greenberg Rosenthal & Costle, LLP and predecessor firms, 1977—. Bd. dir. Greenway Downs Citizens Assn., Falls Church, Va., 1978—79. Mem.: ABA (criminal justice sect., individual rights sect.), ACLU, Va. Coll. Criminal Def. Attys., Va. Trial Lawyers Assn., Alexandria Bar Assn. (chair legis. affairs com. 1984—87). Civil rights, State civil litigation, Criminal. Home: 11631 Quail Ridge Ct Reston VA 20194-1113 Office: Rich Greenberg Rosenthal & Costle LLP 1317 King St Alexandria VA 22314-2928

ROSENTHAL, ILENE GOLDSTEIN, lawyer; b. New Haven, Aug. 27, 1952; d. Sidney Leon and Marian (Goodman) Goldstein; m. Steven Siegmund Rosenthal, Oct. 1, 1983; children: Alexandra M., Eliana D. BA, Wesleyan U., 1974; JD, Georgetown U., 1982. Bar: Calif. 1983, U.S. Dist. Ct. (cen. and no. dists.) Calif. 1983, D.C. 1985, U.S. Ct. Appeals (D.C. cir.) 1985, U.S. Dist. Ct. D.C. 1986. Law clk. to Hon. William P. Gray U.S. Dist. Ct. for Cen. Dist. Caif., L.A., 1982-83; assoc. Wyman, Bautzer, Rothman, Kuchel & Silbert, 1983-84; asst. U.S. Atty. D.C., Washington, 1985-88; minority gen. counsel House Gov. Ops. Com., 1989-91; gen. counsel, dir. litigation Software Publs. Assn., 1991-94; gen. counsel and v.p. for govt. affairs Lightspan Partnership, Inc., 1994-97; pres. New Image Media, LLC, 1997-2000; chair Everybody Wins!, 1995-99, bd. dirs., 1995—; sr. v.p. Lightspan, Inc., 2000—. Bd. dirs. Nat. Coalition for Tech. in Edn. and Tng., 1996—; bd. dirs. Aidan Montessori Sch., Washington. 1998-2001. Contbg. editor Tech. and Learning Mag., 1999—. Office: 2619 Woodley Pl NW Ste 201 Washington DC 20008-1525

ROSENTHAL, KENNETH W. lawyer; b. Frankfurt, Fed. Republic Germany, Nov. 2, 1929; came to U.S., 1944; s. Ludwig and Florence (Koenigsberger) R.; m. Joan Finkelstein, Apr. 10, 1960; children: Jeffrey, David. BA, Syracuse U., 1951; LLB, U. Calif., San Francisco, 1958. Bar: Calif. 1959, U.S. Dist. Ct. (no. dist.) Calif. 1959, U.S. Ct. Appeals (9th cir.) 1959, U.S. Supreme Ct. 1972. Assoc. Jay A. Darwin, San Francisco, 1959-61; ptnr. Darwin, Rosenthal & Leff, 1961-69; pres. Rosenthal & Leff Inc., 1969-89; of counsel Molligan, Cox & Moyer, 1989-98, Cox & Moyer, San Francisco, 1998—. Del. 9th Cir. Jud. Conf., 1986-89. Contbr. numerous articles to profl. jours. Mem. Nat. Bd. Trial Advocacy (cert.), Am. Bd. Trial Advs. (cert.), Calif. Bar. Assn. (legal specialization sect., civic trial advocacy com., mediator, arbitrator 1993—), San Francisco Bar Assn., San Francisco Trial Lawyers Assn. (bd. dirs. 1976-84, pres. 1984). Democrat. Jewish. Avocations: photography, walking. Admiralty, Alternative dispute resolution, Federal civil litigation. Office: Cox & Moyer 703 Market St San Francisco CA 94103-2102

ROSENTHAL, LEE H. federal judge; b. Nov. 30, 1952; m. Gary L. Rosenthal; children: Rebecca, Hannah, Jessica, Rachel. BA in Philosophy with honors, U. Chgo., 1974, JD with honors, 1977. Bar: Tex. 1979. Law clk. to Hon. John R. Brown U.S. Ct. Appeals (5th cir.), 1977-78; assoc. Baker & Botts, 1978-86, ptnr., 1986-92; judge U.S. Dist. Ct. (so. dist.) Tex., 1992—. Vis. com. Law Sch. U. Chgo., 1983-86, 94-97, 99—; mem. Fed. Jud. Conf. Adv. Com. for Fed. Rules of Civil Procedure, 1996—; chair 1999 Fifth Cir. Jud. Conf. Mem. bd. editors Manual for Complex Litigation, 1999—. Mem. devel. com. Tex. Children's Hosp., 1988-92; pres. Epilepsy Assn. Houston/Gulf Coast, 1989-91; trustee Briarwood Sch. Endowment Found., 1991-92; bd. dirs. Epilepsy Found. Am., 1993-98, DePelchin Children's Ctr., 2000—. Fellow Tex. Bar Found.; Mem. ABA, Am. Law Inst. (consultative group for transnat. rules of civil procedure), Texas Bar Assn., Houston Bar Assn. Office: US Dist Ct US Courthouse Rm 11535 515 Rusk St Houston TX 77002-2600

ROSENTHAL, MEYER L(OUIS), lawyer; b. Wilkes-Barre, Pa., May 27, 1944; s. Samuel J. and Lottie G. (Goncher) R.; m. Susan M., Aug. 19, 1967; children: Norman, Bonnie. BA, Rutgers Coll., 1966, JD, 1969. Bar: N.J. 1969, U.S. Dist. Ct. N.J. 1969, Calif. 1975, U.S. Dist. Ct. (cen. dist.) Calif. 1981, U.S. Dist. Ct. (ea. dist.) N.Y. 1980, U.S. Dist. Ct. (so. dist.) N.Y. 1981, U.S. Ct. Appeals (9th cir.) 1981. Law sec. Hon. Leon Milmed N.J. Superior Ct., Newark, 1969-70; assoc. Kaufman & Kaufman, Elizabeth, N.J., 1970-76; ptnr. Trueger & Rosenthal, Morristown, 1976-82; atty. pvt. practice, 1982—. Editor Rutgers Law Rev. Cub scout leader Morris Area Boy Scouts Am., Randolph, N.J., 1980; chmn. Morris City Human Rels. Commn., Morristown, 1992-95, chmn. emeritus, 1999. Recipient Cmty. Hero award Morris County Orgn. Hispanic Affairs, 1996. Mem. Comml. Law League Am., Calif. Bar Assn., N.J. Bar Assn., B'nai B'rith (bd. govs. 1975—, pres. dist. 3 1988-89, Internat. Young Leadership award 1982, Internat. Founders award 1985, nat. commn. anti-defamation league 1992—). State civil litigation, Contracts commercial, Real property. Office: 161 Washington St Morristown NJ 07960-3753 E-mail: meyer@therosenthals.net

ROSENTHAL, STEVEN SIEGMUND, lawyer; b. Cleve., May 22, 1949; s. Fred Siegel and Natalie Josephine Rosenthal; m. Ilene Edwina Goldstein, Oct. 1, 1983; children: Alexandra M., Eliana D. AB, Dartmouth Coll., 1971; JD, Harvard U., 1974. Bar: Fla. 1974, D.C. 1975, U.S. Supreme Ct. 1978, Calif. 1983. Law clk. judge Malcolm R. Wilkey U.S. Ct. Appeals (D.C. cir.), 1974-75; assoc. Covington & Burling, Washington, 1975-80, Morrison & Foerster, Washington, 1980-81, ptnr., 1981-97, Cooper, Carvin & Rosenthal, PLLC, Washington, 1998-2001, Holland & Knight LLP, Washington, 2001—. Lawyer rep. Jud. Conf. D.C. Cir., 1981-83. Pres. Family and Child Services Washington, 1986-88, trustee, 1978—. Mem. ABA, Am. Law Inst., Phi Beta Kappa. Republican. Administrative and regulatory, Federal civil litigation, Government contracts and claims. Office: Holland & Knight LLP 2099 Pennsylvania Ave NW Washington DC 20006-6801

ROSENZWEIG, THEODORE B. lawyer; b. N.Y.C., Apr. 14, 1948; s. Joseph and Elsa Ruth (Davis) R.; m. Barbara Conviser, Jan. 23, 1977; 1 child, Brian Eliott. BA, NYU, 1969; JD, Fordham U., 1973. Bar: N.Y. 1974, U.S. Dist. Ct. (ea. dist.) N.Y. 1976, U.S. Dist. Ct. (so. dist.) N.Y. 1976, U.S. Ct. Appeals (2d cir.) 1977. Asst. dist. atty. Kings County Dist. Atty.'s Office, Bklyn., 1973-79, sr. trial atty. homicide bur., 1978-79; assoc. McAloon & Friedman, P.C., N.Y.C., 1979-82, ptnr., 1983—; mem. faculty Nat. Inst. for Trial Advocacy Program, Benjamin N. Cardozo Sch. of Law, N.Y.C., 1984—. Mem. N.Y. State Bar Assn. (trial lawyers sect.). Democrat. Jewish. State civil litigation, Personal injury. Home: 17 S Morris Ln Scarsdale NY 10583-6015 Office: McAloon & Friedman PC 116 John St Fl 29 New York NY 10038-3498 E-mail: TedRosenzweig@MCF-Esq.com

ROSIC, GEORGE S. lawyer; b. Kenosha, Wis., Dec. 12, 1951; s. Momcilo and Loni R.; m. Mary J. Marselus, June 7, 1976; children: Nicholas Andrew, Gregory George. BA, Knox Coll., 1974; JD, U. Chgo., 1977. Bar: Ill. 1977. Ptnr. Arvey, Hodes, Costello & Burman, Chgo., 1986-91, Wildman, Harrold, Allen & Dixon, Chgo., 1992-94; assoc. gen. counsel MMI Cos., Inc., Deerfield, 1995-2000; ptnr. Michael Best & Friedrich and predecessor firm, Chgo., 2000—. Author: The Illinois Corporation, BNA Corp. Practice Series Portfolio. Mem. ABA, Chgo. Bar Assn. (chair corp. law com. 1995-96), Phi Beta Kappa. Serbian Orthodox. General corporate, Mergers and acquisitions, Securities. Office: Michael Best & Friedrich 401 N Michigan Ave Ste 19 Chicago IL 60611 E-mail: grosic@s-f-law.com

ROSINEK, JEFFREY, judge; b. N.Y.C., Sept. 13, 1941; s. Isidore and Etta (Kramer) R.; m. Sandra Gwen Rosen, Aug. 7, 1977; 1 child, Ian David. BA in History, U. Miami, 1963; postgrad. in polit. sci., JD, 1974. Bar: Fla. 1974. Tchr. Coral Gables (Fla.) High Sch., 1963-78; sole practice Miami, 1974-76; assoc. Tendrich and Todd, 1976-77; ptnr. Todd, Rosinek & Blake, 1984-86; judge Dade County Ct., 1986-89, 11th Jud. Cir., Fla., 1990—, assoc. adminstr. appeal divsn., 1999—; judge Miami Dade County Drug Ct., 1999—. Instr. Boston U., 1975; mem. faculty Fla. Coll. Advanced Jud. Studies, 1992—, Nat. Jud. Coll., 2000—; lectr., presenter in field. Contbr. articles to profl. jours. Chmn. Miami Environ. Rsch. Adv. Com., 1969-73; mem. Miami Beach Tranportation commn., Nat. Bicentennial Competitiion on the Constitution and Bill of Rights com., Dade County Youth Adv. Bd., 1973-75; bd. dirs. U. Miami Law Sch., treas., 1973-75; bd. dirs. U. Miami Law Sch., treas. alumni, jud. dir.; past pres. Dade County Young Dems.; mem. Congl. Civilian Rev. Bd., 1975-90, chmn., 1976-78; bd. dirs., treas. fla. Congl. Com., Legal Svcs. Greater Miami; chmn., 1976-78; chmn. Dade County adv. Coun. Close-Up Found.; Fla. chmn. Porject Concern Internat.; internat. state chmn. Fla. Walk for Mankind, Project Concern, legal adv. com., Kiwanis, 1982-86; v.p. Beth David Congregation, 1982-86; bd. trustees Haven Ctr.; bd. dirs., treas., organizer South Miami-Kendall pro bono project Legal Svc. of Greater Miami, 1983-86; traffic rev. com. Dade County, 1987-92; bd. dirs. Fla. Law Related Edn., 1988—, Adv. Program, 1988—; mem. Miami-Dade County task force for homeless, 1992-94; active Dade Coalition for the Homeless, 1992—, Dade County Homeless Trust, 1993-2001, chmn. criminal justice com.; chmn. Beck Mus. Judaica, 1988—; ednl. dir. Tempel Judea; jud. cir. rep. Dept. corrections "Boot Camp" program, 1994-98; 11th jud. cir. organizer, rep. Homeless Alt. Rehab. Tracking Program, 1994—, rep. Comprehensive Homeless Integration Program (CHIP), 1992-94, chair Fla. 1st Annual Edn. Seminar/Retreat, 1995, Eugent P. Spellman Am. Inn of Ct., 1996—, South Fla. Super Bowl XXXIII Host Com.; 1st v.p. Coral Gables High Sch. Parent-Tchr.-Students Assn., 1995-96, pres., 1996-98. Recipient award Jewish Theol. Sem., 1978, Outstanding Law Student award Merit award Profl. Law Enforcement Assn., appreciation award Liberty City Christian Assn. Mem. ABA (task force reduction of litigation cost and delay 1995—), Dade County Bar Assn., South Miami-Kendall Bar Assn. (past pres.), Coral Gables Bar Assn., Fla. Bar Assn. (jud. nominating procedures com., rules com. family law sec. 1984-87), Miami Beach Bar Assn. (bd. dirs.), Cuban Am. Bar Assn., Dade County Bar (criminal cts. com. 1994—), Chabad of South Dade (bd. dirs. 1999—), Dade Ptnrs., Fla. Conf. Cir. Ct. Judges (criminal justice com. 1995—), Wig and Robe (chancellor 1973-74), Bar and Gavel Soc., U. Miami Law Sch. Alumni Assn. (sec. treas. 1985-87, jud. dir. 1987—), Am. Judges Assn. (bd. govs. 1988-92, sec. 1992-93, 2nd v.p. 1993-94, 1st v.p. 1994-95, pres. 1996-97, chair 32nd Annual Edn. Conf. Miami Beach 1992, mem. Image of Judiciary com., domestic violence com. 1990-96, chair fed. state rels. com. 1994-96, exec. com. 1997, 2000-2001, chair nominations com. 1997, edn.c om. 1998—, chair 38th Annual Edn. Conf. Orlando 1998, coord Close-UP Found. project 1997—), Nat. Ct. Reporters Assn. (strategic com. 1993—), Fla. Assn. Drug Ct. Profls. (charter chair), Biscayne Bay Kiwanis (disting. past pres., lt. gov. Fla. Dist., Major Emphais chmn., pres. 1994—, Kiwanian of Yr. 1983-84), Key Internat. (counselor fla. dist., pres. 1980-81, 94-95, sec. 1995—, Key of Honor 1979, honoree 1984), Kiwanis Internat. (life), Greater Miami C. of C. (Carrefour Housing Corp. for homeless, v.p. permanent housing 1996-98, pres. 1999-2000), Miami-Dade Lions Club (charter mem.). Home: 535 Bird Rd Coral Gables FL 33146-1307 Office: 1351 NW 12th St Miami FL 33125-1644 E-mail: jefaroz@aol.com

ROSKILL, JULIAN WENTWORTH, lawyer; b. London, July 22, 1950; s. Eustace Wentworth and Elizabeth Wallace (Jackson) R.; m. Catherine Elisabeth Garnett, Aug. 30, 1975; children: Matthew, Oliver. Student, Winchester Coll., Eng., 1963-69. Solicitor Allen & Overy, London, 1974-85; ptnr. Rowe & Maw, 1986—. Mem. Law Soc. Eng. and Wales. Avocations: photography, music, tennis. Immigration, naturalization, and customs, Labor. Home: 8 Leigh Rd N5 1SS London England Office: Rowe & Maw 20 Black Friars Ln EC4V 6HD London England Fax: 020 7248 4459. E-mail: jrsokill@roweandmaw.com

ROSKIN, PRESTON EUGENE, lawyer; b. St. Louis, Feb. 20, 1946; s. Chester F. and Evelyn (Kogan) R.; m. Linda Mc Girl, Nov. 28, 1980; children: Eric, Brian, David. BSCE, U. Mo., 1970, JD, 1971. Bar: Mo. 1971, U.S. Ct. Appeals (8th cir.) 1972, U.S. Supreme Ct. 1972. Pvt. practice, Clayton, Mo., 1971-76, 80-83, 85-89; ptnr. Floyd & Roskin, 1976-80, Phelps, Coffin, Roskin, Andreatta & Lorenz, Clayton, 1983-85, Roskin & Newman, 1989-90, Roskin and Leeds, 1994—2001; pvt. practice, 2001—. Mem. ATLA, ABA, Mo. Bar Assn., Mo. Assn. Trial Attys. (bd. govs., exec. com., bd. dirs.), St. Louis Met. Bar Assn., St. Louis County Bar Assn., Ill. Bar Assn., Attys. Motivated for Mo. Jewish. Personal injury, Product liability, Workers' compensation. Home: 9 Woodbridge Park Rd Saint Louis MO 63131-4023 Office: Law Offices of Roskin and Leeds 222 S Central Ave # 1010 Saint Louis MO 63105-3509 E-mail: proskinpc@aol.com

ROSKY, BURTON SEYMOUR, lawyer; b. Chgo., May 28, 1927; s. David T. and Mary W. (Zelkin) R.; m. Leatrice J. Darrow, June 16, 1951; children: David Scott, Bruce Alan. Student, Ill. Inst. Tech., 1944-45; BS, UCLA, 1948; JD, Loyola U., L.A., 1953. Bar: Calif. 1954, U.S. Supreme Ct 1964, U.S. Tax Ct 1964; C.P.A., Calif. Auditor City of L.A., 1948- 51; with Beidner, Temkin & Ziskin (C.P.A.s), L.A., 1951-52; supervising auditor Army Audit Agy., 1952-53; practiced law L.A., Beverly Hills, 1954—; ptnr. Duskin & Rosky, 1972-82, Rosky, Landau & Fox, 1982-93, Rosky, Landau & Stahl, Beverly Hills, 1993-99; pvt. practice, 1999—. Lectr. on tax and bus. problems; judge pro tem Beverly Hills Mcpl. Ct., L.A. Superior Ct.; mem. L.A. Mayor's Community Adv. Council. Contbr. profl. publs. Charter supporting mem. Los Angeles County Mus. Arts; contbg. mem. Assocs. of Smithsonian Instn.; charter mem. Air and Space Mus; mem. Am. Mus. Natural History, L.A. Zoo; supporting mem. L.A. Mus. Natural History; mem. exec. bd. So. Calif. coun. Nat. Fedn. Temple Brotherhoods, mem. nat. exec. bd.; mem. bd. govs. Loyola Sch. Law, L.A. With USNR, 1945-46. Walter Henry Cook fellow Loyola Law Sch. Bd. Govs. Fellow Jewish Chautauqua Soc. (life mem.); mem. Am. Arbitration Assn. (nat. panel arbitrators), Am. Assn. Attys.-CPAs (charter mem. pres. 1968), Calif. Assn. Attys.-CPAs (charter mem., pres. 1963), Calif. Soc. CPAs, Calif., Beverly Hills, Century City, Los Angeles County bar assns., Am. Judicature Soc., Chancellors Assocs. UCLA, Tau Delta Phi, Phi Alpha Delta.; mem. B'nai B'rith. Jewish (mem. exec. bd., pres. temple, pres. brotherhood). Club: Mason. General corporate, Estate planning, Probate. Office: 8383 Wilshire Blvd Beverly Hills CA 90211-2410

ROSNER, JONATHAN LEVI, lawyer; b. N.Y.C., Sept. 4, 1932; s. Oscar S. and Miriam (Reinhardt) R.; m. Lydia Sokol, Dec. 23, 1956; children: Beth, Marianne, Josh. BA, Wesleyan U., Middletown, Conn., 1954; JD, NYU, 1959. Bar: N.Y. 1959, U.S. Dist. Ct. (so. dist.) N.Y. 1962, U.S. Dist. Ct. (ea. dist.) N.Y. 1964, U.S. Ct. Appeals (2d cir.) 1964, U.S. Supreme Ct. 1964, U.S. Dist. Ct. Md. 1969, U.S. Dist. Ct. P.R. 1972, U.S. Ct. Appeals (D.C. cir.) 1976, U.S. Dist. Ct. (ea. dist.) Mich. 1984, U.S. Ct. Appeals (11th cir.) 1984. Law clk. to judge U.S. Dist. Ct. (so. dist.) N.Y., N.Y.C., 1959-60, asst. U.S. atty., 1960-63; ptnr. Rosner, Rosner & McEvoy, 1963-79; pvt. practice, 1979-85; ptnr. Rosner & Murray, 1985—. Adj. prof. law NYU, 1970-83, Pace U., White Plains, N.Y., 1984-86; chief counsel N.Y.C. Spl. Commn. on Power Failure, 1977, dep. commr., gen. counsel N.Y. State Commn. on Criminal Justice and Use of Force, 1985-87. Co-author: How to Prepare Witnesses for Trial, 1985, Cross-Examination of Witnesses, 1989, Impeachment of Witnesses, 1990. Bd. dirs. Westchester Jewish Community Services, 1970-73; trustee Woodlands Community Temple, 1971-76; mem. Wesleyan U. Alumni Assn. (adv. council 1972-79, schs. com. 1964-78, alumni fund class agt. 1954-2000). Mem. ABA, N.Y. State Bar Assn. (com. on grievances 1974-76), Assn. Bar of City of N.Y. (coms. on profl. discipline 1983-87, grievances 1970-74, entertainment 1964-68, 78-82, 93—, ABA-CLE panelist 1976-78), N.Y. County Lawyers Assn., NYU Law Alumni Assn. (bd. dirs. 1965-69, 84-88, 93—), N.Y. County Dist. Attys. Ann. Trial Advocacy Program (faculty 1978-96). Federal civil litigation, State civil litigation, Criminal. Home: 10 Westhaven Ln White Plains NY 10605-5458 Office: Rosner & Murray LLP 1140 Ave of the Ams New York NY 10036 E-mail: jlrosner@aol.com

ROSNER, LEONARD ALLEN, lawyer; b. N.Y.C., Apr. 13, 1967; s. Arnold and Betty (Zimmerman) R.; m. Rachel Stein, Nov. 19, 1994; 1 child, Andrew N. AB in Polit. Sci., AB in Pub. Rels., Syracuse U., 1989, JD cum laude, 1992. Bar: N.Y. 1993. Assoc. Fulreader, Rosenthal, Sullivan, Clifford, Santoro & Kaul, Rochester, N.Y., 1992—. Fin. editor Syracuse Jour. Internat. Law and Commerce, 1991-92. Assigned coun. Monroe County Assigned Coun., Rochester, 1993-94. Mem. N.Y. Bar Assn., Monroe County Bar Assn. Avocations: golfing, reading, television sports, nautilus. Criminal, Family and matrimonial, General practice. Home: 150 Frenchwoods Cir Rochester NY 14618-5251 Office: 1350 Midtown Tower Rochester NY 14604-2010

ROSNER, SETH, lawyer, educator; b. N.Y.C., Jan. 6, 1931; s. Oscar S. and Miriam (Reinhardt) R.; m. Sara Jane Sheldon, Dec. 4, 1970 (div. Mar. 1978); m. Ann E. Del Toro, June 23, 1983; 1 child, Rachel Jones. AB, Wesleyan U., Middletown, Conn., 1952; JD, Columbia U., 1955; LLM in Comparative Law, NYU, 1960; postgrad., U. Paris, 1960-61. Bar: N.Y. 1955, U.S. Dist. Ct. (so. and ea. dists.) N.Y. 1956, U.S. Supreme Ct. 1967. Ptnr. Rosner & Rosner, N.Y.C., 1955-80; sr. ptnr. Marchi Jaffe Cohen Crystal Rosner & Katz, 1981-88; pvt. practice, 1989-97; counsel Jacobs Persinger & Parker, 1997-2001. Adj. prof. NYU Sch. of Law, N.Y.C., 1961-89. Trustee, v.p. exec. com. Fedn. Jewish Philanthropies, N.Y.C., 1977-86; pres., chmn. Jewish Home and Hosp. for Aged, N.Y.C., 1978-86; bd. trustees Wesleyan U. Middletown, Conn., 1977-80; bd. govs. Josephson Inst. of Ethics, Marina Del Rey, Calif., 1986-99, chmn. bd., 2000—; bd. dirs. Saratoga Automobile Mus., Saratoga Springs, N.Y., 1999—. Lt. USN, 1956-59. Fellow Am. Bar Found. (life); mem. ABA (chmn. gen. practice sect. 1980-81, ethics and profl. responsibility com. 1983-89, chmn. professionalism com. 1992-95, chmn. com. on scope, chmn. com. on lawyer competence 1995-97, bd. govs. 1997-2000), Assn. Profl. Responsibility Lawyers (bd. dirs. 1990-96, pres.-elect 1993-94, pres. 1994-95), Assn. of Bar of City of N.Y. (ethics com. 1970-73), N.Y. State Bar Assn. (chmn. gen. practice sect. 1982-83). Avocations: writing, photography, Ferrari automobiles. General corporate, General practice, Professional liability. E-mail: seth@sethrosner.com

ROSOFF, WILLIAM A. lawyer, executive; b. Phila., June 21, 1943; s. Herbert and Estelle (Finkel) R.; m. Beverly Rae Rifkin, Feb. 7, 1970; children: Catherine D., Andrew M. BS with honors, Temple U., 1964; LLB magna cum laude, U. Pa., 1967. Bar: Pa. 1968, U.S. Dist. Ct. (ea. dist.) Pa. 1968. Law clk. U.S. Ct. Appeals (3d cir.), 1967-68; instr. U. Pa. Law Sch., Phila., 1968-69; assoc. Wolf, Block, Schorr & Solis-Cohen, 1969-75, ptnr., 1975-96, chmn. exec. com., 1987-88; also vice chmn. bd. dirs. Advanta Corp., Spring House, Pa., 1996—, pres., 1999—. Trustee RPS Realty Trust, 1990-96, Atlantic Realty Trust, 1996—; guest lectr. confs. and seminars on tax law; mem. tax adv. bd. Commerce Clearing House, 1983-94; mem. legal activities policy bd. Tax Analysts, 1978—; mem. Little, Brown Tax Adv. Bd., 1994-96; chmn. bd. dirs. RMH Telesvcs., Inc., 1997-99. Editor U. Pa. Law Rev., 1965-67; mem. bd. contbg. editors and advisors Jour. Partnership Taxation, 1983-2000; contbr. articles to profl. jours. Bd. dirs., mem. com. on law and social action Phila. coun. Am. Jewish Congress. Fellow Am. Coll. Tax Counsel; mem. Am. Law Inst. (cons. taxation of partnerships 1976-78, assoc. reporter taxation of partnerships, 1978-82, mem. adv. group on fed. income tax project 1982—, cons. taxation of pass-through entities 1995—), Locust Club (dir.), Order of Coif, Beta Gamma Sigma, Beta Alpha Psi. Corporate taxation, Personal income taxation. Office: Advanta Corp Welsh and McKean Rd Spring House PA 19477

ROSOW, MALCOLM BERTRAM, lawyer; b. N.Y.C., Mar. 19, 1922; s. Nelson and Irene (Steiner) R.; m. Carol Joy Sherman, Mar. 9, 1944; children— Michael, Kenneth, Wendy, Heidi. Student CCNY, 1938-40, U. Wis., 1940-43; LL.B., NYU, 1948. Bar: N.Y. 1949, U.S. Dist. Ct. (so. dist.) N.Y. 1949, (ea. dist.) N.Y. 1954, U.S. Dist. Ct. (ea. dist.) Wis. 1982, U.S. Cts. Appeals (2d cir.) 1956, (5th cir.) 1979, (6th cir.) 1980, (1st cir.) 1982, (D.C. cir.) 1981, U.S. Supreme Ct. 1958. Assoc., William L. Standard, N.Y.C., 1949-57, Standard, Weisberg, Harolds & Malament, N.Y.C., 1957-61, Standard, Weisberg & Harolds, 1961-67; ptnr. Standard, Weisberg Heckerling & Rosow, N.Y.C., 1967-81; pres. Standard Weisberg Heckerling & Rosow, P.C., 1981— . Contbr. articles to legal jours. Served to 1st lt. Signal Corps, U.S. Army, 1944-46; ETO. Mem. NYU Law Rev. Alumni Assn. (v.p. 1960-62), N.Y. State Bar Assn., ABA, N.Y. County Lawyers Assn., Internat. Assn. Ins. Lawyers, Def. Research Inst., Maritime Law Assn. U.S., Def. Assn. N.Y. Club: World Trade (World Trade Ctr. N.Y.) (founding mem.). Admiralty, Insurance. Home: 111 Cherry Valley Ave Apt 704 Garden City NY 11530-1574 Office: Standard Weisberg Heckerling & Rosow PC 61 Broadway New York NY 10006-2701

ROSOW, STUART L. lawyer; b. N.Y.C., Mar. 28, 1950; s. Bernard and Lillian (Bonime) R.; m. Amy Berk Kuhn. AB cum laude, Yale U., 1972; JD cum laude, Harvard U., 1975. Law clk. to presiding justice U.S. Ct. Appeals (7th cir.), Chgo., 1975-76; assoc. Paul, Weiss et al, N.Y.C., 1976-79, Kaye, Scholer, Fierman, Hays & Handler, N.Y.C., 1979-84, ptnr., 1984-97, Proskauer Rose LLP, N.Y.C., 1997—. Adj. prof. Columbia Law Sch., N.Y.C., 1998—. Mem. ABA, N.Y. State Bar Assn., Assn. of Bar of City of N.Y. Corporate taxation, Personal income taxation. Office: Proskauer Rose LLP 1585 Broadway Fl 27 New York NY 10036-8299

ROSS, CURTIS BENNETT, lawyer; b. Carbondale, Ill., June 7, 1955; s. Bernard Harris and Marian Frager Ross. BS in Acctg., U. Ill., 1977, JD, 1980. Bar: Ill., 1984. Tax staff Arthur Andersen & Co., Chgo., 1980-82; lawyer Jerome H. Torshen, Ltd., 1983, Curtis Bennett Ross, Chgo., 1984—. Attorney We Are Concerned, Chgo., 1995-99. Mem. Chgo. Bar Assn., CBA Matrimonial Com., Decalogue Soc. Family and matrimonial. Office: 135 S Lasalle Fl 36 Chicago IL 60603-4159

ROSS, DONALD ROE, federal judge; b. Orleans, Nebr., June 8, 1922; s. Roe M. and Leila H. (Reed) R.; m. Janice S. Cook, Aug. 29, 1943; children: Susan Jane, Sharon Kay, Rebecca Lynn, Joan Christine, Donald Dean. JD, U. Nebr., 1948, LLD (hon.), 1990. Bar: Nebr. bar 1948. Practice law, Lexington, Nebr., 1948-53; mayor City of Lexington, 1953; assoc. Swarr, May, Royce, Smith, Andersen & Ross, 1956-70; U.S. atty. Dist. Nebr., 1953-56; gen. counsel Rep. party, Nebr., 1956-58; mem. Rep. Exec. Com. for Nebr., 1952-53; nat. com. mem. Rep. Nat. Com., 1958-70, vice chmn., 1965-70; sr. judge U.S. Ct. Appeals 8th cir., 1971—.

ROSS, ELIZABETH LORRAINE, lawyer; b. Cin., July 21, 1971; d. William Lewis III and Linda Sue Thomas; m. Scott Douglas, July 22, 1995. BA, Bs, Miami U., Oxford, Ohio, 1993; JD, U. Dayton, 1997. Bar: Ohio, U.S. Dist. Ct. (so. dist.) Ohio 1997. Litigation assoc. Porter, Wright, Morris and Arthur, Dayton, Ohio, 1997—. Mem. ABA, Dayton Bar Assn., Phi Beta Kappa. Avocations: golf, running, music. General civil litigation, Government contracts and claims. Office: Porter Wright Morris and Arthur Ste 1600 1 Dayton Ctr Dayton OH 45402-2028

ROSS, GERALD ELLIOTT, lawyer; b. Chatham, Ont., Can., Aug. 9, 1941; s. Sanford Finlay and Helen Letitia Violet (Russell) R.; m. E. Sue Goetz, Dec. 29, 1963 (div. July 1975); m. Diana Guadalupe, Nov. 23, 1975; children: James Russell, Margaret Emily BBA, U. Mich., 1962, MBA, 1963, JD cum laude, 1967. Bar: N.Y. 1968, U.S. Dist. Ct. (so. and ea. dists.) N.Y. 1969, U.S. Ct. Appeals (2d cir.) 1973, U.S. Ct. Appeals (8th cir.) 1973, U.S. Supreme Ct. 1973, U.S. Ct. Appeals (1st cir.) 1983. Assoc. Dewey Ballantine Bushby Palmer & Wood, N.Y.C., 1967-74, Dunnington, Bartholow & Miller, N.Y.C., 1974-77; sr. atty. J.C. Penney Co., 1977-81; pvt. practice Law Offices Gerald Ross, 1981-85; founding ptnr. Fryer, Ross & Gowen, 1986-94, Fryer & Ross, N.Y.C., 1994—. Vestryman Christ and St. Stephen's Ch., N.Y.C., 1981-86, 88-89; trustee Episcopal Diocese of N.Y., 1993—, mem. standing com., 1995-97; bd. dirs. Corp. for the Relief of Widows and Children of Clergymen of the Protestant Episcopal Ch. in the State of N.Y.; pres. 160 West End Owners Corp., 1987—. 1st lt. U.S. Army, 1963-65. Mem. N.Y. State Bar Assn., Assn. of Bar of City of N.Y. (com. profl. judicial ethics, 1996—), Am. Arbitration Assn. (panel constn. arbitrators), Univ. Club, Church Club. Federal civil litigation, General corporate, General practice. Home: 160 W End Ave New York NY 10023-5601 Office: Fryer & Ross 551 5th Ave Rm 1922 New York NY 10176-0173

ROSS, HAROLD ANTHONY, lawyer; b. Kent, Ohio, June 2, 1931; s. Jules and Helen Assumpta (Ferrara) R.; m. Elaine Louise Hunt, July 1, 1961; children: Leslie Ann, Gregory Edward, Jonathan Harold. BA magna cum laude, Case Western Res. U., 1953; JD, Harvard U., 1956. Bar: Ohio 1956. Assoc. Marshman, Hornbeck, Hollington, Steadman & McLaughlin, Cleve., 1961-64; pres. Ross & Kraushaar Co., 1964—. Gen. counsel Brotherhood of Locomotive Engrs., Cleve., 1966—; adv. bd. mem. Ctr. for Advanced Study of Law and Dispute Resolution Procedures, George Mason U. Sch. Law, 2000—. Trustee Citizens League Greater Cleve., 1969-75, 76-82, pres., 1981-82; active Charter Rev. Com. North Olmsted, 1970, 75. With AUS, 1956-58. Mem. ABA (co-chair rwy. and airline labor law sect. 1976-78), Ohio State Bar Assn., Cleve. Bar Assn., Phi Beta Kappa, Delta Sigma Rho, Omicron Delta Kappa. Roman Catholic. Labor. Office: 1548 Standard Bldg 1370 Ontario St Cleveland OH 44113-1701

ROSS, HOWARD PHILIP, lawyer; b. May 10, 1939; s. Bernard and Estelle (Maremont) R.; m. Loretta Teresa Benquil, 1962 (div.); children: Glen Joseph, Cynthia Ann; m. Jennifer Kay Shirley, 1984. BS, U. Ill., 1961; JD, Stetson Coll. Law, 1964. Bar: fla. 1964, U.S. Ct. Appeals (5th cir.) 1965, U.S. Supreme Ct. 1969, U.S. Ct. Appeals (11th cir.) 1981; cert. civil trial lawyer, bus. litigator. Assoc. Parker & Battaglia and predecessor firm, St. Petersburg, Fla., 1964-67; ptnr. Battaglia, Ross, Dicus & Wein, P.A., 1967-87, 1987—, pres., CEO, 1992-99, chmn. bd. dirs., 2000—. Lectr. Stetson Coll. Law, St. Petersburg, 1971-72, adj. prof., 1987. Author: Florida Corporations, 1979; co-author: Managing Discovery in Commercial and Business Litigation, 1993; contbr. articles to profl. jours. Hon. chair St. Petersburg br. Awards Banquet NAACP, 1995; bd. dirs. St. Petersburg Neighborhood Housing Svcs., Inc., 1997, legal counsel, 1997—, pres., 2000—; bd. dirs. Cmty. Alliance, 1997—. Recipient Woman's Svc. League Best Groomed award, 1979, Fla. Bar Merit citation, 1974, Cmty. Svc. award NAACP, 1998, Humanitarian award YMCA of Tampa Bay, 1999. Mem. ABA, Fla. Bar Assn. (chmn. civil trial certification com. 1993-94), St. Petersburg Bar Assn., St. Petersburg Area C. of C. (bd. govs. 1990-95, 2000—, v.p. pub. affairs 1992-93, v.p. membership 1993-94, exec. com. 1992-95, counsel 1994-95, dean entrepreneurial acad. 1996—, treas. 2000—, Mem. of Yr. 1993-94), Citizen Rev. Com. City of St. Petersburg (chmn. subcom. 1992-94, co-chair 1994-97). Republican. Jewish. General civil litigation, Contracts commercial, General corporate. Office: Battaglia Ross Dicus & Wein PA PO Box 41100 980 Tyrone Blvd N Saint Petersburg FL 33710-6382 E-mail: hross@brdwlaw.com

ROSS, JAMES ULRIC, lawyer, accountant, educator; b. Del Rio, Tex., Sept. 14, 1941; s. Stephen Mabrey and Beatrice Jessie (Hyslop) R.; m. Janet S. Calabro, Dec. 28, 1986; children: James Ulric Jr., Ashley Meredith. BA, U. Tex., 1963, JD, 1965. Bar: Tex. 1965, U.S. Tax Ct. 1969; CPA, Tex. Estate tax examiner IRS, Houston, 1965-66; tax acct. Holmes, Raquet, Harris & Shaw, San Antonio, 1966-67; pvt. practice law and acctg. Del Rio and San Antonio, Tex., 1968—. Instr. St. Mary's U., San Antonio, 1973-75; assoc. prof. U. Tex., San Antonio, 1975-99, ret. Contbr. articles on U.S. and Internat. Estate Planning and Taxation to legal and profl. jours. Active Am. Cancer Soc., Residential Mgmt., Inc., Am. Heart Assn. Mem. ABA, Tex. Bar Assn., Tex. Soc. CPAs, San Antonion Bar Assn., San Antonio Estate Planners Coun. Probate, Corporate taxation, Personal income taxation. Home: 3047 Orchard Hl San Antonio TX 78230-3078 Office: 760 Tex Commerce Bank Bldg 7550 IH 10 W San Antonio TX 78229-5803

ROSS, MARK SAMUEL, lawyer, educator, funeral director, writer; b. Newark, June 6, 1957; s. Herbert and Selma Ruth (Feldman) R.; m. Robin Liebman, May 19, 1984; children: Adam Micah, Danielle Leah. BA with honors, Rutgers U., 1979; JD, Benjamin Cardozo Law Sch., 1982; diploma, McAllister Inst. Funeral Svc., 1984. Bar: N.J. 1983, U.S. Dist. Ct. N.J. 1983, N.Y. 1989. V.p. Art/Craft Monuments-Shalom Memls., Union, N.J., 1980—; sec., treas., counsel Menorah Chapels at Milburn, 1983-84; funeral dir. Menorah Chapels at Millburn, 1984—; atty. pvt. practice, 1983—. Counsel Com. for Consumer Protection, Union, 1985—; adj. prof. law Am. Acad.-McAllister Inst., N.Y.C., 1984-85; instr. Jewish law Emanu-El Religious Sch., Westfield, N.J., 1985. Author: (newspaper column) Through My Father's Eyes, 1995—. V.p. Temple Beth Am, Springfield, N.J., 1986-92, pres., 1992-94; counsel Found. Jewish Arts and Heritage, Inc., Union, 1986—. Named Man of Yr. Springfield B'nai B'rith, 1995; recipient Internat. Cmty. Svc. award, B'nai B'rith Internat., 1995. Mem. ABA, N.J. Bar Assn., Union County Bar Assn., B'nai B'rith (pres. 1980-83, Nat. Founders award 1982). Avocations: art, music, photography, golf. Administrative and regulatory, General practice, Probate. Office: 2950 Vauxhall Rd Vauxhall NJ 07088-1246 also: PO Box 641 Millburn NJ 07041-0641

ROSS, MATTHEW, lawyer; b. N.Y.C., Dec. 28, 1953; s. Harvey and Cecile (Shelsky) R.; m. Susan Ruth Goldfarb, Apr. 20, 1986; children: Melissa Danielle, Henry Max, Thomas Frank. BS in Econs., U. Pa., 1975; JD, U. Va., 1978. Bar: N.Y. 1979, U.S. Dist. Ct. (so. dist.) N.Y. 1979. Assoc. Cravath, Swaine & Moore, N.Y.C., 1978-84; prin., assoc. gen. counsel KPMG Peat Marwick LLP, 1984-90; prin., deputy gen. counsel Deloitte & Touche LLP, N.Y.C, 1990—. Mem. ABA (corp. law sect.), N.Y. State Bar Assn. (corp. banking and bus. law sect.), Assn. of Bar of City of N.Y. (corp. law com.), Beta Gamma Sigma. Avocations: basketball, golf, tennis, skiing. Home: 17 Carthage Ln Scarsdale NY 10583-7507 Office: Deloitte & Touche USA LLP 1633 Broadway New York NY 10019-6708

ROSS, MICHAEL AARON, lawyer; b. Newark, Sept. 15, 1941; s. Alexander Ash and Matilda (Blumenthal) R.; m. Leslie Gordon, June 26, 1976; children— Christopher Gordon, Alan Gordon B.A., Franklin and Marshall Coll., 1963; J.D., Columbia U., 1966; M.S. in Econs., U. London, 1967. Bar: N.Y. 1968. Assoc., then ptnr. Shearman & Sterling, N.Y.C., 1967-93; dep. gen. Citigroup, 1993—. Mem. ABA, Am. Law Inst., New York County Lawyers Assn., Assn. of Bar of City of N.Y., Conf. Bd., University Club. Banking, Finance. Office: Citigroup Citigroup 399 Park Ave 3rd Flr New York NY 10043-0001

ROSS, MICHAEL CHARLES, lawyer; BA, U. Va., 1970, JD, 1977. Assoc. Latham & Watkins, 1977-85, ptnr., 1985-93; sr. v.p., gen. counsel, sec. Safeway Inc., Oakland, 1993-2000. Office: Safeway Inc 5918 Stoneridge Mall Rd Pleasanton CA 94588-3229

ROSS, ROGER SCOTT, lawyer; b. Columbus, Ohio, Oct. 25, 1946; s. Donald William and Iris Louise (Smith) R.; m. Lynn Louise Patton, July 29, 1967; 1 child, Anastacia Lynn. Student, Ohio State U., 1964-66; BS in Laws, Western State U., Fullerton, Calif., 1983; JD, Western State U., 1985. Bar: Calif. 1985, U.S. Dist. Ct. (cen. dist.) Calif. 1985. Office mgr. Dial Fin. Co., Buena Park, Calif., 1970-78; asst. br. mgr., loan officer Calif. 1st Bank, Rolling Hills Estates, 1978-79; asst. v.p., loan officer Lloyds Bank, Monterey Park, Calif., 1979-85; pvt. practice law Tustin, 1985-86; ptnr. Anderson & Ross, El Toro, 1986-87; pvt. practice Orange, 1987-90, Bellflower, 1990-94, Anaheim, 1994—. Atty., coach Constnl. Rights Found. of Orange County, 1987—. Mem. AAONMS, ABA, Calif. Bar Assn., L.A. County Bar Assn., Assn. Trial Lawyers Am., Orange County Trial Lawyers Assn., Calif. F&AM, Nat. Forensic Club, Rotary. Republican. Avocations: golf, sailing, tennis. Estate planning, Probate, Real property. Office: 421 N Brookhurst St Ste 126 Anaheim CA 92801-5618

ROSS, WAYNE ANTHONY, lawyer; b. Milw., Feb. 25, 1943; s. Ray E. and Lillian (Steiner) R.; m. Barbara L. Ross, June 22, 1968; children: Gregory, Brian, Timothy, Amy. BA, Marquette U., 1965, JD, 1968. Bar: Wis. 1968, Alaska 1969. Asst. atty. gen. State Alaska, 1968-69; trustee, standing master Superior Ct. Alaska, 1969-73; assoc. Edward J. Reasor & Assocs., Anchorage, 1973-77; prin. Wayne Anthony Ross & Assocs., 1977-83; ptnr. Ross, Gingras & Frenz, Anchorage and Cordova, Alaska, 1983-84, Ross & Gingras, Anchorage and Cordova, 1985; pres. Ross, Gingras and Miner, P.C., Anchorage, 1986-93, Ross and Miner, P.C., Anchorage, 1993—. Col. area def. counsel Alaska State Def. Force; pres. Tyone Mountain Syndicate, Inc. Alaska Rep. Nat. Committeeman, 1992-98; Republican candidate for Gov. of Alaska, 1998, 2002. Decorated knight comdr. Order of Polonia Restituta (Poland), knight Equestrian Order of the Holy Sepulchure of Jerusalem (Vatican). Mem. NRA (bd. dirs. 1980-92, 94—, benefactor), Alaska Bar Assn. (Stanley award), Anchorage Bar Assn., Alaska Gun Collectors Assn. (pres. emeritus), Ohio Gun Colllectors Assn. (hon. life), Smith and Wesson Collectors Assn., 49th Territorial Guard Regiment (pres. 1987-94, 95-96), Alaska Territorial Cavalry (sec. 1991-97, 2001—), Mil. Vehicle Preservation Assn. (v.p. 1994-96), Alaska Peace Officers Assn. Roman Catholic. Criminal, Family and matrimonial, Personal injury. Home: PO Box 101522 Anchorage AK 99510-1522 Office: Ross & Miner 327 E Fireweed Ln Ste 201 Anchorage AK 99503-2110 E-mail: waralaska@alaska.com

ROSS, WILLIAM JARBOE, lawyer, director; b. Oklahoma City, May 9, 1930; s. Walter John and Bertha (Jarboe) R.; m. Mary Lillian Ryan, May 19, 1962; children: Rebecca Anne Roten, Robert Joseph, Molly Kathleen. BBA, U. Okla., 1952, LLB, 1954. Bar: Okla. 1954. Since practiced in, Oklahoma City; asst. municipal counselor Oklahoma City, 1955-60; mem. firm Rainey, Ross, Rice & Binns, 1960—, ptnr., 1965-99. Mem. admissions and grievences com. U.S. Dist. Ct. (we. dist.) Okla. Bd. visitors Coll. of Law U. Okla., St. Anthony's Hosp. Found., Harn Homestead; dir. Ethics and Excellence in Journalism Found., Inasmuch Found. Mem. Okla. Bar Assn., Okla. Heritage Assn. (vice chmn. edn. com.), The Newcomen Soc., Okla. City Golf and Country Club, Econ. Club, Rotary, Phi Alpha Delta, Beta Theta Pi, KC. Estate planning, General practice, Probate. Home: 6923 Avondale Ct Oklahoma City OK 73116-5008

ROSS, WILLIAM ROBERT, lawyer; b. Sundance, Wyo., Aug. 10, 1929; s. James Thomas and Kathryn Melvina (Ormsby) R.; m. Dorothy Evelyn Spencer, Mar. 19, 1951 (dec. July 1980); children: James Bradley, Keith Spencer, Rebecca Ann Ross Duncan; m. Kathleen Riggin Worthington, July 30, 1983. BS in Law, U. Nebr., 1958; LLB, U. Md., 1958. Bar: Wyo. 1958, Colo. 1967. Atty., spl. asst. to solicitor U.S. Dept. of Interior, Washington, 1958-61; atty. Am. Sugar Co., N.Y.C., 1961-64; internat. counsel Gates Rubber Co., Denver, 1964-69; pres. Wexco Internat. Corp., 1969-70; atty., shareholder Lohf & Barnhill, PC, 1970-87; pres., shareholder Lohf, Shaiman & Ross, PC, 1987-93; pvt. practice Littleton, Colo., 1993—. Instr. Law Sch., U. Denver, 1967-73, instr. Bus. Sch., 1970-72. Contbr. articles to profl. law jours. Founding dir., exec. com. World Trade Ctr., Denver, 1989-94. With USAF, 1950-54. Mem. Wyo. State Bar, Colo. Bar Assn., Denver Bar Assn. General corporate, Private international, Legislative. Office: 9425 S Desert Willow Way Littleton CO 80129-5744 E-mail: wrross@pcisys.net

ROSSEEL-JONES, MARY LOUISE, lawyer; b. Detroit, Apr. 19, 1951; d. Rene Octave and Marie Ann (Metcko) Rosseel; m. Mark Christopher Jones, Mar. 16, 1984; 1 child, Kathleen Marie. BA in French with honors, U. Mich., 1973, MA in French, 1976; JD, U. Detroit, 1981. Bar: Mich. 1982, U.S. Ct. Appeals (6th cir.) 1982, U.S. Dist Ct. (ea. dist.) Mich. 1982, U.S. Dist. Ct. (we. dist.) Mich. 1983. Teaching asst. French U. Mich., Ann Arbor, 1974-76; law clk. Johnson, Auld & Valentine, Detroit, 1979-80; assoc. Monaghan, Campbell et al, Bloomfield Hills, Mich., 1981-82; lectr. law U. Clermont, Clermont-Ferrand, France, 1981-82; staff atty. Mich. Nat. Corp., Bloomfield Hills, 1983-85; litigation atty. Am. Motors Corp., Southfield, Mich., 1985-87; staff counsel Chrysler Corp., Auburn Hills, 1987-98; freelance designer, pvt. lang. and piano tutor, eitor, writer; solo law practice, 1998—. Editor: sequel One Life to Give. Recipient Mich. Competitive scholarship, 1969-70, Julia Emanuel scholarship, 1974-75, Henderson House scholarship, 1973, Wayne State Univ. fellow, 1973-74, Univ. Mich., 1974-76. Republican. Roman Catholic. Avocations: classical pianist, interior design. General corporate, Insurance, Personal injury.

ROSSEN, JORDAN, lawyer; b. Detroit, June 13, 1934; s. Nathan Paul and Rebecca (Rizy) R.; m. Susan Friebert, Mar. 24, 1963 (div. June 1972); 1 child, Rebecca; m. M. Elizabeth Bunn, Jan. 3, 1981; children— N. Paul, Jordan David B.A., U. Mich., 1956; J.D., Harvard U., 1959. Bar: Mich. 1960, U.S. Dist. Ct. (ea. dist.) Mich. 1960, U.S. Ct. Appeals (6th cir.) 1966, U.S. Supreme Ct. 1966, U.S. Ct. Appeals (7th cir.) 1974, U.S. Ct. Appeals D.C. cir. 1984, U.S. Ct. Appeals (3rd cir.) 1987, N.Y. 1998, U.S. Dist. Ct. (ea. and so. dists.) N.Y. 1999. Assoc. Sullivan, Elmer, Eames & Moody, Detroit, 1960-62; assoc. Sugar & Schwartz, 1962-64; asst. gen. counsel UAW, 1964-74, assoc. gen. counsel, 1974-83, gen. counsel, 1983-98; of counsel Meyer, Suozzi, English and Klein, N.Y.C., N.Y., 1998—; prof. labor studies Wayne State U., 2000—. Vice pres. N.P. Rossen Agy., Inc., Detroit, 1960-83; gen. counsel Mich. Health & Social Security Research Inst., Inc., Detroit, 1965-83; dir. UAW Job Devel. & Tng. Corp., Detroit, 1984-90. Editor: Mich. Bar Labor Section Publication, 1961-64. Contbr. articles to profl. jours. Pres. Young Democrats, Mich., 1963-65; chmn. Americans for Democratic Action, Mich., 1966-68; chmn. Voter Registration Dem. Party, Mich., 1967 Recipient Human Rights award City of Detroit, 1978 Mem. ABA, Mich. Bar Assn., Nat. Bar Assn., Fed. Bar Assn., Wolverine Bar Assn., Women Lawyers Assn., Lawyers Guild Jewish Administrative and regulatory, Civil rights, Labor. Office: 1350 Broadway Ste 501 New York NY 10018-7705 Fax: 212-239-1311. E-mail: jrossen@msek.com

ROSSI, ANTHONY GERALD, lawyer; b. Warren, Ohio, July 20, 1935; s. Anthony Gerald and Lena (Guarnieri) R.; m. Marilyn J. Fuller, June 22, 1957; children: Diana L., Maribeth, Anthony Gerald III. BS, John Carroll U., 1957; JD, Cath. U. Am., 1961. Bar: Ohio 1961. Ptnr. Guarnieri & Secrest, Warren, 1961—; former acting judge Warren Municipal Ct. Mem. Mahoning-Shenango Estate Planning Coun., 1968—, past sec.; past pres. Warren Olympic Club; past bd. govs. Cath. U. Am. Law Sch. Coun.; past trustee Trumbull Art Guild, Warren Civic Music Assn. Capt. Transp. Corps, AUS, 1957-65. Mem. ABA, Ohio Bar Assn., Trumbull County Bar Assn. (exec. com. 1975—, pres. 1976-77), Am. Arbitration Assn., Ohio State Bar Found., Ohio Motorist Assn. (corp. mem., trustee 1980-86, 92-98), Wolf's Club, KC, Elks, Ohio Acad. of Trial Lawyers. Family and matrimonial, General practice, Health. Home: 2500 Hidden Lakes Dr NE Warren OH 44484-4159 Office: 151 E Market St Warren OH 44481-1102

ROSSI, FAUST F. lawyer, educator; b. 1932; BA, U. Tornoto, 1953; JD, Cornell U., 1960. Bar: N.Y. 1960. Tax trialy atty. Dept. Justice, Washington, 1960-61; sole practice Rochester, N.Y., 1961-66; assoc. prof. Cornell U., Ithaca, 1966-69, prof., 1970—, assoc. dean, 1973-75, Samuel S. Leibowitz prof. trial techniques, 1982—. Vis. prof. Emory U., 1990; cons. report of fed. class actions Am. Coll. of Trial Lawyers, 1971-72; cons. com. on proposed fed. rules of evidence N.Y. Trial Lawyers Assn., 1970; cons., instr. annual seminar N.Y. State Trial Judges, 1970-78; cons., instr. Nat. Inst. for Trial Advocacy, 1974-75, 80-84, 88; cons. N.Y. Law Revision Commn. Project for N.Y. Code of Evidence, 1978-80. Author: Study of the Proposed Federal Rules of Evidence, 1979, Report on Rule 23 Class Actions, 1972, The Federal Rules of Evidence, 1970, Expert Witnesses, 1991; co-author: New York Evidence, 1997; contbr. articles to profl. jours. Lt. j.g. USN. Recipient Jacobsen prize for tchg. trail advocacy, 1992. Mem. Order of Coif. Office: Cornell U Law Sch Myron Taylor Hall Ithaca NY 14853 E-mail: ffr1@cornell.edu

ROSSI, WILLIAM MATTHEW, lawyer; b. Coldwater, Ohio, June 11, 1954; s. Hugh Dominic and Patricia Jean (Putts) R.; m. Constance Sue Streacker, July 21, 1973; children: Bryan Thomas, Lauren Michelle, Alexandria Marie. BA cum laude, Miami U., Oxford, Ohio, 1977; JD magna cum laude, U. Dayton, 1981. Bar: Ohio 1981, U.S. Dist. Ct. (so. dist.) Ohio 1982, U.S. Supreme Ct. 1986, U.S. Ct. Appeals (6th cir.) 1987, Fla. 1991, U.S. Dist. Ct. (so. and mid. dists.) Fla. 1992, U.S. Ct. Appeals (11th cir.) 1992. Assoc. Milliken & Fitton, Hamilton, Ohio, 1981-83; dep. law dir., chief city negotiator City of Middletown, 1984-89; pvt. practice, 1989-92; assoc. Jackson, Lewis, Schnitzler and Krupman, Orlando, Fla., 1992-93; asst. county atty. Sarasota County, 1993—. Bd. dirs. Columbia Inst. Bus., Middletown, 1977-78; lectr. Sawyer Coll., Dayton, 1982-83; small claims referee, 1984-92. Asst. coach Knothole Baseball, Middletown, 1981; bd. dirs. Butler County Mental Health Ctr., Hamilton, 1983-85, Summer Youth Theatre, Middletown, 1985-86; mem. bd. rev. Troop 20 Boy Scouts Am., 1986-87; mem. adv. bd. St. Joseph's Coll. Recipient Am. Jurisprudence award Lawyers Coop. Pub. Co., 1979, 81, Internat. Youth Achievement award Internat. Biog. Ctr. and Am. Biog. Inst., 1982. Mem. ABA, Fla. Bar Assn., Nat. Pub. Employer Labor Rels. Assn., Phi Beta Kappa, Phi Delta Phi (bd. dirs., historian 1979-80). Republican. Roman Catholic. Avocations: golf, travel, writing. State civil litigation, Labor. Home: 6215 Aventura Dr Sarasota FL 34241-9448

ROSSIDES, EUGENE TELEMACHUS, lawyer, writer; b. N.Y.C., Oct. 23, 1927; s. Telemachus and Anna (Maravel) R.; m. Elinor Burcham (div.); 1 child, Gale; m. Aphrodite Macotsin, Dec. 30, 1961; children: Michael, Alexander, Eleni. AB, Columbia U., 1949, JD, 1952. Criminal law investigator Office of Dist. Atty., N.Y.C., 1952; assoc. Rogers & Wells, 1954-56, 61-66, ptnr., 1966-69, 73-92, sr. counsel, 1993—; asst. atty. gen. State of N.Y., 1956-58; asst. to undersec. Dept. Treasury, Washington, 1958-61, asst. sec., 1969-73. Bd. dirs. Sterling Nat. Bank, N.Y.C. Author: U.S. Import Trade Regulation, 2d edit., 1986, Foreign Unfair Competition, 3d edit., 1991, United States Import Trade Law, 1992, also articles; chief import editor Internat. Trade Reporter, Bur. Nat. Affairs, 1980—; editor: The Truman Doctrine of Aid to Greece: A Fifty-Year Retrospective, 1998, Doing Business in Greece, 1996, U.S. Rels. with Greece and Cyprus, 1990—. Mem. Grace Commn., Washington, 1981-82; chmn. nationalities div. Reagan Bush Com., Washington, 1980; campaign mgr. N.Y.C. Nixon for Pres. Com., 1968, Keating for Senator Com., N.Y. State, 1964; bd. dirs. Eisenhower World Affairs Inst., Washington, Am. Hellenic Inst. Inc. Capt. USAF, 1952-60. Recipient Medal for Excellence, Columbia U., 1972, Young Lawyer's award Columbia Law Sch. Alumni Assn., 1972, Silver Anniversary award NCAA, 1974, John Jay award Columbia Coll. Alumni Assn., 1994. Mem. ABA, N.Y. State Bar Assn., Fed. Bar Assn. Republican. Greek Orthodox. Avocations: tennis, photography. Home: 3666 Upton St NW Washington DC 20008-3125 Office: Rogers & Wells 607 14th St NW Ste 900 Washington DC 20005-2000

ROSZKOWSKI, JOSEPH JOHN, lawyer; b. Pawtucket, R.I., Aug. 11, 1938; s. Joseph J. and Anna T. Roszkowski; m. Geraldine J. Szpila, July 2, 1966. BA, Alliance Coll., 1960; JD, Marquette U., 1964. Bar: Wis. 1964, U.S. Dist. Ct. (ea. dist.) Wis. 1964, R.I. 1965. Ptnr. Zimmerman, Roszkowski & Brenner, Woonsocket, R.I., 1965—. Corporator Fogarty Hosp., North Smithfield, RI, 1976—88; counsel Landmark Med. Ctr., 1989—90. Mem. Nat. Ski Patrol, RI, 1974—83; legal counsel R.I. Tuna Tournament, 1975—; bd. dirs. R.I. Legal Svcs., Providence, 1974—87, Legal Aid Soc., Providence, 1985—. Mem. ABA (ho. of dels. 1996—, state del. 2000—, bd. govs. 2001—, commr. Interest on Lawyers' Trust Accounts 1986—), R.I. Bar Found. (pres. 1990-95), R.I. Bar Assn. (pres. 1985-86), Am. Law Inst., Am. Judicature Soc., Fed. Tax Inst. New England (adv. com. 1985-86), R.I. Med. Examiners, U.S. Jaycees (nat. dir. 1968), Am. Acad. Hosp. Attys. Lodge: Rotary (pres. Cumberland, R.I. 1987). Avocations: skiing, sailing, gardening, tennis. Health, Probate, Real property. Home: 1o Little St Cumberland RI 02864-1101 Office: Zimmerman Roszkowski & Brenner 1625 Diamond Hill Rd Woonsocket RI 02895-1541 E-mail: jroskow@aol.com

ROSZKOWSKI, STANLEY JULIAN, retired federal judge; b. Boonville, N.Y., Jan. 27, 1923; s. Joseph and Anna (Christkowski) R.; m. Catherine Mary Claeys, June 19, 1948; children: Mark, Gregory, Dan, John. BS, U. Ill., 1949, JD, 1954. Bar: Ill. 1954. Sales mgr. Warren Petroleum Co., Rockford, Ill., 1954; ptnr. Roszkowski, Paddock, McGreevy & Johnson, 1955-77; judge U.S. Dist. Ct. (we. dist.), Ill., 1977-98; pres. First State Bank, 1963-75, chmn. bd., 1977—; mediator-arbitrator JAMS/ENDISPUTE, Chgo., 1998—. Chmn. Fire and Police Commn., Rockford, 1967-74, commr., 1974— ; chmn. Paul Simon Com., 1972; active Adlai Stevenson III campaign, 1968-71, Winnebago County Citizens for John F. Kennedy, 1962, Winnebago County Dem. Cen. Com., 1962-64; bd. dirs. Sch. of Hope, 1960— ; mem. Ill. Capital Devel. Bd., 1974— . With USAAF, 1943-45. Decorated Air medal with 2 oak leaf clusters.; recipient Pulaski Nat. Heritage award Polish Am. Congress, Chgo., 1982 Mem. ABA, Ill. Bar Assn., Fla. Bar Assn., Winnebago County Bar Assn., Am. Coll. Trial Lawyers, Am. Judicature Soc., Assn. Trial Lawyers Am., Ill. Trial Lawyers Assns., Am. Arbitration Assn. (arbitrator), Fed. Judges Assn. (bd. dirs. 1988—).

ROTCH, JAMES E. lawyer; b. Auburn, Ala., Mar. 26, 1945; s. Elroy B. and Martha (Ellisor) R.; m. Darlene Edwards; children: Jamison B., Susannah R., Amie L. Vaughn. BS, Auburn U., 1967, postgrad., 1967-68; JD, U. Va., 1971. Bar: Ala. 1971, U.S. Dist. Ct. (no. dist.) Ala. 1973. Rsch. asst. Office Instl. Rsch. Auburn (Ala.) U., 1967-68; clk. U.S. Judiciary System, Birmingham, Ala., 1971-72; assoc. Bradley Arant Rose & White LLP, 1971-76; ptnr. Bradley, Arant, Rose & White LLP, 1976—, adminstrv. ptnr., 1990-93. Mem. adv. com. Bioelastics Rsch. Ltd., Birmingham, 1992—, Gov.'s Task Force on Biotechnology, Ala., 1993. Pres. adv. com. Birmingham Mus. Art, 1989-92; bd. dirs. Operation New Birmingham, 1990-91, 95—, co-chmn. cmty. affairs com., mem. exec. com.; Coalition for Better Edn., Birmingham, 1990—; active Boy Scouts Am.; bd. dirs. Birmingham Com. for Olympic Soccer, 1994-96, Ala. Sports Found., 1994-98, Entrepreneurial Ctr. Inc., 1996—; mem. adminstrv. bd. Canterbury United Meth. Ch., 1991-93; chmn. Birmingham Pledge Found., 2000—. Capt. USAR, 1972-78. Mem. ALA, Auburn U. Bar Assn., Birmingham Bar Assn., Internat. Bar Assn., Ala. State Bar Assn., Leadership Birmingham, Leadership Ala., Auburn Coll. Liberal Arts (adv. coun.), U. Va. Alumni Assn., Newcomen Soc., Birmingham Area C. of C. (bd. dirs. 2001), Auburn U. Alumni Assn., Birmingham Venture Club (bd. dirs. 2001), Country Club of Birmingham, Jockey Club, Summit Club (charter), Kiwanis (sec. 1998-99). Methodist. Avocations: horses, bird hunting, cattle farming, golf. General corporate, Mergers and acquisitions, Securities. Office: Bradley Arant Rose & White LLP 2001 Park Pl Ste 1400 Birmingham AL 35203-2736

ROTH, EUGENE, lawyer; b. Wilkes-Barre, Pa., June 28, 1935; s. Max and Rae (Klein) R.; m. Constance D. Smulyan, June 16, 1957; children: Joan Roth Kleinman, Steven P., Jeffrey H., Lawrence W. BS, Wilkes U., 1957; LLB, Pa. State U., 1960. Bar: Pa. 1960, U.S. Dist. Ct. (mid. dist.) Pa. 1961. Assoc. Rosenn, Jenkins & Greenwald LLP, Walkes-Barre, 1960-64, ptnr., 1964—. Mem. Northeastern Pa. Regional bd. 1st Union Bank; bd. dirs. RCN Corp., Commonwealth Telephone Enterprises, Inc.; chmn. Greater Wilkes-Barre Partnership, Inc., 1991-93. Trustee Wilkes U., 1979—, chmn. 1993-98; chmn. United Way of Wyoming Valley, 1983; chmn. annual campaign Osterhout Free Libr. Campaign, 1999; Northeastern Pa. regional bd. dirs. Geiseinger-Wyoming Valley Hosp. Recipient Disting. Pennsylvanian award Phila. C. of C., 1980, Cmty. Svc. award B'nai B'rith, 1994, Disting. Citizen award N.E. Pa. Boy Scouts Am., 1998, Shofar award United Hebrew Inst., 2001; named Outstanding Vol. Fund Raiser Nat. Soc. Fund Raising Exec., 1993. Mem. ABA, Pa. Bar Assn., Luzerne County Law and Libr. Assn., Wilkes-Barre C. of C. (chmn. 1980, vice com. for econ. growth), Wyo. Valley United Jewish Campaign (chmn. 1978 and 1993), B'nai B'rith. Republican. Jewish. Avocations: reading, community svc. Contracts commercial, General corporate, Mergers and acquisitions. Office: Rosenn Jenkins & Greenwald 15 S Franklin St Wilkes Barre PA 18711-0076 E-mail: er@rjglaw.com

ROTH, HADDEN WING, lawyer; b. Oakland, Calif., Feb. 10, 1930; s. Mark and Jane (Haley) R.; m. Alice Becker, Aug., 1987; 1 child, Elizabeth Wing. AA, Coll. Marin, 1949; BA, U. Calif., Berkeley, 1951; JD, U. Calif., San Francisco, 1957. Bar: Calif. 1958, U.S. Dist. Ct. (no. dist.) Calif. 1958, U.S. Ct. Appeals (9th cir.) 1958, U.S. Supreme Ct. 1966. Pvt. practice, San Rafael, 1970—. Judge Marin County Mcpl. Ct., 1966-70; spl. cons. Marin Muni Water Dist., Corte Madera, Calif., County of Marin; atty. Bolinas Pub. Utility Dist., Ross Valley Fire Svc., Tiburon Fire Protection Dist., Town of Ross and San Anselmo, Calif.; hearing officer dist. hosps., 1981—; lectr. law Golden Gate Coll. Law, San Francisco, 1971-73. Chmn. Marin County prison task force, 1973; bd. dirs. Marin Gen. Hosp., 1964-66. Named Outstanding Citizen of Yr., Coll. Marin, 1972. Mem. ABA, Am. Trial Lawyers Assn., Calif. Bar Assn., Marin County Bar Assn., San Francisco Trial Lawyers Assn., Am. Assn. Ind. Investors, Assn. Bus. Trial Lawyers. Avocations: running, weights, reading. Alternative dispute resolution, Appellate, General civil litigation. Office: Hadden Roth Law Offices 1050 Northgate Dr San Rafael CA 94903-2526

ROTH, JANE RICHARDS, federal judge; b. Philadelphia, Pa., June 16, 1935; d. Robert Henry Jr. and Harriett (Kellond) Richards; m. William V. Roth Jr., Oct. 9, 1965; children: William V. III, Katharine K. BA, Smith Coll., 1956; LLB, Harvard U., 1965; LLD (hon.), Widener U., 1986, U. Del., 1994. Bar: Del. 1965, U.S. Dist. Ct. Del. 1966, U.S. Ct. Appeals (3d cir.) 1974. Adminstrv. asst. various fgn. service posts U.S. State Dept., 1956-62; assoc. Richards, Layton & Finger, Wilmington, Del., 1965-73, ptnr., 1973-85; judge U.S. Dist. Ct. Del., 1985-91, U.S. Ct. Appeals (3d cir.), Wilmington, 1991—. Adj. faculty Villanova U. Sch. Law. Hon. chmn. Del. chpt. Arthritis Found., Wilmington; bd. overseers Widener U. Sch. Law; bd. consultors Villanova U. Sch. Law; trustee Hist. Soc. Del. Recipient Nat. Vol. Service citiation Athritis Found., 1982. Fellow Am. Bar Found.; mem. ABA, Fed. Judges Assn., Del. State Bar Assn. Republican. Episcopalian. Office: J Caleb Boggs Fed Bldg 844 King St Rm 5100 Wilmington DE 19801-3519*

ROTH, KENNETH DAVID, lawyer; b. Bklyn., Feb. 12, 1948; s. Ben A. and Sally T. (Dancik) R.; m. Sharon G. Kipness, Aug. 15, 1970; children: Sari Alissa, Scott Aaron. Student Hunter Coll., 1965-67; BA in Polit. Sci., L.I. U., 1970; JD cum laude, Rutgers U., 1973. Bar; N.J. 1973, U.S. Dist. Ct. N.J. 1973, U.S. Ct. Appeals (3d cir.) 1978, U.S. Supreme Ct. 1977. Assoc. Davis & Reberkenny, P.A., Cherry Hill, N.J., 1973-79; shareholder, Davis, Reberkenny & Abramowitz, 1980— , v.p., also dir. assoc. editor Rutgers-Camden Law Jour., 1972-73, mem. exec. com., 1992—; mem. GEMS Landfill Litigation-Generators Steering Com. Mem. ABA, N.J. Bar Assn. (environ. law sect. del. to gen. council), Camden and Burlington County Bar Assn. (trustee 1990-93), Ednl. Negotiators Assn. N.J., N.J. Sch. Bds. Assn., Environ. Law Assn. Democrat. Jewish. Federal civil litigation, Environmental, Real property. Office: Davis Reberkenny & Abramowitz PA 499 Cooper Landing Rd PO Box 5459 Cherry Hill NJ 08034-0480

ROTH, PHILLIP JOSEPH, retired judge; b. Portland, Oreg., Feb. 29, 1920; s. Harry William and Minnie Alice (Segel) R.; m. Ida Lorraine Thomas, Feb. 22, 1957 (div. 1977); children: Phillip Joseph, David Harry; m. Allison Blake Ramsey, Feb. 14, 1978 (div. 1994). BA cum laude, U. Portland, 1943; JD, Lewis and Clark Coll., 1948. Bar: Oreg. 1948, U.S. Dist. Ct. Oreg. 1949, U.S. Ct. Appeals (9th cir.) 1959, U.S. Supreme Ct. 1962. Dep. atty. City of Portland, 1948-50; dep. dist. atty. Multnomah County, Portland, 1950-52; pvt. practice, 1952-64; cir. judge Multnomah County State of Oreg., 1964-94, presiding cir. judge, 1970-71, 76-78. Adj. prof. Lewis & Clark U. Law Sch., Portland, 1978-80, standing com., 1972-90; exec. com. Nat. Conf. State Trial Judges, 1980-91. Author: Sentencing: A View From the Bench, 1973; co-author: The Judicial Immunity Doctrine Today: Between the Bench and a Hard Place, 1984, The Brief Jour.; The Dangerous Erosion of Judicial Immunity, 1989. Mem. Oreg. Legislature, 1952-54; Rep. nominee for Congress, 1956; chmn. Oreg. Rep. Ctrl. Com., 1962-64; adv. bd. Portland Salvation Army, 1976—; mem. bd. overseers Lewis and Clark Coll., 1972-90. Named Alumnus of Yr. U. Portland, 1963, Lewis & Clark Law Sch., 1973. Fellow Am. Bar Found.; mem. ABA (chmn. jud. immunity com. jud. adminstrn. divsn. 1982-90, mem. commn. on standards jud. adminstrn. divsn. 1973-77, chmn. conf. state trial judges 1990-91, HBH Comm. on State Justice Initiatives 1994-98, chmn. jud. adminstrn. divsn. 1994-95), Oreg. Bar Assn. (bd. govs. 1961-64), Multnomah County Bar Assn. (pres. 1959), Am. Judicature Soc., Oreg. Cir. Judges Assn. (pres. 1988-89), U. Portland Alumni Assn. (pres. 1967), Lewis and Clark Coll. Alumni Assn. (prs. 1974-76, 80-81), Multnomah Law Libr. Assn. (bd. dirs.), City Club, Univ. Club, Masons, Shriners, Rotary, B'nai B'rith, Delta Theta Phi. Jewish. Home: 2495 SW 73rd Ave Portland OR 97225-3274

ROTHBERG, GLENDA FAY MORRIS, lawyer; b. Rome, Aug. 7, 1946; d. Glenn Howell and Fay (Givens) Morris; m. Gerald Rothberg, June 18, 1970 (div. Jan. 1989); children: Laura, Abigail. AB, Randolph-Macon Woman's Coll., 1968; JD, Benjamin Cardozo Law Sch., 1985. Bar: N.Y. 1986, U.S. Dist. Ct. (so. and ea. dists.) N.Y. 1987, U.S. Supreme Ct. 1990. Law guardian juvenile rights divsn. Legal Aid Soc., N.Y.C., 1988-91; pvt. practice, 1992—. Faculty dir. Inst. for not-for-profit Mgmt. Columbia Bus. Sch., N.Y.C., 1994-98. Vol. Manhattan Mediation Ctr., N.Y.C., 1996-99; chair legal com. N.Y.C. Comptr. Task Force on Open Adoption, 1999—. Fellow Am. Bar Found.; mem. ABA, Assn. of Bar of City of N.Y. (com. chair 1996-99, mem. coun. on children 1999—). Family and matrimonial, Juvenile. Office: 271 Madison Ave New York NY 10016-1001 E-mail: gmrlaw@aol.com

ROTHBERG, LORETTA SUE, lawyer; b. Miami, Fla., July 8, 1969; d. Lawrence and Judith R. BBA, Hofstra U., 1990; JD, MB, George Washington U., 1994. Bar: N.Y. 1995, D.C. 1996. Atty. Rothberg & Sherman, Bklyn., 1994-96; contract adminstr. ISG, Fairfax, Va., 1996-99, Synergy, Inc., Washington, 1996-98, Maximus, Fairfax, Va., 1998, SRA, Internat., Fairfax, 1998—. Mem. ABA, Nat. Contract Mgmt. Assn. Home: 2726 Ordway St NW Apt 5 Washington DC 20008-5049 E-mail: loretta_rothberg@sra.com

ROTHENBERG, ELLIOT CALVIN, lawyer, author; b. Mpls., Nov. 12, 1939; s. Sam S. and Claire Sylvia (Feller) R.; m. Sally Smalying; children: Sarah, Rebecca, Sam. BA summa cum laude, U. Minn., 1961; JD, Harvard U. (Fulbright fellow), 1964. Bar: Minn. 1966, U.S. Dist. Ct. Minn. 1966, D.C. 1968, U.S. Supreme Ct. 1972, N.Y. 1974, U.S. Ct. Appeals (2d cir.) 1974, U.S. Ct. Appeals (8th cir.) 1975. Assoc. project dir. Brookings Inst., Washington, 1966-67; fgn. svc. officer, legal advisor U.S. Dept. State, 1968-73; Am. Embassy, Saigon; U.S. Mission to the UN; nat. law dir. Anti-Defamation League, N.Y.C., 1973-74; legal dir. Minn. Pub. Interest Rsch. Group, Mpls., 1974-77; pvt. practice law, 1977—. Adj. prof. William Mitchell Coll. Law, St. Paul, 1983—; faculty mem. several nat. comm. law and First Amendment seminars. Author: (with Zelman Cowen) Sir John Latham and Other Papers, 1965, The Taming of the Press: Cohen v. Cowles Media Co., 1999, The Taming of the Press, 1999; contbr. articles to profl. and scholarly jours. and books, newspapers, popular mags. State bd. dirs. YMCA Youth in Govt. Program, 1981-84; v.p. Twin Cities chpt. Am. Jewish Com., 1980-84; mem. Minn. Ho. of Reps., 1978-82, asst. floor leader (whip), 1981-82; pres., dir. North Star Legal Found., 1983—; legal affairs editor Pub. Rsch. Syndicated, 1986—; briefs and oral arguments published in full Landmark Briefs and Arguments of the Supreme Ct. of the U.S., Vol. 200, 1992; mem. citizens adv. com. Voyageurs Nat. Pk., 1979-81. Recipient Legis. Evaluation Assembly Legis. Excellence award, 1980, Vietnam Civilian Svc. medal U.S. Dept. State, 1970, North Star award U. Minn., 1961; Fulbright fellow, 1964-65. Mem. ABA, Minn. Bar Assn., Harvard Law Sch. Assn., Am. Legion, Mensa, Phi Beta Kappa. Jewish. General civil litigation, Communications, Constitutional. Home and Office: 3901 W 25th St Saint Louis Park MN 55416-3803 E-mail: srothenbe@aol.com

ROTHENBERG, GILBERT STEVEN, lawyer, law educator; b. Richmond, Va., Jan. 22, 1951; s. Joseph and Mollie Fay R.; m. Harriet Ann Sherman, Aug., 20, 1972 (div. Dec. 1983); m. Lynn Kay Goldstein, Sept. 20, 1986; 1 child, Arthur C. BA, U. Pa., 1972; JD, Am. U., 1975; LLM in Taxation, Georgetown U., 1979. Bar: Md. 1975, D.C. 1976, U.S. Ct. Appeals (2d cir.) 1975, U.S. Ct. Appeals (7th and D.C. cirs.) 1976, U.S. Ct. Appeals (4th and 9th cirs.) 1977, U.S. Ct. Appeals (1st cir.) 1978, U.S. Ct. Appeals (5th and 11th cirs.) 1981, U.S. Ct. Appeals (10th cir.) 1982, U.S. Supreme Ct. 1979. Atty. appellate sect. Tax Divsn. U.S. Dept. Justice, Washington, 1975-83, reviewer, 1983-88, asst. chief, 1988—. Adj. prof. Am. U. Law Sch., Washington, 1983—. Contbr. articles to profl. publs. Recipient Outstanding Svcs. awards Tax Divsn. U.S. Dept. Justice, 1980, 83, 90, 95, 2000. Mem. Order of Coif. Avocations: golf, racquetball. Home: 7823 Thornfield Ct Fairfax VA 22039-3178 Office: US Dept Justice Tax Div 601 D St NW Washington DC 20004-2904 E-mail: Gilbert.S.Rothenberg@usdoj.gov

ROTHENBERG, KAREN H. dean, law educator; BA, Princeton U., 1973, MPA, 1974; JD, U. Va., 1979. Dean law sch.'s law and health care program U. Md., 2001—, law educator, 2001—. Formerly practiced with Washington D.C. Law firm of Covington and Burling; worked with a variety of health and med. orgns. ; pres. Am. Soc. Law, Medicine and Ethics; lectr. on legal issues in health care; dir. law sch.'s law and health

care program U. Md.; spl. asst. to dir. , 1995—96. Co-editor-in-chief (jours.) Jour. Law, Medicine, and Ethics; co-editor: (book with Elizabeth Thompson) Women and Prenatal Testing: Facing the Challenges of Genetic Technology ;contbr. articles on AIDS, women's health, genetics, right to forego treament . Recipient Joseph Healey Health Law Tchr.'s award, Am. Soc. Law, Medicine and Ethics. Mem.: NIH (sect. on prenatal care, recruitment & ret. of women in clin studies, sect. on ethical, legal and social implications of genetics), Inst. Medicine's Com. (sect. legal and ethical issues for inclusion of women in clin. stud.), Ethics in Reproduction (nat. adv. bd.), Nat. Action Plan Breast Cancer, ABA (coordinating group on bioethics and the law), Nat. Inst. Child & Human Develop. (adv. coun.). Office: U Md Law Sch 515 West Lombard St Baltimore MD 21201 Fax: 410-706-0407. Business E-Mail: krothenberg@law.umaryland.edu*

ROTHMAN, BERNARD, lawyer; b. N.Y.C., Aug. 11, 1932; s. Harry and Rebecca (Fritz) R.; m. Barbara Joan Schaeffer, Aug. 1953; children: Brian, Adam, Helene. BA cum laude, CCNY, 1953; JD, NYU, 1959. Bar: N.Y. 1959, U.S. Dist. Ct. (ea. and so. dists.) N.Y. 1962, U.S. Ct. Appeals (2d cir.) 1965, U.S. Supreme Ct. 1966, U.S. Tax Ct. 1971. Assoc. Held, Telchin & Held, 1961-62; asst. U.S. atty. Dept. Justice, 1962-66; assoc. Edward Gettinger & Peter Gettinger, 1966-68; ptnr. Schwartz, Rothman & Abrams, P.C., 1968-78, Ferster, Bruckman, Wohl, Most & Rothman, LLP, N.Y.C., 1978-98, Law Offices of Bernard Rothman, N.Y.C., 1999—. Acting judge Village of Larchmont, 1982-88, dep. Village atty., 1974-81, former arbitrator Civil Ct., N.Y.C., family disputes panel Am. Arbitration Assn.; guest lectr. domestic rels. and family law on radio and TV, also numerous legal and mental health orgns. Author: Loving and Leaving-Winning at the Business of Divorce, 1998; co-author: Family Law Syracuse Law Rev. of N.Y. Law, 1992, Leaving Home, Family Law Review, 1987; contbr. articles to profl. jours. Mem. exec. bd., past v.p. Westchester Putnam coun. Boy Scouts Am., 1975—; past mem. nat. coun., 1977-81; mem. adv. com. N.Y. State PEACE, 1994—; pres. Congregation B'nai Israel, 1961-63, B'nai Brith, Larchmont chpt., 1981-83. Recipient Silver Beaver award Boy Scouts Am., Wood Badge award. Fellow Am. Acad. Matrimonial Lawyers (bd. govs. N.Y. chpt. 1986-87, 91-93), Interdisciplinary Forum on Mental Health and Family Law (co-chair 1986-97); mem. ABA (family law sect., contbr. Family Adv. Qtrly.), N.Y. State Bar Assn. (exec. com. family law sect. 1982—, co-chmn. com. on mediation and arbitration 1982-88, 93—, com. on legis. 1978-88, com. on child custody 1985-88, com. alt. dispute resolution), Assn. of Bar of City of N.Y. (women in the cts. com. 1996-99), N.Y. State Magistrate Assn., Westchester Magistrate Assn., N.Y. Rd. Runners Club, Limousine 6 Track Club. Democrat. State civil litigation, Family and matrimonial. Address: Law Offices of Bernard Rothman 750 3rd Ave Fl 29 New York NY 10017-2703 E-mail: divorcelawyer@worldnet.att.net

ROTHMAN, DAVID BILL, lawyer; b. N.Y.C., Apr. 25, 1952; s. Julius and Lillian (Halpern) R.; m. Jeanne Marie Hickey, July 7, 1974; children: Jessica Suzanne, Gregory Kozak. BA, U. Fla., 1974, JD, 1977. Bar: Fla. 1977, U.S. Dist. Ct. (so. dist.) Fla. 1980, U.S. Ct. Appeals (5th cir.) 1980, U.S. Supreme Ct. 1981, U.S. Ct. Appeals (11th cir.) 1982, U.S. Dist. Ct. (ea. dist.) Ky. 1985, U.S. Dist. Ct. (mid. dist.) Fla. 1986, cert.: Fla. Bd. , Nat. Bd. Trial Advocacy (criminal trial law). Asst. state atty. Dade County State Atty.'s Office, Miami, Fla., 1977-80; ptnr. Thornton Rothman, P.A., 1980—. Adj. prof. U. Miami Sch. Law, 1995—; com. mem. Fla. Rules Criminal Procedures, 1990-93, metro Dade Ind. Rev. Panel, 1989-97, co-chmn., 1990-91, chmn., 1991-92, 95-97; panel mem. fee arbitration 11th Cir. Ct., 1994-96, co-chair, 1995-96. Mem. ABA, Fla. Bar Assn. (bd. govs. 1999—), Dade County Bar Assn. (criminal ct. com. 1984—, chmn. 1987-90, bd. dirs. 1990-93, treas. 1993-94, sec. 1994-95, v.p. 1995-96, pres. 1997-98), Nat. Assn. Criminal Def. Lawyers, Fla. Assn. Criminal Def. Lawyers (bd. dirs. Miami chpt. 1991—, pres. Miami chpt. 1993-94, statewide sec. 1996-97, treas. 1997-98, v.p. 1998-99, pres.-elect 1999-2000, pres. 2001), Eugene Spellman Inns of Ct. Democrat. Jewish. Avocations: running, weightlifting, reading. Criminal. Home: 9951 SW 127th Ter Miami FL 33176-4833 Office: Thornton & Rothman PA 200 S Biscayne Blvd Ste 2690 Miami FL 33131-5331 E-mail: DBR@ThorntonRothmanLaw.com

ROTHMAN, MICHAEL JUDAH, lawyer; b. Mpls., June 7, 1962; s. Harvey Michael and Elaine Louise (London) R.; m. Shari Latz, Aug. 1, 1993. BA, Carleton Coll., 1984; JD, U. Minn., 1988. Bar: Minn. 1988, U.S. Dist. Ct. Minn. 1988, Calif. 1993, U.S. Dist. Ct. (ctrl. dist.) Calif. 1993, U.S. Ct. Appeals (9th cir.) 1995, U.S. Supreme Ct. 1995. Law clk. to Hon. J. Gary Crippen Minn. Ct. of Appeals, St. Paul, 1988-89; adminstrv. asst. Minn. State Senate, 1989-92; atty. Rubenstein & Perry, L.A., 1993-95, Loeb & Loeb, L.A., 1995-96; ptnr. Barger & Wolen, LLP, 1996—. Vol. atty. F.A.M.E. Ch. and Temple Isaiah Legal Project, L.A., 1994-96. Recipient Best Brief award Regional Internat. Moot Ct. Competition, Colo., 1988. Mem. ABA, Calif. Bar Assn., L.A. County Bar Assn. Democrat. Avocations: golf, running, reading. Administrative and regulatory, General civil litigation, Insurance. Office: Barger & Wolen 515 S Flower St Fl 34 Los Angeles CA 90071-2201

ROTHMAN, MITCHELL LEWIS, lawyer, educator; b. Bronx, N.Y., Mar. 26, 1948; s. Charles Bernard and Edna Marilyn (Schwartz) R. B.A., CUNY, 1969; J.D., Yale U., 1974, Ph.D., 1982. Bar: N.Y. 1975, U.S. Dist. Ct. (no. dist.) N.Y. 1978, Hawaii 1975, U.S. Dist. Ct. Hawaii 1975. Atty. N.Y. State Dept. Environ. Conservation, Albany, 1974; VISTA atty. Legal Aid Soc. Hawaii, Honolulu, 1975; asst. dean, lectr. Syracuse U. Coll. Law, N.Y., 1976-79; assoc. prof. law Hamline U. Sch. Law, St. Paul, 1982— . Contbg. editor pub. edn. div. ABA, 1983— ; contbr. articles to profl. publs. Yale U. fellow, 1979-81; Guggenheim fellow, 1981-82. Office: Hamline University Sch of Law 1536 Hewitt Ave Saint Paul MN 55104-1205

ROTHMAN, ROBERT PIERSON, lawyer; b. Syracuse, N.Y., May 2, 1946; s. R. Raymond and Arlene (Pierson) R.; m. Tovah Guttenplan Rothman, Mar. 26, 1972; children— Arlene Rachel, Aaron Jeffrey, Sarah Michelle. B.A., Pa. State U., 1967; J.D., Syracuse U., 1972. Bar: N.Y. 1973, U.S. Dist. Ct. (no. dist.) N.Y. 1973. Ptnr., Menter, Rudin & Trivelpiece, Syracuse, 1972-78; assoc. Samuel H. Greene, 1978-79; owner, pres. Robert P. Rothman, P.C., Syracuse, 1979— . Officer Syracuse Jewish Fedn., 1980— . Mem. Syracuse Assn. Credit Mgmt. (dir., officer), Mid-York Med. Accts. Mgmt. (dir., officer), Consumer Credit Assn. City of N.Y. Lodges: Syracuse Rotary (found. officer), Temple Soc. of Concord (trustee). Jewish. Bankruptcy, Consumer commercial. Home: 104 Cammot Ln Fayetteville NY 13066-1426 Office: Robert P Rothman PC 107 University Syracuse NY 13210-1004

ROTHSCHILD, DONALD PHILLIP, lawyer, arbitrator; b. Dayton, Ohio, Mar. 31, 1927; s. Leo and Anne (Office) R.; m. Ruth Eckstein, July 7, 1950; children: Nancy Lee, Judy Lynn Hoffman, James Alex. AB, U. Mich., 1950; JD summa cum laude, U. Toledo, 1965; LLM, Harvard U., 1966. Bar: Ohio 1966, D.C. 1970, U.S. Supreme Ct. 1975, R.I. 1989. Teaching fellow Harvard U. Law Sch., Cambridge, Mass., 1965-66; instr. solicitor's office U.S. Dept. Labor, Washington, 1966-67; vis. prof. U. Mich. Law Sch., Ann Arbor, 1976; prof. law George Washington U. Nat. Law Ctr., Washington, 1966-89, emeritus, 1989; prof. law N.Y. Law Sch., 1989-96; dir. Consumer Protection Ctr., 1971—; dir. Inst. Law and Aging, Washington, 1973-89, Ctr. for Community Justice, Washington, 1974-88, Nat. Consumers League, Washington, 1981-87; v.p. Regulatory Alternatives Devel. Corp., Washington, 1982—; cons. Washington Met. Council Govt., 1979-82; mayoral appointee Adv. Com. on Consumer Protection, Washington, 1979-80; chmn. bd. dirs. D.C. Citizens Complaint Ctr., Washington, 1980; counsel Tillinghast, Collins & Graham, Providence, 1989-95, chair human resource group. Co-author: Consumer Protection Text and Materials, 1973; Collective Bargaining and Labor Arbitration, 1979; Fundamentals of Administrative Practice and Procedure, 1981. Contbr. numerous articles to profl. publs. Mem. Fed. Trade Commn. Adv. Council, Washington, 1970. Recipient Community Service award Television Acad., Washington, 1981. Mem. ABA, Nat. Assn. Coll. and Univ. Attys. (Brown U.), Nat. Acad. Arbitrators, Fed. Mediation and Conciliation Service, Am. Arbitration Assn., D.C. Bar Assn., Phi Kappa Phi. Jewish. Office: Shadow Farm Way Unit 4 Wakefield RI 02879-3631

ROTHSTEIN, BARBARA JACOBS, federal judge; b. Bklyn., Feb. 3, 1939; d. Solomon and Pauline Jacobs; m. Ted L. Rothstein, Dec. 28, 1968; 1 child, Daniel. B.A., Cornell U., 1960; LL.B., Harvard U., 1966. Bar: Mass. 1966, Wash. 1969, U.S. Ct. Appeals (9th cir.) 1977, U.S. Dist. Ct. (we. dist.) Wash. 1971, U.S. Supreme Ct. 1975. Pvt. practice law, Boston, 1966-68; asst. atty. gen. State of Wash., 1968-77; judge Superior Ct., Seattle, 1977-80, Fed. Dist. Ct. Western Wash., Seattle, 1980—, chief judge, 1987-94. Faculty Law Sch. U. Wash., 1975-77, Hastings Inst. Trial Advocacy, 1977, N.W. Inst. Trial Advocacy, 1979—; mem. state-fed. com. U.S. Jud. Conf., chair subcom. on health reform. Recipient Matrix Table Women of Yr. award Women in Communication, Judge of the Yr. award Fed. Bar Assn., 1989; King County Wash. Women Lawyers Vanguard Honor, 1995. Mem. ABA (jud. sect.), Am. Judicature Soc., Nat. Assn. Women Judges, Fellows of the Am. Bar, Wash. State Bar Assn., U.S. Jud. Conf. (state-fed. com., health reform subcom.), Phi Beta Kappa, Phi Kappa Phi. Office: US Dist Ct 705 US Courthouse 1010 5th Ave Ste 215 Seattle WA 98104-1189

ROTHSTEIN, PAUL FREDERICK, lawyer, educator; b. Chgo., June 6, 1938; BS, Northwestern U., 1958, LLB, 1961. Bar: Ill. 1962, D.C. 1967, U.S. Supreme Ct. 1975. Instr. U. Mich. Law Sch., 1963; assoc. prof. law U. Tex., 1964-67; mem. Surrey, Karasik, Gould & Greene, Washington, 1967-70; prof. Georgetown U. Law Ctr., 1970—; spl. counsel U.S. Senate Jud. Com. Subcom. on Criminal Laws and Procedures, 1975-77; spl. counsel U.S. Ho. of Reps. Jud. Com. Subcom. on Criminal Law, 1980. Cons. Treasury, 1967-74, HEW, 1970, Commrs. on Uniform State Laws, 1969-75, Nat. Acad. Scis., 1976-77, 95-96, D.C. Law Revision Commn., 1976-78; spkr., coord. numerous legal edn. seminars for judges and lawyers, 1970—. Author: Evidence in a Nutshell, 1970, 2d edit., 1981, 3d edit., 1997, Understanding the New Federal Rules of Evidence, 1973, 74, 75, Federal Rules of Evidence with Practice Comments and Annotations, 1978, 2d edit., 1981, 3d edit., 2001, Cases, Materials and Problems in Evidence, 1986, 2d edit., 1998; contbr. articles on various legal matters to profl. jours.; editor-in-chief Northwestern U. Law Rev., 1960-61. Recipient U. Iowa Legal Edn. award 1974, Disting. Pub. Svc. award Crime Victims Compensation Bd., 1978; other civic and profl. awards; Fulbright scholar, Oxford, Eng., 1962-63. Mem. Fed. Bar Assn. (chmn. fed. rules of evidence com. 1974-77, Disting. Svc. award 1975, nat. coun. 1976-80, chmn. continuing legal edn. com. 1980), D.C. Bar (continuing legal edn. bd. 1980—), ABA (chmn. rules of evidence and criminal procedure com., criminal justice sect. 1984-88), Assn. Am. Law Schs. (sec. evidence sect. 1976, chmn. 1977), Nat. Assn. Criminal Injuries Compensations Bds. (sec. 1977-80), Internat. Assn. Criminal Injuries Compensation Bds. Office: Georgetown U Law Ctr 600 New Jersey Ave NW Washington DC 20001-2022

ROTI, THOMAS DAVID, judge; b. Evanston, Ill., Jan. 20, 1945; s. Sam N. and Theresa S. (Salerno) R.; m. Donna Sumichrast, July 22, 1972; children: Thomas S., Kyle D., Rebecca D., Gregory J. BS, Loyola U., Chgo., 1967, JD cum laude, 1970. Bar: Ill. 1970, U.S. Dist. Ct. (no. dist.) Ill. 1971, U.S. Ct. Appeals (7th cir.) 1971. Sr. law clk. to presiding justice U.S. Dist. Ct. No. Dist. Ill., 1971-72; assoc. Arnstein, Gluck & Lehr, Chgo., 1972-73, Boodell, Sears et al, Chgo., 1973-75; asst. gen. counsel Dominick's Finer Foods, Inc., Northlake, Ill., 1975-77, v.p., gen. counsel, 1977-97; judge Cir. Ct. Cook County, 2000—. Mem. nat. conf. lawyers and econs. com. Food Mktg. Inst., Washington, 1987-97, legis. com. Ill. Retail Mchts. Assn., Chgo., 1987—; dir. NCCJ. Trustee Joint Civic Com. Italian Ams., Chgo., 1986—; mem. Chgo. Coun. EDU-CARE Scholarship Program, 1988. Recipient Am. Jurisprudence award, 1970, Alumni Assn. award Loyola U., 1970. Mem. ABA, Ill. Bar Assn., Chgo. Bar Assn., Am. Corp. Counsel Assn., Chgo. Zool. Soc., Loyola Alumni Assn., Art Inst. Chgo., Phi Alpha Delta, Alpha Signa Nu. Roman Catholic. Home and Office: 5002 Sunset Ct Palatine IL 60067-9047 E-mail: tdroti@mediaone.net

ROUBANES, BARBARA ANN, lawyer; b. Bedford Heights, Ohio, Mar. 9, 1969; d. Harold Dwayne and Kathleen Slater Cabot; m. Matthew Gust Roubanes, Feb. 28, 1998. BA, Otterbein Coll., 1991; postgrad., Oxford (Eng.) U., 1993; JD, Capital U., 1997. Bar: Ohio 1997, U.S. Dist. Ct. (no. and so. dists.) Ohio 1998. Music tchr. Encore Music Studios, Westerville and Dublin, Ohio, 1988-93; pvt. music tchr. Worthington, 1993—98; clk. Ray, Alton & Kirstein Co., LPA, Columbus, 1996-97; assoc. Ray & Alton, LLP, 1997—. Accompanist Sells Mid. Sch. Recipient W. E. Richardson award for outstanding svc. Big Bros./Big Sisters of Columbus and Franklin County, 1996, Five Yr. Vol. Svc. award Big Bros./Big Sisters, 1998. Mem.: ABA, Columbus Bar Assn. (barrister leader program 1998, mentor law sch. liaison com. 1998), Ohio State Bar Assn., Ohio Acad. Trial Lawyers, Franklin County Trial Lawyers Assn., Women Lawyers Franklin County (bd. dirs. 2000—02). Republican. Avocations: flying, music, scuba diving, skiing, training Golden Retrievers. General civil litigation, Personal injury, Product liability. Office: Frank A-Ray Co LPA 175 S 3d St Ste 350 Columbus OH 43215

ROUSE, ROBERT KELLY, JR. judge; b. Lexington, Ky. s. Robert Kelly and Luane (Adams) R.; m. Donna R. Walker, Dec. 21, 1969; children: Kelly B., Erin E. Smith. AA, Daytona Beach (Fla.) C.C., 1966; BS, Fla. State U., 1968; JD, U. Fla., 1974. Bar: Fla. 1975. Ptnr. Regency Talent, Daytona Beach, 1968-69; supr. food divsn. Walt Disney Co., Anaheim, Calif., 1969-70; mgr. restaurants Walt Disney World Co., Orlando, Fla., 1970-71; from assoc. to ptnr. Smalbein, Eubank, Johnson, Rosier & Bussey, P.A., Daytona Beach, 1974-81; ptnr. Smith, Schoder, Rouse & Bouck, P.A., 1981-95; circuit judge State of Fla., 1995—; chief judge Seventh Jud. Cir., 1999—. With USAR, 1969-75. Mem. Am. Bd. Trial Advs., Volusia County Bar Assn. (pres. 1989-90), Volusia Civil Trial Attys. Assn. (pres. 1993-95). Office: Volusia County Courthouse Annex 125 E Orange Ave Ste 307 Daytona Beach FL 32114-4420

ROUSH, CHARLES DOW, lawyer; b. Phoenix, Nov. 18, 1937; s. Dow Ben and Mary Elizabeth (Spalding) R.; m. Carol Ann Carrigan, Aug. 18, 1962 (div. Aug. 1984); m. Cecilia Helen Roush, Dec. 18, 1984; children: Charles Dow Jr., Aileen Marie. LLB, U. Ariz., 1966. Bar: Ariz. 1966, U.S. Ct. Appeals (9th cir.) 1970, U.S. Ct. Appeals (8th cir.) 1980, U.S. Supreme Ct. 1982. Assoc. Lewis & Roca, Phoenix, 1966-70; ptnr. Steiner & Roush, 1970-71; judge Maricopa County Superior Ct., 1971-76; ptnr. Treon, Warnicke & Roush, 1976-86, Roush, McCracken, Guerrero & Miller, Phoenix, 1987—. Instr. Nat. Coll. of State Judiciary, Reno, Nev., 1975-80. Editor Ariz. Law Rev., 1965-66. Lt. col. USAF, 1957-62; with Ariz. Air N.G., 1964-78. Fellow Am. Coll. Trial Lawyers, Internat. Soc. Barristers; mem. ATLA. Avocations: raising, breeding, training, selling, and showing horses and ponies. Office: Roush McCracken Guerrero & Miller 650 N 3rd Ave Phoenix AZ 85003-1523

ROUSH, GEORGE EDGAR, lawyer; b. Tuolumne, Calif., Feb. 29, 1916; s. George Edgar and Ethyl Ruth (Gaskill) R.; m. Sarah Catherine Kragness, Mar. 29, 1944; children— Jane Margaret Roush Melicker, George Edgar III. B.S., U. Calif.-Berkeley, 1940; J.D., N.Y. Law Sch., 1951; life certs. Calif. Community Coll., Sacramento, 1979. Bar: N.Y. 1953, U.S. Ct. Customs and Patent Appeals, 1954, U.S. Supreme Ct. 1970, U.S. Ct. Appeals (fed. cir.) 1982. Patent agt. Philips Labs. Inc., Irvington-on-Hudson, N.Y., 1946-48; patent atty. RCA Labs., Princeton, N.J., 1948-56; div. atty. CBS-Hytran, Danvers, Mass., 1956-57; patent atty. Marchant Calculators, Oakland, Calif., 1957-60, IBM, San Jose, Calif., 1960-82; instr. West Valley Community Coll., Saratoga, Calif., part-time 1979— . Inventor automatic phasing for synchronous radio telegraph systems. Served to lt. col. Signal Corps, U.S. Army, 1940-46. Fellow Internat. Acad. Law and Sci.; mem. IEEE (sr. life mem.), Soc. Wireless Pioneers (life Pioneer mem.), Patent Office Soc. (assoc.), Patent Trademark and Copyright Law Assn. San Francisco. Republican. Episcopalian. Lodge: Kiwanis (pres. Cambrian Park, San Jose 1967). Home: 14660 Big Basin Way Apt B Saratoga CA 95070-6046

ROUSS, RUTH, lawyer; b. Des Moines, May 21, 1914; d. Simon Jacob and Dora (Goldin) R.; m. Dennis O'Rourke, Jan. 21, 1940; children: Susan Jerene, Kathleen Frances, Brian Jay, Dennis Robert, Ruth Elizabeth, Dolores Ann. B.A., Drake U., 1934, J.D., 1937. Bar: Iowa bar 1937, U.S. Supreme Ct. bar 1945, Colo. bar 1946, D.C. bar 1971. Legal counsel to Jay N. Darling, Des Moines, 1937-38; atty. Office of Solicitor, Dept. Agr., 1938-45, asst. to solicitor, 1940-45; practice law Colorado Springs, Colo., 1946—; mem. firm Williams & Rouss, 1946-50, individual practice law, 1950-69; of counsel firm Sutton, Shull & O'Rourke, Colorado Springs and Washington, 1969-72; mem. firm Rouss & O'Rourke, 1972-99, Colorado Springs, 2000—. Dir., sec.-treas. ManExec., Inc. Mem. cast chorus, Colo. Opera Festival, 1976, 78; mem., Colorado Springs Chorale, 1976— . Bd. dirs. Human Relations Commn. City Colorado Springs, 1968-73, chmn., 1971-72; bd. dirs., sec. Colorado Springs Community Planning and Research Council, 1972-78; bd. dirs. Logos, Inc., Colorado Springs, 1972-78, sec., 1976-77, v.p., 1977-78; bd. dirs. Colorado Springs Opera Festival, Colorado Springs World Affairs Council, Urban League of Pikes Peak Region; mem. com. protection human rights Penrose Hosp., adv. council Am. Lung Assn. of Colo., Pikes Peak region; dir., pres., Joseph Henry Edmondson Found.; adv. bd. Care Castle Divsn. Pikes Peak Seniors,El Paso County, Colo. Mem. El Paso County (Colo.) Bar Assn., Colo. Bar Assn., D.C. Bar Assn., Am. Law Inst. (life), Internat. Fedn. Women Lawyers, Women's Forum Colo., Phi Beta Kappa. Estate planning, General practice, Probate. Home: 8 Heather Dr Colorado Springs CO 80906-3114 Office: Box 572 231 E Vermijo Ave Colorado Springs CO 80903-2113

ROUT, ROBERT HOWARD, lawyer; b. Bklyn., Apr. 14, 1927; s. David S. and Shirley (Rosenthal) R.; m. Valerie Marrow, Jan. 27, 1958; children: Robert Howard Jr., W. Christopher, Romanie Marrow. Grad., N.Y. State Maritime Acad., 1947; BA, U. Wis., 1949; JD, Harvard U., 1952. Bar: N.Y. 1953, U.S. Ct. Mil. Appeals 1953, P.R. 1958, U.S. Dist. Ct. P.R. 1958, Conn. 1976, U.S. Ct. Appeals (1st cir.) 1983, U.S. Supreme Ct. 1983. Pvt. practice, N.Y.C., 1955-58, San Juan, P.R., 1958-75; ptnr. Aller & Rout, Lakeville, Conn., 1975—. Chmn. Zoning Bd. Appeals, Salisbury, Conn., 1984-93. Lt. USNR, 1953-55. Mem. Assn. Bar City of N.Y., Colegio de Abogados de P.R., Conn. Bar Assn., Harvard Club (N.Y.). General practice, Probate, Real property. Home: 160 Wells Hill Rd Lakeville CT 06039-2200 Office: Aller & Rout 3 Farnam Rd PO Box 406 Lakeville CT 06039-0406 Office Fax: 860-435-0394. E-mail: therouts@webtv.net

ROUTH, JOHN WILLIAM, lawyer; b. Knoxville, Tenn., Dec. 3, 1957; s. John C. and Mary (Parker) R.; m. Martha Carol Carter, Aug. 6, 1983; children: John Carter, Carol Ann. BA, U. Tenn., 1979, JD, 1983. Bar: Tenn. 1983, U.S. Dist. Ct. (ea. dist.) Tenn. 1983. Assoc. Francis W. Headman, Knoxville, 1983-87, Wm. R. Banks and Assocs., Knoxville, 1987-97; judicial commr. Knox County Gen. Sessions Ct., 1992-94; sole practice law, 1997—. Bd. dirs. Cerebral Palsy Ctr. for Handicapped Adults, Knoxville, 1985-88; chmn. adminstv. bd. Emerald Ave. United Meth. Ch., Knoxville, 1988-90, 98—. Mem. Tenn. Bar Assn., Knoxville Bar Assn., Tenn. Assn. Criminal Def. Lawyers, City Salesman Club (v.p. 1988, sec. 1987, pres. 1998). Methodist. Criminal, General practice, Personal injury. Office: 4611 Old Broadway St Knoxville TN 37918-1784

ROVEN, JOHN DAVID, lawyer; b. N.Y.C., Mar. 16, 1954; s. Philip MOrris and Joyce R.; m. Oct. 25, 1986 (div. July, 1992); children: Melanie, Julia. BA, Coker Coll., 1974; JD, U. S.C., 1981. Bar: S.C. 1981, U.S. Dist. Ct. S.C. 1981, Tex. 1986, U.S. Dist. Ct. (so. dist.) Tex. 1986, Nebr. 1988, U.S. Dist. Ct. (ea. dist.) Tex. 1994. Investigator, law clk. S.C. Atty Gen. Office, Columbia, 1977-81; law clk. U.S. Dist. Ct. S.C., Greenville, 1982-83; assoc. Ness, Motley, Loadholt, Richardson & Poole, PA, Charleston, S.C., 1984-85; ptnr. Jones & Granger, Houston, 1986-95; prin., founder Roven & Assocs., PC, 1995—. Appointed liason counsel FELA Plaintiffs' Com., Asbestos Multi-Dist. Litigation U.S. Dist. Ct. (ea. dist.) Pa. Bd. dirs. Chrysalis Repertory Dance Co., Houston, 1991-94, mem. adv. bd. 1994-98. Recipient Alumnus of Yr. award Coker Coll., Hartsville, S.C., 1984; designated Approved Counsel, Brotherhood Maintenance of Way Employees, Washington, 1989. Fellow ATLA (railroad litigation sect. 1992-94), Acad. Rail Labor Attys. (chmn. occupational disease divsn. 1990-93, Advocate of Yr. 1992). Democrat. Avocations: horse breeding, tng., long distance running. Labor, Product liability, Toxic tort. Office: John Roven & Assocs PC 9575 Katy Fwy Ste 400 Houston TX 77024-1411

ROVINE, ARTHUR WILLIAM, lawyer; b. Phila., Apr. 29, 1937; s. George Isaac and Rosanna (Lipsitz) R.; m. Phyllis Ellen Hamburger, Apr. 7, 1963; children: Joshua, Deborah. AB, U. Pa., 1958; LLB, Harvard U., 1961; PhD, Columbia U., 1966. Bar: D.C. 1964, N.Y. 1984. Assoc. Curtis, Mallet-Prevost, Colt & Mosle, N.Y.C., 1964-66; asst. prof. Cornell U., Ithaca, N.Y., 1966-72; editor Digest of U.S. Practice in International Law U.S. Dept. State, Washington, 1972-75, asst. legal adviser, 1975-81, agt of U.S. Govt. to Iran-U.S. Claims Tribunal The Hague, Netherlands, 1981-83; of counsel Baker & McKenzie, N.Y.C., 1983-85, ptnr., then sr. ptnr., 1985—. Adj. prof. law Georgetown U., Washington, 1977-81; vis. lectr. law Yale U., 1998. Author: The First Fifty Years: The Secretary-General in World Politics, 1920-1970, 1970; editor: Digest of U.S. Practice in International Law, 1973, 74; co-editor: The Case Law of the International Court of Justice, 1968, 1972, 1974, 1976; bd. editors Am. Jour. Internat. Law, 1977-87; also articles on internat. law. Mem. panel on settlement of transnat. bus. disputes, N.Y. panel Ctr. for Pub. Resources; chmn. law subcom. of internat. adv. coun. on profl. edn. Coun. on Internat. Ednl. Exch.; mem. Coun. on Fgn. Rels. Mem. ABA (chmn. internat. law sect. 1985-86, del. to Ho. of Dels. 1988-90), Am. Soc. Internat. Law (cert. of merit 1974, exec. coun. 1975-77, v.p. 1998-99, pres. 2000—), U.S. Coun. for Internat. Bus. (arbitration com.), Am. Arbitration Assn. (panel of arbitrators), Assn. Bar City N.Y. (coun. on internat. affairs). Alternative dispute resolution, Federal civil litigation, Private international. Home: 300 E 56 St New York NY 10022 Office: Baker & McKenzie 805 3rd Ave New York NY 10022-7513 E-mail: arthur.w.rovine@bakernet.com

ROVIRA, LUIS DARIO, state supreme court justice; b. San Juan, P.R., Sept. 8, 1923; s. Peter S. and Mae (Morris) R.; m. Lois Ann Thau, June 25, 1966; children— Douglas, Merilyn. B.A., U. Colo., 1948, LL.B., 1950. Bar: Colo. 1950. Justice Colo. Supreme Ct., Denver, 1979-95, chief justice, 1990-95, ret., 1995. Mem. Pres.'s Com. on Mental Retardation, 1970-71; chmn. State Health Facilities Council, 1967-76; arbiter and mediator Jud. Arbiter Group, Denver. Bd. dirs Children's Hosp.; trustee Temple Buell Found., Denver Found., Harry S. Truman Scholarship Found. With AUS, 1943-46. Mem. ABA, Colo. Bar Assn., Denver Bar Assn. (pres. 1970-71), Colo. Assn. Retarded Children (pres. 1968-70), Alpha Tau Omega, Phi Alpha Delta. Clubs: Athletic (Denver), Country (Denver). Home: 4810 E 6th Ave Denver CO 80220-5137 Office: Judicial Arbiter Group 1601 Blake St Denver CO 80202

ROVNER, DAVID PATRICK RYAN, lawyer; b. Phila., Aug. 6, 1952; s. Edward Isadore and Cecilia C. (Ryan) R. AB, St. Josephs U., 1974; JD, Villanova U., 1977. Bar: Pa. 1977, U.S. Ct. Claims 1978, U.S. Dist. Ct. (ea. dist.) Pa. 1977, U.S. Ct. Appeals (3d cir.) 1978, U.S. Supreme Ct. 1982. Assoc. Krusen, Evans & Byrne, Phila., 1977-80; ptnr. German, Gallagher & Murtagh, 1980-99; pvt. practice Narberth, Pa., 1999—. Editor: Pennsylvania Insurance Law, 1980. Chmn. Lower Merion-Narberth Dem. Com., Ardmore, Pa., 1979; solicitor, past pres. The Neighborhood Club of Bala-Cynwyd, Pa., 1978—. Mem. ABA, Pa. Bar Assn., Phila. Bar Assn., Phila. Trial Lawyers Assn., Phila. Lawyers Club, Founders Club. Democrat. Roman Catholic. Federal civil litigation, State civil litigation, Workers' compensation. Home: 407 Grove Pl Narberth PA 19072-2322 Office: German Gallagher & Murtagh Ste 250 230 Windsor Ave Finpac Bldg Narberth PA 19072-2217 E-mail: drovner@att.net

ROVNER, ILANA KARA DIAMOND, federal judge; b. Riga, Latvia, Aug. 21, 1938; came to U.S., 1939; d. Stanley and Ronny (Medalje) Diamond; m. Richard Nyles Rovner, Mar. 9, 1963; 1 child, Maxwell Rabson. AB, Bryn Mawr Coll., 1960; postgrad., U. London King's Coll., 1961, Georgetown U., 1961-63; JD, Ill. Inst. Tech., 1966; LittD (hon.), Rosary Coll., 1989, Mundelein Coll., 1989; DHL (hon.), Spertus Coll. of Judaica, 1992. Bar: Ill. 1972, U.S. Dist. Ct. (no. dist.) Ill. 1972, U.S. Ct. Appeals (7th cir.) 1977, U.S. Supreme Ct. 1981, Fed. Trial Bar (no. dist.) Ill. 1982. Jud. clk. U.S. Dist. Ct. (no. dist.) Ill., Chgo., 1972-73; asst. U.S. atty. U.S. Atty.'s Office, 1973-77; dep. chief of pub. protection, 1975-76; chief pub. protection, 1976-77; dep. gov., legal counsel Gov. James R. Thompson, Chgo., 1977-84; dist. judge U.S. Dist. Ct. (no. dist.) Ill., 1984-92; cir. judge U.S. Ct. Appeals (7th cir.), 1992—. Mem. Gannon-Proctor Commn. on the Status of Women in Ill., 1982-84; trustee Bryn Mawr Coll., Pa., 1983-89; mem. bd. overseers Ill. Inst. Tech./Kent Coll. Law, 1983—; trustee Ill. Inst. Tech., 1989—; mem. adv. coun. Rush Ctr. for Sports Medicine, Chgo., 1991-96; bd. dirs. Rehab. Inst. Chgo., 1998—; civil justice reform act adv. com. for the 7th cir., Chgo., 1991-95; bd. vis. No. Ill. U. Coll. Law, 1992-94; vis. com. Northwestern U. Sch. Law, 1993-98, U. Chgo. Law Sch., 1993-96, 2000—, 7th cir. race and gender fairness com., 1993—, U.S. Ct. Appeals (7th cir.) fairness com., 1996—, 7th cir. gender study task force, 1995-96, jud. conf. U.S. Com. Ct. Adminstrn. Case Mgmt., 2000—; chair Ill. state selection com., Rhodes Scholarship Trust, 1998, 99. Recipient Spl. Commendation award U.S. Dept. Justice, 1975, Spl. Achievement award 1976, Ann. Nat. Law and Social Justice Leadership award League to Improve the Cmty., 1975, Ann. Guardian Police award, 1977, Profl. Achievement award Ill. Inst. Tech., 1986, Louis Dembitz Brandeis medal for Disting. Legal Svc. Brandeis U., 1993, 1st Woman award, Valparaiso U. Sch. Law, 1993, ORT Women's Am. Cmty. Svc. award, 1987-88, svc. award Spertus Coll. of Judaica, 1987, Ann. award Chgo. Found. for Women, 1990, Arabella Babb Mansfield award Nat. Assn. Women Lawyers, 1998, award Chgo. Attys. Coun. of Hadassah, 1999, 1st Woman award Georgetown U. Law Ctr., 2001; named Today's Chgo. Woman of Yr., 1985, Woman of Achievement Chgo. Women's Club, 1986, others; Hebrew Immigrant Aid Soc. Chgo. 85th Anniversary honoree, 1996; named one of 15 Chgo. Women of the Century, Chgo. Sun-Times, 1999. Mem. Fed. Bar Assn. (pres. Chgo. chpt. 1977-80, treas. Chgo. chpt. 1978-79, sec. Chgo. chpt. 1979-80, 2d v.p. Chgo. chpt. 1980-81, 1st v.p. Chgo. chpt. 1981-82, pres. Chgo. chpt. 1982-83, 2d v.p. 7th cir. 1983-84, v.p. 7th cir. 1984-85), Fed. Judges Assn., Nat. Assn. Women Judges, Women's Bar Assn. Ill. (ann. award 1989, 1st Myra Bradwell Woman of Achievement award 1994), Chgo. Bar Assn. (commendation def. of prisoners com. 1987), Chgo. Coun. Lawyers, Decalogue Soc. of Lawyers (citation of honor 1991, Merit award 1997), Kappa Beta Pi, Phi Alpha Delta (hon.). Republican. Jewish. Office: 219 S Dearborn St Ste 2774 Chicago IL 60604-1803

ROVNER, JACK ALAN, lawyer; b. Boston, May 6, 1946; s. Abraham George and Sarah Rebecca (Miller) R.; m. Sheila Marie Boyle, June 24, 1979; children— Joseph Conahan, Edward Witty, Benjamin Flanagan. B.A., Brandeis U., 1968; J.D. cum laude, Boston U., 1976. Bar: Ill. 1976, U.S. Dist. Ct. (no. dist.) Ill. 1976, U.S. Ct. Appeals (7th and 9th cir.) 1979, U.S. Supreme Ct. 1979. Admin. asst. U.S. EPA, Boston, 1971-73; assoc. Kirkland & Ellis, Chgo., 1976-81, ptnr. 1982-93; pvt. practice, Naperville, Ill., 1993-96; ptnr. Michael, Best & Friedrich, Chgo., 1996—. Served to lt. jr. grade USCG, 1968-71. Article editor Boston U. Law Rev., 1974-76. Mem. ABA (litigation sect., antitrust sect., health law sect.), Am. Health Lawyers Assn., Ill. State Bar Assn., Ill. Assn. Healthcare Attys. Antitrust, Federal civil litigation, Health. Office: 77 W Wacker Dr Ste 4300 Chicago IL 60601-1635

ROWAN, RONALD THOMAS, lawyer; b. Bozeman, Mont., Nov. 6, 1941; s. Lawrence Eugene and Florence M.; m. Katherine Terrell Sponenberg, Sept. 4, 1964; children: Heather, Nicholaus, Matthew. BA, Wichita U., 1964; JD, U. Denver, 1969. Bar: Colo. 1969, U.S. Dist. Ct. Colo. 1969. Asst. city atty. City of Colorado Springs, Colo., 1969-71; asst. dist. atty. 4th Jud. Dist., Colorado Springs, 1971-79; gen. counsel U.S. Olympic Com., Colorado Springs, 1979—, dir. legal affairs, 1986—. Past chmn. CSC, Colorado Springs, 1975—; past chmn. Criminal Justice Adv. Bd., 1983—; past chmn. El Paso Criminal Justice Adv. Com.; bd. dirs. Crimestoppers, 1982-87, past pres. 1985-87, Internat. Anti-counterfeiting Coalition; chmn. Community Corrections Bd., 1981, 86, 87. Mem. ABA, Colo. Bar Assn., El Paso County Trial Lawyers (pres. 1972), El Paso County Bar Assn., U. Denver Law Alumni (chmn.), Colo. Trial Lawyers Assn., Pikes Peak or Bust Rodeo Assn. (Ramrod 1989). Republican. Roman Catholic. General corporate, Entertainment, Sports. Home: 215 Ridge Rd Colorado Springs CO 80904-1460 Office: US Olympic Com One Olympic Plz Colorado Springs CO 80909

ROWDEN, MARCUS AUBREY, lawyer, former government official; b. Detroit, Mar. 13, 1928; s. Louis and Gertrude (Lifsitz) Rosenzweig; m. Justine Leslie Bessman, July 21, 1950; children: Gwen, Stephanie. B.A. in Econs, U. Mich., Ann Arbor, 1950, J.D. with distinction, 1953. Bar: Mich. 1953, D.C. 1978. Trial atty. Dept. Justice, 1953-58; legal advisor U.S. Mission to European Communities, 1959-62; solicitor, assoc. gen. counsel, gen. counsel AEC, 1965-74; commr., chmn. U.S. NRC, Washington, 1975-77; 2tnr. Fried, Frank, Harris, Shriver and Jacobson, 1977—. Served with AUS, 1946-47. Decorated officer Order Legion of Honor Republic of France; Recipient Disting. Service award AEC, 1972 Mem. Am., Fed., Mich., D.C. bar assns., Internat. Nuclear Law Assn., Order of Coif. Home: 7937 Deepwell Dr Bethesda MD 20817-1927 Office: Fried Frank Harris Shriver and Jacobson 1001 Pennsylvania Ave NW Washington DC 20004-2505

ROWE, DAVID WINFIELD, lawyer; b. Chgo., Nov. 7, 1954; s. Bernard John and Gertrude Katherine (Johnson) R.; m. Martha Lynn Plott, June 12, 1977; children: Daniel, Peter. BA, Davidson Coll., 1976; PhD in Psychology, U. Tenn., 1981; JD, U. Mich., 1987. Bar: Colo. 1987, U.S. Dist. Ct. Colo. 1987, U.S. Ct. Appeals (10th cir.) 1987, Nebr. 1989, U.S. Dist. Ct. Nebr. 1989. Vis. asst. prof. Davidson (N.C.) Coll., 1981-82; mental health worker Peninsula Psychiat. Hosp., Louisville, 1982-84; asst. prof. dept. psychology U. Tenn., Knoxville, 1982-84; assoc. Gorsuch, Kirgis, Campbell, Walker & Grover, Denver, 1987-89; NIMH postdoctoral fellow in law and psychology U. Nebr., Lincoln, 1989-91; ptnr. Kinsey, Ridenour, Becker & Kistler, Nebr., 1991—. Mem. interim study group on foster care Health and Human Svcs. com. Nebr. State Legislature, 1990-91; adj. prof. psychology U. Nebr., Lincoln, 1992-94; bd. dirs., past treas. Lincoln Attention Ctr. for Youth; mem. The Mediation Ctr. Author: (with others) Dimensions of Child Advocacy: Advocating for the Child in Protection Proceedings, 1990, Children Under Three in Foster Care, 1991. Exec. com. Lancaster County Rep. Com., 1991-97, chmn., 1993-95; bd. dirs. Lincoln-Lancaster Mental Health Found., 1993—, v.p., 1995-96, pres., 1996-97; mem. Ctrl. Com. Nebr. Rep. Com., 1993-97; deacon Westminster Prebyn. Ch., 1996-99. Mem. ABA, Nebr. Bar Assn. (alternative dispute resolution com. 1990—), Kiwanis (pres. Lincoln 1997-98). Bankruptcy, General civil litigation, Family and matrimonial. Office: Kinsey Ridenour Becker & Kistler 206 S 13th St Lincoln NE 68508-2040 E-mail: drowe@krbklaw.com

ROWE, G. STEVEN, state attorney general, former state legislator; BS, U.S. Mil. Acad.; MBA, U. Utah; JD, U. Maine. Mem. Dist. 30 Maine Ho. of Reps. , 1993-95; mem. Dist. 35 Maine Ho. of Reps., 1995—2001; atty. gen. State of Maine, 2001—. Office: 6 State House Station Augusta ME 04333*

ROWLAND, JOHN ARTHUR, lawyer; b. Joliet, Ill., Mar. 6, 1943; s. John Fornof and Grace Ada (Baskerville) R.; children: Sean B., Keira L. BA, U. Notre Dame, 1965; JD, U. San Francisco, 1968. Bar: Calif. 1969, U.S. Dist. Ct. (no. dist.) Calif. 1982, U.S. Dist. Ct. (ctrl. dist.) Calif. 1998. Asst. dist. atty. San Francisco Dist. Atty.'s Office, 1971-81; assoc. Ropers, Majeski, Kohn and Bentley, San Francisco, 1982—, ptnr., 1985—. Pres., South of Market Boys, San Francisco, 1981. Served to capt. U.S. Army, 1969-71, Korea. Recipient Commendation San Francisco Bd. Suprs., 1981, Merit award Mayor of San Francisco, 1982. Mem. Am. Bd. Trial Advocates. Roman Catholic. General civil litigation, Personal injury. Office: Ropers Majeski Kohn and Bentley 333 Market St Ste 3150 San Francisco CA 94105

ROWLAND, ROBERT ALEXANDER, III, lawyer; b. McAllen, Tex., Apr. 27, 1943; s. Robert Alexander Jr and Margueriete (Gerry) Rowland; m. Victoria Nalle, Apr. 02, 1977; children: Julia Marie, Emily Nalle. BS, Tex. A&M U., 1966; JD, George Washington U., 1972. Bar: Tex 1972, US Dist Ct (so dist) Tex 1973, US Ct Appeals (5th cir) 1973, US Supreme Ct 1976, US Dist Ct (no dist) Tex 1979, US Dist Ct (we dist) Tex 1982, US Dist Ct (ea dist) Tex 1983. Law clk. U.S. Ct. Appeals (5th cir.), Houston, 1973-74; assoc. Vinson & Elkins, 1975-81; ptnr. susman, Godfrey & McGowan, 1982-88; mng. dir. Johnson and Gibbs, 1988-91; ptnr. Hutcheson & Grundy, LLP, 1992-94; chmn., CEO Associated Counsel of Am., 1995—. Bd dirs Vol Ctr, Houston, 1975—84, pres, 1982—83; founding mem, bd dirs Tex Accts and Lawyers for Arts, 1979—92, pres, 1989—91; mem deveop coun Sch Liberal Arts Tex A&M Univ, 1992—; co-chair Mayor's Transition Comt Pakrs City of Houston, 1992—94; bd dirs Contemporary Art Mus Houston, 1974—80, 1991—94, Sarah Campbell Blaffer Gallery of Art Univ Houston, 1989—94, Tex Opera Theater, 1988—89, Houston Parks Bd, 1993—, Nat Recreation and Park Asn, 1992—95, Cult Arts Coun Houston, 1981—86, Park People Inc, 1979—. Capt U.S. Army, 1966—69, Vietnam. Fellow: Houston Bar Found, Tex Bar Found; mem.: Houston Bar Asn (dir 1979—88, secy 1984—85, 2d vpres 1985—86, chmn law and art comt 1984—85), State Bar Tex, Houston Young Lawyers Asn (bd dirs 1975—79, pres 1978—79), River Oaks Country Club, Coronado Club, Phi Delta Phi. Episcopalian. Federal civil litigation, State civil litigation. Home: 2010 Chilton Rd Houston TX 77019-1502 Office: Associated Counsel Am Inc Ste 125 4605 Post Oak Pl Houston TX 77027-9744 E-mail: wickr@swbell.net, rob@associatedcounsel.com

ROWLAND, RONALD LEE, lawyer; b. Columbus, Ohio, Nov. 15, 1947; s. Charles Lossie and Beatrice Gertrude (Lachell) R.; m. Barbara Ann Baird, Mar. 21, 1970; children: Tracy Michelle, Andrew Tyler, Jennifer Kay. B.A., Wittenberg U., 1969; J.D., Ohio State U., 1972; LL.M. in Taxation, U. Fla., 1976. Bar: Ohio 1972, Fla. 1973. Atty., ptnr. Vorys, Sater, Seymour & Pease, Columbus, 1976—; adj. prof. Capital U. Law Sch., Columbus, 1981, 82, 87-90, Grad. Tax Program, 1985-86; chmn. tax com. Ohio Oil and Gas Assn., 1985-95; mem. exec. com. Ohio Small Bus. and Entrepreneurship Coun., 1991-95; chmn. Columbus Investment Interest Group, 1993-95; trustee, sec. Indsl. and Tech. Coun., 1993—. Contbr. papers to confs. Past pres. devel. bd. Children's Hosp., Columbus, 1983-84; trustee Worthington Hills Civic Assn., Ohio, 1983-85. Lt. JAGC, USN, 1972-75. Mem. ABA (partnership taxation com. tax sect.), Fla. Bar, Ohio State Bar Assn., Columbus Bar Assn. (chmn. tax com. 1981-83, chmn. Columbus tax conf. 1983-84), Ind. Petroleum Assn. Am. (tax com.), Worthington Hills Country Club, Athletic Club of Columbus. Roman Catholic. Corporate taxation, Estate taxation, Personal income taxation. Home: 821 Old Woods Rd Columbus OH 43235-1248 Office: Vorys Sater Seymour & Pease PO Box 1008 52 E Gay St Columbus OH 43215-3161

ROWLEY, GLENN HARRY, lawyer; b. Hyannis, Mass., May 16, 1948; s. Harold Frederick and Olive Nellie (Jones) R.; 1 child, Brewster Westgate. BBA, U. Mass., 1970; JD with cum laude, Western New Eng. Coll., 1980. Bar: Mass. 1980, U.S. Dist. Ct. Mass. 1981, U.S. Tax Ct. 1981; cert. elder law atty. Nat. Elder Law Found./ABA. Staff mem. Cape Cod Planning and Econ. Devel. Commn., Barnstable, Mass., 1975-76; staff, estate planning tax dept. Coopers and Lybrand, Springfield, 1980-81; legal assoc. Roberts and Farrell, West Chatham, 1982-84; ptnr. Roberts, Farrell & Rowley, 1984-97; pvt. practice Chatham, Mass., 1997—. Cons. Local Citizen Scholarship Trusts, Harwich and Chatham, Mass., 1985—. Contbr.: (weekly news column) The Cape Codder, The Enterprise, others.; contbr. articles to profl. jours. Founding mem. Brewster (Mass.) Conservation Trust, 1984; elected mem. Brewster Hist. Dist. Com., 1975; adv. bd. The May Inst., The Cape Cod Writers Ctr., Inc. With USN, 1971-74, Iceland. Recipient Am. Jurisprudence awards Lawyers Co-op. Pub. Co., 1978, 79. Mem. Mass. Bar Assn., Ocean Edge Exec. Club, Profl. Writers of Cape Cod, Cape Cod Estate Planning Coun., Nat. Acad. Elder Law Attys., Phi Delta Phi. Avocations: travel, writing. Estate planning, Probate, Estate taxation. Home: Annaniases Knoll/Sheep Pond Brewster MA 02631 Office: The Marketplace PO Box 1489 26 George Ryder Rd S West Chatham MA 02669

ROY, JAMES PARKERSON, lawyer; b. Lafayette, La., Aug. 27, 1951; s. Joseph A. Roy II and Jewell (Parkerson) Lowe; m. Linda Ann Malin, Aug. 1975 (div. 1986); chidlren: John, James Jr., Christopher; m. Virginia R. Roy, 1990. BS, La. State U., 1973, JD, 1976; LLM, Georgetown U., 1977. Bar: La. 1976. Civil trial atty. Domengeaux, Wright, Roy & Edwards, Lafayette, 1976—. Mem. ABA, Assn. Trial Lawyers Am., La. Trial Lawyers Assn. (pres. 1990-91), La. Bar Assn. Democrat. Episcopal. Avocations: hunting, boating, reading, travel. Admiralty, General civil litigation, Personal injury. Office: Domengeaux Wright Roy & Edwards 556 Jefferson St Ste 500 Lafayette LA 70501-6979

ROYAL, CARL ANDREW, lawyer; b. Chgo., Aug. 1, 1949; s. Richard J. and Barbara (Schneider) R.; m. Judith Orahood, Aug. 19, 1972; children: Jennifer, Andrew. BA, Wabash Coll., 1971; JD, Yale U., 1974. Bar: Ill. 1974, U.S. Dist. Ct. (no. dist.) Ill. 1974, U.S. Ct. Appeals (7th cir.) 1981. Assoc. Schiff Hardin & Waite, Chgo., 1974-80, ptnr., 1981-86; gen. counsel Chgo. Merc. Exchange, 1986—. Mem. ABA, Chgo. Bar Assn. (vice chmn. com. on futures regulation law 1988-89, chmn. 1989-90), Futures Industry Assn. (exec. com. law and compliance div.), Chgo. Coun. of Lawyers, CME Club, Phi Beta Kappa. Commodities.

ROZZELL, SCOTT ELLIS, lawyer; b. Texarkana, Tex., Apr. 12, 1949; s. George M. and Dora Mae (Boyett) R.; divorced; children by previous marriage: Stacey Elizabeth, Kimberly Marie. BA, So. Meth. U., 1971; JD, U. Tex., 1975. Bar: Tex. 1975, U.S. Dist. Ct. (so. dist.) Tex. 1975, U.S. Dist. Ct. (no. dist.) Tex. 1977, U.S. Ct. Appeals (1st, 3d, 9th cirs.) 1977, U.S. Ct. Appeals (5th and D.C. cirs.) 1976. Assoc. BakerBotts, LLP, Houston, 1975-82, ptnr., 1983-94, sr. ptnr., 1995-2000; exec. v.p., gen. counsel Center Point Energy, Inc., 2001—. Mem. State of Tex. Aircraft Pooling Bd., 1997—; devel. bd. U. of Tex. Health Sci. Ctr. Houston, 1992—; chair Tex. Commn. for Lawyer Discipline, 2001—. Bd. dirs. Manned Space Flight Edn. Found., Inc., 1997—, Tex. Aviation Hall of Fame, 2001—; vice-chmn. Cancer Counseling Inc., Houston, 1991-92. Fellow Tex. Bar Found. (sustaining life), Houston Bar Found. (sustaining life, bd. dirs. 1991-93, chair 1993), Am. Bar Found.; mem. ABA, State Bar Tex. (bd. dirs. 1997-2000), Houston Bar Assn. (bd. dirs. 1991-95, pres. 1996-97), Fed. Energy Bar Assn., Houston Young Lawyers Assn. (bd. dirs. 1978-82, pres. 1983-84), Plaza Club (bd. dirs. 1995-2001), Coronado Club. Republican. Presbyterian. Avocation: flying vintage airplanes. Administrative and regulatory, Public utilities. Home: 1229 Post Oak Park Houston TX 77027 Office: Reliant Energy Inc PO Box 4567 Houston TX 77210-4567 E-mail: scott-rozzell@relianteneregy.com

RUBENSTEIN, ALLEN IRA, lawyer; b. N.Y.C., Apr. 1, 1942; s. Nathan and Ida (Yankowitz) R.; m. Carole Toby Ballin, Aug. 24, 1963; children: Daniel Stuart, Samuel Philip. BS in Physics, CCNY, 1962; PhD in Physics, MIT, 1967; JD, Boston U., 1974. Bar: N.Y., U.S. Dist. Ct. (so. and ea. dists.) N.Y. 1975, U.S. Ct. Appeals (2d cir.) 1975, U.S. Ct. Appeals (1st and fed. cirs.) 1982. Physicist Stanford (Calif.) U., 1967-69; fellow Weizmann Inst., Rehovoth, Israel, 1969-71; assoc. Kenyon & Kenyon, N.Y.C., 1974-82; ptnr. Gottlieb, Rackman & Reisman, P.C., 1982—. Trustee Beth Israel Anshei Emet, Bklyn. 1981—. Recipient Ward medal CCNY, 1962. Mem. ABA, Am. Phys. Soc., Phi Beta Kappa. Federal civil litigation, Patent, Trademark and copyright. Home: 59 Livingston St Brooklyn NY 11201-4834 E-mail: arubenstein@grr.com, AllenR@alum.mit.edu

RUBENSTEIN, RICHARD EDWARD, law educator; b. N.Y.C., Feb. 24, 1938; s. Harold Simon and Josephine (Feldman) R.; m. Elizabeth Marsh, Aug. 26, 1962 (div. Mar. 1975); children— Alec Louis, Matthew Robert; m. Brenda Libman, Sept. 21, 1975; children: Nicole Hana, Shana Elise. B.A. magna cum laude, Harvard U., 1959; J.D., 1963; M.A., Oxford U. (Eng.), 1961. Bar: D.C. 1964. Assoc. Steptoe & Johnson, Washington, 1963-67; asst. dir. Adlai Stevenson Inst. Internat. Affairs, Chgo., 1967-70; prof. polit. sci. Roosevelt U., Chgo., 1970-79; prof. law Antioch Sch. Law, Washington, 1979— ; adv. cons. Nat. Commn. on Causes and Prevention Violence, Washington, 1968-69; lectr. Ctr. for Legal Studies, Washington, 1980— . Author: Rebels in Eden, 1970, Left Turn, 1973, Alchemists of Revolution, 1987; Editor: Mass Violence in America series, 1968, Great Courtroom Battles, 1974. Coordinator Chgo. Peace Action Coalition, 1970-72. Rhodes scholar Oxford U., 1959-61; Fulbright prof., Aix-en-Provence, France, 1976. Mem. Am. Assn. Polit. Sci., Am. Assn. Rhodes Scholars, Soc. Am. Law Tchrs., Conf. on Critical Legal Studies. Jewish. Home: 4618 Gramlee Cir Fairfax VA 22032-2005

RUBIN, ALLAN AVROM, lawyer, regulatory agency consultant; b. Chgo., Feb. 2, 1916; s. Sol and Sadie (Bloom) R.; m. Harriet Ann Schainis, June 24, 1941; children: Sally Ann Rubin Kovacs, Donald Bruce. AB, U. Mich., 1937, JD, 1939. Bar: Ill. 1939, U.S. Dist. Ct. (no. dist.) Ill. 1939, U.S. Dist. Ct. D.C., U.S. Supreme Ct., Order of Coif. Atty. Randolph Bohrer Law Firm, Chgo., 1939-41; atty., counsel FCC, Washington, 1941-43; chief counsel OPA, 1943-46, regional counsel Chgo., 1946-50; pvt. practice, 1950-52; gen. counsel, exec. v.p. U.S. Brewers Assn., Washington, 1952-82; govt. counsel G. Heileman Brewing Co., 1982-89; pres. Allan A. Rubin, P.C., 1982—. Cons., WOC (Pro Bono), Fed. Emergency Mgmt. Agy., Washington, 1968—; mem. Nat. Def. Exec. Res., Washington, 1968—; dir. legal adv. com. Am. Nat. Metric Coun., 1975-82, chmn., 1979-81. Editor Mich. Law Rev., 1938-39. Mem. ABA, FBA, Ill. Bar Assn., Army and Navy Club, Internat. Club, Order of Coif, Nat. Lawyers Club, Officers Clubs of Mil. Dist. of Washington. Home and Office: 9111 Kittery Ln Bethesda MD 20817-2138 Fax: (301) 365-0334. E-mail: arubin9111@aol.com

RUBIN, BURTON JAY, lawyer, editor; b. Bklyn., Jan. 23, 1946; s. Samuel and Sidell (Greenfield) R.; m. Janice Ann Edelstein, Geb. 17, 1974; 1 child, Jennifer Sidell. AB in Biology, Guilford Coll., Greensboro, N.C., 1966; JD, U. N.C., 1969. Bar: Va. 1971, U.S. Dist. Ct. (ea. dist.) Va. 1997, U.S. Ct. Customs and Patent Appeals 1975. Legal editor labor rels. reporter Bur. Nat. Affairs, Inc., Washington, 1970; asst. editor U.S. Law Week, 1970-74; asst. mng. editor Patent, Trademark and Copyright Jour., 1974-75; mng. editor U.S. Patents Quar., 1975-85; atty. Am. Soc. Travel Agts., 1985-87, gen. counsel, 1987—; pvt. practice, 1990—. Cons. Roundhouse Sq. Psychiat. Ctr., Alexandria, Va. Contbr. articles to profl. jours. Active Fairfax County Water Authority, Va., Fairfax County Police-Citizens Adv. Coun., 1982-83, alt. mem., 1984-85; active Fairfax County Rep. Com., 1982-85, West Springfield Police-Citizens Adv. Com., 1979-85, chmn., 1981; bd. dirs. Bur. Nat. Affairs, 1984-85. Mem. ABA, Am. Soc. Assn. Execs. (legal coun. 1996-2000, vice-chmn. 1997-98, chmn. 1998-99). Office: Am Soc Travel Agts 1101 King St Alexandria VA 22314-2944

RUBIN, HERBERT, lawyer; b. Lisbon, Conn., June 4, 1918; s. Simon and Rose (Berko) R.; m. Rose Luttan, July 6, 1941; children: Barbara, Caroline, Donald. AB, CCNY, 1938; JD, NYU, 1942. Bar: N.Y. 1942, U.S. Dist. Ct. (so. and ea. dists.) N.Y. 1951, U.S. Supreme Ct. 1956, U.S. Ct. Appeals (2d, 3d, 4th, 6th, 9th, 10th, D.C. cirs.). Assoc. Newman & Bisco, 1942; faculty NYU Law Sch., 1946-50, 57-62; prof. creditors' rights Rutgers U. Law Sch., 1949-57; pvt. practice, 1946-56; ptnr. Sereni, Herzfeld & Rubin, and successor Herzfeld & Rubin, N.Y.C., 1956—, sr. ptnr., 1968—. Instr. mil. law, 1944-46; prof. constl. law L.I. U., 1963-68; trustee North Shore L.I. Jewish Hosp. Editor-in-chief NYU Law Rev., 1940-41; bd. editors N.Y. Law Jour., 1971—; contbr. articles to profl. jours. Mem. N.Y. State Banking Bd., 1975-85, N.Y. State Jud. Selection Com., 1975-83, Sen. Moynihan's Jud. Selection Com., 1982—, Sen. Schumer's Jud. Selection Com., 1999—, City Charter Revision Commn., 1998—. 1st lt. Signal Corps, AUS, 1942-46. Recipient award NCCJ, 1967, United Jewish Appeal, 1968, 97, Israel Bonds, 1973, NYU Law Assn. award 1987, Judge Weinfeld award, 1992. Fellow Am. Bar Found.; mem. ABA (mem. coun. N.Y. state), N.Y. State Bar Assn., Queens County Bar Assn. (pres. 1970), Assn. Bar City Of N.Y., Fed. Bar Coun., Jewish Lawyers Guild (award 2001). Jewish. General civil litigation, General corporate, Private international. Office: Herzfeld & Rubin 40 Wall St Fl 54 New York NY 10005-2301

RUBIN, MICHAEL, lawyer; b. Boston, July 19, 1952; m. Andrea L. Peterson, May 29, 1983; children: Peter, Eric, Emily. AB, Brandeis U., 1973; JD, Georgetown U., 1977. Bar: Calif. 1978, U.S. Dist. Ct. (no. dist.) Calif. 1978, U.S. Ct. Appeals (9th cir.) 1978, U.S. Ct. Appeals (5th, 7th, 10th cirs.) 1982, U.S. Supreme Ct. 1984, U.S. Ct. Appeals (D.C. cir.) 1984, U.S. Ct. Appeals (11th cir.) 1987. Teaching fellow Law Sch. Stanford (Calif.) U., 1977-78; law clerk to Hon. Charles B. Renfrew U.S. Dist. Ct. (no. dist.) Calif., San Francisco, 1978-79; law clerk to Hon. James R. Browning U.S. Ct. Appeals (9th cir.), 1979-80; law clerk to Hon. William J. Brennan, Jr. U.S. Supreme Ct., Washington, 1980-81; assoc. Altshuler & Berzon, San Francisco, 1981-85, ptnr., 1985-89, Altshuler, Berzon, Nussbaum, Berzon & Rubin, San Francisco, 1989-2000, Altshuler, Berzon, Nussbaum, Rubin & Demain, San Francisco, 2000—. Civil rights, Federal civil litigation, Labor. Office: Altshuler Berzon Nussbaum Rubin & Demain 177 Post St Ste 300 San Francisco CA 94108-4700 E-mail: mrubin@altshulerberzon.com

RUBIN, MICHAEL HARRY, lawyer, educator; b. Baton Rouge, Jan. 13, 1950; s. Alvin B. and Janice (Ginsberg) R.; m. Ayan J. Liss, June 11, 1972; children: Bethany, Gillian. BA cum laude, Amherst Coll., 1972; JD, La. State U., 1975. Bar: La. 1975, U.S. Ct. Appeals (5th cir.) 1975, U.S. Dist. Ct. (mid., ea. and we. dists.) La. 1976, U.S. Supreme Ct. 1982. Ptnr. Sanders, Downing, Kean & Cazedessus, Baton Rouge, 1983-93, McGlinchey Stafford, Baton Rouge, 1993—. Adj. prof. La. State U. Law

Sch., 1976—. Author: Louisiana Security Devices, Cases, 1981—; contbr. articles to law jours. Mem. Baton Rouge Bar Assn. (pres. 1986-87), La. State Bar Assn. (pres. 2001—), La. Bankers Assn. (past pres.), Baton Rouge Property Lawyers Group (pres. 1982-83), Am. Law Inst., Am. Coll. Real Estate Lawyers. Appellate, Federal civil litigation, Real property. Office: McGlinchey Stafford Lang One American Pl 9th Fl Baton Rouge LA 70825

RUBIN, STEPHEN WAYNE, lawyer; b. N.Y.C., Mar. 29, 1951; s. Oscar R. and Irene J. (Widelok) R.; m. Eileen Grossman, Sept. 23, 1978; children: Ashley G., Camner G. BS, Cornell U., 1973; JD, Columbia U., 1976. Bar: N.Y. 1977, U.S. Dist. Ct. (so. dist.) N.Y. 1977. Assoc. Gordon, Hurwitz & Butowsky, N.Y.C., 1976-79, Feit & Ahrens, N.Y.C., 1979-84, ptnr., 1984-88, Proskauer Rose LLP, N.Y.C., 1989—. Lectr. grad. sch. bus., NYU, 1985-92. Co-contbr. law articles to profl. jours. Nat. pres., sec. Friends of Israel Def. Forces, N.Y.C., 1985-98, mem. nat. bd. dirs., 1985—; vol. firefighter Scarsdale (N.Y.) Fire Dept., 1996—. Mem. ABA, N.Y. State Bar Assn., Assn. of Bar of City of N.Y. General corporate, Securities, Mergers and acquisitions. Office: Proskauer Rose Goetz Mendelsohn 1585 Broadway Fl 27 New York NY 10036-8299

RUBINE, ROBERT SAMUEL, lawyer; b. Rockaway, N.Y., Feb. 28, 1947; s. George and Beatrice (Simon) R.; m. Marilyn Goldberg Rubine, Aug. 15, 1970; children: Seth B., Marisa H. BA, Queens Coll., 1968; JD, Syracuse U., 1971. Bar: N.Y. 1972, Fla. 1975; U.S. Dist. Ct. (ea. and so. dists.) N.Y., 1976; U.S. Supreme Ct. 1976. Trial atty. Legal Aid Soc. Nassau County, Mineola, N.Y., 1971-77; atty. Reifman and Rubine, Jericho, 1977-79; ptnr. Stein, Rubine and Stein, Mineola, 1979-94, Rubine and Rubine, Mineola, 1995—. Adj. prof. C.W. Post Coll., Greenvale, N.Y., 1979-82. Author: (chpt.) Criminal and Civil Investigation Handbook, 1981. Dir. Legal Aid Soc. Nassau County, 1989—, pres., 1994-95, treas., 1996—. Mem. N.Y. State Bar Assn., N.Y. State Assn. Criminal Def. Lawyers, N.Y. State Defenders Assn., Nassau County Bar Assn. Avocation: golf. Criminal, Family and matrimonial, Personal injury. Home: 5 Woodland Rd Oyster Bay NY 11771-3910 Office: Rubine and Rubine PLLC 114 Old Country Rd Mineola NY 11501-4400

RUBINKOWSKI, CONRAD SIGMUND, lawyer, film critic; b. Chgo., July 15, 1951; s. Sigmund Felix and Lee (Zak) R.; m. Kathryn I. Friedli, July 3, 1982; 1 child, Leo Joseph. B.S., Ill. Inst. Tech., 1973; J.D., U. Ill., 1976. Bar: Ill. 1976, U.S. Dist. Ct. (no. dist.) Ill. 1976, U.S. Dist. Ct. (ea. dist.) 1978. Asst. states atty. States Atty.'s Office, Danville, Ill. 1977-80; atty. Joint Com. on Adminstrv. Rules, Springfield, Ill., 1981-83; atty. Ill. Commerce Commn., Springfield, 1983— . Mem. Chili Appreciation Soc. Internat., Amnesty Internat., Phi Delta Phi. Roman Catholic. Lodges: Raccoons (Racoon of Yr. 1988), Mystic Knights of Sea (Exalted Piscator 1986).

RUBINO, VICTOR JOSEPH, academic administrator, lawyer; b. N.Y.C., Dec. 25, 1940; s. Joseph V. and Olympia (Gayda) R.; 1 child, Victor Gayda. BA in Govt., Cornell U., 1962, LLB, 1965. Bar: N.Y. 1965, U.S. Dist. Ct. (so. dist.) N.Y. 1969. Staff atty. Westchester Legal Svcs., White Plains, N.Y., 1968-71; assoc. Squadron Ellenoff Plesent & Lehrer, N.Y.C., 1971; treas., program officer Council on Legal Edn., 1971-79; assoc. dir. Practising Law Inst., 1979-83, exec. dir., 1983—. Democratic candidate for N.Y. State Assembly, 1970; chmn. Rye (N.Y.) Human Rights Commn., 1975-76. Served to capt. U.S. Army, 1966-68. Mem. ABA, Assn. Bar City N.Y. Office: Practising Law Inst 810 7th Ave Fl 26 New York NY 10019-5818

RUBINSTEIN, ESTA, paralegal; b. Jacksonville, Fla., 18 Oct. m. Alan J. Rubinstein. BS in Advt., U. Fla., 1965. Cert. legal asst. Legal asst. R&B, Ft. Myers, Fla., 1979-89; office mgr. R&H, 1989-2000, Goldburg, Rubinstein & Buckley, 1984-86. Dir., cmty. adv. bd. Riverside Bank, N. Ft. Myers; foster care adviser Lee County Ct. System; mem. Smart Growth Task Force for Lee County. Chair N. Ft. Myers LRPC, 1997-99; sec. Women's Polit. Caucus, Ft. Myers, 1996. Avocations: reading, travel.

RUBINSTEIN, FREDERIC ARMAND, lawyer; b. Antwerp, Belgium, Apr. 20, 1931; came to U.S., 1942; s. Samuel N. and Steffa (Warrenreich) R.; m. Susan August, Dec. 24, 1968; 1 child, Nicolas Eric August Rubinstein. BA, Cornell U., 1953, JD, 1955. Bar: N.Y. 1955. Assoc. Law Offices of I. Robert Feinberg, N.Y.C., 1955-60, Guggenheimer & Untermyer, N.Y.C., 1960-65, ptnr., 1965-85, Kelley Drye & Warren LLP, N.Y.C., 1985—. Vice chmn. zoning & planning com. Local Community Bd. # 6, N.Y.C., 1980-86. Mem. ABA (bus. law sect., emerging growth ventures subcom., chmn. 1988-96), Cornell Club of N.Y. General corporate, Mergers and acquisitions, Securities. Office: Kelley Drye & Warren LLP 101 Park Ave New York NY 10178-0002

RUBINSTEIN, KENNETH, lawyer; b. Munich, Germany, Jan. 13, 1947; came to U.S., 1949; s. Jacob and Golda (Turk) R.; m. Shoshana Becker, June 30, 1968; children: Asher, Sharon, Elizabeth Joy. BBA with honors, CCNY, 1968; JD, NYU, 1979. Bar: N.Y. 1980, U.S. Dist. Ct. (so. and ea. dists.) N.Y. 1980, U.S. Supreme Ct. 1996, U.S. Ct. Appeals (2d cir.) 1997, U.S. Tax Ct. 1997. Assoc. Fried, Frank, Harris, Schriver & Jacobson, N.Y.C., 1979-82; pres. Edgemont Devel. Corp., Scarsdale, N.Y., 1983-89; pres., gen. counsel Daniel Equities Corp., White Plains, 1989-91; sr. ptnr. Rubinstein & Rubinstein, LLP, N.Y.C., 1991—. Author: Asset Protection in the New Millenium, 2000, Offshore Asset Protection and the New IRS Traps, 1998, By-Passing the Capital Gains Tax with Charitable Trusts, 1991, Municipal Labor Relations in New York, 1968; contbr. articles to profl. jours. Mem. ABA (probate and tax sect.), N.Y. State Bar Assn. (estate tax sect.), Assn. Bar of City of N.Y. Jewish. Avocations: music, photography, travel. Estate planning, Estate taxation. Office: Rubinstein & Rubinstein LLP 18 E 48th St New York NY 10017 E-mail: krubinstein@assetlawyer.com

RUBRIGHT, JAMES ALFRED, paper and packaging company executive, lawyer; b. Phila., Dec. 17, 1946; s. James Alfred and Helen Lucille (Evans) R. (deceased); m. Mary Elizabeth Angelich, Dec. 30, 1987; children: Noah Michael, Benjamin James, Jami Anne, Nathaniel Drew, James McCurdy, William Angelich. BA, Yale U., 1969; JD, U. Va., 1972. Bar: Ga. 1972. Ptnr. King & Spalding, Atlanta, 1972-94; sr. v.p., gen. counsel Sonat Inc., Birmingham, 1994-97; pres. So. Natural Gas Co. subs. Sonat Inc., 1997-98; exec. v.p. Sonat Inc., 1998-99; CEO Rock-Tenn Co., Norcross, Ga., 1999—. Office: Rock-Tenn Co 504 Thrasher St Norcross GA 30071-1914

RUCKER, DOUGLAS PENDLETON, JR. lawyer; b. Richmond, Va., Dec. 26, 1945; s. Douglas Pendleton and Margaret (Williams) R.; m. Marian F. Copeland; 1 child, Louise Meredith. BA, Hampden-Sydney Coll., 1968; JD, U. Va., 1972. Bar: Va. 1972, D.C. 1986, U.S. Dist. Ct. (ea. and we. dists.) Va. 1972, U.S. Ct. Appeals (4th cir.) 1982, U.S. Supreme Ct. 1982, U.S. Ct. Claims 1995. Assoc. Sands, Anderson, Marks & Miller, Richmond, Va., 1972-76, mem., 1977—, also bd. dirs. Active Lewis Ginter Bot. Garden; mem. adv. com. Richmond Renaissance; active St. John's Episcopal Ch., mem. vestry, 1994—98, register, 1996, jr. warden, 1997, sr. warden, 1998, trustee, 1994—; bd. dirs. Va. Ctr. for the Book Capital chpt. ARC; bd. dirs., vice chmn. James River Devel. Corp. Fellow: ABA, SAR, Am. Bar Found., Va. Law Found. (bd. dirs. 1998—), Va. Bar Assn. (constrn. law chmn. 1992, real estate and bus. law sects., exec. com. 1992—97, pres. 1996), Richmond Bar Assn. (real estate sect., bd. dirs. 1994—97), Soc. Colonial Wars in the State of Va. (dep. gov. gen.), Bar Assn. D.C., Met. Richmond C. of C., Commonwealth Club, Country Club Va., The Twenty-Three Hundred Club. Real property, General civil litigation, Professional liability. Office: Sands Anderson Marks & Miller PO Box 1998 Richmond VA 23218-1998 E-mail: DRucker@sandsanderson.com

RUCKER, ROBERT D. judge; b. Canton, Ga. married; 3 children. BA, Ind. U.; JD, Valparaiso Sch. of Law; LLM, U. Va. Dep. prosecuting atty., Lake County, Ind.; city atty. City of Gary; pvt. practice East Chicago; justice Ind. State Supreme Ct., Indpls., 1999—. Former vice chmn. Ind. Commn. for Continuing Legal Edn. Bd. dirs. Legal Svcs. of N.W. Ind. Decorated Vietnam Vet. Office: State House Rm 312 200 W Washington St Indianapolis IN 46204-2798*

RUDDY, FRANK, former ambassador; b. N.Y.C., Sept. 15, 1937; s. Francis Stephen and Teresa (O'Neil) R.; children: Neil, David, Stephen AB, Holy Cross Coll., 1959; MA, NYU, 1962, LLM, 1967; LLB, Loyola U., New Orleans, 1965; PhD, Cambridge U., Eng., 1969. Bar: D.C., N.Y., Tex., U.S. Supreme Ct. Faculty Cambridge U., 1967-69; asst. gen. counsel USIA, Washington, 1969-72; sr. atty. Office of Telecomm. Policy, White House, 1972-73; dep. gen. counsel USIA, 1973-74; counsel Exxon Corp., Houston, 1974-81; asst. adminstr. AID (with rank asst. sec. state) Dept. State, Washington, 1981-84; U.S. ambassador to Equatorial Guinea, 1984-88; gen. counsel U.S. Dept. Energy, Washington, 1988-89; v.p. Sierra Blanca Devel. Corp., 1989-92; pvt. practice Law Offices of Frank Ruddy, 1992-94. Vis. scholar Johns Hopkins Sch. Advanced Internat. Studies, 1990-94; dep. chmn. UN Referendum for Western Sahara, 1994, Johnston, Rivlin & Foley, Washington, 1995-96, Rivlin & Taylor, et al, 1996-97; ptnr. Ruddy & Muir, Washington, 1998—. Author: International Law in the Enlightenment, 1975; editor: American International Law Cases (series); editor in chief Internat. Lawyer; contbr. articles to legal jours. Bd. dirs. African Devel. Found., Washington, 1983-84, Human Life Internat., 1999—; mem. Coun. of Am. Ambs., Washington, 1988—. Served with USMCR, 1956-61 Mem. ABA (chmn. treaty compliance sect. 1991-93), Am. Soc. Internat. Law, Internat. Law Assn., Hague Acad. Internat. Law Alumni Assn., Oxford and Cambridge Club (London), Dacor House. Republican. Roman Catholic. Nuclear power, Environmental, Private international. Home: 5600 Western Ave Chevy Chase MD 20815-3406 Office: Ruddy and Muir 1730 K Street NW Ste 304 Washington DC 20006 E-mail: global@globalltd.com

RUDEBUSCH, ALICE ANN, lawyer; b. Milw., July 9, 1966; d. Leroy George and Maryann Grace (Carlson) Rudebusch; m. Todd William Nejedlo, May 25, 1991 (div. 1999). BA, Northwestern U., 1988; JD, U. Wis., 1991; Certificat De Langue, Université De Paris, 1986. Bar: Wis. 1991, U.S. Dist. Ct. (we. dist.) Wis. 1991, U.S. Dist. Ct. (ea. dist.) Wis. 1995, U.S. Dist. Ct. (no. dist.) Ill. 1995. Assoc. Hanson Gasiorkiewicz & Weber, S.C., Racine, Wis., 1991-96; ptnr. Hanson & Gasiorkiewicz, S.C., 1997—. Bd. dirs. YWCA, Racine, 1995—2001, sec., 1996—98, pres., 1999—2001; vol. Legal Action of Wis., Kenosha, 1996—97. Mem. State Bar Wis., Wis. Acad. Trial Lawyers, Racine County Bar Assn. General civil litigation, Personal injury, Workers' compensation. Office: Hanson & Gasiorkiewicz SC 2932 Northwestern Ave Racine WI 53404-2249 E-mail: hglawofc@execpc.com

RUDER, DAVID STURTEVANT, lawyer, educator, government official; b. Wausau, Wis., May 25, 1929; s. George Louis and Josephine (Sturtevant) R.; m. Susan M. Small; children: Victoria Chesley, Julia Larson, David Sturtevant II, John Coulter; m stepchildren: Elizabeth Frankel, Rebecca Wilkinson. BA cum laude, Williams Coll., 1951; JD with honors, U. Wis., 1957. Bar: Wis. 1957, Ill. 1962. Of counsel Schiff Hardin & Waite, Chgo., 1971-76; assoc. Quarles & Brady, Milw., 1957-61; asst. prof. law Northwestern U., Chgo., 1961-63, assoc. prof., 1963-65, prof., 1965—, William W. Gurley meml. prof. of law, 1994—, assoc. dean Law Sch., 1965-66, dean Law Sch., 1977-85; chmn. Securities and Exch. Commn., Washington, 1987-89; ptnr. Baker & McKenzie, Chgo., 1990-94, sr. counsel, 1994-99. Cons. Am. Law Inst. Fed. Securities Code; planning dir. Corp. Counsel Inst., 1962-66, 76-77, com. mem., 1962-87, 90—; adv. bd. Ray Garrett Jr. Corp. and Securities Law Inst., 1980-87, 90—; vis. lectr. U. de Liege, 1967; vis. prof. law U. Pa., Phila., 1971; faculty Salzburg Seminar, 1976; mem. legal adv. com. bd. dirs. N.Y. Stock Exch., 1978-82; mem. com. profl. responsibility Ill. Supreme Ct., 1978-87; adv. bd. Securities Regulation Inst., 1978—, chmn., 1994-97; bd. govs. Nat. Assn. Securities Dealers, 1990-93, chmn. Legal Adv. Bd., 1993-96, Arbitration Policy Task Force, 1994-97; trustee Fin. Acctg. Found., 1996—, Internat. Acctg. Stds. Com., 2000—; mem. Internat. Acctg. Stds. Com. Strategy Working Party, 1997-99; chmn. Securities and Exch. Commn. Hist. Soc., 1999—; chmn. Mut. Fund Dirs. Edn. Coun., 1999—. Editor-in-chief: Williams Coll. Record, 1950-51, U. Wis. Law Rev, 1957; editor: Proc. Corp. Counsel Inst, 1962-66; contbr. articles to legal periodicals. 1st lt. AUS, 1951-54. Fellow Am. Bar Found.; mem., com. chmn. ABA (coun. sect. corp. banking and bus. law 1970-74), Chgo. Bar Assn., Wis. Bar Assn., Am. Law Inst., Order of Coif, Comml. Club of Chgo., Econ. Club of Chgo., Gargoyle Soc., Phi Beta Kappa, Phi Delta Pi, Zeta Psi. Home: 325 Orchard Ln Highland Park IL 60035-1939 E-mail: d-ruder@law.northwestern.edu

RUDER, LAWRENCE THEODORE, lawyer; b. Chgo., July 20, 1954; s. Melvin and Phyllis R.; m. Diane F. Freeman, May 17, 1981; children: Dana, Michael, Alexis. BA, U. Ill., 1976; JD, John Marshall Law Sch., 1980. Bar: Ill. 1980. Sr. and founding ptnr. Ruder and Assocs., Chgo., 1980—. Bd. govs. legal com., chmn. bylaws com. Highland Park (Ill.) Cmty. House, 1995—; trustee dist. 112 Edn. Found., Highland Park, 1997—. Ruder scholarship: Hispanic Lawyers Scholarship Fund, 1998. Mem. Assn. Trial Lawyers Am. (mem. product liability sect. 1980—), Ill. Trial Lawyers Assn. (mem. product liability com. 1980—), Ill. State Bar Assn., Chgo. Bar Assn. Office: Ruder and Assocs 221 N Lasalle St Ste 707 Chicago IL 60601-1301 Fax: 312-332-2750. E-mail: ltr@ruderlaw.com

RUDLIN, DAVID ALAN, lawyer; b. Richmond, Va., Nov. 4, 1947; s. Herbert and Dorothy Jean (Durham) R.; m. Judith Bond Faulkner, Oct. 4, 1975; 1 child, Sara Elizabeth. BA with high distinction, U. Va., 1969, JD with honors, 1973. Bar: Va. 1973, U.S. Dist. Ct. (ea. dist.) Va. 1975, U.S. Ct. Appeals (4th cir.) 1975, U.S. Ct. Appeals (10th cir.) 1980, U.S. Ct. Appeals (2d cir.) 1983, U.S. Supreme Ct. 1979. Assoc. gen. counsel U.S. Commn. on Orgn. of Govt. for Conduct Fgn. Policy, Washington, 1973-75; assoc. Hunton & Williams, Richmond, 1975-82, ptnr., 1982—. Adj. faculty civil litigation, appellate practice, libel litigation Duke Univ. Law Sch., Univ. Richmond, T.C. Williams Sch. of Law, Washington and Lee Sch. of Law, William and Mary Sch. of Law, U. Va. Sch. of Law; faculty mem. Boulder and S.E. Regional programs Nat. Inst. Trial Advocacy; faculty mem. Am. Law Inst. ABA. Author: (book chpts.) Toxic Torts: Litigation of Hazardous Substances Cases, 1983, 2d edit., 1992, Federal Litigation Guide, 1989, Corporate Counselor's Guide to Environmental Law, 1989, Sanctions: Rule 11 and Other Powers, 1992, Business and Commercial Litigation in Federal Courts, 1997, Corp. Counsel's Guide to ADR Techniques, 1999, Successful Partnering Between Inside and Outside COunsel, 1999; contbr. articles to profl. jours. and mags., chpts. to books; mem. bd. editl. advisors The Environ. Counselor, Chesterland, Ohio, 1989—, The Toxics Law Reporter, Washington, 1988—. Alumni Metro Leadership Richmond, 1988-89. Mem. ABA (chmn. litig. sect. environ. litig. com. 1985-88, co-chmn. litig. sect. liaison with jud. com. 1988-91, vice-chmn. toxic and hazardous substances and environ. law com. tort and ins. practice sect. 1988-91, co-liaison to standing com. on environ. law from environ. litig. com. litig. sect. 1988-92, dir. div. IV litig. sect. 1991-95, litig. sect. co-chair programs subcom. first amendment and media litig. com. 1993—, mem. litig. sect. task force on specialization 1994—, co-chair litigation sect., 1997, specialization 1994—, mem. litigation sect. task foce on justice sys. 1994—, litigation sect. liaison to ABA jud. administrn. divsn. task force on reducion of litigation cost and delay 1995—, co-chair litigation sect. 1997 ann. meeting Washington 1995-97, chair toxic torts and environ. litigation committee sect. of Environment, Energy and Resources 1997-2000; council mem. litigation sect. 1997-2000, co-chair report card on the litigation section, 2000), Am. Arbitration Assn. (Va. mediation panel 1996—), Va. Bar Assn. (chair joint com. on alt. dispute resolution with Va. State Bar 1991-97, exec. com. mem.), Richmond Bar Assn. (chmn. mem. com. 1988-91, mem. judiciary com. 1991-94, mem. continuing legal edn. com. 1994-96), Va. Assn. Def. Attys., CPR Inst. Dispute Resolution (products liability com. 1988, 97—, judge Ann. Awards in Alt. Dispute Resolution 1990—, mem. panels disting. neutrals Va. 1997—), Va. Bar Assn. (mem. exec. com. 2001), Internat. Assn. Def. Counsel. General civil litigation, Environmental, Libel. Office: Hunton & Williams Riverfront Pla E Tower 951 E Byrd St Ste 200 Richmond VA 23219-4074 Fax: 804-788-8218. E-mail: arudlin@hunton.com

RUDLOFF, WILLIAM JOSEPH, lawyer; b. Bonne Terre, Mo., Feb. 19, 1941; s. Leslie W. and Alta M. (Hogenmiller) R.; m. Rita Howton, Aug. 5, 1965; children: Daniel, Andrea, Leslie, Susan. AB, Western Ky. U., 1961; JD, Vanderbilt U., 1965. Bar: Ky. 1965, Tenn. 1965, U.S. Supreme Ct. 1975, U.S. Ct. Appeals (sixth cir.) 1981. U.S. magistrate Western Dist. Ky., 1971-75. NDEA fellow U. Nebr., 1961-62, U. Ky. fellow. Fellow: Ky. Bar Found. (life; charter); mem.: Am. Bd. Trial Advocates, Am. Counsel Assn., Def. Rsch. Inst., Trial Attys. Am., Am. Coll. Legal Medicine, Ky. Acad. Trial Attys., Internat. Acad. Litigators (diplomate). Federal civil litigation, State civil litigation, Insurance. Home: 126 Broadway St Smiths Grove KY 42171-8258 Office: 553 E Main St Bowling Green KY 42101-2256

RUDMAN, PAUL LEWIS, state supreme court justice; b. Bangor, Maine, Mar. 26, 1935; s. Abraham Moses and Irene (Epstein) R.; m. Inez Lee Kolonel, Oct. 8, 1961; Andrew Isaac, Carole Sue. AB, Yale Coll., 1957; JD, George Washington U. Sch. Law, 1960. Bar: Maine 1960, D.C. 1960; U.S. Dist. Ct. Maine, 1961. Ptnr. Rudman & Winchell, Bangor, 1960-92; justice Maine Supreme Jud. Ct., 1992—. Capt. Maine Air NG, 1960-66. Office: Maine Supreme Jud Ct Penobscot County Courthouse 97 Hammond St Bangor ME 04401*

RUDNICK, ALAN A. management company executive, corporate lawyer; b. Cleve., 1947; BA, U. Chgo., 1969; JD, Case Western Res. U., 1973. Bar: Ohio 1973, Md. 1984, Va. 1988. With Chessie Systems, Inc., 1976-86, asst. treas., 1980-82, asst. v.p. taxation, 1982-84, asst. v.p., treas. taxation, 1984-85; gen. counsel CSX Corp., Richmond, Va., 1985-91, v.p., gen. counsel, corp. sec., 1991—. Adj. prof. Sch. Law, Coll. William and Mary. Mem. ABA, Ohio Bar Assn., Md. Bar Assn., Va. Bar Assn. Office: CSX Corp PO Box 85629 Richmond VA 23285-5629

RUDNICK, MARVIN JACK, lawyer; b. St. Joseph, Mich., Mar. 9, 1948; s. Milton P. and Edna O.R.; m. Cynthia Jane Vanhooser, Sept. 4, 1982; children: Matthew, Andrew. BA, Middlebury Coll., 1970; JD, Syracuse U., 1973. Bar: N.Y. 1973. Corp. atty. Oneida Ltd., N.Y., 1973-76, assoc. counsel, 1976-84, asst. gen. counsel, 1985-86, v.p., sec., gen. counsel, 1986—; mem. adj. faculty Utica Coll., Syracuse U., Utica, N.Y., 1982-84; bd. dirs. Oneida Silversmith's Div. Pres. Sherrill-Kenwood Community Chest, Sherrill, N.Y., 1979-81. With U.S. Army, lt. Res. Mem. ABA, N.Y. State Bar Assn., Madison County Bar Assn., Justinian Soc. Republican. General corporate, Environmental, Trademark and copyright. Office: Oneida Ltd Kenwood Station Adminstrn Bldg Oneida NY 13421

RUDNICK, REBECCA SOPHIE, lawyer, educator; b. Bakersfield, Calif., Nov. 26, 1952; d. Oscar and Sophie Mary (Loven) R.; m. Robert Anthoine, Dec. 2, 1990. BA, Willamette U., Salem, Oreg., 1974; JD, U. Tex., 1978; LLM, NYU, 1984. Bar: Tex. 1978, La. 1979, N.Y. 1980, Calif. 1980. Law clk. to Hon. Charles Schwartz, Jr. U.S. Dist. Ct., New Orleans, 1978-79; assoc. Winthrop, Stimson, Putnam & Roberts, N.Y.C., 1979-85; spl. counsel N.Y. Legis. Tax Study Commn., 1983-84; asst. prof. law Ind. U., Bloomington, 1985-90; assoc. prof. Ind. U. Sch. Law, 1990-94; assoc. prof. law London Law Consortium, Eng., 1994. Vis. assoc. prof. law U. Conn., Hartford, 1984-85; vis. asst. prof. law U. Tex., Austin, 1988; vis. assoc. prof. law U. N.C., Chapel Hill, 1991, Boston U., 1994-95, U. Pa., Phila., 1995-96; prof.-in-residence, IRS, 1991-92; vis. scholar NSW, Australia, 1994, U. Sydney, Australia, 1994; vis. prof. law Seattle U., 1996-97, Wayne State U., 1997, U. Ky., 1998, U. Houston, 1998, Tulane U., 1999, Northwestern Sch. Law, Lewis and Clark Coll., 1999-2000, Boston Coll., 2001, Vt. Law Sch., 2001—. Contbr. articles to profl. jours. Dir., gen. counsel Project GreenHope: Svcs. for Women, N.Y.C., 1980-83; advisor, tech. asst. Internat. Monetary Fund, Washington, 1994. Mem. ABA (tax sect. 1982—, sec. tax sect. passthrough entities task force 1986-88, subcom. chairs for incorps. and CLE/important devel. tax sect., 1989—, corp. tax com. 1989—, tax sect. task force on integration 1990—), Am. Assn. Law Schs. (editor tax sect. newsletter 1987-97), Assn. Bar of City of N.Y. (admiralty com. 1982-85), Internat. Fiscal Assn., Internat. Bar Assn. Office: Vermont Law Sch PO Box 96 Chelsea St S South Royalton VT 05068 E-mail: rrudnick@vermontlaw.edu

RUDOLPH, DANIEL A. lawyer; b. Ann Arbor, Mich., Sept. 7, 1971; BA with distinction, U. Mich., 1992; JD, Georgetown U., 1996. Bar: Md. 1996, D.C. 1998. Assoc. Garson & Assocs., Bethesda, Md. Mem. Md. State Bar Assn., Montgomery County Bar Assn. Real property, Business litigation, Employment litigatio. Office: Garson & Assocs Ste 600 6905 Rockledge Dr Bethesda MD 20814

RUDOLPH, JAMES LEONARD, lawyer; b. Beverly, Mass., Sept. 26, 1950; s. Robert P. and Joyce B. (Yoffa) R.; m. Susan B. Gouchberg, Oct. 31, 1981. B.A., U. Denver, 1972; J.D., Boston Coll., 1975. Bar: Mass. 1975, U.S. Dist. Ct. Mass. 1976, U.S. Ct. Appeals (1st cir.) 1978, U.S. Supreme Ct. 1984. Ptnr. Gargill, Sassoon & Rudolph, Boston, 1976—; bd. dirs. U.S. Trust, Woburn, Mass. Chmn. Swampscott Zoning Bd. Appeals (Mass.), 1984— , mem., 1983— ; v.p. Jewish Rehab. Ctr., Swampscott, 1984—; pres. Camp Kingswood, Bridgton, Maine, 1987— ; chmn. North Shore adv. group Anti-Defamation League. Mem. Boston Bar Assn., Mass. Bar Assn., ABA, Assn. Trial Lawyers Am., Mass. Conveyancers Assn. Jewish. Clubs: Belmont Country (Mass.); Boston Yacht (Marblehead, Mass.). Lodge: Mt. Scopus (Malden, Mass.). Contracts commercial, General corporate, Real property. Office: Gargill Sassoon & Rudolph 92 State St Boston MA 02109-2004

RUDY, ELMER CLYDE, lawyer; b. Elgin, Ill., Apr. 10, 1931; s. Elmer Carl and Bernice (Tobin) R.; m. Margaret L. Meyer, July 5, 1953; children: Lynne, Elizabeth, Paul, Charles, Leslie. BA, Beloit Coll., 1953; LLB, U. Mich., 1958. Bar: Ill. 1958, U.S. Dist. Ct. (no. dist.) Ill. 1959. Assoc. Williams, McCarthy & Kinley, Rockford, Ill., 1958-64; ptnr., mng. ptnr. Williams, McCarthy, Kinley, Rudy & Picha, 1964-81; pres. Williams & McCarthy, P.C., 1982-87, v.p., 1988-2000. Pres. Norill, Inc., Rockford, 1984-91; chmn. bd. Wesley Willows, Inc., 1992-95. Pres. Rockford Mus. Assn., 1983-86, bd. dirs., 1972—; bd. dirs. Coun. of 100, Inc., Rockford, 1985-92. Cpl. U.S. Army, 1953-55. Mem. ABA, Ill. Bar Assn. (chmn. state taxation sect. coun. 1987-88), Winnebago County Bar Assn. (pres. 1980-

81), Am. Judicature Soc., Rotary (dir. local club 1985-89). Republican. Roman Catholic. Avocations: sports, history reading. Administrative and regulatory, General corporate, State and local taxation. Home: 5024 Braewild Rd Rockford IL 61107-1610 Office: Williams & McCarthy PC PO Box 219 Rockford IL 61105-0219

RUEBHAUSEN, OSCAR MELICK, retired lawyer; b. N.Y.C., Aug. 28, 1912; s. Oscar and Eleonora J. (Melick) R.; m. Zelia Krumbhaar Peet, Oct. 31, 1942. AB summa cum laude, Dartmouth Coll., 1934; LLB cum laude, Yale U., 1937. Bar: N.Y. 1938, U.S. Supreme Ct. 1945. Assoc. Debevoise, Stevenson, Plimpton & Page, N.Y.C., 1937-42, Lend-Lease Adminstrn., Washington, 1942-44; gen. counsel Office Sci. Rsch. and Devel., 1944-46; ptnr. Debevoise and Plimpton, 1946-84, presiding ptnr., 1972-81, of counsel, 1984-87; counselor to ednl. instn., 1988-99; retired. Editor: Pension and Retirement Policies in Colleges and Universities, 1990; contbr. articles to profl. jours. Chmn. Commn. on Coll. Retirement, 1984-93; spl. adviser atomic energy to gov. N.Y. State, 1959; vice chmn. N.Y. State adv. com. on atomic energy, 1959-62; chmn. N.Y. State Gov.'s Task Force on protection from radioactive fallout, 1959; mem. Pres.'s Task Force on Sci. Policy, 1969-70, Pres.'s Sci. Adv. Com. Panel on Chems. and Health, 1970-72, Commn. on Critical Choices for Am., 1973-77, adv. com. Carnegie Commn. on Sci., Tech. and Govt., 1988-93; chmn. UN Day, N.Y. State, 1962, chmn. Spl. N.Y. Com. on Ins. Holding Cos., 1967-68; mem. U.S. govt. panel on Privacy and Behavioral Rsch., 1965-66; mem. presdl. panel Chronic Renal Disease, 1966-67; sec., dir. Fund Peaceful Atomic Devel., Inc., 1954-72; dir. Carrie Chapman Catt Meml. Fund, 1948-58; chmn. bd. Bennington Coll., 1957-61, 62-67; trustee Hudson Inst., Inc., 1961-71; trustee Russell Sage Found., chmn. bd., 1965-80; vice-chmn. N.Y.C. Univ. Constrn. Fund, 1966-69; mem. Coun. on Fgn. Rels., Nat. Com. on U.S.-China Rels.; mem. New Sch. Univ. Instl. Policy Com., 1991-2000; bd. dirs. Greenwall Found., 1956-95, chmn., 1982-91, chmn. emeritus, 1991—; bd. dirs. Scripps Clinic and Rsch. Found, 1983-89. Recipient U.S. Presdl. Cert. of Merit, 1948. Mem. ABA, N.Y. State Bar Assn., Yale Law Sch. Assn. (exec. com. and pres. 1960-62, chmn. 1962-64), Assn. of Bar of City of N.Y. (pres. 1980-82, pres. and bd. dirs. fund 1980-82), Order of Coif, Rancho Santa Fe Assn., Century Club (N.Y.C.), River Club (N.Y.C.), Phi Beta Kappa, Sigma Phi Epsilon, Sigma Xi (hon.). Clubs: Century (N.Y.C.), River (N.Y.C.); Rancho Santa Fe Assn. (Calif.). General practice. Home: 450 E 52nd St New York NY 10022-6448

RUEDA, PEDRO ANTONIO, lawyer; b. Madrid, July 25, 1962; JD, U. Complutense de Madrid, 1985; LLM, U. Pa., 1987. From assoc. to ptnr. Gomez-Acebo & Pombo, Madrid, 1987-94; fgn. assoc. Skadden Arps Slate Meagher & Flom, N.Y.C., 1989-90; ptnr. Araoz & Rueda, Madrid, 1994—. Fulbright scholar, 1986. Mem. Madrid Bar Assn. (scholar 1987). Mergers and acquisitions. Office: Araoz & Rueda Castellana 15 Madrid 28046 Spain E-mail: rueda@araraozyruedaabogados.es

RUEGGER, PHILIP T., III, lawyer; b. Plainfield, N.J., Oct. 14, 1949; s. Philip T. Jr. and Gloria Marie (McLaughlin) R.; m. Rebecca Lee Huffman, Aug. 3, 1974; children: Sarah, Britt, Michael. AB, Dartmouth Coll., 1971; JD, U. Va., 1974. Bar: N.Y. 1975. Assoc. Simpson Thacher & Bartlett, N.Y.C., 1974-81, ptnr., 1981—. Chmn. Rye Edn. Fund, Inc. Mem. Assn. Bar City N.Y., Phi Beta Kappa. Clubs: Manursing Island (Rye, N.Y.), Apawamis (Rye). General corporate, Mergers and acquisitions. Home: 275 Grace Church St Rye NY 10580-4201 Office: Simpson Thacher & Bartlett 425 Lexington Ave Fl 15 New York NY 10017-3954 E-mail: pruegger@stblaw.com

RUFE, CYNTHIA MARIE, judge; b. Phila., Oct. 30, 1948; d. Lucien Russell and Antoinette Marie (Galizia) Favata; m. John J. Rufe, Jan. 2, 1999; children: Tiffany Marie, Meredith Anne. BA, Adelphi U., 1970; secondary edn. cert., Bloomsburg State Coll., 1972; JD, SUNY, Buffalo, 1977. Bar: Pa. 1977, U.S. Dist. Ct. (ea. dist.) Pa. 1983, U.S. Ct. Appeals (3d cir.) 1987, U.S. Supreme Ct. 1984. Tchr. Bristol (Pa.) Jr./Sr. H.S., 1970-72; law clk. Div. of Claims, State of N.Y., Buffalo, 1976; asst. pub. defender Bucks County, Doylestown, Pa., 1977-79, dep. pub. defender, 1979-81; pvt. practice Newtown, 1982-93; judge Ct. of Common Pleas, Bucks County, 1994—. Mem. appellate ct. rules com. Supreme Ct. of Pa. Appellate Ct., 1999—; solicitor Children and Youth Agy., Bucks County, 1984-88; spkr., panelist on various law related issues, Bucks County; mem. Conf. State Trial Judges, 1994—, mem. jud. edn., correction and nominating com. juvenile ct. sect. Pres. bd. dirs. Preventive Rehab. Youth and Devel., Bristol, 1978-81; bd. dirs. Reaching-at-Problems Group Home, Chalfont, Pa., 1981-84, Three Arches, Inc., Falls Twp., Pa., 1985, Orgn. to Prevent Teenage Suicide, 1984-93, Youth Svcs., Inc., 1984-93, Today, Inc., 1987-93, Schofield Ford Bridge Reconstrn. Com., 1990-93. Recipient Trial Lawyer's award Erie County Bar Assn., 1977, Four Chaplains Legion of Honor, 1987, M.J. Kirkpatrick Leadership award A Woman's Place, 1999, award Commn. for Social Justice, Sons of Italy, 2000. Mem. Nat. Coun. Juvenile and Family Ct. Judges, Bucks County Bar Assn. (dir. 1983-85, chair criminal law sect. 1987-88, chair bench-bar com. 1988-89, chair membership com. 1983-85, lawyer reaching lawyer com. 1996—), Pa. Bar Assn., Pa. Trial Lawyers Assn., Pa. Coll. Criminal Def. Lawyers, Ill. Bar Assn., Soroptimists (past pres.). Republican. Roman Catholic. Office: Judges Chambers Courthouse Doylestown PA 18901

RUFFNER, CHARLES LOUIS, lawyer; b. Cin., Nov. 7, 1936; s. Joseph H. and Edith (Solomon) R.; m. Mary Ann Kaufman, Jan. 30, 1966 (div. 1993); children: Robin Sue, David Robert; m. Nanette Diemer, Feb. 26, 1995. BSBA in Acctg., U. Fla., 1958; JD cum laude, U. Miami, 1964. Bar: Fla. 1964, U.S. Dist. Ct. (so. and Mid. dists.) Fla. 1964, U.S. Ct. Appeals (5th cir.) 1964, U. S. Ct. Appeals (11th cir.) 1984, U.S. Claims Ct. 1966, U.S. Tax Ct. 1966, U.S. Supreme Ct. 1969; cert. in taxation. Trial atty. tax divsn. Dept. Justice, Washington, 1964-67; pres. Forrest, Ruffner, Traum & Hagen, P.A., Miami, Fla., 1967-78, Ruffner, Hagen & Rifkin, P.A., Miami, 1978-81; tax ptnr. Myers, Kenin, Levinson, Ruffner, Frank & Richards, 1982-84; pres. Charles L. Ruffner, P.A., 1984—. Lectr. Fla. Internat. U., Miami. Author: A Practical Approach to Professional Corporations and Associations, 4 edits., 1970, (column) Tax Talk, Miami Law Rev.; editor Miami Law Rev., 1963-64; contbr. numerous articles on taxation to law jours. Named One of Best Lawyers in Am., 1999-2001. Mem. ABA, Fed. Bar Assn., Fla. Bar (exec. coun. tax sect. 1967-92, 95—, amicus curiae in test case of validity profl. corps.), Dade County Bar Assn., South Fla. Tax Litigation Assn. (chmn. 1986-00), Phi Alpha Delta, Phi Kappa Phi. Corporate taxation, Personal income taxation, State and local taxation. Office: Courvoisier Centre II 601 Brickell Key Dr Ste 507 Miami FL 33131-2652 E-mail: cruff7117@aol.com

RUGGERI, ROBERT EDWARD, lawyer; b. N.Y.C., Sept. 16, 1952; s. Mario Philip and Margaret Gloria (Pascale) R.; m. Mary Beth Thackeray, June 6, 1981. BA, Union Coll., 1974; JD, Antioch U., 1980. Bar: D.C. 1981, N.Y. 1993, U.S. Dist. Ct. D.C. 1982, U.S. Ct. Internat. Trade 1982, U.S. Ct. Appeals (fed. and D.C. cirs.) 1982, U.S. Supreme Ct. 1984. Trainee Commn. European Communities, Brussels, Belgium, 1980-81; legal cons. Secretariat, OECD, Paris, France, 1981-82; assoc. Stewart & Stewart, Washington, 1982-83, Graham and James, Washington, 1984-85, Rogers & Wells, Washington, 1985-92; dep. dir. legal affairs N.Y. State Dept. Environ. Conservation, 1993-94; assoc. counsel SUNY System, Albany, 1994—. Arbitrator NAFTA panels apptd. by U.S., Can., and Mex. govts., 1992—; adj. prof. Georgetown U. Law Ctr., 1988-92. Editor comments Antioch Law Jour., 1979-80. Trustee Schenectady County C.C., 1999—. Fulbright scholar, 1980-81. Mem. ABA, D.C. Bar Assn., Washington Fgn. Law Soc. (sec., treas. 1985-87, bd. govs. 1987-88), Am. Soc. Internat. Law. Roman Catholic. Legislative. Home: 1846 Union St Niskayuna NY 12309-4502 Office: SUNY Office U Counsel Univ Plz Rm S315 Albany NY 12246-0001

RUHM, THOMAS FRANCIS, retired lawyer, investor; b. Bridgeport, Conn., June 8, 1935; s. Herman David and Martica (Sturges) R.; m. Michele Wood, Oct. 5, 1974; children: Wendy Sturges, Thomas Wood. BA, Yale U., 1957; JD, Havard U., 1962. Bar: N.Y. 1963, U.S. Dist. Ct. (so. and ea. dists.) N.Y. 1964, U.S. Ct. Appeals (2d cir.) 1969. Assoc. Shearman & Sterling, N.Y.C., 1962-70; asst. gen. counsel Bessemer Securities Corp., 1970-96, v.p., 1981-96; ret., 1996. Chmn. legal aspects venture capital investing Practicing Law Inst., N.Y. and San Francisco, 1979-81; lectr. on venture capital NYU Grad. Sch., 1986-90, Concordia Coll., Bronxville, N.Y., 1999-2000; expert on fed. securities law, venture capital legal matters, investment tax policy, Fed. Res. monetary policy; witness during 1980s fed. tax hearings; adj. prof. fin. St. John's U., 2000—. Contbg. author: Technology and Economic Policy, 1986; contbr. articles to profl. jours. Commr. upper divsn. Eastchester (N.Y.) Youth Soccer League, 1990-91, coach, 1985-91, dir. coaching 1995-96; sr. warden Christ Ch., Bronxville, N.Y., 1991-94; past v.p. and treas. Bronxville Sch. PTA; treas., bd. dirs. Friends of Bronxville Pub. Libr., 1997-2000; mem. Quogue (N.Y.) Cultural Com., 1998—; mem. Blue Hill Troupe, Ltd., 1972—. Lt. (j.g.) USNR, 1957-59. Mem. Univ. Club, Bronxville Field Club, Quogue Field Club, Quogue Beach Club. Republican. General corporate, Finance, Securities.

RUIZ, VANESSA, state supreme court justice; b. San Jaun, P.R., Mar. 22, 1950; D. Fernando and Irma (Bosch) Ruiz-Suria; m. Eduardo Elejalde, Feb. 11, 1972 (div. Jan. 1982); children: Natalia, Alexia; m. David E. Birenbaum, Oct. 22, 1983; stepchildren: Tracy, Matthew. BA, Wellesley Coll., 1972; JD, Georgetown U., 1975. Bar: D.C. 1972, U.S. Supreme Ct. 1981. Assoc. Fried, Frank, Harris, Shrives & Kampelman, Washington, 1975-83; sr. mgr., counsel Sears World Trade Inc., 1983-94; assoc. judge D.C. Ct. of Appeals, 1994—. Speaker in field. Mem. ABA, Inter-Am. Bar Assn. Office: DC Ct of Appeals 500 Indiana Ave NW Fl 6 Washington DC 20001-2131*

RUIZ-SURIA, FERNANDO, lawyer; b. San Juan, P.R., May 18, 1916; s. Abelardo and Teresa (Suria) R.; m. Irma Bosch, Aug. 18, 1946; children: Fernando, Vanessa, Ivan, Mimi. BA, U. P.R., 1938, LLB, 1940. Bar: P.R. 1941, U.S. Dist. Ct. P.R. 1941, U.S. Ct. Appeals (1st cir.) 1959, U.S. Supreme Ct. 1963, U.S. Ct. Appeals D.C. 1977, Temporary Emergency Ct. Appeals 1980. House counsel Shell Co. Ltd., San Juan, 1942-53; sr. ptnr. Sifre & Ruiz-Suria, San Juan, 1953-67, McConnell Valdes Kelley Sifre Griggs & Ruiz-Suria, San Juan, 1967-81; of counsel McConnell Valdes et al; dir. corps.; mem. jud. confs.; former mem. P.R. Bar Examiners; former mem. Evidence Rules Com. Fellow Am. Coll. Trial Lawyers; mem. Colegio de Abogados de P.R., Sara Bay C. of C., Meadows C. of C., Bird Key Yacht Club (Sarasota, Fla.), Bankers Club (San Juan, P.R.). Roman Catholic. Home: 888 Blvd Of The Arts Apt 1104 Sarasota FL 34236-4832

RULE, CHARLES FREDERICK (RICK RULE), lawyer; b. Nashville, Apr. 28, 1955; s. Frederick Charles and Mary Elizabeth (Malone) R.; m. Ellen Friedland, May 13, 1976 BA, Vanderbilt U., 1978; JD, U. Chgo., 1981. Bar: U.S. Ct. Appeals. (D.C. cir.) 1983. Law clk. U.S. Ct. Appeals (fed. cir.), Washington, 1981-82; spl. asst. to asst. atty. gen. Antitrust div. Dept. Justice, 1982-83, dep. asst. atty. gen. policy planning, 1984-85, acting asst. atty. gen., then dep. asst. atty. gen. regulatory affairs, 1985-86, asst. atty. gen., 1986-89; ptnr. Covington & Burling, 1989-2001, Fried, Frank, Harris, Shriver & Jacobson, Washington, 2001—. Legal, econ. analyst Lexecon, Inc., Chgo., 1979-80 Mem. Bar of D.C. Ct. Appeals, Phi Beta Kappa, Phi Eta Sigma. Republican. Presbyterian Office: Fried Frank Harris Shriver & Jacobson 1001 Pennsylvania Ave Nw Washington DC 20004-2505

RUMAN, SAUL I. lawyer; b. Chgo., May 12, 1925; s. James A. and Pauline (Scharfer) R.; m. Beverlee Mahan, June 17; children: Loral Ruman Conrad, Melissa Ruman Stewart, Elizabeth Ruman Plumlee. BS, Ind. U., 1949, JD with distinction, 1952. Bar: Ind. 1952, U.S. Supreme Ct. 1963, U.S. Dist. Ct. Ind. 1952, U.S. Ct. Appeals (7th cir.) 1962. Atty. pvt. practice, Hammond, Ind., 1952—; mng. ptnr. Ruman, Clements & Holub, P.C., 1990. Former lectr. bus. law Ind. U. N.W.; mem. faculty numerous insts. on law; mem. com. on rules of practice and procedure Supreme Ct. Ind., 1983-92, Ind. Jud. Nominating Commn., 1990; mem. Ind. Supreme Ct. character and fitness com., 1975—. Pres. Ind. U. Sch. Law Alumni Assn., 1972-73, bd. visitors, 1973; bd. advisors N.W. Campus Ind. U., 1973-85, class rep., 1983; faculty Nat. Inst. Trial Advocacy, 1984-86; trustee Ind. Legal Svcs. Fund, 1978, 84. With usn, 1942-45. Fellow Internat. Acad. Trial Lawyers (dir. 1980-86); mem. Ill. Trial Lawyers Assn., Ind. Bar Assn. (chmn. trial lawyers sect. 1970-71), Ind. Trial Lawyers Assn. (emeritus dir., pres. 1980-81, lifetime achievement award 1997), Coll. Fellows, Assn. Trial Lawyers Am., Am. Bd. Trial Advocates, Order of Coif. Federal civil litigation, State civil litigation, Personal injury. Office: 5261 Hohman Ave Hammond IN 46320-1721

RUMBAUGH, CHARLES EARL, arbitrator, mediator, educator, lawyer, speaker, judge; b. San Bernardino, Calif., Mar. 11, 1943; s. Max Elden and Gertrude Maude (Gulker) R.; m. Christina Carol Pinder, Mar. 2, 1968; children: Eckwood, Cynthia, Aaron, Heather. BS, UCLA, 1966; JD, Calif. Western Sch. Law, 1971; cert. in advanced mgmt., U. So. Calif., 1993. Bar: Calif. 1972, U.S. Dist. Ct. (cen. dist.) Calif. U.S. Ct. Appeals (9th cir.), U.S. Supreme Ct. Engr. Westinghouse Electric Corp., Balt., 1966-68; legal counsel Calif. Dept. of Corps., L.A., 1971-77, Hughes Aircraft Co., L.A., 1977-84, asst. to corp. dir. contracts, 1984-89, asst. to corp. v.p. contracts, 1989-95; corp. dir. contracts/pricing Lear Astronics Corp., 1995-97; pres. Ctr. for Conflict Resolution, 1998-99. Arbitrator, mediator, comml., govt. contracts, internat. law, franchise, securities, torts, personal injury, real estate and constrn. panels Am. Arbitration Assn., L.A., San Francisco; EEOC mediator; mem. arbitration and mediation panels ArbitrationWorks, 1994—, Nat. Assn. Security Dealers, Franchise Arbitration & Mediation, Inc., Constrn. ADR, L.A. County Superior Ct., Santa Barbara County Superior Ct.; mem. panel pvt. alt. dispute resolution neutrals U.S. Ct. Fed. Claims; armed svcs. bd. of contract appeals panel of pvt. alt. dispute resolution neutrals, DLA panel of dispute neutrals, also settlement officer U.S. Dist. Ct.; alternative dispute resolution panel World Bank; faculty Calif. State U.; spkr. in field. Mem. editl. bd. Nat. Contract Mgmt. Jour., 1996-00; contbr. articles to profl. jours. Counselor Boy Scouts Am., L.A., 1976—; mem. City of Palos Verdes Estates (Calif.) Citizen's Planning Com., 1986—90; judge pro tem L.A. County Superior Ct , L.A., 1991—2000. Fellow: Nat. Contract Mgmt. Assn. (founder, chmn. alt. dispute resolution com., cert. profl. contracts mgr., nat. bd. advisors, nat. v.p. southwestern region 1993—95, nat. dir. 1992—93, pres. L.A./South Bay chpt. 1991—92, Fellow of Yr. award 1994); mem.: ABA (founder fed. contracts dispute resolution com. dispute resolution sect, forum on franchising, forum on constrn. industry, pub. contract law sect., vice chair strategic alliance com.), FBA (pres. Beverly Hills chpt. 1992—93), Nat. Assn. Purchasing Mgmt. (chair acquisition info.), Soc. Profls. in Dispute Resolution (chmn. internat. sector com. 1996—2000, past bd. dirs. L.A. chpt.), Christian Legal Soc., Aerospace Industries Assn. (chmn. procurement techniques com. 1987—88, chmn. procurement techniques com. 1993—94), State Bar Calif. (franchise law com. vice chair 2001—, Wiley W. Manual pro bono award 1992), Calif. Dispute Resolution Coun. (cons. to qualifications com. 1997—99), Nat. Def. Indsl. Assn. (vice-chmn. west coast legal subcom. 1994—2000, procurement planning com. 1994—). Avocations: camping, skiing, jogging, equestrian. Office: PO Box 2636 Rolling Hills Estates CA 90274 E-mail: adroffice@ieee.org

RUMMAGE, STEPHEN MICHAEL, lawyer; b. Massillon, Ohio, Dec. 27, 1955; s. Robert Everett and Kathleen Patricia (Newman) R.; m. Elizabeth Anne Seivert, Mar. 24, 1979; children: Everett Martin, Carter Kevin. BA in History and English, Stanford U., 1977; JD, U. Calif., Berkeley, 1980. Bar: Wash. 1980, U.S. Dist. Ct. (we. dist.) 1980, U.S. Ct. Appeals (9th cir.) 1983, U.S. Supreme Ct. 1985. Assoc. Davis, Wright et al, Seattle, 1980-85; ptnr. Davis Wright Tremaine, 1986—. Co-author: Employer's Guide to Strike Planning and Prevention, 1985. Mem. Wash. Athletic Club. Democrat. Roman Catholic. Appellate, General civil litigation, Securities. Office: Davis Wright Tremaine 1501 4th Ave Ste 2600 Seattle WA 98101-1688 E-mail: steverummage@dwt.com

RUMMEL, EDGAR FERRAND, retired lawyer; b. New Bern, N.C., June 29, 1929; s. Robert French and Reba Jeanette (Burgess) R.; m. Lillian Hildebrandt, Dec. 28, 1954. BA, Ohio State U., 1955; JD, DePaul U., 1965; LLB, U. London, Eng., 1973; LLM, George Washington U., 1978. Bar: U.S. Dist. Ct. D.C. 1967, U.S. Ct. Appeals (D.C. cir.) 1968, U.S. Supreme Ct. 1971, Md. 1980. Atty.-adviser Dept. Army, Washington, 1971-74, 78, counsel U.S. Army Real Estate Agy., Frankfurt, W.Ger., 1975-77, supervisory atty.-adviser, asst. div. chief Office of Chief of Engrs., Dept. Army, Washington, 1977-83; sr. atty. advisor Office of Judge Advocate Gen., Dept. Army, Washington, 1983-85, trial atty., 1987; spl. asst. U.S. Atty. Dist. Colo., 1985-87, ret. 1987; chmn. mineral leasing com. Dept. Def., 1981-84; mem. Oreg. Nat. Trial Adv. Council, 1983-84. With AUS, 1947-51. Mem. Md. State Bar Assn., Am. Soc. Legal History. Democrat. Episcopalian (vestryman 1981-84). Home: 7812 Adelphi Ct Hyattsville MD 20783-1848

RUMRELL, RICHARD GARY, lawyer; b. Tampa, Fla., Nov. 30, 1945; BA, U. South Fla., 1967; JD with honors, Fla. State U., 1970; LLM, Nottingham Law Sch., 1996. Bar: Fla. 1971, U.S. Dist. Ct. (no. and mid. dists.) Fla. 1972, U.S. Ct. Appeals (5th cir.) 1974, U.S. Supreme Ct. 1976, D.C. 1981, U.S. Dist. Ct. (so. dist.) Fla. Adminstrv. asst. senator Law Chiles, Tallahassee, 1967; legis. intern Fla. Legislature Dept., 1968-69; staff dir. elections Fla. Ho. of Reps., 1971; asst. states atty. 4th Jud. Cir. Fla., Jacksonville, Fla., 1971-74; assoc. Smathers & Thompson, 1975-82; ptnr. Smathers & Rumrell, 1982, Rumrell & Vlcek, Jacksonville, 1985, Rumrell & Johnson, Jacksonville, 1987-95, Rumrell, Costabel & Turk, Jacksonville, Miami, 1995-97, Rumrell, Wagner & Costabel LLP, Jacksonville, Orlando, Miami, 1997—, Alachua, St. Augustine. Chmn. jud. nominating com. 4th Jud. Cir., 1997-98. Author: (with others) Florida: Historical and Contemporary Life in the Sunshine State, 1974. Past pres. port com. Jacksonville Econ. Devel. Council; pres. Mental Health Clinic of Jacksonville, 1981; mem. Jud. Nominating Com., 1982-84; chmn. Pvt. Industry Council, Jacksonville, 1985-86. Mem. ABA (mem. litigation sect.), Fla. Bar Assn. (mem. admiralty law com. 1979-83, bd. of cert.), Jacksonville Bar Assn., Am. Judicature Soc., Maritime Law Assn. U.S. (mem. stevedoring and terminal operators com.), Southeastern Admiralty Law Assn., Nat. Bd. Trial Adv. (certificate), Jacksonville Internat. Trade Assn. (certified), River Club. Democrat. Avocation: fishing. Admiralty, General civil litigation, Personal injury. Office: Rumrell Wagner & Costabel LLP 10151 Deerwood Park Blvd Jacksonville FL 32256-0566 Also: 24 Cathedral Pl Ste 504 Saint Augustine FL 32084 E-mail: rumrell@rumrelllaw.com

RUMSEY, D(AVID) LAKE, JR. lawyer; b. Dallas, Aug. 24, 1944; s. David Lake and Eva Linn (Carter) R. B.A., U. Tex.-Austin, 1970, J.D., 1972. Bar: Ga. 1973, U.S. Dist. Ct. (no. dist.) Ga. 1973, U.S. Ct. Appeals (5th and 11th cirs.) 1973, U.S. Supreme Ct. 1978. Assoc. firm Kutak, Rock & Huie, Atlanta, 1973-78, ptnr., 1978-81; ptnr. firm Mayer, Nations & Rumsey, Atlanta, 1981-82, pvt. practice law, Atlanta, 1982—; adj. prof. Emory Law Sch., 1982—; mem. faculty Nat. Inst. Trial Advocacy, Boulder, Colo., 1982— . Contbr. articles to law jours., chpts. to books. Editor: Masters Advocates' Handbook, 1986. Served with U.S. Army, 1967-69. Decorated Bronze Star medals. Mem. ABA, Assn. Trial Lawyers Am., Atlanta Bar Assn., Def. Rsch. Inst., Atlanta C. of C. (hon. life mem.), Old War Horse Lawyers Club, Ga. Trial Lawyers Assn., State Bar of Ga., Sigma Alpha Epsilon. Federal civil litigation, State civil litigation, Personal injury. Home: 379 Collier Rd NW Atlanta GA 30309-1706 Office: 509 Candler Bldg 127 Peachtree St NE Atlanta GA 30303-1810

RUNCO, WILLIAM JOSEPH, judge; b. Detroit, Jan. 23, 1957; s. Joseph Tony and Rose Mary (Rossi) R.; m. Rhonda Lee Hyde, May 30, 1987; children: Erica, Gabriella, Joseph. BA in Econs., U. Mich., 1979, JD, 1981. Bar: Mich. 1983, U.S. Dist. Ct. (ea. dist.) Mich. 1984. Commr. Wayne County, Detroit, 1981-83; mem. Mich. Ho. Reps., Lansing, 1983-86, 89-91, minority whip, 1983-84; ptnr. Edick, Esper & Runco, Dearborn, Mich., 1985-88, Runco, Tyler & Xuereb, Dearborn, 1988-91; judge 19th Dist. Ct., 1991—. Adj. lectr. U. Mich., Dearborn, 1991—; adj. lectr. Henry Ford C.C., 1996—. Mediator Wayne County Mediation Tribunal, Detroit, 1987-91; del. Rep. Nat. Conv., Detroit, 1980, New Orleans, 1988; mem. Electoral Coll., 1989; mem. citizens adv. com. U. Mich., Dearborn, 1987-89; mem. C.A.S.L. alumni affiliate bd. U. Mich., Dearborn, 1994-97. Mem. ABA, Dearborn Bar Assn., Mich. Dist. Judges Assn. (bd. dirs., pres.), Dearborn Pioneers, Mich. Jud. Conf. (bd. mem., chairperson). Roman Catholic. Avocations: golf, aviation, ice hockey. Office: 19th Dist Ct 16077 Mi Ave Dearborn MI 48126-2999

RUNDIO, LOUIS MICHAEL, JR. lawyer; b. Chgo., Sept. 13, 1943; s. Louis Michael Sr. and Germaine Matilda (Pasternack) R.; m. Ann Marie Bartlett, July 10, 1971; children: Matthew, Melissa. BS in Physics, Loyola U., Chgo., 1965, JD, 1972. Bar: Ill. 1972, U.S. Dist. Ct. (no. dist.) Ill. 1972, U.S. Ct. Appeals (7th cir.) 1974, U.S. Dist. Ct. (ea. dist.) Mich. 1983. Assoc. McDermott, Will & Emery, Chgo., 1972-77, ptnr., 1978—. Served to 1st lt. U.S. Army, 1965-68, Vietnam. Mem. ABA, Chgo. Bar Assn. Federal civil litigation, State civil litigation, Environmental. Home: 676 Skye Ln Barrington IL 60010-5506 Office: McDermott Will & Emery 227 W Monroe St Ste 3100 Chicago IL 60606-5096

RUNDLETT, ELLSWORTH TURNER, III, lawyer; b. Portland, Maine, Jan. 12, 1946; s. Ellsworth Turner II and Esther (Stevens) R.; m. Lisa Warren, Oct. 25, 1964 (div. June 1967); 1 child, Ellsworth Turner IV; m. Jamie Donnelly, June 7, 1982 (div. 1986); m. Marilyn DeJenzano, Aug. 17, 1994. AB cum laude, Bowdoin Coll., 1968; JD, U. Maine, 1973. Bar: Maine 1973, U.S. Dist. Ct. Maine 1973, U.S. Ct. Appeals (1st cir.) 1973; cert. civil trial specialist, Nat. Bd. Trial Advocacy; diplomate Nat. Coll. Advocacy. Bodwoin Coll. intern U.S. Senate, Washington, 1967; law clk. Superior Ct. Maine, Portland, 1972-73; asst. corp. counsel City of Portland, 1973-76; ptnr. Childs, Rundlett, Fifield & Childs, Portland, 1980—. Author: Maximizing Damages in Small Personal Injury Cases, 1991; contbr. legal articles to Maine Bus. Digest, 1978-84. Pres. Pine Tree Alcohol Treatment Ctr., Windham, Maine, 1978-80; trustee Portland Players, Inc., South Portland, Maine, 1977-84, pres., 1985-87. Mem. ATLA, Cumberland County Bar (trustee 1983-84, 86-87, v.p. 1988-90, pres. 1990), Maine Bar Assn. (bd. govs. 1991—), Maine Trial Lawyers

Assn. (pres. 2000-01), U. Maine Law Alumni (bd. dirs. 1984-87, v.p. 1988, pres. 1989, bd. govs. 1991—), Cumberland Club, Portland Club (gov. 1983-86), Bowdoin Club of Portland (pres. 1978). E-mai;l. State civil litigation, General practice, Personal injury. Office: Childs Rundlett & Fifield 257 Deering Ave Portland ME 04103-4858 E-mail: derry@maine.rr.com

RUNFOLA, ROSS THOMAS, lawyer, educator, writer, journalist, poet; b. Buffalo, Aug. 30, 1943; s. Joseph Paul and Isabelle Louise (Santi) R.; children: Jennifer, Ross Thomas; m. Nancy S. Cox, Aug. 10, 1993. BA summa cum laude, SUNY, Buffalo, 1965, MA, 1968, PhD, 1973, JD, 1981. Bar: N.Y. 1982. Prof. social scis. Medaille Coll., Buffalo, 1969—; asst. prof. SUNY, 1970-73; sports columnist Buffalo New Times, 1973-74; co-anchor Sta. WUTV, 1974; reporter Buffalo Courier Express, 1975-76; columnist Spree mag., 1979-82; asst. Erie County Pub. Adminstr., 1981; ptnr. Fiorella, Leiter & Runfola, 1982-86; spl. matrimonial counsel Matusick, Spadafora & Verrastro, 1986-87; ptnr. Siegel, Kelleher & Kahn, 1987—. Dir. Matrimonial Mediation Ctr. Author: Jock: Sports and Male Identity, 1980; contbr. numerous articles to profl. jours.; chief film scriptwriter: Organized Sports: Are They Good for Young People, 1975. Active Mayor's Energy Task Force City of Buffalo, 1973, commn. Human Rights and Cmty. Relations, 2000, Minority task group for 8th judicial dist., 2000, Attica Prison Task Force, N.Y., 1973, Western N.Y. Consortium on Higher Edn., 1974, Erie County (N.Y.) Task Force on Physical Edn. and Recreation for Meeting the needs of the Handicapped, 1974, Instl. Task Force Pvt. Colls. Western N.Y., 1974, Western N.Y. Higher Edn. Task Force, 1975, Legis. Adv. Com. N.Y. State Assembly, 1976, Children's Hosp. Adolescence Program, 1978, Western N.Y. Heart Assn., 1978, Southern Poverty Law Ctr., 1978—, Erie County Dem. Com., 1978—, Step Family Assn. Western N.Y., 1983—, Frontier Dem. Club, 1983—; mem. adv. com. United Way Buffalo, 1991—; bd. dirs. Monsignor Carr Inst., Just Buffalo Lit. Ctr., 1996. Named One of Ten Best Coll. Profs. Western N.Y. Buffalo News, 1987, Prof. of Yr. Medaille Coll., 1998, Leadership Buffalo for Outstanding Leadership and Cmty. Commmitment, 1999; recipient 1st pl. award oral competition Greater Buffalo Poetry Slam, 1998, Social Svcs. award Nat. Conf. for Community and Justice, 1998. Mem. ABA, AAUP, N.Y. State Bar Assn., Erie County Bar Assn. (vice chmn. matrimonial and family law com. 1992—), N.Y. State United Tchrs., N.Y. State Coun. Divorce Mediation, Am. Acad. Family Mediators (designated cons.), Am. Trial Lawyers Assn. Roman Catholic. Avocations: writing, reading, bicycling, cross country skiing. Entertainment, Family and matrimonial. Home: 96 Cleveland Ave Buffalo NY 14222-1610 Office: Siegel Kelleher & Kahn 420 Franklin St Buffalo NY 14202-1302 also: 18 Agassiz Cir Buffalo NY 14214-2601

RUNGE, PATRICK RICHARD, lawyer; b. Iowa City, Oct. 25, 1969; s. Richard Gary and Sally Louise (Cozzolino) R. BSBA in Econs., U. Nebr., Omaha, 1991; JD, Creighton U., 1994. Bar: Nebr. 1994, U.S. Dist. Ct. Nebr. 1994. Prodn. editor U.N.O. Gateway, Omaha, 1990-91; graphic designer Omaha Pub. Power Dist., 1991-97; intern U.S. Dist. Ct., Omaha, 1993; rsch. asst. Creighton U., 1993; sr. cert. law student Creighton Legal Clinic, 1994; atty. Runge Law Office, 1994-95, Runge & Chase, Omaha, 1995—. Pub. defender Winnebago Tribe Nebr., 1996—, Omaha Tribe Nebr., 2000-01. Disting. scholar Omaha (Nebr.) World-Herald, 1987-91; Merit scholar Creighton Law Sch., Omaha, 1991-94. Mem. ABA, Winnebago Bar Assn., Omaha Tribal Bar Assn. Democrat. Lutheran. Constitutional, Criminal, Family and matrimonial. Office: Runge & Chase 7701 Pacific St Ste 323 Omaha NE 68114-5480 E-mail: runge@rungeandchase.com

RUNQUIST, LISA A. lawyer; b. Mpls., Sept. 22, 1952; d. Ralf E. and Violet R. BA, Hamline U., 1973; JD, U. Minn., 1976. Bar: Minn. 1977, Calif. 1978, U.S. Dist. Ct. (ctrl. dist.) Calif. 1985, U.S. Supreme Ct. 1995. Assoc. Caldwell & Toms, L.A., 1978-82; ptnr. Runquist & Flagg, 1982-85; pvt. practice Runquist & Assocs., 1985-99, Runquist & Zybach LLP, L.A., 1999—. Mem. adv. bd. Exempt Orgn. Tax Rev., 1990—, Calif. State U. L.A. Continuing Edn. Acctg. and Tax Program, 1995—. Mem. editorial bd. ABA Bus. Law Today, 1995—; contbr. articles to profl. jours. Mem. ABA (bus. law sect. coun. 1995-99, com. on nonprofit corps. 1986—, chair 1991-95, subcom. current devels. in nonprofit corp. law 1989—, chair 1989-91, subcom. rels. orgns. 1989—, chair 1987-91, 95-98, subcom. legal guidebook for dirs. 1986—, ad hoc com. on info. tech., 1997—, chair 1997-98, co-chair, 1998—, sect. liaison to ABA tech. coun. 1997-2000, subcom. model nonprofit corp. act, partnerships and unincorp. bus. orgns. com. 1987—, state regulation of securities com. 1988-99, exempt orgns. com. 1987—, subcom. religious orgns. 1989—, co-chair 1995-97, subcom. non (c) (3) orgns. 1997—, co-chair 1997—, subcom. guidebook for dirs. of closely held corps. chair 2000—), Calif. Bar Assn. (bus. law sect., nonprofit and unincorp. orgns. com. 1985-92, 93-96, 97—, chair 1989-91), Christian Legal Soc., Ctr. Law and Religious Freedom, Christian Mgmt. Assn. (dir. 1983-89). General corporate, Non-profit and tax-exempt organizations, Securities. Office: 10618 Woodbridge St Toluca Lake CA 91602-2717 E-mail: lisa@runquist.com

RUNYON, BRETT L. lawyer; b. Fresno, Calif., Oct. 20, 1959; AA, Fresno City Coll., 1981; BS, Calif. State U., Fresno, 1982; JD, San Joaquin Coll. Law, 1986. Bar: Calif. 1988, D.C., U.S. Dist. Ct. (ea. dist.), U.S. Ct. Appeals (Fed. cir.) 1998. Atty. Marderosian Oren & Paboojian and predecessor firm, Fresno, 1988—. Arbitrator Fresno County Superior Ct., Fresno County Farm Bur. Mem. ABA, ATLA, Fed. Bar Assn., No. Calif. Assn. Def. Counsel, Fresno County Bar Assn., Delta Theta Phi (meritorious svc. award 1986). Insurance, Product liability, Toxic tort. Office: Marderosian Runyon Cercone & Lehman 1260 Fulton Mall Fresno CA 93721-1916

RUPERT, DONALD WILLIAM, lawyer; b. Clearfield, Pa., Oct. 15, 1946; s. Donald Lee and Dorothy Mae (Bonsall) R.; m. Patricia A. Rupert, June 21, 1969. BS in Chemistry, Miami U., Ohio, 1968; JD, Washburn U., Topeka, 1976. Bar: Tex. 1976, Ill. 1978, U.S. Ct. Appeals (Fed. cir.) 1978, U.S. Dist. Ct. (so. dist.) Tex. 1977, U.S. Ct. Appeals (7th cir.) 1981, U.S. Dist. Ct. (no. dist.) Ill. 1979, U.S. Supreme Ct., 1992. Assoc. Arnold, White & Durkee, Houston, 1976-78, Kirkland & Ellis, Chgo., 1978-83, ptnr., 1983-86; ptnr. Neuman, Williams, Anderson & Olson, Chgo., 1986-90; founding ptnr. Roper & Quigg, 1990-93; ptnr. Keck, Mahin & Cate, Chgo., 1993-96; ptnr. Mayer, Brown & Platt, Chgo., 1996—; cons. USAF, Dayton, Ohio, 1974-81. Contbr. articles to profl. jours. Served to capt. USAF, 1968-74. Miami U. Undergrad. Rsch. fellow, 1967, Grad. Rsch. fellow, 1968. Mem. ABA, Am. Intellectual Property Law Assn., Tex. Bar Assn., Phi Kappa Phi. Democrat. Presbyterian. Federal civil litigation, Intellectual property, Patent. Home: 2519 Park Pl Evanston IL 60201-1315 Office: Mayer Brown & Platt 190 S La Salle St Ste 3100 Chicago IL 60603-3441

RUPORT, SCOTT HENDRICKS, lawyer; b. Nov. 22, 1949; s. Fred Hendricks and Juyne (Kennedy) R.; m. Linda Darlene Smith, Sept. 12, 1970; children: Brittany Lyle, Courtney Kennedy. BSBA, Bowling Green U., 1971; JD, U. Akron, 1974. Bar: Ohio 1974, Pa. 1984, U.S. Dist. Ct. (no. dist.) Ohio 1974, U.S. Ct. Appeals (6th cir.) 1975, U.S. Supreme Ct. 1978; cert. civil trial specialist Nat. Bd. Trial Advocacy. Assoc. Schwab, Sager, Growenburgh, Rothal, Fort, Skidmore & Nukes, Akron, Ohio, 1974-76, Skidmore & George Co. LPA, Akron, 1976-79, Skidmore, Ruport & Haskings, Akron, 1979-83; ptnr. Roderick, Myers & Linton, 1983-85, Ruport Co. LPA, Akron, 1985—. Instr. real estate law U. Akron, 1976-77, adj. asst. prof. constrn. tech. Coll. Engring., 1983—. Capt. Fin. Corps. USAR, 1971-79. Mem. ABA, ATLA, Ohio Bar Assn., Ohio Acad. Trial Lawyers (chmn. civil and bus. litigation sect. 1989), Akron Bar Assn., Beta Gamma Sigma, Sigma Chi. Republican. Presbyterian. Federal civil litigation, State civil litigation, Construction. Office: Ruport Co LPA 3700 Embassy Pkwy Ste 440 Akron OH 44333-8367

RUPP, JOHN PETER, lawyer; b. Westerly, R.I., Dec. 30, 1944; s. Paul P. and Doris T. (Savin) R.; m. Maureen E. O'Bryon, June 30, 1968; children— Megan E., Erin O. B.A., U. Iowa, 1967; J.D., Yale U., 1971. Bar: Maine 1971, D.C. 1971, U.S. Ct. Appeals (1st cir.) 1971. U.S. Ct. Appeals (9th and 4th cirs.) 1975. U.S. Supreme Ct. 1976, U.S. Ct. Appeals (10th cir.) 1977. Law clk. to chief judge First Cir. Ct. Appeals, 1971-72; assoc. Covington & Burling, Washington, 1972-74, ptnr., 1977— ; asst. to solicitor gen. Dept. Justice, Washington, 1974-77; chmn. lawyers com. Children's Def. Fund, Washington, 1983-84. Author: (with others) The Rights of Gays, 1974, 83. Mem. steering com. Americans for Democratic Action, Washington, 1973; credentials judge Democratic Party, 1984. Democrat. Roman Catholic. Mem. ACLU. Administrative and regulatory, Antitrust, Federal civil litigation. Office: Covington & Burling PO Box 7566 1201 Pennsylvania Ave NW Washington DC 20004-2401

RUPPE, ARTHUR MAXWELL, lawyer; b. Boone, N.C., Dec. 15, 1928; s. Arthur Monroe and Floye (Robinson) R.; m. Ruth Marie Ledford; children: Ruth Carol, Sharon Marie, Arthur Maxwell Jr., Susan Lunette. AA, Gardner Webb Coll., 1947; AB, U. N.C., 1950, JD, 1952. Bar: N.C. 1952, U.S. Dist. Ct. (ea. dist.) N.C. 1955, U.S. Ct. Mil. Appeals 1968; cert mediator. Asst. staff, judge advocate U.S. Army, Ft. Bragg, N.C., 1952-55; sole practice Fayetteville, 1955-98; mediator, 1997—. Served to 1st lt. U.S. Army, 1952-55. Mem. ABA, N.C. Bar Assn. (patron), N.C. State Bar Assn., 12 Jud. Dist. Bar Assn., Cumberland County Bar Assn. (pres. 1982-83), K.P. Democrat. Baptist. Avocations: snow ski, tennis. Alternative dispute resolution. Home: 336 Summertime Rd Fayetteville NC 28303-4658

RUPPERT, JOHN LAWRENCE, lawyer; b. Chgo., Oct. 7, 1953; s. Merle Arvin and Loretta Marie (Ford) R.; m. Katharine Marie Tarbox, June 5, 1976. BA, Northwestern U., 1975; JD, U. Denver, 1978; LLM in Taxation, NYU, 1979. Bar: Colo. 1978, U.S. Dist. Ct. Colo. 1978, Ill. 1979, U.S. Tax Ct. 1981. Assoc. Kirkland & Ellis, Denver, 1979-84, ptnr., 1984-88, Ballard, Spahr, Andrews & Ingersoll, Denver, 1988-96; shareholder Brownstein Hyatt Farber & Strickland, P.C., 1996—. Lectr. U. Denver Coll. Law, fall 1984-92; adj. prof. law grad. tax program, 1993-94; sec. Capital Assocs., Inc., 1989-96; sec. Brothers Gourmet Coffees, Inc., 1995-2000; asst. sec. Renaissance Cosmetics, Inc., 1996-98, Rhythms Net Connections Inc., 2000-2001; sec. Skillset Software, Inc., 2000-01; asst. sec. Rhythms NetConnections Inc., 2000-01. Contbr. articles to profl. jours. Mem. ABA, Colo. Bar Assn. (mem. exec. coun. tax sect. 1985-89), Denver Bar Assn. Mergers and acquisitions, Corporate taxation, Personal income taxation. Office: Brownstein Hyatt Farber & Strickland PC 410 17th St Fl 22D Denver CO 80202-4402 E-mail: jruppert@bhfs.com, ruppert53@aol.com

RUSCH, JONATHAN JAY, lawyer; b. Nyack, N.Y., Oct. 16, 1952; s. Thaddeus David and Alice Marjorie (Lewis) R.; m. Doreen Evelyn Lacovara, Aug. 10, 1974; children: Rachel Madeline, Catherine Elizabeth. AB in Pub. Affairs with honors, Princeton U., 1974; MA, U. Va., 1978, JD, 1980. Bar: D.C. 1981, U.S. Dist. Ct. D.C. 1981, U.S. Ct. Appeals (D.C. cir.) 1981, U.S. Ct. Appeals (7th cir.) 1985, U.S. Ct. Appeals (9th cir.) 1990, U.S. Ct. Appeals (5th cir.) 1992, U.S. Supreme Ct. 1992. Assoc. Cleary, Gottlieb, Steen & Hamilton, Washington, 1980-83; spl. asst. to atty. gen. U.S. Dept. Justice, 1983-84; counsel Pres. Commn. on Organized Crime, 1984-86; acting dir., then dir. office of fin. enforcement U.S. Dept. Treasury, 1986-88; trial atty. fraud sect., criminal divsn. U.S. Dept. Justice, 1988-93, asst. spl. counsel House banking facility, 1992, sr. litigation counsel fraud sect., criminal divsn., 1993—, spl. counsel for fraud prevention, criminal divsn., 1998—. Adj. prof. Georgetown U. Law Ctr., 1996—. Recipient Atty. Gen.'s Disting. Svc. award, 1995. Mem. ABA (coun. mem. adminstrv. law sect. 1990-93, chmn. criminal process com. 1987-90, 93-98, chmn. regulatory initiatives com. 1998—), Assn. Am. Law Schs., Tower Club. Home: 4600 Connecticut Ave NW Apt 207 Washington DC 20008-5702 Office: US Dept Justice 1400 New York Ave NW Washington DC 20530 E-mail: jonathan.rusch@worldnet.att.net, Jonathan.Rusch2@usdoj.gov

RUSE, STEVEN DOUGLAS, lawyer; b. Wichita, Kans., Mar. 8, 1950; B.A., U. Kans., 1972; J.D., Creighton U., 1975. Bar: Mo. 1975, U.S. Dist. Ct. (we. dist.) Mo. 1975, Kans. 1982, U.S. Dist. Ct. Kans. 1982. Law clk. to dist. justice U.S. Dist. Ct. Mo., Kansas City, 1975-77; assoc. Shughart, Thomson & Kilroy, Kansas City, 1977-81, ptnr., 1981— . Mem. ABA, Mo. Bar Assn., Kans. Bar Assn. General civil litigation, Insurance. Office: Shughart Thomson & Kilroy 9225 Indian Creek Pky Overland Park KS 66210-2009

RUSH, STEPHEN KENNETH, lawyer; b. Columbus, Ind., Mar. 16, 1942; s. Kenneth E. and Jane (Boyle) R.; m. Nancy Burns, June 19, 1965; children: Jeffrey, Stephanie. BSME, Stanford U., 1965, MSME, 1967; JD, Vanderbilt U., 1976. Bar: Tenn. 1976, U.S. Dist. Ct. (mid. dist.) Tenn. 1977, U.S. Ct. Appeals (6th cir.) 1977. Trustee in bankruptcy U.S. Bankruptcy Ct., Nashville, 1974-75; assoc. Farris, Warfield & Kanady, Nashville, 1976-79, ptnr., 1980-93; ptnr. Sukin Rush Law Group, Nashville, 1993—. Patentee propulsion system for diver. Served to comdr. USN, 1967-73. Mem. ABA, Assn. Trial Lawyers Am., Tenn. Bar Assn., Nashville Bar Assn., Internat. Bar Assn., Internat. Assn. Entertainment Lawyers, Nat. Trust for Hist. Preservation. Federal civil litigation, Entertainment, Libel. Home: RR 5 Franklin TN 37064-9805 Office: Sukin Rush Law Group Third Nat Fin Ctr Ste 2925 Nashville TN 37219

RUSHER, DERWOOD H., II, lawyer; b. Roanoke, Va., Dec. 23, 1954; s. Derwood H. and Edith (McFadden) R.; m. Ashley Simmons, Aug. 15, 1987; children: Paige C, Peyton Clay, Amanda Shelby. BS, Va. Poly. Inst. and State U., 1977; JD, U. Richmond, 1980. Bar: Va. 1980, N.C. 1987, Ga. 1993, U.S. Dist. Ct. (mid. dist.) N.C. 1987, U.S. Dist Ct. (we. dist.) Va. 1987, U.S. Dist. Ct. (ea. dist.) Va. 1988, U.S. Ct. Appeals (4th cir.) 1980, U.S. Ct. Appeals (7th cir.) 1981, U.S. Ct. Appeals (3d, 5th, 6th, 8th, 9th, 10th, 11th, D.C., Fed. cirs.) 1987, U.S. Supreme Ct. 1987, U.S. Dist. Ct. Ariz. 1990, U.S. Dist. Ct. (no. dist.) Ga. 1993. Assoc. Street, Street, Street, Scott & Bowman, Grundy, Va., 1980-81; atty. Standard Oil Co., Chgo., 1981-84, Lexington, Ky., 1984-86; assoc. Womble, Carlyle, Sandridge & Rice, Winston-Salem, N.C., 1986-92; sr. atty. Rollins, Inc., Atlanta, 1992-95; counsel King & Spalding, 1996—. Mem. ABA, Phi Kappa Phi, Phi Delta Phi, Beta Gamma Sigma, Sigma Chi. Methodist. Home: 1320 Northcliff Trace Roswell GA 30076-3274 Office: King & Spalding 191 Peachtree St Atlanta GA 30303-1763

RUSMISEL, STEPHEN R. lawyer; b. N.Y.C., Jan. 27, 1946; s. R. Raymond and Esther Florence (Kutz) R.; m. Beirne Donaldson, Sept. 6, 1980 (div. Jan. 1984); 1 child, Margo Alexander; m. Melissa J. MacLeod, Aug. 24, 1985 (div. Oct. 1996); children: Benjamin William, Eric Scot Kunze, Erin Lea Kunze; m. Teresa R. Paterniti, June 28, 1997; 1 child, Sarah J. Lamendola. AB, Yale U., 1968; JD, U. Va., 1971. Bar: N.Y. 1972, U.S. Ct. Appeals (2d cir.) 1974, U.S. Dist. Ct. (so. dist.) N.Y. 1975. Assoc. Winthrop, Stimson, Putnam & Roberts, N.Y.C., 1971-80, ptnr., 1980-2000, Pillsbury Winthrop LLP, N.Y.C., 2001—. Aux. officer Bedminster Twp. (N.J.) Police, 1976—. Mem. Practicing Law Inst., Am. Arbitration Assn. (arbitrator 1976—), Far Hills Polo Club (Annandale, N.J.), Ausable Club (St. Huberts, N.Y.), Essex Hunt Club (Peapack, N.J.), Phi Delta Phi. Republican. Avocations: polo, flying, carpentry, gardening, poetry. General corporate, Mergers and acquisitions, Securities. Home: Shadowline Farm Bedminster NJ 07921 Office: Pillsbury Winthrop LLP One Battery Park Plz New York NY 10004-1490 E-mail: srusmisel@pillsburywinthrop.com

RUSS, NEIL ANDREW, lawyer; b. Lower Hutt, Wellington, New Zealand, July 22, 1961; s. Arthur Reginald and Robin E. Russ; m. Rachael Dryden; 1 child, Andrew. LLB with honors, Victoria U., Wellington, 1985. BAr: barrister and solicitor High Ct. of New Zealand 1986, solicitor Supreme Ct. of Eng. and Wales 1991. Solicitor Clifford Chance, London, 1988-94; ptnr. Buddle Findlay, Auckland, New Zealand, 1995—. Mem. Inter Pacific Bar Assn. (v.p. tax law com. 1997-2000), Banking Law Assn. (com. 2000), Internat. Fiscal Assn., Taxation Inst. Australia. Avocations: travel, wine, golf, family. Banking, General corporate, Taxation, general. Fax: 64 9 363 0702. E-mail: neil.russ@buddlefindlay.com

RUSSELL, ALLAN DAVID, lawyer, deceased; b. Cleve., May 6, 1924; s. Allan MacGillivray and Marvel (Codling) R.; m. Lois Anne Robinson, June 12, 1947; children: Lisa Anne, Robinson David, Martha Leslie. BA, Yale U., 1945, LLB, 1951. Bar: N.Y. 1952, Conn. 1956, Mass. 1969, U.S. Supreme Ct. 1977. Atty. Sylvania Electric Products, Inc., N.Y.C., 1951-56, div. counsel Batavia, N.Y., 1956-65, sr. counsel, 1965-71; sec., sr. counsel GTE Sylvania Inc., Stamford, Conn., 1971-76; asst. gen. counsel GTE Service Corp., 1976-80, v.p., assoc. gen. counsel staff, 1980-83; pvt. practice Redding, Conn., 1983—. Sec., dir. mktg. subs. Sylvania Entertainment Products Corp., 1961-67; sec. Wilbur B. Driver Co. Dist. leader Rep. Party, New Canaan, Conn., 1955-56; sec. bd. dirs. Youth Found., Inc., 1981-83, bd. dirs., 1985-2001, pres., 2000-01; mem. planning commn., Redding, Conn., 1987-89; mem. Redding Bd. Ethics, 1990-96, chmn., 1992-96; warden Christ Ch. Parish, Redding, 1987-89; bd. dirs. Mark Twain Libr., 1988-94, v.p., 1988-89, pres., 1990-92. With USAAF, 1943-46. Mem. SAR, Assn. of Bar of City of N.Y., Conn. Bar Assn. (exec. com. corp. counsel sect. 1986-90), Am. Soc. Corp. Secs., St. Nicholas Soc., Collie Club Am. Found., Inc. (v.p., dir. 1986-89, pres. 1989-90), Soc. Colonial Wars, Yale Alumni Assn. (sec. local chpt. 1953-56), Yale Club of Danbury (pres. 1990—), Phi Delta Phi. Administrative and regulatory, Antitrust, General corporate. Home: 9 Little River Ln Redding CT 06896-2018 E-mail: adavidfancy14184@aol.com

RUSSELL, C. EDWARD, JR. lawyer; b. Portsmouth, Va., Aug. 19, 1942; BA, Hampden-Sydney Coll., 1964; LLB, Washington & Lee U., 1967. Bar: Va. 1967. Law clk. to Hon. John A. MacKenzie U.S. Dist. Ct. (ea. dist.) Va., 1967-68; atty. Kaufman & Canoles, Norfolk. Mem. ABA (bus. law sect., real property, probate and trust law sect.), Va. State Bar (bus. law sect., real property sect., health law sect.), Va. Bar Assn. (bus. law sect., real estate sect., chmn. young lawyers sect. 1977), Omicron Delta Kappa, Phi Alpha Delta. Contracts commercial, General corporate, Real property. Office: PO Box 13368 Norfolk VA 23506-0368 E-mail: cerussell@kaufcan.com

RUSSELL, CHARLES STEVENS, state supreme court justice, educator; b. Richmond, Va., Feb. 23, 1926; s. Charles Herbert and Nita M. (Stevens) R.; m. Carolyn Elizabeth Abrams, Mar. 18, 1951; children: Charles Stevens Jr., David Tyler. B.A., U. Va., 1946, LL.B., 1948. Bar: Va. 1949, U.S. Dist. Ct. (ea. dist.) Va. 1952, U.S. Ct. Appeals (4th cir.) 1955, U.S. Supreme Ct. 1958. Assoc. Jesse, Phillips, Klinge & Kendrick, Arlington, Va., 1951-57, ptnr., 1957-60, Phillips, Kendrick, Gearheart and Aylor, Arlington, 1960-67; judge 17th Jud. Ct. Va., 1967-82, Supreme Ct. Va., Richmond, 1982-91, ret. Mem. jud. coun. Va., 1977-82; adj. prof. law George Mason U., Arlington, 1977-86, T.C. Williams Sch. Law U. Richmond, 1987-90; mem. exec. com. Va. State Bar, Richmond, 1964-67; mem. faculty Nat. Jud. Coll., Reno, 1980—, Appellate Judges Inst., NYU, 1986—. Mem. Adv. Com. on Youth, Arlington; mem. nat. council of trustees Freedoms Found., Valley Forge, Pa., 1986-91. Served to lt. comdr. USNR, 1944-51. Fellow Am. Bar Found.; mem. ABA, Arlington County Bar Assn., Va. Bar Assn., Richmond Bar Assn., Va. Trial Lawyers Assn., Am. Judicature Soc., Am. Law Inst. (adv. com. on complex litigation 1989-91). Episcopalian. Home: 11 James Falls Dr Richmond VA 23221-3942 Office: Va Supreme Ct PO Box 1315 Richmond VA 23219-1315

RUSSELL, DAN M., JR. federal judge; b. Magee, Miss., Mar. 15, 1913; s. Dan M. and Beulah (Watkins) R.; m. Dorothy Tudury, Dec. 27, 1942; children— Ronald Truett, Dorothy Dale, Richard Brian. B.A., U. Miss., 1935, LL.B., 1937. Bar: Miss. bar 1937. Practice in, Gulfport and Bay St. Louis, Miss.; U.S. judge So. Dist. Miss., 1965—; now sr. judge. Lt. comdr. U.S. Naval Intelligence, 1941-45. Recipient U.S. Supreme Ct. Justice Scalia award, 2000. Founder's Day award Gulfport Rotary Club, 2001. Mem. Miss. Bar Assn., Hancock County Bar Assn., Hancock and Harrison Counties Bar Assn., Bay St. Louis Rotary Club (hon.), Gulfport Rotary Club (hon.), Am. Inns Ct. (hon. Russell-Blass-Walker chpt.), Federalist Soc. (adv. bd. Miss. chpt.), Hancock County C. of C., Tau Kappa Alpha. Club: Rotarian (pres. Bay St. Louis, Miss. 1946). Office: US Dist Ct PO Box 1930 Gulfport MS 39502-1930

RUSSELL, DAVID L. federal judge; b. Sapulpa, Okla., July 7, 1942; s. Lynn and Florence E. (Brown) R.; m. Dana J. Wilson, Apr. 16, 1971; 1 child, Sarah Elizabeth BS, Okla. Bapt. U., 1963; J.D., Okla. U., 1965. Bar: Okla. 1965. Asst. atty. gen. State of Okla., Oklahoma City, 1968-69, legal adviser to gov., 1969-70; legal adviser Senator Dewey Bartlett, Washington, 1973-75; U.S. atty. for Western dist. Okla. Dept. Justice, 1975-77, 81-82; ptnr. Benefield & Russell, Oklahoma City, 1977-81; chief judge U.S. Dist. Ct. (we. dist.) Okla., 1982—. Lt. comdr. JAGC, USN, 1965-68. Selected Outstanding Fed. Ct. Trial judge Okla. Trial Lawyers Assn., 1988. Mem. Okla. Bar Assn., Fed. Bar Assn. (pres. Oklahoma City chpt. 1981), Order of Coif (alumnus mem.). Republican. Methodist. Office: US Dist Ct US Courthouse 200 NW 4th St Oklahoma City OK 73102-3026

RUSSELL, DAVID WILLIAMS, lawyer; b. Lockport, N.Y., Apr. 5, 1945; s. David Lawson and Jean Graves (Williams) R.; m. Frances Yung Chung Chen, May 23, 1970; children: Bayard Chen, Ming Rennick. AB, Dartmouth Coll., 1967, MBA, 1969; JD cum laude, Northwestern U., 1976. Bar: Ill. 1976, Ind. 1983. English tchr. Talledega (Ala.) Coll., summer 1967; math. tchr. Lyndon Inst., Lyndonville, Vt., 1967-68; asst. to pres. for planning Tougaloo (Miss.) Coll., 1969-71, bus. mgr., 1971-73; law clk. Montgomery, McCracken, Walker & Rhoads, Phila., summer 1975; with Winston & Strawn, Chgo., 1976-83; ptnr. Klineman, Rose, Wolf & Wallack, Indpls., 1983-87, Johnson, Smith, Pence, Densborn, Wright & Heath, Indpls., 1987-99, Bose McKinney & Evans, Indpls., 1999—. Cons. Alfred P. Sloan Found., 1972-73; dir. Forum for Internat. Profl. Svcs., 1985—, sec., 1985-88, pres. 1988-89; U.S. Dept. Justice del. to U.S. China Joint Session on Trade, Investment & Econ. Law, Beijing, 1987; leader Ind. Products Trade Fair, Kawachinagano, Japan, 1996; lectr. Ind. law Ind. Gov.'s Trade Mission to Japan, 1986, internat. law Ind. Continuing Legal Edn. Forum, 1986-96, 2000, 01, chmn., 1987, 89, 91, 01; adj. prof. internat. bus. law Ind. U., 1993-95; bd. dirs. Ind. ASEAN Coun., Inc., 1988-93; nat. selection com. Woodrow Wilson Found. Adminstrv. Fellowship Program, 1973-76; vol. Lawyers for Creative Arts, Chgo., 1977-83; dir. World Trade Club of Ind., 1987-93, v.p., 1987-91, pres., 1991-92; dir. Ind. Swiss Found., 1991—; dir. Writer's Ctr., Indpls., 1999—, treas., 2000—; dir. Asian Am. Alliance, 1999—; dir. Ind. Soviet Trade Consortium, 1991-99, sec., 1991-92; v.p., bd. dirs. Ind. Sister Cities, 1988—; dir. Internat. Ctr. Indpls., 1988-92, v.p. 1988-89; Ind. dist. enrollment dir. Dartmouth Coll., 1990-99; dir. Carmel Sister Cities, 1993—, v.p. 1995-96, pres. 1997-99, chmn., 1999—; v.p., gen. coun. Lawrence Durrell Soc., 1993—; mem. bd. advisors Ctr. for Internat. Bus. Edn. and Rsch. Krannert Grad. Sch. Mgmt. Purdue U., 1995—; dir., v.p., gen. coun. Global Crossroads Found., Inc., 1995—;

mem. bd. arbitrators NASD, 1999—; mem. Ind. Dist. Export Coun., 1999—. Woodrow Wilson Found. Adminstrv. fellow, 1969-72. Mem. ABA, ACLU, Ill. Bar Assn., Ind. Bar Assn. (vice chmn. internat. law sect., 1988-90, chmn. 1990-92, co-chmn. written publs. com. 1997-99), Indpls. Bar Assn., Dartmouth Lawyers Assn., Indpls. Assn. Chinese Ams., Chinese Music Soc., Dartmouth Club of Ind. (sec. 1986-87, pres. 1987-88), Internat. Bar Assn., Zeta Psi. Presbyterian. General corporate, Private international, Real property. Home: 10926 Lakeview Dr Carmel IN 46033-3937 Office: Bose McKinney & Evans LLP 2700 First Ind Plz 135 N Pennsylvania St Indianapolis IN 46204-2400

RUSSELL, IRWIN EMANUEL, lawyer; b. N.Y.C., Jan. 24, 1926; m. Suzanne Russell, Nov. 15, 1968. BS in Econs., U. Pa., 1947; JD, Harvard U., 1949. Bar: N.Y. 1949, Calif. 1971. Atty. office chief counsel Wage Stabilization Bd., Washington, 1951-53; pvt. practice N.Y.C., 1954-71; founder, chmn., dir. RAI Rsch. Corp., Hauppage, N.Y., 1954-91; exec. v.p., treas., dir. The Wolper Orgn., Inc., L.A., 1971-76; pvt. practice Beverly Hills, Calif., 1977—. Dir. Walt Disney Co., Burbank, Calif., The Lipper Fund, Inc., N.Y.C. With USAAF, 1944-45. General corporate, Entertainment. Home: 10590 Wilshire Blvd Apt 1402 Los Angeles CA 90024-4563 Office: 9401 Wilshire Blvd Ste 760 Beverly Hills CA 90212-2933

RUSSELL, JAMES FRANKLIN, lawyer; b. Memphis, Mar. 21, 1945; s. Frank Hall and Helen (Brunson) R.; m. Marilyn Land, June 1, 1968 (div. May 1976); children: Mary Helen, Myles Edward; m. Linda Hatcher, July 9, 1977; 1 child, Maggie Abele. BA, Rhodes Coll., 1967; JD, Memphis State U., 1970. Bar: Tenn. 1971, U.S. Dist. Ct. (we. dist.) Tenn. 1971, U.S. Ct. Appeals (6th cir.) 1971, U.S. Dist. Ct. (no. dist.) Miss. 1976, U.S. Ct. Appeals (5th cir.) 1977, U.S. Ct. Appeals (8th cir.) 1987. Assoc. Nelson, Norvell, Wilson, McRae, Ivy & Sevier, Memphis, 1971-75; ptnr. Stanton, Russell & Challen, 1975-78, Russell, Price, Weatherford & Warlick, Memphis, 1978-82, Price, Vance & Criss, Memphis, 1982-85, Apperson, Crump, Duzane & Maxwell, Memphis, 1985-97, 1985-97; cir. ct. judge Divsn. II 30th Jud. Dist., 1997—. V.p. mid-south chpt. Am. Red Cross, Memphis, 1992-94; treas. Epilepsy Found. West Tenn., Memphis, 1992-94. Mem. ABA, Nat. Assn. R.R. Trial Counsel, Internat. Assn. Def. Counsel, Tenn. Bar Assn., Tenn. Def. Lawyers Assn., Memphis Bar Assn. (pres. 1992). Episcopalian. Avocations: golf, snow skiing. Insurance, Transportation, Workers' compensation. Home: 1045 Reed Hooker N Eads TN 38028-6958 Office: Shelby County Courthouse 140 Adams Ave Memphis TN 38103-2000

RUSSELL, MICHAEL JAMES, lawyer; b. Northampton, Mass., May 19, 1958; Cert. in German, U. Vienna, 1979; BA summa cum laude, Gettysburg Coll., 1980; MA, JD, Vanderbilt U., 1984. Bar: Pa. 1984, D.C. 1985, U.S. Supreme Ct. 1995. Rsch. asst. Vanderbilt U., Nashville, 1982-84; legal intern U.S. State Dept., Washington, 1982; law clk. Stewart, Estes & Donnell, Nashville, 1983; atty. U.S. Dept. Agr., Washington, 1984-85; majority counsel subcom. on juvenile justice senate judiciary com. U.S. Senate, 1985-86, minority gen. counsel subcom. on constn., 1987, legis. dir. to Senator Arlen Specter, 1987-90; senate staff mem. Congrl. Crime Caucus, 1987-90; dep. dir. Nat. Inst. Justice U.S. Dept. Justice, Washington, 1990-93, acting dir., 1993-94; pres. Russell & Assocs., 1994-96; sr. pub. safety advisor Corp. Nat. Svc., 1994-96. Dep. chief of staff to Senator Ben Nighthorse Campbell, 1996—. Editorial staff Vanderbilt Jour. Transnat. Law, Nashville, 1982-83, contbr., 1983, rsch. editor, 1983-84 (editor award 1984). Mem. senate staff club, 1985-90, Bush/Quayle Campaign's Crime Adv. Com., 1988, Friends of the Nat. Parks at Gettysburg, Pa., 1989-98; bd. fellows Gettysburg Coll., 1990—; vol. Nat. Constrn. Ctr., Phila., 1990; mem. Bush/Quayle Adminstrn. S.E.S. Assn., 1990-92; Eisenhower Leadership Prize Dinner Com., Eisenhower World Affairs Inst., 1992, 93, mem. com. to celebrate bicentennial of constn., Northampton, Mass., 1987; mem. Bush/Quayle Alumni Assn., 1993—. Recipient Voluntary Svc. award VA, Northampton, 1978, Trustees award Forbes Libr., Northampton, 1989, cert. of appreciation Correctional Edn. Assn., 1991, Phi Alpha Delta, 1989, Fed. Bur. Alcohol, Tobacco and Firearms, 1989, Gettysburg Coll. Career Svcs. Office, 1992, Young Alumni Achievement award Gettysburg Coll., 1992, Wasserstein Fellowship Harvard Law Sch. Office of Pub. Interest Adv., 1995-96. Mem. Am. Soc. Internat. Law, Pa. Soc. of Washington, Phi Beta Kappa, Psi Chi (jr. award 1979). Avocations: racquetball, politics, volunteer svc. Office: Office Senator Ben Nighthorse Campbell 380 Russell Senate Office Bldg Washington DC 20510-0001

RUSSELL, TERRENCE, lawyer; b. Jacksonville, Fla., Sept. 26, 1944; AA, St. Leo Coll., 1964; BA, U. Fla., 1966; JD, Fla. State U., 1968. Bar: Fla. 1969. Law clk. to Hon. W.O. Mehrtens U.S. Dist. Ct. (so. dist.) Fla., 1969; atty. Ruden, McClosky, Smith, Schuster & Russell, P.A., Ft. Lauderdale, Fla. Mem. Fla. Supreme Ct. Appellate Restructure Commn., 1985-86; mem. Fed. Magistrate's merit selection panel, 1985; vice chmn. 17th Jud. Cir. Nominating Commn., 1982-84, chmn., 1985-86; mem. Fla. Supreme Ct. Nominating Commn., 1994—. Bd. govs. Nova U. Law Sch., 1981—; bd. dirs. Broward County Legal Aid Svcs., 1985-86. Mem. ABA (sects. litigation, legal edn.), Fla. Bar (special com. representation of death sentenced inmates 1984-85, bd. govs. 1987-91, pres. 2001-), Broward County Bar Assn. (chmn. special com. legal malpractice ins. 1978, jud. selection and tenure com. 1978-79, bar-bench liaison com. 1978, exec. com. 1980, 81, pres. 1984), No. Broward Bar Assn., Broward County Trial Lawyers Assn., Acad. of Fla. Trial Lawyers (coll. diplomates), Assn. Trial Lawyers Am., Am. Bar Found., Fla. Bar Found. (bd. dirs. 1992-98), Fla. State U. Law Sch. Alumni Assn. (pres. 1986, chmn. 1992-93), Delta Theta Phi, Gold Key. Office: Ruden McClosky et al PO Box 1900 Fort Lauderdale FL 33302-1900*

RUSSELL, THOMAS EDGIE, III, lawyer, construction materials company executive; b. Balt., Nov. 15, 1942; s. Thomas Edgie and Dorothy (Baier) R.; B.A., Wesleyan U., 1964; M.B.A., Wharton Sch., U. Pa., 1966; J.D., U. Md., 1969; m. Anne Woodford, Dec. 28, 1967; children—Catherine Neal, Thomas Edgie IV. Admitted to Md. bar, 1969; law clk. Md. Ct. Appeals, 1969-70; assoc. firm Melnicove, Greenberg & Kaufman, Balt., 1970-73; v.p., gen. counsel Arundel Corp., Balt., 1973-79, v.p. corp. devel., 1979-81, v.p. fin., 1981-84, exec. v.p., 1984— , also dir. Trustee Gilman Sch., Balt.; bd. dirs. Guilford Assn., Balt., Fla. Rock Industries, Helix Health System; chmn. Balt. City Cable TV Commn.; trustee, dir. Union Meml. Hosp., 1986—. Mem. ABA, Md. Bar Assn. Club: Balt. Country. Office: Arundel Corp 110 West Rd Baltimore MD 21204-2316

RUSSIN, JONATHAN, lawyer, consultant; b. Wilkes-Barre, Pa., Oct. 30, 1937; s. Jacob S. and Anne (Wartella) R.; m. Antoinette Stackpole, Oct. 6, 1962; children: Alexander, Andrew, Benjamin, Jacob. BA, Yale U., 1959, LLB, 1963. Bar: D.C. 1963. Guide interpreter Am. Nat. Exhibit, Moscow, 1959; rsch. asst. Law Faculty U. East Africa, Dar es Salaam, Tanganyika, 1961-62; regional legal adviser for Caribbean AID, 1967-69; ptnr. Kirkwood, Kaplan, Russin & Vecchi, Santo Domingo, Dominican Republic, 1969-74, Washington, 1974-78, Kaplan Russin & Vecchi, Madrid, 1978-81, Kaplan Russin & Vecchi, Washington, 1981-92; ptnr., dir. Russian practice group Russin & Vecchi, Moscow, 1992—. Washington rep. for Moscow Patriarchate of Russian Orthodox Ch.; convener adv. coun. Inst. for European, Russian and Eurasian Studies, George Washington U.; mem. adv. bd. Caribbean Am. Directory; trustee St. Nicholas Cathedral, Washington, St. Vladimir's Orthodox Theol. Sem., Crestwood, N.Y., 1985-93; legal adviser Orthodox Ch. in Am. Contbr. articles to profl. jours. Bd. dirs. Delphi Internat., Washington, 1988-2000, Dominican Am. Cultural Inst., Santo Domingo, 1988-92, Nat. Coun. Internat. Visitors, Washington, 1987-93, Fund for Democracy and Devel., Washington, 1993—, MUCIA Global Edn. Group, Inc., 1996—. Recipient Order of St. Vladimir, Moscow Patriarchate, Russian Orthodox Ch., 1991. Mem. ABA, L.Am. Studies Assn., Caribbean Studies Assn., Inter-Am. Bar Assn., Yale Club N.Y., Yale Club Washington. Republican. General corporate, Private international. Office: 815 Connecticut Ave NW Ste 650 Washington DC 20006-4004

RUSSO, DONNA MARIE, lawyer; b. Bklyn., Apr. 22, 1963; d. Frank Francis and Paulette Rita (Pagliaro) R. BA, Fordham U., 1984; JD, Hofstra U., 1986; M in Environ. Law, Vt. Law Sch., 1990. Bar: N.J. 1987, D.C. 1988, N.Y. 1996. Law clk. Staten Island (N.Y.) Dist. Atty., 1983-84, Law Offices of Donald V. Kane, Hempstead, N.Y., 1985-86, U.S. Dept. Health and Human Svcs., N.Y.C., 1985-86; assoc. Holzka, Donahue & Kuhn, Staten Island, 1986-88, Law Office of Philip J. Mattina, S.I., 1988-90, N.J. State Dept. Environ. Protection, Trenton, N.J., 1990-91, Cooper, Rose, & English, Summit and Rumson, 1991—. Mem. ABA, N.J. Bar Assn., N.Y. Bar Assn., D.C. Bar Assn., Essex County Inn of Ct. Environmental, Insurance.

RUSSO, FRANK, lawyer; b. Camden, N.J., Nov. 23, 1953; s. Frank Orlando Russo and Ruth Marie Zebedies; m. Colleen Marie Corr; 2 children. AA, Camden County C.C., 1974; BA, U. S. Fla., 1977; JD, Southwe. U., 1982; grad. Nat. Coll. DUI Def. program, Harvard U., 1997. Bar: Fla. 1985, Colo. 1992. Cert. legal intern then pros. atty. Office State Atty., Clearwater, Fla., 1983-86; pvt. practice St. Petersburg, 1986—. Pres. Meta Progress Inc.; guest lectr. U. S. Fla., St. Petersburg Jr. Coll.; treas. Cir. Ct. Jud. Campaign, 1996. Named Leading Am. Atty. Am. Rsch. Corp., 1998. Mem. Fla. Assn. Criminal Def. Lawyers, Pinellas County Bar Criminal Def. Lawyers Assn., St. Petersburg Bar Assn. Avocations: traveling, mountain biking. Criminal. Office: 11300 4th St N Ste 121 Saint Petersburg FL 33716-2939

RUSSO, ROY R. lawyer; b. Utica, N.Y., July 26, 1936; s. Chester F. and Helen L. (Gacek) R.; m. Ann M. Obernesser, Sept. 19, 1959; children: Andrew F., Susan Elizabeth. BA, Columbia U., 1956; LLB cum laude, Syracuse U., 1959. Bar: N.Y. 1959, D.C. 1967, U.S. Supreme Ct. 1969. Pvt. practice, Washington, 1959—; atty. FCC, 1959-66; ptnr. Cohn and Marks, 1966—; spl. counsel Nat. Cath. Conf. for Interracial Justice, 1984—. Lawyer; b. Utica, N.Y., July 26, 1936; s. Chester F. and Helen L. (Gacek) R.; m. Ann M. Obernesser, Sept. 19, 1959; children: Andrew F., Susan Elizabeth. BA, Columbia U., 1956; LLB cum laude, Syracuse U., 1959. Bar: N.Y. 1959, D.C. 1967, U.S. Supreme Ct. 1969. Pvt. practice law, Washington, 1959—; atty. FCC, Washington, 1959-66; ptnr. Cohn and Marks, Washington, 1966—; spl. counsel Nat. Cath. Conf. for Interracial Justice, Washington, 1984—. Mem. editl. adv. com. The Communications Act: A Legislative History of the Major Amendments 1934-96; mem. adv. bd. Pike and Fischer Comms. Regulation. Founding chmn. Commn. on Social Ministry, Richmond (Va.) Diocese, 1970-74; v.p., bd. dirs. St. Mary's Housing Corp., Annandale, Manassas, Fredericksburg, Ashburn, Va., 1971—; pres., bd. dirs. Caths. for Housing, Inc., 1979-84, Cath. Charities, Arlington (Va.) Diocese, 1980-84. With USAF, 1960-61. Recipient Alumni medal Alumni Fedn. Columbia U., 1994. Mem. ABA, Fed. Communications Bar Assn. (co-chair mass media practice com. 1988-91, nominations com. 1991-92), Computer Law Assn., Internat. Inst. Communications, John Jay Assocs., Soc. Columbia Grads., Columbia U. Club of Washington (sr. v.p. 1989-91, pres. 1991-95), Order of Coif, Phi Alpha Delta. Democrat. Club: Columbia Coll. (Washington) (mem. steering com. 1985—, chmn. Deans' Day program 1988-2000). Mem. editl. adv. com. The Communications Act: A Legislative History of the Major Amendments, 1934-96. Founding chmn. Commn. on Social Ministry, Richmond (Va.) Diocese, 1970-74; v.p., bd. dirs. St. Mary;s Housing Corp., Annandale, Manassas, Fredericksburg and Ashburn, Va., 1971—; pres., bd. dirs. Caths. for Housing, Inc., 1979-84, Cath. Charities, Arlington (Va.) Diocese, 1980-84. With USAF, 1960-61. Recipient Alumni medal Alumni Fedn. Columbia U., 1994. Mem. ABA, Fed. Comms. Bar Assn. (co-chair mass media practice com. 1988-91, nominations com. 1991-92), Computer Law Assn., Internat. Inst. Comms., John Jay Assocs., Soc. Columbia Grads., Columbia U. Club of Washignton (sr. v.p. 1989-91, pres. 1991-95), Columbia Coll. Club of Washingon (mem. steering com. 1985—, chmn. Deans' Day Program 1988-2000), Order of Coif, Phi Alpha Delta. Democrat. Communications. Home: 6528 Bowie Dr Springfield VA 22150-1309 Office: Cohn and Marks 1920 N St NW Ste 300 Washington DC 20036-1622

RUSSO, THOMAS ANTHONY, lawyer; b. N.Y.C., Nov. 6, 1943; s. Lucio F. and Tina (Iarossi) R.: m. Nancy Felipe, June 18, 1966 (div. 1974); m. Janice Davis, June 10, 1977 (div. 1979); m. Marcy C. Appelbaum, June 16, 1985; children: Morgan Danielle and Alexa Anne (twins), Tyler James. BA, Fordham U., 1965; MBA, JD, Cornell U., 1969. Bar: N.Y., 1970, U.S. Ct. Appeals (2d cir.) 1971, U.S. Dist. Ct. (so. and ea. dists.) N.Y. 1971, U.S. Ct. Appeals (7th cir.) 1982. Staff atty. SEC, Washington, 1969-71; assoc. Cadwalader, Wickersham & Taft, N.Y.C., 1971-75; dir. div. trading and markets Commodity Futures Trading Commn., Washington, 1975-77; ptnr. Cadwalader, Wickersham & Taft, N.Y.C., 1977-92, mgmt. com. vice chmn., chief legal officer; mng. dir., mem. op. com. Lehman Bros., 1993—. Vice chmn. bd. trustees Inst. for Fin. Mkts.; bd. dirs. Rev. Securities and Commodities Regulation, N.Y.C., Women's Interart Ctr.; trustee Inst. Internat. Edn., NYU Downtown Hosp., SEC Hist. Soc.; mem. nat. bd. dirs. March of Dimes, The econ. Club, Fgn. Policy Assn. Author: Regulation of the Commodities Futures and Options Markets; co-author: Regulation of Brokers, Dealers and Securities Markets, Supplement Markets; editorial bd. mem. Internat. Jour. Regulatory Law and Practice; practitioner bd. advisors Stanford Jour. of Law.; mem. editl. bd. Futures and Derivatives Law Report. Bd. trustees NYU Downdown Hosp., SEC Hist. Soc. Mem. ABA (mem. futures regulations, exec. coun., adv. com. on fed. regulation of securities, past co-chmn. derivative instruments subcom. of com. on fed. regulation), Assn. of Bar of City of N.Y. (chmn. internat. law sub com. of the com. on commodities regulation 1984-85, chmn. com. commodities regulations 1981-82), D.C. Bar Assn., Econ. Club N.Y. Banking, General corporate, Securities. Office: Lehman Bros Inc 200 Vesey St 10th Fl New York NY 10285-1000 E-mail: trusso1@lehman.com

RUSSON, LEONARD H. state supreme court justice; b. Salt Lake City, May 15, 1933; JD, Utah Coll., 1962. Pvt. practice, Salt Lake City, 1962-84; judge Utah Dist. Ct. (3d dist.), Utah Ct. Appeals; justice Utah Supreme Ct., Salt Lake City, 1995—. Vice chair Utah Bd. Dist. Ct. Judges; mem. Jud. Conduct Commn., Utah Supreme Ct. Adv. Com. on Code of Profl. Conduct. Office: Utah Supreme Ct PO Box 140210 450 S State St Salt Lake City UT 84114-0210*

RUSSONIELLO, JOSEPH PASCAL, lawyer; b. Jersey City, Oct. 12, 1941; s. Sabin G. and Justine B. (Terraciano) R.; m. Moira F. Ward, Aug. 29, 1969. B in Social Sci., Fairfield U., 1963; JD, NYU, 1966. Bar: N.J. 1967, Calif. 1969. Spl. agt. FBI, Washington, 1966-67; dep. dist. atty. City and County San Francisco (Calif.) Dist. Atty. Offices, 1969-75; assoc. Cooley Godward Castro Huddleson & Tatum, San Francisco, 1975-78; U.S. atty. U.S. Dept. Justice (no. dist.) Calif., 1982-90; ptnr. Cooley Godward L.L.P., 1978-82, 90—. Pres., bd. dirs. San Francisco (Calif.) Law Sch., 1996—; analyst KTVU-Ch. 2, Oakland, Calif., 1994—. Pres. Northgate Cottages, Napa, Calif., 1988—; chmn. Catholics for Truth and Justice, San Francisco, 1991—; v.p. Mid-Pacific region Nat. Italian Am. Fedn., 1996-99. Recipient Man of Yr. award NIAF, 1986, Man of Yr. award St. Thomas More Soc., San Francisco, 2000, Assumpta award Trustees St. Mary's Cathedral, 2000, Papal Pro Ecclesia medal, 2000; named Alumni of Yr.-Pub. Sector, NYU Law Sch., 1991. Fellow Am. Coll. Trial Lawyers; mem. Am. bd. Trial Lawyers (adv.), McFetridge Inn of Ct. (barrister). Republican. Avocations: tennis, golf, reading, playing the saxophone. Criminal, Government contracts and claims. Home: 2850 Jackson St San Francisco CA 94115-1146 Office: Cooley Godward LLP 1 Maritime Plz San Francisco CA 94111-3404 E-mail: Russonielloj@cooley.com

RUSSOTTI, PHILIP ANTHONY, lawyer; b. N.Y.C., Mar. 24, 1948; s. Philip Armond and Yolanda (Morelli) R.; m. Mary Wolfe, Jan. 20, 1973 (div. Mar., 1996); children: Thomas, Matthew, Peter; m. Kathleen Kettles, May 25, 1996. BA, Columbia U., 1970; JD, St. John's U., Queens, N.Y., 1973. Bar: N.Y. 1974, U.S. Dist. Ct. (so. dist.) N.Y. 1974, U.S. Dist. Ct. (ea. dist.) N.Y., 1980, U.S. Ct. Appeals (2nd cir.) 1982, U.S. Ct. Appeals (D.C. cir.) 1989, U.S. Ct. Internat. Trade 1986, U.S. Ct. Fed. Claims, 2000, U.S. Supreme Ct., 1997; bd. cert. civil trial atty. Nat. Bd. Trial Advocacy, 1997, U.S. Ct. Fed. Claims, 2000. Bur. chief, Supreme Ct. trial bur. asst. dist. atty. N.Y. County Dist. Atty.'s Office, N.Y.C., 1973-80; pvt. practice, 1980-84; partner Russotti & Barrison, 1985-89, Wingate, Russotti & Shapiro, N.Y.C., 1990—. Lectr. in the field. Gen. counsel Italian Am. Repertory Theatre, N.Y., 1985-90; mem. Prospect Park Alliance, Bklyn., 1996—. Recipient Am. Jurisprudence awards Bancroft Whitney & Lawyers Co-op, 1971, 73. Mem. ABA, ATLA, N.Y. State Bar Assn., N.Y. State Trial Lawyers Assn. Roman Catholic. General civil litigation, Personal injury, Product liability. Home: 433 3rd St Brooklyn NY 11215-2949 Office: Wingate Russotti Shapiro 420 Lexington Ave Rm 2750 New York NY 10170-2793 E-mail: prussotti@yahoo.com

RUST, JOHN HOWSON, JR. lawyer, state legislator; b. May 21, 1947; s. John Howson and Laura Jeanne (Johnson) R.; m. Susan Byrne, Aug. 15, 1970; children: John W., Thomas A., Robert B. BA, U. Va., 1969, JD, 1972. Bar: Va. 1972, U.S. Dist. Ct. (ea. dist.) Va. 1973, U.S. Ct. Appeals (4th cir.) 1975, U.S. Supreme Ct. 1976. Mem. firm Rust & Rust, P.C.; mem. Ho. of Dels., Commonwealth of Va., 1980-82, 96—. Mem. Wilkes Artis, A Profl. Corp., Fairfax, Va.; mem. Ho. of Dels., Commonwealth of Va., 1980-82, 96—. Banking, Federal civil litigation, Contracts commercial. Office: PO Box 460 10370 Main St Fairfax VA 22030-0460 E-mail: johnhr@erols.com

RUTH, BRYCE CLINTON, JR. lawyer; b. Greenwood, Miss., Dec. 19, 1948; s. Bryce Clinton and Kathryn (Arant) R.; m. Martha M. Ruth; children: Lauren Elizabeth, Bryce Clinton III. BS, Delta State U., 1970; JD, Memphis State U., 1979. Bar: Tenn., 1979, U.S. Dist. Ct. (mid. dist.) Tenn. 1979, U.S. Ct. Mil. Appeals 1991, U.S. Ct. Appeals (6th cir.), 1994. Criminal investigation spl. agt. IRS, Memphis and Nashville, 1971-82; asst. dist. atty. Dist. Atty. Office, Gallatin, Tenn., 1982-89; asst. pub. defender Pub. Defender's Office, 1989-90; pvt. practice White House, 1989—; judge City of Cross Plains, Tenn., 1992—; juvenile ct. referee judge Robertson County, 1995-98. Mem. dist. investigating com. dist. VI Tenn. Bd. Law Examiners, 1989—; mem. child enforcement steering com. Asst. Dist. Atty. Office, 1983-84, chmn. legis. subcom., 1985; lectr. in field. Chmn. fin. com. White House First United Meth. Ch., 1983-88, trustee, 1988-90, chmn., 1990; trustee Vol. State Coll. Found., 1993-2000, chmn., 1998-99; bd. dirs. Crime Stoppers of Sumner County, 1989-94; bd. dirs. White House Youth Soccer, 1992-93, coach, 1987-91; bd. dirs. White House Soccer Booster Club, 1996-2000, pres., 1998; bd. dirs. Sumner County CASA, 1992-93; coach Jr. Pro Football, 1980-85; video cameraman for football team White House H.S., 1991—; mem. Leadership Sumner, 1989; bd. dirs. White House Men's Club, 1981-83, 85-88, v.p., 1984, 88, pres., 1985. Lt. col. JAGC, USAR, 1983—. Recipient Disting. Expert award for pistol marksmanship U.S. Treasury, Disting. Svc. award City of White House. Mem. NRA, Tenn. Bar Assn. (del. 1993—, mem. family law code revision commn. 1996—), Sumner County Bar Assn. (chmn. domestic rels. com. 1984-85, v.p. 1998-99, pres. 1999-2000), White House Area C. of C. (bd. dirs. 1990-95, pres. 1993-94), United C. of C. of Sumner County (pres. 1995). Avocations: scuba diving, skiing, golf, hunting, pistol shooting. General civil litigation, Criminal, Family and matrimonial. Office: 3210 Hwy 31W PO Box 68 White House TN 37188-0068 E-mail: bcruthjr@aol.com

RUTH, JOHN NICHOLAS, lawyer, insurance company executive; b. Balt., Feb. 27, 1934; s. John Nicholas and Louise (Hochrein) R.; m. Dolores B. Baumgartner, June 13, 1959; children: John Nicholas, Joan Dolores, Anne Dolores. BSBA, John Hopkins U., 1964; JD, U. Md., 1968. Bar: Md. 1968, U.S. Ct. Appeals (fed. cir.) 1968, U.S. Supreme Ct. 1975. Chief investigator Office of Md. Atty. Gen., Balt., 1967-72, asst. atty. gen., chief consumer protection div., 1972-79; assoc. George W. McManus, Balt., 1979-81; atty. Nationwide Ins. Co., Annapolis, Md., 1981-86, regional claim atty., 1986—; lectr. consumer law U. Md., College Park, 1974—. Mem. Gov.'s Commn. to Study Mechanic Lien Laws, 1977, Commn. to Study Electronic Fund Transfers, 1978; mem. Balt. Neighborhoods, 1977—, bd. dirs., 1978; mem. Wholesome Meat Adv. Council, 1975-79, Fed. Exec. Bd., 1975-79, Met. Council Consumer Agys., 1970-79. Served with USN, 1954-56. Mem. Md. State Bar Assn. Democrat. Roman Catholic. Consumer commercial, Insurance. Home: 301 Halsey Rd Annapolis MD 21401-3218 Office: Nationwide Ins Co 2500 Riva Rd Annapolis MD 21401-7405

RUTHERFORD, CONSTANCE MARY, lawyer; b. San Francisco, Oct. 3, 1948; d. F. James and Barbara (Webster) Rutherford; m. Peter Schofield, Apr. 12, 1969 (div. 1972); m. Bruce Robison, Aug. 12, 1973 (div. 1976); 1 adopted child, Mikhaila. BA, U. Calif., Santa Barbara, 1977; JD, U. Calif., Davis, 1980. Dep. city atty. San Francisco City Atty., 1980-87; dep. county counsel Santa Clara County Counsel, San Jose, Calif., 1988-89, Alameda County Counsel, Oakland, 1989—. Mem. adv. bd. Ct. Apptd. Spl. Advocates, Oakland, 1991—; mem. Alameda County Ednl. Task Force, Oakland, 1999—, chair, 2000—. Bd. dirs. Positive Impact, Oakland, 1985-92, Children of Light, Mill Valley, Calif., 1993-97, Alameda Island Aquatics, 1997-99; vol. Children's Hosp. of Oakland, 1987-91. Democrat. Avocations: reading, thinking, devotion to handicapped child adopted from Russia. Home: 1161 Camino Del Valle Alameda CA 94502-6846 Office: Alameda County Counsel 1221 Oak St Ste 463 Oakland CA 94612-4227

RUTKOFF, ALAN STUART, lawyer; b. Chgo., May 31, 1952; s. Roy and Harriet (Ruskin) R.; m. Mally Zoberman, Dec. 22, 1974; children: Aaron Samuel, Jordana Michal, Robert Nathaniel. BA with high distinction, U. Mich., 1973; JD magna cum laude, Northwestern U., 1976. Bar: Ill. 1976, U.S. Dist. Ct. (no. dist.) Ill. 1976, U.S. Ct. Appeals (7th cir.) 1977, U.S. Ct. Appeals (3d cir.) 1978, U.S. Supreme Ct. 1981, U.S. Ct. Appeals (5th cir.) 1983, U.S. Ct. Appeals (8th cir.) 1990, U.S. Dist. Ct. (we. dist.) Wis. 1996. Assoc. Altheimer & Gray, Chgo., 1976-80; ptnr. Kastel & Rutkoff, 1980-83, Holleb & Coff Ltd., Chgo., 1983-84, McDermott, Will & Emery, Chgo., 1984—. Pres. N. Suburban Synagogue Beth El, Highland Pk., Ill., 1999-2001.. Mem. ABA, Chgo. Bar Assn., Order of Coif. General civil litigation, Labor, Professional liability. Home: 801 Timberhill Rd Highland Park IL 60035-5148 Office: McDermott Will & Emery 227 W Monroe St Ste 3100 Chicago IL 60606-5096 E-mail: arutkoff@mwe.com

RUTLEDGE, ROGER KEITH, lawyer; b. Knoxville, Tenn., Dec. 27, 1946; s. Joseph P. and Jean Mae (Karnes) R.; m. Lily Mee Kin Hee, June 6, 1970; children: Amelia Leilani, Sarah Elizabeth. BA in History with honors, U. N.C., 1968; JD cum laude, Am. U., 1977. Bar: Tenn. 1977, U.S. Dist. Ct. (we. dist.) Tenn. 1978, U.S. Supreme Ct. 1982. Served in U.S. Peace Corps, Nepal, 1968-70; fgn. service officer U.S. Dept. State, Washington and Italy, 1971-76; ptnr. Rutledge & Rutledge, Memphis, 1977—. Pres. Jabez Burns, Inc., 1998-99. Editor fiction Carolina Quar., 1967-68; assoc. editor Am. U. Law Rev., 1976-77. Mem. campaign com.

Albert Gore Jr. U.S. Senate, Shelby County, 1984, for pres. campaign, 1988, 2000; bd. chmn. United Meth. Neighborhood Ctrs., Inc., 1992. Mem. ABA, Tenn. Bar Assn., Memphis Bar Assn. (editor Bar Forum 1986, asst. editor 1987). Democrat. Methodist. General civil litigation, General corporate, General practice. Office: Rutledge & Rutledge 1053 W Rex Rd Memphis TN 38119-3819

RUTSTEIN, DAVID W. lawyer, food products executive; b. N.Y.C., July 7, 1944; s. David and Mazie (Weissman) R.; m. Rena E. Bergsmann, July 19, 1967; children: Sara E., Charles B. BA, U. Pa., 1966; JD with honors, George Washington U., 1969. Bar: Pa. 1969, D.C. 1969. Dep. atty. gen., Pa., 1969-70; ptnr. firm Danzansky, Dickey, Tydings, Quint & Gordon, Washington, 1970-78; sr. v.p., gen. counsel Giant Food, Inc., 1978—; of counsel Venable Law Firm, 2001—. Bd. dirs., chmn., treas. Washington Met. Bd. Trade, Fed. City Council. Bd. dirs., pres. Washington Hebrew Home for Aged, 1989-91; mem. exec. com. Fed. City Coun.; chmn. Agnes and Eugene Meyer Found., Wash. Met. Bd. Trade; trustee Greater Washington Rsch. Ctr. Mem. D.C. Bar Assn., Washington Met. Area Corp. Counsel Assn. (pres. 1986). Jewish. Contracts commercial, General corporate. Home: 9 Greentree Ct Bethesda MD 20817-1440 Office: Giant Food Inc Dept 593 PO Box 1804 Washington DC 20013-1804

RUTTENBERG, HAROLD SEYMOUR, lawyer; b. Chgo., Oct. 27, 1941; s. Irving Norman and Marge Harriet (Roth) R.; children from previous marriage: Adam, Michael, Leslie; m. Marcia Patsy Pritikin, Jan. 3, 1983; children: Sheronna, Aaron. BBA, U. Wis., 1962; JD, Northwestern U., 1965; LLM, Georgetown U., 1968. Bar: Ill. 1965, Minn. 1970, Iowa 1972, U.S. Dist. Ct. (no. dist.) Ill. 1965, U.S. Tax Ct. 1969, U.S. Claims Ct. 1969, U.S. Supreme Ct. 1969. Atty. Office of Chief Counsel Interpretive divsn. IRS, Washington, 1965-69; assoc. Mullin, Galison, Swirnoff & Weinberg, Mpls., 1969-71, Doherty, Rumble & Butler, St. Paul, 1971-72; assoc. gen. counsel Meredith Corp., Des Moines, 1972-83; v.p., gen. counsel Meredith/Burda, 1983-87; v.p., counsel Norwest Bank, 1987-92; ctr. mgr. First Data Resources, 1992-95; pres., compliance officer, CRA officer, security officer human resource dir., Fingerhut Nat. Bank, 1995-97; COO credit card divsn. Am. Nat. Bank of Dekalb (Ill.), 1997-2000, COO processing source internat. underwriting divsn., 2000—. Bd. dirs. Goodwill Industries, Des Moines, 1973-75, Iowa Taxpayers Assn., Des Moines, 1972-87, Bur. for Jewish Living, Des Moines, 1981—, chairperson fin. com., 1986—; v.p. tax com. Iowa Assn. Bus. and Industry, 1986; mem. action coun. Des Moines Ctr. Sci. and Industry, 1975-79, 84—; sec. Greenwood Elem. Sch. PTA, Des Moines, 1982-83; mem. adv. bd. Blank Park Zoo, 1985-87. Mem. Iowa Assn. Bus. and Industry (vice chmn. tax com. 1986-87), Polk-Des Moines Taxpayers Assn. (dir., mem. exec. com. 1985). Independent. General corporate, Immigration, naturalization, and customs, Pension, profit-sharing, and employee benefits. Home: 55 W Delaware Pl Apt 907 Chicago IL 60610-6077 Office: Norwest 6200 Aurora Ave 8430 W Bryn Mawr Ste 720 Chicago IL 60631

RUTTER, MARSHALL ANTHONY, lawyer; b. Pottstown, Pa., Oct. 18, 1931; s. Carroll Lennox and Dorothy (Tagert) R.; m. Winifred Hitz, June 6, 1953 (div. 1970); m. Virginia Ann Hardy, Jan. 30, 1971 (div. 1992); children: Deborah Frances, Gregory Russell, Theodore Thomas; m. Terry Susan Knowles, Dec. 19, 1992. BA, Amherst (Mass.) Coll., 1954; JD, U. Pa., 1959. Bar: Calif 1960. Assoc. O'Melveny & Myers, Los Angeles, 1959-64, Flint & MacKay, Los Angeles, 1964-67, ptnr., 1967-72, Rutter, Hobbs & Davidoff, Los Angeles, 1973—. Bd. dirs. Ojai Festivals Ltd., 2001. Gov. The Music Ctr. of L.A. County, 1978-86, 89-92; bd. dirs. Music Ctr. Operating Co., 1992-96; bd. dirs. Chorus Am., Washington, 1987-96, pres., 1993-95; bd. dirs. L.A. Master Chorale Assn., 1964—, pres., 1980-92, chmn. 1992-96, vice chmn., 1996—; vestryman All Saints Ch., Beverly Hills, Calif., 1983-86, 88-90. Mem. ABA, Assn. Bus. Trial Lawyers (bd. dirs. 1980-82), L.A. County Bar Assn., Beverly Hills Bar Assn., Century City Bar Assn., English-Speaking Union (various offices L.A. chpt. 1963-91), L.A. Jr. C. of C. (bd. dirs. 1964-67). Democrat. Episcopalian. Avocations: classical and choral music, golf. General civil litigation, Environmental, Family and matrimonial. Home: 1045 S Orange Grove Blvd Apt 10 Pasadena CA 91105-1795 Office: Rutter Hobbs & Davidoff Ste 2700 1900 Ave of Stars Los Angeles CA 90067-4508 Fax: 310-286-1728. E-mail: mar@rhdlaw.com

RUTTER, ROBERT PAUL, lawyer; b. Cleve., Apr. 25, 1954; s. Robert Skyles and Mary Jane (Glitz) R.; m. Kathy Alison Deliberato, Dec. 13, 1975; children; Robert, Joe, Kate, Anne. BS in Acctg., Ohio State U., 1975; JD, Case Western Res. U., 1979. Bar: Ohio, 1979; U.S. Dist. Ct. (no. dist.) Ohio 1993, D.C., 1995, U.S. Dist. Ct. (so. dist.) Ind. 1994, U.S. Dist. Ct. (no. dist.) Ind. 1995. Contbr. articles to profl. jours. Mem. Assn. Trial Lawyers Am., Ohio State Bar Assn., Ohio Acad. Trial Lawyers, Cleve. Acad. Trial Lawyers. Insurance, Personal injury. Home: 6591 Beechwood Dr Independence OH 44131-4635 Office: 4700 Rockside Rd Ste 650 Independence OH 44131-2148 E-mail: brutter@mindspring.com

RUTZICK, MARK CHARLES, lawyer; b. St. Paul, Sept. 6, 1948; s. Max Arthur and Bertha (Ward) R.; children by previous marriage: Elizabeth Leslie, Karen Deborah; m. Cynthia Lombardi, Jan. 16, 1994; 1 child, Samuel Ryan. BA, U. Mich., 1970; JD, Harvard U., 1973. Bar: N.Y. 1974, U.S. Supreme Ct. 1977, U.S. Ct. Appeals (9th cir.) 1982, Oreg. 1984, Wash. 1987. Spl. asst. corp. counsel N.Y.C. Housing Adminstrn., 1973-75; assoc. Alexander Hammond P.C., N.Y.C., 1975-76; asst. atty. gen. Office N.Y. State Atty. Gen., 1976-78; atty. Dept. Justice, Washington, 1978-82, spl. litig. counsel, 1982-83, atty.-in-charge field office Portland, Oreg., 1983-86; counsel Preston, Thorgrimson, Shidler, Gates & Ellis, 1986-87, ptnr., 1988-94, LeBoeuf, Lamb, Greene & MacRae, L.L.P., Portland, 1996-99; shareholder Mark C. Rutzick Law Firm, P.C., 1994-96, 99—. Mem. ABA, Oreg. Bar Assn., Wash. State Bar Assn. Administrative and regulatory, Federal civil litigation. Home: 3450 SW Downsview Ter Portland OR 97221-3173 Office: 222 SW Columbia St Ste 1600 Portland OR 97201-6616

RUXIN, PAUL THEODORE, lawyer; b. Cleve., Apr. 14, 1943; s. Charles and Olyn Judith (Koller) R.; m. Joanne Camy, May 25, 1965; children; Marc J., Sarah. BA, Amherst Coll., 1965; LLB, U. Va., 1968. Bar: Ill. 1968, U.S. Dist. Ct. (no. dist.) Ill. 1968, U.S. Ct. Appeals D.C. 1972. Assoc. Isham, Lincoln & Beale, Chgo., 1968-73, ptnr., 1974-77; ptnr., chmn. energy utilities sect. Jones, Day, Reavis & Pogue, Cleve., 1977—. Mem. Hudson Archtl. and Hist. Bd. Rev., 1981-81; mem. Folger Shakespeare Libr. Com., 1999—; exec. bd. Greater Cleve. Boy Scouts Am., 1978-90; bd. dirs. Cleve. chpt. ARC, 1991-97. Mem. ABA, Ohio State Bar Assn. (pub. utilities sect.), Bar Assn. Greater Cleve., Fed. Energy Bar Assn. (com. chmn. 1981), Chgo. Bar Assn., Club at Soc. Ctr., Rowfant Club, Chgo. Club, Caxton Club, Grolier Club. Administrative and regulatory, FERC practice, Public utilities. Office: Jones Day Reavis & Pogue 77 W Wacker Dr Fl 35 Chicago IL 60601-1662 also: 901 Lakeside Ave Cleveland OH 44114-1116 E-mail: paultruxin@jonesday.com

RYAN, DONALD SANFORD, lawyer; b. Little Rock, July 9, 1934; s. John Fergus and Fay (Stuckey) R.; m. Joyce Scarbarough, Dec. 15, 1961; children: William, Thomas, Catherine. BA, Ark. Poly., 1957; JD, U Ark., 1960. Bar: Ark. 1960, Dist., Cir. Cts. Ark. 1960. Atty. Pope, Pratt & Schamburger, Little Rock, 1960-67; instr. Ark. Law Sch., 1965; atty. Dodds, Kidd, Ryan & Moore, 1967—. Fellow Am. Coll. Trial Lawyers; mem. ABA, Ark. Bar Assn., Ark. Trial Lawyers Assn. (pres. 1969-71), Assn. Trial Lawyers Am., Pulaski County Bar Assn.; assoc. Am. Bd. Trial Assocs. Methodist. General practice, Personal injury. Office: Dodds Kidd Ryan & Moore 313 W 2nd St Little Rock AR 72201-2409

RYAN, JAMES E. state attorney general; b. Chgo., Feb. 21, 1946; m. Marie Ryan; children: John, Jim, Matt, Amy, Patrick, Anne marie (dec.). BA in Polit. Sci., Ill. Benedictine Coll., 1968; JD, Ill. Inst. Tech., 1971. Bar: Ill. 1971. Asst. state's atty. criminal divsn. DuPage County State's Atty.'s Office, 1971-74, 1st. asst. state's atty., 1974-76; founder Ryan & Darrah; state's atty. DuPage County State's Atty.'s Office, 1984-94; atty. gen. State of Ill., 1994—. Recipient numerous awards from various orgns. including Nat. Assn. Counties, Alliance Against Intoxicated Motorists; named Lawyer of Yr. DuPage County Bar Assn., 1997. Mem. Ill. State's Attys. Assn. (past pres.; Ezzard Charles award). Republican. Roman Catholic. Office: Office of Atty General 500 S 2nd St Springfield IL 62706-0001

RYAN, JAMES JOSEPH, retired lawyer; b. Cin., June 17, 1929; s. Robert J. and Marian (Hoffman) R.; m. Mary A. Noonan, Nov. 25, 1954; children: Kevin, Timothy, Nora, Daniel. AB, Xavier U., 1951; JD, U. Cin., 1954. Bar: Ohio 1954. Tchr. assoc. Northwestern U., Chgo., 1954-55; ptnr. Dolle, O'Donnell & Cash, Cin., 1958-71, Taft, Stettinius & Hollister, Cin., 1971-99. Lectr. U. Cin. Coll. Law, 1960-65. Chmn. Health Planning Assn. Ohio River Valley, Cin., 1978-85; bd. dirs. Hamilton County Bd. of Mentally Retarded, 1968-80; trustee Resident Home for Mentally Retarded, 1980-97, St. Francis-St. George Hosp. Devel. Coun., 1989-99. Mem. ABA, Ohio Bar Assn., Cin. Bar Assn., Queen City Club, Western Hill Club. Republican. Roman Catholic. Avocations: reading, sports. Estate planning, Corporate taxation, Taxation, general. Home: 5316 Cleves Warsaw Pike Cincinnati OH 45238-3602 Office: 1800 Firstar Tower 425 Walnut St Cincinnati OH 45202-3923

RYAN, JAMES LEO, federal judge; b. Detroit, Nov. 19, 1932; s. Leo Francis and Irene Agnes R.; m. Mary Elizabeth Rogers, Oct. 12, 1957; children: Daniel P., James R., Colleen M. Hansen, Kathleen A. LLB, U. Detroit, 1956, BA, 1992; LLD (hon.), Madonna Coll., 1976, Detroit Coll. Law, 1978, Thomas M. Cooley Law Sch., Lansing, Mich., 1986, U. Detroit Sch. Law, 1986. Justice of peace, Redford Twp., Mich., 1963-66; cir. judge 3d Jud. Circuit Mich., 1966-75; justice Mich. Supreme Ct., 1975-86; judge U.S. Ct. Appeals (6th cir.), 1986—. Faculty Nat. Jud. Coll., Reno. Contbr. article to legal jour. Served with JAGC, USNR, 1957-60; to capt. JAGC, mil. judge Res., 1960-92, ret., 1992. Mem. Fed. Judges Assn., State Bar Mich., Fed. Bar Assn., KC. Office: US Ct Appeals US Courthouse 231 W Lafayette Blvd Detroit MI 48226-2700

RYAN, JOHN DUNCAN, lawyer; b. Portland, Oreg., Dec. 20, 1920; s. Thomas Gough and Virgian Abigail (Hadley) R.; m. Florence A. Ryan, Jan. 30, 1970 (dec. 1987); m. Virginia Kane Wilson, June 15, 1996. BS, Fordham U., 1943; JD, Lewis & Clark Coll., Portland, 1950. Bar: Oreg. 1950. Pvt. practice, Portland, 1950—. Adj. instr. Northwestern Sch. Law Lewis & Clark Coll., 1953-70. Author: (poems) Expressions, 1993, Expressions II, 1995, Expressions III, 1998-99. Sgt. Air Corps, U.S. Army, 1942-46, ETO. Recipient St. Thomas More award Catholic Lawyers for Social Justice, 1993. Mem. ABA (Oreg. delegate 1985-93, chmn. spl. com. on law & literacy 1991-93), Am. Coll. Trial Lawyers, Am. Trial Lawyers Assn., Oreg. State Bar (bd. govs. 1963-67), Oreg. Trial Lawyers Assn. (Trial Lawyer of Yr. 1993), Multnomah County Bar Assn. (Professionalism award 1997), Washington County Bar Assn. Admiralty, Federal civil litigation, General civil litigation. Home and Office: 1206 Circulo Aguilar Rio Rico AZ 85648-3355 and: 503 SW Colony Dr Portland OR 97219-7763 E-mail: ryan98@theriver.com

RYAN, JOSEPH W., JR. lawyer; b. Phila., June 24, 1948; s. Joseph W. Sr. and Marie R. (Hillgrube) R.; m. Mary Pat Law, Sept. 11, 1971; children: Caitlin, Joseph W. III. BA, St. Joseph's U., Phila., 1970; MA, Villanova U., 1971; JD, U. Va., 1978. Bar: Ohio 1978, U.S. Supreme Ct. 1982. Ptnr. Porter, Wright, Morris & Arthur, Columbus, Ohio, 1978—. Lectr. Sch. Dentistry Ohio State U., Columbus, 1982-89, Continuing Legal Edn. Inst., 1984—; mem. trial acad. faculty Internat. Assn. Def. Counsel, Boulder, Colo., 1994. Author: Use of Demonstrative Evidence, 1985; assoc. editor Litigation News, 1986—, editor in chief, 2000—. Trustee Columbus Zool. Assn., 1980-90; bd. dirs. Columbus Speech and Hearing Ctr., 1988-99, pres., 1995-96. Mem. ABA, Ohio State Bar Assn., Columbus Bar Assn., Internat. Assn. Def. Counsel, Am. Arbitration Assn. (panel of arbitrators). Republican. Roman Catholic. General civil litigation, Insurance, Public utilities. Office: Porter Wright Morris & Arthur 41 S High St Ste 30 Columbus OH 43215-6101 E-mail: jryan@porterwright.com

RYAN, LEONARD EAMES, judge; b. Albion, N.Y., July 8, 1930; s. Bernard and Harriet Earle (Fitts) R.; m. Ann Allen, June 18, 1973; 1 child, Thomas Eames Allen-Ryan. Grad., Kent Sch., 1948; AB, U. Pa., 1954; JD, NYU, 1962. Bar: D.C. 1963, N.Y. 1963, U.S. Ct. Appeals (D.C. cir.) 1963, U.S. Dist. Ct. (so. and ea. dists.) N.Y. 1965, U.S. Ct. Appeals (2nd cir.) 1966, U.S. Supreme Ct. 1967. Field engr. constrn. U.S. Steel Fairless Works, Morrisville, Pa., 1951-52; reporter Upper Darby (Pa.) News, 1954; newsman AP, Pitts., Phila., Harrisburg, N.Y.C., 1955-62; reporter, spl. writer on law N.Y. Times, 1962-63; info. adviser corp. hdqrs. IBM, N.Y.C., 1963; trial atty. firm Perrell, Nielsen & Stephens, 1964-66; trial atty. civil rights div. Dept. Justice, Washington, 1966-68; asst. to dir. bus. affairs CBS News, N.Y.C., 1968; program officer Office Govt. and Law, Ford Found., 1968-74; pvt. practice law, cons. pub. affairs, 1974-91; v.p., sec. W. P. Carey & Co., Inc., 1977-83; impartial hearing officer Edn. for All Handicapped Children Act of 1975, 1976-91; per diem adminstrv. law judge N.Y. State Agys., 1976-91; hearing examiner N.Y. State Family Ct., 1980-81; apptd. U.S. adminstv. law judge, 1991; adminstv. law judge Office Hearings and Appeals, San Rafael, Calif., 1991-93, Phila., 1993-94, N.Y.C., 1994—. Arbitrator Small Claims Ct., N.Y.C., 1974-84; bd. dirs. Community Action for Legal Svcs. Inc., N.Y.C., 1971-77, vice-chmn., 1975-77; co-chmn. Citizens Com. to Save Legal Svcs., N.Y.C., 1975-76; bd. dirs. Lower East Side Svc. Ctr., N.Y.C., 1977-89. Author: (with Bernard Ryan Jr.) So You Want to Go Into Journalism, 1963; contbr. articles to profl. jours. Served with USAR, 1950-57. Mem. Am. Judicature Soc., Assn. of Bar of City of N.Y., N.Y. State Bar Assn., St. Elmo Club (Phila.), Heights Casino (Bklyn.). Home: 32 Orange St Brooklyn NY 11201-1634 Office: 111 Livingston St Brooklyn NY 11201-5078

RYAN, ROBERT COLLINS, lawyer; b. Evanston, Ill., Sept. 15, 1953; s. Donald Thomas and Patricia J. (Collins) R.; m. Joanne Kay Holata, Nov. 5, 1983. BA in Econs., BS in Indsl. Engring. with high honors, U. Ill., 1976; JD, Northwestern U., 1979. Bar: Ill. 1979, U.S. Dist. Ct. (no. dist.) Ill. 1980, U.S. Ct. Appeals (Fed. cir.) 1982, U.S. Supreme Ct. 1984, Nev. 1999. Assoc. Allegretti, Newitt, Witcoff & McAndrews, Ltd., Chgo., 1979-83, ptnr., 1983-88; founding ptnr. McAndrews, Held & Malloy, Ltd., 1988-96, of counsel, 1996—; v.p. digital gen. sys., Inc. CNASDAQ DGIT, 2001—. Chief legal and intellectual property officer, exec. v.p. StarGuide Digital Networks, Inc., Reno, 1996-; ; mem. Ian Burns & Assocs., P.C., Reno, 1998—; of counsel Pauley, Petersen, Kinne & Fejer, Hoffman Estates, Ill., 1998—; lectr. engring. law Northwestern U. Tech. Inst., Evanston, Ill., 1981-85, adj. prof. engring. law, 1985-90; lectr. patent law and appellate practice John Marshall Law Sch., 1991-93, adj. prof. patent law and appellate advocacy, 1993—; mem. faculty Nat. Jud. Coll., Reno, Nev., 1998—; mem. alumni bd. mech. and indsl. engring. dept. U. Ill., Urbana, 1996—. Exec. editor Northwestern Jour. Internat. Law & Bus., 1978-79; contbr. articles to profl. jours. Dir. Washoe Assn. Retarded Citizens, Reno, 1997—, sec., 2001—. James scholar U. Ill., 1976. Mem. ABA, Fed. Cir. Bar Assn., Intellectual Property Law Assn. Chgo., Licensing Execs. Soc., Tau Beta Pi, Phi Eta Sigma, Alpha Pi Mu, Phi Kappa Phi. Computer, Patent, Trademark and copyright. Home: 95 Rimfire Cir Reno NV 89509-2989 Office: StarGuide Digital Networks 300 E 2nd St Ste 1510 Reno NV 89501-1591

RYAN, ROBERT DAVIS, lawyer; b. Lynbrook, N.Y., Aug. 14, 1941; s. Thomas Francis and Agnes Frances (Davis) R.; children: John, Daniel, Carolyn. BBA, St. John's U., 1962; JD, Fordham U., 1972. Bar: N.Y. 1973, U.S. Dist. Ct. (so. and ea. dists.) N.Y. 1973, U.S. Ct. Appeals (2d cir.) 1975, U.S. Supreme Ct. 1984. Asst. dist. atty. Westchester County, White Plains, N.Y., 1972-77; assoc. Clark, Gagliardi & Miller, 1977-82; ptnr. Rende, Ryan & Downes, 1982—. Adj. prof. law St. John's U., 1992-95, 99—. Chmn. Cable TV Adv. Com., Lewisboro, N.Y., 1983-99. Mem. Assn. Trial Lawyers Am., N.Y. State Trial Lawyers Assn., Westchester County Bar Assn., N.Y. State Bar Assn. (continuing legal edn. com. trial lawyers sect.), No. Westchester Bar Assn. (bd. govs. 1987-92, pres. 1986-87), White Plains Bar Assn. Republican. Roman Catholic. General civil litigation, Personal injury, Product liability. Home: PO Box 113 Bedford NY 10506-0113 Office: Rende Ryan & Downes 202 Mamaroneck Ave Ste 600 White Plains NY 10601-5312

RYAN, THOMAS J. lawyer; b. Waltham, Mass., Sept. 10, 1945; s. Joseph H. and Mary (Murphy) R.; m. Margaret Atkins, June 21, 1969. BA, St. Lawrence U., 1968; JD with honors, Suffolk U., 1974; LLM in Trade Regulation, NYU, 1977; PMD, Harvard U. , 1982. Bar: Mass. 1974, N.Y 1975, Wis. 1984. Sales rep. Gen. Foods Corp., New Haven, 1969-71, atty., White Plains, N.Y., 1974-76, sr. atty., 1976-77, counsel, 1977-80, sr. counsel, 1980-83; dir. legal svcs. Oscar Mayer Foods Corp., Madison, Wis., 1983-84, v.p., gen. counsel, sec., 1984-94; v.p., gen. counsel Pillsbury Brands, Mpls., 1994—; bd. dirs. Oscar Mayer Found., Madison, 1984-86; mem. allocations com. Dane County United Way, 1984-88, co-chair, 1987-88, bd. dirs. 1991-94; chmn. legal com. Pet Food Inst., 1978-80; chmn. legal com. Am. Meat Inst., 1987-90. Trustee law alumni Suffolk U., 1982-85; alumni rep., admissions office St. Lawrence U., Canton, N.Y., 1983—; v.p. exec. com., bd. dirs. Madison Repertory Theatre, 1989-94, pres., 1993-94; bd. dirs. Red Cross Dane County, 1991-94, Ronald McDonald House, 1992-94, Children's Theatre Co. of Mpls., 1994—, Greater Mpls. Red Cross, 1995—. Mem. ABA (anti-trust and corp. sects., corp. counseling com., Robinson-Patman com.), Am. Corp. Counsel Assn., Wis. State Bar, Sigma Chi (chpt. trustee 1970-83), Harvard Club of N.Y.C., Madison Club, Mpls. Athletic Club, Wayzata Country Club. Administrative and regulatory, General corporate, Private international. Office: The Pillsbury Co 200 S 6th St Ste 200 Minneapolis MN 55402-6005

RYAN, THOMAS PATRICK, lawyer; b. N.Y.C., Dec. 16, 1940; s. Thomas Patrick and Mary Agnes (Hughes) R.; m. Megan Mery, Oct. 1981; children: Judith Ann, Thomas Arthur, Evan Rees, Catherine Maura. BA, St. John's U., Jamaica, N.Y., 1962; MA, U. Notre Dame, 1963; JD, Fordham U., 1973. Bar: N.Y. 1974, U.S. Dist. Ct. (so. and ea. dists.) N.Y. 1976, U.S. Ct. Appeals (2d cir.) 1976. Lectr. Ind. U., South Bend, 1965-70; exec. dir. office of labor relations and collective bargaining N.Y.C. Bd. Edn., 1972-96. Mem. ABA, N.Y. Bar Assn., Am. Arbitration Assn. (com. continuing edn. 1984—). Democrat. Roman Catholic. Avocations: literature, baseball, basketball. Home: 207 Midwood St Brooklyn NY 11225-5058 Office: O'Dwyer & Bernstien 52 Duane St Fl 5 New York NY 10007-1250 E-mail: trodb@hotmail.com

RYAN, THOMAS WILLIAM, lawyer; b. Tulsa, Feb. 16, 1953; s. Dean Lawrence and Helen Ladeen (Steinkierchner) R.; m. Mary Ellen Poxon, Jan. 30, 1973; children: Matthew Alan, Jennifer Erin. BA, U. Houston, 1975, JD, 1978. Bar: Tex. 1978. Ptnr. Hart, Ryan & Pfeffer, Houston, 1978-80; contracts adminstr. Texaco Inc., 1980-85; asst. gen. counsel Total Minatome Corp., 1985-99; gen. counsel, corp. sec. Total Exploration Prodn. USA, Inc., 1999-2001, TotalFinaElf E&P USA, Inc., Houston, 2001—. Coach youth sports YMCA, Houston, 1990-94. Mem. KC (adv. 1985-87), State Bar Tex. Avocations: golf, bowling. FERC practice, Oil, gas, and mineral, Labor. Office: TotalFinaElf E&P USA Inc One Memorial City Plz 800 Gessner Ste 700 Houston TX 77024

RYAN, WILLIAM JOSEPH, JR. lawyer; b. Derby, Conn., Mar. 20, 1951; s. William Joseph and Eleanor (Koon) R.; m. Ann Shirley Wilkinson, June 16, 1973; children— Melissa Ann, William III, Matthew J. B.A. in Psychology cum laude, Fairfield U., 1973; J.D., U. Conn., 1977. Bar: Conn. 1977, U.S. Dist. Ct. Conn. 1977. Sole practice, Derby, 1977-82; ptnr. firm Ryan & Tyma, Derby, 1983-86, Wetmore, Ryan & Tyma, 1986—; bd. dirs. New Haven Legal Assistance, 1981-83. Chmn. profl. div. Valley United Way Campaign, 1988, 89—; mem. Oxford Planning and Zoning Commn., Conn., 1981-82, Oxford Bd. Edn., 1983-87; counsel Town of Oxford, 1987—; v.p. Oxford Republican Town Com., 1984. Mem. Valley Bar Assn. (treas. 1981-82, sec. 1982-83, pres. 1983-84), ABA, Conn. Bar Assn., Assn. Trial Lawyers Am. Roman Catholic. Lodge: Lions (pres. 1984). State civil litigation, General practice, Real property. Home: 10 Crest Rd Oxford CT 06478-1915 Office: Wetmore Ryan & Tyma 231 Coram Ave Shelton CT 06484-3331

RYCE, DONALD THEODORE, lawyer; b. New Orleans, Dec. 15, 1943; s. Donald Theodore and Martha (Herndon) R.; m. Claudine Dianne Walker, July 8, 1984; children: Ted, Martha, Jimmy. BA, U. Fla., 1966, JD, 1968. Bar: Fla. 1968, U.S. Dist. Ct. (so. dist.) Fla. 1972, U.S. Ct. Appeals (5th and 11th cirs.) 1973; approved arbitrator Broward County Sheriff's Office. Jud. law clk. Fla. Dist. Ct. Appeals (4th cir.), West Palm Beach, 1968-70; ptnr. Hogg, Allen, Ryce, Norton & Blue, Miami, Fla., 1970-89, Donald T. Ryce, P.A., Miami, 1989-96, Hogg, Ryce & Hudson, Miami, 1997—99, Hogg, Ryce & Spencer, Miami, 2000—. Co-chmn. liaison com. labor and employment sect. NLRB, Fla., 1990-92, mem. publs. com., 1990-91, exec. coun. labor and employment sect., 1994-98; apptd. missing children adv. bd. Fla. Dept. Law Enforcement, 1996—. Active Fla. Police Chiefs Edn. Rsch. Found.; dir. Jimmy Ryce Ctr. for Victims of Predatory Abduction. Named to Policeman Hall of Fame, 1996, Grand Knight of Order of Michael the Archangel; recipient Leadership award Fla. Police Chiefs Edn. Rsch. Found., 1993. Mem. ABA, Microcomputer Edn. for Employment of the Disabled (bus. adv. coun.), Winter Haven C. of C. (Cmty. Leadership award 1994), Miami Beach C. of C., Coral Gables C. of C., Miami Rotary. Episcopalian. Avocations: tennis, gourmet cooking, biking. General civil litigation, Labor. Office: 333 Arthur Godfrey Rd Ste 714 Miami Beach FL 33140-2716 Fax: 305-532-8386. E-mail: employerlawyer@aol.com

RYDBERG, MARSHA GRIFFIN, lawyer; b. Tampa, Fla., Dec. 11, 1946; d. Jack and Nibia (Santan) Griffin; m. Thomas Henry Rydberg; children: Kristen Elizabeth, Nancy Marshall. BA, Emory U., 1968; JD dum laude, Stetson U., 1976. Bar: Fla. 1976, U.S. Dist. Ct. (mid. dist.) Fla. 1977, U.S. Dist. Ct. (so. dist.) Fla. 1984, U.S. Ct. Appeals (11th cir.) 1977, U.S. Supreme Ct. 1983. Christian youth worker Young Life Campaign, 1968-70; youth dir. First Presbyn. Ch., Tampa, 1970-73; assoc. Gibbons, Tucker, McEwen, Smith Cofer & Taub, 1976-79, Taub & Williams, Tampa, 1979-83; ptnr., 1983-89, Rydberg & Goldstein, P.A., 1989-97, Foley & Lardner, 1997-2000, The Rydberg Law Firm, 2000—. Contbr. articles to profl. jours. Bd. dirs. Jr. League Tampa, 1979-80, chair com. of 100 Greater Tampa C. of C., 1998; atty. 1983-85; pres. Tampa-Hillsborough County Drug Abuse Comprehensive Coord. Office, Inc., 1988-90, chmn. Tampa Downtown Partnership, 1995-96; elder Temple Terrace Presbyn. Ch., Fla., 1982-85; bd. dirs. Fed. Res. Bd. of Atlanta, Jacksonville, 1997—; mem. Tampa Housing Authority Bd., 1994-99. Recipient Bon Sikes Incentive award, Judge Joe Morris award, Am. Jurisprudence awards for excellence in law. Fellow Am. Bar Found., Fla. Bar Found; mem. ABA (com. commendation zoning & property use 1985-88, chair bus. law sect. fin. instn. litig. com. 1992—), Am. Bankruptcy Inst., Fla. Bar (bd. govs., exec. com. 1997—), Fla. Assn. Women Lawyers, Am. Land Title Assn., Ferguson White Inn of Ct., Tampa Bay Bankruptcy Bar Assn., Hillsborough Assn. Women Lawyers, Hillsborough County Bar Assn., (pres. 1991-92, James M. Red McEwen award 1984-85, 87-88, 96-97), Stetson U. Coll. Law

Alumni Assn. (pres. 1993, bd. overseers 1994, adj. prof. banking law), Grater Tampa C. of C. (bd. and exec. com. 1995-2000), Am. and Fla. Land Title Assn., Exchange Club of Tampa (pres. 1998), Phi Alpha Delta (outstanding scholastic achievement award). Democrat. Bankruptcy, Federal civil litigation, State civil litigation. Home: 2606 W Prospect Rd Tampa FL 33629-5358 Office: The Rydberg Law Firm 400 N Tampa St Ste 2630 Tampa FL 33602-5810

RYER, CHARLES WILFRED, lawyer, court administrator; b. Springfield, Mo., July 7, 1940; s. Wilfred Templeton and Rowena Gertrude (Payson) R.; m. Beth Ellen Hadley, July 8, 1967; children— Johannah Kathryn, Matthew Hadley. B.A., Southwest Mo. State U., 1962; J.D., Washington U., 1968; M.S., U. Oreg., 1972. Bar: Mo. 1968, Oreg. 1972. Staff atty. Legal Aid Soc., St. Louis, 1968-69; interviewer Pub. Defender of Santa Clara County, San Jose, Calif., 1969-70; counselor Lane County Juvenile Ct., Eugene, Oreg., 1971-73, supr., 1973-89, asst. dir., 1989—; cons. Alaska Div. Corrections, Anchorage, 1982; instr. State of Oreg. Bd. Police Standards and Tng., Salem, 1976— . Contbr. chpt. to Juvenile Law Handbook, 1982, 91. Served to 1st lt. U.S. Army, 1963-65. Mem. Tchrs. Assn., Sierra. Democrat. Clubs: Royal Scottish Country Dance Soc., Heather and Rose Country Dancers (Eugene). Lodge: Masons. Office: Lane County Juvenile Ct 2411 Centennial Blvd Eugene OR 97401-5805

RYKEN, ROBERT LESLIE, lawyer; b. Yankton, S.D., July 26, 1950; s. Marvin Lyle and Gladys E. (Knutson) R. B.A., U. S.D.-Vermillion, 1972; J.D., Harvard U., 1975. Bar: Ill. 1975, U.S. Dist. Ct. (no. dist.) Ill. 1975, U.S. Tax Ct. 1985. Ptnr., dir. law firm Pope, Ballard, Shepard & Fowle, Ltd., Chgo., 1975— . Mem. jr. governing bd. Chgo. Symphony Orchestra, 1977— . Mem. ABA, Chgo. Bar Assn., Chgo. Estate Planning Council. Democrat. Lutheran. Clubs: Chicago Athletic Assn., Harvard of Chgo., Harvard Law Soc. Ill. Estate planning, Probate, Real property. Home: 616 S Laflin St Unit G Chicago IL 60607-3160 Office: Pope Ballard Shepard & Fowle Ltd 69 W Washington St Chicago IL 60602-3004

RYLAND, WALTER H. lawyer; b. Richmond, Va., Jan. 23, 1943; s. John William and Evelyn (Quillin) R.; m. Madelaine Aerni, July 10, 1976; children: Mark Vanley, Caroline Aerni. BA, Washington & Lee U., 1965, LLB, 1967. Chief dep. atty. gen. Office of the Atty. Gen. of Va., Richmond, 1978-82; ptnr. Williams, Mullen, Christian & Dobbins, 1983—. Counselor, Va. Mus. Fine Arts, Richmond, 1983—; pres. J. Sargeant Reynolds Found., Richmond, 1990; legal adv., Southeastern Legal Found., Atlanta, Ga., 1989—. Co-editor: Racial Preferences in Government Contracting (Nat. Legal Ctr. for the Pub. Interest), 1993. Sec. bd. trustees Washington Internat. U. Va., 1989-91; bd. dirs. Coun. for Am. First Freedom, Richmond, 1988-92; pres. Theatre Va., Richmond, 1987-88; sec. Communication Disorders Found., Richmond, 1986-88, Cultural Art Ctr. and Glen Allen. Mem. ABA, Va. Bar Assn., Richmond Bar Assn. Constitutional, Education and schools, Government contracts and claims. Office: Williams Mullen Clark & Dobbins 2 James Ctr 1021 E Cary St Richmond VA 23219-4000

RYMER, PAMELA ANN, federal judge; b. Knoxville, Tenn., Jan. 6, 1941; AB, Vassar Coll., 1961; LLB, Stanford U., 1964; LLD (hon.), Pepperdine U., 1988. Bar: Calif. 1966, U.S. Ct. Appeals (9th cir.) 1966, U.S. Ct. Appeals (10th cir.), U.S. Supreme Ct. V.p. Rus Walton & Assoc., Los Altos, Calif., 1965-66; Assoc. Lillick McHose & Charles, L.A., 1966-75, ptnr., 1973-75, Toy and Rymer, L.A., 1975-83; judge U.S. Dist. Ct. (cen. dist.) Calif., 1983-89, U.S. Ct. Appeals (9th cir.), L.A., 1989—. Faculty The Nat. Jud. Coll., 1986-88; mem. com. summer ednl. programs Fed. Jud. Ctr., 1987-88, mem. com. appellate judge edn., 1996-99; chair exec. com. 9th Cir. Jud. Conf., 1990; mem. com. criminal law Jud. Conf. U.S., 1988-93, Ad Hoc com. gender-based violence, 1991-94, fed.-state jurisdiction com., 1993-96; mem. commn. on structural alternatives Fed. Cts. Appeals, 1997-98. Mem. editorial bd. The Judges' jour., 1989-91; contbr. articles to profl. jours. and newsletters. Mem. Calif. Postsecondary Edn. Commn., 1974-84, chmn., 1980-84; mem. L.A. Olympic Citizens Adv. Commn.; bd. visitors Stanford U. Law Sch., 1986-99, trustee, 1991—, chair, 1993-96, exec. com., chmn. bd. trustees com. acad. policy, planning and mgmt. and its ad. hoc. com. athletics., chmn. bd. visitors Sch. Law, 1987—; bd. visitors Pepperdine U. Law Sch., 1987—; mem. Edn. Commn. of States Task Force on State Policy and Ind. Higher Edn., 1987-89, Carnegie Commn. Task Force Sci. and Tech. Jud. and Regulatory Decisionmaking, 1990-93, Commn. Substance Abuse Coll. and Univ. Campuses, 1992-94, commn. substance abuse high schs. Ctr. Addiction and Substance Abube Columbia U.; bd. dirs. Constnl. Rights Found., 1985-97, Pacific Coun. Internat. Policy, 1995—, Calif. Higher Edn. Policy Ctr., 1992-97; Jud. Conf. U.S. Com. Fed.-State Jurisdiction, 1993, Com. Criminal Law, 1988-93, ad hoc com. gender based violence, 1991-94; chair exec. com. 9th cir. jud. conf., 1990-94. Recipient Outstanding Trial Jurist award L.A. County Bar Assn., 1988; named David T. Lewis Disting. Jurist-in-Residence U. Utah, 1992. Mem. ABA (task force on civil justice reform 1991-93, mem. coord. com. agenda civil justice reform in Am. 1991), State Bar Calif. (antitrust and trade regulation sect., exec. com. 1990-92), L.A. County Bar Assn. (chmn. antitrust sect. 1981-82, mem. editl. bd. The Judges Jour. 1989-91, mem. com. professionalism 1988—, numerous other coms.), Assn. of Bus. Trial Lawyers (bd. govs. 1990-92), Stanford Alumni Assn., Stanford Law Soc. Soc. Calif., Vassar Club So. Calif. (past pres.). Office: US Ct Appeals 9th Cir US Court of Appeals Bldg 125 S Grand Ave Rm 600 Pasadena CA 91105-1621*

RYNBRANDT, KEVIN ABRAHAM, lawyer; b. Upland, Calif., Nov. 7, 1960; s. Thurman Philip and Marilyn Ruth (Lam) R.; m. Melinda Christine Anderson, June 30, 1984; children: Quentin Thurman, Luke Gordon. BA, Wheaton Coll., 1983; MA, U. Ill., 1985; JD, Vanderbilt U., 1991. Bar: Mich. 1992, U.S. Ct. Appeals (7th cir.) 1994, U.S. Ct. Appeals (6th cir.) 1994, U.S. Dist. Ct. (we. dist.) Mich. 1993, U.S. Dist. Ct. (ctrl. dist.) Ill. 1994, U.S. Dist. Ct. (no., we. and so. dist.) Tex. 1994, U.S. Dist. Ct. Nebr. 1996, U.S. Ct. Appeals (5th cir.) 1997, U.S. Dist. Ct. (ea. dist.) Mich. 1997. Cons. Arthur Andersen & Co., Chgo., 1985-88; law clk. U.S. Dist. Ct (no. dist.) Tex., Dallas, 1991-92; atty. Varnum, Riddering, Schmidt & Howlett LLP, Grand Rapids, Mich., 1992—. Exec. com. Rep. Party, U.S. Congl. 3d Dist., Grand Rapids, 1997—; precinct del. Rep. Party, Ada, Mich., 1997-99; bd. dirs. Jr. Achievement of the Michigan Great Lakes, Inc., 1997—, Am. Youth Soccer Orgn./Region 571 Ada-Cascade. Mem. ABA, Mich. Bar Assn., Grand Rapids Bar Assn. Mem. Reformed Ch. of Am. Avocations: travel, basketball, skiing, reading, golf. Civil rights, General civil litigation, Contracts commercial. Office: Varnum Riddering Schmidt & Howlett LLP 333 Bridge St NW Ste 1300 Grand Rapids MI 49504-5369

RYSKAMP, KENNETH LEE, federal judge; b. 1932; m. Karyl Sonja Ryskamp; 1 child, Cara Leigh. AB, Calvin Coll., 1954; JD, U. Miami, 1956. Bar: Fla. 1956, Mich. 1957, U.S. Supreme Ct. 1970. Law clk. to presiding judge Fla. Ct. Appeals 3d Dist., 1957-59; pvt. practice Miami, Fla., 1959-61; ptnr. Goodwin, Ryskamp, Welcher & Carrier, 1961-84; mng. ptnr. Squire, Sanders & Dempsey, 1984-86; judge U.S. Dist. Ct. (so. dist.) Fla., 1986—. Office: US Dist Ct 701 Clematis St Rm 416 West Palm Beach FL 33401-5112

SAARI, JOHN WILLIAM, JR. lawyer; b. Jersey City, Oct. 12, 1937; s. John William Sr. and Ina Marie (Bain) S.; m. Susan Jo Olson, Aug. 27, 1967 (div. June 1971); m. Marjorie Ann Palm, Nov. 16, 1973. Student, Duke U., 1955-58, U. N.C., 1962-63; JD with honors, Ill. Inst. Tech., Chgo., 1972. Bar: Ill. 1972, U.S. Dist. Ct. (no. dist.) Ill. 1972, Wis. 1980, U.S. Dist. Ct. (ea. and we. dists.) Wis. 1980, U.S. Ct. Appeals (7th cir.) 1972, U.S. Supreme Ct. 1997. Assoc. Yates, Goff, Gustafson & Been, Chgo., 1972-76, Hubbard, Hubbard, O'Brien & Hall, Chgo., 1976-78; atty. Ill. Bell Telephone Co., 1978-79; assoc. Cirilli Law Office, Rhinelander, Wis., 1979-83; pvt. practice, 1983-90; ptnr. Mouw, Saari, Krueger, Paulson & Smith, 1990—. Bd. dirs. Northwoods United Way, 1980-88, pres., 1983-84. With U.S. Army, 1958-61, ETO. Mem. ABA, Ill. Bar Assn., Wis. Bar Assn., Oneida-Vilas-Forest Bar Assn. (pres. 1996-97), Lions (pres. Sugarcamp 1983-84). Avocations: hunting, fishing, baseball, reading, golf. General civil litigation, Insurance, Personal injury. Home: 7279 Arbutus Dr Eagle River WI 54521-9249 Office: Mouw Saari Krueger Paulson Smith 8A W Davenport St Rhinelander WI 54501-3467

SABERS, RICHARD WAYNE, state supreme court justice; b. Salem, S.D., Feb. 12, 1938; s. Emil William and Elrena Veronica (Godfrey) S.; m. Colleen D. Kelley, Aug. 28, 1965 (dec. Feb., 1998); children: Steven Richard, Susan Michelle, Michael Kelley; m. Ellie Schmitz, June 9, 2000. BA in English, St. John's U., Collegeville, Minn., 1960; JD, U. S.D., 1966. Bar: S.D. 1966, U.S. Dist. Ct. S.D. 1966, U.S. Ct. Appeals (8th cir.) 1983. From assoc. to ptnr. Moore, Rasmussen, Sabers & Kading, Sioux Falls, S.D., 1966-86; justice Supreme Ct. S.D., Pierre and Sioux Falls, 1986—. Mem. editorial bd. U. S.D. Law Rev., 1965-66. State rep. March of Dimes, Bismarck, N.D., 1963; bd. dirs. St. Joseph Cathedral, Sioux Falls, 1971-86; trustee, bd. dirs. O'Gorman Found., Sioux Falls, 1978-86; active sch. bd. O'Gorman High Sch., Sioux Falls, 1985-86. Lt. U.S. Army, 1960-63. Named Outstanding Young Religious Leader, Jaycees, Sioux Falls, 1971. Mem. ABA, S.D. Bar Assn., Inst. Jud. Adminstrn., St. John's Alumni Assn. (pres. Sioux Falls chpt. 1975-91). Republican. Roman Catholic. Avocations: tennis, skiing, sailing, sports, wood carving. Home: 1409 E Cedar Ln Sioux Falls SD 57103-4514 Office: SD Supreme Ct 500 E Capitol Ave Pierre SD 57501-5070

SABL, JOHN J. lawyer; b. L.A., June 16, 1951; AB with distinction, Stanford U., 1973, JD, 1976. Bar: Calif. 1976, Ill. 1977. Assoc. Sidley & Austin, Chgo., 1977-83; ptnr. Sidley Austin Brown & Wood, 1983-97, 2000—; exec. v.p., gen. counsel, sec. Conseco, Inc., Carmel, Ind., 1997-2000. Editorial bd. Stanford U. Law Review, 1974-75, assoc. mng. editor, 1975-76. Mem. ABA, Calif. Bar Assn., Ill. Bar Assn., Chgo. Bar Assn. (chmn. securities law commn. 1985-86), Phi Beta Kappa. General corporate, Mergers and acquisitions, Securities. Office: Sidley & Austin Bank One Plz 10 S Dearborn St Chicago IL 60603 E-mail: jsabl@sidley.com

SABRA, STEVEN PETER, lawyer; b. Fall River, Mass., Dec. 1, 1951; s. Peter B. and Eliza J. Sabra; m. Bernadette L. Brown, Sept. 24, 1977. BA in Polit. Sci., Fairfield U., 1973; JD, Duquesne U., 1976. Bar: Mass. 1977, U.S. Dist. Ct. Mass. 1977, U.S. Supreme Ct. 1985. Assoc. Law Offices of Richard N. LaSalle, Fall River, Mass., 1977-80; owner Law Offices of Steven P. Sabra, Somerset, 1980-87, Sabra Law Offices, Somerset, 1987-93, Law Offices Sabra & Aspden. P.A., Somerset, 1993—. Arbitrator accident claims Am. Arbitration Assn., Boston, 1988—; mem. hearing com. Bd. Bar Overseers, Mass., 1988-93; mem. Southeastern Regional Com. of Jud. Nominating Coun., 1995—; corporator Fall River Five Cents Savs. Bank, 1987—; mem. Bd. of Bar Overseers, Mass., 1998—. Chmn., pres. Fall River Port Authority/Fall River Line Pier, Inc., 1992-95. Mem. ABA, ATLA (Pres.'s Club 1998—), Mass. Bar Assn. (bd. delegates 1997-2000), Mass. Acad. Trial Attys., Bristol County Bar Assn. (pres. 1994-95), Fall River Bar Assn. (pres. 1985-87), Mass. Bar Found. Avocation: sports. Personal injury, Workers' compensation. Office: Law Offices Sabra & Aspden 1026 County St Somerset MA 02726-5138 E-mail: stevensabra@aol.com

SACASAS, RENE, lawyer; b. N.Y.C., July 10, 1947; s. Anselmo and Orlanda (Soto) S.; m. Cathy Lee Van Natta, Jan. 24, 1970. BA, Am. U., 1969; JD, Emory U., 1975. Bar: Fla. 1976, U.S. Dist. Ct. (so. dist.) Fla. 1976, U.S. Ct. Appeals (5th cir.) 1976, U.S. Supreme Ct. 1980, U.S. Ct. Appeals (11th cir.) 1983. Law clk. McLarty and Aiken, Atlanta, 1974-76; assoc. Welbaum, Zook, Jones, Williams, Miami, Fla., 1976-79; ptnr. Darrach, Merkin and Sacasas, Miami, 1979-83, Merkin & Sacasas, Miami, 1984-86; of counsel Welbaum, Zook & Jones, Miami, 1986-95; Welbaum, Guernsey, Hingston, Greenleaf & Gregory, Miami, 1996—; asst. prof. bus. law U. Miami, 1985-91, assoc. prof., 1991—, chmn. bus. law dept., 1992—; head master Hecht Residential Coll., 1995-97. Mem. ABA, Fla. Bar Assn. (vice chmn. grievance com. 1981-84), Dade County Bar Assn., Latin Am. C. of C., U.S. Jaycees, Cuban Am. Bar Assn., Iron Arrow, Leadership Fla., Phi Sigma Kappa (ET chpt. pres. 1968), Omicron Delta Kappa, Phi Kappa Phi. Contbr. articles profl. jours. Banking, Private international, Real property. Home: 3790 Kent Ct Miami FL 33133-6137 Office: Welbaum Zook & Jones 901 Ponce De Leon Blvd Coral Gables FL 33134-3073

SACHER, STEVEN JAY, lawyer; b. Cleve., Jan. 28, 1942; s. Albert N. and Cecil P. (Chessin) S.; m. Colleen Marie Gibbons, Nov. 28, 1970; children— Alexander Jerome, Barry Elizabeth, William Paul BS, U. Wis., 1964; JD, U. Chgo., 1967. Bar: D.C. 1968. Assoc. solicitor Employee Retirement Income Security Act U.S. Dept. Labor, Washington, 1974-77; spl. counsel com. on labor and human resources U.S. Senate, 1977-79, gen. counsel, 1980-81; ptnr. Pepper, Hamilton & Scheetz, 1982-88; shareholder Johnson & Wortley, 1988-94; ptnr. Kilpatrick Stockton LLP, 1994—. Adj. prof. law Georgetown U. Law Ctr., 1977; co-chair sr. editors Employee Benefits Law and Annual Supplements, Bur. Nat. Affairs, Washington, 1991-2000. Mem. adv. bd. BNA Pension and Benefits Reporter; mem. editorial bd. Benefits Law Jour., Jour. Pension Planning and Compliance. Founding mem. ERISA Roundtable, Washington. Fellow Coll. Labor and Employment Lawyers. Fellow Coll. Labor and Employment Lawyers, Am. Coll. Employee Benefits Counsel (charter); mem. ABA (mgmt. co-chmn. com. on employee benefits, sect. on labor and employment law 1988-91, chmn. prohibited trans. subcom., com. on employee benefits, sect. on taxation 1986-91), D.C. Bar Assn. Labor, Legislative, Pension, profit-sharing, and employee benefits. Office: Kilpatrick Stockton LLP 607 14th St NW Ste 900 Washington DC 20005 E-mail: ssacher@kilpatrickstockton.com

SACHS, IRVING JOSEPH, lawyer, accountant, pension consultant; b. Chgo., Sept. 12, 1922; s. Philip and Ida (Camras) S.; m. Bettie Taub, June 8, 1947 (dec. Jan. 1964); children— Richard, Melissa, Ilene, Philip; m. 2d Francine Lee Rodbard, Aug. 15, 1965; children— Marc, Jan, Wayne, Jason. B.S. in Acctg., DePaul U., 1948, J.D., 1951. Bar: Ill. 1951; C.P.A., Ill. Sr. ptnr. Sachs, Shapiro & Silver, Chgo. and Skokie, Ill., 1954-65, Sachs, Rosenberg & Kosin, Chgo., 1954-62; sole practice, Chgo. and Highland Park, Ill., 1962-76; pres. Nat. Pension Consultants, Inc., Chgo., 1978-79, Alliance Pension Consultants, Inc., Skokie, 1979— . Served with Signal Corps, U.S. Army, 1943-46, ETO, PTO. Jewish. Office: Alliance Pension Cons Inc 9933 Lawler Ave Suite 505 Skokie IL 60077

SACHS, JOSHUA MICHAEL, lawyer; b. Phila., Apr. 11, 1971; s. Stephen M. and Sandra K. S. BA, Emory U., 1993; JD, Bklyn. Law Sch., 1997. Bar: N.Y., N.J., U.S. Dist. Ct. (so. dist.) N.Y., U.S. Dist. Ct. N.J. Assoc. Klein, Zelman, Rothermel & Dichter, N.Y.C., 1997—. Mediator Bklyn. Legal Svcs., 1996—. Dean's merit scholar Bklyn. Law Sch., 1994; recipient Award for Excellence-Labor Law II CALI, 1997. Mem. ABA, Assn. of the Bar of the City of N.Y., Phi Delta Phi. Avocations: roller hockey, golf, softball. General corporate, Labor. Home: 24 Remsen St Apt 3 Brooklyn NY 11201 Office: Klein Zehman Rothermel & Dichter 485 Madison Ave New York NY 10022

SACK, ROBERT DAVID, judge, educator; b. Phila., Oct. 4, 1939; s. Eugene J. and Sylvia I. (Rivlin) S.; div.; children: Deborah Gail, Suzanne Michelle, David Rivlin; m. Anne K. Hilker, 1989. BA, U. Rochester, 1960; LLB, Columbia U., 1963. Bar: N.Y. 1963. Law clk. to judge Fed. Dist. Ct., Dist. of N.J., 1963-64; assoc. Patterson, Belknap & Webb, N.Y.C., 1964-70; ptnr. Patterson, Belknap, Webb & Tyler, 1970-86, Gibson, Dunn & Crutcher, N.Y.C., 1986-98; sr. assoc. spl. counsel U.S. Ho. of Reps. Impeachment Inquiry, 1974; judge U.S. Ct. Appeals (2d cir.), 1998—. Lectr. Practising Law Inst., 1973-97; lectr. Columbia U. Law Sch., 2001—; mem. adv. bd. Media Law Reporter. Author: Libel, Slander, and Related Problems, 1980, 2nd edit., 1994, CD-ROM edit., 1995, Sack on Defamation -- Libel, Slander, and Related Problems, 3d edit., 1999; co-author: Advertising and Commercial Speech, a First Amendment Guide, 1999; contbr. articles to profl. jours. Chmn. bd. dirs. Nat. Council on Crime and Delinquency, 1982-83; trustee Columbia seminars on media and society Columbia U. Sch. Journalism, 1985-92, N.Y.C. Commn. on Pub. Info. and Comm., 1995-98; v.p., dir. William F. Kerby and Robert S. Potter Fund; bd. visitors Sch. of Law, Columbia U., 1999—. Fellow Am. Bar Found.; mem. ABA (bd. govs. forum com. on comm. law 1980-88), Assn. Bar City N.Y. (chmn. comm. law com. 1986-89). Office: US Circuit Ct for 2d Circuit 40 Foley Sq New York NY 10007-1502

SACK, SYLVAN HANAN, lawyer; b. Phila., Dec. 26, 1932; s. Isidore F. and Mollye (Bellmore) S.; m. Ellen L. Foreman, Aug. 13, 1972; children: Reuben H., Sara I. M.S. in Bus. Adminstrn, Pa. State U., 1956; J.D., U. Balt., 1964. Bar: Md. 1964, U.S. Tax Ct. 1967, U.S. Supreme Ct. 1970; C.P.A., Md. Pvt. practice, Balt., 1967—; assoc. counsel Safety First Club of Md., 1975-78, spl. counsel, 1979—. Gov. Md. chpt. Retinitis Pigmentosa Found., 1974-75 Contbr. articles to profl. jours. Chmn. Indsl. Toxicology NIOSH Function, 1977, Occupational Disease Forum, 1979, OSHA and Diseases in Workplace Seminar, 1981. Mem. Fed. Bar Assn. (gov. chpt. 1968— , chmn. bd. govs. 1969-70, chmn. environ. law program 1984), ABA (chmn. subcom. sect. taxation 1972-75), Md. Bar Assn., Assn. Trial Lawyers Am.; mem. Md. Trial Lawyers Assn. (lectr. toxic torts 1983 conv.) Environmental, Personal injury, Toxic tort. Home: 27 Brightside Ave Baltimore MD 21208-4802

SACKLER, ARTHUR BRIAN, lawyer; b. Utica, N.Y., June 9, 1950; s. Joseph Leon and Leonore (Guttman) S.; m. Linda J. Cimarusti, May 27, 1979; children: Joshua Michael, Jenna Rachel. B.A., Syracuse U., 1970, J.D., 1973; LL.M., Georgetown U., 1979. Bar: N.Y. 1974, D.C. 1975, U.S. Dist. Ct. D.C. 1979, U.S. Supreme Ct. 1979, U.S. Ct. Appeals (D.C. cir.) 1981. Appeals examiner U.S. Civil Service Commn., Washington, 1973-75, atty. advisor, 1975-76, trial atty., 1976-79; gen. counsel Nat. Newspaper Assn., Washington, 1979-82; dir. pub. policy devel. Time Warner, Washington, 1982-92, v.p. law and pub. policy, 1992—; mng. dir. Mailers Coun., 1990—; mem. Joint Washington Media Com., 1979— , Am. Copyright Council, Washington, 1984-86; faculty communications law Practicing Law Inst., 1980, forum com. on communications law seminar, 1980; instr. Am. Press Inst., 1980-82. Editor and contbr.: Federal Laws Affecting Newspapers, 1981; founder, editor newsletter News Media Update, 1979-82; contbr. articles to profl. jours., newspapers. Pres. Birnam Wood Community Assn., Potomac, Md., 1983-84; sec., treas. Potomac Springs Community Assn., Potomac, Md., 1986-87. Mem. ABA (chmn. postal matters com., adminstrv. law sect.), D.C. Bar Assn., Fed. Communications Bar Assn., Fed. Bar Assn., Mag. Pubs. Am. (govt. rels. coun. N.Y.C. 1982-85, 92—), Am. Advt. Fedn. (govt. relations com. Washington 1984—), Direct Mktg. Assn. (govt. relations com. 1986—), Am. Tort Reform Assn. (bd. dirs. 1987-88, corp. steering com. 1986-88), Assn. Am. Pubs. (postal com. N.Y.C. 1983—). Jewish. Clubs: Nat. Press, Bethesda Country. Administrative and regulatory, Legislative. Office: Time Warner Inc 800 Connecticut Ave NW Ste 800 Washington DC 20006-2718

SACKS, IRA STEPHEN, lawyer; b. N.Y.C., Dec. 6, 1948; s. Marvin Leonard and Mildred (Finkelstein) S.; m. Deborah DiNolfo; children: James, Jennifer, Allison, Gillian. BS, MIT, 1970; JD, Georgetown U., 1974. Bar: N.Y. 1975, U.S. Dist. Ct. (so. and ea. dists.) N.Y. 1975, U.S. Ct. Appeals (2d cir.) 1975, U.S. Ct. Appeals (3d cir.) 1984, U.S. Supreme Ct. 1985, U.S. Ct. Appeals (9th cir.) 1986, U.S. Ct. Appeals (11th cir.) 1987, U.S. Ct. Appeals (D.C. and fed. cirs.) 1993. Assoc. Kaye, Scholer, Fierman, Hays & Handler, N.Y.C., 1974-82, ptnr., 1983-87, Fried, Frank, Harris, Shriver & Jacobson, N.Y.C., 1988—. Contbr. articles to profl. jours. NSF fellow, 1970. Mem. ABA, Supreme Ct. Hist. Soc., N.Y. State Bar Assn., Assn. of Bar of City of N.Y. Democrat. Jewish. Avocations: tennis, skiing. Antitrust, Bankruptcy, Trademark and copyright. Home: 105 Old Colony Rd Hartsdale NY 10530-3610 Office: Fried Frank Harris Shriver & Jacobson 1 New York Plz Fl 24 New York NY 10004-1901 E-mail: ira.sacks@ffnsj.com

SAEKS, ALLEN IRVING, lawyer; b. Bemidji, Minn., July 14, 1932; m. Linda J. Levin; 1 child, Adam Charles. BS in Law, U. Minn., 1954, JD, 1956. Bar: Minn. 1956, U.S. Dist. Ct. Minn. 1956, U.S. Ct. Appeals (8th cir.) 1957, U.S. Ct. Appeals (fed. cir.) 1959, U.S. Supreme Ct. 1959, U.S. Ct. Appeals (11th cir.) 1997; cert. civil trial specialist. Asst. U.S. atty. Dept. Justice, St. Paul, 1956-57; assoc. Leonard Street and Deinard, Mpls., 1960-63, ptnr., 1964—. Adj. prof. law U. Minn. Law Sch., 1960-65; chmn. Lawyer Trust Account Bd., Interest on Lawyers Trust Accounts, 1984-87. Chmn. Property Tax Com., 1986-87; bd. dirs. Citizens League, Mpls., 1984-87; pres. Jewish Cmty. Rels. Coun. of Minn. and the Dakotas, 1994-96. 1st lt. JAGC, U.S. Army, 1957-60. Recipient City of Mpls. award, 1996, Lifetime Commitment award Cardozo Soc., 2001. Fellow Am. Bar Found. (life); mem. ABA (commn. on interest on lawyers trust accts. 1990-93), Minn. State Bar Assn., Fund for the Legal Aid Soc. (chmn. 1997-98, Law Day Testimonial award 1996), Hennepin County Bar Assn. (pres. 1983-84), Order of Coif, Phi Delta Phi. Federal civil litigation, Probate, Professional liability. Office: Leonard Street and Deinard 150 S 5th St Ste 2300 Minneapolis MN 55402-4238

SAFA, RACHID P. lawyer; b. Beirut, Lebanon, Aug. 24, 1960; s. Pierre Safa and Nina Karam; m. Altagracia Cristiana Baez, May 26, 1989; childre: Peirre, Gavriela, Michael. BA in Bus. Econs., Am. U., Beirut, Lebanon, 1982; LLM, Georgetown U., 1983; D of Law, Clermont Berrand U., France, 1991. Asst. staff coun. AIG, N.Y.C., 1984-88; regional counsel Schlumberger, Paris, 1988-89, Dubai, United Arab Emirates, 1989-90; sr. assoc. Simmons & Simmons, Paris, 1990-92, Gide in Yrette, Paris, 1992-94; ptnr. Honig Buffat, 1994-98, Jalenques Lecasble, Paris, 1999—. Author: Commercial Banking Law in the Middle East, 1995. Mem. Beirut Bar Assn., N.Y. Bar Assn., Paris Bar Assn. Avocations: reading, tennis, jogging, skiing, gym. Computer, General practice, Private international. Office: Jalenques Lecasble 47 Ave Hoche 75008 Paris France Fax: 33-1-43803159

SAFFELS, DALE EMERSON, federal judge; b. Moline, Kans., Aug. 13, 1921; s. Edwin Clayton and Lillian May (Cook) S.; m. Margaret Elaine Nieman, Apr. 2, 1976; children by previous marriage: Suzanne Saffels Gravitt, Deborah Saffels Godowns, James B.; stepchildren: Lynda Cowger Harris, Christopher Cowger. AB, Emporia State U., 1947; JD cum laude, LLB cum laude, Washburn U., 1949. Bar: Kans. 1949. Pvt. practice law, Garden City, Kans., 1949-71, Topeka, 1971-75, Wichita, Kans., 1975-79; U.S. dist. judge Dist. of Kans., Topeka, 1979—. County atty. Finney County, Kans., 1951-55; chmn. bd. Fed. Home Loan Bank Topeka, 1978-79; mem. Jud. Conf. Com. on Fin. Disclosure, 1993-99. Mem. bd. govs. Sch. Law Washburn U., 1973-85; pres. Kans. Dem. Club, 1957; Dem. nominee Gov. of Kans., 1962; mem. Kans. Ho. of Reps., 1955-63, minority leader, 1961-63; mem. Kans. Corp. Commn., 1967-75, chmn., 1968-75; mem. Kans. Legis. Coun., 1957-63; Kans. rep. Interstate Oil Compact

Commn., 1967-75, 1st vice chmn., 1971-72; pres. Midwest Assn. Regulatory Commn., 1972-73, Midwest Assn. R.R. and Utilities Commrs., 1972-73; trustee Emporia State U. Endowment Assn.; bd. dirs. Nat. Assn. Regulatory Utility Commrs., 1972-75. Maj. Signal Corps U.S. Army, 1942-46. Fellow Am. Bar Found., Kans. Bar Found.; mem. ABA, Kans. Bar Assn., Wichita Bar assn., Am. Judicture Soc., Delta Theta Phi. Lutheran. Office: US Dist Ct 420 Federal Bldg 444 SE Quincy St Topeka KS 66683 Fax: (785) 295-2809

SAFFER, JUDITH MACK, lawyer; b. N.Y.C., June 10, 1942; d. Gilbert and Rose (Elizer) Mack; m. Brian H. Saffer, June 13, 1965; children: Amy, Ian. BA, NYU, 1965, LLB, 1967. Bar: N.Y. 1968, U.S. Ct. Appeals (2d cir.) 1975. Sr. counsel ASCAP, N.Y.C., 1968-86; asst. gen. counsel Broadcast Music, Inc., 1986—. Bd. dirs., v.p. Symphony Space; sec. Found. for Creative Am. Mem. ABA, Am. Intellectual Property Lawyers Assn. (v.p., bd. dirs., sec., coun. intellectual property sect.), Copyright Soc. U.S.A. (past pres.). Federal civil litigation, Labor, Trademark and copyright. Home: 77 Winchip Rd Summit NJ 07901-4142 E-mail: jsaffer@bmi.com

SAFIR, PETER OLIVER, lawyer; b. N.Y.C., Apr. 1, 1945; s. Marshall Phillip and Gladys (Weissberger) S.; m. Ellen Beskind, Jan. 2, 1983; children: Jesse Oliver, Roland Smart, Archie Smart. AB in History, Princeton U., 1967; JD, Yale U., 1972. Bar: N.Y. 1973, D.C. 1975. Assoc. Breed, Abbott & Morgan, N.Y.C., 1972-75; assoc. Kleinfeld Kaplan & Becker, Washington, 1975-78, ptnr., 1979—; prof. lectr. food and drug law George Washington U. Law Sch., 1991—; panelist-moderator Food and Drug Law Inst. programs, Washington, 1979-93. Contbr. articles to profl., trade and law jours. Served with U.S. Army, 1968-71. Mem. ABA (food and drug law sect.). Democrat. Administrative and regulatory, Product liability. Office: Kleinfeld Kaplan & Becker 1140 19th St NW Washington DC 20036-6601

SAFON, DAVID MICHAEL, lawyer; b. Boston, Sept. 6, 1962; s. Kenneth Norman and Barbara Safon; m. Lisa Eileen Spector, Aug. 28, 1988; children: Jennifer, Keith, Noah. BA in Econs. with honors, Coll. William and Mary, 1984; JD cum laude, Cornell U., 1987. Bar: N.Y. 1988, U.S. Dist. Ct. (so. and ea. dists.) N.Y. 1988. Assoc. Proskauer, Rose, Goetz & Mendelsohn, N.Y.C., 1987-89, Benetar, Bernstein, Schair & Stein, N.Y.C., 1989-96, ptnr., 1997—. Contbg. editor: (supplements) Age Discrimination, Employment Discrimination. Mem. ABA (com. on fed. labor stds. legis.), N.Y. State Bar Assn. (labor and employment law sect., com. on labor rels.), Assn. of Bar of City of N.Y., Phi Beta Kappa. Labor. Office: Benetar Bernstein Schair & Stein 330 Madison Ave Fl 39 New York NY 10017-5001

SAFRAN, HUBERT MAYER, lawyer, legislative consultant; b. Salt Lake City, Dec. 25, 1930; s. Joseph J. and Idalla (Aaron) S.; m. Anita E. Shankman, Aug. 10, 1958 (div. Apr. 1977); children: Howard Daniel, Michelle Lynn; m. Marilyn A. Walpin, Aug. 20, 1978. LLB, U. Colo., 1954, JD, 1968. Bar: Colo. 1955. Practice law, Denver, 1955—; ptnr. Safran & Adkins, Denver, 1983-90; pvt. practice Denver, 1990—; mem. Colo. Ho. of Reps., 1965-75, minority whip, 1967-70. Bd. dirs. S.W. Denver Svc. Assn., S.W. Denver YMCA, S.W. Denver Community Ctr., Anti-Defamation League. Mem. Assn. Trial Lawyers Am., Trial Lawyers for Pub. Justice, Am. Arbitration Assn., Colo. Trial Lawyers Assn. (bd. dirs.), Colo. Bar Assn., Denver Bar Assn., Svc. Sta. Dealers Franchise Relationships. Democrat. Jewish. Legislative, Personal injury, Probate. Home: 9531 E Maplewood Cir Englewood CO 80111-7015 Office: 1866 Vine St Denver CO 80206-1122

SAFT, STUART MARK, lawyer; b. N.Y.C., Feb. 17, 1947; s. Stanley and Dorothy (Ligerman) S.; m. Stephanie C. Optekman, June 6, 1970; children: Bradley S., Gordon D. BA, Hofstra U., 1968; JD, Columbia U., 1971. Bar: N.Y. 1972, Fla. 1975, U.S. Dist. Ct. (so. dist.) N.Y. 1975, U.S. Supreme Ct. 1990. Ptnr. Wolf Haldenstern Adler Freeman & Herz, N.Y.C., 1988—. Chmn., bd. dirs. Coun. of N.Y. Coops., N.Y.C., 1981—, N.Y.C. Workforce Investment Bd.; chmn. bd. dirs., CEO Pvt. Industry Coun. of N.Y.C., 1994-2000; bd. dirs. Am. Women's Econ. Devel. Corp., Nat. Assn. Housing Coops., Nat. Coop. Bank, S.L.E. Lupus Found.; adj. asst. prof. NYU, Real Estate Inst. Author: Commercial Real Estate Forms, 3 vols., 1987, Commercial Real Estate Transactions, 1989, Commercial Real Estate Workouts, 1991, Real Estate Development: Strategies for a Changing Market, 1990, Commercial Real Estate Leasing, 1992, Real Estate Investor's Survival Guide, 1992, Commercial Real Estate Financing, 1993, Commercial Real Estate Forms, 2d edit., 7 vols., 1994, Commercial Real Estate Transactions, 2d edit., 1995, Commercial Real Estate Workouts, 2d edit., 1996; contbg. editor: The Real Estate Finance Jour., 1989—; contbr. articles to profl. jours. Served to capt. USAR, 1968-76. Mem. ABA, N.Y. Bar Assn., Fla. Bar Assn. General corporate, Real property. Office: Wolf Haldenstein Adler Freeman & Herz 270 Madison Ave New York NY 10016-0601

SAGE, ALBERT LISTON, III, lawyer, educator; b. Sept. 13, 1947; s. Albert Liston and Dorothy Helen (Barkemeyer) S.; m. Marjorie Leanne Meng, Aug. 28, 1977; children— Stephanie Leanne, Christina Audrey, Albert Liston IV. B.A., Miss. State U., 1969, M.A., 1971; J.D., U. Miss., 1975. Bar: Miss. 1975, U.S. Dist. Ct. (no. dist.) Miss. 1975, U.S. Ct. Appeals (5th cir.) 1977. Assoc., ptnr. Freeland & Gafford, Oxford, Miss., 1975-79; staff atty. Law Research Inst. Law Ctr., U. Miss., Oxford, 1979—; dir. govtl. affairs U. Miss., Oxford, 1987—. Author: Alternatives to Common Law Sovereign Immunity, 1983, A Legal Analysis of Artificial Reef Development, 1986; co-author: A Legal Analysis of Water Management for Mississippi, 1985. Mem. Lafayette County Democratic Exec. Com., 1984. Mem. Miss. Bar Assn., Eastern Mineral Law Found., Rocky Mountain Mineral Law Found., Am. Agrl. Law Assn. Baptist. Lodges: Ducks Unltd. (pres.), Lafayette County Sportsmens Assn. (pres.), Rotary (sec. 1984-85, v.p. 1985-86, pres. 1986-87).

SAGE, LARRY GUY, lawyer; b. Kansas City, Kans., Feb. 21, 1946; s. James Robert and Virginia Mae (Henderson) S.; m. Debbie J. Wilson, Jan. 7, 1989; children: Derek Robert, Bradley Joseph. AA, Yuba Coll., 1966; BA, U. Calif., Berkeley, 1968; JD, U. Calif., Hastings, 1975. Bar: Calif. 1975, U.S. Ct. Mil. Appeals 1976, U.S. Supreme Ct. 1978, Nev. 1986, U.S. Ct. Appeals (fed. cir.) 1986, U.S. Tax Ct. 1986, U.S. Ct. Claims 1986, U.S. Dist. Ct. (no., so., cen. and ea. dists.) Calif. 1987. Atty. Office of Legal Advisor, Nat. Guard Bur., Washington, 1975-76; dep. dist. atty. Ventura County, Calif., 1976-77; assoc. Hathaway, Perrett, Webster, & Powers, Ventura, 1977-80; judge pro tempore Ventura County Superior Ct., 1978-80; dep. county counsel Nevada County, Nevada City, Calif., 1980-83; ptnr. Bass, Bass & Sage, Grass Valley, Calif., 1983-85; supervising dep. dist. atty. Washoe County, Reno, 1986—; instr. bus. law Golden Gate U., 1982-84, U. Nev., Reno, 1986—. Counsel, chmn. bd. Ventura Women's Ctr., 1977-80; bd. dirs. Bullion Fire Protection Dist., 1983-84, ARC, 1982-83; mem. Planning Commn., Santa Paula, Calif., 1978-80; mem. Ventura County Mental Health Adv. Bd., 1978-80; alt. Congressman Barry Goldwater Jr., Norm Shumway. Mem. Calif. Bar. Assn., Nev. State Bar Assn., Nat. Dist. Attys. Assn., Nev. Dist. Attys. Assn., Barristers, Washoe County Bar Assn., Res. Officers Assn., N.G. Assn. U.S., Assn. U.S. Army, 20/30 Club. Republican. Baptist. Criminal. Office: Washoe County Dist Atty 75 Court St Rm 214 Reno NV 89501-1982

SAGER, MADELINE DEAN, lawyer; b. Turlock, Calif., Feb. 9, 1946; d. Paul Kenton and Jean Madeline (Ferguson) Dean; m. Gregory Warren Sager, June, 1970; children: Jeannette Carolyn, Robert Dean. BA, Sacramento State U., 1967; JD, U. Calif., Davis, 1970. Bar: Calif. 1971, U.S. Dist. Ct. (ea. dist.) Calif. 1971, U.S. Dist. Ct. (no. dist.) Calif. 1973. Atty. Blackmon, Isenberg, Moulds & Blicker, Sacramento, 1971-72, Redwood Legal Assistance, Ukiah, Calif., 1972-77, Sager & Sager, Ukiah, Willits, 1977-87, Leonard J. LaCasse, Ukiah, 1990—. Dir. Law Libr. Bd., Ukiah, 1985. Sec. PTA, Calpella, Calif., 1989-90; mem. sch. site coun. Redwood Valley (Calif.) Mid. Sch., 1992-93; treas., dir. Ukiah Dolphin Swim, 1994-97; meet dir. Soroptimist Swim Meet, Ukiah, 1996. Mem. Mendocino County Bar Assn. (pres. 1986), Pacific Swimming (official 1995-98), Music Boosters Ukiah High Sch. Democrat. Presbyterian. Avocations: hiking, camping, music, travel. Insurance, Probate, Real property. Home: PO Box 72 Redwood Valley CA 95470-0072 Office: Leonard J LaCasse 119 S Main St Ukiah CA 95482-4919

SAHID, JOSEPH ROBERT, lawyer; b. Paterson, N.J., Feb. 14, 1944; s. Joseph James and Helen (Vitale) S.; m. Serra Yavuz; children: Annunziata, Joseph, Olivia. BS, Rutgers U., 1965; LLB, U. Va., 1968. Bar: N.Y. 1973, U.S. Dist. Ct. N.Y., U.S. Ct. Appeals (2d and 3d cirs.), U.S. Supreme Ct. Staff mem. Nat. Commn. on Causes and Prevention of Violence, Washington, 1968-69; cons. Pres.'s Commn. on Campus Unrest, 1970; assoc. Cravath, Swaine & Moore, N.Y.C., 1972-77, ptnr., 1977-93, cons., 1994-97; ptnr. Barrack, Rodos & Bacine, 1994-96; pvt. practice, 1996—. Author: Rights in Concord, 1969; co-author: Law and Order Reconsidered, 1969; contbr. articles to profl. jours. Lt. USCG, 1968-72. General civil litigation. Address: 845 3rd Ave Fl 20 New York NY 10022-6601 E-mail: sahid@att.net

ST. AMAND, JANET G. government relations lawyer; b. N.Y.C., Feb. 27, 1953; d. Leonard Marsh and Glenda Weaver St. A.; children: Nikolai, Peter. BA, Arcadia U., 1975; JD, Georgetown U., 1980. Bar: D.C. 1981, N.Y. 1989. Legis. counsel Congressman Jim Coyne, Washington, 1981-83, Congressman Tom Carper, Washington, 1983-85, Sen. John Heinz, Washington, 1985-86, Am. Bankers Assn., Washington, 1986-87; asst. resident counsel J.P. Morgan, N.Y.C., 1987-90; counsel Fin. Svcs. Coun., Washington, 1990-93; fed. dir., counsel Household Internat., 1993—. Mem. Leadership Coun., Salvation Army, 1994—; trustee Arcadia U. (formerly Beaver Coll.), Glenside, Pa., 1999—, alumni bd. dirs., 1995—; mem. Tax Coalition, 1999—. Recipient Mary Armstrong Wolf award Arcadia U., 1999. Mem. Women in Housing & Fin. (bd. dirs. 1991-95, mem. of yr. 1993), Univ. Club, Exchequer Club, Tax Coalition. Presbyn. Avocations: reading, traveling, jogging, politics. Home: 5423 33rd St NW Washington DC 20015 Office: Household Internat 1730 K St NW Ste 1106 Washington DC 20006-3830 E-mail: jgst.amand@household.com

ST. ANTOINE, THEODORE JOSEPH, law educator, arbitrator; b. St. Albans, Vt., May 29, 1929; s. Arthur Joseph and Mary Beatrice (Callery) S.; m. Elizabeth Lloyd Frier, Jan. 2, 1960; children: Arthur, Claire, Paul, Sara. AB, Fordham Coll., 1951; JD, U. Mich., 1954; postgrad., U. London, 1957-58. Bar: Mich. 1954, Ohio 1954, D.C. 1959. Assoc. Squire, Sanders & Dempsey, Cleve., 1954; assoc., ptnr. Woll, Mayer & St. Antoine, Washington, 1958-65; assoc. prof. law U. Mich. Law Sch., Ann Arbor, 1965-69, prof., 1969—, Degan prof., 1981-98, Degan prof. emeritus, 1998—, dean, 1971-78. Pres. Nat. Resource Ctr. for Consumers of Legal Svcs., 1974—78; mem. pub. rev. bd. UAW, 1973—; mem. Mich. Atty. Discipline Bd., 1999—, vice-chmn., 2000—; chmn. UAW-GM Legal Svcs. Plan, 1983—95; Mich. Gov.'s spl. counselor on workers' compensation, 1983—85; reporter Uniform Law Commrs., 1987—92; life mem. Clare Hall, Cambridge (Eng.) U. Co-author: (with R. Smith, L. Merrifield and C. Craver) Labor Relations Law: Cases and Materials, 4th edit., 1968, 10th edit., 1999; editor: The Common Law of the Workplace: The Views of Arbitrators, 1998; contbr. articles to profl. jours. 1st lt. JACG, U.S. Army, 1955-57. Fulbright grantee, London, 1957-58. Mem. ABA (past sec. labor law sect., coun. 1984-92), Am. Bar Found., State Bar Mich. (chmn. labor rels. law sect. 1979-80), Nat. Acad. Arbitrators (bd. govs. 1985-88, v.p. 1994-96, pres. 1999-2000), Internat. Soc. Labor Law and Social Security (U.S. br. exec. bd. 1983—, vice chmn. 1989-95), Am. Arbitration Assn. (bd. dirs. 2000—), Indsl. Rels. Rsch. Assn., Coll. Labor and Employment Lawyers, Order of Coif (life). Democrat. Roman Catholic. Home: 1421 Roxbury Rd Ann Arbor MI 48104-4047 Office: U Mich Law Sch 625 S State St Ann Arbor MI 48109-1215 E-mail: tstanton@umich.edu

ST. CLAIR, DONALD DAVID, lawyer; b. Hammond, Ind., Dec. 30, 1932; s. Victor Peter and Wanda (Rubinska) Small; m. Sergine Anne Oliver, June 6, 1970 (dec. June 1974); m. Beverly Joyce Tipton, Dec. 28, 1987. BS, Ind. U., 1955, MS, 1963, EdD, 1967; JD, U. Toledo, 1992. Bar: Ohio 1992, U.S. Dist. Ct. (no. dist.) Ohio 1993, U.S. Supreme Ct., 1996. Assoc. prof. Western Ky. U. Coll. Edn., Bowling Green, 1967-68, U. Toledo, 1968-77, prof., 1977-92; atty., ptnr. Garand, Bollinger, & St. Clair, Oregon, Ohio, 1992-97; pvt. practice Law Offices Donald D. St. Clair, Toledo, 1997—. Mem. Ohio Coun. Mental Health Ctrs., Columbus, 1978-79; dir. honors programs U. Toledo. Author: (poetry) Daymarks and Beacons, 1983, Impressions from an Afternoon in a Paris Courtroom, 1998; contbr. articles to profl. jours. Organizer Students Toledo Organized for Peace, 1970-71; mem. Lucas County Dem. Party, 1990—. With U.S. Army, 1955-57. Mem. ABA, AAU (nat. bd. dirs. 1973-74), Am. Inns of Ct., Ohio Bar Assn., Toledo Bar Assn., Ohio Acad. Trial Lawyers, Toledo Power Squadron (comdg. officer 1981), Bay View Yacht Club, Ohio Criminal Def. Lawyers Assn., Lucas County Bar Assn., Maumee Valley Criminal Def. Lawyers Assn., Ottawa County Bar Assn., Masons (32 degree), Shriners, Ancient Order Friars, Phi Alpha Delta. Criminal, General practice, Personal injury. Home: 3353 Christie Blvd Toledo OH 43606-2862 Office: 5415 Monroe St Toledo OH 43623-2800 E-mail: stclairlaw@attglobal.net

ST. CLAIR, JOHN GILBERT, lawyer; b. Rupert, Idaho, Sept. 21, 1945; s. Gilbert Clency and Martha Jane (Baker) St. C.; children: Kevin John, Bradley Warren. Student, Champan Coll., 1965; BS in Bus., U. Idaho, 1967, JD, 1970. Bar: Idaho 1970, U.S. Dist. Ct. Idaho 1970. Clk. St. Clair, Hiller, Wood & McGrath C.H., Idaho Falls, Idaho, 1970, assoc., 1974-81, Beard, St. Clair, Gaffney & McNamara PA, Idaho Falls, 1981—. Adv. bd. Idaho State U. Tax Inst., Pocatello, 1977-95, 99—. Bd. dirs. Idaho Cmty. Found., 198-89, Salvation Army, Idaho Falls, 1974-87, Coll. Ea. Idaho Found., Inc., Idaho Falls, 1992. Mem. ABA, Seventh Jud. Dist. Bar Assn., Idaho State Bar Assn., U. Idaho Alumni Assn. (bd. dirs. 1988-91), Idaho Falls Youth Soccer Assn. (bd. dirs. 1982-91), Idaho Falls Country Club (bd. dirs. 1976-79), Rotary (local club 1978-79, 85-90, v.p. 1985-87, pres. 1988-89, U.S. golfing fellowship, bd. dirs. 1990—, pres. 1993-96, exec. sec. 1996—). Republican. Methodist. Alternative dispute resolution, Estate planning, Probate. Home: 1515 Three Fountains Dr Idaho Falls ID 83404-5627 Office: Beard St Clair Gaffney McNamara PA 2105 Coronado St Idaho Falls ID 83404-7495 E-mail: john@idahofallslaw.com

ST. GEORGE, NICHOLAS JAMES, lawyer, manufactured housing company executive; b. Waltham, Mass., Feb. 11, 1939; s. Louis and Rose (Argonti) St. G.; children: Blane Stephen, Nicholas John; m. Eugenia Metzger, July 1965. BA in Econs., Coll. William and Mary, 1960, JD, 1965. Trainee GE Co., Schenectady, 1960; trust rep. Ba. NAt. Bank, Norfolk, 1965-66; group v.p. in charge investment banking dept. Ferguson Enterprises, Newport News, Va., 1977-78; pres., CEO Oakwood Homes Corp., Greensboro, N.C., 1979—, also bd. dirs. Dir. Am. Bankers Ins. Group, First Union Nat. Bank Greensboro, Legg Mason, Inc.; dir. Manufactured Housing Inst.; trustee Marshall-Wythe Sch. Law Coll. William and Mary. Office: Oakwood Homes Corp PO Box 27081 Greensboro NC 27425-7081

SAKAI, PETER A. lawyer; b. McAllen, Tex., Oct. 21, 1954; s. Pete Y. and Rose Marie (Kawahata) S.; m. Raquel M. Dias, Mar. 10, 1982; children: George Y., Elizabeth K. BA, U. Tex., Austin, 1976, JD, 1979. Bar: Tex. 1979. Asst. dist. atty. County of Bexar, San Antonio, 1980-82; pvt. practice, 1983-94; assoc. judge Bexar County Dist. Ct., 1994—. Hearings arbitrator City of San Antonio, 1983-93; judge Mcpl. Ct., City of Elmendorf, Tex., 1985; juvenile assoc. judge 289th Dist. Ct., San Antonio, 1989-94; city atty. City of Leon Valley, Tex., 1986-90. Contbr. to profl. publs. Bd. dirs. Bexar County Juvenile Vols. in Probation, San Antonio, 1983-93; Japan Am. Soc. San Antonio, 1987-89, Cmty. Cultural Arts Orgn., San Antonio, 1987-92, Bexar County Local Devel. Corp., San Antonio, 1989-94. Mem. ABA, State Bar Tex., San Antonio Bar Assn. Avocation: sports. Office: Bexar County Courthouse 100 Dolorosa Rm 205 San Antonio TX 78205-3038

SALACUSE, JESWALD WILLIAM, lawyer, educator; b. Niagara Falls, N.Y., Jan. 28, 1938; s. William L. and Bessie B. (Buzzelli) S.; m. Donna Booth, Oct. 1, 1966; children: William, Maria. Diploma, U. Paris, 1959; AB, Hamilton Coll., 1960; JD, Harvard U., 1963. Bar: N.Y. 1965, Tex. 1980. Lectr. law Ahmadu Bello U., Nigeria, 1963-65; assoc. Conboy, Hewitt, O'Brien & Boardman, N.Y.C., 1965-67; assoc. dir. African Law Ctr., Columbia U., 1967-68; prof., dir. Rsch. Ctr., Nat. Sch. Adminstrn., Zaire, 1968-71; Mid. East regional advisor on law and devel. Ford Found., Beirut, 1971-74, rep. in Sudan, 1974-77; vis. prof. U. Khartoum, Sudan, 1974-77; vis. scholar Harvard Law Sch., 1977-78; prof. law So. Meth. U., Dallas, 1978-86, dean, 1980-86; dean, prof. internat. law Fletcher Sch. Law and Diplomacy, Tufts U., Medford, Mass., 1986-94, Henry J. Braker prof. comml. law, 1994—. Fellow Inst. Advanced Legal Studies, U. London, 1995; vis. prof. Ecole Nat. Ponts et Chaussées, Paris, 1990-95, Inst. Empressa, Madrid, 1995, U. Bristol, U. London Sch. Oriental and African Studies, 1995—; cons. Ford Found., 1978-82, 93, U.S. Dept. State, 1978-80, UN Ctr. on Transnat. Corps., 1988—, Harvard Inst. Internat. Devel., 1990—, Asia Found., 1992, Harvard Law Sch./World Bank Laos Project, 1991-93; with Sri Lanka fin. sector project ISTI/U.S. AID, 1993-94; lectr. Georgetown U. Internat. Law Inst., 1978-94, Panam. U., Mexico City, 1981; chmn. com. on Mid. Ea. law Social Sci. Rsch. Coun., 1978-84; chmn. Coun. Internat. Exch. Scholars, 1987-91; bd. dirs. Boston World Affairs Coun., 1988-95, Emerging Markets Income Funds. I & II, Inc., Global Ptnrs. Income Fund, Inc., Salomon Bros. Worldwide Income Fund, Inc., Asia Tigers Fund, Inc., India Fund, Inc., Emerging Markets Floating Rate Fund, Inc., Mcpl. Advantage Fund, Inc., Mcpl. Ptnrs. Funds I & II, Salomon Bros. High Income Funds I & II, Salomon Bros. 2008 Worldwide Dollar Govt. Term Trust, Mcpl. Ptnrs. Funds I & II; trustee Southwestern Legal Found., 1992—, Am. U. Paris, 1993-97; pres. Internat. Third World Legal Studies Assn., 1987-91; chmn. Inst. Transnat. Arbitration, 1991-93; pres. Assn. Profl. Schs. Internat. Affairs, 1988-89; Fulbright disting. chair in comparative law, Italy, 2000. Author: (with Kasunmu) Nigerian Family Law, 1966, An Introduction to Law in French-Speaking Africa, Vol. I, 1969, Vol. II, 1976, (with Steng) International Business Planning, 1982, Making Global Deals-Negotiating in the International Marketplace, 1991, The Art of Advice, 1994, (video course) Negotiating in Today's World, 1995, The Wise Advisor, 2000; contbr. articles to profl. jours. Mem. ABA, Dallas Bar Found. (trustee 1983-86), Coun. on Fgn. Rels., Am. Law Inst., Am. Soc. Internat. Law, Cosmos Club (Washington). Home: 220 Stone Root Ln Concord MA 01742-4755 Office: Tufts U Fletcher Sch Law-Diplomacy Medford MA 02155 E-mail: jeswald.salacuse@tufts.edu

SALAZAR, KENNETH L. state attorney general; b. Mar. 2, 1955; s. Henry and Emma Salazar; m. Hope Hernandez; children: Melinda, Andrea. BA in Polit. Sci., Colo. Coll., 1977, LLD (hon.), 1993; JD, U. Mich., 1981. Bar: Colo. 1981, U.S. Dist. Ct. Colo. 1981, U.S. Ct. Appeals (10th cir.) 1981, U.S. Supreme Ct. 1999. Farmer, rancher, Conejos County, Colo.; law clk. Colo. Atty. Gen., summer 1979; assoc. Sherman & Howard, Denver, 1981-86; chief legal counsel Office of Gov., 1986-90; exec. dir. Colo. Dept. Natural Resources, 1990-94; dir. Parcel, Mauro, Hultin & Spaanstra, 1994-98; atty. gen. State of Colo., 1999—. Gov.'s rep. State Bd. Equalization, Denver, 1990. Chair Great Outdoors Colo., Denver, 1993-94, Rio Grande Compact Commn., 1995-97, Sangre de Cristo Land Grant Commn., 1993-95; mem. Colo. Water Conservation Bd., Denver, 1990—; mem. City and County of Denver Ethics Panel, 1993; bd. dirs. Denver Cmty. Leadership Forum, 1988; gov.'s rep. State Bd. on Property Tax Equalization, 1987-91; del. Soviet-Am. Young Leadership Dialogue, 1984; bd. dirs. Servicios de la Raza HUD 202 Project, 1985-89, chair, 1986; mem. Am. Israel Friendship League, 1986-89. mem. adv. com. Colo. U. Law Sch. Natural Resources Law Ctr., 1989-92; mem. Western Water Policy Rev. Adv. Commn., 1995-97. Juan Tienda scholar. Mem. ABA, Colo. Bar Assn. (bd. govs. 1989-90, task force to assess the legal profession 1986), Denver Bar Assn. (2d v.p. 1989, chair policy-cmty. rels. subcoms. 1982-84), Hispanic Bar Assn. (ABA task force on opptys. for minorities in legal profession, bd. dirs. 1986-87), Am. Judicature Soc. Avocations: basketball, outdoor activities, politics. Office: State Colo Dept Law 1525 Sherman St Fl 5 Denver CO 80203-1700 E-mail: attorney.general@state.co.us

SALCE, VALERIO, lawyer; b. Rome, Nov. 6, 1968; s. Guido Salce and Alfreda Recanati. LLM, Georgetown U., 1994; JD, U. Rome, 1992. Bar: N.Y. 1995, Italy 1996. Assoc. Studio Legale Tonucci, Rome, 1996, Baker & McKenzie, Rome, 1996—. Avocations: travel, reading, sports. Antitrust, Intellectual property, Mergers and acquisitions. Office: Baker & McKenzie Via Degli Supioni 288 00192 Rome Italy Fax: 3906.3203502. E-mail: valerio.salce@bakernet.com

SALCH, STEVEN CHARLES, lawyer; b. Palm Beach, Fla., Oct. 25, 1943; s. Charles Henry and Helen Louise (Alverson) S.; m. Mary Ann Prim, Oct. 7, 1967; children— Susan Elizabeth, Stuart Trenton B.B.A., So. Meth. U., 1965, J.D., 1968. Bar: Tex. 1968, U.S. Tax Ct. 1969, U.S. Dist. Ct. (so. dist.) Tex. 1969, U.S. Dist. Ct. (ea. dist.) Tex. 1972, U.S. Ct. Appeals (5th cir.) 1969, U.S. Ct. Appeals (fed. cir.) 1982, U.S. Ct. Fed. Claims, 1982. Assoc. Fulbright & Jaworski, Houston, 1968-71, participating assoc., 1971-75, ptnr., 1975—. Co-author: Tax Practice Before the IRS, 1994; contbr. articles to legal jours. Pres. Tealwood Owners Assn., 1982-83, Meml. High Sch. PTA, 1985-86; mem. Tex. PTA (Hon. Life Member award 1986). Mem. ABA (coun. dir. 1985-88, vice chair tax sect. 1988-91, chair elect 1995-96, chair 1996-97), State Bar Tex., Houston Bar Assn., Fed. Bar Assn., Am. Law Inst., Nat. Tax Assn., Am. Coll. Tax Counsel, Internat. Fiscal Assn., Harris County Heritage Soc., Galveston Hist. Found., Smithsonian Assocs., Colonial Williamsburg Found., Am. Bar Found., Southwestern Legal Found., Houston Bar Found., Order of Coif, Beta Alpha Psi, Phi Eta Sigma, Phi Delta Phi. Presbyterian. Clubs: Lakeside Country, Houston Center, Galveston Country, Yacht,Pelican of Galveston, Galveston Artillery. Administrative and regulatory, Private international, Corporate taxation. Home: 342 Tamerlaine Dr Houston TX 77024-6147 Office: Fulbright & Jaworski 1301 Mckinney St Fl 51 Houston TX 77010-3031 E-mail: ssalch@fulbright.com

SALEH, DAVID JOHN, lawyer; b. Buffalo, Apr. 24, 1953; s. Donald Thomas and Joan Barbara (Labaki) S.; m. Elizabeth Catherine Abdella, July 2, 1976; children: Anthony Donald, Amy Madeline, Anne Teresa, Andrew David. BA, SUNY, Buffalo, 1975, JD, 1978. Bar: N.Y. 1979, U.S. Dist. Ct. (we. dist.) N.Y. 1980. Assoc. Jeffrey D. Oshlag, Esq., Batavia, N.Y., 1978-82; ptnr. Oshlag, Saleh & Earl, L.L.P., 1982—; chief counsel, sec. Am. Real Time Svcs., Inc., N.Y.C., 1988-91; atty. Town of Stafford, N.Y., 1994—; town atty. Town of Darien, 2000—. Prosecutor Village of Corfu, N.Y., 1997—; legal counsel City of Batavia Housing Authority, 1982—; atty. Village of Corfu, N.Y., 1981—, Pembroke Ctrl. Sch. Dist., 1985-90; chief counsel Intelligent Quotation Sys. Inc., Norwalk, Conn.,

1987-93; prosecutor Town of Pembroke, 1988—; chief counsel, dir., treas. GB's Country Corners Inc., 1991-93; v.p., chief counsel Marine Ptnrs. Funding, Inc., 1994—; counsel Corfu Fire Dist., 1995—; prosecutor Village of Corfu, N.Y., 1997—; chief counsel Network & Comm. Group, Inc., 1997—; counsel Weston Info. Techs. Inc., others. Mem. staff Buffalo Law Rev., 1976-78. Mem. Pembroke Vol. Fire Dept., 1976-79, Corfu Vol. Fire Dept., 1979—; bd. dirs. Corfu Area Bus. Assn., 1986-87; del. Rep. Caucus; trustee Corfu Free Libr. Assn., 1991—, pres., 1993-96; bd. dirs. St. Jerome Hosp. Found., 1992-98, treas., 1994-98; treas. Genesee Mercy Healthcare Found., Inc., 1996-98; parliamentarian Genesee County Rep. Com., 2000—. Mem. ABA, ATLA, N.Y. Defenders Assn., N.Y. State Bar Assn., Genesee County Bar Assn. (mem. jud. nominations com. for 8th jud. dist. N.Y., chmn. criminal def. com. 1995—), Erie County Bar Assn., N.Y. State Housing Renewal Ofcls., U. Buffalo Alumni Assn. (bd. dirs., v.p. fin. 1997-99, exec. v.p., pres.-elect 1999-2000, pres. 2000—), Lions. Republican. Roman Catholic. General corporate, Criminal, General practice. Home: 54 E Main St Corfu NY 14036-9601 Office: Oshlag Saleh & Earl LLP 432 E Main St Batavia NY 14020-2519 E-mail: djsaleh@aol.com

SALEH, JOHN, lawyer; b. O'Donnell, Tex., June 29, 1928; s. Nahum and Arslie S. BBA, U. Tex., 1950, JD with honors, 1952; cert. U.S. Army Judge Advocate Sch., U. Va., 1953. Bar: Tex. 1952, U.S. Ct. Mil. Appeals, 1953, U.S. Tax Ct. 1954, U.S. Dist. Ct. (no. dist.) Tex. 1956, U.S. Ct. Appeals (5th cir.) 1960, U.S. Supreme Ct. 1961, D.C. 1982. Pvt. practice, Lamesa, Tex., 1954—. Tchg. instr. legal rsch. writing U. Tex. Sch. Law, 1950-52. Mem. editl. bd. Tex. Law Rev., 1951-52. Mem. ABA, ATLA, Tex. Law Rev. Assn. (life), Tex. Bar Assn. (spl. com. to study rev. code criminal procedure 1969-71), D.C. Bar Assn., Tex. Trial Lawyers Assn., Tex. Bar Found., Order of the Coif, The Million Dollar Advocates Forum, Phi Delta Phi. General civil litigation. Home: 605 Doak Odonnell TX 79351 Office: 502 N 1st St Lamesa TX 79331-5406 E-mail: bigjohn@pics.net

SALEM, RICHARD ALLEN, mediator; b. N.Y.C., Aug. 15, 1930; s. Louis H. and Catherine (Levy) S.; m. Greta Waldinger, June 26, 1955; children: Susanne, Peter, Erica. BA in Sociology, Antioch Coll., 1953; MS in Journalism, Columbia U., 1957. Reporter Washington Post, 1957-59; editor, publ. Washington SBIC Newsletter, 1960-62; spl. asst. to dep. dir. for investment Small Bus. Adminstrn., Washington, 1963-64, assoc. dir. Office of Equal Opportunity, 1964-67, regional dir., 1967-68; Midwest dir. Cmty. Rels. Svc. U.S. Dept. Justice, Chgo., 1968-82; pres. Conflict Mgmt. Initiatives, Evanston, Ill., 1982—. Adj. prof. Loyola U., Chgo., 1986-90; mediator Wounded Knee Takeover, 1972, Skokie-Nazi Conflict, 1980. Co-author: Students Guide to Mediation and Law, 1987, Ctr. for Pub. Resources award, 1987; mem. editl. bd. Chgo. Reporter, 1996—; editor: Witness to Genocide - the Children of Rwanda, 2000; contbr. articles to profl. jours. Bd. dirs. Housing Options for Mentally Ill, Evanston, 1997—, Found. Self-Sufficiency Ctrl. Am., 2000—. With U.S. Army, 1953-55. Recipient Outstanding Performance award U.S. Sr. Exec. Svc., 1980. Mem. Soc. Profls. in Dispute Resolution (2d v.p. 1988, bd. dirs. 1982-89, Cmty. Mediation Tng. in South Africa award 1993). Home and Office: 1225 Oak Ave Evanston IL 60202-1220

SALES, JAMES BOHUS, lawyer; b. Weimar, Tex., Aug. 24, 1934; s. Henry B. and Agnes Mary (Pesek) S.; m. Beuna M. Vornsand, June 3, 1956; children: Mark Keith, Debra Lynn, Travis James. BS, U. Tex., 1956, LLB with honors, 1960. Bar: Tex. 1960. Practiced in, Houston, 1960—; sr. ptnr. Fulbright & Jaworski, 1960-00, head litig. dept., 1979-99; ret., 2000. Author: Products Liability in Texas, 1985; co-author: Texas Torts and Remedies, 6 vols., 1986; assoc. editor Tex. Law Rev., 1960; contbr. articles to profl. jours. Trustee South Tex. Coll. Law, 1982-88, 90—, A.A. White Dispute Resolution Ctr., 1991-94; bd. dirs. Tex. Resource Ctr., 1990-97, Tex. Bar Hist. Found., 1990-2001; cir. chair for membership The Supreme Ct. Hist. Soc., 1998-2001. Named among Best Lawyers in Am., 1989—. Fellow Internat. Acad. Trial Lawyers, Am. Coll. Trial Lawyers (state chmn. 1993-96), Am. Bd. Trial Advocates, Am. Bar Found. (sustaining life, state chmn. 1993-98), Tex. Bar Found. (trustee 1991-95, vice-chmn. 1992-93, chmn. 1993-94, chair adv. bd. for planned giving 1994—, sustaining life mem.), Houston Bar Found. (sustaining life, chmn. bd. 1982-83); mem. ABA (ho. of dels. 1984-2003, mem. Commn. on IOLTA 1995-97), FBA, Internat. Assn. Def. Counsel, Nat. Conf. Bar Pres. (coun. 1989-92), So. Conf. Bar, So. Tex. Coll. Trial Advocacy (dir. 1983-87), State Bar Tex. (pres. 1988-89, bd. dirs. 1983-88, chmn. bd. 1985-86), Tex. Assn. Def. Counsel (v.p. 1977-79), Tex. Law Rev. Assn. (bd. dirs. 1996—, pres. 1999-2000), Houston Bar Assn. (officer, bd. dirs. 1970-79, pres.-elect 1979-80, pres. 1980-81), Gulf Coast Legal Found. (bd. dirs. 1982-85), Bar Assn. 5th Fed. Cir., The Forum, Westlake Club (bd. govs. 1980-85), Inns of Ct. (bd. dirs. 1981-84), Order of Coif. Roman Catholic. Home: 10803 Oak Creek St Houston TX 77024-3016 Office: Fulbright & Jaworski 1301 Mckinney St Houston TX 77010-3031 E-mail: jsales@fulbright.com

SALINGER, FRANK MAX, lawyer; b. Landau, Isar, Germany, Dec. 4, 1951; s. Karl and Ingeborg F. (Herold) S.; m. Susan Ann Wagner, May 20, 1978. Student, Columbia Union Coll., Takoma Park, Md., 1969-72; JD, U. Balt., 1975. Bar: Md. 1975, U.S. Dist. Ct. Md. 1975, U.S. Ct. Appeals (4h cir.) 1978, U.S. Tax Ct. 1978, U.S. Ct. Mil. Appeals 1978, U.S. Ct. Appeals (5th cir.) 1982, U.S. Supreme Ct. 1983, U.S. Ct. Appeals (11th cir.) 1984, U.S. Ct. Appeals (9th cir.) 1986, D.C. 1986, U.S. Ct. Appeals (3d cir.) 1989. Pvt. practice, Balt., 1975-77; counsel Md. State Senate, Annapolis, 1975-76; assoc. counsel Am. Fin. Corp., Silver Spring, Md., 1977-78; govt. rels. counsel Truck Trailer Mfrs. Assn., Washington, 1978-80; v.p., gen. counsel, dir. govt. affairs Am. Fin. Svcs. Assocs., 1980-92; v.p. govt. rels. Advanta Corp., Wilmington, Del., 1992—. Co-author: (with Alvin O. Wiese and Robert E. McKew) A Guide to the Consumer Bankruptcy Code, 1989; (with Robert W. Green) State Regulations and Statutes on Consumer Credit, 1989, Federal Consumer Credit Regulations and Statutes, 1989. City councilman, Laurel, Md., 1976-78, zoning commr., 1976-78; chmn. Md. State Young Reps., 1977-78; bd. dirs. Am. Bankruptcy Inst., Washington, 1986-88. Mem. ABA (mem. com. on consumer fin. svcs., subcoms. on interest rate regulation and state regulation), Am. League Lobbyists (chair fin. svcs. sect. 1995-97), Federalist Soc. Law and Pub. Policy, Woodmore Country Club, Capitol Hill Club, Ford's Theatre Soc. Republican. Lutheran. Banking, Consumer commercial, Legislative. Office: Advanta Corp One Righter Pkwy Wilmington DE 19803

SALISBURY, EUGENE W. lawyer, justice; b. Blasdell, N.Y., Mar. 20, 1933; s. W. Dean and Mary I. (Burns) S.; m. Joanne M. Salisbury, July 14, 1950; children: Mark, Ellen, Susan, David, Scott. BA in History and Govt. cum laude, U. Buffalo, 1959, JD cum laude, 1968. Bar: N.Y. 1960, D.C. 1973, U.S. Dist. Ct. (we. and no. dists.) 1961, U.S. Ct. Appeals (2d cir.) 1970, U.S. Ct. Appeals (D.C. cir.) 1973, U.S. Supreme Ct. 1973. Ptnr. Lipsitz, Green, Fahringer, Roll, Salisbury and Cambria, Buffalo, 1960—. Justice Village of Blasdell, 1961-2001; lectr. N.Y. Office Ct. Adminstrn., N.Y.C., 1961—; mem. N.Y. State Commn. on Jud. Conduct, 1989-2001, chmn., 2000-2001. Author: Manual for N.Y. Courts, 1973, Forms for N.Y. Courts, 1977. Capt. U.S. Army, 1948-54, Korea. Decorated Bronze Star, Purple Heart; recipient Citizen of Yr. award Indsl. Rels. Rsch. Assn., 2000; named Jurist of Yr., Erie County Judges and Police Conf., 2001, Magistrate of Yr., Erie County Magistrates Assn., 2001. Mem. ABA (del. spl. ct. sect. 1988-2001), D.C. Bar Assn., Erie County Bar Assn., N.Y. State Bar Assn., World Judges Assn., N.Y. State Magistrates Assn. (pres. 1973, Man of Yr. 1974), N.Y. State Jud. Conf., Upstate N.Y. Labor Adv. Coun., 1995—. Labor. Office: Lipsitz Green Fahringer Roll Salisbury and Cambria 42 Delaware Ave Ste 300 Buffalo NY 14202-3857 E-mail: esalisbury@lipsitzgreen

SALITERMAN, RICHARD ARLEN, lawyer; b. Aug. 3, 1946; s. Leonard Slitz and Dorothy (Sloan) S.; m. Laura Shrager, June 15, 1975; 1 child, Robert Warren. BA summa cum laude, U. Minn., 1968; JD, Columbia U., 1971; LLM, NYU, 1974. Bar: Minn. 1972, D.C. 1974. Mem. legal staff subcom. on antitrust and monopoly U.S. Senate, Washington, 1971-72; acting dir., dep. dir. compliance and enforcement divsn. Fed. Energy Office, N.Y.C., 1974; mil. atty. Presdl. Clemency Bd., White House, Washington, 1975; sr. ptnr. Saliterman & Saliterman, Mpls., 1975—. Adj. prof. law Hamline U., 1976-81. Author: Advising Minnesota Corporations and Other Business Organizations, 4 vols., 1975; chmn. Hennepin County Bar Jour., 1985-87. Trustee, sec. Hopkins Edn. Found.; trustee W. Harry Davis Found., 1990-96; pres. Twin Cities Coun.; mem. nat. bd. dirs. Navy League U.S., Washington, 1997—, nat. judge adv., 2001—. State civil litigation, General corporate, General practice.

SALMAN, ROBERT RONALD, lawyer; b. N.Y., Dec. 26, 1939; s. Samuel L. and Lillian Gertrude (Sincoff) S.; m. Reva Carol Rappaport, June 16, 1963; children: Elyse D. Spiewak, Suzanne A. BA magna cum laude, Columbia Coll., 1961, LLB cum laude, 1964. Bar: N.Y. 1965, U.S. Supreme Ct. 1974, U.S. Ct. Appeals (2nd cir.) 1967, U.S. Ct. Appeals (3rd cir.) 1993, U.S. Ct. Appeals (11th cir.) 1985, U.S. Ct. Appeals (9th cir.) 1979, U.S. Dist. Ct. so. dist., ea. dist.) N.Y. 1969. Assoc. Proskauer, Rose, Goetz & Mendelsohn, N.Y.C., 1964-67; asst. corp. counsel Law Dept. N.Y., 1967-69; assoc. Phillips, Nizer, 1969-73; ptnr. Phillips, Nizer, Benjamin, Krim & Ballon, 1973-87, Reavis & McGrath, N.Y.C., 1987-88, Carter, Ledyard & Milburn, N.Y.C., 1988-94, Phillips & Salman, N.Y.C., 1994-97, Phillips Salman & Stein, N.Y.C., 1997-2000, Duane Morris & Heckscher LLP, N.Y.C., 2001—. Adj. prof. Seton Hall Law Sch., Newark, N.J., 1995-98. Contbr. articles to profl. jours. Pres., founder The Assn. for A Better N.J. Inc., 1991—; pres. Marlboro Jewish Ctr., 1982-84. Recipient NEGEV Builder award Israel Bonds, 1980, Award of Honor UJA Fedn., 1981. Mem. N.Y. State Bar Assn., ABA, Assn. Bar City of N.Y. Avocations: charitable and communal work, baseball, reading, writing. Antitrust, General civil litigation, Entertainment. Office: 111 Broadway New York NY 10006-1901 E-mail: RRSalman@aol.com, RRSalman@DuaneMorris.com

SALO, ANN SEXTON DISTLER, lawyer; b. Indpls., Sept. 2, 1947; d. Harry W. and Ann (Malloy) Distler; m. Donald R. Salo, June 3, 1972 (div. Feb. 1983); 1 child, Eric V. Salo; m. Phillip G. Clark, May 5, 1990; children: Ann Potter Clark, Philip Gray Clark. BA, Purdue U., 1969; JD, George Washington U., 1972; LLM in Taxation, Emory U., 1976. Bar: Ga. 1973, U.S. Dist. Ct. (no. dist.) Ga. 1974. Assoc. Hansell & Post, Atlanta, 1972-78, mng. ptnr., 1978-89; ptnr. Grenwald and Salo, 1989-92, Long, Aldridge & Norman, Atlanta, 1992-95, Salo & Walker, Atlanta, 1995—. Adj. prof. law Emory U., 1983-86; mem. fin. planning adv. bd. Warren Gorham & Lamont, 1988-2000. Author: Estate Planning, 1988. Bd. dirs. Auditory Edn. Ctr., Atlanta, 1987-93, 98-2001; pres. Planned Parenthood of Atlanta, 1984-86; pres. Atlanta Humane Soc., 1990-93. Fellow Am. Coll. Trust and Estate Counsel (state chair 2001—); mem. Atlanta Estate Planning Coun., Atlanta Tax Forum. Estate planning, Probate. Office: Salo & Walker 2968 Lookout Pl NE Atlanta GA 30305-3272 E-mail: adsalo@bellsouth.net

SALOMON, DARRELL JOSEPH, lawyer; b. Feb. 16, 1939; s. Joseph and Rosalie Rita (Pool) S.; m. Christine Mariscal, Apr. 25, 1992; 1 child, Camilla Lind. Student, Georgetown U., 1957-59; BS, U. San Francisco, 1964, JD, 1966. Bar: Calif. 1970, U.S. Dist. Ct. (cen. and no. dists.) Calif. 1970, U.S. Supreme Ct. 1971. Assoc. Offices of Joseph L. Alioto, San Francisco, 1970, 72, 73; dep. city atty. City of San Francisco, 1972; assoc. Salomon & Costello, 1981; ptnr. Hill, Farrer & Burrill, L.A., 1984-87, Arter & Hadden, L.A., 1987-94; assoc. Keck, Mahin & Cate, San Francisco, 1994-96; chmn. Commerce Law Group A Profl. Corp., 1996-99; chief asst. dist. atty. City of San Francisco, 2000; gen. counsel San Francisco Examiner, 2000—. Lectr. law Santa Clara U. Mem. Human Rights Commn. City and County of San Francisco, 1975; mem., past pres. Civil Svc. Commn., San Francisco, 1976-84; trustee San Francisco War Meml. and Performing Arts Ctr., 1984-88; bd. dirs. L.A. Symphony Master Chorale, 1985-87, Marin Symphony Assn., 1995-97. Recipient Disting. Svc. citation United Negro Coll. Fund, 1975; D'alton-Power scholar Georgetown U., 1957. Mem. ABA, Consumer Attys. of Calif. (bd. govs. 1977), Soc. Calif. Pioneers, L.A. Bar Assn., Chit Chat Club, San Francisco Lawyers Club. Antitrust, Intellectual property. Office: San Francisco Examiner 988 Market St San Francisco CA 94124 E-mail: dsalomon@s.f.examiner.com

SALOMON, PHILIPPE M. lawyer; b. N.Y.C., Feb. 4, 1949; BA, Wesleyan U., 1970; JD, Temple U., 1974. Bar: N.Y. 1975, U.S. Supreme Ct. 1978. Mem. Willkie Farr & Gallagher, N.Y.C. Mem. ABA, N.Y. State Bar Assn., Assn. Bar City of N.Y. Federal civil litigation, General civil litigation, State civil litigation. Office: Willkie Farr & Gallagher 787 7th Ave New York NY 10019-6018

SALOOM, KALISTE JOSEPH, JR. lawyer, retired judge; b. Lafayette, La., May 15, 1918; s. Kaliste and Asma Ann (Boustany) S.; m. Yvonne Adelle Nassar, Oct. 19, 1958; children: Kaliste III, Douglas James, Leanne Isabelle, Gregory John. BA with high distinction, U. La., 1939; JD, Tulane U., 1942. Bar: La. 1942. Atty. City of Lafayette, 1948-52; judge City and Juvenile Ct., Lafayette, 1952-93; ret., 1993; of counsel Saloom & Saloom, Lafayette, 1993—. Mem. jud. coun. La. Supreme Ct., 1960-64; bd. dirs. Nat. Ctr. for State Cts., Williamsburg, Va., 1978-84, adv. coun., 1984—, mem. assocs. com., 1986—; judge pro tempore La. Ct. Appeal 3d Cir., 1992; tech. adviser Jud. Adminstrn. of Traffic Cts. mem. adv. com. Nat. Hwy. Traffic Safety Adminstrn., U.S. Dept. Transp., 1977-80, Nat. Com. on Uniform Traffic Laws, 1986; mem. expert panel Drunk Driving Protection Act U.S. Congress, 1989-91. Mem. editl. bd. Tulane Law Rev., 1941; contbr. articles to profl. jours. With U.S. Army, 1942-45. Recipient Civic Cup, City of Lafayette, 1965, Pub. Svc. award U.S. Dept. Transp., 1980, Disting. Jurist award Miss. State U. Pre-Law Soc., 1987, Disting. Svc. award Nat. Ctr. State Cts., 1988, Disting. La. Jurist award La. State Bar Found., 1992, U.S. Supreme Ct. Chief Justice Warren E. Burger Soc. award, 1999. Mem. ABA (Benjamin Flaschner award 1981, vice chair JAD com. on traffic ct. program 1989-99), Am. Judges Assn. (William H. Burnett award 1982), Nat. Coun. Juvenile Ct. Judges, La. City Judges Assn. (past pres.), La. Juvenile Ct. Judges Assn. (past pres.), Am. Judicature Soc. (panel drafting La. children's code 1989-91), U.S. Chief Justice Warren E. Burger Soc. (mem. award 1999), Order of Coif, Equestrian Order of Holy Sepulchre (knight comdr.), Oakbourne Country Club, Rotary (paul Harris fellow), KC. Democrat. Roman Catholic. State civil litigation, Juvenile, Transportation. Home: 502 Marguerite Blvd Lafayette LA 70503-3138 Office: 211 W Main St Lafayette LA 70501-6843

SALOSCHIN, ROBERT L. lawyer; b. N.Y.C., Jan. 15, 1920; s. Bruno Benedix and Edna Saloschin; m. Neita L. Saloschin, Dec. 10, 1949; children: Mary Ann, Joan Janelle. BA, Columbia Coll., 1940; JD, Columbia Law Sch., 1947. Bar: N.Y. 1947, D.C. 1960, Md. 1980, U.S. Supreme Ct. 1956. Pers. adminstr. USN, Washington, 1941-43; atty. Cahill, Gordon, Reindel, N.Y.C., 1947-49, Housing & Home Fin. Agy., Washington, 1950-52, Civil Aeronautics Bd., Washington, 1952-58; atty. Office of Legal Counsel, dir. Office Info. Law U.S. Dept. Justice, 1958-81; of counsel Lerch Early & Brewer, Bethesda, Md., 1981—. Cons. standing com. on law and nat. security ABA, Washington, 1981-91; developed legal strategy for ending racial segregation in interstate bus transp., ICC; mediator for Am. athletics orgns. Olympic Games. Patentee air navigation device; editor: A Short Guide to the Freedom of Information Act, annually, 1974—; editor law rev. Columbia Law Sch., 1947. Organizer, pres. Citizens for Quality Civilization, Inc., Bethesda, 1990—; pres. West Fernwood Citizens Assn., Bethesda, 1962-65; officer North Bethesda Congress of Citizens Assocs., Bethesda, 1965-75. Lt. comdr. USN, WWII. Decorated Air medal with oak leaf cluster. Mem. Ret. Officers Assn., Herring Bay Yacht Club, Phi Beta Kappa. Avocations: coastal cruising, flying, reading, bridge, lecturing in schools. Home: 6603 Lone Oak Dr Bethesda MD 20817-1649

SALTEN, FRANCES CLAIRE, retired lawyer; b. N.Y.C. d. Louis Harold and Minna Eva (Weinberger) Brown; children: Phoebe, Cynthia, Melissa. BA summa cum laude, NYU; MS with honors, Columbia U., 1964; JD magna cum laude, N.Y. Law Sch., 1975. Bar: N.Y. 1976, Fla. 1976, U.S. Dist. Cts. (so. and ea. dist.) N.Y. 1976, U.S. Ct. Appeals (2d cir.) 1979, U.S. Supreme Ct. 1979. Film reviewer Parents Mag., N.Y.C., 1965-68; librarian Port Chester H.S., N.Y., 1964; asst. librarian Iona Coll. Ryan Libr., New Rochelle, 1966-69, SUNY, Purchase, 1969-72; law clk. U.S. Dist. Ct. (So. Dist.) N.Y., N.Y.C., 1975-77; atty. advisor, writer Office of Hearings, Appeals, Social Security Adminstrn. HHS, 1977-85; ret., 1986. Chair Long Beach Drive, Mental Health Assn. Nassau, Mineola, N.Y., 1953; founder, bd. dirs. Long Beach Mental Health Assn., 1954-62; co-founder Long Beach Mental Health Clinic, 1960; co-founder, pres. Profl. Womens Caucus Westchester, 1972; active Womens Rights Com., Westchester Civil Liberties Union, 1971-75. Recipient Deans award N.Y. Law Sch., 1975, Womens Caucus award, 1975, Equitas award, 1975, Corpus Juris Secundum award West Pub. Co., 1975. Mem. ABA (matrimonial and family law com. 1972-79), N.Y. County Lawyers Asn. (womens rights com. 1978-85), N.Y. Womens Bar Assn. (matrimonial and family law com. 1973-80), N.Y. State Bar Assn., Fla. State Bar Assn.

SALTMAN, STUART IVAN, lawyer; b. Holyoke, Mass., Mar. 16, 1940; s. Abraham and Syd Eva (Schultz) S.; m. Sandra Lee, Sept. 19, 1964; children: Jason, Michael, Laura. BS in Polit. Sci., U. Mass., 1961; JD, Case Western Res. U., 1964. Bar: Mass. 1965, Ohio 1965, Pa. 1975. Assoc. gen. counsel Internat. Chem. Workers, Akron, Ohio, 1965; assoc. Metzenbaum, Gaines, Krupansky, Finley & Stern, Cleve., 1965-67; staff U.S. Dept. Labor, 1967-69, NLRB, Cleve., 1969-70; regional atty. EEOC, 1970-75; chief labor counsel Westinghouse Electric Corp., Pitts., 1975-88; chmn. labor law sect. Grigsby, Gaca & Davies, 1988-90; asst. gen. counsel Asea Brown Boveri Power T & D Inc., Coral Springs, Fla., 1990—. Recipient Excellence Hon. award in labor law Case Western Res. U., 1965. Mem. ABA, Allegheny County Bar Assn. (chmn. 1986-88), Masons. Labor. Home: 9045 Lucca St Boynton Beach FL 33437 Office: 4300 Coral Ridge Dr Coral Springs FL 33065 E-mail: stuart.i.saltman@us.abb.com

SALTMARSH, SARA ELIZABETH, lawyer; b. Jacksonville, Fla., Nov. 15, 1956; d. Ernest Olmstead and Anne (Frankenberg) S. Student, Randolph-Macon Woman's Coll., 1974-76; BA in English with honors magna cum laude, Fla. State U., 1978; postgrad., Iowa State U., 1980-81; JD, U. Tex., 1986. Bar: Tex. 1987; cert. family law. Assoc. Ausley & Slaikeu, P.C., Austin, Tex., 1987-90, Law Offices of Edwin J. Terry, Jr., Austin, 1990-92; pvt. practice law, 1992—. Mem. security com. Travis County Commr.'s Ct., 1991-93. Editor: Reference Guide to Travis County Practice, 1991, 92, 93, 95, 96, 97. Bd. dirs. Faith Home for Children with AIDS, 1997-98. Givens Disting. scholar, 1974, Lyndon Baines Johnson Meml. scholar, 1976; recipient Am. Jur. award Wills and Estates, 1986, Marital Relations and Divorce, 1986. Fellow: Tex. Bar Found., Austin Young Lawyers' Assn. Found.; mem.: ABA, Am. Inns of Ct. (barrister 1996—99), Tex. Acad. Family Law Specialists, Tex. Exes, Travis County Bar Assn. (sec.-treas. family law sect. 1989—90, v.p. 1990—91, pres. 1991—92, bd. dirs. 1991—92, chair mentor program com. 1993—94, chair mentor program com. 1996—98), Williamson County Bar Assn., Austin Young Lawyers' Assn. (co-chmn. It's the Law com. 1990—91), Young Lawyers' Assn., Travis County Women Lawyers' Assn., Tex. Ctr. Legal Ethics Professionalism, Fla. State Univ. Alumni Assn. (life), Sierra Club, Phi Beta Kappa, Lambda Iota Tau. Democrat. Avocations: Irish dance, skiing, ice skating, in-line skating, windsurfing, basketry. Alternative dispute resolution, Family and matrimonial. Office: 812 San Antonio St Suite 511 Austin TX 78701

SALTZBURG, STEPHEN ALLAN, law educator, consultant; b. Phila., Sept. 10, 1945; s. Jack Leonard and Mildred (Osgood) Adelman; m. Susan Lee, March 10, 1990; children: Mark Winston, Lisa Marie, Diane Elizabeth, David Lee Mussehl. AB, Dickinson Coll., 1967; JD, U. Pa., 1970. Bar: Calif. 1971, D.C. 1972, Va. 1976. Law clk. U.S. Dist. Ct. (no. dist.) Calif., San Francisco, 1970-71, U.S. Supreme Ct., 1971-72; asst. prof. law sch. U. Va., Charlottesville, 1972-74, assoc. prof., 1974-77, prof., 1977-87, Class of 1962 prof., 1987-90; Howrey prof. trial advocacy, litigation and profl. responsibility George Washington U. Sch. Law, Washington, 1990—. Reporter Alaska Rules of Evidence, 1976-77, Alaska Civil Jury Instrns., 1979-81, Adv. Com. on Rules of Criminal Procedure, 1984-89, Va. Rules on Evidence, 1984-85, Civil Justice Act Adv. Group, U.S. Dist. Ct. D.C., 1992-93, chmn., 1994-99; dep. asst. atty. gen. criminal divsn. U.S. Dept. Justice, 1988-89; mem. adv. com. on Fed. Rules of Criminal Procedure, 1989-95, on Fed. Rules of Evidence, 1992-95; mediator dispute resolution program U.S. Ct. Appeals, 1993—. Author: Evidence in America, 1987, American Criminal Procedure, 6th edit., 2000, Criminal Law: Cases and Materials, 1994, 2d edit., 2000, Evidence: The Objection Method, 1997, Federal Rules of Evidence Manual, 7th edit., 1998, Federal Rules of Evidence Trial Book, 1998, A Modern Approach to Evidence, 2d edit., 1982, Military Rules of Evidence Manual, 4th edit., 1997, Basic Criminal Procedure, 1994, 2d edit., 1997, Military Evidentiary Foundations, 1994, 2d edit., 2000, Trying Cases to Win: Anatomy of a Trial, 1999, Trying Cases to Win: Evidence: Weapons for Winning, 2000, California Federal Evidence Trial Book, 1999, Ohio Rules of Evidence Trial Book, 1999, Washington Evidence Trial Book, 1999. Mem. ABA (chmn. com. on trial advocacy criminal justice sect. 1992-96, task force on Ind. Counsel Act litig. sect. 1997-99, co-chmn. task force on civil trial stds. litig. sect. 1996-97, mem. criminal justice sect. coun. 2000—), Am. Law Inst. Office: George Washington U Law Sch 720 20th St NW Washington DC 20052-0001

SALTZMAN, MICHAEL I. lawyer, educator, author; b. Paterson, N.J., Mar. 1940; s. Edward H. and Frances C. (Bornstein) S.; m. Sandra Leslie Gabrilove, May 20, 1973. A.B., Colgate U., 1961; J.D. Bar: N.Y. 1971, D.C. 1965, Calif. 1974. Trial atty. tax div. U.S. Dept. of Justice, Washington, 1964-69; assoc. Roberts & Holland, N.Y., 1969-70; chief tax unit U.S. Atty's. Office, (so. dist.) N.Y., 1970-72; ptnr. Kaplan, Livingston, Goodwin, Berkowitz & Sellvin, Beverly Hills, Calif., 1972-75; sole practice, N.Y.C., 1975-82; ptnr. Saltzman & Holloran, 1982— ; adj. prof. law NYU. Author: IRS Practice and Procedure, 1981. Mem. ABA, N.Y. State Bar Assn., Assn. Bar City New York, Am. Coll. Tax Counsel. Club: Univ. (N.Y.C.). Federal civil litigation, State civil litigation, Criminal.

SALUP, STEPHEN, lawyer, educator; b. N.Y.C. s. Mannie and Gladys (Friedman) S.; m. Rebecca Scharfmann, June 27, 1983; children: Dana, Stacey, Brett. BA, U. Md., 1962; LLB, NYU, 1965. Bar: N.Y. 1965, Fla. 1976, U.S. Dist. Ct. (so. and ea. dists.) N.Y. 1966. Assoc. Shatzkin and Cooper, N.Y.C., 1965-67; real estate counsel Swift and Co., 1967-69; gen. counsel, dep. adminstr. N.Y.C. Econ. Devel. Adminstrn., 1969-73; assoc. Weisman, Celler, Spett and Madlin, N.Y.C., 1973-74; real estate counsel Nat. Kinney Corp., 1974-84; sr. v.p., gen. counsel Starrett Corp., 1984—. Assoc. prof. St. John's U., N.Y.C., 1976-79, Adelphi U., N.Y.C., 1980. Editor Legal Aspects of Athletic Administration, 1976-78. Active local planning bd., Queens County, N.Y., 1972-76, Cable TV Commn.,

Lawrence, N.Y., 1979-81, Village of North Hills, N.Y.; del. Rep. Jud. Conv., 1968; committeeman Rep. County Com.; adv. bd. Baruch Coll., CUNY. Mem. ABA, Assn. Bar City of N.Y., Lindsay Civic Assn. (v.p. 1970-74). Republican. Jewish. Construction, Labor, Real property. Home: 25 Wimbledon Dr Roslyn NY 11576-3097 Office: Starrett Corp 70 E 55th St New York NY 10022

SALVADOR, TRANQUIL, III, lawyer, educator; b. Quezon City, The Philippines, May 19, 1967; s. Tranquil Phoadaca and Cornelia Santos (Suaverdez) S.; m. Maria Roselle Chua Apasan, May 19, 1967; 1 child, Tranquil Matthew IV. AB in Econs., U. Santo Tomas, The Philippines, 1987; JD, Ateneo de Manila U., The Philippines, 1991. Bar: The Philippines 1992. Legal apprentice Commn. Human Rights, The Philippines, 1988, Structural Alternative Legal Assistance for Grassroots, The Philippines, 1989, Romulo, Mabanta, Buenaventura, Sayoc & de los Angeles, Manila, The Philippines, 1990-92, jr. assoc. The Philippines, 1992-93, sr. assoc. The Philippines, 1997—, jr. assoc. Hong Kong, Hong Kong, 1993. Prof. San Sebastian Coll., The Philippines, 1995—, Far Ea. U., 1994—, Pamantasan ng Lungsod ng Maynila, The Philippines, 2000—; of counsel Cebu Pacific Air, 1995—, United Parcel Svcs., 1996—; mediator Lex Mundi Coll. Mediators, 1995-98; v.p., bd. trustees Balikatang Thalassemia (BA-THA), 2001—. Comdr. Philippine CG, 1998. Mem. Philippine Bar Assn., Integrated Bar of Philippines, Rotary Internat. (charter pres. 2001—). Aviation, General practice, Transportation. Office: Romulo Mabanta et al 8741 Paseo de Rozas 30 Fl Makati City The Philippines Office Fax: 815-3172. E-mail: tranquil@rmbsa.com

SALVADORE, GUIDO RICHARD, lawyer; b. Norton, Mass., Oct. 14, 1927; s. Michele Salvadore and Maria Grazia Costantino; m. Barbara Ann Camparone, Oct. 25, 1958; children: Peter, Richard, Susan, Stephen, Marisa. AB, Brown U., 1951; LLB, Harvard U., 1954. Bar: R.I. 1954, U.S. Dist. Ct. R.I. 1955, U.S. Ct. Appeals (1st cir.) 1996. Atty. Salvadore & Salvadore, Providence; ptnr. Higgins, Cavanagh & Cooney, 1960-90. Dir., pres. Great Am. Nursing Ctrs., Inc., Warwick, R.I., 1969-90. Dir., v.p. R.I. Grand Opera Co., Providence, 1985—. With USN, 1946-48. Mem. ABA, R.I. Bar Assn., Univ. Club, Metacomet Country Club, Brown Faculty Club. Republican. Roman Catholic. Avocations: golfing, basketball, dancing, reading. Contracts commercial, General corporate, Estate planning. Home: 38 Sunset Dr East Greenwich RI 02818-1915 Office: Salvadore & Salvadore 50 Kennedy Plz Providence RI 02903-2393

SALVAN, SHERWOOD ALLEN, lawyer; b. N.Y.C., Dec. 2, 1942; s. Harry and Marie Ann (Deramo) S. BBA, St. Francis Coll., N.Y.C.; MBA, Pace U.; JD, postgrad., NYU. Bar: N.Y. 1969, U.S. Ct. Appeals (2d dist.) 1971, U.S. Dist. Cts. (so. and ea. dist.) N.Y. 1971, U.S. Cir. Ct. (2d cir.) 1972, U.S. Supreme Ct. 1980, D.C. 1981. Tax specialist Haskins & Sells, N.Y.C., 1969-71; sole practice, 1972—. Mem. cen. screening com. first dept. N.Y. Appellate Div., 1977-82; spl. master N.Y. County Supreme Ct., 1977-85; arbitrator Am. Arbitration Assn., 1976-89, N.Y. County and Bronx County Civil Cts., 1976-89; adminstrv. law judge Environ. Control Bd. City of N.Y., 1975-77. Contbr. articles to profl. jours. V.p. N.Y. County Dem. Club, 1980—; jud. del. N.Y. County dems., 1983—. Mem. N.Y. County Lawyers Assn. (chairperson com. word processing 1978-86), Am. Judge Assn., NY Law Sch. Alumni Assn. (bd. dirs. 1984—). State civil litigation, General practice, Personal injury. Home: 526 E 83rd St New York NY 10028-7249 E-mail: woodmanlaw@aol.com

SALVATY, BENJAMIN BENEDICT, lawyer; b. Chgo., Dec. 22, 1940; s. Benjamin Benedict and Marion Therese (Ryan) S.; m. Patircia Louise Recor, Aug. 29, 1964; children: Paul Benedict, Kathleen Anne. BBA, U. Notre Dame, 1962; JD, U. So. Calif., 1965. Bar: Calif. 1966, U.S. Dist. Ct. (no., cen., ea. and so. dists.) Calif., U.S. Ct. Appeals (9th cir.), U.S. Tax Ct., U.S. Supreme Ct. Sr. trial atty. Calif. Dept. Transp., 1966-79; gen. atty. The Atchison, Topeka and Santa Fe Railway Co., 1980-89; sr. ptnr. Hill, Farrer & Burrill, Los Angeles, 1990—. Mem. ABA (litigation sect. urban, state and local govt. law com. on condemnation, zoning and planning com.), Am. Bd. Trial Advs., Am. Judicature Soc., Internat. Right Way Assn., Irish Am. Bar Assn. (bd. dirs. 1985—, treas. 1991, sec. 1992, v.p. 1992-93, pres. 1993-94), Italian Am. Lawyers Assn., State Trial Attys. Assn. (pres. 1975-79), Calif. State Bar (chmn. condemnation com. 1987-88, vice chmn. 1986-87), Pasadena Bar Assn., L.A. County Bar Assn. (condemnation and land valuation com.). Condemnation, Land use and zoning (including planning). Office: Hill Farrer & Burrill LLP One California Plz 37th Fl 300 S Grand Ave Los Angeles CA 90071-3109 Fax: 213-624-4840

SALZBERG, ARTHUR JONATHAN, lawyer; b. Washington, Mar. 21, 1951; s. Samuel Solomon and Rebbeca Ruth (Schechter) S. B.A. cum laude, NYU, 1973; J.D. cum laude, Northwestern U., 1976. Bar: Calif. 1977, D.C. 1979, U.S. Dist. Ct. (cen. dist.) Calif. 1982, U.S. Dist. Ct. (so. dist.) Calif. 1984. Trial atty. Bur. Competition, FTC, Washington, 1976-78; assoc. Brownstein Ziedman & Schomer, Washington, 1978-80; sr. trial atty. Commodity Futures Trading Commn., Washington, 1980-82, br. chief div. of enforcement Western region, Los Angeles, 1982-84, regional counsel Western region, 1984— . Mem. ABA, Calif. Bar Assn., D.C. Bar Assn., Bar Assn. D.C., D.C. Fed Bar Assn. Jewish. Office: Commodity Futures Trading Commn 10850 Wilshire Blvd Ste 370 Los Angeles CA 90024-4315

SALZMAN, GARY SCOTT, lawyer; b. Portchester, N.Y., May 26, 1963; s. David Stuart and Francine (Selenow) S.; m. Suzanne Sansone, Apr. 2, 1990. BBA, U. Miami, 1985, JD, 1988. Bar: Fla. 1988, U.S. Dist. Ct. (so. dist.) 1989, Colo. 1991, U.S. Dist. Ct. (mid. dist.) Fla. 1992, U.S. Ct. Appeals (11th cir.) 1992, U.S. Supreme Ct. 1992; cert. arbitrator and mediator; cert. in bus. litigation, Fla. Assoc. Robinson & Greenberg, PA, Coral Gables, Fla., 1988-89, Buchbinder & Elegant, PA, Miami, 1989, Mishan, Sloto, Hoffman and Greenberg, PA, Miami, 1989-91, Dempsey & Assocs., Winter Park, Fla., 1991-92; pvt. practice, Orlando and Winter Park, 1992-95; ptnr. Marlowe, Appleton, Weatherford & Salzman, Winter Park, 1996-98, Brown, Ward, Salzman & Weiss, P.A., Orlando, 1998—. Comml.,employment and fin. arbitration panelist Am. Arbitration Assn. Mem. ABA, Fla. Bar Assn. (com. rels. with Inst. CPAs 1992-93, bus. litig. com. 1995—), Bus. Exec. Network, Orange County Bar Assn. Finance, Real property. Office: 225 E Robinson St Ste 660 Orlando FL 32801 Fax: 407-425-9596. E-mail: gssalzman@orlandolaw.net

SALZMAN, STANLEY P. lawyer; b. N.Y.C., Jan. 30, 1931; s. George D. and Fanny M. (Pugach) S.; m. Leona Schames, June 18, 1958 (dec. Nov. 1967); m. Marilyn J. Bzura, Feb. 3, 1974; children: Ira J., Mark B., Debra G., Jeffrey M. David, Steven B. David. BA, Bklyn. Coll., 1952; JD, Bklyn. Law Sch., 1955. Bar: N.Y. 1956, U.S. Dist. Ct. (so. and ea. dists.) N.Y. 1960, U.S. Supreme Ct. 1964, U.S. Ct. Appeals (2d cir.) 1966. Assoc. Otterbourg, Steindler, Houston & Rosen, N.Y.C., 1957; ptnr. Venitt, Adler & Salzman, 1958-66, Friesner & Salzman, LLP, Great Neck, N.Y., 1966—. Bd. dirs. Colora Printing Inks Inc., Linden, N.J. State civil litigation, Consumer commercial. Office: Friesner & Salzman LLP 11 Grace Ave PO Box 220700 Great Neck NY 11022-0700 E-mail: legalsps@aol.com

SAM, DAVID, federal judge; b. Hobart, Ind., Aug. 12, 1933; s. Andrew and Flora (Toma) S.; m. Betty Jean Brennan, Feb. 1, 1957; children: Betty Jean, David Dwight, Daniel Scott, Tamara Lynn, Pamela Rae, Daryl Paul, Angie, Sheyla. BS, Brigham Young U., 1957; JD, Utah U., 1960. Bar: Utah 1960, U.S. Dist. Ct. Utah 1966. Sole practice and ptnr., Duchesne, Utah, 1963-76; dist. judge State of Utah, 1976-85; judge U.S. Dist. Ct. Utah, Salt Lake City, 1985-97; chief judge U.S. Dist. Ct., 1997, sr. judge, 1999—. Atty. City of Duchesne, 1963-72; Duchesne County atty., 1966-72; commr. Duchesne, 1972-74; mem. adv. com. Codes of Conduct of Jud. Conf. U.S., 1987-91, Jud. Coun. of 10th Cir., 1991-93; mem. U.S. Del. to Romania, Aug. 1991. Chmn. Jud. Nomination Com. for Cir. Ct. Judge, Provo, Utah, 1983; bd. dirs. Water Resources, Salt Lake City, 1973-76. Served to capt. JAGC, USAF, 1961-63. Named Judge of Yr., Utah State Bar, 1999. Mem. Utah Bar Assn., Supreme Ct. Hist. Soc., Am. Inns of Ct. VII (counselor 1986-89), A. Sherman Christensen Am. Inn of Ct. I (counselor 1989-98), Utah Jud. Conf. (chmn. 1982), Utah Dist. Judges Assn. (pres. 1982-83), Order of Coif (hon. Brigham Young U. chpt.). Mem. LDS Ch. Avocations: beekeeping, reading, sports, cooking chinese food. E-mail: david. Office: US Dist Ct 148 US Courthouse 350 S Main St Ste 150 Salt Lake City UT 84101-2180 E-mail: sam@utd.uscourts.gov

SAMANOWITZ, RONALD ARTHUR, lawyer; b. N.Y.C., June 1, 1944; s. Sam and Thelma (Levin) S.; m. Ann Frieda Weisman, Dec. 18, 1971; 1 child, Samuel. BBA, CUNY, 1965; JD, Bklyn. Law Sch., 1967. Bar: N.Y. 1968, U.S. Dist. Ct. (ea. and so. dists.) N.Y. 1974, U.S. Supreme Ct. 1991. Ptnr. Krakower, Samanowitz & Goldman, N.Y.C., 1968-86, Resnicoff, Samanowitz, Endzweig & Brawer, Great Neck, N.Y., 1986-90, Samanowitz & Endzweig, Great Neck, 1990—. Pres. Greater Fresh Meadows Civic Assn., Flushing, N.Y., 1984-85, award for Civic Svc. 1985, Flower Hill Civic Assn., 1992. Mem. N.Y. State Trial Lawyers Assn. (gov. L.I. divsn.), Brandeis Lawyers Assn. (sec. 1985), Queens Bar Assn. (family law com.), Nassau Bar Assn. (plaintiff roundtable 1988—), Great Neck Lawyers Assn. (past pres., chmn. bd.). Avocation: marathon running. General civil litigation, Family and matrimonial, Real property. Office: Samanowitz & Endzweig 98 Cuttermill Rd Great Neck NY 11021-3006

SAMET, DEE-DEE, lawyer; b. Greensboro, N.C., Sept. 18, 1940; BA, U. Ariz., 1962, JD, 1963. Bar: Ariz. 1964. Ptnr. Samet & Gage, P.C., Tucson, 2001; pvt. practice, 2001—. Arbitrator U.S. Dist. Ct. Ariz., Gender Equality Task Force, 1993; judge pro tem Pima County Superior Ct., 1985—; Ninth Cir. Lawyer rep., 1990-93; mem. Jud. Performance Rev. Commn., 1996-99. Mem. State Bar Ariz. (family law sect., workers compensation sect., trial law sect., co-chair worker's compensation sect. 1988-89, gender bias task force, bd. govs. 1994-97, pres.-elect, pres. 1999-2000), Nat. Panel Arbitrators, Am. Arbitration Assn. (com. on exams., supreme ct. state Ariz. 1984-91), Pima County Bar Assn. (bd. dirs. 1994—), Nat. Assn. Coun. for Children, Ariz. Assn. Coun. for Children, So. Ariz. Fed. Bar Assn. (exec. com. 1995—), So. Ariz. Women Lawyers Assn. (bd. dirs. 1990, pres. 1994-95), Nat. Orgn. Social Security Claimants' Reps. Family and matrimonial, Personal injury, Workers' compensation. Office: Dee-Dee Samet PC 717 N 6th Ave Tucson AZ 85705-8304

SAMOLE, MYRON MICHAEL, lawyer, management consultant; b. Chgo., Nov. 29, 1943; s. Harry Lionel and Bess Miriam (Siegel) S.; m. Sandra Rita Port, Feb. 2, 1967; children— Stacey Ann, Karen Lynn, Rena Mara, David Aaron. Student U. Ill., 1962-65; J.D., DePaul U., 1967; postgrad. John Marshall Lawyers Inst., 1967-69. Bar: Ill. 1967, U.S. Dist. Ct. (no. dist.) Ill. 1968, U.S. Dist. Ct. (so. dist.) Fla. 1989, U.S. Ct. Appeals (7th cir.) 1968, U.S. Ct. Appeals (11th cir.), 2001, Fla. 1981. Pvt. practice, Chgo., 1967-79, Miami, Fla., 1981— ; chmn. bd. Fidelity Electronics and subs., Miami, 1969-83; pres. Fidelity Hearing Instruments, Miami, 1984-86, Samole Enterprises, Inc., Miami, 1986—, Fla. Citrus Tower, Inc., Clermont, 1986—; bd. dirs. Enterprise Bank Fla., Miami, 1985-89, The Sports Collection, Inc., Miami, 1987-94; Bd. dirs. South Dade Greater Miami Jewish Fedn., Young Israel of Kendall, Anshe Emes Congregation. Jewish Vocat. Service scholar U. Ill., Champaign, 1962-65. Mem. ABA, Chgo. Bar Assn., Ill. State Bar Assn., Fla. Bar Assn., Kendall Bar Assn., Dade County Bar Assn., Ill. Trial Lawyers Assn., Miami C. of C., Phi Alpha Delta. Democrat. Lodges: Masons, Shriners. General corporate, Family and matrimonial, General practice. Office: Samole & Berger PA 9700 S Dixie Hwy Ste 1030 Miami FL 33156-2865

SAMPSON, JOHN DAVID, lawyer; b. Lackawanna, N.Y., Feb. 20, 1955; s. Hugh Albert and May (Davidson) Henderson S.; m. Carol Jasen, July 29, 1978; children: Rachel Henderson, Matthew David. BA, Canisius Coll., Buffalo, 1977; JD, Union U., Albany, N.Y., 1982. Bar: N.Y. 1983, Pa. 1998, U.S. Dist. Ct. (we. dist.) N.Y. 1983, U.S. Dist. Ct. (no. dist.) N.Y. 1996. Assoc. Damon & Morey, Buffalo, 1982-87, Lippes Silverstein Mathias & Wexler, Buffalo, 1987-88; ptnr. Walsh & Sampson, PC, 1988-93, Jasen, Jasen & Sampson PC, Buffalo, 1993-99, Underberg & Kessler LLP, Buffalo, 1999—. Paul Harris fellow, 1997. Mem. N.Y. State Bar Assn., Erie County Bar Assn., Def. Rsch. Inst., Rotary Club of Buffalo, Rotary Club of East Aurora (dir. 1993—, pres. 1995-96). Wesleyan Methodist. Avocations: golf, running, skiing. Federal civil litigation, State civil litigation, Personal injury. Home: 44 Elmwood Ave East Aurora NY 14052-2610 Office: Underberg & Kessler LLP 1100 Main Place Tower # 620 Buffalo NY 14202-3711 E-mail: dsampson@underberg-kessler.com

SAMPSON, JOHN J. law educator; b. St. Paul, Sept. 30, 1935; s. J.E. and Margaret A. Sampson; m. Joyce C., Aug. 6, 1940; children: Margaret J., Eleanor H. LLB magna cum laude, U. Minn., 1966. Bar: Calif. 1967, Tex. 1980. Assoc. Morriston-Foerster, San Francisco, 1966-69; asst. gen. counsel U.S. Commn. on Obscenity and Pornography, 1969-70; asst. prof. U. Tex. Sch. Law, Austin, 1970-73, prof., 1973-82, Ben Gardner Sewell prof. law, 1982-86, William Benjamin Wynne prof., 1986—. Bd. dirs. Legal Aid Soc. Central Tex.; lectr., legis. draftsman; reporter Nat. Conf. Commrs. Uniform St. Laws, 1990—. Pres., Minn. Law Rev., 1965-66; contbr. numerous articles to legal publs. Mem. State Bar Tex. (editor family law sect. report 1976—). Office: U Tex Sch Law 727 E 26th St Austin TX 78705-3224 E-mail: jsampson@mail.law.utexas.edu

SAMPSON, WILLIAM ROTH, lawyer; b. Teaneck, N.J., Dec. 11, 1946; s. James and Amelia (Roth) S.; 1 child, Lara; m. Drucilla Jean Mort, Apr. 23, 1988; stepchildren: Andy, Seth. BA in History with honors, U. Kans., 1968, JD, 1971. Bar: Kans. 1971, U.S. Dist. Ct. Kans. 1971, U.S. Ct. Appeals (10th cir.) 1982, U.S. Ct. Claims 1985, U.S. Ct. Appeals (8th cir.) 1992. Assoc. Turner & Balloun, Gt. Bend, Kans., 1971; ptnr. Foulston & Siefkin, Wichita, 1975-86, Shook, Hardy & Bacon, Overland Park, 1987—. Adj. prof. advanced litig. U. Kans., 1994; mem. faculty trial tactics inst. Emory U. Sch. Law, 1994-97; mem. merit selection panel U.S. Dist. Ct. Kans., 1999; lectr., presenter in field. Author: Kansas Trial Handbook, 1997; mem. Kans. Law Rev., 1969-71, editor, 1970-71; contbr. articles to profl. jours. Chmn. stewardship com. Univ. Friends Ch., Wichita, 1984-86; bd. dirs. Friends U. Retirement Corp., Wichita, 1985-87; chmn. capital fund drives Trinity Luth. Ch., Lawrence, Kans., 1990-93, mem. ch. coun., 1990-92; bd. dirs. Lied Ctr. of Kans., 1994-97. Lt. USNR, 1971-75. Named among Best Lawyers in Am. Fellow Am. Bar Found., Kans. Bar Found. (chmn. Kans. coll. advocacy 1986, long-range planning, CLE com. 1987-88, client protection fund commn. 2001—); mem. ABA, Assn. Def. Trial Attys., Kans. Bar Assn., Douglas County Bar Assn., Johnson County Bar Assn. (bench-bar com. 1989-99, Boss of Yr. award 1990), Wichita Bar Assn. (bd. dirs. 1985-86), Am. Bd. Trial Advs. (pres. Kans. chpt. 1990-91, nat. bd. dirs. 1990-91), Internat. Assn. Def. Coun. (faculty mem. trial acad. 1994), Def. Rsch. Inst. (v.p. 2000—, nat. bd. dirs. 1998-2000, Kans. state rep. 1990-98, Exceptional Performance citation 1990, Outstanding State Rep. 1991-92, 94), Kans. Assn. Def. Counsel (pres. 1989-90, legis. coun. 1991, 93, William H. Kahrs Disting. Achievement award 1994), Kans. U. Law Soc. (bd. govs. 1993-96), Am. Inn Ct. (Judge Hugh Means chpt., Master of Bench), Lawrence Country Club, Order of Coif, Delta Sigma Rho, Phi Alpha Theta, Omicron Delta Kappa. Republican. Episcopalian. Avocations: jogging, golf, snow skiing, travel, reading. Federal civil litigation, Intellectual property, Product liability. Office: Shook Hardy & Bacon 9401 Indian Creek Pky Overland Park KS 66210-2005 E-mail: wsampson@shb.com

SAMUEL, RALPH DAVID, lawyer; b. Augusta, Ga., May 8, 1945; s. Ralph and Louise Elizabeth (Wurreschke) S.; m. Lynn Christel Malmgren, June 12, 1971; children: Lynn Britt, Ralph Erik. AB, Dartmouth Coll., 1967; JD, Dickinson Sch. of Law, 1972. Bar: Pa. 1972, U.S. Dist. Ct. (ea. dist.) Pa. 1972, U.S. Ct. Appeals (3d cir.) 1973, U.S. Supreme Ct. 1976. Law clk. to hon. judge John P. Fullam U.S. Dist. Ct. (ea. dist.) Pa., Phila., 1972-74; assoc. MacCoy, Evans & Lewis., 1974-76; ptnr. Samuel and Ballard, P.C., 1976-98; pres., CEO Ralph D. Samuel & Co., P.C., 1998—. Established Samuel Poetry Fellow Dartmouth Coll., Hanover, N.H., 1994. Contbr. articles to profl. jours., poetry to publs. Trustee The George Sch., Newtown, Pa., 1983-90; chmn. bd. dirs. Stapeley in Germantown, 1985-90; mem. Chase Fund Com., 2000; chmn. budget com. Phila. Yearly Meeting of Friends, 1991-93; bd. dirs., mem. fin. com. Phila. Ranger Corps., 1992-94; pres. Cedar Park Neighbors, Phila., 1975-78, West Mt. Airy Neighbors, Phila., 1981-82. Mem. Pa. Soc., Athenaeum of Phila., Sunday Breakfast Club. Mem. Soc. of Friends. Avocations: music, writing, squash, tennis. General civil litigation, Personal injury, Product liability. Office: PO Box 35185 Philadelphia PA 19128-0185 Fax: (215) 849-6859. E-mail: RalphSamuel@RalphSamuel.com

SAMUEL, RAPHAEL, lawyer; b. N.Y.C., Oct. 11, 1946; s. Sam and Sarah R. (Hollenberg) S. BS in Math. magna cum laude, L.I. U., 1968; JD, NYU, 1971. Bar: N.Y. 1972, U.S. Dist. Ct. (so. and ea. dists.) N.Y. 1973, U.S. Ct. Appeals (2d cir.) 1973. Staff atty. N.Y.C. Housing Authority, 1972-78, asst. chief litigation, 1978-83, chief research, opinions and spl. assignments, 1983-87, asst. gen. counse. for spl. projects, 1987-93, assoc. gen. counsel for regulatory affairs, 1993—. Sec. Waterside Tenants Assn., N.Y.C., 1976-78; pres. 130 Water St. Tenants Assn., N.Y.C., 1978-80; sec. 50 8th Ave. Tenants Corp., Bklyn., 1980-83. Served with USNG, 1969-75. Mem. ABA, N.Y. State Bar Assn., Fed. Bar Coun., N.Y. County Lawyers Assn., Nat. Assn. Housing Redevel. Ofcls. Avocations: computer databases, opera, sporting events. Office: NYC Housing Authority 250 Broadway Rm 9047 New York NY 10007-2146 E-mail: section8maven@prodigy.net

SAMUELS, DONALD L. lawyer; b. Washington, May 8, 1961; s. Jack Donald Samuels and Francis Diane (Katcher) Yeoman; m. Linda Marie Tveidt, Aug. 17, 1986. AB, Brown U., 1983; JD, Columbia U., 1986. Bar: Calif. 1986, U.S. Dist. Ct. (cen., no., ea. and so. dists.) Calif. 1988, U.S. Ct. Appeals (9th cir.) 1989, Colo. 1996, U.S. Ct. Appeals (7th cir.) 1996, U.S. Dist. Ct. Colo. 1997, U.S. Ct. Appeals (10th cir.) 1997, Tex. 1998. Law clk., L.A., 1986-87; assoc. Sidley & Austin, 1987-94, ptnr., 1994-95, Samuels & Samuels, L.A., 1995-97; officer, dir., shareholder Ireland & Stapleton, Denver, 1997—. Mem. ABA, Calif. Bar Assn., Colo. Bar Assn., Phi Beta Kappa. Federal civil litigation, State civil litigation, Trademark and copyright. Home: 9931 E Progress Cir Greenwood Vlg CO 80111-3673 Office: Ireland & Stapleton Pryor & Pascoe PC 1675 Broadway Ste 2600 Denver CO 80202-4685 E-mail: dsamuels@irelandstapleton.com

SAMUELS, JANET LEE, lawyer; b. Pitts., July 18, 1953; d. Emerson and Jeanne (Kalish) S.; m. David Arthur Kalow, June 18, 1978; children; Margaret Emily Samuels-Kalow, Jacob Richard Samuels-Kalow, Benjamin Charles Samuels-Kalow. BA with honors, Beloit Coll., 1974; JD, NYU, 1977. Bar: N.Y. 1978, D.C. 1980. Staff atty. SCM Corp., N.Y.C., 1977-80, corp. atty., 1980-83, sr. corp. atty., 1983-85, assoc. gen. counsel Allied Paper div., 1983-86, corp. counsel, 1986, Holtzmann, Wise & Shepard, 1986-88. Mem. N.Y. State Bar Assn., Mortar Board, Phi Beta Kappa. Contracts commercial, General corporate, Securities. E-mail: jlsamuels@hotmail.com

SAMUELS, LAWRENCE ROBERT, lawyer; b. Chgo., June 20, 1946; s. Robert Ernest and Hope Lois (Feldman) S.; m. Marlene Bernstein, June 19, 1983. B.A., U. Chgo., 1968; J.D., Harvard U., 1971. Bar: N.Y. 1972, Ill. 1976, U.S. Dist. Ct. (so. dist.) N.Y. 1973, U.S. Dist. Ct. (no. dist.) Ill. 1976, U.S. Ct. Appeals (2d cir.) 1973, U.S. Ct. Appeals (7th cir.) 1976, U.S. Supreme Ct. 1978. Assoc., Cravath, Swaine & Moore, N.Y.C., 1971-76; assoc. Sonnenschein Carlin Nath & Rosenthal, Chgo., 1976-78, ptnr., 1978-87, ptnr. Ross & Hardies, Chgo., 1987— . Bd. dirs. Loeb Found., Chgo., 1977— ; pres. Men's Council, Mus. Contemporary Art, Chgo., 1983-84. Mem. ABA. Jewish. Club: Metropolitan (Chgo.). Federal civil litigation, State civil litigation, Securities. Home: 1139 W Wellington Ave Chicago IL 60657-4337 Office: Ross & Handies 150 N Michigan Ave Ste 2500 Chicago IL 60601-7569

SAMUELSON, KENNETH LEE, lawyer; b. Natrona Heights, Pa., Aug. 22, 1946; s. Sam and Frances Bernice (Robbins) S.; m. Marlene Ina Rabinowitz, Jan. 1, 1980; children: Heather, Cheryl. BA magna cum laude, U. Pitts., 1968; JD, U. Mich., 1971. Bar: Md. 1972, D.C. 1980, U.S. Dist. Ct. (trial bar) Md. 1984. Assoc. Weinberg & Green, Balt., 1971-73, Dickerson, Nice, Sokol & Horn, Balt., 1973; asst. atty. gen. State of Md., 1973-77; pvt. practice Balt., 1978; ptnr. Linowes and Blocher, Silver Spring (Md.), Washington, 1979-93, Semmes, Bowen & Semmes, Washington, D.C., and Balt., 1993-95, Wilkes Artis, Chartered, Washington, 1995-2001, Deckelbaum Ogens & Raftery, Washington and Md., 2001—. Spkr. in field of telecomms., fin. and real estate. Contbr. articles to profl. jours. Bd. dirs. D.C. Assn. for Retarded Citizens, Inc., 1986—; bd. govs. Wash. Bldg. Congress, 1998—. Mem. ABA (coun. mem. sect. real property, probate and trust law 2000—, moderator various programs), Am. Coll. Real Estate Lawyers (moderator various programs), D.C. Bar (comml. real estate com., chmn. legal opinions project), Md. Bar Assn. (real property, planning and zoning sect., chmn. environ. subcom. legal opinions project 1987-89, litigation sect. 1982-84, chmn. comml. trans. com.), Md. Inst. Continuing Profl. Edn. Lawyers, Am. Arbitration Assn. (arbitrator and mediator), D.C. Bldg. Industry Assn., Washington Assn Realtors, Inc., Nat. Assn. of Corp. Real Estate Execs., Civil Code Drafting Com. of the Russian Legis., Apt. and Office Bldg. Assn. Met. Washington, East Coast Builders Conf., Internat. Coun. Shopping Ctrs. (organized, co-faculty program "univ." 1988, NAFTA 1992, condemnations 1994, leasing 1997, high tech. effects 1998, com. chmn. 1998-99, pub./pvt. partnerships 1999), Montgomery County Bar Assn. (jud. selections com. 1988-90), Phi Beta Kappa, Lambda Alpha. Contracts commercial, Municipal (including bonds), Real property. Office: Deckelbaum Ogens & Raftery # 165 2020 Pennsylvania Ave NW Washington DC 20006 E-mail: ksamuelson@bigfoot.com

SAMUELSON, PAMELA ANN, law educator; b. Seattle, Aug. 4, 1948; d. Peter David and Margaret Susanne (Green) S.; m. Robert J. Glushko, May 7, 1988; 1 child, Robert M. BA in History, U. Hawaii, 1971, MA in Polit. Sci., 1972; JD, Yale U., 1976. Bar: N.Y. 1977, U.S. Dist. Ct. (so. dist.) N.Y. 1977. Rsch. assoc. Vera Inst. of Justice, N.Y.C., 1976-77; assoc. Willkie Farr & Gallagher, 1977-81; prin. investigator Software Engring. Inst., Pitts., 1985-86; asst. prof. Law Sch. U. Pitts., 1981-84, assoc. prof. Law Sch., 1984-87, prof. Law Sch., 1987-96; prof. law and info. mgmt. U. Calif. Law Sch./Sch. Info. Mgmt. and Sys., Berkeley, 1996—. Bd. dirs. Berkeley Ctr. for Law and Tech./U. Calif., Berkeley; vis. prof. Emory Law Sch., Atlanta, 1989-90, Cornell Law Sch., Ithaca, 1995-96; mem. Nat. Rsch. Coun. Study Com. on Intellectual Property Rights and Info. Infrastructure, 1998-2000. Contbr. articles to profl. jours. Bd. dirs. ACLU Greater Pitts., 1983-88, Electronic Frontier Found., 2000—. John D. and Catherine T. MacArthur Found. fellow, 1997, Pub. Policy fellow Electronic Frontier Found., 1997—; recipient Disting. Alumni award U. Hawaii, 2000. Mem. ABA (sci. and tech. sect.), Am. Intellectual Property Law Assn. (subcom. chair 1988-89), Assn. Am. Law Schs. (intellectual property sect.). Democrat. Avocations: gardening, reading. Office: U Calif Berkeley Sch Info Mgmt and Sys 102 South Hall #4600 Berkeley CA 94720-4600 E-mail: pam@sims.berkeley.edu

SANBORN, VON ERIC, lawyer; b. Manchester, N.H., Jan. 19, 1968; s. Duane and Esther (Rush) S.; m. Lisa Kim, Sept. 28, 1996. BA, Boston U., 1991; JD, Albany Law Sch., 1995; LLM in Taxation, Villanova U., 1996. Bar: N.Y. 1997, U.S. Tax Ct 1998. Internat. tax cons. Ernst & Young, Phila., 1997-98; tax assoc. Sheehan, Phinney, Bass & Green, Manchester, N.H., 1998-2000, 2001—. Mem. ABA, N.Y. State Bar Assn., Internat. Fiscal Assn. Avocation: bicycling. Corporate taxation. Office: Bergman Horowitz & Reynolds PO Box 3701 157 Church St PO Box 426 New Haven CT 06502

SANCHEZ, WALTER MARSHALL, lawyer; b. Lake Charles, La., July 3, 1959; s. John Augustine Sanchez and Louise Page Dugas Meyer; m. Frances E. Morgan, Oct. 18, 1986; children: Clare, Madeline, Kate, John. BS, La. State U., Baton Rouge, 1981, JD, 1984. Bar: La. 1984, U.S. Supreme Ct. 1984; bd. cert. family law specialist, La. Bd. of Legal Specialization. Assoc. Godwin, Painter, Roddy, Lorenzi & Watson, Lake Charles, 1985-86; ptnr. Godwin, Roddy, Lorenzi Watson & Sanchez, 1986-90, Lorenzi, Sanchez & Palay, LLP, Lake Charles, 1990—. Vice chmn. La. Indigent Defender Bd., New Orleans, 1994-96; chmn. 14th Jud. Dist. Indigent Defender Bd., Lake Charles, 1987-96; mem. faculty trial advocacy tng. program La. State U. Law Ctr., 1993—; mem. Joint Legis. Com. for Study Indigent Def. Sys., 1996-97; mem. spl. com. to study reinstatement of fault in divorce La. State Law Inst., 1998-2001; apptd. judge pro tempore City Ct. of Sulphur, 1999—. Mem. La. Assn. Criminal Def. Attys. (bd. dirs. 1990—, pres. 1997-98), Am. Mensa, Order of St. Charles. Democrat. Roman Catholic. General civil litigation, Criminal, Family and matrimonial. Office: Lorenzi Sanchez & Palay LLP PO Box 3305 Lake Charles LA 70602-3305

SAND, DAVID BYRON, lawyer; b. Mpls., Jan. 28, 1946; s. William John and Lois E. (Crane) S.; m. June Ann Striffler, Sept. 14, 1969; children—Kristin, Maren, Brandon. BA cum laude, St. Olaf Coll., 1968; JD, Duke U., 1975. Bar: Minn. 1975, U.S. Dist. Ct. Minn. 1976, U.S. Ct. Appeals (8th cir.) 1978. Assoc. Briggs and Morgan, St. Paul, 1975-80, ptnr., Mpls., 1980— ; mem. panel of constrn. industry arbitrators Am. Arbitration Assn., Mpls., 1981— ; commr. North Suburban Cable Commn., 1992—. mem. panel of mediators for Lex Mundi, Chmn. Arden Hills Park & Recreation (Minn.), 1983— ; bd. trustees Hamline Methodist Ch., St. Paul, 1984-92. Lt. (j.g.) USNR, 1969-72. Recipient Svc. award Minn. Bd. Archtl. Engring. and Land Surveying, 1983. Mem. ABA (litigation sect. and forum com. constrn. industry). State civil litigation, Construction. Office: Briggs & Morgan 2400 IDS Ctr 80 S 8th St Ste 2400 Minneapolis MN 55402-2157

SAND, LEONARD B. federal judge; b. N.Y.C., May 24, 1928; B.S., NYU, 1947; LL.B., Harvard, 1951. Bar: N.Y. 1953, U.S. Supreme Ct. 1956, D.C. 1969. Clk. to dist. ct. judge, N.Y., 1952-53; asst. U.S. atty. So. Dist. N.Y., 1953-54; asst. to U.S. Solictor Gen., 1956-59; mem. firm Robinson, Silverman, Pearce, Aronsohn Sand and Berman, N.Y.C., 1960-78; judge U.S. Dist. Ct. So. Dist. N.Y., 1978—, now sr. judge. Adj. prof. law NYU. Note editor: Harvard Law Rev, 1950-51. Del. N.Y. State Constl. Conv., 1967; v.p., treas. Legal Aid Soc. Fellow Am. Coll. Trial Lawyers; mem. ABA, Assn. Bar City N.Y. (v.p.), N.Y. State Bar Assn., Fed. Bar Coun. Office: US Dist Ct US Courthouse 500 Pearl St New York NY 10007-1316

SAND, THOMAS CHARLES, lawyer; b. Portland, Oreg., June 4, 1952; s. Harold Eugene and Marian Anette (Thomas) S.; m. Rhonda Diane Laycoe, June 15, 1974; children: Kendall, Taylor, Justin. Student, Centro des Artes y Lenguas, Cuernavaca, Mex., 1972; BA in English, U. Oreg., 1974; JD, Lewis and Clark Coll., 1977. Bar: Oreg. 1977, U.S. Dist. Ct. Oreg. 1977, U.S. Ct. Appeals (9th cir.) 1984. Assoc. Miller, Nash, LLP, Portland, 1977-84, ptnr., 1984—, mng. ptnr., 1999—. Mem. Oreg. State Bar Com. on Professionalism, 1989, chmn., 1990; dir. young lawyers divsn. Multnomah County Bar Assn., 1980; spl. asst. atty. gen. Wasco County 1983 Gen. Election; speaker in field. Contbr. articles to legal jours. Mem. U.S. Dist. Ct. of Oreg. Hist. Soc., 1990—; bd. dirs. Portland Area coun. Camp Fire, Inc., 1978-90,pres., 1984-86; bd. dirs. Oreg. Indoor Invitational Track Meet, Inc., 1982-84. Recipient Boss of the Yr. award Portland Legal Secs. Assn., 1989. Mem. ABA (securities litigation com., subcom. on broker-dealer litigation), Oreg. Bar Assn., Multnomah Bar Assn. (bd. dirs. task force on structure and orgn. 1989, chmn. com. on professionalism 1988, nominating com. 1986, participating atty. in N.E. legal clin. Vol Lawyers project, award of merit for svc. to profession 1988), Securities Industry Assn. (compliance and legal divsn.), Northwestern Sch. of Law, Lewis and Clark Coll. Alumni Assn. (bd. dirs. 1992, pres. 1997), Valley Comm. Presbyterian Ch., Multnomah Athletic Club, Portland Golf Club. Avocations: golf, guitar, camping, river rafting, children's sports. General civil litigation, Securities. Office: Miller Nash LLP 111 SW 5th Ave Ste 3500 Portland OR 97204-3699

SANDERS, DOUGLAS WARNER, JR. lawyer, municipal judge; b. Oklahoma City, Jan. 13, 1958; s. Douglas Warner Sr. and Jane (Livermore) S.; m. Brenda Gail Cox, Apr. 20, 1990; children: Douglas Warner III, Noel Layne, Jonathan Scott, Stephanie Marie. BS, Okla. State U., 1980; JD, Oklahoma City U., 1983. Bar: Okla., U.S. Dist. Ct. (ea., no. and we. dists.) Okla., U.S. Dist. Ct. (we. dist.) Ark. Assoc. Stipe Law Firm, Oklahoma City, 1983-85; ptnr. Sanders, Sanders & Sullivan, Poteau, Okla., 1985—. Mcpl. judge City of Poteau, 1994—, City of Spiro, Okla., 1994—, Town of Shady Point, Okla., 1994—; mem. Okla. Bd. Bar Examiners, 2000—. Recipient Outstanding Alumnus award Oklahoma City U. Law Sch., 1999. Fellow ABA; mem. Okla. Bar Assn. (bd. govs. 1992-94, v.p. 1997, pres. 1999, Pres.'s award 1997, Disting. Svc. award 1999), LeFlore County Bar Assn. (Pres.'s award 1997). Democrat. Presbyterian. Avocation: golf. General civil litigation, General practice. Home: 900 N Witte St Poteau OK 74953-3636 Office: Sanders Sanders & Sullivan 104 S Church St Poteau OK 74953-3344 E-mail: dougal@clnk.com

SANDERS, EDWIN PERRY BARTLEY, judge; b. Madisonville, Ky., July 12, 1940; s. Virgil Perry and Eunice Jane (Denton) S.; m. Kathryn Walker, Jan. 28, 1967; children: Christopher Charles, Carroll Denton. BS in Bus., Stetson U., 1965, JD, 1968. Bar: Fla. 1968. Ptnr. Ford, Wren and Sanders, 1968-69; mem. Landis, Graham, French, Husfeld and Ford, PA, DeLand, Fla., 1970-83; prof. real estate Stetson U. Sch. Bus. Adminstrn., 1980-83; judge 7th Jud. Cir. Ct. Volusia County, DeLand, Fla., 1983—. With U.S. Army. Mem. Fla. Bar Assn., Volusia County Bar Assn., Lake Beresford Yacht Club, Rotary. Democrat. Episcopalian. Home: 340 Washington Oaks Dr Deland FL 32720-2760 Office: Volusia County Jail Bldg 130 W New York Ave Rm 104 Deland FL 32720-5416 also: PO Box 611 Deland FL 32721-0611

SANDERS, GARY WAYNE, lawyer; b. Wilmington, Del., Dec. 29, 1949; s. Harland Wesley and Anna Marie (Hermanal) S.; m. Cheryl Ann Clark, Aug. 22, 1980. BS, Cal. State Poly. U., 1972; JD, Western State U., 1977. Bar: Calif. 1977. Corp. planner Cert. Grocers, Los Angeles, 1969-74; asst. character coordinator Walt Disney Prodns., Anaheim, Calif., 1968-78; sole practice Seal Beach, 1978-79; v.p., sec., gen. counsel Care Enterprises, Laguna Hills, 1979-88; pvt. practice law Orange, 1988—. Mem. Calif. Bar Assn., Orange County Bar Assn., Nat. Health Lawyers Assn. Republican. Lutheran. Lodges: Elks, Masons. General civil litigation, General corporate, Health. Office: 500 N State College Blvd Orange CA 92868-1604 E-mail: gary@scrhealthlaw.com

SANDERS, HAROLD BAREFOOT, JR. federal judge; b. Dallas, Feb. 5, 1925; s. Harold Barefoot and May Elizabeth (Forrester) S.; m. Jan Scurlock, June 6, 1952; children— Janet Lea, Martha Kay, Mary Frances, Harold Barefoot III. BA, U. Tex., 1949, LLB, 1950. Bar: Tex. bar 1950. U.S. atty. No. Dist. Tex., 1961-65; asst. dep. atty. gen. U.S., 1965-66; asst. atty. gen., 1966-67; legis. counsel to President U.S., 1967-69; partner firm Clark, West, Keller, Sanders & Butler, Dallas, 1969-79; U.S. dist. judge for No. Dist. Tex., 1979—, chief judge, 1989-95. Mem. Tex. Ho. of Reps., 1952-58; Dem. nominee U.S. Senate, 1972. Lt. (j.g.) USNR, World War II. Mem. ABA (chmn. nat. conf. fed. trial judges 1988-89), Fed. Bar Assn. (Disting. Svc. award Dallas 1964), Dallas Bar Assn., State Bar Tex. (jud. conf. U.S. 1989-92, jud. panel on multidistrict litigation 1992-2000), Blue Key, Phi Delta Phi, Phi Delta Theta. Methodist. Office: US Courthouse 1100 Commerce St Ste 15 Dallas TX 75242-1016

SANDERS, RICHARD BROWNING, state supreme court justice; b. Tacoma; 1 child: Laura. BA, U. Wash., 1966, JD, 1969. Assoc. Murray, Scott, McGavick & Graves, Tacoma, 1969, Caplinger & Munn, Seattle, 1971; hearing examiner State Wash., Olympia, 1970; pvt. practice Wash., 1971-95; justice Wash. Supreme Ct., Olympia, 1995—. Adj. prof. U. Wash. Sch. Law; lectr. in field. Contbr. articles to profl. jours. Office: Supreme Court of Washington Temple Justice PO Box 40929 Olympia WA 98504-0929 Fax: (360) 357-2092. E-mail: j_r.sanders@courts.wa.gov

SANDERS, RUSSELL RONALD, lawyer; b. Pitts., May 20, 1956; m. Janice M. Ioli, Aug. 16, 1975; 1 child, Craig D. BA in History, U. Pitts., 1978, JD, 1982. Bar: Pa. 1982, U.S. Dist. Ct. (we. dist.) Pa. 1982, U.S. Ct. Appeals (3d cir.) 1984. Ptnr., shareholder May, Long & Sanders, P.C., Pitts., 1982—. Mem. ABA, Pa. Bar Assn., Allegheny County Bar Assn. Democrat. Roman Catholic. Avocations: hunting, fishing, camping, golf. Bankruptcy, Consumer commercial, General practice. Office: May Long & Sanders PC 600 Grant St Ste 3030 Pittsburgh PA 15219-2712

SANDERSON, DOUGLAS JAY, lawyer; b. Boston, Apr. 21, 1953; s. Warren and Edith S. Sanderson; m. Audrey S. Goldstein, June 6, 1982; children: Scott M.G., Phoebe H.G. BA, Trinity Coll., Hartford, Conn., 1974; JD, George Washington U., 1977. Bar: Va. 1977, D.C. 1978, U.S. Dist. Ct. (ea. dist.) Va. 1978, U.S. Ct. Appeals (4th cir.) 1978. Assoc. Bettius, Rosenberger & Carter, P.C., Fairfax, Va., 1977-82; ptnr. Bettius & Sanderson, P.C. and predecessor firms, 1982-86; prin. Miles & Stockbridge P.C., 1986-95; br. head Miles & Stockbridge, 1989-91; co-owner McCandlish & Lillard, P.C., 1995—. Trustee Cambridge Ctr. Behavioral Studies, Cambridge, 1981-90. Editor: Consumer Protection Reporting Svc., 1976-77. Bd. dirs. Legal Svcs. No. Va., Inc., 1991-97, pres., 1993-95. Mem. ABA, Va. Bar Assn., Fairfax Bar Assn., Ctrl. Fairfax C. of C. (bd. dirs. 1988-93). Avocations: sports, reading. Contracts commercial, Family and matrimonial, Real property. Office: McCandlish & Lillard 11350 Random Hills Rd Ste 500 Fairfax VA 22030-6044

SANDLER, LEWIS HERBSMAN, lawyer, real estate executive; b. N.Y.C., July 2, 1936; s. Samuel Herbsman and Celia (Rubin) S.; m. Viveca M. Lindahl, Sept. 30, 1967 (div. Oct. 1971); 1 child, Stephanie J.; m. Willy Klinkhamer, Oct. 27, 1973; 1 child, Derek J. A.B., Hamilton Coll., 1958; LL.B., Columbia U., 1961. Bar: N.Y. 1962, Tex. 1981. Atty. Port of N.Y., 1961-65, Equitable Life Assurance Co., N.Y.C., 1965-68; assoc. Finley, Kumble, Underberg, Persky & Roth, N.Y.C., 1968-71, ptnr., 1971-73; ptnr. Cohen & Sandler, N.Y.C., 1973-74, Poletti, Freidin, Prasker, Feldman & Gartner, N.Y.C., 1975-77; gen. counsel, gen. ptnr. Southwest Realty, Ltd., Dallas, 1977-92; dir., exec. v.p., sec. gen. counsel SouthWest Property Trust Inc., 1992-96; pres., CEO United Investors Realty Trust, Dallas, 1997—. Bd. govs. Boys Athletic League, N.Y.C., 1976-79. Mem. N.Y. State Bar Assn., Tex. Bar Assn. Real property, Securities. Home: 7156 Helsem Bnd Dallas TX 75230-1946 Office: United Investors Realty Trust 8080 N Central Expy Ste 500 Dallas TX 75206-1812

SANDLER, MICHAEL DAVID, lawyer; b. Los Angeles, Feb. 27, 1946; AB, Stanford U., 1967; JD, Yale U., 1972. Bar: Calif. 1973, D.C. 1973, Wash. 1985. Assoc. Steptoe & Johnson, Washington, 1972-75, 77-79, ptnr., 1980-85; spl. asst. to legal adviser Dept. of State, 1975-77; ptnr. Foster, Pepper & Shefelman, Seattle, 1985-97, Sandler Ahern & McConaughy PLLC, Seattle, 1997—. Adj. prof. law Georgetown U., Washington, 1979, 81-82, U. Wash., Seattle, 1985-92. Vol. Peace Corps, Ethiopia and Ghana, 1968-70. Mem. ABA (chair 1995-96 sect. internat. law and practice). Antitrust, General civil litigation, Private international. Office: Sandler Ahern & McConaughy PLLC 1200 5th Ave Ste 1900 Seattle WA 98101-3135 E-mail: mike@sandlaw.com

SANDLER, ROSS, law educator; b. Milw., Jan. 31, 1939; s. Theodore T. and Laurette (Simons) S.; m. Alice R. Mintzer, Sept. 15, 1968; children: Josephine, Jenny, Dorothy. AB, Dartmouth Coll., 1961; LLB, NYU, 1965. Bar: N.Y. 1965, Fla. 1965. Assoc. atty. Cahill Gordon Reindel & Ohl, N.Y.C., 1965-68; asst. U.S. atty. So. Dist. N.Y., 1968-72; assoc. atty. Trubin Sillcocks Edelman & Knapp, N.Y.C., 1972-75; sr. staff atty. Natural Resources Def. Coun., 1975-81, 83-86; spl. advisor to mayor City of N.Y., 1981-82; exec. dir. Hudson River Found., N.Y.C., 1983-86; commr. N.Y.C. Dept. Transp., 1986-90; ptnr. Jones Day Reavis & Pogue, N.Y.C., 1991-93; law prof. N.Y. Law Sch., 1993—, dir. Ctr. for N.Y.C. law, 1993—; pres. N.Y. Legis. Svc., 1998—. Mem. N.Y.C. Procurement Policy Bd., 1994—; vis. lectr. Yale Law Sch., New Haven, 1977; adj. prof. law NYU Law Sch., 1976-94; chair, mem. N.Y.C. Taxi and Limousine Commn., 1980-90. Co-author: A New Direction in Transit, 1978; columnist Environ. Mag., 1976-80; editor: (jour.) City Law; contbr. book chpt., op-ed columns, articles to profl. jours.; lectr. environ. law, spkr. confs. Trustee Woods Hole (Mass.) Rsch. Ctr., 1983—; mem. exec. com. Hudson River Found., 1986-96; mem. adv. coun. Ctr. Biodiversity and Conservation Am. Mus. Nat. History, 1996—. Recipient Pub. Interest award NYU Law Alumni, 1987, Louis J. Lefkowitz award Fordham Law Sch. Urban Law Jour., 1989, Lifetime Achievement award N.Y. State Bar Assn., 1998. Mem. City Club of N.Y. (chair 1992-93, trustee). Office: NY Law Sch 57 Worth St New York NY 10013-2959

SANDMAN, IRVIN W(ILLIS), lawyer; b. Seattle, Mar. 19, 1954; BA summa cum laude, U. Wash., 1976; JD, UCLA, 1980. Bar: U.S. Dist. Ct. (we. and ea. dists.) Wash. 1980. Prin. Graham & Dunn, Seattle, 1980—. Staff mem. UCLA Law Review. Mem. ABA (vice chair resort and tourism com. 1996-2001, co-chair 2001—), Acad. Hospitality Attys. (charter), Wash. State Hotel and Motel Assn. (govtl. affairs key contact), Wash. State Bar Assn. (chmn. creditor/debtor sect. 1988-90, editor newsletter 1984—, speaker continuing legal edn.). Bankruptcy, Contracts commercial. Office: Graham & Dunn 1420 5th Ave Fl 33 Seattle WA 98101-4087

SANDROCK, SCOTT PAUL, lawyer; b. Massillon, Ohio, Apr. 11, 1953; s. H. Paul and Alvina (Huber) S.; m. Marianne Griffin, Aug. 28, 1976; children: Paul, Christopher. BA, U. Notre Dame, 1975; JD, Ohio State U., 1978. Bar: Ohio 1978, U.S. Dist. Ct. (no. dist.) Ohio, U.S. Ct. Claims, U.S. Ct. Internat. Trade, U.S. Tax Ct., U.S. Ct. Customs and Patent Appeals, U.S. Ct. Mil. Appeals, U.S. Ct. Appeals (6th cir.), U.S. Supreme Ct. From assoc. to ptnr. Black, McCuskey, Souers & Arbaugh, Canton, Ohio, 1978—. Lectr. Malone Coll., 1987—, Mt. Union Coll., 1994—. Author, editor: History of the Canton Jaycees 1934-1984, 1984; also articles. Advancement chmn., Cubmaster Buckeye coun. Boy Scouts Am., 1987-93, asst. scoutmaster, 1991—, Seneca dist. chmn., 1992-94, active numerous coms., 1978—; councilman Village of Navarre, Ohio, 1984-85, chmn. bldgs. and land com., 1984-85; mem. Stark County Regional Planning Commn., 1984-85; trustee Vis. Care Inc., 1982-96, ARC, Canton, 1987-95, chmn. 1993-94; trustee Stark County Parents Anonymous Inc., 1984-88, pres. 1985-87; mem. allocations com. United Way Cen. Stark County, 1990-96; trustee Cmty. Svcs. of Stark County, Inc., 1997—, v.p., 2000—; trustee Canton Cmty. Clinic, 2001—; trustee Canton City Schs. Found., 1998—, pres., 2001—. Recipient Mayor's citation City of Canton, 1985, Merit award Seneca Dist. Boy Scouts Am., 1989, Silver Beaver, Boy Scouts Am.; named one of Outstanding Young Men Am., 1986, 88, 89. Mem. ABA (health law and bus. law sects., franchise forum), Nat. Health Lawyers Assn., Ohio Bar Assn. (computer law com. 1984-93), Ohio state Bar Assn. Coll., Stark County Bar Assn. (disputed fee com., corp. law com., lectr. 1979, 82, 85), Jaycees (Disting. Svc. award, 1993, bd. dirs. 1983-85), Rotary (Canton trustee 1996-99, pres. 1997-98). Republican. Roman Catholic. Club: Notre Dame (Canton) (sec., treas. 1979-87). State civil litigation, General corporate, Franchising. Home: 5443 Echodell Ave NW Canton OH 44708-7476 Office: Black McCuskey Souers & Arbaugh 220 Market Ave S Ste 1000 Canton OH 44702-2171

SANDS, DARRY GENE, lawyer; b. Charleston, Ark., Jan. 4, 1947; s. Anthony Wayne and Marjorie (Elkins) S.; m. Charlotte Moore, Dec. 28, 1968; 1 child, Spencer Justin. BS, U. Ark., 1969; JD, U. Kans., 1974. Bar: Mo. 1974, U.S. Dist. Ct. (we. dist.) Mo. 1974. Dir. Dicus, Davis, Sands & Collins, P.C., Kansas City, Mo., 1991—. Spkr. in field. Contbr. articles to profl. jours. Bd. dirs. Hope House; Camp Mitiog. Mem. ABA, Nat. Assn. Coll. and Univ. Attys., Mo. Bar, Kansas City Met. Bar Assn. (chmn., past chair coll. and univ. law com., local govt. com.), Order of Coif, Lake Quivira Country Club. Democrat. General civil litigation, Education and schools, Labor. Home: 5341 Canterbury Rd Shawnee Mission KS 66205-2612 Office: Dicus Davis Sands & Collins PC 1930 City Center Sq 1100 Main St Kansas City MO 64105-2105 E-mail: dsands@ddsc-law.com

SANDSTROM, DALE VERNON, state supreme court judge; b. Grand Forks, N.D., Mar. 9, 1950; s. Ellis Vernon and Hilde Geneva (Williams) S.; m. Gail Hagerty, Mar. 27, 1993; children: Jack, Carrie, Anne. BA, N.D. State U., 1972; JD, U. N.D., 1975. Bar: N.D. 1975, U.S. Dist. Ct. N.D. 1975, U.S. Ct. Appeals (8th cir.) 1976. Asst. atty. gen., chief consumer fraud and antitrust div. State of N.D., Bismarck, 1975-81, securities commr., 1981-83, pub. svc. commr., 1983-92, pres. commn., 1987-91, justice Supreme Ct., 1992—. Chair N.D. Commn. on Cameras in the Courtroom, 1993—, Joint Procedure Com., 1996—; mem. exec. com. N.D. Jud. Conf., 1995—, chair-elect, 1997-99, chair, 1999-2001; mem. Gov.'s Com. on Security and Privacy, Bismarck, 1975-76, Gov.'s Com. on Refugees, Bismarck, 1976; chmn. Gov's Com. on Comml. Air Transp., Bismarck, 1983-84. Mem. platform com. N.D. Reps., 1972, 76, exec. com., 1972-73, 85-88, dist. chmn., 1981-82; former chmn. bd. deacons Luth. Ch.; mem. ch. coun., exec. com., chmn. legal and constl. rev. com. Evang. Luth Ch. Am., 1993—; mem. exec. bd. dirs., No. Lights Coun., dist. chair Boy Scouts Am., 1998-2000. Named Disting. Eagle Scout, Boy Scouts Am., 1997. Mem. ABA, N.D. Bar Assn., Big Muddy Bar Assn., Nat. Assn. Regulatory Utility Commrs. (electricity com.), N.A. Assn. Securities Adminstrs., Order of De Molay (grand master 1994-95, mem. Internat. Supreme coun., Legion of Honor award), Nat. Eagle Scouts Assn. (regent for life), Shriners, Elks, Eagles, Masons (33d degree, chmn. grand youth com. 1979-87, Youth Leadership award 1986), Bruce M. VanSickle Am. Inn of Court (pres. 1999-2001). Office: State ND Supreme Court Bismarck ND 58505

SANDY, ROBERT EDWARD, JR. lawyer; b. Libertyville, Ill., Feb. 16, 1943; s. Robert Edward and Elizabeth Ann (Carroll) S.; m. Joan Mary Phillips, Apr. 19, 1969; children: Mary Rosanne Phillips-Sandy, John Robert Phillips-Sandy. AB, Harvard U., 1965; JD, U. Chgo., 1968. Bar: Mass. 1969, Maine 1972, U.S. Dist. Ct. Mass. 1970, U.S. Dist. Ct. Maine 1972, U.S. Ct. Appeals (1st cir.) 1994, U.S. Supreme Ct. 1980. Atty. Boston Redevel. Authority, 1969-72; ptnr. Sandy and Sandy, Waterville, Maine, 1972-83, Sherman and Sandy, Waterville, 1983-87; sr. ptnr. Sherman & Sandy, 1987—. Mem. Waterville Bar Assn., Maine Bar Assn., Maine Trial Lawyers Assn., ABA. Avocations: boating, skiing, community theater, Maine Internat. Film Festival. Criminal, Family and matrimonial, General practice. Home: 19 Greenwood Park Waterville ME 04901-4316 Office: Sherman & Sandy 74 Silver St Waterville ME 04901-6524 E-mail: info@shermanandsandy.com

SANETTI, STEPHEN LOUIS, lawyer; b. Flushing, N.Y., June 25, 1949; s. Alfred Julius Sanetti and Yolanda Marie (DiGioia) Boyes; m. Carole Leighton Koller, Sept. 21, 1974; children: Christopher Edward, Dana Harrison. BA in History with honors, Va. Mil. Inst., 1971; JD, Washington and Lee U., 1974. Bar: Conn. 1975, U.S. Ct. Mil. Appeals 1975, U.S. Dist. Ct. Conn. 1978, U.S. Ct. Appeals (2d cir.) 1979, U. S. Supreme Ct. 1980. Litigation atty. Marsh, Day & Calhoun, Bridgeport, Conn., 1978-80; gen. counsel Sturm, Ruger & Co., Southport, 1980—, v.p., 1993-2000, also bd. dirs., 1998-2000, vice chmn., sr. exec. v.p., 2000—. Dir. Product Liability Adv. Coun. Tech. advisor Assn. Firearm and Toolmark Examiners; chmn. legis. & legal affairs com. Sporting Arms & Ammunition Mfrs. Inst., 1993-2001. Served to capt., chief criminal law 1st Cavalry Div. Staff Judge Advocate, U.S. Army, 1975-78. Mem. Am. Acad. Forensic Sci., Def. Rsch. Inst. Republican. Roman Catholic. General civil litigation, General corporate, Product liability. Office: Sturm Ruger & Co Inc 1 Lacey Pl Southport CT 06490-1241

SANFILIPPO, JON WALTER, lawyer; b. Milw., Nov. 10, 1950; s. Joseph Salvator and Jeanne Catherine (Lisinski) S.; m. Pamela Joy Jaeger, July 8, 1972; children: Kerri, Jessica, Jennifer. AS, U. Wis., West Bend, 1972; BS, U. Wis., Milw., 1974, MS, 1978; JD, Marquette U., 1988; postgrad., Nat. Jud. Coll., 1996. Bar: Wis. 1988, U.S. Dist. Ct. (ea. dist.) Wis. 1988, U.S. Ct. Appeals (7th cir.) 1988, U.S. Dist. Ct. (we. dist.) Wis 1989. U.S. Supreme Ct. 1994; cert. elem. tchr., ednl. adminstr., Wis. Collection agt. West Bend Co., 1970-72; educator, athletic dir., coach St. Francis Cabrini, West Bend, 1974-77; clk. of cir. ct. Washington County, 1976-89; ptnr. Schowalter, Edwards & Sanfilippo, S.C., 1989-94; sch. prin.K-8 Campbellsport (Wis.) Sch. Dist., 1994-95; chief dep. clk. Cir. Ct. Milw. County, Milw., 1995—, acting clk., 1997-98; jud. ct. commr. Milw. County, 1997—. Judo tchr. City of West Bend, 1967—; phys. edn. instr., judo coach U. Wis., West Bend, 1992—; fellow ct. exec. devel. program Inst. Ct. Mgmt. Nat. Ctr. State Cts., 1999. Author: Judo for the Physical Educator, 1981, Proper Falling for Education Classes, 1981. Mem. sch. bd. West Bend Sch. Dist., 1979-80; dist. chmn. Wis. Clk. of Cts. Assn., 1976-79, mem. exec. com., 1976-82, 97-98, mem. legis. com., 1982-84, 97-98. Recipient cert. study internat. and Chinese law East Chinese Inst. Politics & Law, Willamette U. Law Sch., Shanghai, People's Republic China, 1988, Black Belt 7th degree U.S. Martial Arts Assn., 2000 Mem. ABA, Nat. Jud. Coll., Nat. Assn. for Ct. Adminstrn., Wis. Bar Assn. (bench/bar com. 1986-88, 97—), Milw. Bar Assn. (cts. com. 1995—, criminal bench/bar com. 1997—, family bench/bar com. 1997—), Washington County Bar Assn., U. Wis.-Washington County Found. Inc. (bd. dirs. 1993-94), Assn. Wis. Sch. Adminstrs., Justinian Soc., Universal Tae Kwon Do Assn. (3d degree Black Belt 1988), U.S. Judo Assn. (6th degree Black Belt 1995), U.S. Martial Arts Assn. (7th degree Black Belt Judo 2000), Rotary (bd. dirs. West Bend Sunrise Club 1990-91, Paul Harris fellow). Roman Catholic. Avocations: Tai Kwon Do, Tai Chi, Judo, photography, model railroading. Office: Milw County Ct House Rm 104 901 N 9th St Milwaukee WI 53233-1425 E-mail: jon.sanfilippo@milwaukee.courts.state.wi.us

SANFORD, BRUCE WILLIAM, lawyer; b. Massena, N.Y., Aug. 5, 1945; s. Doris (Suhrland) Sanford; m. Marilou Green, May 17, 1980; children: Ashley Anne, Barrett William. BA, Hamilton Coll., 1967; JD, NYU, 1970. Bar: N.Y. 1970, Ohio 1971, D.C. 1981, Md. 1985. Staff reporter Wall St. Jour., 1966-67; assoc. Baker and Hostetler, Washington, 1971-79, ptnr., 1979—. Author: Sanford's Synopsis Law of Libel and Privacy, rev. edit., 1991, Libel and Privacy, 2nd edit., 1991, Don't Shoot the Messenger: How Our Growing Hatred of the Media Threatens Free Speech for All of Us, 1999. Trustee Nat. Symphony Orch. Assn.; bd. dirs. Thomas Jefferson 1st Amendment Ctr., U. Va., Charlottesville. Mem. ABA (governing bd., forum com. on communication law, chmn. defamation torts com. 1985-86). Communications. Office: Baker & Hostetler LLP 1050 Connecticut Ave NW Washington DC 20036-5304

SANGMEISTER, GEORGE EDWARD, lawyer, consultant, former congressman; b. Joliet, Ill., Feb. 16, 1931; s. George Conrad and Rose Engaborg (Johnson) S.; m. Doris Marie Hinspeter, Dec. 1, 1951; children: George Kurt, Kimberley Ann. BA, Elmhurst Coll., 1957; LLB, John Marshall Law Sch., 1960, JD, 1970. Bar: Ill. 1960. Ptnr. McKeown, Fitzgerald, Zollner, Buck, Sangmeister & Hutchison, 1969-89; justice of peace, 1961-63; states atty. Will County, 1964-68; mem. Ill. Ho. of Reps., 1972-76, Ill. Senate, 1977-87, 101st-103rd Congresses from 4th (now 11th) Dist. Ill., 1989-95; ret., 1995; cons. McKeown, Fitzgerald, Zollner, Buck, Hutchison, Ruttle and Assocs., 1990—. Chmn. Frankfort Twp. unit Am. Cancer Soc., Will County Emergency Housing Devel. Corp.; past trustee Will County Family Svc. Agy.; past bd. dirs. Joliet Jr. Coll. Found., Joliet Will County Ctr. for Econ. Devel., Silver Cross Found., Silver Cross Hosp. With inf. AUS, 1951-53. Mem. ABA, Ill. Bar Assn., Assn. Trial Lawyers Am., Am. Legion, Frankfort (past pres.), Mokena C. of C., Old Timers Baseball Assn., Lions. Home: 20735 Wolf Rd Mokena IL 60448-8927

SANISLO, PAUL STEVE, lawyer; b. Cleve., Feb. 8, 1927; s. Paul and Bertha (Kasa) S.; m. Mary Ellen P. Conroy, May 7, 1949; 1 child, Susan J. BA, Baldwin-Wallace Coll., 1948; JD, Cleve. State U., 1961. Bar: Ohio 1961, U.S. Dist. Ct. (no. dist.) Ohio 1964. Order clk. Am. Agrl. Chem. Co., Cleve., 1948-52; safety engr. Park Drop Forge Co., 1952-62, personnel mgr., 1954-62; assoc. then ptnr. Spohn & Sanislo, L.P.A., 1962-81; pres., 1981-86; ptnr., pres. Sanislo, Bacevice & Assocs. LPA, Cleve., 1987-98; pres. Sanislo & Assocs. Co. LPA, 1998-2000; of counsel Stewart & Dechant, Cleve., 2000—. Spl. counsel Atty. Gen. Ohio, 1971; arbitrator Am. Arbitration Assn., 1972-78. Mem. Cleve. City Coun., 1964-67; trustee Cleve.-Marshall Law Sch., 1962-63; trustee Cleve.-Marshall Ednl. Found., 1963-68, pres., 1980-83; mem. Solon city Bd. Edn., Ohio, 1972-83, pres., 1974-83; chmn. Solon Charter Rev. Commn., 1971, mem., 2000—; past mem., organizer, legal adv. Solon Drug Abuse Ctr.; mem. Cuyahoga County Dem. Exec. Com.; ward leader 29th Ward Dem. Club, 1965-71, also past pres.; trustee Solon Dem. Ward Club, 1972-75. Recipient Disting. Svc. award City of Solon, 1984, Solon Bd. Edn., 1984, Solon Edn. Assn., 1984. Mem. Bar Assn. Greater Cleve. (Merit Svc. award 1978-79, chmn. workers compensation sect. 1975-96), Ohio Bar Assn., Cuyahoga County Bar Assn., Assn. Trial Lawyers Am., Cleve.-Marshall Law Sch. Alumni Assn. (pres. 1968-69), Hungarian Bus. and Tradesmen's Club (pres. 1967-68), Cleve. Assn. Compensation Attys. (pres. 1973-76). Democrat. Roman Catholic. Avocations: golf, travel. General practice, Personal injury, Workers' compensation. Office: Stewart & DeChant 1440 Standard Bldg Cleveland OH 44113 E-mail: psanislo@stewartdechant.com

SANNER, ROYCE NORMAN, lawyer; b. Lancaster, Minn., Mar. 9, 1931; s. Oscar N. and Clara Sanner; m. Janice L. Sterne, Dec. 27, 1972; children— Michelle Joy, Craig Allen. BS, Minn. State U., Moorhead, 1953; LLB cum laude, U. Minn., 1961. Bar: Minn. 1961, U.S. Dist. Ct. Minn. 1961, U.S. Supreme Ct. 1981. Tchr. English Karlstad (Minn.) High Sch., 1955-57; counsel IDS Life Ins. Co., Mpls., 1961-68, v.p., gen. counsel, 1969-72, exec. v.p., gen. counsel, 1972-77; dir. corp. devel. Am. Express Fin. Advisors, Mpls., 1968-69, v.p., gen. counsel, 1975-78, v.p., 1978-80, v.p., gen. counsel, 1980-82; v.p. law Northwestern Nat. Life Ins. Co., 1982-83, sr. v.p., gen. counsel, sec., 1983-96, ReliaStar Fin. Corp. (formerly known as NWNL Cos., Inc.), Mpls., 1988-96; of counsel Maslon Edelman Borman & Brand, 1996—. Bd. dirs. Fairview Univ. Med. Ctr., Friendship Ventures, Inc., Fraser Cmty. Svcs., Fairview Health Svcs. Served with U.S. Army, 1953-55. Mem. ABA, Minn. Bar Assn., Hennepin County Bar Assn., Fed. Bar Assn., Assn. of Life Ins. Counsel, Minn. Corp. Counsel Assn., Rotary. General corporate, Insurance, Securities. Home: 734 Widsten Cir Wayzata MN 55391-1784 Office: Maslon Edelman Borman & Brand 3300 Wells Fargo Ctr 90 S 7th St Ste 3300 Minneapolis MN 55402-4140 E-mail: rsampls@aol.com

SANS, HENRI LOUIS, JR. lawyer; b. Gardner, Mass., Nov. 11, 1951; s. Henri Louis and Laurette Rolande (Sylvestre) S.; m. Michelle Ann LeBlanc, Aug. 18, 1985. BA, Bates Coll., 1973; JD cum laude, Syracuse U., 1976. Bar: Mass. 1977. Assoc. Francis H. LeBlanc, Gardner, 1977-88; pvt. practice, 1988—. Pres. United Way Gardner, Inc., 1980-83, campaign chmn., 1981-82; pres. Gardner Vis. Nurses Assn., 1981-83; trustee The Gardner Mus., 1986-89; dist. chmn. Bates Coll. Capital Campaign, Lewiston, Maine, 1981; active Annual Alumni Fund Com., 1986-87; trustee Levi Heywood Meml. Libr., 1987—, Henry Heywood Meml. Hospital, 1989—; dir., clk. North County Land Trust, 1992—; bd. dirs., asst. treas. The Health Found. Ctrl. Mass., Inc., 1999—. Mem. No. Worcester County Bar Assn., Greater Gardner C. of C. (Cmty. Svc. award 1982), Order of Coif, Chair City Club Gardner (pres. 1986—), Bates Coll. Club Lewiston. Democrat. Roman Catholic. General corporate, Probate, Real property. Home: 144 Lawrence St Gardner MA 01440-0463 Office: 21 Pleasant St Gardner MA 01440-2608

SANSEVERINO, RAYMOND ANTHONY, lawyer; b. Bklyn., Feb. 16, 1947; s. Raphael and Alice Ann (Camerano) S.; m. Karen Marie Mooney, Aug. 24, 1968 (dec. 1980); children: Deirdre Ann, Stacy Lee; m. Victoria Vent, June 6, 1982 (div. 1995). AB in English Lit., Franklin & Marshall Coll., 1968; JD cum laude, Fordham U., 1972. Bar: N.Y. 1973, U.S. Dist. Ct. (so. and ea. dists.) N.Y. 1973, U.S. Ct. Appeals (2d cir.) 1974, U.S. Supreme Ct. 1986. Assoc. Rogers & Wells, N.Y.C., 1972-75, Corbin & Gordon, N.Y.C., 1975-77; ptnr. Corbin Silverman & Sanseverino LLP, 1978—, mng. ptnr., 1985—. Contbr. articles to profl. jours.; articles editor Fordham Law Rev., 1971-72. Recipient West Pub. Co. prize, 1972. Mem. ABA, Assn. Bar City of N.Y., N.Y. State Bar Assn., Twin Oaks Swim and Tennis Club (bd. dirs. 1981—, pres. 1993—), Alumni Assn. Franklin & Marshall Coll. (bd. dirs. 2001—) Republican. Roman Catholic. Landlord-tenant, Real property. Office: Corbin Silverman Et Al 805 3d Ave New York NY 10022-7513 E-mail: rsanseverino@csslaw.com

SANT, JOHN TALBOT, lawyer; b. Oct. 7, 1932; s. John Francis and Josephine (Williams) S.; m. Almira Steedman Baldwin, Jan. 31, 1959; children: John Talbot Jr., Richard Baldwin, Frank Williams. AB, Princeton U., 1954; LLB, Harvard U., 1957. Bar: Mo. 1957. Assoc. Thompson, Mitchell, Douglas & Neill, St. Louis, 1958-60; atty. McDonnell Aircraft Co., 1960-61; asst. sec., 1961-62; sec., 1962-67, McDonnell Douglas Corp., St. Louis, 1967-76; asst. gen. counsel, 1969-74; corp. v.p. legal, 1974-75; corp. v.p., gen. counsel, 1975-88; bd. dirs., 1978-82; sr. v.p., gen. counsel, 1988-91; ptnr. Bryan Cave, 1991-96; of counsel, 1997. Vestry of St. Michael and St. George, St. Louis, 1979-82, 87-90, 93-95; bd. dirs. Grace Hill Neighborhood Svcs., Inc., St. Louis, 1987-93; pres. Grace Hill Settlement House, 1996-97; mem. transition task force Supt. Elect. of St. Louis Pub. Schs., 1996, found. dir. St. Louis Pub. Schs. Found., chair person Partnership For You, Inc., 2001—. Mem. ABA (pub. contracts sec., coun. 1987-91), Mo. Bar Assn., St. Louis Bar Assn. General corporate. Home: 9 Ridgewood St Saint Louis MO 63124-1849 Office: Bryan Cave 1 Metropolitan Sq Ste 3600 Saint Louis MO 63102-2750

SANTELLE, JAMES LEWIS, prosecutor; b. Milw., Sept. 10, 1958; s. James Nathaniel and Carol Jean (Hasley) S. BA, Marquette Univ., 1980; JD, Univ. Chgo., 1983. Bar: Wis. 1983, U.S. Dist. Ct. (ea. and we. dist.) 1983, U.S. Ct. Appeals (7th cir.) 1983. Clerk Hon. Judge Robert W. Warren , Milw., 1983-85; asst. U.S. atty. Ea. Dist. Wis., 1985—, civil divsn. chief, 1993—99, interim U.S. atty., 2001; prin. dep. dir. Exec. Office U.S. Attys., U.S. Dept. Justice, Washington, 1999—2001. Profl. responsibility com., investigator Wis. Bd. of Attys., 1993—. Editor: The Milw. Lawyer, 1986-92. Bd. dirs. Waukesha County Coun. Alcoholism and Other Drug Abuse, 1993—; citizen counselor Badger Boys State, 1986—; coach Wis. Bar Found. High Sch. Mock Trial Tournament, 1986—. Avocations: running, swimming. Office: US Atty Office 517 E Wisconsin Ave Rm 530 Milwaukee WI 53202-4580*

SANTEMMA, JON NOEL, lawyer; b. Oceanside, N.Y., Dec. 24, 1937; s. Esterino E. and Emilie E. (Davis) S.; m. Lynne Maurer, Dec. 27, 1960 (div. 1987); children: Suzanne, Deborah, Jon E., Christopher Jon; m. Carol Marie Hoffman, July 16, 1988; 1 child, Jessica Noelle. BA, Cornell U., 1960; JD, Fordham U., 1963. Bar: N.Y. 1963, U.S. Ct. Mil. Appeals 1969, U.S. Ct. Claims 1969, U.S. Supreme Ct. 1969, U.S. Dist. Ct. (ea. dist.) N.Y. 1977. Assoc. Parnell Callahan, N.Y.C., 1963-64; assoc. Warburton, Hyman, Deeley & Connolly, Mineola, N.Y., 1964-66; law sec. to adminstrv. judge of Nassau County, 1966-71; pvt. practice, 1971-74, 89—; ptnr. Santemma & Murphy, P.C., 1974-89, Santemma & Deutsch, Mineola, 1993—. Lectr. in field. Trustee Inc. Village of Laurel Hollow, N.Y., 1979-94; mem. Nassau County Rep. Law Com., 1979—; mem. Nassau County Jud. Selection Com., 1992—. Recipient Outstanding Man of Yr. in Law award L.I. U., 1976. Mem. Am. Bar Found., N.Y. Bar Found., N.Y. State Bar Assn. (ho. of dels. 1980-94, 95—, chair condemnation and tax certiorari com. 1997—, exec. com. 1984-85, 89-90, v.p. 1986-88), Nassau County Bar Assn. (pres. 1979-80, Pres.'s award for outstanding svc. 1981), Suffolk County Bar Assn., Assn. Bar City N.Y., Huntington Country Club, Cold Spring Harbor Beach Club, Garden City Golf Club, Ocean Reef Club (Key Largo, Fla.). Federal civil litigation, Condemnation, State and local taxation. Office: 120 Mineola Blvd Mineola NY 11501-4073

SANTOLA, DANIEL RALPH, lawyer; b. Syracuse, N.Y., Oct. 25, 1949; s. Dan D. and Sophie Irene (Podszebka) S.; m. Kathleen Elaine Beach, Aug. 21, 1971; children: Daniel, Jonathan. BA, SUNY, Buffalo, 1971; JD, Union U., Albany, N.Y., 1974. Bar: N.Y. 1975, U.S. Dist. Ct. (no. dist.) N.Y. 1975, U.S. Dist. Ct. Vt. 1986, U.S. Dist. Ct. (we. dist.) N.Y. 1992, U.S. Dist. Ct. (so., ea. dist.) N.Y., 1993. Assoc. Martin Brickman, Esq., Albany, N.Y., 1974-75; assoc. prof. Rensselaer Poly. Inst., Troy, 1976-77, dir. law mgmt. program, 1976-77; assoc. Morris J. Bloomberg, Esq., Albany, 1978-81; ptnr. Bloomberg & Santola, Esq., 1982-87, Powers and Santola, Albany, 1987—. Asst. town atty. Town of Bethlehem, Delmar, N.Y., 1978—. Author: (with others) Products Liability Practice Guide, Medical Equipment, 1988, N.Y. Negligence Guide, Construction Accidents, 1989, Compensating the Catastrophically Injured, 1990, Using SPECT Scans to Show Head Injuries. Mem. N.Y. State Bar Assn. (ho. of dels. 1995—), N.Y. State Trial Lawyers Assn. (past pres. capitol dist. affiliate, bd. dirs. 1988—), Albany County Bar Assn. (pres. 1997), Am. Bd. Trial Advs., N.Y. State Trial Lawyers Inst. (dir. decisions seminar 1984—), Capital Dist. Trial Lawyers Assn. (pres. 1985), Am. Bd. Trial Adv. (Albany chpt., pres. 2000). Republican. Roman Catholic. Avocations: golf, snowboarding, scuba diving. Personal injury, Product liability. Office: Powers and Santola Esq 39 N Pearl St Ste 6 Albany NY 12207-2785 E-mail: DSantola@Powers-Santola.com

SANTONI, CYNTHIA LEE, lawyer; b. Galesburg, Ill. d. Mark Dean and Cleo Berniece Vancil; m. David Wayne Santoni, July 30, 1988 (div. Mar. 1998); children: Mark Vincent, Joseph David, Nicholas Dean. BS, George Mason U., 1980; JD, George Mason U. Sch. Law, 1983. Assoc. Law Office R. Harrison Pledger, McLean, Va., 1983-90; ptnr. Pledger & Santoni, 1990-96; atty., prin. Miles & Stockbridge, 1996—. Charter mem. St. Judes Children's Rsch. Hosp., Annandale, Va., 1992—; mem. Fairfax (Va.) Bar Assn. cir. ct. com., past mem. com. professionalism. Mem. ATLA, Va. Bar Assn., Va. Assn. Def. Attys., Def. Rsch. Inst., ABA Torts, Ins. Practice. Democrat. Avocations: soccer, hockey, fund raising. Personal injury. Office: Miles & Stockbridge 1751 Pinnacle Dr Ste 500 Mc Lean VA 22102-3833

SANTORO, FRANK ANTHONY, lawyer; b. Plainfield, N.J., Dec. 14, 1941; s. Frank V. and Nancy M. (Scavuzzo) S.; m. Patricia Ferrante, Oct. 10, 1964; children— Frank, Jennifer. B.S. in Chemistry, Seton Hall U., 1963, J.D., 1970. Patent atty. Exxon Corp., Linden, N.J., 1970-73; sole practice, South Plainfield, N.J., 1973— ; atty. Planning Bd. Borough South Plainfield, 1971-73; mcpl. prosecutor Borough South Plainfield, 1972. Councilman Borough South Plainfield, 1977-79, mcpl. atty., 1985-93; mcpl. chmn. South Plainfield Republican Orgn., 1981-84. Mem. Middlesex County Bar Assn., UNICO Nat. Roman Catholic. General practice, Probate, Real property. Office: 129 S Plainfield Ave PO Box 272 South Plainfield NJ 07080-0272

SAPP, JOHN RAYMOND, lawyer; b. Lawrence, Kans., June 18, 1944; s. Raymond Olen and Amy (Kerr) S.; m. Linda Lee Tebbe, July 3, 1965; children: Jeffrey, Jennifer, John. BA, U. Kans., 1966; JD, Duke U., 1969. Bar: Wis. 1969, U.S. Dist. Ct. (ea. dist.) Wis. 1969, U.S. Ct. Appeals (7th cir.) 1974, U.S. Ct. Appeals (4th cir.) 1984, U.S. Supreme Ct. 1974. Assoc. Michael, Best & Friedrich, Milw., 1969-76, ptnr., 1976-90, mng. ptnr., 1990—. Dir. Roadrunner Freight Systems, Milw., 1992—. Bd. dirs. Milw. Symphony, 1981-95, mem. exec. com., 1993-95; bd. dirs. Boy Scouts Am., Milw., 1986—, pres. 1990-92; mem. Milw. Arts Bd., 1990, Greater Milw. Com.; bd. dirs. Zool. Soc., 1995—, v.p., 2000—; bd. dirs. Lex Mundi, 1997-2000, mem. exec. com., 1997-2001; bd. dirs. Jr. Achievement Greater Milw., 2001—. Avocations: golf, curling, print collecting. Labor. E-mail: jrsapp@mbf-law.com

SAPP, WALTER WILLIAM, lawyer, energy company executive; b. Linton, Ind., Apr. 21, 1930; s. Walter J. and Nona (Stalcup) S.; m. Eva Kaschner, July 10, 1957 (dec.); children: Karen Elisabeth, Christoph Walter. AB magna cum laude, Harvard, 1951; JD summa cum laude, Ind. U., 1957. Bar: Ind. 1957, N.Y. 1959, Colo. 1966, U.S. Supreme Ct. 1972, Tex. 1977. Pvt. practice, N.Y.C., 1957-60, 63-66; practice in Paris, France, 1960-63, Colorado Springs, 1966-76; assoc. atty. Cahill, Gordon, Reindel & Ohl, Paris, 1960-63, N.Y.C., 1957-60, 63-65, partner, 1966; gen. counsel Colo. Interstate Corp., 1966-76, v.p., 1968-76, sec., 1971-76, sr. v.p., dir., exec. com., 1973-75, exec. v.p., 1975-76; v.p. Coastal States Gas Corp., 1973-76; sr. v.p., gen. counsel Tenneco, Inc., Houston, 1976-92, sec., 1984-86; pvt. practice, 1992—. Editor-in-chief Ind. U. Law Jour., 1956-57. Trustee Houston Ballet, 1982-85, Awty Internat. Sch., 1989-98, 99—, vice-chmn., 1994-97, pres. 1997-98, chmn., 1999—; bd. dirs. Harris County Met. Transit Authority, 1982-84, Houston Internat. Protocol Alliance, 1992-94, Houston Symphony, 1989—, v.p., 1991-94, 2001-; adv. bd. Inst. for Internat. Edn. S.W. region, 1987—, chmn., 1992-94, Internat. and Comparative Law Ctr. Southwestern Legal Found., 1976-92. Lt. USNR, 1951-54. Recipient Chevalier, Ordre Nat. du Mérit, France. Mem. ABA, N.Y. State Bar Assn., Tex. Bar Assn., Assn. of Bar of City of N.Y., Houston Bar Assn., Order of Coif, French-Am. C. of C. (bd. dirs. 1987-92), Alliance Française Houston (bd. dirs. 1989—, v.p. 1991-94, 98—). Mem. United Ch. of Christ. General corporate, Private international, Securities. Office: 1111 Hermann Dr Unit 8B Houston TX 77004-6928

SARASOHN, PETER RADIN, lawyer; b. N.Y.C., Sept. 19, 1944; s. Alvin Norman and Vivian (Radin) S.; m. Patricia A. La Rose, June 15, 1969; children: Amy Sarasohn Spurr, Anne, Adam. JD, Boston U., 1973; BA, U. Mich., 1996. Bar: N.J. 1973, N.Y. 1985. Vol. Peace Corps, Thailand, 1966-68; asst. U.S. atty. U.S. Atty.'s Office, Newark, 1973-77, chief bank fraud divsn., 1976-77; with Ravin Sarasohn Cook Baumgarten Fisch & Rosen, Roseland, N.J., 1978—. Mem. ABA, N.J. Bar Assn. Bankruptcy, General civil litigation, Labor. Office: Ravin Sarasohn Cook Baumgarten Fisch & Rosen 103 Eisenhower Pkwy Roseland NJ 07068-1029

SARAZIN, MARY EILEEN, lawyer; b. Mpls., May 10, 1938; d. Norbert Delos and Alice Mary (Morrison) Sarazin; m. Martin John Timmons, Apr. 4, 1959 (div. Apr. 1995); children: Daniel, Leo, Eileen, John, Kathleen. BS, Coll. St. Catherine, 1959; JD, William Mitchell Coll. Law, 1980. Bar: Minn. 1981, U.S. Dist. Ct. Minn. 1981, U.S. Ct. Appeals (8th cir.) 1985, U.S. Supreme Ct. 1987. VISTA atty. United Handicapped Fedn., Roseville, Minn., 1980-81; sole practice St. Paul, 1981; ptnr. Deretich & Sarazin, 1982—. Atty. State of Minn., 1990-97. Mem.: ABA, Minn. Bar Assn., A.C.R., Ramsey County Bar Assn. Roman Catholic. General practice, Alternative dispute resolution. Home: 8045 Xerxes Ave S Unit 202 Bloomington MN 55431-1061 Office: Deretich and Sarazin PO Box 1662 Saint Paul MN 55101-0662 E-mail: msarazin@aol.com

SARGENTICH, THOMAS OLIVER, law educator, researcher; b. Los Angeles, May 9, 1950; s. Daniel Milo and Margaret Amelia (Lientz) S.; m. Susan Hazard Farnsworth, Jan. 2, 1981. A.B. magna cum laude, Harvard U., 1972, J.D. cum laude, 1977; M.Phil. in Politics, Magdalen Coll., Oxford U., 1974. Bar: D.C. 1978, U.S. Supreme Ct. 1981. Law clk. to judge U.S. Ct. Appeals, Phila., 1977-78; atty.-advisor Office of Legal Counsel, U.S. Dept. Justice, Washington, 1978-83; lectr. Am. U., Washington, 1981, assoc. prof. law, 1983-86, prof. law, 1986—, co-dir. program on law and govt., 1993—; dir. LLM program law and govt., 1998—; adj. prof. law Georgetown U., Washington, 1982; lectr. on adminstrv. and constl. law to various orgs., 1981—; cons. Adminstrv. Conf. U.S., 1986-88, 92-94; reporter Task Force Fed. Judicial Selection Citizens Ind. Cts., 1999; Daniel vis. prof. U. Iowa Coll. Law, 1997. Editor: An Administrative Law Anthology, 1994; contbr. articles in field to legal jours. Mem. Am. U. Fulbright scholarship com., Washington, 1984-94; admissions com. Washington Coll. Law, Am. U., 1983-86, chair appointments com., 1993-94. Recipient Outstanding Performance award U.S. Dept. Justice, 1981; Pauline Ruyle Moore scholar, Am. U., 1989; Elizabeth Payne Cubberly scholar Am. U., 1999; John H. Finley fellow Harvard U., 1972, English-Speaking Union fellow, 1973. Mem. Phi Beta Kappa. E-mail: sargentich@wel.american.edu. Office: Am U Washington Coll Law 4801 Massachusetts Ave NW Washington DC 20016-8196

SARGUS, EDMUND A., JR. judge; b. Wheeling, W.Va., July 2, 1953; s. Edmund A. Sr. and Ann Elizabeth (Kearney) S.; m. Jennifer L. Smart, Jan. 7, 1978; 2 children. AB with honors, Brown U., 1975; JD, Case Western Res. U., 1978. Bar: Ohio 1978, U.S. Dist. Ct. (so. dist.) Ohio 1979, U.S. Dist. Ct. (no. dist.) Ohio 1981, U.S. Ct. Appeals (6th cir.) 1985, U.S. Dist. Ct. (no. dist.) W.Va. 1988, U.S. Ct. Appeals (4th cir.) 1988. Assoc. Cinque, Banker, Linch & White, Bellaire, Ohio, 1978-79, Stanley C. Burech, St. Clairsville, 1980-82; ptnr. Burech & Sargus, 1983-93; U.S. Atty. Dept. of Justice, Columbus, Ohio, 1993-96; dist. judge U.S. Dist. Ct. (so. dist.) Ohio, 1996—. Spl. counsel Ohio Atty. Gen., Columbus, 1979-93; treas. Coalition for Dem. Values, Washington, 1990-93. Solicitor Village of Powhattan Point, Ohio, 1979-93; councilman City of St. Clairsville, 1987-91. Mem. ABA, Ohio Bar Assn. Democrat. Roman Catholic. Office: US Dist Ct 85 Marconi Blvd Columbus OH 43215-2823

SARIS, PATTI BARBARA, federal judge; b. 1951; BA magna cum laude, Radcliffe Coll., 1973; JD cum laude, Harvard U., 1976. Law clerk to Hon. Robert Braucher Mass. Supreme Judicial Ct., 1976-77; atty. Foley Hoag & Eliot, Boston, 1977-79; staff counsel U.S. Senate Judiciary Com., 1979-81; atty. Berman Dittmar & Engel, Boston, 1981-82; chief civil divsn. U.S. Atty.'s Office, 1984-86; U.S. magistrate judge U.S. Dist. Ct. Mass., 1986-89; assoc. justice Mass. Superior Ct., 1989-94; dist. judge U.S. Dist. Ct. Mass., 1994—. Mem. com. on civil rules Supreme Jud. Ct. Comments editor civil rights Civil Liberties Law Rev. Bd. trustees Beth Israel Hosp.; active Wexner Heritage Found. Recipient award Mothers of Murdered Children, 1993, Haskell J. Cohn Disting. Jud. Svc. award Boston Bar Assn.; Nat. Merit scholar, 1969. Mem. Women's Bar, Phi Beta Kappa. Office: US Courthouse Courthouse Way Ste 6130 Boston MA 02210

SARKIA, PETER L. lawyer; b. Helsinki, Finland, Sept. 11, 1967; s. Matti and Seija S. LLM, Uppsala U., Sweden, 1994. Assoc. Lagerlof & Leman, Stockholm, Sweden, 1994-97; sr. assoc. Advokatfirman Hammerskiold & Co., Sweden, 1998—. Banking, Mergers and acquisitions, Securities. Office: Hammerskold & Co Skeppsbron 42 PO Box 2278 103 17 Stockholm Sweden Fax: 46 8 578 450 99. E-mail: peter.sarkia@hammerskiold.se

SARNACKI, MICHAEL THOMAS, lawyer; b. Springfield, Mass., Nov. 13, 1965; s. Robert Michael and Jean Elizabeth S.; m. Kimberly Lynn King, Sept. 9, 1995; children: John Michael, Katherine Margaret. BA, U. Mass., Amherst, 1988; JD, We. New Eng. Coll. Law, 1992. Bar: Mass. 1992, U.S. Dist. Ct. Mass. 1994. Ptnr. Chartier, Ogan, Brady, Shute & Emm, Holyoke, Mass., 1992—. Mem. ABA, Mass. Bar Assn., Hampden County Bar Assn., Springfield Rugby Football Club (dir. 1994—), Elks, Am. Whitewater. Avocations: whitewater kayaking, rugby, running. General civil litigation, Construction, Personal injury. Office: 850 High St Holyoke MA 01040-3767

SARNER, RICHARD ALAN, lawyer; b. Stamford, Conn., Aug. 6, 1955; s. George and Patricia (Sloman) S.; m. Sharyn Frank, Apr. 5, 1986; children: Bryan, Lauren. BA, Dartmouth Coll., 1977; JD, Hofstra U., 1980. Bar: N.Y. 1982, U.S. Dist. Ct. (so. and ea. dists.) N.Y. 1982, U.S. Ct. Appeals (2d cir.) 1985, U.S. Dist. Ct. (no. dist.) N.Y. 1989, Conn. 1990, U.S. Dist. Ct. Conn. 1991, U.S. Supreme Ct. 1991. Assoc. Shea & Gould, N.Y.C., 1980-82, D'Amato & Lynch, N.Y.C., 1982-84, Lowenthal, Landau, Fischer & Ziegler, P.C., N.Y.C., 1984-90; sole practice Stamford, Conn., N.Y.C., Conn., 1990—. Bd. dirs. The Stamford Mus. and Nature Ctr., 1993-99; trustee King & Low-Heywood Thomas Sch., 1994—. Mem. ABA, N.Y. State Bar Assn., Conn. Bar Assn., Stamford/Norwalk Regional Bar Assn., Nat. Network Estate Planning Attys. Democrat. Estate planning, Probate, Estate taxation. Home: 122 Frost Pond Rd Stamford CT 06903-3031 Office: 184 Atlantic St Stamford CT 06901-3518 also: 465 Park Ave Ste 10C New York NY 10022 E-mail: rsarner@aol.com

SARNO, MARIA ERLINDA, lawyer, scientist; b. Manila, Philippines, July 26, 1944; BS in Chemistry magna cum laude, U. Santo Tomas, Philippines, 1967; MS in Chemistry summa cum laude, Calif. State U., Long Beach, 1975; JD cum laude, Western State U., 1993. Bar: Calif. 1994, U.S. Patent Office, 1993. Instr. U. Santo Tomas, Philippines, 1967-68; sr. chemist, analytical rsch. and quality assurance Rachelle Labs., Long Beach, Calif., 1969-74; teaching/rsch. asst. Calif. State U., Long beach, 1971-73; mgr. in charge of radioisotope section Curtis Nuclear Lab., L.A., 1974; assoc. chemist, asst. to dir. quality control Nichols Inst., San Pedro,

Calif., 1974-75; mgr. rsch. and devel. Baxter Healthcare, Hyland, 1975-91; legal coord. sci. affairs Immunotherapy div. Baxter Biotech, Irvine, 1991-93, mgr. regulatory affairs, 1994-95; pvt. law practice, 1994—. Editorial bd: (tech. editor) Western State U. Law Review; Contbr. articles to profl. jours.; patentee in field. Pres. Asian Bus. Assn. Orange County, 2001. Mem. ABA, Los Angeles County Bar Assn., Am. Chem. Soc., Am. Intellectual Property Law Assn., Filipino Am. C. of C. Orange County (asst. treas.). Estate planning, Intellectual property, Patent. Home: 12541 Kenobi Ct Cerritos CA 90703-7756 E-mail: lindasarno@aol.com

SARTAIN, JAMES EDWARD, lawyer; b. Ft. Worth, Feb. 9, 1941; s. James F. and May Belle (Boaz) S.; m. Barbara Hardy, Aug. 17, 1962; 1 child, Bethany Sartain Hughes. BA, Tex. A&M U., 1963; LLB, Baylor U., 1966. Bar: Tex. 1966, U.S. Ct. Mil. Appeals, 1971, U.S. Dist. Ct. (no. dist.) Tex. 1974. Staff atty. Dept. Justice, Washington, 1970-72; staff atty. to U.S. Sen. William L. Scott Fairfax, Va., 1972; pvt. practice Ft. Worth, 1973—; sec. Esprit Comm. Corp., Austin, Tex. Bd. dirs. Ft. Worth Boys Club, 1980-89, Oakwood Cemetery, Ft. Worth, 1979-84; adv. dir. Grady McWhinney Rsch. Found., Abilene, Tex., CAP Initiatives, LLC, Austin, Tex. Capt. arty. U.S. Army, Vietnam. Fellow Coll. State Bar Tex.; mem. ABA, NRA, VFW, Abilene Bar Assn., Baylor Law Alumni Assn., Masons, Phi Delta Phi. Republican. Presbyterian. Consumer commercial, Contracts commercial, General corporate. Home: PO Box 450 Abilene TX 79604-0450

SARTORIUS, PETER S. lawyer; b. Jan. 15, 1947; BA, Williams Coll., 1968; JD, U. Va., 1974. Bar: Pa. 1975. Law clk to Hon. Leonard P. Moore U.S. Ct. Appeals (2nd cir.), 1974-75; ptnr. Morgan, Lewis & Bockius, LLP, Phila. General corporate, Mergers and acquisitions, Securities. Office: Morgan Lewis & Bockius LLP 1701 Market St Philadelphia PA 19103-2903 E-mail: psartorius@morganlewis.com

SASSER, JONATHAN DREW, lawyer; b. Monroe, N.C., Mar. 1, 1956; s. Herman Wallace and Faith Belzora (Harrington) S.; m. Debra A. Smith, Feb. 22, 1994. BA with honors, U. N.C., 1978, JD with honors, 1981. Bar: N.C. 1981, N.Y. 1983, U.S. Dist. Ct. (so. and ea. dists.) N.Y. 1983, U.S. Dist. Ct. (no. dist.) Tex. 1983, U.S. Dist. Ct. (ea. dist.) N.C. 1986, U.S. Ct. Appeals (4th cir.) 1987, U.S. Dist. Ct. (mid. dist.) N.C. 1987, U.S. Supreme Ct. 1988. Law clk. to assoc. justice N.C. Supreme Ct., Raleigh, N.C., 1981-82; assoc. Paul, Weiss, Rifkind, Wharton & Garrison, N.Y.C., 1982-86, Moore & Van Allen and predecessor firm Powe, Porter & Alphin P.A., Durham, N.C., 1986-89; ptnr. Moore & Van Allen, Raleigh, 1990—. Editor: Cellar Door, 1977-78. Dem. precinct chmn., Chapel Hill, N.C., 1976-82. John Motley Morehead Found. fellow, Chapel Hill, 1978; John Motley Morehead Found. scholar, Chapel Hill, 1974. Mem. ABA, N.C. State Bar Assn., N.C. Bar Assn., N.Y. State Bar Assn. Baptist. Avocations: running, triathlons, mountain climbing. Civil rights, Federal civil litigation, State civil litigation. Home: 311 Calvin Rd Raleigh NC 27605-1707 Office: Moore & Van Allen 1 Hannover Sq Ste 1700 Raleigh NC 27601-1794

SASSO, CASSANDRA GAY, lawyer; b. Washington, Feb. 5, 1946; d. Phillip Francis and Lois Aileen (Ayers) S.; m. David John Stephenson, Jr., Feb. 12, 1982; 1 child, Gabriel David. BS magna cum laude, U. Nebr., 1967; MA, U. Calif., Santa Barbara, 1970; JD, Northwestern U., 1974. Bar: Ill., 1974, Colo., 1976. Law clk. Schiff Hardin & Waite, Chgo., 1973; assoc. Sidley & Austin, Chgo., 1974-75; instr. antitrust and securities U. Denver Law Sch., 1978-79, 1985-87; instr. trial practice U. Colo. Law Sch., Boulder, 1983-86; instr. Nat. Inst. Trial Advocacy, 1985—; ptnr., trial lawyer Sherman & Howard, Denver, 1976-91; ptnr. Kutak Rock, Denver, 1991-96; ptnr. Baker & Hostetler, Denver, 1996—. Bd. dirs. Colo. Jud. Inst., 1982-88, v.p. 1984; bd. dirs. Colo. Lawyers Com., Denver, 1980-82, Legal Aid Soc. of Met. Denver, 1981-83; mem. Denver Com. Fgn. Rels., 1981—; chmn. bd. dirs. Colo. ACLU, Denver, 1982-83; mem. steering com. Colo. Lawyers for Nuclear Arms Edn., Denver, 1982-83. Mem. Colo. Womens Bar Assn., Colo. Bar Assn. (bd. govs. 1980-83, ethics com. 1986-95), ABA (securities litigation com. 1988—), Chgo. Council Lawyers (sec. 1974-75), Denver Bar Assn. (bd. trustees 1978-81), Colo. Trial Lawyers Assn. (bd. dirs. 1984-85), Alpha Omicron Pi, Mortar Bd. Democrat. Presbyterian. Home: 3888 W Grambling Dr Denver CO 80236-2444 Office: Baker & Hostetler 303 E 17th Ave Ste 1100 Denver CO 80203-1264

SASSOON, ANDRE GABRIEL, lawyer; b. Cairo, Apr. 13, 1936; came to U.S., 1959; s. Gabriel and Sarine (Tawil) S.; m. Barbara Dee Freedman, Aug. 15, 1965 (div. 2001); children: Daniel, Gabriel, Sarina. GCE, Oxford & Cambridge, England, 1953; JD, Villanova U., 1969; LLM, Harvard U., 1970. Bar: Pa. 1969, N.Y. 1970. Product mgr. Rohm & Haas Co., Phila., 1960-66; law clk. Dist. Atty.'s Office, 1968; assoc. Weil, Gotshal & Manges, N.Y.C., 1970-73; pvt. practice, 1973—; pres., CEO Sterimed Internat., Inc., 1999—. Dir. elem. Youth in Distress, N.Y.C., 1982—; v.p., dir. internat. Anti-Drug Abuse Found., N.Y.C., 1987—; v.p., dir., mem. exec. com. Hebrew Immigrant Aid Soc., N.Y.C., 1977—; internat. sec., gov. bd. internat. govs. World Sephardi Fedn., N.Y.C., 1988—; co-pres., chmn., U.S. com., dir. internat. Jewish Com. for Sephardi '92, N.Y.C., 1989—; mem. N.Y. State Christopher Columbus Quincetenary Commn., Statewide Outreach Com., 1991—; pres., CEO Sterimed Internat., Inc., 1999—. Editor Villanova Law Rev.; contbr. articles to profl. jours. With USAR, 1960-66. Recipient Israel Trade award Govt. of Israel, 1985. Mem. ABA, Am. Arbitration Assn. (panel mem. 1971—), Am. Soc. Internat. Law, Order of the Coif, 0840 Internat. Pvt., 0860 Internat. Pub., SteriMed Internat. (pres. 1999). Private international, Public international. Home: 641 Fifth Ave Apt 30H New York NY 10022 Office: 600 Madison Ave New York NY 10022-1615 E-mail: adnresassoon@aol.com

SATINE, BARRY ROY, lawyer; b. N.Y.C., July 25, 1951; s. Norman S. and Fay (Mekles) S.; m. Janice Bea Halfond, Aug. 4, 1974; children: David, Leah. BA, CCNY, 1972; JD, George Washington U., 1975. Bar: N.Y. 1976, D.C. 1977, U.S. Dist. Ct. (so. dist.) N.Y. 1978, U.S. Supreme Ct. 1979, U.S. Dist. Ct. (ea. dist.) N.Y. 1982, U.S. Ct. Appeals (2d cir.) 1989. Trial atty. U.S. Civil Svc. Commn., Washington, 1975-78; atty. AT&T, N.Y.C., 1978-81, N.Y. Tel. Co., N.Y.C., 1981-82; mem. assoc. Surrey & Morse, 1982-84, ptnr., 1985, Jones, Day, Reavis & Pogue, 1986—. Mem.: Assn. of Bar of City of N.Y. Federal civil litigation, State civil litigation. Office: Jones Day Reavis & Pogue 599 Lexington Ave New York NY 10022-6070 E-mail: barryrsatine@jonesday.com

SATINSKY, BARNETT, lawyer; b. Phila., June 17, 1947; s. Alex and Florence (Talsky) S.; m. Fredda Andrea Wagner, June 17, 1973; children: Meagen, Sara Beth, Jonathan. AB, Brown U., 1969; JD, Villanova U., 1972. Bar: Pa. 1972, U.S. Dist. Ct. (ea. dist) Pa. 1975, U.S. Dist. Ct. (mid. dist.) Pa. 1975, U.S. Ct. Appeals (3d cir.) 1981. Law clk. Phila. Ct. Common Pleas, 1972-73; dep. atty. gen. Pa. Dept. Justice, Harrisburg, 1973-75; 1st asst. counsel Pa. Pub. Utility Commn., 1975-77, chief counsel, 1977; assoc. Fox, Rothschild, O'Brien & Frankel, LLP, Phila., 1978-81; ptnr. Fox, Rothschild, O'Brien & Frankel, 1981—. Children Svcs. Rev. com., United Way Southeast Pa., 1984-86; bd. dirs. ACLU, Harrisburg, 1973-74, Voyage House, Inc., 1994-96. Mem. ABA (pub. utility, labor and employment law sects., employee benefits com. 1984—), Pa. Bar Assn. (labor rels., pub. utility law sects. 1980—, pub. utility law com., governing coun. 1991-93), Phila. Bar Assn. (labor law com. 1980—, chmn. pub. utility law com. 1988-91), Nat. Assn. Coll. and Univ. Attys., Nat. Assn. Regulatory Commrs. (staff subcom. law 1977), Soc. for Human Resource Mgmt., Tau Epsilon Law Soc. Democrat. Jewish. Civil rights, Labor, Public utilities. Office: Fox Rothschild O'Brien & Frankel LLP 2000 Market St Philadelphia PA 19103-3291 E-mail: bsatinsky@frof.com

SATO, GLENN KENJI, lawyer; b. Honolulu, Jan. 6, 1952; s. Nihei and Katherine (Miwa) S.; m. Donna Mae Shiroma, Apr. 4, 1980 (dec. Aug. 1985); m. Nan Sun Oh, Mar. 27, 1987 (dec. Nov. 1997); children: Gavan, Allison, Garrett; m. Sandra K. Kumagai, Nov. 21, 1999. BBA, U. Hawaii, 1975; JD, U. Calif., San Francisco, 1977. Bar: Hawaii 1978, U.S. Dist. Ct. Hawaii, 1978, U.S. Ct. Claims 1990. Assoc. Fujiyama, Duffy & Fujiyama, Honolulu, 1978-80, 83-87, ptnr., 1987-95; stockholder Law Offices of Glenn K. Sato, 1980-82; pres. ISL Svcs., Inc., 1983; ptnr. Sato & Thomas, 1995-98; pvt. practice, 1998—. Vice chmn. Pattern Jury Instrn. Com., State of Hawaii, Honolulu, 1993. Treas. Polit. Action Com., Honolulu, 1993. Mem. Platform Assn., Beta Gamma Sigma. Avocations: golf, hunting, target shooting, surfing. General civil litigation, Consumer commercial, Contracts commercial. Office: Ste 1020 1001 Bishop St Honolulu HI 96813-3481

SATTER, RAYMOND NATHAN, judge; b. Denver, Oct. 19, 1948; s. Charles Herbert and Muriel Vera (Tuller); m. Suzanne Elizabeth Ehlers, May 28, 1977. BA, U. Denver, 1970; JD, Cath. U., 1973. Bar: Colo. 1973, U.S. Dist. Ct. Colo. 1973, U.S. Ct. Appeals (10th cir.) 1973, U.S. Supreme Ct. 1976, U.S. Tax Ct. 1981. Assoc. Wallace, Armatas & Hahn, Denver, 1973-75; ptnr. Tallmadge, Wallace & Hahn, 1975-77; pvt. practice, 1978-87; Denver County judge, 1987—; presiding judge Denver County Ct., 2001—. Gen. counsel Satter Dist., Denver, 1977-78; assoc. mcpl. judge City of Englewood, Colo., 1985-86; mem. Colo. Supreme Ct. Com. on Civil Rules. Pres. Young Artists Orch. Denver, 1985-87; sec. Denver Symphony Assn., 1985-86. Mem. Colo. Bar Assn. (ethics com.), Denver Bar Assn. (bd. trustees 1998-2001, Jud. Excellence award 1992, 95). Avocations: sailing, opera, classical music, fishing, bridge. Office: Denver County Ct 108 City & County Bldg 1437 Bannock St Denver CO 80202-5337 E-mail: rsatter@ci.denver.co.us

SATTERLEE, TERRY JEAN, lawyer; b. Kansas City, Mo., Aug. 28, 1948; d. Charles Woodbury and Francis Jean (Shriver) S.; m. William W. Rice, Jan. 9, 1982; children: Cassandra Jean Rice, Mary Shannon Rice. BA, Kans. U., 1970; JD, U. Mo., 1974. Bar: Mo. 1974. Lawyer Arthur Benson Assocs., Kansas City, Mo., 1974-77, Freilich & Leitner, Kansas City, 1977-78, U.S. Environ. Protection Agy., Kansas City, 1978-83; of counsel Lathrop & Norquist, 1985-87, ptnr., 1987—, mem. exec. com., 1997-2001. Contbr. articles to profl. jours. Chmn. Bd. Zoning Adjustment, Kansas City, 1983-87, Mo. State Pks Adv. Bd., 1997-2001; Kansas City Hazardous Materials com; steering com. COMPASS Met. Planning, Kansas City, 1990-93. Mem. Mo. Bar Assn. (chair environ. com. 1990-93), Kansas City Bar Assn. (environ. com. chmn. 1986-90, v. chair 2000), Mo. C. of C. (natural resource coun. 1990-96, bd. dirs. 1997—, chair 2001), Kansas City C. of C. (environ. com. chmn. 1992), Women's Pub. Svc. Network (named Top 25 US Women in Bus. 2000). Democrat. Episcopalian. Administrative and regulatory, Environmental, Real property. Office: Lathrop & Gage 2345 Grand Blvd Kansas City MO 64108-2612

SAUFER, ISAAC AARON, lawyer; b. Bronx, N.Y., June 16, 1953; s. Solomon and Beatrice (Kanofsky) S.; m. Debra Edith Goldberg, June 26, 1977; children: Suzanne, Nancy, Scott, Daniel, Jonathan. BA, Yeshiva U., N.Y.C., 1975; JD, Bklyn. Law Sch., 1978; LLM in Taxation, NYU, 1982. Bar: N.Y. 1979, N.J. 1986, Fla. 1986, Conn. 1987. Summer intern N.Y. County Dist. Attys. Office, N.Y.C., 1976; legal editor Prentice-Hall, Inc., Englewood Cliffs, N.Y., 1979-80; assoc. Kurzman Karelsen & Frank, LLP, N.Y.C., 1980-85, ptnr., 1986—. Adj. assoc. prof. NYU Sch. Continuing and Profl. Studies, N.Y.C., 1988—; lectr. seminars, 1991, 93, 95, 97, 98, 00. Co-author: (N.Y. real property forms) Bergerman & Roth, 1986-87. Estate planning, Probate, Estate taxation. Office: Kurzman Karelsen & Frank LLP 230 Park Ave Rm 2300 New York NY 10169-2399

SAUFLEY, LEIGH INGALLS, state supreme court justice; m. William Saufley; 2 children. Grad., Maine Sch. Law. Pvt. practice, Ellsworth; asst. counsel U.S. VA; asst., then dep. atty. gen. Maine, 1981-90; justice Maine Supreme Jud. Ct., 1997—. Office: Cumberland County Courthouse PO Box 368 142 Federal St Portland ME 04112-0368*

SAUL, IRA STEPHEN, lawyer; b. West Reading, Pa., Apr. 2, 1949; s. Charles Ryweck and Florence Rebecca (Sussman) S.; m. Elizabeth Claire Barclay, Nov. 30, 1974; children: Barclay Charles, Amanda Emerson. BA, Dickinson Coll., 1971; JD, Am. U., 1975. Bar: Va. 1975, Md. 1988, U.S. Dist. Ct. (ea. dist.) Va. 1976, U.S. Ct. Appeals (4th cir.) 1977, D.C. 1978, U.S. Dist. Ct. D.C. 1978, U.S. Ct. Appeals (D.C. Cir.) 1985. Assoc. Miller, Gattsek, Tavenner, Rosenfeld & Schultz, Bailey's Crossroads, Va., 1975-77; ptnr. Saul & Barclay, Fairfax, Va., 1978—. Mem. No. Va. Apt. Assn. Recipient cert. of Appreciation Inst. Real Estate Mgmt., 1982, 83. Mem. ABA, Assn. Trial Lawyers Am., Fairfax Bar Assn., Va. Trial Lawyers Assn. Republican. State civil litigation, Personal injury, Real property. Office: Saul & Barclay 4114 Leonard Dr Fairfax VA 22030-5118

SAUL, IRVING ISAAC, lawyer; b. July 9, 1929; s. Israel Jacob and Jennie (Green) S.; m. Lita Brown, Dec. 29, 1950; children: Joanne Ilene, Sandra Lynn. BA, Washington and Jefferson Coll., 1949; LLB, U. Pitts., 1952; postgrad., Georgetown U., 1949, Ohio State U., 1951. Bar: Ohio 1952, U.S. Dist. Ct. (so. dist.) Ohio 1954, U.S. Supreme Ct. 1961, U.S. Ct. Appeals (6th cir.) 1966, U.S. Dist. Ct. (no. dist.) Ohio 1967, U.S. Dist. Ct. (ea. dist.) Wis. 1973, U.S. Ct. Appeals (7th cir.) 1978, U.S. Ct. Appeals (4th cir.) 1978, U.S. Ct. Appeals (fed. cir.) 1991. Pvt. practice, Dayton, Ohio, 1952—. Cons. in antitrust litigation; bd. advs. Fed. Civil Practice Abstracts, 1986-88, Ohio Dist. Ct. Rev., 1988—; adj. prof. complex litigation Sch. of Law U. Dayton, 1996-98; lectr. in field. Contbr. articles to profl. jours. James Gillespie Blaine scholar, 1948. Mem. Ohio Bar Assn. (chmn. fed. cts. and practice com. 1977-79, chmn. pvt. enforcement com. 1979-92, bd. govs. antitrust sect. 1982-94), Dayton Bar Assn. (chmn. fed. ct. practice com. 1976-77, 78-80, chmn. com. on judiciary 1987-88), Am. Judicature Soc., Masons (Shriner), Phi Beta Kappa. Jewish. Antitrust, Federal civil litigation, State civil litigation. Office: 113 Bethpolamy Ct Dayton OH 45415-2512

SAUNDERS, BRYAN LESLIE, lawyer; b. Newport News, Va., Apr. 18, 1945; s. Raymond Hayes and Lois Mae (Pair) S.; divorced; children: Kelly Brooke, Justin Lee; m. Anne Mason Dunbar, July 15, 1995. BS, East Tenn. State U., 1967; JD, U. Tenn., 1973. Bar: Va. 1973, U.S. Dist. Ct. (ea. dist.) Va. 1973, U.S. Ct. Appeals (4th cir.) 1991. Lawyer Cogdill & Assocs., Newport News, Va., 1973-76; pvt. practice, 1976—. Commr. in chancery Cir. Ct. of Newport News, 1990-97. Sgt. U.S. Army, 1968-71. Decorated Bronze star, 1971; recipient Outstanding Svc. to Law Enforcement Newport News and Police Dept., 1986. Mem. Va. Bar Assn., Nat. Assn. Criminal Def. Lawyers, Va. Coll. Criminal Def. Attys., Pi Kappa Phi, Pi Gamma Mu. Avocations: chess, bridge, bowling. Criminal, General practice, Juvenile. Office: 728 Thimble Shoals Blvd Ste C Newport News VA 23606-4546 E-mail: bryansaund@aol.com

SAUNDERS, GEORGE LAWTON, JR. lawyer; b. Mulga, Ala., Nov. 8, 1931; s. George Lawton and Ethel Estell (York) S.; children: Kenneth, Ralph, Victoria; m. Terry M. Rose. B.A., U. Ala., 1956; J.D., U. Chgo., 1959. Bar: Ill. 1960. Law clk. to chief judge U.S. Ct. Appeals (5th cir.), Montgomery, Ala., 1959-60; law clk to Justice Hugo L. Black U.S. Supreme Ct., Washington, 1960-62; assoc. Sidley & Austin, Chgo., 1962-67, ptnr., 1967-90; founding ptnr. Saunders & Monroe, 1990—. With USAF, 1951-54. Fellow: ACLA; mem.: ABA, Ill. State Bar Assn., Chgo. Bar Assn., Chgo. Club, Law Club, Point-O-Woods Club, Quadrangle Club, Order of the Coif, Phi Beta Kappa. Democrat. Baptist. Administrative and regulatory, Antitrust, General practice. Home: 179 E Lake Shore Dr Chicago IL 60611-1306 Office: Saunders & Monroe 3160 NBC Tower 455 N Cityfront Plaza Dr Chicago IL 60611-5503

SAUNDERS, LONNA JEANNE, lawyer, newscaster, talk show host; b. Cleve. d. Jack Glenn and Lillian Frances (Newman) Slaby. Student, Dartmouth Coll.; AB in Polit. Sci. with hons., Vassar Coll.; JD, Northwestern U., 1981; cert. advanced study in Mass Media, Stanford U., 1992. Bar: Ill. 1981. News dir., morning news anchor Sta. WKBK-AM, Keene, N.H., 1974-75; reporter Sta. KDKA-AM, Pitts., 1975; pub. affairs dir., news anchor Sta. WJW-AM, Cleve., 1975-76; helicopter traffic reporter WERE-AM Radio, 1976-77; morning news anchor Sta. WBBG-AM, 1978; talk host, news anchor Sta. WIND-AM, Chgo., 1978-82; atty. Arvey, Hodes, Costello & Burman, 1981-82; host, "The Stock Market Observer", news anchor WCIU-TV, 1982-85; staff atty. Better Govt. Assn., 1983-84; news anchor, reporter Sta. WBMX-FM, 1984-86; pvt. practice, 1985—; news anchor Sta. WKQX-FM, 1987. Instr. Columbia Coll., Chgo., 1987-90; guest talk host Sta. WMCA, N.Y.C., 1983, Sta. WMAQ, Chgo., 1988, Sta. WLS, Chgo., 1989, Sta. WWWE, Cleve., 1989, Sta. KVI, Seattle, 1994, WCBM-AM, Balt., 1996, WRC-AM, Wash., D.C., 1997; host, prodr. The Lively Arts, Cablevision Chgo., 1986; talk show host The Lonna Saunders Show, Sta. KIRO-AM, Seattle, 1995-96; news anchor, WTOP-AM Radio, Washington, D.C., 1996-97; talk host, "Today and Tomorrow show", WMAL-AM radio, Washington, D.C., 1997, freelance reporter, CBS Radio Network, N.Y.C., 1995—; writer, General Media, N.Y.C., 1996—; atty. Lawyers for Creative Arts, Chgo., 1985-91; guest columnist Gainesville (Fla.) Sun Newspaper, 1998-99; freelance writer Indians Ink mag., 1998—. Columnist Chgo. Life mag., 1996—; editl. bd. Jour. Criminal Law and Criminology, 1979-81; contbr. articles to profl. jours.; creator pub. affairs program WBBM-AM, Chgo., 1985. Recipient Akron Press Club award for best pub. affairs presentation, 1978; grantee Scripps Howard Found., 1978-81; AFTRA George Heller Meml. scholar, 1980-81. Fellow Am. Bar Found.; mem. ABA (mem. exec. coms. Lawyers and the Arts, Law and Media 1986-92, chmn. exec. com. Law and Media 1990-91, 91-92, Young Lawyers divsn. liaison to Forum Com. on Communications Law 1991-93, Commn. for Partnership Programs 1993-94, regional divsn. chair Forum on Communications Law 1995-96). Roman Catholic. Avocations: theater, piano, baseball. Entertainment, Libel.

SAUNDERS, MARK A. lawyer, consultant; b. N.Y.C., July 9, 1946; s. Phillip George and Florence (Schell) S.; m. Paula Squillante, Sept. 2, 1972; children: David Prescott, Christina Joy. BA cum laude, Fordham U., 1968; JD, U. Va., 1972. Bar: N.Y. 1973, U.S. Dist. Ct. (so. dist.) N.Y.) 1973, U.S. Ct. Appeals (2d cir.) 1974, U.S. Ct. Appeals (D.C. cir.) 1987, U.S. Supreme Ct. 1987. Sr. ptnr. Holland & Knight, N.Y.C.; counsel to corp. fin. and mergers acquisitions depts. Morgan Stanley & Co. Inc., 1975-80; mem. faculty Internat. Law Inst., Washington, 1985—. Mem. comparative law delegation to govt. of People's Rep. of China, 1986; gen. counsel Softstrip Internat. Ltd. subs. Eastman Kodak Co., 1987; mem. adv. bd. Southwestern Legal Found. Author: Amrican Depositary Receipts: An Introduction to U.S. Capital Markets For Foreign Companies, 1993, Fordham Internat. Law Jour., 1993; mng. bd. editors Va. Jour. Internat. Law, 1971-72; cons. editor China Banking and Fin., 1988-92. Chmn. charity benefit Ann. Good Counsel Awards Celebration, 1999, 2000; apptd. fed. adv. bd. nat. polit. action com., 1999; mem. fed. adv. bd. Ann Arbor Polit. Action Com. Jervey fellow in fgn. and comparative law Columbia U. Parker Sch. Internat. Law, 1972. Fellow Am. Coll. Investment Counsel; mem. ABA (coms. fed. securities, regulation and internat. securities matters and fgn. investment in U.S.), Assn. Bar City N.Y., Internat. Bar Assn., Legatus (pres. N.Y.C. chpt. 1998-2000), Phi Beta Kappa. Roman Catholic. General corporate, Private international, Securities. Home: 3 Nutmeg Dr Greenwich CT 06831-3211 Office: Holland & Knight 195 Broadway New York NY 10007-3100 E-mail: msaund@hklaw.com

SAUNDERS, MARTIN JOHNSTON, lawyer; b. Mariemont, Ohio, Feb. 15, 1949; s. Norval and Jane (Johnston) S.; m. Rosanne Clementi; children: Martin Robert, Clare Anne. BA, U. Cin., 1970; JD, Coll. William and Mary, 1973; LLM in Labor Law, NYU, 1974. Bar: Pa. 1974, U.S. Dist. Ct. (we. dist.) Pa. 1974, U.S. Dist. Ct. (we. dist.) Mich. 1990, U.S. Dist. Ct. (no. dist.) Ohio 1999, U.S. Ct. Appeals (3d cir.) 1976, U.S. Ct. Appeals (4th cir.) 1977, U.S. Ct. Appeals (1st cir.) 1981, U.S. Ct. Appeals (7th cir.) 1983, U.S. Ct. Appeals (D.C. cir.) 1990, U.S. Ct. Appeals (6th cir.) 1995, U.S. Supreme Ct. 1978. Intern U.S. Dist. Ct. (we. dist.) Pa., 1972-73; labor counsel Westinghouse Electric Corp., Pitts., 1974-77; ptnr. Thorp, Reed & Armstrong, 1977-94, Jackson Lewis Schnitzler & Krupman, 1995—. Adj. prof. U. Pitts., 1978-94, C.C. Allegheny County, Pitts., 1983-85. Mem. staff William and Mary Law Rev., 1970-73. Served to capt. U.S. Army, 1972-80. Mem. ABA (labor law sect., equal opportunity subcom.), Pa. Chamber Bus. and Industry (human resources com. 1986-95). Republican. Civil rights, Federal civil litigation, Labor. Home: 36 Windsor Rd Pittsburgh PA 15215-1813 Office: Jackson Lewis Schnitzler & Krupman One PPG Pl 28th Fl Pittsburgh PA 15222 E-mail: saunderm@jacksonlewis.com

SAUNDERS, ROBERT M. lawyer; b. N.Y.C., July 31, 1959; s. Herbert L. and Loretta (Tymon) S.; m. Cheryl D. Lambek, Nov. 6, 1988; children: David, Dana. BA, SUNY, Buffalo, 1980; JD, U. Chgo., 1983. Bar: N.Y. 1984, U.S. Dist. Ct. (so. and ea. dists.) N.Y. 1988, Fla. 1995, U.S. Dist. Ct. (so. dist.) Fla. 1995. Assoc. LeBoeuf, Lamb, Leiby & MacRae, N.Y.C., 1983-86, Brown & Wood, N.Y.C., 1986-88, Willkie Farr & Gallagher, N.Y.C., 1988-92, spl. counsel, 1993-95; sole practice Weston, Fla., 1995—. Bankruptcy. Office: 4300 N University Dr Ste C203 Fort Lauderdale FL 33351-6244 Address: 1300 Mancr Ct Fort Lauderdale FL 33326-2818

SAUNDERS, TERRY ROSE, lawyer; b. Phila., July 13, 1942; d. Morton M. and Esther (Hauptman) Rose; m. George Lawton Saunders Jr., Sept. 21, 1975. BA, Barnard Coll., 1964; JD, NYU, 1973. Bar: D.C. 1973, Ill. 1976, U.S. Dist. Ct. (no. dist.) Ill. 1976, U.S. Ct. Appeals (7th cir.) 1976, U.S. Supreme Ct. 1983. Assoc. Williams & Connolly, Washington, 1973-75, Jenner & Block, Chgo., 1975-80, ptnr., 1981-86, Susman, Saunders & Buehler, Chgo., 1987-94; pvt. practice Law Offices of Terry Rose Saunders, 1995—. Author: (with others) Securities Fraud: Litigating Under Rule 10b-5, 1989. Recipient Robert B. McKay award NYU Sch. Law. Mem. ABA (co-chair class actions and derivative suits com. sect. litig. 1992-95, task force on merit selection of judges, co-chair consumer and personal righs itig. com. sect. litig.), Ill. State Bar Assn., Chgo. Bar Assn., Order of Coif, Union League Club. Federal civil litigation, General civil litigation. Office: 30 N La Salle St Chicago IL 60602-2590 E-mail: trslawfirm@aol.com

SAVAGE, EDWARD TURNEY, lawyer; b. Boston, Feb. 14, 1946; s. Arthur Turney and Katrine (Tuttle) S. B.A., Amherst Coll., 1968; M.B.A., Harvard U., 1974, J.D., 1974. Bar: Calif. 1975, N.Y. 1975, U.S. Dist. Ct. (no. dist.) Calif. 1975, U.S. Dist. Ct. (so. dist.) N.Y. 1975, U.S. Ct. Appeals (2nd cir.) N.Y. 1975. Law clk. to presiding judge U.S. Dist. Ct. (no. dist.) Calif., San Francisco, 1974-75; assoc. Cadwalader, Wickersham & Taft, N.Y.C., 1975-77; ptnr. Rosenman & Colin, N.Y.C., 1977-87, Ashinoff, Ross & Korff, N.Y.C., 1988-90, Andrews & Kurth, L.L.P., N.Y.C., 1990—; gen. counsel, v.p. The Marcade Group, Inc., N.Y.C., 1987-88. Pres. Friends of Amherst Athletics, 1979-82. Served to lt. (j.g.) USN, 1968-70; lt. comdr. Res. Recipient Disting. Service award Harvard Bus. Sch., 1974; Amherst Meml. scholar, 1970; Woodroff Simpson fellow, 1971. Mem. Westfield Jaycees. Republican. Presbyterian. Computer, General corporate, Securities. Home: 401 E 88th St Apt 16A New York NY 10128-6634 Office: Andrew & Kurth 425 Lexington Ave # 10 New York NY 10017-3903

SAVAGE, JOHN WILLIAM, lawyer; b. Seattle, Oct. 11, 1951; s. Stanley and Jennie Sabina (Siggstedt) S.; m. Rebecca Lee Abraham, Oct. 1, 1983; children: Bennett William, James Oliver. Student, Lewis and Clark Coll., 1969-71, JD Northwestern Sch. Law, 1977; BA, U. Wash., 1973. Bar: Oreg. 1977, U.S. Dist. Ct. Oreg. 1977, U.S. Ct. Appeals (9th cir.) 1977, U.S. Supreme Ct. Pvt. practice law, Portland, Oreg., 1977-79; ptnr. Bailey, Olstad, Rieke, Geil & Savage, P.C., 1979-80; ptnr., shareholder Rieke, Geil & Savage, P.C., 1980-95; shareholder Rieke & Savage, P.C., 1995—. Mem. Oreg. Literacy Inc., Portland, 1979-85; mem. standing com. City Club, Portland, 1984-88, chmn. law and pub. safety standing com. 1986-87. Recipient award of merit Gerry Spence's Trial Lawyers Coll., 1999. Mem. ABA (chairperson young lawyers sect. Nat. Cmty. Law Week 1983-84, inmate grievance com. 1984-88), Assn. Trial Lawyers Am., Trial Lawyers for Pub. Justice, Oreg. Trial Lawyers Assn., Oreg. Bar Assn. (def. of indigent accused com. 1985-89), Oreg. Criminal Def. Lawyers Assn. (bd. dirs. 1984-86), Multnomah Bar Assn. (v.p. young lawyers sect. 1980, pres.-elect 1981, pres. 1982, Disting. Svc. award, bd. dirs. 1989-92, task force chair 1992-93, jud. selection com. 1998-99, Award of Merit 1994). General civil litigation, Personal injury, Professional liability. Home: 397 Furnace St Lake Oswego OR 97034-3957 Office: Rieke & Savage PC 140 SW Yamhill St Portland OR 97204-3007 E-mail: jwsavage@rieke-savage.com

SAVAGE, MICHAEL, lawyer; b. May 6, 1946; s. Bernard and Mildred (Spitz) Savage; m. Ann Tweedy, Nov. 11, 1990; 1 child Mariana. BA, Yale U., 1968; JD, Georgetown U., 1973. Bar: D.C. 1973, N.Y. 1982, U.S. Supreme Ct. 1976. Assoc. Hedrick & Lane, Washington, 1973—78, ptnr., 1978—82, Gersten, Savage & Kaplowitz, N.Y.C., 1982—. Author: (non-fiction) Everything You Always Wanted to Know About Taxes, 1979, Everything You Always Wanted to Know About Taxes, 4th edit., 1982, Good News, Bad News! A Concise Tax Guide, 1986, Don't Let the IRS Destroy Your Small Business, 1997; editor: (newsletter) Taxes Interpreted, 1980—, Investors Tax Alert, 1982—. Mem.: ABA, D.C. Bar Assn., Authors Guild. Corporate taxation, Estate taxation, Personal income taxation. Home: 101 E 52nd St 9th Fl New York NY 10022-6018 Office: Gersten Savage & Kaplowitz 101 E 52nd St New York NY 10022-6018

SAVAGE, TOY DIXON, JR. lawyer; b. Norfolk, Va., Oct. 12, 1921; s. Toy Dixon and Hildreth Gatewood S.; m. Mary Hunter Hankins, Oct. 19, 1946; children: Tracy G., Toy D. III. BA in Econ., U. Va., 1943, LLB, 1948; LittD (hon.), Ea. Va. Med. Sch., 1995. Assoc., ptnr. Willcox & Savage PC, Norfolk, 1948—. Mem. ho. of dels. Gen. Assembly Va., 1954-63; bd. dirs. Sentara Health Sys., United Cmty. Fund, 1968-73; chmn. Norfolk Found. Distribution Com., Hampton Rds. Areawide Coop. Com., 1963-64, 76-78; trustee Chrysler Mus., Va. Found. for Ind. Coll., Camp Found., North Shore Found., Va. Hist. Soc., Ea. Va. Med. Sch. Found., Va. Mus. Fine Arts, 1975-85; trustee, deacon Freemason St. Bapt. Ch.; mem. Govs. Adv. Bd. on Indsl. Devel., 1983-92; chmn. task force on health care Govs. Commn. on Future of Va., 1984-85; pres. Old Dominion U. Ednl. Found., 1972-73, Med. Ctr. Hosps., 1966-68; vice-chmn. Ea. Va. Med. Authority, 1964-66. Home: 6508 Ocean Front Ave Virginia Beach VA 23451-2056

SAVELKOUL, DONALD CHARLES, retired lawyer; b. Mpls., July 29, 1917; s. Theodore Charles and Edith (Lindgren) S.; m. Mary Joan Holland, May 17, 1941; children: Jeffrey Charles, Jean Marie, Edward Joseph. BA magna cum laude, U. Minn., 1939; JD cum laude, William Mitchell Coll. Law, 1951. Bar: Minn. 1951, U.S. Dist. Ct. Minn. 1952, U.S. Ct. Appeals (8th cir.) 1960, U.S. Supreme Ct. 1971. Adminstrv. work various U.S. govt. depts., including Commerce, War, Labor, Wage Stblzn. Bd., 1940-51; mcpl. judge Fridley, Minn., 1952-53; pvt. practice law Mpls., St. Paul, Fridley, 1951-96; ret., 1997. Chmn. bd. Fridley State Bank, 1962-95; pres. Banrein, Inc., 1962-95, Babbscha Co., 1962-95; mem. faculty William Mitchell Coll. Law, 1952-59, corp. mem., 1956-99; sec. Fridley Recreation and Svc. Co., 1955-97; mem. Minn. Legislature, 1967-69. Mem. Gov.'s Com. Workers Compensation, 1965-67, Gov.'s Adv. Coun. on Employment Security, 1957-60, 62-63; gen. counsel Minn. AFL-CIO Fedn. Labor, 1952-71. 1st lt. AUS, 1943-46. Decorated Bronze Star; recipient Disting. Alumni award Coll. Liberal Arts U. Minn., 1995, Outstanding Alumnus award William Mitchell Coll. Law Alumni/ae Assn., 1997. Mem. ABA, Minn. Bar Assn. (chmn. 1957-58, bd. dirs. 1958-62, 68-69, labor law sect.), Justice William Mitchell Soc., Am. Legion, U. Minn. Pres.'s Club, Phi Beta Kappa. Roman Catholic. Banking, General corporate. Office: 916 Moore Lake Dr W Fridley MN 55432-5148

SAVELL, POLLY CAROLYN, lawyer; b. N.Y.C., Oct. 24, 1960; d. Joel Morton and Elsie Rhea (Crane) S. BA, U. Md., 1982; diploma, Internat. Comp. Law Inst., Paris, 1983; JD, NYU, 1985. Bar: N.Y. 1986. Assoc. corp. and entertainment divsn. Battle Fowler, N.Y.C., 1986-87; atty. Columbia Pictures Entertainment Inc., 1987-89; counsel Turner Broadcasting Sys. Inc., Atlanta, 1989-91; sole practice, 1991-93; asst. gen. counsel WorldCom Inc., N.Y.C., 1993—. Bd. dirs. Eviction Intervention Svcs., Homeless Prevention, Inc. Mem. ABA, Fed. Comm. Bar Assn., Am. Corp. Counsel Assn., Assn. of Bar of City of N.Y. (telecom. law com.). Democrat. Methodist. Contracts commercial, Communications, Private international. Office: WorldCom Inc 380 Madison Ave New York NY 10017-2513

SAVILLE, ROYCE BLAIR, lawyer; b. Cumberland, Md., Aug. 5, 1948; s. E. Blair and Audrey (Cosner) S.; m. Sharon Ann Brinkman, Apr. 3, 1981; children: Melissa Ann, Lauren Ashley, Meagan Elizabeth, Philip Clarke. BA, W.Va. U., 1970, JD, 1974. Bar: W.Va. 1974, U.S. Dist. Ct. (so. and no. dists.) W.Va. 1974. Associate William J. Oates, Jr. Atty. at Law, Romney, W.Va., 1974-75; ptnr. Oates & Saville Attys. at Law, 1975-78; pvt. practice, 1978-99; mng. ptnr. Saville and Davis, PLLC, 1999-2001, Saville and Stewart, PLLC, 2001—. Pres. Potomac Land Co., 1975—; mental hygiene commr. Hampshire County, Romney, 1976—; mcpl. judge City of Romney, 1980-90. Mem. W.Va. Jud. Hearing Bd., Hampshire County Devel. Authority, Romney, Hampshire County Farm Bur., Nat. Trust for Hist. Preservation; dir. Potomac Highlands Travel Coun., Elkins, W.Va., 1984-88; mem. adv. bd. Peterkin Conf. Ctr. of Renewal, Romney, 1988-90; del. W.Va. Dem. Conv., Charleston, 1984; vestryman St. Stephen's Episcopal Ch., Romney, 1984-86. Mem. ABA, ATLA, NRA (life), W.Va. Bar Assn., South Br. Valley Bar Assn. (pres. 1996-97), W.Va. Trial Lawyers Assn., Waterfowl U.S.A. (life), N.Am. Hunting Club (life), McNeill's Rangers SCV (judge adv.), Civil War Preservation Trust, W.Va. Law Sch. Assn. (life), W.Va. U. Alumni Assn. (life), Masons (Clinton Lodge #86), Scottish Rite of Freemasonry, USA Valley of Martinsburg, Orient of W.Va., Osiris Temple AAONMS, Romney chpt. #84 OES, Rotary (Paul Harris fellow), Phi Alpha Delta (life). Democrat. Episcopalian. Avocations: gun collecting, antique collecting, local history. State civil litigation, General practice, Real property. Home: Liberty Hall 276 E Main St Romney WV 26757-1821 also: Mill Island Moorefield WV 26836 Office: 95 W Main St PO Box 2000 Romney WV 26757-2000

SAVITT, SUSAN SCHENKEL, lawyer; b. Bklyn., Aug. 21, 1943; d. Edward Charles and Sylvia (Dlugatch) S.; m. Harvey Savitt, July 2, 1969 (div. 1978); children: Andrew Todd, Daniel Cory. BA magna cum laude, Pa. State U., 1964; JD, Columbia U., 1968. Bar: N.Y. 1968, U.S. Dist. Ct. (so. and ea. dists.) N.Y. 1973, U.S. Tax Ct. 1973, U.S. Ct. Appeals (2d cir.) 1981, U.S. Supreme Ct. 1980, U.S. Dist. Ct. (we. dist.) N.Y. 1996. Atty. Nassau County Legal Svcs., Freeport, N.Y., 1973-74; asst. corp. counsel City of Yonkers, 1977-78; from assoc. to ptnr. Epstein, Becker & Green, P.C., N.Y.C., 1978-94; ptnr. Winston & Strawn, 1994—. Adj. prof. Elizabeth Seton Coll., Yonkers, 1982-83; mem. NYU exec. coun. Met. Ctr. for Ednl. Rsch. Devel. and Tng., 1987-90; mediator Vol. Mediation Panel, U.S. Dist. Ct. (so. dist.) N.Y., 1997—, U.S. Dist. Ct. (ea. dist.) N.Y., 1999—. Mem. Hastings-on-Hudson (N.Y.) Sch. Bd., 1984-93, v.p., 1986, 87-88, pres., 1989-90, 92-93; bd. dirs. Associated Blind, 1993-95, Nat. Child Labor Com., 2001—, Liberal Arts Alumni Coun., Pa. State U., 2001—; bd. dirs. Search for Change, 1996—, sec., 1998—; bd. dirs. Pa. State Profl. Women's Network of N.Y., 1996—, pres., 1998-2000-2000. Mem. ABA (internat. law sect., litigation and labor law sect.), N.Y. State Bar Assn. (labor law sect., comml. litigation sect.), Women's Bar Assn., Fed. Bar Coun., Pa. State Alumni Club (v.p. Westchester County 1985-87), Phi Beta Kappa, Alpha Kappa Delta, Phi Gamma Mu, Pi Kappa Phi. Alternative dispute resolution, Federal civil litigation, Labor. Office: Winston & Strawn 200 Park Ave Rm 4100 New York NY 10166-0005

SAVRANN, RICHARD ALLEN, lawyer; b. Boston, July 29, 1935; s. Abraham B. and Doris (Curhan) S.; m. Diane Barbara Kleven, Dec. 22, 1957; children: Stephen Keith, Russell Clark. BA, Harvard U., 1956, JD, 1959. Bar: Mass. 1959, U.S. Dist. Ct. Mass. 1963, U.S. Ct. Appeals (1st cir.) 1965. Exec. Klev Bro. Mfg., Derry, N.H., 1959-63; assoc. Law Office of Jerome Rappaport, Boston, 1963-68; asst. atty. gen. Commonwealth of Mass., 1968-70; ptnr. Newell, Savrann & Miller, 1970-75; sr. ptnr. Kunian, Savrann & Miller, 1976-81, Singer, Stoneman, Kunian & Kurland, P.C., Boston, 1981-88, Singer, Kunian * Kurland, P.C., Boston, 1988-90; sr. ptnr, Curhan, Kunian, Goshko, Berwick and Savrann, P.C., 1990-92; ptnr. Burns and Levinson, LLP, 1993—. Mem. Andover (Mass.) Housing Authority, 1972-90, chmn., 1984-90; pres. Hospice of Greater Lawrence, North Andover, Mass., 1984; bd. dirs. Boston Latin Sch. Found., 1987, clk., 1992-98; bd. dirs. Comite Internat. de Sci. pour La Santè et l'Environ., Paris, 1993—. Mem. FBA, Fla. Bar, Mass. Bar Assn., Boston Bar Assn., Eastpointe Country Club (Palm Beach Gardens, Fla.), Harvard Club (Andover) (pres. 1985-98). Avocations: golf, opera. General civil litigation, Consumer commercial, Condemnation. Home: 6 Pear Tree Ln Franklin MA 02038-3936 Office: Burns and Levinson 125 Summer St Ste 602 Boston MA 02110-1616 E-mail: rsavrann@b-l.com

SAWICKI, STEPHEN CRAIG, lawyer, mediator; b. Chgo., July 28, 1950; s. Stephen Martin and Helen Jenny Sawicki; m. Mary Kim Gardner, Nov. 19, 1989; children: Stephen, Sara, Adam. BA, U. South Fla., 1973; JD, Samford U., 1977. Bar: Fla. 1977, U.S. Dist. Ct. (mid. dist.) Fla. 1977, U.S. Ct. Appeals (11th cir.) 1983. Banker First Fed. Savs. & Loan, Sarasota, Fla., 1972-73, Sun Bank, Orlando, 1973-74; ptnr. Hendry, Stoner, Sawicki & Brown, 1977—. Mem. panel mediators Fla. Dept. Bus. Regulation, 1990—, Fla. Dept. Ins., 1990—, Manville Personal Injury Settlement Trust, 1990—. Fellow Am. Coll. Civil Trial Mediators (exec. dir. 1996—). Avocations: music, tennis, hiking, sailing, architecture. Alternative dispute resolution, General civil litigation, Personal injury. Office: Hendry Stoner Sawicki and Brown 200 E Robinson St Ste 500 Orlando FL 32801-1956

SAWICKI, ZBIGNIEW PETER, lawyer; b. Hohenfels, Germany, Apr. 13, 1949; came to U.S., 1951; s. Witold and Marianna (Tukiendorf) S.; m. Katheryn Marie Loman, Aug. 19, 1972; children: James, Jeffrey, Jessica, Jason. BSChemE, Purdue U., 1972; MBA, Coll. St. Thomas, St. Paul, 1977; JD, Hamline U., 1980. Bar: Minn. 1980, U.S. Dist. Ct. Minn. 1981, U.S. Ct. Appeals (8th cir.) 1981, U.S. Patent and Trademark Office 1981, U.S. Ct. Appeals (fed. cir.) 1982, Can. Patent Office 1994, Can. Trademark Office 1995. Process engr. 3-M Co., St. Paul, 1973-75; process engrng. supr. Conwed Corp., 1975-77; shareholder, bd. dirs. Kinney & Lange, Mpls., 1980—. Bd. dirs. Orono (Minn.) Hockey Boosters, 1992—. With USAF, 1970-72. Mem. ABA, Am. Intellectual Property Assn., Internat. Trademark Assn., Minn. Intellectual Property Assn. (past treas.), Am. Legion. Intellectual property, Patent, Trademark and copyright. Home: 4510 N Shore Dr Mound MN 55364-9602 Office: Kinney & Lange 312 S 3d St Minneapolis MN 55415-1624 E-mail: zpsawicki@kinney.com

SAWYER, JAMES, lawyer; b. N.Y.C., Feb. 18, 1946; s. Jules and Florence Barbara (Wishnew) S.; m. Margot Peretz, June 8, 1995; children: Kim, Caryn. BA, Adelphi U., 1967; JD, St. Johns U., 1969. Bar: N.Y. 1970, U.S. Dist. Ct. (so. and ea. dists.) N.Y. 1971, U.S. Tax Ct. 1972, U.S. Ct. Appeals (2d cir.) 1972, U.S. Ct. Appeals (1st cir.) 1975, Fla. 1981, U.S. Supreme Ct. 1981. Ptnr. Martin, Van De Walle & Sawyer, Great Neck, N.Y., 1970-81, Hession, Halpern, Bekoff & Sawyer, Mineola, 1982-87, Sawyer, Davis, Halpern and Demetri, Garden City, 1987—. Pres. Temple Or-Elohim, Jericho, N.Y., 1987-89; active Nassau County Med. Malpractice Panel, 1982-86. Mem. ABA, N.Y. State Bar Assn., Nassau County Bar Assn. Jewish. General civil litigation, Personal injury, Probate. Address: Sawyer Davis & Halpern Esq 600 Old Country Rd Rm 330 Garden City NY 11530-2010 E-mail: jsawyer@sawyerlaw.com

SAWYER, THEODORE D(AVID), lawyer; b. Columbus, Ohio, May 2, 1938; s. Theodore Daniel and Elizabeth (Morgan) S.; m. Barbara L. Jones, Aug. 27, 1964; children— Chad, Bret, Andrew. B.A., Ohio State U., 1960; postgrad. Ohio U., 1961-62; J.D., Ohio No. U., 1965. Bar: Ohio 1966, U.S. Dist. Ct. (so. dist.) Ohio 1967, U.S. Ct. Appeals (6th cir.) 1981, U.S. Supreme Ct. 1982. Asst. law dir. City of Springfield (Ohio), 1966; assoc. Potts, Schmidt & Lewis, Columbus, 1966-69; ptnr. Crabbe, Brown, Jones, Potts & Schmidt, 1971, now Crabbe, Brown et al. Pres. Forest Park Civic Assn., Columbus, 1972-73. Mem. ABA, Ohio Assn. Civil Trial Attys. (pres. 1977-78), exec. com. 1973-81), Lawyers Club Columbus (pres. 1979-80), Barristers Club, Columbus Def. Assn. (pres. 1974-75), Def. Rsch. Inst. (regional v.p. 1979-81, bd. dir. 1982-85, def. sec.-treas. 1985-86), Columbus Bar Assn., Ohio State Bar Assn., Internat. Assn. Counsel (chmn. med. malpractice com.), Am. Judicature Soc., Am. Arbitration Assn., Internat. Assn. Def. Counsel, Fedn. Ins. and Corp. Counsel, Creighton Club. Lutheran. Author monograph: (with Mary Picken): Defending the Hospital Emergency Room, 1981. Home: 2026 Guilford Rd Columbus OH 43221-4342 Office: Crabbe Brown et al 500 South Front Ste 1200 Columbus OH 43215-2220

SAWYIER, MICHAEL TOD, lawyer; b. Boston, Jan. 6, 1948; s. Calvin Parker and Fay (Horton) S.; m. Judith Puistonen, June 6, 1968; children: Julianne Patricia, Justine Fay, Alexandra Lee, Sydney Anne Helena. BA, Harvard U., 1969; JD, U. Chgo., 1972; LLM, Yale U., 1973. Bar: Ill. 1972, D.C. 1974, N.Y. 1974, Calif. 1976, Ind. 1983, Tex. 1989, U.S. Dist. Ct. (no. dist.) Ill. 1979, U.S. Ct. Appeals (7th cir.) 1981, U.S. Dist. Ct. (no. and so. dists.) Ind. 1983, U.S. Supreme Ct. 1984. Atty.-adviser Office of Legal Adviser U.S. Dept. State, Washington, 1974-75; assoc. Pillsbury, Madison and Sutro, San Francisco, 1975-77, Baker and McKenzie, Chgo., 1977-79, Foss, Schuman, Drake & Barnard, Chgo., 1979-87; ptnr. Mathewson, Hamblet & Casey, Chgo., 1987-89; ptnr. Sawyier and Stewart, Chgo., 1989—. Dir. Ct. Theatre, Chgo., 1988—. Recipient Paul Cornell prize Hyde Park Hist. Soc., Chgo., 1982. Mem. ABA, Ill. Bar Assn., Chgo. Bar Assn., Ind. Bar Assn., Tex. Bar Assn., Am. Soc. Internat. Law., Chgo. Literary Club, Saddle and Cycle Club, Cliffdwellers Club, Chgo. Club. Bankruptcy, General corporate, Real property. Home: 424 W Melrose St Apt 15A Chicago IL 60657-3862 Address: 53 W Jackson Blvd Ste 1120 Chicago IL 60604-3701

SAX, SPENCER MERIDITH, lawyer; b. Passaic, N.J., June 7, 1955; s. Sander and Sylvia (Manelis) S.; m. Carie Dale Casper, Nov. 4, 1984. BA, Columbia U., 1977; JD, Vanderbilt U., 1980. Bar: Fla. 1980, U.S. Dist. Ct. (so. dist.) Fla. 1980, U.S. Ct. Appeals (5th and 11th cirs.) 1981, U.S. Supreme Ct. 1984. Assoc. Sales & Weissman, P.A., West Palm Beach, Fla., 1980-81, Sachs & Weiss, P.A., Boca Raton, 1981-85; ptnr. Sachs & Sax, P.A., 1985-96, Sachs, Sax & Klein, P.A., Boca Raton, 1996—. Mem. South Palm Beach County Bar Assn. (pres.-elect). State civil litigation, Family and matrimonial, Real property. Office: Sachs Sax & Klein PA 301 Yamato Rd Boca Raton FL 33431-4917

SAXE, DEBORAH CRANDALL, lawyer; b. Lima, Ohio, July 23, 1949; d. Robert Gordon and Lois Barker (Taylor) Crandall; m. Robert Saxe, June 3, 1989; children: Elizabeth Sara, Emily Jane. BA, Pa. State U., 1971; MA, UCLA, 1973, JD, 1978. Bar: Calif. 1978, D.C. 1979, U.S. Dist. Ct. D.C. 1979, U.S. Dist. Ct. (ea. dist.) Calif. 1981, U.S. Dist. Ct. (ctrl. dist.) Calif. 1982, U.S. Dist. Ct. (no. and so. dists.) Calif. 1987, U.S. Ct. Appeals (4th and D.C. cirs.) 1979, U.S. Ct. Appeals (6th cir.) 1985, U.S. Ct. Appeals (8th and 9th cirs.) 1987, U.S. Ct. Appeals (2nd cir.) 1990, U.S. Supreme Ct. 1982, U.S. Dist. Ct. (no. dist.) Ill. 2001, U.S. Ct. Appeals (7th cir.) 2001. Assoc. Seyfarth, Shaw, Fairweather & Geraldson, Washington, 1978-83, Jones, Day, Reavis & Pogue, Washington, 1983-85, L.A., 1985-87, ptnr., 1988-97; shareholder Heller Ehrman White & McAuliffe, 1997—. Judge pro tem, Small Claims Ct., L.A., 1985-88. Co-author: Advising California Employers, 1990, 2d edit., 1995; contbg. editor Employment Discrimination Law, 1989. Bd. dirs. Eisner Pediatric and Family Med. Ctr., L.A., 1990—, chair, 1996-98; bd. dirs. Constitutional Rights Found., 1997—, L.A. County Bar Found., 1997-99. Mem. ABA (labor law sect. 1978—), Calif. Bar Assn. (labor law sect. 1985—), L.A. County Bar Assn. (labor and employment law sect. 1985—, mem. exec. com. 1988—, vice chair 2001—, sec. 1999-2000, treas. 2000-01), Pi Lambda Theta, Phi Beta Kappa. Labor, Pension, profit-sharing, and employee benefits, Wrongful discharge. Office: Heller Ehrman White & McAuliffe 601 S Figueroa St Fl 40 Los Angeles CA 90017-5704 Fax: 213-614-1868. E-mail: dse@hewm.com

SAXL, RICHARD HILDRETH, lawyer; b. Boston, June 3, 1948; s. Erwin Joseph and Lucretia (Hildreth) S. BA, U. Pa., 1970; JD, Rutgers U., Camden, N.J., 1975. Bar: Conn. 1976, U.S. Dist. Ct. Conn. 1976, U.S. Ct. Appeals (2d cir.) 1977. Assoc. Jerry Davidoff, Westport, Conn., 1976-78; ptnr. Davidoff & Saxl, 1979-94; pvt. practice law offices Richard H. Saxl, 1994—; town atty. Fairfield, Conn., 1997-99. Trustee Ridgefield Acad., 1997—. Mem. Fairfield Town Plan and Zoning Commn., 1981-93, chmn., 1991-93; chair Fairfield Land Acquisition com., 1997; mem. Fairfield Charter Revision Commn., 1984-85, 92. Recipient Svc. award, Conn. Fedn. Planning and Zoning Agys., 1993, cert. of commendation, Conn. Jud. Dept. Mem. Conn. Bar Assn., Westport Bar Assn., Pequot Yacht Club. Democrat. Avocations: squash, astronomy. Municipal (including bonds), Probate, Real property. Home: 753 Sasco Hill Rd Fairfield CT 06430-6376 Office: 5 Imperial Ave Westport CT 06880-4302 E-mail: rhsaxl@aol.com

SAXTON, WILLIAM MARVIN, lawyer; b. Joplin, Mo., Feb. 14, 1927; s. Clyde Marvin and Lea Ann (Farnan) S.; m. Helen Grace Klinefelter, June 1, 1974; children: Sherry Lynn, Patricia Ann Painter, William Daniel, Michael Lawrence. A.B., U. Mich., 1949, J.D., 1952. Bar: Mich. Mem. firm Love, Snyder & Lewis, Detroit, 1952-53, Butzel, Long, Detroit, 1953—, dir., chmn., CEO, 1989-96, dir. emeritus, 1997—. Lectr. Inst. Continuing Legal Edn.; sec., bd. dirs. Fritz Broadcasting, Inc., 1983-97; mem. mediation tribunal hearing panel for 3d Jud. Dist. Mich., 1989—, 6th Jud. Dist., 1994—. Trustee Detroit Music Hall Ctr. Soc. for the Performing Arts, 1984-99; trustee Hist. Soc. U.S. Dist. Ct. (ea. dist.) Mich., 1992-95, pres., 1993-95. Recipient Distinguished award Mich. Road Builders Assn., 1987. Master of Bench Emeritus Am. Inn of Court; fellow Am. Coll. Trial Lawyers, Am. Bar Found., Am. Coll. Labor and Employment Lawyers, Mich. Bar Found.; mem. ABA, FBA, Detroit Bar Assn. (dir. 1974-79, Goodnow Pres.'s award 1996), Mich. Bar Assn. (atty. discipline panel, Disting. Svc. award 1998), Detroit Indsl. Rels. Rsch. Assn. (treas. 1980—, v.p. 1982, pres. 1984-85), Mich. Young Lawyers (pres. 1954-55), Am. Law Inst., Indsl. Rels. Rsch. Assn. Am. Arbitration Assn., U.S. 6th Cir. Ct. Appeals (life, mem. jud. conf., mem. bicentennial com.), Am. Inn Ct., Cooley Club, Renaissance Club, Detroit Golf Club (dir. 1983-89), Detroit Athletic Club. Federal civil litigation, State civil litigation, Labor. Office: Butzel Long 150 W Jefferson Ave Ste 900 Detroit MI 48226-4416

SAYLER, ROBERT NELSON, lawyer; b. Kansas City, Mo., June 1, 1940; s. John William and Roberta (Nelson) S.; m. Martha Leith, Aug. 1962; children: Christina, Bentley. BA, Stanford U., 1962; JD, Harvard U., 1965. Bar: U.S. Dist. Ct. D.C. 1966, U.S. Ct. Appeals (D.C. cir.) 1966, U.S. Supreme Ct. 1971, D.C. 1972, U.S. Ct. Appeals (2d cir.) 1977. From assoc. to ptnr. Covington & Burling, Washington, 1965—. V.p. Neighborhood Legal Services, Washington, 1980-82; pres. Legal Aid Soc., Washington, 1983-84. Fellow Am. Bar Found., Am. Coll. Trial Lawyers; mem. ABA (dir. programs, program chmn. 1981, 85, coun., chmn. litigation sect., mem. standing com. on fed. judiciary). Democrat. General civil litigation, Insurance, Intellectual property. Office: Covington & Burling PO Box 7566 1201 Pennsylvania Ave NW Washington DC 20004-2401

SAYLOR, CHARLES HORACE, lawyer; b. Bethlehem, Pa., Jan. 6, 1950; s. Howard James and Florence M. (Glasser) S.; m. Martha Louise Weaver, July 10, 1971; children: Amy Louise, Matthew Charles. BA, Pa. State U., 1971; JD, Dickinson Sch. Law, 1974. Bar: Pa. 1974, U.S. Dist. Ct. (mid. dist.) Pa. 1979. Law clk. Northumberland County Ct. Common Pleas, Sunbury, Pa., 1974-76; assoc. Wiest & Wiest, 1976-79; ptnr. Wiest, Wiest & Saylor, 1979-85, Wiest, Wiest, Saylor & Muolo, Sunbury, 1985-97, Wiest, Saylor, Muolo, Noon and Swinehart, Sunbury, 1998—. Solicitor Twp. of Rush, Pa., 1979—, Twp. of Point, Pa., 1983—, County of Northumberland, 1993-95; instr. Pa. State U., Schuylkill Haven, 1986. Asst. editor Dickinson Law Rev., 1973, Northumberland (Pa.) Legal Jour., 1987—. Trustee Northumberland County Law Libr., 1986—, Priestley-Forsyth Meml. Libr., Northumberland, 1988-93, v.p., 1990-93; coach Am. Youth Soccer Assn., Northumberland, 1988-90; mem. com. YMCA, Sunbury, 1987-98, bd. dirs., 1991—, pres. of bd. dirs., 1997-98, chmn. sustaining campaign, 1992; asst. coach Girls Track and Field, Shikellamy H.S., 1992-93; profls. co-chair United Way, 2000—. Mem. Pa. Bar Assn., Northumberland County Bar Assn. (sec.-treas. 1985-2000, pres. 2001), Pa. Trial Lawyers Assn. Republican. Roman Catholic. Avocations: running, golf. General civil litigation, Personal injury. Home: 233 Honey Locust Ln Northumberland PA 17857-9679 Office: Wiest Saylor Muolo Noon & Swinehart 240244 Market St Sunbury PA 17801-2526

SAYLOR, THOMAS G. state supreme court justice; b. Meyersdale, Pa., Dec. 14, 1946; BA in Govt., U. Va., 1969; JD, Columbia U., 1972. Pvt. practice, 1972-82, 87-93; 1st asst. dist. atty. Somerset County, 1973-76; dir. Pa. Bur. Consumer Protection, 1982-83; 1st dep. atty. gen. Commonwealth of Pa., 1983-87; elected judge Superior Ct. Pa., 1993; elected justice Supreme Ct. Pa., 1997—. Contbr. articles to legal publications. Bd. overseers Widener U. Sch. Law. Mem. ABA, Pa. Bar Assn., Cumberland County Bar Assn., Dauphin County Bar Assn., Appellate Judges Conf. Office: Fulton Bldg 16th Fl 200 N 3d St Harrisburg PA 17101

SAYRE, GEORGE EDWARD, retired lawyer; b. Orange, N.J., June 18, 1935; s. H. Edward and Gertrude (Busch) S.; m. Ann Howard, May 24, 1964 (div. 1974); children— Mark H., Daniel E., Lynn L.; m. Cressey Wallace, Mar. 21, 1982. B.A., Pomona Coll., 1956; LL.B., Stanford U., 1959. Bar: Calif. 1960, U.S. Ct. Appeals (9th cir.) 1960, U.S. Dist. Ct. (no. dist.) Calif. 1960. Acct., Haskins & Sells, San Francisco, 1960; assoc. Sedgwick, Detert, Moran & Arnold, San Francisco, 1961-66, ptnr., 1966-93, ret., 1993. Served with USAF, 1959-60. Republican. Club: St. Francis Yacht (San Francisco) (bd. dirs. 1978-83, sec. 1980-82, rear commodore 1985, vice commodore 1986, commodore 1987), Belvedere Tennis (Tiburon, Calif.). Insurance. Home: PO Box 26641 San Francisco CA 94126-6641

SAYRE, JOHN MARSHALL, lawyer, former government official; b. Boulder, Colo., Nov. 9, 1921; s. Henry Marshall and Lulu M. (Cooper) S.; m. Jean Miller, Aug. 22, 1943; children: Henry M., Charles Franklin, John Marshall Jr., Ann Elizabeth Sayre Taggart (dec.). BA, U. Colo., 1943, JD,

1948. Bar: Colo. 1948, U.S. Dist. Ct. Colo. 1952, U.S. Ct. Appeals (10th cir.) 1964. Law clk. trust dept. Denver Nat. Bank, 1948-49; asst. cashier, trust officer Nat. State Bank of Boulder, 1949-50; ptnr. Ryan, Sayre, Martin, Brotzman, Boulder, 1950-66, Davis, Graham & Stubbs, Denver, 1966-89, of counsel, 1993—; asst. sec. of the Interior for Water and Sci., 1989-93. Bd. dirs. Boulder Sch. Dist. 3, 1951-57; city atty. City of Boulder, 1952-55; gen. counsel Colo. Mcpl. League, 1959-63; prin. counsel No. Colo. Water Conservancy Dist. and mcpl. subdist., 1964-87, spl. counsel, 1987, bd. dirs. dist., 1960-64; former legal counsel Colo. Assn. Commerce and Industry. Lt. (j.g.) USNR, 1943-46, ret. Decorated Purple Heart; recipient William Lee Knous award U. Colo. Law Sch., 1999. Fellow Am. Bar Found. (life), Colo. Bar Found. (life); mem. ABA, Colo. Bar Assn., Boulder County Bar Assn. (pres. 1959), Denver Bar Assn., Nat. Water Resources Assn. (Colo. dir. 1980-89, 93-95, pres. 1984-86), Denver Country Club, Univ. Club, Phi Beta Kappa, Phi Gamma Delta, Phi Delta Phi. Environmental, Real property. Home: 355 Ivanhoe St Denver CO 80220-5841 Office: Davis Graham & Stubbs 1550-17th St Ste 500 Denver CO 80202 E-mail: john.sayre@dgslaw.com

SAYRE, RICHARD LAYTON, lawyer; b. Spokane, Wash., May 21, 1953; s. Charles Layton and Elizabeth Jane (Ward) S.; m. Karen Linda Sayre, Mar. 8, 1979; children: Wendi Sue Stoken, Tracey Lynn Turner. BA, U. Wash., 1976; JD, Gonzaga U., 1979. Bar: Wash. 1979, U.S. Dist. Ct. (ea. and we. dist.) Wash. 1979, U.S. Ct. Appeals (9th cir.) 1986; cert. elder law atty. Nat. Elder Law Found. Deputy prosecuting atty. Spokane County, Spokane, 1979-84; shareholder Underwood, Campbell, Brock & Cerutti, 1984-92, Sayre & Sayre P.S., Spokane, 1992—. Pres. Nat. Acad. Elder Law Attys., Washington, 1995-96; apptd. by Wash. Supreme Ct., Washington Profl. Guardian Cert. Bd. Potentate, trustee El Katif Shrine Temple, Spokane, 1997; bd. govs. Shriner's Hosp. for Children, Spokane, 1993-96; exec. officer Order of DeMolay, Washington, 1993—, internat. supreme coun. Order DeMolay. Recipient Pro Bono award Spokane County Bar Assn., 1991, 99, Recognition of Achievement & Contribution award Lutheran Social Svcs. of Washington, Idaho, 1992, 97, Achievement award Spokane Sexual Assault Ctr., 1997, Disting. Svc. award GOnzaga U., 1997; named Super Lawyer, Washington Law & Politics, 2000, 2001. Mem. Nat. Acad. Elder Law Attys., Spokane Estate Planning Coun. Democrat. Episcopal. Avocations: sailing, skiing. Estate planning, Probate, Legislative. Office: Sayre & Sayre 111 W Cataldo Ave Ste 210 Spokane WA 99201-3203 E-mail: dick@sayrelaw.com

SCACCHETTI, DAVID J. lawyer; b. Newark, July 13, 1956; s. Edmond and Evelyn Scacchetti; m. Marcia Ellen Gessiness, Aug. 31, 1985; children: Gabriella Elise, Olivia Beth. BA in Polit. Sci. with honors, U. Cin., 1978, JD, 1981. Bar: Ohio 1982, U.S. Dist. Ct. (so. dist.) Ohio 1982, U.S. Dist. Ct. (ea. dist.) Ky. 1986, U.S. Dist. Ct. Ariz. 1997. Atty. Edward J. Utz, Esq., Cin., 1982; sole practitioner, 1982-98; atty. Scacchetti & Scacchetti, 1998—. Mem. ATLA, Nat. Assn. Criminal Def. Lawyers, Greater Cin. Criminal Def. Lawyer Assn., Ohio Acad. Trial Lawyers, Ham. County Trial Lawyers Assn., Phi Beta Kappa. Avocations: writing, tennis, Tribal art, guitar, travel. General civil litigation, Criminal, Personal injury. Office: Scacchetti & Scacchetti 601 Main St Fl 3D Cincinnati OH 45202-2519 E-mail: Scaccheti@fuse.net, D.Scacchetti@aol.com

SCAFETTA, JOSEPH, JR. lawyer; b. Chester, Pa., May 10, 1947; s. Giuseppe and Mary (Koslosky) S.; m. Teresa M. Talierco, July 4, 1986; 1 child, Joseph III. BS in Aero. Engring., Pa. State U., 1969; JD, U. Pitts., 1972; M in Patent Law, Georgetown U., 1973; MBA, George Washington U., 1983. Bar: Pa. 1972, U.S. Patent and Trademark Office 1973, D.C. 1978, Va. 1979, U.S. Supreme Ct. 1980, U.S. Ct. Appeals (fed. cir.) 1982. Legal rschr. Arent, Fox, Kintner, Plotkin et al, Washington, 1973; law clk. to presiding judge U.S. Dist. Ct. S.C., Columbia, 1973-74; assoc. Colton & Stone, Arlington, Va., 1975-77, Craig & Antonelli, Washington, 1977-78, Wigman & Cohen, Arlington, 1978-83, Wenderoth, Lind & Ponack, Washington, 1983-86, Cushman, Darby & Cushman, Washington, 1986-87; counsel Russell, Georges & Breneman, Arlington, 1987-91, Young & Thompson, Arlington, 1991-96; pvt. practice, 1996-98; counsel Oblon, Spivak, McClelland, Maier & Neustadt, 1999—. Voting mem. Nat. Commn. for Social Justice, 1995-97. Author: Book Review Copyright Handbook, 1979, The Constitutionality/Unconstitutionality of the Patent Infringement Statute, 1979, (with others) Patents on Microorganisms, 1980; editor: An Intellectual Property Law Primer, 1975; contbr. articles to profl. jours. Mem. Consumer Affairs Commn., Alexandria, Va., 1985-87; charter mem. Christopher Columbus Quincentenary Jubilee Com., 1990-93; chair Va. chpt. Commn. for Social Justice, 1987—; mem. Fairfax County Dem. Com., Falls Church, 1987-89; parliamentarian City Dem. Com., Alexandria, 1985-87. Recipient Robert C. Watson award Am. Patent Law Assn., 1975. Mem.: ABA, Am. Arbitration Assn. (mem. comml. panel), Va. Bar Assn., Am. Intellectual Property Law Assn. (mem. pub. info. com. 1983—2001), D.C. Bar Assn., Patent and Trademark Office Soc., Avanti Italiani (pres. Alexandria chpt. 1981—83), Grand Lodge Va. (state pres. 1993—95), Sons of Italy. Patent, Trademark and copyright. Office: 1755 Jeff Davis Hwy Ste 400 Arlington VA 22202-3530

SCALA, JAMES ROBERT, lawyer; b. Detroit, Oct. 5, 1948; s. Eugene Louis and Edna Ann (Weathers) S.; m. Susan Langford Jones, Feb. 28, 1981; children— James, Elizabeth. A.B. in History, magna cum laude, Georgetown U., 1970; J.D., Columbia U., 1974. Bar: N.Y. 1975, U.S. Dist. Ct. (so. and ea. dists.) N.Y. 1975, U.S. Ct. Appeals (2d cir.) 1975, U.S. Supreme Ct. 1982. Assoc., Dewey, Ballantine, Bushby, Palmer and Wood, N.Y.C., 1974-78, Fried, Frank, et. al., 1978-80, Simpson, Thacher, et. al., 1980-82, Golenbock & Barell, N.Y.C., 1982— . Editor: Columbia Jour. Law and Society Problems, 1973-74. Contbr. articles to profl. jours. Georgetown U. hon. scholar, 1966; Harlan Fiske Stone scholar Columbia U. 1974; Mem. ABA (real property, probate and trust law com. on real estate fin. 1983—), N.Y. State Bar Assn. (real property law sect. com. on real estate fin. and liens, tax sect. coms. on partnerships and income from real property 1983—), Assn. Bar City of N.Y. Episcopalian. Clubs: Columbia, N.Y. Road Runners. Real property, Corporate taxation, Personal income taxation. Office: care Golenbock/Barell 645 5th Ave New York NY 10022-5910

SCALETTA, PHILLIP JASPER, lawyer, educator; b. Sioux City, Iowa, Aug. 20, 1925; s. Phillip and Louise (Pelmulder) S.; m. Helen M. Beedle; children: Phillip R., Cheryl D. Kesler. BS, Morningside Coll., Sioux City, Iowa, 1948; JD, U. Iowa, 1950. Bar: Iowa 1950, U.S. Dist. Ct. Iowa 1950, Ind. 1966, U.S. Supreme Ct. 1968. Ptnr. McKnight and Scaletta, Sioux City, 1950-51; field rep. Farmers Ins. Group, Sioux City, 1951-54, sr. liability examiner, Aurora, Ill., 1954-60; br. claims mgr., Ft. Wayne, Ind., 1960-66; prof. law Purdue U., West Lafayette, Ind., 1966—; dir. profl. masters programs of the Krannet Grad. Sch. of Mgmt. Purdue U., 1987-90; of counsel with Mayfield & Brooks Attys. at Law, 1967—; arbitrator Panel of Arbitrators Am. Arbitration Assn. Co-author: Business Law and Regulatory Environments, 5th edit., 1996, Business Law Workbook, 5th edit., 1996, Foundations of Business Law and Legal Environment, 1986, 4th edit., 1997, Student Workbook and Study Guide, 1986, 4th edit., 1997; contbr. numerous articles to profl. jours. Mem. Ind. Gov's Commn. Individual Privacy, 1975. Recipient Best Tchr. of Yr. award Standard Oil Ind. Found., 1972, Outstanding Tchr. award Purdue U. Alumni Assn., 1974, Most Effective Tchr. award Krannert Grad. Sch. Mgmt. Purdue U., 1991. Mem. Am. Bus. Law Assn. (pres., Sr. Faculty Excellence award 1989), Tippecanoe County Bar Assn., Tri State Bus Law Assn. (past pres.), Midwest Bus. Adminstrn. Assn., Beta Gamma Sigma (bd. govs.). Office: Purdue U 511 Krannert Bldg West Lafayette IN 47907

SCALETTA, PHILLIP RALPH, III, lawyer; b. Iowa City, Dec. 18, 1949; s. Phillip Jasper and Helen M. (Beedle) S.; m. Karen Lynn Scaletta, May 13, 1973; children: Phillip, Anthony, Alexander. BSIM, MS, Purdue U., 1972; JD, Ind. U., 1975. Bar: Ind. 1975, U.S. Dist. Ct. Ind. 1975, Ill. 1993. Assoc. Ice Miller Donadio & Ryan, Indpls., 1975-81, ptnr., 1981—. Contbr. articles to profl. jours. Chmn. Ind. Continuing Legal Edn. Found., Indpls., 1989; mem. Environ. Quality Control Water Com., 1988-98. Mem. Ind. Bar Assn., Indpls. Bar Assn., Def. Rsch. Inst., Internat. Assn. Def. Counsel, Gyro Club Indpls. (v.p. 1992-93, pres. 1993-94, bd. dirs. 1990—). Avocations: golf, skiing, tennis. General civil litigation, Environmental. Home: 7256 Tuliptree Trl Indianapolis IN 46256-2136 Office: Ice Miller 1 American Sq Indianapolis IN 46282-0020

SCALIA, ANTONIN, United States supreme court justice; b. Trenton, N.J., Mar. 11, 1936; s. S. Eugene and Catherine Louise (Panaro) S.; m. Maureen McCarthy, Sept. 10, 1960; children— Ann Forrest, Eugene, John Francis, Catherine Elisabeth, Mary Clare, Paul David, Matthew, Christopher James, Margaret Jane. A.B., Georgetown U., 1957; student, U. Fribourg, Switzerland, 1955-56; LL.B., Harvard, 1960. Bar: Ohio 1962, Va. 1970. Assoc. Jones Day Cockley & Reavis, Cleve., 1961-67; assoc. prof. U. Va. Law Sch., 1967-70; prof. law U. Va., 1970-74; gen. counsel Office Telecommunications Policy, Exec. Office of Pres., 1971-72; chmn. Adminstrv. Conf. U.S., Washington, 1972-74; asst. atty. gen. U.S. Office Legal Counsel, Justice Dept., 1974-77; vis. prof. Georgetown Law Center, 1977, Stanford Law Sch., 1980-81; vis. scholar Am. Enterprise Inst., 1977; prof. law U. Chgo., 1977-82; judge U.S. Ct. Appeals (D.C. cir.), 1982-86; justice U.S. Supreme Ct., Washington, 1986—. Editor: Regulation mag, 1979-82. Sheldon fellow Harvard U., 1960-61 Office: US Supreme Ct Supreme Ct Bldg 1 1st St NE Washington DC 20543-0001*

SCALLY, JOHN JOSEPH, JR. lawyer; b. Glen Ridge, N.J., Feb. 3, 1951; s. John Joseph and Emelia (Passudette) S.; m. Karen Elizabeth Scofield, Aug. 29, 1981; children: Courtney, John. A.B., Muhlenberg Coll., 1973; J.D. Cath. U. Am., 1976. Bar: N.Y. 1977, N.J. 1977, D.C. 1977, U.S. Dist. Ct. N.J. 1977. Assoc. firm Mudge Rose Guthrie & Alexander, N.Y.C., 1976-82; ptnr. firm McCarter & English, Newark, 1982— . Mem. debt mgmt. adv. com. N.J. Local Fin. Bd., Trenton, 1983—; mem. N.J. Gov.'s Commn. on Internat Trade. Pres. No. N.J. chpt. Leukemia Soc. Am., 1989-93; mem. Urban League Essex County, 1987-89. Mem. Nat. Assn. Bond Lawyers, N.J. Mcpl. Attys., Mcpl. Fin. Officers Am., Mcpl. Fin. Officers N.J. Roman Catholic. Clubs: Fiddler's Elbow Country (Bedminster, N.J.); Essex (Newark); World Trade Ctr. (N.Y.C.); N.J. Bond, Baltusrol Golf, Short Hills. Municipal (including bonds). Office: McCarter & English 4 Gateway Ctr PO Box 652 Newark NJ 07101-0652

SCANLON, ROBERT CHARLES, lawyer; b. Orange, N.J., May 25, 1950; s. Robert Alfred and Joyce (Fennimore) S.; m. Kathleen Marie Maginnis, Apr. 7, 1973; children: Elizabeth, Margaret, Marianne. BS, St. Peters Coll., 1972; JD, Gonzaga U., 1976. Bar: Wash. 1977, U.S. Dist. Ct. (ea. dist.) Wash. 1977, U.S. Dist. Ct. (we. dist.) Wash. 1979, U.S. Ct. Appeals (9th cir.) 1980. Assoc. Cooper & Roberts, Spokane, Wash., 1977-81; ptnr. Roberts, DiLuzio & Scanlon, 1981-84; prin. Dellwo, Rudolf & Schroeder PS, 1984-90; with Dellwo, Roberts and Scanlon PS, 1990—. Mem. ABA, Wash. State Bar Assn. (exec. com. family law sect. 1997—, chmn. 1999-2000), Spokane County Bar Assn. (trustee 1981-82, pres. young lawyers sect. 1981-82), Wash. State Trial Lawyers, Assn., Trial Lawyers Am. Republican. Roman Catholic. Consumer commercial, Family and matrimonial, General practice. Home: 3729 W Woodside Ave Spokane WA 99208-4860 Office: Dellwo Roberts Scanlon PS 1124 W Riverside Ave Ste 310 Spokane WA 99201-1109

SCANNELL, TIMOTHY C. lawyer; b. Keene, N.H., Jan. 1, 1966; s. Timothy F. and Kathleen M. Scannell; m. Lynn M. Swanson, June 20, 1992; children: Kieran T., Lars B. Student, Phillips Exeter Acad., 1984; BA, Middlebury Coll., 1988; MPA, U. Mich., 1997; JD, U. Minn., 1997. Bar: N.H. Assoc. McLane, Graf, Raulerson & Middleton, PA, Manchester, N.H., 1997—. Author, editor: Embassy's Complete Boating Guide to Connecticut River, 1989, Embassy's Complete Boating Guide to East Coast of Florida, 1990, Embassy's Complete Boating Guide to Long Island Sound, 1991, Embassy's Complete Boating Guide to Rhode Island and Massachusetts, 1991. Mem. ABA, N.H. Bar Assn., Manchester Bar Assn. Avocations: blues guitar, fiction writing. General corporate, Immigration, naturalization, and customs, Intellectual property. Office: McLane Graf Raulerson & Middleton PA 900 Elm St Manchester NH 03105

SCARMINACH, CHARLES ANTHONY, lawyer; b. Syracuse, N.Y., Feb. 19, 1944; s. John Louis and Lucy (Egnoto) S.; children: John, Catherine, Karen, Charles, Robert. MA, U. Buffalo, 1965; JD, Syracuse U., 1968. Bar: N.Y. 1968, S.C. 1974. Gen. counsel Sea Pines Co., Hilton Head Island, S.C., 1973-78; sole practice, 1978-83; ptnr. Novit & Scarminach, P.A., 1983-93, Novit Scarminach & Williams P.A., Hilton Head Island, 1993—. Bd. dirs. Nations Bank, Hilton Head Island. Chmn. bd. Sea Pines Montessori Sch., Hilton Head Island, 1979-83; bd. dirs. Hilton Head Preparatory Sch., 1984-93, chmn. bd. trustees 1986-93. Maj. U.S. Army, 1968-73. Mem. ABA, S.C. Bar Assn., N.Y. State Bar Assn., Hilton Head Island C. of C. (bd. dirs. 1996-99), Sea Pines Club. Democrat. Roman Catholic. General corporate, General practice, Real property. Home: 10 Wood Duck Ct Hilton Head Island SC 29928-3010 Office: Novit Scarminach & Williams PA PO Box 14 Hilton Head Island SC 29938-0014 E-mail: cscarminach@nswlaw.com

SCEPER, DUANE HAROLD, lawyer; b. Norfolk, Va., Nov. 16, 1946; s. Robert George and Marion Eudora (Hynes) S.; m. Sharon Diane Cramer, July 4, 1981; stepchildren: Karin Stevenson, Diane Stevenson. BS in Law, Western State U., 1979, JD, 1980. Bar: Calif. 1982, U.S. Dist. Ct. (so. dist.) Calif. 1982. Field engr. Memorex/Tex. Instruments, San Diego, 1968-70; computer programmer, 1970-81; atty. Allied Ins. Group, 1981-85; sole practice, 1985-87; ptnr. Paluso & Sceper, 1987—. Cons. computers 1980—; lectr. estate planning various orgns. Patentee in field. Active Com. to Elect King Golden to Congress, San Diego, 1978. Served with USAF, 1965-68. Recipient Am. Jurisprudence award, 1979. Mem. ABA, San Diego County Bar Assn., Assn. Trial Lawyers of Am., Calif. Trial Lawyers Assn., San Diego Trial Lawyers Assn., Am. Subrogation Attys., Assn. of Ins. Def. Counsel, So. Calif. Def. Counsel, Air Commando Assn. (life), Delta Theta Phi. Democrat. State civil litigation, Estate planning, Insurance. Home: 2641 Massachusetts Ave Lemon Grove CA 91945-3149 Office: Paluso & Sceper 1010 2d Ave Ste 1350 San Diego CA 92101

SCHAAB, ARNOLD J. lawyer; b. Newark, 1939; s. Robert George and Pauline Schaab; m. Marcia Stecker, 1964 (div. 1978); children: Emily Diana, Genevieve; m. Patricia Caesar, 1981 (div. 1996); m. Susan McGlamery, 2000. BA, New Sch. U., 1962; LLB, Harvard U., 1965. Bar: N.Y. 1967, U.S. Dist. Ct. (so. and ea. dists.) N.Y. 1967. Assoc. Chadbourne & Parke, N.Y.C., 1966-69; ptnr. Anderson, Kill & Olick, 1969-78; sr. ptnr. Pryor, Cashman, Sherman & Flynn LLP, 1978—. Chmn. Literacy Ptnrs., Inc.; mem. exec. com. Shaker Mus. and Libr., Old Chatham, N.Y.; vis. com. Milano Grad. Sch. Mgmt. and Pub. Policy, New Sch. U. Fulbright scholar Law Faculty U. Paris, 1966. Fellow N.Y. Bar Found., Am. Bar Found.; mem. ABA (vice chair internat. fin. transactions com.), N.Y. State Bar Assn. (chmn. internat. law and practice sect., chmn. spl. com. free trade in the Ams., ho. of dels., fin. com., long range planning com., by-laws com.), Assn. Bar City N.Y. (com. internat. trade, com. fgn. and comparative law), Computer Law Assn., Univ. Club (asst. treas., chmn. fin. com., chmn. audit com.), Doubles, Nat. Arts Club, Archaeol. Inst. Am., Bibl. Archaeology Soc. Contracts commercial, General corporate, Private international. Office: Pryor Cashman Sherman & Flynn 410 Park Ave New York NY 10022-4441

SCHAAF, DOUGLAS ALLAN, lawyer; b. Green Bay, Wis., Nov. 18, 1955; s. Carlton Otto and Fern (Brunette) S.; m. Kathlyn T. Bielke, Feb. 23, 1988. BBA magna cum laude in Internat. Bus., St. Norbert Coll., DePere, Wis., 1978; JD, U. Notre Dame, 1981. Bar: Ill. 1981, Calif. 1987. Assoc. McDermott, Will & Emery, Chgo., 1981-84, Skadden, Arps, Slate, Meagher & Flom, 1984-89; ptnr. Paul Hastings, Janofsky & Walker, L.A., 1989—. Adj. faculty mem. John Marshall Law Sch., 1984-87. Atty. Chgo. Vol. Legal Services, 1984-87; bd. dirs. Orange County Alzheimer's Assn. Mem. Orange County Bar Assn. (chair tax sect. 1994-96). General corporate, Corporate taxation, Personal income taxation. Office: Paul Hastings Janofsky & Walker 695 Town Center Dr Ste 1700 Costa Mesa CA 92626-7191 E-mail: dougschaaf@paalhastings.com

SCHAAP, JACQUELINE, lawyer; b. Haarlem, Netherlands, June 27, 1961; d. Lex and Truus S. Law degree, U. Amsterdam, 1984. Trademark agt. Markgraaf, The Netherlands, 1985-88; ptnr. Boekel de Neree, The Netherlands, 1988—. Author: Promotional Actions, 1997, Trademark Law, 1996; co-author: Intellectual Property, 2000; co-author, editor: Legal Questions on Marketing and Advertising, 1995; contbr. articles to profl. jours. Bd. dirs. theatre group Toneelgroep, Amsterdam. Mem. Dutch Advt. Assn., INTA, ECTA, BMM. Avocation: sports. Communications, Intellectual property, Trademark and copyright. Office: Boekel de Neree PO Box 2508 1000 CM Amsterdam The Netherlands

SCHACHT, RONALD STUART, lawyer; b. Stamford, Conn., Nov. 7, 1932; s. Saul Albert and Faye Dorothy (Gittleman) S.; m. Natalie Helene Goldman, June 17, 1956; children: Patti Ellen, Bonnie Anne, Cindy Joy. B.S., U. Conn., 1954; LL.B., NYU, 1957, LL.M., 1960. Bar: N.Y. 1957, D.C. 1980. Tax atty. IRS, N.Y.C., 1957-62; assoc. Proskauer Rose, LLP, 1962-69, ptnr., 1969—, mng. ptnr., 1981-84, mem. exec. com., 1985-95. Lectr. Practising Law Inst., NYU Inst. Fed. Taxation; adj. asst. prof. Sch. Continuing Edn., NYU, 1970-72. Bd. dirs. Congregation Agudath Shalom, Stamford, 1968-73; mem. com. Fedn. Jewish philanthropies, N.Y.C., 1972-80. Mem. N.Y. State Bar Assn., Assn. of Bar of City of N.Y., N.Y. County Lawyers Assn. (bd. dirs. 1977-83, chmn. ins. com. 1975-85), Newfield Swim Club (bd. dirs. 1967-70, pres. 1979), Phi Kappa Phi, Gamma Chi Epsilon. Democrat. Jewish. Corporate taxation, Estate taxation, Personal income taxation. E-mail: rss6945@aol.com

SCHACHTER, PAUL, lawyer; b. N.Y.C., Feb. 22, 1949; s. David and Blanche (Orris) S. Student, MIT, 1966-68; J.D., Rutgers U., 1974. Bar: N.Y. 1975, P.R. 1976, N.J. 1981, U.S. Dist. Ct. (so. and ea. dists.) N.Y. 1981, U.S. Dist. Ct. N.J. 1981, U.S. Dist. Ct. P.R. 1976, U.S. R.R. Ct. 1982, U.S. Ct. Appeals (1st, 2d, 3d and D.C. cirs.) 1976, U.S. Supreme Ct. 1983. Assoc. David Scribner, Esq., N.Y.C., 1974-75; dir. P.R. Labor Law Project, San Juan, 1975-76; dir. Labor Law Clinic, Rutgers U., 1980-83; ptnr. Escribano & Carreras, Hato Rey, P.R., 1976-77, Reinhardt & Schachter P.C., Newark, N.J., 1983— ; of counsel N.Y. Hotel Trades Council, N.Y.C., 1977-80. Mem. Nat. Lawyers Guild (Chmn. P.R. project 1981-83), Assn. Bar N.Y.C., N.J. Bar Assn., P.R. Bar Assn., AFL-CIO (lawyers coordinating com.). Federal civil litigation, State civil litigation, Labor. Office: Reinhardt & Schachter PC 744 Broad St Newark NJ 07102-3802

SCHADE, GEORGE AUGUST, JR. judge; b. Santurce, P.R., Mar. 3, 1947; s. George August and Carmen Maria (Torres) S.; m. Lillian Marie Hinchman, Mar. 3, 1973; children: Valerie Lillian, Alan Taft. AB, Stanford U., 1968; postgrad., U. Calif., Davis, 1968-69; JD, Am. U., 1971. Bar: Ariz. 1973, U.S. Dist. Ct. Ariz. 1973. Law clk. Ariz. Ct. Appeals, Phoenix, 1972-73; mem. staff Legal Aid Soc. Maricopa County, 1973-75; assoc. firm Machmer, Schlosser & Meitz, 1975-78; sole practice, 1978-80; hearing officer State of Ariz. Dept. Water Resources, 1980-82, 92-95, br. chief, 1983-86, sect. chief, 1986-92; adminstrv. law judge State of Ariz., 1996-2001; spl. master Ariz. Gen. Stream Adjudication, 2001—. Faculty adviser Nat. Jud. Coll., U. Nev., Reno, 1982. Mem. Gov.'s Commn. Ariz. Environment, Phoenix, 1977-83, Gov.'s Ariz.-Mex. Commn., Phoenix, 1978-79; mem. adv. coun. Fed. Bur. Land Mgmt., Phoenix, 1980-82. Served to capt., USAR, 1972-77.

SCHAEFER, DAVID ARNOLD, lawyer; b. Cleve., May 3, 1948; s. Leonard and Maxine V. (Bassett) S.; m. Riki C. Freeman, Aug. 8, 1971; children: Kevin, Lindsey, Traci. BS, Miami U., Oxford, Ohio, 1970; MA, Northwestern U., 1971; JD, Case Western Res. U., 1974. Bar: Ohio 1974, U.S. Dist. Ct. (no. dist.) Ohio 1974, U.S. Ct. Appeals (6th cir.) 1978, U.S. Supreme Ct. 1978. Ptnr. Guren, Merritt et al, 1980-84, Menexch. Friedlander et al, Cleve., 1984-93, McCarthy, Lebit, Crystal & Haiman, Cleve., 1993—. Author: Deposition Strategy, 1981, 2d edit., 1984; contbr. articles to profl. publs. Mem. ABA, Internat. Assn. Def. Counsel, Fed. Bar Assn. (pres. 1992-93), Nat. Inst. Trail Advocacy (faculty), 8th Cir. Jud. Conf. (life). General civil litigation, Product liability. Office: McCarthy Lebit Crystal & Haiman 1800 Midland Bldg 101 W Prospect Ave Ste 1800 Cleveland OH 44115-1027

SCHAEFER, KARL P. lawyer; b. Germany, May 14, 1955; DrJur, Ludwig-Maximilians-U., Munich, Germany, 1982. BAr: munich 1985. Ptnr. Linklaters Ippenhoff & Raedler, Munich, 1993—. Taxation, general. Office: Linklaters Oppenhoff et al Prinzregentenplatz 10 Munich, Bavaria D-81675 Germany Fax: 49-89-41808100. E-mail: karl_schaefer@oppenhoff-raedler.com

SCHAFF, MICHAEL FREDERICK, lawyer; b. Queens, N.Y., Nov. 14, 1957; s. Raymond and Norma S.; m. Robin Barbara Rose, Mar. 17, 1985; children: Rachel Lindsay, Aaron Jacob. BA, Rutgers Coll., New Brunswick, N.J., 1979; MBA, CUNY, 1982; JD, N.Y. Law Sch., N.Y.C., 1982; LLM, Boston U., 1983. Bar: N.Y. and N.J. 1982, Md. 1983, U.S. Dist. Ct. N.J. 1983, U.S. Dist. Ct. Md. 1983, U.S. Tax Ct. 1983. Assoc. Ober, Kaler, Grimes & Shriver, Balt., 1983-84, Greenberg, Dauber & Epstein, Newark, 1984-86, Wilentz, Goldman & Spitzer, Woodbridge, N.J., 1986-91, ptnr., 1991—. Mem. N.J. Legis. Com. for the Study of Pain Mgmt. Contbr. articles to profl. jours. Masters Rsch. fellow, Bernard M. Baruch Coll., 1980. Mem. Am. Health Lawyers Assn. (chair 2001—, vice chmn. physician's orgn. com. 1997-2001, newsletter editor 1997—), N.J. Bar Assn. (chair computer related law com. 1991-93, dir. health and hosp. law sect. 1996—, vice chair 1997-98, chair elect 1998-99, chair 1999-2000), Middlesex County Bar Assn. (chair health and hosp. law com. 1995—), Med. Group Mgmt. Assn., N.J. Med. Group Mgmt. Assn., N.J. Venture Club, Omicron Delta Epsilon. Computer, General corporate, Health. Office: Wilentz Goldman & Spitzer 90 Woodbridge Ctr Dr Woodbridge NJ 07095-1146 E-mail: Schafm@Wilentz.com

SCHAFFER, DEAN AARON, lawyer; b. Lincoln, Nebr., May 17, 1962; s. Edward E. and Sally J. (Schlieter) S.; m. Nancy E. Strieter, Dec. 27, 1986; children: Samantha E., Shannon J. BA, Baylor U., 1984; JD, U. Tex., 1988. Bar: Tex. 1988, U.S. Dist. Ct. (we. dist.) Tex. 1994, U.S. Supreme Ct. 1998. Briefing atty. Tex. Ct. Appeals (3rd cir.), Austin, Tex., 1988-89; assoc. Fulbright & Jaworski L.L.P., 1989-92, participating assoc., 1993-98; chief consumer protection divsn. Office of Atty. Gen. State of Tex., 1999—. Guest lectr. Sch. Law U. Tex., Austin, 1990—; presenter on liability issues in managed care, 1995—. Contbr. articles to profl. publs. Vol. atty. Vol.

Legal Svcs. Ctrl. Tex., Austin, 1991—; bd. dirs. Interfaith Care Alliance, Austin, 1996—, Redeemer Luth. Ch., Austin, 1996—. Recipient Project award of Achievement, young lawyers divsn. ABA, Austin, 1994, Tex. Young Lawyers Assn., 1994, Cert. of merit In-Sch. Scouting Program, Austin, 1996. Fellow Austin Young Lawyers Assn. (pres., bd. dirs.); mem. Travis County Bar Assn. (mem. coun. litigation sect. 1996—, bd. dirs., mem. exec. com.), General civil litigation, Health, Insurance. Home: 7606 Long Point Dr Austin TX 78731-1218 Office: Fulbright & Jaworski LLP 600 Congress Ave Ste 2400 Austin TX 78701-3271

SCHAFFNER, JOAN ELSA, law educator; b. Mineola, N.Y., Apr. 23, 1957; d. George Alvin and Harriette Catherine (Wager) S. BSME, U. So. Calif., 1979, JD, 1990; MSME, MIT, 1981. Bar: Calif. 1990, D.C. 1992. Sr. cons., supr. Energy Mgmt. Assocs., Atlanta, 1981-86; generation analyst Ga. Power Co., 1986-87; assoc. Irell & Manella, L.A., 1990-91; law clk. to Hon. Mariana R. Pfaelzer U.S. Dist. Ct. (ctrl. dist.) Calif., 1991-92; assoc. prof. Nat. Law Ctr., George Washington U., Washington, 1992—. Convener fed. benefits subcom. L.A. working group, gender bias task force U.S. Ct. Appeals (9th cir.), 1991-92. Recipient numerous Am. Jurisprudence awards in Criminal Procedure, Bus. Orgns., and Profl. Responsibility, 1990. Mem. Soc. Am. Law Tchrs., Am. Intellectual Property Law Assn. (editor-in-chief AIPLA Quar. Jour. 1994—), Gaylaw, Animal Legal Def. Fund, Mortar Bd., Order of Laurel, Order of Coif, Phi Kappa Phi, Tau Beta Pi, Pi Tau Sigma. Avocations: percussionist, aerobics. Office: George Washington U Nat Law Ctr 2000 H St NW Washington DC 20006-4234

SCHAFRICK, FREDERICK CRAIG, lawyer; b. Sept. 20, 1948; s. Rudolph Henry and Patricia Eleanor (Zemer) Schafrick; m. Sharon Lee Halpin, May 23, 1981; children: Michael Nile, Nathaniel Henry. AB, U. Mich., 1970, JD , 1973. Bar: D.C. 1973, U.S. Ct. Appeals (D.C. cir.) 1975, U.S. Supreme Ct. 1977. Law clk. U.S. Ct. Appeals (2d cir.), N.Y.C., NY, 1973—74; assoc., then ptnr. Shea & Gardner, Washington, 1974—. Editor (adminstrv.): (law rev.) Mich. Law Rev., 1973. Mem.: ABA, Order of Coif, Phi Beta Kappa. Democrat. Presbyterian. Administrative and regulatory, Appellate, Aviation. Home: 5416 Nebraska Ave NW Washington DC 20015-1350 Office: Shea & Gardner Ste 800 1800 Massachusetts Ave NW Washington DC 20036-1872

SCHALL, ALVIN ANTHONY, federal judge; b. N.Y.C., Apr. 4, 1944; s. Gordon William and Helen (Davis) S.; m. Sharon Frances LeBlanc, Apr. 25, 1970; children: Amanda Lanford, Anthony Davis. BA, Princeton U., 1966; JD, Tulane U., 1969. Bar: N.Y. 1970, U.S. Dist. Ct. (so. and ea. dists.) N.Y. 1973, U.S. Ct. Appeals (2d cir.) 1974, D.C. 1980, U.S. Dist. Ct. D.C. 1991, U.S. Ct. Appeals (D.C. crct.) 1991, U.S. Ct. Fed. Claims 1982, U.S. Ct. Appeals (fed. crct.) 1987, U.S. Supreme Ct. 1989. Assoc. Shearman & Sterling, N.Y.C., 1969-73; asst. U.S. atty. ea. dist. N.Y. Borough of Bklyn., 1973-78, chief appeals divsn., 1977-78; trial atty. civil divsn. U.S. Dept. Justice, Washington, 1978-87, sr. trial counsel, 1986-87, asst. to atty. gen., 1988-92; ptnr. Perlman & Ptnrs., 1987-88; judge U.S. Ct. Appeals (fed. cir.), 1992—. Office: 717 Madison Pl NW Washington DC 20439-0002

SCHALLER, BARRY R. judge; BA, Yale Coll., 1960, JD, 1963. Bar: Conn. 1963, U.S. Dist. Ct. Conn. 1963, U.S. Ct. Appeals (2nd cir.) 1964, U.S. Supreme Ct. 1966. Ptnr. Bronson & Rice, Attys., New Haven, 1963-74; judge Ct. of Common Pleas, Cir. Ct., 1974-78, Superior Ct., State Conn., 1978-92, Appellate Ct., State Conn., 1992—. Counsel to Ho. of Reps., 1969; mem. bd. pardons State of Conn., 1971-74, chair, 1973-74; mem. exec. com. Conn. Planning Com. on Criminal Adminstrn., 1972-74; chair Superior Ct. Benchbook Com., 1985-92; vis. lectr. Yale Coll., 1986, 88; clin. instr. evidence and trial practice Yale Law Sch., 1989—; lectr. W.Va. Magistrates Conf., 1990, Vt. Jud. Coll., 1992, Fla. Jud. Coll., 1993, 94, 96, 99, Ohio Jud. Coll., 1999; faculty Conn. Judges Inst., 1987-90; mem. Superior Ct. Jury Instrn. Com., 1989-92; mem. exec. com. Conn. Ctr. for Jud. Edn., 1989-92; active Superior Ct. Civil Case Mgmt. Task Force; mem. jud. evidence code drafting com. Author: A Vision of American Law: Judging Law, Literature, and the Stories We Tell, 1997; contbr. articles to profl. jours. Assoc. fellow Branford Coll.; adminstrv. co-sec. Yale Class of 1960; mem. adv. com. Fair Haven Mediation Bd., 19980-82; vestry mem., tchr. Trinity Ch., Branford, St. Andrew's Ch., Madison. Recipient book award Quinnipic Law Sch., 1997; Guggenheim fellow Yale Law Sch., 1975-76, 84, 85-86. Fellow Conn. Bar Found. (charter life, fellows adv. com.); mem. ABA (CEELI adv.), Conn. Bar Assn., Hartford County Bar Assn., New Haven County Bar Assn., Conn. Judges Assn. (dir. 1990-92), Am. Judges Assn., Am. Judicature Soc., Am. Law Inst., Yale Law Sch. Assn. (exec. com. 1990-92), Am. Inns of Ct. (bencher 1989-90), Conn. Russian-Am. Rule of Law Program (founder, co-chair), Phi Delta Phi. Office: Appellate Ct State Conn 95 Washington St Hartford CT 06106-4431

SCHALLERT, EDWIN GLENN, lawyer; b. L.A., Aug. 7, 1952; s. William Joseph and Rosemarie Diane (Waggner) S. AB, Stanford U., 1974; JD, MPP, Harvard U., 1981. Bar: N.Y. 1974, U.S. Ct. Appeals (7th cir.) 1986, U.S. Ct. Appeals (2d cir.) 1989, U.S. Dist. Ct. (so. dist.) N.Y. 1975. Legis. aid to U.S. rep. Les Aspin, Washington, 1975-78; law clk. to Hon. J. Skelly Wright, 1981-82; law clk. to Hon. Thurgood Marshall, 1982-83; assoc. Debevoise & Plimpton, N.Y.C., 1983-89, ptnr., 1989—. Mem. Internat. Inst. for Strategic Studies, Coun. Fgn. Rels. (term mem. 1983-88), Phi Beta Kappa. Democrat. Avocation: tennis. Bankruptcy, General civil litigation, Securities. Office: Debevoise & Plimpton 875 3d Ave New York NY 10022-6225

SCHAR, STEPHEN L. lawyer; b. Chgo., Oct. 19, 1945; s. Sidney and Lillian (Lieberman) S.; m. Jessica S. Feit, Aug. 17, 1980; children: Scott Andrew, Elizabeth Loren. BA, U. Chgo., 1967; JD, DePaul U., 1970. Bar: Ill. 1970, U.S. Dist. Ct. (no. dist.) Ill. 1970. Assoc. Aaron, Aaron, Schimberg & Hess, Chgo., 1970-77, ptnr., 1977-80, Aaron, Schimberg, Hess, Rusnak, Deutsch & Gilbert, Chgo., 1980-84, Aaron, Schimberg, Hess & Gilbert, Chgo., 1984, Aaron, Schimberg & Hess, Chgo., 1984, D'Ancona & Pflaum, Chgo., 1985-98; mem. D'Ancona & Pflaum LLC, 1999—. Instr. estate planning Loyola U., Chgo., 1978-79. Bd. dirs. Jewish Children's Bur. Chgo., 1982—, pres., 1996-98; pres. Faulkner Condominium Assn., Chgo., 1980-82, Carl Sandburg Village Homeowners Assn., Chgo., 1981-82. Mem. Ill. Bar Assn., Chgo. Bar Assn. (pres. probate practice divsn. III 1979), Chgo. Estate Planning Coun. Estate planning, Probate, Estate taxation. Home: 2155 Tanglewood Ct Highland Park IL 60035-4231 Office: D'Ancona & Pflaum LLC 111 E Wacker Dr Ste 2800 Chicago IL 60601-4209 E-mail: sschar@dancona.com

SCHARF, ROBERT LEE, retired lawyer; b. May 13, 1920; s. Charles A. and Ethel Virginia (McNabb) S.; m. Jacqueline B. Scharf, Nov. 2, 1940; children: Bonnie Scharf Heald, Mary Ellen Pinero, Robert L. Jr. JD, Loyola U., 1948. Bar: Ill. 1949, Calif. 1972; lifetime teaching credential Calif. C.C. With FBI, 1940-73; dep. city atty. City of L.A., 1973-84; atty. Mitsui Mfrs. Bank, L.A., 1984-85; ret., 1985; former part-time emeritus pro-bono atty. Mental Health Advocacy Office, L.A. Former L.A. County arbitrator; former pro-tem judge Small Claims Ct. 2d lt. U.S. Army, 1944-46. Mem. L.A. County Bar Assn., San Fernando Valley Bar Assn., Soc. Former FBI Agts. Pension, profit-sharing, and employee benefits.

SCHATZ, WILLIAM BONSALL, lawyer; b. McKeesport, Pa., Jan. 18, 1946; s. Carl Frederick and Florence Raye (Hopkins) S.; m. Betty Hurley, Aug. 2, 1970; children: Amanda Raye, Megan Hurley, Michael Hoyt. BBA, Case Western Reserve U., 1968, JD, 1973. Bar: Ohio 1973, U.S. Dist. (no. dist.) Ohio 1973, U.S. Supreme Ct. 1977, U.S. Ct. Appeals (6th cir.) 1984. Asst. dir. law City of Cleve., 1973-77; asst. gen. counsel Northeast Ohio Regional Sewer Dist., Cleve., 1977-78, gen. counsel, 1978—. Speaker on constrn., liability ins., and environ. law. Contbr. articles on constrn., ins., and environ. law to profl. jours. Mem. ABA, Ohio Bar Assn., Assn. Met. Sewerage Agys. (chmn. ins. com. 1985-88, chmn. legal affairs com. 1988-99, bd. dirs. 1999—), Water Environ. Fedn., Cuyahoga County Law Dirs. Assn., Union Club. Club: Chagrin Valley Athletic (Chagrin Falls, Ohio). Home: 40 Park Ln Chagrin Falls OH 44022-2427 Office: NE Ohio Regional Sewer Dist 3826 Euclid Ave Cleveland OH 44115-2504 E-mail: schatzw@neorsd.org

SCHATZKI, GEORGE, law educator; b. 1933; AB, Harvard U., 1955, LLB, 1958, LLM, 1965. Prof. law u. Tex., Austin, 1965-79; dean U. Wash. Sch. Law, Seattle, 1979-82, prof., 1979-84; dean U. Conn. Sch. Law, Hartford, 1984-90, prof., 1994-2000; prof. law Ariz. State U., Tempe, 2000—. Vis. prof. law U. Pa., Phila., 1973-74, Harvard U., Cambridge, Mass., 1977-78; vis. lectr. law Yale U., New Haven, 1993, 96. Co-author: Labor Relations and Social Problems: Collective Bargaining in Private Employment, 1978, Labor and Employment Law, 1988, 2d edit., 1995. Teaching fellow Harvard U., Cambridge, Mass., 1963-65. Office: Ariz State U Coll Law PO Box 877906 Tempe AZ 85287-7906 E-mail: george.schatzki@asu.edu

SCHAUER, FREDERICK FRANKLIN, law educator; b. Newark, Jan. 15, 1946; s. John Adolph and Clara (Balayti) S.; m. Margery Clare Stone, Aug. 25, 1968 (div. June, 1982); m. Virginia Jo Wise, May 25, 1985. AB, Dartmouth Coll., 1967, MBA, 1968; JD, Harvard U., 1972. Bar: Mass. 1972, U.S. Supreme Ct. 1976. Assoc. Fine & Ambrogne, Boston, 1972-74; asst. prof. law W.Va. U., Morgantown, 1974-76, assoc. prof., 1976-78, Coll. William and Mary, Williamsburg, Va., 1978-80, Cutler prof., 1980-83; prof. of law U. Mich., Ann Arbor, 1983-90; Frank Stanton prof. of 1st Amendment Kennedy Sch. of Govt., Harvard U., Cambridge, Mass., 1990—, acad. dean, 1997—. Vis. scholar, mem. faculty law Wolfson Coll. Cambridge (Eng.) U., 1977-78; vis. prof. Law Sch., U. Chgo., 1990; vis. fellow Australian Nat. U., 1993, 98; William Morton Disting. Sr. fellow in humanities Dartmouth Coll., 1991; vis. prof. law Harvard Law Sch., 1996, 97, 2000; Ewald Disting. vis. prof. law U. Va., 1996, vis. prof. govt. Dartmouth Coll., 1997; acad. dean, Frank Stanton prof. first amendment Kennedy Sch. Govt. Harvard U, Cambridge, 1997—. Author: The Law of Obscenity, 1976, Free Speech: A Philosophical Enquiry, 1982 (ABA cert. merit 1983), Supplements to Gunther Constitutional Law, 1983-96, Playing by the Rules: A Philosophical Examination of Rule Based Decision-Making in Law and Life, 1991, The First Amendment: A Reader, 1992, 2d edit., 1995, The Philosophy of Law, 1995; editor: Legal Theory, 1995; contbr. articles to profl. jours. Mem. Atty. Gen.'s Commn. on Pornography, 1985-86. Served with Mass. Army N.G., 1970-71. NEH fellow, summer 1980, Guggenheim fellow, 2001-02. Fellow Am. Acad. Arts and Scis.; mem. Am. Philos. Assn., Am. Soc. for Polit. and Legal Philosophy (v.p. 1996-99), Assn. Am. Law Schs. (chmn. sect. constl. law 1984-86). Office: Kennedy Sch of Govt Harvard U Cambridge MA 02138 E-mail: fred_schauer@harvard.edu

SCHECHTER, DONALD ROBERT, lawyer; b. N.Y.C., Feb. 24, 1946; s. Joseph and Katherine (Beer) S.; m. Roberta Sharon Horowitz, July 3, 1968; children: Elizabeth Anne, Sarah Marilyn. BA, Queens Coll., 1967; JD, Bklyn Law Sch., 1971. Asst. dist. atty. Queens County, Kew Gardens, N.Y., 1971-73; asst. atty. gen. organized crime task force City of N.Y., 1973-74; sole practice Forest Hills, N.Y., 1974—. Legal counsel Centro Civico Colombiano, Jackson Heights, N.Y., 1978—, Fedn. of Merchants and Profls. of Queens, Spanish Orgn., Jackson Heights, 1978—; hearing officer Family Ct., Queens County, Jamaica, N.Y., 1977; consumer counsel Civil Ct., Queens County, 1980. Mem. ABA, N.Y. State Bar Assn., Queens County Bar Assn. (chmn. lawyer placement), Nassau County Bar Assn., Audobon Soc., Sierra Club. Democrat. Jewish. Clubs: Glass Soc. Corvette, N.Y. Mets Dream Week. Lodge: KP. Avocations: antique automobiles, baseball, history, antiques. Criminal, Entertainment, General practice. Office: Ste 1030 80-02 Kew Gardens Rd Kew Gardens NY 11415-3600

SCHEER, JOEL MARTIN, lawyer; b. Bklyn., Dec. 6, 1950; s. Jack H. and Sheila (Gams) S.; m. Linda M. Miller, Aug. 3, 1975; children: Jennie Shayne, Rachel Jayne, Zachary Judd. BA cum laude, Bklyn. Coll., 1972; JD with distinction, Hofstra U., 1975. Bar: Pa. 1975, U.S. Dist. Ct. (ea. dist.) Pa. 1976, U.S. Ct. Appeals (3d cir.) 1986, U.S. Supreme Ct. 1985. Law clk. to judge, Easton, Pa., 1975-76; sole practice, 1976-77; assoc. Fishbone and Refowich, 1977-80; v.p., attu. Fishbone & Scheer, 1980—. Bd. dirs. Lehigh Valley Legal Svcs., Allentown, Pa., 1979-83, Easton Heritage Alliance, 1995—; treas. Easton Area Neighborhood Ctr., 1980-81; pres. Historic Easton, Inc., 1983-85; v.p. B'nai Abraham Synagogue, Easton, 1983-85, pres., 1986-88; mem. exec. bd. Easton Area Econ. Devel. Corp., 1991-92. Mem. Pa. Bar Assn. (ho. of dels. 1999-2000), Northampton County Bar Assn. (bd. govs. 1990-2000, v.p. 1997, pres. 1999), Two Rivers Area C. of C. (v.p. Easton 1989-91, bd. dirs. 1989—). Democrat. Contracts commercial, General practice, Real property. Home: 179 Pennsylvania Ave Easton PA 18042 Office: Fishbone & Scheer 6 S 3rd St Ste 502 Easton PA 18042-4574

SCHEER, MARK JEFFREY, lawyer; b. N.Y.C., Jan. 6, 1962; s. Morton Herbert and Joan Sylvia (Weiss) S.; m. Sheryl Lynn Weinberg, Oct. 24, 1987; children: Matthew Jordan, Danielle Nicole, Lindsay Gayle. BS in Acctg., U. Fla., 1983, M in Acctg., 1984, JD, 1987. Bar: Fla. 1987, U.S. Tax Ct. 1988, U.S. Dist. Ct. (so. dist.) Fla. 1991. Ptnr. Gunster, Yoakley, & Stewart, P.A., Miami, Fla., 1987—. Mem. ABA, AICPA, Fla. Bar Assn., Fla. Isnt. CPAs. Jewish. Bankruptcy, Estate planning, Corporate taxation. Office: 2 S Biscayne Blvd Miami FL 33131-1806 E-mail: mscheer@gunster.com

SCHEIBER, HARRY N. law educator; b. 1935; BA, Columbia U., 1955; MA, Cornell U., 1957, PhD, 1961; MA (hon.), Dartmouth Coll., 1965; D.Jur.Hon., Uppsala U., Sweden, 1998. Instr. to assoc. prof. history Dartmouth Coll., 1960-68, prof., 1968-71; prof. Am. history U. Calif., San Diego, 1971-80; prof. law Boalt Hall, U. Calif., Berkeley, 1980—. Chmn. jurisprudence and social policy program, 1982-84, 90-93, assoc. dean, 1990-93, 96-99; The Stefan Riesenfeld prof., 1991—; vice chair Univ. Academic Senate, 1993-94, chair 1994-95; Fulbright disting. sr. lectr., Australia, 1983, marine affairs coord. Calif. Sea Grant Coll. Program, 1989-2000; vis. rsch. prof. Law Inst. U. Uppsala, Sweden, 1995, hon. prof. DiTella U., Buenos Aires, 1999; cons. Calif. Jud. Coun., 1992-93; acting dir. Ctr. for Study of Law and Soc., 1999—. Co-author, co-author((with L. Friedman)): American Law and the Constitutional Order, 1978co-author: The State and Freedom of Contract, 1998, Law of the Sea: The Common Heritage and Emerging Challenges , 2000, Inter-Allied Conflicts and Ocean Law (1945-1953), 2001, numerous others; editor: Yearbook of the California Supreme Court Historical Society, 1994—;contbr. articles to law revs. and social sci.jours. Chmn. Littleton Griswold Prize Legal History, 1985-88; pres. N.H. Civil Liberties Union, 1969-70; chmn. Project '87 Task Force on Pub. Programs, Washington, 1982-85; dir. Berkeley Seminar on Federalism, 1986-95; cons. judiciary study U.S. Adv. Commn. Intergovernmental Rels., 1985-88; dir. NEH Inst. on Constitutionalism, U. Calif., Berkeley, 1986-87, 88-91. Recipient Sea Grant Colls. award, 1981-83, 84-85, 86—; fellow Ctr. Advanced Study in Behavioral Scis., Stanford Calif., 1967, 71; Guggenheim fellow, 1971, 88; Rockefeller Found. humanities fellow, 1979, NEH fellow, 1985-86; F grantee 1979, 80, 88-89. Fellow U. Calif. Humanities Rsch. Inst., Am. Soc. for Legal History (hon.), Japan Soc. for Promotion of Sci.; mem. Am. Hist. Assn., Orgn. Am. Historians, Agrl. History Soc. (pres. 1978), Econ. History Assn. (trustee 1978-80), Law and Soc. Assn. (trustee 1979-81, 96-99), Nat. Assessment History and Citizenship Edn. (chmn. nat. acad. bd. 1986-87), Marine Affairs and Policy Assn. (bd. dirs. 1991-96), Ocean Governance Study Group (steering com. 1991—), Internat. Coun. Environ. Law, Calif. Supreme Ct. Hist. Soc. (bd. dirs. 1993—, v.p. 1997-98). Office: U Calif Berkeley Law Sch Boalt Hall Berkeley CA 94720-2150 E-mail: scheiber@law.berkeley.edu

SCHEICH, JOHN F. lawyer; b. Bklyn., Aug. 6, 1942; s. Frank A. and Dorothy (O'Hara) S. BA, St. John's U., N.Y.C., 1963, JD, 1966; postgrad., John Marshall Law Sch., Chgo., 1968. Bar: N.Y. 1967, U.S. Ct. Internat. Trade Admission 1969, U.S. Dist. Ct. (ea. and so. dists.) N.Y. 1971, U.S. Ct. Appeals (2nd cir.) 1971, U.S. Supreme Ct. 1975, Pa. 1980. Spl. agt. FBI, U.S. Dept. Justice, Washington, 1966-69; asst. dist. atty. Queens County, Kew Gardens, N.Y., 1969-72; pvt. law practice, Richmond Hill, 1970-76, 79-91; ptnr. Raia & Scheich, P.C., 1976-79; sr. ptnr. Scheich & Goldsmith, P.C., Richmond Hill, Hicksville, N.Y., 1991-95, Scheich, Goldsmith & Dreishpoon, P.C, Richmond Hill, Hicksville, 1996—; mortgage settlement atty. GMAC, N.Y., 1996—. Lectr. estate planning Nat. Bus. Inst., 1994; mem. assigned counsel panel for indigent defendants in major felony and murder cases sth and 11th jud. dists. N.Y. State Supreme Ct., Queens County, 1972—94; lectr. Lawyers in the Classroom, 1979—91; chmn. arbitration panel Civil Ct. City of N.Y., 1981—90; bd. dirs. Ra-Li Brokerage Corp., v.p., 1975—; mem. adv. bd. 1st Am. Title Ins. Co. Am., 1995—; mortgage settlement atty. Gen. Motors Acceptance Corp. N.Y. State, 1996—; trial judge student competition St. John's U. Sch. Law Civil Trial Inst. Student Competition, 0199—. Editor: Conashaugh Courier, 1989-92; mem. editorial bd., 1988-92; contbg. columnist, 1981-89. Mem. Com. for Beautification of East Norwich, Nassau County, L.I., N.Y., 1983—, bd. dirs., 1993-96, pres. 1996—; mem. Holy Name Soc. of Our Lady of Perpetual Help Ch., 1963—, sec., 1965-67, v.p., 1969-71, pres., 1971-73; bd. dirs. Conashaugh Lakes Cmty. Assn., Milford, Pa., 1981-90, organizing mem. Conashaugh Lakes Lot Owners interim com., 1977-81, sec. 1981-82, v.p. 1982-84, pres. 1984-86, past pres. 1986-88; mem. St. Edward the Confessor Sch. Bd., Syosset, N.Y., 1986-90; parish coun. Our Lady of Perpetual Help Roman Cath. Ch., 1976-82, pres. 1978-80, fin. com., adv. to pastor, 1970-82, chmn. fin. com., 1979-82; bd. dirs. Northslope II Homeowners Assn., Shawnee-on-Delaware, Pa., 1988-90, 92-94, 2000—, East Norwich Civic Assn., 1996—; mem. East Norwich Rep. Club, 1982—, bd. dirs. 1984-87, 93—, v.p. 1987-89, pres. 1989-93; nat. trust and estate assoc. Meml. Sloane Kettering Cancer Ctr., N.Y.C., 1994—; active Internat. Wine Ctr., 1985-96, St. Edward the Confessor Ch., Syosset, 1982—, St. Vincent Ch., Dingman Hills, Pa., 1977—, St. Dominic's Ch., Oyster Bay, N.Y., 1982— (apptd. pastor's adv. coun. on estate planning 1998, 99, 00), mem. Legacy Soc. 1998, 99, 00), Lincoln Ctr. Performing Arts, Inc., 1985—, Nat. Rep. Senatorial Com., 1988—, Bravo Soc., 1994—, Concern for Dying, 1984—, Sea Cliff Chamber Players, 1992-99; mem. Nassau County Rep. Com., Town of Oyster Bay, 1993—, St. John Vianney Roman Cath. Ch., St. Petersburg Beach, Fla., 1994—, Non-Resident Fellow, James Beard Found., NYC, 1995—, Performing Arts Ctr. Pinellas County, St. Petersburg, 1994—, Rep. Nat. Senate Adv. Coun., 1997—, Rep. Nat. Com. Chmn.'s Honor Roll, 1997 (cert. Achievement 1998), Pact, Inc. Ruth Eckerd Hall-Richard B. Baumgardner Ctr. for Performing Arts, Clearwater, Fla., 1995—; chmn. tri-centennial celebration com. Village of East Norwich, 1996-97; mem. Fransiscan Ctr. Guild, Tampa, Fla., 1996—, Tilles Ctr. Performing Arts, Inc., Long Island U., Brookville, N.Y., 1997—, adv. coun. estate planning St. Dominic's Ch., 1998, St. Dominic's Legacy Soc., 1998; bd. dirs. Northslope II Homeowners Assn., Shawnee-on-Del., Pa., 2000—; mem. Friends of the Arts, Locust Valley, L.I., N.Y., 1985—. Recipient J. Edgar Hoover award, 1967, award of appreciation, Civil Trial Inst., St. John's U. Sch. of Law, 1991, 95, Disting. Svc. award, 1992, cert. of appreciatin Conashaugh Lakes Cmty. Assn., 1990, Dist. Svc. award Kiwanis Club, 1992, Cert. of Merit for Disting. Svc. award Nassau County Exec. Hon. Thomas Gulotta, 1989, Presdl. Order of Merit award Pres. George Bush, 1991, Order of Merit award Nat. Rep. Senatorial Com., 1994, Cert. Achievement, Rep. Nat. Com., 1998; named one of Best Trial Lawyers in the U.S., Town and Country Mag., 1985; non-resident fellow James Beard Found., N.Y.C., 1995—. Mem. ABA (cert. of appreciation Am. Bar Endowment 1992), ATLA, Pa. State Bar Assn., N.Y. State Bar Assn., Queens County Bar Assn., Nassau County Bar Assn., N.Y. State Trial Lawyers Assn., Ciminal Cts. Bar Assn., Internat. Platform Assn., John Marshall Lawyers Assn. (bd. dirs. 1992—, pres. 1992-97, treas. 1997—), Soc. Former Spl. Agts. of FBI (nat. chpt., L.I. chpt.), N.Y. State Assn. Criminal Def. Lawyers, LeGal Law Assn. (bd. dirs. 2001—, bd. dirs. found. 1995-98, 2001—), St. John's Coll. Alumni Assn., Asst. Dist. Attys. Assn. Queens County, St. John's U. Sch. of Law Alumni Assn., St. John's Prep. Sch. Alumni Assn., Friends of the Arts of Nassau County, Inc., Cath. Lawyers Guild of Queens County, N.Y., KC, Brookhaven Wine Lovers Soc., East Norwich Civic Assn., Sun Island Assn. (bd. dirs. 2001—), Phi Alpha Delta. Avocation: collecting fine wines. General practice, Personal injury, Estate planning. Home: 170 Sugar Toms Ln East Norwich NY 11732-1153 Office: Scheich Goldsmith & Dreishpoon PC 103-42 Lefferts Blvd South Richmond Hill NY 11419-2012 also: 109 Newbridge Rd Hicksville NY 11801-3908 also: 210 Conashaugh Trl Box 4042 Conashaugh Lakes Milford PA 18337

SCHEIDEGGER, KENT STEPHEN, lawyer; b. Arlington, Va., Dec. 31, 1953; s. Paul Francis and Elizabeth (Walker) S.; m. Lada Phasook, April 11, 1981. BS with honors, N.Mex. State U., 1976; JD with distinction, McGeorge Sch. Law, Sacramento, 1982. Bar: Calif. 1982, U.S. Ct. Appeals (9th cir.) 1985, U.S. Supreme Ct., 1987. Commd. nuclear research officer USAF, Sacramento, 1976, advanced through grades to capt., 1982, resigned, 1982; assoc. Neumiller & Beardslee, Stockton, Calif., 1983-84; gen. counsel Calif. Cooler Co., 1984-86; legal dir. Criminal Justice Legal Found., Sacramento, 1986—. Recipient William J. Schafer award for excellence in capital litigation Assn. Govt. Attys. in Capital Litigation. Mem. Federalist Soc. (bd. mem. Sacramento chpt., chmn.-elect criminal law practice group), McGeorge Alumni Assn. (Amicus lex scholar 1981), Order of the Coif. Republican. Office: Criminal Justice Legal Found 2131 L St Sacramento CA 95816-4924

SCHEIGE, STEVEN SHELDON, lawyer; b. N.Y.C., Mar. 15, 1950; s. Manfred Herman and Liba (Miller) S.; m. Fortuna Faye Gorelick, July 8, 1973; children: Robert, Susan-Lisa. BA, Rutgers U., 1972; JD, Georgetown U., 1975. Bar: Md. 1975. From atty.-advisor to asst. chief counsel Occupl. Safety and Health Rev. Commn., Washington, 1975-85, sr. atty., 1985-2001, team leader, 2001—. Spl. project coord. PTA, Montgomery County, Md., 1984; bd. dirs. Temple Israel Congregation, 1994-96, v.p., 1996-97; v.p. Tikvet Israel Congregation, 1997—. Mem. ABA, Md. State Bar Assn., Phi Beta Kappa. Jewish. Office: Occupational Safety and Health Rev Commn 1120 20th St NW Ste 9 Washington DC 20036-3411

SCHEIMAN, EUGENE R. lawyer; b. Bklyn., July 15, 1943; BA, L.I. U., 1966; JD cum laude, Bklyn. Law Sch., 1969. Bar: N.Y. 1970, U.S. Dist. Ct. (so. and ea. dists.) N.Y. 1971, U.S. Ct. Appeals (1st cir.) 1972, U.S. Ct. Appeals (5th cir.) 1973, U.S. Ct. Appeals (4th cir.) 1974, U.S. Supreme Ct. 1976, U.S. Ct. Appeals (2nd cir.) 1977, U.S. Ct. Appeals (fed. cir.), U.S. Ct. Appeals (11th cir.) 1989, U.S. Ct. Appeals (3rd cir.) 1990. Shareholder Buchanan Ingersoll, N.Y.C. Rsch. editor Bklyn. Law Rev., 1968, editor-in-chief, 1969. Mem. ABA (sect. on individual rights and responsibilities, franchise forum), ATLA, N.Y. State Bar Assn., Assn. Bar. City of N.Y. (com. on profl. discipline), Philonomic Honor Soc. Construction, Franchising, Libel. Office: Buchanan Ingersoll PC 140 Broadway New York NY 10005 E-mail: scheimaner@bipc.com

SCHEINHOLTZ, LEONARD LOUIS, lawyer; b. Pitts., June 2, 1927; s. Bernard A. and Marie (Getzel) S.; m. Joan R. Libenson, Aug. 16, 1953; children: Stuart, Nancy, Barry. BA, U. Pa., 1948, MA, 1949; LLB, Columbia U., 1953. Bar: Pa. 1954, U.S. Ct. Appeals (3d cir.) 1959, U.S. Ct. Appeals (6th cir.) 1968, U.S. Supreme Ct. 1972, U.S. Ct. Appeals (4th cir.) 1973, U.S. Ct. Appeals (5th cir.) 1981, U.S. Ct. Appeals (11th cir.) 1991, U.S. Ct. Appeals (2d cir.) 1993. Assoc. Reed, Smith, Shaw & McClay, Pitts., 1953-62, spl. ptnr., 1962-64, gen. ptnr., 1964-97, head labor dept., 1980-86, of counsel, 1997—. Dir. Am. Arbitration Assn., N.Y.C., 1980-96. Author: Exemption Under the Anti-Trust Laws for Joint Employer Activity, 1982, The Arbitrator as Judge and Jury: Another Look at Statutory Law in Arbitration, 1985. Vice chmn. Pa. AAA Fedn., Harrisburg, 1982-85 ; chmn. W. Pa. AAA Motor Club, 1979-82; trustee Montefiore Hosp., Pitts., 1976-79, Nat. Aviary, 1999—; bd. dirs. United Jewish Fedn. Pitts., 1997-2000. Served with USN, 1945-46. Mem. ABA, Pa. Bar Assn., Allegheny County Bar Assn. Republican. Jewish. Labor, Pension, profit-sharing, and employee benefits. Home: 746 Pinoak Rd Pittsburgh PA 15243-1153 Office: Reed Smith Shaw & McClay Mellon Sq 435 6th Ave Pittsburgh PA 15219-1886

SCHEINKMAN, ALAN DAVID, lawyer, legal educator; b. Newark, May 1, 1950; s. Henry R. and Gertrude (Einhorn) S.; m. Deborah Steinberg, July 1, 1978; children: Michael, Rebecca. BA, George Washington U., 1972; JD, St. John's U., Jamaica, N.Y., 1975. Bar: N.Y. 1976, U.S. Dist. Ct. (so. and ea. dists.) N.Y. 1977, U.S. Ct. of Appeals (2d cir.), U.S. Supreme Ct. 1990. Law clk. N.Y. Ct. Appeals, Albany, 1975-77; assoc. Marshall, Bratter, Greene, Allison & Tucker, N.Y.C., 1977-79, Golenbock & Barell, N.Y.C., 1979-82; assoc. prof. law St. John's U., Jamaica, 1983-90; atty. Scheinkman, Fredman & Kosan, LLP, White Plains, N.Y., 1993-97; county atty. Westchester County, 1998-2000; atty. Epstein, Becker & Green, P.C., N.Y.C., 2001—. Assoc. counsel N.Y. State Temporary Commn. to Recodify Family Ct. Act, Albany, 1982; mem. jud. hearing officer adv. com. 9th Jud. Dist., 1981-97; lectr. N.Y. State Ann. Jud. Seminar; adj. prof. Law Sch., Pace U., Rutgers U., St. John's U. Author: Practice Commentaries to McKinney's N.Y. Domestic Rels. Law, 1981—; reporter N.Y. Pattern Jury Instrns.; directing editor McKinney's Texts and Forms. Mem. ABA, N.Y. State Bar Assn. (exec. dir. adminstrn. adjudication task force, com. on appellate ct.). State civil litigation, Family and matrimonial. Home: 26 Chestnut Ridge Rd Armonk NY 10504-3001 Office: Epstein Becker & Green PC 250 Park Ave New York NY 10177 E-mail: ascheinkman@ebglaw.com

SCHELER, BRAD ERIC, lawyer; b. Bklyn., Oct. 11, 1953; s. Bernard and Rita Regina (Miller) S.; m. Amy Ruth Frolick, Mar. 30, 1980; children: Ali M., Maddie H., Zoey B. BA with high honors, Lehigh U., 1974; JD, Hofstra U., 1977. Bar: N.Y. 1978, U.S. Dist. Ct. (so. and ea. dists.) N.Y. 1978. Assoc. Weil, Gotshal & Manges, N.Y.C., 1977-81; sr. ptnr., chmn. bankruptcy and restructuring practice Fried, Frank, Harris, Shriver & Jacobson, 1981—. Rsch. editor Hofstra U. Law Rev., 1975-77. Treas., bus. mgr. Trustees of Gramercy Park, N.Y.C., 1979-87. Fellow Am. Coll. Bankruptcy; mem. ABA (bus. bankruptcy com. corp. banking and bus. law sect., creditors' rights com. litig. sect.), N.Y. State Bar Assn., Assn. Bar City of N.Y. (com. on bankruptcy and corp. reorgn. 1991-94), Sigma Alpha Mu (v.p. 1973). Jewish. Bankruptcy, Contracts commercial, Finance. Home: 94 Larchmont Ave Larchmont NY 10538-3723 Office: Fried Frank Harris 1 New York Plz Fl 23 New York NY 10004-1901 E-mail: Schelbr@ffhsj.com

SCHELLER, ARTHUR MARTIN, JR. law educator; b. Berlin, Wis., Oct. 7, 1927; s. Arthur M. and Ruth M. (Keehn) S.; m. Ann M. Palisin, June 19, 1954; children— Mary, Helen, Arthur, Stephen, Suzanne, Fritz, John, Raissa. B.A., St. Norbert Coll., 1949; J.D., Marquette U., 1954. Bar: Wis. 1954; U.S. Dist. Ct. (ea. dist.) Wis., U.S. Dist. Ct. (no. dist.) Ill. 1960, U.S. Tax Ct. 1983, U.S. Ct. Appeals (7th cir.) 1967. Asst. prof. Loyola U., Chgo., 1958-60; prof. DePaul U., Chgo., 1960-75; prof. John Marshall Law Sch., Chgo., 1975— ; cons. N.E. Ill. Planning Commn., Chgo., 1964-66, Corp. Engrs., 1962-63; lectr. in field, 1979-83. Editor: (with others) Law Manual for Community Organizers, 1970-88. Contbr. articles to profl. publs. Nat. v.p. Cath. Civil Rights League, Milw., 1975-79. Served with USN, 1945-46. Recipient numerous Outstanding Teacher awards. Mem. Wis. Bar Assn., Ill. Bar Assn. Roman Catholic. Club: Union League (Chgo.). Home: 300 Meacham Ave Park Ridge IL 60068-3465 Office: John Marshall Law Sch 315 S Plymouth Ct Chicago IL 60604-3968

SCHEMAN, L. RONALD, lawyer, professional society administrator; b. Aug. 9, 1931; s. Mac and Eleanor (Minkowitz) S.; m. Lynn Cutler; children from a previous marriage: Ann, Corinne, Jennifer, Daniel. BA with distinction cum laude, Dartmouth Coll., 1953; JD, Yale U., 1956. Bar: N.Y., 1956, D.C., 1979. Pvt. practice law, Hartford, Conn., 1957, N.Y.C., 1958-59; fellow Inter-Am. Cultural Conv., Brazil, 1959-61; atty. dept. legal affairs OAS, Washington, 1961-64, planning officer, 1968-70, asst. sec. gen. for mgmt., 1975-84; exec. dir. Pan Am. Devel. Found., 1964-68; pres. Porter Internat. Co., Washington, 1970-75; ptnr. Coudert Bros., 1984-85; exec. dir. Ctr. Advanced Studies of the Americas, 1985-87; ptnr. Kaplan, Russin and Vecchi, 1987-90, Heller, Rosenblatt and Scheman, 1990-93; U.S. exec. dir. Inter-Am. Devel. Bank, Washington, 1993-98; chmn. Internat. Fin. Group, Greenberg, Traurig, 1998-2000; secretariat Inter-Am. Commn. on Human Rights, 1961-64; dir. gen. Inter-Am. Agy. for Cooperation and Devel., 2000—. V.p. fin. Robert R. Nathan Assocs., 1974-75; pub. Soviet Bus. and Trade, 1973-75; dir. Vision mag., 1973-74; assoc. dir. Coun. of Ams., 1976—; adj. prof. internat. orgn. George Washington U., 1979-83. Author: Foundations of Freedom, 1966, The Inter-American Dilemma, 1988, The Alliance for Progress, A Retrospective, 1989; bd. editors Mng. Internat. Devel. quar., 1984-86; contbr. articles on internat. orgn. and inter-Am. affairs to profl. jours. Trustee Inter-Am. Bar Found., 1967-74; trustee Pan Am. Devel. Found., 1987-94, pres., 1976-83; chmn. Mus. of Americas Found., 1998—, Federal City Coun., 1998—; pres. Uruguay—U.S. C. of C., 1999-2000; mem. exec. com. Am. Jewish Com. of Washington; bd. dirs. East-West Trade Coun., 1974-75, Ctr. for Advanced Studies of the Ams., 1984-87. Decorated Order Bernardo O'Higgins (Chile), 1967, Russian Fedn., 1992. Mem. Washington Fgn. Law Soc. (bd. govs. 1965-67, pres. 1968), Am. Fgn. Law Assn. (v.p. 1971), Cosmos Club, Phi Beta Kappa. Public international, International finance, International corporate. Home: Apt W 1027 3003 Van Ness St NW Washington DC 20008-4807 Office: Inter-Am Agy for Cooperation and Devel 1889 F St NW Washington DC 20006-4413

SCHENDEL, WILLIAM BURNETT, lawyer; b. 1948; BA, Swarthmore Coll., 1970; JD, Boston U., 1974. Bar: Alaska 1976, U.S. Dist Ct. Alaska (9th cir.), U.S. Supreme Ct. Ptnr. Schendel & Callahan, Fairbanks, Alaska, 1981—. Pres. Alaska Bar Assn. Mem. ABA, Alaska Bar Assn. (pres. 1998-99). Civil rights, Labor. Office: Schendel & Callahan 613 Cushman St Ste 200 Fairbanks AK 99701-4655

SCHENKLER, BERNARD, lawyer; b. Trani, Italy, Aug. 25, 1948; s. Wolf and Nettie Schenkler; m. Ellen Haberman, Sept. 25, 1977; children: Alan, Sarah. BA, U. Pa., 1970; JD, Columbia U., 1973; diploma in mcpl. law, Rutgers U., 1991. Bar: N.Y. 1974, N.J. 1977, D.C. 1979, U.S. Ct. Appeals (2d cir.) 1975, U.S. Dist. Ct. (so. and ea. dists.) N.Y. 1975, U.S. Tax Ct. 1978, U.S. Ct. Mil. Appeals 1978, U.S. Ct. Appeals (3rd cir.), U.S. Dist. Ct. (no. and we. dists.) N.Y. 1980, U.S. Ct. Claims 1985, U.S. Ct. Internat. Trade 1985, U.S. Ct. Appeals (fed. cir.) 1990, U.S. Ct. Appeals (D.C. cir.) 1990, U.S. Ct. Appeals (4th cir.) 1991, U.S. Ct. Vets. Appeals 1990, U.S. Supreme Ct. 1980. Atty bus. law unit N.Y.C. Human Resources Adminstrn., 1973-76, exec. asst. to gen. counsel, 1977; assoc. Ravin, Sarasohn, Cook, Baumgarten & Fisch, West Orange, N.J., 1978-85; ptnr. Ravin, Sarasohn, Cook, Baumgarten, Fisch & Rosen, Roseland, 1986-2000; of counsel Orloff, Lowenbach, Stifelman & Siegal, P.A., 2000—. Author: Bankruptcy Aspects of Municipal Real Estate Taxation, 1991, Death and Bankruptcy, How the Probate and Bankruptcy Processes Interact, 1994, Close Encounters With the Bankruptcy Code, 1997. Mem. Randolph Twp. (N.J.) Bd. of Ethics, 1978-80. Mem. ABA, N.Y. State Bar Assn., N.J. State Bar Assn., Essex County Bar Assn., D.C. Bar. Jewish. Club: White Meadow Temple Men's Club (Rockaway, N.J.). Avocations: karate (black belt), golf, astronomy. Bankruptcy, State civil litigation, Contracts commercial. Office: Orloff Lowenbach Stifelman & Siegal PA 101 Eisenhower Pkwy Ste 29 Roseland NJ 07068-1082 E-mail: bs@olss.com

SCHER, HOWARD DENNIS, lawyer; b. Ft. Monmouth, N.J., Apr. 23, 1945; s. George Scher and Rita (Eitches) Zar; children: Seth Micah, Eli David. BA, Brandeis U., 1967; JD, Rutgers U., 1971. Bar: Pa. 1971, U.S. Dist. Ct. (ea. dist.) Pa. 1971, U.S. Ct. Appeals (3rd cir.) 1971, U.S. Supreme Ct. 1975. Asst. city solicitor City of Phila., 1971-73; assoc. Goodis, Greenfield, Henry & Edelstein, Phila., 1973-77, Montgomery, McCracken, Walker & Rhoads, Phila., 1977-80, ptnr., 1980-2001; shareholder Buchanan Ingersoll P.C., 2001—. Trustee Fedn. of Jewish Agys. of Greater Phila., 1994—; dir. Akiba Hebrew Acad., Merion, Pa., 1996-98; mem. pres.'s coun. Brandeis U.; pres. Jewish Employment and Vocat. Svcs., 1998—; exec. com. Com. of Seventy. Fellow Am. Coll. Trial Lawyers, Internat. Acad. Trial Lawyers; mem. ABA, Pa. Bar Assn., Phila. Bar Assn., Brandeis U. Alumni Assn. (v.p. 1983-87). Federal civil litigation, State civil litigation. Home: 2222 Locust St Philadelphia PA 19103-5511 Office: Buchanan Ingersoll PC 11 Penn Ctr Ste 14th Fl 1835 Market St Philadelphia PA 19103 Fax: 215-665-8760. E-mail: scherhd@bipc.com

SCHER, IRVING, lawyer; b. N.Y.C., July 22, 1933; s. Charles and Tillie (Ballenberg) S.; m. Amy Lynn Katz, June 8, 1985; 1 child, Sara Katz-Scher. BA, City Coll. N.Y., 1955; JD, Columbia U., 1962. Bar: N.Y. 1963. Assoc. Weil, Gotshal & Manges, N.Y.C., 1962-69, ptnr., 1969—. Adj. prof. NYU Sch. Law, 1972—; co-chmn. ann. anti-trust law inst. Practicing Law Inst., N.Y.C., 1976—; adv. bd. Antitrust and Trade Regulation Reports, 1980—. Editor Columbia Law Rev., 1960-61, revs. editor, 1961-62; editor, co-author: Antitrust Advisor, 4th edit., 1995; contbr. articles to profl. jours. Served as lt. USNR, 1955-59. Recipient Harlan Fiske Stone scholarship Columbia Law Sch., 1960-62, Nat. Scholarship award Columbia Law Sch., 1961-62, Gluck scholarship Columbia Law Sch., 1960-61. Mem. ABA (chmn. antitrust law section 1988-89), N.Y. State Bar Assn. (chmn. antitrust law section 1980-81). Office: Weil Gotshal & Manges 767 5th Ave Fl Concl New York NY 10153-0119 E-mail: Irving.scher@weil.com

SCHER, STANLEY JULES, lawyer; b. Bklyn., Dec. 19, 1929; s. Leo A. and Frances (Goldman) S.; m. Susan Goldman, June 16, 1957; children— William Goldman, Peter Lawrence, Alison Hope. LL.B., Bklyn. Law Sch., 1952. Bar: N.Y. 1954, U.S. Dist. Ct. (so. and ea. dists.) N.Y. 1960, U.S. Supreme Ct. 1970. Ptnr. Tullman, Fisher & Scher, N.Y.C., 1954-62; founder, sr. ptnr. Garbarini & Scher, N.Y.C., 1962— ; med.-legal lectr. physicians, hosps., health-related facilities, 1970— ; mem. faculty N.Y. State Trial Lawyers Assn., 1975— ; lectr. Nassau Acad. Law, 1984, N.Y. State Bar Assn., 1983. Pres. Baker Hill Civic Assn., Great Neck, N.Y., past zone leader Great Neck North Dem. Com., mem. Nat. CIC Orgn., Great Neck. Served with U.S. Army, 1952-54. Mem. ABA, Assn. Trial Lawyers Am., Soc. Med. Jurisprudence, N.Y. State Bar Assn., N.Y. County Lawyers Assn., Queens County Bar Assn., Nassau County Bar Assn. Jewish. Club: Temple Israel Couples (Great Neck, N.Y.) (past pres.). Lodge: B'nai B'rith. Health, Insurance, Personal injury. Home: 59 Essex Rd Great Neck NY 11023-1535 Office: Garbarini & Scher PC Rm 3500 1114 Avenue Of The Americas New York NY 10036-7790

SCHERF, JOHN GEORGE, IV, lawyer; b. Tuscaloosa, Ala., Oct. 12, 1962; s. John G. III and Roberta Cannon (Timmons) S.; m. Lorie Lankford, Feb. 12, 1994; 1 child, Austin Tyler. AA, Okaloosa Walton Jr. Coll., Niceville, Fla., 1983; BA in Psychology, U. West Fla., 1987; JD, Samford U., 1991. Bar: Ala. 1992, U.S. Dist. Ct. (no. dist.) Ala. 1994, U.S. Dist. Ct. (mid. dist.) Ala. 1997, U.S. Dist. Ct. (so. dist.) Ala., 1999. Clk., assoc. Taylor & Taylor, Birmingham, Ala., 1992-93; assoc. Frank S. Buck, P.C., 1993-95; pvt. practice, 1995—. Mem. ATLA, Ala. Bar Assn., Ala. Trial Lawyers Assn., Birmingham Bar Assn. Democrat. Methodist. General civil litigation, Insurance, Personal injury. Home: 1324 Springs Ave Birmingham AL 35242-4862 Office: 1812 28th Ave S # B Birmingham AL 35209-2602 E-mail: smurflaw@aol.com

SCHERLINE, JAY ALAN, lawyer; b. N.Y.C., July 26, 1951; s. Irving Harvey and Shirley (Dauber) S.; m. Lorrie Lipschitz, July 1, 1979. B.S., U. Tampa, 1973; J.D., Vt. Law Sch., 1976. Bar: Pa. 1976, N.J. 1977. Assoc. Rubin & Jaffe, Phila., 1976-77; sole practice, Old Bridge, N.J., 1977-80; ptnr. Scherline & Nowak, Allentown, Pa., 1980— ; prof. Allentown Bus. Sch., 1981-82; lectr. Of counsel Lehigh Valley Polit. Action Com., Allentown, 1983— . Recipient Merit Achievement award Fla. Mental Health Soc., 1973. Mem. ABA, N.J. Bar Assn., Pa. Law Enforcement Offices (assoc.), Lehigh County Bar Assn., Phi Alpha Delta, Delta Sigma Pi. Democrat. Club: ADL (Allentown) (bd dirs.). Lodges: Masons, B'nai B'rith (v.p. 1983-84). General corporate, Insurance, Personal injury. Home: 2824 Rolling Green Pl Macungie PA 18062-1417 Office: 512 W Walnut St Allentown PA 18101-2311 also: 18 Throckmorton Ct Old Bridge NJ 08857-2549

SCHIAVO, PASCO LOUIS, lawyer; b. Hazleton, Pa., June 21, 1937; s. Louis and Josephine (Cortese) S. BA, Lafayette Coll., 1958; JD, U. Pa., 1962. Bar: Pa. 1962, U.S. Dist. Ct. (mid. dist.) Pa. 1965, U.S. Ct. Appeals (3d cir.) 1972, U.S. Supreme Ct. 1970. Assoc. Laputka, Bayless, Ecker & Cohn, Hazleton, 1963-65; asst. dist. atty. Luzerne County, Wilkes-Berre, Pa., 1963-65; pvt. practice Hazleton, 1965—. Mem. disciplinary bd. Supreme Ct. Pa., Harrisburg, 1977-83. Contbr. articles to profl. jours. Pres. Luzerne County Commn. Econ. Opportunity, Wilkes-Barre, 1966-68. Mem. ABA, ATLA, Pa. Bar Assn., Luzerne County Bar Assn., Pa. Trial Lawyers Assn., Am. Judicature Soc., Nat. Bd. Trial Advocacy (diplomate, cert. civil trial advocate). State civil litigation, General practice, Personal injury. Office: 199 N Church St Hazleton PA 18201-5828

SCHIEFELBEIN, LESTER WILLIS, JR. lawyer; b. Feb. 17, 1946; S. Lester Willis and Mary Kathryn (Kelly) S.; m. Linda Ann Boyle, Aug. 15, 1970; children: Tracy, Christy, Lesley, Bryan, Amy. BS, Ariz. State U., 1968; JD, 1971; LLM, George Washington U., 1975. Bar: Calif. 1972, Ariz. 1971, U.S. Supreme Ct. 1976, D.C. 1982. Atty. U.S. Dept. Energy, Washington, 1978-82; counsel Lockheed Electronics Co., Inc., Plainfield, N.J., 1982-88; mem. office of pres., 1986-88; corp. counsel, 1988-89; v.p., chief counsel Lockheed Corp., 1989; chief counsel Lockheed Martin Missles & Space, 1990—. Served to capt., JAGC, USAF, 1971-78, to col. USAFR, 1979-96. Recipient Exceptional Svc. citation U.S. Dept. Energy, 1981, 82. Mem. Fed. bar Assn. (chmn. fsch. and devel. com. 1982—, Disting. Svc. award 1982, 83, 86, vice chmn. internat. procurement com. 1979-81), San Jose Ballet, Los Gatos Nat. Jr. Basketball. General corporate, Government contracts and claims. Office: Lockheed Missiles & Space Co 1111 Lockheed Way Sunnyvale CA 94089-1212

SCHIESSWOHL, CYNTHIA RAE SCHLEGEL, lawyer; b. Colorado Springs, Colo., July 7, 1955; d. Leslie H. and Maime (Kascak) Schlegel; m. Scott Jay Schiesswohl, Aug. 6, 1977; children: Leslie Michelle, Kristen Elizabeth. BA cum laude, So. Meth. U., 1976; JD, U. Colo., 1978; postgrad., U. Denver, 1984. Bar: Colo. 1979, Wyo. 1986, Ind. 1988, U.S. Dist. Ct. Colo. 1979, U.S. Ct. Appeals (10th cir.) 1984, U.S. Supreme Ct. 2000, Utah 2001, U.S. Dist. Ct. Utah 2001; cert. family mediator, 1992, civil mediator 1994. Rsch. clk. City Atty.'s Office, Colorado Springs, Colo., 1976; investigator Pub. Defender's Office, 1976; dep. dist. atty. 4th Jud. Dist. Colo., 1979-81; pvt. practice law Grand Junction, Colo., 1981-82, Denver, 1983-84; assoc. Law Offices of John G. Salmon P.C., 1984-85; pvt. practice Laramie, Wyo., 1985-88, Indpls., 1988-90; of counsel Rund & Wunsch, 1990—2000; dep. prosecuting atty. 53d Jur. Cir. Ind., 2000; pvt. practice Park City, Utah, 2001—. Guest lectr. Pikes Peak C.C., 1980; adj. prof. polit. sci. and speech Butler U., Indpls., 1993-99, spl. asst. to dean for pre-law, 1993-95, asst. dean for pre-profl. svcs., 1995-99. Advisor Explorer Law Post Boy Scouts Am., 1980-81; vol. Girl Scouts Am., 1993-94, Park City Mountain Resort, 2000—, Canyons Resort, 2000—, Leadership Park City, 2000; ex officio mem. ch. devel. com. Ctrl. Rocky Mt. region Christian Ch. (Disciples of Christ), 1986-88; mem. evangelism commn. United Meth. Ch., 1987-88, fin. com. youth and music depts., 1979-81, lay del. Rocky Mountain Ann. Conf., 1986-87, academic tutor youth programs, 1989—, Sunday sch. tchr., 1995-2000; mem. ch. and soc. com. Meridian St. United Meth. Ch., 1989-93, mem. refugee resettlement com., 1990-93; pres. (hon.) United Meth. Women, 1996—2000 mem. ch. choir, 1997—; mem. Park City Singers, 2000—; hearing officer Wyo. Dept. Edn., 1987-88; vol. Project Motivation, Dallas, 1974; chairperson Wyo. Med. Rev. Panel, 1987; lectr. Ind. Pastor's Conf., Rethinking Prisons Conf., 1990, Econ. Edn. for clergy Conf., 1991; bd. dirs. Art Ctr. and Art Assn. Henry County, 1997-2000; trustee New Castle Cmty. Sch. Corp., 1998-2000, sec., 1999-2000, legis. liaison, 1999-2000; mem. exec. panel Henry County YMCA, 2000. Named U. scholar So. Meth. U., 1973. Mem. ABA (internat. law com.), Wyo State Bar, Colo. Bar Assn. (ethics com. 1984-85, long range planning com. 1985-88, chairperson 1986-87), Am. Immigration Lawyers Assn. (sec. Ind. chpt. 1991-92, 93-94, chpt. vice chair 1992-93, asylum liaison 1990-99, chpt. chair 1994-95, bd. govs. 1994-95) Indpls. Bar Assn. (internat. law sect. ethics com. 1990-93), Pi Sigma Alpha (awards com. 1999-2000), Alpha Lambda Delta, Alpha Delta Pi. Republican. General practice, Immigration, naturalization, and customs, Religion. Office: PO Box 981114 Park City UT 84098-1114

SCHIFF, KENNETH EDMUND, lawyer; b. Bklyn., Jan. 29, 1963; s. Jay Bernard and Alma Grace (Scala) S. BA in Fin., N.Y.U., 1984; JD, Bklyn. Law Sch., 1987. Bar: N.J. 1987, N.Y. 1988; registered investment advisor. Assoc. Weil, Gotshal & Manges, N.Y.C., 1987—. Mng. editor Bklyn. Jour. Internat. Law, 1986-87. Mem. ABA, N.Y. Bar Assn., N.Y. County Lawyers Assn. Contracts commercial, General corporate, Securities. Office: Weil Gotshal & Manges 767 5th Ave Fl Concl New York NY 10153-0119

SCHIFFRIN, MICHAEL EDWARD, lawyer; b. N.Y.C., Sept. 24, 1946; s. Isidore and Edna Ruth (Brooks) S.; m. Susan Terry Greenberg, Aug. 28, 1969; children: Joshua Todd, Jessica Brooke. Student, U. Fla., 1964; BA, Hofstra U., 1968; JD, Bklyn. Law Sch., 1972. Bar: N.Y. 1972, Fla. 1974, U.S. Dist. Ct. (so. and mid. dists.) Fla. 1977, U.S. Ct. Appeals (5th cir.) 1975, U.S. Ct. Appeals (11th cir.) 1981. Asst. counsel Fgn. Credit Ins. Assn., N.Y.C., 1973-74; assoc. Law Office of Norman Schwarz, P.A., Miami Beach, Fla., 1974; ptnr. Schwarz & Schiffrin, P.A., 1979-82; assoc. Schultz & Hollander, P.A., Miami, Fla., 1982-84; ptnr. Hollander & Schiffrin, 1984-90, Schiffrin & Cohen, P.A., Miami, 1990-91; prin. Michael Schiffrin & Assocs., P.A., 1992—. Served as 1st lt. U.S. Army, 1972-73. Mem. Miami Beach Bar Assn. (sec. 1979, treas. 1980, 2d v.p. 1981, 1st v.p. 1982, pres. 1984). State civil litigation, Contracts commercial, Trademark and copyright. Office: Michael Schiffrin & Assocs PA 9130 S Dadeland Blvd Suite 1109 2 Datran Ctr Miami FL 33156-1700

SCHIFTER, RICHARD, lawyer; b. Vienna, Austria, July 31, 1923; came to U.S., 1938; s. Paul and Balbina (Blass) S.; m. Lilo Krueger, July 3, 1948; children: Judith, Deborah, Richard P., Barbara, Karen BS in Social Sci. summa cum laude, CCNY, 1943; LLB, Yale U., 1951; DHL (hon.), Hebrew Union Coll., 1992. Bar: Conn. 1951, D.C. 1952, U.S. Supreme Ct. 1954, Md., 1958. Assoc. Fried, Frank, Harris, Shriver & Jacobson, Washington, 1951-57, ptnr., 1957-84; dep. U.S. rep. with rank of ambassador UN Security Council, N.Y.C., 1984-85; asst. sec. of state for human rights and humanitarian affairs Dept. State, Washington, 1985-92; U.S. rep. UN Human Rights Commn., Geneva, 1983-86, 93; spl. asst. to pres., counselor Nat. Security Coun., Washington, 1993-97, spl. adviser to Sec. of State, 1997-2001. Head U.S. del. Conf. on Security and Cooperation in Europe Experts Meeting on Human Rights, Ottawa, Ont., Can., 1985, Dem. Insts., Oslo, 1991; bd. dirs. U.S. Inst. Peace, 1986-92; mem. Congl. Commn. on Security and Cooperation in Europe, 1986-92. V.p., pres. Md. Bd. Edn., Balt., 1959-79; chmn. Md. Gov.'s Commn. on Funding Edn. of Handicapped Children, 1975-77, Md. Values Edn. Commn., 1979-83, Montgomery County Dem. Cen. Com., Md., 1966-70; del. Dem. Nat. Conv., 1968; bd. govs., Nat. Executive Com., 2001—; mem. exec. com. Am. Jewish Com., 1992-93. With U.S. Army, 1943-46, ETO. Recipient Disting. Svc. award Sec. of State, 1992. Mem. Phi Beta Kappa. Democrat. Jewish Home: 6907 Crail Dr Bethesda MD 20817-4723 E-mail: rschifter@aol.com

SCHILD, RAYMOND DOUGLAS, lawyer; b. Chgo., Dec. 20, 1952; s. Stanley Martin and Cassoundra Lee (McArdle) S.; m. Ellen Arthea Carstensen, Oct. 24, 1987; children: Brian Christopher, Melissa Nicole. Student, U.S. Mil. Acad., 1970; BA summa cum laude, De Paul U., 1974, JD magna cum laude, 1982; M in Life Scis., Order of Essenes, 1996. Bar: Ill. 1982, U.S. Dist. Ct. (no. dist.) Ill. 1982, U.S. Ct. Appeals (7th cir.) 1982, Idaho 1989, U.S. Dist. Ct. Idaho 1989, U.S. Ct. Appeals (9th cir.) 1989, U.S. Supreme Ct. 1990. Assoc. Clausen, Miller, Gorman, Caffrey & Witous, Chgo., 1982-84; law clk. to chief judge law divsn. Cir. Ct. Cook County, 1984-85; assoc. John G. Phillips & Assocs., 1985-87, Martin, Chapman, Park & Burkett, Boise, Idaho, 1988-89; pvt. practice, 1989-90; pres. Martin, Chapman, Schild & Lassaw, Chartered, 1990-96; mng. assoc. prelitigation divsn. Litster Law Offices, 2001—. Dir. Behavioral Mgmt. Ctrs.; bd. dirs. Image Concepts Internat., Inc., Boise; lectr. on legal edn. ICLE and NBI, 1993-98. Co-host legal radio talk show KFXD, 1994; legal columnist Idaho Bus. Rev., 1988-96. Mem. adv. bd. Alliance for the Mentally Ill, Boise, 1991—, Parents and Youth Against Drug Abuse, Boise, 1991-92, Bethel Ministries; fair housing adminstr. Sauk Village (Ill.) Govt., 1987-88; instr. Ada County Youth Ct., Boise, 1992—. Schmitt fellow DePaul U., 1974; recipient award of merit Chgo. Law Coalition, 1987. Mem. ATLA, Idaho Trial Lawyers' Assn., Ill. State Bar Assn., Idaho State Bar Assn., Boise Estate Planning Counsel, Shriners (temple atty. 1994—, liaison Crippled Children's Hosp.), Masons (jr. steward 1992). Avocations: tennis, trombone, writing, music. General civil litigation, General corporate, Probate. Office: 6550 W Emerald Ste 108 Boise ID 83704

SCHILLEBEECKX, JAN PAUL, radiologist; b. Geel, Antwerpen, Belgium, July 7, 1948; s. Joseph Schillebeeckx and Christiane Meynen; m. Cathy Irma Vanfleteren, Nov. 6, 1951; children: Fabienne, Joseph. MD, Cath. U., Leuven, 1974. Cert. radiologist. Chmn. med. imaging Imelda Hosp., Bonheiden, Antwerpen, 1980-2000; bd. dirs. Europacs, 2000—. Chmn. Meerkant BVBA, Keerbergen, Belgium, 1985-2000. Comdr. Med. Force, Brussels, 1978-2000. Mem. Belgian Nat. Profl. Soc. Radiology (chmn. 1997-99), Lions Internat. Office: Imelda Ziekenhuis Imeldaan 9 Bonheiden 2820 Antwerpen Belgium E-mail: j.schillebeeckx@kmonet.be, jan.schillebeeckx@imekda.be

SCHILLER, DONALD CHARLES, lawyer; b. Chgo., Dec. 8, 1942; s. Sidney S. and Edith (Lastick) S.; m. Eileen Fagin, June 14, 1964; children— Eric, Jonathan Student, Lake Forest Coll., 1960-63; J.D., DePaul U., 1966. Bar: Ill. 1966, U.S. Dist. Ct. (no. dist.) Ill. 1966, U.S. Supreme Ct. 1972. Ptnr. Schiller, DuCanto & Fleck (formerly Schiller & Schiller and Schiller & DuCanto), Chgo., 1966—. Chair domestic rels. adv.

com. Cir. Ct. Cook County, 1993—2000, exec. com., 1986—93; lectr. in law U. Chgo. Law Sch., 2001—; spkr. profl. confs. Contbr. chpts. and articles to profl. publs. Mem. steering com. on juvenile ct. watching, LWV, 1980-81. Recipient Maurice Weigle award Chgo. Bar Found., 1978, Disting. Alumni award, DePaul U., 1988, various certs. of appreciation profl. groups: named One of Am.'s Best Divorce Lawyers, Town and Country, 1985, 98, The Nat. Law Jour., 1987, The Best Lawyers in Am., 1987—, One of Chgo's. Best Div. Lawyers, Crain's Chgo. Bus., 1981, Today Chgo. Woman, 1985, Inside Chgo. mag., 1988, Chgo. Sun Times, 2000. Fellow Am. Bar Found., Am. Acad. Matrimonial Lawyers (nat. chair continuing legal edn. 1993-94); mem. ABA (bd. govs. 1994-97, chmn. family law sect. 1985-86, Ill. State del. 1980-84, mem. Ho. of Dels. 1984—, editor-in-chief Family Law Newsletter 1977-79; mem. editorial bd., assoc. editor Family Adv. Mag. 1979-84, speaker at confs. and meetings), Ill. Bar Assn. (pres. 1987-88, chmn. family law sect. 1976-77, editor Family Law Bull. 1976-77, bd. govs. 1977-83, treas. 1981-84, v.p. 1984-86, chmn. various coms., lectr., incorporator and pres. Ill. State Bar Assn. Mutual Ins. Co., Inc. 1988-89), Chgo. Bar Assn., Am. Coll. Family Law Trial Lawyers (diplomate). Family and matrimonial. Office: Schiller DuCanto & Fleck 200 N La Salle St Ste 2700 Chicago IL 60601-1098 E-mail: dschiller@sdflaw.com

SCHILLER, HOWARD BARRY, lawyer; b. N.Y.C., Apr. 3, 1949; s. Charles Lawrence and Estelle (Saltzman) S.; m. Bonnie Lee York, June 11, 1972; children: Joshua Garry, Elizabeth York. BA in Religion and History, Wesleyan U., Middletown, Conn., 1971; JD with honors, U. Conn., 1975. Bar: Conn. 1975, U.S. Dist. Ct. Conn. 1975, U.S. Ct. Appeals (2d cir.) 1975, U.S. Supreme Ct. 1980. Staff atty. Conn. Legal Services, Willimantic, 1975-79; pvt. practice, Willimantic, 1979-84, 91-93; ptnr. Shepard & Schiller, Willimantic, 1984-92; prin. Howard B. Schiller, Willimantic, 1992—; atty. Town of Windham, Conn., 1981-84. Bd. dirs. Willimantic YMCA, 1976-82, Windham-Willimantic Cmty. Fed. Credit Union, 1977-79, Natchaug Valley Vis. Nurses Assn., 1985-89, pres. 1986-88; pres. Temple B'nai Israel, Willimantic, 1989-91; active Windham Area Interfaith Ministries, 1995—. Mem. ABA, Assn. Trial Lawyers Am., Conn. Bar Assn., Conn. Trial Lawyers Assn., Nat. Orgn. Social Security Claimants Reps. Democrat. Jewish. Lodge: Masons (master 1980, 94, sec. 1981-93, 95—). State civil litigation, Personal injury, Workers' compensation. Home: 303 North St Willimantic CT 06226-1642 Office: 55 Church St Willimantic CT 06226-2601

SCHIMEL, RICHARD E. lawyer; b. Jersey City, Mar. 2, 1954; s. Albert Samuel and Rose (Schoenfeld) S.; m. Barbara Cheryl Mulitz, Aug. 7, 1983. AB in History, Princeton U., 1975; JD, George Washington U., 1978. Bar: Md. 1978, D.C. 1979, U.S. Dist. Ct. D.C. 1979, U.S. Dist. Ct. Md. 1979, U.S. Ct. Appeals (D.C. cir.) 1979, U.S. Ct. Appeals (4th cir.) 1982. Jud. law clk. Prince George's County Cir. Ct., Upper Marlboro, Md., 1978-79; assoc. Clancy and Pfeifer, Chevy Chase, 1979-82, Budow and Noble PC, Bethesda, 1982—. State civil litigation, Insurance, Personal injury. Home: 9719 Culver St Kensington MD 20895-3654 Office: Budow and Noble PC 7201 Wisconsin Ave Ste 600 Bethesda MD 20814-4849 E-mail: rschimel@budownoble.com

SCHIMMENTI, JOHN JOSEPH, lawyer; b. N.Y.C., Mar. 21, 1938; s. John Marcus and Mae M. (Miranti) S.; m. Mary Elizabeth Sleep, Apr. 18, 1964. B.A., Columbia Coll., 1959; J.D., Georgetown U., 1962, LL.M., 1964. Bar: D.C. 1962, N.Y. 1964, Calif. 1965, U.S. Dist. Ct. (cen. dist.) Calif. 1965, U.S. Ct. Appeals (9th cir.) 1966, U.S. Supreme Ct. 1971. Trial atty. Anti-Trust div. U.S. Dept. Justice, Washington, 1962-64, Lands div., Los Angeles, 1965-67; trial atty. Santa Fe R.R., Los Angeles, 1968-70; ptnr. Schimmenti, Mullins & Berberian, El Segundo, Calif., 1971— . Mem. S.W. Dist. Bar Assn. (pres. 1983), Los Angeles Bar Assn. (condemnation com. 1983), Columbia U. Alumni of So. Calif. (pres. 1978). Republican. Roman Catholic. Club: El Segundo Rotary (pres. 1977). Condemnation. Office: 426 Main St El Segundo CA 90245-3002

SCHINDLER, STEVEN ROY, lawyer; b. N.Y.C., May 21, 1958; s. Jack J. and Gloria Schindler; m. Susan M. Kath, June 14, 1987; children: Alexandra, Emma. BA, Oberlin Coll., 1980; JD, Fordham U., 1985. Bar: N.Y. 1986, U.S. Dist. Ct. (so. and ea. dists.) N.Y. 1986, U.S. Dist. Ct. (no. dist.) N.Y. 1987, U.S. Ct. Appeals (2d cir.) 1996, U.S. Supreme Ct. 1996. Assoc. Burns, Summit, Rovins & Feldesman, N.Y.C., 1985-87, Winthrop, Stimson, Putnam & Roberts, N.Y.C., 1987-96; founding ptnr. Schindler Cohen & Hochman LLP, 1997—. Mem. ABA, Internat. Bar Assn., Assn. Bar City N.Y. Avocations: tennis, hiking, history. Alternative dispute resolution, General civil litigation. Office: Schindler Cohen & Hochman LLP One Liberty Pla 35th Fl New York NY 10006-1404

SCHIRMEISTER, CHARLES F. retired lawyer; b. Jersey City, June 18, 1929; s. Charles F. and Louise P. (Schneider) S.; m. Barbara Jean Fredericks, Feb. 9, 1952; children: Pamela, Charles Bradford. BA, U. Mich., 1951; LLB, Fordham U., 1956. Bar: N.Y. 1956, U.S. Dist. Ct. (so. dist.) N.Y., U.S. Ct. Appeals (2d cir.), U.S. Supreme Ct. 1961. Asst. dist. atty. N.Y. County (N.Y.), 1956-61; assoc. Thelen, Reid & Priest, N.Y.C., 1961-71, ptnr., 1971-94. Chmn. bd. trustees, deacon Cmty. Congrl. Ch., Short Hills, N.J.; trustee Ocean Grove (N.J.) Camp Meeting Assn. Capt. USMC, ret., 1951-53. Mem. Univ. Club (N.Y.C.), Canoe Brook Country Club (Summit, N.J.), Sigma Alpha Epsilon. Republican. Avocations: tennis, oenology, golf. Antitrust, Federal civil litigation, General corporate. Home: 15 Beechcroft Rd Short Hills NJ 07078-1648 Office: Thelen Reid & Priest 40 W 57th St Fl 28 New York NY 10019-4097

SCHIZAS, JENNIFER ANNE, law association administrator; b. Grand Island, Nebr., Aug. 18, 1959; d. John Delano and Jacqueline May (Pieper) S. BJ, U. Nebr., 1982. Rschr. U.S. Senator Carl T. Curtis, Washington, 1978; pub. rels. dir. Nebr. Solar Office, Lincoln, 1979; reporter Sta. WOWT-TV, Omaha, 1980-83; bur. chief Sta. KHAS-TV, Hastings, Nebr., 1983-84; divsn. dir. March of Dimes, Lincoln, 1986-90; exec. dir. Lincoln Arts Coun., 1990-92, Nebr. Food Industry Assn., Lincoln, 1992-93; dir. comm. Nebr. Bar Assn., 1993—. Mem. editor's exch. adv. bd. West Pub. CO., Eagan, Minn., 1995. Mem. Am. Soc. Assn. Execs., Nat. Assn. Bar Execs. (pub. rels. cons. 1995), Nebr. Soc. Assn. Execs. Sertoma Club (v.p.). Democrat. Greek Orthodox. Avocations: running, painting, antique collecting and refinishing. Home: 621 S 30th St Lincoln NE 68510-1427 Office: Nebr Bar Assn 635 S 14th St Lincoln NE 68508-2700 E-mail: jschizas@nebar.com

SCHIZER, ZEVIE BARUCH, lawyer; b. Bklyn., Dec. 19, 1928; s. David and Bertha (Rudavsky) S.; m. Hazel Gerber, Aug. 23, 1962; children: Deborah Gail, Miriam Anne, David Michael. BA magna cum laude, NYU, 1950; JD, Yale U., 1953. Bar: N.Y. 1954, U.S. Dist. Ct. (so. and ea. dist.) N.Y. 1959, U.S. Ct. Appeals (2d cir.) 1959, U.S. Supreme Ct. 1959. Assoc. Guzik & Boukstein, N.Y.C., 1953-54; teaching fellow NYU Sch. Law, 1954-55; assoc. Philips, Nizer, Benjamin & Krim, N.Y.C., 1955-56, Aranow, Brodsky, Einhorn & Dann, N.Y.C., 1956-57; asst. counsel jud. inquiry Appellate Divsn. 2nd Dept., Bklyn., 1957-62; assoc. Hays, Porter, Spanier & Curtis, N.Y.C., 1963-68, ptnr., 1968-85; sec. United Aircraft Products, Inc., Dayton, Ohio, 1970-83; ptnr. Schizer & Schizer, N.Y.C., 1985—. Trustee Bklyn. Pub. Libr., 1966—, pres. 1985-88, N.Y. Young Dem. Club, N.Y.C., 1960-61; trustee East Midwood Jewish Ctr., Bklyn., 1991—. Mem. N.Y. County Lawyers Assn. (mem. profl. ethics com., mem. com. on profl. discipline), Phi Beta Kappa. Democrat. Jewish. General corporate, Probate, Securities. Home: 1134 E 23rd St Brooklyn NY 11210-4519 Office: Schizer & Schizer 3 New York Plz New York NY 10004-2442 E-mail: zschizer@msn.com

SCHLACKS, STEPHEN MARK, lawyer, educator; b. Pittsburg, Kans., Oct. 13, 1955; BA, Austin Coll., Sherman, Tex., 1978; MBA, U. Dallas, 1982; JD, Baylor U., 1986. Bar: Tex. 1987, U.S. Dist. Ct. (so. dist.) Tex. 1987, (no., ea. and we. dists.) Tex. 1988, U.S. Ct. Appeals (5th cir.) 1987, (8th cir.) 1989, U.S. Supreme Ct. 1990. In mgmt. Johnson & Johnson Products, Inc., Sherman, 1978-84; assoc. atty. Wetzel & Assocs., The Woodlands, Tex., 1986-92; ptnr. Hope, Causey & Schlacks, P.C., Conroe, 1992-96, Law Office of Stephen M. Schlacks, The Woodlands, 1996-99, Schlacks, Harrison & Cox PLLC, The Woodlands, 1999—. Adj. faculty North Harris County C.C., Houston, 1990—. Leon Jaworski scholar, 1984, Harcourt Brace Jovanovich scholar, 1986. Mem. Fed. Bar Assn., Montgomery County Bar Assn., Sigma Iota Epsilon, Pi Gamma Mu. Republican. Presbyterian. General civil litigation, Insurance. Home: 66 Racing Cloud Ct The Woodlands TX 77381-5203 Office: 2202 Timberloch Pl Ste 107 The Woodlands TX 77380-1163

SCHLAIN, BARBARA ELLEN, lawyer; b. N.Y.C., May 28, 1948; d. William and Evelyn (Youdelman) S. BA, Wellesley Coll., 1969; MA, Columbia U., 1970; JD, Yale U., 1973. Bar: N.Y. 1974, U.S. Dist. Ct. (so. dist.) N.Y. 1974, U.S. Ct. Appeals (2d cir.) 1975, U.S. Dist. Ct. (ea. dist.) N.Y. 1977. Assoc. firm Donovan Leisure Newton & Irvine, N.Y.C., 1973-76, Graubard Moskovitz McGoldrick Dannett & Horowitz, N.Y.C., 1976-79; atty. McGraw-Hill, Inc., 1979-80, asst. gen. counsel, 1980-86, v.p., assoc. gen. counsel, asst. sec., 1986—. Sec. proprietary rights com. Info. Industry Assn., 1982-83. Author: outlines Practicing Law Inst., 1983, 84, 85, 86, 88; contbr. numerous articles to profl. jours. Bd. dirs., v.p., sec. Dance Rsch. Found., N.Y.C., 1983-86, chmn., 1986-98. Phi Beta Kappa scholar, Durant scholar Wellesley Coll., 1967-69. Mem. ABA, Assn. Am. Pubs. (lawyers com. 1979—), Assn. Bar City N.Y. (comm. law com. 1985-88). General civil litigation, Libel, Trademark and copyright. Office: The McGraw-Hill Companies Inc 1221 Avenue Of The Americas New York NY 10020-1095

SCHLANG, DAVID, real estate executive, lawyer; b. N.Y.C., May 2, 1912; s. Alexander and Blanche (Cohen) S.; m. Arlene Roth, May 9, 1948. LLB, NYU, 1933. Bar: N.Y. 1935, U.S. Dist. Ct. (so. dist.) N.Y. 1940. Individual practice law, 1935-42; sec., pres. Schlang Bros. & Co., Inc., N.Y.C., 1945—. Trustee Brookdale Hosp., Bklyn., 1980—, vice chmn., 1983—; bd. dirs., vice chmn. Samuel Schulman Inst. Nursing and Rehab. of Brookdale Hosp., 1973—, sec. bd. dirs., 1976—; vice chmn. Linroc Nursing Home, 1993—; dir. Legion Meml. Sq., Inc., 1983—; founding mem. U.S. Congl. Adv. Bd. Served with AUS, 1942-45. Decorated Croix de Guerre with palm (France); recipient Conspicious Svc. award State of N.Y., 1965. Mem.: ABA, Criminal Investigation Divsn. Agts. Assn., N.Y. State Bar Assn., N.Y. County Lawyers Assn., Real Estate Bd. N.Y., U.S. Senatorial Club, Met. Club, N.Y. Athletic Club, Woodmere Club. Home: 737 Park Ave New York NY 10021-4256 Office: 67 Wall St New York NY 10005-3101 E-mail: schlang67@aol.com

SCHLAU, PHILIP, retired lawyer; b. N.Y.C., Sept. 25, 1922; s. Joseph and Bella (Brown) S.; m. Florence Schlau, Jan. 31, 1947; children: Stacey, Bethel. BBA cum laude, CCNY, 1943; JD, Harvard U., 1949. Bar: N.Y. 1949, U.S. Dist. Ct. (so. dist.) N.Y. 1950, U.S. Dist. Ct. (ea. dist.) N.Y. 1950, U.S. Ct. Appeals (2d cir.) 1951, U.S. Supreme Ct. 1959. Sr. trial atty. U.S. Fidelity & Guaranty Co., 1950-57; ptnr. Schlau & Nadelson and predecessors, N.Y.C., 1959-70; sr. ptnr. Newman & Schlau PC, 1970-84, Newman, Schlau, Fitch & Burns PC, N.Y.C., 1984-96. Capt. AUS, 1943-46. Mem. ABA, N.Y. State Bar Assn., N.Y. County Lawyers Assn., Def. Rsch. Inst. Federal civil litigation, State civil litigation, Insurance. Home: 201 E 79th St Apt 15H New York NY 10021-0839

SCHLEGEL, DICK REEVES, lawyer, judge; b. Bloomfield, Iowa, Mar. 4, 1922; s. Verne John and Helen Elizabeth (Reeves) S.; m. Maxine Glenn, Apr. 4, 1943; children: Richard R. II, Mary Patricia Wilson, Robert Glenn. BA, U. Iowa, 1948, JD, 1950; LLM, U. Va., 1992. Bar: Iowa 1950. Ptnr. Barnes & Schlegel, Ottumwa, Iowa, 1950-78; judge 8th Jud. Dist. Iowa, 1978-82, Iowa Ct. Appeals, 1982-94, sr. judge, 1994-2000, ret., 2000; of counsel Schlegel Law Firm, Ottumwa, Iowa. With USAF, 1942-50. Decorated Air medal. Mem. ABA, Iowa Bar Assn., Iowa Acad. Trial Lawyers, Assn. Trial Lawyers Iowa, Iowa Judges Assn., Iowa Def. Counsel, Ottumwa Bar Assn., Ottumwa Country Club, Masons. Presbyterian. E-mail: dschlegel@pcsia.net

SCHLEI, NORBERT ANTHONY, lawyer; b. Dayton, Ohio, June 14, 1929; s. William Frank and Norma (Lindsley) S.; m. Jane Moore, Aug. 26, 1950 (div. 1963); children: Anne C. Buczynski, William K., Andrew M.; m. Barbara Lindemann, Mar. 7, 1965 (div. 1981); children: Bradford L., Graham L. (dec. 1995), Norbert L. (dec. 1996), Blake Lindsley, Elizabeth Eldridge; m. Joan Masson, Dec. 29, 1995. BA, Ohio State U., 1950; LLB magna cum laude, Yale U., 1956. Bar: Ohio 1956, Calif. 1958, D.C. 1963, U.S. Supreme Ct. 1963. Law clk. to Justice Harlan U.S. Supreme Ct., 1956-57; assoc. atty. O'Melveny & Myers, L.A., 1957-59; ptnr. Greenberg, Shafton & Schlei, 1959-62; asst. atty. gen. U.S. Dept. Justice, Washington, 1962-66; ptnr. Munger, Tolles, Hills & Rickershauser, 1968-70, Kane, Shulman & Schlei, Washington, 1968-70; ptnr.-in-charge Hughes Hubbard & Reed, L.A., 1972-89; pres., CEO Kahala Capital Corp., Santa Monica, Calif., 1983—; pvt. practice, 1989—. Author: (with M.S. McDougal and others) Studies in World Public Order, 1961 (Am. Soc. Internat. Law ann. book award); State Regulation of Corporate Financial Practices, 1962; editor-in-chief Yale Law Jour., 1955-56. Dem. nominee for Calif. Assembly, 1962, for sec. of state Calif., 1966. Mem. Riviera Country Club (Pacific Palisades, Calif.). Avocations: tennis, golf, skiing, sailing. Federal civil litigation, General corporate, Private international. Office: 2800 28th St Ste 122A Santa Monica CA 90405-2934 Fax: 310-450-0491. E-mail: nas@usinter.net

SCHLEIFENBAUM, ECKHART JOHANNES, lawyer; b. Munich, Sept. 17, 1966; s. Henrich and Dagmar S. Cert., U. Sorbonne, Paris, 1988; Cert. in Polit. Sci. and Internat. Rels., I.E.P., Strasbourg, France, 1991; 1st and 2nd State Exam, U. Regensburg, Germany, 1994, 96, PhD, 1999. Bar: Munich 1999. Rechtsreferender Superior Ct., Regensburg, 1994-96; asst. to prof. Becker Law Faculty, 1994-97; rechtsreferender German Embassy, New Delhi, 1996; assoc. Nörr Stiefenhofer Lutz, Munich, 1999—. Author: Die Auseinandersetzung der Erbengemeinschaft in Italien, 1999. Communications, General corporate, Mergers and acquisitions. Office: Nörr Stiefenhofer Lutz Brienner Str 28 80333 Munich Germany

SCHLESINGER, HARVEY ERWIN, judge; b. June 4, 1940; BA, The Citadel, 1962; JD, U. Richmond, 1965. Bar: Va. 1965, Fla. 1965, U.S. Supreme Ct. 1968. Corp. counsel Seabord Coast Line R.R. Co., Jacksonville, Fla., 1968-70; chief asst. U.S. atty. Mid. Dist. Fla., 1970-75, U.S. magistrage judge, 1975-91, U.S. Dist. judge, 1991—. Adj. prof. U. N. Fla., 1984-91; mem. adv. com. on Fed. Rules of Criminal Procedure to U.S. Supreme Ct., 1986-93; mem. Jud. Conf. Adv. Com. on Adminstrn. of Magistrate Judges Sys., 1996—, chmn., 1998—; chmn. U.S. Dist. Ct. Forms Working Group, Washington, 1983—, Jud. Ct. Ad hoc Com. on Long Range Planning, 1998—, Jud. Conf. Jud. Officers Resources Working Group, 1998-99, 11th Cir. Dist. Judges Assn., 1991—, sec.-treas. 1996- 97, v.p. 1997-98, pres.-elect. 1999-2001, pres. 2001—. Bd. dirs. Pine Castle Ctr. for Mentally Retarded, Jacksonville, 1970-87, pres., 1972-74, chmn. bd. dirs., 1973-74; trustee Pine Castle Found., 1972-76; trustee Congregation Ahavath Chesed, Jacksonville, 1970—, v.p., 1975-80, pres., 1980-82; v.p. S.E. Coun. Union Am. Hebrew Congregations, 1984-88; asst. commr. for exploring N. Fla. Coun. Boy Scouts Am., 1983-86, exec. com., 1986-98, adv. bd., 1998—; mem. Boy Scouts Am. Nat. Jewish Com. on Scouting, Irving, Tex., 1986-93; mem. Fla. Sesquicentennial Commn., 1995-96; trustee River Garden Home for Aged, 1982—, sec., 1985—; co-chmn. bd. govs. Jacksonville chpt. NCCJ, 1983—, presiding co-chmn. 1984-89, nat. bd. trustees, N.Y.C., 1986-93; trustee Jacksonville Cmty. Found., 2000—. Capt. JAGC U.S. Army, 1965-68. Recipient Silver Beaver award Boy Scouts Am., 1986, George Washington Medal Honor, Freedoms Found., Valley Forge, Pa., 1987, Silver Medallion Humanitarian award NCCJ, 1992, Founders award, Fed. Magistrate Judges Assn., 1999, William Green award for profl. excellence U. Richmond Law Sch., 2000. Mem. ABA (fed. rules of evidence and criminal procedure com. 1979-98, Nat. Conf. Spl. Ct. Judges, 1975-90, conf. newsletter editor, 1988-90, Nat. Conf. Fed. Trial Judges, 1990—, chmn. legislation com., 1996-97, Flascher award 1989), Va. Bar Assn., Fla. Bar Assn., Fed. Judges Assn., Jacksonville Bar Assn., Fed. Bar Assn. (pres. Jacksonville chpt. 1974, 75, 81-82), Am. Judicature Soc., Chester Bedell Am. Inns of Ct. (pres. 1992-96), Rotary (Paul Harris fellow, pres. S. Jacksonville club), Masons (past master, past venerable master, knights comdr. of Ct. Honour, 33 degree Scottish Rite bodies), Shrine. Office: 311 W Monroe St PO Box 1740 Jacksonville FL 32201-1740

SCHLESINGER, SANFORD JOEL, lawyer; b. N.Y.C., Feb. 8, 1943; s. Irving and Ruth (Rubin) S.; children: Merideth, Jarrod, Alexandra; m. Suzanne Beth Mangold, 1994; 1 stepchild, Mariel Mangold. BS in Govt. with hons., Columbia U., 1963; JD, Fordham U., 1966. Bar: N.Y. 1966, U.S. Dist. Ct. (so. and ea. dists.) N.Y. 1967, U.S. Ct. Appeals (2d cir.) 1968, U.S. Ct. Internat. Trade 1969, U.S. Tax Ct. 1993, U.S. Supreme Ct. 1978. Assoc. Frankenthaler & Kohn, N.Y.C., 1966-67; asst. atty. gen. trusts and estates bur. charitable found. div. State of N.Y., 1967-69; ptnr. Rose & Schlesinger, 1969-81, Goldshmidt, Oshatz, Powsner & Saft, N.Y.C., 1981-85; ptnr., head trusts and estates dept. Shea & Gould, 1985-93; ptnr., head wills and estates dept. Kaye & Scholer, LLP, 1993—; ptnr. co-chair family owned bus. practice group Kaye Scholer, LLP, 1993—. Adj. faculty Columbia U. Sch. Law, 1989-94; adj. prof. N.Y. Law Sch., 1978—; adj. prof. grad. program in estate planning U. Miami Grad. Sch. Law, 1995—; mem. estate planning adv. com. Practising Law Inst., 1990—; bd. advisors and contbrs. Jour. of S Corp. Taxation, 1989-96; lectr. in field; condr. workshops in field. Author: Estate Planning for the Elderly Client, 1984, Planning for the Elderly or Incapacitated Client, 1993; columnist, mem. editl. bd. Estate Planning mag., 1995—; contbr. articles to profl. jours. Mem. adv. bd. Inst. Fed. Taxation NYU, 1988-96, chmn., 1993-94; mem. legis adv. com. Scarsdale (N.Y.) Sch. Bd., 1981-83, mem. nominating com., 1979-82; pres. dist. 17 N.Y.C. Cmty. Sch. Bd., 1970-71; mem. fin. and estate planning adv. bd. Commerce Clearing House, 1988—; mem. adv. bd. Tax Hotline, 1997—. Fellow Am. Coll. Trust and Estate Counsel (chmn. Downstate N.Y. 2001—); mem. ABA (chmn. social security and other govt. entitlements com. 1990-91, chmn. probate and trust com.-estate planning, drafting charitable giving coms., 1992-94), Internat. Acad. Estate & Trust Law (Academician 1992—), Nat. Acad. Elder Law Attys., Bklyn. Bar Assn., Assn. of Bar of City of N.Y., N.Y. State Bar Assn. (treas. trusts and estates sect. 1991-92, sec. trusts and estates sect. 1992-93, chmn. trusts and estates sect. 1994-95, chmn. exec. com. 1st jud. dist. 1987-91, jour. bd. editors 1995—). Avocations: baseball, writing. Estate planning, Probate, Estate taxation. Office: Kaye Scholer LLP 425 Park Ave New York NY 10022-3506

SCHLEY, MICHAEL DODSON, lawyer; b. Calif., Jan. 4, 1955; m. Donna L. Greene, Jan. 4, 1974; children: Nathaniel, Erica. BA, Westmont Coll., 1977; JD, U. Calif., San Francisco, 1980. Bar: Calif. 1981, D.C. 1984, U.S. Supreme Ct. 1984. Atty. Fed. Home Loan Bank Bd., Washington, 1980-83; gen. counsel Fed. Home Loan Bank Bd. Credit Union, 1981-82; assoc. Fried, Frank et al, Washington, 1983-85; sr. v.p., gen. counsel Fin. Corp. of Santa Barbara, Calif., 1985-90; pvt. practice, 1990—. Mem. adv. bd. Money and Real Estate. Sec. bd. dirs. Found. for Santa Barbara City Coll., Nonprofit Support Ctr., Transition House, Santa Barbara. Mem. ABA (com. on savings insts.), Santa Barbara C. of C. (govt. rev. com.). Republican. Banking.

SCHLIFKE, JAMES STEVEN, lawyer; b. Chgo., Apr. 6, 1948; s. I. Erwin and Marjorie Bergman (Simon) S.; m. Geri Renee Katz, Mar. 2, 1975; children— Adam, Michelle, Alana. B.S. in Gen. Engring., U. Ill., 1970, J.D., 1973. Bar: Ill. 1973, U.S. Patent Office 1977; registered securities rep., options prin. Assoc. Stone Pogrund & Korey, Chgo., 1977-81; gen. counsel Miller Jesser Inc., Chgo., 1981-83; gen. counsel, exec. v.p. Katz, Scher & Co. Inc., Chgo., 1979-83; fl. broker Chgo. Merc. Exch., 1981-86; gen. counsel, dir. compliance, GNP Commodities, Inc., Chgo., 1983-88; pres., gen. counsel, GNP Securities, Chgo., 1983-88; gen. counsel Robbins Trading Co., Chgo., 1988—. Mem. ABA, Ill. State Bar Assn., Chgo. Bar Assn. Home: 2357 Tennyson Ln Highland Park IL 60035-1650

SCHLITTER, STANLEY ALLEN, lawyer; b. Decorah, Iowa, Jan. 27, 1950; s. Joseph Everett and Lillian Helena (Helgerson) S.; m. Sheila Lynn Edwards, Sept. 24, 1977; children: Stephanie Anne, Joseph Allen, John Edward. BS, Iowa State U., 1972; JD, U. Iowa, 1977. Bar: Ill. 1977, U.S. Dist. Ct. (no. dist.) Ill. 1977, U.S. Ct. Appeals (7th cir.) 1981, U.S. Ct. Appeals (Fed. cir.) 1982, D.C. 1989. Assoc. Kirkland & Ellis, Chgo., 1977-84, ptnr., 1984-88, Washington, 1988-91, Jenner & Block, Chgo., 1991—. Mem. ABA, IEEE, Am. Intellectual Property Law Assn. Computer, Patent, Trademark and copyright. Office: Jenner & Block One IBM Plaza Chicago IL 60611-3608

SCHLOSBERG, JONATHAN HARRY, lawyer; b. Johannesburg, Feb. 25, 1953; m. Sheli Hoppenstein, Jan. 10, 1985; hcildren: Tammy, Adam, Gaby. B of Commerce, U. Witwatersrand, Johannesburg, 1974, LLB, 1976, higher diploma income tax, 1979. Dir. Bowman Gilfillan Inc., Johannesburg, 1979—. Mem. Internat. Assn. of Commerce and Econs. Students (trustee), Translator Law Soc., Gautens Law Soc., Transvaal Automobile Club. Avocations: tennis, theatre, films, reading. Contracts commercial, General corporate, Mergers and acquisitions. Office: Bowman Gililan Inc PO Box 785812 Sandton 2146 South Africa Fax: 2711-883-4505

SCHLOSSER, KARIN A. lawyer; b. Rijswijk, The Netherlands; d. Willem Schlosser and Antoninette (Nelissen) S.; m. Heinz Weissenbuehler, Oct. 21, 1998. KD, Luclen Sch. Law, 1982; M in Law, N.Y.U., 1983. Bar: N.Y., 1987. Arbitrator Am. Arbitration Assn., N.Y., 1989—; ptnr. Bigham, Englax, Thomas, and Houston, 1994—. Mem. Am. Arbitration Assn. (bd. dirs.), Maritime Law Assn., European Air Law Assn., Soaring Soc. Am. Avocation: soaring, aviation. Home: 391 Harris Hill Rd Elmira NY 14903-9203 Office: Bigham Englar Jones & Houston 40 Wall St New York NY 10005-2301

SCHLUETER, DAVID ARNOLD, law educator; b. Sioux City, Iowa, Apr. 29, 1946; s. Arnold E. and Helen A. (Dettmann) S.; m. Linda L. Boston, Apr. 22, 1972; children: Jennifer, Jonathan. BA, Tex. A&M U., 1969; JD, Baylor U., 1971; LLM, U. Va., 1981. Bar: Tex. 1971, Dec. 1973, U.S. Ct. Mil. Appeals 1972, U.S. Supreme Ct. 1976. Legal counsel U.S. Supreme Ct., Washington, 1981-83; assoc. dean St. Mary's U., San Antonio, 1984-89, prof. law, 1986—, Hardy prof. trial advocacy, dir. trial advocacy, 2000—; reporter Fed. Adv. Com. on Criminal Rules, 1988—. Chmn. JAG adv. coun., 1974-75. Author: Military Criminal Justice: Practice and Procedure, 1982, 5th edit., 1999; (with others) Military Rules of Evidence Manual, 1981, 4th edit., 1997, Texas Rules of Evidence Manual, 1983, 5th edit., 1998, Texas Evidentiary Foundations, 1992, 2d edit., 1998, Military Evidentiary Foundations, 1994, Military Criminal Procedure Forms, 1997, Federal Evidence Tactics, 1997, Texas Rules of Evidence Trial Book, 2000; editor-in-chief: Emerging Problems Under the Federal Rules of Evidence, 3d edit., 1998; contbr. articles to legal publs.

Maj. JAGC, U.S. Army, 1972-81. Fellow Am. Law Inst., Tex. Bar Found. (life), Am. Bar Found. (life); mem. ABA (vice-chmn. criminal justice sect. coun. 1991-94, vice-chmn. com. on criminal justice and mil. 1983-84, chmn. standing com. on mil. law 1991-92, mem. standing com. on armed forces law, chmn. editl. adv. bd., Criminal Justice Mag., 1989-91), Tex. Bar Assn. Republican. Lutheran. Office: St Marys U Sch Law 1 Camino Santa Maria St San Antonio TX 78228-8500

SCHLUETER, LINDA LEE, law educator; b. L.A., May 12, 1947; d. Dick G. Dulgarian and Lucille J. Boston; m. David A. Schlueter, Apr. 22, 1972; children: Jennifer, Jonathan. BA, U. So. Calif., 1969; JD, Baylor U., 1971. Bar: D.C. 1973, U.S. Supreme Ct. 1976, Ct. Mil. Appeals, 1990, Tex. 1997. Govt. rels. specialist hdqrs. U.S. Postal Svc., Washington, 1973-75; staff atty. Rsch. Group, Inc., Charlottesville, Va., 1979-81; pvt. practice Washington, 1981-83; asst. prof. law Sch. Law St. Mary's U., San Antonio, 1983-87, assoc. prof., 1987-90, prof., 1990-94. Presenter law Tex. Women Scholars Program, Austin, 1986, 87; bd. dirs Inst. for Comparative and Internat. Legal Rsch. Author: Punitive Damages, 1981-89, 4th edit., 2000, ann. suppls., Legal Research Guide: Patterns and Practice, 1986, 4th edit., 2000; editor Cmty. Property Jour., 1986-88, Cmty. Property Alert, 1989-90; editor Modern Legal Sys. Cyclopedia, 20 vols., 1990, ann. suppls. Mem. ABA, Bexar County Women's Bar Assn., San Antonio Conservation Soc., Order of Barristers, Phi Alpha Delta. Republican. Lutheran.

SCHMELZ, BRENDA LEA, legal assistant; b. Washington, June 13, 1958; d. Edward G. and Wilma D. (Hektor) R.; m. Jan M. Schmelz, Oct. 7, 1978; children: Edward L., Brent T. Secretarial sci. cert. with honors, East Ctrl. Coll., Union, Mo., 1977. Sec., paralegal Mittendorf & Mittendorf, Union, 1976-83, Eckelkamp, Eckelkamp, Wood & Kuenzel, Washington, 1983—. Mem. legal secretarial adv. bd. East Ctrl. Coll., 1978, chmn., 1987; mem. legal secretarial adv. bd. State Fair C.C., 1995. Mem. Nat. Assn. Ct. Reporters, Nat. Assn. Legal Secs. (mem. certifying bd. 1997-2000, chmn. 1998-2000, Jett award 1999), Mo. Ct. Reporters Assn., Mo. Assn. Legal Secs. (pres. 1994-96, pres-elect 1992-94, v.p. 1986, 89-91, sec. 1984-86, 89-90, dir. pub. rels. 1987-89, parliamentarian 1998-99, Legal Sec. of Yr. 1987), Franklin County Legal Secs. (pres. 1989-92, Legal Sec. of Yr. 1986, 95), Union of Women Today, Phi Beta Kappa. Republican. Roman Catholic. Home: 1792 Oak Parc Union MO 63084-3607 Office: Eckelkamp Eckelkamp Wood & Kuenzel Bank of Washington Bldg Main & Oak Washington MO 63084

SCHMERTZ, ERIC JOSEPH, lawyer, educator; b. N.Y.C., Dec. 24, 1925; married; 4 children. A.B., Union Coll., 1948, LL.D. (hon.), 1978; cert., Alliance Francaise, Paris, 1948; J.D., NYU, 1954. Bar: N.Y. 1955. Internat. rep. Am. Fedn. State, County and Mcpl. Employees, AFL-CIO, N.Y.C., 1950-52; asst. v.p., dir. labor tribunals Am. Arbitration Assn., 1952-57, 59-60; indsl. relations dir. Metal Textile Corp. subs. Gen. Cable Corp., Roselle, N.J., 1957-59; exec. dir. N.Y. State Bd. Mediation, 1960-62, corp. dir., 1962-68; labor-mgmt. arbitrator, N.Y.C., 1962—; mem. faculty Hofstra U. Sch. Bus., 1962-70; prof. Hofstra U. Sch. Law, 1970—, Edward F. Carlough disting. prof. labor law, 1981-98, dean Sch. Law, 1982-89, disting. prof. emeritus of law, 1998—; of counsel The Dweck Law Firm, N.Y.C., 1999—; commr. labor rels. City of N.Y., 1990-91. Scholar-in-residence Pace U. Sch. Law, 1998—; 1st Beckley lectr. in bus. U. Vt., 1981; bd. dirs. Wilshire Oil Co.; mem. N.Y. State Pub. Employment Rels. Bd., 1991-97; cons. and lectr. in field. Co-author: (with R.L. Greenman) Personnel Administration and the Law, 1978; contbr. chpts. to books, articles to profl. jours., to profl. law confs., seminars and workshops. Mem. numerous civic orgns. Served to lt. USN, 1943-46. Recipient Testimonial award Southeast Republican Club, 1969; Alexander Hamilton award Rep. Law Students Assn.; Eric J. Schmertz Disting. Professorship Pub. Law and Pub. Svc. established Hofstra Law Sch., 1993. Mem. Nat. Acad. Arbitrators, Am. Arbitration Assn. (law com., Whitney North Seymour Sr. medal 1984), Fed. Mediation and Conciliation Svc., N.Y. Mediation Bd., N.J. Mediation Bd., N.J. Pub. Employment Rels. Bd., Hofstra U. Club, Princeton Club. Office: The Dweck Law Firm 230 Park Ave Rm 416 New York NY 10169-0422 E-mail: schmertz@dwecklaw.com

SCHMID, JOHN HENRY, JR. lawyer; b. Erie, Pa., May 11, 1944; s. John Henry Sr. and Margery (St. Lawrence) S.; m. Carol Christine Imig, July 1, 1967; children: Christine Catherine, Heidi Imig. BA, Beloit Coll., 1966; JD, U. Wis., 1969. Bar: Wis. 1969, U.S. Dist. Ct. (we. dist.) Wis. 1969, U.S. Ct. Appeals (7th cir.) 1993, U.S. Supreme Ct. 1993. Sr. ptnr. Axley Brynelson, Madison, Wis., 1969—. Emergency med. technician Village of Maple Bluff, Madison, 1977-84, trustee, 1985-89. Mem. Assn. Def. Trial Attys., Civil Trial Counsel Wis. Avocations: fishing, golf, travel. General civil litigation, Insurance, Workers' compensation. Home: 802 Farwell Dr Madison WI 53704-6034 Office: Axley Brynelson 2 E Mifflin St Madison WI 53703-2889

SCHMIDT, CHARLES EDWARD, lawyer; b. N.Y.C., Oct. 6, 1951; s. Donald J. and Yanina S. (Giera) S.; children: John Charles, Michael Joseph. AB cum laude, Boston Coll., 1972; JD, Fordham U., 1975. Bar: N.Y. 1976, U.S. Supreme Ct. 1982. Law clk. Lilly Sullivan & Purcell, P.C., N.Y.C., 1973-76, assoc., 1976-84, Donovan Maloof Walsh & Kennedy, N.Y.C., 1984-86; ptnr. Kennedy & Lillis, 1986-93, Kennedy Lillis Schmidt & English, 1993—. Mem. ABA, N.Y. State Bar Assn., Maritime Law Assn., Assn. Average Adjusters U.S. (assoc.). Roman Catholic. Admiralty, Federal civil litigation, Insurance. Home: 255 W 108th St Apt 8D1 New York NY 10025-2926 Office: Kennedy Lillis Schmidt & English 100 Maiden Ln Fl 23 New York NY 10038-4816 E-mail: cschmidt@klselaw.com

SCHMIDT, DANIEL EDWARD, IV, lawyer, commercial arbitrator; b. N.Y.C., Dec. 17, 1946; s. Daniel Edward III and Mary (Mannion) S.; m. Gail Kennedy, Sept. 5, 1980; children: Kathryn Kennedy, Michael Kennedy. BA, St. Lawrence U., 1971; postgrad., New Sch., 1972; JD, St. John's U., 1975. Bar: N.Y. 1976; cert. arbitrator. From asst. counsel to assoc. gen. counsel Prudential Property & Casualty, Holmdel, N.J., 1975-81, assoc. gen. counsel, divsn. head, 1981-82; v.p., assoc. gen. counsel, asst. sec. Prudential Reins Co., Newark, 1982-84; dir., v.p., gen. counsel, corp. sec. Scor U.S. Group, N.Y.C., 1984-86, dir., sr. v.p., gen. counsel, corp. sec., 1986-89; dir., exec. com., sr. v.p., gen. counsel, corp. sec. Sorema N.A. Group, 1989-94, dir., exec. com., exec. v.p., group gen. counsel, 1995-99, dir. exec. com., group exec. v.p., chief legal officer, 1999-2000; dep. gen. mgr., gen. counsel, corp. sec. Sorema Internat. Holding, N.V., Groupama, The Netherlands, 1993-96; U.S. counsel, 1996-2000; cons. Sorema NA Group, 2000—. Pvt. practice comml. arbitrator, umpire, Little Silver, N.J., 1987—; reins. lectr., 1986—; pres., bd. dirs. ARIAS (U.S.), N.Y.C. Mem. editl. bd. Arias- U.S. Quar. Presiding judge Ecclesiastical Trial Ct., 1999—2000, Episcopal Diocese of N.J., 1997—; bd. dirs., exec. com. ARC, Monmouth County, Shrewsbury, NJ, 1981—84. With USAR, 1967—70. Mem. ABA, Am. Arbitration Assn. (panel comml. arbitrators, roster of umpires), N.Y. Bar Assn., Assn. Internat. Droit des Assureurs (U.S. chpt.), Bamm Hollow Country Club, Desert Mountain Club. Episcopalian. Avocations: cycling, golf, tennis, skiing. General corporate, Insurance, Securities. Home and Office: Dispute Resolution Svcs Internat 628 Little Silver Point Rd Little Silver NJ 07739-1737 E-mail: dschmidt4@home.com

SCHMIDT, EDWARD CRAIG, lawyer; b. Pitts., Nov. 26, 1947; s. Harold Robert and Bernice (Williams) S.; m. Elizabeth Lowry Rial, Aug. 18, 1973; children: Harold Robert II, Robert Rial. BA, U. Mich., 1969; JD, U. Pitts., 1972. Bar: Pa. 1972, U.S. Dist. Ct. (we. dist.) Pa. 1972, U.S. Ct. Appeals (3d cir.) 1972, U.S. Ct. Appeals (D.C. cir.) 1975, U.S. Supreme Ct. 1981, U.S. Ct. Appeals (9th cir.) 1982, U.S. Ct. Appeals (4th cir.) 1982, U.S. Ct. Appeals (6th cir.) 1987, U.S. Ct. Appeals (2d cir.) 1992, U.S. Ct. Appeals (4th cir.) 1994. Assoc. Rose, Schmidt, Hasley & Di Salle, Pitts., 1972-77, ptnr., 1977-90, Jones, Day, Reavis & Pogue, Pitts., 1990—2001. Mem. adv. com. Superior Ct. Pa., 1978-80; NITA instr. Duquesne U., 1998-99. Co-editor: Antitrust Discovery Handbook-Supplement, 1982; asst. editor: Antitrust Discovery Handbook, 1980; contbr. articles to profl. jours. Bd. dirs. Urban League, Pitts., 1974-77, NITA instr., Duquesne U., 1998, 99. Mem. Supreme Ct. Hist. Soc., Pa. Bar Assn., D.C. Bar Assn., Allegheny County Bar Assn. (pub. reos. com. coun. civil litigation sect. 1977-80), Internat. Acad. Trials Lawyers, Acad. Trial Lawyers Allegheny County (bd. govs. 1980), Western Res. Acad. Alumni Assn. (trustee 1998—). Clubs: Rolling Rock (Ligonier, Pa.), Duquesne (Pitts.), Longue Vue (Pitts.) Republican. Antitrust, Federal civil litigation, Personal injury. Home and Office: 159 Washington St Pittsburgh PA 15218-1351

SCHMIDT, JOSEPH W. lawyer; b. Jeffersontown, Ky., July 6, 1946; s. A.W. and Olivia Ann (Hohl) S.; m. Angela Petchara Apiradee, Dec. 20, 1969; children: Narissa Ann, Suriya Christine. BA in Psychology, Bellarmine Coll., 1969; AB in Commerce, U. Md., Bangkok, 1972; JD, Columbia U., 1975. Bar: N.Y. 1976. Law clk. to presiding judge U.S. Dist. Ct. (so. dist.), N.Y., 1975-76; assoc. Breed, Abbott & Morgan, N.Y.C., 1976-83, ptnr., 1983-93, Whitman Breed Abbott & Morgan, 1993-96, Coudert Bros., N.Y.C., 1996—. Adminstrv. editor Columbia Jour. of Law and Social Problems, 1974-75. Woodrow Wilson fellow, 1968; Harlan Fiske Stone scholar, 1975. Mem. ABA, Assn. of Bar of the City of N.Y., N.Y. Bar Assn., Am. Coll. Investment Counsel. Avocations: skiing, reading. General corporate, Finance, Mergers and acquisitions. Office: Coudert Bros 1114 Ave Of The Americas New York NY 10036-7710 E-mail: schmidtj@coudert.com

SCHMIDT, KATHLEEN MARIE, lawyer; b. Des Moines, June 17, 1953; d. Raymond Driscoll and Hazel Isabelle (Rogers) Poage; m. Dean Everett Johnson, Dec. 21, 1974 (div. Nov. 1983); children: Aaron Dean, Gina Marie; m. Ronald Robert Schmidt, Feb. 7, 1987. BS in Home Econs., U. Nebr., 1974; JD, Creighton U., 1987. Bar: Nebr. 1987, U.S. Dist. Ct. Nebr. 1987, U.S. Ct. Appeals (8th cir.) 1989, U.S. Supreme Ct. 1991. Apprentice printer, journeyman Rochester (Minn.) Post Bull., 1978-82; dir. customer info. Cornhusker Pub. Power Dist., Columbus, Nebr., 1982-83; artist Pamida, Omaha, 1983; offset artist Cornhusker Motor Club, 1983-84; assoc. Lindahl O. Johnson Law Office, 1987-88; pvt. practice, 1988-90; ptnr. Emery, Penke, Blazek & Schmidt, 1990-91; pvt. practice, 1992—. Atty. in condemnation procs. Douglas County Bd. Appraisers, Omaha, 1988-99, Sarpy County Bd. Appraisers, Omaha, 1999—; presenter Nebr. Sch. Bd. Assn., 1991, 92. Mem. Millard Sch. Bd., Omaha, 1989-96, treas. 1991, 92; mem. strategic planning com. Millard Sch. Dist., 1990; mem. Omaha Mayor's Master Plan Com., 1991-94. Named hon. mem. Anderson Mid. Sch., Omaha, 1991; recipient Award of Achievement, Nebr. Sch. Bd. Assn., 1991, 94. Mem. Nebr. Bar Assn., Omaha Bar Assn. (spkrs. bur. 1992—), Nat. Sch. Bd. Assn. (del. federal rels. network 1991-96, cert. recognition 1991). Republican. Lutheran. Family and matrimonial, Juvenile, Probate.

SCHMIDT, L(AIL) WILLIAM, JR. lawyer; b. Thomas, Okla., Nov. 22, 1936; s. Lail William and Violet Kathleen (Kuper) S.; m. Diana Gail (div. May 1986); children: Kimberly Ann, Andrea Michelle; m. Marilyn Sue, Aug. 11, 1990; stepchildren: Leland Darrell Mosby, Jr., Crystal Rachelle Mosby. BA in Psychology, U. Colo., 1959; JD, U. Mich., 1962. Bar: Colo. 1962, U.S. Dist. Ct. Colo. 1964, U.S. Tax Ct. 1971, U.S. Ct. Appeals (10th cir.) 1964. Ptnr. Holland & Hart, Denver, 1962-77, Schmidt, Elrod & Wills, Denver, 1977-85, Moye, Giles, O'Keefe, Vermeire & Gorrell, Denver, 1985-90; of counsel Hill, Held, Metzger, Lofgren & Peele, Dallas, 1989-94; pvt. practice law Denver, 1990-2001; ptnr. Schmidt & Horen LLP, 2001—. Lectr. profl. orgns. Author: How To Live-and Die-with Colorado Probate, 1985, A Practical Guide to the Revocable Living Trust, 1990; contbr. articles to legal jours. Pres. Luth. Med. Ctr. Found., Wheat Ridge, Colo., 1985-89; pres. Rocky Mountain Prison and Drug Found., Denver, 1986—; bd. dirs. Luth. Hosp., Wheat Ridge, 1988-92, Bonfils Blood Ctr. Found., 1995—, Planned Giving Adv. Group of Nat. Jewish Hosp., Denver, 1996-98, St. Joseph Hosp. Found., 1999—; planned giving advisor Aspen Valley Med. Found., 1997—; mktg. and gifts adv. com. The Denver Found., 1998—. Fellow Am. Coll. Trust and Estate Counsel (Colo. chmn. 1981-86); mem. ABA, Am. Judicature Soc., Denver Estate Planning Coun., Rocky Mtn. Estate Planning Coun. (founder, pres. 1970-71), Greater Denver Tax Counsel Assn., Am. Soc. Magicians, Denver Athletic Club, Phi Delta Phi. Republican. Baptist. Avocation: magic. Estate planning, Probate, Estate taxation. Office: 1050 17th St Ste 1700 Denver CO 80265-2077 also: Law Offices Robert L Bolick Ltd 6060 Elton Ave Ste A Las Vegas NV 89107-0100 E-mail: estpln@aol.com

SCHMIDT, MICHAEL FRANCIS, lawyer; b. Detroit, Oct. 5, 1949; s. Carl Howard and Evelyn (Johnson) S.; m. Suzanne Lynn Sofian, June 10, 1977; children: Leslie Marie, Caroline Marie. BS summa cum laude, U. Detroit, 1971, JD magna cum laude, 1975. Bar: Mich. 1975, U.S. Dist. Ct. (ea. dist.) Mich. 1975, U.S. Dist. Ct. (we. dist.) Mich. 1978, U.S. Ct. Appeals (6th cir.) 1981. Assoc. Harvey, Kruse, P.C., Detroit, 1975-79, ptnr., 1979—. Mem. Pres.'s Cabinet, U. Detroit, 1981—. Served with U.S. Army, 1971-77. Mem. Internat. Assn. Def. Counsel, Mich. Assn. Def. Counsel, State Bar Mich., Oakland County Bar Assn., Def. Rsch. Inst., Detroit Athletic Club, Indianwood Golf Club, Beta Gamma Sigma, Alpha Sigma Nu. Roman Catholic. Federal civil litigation, State civil litigation. Office: 1050 Wilshire Dr Ste 320 Troy MI 48084-1526 E-mail: mschmidt@harveykruse.com

SCHMIDT, PAUL JOEL, lawyer; b. Milw., Nov. 25, 1961; s. Joel Schmidt and Mary Bierlein. BA, Colo. Coll., 1985; postgrad. U. Mich., 1986-88; JD, U. Colo., 1992. Bar: Colo. 1992, U.S. Dist. Ct. Colo. 1993. Assoc. Crane, Leake, Casey et al, Durango, Colo., 1993-95; dep. dist. atty. 6th Jud. Dist., 1995—. Actor Project A Jacky Chan H.K., 1983. Regional coord. Access Fund, Four Corners, 1993-95. Chinese Studies fellow U. Mich., 1987-88. Avocations: mountaineering, rock climbing, hiking, mountain-biking, skiing. Office: Office Dist Atty 1060 E 2d Ave Durango CO 81301

SCHMIDT, RICHARD MARTEN, JR. lawyer; b. Winfield, Kans., Aug. 2, 1924; s. Richard M. and Ida (Marten) S.; m. Ann Downing, Jan. 2, 1948; children: Eric, Gregory, Rolf (dec.), Heidi. AB, U. Denver, 1945, JD, 1948. Bar: Colo. 1948, D.C. 1968. Dep. dist. atty., City and County of Denver, 1949-50; mem. firm McComb, Zarlengo, Mott & Schmidt, Denver, 1950-54; ptnr. Schmidt & Van Cise (and predecessor), 1954-65; gen. counsel USIA, 1965-68; of counsel Cohn and Marks, Washington, 1969—. Counsel spl. agrl. investigating subcom. Counsel Am. Soc. Newspaper Editors, 1968—; mem. Gov.'s Coun. Local Govt., Colo., 1963-64; chmn. Mayor's Jud. Adv. Com., Denver, 1963-64, Gov.'s Supreme Ct. Nominating Com., 1964-65; mem. Gov.'s Oil Shale Adv. Com., 1963-65, Colo. Commn. on Higher Edn., 1965; mem. bd. Nat. Press Found., 1993—. Trustee U. Denver (life). Mem. ABA (chmn. standing com. on assn. comms. 1969-73, chmn. forum com. on comms. 1979-81, co-chmn. nat. conf. lawyers and reps. of media 1984-89, mem. commn. on lawyer advt. 1964-68), Colo. Bar Assn. (gov.), Denver Bar Assn. (pres. 1963-64), D.C. Bar Assn., Cosmos Club (Washington). Episcopalian. Home: 115 5th St SE Washington DC 20003-1123 Office: Cohn and Marks Cohn and Marks 1920 N St NW Ste 300 Washington DC 20036-1622 E-mail: rms@cohmarks.com

SCHMIDT, WAYNE WALTER, law association executive; b. St. Louis, Feb. 8, 1941; s. Warren W. and Geneva N. (Walker) S.; children: Andrew M., Nancy K. Diploma in English and comparative law, City of London Coll., 1963; BA, U. N.Mex., 1964; JD, Oklahoma City U., 1966; LLM, Northwestern U., 1974. Bar: N.Mex. 1966, Ill. 1968, D.C. 1970, N.Y. 1982. Dir. police legal advisor program Northwestern U., 1968-70; counsel Internat. Assn. Chiefs of Police, 1970-73; exec. dir. Am. for Effective Law Enforcement, Inc., Chgo., 1973—; pres. Pub. Safety Pers. Rsch. Inst., 1974—, Govt. Employment Rsch. Inst., Inc., 1986-89, Lauterbrunnen Properties, 1990-93; dir. Comprehensive Ensurers Market Syndicate, Inc., 1984-91, 93-94, Capital Exch. Mgmt., Inc., 1988-91. Cons. Uniform Code of Criminal Procedure. Co-author: Legal Aspects of Criminal Evidence, 1978, Introduction to Criminal Evidence, 1982, Introduction to Criminal Evidence and Court Procedure, 1987, 3d edit. 1995; editor Fire and Police Pers. Reporter, 1975—, Pub. Employment Health Law and Benefits, 1986-89, Fire and Police Ann. Case Digest, 1984—. Served with U.S. Army, 1966-67. Mem. ABA (liaison to criminal justice coun. 1973—), Internat. Assn. Chiefs of Police (vice chair legis. com. 1988—). Office: Am Effective Law Enforcement Legal Ctr 841 W Touhy Ave Park Ridge IL 60068-3351 E-mail: aele@aol.com

SCHMIDT, WILLIAM ARTHUR, JR. lawyer; b. Cleve., Oct. 2, 1939; s. William Arthur and Caroline (Jäger) S.; m. Gerilyn Pearl Smith, Sept. 30, 1967; children: Deborah, Dawn, Jennifer. BSBA, Kent State U., 1962; JD, Cleve. State U., 1968. Bar: Ohio 1968, Ill. 1990. Contract specialist NASA-Lewis, Cleve., 1962-66, procurement analyst, 1967-68; atty. Def. Logistics Agy., Alexandria, Va., 1968-73; assoc. counsel Naval Sea Sys. Command, Arlington, 1973-75; procurement policy analyst Energy R & D Adminstrn., Germantown, Md., 1975-76; sr. atty. U.S. Dept. Energy, 1976-78, counsel spl. projects Oak Ridge, Tenn., 1978-83; judge Agr. Bd. Contract Appeals, Washington, 1983-87; judge Bd. Contract Appeals HUD, 1987; chief legal counsel Fermilab, Batavia, Ill., 1987-92; gen. counsel Univ. Rsch. Assn., Inc., Washington, 1992—. Co-author: (NASA handbook) R & D Business Practices, 1968. Mem. Fed. Bar Assn. (past pres. East Tenn. 1978-83, 25 Yr. Svc. award 1994), Ill. Bar Assn., Bd. Contract Appeals Judges Assn. (dir.-sec. 1986-88), Sr. Execs. Assn., Delta Theta Phi (dist. chancellor 1978-83), Sigma Chi. Republican. Lutheran. Avocations: classic cars, Civil War history. General corporate, Government contracts and claims, Non-profit and tax-exempt organizations. Home: 7209 Bloomsbury Ln Spotsylvania VA 22553-1944 Office: Univ Rsch Assn Inc 1111 19th St NW Ste 400 Washington DC 20036-3627

SCHMITT, WILLIAM ALLEN, lawyer; b. Louisville, Aug. 29, 1909; s. Michael Joseph and Naoma Katherine Schmitt; m. Dorothy S. Turner, June 12, 1936 (dec. Feb. 1998); 1 child, Selene S. Kaelin. Student, U. Louisville, 1933. Bar: Ky. 1936, U.S. Dist. Ct. (we. dist.) Ky. 1936, N.C. 1997. Pvt. practice law, Louisville, 1936—; assoc. atty. Schmitt & Schmitt, 1936-60; judge Jefferson County Probate Ct., 1962-70; alcohol beverage control adminstr. Jefferson County Govt., 1962-70; law ptnr. Schmitt & Sandmann, 1968-74; pvt. practice law, 1974—, Jamestown, N.C., 1997—. Author: Kentucky Probate, 1980, 2nd edit., 1997; contbr. articles to profl. jours. Election poll judge various gen. elections, Louisville; active Muir Chapel United Meth. Ch.; pres. Wildwood Country Club, 1964, Legal Aid Soc., Louisville, 1968. Lt. USN, 1944-46. Inductee Ky. Tennis Hall of Fame, 1993. Mem. ABA, ATLA, Am. Arbitration Assn. (arbitration panelist 1983—, cert. mediator 1985—), Nat. Assn. Securities Dealers (arbitration panelist 1990—, cert. mediator 1994—), Am. Coll. Trust and Estate Counsel (state chmn. 1978-83), Ky. Bar Assn. (life, spkr. at seminars and convs. 1960-80, pres. 1970-71, probate com. 1970-86, chmn. 1977-81, trustee 1971-86, chmn. 1978-86, clients indemnity fund), N.C. State Bar Assn., N.C. State Bar, Fla. Acad. Cert. Mediators, Louisville Bar Assn. (spkr. at seminars 1960-80, pres. 1966, chmn. probate com. 1974-79, various meritorious svc. awards 1966-75). Avocation: tennis. Estate planning, Personal injury, Probate. Home: 109 Sagewood Rd Jamestown NC 27282-9489 Office: PO Box 997 Jamestown NC 27282-0997 also: 500 Ky Home Life Bldg 239 S 5th St Louisville KY 40202-3213 E-mail: waschmitt@northstate.net

SCHMITZ, FRANCIS DAVID, lawyer; b. Milw., July 13, 1950; s. Joseph Francis and Helen Julia (Rudzik) S.; m. Elizabeth Ann Brinker, Dec. 12, 1975; children: Sarah, Catherine. BA, St. Norbert Coll., 1972; MBA, So. Ill. U., 1975; JD, Marquette U., 1983. Bar: Wis. 1983, U.S. Dist. Ct. (ea. and we. dists.) Wis. 1983, U.S. Ct. Appeals (7th cir.) 1985. Law clk. to judge U.S. Ct. Appeals (7th cir.), Chgo., 1983-84; asst. U.S. atty. for ea. dist. Wis. U.S. Dept. Justice, Milw., 1984—, chief criminal divsn., 1993-96, chief econ. crimes, 1996-98, chief civil divsn., 1999—. Capt. U.S. Army, 1973-80, col. USAR, 1980—. Mem. State Bar Wis., Assn. U.S. Army, Habitat for Humanity. Roman Catholic. Avocations: flyfishing, golf. Office: Office US Atty 517 E Wisconsin Ave Milwaukee WI 53202-4500

SCHMOLL, HARRY F., JR. lawyer, educator; b. Somers Point, N.J., Jan. 20, 1939; s. Harry F. Sr. and Margaret E. S.; m. Rita L. Miescier, Aug. 29, 1977. BS, Rider Coll., 1960; JD, Temple U., 1967. Bar: Pa., D.C. 1969, N.J. 1975. With claims dept. Social Security Adminstrn., Phila., 1960-67; staff atty. Pa. State U., State College, 1968-69, instr. criminal justice University Park, 1969-74; regional dir. Pa. Crime Commn., State College, 1969-70; campaign aide U.S. Senator Scott Hugh, Harrisburg, Pa., 1970; pvt. practice law State College, 1970-74, Manahawkin, N.J., 1975-96; prof. criminal justice, bus. law Burlington County Coll., Pemberton, 1974—; pres. elect edn. assn., 1992-93, 96-97; pres. edn. assn., 1993-94, 97-98. Judge mcpl. ct., Stafford Twp., 1982-85. Author: New Jersey Criminal Law Workbook, 1976, 2nd edit., 1979, Absecon Diary of Margie Roth, 1933-37, 2000. Former gen.counsel german Heritage Coun. N.J., Inc.; mem. Barnegat Twp. Rent Control Bd., 1991, Barnegat Twp. Zoning Bd., 1994; mem. fund distbn. com. United Way of Burlington County, N.J., 1987—; trustee H.B. Smith Indsl. Village Conservacny, 1988—; mem. Stafford Twp. Com., 1979-81; dep. mayor, 1979. Mem. Pa. Bar assn., N.J. Bar Assn., German-Am. Club So. Ocean County (past pres.), Tri-State Jazz Soc. (bd. dirs.). General practice, Personal injury, Probate. E-mail: hschmoll@home.com

SCHMUDDE, LEE GENE, corporate lawyer; b. Harvey, Ill., Apr. 13, 1950; s. Kenneth H. and Jean E. (Alexander) S.; m. Mariann Verscharen, June 25, 1976; 1 child, Leighanne K. BA summa cum laude, Cornell Coll., Mount Vernon, Iowa, 1972; JD, Duke U., 1975. Bar: Fla. 1975, U.S. Dist. Ct. (ctrl. dist.) Fla. 1975. Law clk. to Chief Judge Joseph P. McNulty 2d Dist. Ct. Appeals, Lakeland, Fla., 1975-76; atty. Peterson, Myers, Lake Wales, 1976-78; v.p. legal and environ. affairs Walt Disney World Co., Orlando. Lectr. ABA, Fla. Bar, Orange County Bar Assn., Def. Lawyers Assn. Contbr. articles to Fla. Bar Jour. Bd. dirs., treas. Fla. Symphony Orch., Orlando, 1997; bd. dirs. Children's Home Soc., 1981-85; mem. adv. bd. Jr. Achievement, 1995—; chmn. Fla. Self-Ins. Guaranty ASsn., 1985, 93, bd. dirs., 1985—. Mem. Fla. Bar Assn. (lectr.), Am. Zoo and Aquarium Assn., U.S. C. of C. (Outstanding Young Man of Am. 1975), Fla. C. of C. (jud. and tort reform adv. bd. 2000—), Fla. Assn. Self-Insurers (bd. dirs. 1984-85), Ctrl. Fla. Hist. Soc. (bd. dirs. 2000—), Phi Beta Kappa. Avocations: tennis, basketball, sport fishing. Administrative and regulatory, General corporate, Environmental. Office: Walt Disney World Co PO Box 10 000 Lake Buena Vista FL 32830-1000

SCHMULTS, EDWARD CHARLES, lawyer, corporate and philanthropic administrator; b. Paterson, N.J., Feb. 6, 1931; s. Edward M. and Mildred (Moore) S.; m. Diane E. Beers, Apr. 23, 1960; children: Alison C., Edward M., Robert C. BS, Yale U., 1953; JD, Harvard U., 1958. Bar: N.Y. 1959, D.C. 1974. Assoc. White & Case, N.Y.C., 1958-65, ptnr., 1965-73, 77-81; gen. counsel Treasury Dept., Washington, 1973-74, undersec.,

1974-75; dep. counsel to Pres. U.S., 1975-76; dep. atty. gen. of U.S. Dept. Justice, Washington, 1981-84; sr. v.p. external rels., gen. counsel GTE Corp., Stamford, Conn., 1984-94. Lectr. securities laws. Bd. dirs. Green-Point Fin. Corp., Germany Fund, Ctrl. European Equity Fund, Deutsche Asset Mgmt. VIT Funds; chmn. bd. trustees Edna McConnell Clark Found. Served to 1st lt. USMC, 1953-55; capt. USMCR. Mem. Am. Bar Assn., Assn. Bar City N.Y., Adminstrv. Conf. U.S. (council 1977-84), Sakonnet Golf Club, Met. Club.

SCHNEE, CARL, lawyer, former prosecutor; BA, Muhlenberg Coll.; JD, Villanova U.; MA in Liberal Studies, U. Del., 2000. Bar: Del. 1962. Asst. pub. defender, 1965-69; former sr. ptnr. Prickett, Jones, Elliot, Kristol and Schnee; U.S. atty. Del. dist. U.S. Dept. Justice, 1999—2001; ptnr. Duane, Morris & Heckscher, Wilmington, Del., 2001—. Mem. Del. Bar. Office: 1100 N Market St Ste 1200 Wilmington DE 19801-1160*

SCHNEEBAUM, STEVEN MARC, lawyer; b. N.Y.C., Oct. 29, 1948; s. Harry and Nathalie (Maharam) S.; m. Karen McGovern, Aug. 20, 1972; children: Megan A., Rachel C. BA, Yale U., 1969; MA, Oberlin Coll., 1970; BA, Oxford U., Eng., 1976; MCL, George Washington U., 1978. Bar: D.C. 1978, U.S. Dist. Ct. D.C. 1978, U.S. Ct. Appeals (D.C. cir.) 1980, U.S. Ct. Internat. Trade 1981, U.S. Ct. Appeals (10th cir.) 1981, U.S. Ct. Appeals (7th cir.) 1982, U.S. Ct. Claims 1983, U.S. Ct. Appeals (fed. cir.) 1984, U.S. Ct. Appeals (4th cir.) 1985, U.S. Ct. Appeals (9th cir.) 1987, U.S. Ct. Appeals (3d cir.) 1989, U.S. Dist. Ct. Md. (trial bar) 1987., U.S. Supreme Ct. 1989, U.S. Ct. Appeals (5th cir.) 1992, U.S. Ct. Appeals (11th cir.) 1993. Assoc. Patton, Boggs & Blow, Washington, 1978-83, ptnr., 1983—. Prof. law , lectr. Am. U., Washington, 1988-90, Johns Hopkins Sch. Advanced Internat. Studies, Washington, 1990—, Nat. Law Ctr. George Washington U., Washington, 1992—, U.S. Ct. Appeals (6th ctr. 1999), (2d ctr. 2000). Contbr. articles to profl. jours. Bd. dirs. Legal Counsel for the Elderly, Washington, 1982-87, vice chmn., 1986, chmn., 1987; bd. dirs. Internat. Human Rights Law Group, Washington, 1982-96, treas., 1990—, bd. dir. Archdiocesan Legal Netowrk, 1989— (chmn. elect 2001). Recipient Cert. Appreciation D.C. Bar, 1984, Pro Bono award Internat. Human Rights Law Group, 1986. Mem. ABA, Fed. Bar Assn., Am. Soc. Internat. Law (bd. rev. and devel. 1988-92), Washington Fgn. Law Soc. Federal civil litigation, Private international, Public international.

SCHNEIDER, ELAINE CAROL, lawyer, researcher, writer; b. Mpls., Aug. 28, 1957; d. Allan William and Deborah G. Schneider; m. William Mack Olivé, Oct. 10, 1987 (div. July 1996); 1 child, Vanessa Inez Olivè. BA, U. Minn., 1979; JD, William Mitchell Coll. Law, St. Paul, 1982. Bar: N.Mex. 1984, Minn. 1998, D.C. 1999. Assoc. Settles, Kalamarides & Assocs., Anchorage, 1982, Dickson, Evans & Esch, Anchorage, 1982; legal rschr. John Hanson, 1983, 1983; acct. rep. Westlaw Svcs., Inc., Albuquerque, 1984, sales rep. New Orleans, 1985-86; libr. sales rep. West Pub. Co., Spokane, Wash., 1986-87, reference atty. St. Paul, 1988-97, product mgr., 1997-2001; pvt. practice Mpls. Ethics adv. bd. N.Mex. Bar, Albuquerque, 1984-85; midwest regional conf. com. Am. Immigration Lawyers Assn., 2000. Author: Substantive Judicial Law Outline of Habeas Corpus, 1984, What They Don't Teach You in the Bar Review Course, 1991, Challenging an Incredibility Finding on Appeal, An Incredibility Paradigm, 2001; mem. law rev. staff William Mitchell Coll. Law, 1980-81. Atty. immigration and naturalization law Minn. Advocates for Human Rights, Refugee and Immigrant Project. Recipient Vol. Pro Bono Atty. award, 15th Ann. Minn. Advocates for Human Rights, 1999. Mem. Phi Beta Kappa. Avocations: ventriloquism, skiing, swimming, travel, languages. Immigration, naturalization, and customs. Office: 701 4th Ave S Ste 500 Minneapolis MN 55415-1810 E-mail: avocatecs@aol.com

SCHNEIDER, ELIZABETH KELLEY, law librarian; b. Bloomington, Ill., July 10, 1946; d. George Raymond and Lucille Genvieve (Sutter) Kelley; m. John James Schneider, Aug. 21, 1982. BA in History, Wesleyan U., Ill., 1968; MLS, U. Minn., 1969; JD, William Mitchell Coll. of Law, 1973; LLM in Health Law, St. Louis U., 1997. Bar: Minn. 1974, U.S. Dist. Ct. Minn. 1995. Librarian Ramsy County Law Library, St. Paul, 1971-73; asst. law librarian U. of Akron (Ohio) Coll. of Law, 1973-74; prof. law, librarian Hamline U. Sch. Law, St. Paul, 1974-81; dir. Maricopa County Law Library, Phoenix, 1981-91; assoc. dir. law libr., asst. prof. Tex. Tech. Sch. Law, 1992-2000. Instr. legal research Ariz. Legal Secs. Assn., 1982, Phoenix Coll., 1982-85, Ariz. State Library Assn., 1984. Mem. ABA, Am. Assn. Law Libraries, Ariz. Assn. Law Libraries (pres. 1985-86), Ariz. Women Lawyers Assn., Desert Sun Aux., Nat. Assistance League (sec. 1985-86, chmn. 1986-87), Southwestern Assn. of Law Libr. (sec. 1987-90, v.p. 1990-91), Legal Info. Svcs. to the Pub. (chair 1988-89), Alpha Gamma Delta (pres. 1985-86). E-mial. Office: Plattner Schneidman & Schneider Sch Law 1707 E Highland Ste 190 Phoenix AZ 75016 E-mail: eksphx@yahoo.com

SCHNEIDER, KAREN BUSH, lawyer, educator; b. Lansing, Mich., Mar. 17, 1951; d. Gerard Joseph and Emily Virginia (Szoka) Bush; 1 child, Emily Margaret. BA magna cum laude, U. Notre Dame, 1973, JD, 1976. Bar: Mich. 1976, U.S. Dist. Ct. (we. dist.) Mich. 1976, U.S. Dist. Ct. (ea. dist.) Mich. 1981. From assoc. to ptnr. Foster, Swift, Collins & Smith P.C., Lansing, 1976-88; ptnr. White, Schneider Baird Young & Chiodini, P.C., Okemos, Mich., 1988—, pres., 1994-97, 99—. Adj. prof. Thomas M. Cooley Law Sch., Lansing, 1985—, vis. prof., 1988-89; mem. jud. qualifications com. State Bar Mich., 1987-91; arbitrator, Mich. Employment Rels. Commn., 1990—. Contbr. legal briefs to profl jours., quarterly articles to Greater Lansing Bus. Monthly mag., Lansing. Mem. adv. coun. Wharton Ctr., 2001—. Recipient Frederick Griffiths award for Tchg. Excellence Thomas M. Cooley Law Sch., 2000. Fellow Mich. State Bar Found.; mem. Am. Arbitration Assn. (labor arbitrator 1985—), Ingham County Bar Assn. (bd. dirs., sec. 1982-83, pubs. com. 1983-85, chmn. pubs. com. 1984-85), Am. Lung Assn. Mich. (bd. dirs. 1985-89, chmn. pers. com. 1986-89), U. Notre Dame Alumni Assn. of Lansing (sec. 1979-80, pres. 1980-81, pub. rels. officer 1981-82, v.p. 1983-85), Capital Area Humane Soc. (bd. dirs. 1984-90, corr. sec. 1984, rec. sec. 1985, fundraising chmn. 1985-90, pres. 1986), State Bar of Mich. (continuing edn. com. 1997—, Biennial Diana award for profl. and cmty. svc. 1999). Roman Catholic. Avocations: fitness swimming, gourmet cooking. Civil rights, Labor. Home: 16717 Thorngate Rd East Lansing MI 48823-9772 Office: White Schneider Baird Young & Chiodini PC 2300 Jolly Oak Rd Okemos MI 48864-3546 E-mail: Kschneider@wsbyc.com

SCHNEIDER, LAZ LEVKOFF, lawyer; b. Columbia, S.C., Mar. 15, 1939; s. Philip L. and Dorothy Harriet (Levkoff) S.; m. Ellen Linda Shiffrin, Dec. 12, 1968; 1 child, David Allen. BA, Yale U., 1961, LLB, 1964; LLM, NYU, 1965. Bar: D.C. 1965, N.Y. 1965, Fla. 1970. Assoc. Fulton, Walter & Duncombe, N.Y.C., 1965-67, Roseman, Colin Kaye Petschek Freund & Emil, N.Y.C., 1967-69, Kronish, Lieb, Weiner, Shainswit & Hellman, N.Y.C., 1969-70; ptnr. Ruden Barnett McClosky & Schuster, Ft. Lauderdale, Fla., 1970-80, Sherr, Tiballi, Fayne & Schneider, Ft. Lauderdale, 1986-91, Berger Singerman, Ft. Lauderdale, 1991—; pvt. practice, 1980-86. Bd. dirs. Ocean Biochem. Inc. Grad. editor Tax Law Rev., 1964-65. Exec. com. Fla. regional bd. Anti Defamation League, 1972—. Mem. Fla. Bar Assn., Broward County Bar Assn. (chmn. sect. corp. bus. and banking law 1978-80), Yale Club (pres. 1977-79). Jewish. General corporate, Securities. Office: 350 E Las Olas Blvd Ste 1000 Fort Lauderdale FL 33301-4215 E-mail: Lschneider@bergersingerman.com, lazsch@att.net

SCHNEIDER, MAHLON C. lawyer; b. 1939; BA, U. Minn., 1962, law degree, 1964. Bar: Minn. 1965. Atty. Green Giant Co., 1980, Pillsbury, 1980-84, v.p., gen. counsel foods divsn., 1984-89; corp. atty. Geo. A. Hormel & Co., Austin, Minn., 1989-90, v.p., gen. counsel, 1990-99, sr. v.p. external affairs, gen. counsel, 1999—. Contracts commercial, Product liability. Office: Hormel Foods Corp 1 Hormel Pl Austin MN 55912-3680

SCHNEIDER, PAM HORVITZ, lawyer; b. Cleve., Nov. 29, 1951; m. Milton S. Schneider, June 30, 1973; 1 child, Sarah Anne. BA, U. Pa., 1973; JD, Columbia U., 1976. Bar: N.Y. 1977, Pa. 1979. Assoc. White & Case, N.Y.C., 1976-78, Drinker Biddle & Reath LLP, Phila., 1978-84, ptnr., 1984-2001; founding ptnr. Gadsden Schneider & Woodward LLP, King of Prussia, Pa., 2001—. Contbr. articles to profl. jours. Fellow Am. Coll. Trust and Estate Counsel (past regent); mem. ABA (past chair, real property probate and trust law sect.), Internat. Acad. Estate and Trust Law (academician). Estate planning, Probate, Estate taxation. Office: Gadsden Schneider & Woodward LLP The Merion Bldg 700 S Henderson Rd Ste 345 King Of Prussia PA 19406 E-mail: pschneider@gsw-llp.com

SCHNEIDER, RICHARD GRAHAM, lawyer; b. Bryn Mawr, Pa., Aug. 2, 1930; s. Vincent Bernard and Marion Scott (Graham) S.; m. Margaret Peter Fritz, Feb. 15, 1958; children: Margaret W., Richard Graham, John F. BA, Yale U., 1952; JD, U. Pa., 1957. Bar: Pa. 1958. Assoc. Dechert Price & Rhoads, Phila., 1957-66, ptnr., 1966-95; of counsel, 1995—. Case editor U. Pa. Law Rev., 1956-57. Trustee Baldwin Sch., Bryn Mawr, 1971-79; trustee Episcopal Acad., Merion, Pa., 1976-83. 1st lt. USAF, 1952-54, PTO. Mem. ABA, Pa. Bar Assn., Phila. Bar Assn., Order of Coif, Merion Cricket Club, Merion Golf Club (sec. 1997—), Yale Club (pres. 1966-68). Republican. Presbyterian. Antitrust, General civil litigation. Office: Dechert Price & Rhoads 4000 Bell Atlantic Tower 1717 Arch St Lbby 3 Philadelphia PA 19103-2713 E-mail: gladwyue@aol.com

SCHNEIDER, ROBERT JEROME, lawyer; b. Cin., June 22, 1947; s. Jerome William and Agnes (Moehringer) S.; m. Janice Loraine Eckhoff, Dec. 13, 1968; children: Aaron Haisley, Jared Alan, Margot Laraine. BSME, U. Cin., 1970, JD, 1973. Bar: Ill. 1973, U.S. Dist. Ct. (no. dist.) Ill. 1973, U.S. Ct. Appeals (7th cir.) 1973, U.S. Ct. Appeals (fed. cir.) 1973. Ptnr. Mason, Kolehmainen, Rathburn & Wyss, Chgo., 1973-82; ptnr., asst. chmn. patents, chmn. intellect. property dept. McDermott, Will & Emery, 1982-94; chmn. intellectual property dept. Chapman & Cutler, 1995—. Mem. ABA, ASME, Ill. Bar Assn., Chgo. Bar Assn., Licensing Execs. Soc., Intellectual Property Law Assn. Chgo. (sec. 1981-83), Fedn. Internat. des Conseils en Proriete Industrielle, Assn. Internationale pour la Protection de la Propertièté Industrielle, Internat. Trademark Assn., Internat. Trade Commn. Trial Lawyers Assn., Am. Intellectual Property Law Assn., Tower Club (bd. govs. 1988—, v.p. 1994-95, pres. 1995—), Univ. Club Chgo. Republican. Roman Catholic. Federal civil litigation, Patent, Trademark and copyright. Home: 1609 Asbury Ave Winnetka IL 60093-1303 Office: Chapman & Cutler Chicago IL 60601 Fax: 530-464-2529. E-mail: iplaw@chapman.com

SCHNEIDER, THOMAS PAUL, foundation administrator; b. June 5, 1947; s. Milton and Gloria (Bocaner) S.; m. Susan G. Stein, May 31, 1987; children: Rachel Jenny, Daniel Joshua. BA with honors, JD, U. Wis., 1972. Atty. U.S. Dept. Justice, Milw., 1993-2001; exec. dir. youth svcs. COA Youth & Family Ctrs., 2001—. Mem. Wis. Bar Assn. Democrat. Jewish. Office: COA Youth & Family Ctrs 909 E North Ave Milwaukee WI 53212 E-mail: tomcoa@execpc.com

SCHNURMAN, ALAN JOSEPH, lawyer; b. N.Y.C., July 1, 1945; s. Albert and Ruth (Sirota) S.; m. Judith Bernstein, Mar. 31, 1974; children—Michele, David. B.S. in Acctg., Bklyn. Coll., 1967; J.D., N.Y. Law Sch., 1971. Bar: N.Y. 1972, U.S. Ct. Appeals (2d cir.) 1973, U.S. Dist. Ct. (ea. and so. dists.) N.Y. 1974, U.S. Supreme Ct. 1976. Acct. tax dept. Arthur Andersen & Co., N.Y.C., 1971-72; sole practice, N.Y.C., 1972-80; ptnr. Zalman & Schnurman, N.Y.C., 1980—; chmn. arbitration panels N.Y. Civil Ct., 1983—; moderator in field. Host Lawline syndicated cable TV program, 1983—; assoc. editor N.Y. State Trial Lawyers Quar., 1981. Mem. ABA, Am. Judges Assn., N.Y. State Bar Assn., Assn. Trial Lawyers Am., N.Y. State Trial Lawyers Assn. (bd. dirs. 1988—), Assn. Trial Lawyers N.Y.C. (bd. dirs. 1986—, v.p., chmn. continuing legal edn. 1988—), N.Y. County Lawyers Assn., Assn. of Bar of City of N.Y. (supreme ct. com. 1989—), N.Y. Law Sch. Alumni Assn. (bd. dirs. 1983—). Democrat. Jewish. State civil litigation, Insurance, Personal injury. Home: 870 United Nations Plz Apt 20E New York NY 10017-1819 Office: Zalman & Schnurman 63 Wall St Fl 27 New York NY 10005-3062

SCHOBER, THOMAS LEONARD, lawyer; b. Green Bay, Wis., Jan. 5, 1946; s. Leonard M. and Ruth (Christoph) S.; m. Suzan C. Murray, Sept. 5, 1981. BA, Northwestern U., 1968; JD, U. Wis., 1973. Bar: Wis. 1973; cert. civil advocate Nat. Bd. Trial Advocacy; cert. mediator. Assoc. Trowbridge Law Firm, Green Bay, 1973-81; ptnr. Schober & Ulatowski, 1981—. Chmn. bd. atty.'s profl. responsibility com. Dist. 14, Supreme Ct. Wis., 1985-96. Pres. YMCA, Green Bay, 1984-85. Served as sgt. U.S. Army, 1968-70, Vietnam. Mem. ABA, Wis. Bar Assn., Def. Research Inst., Trucking Industry Def. Assn. State civil litigation, Insurance, Transportation. Office: PO Box 1780 Green Bay WI 54305-1780 E-mail: tomLS@sulaw.com

SCHOCHET, HARVEY S. lawyer; b. Balt., May 24, 1948; s. Nathan and Silvia (Shostack) S.; m. Kathleen Kerr, Nov. 25, 1976; children: John, Joanna. BS with highest honors, U. Md., 1971; JD, Georgetown U., 1974. Bar: Calif. 1974, U.S. Dist. Ct. (no. dist.) Calif. 1974; CPA, Md. 1971; Assoc. firm Dinkelspiel, Pelavin, Steefel & Levitt, San Francisco, 1974-80; ptnr. Steefel, Levitt & Weiss, San Francisco, 1981— ; bd. dirs. Am. Bankruptcy Inst., Washington, 1983— . Author: Tender Offers, 1974; Setoffs, 1981-84, 88; DIP Financing 1981. Editor: International Bankruptcy, 1983; Georgetown U. Law Jour., 1974. Mem. ABA (bus. bankruptcy com. 1975— , one of Best Lawyers in Am., 1987). Banking, Bankruptcy. Office: Steefel Levitt & Weiss 29th Flr One Embarcadero Ctr San Francisco CA 94111

SCHOCHOR, JONATHAN, lawyer, educator; b. Suffern, N.Y., Sept. 9, 1946; s. Abraham and Betty (Hechtor) S.; m. Joan Elaine Brown, May 31, 1970; children: Lauren Aimee, Daniel Ross. BA, Pa. State U., 1968; JD, Am. U., 1971. Bar: D.C. 1971, U.S. Dist. Ct. D.C. 1971, U.S. Ct. Appeals (D.C. cir.) 1971, Md. 1974, U.S. Dist. Ct. Md. 1974, U.S. Supreme Ct. 1986. Assoc. McKenna, Wilkinson & Kittner, Washington, 1970-74, Ellin & Baker, Balt., 1974-84; ptnr. Schochor, Federico & Staton, 1984—. Lectr. in law; expert witness to state legis. Assoc. editor-in-chief Am. U. Law Rev., 1970-71. Mem. ABA, ATLA (state del. 1991, state gov. 1992-95), Am. Bd. Trial Advs. (membership com. 1994—), Am. Bd. Trial Advs., Am. Judicature Soc., Md. State Bar Assn. (spl. com. on health claims arbitration 1983), Md. Trial Lawyers Assn. (bd. govs. 1986-87, mem. legis. com. 1985-88, chmn. legis. com. 1986-87, sec. 1987-88, exec. com. 1987-92, v.p. 1987-88, pres.-elect 1989, pres. 1990-91), Balt. City Bar Assn. (legis com. 1986-87, spl. com. on tort reform 1986, medicolegal com. 1989-90, cir. ct. for Balt. City task force-civil document mgmt. sys. 1994-95), Bar Assn. D.C., Internat. Platform Assn., Phi Alpha Delta. Federal civil litigation, State civil litigation, Personal injury. Office: Schochor Federico & Staton PA 1211 Saint Paul St Baltimore MD 21202-2783

SCHOENBORN, DANIEL LEONARD, lawyer; b. Buffalo, Oct. 28, 1947; s. Leonard Schoenborn and Ann Milne (Finlayson) McClive; m. Theresa Marranca, July 20, 1968; children: Jeffrey, Sean, Marla. BA, SUNY, Buffalo, 1969; JD, SUNY, 1972. Bar: N.Y. 1973, U.S. Dist. Ct. (we. dist.) N.Y. 1975, U.S. Ct. Appeals (2d cir.) 1975, U.S. Supreme Ct. 1978. Assoc. C. Spinner, Buffalo, 1972-73; ptnr. DeMarie & Schoenborn, P.C., 1973—. Chmn. com. Cub Scouts Pack 248 Boy Scouts Am., Elma, N.Y., 1981-82; trustee Leukemia Soc. Am., Buffalo, 1981-87, v.p., 1982-86; sponsor Elma, Marilla, Wales Sports Inc., Elma, 1981—, bd. dirs. 1988-90. Mem. ABA (ins. practice com.), Erie County Bar Assn. (chmn. com. 1980—, dir. 1991—), N.Y. State Bar Assn., N.Y. State Trial Law Assn. (negligence com. 1985—), Erie County Trial Lawyers Assn., Kiwanis (sec. 1988-90, pres. 1996-98). Republican. Roman Catholic. General civil litigation, Insurance, Personal injury. Office: DeMarie & Schoenborn PC 800 Convention Tower Buffalo NY 14202-3174

SCHOENE, FRIEDRICH TOBIAS, lawyer; b. Goettingen, Germany, May 20, 1966; s. Albrecht and Dagmar (Haver) S.; m. Louisa Gräfin zu Innhausen and Knyphausen, Aug. 11, 2000. Degree in law, U. Heidelberg, Muenster and Goettingen, Germany. Bar: Berlin 1996. Assoc. Oppenhoff & Raedler, Berlin, Germany, 1996-99; jr. ptnr. Oppenhoff & Raedler Linklaters & Alliance, Germany, 1999-2000; ptnr. Hogan & Hartson Raue LLP, Germany, 2001—. Vis. lawyer S. Horowitz & Co., Tel Aviv, 1998—99. Mem.: German-Israeli Lawyers' Assn. (bd. dirs. 1998—2001), Order St. John (knight 1998—). Appellate, General civil litigation, General corporate. Office: Hogan & Hartson Raue LLP Potsdamer Platz 1 Berlin 10785 Germany E-mail: FTSchoene@hhlaw.com

SCHOENE, KATHLEEN SNYDER, lawyer; b. Glen Ridge, N.J., July 24, 1953; d. John Kent and Margaret Ann (Bronder) Snyder. BA, Grinnell Coll., 1974; MS, So. Conn. State Coll., 1976; JD, Washington U., St. Louis, 1982. Bar: Mo. 1982, U.S. Dist. Ct. (we. and ea. dists.) Mo. 1982, Ill. 1983. Head libr. Mo. Hist. Soc., St. Louis, 1976-79; assoc. Peper, Martin, Jensen, Maichel & Hetlage, 1982-88, ptnr., 1989-98, Armstrong Teasdale LLP, St. Louis, 1998—. Bd. dirs. Legal Svcs. of Eastern Mo. Author: (with others) Missouri Corporation Law and Practice, 1985, Missouri Business Organizations, 1998; contbr. articles to profl. jours. Trustee Grinnell (Iowa) Coll., ex officio voting mem., 1991-93; bd. dirs. Jr. League St. Louis, 1995-96, Leadership Ctr. Greater St. Louis, 1995-96, FOCUS St. Louis, 1996-2001, exec. com., 1997-99; active St. Louis Forum, 1997—, Herbert Hoover Boys and Girls Club, St. Louis, 1999—. Mem. ABA, Nat. Conf. Bar Founds. (trustee 1996-2000, pres. elect 1997-98, pres. 1998-99), The Mo. Bar (bd. govs. 1997-99, chair bus. law com. 2000—), Ill. State Bar Assn., Bar Assn. Met. St. Louis (treas. 1991-92, sec. 1992-93, v.p. 1993-94, pres.-elect 1994-95, pres. 1995-96, chair small bus. com. 1987-88, exec. com. 1988-96, chair bus. law sect. 1988-89, mem. exec. com. young lawyers sect. 1988-90), St. Louis Bar Found. (bd. dirs. 1994-2000, v.p. 1995-96, pres. 1996-98). General corporate, Health, Securities. Home: 7824 Cornell Ave Saint Louis MO 63130-3701 Office: Armstrong Teasdale One Metropolitan Sq Saint Louis MO 63102 E-mail: kschoene@armstrongteasdale.com

SCHOENFELD, BARBARA BRAUN, lawyer, investment executive; b. Phila., Apr. 17, 1953; d. Irving Leon Braun and Virginia (Parker) Sand; m. Larry Jay Schoenfeld, June 29, 1975; children: Alexander, Gordon, Max. BA cum laude, U. Pa., 1974, M in City Planning, Social Work, 1977; JD, Boston U., 1982. Bar: R.I. 1982, U.S. Dist. Ct. R.I. 1982. Assoc. planner Del. Valley Hosp. Council, Phila., 1978-79; summer assoc. Tillinghast, Collins & Graham, Providence, 1980, 81; assoc. Edwards & Angell, 1982-86, Ropes & Gray, Providence, 1986-92; dep. treas., gen. counsel State of R.I., 1993-99; v.p. Brown Bros. Harriman & Co., Boston, 1999—. Chmn., bd. dirs. Com. Women's Health Concerns, Phila., 1978-79; bd. dirs. Jewish Family Svc., Providence, 1982-88, Jewish Fedn. of R.I., 1989-91; assoc. treas. Jewish Cmty. Ctr. of R.I.; bd. of assocs. Alumni Trustees U. Pa.; chmn. admissions com. U. Pa. Alumni Club, Providence, 1982-95; trustee The Wheeler Sch., 1994—. Mem. ABA, R.I. Bar Assn., Ledgemont Country Club (Seekonk, Mass.). Democrat. Jewish. Avocations: skiing, travel, French. Office: Brown Bros Harriman & Co 40 Water St Boston MA 02109-3661 E-mail: bbsprov@aol.com

SCHOENFELD, HOWARD ALLEN, lawyer; b. N.Y.C., Apr. 17, 1948; s. Irving and Muriel (Levy) S.; m. Paula Simon; 1 child, Haley Rebecca. BA, U. Pa., 1970; JD, Georgetown U., 1973. Bar: Md. 1973, U.S. Dist. Ct. Md. 1973, Wis. 1976, U.S. Dist. Ct. (ea. dist.) Wis. 1976, U.S. Dist. Ct. (we. dist.) Wis. 1987. Law clk. Md. Ct. Appeals, 1973-74; assoc. Gordon, Feinblatt, Rothman, Hoffberger & Hollander, Balt., 1974-76; ptnr. Trebon & Schoenfeld, Milw., 1976-85, Godfrey & Kahn, Milw., 1985—. Chmn. John Anderson Campiagn for Pres., Wis., 1980; pres. Milw. Jewish Coun., 1987-89, mem., 1983—. Recipient Young Leadership award Milw. Jewish Fedn., 1983. Mem. ABA, Wis. Bar Assn., Milw. Bar Assn. Banking, Bankruptcy, Contracts commercial. Office: Godfrey & Kahn 780 N Water St Ste 1500 Milwaukee WI 53202-3590 E-mail: haschoen@gklaw.com, hasreorg@aol.com

SCHOENFELD, MICHAEL P. lawyer; b. Oct. 17, 1935; s. Jack and Anne Schoenfeld; m. Helen Schorr, Apr. 3, 1960; childrne: Daniel, Steven, Tracy. BS in Acctg., NYU, 1955; LLB, LLD, Fordham U., 1958. Bar: N.Y. 1959, U.S. Supreme Ct. 1963. Coun. Am. Home Assurance Co., N.Y.C., 1958-62; ptnr. Schoenfeld & Schoenfeld, Melville, N.Y., 1959—. V.p. Interstate Brokerage Corp., 1965-84, pres., 1984—; ptnr. Melville Realty Co., 1977—; legal adv. various bus. orgns. V.p., trustee Temple Beth David, Commack, N.Y., 1972-75; chmn. Cmty. Action Com. of Dix Hills and Commack, 1970-72, Dix Hills Planning Bd., 1972-74; treas. Dix Hills Rep. Club, 1976-80; mem. Huntington (N.Y.) Zoning Bd. Appeals, 1980-91, chmn., 1986-89. Recipient United Jerusalem award Israel Bond Drive, 1977, City of Hope Svc. award, George Bacon award Fordham Law Sch. Mem. N.Y. State Bar Assn., Suffolk County Bar Assn. Insurance, Personal injury, Product liability. Home: 14 Clayton Dr Dix Hills NY 11746-5517 Office: 999 Walt Whitman Rd Melville NY 11747-3007

SCHOENFIELD, RICK MERRILL, lawyer; b. Chgo., July 21, 1951; s. Herbert and Bernice (Krichilsky) S. BA, Northwestern U., 1973, JD cum laude, 1976; cert., Nat. Inst. Trial Advocacy, Chgo., 1979. Bar: Ill. 1976, U.S. Dist. Ct. (no. dist.) Ill. 1977, U.S. Ct. Appeals (7th cir.) 1979, U.S. Ct. Appeals (4th cir.) 1984, U.S. Supreme Ct. 1984, U.S. Dist. Ct. (ea. dist.) Wis. 1987. Assoc. Ettinger & Lake, Chgo., 1976-79, Ettinger & Assocs., Ltd., Chgo., 1979-81; ptnr. Ettinger & Schoenfield, 1981-92, Schoenfield, Swartzman & Massin, Chgo., 1992—. Instr. De Paul Law Sch., Chgo., 1977-78, Chgo.-Kent Coll. Law, 1989—, U. Ill. Chgo., 1991-94. Co-author Legal Negotiations: Gettin Maximum Results, 1988, The McGraw Hill 26 Hour Negotiation Course, 1991. Recipient award for Pro Bono Litigation, Operation Lakewatch, Chgo., 1983. Mem. Nat. Resources Def. Council. Environmental, Personal injury, Toxic tort. Office: Schoenfield Swartzman & Massin 55 W Monroe St Ste 3460 Chicago IL 60603-5010 E-mail: rschoenfield@ameritech.net

SCHOENWALD, MAURICE LOUIS, retired lawyer; b. N.Y.C., Mar. 30, 1920; s. Jacob and Gertrude (Maier) S.; m. Susan Zysman, Nov. 4, 1943; children: David, Beth, Robin. BA, NYU, 1943; JD, Case Western Res. U., 1947. Bar: N.Y. 1947, Fla. 1978, U.S. Dist. Ct. (so. dist.) N.Y. 1950, U.S. Dist. Ct. (ctrl. dist.) Fla. 1980, U.S. Ct. Appeals (11th dist.) Ga. 1986. Pvt. practice, N.Y.C., 1948-80. Pres. New Alternatives Fund, Melville, N.Y.,

1982—, Accrued Equities Inc., fin. advisor, since 1954; prin. broker dealer; mem. faculty Hofstra U., 1968-69. Author: Investment Contracts, 1982, (handbook) Wealth Management, 1974. Bd. dirs. ACLU, Sarasota, Fla., 1984-86. Lt. (j.g.) USN, 1942-45. Fellow Acad. Matrimonial Lawyers, Sarasota Sailing Squadron. Democrat. Family and matrimonial, General practice, Securities.

SCHOETTLE, FERDINAND P. legal educator; b. Phila., Aug. 17, 1933; s. Ferdinand P. and Helen Louise (White) S.; m. E. Bok, Feb. 13, 1965 (div. 1976); m. D. Jean Thomson, Nov. 24, 1979 (div. 1982); children—Michael, Derek. B.A. in History, Princeton U., 1955; LL.D., Harvard U., 1960, M.A. in Econs., 1978, Ph.D., 1983. Bar: Pa. 1961, Minn. 1968. Asst., U.S. Senator J.S. Clark, Washington, 1961-62; assoc. Morgan, Lewis & Bockius, Phila., 1963-67; prof. law U. Minn. Law Sch., Mpls., 1967— ; vis. prof. Harvard U., 1972-74, Uppsala U., Sweden, 1984; guest scholar Brookings Inst., Washington, 1992-93. Co-author: State and Local Taxes, 1974; editor: Tax Policy Notes, 1993—; contbr. articles to profl. jours. Served to lt. USN, 1955-57. Mem. sailing U.S. Olympic Team, 1956, 60. Mem. ABA (chmn. taxes and revenue com. 1979-82), Am. Law Inst. Home: 3104 Dumbarton Ave NW Washington DC 20007-3308 Office: U Minn Sch Law Minneapolis MN 55455

SCHOFIELD, ANTHONY WAYNE, judge; b. Farmington, N.Mex., Mar. 5, 1949; s. Aldred Edward and Margueriete (Knudsen) S.; m. Rebecca Ann Rosecrans, May 11, 1971; children: Josie, Matthew Paul, Peter Christian, Addie, Joshua James, M. Thomas, Jacob L., Daniel Z. BA, Brigham Young U., 1973, JD, 1976. Bar: Utah 1976, U.S. Dist. Ct. Utah 1976, U.S. Ct. Appeals (7th and 10th cirs.) 1977. Law clk. to hon. judge A. Sherman Christansen U.S. Dist. Ct. Utah, Salt Lake City, 1976-77; assoc. Ferenz, Bramhall, Williams & Gruskin, Agana, Guam, 1977-79; pvt. practice American Fork, Utah, 1979-80; assoc. Jardine, Linebaugh, Brown & Dunn, Salt Lake City, 1980-81; mem., dir. Ray, Quinney & Nebeker, Provo, Utah; judge 4th Jud. Dist. Ct., 1993—. Bishop Mormon Ch., American Fork, 1985-88; commr. American Fork City Planning Commn., 1980-85; trustee American Fork Hosp., 1984-93. Mem. Cen. Utah Bar Assn. (pres. 1987, 91). Avocations: photography, music. Office: 125 N 100 W Provo UT 84601-2849

SCHOLL, DAVID ALLEN, former federal judge, lawyer; b. Bethlehem, Pa., Aug. 20, 1944; s. George Raymond and Beatrice Roberta (Weaver) S.; m. Cynthia Ann Schuler Vetere, June, 1966 (div. 1972); m. Portia Elizabeth White, May 26, 1973; children: Tracy, Xavier; 1 stepchild, Sierra Milan. AB, Franklin & Marshall Coll., 1966; JD, Villanova U., 1969. Bar: Pa. 1969, U.S. Dist. Ct. (ea. dist.) 1970, U.S. Ct. Appeals (3d cir.) 1971, U.S. Tax Ct. 1975, U.S. Supreme Ct. 1975. Staff atty. Community Legal Services, Inc., Phila., 1969-73, 77-80; exec. dir. Delaware County Legal Assistance Assn., Chester, Pa., 1973-76; mng. atty. Lehigh Valley Legal Services, Bethelehem, Allentown, 1980-86; judge U.S. Bankruptcy Ct., Phila., 1986-94, chief judge, 1994-99, judge, 1999-2000. Bd. dirs. Phila. Vols. for Indigent Program, 1988—94, Consumer Bankruptcy Assistance Project, 1992—98, 2000—. Recipient Joseph Harris award Ba'Hais of Lehigh Valley, Bethelehem, 1984, Vol. of Yr. award Temple LEAP Program, 1997. Mem. Pa. Bar Assn. (chairperson consumer law commn., 1983-86), Northampton County Bar Assn. Avocations: baseball, rock music. Office: Ste 309 200 E State St Media PA 19063 Fax: 610-565-1201. E-mail: judgescholl@redeptionlawcenter.com

SCHOLL, JUDITH LOIS, lawyer; b. N.Y.C., Nov. 2, 1949; d. Harry and Deena (Isreal) Teitelbaum; m. Frederick William Scholl, May 23, 1978. B.A., SUNY, 1971; J.D., Bklyn. Law Sch., 1974; LL.M., NYU, 1979. Bar: N.Y. 1976, U.S. Dist. Ct. (so. dist.) N.Y. 1981. Assoc. prof. law Del. Law Sch., Wilmington, 1975-79; contracts coordinator, adminstr. Optical Info. System, Exxon Enterprises, Inc., Elmsford, N.Y., 1977-79; assoc. prof. law Touro Law Sch., N.Y.C., 1980— ; v.p., gen. counsel, gen. mgr., dir. Godenoll Tech. Corp., Yonkers, N.Y., 1980— ; tutor Kingston Study group for disadvantaged, N.Y., 1968-69; atty. pro bono publico court case, N.Y.C., 1981-82, executor and trustee of charitable estate and trust, 1984— . Named Outstanding Tchr., Del. Law Sch. Students, Wilmington, 1976. Mem. Order of Barristers, ABA, Westchester Women's Bar Assn., Phi Alpha Delta. Home: 2575 Palisade Ave Bronx NY 10463-6101 Office: Codenoll Tech Corp 1086 N Broadway Yonkers NY 10701-1107

SCHOLL, STEPHEN GERRARD, lawyer; b. Houston, June 29, 1948; s. Al Cleveland and Jeanne Gladys (Gerrard) S.; m. Deborah Ann Pasek, Feb. 14, 1988; 1 child, Madeline Morgan. BA in Polit. Sci., U. Mo., 1970, JD, 1973. Bar: Mo. 1973, U.S. Dist. Ct. (we. dist.) Mo. 1973, U.S. Dist. Ct. (so. dist.) Tex. 1989, U.S. Ct. Appeals (8th cir.) 1980, U.S. Ct. Appeals (5th cir. 1989); cert. in civil trial law. Assoc., ptnr. Popham, Conway, Sweeny, Fremont & Bunschu PC, Kansas City, Mo., 1973-78, Linde, Thomson, Fairchild, Langworthy, Kohn & Van Dyke PC, Kansas City, 1978-86; ptnr., shareholder Dotson & Scofield, Houston, 1986-90, Hirsch & Westheimer PC, Houston, 1990—. Adj. prof. U. Houston Law Ctr., 1989-96. Contbr. articles to profl. jours. Mem. ABA (litigation sect.), Nat. Inst. Trial Advocacy, Mo. Bar Assn. Contracts commercial, Personal injury, Transportation. Home: 849 Harvard St Apt A Houston TX 77007-1644 Office: Hirsch & Westheimer PC 700 Louisiana St Fl 25 Houston TX 77002-2700 E-mail: sscholl@hirschwest.com

SCHOLLANDER, WENDELL LESLIE, JR. lawyer; BS, U. Pa., 1966, MBA, 1968; postgrad., Stetson U., 1969-70; JD, Duke U., 1972. Bar: N.C. 1977, Tenn. 1972, Fla. 1987. With Container Corp. Am., Fernandina, Fla., 1968-69; assoc. Miller, Martin, Chattanooga, 1972-75; asst. counsel R.J. Reynolds Industries, Inc., 1975-78, assoc. counsel, 1978-79, sr. assoc. counsel, 1979-82, sr. counsel, 1982-85; gen. counsel RJR Archer, Inc., Winston-Salem, N.C., 1979-85; of counsel Finger, Parker & Avram, 1985-87; ptnr. Schollander, 1987—. Gen. counsel Splty. Tobacco Council, 1985-87. Mem. ABA, N.C. Bar Assn., Forsyth County Bar Assn., Mensa, SAR, Phi Delta Phi, Kappa Sigma. Presbyterian. Bankruptcy, General corporate, Franchising. Office: 2000 W 1st St Ste 509 Winston Salem NC 27104-4225

SCHON, ALAN WALLACE, lawyer, actor; b. Mpls., Nov. 27, 1946; s. Hubert Adelbert and Jennie (Jamieson) S.; m. Linda Kay Long, June 14, 1969; 1 child, Cynthia Anne. BA, U. Minn., 1969; JD, William and Mary Coll., 1973; grad. Command & Gen. Staff Coll., U.S. Army, 1984. Bar: Minn. 1973, U.S. Dist. Ct. Minn., Alaska 1986, U.S. Dist. Ct. Alaska, U.S. Ct. Appeals (9th cir.) 1988, Va. 1995. Prin. Schon Law Office, Fairbanks, Alaska, 1986-94; owner, pub. Nordland Pub. Co., Hampton, Va., 1991-94; dep. city atty. mcpl. bonds, environ. law, pub.-pvt. econ. devel. funding environ. law City of Hampton, 1994-99. Nationwide environ. group mgr. Delphi Info. Network, Gen. Videotex Corp., Cambridge, Mass., 1991-94; ind. assoc. Pre-Paid Legal Svcs. Inc., 1999—. Author, pub. EnvironLaw, 1991-94; editor William and Mary Law Rev., 1970-73; stage, film and TV actor; screenwriter: Operation Desert Fire, 1997, Operation Firestorm, 1998. Dir. Alaska State Fair, Fairbanks, 1987-91, Fairbanks Light Opera Theater, Fairbanks, 1991-94; dir., v.p. bus. and fin. Williamsburg (Va.) Players Theater, 2000—; dir., sec. Riding for Am., Inc., 1993-97; dir. Interior Alaska Econ. Devel. Ctr., 1993-94. Maj. U.S. Army, 1974-86. Mem. Fairbanks C. of C. (chmn. environ. concerns com. 1992-94). Avocations: outdoor sports, arts. Home and Office: 389 River Forest Rd Virginia Beach VA 23454-3288

SCHON, STEVEN ELIOT, lawyer; b. Detroit, Jan. 29, 1951; s. William and Betty Ruth (Conn) S. BA with distinction, U. Mich., 1972, JD magna cum laude, 1976. Bar: Calif. 1977, U.S. Dist. Ct. (no. dist.) Calif. 1977, U.S. Ct. Appeals (7th and 9th cirs.) 1979. Law clk. to Hon. J. Edward Lumbard, U.S. Ct. Appeals (2d cir.), N.Y.C., 1976-77; assoc. Howard, Rice Nemerovski, Canady, Robertson & Falk, San Francisco, 1977-82, mem., 1982—, also dir. Articles editor U. Mich. Law Rev., 1975-76. Angell scholar U. Mich., Ann Arbor, 1979-82. Mem. ABA (litigation sect.), Calif. Bar, San Francisco Bar Assn., Order of Coif, Phi Beta Kappa, Phi Delta Phi. Antitrust, Federal civil litigation, State civil litigation. Office: Howard Rice Nemerovski 7th Fl 3 Embarcadero Ctr Ste 7 San Francisco CA 94111-4074 E-mail: sschon@hrice.com

SCHOOLEY, VERN DEAN, lawyer, real estate developer; b. Reed City, Mich., Sept. 26, 1937; s. Clinton D. and Agnes Schooley; m. Tricia M. Reschke, Nov. 27, 1976; 1 child, Kelly Ann. BSME, Mich. State U., 1961; JD, U. San Diego, 1966. Bar: Calif., U.S. Patent Office. Design engr. Boeing Aircraft, Renton, Wash., 1962, Gen. Dynamics Astronotics, San Diego, 1962-66; assoc. Fulwider, Patton, Lee & Utecht, LLP, Long Beach, Calif., 1966-73, ptnr., mgr., 1973—. Mem. Long Beach Bar Assn. (bd. govs. 1986-87, pres. 1990, Atty. of Yr. 1996), Inn of Ct. (pres. Joseph A. Ball/Clarence S. Hunt chpt.), Am. Inn of Ct. (bd. trustees 1998, 2000), Am. Internat. Property Assn. Avocations: tennis, snow skiing. Office: Fulwider Patton Lee & Utecht LLP 200 Oceangate Ste 1550 Long Beach CA 90802-4335 E-mail: vschooley@fulpat.com

SCHOONHOVEN, RAY JAMES, retired lawyer; b. Elgin, Ill., May 24, 1921; s. Ray Covey and Rosina Madeline (Schram) (White) S.; m. Marie Theresa Dunn, Dec. 11, 1943; children: Marie Kathleen "Kamie", Ray James, Jr., Pamela Suzanne, John Philip, Rose Lynn. B.S.C., U. Notre Dame, 1943; J.D., Northwestern U., 1948. Bar: Ill. 1949, U.S. Supreme Ct. 1954, D.C. 1973, U.S. Ct. Mil. Appeals 1954. Assoc. Seyfarth, Shaw Fairweather & Geraldson, Chgo., 1949-57; ptnr. Seyfarth, Shaw Fairweather & Geraldson now Seyfarth Shaw, 1957-92; ret. Chief rulings and ops. br. Wage Stabilization Bd. Region VII, Chgo., 1951-52 Book rev. editor: Ill. Law Rev., 1948. Served to lt.comdr. USNR, 1942-62. Mem. ABA, Ill. State Bar Assn., Chgo. Bar Assn., D.C. Bar Assn., Chgo. Athletic Assn., Univ. Club. Chgo., Fed. Bar Assn., Order of Coif. Republican. Roman Catholic. Administrative and regulatory, Labor. Home: 1182 Lynette Dr Lake Forest IL 60045-4601 Office: Seyfarth Shaw 55 E Monroe St Ste 4200 Chicago IL 60603-5863

SCHOONMAKER, SAMUEL VAIL, III, lawyer; b. Newburgh, N.Y., Sept. 1, 1935; s. Samuel V. Jr. and Catherine (Wilson) S.; m. Carolyn Peters, Sept. 18, 1965; children: Samuel V. IV, Frederick P. BA magna cum laude, Yale U., 1958, JD, 1961. Bar: Conn. 1961, U.S. Dist. Ct. Conn. 1961, U.S. Dist. Ct. (so. and ea. dist.) N.Y. 1964, U.S. Ct. Appeals (2d cir.) 1964, U.S. Supreme Ct. 1965. Assoc. Cummings & Lockwood, Stamford, Conn., 1961-70, co-mng. ptnr., 1987-90, mng. ptnr., 1990-94, chmn. exec. com., 1987-96; founder, pres. Schoonmaker George & Colin, P.C., Greenwich, 1996—. State trial referee Conn. Superior Ct., 1989; pres. Schoonmaker Family Assn., New Paltz, N.Y., 1975-77. Sr. topical editor Conn. Bar Jour., 1977-81; mem. editl. bd. Fairshare and Am. Jour. Family Law, 1992—; contbr. articles to profl. jours. Chmn. Conn. Child Support Commn., 1984-86; mem. Conn. Family Support Com., 1986-90; mem. Darien (Conn.) Rep. Town Com., 1974-76, rep. town meeting, 1990-98; pres. Youth Tennis Found. New Eng., Needham, Mass., 1975-77; pres. New Eng. Lawn Tennis Assn., 1977-79 (Man of Yr. award 1979); pres., trustee Huegenot Hist. Soc., 1999—. Fellow Am. Acad. Matrimonial Lawyers Conn. (bd. mgrs., Disting. Svc. award 1988), Internat. Acad. Matrimonial Lawyers, Am. Bar Found.; mem. ABA (chmn. family law sect. 1982-83), Conn. Bar Assn. (chmn. family law sect. 1971-74), Conn. Bus. and Industry Assn. (bd. dirs. 1993-98), S.W. Conn. Bus. and Industry Assn. (bd. dirs. 1990-97), Pub. Defenders Assn. (chmn.), Wee Burn Country Club (Darien, Conn., asst. sec.), Yale Club (N.Y.C.), Phi Beta Kappa. Avocation: tennis, platform tennis. Family and matrimonial. Home: 231 Old Kings Hwy S Darien CT 06820-5931 Office: Schoonmaker George & Colin PC PO Box 5059 81 Holly Hill Ln Greenwich CT 06831-5059

SCHOR, LAURENCE, lawyer; b. Bklyn., May 3, 1942; s. Julius and Ruth (Zackowitz) S.; m. Susan Leslie Gurevitz, Dec. 26, 1965; children: Meredith Nan, Joseph Sanford, Wendy Claire, Samuel Julius. BBA, So. Meth. U., 1963; JD, U. Tex., 1966; LLM, George Washington U., 1972. Bar: Tex. 1966, D.C. 1971, Md. 1993.; U.S. Ct. Appeals (D.C., 4th, 5th, 11th cirs.). Atty. NASA, Huntsville, Ala., 1966-68; asst. gen. counsel NASA support U.S. Army C.E., Washington, 1968-70; assoc. Sellers, Conner & Cuneo, 1970-73; from assoc. to ptnr. Max E. Greenberg, Trayman, Cantor, Reiss & Blasky, 1974-80; ptnr. Schnader, Harrison, Segal & Lewis, 1981-91, ptnr.-in-charge, 1986-88; mem. Miller & Chevalier, 1991-93; ptnr. Smith, Somerville & Case, LLC, 1993-96, McManus, Schor, Asmar & Darden, LLP, Washington, 1997—. Lectr. George Washington U., others. Author: The Right to Stop Work, 1991; author: (manual) Delays, Suspensions and Acceleration, Workplace Safety and Health in the 1990's, 1992; author: Claims Against Bonding Companys, Construction Contractors' Handbook of Business and Law, 1992, How to File a Federal Contract Claim, 1998; co-author: Suing a Government: Special Considerations for Book Construction Disputes: Representing the Contractor, 3d edit., 2001; author, editor 50 State Lien and Bond Laws, 1993—2001, Vol. 3 Form Book rewrite, 2000, editor update, 2001;contbr. chapters to books. Founder, pres. Manor Lake Civic Assn., Montgomery County, 1969-71; precinct chmn. Montgomery County Dems., 1972-76; mem. D.C. City Coun. Procurement Reform Task Force, 1995-96. Mem. ABA (chmn. region III pub. contract law sect., 1982-88, chmn. constrn. com. 1986-90, sect. budget and fin. 1990-95), D.C. Bar Assn. (chmn. divsn. 10 govt. contracts and litigation, 1981-85), Fed. Bar Assn., Am. Coll. Constrn. Lawyers (founder, bd. dirs., treas. 1996-2000, pres. elect 2000, pres. 2001—), B'nai B'rith Youth Orgn (adult adv. bd. 2001—), Phi Alpha Delta (pres. T.C. Clark chpt. 1965-66). Jewish. Avocations: reading, travel. Federal civil litigation, Construction, Government contracts and claims. Home: 7021 Mountain Gate Dr Bethesda MD 20817-3913 Office: McManus Schor Asmar & Darden LLP 1301 Connecticut Ave NW Fl 6 Washington DC 20036-1815 E-mail: lschor@msadlaw.com

SCHOR, SUZI, lawyer, psychologist; b. Chgo., Feb. 1, 1947; d. Samuel S. and Dorothy Helen (Hineline); 1 child, Kate. BSBA, Ind. U., 1964; JD, Northwestern U., 1970, U. Palmer's Green, London, 1971; PhD in Fine Arts (hon.), U. Nev., PhD in Clin. Psychology, 1989, Kensington U., 1989. Bar: Ill., 1971. Pvt. practice, L.A., 1971-80; v.p. legal affairs Little Gypzy Mgmt., Inc., Beverly Hills, Calif., 1980—; trust officer, pvt. fiduciary svcs. Bank of Am., L.A. Mem. Pres.'s Coun. on Alcoholism. Author: 13th Step to Death, 1995; contbg. author Wine and Dine Mag.; contbr. articles to profl. jours. Bd. dirs. Nat. Ctr. for Hyperactive Children, L.A., 1989-91, sec. Rainbow Guild Cancer Charity, L.A., 1985-89, ind. cons. Jewish Legal Aid, L.A., 1988—; campaign coord. advisor Dem. Nat. Campaign, L.A., 1990, 94, 2000; donor mem. L.A. Coun. on World Affairs. Recipient Poet of Yr. award Nat. Libr. and Assn. of Poetry, 1995, 98. Mem. ABA (criminal justice com. 1994), AAUW, NAADAC, CAADAC, L.A. Breakfast Club (chmn. entertainment 1988-90), Rotary, Mensa, Beverly Hills Bar Assn., Century City Bar Assn. Jewish. Avocations: singing, skiing, writing. General civil litigation, Criminal, Entertainment.

SCHORLING, WILLIAM HARRISON, lawyer; b. Ann Arbor, Mich., Jan. 7, 1949; s. Otis William Schorling and Ruthann (Bales) Schorling Moorehead; m. Lynne Ann Newcomb, June 1, 1974; children: Katherine Pearce, Ann Oury, John Roberts. BA cum laude, Denison U., 1971; JD cum laude, U. Mich., 1975. Bar: Pa. 1975, U.S. Ct. Appeals (3d cir.) 1977, N.J. 1998. Ptnr. Eckert, Seamans, Cherin & Mellott, Pitts., 1984-89, Klett Rooney Lieber & Schorling, PC, Pitts., 1989—. Lectr. Pa. Bar Inst., Harrisburg, 1983—, Comml. Law League, N.Y.C., 1984—, Profl. Edn. Systems, Inc., Eau Claire, Wis., 1986—, Southwest Legal Found., Dallas, 1994—; founders' coun. Comml. Fin. Assn. Edn. Found., 1991—; bd. dirs. Consumer Bankruptcy Assistance Project. Contbr. articles to profl. jours. Trustee Pa. Acad. Fine Arts. Fellow Am. Coll. Bankruptcy, Am. Bar Found.; mem. ABA (bus. law section coun. 2000—, chmn. bus. bankruptcy com. 1996-99, lectr. 1988—), Am. Banker Inst. (lectr. 1994—), Phila. Bar Assn. (lectr. 1996—), E. Dist. Bankruptcy Conf., Pa. Bar Assn. (lectr. 1983—), Allegheny County Bar Assn. (chmn. bankruptcy and comml. law sect. 1991), The Com. of Seventy (vice chair), Longue Vue Club, Duquesne Club, Pyramid Club, Pa. Soc., Bedens Brook Club. Presbyterian. Bankruptcy, Contracts commercial. Home: 12 Scudder Ct Pennington NJ 08534-2325 Office: Klett Rooney Lieber & Schorling 2 Logan Sq Fl 12 Philadelphia PA 19103-2707

SCHORR, BRIAN LEWIS, lawyer, business executive; b. N.Y.C., Oct. 5, 1958; s. Philip I. and Hannah Schorr; m. Amy B. Horowitz, Aug. 19, 1984; 2 children. BA magna cum laude, MA, Wesleyan U., Middletown, Conn., 1979; JD, NYU, 1982. Bar: N.Y. 1983, D.C. 1985, U.S. Supreme Ct. 1988. Assoc. Paul, Weiss, Rifkind, Wharton & Garrison, N.Y.C., 1982-90, ptnr., 1991-94; exec. v.p., gen. counsel Triarc Cos., Inc., 1994—. Mem. bd. advisors Jour. Ltd. Liability Cos., 1994-98; lectr. CLE programs. Author: Schorr on New York Limited Liability Companies and Partnerships, 1994; contbr. articles to legal jours. Vice pres. Bronx (N.Y.) H.S. Sci. Endowment Fund, Inc. Mem. ABA, N.Y. State Bar Assn., Assn. Bar City N.Y. (chmn. com. on corp. law 1993-96, co-chmn. joint drafting com. N.Y. ltd. liability co. law), Tri Bar Opinion Com., Bronx H.S. Sci. Alumni Assn. (trustee). Finance, Mergers and acquisitions, Securities. Office: Triarc Cos Inc 280 Park Ave New York NY 10017-1216

SCHOTT, CLIFFORD JOSEPH, lawyer; b. Newark, July 28, 1926; s. Clifford J. and Sally V. (Donnelly) S.; m. Nancybelle MacDonnell, July 22, 1951; children: Christylee, Clifford, Sally, Steven, Craig. Student, Upsala U., 1949-51; grad., U. Miami, 1952, JD, 1954. Bar: Fla. 1955, U.S. Dist. Ct. (so. dist.) Fla. 1956, U.S. Ct. Appeals (5th cir.) 1959, U.S. Ct. Appeals (11th cir.) 1981, U.S. Tax Ct. 1973, Fla. RR and Pub. Utilities Commn. 1963, U.S. Supreme Ct. 1968. Assoc. Holladay & Swann, Miami, Fla., 1955-56; ptnr. Hastings, Thomas & Sheppard, 1956-57; asst. gen. counsel Dade County Port Auth., 1957-60; atty., negotiator Eastern Airlines, Inc., 1960-63; assoc. Carver, Langston & Massey, Lakeland, Fla., 1963-66; ptnr. Wendel & Schott, 1966-68; pvt. practice, 1968-83; sr. ptnr. Schott & Dale, P.A., 1983-89; pvt. practice Fla., 1989-99; ret., 1999—. Mcpl. judge City of Lakeland, 1967-68; asst. county solicitor County of Polk, Bartow, Fla., 1967-69. Pres., Polk County Assn. Retarded Children, Lakeland, 1966-67, com. chmn., 1967; counsel Ch. of the Resurrection, Lakeland; bd. dirs. St. Joseph's Sch., Lakeland, 1973. With USAAF, 1944-46, ETO. Mem. ABA, ATLA, Fla. Bar Assn., Lakeland Bar Assn., Polk County Trial Lawyers Assn. (adv. com. 1983—), Fla. Def. Lawyers Assn. (bd. dirs. 1985—), 10th Judicial Cir. Bar, Lakeland C. of C. (aviation adv. com.), Am. Legion (judge adv. 1978), Rotary (pres. 1969-70), KC (dep. grand knight 1973), Phi Alpha Delta. Republican. Roman Catholic. Avocations: tennis, fishing, squash, travel, reading. Federal civil litigation, General civil litigation, Personal injury. Home: 111 Florida Shores Blvd Daytona Beach Shores FL 32118-5629

SCHOTTELKOTTE, MICHAEL ROGER, lawyer, judge; b. Cin., Aug. 26, 1947; s. Roger J. and Regina R. (Buescher) S. BS, Seton Hall U., 1969; JD, U. Colo., 1972. Bar: Colo. 1972, U.S. Dist. Ct. Colo. 1972, U.S. Ct. Appeals (10th cir.) 1972. Assoc. Brown and Brown, Delta, Colo., 1972-77, ptnr., 1977—. Mcpl. judge City of Delta, 1974-93. Mem. Kiwanis (pres. Delta club 1977). Republican. Roman Catholic. Consumer commercial, Probate, Real property. Office: Brown Schottelkotte & Tweedell PO Box 43 550 Palmer St Delta CO 81416-1720

SCHOUMACHER, BRUCE HERBERT, lawyer; b. Chgo., May 23, 1940; s. Herbert Edward and Mildred Helen (Wagner) S.; m. Alicia Wesley Sanchez, Nov. 4, 1967; children: Liana Cristina, Janina Maria. BS, Northwestern U., 1961; MBA, U. Chgo., 1963, JD, 1966. Bar: Nebr. 1966, U.S. Dist. Ct. Nebr. 1966, Ill. 1971, U.S. Dist. Ct. (no. dist.) Ill. 1971, U.S. Ct. Appeals (7th cir.) 1979, U.S. Supreme Ct. 1982, U.S. Ct. Fed. Claims 1986. Assoc. Luebs, Tracy & Huebner, Grand Island, Nebr., 1966-67, McDermott, Will & Emery, Chgo., 1971-76, ptnr., 1976-89, Querrey & Harrow, Ltd., Chgo., 1989—. Instr. bus. adminstrn. Bellevue Coll., Nebr., 1967-70; lectr. U. Md., Overseas Program, 1970. Author: Engineers and the Law: An Overview, 1986; contbg. author: Construction Law, 1986, Construction Law Handbook, 1999; co-author: Successful Business Plans for Architects, 1992; contbr. articles to profl. jours. Served to capt. USAF, 1967-71, Vietnam. Decorated Bronze Star, 1971. Fellow Am. Coll. Constrn. Lawyers; mem. ABA, AIA (profl. affiliate), Nebr. Bar Assn., Ill. State Bar Assn. (ad hoc com. large law firms 1992-98, chmn. membership and bar activities com. 1988-89, coun. ins. law sect. 1986-91, mem. spl. com. on computerized legal rsch. 1986-87), Chgo. Bar Assn. (chmn. fed. civil procedure com. 1982-83), Def. Rsch. Inst., Ill. Assn. Def. Trial Counsel, Chgo. Bldg. Congress (bd. dirs. 1985—, sec. 1987-89, 95—, v.p. 1989-91), Western Soc. Engrs. (assoc.), The Lawyers Club of Chgo., Tower Club (Chgo.), Univ. Club Chgo., Pi Kappa Alpha, Phi Delta Phi. Republican. Methodist. Federal civil litigation, State civil litigation, Construction. Office: Querrey & Harrow Ltd 175 W Jackson Blvd Ste 1600 Chicago IL 60604-2827

SCHRADER, ALFRED EUGENE, lawyer; b. Nov. 1, 1953; s. Louis Clement and Helen Mae (Eberz) S.; m. Debra Susanne Britt-Garrett, Aug. 12, 1997. BA in Polit. Sci. magna cum laude, Kent State U., 1975; JD, Ohio State U., 1978. Bar: Ohio 1978, U.S. Dist. Ct. (no. dist.) Ohio 1978, U.S. Ct. Appeals (6th cir.) 1985, U.S. Supreme Ct. 1985. Dep. clk. Summit County Clk. of Cts., Akron, 1972-74; pvt. practice law, 1978—; spl. counsel Bath Twp., Ohio, 1980-92, 95-98. Spkr. Akron Bar Assn.-Akron Univ. Sch. Law CLE Seminars. Trustee Springfield Twp., Ohio, 1973—, pres., 1975, 79, 82, 88, 90, 95-96, 2000—; v.p. Springfield-Akron Joint Econ. Devel. Dist., 1995-97, pres., 1997-2001; mem. adv. com. Cmty. Devel. Block, Summit County, 1985-97, Twinsburg Twp. tax abatement counsel, 1994—, Summit County Annexation Com., 1981-85; mem. Summit County Jail Study Commn., 1983, 84; mem. adv. bd. Springfield Schs., 1975; acting law dir. City of Streetsboro, Portage County, Ohio, 1997; rep. numerous twps. State of Ohio on land use planning, annexation, revenue sharing, zoning and local govt. law matters. Mem. ATLA, Akron Bar Assn. (v.p. legis. com. 1981-82, v.p. local govt. sect. 1992-93, chair local govt. sect. 1993-95), Ohio Acad. Trial Lawyers, Ohio Bar Assn., Summit County Twp. Assn. (exec. com. 1983—), Ohio Twp. Assn., Risk Mgmt. Authority (bd. dirs. 1996—, sec. 1997-2000, pres. 2000—), Nat. Assn. Town and Twp. Attys. (bd. dirs. Ohio chpt. 1986, sec. 1987-93, v.p. 1993-97). Democrat. Roman Catholic. Fax: 330 762 2255. Land use and zoning (including planning), Municipal (including bonds), Personal injury. Home: 3344 Brunk Rd Akron OH 44312-3710 Office: Schrader Romanoski Stevenson and Grant 441 Wolf Ledges Pky Ste 400 Akron OH 44311-1039 Fax: (330) 762-2255. E-mail: attysrsg@aol.com

SCHRAFF, PAUL ALBERT, lawyer; b. Cleve., July 2, 1949; s. Albert G. and Patricia M. S.; m. Deborah L. DuVall, June 17, 1978; children: Christopher L., Devin P. BS in Computer Sci., U. Dayton, 1971; MBA, Cleve. State U., 1973, JD summa cum laude, 1977. Bar: Ohio 1977, U.S. Dist. Ct. (no. dist.) Ohio 1978, Fla. 1978, Hawaii 1981, U.S. Dist. Ct. Hawaii 1981, U.S. Ct. Appeals (9th cir.) 1985. Assoc. Ford, Whitney, Crump & Schulz, Cleve., 1977-81, Carlsmith & Dwyer, Honolulu, 1981-83; cons. Coopers & Lybrand, 1983-84; assoc. Dwyer Schraff Meyer Jossem & Bushnell, 1985-87; dir. Dwyer Schraff Meyer Jossem & Bushnell and predecessors, 1987—. Contbr. remedies chpt. Hawaii Commerical Real Estate Manual, 1997. Mem. ABA, Ohio Bar Assn., Hawaii Bar Assn., Fla. Bar Assn., Assn. Info. Tech. Profls. (legis. liaison 1985—), Am. Arbitration Assn. Federal civil litigation, State civil litigation, Computer. Office: Dwyer Schraff Meyer et al 900 Fort Street Mall Ste 1800 Honolulu HI 96813-3715 Business E-Mail: pschraff@dwyerlaw.com

SCHRAMM, PAUL HOWARD, lawyer; b. St. Louis, Oct. 6, 1933; s. Benjamin Jacob and Frieda Sylvia (Goruch) S.; m. Sue-Ann Batson; children: Scott Lyon, Dean Andrew, Thomas Edward, Jeremy Arthur Savran. AB, U. Mo., 1955, JD, 1958. Bar: Mo. 1958, U.S. Dist. Ct. (ea. dist.) Mo. 1963, U.S. Ct. Appeals (8th cir.) 1967, U.S. Tax Ct. 1970, U.S. Supreme Ct. 1972, U.S. Dist. Ct. (ea. dist.) Wis., 1988. Ptnr. Schramm & Schramm, St. Louis, 1959-61, Schramm & Morganstern, St. Louis, 1970-76, Schramm, Pines & Marshall, St. Louis, 1977-79, Schramm, Newman, Pines & Freyman, St. Louis, 1979-82, Schramm, Pines & Spewak, St. Louis, 1983-85, Schramm & Pines, L.L.C., St. Louis, 1985-2000, Edwards, Singer, Schramm, Watkins & Spoeneman, L.L.P., St. Louis, 2000—. Pros. atty. City of Ellisville, Mo., 1973-77; judge Ellisville mcpl. div. St. Louis County Cir. Ct., 1977-83; teaching faculty trial advocacy Harvard Law Sch., 1991. Mem. Bar Assn. Met. St. Louis (exec. com. 1976-77, chmn. county sect. 1976-77), St. Louis County Bar Assn. (chmn. lawyers reference service 1971, cir. ct. jud. com. 1970), Phi Delta Phi. Club: University (St. Louis). Avocations: music, sports, reading. General civil litigation, General corporate, Family and matrimonial. Home: 7507 Byron Pl Saint Louis MO 63105-2703 Office: Edwards Singer Schramm Watkins & Spoeneman LLP 1600 Clayton Ctr 120 S Central Ave Ste 1600 Saint Louis MO 63105-1798

SCHRANDT, CURTIS LEON, lawyer, securities analyst, financial advisor; b. Van Nuys, Calif., Nov. 21, 1957; s. Edward Leon and Ethel Jeannine (Thompson) S. BS in Bus. Mgmt. summa cum laude, U. Utah, 1992, BA in Bus. Fin., 1993; JD cum laude, Quinnipiac U. Sch. Law, 1996. Bar: Conn. 1996, N.Y. 1998, D.C. 1999; CFA. Owner Friends-Exotic Pets, Salt Lake City and Orem, Utah, 1978-89; mgr. ZCMI Dept. Stores, Salt Lake City, 1991-93; ptnr. Hersh & Fowler-Cruz, White Plains, N.Y., 1996-98; owner Law Offices of Curtis Schrandt, Stratford, Conn., 1998—, CLS Enterprises, Stratford, 1996—. Fin. chmn. Hersh & Fowler-Cruz, 1996-98. Mng. editor Quinnipiac Law Rev., 1995-96 (Disting. Svc. award 1996). Mem. ABA, Conn. Bar Assn., N.Y. Bar Assn., D.C. Bar Assn. Office: Law Offices Curtis Schrandt 803 Stratford Ave Stratford CT 06615-6350 Fax: 303-975-6304. E-mail: cschrandt@lawyer.com

SCHRECK, ROBERT A., JR. lawyer; b. Buffalo; BS in Bus. Adminstrn., Georgetown U., 1974; MBA, Northwestern U., 1975, JD, 1978. Bar: Ill. 1978. Ptnr. McDermott, Will & Emery, Chgo., 1978—. Mem. ABA. General corporate, Securities, Acquisitions. Office: McDermott Will & Emery 227 W Monroe St Ste 3100 Chicago IL 60606-5096 E-mail: rschreck@mwe.com

SCHRECK, ROBERT J. lawyer; b. Buffalo, Jan. 5, 1956; s. Frank Joseph and Rachel Ann (Catalano) S.; m. Pamela Sheehan, Aug. 13, 1983; children: Robert F., Michael F. BA, SUNY at Buffalo, 1977, JD, 1981. Bar: N.Y. State 1982, U.S. Dist. Ct. (we. dist.) N.Y. 1982, U.S. Supreme Ct. 1987. Asst. dist. atty. Erie County Dist. Atty.'s Office, Buffalo, 1981-84; ptnr. Mattar & D'Agostino, LLP, 1984—. Lectr. Better Bus. Bur., Buffalo, 1986-2001; chmn. rev. com. Erie County Assigned Coun., Buffalo, 1995—. Committeeman Erie County Rep. com., Buffalo, 1989—; vice chmn. Erie County Coordinating Coun. on Children & Families, Buffalo, 1991-94; dir. Am. Heart Assn., Western N.Y., 1996-99, St. Joseph's Collegiate Instn., Buffalo, 1997, Buffalo Diocese Vicariate, Western N.Y., 1997; councilman St. Benedict's Cath. Ch. Parish Counsel, Buffalo, 1996-98; coach Ctrl. Amherst (N.Y.) Little League, 1996—; gen. mgr. Amherst Youth Hockey AAA Travel Team; pres. Ronald McDonald House, Buffalo, 1997-98. Recipient Connelly Trial Technique award U. Buffalo, 1981. Mem. ABA, N.Y. State Bar Assn., Erie County Bar Assn., Judges & Police Execs. Conf. of Erie County, Nat. Assn. of Watch and Clock Collectors, Brookfield Country Club, West Side Rowing Club, Western N.Y. Cert. Football Ofcls. Assn. (parliamentarian 1989—). Republican. Roman Catholic. Avocation: high sch. football ofcl. Criminal, Family and matrimonial, Personal injury. Home: 105 Audubon Dr Snyder NY 14226-4078 Office: Mattar & D'Agostino LLP 17 Court St Ste 600 Buffalo NY 14202-3294 E-mail: attorney@mattar-dagostino.com

SCHRECKENGAST, WILLIAM OWEN, lawyer; b. Greenwood, Ind., Oct. 14, 1926; s. Vernon Edward and Marthena O. (Mullinix) S.; m. Helen Margaret Sheppard, Nov. 11, 1949 (div.); children: Pamela, Sandra, James, John; m. Virginia Thompson, Mar. 14, 1990. LLB, Ind. U., 1956. Bar: Ind. 1956, U.S. Ct. Appeals (7th cir.) 1956, U.S. Dist. Ct. (so. dist.) Ind. 1956, U.S. Supreme Ct. 1967. Ptnr. Kitley, Pontius & Schreckengast, Beech Grove, Ind., 1957-59, Kitley & Schreckengast, Beech Grove, 1959-63, 78-82, Kitley, Schreckengast & Davis, Beech Grove, 1963-78, Schreckengast & Lovern, Indpls., 1982-88, Schreckengast Lovern & Helm, Indpls., 1988—. Chmn. Ind. campaign John Walsh for Sec. of State, Indls., 1958; chmn. ward Beech Grove Dems., 1958-60. Served to 1st sgt. U.S. Army, 1944-46, PTO. Mem. ABA, Ind. Bar Assn. (bd. mgrs. 1973-74, pres. citation 1974, pres. trial lawyer sect. 1977-78), Ind. Def. Lawyers Assn. (diplomat), Am. Judicature Soc., Nat. Inst. Trial Advocacy (teaching faculty 1980-85), Platform Soc. Republican. Club: Hillview Country (Franklin, Ind.). Lodge: Masons. Avocations: golf, flying. State civil litigation, Insurance, Personal injury. Home: 8026 Singleton St Indianapolis IN 46227-2568 Office: Schreckengast Lovern & Helm 8007 S Meridian St Ste 1 Indianapolis IN 46217-2922

SCHREIBER, ALAN HICKMAN, lawyer; b. Muncie, Ind., Apr. 4, 1944; s. Ephriam and Clarrisa (Hickman) S.; m. Phyllis Jean Chamberlain, Dec. 22, 1972; children: Jennifer Aline, Brett Justin. Student, DePauw U., 1962-64; BS in Bus., Ind. U., 1966, JD, 1969. Bar: Fla. 1971, U.S. Dist. Ct. (so. dist.) Fla. Asst. State Atty.'s Office, Ft. Lauderdale, Fla., 1971-76; pub. defender 17th Jud. Cir., 1976—. Cons. Fla. Bar News on Criminal Law, 1982; lobbyist for indigent funding, Fla., 1980—; apptd. to Supreme Ct. Com. on Racial and Ethic Bias; co-chair Chiles-MacKay task force on criminal justice. Contbr. articles to profl. jours. Mem. Dem. Exec. Com., Ft. Lauderdale, 1980; mem. Plantation Dem. Club, 1983; campaign chmn. Goldstein for Atty. Gen. Fla., 1982. Named Young Dem. of Yr., Broward County Young Dems., 1980; Man of Yr., Jewish War Vets., 1982; recipient B'nai B'rith Pub. Servant award, 1990. Mem. Fla. Bar Assn., Broward County Bar Assn., ABA, Nat. Legal Aid Defenders Assn., Phi Alpha Delta. Criminal. Home: 885 Orchid Dr Fort Lauderdale FL 33317-1221 Office: 201 SE 6th St Fort Lauderdale FL 33301-3303

SCHREIBER, DAVID M. lawyer, judge; b. Kansas City, Mo., Aug. 13, 1937; s. William and Hinda Gold Schreiber; m. Adrienne Rennie Ehre, May 31, 1959; children: Beth F., Kathy L. JD, LLB, U. Ariz., 1962; cert. jud. devel. adminstrv. law, Nat. Jud. Coll., 1997. Bar: Ariz., 1962, Nev., 1968, U.S. Ct. Appeals (9th cir.), 1978, U.S. Dist. Ct., 1968, U.S. Supreme Ct., 1972. Pvt. practice, Tucson, 1962-64; hearings officer, referee Indsl. Commn. Ariz., Phoenix, 1964-67; asst. v.p., house counsel First Western Savings & Loan, Las Vegas, Nev., 1967-69; chief dep. pub. defender Clark County Pub. Defenders Office, 1969-71; chief dep. dist. atty., counsel Nev. Juvenile Ct., 1971-76; pvt. practice, 1976-92; adminstrv. law judge State of Nev., Dept. Motor Vechiles and Pub. Safety, 1992—. Chmn. Cmty. Devel. Adv. com., Clark County, Nev., 1995-96. Recipient Law Enforcement Commendation medal Nat. Soc. Sons Am. Revolution, 1995 Mem. Nat. Assn. Adminstrv. Law Judges. Avocations: classical music, collecting art, politics. Home: 3310 Brookfield Dr Las Vegas NV 89120-1969 Office: State Nev Dept Motor Vechiles 2701 E Sahara Ave Las Vegas NV 89104-4119

SCHREIBER, JOHN T. lawyer; b. N.Y.C., Mar. 30, 1960; s. Toby Schreiber and Morley Ann (Perrish) Clark; m. Theresa Ann Sawyer, Aug. 11, 1984; children: Zoe Cassandra Bloch Schreiber, Alana Nichole Perrish Schreiber. BA Politics, Brandeis U., 1982; JD, Santa Clara U., 1986. Bar: Calif. 1987; U.S. Dist. Ct. (no. dist.) Calif. 1987; U.S. Dist. Ct. (ea. dist.) Calif. 1990; U.S. Ct. Appeals (9th cir.) 1989. Assoc. Law Offices of Wm. D. McHugh, San Jose, Calif., 1987-88, Hallgrimson, McNichols, McCann & Inderbitzen, Pleasanton, 1989-92; pvt. practice Walnut Creek, 1993—. Bd. dirs. East Bay Depot for Creative Re-use, Oakland. Field coord. Cen. Contra Costa County, Tom Bradley Campaign for Govs., Concord, Calif., 1982, Clinton-Gore Campaign, Walnut Creek, Calif., 1992; mem. Ask-A-Lawyer Program Contra Costa Legal Svcs. Found., Richmond, Calif., 1992—; co-chair Clinton-Gore Contra Costa County, 1996. Mem. ABA, Contra Costa Bar Assn. (program dir. appellate sect. 1993-95, pres. appellate sect. 1995-96), MCLE com. 1995—), Santa Clara Bar Assn., Am. Israeli Polit. Action Com. Avocations: reading, golf, softball, movies, exercising. General civil litigation. Office: 961 Ygnacio Valley Rd Walnut Creek CA 94596-3825

SCHREIBER, SALLY ANN, lawyer; b. El Paso, Tex., July 23, 1951; d. Warren Thomas and Joyce (Honey) S.; children: Amanda Honey, Ryan Thorp Luther. BBA, U. N.Mex., 1973; JD, Stanford U., 1976. Bar: Calif. 1976, Tex. 1977. Assoc. Johnson & Swanson, Dallas, 1976-81, ptnr., 1981-89; mem. firm Johnson & Gibbs, P.C., 1989-93; of counsel Cox & Smith, Inc., 1993-94; shareholder Munsch Hardt Kopf & Harr, P.C., 1994—. Spkr. Advanced Mgmt. Rsch. Internat., Dallas, 1984, U. Tex., Austin, 1984, 89, 91, 93, 99, 2000, Houston, 1994, Dallas, 1995, San Antonio, 1998, 2001, State Bar of Tex., Dallas, 1989, Lubbock, Arlington, San Antonio, 1990, Houston, 1994, South Tex. Coll. Law, Houston, 1990, 94, U. Houston, 1996, 97, Dallas, 1996, 97, Dallas Bus. Jour., 1997, Pres.'s Forum, Dallas, 1998, 2000, 01, North Dallas C. of C., Dallas, 1998. Editor Stanford U. Law Rev., 1975-76; co-author paper Internat. Bar Assn., 1986. Bd. dirs. The Lyric Opera of Dallas, 1982-86, bd. trustees, 1986-90; mem. law sch. bd. vis. Stanford (Calif.) U., 1981-84; dir. Tex. Bus. Law Found., 1989—, treas. 1994-96, sec. 1996—. Mem. ABA, Tex. Bar Assn. (corp. law com. 1981—, vice chair 1993-97, chair 1997-2001, ptnrship. law com. 1985—, ltd. liability company com. 1992—, opinion com. 1989-98, codification com. 1997—, bus. law sect. coun. 1996—), Calif. Bar Assn., Dallas Bar Assn. General corporate, Securities. Home: 2737 Purdue Ave Dallas TX 75225-7910 Office: Munsch Hardt Kopf & Harr PC 4000 Fountain Pl 1445 Ross Ave Ste 4000 Dallas TX 75202-2790 E-mail: sschreiber@munsch.com

SCHREMPP, WARREN C. lawyer; b. Omaha, Jan. 29, 1919; s. Charles F. and Josephine I. (Brady) S.; m. Elizabeth K. Murphy; children: Warren C., Erich Kevin. PhB, Creighton U., 1940, JD, 1943. Bar: Nebr. Ptnr. Warren C. Schrempp & Assocs., Omaha; asst. U.S. dist. atty. State of Nebr., 1945-48. Author: The New Voice of the Sixth, 1965; The Eavesdrop Menace, 1967; The Damage Argument, 1976. Fellow Internat. Soc. Barristers, Iowa Acad Trial Lawyers (hon.); mem. Nebr. Assn. Trial Attys. (pres. 1962-63), Assn. Trial Lawyers Am. (bd. govs.), ABA, Nebr. Bar Assn., Am. Bd. Trial Advocates (diplomate, named Best Lawyers in Am.), Trial Lawyers for Pub. Justice (bd. dirs. 1992). Roman Catholic. Personal injury. Home: 700 S 89th St Omaha NE 68114-4230 Office: Inns of Ct Bldg 617 N 90th St Omaha NE 68114-2821

SCHRIMP, ROGER MARTIN, lawyer; b. Stockton, Calif., May 26, 1941; s. Clarence and Mary Helen (Martin) S; m. Delsie Louise Canapa, July 7, 1963; children: Angela and Christine. AA with honors, Stockton C.C., 1961; AB with honors, U. Calif., Berkeley, 1963, JD, 1966; LLM, U. Pacific, 1982. Bar: Calif. 1966, U.S. Dist. Ct. (no., ctrl., and ea. dist.) Calif. 1967, U.S. Tax Ct. 1978, U.S. Supreme Ct. 1978, U.S. Claims Ct. 1981. Ptnr. Law Offices of Stockton & Schrimp, Modesto, Calif., 1966-86; private practice Law Offices of Roger M. Schrimp, 1986-90; ptnr. Law Offices of Damrell, Nelson, Schrimp, Pallios & Ladine, 1990—. Bd. gov.s Calif. C.C., pres., chmn. econ. Devel. and vocat. edn. com., 1996—; founder, chmn. bd. Oak Valley Cmty. Bank, Oakdale, Calif. 1991—; chair Joint Adv. com. Vocational Edn., Calif. Bd. Edn.; mem. Calif. State U. Joint Standing com. Yosemite area council bd. Boy Scouts Am., 1967—, nat. council, 1986-93, council pres., 1986-87, exec. bd. mem., 1967—, western region bd. mem., 1990-98, area III v.p., 1990-95, area III pres. 1995—, western region exec. bd. 1995—; exec. com. Oak Valley Dist. Cmty. Hosp. Found., 1976-94, bd. trustees, 1970-94; chmn. Oakdale Airport Commn., 1974-88, commn. mem. 1970-88; bd. trustees Oakdale Elem. Sch. Dist., 1972-80; bd. dir. Am. Cancer Soc., Stanislaus/Tuolumne Br., 1967-80, pres., 1970-71; vice-chmn. culture commn. City of Modesto, 1989-93, mem., 1986-93; mem. Calif. Postsecondary Edn. Commn. (western region v.p. finance 1998—). Mem. ABA (com. agr., taxation section), State Bar Calif., Assn. Trial Lawyers Am., Calif. Trial Lawyers Assn., Stanislaus County Bar Assn. (pres. 1993-94), Am. Judicature Soc., Northern Calif. Assn. Def. Counsel, Def. Rsch. Inst., Lawyers-Pilot Assn., Oakdale Rotary Club (pres. 1980-81), Medesto Lions "500" Club (pres. 1973-74), Rancheros Visitadores, El Viage de Portola, Oakdale Shrine Club (pres. 1975), Oakdale Dinner Club (pres. 1970-71), Calif. Cattlemen's Assn. (bd. dir. 1994-97), San Joaquin/Stanislaus Cattlemen's Assn., Knights Ferry Lodge #112, Morning Star Lodge #68, McHenry Mansion Found., McHenry Mus. Found., Modesto Shrine Club, Internat. Order St. Hubertus, Univ. Calif. Alumni, Million Doallar Advocates Forum, Univ. Calif. Berkeley Boalt Hall Alumni Assn. (bd. dir. 1994—), Airplane Owners and Pilots Assn., Oakdale Sportsmen's Club. Republican. State civil litigation, Taxation, general. Office: Damrell Nelson Schrimp Pallios & Ladine 1610 I St Fl 5 Modesto CA 95354-1122

SCHRODER, JACK SPALDING, JR. lawyer; b. Atlanta, July 10, 1948; s. Jack Spalding Sr. and Van (Spalding) S.; m. Karen Keyworth, Sept. 1, 1973; children: Jack Spalding III, James Edward. BA, Emory U., 1970; JD, U. Ga., 1973. Bar: Ga. 1973, U.S. Dist. Ct. (no. dist.) Ga. 1973, U.S. Ct. Appeals (5th cir.) 1973, U.S. Ct. Appeals (11th cir.) 1982. Assoc. Alston & Bird, Atlanta, 1973-78, ptnr., 1978—. Author: Credentialing: Strategies for a Changing Environment/BNA's Health Law and Business Series, 1996; co-editor, contbg. author: Georgia Hospital Law manual, 1979, 84,92. Bd. dirs. Rsch. Atlanta, 1996-2000, pres., 1999; participant Leadership Ga., Atlanta, 1986. United Way (chmn. legal divsn.), Atlanta, 1980; vice chair Hosps. and Health Systems Law Inst., 2001—. Mem. ABA (vice chmn. medicine and law com. 1989-90), Am. Health Lawyers Assn. (bd. dirs. 1994-99, chmn. med. staff and physician rels. com. 1991-94), Ga. Acad. Healthcare Attys. (pres. 1981-82), State Bar Ga. (bd. govs. 1987-89), Atlanta Coun. Younger Lawyers (pres. 1977-78), Atlanta Bar Assn. (pres. 1982-83), Atlanta Bar Found. (pres. 1991-95). Health. Office: Alston & Bird 1 Atlantic Ctr 1201 W Peachtree St NW Atlanta GA 30309-3424 E-mail: jschroder@alston.com

SCHROEDER, EDWIN MAHER, law educator; b. New Orleans, June 25, 1937; s. Edwin Charles and Lucille Mary (Maher) S.; m. Marietta Louise DeFazio, Aug. 1, 1936; children: Edwin Charles II, Jonathan David, Margaret Louise. AA, St. Joseph Sem., St. Benedict, La., 1957; PhB, Gregorian U., Rome, 1959; JD, Tulane U., 1964; MS, Fla. State U., 1970. Bar: Mass. 1964. Asst. prof. law U. Conn., 1965-68; asst. prof., asst. law libr. U. Tex., 1968-69; asst. prof. Fla. State U., 1969-71, assoc. prof., 1971-75, prof., 1975—, dir. Law Libr., 1969—, asst. dean Coll. Law, 1979-83, assoc. dean Coll. Law, 1983-93. Mem. ABA, Am. Assn. Law Librs. (v.p. Southwestern chpt. 1983-84, pres. 1984-85), Order of Coif, Beta Phi Mu. Roman Catholic. Home: 806 Middlebrooks Cir Tallahassee FL 32312-2439 Office: Fla State U Coll Law Law Libr Tallahassee FL 32306-1600 E-mail: eschroed@law.fsu.edu

SCHROEDER, ERIC PETER, lawyer; b. Floral Park, N.Y., July 20, 1970; s. Fredric G. and Linda M. Schroeder. BA, Duke U., 1992; JD, Vanderbilt U., 1996. Bar: Ga. 1997, U.S. Dist. Ct. (no. dist.) Ga. 1997, U.S. Ct. Appeals (11th cir.) 1998. Law clk. Hon. William C. O'Kelley, U.S. Dist. Ct. (no. dist.) Ga., Atlanta, 1996-97; atty. Powell, Goldstein, Frazer & Murphy, 1997—. Mem. planning com. Ga. Bar Media Jud. Conf., 1999, 2000. Articles editor Vanderbilt Law Rev., 1995-96; mem. editl. bd. INTA The Trademark Reporter, 2000—. Active Boys and Girls Club of Am., Atlanta, 1998-00; vol. Ga. Vol. Lawyers for the Arts, Atlanta, 1998; lawyer Anti-Defamation League, Atlanta, 1998. Mem. Atlanta Bar Assn., U.S. Copyright Soc., Internat. Trademark Assn., Order of Coif, Lamar Inn of Ct. Constitutional, Libel, Trademark and copyright. Home: 977 North Ave Atlanta GA 30306-4701 Office: Powell Goldstein Frazer & Murphy 191 Peachtree St Atlanta GA 30303 E-mail: eschroeder@pgfm.com

SCHROEDER, GERALD FRANK, state supreme court justice; b. Boise, Idaho, Sept. 13, 1939; s. Frank Frederick and Josephine Ivy (Lucas) S.; m. Carole Ann McKenna, 1967; children: Karl Casteel, Erich Frank. BA magna cum laude, Coll. of Idaho (now Albertson Coll. of Idaho), 1961; JD, Harvard U., 1964. Bar: Idaho 1965. Assoc. Moffatt, Thomas, Barrett & Blanton, Boise, 1965-66; pvt. practice, 1966-67; asst. U.S. atty. Dept. Justice, 1967-69; judge Ada County Probate Ct., 1969-71; magistrate State of Idaho, 1971-75; dist. judge U.S. Dist. Ct. (4th dist.) Idaho, 1975-95; justice Idaho Supreme Ct., 1995—. Instr. Boise Bar Rev., 1973—; adj. faculty law Boise State U., 1986-95; former mem. Gov. Coun. on Crime and Delinquency. Author: Idaho Probate Procedure, 1971; (novel) Triangle of the Sons-Phenomena, 1983; contbr. chpt. to history text. Bd. dirs. Boise Philharm. Assn., 1978-81; adminstrv. and dist. judge 4th dist. State of Idaho, 1985-95. Toll fellow Nat. Coun. State Govt., 1990. Mem. Idaho Bar Assn., Boise Racquet and Swim Club (pres. bd. dirs. 1991-93).

SCHROEDER, JAMES WHITE, lawyer; b. Elmhurst, Ill., Apr. 19, 1936; s. Paul W. and Thelma C. (White) S.; m. Patricia N. Scott, Aug. 18, 1962; children: Scott W. and Jamie C. BA, Princeton U., 1958; JD, Harvard U., 1964. Bar: Colo. 1964, U.S. Dist. Ct. Colo. 1964, U.S. Ct. Appeals (10th cir.) 1965, U.S. Supreme Ct. 1972, U.S. Dist. Ct. D.C. 1973, U.S. Ct. Appeals (D.C. cir.) 1974, U.S. Ct. Appeals (8th cir.) 1977, U.S. Ct. Appeals (3d cir.) 1981, U.S. Claims Ct. 1983, U.S. Ct. Appeals (fed. cir.) 1983. Ptnr. Moseley, Wells & Schroeder, Denver, 1965-72, Kaplan Russin & Vecchi, Washington, 1973-92; counsel Whitman & Ransom, 1992-93; dep. under sec. U.S. Dept. Agr., 1993-2001. Arbitrator Am. Arbitration Assn. Active Ams. for Democratic Action, Smithsonian Instn. Lt. USNR, 1958-64. Am. Field Svc. scholar 1953, NROTC scholar, 1954. Mem. ABA, Fed. Bar Assn., Denver Bar Assn., Colo. Bar Assn., D.C. Bar Assn., Cap and Gown Club, Lincoln's Inn Club, City Club Denver (pres. 1972), Princeton Club Washington (pres. 1982-84). Democrat. Home: 4102 Lester Ct Alexandria VA 22311-1121

SCHROEDER, LEILA OBIER, retired law educator; b. Plaquemine, La., July 11, 1925; d. William Prentiss and Daisy Lavinia (Mays) Obier; divorced; 1 child, James Michael Cutshaw; m. Martin Charles Schroeder Jr., Sept. 19, 1969. BA, Newcomb Coll., 1946; MSW, La. State U., 1953, JD, 1965. Bar: La. 1965. Exec. dir. Evangeline Area Guidance Ctr. La. Dept. Hosps., Lafayette, 1955-57, dir. social services dept. East La. State Hosp. Jackson, 1957-60, cons. psychiat. social work Baton Rouge, 1960-61; research assoc. La. State U., 1965-68, asst. prof., 1968-73, assoc. prof., 1973-80, prof., 1980-96; ret., 1996. Author: The Legal Environment of Social Work, 1982, The Legal Environment of Social Work, 1995; contbr. articles to profl. jours. Fellow Am. Orthopsychiat. Assn.; mem. ABA, Nat. Assn. Social Workers, Acad. Cert. Social Workers, La. State Bar Assn., Baton Rouge Bar Assn. Home: 4336 Oxford Ave Baton Rouge LA 70808-4651

SCHROEDER, MARY MURPHY, federal judge; b. Boulder, Colo., Dec. 4, 1940; d. Richard and Theresa (Kahn) Murphy; m. Milton R. Schroeder, Oct. 15, 1965; children: Caroline Theresa, Katherine Emily. B.A., Swarthmore Coll., 1962; J.D., U. Chgo., 1965. Bar: Ill. 1966, D.C. 1966, Ariz. 1970. Trial atty. Dept. Justice, Washington, 1965-69; law clk. Hon. Jesse Udall, Ariz. Supreme Ct., 1970; mem. firm Lewis and Roca, Phoenix, 1971-75; judge Ariz. Ct. Appeals, 1975-79, U.S. Ct. Appeals (9th cir.), Phoenix, 1979-2000, chief judge, 2000—. Vis. instr. Ariz. State U. Coll. Law, 1976, 77, 78 Contbr. articles to profl. jours. Mem. ABA (Margaret Brent award 2001), Ariz. Bar Assn., Fed. Bar Assn., Am. Law Inst. (coun. mem.), Am. Judicature Soc., Soroptimists. Office: US Ct Appeals 9th Cir US Courthouse Ste 610 401 W Washington St SPC-54 Phoenix AZ 85003-2156 Fax: (602) 322-7329. E-mail: mary_schroeder@ca9.uscourts.gov

SCHROEDER, VAN ACE, lawyer; b. Lincoln, Nebr., Feb. 8, 1952; s. Clark Eugene and Shirley Mae (Suddarth) S.; m. Ann Marie Wallace, Nov. 20, 1982; children: Stephen C., Michael W. B.A., U. Nebr.-Lincoln, 1974, J.D., 1977. Bar: Nebr. 1977, U.S. Dist. Ct. Nebr. 1977, U.S. Ct. Appeals (8th cir.) 1987, U.S. Supreme Ct. 1994. Assoc. atty. Weber Law Offices, Bellevue, Nebr., 1977-80, Pelton Law Offices, Bellevue, 1980-82; assoc. Pelton, Bertolini, Schroeder, Veith & Blount, Bellevue, 1982-89, ptnr. Bertolini, Schroeder & Blount, 1989—; atty. coach Nebr. Mock Trial Project, Omaha Bryan High Sch., 1983, Bellevue E. High Sch., 1984-92. Recipient Am. Jurisprudence award Bancroft-Whitney Co., 1977; named to Outstanding Young Men of Am., 1985. Mem. ABA, Am. Trial Lawyers Assn., Nebr. Bar Assn., Nebr. Assn. Trial Attys., Nebr. 2d Jud. Dist. Bar Assn., Omaha Bar Assn., Sarpy County Bar Assn. Democrat. Lodge: Eagles. Family and matrimonial, General practice, Personal injury. Office: Bertolini Schroeder & Blount 1620 Wilshire Dr Ste 250 Bellevue NE 68005-6600

SCHROEDER, WALTER ALLEN, lawyer, banker; b. San Francisco, July 29, 1954; s. Carl Walter and Mary (Lee) S.; m. Andrea Maggie Paull, June 3, 1994. BS in Bus. Adminstrn., Georgetown U., 1976; JD, U. Houston, 1979. Bar: Tex. 1979, D.C. 1984, U.S. Dist. Ct. (no. dist.) Tex. 1979, U.S. Dist. Ct. (so. dist.) Tex. 1980, U.S. Dist. Ct. (we. dist.) Tex. 1982, U.S. Ct. Appeals (5th cir.) 1980, U.S. Ct. Appeals (11th cir.) 1981, U.S. Ct. Appeals (D.C. cir.) 1987, U.S. Supreme Ct. 1984. Asst. treas. G.U. Fed. Credit Union, Washington, 1976-77; asst. to pres. U.S.E. Credit Union, Houston, 1977-79; analyst Banc Systems, Inc., 1979; briefing atty. Tex. Ct. Civil Appeals, Ft. Worth, 1979-80; asst. counsel Am. Ins. Assn., Houston, 1980-81; atty. Rolston & Hausler, 1981-85, Chamberlain, Hrdlicka, White, Johnson & Williams, 1985-86, Holrah, Lange & Thoma, 1986-87, Eikenburg & Stiles, 1987-89; v.p., sr. atty. First City Tex.-Houston, N.A., 1989-91; ptnr. Schroeder, Walthall & Neville, LLP, Houston, 1991—; apptd. assoc. judce Mcpl. Ct., City of Houston, 1995—. Bd. dirs., v.p. Victorian Owners Assn., Inc., 1989—; v.p. Park Regency Coun. C-owners, pres., 1985-86, bd. dirs., 1985-86, 87-90. Contbr. articles

to profl. jours. Trustee Found. Amateur Radio, Inc., Washington, 1972-76, chmn. audit com., 1975-76; treas. Houston Echo Soc., 1979; mem. Ethics Commn., City of Houston, 1991-95, chmn., 1992-95. Mem. ABA, D.C. Bar Assn., Houston Bar Assn., State Bar Tex., Tex. Assn. Bank Counsel (co-chmn. corp. counsel sect. 1989-90). Republican. Lutheran. Banking, Contracts commercial, Real property. Office: Ste 1111 1111 North Loop West Houston TX 77008 E-mail: schroeder@swnlaw.com

SCHROER, GENE ELDON, lawyer; b. Randolph, Kans., Aug. 29, 1927; s. Harry Edward and Florence Lillian (Schwartz) S.; m. Edith Grace Kintner, Apr. 7, 1956 (div.); children: Kenneth G., Rebecca J., Sonya J., Connie J.; m. Anne Oliver; 1 child, Edward G. AB, LLB, Washburn U., 1957. Bar: Kans. 1957, U.S. Dist. Ct. Kans. 1957, U.S. Ct. Appeals (10th cir.) 1970, U.S. Supreme Ct. 1983. Pvt. practice, Topeka, 1957-68; ptnr. Schroer, Rice, P.A., 1968—, pres., 1970—, also bd. dirs. Contbr. articles to profl. jours. and chpts. to books. Supr. Shawnee County Soil Conservation Dist., Topeka, 1968-84. With U.S. Army, 1951-53. Mem. ABA, Kans. Bar Assn., Assn. Trial Lawyers Am. (gov. 1976-79, seminar lectr. 1973—, chmn. tort sect. 1974-75, instr. Nat. Coll. Adv. 1978, 81-88), Kans. Trial Lawyers Assn. (gov. 1972—, seminar lectr. 1974—, pres. 1974-75), Nat. Bd. Trial Advocacy (sustaining founder), N.Y. Acad. Sci., Am. Bd. Trial Advs. (sec., treas. Kans. chpt. 1990-91, pres. 1991-92), Civil Justice Found. (founding sponsor), Trial Lawyers for Pub. Justice (bd. dirs. 1982-96). Democrat. Methodist. Federal civil litigation, State civil litigation, Personal injury. Office: Schroer Rice PA 115 SE 7th St Topeka KS 66603-3901 E-mail: gschroer@schroerrice.com

SCHROPP, JAMES HOWARD, lawyer; b. Lebanon, Pa., June 20, 1943; Work e-mail: schroja@ffhsj.com. s. Howard J. and Maud E. (Parker) S.; m. Jo Ann Simpson, Sept. 4, 1965; children: James A., John C., Jeffrey M., Jeremy M. BA, U. Richmond, 1965; JD, Georgetown U., 1973. Bar: D.C. 1973, U.S. Supreme Ct. 1980. Asst. gen. counsel SEC, Washington, 1973-79; ptnr. Fried, Frank, Harris, Shriver & Jacobson, 1979—. Adj. prof. Georgetown U., Washington, 1982-86; mem. faculty Na.t Inst. for Trial Advocacy. Mem. ABA (discovery com. litigation sect. 1984-86, tender offer litigation subcom. corp. banking and bus. law sect. 1985-86, task force on broker-dealer compliance supervisory procedures 1987-89). Federal civil litigation, General corporate, Securities. Office: Fried Frank Harris Shriver & Jacobson 1001 Pennsylvania Ave NW Washington DC 20004-2505

SCHROTH, PETER W(ILLIAM), lawyer, management and law educator; b. Camden, N.J., July 24, 1946; s. Walter and Patricia Anne (Page) S.; children: Laura Salome Erickson-Schroth, Julia James. AB, Shimer Coll., 1966; JD, U. Chgo., 1969; M in Comparative Law, U.Chgo., 1971; SJD, U. Mich., 1979; postgrad., U. Freiburg, Fed. Republic Germany, Faculté Internationale pour l'Enseignement de Droit Comparé; MBA, Rensselaer Poly. Inst., 1988; DHL, Shimer Coll., 2000; MSc, Sch. Oriental and African Studies, 2000. Bar: Ill. 1969, N.Y. 1979, Conn. 1985, Mass. 1990; solicitor Supreme Ct. England and Wales 1995. Asst. prof. So. Meth. U., 1973-77; fellow in law and humanities Harvard U., 1976-77, vis. scholar, 1980-81; assoc. prof. N.Y. Law Sch., 1977-81; prof. law Hamline U., St. Paul, 1981-83; dep. gen. counsel Equator Bank Ltd., 1984-87; v.p., dep. gen. counsel Equator Holdings Ltd., 1987-94, v.p., gen. counsel, 1994-2000. Adj. prof. law U. Conn., 1985-86, Western New Eng. Coll., 1988—, adj. prof. of mgmt. Rensselaer Poly. Inst., 1988-98, prof., 1999—, dir. Ctr. for Global Bus. Studies, 2000—. Author: Foreign Investment in the United States, 2d edit., 1977; (with Stiefel) Products Liability: European Proposals and American Experience, 1981, Doing Business in Sub-Saharan Africa, 1991; bd. editors Am. Jour. Comparative Law, 1981-84, 91—; mem. editl. bd. Conn. Bar Jour., 1988—, sr. editor, 1993-2000, editor-in-chief, 2000—; mem. editl. bd. N.Y. Internat. Law Rev.; mem. editl. rev. bd. Jour. Bus. in Developing Nations, 1996-2000, editor, 2000—; contbr. articles to profl. jours. Mem. ABA (editor in chief ABA Environ. Law Symposium 1980-82), Am. Soc. Comparative Law (bd. dirs. 1978-84, 91—), Am. Fgn. Law Assn., Internat. Bar Assn., Internat. Law Assn. (com. multinat. banking), Acad. Internat. Bus., Conn. Civil Liberties Union (bd. dirs. 1985-92), Environ. Law Inst. (assoc.), Columbia U. Peace Seminar (assoc.), Hartford Club (bd. govs. 1995-98), Am. Corp. Counsel Assn. (pres. Conn. chpt.1997-2000), Conn. Bar Assn. (chair sect. of internat. law 1997-2000). Banking, Private international. Office: Rensselaer Poly Inst Lally Sch Mgmt and Tech 275 Windsor St Hartford CT 06120-2910

SCHUBERT, BLAKE H. lawyer, investor; b. Wheeling, W.Va., Apr. 21, 1939; s. John Arnold and Esther Elizabeth (Masters) S.; m. Carol Jean Cramp, Jan. 13, 1962; children: Cheryl Lynn, Charles Bradley, Elisabeth Anne. BA, Ohio Wesleyan U., 1961; JD, U. Chgo., 1964. Bar: Ill. 1964, U.S. Dist. Ct. (no. dist.) Ill. 1968, U.S. Tax Ct. 1994. Atty., Brunswick Corp., Chgo., 1964-68; asst. group counsel FMC Corp., Chgo., 1968-73; gen. counsel Dresser Tool Group, Chgo., 1973-79; chmn. Schubert Securities Corp., Oak Park, Ill., 1979-84, Inter-Am. Investments, Inc., Oak Park, 1980—; gen. ptnr. Investment Trust Ltd., St. Petersburg, Fla., 1981-91, Inter-Am. Fund, Oak Park, 1982-91, Inter-Am. Fund I, Oak Park, 1982-91, Inter-Am. Fund II, Oak Park, 1984-89; chmn. Compath Video Corp., Oak Park, 1984-85; lectr. Am. Inst. Banking, 1965, Chgo. Inst. Fin. Studies, 1984-85. Chmn. 1st United Ch. Endowment Fund, Oak Park, 1975-80, Park Forest Co-op. (Ill.), 1966-70; mem. Chgo. Bd. Options Exch., 1979-83. Recipient Bancroft-Whitney Prize U. Chgo., 1964. Author: The Well-Kept Secrets of Investing, 1982. General civil litigation, Securities, Taxation, general. Home and Office: 522 Linden Ave Oak Park IL 60302-1659

SCHUCHART, FREDERICK MARK, lawyer; b. San Francisco, Sept. 24, 1945; s. Frederick Francis and Florence (Rogers) S.; m. Katharine Jeanne Murray, Aug. 28, 1970; children: Marisa Renee, Christopher Paul. BS in Pharmacy, Wash. State U., 1968; JD, Gonzaga U., 1974. Bar: Wash. 1974, U.S. Dist. Ct. (ea. dist.) Wash. 1974, U.S. Ct. Appeals (9th cir.) 1979. Assoc. Schuchart, Violette & Spokane, 1974—. Mem. ABA, Wash. State Bar Assn., Wash. State Pharm. Assn., Eagles. Democrat. Lutheran. Family and matrimonial, Personal injury, Probate. Home: S 8105 Hilby Rd Spokane WA 99223 Office: Schuchart & Viollette N 4407 N Division St Ste 714 Spokane WA 99207-1600

SCHUCK, CARL JOSEPH, lawyer; b. Phila., Nov. 21, 1915; s. Joseph and Christina (Schadl) S.; m. Mary Elizabeth Box, June 7, 1941; children: Mary Ann (dec.), John, James, Catherine, Christopher. BS, St. Mary's Coll., 1937; postgrad., U. So. Calif., 1937-38; JD, Georgetown U., 1941. Bar: D.C. 1940, Calif. 1943, U.S. Supreme Ct. 1952. Atty. Dept. Justice, Washington, 1940-42, Alien Property Custodian, San Francisco, 1942-44, Overton, Lyman & Prince, L.A., 1944-47, mem. firm 1947-79, profl. corp. mem. firm, 1979-85. Lectr. Practising Law Inst., 1973; Del. 9th Cir. Jud. Conf., 1963-80, chmn. lawyer-dels. com., 1972, mem. exec. com., 1976-80, chmn. exec. com., 1977-78, mem. sr. adv. bd., 1989-95; mem. disciplinary bd. State Bar Calif., 1970-71. Fellow Am. Coll. Trial Lawyers (chmn. com. on complex litigation 1979-81, regent 1981-85), L.A. County Bar Assn. (trustee 1974-76), Phi Alpha Delta. Club: Chancery (pres. 1984-85). Antitrust, Federal civil litigation, State civil litigation. Home and Office: 16916 Hierba Dr Apt 254 San Diego CA 92128-2679

SCHUETTE, CHARLES A. lawyer; b. Columbus, Ind., Feb. 24, 1942; BBA, U. Okla., 1964, JD, 1967. Bar: Okla. 1967, Fla. 1970, U.S. Supreme Ct. 1979, U.S. Dist. Ct. (so. dist.) Fla. 1982, U.S. Dist. Ct. (mid. dist.) Fla. 1982. Chmn., CEO Akerman, Senterfitt & Eidson P.A. Fellow Am. Bar Found.; mem. ABA, Fla. Bar, Okla. Bar Assn., Dade County Bar Assn. Contracts commercial, Public international, Real property. Office: Akerman Senterfitt & Eidson PA 1 SE 3rd Ave Fl Miami FL 33131-1700

SCHULER, ALISON KAY, lawyer; b. West Point, N.Y., Oct. 1, 1948; d. Richard Hamilton and Irma (Sanken) S.; m. Lyman Gage Sandy, Mar. 30, 1974; 1 child, Theodore. AB cum laude, Radcliffe Coll., 1969; JD, Harvard U., 1972. Bar: Va. 1973, D.C. 1974, N.Mex. 1975. Assoc. Hunton & Williams, Richmond, Va., 1972-75; asst. U.S. atty. U.S. Atty.'s Office, Albuquerque, 1975-78; adj. prof. law U. N.Mex., 1983-85, 90, 98—; ptnr. Sutin, Thayer & Browne, Albuquerque, 1978-85, Montgomery & Andrews, P.A., Albuquerque, 1985-88; sole practice, 1988—. Bd. dirs. Am. Diabetes Assn., Albuquerque, 1980-85, chmn. bd. dirs., 1984-85; bd. dirs. June Music Festival, 1980-95, pres., 1983-85, 93-94; bd. dirs. Albuquerque Conservation Trust, 1986-90, N.Mex. Osteo. Found., 1993-96; chairperson Albuquerque Com. Fgn. Rels., 1984-85; mem. N.Mex. Internat. Trade and Investment Coun., Inc., 1986—; mem. coun. St. Lukes Luth. Ch., 1976-80, 82-84, 91-96, v.p., 1978-80, 82-84, pres., 1994-95, chartered org. rep. troop 444, Boy Scouts Am., 1997—, mem. nominating com., mem.-at-large dist. com. Sandia dist., 1998—, dist. vice chmn., 1999—, v.p. Great S.W. coun., 2001—. Recipient Award of Merit, Sandia Dist., 2000, Tng. award, 2000. Mem. Fed. Bar Assn. (coord.), ABA, Va. Bar Assn., N.Mex. Bar Assn. (chmn. corp., banking and bus. law 1982-83, bd. dirs. internat. and immigration law sect. 1987-95, chmn. 1993-94), Harvard U. Alumni Assn. (mem. fund campaign, regional dir. 1984-86, v.p. 1986-89, chmn. clubs com. 1985-88, chmn. communications com. 1988-91), Radcliffe Coll. Alumnae Assn. Bd. Mgmt. (regional dir. 1984-87, chmn. comms. com. 1988-91), Harvard-Radcliffe Club (pres. 1980-84). General corporate, Private international, Securities. Home: 632 Cougar Loop NE Albuquerque NM 87122-1808 Office: 4300 San Mateo Blvd NE Ste B380 Albuquerque NM 87110-8401 E-mail: akschuler@aol.com

SCHULER, WALTER E. lawyer; b. Memphis, Sept. 8, 1962; s. James D. and Clare A. Schuler. BBA magna cum laude, U. Memphis, 1993; JD cum laude with cert. in health law with hons., St. Louis U., 1996. Bar: Tenn. 1996, U.S. Dist. Ct. (Western Dist.) Tenn. 1996, U.S. Ct. Appeals (6th cir.), 1998. Assoc. The Bogatin Law Firm, PLC, Memphis, 1996—. Contbr. articles to profl. jours., chpt. to book. Sgt. (E-5), U.S. Army, 1985-90, staff sgt. (E-6) USAR, 1990-93. Recipient Commendation Medal-1st Oak Leaf Cluster, U.S. Army, 1989, Army Achievement Medal-2nd Oak Leaf Cluster, 1989, Nat. Def. Svc. Med., 1992. Mem. Am. Health Lawyers Assn., ABA, Tenn. Bar Assn., Memphis Bar Assn. General civil litigation, General corporate, Health. Office: Bogatin Law Firm PLC Ste 300 International Place Dr Memphis TN 38120

SCHULHOFER, STEPHEN JOSEPH, law educator, consultant; b. N.Y.C., Aug. 20, 1942; s. Joseph and Myrelle S.; m. Laurie Wohl, May 28, 1975; children: Samuel, Jonah. AB, Princeton U., 1964; LLB, Harvard U., 1967. Bar: D.C. 1968, U.S. Dist. Ct. (ea. dist.) Pa. 1973, U.S. Supreme Ct. 1973. Law clk. U.S. Supreme Ct., Washington, 1967-69; assoc. Coudert Freres, Paris, 1969-72; prof. law U. Pa., Phila., 1972-86; prof. U. Chgo., 1986—. speedy trial reporter U.S. Dist. Ct., Wilmington, Del., 1975-80; cons. U.S. EPA, Washington, 1977-78, U.S. Sentencing Commn., Washington, 1987-94. Author: Unwanted Sex: The Culture of Intimidation and the Failure of Law, 1998; Prosecutorial Discretion and Federal Sentencing Reform, 1979. Editor: Criminal Law and its Processes, 1983, 89, 95; contbr. articles to profl. jours. Trustee, Community Legal Services, Inc., Phila., 1981-86. Walter Meyer grantee Am. Bar Found., 1984. Mem. ACLU (Ill. bd. dirs. 1993-97), Law and Soc. Assn. Office: U Chgo Law Sch 1111 E 60th St Chicago IL 60637-2776

SCHULLER, STEPHEN ARTHUR, lawyer; b. Wilmington, N.C., 1951; s. Reinhold S. and Gisela (Krause) S.; m. Linda Joy McIntosh, 1977; 1 child. BA, Northwestern U., 1973; JD, U. Tulsa, 1976. Bar: Okla. 1976, U.S. Dist. Ct. (no. dist.) Okla. 1976, Ill. 1977, U.S. Ct. Appeals (10th cir.) 1993. Corp. atty. Roper Corp., Kankakee, Ill., 1977; assoc. Prichard, Norman, Reed & Wohlgemuth, Tulsa, 1977-82; ptnr. Prichard, Norman & Wohlgemuth, 1982-83, Barrow, Gaddis, Griffith & Grimm, Tulsa, 1983-91; pvt. practice law, 1991-95; ptnr. Schuller & Mills, 1995-98, Boone, Smith, Davis, Hurst & Dickman, Tulsa, 1998—. Trustee Employees' Retirement System Tulsa County, 1990—, co-chairperson Dist. 6 planning team, 1989-92; mem. sales tax overview com. City of Tulsa, 1991-94. Mem. ABA, Okla. Bar Assn. (bd. dirs. real property sect. 1983-93, chmn. 1986), Tulsa County Bar Assn., Tulsa Title and Probate Lawyers Assn. (dir. 1986-89, pres. 1989) Contracts commercial, Land use and zoning (including planning), Real property. Office: 100 W 5th St Ste 500 Tulsa OK 74103-4288 E-mail: sschuller@boonesmith.com

SCHULMAN, JERRY ALLEN, lawyer; b. Chgo., May 15, 1944; s. Harold and Florence (Gross) S.; m. Mary Falat, June 23, 1974; children: Michael, Jonathan, Melissa. BS in Chem. Engring., Ill. Inst. Tech., 1972; JD, Loyola U., Chgo., 1973. Bar: Ill. 1973, U.S. Dist. Ct. (no. dist.) Ill. 1973, U.S. Ct. Customs and Patent Appeals, 1976, U.S. Ct. Appeals (fed. cir.) 1983, U.S. Dist. Ct. (no. dist.) N.Y. 1988. Assoc. Alter & Weiss, Chgo., 1973-82, Wallenstein, Wagner, Chgo., 1982-83, ptnr. Epton, Mullin & Druth, Ltd., Chgo., 1983-89; of counsel Seyfarth, Shaw, Fairweather and Geraldson, Chgo., 1989—; vol. Lawyers for the Creative Arts, Chgo., 1976— . Midwest fin. dir. The Holiday Project, San Francisco, 1982-83. Served with USAR, 1976-84. Mem. ABA, Patent Law Assn. Chgo., Chgo. Bar Assn. (chmn. patents, trademarks and copyrights 1985-86, chmn. adoption law 1987-88). Office: Seyfarth Shaw Fairweather and Geraldson 55 E Monroe St Ste 4200 Chicago IL 60603-5863

SCHULMAN, ROBERT S. lawyer; b. N.Y.C., July 9, 1941; s. Donald Benedict and Edythe (Smythe) S.; m. Susan Jan Von Helbig, Sept. 18, 1974; children: Elizabeth Jane, Jennifer Lynn. BA, Rutgers U., New Brunswick, 1963; JD cum laude, Rutgers U., Newark, 1966. Bar: N.J. 1967, Calif. 1976, U.S. Dist. Ct. N.J. 1967, U.S. Supreme Ct. 1970, U.S. Dist. Cts. (ctrl., no., so., ea., dists.) Calif. 1976, U.S. Ct. Appeals (9th cir.) Calif. 1976. With Pitney, Hardin & Kipp, Newark, 1966-74; dept. atty. gen. Office of N.J. Atty. Gen., Trenton, 1974-75; assoc. Cox, Castle & Nicholson, L.A., 1976-80; ptnr. Zobrist, Garner & Garrett, 1980-83, Stephens, Berg, Lasater & Schulman, L.A., 1984-91, Crosby, Heafey, Roach & May, L.A., 1991—. Atty. Bd. of Edn., Fairview, N.J., 1972, Bd. of Adjustment, Fairview, N.J., 1971-73. Contbr. articles to profl. jours. Dir. Deafwest Theatre, L.A., Calif., 1991-97. Mem. State Bar of Calif., Calif. Club. Republican. Congregationalist. General civil litigation, Insurance. Home: 905 Wiladonda Dr La Canada Flintridge CA 91011-3825 Office: Crosby Heafey Roach & May 355 S Grand Ave 29th Fl Los Angeles CA 90071

SCHULMAN, STEVEN GARY, lawyer; b. Gloversville, N.Y., June 10, 1951; s. Jacob and Selma Pearl (Shapiro) S. BA magna cum laude, Williams Coll., 1973; MA, Tufts U., 1975, MALD, 1976; JD with honors, U. Chgo., 1980. Bar: N.Y. 1981, D.C. 1981, U.S. Dist. Ct. (so. dist.) N.Y. 1981. Law clk. to Hon. Robert L. Kunzig U.S. Ct. Claims, Washington, 1980-81; with Milberg Weiss Bershad Hynes & Lerach, LLP, N.Y.C., ptnr. Mem. ABA, ATLA, N.Y. State Bar Assn., D.C. Bar Assn., Assn. of Bar of City of N.Y., Phi Beta Kappa. Federal civil litigation, Securities. Office: One Penn Plz 49th Fl New York NY 10110-0165

SCHULT, THOMAS P. lawyer; b. Great Falls, Mont., Sept. 12, 1954; s. Peter Henry and Louise (de Russy) S.; m. Margo C. Soulé, Sept. 18, 1982. BS in Russian History, U. Va., 1976, JD, 1979. Bar: U.S. Dist. Ct. (we. dist.) Mo. 1979, U.S. Ct. Appeals (10th cir.) 1983, U.S. Ct. Appeals (7th, 8th and llth cirs.) 1984, U.S. Ct. Appeals (5th cir.) 1985, U.S. Supreme Ct. 1987, U.S. Ct. Appeals (9th cir.) 1988. Ptnr. Lathrop Koontz & Norquist, Kansas City, Mo., 1979-89, Bryan Cave, Kansas City, 1989-94; Stinson, Mag & Fizzell, 1994-2001; ptnr. Berkowitz Feldmiller, 2001—. Committeeman Jackson County Reps., Kansas City, 1984—. Mem. ABA (products liability com.), Products Liability Adv. Coun., Mo. Bar Assn. (lectr. continuing legal edn.), Fedn. of Ins. and Corporate Counsel, Def. Rsch. Inst. Episcopalian. Federal civil litigation, State civil litigation. Office: Stinson Mag & Fizzell 1201 Walnut St Ste 2800 Kansas City MO 64106-2117

SCHULTE, BRUCE JOHN, lawyer; b. Burlington, Iowa, June 27, 1953; s. James Andrew and Julia Germaine (Van Dale) S.; m. Mary E. Guest, July 1984 (div. Feb. 1995); children: James, John; m. Catherine Tobben, 2001. BA in Am. Studies, U. Notre Dame, 1975; JD, U. Iowa, 1978. Bar: Iowa 1978, U.S. Dist. Ct. (so. dist.) Iowa 1979, U.S. Ct. Appeals (8th cir.) 1982, Minn. 1988, U.S. Dist. Ct. Minn. 1988, Ill. 1989. Law clk. Justice K. David Harris Supreme Ct. Iowa, Des Moines, 1978-79; ptnr. Dailey, Ruther, Bauer, Schulte & Hahn, Burlington, Iowa, 1979-87; atty. Bennett, Ingvaldson & McInerny, Mpls., 1988; gen. counsel Blackwood Corp., St. Paul, 1988-89; publs. editor Nat. Inst. for Trial Advocacy-U. Notre Dame, Ind., 1989-91; asst. dean pub. affairs Chgo. (Ill.) Kent Coll. Law, 1991-94; dep. dir. assoc. rels. West Pub., Eagan, Minn., 1995-97; dir. mktg., v.p. acad. consulting Performance Comm. Group, Chgo., 1997-2001. Key person com. ATLA, 1984-88; mem. commn. on jud. dists. Supreme Ct. Iowa, 1987-88; publs. com. Nat. Law Firm Mktg. Assn., 1993-94. Author: Persuasive Expert Testimony, 1990, Laser Disc Technology in the Courtroom, 1990; editor: Cases and Materials on Evidence, 1991, Modern State and Federal Evidence, 1991, Problems and Cases for Legal Writing, 1991. Mem. state ctrl. com. Iowa Dem. party, 1984-88; devel. com. Frances Xavier Ward Sch., Chgo., 1993—; mem. cmty. task force Chgo. (Ill.) Downtown Circulator Project, 1994-96; v.p. pub. affairs U. Notre Dame Alumni Class of 1975. Notre Dame scholar U. Notre Dame, Ind., 1971-72; recipient Spectra award Internat. Assn. Bus. Communicators, 1993, Silver Trumpet, Publicity Club Chgo., 1994. Mem. ABA (mem. tech. com. lawyers conf. jud. adminstrn. divsn. 1995—, vice chair task force on image of judiciary 2000—), Ill. Bar Assn. (mem. standing com. legal edn. and admission to bar 1993-97), Chgo. Bar Assn. (mem. law office tech. com. 1995-97), Assn. Am. Law Schs., Chgo. Pub. Rels. Forum (treas. 1997), Notre Dame Club Chgo. (co-chair Hesburgh Forum com. 1993-98, trustee 1995-98, sec. 1997-98), Nat. Soc. Fundraising Profls. (cert. fundraising profl., Midwest conf. steering com. 1997-99), Execs. Club of Chgo. (co-chair standing com. on edn. and pub. svc.). Avocations: sailing, choir, gardening, skiing. State civil litigation. Home: 816 Main St Evanston IL 60602 E-mail: brucejschulte@aol.com

SCHULTE, JEFFREY LEWIS, lawyer; b. N.Y.C., July 24, 1949; s. Irving and Ruth (Stein) S.; m. Elizabeth Ewan Kaiser, Aug. 13, 1977; children: Andrew Riggs, Ian Garretson, Elizabeth Alexandra. BA, Williams Coll., 1971; postgrad., Harvard U., 1971-72; JD, Yale U., 1976. Bar: Pa. 1978, Ga. 1993. Law clk. to hon. John J. Gibbons U.S. Ct. Appeals (3d cir.), Newark, 1976-77; assoc. Schnader, Harrison, Segal & Lewis, Phila., 1977-84, ptnr., 1985-92, founding ptnr. Atlanta, 1992-98, exec. com., 1994-98; ptnr. Morris, Manning & Martin, 1998—. Nat. steering com. lawyers com. to end "Pay-to-Play." Contbr. articles to profl. jours. Trustee Ga. Shakespeare Festival, 1997-99; bd. dirs. North Ardmore (Pa.) Civic Assn., pres., 1990; bd. dirs. Main Line YMCA, chmn., 1989-91. Mem.: ABA, Pa. Bar Assn., State Bar Ga., Phila. Bar Assn., Atlanta Bar Assn. (chmn. comm. and media rels. com.), Atlanta Venture Forum, Bus. and Tech. Alliance, Yale Club of Ga. (bd. dirs. 1996—, pres. 2000—01, chmn. of bd. 2001—02), Williams Club Atlanta, Marion Cricket Club, Williams Club N.Y.C., Weekapaug Yacht Club R.I., Weekapaug Tennis Club, Phi Beta Kappa. Finance, Mergers and acquisitions, Securities. Office: Morris Manning & Martin Atlanta Financial Center 3343 Peachtree Rd NE Ste 1600 Atlanta GA 30326-1044 E-mail: jls@mmmlaw.com

SCHULTZ, DENNIS BERNARD, lawyer; b. Detroit, Oct. 15, 1946; s. Bernard George and Madeline Laverne (Riffenberg) S.; m. Andi Lynn Leslie, Apr. 18, 1967; 1 child, Karanne Anne. BS, Wayne State U., 1970; JD, Mich. State U., 1977. Bar: Mich. 1977, U.S. Dist. Ct. (ea. and we. dist.) Mich., U.S. Ct. Appeals (6th cir.), U.S. Dist. Ct. (we. dist.) Pa. V.p. Barkay Bldg. Co., Ferndale, Mich., to 1976; law clk. Hon. George N. Bashara, Mich. Ct. Appeals, Detroit, 1977; shareholder Butzel Long, 1978—. Editor Detroit Coll. Law Rev., 1977. Detroit Coll. Law Alumni Assn. scholar, 1976, Mich. Consolidated Gas Co. scholar, 1977. Mem. Detroit Bar Assn., Mich. Bar Assn. Republican. Roman Catholic. Avocations: boating, biking, golf. General civil litigation, Contracts commercial, Construction.

SCHULTZ, LOUIS WILLIAM, retired judge; b. Deep River, Iowa, Mar. 24, 1927; s. M. Louis and Esther Louise (Behrens) S.; m. D. Jean Stephen, Nov. 6, 1949; children: Marcia, Mark, Paul. Student, Central Coll., Pella, Iowa, 1944-45, 46-47; LLB, Drake U., Des Moines, 1949. Bar: Iowa. Claims supr. Iowa Farm Mut. Ins. Co., Des Moines, 1949-55; partner firm Harned, Schultz & McMeen, Marengo, Iowa, 1955-71; judge Iowa Dist. Ct. (6th dist.), 1971-80; justice Iowa Supreme Ct., 1980-93; county atty. Iowa County, 1960-68; ret., 1993. Served with USNR, 1945-46. Mem. Am. Bar Assn., Iowa Bar Assn. (bd. govs.), Iowa Judges Assn. (pres.)

SCHULTZ, RICHARD ALLEN, lawyer, farmer; b. Emporia, Kans., Jan. 3, 1939; s. Ebur Samuel and Opal Mae (Porter) S.; m. Esther Marie Strafuss, May 8, 1971; children: William Allen, Bryan Lee. BS in Indsl. Mgmt., U. Kans., 1961; JD, Washburn U. Topeka, 1970. Bar: Kans. 1971. Sole practice law, Topeka, 1970—. Dep. dir. Kans. Govs. Com. Criminal Adminstrn., 1971-73; asst. jud. adminstr. Kans. Supreme Ct., 1973-76; ct. adminstr. 3d Jud. Dist., Kans., 1976-83; dep. sec. Dept. Corrections State of Kans., Topeka, 1983-88. Exec. bd. Topeka YMCA; dist. officer Jayhawk Area Boy Scouts Am., Nat. Eagle Scout Assn.; dir. Kans. Vets. Found., Inc. Lt. USN, 1961-67. Decorated commendation award USN. Mem. ABA, Topeka Bar Assn. (Liberty Bell award 1983), Kans. Bar Assn., Am. Legion, Vietnam Vets Am., Phi Alpha Delta, Alpha Tau Omega. Democrat. Methodist. Criminal, General practice. Office: 3109 SW Stone Ave Topeka KS 66614-2821

SCHULTZE, PASCAL, lawyer; b. Strasbourg, France, Jan. 24, 1966; s. Heinz and Marguerte Schultze; m. Sybile Girard, Sept. 2, 2000. Lic. AES, U. Strasbourg, 1987, Maitraise de Deat des Affairs, 1988; DESS de Deat Fiscal, U. Dijon, France, 1989. Tax cons. Arthur Andersen, Luxembourg, 1989-91; tax lawyer Price Waterhouse, Paris, 1991-95; tax specialist Hewlett Packard, Böblingen, Germany, 1995-98; jr. ptnr. Haarmann Hemmelrath, Paris, 1998—. Real property, Corporate taxation. Office: Haarmann Hemmelrath 23 Rue Balzac F 75406 Paris Cedex 8 France Fax: 01.53.53.02.81. E-mail: pascal_schultze@hhp.de

SCHULZ, BRADLEY NICHOLAS, lawyer; b. Staten Island, N.Y., July 1, 1959; s. George Robert Jr. and Mary Jane (Fazakerley) S. BA, Wake Forest U., 1981; JD, N.Y. Law Sch., 1984. Bar: N.Y. 1985, N.C. 1985, N.J. 1985, U.S. Dist. Ct. (ea. dist.) N.C. 1985, U.S. Dist. Ct. (so. dist.) N.Y. 1985. Assoc. Mast, Tew, Armstrong & Morris, P.A., Smithfield, N.C., 1984-85; ptnr. Mast, Schulz Mast Mills & Stem, P.A., 1986-97, mng. ptnr., 1998—. Chmn. Young Republicans, Johnston County, Smithfield, 1988. Hankins scholar Wake Forest U., 1977-8l, N.Y. Law Sch. scholar, l98l-84. Mem. ABA, N.C. Bar Assn., N.Y. Bar Assn., N.J. Bar Assn., N.C. Acad. Trial Lawyers, Johnston County Bar Assn., Theta Chi Fraternity. Republican. Episcopalian. Avocations: yachting, sailing, skiing. General civil litigation, Insurance, Personal injury. Home: 946 Debro Rd Kenly NC 27542-9725 Office: Mast Schulz Mast Mills & Stem PA PO Box 119 Smithfield NC 27577-0119 E-mail: Brad@mastschulz.com

SCHULZ, KEITH DONALD, corporate lawyer; b. Burlington, Iowa, Dec. 20, 1938; s. Henry Carl and Laura Iral (Bowlin) S.; m. Emily Brook Roane, Apr. 19, 1985; children: Keith Jr., Sarah, Christine, Stefan. BA, U. Iowa, 1960, JD, 1963. Bar: Iowa 1963, Ill. 1966, Wis., 1990. Dep. Sec. of State, State of Iowa, Des Moines, 1965-66; atty. AT&T, Chgo., 1966-67; sec., gen. counsel Borg-Warner Acceptance Corp., 1967-74; asst. gen. counsel Borg-Warner Corp., 1974-84, v.p., gen. counsel, 1984-88; of counsel Bell, Boyd & Lloyd, 1988—. Chmn., CEO Downtown Ptnrs., Inc., 1995-96. Contbr. articles to Harvard Bus. Rev., Jour. for Corp. Growth. Chmn. bd. dirs. Vol. Legal Svcs. Found., Chgo., 1984-91; bd. dirs. Southeast Iowa Symphony Orch., pres., 1998-2000, Heritage Trust Found. Mem. Iowa Bar Assn., Chgo. Bar Assn. (chmn. corp. law depts. com. 1983-84), Wis. Bar Assn., Assn. of Gen. Counsel, Am. Soc. Corp. Secs., Law Club of Chgo. Clubs: University, Economic (Chgo.). Avocations: tennis, bicycling, skiing. General corporate, Finance, Mergers and acquisitions. Office: Bell Boyd & Lloyd 70 W Madison St Ste 3300 Chicago IL 60602-4284 E-mail: KDons@aol.com

SCHULZ, WILLIAM JOHN, lawyer, financial company executive; b. Pitts., Pa., Nov. 4, 1946; s. Theron Paul and Jeanne Mary (Enright) S.; m. Jane Ellen Burgess, July 29, 1967; children— Bryan, David, Kevin. B.S., U. Wis.-Oshkosh, 1968; J.D., U. Wis., Madison, 1971. Bar: Wis. 1971, Mich. 1971. Corp. atty. to sr. atty. corp. fin. Ford Motor Co., Detroit, 1971-80; sr. atty. First Wis. Corp., Milw., 1980-82, asst. gen. counsel, 1982-83, v.p., sec., dep. gen. counsel, 1983-86; 1st v.p., sec.. dep. gen. counsel, 1986—. instr. bus. law Keller Grad. Sch. Mgmt., Milw., 1983-90. Mem. Wauwatosa Sch. Bd., 1984-90. Mem. Am. Soc. Corp. Secs. Banking, General corporate, Securities. Home: 965 Jonquil Ct Brookfield WI 53045-5906 Office: Firstar Corp 777 E Wisconsin Ave Milwaukee WI 53202-5300

SCHULZE, ERIC WILLIAM, lawyer, legal publications editor, publisher; b. Libertyville, Ill., July 8, 1952; s. Robert Carl and Barbara (Mayo) S. BA, U. Tex., 1973, JD, 1977. Bar: Tex. 1977, U.S. Dist. Ct. (we. dist.) Tex. 1987, U.S. Ct. Appeals (5th cir.) 1987, U.S. Dist. Ct. (ea. and so. dists.) Tex. 1988, U.S. Dist. Ct. (no. dist.) Tex. 1989, U.S. Supreme Ct. 1989; bd. cert. civil appellate law Tex. Bd. Legal Specialization, 1990—. Rsch. asst. U. Tex., Austin, 1978; legis. aide Tex. Ho. of Reps., Austin, 1979-81; editor Tex. Sch. Law News, Austin, 1982-85; assoc. Hairston, Walsh & Anderson, Austin, 1986-87; ptnr. Walsh, Anderson, Brown, Schulze & Aldridge, Austin, 1988—, mng. ptnr., 1993—; editor Tex. Sch. Adminstrs. Legal Digest, Austin, 1986-92, co-pub., 1991—, mng. editor, 1992—. Editor: (legal reference books) Texas Education Code Annotated, 1982-85; editl. adv. com. West's Edn. Law Reporter, 1996—. Del. Tex. State Democratic Conv., 1982, Travis County Dem. Conv., 1982, 84, 86. Recipient Merit award for pubs. Internat. Assn. Bus. Communicators-Austin br., 1983, Merit award for authorship Coll. of State Bar Tex., 1992. Mem. Fed. Bar Assn., Am. Bar Assn., Tex. Bar Assn., Travis County Bar Assn., Bar Assn. of 5th Cir., Defense Rsch. Inst., Nat. Council Sch. Attys., Tex. Council Sch. Attys., Edn. Law Assn., Toastmasters (pres. Capital City chpt. 1995). Appellate, Civil rights, Education and schools. Home: 3416 Mount Bonnell Cir Austin TX 78731-5745 Office: Walsh Anderson Brown Schulze & Aldridge PO Box 2156 Austin TX 78768-2156

SCHUM, RANDOLPH EDGAR, lawyer; b. Brantford, Ont., Can., Apr. 9, 1948, came to U.S., 1963, naturalized, 1969; s. Walter O. and Anne M. (Wasatti) S. AB in Polit Sci., St. Louis U., 1969, JD cum laude, 1973. Bar: Mo. 1973, Ill. 1974, Colo. 1979, Minn. 1983, U.S. Supreme Ct. 1984, U.S. Ct. Appeals (7th cir.) 1976, U.S. Ct. Appeals (8th cir.) 1974; U.S. Ct. Appeals (5th cir.) 1988, U.S. Ct. Appeals (10th cir. 1990). Assoc. Fordyce & Mayne, Clayton, Mo., 1973-75, Pope & Driemeyer, Belleville, Ill., 1975-79, Allen, Metcalf, Rogers & Vahrenwald, Ft. Collins, Colo., 1979-80, Paul L. Pratt, P.C., East Alton, Ill., 1980-84; ptnr. Blunt & Schum, Edwardsville, Ill., 1984—; chmn. Consumer Adv. Bd., St. Louis, 1971-73. Editor St. Louis U. Law Sch. Jour., 1972-73. With USAR, 1969-75. Mem. Acad. Rail Law Attys., Ill. Trial Lawyers Assn., Colo. Trial Lawyers Assn., Mo. Bar Assn., Madison County Bar Assn. Federal civil litigation, State civil litigation, Personal injury. Home: 9 Fairway Dr Edwardsville IL 62025-3611 Office: Blunt & Schum PO Box 373 Edwardsville IL 62025-0373

SCHUMACHER, HARRY RICHARD, lawyer; b. Bklyn., June 21, 1930; s. Henry Richard and Martha (Hagenbucher) S.; m. Mary Channing Stokes, Nov. 23, 1963 (dec. Feb. 1980); m. Katherine E. Ware, June 8, 1991; children: Richard, Garry. B.A., Yale U., 1951; J.D. magna cum laude, Harvard U., 1958. Bar: N.Y. 1959, U.S. Supreme Ct. 1964. Assoc. firm Cahill Gordon & Reindel and predecessor firms, N.Y.C., 1958-67, ptnr., 1968-97. Chmn. Legal Svcs. for N.Y.C., Inc., 1994—; dir. New York Legislative Svcs., 2000—. Mem. Manhattan Borough Pres.'s Community Planning Bd. 6, 1962-66; Democratic candidate for N.Y. State Assembly, 1962, 63; bd. dirs. Incarnation Camp, Ivoryton, Conn., 1961-72. Served to lt. (j.g.), USNR, 1951-54. Mem. ABA, N.Y. State Bar Assn. (mem. ho. dels. 1990-94, 2001—), Assn. of Bar of City of N.Y., Fed. Communications Bar Assn., N.Y. County Lawyers Assn. (bd. dirs. 1987-93, 96-99), Am. Judicature Soc. Episcopalian (warden). Clubs: Union, Yale (N.Y.C.). Administrative and regulatory, Federal civil litigation. Home: 47 E 88th St New York NY 10128-1152 Office: Cahill Gordon & Reindel 80 Pine St Fl 16 New York NY 10005-1790

SCHUMACHER, PAUL MAYNARD, lawyer; b. Columbus, Nebr., Apr. 4, 1951; s. Maynard Mathew and Rita Bell (Jarosz) S.; m. Michele Suzanne Gassé, June 26, 1976; children: Nicole Suzanne, Kristen Paulette. AA, Platte Coll., 1971; BS, Fort Hays U., 1973; JD, Georgetown U., 1976. Bar: Fla. 1976, Nebr. 1977, U.S. Dist. Ct. Nebr. 1977. Mem. staff U.S. Senate, Washington, 1974-76; sole practice Miami, Fla. and Columbus, 1976—; v.p. Community Lottery Systems, Inc., Columbus, 1990-92, pres., 1992—. V.p. Megavision Corp., Columbus, 1976—. Treas. prin. Rep. campaign com. U.S. Senate Candidate, Lincoln, Nebr., 1978-79; atty. Platte County, Columbus, 1979-87; chmn. Platte county Reps., 1988-94; mem. Nebr. Rep. State Ctrl. Com., 1994-96, 2000—; CEO Lotto Nebr., 1992—; CEO Cmty. Internet Sys., Inc., 1995-98, bd. dirs., 1995—. Mem. Nebr. Bar Assn., Fla. Bar Assn., Platte County Bar Assn. (pres. 1992-93), Internat. Platform Assn., N.Am. Gaming Regulators Assn. (internat. gaming com.), Rotary, Elks. Roman Catholic. Avocation: physics. Home: 6255 Meyer Rd Columbus NE 68601-8044 Office: PO Box 122 Columbus NE 68602-0122 E-mail: pschumac@megavision.com

SCHUMACHER, STEPHEN JOSEPH, lawyer, educator; b. L.A., Feb. 5, 1942; s. Joseph Charles and Theresa Isabel (Flynn) S.; m. Jeanne Keller Schumacher, Sept. 29, 1990; children by previous marriage: William Scott, Stacey Elizabeth. AB, U. So. Calif., 1963; JD, Hastings Coll. Law, U. Calif., 1967; LLM in Taxation, NYU, 1969. Bar: Calif. 1968. Assoc. Stephens, Jones, LaFever & Smith, L.A., 1967-68, Wenke, Kemble & Burge, 1970-73; ptnr. Wenke, Taylor, Schumacher & Evans, Santa Ana, Calif., 1974-79, Schumacher & Evans, Costa Mesa, 1979-87; sole practice Orange County, 1987—. Instr. real estate taxation U. Calif.-Irvine, 1980-83. Bd. dirs. Orange County Opportunities Industrialization Ctr., 1973-75. Mem. ABA, Calif. Bar Assn., Orange County Bar Assn., Balboa Bay Club. Estate planning, Corporate taxation, Personal income taxation. Office: 4340 Campus Dr Ste 100 Newport Beach CA 92660-1812 E-mail: sjschu42@hotmail.com

SCHUMAN, WILLIAM PAUL, lawyer; b. Chgo., May 6, 1954; s. Alvin W. and Gloria (Kayner) S.; m. Caryn Gutmann, Dec. 20, 1980; children: Lindsey J., Lisa A., Jamie L. BBA, U. Mich., 1976; JD, Harvard U., 1979. Bar: U.S. Dist. Ct. (no. dist.) Ill. 1979. Assoc. McDermott, Will & Emery, Chgo., 1979-84, ptnr., 1985—. Mem. ABA, Ill. Bar Assn., Chgo. Bar Assn. Avocations: softball, golf, basketball. Federal civil litigation, Securities, General civil litigation. Home: 1863 Clavey Rd Highland Park IL 60035-4373 Office: McDermott Will & Emery 227 W Monroe St Ste 3100 Chicago IL 60606-5096 E-mail: wschuman@mwe.com

SCHUPBACH, ARTHUR CHRISTOPHER, lawyer; b. N.Y.C., July 6, 1948; s. Arthur Charles and Margaret Agnes (Plunkett) S.; m. Eileen Patricia O'Shea, Oct. 20, 1973; children— Arthur, Megan, Kristin, Brian. B.A., Fordham Coll., 1970; J.D., NYU, 1973. Bar: N.Y. 1974, U.S. Dist. Ct. (so. and ea. dists.) N.Y. 1974, U.S. Ct. Appeals (2d cir.) 1979, U.S. Supreme Ct. 1979, U.S. Tax Ct. 1982. Assoc. Redmond & Pollio, P.C. (formerly Manning, Carey, Redmond & Tully and Manning, Carey & Redmond,) Garden City, N.Y., 1973— . Mem. ABA, N.Y. State Bar Assn., Nassau County Bar Assn. Republican. Roman Catholic. Banking, General practice, Real property. Office: Redmond & Pollio PC 1461 Franklin Ave Garden City NY 11530-1648

SCHUPP, ROBERT WARREN, law educator; b. Miami Beach, Fla., Jan. 21, 1947; s. Frederick Anthony Schupp and Mary June (Barefoot) Schupp Goodall. B.S. in Mgmt., U. Fla., 1969, J.D., 1973. Bar: Fla. 1973, U.S. Dist. Ct. (mid. dist.) Fla. 1974. Instr. Fla. Jr. Coll., Jacksonville, 1972-73; assoc. prof. U. N. Fla., Jacksonville, 1973—; cons. Sears, Roebuck & Co., Inc., 1974. Contbr. articles to legal jours. Participant Leadership Jacksonville, 1979. Recipient Fla. Disting. Service medal Fla. N.G., 1981. Mem. Fla. Bar Assn., Beta Gamma Sigma, Delta Sigma Pi. Republican. Office: U N Fla 4567 Saint Johns Bluff Rd S Jacksonville FL 32224-2646

SCHUR, GERALD, lawyer; b. Chgo., Apr. 14, 1935; s. John A. and Esther K. S.; m. Sandra Schur, Oct. 26, 1958; children: Andrea Joy Levy, Robert L., David I. BSChemE, Purdue U., 1957; JD, John Marshall U., 1963, M in Patent Law, 1968. Bar: Ill. 1963, U.S. Dist. Ct. (no. dist.) Ill. 1963, U.S. Ct. Appeals (7th cir.) 1979, U.S. Ct. Appeals (fed. cir.) 1978, U.S. Patent and Trademark Office 1964. Engr. Velsicol Chem. Corp., Chgo., 1957-59, patent asst., 1959-63, patent atty., 1963-67; div. patent counsel SCM Corp., N.Y.C., 1967-71; assoc. Arnstein, Gluck, et al., Chgo., 1971-75, ptnr., 1975-84; prin. Welsh & Katz, Ltd., 1984—. Pres. Mens Club, North Suburban Synagogue Beth El, Highland Park, Ill., 1973-74. With Army N.G., 1957-63. Mem. ABA, Ill. State Bar Assn., Patent Law Assn. Chgo. (chmn. com. 1984—), North Suburban Bar Assn., Am. Intellectual Property Law Assn., Decalogue Soc. Chgo. (pres. 1999-2000). Intellectual property, Patent, Trademark and copyright. Office: Welsh & Katz Ltd 120 S Riverside Plz # 22 Chicago IL 60606-3913

SCHUSTER, PHILIP FREDERICK , II, lawyer, writer; b. Denver, Aug. 26, 1945; s. Philip Frederick and Ruth Elizabeth (Robar) S.; m. Barbara Lynn Nordquist, June 7, 1975; children: Philip Christian, Matthew Dale. BA, U. Wash., 1967; JD, Willamette U., 1972. Bar: Oreg. 1972, U.S. Dist. Ct. Oreg. 1974, U.S. Ct. Appeals (9th cir.) 1986, D.C. 2001, U.S. Supreme Ct. 1986. Dep. dist. atty. Multnomah County, Portland, Oreg., 1972; title examiner Pioneer Nat. Title Co., 1973-74; assoc. Buss, Leichner et al, 1975-76; from assoc. to ptnr. Kitson & Bond, 1976-77; pvt. practice, 1977-95; ptnr. Dierking and Schuster, 1996—; adj. prof. law Lewis & Clark Coll., 2002. Arbitrator Multnomah County Arbitration Program, 1985—; student mentor Portland Pub. Schs., 1988—. Author: The Indian Water Slide, 1999; contbg. author OSB CLE Publ., Family Law; contbr. articles to profl. jours. Organizer Legal Aid Svcs. for Community Clinics, Salem, Oreg. and Seattle, 1969-73; Dem. committeeman, Seattle, 1965-70; judge Oreg. State Bar and Classroom Law Project, H.S. Mock Trial Competition, 1988—. Mem. ABA, ATLA, NAACP (exec. bd. Portland, Oreg. chpt. 1979-98), ACLU, Multnomah Bar Assn. (Vol. Lawyers Project), Internat. Platform Assn., Alpha Phi Alpha. Avocations: river drifting, camping, swimming, walking, writing. Personal injury, Real property, Workers' compensation. Office: 3565 NE Broadway St Portland OR 97232-1820 E-mail: schuster@pcez.com

SCHUSTER, ROBERT PARKS, lawyer; b. St. Louis, Oct. 25, 1945; s. William Thomas Schuster and Carolyn Cornforth (Daugherty) Hathaway; 1 child, Susan Michele. AB, Yale U., 1967; JD with honors, U. Wyo., 1970; LLM, Harvard U., 1971. Bar: Wyo. 1971, U.S. Ct. Appeals (10th cir.) 1979, U.S. Supreme Ct. 1984, Utah 1990. Dep. county atty. County of Natrona, Casper, Wyo., 1971-73; pvt. practice law, 1973-76; assoc. Spence & Moriarity, 1976-78; ptnr. Spence, Moriarity & Schuster, Jackson, Wyo., 1978—. Trustee U. Wyo., 1985-89; Wyo. Dem. nominee for U.S. Ho. of Reps., 1994; polit. columnist Casper Star Tribune, 1987-94; pres. United Way Natrona County, 1974; bd. dirs. Dancers Workshop, 1981-83; chair Wyo. selection com. Rhodes Scholarship, 1989-98; mem. bd. visitors Coll. Arts and Scis., U. Wyo., 1991-2000; mem. Dem. Nat. Com., 1992-2000; chair Wyo. Pub. Policy Forum, 1992-98; mem. Wind River Reservation Econ. Adv. Coun., 1998-99. Ford Found. Urban Law fellow, 1970-71. Mem. ABA, ATLA, Wyo. Trial Lawyers Assn. Federal civil litigation, State civil litigation. Home: PO Box 548 Jackson WY 83001-0548 Office: Spence Moriarity & Schuster 15 S Jackson St Jackson WY 83001

SCHUTT, WALTER EUGENE, lawyer; b. Cleve., July 27, 1917; s. Erle Minchin and Elizabeth (Eastman) S.; m. Dorothy Louise Gilbert, Apr. 18, 1942 (dec. Mar. 2000); children: Gretchen Sue, Stephen David, Elizabeth Ann, Robert Barclay. AB, Miami U., Oxford, Ohio, 1939; JD, U. Cin., 1948. Bar: Ohio 1948, U.S. Dist. Ct. (so. dist.) Ohio 1953, U.S. Supreme Ct. 1962, U.S. Tax Ct. 1983, U.S. Ct. Appeals (6th cir.) 1986. Pvt. practice, Wilmington, Ohio, 1948—; city solicitor, 1950-53. Mem. Wilmington Bd. Edn., 1958-65; chmn. Clinton County chpt. ARC, 1951-53; Wilmington chmn. Cin. Symphony Orch. Area Artists Series, 1969-71; trustee Wilmington Coll., 1962-74, sec. 1966-74; trustee Quaker Hill Found., Richmond, Ind., 1970-75, Friends Fellowship Cmty. Inc., 1986-93; rep. U.S. preparations com. 6th Internat. Assembly World Coun. of Chs., 1982. 1st lt. USAAF, 1943-46. Decorated DFC; recipient Disting. Svc. award Wilmington Jr. C. of C., 1953. Mem. Am. Bar Assn. (arms control and disarmament com. 1977-80), Ohio State Bar Assn., Clinton County Bar Assn. (past pres.), World Peace Through Law Ctr. Mem. Soc. of Friends (presiding clk. Friends United Meeting 1978-81, rep. to bd. Nat. Coun. Chs. of Christ 1985-96, presiding clk. Friends com. on nat. legis. 1984-87), Rotary. General practice, Non-profit and tax-exempt organizations, Probate. Home: 81 Columbus St Wilmington OH 45177-1801 Office: Thorne Bldg 36 1/2 N South St Wilmington OH 45177-2361

SCHUTZ, RONALD JAMES, lawyer; b. Adrian, Minn., Nov. 15, 1955; s. Harold Henry and Joanne Dorothy (Peters) S.; m. Janet Jayne Jensen, June 4, 1977; children— Matthew, Erik, Kristin. B.S. in Mech. Engring., Marquette U., 1978; J.D., U. Minn., 1981. Bar: Minn. 1981, U.S. Dist. Ct. Minn. 1981, U.S. Ct. Mil. Appeals 1984, U.S. Supreme Ct. 1986. Commd. capt. U.S. Army, 1981; atty. JAGC, Ft. Ord, Calif., 1981-85; atty. Merchant & Gould, Mpls., 1985-87, Robins, Zelle, Larson & Kaplan, Mpls., 1987—; lectr. U. Minn. Law Sch., 1986-87. Contbr. articles to profl. jours. Mem. N.W. Suburbs Cable Commn. Recipient Army Achievement medal, 1983, 84. Mem. ABA, Minn. Bar Assn., Judge Advocates Assn., Assn. Trial Lawyers Am. Republican. Office: 800 Lasalle Ave Minneapolis MN 55402-2006

SCHUTZ, SIGMUND D. lawyer; b. N.Y.C., Dec. 4, 1972; s. James Scott and Judith Ann (Arseneault) S. BA, Colby Coll., 1994; JD, Cornell U., 1997. Bar: Maine 1997, U.S. Dist. Ct. Maine 1997, N.Y. 1998. Assoc. Preti, Flaherty, Beliveau & Pachios, Portland, Maine, 1997—. Mem. exec. bd. Environ. Bus. Coun. Maine, Portland, 1998—; mem. Environ. Tech. bd., Maine Tech. Inst. Vol. atty. Vol. Lawyers Project, Portland, 1997-2001; vol. tchr. Jr. Achievement Maine, Portland, 1997. Mem. ABA, Maine Bar Assn., Am. Red Cross (mem. bd., chair strategic planning com., Portland chpt.). General civil litigation, Environmental. Office: Preti Flaherty Et Al One City Ctr Portland ME 04112

SCHUYLER, MARILYNN L. lawyer, mediator, government administrator; b. Lubbock, Tex., July 25, 1965; d. Donald Lee and Nannette Lynn Schuyler. BA in Econs., U. Calif., Berkeley, 1987; JD, Georgetown U., 1996. Field mgr. U.S. Dept. Labor, Bur. Labor Stats., San Francisco, 1987-92, sr. field economist, 1992, economist, 1992-95; Affirmative Action officer-Adminstrn., U.S. Dept. Labor, Washington, 1995-96, civil rights officer San Francisco, 1996-97, compliance officer liaison OFCCP, 1997-98, asst. dist. dir. Oakland, 1998—. Reader/grader Calif. Bar Assn., San Francicso, 1998—; mem. Commn. on LL-T Affairs, Takoma Park, Md., 1994-96; mem. Commn. on Status of Women, Berkeley, Calif., 1991-92. Recipient Am. Jurisprudence award, 1994; Olin Law and Econs. fellow, 1994-95. Mem. Soc. for Profls. in Dispute Resolution, Ninety-Nines, Toastmasters (v.p.). Avocation: flying. Home: PO Box 1049 Alameda CA 94501-0105

SCHWAAB, RICHARD LEWIS, lawyer, educator; b. Oconomowoc, Wis., Nov. 15, 1945; s. Thomas L. and Phyllis N. (Lord) S.; m. Lynn Louise Howie; children: Amy, William, Andrew, Matthew. BSChemE, U. Wis., 1967; JD with honors, George Washington U., 1971, LLM in Internat. Law with highest honors, 1979. Bar: Va. 1971, U.S. Dist. Ct. (ea. dist.) Va. 1979, U.S. Supreme Ct. 1980, U.S. Ct. Appeals (fed. cir.) 1982, D.C. 1998. Ptnr. Stepno, Schwaab & Linn, Arlington, 1974-78, Schwartz, Jeffrey, Schwaab, Mack, Blumenthal & Evans, P.C., Alexandria, 1978-88; ptnr. in charge, chair dept. intellectual property Foley & Lardner, Washington, 1988-99; ptnr. Foley & Lardner, 1999—. Lectr. law George Washington U., 1978-88, George Mason U., 1989—. Max Planck Inst. Fgn. and Internat. Patent, Copyright and Competition Law fellow, 1971-72. Co-author Patent Practice, 6 vols., 1976-99, International Patent Law: EPC & PCT, 3 vols., 1978; Intellectual Property Protection for Biotechnology Worldwide, 1987; contbr. articles to profl. jours. Mem. ABA, Am. Intellectual Property Law Assn., Va. State Bar (gov. 1974-78), Am. Soc. Internat. Law, Internat. Patent and Trademark Assn., Internat. Fedn. Indsl. Property Attys., Christian Legal Soc., Phi Kappa Phi, Tau Beta Pi. Private international, Patent, Trademark and copyright. Home: 34205 Nashotah Rd Nashotah WI 53058-9534 Office: Foley & Lardner 3000 K St NW Ste 500 Washington DC 20007-5143 E-mail: rschwaab@foleylaw.com

SCHWAB, ARTHUR JAMES, lawyer; b. Pitts., Dec. 7, 1946; s. Earl Walter and Helen Alice (Gascoine) S.; m. Karen Jenny, Sept. 2, 1967; children: John Arthur, Ellen Katherine, David Earl. Student, Muskingum Coll., 1964-65; AB, Grove City Coll., 1968; JD, U. Va., 1972. Bar: Pa. 1972, N.J. 1985, U.S. Dist. Ct. (we. dist.) Pa. 1972, U.S. Dist. Ct. (ea dist.) Pa. 1978, U.S. Dist. Ct. (no. dist.) Ohio 1979, U.S. Dist. Ct. S.C. 1980, U.S. Dist. Ct. N.Mex. 1981, U.S. Dist. Ct. Mass. 1984, U.S. Dist. Ct. N.J. 1984, U.S. Ct. Appeals (3d cir.) 1972, U.S. Ct. Appeals (11th cir.) 1982, U.S. Ct. Appeals (4th cir.) 1982, U.S. Ct. Appeals (8th cir.) 1991, U.S. Ct. Appeals (9th cir.) 1995, U.S. Supreme Ct. 1975. Ptnr. Reed, Smith, Shaw and McClay, Pitts., 1973-90; ptnr., chair of litigation Buchanan Ingersoll, 1990-99, chief counsel complex litig., 2000—. Faculty U. Va. Trial Advocacy Program. Mem. editorial bd. Va. Law Rev., Sch. Law U. Va., Charlottesville, 1972. Bd. dirs. Grove City (Pa.) Coll. Mem. Pa. Bar Assn. (past chair civil litigation sect.), Acad. Trial Lawyers Allegheny County (past mem. bd. dirs.), Allegheny County Bar Assn., (past chair civil litigation sect.), Am. Inns of Ct. (past pres. Pitts. chpt.), Duquesne Club. Republican. Presbyterian. Federal civil litigation, Computer, Trademark and copyright. Home: 3000 Old Orchard Ct Gibsonia PA 15044-6072 Office: Buchanan Ingersoll One Oxford Ctr 301 Grant St Fl 20 Pittsburgh PA 15219-1410

SCHWAB, HAROLD LEE, lawyer; b. N.Y.C., Feb. 5, 1932; s. Harold Walter and Beatrice (Braverman) S.; m. Rowena Vivian Strauss, June 12, 1953; children: Andrew, Lisa, James. BA, Harvard Coll., 1953; LLB, Boston Coll., 1956. Bar: N.Y. 1957, U.S. Ct. Mil. Appeals 1958, U.S. Dist. Cts. (so. and ea. dists.) N.Y. 1967, U.S. Dist. Ct. (no. dist.) N.Y. 1974, U.S. Dist. Ct. (we. dist.) N.Y. 1988, U.S. Dist. Ct. Conn. 1995, U.S. Dist. Ct. (ea. and we. dists.) Ark. 2000, U.S. Ct. Appeals (2d cir.) 1971, U.S. Ct. Appeals (D.C. cir.) 1986, U.S. Ct. Appelas (11th cir.) 1988, U.S. Ct. Appeals (5th cir.) 1991, U.S. Supreme Ct. 1971. V.p. H.W. Schwab Textile Corp., N.Y.C., 1959-60; assoc. Emile Z. Berman & A. Harold Frost, 1960-67, ptnr., 1967-74; sr. ptnr. Lester Schwab Katz & Dwyer, 1974—. Lectr. N.Y. Jud. Seminars, N.Y. State Bar Assn., N.Y. County Lawyers Assn. Contbr. articles to legal jours.; mem. editl. bd. Jour. Products and Toxics Liability, 1976-96. Served to lt. col. USAFR. Fellow Internat. Acad. Trial Lawyers; mem. ABA, ASTM, SAE, Assn. Advancement of Automotive Medicine, Product Liability Adv. Coun., N.Y. State Bar Assn. (chmn. trial lawyers sect. 1980-81, editor sect. newsletter 1981-84), Am. Bd. Trial Advs. (pres. N.Y. chpt. 1982-83), Fedn. Ins. and Corp. Counsel (v.p. 1979-80), N.Y. State Trial Lawyers Assn., Def. Assn. N.Y., Harvard Club N.Y., Downtown Assn. Federal civil litigation, State civil litigation, Product liability. Home: 205 Beach 142 St Neponsit NY 11694 Office: Lester Schwab Katz & Dwyer 120 Broadway Fl 38 New York NY 10271-0071

SCHWAB, HOWARD JOEL, judge; b. Charleston, W.Va., Feb. 13, 1943; s. Joseph Simon and Gertrude (Hadas) S.; m. Michelle Roberts, July 4, 1970; children: Joshua Raphael, Bethany Alexis. BA in History with honors, UCLA, 1964, JD, 1967. Bar: Calif. 1968, U.S. Dist. Ct. (cen. dist.) Calif. 1968, U.S. Ct. Appeals (9th cir.) 1970, U.S. Supreme Ct. 1972. Clk. legal adminstrn. Litton Industries, L.A., 1967-68; dep. city atty., 1968-69; dep. atty. gen. State of Calif., 1969-84; judge Mcpl. Ct. L.A. Jud. Dist., 1984-85; judge Superior Ct. Superior Ct. L.A. County, L.A., 1985—. Mem. faculty Berkeley (Calif.) Judicial Coll., 1987—. Contbr. articles to profl. jours. Recipient CDAA William E. James award Calif. Dist. Atty.'s Assn., 1981. Mem. San Fernando Valley Bar Assn., Inn. of Ct., Phi Alpha Delta. Democrat. Jewish. Avocations: history, book collecting. Office: LA Superior Ct 900 3rd St San Fernando CA 91340-2935

SCHWAB, NELSON, JR. lawyer; b. Cin., July 19, 1918; s. Nelson Sr. and Frances Marie (Carlile) S.; m. Elizabeth Bakhaus (div.); m. Sylvia Lambert; children: Nelson III, Richard O. BA, Yale U., 1940; LLB, Harvard U., 1943. Bar: Ohio 1947. Ptnr. Graydon Head & Ritchey, Cin., 1947-95; sr. counsel, 1995—. Bd. dirs. Rotex, Inc., Ralph J. Stolle co., Security Rug Cleaning Co., Yoder Die Casting Corp. Grants Review Com. The Greater Cin. Found.; mem. Cin. Pub. Schs. Degration Task Force; former chmn. bd. Vol. Lawyers for the Poor Found.; trustee Cin. Scholarship Found., FISC; adv. bd. Cin. Playhouse in the Park; ; past mem., sec. Cin. Bus. Com., 1977-88, mm. Schs. Task Force; past mem. Cin. City Mgr.'s Working Rev. Com. 2000 Plan, chmn. Reconstituted 2000 Plan Rev. Com., 1990; pres. Greater Cin. C. of C., 1973; chmn. Greater Cin. Ednl. TV, 1965-70, hon. trustee; chmn. Cincinnati and Hamilton County Am. Red Cross, 1955-57, hon. trustee; incorporator United Appeal, 1955; mem. Cin. Sch. Bd., 1959-64. Honoree Greater Cin. Region NCCJ, 1990; Great Living Cincinnatian Grater Cin. C. of C., 1991 Mem. 6th Cir. Jud. Conf., Cin. Country Club (past bd. dirs., sec.), Commonwealth Club (past pres.),

Comml. Club, Recess Club (past pres.), Gyro Club (past pres.), Queen City Club, Queen City Optimists (past pres.), Cin. Yale Club (past pres.), Lincoln's Inn Soc., Delta Kappa Epsilon. General corporate, Estate planning, General practice. Home: 2470 W Rookwood Ct Cincinnati OH 45208-3321 Office: Graydon Head & Ritchey 511 Walnut St # 53D Cincinnati OH 45202-3115

SCHWAB, STEPHEN WAYNE, lawyer; b. Washington, Jan. 25, 1956; s. A. Wayne and Elizabeth (Parsons) S.; m. Debora Zellner, May 26, 1979; children: Benjamin Earl, Jason Edward. BA, Northwestern U., 1979; JD, Pa. State U., 1982. Bar: Ill. 1982, U.S. Dist. Ct. (no. dist.) Ill. 1983, U.S. Ct. Appeals (7th cir.) 1985, U.S. Ct. Claims 1986, U.S. Supreme Ct. 1989, U.S. Ct. Appeals (9th cir.) 1991, D.C. Assoc. Pretzel & Stouffer, Chgo., 1982-85; ptnr. Piper Marbury Rudnick & Wolfe, 1985—. Author: Retaliatory Discharge-Insurable or Not?, 1985, Amreco: A Step Towards International Rehabilitations, 1988, Onset of an Offset Revolution: The Application of Set-Off in Insurance Insolvencies, 1990, Cross Border Insurance Insolvencies: The Search for a Forum Concursus, 1991, An Overview of United States Reinsurance Regulation and Proposals for Reform, 1992, Supreme Court Decides Superpriority Case, 1993, Contingent Claims: Has Their Time Finally Come?, 1994, Insurance Company Receiverships: What Does the Future Hold?. 1994, Should Receivers Sell, or Just Collect, Insurer Shells?, 1994, Caught Between Rocks and Hard Places: The Plight of Reinsurance Intermediaries Under U.S. and English Law, 1995, 96, Banks Selling Annuities May Cause a Turf Battle, 1995, Receiverships, 1995, Reinsurer Liability for Contingent Claims, 1997, Beware Common Account Reinsurance, 1997; contbr. articles to profl.jours. Mem. ABA, Internat. Bar Assn., Ill. Bar Assn., Chgo. Bar Assn., Wigmore Inn of Ct., Order of Barristers, Phi Eta Sigma. Lutheran. E-maol. Federal civil litigation, State civil litigation, Insurance. Office: Piper Marbury Rudnick & Wolfe 203 N La Salle St Fl 18 Chicago IL 60601-1210 E-mail: Stephen.schwab@piperrudnick.com

SCHWAB, TERRANCE W. lawyer; b. Pitts., May 19, 1940; m. Eileen Caulfield, Jan. 4, 1969; children: Matthew Caulfield, Catherine Grimley, Claire Gillespie. BA magna cum laude, Harvard U., 1962; LLB cum laude, Columbia U., 1966. Assoc. Milbank, Tweed, Hadley & McCloy, N.Y.C., 1966-70, Kelley, Drye & Warren, N.Y.C., 1970-74, ptnr., 1975-96; sr. v.p., gen. counsel global fin. and investment banking The Sanwa Bank Ltd., 1996—. Lectr. various profl. orgns. Assoc. editor: Law Practice of Alexander Hamilton, 1964-1980; contbr. articles to profl. jours. Trustee, sec. Caramoor Ctr. for Music and Arts, Katonah, N.Y., 1971—; trustee Sch. of Convent of Sacred Heart, N.Y.C., 1987—, chmn., 1990-93. Mem. ABA, N.Y. State Bar Assn., Assn. of Bar of City of N.Y., Harvard Club. Banking, Contracts commercial, Private international. Office: The Sanwa Bank Ltd 55 E 52nd St Fl 24 New York NY 10055

SCHWABE, GEORGE BLAINE, III, lawyer; b. Tulsa, Oct. 10, 1947; s. George Blaine Jr. and Marguerite Irene (Williams) S.; m. Jann Lee Schoonover, July 28, 1972; 1 child, George Blaine IV. BBA, U. Okla., 1970, JD, 1974. Bar: Maine 2001, U.S. Ct. Appeals (10th cir.) 1974, Okla. 1974, U.S. Dist. Ct. (we. dist.) Okla. 1974, U.S. Dist. Ct. (no. dist.) Okla. 1985, U.S. Dist. Ct. (ea. dist.) 1998, U.S. Supreme Ct. 1991, Maine 2001. From assoc. to ptnr. Crowe & Dunlevy, Oklahoma City, 1974-82; ptnr., dir. Mock, Schwabe, Waldo, Elder, Reeves & Bryant, 1982-96; shareholder, dir. Gable Gotwals Mock Schwabe, 1996-98; member Mock, Schwabe, Waldo, Elder, Reeves & Bryant, 1998—. Adj. prof. law Oklahome City U.; lectr. in field. Capt. USAR. Fellow Am. Coll. Bankruptcy; mem. ABA (bus. bankruptcy com. sect. bus. law), Okla. Bar Assn., Bankruptcy and Reorganization Sect. (pres. 1987-88, bd. dirs. 1985—), Okla. City Golf & Country Club, Rotary. Republican. Mem. Christian Ch. Avocations: golf, snow and water skiing, tennis, travel. Bankruptcy, Consumer commercial, Contracts commercial. Office: Mock Schwabe et al 2 Leadership Sq 14th Fl 211 N Robinson Ave Oklahoma City OK 73102-7109 E-mail: gschwabe@mswerb.com

SCHWABE, JOHN BENNETT, II, lawyer; b. June 14, 1946; s. Leonard Wesley and Hazel Fern (Crouch) Schwabe. AB, U. Mo., Columbia; JD, U. Mo., Columbia, 1970. Bar: Mo. 1970, U.S. Dist. Ct. (we. dist.) Mo. 1970, U.S. Ct. Mil. Appeals 1971, U.S. Supreme Ct. 1973; ordained minister. Pvt. practice, Columbia, Mo., 1974—, St. Louis, 1984—96. Mem. Friends of Music, Columbia, Mo., 1979—; bd. dir. Mo. Symphony Soc., 1984—85; trustee, lay leader, mem. adminstrv. bd. Wilkes Blvd. United Meth. Ch., 1974—79, chmn. pastor-parish rels. com., 1984—85; minister, founder John Schwabe Ministries. Capt. JAGC USAF, 1970—74. Mem.: ABA, Boone County Bar Assn. (sec. 1977—79), Met. St. Louis Mo. Assn. Trial Attys., Personal Injury Lawyers Assn., Lawyers Assn. St. Louis, Columbia C. of C., Am. Legion, Phi Delta Phi. Methodist. State civil litigation, Personal injury, Workers' compensation. Office: John B Schwabe II Law Firm Schwabe Bldg 2 E Walnut St Columbia MO 65203-4163

SCHWAGER, LINDA HELEN, lawyer, councilwoman; b. Bronx, N.Y., Dec. 30, 1948; d. Joseph David and Rose Polonetsky; m. Steven Schwager, Aug. 15, 1971; children: Russell, Mark, Eric. BA, Queens Coll., Flushing, N.Y., 1970; MS, Bklyn. Coll., 1973; JD, CUNY, Flushing, 1995. Bar: N.J. 1996, N.Y. 1997, D.C. 1998, U.S. Supreme Ct. 1999. Tchr. Pub. Sch. 274, Bklyn., 1970-75; retail bus. owner Party Emporium, Oakland, N.J., 1985-92; pvt. practice, 1996—; councilwoman Borough of Oakland, 1991-99. Co-feature editor Bergen Barrister mag., 1998—. Chairperson Rep. party Borough of Oakland, 1980. Named Oakland Woman of Yr. Woman's Club of Oakland, 1989, Woman of Yr. Oakland C. of C., 1996; Paul Harris fellow Oakland-Franlin Lakes Rotary Club, 1999. Mem. N.J. Bar Assn., N.Y. Bar Assn., D.C. Bar Assn., Bergen County Bar Assn. (membership legal svcs. bd. 1995), Women Lawyer in Berger County (newsletter editor 1996—). Jewish. Office: 413 Ramapo Valley Rd Oakland NJ 07436-2707 E-mail: lin822@aol.com

SCHWARCZ, STEVEN LANCE, law educator, lawyer; b. N.Y.C., Nov. 10, 1949; s. Charles and Elinor Schwarcz; m. Susan Beth Kolodny, Aug. 24, 1975; children: Daniel Benjamin, Rebekah Mara. BS summa cum laude in Aero. Engring., NYU, 1971; JD, Columbia U., 1974. Bar: N.Y. 1971, U.S. Dist. Ct. (so. dist.) N.Y. 1975. Assoc. Shearman & Sterling, N.Y.C., 1974-82, ptnr., 1983-89; ptnr., chmn. structured fin. Kaye, Scholer, Fierman, Hays & Handler, 1989-96; prof. Duke U. Sch. Law, Durham, N.C., 1996—; spl. counsel Kaye, Scholer, Fierman, Hays & Handler, 1989—96; 2d faculty dir. Duke Global Capital Markets Ctr. Adj. prof. law Yeshiva U., Benjamin N. Cardozo Sch. Law, N.Y.C., 1983-92; vis. lectr. Yale Law Sch., 1992-96; lectr. Columbia Law Sch., 1992-96. Contbr. articles to profl. jours. Chmn. Friends of the Eldridge St. Synagogue, N.Y.C., 1979—, Legis. Drafting Rsch. Fund. George Granger Brown scholar, 1971; NSF grantee in Math., 1969. Fellow Am. Coll. Comml. Fin. Lawyers; mem. Am. Law Inst., Assn. of Bar of City of N.Y. (environ. law com. 1975-78, nuc. tech. com. 1979-81, sci. and law com. 1985—, chmn. 1987—), Am. Law and Econs. Assn., Tau Beta Pi, Sigma Gamma Tau. Jewish. Office: Duke U Sch Law Box 90360 Science Dr & Towerview Rd Durham NC 27708 E-mail: schwarcz@law.duke.edu

SCHWARTZ, ALLEN G. federal judge; b. Bklyn., Aug. 23, 1934; s. Herbert and Florence (Safier) S.; m. Joan Ruth Teitel, Jan. 17, 1965; children: David Aaron, Rachel Ann, Deborah Eve. BBA, CCNY, 1955; LLB, U. Pa., 1958. Bar: N.Y. 1958. Asst. dist. atty. Office of Dist. Atty., N.Y. County, 1959-62; assoc. firm Paskus Gordon & Hyman, N.Y.C., 1962-65; ptnr. firm Koch Lankenau Schwartz & Kovner, 1965-69, Dornbush Mensch Mandelstam & Schwartz, N.Y.C., 1969-75; mem. Schwartz & Schreiber, P.C., 1975-77; corp. counsel City of N.Y., 1978-81; mem. Schwartz Klink & Schreiber, P.C., 1982-87; ptnr. Proskauer Rose Goetz & Mendelsohn, N.Y.C., 1987-94; judge U.S. Dist. Ct. (so. dist.) N.Y., 1994—. Mem. ex officio N.Y.C. Bd. Ethics, 1978-81; pro bono sports commr. City of N.Y., 1982-83. Research editor: U. Pa. Law Rev, 1957-58. Recipient Award of Achievement, Sch. Bus. Alumni, Soc. of the City Coll., 1981, Hogan-Morganthau Assocs. award, 1980, Corp. Coun. ann. award, 1995, Frank S. Hogan Assocs. award, 1995, Pres.'s medal Baruch Coll., 2001. Office: US Courthouse 500 Pearl St Rm 1350 New York NY 10007-1316 E-mail: allen_g._schwartz@nysd.uscourts.gov

SCHWARTZ, BARRY FREDRIC, lawyer, diversified holding company executive; b. Phila., Apr. 16, 1949; s. Albert and Evelyn (Strauss) S.; m. Sherry L. Handsman, Mar. 21, 1985; children: Fanny Rose, Abraham David. AB cum laude, Kenyon Coll., 1970; JD, Georgetown U., 1974. Bar: Pa. 1974, Ill. 1974, N.Y. 1992, U.S. Dist. Ct. (ea. dist.) Pa. 1974, U.S. Dist. Ct. (no. dist.) Ill. 1975, U.S. Dist. Ct. (so. dist.) N.Y. 1992, U.S. Ct. Appeals (7th cir.) 1977, U.S. Ct. Appeals (3d cir.) 1978, U.S. Ct. Appeals (4th cir.) 1979, U.S. Ct. Appeals (6th cir.) 1981, U.S. Supreme Ct. 1981, N.Y. 1992. Assoc. Sachnoff, Schrager, Jones & Weaver, Chgo., 1974-76; ptnr. Wolf, Block, Schorr & Solis-Cohen, Phila., 1976-89; exec. v.p. gen. counsel MacAndrews & Forbes Holdings, Inc., N.Y.C., 1989—. Trustee Kenyon Coll.; v.p. Temple Sholom. Federal civil litigation, Mergers and acquisitions, Securities. Home: 16 Brookside Park Greenwich CT 06831-5316 Office: MacAndrews & Forbes Holdings Inc 35 E 62nd St New York NY 10021-8032

SCHWARTZ, BARRY STEVEN, lawyer; b. Bklyn., Mar. 12, 1950; s. Joseph and Helen (Lipkin) S.; m. Sherry Licht Cooper, Feb. 18, 1984; 1 child, Jennifer. BA, NYU, 1972; JD, Cath. U. Am., 1975. Bar: N.Y. 1976, U.S. Dist. Ct. (so. dist.) 1976, N.J. 1979, U.S. Ct. Appeals (2d cir.) 1988. Assoc. Seavey, Fingerit & Vogel, N.Y.C., 1976-81; pvt. practice law, 1980—; of counsel Seavey, Vogel & Oziel, LLP, 1992-98, Seavey, Vogel & Oziel, N.Y.C., 1998—. Atty. West New York (N.J.) Rent Control Board, 1984-86. Assoc. editor Cath. U. Law Rev., 1974-75. Mem. ABA, N.Y. State Bar Assn., Masons (master Audubon-Gotham club 1986). Avocations: music, reading, travel, computers. General civil litigation, Landlord-tenant, Real property. Home: 6 Corn Mill Ct Saddle River NJ 07458-1232 Office: 119 W 57th St New York NY 10019-2303 E-mail: bssesq@msn.com

SCHWARTZ, BERNARD JULIAN, lawyer; b. Edmonton, Alberta, Can., July 29, 1960; came to U.S., 1982; s. Sol and Anne (Motkovich) S. BA, U. Alberta, 1981; JD, McGeorge Sch. Law, 1986. Bar: U.S. Supreme Ct. 1991. Atty. Ropers, Majeski, San Francisco, 1987-88, Riverside County Pub. Defenders, Riverside, Calif., 1988-89; pvt. practice, 1990—. Coach Riverside County H.S. Mock Trial Team, 1990, 96, 97. Mem. Calif. Attys. Criminal Justice, Calif. Pub. Defenders Assn., Riverside County Bar Assn. Criminal. Home: 6157 Hillary Ct Riverside CA 92506-2139

SCHWARTZ, BRUCE S. lawyer; b. Phila., Feb. 6, 1939; s. Sidney and Betty Rudin (Taub) S.; m. Marilyn Brownstein, Feb. 28, 1976; children— Cydney, Billie Samantha, Michael Steven. B.S., Phila. Coll. Textiles & Scis., 1960; J.D., U. Miami, Fla., 1963. Bar: Fla. 1963, U.S. Supreme Ct. 1971; cert. civil trial practice lawyer. Ptnr. Linet, Schwartz & Klein, North Miami Beach, Fla., 1963-70, Schwartz, Steinhardt, Weiss & Weinstein, P.A., North Miami Beach, 1970— ; mcpl. judge City of North Miami Beach, 1971-75; rep. to Fla. Patient's Compensation Fund, Fla. Bar. Mem. Assn. Trial Lawyers Am., Acad. Fla. Trial Lawyers (bd. dirs. 1973-75, Coll. Diplomates 1979—), Def. Research Inst., North Dade Bar Assn. (pres. 1970-71). Personal injury. Home: 11111 Biscayne Blvd Miami FL 33181-3404 Office: 2216 Fisher Island Dr Miami FL 33109-0067

SCHWARTZ, CHARLES, JR. federal judge; b. New Orleans, Aug. 20, 1922; s. Charles and Sophie (Hess) S.; m. Patricia May, Aug. 31, 1950 (dec.); children: Priscilla May, John Putney. BA, Tulane U., 1943, JD, 1947. Bar: La. 1947. Ptnr. Guste, Barnett & Little, 1947-70; practiced in New Orleans, until 1976; ptnr. firm Little, Schwartz & Dussom, 1970-76; dist. counsel Gulf Coast dist. U.S. Maritime Adminstrn., 1953-62; judge U.S. Dist. Ct. (ea. dist.) La., New Orleans, 1976-91, sr. judge, 1991—. Mem. Fgn. Itelligence Surveillance Ct., 1992-98; prof. Tulane U. Law Sch., 1977-99; lectr. continuing law insts., 1974-75; mem. Jud. Conf. Com. U.S. on implementation of jury system, 1981-85; mem. permanent adv. bd. Tulane Admiralty Law Inst., 1984—. Bd. editors Tulane Law Rev. Pres. New Orleans unit Am. Cancer Soc., 1956-57; v.p., chmn. budget com. United Fund Greater New Orleans Area, 1959-61, trustee, 1953-65; bd. dirs. Cancer Assn. Greater New Orleans, 1958— , pres., 1958-59, 72-73; bd. dirs. United Cancer Council, 1963-85, pres., 1971-73; mem. com. on grants to agencies Community Chest, 1965-87; men's adv. com. League Women Voters, 1966-68; chmn. com. admissions of program devel. and coordination com. United Way Greater New Orleans, 1974-77; mem. comml. panel Am. Arbitration Assn., 1974-76; bd. dirs. Willow Wood Home, 1979-85, 1989-92; bd. mgrs. Touro Infirmary, 1992—; trustee Metairie Park Country Day Sch., 1977-83; mem. La. Republican Central Com., 1961-76; mem. Orleans Parish Rep. Exec. Com., 1960-75, chmn., 1964-75; mem. Jefferson Parish Rep. Exec. Com., 1975-76; del. Rep. Nat. Conv., 1960, 64, 68; mem. nat. budget and consultation com. United Community Funds and Coun. of Am., 1961; bd. dirs. Community Svcs. Coun., 1971-73. Served to 2d lt. AUS, 1943-46; maj. U.S. Army Res.; ret. Mem. La. Bar Assn. New Orleans Bar Assn. (legis. com. 1970-75), Fed. Bar Assn., Fgn. Rels. Assn. New Orleans (bd. dirs. 1957-61), 5th Cir. Dist. Judges Assn. (pres. 1984-85), Lakewood Country Club (bd. dirs. 1967-68, pres. 1975-77). Office: 219 Northline Metairie LA 70005-4447

SCHWARTZ, CHARLES WALTER, lawyer; b. Brenham, Tex., Dec. 27, 1953; s. Walter C. and Annie (Kuehn) S.; m. Kay Anne Kern, Sept. 24, 1996. BS, U. Tex., 1975, MA, 1980, JD, 1977; LLM, Harvard U., 1980. Bar: Tex. 1977; bd. cert. civil appellate law Tex. Bd. Legal Specialization. Law clk. U.S. Ct. Appeals (5th cir.), Austin, Tex., 1977-79; assoc. Vinson & Elkins L.L.P., Houston, 1980-86, ptnr., 1986—. Contbr. articles to law revs. Fellow Coll. of State Bar of Tex.; mem. ABA, Tex. Bar Assn. (former chmn. grievance com. 1993-99), Tex. Bar Found., Houston Bar Found., Houston Bar Assn., Am. Law Inst., Tex. Law Rev. Assn., Bar Assn. of 5th Cir. Fellow Tex. Bar Found. (life), Houston Bar Found., Coll. State Bar of Tex.; mem. ABA, State Bar Tex. (former chmn. grievance com. 1993-99, bd. dirs. 2000—, mem. exec. com. 2001—), Houston Bar Assn., Am. Law Inst., Tex. Law Rev. Assn., Bar Assn. 5th Cir. Appellate, Federal civil litigation, Securities. Home: 2154 Chilton Rd Houston TX 77019 Office: Vinson & Elkins LLP 2300 First City Tower 1001 Fannin St Houston TX 77002-6760 E-mail: cschwartz@velaw.com

SCHWARTZ, DONALD LEE, lawyer; b. Milw., Dec. 8, 1948; s. Bernard L. and Ruth M. (Marshall) S.; m. Susan J. Dunst, June 5, 1971; children: Stephanie Jane, Cheryl Ruth. BA, Macalester Coll., 1971; JD, U. Chgo., 1974. Bar: Ill. 1974. Assoc. Sidley & Austin, Chgo., 1974-80, ptnr., 1980-88, Latham & Watkins, Chgo., 1988—. Chmn. Ill. Conservative Union, 1979-81, bd. dirs. 1977-85. Served with U.S. Army, 1971-77. Mem. ABA (uniform comml. code com., comml. fin. svcs. commn.), Ill. Bar Assn. (sec. coun. banking and bankuprtcy sect. 1982-83), Chgo. Bar Assn. (chmn. comml. law com. 1980-81, fin. insts. com. 1982-83), Ivanhoe Country Club, Sea Pines Country Club, Met. Club. Republican. Episcopalian. Avocation: golf. Banking, Bankruptcy, Contracts commercial. Home: 191 Park Ave Glencoe IL 60022-1351 Office: Latham & Watkins Ste 5800 Sears Tower Chicago IL 60606 E-mail: Donald.schwartz@lw.com

SCHWARTZ, EDWARD ARTHUR, lawyer; b. Boston, Sept. 27, 1937; s. Abe and Sophie (Gottheim) S.; m. Sheila Kauffman, Apr. 5, 1997; children: Eric Allen, Jeffrey Michael. AB, Oberlin Coll., 1959; LLB, Boston Coll., 1962; postgrad., Am. U., 1958-59, Northeastern U., 1970; postgrad. exec. program, Stanford U., 1979. Bar: Conn. 1962, Mass. 1965. Legal intern Office Atty. Gen. Commonwealth of Mass., 1961; assoc. Schatz & Schatz, Hartford, Conn., 1962-65, Cohn, Reimer & Pollack, Boston, 1965-67; v.p., gen. coun., sec. Digital Equipment Corp., Maynard, Mass., 1967-88; pres. New Eng. Legal Found., Boston, 1990-98. Vis. prof. law Boston Coll., 1986, adj. prof., 1987-89 bd. dirs. SatelLife Corp.; bd. advisors Buffalo Hill Hist. Ctr. Editor Boston Coll. Indsl. and Comml. Law Rev, 1960-62, Ann. Survey Mass. Law, 1960-62. Chair, bd. trustees Rural Land Found. Mem. ABA, Mass. Bar Assn., Boston Bar Assn. General corporate. Home: 62 Todd Pond Rd Lincoln MA 01773-3808

SCHWARTZ, ESTAR ALMA, lawyer; b. Bklyn., June 29, 1950; d. Henry Israel and Elaine Florence (Scheiner) Sutel; m. Lawrence Gerald Schwartz, June 28, 1976 (div. Dec. 1977); 1 child, Joshua (dec.); m. James Frances Edward Stuart, Sept. 25, 1999. JD, N.Y.U., 1980. owner Estaris Paralegal Svc., Flushing, N.Y., 1992—. Mgr., ptnr. Scheiner, Scheiner, DeVito & Wytte, N.Y.C., 1966-81; fed. govt., social security fraud specialist DHHS, OI, OIG, SSFIS, 1982-83; pensions Todtman, Epstein, et al, 1983-85; office mgr., sec. Sills, Beck, Cummis, 1985-86; office mgr., bookkeeper Philip, Birnbaum & Assocs., 1986-87; office mgr., sec. Stanley Posses, Esq., Queens, N.Y., 1989-90. Owner Sutel Creative Mgmt. Agy., Flushing, N.Y., 1999—. Democrat. Jewish. Avocations: needlepoint, horseback riding, tennis, bowling, writing children's stories. Pension, profit-sharing, and employee benefits, Personal injury, Product liability. Home and Office: 67-20 Parsons Blvd Apt 2A Flushing NY 11365-2960 E-mail: Sutel@email.com, sutell@aol.com

SCHWARTZ, HOWARD J. lawyer; b. N.Y.C., July 17, 1946; s. Joseph and Fay S.; m. Kathryn Brancati; children: Hania, Bethany, Christopher. BA, Muhlenberg Coll., 1968; JD, NYU, 1972. Atty. Rabinowitz, Boudin & Standard, N.Y.C., 1973-74, Legal Aid Soc., N.Y.C., 1974-77; ptnr. Schwartz & Sands, 1977-79, Robinson, Perlman & Kirschner, N.Y.C., 1979-86, Davis & Gilbert, N.Y.C., 1986-92; prin. Porzio, Bromberg & Newman, Morristown, N.J., 1993—. Contbr. articles to profl. jours. Coach Montville Recreation Dept., N.J., 1993—. Mem. ABA, N.Y. State Bar Assn., N.J. State Bar Assn., Internat. Assn. Defense Counsel, Inns of Ct. Avocations: skiing, tennis. Entertainment, Intellectual property, Trademark and copyright. Office: Porzio Bromberg & Newman 163 Madison Ave Morristown NJ 07960-7324

SCHWARTZ, JAMES EVAN, lawyer; b. N.Y.C., June 16, 1956; s. Louis and Elaine Florence (Friedman) S.; m. Susan Lea Cohen, Nov. 18, 1989; children: Jessica, Deborah, Andrew. BA, U. Pa., 1978; JD, Duke U., 1981. Bar: N.Y. 1982, U.S. Dist. Ct. (so. and ea. dists.) N.Y. 1987. Assoc. Bell, Kalnick, Beckman, Klee & Green, N.Y.C., 1981-83, Goldschmidt, Fredericks & Oshatz, N.Y.C., 1983-84, Jarblum, Solomon & Fornari, P.C., N.Y.C., 1984-86, Liebman, Adolf & Charme, P.C., N.Y.C., 1986-87, Carb, Luria, Cook & Kufeld, N.Y.C., 1987-95; ptnr. Carb, Luria, Glassner, Cook & Kufeld, 1995—. Arbitrator Civil Ct. of City of N.Y. Mem. ABA, Assn. of Bar of City of N.Y. Democrat. Jewish. Avocations: skiing, running, tennis, numismatics. General civil litigation, Contracts commercial, Real property. Home: 16 Carriage House Ln Mamaroneck NY 10543-1004 Office: Carb Luria Cook & Kufeld LLP 521 5th Ave New York NY 10175-0003

SCHWARTZ, JEFFREY BYRON, lawyer; b. Phila., Dec. 3, 1940; s. Carl Sidney and Tessie Claire (Cohen) S.; m. Joan S. Weinman, Aug. 4, 1963; children: Kevin, Jill. BS, Pa. State U., 1962; JD, U. Pa., 1965; MBA, Am. U., 1967. Bar: Pa. 1965, D.C. 1968, La. 1969. Staff acct. Price Waterhouse & Co., Washington, 1962; trial atty. SEC, 1965-68; sr. atty. New Orleans Legal Assistance, 1968-70; gen. counsel Nat. Tenants Orgn., Washington, 1970-73; litigation atty. Nat. Health and Environ. Law Project, 1971-74; chief counsel Pa. Dept. Health, Harrisburg, 1974-79; ptnr. Berriman & Schwartz, King of Prussia, Pa., 1979-85; sr. ptnr. Wolf, Block, Schorr & Solis-Cohen, Phila., 1985-92; ptnr. Cohen, Shapiro, Polisher, Shiekman & Cohen, 1992-95, Fox Rothschild, O'Brien & Frankel, LLP, Phila., 1995-99; sr. legal advisor USAID Assistance Program Bulgarian Securities and Stock Exch. Commn., 1999—. Guest lectr. on welfare and health law U. Pa. Sch. Law, Tulane U. Law Sch., Wayne State U. Law Sch. and Georgetown U. Law Sch.; instr. Catholic U. Am. Law Sch., 1972-73; course planner Pa. Bar Inst., 1980—. Contbr. articles to profl. jours. Reginald Heber Smith fellow, 1968-70. Mem. Am. Soc. Hosp. Attys., Am. Health Lawyers Assn. (dir.), Pa. Soc. Hosp. Attys. (pres. 1983-85, bd. dirs. 1983-89), Hosp. Attys. Southeastern Pa., Am. Pub. Health Assn. (chmn. health law com. 1978-81), Pa. Bar Assn., D.C. Bar Assn. Democrat. Jewish. Federal civil litigation, State civil litigation, Health. Home: 10 Radcliff Rd Bala Cynwyd PA 19004-2631

SCHWARTZ, LAWRENCE B. lawyer, accountant, banker; b. Bridgeport, Conn., May 17, 1929; s. Joseph A. and Augusta J. (Josephson) S.; m. Valerie Markman, July 13, 1972; children— David, Roberta, Richard. B.S. in Econs., Wharton Sch., U. Pa. 1951; J.D., U. Conn. 1954. Bar: Conn. 1954, U.S. Dist. Ct. Conn. 1955, U.S. Tax Ct. 1956. Ptnr. Gladstone, Schwartz, Baroff & Blum, Bridgeport, 1962; chmn. bd., chmn. exec. com. Lafayette Bank and Trust Co., Bridgeport, 1965— , also dir.; treas. Town of Trumbull, Conn., 1958, Trumbull Sch. Lunch Program, 1958-60; sec. Conn. Bd. Pardons, Hartford, 1972-78; co-chmn. bd. Constn. Bancorp of New Eng. Inc. Recipient Gold medal Conn. Soc. C.P.A.s, 1954. Mem. Conn. Bar Assn., ABA, Assn. Trial Lawyers Am., Profl. Orgn. Attys. and C.P.A.s. Jewish. Clubs: Algonquin (Bridgeport); Rolling Hills Country (Wilton, Conn.); Frenchmen's Creek Golf, Yacht and Country; Palm Beach (Fla.) Gardens. Lodge: Odd Fellows. Banking, Real property, Corporate taxation. Home: 525 S Flagler Dr Apt 26C West Palm Beach FL 33401-5901 Office: Gladstone Schwartz Baroff 1087 Broad St Bridgeport CT 06604-4261 also: Constitution Bancorp 1643 Post Rd Fairfield CT 06430-5910

SCHWARTZ, LEONARD JAY, lawyer; b. San Antonio, Sept. 23, 1943; s. Oscar S. and Ethel (Eastman) S.; m. Sandra E. Eichelbaum, July 4, 1965; 1 child, Michele Fay. BBA, U. Tex., 1965, JD, 1968. Bar: Tex. 1968, Ohio 1971, U.S. Supreme Ct. 1971, U.S. Dist. Ct. (no., ea., wes. and so. dists.) Tex., U.S. Dist. Cts. (no. and so. dists.) Ohio, U.S. Dist. Ct. Nebr., U.S. Ct. Appeals (5th, 6th, 7th and 11th cirs.). Assoc. Roberts & Holland, N.Y.C., 1968-70; ptnr. Rigely, Schwartz & Fagan, San Antonio, 1970-71; staff counsel ACLU of Ohio, Columbus, 1971-74; ptnr. Schwartz & Fishman, 1974-79; elections counsel to sec. of state State of Ohio, 1979-80; ptnr. Waterman & Schwartz and successor firms, Austin, Tex., 1981-85; mng. dir. Schwartz & Eichelbaum, PC, Austin and other cities, 1985-99, 2000—, shareholder Austin, various locations, 1985—. Gen. counsel various sch. dists., cities and counties; adj. prof. law U. Tex. Sch. Law, Austin; labor and employment law cons. and sch. law Tex. Assn. Sch. Adminstrs; condr. workshops in field; mem. com. on fed. judiciary rels. Tex. Bar. Contbr. articles to profl. jours. Mem. chancellor's coun. U. Tex. Sys.; mem. U. Tex. Pres.'s Assocs., Littlefield Soc., Sch. of Law Keeton Fellows. Recipient Outstanding Tchg. Quiz Master award U. Tex. Sch. Law, 1968. Fellow Tex. Bar Found.; mem. ABA, FBA, Tex. Bar Assn., Bar Assn. 5th Cir., Phi Delta Phi. Democrat. Jewish. Administrative and regulatory, Federal civil litigation, Labor. Office: Schwartz & Eichelbaum PC 4201 W Parmer Ln Ste 100 Austin TX 78727 Fax: 512-472-2599. E-mail: lschwartz@edlaw.com

SCHWARTZ, MILTON LEWIS, federal judge; b. Oakland, Calif., Jan. 20, 1920; s. Colman and Selma (Lavenson) S.; m. Barbara Ann Moore, May 15, 1942; children: Dirk L., Tracy Ann, Damon M., Brooke. A.B., U. Calif. at Berkeley, 1941, J.D., 1948. Bar: Calif. bar 1949. Rsch. asst. 3d Dist. Ct. Appeal, Sacramento, 1948; dep. dist. atty., 1949-51; practice in Sacramento, 1951-79; partner McDonough, Holland, Schwartz & Allen, 1953-79; U.S. dist. judge Eastern Dist. Calif., U.S. Dist. Ct., Calif., 1979-90, sr. judge, 1990—. Prof. law McGeorge Coll. Law, Sacramento, 1952-55; mem. Com. Bar Examiners Calif., 1971-75 Pres. Bd. Edn. Sacramento City Sch. Dist., 1961; v.p. Calif. Bd. Edn., 1967-68; trustee Sutterville Heights Sch. Dist. Served to maj. 40th Inf. Divsn. AUS, 1942-46, PTO. Named Sacramento County Judge of Yr., 1990; Milton L. Schwartz Am. Inn of Court named in his honor, Davis, Calif. Fellow Am. Coll. Trial Lawyers; mem. State Bar Calif., Am. Bar Assn., Am. Bd. Trial Advocates, Anthony M. Kennedy Am. Inn of Ct. (pres. 1988-90, pres. emeritus 1990—). Office: US Dist Ct Rm 15 200 501 I St Sacramento CA 95814

SCHWARTZ, PHILIP, lawyer; b. June 7, 1930; s. Louis and Kate (Brodsky) S.; m. Iris M. Ballin, Nov. 28, 1953 (div. 1979); children: David, Elyse, Donna; m. Monique W. Wagner, July 26, 1982 (div. 1991); m. Carol J. Pruett, Aug. 14, 1992. BA, George Washington U., 1952, JD, 1959; LLM in Taxation, Georgetown U., 1961; postgrad., U. Paris, London Sch. Econs., Harvard U. Bar: Va. 1959, D.C. 1966, U.S. Tax Ct. 1966, U.S. Ct. Appeals (D.C. cir.) 1966, U.S. Ct. Mil. Appeals 1966, U.S. Supreme Ct. 1966, U.S. Ct. Appeals (4th cir.) 1982, U.S. Ct. Internat. Trade 1988, N.Am. Coun. London Ct. Internat. Arbitration 1988. Sr. intelligence analyst Nat. Security Agy., Washington, 1952-54, 56-63; assoc. Varoutsos, Koutolakos & Arthur, Arlington, Va., 1963-67; ptnr. Schwartz & Ellis, Ltd., 1968—. Instr. No. Va. Life Underwriters Tng. Coun., 1974, No. Va. Paralegal Inst., Arlington, 1976; moot ct. judge George Washington U., Washington, Georgetown U., Washington, Jessup Internat. Law Competition; commr. Chancery Arlington Cir. Ct., judge Pro Tempo; spkr. in field. Contbr. articles to profl. jours. Mem. U.S. Sec. of State adv. com. on pvt. internat. law, Arlington County Bd. Zoning Appeals, 1972-85, Arlington County Coun. Human Rels., 1973; del. to vogue conf. pvt. internat. law; bd. dirs. Jewish Cmty. Ctr. Greater Washington, 1975. With M.I., U.S. Army, 1954-56. Master Barrister Am. Inns of Ct.; fellow Internat. Acad. Matrimonial Lawyers (pres. 1996-97), Am. Acad. Matrimonial Lawyers (bd. govs., v.p.); mem. ABA (chmn. family law sect. com. internat. laws 1983-86, chmn. internat. law sect. com. enforcement fgn. judgments), Internat. Bar Assn. (chmn. family law divsn. 1988-92, governing coun. gen. practice sect., liaison officer to IMF), Va. Trial Lawyers Assn. (instr. 1984), Assn. Trial Lawyers Am. (vice chmn. internat. practice sect.), Va. State Bar (bd. govs. internat. law sect., liaison to ABA internat. law sect., spl. com. reducing litigation delay and costs), Calif. Bar Assn. (internat. law sect.), N.Y. State Bar Assn. (internat. law, family law sect.), D.C. Bar (internat. law, family law sect.), Arlington County Bar Assn. (cts. com., legis. com., jud. selection com.), Fairfax County Bar Assn. (family law and internat. law sects.), Brit. Inst. Internat. and Comparative Law, Am. Soc. Internat. Law, World Assn. Lawyers, Union Internationale des Avocats, Inter-Am. Bar Assn., Internat. Soc. Family Law, Solicitors Family Law Assn., Soc. English and Am. Lawyers, Am. Fgn. Law Assn., Internat. Law Assn., Asia-Pacific Lawyers Assn., Arlington Jaycees, Kiwanis, Phi Epsilon Pi, Delta Phi Epsilon, Phi Delta Phi. General corporate, Family and matrimonial, Private international. Office: Schwartz & Ellis Ltd 6950 Fairfax Dr Arlington VA 22213-1012 Fax: 703-534-0329. E-mail: schwellis@aol.com

SCHWARTZ, RENEE GERSTLER, lawyer; b. Bklyn., June 18, 1933; d. Samuel and Lillian (Neulander) Gerstler; m. Alfred L. Schwartz, July 30, 1955; children: Carolyn Susan, Deborah Jane. AB, Bklyn. Coll., 1953; LLB, Columbia U., 1955. Bar: N.Y. 1956, U.S. Dist. Ct. (so. and ea. dists.) N.Y. 1956, U.S. Ct. Appeals (2d cir.) 1956, U.S. Dist. Ct. D.C. 1983, U.S. Supreme Ct. 1986. Assoc. Botein, Hays & Sklar, N.Y.C., 1955-64, ptnr., 1965-89, Kronish, Lieb, Weiner & Hellman, N.Y.C., 1990—. Bd. dirs. New Land Found., N.Y.C., 1965—. Mem. Bar Assn. City of N.Y. Family and matrimonial, Libel, Public utilities. Home: 115 Central Park W New York NY 10023-4153 Office: Kronish Lieb Weiner & Hellman 1114 Avenue Of The Americas New York NY 10036-7703 E-mail: rschwartz@klwhllp.com

SCHWARTZ, ROBERT H. lawyer; b. Detroit, Apr. 7, 1948; s. Earl M. and Betty (Kert) S.; m. Linda, June 13, 1971. BA, Wayne State U., 1969, JD, 1972. Bar: Mich. 1972, U.S. Dist. Ct. Mich. 1972, U.S. Tax Ct. 1980, U.S. Ct. Appeals, U.S. Supreme Ct., U.S. Ct. Appeals. Assoc. Garan, Lucow, Miller, Detroit, 1972-73; sole practice Southfield, Mich., 1973-75, 80-84; atty. Barr & Schwartz, 1975-77; ptnr. Gourwitz, Barr & Schwartz, 1977-80; with Raymond & Prokop P.C., 1984—, pres., mng. ptnr., 1997—. Pres., Jewish Nat. Fund Metro. Detroit, 1997—. Mem. Mich. Bar Assn. (mem. comml. litigations), Mich. Health Care Lawyers (pres. 1985), Oakland County Bar Assn., Healthcare Fin. Mgmt. Assn. (co-chair law com.), Am. Health Lawyers Assn., Med. Group Mgmt. Assn. (co-chair tech. subcommitee Health Law Section), Mich. State Bar. Avocations: photography, baseball. State civil litigation, General corporate, Health. Office: Raymond & Prokop PC 4th Fl PO Box 5058 26300 Northwestern Hwy Southfield MI 48086-5058 E-mail: rschwartz@raypro.com

SCHWARTZ, ROBERT S. lawyer; b. Columbus, Ohio, Sept. 22, 1947; s. Stanley and Miriam (Golin) S.; m. Nancy R. Krasa, Apr. 20, 1980; children— Hannah, Lila, William. B.A., U. Chgo., 1970; M.A., U. Mich., 1971; J.D., Ohio State U., 1975. Bar: N.Y. 1976, U.S. Dist. Ct. (so. dist.) N.Y. 1976, Ohio 1986. Assoc. Fried, Frank, Harris et al, N.Y.C., 1975-79; atty. Marsh & McLennan Cos., Inc., 1979-84, sr. atty., 1984-85; assoc. Schwartz, Kelm, Warren & Rubenstein, Columbus, 1985-86, ptnr., 1987—; adj. assoc. prof. NYU, 1983-85. Mem. ABA, N.Y. State Bar Assn., Ohio Bar Assn., Columbus Bar Assn. General corporate, Insurance, Securities. Office: Schwartz Kelm Warren & Rubenstein 41 S High St Columbus OH 43215-6101

SCHWARTZ, ROGER ALAN, judge; b. N.Y.C., May 2, 1945; s. George Martin Ronald and Claire Marie (Dorsch) S.; m. Carmela Patricia Gillan, Sept. 29, 1979 (div.); 1 child, Julia Claire. BA, Muhlenberg Coll., 1967; JD, Temple U., 1973, M in Labor Law, 1976, MPA, 1979; disting. grad., U.S. Army Command and Gen. Staff Coll.; MA in History summa cum laude, U. Scranton, 1997; postgrad. studies, Marywood U., 1997—. Bar: Pa. 1973, N.Y. 1982, D.C. 1976, U.S. Dist. Ct. (ea. dist.) Pa. 1973, U.S. Ct. Appeals (3d cir.) 1976, U.S. Mil. Appeals 1981, U.S. Ct. Appeals (Fed cir.) 1986, U.S. Supreme Ct, 1976. Personnel mgmt. specialist CSC, Phila., 1973-74, asst. appeals officer, 1974-78; sr. adminstrv. judge U.S. Merit Systems Protection Bd., 1979-89; adminstrv. law judge Social Security Adminstrn., Wilkes-Barre, Pa., 1989—. Arbitrator Phila. Ct. Common Pleas, 1973-89; asst. prof. Inst. for Paralegal Tng., Phila., 1976-77. With U.S. Army, 1968-70, Vietnam, Persian Gulf War, 1990; col. JAGC Res. Decorated Bronze Star, Purple Heart, Nat. Svc. medal with svc. star, Meritorious Svc. medal with one oak leaf cluster, Meritorious Achievement medal with 1 oak leaf cluster, Army Commendation medal with 4 oak leaf clusters. Mem. ABA, Phila. Bar Assn., Am. Judicature Soc., Am. Arbitration Assn., Res. Officers Assn. (Pa. state sec. 1996-97), Assn. Adminstrv. Law Judges (v.p. region III), Rotary (bd. dirs. Wilkes Barre chpt.). Avocations: piano, computers, billiards. Office: Social Security Adminstrn Office Hearings & Appeals 7 N Wilkes Barre Blvd Wilkes Barre PA 18702-5249 E-mail: rogschwa@infi.net

SCHWARTZ, STEPHEN JAY, lawyer; b. Bklyn., May 28, 1947; s. Morris and Muriel (Scherr) S. BA, Queens Coll., 1969; JD, Bklyn. Law Sch., 1973. Bar: N.Y. 1974, U.S. Dist. Ct. (ea. and so. dists.) N.Y. 1974. Assoc. Aaron J. Broder & F. Lee Bailey, N.Y.C., 1973-74, Harry Grossmun, N.Y.C., 1974-78, Paul A. Gritz, Bklyn., 1978-80; ptnr. Schwartz, Dicker & Gutstein, N.Y.C., 1980-88, Schwartz, Gutstein & Assocs., N.Y.C., 1988—; gen. counsel Hubert Lanz, Inc., Munich, W.Ger., 1980—; bd. dirs. Penstone, Ltd., London; cons. SDVB, Ltd., Graz, Austria; gen. counsel The Am. Theatre Collection, Inc., The Am. Play Co., Authors Research Co. Inc. Mem. ABA, N.Y. Chamber Commerce and Industry, N.Y. State Bar Assn., Queens County Bar Assn. General corporate, Private international, Personal injury. Office: 271 Madison Ave Ste 1800 New York NY 10016-1001

SCHWARTZ, STEVEN T. lawyer; b. Montizello, N.Y., Aug. 25, 1960; s. Arnold Schwartz and Harriet Phyllis Karp. AA, Nassau C.C., 1987; BA, SUNY, Buffalo, 1991; JD, Bklyn. Law Sch., 1995. Bar: U.S. Dist. Ct. N.J. 1996, N.Y. 1997, U.S. Dist. Ct. (ea. dist.) N.Y. 1997, U.S. Dist. Ct. (so. dist.) N.Y. 1997. With Schweider Kleiwick Weitz Darmashek & Shrot, N.Y.C. Mem. Assn. of Trial Lawyers of Am., N.Y. State Trial Lawyers Assn. Jewish. Personal injury, Product liability, Toxic tort. Office: Schweider Kleiwick Weitz Darmashek & Shrot 223 Broadway Woolworth Bldg New York NY 10279

SCHWARTZ, STUART RANDALL, lawyer; b. Chgo., Feb. 7, 1949; s. Samuel Louis and Marion (Kogon) S.; m. Gayle Ann Jackson, Sept. 15, 1973; children: Sarah, Susan. B.A. in Econ., U. Pa., 1970; J.D. cum laude, Northwestern U., 1973. Bar: Ill. 1973, Fla. 1983, U.S. Dist. Ct. (no. dist.) Ill. 1973. Atty. Merc. Fin. Corp., Chgo., 1973-74, Borg-Warner Corp., Chgo., 1974-77; v.p., asst. gen. counsel Assocs. Comml. Corp., Chgo., 1977-83; assoc. Jacobs, Robbins, Gaynor, Burton, Hampp, Burns, Bronstein & Shasteen P.A., St. Petersburg, Fla., 1983-86; v.p., asst. gen. counsel Sanwa Bus. Credit Corp., Chgo., 1986—. Served to sgt. USAR, 1970-76. Mem. ABA (comml. fin. services com.). Jewish. Bankruptcy, Consumer commercial, Contracts commercial. Home: 1145 Jeffery Ct N Northbrook IL 60062-4658 Office: Sanwa Bus Credit Corp 1 S Wacker Dr Chicago IL 60606-4614

SCHWARTZ, WILLIAM, lawyer, educator; b. Providence, May 6, 1933; s. Morris Victor and Martha (Glassman) S.; m. Bernice Konigsberg, Jan. 13, 1957; children: Alan Gershon, Robin Libby. AA, Boston U., 1952, JD magna cum laude, 1955, MA, 1960; postgrad., Harvard Law Sch., 1955-56; LHD (hon.), Hebrew Coll., 1996, Yeshiva U., 1998. Bar: D.C. 1956, Mass. 1962, N.Y. 1989. Prof. law Boston U., 1955-91, Fletcher prof. law, 1968-70, Roscoe Pound prof. law, 1970-73, dean Sch. of Law, 1980-88, dir. Ctr. for Estate Planning, 1988-91; univ. prof. Yeshiva U., N.Y.C., 1991—; of counsel Swartz & Swartz, 1973-80; v.p. for acad. affairs, chief acad. officer Yeshiva U., N.Y.C., 1993-98; counsel Cadwalader, Wickersham and Taft, N.Y.C., Washington, Charlotte, London, 1988—; mem. faculty Frances Glessner Lee Inst., Harvard Med. Sch., Nat. Coll. Probate Judges, 1970, 77, 78, 79, 88; gen. dir. Assn. Trial Lawyers Am., 1968-73; reporter New Eng. Trial Judges Conf., 1965-67; participant Nat. Met. Cts. Conf., 1968; dir. Mass. Probate Study, 1976—; chmn. spl. com. on police procedures City of Boston, 1989, 91. Bd. dirs. UST Corp., chmn. of co., 1993-94, chmn. bd. dirs., 1996-2000; bd. dirs. Viacom Inc., Viacom Internat. Inc.; chmn. compensation com., mem. adv. com. WCI Steel, Inc., Ambient; mem. legal adv. bd. N.Y. Stock Exch. Author: Future Interests and Estate Planning, 1965, 77, 81, 86, Comparative Negligence, 1970, A Products Liability Primer, 1970, Civil Trial Practice Manual, 1972, New Vistas in Litigation, 1973, Massachusetts Pleading and Practice, 7 vols., 1974-80, Estate Planning and Living Trusts, 1990, The Convention Method: The Unused Amending Superhighway, 1995, Jewish Law and Contemporary Dilemmas and Problems, 1997, Does Time Heal All Wrongs?, 1999, others; note editor: Boston U. Law Rev., 1954-55; property editor: Annual Survey of Mass. Law, 1960—; contbr. articles to legal jours. Bd. dirs. Kerry Found.; trustee Hebrew Coll., 1975—, Salve Regina Univ.; rep. Office Public Info., UN, 1968-73; chmn. legal adv. panel Nat. Commn. Med. Malpractice, 1972-73; examiner of titles Commonwealth of Mass., 1964—; spl. counsel Mass. Bay Transp. Authority, 1979; trustee Yeshiva U.; pres. Fifth Ave. Synagogue, N.Y.C., 1997-2001, hon. pres., 2001—. Recipient Homer Albers award Boston U., 1955, John Ordronaux prize, 1955; Disting. Service award Religious Zionists Am., 1977; William W. Treat award; William O. Douglas award. Fellow Am. Coll. Probate Counsel; mem. ABA, Am. Law Inst., Mass. Bar Assn. (chmn. task force tort liability), N.Y. State Bar Assn., Assn. Bar City N.Y., Nat. Coll. Probate Judges (hon. mem.), Phi Beta Kappa. Office: 100 Maiden Ln New York NY 10038-4818

SCHWARTZEL, CHARLES BOONE, lawyer; b. Louisville, Jan. 4, 1950; s. Charles Joseph and Rosemary Jane (Redens) S.; m. Rose Marie Carlisi, June 20, 1980; children: Sally Ann, Charles Gerard. BA, Vanderbilt U., 1972; JD, U. Tex., 1975. Bar: Tex. 1975. Atty. Vinson & Elkins L.L.P., Houston, 1975-98, ptnr., 1983-98; pvt. practice, 1998—. Contbr. articles to profl. jours. Councilman City of West University Place, Tex., 1985-89. Fellow Am. Coll. Trust and Estate Counsel; mem. Tex. Bar Assn. Roman Catholic. Estate planning, Probate, Estate taxation. Office: Attorney at Law 1010 Lamar St Ste 1520 Houston TX 77002-6315

SCHWARTZMAN, ANDREW JAY, lawyer; b. N.Y.C., Oct. 4, 1946; s. Joel Jay and Theresa (Greenhauff) S.; m. Linda Lazarus, June 8, 1986. AB, U. Pa., 1968, JD, 1971. Bar: N.Y. 1972, D.C. 1974, Temporary Emergency Ct. Appeals 1977, U.S. Dist. Ct. D.C. 1978, U.S. Ct. Appeals (D.C. cir.) 1981, U.S. Ct. Appeals (2d cir.) 1987, U.S. Ct. Appeals (4th, 7th, 8th, 9th cirs.) 1991, U.S. Supreme Ct. 1980. Staff cousnel United Ch. of Christ Office of Comm., N.Y.C., 1971-74; atty. adviser Fed. Energy Office, Washington, 1974-77; sr. atty. adviser U.S. Dept. Energy, 1977-78; bd. dirs. Safe Energy Comms. Coun., pres. bd. dirs., 1989—; dir. Media Access Project, Washington, 1978-96, pres., CEO, 1996—. Mem. adv. panel Study on Comms. Systems for an Info. Age, Office of Tech. Assessment; mem. adv. bd. Ctr. for Democracy and Tech., 1996—, Office Tech. Assessment; lectr. Fairleigh Dickinson U., 1972-73; bd. dirs. Telecommunications Research Action Ctr.; mem. comms. coun. forum Aspen Inst. on Comms. and Soc., 1992—; mem. bd. dirs. Min. Media and Telecomms. Coalition, 1994—; mem. adv. bd. Nat. Inst. Entertainment and Media Law, Southwestern U. Sch. Law, 2000—. Contbg. author: Les Brown's Dictionary of Television, 3d edit., Ency. of the Consumer Movement, 1997; contbr. articles to legal jours. Recipient Everett Parker award United Ch. of Christ, 1994. Mem. ABA, Fed. Comms. Bar Assn., U. Pa. Alumni Assn. Home: 3624 Military Rd NW Washington DC 20015-1724 Office: Media Access Project 950 18th St NW Ste 220 Washington DC 20006-5515

SCHWARTZMAN, ROBIN BERMAN, lawyer; b. Mobile, Ala., Aug. 22, 1941; d. Hyman E. and Lillian (Cooperman) B.; m. Edward Schwartzman, May 21, 1971 (div. 1994); 1 child, Daniel Berman. BA, Bryn Mawr Coll., 1961; MA, Harvard U., 1963; JD, NYU, 1975. Bar: N.Y. 1976, D.C. 1982. Rsch. analyst, Slavic reference libr. and area specialist for Yugoslavia, U.S. Library of Congress, 1965-67; reference libr. and archivist Council Fgn. Relations, N.Y.C., 1967-70; program officer Internat. Rsch. and Exchange Bd., N.Y.C., 1970-72; assoc. Morgan, Lewis & Bockius, N.Y.C., 1975-77; assoc. Fried, Frank, Harris, Shriver & Jacobson, N.Y.C., 1977-79; deputy dir. Bur. Trade Regulation U.S. Dept. Commerce, Washington, 1979-81; sr. atty. Burlington Industries, Greensboro, N.C., 1984-87, asst. gen. counsel, 1987-88; of counsel Heron, Burchette, Ruckert & Rothwell, Washington, 1988-90; sr. atty. Weadon & Assocs, Washington, 1991-92; assoc. atty. Dickstein, Shapiro & Morin, Washington, 1992-93; sr. legal & regulatory officer U.S. Agy. Internat. Devel. Bur. of Europe and New Ind. States, Washington, 1993-96, dep. dir. office privatization, Kiev, Ukraine, 1997; atty. and internat. trade and devel. cons., 1997—; adj. asst. prof. U. Md., 1998—. Contbr. articles to profl. jours. Carnegie Scholarship for Study in Soviet Union, Bryn Mawr Coll., 1960, Woodrow Wilson fellow, Harvard U., 1961-62, Nat. Def. Fgn. Lang. fellow, Harvard U., 1962-64, Jr. fellow Ctr. for Internat. Studies NYU Sch. Law, 1974-75. Mem. ABA (sect. internat. law, com. NIS law, coord. Ukraine, com. Ctrl. European law; sect. govt. and pub. sector lawyers, jour. com., 1996—), Women in Internat. Trade, Exec. Women in Govt. (vice chmn. 1981), Fed. Bar Assn. (steering com. democracy devel. initiative 1991-93) . Democrat. Jewish. General corporate, Private international, Pension, profit-sharing, and employee benefits. Home and Office: 5510 Surrey St Chevy Chase MD 20815-5524

SCHWARZ, CARL A., JR. lawyer; b. N.Y.C., Apr. 27, 1936; s. Carl A. and Genevieve C. Byrne; m. Maryellen McG., Apr. 30, 1966; children: Peter Thomas, Elizabeth Anne. BS, Fordham U., 1957, JD, 1960. Bar: N.Y. 1960, U.S. Dist. Ct. (so., ea., we. and D.C. dists.) N.Y. 1960, U.S. Ct. Appeals (2d cir.) 1960, U.S. Supreme Ct. 1965. Ptnr. Schwarz & DeMarco, Garden City, N.Y. Chmn., bd. trustees N.Y. Sch. Interior Design. Trustee Cath. Charities; Capt. USAF, 1961-65. Mem. Manhasset Bay Yacht Club (vice commodore), Order of Malta. Roman Catholic. Labor, Pension, profit-sharing, and employee benefits. Office: Schwarz & DeMarco LLP 1225 Franklin Ave Garden City NY 11530-1691

SCHWARZ, HARRY HEINZ, lawyer; b. Cologne, Germany, May 13, 1924; s. Fritz Seigfried and Alma S.; m. Annette Louise Rudolph Schwarz; children: Jonathan, Allan, Michael. BA, Witwatersrand U., 1946, LLB, 1949; PhD, Stellenbosch U., 1993, U. Judaism, L.A., 1994. Capt. SAAF, South Africa, 1943-45; lawyer Law Soc., 1949—; advocate Soc. of Advocates, 1953-64; mem. of counsel Goosecrest, Tresoceal, 1958-74, mem. of Parliament South Africa, 1974-91; ambassador to U.S. For South Africa, Washington, 1991-94; colonel SAAF, South Africa, 1991—. City loueille, Johannesburg City Counsel, South Africa, 1951-58; CEO Western Merchant Bank, South Africa, 1969-74; advisor Alzia Guap Straas Hanes & Feld, Washington, 1994-2000; cons. Hofmeyer, South Africa, 1994—. Author: Poverty Goodes Freedom; contbr. articles to profl. jours. Councillor City Counsel, 1951-58; M.P.C. State Goosecrest, 1958-74; MP Central Pastrell, 1974-91; ambassador Diplomatic Foocp Afgain, Washington, 1991-94. Col. South Africa Air Force, 1991-2000. Capt. 1943-45. Recipient Dal Granes award U. Vancouver. Fellow Inst. Dirs., 1991—; mem. Traward Law Soc., 1949—. Avocations: literature, music, sports, politics. Banking, Estate planning, Estate taxation. Office: Hofmeyer 6 Sandocon Valley Crescent Johannesburg 2196 South Africa E-mail: harrys@hofmeyer.com

SCHWARZ, JAMES HAROLD, lawyer; b. Hammond, Ind., Dec. 7, 1954; s. Arthur Martin and Agnes (Sternbach) S.; m. Sandra Ellen Gelman, July 30, 1978; children: Jacqueline, Shana, Jonathan. BS, Ind. U., 1977; JD, Ind. U., Indpls., 1980. Bar: Ind. 1980, U.S. Dist. Ct. (so.dist.) Ind. 1980, U.S. Tax Ct. 1989. Assoc. Ice, Miller, Donadio & Ryan, Indpls., 1980-83, Bayh, Tabbert & Capehart, Indpls., 1983, Dann, Pecar, Newman & Kleiman, Indpls., 1983-86, ptnr., 1986—. Bd. dirs. Bur. Jewish Edn., Indpls., 1985-98, Jewish Fedn. Gtr. Indpls., Inc., 1995—. Mem. ABA, Ind. Bar Assn., Indpls. Bar Assn, Am. Coll. of Real Estate Lawyers, Nat. Assn. Bond Lawyers. General corporate, Real property, Corporate taxation. Home: 8907 Spicewood Ct Indianapolis IN 46260-1545 Office: PO Box 82008 Indianapolis IN 46282-2008

SCHWARZ, MICHAEL, lawyer; b. Brookline, Mass., Oct. 19, 1952; s. Jules Lewis and Estelle (Kosberg) S.; m. Rebecca Handy; 1 child, Patrick Joshua Charles. BA magna cum laude, U. No. Colo., 1975; postgrad., U. N.Mex., 1977, JD, 1980; reader in Negligence Law, Oxford U., 1978; diploma in Legal Studies, Cambridge U., 1981. Bar: N.Mex. 1980, U.S. Dist. Ct. N.Mex. 1980, U.S. Ct. Appeals (10th, D.C., and Fed. cirs.) 1982, U.S. Ct. Internat. Trade, 1982, U.S. Tax Ct. 1982, N.Y. 1987, U.S. Supreme Ct. 1983. Vol. VISTA, Albuquerque, 1975-77; rsch. fellow N.Mex. Legal Support Project, 1978-79; supr. law Cambridge (Eng.) U., 1980-81; law clk. to chief justice Supreme Ct. N.Mex., Santa Fe, 1981-82; pvt. practice, 1982—. Spl. pros. City of Santa Fe, 1985, spl. asst. atty. gen., 1986-88; mem. west editl. adv. com. Social Security Reporting Svc., 1983-95; mem. N.Mex. Supreme Ct. Com. Profl. Responsibility, 1990—, chmn., 1998—. Author: New Mexico Appellate Manual, 1990, 2d edit., 1996; contbr. articles to profl. jours. Vice dir. Colo. Pub. Interest Rsch. Group, 1974; scoutmaster Great S.W. Area coun. Boy Scouts Am., 1977-79; mem. N.Mex. Acupuncture Lic. Bd., 1983; level 1 referee, assoc. coach U.S. Hockey Team. Recipient Cert. of Appreciation Cambridge U., 1981, Nathan Burke Meml. award, 1980, N.Mex. Supreme Ct. Cert. Recognition, 1992, 93, 95, N.Mex. Supreme Ct. Cert. Appreciation Outstanding Svc. to Legal Sys., 2001. Mem. ABA (litig. com. on profl. responsibility, litig. com. on pretrial practice and discovery, 10th cir. editor 1998, mem. Ctr. Profl. Responsibility), ATLA, ACLU, Bar Assn. U.S. Dist. Ct. Dist. N.Mex., State Bar N.Y., N.Mex. State Bar (bd. dirs. employment law sect. 1990-96, chmn. 1990-91, bd. dirs. 1999-2001), Santa Fe Trailrunners Hockey Assn. (bd. dirs. 2001—). Civil rights, Federal civil litigation, State civil litigation. Home and Office: PO Box 1656 Santa Fe NM 87504-1656 E-mail: barristr@nm.net

SCHWARZER, WILLIAM W, federal judge; b. Berlin, Apr. 30, 1925; came to U.S., 1938, naturalized, 1944; s. John F. and Edith M. (Daniel) S.; m. Anne Halbersleben, Feb. 2, 1951; children: Jane Elizabeth, Andrew William. AB cum laude, U. So. Calif., 1948; LLB cum laude, Harvard U., 1951. Bar: Calif. 1953, U.S. Supreme Ct. 1967. Teaching fellow Harvard U. Law Sch., 1951-52; asso. firm McCutchen, Doyle, Brown & Enersen, San Francisco, 1952-60, ptnr., 1960-76; judge U.S. Dist. Ct (no. dist) Calif., San Francisco, 1976—; dir. Fed. Jud. Ctr., Washington, 1990-95. Sr. counsel Pres.'s Commn. on CIA Activities Within the U.S., 1975; chmn. U.S. Jud. Conf. Com. Fed.-State Jurisdiction, 1987-90; mem. faculty Nat. Inst. Trial Advocacy, Fed. Jud. Ctr., All-ABA, U.S.-Can. Legal Exch., 1987, Anglo-U.S. Jud. Exch., 1994-95, Salzburg Seminar on Am. Studies; disting. prof. Hastings Coll. Law U. Calif. Author: Managing Antitrust and Other Complex Litigation, 1982, Civil Discovery and Manadatory Disclosure, 1994, Federal Civil Procedure Before Trial, 1994; contbr. articles to legal publs., aviation jours. Trustee World Affairs Coun. No. Calif., 1961-88; chmn. bd. trustees Marin Country Day Sch., 1963-66; mem. Marin County Aviation Commn., 1969-76; mem. vis. com. Harvard Law Sch., 1981-86. Served with Intelligence, U.S. Army, 1943-46. Fellow Am. Coll. Trial Lawyers (S. Gates award 1992), Am. Bar Found.; mem. ABA (Meador Rosenberg award 1995), Am. Law Inst., San Francisco Bar Assn., State Bar Calif., Coun. Fgn. Rels. Office: 450 Golden Gate Ave San Francisco CA 94102-3661

SCHWARZSCHILD, PATRICIA MICHAELSON, lawyer; b. Washington, Jan. 15, 1950; d. Louis LeRoy and Katherine Ann (Elmore) Michaelson; m. William Harry Schwarzschild, June 9, 1973 (div.); children— W.H., Michael Todd. B.S., Va. Tech. U., 1972; J.D., Vanderbilt U., 1975. Bar: Va. 1975, U.S. Dist. Ct. (ea. dist.) Va. 1975, U.S. Ct. Appeals (4th cir.) 1981. Staff atty. Va. State Corp. Commn., Richmond, 1975-77; assoc. McGuire, Woods & Battle, Richmond, 1977-81; ptnr. Hunton & Williams, Richmond, 1981—. mem. exec. com., bd. dirs. Va. Capital Representation Resouce Ctr. Bd. dirs. YMCA, Richmond, 1977-83, Richmond Children's Mus., 1980-81, Va. Fedn. Planned Parenthood, Richmond, 1983-86. Fellow Va. Law Found. (exec. coun.); mem. ABA (council on issues affecting legal profession), Va. Bar Assn. (chmn. membership com. 1982-84, bd. govs. litigation section), Va. Bar (fellow young lawyers sect.), Am. Judicature Soc. Club: Westwood Racquet. Office: Hunton & Williams E Tower Riverfront Plz PO Box 1535 Richmond VA 23218-1535

SCHWED, PETER GREGORY, lawyer; b. N.Y.C., Feb. 24, 1952; s. Peter and Antonia (Holding) S.; m. Margaret Allen Peters, Feb. 18, 1984; children: Sarah Holding, Robert Griffin. B.A. summa cum laude, Princeton U., 1973; J.D., Columbia U., 1976. Bar: N.Y. 1977, U.S. Dist. Ct. (so. dist.) N.Y. 1978, U.S. Dist. Ct. (ea. dist.) N.Y. 1978, U.S. Ct. Appeals (2d cir.) 1985. Assoc. Kaye, Scholer, Fierman, Hays & Handler, N.Y.C., 1976-79, Gelberg & Abrams, N.Y.C., 1979-81, Kramer, Levin, Nessen, Kamin & Frankel, N.Y.C., 1981-83; ptnr. Bernstein, Obstfeld & Schwed, P.C., N.Y.C., 1983-86, Austrian, Lance & Stewart P.C., N.Y.C., 1986-87; ptnr. Graham & James, N.Y.C., 1987—, mng. ptnr. N.Y. office, mem. firmwide exec. com., 1990-92. Co-author: Creditors' Rights Handbook, 1982. Harlan Fiske Stone scholar Columbia U. Sch. Law, N.Y.C., 1975-76. Mem. N.Y. State Bar Assn., Assn. Bar City N.Y., Phi Beta Kappa. Bankruptcy, Federal civil litigation. Office: Graham & James 885 3rd Ave Fl 24 New York NY 10022-4834

SCHWELB, FRANK ERNEST, district judge; b. Prague, Czechoslovakia, June 24, 1932; came to U.S., 1947; s. Egon and Caroline (Redisch) S.; m. Taffy Wurzburg, Apr. 9, 1988. BA, Yale U., 1949-53; LLB, Harvard U., 1958. Bar: N.Y. Ct. Appeals 1958, U.S. Dist. Ct. (so. and ea. dists.) N.Y. 1960, U.S. Ct. Appeals (2d cir.) 1961, U.S. Supreme Ct. 1965, U.S. Ct. Appeals (4th cir.) 1968, D.C., D.C. Ct. Appeals, U.S. Dist. Ct. D.C. 1972. Assoc. Mudge, Stern, Baldwin & Todd, N.Y.C., 1958-62; trial atty. Civil Rights Div. U.S. Dept. Justice, Washington, 1962-79, chief eastern sect., 1969, chief housing sect., 1969-79, spl. counsel for litigation, 1979; spl. counsel rev. panel on new drug regulation HEW, 1976-77; assoc. judge Superior Ct. D.C., 1979-88, D.C. Ct. Appeals, Washington, 1988—. Instr. various legal edn. activities. Contbr. articles to profl. jours. With U.S. Army, 1955-57. Recipient Younger Fed. Lawyer award, Fed. Bar Assn., 1967. Mem. Bar Assn. D.C., World Peace Through Law Ctr., World Assn. Judges, Czechoslovak-Am. Orgns., De Tocqueville Soc., Order of the Battered Boot. Avocations: tennis, table tennis, sports, Gilbert and Sullivan operettas, Shakespeare. Home: 4879 Potomac Ave NW Washington DC 20007-1539 Office: DC Ct Appeals 500 Indiana Ave NW Washington DC 20001-2138 E-mail: fschwelb@dcca.state.dc.us

SCHWENDIMAN, STEPHEN GLENN, lawyer; b. Freeport, Ill., Apr. 2, 1948; s. Glenn and Helen (Snow) S.; m. Carolee Kulinsky, Sept. 3, 1971; children: Larah, Stephen, Karissa, Jeremy. BA, Brigham Young U., 1972; JD, U. Utah, 1975. Bar: Utah 1975. Asst. atty. gen. Utah, Salt Lake City, 1975—. Divsn. chief, 1983-89. Voting dist. vice chmn. Rep. Com., Salt Lake City, 1982-84, voting dist. chmn., 1988-90; scoutmaster, Boy Scouts Am., 1981-84, roundtable commr. Evergreen dist., 1980-84, asst. dist. commr., 183-85, dist. commr., 1985-89, dist. chmn., 1990-94, nat. jamboree scoutmaster, 1989, 97, dist. merit award, 1981, Silver Beaver award, 1990. Mem. Utah Bar Assn. Mormon. Office: Utah Atty Gen 160 E 300 S Salt Lake City UT 84111-2316

SCHWENKE, ROGER DEAN, lawyer; b. Washington, Oct. 18, 1944; s. Clarence Raymond and Virginia Ruth (Gould) S.; m. Carol Lynne Flenniken, Nov. 29, 1980; 1 child: Matthew Robert; stepchildren: Tracy L. Wolf Dickey, Mary M. Wolf. BA, Ohio State U., 1966; JD with honors, U. Fla., 1969. Bar: Fla. 1970. Instr. Coll. Law U. Fla., Gainesville, 1969-70; assoc. Carlton, Fields, Ward, Emmanuel, Smith & Cutler P.A., Tampa, Fla., 1970-74, ptnr., 1975—; adminstr., dept. head Real Estate, Environ. and Land Use Dept., 1978—. Adj. prof. Coll. Law, Stetson U., St. Petersburg, Fla., 1979-80; mem. faculty U. Miami Coll. of Law Master of Law's in Real Estate Devel. Program, 1994-96. Author chpt. in Environmental Regulation and Litigation in Florida, 1987, chpt. in Florida Real Property Complex Transactions, 1997, 2000; contbr. articles to profl. jours., chpt. to book. Mem. diocesan coun. Episc. Diocese SW Fla., 1978-86, mem. standing com., 1989-92, chief judge Eccles. Ct., 1996—. Recipient Gertrude Brick Law Rev. prize U. Fla., 1969. Fellow Am. Coll. Real Estate Lawyers (bd. govs. 1985-88), Am. Law Inst.; mem. ABA (standing com. on environ. law 1980—, coun. real property sect. 1988-95), Fla. Bar Assn., Air & Waste Mgmt. Assn., Order of Coif, Greater Tampa C. of C. (chmn. environ. coun. 1980-81), Tampa Club. Democrat. Contracts commercial, Environmental, Real property. Office: Carlton Fields PO Box 3239 Tampa FL 33601-3239 Fax: 813-229-4133. E-mail: rschwenke@carltonfields.com

SCHWIEBERT, MARK WILLIAM, lawyer, mayor; b. Rock Island, Ill., Aug. 2, 1950; s. Lloyd Alvin and Olive (Johnson) S.; m. Deborah L. Johnson, Oct. 10, 1987. BA, Augustana Coll., Rock Island, 1972; JD, Drake U., 1975, MA, 1976. Bar: Ill. 1975, U.S. Dist. Ct. (ctrl. dist.) Ill. 1977, Iowa 1999, U.S. Supreme Ct. 1999. Ptnr. Schwiebert & Schwiebert, Moline, Ill., 1975—. Probate law lectr. Marycrest Coll., Davenport, Iowa, 1976-77; chmn. elected ofcls. com. Ill. Quad Cities Joint Purchasing Coun.; bd. dirs. Rock Island Econ. Growth Corp., 1982—; bd. dirs., chmn. transp. policy com. Bi-State Regional Comm.; mem. exec. com. Quad-Cities Devel. Group. Mem. No. Ill. Luth. Synod Coun., 1987-90. Named One of 10 Outstanding Young Men Quad Cities, Quad City Times, 1984; recipient Outstanding Svc. award Ill. Quad Cities Commerce Com., 1990, Rock Island Jaycees, 1991. Mem. ABA, Ill. Bar Assn. (com. on profl. competence 1980-87, cert. of Appreciaiton 1987), Rock Island Bar Assn., Rotary (Paul Harris fellow 1992), Kiwanis (bd. dirs. 1986-89, Layperson of yr. and Spiritual Aims award 1989). Avocations: writing, watercolor painting, running, tennis. Family and matrimonial, General practice, Real property. Office: Schwiebert & Schwiebert 501 15th St Ste 605 Moline IL 61265-2135

SCIALABBA, DONALD JOSEPH, lawyer; b. N.Y.C., Aug. 4, 1950; s. Angelo Joseph and Sarah Scialabba; m. Lorraine Anne Capizzi, June 20, 1976; children: Christopher, Daniel, Laura. BS in Econs., CCNY, 1973; JD, Seton Hall U., 1980. Bar: N.Y. 1981, U.S. Dist. Ct. (ea. and so. dists.) N.Y. 1982, U.S. Ct. Appeals (2d cir.) 1994. Assoc. Costello & Shea, N.Y.C., 1981-88; ptnr. Costello Shea & Gaffney, 1989-2000; assoc. Meiselman, Denlea, Packman & Eberz, P.C., White Plains, N.Y., 2000—. Mem. N.Y. County Lawyers Assn. Avocations: golf, woodworking, photography. Appellate, Personal injury, Product liability. Office: Meiselman Denlea Packman & Eberz PC & Eberz PC 1311 Mamaroneck Ave White Plains NY 10605-5221 E-mail: info@mdpelaw.com

SCIPIONE, RICHARD STEPHEN, insurance company executive, lawyer, retired; b. Newton, Mass., Aug. 27, 1937; BA, Harvard U., 1959; LLB, Boston U., 1962. Bar: Mass. 1962. Atty. John Hancock Mut. Life Ins. Co., Boston, 1965-69, asst. counsel, 1969-74, assoc. counsel, 1975-79, sr. assoc. counsel, 1980-82, 2d v.p., counsel, 1982-84, v.p. gen. solicitor, 1984-85, sr. v.p. and gen. solicitor, 1986-87, gen. counsel, 1987-2000, ret., 2000. Bd. dirs. New England Legal Found., John Hancock Advisers/Distbrs. Capt. U.S. Army, 1962-65. Mem. ABA (dir. New Eng. coun.), Assn. Life Ins. Counsel (gov. 1994-98), Chatham Yacht Club, South Shore Country Club.

SCIRICA, ANTHONY JOSEPH, federal judge; b. Norristown, Pa., Dec. 16, 1940; s. A. Benjamin and Anna (Sclafani) S.; m. Susan Morgan, May 6, 1966; children— Benjamin, Sara B.A., Wesleyan U., 1962; J.D., U. Mich., 1965; postgrad., Central U., Caracas, Venezuela, 1966. Bar: Pa., 1966, U.S. Dist. Ct. (ea. dist.) Pa., 1984, U.S. Ct. Appeals (3d cir.), 1987. Ptnr. McGrory, Scirica, Wentz & Fernandez, Norristown, Pa., 1966-80; asst. dist. atty. Montgomery County, 1967-69; mem. Pa. Ho. of Reps, Harrisburg, 1971-79; judge Montgomery County Ct. Common Pleas, Pa., 1980-84, U.S. Dist. Ct. (ea. dist.) Pa., Phila., 1984-87, U.S. Ct. Appeals (3d cir.), 1987—. Chmn. Pa. Sentencing Commn., 1980-85 Fulbright scholar Central U., Caracas, Venezuela, 1966 Mem. Montgomery Bar Assn., Pa. Bar Assn., ABA Roman Catholic Office: US Courthouse 601 Market St Rm 22614 Philadelphia PA 19106-1715

SCLAFANI, FRANCES ANN, lawyer, federal agency executive; b. N.Y.C., Aug. 25, 1949; d. Joseph John and Clementina Theresa (Polite) S. BA (hon.), St. John's U., 1971, JD, 1974. Bar: N.Y. 1975, U.S. Dist. Ct. (ea. and so. dists.) N.Y., 1975, U.S. Ct. Appeals (2d cir.) 1975, U.S. Supreme Ct. 1978, U.S. Dist. Ct. D.C. 1987, U.S. Ct. Appeals (D.C. cir.) 1987. Spl. congl. asst. U.S. Congress, Washington, 1971; asst. dist. atty. County of Suffolk (N.Y.), Riverhead, 1974-86; assoc. dir. U.S Office Personnel Mgmt., Washington, 1986—; head of Office Fed. Investigations, Washington, 1986—; bd. fgn. svc. Dept. State, Washington, 1986-90; bd. dirs. Fed. Law Enforcement Tng. Ctr., Glynco, Ga., 1986—; dep. chief Felony Trial Bur., 1981-82, Major Offense Bur., 1982-83. Rep. candidate for N.Y. state atty. gen., 1982; commr. President's Commn. on Organized Crime, Washington, 1983-86, mem. com. on narcotics control and interdiction, 1984-86; rep. to Western Hemisphere Conf. on Narcotics Control, Washington, 1985; faculty U.S. Dept. of Justice Ann. Internat. Drug Traffickers Prosecution Conf., 1983. Recipient award for svc.to victims rights Decision for Women in Commerce and Professions, 1984. Mem. ABA (asst. sec. criminal justice sect. 1980-82), Nat. Dist. Attys. Assn. (assoc. dir. 1980-86), D.C Bar Assn., N.Y. Bar Assn. Roman Catholic. Office: Office of Pers Mgmt Investigations Group 1900 E St NW Washington DC 20415-0002

SCOFIELD, DAVID WILLSON, lawyer; b. Hartford, Conn., Oct. 17, 1957; s. Leslie Willson and Daphne Winifred (York) S. AB, Cornell U., 1979; JD, U. Utah, 1983. Bar: Utah 1983, U.S. Dist. Ct. Utah 1983, U.S. Dist. Ct. Ariz. 1993, U.S. Dist. Ct. Hawaii 1995, U.S. Ct. Appeals (10th cir.) 1990, U.S. Ct. Appeals (9th cir.) 1995, U.S. Supreme Ct. 1996, U.S. Ct. Claims, 1997. Assoc. Parsons & Crowther, Salt Lake City, 1983-87, Callister, Duncan & Nebeker, Salt Lake City, 1987-89, ptnr., 1989-92; founding ptnr. Parsons, Davies, Kinghorn & Peters, 1992-96, pres., 1996-97. Author: Trial Handbook for Utah Lawyers, 1994; mem. Utah Law Rev., 1981-83; contbr. articles to legal jours. Bd. dirs. Westminster Coll. Found., 1994-96, chmn. cultivation com., 1995-96. Named to Outstanding Young Men of Am., 1986. Mem. ABA, Assn. Trial Lawyers Am., Utah Trial Lawyers Assn., Salt Lake County Bar Assn., Zeta Psi. Congregationalist. Avocations: American history, writing, sports. Federal civil litigation, General civil litigation, General practice. Home: 2331 Scenic Dr Salt Lake City UT 84109-1432 Office: Parsons Davies Kinghorn & Peters 185 S State St Ste 700 Salt Lake City UT 84111-1550 E-mail: dws@pdkplaw.com

SCOFIELD, LOUIS M., JR. lawyer; b. Brownsville, Tex., Jan. 14, 1952; s. Louis M. and Betsy Lee (Aiken) S.; children: Christopher, Nicholas, Emma. BS in Geology with highest honors and high distinction, U. Mich., 1974; JD with honors, U. Tex., 1977. Bar: Tex. 1977, U.S. Dist. Ct. (ea. and so. dists.) Tex., U.S. Ct. Appeals (5th cir.) 1981, U.S. Supreme Ct. 1984. Ptnr. Mehaffy & Weber, Beaumont, Tex., 1982—. Spkr. CNA Ins., Dallas, Jefferson County Ins. Adjusters, S.E. Tex. Ind. Ins. Agts., Gulf Ins. Co., Dallas, Employers Casualty Co., Beaumont, Tex. Employment Commn., Jefferson County Young Lawyers Assn., Jefferson County Bar Assn., South Tex. Coll. of Law, John Gray Inst., Lamar U., 1991, Tex. Assn. Def. Counsel, 1991; cert. arbitrator Nat. Panel of Consumer Arbitrators; arbitrator BBB; presenter Forest Park H.S., Martin Elem. Sch., St. Anne's Sch. Contbr. articles to profl. jours.; columnist Jefferson County Bar Jour. Patron Beaumont Heritage Soc., John J. French Mus.; bd. dirs. Beaumont Heritage Soc., 1983-84, mem. endowment fund com., 1988; chmn. lawyers divsn. United Appeals Campaign, 1984; grand patron Jr. League of Beaumont, 1989, 90. Fellow: Tex. Bar Found. (life), State Bar of Tex. (mentors com. 1995); mem.: ABA (contbg. editor newsletter products, vice chmn.gen liability and consumer laws com.), Assn. Defense Trial Attys. (chmn. Tex. membership com., chmn. Ctrl. U.S. region 2000—, exec. coun. 1999—2002), Tex. Assn. Defense Counsel (dir. at large 1986—87, v.p. 1987—89, adminstrv. v.p. 1989—90, program chmn. San Diego 1989), Def. Rsch. Inst., Am. Judicature Soc., Jefferson County Bar Assn. (disaster relief project 1979, outstanding young lawyer's com. 1980), Beaumont County Country Club, Phi Beta Kappa. Democrat. Episcopalian. Avocations: golf, reading, fishing. General civil litigation, Insurance, Personal injury. Home: 4790 Littlefield St Beaumont TX 77706-7748 Office: Mehaffy & Weber PO Box 16 Beaumont TX 77704-0016

SCOGLAND, WILLIAM LEE, lawyer; b. Moline, Ill., Apr. 2, 1949; s. Maurice William and Harriet Rebecca S.; m. Victoria Lynn Whitham, Oct. 9, 1976; 1 child, Thomas. BA magna cum laude, Augustana Coll., 1971; JD cum laude, Harvard U., 1975. Bar: Ill. 1975, U.S. Dist. Ct. (no. dist.) Ill. 1975. Assoc. Wildman, Harrold, Allen & Dixon, Chgo., 1975-77, Hughes Hubbard & Reed, Milw., 1977-81; from assoc. to ptnr. Jenner & Block, Chgo., 1981—. Author: Fiduciary Duty: What Does It Mean?, 1989; co-author Employee Benefits Law, 1987. Mem. Phi Beta Kappa, Omicron Delta Kappa. Republican. Mergers and acquisitions, Pension, profit-sharing, and employee benefits. Office: Jenner & Block One IBM Plz Fl 4000 Chicago IL 60611-7603

SCOTT, ALAN FULTON, JR. lawyer; b. Phila., Mar. 26, 1945; s. Alan Fulton and Elizabeth (Reed) S.; m. Kitty Kimball, Jan. 26, 1966; children— Kathryn Elizabeth, Alan Fulton III, Sarah Kimball. B.A. in English, U. N.C., 1967; J.D., U. Tulsa, 1970. Bar: Fla. 1970, D.C. 1982, U.S. Dist. Ct. (mid. dist.) Fla. 1971, U.S. Ct. Appeals (5th cir.) 1972. Shareholder Markel, Scott, McDonough & O'Neal, Orlando, Fla., 1970-82; ptnr. Brackett, Cook, Sned, Welch & Scott, West Palm Beach, Fla., 1982-87, Scott, Henderson, Powers & Dufresne, 1987—. Mem. ABA, Acad. Fla. Title Lawyers, Internat. Law Com. Fla., Def. Rsch. Inst., West Palm Beach C. of C., Bear Lakes Country Club. Republican. Episcopalian. Contracts commercial, Construction, Personal injury. Address: 25 Lexington Ln W Apt F Palm Beach Gardens FL 33418-7108

SCOTT, BRIAN DAVID, lawyer; b. Spokane, Wash., Sept. 30, 1946; s. Dick E. and Helene L. (Johnson) S.; m. Lynita G. Muzzall, Sept. 9, 1972; children: D. Alexander, Rachel E., S. Andrew. BA, U. Wash., 1968; JD, U. Wis., 1972. Bar: Wis. 1972, Wash. 1972, U.S. Dist. Ct. (we. dist.) Wash. 1972, U.S. Dist. Ct. (we. dist.) Wis. 1972. Asst. atty. gen. Wash. State Atty. Gen.'s Office, Seattle, 1972-74; assoc. Jackson, Ulvestad, Goodwin, Grutz, 1974-81; ptnr. Goodwin, Grutz & Scott, 1981-96, Grutz, Scott & Kinney, Seattle, 1996-99, Grutz, Scott, Kinney & Fjelstad, Seattle, 1999—. Mem. ATLA, Wash. Trial Lawyers Assn., Wash. Athletic Club. Democrat. Avocations: boating, skiing, travel. Personal injury, Product liability, Workers' compensation. Home: 158 Prospect St Seattle WA 98109-3750 Office: Grutz Scott Kinney & Fjelstad 600 University St Ste 1928 Seattle WA 98101-4178 E-mail: scott@gskf-law.com

SCOTT, DAVID RODICK, lawyer, legal educator; b. Phila., Dec. 30, 1938; s. Ernest and Lydia Wister (tunis) S.; m. Ruth Erskine Wardle, Aug. 20, 1966; children: Cintra W., D. Rodman. AB magna cum laude, Harvard U., 1960, JD, 1965; MA, Cambridge U., 1962. Bar: Pa. 1966, D.C. 1977, U.S. Dist. Ct. (ea. dist.) Pa. 1966, U.S. Ct. Appeals (3rd cir.) 1966, U.S. Ct. Appeals (D.C. cir.) 1977, U.S. Supreme Ct. 1977. Law clk. to assoc. justice Supreme Ct. Pa., Phila., 1965-66; assoc. Pepper, Hamilton & Scheetz, 1966-69, 72-76; asst. dist. atty. City of Phila., 1970-72; sr. trial atty. criminal divsn. U.S. Dept. Justice, Washington, 1976-80; chief counsel, acting dir. Office Govt. Ethics, 1980-84; univ. counsel Rutgers U., New Brunswick, N.J., 1984—. Acting dir. U.S. Office Govt. Ethics, 1982-83; tchr., lectr. in law Cath. U. Am., Washington, 1977-81, Inst. Paralegal Tng., Phila., 1970-74; instr. faculty of arts and scis. Rutgers U.; lectr. in field. Contbr. chpts. to textbooks, articles to profl. jours. Trustee United Way Greater Mercer County, 1990—, Princeton Area Cmty. Found., Inc., 1991—; bd. mgrs. Episc. Acad., Merion, Pa., 1970-74. Keasbey Found. fellow, 1960-62. Mem ABA, Pa. Bar Assn., Nat. Assn. Coll. and Univ. Attys. (bd. dirs. 1993-96), Am. Friends Cambridge U. (head N.J. chpt. 1987-93). General corporate, Education and schools. Home: 255 Russell Rd Princeton NJ 08540-6733 Office: Rutgers U Office of Univ Counsel Winants Hall New Brunswick NJ 08901 E-mail: scott@oldqueens.rutgers.edu

SCOTT, DORIS PETERSEN, lawyer; b. June 22, 1925; d. David Steele and Leslie Helena (Suit) Petersen; m. Charles Lurman Scott, Aug. 30, 1947; children: Charles L., David Steele. Student, Coll. of Notre Dame of Md., 1945; JD, U. Md., 1949. Bar: Md. 1949, U.S. Dist. Ct. Md. 1955, U.S. Ct. Appeals (4th cir.) 1956. Assoc. Callahan & Caldwell, Balt., 1949—51; pvt. practice Elkton, 1951—82; ptnr. Scott & Scott, 1983—. Atty., Cecil County Bd. Edn., 1954; dir. Cecil Fed. Savingss & Loan Assn.; trustee Deferred Compensation Bd., State of Md., 1975—79. Mem.: ABA, Md. State Bar Assn. (past mem. bd. govs.), Cecil County Bar Assn. (past pres.), Susquehana Law League, Balt. Country Club. Democrat. Episcopalian. Personal injury, Probate, Real property. Office: 109 E Main St Elkton MD 21921-5906

SCOTT, G. JUDSON, JR. lawyer; b. Phila., Nov. 16, 1945; s. Gerald Judson and Jean Louise (Evans) S.; m. Ildiko Kalman, Mar. 21, 1971; children: Nathan Emory, Lauren Jean. AA, Foothill Jr. Coll., Los Altos, Calif., 1965; BA, U. Calif., Santa Barbara, 1968; JD cum laude, U. Santa Clara, 1975. Bar: Calif. 1975, U.S. Dist. Ct. (no. dist.) Calif. 1975, U.S. Ct. Appeals (9th cir.) 1975, U.S. Supreme Ct. 1981. Assoc. Feldman, Waldman & Kline, San Francisco, 1975-76, Law Offices John Wynne Herron, San Francisco, 1976-80; of counsel firm Haines & Walker, Livermore, 1980; ptnr. Haines Walker & Scott, 1980-84; officer, dir., shareholder firm Smith, Etnire, Polson and Scott, Pleasanton, Calif., 1984-88; pvt. practice, 1988—. Judge pro tem Livermore-Pleasanton Mcpl. Ct., 1981-83; settlement commr. Alameda County Superior Ct., 1994—; lectr. Calif. Continuing Edn. of Bar. Contbg. author: Attorney's Guide to Restitution, 1976; editor: The Bottom Line, 1989-91. Pres. Walnut Creek Open Space Found., Calif., 1981-83. Rear adm. USNR, 1968-2001. Mem. ATLA (sustaining), Consumer Attys. Calif. (reviewer of pending Calif. legis.), Am. Coll. Barristers (sr. counsel), Ea. Alameda County Bar Assn. (v.p. 1981-82), Calif. State Bar (mem. standing com. on lawyer referral svcs. 1985-88, mem. exec. com. law practice mgmt. sec. 1988-93, chair 1992-93), Alameda County Bar Assn. (chmn. law office econs. com. 1986-87, mem. jud. nomination evaluation com. 1996-97, bd. dirs. 1997-98, v.p. 1999, pres.-elect 2000, pres. 2001, chair task force 1997), Alameda-Contra Costa County Trial Lawyers Assn., Livermore C. of C. (past chmn. growth study 1983), Pleasanton C. of C., Million Dollar Advs. Forum. Republican. Episcopalian. General civil litigation, Insurance, Personal injury. Office: 6140 Stoneridge Mall Rd Ste 125 Pleasanton CA 94588-3233

SCOTT, GREGORY KELLAM, judge trial referee, former state supreme court justice, lawyer; b. San Francisco, July 30, 1943; s. Robert and Althea Delores Scott; m. Carolyn Weatherly, Apr. 10, 1971; children: Joshua Weatherly, Elijah Kellam. BS in Environ. Sci., Rutgers U., 1970, EdM in Urban Studies, 1971; JD cum laude, Ind. U., Indpls., 1977. Asst. dean resident instrn. Cook Coll. Rutgers U., 1972-75; trial atty. U.S. SEC, Denver, 1977-79; gen. counsel Blinder, Robinson & Co., Inc., 1979-80; asst. prof. coll. law U. Denver, 1980-85, assoc. prof., 1985-93, prof. emeritus, 1993—, chair bus. planning program, 1986-89, 92-93; justice Colo. Supreme Ct., Denver, 1993-2000; gen. counselor Kaiser-Hill Co., Golden, 2000—; judge trial referee Colo. Supreme Ct., 2000. Of counsel Moore, Smith & Bryant, Indpls., 1987-90; v.p., gen. counsel Comml. Energies, Inc., 1990-91; presenter in field. Author: (with others) Structuring Mergers and Acquisitions in Colorado, 1985, Airport Law and Regulation, 1991, Racism and Underclass in America, 1991; contbr. articles to profl. jours. Mem. ABA, Nat. Bar Assn., Nat. Assn. Securities Dealers, Inc., Nat. Arbitration Panel (arbitrator), Colo. Bar Found., Sam Cary Bar Assn., Am. Inn Ct. (founding mem. Judge Alfred A. Arraj inn). Avocations: golfing, reading, traveling. Office: Kaiser-Hill Co LLC Rocky Flats Environ Tech Site 10808 Hwy 93 Unit B Golden CO 80403-8200

SCOTT, ISAAC ALEXANDER, JR. lawyer; b. Little Rock, Aug. 23, 1934; s. Isaac A and Sherwin B (Gilbert) Scott; m. Elaine Hoffman, Aug. 24, 1957; children: Melissa E, Caitlin, Bronwen. AB, Harvard U., 1956; LLB, U. Ark., Fayetteville, 1959. Bar: Ark 1959. Law clk. U.S. Dist. Ct., 1960-61; assoc. Chowning, Mitchell, Hamilton & Burrow, 1961-65, Wright, Lindsey & Jennings, Little Rock, 1965-66, ptnr., 1967—, mng. ptnr., 1985-86. Co-author: (book) Lender's Liability in Arkansas and a Review of the Uniform Commercial Code. Pres Chamber Music Soc Little Rock; bd dirs Ark Reparatory Theatre, pres, 1996—97; mem 50 for the Future, Little Rock, 1997—; bd dirs Urban League Greater Little Rock, Univ Ark Found Inc, 1996—98, Downtown Partnership; Ark Bus and Educ Alliance. With U.S. Army, 1959—62. Fellow: Am Col Bankruptcy; mem.: Ark Bar Asn (mem house delegs 1972—75), Pulaski County Bar Asn (incorporator, bd dirs legal aid bur 1967—69, pres 1997—98, Lawyers Citizen Award 2000—01), Book Club, Little Rock Club, Capitol Club, Harvard Club Ark (pres). Bankruptcy, Federal civil litigation, Contracts commercial. Office: Bank of Am Bldg 200 W Capitol Ave Ste 2200 Little Rock AR 72201-3627 E-mail: iscott@WLJ.com

SCOTT, JOHN JOSEPH, lawyer; b. Chgo., Dec. 30, 1950; s. John Joseph and Alice (Pierzhala) S.; m. Maria Crawford, Aug. 17, 1974. BA, Yale U., 1972; JD, U. Chgo., 1975. Bar: Ill. 1975, U.S. Dist. Ct. (no. dist.) Ill. 1976. Assoc. Kirkland & Ellis, Chgo., 1975-82, ptnr., 1982-91; asst. gen. counsel CF Industries, Inc., Long Grove, Ill., 1991—. Mem. ABA, Chgo. Bar Assn., Am. Soc. Corp. Secs., Order of Coif. Roman Catholic. Avocations: reading, swimming, bike riding, playing tennis. General corporate, Finance, Securities. Office: CF Industries Inc One Salem Lake Dr Lake Zurich IL 60047-8401

SCOTT, JOHN ROLAND, business law educator; b. Wichita Falls, Tex, May 13, 1937; s. John and Margaret S.; m. Joan Carol Redding, Sept. 5, 1959; 1 child, John Howard. Llb, Baylor Sch. Law, Waco, Tex., 1962. Bar: Tex. 1962, Alaska 1970, Tex., 1965, U.S. Dist. Ct. (we. dist.), U.S. Dist. Ct. Alaska 1975. Assoc. litigation sect. Lynch & Chappell, Midland, Tex., 1962-65; regional atty. Atlantic Richfield Co., 1965-79; sr. atty. Anchorage, 1969-77, Dallas, 1977-80; v.p., assoc. gen. counsel Mitchell Energy & Devel. Corp., Houston, 1980-82; asst. gen. counsel Hunt Oil Co., Dallas, 1982-84, v.p., chief counsel, 1984-91, sr. v.p. gen. counsel, 1994-2001; adj. prof. bus. law Dallas Bapt. U., 2001—. Bar examiner in Alaska, 1974-77 Mem. State Bar Tex. (lectr.), Dallas Bar Assn., ABA, Phi Alpha Delta. Republican. Office: 3801 Hanover Ave Dallas TX 75225-7471 E-mail: jorosc13@aol.com

SCOTT, JOHN TONER, lawyer; b. Indpls., July 12, 1935; s. John Elmer and Jane (Toner) S.; m. Ann Cecelia Drilling, Sept. 9, 1961; children: Jeffrey, John, Greg. B.S. in Acctg., Ind. U., 1958, LL.B., 1961. Bar: Ind. 1961, U.S. Dist. Ct. (so. dist.) Ind. 1961, U.S. Supreme Ct. 1969, U.S. Dist. Ct. (no. dist.) Ind. 1979. Assoc., Peck, Scott & Shine, Anderson, Ind., 1963-68, Scott & Shine, Anderson, 1968-70; ptnr.Scott & Scott, Anderson, 1970—; editor, pub. Anderson Herald, 1981-86; pres. Shadow Trails, Inc., 1965-80; asst. city atty. City of Anderson, 1968-71. Pres. United Nations Assn., Anderson, 1964-70; mem. Family Service Madison County, Anderson, 1964-68, pres. 1967; mem. Urban League of Madison County, Anderson, 1973-77, pres. 1976-77; dist. chmn. Hillis for Congress Com., 1970-80; bd. dirs. ARC, Anderson, 1981-82, 88-94, 97—, v.p., 1981, pres. 1993; del. Ind. State Republican Conv., Indpls., 1970, 72, 74, 76, 78, 80, 82, 92; del. Ho. Dels., Madison County, 1980-89; active Maplewood Cemetery Bd., 1996—. Served to capt. U.S. Army, 1961-63. Mem.

Madison County Bar Assn. (pres. 1970-71), Ind. State Bar Assn. (past com. chmn., del. Madison County 1980-97), Assn. Ins. Attys., Ind. Trial Lawyers Assn., Ind. Defense Lawyers Assn. (com. chmn.), Internat. Platform Assn., Anderson C. of C., Blue Key, Sigma Delta Chi, Alpha Kappa Psi (treas. 1957-58), Delta Theta Phi (sec.-treas. 1960-61), Phi Gamma Delta (pres. Anderson chpt. 1971, 1986-93, dir. Ind. U. Alumni Assn., Madison County 1993-98, pres. 1996-97). Presbyterian. Club: Lincoln. Lodge: Sertoma (v.p., bd. dirs. Anderson chpt. 1966-68). Family and matrimonial, Personal injury, Probate. Home: 928 Winding Way Anderson IN 46011-1629 Office: Scott & Scott Ste 931 Merdian St Anderson IN 46016

SCOTT, JOSEPH MITCHELL, JR. lawyer, judge; b. Lexington, Ky., Sept. 1, 1946; s. Joseph Mitchell and Marjorie Louise (Rush) S.; m. Patricia Ann Thompson, Aug. 2, 1980; children: Rush Thompson, Jane Mitchell. BBA in Acctg., U. Notre Dame, 1968; JD, U. Ky., 1971. Bar: Ky. 1971, U.S. Ct. Appeals (6th cir.) 1984. Ptnr. Stoll, Keenon & Park, Lexington, 1971-99; judge U.S. Bankruptcy Ct., Ky., 1999—. 1st lt. U.S. Army, 1968-71. Banking, Bankruptcy, Contracts commercial. Office: PO Box 1111 Lexington KY 40588-1111

SCOTT, KATHRYN FENDERSON, lawyer; b. Augusta, Ga., June 6, 1970; d. Robert Thomas Fenderson and Christine (Cunningham) Cormier; m. Charles Dean Scott. BA, Eckerd Coll., St. Petersburg, Fla., 1992; JD, Stetson U., St. Petersburg, 1995. Bar: Fla. 1995, U.S. Dist. Ct. (mid. dist.) Fla. 1995, U.S. Ct. Appeals (11th cir.) 1997. Assoc. Govan, Burns & Jones, St. Petersburg, 1995-97; ptnr. Scott & Fenderson, 1997—. Editl. bd. Paraclete, St. Petersburg Bar Assn., 1996-99; mentor program Stetson U. Coll. Law, St. Petersburg, 1996—. Recipient Am. Jurisprudence award Lawyer's Coop. Pub., 1992. Mem. ABA, Assn. Trial Lawyers Am., Assn. Fla. Trial Lawyers, St. Petersburg Bar Assn., Clearwater Bar Assn. Criminal, Family and matrimonial, Personal injury. Office: Scott and Fenderson 4554 Central Ave Ste L Saint Petersburg FL 33711-1046 Fax: 727-321-4499. E-mail: fenderlaw@aol.com

SCOTT, LEWIS KELLY, lawyer; b. Scottsbluff, Nebr., Sept. 12, 1928; s. Clrnce Kelly and Laura (Duerner) S.; m. Janice Lee Gildow, Dec. 27, 1950 (dec. Mar. 1979); 1 child, Kelly Faith. BA, Stanford U., 1950, LLB, 1952. Bar: Calif. 1952, Oreg. 1953, U.S. Dist. Ct. Oreg. 1953, U.S. Ct. Appeals (9th cir.) 1958, U.S. Supreme Ct. 1983. Assoc. Spears, Lubersky, Campbell, Bledsoe, Anderson & Young, and predecessor firms, Portland, Oreg., 1956-60, ptnr., 1960—. Construction, Labor. Home: 1559 SW Mary Failing Dr Portland OR 97219-8392 Office: Lane Powell Spears Lubersky 520 SW Yamhill St Ste 800 Portland OR 97204-1331

SCOTT, PETER BRYAN, lawyer; b. St. Louis, Nov. 11, 1947; s. gilbert Franklin and Besse Jean (Fudge) S.; children: Lindsay W., Sarah W., Peter B. Jr. AB, Drury Coll., 1969; JD, Washington U., St. Louis, 1972, LLM, 1980. Bar: Mo. 1972, Colo. 1980; diplomate Ct. Practice Inst.; accredited estate planner, advanced wealth specialist planner. Pvt. practice, St. Louis, 1972-80; assoc. McKie and Assocs., Denver, 1980-81; ptnr. Scott and Chesteen, P.C., 1981-84, Veto & Scott, Denver, 1984-92; pvt. practice, 1992—. Tchr. Denver Paralegal Inst., Red Rocks C.C. Mem. Evergreen Christian Ch., Disciples of Christ. Capt. USAR, 1971-79. Mem. ABA, Mo. Bar Assn., Colo. Bar Assn., 1st Jud. Dist. Bar Assn. Republican. General corporate, Estate planning, Probate. Home: 6305 W 6th Ave Unit C18 Lakewood CO 80214-2359 Office: Ste 2-103 777 S Wadsworth Blvd Lakewood CO 80226

SCOTT, ROBERT EDWIN, dean, law educator; b. Nagpur, India, Feb. 25, 1944; came to U.S., 1955; s. Roland Waldeck and Carol (Culver) S.; m. Elizabeth (Loch) Shumaker, Aug. 14, 1965; children: Christina Elaine, Robert Adam. BA, Oberlin (Ohio) Coll., 1965; JD, Coll. of William and Mary, 1968; LLM, U. Mich., 1969, SJD, 1973. Bar: Va. 1968. From asst. to prof. Law Sch. Coll. of William and Mary, Williamsburg, Va., 1969-74; prof. law Sch. of Law U. Va., Charlottesville, 1974-82, Lewis F. Powell, Jr. prof. Sch. of Law, 1982—, dean and Arnold H. Leon prof., 1991—. Author: Commercial Transactions, 1982, 91, Sales Law and the Contracting Process, 1982, 91, Contract Law and Theory, 1988, 93, Payment Systems and Credit Instruments, 1996. Fellow Am. Bar Found., Am. Acad. Arts and Scis.; mem. Va. Bar. Democrat. Methodist. Home: 1109 Hilltop Rd Charlottesville VA 22903-1220 Office: U Va Sch of Law Charlottesville VA 22903

SCOTT, ROBERT GENE, lawyer; b. Montague, Mass., Aug. 29, 1951; s. Edwin Ray and Barbara Agnes (Painchaud) S.; m. Laura Beth Williams, May 27, 1978; children: Jason Robert, Amanda Marie, Leah Beth. BS, U. Notre Dame, 1973, MS, 1975; postgrad., U. Tex., 1975-76; JD, U. Notre Dame, 1980. Bar: Ind. 1980, U.S. Dist. Ct. (no. dist.) Ind. 1980, U.S. Patent Office 1980, Mo. 1981, U.S. Dist. Ct. (we. dist.) Mo. 1981, U.S. Ct. Appeals (11th cir.) 1986, U.S. Ct. Appeals (8th cir.) 1987, U.S. Ct. Appeals (10th cir.) 1987, Kans. 1989, U.S. Dist. Ct. Kans. 1989, U.S. Supreme Ct. 1999. Asst. women's basketball coach U. Notre Dame, Ind., 1977-80; assoc. atty. Oltsch, Knoblock & Hall, South Bend, 1980-81; atty. Swanson, Midgley et al, Kansas City, Mo., 1981-82; exec. adminstr. Coun. of Fleet Specialists, Shawnee Mission, Kans., 1982-83; atty. Levy and Craig, Kansas City, Mo., 1983-89, Turner, Vader & Koch, Chartered, 1989-93; pvt. practice, 1993-95, 98; atty. Neill, Scott, Terrill & Embree, LLC, Lenexa, Kans., 1996-98; pvt. practice, 1998—. Mem. Equilaw panel arbitrators Panel Arbitrators, U.S. Dist. Ct. (we. dist.) Mo. Precinct committeeman Johnson County Rep. Party, Kans., 1983-84. Mem. ABA, Ind. Bar Assn., Mo. Bar Assn., Kansas City Bar Assn., Kansas City Lawyers Assn., Kans. Bar Assn., Wyandotte County Bar Assn., Johnson County Bar Assn., Am. Arbitration Assn. (mem. panel of arbitrators, constrn. arbitrator adv. bd.), Nat. Assn. Security Dealers (panel arbitrators, complex litigation panel), Nat. Arbitration Forum (panel of arbitrators), Notre Dame Club of Kansas City (pres. 1985-86), S.W. United Soccer Club of Kans. (pres. 1994-96), Heartland Soccer Assn. (v.p. 1997—). Republican. Roman Catholic. General civil litigation, Trademark and copyright, Workers' compensation. Office: 303 E Poplar Olathe KS 66061 E-mail: bob@rscottlaw.com

SCOTT, THEODORE R. lawyer; b. Mount Vernon, Ill., Dec. 7, 1924; s. Theodore R. and Beulah (Flannigan) S.; children: Anne Laurence, Sarah Buckland, Daniel, Barbara Gomon. AB, U. Ill., 1947, JD, 1949. Bar: Ill. 1950. Law clk. to judge U.S. Ct. Appeals, 1949-51; pvt. practice Chgo., 1950—; assoc. Spaulding Glass, 1951-53, Loftus, Lucas & Hammand, 1953-58, Ooms, McDougall, Williams & Hersh, 1958-60; ptnr. McDougall, Hersh & Scott, Chgo., 1960-87; of counsel Jones, Day, Reavis & Pogue, 1987-97, Rockey, Milnamow & Katz, 1998—. 2nd lt. USAAF, 1943-45. Decorated Air medal. Fellow Am. Coll. Trial Lawyers; mem. ABA, Ill. Bar Assn., Chgo. Bar Assn., 7th Cir. Bar Assn. (past pres.), Legal Club Chgo., Law Club Chgo., Patent Law Assn. Chgo. (past pres.), Union League Club, Exmoor Country Club (Highland Park, Ill.), Phi Beta Kappa. E-mail: tsb24nav2aol.com. Federal civil litigation, Patent, Trademark and copyright. Home: 1569 Woodvale Ave Deerfield IL 60015-2350

SCOTT, THOMAS EMERSON, JR. lawyer, former prosecutor; b. Pittsburg, Penn., Apr. 27, 1948; s. Thomas Emerson Sr. and Marie (Ebel) S.; m. Ginger Claud, Mar. 1978 (div. Aug. 1980); m. Joyce Newman, Aug. 6, 1983. BA in Econs. cum laude, U. Miami, 1969, JD cum laude, 1972; LLM, U. Va., 1989. Bar: Fla. 1972, U.S. Dist. Ct. (so. dist.) Fla. 1972, U.S. Ct. Appeals (5th and 11th cirs.) 1972. Law clk. to cir. judge 11th jud. cir. ct., State of Fla., Dade County, 1970-71; assoc. Bradford, Williams, McKay, Kimbrell, Hamann & Jennings, P.A., Miami, Fla., 1972-76, mem. firm, 1977-79; assoc. Huebner, Shaw & Burrell, Ft. Lauderdale, 1976-77; cir. judge 11th jud. cir. State of Fla., Miami, 1979-84; ptnr. Kimbrell, Hamann, Jennings, Womack, Carlson & Kniskern P.A., 1984-85, Steel Hector & Davis, Miami, Fla., 1990—; judge U.S. Dist. Ct. (so. dist.) Fla., 1985-90; U.S. atty U.S. So. Dist., Fla., 1997-99; ptnr. Shook Hardy & Bacon, Miami, 1999—. Chmn. security com. U.S. Dist. Ct., so. dist. Fla.; instr. litigation skills U. Miami, Coral Gables, 1984-86; instr. Nita program U. Fla.; instr. trial advocacy program Nova U.; instr. profl. responsibility and product liability St. Thomas U. Contbr. articles to profl. jours. Served to 1st lt. USAR, 1969—. Mem. ABA (co-chmn. com. on discovery litigation sect.), Fla. Bar Assn. (chmn. standing com. on professionalism, past chmn. CLE trial advocacy program), Dade County Bar Assn. (Outstanding Jurist award Young Lawyers' sect.), U.S. Dist. Judges' Assn., Product Liability Adv. Coun. Found. Republican. Roman Catholic. Avocations: running, collectibles. State civil litigation, Criminal, Product liability. Office: Shook Hardy & Bacon 201 S Biscayne Blvd Ste 2400 Miami FL 33131-4313 E-mail: tscott@shb.com*

SCOTT, W. WARREN, lawyer; b. Wurtzburg, Hesse, Germany, Oct. 19, 1952; s. Willard Warren and Justine S.; m. Bettina Arndt, June 21, 1986; children: Jesse, Taylor, Cameron. BA, Georgetown U., 1974; JD, U. Chgo., 1978. Bar: Calif. 1978, N.Y. 1979, New South Wales 1998. Assoc. Gravath Swaine & Moore, N.Y., 1979-82, Coudert Bros., London and N.Y., 1982-87; ptnr. N.Y., 1987-91, Sydney, 1991—. Mem. Australia-Israel C. of C., U. Club (N.Y.), Tattersalls Club. Office: Coudert Bros 1 Macquarie Pl Level 8 The Galeway Sydney NSW 2000 Australia Fax: 612-9830-7117. E-mail: warren.scott@sydney.coudert.com

SCOTT, WINDIE OLIVIA, lawyer; b. Mobile, Ala., Sept. 27, 1952; d. Clifford A. and Vivian (Pugh) S. B.A. in Polit. Sci., Calif. Poly. U., 1974; JD, U. Calif.-Davis, 1977. Bar: Calif. 1979. Grad. student asst. State of Calif., Sacramento, 1979, legal counsel Bd. Equalization, 1979-81, staff counsel I, dept. gen. svc., 1981-84, sr. staff counsel Office of Contr. Gray Davis, 1984—; dir. Centro de Legal, Sacramento, 1984. Mem. Black Women's Network, Sacramento, 1983—; treas. local chpt. Pan Hellenic Council, 1983—. Named One of Sacramento's 100 Most Influential Blacks, Sacramento Observer Newspapers, 1984, Outstanding Woman of Yr. YWCA, 1990; recipient Outstanding Businesswoman award Iota Lambda, 1991. Mem. Wiley Manuel Bar Assn. (pres. 1984—, Outstanding Service award, 1983, Unity award 1990), Black Am. Polit. Assn. Calif., Women Lawyers of Sacramento (pres. 1989, past pres. award 1990), Calif. Assn. Black Lawyers (bd. dirs. 1980—), Sacramento County Bar Assn. (bd. dirs. 1988—, exec. com., state bar conf. dels. 1990—), Alpha Kappa Alpha. Democrat. Roman Catholic. Office: Office Contr Gray Davis 1020 N St Ste 128 Sacramento CA 95814-5687

SCOULAR, ROBERT FRANK, lawyer; b. Del Norte, Colo., July 9, 1942; s. Duane William and Marie Josephine (Moloney) S.; m. Donna V. Scoular, June 3, 1967; children— Bryan T., Sean D., Bradley R. B.S. in Aero. Engring., St. Louis U., 1964, J.D., 1968. Bar: Mo. 1968, Colo. 1968, N.D. 1968, U.S. Supreme Ct. 1972, Calif. 1979. Law clk. to chief judge U.S. Ct. Appeals (8th cir.), 1968-69; ptnr. Bryan, Cave, McPheeters & McRoberts, St. Louis, 1969-89, mng. ptnr. Los Angeles, 1979-84, exec. com., 1984-85, sect. leader tech., computer and intellectual property law, 1985-89; ptnr. Sonnenschein, Nath, Rosenthal, Chgo., 1990—, mng. ptnr. L.A., 1990—, mem. policy and planning com., 1995—. Co-leader intellectual property practice, 1990-98; dir. Mo. Lawyers Credit Union, 1978-79. Contbr. articles to profl. jours. Bd. dirs. St. Louis Bar Found., 1975-76, 79; bd. dirs., vice chmn. L.A. Area Coun. Boy Scouts Am.; league commr. Am. Youth Soccer Orgn.; mem. alumni coun. St. Louis U., 1979-82, dean's coun. Sch. Law, 2000—; hon. dean Dubourg Soc. Recipient Nat. Disting. Eagle Scout award. Mem. ABA (nat. dir. young lawyers div. 1977-78), Am. Judicature Soc., Bar Assn. Met. St. Louis (v.p. 1978-79, sec. 1979, chmn. young lawyers sect. 1975-76), Los Angeles County Bar Assn., Assn. Bus. Trial Lawyers, Calif. Bar. Assn., Mo. Bar (chmn. young lawyers sect. 1976-77, disting. svc. award), Computer Law Assn., Fed. Bar Assn., Dubourg Soc. (hon. dean). General civil litigation, Government contracts and claims, Intellectual property. Home: 1505 Lower Paseo La Cresta Palos Verdes Peninsula CA 90274-2066 Office: Sonnenschein Nath & Rosenthal 601 S Figueroa St Ste 1500 Los Angeles CA 90017-5720

SCOVILLE, LAURENCE MCCONWAY, JR. arbitrator, mediator; b. Brunswick, Ga., Sept. 24, 1936; s. Laurence McConway and Mary (Williams) S.; m. Lynn Bayne Johnston, Aug. 20, 1960; children: Evelyn Mary, Laurence M. III, Robert J. AB, Dartmouth Coll., 1958; LLB, U. Mich., 1961. Bar: Mich. 1961, U.S. Dist. Ct. (ea. and we. dists.) Mich. 1961, U.S. Ct. Appeals (6th cir.) 1972, U.S. Supreme Ct. 1986. Assoc. Clark, Klein & Beaumont, Detroit, 1961-68, ptnr., 1968-95, mem. exec. com., 1976-95, chmn., 1990-95; mem. Clark Hill PLC, 1996-97, of counsel, 1998. Bd. dirs. The Detroit Legal News, 1989—; chmn. rules com. U.S. Dist. Ct. (ea. dist.) Mich., Detroit, 1988-92. Author: Construction Litigation: Representing the Contractor, 1986, 91. Bd. dirs., exec. com. Detroit Econ. Growth Corp., 1990-98; bd. dirs. Stratford Festival Am., 1997—, chmn. 1999—; bd. govs. Stratford Shakespearean Festival, 1996—; founder, chmn. Mich. Mems. of the Stratford Festival, 1998-2000. bd. dirs. 1998- Mem. Nat. Assn. Sec. Dealers (mediator, arbitrator), State Bar Mich., CPR Inst. Dispute Resolution (panel of disting. neutrals), Am. Arbitration Assn. (mediator, nat. panel arbitrators, large complex case program), Am. Soc. Employers (bd. dirs. 1993-98), Dartmouth Lawyers Assn., Dartmouth Rowing Club (bd. stewards 1988-97), Met. Affairs Coalition (bd. dirs. 1992-98, vice chmn. 1995-98), Econ. Club Detroit (sec. 1988-95, bd. dirs. 1994-99), Detroit Club (bd. dirs. 1989-94, pres. 1993-94), Country Club Detroit, Dataw Island Club. Avocations: tennis, hunting, fishing, theatre, golf. Home: RR2 Beach O'Pines Box 30 Grand Bend ON Canada N0M 1T0 Office: 24 Reeve Ct Saint Helena Island SC 29920 E-mail: larlyn@islc.net

SCOWCROFT, JEROME CHILWELL, lawyer; b. Pocatello, Idaho, May 17, 1947; s. Harold and Alberta Mary (Chilwell) S.; m. Corinne Gail Cox, Mar. 12, 1983; children: Jason Trevor, Brian Jonathan. BA, Stanford U., 1969; M in Research Psychology, U. Calif., San Diego, 1973; JD, Duke U., 1978. Bar: N.Y. 1980, Wash. 1986. Assoc. Haight, Gardner, Poor & Havens, N.Y.C., 1978-81, Schwabe, Williamson & Wyatt, Seattle, 1985—; editor, legal advisor Lamorte, Burns & Co., N.Y.C. and Greenwich, Conn., 1981-85. Lectr. in admiralty law U. Wash., 1988-89, adj. prof., 1988—. Bd. advisors Maritime Adv. Svcs., Arbitration Award Digest, 1981—; contbg. editor U.S. Maritime Arbitration, Internat. Congress Comml. Arbitration, 1983—; case editor Jour. of Maritime Law and Commerce, 1987—; contbr. articles to profl. jours. With U.S. Army, 1970-72. Fellow HEW, 1975-76. Mem. ABA, Maritime Law Assn. U.S. (vice chmn. carriage of goods com. 1991—), Seattle World Trade Club, Propeller Club. Republican. Episcopalian. Avocations: math., photography, tennis, hiking. Admiralty, Contracts commercial, Private international. Home: 2524 Sahalee Dr E Redmond WA 98074-6357 Office: Schwabe Williamson & Wyatt 1420 5th Ave Ste 3500 Redmond WA 98053

SCRIGGINS, LARRY PALMER, lawyer, director; b. Englewood, N.J., Nov. 27, 1936; s. Thomas Dalby and M. Patricia (Fowler) S.; m. Victoria Jackola, Feb. 17, 1979; children: Elizabeth J., Thomas P. AB, Middlebury Coll., 1958; JD, U. Chgo., 1961. Bar: Md. 1962. Law clk. to chief judge Md. Ct. Appeals, 1962; assoc. Piper & Marbury, L.L.P., Balt., 1962-69, ptnr., 1969-98, vice chmn., 1988-93, mem. exec. com., CFO, 1993-98; sr. counsel Piper Marbury Rudnick & Wolfe LLP, 1999-2001, ptnr. emeritus, 2001—. Mem. legal adv. com. N.Y. Stock Exch., 1992-96; bd. dirs. USF & G Corp., 1979-98, Center Stage Assocs., 1979-89, Balt. Choral Arts Soc., 1979-96, Balt. Conv. Bur., 1982-95, YMCA of Greater Balt., 1987-94, Fund for Ednl. Excellence, 1990-98, chmn. bd. trustees, 1993-98; bd. dirs. Nat. Aquarium in Balt., bd. govs. 1987-93; bd. dirs. Balt. Symphony Orchestra, 1996-2001. Contbr. articles to profl. jours. Fellow Am. Bar Found.; mem. AICPA (planning com. 1989-92), Md. Bar Assn. (coun. 1976-78, chmn. 1977-78, mem. com. on corp. laws 1981-84), ABA (sect. on bus. law coun. 1972-76, chair 1991-92, vice chair and editor-in-chief The Bus. Lawyer 1989-90, chmn. law and acctg. com. 1985-88, chmn. com. corp. laws 1996-2000, chmn. ad hoc com. on ethics 2000 1999—), Internat. Bar Assn., Am. Judicature Soc., Am. Law Inst., Task Force on Fin. Instruments, Fin. Acctg. Stds. Bd. General corporate, Finance, Securities. Home: 13663 E Columbine Dr Scottsdale AZ 85259-3752 Office: Piper Marbury Rudnick & Wolfe LLP 6225 Smith Ave Baltimore MD 21209-3600 E-mail: larry.scriggins@piperrudnick.com

SCRIVEN, JOHN G. retired lawyer, chemical company executive; Bar: Mich. 1993. Sr. staff counsel Dow Europe S.A., 1981-83; gen. counsel Dow Chem. Co., Midland, Mich., 1983-86, v.p., gen. counsel, 1986-2000, v.p., gen. counsel, sec., 1986-2000; ret., 2000. Office: Dow Chem Co 2030 Dow Ctr Midland MI 48674-0001

SCRIVEN, WAYNE MARCUS, lawyer; b. Sumter, S.C., Aug. 31, 1953; s. Philip Roosevelt and Sarah Ella (Pringle) S. BA in History Edn. cum laude, Va. Union U., 1975; JD, Golden Gate U. Sch. of Law, 1979. Bar: Va. 1980, U.S. Dist. Ct. (ea. dist.) Va. 1980, U.S. Ct. Appeals (4th cir.) 1980, S.C. 1982, U.S. Dist. Ct. S.C. 1982, U.S. Supreme Ct. 1984, Calif. 1987, U.S. Dist. Ct. (no. dist.) Calif. 1986, U.S. Ct. Appeals (9th cir.) 1986, D.C. 1993, U.S. Dist. Ct. D.C. 1994, U.S. Dist. Ct. Md. 1994, U.S. Ct. Appeals (fed. cir.) 1994, D.C. Directing atty. Petersburg (Va.) Legal Aid Soc., 1980-81; staff atty. Carolina Regional Legal Svcs. Corp., Florence, S.C., 1981-82; solo practice atty., 1982-85, Richmond, Va., 1985-86, San Francisco, 1986-93, Washington, 1993—. Contract atty. Neighborhood Legal Asst. Program, Marion, S.C., 1982-83, pro bonocontract atty., 1983-85, Carolina Regional Legal Svcs. Corp., Florence, 1983-85, Bar Assn. of San Francisco, 1987-93; notary public, S.C., 1981-91, Va., 1986-91. Bd. dirs. Young Men's Christian Assn., Florence, 1982-83, Pee Dee Crisis Ctr., Florence, 1983-84, San Francisco Neighborhood Legal Asst. Program, 1992-93. Named one of Outstanding Young Men of Am., U.S. Jaycees, 1982; recipient Outstanding Lawyer in Pub. Svc., Bar Assn. San Francisco, 1988-91. Mem. ABA, Washington Bar Assn., Assn. Trial Lawyers of Am., U.S. Supreme Ct. Hist. Soc. Baptist. Avocations: fishing, guitar playing, nature trail walking. General practice, Labor, Personal injury. Office: Scriven & Assocs 7900 Sudley Rd Ste 420 Manassas VA 20109 also: Scriven & Assocs 1225 Eye St NW Ste 500 Washington DC 20005-3914 Fax: (703) 369-7158. E-mail: Wayne-Marcus-Scriven@abanet.org

SCRIVNER, THOMAS WILLIAM, lawyer; b. Madison, Wis., Sept. 10, 1948; s. William H. and Jane (Gehrz) S.; m. Meredith Burke, Aug. 16, 1980; children: Allison, David. AB, Duke U., 1970, MAT, 1972; JD, U. Wis., 1977. Assoc. Michael, Best & Friedrich LLP, Milw., 1978-85, ptnr., 1985—. Mem. ABA, Wis. Bar Assn., Milw. Bar Assn. (labor sect.), Corp. Practice Inst. (pres. 1989-92). Episcopalian. Administrative and regulatory, Labor. Home: 4626 N Cramer St Milwaukee WI 53211-1203 Office: Michael Best & Friedrich LLP 100 E Wisconsin Ave Ste 3300 Milwaukee WI 53202-4108

SCROGGS, LARRY KENNETH, lawyer, state legislator; b. Beebe, Ark., Oct. 8, 1941; s. Kenneth Chalmers and Mildred Lorene (McDonald) S.; m. Mary Patricia Rushing, Aug. 25, 1967; children: Larry Kenneth Jr., James Kevin, Michael Kyle. BA, Harding U., 1963; JD, Vanderbilt U., 1971. Bar: Tenn. 1971, U.S. Dist. Ct. (we. dist.) Tenn. 1971, U.S. Ct. Appeals (8th cir.) 1982, U.S. Ct. Appeals (6th cir.) 1989, U.S. Supreme Ct. 1981. Assoc. Law Firm of Leo Bearman, Memphis, 1971-72, Holt, Batchelor, Spicer, Memphis, 1972-76, ptnr., 1976-80, Less & Scroggs, Memphis, 1980-92; pvt. practice, Germantown, Tenn., 1992-96; ptnr. Scroggs & Rogers, Collierville, 1997—; mem. Tenn. Ho. of Reps., Nashville, 1997—. Mcpl. ct. judge City of Germantown, 1980-86; atty. for County Trustee, Shelby County, Memphis, 1990—. Mem. campaign steering com. George Bush for Pres., Memphis, 1987-92; vol. Ed Bryant for Congress campaign, Memphis, 1994, Don Sundquist for Gov. campaign, Memphis, 1994. Lt. U.S. Navy, 1964-67, Vietnam. Mem. ABA, Tenn. Bar Assn., Memphis Bar Assn. (bd. dirs. 1990-91). Republican. Mem. Ch. of Christ. Avocations: photography, boating, tennis. Federal civil litigation, State civil litigation, Construction. Office: Scroggs & Rogers 110 E Mulberry St Ste 200 Collierville TN 38017-2675

SCUDDER, CHARLES SEELYE KELLGREN, lawyer; b. London, Feb. 20, 1947; came to U.S., 1964; s. Evarts Seelye and Henrica Antonina (Kellgren) S.; m. Jannette Harris Ericson, June 20, 1970; children: John Whitney, Jocelyn Seelye, Ansley Harris. BA, Yale U., 1968; BA in Law with 2d class honors, Oxford U., 1973; JD with honors, U. Conn., 1975; MA (hon.), Oxford U., 1980. Bar: N.Y. 1976, U.S. Dist. Ct. N.Y. 1976. Assoc., Winthrop Stimson Putnam & Roberts, N.Y.C., 1975-81; sr. counsel Conoco Inc., Wilmington, Del., 1981-87; v.p. and assoc. gen. counsel Unisys Corp., Blue Bell, Pa., 1987—. With U.S. Army, 1968-71. Editor Conn. Law Review, 1974. Mem. ABA (subcom. on multinat. corps.), N.Y. State Bar Assn., Am. Corp. Counsel Assn. Republican. General corporate, Private international, Securities. Office: Unisys Corp Township Line Blue Bell PA 19424-0001

SCUDDER, THEODORE TOWNSEND, III, lawyer; b. Oak Park, Ill., June 26, 1939; s. Theodore Townsend Jr. and Joan (Kerr) S.; m. Eileen Hesmondhalgh, May 31, 1974; children: Coraline Sarah, Robert Cameron. AB, Harvard U., 1961; JD, U. Mich., 1964; postgrad. John Marshall Law Sch., 1965-67, Northwestern Law Sch., 1971. Bar: Ill. 1964, U.S. Dist. Ct. (no. dist.) Ill. 1965. Ct. reporter Ill. Army N.G., Chgo., 1964-70; assoc. Willian, Brinks, Olds, Hofer, Chgo., 1963-67, Wilson & McIlvaine, Chgo., 1967-68, Jacobs, Williams & Montgomery, Chgo., 1968-70, asst. U.S. atty. U.S. Dept. Justice, Chgo., 1970-79; ptnr. Ruff Weidenaar & Reidy, Chgo., 1979-87; sole practice, Hoffman Estates, Ill. 1987—; trustee, counsel Pacific Garden Mission, Chgo., 1967— ; advisor Ill. Selective Svc., Springfield, 1973-79. Editor: Pike-Schaefer Dialog, 1969. Canvasser, Republican Party, Chgo., 1964-67. NEH scholar U. Wis., 1974. Mem. ABA, Christian Legal Soc. (bd. dirs. 1965-67), Am. Judicature Soc., Ill. Bar Assn., Chgo. Bar Assn., Harvard Club (asst. treas. 1968-72). Philadelphia Soc. Episcopalian. Federal civil litigation, Personal injury, Trademark and copyright. Home: 362 Marion Ave Glen Ellyn IL 60137-4014 Office: 35 E Wacker Dr Ste 2800 Chicago IL 60601-2308

SCULLIN, FREDERICK JAMES, JR. federal judge; b. Syracuse, N.Y., Nov. 5, 1939; s. Frederick James and Cleora M. (Fellows) S.; m. Veronica Terek Sauro, Aug. 31, 1984; children: Mary Margaret, Kathleen Susan, Kellie Anne, Rebecca Rose; 1 stepchild, Angel Jenette Sauro. B.S. in Econs., Niagara U., 1961; LL.B., Syracuse U., 1964. Bar: N.Y. 1964, Fla. 1976, U.S. Dist. Ct. (no. dist.) N.Y. 1967, U.S. Supreme Ct. 1971. Assoc. Germain & Germain, Syracuse, 1967-68; asst. dist. atty. Onondaga County, 1968-71; asst. atty. gen. N.Y. State Organized Crime Task Force, 1971-78, dir. regional office, 1974-78; chief prosecutor, dir. Gov.'s Council on Organized Crime State of Fla., Tallahassee, 1978—; sole practice Syracuse, 1979-82; U.S. atty. for No. Dist. N.Y., 1982-92; judge U.S. Dist. Ct. (no. dist.) N.Y., 1992—, chief judge. With U.S. Army, 1964-67, Vietnam; col. USAR. Decorated Air medal, Bronze Star; Cross of Gallantry (Vietnam) Mem. Am. Judicature Soc., Fla. Bar Assn., Fed. Bar Assn., Fed. Bar Coun., Onon City Bar Assn. Office: US Dist Ct US Courthouse 100 S Clinton St Syracuse NY 13261-6100 E-mail: fscullin@nynd.uscourts.gov

SCULLY, ROGER TEHAN, II, lawyer; b. Washington, Jan. 10, 1948; s. James Henry and Marietta (Maguire) S.; m. Martha Anne Seebach, Dec. 29, 1979. BS, U. Md., 1977; JD, Cath. U., 1980. Bar: Md. 1980, D.C. 1981, U.S. Tax Ct. 1982, U.S. Supreme Ct. 1988. V.p. Bogley Related Cos., Rockville, Md., 1971-75; law clk. to presiding justice Superior Ct. of D.C., Washington, 1979-81; assoc. Lerch, Early & Roseman, Bethesda, Md., 1981-82; gen. counsel Laszlo N. Tauber, M.D. & Assocs., 1982-94, Jefferson Meml. Hosp., Alexandria, Va., 1982-94; spl. counsel Venable, Baetjer, Howard & Civiletti, Washington, 1991-96. Cons. in real estate Order of Friar Minor, N.Y.C., 1977—; lectr. Mortgage Bankers Assn., Washington, 1984—; bd. dirs. Nozzoli Constrn. Co., Washington; exec. com., spl. counsel to bd. dirs., bd. dirs. Chromachron Technology Corp., Toronto; bd. dirs. MusicWorks, N.Y.C.; vice chair Sayett Tech., Inc., Rochester, N.Y.; vice chair, bd. dirs., exec. com. MediaShow, Inc., Rochester. Author: (with Quarles & Howard) Summary Adjudication Dispositive Motions and Summary Trials, 1991. Mem. pres.'s coun. St. Bonaventure U., Olean, N.Y., 1995—, chmn. pres.'s coun., 1986-95; trustee Belmont Abbey Coll., Charlotte, N.C., 1993-95, Edmund Burke Sch., Washington, 1984—; bd. dirs. Nat. Children's Choir, Washington, 1980-94. Recipient First Order Affiliation Order of Friars Minor, 1985; named one of Outstanding Young Men in Am., 1982. Fellow D.C. Bar Assn.; mem. ABA, ATLA, FBA, Md. Bar Assn. (chmn. corp. counsel sect.), Am. Judicature Soc., Assn. Governing Bd. of Univs. and Colls., Am. Inns of Ct., Irish Legal Soc., Selden Soc., U.S. Jud. Conf. of 4th Cir. (permanent mem.), U.S. Jud. Conf. Fed. Cir. (del.), Jud. Conf. of D.C. (del.). Republican. Roman Catholic. Contracts commercial, Private international, Real property. Home: 10923 Wickshire Way North Bethesda MD 20852-3220 Office: 7712 Greentree Rd West Bethesda MD 20817-1428 E-mail: Scullyhome@MyMailstation.com

SCURO, JOSEPH E., JR. lawyer; b. Jersey City, Mar. 28, 1948; s. Joseph E. and Phyllis (Amato) S.; m. Virginia Ruth Shaw. BA with honors, Manhattan Coll., 1970; JD, Ohio State U., 1972. Bar: Tex., Ohio, U.S. Dist. Cts., U.S. Ct. Appeals (5th and 10th cir.), U.S. Tax Ct., U.S. Mil. Appeals, U.S. Supreme Ct. Asst. atty. gen. Ohio, 1973-81; chief legal counsel Ohio State Hwy. Patrol, 1975-81; practice law, 1973—; of counsel Nicholas & Barrera, San Antonio and Dallas, 1982-90; counsel to San Antonio, Dallas and Grapevine Police Officers Assns, Combined Law Enforcement Assn. Tex., Alamo Heights Police Officers Assn., Tex. Mcpl. League; former legal adviser, spl. counsel to cities of San Marcos, New Braunfels, Balcones Heights, La Vernia, Poteet, Laredo, Odessa, Dilley, Hondo, Highland Park, Kyle, Universal City, Del Rio, Greenville, Galveston, Arlington, Austin and others; former spl. counsel on tng. San Antonio Police Dept.; former counsel to Bexar County Constable's Assn.; condr. seminars. Contbr. articles on police and law enforcement to profl. jours. Bd. dirs. Nat. Hispanic Arts Endowment. Served to capt. USAF, 1970-75. Fellow Southwestern Legal Found. (sec. 1986-91); mem. ABA, Tex. Bar Assn., Ohio Bar Assn., San Antonio Bar Assn., Columbus (Ohio) Bar Assn., Am. Trial Lawyers Assn., Police Exec. Research Forum, Internat. Assn. Chiefs of Police (legal officer sect.), Ams. for Effective Law Enforcement (bd. advs.), Southwestern Law Enforcement Inst. (bd. advs.), Internat. Soc. Law Enforcement and Criminal Justice Instrs., Fed. Criminal Investigators Assn. (hon.), Ohio Assn. Polygraph Examiners (hon.). Republican. Presbyterian. Federal civil litigation, State civil litigation, Criminal. Office: Main Place Station PO Box 50966 Dallas TX 75250-0966

SCZUDLO, WALTER JOSEPH, lawyer; b. Fairbanks, Alaska; s. Walter and Dolores J. Sczudlo; children: Lauren Hall, Elizabeth Fairbanks, Walter Christopher; m. Rebecca Grey Tucker. AB, Middlebury Coll., 1975; JD, Golden Gate U., 1979; LLM, Georgetown U., 1987; postgrad., U. Calif., Santa Barbara, 1972, Tulane U., 1971-72, Vt. Law Sch., 1976-77. Bar: Alaska 1979, Calif. 1980, D.C. 1986, U.S. Ct. Appeals (9th cir.) 1980, U.S. Ct. Appeals (D.C. cir.) 1986, U.S. Dist. Cts. (no., cen., ea. and so. dists.) Calif., U.S. Dist. Ct. Alaska, U.S. Ct. Claims, U.S. Tax Ct. Law clk. to presiding justice Alaska Supreme Ct., 1978-79; assoc. atty. Merdes, Schaible, Staley and Delisio, Anchorage, 1979-82; legis. dir., gen. counsel U.S. Senator Murkowski, Washington, 1982-84; sr. tax assoc. Schramm and Raddue, Santa Barbara, Calif., 1984-85; dir. congl. rels., counsel Natural Gas Supply Assn., Washington, 1985-88; Washington counsel Shell Oil Co., 1988-96; v.p., Washington counsel Intercontinental Energy Corp., 1996-99; gen. counsel, vice pres. pub. affairs and comms. Assn. Fundraising Profls., Washington, 1999—; prin. ptnr. WEBK Broadcasting 105.3 FM, Killington, Vt., 1985—. Dir. Sun's Edge, Inc., Santa Barbara, 1987—, Natural Gas Roundtable, Washington, 1987—. Author: (with other) Washington Legal Foundation, 1988. Com. chmn. Steve Cowper for Gov., Anchorage, 1982. Recipient Am. Jurisprudence award Bancroft-Whitney Pub. Co., 1978. Roman Catholic. Avocations: mountaineering, cross-country skiing, tennis. FERC practice, Legislative, Corporate taxation. Home: 6700 Loring Ct Bethesda MD 20817-3148 Office: AFP 1101 King St Ste 700 Alexandria VA 22314-2944 E-mail: wsczudlo@AFPNET.org

SEABOLT, RICHARD L. lawyer; b. Chgo., Aug. 28, 1949; BGS with distinction, U. Mich., 1971; JD, U. Calif., Hastings, 1975. Bar: Calif. 1975. With Hancock, Rothert & Bunshoft, San Francisco, 1975—, ptnr., 1981—. Pres. Def. Seminar Assocs., 1992—; exec. com., chmn. Commn. Jury Instrn., litig. sect. State Bar Calif. Frequent speaker and author profl. jours., Large Complex Case Panel-Constrn., Am. Arbitration Assn. Mem. ABA, State Bar Calif., Bar Assn. San Francisco. Appellate, General civil litigation, Contracts commercial. Office: Hancock Rothert & Bunshoft LLP Four Embarcadero Ctr San Francisco CA 94111-4106 Fax: 415-955-2599. E-mail: rlseabolt@hrblaw.com

SEABURG, JEAN, lawyer; b. Mpls., May 3, 1935; d. Gunnar Fredrick and Lorraine Elise (Otto) Dahlstrom; m. Paul A. Seaburg, July 27, 1957 (div. Jan. 1973); children— Mark David, Gunnar Paul; m. Richard J. Lee, Feb. 24, 1984 (dec. June 1986). Student U. Minn., 1953-57; B.S.C.E., Marquette U., 1967, J.D., 1974. Bar: Wis. 1974, Minn. 1986, U.S. Dist. Ct. (ea. and we. dists.) Wis. 1974, U.S. Dist. Ct. Minn. 1986, U.S. Patent Office 1986, U.S. Dist. Ct. (no. dist.) N.Y. 1989, U.S. Ct. Appeals (1st, 10th and 11th cirs.) 1989; registered profl. engr., Wis., Minn. Engr., Howard, Needles, Tammen & Bergendoff, Milw., 1967-71; law clk. Habush, Habush & Davis, Milw., 1973-74, assoc., 1974-77, ptnr., 1977-86; assoc. James E. Olds, Ltd., Mpls., 1986—. Mem. ABA, ASCE, Assn. Trial Lawyers Am., Nat. Soc. Profl. Engrs. Lutheran. Federal civil litigation, Patent, Personal injury. Office: 4135 Brunswick Ave S Saint Louis Park MN 55416-3132

SEAGLE, J. HAROLD, lawyer; b. Marion, N.C., May 9, 1947; s. Rufus James and Alma Rhoda (McMahan) S.; m. Linda Jean Cranford, June 3, 1967; 1 child, James Mark. BA, U. N.C., 1973, JD, 1977. Bar: N.C. 1977; U.S. Dist. Ct. (ea., middle, we. dists.) N.C. 1977, 88, 92; U.S. Ct Appeals (4th cir.) 1982; U.S. Supreme Ct. 1982. Assoc. atty. Rountree & Newton, Wilmington, N.C., 1977-79; ptnr. Rountree & Seagle, L.L.P., 1979—. Past pres. Fifth Jud. Dist. Bar. Bd. trustees and bd. deacons Winter Park Baptist Ch.; past moderator Wilmington Baptist Assn.; bd. dirs. Rescue Mission of Cape Fear; past adv. Bd. Coastal Bioethics Network; past chmn. annual fund drive Am. Cancer Soc.; past sect. chmn. Cape Fear United Way. Mem.: New Hanover County Bar Assn. (co-chair grievance com.), N.C. Bar Assn., N.C. State Bar, N.C. Acad. Trial Lawyers, N.C. Coll. of Advocacy, Southeastern Admiralty Law Inst. (chmn.), Maritime Law Assn. of U.S. (proctor), N.C. Bar Coun. of Pres. Wilmington Inns of Ct. (exec. com., master). Avocations: acoustic guitar, motorcycle racing. Admiralty, General civil litigation, Environmental. Office: Rountree & Seagle LLP 2419 Market St Wilmington NC 28403-1135 E-mail: hseagle@rountreeseagle.com

SEAGULL, KEITH ALLEN, lawyer; b. Milw., Apr. 19, 1957; s. Louis and Helen Ann S.; m. Asma Parveen, Nov. 20, 1994; 1 stepchild, Samia; 1 child, Sasha Y. BS, U. Wis., Milw., 1977; JD, Southwestern U., L.A., 1981; cert. atendance, Cambridge U., 1981. Bar: Calif. 1990; cert. specialist workers' compensation State Bar Calif. Bd. Legal Specialization. Law clerk Law Offices Steven M. Hanna, Fullerton, Calif., 1981-85; asst. office mgr. Joe Kay Design & Constrn., 1985-89; adjuster Wausau Ins., Pasadena, 1989-90; atty., adjuster Springfield Ins., Covina, 1990-91; atty. Law Offices Rose, Klein & Marias, L.A., 1991, Stephen G. Krutzsch & Assocs., ITT Hartford Ins., Brea, Calif., 1991-94, Law Office James Max Stewart, Temecula, 1994-95; prin. Law Offices Keith A. Seagull, Pomona, 1995—. Mem. ABA, Calif. Applicants' Attys. Assn., Eastern Bar Assn. L.A. County, Masons. Avocations: sailing, world religions, walking, music, politics. Workers' compensation.

SEAMAN, ROBERT E., III, lawyer; b. Chgo., Apr. 2, 1947; s. Robert E. II and Rae June (Blair) S.; children: Kimberly Desiree, Charissa Alaine, Robert E. IV, Jason Robert. BA in Polit. Sci., The Citadel, 1969; JD, U. Va., 1972; postdoctoral, N.Y. Inst. Fin., 1975-77, Harvard U., 1979. Bar: N.Y. 1975, S.C. 1978, U.S. Dist. Ct. (so. dist.) N.Y. 1975, U.S. Tax Ct. 1980, U.S. Ct. Appeals (2nd cir.) 1975, U.S. Ct. Appeals (4th cir.) 1979, U.S. Supreme Ct. 1979, U.S. Ct. Mil. Appeals 1980. Assoc. Breed, Abbott & Morgan, N.Y.C., 1972-74; v.p.-legal, asst. sec. Paine, Webber, Jackson & Curtis Inc. and subs., 1974-77, asst. to chmn. bd. PaineWebber Inc., 1974-77; assoc. gen. counsel Col. Life and Accident Ins. Co., Columbia, S.C., 1977-80; sole practice, 1980—. Gen. counsel Jacom Computer Services, Inc., Northvale, N.J., 1977—; chmn. The dorchester Group, 1987—; bd. dirs., gen. counsel Internat. Chem. Cons., Ltd., 1983-88; pres. Titan Trading Co., Inc., Columbia, 1984-86, Comptel Data Sys., 1984—; chief exec. officer, pub. Up2Date Market Adv. Service, Columbia, 1985-87; chmn. bd., CEO Race Mktg. Assocs. Inc.; lectr. various ednl. instns. Co-author: How to Use the Relative Strength Index to Increase Trading Profits, 1986, Legal Issues in the Leasing Process, 1991; editor in chief: The Reading Guide and Virginia Law School Outline Series, 1971-72; sr. editor Va. Law Weekly, 1970-72; contbr. articles to profl. jours. Student senator S.C. Legislature, 1968-69; mem. coll. presdl. adv. com., state dir. Collegiate Counsel of UN, 1968-69; trustee Faith United Meth. Ch.; coord. phon-a-thon campaign Midlands S.C. youth div. YMCA, 1980-82; class chmn. Citadel Devel. Found., 1980; chpt. chmn., campaign adv. com. chmn., vice chmn. exec. com. Midlands chpt. March of Dimes, 1978-81; mem. task force Greater Columbia C. of C.; vice chmn. bd. KIDS North Jersey, 1990-94; founder, chmn. The Millennium Found., 1992—. Served capt. M.I., inf. U.S. Army, 1972 -77, Res., 1977-83. Robert R. McCormick scholar McCormick Found., and Chgo. Tribune, 1965-69, DuPont scholar U. Va., 1969-72; winner Estate Planning contest 1st Nat. Bank Chgo., 1971; recipient Leadership award Citadel Devel. Found., 1979-80, named Young Man of Yr., S.C. Greater Met. Area Jaycees, 1980; recipient Recognition award Nat. March of Dimes, 1981; named Knight Comdr., Grand Cross, Min. Fin. and Advocar Gen., Order St. John Knights of Malta. Mem. Assn. of Bar of City of N.Y., ABA (state regulation of securities com., subcom. on oil and gas, subcom. on regulation of equipment leasing, securities industry assn. compliance divsn. 1974-77), Am. Assn. Equipment Lessors, Info. Tech. Resellers Assn., NYSE, AMEX, Nat. Assn. Securities Dealers (registered rep.), Commodities Futures Trading Commn. (registered prin.), N.Y. Bar Assn., S.C. Bar Assn., Citadel Brigadier Club (bd. dirs.), Ill. Citadel Club (pres.), Knights of Malta (Knighted and designated Knight Comdr., Grand Cross, Minister of Fin. and Avocar Gen. Order of St. John), Pi Sigma Alpha; Clubs: Yale Club N.Y.C., Rockland Country Club, Com. of 100 Club, Met. Bus. Club, Palmetto Soc., Toastmasters (pres. Lexington chpt., ann. impromptu speech contest champion, Toastmaster of Yr. 1979). Contracts commercial, Finance, Securities. Office: 560 Route 303 Orangeburg NY 10962-1314

SEAR, MOREY LEONARD, federal judge, educator; b. New Orleans, Feb. 26, 1929; s. William and Yetty (Streiffer) S.; m. Lee Edrehi, May 26, 1951; children: William Sear II, Jane Lee. JD, Tulane U., 1950, LLD (hon.), 1999. Bar: La. 1950. Asst. dist. atty., Parish Orleans, 1952-55; individual practice law Stahl & Sear, New Orleans, 1955-71; spl. counsel New Orleans Aviation Bd., 1956-60; magistrate U.S. Dist. Ct. (ea. dist.) La., 1971-76, judge, 1976—, chief judge, 1992-99; judge Temp. Emergency Ct. of Appeals, 1982-87. Adj. prof. Tulane U. Coll. Law; former chmn. com. on adminstrn. of bankruptcy sys., former chmn. adv. com. on bankruptcy rules, former mem. com. on adminstrn. of fed. magistrate sys. Jud. Conf. U.S., mem. jud. panel on multidist. litigation; former mem. Jud. Conf. of U.S. and Its Exec. Com.; former mem. cir. coun. 5th Cir. of U.S.; founding dir. River Oaks Pvt. Psychiat. Hosp., 1968. Pres. Congregation Temple Sinai, 1977-79; bd. govs. Tulane Med. Ctr., 1977—; former chmn. Tulane Med. Ctr. Hosp. and Clinic, 1980-85. Decorated Order of Vasco Nunez de Balboa (Panama) with grade of grand ofcl. Mem. ABA, La. Bar Assn., New Orleans Bar Assn., Order of Barristers, Order of the Coif (hon.). Office: US Dist Ct C-256 US Courthouse 500 Camp St New Orleans LA 70130-3313

SEARCY, WILLIAM NELSON, lawyer, director; b. Moultire, Ga., June 26, 1942; s. Floyd Hartsfield and Anna (Pidcock) S.; m. Camille Heery, June 17, 1967; 1 child, Amelia Ashburn. AB, U. Ga., 1964, JD, 1967; LLM in Taxation, Washington U., St. Louis, 1968. Bar: Ga. 1967, U.S. Dist. Ct. (so. dist.) Ga. 1970, U.S. Ct. Appeals (5th and 11th cirs.) 1976, U.S. Tax Ct. Assoc. Bouhan, Williams & Levy, Savannah, Ga., 1970-73; ptnr. Brannen, Searcy & Smith, 1973—. Chmn. bd. dirs. Citizens Bank, Cairo, Ga., 1993—; sec. Am. Fed. Savs. and Loan Assn., 1978-81; mem. adv. bd. Liberty Svgs. Bank, 1984-88. Pres. Chatham-Savannah Voluntary Action Ctr., Inc., 1978-80. Served to brig. Ga. ANG, 1967—. Mem. ABA (sec. spl. liaison tax com. S.E. region 1983-84, chmn. 1984-85), State Bar Ga. (chmn. sect. taxation 1983-84, mem.-at-large exec. coun. Young Lawyers sect. 1975-78, chmn. conf. with Ga. Soc. CPA's 1979-81, Ga. commn. on continuing lawyer competency 1989-95, vice chmn. 1995), Savannah Bar Assn. (pres. Younger Lawyers sect. 1975-76), Am. Judicature Soc., Savannah Estate Planning Coun., Inst. Continuity Legal End., Rotary, Oglethorpe Club, Savannah Golf Club, Georgian Club. Banking, General corporate, Estate planning. Office: PO Box 8002 Savannah GA 31412-8002

SEARS, ALAN EDWARD, lawyer; b. Chattanooga, Oct. 31, 1951; s. Edward Lee and Anna Maria (Shepperd) S.; m. Paula Scott Lebeau, Nov. 11, 1988; children: Kelley, Shelby, Anna Marie, Rebecca, Isaiah, Isabella. BA, U. Ky., 1974; JD, U. Louisville, 1977. Bar: Ky. 1977, U.S. Supreme Ct. 1980, Ariz. 1987, D.C. 1989, Calif. 1990, U.S. Dist. Ct. (we. and ea. dists.) Ky., U.S. Dist. Ct. Ariz., U.S. Dist. Ct. D.C., U.S. Ct. Appeals (D.C., 4th, 5th, 6th, 7th, 9th, 11th and D.C. cirs.), U.S. Tax Ct., U.S. Dist. Ct. (ctrl. & so. dists.) Calif. Asst. corp. counsel City of Ashland, Ky., 1977-78; assoc. Johnson, Dunnagan & Martin, Ashland, 1977-79, Amshoff & Amshoff, Louisville, 1979-81; chief criminal div., asst. U.S. atty. U.S. Dept. Justice, 1981-85, exec. dir. atty. gens. commn. on pornography Washington, 1985-86; assoc. solicitor U.S. Dept. Interior, 1986-87; exec. dir. Children's Legal Found., Phoenix, 1987-90; assoc. Snell & Wilmer, 1990; exec. dir., gen. counsel Nat. Family Legal Found., 1990-91; asst. U.S. atty. U.S. Dept. Justice, 1991-93; pres., gen. counsel Alliance Def. Fund, 1993—. Cons. and pub. speaker to numerous organizations. Co-author: Time, Place & Manner Regulation, 1989, Prosecution & Trial of Obscenity Case, 1988; contbr. chpts. to books. Bd. dirs. Ariz. Family Rsch. Inst. Phoenix, 1988-92, Lincoln Caucus Ednl. Corp., Phoenix, 1990—, Nat. Family Legal Found., Phoenix, 1991—; precinct capt. Rep. Party, 1979-81, legis. dist. chmn., 1980-81; mem. campaign staff Gov. Louie Nunn, 1979, and Senator Cook for U.S. Senate, 1974, other party activities. Mem. ABA, Ariz. Lawyers Div. Federalist Soc. (dir. 1988—), Calif. Bar Assn., Ariz. Bar Assn., Ky. Bar Assn., D.C. Bar Assn. Constitutional. Office: Alliance Def Fund 8960 E Raintree Dr #300 Scottsdale AZ 85260

SEARS, JOHN WINTHROP, lawyer; b. Boston, Dec. 18, 1930; s. Richard Dudley and Frederica Fulton (Leser) S.; m. Catherine Coolidge, 1965 (div. 1970). AB magna cum laude, Harvard U., 1952, JD, 1959; MLitt, Oxford U., 1957. Bar: Mass. 1959, U.S. Dist. Ct. Mass. 1982. Rep. Brown Bros. Harriman, N.Y.C., 1959-63, Boston, 1963-66; mem. Mass. Ho. Reps., 1965-68; sheriff Suffolk County, Mass., 1968-69; chmn. Boston Fin. Commn., 1969-70, Met. Dist. Commn., 1970-75; councilor-at-large Boston City Coun., 1980-82; trustee Sears Office, Boston, 1975—. Contbr. articles to profl. jours. Apptd. bd. dirs. Fulbright Scholarship, 1991-93; trustee Christ's Ch., Longwood, Brookline, Mass., 1965—, Sears Trusts, Boston, 1975—; hon. trustee J. F. Kennedy Libr., 1991—; bd. dirs. Am. Mus. Textile Heritage, 1987-97, Shirley-Eustis Assoc., Environ. League, Mass., 1994-97; Rep. candidate Sec. State, Mass., 1978, Gov. of Mass., 1982; vice chmn. Ward 5 Rep. Com., 1965-69, 75-85; chmn. Rep. State Com., 1975-76, mem., 1980-85; del. Rep. Nat. Conv., 1968, 76, State Conv., 1966-92; mem. U.S. Electoral Coll., 1984; bd. dirs. United South End Settlements, 1966—, chmn., 1977-78. Lt. comdr. USNR, 1952-54, 61-62. Recipient Outstanding Pub. Servant award Mass. Legis. Assn., 1975; Rhodes scholar, 1955 Mem. Mass. Bar Assn., New Eng. Hist. and Geneal. Soc. (bd. dirs., councillor 1977-82), Mass. Hist. Soc., Handel and Haydn Soc. (gov. 1982-87), Signet Soc., Boston Atheneum, Tennis and Racquet Club, Somerset Club, The Country Club (Brookline), St. Botolph Club, Wednesday Evening Club of 1777, Thursday Evening Club of 1846 (pres. 1999), Spee Club (Cambridge chpt., pres., trustee), Phi Beta Kappa. Republican. Home: 7 Acorn St Boston MA 02108-3501

SEARS, KELLEY DEAN, lawyer; b. Milan, Mo., July 27, 1946; s. Floyd and Vera Colleen (Kelley) S.; m. Marsha Ann Baxter, May 30, 1970; 1 child, Connor Jay. B.S. in Acctg., U. Kans., 1969, J.D., 1974. Bar: Mo. 1974, U.S. Dist. Ct. (we. dist.) Mo. 1974, U.S. Ct. Appeals (8th cir.) 1974. Assoc. Smith, Gill, Fisher & Butts, Kansas City, Mo., 1974-79, Stubbs & Mann, Kansas City, 1979-82; ptnr. Cooling, Herbers & Sears, Kansas City, 1982— ; instr. U. Mo.-Kansas City, 1981-83. Served with U.S. Army, 1969-71, Vietnam. Mem. ABA, Kansas City Bar Assn., Lawyer Assn. Kansas City. Republican. Methodist. State civil litigation, General practice, Labor. Home: 221 NW Shagbark St Lees Summit MO 64064-1445 Office: 2400 City Ctr Sq 1100 Main PO Box 26770 Kansas City MO 64196-6770

SEAVER, JEFFREY MARK, SR. lawyer; b. Hartford, Conn., Feb. 4, 1960; s. Herbert Lawrence and Mary Muriel S.; m. Brenda Colette Seaver, June 23, 1983; children: Arielle, Lunden, Jared. B in Gen. Studies, La. Tech. U., 1988; JD, So. Univ. Law Ctr., Baton Rouge, 1997. Bar: La. 1997. With USAF, 1977-89, advanced through grades to tech. sgt., 1987, inflight refueling technician La., 1977-89; dir. tng. FDIC, Washington, 1990-94; mng. ptnr. Seaver Law Firm, Baton Rouge, 1997—. Bd. dirs. Krewe of Orion, Baton Rouge. Author: Career Transition and Placement Training Manual, 1994. Recipient pro-bono award Baton Rouge Bar Assn., 1998. Mem. ABA, Assn. Trial Lawyers Am., La. Trial Lawyers Assn., La. State Bar, Baton Rouge Bar, Baton Rouge C. of C. Republican. Roman Catholic. Avocations: hunting, fishing. Home: 10919 Major Oaks Dr Baton Rouge LA 70815-5445 Office: Seaver Law Firm LLC 2833 Brakley Dr Ste A Baton Rouge LA 70816-2329 E-mail: jeffseaver@seaverlawfirm.com

SEAVER, ROBERT LESLIE, retired law educator; b. Brockton, Mass., June 13, 1937; s. Russell Bradford and Lois (Marchant) S.; m. Marjorie V. Rote, Aug. 21, 1960 (div. 1974); children: Kimberly, Eric, Kristen; m. Elizabeth A. Horwitz, May 22, 1984. AB cum laude, Tufts U., Medford, Mass., 1958; JD, U. Chgo., 1964. Bar: Ohio 1964, U.S. Ct. Appeals (6th cir.) 1964, U.S. Dist. Ct. (so. dist.) Ohio 1965. Assoc. Taft, Stettinius and Hollister, Cin., 1964-66; v.p., sec., gen. counsel IDI Mgmt. Inc., 1966-74; pvt. practice, 1974-75; prof. law emeritus No. Ky. U. Salmon P. Chase Coll. Law, Highland Heights, 1975—; of counsel Cors & Bassett, Cin., 1993-99; ret., 1999. Cons. in field, 1975—. Author/editor: Ohio Corporation Law, 1988; contbr. chpts. to books. Advisor subcom. on pvt. corps of Ky. Commn. on Constl. Rev., 1987. With USMC, 1958-61. Recipient Justice Robert O. Lukowsky award of Excellence Chase Law Sch. Student Bar Assn., 1986. Mem. Ohio Bar Assn. Republican. Unitarian. Avocations: duplicate bridge (life master), history. Home: 826 Woodscene Ct Cincinnati OH 45230-4334 Office: Northern Kentucky U Salmon Chase Coll Law Highland Heights KY 41099 E-mail: rseaver@cinci.rr.com

SEAWELL, DONALD RAY, lawyer, publisher, arts center executive, producer; b. Jonesboro, N.C., Aug. 1, 1912; s. A.A.F. and Bertha (Smith) S.; m. Eugenia Rawls, Apr. 5, 1941; children: Brook Ashley, Donald Brockman. AB, U. N.C., 1933, JD, 1936, DLitt, 1980; LHD, U. No. Colo., 1978. Bar: N.C. 1936, N.Y. 1947. With SEC, 1939-41, 45-47, Dept. Justice, 1942-43; chmn. bd., dir., pub., pres. Denver Post, 1966-81; chmn. bd., dir. Gravure West, L.A., 1966-81; dir. Swan Prodns., London; of counsel firm Bernstein, Seawell, Kove & Maltin, N.Y.C., 1979—; chmn. bd., chief exec. officer Denver Ctr. for Performing Arts, 1972—. Ptnr. Bonfils-Seawell Enterprises, N.Y.C.; bd. vis. U. N.C. Chmn. bd. ANTA, 1965—; mem. theatre panel Nat. Coun. Arts, 1970-74; bd. govs. Royal Shakespeare Theatre, Eng.; trustee Am. Acad. Dramatic Arts, 1967—, Hofstra U., 1968-69, Cen. City Opera Assn., Denver Symphony; bd. dirs., chmn. exec. com. 0ir Force Acad. Found., Nat. Ints. Outdoor Drama, Walter Hampden Meml. Library, Hammond Mus.; pres. Helen G. Bonfils Found., 1972-97, pres. emeritus, 1997—, chmn. fin. com., 1997—, Denver Opera Found., 1997—; dir. Found. for Denver Ctr. for Performing Arts, Population Crisis Com., pres. 1982-91; bd. dirs. Family Health Internat., Found. for Internat. Family Health; bd. visitors N.C. Sch. Arts, 1992-98; pres. Frederick G. Bonfils Found., 1972-92; chmn. Civilian Mil. Inst. Recipient Am. Acad. Achievement award, 1980, Tony award for producing On Your Toes, 1983, Voice Rsch. and Awareness award Voice Found., 1983, Arts and Entertainment Cable Network award, 1987, Third Millenium Leadership award Am. Diabetes Assn., 1996, Colo. Tourism Hall of Fame award, 1999, Thomas Degaetani award U.S. Inst. for Theatre Tech., 2000, Benjamin F. Stapleton, Jr. award, 2000, Mayor's Millennium award, 2000, Downtown Denver award for Tantalus, 2001. Mem. Bucks Club (London), Dutch Treat Club (N.Y.C.), Denver Country Club, Denver Club, Cherry Hills Country Club, Mile High Club (Denver), Garden of Gods Club (Colorado Springs, Colo.). Office: Denver Ctr for Performing Arts 1050 13th St Denver CO 80204-2157 E-mail: geary@dcpa.org

SEAY, J. DAVID, lawyer, educator; b. Frederick, Okla., Jan. 31, 1951; s. Joe Dwight and Ruth Roselle (Dulany) S.; m. Anita Busby Dec. 22, 1971. B.A., Oklahoma City U., 1973; J.D., Cath. U. Am., 1977. Bar: Mass. 1977, N.Y. 1982. Mem. policy staff Cost of Living Council, Washington, 1973-74; staff exec. John Hancock Life Ins. Co., Boston, 1977-79; sec., counsel United Hosp. Fund, N.Y.C., from 1979, v.p., 1985— ; adj. faculty Benjamin Cardozo Law Sch., N.Y.C., 1984, New Sch. Univ., 1987—, N.Y. Med. Coll., 1991—; bd. dirs. N.Y. Bus. Group on Health, 1984, N.Y. Nonprofit Coordinating Com., 1986, Profl. Exam. Svc., Forum for Health Planning, Inst. for Cmty. Living, Nat. Ctr. on Philanthropy and Law. Wooten scholar, 1969; Columbus Sch. Law scholar, 1974. Fellow N.Y. Acad. Medicine; mem. N.Y. State Bar Assn., Mass. Bar Assn., Am. Health Lawyers Assn., Am. Acad. Law and Medicine, N.Y. Acad. Medicine, University Club. Democrat. General corporate, Health. Home: PO Box 245 North Chatham NY 12132-0245 Office: United Hosp Fund Empire State Bldg 350 5th Ave Lowr 23 New York NY 10118-0110

SEBASTIAN, ARI-BEN CALLEJA, lawyer; b. Manila, The Philippines, Feb. 23, 1961; s. Florante Santos and Celia (Calleja) S.; m. Pilar Juliana Schramm Cayetano, July 14, 1994; children: Maxine Selina, Nadine Sandra, Gabriel C. AB, U. Philippines, 1982, LLB, 1986. Bar: The Philippines 1987. Confidential assoc. Office Justice, Pronove, The Philippines, 1986-87; assoc. Siguion Reyna Montecillo & Ongsiako, The Philippines, 1987-95; mng. ptnr. Cayetano Sebastian Ata Dado & Cruz, Manila, The Philippines, 1995—. Bd. dirs. Bases Conversion Devel. Authority, sec., 1998-99, Elcom Internat. Resources Inc., sec., 1999—.asst. gen. counsel Ayala Alabang Country Club, The Philippines, 1996-98. Office: Caytano Sebastian Dado Cruz Fl 12 116 Tordesillas St Manila The Philippines

SEBRIS, ROBERT, JR. lawyer; b. N.Y.C., May 20, 1950; s. Robert and Ruth (Kagis) S.; m. S. Lawson Hollweg, Sept. 8, 1973; children: Jared Matthew, Bryan Taylor. BS in Indsl. Labor Rels., Cornell U., 1972; JD, George Washington U., 1978. Bar: D.C. 1978, Wash. 1980. Labor rels. specialist Onondaya County Office labor rels., Syracuse, N.Y., 1973-74, U.S. Dept. Labor, Washington, 1972-75; labor rels. mgr. U.S. Treasury Dept., 1975-78; employee rels. mgr., 1978-80; assoc. Davis, Wright, Todd, Riese & Jones, Seattle, 1980-84; ptnr. Davis, Wright, Tremain, Bellevue, Wash., 1985-92, Sebris Busto, P.S., Bellvue, 1992—. Expert witness T.E.A.M. Act Amendments NLRA U.S. Senate hearing, 1997. Co-Author: Employer's Guide to Strike Planning, 1985; contbr. articles to profl. jours. Mem. Bellevue C.C. Found., 1988-95, pres., 1995-96; chair employment law cert. program U. Wash. Law Sch., 1996-97. Mem. ABA (health law forum, labor and employment law sect., com. on employee rights), Wash. Bar Assn., D.C. Bar Assn., Seattle/King County Bar Assn. (chmn. labor law sect. 1991-92), Pacific Coast Labor Law Conf. (planning com. 1980-93, chmn. 1991-92), Am. Health Lawyers Assn., Soc. Human Resource Mgmt. Avocations: golf, soccer, coaching youth sports. Alternative dispute resolution, Labor. Home: 16301 Mink Rd NE Woodinville WA 98072-9463 Office: Sebris Busto PS Ste 325 14205 SE 36th St Bellevue WA 98006 E-mail: rsebris@sebrisbusto.com

SECHRIEST, MARY PAULINE, lawyer; b. Durham, N.C., Sept. 2, 1951; d. Stuart Wilson and Carolyn Frazier (Tuck) S. BA, U. N.C., 1973, JD, 1976. Bar: N.C. 1976. Assoc. William E. Butner, Hickory, N.C., 1977-79; asst. to vice chancellor for adminstrn. U. N.C., Chapel Hill, 1979-80, legal adviser to the spl. asst. to chancellor, 1980-88, assoc. univ. counsel, 1988—. Mem. ABA, N.C. State Bar, N.C. Bar Assn. (edn. law sect. coun. 1989-92), Orange County Bar Assn., Phi Beta Kappa. Democrat. Episcopalian. Avocations: needlework, music, writing. Home: 2701 Homestead Rd Apt 1015 Chapel Hill NC 27516-8758 Office: U NC C B 9150 Chapel Hill NC 27599-9150

SECOLA, JOSEPH PAUL, lawyer; b. Hartford, Conn., May 18, 1959; s. Pasquale Anthony and Anna Maria; m. Mary Alice Ipavich, June 20, 1982; children: Peter, Sharon, Mary Joy, Timothy, Paul, Andrew. BA in History, Fairfield U., 1981; JD, Oral Robert U., 1984. Bar: Conn. 1984, N.Y. 1985, U.S. Dist. Ct. Conn. 1985, Va. 1986, U.S. Dist. Ct. (so. dist.) N.Y. 1988, U.S. Ct. Appeals (2d cir.) 1989, U.S. Supreme Ct. 1990, U.S. Dist. Ct. (we. dist.) N.Y. 1996. Pvt. practice, Brookfield, Conn., 1984—. Mem. bd. edn. City of Milford, Conn., 1989-90, Greater Danbury (Conn.) Cath. Elem. Schs., 1992-96 Mem. Nat. Employment Lawyers Assn., Am. Trial Lawyers Assn., Conn. Trial Lawyers Assn., Conn. Bar Assn., Conn. Employment Lawyers Assn., Litchfield County Bar Assn., Greater Danbury Bar Assn. Republican. Roman Catholic. Avocations: sports, N.Y. Yankees. Appellate, General civil litigation, Personal injury. Office: Ste 500 67 Federal Rd Bldg A Brookfield CT 06804-2538 Fax: (203) 740-2355. E-mail: jpsecolalaw@aol.com

SEE, HAROLD FREND, judge, law educator; b. Chgo., Nov. 7, 1943; s. Harold Frend and Corinne Louise (Rachau) S.; m. Brenda Jane Childs, Dec. 2, 1978; children: Callie Suzanne, Garrett Brittain; children by previous marriage: Mary Elisabeth, Eric Palmer. Student, U. Chgo., 1962-63; BA, Emporia State U., 1966; MS, Iowa State U., 1969; JD, U. Iowa, 1973. Bar: Ill. 1973, U.S. Dist. Ct. (no. dist.) Ill. 1973, Ala. 1981, U.S. Ct. Appeals (fed. cir.) 1991; U.S. Supreme Ct. Instr. econs. Iowa State U., Ames, 1967-69; asst. prof. econs. Ill. State U., Normal, 1969-70; assoc. Sidley & Austin, Chgo., 1973-76; assoc. prof. law U. Ala., Tuscaloosa, 1976-78, prof., 1978-97; justice Supreme Ct. Ala., 1997—. Contbr. to books, also articles and book reviews. Mem. ABA, Ala. Bar Assn., Am. Econ. Assn., Am. Law and Econs. Assn., Soc. Profls. in Dispute Resolution, Am. Law Inst., Ala. Law Inst. Baptist. Office: Supreme Ct Ala 300 Dexter Ave Montgomery AL 36104-3741

SEEGAL, JOHN FRANKLIN, lawyer; b. Newton, Mass., May 21, 1946; s. Samuel Melbourne and Martha (Lewenberg) S.; m. Barbara Ellen Wayne, Apr. 2, 1982; children: Sarah Rachel, Laura Rose. BA, Harvard U., MBA, JD, Harvard U., 1973. Assoc. Orrick, Herrington & Sutcliffe, LLP, San Francisco, 1973-78, ptnr., 1979—. Co-chmn. Inst. on Securities Regulation, 2001—. Mem. ABA, Calif. Bar Assn. Republican. Jewish. General corporate, Securities. Office: Orrick Herrington & Sutcliffe LLP 400 Sansome St San Francisco CA 94111-3143

SEEGER, EDWIN HOWARD, lawyer; b. N.Y.C., Aug. 6, 1930; s. Harold E. and Anne (Galves) S.; m. Frances Cheatham, Mar. 26, 1956; 1 child, Elizabeth Francesca. BA, Johns Hopkins U., 1951, MA, 1953; JD, George Washington U., 1956. Bar: D.C. 1956. Assoc. firm Covington & Burling, Washington, 1956-61; asst. adminstr., gen. counsel Nat. Capital Transp. Agy., Washington, 1961-64; mng. ptnr. Prather Seeger Doolittle & Farmer, Washington, 1964-94; mng. ptnr. Vedder, Price, Kaufman, Kannholz, Day, Washington, 1994-96, Seeger, Potter, Richardson, Luxton, Joselon & Brooks, 1996—. Mem. ABA, Fed. Bar Assn. Clubs: Metropolitan, University (Washington). General corporate, Environmental, Foreign trade. Home: 213 S Fairfax St Alexandria VA 22314-3303 Office: Seeger Potter Richardson Luxton Joselow & Brooks 2121 K St NW Washington DC 20037-1801

SEGALL, JAMES ARNOLD, lawyer; b. Columbus, Ohio, Aug. 19, 1956; s. Arthur and Greta Helene (Cohen) S.; m. Janice Faye Wiesen, Mar. 14, 1981; children: Gayle Helene, Aryn Michelle, Craig Lawrence. BA, Coll. of William and Mary, 1978; JD, Washington and Lee U., 1981. Bar: Va. 1981, U.S. Dist. Ct. (ea. dist.) Va. 1981. Assoc. Phelps & King P.C., Newport News, Va., 1981-84, Buxton & Lasris P.C., Yorktown, 1984-85; sole practice Newport News, 1985-89; pres. James A. Segall & Assocs., 1990-91, James A. Segall & Assocs., P.C., 1991-92, Segall & Moody, Newport News, 1992-98; ptnr. Krinick, Segall, Moody & Lewis, Va., 1998-2000, Krinick, Segall, Moody, Lewis & Allen, Newport News, 2001—. Lectr. Hampton Roads Regional Acad. Criminal Justice, 1986-89. Bd. dirs. ct.-apptd. Spl. Adv. Program, Newport News, 1986-87, Hamton-Newport News Cmty. Svcs. Bd., 1993—, treas., 1995-96, 99—, vice-chair, 1996-97, chair 1997-99; participant coop. office edn. program Newport News Pub. Schs., 1987-90; lectr. vol. programs 7th Dist. Ct. Svc. Unit, 1986-89; active City Newport News Adv. TV Commn., 1990-93, Newport News Dem. City Com., 1990-91; bd. dirs. Rodef Sholom Temple, 1992-94, United Jewish Comty., the Va. Peninsula, Inc., 1990—, chmn. spl. activities and fundraising com., 1990-91, chmn. bylaws com., 1992-93, 95—, campaign coun., 1995—, cmty. rels. coun., 1995-98, v.p. human svcs., 1998-2000, sunday school teacher, Rodef Sholom Temple, 2001-. Mem. Newport News Bar Assn., Va. Trial Lawyers Assn., Va. Coll. Criminal Def., B'nai B'rith (pres. 1989-91), Ruritan (sec. 1985-87), Moose. Avocations: computers, history, philosophy. General corporate, Family and matrimonial, Personal injury. Home: 306 Dogwood Dr Newport News VA 23606-3728 Office: Krinick Segall Moody Lewis & Allen 525 Oyster Point Rd Newport News VA 23602-6014

SEGALLA, THOMAS FRANCIS, lawyer; b. Lee, Mass., Apr. 7, 1943; s. Stanley John and Ann (Finnegan) S.; m. Mary Louise, May 7, 1967. BBA cum laude, U. Miami, Coral Gables, Fla., 1965; JD cum laude, SUNY-Buffalo, 1972. Bar: N.Y. 1973, U.S. Dist. Ct. (we.dist.) N.Y. 1973, U.S. Supreme Ct. 1983. Prodn. mgr. UniRoyal Inc., Naugatuck, Conn., 1966-69; law asst. N.Y. Atty. Gen., Buffalo, 1971; ptnr. Saperston & Day, PC, 1972-2001, Goldberg Segalla, Buffalo, 2001—. Lectr. Erie C.C., Buffalo, 1970-73, Ins. Agts., Syracuse, N.Y., 1971— , Bryant & Stratton Inst., Buffalo, 1975; assoc. prof. SUNY, 1985—. Editor SUNY Buffalo Law Rev., 1971-72. Mem. Shea's Buffalo, 1983. Mem. ABA, Def. Rsch. Inst., Erie County Bar Assn. Internat. Platform Assn., Fed. Insurance and Corp. Counsel, Internat. Bar ASsn., Internat. Assn. Def. Counsel, Kappa Sigma (pres. Miami 1964-65). Roman Catholic. Federal civil litigation, State civil litigation, Insurance. Home: 25 Westfield Rd Buffalo NY 14226-3492 Office: Goldberg Segalla 120 Delaware Ave Buffalo NY 14202-1486

SEGEL, KAREN LYNN JOSEPH, lawyer, taxation specialist; b. Youngstown, Ohio, Jan. 15, 1947; d. Samuel Dennis and Helen Anita Joseph; m. Alvin Gerald Segel, June 9, 1968 (div. Sept. 1976); 1 child, Adam James. BA in Soviet and East European Studies, Boston U., 1968; JD, Southwestern U., 1975. Bar: Calif., 1996, U.S. Tax Ct., 1996, U.S. Dist. Ct. (cen. dist.) Calif., 1996, U.S. Ct. Appeals (9th cir.), 1997. Adminstrv. asst. Olds Brunel & Co., N.Y.C., 1968-69, U.S. Banknote Corp., N.Y.C., 1969-70; tax acct. S.N. Chilkov & Co. CPA's, Beverly Hills, Calif., 1971-74; intern Calif. Corps. Commr., 1975; tax. sr. Oppenheim Appel & Dixon CPA's, L.A., 1978, Fox, Westheimer & Co. CPA's, L.A., 1978, Zebrak, Levine & Mepos CPA's, L.A., 1979; ind. cons. acctg., taxation specialist Beverly Hills, 1980—. Settlement officer L.A. County Superior Ct., 2000; law student mentor Southwestern U., 1996-2000, tax moot ct. judge, 1997; settlement officer Beverly Hills Mcpl. Ct. Editorial adv. bd. Am. Biog. Inst. High sch. amb. to Europe People-to-People Orgn., 1963. Mem. Calif. State Bar, Women's Inner Circle of Achievement, Complex Litig. Inns of Ct., L.A. County Bar Assn, Beverly Hills Tinseltown Rose Soc. Avocations: collecting seashells, lhasa apso dog breeding, art, travel, music. E-mail: kjslaw@earthlink.net

SEGLUND, BRUCE RICHARD, lawyer; b. Lansing, Mich., June 3, 1950; s. Richard Oswald and Josephine Ann (Kraus) S.; m. Connie Sue Roberts, June 19, 1970; children: Jennifer Lynne, Nicole Marie. BS, Mich. State U., 1973; JD, Thomas M. Cooley Law Sch., 1979. Bar: Mich. 1981, U.S. DIst. Ct. (ea. dist.) Mich. 1981. Assoc. Michael W. Reeds, P.C., Walled Lake, Mich., 1981-82; sole practice, 1982-85; ptnr. Mick and Seglund, 1985-89, Connelly, Crowley, Groth and Seglund, Walled Lake, 1989—. Mem. Mich. Bar Assn. (mem. character and fitness com. dist. J 1988-2000), Oakland County Bar Assn. (lectr. 1984), Mich. Jaycees (pres. Walled Lake 1982-83, execllence award 1982-83, pres. of yr. 1982-83), Walled Lake C. of C. (bd. dirs. scholarship fund 1985-88). Roman Catholic. Lodge: KC (adv. 1982-94). General corporate, Labor, Municipal (including bonds). Home: 8618 Buffalo Dr Commerce Township MI 48382-3408 Office: Connelly Crowley Groth & Seglund 2410 S Commerce Rd Walled Lake MI 48390-2129 E-mail: ccgs@ismi.net

SEIBEL, ROBERT FRANKLIN, law educator; b. N.Y.C., Sept. 26, 1946; s. Sam and Blanche (Marcus) S.; m. Kathleen M. Costello, June 9, 1974. AB, Bowdoin Coll., 1968; JD, Northeastern U., 1971. Bar: Mass. 1971, Ill. 1979, U.S. Dist. Ct. (no. dist.) Ill. 1979, Iowa 1980, U.S. Dist. Ct. (so. dist.) Iowa 1980, Maine 1981, U.S. Dist. Ct. Maine 1981, N.Y. 1989. Assoc. Ropes & Gray, Boston, 1971-79; clin. prof. law Chgo. Kent Coll. Law, 1979-80; assoc. prof., exec. dir. clinic Drake Law Sch., Des Moines, 1980-81; assoc. prof. law U. Maine, Portland, 1981-85; vis. lectr. law Cornell U., Ithaca, N.Y., 1986-87, sr. lectr., 1986—, assoc. dir. clinic, 1986-89; bd. dirs. Legal Svcs. of Iowa, 1980-81, Polk County Legal Aid, Des Moines, 1980-81; cons. Home Equity Conv. Task Force, Maine, 1983-84, Maine Bar Legal Aid Commn., 1983-84; bd dirs. Community Dispute Resolution Ctr., Ithaca, N.Y., 1986—, Cornell Ctr. for Religion, Ethics and Social Policy, 1988-90; bd. dirs. Clin. Legal Edn. Assn., 1992—. Office: Cornell U Legal Aid Clinc Myron Taylor Hall Ithaca NY 14853

SEIDEL, ARTHUR HARRIS, lawyer; b. N.Y.C., May 25, 1923; s. Philip and Pearl (Geller) S.; m. Raquel Eliovich, Aug. 21, 1949; children: Stephen A., Paul B., Mary Beth Sharp. B.S., CCNY, 1942; A.M., U. Mich., 1943; J.D. with honors, George Washington U., 1949. Bar: D.C. 1949, Pa. 1956, N.Y. 1957. Atty. patent dept. Gulf Oil Corp., Washington and Pitts., 1947-52; individual practice law, 1952-64; sr. ptnr. firm Seidel & Gonda, 1964-68, Seidel, Gonda & Goldhammer (P.C.), Phila., 1968-72, pres., 1972-84, Seidel, Gonda, Goldhammer & Abbott, P.C., Phila., 1984-88, Seidel, Gonda, Lavorgna & Monaco, Phila., 1988-2001; of counsel Drinker, Biddle & Reath, 2001—. Lectr. in Intellectual Property Temple U. Law Sch., 1973-86, Am. Law Inst. Editor: George Washington Law Rev, 1949; author: (with others) Trademark Practice, 2 vols, 1963, Monographs on Patent Law and Practice, 5th edit, 1993, Trademarks and Copyrights, 6th edit., 1992, Trade Secrets and Employment Agreements 3d edit, 1995; also articles. Mem. Adv. Com. for Restatement of Law of Unfair Competition. Mem. ABA, Am. Law Inst., Pa. Bar Assn., Phila. Bar Assn., Am. Intellectual Property Law Assn., Phila. Intellectual Property Law Assn., Order of Coif. Patent, Trademark and copyright. Home: 904 Centennial Rd Narberth PA 19072-1408 Office: Drinker Biddle & Reath LLP One Logan Sq Philadelphia PA 19103 E-mail: seidelah@dbr.com

SEIDEL, RICHARD STEPHEN, lawyer; b. Phila., Jan. 3, 1965; s. Gary Leonard and Judith Lee Seidel; m. Jodi Helene Woodin, May 14, 1992; children: Hallie Alexa, Jamie Morgan. BA in Criminal Justice cum laude, Temple U., 1986, JD cum laude, 1989. Bar: N.J. 1989, Pa. 1989, U.S. Dist. Ct. (ea. dist.) Pa. 1989, U.S. Ct. Appeals (3rd cir.) 1990. Assoc. Mesirov, Gelman, Jaffe, Cramer & Jamieson, Phila., 1989-94, Daniels, Saltz, Mongoluzzi & Barrett, Phila., 1994-96, Bernstein, Silver & Agins, Phila., 1996-98; ptnr. Agins, Haaz & Seidel, LLP, 1998—. Presenter in field. Contbr. articles to profl. jours. Fellow Acad. Advocacy Temple U. Sch. Law, Phila., 1997. Mem. ABA, ATLA (student trial advocacy competition judge), Phila. Trial Lawyers Assn. (bd. dirs. 1997—, bar elections com., young lawyers com., Musmanno com.), Pa. Bar Assn., Phila. Bar Assn. (state civil com., state civil sub-com. on the Phila. discovery ct., state civil sub-com. on ABA civil trial practice stds., state civil mentoring program, medico-legal com., young lawyers divsn. H.S. mock trial competition, young lawyers divsn. law firm liaison, legal line vol.), Phila. Bar Found. Avocations: golf, music, sports. Personal injury, Product liability, Professional liability. Office: Agins Haaz & Seidel LLP 1604 Locust St Fl 3 Philadelphia PA 19103-6305

SEIDEL, SELVYN, lawyer, educator; b. Long Branch, N.J., Nov. 6, 1942; s. Abraham and Anita (Stoller) S.; m. Deborah Lew, June 21, 1970; 1 child, Emily. BA, U. Chgo., 1964; JD, U. Calif., Berkeley, 1967; diploma in law, Oxford U., 1968. Bar: N.Y. 1970, D.C. Ct. Appeals 1982. Ptnr. Latham & Watkins, N.Y.C., 1984—. Adj. prof. Sch. Law, NYU, 1974-85; instr. Practicing Law Inst., 1980-81, 84. Contbr. articles to profl. jours. Bd. dirs. Citizen Scholarship Fund Am., 1995—. Mem. ABA, N.Y. County Bar Assn., N.Y.C. Bar Assn. (mem. fed. cts. com. 1982-85, internat. law com. 1989-92, 95-96, art law com. 1997-2000), Boalt Hall Alumni Assn. (bd. dirs. 1980-82). Federal civil litigation, Private international. Office: Latham & Watkins 885 3rd Ave Fl 9 New York NY 10022-4834 E-mail: selvyn.seidel@lw.com

SEIDEN, ANDY, lawyer; b. N.Y.C., Sept. 16, 1956; s. Stanley and Dorothy Rose. BS in Indsl. and Labor Rels., Cornell U., 1978; vis. student, Harvard Law Sch., 1980-81; JD, U. Calif., Berkeley, 1981. Bar: Calif. 1981, N.Y. 1993. Assoc. Donovan Leisure Newton & Irvine, L.A., 1981-85, Curtis Mallet-Prevost Colt & Mosle, N.Y.C., 1987-89, Pettit & Martin, San Francisco, 1989-91; pvt. practice, 1991-93; ptnr. Whitehead & Porter, 1993-95; v.p. bus. devel. and bus. affairs, gen. counsel Big Top Prodns., 1995-96; v.p. bus. and legal affairs Walt Disney Feature Animation, Burbank, Calif., 1997-98; pres. Leapfrog Cyberspace Navigators, L.A., 1998-2000; of counsel Loeb & Loeb, 2000—. Bd. dirs. L.A. League of Conservation Voters, L.A., 1983-85. Mem. ABA (com. on negotiated acquisitions 1994-96), Phi Kappa Phi. Democrat. Avocations: world travel, skiing, cultural anthropology. Contracts commercial, Entertainment, Intellectual property. Office: Ste 2200 10100 Santa Monica Blvd Los Angeles CA 90067

SEIDEN, STEVEN JAY, lawyer; b. N.Y.C., June 21, 1960; s. Martin S. and Rita (Glazer) S.; m. Kathryn LaRussa, Sept. 30, 1984; children: Robert B., Daniel M., Michael J. BA, SUNY, Oneonta, 1981; JD, Hofstra U., 1984. Bar: N.Y. 1985, U.S. Dist. Ct. (ea. and so. dists.) N.Y. 1985, U.S. Supreme Ct. 1995, U.S. Ct. Appeals (fed. cir.) 1995, U.S. Ct. Fed. Claims 1995, U.S. Ct. Appeals for the Armed Forces, 1995. Assoc. Shapiro, Baines,Saasto & Shainwald, Mineola, N.Y., 1984-88; ptnr. Seiden & Kaufman, Carle Place, 1988-93, 95—, Seiden, Kaufman, & Bosek, Carle Place, 1993-95. Mem. ABA, N.Y. State Bar Assn., N.Y. State Trial Lawyers Assn., Assn. Trial Lawyers Am., Nassau County Bar Assn., L.I. Trial Lawyers Assn. (bd. dirs.), Civil Justice Found. (founding sponsor). Jewish. Personal injury. Office: Seiden & Kaufman 1 Old Country Rd Ste 114 Carle Place NY 11514-1821

SEIDENWURM, RICHARD LEWIS, lawyer; b. N.Y.C., Feb. 1, 1941; s. Jesse and Lillian (Epstein) S.; m. Carol Ann Wender, Aug. 14, 1965; children: Amy, Robert. BA, Williams Coll., 1962; JD, Columbia U., 1965. Bar: N.Y. 1966, Calif. 1973, U.S. Dist. Ct. (so. and ea. dists.) N.Y. 1966, U.S. Dist. Ct. (so. dist.) Calif. 1973. Assoc. counsel OEO, Washington, 1965-66; assoc. Davis Polk & Wardwell, N.Y.C., 1966-72; ptnr. Solomon, Ward, Seidenwurm & Smith and predecessor firms, San Diego, 1973—. Mem. State Bar Calif. (lectr. continuing edn. divsn. 1980, 83, 85). Home: 4597 Vista De La Patria Del Mar CA 92014-4151 Office: Solomon Ward Seidenwurm & Smith 401 B St Ste 1200 San Diego CA 92101-4295 E-mail: rseidenwurm@swsslaw.com

SEIDLER, B(ERNARD) ALAN, lawyer; b. N.Y.C., Nov. 26, 1946; s. Aaron H. and Ethel T. (Berkowitz) S.; m. Lynne Aubrey, Jan. 21, 1978; children: Jacob A., Morgan H., Lily R. BA, Colgate U., 1968; JD, Seton Hall U., 1972. Bar: N.Y. 1973, U.S. Dist. Ct. (ea., no. and so. dists.) N.Y. 1975, U.S. Ct. Appeals (2d cir.) 1976, U.S. Ct Appeals (3d cir.) 1984, U.S. Supreme Ct. 1977. Staff atty. N.Y. Legal Aid Soc., N.Y.C., 1972-75; sole practitioner N.Y.C. and Nyack, N.Y., 1975—. Mem. Snedens Landing Tennis Assn. (Palisades, N.Y.), Palisades Swim Club (pres.). General civil litigation, Criminal, Probate. Office: 127 S Broadway Nyack NY 10960-4433

SEIDMAN, JENNIFER L. lawyer; b. West Palm Beach, Fla., Oct. 15, 1970; d. Alfred Joseph and Dorothy Dolce. BS, Fla. State U., 1991; JD, Stetson Coll. Law, 1995. Assoc. Gunster, Yoakley, Valdes-Fauli & Stewart, West Palm Beach, 1995-97, Foley & Lardner, West Palm Beach, 1997-99; asst. gen. counsel Catalfumo Constrn. & Devel., Palm Beach Gardens, Fla., 1999—. Office: Catalfumo Constrn & Devel 4300 Catalfumo Way Palm Beach Gardens FL 33410-4248 E-mail: jseidman@catalfumo.com

SEIFERT, LUKE MICHAEL, lawyer; b. Smyrna, Tenn., Apr. 8, 1957; s. Donald R. and Joan (Clemas) S.; m. Kathleen Louise Schaffer, Aug. 1, 1980; children: Joseph, Nicholas, Peter, Rachel. BA, Creighton U., 1979; JD, William Mitchell Sch. of Law, St. Paul, 1983. Bar: U.S. Dist. Ct. Minn., Minn. Page Minn. Ho. of Reps., St. Paul, 1980, com. adminstr., 1981-82; assoc. Holmen Law Office, St. Cloud, Minn., 1983-87; pvt. practice, 1987-98; assoc. Quinlivan Law Firm, 1998—. Mem. ABA, Minn. Bar Assn., Minn. Trial Lawyers Assn., Minn. Def. Lawyers Assn., Stearns Benton Bar Assn. (sec., treas. 1986-87, v.p. 1987-88, pres. 1988-89), K.C. (guard 1986-87, advocate 1987-90), Delta Theta Phi. Criminal, Personal injury, Workers' compensation. Home: 1305 W Oakes Dr Saint Cloud MN 56303-0741 Office: Quinlivan Hughes Law Firm PO Box 1008 600 Wells Fargo Ctr Saint Cloud MN 56302 E-mail: lseifert@quinlivan.com

SEIFERT, STEPHEN WAYNE, lawyer, performing arts executive; b. Washington, May 25, 1957; s. Arthur John and Frances E. (Smith) S. BA summa cum laude, Yale U., 1979; JD, Stanford U., 1982. Bar: Colo. 1982, U.S. Dist. Ct. Colo. 1982, U.S. Ct. Appeals (10th cir.) 1982, U.S. Ct. Appeals (5th cir.) 1987, U.S. Supreme Ct. 1988. Ptnr., Fairfield and Woods P.C., Denver, 1982-98; mng. dir. Fairfield & Woods P.C., 1990-92, 95-96; chmn. bd. dirs. Opera Colo., 1989-92, pres., exec. dir., 1997-2001. Author: Colorado Creditors' Remedies--Debtors' Relief, 1990; contbg. author: Colorado Methods of Practice; contbr. articles to profl. jours. Trustee Denver Metro C. of C., Denver Pub. Libr. Friends Found., Yale-Harvard Regatta Com., Allied Arts Inc., Rocky Mt. Region Inst. Internat. Edn.; mem. adv. bd. program in health care ethics, humanities and law U. Colo. Health Scis. Ctr.; mem. chancellor's scholars and leaders coun. U. Colo., Denver. Mem. Law Club Denver (v.p. 1992-93, pres. 1993-94), Univ. Club, Phi Beta Kappa. Bankruptcy, General civil litigation, Contracts commercial.

SEIFERT, THOMAS LLOYD, lawyer; b. Boston, June 6, 1940; s. Ralph Frederick and Hazel Bell (Harrington) S.; m. Ann Cecelia Berg, June 19, 1965. BS cum laude, Ind. U., 1962, JD cum laude, 1965. Bar: Ill. 1965, Ind. 1965, N.Y. 1979. Assoc. law firm Keck, Mahin & Cate, Chgo., 1965-67; atty. Essex Group, Inc., Ft. Wayne, Ind., 1967-70, Amoco Corp., Chgo., 1970-73; assoc. gen. counsel, asst. sec. Canteen Corp., 1973-75; sec., gen. counsel The Marmon Group, Inc. (and predecessor cos.), 1975-78; v.p., gen. counsel, sec. Hanson Industries, Inc., N.Y.C., 1978-82; sr. v.p. law, chief fin. officer Petrie Stores Corp., 1982-83; mem. Finley, Kumble, Wagner, Heine, Underberg, Manley, Myerson & Casey, 1983-87, Paul, Weiss, Rifkind, Wharton & Garrison, N.Y.C., 1987-91; gen. counsel, chief legal officer Sterling Grace Capital Mgmt., L.P. and affiliated cos., 1991—. Note editor Ind. Law Jour., 1964-65. Named to Ind. Track and Cross Country Hall of Fame, 1993. Mem. ABA, N.Y. State Bar Assn., Order of Coif, The Creek, Beta Gamma Sigma. General corporate, Mergers and acquisitions, Real property. Home: Museum Tower 15 W 53d St Apt 31 E New York NY 10019-5401 Office: Sterling Grace Capital Mgmt 515 Madison Ave Ste 2600 New York NY 10022-5403 E-mail: rumpole800@aol.com, tlseifert@msn.com

SEIFF, ERIC A. lawyer; b. Mt. Vernon, N.Y., Apr. 25, 1933; s. Arthur N. and Mathilde (Cohen) S.; m. Sari Ginsburg, June 26, 1960 (div. Oct. 1983); children: Judith C., E. Kenneth, Dean A.; m. Meredith Feinman, Jan. 15, 1984; children: Abigail, Sarah. BA, Yale U., 1955; LLB, Columbia U., 1958. Bar: N.Y. 1958, U.S. Dist. Ct. (so. dist.) N.Y. 1960, U.S. Dist. Ct. (ea. dist.) N.Y. 1981, U.S. Ct. Appeals (2d cir.) 1965, U.S. Supreme Ct. 1967.

Assoc. Bower and O'Connor, N.Y.C., 1959-60, Yellin, Kramer & Levy, N.Y.C., 1961; asst. dist. atty. N.Y.C. Dist. Atty.'s Office, 1962-67; asst. counsel Agy. for Internat. Devel., Washington, 1967-70, counsel Rio de Janeiro, 1970-72; gen. counsel N.Y. State Divsn. Criminal Justice Svcs., 1972-74; dep. chief atty. Legal Aid Soc. Criminal Def., N.Y.C., 1974-75; first dep. commr. N.Y. State Investigation Commn., 1975-77, chmn., 1977-79; ptnr. Seiff, Kretz & Maffeo (formerly Scoppetta & Seiff), 1981—; spl. dist. atty. Bronx County, 1986-89. Spl. asst. atty. gen. State of N.Y., Gov.'s Task Force Investigating Conduct of Attica Prosecutions, 1975. Bd. dirs. Legal Aid Soc., N.Y.C., 1994-2000; Prisoners' Legal Svcs., N.Y.C., 1989—, Lawyers Fund for Client Protection, N.Y., 1980—. Recipient Frank S. Hogan Meml. award Frank S. Hogan Assn., 1994. Mem. N.Y. Criminal Bar Assn. (bd. dirs. 1980—, past pres.), Bar Assn. City N.Y. (chmn. project on the homeless 1999—). General civil litigation, Criminal, Family and matrimonial. Office: Seiff Kretz & Maffeo 645 Madison Ave New York NY 10022-1010

SEIGEL, JAN KEARNEY, lawyer; b. Bayonne, N.J., Feb. 7, 1947; s. Max and Margaret (Kearney) S.; m. Judy L. Mascuch, Aug. 29, 1971; children: Margaret, Emily, Jonas, Luke. BSBA, Georgetown U., 1968, JD, 1971; LLM in Taxation, NYU, 1974. Bar: N.J. 1971, D.C. 1972, Ga. 1972, U.S. Ct. Appeals (3d cir.) 1979, U.S. Supreme Ct. 1979. Law sec. to Hon. Theodore Rosenberg Superior Ct. of N.J., Paterson, 1971-72; asst. prosecutor Passaic County Pros.'s Office, 1972-76; pvt. practice Ridgewood, 1976-98; sr. ptnr. Seigel & Mongiardo, P.C., N.J., 1990—. Mem. faculty William Paterson Coll., 1974-79; lectr. N.J. Inst. for Continuing Edn., 1981—, N.J. State Bar and various county bar assns. Recipient Police Hon. Legion award Police Chiefs Assn. of N.J., 1980. Mem. ABA (rep. of N.J. young lawyers divsn. 1980-82), N.J. State Bar Assn. (Young Lawyer of Yr. award 1983, bd. trustees 1978-79), Passaic County Bar Assn. (bd. trustees 1973-81), Bergen County Bar Assn. Criminal, Personal injury. Office: Seigel & Mongiardo 505 Goffle Rd Ridgewood NJ 07450-4027

SEIGEL, STUART EVAN, lawyer; b. N.Y.C., Mar. 25, 1933; s. Philip Herman and Betty Sarah (Leventhal) S.; m. Joyce Roberta Meyers (div.); children: Charles Meyers, Lee Bennett, Suzanne Marcie; m. Sherry Diane Jackson,Sept. 24, 1989. BS, N.Y. U., 1953, LLB, 1957; LLM in Taxation, Georgetown U., 1960. Bar: N.Y. 1958, D.C. 1958. Atty. Office Chief Counsel, IRS, Washington, 1957-65, Office Tax Legis. Counsel, Dept. Treasury, Washington, 1965-69, assoc. tax legis. counsel, 1968-69; ptnr. firm Cohen and Uretz, Washington, 1969-77; chief counsel IRS, 1977-79; ptnr. firm Williams and Connolly, 1979-89, Arnold and Porter, N.Y.C., 1989—. Lectr. George Washington U. Sch. Law, 1970-73; adj. prof. law Antioch Sch. Law, 1973-76, Georgetown U. Sch. Law, 1981. Mem. ABA, Am. Law Inst., Am. Coll. Tax Counsel, N.Y. State Bar Assn. Club: Metropolitan (Washington). E-mail: stuart. General corporate, Corporate taxation, Taxation, general. Office: Arnold and Porter 399 Park Ave New York NY 10022-4690 E-mail: seigel@aporter.com

SEILER, JAMES ELMER, judge; b. LaCrosse, Wis., Sept. 2, 1946; s. Elmer Bernard and Margaret Theresa (Mader) S.; m. Sonia Gonzales, Feb. 9, 1968; children: Rebecca, Cristina. BA, U. Wis., LaCrosse, 1968; JD, U. Wis., 1973. Bar: Wis. 1973, Minn. 1981, U.S. Supreme Ct. 1985, Mo. 1986. Pvt. practice, Balsam Lake, Wis., 1973-81; in-house counsel Farm Credit Banks, St. Paul, 1981-85; corp. counsel Hussmann Corp., St. Louis, 1985-94; adminstrv. law judge Social Security, Evansville, Ind., 1994-95, Office of Hearings and Appeals, Creve Coeur, Mo., 1995—; chief adminstrv. law judge Hearing Office, 1997—. Candidate Dist. Atty., Polk County, Wis., 1980. With U.S. Army, 1969-71. Avocations: soccer coach, swimming, water skiing, running. Home: 18 Harbor Point Ct Lake Saint Louis MO 63367-1336 Office: 11475 Olde Cabin Rd Saint Louis MO 63141-7130

SEITELMAN, MARK ELIAS, lawyer; b. N.Y.C., Apr. 14, 1955; s. Leo Henry and Pearl (Elias) S. BA, Bklyn. Coll., 1976; JD, Bklyn. Law Sch., 1979. Bar: N.Y. 1980, U.S. Dist. Ct. (ea., so., and we. dists.) N.Y. 1980, U.S. Supreme Ct. 1995, U.S. Ct. Mil. Appeals, 1995. Law asst. Criminal Ct., Bklyn., 1979; law clk. to Hon. Justice Aaron D. Bernstein N.Y. Supreme Ct., 1980; assoc. Lester, Schwab, Katz & Dwyer, N.Y.C., 1981-87, Weg and Myers, 1987-88, Kroll & Tract, 1988-90; pvt. practice N.Y.C., 1990—. Appeared on WABC TV Eyewitness News; interviewed by N.Y. Daily News, N.Y. Newsday. Mem. ABA, ATLA (sustaining mem. motor vehicle and small practice sect.), N.Y. State Bar Assn., N.Y. County Bar Assn. (ins. and supreme ct. coms.), N.Y. State Trial Lawyers Assn. (sustaining mem., bd. dirs., mem. spkrs. bur., conv. com., legis. com., contbg. editor Trial Lawyers Quar.), N.Y. State Trial Lawyers Inst. (CLE program chmn., lectr.), Bklyn. Bar Assn. (legis. com., employment law com.). Insurance, Personal injury, Product liability. Office: 111 Broadway 9th Fl New York NY 10006

SEITMAN, JOHN MICHAEL, lawyer, arbitrator, mediator; b. Bloomington, Ill., Feb. 9, 1942; BS, U. Ill., 1964, JD, 1966. Bar: Calif., U.S. Dist. Ct. (so., cen., no. and ea. dists.) Calif., U.S. Ct. Appeals (9th cir.). Prin. Lindley, Lazar & Scales, San Diego, 1966-97. Lectr. in continuing legal edn. Bd. dirs. San Diego County Bar Found., 1983-89, treas., 1983-84, pres., 1988-89; del. to 9th Cir. Jud. Conf., 1986, 88. Fellow Am. Bar Found.; mem. ABA, State Bar Calif. (pres. 1991-92), San Diego County Bar Assn. (pres. 1986). General civil litigation, Consumer commercial, General practice. Office: PO Box 2156 Del Mar CA 92014-1456

SEITZ, PATRICIA ANN, lawyer; b. Washington, Sept. 2, 1946; d. Richard J. and Bettie Jean (Merrill) S.; m. Alan Graham Greer, Aug. 14, 1981. BA in History cum laude, Kans. State U., 1968; JD, Georgetown U., 1973. Bar: Fla. 1973, D.C. 1975, U.S. Dist. Ct. (no., mid., so. dists., trial bar) Fla., U.S. Ct. Appeals (5th and eleventh cir.), U.S. Supreme Ct. Reporter Dallas Times Herald, Washington, 1970-73; law clk. to Hon. Charles R. Richey U.S. Dist. Ct., 1973-74; assoc. Steel, Hector & Davis, Miami, Fla., 1974-79, ptnr., 1980-96; dir. office legal counsel Office of Nat. Drug Control Policy, Exec. Office of Pres., Washington, 1996-97; judge U.S. Dist. Ct. (so. dist.) Fla., 1998—. Adj. faculty U. Miami Law Sch., Coral Gables, Fla., 1984-88; faculty Nat. Inst. Trial Advocacy, Boulder, Colo., 1982, 83, 95, Chapel Hill, N.C., 1984, 87. Fla. region, 1989; lectr. in field. Contbr. numerous articles to law jours. Mem. Dade Munroe Mental Health Bd., Miami, 1982-84, United Way of Greater Miami comty. devel. com., 1984-87; chmn. family abuse task force United Way of Greater Miami, 1986; chmn. devel. com. Miami City Ballet, 1986-87, bd. dirs., 1986-90. Fellow Am. Bar Found., Am. Bd. Trial Advocacy, Internat. Soc. Barristers; mem. ABA (chmn. various coms. 1979-85, Ho. Dels. 1992-96), Am. Arbitration Assn. (nat. bd. dirs. 1995-97, complex case panel arbitrator), The Fla. Bar (bd. govs. young lawyer divsn. 1981-82, bd. govs. 1986-92, pres. 1993-94, bd. cert. civil trial), Fla. Assn. Women Lawyers, Dade County Bar Assn. (pub. interest law bank). Roman Catholic. Avocations: travel, art. Office: Fed Courthouse Square 301 N Miami Ave Fl 5 Miami FL 33128-7702

SEITZINGER, EDWARD FRANCIS, lawyer; b. Mapleton, Iowa, Apr. 3, 1916; s. John and Catherine Emma (Griffin) S.; m. Marian Bernice Westerberg, June 27, 1943; 1 child, Pam Kathleen. Student Iowa State U., 1935-36, 37-38; B.S., S.D. State U., 1942; J.D. cum laude, U. Iowa, 1947. Bar: Iowa 1947, U.S. Supreme Ct. 1955. Counsel Iowa Farm Bur. Fedn. and Affiliated Cos., 1947-58, asst. gen. counsel, 1958-78, gen. counsel, 1978-82; mem. Iowa Merit Employment Commn., 1982-87, Alcoholic Beverage Comm., 1987—. Bd. dirs. Legal Aid Soc. Polk County, Iowa, 1970-72; trustee Lutheran Home for Aging, 1967-75. Served with U.S. Army, World War II. Mem. ABA, Iowa State Bar Assn. (bd. govs. 1972-73, 73-75), Polk County Bar Assn. (pres. 1969-70), Def. Research Inst. (bd. dirs. 1968-75, v.p. pub. relations 1968-71, v.p. adminstr. 1972-73, pres. 1973-74, chmn. 1974-75), Nat. Conf. Local Def. Groups (chmn. 1973-77), Nat. Assn. Ind. Insurers, Fedn. Ins. Counsel (v.p. 1968-69, bd. dirs. 1970-72, v.p. 1974-75), Internat. Assn. Ins. Counsel, Iowa Def. Counsel Assn. (1st pres. 1964-65, bd. dirs. 1964—), Iowa Conf. Bar Assn. Presidents (bd. dirs. 1969-71, v.p. 1971-73, pres. 1974-79), Iowa Life Ins. Assn. (v.p. 1980-82, bd. dirs. 1979-82), Am. Council Life Ins., Nat. Rifle Assn., Iowa Farm Bur. Fedn., Am. Farm Bur. Fedn. Republican. Lutheran. Clubs: Des Moines Golf & Country, Des Moines. Lodges: Masons, Shriners. General corporate, General practice, Insurance. Home: 13399 29th Dr Des Moines IA 50323-2115

SELBY, LELAND CLAY, lawyer; b. Granite City, Ill., July 4, 1944; s. William Edward and Agnes (Newell) S.; m. Diane Schryver, Aug. 20, 1966; children: Leland Clay, Timothy Schryver, Amanda Elizabeth. BA, U. Richmond, 1966; LLB, U. Va., 1969. Bar: Conn. 1969, N.Y. 1989. Assoc. Hirschberg, Pettengill & Strong, Greenwich, Conn., 1969-74; ptnr. Hirschberg, Pettengill, Strong & Nagle, 1974-78, Whitman & Ransom, Greenwich, 1978-93, Whitman Breed Abbott & Morgan, Greenwich, 1993-95; mem. Fogarty Cohen Selby & Nemiroff LLC, 1995—. Bd. dirs., v.p. Stamford (Conn.) Ctr. for Arts, 1989—; chmn. bd. govs. Greenwich Found. for Cmty. Gifts, 1980-90; pres. United Way of Greenwich, 1978-80; bd. dirs. Retirement Sys., Town of Greenwich, 1993-2001, Greenwich Symphony Orch., 1986-95. Named Greenwich Young Man of Yr., Greenwich Jaycees, 1974. Fellow Am. Coll. Trust and Estate Counsel; mem. ABA, Conn. Bar Assn., N.Y. State Bar Assn., Greenwich Bar Assn., Preston Mountain Club (sec. 1999—), Riverside Yacht Club, Va. Club of N.Y.C., Harpoon Club of Greenwich. Episcopalian. Avocations: fly fishing, sporting clays, hiking, reading, travel. Estate planning, Probate, Estate taxation. Home: One Pinecrest Rd Riverside CT 06878 Office: Fogarty Cohen Selby & Nemiroff 88 Field Point Rd Greenwich CT 06830-6468

SELIG, JOEL LOUIS, lawyer, educator; b. Boston, Apr. 12, 1944; s. William Max and Ruth Horton (Berger) S.; m. Ruth Mildred Osterweis, Oct. 6, 1968; children— William Osterweis, Deborah Osterweis. A.B., Harvard U., 1965, J.D., 1968. Bar: Mass. 1968, U.S. Dist. Ct. Mass. 1969, U.S. Supreme Ct. 1973, U.S. Ct. Appeals (9th cir.) 1974, U.S. Ct. Appeals (D.C. cir.) 1974, U.S. Ct. Appeals (5th cir.) 1975, D.C. 1976, U.S. Ct. Appeals (6th cir.) 1976, U.S. Dist. Ct. D.C. 1976, U.S. Ct. Appeals (10th cir.) 1977, U.S. Ct. Appeals (11th cir.) 1981. Atty. Mass. Law Reform Inst., Boston, 1969; atty., employment sect., civil rights div. Dept. Justice, Washington, 1969-73, atty., appellate sect., 1977-78, dep. chief, housing and credit sect., 1978-79, dep. chief, gen. litigation sect., 1979-82, sr. trial atty., fed. enforcement sect., 1982-83; dir. govt. employment discrimination project Lawyers' Com. for Civil Rights Under Law, Washington, 1973-77; vis. prof. law U. Wyo. Coll. Law, Laramie, 1983-84, prof. law, 1984—, centennial disting. prof. of law, 1992-95; temporary recorder Supreme Ct. Wyo. Permanent Rules Adv. Com., 1983-84, reporter, 1984— . Office: Univ Wyo Coll Law University Station PO Box 3035 Laramie WY 82071-3035

SELIGMAN, DELICE, lawyer; b. Worcester, Mass. m. Frederick Seligman. AB, MA, Clark U.; JD, NYU, 1971. Bar: N.Y. 1972, U.S. Dist. Ct. (so. and ea. dists.) N.Y. 1973, U.S. Supreme Ct. 1979. Assoc. Legal Aid Soc. Nassau County, Mineola, N.Y., 1972-76; ptnr. Seligman, Stein & Abromowitz, Garden City, 1976-86, Seligman & Seligman, N.Y.C., N.Y., 1986—. Legal counsel Contemporary Sculptors, Roslyn, N.Y., 1987-90, Artists Network Great Neck, N.Y., 1987-90, Woodstock Animal Rights Movement, Legal Action for Animals, Stop Graffiti Now, Inc.; pres. Wildlife Legal Action, Inc. Bd. dirs. For Our Children and Us, Hicksville, N.Y., 1985—; pres. Vol. Lawyers for Animal Rights, 2001—, Animal Advocates, Inc., 1999—. Mem. Nassau Women's Bar Assn. (pres. 1982-83), Bar Assn. Nassau County (chair arts com. 1984-85), Phi Alpha Delta. Entertainment, Art. Home: Runge Rd Shokan NY 12481 Office: 26 Broadway New York NY 10004-1703 also: Seligman & Seligman 70 Main St Kingston NY 12401-3802

SELIGMAN, FREDERICK, lawyer; b. Bklyn. s. Martin and Florence (Alperin) S.; m. Delice Felice. AB, Clark U., 1957; JD, N.Y. Law Sch., 1972. Bar: N.Y. 1973, U.S. Dist. Ct. (so. and ea. dists.) N.Y. 1974, U.S. Tax Ct. 1974, U.S. Ct. Appeals (2d cir.) 1975, U.S. Supreme Ct. 1979. Atty. N.Y.C. (N.Y.) Police Dept., 1972-73; asst. dist. atty. N.Y. County, N.Y.C., 1973-79; pvt. practice, 1980-85; ptnr. Seligman & Seligman, 1986—. Mem. N.Y. Criminal Bar Assn., N.Y. State Defenders Assn. Criminal, General practice. Home: Runge Rd Shokan NY 12481 Office: Seligman & Seligman 26 Broadway New York NY 10004-1703

SELIGMAN, JOEL, dean; b. N.Y.C., Jan. 11, 1950; s. Selig Jacob and Muriel (Bienstock) S.; m. Friederike Felber, July 30, 1981; children: Andrea, Peter. AB magna cum laude, UCLA, 1971; JD, Harvard U., 1974. Bar: Calif. 1975. Atty., writer Corp. Accountability Rsch. Group, Washington, 1974-77; prof. law Northeastern U. Law Sch., 1977-83, George Washington U., 1983-86, U. Mich., Ann Arbor, 1986-95; dean law U. Ariz., Tucson, 1995-99; dean sch. law Washington U., St. Louis, 1999—. Cons. Fed. Trade Commn., 1979-82, Dept. Transp., 1983, Office Tech. Assessment, 1988-89; chair adv. com. on mkt. info. SEC, 2000—; reporter Nat. Conf. of Commrs. on Uniform State Laws, Uniform Securities Act, 2001. Author (with others) Constitutionalizing the Corporation: The Case for the Federal Chartering of Giant Corporations, 1976, The High Citadel: The Influence of Harvard Law School, 1978, The Transformation of Wall Street: A History of the Securities and Exchange Commission and Modern Corporate Finance, 1982, The SEC and the Future of Finance, 1985, (multi-volume) Securities Regulation; contbr. articles to profl. jours. Mem. State Bar Calif., Am. Law Inst. (adv. com., advisor corp. governance project), AICPAs (profl. ethics exec. com. 2000—). Office: Wash U Sch Law CB 1120 1 Brookings Dr Saint Louis MO 63130-4862

SELIGMANN, WILLIAM ROBERT, lawyer, author; b. Davenport, Iowa, Oct. 10, 1956; s. William Albert and Barbara Joyce (Carmichael) S.; m. Carole Lee Francis; children: D Anna, Matthew. BA, U. Calif., Santa Barbara, 1979; JD, Santa Clara U., 1982. Bar: Calif. 1983, U.S. Dist. Ct. (no. dist.) Calif. 1983. Assoc. Office of J.R. Dempster, Cupertino, Calif., 1983-85; city atty. City of Campbell, 1985—; ptnr. Dempster, Seligmann & Raineri, Los Gatos, 1985—2001, pvt. practice, 2001—. Judge pro tem, Santa Clara County, 1992—. Bd. dirs. Los Gatos C. of C. Mem. Santa Clara County Bar Assn. (civil practice com., judiciary com., exec. bd. pub. law sect.), State Bar of Calif. (exec. bd. pub. law section, 2001—). Avocations; cross country skiing, scuba diving, swimming, writing, Aikido. General civil litigation, Land use and zoning (including planning), Real property. Office: Dempster Seligmann & Raineri 455 Los Gatos Blvd Ste 111 Los Gatos CA 95032-5523 E-mail: bill@soutbaylaw.com

SELINGER, CARL M. legal educator, dean; b. 1934. B.A., U. Calif.-Berkeley, 1955; J.D., Harvard U., 1958. Bar: Calif. 1958, Hawaii 1976, Mich. 1980, W.Va. 1983. Pvt. practice, Calif., 1958-59; teaching fellow Harvard U., Cambridge, Mass., 1960-61; prof. law Albany (N.Y.) Coll., 1961-63, U. N.Mex., Albuquerque, 1963-68; acad. dean Bard Coll., Annandale-on-Hudson, N.Y., 1968-75; prof. sch. law, assoc. dean U. Hawaii, Honolulu, 1975-79; dean Sch. Law, U. Detroit, 1979-82; dean Coll. Law, W.Va. U., Morgantown, 1982— ; cons. Office: WVa U Coll Law Morgantown WV 26506

SELINGER, JERRY ROBIN, lawyer; b. Peekskill, N.Y., Nov. 3, 1947; s. Philip R. and Helen D. (Klein) S.; m. Barbara D. Wax, Aug. 2, 1969; children: Elise, Scott. BS in Engring. Sci., SUNY, Buffalo, 1969; MS, Columbia U., 1971; JD, George Washington U., 1975. Bar: Md. 1975, D.C. 1976, U.S. Ct. Appeals (fed. cir.) 1977, U.S. Supreme Ct. 1978, Tex. 1980, U.S. Ct. Appeals (5th and 11th cirs.) 1981, U.S. Ct. Appeals (3d cir.) 1982. Atty. Arent, Fox, Kintner, Plotkin & Kahn, Washington, 1975-79, Richards, Harris & Medlock, Dallas, 1979-82; mem., dir. Baker, Mills & Glast, 1982-90; ptnr. Vinson & Elkins LLP, 1990-97; shareholder Jenkens & Gilchrist, 1997—. Contbr. articles to profl. jours. Mem. ABA, Tex. Bar Assn. (chair intellectual property law sect. 1996-97, bd. dirs. 1998-2001), Dallas Bar Assn. (bd. dirs. 1995-96), Tex. Young Lawyers Assn. (bd. dirs. 1984-86, Pres. award 1986), Am. Intellectual Property Law Assn., Dallas Assn. Young Lawyers (sec. 1983, treas. 1984), Order of Coif, Phi Delta Phi. Federal civil litigation, State civil litigation, Trademark and copyright. Home: 10414 Woodford Dr Dallas TX 75229-6317 Office: Jenkens & Gilchrist 1445 Ross Ave Ste 3200 Dallas TX 75202-2785 E-mail: jselinger@jenkens.com

SELLERS, BARBARA JACKSON, federal judge; b. Richmond, Va., Oct. 3, 1940; m. Richard F. Sellers; children: Elizabeth M., Anne W., Catherine A. Attended, Baldwin-Wallace Coll., 1958-60; BA cum laude, Ohio State U., 1962; JD magna cum laude, Capital U. Law Sch., Columbus, Ohio, 1979. Bar: Ohio 1979, U.S. Dist. Ct. (so. dist.) Ohio 1981, U.S. Ct. Appeals (6th cir.), 1986. Jud. law clk. Hon. Robert J. Sidman, U.S. Bankruptcy Judge, Columbus, Ohio, 1979-81; assoc. Lasky & Semons, 1981-82; jud. law clk. to Hon. Thomas M. Herbert, U.S. Bankruptcy Ct., 1982-84; assoc. Baker & Hostetler, 1984-86; U.S. bankruptcy judge So. Dist. Ohio, 1986—. Lectr. on bankruptcy univs., insts., assns. Recipient Am. Jurisprudence prize contracts and criminal law, 1975-76, evidence and property, 1976-77, Corpus Juris Secundum awards, 1975-76, 76-77. Mem. Columbus Bar Assn., Am. Bankruptcy Inst., Nat. Conf. Bankruptcy Judges, Order of Curia, Phi Beta Kappa. Office: US Bankruptcy Ct 170 N High St Columbus OH 43215-2403 E-mail: barbara_j._sellers@ck6.uscourts.gov

SELLERS, CAROL, lawyer; b. Durham, N.C., Mar. 2, 1943; d. George Grover and Mae (Savage) Sellers; m. James K. Herbert, Nov. 13, 1980; children— John, Kathie, Paul, Barry. B.A., Duke U., 1964; J.D. cum laude, Whittier Sch. Law, 1976. Bar: Calif. 1976. Tchr. high sch. English, Heber, Utah, 1964-67; founder, exec. dir. Fremont Scholastic Inst., Salt Lake City, 1967-71; adminstr. Office of Dean, Whittier Sch. Law, Los Angeles, 1973-76; assoc. Katz, Granof, Palarz, Beverly Hills, Calif., 1976-78; dir. Western div. Harcourt Brace Jovanovich Legal and Profl. Publs., 1977-81, pres., exec. dir. Harcourt Brace Jovanovich Multistate Workshop, 1981— ; dean San Joaquin Coll. Law, 1982— ; lectr. women in legal and bus. professions. Angier B. Duke scholar, 1961-64; Beverly Rubens Gordon scholar, 1972-76. Mem. Beverly Hills Bar Assn., Fresno County Bar Assn., Assn. Women and Law Com. (1st chmn. 1977), ABA. Office: 11801 W Olympic St Suite 7 Los Angeles CA 93704

SELTZER, JEFFREY LLOYD, diversified financial services company executive; b. Bklyn., July 27, 1956; s. Bernard and Sue (Harris) S.; m. Ana Isabel Sifre, Sept. 2, 1985; children: Ian Alexander, Pamela Allison. BS in Econs. cum laude, U. Pa., 1978; JD, Georgetown U., 1981. Bar: N.Y. 1982. Assoc. Austrian, Lance & Stewart, N.Y.C., 1981-85; assoc. gen. counsel, asst. v.p. Shearson Lehman Bros., 1986; mng. dir. Lehman Bros., 1986-94; dep. chmn., mng. dir. CIBC Oppenheimer Corp., 1994-99; exec. v.p., COO Adirondack Trading Ptnrs., 1999—, Exch. Tech. Corp., 2000—. Spl. prof. law Hofstra U., 1999—. Author: The U.S. Greeting Card Market, 1977, Starting and Organizing a Business, 1984, Swap Risk Management: A Primer, 1988, A View for the Top: The Role of the Board of Directors and Senior Management in the Derivatives Business, 1995, Financial Strategy Roundtable: Derivatives, 1995. Mem. Nat. Policy Forum, 1994-97; mem. securities industry coalition Bush-Quayle campaign, 1992; mem. U.S. Trade Adv. Com. on Svc. Industries, Washington, 1990-94; small bus. adv. coun. Rep. Nat. Com., Washington, 1984-90; nat. adv. coun. U.S. SBA, 1982-87; advisor Friends of Giuliani, N.Y.C., 1989, New Yorkers for Lew Lehrman, N.Y.C., 1981-82; policy analyst Reagan-Bush Com., Arlington, Va., 1980; dir. Nassau County Sports Commn., 1997—, mem. exec. com.; mem. fiscal mgmt. adv. bd. County of Nassau, 1997-99; mem. adv. bd. Huntsman Program on Internat. Studies and Bus., U. Pa., 1997—; chmn. Class 1978 fundraising U. Pa., 1997—; vice chmn., trustee Inst. Internat. Bankers, 1998-99. Recipient Disting. Alumnus award W. C. Mepham H.S., 1994. Mem. ABA, Re. Nat. Lawyers Assn., Federalist Soc., Ctr. for Study of Presidency, Securities Industry Assn. (chmn. swap and derivative products com. 1990-94). Home: 3 Yates Ln Jericho NY 11753-1418 Office: 45 Rockefeller Plz Ste 3201 New York NY 10111-3299

SELYA, BRUCE MARSHALL, federal judge; b. Providence, May 27, 1934; s. Herman C. and Betty (Brier) S.; children: Dawn Meredith Selya Sherman, Lori Ann BA magna cum laude, Harvard U., 1955, JD magna cum laude, 1958. Bar: D.C. 1958, R.I. 1960. Law clk. U.S. Dist. Ct. R.I., Providence, 1958-60; assoc. Gunning & LaFazia, 1960-62; ptnr. Gunning, LaFazia, Gnys & Selya, 1963-74, Selya & Iannuccillo, Providence, 1974-82; judge U.S. Dist. Ct. R.I., 1982-86, U.S. Ct. Appeals (1st cir.), Providence, 1986—. Judge Lincoln Probate Ct., R.I., 1965-72; mem. R.I. Jud. Council, 1964-72, sec., 1965-70, chmn., 1971-72; mem. Gov.'s Commn. on Crime and Adminstrn. Justice, 1967-69; del. Nat. Conf. on Revisions to Fed. Appellate Practice, 1968-82; mem. various spl. govtl. commns. and adv. groups Chmn. bd. trustees Bryant Coll., Smithfield, R.I., 1986-92; bd. dirs. Lifespan Health Sys., chmn. bd. dirs., 1994—, mem. bd. trustees R.I. Hosp. subs. Recipient Louis Dembitz Brandeis medal for disting. legal svc. Brandeis U., 1988, Neil Houston award Justice Assistance of Am., 1992. Mem. ABA, FBA, Fed. Judges Assn., R.I. Bar Assn. (chmn. various coms.), R.I. Bar Found., U.S. Jud. Conf. (mem. com. on jud. br.), Am. Arbitration Assn., Am. Judicature Soc. (bd. dirs.). Jewish Home: 224 George St Providence RI 02906-3115 Office: US Ct Appeals US Courthouse 1 Exchange Terr Rm 311 Providence RI 02903*

SEMAYA, FRANCINE LEVITT, lawyer; b. N.Y.C., Mar. 26, 1951; d. Julie and Ann (Tannenbaum) Levitt; m. Richard Semaya, Aug. 3, 1975; children: Stefanie Rachel, David Steven, Scott Brian. BA magna cum laude, Bklyn. Coll., 1973, MS magna cum laude, 1975; JD cum laude, N.Y. Law Sch., 1982. Bar: N.Y. 1983, U.S. Dist. Ct. (ea. and so. dists.) N.Y. 1983, U.S. Supreme Ct. 2000. Sr. legal analyst, atty. Am. Internat. Group, Inc., N.Y.C., 1977-83; assoc. counsel, asst. v.p. Beneficial Ins. Group, Inc. (formerly Benico, Inc.), Peapack, N.J., 1983-87; v.p., counsel Am. Centennial Ins. Co., 1985-87; legal/reins. cons., 1987; counsel reins. Integrity Ins. Co. in Liquidation, Paramus, N.J., 1988-91; ptnr. Werner & Kennedy, N.Y.C., 1991-99; sr. ptnr. Cozen O'Connor, 1999—. Spkr. in field. Editor: Law and Practice of Insurance Insolvency Revisited, 1989, 99, State of Insurance Regulation: Today and Tomorrow, 1991; contbg. editor Reference Handbook Ins. Co. Insolvency, 3rd edit., 1993, 4th edit., 1999; contbr. numerous articles to profl. jours. Mem. ABA (sect. del. to ho. dels. 1998—, tort and ins. practice sect. coun. 1994-97, chmn. task force on ins. insolvency 1995-2000, chmn. professionalism com. 1997-98, chmn. pub. regulation of ins. law com. 1990-91, chair pub. rels. com. 1993-94, co-editor State Regulation Ins. 1991), N.Y. State Bar Assn., Practicing Law Inst. (ins. law adv. com. 1995—), Assn. Bar City N.Y. (ins. law com.), Fedn. Regulatory Counsel, Phi Beta Kappa. Avocations: reading, travel. Administrative and regulatory, Banking, Insurance. Office: Cozen O'Connor 16 Fl 45 Broadway Atrium New York NY 10006-3007 E-mail: fsemaya@cozen.com

SEMEL, MARTIN IRA, lawyer; b. N.Y.C., June 26, 1934; s. Joseph and Clara (Rosenblatt) S.; m. Barbara Peltz, June 14, 1956; children: Deborah, Richard, Rhonda. BA, Cornell U., 1956, LLD, 1959. Bar: N.Y. 1959, U.S. Dist. Ct. (so. dist.) N.Y. 1963, U.S. Ct. Appeals (2d cir.) 1963, U.S. Supreme Ct. 1964. Assoc., Bierman & Lass, N.Y.C., 1959-62; sole practice, N.Y.C., 1963-64; ptnr. Semel & Patrusky, 1964-69, Semel, Patrusky & Buchsbaum, N.Y.C., 1969-89, Semel & Patrusky, N.Y.C., 1989—. Served as 1st lt. U.S. Army, 1957-63 Res. Mem. N.Y. State Bar Assn., N.Y. State Trial Lawyers Assn., Nat. Bar Assn., Am. Trial Lawyers Assn. Jewish. Admiralty, General corporate, Real property. Home: 250 Pepperidge Rd Hewlett NY 11557-2749 Office: Semel Patrusky & Buchsbaum 22 Jericho Tpke # 241 Jericho NY 11753-1039

SEMPLE, JAMES WILLIAM, lawyer; b. Phila., Nov. 18, 1943; s. Calvin James and Marie (Robinson) S.; m. Ellen Burns, Nov. 26, 1966; children: Megan Semple Greenberg, Luke Robinson. AB, St. Josephs U., Phila., 1965; JD, Villanova U., 1974. Bar: Del. 1974, U.S. Dist. Ct. Del. 1974, D.C. 1975, U.S. Ct. Appeals (3d cir.) 1982, U.S. Tax Ct. 1996. Ptnr. Morris, James, Hitchens & Williams, Wilmington, 1983—. Lectr. numerous seminars; mediator Superior Ct. Voluntary Mediation Program. Mem. ABA, Am. Bd. Trial Advs., Fedn. Ins. and Corp. Counsel, Am. Judicature Soc., Am. Soc. Law and Medicine, Assn. Internat. de Droit d'Assurance. General civil litigation, Contracts commercial, Insurance. Office: Morris James Hitchens & Williams PO Box 2306 Wilmington DE 19899-2306 E-mail: jsemple@morrisjames.com

SENDEROWITZ, STEPHEN JAY, lawyer; b. Allentown, Pa., Apr. 13, 1949; s. Robert B. and Ralpha Iris (Becker) S.; m. Carol Jean Wintner, Apr. 29, 1977. B.A., Northwestern U., 1971, J.D., 1974. Bar: Ill. 1974, U.S. Dist. Ct. (no. dist.) Ill. 1974, U.S. Ct. Appeals (7th cir.) 1974. Trial atty. EEOC, Chgo., 1974-75; asst. U.S. atty. Dept. Justice, Chgo., 1975-83, dep. chief criminal div., 1979-83, dep. chief spl. prosecution div., 1983; sole practice, 1985-86, ptnr. Stone, McGuire & Benjamin, Chgo., 1986—; Becker and Tenenbaum, Chgo., 1987, chmn. U.S. Atty. Gen.'s Econ. Crime Council Com. on Commodity Fraud, Washington, 1983; lectr. fraud sect. FBI, Dept. Justice, 1980-83. Recipient Spl. Achievement award Dept. Justice, 1978, 79, 80, 81. Club: Union League (Chgo.). Federal civil litigation, Criminal, Commodities. Office: Becker and Tenenbaum 200 S Michigan Ave Fl 10 Chicago IL 60604-2404

SENNET, CHARLES JOSEPH, lawyer; b. Buffalo, Aug. 7, 1952; s. Saunders M. and Muriel S. (Rotenberg) S. AB magna cum laude, Cornell U., 1974; JD with high honors, George Washington U., 1979. Bar: Ill. 1979, U.S. Dist. Ct. (no. dist.) Ill. 1979, U.S. Ct. Appeals (7th cir.) 1982, U.S. Ct. Appeals (D.C. cir.) 1993. Assoc. Reuben & Proctor, Chgo., 1979-83; assoc. counsel Tribune Co., 1984-91, sr. counsel, 1991—. Adj. faculty Medill Sch. Journalism, Northwestern U., 1991-94; co-chair Television Music Lic. Com., 1995—. Contbr. articles to profl. jours. Mem. ABA (spkr. 1984-88, 91-97, 2000—, mem. gov. bd. Forum on Comms. Law 1995-98), NATAS, Ill. Bar Assn. (chmn. media law com. 1989-91), Chgo. Bar Assn., Fed. Comms. Bar Assn. Communications, Entertainment, Libel. Office: Tribune Co 435 N Michigan Ave Chicago IL 60611-4066

SENSENICH, ILA JEANNE, judge; b. Pitts., Mar. 6, 1939; d. Louis E. and Evelyn Margaret S. BA, Westminster Coll., 1961; JD, Dickinson Sch. Law, 1964, JD (hon.), 1994. Bar: Pa. 1964. Assoc. Stewart, Belden, Sensenich and Harrington, Greensburg, Pa., 1964-70; asst. pub. defender Westmoreland (Pa.) County, 1970-71; U.S. magistrate judge We. Dist. Pa., Pitts., 1971—. Adj. prof. law Duquesne U., 1982-87. Author: Compendium of the Law of Prisiner's Rights, 1979; contbr. articles to profl. jour. Trustee emeritus Dickinson Sch. Law. Vis. fellow Daniel & Florence Guggenheim program in criminal justice Yale Law Sch., 1976-77. Mem. ABA, Fed. Magistrate Judges Assn. (sec. 1979-81, 88-89, treas. 1989-90, 2d v.p. 1990-91, pres.-elect 1992-93, pres. 1993-94), Pa. Bar Assn., Allegheny County Bar Assn. (fed. ct. sect.), Nat. Assn. Women Judges, Westmoreland County Bar Assn., Allegheny County Bar Assn. (fed. sect., com. women in law), Womens Bar Assn. We. Pa., Am. Judicature Soc. Democrat. Presbyterian. Avocations: skiing, sailing, bicycling, classical music, cooking. Office: 518B US PO And Courthouse Pittsburgh PA 15219

SENTELLE, DAVID BRYAN, federal judge; b. Canton, N.C., Feb. 12, 1943; s. Horace Richard, Jr. and Maude (Ray) S.; m. Jane LaRue Oldham, June 19, 1965; children: Sharon Sentelle Lewis, Regan Sentelle Herman, Rebecca Sentelle Acheson. AB, U. N.C., 1965, JD with honors, 1968. Bar: N.C. 1968, U.S. Dist. Ct. (we. dist.) N.C. 1969, U.S. Ct. Appeals (4th cir.) 1970. Assoc. Uzzell & Dumont, Asheville, N.C., 1968-70; asst. U.S. atty. City of Charlotte, 1970-74, dist. judge, 1974-77; ptnr. Tucker, Hicks, Sentelle, Moon & Hodge, P.A., Charlotte, 1977-85; judge U.S. Dist. Ct. (we. dist.) N.C., 1985-87, U.S. Ct. Appeals D.C., 1987—. Adj. prof. Fla. State U. Coll. Law; presiding judge Spl. Divsn. for Appointment of Ind. Counsels, 1992—. Contbr. articles to profl. jours. Chmn. Mecklenburg County Rep. Com., 1978-80; chmn. N.C. State Rep. Conv., 1979-80; pres. Am. Inns of Ct. Found. Dameron fellow, 1967 Mem. Mecklenburg County Bar Assn., Edward Bennett Williams Inn of Ct. (pres.). Baptist. Lodges: Masons, Scottish Rite, Shriners. Office: US Court of Appeals 333 Constitution Ave NW Washington DC 20001-2866

SENTER, LYONEL THOMAS, JR. federal judge; b. Fulton, Miss., July 30, 1933; s. L. T. and Eva Lee (Jetton) S.; married. B.S., U. So. Miss., 1956; LL.B., U. Miss., 1959. Bar: Miss. 1959. County pros. atty., 1960-64; U.S. commr., 1966-68; judge Miss. Circuit Ct., Circuit 1, 1968-80, U.S. Dist. Ct. (no. dist.) Miss., 1980-82, chief judge, 1982-98, sr. judge, 1998—. Mem. Miss. State Bar Democrat. Office: US Dist Ct PO Box 925 Aberdeen MS 39730-0925

SERBIN, RICHARD MARTIN, lawyer; b. Pitts., Dec. 21, 1947; s. Bernard Serbin and Ella (Stone) Kublanov; m. Francie M. Buncher, June 2, 1974; children: Lawrence B., Haley E., Joshua H. BA, U. Pitts., 1970; JD, Duquesne U., 1974. Bar: Pa. 1974, N.C. 1996, U.S. Dist. Ct. (mid. dist.) Pa. 1974, U.S. Dist. Ct. (we. dist.) Pa. 1980, U.S. Ct. Appeals (3d cir.) 1981, U.S. Supreme Ct. 1985; cert. Nat. Bd. Trial Advocacy (civil). Assoc. Barron & Zimmerman, Lewistown, Pa., 1974-77; ptnr. Mullen, Casanave, Carpenter & Serbin, Altoona, 1977-81, Levine, Reese & Serbin, Altoona, 1982-97, Reese, Serbin, Kovacs & Nypaver, Altoona, 1997—. Asst. dist. atty. Juniata County, Mifflintown, Pa., 1976-77; instr. Pa. State U., Altoona, 1979-83, 89; adj. settlement judge for Western Dist. Ct., Pa. Bd. dirs. Jewish Fedn., Altoona, 1980-89, Temple Beth Israel, Altoona, 1983-86, Pleasant Valley Community Living, 1982-86, Big Brothers/Sisters of Blair County, 1987-95; mem. Big Brothers and Friends of Boys, 1978-80. Mem. ABA, ATLA, Pa. Trial Lawyers Assn. (bd. govs. 1988-90), Blair County Bar Assn., Million Dollar Advocates Forum. Democrat. Jewish. Avocations: tennis, skiing. General civil litigation, State civil litigation, Personal injury. Office: Reese Serbin Kovacs & Nypaver 85 Logan Blvd Altoona PA 16602-3123

SERCARZ, MAURICE HENRI, lawyer; b. N.Y.C., Sept. 11, 1949; s. Leon L. and Gisele (Sercarz) S. B.A., Wesleyan U., Middletown, Conn., 1971; J.D., U. N.C., 1976. Bar: N.Y. 1977, U.S. Dist. Ct. (ea. and so. dists.) N.Y. 1979, U.S. Ct. Appeals (2d cir.) 1981. Staff atty. supr. criminal def. div. Legal Aid Soc., N.Y.C., 1976-81; sole practice, N.Y.C., 1981; assoc., then ptnr. Kalik, Rosoff, Maron & Sercarz, N.Y.C., 1981— ; tchr. trial advocacy clin. program Benjamin Cordozo Law Sch., N.Y.C., 1984. Mem. N.Y. County Lawyers Assn., Nat. Coll. Criminal Def. Lawyers, Kings County Criminal Bar Assn. Criminal.

SERCHUK, IVAN, lawyer; b. N.Y.C., Oct. 13, 1935; s. Israel and Freda (Davis) S.; children: Camille, Bruce Mead, Vance Foster. BA, Columbia U., 1957, LLB, 1960. Bar: N.Y. 1961, U.S. Dist. Ct. (so. dist.) N.Y. 1963, U.S. Ct. Appeals (2d cir.) 1964, U.S. Tax Ct. 1966. Law clk. to judge U.S. Dist. Ct. (so. dist.) N.Y., N.Y., 1961-63; assoc. Kaye, Scholer, Fierman, Hays & Handler, 1963-68; dep. supt., counsel N.Y. State Banking Dept., N.Y.C., Albany, 1968-71; mem. Berle & Berle, 1972-73; spl. counsel N.Y. State Senate Banks Com., 1972; mem. Serchuk & Zelermyer LLP, White Plains, N.Y., 1976—. Lectr. Practising Law Inst., 1968-71. Mem. N.Y. State Bar Assn., Assn. of Bar of City of N.Y. Banking, General corporate, Mergers and acquisitions. Home: Mead St Waccabuc NY 10597 Office: Serchuk & Zelermyer LLP 81 Main St White Plains NY 10601-1711 E-mail: iserchuk@s-zlaw.com

SERENA, C. DAVID, lawyer; b. McKeesport, Pa., July 20, 1940; s. Chester David and Dorothy Grace (Furst) S.; 1 child, Anthony David. J.D., Southwestern U., 1968. Bar: Calif. 1969, U.S. Dist. Ct. (cen. dist.) Calif. 1969, U.S. Supreme Ct. 1972, U.S. Ct. Appeals, 9th cir. 1972, U.S. Dist. Ct. (so. dist.) Calif. 1975, U.S. Dist. Ct. (no. and ea. dists.) Calif. 1981. Policeman, sgt. of police Los Angeles Police Dept., 1961-69; mem. Cadoo, Tretheway, McGinn & Morgan, Marina Del Rey, Calif., 1969-81, Cadoo, Tretheway, McGinn & Serena, Marina Del Rey, 1982— ; instr. Marymount Coll., Palos Verdes, Calif., 1973-74; planning commr. City of Carson, Calif., 1975-76; sec., dir. Calif. Standard Indemnity, Encino, Calif., 1982— . Mem. Marina Del Rey Bar Assn. (bd. dirs. 1975-79), Los Angeles County Bar Assn. Republican. Club: Marina City. State civil litigation, Insurance, Personal injury. Office: Cadoo Tretheway McGinn & Serena 4560 Admiralty Way Ste 110 Marina Del Rey CA 90292-5424

SERKA, PHILIP ANGELO, lawyer, educator; b. Tacoma, Oct. 29, 1952; s. Joseph and Mary Phyllis (Lovrovich) S.; m. Mary Margaret Foote, May 24, 1975; children: Bradley Philip, Lindsay Dumica. AA, Tacoma C.C., 1971; BA, U. Wash., 1973; JD, U. Puget Sound, 1976. Bar: Wash. 1979, U.S. Dist. Ct. (we. dist.) Wash. 1979. Dep. prosecutor Whatcom County, Bellingham, Wash., 1976-80; assoc. Flynn, Adelstein, Sharpe, 1980-82; ptnr. Adelstein, Sharpe & Serka, 1984—. Lectr. environ. law and zoning Western Wash. U., Bellingham, 1979, 83, 84; chmn. bd. dirs., Northcoast Credit Union, 1999—. Mem. Bellingham Mcpl. Appeals and Code Rev. Bd., 1979-84, chmn., 1979-83; bd. dirs. Whatcom County-Bellingham Vis. and Conv. Bur., 1986—, pres., 1987-88; bd. dirs., North Puget Sound br. Arthritis Found., 1996-2000. Mem. Wash. State Bar Assn. (environ. and land use law sect., lectr. at seminar 1986), Wash. State Trial Lawyers Assn., Wash. State Prosecutors Assn. (com. land use legis. 1978-80), Bellingham-Whatcom County C. of C. (bd. dirs. 1999—), Bellingham C. of C. (devel. area recreational entertainment divsn. pageant scholarship com. 1983). Environmental, General practice, Real property. Home: 5006 Silver Beach Ave Bellingham WA 98226-9471 Office: Adelstein Sharpe & Serka 400 N Commercial St Bellingham WA 98225-4003 E-mail: pserka@adelstein.com

SERNA, PATRICIO, state supreme court chief justice; b. Reserve, N.Mex., Aug. 26, 1939; m. Eloise Serna; 1 stepchild, John Herrera; children: Elena Patricia, Anna Alicia. BSBA with honors, U. Albuquerque, 1962; JD, U. Denver, 1970; LLM, Harvard U., 1971; postgrad., Nat. Jud. Coll., 1985, 90, 92, 94. Bar: N.Mex. 1970, Colo. 1971, U.S. Dist. Ct. N.Mex. 1970. Probation and parole officer State of N.Mex., Santa Fe, Las Cruces, 1966-67; spl. asst. to commn. mem. Equal Opportunity Commn., Washington, 1971-75; asst. atty. gen. State of N.Mex., Santa Fe, 1975-79; pvt. practice, 1979-85; dist. judge First Jud. Dist., 1985-96; supreme ct. justice N.Mex. Supreme Ct., 1996-01, chief justice, 2001—. Adj. prof. law Georgetown U., Washington, 1973, Cath. U., Washington, 1974-75; faculty advisor Nat. Jud. Coll., Reno, 1987. Exhibited at N.Mex. Mus. Fine Arts, Gov.'s Gallery, Santa Fe. Active Citizens Organized for Real Edn., Santa Fe, No. N.Mex. Martin Luther King Jr. State Holiday Commn., Santa Fe; past bd. dirs. Santa Fe Group Homes Inc. With U.S. Army, 1963-65. Mem. N.Mex. Bar Assn., N.Mex. Hispanic Bar Assn., Nat. Hispanic Bar Assn., Nat. Coun. Juvenile and Family Ct. Judges, No. N.Mex. Am. Inns of Ct., Santa Fe Bar Assn., Elks, Fraternal Order of Eagles, Fraternal Order of Police, Phi Alpha Delta. Avocations: hiking, fishing, ping pong, chess, painting. Office: NMex Supreme Ct PO Box 848 Santa Fe NM 87504-0848

SERNETT, RICHARD PATRICK, lawyer, consultant; b. Mason City, Iowa, Sept. 8, 1938; s. Edward Frank and Loretta M. (Cavanaugh) S.; m. Janet Ellen Ward, Apr. 20, 1963; children: Susan Ellen, Thomas Ward, Stephen Edward, Katherine Anne. BBA, U. Iowa, 1960, JD, 1963. Bar: Iowa 1963, Ill. 1965, U.S. Dist. Ct. (no. dist.) Ill. 1965, U.S. Supreme Ct. 1971. House counsel, asst. sec. Scott, Foresman & Co., Glenview, Ill., 1963-70, sec., legal officer, 1970-80; v.p., law sec. SFN Cos., Inc., 1980-83, sr. v.p., sec., gen. counsel, 1983-85, exec. v.p., gen. counsel, 1985-87; pvt. practice Northbrook, Ill., 1988-90; v.p., sec., gen. counsel Macmillan/McGraw-Hill Sch. Pub. Co., 1990-92; v.p. Bert Early Assoc., Chgo., 1992-93; ptnr. Sernett & Blake, Northfield, Ill., 1993-95; ret., 1995. Mem. U.S. Dept. State Adv. Panel on Internat. Copyright, 1972-75. Chmn. bd. dirs. Iowa State U., Broadcasting Co., 1987-94. Mem. ABA (chmn. copyright div. 1972-73, com. on copyright legis. 1967-68, 69-70, com. on copyright office affairs 1966-67, 79-81, com. on program for revision copyright law 1971-72), Am. Intellectual Property Law Assn., Am. Soc. Corp. Secs., Ill. Bar Assn. (chmn. copyright com. 1971-72), Chgo. Bar Assn., Patent Law Assn. Chgo. (bbd. mgrs. 1979-82, chmn. copyright law com. 1972-73, 77-78), Copyright Soc. U.S.A. (trustee 1972-75, 77-80), North Shore Country Club (Glenview, Ill.), Wyndemere Country Club (Naples, Fla.), Met. Club Chgo. General corporate, Mergers and acquisitions, Trademark and copyright. Home: 2579 Fairford Ln Northbrook IL 60062-8101

SEROTA, IRVING, lawyer; b. Bklyn., Nov. 17, 1931; s. Albert and Florence (Forman) S.; m. Annette Kupperman, Nov. 27, 1955; children—Lois G., Stuart D. LL.B., Bklyn. Law Sch., 1954. Bar: N.Y. 1954, U.S. Dist. Ct. (so. and ea. dists.) N.Y. 1959, U.S. Supreme Ct. 1971. Sole practice, N.Y., 1954-59; ptnr. Kaufman & Serota P.C., N.Y.C., 1959— , Kantor & Serota P.C., N.Y.C., 1973-83. Mem. N.Y. State Bar Assn., N.Y. County Lawyers Assn. Lodge: K.P. (chancellor 1962-63). Contracts commercial, General practice, Probate. Office: Kaufman & Serota PC 225 Broadway New York NY 10007-3001 E-mail: irvser@aol.com

SEROTA, JAMES IAN, lawyer; b. Chgo., Oct. 20, 1946; s. Louis Henry and Phyllis Estelle (Horner) S.; m. Susan Perlstadt, May 7, 1972; children: Daniel Louis, Jonathan Mark. AB, Washington U., St. Louis, 1968; JD cum laude, Northwestern U., 1971. Bar: Ill. 1971, U.S. Dist. Ct. (no. dist.) Ill. 1972, D.C. 1978, U.S. Supreme Ct. 1978, U.S. Ct. Appeals (D.C. cir.) 1978, U.S. Dist. Ct. (D.C. dist.), U.S. Ct. Claims 1980, N.Y. 1981, U.S. Dist. Ct. (so. and ea. dists.) N.Y. 1981, U.S. Ct. Appeals (2d cir.) 1983. Trial atty. Antitrust div. U.S. Dept. Justice, Washington, 1971-77; assoc. Bell, Boyd & Lloyd, 1977-81; ptnr. Werner, Kennedy & French, N.Y.C., 1982-85, Levitsky & Serota, 1985-86, Huber, Lawrence & Abell, N.Y.C., 1987-98, Vinson & Elkins, 1998—. Contbr. articles to profl. jours.; editor Law Rev. Northwestern U.; law bd., antitrust columnist CCH Power and Telecom Law jour. Recipient Spl. Achievement award U.S. Dept. Justice, 1976. Mem. ABA (chmn. ins. industry com. 1987-90, vice chair program com. 1990-91, chair annual mtg. program 1991-94, chair fuel & energy com. 1994-97, coun. 1997-2000), N.Y. State Bar Assn., Assn. of Bar of City of N.Y. (antitrust and trade regulation com. 1988-91), Fed. Bar Council. Antitrust, Federal civil litigation. E-mail: jserota@velaw.com

SEROTA, SUSAN PERLSTADT, lawyer, educator; b. Chgo., Sept. 10, 1945; d. Sidney Morris and Mildred (Penn) Perlstadt; m. James Ian Serota, May 7, 1972; children: Daniel Louis, Jonathan Mark. AB, U. Mich., 1967; JD, NYU, 1971. Bar: Ill. 1971, D.C. 1972, N.Y. 1981, U.S. Dist. Ct. (no. dist.) Ill. 1971, U.S. Dist. Ct. (so. dist.) N.Y. 1981, U.S. Dist. Ct. (ea. dist.) N.Y. 1985, U.S. Ct. Claims 1972, U.S. Tax Ct. 1972, U.S. Ct. Appeals (D.C. cir.) 1972. Ptnr. Pillsbury Winthrop LLP, N.Y.C., 1982—. Adj. prof. Sch. Law, Georgetown U., Washington, 1974-75; mem. faculty Practicing Law Inst., N.Y.C., 1983—. Editor: ERISA Fiduciary Law, 1995, Supplement, 1998; assoc. editor Exec. Compensation Jour., 1973-75; dep. editor Tax Mgmt., Estate and Gift Taxation and Exec. Compensation, 1973-75; mem. editl. adv. bd. Benefits Law Jour., 1988—, Tax Mgmt. Compensation Jour., 1993—; mem. bd. editor ERISA and Benefits Law Jour., 1992—; contbr. articles to profl. jours. Fellow Am. Coll. Tax Counsel, Am. Coll. of Employee Benefits Counsel (dir., charter fellow); mem. ABA (chmn. joint com. employee benefits 1987-88, taxation sect. 1991-92, vice-chair taxation sect. 1999—), Internat. Pension and Employee Benefits Lawyers Assn. (co-chair 1993-95), N.Y. State Bar Assn. (exec. com. tax sect. 1988-92), Am. Bar Retirement Assn. (dir. 1994—, pres. 1999-2000). Democrat. Mergers and acquisitions, Pension, profit-sharing, and employee benefits, Taxation, general. Office: Pillsbury Winthrop LLP One Battery Park Pla New York NY 10004-1490 E-mail: sserota@pillsburywinthrop.com

SEROTTA, JUDD ADAM, lawyer; b. Phila. s. Howard Lawrence and Carol Fay Hecht Serotta; m. Linda Jo Albers, Aug. 13, 1998. BA, Dartmouth Coll., 1994; JD, Harvard U., 1997. Bar: Pa. 1997, N.J. 1997, U.S. Dist. Ct. (ea. dist.) Pa. 1998. Assoc. Wolf, Block, Schorr & Solis-Cohen LLP, Phila., 1997—. Mem. leadership devel. program Am. Jewish Com., Phila., 1998—, Young Leadership Coun. Jewish Fedn., Phila., 1998—. Mem. ABA, Pa. Bar Assn., Phila. Bar Assn., Mendelssohn Club (tenor I 1997—). Republican. Jewish. Avocations: music, politics, travel, film, sports. General civil litigation, Constitutional, Legislative. Office: Wolf Block Schorr & Solis-Cohen LLP 12 Fl Packard Bldg 111 S 15th St Philadelphia PA 19102

SERRES, GREGORY A. prosecutor; BBA, Texas A&M U.; JD, Baylor U., 1986. Prosecutor Harris Co. Dist. Atty. Office , Tex., 1987—92; asst. US atty. US Dept. Justice, Southern Dist., 1992—95, chief, Special Prosecutions Div., 1995—98, first asst. US atty., 1998—2001, US atty., 2001—. Grantee Nat. Merit Scholar, Lechner Fellowship. Office: US Attorney Southern Dist of Tex PO Box 61129 Houston TX 77208 Fax: 713-567-3389*

SERRETTE, CATHY HOLLENBERG, lawyer; b. Scranton, Pa., Apr. 28, 1954; d. Herbert Saul and Lee (Weisberger) Hollenberg; m. Dennis Louis Serrette, July 27, 1985; children: Kyle Malcolm, Desmond Harold, Malcolm Mandela. BS summa cum laude, U. Pitts., 1975; JD, George Washington U., 1980; LLM in Internat. Legal Studies, Am. U., 1991. Bar: N.Y. 1980, D.C. 1986, Md. 1986, U.S. Dist. Ct. D.C. 1987. Assoc. Advs. for Children, N.Y.C., 1980-81; ptnr. Kresky, Sinawski & Hollenberg, 1981-84; legis. dir. Congressman Savage, Washington, 1985-86; pvt. practice Oxon Hill, Md., 1987—; master for domestic causes Cir. Ct. Prince George's County, 2001—. V.p. Law Found. of Prince Georges County, Inc., 1996—; co-legal dir. ACLU, Prince Georges County chpt. Writer ABA Commn. on the Disabled, 1978-79. Co-chairperson edn. com. NAACP, Prince Georges County, Md., 1987-88; chairperson parent's adv. com. Apple Grove Elem. Sch., 1987-88; co-coord. 26th legis. dist. Prince Georges County Rainbow Coalition, 1988; bd. dirs. Prince Georges County chpt. ACLU, 1994—, Prince Georges County Law Found., 1995—, treas. Mem. Nat. Lawyers Guild (D.C. chpt. chair So. Africa com. exec. bd., pres. South African Women's Day com. 1988—), D.C. Bar Assn., Md. Bar Assn., Prince Georges County Bar Assn., Md. Women's Bar Assn., Phi Beta Kappa. Jewish. Avocations: skiing, horseback riding, swimming, tennis. General civil litigation, Criminal, Family and matrimonial. Home: 1809 Clayton Dr Oxon Hill MD 20745-3724 Office: Hollenberg Serrette & McDermott 6192 Oxon Hill Rd Ste 511 Oxon Hill MD 20745-3142

SERRING, MICHAEL, lawyer; b. Frederiksberg, Denmark, Apr. 13, 1960; s. Rikard and Erna Lilly Serring; m. Lisbeth Fahlgren, May 4, 1990; 1 child, Ann-Sophie. Degree in Law, U. Copenhagen, 1984. Bar: Denmark 1987, Supreme Ct. Denmark 1992. Tutor Copenhagen U., 1985-88; with Bech Bruun Dragsted, Copenhagen, Denmark, 1993—, ptnr. Denmark, 1996—. Contbr. chpt. to book. Mem. Danish Bar Assn. (insolvency com. 1997—, course orgn. com. 1997—), Kuratorforeningen. Bankruptcy, Consumer commercial. Office: Bech Bruun Dragsted 3 Norre Farimagsgade DK 1364 Copenhagen Denmark Office Fax: 45 33 15 25 55. E-mail: michael.serring@bechbruundragsted.com

SERRITELLA, WILLIAM DAVID, lawyer; b. Chgo., May 16, 1946; s. William V. and Josephine Dolores (Scalise) S. JD, U. Ill., Champaign, 1971. Bar: Ill. 1971, U.S. Dist. Ct. (no. and cen. dists.) Ill. 1972, U.S. Dist. Ct. (ea. and we. dists.) Wis. 1995, U.S. Ct. Appeals (7th cir.) 1974, U.S. Supreme Ct. 1979, U.S. Dist. Ct. (so. dist.) Ind. 1997. Law clk. U.S. Dist. Ct., Danville, Ill., 1971-72; ptnr. Ross & Hardies, Chgo., 1972—. Arbitrator Am. Arbitration Assn. Mem. ABA, Ill. Bar Assn., Chgo. Bar Assn., Nat. Assn. R.R. Trial Counsel (Ill.), Soc. Trial Lawyers, Defense Rsch. Inst., Legal Club, Trial Lawyers Club (Chgo.). Federal civil litigation, State civil litigation, Personal injury. Office: Ross & Hardies 150 N Michigan Ave Ste 2500 Chicago IL 60601-7567 E-mail: williamserritella@ross-hardies.com

SERUMGARD, JOHN R. lawyer; b. Rolla, N.D., June 11, 1944; s. John R. and Antoinette R. (Bedard) S.; m. K. Laura Wippich, June 9, 1969; children: Jennie Lynn, John Matthew, Kristen Leigh. AB, Georgetown U., 1966, JD, 1969, LLM, 1974. Bar: Ill. 1969, D.C. 1980, U.S. Supreme Ct. 1975. Staff asst. Office U.S. Rep. Fred Schwengel, 1967-68; legal editor labor svcs. Bur. Nat. Affairs, Inc., Washington, 1968-70; labor atty. U.S. C. of C., 1972-75; v.p. labor rels. Rubber Mfrs. Assn., 1975—, sr. v.p., 1998-99, exec. v.p., 1999—. Treas. Rubber Mfrs. Assn., Washington, 1981-89; treas. Natural Rubber Shippers Assn., Inc., 1981-89; chmn. Scrap Tire Mgmt. Coun., 1990—. Bd. dirs. Riverside Manor Civic Assn., 1979-80. Capt. U.S. Army, 1970-72. Mem. ABA, D.C. Bar Assn., Indsl. Rels. Rsch. Assn., River Bend Golf and Country Club (Great Falls, Va.), Farragut Square Club (Washington). Labor, Corporate taxation. E-mail: john@rma.org

SERVICE, JOHN GREGORY, law educator; b. Batesville, Ind., May 30, 1949; s. Henry David and Martha Geneva (Ennis) S.; m. Rosemarie Pinkocze, June 16, 1974; children: Patrick David, Kimberly Marie. AA, Broward Jr. Coll., 1969; BBA, Fla. Atlantic U., 1971; JD, U. Miami, 1974. Bar: Fla. 1974, U.S. Dist. Ct. (so. dist.) Fla. 1976. Claims adjuster Allstate Ins. Co., Coconut Creek, Fla., 1975; atty. Legal Aid Svc. Broward County, Inc., Ft. Lauderdale, 1975-77; house counsel Liberty Mut. Ins. Co., 1977-78; prof. law and econs. Broward C.C., Coconut Creek, 1978—. Adj. prof. Palm Beach Jr. Coll., Boca Raton, Fla., 1982—, Coll. of Boca Raton, 1983—; cons. on hotel and motel liability problems, Delray Beach, Fla.; mediator Fla. Dept. of Ins. Program. Co-author: The Police Use of Force, 1981, Security Litigations and Related Matters, 1982, Hotel-Motel Law: A Primer on Innkeeper Liability, 1983, Security for Hotels and Motels: A Perspective on Liabilities, 1986; contbr. articles on hotel-motel law and liability problems to legal jours. Mem. Fla. Bar Assn., Nat. Assn. Securities Dealers (arbitrator, mediator). Republican. Methodist. Home: 7020 NW 5th Ave Boca Raton FL 33487-2381 Office: Broward Community College 1000 Coconut Creek Blvd Pompano Beach FL 33066-1697 E-mail: GService@Broward.cc.fl.us, JGService@aol.com

SESSIONS, JEFFERSON BEAUREGARD, III, senator; b. Hybart, Ala., Dec. 24, 1946; s. Jefferson Beauregard and Abbie (Powe) S.; m. Mary Montgomery Blackshear, Aug. 9, 1969; children: Mary Abigail, Ruth Blackshear, Samuel Turner BA, Huntingdon Coll., Montgomery, Ala., 1969; JD, U. Ala., 1973. Bar: Ala. 1973. Assoc. Guin, Bouldin & Porch, Russellville, Ala., 1973-75; asst. U.S. atty. U.S. Dept. Justice, Mobile, 1975-77, U.S. atty., 1981-93; assoc., ptnr. Stockman & Bedsole Attys., 1977-81; ptnr. Stockman, Bedsole & Sessions, 1993-94; atty. gen. State of Ala., 1996; U.S. senator from Ala., 1997—. Mem. U.S. atty. gen.'s. adv. com., 1987-89, vice-chmn. 1989; mem. judiciary, health, edn., labor & pensions armed svcs. coms. Presdl. elector State of Ala., 1972; trustee, mem. exec. com. Mobile Bay Area Partnership for Youth, 1981-95; chmn. adminstrv. bd. Ashland Pl. United Meth. Ch., Mobile, 1982; 1st v.p. Mobile Lions Club, 1993-94. Capt. USAR, 1975-85 Recipient U.S. Atty. Gen's. award for significant achievements in the war against drug trafficking U.S. Atty. Gen. William P. Barr, 1992. Mem. ABA, Ala. Bar Assn., Mobile Bar Assn. Home: 1119 Hillcrest Xing E Mobile AL 36695-4505 Office: 493 Senate Russell Office Bldg Washington DC 20510-0001 E-mail: senator@sessions.senate.gov

SESSIONS, WILLIAM STEELE, former government official, lawyer; b. Ft. Smith, Ark., May 27, 1930; s. Will Anderson and Edith A. (Steele) S.; m. Alice Lewis, Oct. 5, 1952; children: William Lewis, Mark Gregory, Peter Anderson, Sara Anne. BA, Baylor U., 1956, LLB, 1958; hon. degree, John C. Marshall Law Sch., St. Mary's U., 1989; LLD (hon.), Dickinson Coll., 1988, Flager Coll., 1990, Davis & Elkins Coll., 1992, McMurry U., 1997. Bar: Tex. 1959; U.S. Dist Ct. (Western Dist.) Tex.; Ct. Appeals (5th Cir.). Ptnr. McGregor & Sessions, Waco, Tex., 1959-61; assoc. Tirey, McLaughlin, Gorin & Tirey, 1961-63; ptnr. Haley, Fulbright, Winniford, Sessions & Bice, 1963-69; sect. chief, govt. ops sect. criminal divsn. U.S. Dept. Justice, Washington, 1969-71; U.S. atty. U.S. Dept Justice, U.S. Dist. Ct., (we. dist), San Antonio, 1971-74; dist. judge U.S. Dist. Ct. (we. dist.) Tex., 1974-87, chief judge, 1980-87; dir. FBI, Washington, 1987-93; ptnr. Sessions & Sessions, San Antonio, 1995-2000, Holland & Knight, LLP, San Antonio, 2000—. Bd. dirs. Fed. Jud. Ctr., Washington, chmn. bench book com., 1981—; mem. Tex. Commn. on Judicial Efficiency, 1995, Tex. Commn. on a Representative Student Body, 1998. Contbr. articles to profl. jours. Active Dr. Martin Luther King Jr. Fed. Holiday Commn., 1991-96, hon. bd. dirs., 1993-94; bd. trustees Nat. Environ. Edn. & Tng. Found., Inc., 2001—. Lt. USAF, 1951-55; capt. USAFR, Recipient Rosewood Gavel award St. Mary's U. Sch. Law, San Antonio, 1982, Disting. Alumni award Baylor U., Golden Plate award Am. Acad. Achievement, 1988, Law Enforcement Leadership award Assn. Fed. Investigators, 1989, medal of honor DAR, 1989, Disting. Eagle Scout award Boy Scouts Am., 1990, Person of Yr. award Am. Soc. for Indsl. Security, 1990, Magna Charta award Baronial Order of Magna Charta, 1990; named Lawyer of Yr., Baylor Law Sch., 1988, Father of Yr., Nat. Fathers Day Com., 1988, Ellis Island Congl. Medal of Honor, 1992; inducted into Eagle Scout Hall of Fame, 1998. Fellow ABA (chmn. spl. com. on judicial independence 1997—, Nat. Law Day chmn. 2000); mem. Jud. Conf. U.S. (com. on ct. adminstrn., chmn. jud. improvements subcom. 1983-85, ad hoc com. on automation to subcom. 1984-87, mem. ad hoc ct. reporter com. 1984-87), San Antonio Bar Assn. (bd. dirs. 1973-74), Fed. Bar Assn. (pres. San Antonio sect. 1974), Am. Judicature Soc. (exec. com. 1982-84), Dist. Judges Assn. of 5th Cir. (pres. 1982-83), State Bar of Tex. (chmn. com. to develop procedures for cert. state law questions to Supreme Ct. by Fed. Cts. 1983-85), Waco McLennan County Bar Assn. (pres. 1968), San Antonio Inns of Ct. (pres. 1986), William S. Sessions Inns of Ct. Republican. Methodist Avocations: hiking, climbing, canoeing. Office: Holland & Knight LLP Ste 100 2099 Pennsylvania Ave NW Washington DC 20006 Fax: (202) 955-5564. E-mail: wsession@hklaw.com

SESTRIC, ANTHONY JAMES, lawyer; b. St. Louis, June 27, 1940; s. Anton and Marie (Gasparovic) S.; m. Carol F. Bowman, Nov. 24, 1966; children: Laura Antonette, Holly Nicole, Michael Anthony. Student, Georgetown U., 1958-62; JD, Mo. U., 1965. Bar: Mo. 1965, Minn. 1996, U.S. Ct. Appeals (8th cir.) 1965, U.S. Ct. Appeals (7th cir.) 1984, U.S. Dist. Ct. Mo. 1966, U.S. Dist. Ct. (no dist.) Tex. 1985, U.S. Dist. Ct. Ill. 1994, U.S. Tax Ct. 1969, U.S. Supreme Ct. 1970, U.S. Claims Ct. 1986. Law clk. U.S. Dist. Ct., St. Louis, 1965-66; ptnr. Sestric, McGhee & Miller, 1966-77, Fordyce and Mayne, 1977-78, Sestric & Garvey, 1978-96, Sestric Law Firm, St. Louis, 1996—. Spl. asst. to Mo. atty. gen., St. Louis, 1968, spl. asst. circuit atty., 2001—; mem. Fed. Jud. Selection Commn., 1993, U.S. Jud. Selection Commn., 1993-94; gen. chmn. 22nd jud. cir. bar com., 1995, mem. Region XI disciplinary com., 2001—. Contbr. articles to profl. jours. Hearing officer St. Louis Met. Police Dept.; active St. Louis Air Pollution Bd. Appeals and Varience Rev., 1966-73, chmn., 1968-73; active St. Louis Airport Commn., 1975-76; dist. vice-chmn. Boy Scouts Am., 1970-76; bd. dirs. Full Achievement, Inc., 1970-77, Legal Aid Soc. St. Louis, 1976-77, Law Libr. Assn. St. Louis, 1976-78, Thomas Dunn Memls., 1995-98, Marquette Learning Ctr., 1995-98; v.p. bd. St. Elizabeth Acad., 1985-86 Mem. ABA (state chmn. judiciary com. 1973-75, cir. chmn. com. condemnation, zoning and property use 1975-77, standing com. bar activities 1982-88), Nat. Conf. Bar Pres.'s (exec. coun. 1987-90), Mo. Bar Assn. (vice-chmn. young lawyers sect. 1973-76, bd. govs. 1974-77, chmn. law practice mgmt. com. 1997-99), Bar Assn. Met. St. Louis (chmn. young lawyers sect. 1974-75, exec. com. 1974-83, 94-95, pres. 1981-82, bd. govs. 1995-98, chmn. survey com. 1999). Federal civil litigation, State civil litigation, Estate planning. Home: 3967 Holly Hills Blvd Saint Louis MO 63116-3135 Office: Sestric Law Firm 801 N 2nd St Saint Louis MO 63102-2560 E-mail: ajsestric@juno.com

SETRAKIAN, BERGE, lawyer; b. Beirut, Lebanon, Apr. 14, 1949; came to U.S. 1976; s. Hemayak and Arminee S.; m. Vera L. Nazarian, Nov. 22, 1975; children: Ani, Lara. Diplome d'Etudes de Doctorat, U. Lyons, France, 1973; Diplome d'Etudes de Doctorat Droit Compare, F.I.E.D.C., Strasbourg, France, 1974; Licence en Droit Francais, Licence en Droit Libanais, U. St. Joseph, 1972. Bar: Beirut 1972, N.Y. 1983. Assoc. Tyan & Setrakian, Beirut, 1972-76; ptnr. Whitman & Ransom, N.Y.C., 1976-93, Whitman, Breed, Abbott & Morgan, N.Y.C., 1993-2000, Winston & Strawn, N.Y.C., 2000—. Bd. dirs. Cedars Bank, Calif., 1987—, Bank Audi, U.S.A., 1991; fgn. law cons., N.Y., 1978. Bd. dirs., v.p., sec. Armenian Gen. Benevolent Union, N.Y.C., 1977—; pres. Worldwide Youth orgns., 1978—; bd. dirs. Armenian Assy. of Am., Washington, 1978-87; bd. dirs. Am. Task Force for Lebanon, 1988—; bd. dirs. Am. U. Armenia, 1992—. Mem. ABA, N.Y. Bar Assn., Beirut Bar Assn., U.K. Law Soc., Am. Fgn. Law Assn., Englewood Field Club. Banking, Contracts commercial, Private international. Office: Winston & Strawn 200 Park Ave New York NY 10166-0005 E-mail: bsetraki@winston.com

SETTLAGE, STEVEN PAUL, lawyer; b. Nashville, Tenn., April 29, 1951; s. Paul Herman and Doris Ruby (Taylor) S.; m. Diane Marie Ribblett, Aug. 11, 1973; children: Christine Marie, Matthew Steven, Jessica Lauren, Joshua Taylor. BS, Vanderbilt U., 1973; JD, Washington and Lee U., 1976. Bar: Va. 1976. Assoc. Hirschler, Fleischer, Weinberg, Cox & Allen, Richmond, Va., 1976-81, ptnr., chmn. real estate sect., 1981-86; exec. v.p. Rowe Devel. Co., 1986-88; pres. Rowe Devel. Co., 1988—; lectr. Va. Law Found., Charlottesville, 1982. Author: Landlord Tenant Law and Practie, 1978, 84; Real Estate Financing in the '80s, 1982. Trustee Christ the King Lutheran Ch., Richmond, 1982- 83. Mem. Va. State Bar Assn. (real estate com.), ABA, Richmond Bar Assn. (exec. com. real estate sect. 1981-82), Phi Alpha Delta. General corporate, Landlord-tenant, Real property. Home: 3811 Old Gun Rd W Midlothian VA 23113-2020 Office: Rowe Development Co PO Box 32136 Glen Allen VA 23060

SETTLE, CANDICE A. lawyer; b. Fort Smith, Ark., July 26, 1972; d. George M. and Mary L. Cabaniss; m. Kiley Settle, Aug. 7, 1993 (div. Aug. 1998); 1 child, Taryn. Assoc. Orgain Bell & Tucker, Beaumont, Tex., 1997-98, Bagby Law Firm, Van Buren, Ark., 1998; atty. Crawford County Dep. Pub. Def., 1998—; pvt. practice, 1998—. Bd. dirs. Western Ark. Legal Svcs., Fort Smith. Bd. dirs. Vol. Atty. Project, Fort Smith, 1998—. Mem. Bus. and Profl. Women, Sertoma Club. Baptist. Office: PO Box 1695 8 South 6th St Van Buren AR 72957

SETTLE, ERIC LAWRENCE, lawyer; b. N.Y.C., July 28, 1961; s. Elliott Titus and Thelma (Radzvill) S.; m. Robin Marks, Aug. 23, 1986; children: Adam Harrison, Alexander Howard. AB cum laude, Colgate U., 1983; JD with honors, George Washington U., 1986. Bar: Pa. 1986, U.S. Dist. Ct. (ea. dist.) Pa. 1987, U.S. Dist. Ct. (mid. dist.) Pa. 1995, U.S. Ct. Appeals (3d cir.) 1992, U.S. Supreme Ct. 1995. Assoc. Wolf, Block, Schorr & Solis-Cohen, Phila., 1986-90, Fox, Rothschild, O'Brien & Frankel, Phila., 1990-95; dep. gen. counsel to gov. Commonwealth of Pa., 1995-97; regional gen. counsel Aetna (now Aetna Inc.), Blue Bell, Pa., 1997—. Trustee Colgate U., Hamilton, N.Y., 1983-86, Bryn Mawr Rehab. Hosp., 1993-94; pres. Riverview Condominium Assn., Phila., 1991-93; counsel Craig Snyder for U.S. Congress, Phila., 1992. George Cobb fellow Colgate U., 1981, 82. Mem. ABA (young lawyers divsn., career issues com. 1992-93), Pa. Bar Assn. (exec. com. young lawyers divsn. 1992-93), Phila. Bar Assn. (young lawyers sect. exec. com. 1990-92, dir. bar edn. ctr. 1993-95, trustee Phila. Bar Found., 1994), Phi Alpha Delta (marshal 1984-85). Administrative and regulatory, Health. Home: 1148 N Woodbine Ave Narberth PA 19072-1245 Office: Aetna Inc Law Dept 980 Jolly Rd # U19A Blue Bell PA 19422-1904 E-mail: settleel@aetna.com

SETZLER, EDWARD ALLAN, lawyer; b. Kansas City, Mo., Nov. 3, 1933; s. Edward A. and Margaret (Parshall) S.; m. Helga E. Friedemann, May 20, 1972; children: Christina, Ingrid, Kirstin. BA, U. Kans., 1955; JD, U. Wis., 1962. Bar: Mo. 1962, U.S. Tax Ct. 1962. Assoc. Spencer, Fane, Britt & Browne, Kansas City, 1962-67, ptnr., 1968-2000, mng. ptnr., 1974-77, 78-82, chmn. trust and estate sect., 1974-2000; ptnr. Husch & Eppenberger, LLC, 2000—. Lectr. CLE programs U. Mo. and Kansas City Sch. Law, 1983-95; mem. Jackson County Probate Manual Com., 1988; Mo. rep. to joint editl. bd. Uniform Probate Code, 1989-99. Co-author: (book) Missouri Estate Administration, 1984, supplements, 1987—2001; co-author, co-editor: Understanding Living Trusts, 1990, expanded edit., 2001. Amb., bd. govs., bd. dirs., chmn. found. com. Am. Royal, 1982—; mem. planning giving com., bus. coun. Nelson Atkins Mus. Art, 1984—; mem. deferred giving com. Children's Mercy Hosp., 1991—; mem. Kansas City Estate Planning Symposium Com., 1984-92, chmn., 1991; mem. adv. com. Greater Kansas City Cmty. Found., 2000—. Fellow Am. Coll. Trust and Estate Counsel (state chmn. 1992-97, mem. state membership com. 1986-2001); mem. ABA, Mo. Bar Assn. (lectr., vice chmn. probate and estate planning com. 1994-97), Kansas City Met. Bar Assn. (lectr., chmn. probate and trust 1979, 92, vice chmn. 1983-85, 91, legis. rev. com. 1991-95), Estate Planning Soc. Kansas City (co-founder 1965, pres. 1983-84, dir. 1984-85, mem. social com. 1968—), Order of Coif, Sigma Chi, Phi Delta Phi. Estate planning, Probate, Estate taxation. Office: 1200 Main St Ste 1700 Kansas City MO 64105-2100 Fax: 816-421-0596. E-mail: edward.setzler@husch.com

SEVERAID, RONALD HAROLD, lawyer; b. Berkeley, Calif., July 13, 1951; s. J. Harold and Irene Ann (Clark) S.; m. Peggy R. Chappus. BA, U. Calif., Davis, 1973; JD, Georgetown U., 1977. Bar: Calif. 1977, D.C. 1979, U.S. Dist. Ct. (ea. and ctrl. dists.) Calif. 1977. Assoc. Kindel & Anderson, L.A., 1977-79; exec. v.p., gen. counsel Pacific Mktg. Devel., Sacramento, 1979-80, pres., 1980-81; sec. Aaron-Ross Corp., Glendora, Calif., 1983-84; sole practice Sacramento, 1979-84; sr. atty. Severaid & Seegmiller, 1984-94; ptnr. Severaid & Nauman, 1994-96; sole practice, 1997—. Co-editor Internat. Cts. of Justice Opinion Briefs, 1978; sr. topics editor Law and Policy in Internat. Bus., 1975-76; contbr. articles to profl. jours. Pres. Pacifica Villas Homeowners Assn., 1978-79. Mem. ABA, Calif. State Bar Assn., Sacramento County Bar Assn., Cmty. Assns. Inst. (pres. Calif. North chpt. 1988-89, mem. Calif. legis. action com., chmn. subcom. assessments and lien rights 1990, legis. chair 1991-93, chmn. 1993-94), Calif. Trustees Assn. State civil litigation, General corporate, Real property. Office: Severaid Law Office 1805 Tribute Rd Ste J Sacramento CA 95815-4303

SEVEY, JACK CHARLES, lawyer; b. Sacramento, June 5, 1938; s. Cecil Alvin and Virginia Lutisha S.; m. Roberta Rae Rossi; children: Jack C. Jr., Jeffrey C., Kristin M., James C., Kara M. AA, Sacramento Jr. Coll., 1959; BA, U. Calif., Berkeley, 1961; LLB, U. San Francisco, 1964. Bar: U.S. Dist. Ct. (no. dist.) Calif. 1965, U.S. Ct. Appeals (9th cir.), U.S. Supreme Ct. Assoc. O'Conner & Lewis, Sacramento, 1965-68; ptnr. O'Conner & Sevey, 1968-78, Gessford, Sevey & Alpar, Sacramento, 1978-83, Sevey & Alpar, Sacramento, 1983-90, Crow Law Firm Inc., Sacramento, 1990—. Named Adv. of Yr., Sacramento Consumer Attys., 1995. Fellow Am. Coll. Trial Lawyers; mem. Am. Bd. Trial Advs. (pres. Sacramento chpt. 1993). Personal injury. Office: Crow Law Firm 700 E St Sacramento CA 95814-1209

SEVIER, ERNEST YOULE, lawyer; b. Sacramento, June 20, 1932; s. Ernest and Helen Faye (McDonald) S.; m. Constance McKenna, Apr. 12, 1969; children: Carolyn Stewart, Katherine Danielle. A.B., Stanford U., 1954, J.D., 1956. Bar: Calif. 1956, U.S. Supreme Ct. 1965. Asso. mem. firm Sedgwick, Detert, Moran & Arnold, San Francisco, 1958-62; mem. firm Severson & Werson, 1962-99. Served with USAF, 1956-57. Fellow Am. Bar Found.; mem. ABA (chmn. tort and ins. practice sect. 1982-83, exec. coun. 1976-84, chmn. standing com. on assoc. comms. 1988-90, chmn. coord. com. on Outreach to Pub. 1989-90, chmn. standing com. on lawyers responsibility for client protection 1991-94, commn. on non-lawyer practice 1992-95), Calif. Bar Assn. Office: Severson & Werson 1 Embarcadero Ctr Fl 26 San Francisco CA 94111-3715

SEWARD, GEORGE CHESTER, lawyer; b. Omaha, Aug. 4, 1910; s. George Francis and Ada Leona (Rugh) S.; m. Carroll Frances McKay, Dec. 12, 1936 (dec. 1991); children: Gordon Day, Patricia McKay (Mrs. Dryden G. Liddle), James Pickett, Deborah Carroll (Mrs. R. Thomas Coleman). BA, U. Va., 1933, LLB, 1936. Bar: Va. 1935, N.Y., Ky., D.C., U.S. Supreme Ct. With Shearman & Sterling, N.Y.C., 1936-53, Seward & Kissel, N.Y.C., 1953—. Dir. Witherbee Sherman Corp., 1952-66, pres. 1964-66, Howmet Corp., 1955-75, Chas. P. Young Co., 1965-72, Howmedica Inc., 1970-72, Benson Mines, Inc., 1980-85; trustee Benson Iron Ore Trust, 1969-80. Author: Basic Corporate Practice, 1977, Seward and Related Families, 1994; co-author: Model Business Corporation Act Annotated, 1960, We Remember Carroll, 1992. Trustee Arts and Scis. Coun. U. Va., 1983-93, pres., 1991-93; trustee Edwin Gould Found. for Children, 1955-96, Nature Conservancy of Ea. L.I., 1969-80, N.Y. Geneal. and Biog. Soc. Named to Louisville Male H.S. Alumni Assn. Hall of Fame, 1991; commd. Ky. Col., 1993. Fellow Am. Bar Found. (chmn. model corp. acts com. 1956-65), N.Y. State Bar Found.; mem. Internat. Bar Assn. (hon. life pres., hon. pres., founder sect. on bus. law, lectr. series named in his honor, New Delhi 1988, Lisbon 1992, Budapest 1993, Geneva 1994), ABA (chmn. bus. law sect. 1958-59, chmn. sect. com. corp. laws 1952-58, chmn. sect. banking com. 1960-61, mem. ho. of dels. 1959-60, 63-74, mem. joint com. with Am. Law Inst. on continuing legal edn. 1965-74), Athenaeum Lit. Assn. (Louisville), Downtown Assn. (N.Y.C.), Knickerbocker Club, N.Y. Yacht Club, Univ. Club (Chgo.), Met. Club (Washington), Bohemian Club (San Francisco), Gardiner's Bay Country Club (Shelter Island, N.Y.), Greencroft Club (Charlottesville, Va.), Cum Laude Soc., Raven Soc., Order of Coif, Phi Beta Kappa Fellows (pres. 1969-75), Phi Beta Kappa, Theta Chi, Delta Sigma Rho. General corporate, Finance, Private international. Home: 48 Greenacres Ave Scarsdale NY 10583-1436 Office: Seward & Kissel One Battery Park Plz New York NY 10004 also: Internat Bar Assn 271 Regent St London W1R 7PA England

SEWELL, CAMERON DEE, lawyer; b. Dallas, Aug. 29, 1947; s. William Albert and Sylvia DeLeon (Harman) S.; m. Sandra Morris, Aug. 23, 1968; children: Paul, David, Laurie. BA, U. Tex., 1968; JD, 1970. Bar: Tex. 1971, U.S. Dist. Ct. (no. dist.) Tex. 1977, U.S. Tax Ct. 1972, U.S. Ct. Appeals (5th cir.) 1981. Assoc. Stroud & Smith, Dallas, 1971-76, ptnr., 1976-84, mng. ptnr., 1983-84; ptnr. Vial, Hamilton, Koch & Knox, Dallas, 1984-92; ptnr., True, Rohde & Sewell, Dallas, 1992—. Trustee sch. bd. Lancaster Ind. Sch. Dist., Tex., 1983-92; chmn. civil svc. commn. City of Lancaster, Tex., 1995—. Mem. ABA, Tex. Bar Assn., Dallas Bar Assn. Baptist. General corporate, Oil, gas, and mineral, Corporate taxation. Home: 214 Creekwood Dr Lancaster TX 75146-3404

SEXTON, DAVID FARRINGTON, lawyer, investment banking executive; b. Montclair, N.J., Aug. 20, 1943; s. Dorrance and Marjorie (McComb) S.; m. Ann Hemelright, Feb. 27, 1971; children: James, Ashley, Christopher. AB cum laude, Princeton U., 1966; JD cum laude, U. Pa., 1972. Bar: N.Y. 1972. Assoc. Sullivan & Cromwell, N.Y.C., 1972-77; with First Boston Corp., 1977-90, v.p., gen. counsel, 1980-83, mng. dir., gen. counsel, 1983-86; mng. dir., pres. First Boston Internat. Ltd., 1986-90; sr. exec. v.p., dir. Yamaichi Internat. (America), Inc., N.Y.C., 1990-95, vice-chmn., 1995-98; pres., CEO The Farrington Group, LLC, 1998—. Bd.dirs. Yamaichi (Am.) Holdings, Inc., Yamaichi (Am.) Fin., Inc.; adj. prof. law Fordham U., 1985-86; mem. U.S.-Japan Friendship Commn., Washington, 1990-94, chmn. fin. adv. com., 1994—. Lt. USNR, 1966-69. Mem. Assn. Bar City N.Y., Racquet and Tennis Club, N.Y. Yacht Club, Ivy Club, Bucks Harbor Yacht Club (bd. govs. 1991—), The Nat. Assn. of Japan Am. Socs. (bd. dirs. 1998—). Republican. Presbyterian. General corporate, Securities.

SEXTON, JOHN EDWARD, lawyer, dean, law educator; b. Bklyn., Sept. 29, 1942; s. John Edward and Catherine (Humann) S.; m. Lisa Ellen Goldberg; children: Jed, Katherine. BA, Fordham U., 1963, PhD, 1978; JD, Harvard U., 1979. Bar: N.Y. 1981, U.S. Supreme Ct. 1984. Prof. religion St. Francis Coll., Bklyn., 1965-75; law clk. U.S. Ct. Appeals, Washington, 1979, 80, U.S. Supreme Ct., Washingtont, 1980-81; prof. law NYU, N.Y.C., 1981—, dean law sch., 1988—. Dir. Washington Sq. Legal Services, N.Y.C., 1983—, Pub. Interest Law Found., N.Y.C., 1983-85. Author: A Managerial Model of the Supreme Court, 1985, Federal Jury Instructions-Civil, 1985, How Free Are We? A Study of the Constitution, 1985, Cases and Materials in Civil Procedure, 1988. Dir. Root-Tilden Scholarship Program, 1984-88. Mem. Assn. of Am. Law Schs. (pres. 1997-98). Home: 29 Washington Sq W New York NY 10011-9180 Office: NYU Law Sch 40 Washington Sq S New York NY 10012-1099*

SEYBERT, JOANNA, federal judge; b. Bklyn., Sept. 18, 1946; BA, U. Cin., 1967; JD, St. John's U., 1971. Bar: N.Y. 1972, U.S. Dist. Ct. (ea. and so. dists.) N.Y. 1973. Trial staff atty. Legal Aid Soc., N.Y.C., 1971-73, sr. staff atty. Mineola, N.Y., 1976-80; sr. trial atty. Fed. Defender Svc., Bklyn., 1973-75; bur. chief Nassau County Atty's Office, Mineola, 1980-87; judge Nassau County Dist. Ct., Hempstead, N.Y., 1987-92, Nassau County Ct., Mineola, 1992-94, U.S. Dist. Ct. (ea. dist.) N.Y., Uniondale, 1994—. Mem. Internat. Assn. Judges (del.e), Bar Assn. Nassau County, Theodore Rooelt A. Inns of Ct. (past pres.), Fed. Judges Assn., Nassau Lawyeräs Assn. (pas pres.). Office: 1034 Federal Plz Central Islip NY 11722-4443

SEYMOUR, BARBARA LAVERNE, lawyer; b. Columbia, S.C., July 9, 1953; d. Leroy Semon and Barbara Lucile (Youngblood) Seymour. BS, S.C. State Coll., 1975; JD, Georgetown U., 1979; MBA, Harvard U., 1985. Bar: S.C. 1979, Tex. 1984, U.S. Dist. Ct. (ea. dist.) Tex. 1983, U.S. Dist. Ct. (so. dist.) Tex. 1985, U.S. Tax Ct. 1986, U.S. Claims Ct. 1991. Tax atty. Texaco Inc., White Plains, N.Y., 1979-80, Houston, 1980-98; exec. asst. Office of the CFO-Gen. Counsel, Equilon Enterprises LLC, 1998-99, asst. sec., counsel, 1999—. Mem. IRS Commr.'s Adv. Group, 1995-97; mem. Simplified Tax and Wage Reporting Sys. Working Group, 1994-97; loaned exec. for task force to audit Tex. Employment Commn. by Gov. of Tex., 1987-88. Troop leader Girl Scouts U.S., White Plains, 1979-80, asst. troop leader, Houston, 1981-82; bd. dirs. Sickle Cell Disease Rsch. Found. Tex., Houston, 1986-92, treas., 1986-88, pres., 1988-90, chair 25th ann. gala, 1996; vol. allocation panel United Way of the Tex. Gulf Coast; bd. dirs. Found. for Main St., Sandra Organ Dance Co., v.p., 2000—; mem. Black Exec. Exch. program Nat. Urban League 1980-; bd. dirs., exec. com. Houston Area Urban League, 1995-2001, 3d v.p., 1998-2000,1st v.p., 2000-2001, chair 1997 Equal Opportunity Day Dinner, co-chair Host Com., 99; bd. dirs., asst. treas. Sheila Jackson Lee for Congress, 1995-97; Nat. Urban League Conf. Named one of 50 Outstanding Young Leaders of the Future, Ebony Mag., 1983; recipient Disting. Bus. Alumnus award S.C. State Coll., 1991, Eagle award Nat. Eagle Leadership Inst., 1995; selected for Leadership Houston, Leadership Am., 1990; finalist Five Outstanding Young Houstonians award Jaycees, 1988, one of 10 Foremost Fashionables in Houston, Alpha Kappa Alpha, 1994; named 2001's ABC channel 13 Woman of Distinction. Mem. ABA (environ. tax com., employment tax com.), Houston Black Women Lawyers Assn. (sec. 1981-82, treas. 1982-83), Houston Bus. Forum (bd. dirs. 1983, 87-90, treas. 1988-89, sec. 1989-90), Nat. Bar Assn. (com. chmn. 1982-83), S.C. Bar Assn., Tex. Bar Assn., Harvard U. Bus. Sch. Black Alumni Assn. (historian 1985-86), Black Law Alumni Coun. of Georgetown U. Law Ctr., W.J. Durham Soc., The Links, Inc. (v.p. Houston chpt. 1996-2000, pres. 2000—, chair 1995 Cotillion), Alpha Kappa Alpha. Democrat. Roman Catholic. Roman Catholic. Pension, profit-sharing, and employee benefits, Corporate taxation, State and local taxation. Office: Equilon Enterprises LLC 1100 Louisiana St Ste 1066 Houston TX 77002-5220 E-mail: blseymour@equilon.com

SEYMOUR, DONALD EDWARD, lawyer; b. Pitts., May 26, 1946; s. Robert Edward and Hazel (Dixon) S. B.A., Denison U., 1967; J.D., U. Mich., 1970. Bar: Pa. 1970. Assoc. Kirkpatrick & Lockhart, Pitts., 1970-79, ptnr., 1979— . Mem. ABA, Pa. Bar Assn., Allegheny County Bar Assn. Federal civil litigation, State civil litigation. Office: Kirkpatrick & Lockhart 1500 Oliver Building Pittsburgh PA 15222-2312

SEYMOUR, MARY FRANCES, lawyer; b. Durand, Wis., Oct. 20, 1948; d. Marshall Willard and Alice Roberta (Smith) Thompson; m. Marshall Warren Seymour, June 6, 1970; 1 foster child, Nghia Pham. BS, U. Wis., LaCrosse, 1970; JD, William Mitchell Coll., 1979. Bar: Minn. 1979, U.S. Dist. Ct. Minn. 1979, U.S. Ct. Appeals (8th cir.) 1979, U.S. Supreme Ct. 1986. With Cochrane and Bresnahan, P.A., St. Paul, 1979-94, Loper & Seymour, P.A., 1994—. Mem. ABA, Minn. Bar Assn., Ramsey County Bar Assn. Federal civil litigation, General civil litigation, State civil litigation. Office: Loper & Seymour PA 24 4th St E Saint Paul MN 55101-1002 E-mail: maryfseymour@msn.com

SEYMOUR, MCNEIL VERNAM, lawyer; b. St. Paul, Dec. 21, 1934; s. McNeil Vernam and Katharine Grace (Klein) S.; children: Margaret, McNeil Vernam, James, Benjamin; m. Mary Katherine Velner, May 15, 1993. AB, Princeton U., 1957; JD, U. Chgo., 1960. Bar: Minn. 1960, U.S. Dist. Ct. Minn. 1960. Mem. Seymour & Seymour, St. Paul, 1960-71; mem. firm Briggs & Morgan, 1971—, ptnr., 1976—. Trustee, treas. Oakland Cemetery Assn.; bd. dirs. Thomas Irvine Dodge Found.; pres., treas. White Bear Unitarian Ch., 1964-65; sec., bd. dirs. Ramsey County Law Libr.,

1972-76. With U.S. Army, 1960-62. Mem. Minn. Bar Assn., Ramsey County Bar Assn., Somerset Country Club. Republican. Unitarian. Estate planning, Probate, Estate taxation. Home: 886 S Highview Cir Mendota Heights MN 55118-3686 Office: Briggs & Morgan W-2200 1st Nat Bank Bldg Saint Paul MN 55101 E-mail: Seymcn@Briggs.com

SEYMOUR, STEPHANIE KULP, federal judge; b. Battle Creek, Mich., Oct. 16, 1940; d. Francis Bruce and Frances Cecelia (Bria) Kulp; m. R. Thomas Seymour, June 10, 1972; children: Bart, Bria, Sara, Anna. BA magna cum laude, Smith Coll., 1962; JD, Harvard U., 1965. Bar: Okla. 1965. Practice, Boston, 1965-66, Tulsa, 1966-67, Houston, 1968-69; assoc. Doerner, Stuart, Saunders, Daniel & Anderson, Tulsa, 1971-75, ptnr., 1975-79; judge U.S. Ct. Appeals (10th cir.) Okla., 1979-94, 2000—, chief judge, 1994-2000. Assoc. bar examiner Okla. Bar Assn., 1973-79; trustee Tulsa County Law Library, 1977-78; mem. U.S. Jud. Conf., 1994—, com. defender svcs., 1985-91, chmn., 1987-91, com. to review cir. council conduct and disability, 1996—; mem. joint fed. tribal rels. com. for 9th and 10th cirs., 1993—, Okla. State Fed. tribal judicial council, 1993—. Mem. various task forces Tulsa Human Rights Commn., 1972-76, legal adv. panel Tulsa Task Force Battered Women, 1971-77. Mem. Am. Bar Assn., Okla. Bar Assn., Tulsa County Bar Assn., Phi Beta Kappa. Office: US Courthouse 333 W 4th St Ste 4-562 Tulsa OK 74103-3819*

SEYMOUR, STEVEN WAYNE, lawyer; b. Ft. Dodge, Iowa, Nov. 28, 1945; s. Byron Horatio and Ruth Phyllis (Heins) S.; m. Charlotte Sue Ziesman, Sept. 6, 1969; children: Jeffrey Charles, Todd William. BA, U. Iowa, 1968; postgrad., U. Tubingen (W.Ger.), 1971-72; JD, Willamette U., 1975. Bar: Oreg. 1975, U.S. Dist. Ct. Oreg. 1980, U.S. Ct. Appeals (9th cir.) 1984. Law clk. Oreg. Legislature, Salem, 1974-75; dep. dist. atty. Multnomah County, Portland, Oreg., 1975-80; assoc. Samuels Samuels Yoelin & Weiner, 1980-83, ptnr., 1983—. Mem. budget adv. com. City of Portland, 1977; pres. Grant Park Neighborhood Assn., 1980-83; mem. Portland City Club, 1983-84; chmn. governing bd. First United Methodist Ch., Portland, 1984; active local Boy Scouts Am. Served with U.S. Army, 1969-72, Germany. Mem. ABA (litigation sect., trial practice com.), Oreg. Bar Assn. (exec. com., treas. 1985-87, sec. 1987-88), Multnomah County Bar Assn., Internat. Assn. Arson Investigators. Methodist. Club: Willamette Sail. Avocations. Federal civil litigation, State civil litigation, Labor. Office: Samuels Yoelin Kantor Seymour & Spinrad LLP 4640 SW Macadam Ave Ste 200 Portland OR 97201-4278 E-mail: sws@samuelslaw.com

SFEKAS, STEPHEN JAMES, lawyer, educator; b. Balt., Feb. 12, 1947; s. James Stephen and Lee (Mesologites) S.; m. Joanne Lorraine Murphy, May 27, 1973; children: James Stephen, Andrew Edward Stephen, Christina Marie; m. Elizabeth Ruff, Nov. 1, 1997. BS in Fgn. Svc., Georgetown U., 1968, JD, 1973; MA, Yale U., 1972. Bar: Md. 1973, U.S. Dist. Ct. Md. 1974, U.S. Ct. Appeals (4th cir.) 1974. Law clk. U.S. Dist. Ct., Balt., 1973-74; assoc. firm Frank, Bernstein, Conaway & Goldman, 1974-75; asst. atty. gen. State of Md., 1975-81; assoc. firm Tydings & Rosenberg, 1981-82, ptnr., 1983-86; with firm Miles & Stockbridge, 1986-90; ptnr. Weinberg & Green, 1991-98; now Saul & Ewing, LLP, 1998—. Instr. legal writing C.C. Balt., 1976-79; instr. legal ethics Goucher Coll., Balt., 1979; adj. prof. adminstrv. law U. Md., Balt., 1981-93, health, 1993—, law sch. U. Balt., 1993—. Editor Georgetown Law Jour., 1972-73; contbr. articles to legal publs. Bd. dirs. Md. region NCCJ, 1981-89, co-chmn. Md. region, 1986-89; mem. Piraeus Sister City Com., City of Balt., 1983-89; mem. parish coun. Greek Orthodox Cathedral of Annunciation, Balt., 1981-84; mem. internat. com. Balt. region ARC, 1984-85; mem. adv. com. on bread for the world Dept. Ch. and Soc., Greek Orthodox Archdiocese North and S.Am., 1984—; pres. Greek Orthodox Counseling and Social Svcs. of Balt., 1984-88; bd. dirs. Orthodox Christian Laity, 1990—, Ctrl. Md. Ecumenical Coun., 1991—, Balt. Assn. for Retarded Citizens; mem. bylaw com. Girl Scouts Ctrl. Md., 1989-91, Md. Leadership Program, 1997; mem. pres.'s adv. coun. U. Md., Baltimore County. Danforth fellow, Woodrow Wilson fellow, WHO fellow, London, 1979. Fellow Md. Bar Found., Soc. for Values in Higher Edn.; mem. ABA (Grant Morris fellow 1979, forum com. on health law), Md. Bar Assn., Bar Assn. Balt. City, Am. Health Lawyers Assn., Am. Soc. Hosp. Attys. Democrat. Administrative and regulatory, Federal civil litigation, Health. Office: Saul & Ewing LLP 100 S Charles St Baltimore MD 21201-2725 E-mail: ssfekas@saul.com

SGANZERLA, ANDREA BENEDETIO, lawyer; b. Milano, Lombardia, Italy, Nov. 8, 1960; s. Mario Sganzerla and Liú Reali; m. Vittoria Lodi, July 13, 1996; 1 child, Alessandro. Degree in law, U. Milano, 1985. Cert. specialist in arbitration, specialist in European cmty. law. Ptnr. Studio Associato, Milano, 1986-94; owner, ptnr. Studio Legale, 1995—. Cons. Confindustria, Milano, 1993; journalist; dir. Nat. Tech. Rev., 1993. Contbr. articles to profl. jours. With Italian Army, 1984-85. Mem. Italian Internat., European Cmty. Relationships Commn. Avocations: skiing, parachuting, tennis. Contracts commercial. Office: Studio Legale Sganzerla Via A Sangiorgio 15 20145 Milano Italy Home Fax: 024817146; Office Fax: 024817146. E-mail: studiosganzer@tiscalinet.it

SHABAZ, JOHN C. federal judge; b. West Allis, Wis., June 25, 1931; s. Cyrus D. and Harriet T. Shabaz; children: Scott J., Jeffrey J., Emily D., John D. BS in Polit. Sci., U. Wis., 1999; LLB, Marquette U., 1957. Pvt. practice law, West Allis, Wis., 1957-81; mem. Wis. Assembly, 1965-81; judge U.S. Dist. Ct. (we. dist.) Wis., 1981-96, chief judge, 1996-2001. With U.S. Army, 1954-64. Office: US Dist Ct PO Box 591 Madison WI 53701-0591

SHACHOK, MARY ELLEN, lawyer; b. Lynn, Apr. 28, 1961; d. Richard Arnold and Mary Theresa (O'Reilly) S.; 1 child, Shannon Marie. BA in Psychology cum laude, Salem State Coll., 1983; JD, Suffolk U., 1987. Bar: Mass., U.S. Dist. Ct. Mass. Assoc. Law Office Gary S. Sackrider, Salem, Mass., 1987-91, Law Office Ronald Rainer, Boston, 1990-91; pvt. practice Salem, 1991—. Cons. atty. Advocates for Better Child Support, Peabody, Mass., 1993-94, Assn. Child Support Enforcement, Peabody, 1994-95. Mem. Mass. Bar Assn., Essex County Bar Assn., North Shore Women's Lawyer Assn., Phi Delta Phi. Roman Catholic. Avocations: music, travel, dance, roller blading, reading. General civil litigation, Personal injury, Probate. Office: 19 North St Salem MA 01970-3957

SHACTER, DAVID MERVYN, lawyer; b. Toronto, Ont., Can., Jan. 17, 1941; s. Nathan and Tillie Anne (Schwartz) S. BA, U. Toronto, 1963; JD, Southwestern U., 1967. Bar: Calif. 1968, U.S. Ct. Appeals (9th cir.) 1969, U.S. Supreme Ct. 1982. Law clk., staff atty. Legal Aid Found., Long Beach, Calif., 1967-70; asst. city atty. City of Beverly Hills, 1970; ptnr. Shacter & Berg, Beverly Hills, 1971-83, Selwyn, Capalbo, Lowenthal & Shacter Profl. Law Corp., 1984-99; pvt. practice, 1999—. Del. State Bar Conf. Dels., 1976—; lectr. Calif. Continuing Edn. of Bar, 1977, 82, 83, 86; judge pro tem L.A. and Beverly Hills mcpl. cts.; arbitrator L.A. Superior Ct., 1983—, also judge pro tem; disciplinary examiner Calif. State Bar, 1986. Bd. dirs. and pres. Los Angeles Soc. Prevention Cruelty to Animals, 1979-89. Mem. Nat. Assn. of Securities Dealers (Dispute Resolution Dept., arbitrator, 1998—), Beverly Hills Bar Assn. (bd. govs. 1985—, editor-in-chief jour., sec. 1987-88, treas. 1988-89, v.p. 1989-90, pres.-elect 1990-91, pres. 1991-92), Beverly Hills Bar Found. (pres. 1995—, bd. govs. 1998—), Am. Arbitration Assn. (nat. panel arbitrators, neutral arbitrator, panel chmn.), City of Hope Med. Ctr. Aux., Wilshire C. of C. (bd. dirs., gen. counsel 1985-87). General civil litigation, Estate planning, Personal injury. Office: 2566 Overland Ave Ste 550 Los Angeles CA 90064-3371 E-mail: david@shacter.org

SHADDIX, JAMES W. lawyer; b. 1946; BBA, U. Tex., 1968, JD, 1971. Bar: Tex. 1971. With U.S. Treasury-IRS, 1972-77; atty. Pennzoil Co., 1977-79, asst. gen. counsel, 1977-90, gen. counsel, 1990-98; gen. cousnel Pennzoil-Quaker State Co., 1998—. General corporate, Oil, gas, and mineral, Labor. Office: Pennzoil-Quaker State Co PO Box 2967 Houston TX 77252-2967

SHADDOCK, WILLIAM CHARLES, lawyer; b. Orange, Tex., Aug. 25, 1951; s. Carroll Bitting and Hulda Martha (Gaertner) S.; m. Kim Lei McDonald, Mar. 27, 1982; children: William Charles, Andrew Christopher. B.B.A., Tex. Christian U., 1973; M.B.A., So. Meth. U., 1974; J.D., Baylor U., 1977. Bar: Tex. 1977, U.S. Dist. Ct. (no. dist.) Tex. 1980. Assoc. Turner Hitchins, Webb, McInerney & Strother, Dallas, 1977-83; gen. counsel, v.p. Shaddock & Cook Developers, Inc., Dallas, 1983-88; ptnr. Shaddock, Cook & Shaddock, Dallas, 1988—; dir. Preston North Nat. Bank, Dallas; bd. dirs. The Colony Municipal Utility Dist., 1974-76. Mem. ABA, Dallas Bar Assn., Tex. Christian U. Alumni Assn. (bd. dirs. 1981-84), Sigma Chi. Contbr. article to profl. jours. Republican. Lutheran. Club: Downtown Dallas Rotary. State civil litigation, General corporate, Real property. Home: 5216 Corinthian Bay Dr Plano TX 75093-4029 Office: Shaddock Cook & Shaddock 1900 Preston Rd Ste 267 Plano TX 75093-3604

SHADDOCK, WILLIAM EDWARD, JR. lawyer; b. Lake Charles, La., Jan. 18, 1938; s. William Edward Shaddock and Edith (Burton) Plauche; m. Winifred Craig Gorham, Aug. 2, 1958; children: Stephen Gorham, Mary Craig, Nancy Edith. BS, La. State U., 1960, JD, 1963. Bar: La. 1963, U.S. Dist. Ct. (we. dist.) La. 1964, U.S. Supreme Ct. 1968, U.S. Ct. Appeals (5th cir.) 1981; cert. specialist in estate planning and adminstrn. La. Bd. Legal Specialization. Assoc. Plauche & Stockwell, Lake Charles, La., 1963-66; ptnr. Stockwell, Sievert, Viccellio, Clements & Shaddock, L.L.P., 1966—. Fellow Am. Coll. Trusts and Estates Counsel. Republican. Methodist. Avocations: fishing, hunting, photography. Oil, gas, and mineral, Estate planning, Probate. Office: Stockwell Sievert Viccellio Clements & Shaddock LLP PO Box 2900 One Lakeside Plz 4th Fl Lake Charles LA 70602 E-mail: weshaddock@ssvcs.com

SHADLEY, SUE ANN, lawyer; b. Crawfordsville, Ind., Feb. 10, 1952; d. Kenneth Woodrow Shadley and Wilma Grace (Myer) Wilkinson; m. Michael Allen Hart, Feb. 4, 1984. B.S., Purdue U., 1974; J.D., Ind. U., 1977. Bar: Ind. 1977. Atty. Ind. U. Student Loan Adminstrn., Bloomington, 1977-78; legal analyst Ind. Air Pollution Control Div., Indpls., 1978-82; legal analyst, adminstrv. law judge Ind. Dept. Natural Resources, Div. Reclamation, Indpls., 1982— . Mem. ABA, Ind. Bar Assn. Office: Div Reclamation 309 W Washington St Ste 201 Indianapolis IN 46204-2721

SHADOAN, WILLIAM LEWIS, judge; b. Galesburg, Ill., July 12, 1931; s. William Parker and Hortense (Lewis) S.; m. Katherine E. Thomson, 1961; children: Ann-Wayne Harlan, Kate, Tom. BS, U. Ky., 1955; JD, U. Louisville, 1961. Bar: Ky. 1961, U.S. Dist. Ct. (we. dist.) Ky. 1961. City atty., Wickliffe, Ky., 1963; county atty. Ballard County, 1963-76; chief regional judge 1st cir. Wickliffe, 1983—. Chmn. Ballard County Dem. Party, 1963; trustee Meth. Ch., Wickliffe, 1961-84; advisor Selective Svc., Peducah, Ky., 1968; chmn. Wickliffe C. of C., 1967-71; mem. exec. com. Ky. Hist. Soc., Frankfort; vice chmn. Ky. Cert. of Need and Lic. Bd., 1973-84; named assoc. justice Ky. Surpeme Ct., 1984. Capt. U.S. Army, 1955-59. Mem. ABA, Ky. Health Systems Assn. (vice chmn. 1976-82), Ky. Bar Assn. (Outstanding Judge 1997), Assn. Trial Lawyers Am., Ky. County Ofcls. Bd. (chmn. 1976-80), Miss. River Commn. (chmn. 1976-83), Ky. County Attys. Assn. (pres. 1966-77), First Dist. Bar Assn. (pres.), Masons (Wickliffe, 32 degree), Shriners (Madisonville, Ky.), Orer Ea Star, Elks. Home: RR 2 Wickliffe KY 42087-9804 Office: Ballard Courthouse 4th St Wickliffe KY 42087

SHADUR, MILTON IRVING, judge; b. St. Paul, June 25, 1924; s. Harris and Mary (Kaplan) S.; m. Eleanor Pilka, Mar. 30, 1946; children: Robert, Karen, Beth. B.S., U. Chgo., 1943, J.D. cum laude, 1949. Bar: Ill. 1949, U.S. Supreme Ct. 1957. Pvt. practice practice, Chgo., 1949-80; assoc. Goldberg, Devoe & Brussell, 1949-51; ptnr. Shadur, Krupp & Miller and predecessor firms, 1951-80; judge U.S. Dist. Ct. (no. dist.) Ill., Chgo., 1980-92, sr. judge, 1992—. Commr. Ill. Supreme Ct. Character and Fitness, 1961-72, chmn., 1971; gen. counsel Ill. Jud. Inquiry Bd., 1975-80; chmn. adv. com. on evidence rules to Jud. Conf. of U.S., 1999—, mem. adv. com., 1992-99. Editor-in-chief: U. Chgo. Law Rev., 1948-49. Chmn. visiting com. U. Chgo. Law Sch., 1971-76, mem. vis. com., 1989-92, 99—; bd. dirs. Legal Assistance Found. Chgo., 1972-78; trustee Village of Glencoe, 1969-74, Ravinia Festival Assn., 1976-93, exec. com. 1983-93, vice chmn. 1989-93, life trustee, 1994—. Lt. (j.g.) USNR, 1943-46. Fellow Am. Bar Found.; mem. ABA (spl. com. on youth edn. for citizenship 1975-79), Ill. State Bar Assn. (joint com. on rules of jud. conduct 1974), Chgo. Bar Assn. (chmn. legis. com. 1963-65, jud. com. 1970-71, profl. ethics com. 1975-76, sec. 1967-69), Chgo. Council Lawyers, Order of Coif Office: US Dist Ct 219 S Dearborn St Ste 2388 Chicago IL 60604-1800

SHAEVSKY, MARK, lawyer; b. Harbin, Manchuria, China, Dec. 2, 1935; came to U.S., 1938, naturalized, 1944; s. Tolio and Rae (Weinstein) S.; m. Lois Ann Levi, Aug. 2, 1964; children: Thomas Lyle, Lawrence Keith. Student, Wayne State U., 1952-53; BA with highest distinction, U. Mich., 1956, JD with highest distinction, 1959. Bar: Mich. 1959. Law clerk to presiding judge U.S. Dist. Ct., Detroit, 1960-61; assoc. Honigman Miller Schwartz & Cohn, 1961-64; ptnr. Honigman, Miller, Schwartz & Cohn, 1965-69, sr. ptnr., 1969—. Instr. law Wayne State U. Law Sch., Detroit, 1961-64; comml. arbitrator Am. Arbitration Assn., Detroit; bd. dirs. Charter One Fin. Inc., Charter One Bank. Contbr. Wayne State U. Law Rev., U. Mich. Law Rev., 1957-59, asst. editor, 1958-59. Dir. Detroit Mens Orgn. of Rehab. through Tng., 1969-79; mem. exec. bd. Am. Jewish Com., Detroit, 1965-74; trustee Jewish Vocat. Svcs., Detroit, 1973-76; sec., dir. Am. Friends Hebrew Univ., Detroit, 1976-84; mem. capital needs com. Jewish Welfare Fedn., Detroit, 1986-97; trustee William Beaumont Hosp., 1997—, Beaumont Found., 1997—; dir. Shaevsky Family Found., 2000—. With U.S. Army, 1959-60. Burton Abstract fellow, 1959. Mem. ABA, Mich. Bar Assn., Franklin Hills Country Club, Detroit Athletic Club, Order of the Coif, Phi Beta Kappa. General corporate, Real property, Securities. Home: The Hills of Lone Pine 4750 N Chipping Gln Bloomfield Hills MI 48302-2390 Office: Honigman Miller Schwartz & Cohn 2290 First National Bldg Detroit MI 48226 E-mail: mzs@honigman.com

SHAFER, ROBERT TINSLEY, JR. judge; b. Cin., Sept. 11, 1929; s. Robert Tinsley and Grace Elizabeth (Welsh) S.; m. Barbara Jean Hough, Dec. 27, 1950; children: Richard Hough, Janet Lee Shafer Davis, Charles Welsh. BA, Coll. of Wooster, 1951; JD, U. Cin., 1956. Bar: Fla. 1956, U.S. Ct. Appeals (5th cir.) 1963, U.S. Dist. Ct. (so. dist.) Fla. 1961, U.S. Supreme Ct. 1965. Asst. trust officer 1st Nat. Bank, Ft. Myers, Fla., 1956-57; ptnr. Henderson, Franklin, Starnes & Holt, P.A., 1957-77; cir. judge 20th Jud. Cir. State of Fla., 1977-92, chief cir. judge, 1985-89, sr. judge, 1992—. Mem. com. for ret. and sr. judges Nat. Conf. State Trial Judges. Contbr. article to Corp. Law, 1955-56 (Goldsmith Corp. Law prize, 1956). Elder Covenant Presbyn. Ch., 1982-85; mem. jud. commn. Fla. Presbyn. Synod, 1960-63; chmn. Lee County chpt. Red Cross, Ft. Myers, 1963; chair Permanent Judicial Commn., Peace River Presbytery, Presbyn. Ch. U.S.A. 2nd lt. USMCR, 1951-53, PTO, Korea. Mem. ABA, Fla. Conf. Cir. Judges (exec. com. 1986-88), Fla. Bar Assn. (bd. govs. Jr. Bar sect. 1961-64), Lee County Bar Assn. (pres. 1968), Am. Judges Assn., Am. Judicature Soc., Nat. Conf. Met. Cts. Calusa Inn of Ct. Republican. Avocations: bicycling, travel, reading, walking. Home: 2704 Shriver Dr Fort Myers FL 33901-5931

SHAFFER, CHARLES ALAN, lawyer; b. Wilkes-Barre, Pa., July 22, 1938; s. Joseph and Irene G. (Murzin) S.; m. Barbara A. Kurlancheek, July 30, 1961; children— Jonathan David, Susan Deborah. BS in Econs., U. Pa., 1960, JD, 1963. Bar: Pa. 1963, U.S. Dist. Ct. (mid. dist.) Pa. 1968, U.S. Ct. Appeals (3d cir.) 1975, U.S. Supreme Ct. 1976; diplomate Nat. Bd. Trial Advocacy; cert. civil trial adv. Sole practice, 1963-68; asst. pub. defender Luzerne County, Pa., 1965-67; law clk. Ct. Common Pleas of Luzerne County, 1967-69; 1st clk. of Orphans' Ct., dep. register of wills, 1972-83; ptnr. Flanigan, Doran, Biscontini & Shaffer, Wilkes-Barre, 1968-86, Mahler, Shaffer & Pugliese, 1986—; mem. faculty Wilkes Coll., 1964-70; lectr. Pa. Bar Inst., 1988; nat. panel arbitrators Am. Arbitration Assn.; Pa. coun. mediators; cert. mediator U.S. Dist. Ct. spl. trial master Ct. of Common Pleas, Pa. Contbr. articles to profl. jours. Bd. dirs. Jewish Community Ctr., Wilkes-Barre, 1970-76; pres. United Rehab. Services, Inc., 1970-72; treas., bd. dirs. Temple B'nai B'rith, Kingston, Pa., 1980; incorporator, bd. dirs. Health Services Agy. Northeastern Pa. Mem. Luzerne County Bar Assn. (pres. 1998-2000), Pa. Bar Assn. (judicial adminstrn. com. and dispute resolution com.), ABA (litig. sect. com. on trial practice), Pa. Trial Lawyers Assn., ATLA, Pa. Def. Rsch. Inst., Westmoreland (Wilkes-Barre) Club. Avocations: skiing, photography, science fiction. Home e-mail: cas866@aol.com; office e-mail: cshaffer@usnetway.com. General civil litigation, Insurance, Personal injury. Home: 866 Nandy Dr Kingston PA 18704-5608 Office: Mahler Shaffer & Pugliese 575 Pierce St Ste 500 Kingston PA 18704-5754

SHAFFER, DAVID JAMES, lawyer; b. Springfield, Ohio, July 30, 1958; s. Frank James Shaffer and Martha Isabelle (Hardman) Matthews; children: Brynn Danielle, Jedediah Clay. BA, Wittenberg U., 1980; JD, Stanford U., 1983. Bar: Calif. 1984, U.S. Dist. Ct. (no. and ea. dists.) Calif. 1984, U.S. Ct. Appeals (9th cir.) 1984, U.S. Dist. Ct. (so. dist.) Calif. 1985, U.S. Dist. Ct. (we. dist.) Wash. 1986, D.C. 1988, U.S. Dist. Ct. D.C. 1988, U.S. Ct. Appeals (D.C. cir.) 1988, U.S. Dist. Ct. (no. dist.) Tex. 1991, U.S. Supreme Ct. 1993, Md. 1994, U.S. Dist. Ct. Md. 1997. Supr. field ops. U.S. Census Bur., Columbus, Ohio, 1980; legal intern Natural Resources Def. Coun., Inc., San Francisco, 1982-83; assoc. Gibson, Dunn & Crutcher, San Jose, Calif., 1983; law clk. to Judge Betty B. Fletcher, U.S. Ct. Appeals for 9th Cir., Seattle, 1983-84; assoc. Gibson, Dunn & Crutcher, San Jose, 1984-87, Arnold & Porter, Washington, 1987-92; ptnr. Semmes, Bowen & Semmes, 1992-94, Arter & Hadden, Washington, 1995-99, Thelen Reid & Priest LLP, Washington, 1999—. Contbr. articles to profl. and legal jours. Campaign mgr. Clark County Dem. Party, Springfield, 1978-80; organizer Citizens for Sensible County Planning, Fairfax, Va., 1989-94. Alumni scholar Wittenberg U., 1976. Mem. ABA, FBA (chmn. EEO com. 1992-94, individual rights and responsibilities 1994-95, co-chmn. alt. dispute resolution 1995-96, mem. governing bd. labor law and labor rels. sect., editor newsletter Labouring Oar, Outstanding Svc. award 1992), D.C. Bar Assn., Calif. Bar Assn., Order of Coif. Avocations: music, hiking, nature study. Civil rights, General civil litigation, Labor. Office: Thelen Reid & Priest LLP 701 Pennsylvania Ave NW Washington DC 20004-2608 E-mail: dshaffer@thelenreid.com

SHAFFER, RICHARD JAMES, lawyer, former manufacturing company executive; b. Pe Ell, Wash., Jan. 26, 1931; s. Richard Humphrys and Laura Rose (Faas) S.; m. Donna M. Smith, May 13, 1956; children: Leslie Lauren Shaffer Litsinger, Stephanie Jane Athenton. B.A., U. Wash.; LL.B., Southwestern U. Bar: Calif. Vice pres., gen. counsel, sec. NI, Inc., Long Beach, Calif., 1974-89; gen. counsel Masco Bldg. Products Corp., 1985-89; pvt. practice, Huntington Beach, Calif., 1989—. Mem. ltd. liability co. drafting com. and task force Calif. State Bar, 1992-94; lectr. on ltd. liability cos. Trustee Ocean View Sch. Dist., 1965-73, pres., 1966, 73; mem. fin. adv. com. Orange Coast Coll., 1966; mem. Long Beach Local Devel. Corp., 1978-89, Calif. Senate Commn. on Corp. Governance, Shareholders' Rights and Securities Transactions, 1986-97, chmn. drafting com. ltd. liability co. act for senate com., 1991-93; mem. City of Huntington Beach Pers. Commn., 1996-98; bd. dirs. Huntington Beach Libr. Patrons, 1996-98. Mem. ABA, Nat. Assn. Securities Dealers (bd. arbitrators), Calif. Bar Assn. (exec. com. corp. law dept. com. bus. sect. 1981-88), Orange County Bar Assn., Huntington Harbour Yacht Club, Wanderlust Skiers of Huntington Harbour (pres.). General corporate, Finance, Real property.

SHAFFER, ROBERTA IVY, law librarian; b. Oceanside, N.Y., Nov. 27, 1953; d. Joseph Ceicel and Gladys (Dellerson) S.; m. Robert Maman, Aug. 14, 1995. AB in Econs., Vassar Coll., 1973; M of Librarianship, Emory U., 1975; JD, Tulane U., 1980; cert. in arts mgmt., Am. U., 1987. Bar: Tex. 1982, U.S. Dist. Ct. (so. dist.) Tex., U.S. Ct. Appeals (5th cir.), U.S. Supreme Ct. Dir. legal communications U. Houston Law Ctr., 1980-84, assoc. dir. law and tech., 1982-84; spl. asst. to law libr. Libr. of Congress, Washington, 1984-87; Fulbright sr. researcher Tel Aviv Faculty Law, 1987-88; pvt. practice cons. Washington, 1988-89; dir. devel. Washington Project for the Arts, 1989; acting libr. dir. George Washington U. Law Ctr., Washington, 1990; asst. dean U. Washington, Seattle, 1990-91; dir. libr. svcs. Covington & Burling, Washington, 1991-99; dean Grad. Sch. Libr. and Info. Sci. U. Tex., Austin, 1999-2001; with The Spl. Librs. Assn., Washington, 2001—. Cons. Coca-Cola Co., Atlanta, 1975-76, Research Info. Service, Houston, 1982-84; edn. rep. Westlaw, St. Paul, 1982-83. Bd. dirs. Austin Visual Artists Assn. Mem. ABA, Am. Assn. Law Librs., Internat. Assn. Law Librs. (sec. 1992-95, v.p. 1995-2000). Avocation: swimming, archeology, jewelry design. Office: The Spl Libr Assn $m 564 1700 8th St NW Washington DC 20009-2514 E-mail: roberta@sla.org

SHAFFERT, KURT, retired lawyer, chemical engineer; b. Vienna, July 20, 1929; s. Rudolph nee Schafranik and Irma (Altar) S.; m. Judith Pytel, June 12, 1955; children: Elona Ruth, Robin Laurette. BChemE, CCNY, 1951; LLB cum laude, NYU, 1963. Bar: N.Y. 1963, D.C. 1965, U.S. Supreme Ct. 1967, U.S. Patent and Trademark Office 1964. Chem. engr. Diamond Alkali Co., Newark, 1951-54; process devel. engr. Am. Cyanamid Co., Stamford, Conn., 1957-59; patent liaison engr. Uniroyal Inc., 1959-63; assoc. Arthur, Dry & Kalish, N.Y.C., 1963-66, Office of Robert F. Conrad, Washington, 1966-69; sr. ptrn. Shaffert, Miller & Browne, 1970-74; sr. trial atty. intellectual property sect. Antitrust divsn. Dept. of Justice, 1974-85, professions and intellectual property sect., 1985-94, intellectual property guidelines task force, 1994, civil task force, 1994-2000; ret., 2000. Mem. Bethesda-Chevy Chase Jewish Comm. Group, 1965, pres., 1973-74, v.p. 1972-73, treas. 1971-72; mem. Jewish Comm. Ctr. of Greater Wash., 1970-78, bd. dirs., 1973-78; provided tape recorded Holocaust recollections for Stephen Spielberg Holocaust Archive Survivors of the Shoa Visual History Found., 1998. With U.S. Army, 1955-56. Mem. ABA (antitrust sect., patent, trademark and copyright sect.), Profl. Assn. Antitrust Divsn. Dept. of Justice (pres. 1978-79), Bar Assn. D.C. (council del. 1972-74), D.C. Bar Assn.

SHAHEEN, MICHAEL EDMUND, JR. lawyer, government official; b. Boston, Aug. 5, 1940; s. Michael Edmund and Dorothy Wallace (Cameron) S.; m. Polly Adair Dammann, Sept. 11, 1976; children: Michael Edmund, Timothy Andrew. BA, Yale U., 1962; LLB, Vanderbilt U., 1965. Bar: Tenn. 1968. Dir. ann. capital support fund, instr. physics Memphis U. Sch., 1965-66; law clk. Judge Robert M. McRae, Jr., Memphis, 1966-68; pvt. practice Tenn., Miss., 1968-73; dep. chief voting and public accomodations sect. Dept. Justice, Washington, 1973-74, dep. chief fed. programs sect., civil rights divsn., 1974-75; counsel to Atty. Gen. for Intelligence, 1975; spl. adv. to atty. gen., counsel, dir. Office Profl. Responsibility, 1975-98; spl. counsel to commr. IRS, Washington, 1998-2000; chief spl. counsel Office of Spl. Rev. Office of Ind. Counsel, 1998-2000; chief counsel Commn. on Advancement of Fed. Law Enforcement, 1998-2000; prin. sr. counselor to commr. IRS, U.S. Dept. Treasury, 2000—; dir., chief inves-

tigative counsel Atty. Gen. Commn. to Rev. FBI Security Programs & Sys., 2001—. Mayor, Como, Miss., 1970-73; pres. Como Resources, Inc., 1971-72; mcpl. judge, Como, 1970-73; chmn. Como Indsl. Devel. Commn., 1970-73 Mem. Phi Delta Phi, Zeta Psi. Office: Internal Rev Svc 1111 Constitution Ave NW Washington DC 20224-0001

SHAIKUN, MICHAEL GARY, lawyer; b. Ky., Mar. 17, 1942; s. Leon J. and Cleo (Taub) S.; m. Phyllis Miriam Cohen, Aug. 21, 1964; children: Benjamin, Stephanie, Alissa. BS in Econs. with highest honors, U. Pa., 1963; JD, Harvard U., 1966. Bar: Ky. 1966, U.S. Dist. Ct. (we. dist.) Ky. 1966. Assoc. Greenebaum Doll & McDonald PLLC, Louisville, 1966-69, mem., 1970—. Contbr. articles to profl. jours. Bd. dirs. Jewish Cmty. Fedn. Louisville, 1971—, past pres.; past chmn. Found. for Planned Giving, Jewish Cmty. Fedn., Louisville; bd. dirs., chmn. fin. devel. YMCA Safe Place Svcs., 1995—. Mem. ABA, Ky. Bar Assn., Louisville Bar Assn. Democrat. Jewish. Avocation: computers. Bankruptcy, Contracts commercial, Real property. Home: 5907 Burlington Ave Louisville KY 40222-6118 Office: Greenebaum Doll & McDonald PLLC 3300 National City Tower Louisville KY 40202 E-mail: MGS@gdm.com

SHAINES, ROBERT ARTHUR, lawyer; b. Newburyport, Mass., Nov. 24, 1929; s. Edward I. and Ruth Helena (Diamond) Shaines; m. Gladys Breger, Dec. 1954 (div. Sept. 1984); children:-Stephanie, Pamela, Kate; m. Denise Kelly, Dec. 30, 1984. Student, U. N.H., 1949; JD cum laude, Boston U., 1951. Assoc. Lobel & Lobel, Boston, 1954; ptnr. Reinhart & Shaines, Portsmouth, N.H., 1954-56, Shaines Brown, Portsmouth, 1956-66, Robert A. Shaines & Assocs., Portsmouth, 1966-70, Shaines, Madrigan & McEachern, Portsmouth, 1970-85, Shaines & McEachern, Portsmouth, 1985—. Pres. Strawberry Banke, Inc., Portsmouth, 1977-80. Mayor City of Portsmouth, 1960-61; councilman City of Portsmouth, 1958-67; police commr. City of Portsmouth, 1980-81. Served as capt. USAF, 1950-54, Korea. Mem. N.H. Bar Assn. (sec. 1973-75, gov. at large 1976-79, chmn. prepaid legal services com. 1976-79), Portsmouth Bar Assn. (pres. 1963), Rockingham Bar Assn. (pres. 1972). Federal civil litigation, State civil litigation, General corporate. Home: 81 Garland Rd Rye NH 03870-2505 Office: Shaines & McEachern 25 Maplewood Ave Portsmouth NH 03801-3707 E-mail: rsha8125@cs.com

SHAMAN, JEFFREY M. law educator; b. Pitts., June 29, 1941; s. Marvin Arthur and Florence Paula (Sivitz) S.; m. Susan Schwartz, Aug. 14, 1966; children: Craig Barrett, Blair Justin. BA, Pa. State U., 1964; JD, U. So. Calif., 1967; LLM, Georgetown U., 1971. Atty. CAB, Washington, 1967-68; atty. HEW, Washington, 1968-70; prof. U. Akron Sch. Law, 1971-73; prof. DePaul U. Coll. Law, Chgo., 1973—; dir. Ctr. for Jud. Conduct Orgns., 1984-90, DePaul U. Ctr. for Ch.-State Studies, 1986—. Co-author: Judicial Conduct and Ethics, 1990, 2nd edit. 1995, Judicial Disqualification—An Empirical Study of Judicial Practices and Attitudes, 1995. sr. editor Cogitations, 1983-86; contbr. articles to profl. jours. Bd. dirs., v.p. policy ACLU, Chgo., 1986-90, pres., 1990-93; bd. legal advisers Ctr. for Ch.-State Studies, 1990-97. Fellow Am. Judicature Soc. (sr.), Wicklander Prof. of Profl. Ethics; mem. ABA, Am. Soc. Legal History, Assn. Am. Law Schs., Am. Law Inst., Inst. for Internat. Human Rights (bd. dirs.), Alpha Delta Sigma. Office: DePaul U Coll Law 25 E Jackson Blvd Chicago IL 60604-2289

SHAMBAUGH, STEPHEN WARD, lawyer; b. South Bend, Ind., Aug. 4, 1920; s. Marion Clyde and Anna Violet (Stephens) S.; m. Marilyn Louise Pyle (dec. 1993); children: Susan Wynne Shambaugh Hinkle (dec. 1998), Kathleen Louise Shambaugh Thompson. Student, San Jose State Tchrs. Coll., 1938-40, U. Ark., 1951; LLB, U. Tulsa, 1954. Bar: Okla. 1954, Colo. 1964. Mem. staff Reading & Bates, Inc., Tulsa, 1951-54; v.p., gen. mgr., legal counsel Reading & Bates Drilling Co. Ltd., Calgary, Alta., Can., 1954-61; sr. ptnr. Bowman, Shambaugh, Geissinger & Wright, Denver, 1964-81; sole practice, 1981-97; now ret. Dir., fin. counsel various corps. Col. USAF ret. Mem. Colo. Bar Assn., Okla. Bar Assn., P-51 Mustang Pilots Assn., Masons, Elks, Phi Alpha Delta. Banking, General corporate, Oil, gas, and mineral.

SHAMIS, EDWARD ANTHONY, JR. lawyer; b. Pensacola, Fla., Dec. 12, 1949; s. Edward Anthony Sr. and Mona Kathryn (McLaughlin) S.; m. Elizabeth Handley, Jan. 24, 1971; children: Ashley Vera, Edward Anthony III. BS, La. State U., 1972, JD, 1974. Bar: La. 1974, U.S. Dist. Ct. (ea. dist.) La. 1975, U.S. Tax Ct. 1981, U.S. Ct. Appeals (5th cir.) 1982, U.S. Supreme Ct. 1983. Pvt. practice, Slidell, La., 1974—. Spl. counsel to Slidell City Coun., 1984—. Bd. dirs. Pope John H.S., Slidell, 1988-90, Children's Wish Endowment Fund, Inc. (formerly Northshore Children's Endowment Fund) 1991—; mem., pres. St. Tammany Assn. for Children with Learning Disabilities, Slidell, 1976-81; chmn. Slidell Bd. Zoning Adjustments, 1976-81; past mem. Boys Club; past mem. and chmn. St. Tammany Parish Ethics Commn. Mem. ATLA, La. Bar Assn. (hos. of dels. 1985-86, 88-89, 89-90, 94-97), St. Tammany Bar Assn., Slidell Bar Assn. (pres. 1978-79), La. Trial Lawyers Assn. (pres.'s adv. coun. 1980-81, 84-85, 89-90, 95-96). Republican. Avocations: hunting, computers, fishing, boating. Federal civil litigation, State civil litigation, Personal injury. Office: 486 Brownswitch Rd Slidell LA 70458-1102 E-mail: EShamisjr@aol.com

SHANAHAN, THOMAS M. judge; b. Omaha, May 5, 1934; m. Jane Estelle Lodge, Aug. 4, 1956; children: Catherine Shanahan Trofholz, Thomas M. II, Mary Elizabeth, Timothy F. A.B. magna cum laude, U. Notre Dame, 1956; J.D., Georgetown U., 1959. Bar: Nebr., Wyo. Mem. McGinley, Lane, Mueller, Shanahan, O'Donnell & Merritt, Ogallala, Nebr.; assoc. justice Nebr. Supreme Ct., Lincoln, 1983-93; judge U.S. Dist. Ct. Nebr., Omaha, 1993—. Office: US Dist Ct 111 S 18th Plz Ste 3141 Omaha NE 68102

SHANDELL, RICHARD ELLIOT, lawyer; b. N.Y.C., Dec. 23, 1932; s. Edward and Dorothy (Glass) S.; m. Helene Hicken, Aug. 28, 1954; children: Andrea, Thomas, Deborah. BS in Econs., U. Pa., 1953; JD, Columbia U., 1956. Bar: N.Y. 1957. Ptnr. Katz, Shandell, Katz & Erasmous, N.Y.C, Glaser, Shandell & Blitz, N.Y.C, 1981—, Shandell Blitz Blitz Bookson & Kern LLP, N.Y.C. Author: The Preparation and Trial of Medical Malpractice Cases, 1981; contbg. author: Medical Malpractice: Strategic and Practical Principles 1986. Mem. Assn. Trial Lawyers Am. (gov.), N.Y. State Trial Lawyers Assn. (past pres.). Personal injury, Product liability. Home: 325 W 86th St New York NY 10024 Office: Shandell Blitz Blitz Glass Bookson & Kern LLP 150 Broadway New York NY 10038-4381

SHANE, PETER MILO, law educator; b. Oceanside, N.Y., July 12, 1952; s. Albert and Ann (Semanoff) S.; m. Martha Elisabeth Chamallas, June 27, 1981; 1 child: Elisabeth Ann. AB, Harvard U., 1974; JD, Yale U., 1977. Bar: N.Y. 1978, U.S. Ct. Appeals (5th cir.) 1978, D.C. 1979, U.S. Ct. Appeals (8th cir.) 1983, U.S. Supreme Ct. 1984, Pa. 1995. Law clk. to judge U.S. Ct. Appeals (5th cir.), New Orleans, 1977-78; atty., advisor office of legal counsel U.S. Dept. Justice, Washington, 1978-81; asst. gen. counsel Office of Mgmt. and Budget, 1981; assoc. prof. law U. Iowa, Iowa City, 1981-85, prof., 1985-94; dean U. Pitts., 1994-98, prof., 1994—. Adj. lectr. Am. U., Washington, D.C., 1979-80; vis. prof. law Duke U., Durham, N.C., 1986, Boston Coll., Newton, Mass., 1999, Villanova (Pa.) U., 1999; cons. U.S. Dept. Edn., Washington, D.C., 1980, MacArthur Justice Found., Chgo., 1987; active Adminstrv. Conf. U.S., 1991, pub. mem., 1995; cons. Nat. Commn. Jud. Discipline and Removal, 1992-93; cooperating atty. Iowa Civil Liberties Union, Des Moines, 1982-94, bd. dirs., 1987-89; active Coun. on Legal Edn. Opportunity, 1996—; reporter Civil Justice Adv. Group, U.S. Dist. Ct. (we. dist.) Pa. Author: (with H.H. Bruff) The Law of Presidential Power: Cases and Materials, 1988, (with J. Mashaw and R. Merrill) Administrative Law: The American Public Law System, 1992, (with H.H. Bruff) Separation of Powers Law, 1996. Mem. Dem. cen. com. Johnson County, Iowa, 1982-88. Recipient citation for outstanding svc. Pa. House of Reps., 1998; named Young Leader of Higher Edn., Am. Assn. Higher Edn., 1998; Old Gold Summer fellow U. Iowa, 1981-84, Mellon Found. fellow, 1982. Mem. ABA (coun. sect. adminstrv. law and regulatory practice 1993-96, chmn. com. on govt. orgn. and separation of powers 1987-91), Assn. Am. Law Schs. (chair adminstrv. law 1990, chair remedies 1992, chair law sch. deans 1997), Am. Law Inst. Jewish. Office: U Pitts Sch Law 3900 Forbes Ave Pittsburgh PA 15213

SHANK, SUZANNE ADAMS, lawyer; b. Kansas City, Mo., Nov. 13, 1946; d. Howard Howe and Bettie Ann (Winkler) Hettick; m. Martin Smoler, May 18, 1991. BJ, U. Mo., 1972; MPA in Health Adminstrn., JD, U. Mo., 1982. Bar: Mo. 1982, U.S. Dist. Ct. (we. dist.) Mo. 1982. Journalist U. Kans. Med. Ctr., Kansas City, 1972-73; asst. editor Am. Family Physician, Mo., 1973-75; exec. dir. Lambert Med. Clinic, 1975-80; assoc. Shughart, Thomson & Kilroy, 1982-85; v.p. GE/Employers Reins. Corp., Overland Park, Kans., 1985-2000; sr. v.p. Attys. Liability Assurance Soc., Chgo., 2000—. Mem. Friends of Zoo, Kansas City, Mo., 1981—, Menorah Med. Ctr. Aux., Kansas City, 1982—, Women's Vision Internat., Kansas City, Mo., 1999—; mem. Internat. Rels. Coun., 1999—. Mem. ABA, Mo. Bar Assn., Kansas City Bar Assn. (chmn. ins. law com.), Soc. Profl. Journalists, Soc. CPCU (rsch. com.), Com. to Protect Journalists, Kappa Tau alpha. Contracts commercial, General corporate, Insurance. Home: 2703 W 66th Ter Shawnee Mission KS 66208-1810 Office: Attorneys Liability Assurance Soc 311 S Wacker 5700 Chicago IL 60606

SHANK, WILLIAM O. lawyer; b. Hamilton, Ohio, Jan. 11, 1924; s. Horace Cooper and Bonnie (Winn) S.; m. Shirleen Allison, June 25, 1949; children— Allison Kay, Kristin Elizabeth. BA, Miami U., Oxford, O., 1947; JD, Yale, 1950. Bar: Ohio, Ill., U.S. Supreme Ct. Pvt. practice, Hamilton, Ohio, 1951-55, Chgo., 1955—; mem. firm Shank, Briede & Spoerl, Hamilton, Ohio, 1951-55; assoc. Lord, Bissell & Brook, Chgo., 1955-58; atty. Chemetron Corp., 1958-60, sr. atty., 1960-61, gen. atty., asst. sec., 1961-71, sec., gen. counsel, 1971-78; v.p., gen. counsel, sec. Walgreen Co., Deerfield, Ill., 1978-89; ptnr. Burditt & Radzius, Chartered, Chgo., 1989-98; exec. v.p. Internat. Bus. Resources, Inc., 1993—; ptnr. Williams Montgomery & John Ltd., 1998—. Mem. bus. adv. coun. Miami U., Oxford, Ohio, 1975—; arbitrator 19th Jud. Cir., Ill., 1995—; adv. bd. eLawForum, Washington, 1999—. Bd. dirs. Coun. for Cmty. Svcs. Met. Chgo., 1973-77; trustee Libr. Internat. Rels., 1971-78; bd. dirs. Chgo. Civic Fedn., 1984-89, Walgreen Drug Stores Hist. Found., 1990—; mem. Chgo. Crime Commn., 1985-89. 1st lt., pilot 8th Air Force, USAAF, World War II, ETO. Fellow Am. Bar Found. (life); mem. ABA (com. corp. gen. counsel), Ill. State Bar Assn., Chgo. Bar Assn. (chmn. com. on corp. law depts. 1971-72, 89-90), Am. Soc. Corp. Secs. (pres. Chgo. regional group 1983-84, nat. bd. dirs. 1984-87), Yale U. Law Sch. Assn. (past pres. Ill. Alumni, exec. com. New Haven), Walgreen Alumni Assn. (pres. 1992-94), Legal Club (pres. 1979-80), Law Club, Lawyers Club (Chgo.), Univ. Club, Econ. Club, Yale Club of Chgo., Omicron Delta Kappa, Phi Delta Phi, Sigma Chi. General civil litigation, General corporate, Estate planning. Home: 755 S Shore Dr Crystal Lake IL 60014-5530 Office: Williams Montgomery & John Ltd 20 N Wacker Dr Ste 2100 Chicago IL 60606 E-mail: wos@willmont.com

SHANKS, HERSHEL, editor, writer; b. Sharon, Pa., Mar. 8, 1930; s. Martin and Mildred (Freedman) S.; m. Judith Alexander Weil, Feb. 20, 1966; children: Elizabeth Jean, Julia Emily. BA, Haverford (Pa.) Coll., 1952; MA, Columbia, 1953; LLB, Harvard, 1956. Bar: D.C. 1956. Trial atty. Dept. Justice, 1956-59; pvt. practice Washington, 1959-88; ptnr. Glassie, Pewett, Beebe & Shanks, 1964-88; editor Bibl. Archaeology Rev., Washington, 1975—. Pres. Bibl. Archaeology Soc., 1974—, Jewish Ednl. Ventures Inc., 1987—. Author: The Art and Craft of Judging, 1968, The City of David, 1973, Judaism in Stone, 1979, Jerusalem--An Archaeological Biography, 1995, The Mystery and Meaning of the Dead Sea Scolls, 1998, also articles; co-editor: Recent Archaeology in the Land of Israel, 1984; editor: Ancient Israel, A Short History, 1988, revised edit., 1999, Christianity and Rabbinic Judaism, 1992, Understanding the Dead Sea Scrolls, 1992; editor Bible Rev., 1985—, Moment mag., 1987—, Archaeology Odyssey, 1998—. Mem. ABA, D.C. Bar Assn., Am. Schs. Oriental Rsch., Nat. Press Club, Cosmos Club, Phi Beta Kappa. Home: 5208 38th St NW Washington DC 20015-1812 Office: Bibl Archaeology Soc 4710 41st St NW Washington DC 20016-1706 E-mail: hshanks@bib-arch.org

SHANKS, WILLIAM ENNIS, JR. lawyer; b. Jackson, Miss., Sept. 5, 1950; s. William Ennis and Alice Josephine (Crisler) S.; m. Jean F. Steinschneider, Sept. 7, 1974; 1 child, William E. III. B.A., Harvard U., 1972; J.D. cum laude, Emory U., 1976; LL.M. with highest honors in Taxation, Ala. U., 1979. Bar: Ga. 1976, Ala. 1976, Ptnr. Balch & Bingham, Birmingham, Ala., LLP, 1976—. Bd. dirs. Birmingham Festival Theatre, 1980-88, treas., 1980-84; trustee Creative Montessori Sch., 1995—. Mem. Birmingham Estate Planning Council, Birmingham Employee Benefit Forum, Birmingham Profit Sharing Group, ABA, Summit Club, Exch. Club (bd. dirs. 1984-85, sec. 1985-86, v.p. 1985-86, pres. 1986-87), Harvard Club Birmingham (v.p. 1996-98, pres. 1998-99), Order of Coif. Presbyterian. Estate planning, Pension, profit-sharing, and employee benefits, Corporate taxation. Home: 4516 Old Leeds Rd Birmingham AL 35213-3304 Office: Balch & Bingham 600 18th St N Birmingham AL 35203-2206

SHANMAN, JAMES ALAN, lawyer; b. Cin., Aug. 1, 1942; s. Jerome D. and Mildred Louise (Bloch) S.; m. Marilyn Louise Glassman, June 11, 1972; 1 child, Ellen Joan. BS, U. Pa., 1963; JD, Yale U., 1966. Bar: N.Y. 1967, U.S. Ct. Mil. Appeals 1971, U.S. Supreme Ct. 1971, U.S. Ct. Appeals (2d cir.) 1972, U.S. Dist. Ct. (so. and ea. dists.) N.Y. 1972, U.S. Ct. Internat. Trade 1976, U.S. Ct. Appeals (fed. cir.) 1987, U.S. Dist. Ct. (ea. dist.) Mich. 1989, U.S. Ct. Appeals (7th cir.) 1999. Assoc. Cahill Gordon & Reindel, N.Y.C., 1971-74, Freeman, Meade, Wasserman, Sharfman & Schneider, N.Y.C., 1974-76; mem. firm Sharfman, Shanman, Poret & Siviglia, P.C., 1976-95; ptnr. Camhy Karlinsky & Stein LLP, 1995-96; mem. firm Sharfman, Siviglia, Poret, Kook, Ross & Shanman, P.C., 1996-98; ptnr. Edwards & Angell, LLP, 1998—. Speaker on reins. law topics. Capt. USAF, 1966-71. Mem.: ARIAS.US (cert. arbitrator), ABA, N.Y. State Bar Assn., Assn. of Bar of City of N.Y. (com. ins. law 1985—88, com. ins. law 1990—92, com. ins. law 1998—2001, com. profl. liability ins. 1988—92, com. on assn. ins. plans 1989—), Am. Arbitration Assn. (comml. panel arbitrators 1980—), Confrérie de la Chaine Rôtisseurs, Bailliage de Conn. Federal civil litigation, State civil litigation, Insurance. Office: Edwards & Angell LLP 750 Lexington Ave New York NY 10022-1253 E-mail: jshanman@ealaw.com

SHANNAHAN, WILLIAM PAUL, lawyer; b. Detroit, Nov. 21, 1934; s. William and Jean (Boyle) S.; m. Saracia L. Price, Sept. 24, 1983; children: MeglynAnne, Michael-Padraic. AB, U. Detroit, 1956; JD, Georgetown U., 1958. Bar: D.C. 1958, Mich. 1958, Calif. 1962. Ptnr. Higgs, Fletcher & Mack, La Jolla, Calif., 1967-81, Aylward, Kintz, et al, La Jolla, 1981-87, pvt. practice, La Jolla, 1987—. With U.S. Army, 1959-60. Democrat. Roman Catholic. Probate, Taxation, general. Office: 1200 Prospect St Ste 425 La Jolla CA 92037-3660

SHANNON, JOEL INGRAM, lawyer; b. Wharton, Tex., May 2, 1946; s. Carl Steen and Leonora (Hudgins) S.; children— Rebecca, Rachael, Robin; m. Margaret Barrett Martin, 1988; 1 stepchild, Trevor Martin. B.A., U. Tex., 1968, J.D., 1970. Bar: Tex. 1971; cert. in comml. real property. Law clk. Supreme Ct. Tex., Austin, 1971-72; assoc. Andrews & Kurth, Houston, 1972-78, ptnr., 1978—; adj. prof. sch. law U. Tex., 1992. Founding trustee, exec chmn. Episcopal High Sch., Houston, 1983— . Democrat. Episcopalian. Banking, Real property. Office: Andrews & Kurth 4200 Texas Commerce Tower Houston TX 77002

SHANNON, JOHN SANFORD, lawyer, retired railway executive; b. Tampa, Fla., Feb. 8, 1931; s. George Thomas and Ruth Evangeline (Garrett) S.; m. Elizabeth Howe, Sept. 22, 1962; children: Scott Howe, Elizabeth Garrett, Sandra Denison. AB, Roanoke Coll., 1952; JD, U. Va., 1955. Bar: Va. 1955. Assoc. Hunton Williams Gay Powell & Gibson, Richmond, Va., 1955-56; solicitor Norfolk & Western Ry., Roanoke, 1956-60, asst. gen. solicitor, 1960-64, gen. atty., 1964-65, gen. solicitor, 1965-68, gen. counsel, 1968-69, v.p. law, 1969-80, sr. v.p. law, 1980-82; exec. v.p. law Norfolk (Va.) So. Corp., 1982-96, ret., 1996. Bd. dirs. Norfolk So. Ry. Co., Pocahontas Land Corp., Va. Holding Corp., Norfolk and Western Ry. Co. Editor-in-chief: Va. Law Rev, 1954-55. Chancellor Episcopal Diocese Southwestern Va., 1974-82; pres. bd. trustees North Cross Sch., Roanoke, 1973-82; trustee, past chmn. exec. com. Roanoke Coll., Salem, Va.; bd. dirs. Legal Aid Soc., Roanoke Valley, 1969-80, pres., 1970-79; trustee Chrysler Mus., Norfolk, 1982-94, Norfolk Acad., 1987-99. Mem. Va. Bar Assn., Norfolk and Portsmouth Bar Assn., Shenandoah Club, Roanoke Country Club, Norfolk Yacht and Country Club, Harbor Club, Order of Coif, Sigma Xi, Omicron Delta Kappa, Phi Delta Phi. Home: 7633 Argyle Ave Norfolk VA 23505-1701

SHANNON, MALCOLM LLOYD, JR. lawyer, educator; b. Phila., Jan. 27, 1946; m. Jeanne Marie Halle, Dec. 28, 1974; children: Travis Alan, Kate Meredith. BBA, U. N.Mex., 1968, JD, 1971. Bar: N.Mex. 1971, U.S. Supreme Ct. 1976, Tex. 1981, Colo. 1984, Calif. 1986. Counsel Gen. Atomics, 1991—. Lectr. mining and pub. land law U. N.Mex. Adv. com. solar energy application Tech. Vocat. Inst. of Albuquerque Pub. Schs., 1976; judge N.Mex. State Sci. Fair 1978-80; mem. ednl. accountability com. Cherry Creek Sch. Dist., 1984-86; bd. dirs. Denver U./Pioneer Jr. Hockey Assn., 1991-94. Author publs. in field. Mem. ABA, Am. Corp. Counsel Assn. Republican. Roman Catholic. General corporate, Oil, gas, and mineral, Real property. Home: 6199 S Jamaica Ct Englewood CO 80111-5714 Office: 7800 E Dorado Pl Ste 200 Englewood CO 80111

SHANNON, MARGARET ANNE, lawyer; b. Detroit, July 6, 1945; d. Johannes Jacob and Vera Marie (Spade) Van De Graaf; m. Robert Selby Shannon, Feb. 4, 1967. Student, Brown U., 1963-65; BA in History, Wayne State U., 1966, JD, 1973. Bar: Mich. 1973. Housing aide City of Detroit, 1967-68; employment supr. Sinai Hosp., Detroit, 1968-69; assoc. gen. counsel regulatory affairs Blue Cross Blue Shield Mich., 1969-80; ptnr. Honigman Miller Schwartz and Cohn, 1980-95, of counsel, 1996—. Nat. Merit scholar, 1963-66. Mem. ABA (vice-chmn. pub. regulation of ins. law com. 1981-82), Mich. State Bar (chmn. health care com. 1991, 92, co-chmn. payor subcom. health law sect.), Nat. Health Lawyers Assn., U. Liggett Sch. Alumni (bd. govs.). Administrative and regulatory, Health. Home: 2003 Shorepointe Ln Grosse Pointe MI 48236-1060 Office: Honigman Miller Schwartz and Cohn 2290 First National Bldg Detroit MI 48226-3583 E-mail: mshannon@honigman.com

SHANNONHOUSE, ROYAL GRAHAM, III, lawyer, educator; b. New Bern, N.C., May 18, 1929; s. Royal Graham and Mary Sue (Poe) S.; m. Myra Welsh, July 5, 1952; children: Royal Graham IV, William Welsh, Elliott McCarten. BA, U. N.C., 1950, JD with honors, 1955. Bar: N.C. 1955, U.S. Dist. Ct. (ea. dist.) N.C. 1967, U.S. Ct. Appeals (4th cir.) 1969, U.S. Dist. Ct. Md. 1974, Md. 1988. Asst. dir. Inst. of Govt., Chapel Hill, N.C., 1955-60; asst. prof. law U. Ga., Athens, 1960-65; sole practice Rocky Mount, N.C., 1965-69; prof. law U. Balt., 1969-83; counsel Blumenthal, Wayson, Downs & Offutt P.A., Annapolis, Md., 1983-93; ptnr. Dalnekoff & Mason, P.A., 1994—. Instr. Police Acad., Balt., 1970-74, Md. Bar Rev., Balt., 1973-74; speaker Harford Co. Vestry Assn., 1973, Waxter Sr. Citizens Ctr., 1974-75, Montgomery Coll. Forum, 1975; reporter Md. Jud. Conf., 1973-74, U.S. Dist. Ct. Md., Balt., 1976-80, Speedy Trial Act; adj. prof. law U. Balt., 1983-93. Contbr. articles to profl. jours. Cons. Mayor's Council Criminal Justice, 1976. Served with USNR, 1950-52, Korea. Democrat. Episcopalian. Avocation: studying law. Land use and zoning (including planning), Probate, Real property. Office: 2448 Holly Ave Ste 301 Annapolis MD 21401-3177 E-mail: rshannonhousepc@dellepro.com

SHAPIRO, ALVIN DALE, lawyer; b. N.Y.C., Apr. 30, 1930; s. Samuel and Fannie (Korman) S.; m. Patricia Nan Swaden, Nov. 8, 1959; children: Peter, Julia, Molly, Anthony. BS, U. Mo., 1951; LLB, Yale U., 1958. Bar: Fla. 1958, Mo. 1959, U.S. Supreme Ct. 1966. Assoc. Sams, Anderson & Assocs., Miami, Fla., 1958-59; ptnr. Stinson, Mag & Fizzell, Kansas City, Mo., 1959-80; sole practice, 1980-95; ptnr. Shapiro, Manson & Karbank, 1996—. Mem. Yale Law Sch. Exec. Com., 1982-87. Exec. bd. dirs., v.p. Hyman Brand Hebrew Acad., Kansas City, 1966—; bd. dirs. Beth Shalom Congregation, Kansas City, 1970—. Served with USN 1951-55. Mem. ABA, Mo. Bar Assn., Fla. Bar Assn. Democrat. Jewish. Club: Yale. Federal civil litigation, State civil litigation, General practice. Home: 816 W 52nd Ter Kansas City MO 64112-2322 Office: 1200 Main St Kansas City MO 64105-2122

SHAPIRO, BENJAMIN LOUIS, lawyer, association administrator; b. N.Y.C., June 5, 1943; s. Leonard and Henrietta (Cohen) S. BA, L.I. U., 1966; JD, New Eng. Law Sch., 1972; LLM, NYU, 1973. Bar: Mass. 1975, U.S. Dist. Ct. Mass. 1975, U.S. Ct. Appeals (1st cir.) 1975. Ct. planner Govs. Commn. on Adminstrn. Justice, Montpelier, Vt., 1973-74; staff atty. Nat. Ctr. for State Cts., Boston, 1974-76; regional counsel U.S. Dept. Justice Law Enforcement Assistance Adminstrn., 1976-77, ct. specialist, 1977-80, exec. asst. to adminstr., 1980-81; atty. advisor U.S. Dept. Justice/Office Justice Assistance, 1981-82; program mgr., dep. asst. adminstr. Office Juvenile Justice and Delinquency Prevention, 1982-89; exec. dir. Mass. Dist. Atty. Assn., 1989-95; sr. cons. justice programs Capital Assocs., Rockville, Md., 1995, Dyncorp LLC, Reston, Va., 1996; gen. counsel house post audit and oversight com. Ho. of Reps., Boston, 1997—. Chmn. host com. Nat. Salute to Vietnam Vets., v.p. D.C. Chpt. Vietnam Vets. Am., 1982; presenter Internat. Symposium on Seriously Troubled Youth, Princeton U., 1986. Asst. editor-in-chief New Eng. Law Rev. Pres. Nat. Assn. Justice info. Sys. With U.S. Army, 1966-69. Mem. Nat. Dist. Attys. Assn. (bd. dirs.). Democrat. Jewish. Home: 2001 Marina Dr Apt 610 North Quincy MA 02171-1544

SHAPIRO, DAVID L. lawyer; b. Corsicana, Tex., May 19, 1936; s. Harry and Alice (Laibovitz) S. BA, U. Tex., 1967; JD, St. Mary's U., 1970. Bar: Tex. 1970, U.S. Dist. Ct. (we. dist.) Tex. 1972, U.S. Supreme Ct. 1975, U.S. Ct. Appeals (5th cir.) 1981. Assoc. Law Office Jim S. Phelps, Houston, 1971; pvt. practice, Austin, 1972—. Spl. counsel com. human resources Tex. Ho. Reps., Austin, 1973-74; counsel subcom. health svcs. Tex. Senate, Austin, 1983-87. With U.S. Army, 1959-61. Mem. State Bar Tex. (chmn. lawyer referral svc. com. 1980-82, adminstrn. of justice com. 1990-93, jury svc. com. 1998—, contbr. Media Law Handbook supplement 1986), Travis County Bar Assn. (sec.-treas. 1977-78, dir. 1979, pres. family law sect. 1980-81), Coll. of State Bar of Tex., Austin Criminal Def. Lawyers Assn., Travis County Bar Assn. Democrat. Avocations: automobiles, reading. State civil litigation, Criminal, Family and matrimonial. Office: 1200 San Antonio St Austin TX 78701-1834 E-mail: dave.shapiro@senate.state.tx.us

SHAPIRO, DAVID W. prosecutor; Graduate, State U. NY, Binghamton; JD, State U. NY , Buffalo. Fed. Prosecutor Eastern Dist., NY, 1986—92, chief organized crime unit; Fed. Prosecutor Dist. of Ariz., 1992—94; chief Appellate Div. Northern Dist. , Calif., 1994—2001, chief Criminal Div., 1994—2001, U.S. Atty., 2001—. Office: US Attorney 450 Golden Gate Ave Box 36055 San Francisco CA 94102 Fax: 415-436-7234*

SHAPIRO, EDWIN HENRY, lawyer; b. Chgo., Mar. 12, 1938; s. Irving and Esther (Mikell) S.; m. Lesley Dahlin, Dec. 27, 1959; children: Craig, Cori. BS in Acctg., U. Ill., 1959; JD, Northwestern U., 1963. Bar: Ill. 1963, U.S. Dist. Ct. (no. dist.) Ill. 1970, U.S. Supreme Ct. 1979. Tax acct. Arthur Andersen & Co., Chgo., 1962-67; ptnr. Rosenfeld, Rotenberg, Hafron & Shapiro, Schaumburg, Ill., 1967—. Mem. ABA, Ill. Bar Assn., N.W. Suburban Bar Assn. (pres. 1985-86), Tau Epsilon Phi. Avocations: swimming, travel. State civil litigation, Real property. Office: 1111 N Plaza Dr Ste 570 Schaumburg IL 60173-4992 E-mail: rrhs2@aol.com

SHAPIRO, GARY JOHN, lawyer; b. San Francisco, Oct. 4, 1941; s. Herbert H. and Raye (Wall) S.; m. Dana Bloom, July 5, 1964; children: Karen Hillary, Anne S. Mulvaney. BS, U. Calif.-Berkeley, 1963, JD, 1966. Bar: Calif. 1966, Fed. Dist. Ct. 1967, U.S. Ct. Appeals 1967. Law clk. Oliver D. Hamlin, U.S. Ct. Appeals, 9th Cir., 1966-67; assoc. Dinkelspiel & Dinkelspiel, San Francisco, 1967-69; ptnr. firm Buchman, Kass & Shapiro, Profl. Corp., Oakland, Calif., 1970-75; of counsel Steefel, Levitt & Weiss, 1985—. Judge pro tem Alameda County Mcpl. Ct., San Leandro-Hayward Jud. Dist., 1972; ptnr. Shapiro Assocs., Mill Valley; mem. faculty San Francisco Law Sch., 1968-71; mem. faculty John F. Kennedy U. Sch. Law, Sch. Bus. Adminstrn., 1977-79, Am. Coll., Bryn Mawr, Pa., 1977-79, Golden Gate U. Grad. Sch. Banking, Fin. and Real Estate, 1979-81; lectr. various tax and real estate seminars. Contbr. articles to legal jours. Bd. dirs., pres. Endowment Found. of Jewish Welfare Fedn., 1985-87; bd. dirs., treas. Jewish Family Svc. Agy., Alameda County; bd. dirs. Am. Friends Shaare Zedak Hosp., Am. Friends Ben Gurim U., Jewish Fedn. Greater East Bay, Jewish Nat. Fund, Temple Emanu-El, San Francisco, 1989-95; pres. Estate Planning Coun. of East Bay, 1980; trustee, sec. Jacques and Esther Reutlinger Found.; trustee Helzel Family Found., trustee, vice chair, chair finance comm. Pacific Grad. Sch. Pschology; trustee St. Francis Hosp. Found., chair inv. com. Mem. ABA, Am. Israel Pub. Affairs Com. of No. Calif. (bd. dirs., vice chmn., nat. exec. com.), Bar Assn. San Francisco, Order of Coif, Concordia-Argonaut Club, Lake Merced Club, Troon Club, Judah L. Mognes Mus (trustee, pres.), Hewbrew Free Lan Assn (bd. dir.). Republican. Jewish. Office: One Embacadero Center 29th Floor San Francisco CA 94111 E-mail: shapirog@alumni.haas.org

SHAPIRO, GEORGE HOWARD, retired lawyer; b. St. Louis, Nov. 10, 1936; s. Isadore T. and Alice (Schucart) S.; m. Mary Kenney Leonard, 1977 (div. 1994); m. Ray Ann Kremer, 1999; 1 child, Ellen. BA, Harvard U., 1958, LLB, 1961; postgrad., London Sch. Econs., 1961-62. Bar: Ga. 1960, D.C. 1963. Atty. U.S. Dept. Labor, Washington, 1962-63; assoc. Arent Fox Kintner Plotkin & Kahn, 1963-69, ptnr., 1970-99; ret., 2000. Co-author: 'Cable Speech' The Case for First Amendment Protection, 1983; editor: New Program Opportunities in the Electronic Media, 1983, Current Developments in CATV, 1981. With USAR, 1962-68. Frank Knox Meml. fellow Harvard U., 1961-62. Mem. D.C. Bar Assn., Fed. Communications Bar Assn. Democrat. Jewish. Avocation: skiing. Federal civil litigation, Communications, Constitutional. Home: Apt 906 3180 Mathieson Dr NE Atlanta GA 30305-1834 E-mail: GHSinATL@aol.com

SHAPIRO, HOWARD ALAN, retired lawyer; b. Albany, N.Y., May 12, 1932; s. Ralph and Estelle (Warshak) S.; m. Eleanor Siegel, June 20, 1954; children: David Todd, Andrew Neil, Diane Graser. AB magna cum laude, Harvard U., 1953, LLB magna cum laude, 1956. Bar: N.Y. 1956. Assoc. Proskauer Rose Goetz & Mendelsohn, N.Y.C., 1956-65, ptnr., 1965-97. Lectr. Practicing Law Inst., 1971-79. Editor Harvard Law Rev., 1954-56, note editor, 1955-56. Banking, General corporate, Securities.

SHAPIRO, IRVING, law educator, author; b. N.Y.C., Aug. 23, 1917; s. Isidor and Bessie (Hecht) S.; m. Rosalind Leonora Roth, Sept. 14, 1941; children— Deanne, Susan, Joyce. B.A., NYU, 1946, J.D., 1942. Bar: N.Y. 1943. Spl. asst. to adminstrv. judge N.Y. Supreme Ct., Bklyn., 1949-74; prof. St. John's U., Jamaica, N.Y., 1974— ; dir. programs Ct. Careers, N.Y.C., 1960— ; arbitrator Small Claims Ct., N.Y.C., 1977— . Author: Dictionary of Legal Terms, 1969; New Dictionary of Legal Terms, 1984. Editor N.Y. Statutes, 1963-73. Contbr. articles to law jours. Served with U.S. Army, 1943-46. Decorated Army Commendation medal. Fellow Inst. for Ct. Mgmt.; mem. Criminal Justice Educators Assn. Democrat. Jewish. Office: St Johns U Bent Hl # 425 Jamaica NY 11439-0001

SHAPIRO, JAMES EDWARD, judge; b. Chgo., May 28, 1930; BS, U. Wis., 1951; JD, Harvard U., 1954. Bar: Wis. 1956, U.S. Dist. Ct. (ea. dist.) Wis. 1956, U.S. Ct. Appeals (7th cir.) 1962, U.S. Supreme Ct. 1971. Sole practice, Milw., 1956-57; resident house counsel Nat. Presto Industries, Eau Claire, Wis., 1957-60; ptnr. Bratt & Shapiro, Milw., 1960-64; sole practice, 1964-74; ptnr. Frank, Hiller & Shapiro, 1974-82; judge U.S. Bankruptcy Ct., 1982—, chief judge, 1996-2000. Mem. Bayside Bd. Appeals, Wis., 1969-77; Milw. county ct. commr., 1969-78; dir. Milw. Legal Aid Soc., 1969-77. Served to 1st lt. U.S. Army, 1954-56. Jewish. Office: US Courthouse 140 Fed Bldg 517 E Wisconsin Ave Milwaukee WI 53202-4500 E-mail: james_e_shapiro@wieb.uscourts.gov

SHAPIRO, MICHAEL HENRY, government executive; b. Bayonne, N.J., Sept. 23, 1948; s. William and Sophie (Slotkin) S. BS, Lehigh U., 1970; MS, Harvard U., 1972, PhD, 1976. Assoc. prof. Harvard U., Cambridge, Mass., 1976-82, analyst, 1980-81, br. chief, 1981-83, dir. econs. and tech. divsn., 1983-89; dep. asst. adminstr., air and radiation U.S. EPA, Washington, 1989-93, dir. office of solid waste, 1993-99, dep. asst. adminstr., solid waste and emergency response, 1999—. Office: EPA # 5101 1200 Pennsylvania Ave NW Washington DC 20460-0002

SHAPIRO, NELSON HIRSH, lawyer; b. Feb. 3, 1928; s. Arthur and Anna (Zenitz) S.; m. Helen Lenora Sykes, June 27, 1948; children: Ronald Evan, Mitchell Wayne, Jeffrey Mark, Julie Beth. BEE, Johns Hopkins U., 1948; JD, George Washington U., 1952. Bar: D.C. 1952, Va. 1981. Patent examiner U.S. Patent Office, 1948-50; patent advisor U.S. Signal Corps, 1950-52; mem. Shapiro & Shapiro, Arlington, Va., 1952-98, Vorys, Sater, Seymour and Pease LLP, Washington, 1998-2001, Miles & Stockbridge, McLean, Va., 2001—. Patentee; contbr. articles to legal publs. and Ency. of Patent Practice and Invention Mgmt., 1964. Mem. ABA, Am. Patent Law Assn., Bar Assn. D.C., Order of Coif, Tau Beta Pi. Patent, Trademark and copyright. Home: 7001 Old Cabin Ln Rockville MD 20852-4531 Office: Miles & Stockbridge 1751 Pinnacle Dr Ste 500 Mc Lean VA 22067-3833 E-mail: nshapiro@milesstockbridge.com

SHAPIRO, PHILIP ALAN, lawyer; b. Chgo., May 14, 1940; s. Joe and Nettie (Costin) S.; m. Joyce Barbara Chapnick, May 29, 1966; children: David Ian, Russell Scott, Mindi Jennifer. AA, Wilson Coll., 1960; BS in Fin., So. Ill. U., 1965; MBA, Nat. Univ., San Diego, Calif., 1975; MBA in Mktg. with distinction, San Diego State U., San Diego, 1977; JD, JD, Western State U., 1985. Bar: Calif. 1988. Spl. agt. U.S. Secret Svc., Washington, 1965-67, Chgo., 1967-77; mgr. divsn. sales Roche Labs. divsn. Hoffman-La Roche, Inc.; account exec. Cellular Comm., Inc., San Diego, 1985; with Complete Comm., 1983—; assoc. Law Office Jeffrey S. Schwartz, 1988-91; pvt. practice, 1991—. Chair gen. and solo practice section State Bar of Calif.; editor law rev. Western State U. Coll. Law. Editor law rev. Western State U. Coll. Law. Mem. Spreckes Elem. Sch. Adv. Bd., San Diego, 1976-77; mem. University City Town Coun., San Diego, 1977; pres. Congregation Beth El, La Jolla, Calif., 1976-79. With USMC, 1958-60. Recipient Award of Merit, U.S. Treasury Dept., 1965, Israel Solidarity award, 1977, U. of Judaism award, 1978, Wiley W. Manuel award State Bar Calif., 1990, 91. Mem. ABA (vice chmn. gen. practice sect.), Calif. Trial Lawyers Assn., San Diego County Bar Assn., San Diego Trial Lawyers Assn., State Bar Calif. (exec. com. gen. practice sect.), San Diego Bus. Referrals (pres. 1998-99). Bankruptcy, General practice, Personal injury. Office: PO Box 178475 San Diego CA 92177-8475 Fax: 858-483-4639. E-mail: pshaplaw@san.rr.com

SHAPIRO, ROBERT, lawyer; b. Plainfield, N.J., Sept. 2, 1942; BS in Fin., UCLA, 1965; JD, Loyola U., L.A., 1968. Bar: Calif. 1969, U.S. Ct. Appeals (9th cir.) 1972, U.S. Dist. Ct. (cen., no. & so. dists.) Calif. 1982. Dep. dist. atty. Office of Dist. Atty., L.A., 1969-72; sole practice, 1972-87, 88—; of counsel Bushkin, Gaims, Gaines, Jonas, 1987-88; Christensen, Miller, Fink & Jacobs, 1988-95; ptnr. Christensen, Miller, Fink, Jacobs, Glaser, Weil & Shapiro, 1995—. Author: Search for Justice, 1996, Misconception, 2001. Recipient Am. Jurisprudence award Bancroft Whitney, 1969. Mem. Nat. Assn. Criminal Def. Lawyers, Calif. Attys. for Criminal Justice, Trial Lawyers for Pub. Justice (founder 1982), Century City Bar Assn. (Best Criminal Def. Atty. 1993). General civil litigation, Criminal. Office: 2121 Avenue Of The Stars Fl 19 Los Angeles CA 90067-5010

SHAPIRO, SANDRA, lawyer; b. Providence, Oct. 17, 1944; d. Emil and Sarah (Cohen) S. AB magna cum laude, Bryn Mawr Coll., Pa., 1966; LLB magna cum laude, U. Pa., 1969. Bar: Mass. 1970, U.S. Dist. Ct. Mass. 1971, U.S. Ct. Appeals (1st cir.) 1972, U.S. Supreme Ct. 1980. Law clk. U.S. Ct. Appeals (1st cir.), Boston, 1969-70; assoc. Foley, Hoag & Eliot LLP, 1970-75, ptnr., 1976—. Mem. bd. bar overseers Mass. Supreme Judicial Ct., 1988-92, mem. gender bias study com., 1986-89. Contbr. articles to profl. jours. Bd. dirs. Patriots' Trail coun. Girl Scouts U.S., 1994-97; mem. bd. overseers Boston Lyric Opera, 1993—, New England Conservatory of Music, 1995—, Celebrity Series of Boston, 1997—. Woodrow Wilson fellow, 1966. Mem.: ABA (ethics, profl. and pub. edn. com. 1994—), Women's Bar Assn. Mass. (pres. 1985—86), New Eng. Women in Real Estate, Nat. Women's Law Ctr. Network, Mass. Bar Assn. (chmn. real property sect. coun., com. on profl. ethics), Boston Bar Assn. (mem. coun.), U. Pa. Law Sch. Alumni Assn. (bd. mgrs. 1990—94), Boston Club, Order of Coif. Contracts commercial, Land use and zoning (including planning), Real property. Office: Foley Hoag & Eliot LLP 1 Post Office Sq Boston MA 02109-2170 E-mail: sshapiro@fhe.com

SHARE, RICHARD HUDSON, lawyer; b. Mpls., Sept. 6, 1938; s. Jerome and Millicent S.; m. Carolee Martin, 1970; children: Mark Lowell, Gregory Martin, Jennifer Hillary, Ashley. BS, UCLA, 1960; JD, U. So. Calif., 1963. Bar: Calif. Sup. Ct. 1964, U.S. Dist. Ct. (cen. and so. dists.) Calif., U.S. Supreme Ct. 1974. Field agt. IRS, 1960-63; mem. law divsn., asst. sec. Avco Fin. Svcs., 1963-72; founder Frandzel and Share, A Law Corp., L.A., 1972-99, Richard Hudson Share & Assocs., 1999—. Lectr. Nat. Bus. Inst., Creditor's Rights; adj. prof. Loloya Law Sch., 1999. Pub. N.Mex. Bus. Jour., 2001. Mem. Calif. Bankers Assn. Banking, Consumer commercial, Contracts commercial. Office: PO Box 1003 Pacific Palisades CA 90272-1003 also: 150 N Santa Anita Ave Ste 530 Arcadia CA 91006-3127 E-mail: sharelaw@aol.com

SHARETT, ALAN RICHARD, lawyer, environmental and disability litigator, mediator and arbitrator, law educator; b. Hammond, Ind., Apr. 15, 1943; s. Henry S. and Frances (Givel) Smulevitz; children: Lauren Ruth, Charles Daniel; m. Cherie Ann Vick, Oct. 15, 1993. Student, Ind. U., 1962-65; JD, DePaul U., 1968; advanced postgrad. legal edn., U. Mich. and U. Chgo., 1970-71; postgrad., Fla. Internat. U., 1999-2000; cert. mediator, Am. Arbitration Assn., 1994; cert. tng. and human resource devel., Fla. Internat. U., 2000. Bar: Ind. 1969, N.Y. 1975, U. S. Ct. Appeals (2d cir.) 1975, U.S. Ct. Appeals (7th cir.) 1974, U.S. Supreme Ct. 1973. Assoc. World Peace Through Law Ctr., Washington, 1967-68, Call, Call, Borns and Theodoros, Gary, Ind., 1969-71; judge protem Gary City Ct., 1970-71; environ. dist. atty. 31st Jud. Cir., Lake County, Ind., 1971-75; counsel Dunes Nat. Lakeshore Group, 1971-75; mem. Cohan, Cohan and Smulevitz, 1971-75; town atty. Independence Hill, Ind., 1974-75; judge pro tem Superior Ct., Lake County, 1971-75; pvt. practice Flushing, N.Y., 1980-82, Miami Beach, Fla., 1988—; lead trial counsel, chmn. lawyers panel No. Ind. ACLU, 1969-71; liaison trial counsel Lake County and Ind. State Health Depts., and Atty. Gen., 1971-75. Professorial dir. NYU Pub. Liability Inst., N.Y.C., 1975-76; speaker, guest lectr., adj. faculty ATLA, Ind. U., Purdue U., NYU, Ind. U., De Paul U., Valparaiso U., St. Joseph Coll., U. Miami; coll. paralegal instr., 1970-89; adj. faculty prof. constl. law Union Inst., Miami, Cin., 1990-92; adj. prof. environ. litigation and alternative dispute resolution Ward Stone Coll., Miami, 1994; guest prof. internat. environ. law Dept. Internat. and Comparative Law, hemispheric Interam., U. Miami, 1992—; mem. adv. panel, seminar speaker on internat. environ. law Interam. Dialogue on Water Mgmt., 1993; speaker on environ. transactions and litigation, North Dade county Fla. Bar Assn., 1995—; seminar speaker on environ. politics, U. Miami Dept. Environ. Sci., 1995—; mem. Nat. Dist. Attys. Assn., 1972-75, mem. environ. protection com.; pres. ESI Group, Nat. Environ. Responsibility Cons. Inc. Editor-in-chief DePaul U. The Summons, 1967-68; mem. staff DePaul Law Rev., 1968; contbr. articles to profl. jours. Gen. counsel Marjory Stoneman Douglas Friends of Everglades, 1992-93; asst. atty. gen., chair fed. and constnl. practice litigation group N.Y. State, N.Y.C., 1976-78; mem. Coalition Fla. Save Our Everglades Program; diplomate, vice chancellor Law-Sci. Acad. Am., 1967. Recipient Honors award in forensic litigation Law-Sci. Acad. Am., 1967. Mem. ABA (nat. article editor law student divsn. 1967-68, nat. com. environ. litigation, com. fed. procedures, com. toxic torts, hazardous substances and environ. law, com. energy resources law, com. internat. environ. law, com. internat. litigation, environ. interest group, sect. natural resources, energy and environ. law, judge negotiation competition championship round, law student divsn., midyr. meeting 1995, sect. sci. and tech., biotech. com., environ. law and pub. health com., standing com. sci. evidence, spl. com. legal edn., nat. toxic and hazardous substances and environ. law com., sect. tort and ins. practice, corp. gen. counsel com., non-profit orgns. com., media law and defamation torts com., tort and hazardous substances and environ. law com.), AAAS (physics, math, astronomy), Judicature Soc., Nat. Orgn. Social Security Claimants Reps. (sustaining), Am. Arbitration Assn. (cert. program in mediation 1993), ASTD, Soc. Human Resource Mgmt., Assn. Bar City N.Y., N.Y. County Lawyers Assn. (com. on fed. cts. 1977-82), ATLA (nat. coms. toxic, environ. and pharm. torts, environ. litigation), Environ. Law Inst., Am. Immigration Lawyers Assn., Ill. State Bar Assn. (staff editor 1967-68), N.Y. State Bar Assn. (environ. law sect., family law sect.), Ind. State Bar Assn. (environ. law sect., internat. law sect., trial practice sect.), Fla. Assn. Environ. Profls., Greater Miami C. of C. (trustee 1993-94, com. environ. awareness, environ. econs., biomed. exch., planning and growth mgmt., internat. econ. devel., bus. and industry econs. devel., govtl. affairs, ins., internat. banking, Europe/Pacific), N.Y. Acad. Sci., The Planetary Soc., Astron. Soc. of Pacific, Am. Acad. Poets, Soc. Cross Astron. Soc., The Planetary Soc., Astron. Soc. Environmental, Health, Labor. Office: ESI Group Nat Environ Responsibility Cons Inc 14630 Bull Run Rd Ste 213 Miami Lakes FL 33014-2017 E-mail: arsharett@mindspring.com

SHARFMAN, STEPHEN L. lawyer; b. 1944; AB, George Washington U., 1966; JD, Georgetown U., 1969. Bar: D.C. 1970. Asst. gen. coun. Met. Area Transit Comn., Washington; gen. counsel Postal Rate Commn. Bd dir. Danbury Forest Civic Assn.; Lakeside Village Cmty. Assn; Oak Marr Homeowners Assn. Office: Office Gen Counsel 1333 H St NW Washington DC 20268-0001 E-mail: sharfman@prc.gov

SHARMA, HARRISH KUMAR, lawyer; b. Delhi, India, Aug. 28, 1950; s. Ramkishan Lal and Janki Devi Sharma; m. Chander Kanta, Dec. 5, 1975; children: Alka, Meena, Ashish. Grad., Delhi U., 1977; degree in law, MMH Coll., Ghaziabad, India, 1990; postgrad., Anamalai (India) U., 1986; LLM, Meerut (India) U., 1992. Cert. in labor law, personnel mgmt. and indsl. rels. Bhartiyavidya Bhawan, Bombay, 1987; cert. in supervision Nat. Productivity Coun., New Delhi, 1984; cert. in rural journalism Indian Inst. Mass. Comm., New Delhi, 1985. Legal asst. Delhi Vidyat Bd., 1970-90; lawyer Supreme Ct. India, Delhi, 1991—. Advocate and legal cons., Delhi, 1991—. Bd. dirs. Indian Fedn. Sm. and Med. Newspapers, New Delhi, 1990— (Selfless Svc. award 1995); sec. Hitkari Parishad, Sonepat, India, 1990—; chief trustee Ram-Janki Trust, Sonepat, 1999. Recipient award of Honor, Rotary, Zonevi, 1998. Mem. Bar Assn. India (life), Supreme Ct. Bar Assn., Delhi High Ct. Bar Assn., Delhi Bar Assn. Avocations: travel, reading. Home: 1538 Housing Colony Sect 14 Haryana Songpat 131001 India E-mail: sonepat@yahoo.com

SHARP, REX ARTHUR, lawyer; b. Liberal, Kans., Jan. 1, 1960; s. Gene Hugh and Jo Ann (King) S.; m. Lori Renee Lewis, May 23, 1987; children: Lori Alexandra, Lewis Arthur, William Hugh. Student, U. Okla., 1978-79; AB in Econs. with honors & distinction, Stanford U., 1982; JD cum laude, U. Mich., 1985. Bar: Tex. 1985, Kans. 1985, Okla. 1986, Colo. 1988, Mo. 2000, U.S. Dist. Ct. (so. and no. dists.) Tex., U.S. Dist. Ct. (we. and no. dists.) Okla., U.S. Dist. Ct. Kans., U.S. Dist Ct. (we. dist.) Mo. , U.S. Ct. Appeals (10th cir.), U.S. Supreme Ct.; civil trial cert. N.B.T.A. Litigation assoc. Fulbright & Jaworski, Houston, 1985-87; assoc. Neubauer, Sharp, McQueen, Dreiling & Morain, Liberal, 1987-89; ptnr. McKinley, Sharp, McQueen, Dreiling, Morain & Tate, P.A., 1989-97, Husch & Eppenberger, Kansas City, Mo., 1997-2000, Sharp Law LLC, Prairie Village, Kans., 2000; stockholder Gunderson, Sharp, Trout & Rhein, P.C., 2000—. Asst. city atty. City of Liberal, 1988-93, city atty., 1993-97. Avocation: golf. General civil litigation, General practice, Personal injury. Office: Gunderson Sharp Trout & Rhein PC 4121 W 83d St Ste 256 Prairie Village KS 66208 Fax: 913-901-0419. E-mail: rexsharp@birch.net

SHARPE, CALVIN WILLIAM, law educator, arbitrator; b. Greensboro, N.C., Feb. 22, 1945; s. Ralph David and Mildred (Johnson) S.; m. Maya Annette Hall, Jan. 25, 1970 (div. Oct. 1975); 1 child, Kabral; m. Janice M. Jones, Apr. 13, 1978; children: Melanie, Stevie. BA, Clark Coll., 1967; postgrad., Oberlin Coll., 1968; MA, Chgo. Theol. Sem., 1996; JD, Northwestern U., Chgo., 1974. Bar: Ill. 1974. Tchr. elem. sch. N.Y. Sch. System, Bklyn., 1968-69; dir. homework study ctr. Ocean Hill Brownsville, 1969; investigator Ill. Gov.'s Task Force on Cook County Property Tax, Chgo., 1972-73; law clk. to judge Hubert L. Will U.S. Dist. Ct. (no. dist.) Ill., 1974-76; assoc. Cotton, Watt, Jones, King & Bowlus, 1976-77; trial atty. NLRB, Winston-Salem, N.C., 1977-81; asst. prof. U. Va., 1981-84; assoc. prof. Case Western Res. U., Cleve., 1984-88, prof., 1988—, John Deaver Drinko-Baker & Hostetler prof. law, 1999—, acad. dean, 1991-92. Exec. bd. Pub. Sector Labor Rels. Assn., Ohio, 1986—; chmn. evidence sect. Assn. Am. Law Schs., 1987-88; mem. Am. Labor Law Project to Soviet Union and Western Europe-People to People, 1988; mem. Youth Svcs. Adv. Bd. of the Cuyahoga County Juvenile Ct., 1989-91; cons. So. African Commn. on Concilation, Mediation and Arbitration, 1998—. Co-author: Understanding Labor Law, 1999. Bd. trustees Cleve. Hearing and Speech Ctr., 1985-88; bd. dirs. Garrett-Evang. Theol. Sem., 1999—, Cleve. Pub. Radio, 1993-94. Mem. Soc. Profls. in Dispute Resolution, Internat. Soc. Labor Law and Social Security, Indsl. Rels. Rsch. Assn. (convener and first chair labor and employment law sect. 1995-97), Nat. Acad. Arbitrators (bd. govs. 2001—). Office: Case Western Res U Law Sch 11075 East Blvd Cleveland OH 44106-5409

SHARPE, JAMES SHELBY, lawyer; b. Ft. Worth, Sept. 11, 1940; s. James Henry and Wanzel (Vanderbilt) S.; m. Martha Moudy Holland, June 9, 1962; children: Marthanne Freeman, Caren Sharp, Stephen. BA, U. Tex., 1962, JD, 1965. Bar: Tex. 1965, U.S. Dist. Ct. (no. dist.) Tex. 1966, U.S. Dist. Ct. (ea. dist.) Tex. 1993, U.S. Ct. Appeals (5th and 6th cirs.) 1982, U.S. Ct. Appeals (fed. cir.) 1983, U.S. Ct. Appeals (10th cir.) 1992, U.S. Supreme Ct. 1972. Briefing atty. for chief justice Supreme Ct. of Tex., Austin, 1965-66; ptnr. Brown, Herman, Scott, Dean & Miles, Ft. Worth, 1966-84, Gandy Michener Swindle Whitaker & Pratt, Ft. Worth, 1984-87; shareholder Sharpe & Tillman, 1988—. Adj. prof. polit. sci. Tex. Christian U., Ft. Worth, 1969-79, Dallas Bapt. U., 1987, 1992-94; gen. counsel U.S.A. Radio Network, Internat. Christian Media, Denton Pub. Co. Pres. Ft. Worth-Tarrant County Jr. Bar, 1969-70, bd. dirs., 1968, sec., 1968, v.p., 1968-69; head marshal USA-USSR Track and Field Championships, Ft. Worth, USA-USSR Jr. Track and Field Championships, Austin, Tex., Relays, Austin, 1963—, NCAA Nat. Track and Field Championships, 1976, 80, 85, 92, 95, S.W. Conf. Indoor Track and Field Championships, 1987-96, Olympic Festival, San Antonio, 1993, Colorado Springs, 1995; 12 time head marshal S.W. Conf. Track and Field Championships, Big 12 Outdoor Conf. Track and Field Championship, 1997, 98, 99, 2001, head marshall 2000 Olympic Trials in Track and Field. USA/Mobil Track Championship, 1994, 95; USA Nat. Jr. Track Championship, 1994, 95, 98, 99, USA Track and Field Track Championship, 1997, 2001, Master's Nat. Track and Field Nat. Championship, 1996, 98. Mem. ABA, State Bar of Tex. (dist. 7-A grievance com. 1983-85, com. adminstrn. of justice 1985-92, com. on ct. rules 1992—, chmn. 1992-93, 93-94). Baptist. General civil litigation, Constitutional, Libel. Office: Sharpe & Tillman 6100 Western Pl Ste 901 Fort Worth TX 76107-4679 E-mail: utlawman@aol.com

SHARPE, ROBERT FRANCIS, JR. lawyer; b. Long Branch, N.J., Mar. 9, 1952; s. Robert Francis and Audrey Carolyn (Rembe) S.; 1 child, Robert Francis III; m. Maria S. Renna, Sept. 9, 2000. BA, DePauw U., 1975; BSE, Purdue U., 1975; JD, Wake Forest U., 1978. Bar: N.C. 1978. Atty. Capital Synergistics Corp., Winston-Salem, N.C., 1977-80; asst. counsel R.J. Reynolds Industries, 1980-82, assoc. counsel, 1983-85, counsel, 1985-86; corp. and comml. counsel R.J. Reynolds Tobacco Co., 1986-87; sr. counsel, asst. sec. R.J. Reynolds Nabisco, Inc., Atlanta, 1987-88, asst. gen. counsel, asst sec., 1989-93, v.p., sec., gen. counsel, 1996-97; v.p. mergers and acquisitions Tyco Internat., 1994-95; sr. v.p. pub. affairs & gen. coun. PepsiCo, Inc., Purchase, N.Y., 1998—. Bd. dirs. Whitman Corp., Pepsi Bottling Group. Active Jr. Achievement, U.S. C. of C. Bd. dirs. Whitman Corp., Pepsi Bottling Group. Mem. ABA, N.C. Bar Assn., Am. Corp. Counsel Assn. Republican. Episcopalian. Avocations: golf, fishing. Contracts commercial, General corporate, Securities. Office: PepsiCo Inc 700 Anderson Hill Rd Purchase NY 10577-1444

SHARTS, JOHN EDWIN, III, lawyer; b. Cin., Feb. 14, 1948; s. John Edwin Jr. and Dorothy May (Kinder) S.; m. Martha Ann Meloy, Aug. 8, 1975; children: Megan Elizabeth, Jessica Anne. BA in Chemistry, U. Cin., 1970; JD, U. No. Ky., 1974. Bar: Ohio 1974, U.S. Dist. Ct. (so. dist.) Ohio 1975. Ptnr. Lawson & Sharts, Springboro, Ohio, 1974-89; city prosecutor City of Springboro, 1989—; sole practice, 1989—. Trustee Warren County Mental Health, Ohio, 1982-84. Mem. Ohio State Bar Assn., ABA, Assn. Trial Lawyers Am., Assn. Trial Lawyers Ohio, Warren County Bar Assn. (past treas.). Republican. Presbyterian. State civil litigation, Consumer commercial, General practice. Office: PO Box 350 Springboro OH 45066-0350

SHATTUCK, CATHIE ANN, lawyer, former government official; b. Salt Lake City, July 18, 1945; d. Robert Ashley S. and Lillian Culp (Shattuck). B.A., U. Nebr., 1967, J.D., 1970. Bar: Nebr. 1970, U.S. Dist. Ct. Nebr. 1970, Colo. 1971, U.S. Dist. Ct. Colo. 1971, U.S. Supreme Ct. 1974, U.S. Ct. Appeals (10th cir.) 1977, U.S. Dist. Ct. D.C. 1984, U.S. Ct. Appeals (D.C. cir.) 1984. V.p., gen. mgr. Shattuck Farms, Hastings, Nebr., 1967-70; asst. project dir. atty. Colo. Civil Rights Commn., Denver, 1970-72; trial atty. Equal Employment Opportunity Commn., 1973-77, vice chmn. Washington, 1982-84; pvt. practice law Denver, 1977-81; mem. Fgn. Svc. Bd., Washington, 1982-84, Presdl. Personnel Task Force, Washington, 1982-84; ptnr. Epstein, Becker & Green, L.A. and Washington, 1984—. Lectr. Colo. Continuing Legal Edn. Author: Employer's Guide to Controlling Sexual Harrassment, 1992; mem. editorial bd. The Practical Litigator, 1988—. Bd. dirs. KGNU Pub. Radio, Boulder, Colo., 1979, Denver Exchange, 1980-81, YWCA Met. Denver, 1979-81. Recipient Nebr. Young Career Woman Bus. and Profl. Women, 1967; recipient Outstanding Nebraskan Daily Nebraskan, Lincoln, 1967 Fellow Am. Coll. of Labor and Employment Lawyers; mem. ABA (mgmt. chair labor and employment law sect. com. on immigration law 1988-90, mgmt. chair com. on legis. devels. 1990-93), Nebr. Bar Assn., Colo. Bar Assn., Colo. Women's Bar Assn., D.C. Bar Assn., Nat. Women's Coalition, Delta Sigma Rho, Tau Kappa Alpha, Pi Sigma Alpha, Alpha Xi Delta, Denver Club. Administrative and regulatory, Civil rights, Juvenile.

SHATTUCK, GARY G. lawyer; b. Nashua, N.H., 1950; m. Katherine H. Catlin, 1972. BA, U. Colo., 1972; JD magna cum laude, Vt. Law Sch., 1987. Bar: Vt. 1987, U.S. Dist. Ct. Vt. 1987, U.S. Ct. Appeals (2d cir.) 1992. Dep. sheriff Boulder County Sheriff's Dept., Boulder, Colo., 1973-75; patrol comdr. Vt. State Police, Waterbury, 1975-87; litigation assoc. Reiber, Kenlan, Schweibert & Hall, P.C., Rutland, Vt., 1987-89; asst. atty. gen. Office of Atty. Gen., Montpelier, 1989-91; suprvising atty. Vt. Drug Task Force, 1989-91; asst. U.S. atty. Organized Crime Drug Enforcement Task Force, U.S. Dept. Justice, Burlington, Vt., 1991—. Adj. prof. Castleton (Vt.) State Coll., 1997-98; U.S. Dept. Justice legal advisor to UN Mission in Kosovo, Pristina, 2000, Sarajevo, Bosnia-Herzegovina, 2001. Bd. dirs. Rutland Mental Health, 1991; citizen's adv. com. Rutland Solid Waste Dist., 1987; del. Nat. Assn. Asst. U.S. Attys., 1994-99; bd. dirs. Vt. Archeol. Soc., 1998-99. Recipient Atty. Gen. Janet Reno Spl. Achievement award, 1993, award Dept. Justice for svc. in Kosovo. Mem. Lake Champlain Maritime Mus., Inst. Nautical Archaeology, Nat. Trust Historic Preservation, New Eng. Narcotic Enforcement Officers Assn. (award 2001). Office: Office of US Atty PO Box 570 Burlington VT 05402-0570 E-mail: garyshattuck@hotmail.com

SHAW, ABELINA MADRID, state official, lawyer; b. Lihue, Hawaii, Apr. 13, 1947; d. Venancio and Rosenda (Pasion) Madrid; m. Cuyler Eaton Shaw, Nov. 22, 1977; 1 child, Renee Nalani. BEd, U. Hawaii, 1970, MA, 1972, JD, 1976. Bar: Hawaii 1977. Grad. teaching asst. dept. speech communication U. Hawaii, Honolulu, 1970-71, adminstrv. asst. PEACE Satellite, 1971-72, instr., dept. speech communication, 1972-73; speech writer Office of Speaker State of Hawaii Legislature, Honolulu, 1973; law clk. Ashford & Wriston, Honolulu, 1974, Legal Aid Soc. Hawaii, Lihue, 1975, Hawaii Supreme Ctr., Honolulu, 1976; dep. atty. gen. State of Hawaii, Honolulu, 1977, spl. asst. to gov., 1979, dep. dir. Dept. Health, 1980-87, ct. staff atty. Supreme Ct. of Hawaii, 1987—. Mem. Health and Community Services Council, Honolulu, 1984; del. Democratic State Conv., Hawaii, 1982, 84. Mem. Hawaii Bar Assn., Bus. and Profl. Women of Am., Zonta. Roman Catholic. Home: 3783 Kumulani Pl Honolulu HI 96822-1113 Office: State Hawaii Dept Health 1250 Punchbowl St Honolulu HI 96813

SHAW, BARRY N. lawyer; b. Newark, July 31, 1940; s. Harry G. and Evelyn (Kruger) S.; m. Cheryl Lynn Rosen, Mar. 24, 1963; children: Jennifer B., Jonathan M. BS in Acctg., Rutgers U., 1962, LLB, 1965. Bar: Pa. 1966, N.J. 1974, U.S. Supreme Ct. 1988, Oreg. 1996; CPA, Pa. With Coopers & Lybrand, Phila., 1965-68; corp. counsel Lincoln Bank, 1968-72, Waste Resources Corp., Phila., 1972-74; ptnr. Spivack, Dranoff & Shaw, 1974-75, Dranoff & Shaw, Phila., 1975-79, Jubanyik, Varbalow Tedesco Shaw & Shaffer, Cherry Hill, N.J., 1979-95, Dilworth, Paxson, Kalish & Kauffman (successor firm), Cherry Hill, 1995-97, Davis, Gilstrap, Hearn & Shaw PC, Ashland, Oreg., 1997-2000, Grantland, Blodgett & Shaw, LLP, Medford, 2000—. Lectr. in banking and real estate law. Author: Selected Decisions in Lender Liability Law, 1990, Environmental Lender Liability, 1992. Chmn. Shamong Twp. (N.J.) Planning Bd., 1990-93, Local Civic Assn.; active Shamong Twp. Com., 1993-97; mayor Shamong Twp., 1995; sec. Pinelands Mcpl. (Mayors') Coun., 1996-97. Mem. Oreg. State Bar, Jackson County Bar Assn., Rotary (pres. 2001-2002). Republican. Avocations: farming, writing. Contracts commercial, General corporate, Probate. Office: Grantland Blodgett & Shaw LLP 1818 E McAndrew Rd Medford OR 97504 Fax: 541-770-1290. E-mail: bshaw@mighty.net

SHAW, CHARLES ALEXANDER, judge; b. Jackson, Tenn., Dec. 31, 1944; s. Alvis and Sarah S.; m. Kathleen Ingram, Aug. 17, 1969; 1 child, Bryan Ingram. BA, Harris Stowe State Coll., 1966; MBA, U. Mo., 1971; JD, Cath. U. Am., 1974. Bar: D.C. 1975, Mo. 1975, U.S. Ct. Appeals (8th and D.C. cirs.) 1975, U.S. Dist. Ct. (ea. dist.) Mo. 1976, U.S. Ct. Appeals (6th and 7th cirs.) 1976. Tchr. St. Louis Pub. Schs., 1966-69, D.C. Pub. Schs., Washington, 1969-71; law clk. U.S. Dept. Justice, 1972-73, NLRB, Washington, 1973-74, atty., 1974-76; assoc. Lashly, Caruthers, Theis, Rava & Hamel, St. Louis, 1976-80, asst. U.S. atty., 1980-87; judge Mo. Cir. Ct., 1987-94, asst. presiding judge, 1993-94; judge U.S. Dist. Ct., 1994—. Hearing officer Office of the Mayor, Washington, 1973-74; instr. U. Mo., St. Louis, 1980-81. State bd. dirs. United Negro Coll. Fund, St. Louis, 1979-83; trustee St. Louis Art Mus., 1979-82, 89-96; bd. dirs. Arts and Edn. Coun., 1992-96, Metro Golf Assn., 1993-2000, Landmarks Assn., St. Louis, 1980-82. Danforth Found. fellow, 1978-79; Cath. U. Am. scholar, 1971-74. Mem. D.C. Bar Assn., Mo. Bar Assn., Mound City Bar Assn., Bar Assn. Metro. St. Louis, Harris-Stowe State Coll. Alumni Assn. (bd. dirs., Disting. Alumni 1988), Nat. Assn. Guardsmen (sec. St. Louis chpt. 1999-2001), Phi Alpha Delta (svc. award 1973-74), Sigma Pi Phi (pres. St. Louis chpt. 1999-2001). Avocation: golf. Office: 111 S 10th St Saint Louis MO 63102

SHAW, CHERYL D. lawyer; b. Kansas City, Mo., Aug. 18, 1958; Grad., Cerritos Coll., 1991; JD cum laude, Whittier Coll., 1997. Bar: Calif. 1997, U.S. Dist. Ct. (ctrl. dist.) Calif. 1997. Tchg. fellow Whittier (Calif.) Coll., 1995-96; assoc. Wasserman, Comden & Casselman, L.L.P., Tarzana, Calif., 1997—. Founder, chief fin. dir. Whittier Legal Rels. Honors Bd. Mng. editor Whittier Law Rev., 1996-97. Mem. State Bar Calif. Office: Wasserman Comden & Casselman PO Box 7033 5567 Reseda Blvd Ste 330 Tarzana CA 91357-7033

SHAW, ELIZABETH ORR, lawyer; b. Monona, Iowa, Oct. 2, 1923; d. Harold Topliff and Hazel (Kean) Orr; m. Donald Hardy Shaw, Aug. 16, 1946; children: Elizabeth Ann, Andrew Hardy, Anthony Orr. AB, Drake U., 1945; postgrad., U. Minn., 1945-46; JD, U. Iowa, 1948. Bar: Ill. 1949, Iowa 1956. Assoc. Lord Bissell & Brook, Chgo., 1949-52; pvt. practice law Arlington Heights, Ill., 1952-56; ptnr. Wood & Shaw, Davenport, Iowa, 1968-72; mem. Iowa Ho. of Reps., Des Moines, 1967-72, Iowa Senate, Des Moines, 1972-77; county atty. Scott County, Davenport, 1977-78; corp. atty. Deere & Co., Moline, Ill., 1979-89; pvt. practice Davenport, 1990-98; ret., 1999. Mem. Scott County Bar Assn. (com. chmn. 1970-72), Iowa State Bar Assn. (chmn. family law com. 1970-76), Order of Coif, Phi Beta Kappa, Kappa Kappa Gamma, PEO. Republican. Mem. United Ch. of Christ. Administrative and regulatory, General corporate, Environmental. Home and Office: 29 Hillcrest Ave Davenport IA 52803-3726 E-mail: dhsiwg@aol.com

SHAW, L. EDWARD, JR. lawyer; b. Elmira, N.Y., July 30, 1944; s. L. Edward and Virginia Anne (O'Leary) S.; m. Irene Ryan; children: Christopher, Hope, Hillary, Julia, Rory B.A. in Econs., Georgetown U., Washington, 1966; J.D., Yale U., New Haven, 1969. Bar: N.Y. 1969. Assoc. Milbank, Tweed, Hadley & McCloy, N.Y.C., 1969-77, ptnr., 1977-83; sr. v.p., gen. counsel Chase Manhattan Corp., 1983-85, exec. v.p., gen. counsel, 1985-96; vice chmn., gen. counsel Natwest Markets, 1996-97, pres., 1997-99; gen. counsel Aetna Inc., 1999—. Mem. Assn. Bar City N.Y., Winged Foot Golf Club, Phi Beta Kappa. Roman Catholic. Avocations: youth athletics, golf. Office: Aetna Inc RC4B 151 Farmington Ave Hartford CT 06156-3124 E-mail: ShawJL@aetna.com

SHAW, LEANDER JERRY, JR. state supreme court justice; b. Salem, Va., Sept. 6, 1930; s. Leander J. and Margaret S. BA, W.Va. State Coll., 1952, LLD (hon.), 1986; JD, Howard U., 1957; PhD (hon.) in Pub. Affairs, Fla. Internat. U., 1990; LLD (hon.), Nova Law Sch., 1991, Washington & Lee Law Sch., 1991. Asst. prof. law Fla. A&M U., 1957-60; sole practice Jacksonville, Fla., 1960-69, 72-74; asst. pub. defender, 1965-69; asst. state's atty. Fla., 1969-72; judge Fla. Indsl. Relations Commn., 1974-79, Fla. Ct. Appeals (1st dist.), 1979-83; justice Fla. Supreme Ct., Tallahassee, 1983—, chief justice, 1990-92. Office: Fla Supreme Ct Supreme Ct Bldg 500 S Duval St Tallahassee FL 32399-6556 E-mail: SupremeCourt@FLCOURTS.ORG

SHAW, ROBERT BERNARD, lawyer; b. Newark, Jan. 26, 1934; s. Nathan and Serena Shaw; m. Sydelle Mae Resnick, Feb. 8, 1958; children: Howard, Lisa, Michael. BS, NYU, 1955; JD, Bklyn. Law Sch., 1958. Bar: N.Y. 1959, U.S. Dist. Ct. (so. and ea. dists.) N.Y. 1960. Ptnr. Shaw & Meyer, N.Y.C., 1959-61; pvt. practice, 1961-70, 74—; ptnr. Shaw, Issler & Rosenberg, 1970-74. Past pres. Past Capts. Assn. USCG Aux. Mem. N.Y. State Bar Assn., Nassau County Bar Assn., City of N.Y. Police Res. Assn. (bd. dirs. 1997—, v.p. legal affairs). General civil litigation, Family and matrimonial. Office: 630 3rd Ave New York NY 10017-6705 E-mail: rbshawlaw@aol.com

SHAY, DAVID EUGENE, lawyer; b. Scranton, Pa., Nov. 9, 1962; s. Howard E. Jr. and Arlene (Pace) S.; m. Kimberly R. Grow, June 22, 1985; children: Daniel E., Andrew W., Matthew D. BS in Journalism, Kans. U., 1984, JD, 1988. Bar: Mo. 1988, U.S. Dist. Ct. (we. dist.) Mo. 1988, U.S. Ct. Appeals (5th and 8th cirs.) 1991, U.S. Dist. Ct. Kans. 2000. Reporter KDXE, Sulphur Springs, Tex., 1984, KTTR/KZNN, Inc., Rolla, Mo., 1984-85; shareholder Shughart, Thomson & Kilroy, P.C., Kansas City, 1988-99, Seigfreid, Bingham, Levy, Selzer & Gee, P.C., Kansas City, 1999—. Contbr. articles to profl. publs., chpt. to Mo. Bar Deskbook, 1991, 97. Mem. The Christian Ch. of Greater Kansas City, ministerial ethics com., 1999—; moderator Blue Valley Christian Ch. Mem. ABA, Mo. Bar Assn. (chair environ. and energy law com. 1995-97), Lawyers Assn. Kansas City (bd. dirs. 2000—, young lawyers sect. bd. dirs. 1991-97, young lawyers sect. officer 1993-97, young lawyers sect. pres. 1996-97), Kansas City Met. Bar Assn., Lawyers Encouraging Acad. Performance (dir. 1996-97), Order of Coif, Phi Kappa Phi. Republican. Mem. Christian Ch. (Disciples of Christ). General civil litigation, Environmental, Insurance. Office: Seigfreid Bingham et al 2800 Commerce Twr 911 Main St Ste 2800 Kansas City MO 64105-2069 E-mail: dshay@sblsg.com

SHAY-BYRNE, OLIVIA, lawyer; b. Trenton, N.J., Aug. 14, 1957; d. Stewart and Elizabeth (Sherrill) B. Student, Vanderbilt U., 1975-76; BA, Bowdoin Coll., 1979; JD, U. Toledo, 1982; LLM in Taxation, Georgetown U., 1987. Bar: Tex. 1982, Ohio 1984, Md. 1985. Assoc. Whiteford, Taylor & Preston, Balt., 1984-87, Linowes & Blocher, Silver Spring, Md., 1987-90; ptnr. Weinberg & Jacobs, Rockville, 1990-96, Sutherland Asbill & Brenna LLP, Rockville, 1996-99, Sutherland Asbue & Brenna, Washington, 1999—. Author: The At-Risk Rules Under the Tax Reform Act of 1986, The Door Closes on Tax Motivated Investments, IRS Issues New Guidelines for Management Contracts Used for Facilities Financed with Tax Exempt Bonds, 1993, RRA '93 Loosens Real Estate Rules for Exempt Organizations, 1993; contbr. articles to profl. jours. Mem. Tax Coun. for State of Md., Leadership Montgomery, 1996; bd. dirs. Bethesda Acad. Performing Arts, Inst. for In Vitro Scis., Inc.; chair GULC Nat. Tax Exempt Bond Conf., 1997. Mem. ABA (exempt orgn. com. taxation sect. 1991—), Md. Bar Assn. (coun. taxation sect.), Balt. City Bar Assn. (chmn. speakers bur. young lawyers sect.), Lawyers for Arts Washington, Comml. Real Estate Woman (bd. dirs., pres.), Profls. for Strathmore Hall (co-chmn.), D.C. Bowdoin Coll. Alumni Assn. (pres. 1992—), Howard County C. of C. (legis. com. 1989), Rotary. General corporate, Corporate taxation, Taxation, general. Home: 1811 Brentridge St Vienna VA 22182-2579 Office: Sutherland Asbill & Brennan LLP 1275 Pennsylvania Ave NW Washington DC 20004-2404

SHEA, DAVID MICHAEL, state supreme court justice; b. Hartford, July 1, 1922; s. Michael Peter and Margaret (Agnes) S.; m. Rosemary Anne Sasseen, Apr. 28, 1956; children: Susan, Kathleen, Margaret, Rosemary, Christina, Michael, Maura, Julie BA, Wesleyan U., 1944; LLB, Yale U., 1948. Bar: Conn. 1948. Assoc. Tunick & Ferris, Greenwich, Conn., 1948-49; assoc. Bailey & Wechsler, Hartford, 1949-57; ptnr. Bailey, Wechsler & Shea, 1957-65; judge Conn. Superior Ct., 1966-81; justice Conn. Supreme Ct., 1981-92, state judge referee, 1992—. Served with U.S. Army, 1943-46 Democrat. Roman Catholic Office: Conn Superior Ct 95 Washington St Hartford CT 06106-4431

SHEA, EDWARD EMMETT, lawyer, educator, author; b. Detroit, May 29, 1932; s. Edward Francis and Margaret Kathleen (Downey) S.; m. Ann Marie Conley, Aug. 28, 1957; children: Michael, Maura, Ellen. AB, U. Detroit, 1954; JD, U. Mich., 1957. Bar: Mich. 1957, Fla. 1959, N.Y. 1961. Assoc. Simpson Thacher & Bartlett, N.Y.C., 1960-63, Dykema, Wheat, Spencer, Detroit, 1963-69, Cadwalader Wickersham & Taft, N.Y.C., 1969-71; v.p., gen. counsel, chmn. Reichhold Chems., White Plains, N.Y., 1971-81; adj. prof. Pace U. Grad. Sch. Bus., N.Y.C., 1982—; counsel, ptnr. Windels, Marx, Lane & Mittendorf, 1982-84; ptnr. Windels, Marx, Davies & Ives, 1986—; sr. v.p., gen. counsel GAF Corp., 1984-86. Sec. Peridot Chems., 1988-97; lectr. N.Y. Inst. Fin., 1995—. Author: An Introduction to the U.S. Environmental Laws, 1995, The Lead Regulation Handbook, 1996, The McGraw-Hill Guidebook to Acquiring and Divesting Businesses, 1998; editor: The Acquisitions Yearbook, 1991-93; contbr. articles to profl. jours. Mem. adv. bd. N.Y. State Small Bus. Ctr. Program, 1988-93. 1st lt. JAGC, USAF, 1957-60. Mem. N.Y. Athletic Club. Environmental, Finance, Private international. Office: Windels Marx Lane & Mittendorf 156 W 56th St Fl 23 New York NY 10019-3867 E-mail: eshea@windelsmarx.com

SHEA, EDWARD FRANCIS, federal judge; b. Malden, Mass., June 6, 1942; s. Leo John and Genevieve (Lee) S.; m. Marguerite Mary DeRenne, Oct. 29, 1960; children: Kathryn, Marilou, Jacqueline Jeanne, Edward Francis. BS in Edn., Boston State U., 1965; JD, Georgetown U., 1970. Bar: Wash. 1971. Law clk. Wash. State Ct. Appeals, Tacoma, 1970-71; ptnr. Peterson, Taylor, Day & Shea, Pasco, Wash., 1971-79, Shea, Kuffel, Lindsay & Flynn, Pasco, 1979-87, Shea, Kuffel & Klashke, Pasco, 1987-96, Shea, Kuffel, Klashke & Shea, Pasco, 1997-98; apptd. judge U.S. Dist. Ct. (ea. dist.) Wash., Richland, 1998—. Cjwyer; b. Malden, Mass., June 6, 1942; s. Leo John and Genevieve (Lee) S.; m. Marguerite Mary DeRenne, Oct. 29, 1960; children— Kathryn, Marilou, Jacqueline Jeanne, Edward Francis. B.S. in Edn., Boston State U., 1965; J.D., Georgetown U., 1970. Bar: Wash. 1971. Law clk. Wash. State Ct. Appeals, Tacoma, 1970-71; ptnr. Peterson, Taylor, Day & Shea, Pasco, Wash., 1971-79, Shea, Kuffel, Lindsay & Flynn, Pasco, 1979-87, Shea, Kuffel & Kloshke, 1987-96, Shea, Kuffel, Kloshke & Shea, 1997—. Chmn., Pasco Centennial Com., 1983-84; bd. dirs. Fund for Edn. Activities, Pasco, 1981-83. Mem. Wash. State Trial Lawyers (gov. 1973-74, 81-83), ABA (chmn. bd. editors Barrister Mag. 1977-79, ho. of dels. 1979, 89-94), Wash. State Bar Assn. (bd. govs. 1986-89, pres. 1995-96). Chmn., Pasco Centennial Com., 1983-84. Mem. ABA (chmn. bd. editors Barrister Mag. 1977-79, ho. of dels. 1979, 89-94), Wash. State Trial Lawyers (gov. 1973-74, 81-83), Wash. State Bar Assn.(bd. govs. 1986-89, pres. 1995-96). Office: U S District Ct 825 Jadwin Ave Ste 190 Richland WA 99352 E-mail: ed_shea@waep.uscourts.gov

SHEA, GERALD MACDONALD, lawyer; b. N.Y.C., Nov. 10, 1942; s. John Anthony and Grace (Deery) S.; m. Claire Marie Antoinette Elisabeth de Gramont, Dec. 5, 1981; children— Penelope Mahot de la Querantonnais, Sebastian John Andrew, Alexander George Edward. B.A., Yale U., 1964; J.D., Columbia U., 1967. Bar: N.Y. 1968. Assoc. Debevoise & Plimpton, N.Y.C., 1967-72, 75-76, Paris, France, 1972-75, internat. counsel, Paris, 1987—; sr. counsel Mobil Oil Corp., N.Y.C., 1976-83; v.p., gen. counsel Mobil Saudi Arabia Inc., Jeddah, 1983-87; internat. counsel Debevoise and Plimpton, Paris, 1987. Jerome Michael scholar, 1966. Mem. Assn. Bar City N.Y. Club: Racquet and Tennis (N.Y.C.). General corporate, Private international, Mergers and acquisitions. Office: Mobil Saudi Arabia Inc Jeddah Saudi Arabia

SHEA, JAMES WILLIAM, lawyer; b. N.Y.C., July 10, 1936; s. William P. and Mildred E. (McCaffrey) S.; m. Ann Marie Byrne, June 6, 1964; children: James T., Kathleen A., Tracy A. BS, St. Peters Coll., 1957; JD, Fordham U., 1962; LLM in Taxation, NYU, 1965. Bar: N.Y. 1962, U.S. Dist. Ct. (so. and ea. dists.) N.Y. 1966, U.S. Supreme Ct. 1967. Revenue agent U.S. Treasury Dept., N.Y.C., 1961-63; tax atty. Kennecott Copper Corp., 1963-67; tax counsel CBS Inc., 1968-71; ptnr. Hunton & Williams and predecessor firm Conboy, Hewitt, O'Brien & Boardman, 1971—. Bd. dirs. Victory Van Lines Inc., N.Y.C. Rep. committeeman, Staten Island, N.Y., 1980; mem. adv. com. tax and fin. N.Y. State Charter Commn. City of S.I. Served to 1st lt. U.S. Army, 1957-61, to capt. USAR, 1962-72. Mem. ABA, N.Y. State Bar Assn., Richmond County Country Club S.I. (sec. 1993-96, v.p. 1996-98, pres. 1998-2000, bd. dirs. 1993—). Republican. Roman Catholic. E-mail: jshea.hunton.com. Probate, Personal income taxation, State and local taxation. Home: 399 Tysens Ln Staten Island NY 10306-2844 Office: Hunton & Williams 200 Park Ave Rm 4400 New York NY 10166-0091

SHEA, PATRICK A. lawyer, educator; b. Salt Lake City, Feb. 28, 1948; s. Edward J. and Ramona (Kilpack) S.; m. Deborah Fae Kern, Sept. 1, 1980; children: Michael, Paul. BA, Stanford U., 1970; MA, Oxford U., Eng., 1972; JD, Harvard U., 1975. Bar: Utah 1976, D.C. 1979. Mem. profl. staff majority leader's office U.S. Senate, 1971, asst. staff dir. intelligence com., 1975-76; assoc. VanCott, Bagley, Salt Lake City, 1976-79, ptnr., 1980-87; counsel fgn. relations com. U.S. Senate, 1979-80; gen. counsel KUTV, Comm. Investment Corp., Standard Comm.; dir. Bur. of Land Mgmt. Dept. of Interior, 1997-98; dep., asst. sec. interior Land & Minerals Mgmt., 1998-2000; of counsel Ballard, Spahr, Andrews & Ingersoll LLP, Salt Lake City, 2000—. Cons. judiciary com. U.S. Ho. of Reps., 1972-73; adj. prof. polit. sci. U. Utah, Salt Lake City, 1981-97. Chmn. Utah Democratic Party, Salt Lake City, 1983-85; v.p. Tomorrow-Today Found., Salt Lake City, 1982-84. Mem. Am. Rhodes Scholar Assn., Utah Bar Assn., D.C. Bar Assn., Stanford Alumni Assn. (pres.-elect 1983-84). Roman Catholic. Club: Alta. Federal civil litigation, Entertainment, Libel. Office: Ballard Spahr Andrews & Ingersoll LLP One Utah Ctr Ste 600 201 S Main St Salt Lake City UT 84111-2221 Fax: 202-208-3144. E-mail: sheap@ballardspahr.com

SHEACH, ANDREW JONATHAN, lawyer; b. Ilford, Essex, Eng., Apr. 7, 1963; BA in Law with honors, Cambridge U., Eng., 1984. Trainee solicitor Cameron Markby, London, 1985-87, solicitor, 1987-93; ptnr. CMS Cameron McKenna, 1993—. General corporate, Mergers and acquisitions. Office: CMS Cameron McKenna 160 Aldersgate St EC1A 4DD London England Fax: 00 44 207 367 2000. E-mail: ajs@cmck.com

SHEAFFER, WILLIAM JAY, lawyer; b. Carlisle, Pa., Jan. 18, 1948; s. Raymond Jay and Barbara Jean (Bell) S.; m. Carol Ann Madison, Jan. 5, 1974. BA cum laude, U. Cen. Fla., 1975; JD, Nova U., 1978. Bar: Fla. 1978, U.S. Dist. Ct. (mid. dist.) Fla. 1979, U.S. Dist. Ct. (so. and no. dists.) Fla. 1981, U.S. Ct. Appeals (5th and 11th cirs.) 1981, U.S. Supreme Ct. 1983. Atty. State of Fla., Orlando, 1978-79; pvt. practice, 1979—. Apptd. to merit selection panel to consider U.S. Magistrate Judge Applicants, 1995, 97, 99. Pres. City Coun. Edgewood, Fla., 2000—; served to ensign class 4 USN, 1967-71. Mem. ABA, NACDL, Fla. Bar Assn. (cert. criminal trial specialist, vice chmn. 9th judicial cir. grievance com. 1997, 98), Orange County Bar Assn. (Guardian Ad Litem of Yr. 1994, award of excellence 1995), Fed. Bar Assns., Fla. Assn. Criminal Def. Lawyers Inc., Fed. Trial Lawyers Assn., Am. Inns of Ct. (ctrl. Fla. master), Tiger Bay Club. Democrat. Avocations: boating, running, skiing, scuba diving, golf. Administrative and regulatory, Appellate, Criminal. Office: 609 E Central Blvd Orlando FL 32801-2916 Fax: 407-648-0683. E-mail: defenselaw@prodigy.net

SHEAHAN, MICHAEL JOHN, lawyer; b. St. Paul, Jan. 27, 1934; s. Louis Patrick and Evelyn Sylvia (Frediani) S.; m. Charlene Ruth Schermerhorn, Nov. 5, 1960; children: John M., Mark W., Stephen P. B.S., U. Minn.-Mpls., 1960, LL.B., 1961. Bar: Minn. 1961, U.S. Dist. Ct. Minn. 1964. Assoc. T. O. Kachelmacher, Mpls., 1961; ptnr. Cummins, Gislason, & Sheahan, Ltd., St. Paul, 1973-76, Peterson, Gray & Sheahan, Ltd., St. Paul, 1976-85; prin. Michael J. Sheahan, P.A., 1985—. Chmn. Ramsey County Bar Fund, St. Paul, 1983-84. Mem., sec. St. Paul City Charter Commn., 1976-80; dean Acad. Cert. Trial Lawyers Minn., 1995-96. Trustee, St. Thomas Acad., St. Paul, 1983-95. Served with U.S. Army, 1955-57. Named Minn. Super Lawyer, Minn. Law and Politics mag., 1998. Mem. Minn. Trial Lawyers Assn. (dir.), Ramsey County Bar Assn., ABA, Minn. State Bar Assn., Nat. Bd. Trial Advocacy, Phi Delta Phi. Roman Catholic. Clubs: St. Paul Athletic (past. sec., dir.), Pool & Yacht, Optimists (past pres.), Gyro. General corporate, Personal injury, Probate. Home: 8160 Emerald Ln Saint Paul MN 55125-3325 Office: Michael J Sheahan PA 3900 Northwoods Dr Ste 250 Saint Paul MN 55112-6991

SHEAHAN, ROBERT EMMETT, lawyer, consultant; b. Chgo., May 20, 1942; s. Robert Emmett and Lola Jean (Moore) S.; m. Pati Smith, Mar. 20, 1991. BA, Ill. Wesleyan U., 1964; JD, Duke U., 1967; MBA, U. Chgo., 1970. Bar: Ill. 1967, La. 1975, N.C. 1978. Vol. VISTA, N.Y.C., 1967-68; trial atty. NLRB, Milw., New Orleans, 1970-75; ptnr. Jones, Walker, Waechter, Poitevent, Carrere & Denegre, New Orleans, 1975-78; pvt. practice High Point, N.C., 1978—. Bd. dirs. Inst. for Effective Mgmt., Bus. Publs. Inst. Author: Employees and Drug Abuse: An Employer's Handbook, 1994, The Encyclopedia of Drugs in the Workplace, Labor and Employment Law in North Carolina, 1991, Personnel and Employment Law in North Carolina, 1992, Desk Book of Labor and Employment Law for Healthcare Employers' Desk Manual, 1995, North Carolina Lawyers' Desk Book; contbg. author: The Developing Labor Law, 1975—; editor: The World of Personnel; contbg. editor: Employee Testing and the Law;

contbr. periodic supplements N.C. Gen. Practice Deskbook, 1992—. Bd. dirs. High Point United Way, 1979-83; mem. congl. action com. High Point C. of C., chmn., 1991—, bd. dirs., 1996—. Mem. ABA, N.C. Bar Assn., High Point Bar Assn., Ill. Bar Assn., La. Bar Assn., Sedgefield (N.C.) Country Club, String and Splinter Club, Island Club. Republican. Roman Catholic. Labor. Home: 8 Sabal Palm Ct Bald Head Island NC Office: Eastchester Office Ctr 603 Eastchester Dr Ste B High Point NC 27262-7647

SHEARER, DEAN PAUL, lawyer; b. Waco, Tex., Aug. 30, 1960; s. Clyde Paul and Elaine Shearer; m. Linda Hallene, May 22, 1982; children: Stephanie Ann, John Paul. Student, U. Houston, 1978-81; BS, U. Houston-Clear Lake, 1982; JD, South Tex. Coll. Law, Houston, 1989. Bar: Tex. 1989; bd. cert. in estate planning and probate. Atty. Babchick Cohen & Shearer P.C., Houston, 1989—. Adj. prof. U. Houston-Clear lake 1991-97; instr. Exec. Devel. program U. Houston Coll. Bus. Adminstrn. 1997—. Trustee, v.p. Clear Lake City Cmty. Assn., 1992-94; asst. den leader Boy Scouts Am., Houston, 1995-96; team mgr. Bay Area Youth Sports, Houston, 1994-99; vol. Jr. Achievement, 1994, Habitat for Humanity, 1995, 97, YMCA, 1997, 99. Mem. Houston Bar Assn. (co-chair campaign for homeless com. 1998-99, chair speakers bur. 1999—, continuing legal edn. com. 1997-98), State Bar Tex., State Bar Coll. Roman Catholic. Avocations: motorcycling, boating, bicycling. Estate planning, Probate, Estate taxation. Home: 810 Heathgate Dr Houston TX 77062-2624 Office: Babchick Cohen & Shearer PC 4615 Post Oak Place Dr Ste 279 Houston TX 77027-9753

SHEARING, MIRIAM, state supreme court justice; b. Waverly, N.Y., Feb. 24, 1935; BA, Cornell U., 1956; JD, Boston Coll., 1964. Bar: Calif. 1965, Nev. 1969. Justice of peace Las Vegas Justice Ct., 1977-81; judge Nev. Dist. Ct., 1983-92, chief judge, 1986; justice Nevada Supreme Ct., Carson City, 1993-97, chief justice, 1997—. Mem. ABA, Am. Judicature Soc. (chair 2001-), Nev. Judges Assn. (sec. 1978), Nev. Dist. Ct. Judges Assn. (sec. 1984-85, pres. 1986-87), State Bar Nev., State Bar Calif., Clark County Bar Assn. Democrat. E-mail: shearing@nvcourts.state.nv.us

SHEBLE, WALTER FRANKLIN, retired lawyer; b. Chestnut Hill, Pa., Sept. 14, 1926; s. Franklin and Harriett Elizabeth (Smith) S.; m. Nancy Altemus, July 7, 1956; 3 children. AB, Princeton U., 1948; JD, George Washington U., 1952, LLM, 1953. Bar: U.S. Dist. Ct. D.C. 1952, U.S. Ct. Appeals D.C. 1952, U.S. Supreme Ct. 1953, U.S. Ct. Appeals Md. 1960. Assoc. Hudson & Creyke, Washington, 1953-56, H. William Tanaka, Washington, 1956-61, 63-66; cons. Office of Pres., 1961-63; spl. asst. to postmaster gen., U.S. rep. Univ. Postal Union, Bern, Switzerland, 1966-70; spl. asst. to gen. counsel Interam. Devel. Bank, Washington, 1970-88. Trustee New Eng. Coll. Mem. bd. mgrs. Chevy Chase Village, 1985-89; pres. Parents Assn. Nat. Cathedral Sch., 1969-70, mem. governing bd. 1970. Mem. ABA (exec. coun. gen. practice sect. 1982-87), Bar Assn. D.C., Colonial Club, Barristers Club, Met. Club, Chevy Chase Club. Avocations: gardening, surf fishing. General practice, Public international, Legislative. Office: 7700 Old Georgetown Rd Ste 800 Bethesda MD 20814-6100

SHECTER, HOWARD L. lawyer; b. Boston, May 13, 1943; AB, Harvard U., 1965; JD, U. Pa., 1968. Bar: Pa. 1968, N.Y. 1996. Assoc. Morgan, Lewis & Bockius LLP, Phila., 1968-73, ptnr. N.Y.C., 1973—. General corporate, Private international, Mergers and acquisitions. Office: Morgan Lewis & Bockius LLP 101 Park Ave New York NY 10178-0060

SHEEHAN, KENNETH EDWARD, lawyer, business executive; b. N.Y.C., Aug. 12, 1946; s. William Arvis and Anne (Murphy) S.; m. Julie Babka, Aug. 16, 1969 (div. 1980); children— Megan, Kristen, Elaine; m. Cynthia Leigh Davis, Sept. 10, 1982; children: Abigail Elizabeth, Kenneth Brendan. B.S. in Bus. Adminstrn., Georgetown U. 1968; postgrad. U. Akron, 1968-69; J.D., Fordham U., 1972. Bar: N.Y. 1973, N.J. 1973, U.S. Dist. Ct. (so. and ea. dists.) N.Y. 1973, U.S. Ct. Appeals (2d cir.) 1973, U.S. Ct. Appeals (3rd cir.) 1973, U.S. Supreme Ct. 1976. Assoc., Kirlin, Campbell & Keating, N.Y.C., 1973-76, ptnr., 1976; counsel Am. Bur. Shipping N.Y.C., 1976-77, v.p., gen. counsel, 1977-88, ptnr. Chazen & Sheehan, N.Y.C., 1988— ; dir., office-in-charge Marine and Indsl. Ins., Hamilton, Bermuda, 1982— , ABS Boiler and Marine Ins., Burlington, Vt., 1982— ; dir., v.p., gen. counsel ABS Group Cos., N.Y.C., 1978— , ABS Worldwide Tech. Svcs., Inc., 1978, ABS Properties, Inc., 1978, Armory Properties, Ltd., 1981; frequent expert witness before congress, mcht. marine safety and liability. Contbr. articles to profl. pubs. With N.Y. Army N.G., 19770-76. Mem. ABA (speaker ABA Ann. Convs. 1988 and 1989 div. of sci. and tech.), Maritime Law Assn., Assn. of Bar of City of N.Y., Soc. Naval Architects, N.Y. State Bar Assn., N.J. State Bar Assn., N.Y. County Lawyers Assn., Essex Fells Country Club (N.J.), Whitehall Lunch Club (N.Y.C.). Home: PO Box 8152 Fort Myers FL 33908-0121 Office: Chazen & Sheehan 122 E 42nd St Fl 43 New York NY 10168-4399 also: 45 Eisenhower Dr Paramus NJ 07652-1416

SHEEHAN, ROBERT C. lawyer; b. N.Y.C., Oct. 12, 1944; s. John Edward and Mary Elizabeth (Trede) S.; m. Elizabeth Mary Mammen, Aug. 17, 1968; children: Elizabeth, Robert, William. BA, Boston Coll., 1966; LLB, Univ. Pa., Phila., 1969. Bar: N.Y. 1970. Ptnr. Skadden, Arps, Slate, Meagher & Flom LLP, N.Y.C., 1978—, exec. ptnr., 1994—. Banking, General corporate, Mergers and acquisitions. Office: Skadden Arps Slate Meagher Flom LLP 4 Times Sq New York NY 10036-6595

SHEFTMAN, HOWARD STEPHEN, lawyer; b. Columbia, S.C., May 20, 1949; s. Nathan and Rena Mae (Kantor) S.; children from a previous marriage: Amanda Elaine, Emily Catherine; m. Karyn L. Jenkins. BS in Bus. Adminstrn., U. S.C., 1971, JD, 1974. Bar: S.C. 1974, U.S. Dist. Ct. 1975, U.S. Ct. Appeals (4th cir.) 1982. Assoc. Kirkland, Taylor & Wilson, West Columbia, S.C., 1974-75; ptnr. Sheftman, Oswald & Holland, 1975-77, Finkel & Altman, LLC, Columbia, 1977—. Mem. S.C. Bar Assn. (chmn. practice and procedure com. 1999-2001), S.C. Trial Lawyers Assn. (chmn. domestic rels. sect. 1982-83, bd. govs. 1987-93, 94-98), Richland Bar Assn., Met. Sertoma Club (pres. 1986-87). Jewish. Federal civil litigation, State civil litigation, Family and matrimonial. Office: Finkel & Altman LLC PO Box 1799 Columbia SC 29202-1799 E-mail: hsheftman@finkellaw.com

SHEHAN, WAYNE CHARLES, lawyer; b. Miami, Fla., Nov. 25, 1944; s. Joseph L. Shehan and Louise A. Salloum; m. Sherrin M. Graham, May 21, 1981; children: Christopher, Kevin. BS, U. Detroit, 1966, JD, 1969. Bar: Mich. 1969. Prin. Wayne C. Shehan, P.C., St. Clair Shores, Mich., 1969—. Prof. U. Detroit, 1969-70; mediator Macomb County Cir. Ct., Mt. Clemens, Mich., 1988—; lectr. People's Law Sch., St. Clair Shores, 1987—. Precinct del. Macomb County Rep. Party, St. Clair Shores, 1974-80. Mem. State Bar Mich., Macomb County Bar Assn. (speakers bur.), Macomb County Trial Lawyers Assn. Avocations: skiing, tennis, bicycling, platform tennis, ice hockey. Criminal, Family and matrimonial, Probate. Office: 22420 Greater Mack Ave Saint Clair Shores MI 48080-2012 E-mail: wshehan0@ameritech.net

SHEILS, DENIS FRANCIS, lawyer; b. Ridgewood, N.J., Apr. 7, 1961; s. Denis Francis and Anna Marie (Clifford) S.; m. Harriet A. Bonawitz, Sept. 17, 1988; 1 child, Denis F. BA, La Salle Coll., 1983; JD, Fordham U., 1986. Bar: N.Y. 1987, Pa. 1987, U.S. Dist. Ct. (ea. dist.) Pa. 1987, U.S. Ct. Appeals (3d cir.) 1987, U.S. Dist. Ct. (so. and ea. dists.) N.Y. 1992, U.S. Supreme Ct. 1994, U.S. Dist. Ct. (no. dist.) N.Y. 1997, U.S. Ct. Appeals (2d cir.) 1999. Assoc. Kohn, Swift & Graf, PC, Phila., 1987-97, shareholder, 1997—. Active Lower Makefield Twp. Cable TV Adv. Bd. Mem. AAAS, ABA, Phila. Bar Assn. Roman Catholic. Federal civil litigation, General civil litigation, State civil litigation. Home: 2124 Ashley Rd Newtown PA 18940-3737 Office: Kohn Swift & Graf PC 21st Fl One South Broad St Philadelphia PA 19107 E-mail: dsheils@kohnswift.com

SHEILS, JAMES BERNARD, lawyer; b. New Rochelle, N.Y., May 18, 1950; s. Richard Anthony and Jeanne Bernadette (Berrigan) S.; m. Cheryl Ann Girouard, Aug. 19, 1973; children— Siobhan, Caitrin, Daniel. A.B. with honors, Holy Cross Coll., 1972; J.D., Boston Coll., 1975. Bar: Mass. 1975, U.S. Dist. Ct. Mass 1977, U.S. Supreme Ct. 1983. Assoc. Kamberg, Berman, Gold & West, P.C., Springfield, 1975-80, ptnr., 1980-85; ptnr. Shatz, Schwartz & Fentin, 1985—; dir. Springfield Leadership Inst., 1979— . Author: What the General Practitioner Needs to Know About Consumer Protection, 1982; (with others) Don't Get Left Picking Up the Check; Negotiable Instruments Under UCC, 1984. Contbr. editor: Massachusetts Collection Law, 1984. Mem. Zoning Bd. Appeals, East Longmeadow, Mass., 1983-87 , chmn. 1985-87 ; bd. dirs. Goodwill Industries of Springfield/Hartford, 1980—, chmn. 1988—; mem. Democratic Town Com., East Longmeadow, 1981— . Mem. ABA, Mass. Bar Assn., Hampden County Bar Assn., Assn. Comml. Fin. Attys., Smaller Bus. Assn. New Eng. (bd. dirs. 1983-87), bd. trustees Mount St. Vincent Nursing Home, 1988—. Banking, Contracts commercial. Home: 170 Tanglewood Dr East Longmeadow MA 01028-2641 Office: 1441 Main St Springfield MA 01103-1406

SHEIMAN, RONALD LEE, lawyer; b. Bridgeport, Conn., Apr. 26, 1948; s. Samuel Charles and Rita Doris S.; m. Deborah Joy Lovitky, Oct. 16, 1971; children: Jill, Laura. BA, U. Mich., 1970; JD, U. Conn., 1973; LLM in Taxation, NYU, 1974. Bar: Conn. 1973, U.S. Ct. Appeals (2d cir.) 1975, U.S. Dist. Ct. Conn. 1975, U.S. Tax Ct. 1975, U.S. Supreme Ct. 1977, D.C. 1978, N.Y. 1981. Sr. tax atty. Office of Regional Counsel IRS, Phila., 1974-78; pvt. practice Westport, Conn., 1978—. Mdm. adv. bd. Early Childhood Resource and Info. Ctr., N.Y. Pub. Libr., N.Y.C., 1984. Mem. ABA, Fed. Bar Assn., Conn. Bar Assn. Corporate taxation, Estate taxation, Personal income taxation. Home: 128 Random Rd Fairfield CT 06432-1408 Office: 1804 Post Rd E Westport CT 06880-5607

SHEINFELD, MYRON M. lawyer, educator; b. Mass., Mar. 18, 1930; s. Robert and Sadye (Rosenberg) S.; m. Christina Trzcinski, Mar. 30, 1985; children: Scott, Tom. BA, Tulane U., 1951; JD, U. Mich., 1954. Bar: Mich. 1954, Tex. 1956. Rschr. Legis. Rsch. Inst., U. Mich., 1954; asst. U. S. atty. So. Dist. Tex., 1958-60; law clk. U.S. Dist. Judge, 1960-61; ptnr. Strickland, Gordon & Sheinfeld, Houston, 1961-68; shareholder, of counsel Sheinfeld, Maley & Kay, P.C., 1968-96, counsel to firm, 1006—. Adj. prof. law U. Tex.; mem. Nat. Bankruptcy Conf.; former chmn. Tex. Bankruptcy Adv. Commn.; bd. dirs. Nabors Industries, Third Ave. Value Fund, Inc., Anchor Glass Container Corp.; mem. Tex. Bd. Legal Specialization. Bd. editors Practical Lawyer; contbr. articles to profl. jours. With JAG U.S. Army, 1955-58. Fellow Am. Coll. Bankrupcty (bd. dirs.); mem. State Bar Tex., Houston Ctr. Club (bd. dirs.), Phi Beta Kappa, Phi Sigma Alpha. Bankruptcy, Mergers and acquisitions, Taxation, general. Office: Akin Gump Strauss Hauer & Feld Pennzoil Place-South Tower 711 Louisiana StreetSte 1900 Houston TX 77002 E-mail: msheinfe@smklaw.com

SHELDON, J. MICHAEL, lawyer, educator; b. Mt. Carmel, Pa., Sept. 1, 1951; s. Lloyd Loomis and Helen Roberta (Sosnoski) S. AA, Harrisburg (Pa.) Community Coll., 1978; BS, Pa. State U., 1980; M in Journalism, Temple U., 1991; JD, Widener U. Sch. Law, 1996. News announcer Sta. WNUE-AM, Ft. Walton Beach, Fla., 1974-76, Sta. WFEC-AM, Harrisburg, 1977-78; announcer Sta. WCMB-AM, Wormleysburg, Pa., 1979-80; writer newspaper Pa. Beacon, Harrisburg, 1982-85; media specialist Commonwealth Media Svcs., 1982-86; dir. communications Pa. Poultry Fedn., 1986-89; news anchor Sta. WGAL-TV, Lancaster, Pa., 1989-90; dir. pub. rels. Profl. Ins. Agts. - Pa., Md., Del., Mechanicsburg, 1990-92; v.p. comm. and mktg. United Way of the Capital Region, Harrisburg, 1992-93, Widener U. Sch. of Law, 1994-96; pres. Open Mike Comm., Harrisburg, 1994—. Mem. adj. faculty dept. journalism Temple U., 1992; mem. faculty dept. humanities Pa. State U., 1995-97, 99—. Contbg. author: Pa. 12th Annual Civil Litigation Update, Spoliation of Evidence: Why You Can't Have Your Cake and Eat it Too, 1999; contbg. editor: A Practical Guidebook to Massachusetts Aviation Law, 1999; Contbr. articles to profl. jours. Pub. rels. advisor Cen. Pa. Leukemia Soc., Harrisburg, 1989-90; media advisor Polit. Campaign, Hershey, Pa., 1990. With USAF, 1969-73. Mem. Vets. of Foreign War (life), Am. Legion, Knights of Columbus, Chi Gamma Iota, Delta Tau Kappa. Republican. Roman Catholic. Avocations: motorcycles, music, electronics, martial arts. Office: 6059 Allentown Blvd Harrisburg PA 17112-2672

SHELDON, ROBERT RYEL, lawyer; b. Bridgeport, Conn., Feb. 18, 1949; s. Frederick C. and Mary E. (Quinn) S.; m. Deborah J. Goodwin, Apr. 10, 1976; children— Jeffrey D., Christopher R. B.A. in History, Coll. Holy Cross, 1971; J.D., U. Conn., 1974. Bar: Conn. 1974, U.S. Dist. Ct. Conn. 1974, U.S. Ct. Appeals (2d cir.) 1975. Assoc., Tremont and Green, Bridgeport, 1974-81; ptnr. T. Paul Tremont, P.C., Bridgeport, 1981-83, Tremont Yuditski and Sheldon, P.C., Bridgeport, 1983— ; lectr. workers' compensation law Conn. Bar Assn., 1981, 86, Conn. Trial Lawyers Assn., 1980, 82, 86—. Recipient Am. Jurisprudence award Bancroft-Whitney Co./Lawyers Coop. Pub. Co., 1972. Mem. ABA, Am. Trial Lawyers Assn., Conn. Bar Assn., Conn. Trial Lawyers Assn., Bridgeport Bar Assn. Roman Catholic. Club: Holy Cross (Fairfield County, Conn.) (v.p. 1981-83). Federal civil litigation, State civil litigation, Personal injury. Home: 895 Galloping Hill Rd Fairfield CT 06430-7128 Office: Tremont Yuditski and Sheldon PC 64 Lyon Ter Bridgeport CT 06604-4022

SHELL, LOUIS CALVIN, lawyer; b. Dinwiddie County, Va., Dec. 8, 1925; s. Roger LaFayette and Susie Ann (Hill) S.; m. Barbara Marie Pamplin, Aug. 5, 1950; children: Pamela Shell Baskervill, Patricia Shell Caulkins. BA, U. Va., 1946, LLB, 1947. Bar: Va. 1947. Sr. trial atty. Shell, Johnson, Andrews Baskervill & Petersburg. Va. chmn. Petersburg Electoral Bd., 1952, vice mayor city coun., 1957-60; trustee Petersburg Dist. United Meth. Ch. Named Outstanding Young Man, Petersburg Jr. C. of C., 1956. Fellow Am. Coll. Trial Lawyers; mem. Petersburg Bar Assn., Va. State Bar Assn. (coun. 1972-75), Kiwanis. State civil litigation, Personal injury. Home: 10813 Lakeview Dr Petersburg VA 23805-7152 Office: Shell Johnson Andrews & Baskervill PO Box 3090 Petersburg VA 23805-3090

SHELLEY, SUSANNE MARY, lawyer, mathematics educator; b. Vienna, Austria, Feb. 2, 1928; came to U.S., 1946; d. Joseph and Paula (Grunbaum) Langer; m. Robert E. Shelley, July 21, 1946; children: Frances S. MacCallum, Mark Robert. BA, Calif. State U., Sacramento, 1961, MA, 1963; JD, U. Pacific, 1980. Bar: Calif. 1980, U.S. Dist. Ct. (ea. dist.) Calif. 1980. Tchr. math. Johnson High Sch., Sacramento, 1961-65; prof. math. Sacramento City Coll., 1965-84; gen. counsel Los Rios Community Coll. Dist., Sacramento, 1984-94, Johnson, Schachter, & Collins, Sacramento, 1994—. Author 13 math. textbooks. Named Outstanding Educator, Sacramento City Coll., 1967. Mem. ABA, Calif. State Bar Assn., Sacramento County Bar Assn., Order of Coif. Republican. Roman Catholic. Government contracts and claims, Labor. Home: 28 Shoreline Cir Sacramento CA 95831-2112 Office: Johnson Schachter & Collins 2180 Harvard St Ste 560 Sacramento CA 95815-3326

SHELTON, DOROTHY DIEHL REES, lawyer; b. Manila, 16 Sept. came to U.S., 1945; d. William Walter John and Hedwig Diehl; m. Charles W. Rees, Jr., June 15, (div. 1971); children: Jane Rees Stebbins, John B., Anne Rees Slack, David C.,; m. Thomas C. Shelton, Mar. 4, 1977. BA in Music, Stanford Univ.; JD, Western State Univ. Coll. Law. Bar: Calif. U.S. Dist. Ct. (so. dist.) Calif. Pvt. practice, San Diego, 1977—. Mem. ABA, Calif. State Bar, San Diego County Bar Assn., Consumer Attys. San Diego, Stanford U. Alumni Assn., Jr. League San Diego, Gt. Pyrenees Club Am., Dachshund Club Am., Nu Beta Epsilon. Avocations: gardening, reading, Great Pyrenees dogs. General civil litigation, Criminal, Personal injury. Office: 110 W C St Ste 711 San Diego CA 92101-3906

SHELTON, GREGORY DOUGLAS, lawyer; b. Reno, May 25, 1968; s. Terry Douglas Shelton and Molly Ann McNees; m. Jeanmarie Harrison, June 14, 1997. BA in Philosophy magna cum laude, U. Mass., 1994; JD cum laude, Vt. Law Sch., 1997. Bar: N.Y. 1998. Assoc. Shoeman, Marsh & Updike, N.Y.C., 1997-98, Skadden, Arps, Slate, Meagher & Flom LLP, N.Y.C., 1998—. Mem. superior jurisdiction com. N.Y. State Cts., N.Y.C., 1998—. Mem. sr. editl. bd., bus. mgr. Vt. Law Rev., 1996-97. Mem. Assn. Bar City N.Y. Product liability. Home: 33-43 14th St # 3B Queens NY 11106 Office: Skadden Arps Slate Meagher & Flom 919 3d Ave New York NY 10022

SHEN, MICHAEL, lawyer; b. Nanking, Jiangsu, Peoples Republic of China, Aug. 15, 1948; came to U.S. 1951; s. James Cheng Yee and Grace (Pai) S.; m. Marina Manese (div.); m. Pamela Nan Bradford, Aug. 12, 1983; 1 child, Jessica Li. BA, U. Chgo., 1969; MA, U. Pa., 1970; JD, Rutgers U., 1979. Bar: U.S. Dist. Ct. N.J. 1979, N.Y. 1980, U.S. Dist. Ct. (so., no. and ea. dists.) N.Y. 1980, N.J. 1981, U.S. Ct. Appeals (2d cir.) 1987, U.S. Supreme Ct. 1988, U.S. Ct. Appeals (3rd cir.) 1996. Staff atty. Bedford Stuyvesant Legal Svcs., Bklyn., 1979-80, Com. for Interns and Residents, N.Y.C., 1980-81; ptnr. Shneyer & Shen, P.C., N.Y.C. 1981—. Pres. bd. dirs. Asian Am. Legal Def. and Edn. Fund, N.Y.c.; of counsel 318 Restaurant Workers Union, N.Y.C., 1984—. Bd. dirs. Nat. Asian Pacific Am. Legal Consortium, N.Y.C., Nat. Employment Law Project; past bd. dirs. N.Y. Civil Liberties Union, N.Y.C., 1987-98. Mem. Internat. Platform Assn., Nat. Employees Lawyers Assn., N.Y. State Bar Assn., N.Y. County Bar Assn., Nat. Lawyers Guild. Avocations: arts, reading. Civil rights, Labor, Workers' compensation. Office: Shneyer & Shen PC 2109 Broadway Ste 206 New York NY 10023-2106 also: 1085 Cambridge Rd Teaneck NJ 07666-1901 E-mail: shenlaw@compuserve.com

SHENEFIELD, JOHN HALE, lawyer; b. Toledo, Jan. 23, 1939; s. Hale Thurel and Norma (Bird) S.; m. Judy Simmons, June 16, 1984; children: Stephen Hale, Christopher Newcomb. AB, Harvard U., 1960, LLB, 1965. Bar: Va. 1966, D.C. 1966. Assoc. to ptnr. Hunton & Williams, Richmond, Va., 1965-71, 71-77; dep. asst. atty. gen. antitrust div. Dept. Justice, Washington, 1977, asst. atty. gen., 1977-79, assoc. atty. gen., 1979-81; ptnr. Milbank, Tweed, Hadley & McCloy, 1981-86, Morgan, Lewis & Bockius, Washington, 1986—, chmn., 1995-98. Assoc. prof. law U. Richmond, 1975; prof. law Georgetown Law Ctr., 1981-83; chmn. Nat. Commn. for Rev. Antitrust Law and Procedures, 1978-79. Co-author The Antitrust Laws - A Primer, 3d edit., 1998; contbr. articles on law to profl. jours. Sec. Va. Dem. Com., 1970-72, treas., 1976-77; chmn. Richmond Dem. Party, 1975-77; bd. govs. St. Albans Sch., 1983-90, 97-2000, chmn. 1988-90; mem. chpt. Washington Cathedral, 1988-98, 2000—; pres. Nat. Cathedral Assn., 1993-96; chmn. Va. Racing Commn., 1989-97. 2d lt. U.S. Army, 1961-62; to capt. Res., 1965. Mem. ABA, Va. Bar Assn. Antitrust, Federal civil litigation. Home: 220 Carrwood Rd Great Falls VA 22066-3721 Office: Morgan Lewis & Bockius 1800 M St NW Lbby 6 Washington DC 20036-5828

SHENK, GEORGE H. lawyer; b. N.Y.C., Sept. 10, 1943; BA, Princeton U., 1965; M in Internat. Affairs, Columbia U., 1967; JD, Yale U., 1970. Bar: N.Y. 1971, Calif. 1985. Assoc. Coudert Bros., Paris, 1970, N.Y.C., 1970-73, Hong Kong, 1973-75, Tokyo, 1975-78, ptnr. N.Y.C., 1978-91, San Francisco, 1991-94, Heller Ehrman, White & McAuliffe, 1994—. Exec. dir. San Francisco Com. on Fgn. Rels. Contbr. articles to publs. Mem. Bar Assn. City of N.Y., Calif. State Bar Assn., Coun. Fgn. Rels., Pacific Coun. on Internat. Policy. Banking, General corporate, Private international. Office: Heller Ehrman White & McAuliffe 333 Bush St San Francisco CA 94104-2806

SHENKER, JOSEPH C. lawyer; b. N.Y.C., Nov. 6, 1956; BS in Acctg., CUNY, 1977; JD, Columbia U., 1980. Bar: N.Y. 1981, U.S. Dist. Ct. (ea. and so. dists.) N.Y 1981, U.S. Claims Ct. 1982, U.S. Tax Ct. 1982, U.S. Supreme Ct. 1988. Assoc. Sullivan & Cromwell, N.Y.C., 1980-86, ptnr., 1986—. Contbr. articles to profl. jours. Bd. dirs. Am. Friends of Yeshivat Kerem B'yavneh, Inc., Rabbinical Sem. of Am., Jewish Cmty. Rels. Coun. N.Y., Inc., Met. N.Y. Coordinating Coun. on Jewish Poverty, Inc. Fellow Am. Bar Found.; mem. ABA, N.Y. State Bar Assn., Assn. Bar City N.Y. General corporate, Real property, Securities. Office: Sullivan & Cromwell 125 Broad St Fl 33 New York NY 10004-2400 E-mail: shenkerj@sullcrom.com

SHENKO, WILLIAM EDWARD, JR. lawyer; b. Sioux Falls, S.D., July 1, 1954; s. William Edward and Jeanette Elizabeth Shenko; m. Linda Mulford, Nov. 21, 1981. AA, Edison C.C., Ft. Myers, Fla., 1975; BA, U. South Fla., 1977; JD, Stetson U., 1980. Bar: Fla. 1980, U.S. Dist. Ct. (mid. dist.) Fla. 1980, U.S. Dist. Ct. (so. dist.) Fla. 1982. Legal intern Organized Crime Unit, 6th Cir., Clearwater, Fla., 1980; asst. state atty. 20th Cir. of Fla. Juvenile Divsn., Ft. Myers, 1980, Lee County Commrs., Ft. Myers, 1980, Felony Divsn., 20th Cir., Ft. Myers, 1981; assoc. Alderman and Gerald, 1981-85; assoc., ptnr. Echols Cotter & Shenko, Ft. Myers Beach, Fla., 1985-95; pres. William E. Shenko, Jr. P.A., 1995—. Counsel Ft. Myers Beach Bd. Realtors, 1984, 94, 95, 96, Iona Mcgregor Fire Dist., Ft. Myers, 1984—; spl. master City of Sanibel, Fla., 1995-96; bd. dirs. Pink Shell VV Condo Assn., Ft. Myers Beach, 1988-93, pres., 1992-93. Founder Ft. Myers Beach Incorporation Com., 1993; mem. bd. rev. Eagle Scouts, Ft. Myers, 1994-97; bd. dirs. Ft. Myers Beach Voters Assn., 1994-96. Mem. Ft. Myers and Beach C. of C., Marathon Yacht Club, Ft. Myers Bd. Realtors, Bonita Springs Bd. Realtors. Republican. Roman Catholic. Avocation: sailing. Government contracts and claims, Probate, Real property. Office: 1661 Estero Blvd Ste 24 Fort Myers Beach FL 33931 E-mail: beachlaw@flash.net

SHENTOV, OGNJAN V. lawyer, researcher; b. Sofia, Bulgaria, Aug. 22, 1958; came to U.S., 1986; s. Varban Petrov and Lalka Stoinova Shentov; m. Lubima Galinova Kalinkova, Feb. 14, 1994. BS, Tech. U., Sofia, 1984; MS, U. Calif., Santa Barbara, 1988, PhD, 1991; JD, N.Y. Law Sch., 1997. Bar: N.Y. 1998, U.S. Dist. Ct. (ea. and so. dists.) N.Y. 1998, U.S. Ct. Appeals (fed. cir.) 1998. Tchg. and rsch. asst. U. Calif., 1986-91; postdoctoral rsch. asst. SUNY, Stony Brook, 1991-97; assoc. Pennie & Edmonds LLP, N.Y.C., 1997—. Co-author: Handbook for Dip. Sig. Proc., 1991; contbr. articles to profl. jours. Me. IEEE. Federal civil litigation, Intellectual property, Patent. Office: Pennie & Edmomds LLP 1155 Ave of Americas New York NY 10036

SHEPARD, RANDALL TERRY, state supreme court chief justice; b. Lafayette, Ind., Dec. 24, 1946; s. Richard Schilling and Dorothy Ione (Donlen) S.; m. Amy Wynne MacDonell, May 7, 1988; one child, Martha MacDonell. AB cum laude, Princeton U., 1969; JD, Yale U., 1972; LLM, U. Va., 1995; LLD (hon.), U. So. Ind., 1995. Bar: Ind. 1972, U.S. Dist. Ct. (so. dist.) Ind. 1972. Spl. asst. to under sec. U.S. Dept. Transp., Washington, 1972-74; exec. asst. to mayor City of Evansville, Ind., 1974-79; judge

Vanderburgh Superior Ct., Evansville, 1980-85; assoc. justice Ind. Supreme Ct., Indpls., 1985-87, chief justice, 1987—. Instr. U. Evansville, 1975-78, Indiana U., 1995, 99 Author: Preservation Rules and Regulations, 1980; contbr. articles to profl. publs. Bd. advisors Nat. Trust for Hist. Preservation, 1980-87, chmn. bd. advisors, 1983-85, trustee, 1987-96; dir. Hist. Landmarks Found. Ind., 1983—, chmn., 1989-92, hon. chmn., 1992—; chmn. State Student Assistance Commn. on Ind., 1981-85; chmn. Ind. Commn. on Bicentennial of U.S. Constn., 1986-91; vice chmn. Vanderburgh County Rep. Ctrl. Com., 1977-80. Recipient Friend of Media award Cardinal States chpt. Sigma Delta Chi, 1979, Disting. Svc. award Evansville Jaycees, 1982, Herbert Harley award Am. Judicature Soc., 1992. Mem. ABA (coun. mem. sect. on legal edn. 1991—, chair sect. on legal edn. 1997—, immediate past chair appellate judges conf. 1997-98), Ind. Bar Assn., Ind. Judges Assn., Princeton Club (N.Y.), Capitol Hill Club (Washington), Columbia Club (Indpls.). Republican. Methodist. Home: 3644 Totem Ln Indianapolis IN 46208-4171 Office: Ind Supreme Ct 304 State House Indianapolis IN 46204-2213

SHEPHERD, JOHN FREDERIC, lawyer; b. Oak Park, Ill., May 22, 1954; s. James Frederic Shepherd and Margaret Joanne (Crotchett) Woollen; children: Eliza Marion, Justine Catherine. AB magna cum laude, Dartmouth Coll., Hanover, N.H., 1976; JD, U. Denver, 1979. Bar: Colo. 1979, U.S. Dist. Ct. Colo. 1979, D.C. 1981, U.S. Dist. Ct. D.C. 1981, U.S. Ct. Appeals (10th cir.) 1981, U.S. Ct. Appeals (D.C. cir.) 1982, U.S. Ct. Appeals (9th cir.) 1990, U.S. Supreme Ct. 1984. Assoc. Holland & Hart, Denver, 1979-81, Washington, 1981-85, ptnr., 1985-87, Denver, 1987—; natural resources disting. practitioner in residence U. Denver Coll. Law, 1998. Reporter Mineral Law Newsletter, 1985-92. Mem. 50 for Colo., Denver, 1989. Mem. ABA (chmn. pub. lands and land use com. 1991-93, mem. coun. for sect. of natural resources energy and environ. law 1993-96), Rocky Mountain Mineral Law Found. (mem. long-range planning com. 1988—, trustee 1993-95), Dartmouth Alumni Club (pres. Washington chpt. 1985-86, trustee Rocky Mt. chpt., 1998—), Denver Athletic Club. Avocations: flyfishing, basketball, running. Oil, gas, and mineral, Environmental, Natural resources. Home: 320 Clermont St Pkwy Denver CO 80220-5642 Office: Holland & Hart 555 17th St Ste 3200 Denver CO 80202-3950 E-mail: JShepherd@Hollandhart.com

SHEPHERD, JOHN MICHAEL, lawyer; b. St. Louis, Aug. 1, 1955; s. John Calvin and Bernice Florence (Hines) S.; m. Deborah Tremaine Fenton, Oct. 10, 1981; children: Elizabeth White, Katherine Tremaine. BA, Stanford U., 1977; JD, U. Mich., 1980. Bar: Calif. 1981, D.C. 1991, U.S. Dist. Ct. (no. dist.) Calif. 1981. Assoc. McCutchen, Doyle, Brown & Enersen, San Francisco, 1980-82; spl. asst. to asst. atty. gen. U.S. Dept. Justice, Washington, 1982-84, dep. asst. atty gen., 1984-86; assoc. counsel to The President The White House, 1986-87; sr. dep. comptroller of the currency Dept. Treasury, 1987-91; spl. counsel Sullivan & Cromwell, N.Y.C., 1991-93, Washington, 1993; exec. v.p., gen. counsel Shawmut Nat. Corp., Boston, 1993-95; ptnr. Brobeck, Phleger & Harrison LLP, San Francisco, 1995-2000; exec. v.p., gen. counsel and sec. Bank of New York Co., Inc., N.Y.C., 2001—. Chmn. fin. svcs. and insolvency group, 1996-97, mem. policy com., 1997-2000; bd. dirs. Wilson Coun. Contbr. articles to profl. jours. Asst. dir. policy Reagan-Bush Presdl. Transition Team, Washington, 1980-81; bd. dirs. Reagan Dep. Asst. Secs., Washington, 1985-90; trustee New Eng. Aquarium, 1994-96. Named one of Outstanding Young Men Am., U.S. Jaycees, 1984; Wardack Research fellow Washington U., 1976. Mem. ABA (chmn. fin. markets and ins. com., antitrust law sect. 1992-95, mem. banking law com. 1983—, vice chair 1998—, chmn. bank holding co. acquisitions subcom. 1995-98, bus. law sect., standing com. on law and nat. security 1984-96), D.C. Bar Assn., New Eng. Legal Found. (bd. dirs. 1994-96), Pacific Coun. Internat. Policy, Chevy Chase Club, Univ. Club, Met. Club, Olympic Club, Wilson Coun. Woodrow Wilson Internat. Ctr. for Scholars, 2000—. Office: Bank of NY Co Inc One Wall St New York NY 10286 E-mail: mshepherd@bankofny.com

SHEPPARD, BERTON SCOTT, lawyer; b. Zanesville, Ohio, Aug. 6, 1936; s. Isaac and Ruth (Scott) S.; m. Regina Polka, Oct. 6, 1962; children: Kristina M., Cynthia A. BS in Agr. Engring., Mich. State U., 1958; JD, Northwestern U., 1961. Bar: Ill. 1962, U.S. Dist. Ct. (no. dist.) Ill. 1962, U.S. Dist. Ct. Md. 1965, U.S. Ct. Appeals (4th cir.) 1970, U.S. Ct. Appeals (7th cir.) 1974, U.S. Ct. Appeals (fed. cir.) 1982, U.S. Ct. Customs and Patent Appeals 1976, U.S. Supreme Ct. 1976. With Leydig, Voit & Mayer, Ltd. and predecessor firms, Chgo., 1959-62, assoc., 1962-70, ptnr., 1971-2000, of counsel, 2001—. Mem. editl. bd. Northwestern Law Rev., 1960-61. With USAR, 1961. Mich. State U. scholar, 1954-58, Hardy scholar Northwestern U., 1958-61. Mem. ABA, Am. Intellectual Property Law Assn., Fed. Cir. Bar Assn., Fed. Bar Assn., Intellectual Property Law Assn. Chgo., Lawyers Club Chgo. Republican. Federal civil litigation, Patent, Trademark and copyright. Office: Leydig Voit & Mayer 2 Prudential Plz Ste 4900 Chicago IL 60601 E-mail: bertons@aol.com

SHER, LEOPOLD ZANGWILL, lawyer; b. New Orleans, May 1, 1953; s. Joseph and Rachel (Israelowiec) S.; m. Karen Baumgarten, June 7, 1975; children: Rose Sarah, Samantha Jill. BA, Tulane U., 1974, JD, 1976. Bar: La., U.S. Dist. Ct. (ea. dist.) La., U.S. Ct. Appeals (5th cir.), U.S. Supreme Ct. Mem. Sher Garner Cahill Richter, Klein McAlister & Hilbert LLC, New Orleans, 1999—. Mem. Leman-Stern Young Leadership Tng., New Orleans, 1980, Met. Area Com. Young Leadership Tng./Leadership Forum, New Orleans, 1982; chmn. Preservation Action Tax Task Force, La., 1985-86. Mem. ABA (chmn. real estate fin. subcom. of comml. fin. svcs. com. of bus. law sect., mem. supervisory coun. Group H, real property sect.), Am. Bar Found., Am. Coll. Mortgage Attys., Anglo-Am. Real Property Inst. (bd. govs.), Am. Coll. Comml. Fin. Lawyer, Am. Land Title Assn. (lenders counsel group), Am. Coll. Real Estate Lawyers (bd. govs., treas.), La. Bar Assn., Am. Arbitration Assn., Internat. Coun. Shopping Ctrs., Acad. Hospitality Attys., Assn. Comml. Fin. Attys., Am. Bankruptcy Inst. Democrat. Jewish. Contracts commercial, Landlord-tenant, Real property. Home: 5500 Marcia Ave New Orleans LA 70124-1055 Office: Klein McAlister & Hilbert Sher Garner Cahill Richter 909 Poydras St 28th Fl New Orleans LA 70112 E-mail: isher@shergarner.com

SHERA TAYLOR, DIANA MARIE, judge, lawyer; b. El Paso, Tex. Paralegal Cert., San Francisco State U., 1983, BA, 1986; JD, Golden Gate U., San Francisco, 1992. Bar: Calif. 1993, Oreg. 1995, U.S. Dist. Ct. (no. dist.) Calif. 1993. Atty. Berding & Weil, Alamo, Calf., 1993-95; sole practitioner St. Helens, Oreg., 1996—; judge Columbia City (Oreg.) Mcpl. Ct., 1996—. Bd. dirs., treas. Columbia County Legal Aid, St. Helens, 1997—; mediator Multnomah County Small Claims, Portland, Oreg., 1998—. Author newsletter Legalese Demystified, 1997—. Bd. dirs. Columbia Cmty. Mental Health Agy., St. Helens, 1998—; mem. adv. com. Area Agy. on Aging, St. Helens, 1997—; legal advisor Women's Resource Ctr., St. Helens, 1996—. Mem. ABA, Oreg. Mcpl. Judges Assn., Nat. Judges Assn., Oreg. Women Lawyers, Kiwanis Internat. Office: PO Box 232 Saint Helens OR 97051-0232

SHERBY, KATHLEEN REILLY, lawyer; b. St. Louis, Apr. 5, 1947; d. John Victor and Florian Sylvia (Frederick) Reilly; m. James Wilson Sherby, May 17, 1975; children: Michael R.R., William J.R., David J.R. AB magna cum laude, St. Louis U., 1969, JD magna cum laude, 1976. Bar: Mo. 1976. Assoc. Bryan Cave, St. Louis, 1976-85; ptnr. Bryan Cave LLP, 1985—. Contbr. articles to profl. jours. Bd. dirs Jr. League, St. Louis, 1989-90, St. Louis Forum, 1992-99, pres., 1995-97; chmn. Bequest and Gift Coun. of St. Louis U., 1997-99; jr. warden Ch. of St. Michael and St. George, 1998-2000; bd. dirs. Bistate chpt. ARC, 2000—; bd. trustees St. Louis Sci. Ctr., 2000—. Fellow Am. Coll. Trust and Estate Coun. (regent 1997—), Estate Planning Coun. of St. Louis (pres. 1986-87), Bar Assn. Met. St. Louis (chmn. probate sect. 1986-87), Mo. Bar Assn. (chmn. probate and trust com. 1996-98, chmn. probate law revision subcom. 1988-96). Episcopalian. Estate planning, Probate, Estate taxation. Home: 47 Crestwood Dr Saint Louis MO 63105-3032 Office: Bryan Cave LLP 1 Metropolitan Sq Ste 3600 Saint Louis MO 63102-2733

SHERER, SAMUEL AYERS, lawyer, urban planning consultant; b. Warwick, N.Y., June 17, 1944; s. Ernest Thompson and Helen (Ayers) S.; m. Dewi Sudewinahidah, June 28, 1980 (dec. Dec. 2000). AB magna cum laude, Oberlin Coll., 1966; JD, Harvard U., 1970; M in City Planning, MIT, 1970. Bar: D.C. 1972, U.S. Supreme Ct. 1979. Atty., advisor HUD, Boston, 1970; sr. cons. McClaughry Assoc., Washington, 1970-71, 74-76; cons. Urban Inst., 1971-72; atty., urban planner IBRD Jakarta (Indonesia) Urban Devel. Study, 1972-74; atty., advisor Office Minority Bus. U.S. Dept. Commerce, Washington, 1976-77; ptnr. Topping & Sherer, 1977-90; pres. Sherer-Axelrod-Monacelli, Inc., Cambridge, Mass., 1978-99; prin. The Washington Team, Inc., 1992—, Richardson & Sherer, LLC, 2000—. Bd. dirs. EnviroClean Solutions, Inc., The Urban Agr. Network; rep. Internat. Devel. Law Inst., Washington, 1983-90; sr. fellow Climate Inst., 1988—; cons. in field. Co-author: Urban Land Use in Egypt, 1977; editor: Important Laws and Regulations Regarding Land, Housing and Urban Development in the Arab Republic of Egypt, 1977, Important Laws and Regulations Regarding Land, Housing and Urban Development in the Hashemite Kingdom of Jordan, 1981. Bd. dirs. MIT Enterprise Forum of Washington-Balt., 1980-82; mem. D.C. Rep. Cent. Com., 1984-88; mem. nat. governing bd. Ripon Soc., Washington, 1977-83. Urban Studies fellow HUD, 1969-70. Mem. ABA, D.C. Bar Assn., Am. Planning Assn., The Am. Soc. of Internat. Law, Asia Soc., Phi Beta Kappa. Avocations: tennis, reading. Environmental, Public international, Land use and zoning (including planning). Home: 4600 Connecticut Ave NW Apt 205 Washington DC 20008-5702 Office: 7 Brookes Ave Gaithersburg MD 20877-2754 E-mail: washteam@aol.com

SHERIDAN, JOHN ROBERT, lawyer; b. Upland, Pa., Oct. 8, 1944; s. John Paul and Theresa Valerie (Dawson) S.; m. Barbara Ann Bigelow, Aug. 18, 1973; children— Daniel, Timothy. B.A., U. Del., 1966; J.D., U. Balt., 1972. Bar: Pa. 1973, Del. 1975, U.S. Dist. Ct. Del. 1976. Law clk. Herlihy & Herlihy, Wilmington, Del., 1971-72; asst. city solicitor Wilmington, 1973— . Pres., Forty Acres Restoration, Inc., Wilmington, 1975-81; staff mem. Maloney for U.S. Senate, Wilmington, 1976; mem. City Democratic Com., Wilmington, 1977— ; alt. del. State Dem. Conv., Del., 1984, regular del., 1988; mem. Frawley for Wilmington, 1984, 88, Citizens for Biden, 1980—. Served with USAR, 1966-72. Mem. ABA, Pa. Bar Assn., Del. Bar Assn., Am. Mgmt. Assn., Del. Assn. Pub. Adminstrs., Internat. Plaform Assn., Sierra Club. Democrat. Roman Catholic. Home: 1611 Mt Salem Ln Wilmington DE 19806-1134 Office: Office of City Solicitor 800 N French St Wilmington DE 19801-3590

SHERIDAN, PETER LOUIS, solicitor; b. Singapore, Singapore, Mar. 19, 1958; s. Lee and Margaret S.; m. Helen Frances Dudley, Feb. 9, 1993; children: Anna, Katherine. BA with honors, Oxford U., Eng., 1980. Cert. solicitor Eng., Wales, 1994. Articled clk. Loosemores, Cardiff, Wales, 1981-84; solicitor Phillips & Buck, Wales, 1984-85, Cameron Markby, London, 1985-93; solicitor, ptnr. Shadbolt & Co., Reigate, Eng., 1992—. Author: Construction and Engineering Arbitration, 1999 (Brit. Constrn. Industry Lit. award 1999); contbr. articles to profl. jours. Mem. Soc. Constrn. Law, Law Soc., Arbitration Club. Office: Shadbolt & Co Chatham Ct Leibourne Rd Surrey Reigate RH2 7LD England

SHERIFF, SEYMOUR, retired lawyer; b. Rye, N.Y., Aug. 22, 1917; s. Michael and Anna (Rosenfeld) S.; m. Selene Gloria Wolf, Oct. 15, 1950; children: Steven, Susan, Ellen, Carol. BSS cum laude, CCNY, 1935; JD cum laude, Yale U., 1938. Bar: D.C. 1938, N.Y. 1938, Md. 1957. Pvt. practice, Washington, 1938-58; sr. ptnr. Gardner, Morrison, Sheriff & Beddow, 1958-2000; ret., 2000. With AUS, 1942-45. Decorated Legion of Merit. Mem. Order of Coif, Phi Beta Kappa. General corporate.

SHERK, GEORGE WILLIAM, lawyer; b. Washington, June 23, 1949; s. George William Sr. and Lorraine Martha (Meyer) S. AA, St. Louis C.C., 1970; BA, Colo. State U., 1972, MA, 1974; JD, U. Denver, 1978. Bar: Am. Samoa 1978, Colo. 1979, U.S. Dist. Ct. Colo. 1979, U.S. Ct. Claims 1984, U.S. Supreme Ct. 1985. Cons. office of legis. counsel Govt. of Am. Samoa, Pago Pago, 1978-79; atty. advisor western area power adminstrn. U.S. Dept. Energy, Colo., 1979-80; pvt. practice law Denver, 1980-82; staff assoc. Nat. Conf. State Legis., 1980-82; spl. asst. office of water policy U.S. Dept. Interior, Washington, 1982-83; atty. land and natural resources div. U.S. Dept. Justice, 1984-90; of counsel Will & Muys, 1990-93; pvt. practice Alexandria, Va., 1993—. Vis. scholar U. Wyo. Coll. Law, 1993; vis. prof. Ga. State U. Coll. Law, 1994-95, Ga. State U. Policy Rsch. Ctr., 1995-96; assoc. professorial lectr. George Washington U. Sch. Engring. and Applied Sci., Washington, 1997—; hon. assoc. water law and policy programme Ctr. for Energy, Petroleum and Mineral Law Policy, U. Dundee, Scotland, 1998—; lectr. various colls. and univs.; mem. assoc. faculty Va. Inst. Marine Sci., Coll. of William and Mary, Gloucester Pt., Va., 1989-94; dep. dir. Ctr. Risk Sci. & Pub. Health Sch. Pub. Health & Health Svcs. George Washington U., 2000-01. Author, co-author or editor numerous books and articles on water law and alternative energy law; book review editor Rivers: Studies in the Science, Environmental Policy and Law of Instream Flow, 1989-2000. Mem. ABA, ASCE, Water Environ. Fedn., State Bar Colo. Avocations: automobile racing and rallying, sports, reading, outdoor activites, sailing. Federal civil litigation, Environmental, Real property. Home and Office: 801 N Pitt St # 1708 Alexandria VA 22314-1765 E-mail: gwsherk@hzolaw.com

SHERK, KENNETH JOHN, lawyer; b. Ida Grove, Iowa, Feb. 27, 1933; s. John and Dorothy (Myers) Sherk; children: Karin Fulton, Katrina, Keith, Kyle. BSC, U. Iowa, 1955; JD, George Washington U., 1961. Bar: Ariz. 1962, U.S. Dist. Ct. Ariz. 1962, U.S. Ct. Appeals (9th cir.) 1966, U.S. Supreme Ct. 1974. Assoc. Moore & Romley, Phoenix, 1962-67, ptnr., 1967-79, Romley & Sherk, Phoenix, 1979-85; dir. Fennemore Craig, 1985—. 1st lt. U.S. Army, 1955-58, Korea. Recipient Profl. Achievement Svcs. award George Washington Law Assn., 1986, Ariz. Judges Assn., 1989, Disting. Svc. award Phoenix Assn. Def. Counsel, 1990; named Mem. of Yr. State Bar of Ariz., 1994. Fellow Am. Coll. Trial Lawyers, Am. Acad. Appellate Lawyers, Am. Bar Found., Ariz. Bar Found. (Walter E. Craig award 1999); mem. ABA (ho. of dels. 1990-93), Ariz. Bar Assn. (pres. 1985-86), Maricopa County Bar Assn. (pres. 1978-79). Republican. Congregational. Avocations: fishing, hiking, bicycling. General civil litigation, Personal injury. Home: 1554 W Las Palmaritas Dr Phoenix AZ 85021-5429 Office: Fennemore Craig 3003 N Central Ave Ste 2600 Phoenix AZ 85012-2913

SHERLING, FRED W. b. Dec. 22, 1933; s. Weaver V. and Ruth M. (Bowen) S.; m. Camille Margaret Brochetto, Nov. 29, 1969; children: Charlotte, Sharon, Cheryl. BS in Chem. Engring., U. Tenn., 1957; LLB, George Washington U., 1961. Bar: U.S. Ct. Appeals (D.C. cir.) 1963, U.S. Ct. Customs and Patent Appeals 1963, U.S. Ct. Appeals (fed. cir.), 1982, U.S. Supreme Ct. 1982. Patent examiner U.S. Patent Office, Washington, 1957-63; assoc. solicitor, 1963-86; sole practice, 1986—. Mem. patent Office Soc. Baptist. E-mail: camilla88@aol.com

SHERMAN, CARL LEON, lawyer; b. Pitts., Sept. 3, 1945; s. Julius Louis Sherman and Ida Sherman Cohodas; m. Selma Bonderow, Oct. 14, 1973; children: Alyssa B., Dana B. BA, U. Pitts., 1967, JD, 1970. Bar: Pa. 1970, U.S. Supreme Ct. 1974. Law clk. Allegheny-Ct. Common Pleas, Pitts., 1970-71; sole practice, 1971-73; ptnr. Miller & Sherman, 1974-77; assoc. Tucker Arensberg et al, 1977-79, ptnr., 1979-85, Sherman & Picadio, Pitts., 1985-90, Sable, Makaroff, Sherman & Gusky, Pitts., 1990-91, C. Leon Sherman & Assocs. P.C., Pitts., 1992—. Bd. dirs. Am. Wind Symphony, Pitts., 1974-82; mem. Ross Twp. Planning Commn., Pitts., 1976-78, chmn., 1978-80. Mem.: Pa. Bar Assn., Allegheny County Bar Assn., Fedn. Ins. and Corp. Counsel, Def. Rsch. Inst. Club: Rivers (Pitts.). Avocations: sports, exercising. Federal civil litigation, State civil litigation. Office: C Leon Sherman & Assocs PC Grant Building Fl 16 Pittsburgh PA 15219-2203 E-mail: sherman@clshermanlaw.com

SHERMAN, EDWARD FRANCIS, dean, law educator; b. El Paso, Tex., July 5, 1937; s. Raphael Eugene and Mary (Stedmond) S.; m. Alice Theresa hammer, FEb. 23, 1963; children: Edward F. Jr., Paul. BA, Georgetown U., 1959; MA, U. Tex., El Paso, 1962, 67; LLB, Harvard U., 1962, SJD, 1981. Bar: Tex. 1962, Ind. 1976. Aide to gov. Nev., state govt. fellow, Carson City, 1962; law clk. judge U.S. Dist. Ct. (we. dist.), El Paso, Tex., 1963; ptnr. Mayfield, Broaddus & Perrenot, 1963-65; tchg. fellow Law Sch. Harvard U., Cambridge, Mass., 1967-69; prof. Sch. Law Ind. U., Bloomington, 1969-77; Edward Clark Centennial prof. U. Tex., Austin, 1977-96; prof., dean Tulane U. Law Sch., 1996—. Fulbright prof. Trinity Coll., Dublin, 1973-74; vis. prof. Stanford Law Sch., 1977; counsel Tex. County Jail Litigation, 1978-85; bd. dirs., officer Travis County Dispute Resolution, 1993—; mem. arbitrtor panel, course dir. Internat. Ctrs. Arbitration. Co-author: The Military in American Society, 1979, Complex Litigation, 1985, 3d edit., 1998, Processes of Dispute Resolution, 1989, 2d edit., 1996, Civil Procedure: A Modern Approach, 1989, 3d edit., 2000, Rau & Sherman & Shannon's Texas ADR and Arbitration Statutes, 1994, 3d edit., 1999. Capt. U.S. Army, 1965-67, lt. col. Res., 1970-90. Fellow Tex. Bar Found.; mem. ABA (reporter civil justice improvements project 1993, offer of judgement task force 1995, com. on pro bono and pub. svc. 1997—), Am. Arbitration Assn. (arbitrator panel), AAUP (gen. counsel 1986-88), Am. Law Inst., Tex. State Bar Assn. (alternative dispute resolution com. 1985-96, chair pattern jury charge com. 1983-94, Evans award for excellence in dispute resolution 1998), Tex. Civil Liberties Union (gen. counsel 1985-91), La. Law Inst., La. State Bar (bd. govs. 1997-99, com. on codes of lawyer and jud. conduct 1999—, com. on multi-juris. practice 2000—); La. Bar Found. (jud. liason com. 1999—), Assn. Am. Law Schs. (chmn. Sect. Litigation 1999, chmn. Sect. ADR 1995, com. on clin. legal edn. 1999—. Home: 21 Newcomb Blvd New Orleans LA 70118-5527 Office: Tulane Law Sch 6329 Freret St New Orleans LA 70118-6231

SHERMAN, FREDERICK HOOD, lawyer; b. Deming, N.Mex., Aug. 9, 1947; s. Benjamin and Helen (Hood) S.; m. Janie Carol Jontz, Oct. 23, 1973; children: Jerah Elizabeth, Frederick Jakub. BBA, Southern Meth. U., 1970, JD, 1972. Bar: Tex. 1972, N.Mex. 1973, U.S. Dist. Ct. N.Mex. 1973, U.S. Dist. Ct. (we. dist.) Tex. 1974, U.S. Supreme Ct. 1979; cert. mediator. Assoc. Sherman & Sherman, Deming, 1973-74, ptnr., 1974-78, prin., 1978—, owner, 1998—. Assoc. prof. Western N.Mex. U., Silver City, 1975-77; mem. specialization com. N.Mex. Supreme Ct., 1986-94; liaison N.Mex. Supreme Ct and Workers Compensation Bd., 1991-94; mem. jud. selection com. State Bar N.Mex., 1985-88, legal retreat com., 1986-88, co-chair, 1986-87, alternative dispute resolution com., 1980-91; apptd. guardian of assets State Fiscal Acctg. State N.Mex., 1992—; state coord. Nat. Bd. Trial Advocates for Bd. Cert. of Trial Specialist, 1994-98. Contbr. articles to profl. jours. Chmn. Luna County Planning Commn., Deming, 1976-78; apptd. visitor to U. N.Mex. Law Sch., 1983—; treas. Luna County Econ. Devel. PSS, 1987-88, also bd. dirs.; bd. dirs. Luna County Hosp., 1991-94; bd. mem. Deming Pub. Sch., 1991-94, pres., 1991-92, elected bd. mem. 1991-95; chmn. bd. dirs. Luna County Charitable Found., 1991—; hon. dir. Deming Art Coun., 1989—; pres. Luna County Sch. Bd., 1991-92; pres., chmn. of the bd. Sherman Family Charitable Found., 1991—; mem. N. Mex. High Sch. Task Force, 1993-94. Recipient Svc. award N.Mex. Bd. Legal Specialization, 1994. Mem. ATLA (del. 2000—, Notably Large award 1983, 84, 85, state del. 2000—), N.Mex. Trial Lawyers Assn. (bd. dirs. 1986—, sec. 1989, 97, designated mentor in personal injury/auto and social security 1998—, officer 1997-98, Amicus Curiae award, 1991), N.Mex. Bar Assn., State Bar N.Mex. (commr. 1978-86, com. on alt. dispute resolutions practice 1980-90, jud. selection com. 1985, com. for legal retreat 1989, Outstanding Svc. award, 1986, 94 and Dedication award 1986, med. review com. 2000, arbitration com. 2000), Tex. Bar Assn., 6th Jud. Bar Assn., Am. Inns. of Ct. (master atty. 1995—, officer 1997—), Coll. State Bar Tex. (pro bono, 1995—), Col. Albert Fountain Inns. of Court (charter), Supreme Ct. Com. on Professionalism. Democrat. Roman Catholic. Avocations: skiing, investments, camping, farming, wine making. General civil litigation, Pension, profit-sharing, and employee benefits, Personal injury. Office: Sherman & Sherman PO Box 850 Deming NM 88031-0850

SHERMAN, GERALD HOWARD, lawyer, educator; b. N.Y.C., Aug. 29, 1932; s. Abraham and Jean (Rose) S.; m. Lola Barbara Kay, Mar. 19, 1961; children: Jonathan, Ann. BBA, CCNY, 1953; LLB, Harvard U., 1958. Bar: N.Y. 1959, D.C. 1960. Mem. firm Cooper & Silverstein, Washington, 1958-61; ptnr. Silverstein & Mullens, 1961-99; shareholder Buchanan Ingersoll, P.C., 2000—. Adj. prof. Georgetown U. Law Center, 1974-87, also mem. Adv. Bd. Tax Mgmt., 1960—, BNA Pension Reporter, 1975-81. Bd. dirs., v.p. Jewish Found. for Group Homes, 1982-90; bd. dirs. Am. Digestive Disease Soc., 1983-87, Washington Conservatory Music, 1995—. Mem. ABA, Bar Assn. D.C. Corporate taxation, Estate taxation, Personal income taxation. Home: 3804 Klingle Pl NW Washington DC 20016-5433 Office: 1776 K St NW Washington DC 20006-2304

SHERMAN, IAN MATTHEW, lawyer; b. Chgo., Apr. 30, 1953; s. George and Vivian K. (Soffran) S.; m. Barbara Jan Smiley, Aug. 6, 1978; children: Wendy Joyce, Wesley Jacob, David Scott. AB, U. Ill., 1975; JD, Boston U., 1978. Bar: Ill. 1978, U.S. Dist. Ct. (no. dist.) Ill. 1978, U.S. Dist. Ct. (ea. dist.) Wis. 1995, U.S. Dist. Ct. (no. dist.) Ind. 2000, U.S. Ct. Appeals (7th cir.) 1984. Ptnr. Rooks, Pitts & Poust, Chgo., 1978—. Lectr. in field. Contbr. articles to profl. jours. Participant Youth Motivation Program Chgo. Pub. H.S., 1982; pro bono Am. Jewish Congress, 1992—; vol. Legal Svcs. Inst., Chgo., 1982—; bd. dirs. The Vol. Ctr., 1986—90, chmn. fin. com., 1986—87, sec., 1987—88, pres., 1988—89. Mem.: Soc. Trial Lawyers, Ill. Assn. Healthcare Attys. (chmn.), Ill. State Bar Assn. (standing com. profl. conduct), Chgo. Bar Assn. (chmn. med.-legal rels. com. 2001—, cert. appreciation 1983), Phi Beta Kappa, Phi Kappa Phi. General civil litigation, Personal injury, Professional liability. Home: 923 Oak St Winnetka IL 60093-2440 Office: Rooks Pitts Poust 10 S Wacker Dr Ste 2300 Chicago IL 60606-7407 E-mail: isherman@rookspitts.com

SHERMAN, JOSEPH ALLEN, JR. lawyer; b. St. Joseph, Mo., Sept. 18, 1929; s. Joseph Allen and Faye Louise (Anthony) S.; m. Mary Jane Phipps, July 2, 1949; children: Joseph Allen, David Phipps, Mark Eden, John William. LLB, U. Mo.-Kansas City, 1955. Bar: Mo. 1956, U.S. Dist. Ct. (we. dist.) Mo. 1961, U.S. Ct. Apls. (8th and 5th cirs.) 1975, U.S. Sup. Ct. 1977, U.S. Ct. Apls. (10th cir.) 1978. Claims atty. Western Casualty & Surety Co., Kansas City, Mo., 1955-56; spl. agt. FBI, San Francisco, 1956-57; home office rep. Prudential Ins. Co., Kansas City, Mo., 1957-59; assoc. Deacy & Deacy, Kansas City, after 1959, ptnr., to 1967; ptnr. Jackson, Barker & Sherman, Kansas City, 1967-69, Jackson & Sherman, Kansas City, 1969-83; pres. Sherman Wickens Lysaught, P.C., Kansas City, 1983-91; pres. Sherman, Wickens & Lysaught, P.C. 1989-91, Sherman, Taff & Bangert, P.C., 1991-93; of counsel Sherman, Taft & Bangert, P.C.,

1993—. lectr. continuing legal edn. Mem. Bd. Edn. Elem. Sch. Dist. 49, Shawnee Mission, Kans., 1963-69, pres., 1967-68; mem. Bd. Edn. Shawnee Mission Unified Sch. Dist. 512, 1969-70; mem. City Plan Commn., Weatherby Lake, Mo., 1973-91. Recipient Gavel award Def. Research Inst., 1984. Fellow Internat. Acad. Trial Lawyers, Internat. Soc. Barristers; mem. Internat. Assn. Def. Counsel, Def. Research Inst. (pres. 1982, chmn. bd. 1983, hon. chmn. bd. 1984), Western Mo. Orgn. Def. Lawyers (pres. 1973-74), Kansas City Metro. Bar Assn. (pres. 1976-77). Republican. Presbyterian. Club: Kansas City. Federal civil litigation, State civil litigation, Personal injury. Home: 10009 NW 75th St Weatherby Lake MO 64152-1752 Office: Sherman Taff & Bangert PC Top City Center S1 PO Box 26530 Kansas City MO 64196-6530

SHERMAN, LAWRENCE JAY, lawyer; b. Pitts., May 20, 1942; s. Ben E. and Leonora C. (Weill) S.; m. Iris Shapiro, Aug. 19, 1967; children: Rachel L., Jessica S. BA in Polit. Sci. with honors, U. Pitts., 1963; JD, U. Mich., 1966. Bar: D.C. 1967, Calif. 1967, Md. 1984, U.S. Dist. Ct. D.C., U.S. Dist. Ct. Md., U.S. Claims Ct., U.S. Ct. Appeals (D.C., 1st, 3rd, 4th, 5th and 6th cir.). Appellate atty. NLRB, Washington, 1966-69; assoc. Cohen & Berfield, 1969-70; exec. dir. Migrant Legal Action Program, 1970-75; assoc. Lichtman, Abeles, Anker & Nagle, P.C., 1975-77; pvt. practice, 1977-81; ptnr. Sherman & Ladidus, 1981-86; counsel Deso, Thomas, Spevack, Weitzman & Rost PC, 1991-2000; ptnr. Brown & Sherman, LLP, 2000—. Adj. prof. George Meany Ctr. for Labor Studies, Silver Spring, Md. 1988-2000; prin. Mng. Human Resources For 21st Century, Washington, 1990-99. Contbr. articles to profl. jours. Fellow Am. Bd. Trial Advocates; mem. ABA (labor and employment law sect., litig. sect.), D.C. Bar (labor and employment law sect., litig. sect., co-chmn. steering com., 1981-85, labor law sect. 1978-84, co-chmn. labor law sect. 1983-84, lawyers coord. com.), Met. Lawyers Assn., Md. Lawyers Assn., Nat. Employment Lawyers Assn. Democrat. Avocations: tennis, racquetball, running, travel, reading. Civil rights, General civil litigation, Labor. Office: Brown & Sherman LLP 1400 K St NW Ste 1000 Washington DC 20005-2403 E-mail: jdlarry@aol.com

SHERMAN, LESTER IVAN, retired lawyer; b. Flagler, Colo., June 1, 1936; s. Lester B. and Helen E. S.; m. Lois E. Hafling, July 19, 1958 (div. Mar. 1986); children: Kathi, Scott, Brett; m. Kay A. Swanson, Dec. 21, 1993. Student, Colo. State U., 1954-55; BSBA, U. Denver, 1958, JD, 1961. Bar: Colo. 1961, U.S. Dist. Ct. Colo. 1961. Pvt. practice, Durango, Colo., 1965-67, 79-81, 1986-97; ret., 1997; ptnr. Hamilton, Sherman, Hamilton & Shand, P.C., 1967-78, Sherman, Rhodes & Wright, P.C., Durango, 1981-86; judge La Plata County (Colo.) Ct., 1966-76. Cons. in field; mem. Colo. Commn. on Jud. Qualifications, 1974-76. Mem. La Plata County Bd. for Mentally Retarded and Seriously Handicapped, Inc., 1968-75, pres., 1970-73; bd. dirs. Colo. County Judges Assn., 1973-74. Mem. S.W. Colo. Bar (pres. 1969-70), Colo. Bar Assn. (gov. 1970-72, 74-76), ABA, Petroleum Club, Elks, Phi Delta Phi, Sigma Chi. Republican. General corporate, Estate planning, Real property. Home: 320 N Skylane Dr Durango CO 81303-6040

SHERMAN, MARTIN PETER, lawyer; b. N.Y.C., May 2, 1940; m. Susan Randall, Feb. 16, 1969; children: David, Timothy, Peter. BA, UCLA, 1961; JD, U. Chgo., 1964; LLM, U. So. Calif., 1969. Bar: Calif. 1965, Pa. 1972. Law clk. L.A. Superior Ct., 1964-65; dep. county counsel L.A. County, 1965-66; atty. Antipoverty Program, Ventura, San Francisco and L.A., 1966-69; counsel Atlantic Richfield Co., L.A. and Phila., 1969-73; asst. gen. counsel Ampex Corp., Redwood City, Calif., 1973-87, corp. counsel Amgen, Inc., Thousand Oaks, Calif., 1987-88; sr. atty., Intel Corp., Santa Clara, 1988-95; spl. counsel Tomlinson, Zisko, Morosoli & Maser, Palo Alto, Calif., 1995-97. Mem. ABA. Contbr. articles to law jour. Antitrust, Computer, Intellectual property. Office: 1131 Stanley Way Palo Alto CA 94303-2915

SHERMAN, ROBERT TAYLOR, JR. lawyer; b. Little Rock, July 26, 1952; s. Robert Taylor and Mary Lisbeth (Doak) S.; children: Robert Taylor III, Kathleen Malloy, Leigh Michele; m. Linda Jean Clark, May 17, 1987; 1 child, Jeremy Ryan. BA, So. Meth. U., 1974; JD, U. Tex., 1977. Bar: Tex. 1977, U.S. Dist. Ct. (so. dist.) Tex. 1978, U.S. Ct. Appeals (5th cir.) 1979. Atty. Conoco Inc., Houston, 1977-79, Fluor Corp., Houston, 1979-81, Global Marine Drilling Co., Houston, 1982-83; gen. counsel WellTech, Inc., Houston, 1981-82; assoc. Watt & White, Houston, 1983-85; asst. gen. counsel CRS Sirrine Inc., Houston, 1985-86, v.p. adminstrn., gen. counsel, CRSS Capitol Inc., Houston, 1986—. Recipient E. Ernest Goldstein award Tex. Internat. Law Jour., 1977. Mem. ABA, Houston Bar Assn. (exec. council sect. of internat. law 1983—), Maritime Law Assn. (proctor in admiralty), Houston Young Lawyers Assn. (bd. dirs. 1982-84), State Bar of Tex. (chmn. com. on multi-nat. corps. sect. of internat. law 1984-86). Republican. Episcopalian. Construction, Insurance, Private international. Home: 2231 Pine Island Rd Minnetonka MN 55305-2424 Office: CRSS Capital Inc 1177 W Loop S #900 Houston TX 77027

SHERMAN, VICTOR, lawyer; b. Indpls., Aug. 28, 1951; s. Marshall and Sara Lee Sherman; m. Claudia Ann Cron, Oct. 8, 1988; children: Mark, Daniel, Miles, Oliver, Luke. BS, UCLA, 1962; LLB, U. Calif., Berkeley, 1965. Bar: Calif. 1966, Conn. 1996, U.S. Ct. Appeals (9th cir.) 1971, U.S. Supreme Ct. 1996. Ptnr. Nasatir, Sherman & Hirsch, L.A., 1970-83, Main St. Law Bldg., Santa Monica, Calif., 1984—; mng. ptnr. Sherman & Sherman, 1984—. Speaker, founder Advanced Criminal Law Seminar, Aspen, Colo., 1981—. Pvt. 1st class U.S. Army, 1960-67. Mem. Nat. Assn. Criminal Def. Lawyers (life). Office: Sherman & Sherman 2115 Main St Santa Monica CA 90405-2215

SHERMAN, WILLIAM FARRAR, lawyer, former state legislator; b. Little Rock, Sept. 12, 1937; s. Lincoln Farrar and Nancy (Lowe) S.; m. Carole Lynn Williams, Sept. 2, 1967; children: John, Anna, Lucy. BA in History, U. Ark.-Fayetteville, 1960; LLB, U. Va., 1964. Bar: Ark. 1964, U.S. Supreme Ct. 1970. Assoc. Smith, Williams, Friday & Bowen, Little Rock, 1964-66; asst. U.S. atty. Ea. Dist. Ark., 1966-69, Ark. Securities Commr., Little Rock, 1969-71; ptnr. Jacoway, Sherman & Pence, 1971—. Legal counsel Voice of the Retarded, 1991-2001, BBB Ark., 1971-2001; mem. Ark. Ho. of Reps., 1974-84; spl. assoc. justice Supreme Ct., 1991; del. Constnl. Conv. Ark., 1979. With U.S. Army, 1960-61, now brig. gen. U.S. Army ret. Mem. ABA, Ark. Bar Assn., Pulaski County Bar Assn., Ark. Bar Found. Democrat. Methodist. General practice, Legislative, Military. Office: 221 W 2nd St Little Rock AR 72201-2505 E-mail: clsherman@aristotle.net

SHERR, MORRIS MAX, retired lawyer; b. Marysville, Calif., Mar. 3, 1930; s. Alfred and Alice Carrie (Peters) S.; m. Bobbie Gray, June 27, 1954; children: David, Rodney. BA, Calif. State U., 1952; JD, U. Calif., San Francisco, 1956. Bar: Calif. 1956. Prin. elem. sch., Stanislaus County, Calif., 1952-54; instr. Golden Gate Coll., 1954-55, Calif. State U., San Francisco, 1955-56, asst. prof. Fresno, 1956-59; assoc. Thompson & Rose, CPAs, 1959-61; ptnr. Blumberg, Sherr & Kerkorian, 1961-84; prin. Morris M. Sherr & Assocs., 1984—, ret., 1999. Mem. adv. coun. St. Agnes Hosp. Found., 1978-83; mem. bd. deacons Evang. Free Ch. of Fresno, 1992—, mem. fin. com., 1995—. Mem. AICPA, Fresno Estate Planning Coun. (dir. 1977-79), Fresno County Bar, Christian Legal Soc., Calif. State Bar (cert. tax specialist), Am. Bapt. Chs. of West (moderator), Elks, Masons, Shriners. Baptist (chmn. trustees 1967-69, deacon 1969-73). Probate, Estate taxation, Taxation, general. Office: 6051 N Fresno St Ste 200 Fresno CA 93710-5280

SHERRER, CHARLES WILLIAM, lawyer, writer; b. Denton, Kans., July 24, 1922; s. Charles Eric and Pearl Bearl (McClellan) S.; m. Marion Sylva Webb, Aug. 27, 1948; children— Gary L., Carol J. Sherrer McGehee. B.S., U. Kans., 1948; J.D., U. Mo.-Kansas City, 1951. Bar: Mo. 1950, Kans. 1958, U.S. Supreme Ct. 1959. Atty., U.S. Army C.E., 1955-88 ; div. counsel South Pacific div., Lafayette, Calif., 1973-88 . Served with AUS, 1942-45; to 1st lt., 1950-52. Mem. ABA, Fed. Bar Assn., Mensa, Soc. Am. Mil. Engrs. Author: (with Sherrer) Ethical and Professional Standards for Academic Psychologists and Counsellors, 1980: contbr. articles to legal jours. Antitrust, Government contracts and claims, Labor. Home: 3933 Woodside Ct Lafayette CA 94549-3413

SHERTZER, GEORGE EDWIN, lawyer; b. Hershey, Pa., June 9, 1928; s. Lester and Edna (Weaver) S.; m. Margaret Delano, Oct. 6, 1957; children: John D., Anne E. BA, Yale U., 1950; LLB, Columbia U., 1953. Bar: N.Y. 1957, Conn. 1985. Assoc. Winthrop, Stimson, Putnam & Roberts, N.Y.C., 1955-59; asst. counsel GTE Svc. Corp., Stamford, Conn., 1959-66, gen. atty., 1966-69, GTE Corp., Stamford, 1969-72, gen. counsel, 1972-83, v.p., 1969-76, sr. v.p., 1976-83; adj. prof. Vt. Law Sch., 1987—. Fellow Am. Bar Found. (life). Administrative and regulatory, General corporate, Public utilities. Home: 111 Maywood Rd Norwalk CT 06850-4424

SHERWOOD, ARTHUR LAWRENCE, lawyer; b. L.A., Jan. 25, 1943; s. Allen Joseph and Edith (Ziff) S.; m. Frances Merele, May 1, 1970; children: David, Chester. BA magna cum laude, U. Calif., Berkeley, 1964; MS, U. Chgo., 1965; JD cum laude, Harvard U., 1968. Bar: Calif. 1969, US. dist. cts. (cen. dist.) Calif. 1968 (no. dist.) Calif. 1971 (so. dist.) Calif. 1973 (ea. dist.) Calif. 1973, U.S. Ct. Appeals (9th cir.) 1973, U.S. Ct. Appeals (D.C. cir.) 1991, U.S. Supreme Ct., 1980. Instr. UCLA Law Sch., 1968-69; assoc. Gibson, Dunn & Crutcher, L.A., 1968-75, ptnr., 1975-98; judge pro tem L.A. Mcpl. and Superior Ct., 1980-98, of counsel 1998—; instr. law, UCLA, 1968-69, arbitrator N.Y. Stock Exchange., Nat. Futures Assn. Co-author: Civil Procedure During Trial, 1995, Civil Procedure Before Trial, 1990; contbr articles to profl. jours. NASA fellow U. Chgo., 1964-65; chmn. Far Ea. Art Coun., L.A. County Mus. Art, 1992-97. Mem. ABA, L.A. County Bar Assn., Calif. Bar Assn., Phi Beta Kappa. Republican. Avocations: art, 18th century Am. history. Antitrust, General civil litigation, Securities. Office: 300 N Swall Dr Unit 305 Beverly Hills CA 90211-4733

SHERWOOD, DEVON FREDRICK, lawyer; b. Hanibal, Mo., June 20, 1943; s. Malcolm and Virginia Dolores (Gresham) S.; m. Stephanie Jan Wanner, Dec. 26, 1963 (div. Feb. 1976); children: Leslie, Jennifer, Stuart; m. Wanda Lee Mullins, May 17, 1977. AB, U. Mo., 1965, JD, 1968. Bar: Mo. 1968, U.S. Dist. Ct. (we. dist.) Mo. Assoc. Lilley & Cowan, Springfield, Mo., 1968-69, Donald Bonacker, Springfield, 1969-72; sr. ptnr. Sherwood & Bruer, Springfield, 1972-77; sole practice, Springfield, 1977-80; sr. ptnr. Sherwood, Honecker & Bender, Springfield, 1980— ; city atty. Fair Grove, Mo., 1973-76. Bd. editors Mo. Law Rev., 1967-68. Elder deacon National Avenue Christian Ch., Springfield, 1969-74; del. Springfield Area Council Chs., 1971-74. Recipient Lon O. Hocker Outstanding Trial Lawyers award Mo. Bar Found. Mem. ATLA, Mo. Bar Assn., Springfield Met. Bar Assn., Mo. Assn. Trial Lawyers, Phi Delta Phi. Republican. General civil litigation, Criminal, Family and matrimonial. Home: 3675 W Sexton Dr Springfield MO 65810-1023 Office: Sherwood Honecker & Bender 155 Park Central Sq Springfield MO 65806-1322

SHERZER, HARVEY GERALD, lawyer; b. Phila., May 19, 1944; s. Leon and Rose (Levin) S.; m. Susan Bell, Mar. 28, 1971; children: Sheri Ann, David Lloyd. BA, Temple U., 1965; JD with honors, George Washington U., 1968. Bar: D.C. 1970, U.S. Ct. Appeals (D.C. cir.) 1970, U.S. Ct. Fed. Claims 1970, U.S. Ct. Appeals (fed. cir.) 1970, U.S. Supreme Ct. 1974. Law clk. to trial judges U.S. Ct. Fed. Claims, Washington, 1968-69; law clk. to chief judge U.S. Ct. Appeals for Fed. Cir., 1969-70; assoc. Sellers, Conner & Cuneo, 1970-75, ptnr., 1975-80, McKenna, Conner & Cuneo, Washington, 1980-82, Pettit & Martin, Washington, 1982-85, Howrey & Simon, Washington, 1985-2000, Howrey Simon Arnold & White, Washington, 2000—. Adv. bd. The Govt. Contractor, 1996-99. Author: (with others) A Complete Guide to the Department of Defense Voluntary Disclosure Program, 1996; contbr. articles to profl. jours. Government contracts and claims, Private international. Office: Howrey Simon Arnold & White 1299 Pennsylvania Ave NW Ste 1 Washington DC 20004-2400 E-mail: sherzharv@aol.com

SHESTACK, JEROME JOSEPH, lawyer; b. Atlantic City, Feb. 11, 1925; s. Isidore and Olga (Shankman) S.; m. Marciarose Schleifer, Jan. 28, 1951; children: Jonathan Michael, Jennifer. AB, U. Pa., 1944; LLB, Harvard U., 1949; LLD (hon.), Dickinson Coll. Law, 1997, Stetson Sch. of Law, 1998, Whittier Coll. Law, 1998. Bar: Ill. 1950, Pa. 1952. Teaching fellow Northwestern U. Law Sch., Chgo., 1949-50; asst. prof. law, faculty editor La. State Law Sch., Baton Rouge, 1950-52; dep. city solicitor City of Phila., 1952, 1st dep. solicitor, 1952-55; ptnr. Schnader, Harrison, Segal & Lewis, Phila. and Washington, 1956-91, Wolf, Block, Schorr & Solis-Cohen, Phila., 1991—. Adj. prof. law U. Pa., 1956; U.S. amb. to UN Human Rights Commn., 1979-80; U.S. del. to ECOSOC, UN, 1980; sr. U.S. del. to Helsinki Accords Conf., 1979-80; mem. U.S. Commn. on Improving Effectiveness of UN, 1989—; chmn . Internat. League Human Rights, 1973-94, hon. chmn., 1994—, U.S. del. to CSCE Conf., Moscow, 1991; founder, chmn. Lawyers Com. Internat. Human Rights, 1978-80, Jacob Blaustein Inst. Human Rights, 1988-92; mem. nat. adv. com. legal svcs. OEO, 1965-72; bd. dirs., exec. com. Laywers Com. Civil Rights; mem. coun. Holocaust Mus.. 1999—, exec. com., chair com. on conscience. Editor: (with others) Rights of Americans, 1971, Human Rights, 1979, International Human Rights, 1985, Bill of Rights: A Bicentennial View, 1991, Understanding Human Rights, 1992, Thomas Jefferson: Lawyer, 1993, Francis Scott Key, 1994, Abraham Lincoln, Circuit Lawyer, 1994, The Holocaust, 1997, Moral Foundations of Human Rights, 1997, The Philosophy of Human Rights, 1997, W.B. Yeats, Poet of Passionate Intensity, 1997. Mem. exec. com. Nat. Legal Aid and Defender Assn., 1970-80; trustee Eleanor and Franklin Roosevelt Inst., 1986—; bd. govs. Tel Aviv U., 1983—, Hebrew U., 1969—; v.p. Am. Jewish Com., 1984-89; chmn. bd. dirs. Am. Poetry Ctr., 1976-91; trustee Free Libr. Phila., vice chmn., 1989-96. With USNR, 1943-46. Rubin fellow Columbia U. Law Sch., 1984; hon. fellow U. Pa. Law Sch., 1980. Mem. ABA (ho. of dels. 1971-73, 77—, mem. jud. com. 1985-90, bd. govs. 1992-95, exec. com. 1994-95, pres. elect 1996, pres. 1997-98, pres. ALI-ABA 1997-98), Internat. Bar Assn. (chmn. com. on human rights 1990-94, chmn. com. profl. ethics 2000—), Internat. Acad. Trial Lawyers, Am. Soc. Internat. Law (exec. com. 1993-95, internat. com. jurists exec. com. 1998—), Am. Law Inst., Am. Arbitration Assn. (bd. dirs. 1999—), Am. Coll. Trial Lawyers, Am. Acad. Appellate Lawyers, Internat. Assn. Jewish Lawyers and Jurists (Am. Soc. pres. 2000—), Order of Coif., Am. Soc. Internat. Law, Nat. Conf. Bar Found. (bd. dirs. 1998—). Antitrust, Libel, Securities. Home: Parkway House 2201 Pennsylvania Ave Philadelphia PA 19130-3513 Office: Wolf Block Schorr & Solis-Cohen 1650 Arch St Fl 20 Philadelphia PA 19103-2029 E-mail: jshestack@wolfblock.com

SHETTY, NISHITH KUMARE, lawyer; b. Udipi, Mangalore, India, June 6, 1971; s. Narshim Babu and Shobha Narshim Shetty. LLB with honors, Nat. U. Singapore, Singapore, 1994. Bar: Supreme Ct. Singapore, Supreme Ct. Eng. and Wales. Assoc. Messrs Wong Partnership, Singapore, 1995-2000, ptnr., 2001—. Mem. Law Soc. Singapore, Law Soc. Eng. and Wales. General civil litigation, Alternative dispute resolution, Construction, Libel. Office: Messrs Wong Partnership 80 Raffles Pl #58-01 UOB Plz 1 048624 Singapore Singapore

SHIEBER, WILLIAM J. lawyer; b. White Plains, N.Y., June 11, 1960; s. Benjamin M. and Phyllis Carol (Chodos) S. BA, Earlham Coll., 1982; JD, Yale U., 1988. Bar: Va. 1990, U.S. Dist. Ct. (ea. dist.) Va. 1990, D.C. 1991, U.S. Dist. Ct. D.C. 1991, U.S. Ct. Appeals (4th and D.C. cirs.) 1992. Law clk. to Judge T.S. Ellis III U.S. Dist. Ct. (ea. dist.) Va., 1988-89; assoc. Covington & Burlington, Washington, 1989-97; of counsel Arent Fox Kintner Plotkin & Kahn, 1998—. Editor Yale Law and Policy Rev., 1987, Yale Law Jour., 1988; mng. editor Yale Jour. Law and the Humanities, 1988. Mem. ABA, Va. State Bar Assn., D.C. Bar Assn. Antitrust, General civil litigation, Intellectual property. Office: Arent Fox Kintner Plotkin & Kahn 1050 Connecticut Ave NW Ste 500 Washington DC 20036-5303

SHIELDS, CRAIG M. lawyer; b. Oceanside, N.Y., Nov. 28, 1941; s. John Anderson and Lillian Ethel (Hagen) S.; m. Candia Atwater Shields, July 13, 1963 (div. 1985); children: Mark, Christopher, Evan; m. Norma Magor Peters, Apr. 25, 1998. Bar: N.Y. 1967, U.S. Dist. Ct. (so. and ea. dists.) N.Y. 1967, U.S. Ct. Appeals (2d cir.) 1967, U.S. Supreme Ct. 1976. Assoc. Clark, Carr & Ellis, N.Y.C., 1966-69; ptnr. Borden & Ball, 1969-76, Sage, Gray, Todd & Sims, N.Y.C., 1976-80; counsel Conboy, Hewitt, O'Brien & Boardman, 1980-83; ptnr. Collier, Cohen, Shields & Bock, 1983-92, Quinn & Suhr, White Plains, N.Y., 1992-95; v.p., gen. counsel United Vanguard Homes, Inc., Glen Cove, 1992—. Contbr. articles to profl. jours. Bd. dirs. Group House of Port Washington (N.Y.) Inc., 1973-85, Children's House, Inc., Mineola, N.Y., 1985-89, Resources for Program Devel., Inc., Port Washington, 1982—; pres. Port Washington Community Action Coun., 1968-69; committeeman Dem. Party, Port Washington, 1967-71. Mem. ABA, Assn. of Bar of City of New York, N.Y.State Bar Assn. Democrat. Methodist. General corporate, Securities. Home: 103 E 86th St Apt 7A New York NY 10028-1058 Office: United Vanguard Homes Inc 4 Cedar Swamp Rd Glen Cove NY 11542-3744 E-mail: afeck@uvhco.com

SHIELDS, LLOYD NOBLE, lawyer; b. Longview, Tex., Dec. 11, 1951; s. Lloyd Leon and Carolyn Lynch (Noble) S.; m. Lynn Ellen Hufft, June 15, 1974; children— Carolyn Elise, Ellen Lynch, Audrie Menville. B. Arch., Tulane U., 1974, J.D., 1977. Bar: La. 1977, U.S. Dist. Ct. (ea., we. and mid. dists.) La., U.S. Ct. Appeals (5th cir.) 1978, U.S. Patent Office 1981. Law clk. Civil Dist. Ct., New Orleans, 1977-78; assoc. Deutsch, Kerrigan & Stiles, New Orleans, 1978-79; ptnr. Simon, Peragine, Smith & Redfearn, New Orleans, 1979— ; instr. New Orleans Bar Review, Inc., 1980— , Loyola U. Law Sch., 1987—. Bd. dirs. Preservation Resource Ctr., New Orleans, 1983—, pres. 1986-88; pres. Operation Comeback Inc. 1988—. Mem. ABA (chmn. automobile law com. torts and ins. practice sect. 1984-85), Am. Arbitration Assn. (constrn. industry panel). Presbyterian. General civil litigation, Construction. Office: Simon Peragine Smith & Redfearn 1100 Poydras St Fl 30 New Orleans LA 70163-1101

SHIELDS, WILLIAM GILBERT, lawyer; b. Charleston, W.Va., June 11, 1945; s. Alston Burkley and Marguerite Louise (Gilbert) S.; m. Linda Jeanne May, Oct. 4, 1968; children— William Gilbert, Jr. and Robert Alston. B.A., U. N.C., 1967; J.D., U. Va., 1974. Bar: Va. 1974, U.S. Dist. Ct. (ea. and we. dists.) Va. 1975, U.S. Ct. Appeals (4th cir.) 1975, U.S. Supreme Ct. 1980. Law clk. Supreme Ct. of Va., Richmond, 1974-75; assoc. atty. May, Miller & Parsons, Richmond, 1975-78; ptnr. Beale, Eichner, Wright, Denton & Shields, Richmond, 1978-83, Anderson, Parkerson & Shields, Richmond, 1983— ; guest lectr. Va. Commonwealth U., Richmond, 1978-81, Va. Welfare Dept., Richmond, 1984— , tort seminar Va. Trial Lawyers Assn., 1987—. Chmn., Central Richmond Jaycee's Venereal Disease Project, 1975; mem. Richmond Democratic Com., 1978-79; vol. for Juvenile and Domestic Relations Ct. After Care Program, 1978-81; mem. parish council St. Peters Ch., Richmond, 1979-81. Served to 1st lt. U.S. Army, 1968-72. Named An Outstanding Young Man of Am., Jaycees, 1976, 80. Mem. Richmond Trial Lawyers Assn. (treas. 1987-88, sec. 1988-89). Roman Catholic. Family and matrimonial, Personal injury. Home: 13531 Kingsmill Rd Midlothian VA 23113-3883 Office: Anderson Parkerson Shields PO Box 7439 3437 W Cary St Richmond VA 23221

SHIENTAG, FLORENCE PERLOW, lawyer; b. N.Y.C. d. David and Ester (Germane) Perlow; m. Bernard L. Shientag, June 8, 1938. BS, NYU, 1940, LLB, 1933, JD, 1940. Bar: Fla. 1976, N.Y. Law aide Thomas E. Dewey, 1937; law sec. Mayor La Guardia, 1939-42; justice Domestic Relations Ct., 1941-42; mem. Tchrs. Retirement Bd., N.Y.C., 1942-46; asst. U.S. atty. So. dist. N.Y., 1943-53; cir. ct. mediator Fla. Supreme Ct., 1992; pvt. practice N.Y.C., 1960—, Palm Beach, Fla., 1976—. Lectr. on internat. divorce; mem. Nat. Commn. on Wiretapping and Electronic Surveillance, 1973—, Task Force on Women in Cts., 1985-86. Contbr. articles to profl. jours. Candidate N.Y. State Senate, 1954; bd. dirs. UN Devel. Corp., 1972-95, Franklin and Eleanor Roosevelt Inst., 1985—; bd. dirs., assoc. treas. YM and YWHA; hon. commr. commerce, N.Y.C. Mem. ABA, Fed. Bar Assn. (exec. com.), Internat. Bar Assn., N.Y. Women's Bar Assn. (pres., dir., Life Time Achievement award 1994), N.Y. State Bar Assn., N.Y.C. Bar Assn. (chmn. law and art sect.), N.Y. County Lawyers Assn. (dir.), Nat. Assn. Women LAwyers (sec.). Home: 737 Park Ave New York NY 10021-4256

SHIGETOMI, KEITH SHIGEO, lawyer; b. Honolulu, Oct. 16, 1956; s. Samson Shigeru and Doris (Ogawa) S.; m. Ann Keiko Furutomo, Oct. 29, 1985; children: Samson Shigeru II, Marisa Mae. BSBA magna cum laude, Drake U., 1978; JD, U. Hawaii, 1983. Bar: Hawaii, 1983, U.S. Dist. Ct. Hawaii 1983, U.S. Ct. Appeals (9th cir.) 1986. Dep. pub. defender Office of Pub. Defender, Honolulu, 1983-88; pvt. practice, 1988-90, 94—; ptnr. Shigetomi & Thompson, 1990-94. Ind. grand jury counsel Cir. Ct., State of Hawaii, Honolulu, 1988-89. Finalist Three Outstanding Young Persons Hawaii Jaycees, 1994; named Criminal Def. Lawyer of Yr. Consumer Bus. Rev., 1996, 97, 99. Mem. Hawaii Bar Assn., Nat. Asian Pacific Bar Assn., Beta Gamma Sigma, Beta Alpha Psi, Phi Eta Sigma. Criminal, Juvenile, Personal injury. Office: 711 Kapiolani Blvd Ste 1440 Honolulu HI 96813-5238

SHIHATA, IBRAHIM FAHMY IBRAHIM, retired bank executive, lawyer, writer; b. Damietta, Egypt, Aug. 19, 1937; s. Ibrahim and Neamat (El Ashmawy) S.; m. Samia S. Farid, June 18, 1967; children: Sharif, Yasmine, Nadia. LL.B., U. Cairo, 1957, diploma in pub. law and fin., 1958, diploma in pvt. law, 1959; S.J.D., Harvard U., 1964; LLD (hon.), U. Dundee, Scotland, 1995, U. Paris Panthéon, Sorbonne, France, 1996, Am. U., Cairo, 2000. Mem. Conseil d'Etat, UAR, 1957-60, Tech. Bur. of Pres., Egypt, 1959-60; from lectr. to assoc. prof. internat. law Ain-Shams U., Cairo, 1964-66, 70-72; legal adviser Kuwait Fund for Arab Econ. Devel., 1966-70, 72-76; dir. gen. OPEC Fund for Internat. Devel., Vienna, 1976-83; exec. dir. Internat. Fund for Agrl. Devel., Rome, 1977-83; sr. v.p., gen. counsel World Bank, Washington, 1983-98; ret., 1998. Sec. gen. Internat. Ctr. Settlement of Investment Disputes, Washington, 1983—; chmn. bd. Internat. Devel. Law Inst., Rome, 1983—; chmn. Egyptian Ctr. Econ. Studies, Cairo, 1999—; bd. dirs. Internat. Fertilizer Devel. Ctr., Muscle Shoals, Ala., 1979-84, Vienna Devel. Inst.; mem. exec. coun. Am. Soc. Internat. Law, Washington, 1984-87; adv. com. Rsch. Ctr. Internat. Law, Cambridge, Eng., 1985—; founding adv., bd. dirs. Inst. Transnat. Arbitration, Houston, 1986—; hon. fellow Inst. Advance Legal Studies, U. London. Author: The Power of the International Court to Determine Its Own Jurisdiction, 1965, International Air and Space Law, 1966, International Economic Joint Ventures, 1969, International Guarantee for Foreign Investments, 1971, Treatment of Foreign Investments in Egypt, 1972, Secure and Recognized Boundaries, 1974, The Arab Oil Embargo, 1975, The Other Face of OPEC, 1982, The OPEC Fund for International Development-The Formative Years, 1983, A Program for Tomorrow-Challenges and Prospects of the Egyptian Economy in a Changing World,

1987, MIGA and Foreign Investment, 1988, The European Bank for Reconstruction and Development, 1990, The World Bank and the Arab World, 1990, The World Bank and in a Changing World, vol. 1, 1991, Legal Treatment of Foreign Investment: The World Bank Guidelines, 1993, Towards Comprehensive Reforms, 1993, The World Bank Inspection Panel, 1994, 2d edit., rev. 1999, The World Bank in a Changing World, vol. 1, 1991, vol. 2, 1995, vol. 3, 1999, Complementary Reform: Essays on Legal, Judicial and Other Institutional Reform Supported by the World Bank, 1997; editor ICSID Rev.-Fgn. Investment Law Jour. Sr. v.p. IBRD, 1983-99, v.p., 1983-98. Decorated Grosses Silbernes Ehrenzeichen am Bande fuer Verdienste um die Republik Oesterreich (Australia), 1983; recipient Babcock prize, 1964, Kuwait prize for sci. progress in social scis., 1983. Mem. Am. Soc. Internat. Law, Institut de Droit Internat. (Geneva), Social Scis. Acad. (Chile). E-mail: ibrahimy19@yahoo.com

SHIMER, SUSAN ROSENTHAL, lawyer; b. Vienna, Austria, Mar. 17, 1937; came to U.S., 1940; d. Carl August and Else (Spitz) Rosenthal; m. Zachary Shimer, Feb. 26, 1961; children: Jennifer Rosann, Robert Jay. AB, Barnard Coll., 1957; JD, U. Mich., 1960. Bar: N.Y. 1961 U.S. Dist. Ct. (so. dist.) N.Y. 1964, U.S. Ct. Apls. (2d cir.) 1967, U.S. Supreme Ct. 1968. Trial atty. U.S. Dept. Justice, Washington, 1960-62; atty. U.S. Dept. HEW, N.Y.C., 1962-64; assoc. Chadbourne, Parke, Whiteside & Wolff, N.Y.C., 1964-71, cons., 1972-75; adj. antitrust law Pace Law Sch., White Plains, N.Y., 1978-80; town justice Town of North Castle, Armonk, N.Y., 1976—. Asst. editor U. Mich. Law Rev., 1959-60. Chmn. enforcement adjucation subcom. Stop DWI Bd. of Westchester, White Plains, 1982-86, Runaway and Homeless Youth Adv. Commn., White Plains, 1984; bd. dirs. Children's Assn. Westchester, 1983-85; pres. North Castle Hist. Soc., 1986-89. Mem. Westchester County Magistrates Assn. (bd. dirs. 1982—, pres. 1986), Westchester County Bar Assn., N.Y. State Magistrates Assn. (bd. dirs. 1985-88). Democrat. E-mail: zsshimer@earthlink.net. Home: 16 Pond Ln Armonk NY 10504-2633 Office: Town of North Castle 15 Bedford Rd Armonk NY 10504-1802

SHIMOMURA, FLOYD DUDLEY, lawyer, educator; b. Sacramento, Calif., Mar. 13, 1948; s. Ben Hiroyuki and Lois Miyeko (Morimoto) S.; m. Ruth Ann Aoki, Apr. 4, 1971; children— Mark, Lisa. B.S., U. Calif.-Davis, 1970, J.D., 1973. Bar: Calif., 1973. Dep. atty. gen. State of Calif., Sacramento, 1973-81; prof. law U. Calif.-Davis, 1981— . Nat. v.p. Japanese Am. Citizens League, San Francisco, 1978-82, nat. pres., 1982-84; planning commr. City of Woodland, Calif., 1978-82. Mem. State Bar Calif., Orgn. Calif. State Dep. Attys. Gen., Order of Coif, Phi Beta Kappa, Phi Kappa Phi. Democrat. Home: 719 Fairview Dr Woodland CA 95695-6805 Office: Sch of Law Univ Calif Davis CA 95616

SHIMPOCK, KATHY ELIZABETH, lawyer, writer; b. Mooresville, N.C., July 20, 1952; d. Charles Walter and Minna Ethel (McLean) S.; m. David Edward Vieweg, Sept. 3, 1983 (div. Mar. 1997); children: Jessica Kim Vieweg, Jayme Elise Kyung Vieweg. BA, Colo. Coll., 1973; JD, U. Wyo., 1977; MLL, U. Denver, 1979; MBA, Ariz. State U., 1992. Bar: Ariz. 1977. Asst. librarian Stanford (Calif.) U. Coll. Law, 1979-82; law librarian, asst. prof. law U. Bridgeport (Conn.) Coll. Law, 1982-83; dir. Law Libr. Adminstrv. Svcs., Mountain View, Calif., 1983-85; exec. asst. to dean Ariz. State U. Coll. Law, Tempe, 1985-87; dir. Law Libr. Adminstrv. Svcs., Mesa, Ariz., 1987-95; dir. libr. svcs. Jennings, Strouss & Salmon, Phoenix, 1988-89; dir. rsch. svcs. O'Connor, Cavanagh et al, 1989-95; pres. Juris Rsch., Mesa, 1995-96; counsel Muchmore & Wallwork, Phoenix, 1995-98; pres. Juris Rsch., Tempe, 1998—. Adv. bd. West Pub. Co., St. Paul, 1991-94; mediator Alternative Dispute Resolution Program, Maricopa County, Ariz. Author: Business Research Handbook: Methods and Sources for Lawyers and Business Professionals, 1996—; co-author: Arizona Legal Research Guide, 1992; contbr. chpts. to books, articles to profl. jours.; bi-monthly columnist AzALL News, 1996-97, Legal Assistant Today, 1993-96; contbr. book revs. to Libr. Jour., Legal Info. Alert, 1993-98; editor Southwest Assn. Law Librs. Bull., 1990, Ariz. State U. Coll. Law Law Forum, 1986, Juris Rsch. E-line, 1999—. Rsch. atty. Comml. Law Project for the Ukraine, Phoenix, 1995-96. Mem. ABA (co-chair law practice mgmt. environ. divsn. 1996-99), Am. Assn. Law Librs. (chair 1994-95), Ariz. Assn. Law Librs. (pres. 1996-97, pres.'s award 1997, Disting. Mem. award 1998), State Bar of Ariz. (chair 1996-98, 2001—, Cont. Legal Edn. award 1998), Ariz. Women Lawyers Assn. (steering com. 1998-2000). Democrat. Unity. Avocations: reading, yoga, painting, drawing. Environmental, Intellectual property, Labor. Office: Juris Rsch PO Box 2157 Tempe AZ 85280-2157 E-mail: kshimpock@jurisresearch.com

SHINDLER, DONALD A. lawyer; b. New Orleans, Oct. 15, 1946; s. Alan and Isolene (Levy) S.; m. Laura Epstein, 1969; children: Jay, Susan. BSBA, Washington U., St. Louis, 1968; JD, Tulane U., 1971. Bar: La. 1971, U.S. Dist. Ct. (ea. dist.) La. 1971, U.S. Tax Ct. 1974, Ill. 1975, U.S. Dist. Ct. (no. dist.) Ill. 1975; CPA, La.; lic. real estate broker, Ill. Assoc. Pope, Ballard, Shepard & Fowle, Chgo., 1975-78, Rudnick & Wolfe, Chgo., 1978-81, ptnr., 1981-99; gen. counsel America's Second Harvest Nat. Food Bank Network, 1998-2000; ptnr. Piper Marbury Rudnick & Wolfe, Chgo., 1999—. Seminar lectr. ABA, Chgo. Bar Assn., Ill. Inst. CLE, Profl. Edn. Sys., Inc., Internat. Assn. Corp. Real Estate Execs., Urban Land Inst., Am. Corp. Counsel Assn., Bldg. Owners and Mgrs. Assn., Internat. Assn. of Attys. and Execs. in Corp. Real Estate, others. Contbr. articles on real estate to legal jours. Trustee Glencoe (Ill.) Pub. Libr., 1981-87, pres., 1986-87; alumni bd. govs. Washington U., 1992-93; mem. Glencoe Zoning Commn./Bd. Appeals, 1994-2000. Lt. JAGC, USNR, 1971-75. Mem. ABA, La. State Bar Assn., Chgo. Bar Assn. (com. chmn. 1979-80, 83-84, 90-94, 96-99, editor land trust seminars 1984-96), Urban Land Inst. (mem. steering com. Chgo. dist. coun.), Internat. Assn. Corp. Real Estate Execs. (pres. Chgo. chpt. 1997-98, dir. 1991—), Internat. Assn. Attys. and Execs. in Corp. Real Estate, Union League Club (chair real estate group 1993-96), Order of Coif, Beta Gamma Sigma, Omicron Delta Kappa. General corporate, Environmental, Real property. Office: Piper Marbury Rudnick & Wolfe Ste 1800 203 N La Salle St Ste 1800 Chicago IL 60601-1210 E-mail: donald.shindler@piperrudnick.com

SHINKLE, JOHN THOMAS, lawyer; b. Albany, N.Y., May 9, 1946; s. Robert Thomas and Margery Joan (Kneip) S.; m. Csilla Elizabeth Bekasy, Sept. 2, 1967; children: Reka, Ildiko. BA, Yale U., 1967; JD, Harvard U., 1970. Bar: D.C. 1971, N.Y. 1983, U.S. Supreme Ct. 1974. Law clk. U.S. Ct. Appeals for D.C. Circuit, Washington, 1970-71; assoc. Caplin & Drysdale, 1971-77, ptnr., 1977-80; assoc. dir. divsn. corp. fin. SEC, 1980-81, dep. gen. counsel, 1981-82; gen. counsel Salomon Bros. Inc., N.Y.C., 1982-94, v.p., 1982-87, dir., 1988-94, Asia Pacific legal and compliance dir., 1995; mng. dir. Salomon Bros., Hong Kong, 1996-97, Salomon Smith Barney, Hong Kong, 1997—. Contbr. articles to profl. jours. Mem. ABA, Assn. Bar City N.Y., Securities Industry Assn. (chmn. fed. regulation com. 1989-91), Futures Industry Assn. (dir. 1989-97), Downtown Athletic Club (N.Y.C.). General corporate, Private international, Securities. Home: 2703B Queen's Garden 9 Old Peak Rd Hong Kong China Office: Salomon Smith Barney 3 Exchange Sq Fl 20 Hong Kong China

SHINN, CLINTON WESLEY, lawyer; b. Haworth, Okla., Mar. 7, 1947; s. Clinton Elmo and Mary Lucille (Dowdy) S.; m. Catherine Borne; children: Laura Kathryn, Clinton Wesley, Timothy Daniel. BS, McNeese State U., 1969; JD, Tulane U., 1972; LLM, Harvard U., 1973. Bar: La. 1972, U.S. Dist. Ct. (ea. dist.) La. 1975, U.S. Dist. Ct. (we. dist.) La. 1980, U.S. Ct. Appeals (5th cir.) 1981, U.S. Ct. Appeals (11th cir.) 1982, U.S. Tax Ct. (1982). Asst. prof. law Tulane U., New Orleans, 1973-75; assoc. Stone, Pigman et al, 1975-78, ptnr., 1979-97, Gill & Shinn, LLC, Covington, La., 1998-2000, of counsel, 2000—; assoc. prof. law Appalachian Sch. Law, 1999—. Faculty advisor, 1974-75, editor in chief Tulane Law Rev., 1971-72, ASL Federalist Soc., 1999—, ASL Student Bar Assn., 2000—. Editor in chief Tulane Law Rev., 1971-72 Co-founder, bd. dirs. Childhood Cancer Families Network, 1987-90; co-founder Camp Challenge, 1988; team leader Campaign for Caring, Children's Hosp., New Orleans, 1989-91; bd. dirs. Christ Episcopal Sch., Covington, 1988-91, chmn. long-range planning, 1990-91, exec. com., 1989-91, chmn. legal com., 1989-91, chmn. admissions/recruitment com., 1988-90, mem. headmaster search com., 1993; bd. dirs. Greater New Orleans YMCA, 1989-98, 99-2000, exec. com., 1991-98, asst. sec., 1994-95, sec., 1996-98, mem. fin. com., 1994-98, exec. dir. search com., 1996, 2d vice-chair, 1998; mem. Leadership Coun., 1997-98; active Indian Guides/Princesses; bd. dirs. West St. Tammany YMCA, 1987-95, exec. com., 1988-95, bd. chmn., 1989-90, 92-93; bd. dirs. Christwood, 1992—, bd. v.p., 1997-99; bd. dirs. La. Air & Waste Mgmt. Assn., 1993-99; chmn. corp. rels. com., 1992-93, vice-chmn., 1996-97, chair, 1997-98, past chair, 1998-99. Co-recipient Pals of the Yr. award Greater New Orleans YMCA Indian Guides/Princesses, 1987-88; named Vol. of Yr. West St. Tammany YMCA, 1990, 92, Ill. Prof. of Yr., Appalachian Sch. Law, 1999-01. Fellow Am. Coll. Trust and Estate Counsel, La. Bar Found., Northshore Estate Planning Coun.; mem. ABA, Nat. Assn. Securities Dealers (bd. arbitrators), Nat. Wildlife Fedn. (life), La. Bar Assn., La. Forestry Assn., New Orleans Estate Planning Coun., Air and Waste Mgmt. Assn., Order of Coif, Nat. Commn. for Planning Giving (New Orleans chpt.), Federalist Soc. (faculty advisor), Student Bar Assn. (faculty advisor 2000—). Avocations: backpacking, gardening. General corporate, Environmental, Probate. Home: PO Box 694 Grundy VA 24614-0694 Office: Gill & Shinn LLC 109 Northpark Blvd Ste 201 Covington LA 70433-5080 also: Appalachian Sch Law PO Box 2825 Grundy VA 24614-2825

SHIPLEY, DAVID ELLIOTT, dean, lawyer; b. Urbana, Ill., Oct. 3, 1950; s. James Ross and Dorothy Jean (Elliott) S.; m. Virginia Florence Coleman, May 24, 1980; 1 child, Shannon C. BA, Oberlin Coll., 1972; JD, U. Chgo., 1975. Bar: R.I. 1975. Assoc. Tillinghast, Collins & Graham, Providence, 1975-77; asst. prof. U. S.C. Sch. Law, Columbia, 1977-81, assoc. prof., 1981-85, prof., 1985-90, assoc. dean, 1989-90; dean U. Miss. Sch. Law, University, 1990-93, U. Ky. Coll. Law, Lexington, 1993-98; dean Sch. Law U. Ga., Athens, 1998—. Vis. prof. Coll. William and Mary, Williamsburg, Va., 1983-84, Ohio State U. Coll. Law, Columbus, 1986-87. Author: South Carolina Administrative Law, 1983, 2d edit., 1989; co-author Copyright Law, 1992. Pres. Shandon Neighborhood Assn., Columbia, 1988-90. Named Prof. of Yr., U. S.C. Sch. Law, 1990, faculty scholar, 1989-90. Mem. ABA, R.I. Bar Assn., S.C. Bar Assn. (assoc.). Methodist. Avocations: running, yardwork, gardening, reading. Home: 475 River Bottom Rd Athens GA 30606-6430 Office: U Ga Sch Law Athens GA 30602-6012*

SHIPP, DAN SHACKELFORD, lawyer; b. Yazoo City, Miss., Jan. 6, 1946; s. Dan Hugh and Anora Nona (Shackelford) A.; m. Carolyn Julie Perry, Nov. 30, 1974; children: Perry Lee, Clay Alexander. AA, Holmes Jr. Coll., 1966; BA, Miss. State U., 1968; JD, U. Miss., 1971. Bar: Miss. 1971, U.S. Dist. Ct. (no. dist.) Miss. 1971, U.S. Dist. Ct. (so. dist.) Miss. 1976, Colo. 1986, U.S. Ct. Appeals (5th cir.) 1982, U.S. Ct. Appeals (10th cir.) 1986, U.S. Dist. Ct. Colo. 1986. Pvt. practice, Yazoo City, Miss., 1974-83, Aspen, 1986—. Speaker in field. Recipient Master Advocate Cert. award Notre Dame Law Sch., 1993. Mem. ABA, Colo. Trial Lawyers Assn. (bd. dirs. 1986-88), Assn. Trial Lawyers Am., Colo. Bar Assn., Toastmasters Internat. Maroon Creek Club. Avocations: hunting, archery, traveling. General civil litigation, General practice, Personal injury. Office: 407 J AABC PO Box 8629 Aspen CO 81612-8629 Fax: 970-925-1599. E-mail: grand@rof.net

SHIPP, ROSE LEVADA, lawyer; b. Jersey City, N.J., Sept. 24, 1934; d. Anthony and Joyce Waldean (Gilbert) DeGregorio; m. David Crenshaw Shipp, Sept. 11, 1954; children: David Anthony (dec.) Sallie Dean, Daniel Linwood. BA magna cum laude, U. Louisville, Ky., 1970, JD, 1972. Bar: Ky. 1973. Student intern U.S. Atty.'s Office, Louisville, 1971-72; solo practice, Louisville, 1973-76, Taylorsville, Ky., 1979-86; asst. Commonwealth's atty., Louisville, 1976-78. Mem. Young Reps. Am., Louisville, 1968-72; treas., v.p. Republican Attys. of Louisville, 1973-75; precinct capt., 1974-75; audio tester Head Start, Louisville, 1964-65; Pres., Woodcock Honor Soc., U. Louisville, 1973. Mem. Ky. Bar Assn. Home: 2781 Maple Rd Louisville KY 40205-1735 Office: Rose Levada Shipp Atty at Law PO Box 483 Main St 2781 Maple Rd Louisville KY 40205-1735

SHIPPEY, SANDRA LEE, lawyer; b. Casper, Wyo., June 24, 1957; d. Virgil Carr and Doris Louise (Conklin) McClintock; m. Ojars Herberts Ozols, Sept. 2, 1978 (div.); children: Michael Ojars, Sara Ann, Brian Christopher; m. James Robert Shippey, Jan. 13, 1991; 1 child, Matthew James. BA with distinction, U. Colo., 1978; JD magna cum laude, Boston U., 1982. Bar: Colo. 1982, U.S. Dist. Ct. Colo. 1985. Assoc. Cohen, Brame & Smith, Denver, 1983-84, Parcel, Meyer, Schwartz, Ruttum & Mauro, Denver, 1984-85, Mayer, Brown & Platt, Denver, 1985-87; counsel western ops. GE Capital Corp., San Diego, 1987-94; assoc. Page, Polin, Busch & Boatwright, 1994-95; v.p., gen. counsel First Comml. Corp., 1995-96; legal counsel NextWave Telecom Inc., 1996-98; ptnr. Procopio, Cory, Hargreaves and Savitch, LLP, 1998—. Active Pop Warner football and cheerleading; bd. dirs. San Diego Christian Found., 2001—. Mem. Phi Beta Kappa, Phi Delta Phi. Republican. Mem. Ch. of Christ. Avocations: tennis, golf, photography. Banking, General corporate, Finance. Home: 15839 Big Springs Way San Diego CA 92127-2034 Office: Procopio Cory Et Al 530 B St Ste 2100 San Diego CA 92101-4496 E-mail: sls@procopio.com

SHIRBIN, JOHN MARTIN, lawyer; b. Sydney, Dec. 21, 1950; s. John Dalley and Dorothy S.; m. Glenda Gaye Beckett; children: James, Andrew, Juliet. BA, U. Sydney, 1973; LLB, 1975. Bar: solicitor Supreme Ct. New South Wales. Pntr. Clayton Utz, Sydney, 1979—; mng. ptnr., 1987-90; chair bd. dirs., 2000. Finance, Government contracts and claims, Public utilities. Home: 35 Dettmann Ave Longueville NSW 2066 Australia Office: Clayton Utz 1 O'Connell St Sydney NSW Australia Home Fax: 612 94186738; Office Fax: 612 9251 7832. E-mail: jshirbin@claytonutz.com

SHIRE, HAROLD RAYMOND, law educator, writer, scientist; b. Denver, Nov. 23, 1910; s. Samuel Newport and Rose Betty (Herman) S.; m. Cecilia Goldhaar, May 9, 1973; children: David, Darcy, Esti. MBA, Pepperdine U., 1972, LLD (hon.), 1975; JD, Southwestern U., L.A., 1974; M in Liberal Arts, U. So. Calif., 1977; PhD in Human Behavior, U.S. Internat. U., San Diego, 1980. Bar: Calif. 1937, U.S. Dist. Ct. (so. dist.) Calif. 1939, U.S. Supreme Ct. 1978. Dep. dist. atty. L.A. County, Calif., 1937-38; asst. U.S. atty. So. Dist. Calif., L.A. and San Diego, 1939-42; pvt. practice L.A., 1946-56; pres., chmn. bd. Gen. Connectors Corp., U.S. and Eng., 1956-73; prof. mgmt. and law Pepperdine U., Malibu, Calif., 1974-75, U.S. Internat. U., San Diego, 1980-83; dir. Bestobell Aviation, Eng., 1970-74. Author: Cha No Yu and Symbolic Interactionism: Method of Predicting Japanese Behavior, 1980, The Tea Ceremony, 1984. Patentee aerospace pneumatics; invented flexible connectors; designed, manufactured flexible integrity systems. Advisor U. S.C. Gerontology Andrus Ctr., pre-retirement tng., 1976-80; bd. dirs. Pepperdine U., 1974-80; nat. bd. govs. Union Orthodox Jewish Congregations Am., 1973—; mem. Rep. Nat. Com.; pres. Jewish Nat. Fund Legion of Honor, 1991—; mem. Presdl. Roundtable, Washington, 1989-97; mem. Inner Cir., Pres. Regan and Bush, 1989-92; life mem. Rep. Nat. Com. With U.S. Army, 1942-46. Decorated chevalier du vieux moulin (France); companion Royal Aero. Soc. (U.K.); recipient Tea Name Grand Master Soshitsu Sen XV Urasenke Sch., Kyoto, Japan, 1976, Medal of Honor Jewish Nat. Fund, Legion of Honor, 1991, U.S. Senate Medal of Freedom. Mem. ABA, Am. Welding Soc., Soc. Material and Process Engrs., Am. Legion (svc. officer China #1 Shanghai), Calif. Symphony Soc. (pres. 1998—), Masons (32 degree, Hiram award 1994), Royal Arch, Shrine, Legion of Honor Jewish Nat. Fund (nat. chmn. bd. 1999). Achievements include design and manufacture of fluidic systems flexible integrity for Saturn IV and welding in Apollo XI landing on moon, 1969. Office: PO Box 1352 Beverly Hills CA 90213-1352

SHIRLEY, ROBERT BRYCE, lawyer; b. Morehead City, Calif., Feb. 5, 1951; s. Robert Wayne and JoAnne Elaine (Shook) S.; m. Marilyn Jeanette Roy, June 30, 1973; children: Robert Wayne, James Roy, Emma Kate. BA, Stanford U., 1973, MBA, JD, Stanford U., 1977. Bar: Calif. 1977, Ohio 1981, U.S. Dist. Ct. (ctrl. dist.) Calif. 1978, U.S. Dist. Ct. (no. dist.) Ohio 1984, U.S. Dist. Ct. (so. dist.) Ohio 1985. Assoc. McKenna & Fitting, L.A., 1977-79; gen. counsel The Way Internat., New Knoxville, Ohio, 1980-85; ptnr. Morrison & Shirley, Irvine, Calif., 1985-87; sr. atty. Taco Bell Corp., 1988-92, corp. counsel, 1993, mng. counsel, 1994—. Mem. ABA, Calif. Bar Assn., Am. Corp. Counsel Assn., Internat. Assn. Corp. Real Estate Execs., Internat. Coun. Shopping Ctrs., Internat. Assn. Attys. and Execs. in Corp. Real Estate (dir.). Republican. Avocaitons: skiing, fishing, backpacking. General corporate, Real property. Home: 7 La Dera Irvine CA 92620-1947 Office: Taco Bell Corp 17901 Von Karman Ave Irvine CA 92614-6221 E-mail: bshirley@tacobell.com

SHIRTZ, JOSEPH FRANK, lawyer, consultant; b. Yeadon, PA, June 26, 1959; s. Raymond Loren and Ann Gredel (Lutz) S.; m. Catherine Irene Enright, Sept. 6, 1987; children: Ryan, Erin. BSME, U. Ala., Tuscaloosa, 1981; JD, Villanova, 1984. Bar: Pa. 1984, N.Y. 1985, N.J. 1986, U.S. Dist. Ct. N.J. 1986, U.S. Patent Office 1985, U.S. Ct. Appeals (fed. cir.) 1986. Law clk. Ct. of Common Pleas, Norristown, Pa., 1983; assoc. Pennie & Edmonds, N.Y.C., 1984-87; patent atty. Johnson & Johnson, New Brunswick, N.J., 1987-94, supervisory atty., 1994-98, assoc. patent counsel, 1998—. Mem. N.J., N.Y. Intellectual Property Law Assn. Patent, Taxation, general. Office: Johnson & Johnson One Johnson & Johnson Plaza New Brunswick NJ 08933-0001

SHMUKLER, STANFORD, lawyer; b. Phila., June 16, 1930; s. Samuel and Tessye (Dounne) S.; m. Anita Golove, Mar. 21, 1951; children: Jodie Lynne Shmukler Girsh, Joel Mark, Steven David. BS in Econs., U. Pa., 1951, JD, 1954. Bar: D.C. 1954, Pa. 1955, U.S. Ct. Appeals (2d cir.) 1959, U.S. Supreme Ct. 1959, U.S. Ct. Appeals (3d cir.) 1960, U.S. Ct. Mil. Appeals 1966. Atty. U.S. Bur. Pub. Roads, 1954-55, cons., 1955-57; sole practice Phila., 1955—. Lectr. Temple U. Law Sch., 1975-78; mem., past sec., exec. dir. crminal procedural rules com. Pa. Supreme Ct., 1971-87; mem. lawyers adv. com. Ct. Appeals for 3d cir., 1977-80, selection com. Criminal Justice Act Panel, 1979-84; chmn. selection com. Phila. Bar Ct. Appointments, 1988-91. Contbr. articles to profl. jours. Bd. dirs. Ecumenical Halfway House, 1967-71; bd. mgrs. Alumni Assn., Ctrl. High Sch., Phila. Served to col. JAGC, USAR, from 1955 (ret.). Recipient Phila. Bar Assn. Criminal Justice Sect. award, 1977, Justice Thurgood Marshall award, 1992; Legion of Honor, Chapel of the Four Chpalains, 1983. Mem. ABA, Pa. Bar Assn., Phila. Bar Assn. (bd. govs. 1971-73, past chmn. criminal justice com. and mil. justice com.), Fed. Bar Assn. (chmn. criminal law com. adminstrn. justice sect., co-chmn. criminal law com. Phila. chpt., Leadership award Phila. 1991, 94), Pa. Assn. Criminal Def. Lawyers, Nat. Assn. Criminal Def. Lawyers., Justice Lodge, B'nai B'rith. Democrat. Jewish. Appellate, Criminal, Military. Home: 1400 Melrose Ave Melrose Park PA 19027-3155 E-mail: SSESQ1@aol.com

SHOAFF, THOMAS MITCHELL, lawyer; b. Ft. Wayne, Ind., Aug. 21, 1941; s. John D. and Agnes H. (Hanna) S.; m. Eunice Swedberg, Feb. 7, 1970; children: Andrew, Nathaniel, Matthew-John. BA, Williams Coll., 1964; JD, Vanderbilt U., 1967. Bar: Ind. 1968. Assoc. Isham, Lincoln & Beale, Chgo., 1967-68; ptnr. Baker & Daniels, Ft. Wayne, Ind., 1968—. Bd. dirs. Weaver Popcorn Co., Inc., Ft. Wayne, Dreibelbiss Title Co., Inc., Ft. Wayne, Am. Steel Investment Corp., Ft. Wayne. Bd. dirs. McMillen Found., Ft. Wayne, Wilson Found., Ft. Wayne. Mem. ABA, Allen County Bar Assn., Ind. State Bar Assn. Presbyterian. Avocations: golf, sailing. General corporate. Office: Baker & Daniels 111 E Wayne St Ste 800 Fort Wayne IN 46802-2603

SHOCKEY, GARY LEE, lawyer; b. Casper, Wyo., Sept. 25, 1950; s. Bernis L. and Shirley E. (Diehl) S.; m. Dona K. Galles, June 1, 1979; children: Amber, Jeremy, Kimberly. AB in Polit. Sci. and Sociology, Yale U., 1973; JD, U. Wyo., 1976. Bar: Wyo. 1976, U.S. Dist. Ct. Wyo. 1976, U.S. Ct. Appeals (10th cir.) 1984, U.S. Ct. Appeals (9th cir.) 1988, U.S. Claims Ct. 1989, U.S. Supreme Ct. 1989, U.S. Ct. Appeals (fed. cir.) 1993, U.S. Dist. Ct. Ariz 1994. Pub. defender State of Wyo. and City of Casper, 1976-78; sole practice Casper, 1976-79; assoc. Spence, Moriarity & Schuster, Casper and Jackson, Wyo., 1978-82, ptnr. Jackson, 1982—. Mem. ABA, Wyo. State Bar (continuing legal edn. com. 1984-85, law and legis. reform com. 1986-88), Assn. Trial Lawyers Am., Wyo. Trial Lawyer's Assn. (bd. dirs. 1984-90). E-mail: g. Federal civil litigation, State civil litigation, Personal injury. Office: Spence Moriarity & Schuster PO Box 548 Jackson WY 83001-0548 E-mail: shockey@smswy.com

SHOFF, PATRICIA ANN, lawyer; b. Colby, Kans., Sept. 27, 1948; d. Clarence O. and Clara C. (Ortbal) Shoff; m. Thomas E. Salsbery, Oct. 6, 1979; children: Emily Anne, Edward Philip. BA with honors, U. Iowa, 1970, JD with distinction, 1973. Bar: Iowa 1973, U.S Dist. Ct. (no. and so. dists.) Iowa 1974. Law clk. Supreme Ct. of Iowa, Des Moines, 1973-74; assoc. Thoma Schoenthal Davis, Hockenberg & Wine, 1974-79; ptnr., shareholder Davis, Brown, Koehn, Shors & Roberts, P.C., 1979—. Sec. bd. dirs. Iowa's Children and Families, 1980-91, v.p. 1981-82, pres. 1982-83, Very Spl. Arts Iowa, 1988-93, sec. 1990, chair pers. com., 1990-92, pres. 1992, chair resource devel. com. 1992—; mem. Gov.'s Com. Child Abuse Prevention, 1982-92, chair 1987-92; co-chair fundraising com. Hospice of Ctrl. Iowa, 1983-85; pub. rels. com. mem. St. Augustin's Ch., 1986-87; exec. bd. Mid-Iowa Coun. Boy Scouts Am., 1988—, nominating com., 1989-91, Homestead bd. dirs., 1993, pres.-elect, 1994, pres., 1995. Mem. ABA (family law sect., labor, employment law sect.), AAUW (juvenile justice com. 1974-76), Iowa Law Sch. Found. (bd. dirs. 1992—), Iowa State Bar Assn. (young lawyers sect., family law com. 1979-81, membership com. 1979-81, chair legal aid com. 1981-85, labor and employment law com. 1991-92, bd. govs. 1995—others), Iowa Supreme Ct. Bd. Law Examiners (vice-chair 1991-95), Polk County Bar Assn. (treas. 1989-92, v.p. 1992-93, pres. elect 1993, pres. 1994, Merit award 1990), Womens Fedn. Lawyers, Greater Des Moines C. of C. Fedn. (bd. dirs. 1984-85, bur. econ. devel. com. 1985—, exec. call com. 1985—), Polk County Women Attys., Iowa Orgn. Women Attys., Greater Des Moines C. of C. Leadership Inst. (pres. bd. govs. 1984-85, alumni orgn. 1984—), Jr. League (adv. planning 1983-84, placement advisor 1986-87, grants com. 1988), Phi Delta Phi. Democrat. Roman Catholic. Family and matrimonial, Labor, Workers' compensation. Office: Davis Brown Koehn Shors & Roberts 2500 Fin Ctr 666 Walnut St Des Moines IA 50309-3904 E-mail: pas@lawiowa.com

SHOMETTE, DONNA M. DIXSON, paralegal; b. Munich, Germany, Dec. 17, 1963; d. Thomas Joe and Maria Theresia (Meier) Pitts-Gibbs; m. Ben J. Dixson Jr., Sept 29, 1984 (div.); m. C. Douglas Shomette, Dec. 05, 1995. Student, La. State U., 1982-83, 91, Collin Co. Cmty. Coll., 1998. Cert. fligth attendant, Continental Airlines, 1991. Fashion designer, Dallas, 1985-87, 92; medical paralegal, 1993-95; freelance paralegal, 1997—.

Legal student Southeastern Paralegal Inst., Dallas, 1994-95. Recipient Editors Choice award, Internat. Soc. Poetry, 1995. Mem. ABA, State Bar Tex., Am. Trial Lawyers Assn., Nat. Assn. Legal Assts., Dallas Opera Guild, Dallas Mus. Art, Dallas Arboretum. Avocations: music, poetry, art, skiing, gardening. Home: 320 Hackberry St Lockhart TX 78644-3027

SHOOK, ANN JONES, lawyer; b. Canton, Ohio, Apr. 18, 1925; d. William M. and Lura (Pontius) Jones; m. Gene E. Shook Sr., Nov. 30, 1956; children: Scott, William, Gene Edwin Jr. AB, Wittenberg U., 1947; LLB, William McKinley Law Sch., 1955. Bar: Ohio 1956, U.S. Dist. Ct. (no. dist.) Ohio 1961, U.S. Ct. Appeals (6th cir.) 1981. Cost acct. Hoover Co., North Canton, Ohio, 1947-51; asst. sec. Stark County Prosecutor's Office, Canton, 1951-53; ins. adjuster Traveler's Ins. Co., 1953-56; ptnr. Shook & Shook, Toledo, 1958-62, North Olmsted, Ohio, 1962—. Mem. at large coun. Olmsted Community Ch., Olmsted Falls, Ohio, 1987-90; chmn. ways and means com. North Olmsted PTA, 1968; area chmn. United Way Appeal, North Olmsted, 1963; v.p. LWV, Toledo, 1960-62. Mem. Cleve. Bar Assn. Avocations: reading, boating, dancing, fitness. Estate planning, Probate, Personal income taxation. E-mail: shooklaw@worldnet.att.net

SHORE, MICHAEL ALLAN, lawyer, accountant; b. Cleve., Dec. 6, 1931; s. Herman and Genevieve Elizabeth (Cohen) S.; m. M. Kay Shore; children: Debbie S. George, Steven J. BS in Econs., U. Pa., 1953; JD, Cleve. State U., 1959; postgrad., Case Western Res. U. Bar: Ohio, U.S. Supreme Ct.; CPA, Ohio, N.Y. Prin. Michael A. Shore Co., L.P.A., Cleve.; pres., ptnr. Shore, Shirley & Co., CPAs. Dir. various corps.; lectr. taxation Case Western Res. U., Cleve.; acting judge Shaker Heights Municipal Ct., 1983—; arbitrator Am. Arbitration Assn. Served with U.S. Army, 1953-55. Mem. Ohio Bar Assn., Cleve. Bar Assn., AICPA, Am. Assn. Atty.-CPAs, Masons. Republican. Jewish. General corporate, Probate, Taxation, general. Office: 23230 Chagrin Blvd Cleveland OH 44122-5402

SHORES, JANIE LEDLOW, retired state supreme court justice; b. Georgiana, Ala., Apr. 30, 1932; d. John Wesley and Willie (Scott) Ledlow; m. James L. Shores, Jr., May 12, 1962; 1 child, Laura Scott. J.D., U. Ala., Tuscaloosa, 1959; AB, Samford U., 1968; LLM, U. Va., 1992. Bar: Ala. 1959. Pvt. practice, Selma, 1959; mem. legal dept. Liberty Nat. Life Ins. Co., Birmingham, Ala., 1962-66; assoc. prof. law Cumberland Sch. Law, Samford U., 1966-74; assoc. justice Supreme Ct. Ala., 1975-99. Legal adviser Ala. Constn. Revision Commn., 1973; mem. Nat. Adv. Coun. State Ct. Planning, 1976—. Contbr. articles to legal jours. Bd. dirs. State Justice Inst., 1995-98. Mem. Am. Bar Assn., Am. Judicature Soc., Farrah Order Jurisprudence. Democrat. Episcopalian. Office: Ala Supreme Ct Rm 520 Jefferson County Courthouse Birmingham AL 35203

SHORS, JOHN D. lawyer; b. Ft. Dodge, Iowa, July 21, 1937; s. George A. and Catherine (Shaw) S.; m. Patricia Ann Percival, Oct. 7, 1967; children: John, Tom, Matt, Luke. BSEE, Iowa State U., 1959; JD, U. Iowa, 1964. Bar: Iowa, U.S. Supreme Ct. Assoc. then shareholder Davis, Brown, Koehn, Shors & Roberts, P.C., Des Moines, 1964—. Co-author: Closely Held Corporations in Business and Estate Planning, 1982. Pres. Mercy Hosp. Found., Des Moines, 1981-84; chair Iowa State U. Found., Ames, 1989-92; bd. dirs. Mercy Housing, Denver, 1992—. Cpl. U.S. Army, 1960-61. Recipient Iowa State U. Alumni medal, YLS Merit award Iowa State Bar Assn. Mem. Iowa State Bar Assn. (pres. 1992) Iowa Women Profl. Corp. (Good Guy award 1987), Iowa Rsch. Coun. (bd. dirs. 1994—), Am. Judicature Soc. (bd. dirs. 1974-79), Polk County Bar Assn. (pres. 1986), Rotary (Des Moines chpt.), DM Club, Glenoaks C.C. Republican. Roman Catholic. Office: Davis Brown Koehn Shors & Roberts PC 666 Walnut St Ste 2500 Des Moines IA 50309-3904 E-mail: johnshors@lawiowa.com

SHORT, JOEL BRADLEY, lawyer, software publisher; b. Birmingham, Ala., Dec. 27, 1941; s. Forrest Edwin and Laura Elizabeth (Bradley) S.; m. Georgianna Pohl, June 5, 1965 (div. Apr. 1973); m. Nancy Ann Harty, Dec. 17, 1977; children: Christopher Bradley, Matthew Douglas. BA, U. Colo., 1963, LLB, 1966, JD, 1968. Bar: Kans. 1966, U.S. Dist. Ct. Kans. 1966, U.S. Ct. Appeals (10th cir.) 1975, U.S. Supreme Ct. 1976. Ptnr. Short & Short, Attys., Fort Scott, Kans., 1966-77, Nugent & Short, Overland Park, 1977-83; pvt. practice J. Bradley Short & Assoc., 1983-91; ptnr. Short & Borth, 1991—; owner Bradley Software. Mem. tech. adv. com. Kans. Jud. Coun., Topeka, 1991-95. Contbg. author: Practitioner's Guide to Kansas Family Law, 1997. 1st lt. U.S. Army, 1967-73. Fellow Am. Acad. Matrimonial Lawyers; mem. Johnson County Bar Assn. (ethics com. 1983-98, family law com. 1983—). Avocation: sailing. Family and matrimonial. Office: Short and Borth 32/1111 Corporate Woods 9225 Indian Creek Pkwy Overland Park KS 66210-2009 E-mail: brad@shortandborth.com

SHORT, SKIP, lawyer; b. N.Y.C., July 13, 1951; s. Albert Joseph and Gertrude B. (Johnson) S.; m. Linda Marie Short; children: Sabrina Shiva, Salim Albert, Anjelica Lynn. BA, Fordham Coll., 1972; JD, Georgetown U., 1975. Bar: N.Y. 1976, D.C. 1979, U.S. Dist. Ct. (ea. dist.) N.Y. 1976, U.S. Dist. Ct. (so. dist.) N.Y. 1978, U.S. Ct. Appeals (1st and D.C. cirs.) 1983, U.S. Supreme Ct. 1984. Sole practice, N.Y.C., 1975-79; ptnr. Short & Billy, 1979—. Cons. ins. seminars, 1978—; arbitrator N.Y. Civil Ct., 1981-93; adminstrv. law judge N.Y. Environ. Control Bd., 1980-82; arbitrator comml., no-fault, internat. and uninsured motorist tribunals Am. Arbitration Assn., N.Y.C., 1981—, mem. law com., 1991-93, mem. arbitrator screening com., 1992-99, panels membership and arbitration rules subcom., 1993-98; arbitrator U.S. Dist. Ct. (ea. dist.) N.Y., 1986—; spl. master N.Y. Supreme Ct., 1988—, N.Y. Civil Ct., 1994—; spkr. Am. Arbitration Tng. Seminar, 1991, 93, 94, N.Y. St. Bar Assn. Continuing Legal Edn. Project, 1992, N.Y. State Trial Lawyers Assn., 1996. Author: First Party Claims, 1979; co-author: First Party Claims Under the New York Comprehensive Aubomobile Reparations Act, 3d edit., 1984; contbg. author: New York Insurance Law Treatise, 1991, Insurance Law Practice, 2001. Spl. envoy Internat. Human Rights Found., 1986-87. Mem. N.Y. State Bar Assn. (spkr. continuing legal edn. program), N.Y. County Lawyers Assn. (spl. Masters com.). Federal civil litigation, Insurance, Private international. Office: Short & Billy 217 Broadway New York NY 10007-2909 E-mail: skipshort@datatone.com

SHORT, TIMOTHY ALLEN, lawyer; b. Russell, Kans., July 17, 1952; d. H. Francis and Ruth (Teeter) Short; m. Barbara Diane Phillips, June 30, 1979; children: Justin Corey, Kisha Erin. BA in Speech Communication, Kans. U., 1974, JD, 1977. Bar: Kans. 1977. Atty. Fred Spigarelli, P.A., Pitts., 1976-82; ptnr. Spigarelli, McLane & Short, 1982—. Mem. ABA, Assn. Trial Lawyers Am., Kans. Bar Assn., Kans. Trial Lawyers Assn. (bd. govs. 1987—, exec. bd. 1990—, parliamentarian 1991-92), Southeast Kans. Bar Assn., Crawford County Bar Assn. (sec. 1979). Democrat. Presbyterian. Avocations: canoeing, softball, computers, basketball. State civil litigation, Personal injury, Workers' compensation. Home: 601 W Kansas St Pittsburg KS 66762-4923 Office: Spigarelli McLane & Short PO Box 1447 PO Box 1449 Pittsburg KS 66762-1449

SHORTER, JAMES RUSSELL, JR. lawyer; b. N.Y.C., June 10, 1946; s. James Russell and Helen (Ibert) S. AB, Columbia Coll., 1968; JD, Harvard U., 1975; LLM in Taxation, NYU, 1979. Bar: N.Y. 1976, U.S. Dist. Ct. (so. and ea. dists.) N.Y. 1976, U.S. Tax Ct. 1987. Assoc. Thacher Proffitt & Wood, N.Y.C., 1975-84, ptnr., 1984—. Capt. USNR, 1968-98. Mem. ABA (tax, bus. law sect.). Republican. Club: Harvard (N.Y.C.). Personal income taxation, Taxation, general. Home: 345 E 80th St Apt 26C New York NY 10021-0671 Office: Thacher Proffitt & Wood 11 W 42nd St 11th Fl New York NY 10036 E-mail: jshorter@tpwlaw.com

SHORTRIDGE, JUDY BETH, lawyer; b. Johnson City, Tenn., Feb. 17, 1954; d. George Edd and Anna Louise (Salmon) Copenhaver; m. Michael L. Shortridge, July 27, 1984; children: Sarah Elizabeth, Alexander Blake. BA, Va. Poly. Inst. and State U., 1976; MEd, U. Va., 1982; JD, U. Tenn., 1989. Bar: Va. 1990, U.S. Dist. Ct. (we. dist.) Va. 1990, Ea. Dist. Tenn., 1995. Tchr. Stafford County (Va.) Sch. System, 1976-84, Wise County (Va.) Sch. System, 1984-86; ptnr. Shortridge & Shortridge, P.C., Norton, Va., 1990—. Recipient Am. Jurisprudence award U. Tenn., 1989. Mem. Va. Bar Assn. Administrative and regulatory, Insurance, Personal injury. Home: 340 Winterham Dr Abingdon VA 24211-3800 Office: Shortridge & Shortridge PC 18 7th St NW Ste 300 Norton VA 24273-1946

SHORTZ, RICHARD ALAN, lawyer; b. Chgo., Mar. 11, 1945; s. Lyle A. and Wilma Warner (Wildes) S.; m. Jennifer A. Harrell; children: Eric, Heidi. BS, Ind. U., 1967; JD, Harvard U., 1970. Bar: Calif. 1971, U.S. Supreme Ct. 1980. Assoc. Gibson, Dunn & Crutcher, L.A., 1970-73; sr. v.p., gen. counsel, sec. Tosco Corp., 1973-83; ptnr. Jones, Day, Reavis & Pogue, 1983-95, Rogers & Wells, L.A., 1995-97, Morgan Lewis & Bockius, L.A., 1997—. Mem. L.A. World Affairs Inst., 1983—, Town Hall L.A., 1983—. 2nd lt. U.S. Army, 1970-71. Mem. ABA, L.A. Bar Assn., Calif. Bar Assn., Calif. Club, Beach Club (Santa Monica, Calif.), L.A. Country Club. Republican. Episcopalian. FERC practice, Finance, Securities. Home: 1343 Pavia Pl Pacific Palisades CA 90272-4047 Office: Morgan Lewis & Bockius 300 S Grand Ave Ste 2200 Los Angeles CA 90071-3132 E-mail: rshortz@morganlewis.com

SHOSS, CYNTHIA RENÉE, lawyer; b. Cape Girardeau, Mo., Nov. 29, 1950; d. Milton and Carroll Jane (Duncan) S.; m. David Goodwin Watson, Apr. 13, 1986; 1 child, Lucy J. Watson. BA cum laude, Newcomb Coll., 1971; JD, Tulane U., 1974; LLM in Taxation, NYU, 1980. Bar: La. 1974, Mo. 1977, Ill. 1978, N.Y. 1990. Law clk. to assoc. and chief justices La. Supreme Ct., New Orleans, 1974-76; assoc. Stone, Pigman et al, 1976-77, Lewis & Rice, St. Louis, 1977-79, Curtis, Mallet-Prevost, et al, N.Y.C., 1980-82; ptnr. LeBoeuf, Lamb, Greene & MacRae, L.L.P., 1982—; mng. ptnr. London office LeBoeuf, Lamb, Leiby & MacRae, 1987-89. Assoc. editor Tulane Law Rev., 1972-74; frequent speaker before profl. orgns. and assns. Contbr. articles to profl. jours. Mem. Westchester County Airport Adv. Bd. Mem. ABA, Am. Mgmt. Assn. (ins. and risk mgmt. coun.), Corp. Bar Westchester and Fairfield, Power of Atty., Inc. (chair, bd. dirs.). Insurance, Corporate taxation, International taxation. Office: LeBoeuf Lamb Greene Et Al 125 W 55th St New York NY 10019-5369

SHOTWELL, CHARLES BLAND, lawyer, retired air force officer, educator; b. Tucson, Jan. 10, 1955; s. William Bedford and Pauline Shotwell; m. Jeannene V. Brooks, Aug. 10, 1988. BA, U. Puget Sound, 1977, JD, 1980; LLM in Internat. Law, Am. U., 1991. Bar: Hawaii 1980, U.S. Dist. Ct. Hawaii 1980, U.S. Ct. Mil. Appeals 1981, D.C. 1989, U.S. Ct. Appeals D.C. 1989. Commd. 2d lt. USAF, 1980, advanced through grades to lt. col., 1994, chief civil law Mich., 1980-83, mil. justice reviewer Sembach Air Base, Fed. Republic Germany, 1983-84, area def. counsel Fed. Republic Germany, 1984-85, desk officer Internat. Negotiations Div., Ramstein Air Base, Fed. Republic Germany, 1985-88, chief legis. sect., dir. internat. programs Pentagon, Washington, 1988-91; assoc. prof. USAF Acad., 1992-95; Europe affairs advisor Joint Chiefs Staff NATO, Washington, 1995-98; sr. mil. fellow Inst. Nat. Strategic Studies, 1998—; sr. security advisor DynCorps, Alexandria, Va. Adj. instr. aviation law and ins. Embry-Riddle Aero. U., Ramstein Air Base, 1985-88; USAF Nat. Def. fellow Tufts U., 1991-92; internat. politico-mil. planner U.S. Joint Staff, 1995-98; sr. mil. fellow Inst. Nat. Strategic Studies, Nat. Def. U., 1998-2000. Newsletter editor; contbr. to profl. publs. Mem. ABA, Hawaii State Bar Assn., D.C. Bar Assn., Air Force Assn. Avocations: skiing, running. Home: 5746 Union Mill Rd Apt 470 Clifton VA 20124-1088

SHREVE, GENE RUSSELL, law educator; b. San Diego, Aug. 6, 1943; s. Ronald D. and Hazel (Shepherd) S.; m. Marguerite Russell, May 26, 1973. AB with honors, U. Okla., 1965; LLB, Harvard U., 1968, LLM, 1975. Bar: Mass. 1969, Vt. 1981. Appellate atty. and state extradition hearing examiner Office of Mass. Atty Gen., 1968-69; law clk. U.S. Dist. Ct., Dallas, 1969-70; staff and supervising atty. Boston Legal Assistance Project, 1970-73; assoc. prof. Vt. Law Sch., Royalton, 1975-81; vis. assoc. prof. George Washington U., Washington, 1981-83; assoc. prof. law N.Y. Law Sch., N.Y.C., 1983-84, prof., 1984-87; vis. prof. law Ind. U., Bloomington, 1986, prof., 1987-94, Ira C. Batman faculty fellow, 1988-89, Charles L. Whistler faculty fellow, dir. grad. studies, 1992-93, Richard S. Melvin Prof. Law, 1994—. Author: A Conflict of Laws Anthology, 1997; co-author: Understanding Civil Procedure, 2d edit., 1994; mem. editl. bd. Am. Jour. Comparative Law, 1994—, Jour. Legal Edn., 1998—; contbr. numerous articles to legal jours. Mem. Am. Law Inst., Am. Soc. for Pol. and Legal Phil., Assn. Am. Law Schs. (civil procedure sect. chair 1997, conflict of laws sect. chair 1998). Democrat. Episcopalian. Office: Ind U Sch Law Bloomington IN 47405

SHROYER, THOMAS JEROME, lawyer; b. Morris, Minn., Mar. 18, 1952; s. Virgil Ernest and Muriel June (Hanson) S.; m. Nan Kenwood Sorensen, June 30, 1979; children: Eric Sorensen, Peter Thomas. BA in Polit. Sci., U. Minn., 1974, JD, 1977. Cert. civil trial specialist Minn. State Bar Assn. With Thoma, Schoenthal, Des Moines, 1977-78; assoc. Chadwick Johnson & Bridell, Bloom, Minn., 1978-80; shareholder, bd. dirs., pres., CEO Moss & Barnett, Mpls., 1980—. Author: Accountant Liability, 1991. Federal civil litigation, State civil litigation. Address: 90 S 7th St 4800 Wells Fargo Ctr Minneapolis MN 55402-3903

SHUGHART, DONALD LOUIS, lawyer; b. Kansas City, Mo., Aug. 12, 1926; s. Henry M. and Dora M. (O'Leary) Shughart; m. Mary I. Shughart, July 25, 1953; children: Susan C. Hogsett, Nancy J. Goede. AB, U. Mo., Columbia, 1949, JD, 1951. Bar: Mo. 1951, U.S. Dist. Ct. (we. dist.) Mo. 1951, U.S. Tax Ct. 1979. With Shughart, Thompson & Kilroy, PC, Kansas City, Mo., 1951—. Mem. Mo. Motor Carriers Assn. Planned giving com. Rockhurst U.; adv. bd. St. Joseph Hosp. With AC, U.S. Army, 1944-47. Mem. Kansas City Bar Assn. (chmn. bus. orgns. com. 1990-91), Mo. Bar Assn. (chmn. corp. com. 1980-81, 82-83), Lawyers Assn. Kansas City, Am. Judicature Soc., Mo. Orgn. Def. Lawyers (pres. 1971-72), U. Mo. Law Soc., Phi Delta Phi, Sigma Chi. Republican. Roman Catholic. General corporate, Estate planning. Home: 1242 W 67th Ter Kansas City MO 64113-1941 Office: Shug Thom Kilroy 12 Wyandotte Pla 120 W 12th St Kansas City MO 64105-1917

SHULMAN, MARGARET ALEX RABINOVICH, lawyer, musician; b. St. Petersburg, Russia, Jan. 15, 1972; came to U.S., 1991; d. Alexander Davidovich and Eleonora Kirillovna (Yelekoyeva) Rabinovich; m. Dmitry Shulman, Dec. 28, 1996; 1 child, Alan Michael. Student, Mus. Coll. at St. Petersburg, 1987-90; BA in Music and Psychology, U. Mich., 1994; JD cum laude, Wayne State U., 1997. Bar: Mich. 1997. Prin. flutist Orch. Classica, St. Petersburg, 1990; music tchr. Classical Music Sch., Farmington Hills, Mich., 1991-94; flutist Temple Israel, West Bloomfield, 1991—; atty. Butzel Long, P.C., Detroit, 1997—. Dir. Washtnaw Literacy, Ann Arbor, 1999. Editor Wayne Law Rev. Jour., 1995-97. Mem. Internat. Visitors Coun. Met. Detroit, 1998—. Mem. ABA, State Bar Mich., Order of Coif. Avocations: music, studying foreign languages. Home: 2414 Foxway Dr Ann Arbor MI 48105-9667 Office: Butzel Long PC 150 W Jefferson Ave Ste 900 Detroit MI 48226-4416

SHULMISTER, M(ORRIS) ROSS, lawyer; b. Atlanta, Jan. 6, 1940; s. Morris and Kathryn Sybella (Baker) S.; m. Benita Vee Rosin, Dec. 16, 1974. BEE, U. Fla., 1962, JD, 1973. Bar: Fla. 1973, U.S. Dist. Ct. (so. dist.) Fla. 1974, U.S. Dist. Ct. (mid. dist.) Fla. 1985, U.S. Ct. Appeals (5th and 11th cirs.) 1981. Pvt. practice, Broward County, Fla., Ft. Lauderdale, 1974-98, Pompano Beach, 1998—. Spl. master for code enforcement, Pompano Beach, Fla., 1991-92. Mem. Broward County Consumer Protection Bd., 1983-2001, chmn., 1999-2000; chmn. Charter Review Bd., Pompano Beach, Fla., 1994-97; dir. South Pompano Civic Assn., 1989-2000, v.p., 1989, pres., 1992-98. Lt. col. USAF, 1964-70, ret., USAFR, 1970-93. Mem. Fla. Bar (mem. constrn. law subcom., civil trial cert. 1984-99), Broward County Bar Assn. General civil litigation, Construction, Probate. Office: 590 SE 12th St Pompano Beach FL 33060-9409

SHULTS-DAVIS, LOIS BUNTON, lawyer; b. Elkton, Md., Sept. 29, 1957; d. Asa Grant Bunton and Carolyn Elizabeth Bunton Pate; m. David Reed Shults (Dec. 8, 1979 (div. Sept. 1990); children: Kenneth Grant, Joseph David, Lawrence Scott; m. Michael Howard Davis, June 14, 1992. BS, East Tenn. State U., 1977; JD, U. Tenn., 1980. Bar: Tenn. 1980, U.S. Dist. Ct. (ea. dist.) Tenn. 1985. Assoc. Jenkins & Jenkins, Knoxville, Tenn., 1980-82, R.O. Smith Law Offices, Erwin, 1982-85; ptnr. Shults & Shults, 1985—. Gen. counsel Erwin Nat. Bank, 1985—; town atty., Unicoi, Tenn., 1999; Tenn. Supreme Ct. listed mediator; hearing officer Tenn. Supreme Ct. Bd. Profl. Responsibility Bd., 2001. Bd. dirs. Unicoi County Heritage Mus., Erwin, 1986-87, Unicoi County Ambulance Authority, Erwin, 1990-91, YMCA, Erwin, 1991-94; pres. Unicoi Elem. PTO, 1994, Unicoi County Mid. Sch. PTA, 1997; Tenn. Young Lawyers mock trial competition coach, 1993, 95-2001; Scales program vol., 1998. Recipient Contbn. to Edn. award Unicoi County Sch. Bd., 1994, 98. Mem. Female Attys. of Mountain Empire, DAR (regent 1990-92), Internat. Platform Speakers Assn. Republican. Methodist. Avocations: snow skiing, reading, travel, gardening, home improvement. Family and matrimonial, Probate, Real property. Home: 314 Greenbriar Dr Unicoi TN 37692-9748 Office: Shults & Shults 111 Gay St Erwin TN 37650-1227

SHULTZ, DANA HOWARD, lawyer, consultant; b. Nov. 10, 1949; s. Morris and Shirley (Gorman) S.; m. Chany Peggy Jakubowitz, Aug. 11, 1974. BA in Computer and Comm. Sci., U. Mich., 1971; JD, U. Calif-Berkeley, 1977. Bar: Calif, 1977, U.S. Dist. Ct. (no. dist.) Calif. 1977. Sr. staff atty. Mead Data Central, San Francisco, 1977-82; gen. counsel Baron Data Systems, San Leandro, Calif., 1982-85; western region mktg. mgr. Document Automation Corp., 1985-88; cons. Ziegler Ross Inc., San Francisco, 1990-92; prin. Dana Shultz & Assocs., Oakland, Calif., 1992-2000; v.p., legal counsel Visa Internat. Svc. Assn., 2000—. Bd. dirs. Cmty. Hospice East Bay, Berkeley, 1982-84. Mem. State Bar Calif., Computer Law Assn., Inst. Mgmt. Cons. (No. Calif. bd. mem. 1994-99), Piedmont Swim Club (pres. 1992-94). Home: 160 Bell Ave Piedmont CA 94611-3404 Office: Dana Internat Svc Assn PO Box 8999 San Francisco CA 94128-8999

SHULTZ, DONALD RICHARD, lawyer; b. Mitchell, S.D., Sept. 14, 1930; s. Milo W. and Ruth Ida (Train) S.; m. Frankie Joan Swett, Sept. 6, 1953; children: Jay C., Joni Jull, Jan Susan. JD, U. S.D., 1954. Bar: S.D. 1954. Mem. Lynn, Jackson, Shultz & Lebrun, Rapid City & Sioux Falls, S.D., 1956—. Served with U.S. Army, 1954-56. Mem. Am. Bd. Trial Advocates (nat. pres. 1993), Am. Coll. Trial Lawyers, Internat. Acad. Trial Lawyers, Internat. Soc. Barristers, S.D. State Bar (pres. 1984-85). Alternative dispute resolution, Federal civil litigation, General civil litigation. Home and Office: PO Box 8110 Rapid City SD 57709-8110 E-mail: dshultz@lynnjackson.com

SHULTZ, JOHN DAVID, lawyer; b. L.A., Oct. 9, 1939; s. Edward Patterson and Jane Elizabeth (Taylor) Schultz; m. Joanne Person, June 22, 1968; children: David Taylor Schultz, Steven Matthew Schultz. Student, Harvard Coll., 1960—61; BA, U. Ariz., 1964; JD, Boalt Hall, U. Calif., Berkeley, 1967. Bar: N.Y. 1968, Calif. 1978. Assoc. Cadwalader, Wickersham & Taft, N.Y.C., 1968—77; ptnr. Lawler, Felix & Hall, L.A., 1977—83, mem. exec. com., chmn. planning com., co-chmn. recruiting and hiring com.; ptnr. Morgan, Lewis & Bockius, 1983—, chmn. mgmt. com., mem. lateral entry com., chmn. profl. evaluation com., chmn. practice devel. com., chmn. recruiting com. Mem. adv. bd. Internat. and Comparative Law Ctr., Southwestern Legal Found., 1981—; active Practicing Law Inst. Adv. Bd., Corp. and Securities Law, 1992—; Trustee St. Thomas Ch., N.Y.C., 1969—72, Shore Acres Point Corp., Mamaroneck, NY, 1975—77. Mem.: ABA, Assn. Bar City of N.Y., State Bar Calif., N.Y. State Bar Assn., Jonathan Club (L.A.), Phi Delta Phi, Sigma Chi. Episcopalian. General corporate, Mergers and acquisitions. Office: Morgan Lewis & Bockius LLP 300 S Grand Ave Ste 22 Los Angeles CA 90071-3109

SHUMAKER, HAROLD DENNIS, lawyer; b. Richmond, Va., July 8, 1946; s. Milton and Virginia (Grossman) S.; m. Lucy Jane Light, May 23, 1969. BS, U. Ala., 1969; JD, New England Sch. Law, 1983. Bar: Pa. 1983, U.S. dist. Ct. (mid. dist.) Pa. 1988. From br. fin. mgr. to regional fin. mgr. Sperry Univac, Harrisburg, Pa., 1970-80; sr. project adminstr. IOCS, Inc., Waltham, Mass., 1980-83; assoc. Sponaugle & Sponaugle, P.C., Lancaster, Pa., 1983-84; pres., gen. counsel, dir. Horizon Technologies, Inc., Marietta, 1984—; sr. staff atty. Commodore Bus. Machines, Inc., West Chester, 1985-87; pvt. practice Marietta, 1987—. Pres. Marietta-Maytown East Donegal Bicentennial, 1974-76, Marietta Restoration Assn., 1976; chmn. Marietta Housing Hearing Bd., 1984-2001; chmn. Marietta Planning Commn., 1996—. With USNG, 1969-75. Mem. ABA, Pa. Bar Assn. (mem. unauthorized practice law com 1996-, elder law com. 2000-), Lancaster Bar Assn., Ctrl. Pa. U. Ala. Alumni Assn. (v.p. 1985-86, 95-96, 2000-01, pres. 1999-2000), Lions (pres. 1977-78, 89-90, 97-98, v.p. 1988-89, 93-97, bd. dirs. 1990—, Melvin Jones fellow for humanitarian work 1998). Democrat. Jewish. General corporate, Probate, Real property. Home and Office: 402 W Market St Marietta PA 17547-1205 E-mail: hdshumaker@dejazzd.com

SHUMAKER, ROGER LEE, lawyer; b. Sept. 6, 1950; s. Donald E. and Helen Jeannette (Gary) Shumaker; m. Cheralyn Jean Fee, Aug. 28, 1971; children: Donald Lawrence, William Lee, Cristin Leigh. BA, Manchester Coll., 1972; JD, Case Western Res. U., 1976. Bar: Ind. 1976, Ohio 1976. Assoc. Kiefer, Knecht, Rees, Meyer & Miller, Cleve., 1976—79; ptnr. Knecht, Rees, Meyer, Mekedis & Shumaker, 1979—86; shareholder McDonald, Hopkins Burke & Habar, L.P.A., 1986—. Trustee Manchester Coll., Ind., 1983—87, Ohio Presbyn. Retirement Svcs. Found., 1992—97, 1997sec., 1995—97. Mem. Breckenridge Village Coun., Ohio Presbyn. Cmtys., Willoughby, Ohio, 1981—97; mem. adv. com. Salvation Army Adv. Bd., Cleve., 1986—, sec., 1998—2000, vice chmn., 2000—; faculty mem. Notre Dame Estate Planning Inst., 1986, 1990. Fellow: Am. Coll. Trust & Estate Counsel (tech. in the practice com. 1989—); mem.: ABA (chmn. software evaluation com. 1983—85, chmn. com. on tech. and econs. in probate and planning 1985—89, mem. coun. sect. real property, probate and trust law 1991—, software editor Planning and Probate 1991—97, software coord. commn. legal tech. 1992—96), Ohio State Bar Assn., Bar Assn. Greater Cleve. (chmn. estate planning inst. 1983), Estate Planning Coun. (chmn. program com. 1987, treas. 1988, sec. 1989, v.p. 1990, pres. 1991). Democrat. Methodist. General corporate, Probate, Estate taxation. Office: McDonald Hopkins Burke & Haber Co LPA 2100 Bank One Ctr 600 Superior Ave E Ste 2100 Cleveland OH 44114-2653

SHUMAN, MARK PATRICK, lawyer, economist; b. Lawton, Okla., Jan. 22, 1952; s. Billy Joe and Jeane (Keating) Shuman. BA in Econs., U. Colo., 1975, MA in Econs., 1977, postgrad., 1978, JD, 1980. Bar: Colo. 1980, Wyo. 1990. Assoc. Brenman, Raskin, Friedlob & Tenenbaum, Denver,

1980-85, ptnr., 1986-87; gen. counsel, sec. Matrix Membranes Inc., Wheat Ridge, Colo., 1987-90; pvt. practice Riverton, Wyo., 1990-92; atty.-advisor divsn. corp. fin. U.S. Securities and Exch. Commn., 1992-96; spl. counselotfice assoc. dir. ops. U.S. SEC, 1997—. Bd. dirs. Community Tech. Skills Ctr., 1988-90, v.p. 1989, pres. 1990. Mem. ABA, Colo. Bar Assn. (chmn. uniform state law com. 1986, mem. ad hoc com. for revision of Colo. Revised Uniform Ltd. Partnership Act 1986), Aurora Bar Assn., Wyo. Bar Assn. General corporate, Environmental, Securities. Home: 4412 Eastwood Ct Fairfax VA 22032 Office: 450 Fifth St NW Stop 4-6 Washington DC 20549 E-mail: shumanm@sec.gov

SHURN, PETER JOSEPH, III, lawyer; b. Queens, N.Y., Aug. 30, 1946; s. Peter J. Jr. and Vivienne M. (Tagliarino) S.; m. Ingrid Kelbert; children: Steven Douglas, Vanessa Leigh, David Michael. BSEE magna cum laude, Poly. Inst. Bklyn., 1974; JD magna cum laude, New Eng. Sch. Law, 1977; LLM in Patent and Trade Regulation Law, George Washington U., 1981. Bar: N.C. 1977, Va. 1979, Tex. 1982. Rsch. scientist GTE Labs., 1965-77; sole practice Raleigh, N.C., 1977-78; assoc. Burns, Doane, Swecker & Mathis, Alexandria, Va., 1978-80; tech. advisor to judge U.S. Ct. Appeals (fed. cir.), 1980-81; ptnr. Arnold, White & Durkee, Houston, 1981-2000, Howrey, Simon, Arnold and White LLP, Houston, 2000—. Adj. prof. South Tex. Coll. Law, 1984-88, 2000—; invited mem. nat. panel neutrals Am. Arbitration Assn., 1993—; arbitrator Nat. Patent Bd., 1999—. Contbr. articles to profl. jours. With U.S. Army, 1966-68. Fellow Houston Bar Found. (life), Coll. State Bar Tex.; mem. ABA, ATLA, IEEE, Houston Bar Assn., Am. Patent Law Assn. (Robert C. Watson award 1981), Houston Patent Law Assn., Sigma Xi. Alternative dispute resolution, Federal civil litigation, Intellectual property. Office: Howrey Simon Arnold & White LLP 750 Bering Dr Houston TX 77057-2149 also: PO Box 4433 Houston TX 77210-4433

SHURTLEFF, MARK L. state attorney general; BA, Brigham Young U.; JD, U. Utah. Officer, atty. JAG USN, 1985—90; pvt. practice in law Calif., 1990—93; asst. atty. gen. State of Utah, 1993—97; dep. county atty. Salt Lake County, 1997—98; commr. Salt Lake County Commn., 1999—2000, chmn., 2000; atty. gen. State of Utah, 2001—. Leader Boy Scout troops, 1980—; anti-drug lectr., at-risk youth mentor. Office: State Capitol Bldg Rm 236 Salt Lake City UT 84114*

SIDAMON-ERISTOFF, CONSTANTINE, lawyer; b. N.Y.C., June 28, 1930; s. Simon C. and Anne Huntington (Tracy) Sidamon-E.; m. Anne Phipps, June 29, 1957; children: Simon, Elizabeth, Andrew. B.S.E. in Geol. Engring, Princeton U., 1952; LL.B., Columbia U., 1957. Clk., then assoc. firm Kelley Drye Newhall Maginnes & Warren, N.Y.C., 1957-64; individual practice law, 1964-65, 74-77; exec. asst. to Congressman John V. Lindsay, 1964-65; city coordinator Lindsay Mayoral Campaign, N.Y.C., 1965; asst. to mayor City of N.Y., 1966, commr. hwys., 1967-68, transp. adminstr., 1968-73; ptnr. Sidamon-Eristoff, Morrison, Warren, & Ecker, N.Y.C., 1978-83; counsel Morrison & de Roos, 1984-88; pvt. practice N.Y.C., 1988-89; regional adminstr. Region II EPA, 1989-93; of counsel Patterson, Belknap, Webb & Tyler, 1993-99, Lacher & Lovell-Taylor P.C., N.Y.C., 1999—. Mem. N.Y. State Met. Transp. Authority Bd., 1999—; commr. N.Y. State Jud. Commn. on Minorities, 1987—91; mem. Gov.'s Coun. on Hudson River Valley Greenway, 1989—89; trustee United Mut. Savs. Bank, N.Y.C., 1979—82, Phipps Houses, N.Y.C., 1974—, chmn., 1986—2001, chmn. emeritus, 2001—. Hon. trustee Am. the Beautiful Fund, Washington, 1985—97; chmn. Audubon Soc. N.Y., 1999—; trustee Allaverdy Found., N.Y.C., 1962—, Am. Farm Sch., Thessaloniki, Greece, 1973—79, Carnegie Hall, N.Y.C., 1967—92, Millbrook (N.Y.) Sch., 1971—89, hon. trustee, 1989—, Orange County (N.Y.) Citizens Found., 1974—81; bd. dirs., mem. exec. com. Mid-Hudson Pattern for Progress, Poughkeepsie, NY, 1975—89, chmn., 1981—85; bd. dirs. Coun. on Mcpl. Performance, N.Y.C., 1979—87, chmn., 1981—85, vice chmn., 1986—87; mem. Orange County (N.Y.) Planning Bd., 1997—; N.Y. State Rep. committeeman, 1980—89; bd. dirs. Tolstoy Found., N.Y.C., 1975—, chmn., bd. dirs., 1979—89, 1994—; bd. dirs. Caramoor Ctr. Music and Arts, Katonah, NY, 1961—80; chmn., bd. dirs. Boyce Thompson Inst. for Plant Rsch., Ithaca, 1994—. Decorated Bronze Star; co-recipient Civic Leadership award (with wife), Citizens Union, 1997, Force for Nature award (with wife), Natural Resources Def. Coun., 1999, Environ. Leadership award (with wife), Nat. Audubon Soc., 2001; recipient Honor award, Kings County chpt. N.Y. State Soc. Profl. Engrs., 1969, Greater N.Y. coun. Girls Scouts U.S., 1973, Bd. Leadership award, Coun. Mcpl. Performance, 1984, Transp. Manof Yr. award, Greater N.Y. March of Dimes, 1985, award of excellence, Mid-Hudson Pattern for Progress, 1990, Honor award, Nat. and N.Y. Parks and Conservation Assn., 1992, Bronze medal, USEPA, 1993. Mem. ABA, N.Y. State Bar Assn., Assn. of Bar of City of N.Y., N.Y. County Lawyers Assn., Kent Moot Ct., AIME, Phi Delta Phi, Delta Psi. Eastern Orthodox. Clubs: Century Assn. (N.Y.C.), Knickerbocker (N.Y.C.), Racquet and Tennis (N.Y.C.). Office: Lacher & Lovell-Taylor PC 6th Fl 770 Lexington Ave New York NY 10021-8165 E-mail: cseristoff@lltlaw.com, ananouri@aol.com

SIDDALL, MICHAEL SHERIDAN, lawyer; b. Milw., Jan. 5, 1948; s. James Joseph and Mary Elizabeth (Lynch) S. BS, U. Wis., Oshkosh, 1972; JD, Drake U., 1974. Bar: Wis. 1974, U.S. Dist. Ct. (ea. and we. dists.) Wis. 1975. Ptnr. Herrling, Clark, Hartzheim & Siddall Ltd., Appleton, Wis., 1974—. Atty. chmn. Wis. Patients Compensation Panel, Appleton, 1980—; instr. U. Wis. Law Sch., Madison, 1981—. Served to sgt. paratrooper, U.S. Army, 1967-69, Vietnam. Mem. ABA (tort and ins. practice sect.), Assn. Trial Lawyers Am., Wis. Acad. Trial Lawyers, Am. Arbitration Assn. (arbitrator), Nat. Bd. Trial Adv. (cert. civil trial adv. specialist). State civil litigation, Insurance, Personal injury. Home: 125 Pine Ct Appleton WI 54914-1983 Office: 800 N Lynndale Dr Appleton WI 54914-3028 E-mail: msiddall@herringclark.com

SIDES, JACK DAVIS, JR. lawyer; b. Dallas, Sept. 18, 1939; s. Jack Davis Sr. and Edith Eugenia (Lowrie) S.; m. Nancy Pauline Cantwell, July 22, 1967 (div. Sept. 1976); children: Mary Katharine, Jack Davis III; m. Laura Gail Miller, Aug. 2, 1979; children: Susan Ashley, Stacy Anne. BBA, U. Tex., 1962, JD with honors, 1963. Bar: Tex. 1963. Assoc. Jackson, Walker, et al, Dallas, 1963-67, White, McElroy, White, Sides & Rector, Dallas, 1968-78; sole practice, 1978—. Editor: U. Tex. Law Review, 1963. With USAFNG, 1963-69. Fellow Dallas Bar Found., Tex. Bar Found. (life); mem. ABA, Tex. Bar Assn. (grievance subcom. 1979-86), Dallas Bar Assn. (ethics com. 1973-77, jud. com. 1988—), Tex. Assn. Def. Counsel, Dallas Assn. Def. Counsel (sec. 1973-74). Republican. Methodist. Club: Brook Hollow Golf (Dallas). Avocations: reading, tennis, exercising. Federal civil litigation, State civil litigation. Office: 2301 Cedar Springs Rd Ste 350 Dallas TX 75201-7803 E-mail: jacksides@aol.com

SIDMAN, ROBERT JOHN, lawyer; b. Cleve., Aug. 4, 1943; s. Charles Frances and Louise (Eckert) S.; m. Mary Mato, July 29, 1967; children: Christa Mary, Alicia Mary. BA, Benedictine Coll., 1965; JD, U. Notre Dame, 1968. Bar: Ohio 1968, U.S. Dist. Ct. (so. dist.) Ohio 1970, U.S. Ct. Appeals (6th cir.) 1971, U.S. Supreme Ct. 1971. Law clk. U.S. Dist. Ct. (so. dist.) Ohio, Columbus, 1968-70; assoc. Mayer, Tingley & Hurd, 1970-75; judge Bankruptcy Ct. U.S. Dist. Ct. (so. dist.) Ohio, 1975-82; ptnr. Vorys, Sater, Seymour & Pease, 1982—. Prof. Ohio State U. Law Sch., Columbus, 1984, 85, 86. Mem. Nat. Conf. Bankruptcy Judges (bd. dirs. 1981-82), Assn. Former Bankruptcy Judges (bd. dirs. 1983-89, treas. 1986-87, pres. 1988-89). Bankruptcy, Federal civil litigation, Contracts commercial. Office: Vorys Sater Seymour & Pease PO Box 1008 52 E Gay St Columbus OH 43215-3161 E-mail: rjsidman@vssp.com, rsidman843@aol.com

SIEDZIKOWSKI, HENRY FRANCIS, lawyer; b. Chester, Pa., Dec. 27, 1953; s. Henry W. and Virginia (Szymanski) S. BA cum laude, Juniata Coll., 1975; JD magna cum laude, Villanova U., 1979. Bar: Pa. 1979, U.S. Dist. Ct. (ea. dist.) Pa. 1979, U.S. Ct. Appeals (3d cir.) 1979, U.S. Ct. Appeals (8th cir.) 1981, U.S. Dist. Ct. (we. dist.) Pa. 1986. Assoc. Dilworth, Paxson, Kalish & Kauffman, Phila., 1979-86; ptnr. Baskin Flaherty Elliott & Mannino P.C., 1986-90, Elliott Bray & Riley, Phila., 1990-92, Elliott, Vanaskie & Riley, 1992-94, Elliot, Reihner, Siedzikowski & Egan, 1994—. Mem. hearing com. disciplinary bd. Supreme Ct. Pa., 1985-91. Mem. ABA (chmn. Lanham act subcom. of bus. torts com. of litigation sect. 1986—, rotating editor newsletter of antitrust sect. franchisee com.), Pa. Bar Assn., Phila. Bar Assn. (chmn. subcom. disciplinary rules for profl. responsibility com. 1984-90). Democrat. Roman Catholic. Bankruptcy, Federal civil litigation, Franchising. Office: Elliott Reihner et al 925 Harvest Dr Blue Bell PA 19422-1956 E-mail: hfs@erse.com

SIEGAL, JOEL DAVIS, lawyer; b. Plainfield, N.J., Feb. 9, 1937; s. Samuel and Florence (Ravitz) S.; m. Ronny J. Greenwald, Oct. 16, 1972; children: Samuel Jesse, Evan Charles. BA in Polit. Sci., U. Pa., 1958; JD, Yale U., 1961; MA in Internat. Rels., U. Stockholm, 1963. Bar: N.J., 1962, N.Y., 1965; U.S. Dist. Ct. N.J., 1962, U.S. Ct. Appeals (3rd cir.), 1963, U.S. Supreme Ct., N.Y., 1969, U.S. Dist. Ct. (so. and ea. dist.) N.Y., 1975. Law clk. to Hon. Arthur S. Lane, Newark, 1961-62; law clk. to Hon. Phillip Forman, 1963-64; assoc. Hellring Lindeman Goldstein & Siegal, Newark, 1967-70, ptnr., 1970—. Commr. Nat. Conf. Commrs. on Uniform Laws, 1991-98; mem. U.S. Dist. Ct. Adv. Bd., Newark, 1991-92. Contbr. articles to profl. jours. Mcpl. chmn. Dem. Party, Borough of Alpine, N.J., 1983-86. Fellow Am. Bar Found.; mem. ABA, N.J. Bar Assn., Essex County Bar Assn., Assn. Fed. Bar N.J. (nat. del. N.J. 1974, pres. 1990-92, adv. bd. 1993—), Harmonie Club of N.Y.C. Democrat. Jewish. General civil litigation, Family and matrimonial. Office: Hellring Lindeman Goldstein Siegal 1 Gateway Ctr Fl 8 Newark NJ 07102-5386 Fax: (973) 621-7406. E-mail: jdsiegal@hlgslaw.com

SIEGAN, BERNARD HERBERT, lawyer, educator; b. Chgo., July 28, 1924; s. David and Jeannette S.; m. Sharon Goldberg, June 15, 1952 (dec. Feb. 1985); m. Shelley Zifferblatt, Nov. 19, 1995. AA, Herzl. Jr. Coll., Chgo., 1943, 46; Student, Roosevelt Coll., Chgo., 1946-47; J.D., U. Chgo., 1949. Bar: Ill. 1950. Practiced in, Chgo.; partner firm Siegan & Karlin, 1952-73; pres., sec. various small corps. and gen. partner in partnerships engaged in real estate ownership and devel., 1955-70; weekly columnist Freedom newspaper chain, other papers, 1974-79. Cons. law and econs. program U. Chgo. Law Sch., 1970-73; adj. prof. law U. San Diego Law Sch., 1973-74, Disting. prof., 1975—; adj. scholar Cato Inst., Washington, 1991—, Heritage Found., 1992—; cons. windfalls and wipeouts project HUD, 1973-74; cons. FTC, 1985-86, U.S. Justice Dept., dir. constl. bibliog. project, 1986-88; keynote speaker 5th Internat. Conf. on Urbanism, Porto Alegre, Brazil, 1989; nominated by Pres. Reagan to U.S. Ct. Appeals (9th cir.) Feb. 2, 1987, confirmation denied July 14, 1988 by party line vote Senate Judiciary Com. Author: Land Use Without Zoning, 1972, Spanish edit., 1995, Other People's Property, 1976, Economic Liberties and the Constitution, 1980, The Supreme Court's Constitution: An Inquiry Into Judicial Review and Its Impact on Society, 1987, Drafting a Constitution for a Nation or Republic Emerging into Freedom, 1992, 2d edit., 1994, Portuguese, Ukrainian, Polish and Spanish edits., 1993, Property and Freedom: The Constitution, Supreme Court and Land Use Regulation, 1997, Adapting a Constitution to Protect Freedom and Provide Abundance (in Bulgarian), 1998, Property Rights: From Magna Carta to the Fourteenth Amendment, 2001; editor: Planning without Prices, 1977, The Interaction of Economics and the Law, 1977, Regulation, Economics and the Law, 1979, Government, Regulation and the Economy, 1980. Mem. pres.-elect's Task Force on Housing, 1980-81; mem. Pres.'s Commn. on Housing, 1981-82; mem. Nat. Commn. on bicentennial of U.S. Constn., 1985-91; chmn. adv. com. Affordable Housing Conf., San Diego, 1985, Rights of Regulated Conf., Coronado, Calif., 1976; chmn. Conf. on the Taking Issue, 1976; mem. Houston Regional Urban Design Team, Study of Houston, 1990; mem. U.S. team Bulgarian Econ. Growth and Transition Project, 1990; mem. devel. bd. Mingei Internat. Mus. World Folk Art, 1981-84. Served with AUS, 1943-46. Research fellow law and econs. U. Chgo. Law Sch., 1968-69; Urban Land Inst. research fellow, 1976-86; recipient Leander J. Monks Meml. Fund award Inst. Humane Studies, 1972, George Washington medal Freedom Founds. at Valley Forge, 1981, Spl. award Liberal Inst. of Rio Grande do Sul, Porto Alegre, Brazil, 1989, Thorsnes award for outstanding legal scholarship, 1998; named Univ. Prof., U. San Diego, 1997-98. Home: 6005 Camino De La Costa La Jolla CA 92037-6519

SIEGEL, BERNARD LOUIS, lawyer; b. Pitts., Sept. 15, 1938; s. Ralph Robert and Frieda Sara (Stein) S.; m. Marcia Margolis, Sept. 3, 1961 (div. Aug. 1983); children: Jonathan, Sharon; m. Susan Erickson, Aug. 31, 1997 (div. June 2001). BA, Brandeis U., 1960; JD, Harvard U., 1963. Bar: Pa. 1964, U.S. Dist. Ct. (we. dist.) Pa. 1964, U.S. Dist. Ct. (ea. dist.) Pa. 1985, U.S. Ct. Appeals (3d cir.) 1985, U.S. Supreme Ct. 1985. Assoc. Silin, Eckert & Burke, Erie, Pa., 1963-66; ptnr. Silin, Eckert, Burke & Siegel, 1966-73; 1st asst. dist. atty. Erie County, 1972-76; dep. atty. gen. Pa. Dept. Justice, Phila., 1976-78; dep. dist. atty. Dist. Atty. of Phila., 1978-86; pvt. practice Phila., 1986—. Adj. prof. La Salle U., Phila., 1986-98; lectr. Fed. Law Enforcement Tng. Ctr., Glynco, Ga., 1986-97, Mercyhurst Coll., Erie, 1974-76, Nat. Coll. Dist. Attys., Houston, 1978-85; adj. prof. Temple U. law sch., 1995—; mem. criminal rules com. Pa. Supreme Ct., Phila., 1976-85; commr. Pa. Crime Commn., Harrisburg, 1976-79. Author: (with others) Pennsylvania Grand Jury Practice, 1983, By No Extraordinary Means, 1986. Mem. ABA, Nat. Assn. Criminal Def. Lawyers, Pa. Assn. Criminal Def. Lawyers (bd. dirs. 1988—), Pa. Bar Assn. (chmn. criminal law sect. 1988-91), Phila. Bar Assn. (chmn. criminal justice sect. 1990-91). Democrat. Jewish. Avocations: bicycling, reading, hiking. Criminal. Office: 1515 Market St Ste 1915 Philadelphia PA 19102-1920 E-mail: blsesq@snip.net

SIEGEL, CORDELL, lawyer; b. St. Louis, May 23, 1941; s. Ben and Ann (Gornstein) S.; m. Helene Beverly Spector, Aug. 15, 1965; children: Craig, Julie. BSc magna cum laude, St. Louis U., 1964, JD cum laude, 1966. Bar: Mo. 1966. Assoc. Morris A. Shenker, St. Louis, 1966-84; mem. Susman, Schermer, Rimmel & Shifrin LLC, 1984-2000; prin. Frankel, Rubin, Bond & Dubin PC, 2001—. Instr. law St. Louis U., 1966-68. Coord. St. Louis Commn. on Crime and Law Enforcement, 1969-73; region 5 jud. standing and tech. adv. com. Mo. Coun. Criminal Justice, 1974-75. Mem. ABA, Assn. Trial Lawyers Am., Mo. Bar Assn., Met. Bar Assn. St. Louis, Lawyers Assn. St. Louis, St. Louis County Bar Assn., Order of Woolsack, Beta Gamma Sigma, Alpha Sigma Nu. Jewish. General civil litigation, Family and matrimonial, Personal injury. Home: 14412 Tealcrest Dr Chesterfield MO 63017-2314 Office: Frankel Rubin Bond & Dubin PC 231 S Bemiston Ste 1111 Saint Louis MO 63105-1914 Fax: 314-726-5837

SIEGEL, EDWARD, lawyer; b. Asbury Park, N.J., Jan. 15, 1931; s. Nathan Albert and Fannie Siegel; m. Helen Dorothy Haber, Aug. 29, 1954; children: Sharon, Frances. BA, U. Fla., 1952, JD, 1955. Bar: Fla. 1955. Spl. asst. atty. gen. Office Atty. Gen. Fla., Tallahassee, 1955; ptnr. Adams, Rothstein & Siegel, Jacksonville, Fla., 1957-90. Author: How to Avoid Lawyers, 1969, Defend Yourself! The Moneysworth Legal Advisor, 1972, Just Like a Lawyer, 1993; mem. editorial bd. Fla. Bar Jour., 1979-86. Bd. dirs. Jacksonville Jewish Ctr., 1968-70; bd. dirs., v.p. Jewish Family and Children's Svcs., 1970-75; trustee Jacksonville Libr. Bd., 1978-82. Served as 1st lt. USAF, 1955-57. Mem. ABA, Fla. Bar Assn., Jacksonville Bar Assn. (chmn. fee arbitration com. 1976-77), Blue Key, Order of Coif, Phi Beta Kappa. Democrat. Consumer commercial, Family and matrimonial, Real property. Home: 6855 San Sabastian Ave Jacksonville FL 32217-2731

SIEGEL, HOWARD JEROME, lawyer; b. Chgo., July 29, 1942; s. Leonard and Idele (Lehrner) S.; m. Diane L. Gerber; children: Sari D., Allison J., James G. BS, U. Ill., 1963; JD, Northwestern U., 1966. Bar: Ill. 1966, U.S. Dist. Ct. (no. dist.) Ill. 1967. Assoc. Ancel, Stonesifer & Glink, Chgo., 1966-70; ptnr. Goldstine & Siegel, Summit, Ill., 1970-75; sole practice Chgo., 1975-77; pres. Wexler, Siegel & Shaw, Ltd., 1978-82; ptnr. Keck, Mahin & Cate, 1982-95, Neal Gerber & Eisenberg, Chgo., 1995-99; counsel Fagel & Haber, 1999—. Bd. dirs. various corps. Mem. ABA, Chgo. Bar Assn., Ill. Bar Assn., Standard Club (Chgo.), Twin Orchard Country Club (Long Grove, Ill.). General corporate, Real property. Office: FabelHaberLLC 55 E Monroe 40th Fl Chicago IL 60603 E-mail: hsiegel@fagelhaber.com

SIEGEL, JEFFREY NORTON, lawyer; b. N.Y.C., Nov. 27, 1942; s. George Siegel and Rose (Friedman) Gerber; m. Judith Sharon Chused, June 11, 1966; children: Linda. AB, Brown U., 1964; LLB, Harvard U., 1967. Bar: N.Y. 1968. Assoc., ptnr. Golenbock & Barell, N.Y.C., 1967-89; ptnr. Whitman & Ransom, 1990-93, Shack Siegel Katz Flaherty & Goodman P.C., N.Y.C., 1993—. Mem. bus. com. The Jewish Mus. Mem. ABA, Assn. Bar City N.Y. (com. securities regulation 1987-90, com. profl. responsibility 179-84), Phi Beta Kappa. General corporate, Mergers and acquisitions, Securities. Home: 975 Park Ave New York NY 10028-0323 Office: Shack Siegel Katz Flaherty & Goodman PC 530 5th Ave New York NY 10036-5101

SIEGEL, JULIAN LEE, lawyer; b. Washington, July 22, 1928; s. Harry Alec and Etta (Schofer) S. BS, George Washington U., 1954, JD, 1959. Bar: D.C. 1960, U.S. Ct. Appeals (D.C. cir.) 1960, Mass. 1969, U.S. Supreme Ct. 1980, U.S. Ct. Appeals (fed. cir.) 1982; registered patent atty. U.S. Patent and Trademark Office. Mathematician U.S. Naval Obs., Washington, 1954-62; patent atty. USAF, Waltham, Mass., 1962-76, Hanscom AFB, 1976-97; chief patent and data br. Electronics Sys. Ct., 1997—. Chief intellectual property law. With USN, 1946-48. Mem. Boston Patent Law Assn., North Medford Club (pres. 1976-78). Republican. Home: 56 Fifer Ln Lexington MA 02420-1225 Office: ESC/JAZ 40 Wright St Hanscom AFB MA 01731-2903 E-mail: julian.siegel@hanscom.af.mil

SIEGEL, KENNETH ERIC, lawyer; b. Pitts., June 1, 1947; s. Abraham and Cecelia June (Kholas) S.; m. Maryann Therese Fitzgerald, May 1970; children— Eric Kenneth, Deborah Kathleen, Kevin Marc. B.S. in Bus. Adminstrn., Duquesne U., 1969; J.D., Temple U., 1972. Bar: Pa. 1972, U.S. Ct. Appeals (2d cir.) 1981, U.S. Ct. Appeals (5th cir.) 1980, U.S. Ct. Appeals (7th cir.) 1979, U.S. Ct. Appeals (8th cir.) 1983, U.S. Ct. Appeals (9th cir.) 1980, U.S. Ct. Appeals (10th cir.) 1980, U.S. Ct. Appeals (11th cir.) 1984, U.S. Ct. Appeals (D.C. cir.) 1978, U.S. Supreme Ct. 1980. Trial atty. bur. enforcement ICC, Washington, 1972-76; atty. office gen. counsel U.S. Gen. Acctg. Office, Washington, 1976-77; counsel Am. Trucking Assn., Inc., Washington, 1977— . Editor: Assn. Transp. Practitioners Jour. Coach and Officer, Sterling Youth Soccer Assn., Va., 1984. Mem. ABA, Pa. Bar Assn., Assn. Transp. Practitioners. Administrative and regulatory, General corporate, Transportation. Home: 1074 Tottenham Ct Sterling VA 20164-4820 Office: Law Dept Am Trucking Assn Inc & Am Trucking Assn Ligation Ctr 2200 Mill Rd Alexandria VA 22314-4654

SIEGEL, LISA BETH, lawyer, accountant; b. Hollywood, Fla., Aug. 30, 1963; d. Jerry and Laura (Rowen) S. BS in Acctg., U. Fla., 1985; JD, Nova Southeastern U., 1995. Bar: Fla. 1995; CPA, Fla. Acct. various firms, Fla. and N.Y., 1985-92; assoc. Belson & Lewis, Boca Raton, Fla., 1998—. Mem. editl. bd. Nova Law Rev. Mem. AICPAs, Fla. Inst. CPAs, Fla. Bar Assn., Am. Assn. Attys. and CPAs. Office: Belson & Lewis Attys at Law 2000 Glades Rd Ste 306 Boca Raton FL 33431-8504

SIEGEL, MARK JORDAN, lawyer; b. Dallas, Feb. 22, 1949; s. Jack H. and Zelda (Sikora) S.; m. Linda Siegel; children: Jenna, Jason, Jordan. BS in Psychology, North Tex. State U., 1972; JD, South Tex. Coll. Law, 1977. Bar: Tex. 1977, U.S. Dist. Ct. (no. dist.) Tex. 1980, U.S. Ct. Appeals (11th and 5th cirs.) 1982, U.S. Supreme Ct. 1982. Pvt. practice, Dallas, 1977-87. Bd. dirs. Scotch Corp., Dallas. Sponsor Civil Justice Found.; mem. North Dallas 40. Named one of Outstanding Young Men of Am. Mem. ATLA, Tex. Trial Lawyers Assn., Dallas Trial Lawyers Assn., Nat. Bd. Tril Advocacy (cert. civil trial specialist), Tex. Bd. Legal Specialization (cert. civl. trial law). State civil litigation, Personal injury. Office: 3607 Fairmount St Dallas TX 75219-4710 E-mail: mjs@siegellegal.com

SIEGEL, PAUL, judge; b. Troy, N.Y., May 7, 1938; s. Benjamin and Mary (Silverman) S.; 1 child, Mark Aron; m. Janique Auvertin, Apr. 30, 1994. BS in Physics magna cum laude, U. Miami, 1958, LLB cum laude, 1962. Bar: Fla. 1963, D.C. 1964, U.S. Supreme Ct. 1967, U.S. Ct. Appeals (5th cir.) 1967, U.S. Ct. Appeals (11th cir.) 1982; cert. civil trial lawyer Fla. Bar. Mem. gen. counsel's office AEC, Washington, 1962-65; ptnr. Sinclair, Louis, Siegel, Heath, Nussbaum & Zavertnik, P.A., Miami, Fla., 1972-91; judge Dade County Cir. Ct., 1991—. Editor in chief, exec. editor U. Miami Law Rev. Chmn. bd. dirs. Alliance Francaise of Dade County, 1983-87, pres., 1990-92; pres. Pro-Mozart Soc. Greater Miami, 1984-92. Home: 235 E San Marino Dr Miami FL 33139-1151 Office: Dade County Courthouse 73 W Flagler St Ste 412 Miami FL 33130-1707 E-mail: psiegel@jud11.flcourts.org

SIEGEL, SARAH ANN, lawyer; b. Providence, Aug. 29, 1956; BA in History cum laude, Brandeis U., 1978; JD, Washington U., St. Louis, 1981. Bar: Mo. 1982, U.S. Dist. Ct. (ea. dist.) Mo. 1983. Assoc. atty., St. Louis, 1982-83; staff atty. Land Clearance for Redevel. Authority, 1983-85, gen. counsel, 1985-88, Econ. Devel. Corp., St. Louis, 1988-90, St. Louis Devel. Corp., 1990-91; spl. counsel for devel. City of St. Louis, 1991-92; assoc. Suelthaus & Walsh, P.C., St. Louis, 1992-95, prin., 1995-99; v.p., gen. counsel Dierbergs Mkts. Inc., 1999—. Pres. Central Reform Congregation, St. Louis, 1991-93, v.p., 1989-91, bd. dirs. 1987-89; bd. dirs. St. Louis Art Fair, 2001—, Friends of the Sheldon Concert Hall, 1997—. Mem. ABA, Mo. Bar Assn. (vice chair com. on eminent domain 1990-91, steering com. 1987-89, 95-96), Women's Lawyer Assn. (bd. dirs. 1985-90, v.p. 1989-90), Am. Corp. Counsel Assn. Avocations: hiking, swimming. General corporate, Real property, Alternative dispute. E-mail: siegels@dierbergs.com

SIEGEL, STANLEY, lawyer, educator; b. N.Y.C., Mar. 2, 1941; s. David Aaron and Rose (Minsky) S. B.S. summa cum laude, NYU, 1960; J.D. magna cum laude, Harvard U., 1963. Bar: N.Y. 1963, D.C. 1964, Mich. 1970, Calif. 1976; CPA, Md. Atty. Office Sec. of Air Force, 1963-66; asst. prof. law U. Mich., Ann Arbor, 1966-69, assoc. prof., 1969-71, prof., 1971-74; ptnr. Honigman, Miller, Schwartz & Cohn, Detroit, 1974-76; prof. law UCLA, 1976-86, NYU, 1986—, assoc. dean, 1987-89. Vis. prof. Stanford Law Sch., 1973, Ctrl. European U., Budapest, 1993—, U. Konstanz, Germany, 1996, Tel Aviv U., 1998; fellow Max-Planck Inst., Hamburg, 1988; cons. reorgn. U.S. Postal Svc., 1969-71; exec. sec. Mich. Law Revision Commn., 1973; mem. bd. examiners AICPA, 1980-83; mem. editl. bd. Lexis Electronic Author's Press, 1996-98. Author: (with Schulman and Moscow) Michigan Business Corporations, 1979, (with Conard and Knauss) Enterprise Organization, 4th edit., 1987, (with D. Siegel)

Accounting and Financial Disclosure: A Guide to Basic Concepts, 1983, (with others) Swiss Company Law, 1996. Served to capt. USAF, 1963-66. Mem. ABA, D.C. Bar Assn., Calif. Bar Assn., Assn. of Bar of City of N.Y., Am. Law Inst., AICPA. Office: NYU Law Sch 40 Washington Sq S New York NY 10012-1099 E-mail: stanleysiegel@nyu.edu

SIEGEL, STEVEN RICHARD, lawyer; b. Lynn, Mass., June 18, 1944; s. Henry William and Marcy (Starr) S.; AB, Bowdoin Coll., 1965; JD, NYU, 1968; m. Sherry Garber, Aug. 26, 1966; children: Matthew, Julie. Bar: Mass. 1968. Assoc., Mintz, Levin, Cohn, Ferris, Glovsky and Popeo, P.C., 1968-71; ptnr. Topkins, Gaffin, Siegel & Krattenmaker, P.C., Boston, 1971-73; v.p. SCA Svcs., 1973-79; v.p., gen. counsel, v.p. adminstrn. Instrumentation Lab., Inc., Lexington, Mass., 1979-83; v.p., gen. counsel, sec. Docktor Pet Ctrs., Inc., First Internat. Svc. Corp. d/b/a Command Performance, 1983-88, Nutrient Cosmetics, Ltd. d/b/a "I" Natural Cosmetics, 1983-88; v.p. Rohammer Corp., Boston, 1988-90; ptnr. Wayne, Lazares, Chappell, P.C., Boston, 1990—; chmn. DD U.K. Ltd. Mem. ABA, Dunkin Donuts Am. Franchise Assn. (chmn. 1993—), Assn. Corp. Growth (past pres. Boston chpt.), Mass. Bar Assn., Boston Bar Assn., Dunkin Donuts Ind. Franchise Owners Assn. (pres. 1992—). General corporate, Franchising. Home: 6 Old Coach Rd Sudbury MA 01776-1316 Office: 200 State St Boston MA 02109-2605

SIEGER, JOHN ANTHONY, lawyer; b. Chgo., Sept. 1, 1942; s. Joseph F. and Alice J. (Hayes) S.; m. Mary K. Heffernan, Feb. 19, 1966; children—Maggie, Kerry, Matt, Bill, Mike. B.A., U. Notre Dame, 1964; J.D., Georgetown U., 1967. Bar: Ill. 1967, U.S. Dist. Ct. (no. dist.) Ill. 1967, U.S. Ct. Appeals (5th cir.) 1973, Tex. 1974, U.S. Dist. Ct. (so. dist.) Tex. 1984. Atty., U.S. Dept. Labor, Chgo., 1967-70, Texaco Inc., Chgo., 1970-71, Houston, 1971-78; atty., sr. atty., assoc. gen. atty. Panhandle Eastern Corp., Houston, 1978-82, gen. atty., 1982-86, v.p., gen. counsel, 1986-89, sr. v.p., gen. counsel, 1989—. Mem. exec. com. Harris County Democratic party, Houston, 1982-85; election judge City of Hunters Creek Village, Tex., 1982-83. Research fellow Southwestern Legal Found., 1986—. Mem. Chgo. Bar Assn., State Bar Tex. (committeeman 1982-89). Roman Catholic. Antitrust, Federal civil litigation, General corporate. Office: Panhandle Ea Corp 5400 Westheimer Ct PO Box 1642 Houston TX 77251-1642

SIEGFRIED, DAVID CHARLES, retired lawyer; b. N.Y.C., Feb. 15, 1942; s. Charles Albert and Marjorie Claire (Young) S.; m. Meri Stephanie Smith; children: Karin Elisabeth, Christine Elise. AB summa cum laude, Princeton U., 1964; JD, Harvard U., 1967. Bar: N.Y. 1970. Assoc. Milbank, Tweed, Hadley & McCloy, N.Y.C., 1968-76, ptnr. 1977-79, 83-85, 88-98, resident ptnr. Hong Kong and Singapore, 1979-83, 85-88. Bd. dirs. PALS; speaker in field. Bd. dirs. Cmty. Agys. Corp. N.J., Inc., v.p. found. 1st lt. USAR, 1967-74. Mem.: ABA, N.Y. State Bar Assn., Assn. of Bar of City of N.Y., Millburn N.J. Hist. Preservation Commn. (vice chmn.), Millburn-Short Hills Hist. Soc. (pres.), Princeton U. (exec. com. alumni coun.). Congregationalist. Clubs: Princeton (New York), Short Hills (N.J.), Am. (Hong Kong/Singapore), Tanglin (Singapore), Cricket. Avocations: running, tennis, historic reading. Banking, Contracts commercial, Private international. Home: 30 Western Dr Short Hills NJ 07078-3230

SIEKMAN, THOMAS CLEMENT, lawyer; b. Somerville, Mass., Sept. 22, 1941; s. Aloysius C. and Estelle M. (Forte) S.; children: Michael T., James T., Amy K. BS in Engring., Merrimack Coll., 1963; JD, Villanova U., 1966. Bar: Mass. 1966, U.S. Dist. Ct. Mass. 1969. Patent atty. Bethlehem (Pa.) Steel, 1966-68, Mohawk Data Scis., Stoneham, Mass., 1968-72, Chittick, Thompson & Pfund, Boston, 1972-73; from patent atty. to v.p. and gen. counsel Digital Equipment Corp., Maynard, 1973-98; Sr. v.p., gen. coun., sec. Compaq Computer Corp., 1998—. Bd. dirs., chmn. N.E. Legal Found. Trustee Mass. Taxpayers Found., Merrimack Coll.; mem. New Eng. Legal Found.; mem. Houston cmty. adv. bd. Teach Am.; bd. dirs. Houston African-Am. Mus. Mem. ABA, Am. Corp. Counsel Assn., Assn. Gen. Counsel. Avocations: squash, skiing. Home: 3435 Westheimer # 1707 Houston TX 77027 Office: Compaq Computer Corp PO Box 692000 Houston TX 77269-2000 Home Fax: 713-599-0953; Office Fax: (281) 518-8209. E-mail: tom.siekman@compaq.com

SIFFERT, JOHN SAND, lawyer, educator, writer; b. N.Y.C., Mar. 26, 1947; s. Robert Spencer and Miriam (Sand) S.; m. Goldie Alfasi-Siffert, June 1, 1975; children: David Alfasi, Matthew Alfasi. BA, Amherst Coll., 1969; JD, Columbia U., 1972. Bar: N.Y. 1973, U.S. Dist. Ct. (so. dist.) N.Y. 1974, (ea. dist.) N.Y. 1974, U.S. Ct. Appeals (2d cir.) 1974, U.S. Supreme Ct. 1979. Law clk. to Hon. Murray I. Gurfein U.S. Dist. Ct. (so. dist.) N.Y., 1972-74; asst. U.S. atty. (so. dist.) N.Y., 1974-79; ptnr. Fulop & Hardee and predcessor firm Barovick, Konecky et al, N.Y.C., 1979-83, Lankler & Siffert, N.Y.C., 1983-84, Lankler, Siffert & Wohl, N.Y.C., 1984—. Adj. prof. NYU, 1979—; mem. adv. coun. procurement policy bd. City of N.Y., 1991-95; bd. dirs. N.Y.C. Off-Track-Betting, 1995—, NYLPI, 1998—; spl. master First Dept. Appellate Divsn., 1999—. Co-author: Business Crime, 1981, Modern Federal Jury Instructions-Criminal, Modern Federal Jury Instructions-Civil. Fellow: Am. Coll. Trial Lawyers (chair com. on admission to fellowship 2001—); mem.: ABA, N.Y. State Bar Assn., Assn. of Bar of City of N.Y., Fed. Bar Coun. (pres. Inns of Ct. 2001—). Democrat. Jewish. Federal civil litigation, State civil litigation, Criminal. Office: Lankler Siffert & Wohl 500 5th Ave Fl 33 New York NY 10110-3398 E-mail: jsiffert@lswlaw.com

SIFTON, CHARLES PROCTOR, federal judge; b. N.Y.C., Mar. 18, 1935; s. Paul F. and Claire G. S.; m. Susan Scott Rowland, May 20, 1986; children: Samuel, Tobias, John. A.B., Harvard U., 1957; LL.B., Columbia U., 1961. Bar: N.Y. 1961. Assoc. Cadwalader, Wickersham & Taft, 1961-62, 64-66; staff atty. U.S. Senate Fgn. Rels. Com., 1962-63; asst. U.S. atty. N.Y.C., 1966-69; ptnr. LeBoeuf, Lamb, Leiby and MacRae, 1969-77; judge U.S. Dist. Ct. (ea. dist.) N.Y., Bklyn., 1977—, chief judge, 1995-2000, sr. judge, 2000—. Mem. Bar Assn. City of N.Y., Jud. Conf. U.S. Office: US Dist Ct US Courthouse 225 Cadman Plz E Rm 244 Brooklyn NY 11201-1818

SIGETY, CHARLES EDWARD, lawyer, family business consultant; b. N.Y.C., Oct. 10, 1922; s. Charles and Anna (Toth) S.; m. Katharine K. Snell, July 17, 1948; children: Charles, Katharine, Robert, Cornelius, Elizabeth. BS, Columbia U., 1944; MBA, Harvard U., 1947; LLB, Yale U., 1951; LHD (hon.), Cazenovia Coll., 1994. Bar: N.Y. 1952, D.C. 1958. With Bankers Trust Co., 1939-42; instr. adminstrv. engring. Pratt Inst., 1948; instr. econs. Yale U., 1948-50; vis. lectr. acctg. Sch. Gen. Studies Columbia U., N.Y.C., 1948-50, 52; rapporteur com. fed. taxation for U.S. coun. Internat. C. of C., 1952-53; asst. to com. fed. taxation Am. Inst. Accts., 1950-53; with Compton Advt. Agy., N.Y.C., 1954; vis. lectr. law Yale U., 1952; pvt. practice law N.Y.C., 1952-67; pres., dir. Video Vittles, Inc., 1953-67; dep. commr. FHA, 1955-57; of counsel Javits and Javits, 1959-60; 1st asst. atty. gen. N.Y., 1958-59; dir., mem. exec. com. Gotham Bank, N.Y.C., 1961-63; dir. N.Y. State Housing Fin. Agy., 1962-63; chmn. Met. Ski Slopes, Inc., N.Y.C., 1962-65; pres., exec. adminstr. Florence Nightingale Health Ctr., 1965-85; dir. Schaerer AG, Wabern, Switzerland, 1982-88; chmn. Kenbar Group, N.Y.C., 1997—, Internat. Bioimmune Sys., Inc., Great Neck, N.Y., 1999—. Professorial lectr. Sch. Architecture, Pratt Inst., N.Y.C., 1962-66; mem. Sigety Assocs., cons. in housing mortgage financing and urban renewal, 1957-67; ho. cons. Govt. of Peru, 1956; mem. missions to Hungary, Poland, Fed. Republic Germany, Malta, Czechoslovakia, Russia, Israel, Overseas Pvt. Investment Corp., 1990-92; owner, operator Peppermill Farms, Pipersville, Pa., 1956—. Bd. dirs., sec., v.p., treas. Nat. Coun. Health Ctrs., 1969-85; bd. dirs. Am.-Hungarian Found., 1974-76, Pritikin Rsch. Found., 1991—, Stratford Arms Condo Assn., 1992-93, Global Leadership Inst., 1993—; founding mem., bd. dirs., Natl. Assn. for Continence, 1982—, trustee Cazenovia (N.Y.) Coll., 1981—, Delaware Valley Coll. Sci. and Agr., Doylestown, Pa., 1998—; trustee, v.p. Woodmere Art Mus. Phila., 2000—, Navy Supply Corps Found., Athens, Ga., 2000—; del. White House Conf. on Aging, 1971, White House Conf. on Mgmt. Tng. and Market Econs. Edn. in Ctrl. and Ea. Europe, 1991; bd. visitors Lander Coll., U. S.C., Greenwood, 1982-84; mem. fin. com. World Games, Santa Clara, 1981, London, 1985, Karlsruhe, 1989, The Hague, 1993, Confrerie des Chevaliers du Tastevin, Confrerie de la Chaine des Rotisseurs, Wine and Food Soc., Wednesday 10. Lt. (j.g.) Supply Corps, USNR, 1942-46. Recipient President's medal Cazenovia Coll., 1990, George Washington laureate Am. Hungarian Found., 1996; named Prin. for Day, Townsend Harris H.S. N.Y.C. Bd. Edn., 1997-2001, Disting. Alumnus U.S. Navy Supply Corps Sch., Athens, Ga., 1998; Baker scholar Harvard U., 1947. Mem. DOCA (Defense Orientation Conf. Assn.). Presbyterian. E-mail: sigety@msn.com

SIGMOND, CAROL ANN, lawyer; b. Phila., Jan. 9, 1951; d. Irwin and Mary Florence (Vollmer) S. BA, Grinnell Coll., 1972; JD, Cath. U., 1975. Bar: Va. 1975, D.C. 1980, Md. 1988, N.Y. 1990, U.S. Dist. Ct. (ea. dist.) Va. 1975, U.S. Dist. Ct. (so. and ea. dist.) N.Y. 1991, U.S. Ct. Appeals (4th cir.) 1976, U.S. Ct. Appeals (fed. cir.) 1987. Asst. gen. counsel Washington Met. Area Transit Authority, 1978-85; acting assoc. gen. counsel for appeals and gen. law, 1985-86; assoc. Patterson, Belknap, Webb & Tyler, Washington, 1986-89, Berman, Paley, Goldstein & Kannry, N.Y.C., 1991-93; prin. Law Offices of Carol A. Sigmond, 1993-97; of counsel Pollack & Greene, LLP, 1998-2000; pvt. practice, 2000—. Mem. Women's Nat. Dem. Club. Active Womens Nat. Dem. Club. Mem. ABA, D.C. Bar Assn., Arlington County Bar Assn., Va. State Bar Assn., Md. State Bar Assn. Democrat. Mem. LDS. Avocations: piano, bridge. General civil litigation, Construction. Office: 733 3d Ave Fl7 New York NY 10017

SIGMOND, RICHARD BRIAN, lawyer; b. Phila., Dec. 7, 1944; s. Joseph and Jean (Nissman) S.; children: Michael, Catherine, Alina; m. Susan Helen Peteraf, Dec. 24, 1984. BS, Phila. Coll. Textiles & Sci., 1966; JD, Temple U., 1969. Bar: Pa. 1969, U.S. Supreme Ct. 1973, U.S. Dist. Ct. (ea. dist.) Pa. 1975, U.S. Ct. Appeals (3d cir.) 1975, N.Y. 1982, D.C. 1995. Atty. Pub. Defender Assn., Phila., 1969-70; ptnr. Meranze, Katz, Spear & Wilderman, 1970-84; sr. ptnr. Spear, Wilderman, Sigmond, Borish & Endy, 1985-89, Sagot, Jennings & Sigmond, Phila., 1989—; gen. counsel Internat. Brotherhood Painters and Allied Trades, 1997-2000. Chmn., bd. dirs. Gatehouse Phila., 1972-83; lectr. Pvt. Industry Coun., Phila., 1985—, labor studies div., Pa. State U., 1978-82, 85-86; gen. counsel Stabilization Agreement, Sheet Metal Industry Trust Fund, 1994—, Internat. Painters and Allied Trades Industry Pension Fund, 1997—. Mem. ABA (labor law com., litigation com.), AFL-CIO (lawyers coordinating com.), Pa. Bar Assn. (labor law com.), Phila. Bar Assn. (labor com.), Phi Alpha Delta. Avocations: sailing, writing. Federal civil litigation, Labor, Pension, profit-sharing, and employee benefits. Office: Penn Mutual Towers 510 Walnut St Fl 16 Philadelphia PA 19106-3601

SIGUENZA, PETER CHARLES, JR. territory supreme court justice; b. July 1, 1951; s. Peter C. and Barbara L. (Bordallo) S.; m. Joleen Taitano Rios, Dec. 6, 1969; 1 child, Dawn. BA, Calif. State U., 1976; JD, U. of the Pacific, 1980. Bar: Calif. 1981, Guam 1981, U.S. Ct. Appeals (9th cir.), Commonwealth No. Marianas 1983. Pvt. practice Klemm, Blair & Barusch; staff atty. Guam Legal Svcs. Corp.; clk. Superior Ct. Guam; libr. Calif. Ct. Appeal; judge Guam Superior Ct., Agana, 1984-96; justice Supreme Ct. Guam, 1999—2001; chief justice Guam Supreme Ct., 1996—99, 2001—. Designated judge Dist. Ct. Guam, Supreme Ct. Federated States Micronesia; chair bd. trustees Father Duenas Meml. Sch., 1991; chair rules commn. Supreme Ct. Guam, 1993. Mem. ABA, Am. Judges Assn. Office: Supreme Ct of Guam Judiciary Bldg 120 W O'Brien Dr Hagatna GU 96910-5174*

SIINO, SALVATORE G. lawyer; b. Newark, Oct. 21, 1972; s. Joseph and Frances Siino. BA in Econs., Georgetown U., 1993; JD, George Washington U., 1997. Bar: N.Y., N.J. Assoc. Pitney, Hardin, Kipp & Szuch, Morristown, N.J., 1997—. General corporate, Mergers and acquisitions, Securities. Office: Pitney Hardin Kipp & Szuch 200 Campus Dr Florham Park NJ 07932

SILBER, ALAN, lawyer; b. Newark, Oct. 21, 1938; s. Charles and Hermine (Hahn) S.; m. Dana Slater, July 5, 1996; 1 child, Laramie. BA, Duke U., 1960; LLB, Columbia U., 1965. Bar: N.J. 1965, U.S. Supreme Ct. 1965, Calif. 1972, U.S. Dist. Ct. (no. dist.) Calif. 1972, U.S. Ct. Appeals (9th cir.) 1972, N.Y. 1982, U.S. Ct. Appeals (2d, 3d, 4th, 6th cirs.) 1982, U.S. Dist. Ct. N.J. 1982, U.S. Dist. Ct. Hawaii 1982, U.S. Dist. Ct. (so., ea., and no. dists.) N.Y. 1982. Ptnr. Podvey Sachs Catenaci & Silber, Newark, 1980-82, Silber & Rubin, N.Y.C., 1982-87, Hayden & Silber, Weehawken, N.J., 1988—. Bd. advisors Drug Policy Found., Washington, 1987—, The Vol. Com. of Lawyers, N.Y.C., 1997. Mem. Assn. Criminal Def. Lawyers N.J. (pres. 1992-93, founding mem.), Nat. Assn. Criminal Def. Lawyers (regional coord., 3d cir. strike force 1993—). Democrat. Jewish. Avocation: running. Appellate, General civil litigation, Criminal. Home: 160 W 16th St New York NY 10011-6285 Office: Hayden & Silber 500 Frank W Burr Blvd Teaneck NJ 07666-6802

SILBERGELD, ARTHUR F. lawyer; b. St. Louis, June 1, 1942; s. David and Sabina (Silbergeld) S.; m. Carol Ann Schwartz, may 1, 1970; children: Diana Lauren, Julia Kay. BA, U. Mich., 1968; M in City Planning, U. Pa., 1971; JD, Temple U., 1975. Bar: N.Y. 1976, Calif. 1978, D.C. 1983, U.S. Ct. Appeals (2nd cir.), U.S. Ct. Appeals (9th cir.), U.S. Ct. Appeals (D.C. cir.), U.S. Supreme Ct. 1999. Assoc. Vladeck, Elias, Vladeck & Lewis, N.Y.C., 1975-77; field atty. NLRB, L.A., 1977-78; ptnr., head employment law practice group McKenna, Conner & Cuneo, 1978-89; ptnr. Graham & James, 1990-96; labor ptnr. Sonnenschein Nath & Rosenthal, 1996-99; ptnr. Proskauer Rose LLP, 1999—. Instr. extension divsn. UCLA, 1981-89. Author: Doing Business in California: An Employment Law Handbook, 2nd edit., 1997, Advising California Employers, 1990, 91, 93, 94, 95 supplements; contbr. articles to profl. jours. Founding mem. L.A. Mus. Contemporary Art; bd. dirs. Bay Cities unit Am. Cancer Soc., Calif., 1981-85, Jewish Family Svc., L.A., 1981-85, So. Calif. Employers Roundtable, Leadership coun., So. Poverty Law Ctr., L.A., Child Devel. Ctr., 1998—, Leadership Task Force, Drs. Without Borders; pres. Mo. Valley Fedn. of Temple Youth, 1959-60. Mem. L.A. County Bar Assn. (chair labor and employment law sect. 1999-2000, trustee 2000-01), Mus. Modern Art (N.Y.C.), Aperture Found. Labor. Office: Proskauer Rose LLP 2049 Century Park E Fl 32 Los Angeles CA 90067-3101

SILBERMAN, ALAN HARVEY, lawyer; b. Chgo., Oct. 22, 1940; s. Milton J. and Mollie E. (Hymanson) S.; m. Margaret Judith Auslander, Nov. 17, 1968; children: Elena, Mark. BA with distinction, Northwestern U., 1961; LLB, Yale U., 1964. Bar: Ill. 1964, U.S. Dist. Ct. (no. dist.) Ill. 1966, U.S. Ct. Appeals (7th cir.) 1970, (5th and 9th cir.) 1977, (D.C. cir.) 1979, (4th cir.) 1980, (11th cir.) 1981, (3rd cir.) 1982, (8th and 10th cirs.) 1993, U.S. Supreme Ct. 1978. Law clk. U.S. Dist. Ct., Chgo., 1964-66; assoc. Sonnenschein Nath & Rosenthal, 1964-71, ptnr., 1972—. Mem. antitrust adv. bd. Bur. Nat. Affairs, Washington, 1985—; mem. Ill. Atty. Gen. Franchise Adv. Bd., 1996—. Contbr. articles to profl. jours. Bd. dirs., v.p., sec. Camp Ramah in Wisc., Inc., Chgo., 1966-86, pres., 1986-94; bd. dirs. Nat. Ramah Commn., Inc. of Jewish Theol. Sem. Am., N.Y.C., 1970—, v.p., 1986-94, pres., 1994-99, sr. v.p., 1999—; mem. U.S. del. 33d World Zionist Congress, Jerusalem, 1997. Mem. ABA (chmn. antitrust sect. FTC com. 1981-83, chmn. nat. insts. 1983-85, mem. coun. antitrust sect. 1985-88, fin. officer 1988-90, sect. del. ho. of dels. 1990-92, chmn.-elect 1992-93, chmn. 1993-94), Ill. Bar Assn. (chmn. antitrust sect. 1975-76), Northwestern U. 1851 Soc. (chair 1994-97). Antitrust. Home: 430 Oakdale Ave Glencoe IL 60022-2113 Office: Sonnenschein Nath 233 S Wacker Dr Ste 8000 Chicago IL 60606-6491

SILBERMAN, CURT C. lawyer; b. Wuerzburg, Fed. Republic Germany, May 23, 1908; came to the U.S., 1938, naturalized, 1944; s. Adolf and Ida (Rosenbusch) S.; m. Else Kleemann, 1935. Student, U. Berlin, U. Munich; JD summa cum laude, Wuerzburg U., 1931, Rutgers U., 1947; Dr. (hon.), Middlebury Coll., 1997. Bar: N.J. 1948, U.S. Supreme Ct. 1957. Pvt. practice internat. pvt. law, West Orange, N.J., 1948—. Lectr. internat. pvt. law, 1954, 81, 82, 87, 91, 95; prin. guest lectr. at Univ.'s 400th anniversary U. Wuerzburg, 1982. Contbr. articles to legal jours. Pres. Am. Fedn. Jews from Ctrl. Europe, N.Y., 1962-86, chmn. bd., 1986—; past pres. Jewish Philanthropic Fund of 1933, Inc., N.Y., 1971-87, chmn. bd., 1987—; trustee Leo Baeck Inst., N.Y., 1962—, N.Y. Found. Nursing Homes, Inc.; hon. trustee Jewish Family Svc. of Metro-West, N.J.; past co-chmn. Coun. Jews from Germany, 1974-98; chmn. Rsch. Found. for Jewish Immigration, Inc., N.Y.; past bd. dirs. Conf. on Jewish Material Claims Against Germany. Recipient Golden Doctoral Diploma, U. Wuerzburg Law Faculty, 1982, Festschrift dedicated to him by Am. Fedn. Jews from Ctrl. Europe in N.Y., 1969; recipient Pub. Svc. medal. Mem. N.J. Bar Assn. (chmn. com. comparative jurisprudence 1966-73, chmn. com. internat. trade 1974-78), Essex County Bar Assn., Am. Coun. on Germany, Internat. Biographical Dictionary of Ctrl. European Emigres (adv. bd.). Private international.

SILBERMAN, JOHN ALAN, lawyer; b. Balt., Sept. 20, 1951; s. Ronnie A. and Dovera (Gogel) S. BA, Northwestern U., 1973; JD, Harvard U., 1976. Bar: N.Y. 1977, U.S. Dist. Ct. (so. and ea. dists.) N.Y. 1977. Assoc. Paul, Weiss, Rifkind, Wharton & Garrison, N.Y.C., 1976-84, ptnr., 1985-96; prin. John Silberman Assocs., 1996—. Bd. dirs., Pres.'s adv. coun. on the Arts John F. Kennedy Ctr., Washington, 1998—, Found. for Contemporary Performance Arts, N.Y.C., 1998—. Entertainment, Estate planning, Probate. Office: John Silberman Assocs PC 145 E 57th St New York NY 10022-2141

SILBERMAN, LAURENCE HIRSCH, federal judge; b. York, Pa., Oct. 12, 1935; s. William and Anna (Hirsch) S.; m. Rosalie G. Gaull, Apr. 28, 1957; children: Robert Stephen, Katherine DeBoer Balaban, Anne Gaull Otis. BA, Dartmouth Coll., 1957; LLB, Harvard U., 1961. Bar: Hawaii 1962, D.C. 1973. Assoc. Moore, Torkildson & Rice and Quinn & Moore, Honolulu, 1961-64; ptnr. Moore, Silberman & Schulze, 1964-67; atty. appellate divsn. gen. counsel's office NLRB, Washington, 1967-69; solicitor of labor U.S. Dept. Labor, 1969-70, undersec. labor, 1970-73; ptnr. Steptoe & Johnson, 1973-74; dep. atty. gen. U.S., 1974-75; amb. to Yugoslavia, 1975-77; mng. ptnr. Morrison & Foerster, Washington, 1978-79, 83-85; exec. v.p. Crocker Nat. Bank, San Francisco, 1979-83; judge U.S. Ct. Appeals (D.C. cir.), Washington, 1985—. Lectr. labor law and legis. U. Hawaii, 1962—63; adj. prof. adminstrv. law Georgetown U., Washington, 1987—94, Washington, 1997, Washington, 1999—2001, NYU, 1995, 96, Harvard U., 1998; lectr. labor law Georgetown U., Washington, 2001; Pres.' spl. envoy on ILO affairs, 1976; gen. adv. com. on Arms Control and Disarmament, 1981—85; mem. Def. Policy Bd., 1981—85; vice-chmn. State Dept.'s Commn. on Security and Econ. Assistance, 1983—84. Bd. dirs. Com. on Present Danger, 1978-85, Inst. for Ednl. Affairs, 1981-85; vice chmn. adv. coun. on gen. govt. Rep. Nat. Com., 1977-80. With AUS, 1957-58. Am. Enterprise Inst. sr. fellow, 1977-78, vis. fellow 1978-85. Mem. U.S. Fgn. Intelligence Surveillance Act Ct. of Rev., Coun. on Fgn. Rels.

SILER, EUGENE EDWARD, JR. federal judge; b. Williamsburg, Ky., Oct. 19, 1936; s. Eugene Edward and Lowell (Jones) S.; m. Christy Dyanne Minnich, Oct. 18, 1969; children— Eugene Edward, Adam Troy. B.A. cum laude, Vanderbilt U., 1958; LL.B., U. Va., 1963; LL.M., Georgetown U., 1964. Bar: Ky. 1963, Va. 1963, D.C. 1963. Individual practice law, Williamsburg, 1964-65; atty. Whitley County, Ky., 1965-70; U.S. atty. Eastern Dist. Ky., Lexington, 1970-75; judge U.S. Dist. Ct., Eastern and Western Dists., Ky., 1975-91; chief judge Eastern Dist., 1984-91; judge U.S. Ct. Appeals (6th cir.), 1991—. Campaign co-chmn. Congressman Tim L. Carter, 1966, 5th Congl. Dist.; campaign co-chmn. U.S. Senator J.S. Cooper, 1966; trustee Cumberland Coll., Williamsburg, 1965-73, 80-88; 1st v.p. Ky. Bapt. Convention, 1986-87; bd. dirs. Bapt. Healthcare Systems Inc., 1990—. Served with USN, 1958-60, with Res. 1960-83. E. Barrett Prettyman fellow, 1963-64; recipient medal Freedom's Found., 1968 Mem. FBA, Ky. Bar Assn. (Judge of Yr. award 1992), D.C. Bar Assn., Va. State Bar. Republican. Baptist. Home: PO Box 129 Williamsburg KY 40769-0129 Office: US Ct Appeals 1380 W 5th St Ste 200 London KY 40741-1615*

SILETS, HARVEY MARVIN, lawyer; b. Chgo., Aug. 25, 1931; s. Joseph Lazarus and Sylvia Silets; m. Elaine L. Gordon, June 25, 1961; children: Hayden Leigh, Jonathan Lazarus (dec.), Alexandra Rose. BS cum laude, DePaul U., 1952; JD (Frederick Leicke scholar), U. Mich., 1955. Bar: Ill. 1955, U.S. Dist. Ct. (no. dist.) Ill. 1955, N.Y. 1956, U.S. Tax Ct. 1957, U.S. Ct. Mil. Appeals 1957, U.S. Ct. Appeals (7th cir.) 1958, U.S. Supreme Ct. 1959, U.S. Ct. Appeals (6th cir.) 1965, U.S. Ct. Appeals (2d cir.) 1971, U.S. Ct. Appeals (5th cir.) 1972, U.S. Ct. Appeals (11th cir.). Assoc. Paul, Weiss, Rifkind, Wharton & Garrison, N.Y.C., 1955-56; asst. atty. U.S. Dist. Ct. (no. dist.) Ill., 1958-60; chief tax atty. U.S. Atty. No. Dist. Ill., Chgo., 1960-62; ptnr. Harris, Burman & Silets, 1962-79, Silets & Martin, Ltd., Chgo., 1979-92, Katten Muchin Zavis, Chgo., 1992—. Asst. advance tng. program IRS, U. Mich., 1952-53; law lectr. advance fed. taxation John Marshall Law Sch., 1962-66; adj. prof. taxation Chgo.-Kent Coll. Law, 1985—; gen. counsel Nat. Treasury Employees Union, 1968-92; mem. adv. com. tax litigation U.S. Dept. Justice, 1979-82; mem. Tax Reform Com., State of Ill., 1982-83; mem. Speedy Trial Act Planning Group U.S. Dist. Ct. (no. dist.) Ill., 1976-79; mem. civil justice reform act adv. com. U.S. Dist. Ct. (no. dist.) Ill., 1991-94; lectr. in field. Contbr. articles to profl. jours. Trustee Latin Sch., Chgo., 1970-76; active Chgo. Crime Commn., 1975-93, Govv.'s Commn. Reform Tax Laws, Ill., 1982-83. With AUS, 1956-58. Fellow Am. Coll. Trial Lawyers (chmn. com. on fed. rules of criminal procedure 1982-91, fed. rules of evidence com. 1988-93, jud. com., fed. criminal procedures com., Upstate Ill. com. chmn. 1990-91), Am. Coll. Tax Counsel, Internat. Acad. Trial Lawyers, Soc. Advanced Legal Studies; mem. ABA (active various coms.), Bar Assn. 7th Fed. Cir. (chmn. com. criminal law and procedure 1972-82, bd. govs. 1983-86, sec. 1986-88, v.p. 1989-90, pres. 1990-91), NACDL, FBA (bd. dirs. 1971—, pres. 1977-78, v.p. 1976-77, sec. 1975-76, treas. 1974-75, active various coms.), Chgo. Bar Assn. (tax com. 1958-66, com. devel. law 1966-72, 78-88, com. fed. taxation 1968—, com. evaluation candidates 1978-80, exec. com. tax sect. 1994—), Am. Bd. Criminal Def. Lawyers, Decalogue Soc. Lawyers, Bar Assn. N.Y. City, Standard Club, Cliff Dwellers Club, Chgo. Club, Phi Alpha delta, Pi Gamma Mu. General corporate, Criminal, Taxation, general. Office: Katten Muchin Zavis 525 W Monroe St Ste 1300 Chicago IL 60661-3647 E-mail: hsilets@kmz.com

SILKENAT, JAMES ROBERT, lawyer; b. Salina, Kans., Aug. 2, 1947; s. Ernest E. and Mildred R. (Iman) S.; children: David Andrew, Katherine Anne. BA, Drury Coll., 1969; JD, U. Chgo., 1972; LLM, NYU, 1978. Bar: N.Y. 1973, D.C. 1980. Assoc. Cravath, Swaine & Moore, N.Y.C., 1972-80; counsel Internat. Fin. Corp., Washington, 1980-86; ptnr. Morgan, Lewis & Bockius, N.Y.C., 1986-89, Morrison & Foerster, N.Y.C., 1989-92, Pillsbury, Winthrop, N.Y.C., 1992—. Chmn. Council N.Y. Law Assocs.,

1978-79, Lawyers Com. Internat. Human Rights, 1978-80. Editor ABA Guide to Fng. Law Firms, Moscow Conf. on Law Bilateral Econ. Rels., ABA Guide to Internat. Bus. Negotiations; contbr. articles to profl. jours. Capt. U.S. Army, 1972-73. Fellow NEH, 1977, U.S. Dept. State, 1981. Fellow Am. Bar Found.; mem. ABA (chmn. internat. law and practice sect. 1989-90, chmn. sect. officer's conf. 1990-92, mem. ho. of dels. 1989—, bd. govs. 1994-97). General corporate, Finance, Private international. Office: Pillsbury Winthrop One Battery Park Plz New York NY 10004

SILLER, STEPHEN I. lawyer; b. May 8, 1949; m. Helen Seewald, June 6, 1971. BA, Bklyn. Coll., 1970, JD cum laude, 1973; LLM, NYU, 1978. Bar: N.Y. 1974, U.S. Dist. Ct. (so. and ea. dists.) N.Y. 1974, U.S. Ct. Appeals (2d cir.) 1974. Assoc. Fried, Frank, Harris, Shriver & Jacobson, N.Y.C., 1973-78, Feit & Ahrens, N.Y.C., 1978-80, ptnr., 1981-87; founder, sr. ptnr. Siller Wilk LLP, 1987—. Mem. ABA (partnership law com., negotiated acquisitions com.), Internat. Bar Assn., Assn. Bar City of N.Y. (transp. com. 1978—, U.S. in global economy com. 1996-97). General corporate, Mergers and acquisitions, Securities. Office: Siller Wilk LLP 747 3rd Ave Fl 38 New York NY 10017-2803 E-mail: ssiller@sillerwilk.com

SILLS, NANCY MINTZ, lawyer; b. N.Y.C., Nov. 3, 1941; d. Samuel and Selma (Kahn) Mintz; m. Stephen J. Sills, Apr. 17, 1966; children: Eric Howard, Ronnie Lynne Sills Lindberg. BA, U. Wis., 1962; JD cum laude, Union U., 1976. Bar: N.Y. 1977, U.S. Dist. Ct. (no. dist.) N.Y. 1977, U.S. Tax Ct. 1984. Asst. editor fin. news Newsweek mag., N.Y.C., 1962-65; staff writer, reporter Forbes mag., 1965; rsch. assoc. pub. rels. Ea. Airlines, 1965-67; asst. editor Harper & Row, 1968-69; freelance writer, editor N.Y.C., Albany, 1967-70; confidential law sec. N.Y. State Supreme Ct., Albany, 1976-79; assoc. Whiteman, Osterman & Hanna, 1979-81, Martin, Noonan, Hislop, Troue & Shudt, Albany, 1981-83; ptnr. Martin, Shudt, Wallace & Sills, 1984; of counsel Krolick and DeGraff, 1984-89; ptnr. Hodgson, Russ, Andrews, Woods & Goodyear, 1990-91; pvt. practice, 1991—; of counsel Lemery & Reid, Albany and Glens Falls, N.Y., 1993-94. Asst. counsel N.Y. State Senate, 1983-88; cons. The Ayco Corp., 1975; jud. screening com. Third Jud. Dept., 1997—. Editor: Reforming American Education, 1969, Up From Poverty, 1968; rschr.: The Negro Revolution in America, 1963; contbr. articles to mags. Bd. dirs. Jewish Philanthropies Endowment, 1983-86, United Jewish Fedn. N.E. N.Y. Endowment Fund, 1992-96, Daus. Sarah Found., 1994-97, Albany Jewish Cmty. Ctr., 1984-87; mem. Guilderland (N.Y.) Conservation Adv. Coun., 1993-96; mem. planned giving tech. adv. com. Albany Law Sch., Union U., 1991-95, chmn., 1992-95; mem. regional cabinet State of Israel Bonds Devel. Corp. for Israel, 1991-92; surrogate decision making com. N.Y. State Commn. Quality of Care for Mentally Disabled. Mem. ABA, N.Y. State Bar Assn., Albany County Bar Assn., N.Y. Criminal and Civil Cts. Bar Assn. (dir. 2000-), Estate Planning Coun. Ea. N.Y., Aux. Albany County Med. Soc., Capital Dist. Trial Lawyers Assn., Capital Dist. Women's Bar Assn., Phi Beta Kappa, Sigma Epsilon Sigma. Republican. Estate planning, General practice, Probate. Home: 16 Hiawatha Dr Guilderland NY 12084-9526 Office: 126 State St Albany NY 12207-1637 E-mail: nmsills@capital.net

SILSBY, PAULA, prosecutor; U.S. atty. Dist. Maine U.S. Dept. Justice. Office: PO Box 9718 Portland ME 04104*

SILVA, EUGENE JOSEPH, lawyer; b. Gloucester, Mass., May 23, 1942; s. Edward Joseph and Rose (Lebre) S.; m. Nancy Blue-Pearson, Jan. 8, 1972; children: Eugene Joseph II, Michael Joseph. BS with honors, Maine Maritime Acad., 1964; JD, U. Notre Dame, 1972. Bar: Calif. 1972, U.S. Dist. Ct. (so. and cen. dists.) Calif. 1972, Tex. 1977, U.S. Dist. Ct. (so. and ea. dists.) Tex. 1978, U.S. Ct. Appeals (5th, 2d and 11th cirs.) 1978, U.S. Supreme Ct. 1981; lic. Master Mariner. Assoc. Luce, Forward, Hamilton & Scripps, San Diego, 1972-77, Vinson & Elkins, Houston, 1977-79, ptnr., 1980—. Bd. dirs. Cabrillo Festival Inc., San Diego, 1974-77, San Jose Clinic, Inc., 1990—, pres. 1993-95; bd. dirs. Portuguese Heritage Scholarship Found., 1995—, St. Joseph Hosp. Found., 1996—. Decorated Knight Comdr. Equestrian Order of Holy Sepulchre of Jerusalem; recipient Outstanding Alumni award Maine Maritime Acad., 1990. Mem. Houston Bar Assn., Calif. Bar Assn., Tex. Bar Assn., Internat. Bar Assn., Grays Inn U. Notre Dame Sch. Law (pres. 1970-72), Southeastern Admiralty Law Inst., Maritime Law Assn. U.S. (proctor in admiralty 1974—), Portuguese Union Calif. (bd. dirs. 1973-74), Portuguese Am. League San Diego (pres. 1974-75), Portuguese Am. Leadership Coun. U.S., Asia-Pacific Lawyers Assn., Notre Dame Club (pres. San Diego chpt. 1976-77), The Naval Club (London). Roman Catholic. Admiralty, Federal civil litigation, Private international. Home: 8 Smithdale Estates Dr Houston TX 77024-6600 Office: Vinson & Elkins 2300 First City Tower 1001 Fannin St Ste 3300 Houston TX 77002-6706

SILVER, ALAN IRVING, lawyer; b. St. Paul, Sept. 17, 1949; s. Sherman J. Silver and Muriel (Bernstein) Brawerman; m. Janice Lynn Gleekel, July 8, 1973; children: Stephen, Amy. BA cum laude, U. Minn., 1971, JD cum laude, 1975. Bar: Minn. 1975, U.S. Dist. Ct. Minn. 1975, U.S. Dist. Ct. (ea. dist.) Wis. 1975, U.S. Ct. Appeals 8th and 10th cirs.) 1975. Assoc. Doherty, Rumble & Butler, P.A., Mpls., 1975-80, ptnr. St. Paul, 1980-99, Bassford, Lockhart, Truesdell & Briggs, P.A., Mpls., 1999—. Mem. 2d Jud. Dist. Ethics Com., St. Paul, 1985-88, 4th Jud. Dist. Ethics Com., Mpls., 1990-97. Author numerous continuing edn. seminar material. Vol. atty. Legal Assistance Ramsey County, St. Paul, 1975-82; mem. St. Louis Park (Minn.) Sch. Bd., 1993-99, chair, 1995-97; mem. St. Louis Park Human Rights Commn., 1987-91; chmn. site mgmt. coun. Susan Lindgren Sch., St. Louis Park, 1986-93; bd. dirs. Jewish Cmty. Rels. Coun., Anti-Defamation League Minn. and Dakotas, 1987-93, 97—, treas., 1992-93. Mem. ABA, Minn. Bar Assn. (exec. bd. antitrust sect. 1984), Hennepin County Bar Assn. Avocations: running, guitar, reading. Antitrust, Federal civil litigation, General civil litigation. Home: 4320 W 25th St Minneapolis MN 55416-3841 Office: Bassford Lockhart Truesdell & Briggs PA 3550 Multifoods Tower 33 S 6th St Minneapolis MN 55402-1501 E-mail: alans@email.bassford.com

SILVER, BARRY MORRIS, lawyer, lay preacher; b. Mt. Vernon, N.Y., Nov. 18, 1956; s. Samuel Manuel and Elaine Martha (Shapiro) S. BA, Fla. Atlantic U., 1979; JD, Nova U., 1983. Bar: Fla. 1983. Law clk. to presiding justice 4th Dist. Ct. Appeals, West Palm Beach, Fla., 1982-83; pvt. practice Boca Raton, 1983—; sole practice, 1986—. Tchr. Hebrew and religion Temple Beth El, Boca Raton, 1979-84; tchr. bilingual edn. Palm Beach County Schs., Delray Beach, Fla., 1981-83; faculty Palm Beach Jr. Coll., Boca Raton, 1990—; atty. NOW, South Palm Beach County; mem. Fla. Ho. Reps., 1997-98. Vol. Haitian Refugee Ctr., Miami, 1982. Mem. Fla. Bar Assn., Palm Beach County Bar Assn., Sierra. Democrat. Jewish. Avocations: languages, tennis, Frisbee, chess, backgammon. Civil rights, General civil litigation, Personal injury. Home: 6362 Walk Cir Boca Raton FL 33431 Office: 7777 Glades Rd Ste 308 Boca Raton FL 33434-4150 E-mail: barryboca@aol.com

SILVER, HARRY R. lawyer; b. Phila., Aug. 8, 1946; s. Jerome Benjamin Silver and Josephine Sandler (Steinberg) Furr; m. Jessica Dunsay, Nov. 23, 1972; children: Gregory, Alexander. BA, Temple U., 1968; JD, Columbia U., 1971. Bar: N.Y. 1972, D.C. 1973, U.S. Dist. Ct. D.C., U.S. Ct. Claims, U.S. Ct. Appeals (1st, 4th, 5th, 7th, 8th, 9th, 10th, fed. and D.C. cirs.), U.S. Supreme Ct. Law clk. to Hon. Harold R. Medina, U.S. Ct. Appeals (2d cir.), N.Y.C., 1971-72; assoc. Arent, Fox, Kintner, Plotkin & Kahn, Washington, 1972-74; atty. U.S. Dept. Justice, 1974-77, U.S. Dept. Energy, Washington, 1977-78; assoc. Akin, Gump, Strauss, Hauer & Feld, 1978-81, ptnr., 1981-88, Oppenheimer, Wolff & Donelly, Washington, 1988-91, Davis Wright Tremaine, Washington, 1991-94, Ober, Kaler, Grimes & Shriver, Washington, 1994—. Mem. ABA, Fed. Bar Assn. Avocations: running, music, travel. Administrative and regulatory, Federal civil litigation, Government contracts and claims. Home: 6829 Wilson Ln Bethesda MD 20817-4948 Office: Ober Kaler Grimes & Shriver 1401 H St NW Ste 500 Washington DC 20005-2175 E-mail: hrsilver@ober.com

SILVER, PAUL ALLEN, lawyer; b. Providence, Mar. 1, 1950; s. Caroll M. and Gail (Arkin) S.; m. Katherine C. Haspel, June 22, 1975; children: Andrew Haspel, Nathaniel Haspel. AB, Harvard U., 1972; JD, Boston U., 1975. Bar: R.I. 1975, U.S. Dist. Ct. R.I. 1975, Mass. 1985. Assoc. firm Hinckley, Allen, Salisbury & Parsons, Providence, 1975-81; ptnr. Hinckley, Allen & Snyder, Providence, 1981—; faculty MS in Taxation Program, Bryant Coll., North Smithfield, R.I., 1982. Author: Cheap Eats, 1972, 2d edit., 73, 3d edit., 75. Bd. dirs. Travelers Aid Soc. of R.I., Providence, 1983-89, 95—; pres., 1986-89; bd. dirs. Ronald McDonald House, 1987-95, Camp Ruggles, 1991—; bd. trustees Providence Athenaeum, 1995—; active Planned Giving Coun. of R.I. Mem. ABA, R.I. Bar Assn., Estate Planning Coun. of R.I., Moses Brown Sch. Alumni Assn. (bd. dirs. 1984—), Internat. Assn. Fin. Planning (bd. dirs. R.I. chpt. 1986-95). Jewish. Avocations: finance, business. Estate planning, Probate, Personal income taxation. Home: 310 Olney St Providence RI 02906-2326 Office: Hinckley Allen & Snyder 1500 Fleet Ctr Providence RI 02903-2319

SILVERBERG, JAY LLOYD, lawyer; b. N.Y., Oct. 1, 1961; s. Sheldon and Elissa (Nenner) S.; children: Jennifer, Rebecca, Sabrina. BA, Brandeis U., 1983; JD, Boston U., 1986. Bar: N.Y. 1987, N.J. 1987, U.S. Dist. Ct. (so. dist.) N.Y. 1990, U.S. Dist. Ct. (ea. dist.) N.Y. 1991. Assoc. McCarter & English, Newark, 1986-87, Proskauer Rose, N.Y.C., 1987-91; mem. Silverberg, Stonehill & Goldsmith, P.C., 1991—. Lectr. Nat. Assn. Credit Mgmt., Columbia U. Sch. Bus., 1996. Editor: Annual Review of Banking Law, 1986. Paul J. Liacos scholar Boston U. Sch. Law, 1985, G. Joseph Tauro scholar, 1984. Mem. N.Y. Inst. Credit, Manhattan Credit Club (pres. 1998), Turnaround Mgmt. Assn. Bankruptcy, Contracts commercial, General corporate. Office: Silverberg Stonehill & Goldsmith PC 111 W 40th St New York NY 10018-0968 E-mail: JLSilverberg@SSGPC.com

SILVERBERG, MARK VICTOR, lawyer, educator; b. Akron, Ohio, Sept. 26, 1957; s. Alvin Harold and Marilyn (Bierman) S.; m. Marsha Phyllis Mermelstein, Aug. 11, 1979; childern: Samantha Michele, Marissa Jill. BS, Rider Coll., 1979; JD, Pace U., 1983. Bar: N.J. 1983, N.Y. 1984, U.S. Dist. Ct. (so. dist.) N.Y., U.S. Dist. Ct. N.J. Atty. Met. Life Ins. Co., N.Y.C., 1983-84; corp. counsel H & N Chem. Co., Totowa, N.J., 1984-85; pvt. practice East Brunswick, 1985-90; gen. coun. East Coast Title Ins., 1990-91; sr. v.p. New Century Mortgage Corp., 1991—; CEO M&M Propery Corp.; sec./treas. Century Mortgage Svcs., Inc. Prof. law Middlesex County Coll., Edison, N.J., 1985—, Mercer County Coll., Trenton, N.J., 1985—, Upsala Coll., East Orange, N.J., 1991—. Mem. ABA (real estate, probate and property law sect., corp. law sect.), N.Y. State Bar Assn., N.J. Bar Assn. (real estate, probate and property law sect., corp. law sect.), Middlesex County Bar Assn., Rotary. Republican. Jewish. Avocations: basketball, golf, hockey, woodworking, gardening. General corporate, Probate, Real property.

SILVERBERG, STEVEN MARK, lawyer; b. Bklyn., June 7, 1947; m. Arlene Leopold, July 4, 1971; 2 children. BA, Bklyn. Coll., 1969; JD, NYU, 1972. Bar: N.Y. 1973, U.S. Dist. Ct. (so. and ea. dists.) N.Y. 1974, U.S. Supreme Ct. 1976, U.S. Ct. Appeals (2nd cir.) 1978. Asst. dist. atty. Kings County Dist. Atty., Bklyn., 1972-75; dep. town. atty. Town of Greenburgh, N.Y., 1975-79; ptnr. Stowell, Kelly & Silverberg, White Plains, 1979-83, Hoffman, Silverberg & Wachtell, Elmsford, 1983-86, Hoffman, Silverberg, Wachtell & Koster, White Plains, 1986-89; pvt. practice, 1989-92; ptnr. Kirkpatrick & Silverberg LLP, 1993-00, Wilson, Elser, Moskowitz, Edelman & Dicker LLP, White Plains, 2001—. Adj. assoc. prof. N.Y. Law Sch., 1990-93. Co-author: Wetlands and Coastal Zone Regulations and Compliance, 1993; contbr. to profl. publs. Counsel Greenburgh Housing Authority, 1979-84, Town of Mamaroneck, N.Y., 1984-96, Village of Mamaroneck, 1999—, planning and zoning bd. Town of Haverstraw, 2001—; bd. dirs. Temple Beth Torah, Upper Nyack, N.Y., 1977-89, 2000—, pres. 1984-86; bd. dirs. N.J. West Hudson Valley Region Union of Am. Hebrew Congregations, 1986-88, Westchester Mcpl. Planning Fedn. Mem. ABA, N.Y. State Bar Assn., Westchester County Bar Assn. (chair environtl. law com. 1997—). General corporate, Environmental, Real property. Office: Wilson Elser Moskowitz Edelman & Dicker LLP 3 Gannett Dr White Plains NY 10604

SILVERMAN, ALAN HENRY, lawyer; b. N.Y.C., Feb. 18, 1954; s. Melvin H. and Florence (Green) S.; m. Gretchen E. Freeman, May 25, 1986; children: Willa C.F., Gordon H.F. BA summa cum laude, Hamilton Coll., 1976; MBA, JD, U. Pa., 1980. Bar: N.Y. 1981, U.S. Dist. Ct. (so. and ea. dist.) N.Y. 1981, U.S. Ct. Internat. Trade 1981, D.C. 1986, U.S. Supreme Ct. 1990. Assoc. Hughes, Hubbard & Reed, N.Y.C., 1980-84; asst. counsel Newsweek, Inc., 1984-86; v.p., gen. counsel, sec., dir. adminstrn. Cable One, Inc., Phoenix, 1986—. Contbr. articles to profl. jours. Mem. prevention adv. com. Gov. Pa. Justice Commn., 1975-79; bd. dirs. Lawyers' Alliance for N.Y., 1982-85, N.Y. Lawyers Pub. Interest, 1983-85, Nat. Assn. JD-MBA Profls., 1983-85, Bus. Vols. for Arts, Inc., Phoenix, 1989-93, Ariz. Vol. Lawyers for the Arts, Inc., 1994-97, First Amendment Coalition Ariz., Inc., 1991—; mem. Maricopa County Citizens Jud. Adv. Coun., 1990-93; mem. citizens' bond com. City of Phoenix, 2000. Mem. ABA, Assn. of Bar of City of N.Y., D.C. Bar Assn., Phi Beta Kappa. Communications, Entertainment, Libel. Home: 5833 N 30th St Phoenix AZ 85016-2401 Office: Cable One Inc 1314 N 3d St Phoenix AZ 85004 E-mail: alan.silverman@cableone.net

SILVERMAN, ARNOLD BARRY, lawyer; b. Sept. 1, 1937; s. Frank and Lillian Lena (Linder) S.; m. Susan L. Levin, Aug. 7, 1960; children: Michael Eric, Lee Oren. B of Engring. Sci., Johns Hopkins U., 1959; LLB cum laude, U. Pitts., 1962. Bar: U.S. Dist. Ct. (we. dist.) Pa. 1963, Pa. 1964, U.S. Patent and Trademark Office 1965, U.S. Supreme Ct. 1967, Can. Patent Office 1968, U.S. Ct. Claims 1975, U.S. Ct. Appeals (3d cir.) 1982, U.S. Ct. Appeals (fed. cir.) 1985. Patent atty. Alcoa, New Kensington, Pa., 1962-67, 68-72, sr. patent atty., 1972-76; ptnr. Price and Silverman, Pitts., 1967-68; v.p., gen. patent counsel Joy Mfg. Co., 1976-80; ptnr. Murray Silverman & Keck, 1980-81, Buell, Blenko, Ziesenheim & Beck, Pitts., 1984; ptnr. intellectual property dept. Eckert, Seamans, Cherin & Mellott, 1984—, chmn., 1992—, chmn. info. tech. practice group, 1992-97; spl. asst. atty. gen. State of W.Va., 1985—; spl. counsel patents U. Pitts., 1975—. Spkr. on patents, trademarks, copyright, computer law; nat. panel of arbiters Am. Arbitration Assn., 1987—. Contbr. articles to profl. jours. Mem. Churchill CSC (Pa.), 1967-90, chmn., 1975-90; mem. Pitts. law com. Anti-Defamation League, 1981—, regional adv. bd., 1982—, ch-chmn. Pitts. region ann. dinner, 1983, mem. chmn. by-laws com., 1983; bd. govs. Slippery Rock U. Found., 1985-91; Pitts. steering com. MIT Enterprise Forum, 1986-87. With U.S. Army, 1963-64. Recipient Am. Spirit Honor medal, Ft. Knox, 1963, Mem. ABA, ASME, Allegheny County Bar Assn. (chmn. pub. rels. com. 1978-80, vice-chmn. intellectual property sect. 1981-83, chmn. 1984-85), Pitts. Patent Law Assn. (chmn. pub. rels. com., 1968-69, chmn. patent laws com., 1970-72, chmn. nominating com., 1973, chmn. legis. action com., 1975-76, bd. mgrs. 1974-88, newsletter editor 1974-88, sec.-treas. 1976-84, v.p. 1984-85, pres. 1985-86, pub. rels. com. 1994-95, program com. 1995-96), Am. Intellectual Property Law Assn. (membership com. 1985-88, pub. rels. com. 1994—), U.S. Trademark Assn. (chmn. task force on advt. agys. 1981, membership com. 1987-89), D.C. Bar Assn., Pa. Bar Assn. (co-chmn. sports/entertainment com. 2001—), Nat. Assn. Coll. and Univ. Attys., Am. Chem. Soc. (chemistry and the law sect.), Licensing Execs. Soc. (co-chmn. Pitts. chpt. 1994-96), Brit. Inst. Chartered Patent Agts. (fgn. mem.), Johns Hopkins U. Alumni Assn. (chmn. publicity com. 1963-66, exec. com. 1966-87, v.p. 1969-70, pres. 1971-72, nat. alumni coun. 1989-92), Johns Hopkins Soc. Engring. Alumni (coun. mem. 2000—), U. Pitts. Gen. Alumni Assn. (life; bd. dirs. 2001—), U. Pitts. Law Alumni Assn. (bd. dirs. 1992-97, treas. 1997-98, v.p. 1998-99, pres.-elect 1999-2000, pres. 2001—), Robert Bruce Assn. Law Fellows (life), Golden Panthers, Stratford Cmty. Assn. (v.p. 1966-67, gov. 1966-70, pres. 1967-68), Mensa (fellow, lawyers in Mensa 1978—, nat. assoc. counsel patents and trademarks copyrights 1980-82, inventors' spl. interest group 1980-86), Intertel (treas. Pitts. Forum 1983—), Duquesne Club, Order of Coif, Tau Epsilon Rho, Psi Chi. Republican. Jewish. Computer, Patent, Trademark and copyright. Home: 2019 High Pointe Ct Murrysville PA 15668-8515 Office: 600 Grant St 44th Fl Pittsburgh PA 15219-2703 E-mail: arnie@telerama.lm.com, abs@escm.com

SILVERMAN, ARTHUR CHARLES, lawyer; b. Lewiston, Maine, June 13, 1938; s. Louis A. and Frances Edith (Brownstone) S.; BS in Elec. Engring., BS in Indsl. Mgmt., MIT, 1961; JD, Columbia U., 1964; m. Donna Linda Zolov, June 18, 1961; children: Leonard Stephen, Daniel Edward. Bar: N.Y. 1965, U.S. Supreme Ct. 1971. Engr., engring. asst. Gen. Electric Co., Pittsfield, Mass. and Phila., 1958-62; assoc. Baer & Marks, N.Y.C., 1965-68; assoc. Golenbock and Barell, N.Y.C., 1968-72, ptnr., 1972-89; ptnr. Reid & Priest LLP, N.Y.C., 1989-98, dep. chair, 1996-98; ptnr. Thelen Reid & Priest LLP, N.Y.C., 1998—. Treas., trustee Ramaz Sch., 1977-84, vice chmn., 1984-85, 86-88, chmn., 1988-92, hon. chmn., 1992—; bd. govs. MIT Hillel Found., 1979-84; mem. Bd. Jewish Edn. of City of N.Y., 1981-84; mem. exec. com. Nat. Jewish Ctr. for Learning and Leadership, 1984-90. Mem. IEEE, ABA, NSPE, N.Y. State Bar Assn., Fed. Bar Council, Assn. Bar City N.Y., N.Y. Soc. Architects, Internat. Bar Assn., Inter-Pacific Bar Assn., Constrn. Mgmt. Inst., Constrn. Specifications Inst. General civil litigation, Construction, Real property. Home: 200 E 74th St New York NY 10021-3618 Office: Thelen Reid & Priest LLP 40 W 57th St New York NY 10019-4097

SILVERMAN, BARRY G. federal judge; b. N.Y.C., Oct. 11, 1951; 1 child, Bagel Ann. BA summa cum laude, Ariz. State U., 1973, JD, 1976. Bar: Ariz. 1976, U.S. Dist. Ct. Ariz. 1976, U.S. Ct. Appeals (9th cir.) 1976, U.S. Supreme Ct. 1980. Asst. city prosecutor, Phoenix, 1976-77; dep. atty. Maricopa County, 1977-79; ct. commr., 1979-84; judge, 1984-95, Superior Ct. Ariz. Maricopa County, 1995; apptd. magistrate judge U.S. Dist. Ct. Ariz., 1995; judge U.S. Ct. Appeals 9th cir., 1998—. Instr. constnl. law Coll. Law, Ariz. State U., spring, 1983, adj. prof. advanced criminal procedure, spring 1989; lectr. comty. property BAR/BRI Ariz., Idaho and Nev. Bar Rev. Courses , 1989—; mem. Ariz. Supreme Ct. Com. on Jud. Edn. and Tng., 1988—. Recipient Exel award Soc. Nat. Assn. Publs., 1992. Mem. ABA, State Bar Ariz., Maricopa County Bar Assn. (Henry Stevens award 1991). Avocations: magic, beagles, baseball, wine tasting. Office: 401 W Washington St SPC 78 Phoenix AZ 85003

SILVERMAN, MOSES, lawyer; b. Bklyn., Mar. 3, 1948; s. Bernard and Anne Silverman; m. Betty B. Robbins, Jan. 19, 1980; children: Benjamin, Rachel. AB, Colby Coll., 1969; JD, NYU, 1973. Bar: N.Y. 1974, U.S. Dist. Ct. (so. and ea. dists.) N.Y. 1974, U.S. Ct. Appeals (2d cir.) 1974, U.S. Ct. Appeals (D.C. cir.) 1977, U.S. Supreme Ct. 1977, D.C. 1982, U.S. Ct. Appeals (fed. cir.) 1985, U.S. Ct. Appeals (11th cir.), 1986 . Assoc. Paul, Weiss, Rifkind, Wharton & Garrison, N.Y.C., 1973-81, ptnr., 1981—. Vol. U.S. Peace Corps., Istanbul, Turkey, 1969-70; bd. dirs. Legal Aid Soc., 1998—, Vols. Legal Svcs. Mem. ABA, Assn. of Bar of City of N.Y. Antitrust, Federal civil litigation, State civil litigation. Home: 7 Gracie Sq New York NY 10028-8001 Office: Paul Weiss Rifkind Wharton & Garrison 1285 Ave of Americas Rm 202 New York NY 10019-6028 E-mail: msilverman@paulweiss.com

SILVERS, EILEEN S. lawyer; b. N.Y.C., Sept. 21, 1948; d. Sidney and Ethel Lynne (Starobin) Swertloff; m. Richard J. Bronstein; children: Steven Jay, Sharron Roth. BA magna cum laude, SUNY, Buffalo, 1970; JD, Columbia U., 1975. Bar: N.Y. 1977, U.S. Tax Ct. 1981, U.S. Ct. Claims 1983, D.C. 1984. Assoc. Paul, Weiss, Rifkind, Wharton & Garrison, N.Y.C., 1975-83, ptnr., 1983-94; v.p. taxes Bristol-Myers Squibb Co., 1994—. Mem. tax com. Nat. Fgn. Trade Coun. (steering com.); tax subcom. PhRMA; exec. com. PRUSA. Mem. tax coun. Mfrs. Alliance; bd. dirs. The Tax Coun. Mem. ABA (tax sect.), N.Y. State Bar Assn. (chmn. persona 1 income com. tax sect. 1983-85, exec. com. 1982-85, 90-91), Internat. Fiscal Assn., Tax Execs. Inst. Corporate taxation, Personal income taxation, International taxation. Home: 20 Mountain Peak Rd Chappaqua NY 10514-2110 Office: Bristol-Myers Squibb Co 345 Park Ave New York NY 10154-0004

SILVERTHORN, ROBERT STERNER, JR. lawyer; b. Oklahoma City, Dec. 22, 1948; s. Robert Sterner and Marilyn I. Silverthorn; m. Mary Russell Cofer, June 26, 1982; children: Robert Sterner III, Christine Elizabeth. BA, Dickinson Coll., 1969; JD, U. Louisville, 1974; postgrad., Nat. Def. U., 1988, U.S. Army War Coll., 1989, 93. Bar: Ky. 1975, U.S. Dist. Ct. (we. dist.) Ky. 1975, U.S. Tax Ct. 1975, U.S. Dist. Ct. (ea. dist.) Ky. 1980, U.S. Dist. Ct. (so. dist.) Tex. 1981, U.S. Dist. Ct. (no. dist.) Ohio 1983, U.S. Dist. Ct. (so. dist.) Ind. 1993, U.S. Supreme Ct. 1983. Pvt. practice, Louisville, 1975; assoc. Pallo White & O'Conner, Louisville, 1975-76, Hargadon Lenihan & Harbolt, Louisville, 1976-82; ptnr. White Diamond & Silverthorn, Louisville, 1982-83; of counsel Nutt & Mayer, Louisville, 1983-91; mng. ptnr. Morris, Silverthorn & Dutton, Louisville, 1991-92, Silverhorn Law Offices, 1993—; commd. 2d lt. U.S. Army, 1970, advanced through grades to col., 1991, comdr. 1st Brigade 100th Divsn., 1993—; bd. dirs. Energy Buyers Svc. Corp., Houston, 1980-85, 92-93, Maroco Leasing, Inc., Louisville; repeat guest radio talk show Ask the Lawyers Sta. WHAS. Pres. Windhurst Acres Homeowners Assn., St. Matthews, Ky., 1981-85. Bd. dirs. Boy Scouts of Am. Cherokee Dist. Decorated Meritorious Svc. medal with 2 oak leaf clusters, Bronze Star with 1 oak leaf cluster, Air medal, Army Commendation medal with 3 oak leaf clusters, Army Achievement medal; recipient Constl. Book award U. Louisville, 1975. Mem. ABA (vice chair litigation, tort ins., litigation com. gen. practice sect.), Ky. Bar Assn., Louisville Bar Assn., Ky. Acad. Trial Attys., Res. Officers Assn., Assn. of Century (pres. 1993—), Assn. U.S. Army, chmn. Louisville Armed Forces Day com. 1986-88, Louisville Area C. of C. (mil. affairs com.), Hurstbourne Country Club, Jefferson Club, Club of Jeffersontown, Ky., Masons, Rotary (pres. 1995—), Delta Theta Phi (dean), Sigma Chi. Methodist. Family and matrimonial, Personal injury, Real property. Home: 1724 Edenside Ave # 2 Louisville KY 40204-1520 Office: Silverthorn Law Offices 455 S 4th Ave Ste 1200 Louisville KY 40202-2512

SIMANDLE, JEROME B. federal judge; b. Binghamton, N.Y., Apr. 29, 1949; s. Paul R. Sr. and Mary F. Simandle; married; children: Roy C., Liza Jane. BSE magna cum laude, Princeton U., 1971; JD, U. Pa., 1976; diploma in Social Scis., U. Stockholm, 1974-75. Bar: Pa. 1977, N.J. 1978. Law clk. to Hon. John F. Gerry U.S. Dist. Ct., N.J., 1976-78; asst. U.S. atty. Dist. N.J., 1978-83; U.S. magistrate judge U.S. Dist. Ct., N.J., 1983-92, judge, 1992—. Mem. lawyers adv. com. U.S. Dist. Ct. N.J., 1984-95; ct. adminstrn. case mgmt. com. Jud. Conf. U.S., 1991-97; mem. CPR Inst. for Dispute Resolution Commn. on Ethics and Stds. in Alternative Dispute Resolution, 1996—. Internat. grad. fellow Rotary Found., 1974-75. Fellow Am. Bar Found.; mem. ABA, Fed. Judges Assn. (bd. dirs. 1997—), Am. Judicature Soc., Camden County Bar Assn., Camden Inn of Ct. (master 1987—, program chmn. 1990-93, vice chmn. 1996—). Office: US Dist Ct US Courthouse One John F Gerry Plz Camden NJ 08101-0888

SIMBURG, MELVYN JAY, lawyer; b. San Francisco, June 15, 1946; s. Earl J. and Pearl Estelle (Garmaise) S.; m. Barbara Sherri Frost, Jan. 1, 1981; 2 children. AB, U. Calif., Berkeley, 1968; JD, M in Internat. Affairs, Columbia U., 1972. Bar: Wash. 1972, U.S. Ct. Appeals (9th cir.) 1972. Assoc. Perkins Coie, Seattle, 1972-76; pvt. practice, 1976-81; pres. Melvyn Jay Simburg, P.S., A Profl. Svc. Corp., 1981-83, Simburg, Ketter, Sheppard & Purdy, LLP, Seattle, 1983—. Adj. prof. Law Sch., U. Puget Sound (now Seattle U.), Tacoma, 1972-74; chmn. ann. seminar on U.S. Can. bus. trans. of Bar Assn. B.C. and Wash. State. Contbr. articles to profl. jours. Former pres. Leschi Improvement Coun., Seattle; active Seattle Film Soc., Seattle Art Mus. Mem. ABA (com. on internat. intellectual property rights, sect. internat. law and practice, com. on internat. bus. law, sect. bus. law), Wash. State Bar Assn. (chmn. sect. internat. law and practice 1986-87), Seattle-King County Bar Assn. (past chmn. sect. internat. and comparative law), World Trade Club Seattle (bd. dirs. 1983-86), World Affairs Coun. Seattle, Seattle C. of C. (vice chmn. internat. trade and devel. com. 1984-86). General civil litigation, Intellectual property, Private international. Home: 235 Lake Dell Ave Seattle WA 98122-6310 Fax: 206-223-3929. E-mail: msimburg@sksp.com

SIMKANICH, JOHN JOSEPH, lawyer, engineer; b. Clairton, Pa., 1941; BSEE, Drexel Inst. Tech., 1964; MSEE, Purdue U., 1966; JD, George Washington U., 1972. Bar: U.S. Patent Office 1970, Pa. 1973, U.S. dist. Ct. (ea. dist.) Pa. 1977, U.S. Supreme Ct. 1977, U.S. Ct. Appeals (Fed. cir.) 1982, U.S. Ct. Appeals (3d cir.) 1992. Elec. engr. U.S. Steel Co., 1963-65; engr. Westinghouse Aerospace, Balt., 1966-69; sys. developer TRW Sys. Inc., Washington, 1969-70; patent atty. Burroughs Corp., Paoli, Pa., 1970-74, Johnson & Johnson, New Brunswick, N.J., 1974-77; pvt. practice intellectual property law Newtown, Pa., 1977—. Adv. Soup, Inc., Washington, 1970-72; introduced to FTC truth-in-advt. law; presenter in field. Patentee in field; product developer and licensing; analog and digital computer designer, programmer. Mem. IEEE (sr.), Pa. Bar Assn., Bucks County Bar Assn., Phila. Intellectual Property Law Assn., Am. Intellectual Property Law Assn., Delta Theta Phi, Eta Kappa Nu. Roman Catholic. Republican. Computer, Patent, Trademark and copyright. Office: PO Box 671 Newtown PA 18940-0671

SIMMENS, ADAM, lawyer; b. Phila., July 12, 1966; s. Harvey and Joyce Simmens; m. Michelle Joy Ferman, May 23, 1999. BS in Acctg., Drexel U.; JD, Widener U., 1996. Sole practice, Phila., 1998—. Home: PO Box 189 Flourtown PA 19038 Office: 1135 E Erie Ave Philadelphia PA 19124

SIMMONS, BRYAN JOHN, lawyer; b. Springfield, Pa., Sept. 12, 1955; s. Alfred John and Priscilla Theresa (O'Donnell) S.; m. Carol Lynn Hoffman, Aug. 11, 1979; children: Brett, Kristen. BS in Meteorology, Pa. State U., 1977; JD, Dickinson Law Sch., 1981. Bar: Pa. 1981, U.S. Dist. Ct. (mid. dist.) 1982, U.S. Ct. Appeals (3d cir.) 1982. Law clk. Lancaster County (Pa.) Ct. of Common Pleas, 1981-82; counsel Hershey (Pa.) Foods Corp., 1982—. Tristee Elizabethtown (Pa.) Pub. Libr., 1985—, pres., 1992-98. Mem. ABA, Pa. Bar Assn., Lancaster County Bar Assn., Licensing Execs. Soc., Nat. Weather Assn., Lancaster County Conservancy, Lancaster Aquatic Club (bd. dirs. 1999—). Avocations: fishing, softball. Environmental, Private international, Patent. Home: 1104 Sheaffer Rd Elizabethtown PA 17022-9214 Office: Hershey Foods Corp 100 Crystal A Dr Unit 8 Hershey PA 17033-9702 E-mail: BJSimmons@hersheys.com

SIMMONS, CHARLES BEDFORD, JR. lawyer; b. Greenville, S.C., Dec. 4, 1956; s. Charles Bedford and Mary Margaret (Mason) S.; children: Charles B. III, Elizabeth S., Mason W. AA magna cum laude, Spartanburg Meth. Coll., 1977; BS magna cum laude, E. Tenn. State U., 1979; JD, U. S.C., 1982. Bar: S.C. 1982, U.S. Dist. Ct. S.C. 1983, U.S. Ct. Appeals (4th cir.) 1986. Law clk. to presiding justice S.C. Cir. Ct., Greenville, 1982-83; with Carter Law Firm, 1983-86; ptnr. Wilkins, Nelson, Kittredge & Simmons, 1986-89; civil ct. judge, 1989—; presiding judge 13th Circuit Drug Ct. Mem. bench-bar com. S.C. Supreme Ct., 1992-97; presiding judge 13th cir. Drug Ct. Mem. adv. com. paralegal program Greenville Tech. Coll., 1989-97, chmn., 1990-91; mem. Friends of 200 Adv. Bd., 1991-99. Named Big Brother of Yr., Big Bros.-Big Sisters, 1988; recipient Svc. to Manking award Rotary Club, 1989, Outstanding Young Disting. Svc. award Greenville Jaycees, 1990-91. Mem. S.C. Bar Assn. (young lawyer liason 1985-89, named Outstanding Young Lawyer of Yr. 1989), Greenville Bar Assn., Assn. Trial Lawyers Am., S.C. Trial Lawyers Assn., Greenville Young Lawyers (pres. 1988—), Gamma Beta Phi, Pi Gamma Mu, Phi Delta Phi. Republican. Presbyterian. Clubs: Greenville City, Textile (v.p. 1985-87), Revelers (Greenville). Home: 11 W Hillcrest Dr Greenville SC 29609-4615 Office: Ste 207 County Courthouse Greenville SC 29601

SIMMONS, DANIEL DAVID, lawyer; b. Adelaide, Australia, Nov. 27, 1969; s. David Winston and Simone Simmons; m. Melissa Anne Bresnahan, June 11, 2000. LLB with honors, Bond U., Queensland, Australia, 1991; BEc, U. Adelaide, Australia, 1992; GDLP, U. South Australia, 1992. Bar: High Ct. of Australia 1992, Supreme Ct. of South Australia 1992, Supreme Ct. of NSW, 1995. Solicitor Thomson Playford (formerly Thomsons), Adelaide, 1992-95; assoc. Atanaskovic Hartnell, Sydney, 1995-98, ptnr., 1998—. Author in field. Communications, General corporate, Mergers and acquisitions. Office: Atanaskovic Hartnell Level 10 75-85 Elizabeth St Sydney NSW 2000 Australia Fax: 612 9777 8777. E-mail: dds@ah.com.au

SIMMONS, DOREEN ANNE, lawyer; b. Dec. 22, 1949; d. Samuel and Gloria (Jensen) Buranich; m. Harvey O. Simmons III, Oct. 12, 1974; children: Olivia, Grace, Harvey. BA, Purdue U., 1971; J.D., Union U., 1974. Bar: N.y. 1975, U.S. Dist. Ct. (No. and we. dist.) N.Y. Sr. asst. dist. atty. Onondaga County (N.Y.), Syracuse, 1975-80; ptnr. Hancock & Estabrook, 1980—. Mem. com. on character and fitness 5th Jd. Dist. N.Y. State Appellate Div., 198 4— . Mem. NYS Bar Found., Christian Bros. Acad. (bd. sec.). Federal civil litigation, State civil litigation, Environmental. Office: Hancock & Estabrook Mony Tower I PO Box 4976 Syracuse NY 13221-4976

SIMMONS, HARVEY OWEN, III, lawyer; b. Schenectady, N.Y., Nov. 20, 1948; s. Harvey Owen and Mary Elizabeth (Wall) S.; m. Doreen Anne Buranich, Oct. 12, 1974; children— Olivia Mary, Grace Catherine, Harvey O. Simmour IV. B.S. in Fgn. Service, Georgetown U., 1970; J.D., Union U., 1973; LL.M., NYU, 1984. Bar: N.Y. 1974. System atty. Niagara Mohawk Power, Syracuse, N.Y., 1977-80; asst. gen. counsel, asst. sec. Goulds Pumps, Inc., Seneca Falls, N.Y., 1980-86, gen. counsel, sec. Crucible Materials Corp., Syracuse, N.Y., 1986—. LTC USAR, 1970-77, ret. Decorated Army Commendation medal; Georgetown U. scholar, 1966-70, scholar, Union U., 1970-73. Mem. N.Y. State Bar Assn. Republican. Roman Catholic. General corporate. Home: 38 W Lake St Skaneateles NY 13152-1406 Office: Crucible Materials Inc PO Box 977 Syracuse NY 13201-0977

SIMMONS, JAMES CHARLES, lawyer; b. N.Y.C., June 5, 1935; s. James Knight and Helen (Bielefeld) S.; m. Carolyn Ann Edwards, June 12, 1957; children: James M., Shawn M. Dzielawa. BSMetE, Lehigh U., 1957; JD, Duquesne U., 1965. Bar: Pa. 1965, U.S. Dist. Ct. (we. dist.) Pa. 1965, (ea. dist.), 2001; U.S. Ct. Appeals (3rd cir.) 1965, U.S. Ct. Appeals (fed. cir.) 1977. Metall. engr. Crucible Steel Co. Am., Midland, Pa., 1957-66, atty. Pitts., 1966-67; contract adminstr. Nuclear Materials & Equipment Corp., Apollo, Pa., 1967-69; patent atty. Bausch & Lomb, Rochester, N.Y., 1969-94; asst. gen. patent counsel Air Products and Chem., Inc., Allentown, Pa., 1994-97; sr. atty. Ratner & Prestia, Valley Forge, 1994-97, ptnr. Allentown, 1997—. Mem. ABA (com. chair Invention Com., 2001-), Am. Intellectual Property Law Assn. (sec. 1993-96; com. chair Invention Issue Com. 2001-) Pa. Bar Assn., Fed. Cir. Bar Assn., Phila. Intellectual Property Law Assn., Bar Assn. Lehigh County, Benjamin Franklin Am. Inn of Ct. Intellectual property, Patent, Trademark and copyright. Office: Ratner & Prestia 5100 W Tilghman St Ste 265 Allentown PA 18104-9141 E-mail: jcsimmons@ratnerprestia.com

SIMMONS, KERMIT MIXON, lawyer; b. Winnfield, La., Oct. 7, 1935; s. Kermit Carson and Mamie Rose (Mixon) S.; m. Nina Underwood, Jan. 30, 1960; children— Kermit Mixon, Susan Elizabeth, Alfred Lee. B.A., La. Tech. U., 1956; J.D., La. State U., 1959. Bar: La. 1959, U.S. Dist. Ct. (we. dist.) La. 1965, U.S. Ct. Appeals (5th cir.) 1965. Law clk. La. 2d Cir. Ct. Appeals, Shreveport, 1961-62; assoc. Lowe & Benton, Minden, La., 1962-63; ptnr. Peters & Simmons, Winnfield, La., 1963-69; sole practice, Winnfield, 1969-74; ptnr. Simmons & Derr, Winnfield, 1974— ; 1st asst. 8th Jud. Dist. Atty., Winnfield, 1965-89; chmn. spl. com. malpractice ins. La. Bar, 1984-85. Trustee Winn Parish Bd. Library Trustees, 1966—. Mem. La. Trial Lawyers Assn., La. Bar Assn. (ho. of dels. 1988—), Winn Parish Bar Assn. (pres. 1981—). Lodges: Rotary (pres. Winnfield 1967), Masons. Banking, State civil litigation, Probate. Home: Simmons & Derr 200 Church Winnfield LA 71483

SIMMONS, PETER, law and urban planning educator; b. N.Y.C., July 19, 1931; s. Michael L. and Mary A. S.; m. Ruth J. Tanfield, Jan. 28, 1951; children: Sam, Lizzard. A.B., U. Calif., Berkeley, 1953, LL.B., 1956; postgrad. (Alvord fellow), U. Wis., 1956-58. Prof. SUNY, Buffalo, 1963-67; mem. faculty Ohio State U., 1967-75, U. Ill., 1972, Case Western Res. U., 1974-75; prof. law and urban planning Rutgers U. Coll. Law, Newark, 1975—, dean, 1975-93; university prof. Rutgers U., 1993—. Contbr. articles to profl. jours. Mem. Ohio Housing Commn., 1972-74; commr. Ohio Reclamation Rev. Bd., 1974-75; chmn. N.J. Criminal Disposition Commn., 1983-84; mem. N.J. Law Revision Commn., 1987—. Mem. Am. Planning Assn., Urban Land Inst., Am. Law Inst., AAUP (nat. council 1973-75). Office: Rutgers U Law Sch 15 Washington St Newark NJ 07102-3192 E-mail: psimmons@andromedalrutgers.edu

SIMMONS, PETER LAWRENCE, lawyer; b. N.Y.C., May 1, 1965; s. John Derek and Rosalind (Wellish) S. AB magna cum laude, Columbia U., 1985, JD, 1987. Bar: N.Y. 1987, U.S. Dist. Ct. (so. and ea. dists.) N.Y. 1988, U.S. Ct. Internat. Trade 1991, U.S. Spreme Ct. 1991, U.S. Ct. Appeals (2d cir.) 1992, U.S. Ct. Appeals (1st cir.) 1993. Law clk. to Hon. Lawrence W. Pierce U.S. Ct. Appeals (2d cir.), N.Y.C., 1987-88; assoc. Fried, Frank, Harris, Shriver & Jacobson, 1988-94, ptnr., 1994—. Treas., sr. editor Columbia Law Rev., 1985-87. Harlan Fiske Stone scholar, 1985-87. Mem. ABA, Fed. Bar Coun., N.Y. Bar Assn., Assn. of Bar of City of N.Y. (profl. responsibility com. 1998—, civil rights com. 1989-92), Phi Beta Kappa. General civil litigation. Home: 203 E 72nd St Apt 20A New York NY 10021-4551 Office: Fried Frank Harris Shriver & Jacobson 1 New York Plz Fl 22 New York NY 10004-1980 E-mail: peter.simmons@ffhsj.com

SIMMONS, SHERWIN PALMER, lawyer; b. Bowling Green, Ky., Jan. 19, 1931; AB, Columbia U., 1952, LLB, 1954, JD, 1969. Bar: Tenn. 1954, Fla. 1957. Assoc. Fowler, White, Collins, Gillen, Humkey & Trenam, Tampa, Fla., 1956-60, ptnr., 1960-70, Trenam, Simmons, Kemker, Scharf & Barkin, Tampa, 1970-77; stockholder, pres. Trenam, Simmons, Kemker, Scharf, Barkin, Frye & O'Neill, PA, 1977-94; ptnr., chair tax group Steel Hector & Davis, LLP, Miami, Fla., 1994—. Atty. adv. U.S. Tax Ct., Washington, 1954-56, mem. nominating commn., 1978-81; mem. adv. group Commr. of IRS, 1978-79, 89-90, U.S. Dept. Justice, 1979-80; adj. prof. U. Miami, 1995—. Author: Federal Taxation of Life Insurance, 1966; bd. of advisors mag. The Tax Times, 1986-87; contbr. articles to legal jours. Trustee Hillsborough County Soc. Crippled Children & Adults, 1956-65, pres., 1960-61; treas., chmn. Hillsborough County Pub. Edn. Study Commn., 1965-66; mem. adv. bd. Salvation Army, 1959-62, 64-66, sec., 1960-61; chmn., bd. dirs. The Fla. Orch., 1987-89; founding trustee, pres. Am. Tax Policy Inst., 1996-99; trustee Tampa Bay Performing Arts Ctr., Inc., 1984-93, program adv. com., 1985-89, investment com., 1986-91. Fellow Am. Coll. Trust and Estate Counsel (bd. regents 1982-88), Am. Bar Found. (fellow 1969—, devel. com. 1992-94), Am. Coll. Tax Counsel (regent 1987-93, vice chmn. 1989-91, chmn. 1991-93); mem. ABA (vice chmn. adminstrn. taxation sect. 1972-75, chmn. 1975-76, ho. of dels. 1985-90, bd. govs. 1990-93, chmn. bd. govs. fin. com. 1992-93, chmn. commn. on multidisciplinary practice 1998-2000), Am. Bar Retirement Assn. (bd. dirs. 1984-90, v.p. 1987-88, pres. 1988-89), Am. Law Network ABA-Am. Law Inst. (com. continuing profl. edn. 1973—), FBA, Fla. Bar Assn. (chmn. taxation sect. 1964-65), Am. Judicature Soc., So. Fed. Tax Inst. (trustee, pres. 1974, chmn. 1975 trustee emeritus 1999—), Internat. Acad. Estate and Trust Law, Internat. Fiscal Assn., Am. Law Inst. (mem. coun. 1985—, exec. com. 1994-97, 99—, mem. com. 1997—, chmn. 1999—). Corporate taxation, Estate taxation, Taxation, general. Office: 200 S Biscayne Blvd Ste 4100 Miami FL 33131-2362 E-mail: 815home@msn.com, spstax@steelhector.com

SIMMONS, STEPHEN JUDSON, lawyer; b. Columbus, Ohio, Feb. 19, 1946; s. Samuel A. and Jane A. (McGrath) S.; m. Claire Maxine Schriber, Aug. 15, 1970; children: Darren, Judson. BA, Ohio State U., 1968; JD, U. Cin., 1972. Bar: Ohio 1973, Tex. 1982. Sr. law clk. U.S. Dist. Ct. (ea. dist.) Tenn., Knoxville, 1972-74; asst. atty. gen. Office of Atty. of Ohio, Columbus, 1974-75; assoc. McGrath & Shirey, 1975; corp. counsel Wendys, Inc., 1975-79; sr. v.p., gen. counsel Precision Tune, Inc., Beaumont, Tex., 1979-87, also dir.; sr. v.p. adminstrn., dir. Kwik-Kopy Corp., Cypress, Tex., 1988-90; v.p. Deli Mgmt., Inc., 1990-94; pvt. practice Houston, 1994—. Bd. editors U. Cin. Law Rev., 1971-72. Mem. Tex. Bar Assn. Roman Catholic. General corporate, Franchising, Real property. Home: 13603 Balmore Cir Houston TX 77069-2703 Office: 3845 Fm 1960 Rd W Ste 250 Houston TX 77068-3548 Fax: 281-586-0088. E-mail: sjsimmons@aol.com

SIMON, BRUCE HARVEY, lawyer; b. N.Y.C., Dec. 27, 1934; s. Morris and Pearl (Mandelstein) S.; m. Arlene Bartfield, June 16, 1957; children: Douglas, Charles, Rachel. BA, Bklyn. Coll., 1956; LLB, Harvard U., 1959. Bar: N.Y. 1961, U.S. Ct. Appeals (2d, 3d, 4th and 5th cirs.) U.S. Dist. Ct. (so., ea. and no. dists.) N.Y. Assoc. Cohen & Weiss, N.Y.C., 1960-66; ptnr. Cohen, Weiss & Simon, 1966—. Mem. N.Y.C. Bd. Collective Bargaining; bd. dirs. AFL-CIO Lawyers Coordinating Com., 1982—; disting. practitioner in residence Cornell Law Sch., 1995. Contbr. articles to legal publs. Served with U.S. Army, 1959-60. Mem. ABA, Fed. Bar Coun. Democrat. Jewish. Bankruptcy, Labor, Pension, profit-sharing, and employee benefits. Office: Cohen Weiss & Simon 330 W 42nd St Fl 25 New York NY 10036-6976 E-mail: bsimon@cwsny.com

SIMON, DAVID ROBERT, lawyer; b. Newton, Mass., June 21, 1934; m. Myrna B. Kiner, June 28, 1959; children— Marianne, Geoffrey. A.B., Harvard U., 1956, LL.B., 1960. Bar: Mass. 1960, N.J. 1963, N.Y. 1980. Law sec. to judge U.S. Dist. Ct., Newark, 1961-63; assoc. Newark Law Firm, 1964-68; ptnr. Simon & Allen, Newark, 1968-86; ptnr. Kirsten, Simon, Friedman, Allen, Cherin & Linken, Newark, 1987-89; ptnr. Whitman & Ransom, Newark, 1989-93; sole practitioner, 1994—. Served with USAR, 1956-64. Mem. ABA, N.J. State Bar Assn., Essex County Bar Assn. Antitrust, Federal civil litigation, State civil litigation. Home: 875 Fifth Ave 11E New York NY 10021-4952 Office: One Riverfront Plz Newark NJ 07102

SIMON, H(UEY) PAUL, lawyer; b. Lafayette, La., Oct. 19, 1923; s. Jules and Ida (Rogére) S.; m. Carolyn Perkins, Aug. 6, 1949 (dec. Dec. 1999); 1 child, John Clark. B.S., U. Southwestern La., 1943; J.D., Tulane U., 1947. Bar: La. 1947; CPA, La. 1947. Pvt. practice, New Orleans, 1947—; asst. prof. advanced acctg. and taxation U. Southwestern La., 1944-45; staff acct. Haskins & Sells (now Deloitte & Touche), New Orleans, 1945-53, prin., 1953-57; ptnr. Deutsch, Kerrigan & Stiles, 1957-79; sr. founding ptnr. Simon, Peragine, Smith & Redfearn, 1979—. Mem. New Orleans Bd. Trade. Author: Community Property and Liability for Funeral Expenses of Deceased Spouse, 1946, Income Tax Deductibility of Attorney's Fees in Action in Boundary, 1946, Fair Labor Standards Act and Employee's Waiver of Liquidated Damages, 1946, Louisiana Income Tax Law, 1956, Changes Effected by the Louisiana Trust Code, 1965, Gifts to Minors and the Parent's Obligation of Support, 1968; co-author: Deductions—Business or Hobby, 1975, Role of Attorney in IRS Tax Return Examination, 1978; assoc. editor: The Louisiana CPA, 1956-60; mem. bd. editors Tulane Law Rev., 1945-46, adv. bd. editors, 1992—; estates, gifts and trusts editor The Tax Times, 1986-87. Bd. dirs., mem. fin. com. World Trade Ctr., 1985-86; mem. New Orleans Met. Crime Commn., Coun. for a Better La., New Orleans Met. Area Com., Bur. Govtl. Rsch., Pub. Affairs Rsch. Coun.; co-chmn. NYU Tax Conf., New Orleans, 1976; mem. dean's coun. Tulane U. Law Sch. Fellow Am. Coll. Tax Counsel; mem. ABA (com. ct. procedure tax sect. 1958—), AICPA, La. Bar Assn. (com. on legis. and adminstrv. practice 1966-70, bd. cert. tax atty.), New Orleans Bar Assn., Internat. Bar Assn. (com. on securities issues and trading 1970-88), Am. Judicature Soc., Soc. La. CPAs, New Orleans Assn. Notaries, Tulane U. Alumni Assn., New Orleans C. of C. (coun. 1952-66), Tulane Tax Inst. (program com. 1960-96), Internat. House (bd. dirs. 1976-79, 82-85), Internat. Platform Assn., City Energy Club, Press Club, New Orleans Country Club, Phi Delta Phi (past pres. New Orleans chpt.), Sigma Pi Alpha. Roman Catholic. General corporate, Estate planning, Corporate taxation. Home: 6075 Canal Blvd New Orleans LA 70124-2936 Office: 30th Fl Energy Ctr New Orleans LA 70163 E-mail: hpsimon@aol.com, hpsimon@spsr-law.com

SIMON, JAMES LOWELL, lawyer; b. Nov. 8, 1944; s. K. Lowell and Elizabeth Ann (Unholz) S.; m. RuthAnn Beck, July 4, 1997; children: Heather Lyn Small, Brandon James; stepchildren: Gary G. Mower, Richard M. Nazareth II, Juliet A. Nazareth. Student, U. Ill., 1962-63, JD with honors, 1975; BSEE magna cum laude, Bradley U., 1967. Bar: Fla. 1975, Utah 1999, U.S. Dist. Ct. (mid. dist.) Fla. 1976, U.S. Ct. Appeals (11th cir.) 1981, U.S. Patent Office 1983, U.S. Dist. Ct. Utah 1999. Engr. Pan Am. World Airways, Cape Kennedy, Fla., 1967-68; assoc. Akerman, Senterfitt & Eidson, Orlando, 1975-80; ptnr. Bogin, Munns, Munns & Simon, 1980-87, Holland & Knight, LLP, 1987-99; corp. counsel Agilent Technologies, Palo Alto, Calif., 2000—. With Seminole County Sch. Adv. Coun., Fla., 1981-88, chmn., 1982, 83; with Forest City Local Sch. Adv. Com., Altamonte Springs, Fla., 1981-84, Code Enforcement Bd., Altamonte Springs, 1983-84, Cen. Bus. Dist. Study com., Altamonte Springs, 1983-85, Rep. Coun. of '76, Seminole County, 1982-87; mem. Seminole County Libr. Adv. Bd., 1989-92, sec., 1990, pres., 1991, Seminole County Citizens for Quality Edn., 1990-92; mem. Seminole County Sch. Dist. Strategic Planning Com., 1991-99, Leadership Orlando Alumni, 1992-99; bd. dirs. Found. for Seminole County Pub. Schs., Inc., 1992-95, chmn., 1993-94; bd. dirs. Greater Seminole C. of C., 1993; active Lake Brantley H.S. Band Boosters, 1995-2000, Lake Brantley H.S. PTSA, 1995-2000, Chorus Boosters, 1997, Leadership Club-Heart of Fla. United Way, 1997; sponsor concerts Orlando Philharm. Orch. for Boys and Girls Clubs. Cen. Fla., 1996-97; regional dir. region 5 Holocaust Remembrance Project, 1997-99. Capt. USAF, 1968-72. Mem. ABA, Orange County Bar Assn. (jud. rels. com. 1982-83, fee arbitration com. 1983-99), Greater Orlando C. of C., Seminole County Bar Assn. (sec. trial lawyers sect. 1993-94), U. Ill. Alumni Club, Phi Kappa Phi, Tau Beta Pi, Sigma Tau, Eta Kappa Nu. Republican. E-mail: jim. Intellectual property, Patent, Trademark and copyright. Home: 1675 Tupolo Dr San Jose CA 95124-4754 E-mail: simon@agilent.com

SIMON, JOHN GERALD, law educator; b. N.Y.C., Sept. 19, 1928; s. Robert Alfred and Madeleine (Marshall) S.; m. Claire Aloise Bising, June 14, 1958; 1 son, John Kirby (dec.). Grad., Ethical Culture Schs., 1946; AB, Harvard U., 1950; LLB, Yale U., 1953; LLD (hon.), Ind. U., 1989. Bar: N.Y. 1953. Asst. to gen. counsel Office Sec. Army, 1956-58; with firm Paul, Weiss, Rifkind, Wharton & Garrison, N.Y.C., 1958-62; mem. faculty Yale Law Sch., 1962—, prof. law, 1967-76, Augustus Lines prof. law, 1976—, dep. dean, 1985-90, acting dean, 1991; dir., co-chmn. program on non-profit orgns. Yale U., 1977-88. Author: (with Powers and Gunnemann) The Ethical Investor, 1972. Pres. Taconic Found., 1967—; trustee, sec. Potomac Inst., 1961-93; mem. grad. bd. Harvard Crimson, 1950—; chmn. bd. dirs. Coop. Assistance Fund, 1970-76, vice chmn., 1977—; mem. governing coun. Rockefeller Archives Ctr., 1982-86; trustee The Found. Ctr., 1983-92, Open Soc. Inst.-N.Y., 1996—. 1st lt. U.S. Army, 1953-5 6. Recipient Certificate of Achievement Dept. Army, 1956 Mem. Phi Beta Kappa. Office: Yale U Law Sch PO Box 208215 New Haven CT 06520-8215

SIMON, M. DANIEL, lawyer; b. London, England, Mar. 15, 1965; s. John J. and Sarah Simon. BSc (with 1st class honors), U. Sussex, UK, 1988; LLD, College of Law, London, 1991. solicitor of the Supreme Court of England and Wales. Trainee Forsyte Kerman Solicitors, London, U.K, 1991-93, solicitor U.K, 1993-98, Paisner & Co., London, U.K, 1999, ptnr. U.K, 1999—. Contbr. articles to profl. jours. Dir. treas. Forest Sch. Camps (Children's Charity), 1990—; trustee Juliet Gomperts Memorial Trust (Art Charity), 1990—. Mem. Charity Law Assn., Internat. Bar Assn., European Assn. Planned Giving. Avocations: cycling, camping, croquet. Estate planning, Probate, Estate taxation. Office: Paisner & Co. 154 Fleet Street EC4A 2SO London England Fax: 020 7353 8621. E-mail: dsimon@paisner.co.uk

SIMON, MICHAEL SCOTT, lawyer; b. Bronx, N.Y., Feb. 9, 1954; s. Philip and Miriam C. (Feller) S.; m. Elayne Robin Baer, May 26, 1974; children: Joshua Seth, Sarah Emily, Rachel Melissa. BA, SUNY, Stony Brook, 1976; JD, Boston U., 1979. Bar: N.Y. 1980, U.S. Dist. Ct. (ea. and so. dists.) N.Y. 1980, U.S. Ct. Appeals (2d cir.) 1981, U.S. Tax Ct. 1983, U.S. Supreme Ct. 1983; Fla. 1987. Asst. corp. counsel N.Y.C. Law Dept., 1979-82; assoc. Tenzer, Greenblatt, Fallon & Kaplan, N.Y.C., 1982-88; ptnr. Tenzer, Greenblatt L.L.P., 1989-99, Blank Rome Tenzer Greenblatt, LLP, N.Y.C., 2000—. Mem. ABA, N.Y. State Bar Assn., Fla. Bar Assn., N.Y. County Lawyers Assn., Assn. Bar City N.Y., Pi Sigma Alpha. Avocations: travel, music. State civil litigation, Landlord-tenant, Real property. Home: 4 Talon Way Dix Hills NY 11746-6239 Office: Blank Rome Tenzer Greenblatt LLP 405 Lexington Ave New York NY 10174-0002 E-mail: msimon@blankrome.com

SIMON, NANCY RUTH, lawyer; b. Gary, Ind. BSEE, Iowa State U., 1985; MBA, U. Dallas, 1988; JD, So. Meth. U., 1991. Bar: Tex. 1991, Calif. 1994; registered to practice before U.S. Patent and Trademark Office 1992. Elec. engr. Tex. Instruments, Dallas, 1986-88; law clk. to pvt. law firms, 1989-91; law clk. U.S. Attys. Office, 1991; assoc. Felsman, Bradley, Gunter & Dillon, LLP, Ft. Worth, 1991-93; patent counsel Apple Computer, Inc., Cupertino, Calif., 1993-2000; ptnr. Simon & Koerner, LLP, 2000—. Realtor Coldwell Banker, San Jose, Calif, 1997-98. Co-author: Attorneys' Fees in IPL Cases; mem. So. Meth. U. Law Rev. Jour. of Air Law and Commerce, 1990-91. Mem. ABA, Am. Intellectual Property Law Assn., State Bar Tex., State Bar Calif., San Francisco Bay Area Intellectual

Property Am. Inn of Ct., Mensa Iowa State U. Student Alumni Assn. (mem. career awareness com. 1984-85), Sigma Iota Epsilon, Zeta Tau Alpha (social chmn. 1982-83, house mgr. 1983-84, chmn. jud. bd. 1984-85), Phi Delta Phi. Avocations: reading, music, scuba diving. Computer, Intellectual property, Patent. Office: Simon & Koerner LLP 10052 Pasadena Ave Ste B Cupertino CA 95014-5945

SIMON, SEYMOUR, lawyer, former state supreme court justice; b. Chgo., Aug. 10, 1915; s. Ben and Gertrude (Rusky) S.; m. Roslyn Schultz Biel, May 26, 1954; children: John B., Nancy Simon Cooper, Anthony Biel. BS, Northwestern U., 1935, JD, 1938; LLD (hon.), John Marshall Law Sch., 1982, North Park Coll., 1986, Northwestern U., 1987. Bar: Ill. 1938. Spl. atty. Dept. Justice, 1938-42; practice law Chgo., 1946-74; judge Ill. Appellate Ct., 1974-80; presiding justice Ill. Appellate Ct. (1st Dist., 3d Div.), 1977, 79; justice Ill. Supreme Ct., 1980-88; ptnr. Piper Marbury Rudnick & Wolfe and predecessor firm, Chgo., 1988—. Former chmn. Ill. Low-Level Radioactive Waste Disposal Facility Siting Commn.; former dir. Nat. Gen. Corp., Bantam Books, Grosset & Dunlap, Inc., Gt. Am. Ins. Corp. Mem. Cook County Bd. Commrs., 1961-66, pres., 1962-66; pres. Cook County Forest Preserve Dist., 1962-66; mem. Pub. Bldg. Commn., City Chgo., 1962-67; Alderman 40th ward, Chgo., 1955-61, 67-74; Democratic ward committeeman, 1960-74; bd. dirs. Schwab Rehab. Hosp., 1961-71, Swedish Covenant Hosp., 1969-75. With USNR, 1942-45. Decorated Legion of Merit; recipient 9th Ann. Pub. Svc. award Tau Epsilon Rho, 1963, Hubert L. Will award Am. Vets. Com., 1983, award of merit Decalogue Soc. Lawyers, 1986, Judge Learned Hand award Am. Jewish Com., 1994, Frances Feinberg Meml. Crown award Associated Talmud Torahs of Chgo., 1995, Bill of Rights in Action award Constl. Rights Found., 1997, Civic Contbn. award LWV Chgo., 2000; named to Sr. Citizen's Hall of Fame, City of Chgo., 1989, Hall of Fame Jewish Comty. Ctrs. Chgo., 1989, Laureate Lincoln Acad. Ill., 1997, Chgo. Coun. Lawyers and the Appleseed Fund Justice Commitment to Justice award, 1998. Mem. ABA, Ill. Bar Assn., Chgo. Bar Assn., Chgo. Hist. Soc., Decalogue Soc. Lawyers (Merit award 1986), Izaak Walton League, Chgo. Hort. Soc., Comml. Club Chgo., Std. Club, Variety Club, Order of Coif, Phi Beta Kappa, Phi Beta Kappa Assocs. Administrative and regulatory, Antitrust, General civil litigation. Home: 1555 N Astor St Chicago IL 60610-1673 Office: Piper Marbury Rudnich & Wolfe 203 N La Salle St Ste 1800 Chicago IL 60601-1210

SIMONE, JOSEPH R. lawyer; b. N.Y.C., Jan. 7, 1949; m. Virginia E. Simone, May 29, 1971; children: Jacquelyn, Robert. BA cum laude, Queens Coll., 1971; LLM in Taxation, NYU, 1977; JD cum laude, Fordham U., 1974. Bar: N.Y. 1975, U.S. Dist. Ct. (so. dist.) N.Y. 1975, U.S. Ct. Appeals (2d cir.) 1975. Ptnr. Patterson, Belknap, Webb & Tyler, N.Y.C., 1982-88, Schulte, Roth & Zabel, N.Y.C., 1988—; spl. prof. law Hofstra U. Sch. Law, 1998-2001. Author: (textbooks) Pension Answer Book, 5th edit., 1990, Essential Facts: Pension and Profit-sharing Plans, 1999; editl. advisor Jour. of Pension Planning. Mem. Am. Arbitration Assn. (panel on multi-employer pension plans, employee benefits law adv. com, co-chair symposium employee benefits), Phi Beta Kappa. Pension, profit-sharing, and employee benefits. Office: Schulte Roth & Zabel 919 3rd Ave Fl 19 New York NY 10022-4774 E-mail: joseph.simone@srz.com

SIMONS, BARBARA M. lawyer; b. N.Y.C., Feb. 7, 1929; d. Samuel A. and Minnie (Mankes) Malitz; m. Morton L. Simons, Sept. 2, 1951; 1 child, Claudia. BA, U. Mich., 1950, JD, 1952. Bar: N.Y. 1953, U.S. Supreme Ct. 1963, U.S. Ct. Appeals (D.C. cir.) 1971, (5th cir.) 1992, (1st cir.) 1994. Ptnr. Simons & Simons, Washington, 1962—. Pres. Forest Hills Citizens Assn., Washington, 1998—; past pres. D.C. chpt. U. Mich. Alumnae, Washington. Alumnae scholar U. Mich., 1946-50. Mem. Washington Coun. Lawyers, Nat. Partnership Women & Families, Sierra Club, Nat. Symphony Orch. Assn., Phi Beta Kappa, Phi Kappa Phi, Alpha Lambda Delta. Administrative and regulatory, FERC practice, Public utilities. Office: Simons & Simons 5025 Linnean Ave NW Washington DC 20008-2042

SIMONS, RICHARD DUNCAN, lawyer, retired judge; b. Niagara Falls, N.Y., Mar. 23, 1927; s. William Taylor and Sybil Irene (Swick) S.; m. Muriel (Penny) E. Genung, June 9, 1951 (dec. 1992); m. Esther (Esi) Turkington Tremblay, May 21, 1994; children: Ross T., Scott R., Kathryn E., Linda A. AB, Colgate U., 1949; LLB, U. Mich., 1952; LLD (hon.), Albany Law Sch., 1983. Bar: N.Y. 1952. Pvt. practice, Rome, 1952-63; asst. corp. counsel City of Rome, 1955-58, corp. counsel, 1960-63; justice 5th jud. dist. N.Y. Supreme Ct., 1964-83, assoc. justice appellate divsn. 3d dept., 1971-72, assoc. justice appellate divsn. 4th dept., 1973-82; assoc. judge N.Y. Ct. Appeals, 1983-96, acting chief judge, 1992-93; counsel McMahon, Grow & Getty, Rome, 1997-00; dir. N.Y. State Capital Defender Office, 1997-2000; chief appellate judge Oneida Indian Nation, 1997—. Jurist in residence Syracuse U. Law Sch., 1998; mem. Law Sch. Admission Svcs., Bar Passage Study Com. Editorial staff: N.Y. Pattern Jury Instructions, 1979-83. Chmn. Republican City Com., 1958-62; vice chmn. Oneida County Rep. Com., 1958-62; bd. mgrs. Rome Hosp. and Murphy Meml. Hosp., 1953; mem. Chief Judge's Commn. on Fiduciary Appointments, Chief Judge's Com. to Promote Trust and Confidence in the Legal Sys., N.Y. Fair Elections Project, Inc., Campaign for Effective Justice. Served with USN, World War II. NEH fellow U. Va. Law Sch., 1979 Fellow Am. Bar Found., N.Y. State Bar Found. (chmn. 1997-98); mem. ABA, N.Y. State Bar Assn. (chair task force on ct. reorganization 1999-2000, Disting. Svc. award 2000), Oneida County Bar Assn., Rome Bar Assn., Am. Law Inst., Inst. Jud. Adminstrn. Home: 6520 Pillmore Cir Rome NY 13440-7337 Office: McMahon Grow & Getty 301 N Washington St Ste 4 Rome NY 13440-5152

SIMONSEN, GREGORY MARK, lawyer, bishop; b. Salt Lake City, June 20, 1957; s. Robert Merrill and Mary Jeannette (Facer) S.; m. Laurel Lee Bunker, Mar. 2, 1979; children: Scott Elden, Collin Robert, Logan David, Rachel Lea. BS magna cum laude, U. Utah, 1982, JD, 1985. Bar: Utah 1985, U.S. Dist. Ct. Utah 1985, U.S. Ct. Appeals (10th cir.) 1985. Assoc. Fox, Edwards, Gardiner & Brown, Salt Lake City, 1985-87, Edwards, McCoy & Kennedy, Salt Lake City, 1987-90, ptnr., 1990-91, Fetzer, Hendrickson & Simonsen, Salt Lake City, 1991—. Bd. dirs. Salt Lake City Rape Crisis Ctr., 1986-87; gen. ptnr. Simpar Assocs.; elected del. Salt Lake County Conv., 1990, Rep. State Conv., 1992. Richard Leary scholar, 1983-85. Mem. ABA, Utah Bar Assn., Salt Lake County Bar Assn. Republican. Mormon. Avocations: horseback riding, ranching. Environmental, Real property.

SIMONTON, ROBERT BENNET, lawyer; b. N.Y.C., Feb. 23, 1933; s. Theodore E. and Beulah H. (Hulsebus) S.; m. Tanya Wood, Aug. 24, 1957; children: Sheri, Robert B. Jr., Scott S. Student, Amherst Coll., 1950-52; BS in Engring., Columbia U., 1954; LLB, Syracuse U., 1959. Bar: N.Y. 1959. Patent agt., atty. Theodore E. Simonton, Cazenovia, N.Y., 1956-60; assoc. Hancock, Dorr, Ryan and Shove, Syracuse, 1960-64; staff atty. Bristol-Myers Co., 1967, counsel, 1967-71, v.p., counsel Bristol Labs., 1971-74; v.p., sec., gen. counsel Crouse Hinds Co., 1974-75; staff atty. Sterling Drug Inc., N.Y.C., 1975-78, sec., asst. gen. counsel, 1978-88; small bus. cons., 1988—. Adj. prof. U. Bridgeport (Conn.) Law Sch., 1988-90; trustee Syracuse Savs. Bank, 1973-76. Bd. govs. Citizens' Found., Syracuse, 1969-70; bd. dirs. Urban League of Syracuse, 1967-72, pres., 1967-71, chmn., 1971-72; bd. visitors Syracuse U. Coll. Law, 1968—; bd. dirs. Graham Windham, also sec., 1986-88, Goodwill Industries, Coastal Empire, 1992-98, treas., 1993-95; treas. Landings Assn. Inc., 1994-96; bd. trustees Manlius Pub. Hill Sch., 1962-75, chmn., 1971-74; vol. Ga. Legal Svcs., 1998—. Served with U.S. Army, 1954-56. Recipient Justinian Honor Soc. award Syracuse U. Coll. Law, 1959. Antitrust, General corporate, Pension, profit-sharing, and employee benefits.

SIMPSON, CHARLES R., III, judge; b. Cleve., July 8, 1945; s. Charles Ralph and Anne M. Simpson; married; 3 children. BA, U. Louisville, 1967, JD, 1970. Bar: Ky. 1970, U.S. Dist. Ct. (we. dist.) Ky. 1971, U.S. Cir. Ct. (6th cir.) 1985. With Rubin, Trautwein & Hays, Louisville, 1971-75, Levin, Yussman & Simpson, Louisville, 1975-77; judge U.S. Dist. Ct. (we. dist.) Ky., 1986—, now chief judge; pvt. practice, 1977-86. Part-time staff counsel Jefferson County Judge/Exec., 1978-84; adminstr. Jefferson County Alcoholic Beverage Control, 1983-84; city clk. City of Rolling Fields, 1985-86. Roman Catholic. Office: We Dist Ct Ky 247 US Courthouse 601 W Broadway Louisville KY 40202-2238 E-mail: judgesimpson@kywd.vscourts.gov

SIMPSON, DANIEL REID, lawyer, mediator; b. Glen Alpine, N.C., Feb. 20, 1927; s. James R. and Margaret Ethel (Newton) S.; m. Mary Alice Leonard, Feb. 25, 1930; children: Mary Simpson Beyer, Ethel B. Simpson Todd, James R., II. BS, Wake Forest U., 1949, LLB, 1951. Bar: N.C. 1951, U.S. Dist. Ct. (we. dist.) N.C. 1951, U.S. Ct. Appeals (4th and 5th cirs.) 1980; cert. mediator. Former ptnr. Simpson Aycock PA, Morganton, N.C.; of counsel Simpson, Simpson & Viney, P.A. Bd. dirs. 1st Union Nat. Bank, Morganton, N.C. Mem. N.C. Ho. of Reps., 1959-65; mem. N.C. Senate, 1984-96; del. Rep. Nat. Conv., 1968, 76; mem. N.C. Rep. Exec. Com. Served with AUS, 1943-45, PTO. Recipient Guardian Small Bus. award Order of Longleaf Pine; named to NRA Legion of Honor; sports complex named in his honor by Town of Glen Alpine, N.C. Mem. N.C. Bar Assn., Burke County Bar Assn., Masons. Baptist. General corporate, Franchising. Home: 2358 E Point Rd Nebo NC 28761-9694 Office: Simpson Simpson & Viney PA 204 E Mcdowell St Morganton NC 28655-3545 also: PO Box 1329 Morganton NC 28680-1329

SIMPSON, JAMES MARLON, JR. lawyer; b. Little Rock, June 9, 1952; s. James Marlon Sr. and Wanda Louise (Garrison) S. m. Karen Brooks, Dec. 30, 1977. B.S., U. Ark., 1974, J.D., 1976. Bar: U.S. Dist. Ct. (ea. and we. dists.) Ark. 1977, U.S. Ct. Appeals (8th cir.) 1977. Ptnr. Friday, Eldredge & Clark, Little Rock, 1976— . Contbr. articles to legal publs. Mem. ABA, Ark. Bar Assn. (ho. of dels. 1983—), Pulaski County Bar Assn, Am. and Ark. Bd. Trial Advocates, Internat. Assn. of Defense Counsel, Ark. Assn. Defense Counsel. Republican. Baptist. Lodge: Rotary. Antitrust, Federal civil litigation, State civil litigation. Home: 30 River Ridge Cir Little Rock AR 72227-1502 Office: Friday Eldredge & Clark 2000 First Commercial Bldg Little Rock AR 72201

SIMPSON, JOHN M. lawyer; b. Ponca City, Okla., Sept. 26, 1950; AB, Harvard U., 1972; JD, Columbia U., 1978. Bar: D.C. 1979, N.C. 1988. Mem. Fulbright & Jaworski L.L.P., Washington. Office: Fulbright & Jaworski LLP Market Square 801 Pennsylvania Ave NW Washington DC 20004-2615 E-mail: jsimpson@fulbright.com

SIMPSON, LYLE LEE, lawyer; b. Des Moines, Oct. 15, 1937; s. R. Clair and Martha B. (Accola) S. BA, Drake U., 1960, JD, 1963. Bar: Iowa 1963, U.S. Dist. Ct. (so. and no. dists.) Iowa 1963, U.S. Ct. Appeals (8th cir.) 1963, U.S. Tax Ct. 1963, U.S. Supreme Ct. 1970, U.S. Ct. Mil. Appeals 1972. Pvt. practice, Des Moines, 1963; mem. Beving and Swanson, 1964-68; sr. ptnr. Peddicord, Simpson & Sutphin, 1968-83; pres. Dreher, Simpson & Jensen, PC, 1984—. Gen. counsel campaign com. Gov. Iowa, 1978-98. Contbr. articles to profl. jours. Chmn. bd. trustees Broadlawns Med. Ctr., 1974-80; mem. Iowa Inaugural Com., 1983, 87, 89, 91, 95; bd. dirs. YMCA Boys Camp, 1967-86, Home, Inc., 1981-85, Project H.E.L.P.E.R., 1983-87, Batten Found.; pres., bd. dirs. Polk County Health Svcs., 1972-88; chmn. Iowa Health Facilities Coun., 1988-93; pres. First Unitarian Ch., 1958-70, Iowa Humanities Bd., 1988-94, Humanist Found., 1980—, East High Alumni Found., 1992—; treas. Iowa Humanities Found., 1994-99, vice-chmn., Iowa Health Found.; investment com., fin. com. Iowa Health Sys., 2000—. Recipient Oren E. Scott award, Class of 1915 award in liberal arts Drake U., 1960. Mem. ABA, Iowa Bar Assn., Polk County Bar Assn., Am. Arbitration Assn., Am. Humanist Assn. (pres. 1979-89), Prairie Club (pres. 1992), Morning Club (pres. 1965), Le Chevaliers de vin Club (pres. 1976-85), YMCA Heritage Club (pres.), Masons, Scottish Rite (Shriner, 33 degree), Rotary. Republican. Congregationalist. General corporate, Estate planning, Real property. Address: 1500 Hub Tower Des Moines IA 50309-3940 E-mail: lsimpson@dreherlaw.com

SIMPSON, RUSSELL AVINGTON, retired law firm administrator; b. Greybull, Wyo., June 19, 1935; s. William Avington and Margaret E. (Draper) S.; m. Margarita A. del Valle, Dec. 19, 1960; children: Margaret E., Robert A., Alexandra P., Christina M. BS with honors, U. Wyo., 1957; LLB, Harvard U., 1965. Bar: Tex. 1965, Mass. 1966. Assoc. Bonilla, de Pena, Read & Bonilla, Corpus Christi, Tex., 1965-66; asst. dean, dir. admissions Harvard Law Sch., Cambridge, Mass., 1966-75, asst. dean, dir. fin. aid, 1972-78, asst. dean for fin. and gen. adminstrn., 1978-84; dir. adminstrn. Hill & Barlow, Boston, 1984-90; v.p., treas. The Archs. Collaborative, Cambridge, 1991-92, ret., 1992. Chmn. devel. com. Law Sch. Data Assembly Service, 1969; pres. bd. dirs. Law Sch. Admissions Services, Newtown, Pa., 1979-80, bd. dirs., 1989-91; trustee Law Sch. Admission Coun., 1968-70, 72-78, 81-82, chmn. svcs. com. 1972-74, chmn. test devel. and rsch. 1976-78; founder Grad. and Profl. Sch. Fin. Aid Coun. Mem. Belmont (Mass.) Town Meeting, 1975-96, Belmont Sch. Com., 1977-83. Capt. USAF, 1957-62. Mem. Tex. Bar Assn., Rotary (bd. dirs. Belmont 1978-80), Phi Kappa Phi. Democrat. Home: 49 Elizabeth Rd Belmont MA 02478-3819 E-mail: russsmpsn@earthlink,net

SIMPSON, RUSSELL GORDON, lawyer, former mayor, counselor to not-for-profit organizations; b. Springfield, Mass., May 22, 1927; s. Archer Roberts and Maude Ethel (Gordon) S.; m. Bickley S. Flower, Sept. 11, 1954; children: Barbara G., Elisabeth Pires-Fernandes, Helen Blair. BA, Yale U., 1951; JD, Boston U., 1956; postgrad., Parker Sch. Internat. Law, 1962. Bar: Mass. 1956, U.S. Dist. Ct. (fed. dist.) Mass. 1957, U.S. Ct. Appeals (2d cir.) 1958, U.S. Supreme Ct. 1980. Advt. mgr. Burden Bryant Co., Springfield, 1951-53; assoc. Goodwin, Procter & Hoar, Boston, 1956-64, ptnr., 1965-87, of counsel, 1987—. Sr. advisor to pres. World Learning, Inc., Brattleboro, Vt., 1988-89, exec. v.p., 1989-90, sr. v.p., 1990-91, trustee, 1991—, exec. com., 1994—; trustee, mem. exec. com., Save the Children Fedn., Westport, Conn., 1995—; mem. exec. group Internat. Save the Children Alliance, Geneva, Switzerland and London, Eng., 1996—; dir., vice chmn., mem. exec. com., Cmty. Found. Palm Beach and Martin Counties, West Palm Beach, Fla., 1994-2000; counselor to not-for-profit orgns., 1991-2000. Author: The Lawyer's Basic Corporate Practice Manual, 1971, rev. edit., 1978, 84, 87. Mayor Jupiter Island, Fla., 1993-99; hon. consul New Eng. of Bolivia, 1958-82, mem. spl. com. to revise Mass. Corrupt Practices Act, 1961-62; bd. govs. Jupiter Island Club, 2000—; mem. blue ribbon commn. Martin County Fla. Econ. Coun. Named Outstanding Young Man of Greater Boston, 1963. Fellow Am. Bar Found., Mass. Bar Found.; mem. Mass. Bar Assn. (chmn. banking and bus. law sect. 1980-83, bd. dels., exec. com. 1983-87, v.p. 1985-87), ABA (corp. banking and bus. law sect., com. on law firms, co-chmn. com. on law firm governance, panel on corp. law ednl. programs), Hobe Sound Yacht Club (gov., sec. 2001—). Home: 101 Harbor Way PO Box 1106 Hobe Sound FL 33475-1106

SIMPSON, STEVEN DREXELL, lawyer; b. Sturgis, Mich., Sept. 20, 1953; s. Rex and Lorraine Simpson; m. Peggy Deibert, Apr. 28, 1979; children: Andrew Drexell, Christine Elizabeth, Marianne Tyner. BA, Hillsdale (Mich.) Coll., 1975; JD, Wake Forest U., 1978; LLM in Taxation, Georgetown U., 1981. Bar: Fla. 1978, D.C. 1980, N.C. 1984. Assoc. Bradford, Williams et al, Miami, Fla., 1978-80, Webster & Chamberlain, Washington, 1980-82, Fisher, Wayland et al, Washington, 1982-84, Maupin, Taylor & Ellis, P.A., Raleigh, N.C., 1984-98; ptnr. Law Offices of Steven D. Simpson P.A., 1998—. Author: Taxation of Broadcasters, 1984, Tax-Exempt Organizations: Organizational and Operational Requirements, 2000, Taxable Expenditures, 2000, Tax Compliance for Tax-Exempt Organizations, 2000, Tax-Exempt Organizations: Reporting, Disclosure and Other Procedural Aspects, 2000; contbr. articles to profl. jours. Mem. ABA (exemp orgns. com.). Republican. Methodist. Avocations: golf, running. Health, Non-profit and tax-exempt organizations, Taxation, general. Home: 409 Hillandale Dr Raleigh NC 27609-7036 Office: Landmark Center II 4601 Six Forks Rd Ste 530 Raleigh NC 27609-5286 E-mail: s.simpsonlaw@verizon.net

SIMS, REBECCA LITTLETON, lawyer; b. Macon, Ga., May 24, 1957; d. William Harvey and Carlan Patricia (Hammond) Littleton; m. Charles Neil Sims, Jr., Dec. 29, 1984; children: Charles Neil III, William Vickers, Caroline Greer. Student, Tex. A&M U., 1977, Baylor U., 1978, U. South, 1979; JD, Baylor U., 1981; BA in Polit. Sci. with honors, U. South, 1979. Bar: Ga. 1983, U.S. Dist. Ct. (so. dist.) Ga. 1984, U.S. Dist. Ct. (no. dist.) Ga. 1985, U.S. Dist. Ct. (mid. dist.) Ga. 1992, U.S. Supreme Ct. 2001. Law clk., Waco, Tex., 1981, Waycross Jud. Cir., Waycross and Douglas, Ga., 1982-83; asst. dist. atty. Waycross cir. Dist. Atty.'s Office, Douglas, 1983-84; spl. asst. to atty. gen. Dept. Family and Children's Svcs., Coffee County, 1988-90; pvt. practice Douglas, 1985-92; state ct. solicitor Coffee County, Ga., 1989-96; in-house counsel Sims Funeral Home, 1997-99; instr. polit. sci. South Ga. Coll., Douglas, 2000—. Mem Bar of United States Supreme Ct., 2001. Mem. altar guild St. Andrew's Episcopal Ch., Douglas, 1983-90, 2000—, vestryman, clk. of vestry, 1986-88; bd. dirs. Shelter for Abused Women, Waycross, 1986-87; trustee Diocese of Ga., U. South, Savannah, 1988-91; mem. First Meth. Ch., Douglas, Ga., 1991-99, United Meth. Women Cir. # 8, 1991-98; dir. Vacation Bible Sch., 1997, 98; legis. aid Charles Neil Sims, Jr., Ga. Ho. Reps., 1997—. Mem. State Bar Ga., Acad. Boosters Club (awards chmn. 1997-98), Beta Sigma Phi (pres. 1997-98). Avocations: gardening, reading, needlework, cooking, antiques. Criminal, Family and matrimonial, Probate. Office: PO Box 2352 Douglas GA 31534-2352 E-mail: rsims@mail.sgc.peachnet.edu, arcades57@aol.com

SIMS, ROGER W. lawyer; b. Cleve., Aug. 3, 1950; BA with high honors, U. Fla., 1972, JD, 1974. Bar: Fla. 1975. Mem. Holland & Knight, Orlando, Fla. Mem. Moot Ct. U. Fla.; contbr. to profl mags and jours. Mem. ABA (mem. standing com. on environ. law 2000—), Fla. Bar Assn. (chmn. environ., land use law sect. 1988-89), Phi Beta Kappa, Phi Kappa Phi, Omicron Delta Kappa, Phi Alpha Delta, Fla. Blue Key. Administrative and regulatory, Environmental, Real property. Office: Holland & Knight PO Box 1526 200 S Orange Ave Ste 2600 Orlando FL 32801-3453

SIMS, VICTOR DWAYNE, lawyer; b. Middletown, Ohio, Aug. 1, 1959; s. Gerald Clifton and Ethel Ree (Bruce) S. Student, Am. U., 1980; BA, Heidelberg Coll., 1981; JD, Howard U., 1987. Bar: Ohio, 1989; U.S. Dist. Ct. (so. dist.) Ohio, 1990. Congl. intern U.S. Congress, Washington, 1980; fundraiser Telecommunications Rsch. and Action Ctr., 1984; assoc. Leslie I. Gaines & Assoc., Cin., 1989-91; pvt. practice Sims and Assocs., 1991—. Mng. atty. Leslie I. Gaines & Assoc., 1990—; ptnr. Sims and Asmah Law Firm. Author poetry. Mem. ABA, Ohio Bar Assn., Cin. Bar Assn. Avocations: writing, music, current events. Criminal, Family and matrimonial, General practice. Office: Centennial Plaza III #850 895 Central Ave Cincinnati OH 45202

SIMSON, GARY JOSEPH, law educator, educator; b. Newark, Mar. 18, 1950; s. Marvin and Mildred (Silberg) S.; m. Rosalind Slivka, Aug. 15, 1971; children: Nathaniel, Jennie Anne. BA, Yale Coll., 1971; JD, Yale U., 1974. Bar: Conn. 1974, N.Y. 1980. Law clk. to judge U.S. Ct. Appeals 2d Cir., 1974-75; from asst. prof. law to prof. law U. Tex., 1975-80; prof. law Cornell U., Ithaca, N.Y., 1980-97, prof. law, assoc. dean, 1997—. Vis. prof. law Cornell U., Ithaca, 1979-80, U. Calif., Berkeley, 1986; chmn. adv. bd. law casebook series Carolina Acad. Press. Author: Issues and Perspectives in Conflict of Laws, 1985, 3d edit., 1997; contbr. articles to profl. jours. Mem. ABA, ACLU, Phi Beta Kappa. Office: Cornell U Law Sch Myron Taylor Hall Ithaca NY 14853 E-mail: simson@law.mail.cornell.edu

SINAK, DAVID LOUIS, lawyer; b. Detroit, Oct. 3, 1953; s. Joseph and Edwina Mae (Collarini) S.; m. Elisabeth Crook; children: Jeffrey David, Margaret Louise, Slade Henry. BA, U. Notre Dame, 1975; student, London Sch. Econs., 1975-76; JD, Boston Coll., 1979. Bar: Tex. 1979, U.S. Ct. Claims 1981, U.S. Tax Ct. 1981, U.S. Dist. Ct. (no. dist.) Tex. 1984, U.S. Ct. Appeals (fed. cir.) 1982, U.S. Ct. Appeals (5th cir.) 1984. Assoc. Hughes and Luce (formerly Hughes and Hill), Dallas, 1979-84; ptnr. Hughes and Luce, L.L.P. (formerly Hughes and Hill), 1984—. Speaker on taxes to tax insts., law insts. and assns. and legal founds., 1981—. Mem. ABA, Tex. Bar Assn., Dallas Bar Assn. Corporate taxation, Taxation, general, Personal income taxation. Office: Hughes and Luce LLP 1717 Main St Ste 2800 Dallas TX 75201-4685 E-mail: sinakd@hughesluce.com

SINAS, GEORGE THOMAS, lawyer; b. Detroit, June 1, 1950; s. Thomas George and Martha (Gikas) S.; m. Sheryl Ann Hogan, June 24, 1972; children— Thomas, Stephen. B.A. in Polit. Sci., U. Mich., 1972; J.D., Wayne State U., 1975. Bar: Mich. 1975, U.S. Dist. Ct. (ea. dist.) Mich. 1976, U.S. Ct. Appeals (6th cir.) 1976, U.S. Dist. Ct. (we. dist.) Mich. 1980. Ptnr. Sinas, Dramis, Brake, Boughton, McIntyre & Reisig, P.C., Lansing, Mich., 1975—; faculty Mich. Jud. Inst., 1979— ; mediator Ingham Cir. Cts., 1980—; mem. Supreme Ct. Com. on Standard Jury Instructions, Detroit, 1984—. Author: Michigan No Fault Auto Insurance Decisions, 1978 (Mich. Trial Lawyers Assn. Spl. award 1979). Chair State Bar of Mich. Negligence Law Section, 1989-90. Mem. Mich. Trial Lawyers Assn. (pres. 1982-83), Assn. Trial Lawyers Am. (nat. gov. 1984-90). Insurance, Personal injury. Office: 520 Seymour Ave Lansing MI 48933-1118

SINCLAIR, JULIE MOORES WILLIAMS, law librarian, consultant; b. Montgomery, Ala., May 2, 1954; d. Benjamin Buford and Marilyn Moores (Simpson) Williams; m. Winfield James Sinclair, Dec. 16, 1978. BA, U. of South, 1976; MLS, U. Ala., Tuscaloosa, 1977; JD, Washington U., St. Louis, 1987. Bar: Ala. 1989, U.S. Dist. Ct. (no. dist.) Ala. 1989. Serials libr. Ala. Dept. Archives and History, Montgomery, 1977; cataloguing libr. Ala. Pub. Libr. Svc., 1978; league libr. Ala. League Municipalities, 1978-84; asst. libr. Mo. Ct. Appeals, St. Louis, 1984-86, law clk., 1987-88; cons. Law Libr. Cons., Birmingham, Ala., 1988—; librarian Thomas Goode Jones Sch. of Law Library. Contbr. numerous articles to profl. jours. Mem. Ala. Bar Assn., Ala. Libr. Assn., Am. Assn. Law Librs., Law Libr. Assn. Ala. (charter, v.p. 1992-93, pres. 1993-94), Ala. Fedn. Bus. and Profl. Women (pres. 1997-98), Order of Gownsmen, Phi Alpha Theta. Episcopalian. Avocations: travel and sightseeing, reading, attending theatre, especially Shakespeare. Office: Law Libr Svcs Cons 3045 Independence Dr Ste D Birmingham AL 35209-4170 E-mail: jmwsinclair@mindspring.com, jsinclair@faulkner.edu

SING, WILLIAM BENDER, lawyer; b. Houston, Oct. 16, 1947; s. William Bender Sr. and Alice Irene S.; m. Doris Anne Spradley, Sept. 1, 1967; children: Erin Elaine, Emily Elizabeth. BS cum laude, U. Houston, 1968, JD magna cum laude, 1971; MLA, U. St. Thomas, 1995. Bar: Tex. 1971. Assoc. Fulbright & Jaworski, LLP, Houston, 1973-80, ptnr., 1980—. Elder, trustee St. Andrew's Presbyn. Ch., Houston; past pres., bd. dirs. St. Andrew's Presbyn. Sch., Houston; past pres. Houston C.C. Place Civic

Assn. 1st lt. U.S. Army, 1971-73. Mem. ABA, Tex. Bar Assn., Houston Bar Assn., Order of the Barons Law Honor Soc., U. Houston Alumni Orgn. (life), Phi Delta Phi (life), Phi Kappa Phi, Omicron Delta Epsilon. Presbyterian. Avocation: reading history and literature. Bankruptcy, Real property. Office: Fulbright & Jaworski LLP 1301 Mckinney St Houston TX 77010-3031

SINGER, DANIEL MORRIS, lawyer; b. Bklyn., Oct. 10, 1930; s. Samuel W. and Fannie G. (Sabloff) S.; m. Maxine Frank, June 15, 1952; children: Amy E., Ellen R., David B., Stephanie F. BA with honors, Swarthmore Coll., 1951; LLB, Yale U., 1954. Bar: N.Y. 1956, U.S. Dist. Ct. D.C. 1957, U.S. Ct. Appeals (D.C. cir.) 1957, U.S. Supreme Ct. 1959. Motions clk. U.S. Ct. Appeals for D.C. Circuit, Washington, 1956-57, law clk. to Judge George T. Washington, 1957-58; assoc. Fried, Frank, Harris, Shriver & Jacobson, 1958-64, ptnr., 1965-87, counsel, 1987—. Arbitrator complex comml. case and constrn. nat. panels; mediator US Dist. Ct., Washington; vol. atty. Lawyers Com. for Civil Rights Under Law, 1965, 66; mem. exec. com. Washington Lawyers Com. for Civil Rights Under Law, 1973—; spl. asst. corp. counsel, D.C., 1995-2000. Bd. mgrs. Swarthmore Coll., 1987-91; bd. dirs., sec.-treas. Nat. Com. Tithing in Investment, 1964-65; dir., sec.-treas. Coun. for a Livable World, 1962-64; mem. governing coun., mem. exec. com. Am. Jewish Congress, 1986-96, v.p., 1988-92; dir. Am. Soc. for Protection of Nature in Israel, 1986—; bd. dirs. D.C. Developing Families Ctr., 1999—; bd. dirs. D.C. Appleseed Ctr., 1996—, pres., 2000. With Signal Corps, U.S. Army, 1954-56. Mem. ABA, D.C. Bar. Home: 5410 39th St NW Washington DC 20015-2902 Office: Fried Frank Harris Shriver 1001 Pennsylvania Ave NW Washington DC 20004-2596 E-mail: daniel.singer@ffhsj.com

SINGER, GARY JAMES, lawyer; b. L.A., Oct. 8, 1952; s. Stanley Merle and Ernestine Alice (Brandstatter) S.; m. Melanie Carol Rabin, Mar. 19, 1978; children: Brian, Kimberly, Andrew. BA, U. Calif., Irvine, 1974; JD, Loyola U., 1977. Bar: Calif. 1977, U.S. Dist. Ct. (fed. dist.) 1978. Assoc. O'Melveny & Myers, L.A., Newport Beach, Calif., 1977-84, ptnr., 1985—. Bd. dirs. Irvine Barclay Theatre, UC Irvine Found. Avocations: golf, skiing, reading. General corporate, Securities. Office: O'Melveny & Myers 610 Newport Center Dr Ste 1700 Newport Beach CA 92660-6429

SINGER, JEFFREY, lawyer; b. Bklyn., Apr. 5, 1955; s. Stanley and May Singer; m. Carol Joan Gilbert, Nov. 23, 1991; 1 child, Tori Hannah; step-children: Matthew Hollander, Michael Hollander. BA, SUNY at Stony Brook, 1976; JD, Bklyn. Law Sch., 1979. Bar: N.Y. 1980, U.S. Dist. Ct. (so. dist. and ea. dist.) N.Y. 1980, U.S. Ct. Appeals (2d cir.) 1982, U.S. Supreme Ct. 1984. Law clk. Segan, Culhane, Nemerov & Geen P.C., N.Y.C., 1977-79, assoc., 1980-86, ptnr., 1986—. Mem. Am. Trial Lawyers Assn., N.Y. State Trial Lawyers, Assn. of Bar of City of N.Y. Avocations: scuba diving, golf, wine collecting. E-mial. Personal injury, Product liability. Office: Segan Nemerov & Singer PC 112 Madison Ave Fl 6 New York NY 10016-7416 E-mail: jsinger@snslaw.com

SINGER, MICHAEL HOWARD, lawyer; b. N.Y.C., Nov. 22, 1941; s. Jack and Etta (Appelbaum) S.; m. Saundra Jean Kupperman, June 1, 1962; children: Allison Jill, Pamela Faith. BS in Econs., U. Pa., 1962; JD, NYU, 1965, LLM in Taxation, 1968. Bar: N.Y. 1965, U.S. Ct. Claims 1968, U.S. Supreme Ct. 1969, U.S. Ct. Appeals (6th cir.) 1970, D.C. 1972, U.S. Tax Ct. 1972, Nev. 1973, U.S. Ct. Appeals (9th cir.) 1973. Law asst. Appellate Term Supreme Ct., N.Y.C., 1965-68; trial lawyer Ct. Claims Tax Div., Washington, 1968-72; tax lawyer Beckley, DeLanoy & Jemison, Las Vegas, 1972-74; ptnr. Oshins, Singer, Segal & Morris, 1974-87; pvt. practice, 1987; ptnr. Michael H. Singer Ltd., 1987-96, Singer, Brown, and Barringer, LLC, Las Vegas, 1996-99, Singer & Brown, LLC, 1999—. Settlement judge Nev. Supreme Ct., 1997—. Pres. Las Vegas chpt. NCCJ, 1980-82. Mem. ABA, ABI, Nev. Bar Assn., Las Vegas Country Club (bd. dirs. 1999—). Democrat. Jewish. Avocations: golf, tennis. Contracts commercial, General corporate, Real property. Home: 4458 Los Reyes Ct Las Vegas NV 89121-5341 Office: Singer & Brown LLC 520 S 4th St Fl 2 Las Vegas NV 89101-6524 E-mail: mhsinger@lvcm.com

SINGER, MYER R(ICHARD), lawyer; b. Everett, Mass., Oct. 24, 1938; s. Nathan and Celia (Rudin) S.; m. Elaine Doris Ginesky, June 17, 1962; children: Andrew L., Stephen D., Jocelyn G. BSBA, Boston U., 1960, LLB, 1963. Bar: Mass. 1963, U.S. Ct. Appeals (1st cir.) 1963. Atty. Boston Legal Aid Soc., 1963-64; pvt. practice Dennis Port, Mass., 1965—. Trustee, corporator, mem. bd. investment Cape Cod Five Cents Savs. bank, Harwich Port, Mass.; trustee Cape Cod Mus. of Natural History, 2001—; faculty Mass. Continuing Legal Edn., Inc., 1985, 1990—98; program chmn. Real Estate Devel. Cape Cod-Mass. Bar Inst., 1999. Co-author: Creation and Care of Condominiums, 1985, Everything You Need to Know About the Cape Cod Commission Act, 1990; speaker in field. Pres. Dennis Yarmouth Band Parents, 1986—87; mem. adv. bd. Cape Mus. Fine Arts, Dennis, 1988—96; former trustee Cape Code Synagogue; mem., clk. Yarmouth (Mass.) Zoning Bd. Appeals, 1980—86; former bd. dirs. Cape Cod and Island chpt. of Mass. Heart Assn.; former pres. Legal Svcs. of Cape Cod and Island, Inc. Mem. ABA, Mass. Bar Assn. (chmn. bar assn. program real estate devel. Cape Cod 1999), Barnstable County Bar Assn. (mem. exec. com. 1999—). Avocations: boating, photography. Land use and zoning (including planning), Real property. Home: 238 Greenland Circle East Dennis MA 02641-1302 Office: PO Box 67 26 Upper County Rd Dennis Port MA 02639-0067 E-mail: singerlaw@capcod.net

SINGER-FRANKES, DEBORAH, lawyer; d. David Juris and Linda (Cohen) F.; m. Chaim Singer-Frankes, Jan. 5, 1992. BA in Govt., Cornell U., 1989; JD, U. Calif. Sch. of Law, 1994. Bar: Calif., 1996. Trial atty. Aux. Legal Svcs., Inc., L.A., 1996-99; assoc. L.A. County Counsel, Monterey Park, Calif., 1999—. Mem. L.A. County Bar Assn. Office: Office Co Counsel 201 Centre Plaza Dr Ste 1 Monterey Park CA 91754-2142

SINGLETARY, ALVIN D. lawyer; b. Sept. 27, 1942; s. Alvin E. and Alice (Pastoret) Singletary; m. Judy Louise Singletary, Dec. 03, 1983; children: Kimberly Dawn, Shane David, Kelly Diane. BA, La. State U., 1964; JD, Loyola U., New Orleans, 1969. Bar: La. 1969, U.S. Dist. Ct. (ea. dist.) La. 1972, U.S. Ct. Appeals (5th cir.) 1972, U.S. Ct. Appeals (11 cir.) 1981, U.S. Ct. Internat. Trade 1981, U.S. Ct. Customs and Patent Appeals 1982, U.S. Supreme Ct. 1978. Instr. Delgado Coll., New Orleans, 1976—77; sole practice Slidell, 1970—. Spl. asst. dist. atty 22d Judicial Dist. Ct. , Parish of St. Tammany, La.; sec., treas. St. Tammany Pub. Trust Fin. Authority, 1978—. Chmn. sustaining membership enrollment Cypress dist. Boy Scouts Am., 1989—; treas. Slidell Centennial commn.; councilman-at-large City of Slidell, 1978—, interim mayor, 1985; mem. Dem. State Ctrl. Com., 1978—82; mem. Rep. State Ctrl. Com. Dist. 76, La., 1996—; del. La.Constl. Conv., 1972—73; chmn. Together We Build Program First Baptist Ch. of Slidell, La.; bd. dir. St. Tammany Coun. on Aging. Mem.: Lions, Delta Theta Phi. Baptist. General practice, Probate, Real property. Office: PO Box 1158 Slidell LA 70459-1158

SINGLETON, JAMES KEITH, federal judge; b. Oakland, Calif., Jan. 27, 1939; s. James K. and Irene Elisabeth (Lilly) S.; m. Sandra Claire Hoskins, Oct. 15, 1966; children: Matthew David, Michael Keith. Student, U. Santa Clara, 1957-58; AB in Polit. Sci., U. Calif., Berkeley, 1961, LLB, 1964. Bar: Calif. 1965, Alaska, 1965. Assoc. Delaney Wiles Moore and Hayes, Anchorage, 1963, 65-68, Law Offices Roger Cremo, Anchorage, 1968-70; judge Alaska Superior Ct., 1970-80, Alaska Ct. Appeals, Anchorage, 1980-90, U.S. Dist. Ct. for Alaska, Anchorage, 1990-95, chief judge, 1995—. Chmn. Alaska Local Boundary Commn., Anchorage, 1966-69. Chmn. 3d Dist. Rep. Com., Anchorage, 1969-70. Mem. ABA, Alaska Bar Assn., Phi Delta Phi, Tau Kappa Epsilon. Office: US Dist Ct 222 W 7th Ave Unit 41 Anchorage AK 99513-7504

SINGLETON, JOHN ROBINSON, lawyer; b. Calgary, Alta., Can., May 16, 1945; s. Fredrick Bowden and Doreen Marion (Robinson) S. BA, U. Alta., 1966, LLB, 1969; LLM, London Sch. Econs. and Polit. Sci., 1971. Bar: Atla. 1971, N.W.T. 1978, Sask. 1981, B.C. 1982, Y.T. 1984. Assoc. Milner & Steer, Edmonton, Alta., 1969-74, ptnr., 1974-81; owner, operator Singleton & Co., Vancouver, B.C., Calgary and Admonton, Alta, 1982-86; ptnr. Singleton & Urquhart, Vancouver, B.C., Calgary and Edmonton, Alta., 1986—. Pres., Edmonton Symphony Soc., 1979-80, bd. dirs., 1977-79. Mem. Can. Bar Assn. (exec. com. 1978-81, chmn. constrn. law sect. 1986—), Law Soc. B.C., Law Soc. Atla., Law Soc. Sask., Law Soc. Yukon, Law Soc. N.W. Ter. Office: 590 First Edmonton Pl Edmonton AB Canada V6Z 2K8

SINGLETON, SARAH MICHAEL, lawyer; b. Ann Arbor, Mich., Apr. 2, 1949; d. Palmer Christie and Susan (Ballard) S. B.A., Sarah Lawrence Coll., 1971; J.D., Ind. U., 1974. Bar: N. Mex. 1974, U.S. Dist. Ct. N.Mex. 1974, U.S. Ct. Appeals (10th cir.) 1976, U.S. Supreme Ct. 1978. Asst. appellate defender Pub. Defender Office, Santa Fe, N.Mex., 1974-76; ptnr. Pickard & Singleton, Santa Fe, 1976-81; sole practice, Santa Fe, 1981-85; shareholder Montgomery & Andrews, P.A., Santa Fe, 1985— ; bd. visitors U. N.Mex. Sch. Law, 1983— . Contbr. to Women & The Law: The Situation in New Mexico, 1975, also articles; editor (with Pamela B. Minzner) Women's Legal Rights Newsletter, 1983. Pres. bd. trustees No. N.Mex. Legal Services, 1982; chmn. N.Mex. Bd. Bar Examiners, 1983-87 (outstanding service to the ct. and judiciary award 1986). Mem. ABA, State Bar N.Mex. (Outstanding Contbn. award 1983), 1st Jud. Dist. Bar Assn. (pres. 1978). Democrat. Club: Blue Sox Softball (coach 1984). Federal civil litigation, State civil litigation. Office: Montgomery & Andrews PA PO Box 2307 Santa Fe NM 87504-2307

SINK, ROBERT C. lawyer; b. Racine, Wis., 1938; AB, Duke U., 1959, LLB, 1965. Bar: N.C. 1965. Ptnr. Robinson, Bradshaw & Hinson, P.A., Charlotte, N.C., 1965—. Assoc. editor Duke Law Jour., 1964-65. Trustee Pub. Libr. Charlotte and Mecklenburg County, 1985-90, chmn., 1989-90; bd. dirs. Mus. New South, 1991-97, chmn., 1996-97. Lt. USN, 1959-62, USNR. Mem. ABA (ho. dels. 2001—), N.C. State Bar (councilor 1988-96, v.p. 1997, pres.-elect 1997-98, pres. 1998-99), Mecklenburg County Bar (pres. 1986-87), Order of Coif, Phi Beta Kappa. Construction, Government contracts and claims, Real property. Office: Robinson Bradshaw & Hinson PA 101 N Tryon St Ste 1900 Charlotte NC 28246-0103

SINN, DAVID RANDALL, lawyer; b. Peoria, Ill., July 28, 1950; s. Edgar Christian and Esther May (Moore) S.; m. Connie J. Wunder, Aug. 15, 1970; children— Natalie, Rachel, Julia, David J. B.S., Western Ill. U., 1973; J.D., U. Tenn, 1976. Bar: Ill. 1976, U.S. Dist. Ct. (cen. dist.) Ill. 1979; v.p. Sinn Oil Co., East Peoria, Ill., 1976-79; assoc. Heyl, Royster, Voelker & Allen, Peoria, 1979-84, ptnr., 1984— ; def. counsel State of Ill.; lectr. Coll. St. Francis, Joliet, Ill., 1986—. Author: Medical Malpractice. Bd. dirs. Samaritan Ctr., Peoria, 1980-87. Served with USAR, 1970-76. Ill. State scholar, 1968. Mem. ABA, Ill. State Bar Assn., Peoria County Bar Assn. Mem. Christian Ch. (Disciples of Christ). Club: Willow Knolls (Peoria). Federal civil litigation, State civil litigation, Personal injury. Office: Heyl Royster Voelker & Allen 124 SW Adams St Ste 600 Peoria IL 61602-1352

SINNOTT, JOHN PATRICK, lawyer, educator; b. Bklyn., Aug. 17, 1931; s. John Patrick and Elizabeth Muriel (Zinkand) Sinnott; m. Rose Marie Yuppa, May 30, 1959; children: James Alexander, Jessica Michelle. BS, U.S. Naval Acad., 1953; MS, USAF Inst. Tech., 1956; JD, No. Ky. U., 1960. Bar: Ohio 1961, NY 1963, NJ 1970, Ga 2000, US Patent Office 1963, US Supreme Ct 1977. Assoc. Brumbaugh, Graves, Donohue & Raymond, N.Y.C., 1961-63; patent atty. Bell Tel. Labs., Murray Hill, N.J., 1963-64, Schlumberger Ltd., N.Y.C., 1964-71; asst. chief patent counsel Babcock & Wilcox, 1971-79; chief patent and trademark counsel Am. Std. Inc., 1979-92; of counsel Morgan & Finnegan, 1992-99, Langdale, Vallotton, Linahan & Wetherington, L.L.P., Valdosta, Ga., 2000—. Adj lectr NJ Inst Technology, Newark, 1974—89; adj prof Seton Hall Univ Sch Law, Newark, 1989—98. Author: (book) Counterfeit Goods Suppression, 1998, World Patent Law and Practice, Vols 2-2P, 1999, A Practical Guide to Document Authentication, 2001;contbr. articles to profl jours. Mem. local Selective Serv Bd., Plainfield, NJ, 1971; bd dirs New Providence Community Swimming Pool, 1970. Capt. USAF, 1953—61. Decorated Legion of Merit, others. Mem. N.Y. Intellectual Property Law Assn. (bd. dirs. 1974-76), Squadron A Club, Cosmos. Republican. Roman Catholic. Patent, Trademark and copyright. Home: 2517 Rolling Rd Valdosta GA 31602-1244 Fax: (229) 244-9646. E-mail: specan23@aol.com

SINOR, HOWARD EARL, JR. lawyer; b. New Orleans, Sept. 6, 1949; s. Howard E. and Beverly M. (Bourgeois) S.; children: Sally, Vera Sue, Sarah, Sadie. BA with honors, U. New Orleans, 1971; JD cum laude, Harvard U., 1975. Bar: La. 1975, U.S. Supreme Ct. 1983, U.S. Ct. Appeals (3rd, 5th and 11th cir.), U.S. Dist. Ct. (ea., middle, we.) Dist. La. Ptnr. Jones, Walker, Waechter, Poitevent, Carrere & Denegre, 1975-98, Gordon, Arata, McCollam, Duplantis & Eagan, New Orleans, 1999—. Contbg. author: La. Appellate Practice Handbook, 1990, 97; editor: CLE Manual of Recent Developments, 1985; contbr. articles to profl. jours. Recipient Pres.'s award, La. State Bar Assn., 1987. Fellow La. Bar Found.; mem. ABA, FBA, La. State Bar Assn. (chmn. antitrust sect. 1987-89). Avocations: golf, hiking. General civil litigation, Construction, Environmental. Office: Gordon Arata et al 201 Saint Charles Ave Fl 40 New Orleans LA 70170-4000

SISKE, ROGER CHARLES, lawyer; b. Starkville, Miss., Mar. 2, 1944; s. Lester L. and Helen (Cagan) S.; m. Regina Markunas, May 31, 1969; children: Kelly, Jennifer, Kimberly. BS in Fin. with honors, Ohio State U., 1966; JD magna cum laude, U. Mich., 1969. Bar: Ill. 1969. Assoc. Sonnenschein Nath & Rosenthal, Chgo., 1969-78, ptnr., 1978—. Chmn. nat. employee benefits and exec. compensation dept. Served to capt. U.S. Army, 1970-71. Decorated Bronze Star. Fellow Am. Coll. Employee Benefits Counsel (charter); mem. ABA (past chmn. tax sect. employee benefits com., past chmn. joint com. on employee benefits and exec. compensation and bus. law sect., employee benefits and exec. compensation com.), Chgo. Bar Assn. (past chmn. employee benefits com., mem. exec. coun. of tax com.), past chmn. employee benefits coun. ISBA, Order of Coif (editor law review), Phi Alpha Kappa. Republican. Pension, profit-sharing, and employee benefits, Corporate taxation, Estate taxation. Office: Sonnenschein Nath Rosenthal 233 S Wacker Dr Ste 8000 Chicago IL 60606-6491

SISSEL, GEORGE ALLEN, manufacturing executive, lawyer; b. Chgo., July 30, 1936; s. William Worth and Hannah Ruth (Harlan) S.; m. Mary Ruth Runsvold, Oct. 5, 1968; children: Jenifer Ruth, Gregory Allen. B.S. in Elec. Engring., U. Colo., 1958; J.D. cum laude, U. Minn., 1966. Bar: Colo. 1966, Ind. 1973, U.S. Supreme Ct. 1981. Assoc. Sherman & Howard, Denver, 1966-70; with Ball Corp., Broomfield, Colo., 1970—, assoc. gen. counsel, 1974-78, gen. counsel, 1978-95, corp. sec., 1980-95, v.p., 1981-87, sr. v.p., 1987-95, pres., 1995-98, CEO, 1995-2001, chmn. bd., 1996—, also bd. dirs. Bd. advisors First Chgo. Equity Capital, 1995—; bd. dirs. First Merchants Corp. Assoc. editor: U. Minn. Law Rev., 1965-66. Served with USN, 1958-63. Mem. ABA, Can. Mfrs. Inst. (bd. dirs., chmn.), Nat. Assn. Mfrs. (bd. dirs.), Colo. Bar Assn., Colo. Assn. Commerce & Industry, Order of Coif, MIT Soc. Sr. Execs., (bd. govs. 1987-95), Sigma Chi, Sigma Tau, Eta Kappa Nu. Methodist. Lodge: Rotary.

SITES, JAMES PHILIP, lawyer, consul; b. Detroit, Sept. 17, 1948; s. James Neil and Inger Marie (Krogh) S.; m. Barbara Teresa Mazurek, Apr. 9, 1978; children: Philip Erling, Teresa Elizabeth. Student, U. Oslo, Norway, 1968-69; BA, Haverford Coll., 1970; JD, Georgetown U., 1973, ML in Taxation, 1979. Bar: Md. 1973, D.C. 1974, U.S. Supreme Ct. 1978, Mont. 1984, U.S. Tax Ct. 1984, U.S. Dist. Ct. Mont. 1984, U.S. Ct. Appeals (9th cir.) 1988. Law clk. to Hon. James C. Morton, Jr. Ct. Spl. Appeals Md., Annapolis, 1974-75; law clk. to Hon. Orman W. Ketcham Superior Ct. D.C., Washington, 1975-76; gen. atty. U.S. Immigration & Naturalization Svc., 1976-77; trial atty. tax divsn. U.S. Dept. Justice, 1977-84; ptnr. Crowley, Haughey, Hanson, Toole & Dietrich, Billings, Mont., 1984—; consul for Govt. of Norway State of Mont., 1987—. Instr. Norwegian Ea. Mont. Coll., 1987-88, Sons of Norway, 1989—, instr. polit. sci. Mont. State U., Billings, 1997—; v.p. Scandinavian Studies Found., 1989—; bd. dirs. Billings Com. on Fgn. Rels., Festival of Cultures; mem. Mont. Coun. for Internat. Visitors, The Norsemen's Fedn. Chmn. local exec. bd. Mont. State U., Billings, 1993—. Decorated knight 1st class Royal Norwegian Order of Merit; U. Oslo scholar, 1969. Mem. Md. Bar Assn., Mont. State Bar (co-chmn. com. on income and property taxes 1987-91, chair tax and probate sect. 1991-92, chair tax litigation subcom. 1992—), D.C. Bar Assn., Am. Immigration Lawyers Assn., Norwegian-Am. C. of C., Billings C. of C. (bd. dirs. 1998—, chair-elect), Hilands Golf Club, Kenwood Golf and Country Club, Billings Stamp Club, Elks, Masons. Avocations: philately, sports card collecting, hiking, Nordic skiing. Administrative and regulatory, Immigration, naturalization, and customs, State and local taxation. Office: Crowley Haughey Hanson Toole & Dietrich Consulate for Norway 490 N 31st St Billings MT 59101-1256

SITES, RICHARD LOREN, lawyer; b. Feb. 16, 1948; s. Loren Richard and Frances Mary (Tellaro) Sites; m. Karen Ann Heazlit, Oct. 06, 1979; children: Brian, David. BA, Coll. Wooster, 1970; JD, U. Denver, 1973, MS, 1975. Bar: Colo. 1973, Ohio 1975, U.S. Dist. Ct. 1973, U.S. Supreme Ct. 1977; cert. health care fin. mgmt. Ohio State U., 1984. Sole practice, Columbus, Ohio, 1973—; atty. HHS, 1975—85, Ohio Hosp. Assn., Columbus, 1985—. Assoc. grad. faculty, academic adv. Ctrl. Mich. U., 1992—. Contbr. articles to profl. jours. Co-founder FAMOHIO, Inc., 1992, pres., 1996—98; leader Boy Scouts Am., 1992—; alumni admissions rep. Coll. Wooster, Ohio, 1979—85, fund raiser, 1984; v.p. Sycamore Hills Residents Assn., Columbus, 1983, pres., 1984. Recipient Spl. Contbn. award, Ohio Soc. for Hosp. Engring., 1988. Office: Ohio Hosp Assn 155 E Broad St Fl 15 Columbus OH 43215-3609

SIVERD, ROBERT JOSEPH, lawyer; b. July 27, 1948; s. Clifford David and Elizabeth Ann (Klink) S.; m. Bonita Marie Shulock, Jan. 8, 1972; children: Robert J. Jr., Veronica Leigh. AB in French, Georgetown U., 1970, JD, 1973; postgrad., The Sorbonne, Paris, 1969. Bar: N.Y. 1974, U.S. Dist. Ct. (so. and ea. dists.) N.Y. 1974, U.S. Ct. Appeals (2d cir.) 1974, U.S. Supreme Ct. 1980, U.S. Dist. Ct. (ea. dist.) Pa. 1984, U.S. Ct. Appeals (3d cir.) 1984, U.S. Ct. Appeals (6th cir.) 1985, Ohio 1991, Ky. 1992. Assoc. Donovan Leisure Newton & Irvine, N.Y.C., 1973-83; staff v.p., litigation counsel Am. Fin. Group, Inc., Greenwich, Conn., 1983-85, v.p. litigation counsel, 1986-87, v.p. assoc. gen. counsel Cin., 1987-92; sr. v.p., gen. counsel and sec. Gen. Cable Corp., 1992-94, exec. v.p., gen. counsel and sec., 1994—. Mem. ABA, Assn. of Bar of City of N.Y., Ky. Bar Assn. Republican. Antitrust, Federal civil litigation, General corporate. Office: Gen Cable Corp 4 Tesseneer Dr Newport KY 41076-9167

SIVITZ, WILLIAM DAVID, lawyer, industrial manufacturing company executive; b. Cin., Apr. 2, 1943; s. Aaron and Mary Sivitz; m. Hilary Falk, Apr. 5, 1975; children— Carolyn, Owen, Hilary. B.A., Northwestern U., 1961; LL.D. cum laude, George Washington U., 1965. Bar: Ohio 1969, Mass. 1969, N.H. 1975. Atty. W. R. Grace, N.Y.C., 1969-72; asst. gen. counsel Wheelabrator-Frye, N.Y.C., 1972-75, Hampton, N.H., 1975-77; exec. v.p., gen. counsel Chase REIT/Triton Group Ltd., N.Y.C., 1977-84; v.p., gen. counsel The Pullman Co., Princeton, N.J., 1984— ; cons. Triton Group Ltd., N.Y.C., 1984— ; dir. Fifth Avenue Cards Inc., N.Y.C., 1095 Park Corp., N.Y.C. Office: The Pullman-Peabody Co 182 Nassau St Princeton NJ 08542-7000

SIX, FRED N. state supreme court justice; b. Independence, Mo., Apr. 20, 1929; AB, U. Kans., 1951, JD with honors, 1956; LLM in Judicial Process, U. Va., 1990. Bar: Kans. 1956. Asst. atty. gen. State of Kans., 1957-58; pvt. practice Lawrence, Kans., 1958-87; judge Kans. Ct. Appeals, 1987-88; justice Kans. Supreme Ct., Topeka, 1988—. Editor-in-chief U. Kans. Law Review, 1955-56; lectr. on law Washburn U. Sch. Law, 1957-58, U. Kans., 1975-76. Served with USMC, 1951-53; USMCR, 1957-62. Recipient Disting. Alumnus award U. Kans. Sch. Law, 1994. Fellow Am. Bar Found. (chmn. Kans. chpt. 1983-87); mem. ABA (jud. adminstrn. divsn.), Am. Judicature Soc., Kans. Bar Assn., Kans. Bar Found., Kans. Law Soc. (pres. 1970-72), Kans. Inn of Ct. (pres. 1993-94), Order of Coif, Phi Delta Phi. Office: Kans Supreme Ct 374 Kansas JudICIAL Center 301 SW 10th Ave Topeka KS 66612-1502 E-mail: fsix@kscourts.org

SKAGGS, SANFORD MERLE, lawyer; b. Berkeley, Calif., Oct. 24, 1939; s. Sherman G. and Barbara Jewel (Stinson) S.; m. Sharon Ann Barnes, Sept. 3, 1976; children: Stephen, Paula Ferry, Barbara Gallagher, Darren Peterson. BA, U. Calif., Berkeley, 1961; JD, U. Calif., 1964. Bar: Calif. 1965. Atty. Pacific Gas and Electric Co., San Francisco, 1964-73; gen. counsel Pacific Gas Transmission Co., 1973-75; ptnr. Van Voorhis & Skaggs, Walnut Creek, Calif., 1975-85, McCutchen, Doyle, Brown & Enersen, San Francisco and Walnut Creek, 1985—. Mem.Calif. Law Revision Commn., 1990—, chmn. 1993; dir. John Muir/Mt. Diablo Health Sys., 1996—. Councilman City of Walnut Creek, 1972-78, mayor 1974-75, 76-77; bd. dirs. East Bay Mcpl. Utility Dist., 1978-90, pres., 1982-90. Mem. Calif. State Bar Assn., Contra Costa County Bar Assn., Urban Land Inst., Lambda Alpha, Alpha Delta Phi, Phi Delta Phi. Republican. State civil litigation, Condemnation, Land use and zoning (including planning). Office: McCutchen Doyle Brown & Enersen 1333 N California Blvd Ste 210 Walnut Creek CA 94596-4585

SKALL, GREGG P. lawyer; b. El Paso, Tex., Mar. 28, 1944; s. Ben Milton and Lottie (Berger) S.; m. Monte Kaye Leake, June 27, 1971; 1 child, Brandon Cornell. BS, Ohio State U., 1966; JD, U. Cin., 1969. Bar: Ohio 1969, D.C. 1971, D.C. Dist. Ct. 1971, U.S. Dist. Ct. (no. dist.) Ohio 1972, D.C. Ct. Appeals 1971, U.S. Supreme Ct. 1978. Atty. gen. State of Ohio, Cleve., summer 1967; intern U.S. Dept. Justice, div. Civil Rights, Washington, summer 1968; tax law specialist IRS, 1969; gen. atty. FCC, 1970-72; ptnr. Garber, Simon, Haiman, Gutfeld, Werthiemer & Friedman, Cleve., 1972-75; acting gen. counsel Office Telecommunications Policy Exec. Office of the Pres. of the U.S., Washington, 1975-78; chief counsel Nat. Telecommunications and Info. Adminstrn., 1978-80; ptnr. Blum, Nash & Railsback, 1980-84, Baker & Hostetler, Washington, 1984-91, Pepper & Corazzini LLP, Washington, 1991—. Professorial lectr. telecomms. law and regulatory policy George Washington U., Washington, 1978-80; mem. adv. bd. Pike & Fischer Radio Regulation, 1991—; comms. counsel to Minn., Calif. and Nev. Broadcasters Assns., 1990—. Co-author: The Broadcaster's Survival Guide: A Handbook of FCC Rules and Regulations for Radio and TV Stations, 1988; contbr. articles to law jours. Mem. Fed.

Bar Assn. (chmn. regulated industries com. 1979-81), ABA, Fed. Communications Bar Assn., Minn. Broadcasters Assn., Calif. Broadcasters Assn. Lodge: Masons. Administrative and regulatory, Communications, Computer. Office: Pepper & Corazzini 200 Montgomery Bldg 1776 K St NW Ste 200 Washington DC 20006-2364 E-mail: gps@commlaw.com

SKANCKE, NANCY J. lawyer; b. Mar. 24, 1950; d. Frank Benson and LaVerne (Bloomberg) Hubbard; m. Steven Lynn Skancke, Nov. 29, 1975; children: Matthew David, Carolyn Elizabeth. BS in Math. (hon.), Purdue U., 1972; JD (hon.), George Washington U., 1975. Bar: Va. 1975, D.C. 1975, U.S. Ct. Appeals (5th, D.C. 11th cirs.), U.S Supreme Ct., U.S. Ct. Fed. Claims, U.S. Dist. Ct., D.C. Assoc. Ross, Marsh & Foster, Washington, 1975-80; ptnr., 1980-92; mem. mgmt. com., 1981-84; chmn. profl. devel. com., 1989-92; ptnr. Baller Hammett, Washington, 1992-93, Grammer, Kissel, Robbins & Skancke, 1993-96, Grammer, Kissel, Robbins, Sjancke & Edwards, 1996-2000, GKRSE, 2000—. Bd. dirs. Found. of Energy Law Jour. Contbr. articles to profl. jours. Master Prettyman-Leventhal Am. Inns of Ct., 1988—2001, pres., 1992—93; chmn. D.C. Metro Area coun. Am. Inns of Ct., 1992—99, chmn. nat. ann. meeting, 1994. Fellow: Am. Bar Found.; mem.: ABA (sect. of natural resources and energy law, sect. of adminstrv. and reg), Energy Bar Assn. (bd. dirs. 1985—88, chmn. jud. rev. com. 1990—91, chmn. jud. rev. com. 1996—98, chmn. ethics com. 2001—). Administrative and regulatory, Contracts commercial, FERC practice. Home: 833 Nethercliffe Hall Rd Great Falls VA 22066-2717 Office: Law Offices of GKRSE Ste 330 1500 K St NW Washington DC 20005 E-mail: njskance@gkrse-law.com

SKARE, ROBERT MARTIN, lawyer, director; b. Jan. 13, 1930; s. Martin Samuel and Verna Adelle (Forseth) S.; m. Marilyn Hutchinson, Aug. 28, 1954; children: Randolph, Robertson, Rodger, Richard. Student, St. Olaf Coll., 1947-48; BS, U. Minn., 1951, JD, 1954. Bar: Minn. 1956. Clk. Minn. Supreme Ct., 1953-54; assoc. Best and Flanagan, Mpls., 1956-60, ptnr., 1960-90, sr. ptnr., 1970-90, of counsel, 1990—. Founder, dir., gen. counsel, v.p. Luth. Brotherhood Mut. Funds, Mpls., 1969—93; corp. mcpl. counsel City of Golden Valley, Minn., 1963—88; bd. dirs. Norwest Bank Minn.-Wells Fargo Cmty. Bd., 1972—93, Vesper Soc. Group, San Francisco, 1985—; Son of Heaven, Inc.bd. dirs. Seattle, Wash., 1987—91, Aspen Inst. Cmty. Forum, 1997—, Nat. Coun. Search Inst. Youth Initiative, 1998—; nat. pres. Luth. Human Rels. Assn. Am., 1977—79; founder, dir. Episc. Found. of Aspen, Vinland Nat. Ctr.; founder Westwood Luth. Found. Trustee Am. Luth. Ch.; mem. bd. mgmt. U. Minn. YMCA. Recipient Pres. award Luth. Human Rels. Assn. Am., 1979, Presdl. Awd., Search Inst., 1997. Mem. ABA, Minn. State Bar Assn., Hennepin County Bar Assn., U. Minn. Alumni Club (charter), Mpls. Club, Torske Klubben, Sigma Alpha Epsilon (Disting. Alumni Svc. award 1978). Home: 780 Mountain Laurel Dr Aspen CO 81611-2344 Office: 4000 US Bank Pl Minneapolis MN 55402-4331

SKELLY, JOSEPH GORDON, lawyer; b. Oil City, Pa., June 2, 1935; s. Daniel Joseph and Ruth Mary (Mansfield) S.; m. Barbara Ossoff, Apr. 30, 1966; children— Mame, Meghan, Stephen. B.S., U. Notre Dame, 1957; J.D., Villanova U., 1962. Bar: Pa. 1963, U.S. Supreme Ct. 1967, U.S. Ct. Appeals (3d cir.) 1967, U.S. dist. ct. (ea. dist.) Pa. 1969, U.S. dist. ct. (mid. dist.) Pa. 1970. Assoc., Breene, Frame & Magee, Oil City, Pa., 1963-67; founding ptnr. Ball, Skelly, Murren & Connell and predecessor firm Ball & Skelly, Harrisburg, 1968—; lectr. ethics seminars Pa. Bar Inst., ethics com. Holy Spirit Hosp. Past bd. dirs. Keystone council Boy Scouts Am. Recipient Silver Beaver award Boy Scouts Am. Mem. Pa. Bar Assn. (immediate past chmn., chair Professionalism Com., Spl. Achievement award, 1995), Dauphin County Bar Assn., Pa. Trial Lawyers Assn., Lawyers Concerned For Lawyers, Inc. (bd. dirs.). Republican. Administrative and regulatory, General civil litigation, General practice. Office: PO Box 1108 511 N 2d St Harrisburg PA 17108

SKELTON, BYRON GEORGE, federal judge; b. Florence, Tex., Sept. 1, 1905; s. Clarence Edgar and Avis (Bowmer) S.; m. Ruth Alice Thomas, Nov. 28, 1931; children: Sue, Sandra. Student, Baylor U., 1923-24; AB, U. Tex., 1927, MA, 1928, LLB, 1931. Bar: Tex. 1931, Circuit Ct. Appeals 1937, U.S. Supreme Ct. 1946, FCC 1950, Tax Ct. U.S 1952, U.S. Treasury Dept 1952, ICC 1953. Practice of law, Temple, Tex., 1931-66; partner Saulsbury & Skelton, 1934-42, Saulsbury, Skelton, Everton, Bowmer & Courtney, 1944-55, Skelton, Bowmer & Courtney, 1955-66; judge U.S. Ct. Claims, Washington, 1966-77, sr. fed. judge, 1977-82, U.S. Ct. Appeals (fed. cir.), Washington, 1982—. County atty., Bell County, Tex., 1934-38; spl. asst. U.S. amb. to Argentina, 1942-45; city atty., Temple, 1945-60; dir. First Nat. Bank of Temple. Dem. nat. committeeman for Tex., 1956-64; del. Dem. Nat. Conv., 1948, 56, 60, 64; del. Tex. Dem. Conv., 1946, 48, 50, 52, 54, 56, 58, 60, 62, 64, vice chmn., 1948, 58; chmn. Dem. Adv. Coun. of Tex., 1955-57; former pres. Temple YMCA; pres. Temple Indsl. Found., 1966. Appointed Ky. Col. and Adm. in Tex. Navy, 1959; recipient Legion of Honor DeMolay, 1980, Temple Outstanding Citizen award, 1984. Mem. ABA, State Bar Tex., Bell-Lampasas and Mills Counties Bar Assn. (past pres.), Am. Law Inst., Am. Judicature Soc., Temple C. of C. (past pres., dir.), Ex-Students' Assn. U. Tex. (past pres., mem. exec.coun.), Gen. Soc. Mayflower Descs., Masons (past worshipful master), Shriners, Kiwanis (past pres.), Phi Beta Kappa, Pi Sigma Alpha, Sigma Delta Pi, Delta Theta Phi. Democrat. Methodist. Home: 1101 Dakota Dr Temple TX 76504-4905 Office: US Ct Appeals 305 Fed Bldg Temple TX 76501

SKIGEN, PATRICIA SUE, lawyer; b. Springfield, Mass., June 16, 1942; d. David P. and Gertrude H. (Hirschhaut) Skigen; m. Irwin J. Sugarman, May 1973 (div. Nov. 1994); 1 child Alexander David Sugarman ; m. Gary W. Guttman, May 2001. BA with distinction, Cornell U., 1964; LLB, Yale U., 1968. Bar: N.Y. 1968, U.S. Dist. Ct. (so. dist.) N.Y. 1969. Law clk. Anderson, Mori & Rabinowitz, Tokyo, 1966-67; assoc. Rosenman Colin Kaye Petschek Freund & Emil, N.Y.C., 1968-70, Willkie Farr & Gallagher, N.Y.C., 1970-75, ptnr., 1977-95; v.p., corp. fin. group legal dept. Chase Manhattan Bank, 1995—. Dep. supt., gen. counsel N.Y. State Banking Dept., N.Y.C., 1975-77, 1st dep. supt. banks, 1977; adj. prof. Benjamin Cardozo Law Sch. Yeshiva U., 1979. Contbr. articles to profl. jours. Cornell U. Dean's scholar, 1960-64, Regent's scholar, 1960-64, Yale Law Sch. scholar, 1964-68. Mem. ABA (corp. banking and bus. law sect.), Assn. of Bar of City of N.Y. (chmn. com. banking 1991-94, long range planning com. 1994-96, audit com. 1995—), Phi Beta Kappa, Phi Kappa Phi. Banking, General corporate, Mergers and acquisitions. Office: JP Morgan Chase and Co 270 Park Ave Fl 40 New York NY 10017-2014

SKILLERN, FRANK FLETCHER, law educator; b. Sept. 26, 1942; s. Will T. and Vera Catherine (Ryberg) S.; m. Susan Schlaefer, Sept. 3, 1966; children: Nathan Edward, Leah Catherine. AB, U. Chgo., 1964; JD, U. Denver, 1966; LLM, U. Mich., 1969. Bar: Colo. 1967, Tex. 1978. Pvt. practice law, Denver, 1967; gen. atty. Maritime Adminstrn., Washington, 1967-68; asst. prof. law Ohio No. U., 1969-71, Tex. Tech U., Lubbock, 1971-73, assoc. prof. law, 1973-75, prof. law, 1975—. Vis. prof. U. Tex. Law Sch., summer 1979, U. Ark. Law Sch., 1979-80, U. Tulsa Coll. Law, 1981-82; cons. and speaker in field. Author: Environmental Protection: The Legal Framework, 1981, 2d edit. published as Environmental Protection Deskbook, 1995, Regulation of Water and Sewer Utilities, 1989, Texas Water Law, Vol. I, 1988, rev. edit., 1992, Vol. II, 1991; contbr. chpts. to Powell on Real Property, Zoning and Land Use Controls, others; author cong. procs. and numerous articles. Mem. ABA (mem. publs. com. Sect. Natural Resources Law 1984—, vice chair internat. environ. law com. Sect. Natural Resources Law 1987). Office: Tex Tech U Sch Law PO Box 40004 Lubbock TX 79409-0004

SKILLING, RAYMOND INWOOD, lawyer; b. Enniskillen, U.K., July 14, 1939; s. Dane and Elizabeth (Burleigh) S.; m. Alice Mae Welsh, Aug. 14, 1982; 1 child by previous marriage, Keith A. F. LLB, Queen's U., Belfast, U.K., 1961; JD, U. Chgo., 1962. Solicitor English Supreme Ct. 1966. Bar: Ill 1974. Assoc. Clifford-Turner (now Clifford Chance), London, 1963-69, ptnr., 1969-76; exec. v.p., chief counsel Aon Corp. (and predecessor cos.), Chgo., 1976—. Bd. dirs. Aon Corp. (and predecessor cos.). Commonwealth fellow, U. Chgo., 1961-62, Bigelow teaching fellow U. Chgo. Law Sch., 1962-63; Fulbright scholar U.S. Ednl. Commn., London, 1961-63; recipient McKane medal Queen's U., Belfast, 1961. Mem. ABA, Ill. Bar Assn., Chgo. Bar Assn., The Casino Chgo., Chgo. Club, Econ. Club Chgo., Racquet Club Chgo., Bucks Club London, The Carlton Club London, The City of London Club. Office: Aon Corp Aon Ctr 200 E Randolph Chicago IL 60601

SKILTON, ROBERT HENRY, law educator, lawyer; b. Phila., Jan. 17, 1909; s. Robert Henry and Margaret Thompson (Beaton) S.; m. Margaret Rittenhouse Neisser, Aug. 22, 1936; children— Robert Henry, III, John Singleton, Margaret Anne, David Hamilton. A.B., U. of Pa., 1930, M.A., 1931, LL.B., 1934, Ph.D., 1943. Bar: Pa. 1934, Wis. 1962, U.S. Supreme Ct. 1945. Inst. in English Swarthmore Coll., Pa., 1930-31; assoc. Edmonds Obermayer Rebmann, Phila. Pa., 1934-37; instr. asst. to assoc. prof., Wharton Sch. U. of Pa., 1937-53; assoc. prof. to prof. Law Sch. U. of Wis., Madison, 1953-76; vis. prof. Southern Ill. Law Sch., 1976, 78-79, 80-81, 81-83, McGeorge Sch. of Law, Sacramento, Calif., 1977-78, Williamette Coll. of Law, Salem, Oreg., 1979, Wayne State Law Sch., Detroit, 1981-82, U. of Wis. Law Sch., 1983-84. Author: Government and the Mortgage Debtor, 1929-39, 1943, Industrial Discipline and the Arbitration process, 1952. Editor: Annals on Our Servicemen and Economic Security, 1942. Contbr. articles to prof. jours. Served to lt., USN, 1943-46. Mem. ABA, Wis. Bar Assn. Home: 4106 Cherokee Dr Madison WI 53711-3031

SKINNER, MICHAEL DAVID, lawyer; b. Jan. 5, 1950; s. Roger Gilman and Jerry Ann (Sneed) S.; m. Janet Louise Horaist, Jan. 7, 1978. JD, La. State U., 1976. Bar: La. 1977, U.S. Dist. Ct. (we. dist.) La. 1978, U.S. Ct. Appeals (5th and 11th cirs.) 1978, U.S. Dist. Ct. (mid. dist.) La. 1982, U.S. Supreme Ct. 1982, U.S. Dist. Ct. (so. dist.) Tex. 1983. Pvt. practice, Lafayette, La., 1976-84; ptnr. Guilliot, Skinner & Everett, 1984-86, Goode, Skinner & Hawkland, 1986-93; U.S. atty. West Dist. La., 1993-2000. Mem. Downtown Lafayette Unltd., Lafayette, 1984; bd. dirs. Assn. Culturelle de la Louisiane, Lafayette, 1984. Mem. La. State Bar Assn. (mem. ho. of dels.). Democrat. General corporate, Criminal, Real property. Office: Onebane Bernard Torian Diaz McNamara & Abell Ste 600 Versailles Ctr 102 Versailles Blvd Lafayette LA 70502*

SKINNER, WALTER JAY, federal judge; b. Washington, Sept. 12, 1927; s. Frederick Snowden and Mary Waterman (Comstock) S.; m. Sylvia Henderson, Aug. 12, 1950; 4 children. A.B., Harvard, 1948; J.D., 1952. Bar: Mass. 1952, U.S. Dist. Ct. 1954. Assoc. firm Gaston, Snow, Rice & Boyd, Boston, 1952-57; pvt. practice law Scituate, Mass., 1957-63; asst. dist. atty. Plymouth County, 1957-63; town counsel Scituate, 1957-63; asst. atty. gen., chief Criminal Div., Commonwealth of Mass., 1963-65; mem. firm Wardwell, Allen, McLaughlin & Skinner, Boston, 1965-74; judge U.S. Dist. Ct. of Mass., 1974—; sr. status, 1992—. Bd. dirs. Douglas A. Thom Clinic, 1966-70. Mem. Mass. Bar Assn., Boston Bar Assn. Office: US Dist Ct 1 Courthouse Way Boston MA 02210-3002

SKIRNICK, ROBERT ANDREW, lawyer; b. Chgo., Apr. 23, 1938; s. Andrew and Stella (Sanders) S.; children: Rebecca, David; m. Maria Ann Castellano, Oct. 4, 1974; 1 child, Gabriella. BA, Roosevelt U., 1961; JD, U. Chgo., 1966. Bar: U.S. Dist. Ct. (no. dist.) Ill. 1966, U.S. Ct. Appeals (7th cir.) 1968, U.S. Supreme Ct. 1970, U.S. Ct. Appeals (5th and 9th cirs.) 1982, N.Y. 1982, U.S. Ct. Appeals (3rd cir.) 1983, U.S. Dist. Ct. (ea. dist.) Mich. 1988, (so. and ea. dists.) N.Y. 1989, U.S. Ct. Appeals (2nd cir.) 1990, U.S. Dist. Ct. (no. dist.) Calif. 1992, U.S. Ct. Appeals (11th Cir.) 1992, U.S. Dist. Ct. (so. dist.) Tex. 1992, U.S. Dist. Ct. Ariz. 1993. Atty. office gen. counsel honors program HEW, Washington, 1966-68; ptnr. Fortes, Eiger, Epstein & Skirnick, Chgo., 1975-77, Much, Shelist, Freed, Chgo., 1977-79, Wolf, Popper, Ross, Wolf & Jones, N.Y.C., 1979-87, Kaplan, Kilsheimer & Foley, N.Y.C., 1988-89, Wechsler, Skirnick, Harwood, Halebian & Feffer, N.Y.C., 1989-95, Lovell & Skirnick, LLP, N.Y.C., 1995-97, Meredith Cohen Greenfogel & Skirnick, P.C., N.Y.C., 1997—. Instr. NYU, 1979-80; cons. Nat. Legal Aid and Def. Assn., Chgo., 1968-69; spl. asst. atty. gen. Ill. Atty Gen. Office, Chgo., 1972-73; spl. antitrust counsel State of Conn., 1976-77; mem. adv. bd. Small Bus. Legal Def. Commn., San Francisco, 1982—; lectr. Practicing Law Inst., N.Y.C., 1986-87; spl. master So. Dist. N.Y., 1988-91; ct. appted co-lead counsel NASDAQ market makers antitrust litigation, 1994—. Author: (with others) Federal Subject Matter Jurisdiction of U.S. District Courts, Federal Civil Practice, 1974, Antitrust Class Actions-Twenty Years Under Rule 23, 1986, The State Court Class Action-A Potpourri of Difference in the ABA Forum, Summer 1985; contbg. author: Multiparty Bargaining in Class Actions, Attorneys' Practice Guide to Negotiations, 2d edit., 1996; bd. editors Ill. Bar Antitrust Newsletter, 1969-73; topic and articles editor Jour. Forum Com. on Franchising, 1981-86. Atty. Office Gen. Counsel Honors Program, U.S. Dept. HEW, 1966-68; chmn. Ill. Legis. Com. Antitrust Section Ill. Bar., 1970-71; Topic and Articles Editor, Jour. Forum Com. on Franchising, 1981-86. Mem. ABA (co-chair securities law subcom., litigation sect. 1987, mem. com. on regulation of futures and derivative instruments, mem. forum com. on franchising), ATLA, Fed. Bar Coun. (mem. com. on second cir cts. 1983-86), N.Y. State Bar Assn. (mem. class action com.), N.Y. State Trial Lawyers Assn., Ill. Bar Assn. (chmn. antitrust sect. Ill. legis. com. 1970-71), Nat. Assn. for Pub. Interest Law Fellowships (mem. exec. com., mem. selection com., mem. investment and fin. com., bd. dirs. 1991-97, v.p. 1994-97, mem. budget com. 1998—, nomination and election coms. 1998—, bd. of dirs. 1997—), Nat. Assn. Pub. Interest Law (mem. fin. and investment com. 1998—, nomination and election com. 1998-99, chair, nominations and elections com., 1999—, bd. dirs. 1997—), Washington, Navy League of U.S. (N.Y. coun., mem. jour. com. 1995-97), Carlton Club, Plandome Country Club. Antitrust, Federal civil litigation, Securities. Office: Meredith Cohen Greenfogel & Skirnick 63 Wall St New York NY 10005-3001

SKJOLD, BENJAMIN R. lawyer, financial consultant; b. Mpls., Mar. 10, 1970; s. Stephen Arthur and Mary Earl Beran S.; m. Kara Nicole Theis. BA, Macalester Coll., 1992; JD, Chgo.-Kent Coll. of Law, 1997. Bar: Ill., U.S. Dist. Ct. (no. dist.) Ill. Lawyer Law Offices of Donald S. Nathan, Chgo., 1997—. Mem. Union League Club of Chgo. Avocations: golf, reading. Civil rights, General civil litigation, Personal injury. Home: 406 Lee #2 Evanston IL 60202 Office: Law Offices of Donald S Nathan 221 N LaSalle #726 Chicago IL 60601

SKLAR, ALAN CURTIS, lawyer; b. N.Y.C., Aug. 19, 1959; s. Jerry and Martha (Kolin) S.; m. Linda Susan Catalan, Dec. 26, 1982; twins: Daniel Jay and Jennifer Rachel. BA summa cum laude, U. Pa., 1980, JD, 1982. Bar: Calif., Nev. Assoc. Wolf Block Schorr & Solis-Cohen, Phila., 1980, 81, Rifkind & Sterling, Beverly Hills, Calif., 1982-84, Mitchell Silberberg & Knupp, L.A., 1984-86; mng. dir. Coastal Investment Group, Beverly Hills, 1986-89; ptnr. Warren Clark & Sklar (and predecessor), L.A., 1989—, Gordon & Silver, Las Vegas, Nev., 1991-95, Sklar Warren Conway & Williams LLP, Las Vegas, 1995—. Bd. dirs. Consolidated Mgmt., Inc., N.Y.C., L.A., Las Vegas. Author: Tactics and Techniques Mergers and Acquisitions, 1985, Recent Developments in Mergers and Acquisitions, 1985, California Corporate Securities Laws, 1985, Secured Real Estate Transactions, 1993. Bd. trustees Las Vegas Bowl Organizing Com., 1995, 96, So. Nev. Housing Corp., 1995—; mem. U. Pa. Alumni Secondary Sch. Com., 1998—; counsel Chabed of So. Nev., Las Vegas, 1991-2000. Named Top Corp. Atty., Nev. Bus. Jour. Mem. ABA, State Bar Nev., State Bar Calif., TPC Summerlin Country Club, World Zionist Orgn., Phi Beta Kappa, Phi Alpha Theta. Democrat. Jewish. Office: Sklar Warren Conway & Williams LLP 221 N Buffalo Dr Las Vegas NV 89145-0303 E-mail: asklar@sklar-law.com

SKLAR, WILFORD NATHANIEL, retired lawyer, real estate broker; b. Salt Lake City, Dec. 13, 1916; s. Benjamin B. Sklar and Blanche Blau; m. Sarah Cohen, Jan. 16, 1945 (dec. Dec. 2000); children: Beth-Lynn, Teri Helene (dec.) BBA, U. Pitts., 1942; JD, Southwestern Sch. Law, 1960. Bar: Calif. 1960, U.S. Dist. Ct. Calif. 1962, U.S. Supreme Ct. 1965. Pvt. practice, Riverside, Calif., 1960-98; ret., 1998. Co-pub. worker's compensation books. Co-comdr. mil. affairs com. March AFB, Calif.; active Riverside Family Svcs., 1965-85. Sgt. USAF, 1942-46. Mem. B'nai B'rith (Akiba Dist. award 1970, 74), Riverside Jewish War Vets. Democrat. Jewish. Avocations: golf, coin collecting, real estate investments. Home: 5904 Copperfield Ave Riverside CA 92506-4510

SKLAR, WILLIAM PAUL, lawyer, educator; b. N.Y.C., Sept. 10, 1958; s. Morris and Helen (Meyers) S.; m. Lori Ann Hodges, Jan. 5, 1985. BBA magna cum laude, U. Miami, 1977, JD, 1980. Bar: Fla. 1980, N.Y. 1986, U.S. Dist. Ct. (so. dist.) Fla. 1981, U.S. Tax Ct. 1980, U.S. Ct. Appeals (5th cir.) 1980, U.S. Ct. Appeals (11th cir.) 1981. Assoc. Wood, Cobb, Murphy & Craig, West Palm Beach, Fla., 1980-85, ptnr., 1985-88, Foley & Lardner, West Palm Beach, 1989—, ptnr.-in-charge, 1995—. Chmn. Fla. Real Estate Dept., 1991—; adj. prof. law Sch. Law, U. Miami, Coral Gables, Fla., 1980—; dir. Inst. on Condo. and Cluster Devels., Inst. on Real Property Law, 1986—. Co-author: Cases and Materials in Condominium and Cluster Developments, 1980; author, co-editor; Florida Real Estate Transactions, 1983; contbr. articles to profl. jours. Atty. adv. bd. Morse Geriatric Ctr., West Palm Beach, 1984-88. Mem. ABA (chmn. subcom. on condominium and coop. housing sect. gen. practice 1983-88), Fla. Bar (com. condominium and planned devels. 1980—, bd. cert. real estate lawyer 1994, exec. coun. mem. real property, probate and trust law sect. 1997—), Palm Beach County Bar Assn., Coll. Cmty. Assn. Lawyers, Phi Delta Phi, Pi Sigma Alpha. Republican. Avocations: travel, tennis. Land use and zoning (including planning), Real property. Home: 7238 Montrico Dr Boca Raton FL 33433-6930 Office: Foley & Lardner West Tower 777 S Flagler Dr Ste 901 West Palm Beach FL 33401-6161

SKOGLUND, MARILYN, state supreme court justice; b. Chgo., Aug. 28, 1946; BA, So. Ill. U., 1971; clerkship, 1977-81. Bar: Vt. 1981, U.S. Dist. Ct. Vt. 1981, U.S. Ct. Appeals (2d cir.) 1983. Asst. atty. gen. Civil Law Divsn., 1981-88, chief, 1988-93, Pub. Protection Divsn., 1993-94; judge Vt. Dist. Ct., 1994-97; assoc. justice Vt. Supreme Ct., 1997—. Office: Vt Supreme Ct 109 State St Montpelier VT 05609-0001

SKOLNICK, S. HAROLD, lawyer; b. Woonsocket, R.I., June 17, 1915; s. David and Elsie (Silberman) S.; m. Shirley Marshall. AB cum laude, Amherst Coll., 1936; JD, Boston U., 1940. Bar: R.I. 1940, U.S. Supreme Ct. 1946, D.C. 1947, Fla. 1952, U.S. Dist. Ct. (so. dist.) Fla. 1953, U.S. Ct. Appeals (5th cir.) 1960, U.S. Ct. Appeals (11th cir.) 1981. Atty. Dept. of War, Washington, 1940-42; asst. gen. counsel, asst. chief legal dept. Office Chief Ordnance, Dept. of Army, 1947-50; assoc. Francis I. McCanna, Providence, 1951-52; ptnr. French & Skolnick, Miami, Fla., 1953-60; sole practice, 1961—. Served to lt. col. U.S. Army, 1942-47. Mem. ABA, Am. Judicature Soc., Nat. Def. Indsl. Assn. (life), R.I. Bar Assn., D.C. Bar Assn., Dade County Bar Assn., Estate Planning Coun. Greater Miami, Masons, Shriners. Insurance, Probate. Home and Office: 6521 SW 122d St Miami FL 33156-5550

SKOLROOD, ROBERT KENNETH, lawyer; b. Stockton, Ill., May 17, 1928; s. Myron Clifford and Lola Mae (Lincicum) S.; m. Marilyn Jean Riegel, June 18, 1955; children: Cynthia, Mark, Kent, Richard. BA, Ohio Wesleyan U., 1952; JD, U. Chgo., 1957. Bar: Ill. 1957, Okla. 1981, D.C. 1987, U.S. Supreme Ct., 1982, Va. 1985, U.S. Dist. Ct. (no. dist.) Ill. 1959, U.S. Ct. Appeals (7th cir.) 1970, U.S. Dist. Ct. (no. dist.) Okla. 1982, U.S. Dist. Ct. Nebr. 1985, U.S. Dist. Ct. (so. dist.) Ala. 1986, U.S. Dist. Ct. (so. dist.) N.Y. 1986, U.S. Dist. Ct. (ea. and we. dists.) Va. 1986, U.S. Ct. Appeals (2nd, 4th, 6th, 7th, 8th 10th and 11th cirs.) 1986, U.S. Dist. Ct. D.C. 1987, Ptnr. Reno, Zahm, Folgate, Skolrood, Lindberg & Powell, Rockford, Ill., 1957-80; prof. O.W. Coburn Sch. Law, Oral Roberts U., Tulsa, 1980-81, gen. counsel, 1980-84; exec. dir., gen. counsel Nat. Legal Found., Virginia Beach, Va., 1984-95; with Law Firm of Scogins & Skolrood, Roanoke, Va., 1995—. Contbr. articles to legal jours.; lead counsel on several major constitutional cases. Pres., John Ericsson Rep. Club, 1964; trustee No. Ill. conf. United Meth. Ch., 1957-74, chmn., 1972-74; pres. Ill. Home and Aid Soc.; mem. Evangelical Free Ch. Served with U.S. Army, 1952-54, Korea. Fellow Am. Coll. Trial Lawyers; mem. Ill. Bar Assn., Okla. Bar Assn., Va., Bar Assn., Dist of Columbia Bar Assn, ATLA, Va. Trial Lawyers Assn., Tex. Trial Lawyers Assn., Ill. Trial Lawyers Assn., Okla. Trial Lawyers Assn., Christian Educators Assn. Internat. (bd. reference), Kappa Delta Pi, Pi Sigma Kappa. E-mail: skolrood@prodigy.net. Home: 5217 Dresden Ln Roanoke VA 24012-8576 Office: Scogins & Skolrood 3243 Electric Rd Ste 1A Roanoke VA 24018-6440

SKOPIL, OTTO RICHARD, JR. federal judge; b. Portland, Oreg., June 3, 1919; s. Otto Richard and Freda Martha (Boetticher) S.; m. Janet Rae Lundy, July 27, 1956; children: Otto Richard III, Casey Robert, Shannon Ida, Molly Jo. BA in Econs., Willamette U., 1941, LLB, 1946, LLD (hon.), 1983. Bar: Oreg. 1946, IRS, U.S. Treasury Dept., U.S. Dist. Ct. Oreg., U.S. Ct. Appeals (9th cir.), U.S. Supreme Ct. 1946. Assoc. Skopil & Skopil, 1946-51; ptnr. Williams, Skopil, Miller & Beck (and predecessors), Salem, Oreg., 1951-72; judge U.S. Dist. Ct., Portland, 1972-79, chief judge, 1976-79; judge U.S. Ct. Appeals (9th cir.), Portland, 1979—, now sr. judge. Chmn. com. adminstrn. of fed. magistrate sys. U.S. Jud. Conf., 1980-86; co-founder Oreg. chpt. Am. Leadership Forum; chmn. 9th cir. Jud. Coun. Magistrates Adv. Com., 1988-91; chmn. U.S. Jud. Conf. Long Range Planning Com., 1990-95. Hi-Y adviser Salem YMCA, 1951-52; appeal agt. SSS, Marion County (Oreg.) Draft Bd., 1953-66; master of ceremonies 1st Gov.'s Prayer Breakfast for State Oreg., 1959; mem. citizens adv. com., City of Salem, 1970-71; chmn. Gov.'s Com. on Staffing Mental Instns., 1969-70; pres., bd. dirs. Marion County Tb and Health Assn., 1958-61; bd. dirs. Willamette Valley Camp Fire Girls, 1946-56, Internat. Christian Leadership, 1959, Fed. Jud. Ctr., 1979; trustee Willamette U., 1969-71; elder Mt. Park Ch., 1979-81. Served to lt. USNR, 1942-46. Recipient Oreg. Legal Citizen of Yr. award, 1986, Disting. Alumni award Willamette U. Sch. Law, 1988. Mem. ABA, Oreg. Bar Assn. (bd. govs.), Marion County Bar Assn., Am. Judicature Soc., Oreg. Assn. Def. Counsel (dir.), Def. Research Inst., Assn. Ins. Attys. U.S. and Can. (Oreg. rep. 1970), Internat. Soc. Barristers, Prayer Breakfast Movement (fellowship council). Clubs: Salem, Exchange (pres. 1947), Illahe Hills Country (pres., dir. 1964-67). Office: Sr Circuit Judge 827 US Courthouse 1000 SW 3rd Ave Portland OR 97204-2930

SKREIN, STEPHEN PETER MICHAEL, lawyer; b. Eng. AM, U. So. Calif.; MA, Oxford U. Bar: Eng. and Wales. Trainee solicitor Richards Butler, London, 1971-73, asst. solicitor, 1973-76, ptnr., 1976—. Freeman City of London. Mem. City of London Solicitors Co. (liveryman), Law Soc., Internat. Trademark Assn., Internat. Bar Assn. Communications, Libel, Trademark and copyright. Office: Richards Butler Beaufort Ho 15 St Botolph St London EC3A 7EE England

SKRETNY, WILLIAM MARION, federal judge; b. Buffalo, Mar. 8, 1945; s. William S. and Rita E. (Wyroski) S.; m. Carol Ann Skretny; 3 children. AB, Canisius Coll., 1966; JD, Howard U., 1969; LLM, Northwestern U., 1972. Bar: Ill. 1969, U.S. Dist. Ct. (no. dist) Ill. 1969, N.Y. 1972, U.S. Ct. Appeals (7th cir.) 1972, U.S. Dist. Ct. (we. dist.) N.Y. 1973, U.S. Ct. Appeals (2d cir.) 1976, U.S. Supreme Ct. 1980. Asst. U.S. atty. Office of U.S. Atty. No. Dist. Ill., Chgo., 1971-73, Office of U.S. Atty. We. Dist. N.Y., Buffalo, 1973-81, 1st asst., 1975-81; gen. ptnr. Duke, Holzman, Yaeger & Radlin, 1981-83; 1st dep. dist. atty. Office Dist. Atty Erie County, 1983-88; with Gross, Shuman, Brizdle and Gillfillan, PC, 1988, Cox, Barrell, Buffalo, 1989-90; judge U.S. Dist. Ct. (we. dist.) N.Y., 1990—. Mem. jud. conf. com. on security and facilities, 1994, chair subcom. on planning and space mgmt., com. liaison for long range planning. Bd. dirs. Sudden Infant Death Found. We. N.Y., 1979, Cerebral Palsy Foun. We. N.Y., 1985; chmn. major corps. divsn. Studio Arena Theatre, Buffalo, 1982; chmn. Polish Culture, Canisius Coll., 1985, trustee, 1989; pres. Canisius Coll. Alumni Assn., 1989; regional chmn. Cath. Charities Appeal, 1986-87. Named Citizen of Yr. Am Pol Eagle Newspaper, 1977, 90, Disting. Grad. Nat. Cath. Edn. Assn. Dept. Elem. Sch., 1991, Disting. Alumnus Canisius Coll., 1993; named to Wall of Fame Law Sch. Northwestern U. Mem. ABA, Fed. Judges Assn., Bar Assn. of Erie County, Di Gamma, Phi Alpha Delta. Republican. Roman Catholic. Office: US District Court 68 Court St Rm 507 Buffalo NY 14202-3405

SKULINA, THOMAS RAYMOND, lawyer; b. Cleve., Sept. 14, 1933; s. John J. and Mary B. (Vesely) S. AB, John Carroll U., 1955; JD, Case Western Res. U., 1959, LLM, 1962. Bar: Ohio 1959, U.S. Supreme Ct. 1964, ICC 1965. Ptnr. Skulina & Stringer, Cleve., 1967-72, Riemer Oberdank & Skulina, Cleve., 1978-81, Skulina, Fillo, Walters & Negrelli, 1981-86, Skulina & McKeon, Cleve., 1986-90, Skulina & Hill, Cleve., 1990-97; atty. Penn Ctrl. Transp. Co., 1960-65, asst. gen. atty., 1965-78, trial counsel, 1965-76; with Consol. Rail Corp., 1976-78; pvt. practice Cleve., 1997—. Tchr. comml. law Practicing Law Inst., N.Y.C., 1970; practicing labor arbitrator Fed. Mediation and Conciliation Svc., 1990—; arbitrator Mcpl. Securities Rulemaking Bd., 1994-98, N.Y. Stock Exch., 1995—, NASD, 1996—; mediator NASD, 1997—, AAA Comml., 1997—; mediator vol. panel EEOC, 1997-99, contract panel, 1999-2000, v.p., 2000—, contract, 2001—; arbitrator Better Bus. Bur., 2000—. Contbr. articles to legal jours. Income tax and fed. fund coord. City of Warrensville Heights, Ohio, 1970-77; spl. counsel City of North Olmstead, Ohio, 1971-75, spl. counsel to Ohio Atty. Gen., 1983-93, Cleve. Charter Rev. Commn., 1988; pres. Civil Svc. Commn., Cleve., 1977-86, referee, 1986—; fact-finder State Employees Rels. Bd., Ohio, 1986—; hearing officer Human Resource Commn., Summit County, Ohio, 2000—. With U.S. Army, 1959. Mem. ABA (R.R. and motor carrier com. 1988-96, jr. chmn. 1989-96, alt. dispute resolution com. 1998—), FBA, Assn. Conflict Resolution, Cleve. Bar Assn. (grievance com. 1987-93, chmn. 1997-98, trustee 1993-96, ADR com. 1997—), Ohio Bar Assn. (bd. govs. litigation sect. 1986-98, negligence law com. 1989-96, ethics and profl. responsibility com. 1990-91, alt. dispute resolution com. 1996—), Am. Arbitration Assn. (practicing labor arbitrator 1987—), Nat. Assn. R.R. Trial Counsel, Internat. Assn. Law and Sci., Pub. Sector Labor Rels. Assn., Internat. Indsl. Rels. Rsch. Assn. Democrat. Roman Catholic. Alternative dispute resolution, Federal civil litigation, Transportation. Home: 3162 W 165th St Cleveland OH 44111-1016 Office: 24803 Detroit Rd Cleveland OH 44145-2553 E-mail: tskulina@aol.com

SKWARYK, ROBERT FRANCIS, judge; b. Erie, Pa., Nov. 4, 1948; s. Frank and Gloria (Hinkle) S. BS, Pa. State U., 1973; JD, U. Kans., 1977. Bar: Pa. 1977, U.S. Dist. Ct. (we. dist.) Pa. 1977. Legal intern legal svcs. Clallum and Jefferson Counties, Port Angeles, Wash., 1977; assoc. Galbo, McNelis, Restifo & Held, Erie, 1977-80; instr. bus. law Behrend Coll. Pa. State U., 1978-80; appeals referee Commonwealth of Pa., Harrisburg and Pottsville, 1981, Pitts. and Erie, 1985-88, adminstrv. law judge Allentown, 1988-96, Pitts., 1996—. Contbg. author ct. opinions Pa. Liquor Control Bd., 1988—. Mem. Behrend Coll. Soccer Alumni Assn., Erie, 1974-90. Sgt. USMC, 1967-70, lt. (j.g.) USN, 1981-85, lt. USNR, 1986-92, Saudi Arabia, lt. comdr. USNR, 1992-98, comdr., 1998—. Mem. ABA, Pa. State Bar Assn., Erie County Bar Assn., Pa. Conf. Adminstrv. Law Judges, First Marine Air Wing Assn., Pa. State U. Alumni Assn. Avocations: soccer, flying, orienteering. Home: 833 Greentree Rd Apt 2-6 Pittsburgh PA 15220-3418 Office: Commonwealth Pa Office Adminstrv Law Judge 875 Greentree Rd Pittsburgh PA 15220-3508

SLACK, JOHN MARK, III, lawyer; b. Charleston, W.Va., Sept. 15, 1942; s. John Mark and Frances (Reid) S.; m. Barbara Henderson, Sept. 21, 1963; children— John Mark IV, Jeanne Reid. B.A., U. N.C.-Chapel Hill, 1965; J.D., U. Tenn.-Knoxville, 1969. Bar: W.Va. 1969, U.S. Dist. Ct. (so. and no. dists.) W.Va. 1970, U.S. Ct. Appeals (4th cir.) 1970, U.S Supreme Ct. 1974. Assoc., Jackson Kelly Holt & O'Farrell, Charleston, 1969-76, ptnr., 1976— . Democrat. Lodges: Masons, Shriners, Jesters. Federal civil litigation, State civil litigation, Labor. Office: Jackson & Kelly PO Box 553 Charleston WV 25322-0553

SLADE, JEFFREY CHRISTOPHER, lawyer; b. Los Angeles, June 4, 1946; s. Sherman Richard and Afton Audre (Johnson) S.; m. Ruth Anne Diem, Mar. 5, 1983; 1 child, Katharine Anne. BA, Pomona Coll., 1967; MDiv., Union Theol. Sem., 1970; JD cum laude, NYU, 1976. Bar: N.Y. 1977, U.S. Dist. Ct. (so. and ea. dists.) N.Y. 1978, U.S. Dist. Ct. (no. dist.) Tex. 1978, Tex. 1979, U.S. Ct. Appeals (5th cir.) 1979, U.S. Dist. Ct. (ea. dist.) Ky. 1985, U.S. Ct. Appeals (2d and 3rd cirs.) 1985, U.S. Supreme Ct. 1985, U.S. Ct. Appeals (6th cir.) 1986. Law clk. to judge Charles H. Tenney U.S. Dist. Ct. (so. dist.), N.Y.C., 1976-78; assoc. Akin, Gump, Strauss, Hauer & Feld, Dallas, 1978-80, Paul, Weiss, Rifkind et al, N.Y.C., 1980-84; ptnr. Leventhal & Slade, 1984-99; prin. Slade & Assocs., P.C., 2000—. Author: Electoral Conditions in Guyana, An America's Watch Report, 1990. Chmn. church coun., The Riverside Ch., N.Y.C., 1992-96. Mem.: N.Y. State Bar Assn. Federal civil litigation, State civil litigation, Criminal. Office: Slade & Assocs PC 11 Vestry St 5th Fl New York NY 10013 E-mail: jslade@sladelaw.com

SLADE, LYNN HEYER, lawyer; b. Santa Fe, Jan. 29, 1948; m. Susan Zimmerman, 1 child, Benjamin, 1 child from a previous marriage, Jessica. BA in Econs., U. N.Mex., 1973, JD, 1976. Bar: N.Mex. 1976, U.S. Dist. Ct. N.Mex. 1976, U.S. Ct. Appeals (10th cir.) 1978, U.S. Ct. Appeals (D.C. cir.) 1984, U.S. Supreme Ct. 1984. Ptnr. Modrall, Sperling, Roehl, Harris & Sisk, PA, Albuquerque, 1976—. Adj. prof. U. N.Mex. Sch. Law, Albuquerque, 1990. Editor N.Mex. Law Rev., 1975-76; contbr. articles to profl. jours. Trustee-at-large Rocky Mountain Min. L. Found., 1995-97; bd. dirs. N.Mex. First, 1999—, chair nominating and membership com., 2001—. Fellow N.Mex. Bar Found.; mem. ABA (sect. of environ., energy and resources, membership officer 1998-2000, chair com. on Native Am. natural resources 1991-94, coun. mem. 1995-98, mem. sects. litigation, dispute resolution, internat. law, pub. utilities and comm., and transp. law), N.Mex. State Bar (chair, bd. dirs. sect. of natural resources 1983-87, bd. dirs. Indian law sect. 1987-90). Environmental, Native American, Natural resources. Home: 143 Olguin Rd Corrales NM 87048-6930 Office: Modrall Sperling Roehl Harris & Sisk PA 500 4th St NW Ste 1000 Albuquerque NM 87102-2186 E-mail: lslade@modrall.com

SLADKUS, HARVEY IRA, lawyer; b. Mar. 5, 1929; s. Samuel Harold and Charlotte Dorothy Sladkus; m. Harriet Marcia Barske, Nov. 26, 1967 (div.); children: Steven David, Jeffrey Brandon; m. Roberta Frances Pope, Oct. 24, 1986. AB, Syracuse U., 1950; JD, NYU, 1961. Bar: N.Y. 1962, Conn. 1981, U.S. Supreme Ct. 1967. Assoc. Morris Ploscowe, N.Y.C., 1961-66; pvt. practice, 1968-95, 97—; ptnr. Dweck & Sladkus and Feiden, Dweck & Sladkus, 1968-95, Dweck & Sladkus, LLP, 1996, Harvey I. Sladkus, P.C., 1997—. Small claims arbitrator Civil Ct. City of N.Y., 1977—; adj. prof. law Benjamin N. Cardozo Sch. Law, 1994—95; lectr. family and matrimonial law. Contbg. author: Practice Under New York's Matrimonial Law, 1971-79; contbr. columnist It's The Law, Suffolk Times, 1999—; editor-in-chief Family Law Practice, 1982; contbr. articles to profl. jours. 1st lt. U.S. Army, 1952-53, Korea. Decorated Bronze Star; recipient George Washington Honor medal Freedoms Found., Valley Forge, 1953, War Svc. medal Korean Govt. Mem. N.Y. State Bar Assn., Assn. Bar City N.Y., Am. Acad. Matrimonial Lawyers, Internat. Acad. Matrimonial Lawyers, Am. Judges Assn., Am. Arbitration Assn. (nat. panel arbitrators), Suffolk County Bar Assn. Jewish. Federal civil litigation, State civil litigation, Family and matrimonial. Office: 425 Park Ave New York NY 10022-3506 E-mail: harvey.sladkus@verizon.net

SLAVIK, DONALD HARLAN, lawyer; b. Milw., June 17, 1956; s. Donald Jean and Sally Ann (Croy) S.; m. Cynthia Sue Barfknecht, Jan 5, 1980. BS in Nuclear Engring., U. Wis., 1978, JD, 1981. Bar: Wis. 1981, U.S. Dist. Ct. (ea. and we. dists.) Wis. 1981. Mem. Habush, Habush & Rottier, Milw., 1981—. Lectr. engring. extension U. Wis., Madison, 1985-95. Author: (with others) Anatomy of a Roof Crush Case, 1985, Seat Belt Handbook, 1987, Crashworthiness, 1989, 98; contbr. articles to profl. jours. Mem. Assn. Trial Lawyers Am. (co-chair exch. com. 1986-87, 91-93, chmn. computer law office tech. 1993-97, 2000—), Wis. Bar Assn., Attys. Info. Exch. Group (bd. dirs., exec. com. 1987—, lectr. 1987—, pres. 2001-2003), Assn. for Advancement of Automotive Medicine (sci. program com. 1996-2001). Personal injury, Product liability. Office: Habush Habush Davis & Rottier Ste 2300 777 E Wisconsin Ave Milwaukee WI 53202-5381

SLAVIN, HOWARD LESLIE, lawyer, real estate broker, law educator, judge; b. Bklyn., Aug. 13, 1951; s. Benjamin David and Pauline (Rothenberg) S.; m. Rhea Englander, Feb. 16, 1986. BA, SUNY, Stony Brook, 1972; MS, U. Utah, 1975; JD, U. Denver, 1978. Bar: Colo. 1979, U.S. Dist. Ct. Colo. 1979, U.S. Ct. Appeals (10th cir.) 1985. Assoc. Law Offices of Arthur M. Frazin, Denver, 1979-82; sole practice, 1982-86, 89-96; ptnr. Slavin & Donnelly, 1986-89; magistrate county ct. City and County of Denver, 1989—; referee, arbitrator Douglas County Bd. Equalization, 1990—; referee Jefferson County Bd. Equalization, 1993—. Investigator, subcontractor USDA, Denver, 1983-85; instr. Denver Paralegal Inst., 1982-85; mediator Ctr. for Dispute Resolution, Denver, 1980. Lectr. Community Assn. Inst., Denver, 1986; mentor U. Denver Alumni Mentor Program, 1986. N.Y. Bd. Regents scholar, 1968-72; N.Y. State Dept. Labor grantee, 1974-75. Mem. Colo. Bar Assn., Denver Bar Assn. Jewish. Avocations: jazz guitar, piano. Bankruptcy, Contracts commercial, Real property. Office: Denver County Ct Rm 108 City & County Bldg 1437 Bannock St Denver CO 80202-5337

SLAYDON, KATHLEEN AMELIA, lawyer; b. Ft. Worth, June 1, 1951; d. A. Glynn and E. Jeanne (Miller) S.; m. John Mayer. BA, Rice U., 1973; JD, U. Tex., 1976. Bar: Tex. 1977, U.S. Dist. Ct. (so. dist.) Tex. 1978, U.S. Ct. Appeals (5th cir.) 1978, U.S. Ct. Appeals (11th cir.) 1981, U.S. Dist. Ct. (we. dist.) Tex. 1984, U.S. Supreme Ct. 1989. Assoc. Reynolds, Allen Cook, Houston, 1977-78; assoc. Ross, Banks, May Cron & Cavin, Houston, 1978-83, ptnr., 1983-89; litigation atty., liquidation div. FDIC, 1989—; speaker continuing legal edn. State Bar Tex., 1983-89. Mem. Tex. Assn. Bank Counsel, State Bar Assn. Tex., Houston Bar Assn., Rice U. Alumni Assn. (chairperson fund drive 1973). Banking, Bankruptcy, Contracts commercial. Home: 725 E Creekside Dr Houston TX 77024-3239

SLAYTON, JOHN HOWARD, lawyer, trust company executive; b. Sparta, Wis., July 6, 1955; s. Rex Gordon and Elizabeth (Ward) S.; m. Judith Hughes. BA in Polit. Sci. cum laude, Marquette U., 1977; JD cum laude, George Washington U., 1980, MBA in Fin., 1982; LLM in Taxation, Georgetown U., 1986. Bar: D.C. 1981, U.S. Ct. Appeals (D.C. cir.) 1981, U.S. Dist. Ct. (D.C. dist.) 1981, Va. 1993. Assoc. Metzger, Shadyac & Schwarz, Washington, 1980-83, Pillsbury, Madison & Sutro, Washington, 1983-87, Leland & Assocs., Inc., Washington, 1987-95; pres., CEO The Trust Co. of the South, Burlington, N.C., 1996—. Instr. real estate syndication, Arlington (Va.) County Continuing Edn./Realty Bd., 1982; cons., Washington, 1995-96. Contbr. articles to profl. jours. Mem.: ABA (chmn. trusts and investments subcom. of banking com., com. fed. regulation of securities), Va. Bar Assn., D.C. Bar Assn., N.C. Bar Assn. Roman Catholic. General corporate, Securities, Corporate taxation. Office: The Trust Co of the South 3041 S Church St Burlington NC 27215-5154 E-mail: jslayton@tcts.com

SLEDGE, JAMES SCOTT, judge; b. Gadsden, Ala., July 20, 1947; s. L. Lee and Kathryn (Privott) S.; m. Joan Nichols, Dec. 27, 1969; children: Joanna Scott, Dorothy Privott. BA, Auburn U., 1969; JD, U. Ala., 1974, postgrad., 1989. Bar: Ala. 1974, U.S. Ct. Appeals (5th cir.) 1975, U.S. Ct. Appeals (11th cir.) 1981. Ptnr. Inzer, Suttle, Swann & Stivender, P.A., Gadsden, 1975-91; judge U.S. Bankruptcy Ct. No. Dist. Ala., 1991—; chair Nat. Conf. Fed. Judges, 2000—. Instr. U. Ala., Gadsden, 1975-77, Gadsden State C.C., 1989-90. Lay min., vestryman Holy Comforter Episc. Ch., Gadsden, 1976—, sr. warden, 2000; exec. com. Ala. Coun. on the Arts, 1994—; incorporator Episc. Day Sch., Gadsden, 1976, Kyle Home for Devel. Disadvantaged, Gadsden, 1979; bd. dirs. Salvation Army, 1984-91, Etowah County Health Dept., 1975-91, Episc. Day Sch., 1992-96, Gadsden Symphony, 1993-96; mem. Ala. Dem. Exec. Com., 1990-91, Etowah County Dem. Exec. Com., 1984-91; founder Gadsden Cultural Arts Found., 1983, chmn., 1986-91. Capt. U.S. Army, 1969-71, Vietnam. Decorated Legion of Honor (Vietnam); recipient Gov.'s award for art Ala. Coun. of Arts, 1993. Mem. ABA (publs. chair 1997, 98, vice chair jud. divsn. 2000), Gadsden-Etowah C. of C. (gen. counsel, v.p., bd. dirs. 1986-93), Kiwanis (bd. dirs. 1981-84), Phi Kappa Phi, Phi Eta Sigma. Home: 435 Turrentine Ave Gadsden AL 35901-4059

SLEET, GREGORY M. lawyer, judge; b. N.Y.C. m. Mary Sleet; children: Moneta, Kelsi. BA in Polit. Sci. cum laude, Hampton U., 1973; JD, Rutgers U., 1976. Bar: Del., N.Y., Pa., U.S. Dist. Ct. (ea. dist.) Pa., U.S. Dist. Ct. (ea. dist.) Del., U.S. Ct. Appeals (3d cir.). Pvt. practice, Phila.; dep. atty. gen. State of Del.; in-house counsel Hercules Inc.; dep. atty. gen. U.S. Dist. Ct., Del.; U.S. atty. U.S. Dist. Ct. (ea. dist.), 1994—, judge, 1998—. Mem. Atty. Gen. Janet Reno's adv. com., 1995-97, vice-chair, 1996—. Bd. overseers Widener U. Sch. of Law. Recipient Disting. Svc. award NAACP, 1994. Office: US Courthouse Lockbox 19 844 King St Wilmington DE 19801-3519

SLEIGH, RUSSELL HOWARD PHALF, lawyer; b. Grimsby, Eng., Mar. 16, 1949; BA, Merton Coll., Oxford, Eng., 1970. Solicitor Lovell, White & King, London, 1973-77, N.Y.C., 1977-80, ptnr. London, 1980-90, Lovell, White & Durrant, Paris, 1990-93, London, 1993—, mng. ptnr. litigation, 1997—. Banking, Private international. Office: Lovells 65 Holborn Viaduct London ECIA2DY England E-mail: russell.sleigh@lovells.com

SLEIK, THOMAS SCOTT, lawyer; b. La Crosse, Wis., Feb. 24, 1947; s. John Thomas and Marion Gladys (Johnson) S.; m. Judith Mattson, Aug. 24, 1968; children: Jennifer, Julia, Joanna. BS, Marquette U., 1969, JD, 1971. Bar: Wis. 1971, U.S. Dist. Ct. (we. dist.) Wis. 1971. Assoc. Hale Skemp Hanson Skemp & Sleik, La Crosse, 1971-74, ptnr., 1975—. State pres. Boy Scouts Am., 1981-83, bd. dirs. Gateway Area Coun., 1973-99, pres., 1980-81; trustee La Crosse Pub. Libr., 1981—; bd. dirs. Children's Mus. of LaCrosse, Greater La Crosse Area United Way, 1985-92, campaign chmn., 1986, pres., 1987; mem. Sch. Dist. La Crosse Bd. Edn., 1973-77, v.p., 1977. Fellow Am. Acad. Matrimonial Lawyers (pres. Wis. chpt. 1999-2000); mem. ABA, State Bar Wis. (bd. govs. 1987-94, pres. 1992-93, spkr. litigation sect. and family law seminars), La Crosse County Bar Assn. Roman Catholic. State civil litigation, Family and matrimonial, Labor. Home: 4082 Glenhaven Dr La Crosse WI 54601-7503 Office: Hale Skemp Hanson Skemp & Sleik 505 King St Ste 300 La Crosse WI 54601-4062

SLEMMER, CARL WEBER, JR. retired lawyer; b. Camden, N.J., Mar. 28, 1923; s. Carl and Annetta (Donner) S.; m. Renée Jeannette Kinsey, Oct. 11, 1952; children: Michael, John, Sandra. BS, Muhlenberg Coll., 1948; JD, Temple U., 1963. Bar: N.J. 1972, Pa. 1972, U.S. Dist. Ct. N.J. 1972, Fla. 1974. Various pers. positions RCA, Camden, 1950-55; mgr. labor rels. Allied Chem. Corp., Morristown, N.J., 1955-67; dir. employee rels. Exide Corp., Phila., 1967-82; pvt. practice Cherry Hill, N.J., 1982-83; dir. labor rels. Columbia U., N.Y.C., 1983-89; mgr. tax office H & R Block, Marlton, N.J., 1991-93; ret., 1993. Mem. labor coun. U. Pa., Phila., 1967-82. Lt. (j.g.) USN, 1943-46, PTO. Republican. Presbyterian. Avocations: tennis, reading, travel, legal research. Home: 888 Heritage Rd Moorestown NJ 08057-1330 E-mail: carlslemmer@cs.com

SLEURINK, PAUL H. laywer; b. Amsterdam, Apr. 25, 1957; s. Herman and Henriette (Gruter) S.; m. Jetty Elja Algra, Dec. 15, 1987; children: Eline, Isabelle, Anne-Macike. M in Law, Leyden (The Netherlands) U.; LLM in Tax Law. Tax inspector, The Netherlands, 1982-86; assoc. Loyens Vollamaans, Amsterdam, 1986-90; ptnr. N.Y.C., 1990-96, Amsterdam, 1996-98, Loyens-Loeff and predecessor firm, London, 1998—. Corporate taxation. Home: 27 Sumner Pl SW7 3NT London England Office: Loyen-Loeff 26 Throgmorton St London EC4N 6NQ England Fax: 78263080. E-mail: paul.sleurink@loyensloeff

SLEWETT, ROBERT DAVID, lawyer; b. N.Y.C., June 4, 1945; s. Nathan and Evelyn (Miller) S.; m. Sheila Faith Winkler, Jan. 27, 1973; children: Gregory, Danielle. BA in Pub. Affairs, George Washington U., 1967; JD, Cornell U., 1970. Bar: Fla. 1970. Mem. Smith and Mandler, Miami Beach, Fla., 1970-73; with Robert D. Slewett, Atty. at Law, 1973-87; ptnr. Steinberg, Slewett & Yaffe, 1987-98, Robert D. Slewett, P.A., Miami Beach, 1998—. Lectr. in probate and medicaid field. Exec. v.p., gen. counsel Nat. Parkinson Found., Miami, Fla., 1993—; bd. dirs., legal counsel Boystown of Jerusalem Found. Am., N.Y.C., 1993—; mem. Dade County Estate Planning Coun., Heritage Soc. Miami Jewish Home and Hosp. Named One of Leading Fla. Attys. in Field of Trusts and Estates. Mem. Nat. Acad. Elder Lawyers, Fla. Bar Assn. (probate litigation com., probate rules com. 2000—), Dade County Bar Assn. (chmn. spl. needs trust com.), Estate Planning Coun. Dade County. Estate planning, Probate, Real property. Home: 2235 NE 204th St Miami FL 33180-1311 Office: 801 NE 167 St Fl 2 North Miami Beach FL 33162 Fax: 305-455-2049. E-mail: slewlaw@msn.com

SLICKER, FREDERICK KENT, lawyer; b. Tulsa, Aug. 21, 1943; s. James Floyd and Lucille Geneva (Nordling) S.; children: Laura, Kipp. BA, U. Kans., 1965, JD with highest distinction, 1968; LLM, Harvard U., 1973. Bar: Kans. 1968, U.S. Ct. Mil. Appeals 1968, U.S. Supreme Ct. 1972, Tex. 1973, Okla. 1980. Assoc. Jackson, Walker, Winstead, Cantwell & Miller, Dallas, 1973-76, Worsham, Forsythe & Sampels, 1977-80, ptnr., 1980; assoc. Hall, Estill, Hardwick, Gable, Collingsworth & Nelson, Tulsa, 1980-81, mem., 1982-86; ptnr. Baker, Hoster, McSpadden, Clark, Rasure & Slicker, 1986-91; pvt. practice, 1991-92; shareholder Sneed Lang Adams & Barnett, 1992-96; pvt. practice law, 1996-2000; prin. founder Slicker & Alberty PC, 2000—. Gen. counsel Image Analysis, Inc., Centrex, Inc., NUBAR, Inc. Author: A Practical Guide to Church Bond Financing, 1985, Angels All Around, 1999. Vice chmn. bd. trustees, chmn. admnstrv. bd., chmn. fin. com., treas. 1st United Meth. Ch., Tulsa; mem. task force Tulsa area Promise Keepers; founder Tulsa Men's Ministries Inc. Capt. U.S. Army, 1965-72. Mem. ABA, Okla. Bar Assn., Order of Coif. Democrat. Avocation: Christian men's ministries. Franchising, Mergers and acquisitions, Securities. Office: 4444 E 66th Ste #201 Tulsa OK 74136-4206 Fax: 918-496-9024. E-mail: fslicker@swbell.com

SLIGER, HERBERT JACQUEMIN, JR. lawyer; b. Urbana, Ill., Nov. 21, 1948; s. Herbert Jacquemin and Marina (Mantia) S.; m. Sandra Ann Ratti, May 3, 1996; children: Lauren Christine, Matthew Ryan, Nicholas Adam, Claire Nicole, Adam Gregory. BS in Fin., U. Ill., 1970; JD, U. Ariz., 1974. Bar: Ariz. 1974, Ill. 1975, U.S. Supreme Ct. 1983, Okla. 1984, U.S. Ct. Appeals (7th cir.) 1980, U.S. Tax Ct. 1980; CPA, Okla. Lawyer Charles W. Phillips Law Offices, Harrisburg, Ill., 1974-75; trust counsel Magna Trust Co., F/K/A Millikin Nat. Bank, Decatur, 1976-80, First of America Trust Co., Springfield, 1980-83; trust counsel personal fin. svcs. group First Interstate Bank Okla. NA, Oklahoma City, 1983-86; mgr. employee benefits trust dept. First Interstate Bank of Okla., NA, 1986-89; v.p., pension counsel Star Bank, NA, Cin., Cin., 1989-90; asst. gen. counsel Bank One Ariz. Corp., Phoenix, 1990-95; asst. gen. counsel, nat. practice group head Banc One Corp., Columbus, Ohio, 1995-98, state gen. counsel Phoenix, 1996-97; sec. of bd. and cashier Bank One, Ariz. NA, 1996-97; sec. of bd. and statutory agt. Banc One Ariz. Corp., 1996-97; sec. bd. Bank One Trust Co. N.A., Columbus, 1996—; asst. gen. counsel, trust counsel practice group head law dept. Bank One Corp., Chgo., 1999—. Co-chmn. Nat. Conf. Lawyers and Corp. Fiduciaries, 1992-94; instr. Chaminade U. Hawaii, Hawaii Tax Inst., 1999. Contbr. articles to profl. jours. Mem. ABA (sect. bus. law, banking law com., trust and investment svcs. subcom. 1991-99, sect. real property, probate and trust law 1974—, fiduciary income taxation subcom. 1994—, fiduciary environ. problems com. 1993-99, sect. of taxation, employee benefits com. 1991—), State Bar of Ariz., Okla. Bar Assn., Am. Bankers Assn. (chmn. trust counsel com. 1992-94, mem. and head of fiduciary law dept. Nat./Grad. Trust Sch. Bd. of Faculty Advisors 1994-95, faculty mem. teaching "fiduciary duties under ERISA" Nat. Employee Benefit Trust Sch. 1994-96, spokesman Environ. Risk Task Force 1994-95, mem. trust and investment divsn. exec. com. 1992-94, mini-adv. bd. chairperson trusts and estates 1995-99), Nat. Conf. Lawyers and Corp. Fiduciaries (co-chmn. 1992-94). Roman Catholic. Avocations: phys. fitness, original print collecting. Estate planning, Pension, profit-sharing, and employee benefits, Taxation, general.

SLIVE, STEVEN HOWARD, lawyer; b. Queens, N.Y., July 1, 1950; s. Theodore Hertzel and Jean Rhoda (Blatt) S.; m. Harriet Weinmann, Sept. 3, 1982. BGS, Ohio U., 1972; JD, Cleve. State U., 1976. Bar: Ohio 1976. Dir. legal clinic Free Med. Clinic Greater Cleve., 1977-81; ptnr. Slive & Slive, Cleve., 1981—. Adv. bd. Cuyahoga County Juvenile Ct., 1984—. Trustee Guardian Ad Litem Adv. Bd. Cuyahoga County, Cleve., 1982-84, Cleve. State U.; adv. bd. Domestic Rels. Ct., Cuyahoga County Juvenile Ct., 1984—; vol. atty. Free Med. Clinic Greater Cleve., 1981—; advocacy com. Divorce Equity, Inc.; bd. dirs. ACLU, 1983-84. Mem. Ohio State Bar Assn., Greater Cleve. Bar Assn. (treas. family law sect.), Cuyahoga County Bar Assn., Cleve. Marshall Coll. Law Alumni Assn. (trustee 1984—). Democrat. Avocations: basketball, jogging, photography. General civil litigation, Family and matrimonial, General practice.

SLIVKA, MICHAEL ANDREW, lawyer; b. Ambridge, Pa., Jan. 14, 1955; s. Andrew and Veronica (Yanko) S. AB in Psychology, Cornell U., 1977; JD, U. Miami, 1980. Bar: Fla. 1980, U.S. Dist. Ct. (so. dist.) Fla. 1981, U.S. Ct. Appeals (5th cir.) 1981, U.S. Ct. Appeals (11th cir.) 1981, Colo. 1997, U.S. Dist. Ct. Colo. 1999; cert. arbitrator. Pvt. practice, Ft. Lauderdale, Fla., 1990-99; pvt. prac. Colorado Spgs., CO, 1999—. Bd. dirs. Peak Venture Group. Precinct capt., exec. com. Broward County Rep. Party, 1991-92; v.p. West Broward Rep. Club, 1991-92; sec. North Dade/South Broward Estate Planning Coun., 1991-92. Albert C. Murphy scholar Cornell U., 1973. Mem. Fla. Bar Assn. (young lawyers sect., mem. collection forms com. 1983-85, bicentennial com. 1987), Bankruptcy Bar

Assn., Assn. for Objective Law, El Paso County Bar Assn., Weston Area Jaycees (past sec.). Republican. Avocations: Objectivist philosophy, weightlifting, motorcycling, gardening. Bankruptcy, General civil litigation, Personal injury. Home and Office: 225 Thames Dr Colorado Springs CO 80906-5952 Fax: 719-576-6963. E-mail: michael@qwest.net

SLOAN, F(RANK) BLAINE, law educator; b. Geneva, Jan. 3, 1920; s. Charles Porter and Lillian Josephine (Stiefer) S.; m. Patricia Sand, Sept. 2, 1944; children: DeAnne Sloan Riddle, Michael Blaine, Charles Porter. AB with high distinction, U. Nebr., 1942, LLB cum laude, 1946; LLM in Internat. Law, Columbia U., 1947. Bar: Nebr. 1946, N.Y. 1947. Asst. to spl. counsel Intergovtl. Com. for Refugees, 1947; mem. Office Legal Affairs UN Secretariat, N.Y.C., 1948-78; gen. counsel Relief and Works Agy. Palestine Refugees, Beirut, 1958-60; dir. gen. legal divsn., dep. to the legal counsel UN Legal Office, N.Y.C., 1966-78, rep. of Sec. Gen. to UN Commn. Internat. Trade Law, 1969-78, rep. to Legal Sub-com. on Outer Space, 1966-78; rep. UN Del. Vietnam Conf., Paris, 1973; rep. UN Conf. on Carriage of Goods by Sea Hamburg, 1978; prof. internat. law orgn. and water law Pace U., 1978-87, prof. emeritus, 1987—. Law lectr. Blaine Sloan Internat., 1988—. Author: United Nations General Assembly Resolutions in Our Changing World, 1991; contbr. articles to legal jours. Cons. UN Office of Legal Affairs, 1983-84, UN Water Resources Br., 1983; supervisory com., Pace Peace Ctr.; legal advisor Korean Missions, 1951, 53, UNTSO, Jerusalem, 1952, UNEF I, Gaza, 1957-58; prin. sec.UN Commn. to investigate Sec.-Gen. Hammarskjold's crash, 1961-62. Navigator AC, U.S. Army, 1943-46 Decorated Air medal. Mem. Am. Soc. Internat. Law, Am. Acad. Polit. and Social Sci., Am. Arbitration Assn. (panel of arbitrators), Order of Coif, Phi Beta Kappa, Phi Alpha Delta (hon.). Republican. Roman Catholic. Home: HCR-68 Box 72 Foxwind-Forbes Park Fort Garland CO 81133 Office: 78 N Broadway White Plains NY 10603-3710 also: 375 Soubry Pl Forbes Park Fort Garland CO 81133

SLOCA, STEVEN LANE, lawyer; b. Plainfield, N.J., Dec. 18, 1944; s. Charles and Maureen (Rushmore) S.; children: Lee M. H., Andrew C. BA summa cum laude with highest distinct, Dartmouth Coll., 1966; LLB, Yale U., 1969. Bar: Calif. 1970, U.S. Dist. Ct. (ctrl. dist.) Calif. 1970, U.S. Ct. Appeals (9th cir.) 1976. Assoc. Irell & Manella, L.A., 1969-77, ptnr., 1977—. Instr. trial advocacy Yale U., New Haven, 1968-69. Editor: Yale Law Your., 1967-69. Served to capt. U.S. Army, 1970-71, Vietnam. Mem. ABA (sect. on litigation), State Bar Calif. (sect. on real property), Assn. Bus. Trial Lawyers, Beverly Hills Bar Assn. (mem. exec. com., ADR sec., coord. settlement officer program), Dartmouth Lawyers Assn., Order of Coif, Phi Beta Kappa. Democrat. Methodist. Administrative and regulatory, State civil litigation, Real property. Home: 4334 Huntley Ave Culver City CA 90230-4719 Office: Irell & Manella 1800 Avenue Of The Stars Los Angeles CA 90067-4212

SLOMAN, MARVIN SHERK, lawyer; b. Fort Worth, Apr. 17, 1925; s. Richard Jack and Lucy Janette (Sherk) S.; m. Margaret Jane Dinwiddie, Apr. 11, 1953; children: Lucy Carter, Richard Dinwiddie. BA, U. Tex., 1948; LLB with honors, 1950. Bar: Tex. 1950, N.Y. 1951. Assoc. Sullivan & Cromwell, N.Y.C., 1950-56, Carrington, Coleman, Sloman & Blumenthal LLP and predecessor, Dallas, 1956-60, ptnr., 1960-97; sr. counsel, 1998—. Appellate, General civil litigation, General practice. Office: Carrington Coleman Sloman & Blumenthal LLP 200 Crescent Ct Ste 1500 Dallas TX 75201-1848

SLOVENKO, RALPH, law educator; b. New Orleans, Nov. 4, 1926; s. Sam and Clara (Roitman) S. B.E., Tulane U., 1948, LL.B., 1953, M.A., 1960, Ph.D., 1965. Bar: La. 1953, Kans. 1965, Mich. 1969. Prof. law Tulane U., 1954-64, dept. psychiatry Sch. Medicine, 1960-65, U. Kans. Law Sch. and Menninger Found., 1965-67, Wayne State U. Law Sch., 1969—; vis. Road Eminent scholar U. Fla. Coll. Law, 1991. Editor-in-Chief Tulane Law Rev., 1952-53; editor Tulane Hullaballo, 1950; assoc. editor Bull. Am. Acad. Psychiatry and Law; bd. editors Jour. Psychiatry and Law; mem. editorial bd. Behavioral Scis. and the Law; mem. editorial bd. Medicine and Law/An Internat. Jour.; mem. rev. bd. Hosp. and Community Psychiatry. Author: Psychiatry and Law, 1973; Tragicomedy in Court Opinions, 1974; Handbook of Criminal Procedures and Forms, 1967; Civil Code of Louisiana and Ancillaries, 2d edit., 1981, Psychiatry and Criminal Culpability, 1995, Psychotherapy and Confidentiality, 1998; others; contbr. articles to law jours., chpts. in books. Served with USNR, 1944-45. Recipient Manfred Guttmacher award Am. Psychiat. Assn., 1974, Amicus award Am. Acad. Psychiatry and Law, 1986; Fulbright scholar, France, 1955, Amicus award Am. Acad. Psychiatry Law, 1986. Mem. ABA (mem. task force criminal justice mental health standards project 1981-83), Am. Orthopsychiat. Assn. (past bd. dirs.), Am. Acad. Psychoanalysis (com. on confidentiality, com. on nat. health ins.), Acad. Psychosomatic Medicine (legal com.), Assn. Am. Law Schs. (com. law and medicine), La. Assn. Mental Health, Kans. Bar Assn., La. Bar Assn., New Orleans Bar Assn., Mich. Bar Assn., Am. Assn. Marriage and Family Counselors, Internat. Acad. Forensic Psychology, Inter-Am. Bar Assn., Internat. Assn. Criminal Law, Am. Soc. Criminology, So. Soc. Philosophy and Psychology, Am. Acad. Forensic Scis. Fax: 313-577-2620. Office: Wayne State U Law Sch Detroit MI 48202

SLOVITER, DOLORES KORMAN, federal judge; b. Phila., Sept. 5, 1932; d. David and Tillie Korman; m. Henry A. Sloviter, Apr. 3, 1969; 1 dau., Vikki Amanda. AB in Econs. with distinction, Temple U., 1953, LHD (hon.), 1986; LLB magna cum laude, U. Pa., 1956; LLD (hon.), The Dickinson Sch. Law, 1984, U. Richmond, 1992; LL.D. (hon.), Widener U., 1994. Bar: Pa. 1957. Assoc., then ptnr. Dilworth, Paxson, Kalish, Kohn & Levy, Phila., 1956-69; mem. firm Harold E. Kohn (P.A.), 1969-72; assoc. prof., then prof. law Temple U. Law Sch., 1972-79; judge U.S. Ct. Appeals (3d cir.), 1979—, chief judge, 1991-98. Mem. bd. overseers U. Pa. Law Sch., 1993-99; bd. dirs. Nat. Constitution Ctr., 1998—. Mem. S.E. region Pa. Gov.'s Conf. on Aging, 1976-79, Com. of 70, 1976-79; trustee Jewish Publ. Soc. Am., 1983-89; Jud. Conf. of U.S., 1991-98, U.S. com. Bicentennial Constn., 1987-90, com. on Rules of Practice and Procedure, 1990-93. Recipient Juliette Low medal Girl Scouts Greater Phila., Inc., 1990, Honor award Girls High Alumnae Assn., 1991, Jud. award Pa. Bar Assn., 1994, U. Pa. James Wilson award, 1996, Temple U. Cert. of Honor award, 1996; Disting. Fulbright scholar, Chile, 1990. Mem. ABA, Fed. Bar Assn., Fed. Judges Assn., Am. Law Inst., Nat. Assn. Women Judges, Am. Judicature Soc. (bd. dirs. 1990-95), Phila. Bar Assn. (gov. 1976-78, Sandra Day O'Connor award 1997), Order of Coif (pres. U. Pa. chpt. 1975-77), Phi Beta Kappa. Office: US Ct Appeals 18614 US Courthouse 601 Market St Philadelphia PA 19106-1713

SLUTZKY, LORENCE HARLEY, lawyer; b. Chgo., Jan. 27, 1946; s. Nathan and Gertrude (Rosenholtz) S.; m. Linda Kay Day, Feb. 1, 1970; children— Brian Adam, Michael Aaron. B.S. in Acctg., So. Ill. U., 1968; postgrad. U. Exeter, Eng., 1971; J.D., John Marshall Law Sch., 1972. Bar: Ill. 1972, Fla. 1972, U.S. Dist. Ct. (no. dist.) Ill. 1972, U.S. Ct. Appeals (7th cir.) 1972, U.S. Supreme Ct. 1976. Law clk. U.S. Dist. Ct. (no. dist.) Ill., Chgo., 1972-73; atty. State's Atty.'s Office, Cook County, Ill., 1973-76; ptnr. Robbins, Schwartz, Nicholas, Lifton & Taylor Ltd., Chgo., Decator, Ill., 1976—; arbitrator Am. Arbitration Assn., Chgo., 1974—. Author: Construction Litigation, 1984. Contbr. articles on archtl./engr. liability to profl. jours. Mem. ABA, Ill. State Bar Assn., Chgo. Bar Assn., Fla. Bar Assn. Construction, Education and schools, Labor. Home: 2306 Carrington Way Glenview IL 60025-1011 Office: Robbins Schwartz Nicholas Lifton & Taylor Ltd 29 N La Salle St Chicago IL 60602-2601

SMAIL, LAURENCE MITCHELL, lawyer, educator; b. May 2, 1937; s. Samuel Percy and Kathryn Jeanette (Mitchell) S.; m. Katherine Sylvia Carr, Nov. 30, 1964; 1 child, Leslie Anne. BA, Washington and Lee U., 1959, JD, 1962; MBA, Coll. William and Mary, 1973. Bar: Va. 1964, U.S. Ct. Claims 1967, U.S. Supreme Ct. 1968, U.S. Ct. Appeals (Fed. cir.) 1982; cert. profl. contracts mgr. Assoc. Hoyle & Short, Newport News, Va., 1965-66; atty. advisor USAAV Labs., Ft. Eustis, 1966-74; counsel SUPSHIP, Newport News, 1974, U.S. Army Aviation Applied Tech. Directorate, Ft. Eustis, 1974-99; dir. 1st advisor Fed. Credit Union, 1973—. Adj. prof. Fla. Tech., 1976—, asst. prof. mgmt.; pres. Med. Security Card, Inc., Newport News, 1995—; chmn. legal issues com. Fed. Lab. Consortium, 1993—94. Contbr. articles to profl. jours. Pres. Brentwood Civic League, 1969; chmn. Newport News Taxpayers Assn., 1973. Served to capt. U.S. Army, 1962-65. Fellow Nat. Contract Mgmt. Assn. (nat. v.p. 1979-80), Am. Helicopter Soc., Fed. Bar Assn., Va. Bar Assn., Phi Delta Phi, Phi Gamma Delta, Warwick Yacht Club, Pegasus Club (past pres.). Republican. Presbyterian. Home: 507 Beech Dr Newport News VA 23601-3109 Office: Fla Tech Hampton Rds Grad Ctr Bldg 1708 Fort Eustis VA 23604 E-mail: l-smail@home.com

SMALL, ALDEN THOMAS, judge; b. Columbia, S.C., Oct. 4, 1943; s. Alden Killin and Shirley Edna (Eldridge) S.; m. Judy Jo Worley, June 25, 1966; children: Benjamin, Jane. AB, Duke U., 1965; JD, Wake Forest U., 1969. Bar: N.C. 1969. Asst. v.p. First Union Corp., Greensboro, N.C., 1969-72; assoc. dir., gen. counsel Cmty. Enterprise Devel. Corp. Alaska, Anchorage, 1972-73; v.p., assoc. gen. counsel First Union Corp., Raleigh, N.C., 1973-82; judge U.S. Bankruptcy Ct., 1982—, chief judge, 1992-99. Bd. govs. Nat. Conf. of Bankruptcy Judges, 1987-90; adj. prof. law Campbell U. Sch. Law, 1980-82; bd. dirs. Am. Bankruptcy Inst., 1989-95, Fed. Jud. Ctr., 1997—; sec. Nat. Conf. Bankruptcy Judges, 1998—, pres.-elect, 1999, pres., 2000—; chmn. Nat. Conf. Bankruptcy Judges Ednl. Endowment, 1993-94; mem. long range planning com. U.S. Judicial Conf., 1991-95, adv. com. bankruptcy rules, 1996-99, chair adv. com. on bankruptcy rules, 2000—; mem. Bd. Fed. Jud. Ctr., 1997-2001; faculty Nat. Comml. Lending Sch., 1981-82; cons. Nat. Coalition for Bankruptcy Reform, 1981-82. Contbg. editor Norton Bankruptcy Law and Practice. Mem. ABA, Am. Coll. Bankruptcy, Am. Bankers Assn. (bankruptcy task force 1980-82), N.C. Bankers Assn. (bank counsel com. 1980-82), N.C. Bar Assn. (bankruptcy coun.), Kappa Sigma, Phi Alpha Delta. Republican. Office: US Bankruptcy Ct PO Box 2747 Raleigh NC 27602-2747

SMALL, CLARENCE MERILTON, JR. lawyer; b. Birmingham, Ala., July 24, 1934; s. Clarence Merilton and Elva (Roberts) S.; m. Jean Russell, Nov. 18, 1935; children: William Stephen, Elizabeth Ann, Laura Carol. BS, Auburn U., 1956; LLB, U. Ala., 1961. Assoc. Christian & Small, Birmingham, 1961—. Served to 1st lt., arty. AUS, to capt. JAGC. Fellow Am. Bar Found., Internat. Acad. Trial Lawyers, Am. Coll. Trial Lawyers, Ala. Law Found.; mem. ABA (ho. of dels. 1984-86), Ala. Bar Assn. (pres. 1992-93), Birmingham Bar Assn. (pres. 1979), Ala. Def. Lawyers Assn., Internat. Assn. Def. Counsel. Office: 1800 Financial Ctr Birmingham AL 35203-4611 E-mail: cmsmall@csattorneys.com

SMALL, JONATHAN ANDREW, lawyer; b. Balt., June 30, 1959; s. Marvin Myron and Suzanne (Bierstock) S. AA, Foothill Jr. Coll., 1980; BS in Math. with honors, Calif. Poly. State U., 1983; JD, U. Santa Clara, 1986. Bar: Calif. 1987, U.S. Dist. Ct. (no. and so. dists.) Calif. 1987, U.S. Patent Office 1987, U.S. Ct. Appeals (fed. cir.) 1987. Patent atty. Townsend & Townsend, San Francisco, 1986-89; counsel Xerox Corp., Palo Alto, Calif., 1989-92, 97-00, assoc. gen. patent counsel, 1999-2000; assoc. Weil, Gotshal & Manges, Menlo Park, 1992-93; gen. counsel Komag Inc., Milpitas, 1993-97, Calient Networks, Inc. (formerly Chromisys, Inc.), San Jose, 2000—. Editor-in-chief Santa Clara Computer and High-Tech. Law Jour., 1985-86; contbr. articles to legal jours. Mem. ABA (chair intellectual property sect., elect. filing), Am. Intellectual Property Law Assn. Avocations: bicycle touring, kayaking. Consumer commercial, Intellectual property, Patent. Office: Calient Networks Inc 5853 Rue Ferrari San Jose CA 95138

SMALL, JONATHAN ANDREW, lawyer; b. N.Y.C., Dec. 26, 1942; s. Milton and Teresa Markell (Joseph) S.; m. Cornelia Mendenhall, June 8, 1969; children: Anne, Katherine. BA, Brown U., 1964; student, U. Paris, 1962-63; LLB, Harvard U., 1967; MA, Fletcher Sch. of Law and Diplomacy, 1968; LLM, NYU, 1974. Bar: N.Y. 1967. VISTA vol., Washington and Cambridge, Mass., 1968; law clk. to judge U.S. Ct. Appeals (2d cir.), 1968-69; assoc. Debevoise & Plimpton, N.Y.C., 1969-75, ptnr., 1976-99; pres. Nonprofit Coord. Com. N.Y., 2000—. Cons. Spl. Task Force of N.Y. State Taxation, 1976 Trustee Brearley Sch., 1985-95; bd. dirs. Nonprofit Coordinating Com. of N.Y., 1985—, Muscular Dystrophy Assn., 1986-88, Human Svcs. Coun. N.Y.C., Inc., 2000—, Investor Responsibility Rsch. Ctr., Inc., 2000—, Lawyers Alliance for N.Y., 2000—, U.S. Com. fo the UN Population Fund, 2000—. Mem. ABA, N.Y. State Bar Assn. (chmn. tax sect. com. exempt orgns. 1980-82, co-chmn., 1995), Assn. Bar City N.Y., Nonprofit Forum, Phi Beta Kappa. Non-profit and tax-exempt organizations, Corporate taxation, Personal income taxation. Home: 60 E End Ave New York NY 10028-7907 Office: Nonprofit Coord Com of NY 1350 Broadway Rm 1801 New York NY 10018-7718

SMART, ALLEN RICH, II, lawyer; b. Chgo., July 3, 1934; s. Jackson W. Smart and Dorothy (Byrnes) Bowles. Student, Deerfield Acad., 1949-52; AB magna cum laude, Princeton U., 1956; LLB, Harvard U., 1961. Bar: Ill. 1961. Assoc. Bell Boyd & Lloyd, Chgo., 1961-69, ptnr., 1970-91, of counsel, 1992—. Bd. dirs. Rec. for Blind, Inc., Chgo., 1984-95, vice-chmn., 1987-90; co-chmn. zoning com. Old Town Triangle Assn., Chgo., 1987-94; bd. dirs. Lawrence Hall Sch. for Boys, 1965-70, Old Masters Soc., Art Inst., 1987—; governing mem. Orchestral Assn. Lt. USNR, 1956-58. Mem. ABA, Ill. Bar Assn., Chgo. Bar Assn., Infant Welfare Soc. Chgo. (bd. dirs. 1971-95, pres. 1982-86), Friends of the Parks Chgo. (bd. dirs. 1986—), Renaissance Soc. Chgo. (bd. dirs. 1988—), University (bd. dirs. 1986-89), Arts, Legal, Law, Economic clubs of Chgo. Home: 1732 N North Park Ave Chicago IL 60614-5710 Office: Bell Boyd & Lloyd 3200 Three First Nat Pl Chicago IL 60602

SMARTT, JOHN MADISON, lawyer; b. Smartt, Tenn., Feb. 24, 1919; s. Robert White and Sarah Alma (Roggli) S.; BS, U. Tenn., 1942, JD, 1948; m. Harriet Chapin, June 9, 1943; children: John Madison, Jane (Mrs. Roy D. Stroud), Douglas A., Robert W., III. Bar: Tenn. 1948, U.S. Dist. Ct. (ea. dist.) Tenn. 1969; alumni dir. U. Tenn., Knoxville, 1948-69, ptnr. Fowler & Robertson, Knoxville, 1969-83; of counsel Ambrose, Wilson, Grimm & Durand, Knoxville, 1983—; coordinator Tenn. Law Inst., Knoxville, 1972—. Bd. dirs. United Way of Greater Knoxville, 1984; life mem. 6th Circuit Jud. Conf. Capt. AUS, 1942-46; lt. col. Res. Mem. Great Smokey Mt. Conservation Assn. (pres. 1978), Tenn. Bar Found., Kiwanis, Phi Delta Phi. Democrat. Presbyterian (mem. session 1970-73). Avocations: hiking, running, singing. Home: 4603 Holston Hills Rd Knoxville TN 37914-5007 Office: Ambrose Wilson Grimm & Durand PO Box 2466 Knoxville TN 37901-2466

SMAY, STEPHEN LEROY, association executive, lawyer; b. Sioux City, Iowa, May 16, 1944; s. John LeRoy and Mary Louise (Sargent) S. B.A., Drake U., 1966; J.D., U. Mich., 1968. Asst. prof. bus. law Mich. State U., East Lansing, 1968-70; assoc. atty. Cleary, Gottlieb, et al, N.Y.C., 1970-72; asst. to pres. Council on Fgn. Relations, N.Y.C., 1972-73; grant dir. ABA, Chgo., 1974-77; exec. dir. State Bar Wis., Madison, 1978— . Office: State Bar Wis 402 W Wilson St PO Box 7158 Madison WI 53707-7158

SMEAD, BURTON ARMSTRONG, JR. retired lawyer; b. Denver, July 29, 1913; s. Burton Armstrong and Lola (Lewis) S.; m. Josephine McKittrick, Mar. 27, 1943 children: Amanda Armstrong, Sydney Hall. BA, U. Denver, 1934, JD, 1950; grad., Pacific Coast Bank Trust Sch., 1955. With Wells Fargo Denver (formerly Denver Nat. Bank), 1934-78, trust officer, 1955-70; v.p., trust officer Norwest Bank Denver (now Wells Fargo), 1970-78; of counsel Buchanan Neville & Stouffer, Lakewood, Colo., 1985-99. Author: History of the Twelfth Field Artillery Battalion in the European Theater of Operations, 1944-45, Captain Smead's Letters to Home, 1944-45; editor: Colorado Wills and Estates, 1965. Pres., trustee Stebbins Orphans Home Assn., resigned, 1998; chmn. bd. dirs. Colo. divsn. Am. Cancer Soc., 1961-68. Maj. U.S. Army, 1941-45, ETO. Decorated Bronze Star; Croix de Guerre (France). Mem. Colo. Bar Assn. (treas. 1970-88, chmn. probate and trust law sect. 1967-68, exec. coun., bd. govs. 1970-88, coun. bd. govs. 1970-88, hon. 1989—, award of merit 1979), Denver Bar Assn., Denver Estate Planning Coun. (co-founder, pres. 1971-72), Univ. Club (Denver). Republican. Episcopalian. Home and Office: 111 Emerson St Apt 1143 Denver CO 80218-3790

SMEDINGHOFF, THOMAS J. lawyer; b. Chgo., July 15, 1951; s. John A. and Dorothy M. Smedinghoff; m. Mary Beth Smedinghof. BA in Math., Knox Coll., 1973; JD, U. Mich., 1978. Bar: Ill. 1978, U.S. Dist. Ct. (no. dist.) Ill. 1978. Assoc. McBride, Baker & Coles and predecessor McBride & Baker, Chgo., 1978-84, ptnr., 1985-99, Baker & McKenzie, Chgo., 1999—. Adj. prof. computer law John Marshall Law Sch., Chgo.; chair Ill. Commn. on Electronic Commerce and Crime, 1996—; mem. U.S. Del. to UN Commn. on Internat. Trade Law. Author: Online Law, 1996. Mem. ABA (chair electronic commerce divsn. 1995—). Computer, General corporate, Intellectual property. Office: Baker & McKenzie 130 E Randolph St Ste 3700 Chicago IL 60601-6342 E-mail: smedinghoff@bakernet.com

SMEGAL, THOMAS FRANK, JR. lawyer; b. Eveleth, Minn., June 15, 1935; s. Thomas Frank and Genevieve (Andreachi) S.; m. Susan Jane Stanton, May 28, 1966; children: Thomas Frank, Elizabeth Jane. BS in Chem. Engring., Mich. Technol. U., 1957; JD, George Washington U., 1961. Bar: Va. 1961, D.C. 1961, Calif. 1964, U.S. Supreme Ct. 1976. Patent examiner U.S. Patent Office, Washington, 1957-61; staff patent atty. Shell Devel. Co., San Francisco, 1962-65; patent atty. Townsend and Townsend, 1965-91, mng. ptnr., 1974-89; sr. ptnr. Graham and James, 1992-97; pres., ptnr. Knobbe, Martens, Olson & Bear, 1997—. Mem. U.S. del. to Paris Conv. for Protection of Indsl. Property; mem. adv. com. Ct. of Appeals for Fed. Cir., 1992-96. Contbr. articles to profl. jours. Pres. bd. dirs. Legal Aid Soc. San Francisco, 1982-84, Youth Law Ctr., 1973-84; bd. dirs. Nat. Ctr. for Youth Law, 1978-84, San Francisco Lawyers Com. for Urban Affairs, 1972—, Legal Svcs. for Children, 1980-88; bd. dirs., presdl. nominee Legal Svcs. Corp., 1984-90, 93—. Capt. Chem. Corps, U.S. Army, 1961-62. Recipient St. Thomas More award, 1982. Mem. ABA (chmn. PTC sect. 1990-91, ho. of dels. 1988-2000, mem. standing com. Legal Aid and Indigent Defendants 1991-94, chair sect. officer conf. 1992-94, bd. govs. 1994-97, standing com. on Pro Bono and Pub. Svc. 1997-2001, standing com. on Gavel awards 2001—), Intellectual Property Law Assn. (chmn. nat. coun. 1989), Nat. Inventors Hall of Fame (pres. 1988), Calif. Bar Assn. (v.p. bd. dirs. 1986-87), Am. Patent Law Assn. (pres. 1986), Internat. Assn. Intellectual Property Lawyers (pres. 1995—), Bar Assn. San Francisco (pres. 1979), Patent Law Assn. San Francisco (pres. 1974), World Trade Club, Olympic Club, Golden Gate Breakfast Club, Claremont Club (Berkeley). Republican. Roman Catholic. Patent, Trademark and copyright. Office: Knobbe Martens Olson & Bear 201 California St Ste 1150 San Francisco CA 94111-5002 E-mail: tsmegal@kmob.com

SMILEY, GUY IAN, lawyer; b. N.Y.C., July 30, 1938; s. Edward and Minerva June (Silverman) S.; m. Constance Ann Rodbell, July 30, 1967; children: Erica, Andrew. BA, Cornell U., 1960; JD, Columbia U., 1963. Bar: N.Y 1964, U.S. Dist. Ct. (so. dist.) N.Y. 1965, U.S. Dist. Ct. (ea. dist.) N.Y. 1965, U.S. Ct. Appeals (2d cir.) 1967, U.S. Supreme Ct. 1970. Assoc. Law Offices of Harry H. Lipsig, N.Y.C., 1964-68; ptnr. Smiley & Smiley LLP (formerly Smiley, Schwartz & Captain), 1968—. Arbitrator Am. Arbitration Assn., N.Y. 1974—, Civil Ct. City of N.Y., 1974-80; co-chmn. Combined Jud. Screening Panel City of N.Y., 1983—. Contbr.: (book) The Lawyers Secretary, 1972. V.p., gen. counsel Westchester Emergency Communications Assn., White Plains, N.Y., 1979—; vol. counsel Am. Radio Relay League, 1983—. Served to lt. (JAGC) USN 1966-70. Mem. Assn. Trial Lawyers Am. (sustaining), N.Y. State Trial Lawyers Assn. (mem. legis. com., 1979-85, bd. dirs. 1982—, editor-in-chief newsletter, 1984—, dep. treas. 1986), Jewish Lawyers Guild (sec. 1984—). Avocations: amateur radio, tennis, skiing. Federal civil litigation, State civil litigation, Personal injury. Home: 425 E 58th St New York NY 10022-2300 Office: Smiley & Smiley LLP 60 E 42nd St Rm 950 New York NY 10165-0999 E-mail: gsmiley@smileylaw.com

SMILEY, STANLEY ROBERT, lawyer; b. N.Y.C., Feb. 19, 1947; s. Arthur and Rose Smiley; m. Anita Kape, June 28, 1970; children: Wayne Alan, Lori Patricia. BA, SUNY, Buffalo, 1968; JD, St. John's U., 1971. Bar: N.Y. 1971, Calif. 1977, U.S. Tax Ct. 1972, U.S. Ct. Mil. Appeals 1972, U.S. Ct. Appeals (9th cir.) 1979, U.S. Dist. Ct. (cen. dist.) Calif. 1978, U.S. Dist. Ct. (no. so. and ea. dists.) Calif., 1979. Atty., Office of Chief Counsel, IRS, Newark, 1971-72, L.A., 1976-78; ptnr. McLaughlin and Irvin, L.A., Calif., 1978-95; ptnr. St. John, Smiley & Zamost, L.A., 1995-97; of counsel St. John, Wallce, Brennan and Folan, Torrance, 1997—; guest instr. U. Md., Madrid, 1974-76. With JAGC, USAF, 1972-76. Mem. ABA (com. tax ct. procedure 1981—), State Bar N.Y., State Bar Calif., L.A. County Bar Assn., Bar Assn. San Francisco, Phi Delta Phi. Assoc. editor St. John's Law Rev., 1969-71. Pension, profit-sharing, and employee benefits, Probate, Corporate taxation. Home: 2525 Camino Del Sol Fullerton CA 92833-4826 Office: 21515 Hawthorne Blvd Ste 840 Torrance CA 90503-6507

SMILLIE, DOUGLAS JAMES, lawyer; b. Glen Ridge, N.J., Aug. 16, 1956; s. James and Nancy (Albright) S.; m. Nancy Marie McKenna, Jan. 27, 1990; children: Sara Grace, Jeffrey Douglas, Heather Patricia. BA in Polit. Sci. cum laude, Muhlenberg Coll., 1978; JD, Villanova U., 1982. Bar: Pa. 1982, U.S. Dist. Ct. (ea. dist.) Pa. 1982, U.S. Ct. Appeals (3d cir.) 1983, N.J. 1984, U.S. Dist. Ct. N.J. 1984, U.S. Dist. Ct. (mid. dist.) Pa. 1995. Assoc. Clark, Ladner, Fortenbaugh & Young, Phila., 1982-90, ptnr., 1991-96; shareholder, v.p., chair litigation sect. Fitzpatrick Lentz & Bubba, P.C., Center Valley, Pa., 1996—. Lectr. bus. bankruptcy Lehigh-Carbon C.C., 1999. Author: When Worlds Collide: The Impact of the Bankruptcy Stay on Environmental Clean-Up Litigation, 1989, The Absolute Priority Rule: Catch 22 for Reorganizing Closely-Held Businesses, 1992; editor (newsletter) Environ. Impact, 1985-96; contbr. articles to profl. jours. Recipient Rev. Joseph Williams award. Mem. ABA (litigation sect.), Nat. Bus. Inst. (seminar spkr. 1991, 99), Am. Bankruptcy Inst. (seminar spkr. 1986), Turnaround Mgmt. Assn., Comml. Law League Am. (bankruptcy and insolvency sect., creditors rights sect.), Assn. Comml. Fin. Attys., Robert Morris Assocs. (seminar spkr. 1995), N.J. Bar Assn. (bankruptcy sect., environ. law sect.), Phila. Bar Assn. (Ea. Dist. Bankruptcy Conf.), Lehigh County Bar Assn. Avocation: Second City Troop Rugby Football Club. Bankruptcy, General civil litigation, Contracts commercial. Office: Fitzpatrick Lentz & Bubba PO Box 219 Stabler Corp Ctr 4001 Schoolhouse Ln Center Valley PA 18034-0219 Fax: 610-797-6663. E-mail: dsmillie@flblaw.com

SMITH, ARTHUR B., JR. lawyer; b. Abilene, Tex., Sept. 11, 1944; s. Arthur B. and Florence B. (Baker) S.; m. Tracey L. Truesdale, 1999; children: Arthur C., Sarah R. BS, Cornell U., 1966; JD, U. Chgo., 1969. Bar: Ill. 1969, N.Y. 1976. Assoc. Vedder, Price, Kaufman & Kammholz, Chgo., 1969-74; asst. prof. labor law N.Y. State Sch. Indls. and Labor Rels., Cornell U., 1975-77; ptnr. Vedder, Price, Kaufman & Kammholz, Chgo., 1977-86; founding mem. Murphy, Smith & Polk, 1986-98; shareholder Ogletree & Deakins, 1999—. Guest. lectr. Northwestern U. Grad. Sch. Mgmt., 1979, Sch. Law, spring 1980; mem. hearing bd. Ill. Atty. Registration and Disciplinary Commn. Author: Employment Discrimination Law Cases and Materials, 5th edit., 2000, Construction Labor Relations, 1984, supplement, 1993; co-editor-in-chief: 1976 Annual Supplement to Morris, The Developing Labor Law, 1977; asst. editor: The Developing Labor Law, 4th edit., 2000; contbr. articles to profl. jours. Recipient award for highest degree of dedication and excellence in tchg. N.Y. State Sch. Indsl. and Labor Rels., Cornell U., 1977. Fellow Coll. Labor and Employment Lawyers; mem. ABA (co-chmn. com. on devel. law under Nat. Labor Rels. Act, Sect. Labor Rels. Law 1976-77), N.Y. State Bar Assn., Phi Eta Sigma, Phi Kappa Phi, Chgo. Athletic Assn., Mid-Day Club. Presbyterian. Administrative and regulatory, Federal civil litigation, Labor. Office: Ogletree Deakins et al 2 First National Plz Fl 25 Chicago IL 60603 E-mail: Arthur.Smith@odnss.com

SMITH, ARTHUR LEE, lawyer; b. Davenport, Iowa, Dec. 19, 1941; s. Harry Arthur Smith and Ethel (Hoffman) Duerre; m. Georgia Mills, June 12, 1965 (dec. Jan. 1984); m. Jean Bowler, Aug. 04, 1984; children: Juliana, Christopher, Andrew. BA, Augustana Coll., Rock Island, Ill., 1964; MA, Am. U., 1968; JD, Washington U., St. Louis, 1971. Bar: Mo 1971, DC 1983. Telegraph editor Davenport Morning Democrat, 1962-64; ptnr. Peper Martin Jensen Maichel & Hetlage, 1971-95, Husch & Eppenberger, St. Louis, 1995—. Arbitrator Nat Asn Security Dealers, 1980—, Am Arbit Asn. 1980—. Columnist: St Louis Lawyer. Lt USN, 1964—68. Mem.: ABA, DC Bar Asn (chmn law practice mgt 1990—91), Mo Bar Asn (chair admin law comt 1995—97, vice-chair ins programs comt 1981—83, vice-chair antitrust comt 1981—83), P Buckley Moss Soc (dir 1994—, vpres 1998—2000, exec vpres 2001—), Bar Asn Metropolitan St Louis (chmn law mgt comt 1993—96, chair technology comt 1996—99, Pres's award Exceptional Serv 1995), Order Coif. Federal civil litigation, Public utilities, Securities. Home: 1320 Chesterfield Estate Dr Chesterfield MO 63005-4400 Office: Husch & Eppenberger 100 N Broadway Ste 1300 Saint Louis MO 63102-2789 E-mail: arthur.smith@husch.com

SMITH, BRIAN WILLIAM, lawyer, former government official; b. N.Y.C., Feb. 3, 1947; s. William Francis and Dorothy Edwina (Vogel) S.; m. Donna Jean Holverson, Apr. 24, 1976; children: Mark Holverson, Lauren Elizabeth. BA, St. John's U., N.Y.C., 1968, JD, 1971; MS, Columbia U., 1981. Bar: N.Y. 1972, D.C. 1975, U.S. Dist. Ct. (ea. and so. dists.) N.Y. 1975, U.S. Supreme Ct. 1976, U.S. Dist. Ct. D.C. 1986. Atty. Am. Express Co., N.Y.C., 1970-73, CIT Fin. Corp., N.Y.C., 1973-74; assoc. counsel, mng. atty. Interbank Card Assn. (named changed to Master Card Internat., Inc.), 1974-75, sr. v.p., corp. sec., gen. counsel, 1975-82; chief counsel Compt. of Currency, Washington, 1982-84; ptnr. Stroock & Stroock & Lavan, 1984-92, mng. ptnr., 1986-92; ptnr. Mayer, Brown & Platt, Washington and N.Y.C., 1992—. Lectr. fin. industry. Editor: (Book) Bank Investment Products Deskbook, 1995—2001, E-Commerce in Financial Products and Services, 2001—, Bank Investment Products Deskbook, 1995—2001, E-Commerce, Financial Products and Services, 2001. Capt., USAR, 1970-78. Mem. ABA, N.Y. State Bar Assn., D.C. Bar Assn., Assn. Bar City N.Y., Fed. Bar Assn., N.Y. Athletic Club, Met. Club (N.Y.), Met. Club (Washington). Antitrust, Banking, General corporate. Home: 35 W Lenox St Chevy Chase MD 20815-4208 Office: Mayer Brown & Platt 1909 K St NW Washington DC 20006-1152 E-mail: bsmith@mayerbrown.com

SMITH, BRUCE ARTHUR, lawyer; b. Terre Haute, Ind., Jan. 4, 1952; s. Wayne Coakley and Stella Inez S.; m. Lora L. Smith, May 16, 1992; children: Ashley Nicole, Haley Marie, Nathan Wayne. BS, Ind. State U., 1973; JD cum laude, Ind. U., 1976. Bar: Ind. 1976, U.S. Dist. Ct. (so. dist.) Ind. 1976, U.S. Tax Ct. 1977, Ill. 1984, U.S. Supreme Ct. 1983; cert. in bus. bankruptcy law and consumer bankruptcy law Am. Bd. Cert. Ptnr. Sturm, Smith & Parmenter, Vincennes, Ind., 1976—. Instr. paralegal edn. Vincennes U., 1977-81, mem. adv. bd. edn. small bus. edn., 1984-86; dep. pros. atty. Knox County Prosecutor's Office, Vincennes, 1976-82. Mem. ABA, Ind. Bar Assn. (chair bankruptcy law sect., 1994-95), Ill. Bar Assn., Knox County Bar Assn. (pres. 1982-83), Assn. Trial Lawyers Am., Ind. Trial Lawyers Assn., Knox County C. of C. (bd. dirs., pres. 1985-86), Vincennes Area C. of C. (bd. dirs., pres. 1985-86), instr. Ind. Continuing Legal Edn. Forum, 1995, 97, Phi Delta Phi. Lodges: Kiwanis (pres. 1981-82), Elks (exalted ruler 1983-84). Banking, Bankruptcy, Contracts commercial. Home: 3328 Deer Creek Dr Vincennes IN 47591-9600 Office: Sturm Smith & Parmenter 302 Main St PO Box 393 Vincennes IN 47591-0393

SMITH, CAROL ANN, lawyer; b. Birmingham, Ala., Apr. 23, 1949; d. James William and Mildred Viola (Ferguson) S. BA, Birmingham So. Coll., 1971; JD, U. Ala., Tuscaloosa, 1975; LL.M., NYU, 1977. Bar: Ala. 1975, U.S. Dist. Ct. (no. dist.) Ala. 1977, U.S. Dist. Ct. (mid. dist.) Ala. 1976, U.S. Ct. Appeals (11th cir.) 1981, U.S. Ct. Appeals (5th cir.) 1979, U.S. Dist. Ct. (so. dist.) Ala. 1986. Law clk. Ala. Supreme Ct., Montgomery, 1975-76; assoc. Lange, Simpson, Robinson & Somerville, Birmingham, 1977-81; assoc. Starnes & Atchison, Birmingham, 1981-83, ptnr., 1983— . Editorial bd. Ala. Law Rev., 1973-75. Mem. bd. mgmt. Metro YMCA, Birmingham, 1984-90, exec. com., 1989. Mem. Birmingham Bar Assn. (pres. 1996-97, pres. young lawyers sect. 1984), Ala. Bar Inst. for Continuing Legal Edn. (exec. com. 1979—), Ala. Def. Lawyers Assn. (sec., treas. 1996, pres. 1997—, bd. dirs. 1988-90), Ala. Bar Assn. (editorial bd. The Ala. Lawyer 1979-88, assoc. editor 1984-88, exec. com. young lawyers sect. 1983-84), Phi Beta Kappa. Methodist. Federal civil litigation, State civil litigation, Insurance. Home: 4341 Old Brook Trl Birmingham AL 35243-4049 Office: Starnes & Atchison 7th Fl PO Box 598512 One Brookwood Pl Birmingham AL 35259-8512

SMITH, CAROL J. legal secretary, medical transcriptionist; b. Camden, N.J., May 22, 1943; d. Rogers Marsh and Jeannette Alfretta (MacAchren) Smith; m. Christopher Leo Glennon III, June 27, 1964 (div. Dec. 1974); children: Jeannette Ann Glennon, Rogers Smith Glennon. Grad., Katherine Gibbs Sch., Montclair, N.J., 1963. Cert. paralegal. Pvt. sec. Brakemaster Sales Corp./RJ Truck Components, Haddonfield, N.J., 1970-77; sec. to h.s. prin., sec. to supr. Bd. Edn., 1977-79; legal sec. Green, Lundgren & Ryan, 1979-85, Robert Messick, Esq., Haddonfield, 1985-86; sec. archtl. firm Charles Weiler Assocs., 1986-87; legal sec. Tomlin, Clark & Hopkin, 1987-97; legal sec. to three attys. to 3 attys., Cherry Hill, N.J., 1998; legal sec. Frederick W. Hardt, Esq., Moorestown, 1999—. Police officer and sec. Aux. Police, Haddonfield, 1984—; coord., sec., treas. Crime Watch, Haddonfield, 1979—; bd. sec. Haddonfield Planning Bd., 1980s; mem. Juvenile Conf. Commn., Haddonfield, 1987-99. Mem. Colonial Dames XVII, Daus. Am. Colonists, Daus. of 1812 (sec.-treas.), Ladies of Grand Army of Republic (sec.-treas), UDC (sec.), French Huguenot Soc., Order Eastern Star, Am. Legion Aux. (pres., sec.), DAR. Republican. Presbyterian. Avocations: reading, genealogy, needlework, plants, animals. Home: 33 Colonial Ave Haddonfield NJ 08033-1503 E-mail: ECHELONCJS@aol.com

SMITH, CAROLE DIANNE, lawyer, editor, writer, product developer; b. Seattle, June 12, 1945; d. Glaude Francis and Elaine Claire (Finkenstein) S.; m. Stephen Bruce Presser, June 18, 1968 (div. June 1987); children: David Carter, Elisabeth Catherine. AB cum laude, Harvard U., Radcliffe Coll., 1968; JD, Georgetown U., 1974. Bar: Pa. 1974. Law clk. Hon. Judith Jamison, Phila., 1974-75; assoc. Gratz, Tate, Spiegel, Ervin & Ruthrouff, 1975-76; freelance editor, writer Evanston, Ill., 1983-87; editor Ill. Inst. Tech., Chgo., 1987-88; mng. editor LawLetters, Inc., 1988-89; editor ABA, 1989-95; product devel. dir. Gt. Lakes divsn. Lawyers Coop. Pub., Deerfield, Ill., 1995-96; product devel. mgr. Midwest Market Ctr. West Group, 1996-97; mgr acquisitions, bus. and fin. group CCH, Inc., Riverwoods, 1997—. Author Jour. of Legal Medicine, 1975, Selling and the Law: Advertising and Promotion, 1987; (under pseudonym Sarah Toast) 71 children's books and stories, 1994-2000; editor The Brief, 1990-95, Criminal Justice, 1989-90, 92-95 (Gen. Excellence award Soc. Nat. Assn. Pubs. 1990, Feature Article award-bronze Soc. Nat. Assn. Pubs. 1994), Franchise Law Jour., 1995; editor-in-chief The Brief, ABA Tort and Ins. Practice Sect., 1998-2000; mem. editl. bd. The Brief, ABA Tort and Ins. Practice Sect., 1995-2000. Dir. Radcliffe Club of Chgo., 1990-93; mem. parents council Latin Sch. Chgo., 1995-96. Mem. ABA. Office: CCH Inc Bus and Fin Group 2700 Lake Cook Rd Riverwoods IL 60015-3867 E-mail: smithca@cch.com

SMITH, CHARLES Z. state supreme court justice; b. Lakeland, Fla., Feb. 23, 1927; s. John R. and Eva (Love) S.; m. Eleanor Jane Martinez, Aug. 20, 1955; children: Carlos M., Michael O., Stephen P., Felica L. BS, Temple U., 1952; JD, U. Wash., 1955. Bar: Wash. 1955. Law clk. Wash. Supreme Ct., Olympia, 1955-56; dep. pros. atty., asst. chief criminal div. King County, Seattle, 1956-60; ptnr. Bianchi, Smith & Tobin, 1960-61; spl. asst. to atty. gen. criminal div. U.S. Dept. Justice, Washington, 1961-64; judge criminal dept. Seattle Mcpl. Ct., 1965-66; judge Superior Ct. King County, 1966-73; former assoc. dean, prof. law U. Wash., 1973; now justice Wash. Supreme Ct., Olympia. Mem. adv. bd. NAACP, Seattle Urban League, Wash. State Literacy Coun., Boys Club, Wash. Citizens for Migrant Affairs, Medina Children's Svc., Children's Home Soc. Wash., Seattle Better Bus. Bur., Seattle Foundation, Seattle Symphony Orch., Seattle Opera Assn., Community Svc. Ctr. for Deaf and Hard of Hearing, Seattle U., Seattle Sexual Assault Ctr., Seattle Psychoanalytic Inst., The Little Sch., Linfield Coll., Japanese Am. Citizens League, Kawabe Meml. Hous, Puget Counseling Ctr, Am. Cancer Soc., Hutchinson Cancer Rsch. Ctr., Robert Chinn Found.; pres. Am. Bapt. Chs. U.S.A., 1976-77, U.S. Commn. on Internat. Religious Freedom, 1999-2000. lt. col. ret. USMCR Mem. ABA, Am. Judicature Soc., Washington Bar Assn., Seattle-King County Bar Assn., Order of Coif., Phi Alpha Delta, Alpha Phi Alpha. Office: Wash Supreme Ct Temple of Justice PO Box 40929 Olympia WA 98504-0929

SMITH, D. BROOKS, federal judge; b. 1951; BA, Franklin and Marshall Coll., 1973; JD, Dickinson Sch. Law, 1976. Pvt. practice Jubelirer, Carothers, Krier, Halpern & Smith, Altoona, Pa., 1976-84; judge Ct. Common Pleas of Blair County, 1984-88, U.S. Dist. Ct. (we. dist.) Pa., 1988—, chief judge, 2001—. Asst. dist. atty. Blair County, part-time, 1977-79, spl. prosecutor, 1981-83, dist. atty. part-time, 1983-84; instr. Pa. State U., Altoona campus, 1977—, St. Francis Coll., 1986—; adv. com. on criminal rules U.S. Jud. Conf., 1993-99. Trustee St. Francis Coll. Mem. Am. Law Inst., Pa. Bar Assn., Am. Judicature Soc., Pa. Soc., Amen Corner, Blair County Game, Fish and Forestry Assn., Fed. Judges Assn. (bd. dirs. 1993-97), Am. Law Inst., Inns of Ct., Allegheny County Bar Assn., Pi Gamma Mu. Office: US Courthouse 319 Washington St Ste 104 Johnstown PA 15901-1624

SMITH, DANIEL CLIFFORD, lawyer; b. Cin., Aug. 9, 1936; s. Clifford John and Vivian Aileen (Stone) S.; m. Carroll Cunningham; children: Edward, Andrew, Scott. BS, Ariz. State U., 1960; postgrad., George Washington U., 1961-62; JD, Am. U., 1965. Bar: D.C. 1965, U.S. Ct. Appeals (D.C. cir.) 1966, U.S. Ct. Appeals (Fed. cir.), U.S. Dist. Ct. D.C. 1966, Va. 1967, U.S. Supreme Ct. 1969, U.S. Ct. Appeals (4th cir., 5th cir., 6th cir., 7th cir., 9th cir., 11th cir.), U.S. Ct. Claims, U.S. Ct. Customs and Patent Appeals, U.S. Tax Ct. Assoc. Alpern & Feissner, Washington, 1963-66; atty. FTC, 1966-70; ptnr. Arent, Fox, Kintner, Plotkin & Kahn, 1970-93, Canfield & Smith, Washington, 1993—. Pres., dir. Country Pl. Citizens Assn., Inc., 1974-77; bd. dirs. Sea Watch Condominium, Ocean City, Md., 1978—, treas., 1982-86, pres. 1986—; active Supreme Ct. Hist. Soc., The Federalist Soc., Smithsonian Inst. Assocs., Ariz. State Soc. Served with USMC. Mem. D.C. Bar Assn. 9dr. 1974-76, chmn. consumer protection com. 1972-74, chmn. D.C. affairs sect. 1975-76), Va. State Bar Assn., ABA, Fed. Bar Assn., Assn. Trial Lawyers Am., Nat. Field Selling Assn. (gen. counsel), Ariz. State U. Alumni Assn., Rotary Club (pres. 1987-88, 96-97), Optimist (pres. 1972-73), Internat. Town and Country Club (dir. 1969-73), Masons, Delta Theta Phi. Administrative and regulatory, Antitrust, Federal civil litigation. Office: Canfield & Smith Fed Bar Bldg 1815 H St NW Ste 1001 Washington DC 20006-3604

SMITH, DANIEL LYNN, lawyer; b. Ottawa, Kans., June 22, 1952; s. Daniel H. and Mary K. (Lynn) S.; m. Alana A. Windhorst, Aug. 15, 1981; children: Tricia, Lauran, Alexa. BA, U. Kans., 1973; JD, Duke U., 1976. Bar: Kans. 1976, U.S. Dist. Ct. Kans. 1976, U.S. Ct. Appeals (10th cir.) 1977, U.S. Tax Ct. 1977. Assoc. Bronston Law Offices, Overland Park, Kans., 1976-78; ptnr. Oliver, Smith & Oliver, 1978-80, Bronston and Smith, Overland Park, 1981-92, Ankerholz & Smith, Overland Park, Kans., 1992—; pvt. practice Westwood, 1980-81. Mem. Kans. Bar Assn., Kans. Trial Lawyers Assn. (bd. govs. 1981—), Civil War Roundtable Kansas City, Phi Beta Kappa. General civil litigation, Personal injury, Workers' compensation. Home: 10075 Goodman Dr Shawnee Mission KS 66212-3432 Office: Ankerholz & Smith 6900 College Blvd Overland Park KS 66211-1547

SMITH, DANIEL TIMOTHY, lawyer; b. Denver, July 20, 1948; s. Harold Kennedy and Dorothy (Gannon) S. BA, Duke U., 1970; JD, U. Denver, 1973. Bar: Colo. 1973, U.S. Dist. Ct. Colo. 1973, U.S. Ct. Appeals (10th cir.), U.S. Supreme Ct. 1979, U.S. Ct. Claims 1979. Dep. dist. atty. Denver Dist. Atty. Office, 1973-74; spl. asst. atty. gen. Colo. Atty. Gen.'s Office, Denver, 1973-74; asst. U.S. atty. Dist. of Colo., 1974-76; ptnr. Wiggins & Smith P.C., 1977-87; pvt. practice, 1987—. Chmn. fundraising Am. Cancer Soc., Denver., 1992-93; mem. golf com. Am. Heart Assn., Denver, 1988—. Mem. ABA, Colo. Criminal Def. Bar (sec. 1979-81). Avocation: golf. General civil litigation, Criminal. Office: 1900 Grant St Ste 580 Denver CO 80203-4346

SMITH, DAVID BURNELL, lawyer; b. Charleston, W.Va., Apr. 8, 1941; s. Ernest Dayton and Nellie Dale (Tyler) S.; m. Rita J. Hughes, Sept. 25, 1967. BA, U. Charleston, 1967; JD, U. Balt., 1972; MJS, U. Nev., 1995. Bar: Colo. 1972, Md. 1972, U.S. Supreme Ct. 1980, Ariz. 1983, U.S. Dist. Ct. Md. 1972, U.S. Dist. Ct. Colo. 1972, U.S. Ct. Appeals (4th Cir.) 1972, U.S. Ct. Appeals (9th cir. 1972, U.S. Ct. Appeals (10th cir.) 1983. Sales rep. Gulf Oil, Washington, 1967-72; pvt. practice Littleton, Colo., 1972-83, Glendale, Ariz., 1983-86, Phoenix, 1986-88, Scottsdale, Ariz., 1988—. Pro-tempore judge Wickenburg Mcpl. Ct., 1986—; presiding judge Peoria (Ariz.) Mcpl. Ct., 1987-94, Cave Creek Mcpl. Ct., 1995-98. Appeared as actor in movie Dead Girls Don't Tango, 1990. V.p. South Jefferson County Reps., Lakewood, Colo., 1979, pres., 1990; candidate Dist. 6 for Congress; pres. Ariz. Rep. Assembly Dist. 28. Served with USCG, 1959-66. Mem. ATLA, Nat. Assn. Criminal Lawyers, Am. Judicature Soc., ABA (vice-chmn. family law 1983), Nat. Assn. Criminal Def. Attys., Ariz. Magistrates Assn., Colo. Bar Assn., Ariz. Bar Assn., Md. Bar Assn., Colo. Trial Lawyers Assn., Maricopa County Bar Assn., Scottsdale Bar Assn. (bd. dirs., sec. 1996—), Masons, Shriners, Elks. State civil litigation, Criminal, Personal injury. Home: PO Box 5145 36418 N Wildflower Rd Carefree AZ 85377-5145 Office: 4310 N 75th St Scottsdale AZ 85251-3578 E-mail: dbsattyatlaw@cs.com

SMITH, DAVID JAMES, corporate lawyer; Asst. sec. Archer Daniels Midland, Decatur, Ill., 1988-97, asst. gen. counsel, 1995-97, v.p., sec. gen. counsel, 1997—. Office: Archer Daniels Midland Co 4666 E Faries Pkwy Decatur IL 62526-5666

SMITH, DAVID ROBINSON, lawyer; b. Loveland, Ohio, Sept. 27, 1946; s. William E. and Mamie (Robinson) S.; m. Wessylyne French, Apr. 12, 1969; 1 child, Kimberly. BA, Central State U., 1969; JD, DePaul U., 1974. Bar: Ill. 1975. Asst. chief counsel U.S. Dept. Energy, Argonne, Ill., 1972-83; ptnr. Cole & Smith, Chgo., 1983-85; corp. v.p., gen. counsel, sec. Maxima Corp., Rockville, Md. Mem. ABA (state chmn. pub. contract law 1984), Nat. Bar Assn., Ill. Bar Assn., Nat. Contract Mgmt. Assn. (seminar chmn. 1984), Alpha Phi Alpha. Baptist. General corporate, Government contracts and claims. Home: 3527 Laurel Leaf Ln Fairfax VA 22031-3212 Office: The Maxima Corp 2101 E Jefferson St Rockville MD 20852-4908

SMITH, DEIRDRE O'MEARA, lawyer; b. N.Y.C., June 2, 1946; d. Thomas Francis and Mary Veronica (Meehan) O'Meara; children: Thomas Brady Ahr, Andrew Travers Ahr; m. Gerald Monroe Smith, Aug. 15, 1992. BA cum laude, Trinity Coll., 1968; MEd, Va. Commonwealth U., 1976; JD, U. Mo., 1982. Bar: Mo. 1982, U.S. Dist. Ct. (we. dist.) Mo. 1982. Tchr. Prince George's County Schs., Md., 1968-70, St. Michael's Sch., Richmond, Va., 1976-78; staff lawyer Mo. Supreme Ct., Jefferson City, 1982-83; gen. counsel State of Mo. Detention Facilities Commn., 1983, State of Mo. Jud. Fin. Commn., Jefferson City, 1983-85; clk. of the ct. Mo. Ct. Appeals Eastern Dist., St. Louis, 1985-98. Bd. dirs. Downtown St. Louis, 1994-95. Recipient Acad. Excellence award in environ. law U. Mo. Sch. Law, 1981; disting. fellow St. Louis Bar Found. Fellow Am. Bar Found., Mo. Bar Found.; mem. ABA (jud. divsn. lawyers conf., exec. com. 1997-2000), Nat. Conf. Bar Pres., Nat. Conf. Bar Founds., Mo. Bar Assn. (Mo. Client Security Security Trust Fund bd. dirs. 1991-95, chmn. 1995-96), St. Louis County Bar Assn., Lawyers Assn. St. Louis (Outstanding Svc. award 1998), Met. St. Louis Bar Assn. (exec. com. 1988-96, pres. 1994-95), St. Louis Bar Found. (bd. dirs. 1989-96, pres. 1995-96), St. Louis Women Lawyers Assn. (bd. dirs. 1989-94, pres. 1992-93), Am. Judicature Soc. (bd. dirs. 1990-94, bd. exec. com. 1993—, v.p. 1995-97, sec. 1997-99, treas. 1999-2001, pres. 2001—), Nat. Conf. Appellate Ct. Clks. (exec. com. 1990-92), Media Club St. Louis (bd. dirs.), Phi Delta Phi. Roman Catholic.

SMITH, DUNCAN CAMPBELL, III, lawyer; b. Dover, N.J., Aug. 12, 1947; s. Duncan C. and Dorothy H. (Sarles) S.; m. Sherry A. Fisher, Dec. 27, 1968; children— Scot D., Amanda J. B.A., Drew U., 1969; J.D., Coll. William and Mary, 1976. Bar: Va. 1976, D.C. 1980, U.S. Ct. Mil. Appeals 1976, U.S. Supreme Ct. 1980. Law specialist USCG Hdqtrs., Washington, 1976-78; atty.-advisor Dept. Treasury, Washington, 1978-80; minority counsel Mcht. Marine and Fisheries Com., U.S. Ho. of Reps., Washington, 1980-86, chief minority counsel Merch. Marine and Fishery com. U.S. Ho. of Reps., Washington, 1986-90; ptnr. Dyer, Ellis, & Joseph, Washington, 1990—. Served to capt. USCGR, 1978—. Decorated Nat. Def. Svc. medal, Coast Guard Achievement medal, Armed Forces Res. medal, Spl. Ops. Svc. Ribbon. Mem. Fed. Bar Assn. (chmn. young lawyers div. 1979-80, asst. editor 1980-83), Va. Bar Assn., D.C. Bar Assn., Maritime Law Assn., Omicron Delta Epsilon. Office: Dyer Ellis & Joseph Ste 1100 600 New Hampshire Ave NW Washington DC 20037-2485

SMITH, DWIGHT CHICHESTER, III, lawyer; b. Ft. Meade, Md., June 24, 1955; s. Dwight Chichester Jr. and Rachel (Stryker) S.; m. Mindy L. Kotler, Aug. 18, 1985; children: Dwight C. IV, Cornelia R. BA, Yale U., 1977, JD, 1981. Bar: D.C. 1982, N.Y. 1982. Para-legal House Ethics Com., Washington, 1977-78; law clk. to Hon. Hugh Bownes U.S. Ct. Appeals (1st cir.), Concord, N.H., 1981-82; assoc. Kaye, Scholer, Fierman, Hays & Handler, Washington, 1982-84, Covington & Burling, Washington, 1984-90; dep. chief counsel for legal policy Office of Thrift Supervision, Dept. of Treasury, 1990-94, dep. chief counsel for bus. transactions, 1995-99; counsel Alston & Bird LLP, 1999—. Article and book rev. editor Yale Law jour., 1980-81; contbr. articles to profl. jours. Mem. Potomac Boat Club, City Tavern Club. Presbyterian. Avocation: rowing. Home: 1606 32nd St NW Washington DC 20007-2930 Office: Alston & Bird LLP North Bldg 11th Fl 601 Pennsylvania Ave NW Washington DC 20004-2601 E-mail: dcsmith@alston.com

SMITH, EDWIN DUDLEY, lawyer; b. N.Y.C., Oct. 4, 1936; s. Edwin Dudley Jr. and Mary Jane (Bannigan) S.; m. Joan Joyce Mortenson, June 29, 1963; children: Edwin Dudley V, Patrick Townshend. BA, U. Kans., 1960, JD, 1963. Bar: Kans. 1963, Mo. 1992, U.S. Dist. Ct. Kans. 1963, U.S. Ct. Appeals (10th cir.) 1967, U.S. Supreme Ct. 1972, U.S. Dist. Ct. (we. dist.) Mo., 1998. Assoc. Fisher Patterson Sayler & Summers, Topeka, 1963-66; ptnr. Fisher Patterson Sayler & Smith, L.L.P., Topeka, Overland Park, 1966—. Contbg. author: Pharmacy Law Annual, 1991. Chpt. advisor Tau Kappa Epsilon Frat., 1988-93; mem. adv. bd. Florence Crittenton Svcs., Topeka, 1988-91; chmn. legis. com. U.S. Swimming, 1986-90; chmn. Missouri Valley Swimming, 1987-89. Fellow Kans. Bar Found.; mem. ABA, Kans. Bar Assn. (bd. govs. 1986-92, Outstanding Svc. award 1978), Topeka Bar Assn., Johnson County Bar Assn., Kansas City Met. Bar Assn., Internat. Assn. Def. Counsel, Am. Judicature Soc. (bd. dirs. 1984-89), Am. Bd. Trial Adv. (pres. Kans. chpt. 1989-90), Kans. Assn. Def. Counsel, Def. Rsch. Inst., Am. Soc. Pharmacy Law. Avocation: photography. General civil litigation, Personal injury, Professional liability. Home: 4344 W 124th Ter Leawood KS 66209-2277 Office: Fisher Patterson Sayler & Smith LLP 51 Corporate Woods Ste 300 9393 W 110th St Shawnee Mission KS 66210 also: Fisher Patterson Sayler & Smith LLP 3550 SW 5th St Topeka KS 66606-1998 E-mail: dsmith@fisherpatterson.com

SMITH, EDWIN ERIC, lawyer; b. Louisville, Sept. 29, 1946; s. Lester Henry and Nancy Joy (Heyman) S.; m. Katharine Case Thomson, Aug. 16, 1969; children: Benjamin Clark, George Lewis, Andrew Laurence. BA, Yale U., 1968; JD, Harvard Law Sch., 1974. Bar: Mass. 1974, U.S. Dist. Ct. Mass. 1974. Assoc. Bingham Dana LLP, Boston, 1974-81, ptnr., 1981—. Lectr. in field; Mass. commr. on uniform state laws; mem. uniform comml. code articles 5 and 9 drafting com.; chmn. uniform comml. code payments article divsn. drafting com.; U.S. del. to receivables assignment working group UN Commn. on Internat. Trade Law. Lt. USNR, 1969-71. Recipient Achievement Medal USN, 1971. Mem. ABA (chmn. uniform comml. code com. bus. law sect. 1995-99, advisor to the permanent editl. bd. uniform comml. code 1999—), Am. Law Inst. (Uniform Comml. Code article 9 study com.), Am. Coll. Comml. Fin. Lawyers (v.p.), Assn. Comml. Fin. Attys. Banking, Bankruptcy, Contracts commercial. Home: 4 Chiltern Rd Weston MA 02493-2714 Office: Bingham Dana LLP 150 Federal St Boston MA 02110-1713 E-mail: eesmith@bingham.com

SMITH, EDWIN LLOYD, lawyer; b. Bklyn., Mar. 28, 1944. BA, NYU, 1965; JD, Bklyn. Law Sch., 1968. Bar: N.Y. 1968, U.S. Dist. Ct. (so. and ea. dists.) N.Y. 1973, U.S. Ct. Appeals (2d cir.) 1975. Atty. Atlantic Mut. Ins. Co., N.Y.C., 1968-69; assoc. Shatzkin & Cooper, N.Y.C., 1969-72, Lanzone & Assocs., N.Y.C., 1972-78; prin. Edwin L. Smith, N.Y.C.,

1978-81; ptnr. Smith & Laquercia, N.Y.C., 1981-83, prin., 1983—. Contbr. articles to ins. and legal jours. Mem. N.Y. State Bar Assn., N.Y. County Lawyers Assn., Assn. Trial Lawyers Am., Def. Research Inst. State civil litigation, General practice, Insurance. Office: Smith & Laquercia PC 291 Broadway New York NY 10007-1814

SMITH, ELEANOR VAN LAW, paralegal; b. Richmond, Va., Aug. 11, 1964; d. William Preston Jr. and Priscilla Norris Smith. AS, U. S.C., Columbia, 1985, BA in Interdisciplinary Studies, 1986; Paralegal Cert., Nat. Ctr. Paralegal Tng., Atlanta, 1987. Sales assoc. Ship n' Shore, Columbia, 1984-85, The Ltd., Columbia, 1985-86; office asst. Universal Printing, Charleston, S.C., 1986-87; sales assoc. Evelyn Rubin, 1987; paralegal First Union Nat. Bank, Atlanta, 1988-89, L.J. Hooker Devel., Atlanta, 1989-90; sr. paralegal James Lang La Salle Americas, Inc., 1990—. Participant Habitat for Humanity, Atlanta, 1993-95, Multiple Sclerosis Soc., Atlanta, 1994-95, Osteoporosis Soc., Atlanta, 1997, Ptnr. for Spl. Olympics, 1999. Mem. Internat. Collectors Soc., Carolina Merchandising Club (sec. 1985-86), Delta Delta Delta. Republican. Episcopalian. Avocations: travel, tennis, cooking, knitting, exercise. Home: 838 Preston Woods Trl Dunwoody GA 30338-5432 Office: Jones Lang La Salle 3500 Piedmont Rd NE Ste 600 Atlanta GA 30305-1507

SMITH, FRANK LEONARD, III, lawyer; b. Albuquerque, Oct. 16, 1946; s. Frank Leonard, Jr. and Mary Frances (Wilson) S.; LL.B., Armstrong Coll., Berkeley, Calif., 1973, M.B.A., 1977; m. Sandra Terepka. Admitted to Calif. bar, 1974; asso. firm Graves & Mallory, Oakland, Calif., 1973-74; ptnr. firm Bradley & Smith, Vallejo, Napa, Calif., 1974— . Pres., Vallejo Symphony, Marin County Commuters Assn., Calif. Young Republicans of Solano County; treas. San Francisco Annex; bd. dirs. Silverado council Boy Scouts Am., Solano County YMCA. Recipient Am. Jurisprudence award Armstrong Law Sch., 1973. Mem. Am. Bar Assn., Calif. Trial Lawyers Assn. Republican. Roman Catholic. Club: Silverado Country. Contbr. legal articles to Update Mag., 1978, 79. Home: 2060 Big Ranch Rd Napa CA 94558-2403 Office: 521 Georgia St Vallejo CA 94590-6006

SMITH, FRANK TUPPER, lawyer; b. May 21, 1929; s. Frank T. and Mary Elizabeth Smith; m. Jill A. Jacobsen, Mar. 9, 1957; children: Delia, Lisa Noel, Kathryn. BA, Columbia Coll., 1951; JD, Columbia U., 1954; MBA, NYU, 1963. Bar: N.Y. 1956, Calif. 1966, Tex. 1974, U.S. Supreme Ct. 1963; cert. estate planning and probate law specialist, Tex. Assoc. Vaughn & Lyons, N.Y.C., 1956-60, Edward R. Peckerman, N.Y.C., 1960-63; v.p. Bank of Calif., San Francisco, 1963-69; assoc. Paul Hastings Janofsky & Walker, L.A., 1969-72; v.p., trust officer Republic Nat. Bank, Dallas, 1972-74; ptnr. Smith, Miller & Carlton, 1975-87; sr. ptnr. Frank Tupper Smith & Assocs. PC, 1987—. Lectr. estate and tax planning U. Tex., Dallas, Dallas Community Coll. Dist. Bd. dirs. Am. Heart Assn., 1979-82, Tex. chmn. planned giving com., 1980-82, nat. chmn. planned giving com., 1983-86; bd. dirs., v.p. fund raising Brain/Behavior Ctr., 1992—; bd. dirs. Planned Living Assistance Network North Tex., Inc., 1996-2000. With AUS, 1954-56. Mem. ABA, Calif. State Bar Assn., Tex. State Bar Assn., Dallas Bar Assn., Columbia U. North Tex. Club (pres. 1980-86), Univ. Club, Rush Creek Yacht Club. Estate planning, Probate, Estate taxation. Home: 3975 High Summit Dr Dallas TX 75244-6623 Office: 3860 W Northwest Hwy Dallas TX 75220-5183 E-mail: tuppertalk@yahoo.com

SMITH, GEORGE BUNDY, state supreme court justice; b. New Orleans, Apr. 7, 1937; m. Alene L. Smith; children: George, Jr., Beth Beatrice. Cert. Polit. Studies, Institut d'Etudes Politiques, Paris, 1958; BA, Yale U., 1959, JD, 1962; MA in Polit. Sci., NYU, 1967, PhD, 1974; M od Jud. Process, U. Va., 2001. temp. judge Family Ct. N.Y. State, Crimal Ct. N.Y.C. Staff atty. NAACP, 1962-64; law sec. to Hon. Jawn Sandifer, 1964-67; law sec. to Hon., Edward Dudley, 1967-71; law sect. to Hon. Harold Stevens, 1972-74; adminstr. model cities City of N.Y., 1974-75; interim judge Civil Ct. N.Y.C., 1975-76, judge, 1976-79, N.Y. State Supreme Ct., 1980-86, assoc. justice appellate divsn., 1st dept., 1987-92; assoc. judge N.Y. State Ct. Appeals, 1992—. Apptd. mem. N.Y. State Ethics Commn. Unified Ct. System; adj. prof. law Fordham U., 1981—. Author: (with Alene L. Smith) You Decide: Applying the Bill of Rights to Real Cases; contbr. articles to profl. jours. Trustee Grace Congl. Ch., Harlem, N.Y., Horace Mann-Barnard Sch., Bronx, N.Y., 1977-99; bd. dirs. Harlem-Dowling Westside Ctr. for Children and Family Svcs., N.Y.C.; former alumni trustee Phillips Acad., Andover, Mass.; former trustee Horace Mann-Barnard Sch., Bronx. Mem. Met. Black Bar Assn. (founding, former pres. Harlem Lawyers Assn., bd. dirs., chmn. 1984-88), Assn. of Bar of City of N.Y. (v.p. 1988-89), Judicial Friends. Office: NY Court Appeals 29th Fl 61 Broadway Rm 2900 New York NY 10006-2802 also: Ct of Appeals Hall 20 Eagle St Albany NY 12207-1009

SMITH, GEORGE CURTIS, judge; b. Columbus, Ohio, Aug. 8, 1935; s. George B. and Dorothy R. Smith; m. Barbara Jean Wood, July 10, 1963; children: Curtis, Geoffrey, Elizabeth Ann. BA, Ohio State U., 1957, JD, 1959. Bar: Ohio 1959, U.S. Dist. Ct. (so. dist.) Ohio 1987. Asst. city atty. City of Columbus, 1959-62; exec. asst. to Mayor of Columbus, 1962-63; asst. atty. gen. State of Ohio, 1964; chief counsel to pros. atty. Franklin County, Ohio, 1965-70; pros. atty., 1971-80; judge Franklin County Mcpl. Ct., Columbus, 1980-85, Franklin County Common Pleas Ct., 1985-87. Mem. Ohio Bicentennial Com. 2003; mem. Ohio Supreme Ct. Coun. on Victims Rights; judge in residence Law Sch. U. Cin.; chair Fed. Ct. Case Settlement Svc.; faculty Ohio Jud. Coll., Litig. Practice Inst.; chmn., Fed. Bench-Bar Conf.; lectr. ABA Anti-Trust Sec.; alumni spkr. law graduation Ohio State U.; pres. Young Rep. Club; chmn. Perry Group, Put-in-Bay, 2000; exec. com. Franklin County Rep. Party, 1971-80. Elder Presbyn. Ch. Recipient Superior Jud. Svc. award Supreme Ct. Ohio. Mem. Ohio Pros. Attys. Assn. (pres., Ohio Pros. of Yr. Award of Hon. Leadership award), Columbus Bar Assn., Columbus Bar Found., Columbus Athletic Club (pres., dir.), Lawyers Club of Columbus, Masons (33d degree), Shriners. Office: 85 Marconi Blvd Columbus OH 43215-2823

SMITH, GLEE SIDNEY, JR. lawyer; b. Rozel, Kans., Apr. 29, 1921; s. Glee S. and Bernice M. (Augustine) S.; m. Geraldine B. Buhler, Dec. 14, 1943; children: Glee S., Stephen B., Susan K. AB, U. Kans., 1943, JD, 1947. Bar: Kans. 1947, U.S. Dist. Ct. 1951, U.S. Supreme Ct. 1973, U.S. Ct. Mil. Appeals 1988. Ptnr. Smith Burnett & Larson, Lanred, Kans., 1947—. Of counsel Barber, Emerson et. al., Lawrence, Kans., 1992—, Kans. state senator, 1957-73, pres. Senate, 1965-73; mem. Kans. Bd. Regents, 1975-83, pres., 1976; bd. govs. Kans. U. Law Soc., 1967—; mem. Kans. Jud. Coun., 1963-65; county atty. Pawnee County, 1949-53; mem. bd. edn. Larned, 1951-63; Kans. commr. Nat. Conf. Commn. on Uniform State Laws, 1963—; bd. dirs. Nat. Legal Svcs. Corp., 1975-79. Served to 1st lt. U.S. Army Air Corps, 1943-45. Recipient disting. svc. award U. Kans. Law Sch., 1976; disting. svc. citation U. Kans., 1984. Fellow Am. Coll. Probate Counsel, Am. Bar Found.; mem. ABA (bd. of govs. 1987-90, chmn. ops. com. 1989-90, exec. com. 1989-90, chmn. task force on solo and small firm practitioners 1990-91, chmn. com. on solo and small firm practitioners 1992-94, chmn. task force on applying fed. legis. to congress 1994-96), Kans. Bar Assn. (del. to ABA ho. of dels. 1982-92, bd. govs. 1982-92, leadership award 1973, medal of distinction 1993), Southwest Kans. Bar Assn., Am. Jud. Soc., Kiwanis, Masons, Rotary. Republican. Presbyterian. General practice, Probate, Estate taxation. Home: 4313 Quail Pointe Rd Lawrence KS 66047-1966 E-mail: gsmith@eagle.cc.ukans.edu

SMITH, GREGORY BUTLER, lawyer; b. Muncie, Ind., June 20, 1946; AB, Ind. U., 1968; JD, Ind. U., 1971. Bar: Ind. 1971, U.S. Dist. Ct. (so. dist.) Ind. 1971, U.S. Dist. Ct. (so. dist.) Ill. 1978. Ptnr., Smith & Smith, Muncie, 1971—; dep. prosecutor Delaware County, Muncie, 1971-72. Contbr. articles to profl. jours. Mem. East Cen. Ind. Estate Planning Council, Muncie, 1980-88; pres. Muncie Common Council, 1981; bd. dirs. Muncie Transit System, 1983-96. Mem. Ind. Bar Assn., Muncie Bar Assn. (pres. 1980-81), Am. Pub. Transit Assn. (legal affairs com.), Soc. Profl. Dispute Resolution (pres. Ind. chpt. 1994-95), Phi Alpha Delta, Sigma Iota Epsilon. Lodge: Kiwanis. General practice, Probate. Office: Smith & Smith Law Offices PO Box 236 Muncie IN 47308-0236

SMITH, GREGORY DALE, lawyer, judge; b. Knoxville, Feb. 1, 1963; s. James C. and Essie Pearl (Norman) S.; m. Cynthia Luckett, Oct. 15, 1988; children: Leora, Philip. BS, Middle Tenn. State U., 1985; JD, Cumberland Law Sch., 1988. Bar: Tenn., U.S. Supreme Ct., U.S. Ct. Appeals (fed. crct.), U.S. Ct. Mil. Appeals, U.S. Dist. Ct. (mid., ea. and we. dists.) Tenn., Army Ct. of Mil. Rev., U.S. Ct. Vet. Appeals. Mcpl. magistrate City of Birmingham, Ala., 1987-88; assoc. Marks, Marks & Shell, Clarksville, Tenn., 1988-89; juvenile referee Montgomery County Juvenile Ct., 1992-95; assoc. Richardson & Richardson, 1989-93; pvt. practice, 1993—. Adj. prof. Austin Peay State U., Clarksville, 1989—; lectr. in field; hearing officer Tenn. Bd. Profl., 1993—; mcpl. judge, Pleasant View, Tenn., 1997—. Author: The TACDL Guide to Defending Juvenile Cases in Tennessee, 1993; co-author: Juvenile Courts in Tennessee, 1998; contbr. articles to profl. jours. Bd. dirs. United Way of Clarksville and Montgomery County, 1992—, Treehouse Daycare Ctr., 1991-95, sec., 1992, v.p., 1993, pres. 1994; Leadership Clarksville; participant UN conf. juvenile drug prevention, 1994. Named Internat. Man of the Yr. Internat. Biog. Ctr., Cambridge, Eng., 1992, Outstanding Young Alumnus, Middle Tenn. State U., 1999. Mem. ABA (juvenile justice com. nat. chmn. 1990-92, nat. vice chmn. litigation 1992-93), Tenn. Assn. Criminal Def. Lawyers (chmn. juvenile justice com. 1991-95, chmn. ethics com. 1995-97—), Montgomery County Young Lawyers (pres. 1991—), Tenn.Bar Assn. (assoc. gen. counsel 1995-2001, Pro Bono Atty. of Yr. 2001), Tenn. Young Lawyers Conf. (bd. dirs. 1992-94). Democrat. Criminal, General practice, Juvenile. Office: 331 Franklin St Ste 1 Clarksville TN 37040-3448 E-mail: gregorydsmith@prodigy.net

SMITH, GREGORY HAYES, lawyer; b. Concord, N.H., Apr. 5, 1946; s. Erville Hayes and Natalie Smith; children: Geoffrey Hayes, Stuart Blodgett. BA in Chemistry, U. N.H., 1969; JD, U. Maine, 1973. Bar: N.H. 1973, U.S. Supreme Ct. 1979. Asst. atty. gen. State of N.H., Concord, 1973-78; chief Criminal Justice div. N.H., 1976-78; dep. atty. gen. State of N.H., Concord, 1978-80, atty. gen., 1980-84; ptnr. McLane Graf et al, 1984—. Chmn. N.H. Jud Coun., Concord, 1984—. Editor, co-author: N.H. Environmental Law Handbook. Mem. N.H. Crime Commn., 1980-84, Gov.'s Task Force on Drunk Driving, 1982; chmn. Gov.'s Commn. on Gambling, 1982, Leadership Manchester, 1986—, N.H. Police Standards and Tng. Coun., 1980-84; mem. Environ. Ins. Risk Study Commn., 1987—. Fellow N.H. Bar Assn.; mem. ABA, Merrimack County Bar Assn., Manchester Bar Assn., U. Maine Law Sch. Alumni Assn. (bd. dirs. 1986—), Nat. Assn. Atty. Gen., Greater Manchester C. of C. Found. (bd. dirs. 1987—). Office: McLane Graf et al 15 N Main St Concord NH 03301-4945 E-mail: gsmith@mclane.com

SMITH, H(AROLD) LAWRENCE, lawyer; b. Evergreen Park, Ill., June 27, 1932; s. Harold Lawrence and Lorna Catherine (White) S.; m. Madonna Jeanne Koehl, June 9, 1956 (div. 1968); children: Lawrence Kirby, Sandra, Michele, Makonna Clare Galloway; m. Nancy Leigh Baum, May 2, 1970 (dec. 1983); m. Louise Fredericka Jeffrey, Nov 2, 1984 (div. 1994); m. Marianne Lorraine Laug, Apr. 19, 1997. BS, US Naval Acad., 1956; JD, John Marshall Law Sch., 1965. Bar: Ill. 1965, Mich. 1986, U.S. Dist. Ct. (no. dist.) Ill. 1965, U.S. Ct. Appeals (7th cir.) 1967, U.S. Ct. of Customs and Patent Appeals, 1976, U.S. Ct. Appeals (fed. cir.) 1982, U.S. Patent and Trademark Office 1968. Asst. prof. naval sci. U. Notre Dame, 1960-61; tech. asst. Langner, Parry, Card & Langner, Chgo., 1961-65, assoc., 1965-69; patent atty. Borg-Warner Corp., 1970-74; sr. patent atty. Continental Can Co., Inc., Chgo. and Oak Brook, Ill., 1974-82, asst. gen. counsel Stamford and Norwalk, Conn., 1982-86; ptnr. Varnum, Riddering, Schmidt & Howlett, Grand Rapids, Mich., 1986-96, counsel, 1996-97; ptnr. Rader, Rishman, Grauer & McGarry, 1997—. Adj. prof. patent law Cooley Law Sch., 1991—. Served to lt. USN, 1956-61. Fellow Mich. State Bar Found.; mem. Intellectual Property Law Assn. Chgo., Chartered Inst. Patent Agts. (London), World Affairs Coun. Western Mich. (dir. 1996—), treas. 1998-99), Internat. Platform Assn., Peninsular Club. Antitrust, Patent, Trademark and copyright. Office: Rader Fishman Grauer & McGarry 171 Monroe Ave NW Ste 600 Grand Rapids MI 49503-2634 E-mail: hls@raderfishman.com

SMITH, HERMAN EUGENE, lawyer; b. Ceredo, W.Va., Sept. 12, 1926; s. Leonard P. and Evelyn J. (Melson) S.; m. Charlotte Virginia Toney, July 13, 1945; children— Mary, Herman, Michael W. Student Marshall U., 1944-47; B.S. in Mech. Engring., Va. Poly, Inst. and State U., 1949; J.D., John Marshall Law Sch., 1961. Bar: Ill. 1961, U.S. Dist. Ct. (no. dist.) Ill. 1981, U.S. Supreme Ct. 1976. Engr. Bituminous Coal Research, Inc., Huntington, W.Va., 1949-51; engr. Goodman Mfg. Co., Chgo., 1951-61, house counsel, 1961-64; patent atty. Borg Warner Corp., Chgo., 1964-78; fgn. patent dir., 1978-87; ret., 1987. Mem. health council Village of Park Forest, Ill., 1977-82, mem. profl. adv. com., 1976-82. Served wtih U.S. Army, 1945-46, PTO. Mem. ABA, Am. Intellectual Property Law Assn., Ill. State Bar Assn., Patent Law Assn. Chgo. (chmn. fgn. patent com.). Lodge: Kiwanis. Patent. Office: Borg Warner Corp 200 S Michigan Ave Ste 1700 Chicago IL 60604-2460

SMITH, JACK DAVID, lawyer; b. Honolulu, Jan. 4, 1946; s. Jack David and Gloria June (Slater) S.; m. Mary Elizabeth Zasadny, Sept. 17, 1977; children: Amy Elizabeth, Amanda Marie. BA in Polit. Sci., George Washington U., 1968, JD, 1971. Bar: Va. 1971, U.S. Ct. Mil. Appeals 1971, U.S. Ct. Appeals (1st and D.C. cirs.) 1975, U.S. Ct. Appeals (2d and 7th cirs.) 1976, U.S. Supreme Ct. 1976, D.C. 1986. Atty. litig. div. FCC, Washington, 1974-81, dept. chief common carrier bur., 1981-83, chief common carrier bur., 1983-84, gen. counsel, 1984-86; dep. gen. counsel Fed. Home Loan Bank Bd., 1986-89, Fed. Deposit Ins. Corp., Washington, 1989—. Served to capt. USMC, 1971-74. Mem. Va. Bar Assn., D.C. Bar Assn. Avocations: tennis, running, skiing. Home: 7824 Telegraph Rd Alexandria VA 22315-3701 Office: Fed Deposit Ins Corp 550 17th St NW Washington DC 20429-0002 E-mail: jsmith@fdic.gov

SMITH, JAMES A. lawyer; b. Akron, Ohio, June 11, 1930; s. Barton H. and Myrna S. (Young) S.; m. Melda I. Perry, Jan. 17, 1959; children: Hugh, Sarah Louise. AB, Western Res. U., 1952; postgrad., Columbia U., 1954-56, LLB, 1961; postgrad., Yale U., 1956-58. Bar: Ohio 1961, U.S. Dist. Ct. (no. dist.) Ohio 1963, U.S. Ct. Appeals (6th cir.) 1973, U.S. Supreme Ct. 1974, U.S. Ct. Appeals (11th cir.) 1983, U.S. Ct. Appeals (D.C. cir.) 1984. Assoc. Squire, Sanders and Dempsey, Cleve., 1961-70, ptnr., 1970-91, counsel, 1991-96; adj. prof. Case Western Res. U. Sch. Law, 1997-98, ret. Mem. spl. adv. com. Nat. Conf. Commrs. on Uniform State Laws, 1972-74. Trustee Chagrin Falls Park Cmty. Ctr., 1968-78, Greater Cleve. Neighborhood Ctrs. Assn., 1973-78, Legal Aid Soc. Cleve., 1977-80, Cleve. Inst. Music, 1994—; mem. Charter Rev. Commn., Chagrin Falls, 1966. Lt. (j.g.) USNR, 1952-54. Fellow Am. Coll. Trial Lawyers; mem. ABA, Ohio Bar Assn., Cleve. Bar Assn. (trustee 1988-92), U.S. Ct. Appeals for 6th Cir. Jud. Conf. (life), Ohio Ct. Appeals for 8th Jud. Dist. Conf. (life), Ct. of Nisi Prius (clk. 1975-76, judge 1994-95), Phi Beta Kappa, Omicron Delta Kappa, Delta Sigma Rho. Democrat. Federal civil litigation, General civil litigation, State civil litigation.

SMITH, JAMES ALBERT, lawyer; b. Jackson, Mich., May 12, 1942; s. J. William and Mary Barbara (Browning) S.; m. Lucia S. Santini, Aug. 14, 1965; children: Matthew Browning, Aaron Michael, Rachel Elizabeth. BA, U. Mich., 1964, JD, 1967. Bar: Mich. 1968, U.S. Dist. Ct. (ea. dist.) Mich., U.S. Ct. Appeals (6th and D.C. cirs.), U.S. Supreme Ct. Assoc. Bodman, Longley & Dahling, Detroit, 1967-75, ptnr., 1975—. Mem. panel Atty. Discipline Bd., Wayne County, Mich., 1987—; arbitrator Am. Arbitration Assn., 1975—; mem. Banking Commrs. com. on Contested Case Adminstrn., 1978. Mem. pro bono referral group Call For Action, Detroit, 1982—. Mem. ABA, State Bar Mich., Detroit Bar Assn. Roman Catholic. Avocations: sailing, travel. Federal civil litigation, Insurance, Public utilities. Office: Bodman Longley & Dahling 100 Renaissance Ctr Ste 34 Detroit MI 48243-1001

SMITH, JAMES ALEXANDER, JR. lawyer; b. Highland Park, Ill., Nov. 14, 1948; s. James Alexander and Dorothy (Banker) S.; m. Susan Wilcox Thomas, Dec. 27, 1982; children: Deirdre, Kara. BA cum laude, U. Notre Dame, 1970; JD, Cornell U., 1973. Bar: Wash. 1973, U.S. Dist. Ct. (ea. and we. dists.) Wash. 1973, U.S. Ct. Appeals (9th cir.) 1984, U.S. Supreme Ct. 1984. Assoc. Bogle & Gates, Seattle, 1973-78, ptnr., 1978-82, Perey & Smith, Seattle, 1982-86; mem. Smith & Leary, 1986-2000, Smith & Hennessey, Seattle, 2000—. Mem. Civil Justice Reform Act. Adv. Com., 1999—. Rsch. editor Cornell U. Law Rev., 1972-73. Bd. dirs. Children's Montessori Sch., Bainbridge Island, Wash., 1981-88, South Bainbridge Cmty. Assn., 1990-96, 99—. Mem. ATLA, ABA (litigation and ADR sect.), Wash. State Bar Assn. (trustee trial practice sect. 1983-86), Fed. Bar Assn. (chair ADR Task Force 1995-96, chair ADR com. 1995—, v.p. 2000—), Wash. State Trial Lawyers Assn., Sports Lawyers Assn., Internat. Soc. Barristers, Am. Arbitration Assn., Wing Point Country Club, Notre Dame Club (bd. dirs. 1977-78), Seattle Yacht Club. Roman Catholic. Avocations: soccer, outdoor sports, sailing, creative writing. Alternative dispute resolution, Federal civil litigation, State civil litigation. Home: 10672 NE Country Club Rd Bainbridge Island WA 98110-2336 Office: Smith & Leary 316 Occidental Ave S Suite 500 Seattle WA 98104

SMITH, JAMES BARRY, lawyer; b. N.Y.C., Feb. 28, 1947; s. Irving and Vera (Donaghy) S.; m. Kathleen O'Connor, May 28, 1977; children: Jennifer, Kelly. BA in Econs., Colgate U., 1968; JD, Boston U., 1974. Assoc. McDermott, Will & Emery, Chgo., 1974-78, Ungaretti & Harris, Chgo., 1978-80, ptnr., 1980, head real estate dept., 1988. Lt. U.S. Navy, 1968-70. Mem. Chgo. Bar Assn., Chgo. Mortgage Atty. Assn. Avocations: sports, reading, travel. Real property. Office: Ungaretti & Harris 3500 Three First Nat Pla Chicago IL 60602 E-mail: jbsmith@uhlaw.com

SMITH, JAMES IGNATIUS, III, bar association executive; b. Grosse Pointe, Mich., May 23, 1931; s. James I. and Jacqueline Mary (Moran) S.; m. Deborah L. Eyler, Mar. 17, 1983. BS, U. Notre Dame, 1953. Sales mgr., gen. mgr. Esmeralda Canning Co., Circleville, Ohio, 1955-57; gen. reporter The Herald, Circleville, 1957-60; asst. exec. sec., dir. pub. rels. Ohio State Bar Assn., Columbus, 1960-62; exec. dir. Allegheny County Bar Assn., Pitts., 1963—; pres. Profl. Seminars and Designs, Pitts., 1972—. Editor: (mng.) Pittsburgh Legal Jour., The Allegheny Lawyer. Chmn. Reapportionement com., Bethel Park, Pa., 1969-71; dir. Mt. Lebanon Little League, 1989—. Served with U.S. Army, 1953-55. Recipient Journalism award Ohio State Bar Assn., Columbus, 1959; named Man of Yr., Notre Dame Club Pitts., 1972, Man of Yr. State of Israel Bonds Tri-State Area, 1988. Mem. Nat. Assn. Bar Execs. (pres. 1977-78), Legal Svcs. Assn. (bd. dirs., 1st sec. 1966—), Pitts. Soc. Assn. Execs. (pres. 1973-74), Assn. Continuing Legal Edn. Adminstrs., Pitts. C. of C., Pitts. Press Club, Notre Dame Club (pres. 1970-71), Serra Club (dir. 1971-72), Elks. Democrat. Roman Catholic. Home: 350 Jonquil Pl Pittsburgh PA 15228-2562 Office: Allegheny County Bar Assn Koppers Building Fl 4 Pittsburgh PA 15219-1826

SMITH, JAMES W., JR. state supreme court justice; b. Louisville, Oct. 28, 1943; BS, U. So. Miss., 1965; JD, Jackson Sch. Law, 1972; MEd with honors, Miss. Coll., 1973. Bar: Miss. 1972, U.S. Dist. Ct. (no. and so. dists.) Miss. 1973, U.S. Ct. Appeals (5th cir.) 1974. Pvt. practice, Pearl, 1972-78, Brandon, 1979-80; prosecuting atty. City of Pearl, 1973-80; prosecutor Rankin County, 1976; dist. atty. 20th Jud. Dist., 1977-82; judge Rankin County, 1982-92; Supreme Ct. justice Cen. Dist., 1993—. Instr. courtroom procedure and testifying Miss. Law Enforcement Tng. Acad., 1980-91. With U.S. Army, 1966-69. Named Wildlife Conservationist of Yr. Rankin County, 1988; recipient Outstanding Positive Role Model for Today's Youth award, 1991, Child Forever award Miss. Voices of Children and Youth, 1992, You've Made a Difference award, 1995, Alumnus of Yr. award Hinds C.C., 1996. Fellow Miss. Bar Found. (bd. dirs. 1998); mem. Miss. State Bar Assn., Rankin County Bar Assn., Nat. Wildlife Fedn., Nat. Wild Turkey Fedn., Ducks Unltd., Am. Legion, Rotary. Office: Carroll Gartin Justice Bldg PO Box 117 Jackson MS 39205-0117

SMITH, JEFFREY MICHAEL, lawyer; b. Mpls., July 9, 1947; s. Philip and Gertrude E. (Miller) S.; 1 son, Brandon Michael. Student, U. Malaya, 1967-68; BA cum laude, U. Minn., 1970, JD magna cum laude, 1973. Bar: Ga. 1973. Assoc. Powell, Goldstein, Frazier & Murphy, 1973-76; ptnr. Rogers & Hardin, 1976-79, Bondurant, Stephenson & Smith, 1979-85, Arnall, Golden & Gregory, 1985-92, Katz, Smith & Cohen, 1992-98; shareholder Greenberg Traurig, 1998—. Vis. lectr. Duke U., 1976-77, 79-80, 89-93; adj. prof. Emory U., 1976-79, 81-82; lectr. Vanderbilt U., 1977-82. Co-author: Preventing Legal Malpractice, 1999, Legal Malpractice, 1999. Bd. visitors Law Sch. U. Minn., 1976-82. Mem. ABA (vice-chmn. com. profl. liability 1980-82, mem. standing com. lawyers's profl. liability 1981-85, chmn. 1985-87, standing com. lawyer competency 1993-95), State Bar Ga. (chmn. profl. liability and ins. com. 1978-89, trustee Inst. Cont. Legal Edn. in Ga. 1979-80), Order of the Coif, Phi Beta Kappa. Entertainment, Professional liability. Home: 145 15th St NE Apt 811 Atlanta GA 30309-3559 Office: Greenberg Traurig 3290 Northside Dr Ste 400 Atlanta GA 30327

SMITH, JERRY EDWIN, federal judge; b. Del Rio, Tex., Nov. 7, 1946; s. Lemuel Edwin and Ruth Irene (Henderson) S.; m. Mary Jane Blackburn, June 4, 1977; children: Clark, Ruth Ann, J.J. BA, Yale U., 1969, JD, 1972. Bar: Tex. 1972. Law clk. to judge U.S. Dist. Ct. (no. dist.) Tex., Lubbock, 1972-73; assoc. then ptnr. Fulbright & Jaworski, Houston, 1973-84; city atty. City of Houston, 1984-88; cir. judge U.S. Ct. Appeals (5th cir.), Houston, 1988—. Chmn. Harris County Rep. Party, Houston, 1977-78; committeeman State Rep. Exec. Com., Tex., 1976-88. Mem. State Bar Tex., Houston Bar Assn. Methodist. Office: US Ct Appeals US Courthouse 515 Rusk St Ste 12621 Houston TX 77002-2603*

SMITH, JOHN KERWIN, lawyer; b. Oct. 18, 1926; 1 child, Cynthia. BA, Stanford U.; LLB, Hastings Coll. Law. Ptnr. Haley, Purchio, Sakai & Smith, Hayward, Calif. Bd. dirs. Berkeley Asphalt, Mission Valley Ready-Mix, Coliseum Found., Mission Valley Rock, Rowell Ranch Rodeo, Hastings Coll. Law (alumnus of yr. award 1989). Gen. ptnr. Oak Hills Apts., City Ctr. Commercial, Creekwood I and II Apts.; Road Parks commn. 1957; city coun. 1959-66, mayor 1966-70; chmn. Alameda County Mayors conf. 1968, revenue taxation com. League Calif. Cities, 1968; vice chmn. Oakland-Alameda County Coliseum; vol. Hastings 1066 Found. (pres., vol. svc. award 1990), Martin Kauffman 100 Club; bd. dirs. Hastings Coll. of Law, 1999—. Mem. ABA, Calif. Bar Assn., Alameda County Bar Assn., Am. Judicature Soc., Rotary. Probate, Real property. Office: Haley Purchio Sakai & Smith 22320 Foothill Blvd Ste 620 Hayward CA 94541-2700 E-mail: hpssckb@aol.com

SMITH, JOSEPH PHILIP, lawyer; b. Jackson, Tenn., June 14, 1944; s. William Benjamin and Virginia Marie (Carey) S.; m. Deborah J. Smith, Dec. 22, 1972; 1 child, Virginia Louise. BA, U. Miss., 1967, JD, 1975; MEd, U. So. Miss., 1977; EdD, U. Memphis, 1998. Bar: Miss. 1975, Tex. 1979, Tenn. 1995, U.S. Dist. Ct. (no. dist.) Miss. 1975, U.S. Dist. Ct. (no. dist.) Tex. 1982, N.Mex. 1991, Colo. 1991, U.S. Dist. Ct. N.Mex. 1993, U.S. Dist. Ct. Colo. 1993, U.S. Ct. Appeals (10th cir.) 1993. Tchr. math. Marks (Miss.) Jr. H.S., 1971-73; asst. prof. ednl. law U. N.D. , 1997—98; tchr., then asst. prin. Biloxi (Miss.) City Schs., 1975-78; oil and gas landman Modling & Assocs., 1978-79; assoc., then ptnr. Byrnes, Myers, Adair, Campbell & Sinex, Houston, 1979-85; farmer Quitman County, Miss., 1988-90; pvt. practice Memphis, Marks, and Raton, Tenn., Miss., and N.Mex, 1985-2000; dep. dist. atty. 8th Jud. Dist. N.Mex., Taos, 2000—. Mem. Archdiocese of Santa Fe Sch. Bd., 1991-92. Capt. USAF, 1967-71. Mem. ABA, Tenn. Bar Assn., Memphis Bar Assn., Miss. Pub. Defender Assn. (treas. 1988-90), Philmont Staff Assn. (life), Rotary (pres., sec. Marks club 1985-90, mem. Raton club 1990-91). Republican. Roman Catholic. Home: PO Box 1178 Taos NM 87571 E-mail: jpsmith@da.state.nm.us

SMITH, JULES LOUIS, lawyer; b. N.Y.C., Oct. 7, 1947; s. Henry Newman and Leonora (Fuerth) S.; m. Alexandra Remington Northrop, Feb. 15, 1986. BS, Syracuse U., 1969, JD, 1971. Bar: N.Y. 1972, U.S. Dist. Ct. (no. dist.) N.Y. 1972, U.S. Dist. Ct. (we. dist.) N.Y. 1973, U.S. Ct. Appeals (2d cir.) 1975, U.S. Supreme Ct. 1982. Assoc. Blitman and King LLP, Syracuse, N.Y., 1971-77, ptnr., 1977-88, resident ptnr., 1988—. Lectr. to legal and profl. assns., confs., colls., 1980—, including AFL-CIO Union Lawyers Conf., 1991, ABA Labor and Employment Law, 1992, 25th Pacific Coast Labor Law Conf., 1992, ABA Satellite Seminar, 1992, N.Y. State Bar Assn. Labor and Employment Law Sect. Ann. Meeting, 1993; lectr. Inst. Indsl. Labor Rels.; mem. N.Y. State Bar Assn. Task Force on Adminstrv. Hearings, Albany, 1986—; bd. advisors LeMoyne Inst. Labor Rels., LeMoyne Coll., Syracuse Inst. Labor Rels.; mem. exec. bd. Greater Mem. editl. bd. Syracuse Law Rev., 1970-71; contbr. articles to legal publs. Sec. Onondaga Neighborhood Legal Svcs., 1978, pres., 1979, v.p. bd. dirs., 1983-87; chair Prevention Ptnrs., 1994-97, pres. 1994-96; co-chair legal divsn. fund raising activities Syracuse Symphony Orch., 1985-86; bd. dirs. fundraising activities Am. Heart Assn., 1985-86; bd. dirs. Greater Rochester Fights Back, 1990-92, vice chair, 1992-93, chair, 1994; pres. Prevention Ptnrs., 1994-96, bd. dirs., 1999—; bd. dirs. United Way Greater Rochester, Cmty. Legal Intake Project, 1998—; v.p. Rochester Com. on Fgn. Rels., 1990-94. Fellow N.Y. Bar Found.; mem. ABA (union chmn. EEO com. labor and employment law sect. 1985-88, co-chairperson labor and employment law sect., mem. ad hoc com. to comment on EEO com. Ams. with Disabilities Act regulations, Coll. of Labor and Employment Lawyers award 1996), FBA, N.Y. State Bar Assn. (chmn. membership and fin. com. 1980-83, mem. spl. com. on specialization 1983-85, chmn. labor and employment law sect. 1984-85, mem. ho. dels. 1989-92), Onondaga County Bar Assn., Monroe County Bar Assn., N.Y. State Trial Lawyers Assn., Am. Trial Lawyers Assn., Fed. Bar Coun., Indsl. Rels. Rsch. Assn., Assn. Ctrl. N.Y. (co-founder, v.p. 1981), Justinian Honor Soc., Order of Coif. Democrat. Jewish. Avocations: skiing, running, cooking, reading. Federal civil litigation, General civil litigation, Labor. Office: Blitman and King LLP 16 Main St W Ste 207 Rochester NY 14614-1601

SMITH, KEVIN HOPKINS, lawyer; b. Phoenixville, Pa., Jan. 29, 1953; s. Roland and Florence Helen (Hopkins) S.; m. Janet Arlene Nicholson, June 27, 1981; children: Dustin Lofland, Laura Nicholson. BA in Polit. Sci., Pa. State U., 1974; JD, Georgetown U., 1977. Bar: Pa. 1977, U.S. Dist. Ct. (ea. dist.) Pa. 1977, U.S. Supreme Ct. 1984, U.S. Ct. Appeals (3d cir.) 1988. Assoc. Liebert, Short, FitzPatrick & Lavin, Phila., 1977-79; atty. Fed. Election Commn., Washington, 1979-80; counsel Am. Gas Assn., Arlington, Va., 1980-83; ptnr. Baer & Smith, Phoenixville, 1983-87; pvt. practice Kimberton, Pa., 1987—. Solid waste hearing officer Chester County, Pa., 1993-96. Editor Am. Criminal Law Rev., 1976-77, Regulation of the Gas Industry, 1982-83. Councilman Borough of Phoenixville, 1986-88; committeeman Chester County Rep. Orgn., 1986-88, 90-96; asst. gen. counsel Pa. Young Reps., 1988-90; gen. counsel Chester County Young Reps., 1985-90; vice chmn. Area 6 Rep. Com., 1990-94; state committeeman Rep. Party Pa., 1994-96; parliamentary counsel Chester County Rep. Com., 1994-95. Mem. Phoenixville Area C. of C. (exec. com. 1986-91, bd. dirs. 1985-91, legis. com. 1988-91), Chester County C. of C. (bd. dirs. 1990-91, legis. com. 1990-91). Estate planning, Probate, Real property. Home: 2600 Fairview Dr Alexandria VA 22306-6405 Office: 2600 Fairview Dr Alexandria VA 22306-6405

SMITH, LARRY VAN, lawyer; b. Dallas, Aug. 22, 1947; s. Chester Cleo and Ann (Simmel) S.; m. Andrea Vaughan, Nov. 13, 1976; children—Elizabeth, Jordan. B.A., So. Methodist U., 1969, J.D., 1973. Bar: Tex. 1973. Ptnr., Locke, Purnell, Rain, Harrell (and predecessor firms), Dallas, 1973— . Served with USNG, 1969-75. Protestant. Banking, Construction, Real property. Home: 4701 Kelsey Rd Dallas TX 75229-6507 Office: Locke Purnell Rain Harrell 2200 Ross Ave Ste 2200 Dallas TX 75201-6776

SMITH, LAUREN ASHLEY, lawyer, journalist, clergyman, physicist; b. Clinton, Iowa, Nov. 30, 1924; s. William Thomas Roy and Ethel (Cook) S.; m. Barbara Ann Mills, Aug. 22, 1947; children: Christopher A., Laura Nan Smith Pringle, William Thomas Roy II. BS, U. Minn., 1946, JD, 1949; postgrad., U. Chgo., 1943-49; MDiv, McCormick Theol. Sem., 1950; postgrad., U. Iowa, 1992. Bar: Colo. 1957, Iowa 1959, Ill. 1963, Minn. 1983, U.S. Supreme Ct. 1967; ordained to ministry Presbyn. Ch., 1950. Pastor Presbyn. Ch., Fredonia, Kans., 1950-52, Lamar, Colo., 1952-57, Congl. Ch., Clinton, 1975-80; editor The Comml., Pine Bluff, Ark., 1957-58; ptnr. Schoenauer Smith & Fullerton ASP, Clinton, 1995—. CEO LASCO Pub. Group, Clinton, 1995—; CEO, founder Interlink for the Internet Generation; internat. conferee Stanley Found., Warrenton, Va., 1963—72; legal observer, USSR, 1978; co-sponsor All India Renewable Energy Conf., Bangalore, 1981; law sch. conferee U. Minn., China, 1983; lectr. law, religion, physics, nat. policy U. Wis., 2001. Author: (jurisprudence treatise) Forma Dat Esse Rel, 1975, (monograph) First Strike Option, 1983; co-author: India On to New Horizons, 1989; columnist Crow Call, 1968—; co-editor Press and News of India, 1978-82; pub. Crow Call; pseudonym Christopher Crow, 1981—; writer BBC World Svc., London; editor Asian Econ. Cmty. Jour.; contbr. articles to religious publs. Minister-at-large Presbyn. Ch. U.S.A., Iowa, 1987—; bd. dirs. Iowa divsn. UN Assn. U.S.A., Iowa City, 1970-85; fellow Molecular Nanotechnology Foresight Inst., Palo Alto, Calif.; Franciscans United Nations Non Govt. Orgn.; assoc. Westar Inst. (The Jesus Seminar), Santa Rosa, Calif., 1997; active Quad City Estate Planning Coun.; founder, CEO Interlink relating quantum mechanics and religion. Mem. Iowa Bar Assn., Ill. Bar Assn., St. Andrews Soc., Clinton County Bar Assn. (pres. 1968, Best in Iowa citation), Clinton Ministerial Assn., Samaritan Health Systems Chaplain Corps. (pres.), European Soc. for Study of Sci. and Religion, Quad City Estate Planning Coun., Quaker Internat. Yokefellow, Nat. Network for New Spiritual Formation Presbyn. Ch. USA, Franciscans Internat., City Club of Quad Cities (bd. dirs.).

SMITH, LAVENSKI R. (VENCE SMITH), former state supreme court justice; m. Trendle Smith; 2 children. JD, U. Ark., 1987. Pvt. practice, Springdale, 1991-94; staff lawyer Ozark Legal Svcs., 1987-91; asst. prof. John Brown U., 1994-96; interim assoc. justice Ark. State Supreme Ct., 1999—2000. Bd. dirs. N.W. Ark. Christian Justice Ctr.; trainer Ptnrs. for Family Tng., 1993-96; chmn. Ark. Pub. Svc. Commn., 1996-98. Republican. Office: Ark Supreme Ct Justice Bldg 625 Marshall St Little Rock AR 72201-1054*

SMITH, LAWRENCE SHANNON, lawyer; b. Dallas, Oct. 6, 1943; s. Lawrence Shannon and Joan (Smith) S. B.A., U. Tex., 1965, J.D., 1970. Bar: Tex. 1970, U.S. Tax Ct. 1970, U.S. Supreme Ct. 1974; cert. adminstrv. law. Shareholder Small, Craig, & Werkenthin, Austin, Tex., 1970-95; ptnr. Smith, Majcher & Mudge, Austin, 1995—. 1st. lt. U.S. Army, 1966-68, Korea. Administrative and regulatory, Environmental, Public utilities. Office: Smith Majcher & Mudge LLP 816 Congress Ave Ste 1270 Austin TX 78701-2476

SMITH, LESLIE CLARK, lawyer; b. Balt., July 15, 1941; s. Leslie McClure and Evelyn (Clark) S.; m. Judy Smith, Feb. 6, 1988; children—Gerre Ann, Randy Lee. B.A., Vanderbilt U., 1962; J.D., U. Ky., 1971; LL.M., U. Western Australia, 1978. Bar: N.Mex. 1971, U.S. Dist. Ct. N.Mex. 1971, U.S. Tax Ct. 1972, U.S. Supreme Ct. 1975, U.S. Ct. Appeals (10th cir.) 1982. Ptnr. firm Buhler, Smith, Fitch & Stout, Truth or Consequences, N.Mex., 1971-76, Smith & Filosa, Truth or Consequences, 1976-89; dist. judge 7th Jud. Dist., Socorro, N.Mex., 1989—; dir. 1st Sierra Nat. Bank; instr. U. Western Australia, Perth, 1975. Contbr. articles to profl. jours. Articles editor U. Ky. Law Rev., 1970-71. Pres. Fiesta Bd., Truth or Consequences, 1982, 87, mem. Bd. Bar Commrs., 1986-89. Capt. USAF, 1962-68, Vietnam, Congo, Dominican Republic. Mem. N.Mex. Trial Lawyers (bd. dirs. 1982-89), Assn. Trial Lawyers Am., N.Mex. Bar Assn. (mem. bd. bar commrs., N.Mex. Supreme Ct. com. on civil rules, bd. dirs. criminal sect. 1982-88, judiciary com. 1982-88). Episcopalian. Club: Rotary (pres. Truth or Consequences 1983). Banking, State civil litigation, General practice. Home: 718 Palo Verde Dr Truth Or Consequences NM 87901-1532 Office: Dist Ct PO Box 1127 Socorro NM 87801-1127

SMITH, LESTER V., JR. lawyer, educator; b. Mt. Pleasant, Pa., May 10, 1940; s. Lester V. and Margaret (Kurtz) S.; m. Nadine A. Wooley; children: Julia, Ann Marie. AB, Duke U., 1962; JD, U. N.C., 1965. Bar: N.C. 1965, Iowa 1970, Ill. 1972, Oreg. 1973, U.S. Dist. Ct. Oreg. 1973, U.S. Dist. Ct. (no. dist.) Ill. 1969, U.S. Dist. Ct. (so. dist.) Ill. 1970, U.S. Ct. Appeals (9th cir.) 1975, U.S. Supreme Ct. 1981. Atty. NLRB, Peoria, Ill., 1965-66, 69-78; spl. trial counsel U.S. Army, Germany, 1966-69; assoc. Davies, Biggs, Strayer, Stoel & Boley, Portland, Oreg., 1973-77; founder, ptnr. Bullard, Korshoj, Smith & Jernstedt, 1977-2000, Bullard, Smith, Jernstedt & Harnish, Portland, 2000—. Lectr., instr. Bus. Sch. U. Md., W.Ger., 1966-69, Lewis and Clark Sch. Law, Portland, 1983-87. Sect. editor Advising Oreg. Bus., 1984; contbr. articles to profl. jours. Chmn. Dorchester Conf., Seaside, Oreg., 1981. Capt. U.S. Army, 1966-69. Mem. ABA (labor law sect.), Ill. Bar Assn., Oreg. State Bar Assn. (chmn. labor rels. sect. 1982-83), Multnomah County Bar Assn., Duke U. Alumni Assn. (chmn. Oreg. area 1980—), Multnomah Athletic Club (trustee 1984-87, pres. 1986-87), Oreg. Rd. Runners Club (pres. 1981-84, marathon dir. 1982—). Labor. Home: 2744 SW Sherwood Dr Portland OR 97201-2251 Office: Bullard Smith Kernsted Harnish Bullard Korshoj Smith & Jernstedt 1000 SW Broadway Ste 1000 Portland OR 97205-3062 E-mail: lsmith@bullardlaw.com

SMITH, LOREN ALLAN, federal judge; b. Chgo., Dec. 22, 1944; m. Catherine Yore; children: Loren Jr., Adam (dec.). BA in Polit. Sci., Northwestern U., 1966, JD, 1969; LLD (hon.), John Marshall Law Sch., 1995, Capitol U. Law Sch., 1996, Campbell U., 1997. Bar: Ill. 1970, U.S. Ct. Mil. Appeals 1973, U.S. Ct. Appeals (D.C. cir.) 1974, U.S. Supreme Ct. 1974, U.S. Ct. Claims, 1985, U.S. Ct. Appeals (fed. cir.) 1986, U.S. Ct. Fed. Claims. Host nightly radio talk show What's Best for America?, 1972; cons. Sidney & Austin, Chgo., 1972-73; gen. atty. FCC, 1973; asst. to spl. counsel to the pres. White House, Washington, 1973-74; spl. asst. U.S. Atty., D.C., 1974-75; chief counsel Reagan for Pres. campaigns, 1976, 80; prof. Del. Law Sch., 1976-84; dep. dir. Office Exec. Br. Mgmt. Presdl. Transition, 1980-81; chmn. Adminstrv. Conf. U.S., 1981-85; appointed judge U.S. Ct. Fed. Claims, Washington, 1985, designated chief judge, 1986-2000; sr. judge, 2000—. Prof. law Del. Law Sch., 1976-84; adj. prof. Internat. Law Sch., 1973-74, Georgetown U. Law Ctr., 1992—, Washing Coll. Law, Am. U., 1996, Columbus Sch. Law, Cath. U. Am., 1996—, George Mason U. Sch. Law, 1998—; past mem. Pres.'s Cabinet Coun. on Legal Policy, Pres.' Cabinet Coun. on Mgmt. and Adminstrn.; chmn. Coun. Ind. Regulatory Agys.; served as disting. jurist in residence U. Denver; Allen chair U. Richmond Sch. Law, 1995. Co-author: Black America and Organized Labor: A Fair Deal?, 1979; contbr. articles to profl. jours. Adv. bd. mem. WETA Pub. Radio Cmty. Adv. Bd. Recipient Presdl. medal Cath. U. Am. Law Sch., 1993, Romanian medal of justice Romanian Min. of Justice, 1995, Ronald Reagan Pub. Svc. award Nat. Property Rights Conf., 1997. Mem. Bar Assn. D.C. (hon. mem., judicial honoree award 1997), Univ. Club (Washington, named club mem. of the yr. 1991, chmn. entertainment com., centennial com.). Republican. Jewish. Office: US Ct of Fed Claims 717 Madison Pl NW Washington DC 20439-0002

SMITH, MARK P. foundation executive; b. Charleston, W.Va., July 27, 1949; s. Bernard Henry and Josephine (Polan) S.; m. Jane Stephens, May 6, 1978; children: Stephen Noble, Allison Baxter. B.A., Princeton U., 1971; J.D., Yale U., 1978. Asst. to exec. dir. ABA, Chgo., 1976-79; exec. dir. W.Va. State Bar, Charleston, 1979-88; v.p. Southwestern Legal Found., Richardson, Tex., 1996— (dir. Inst. for Transnational Arbitration, 1993-98); dir. Mcpl. Legal Studies Ctr., 1998—; sec. W.Va. Legal Services Plan, Inc., Charleston, 1987-88; treas. Found. for Youth and Govt., Charleston, 1983-88; pres. Saigling Elem. Sch., PTA, 1991-92; lectr. U. Tex., Dallas, 1990-94. Pres., bd. dirs. Coalition for Homeless, Charleston, 1986-87; sec. W.Va. Coalition for the Homeless, 1986-87; v.p. Volunteer Ctr. Collin County, 2000—. Mem. Nat. Assn. Bar Execs. (chmn. continuing edn. com. 1981-82, mem. exec. com. 1984-86). Office: The Southwestern Legal Found PO Box 830707 Richardson TX 75083-0707

SMITH, MILTON CLARK, JR. lawyer; b. Dallas, Apr. 5, 1940; s. Milton C. and Virginia (Terry) S.; m. Carol Ann Brinsmade, Aug. 23, 1963; children: Mollye Catherine, Patricia Clark. BBA, U. Tex., 1963, JD, 1966. Bar: Tex. 1966, U.S. Dist. Ct. (so. dist.) Tex. 1966, U.S. Dist. Ct. (no. dist.) Tex. 1972. Jr. ptnr. Cox, Wilson, Duncan & Clendenin, Brownsville, Tex., 1966-68; assoc. Wade & Thomas, Dallas, 1968; v.p. Bonanza Internat. Devel. Co., 1968-71; corp. counsel Steak and Ale Restaurants Am., Inc., 1971-72; ptnr. Johnson, Blakeley, Johnson, Smith & Clark, 1972—. Fellow Tex. Bar Found.; mem. State Bar Tex., Dallas Bar Assn. Republican. Episcopalian. General corporate, Probate, Real property. Home: 4135 Normandy Ave Dallas TX 75205-2037 Office: Johnson & McElroy LLP 5500 Preston Rd Ste 370 Dallas TX 75205-2675

SMITH, MORTON ALAN, lawyer; b. N.Y.C., Mar. 13, 1931; s. David and Augusta S.; m. Nancy, July 2, 1954 (div. July 1974); children: Robynn, Jeffrey, Richard; m. Jane Saffir, June 10, 1979; children: Michael, Richard. BA, U. Fla., 1953; LLD with honors, U. N.C., 1956. Bar: N.Y. 1957, D.C. 1957. Spl. trial atty. Office Chief Counsel IRS, Phila., 1956-58; spl. asst. U.S. Atty. Dist. N.J., 1957; law clk. to judge U.S. Tax Ct., Washington, 1958-60; assoc. Kaye Scholer, N.Y.C., 1960-62, Saul Silverman, N.Y.C., 1962-67; sr. ptnr. Hall, Dickler, Lawler, Kent & Friedman, 1967—. Bd. dirs. Eden Park Health Corp., Albany, N.Y. Contbr. articles to profl. jours. V.p. Rye Brook (N.Y.) Bd. Edn., 1968-73; organizer of incorporation of Village of Rye Brook, 1982, now spl. counsel; bd. dirs. Herbert Birch Sch. for Exceptional Children, N.Y.C., Westchester County United Way, 1991; leadership chmn. United Way Campaign, Rye Brook, 1989-91; mem. Westchester County Housing Implementation Commn.; bd. dirs. Eden Park Health Svcs., Albany, N.Y.; pres. Bocaire Home Owners Assn., Boca Raton, Fla. Mem. ABA (tax sec.). Avocations: golf, skiing, tennis, gardening, reading. Criminal, Taxation, general. Office: Hall Dickler Lawler Kent & Friedman 909 3rd Ave New York NY 10022-4731 E-mail: msmith@halldickler.com

SMITH, PATRICIA A. lawyer, author; b. Staten Island, N.Y., May 11, 1956; BA, Bklyn. Coll., 1978; JD, Bklyn. Law Sch., 1986. Bar: N.Y. 1987, U.S. Dist. Ct. (so. and ea. dists.) N.Y. 1988, U.S. Supreme Ct. 1991. Atty. City of N.Y., 1988-90; assoc. for an ins. def. firm, N.Y.C., 1990-96; ptnr. Smith Abbot, L.L.P., 1996—. Co-author: The Preparation and Trial of Medical Malpractice Cases, 1990; contbr. articles to profl. jours. Mem. Women's Bar Assn. State N.Y. (pres. Staten Island chpt. 1989-90), N.Y. County Lawyers Assn. Democrat. Roman Catholic. Avocations: skiing, photography. Personal injury, Product liability.

SMITH, RALPH HARRISON, lawyer; b. Albuquerque, Nov. 2, 1951; s. Robert Tatum and Harriet Smith; m. Helen Elizabeth Oakley, July 13, 1974; children: Harrison, William, Robert. BA, Washington and Lee U., 1973; MA, Oxford U., 1976; JD, Yale, 1979. Bar: D.C. 1979, Ala. 1982. Assoc. atty. Convington & Burling, Washington, 1979-82, Cabaniss, Johnston, Gardner, Dumas & O'Neal, Birmingham, Ala., 1982-84; ptnr. Johnston, Barton, Proctor & Powell LLP, 1984—. Pres.'s adv. coun. Birmingham So. Coll., 1987-88; mem. leadership coun. U. Ala., Birmingham, 1988-91, Med. Clinics Bd., Birmingham, 1997; dir. Bham Comm. on Fgn. Rels., Birmingham, 1996—; selection com. Rhodes Scholarship, 1982-87, 98—. Trustee Highland's Day Sch., Birmingham, 1985-89; pres. bd. St. Martin's in the Pines Nursing Home, Birmingham, 1990; dir. Ala. Sch. Fine Arts Found., Birmingham, 1993-98; mem. Leadership Birmingham, 1988, mems. coun., 1998—; chancellor Episcopal Diocese of Ala., 2000-. Recipient Rhodes scholarship Rhodes Trust, 1973. Mem. Birmingham Bar Assn., D.C. Bar Assn. (trustee), Birmingham C. of C., Rotary Club of Birmingham (dir., v.p. 1989-91, 90-91, 2001-). Episcopalian. General corporate, Health, Private international. Home: 3519 Country Club Rd Birmingham AL 35213-2826 Office: Johnston Barton Procter & Powell LLP 1901 6th Ave N Ste 2900 Birmingham AL 35203-2622 E-mail: rhs@jbpp.com

SMITH, RALPH WESLEY, JR. retired federal judge; b. Ghent, N.Y., July 16, 1936; s. Ralph Wesley and Kathleen S. (Callahan) S.; m. Nancy Ann Fetzer, Dec. 30, 1961 (div. 1981); children: Mark Owen, Tara Denise, Todd Kendall; m. Barbara Anne Milian, Nov. 8, 1982; stepchildren: Kim Highter, Jeffrey Highter, Eric Highter. Student, Sorbonne, U. Paris, Paris, 1954-55; BA, Yale U., 1956; LLB, Albany Law Sch., 1966. Bar: N.Y. 1966, U.S. Dist. Ct. (no. dist.) N.Y. 1966. Assoc. Hinman, Straub Law Firm, Albany, N.Y., 1966-69; chief asst. dist. atty. Albany County, 1969-73, dist. atty., 1974; regional dir. state nursing home investigation Asst. Atty. Gen., Albany, 1975-77; dir. State Organized Crime Task Force, 1978-82; U.S. magistrate judge U.S. Dist. Ct. (no. dist.) N.Y., Albany, 1982-2001. Judge moot ct. Albany Law Sch., 1983-2001; lectr. N.Y. State Bar Assn., 1985—, Am. Inns of Ct., 1994-99. Capt. (ret.) USNR, 1957-82. Mem. Fed. Magistrate Judges Assn. (dir. 2d cir. 1992-99), Columbia County Magistrates Assn. Republican. Roman Catholic. Avocations: fishing, bicycling, skiing, camping. Home: 40 Wequasset Rd Harwich Port MA 02646

SMITH, RICHARD MULDROW, lawyer; b. Jefferson City, Mo., Sept. 2, 1939; s. Elmer Clyde and Mary (Muldrow) S.; children: Stephen, Michael. JD, U. Ark., 1963; postgrad., U. Ill., 1963-64. Bar: Ark. 1963, D.C. 1980, U.S. Ct. Appeals (D.C. cir.) 1980, U.S. Supreme Ct. 1980. Asst. prof. U. N.C., Chapel Hill, 1964-67, assoc. prof., 1967-73, prof., 1973-79; spl. counsel FPC, Washington, 1976-77; mem. White House Energy Policy Staff, 1978-79; dir. Office of Policy Coordination, Dept. of Energy, 1978-79; ptnr. Mayer, Brown & Platt, 1979-91; pres. Little Creek Marina Inc., Norfolk, Va., 1992—. Author: (with others) North Carolina Uniform Commercial Code Forms Annotated, 2 vols., 1967. Mem. ABA (pub. utility law sect., coun. mem. 1985-88, chmn. gas com. 1988-89, chmn. publ. com. 1989-91). Contracts commercial, FERC practice, Public utilities. Home: 4725 Bradston Rd Virginia Beach VA 23455 Office: 4801 Pretty Lake Ave Norfolk VA 23518-2005

SMITH, RICHARD WENDELL, lawyer; b. Lincoln, Nebr., May 29, 1912; s. Walter Charles and Mary Frances (Goodale) S.; m. Patricia Adelle Lahr, Apr. 8, 1947; children: Laurie Patricia, Barton Richard. AB, Nebr. Wesleyan U., 1933; JD, Harvard U., 1938. Bar: Nebr. 1938, U.S. Dist. Ct. Nebr. 1938, U.S. Ct. Claims 1949, U.S. Ct. Appeals (7th and 8th Fed. cirs.), U.S. Supreme Ct. 1955. Spl. agt. FBI, Dept. Justice, Washington, 1942-44; ptnr. Woods and Aitken, Lincoln; apptd. by U.S. Dist Ct. as trustee in reorgn. of Am. Buslines, Inc., 1954-58; lectr. constrn. law Fed. Publs., Washington, 1974-96. Contbr. articles to profl. jours. Bd. dirs., sec., life mem. Nebr. Wesleyan U., Lincoln, 1958-74; sec. Harvard Schs. and Scholarship Com., Lincoln, 1948—; trustee Nebr. Art Assn., Lincoln, 1984-86; bd. dirs. Lincoln Symphony Orch. Assn., Lincoln Community Theater, 1982-87. Served to lt. USNR, 1944-46. Mem. ABA (governing com. forum on constrn. industry 1983-89), Nebr. Bar Assn. Republican. Lodge: Rotary (pres. 1981-82). Construction, Government contracts and claims, Probate. Home: 916 Fall Creek Rd Lincoln NE 68510-3837 Office: Woods & Aitken 301 S 13th St Ste 500 Lincoln NE 68508-2578

SMITH, ROBERT BLAKEMAN, lawyer; b. Mt. Vernon, N.Y., June 18, 1949; s. William Blakeman and Helen Theresa (Curley) S.; m. Laura Lindley Brock, July 18, 1987; children: Morgan Lindley, Justin Pierce. BS, Rensselaer Poly. Inst., 1971, ME, 1973; JD, Boston U., 1976. Bar: N.Y. 1977, U.S. Dist. Ct. (so. and ea. dists.) N.Y. 1977, U.S. Dist. Ct. (no. dist.) N.Y. 1981, U.S. Dist. Ct. Ariz. 1992, U.S. Patent and Trademark Office 1977, U.S. Ct. Appeals (7th cir.) 1979, U.S. Ct. Appeals (fed. cir.) 1982, U.S. Supreme Ct. 1981. Assoc. Brumbaugh, Graves, Donohue & Raymond, N.Y.C., 1976-84, ptnr., 1984-89; of counsel White & Case, 1989-99, Skadden, Arps, Slate, Meagher & Flom, N.Y.C., 1999—. Lectr. IEEE, N.Y.C., 1983-88, Practising Law Inst., 1990-99. Trustee Delta Phi Found., Ithaca, N.Y., 1978-86, St. Elmo Found., Pearl River, N.Y., 1986—. Mem. N.Y. Intellectual Property Law Assn., Am. Intellectual Property Law Assn. Patent, Trademark and copyright. Home: 100 Riverside Dr New York NY 10024-4822 Office: Skadden Arps Slate Meagher & Flom Four Times Sq New York NY 10036-6522 E-mail: Robsmith@SKadden.com

SMITH, ROBERT EVERETT, lawyer; b. N.Y.C., Mar. 15, 1936; s. Arthur L. and Augusta (Cohen) S.; m. Emily Lucille Lehman, July 17, 1960; children: Amy, Karen, Victoria. BA, Dartmouth Coll., 1957; LLB, Harvard U., 1960. Bar: N.Y. 1960, U.S. Dist. Ct. (so. dist.) N.Y. 1962, U.S. Ct. Appeals (2d cir.) 1963, U.S. Supreme Ct. 1967, U.S. Dist. Ct. (ea. dist.) N.Y. 1969, U.S. Ct. Appeals (3d cir.) 1982, U.S. Ct. Appeals (9th cir.) 1988. Assoc. Paul, Weiss, Rifkind, Wharton & Garrison, N.Y.C., 1960-65; from assoc. to ptnr. Baar, Bennett & Fullen, 1965-74; ptnr. Guggenheimer & Untermyer, 1974-85, Rosenman & Colin LLP, N.Y.C., 1985-98, chmn., 1994-97, counsel, 1998—. With U.S. Army, 1961-64. Mem. ABA, N.Y. State Bar Assn., Assn. of Bar of City of N.Y., Fed. Bar Coun., N.Y. County Lawyers Assn., Am. Arbitration Assn. (nat. panel arbitrators), The Am. Law Inst. Federal civil litigation, State civil litigation, General corporate. Office: Rosenman & Colin LLP 575 Madison Ave Fl 26 New York NY 10022-2585 E-mail: resmith@rosenman.com

SMITH, R(OBERT) MICHAEL, lawyer; b. Cin., Nov. 25, 1951; s. Barney and Jean (Maloney) S.; m. Leslie Y. Straub. BA in Polit. Sci., U. Cin., 1982; JD, Ohio State U., 1985. Bar: Ohio 1985, U.S. Dist. Ct. (so. dist.) Ohio 1992, U.S. Supreme Ct. 1992. Law clk. to Justice Holmes Ohio Supreme Ct., Columbus, 1985-89; sr. staff atty., referee, editor Ohio Ct. Claims, 1989-94. Instr. law Ohio State U., 1985—, instr. continuing edn. courses, 1990—. Incorporator, trustee various non-profit orgns., Cin. and Columbus; pres. So. Bapt. Messianic Fellowship, 1994-97; 2d v.p. Ohio So. Bapt. Conv. Republican. Avocations: target shooting, writing, running. Home: 4325 Kinloch Rd Louisville KY 40207-2853 Office: 4325 Kinloch Rd Louisville KY 40207-2853

SMITH, ROBERT MICHAEL, lawyer, mediator, arbitrator; b. Boston, Nov. 4, 1940; s. Sydney and Minnie (Appel) S.; m. Catherine Kersey, Apr. 14, 1981 (dec. 1983); m. Clarissa Redmond, Feb. 11, 1999. AB cum laude, Harvard Coll., 1962; diploma, Centro de Estudos de Espanol, Barcelona, 1963; MA in Internat. Affairs, Columbia U., 1964, MS in Journalism with high honors, 1965; JD, Yale U., 1975. Bar: Calif., N.Y., D.C., U.S. Supreme Ct.; solicitor Supreme Ct. of Eng. and Wales; accredited mediator Hong Kong Internat. Arbitration Ctr.; chartered arbitrator, Eng. Intern in econ. devel. UN, Geneva, 1964; corr. Time Mag., N.Y.C., 1965-66, The N.Y. Times, Washington, 1968-72, 75-76; atty. Heller, Ehrman, White & McAuliffe, San Francisco, 1976-78; spl. asst. Office of Atty. Gen. of U.S., Washington, 1979-80; dir. Office Pub. Affairs U.S. Dept. Justice, 1979-80; mem. U.S. delegation U.S. v. Iran Internat. Ct. of Justice, The Hague, 1980; asst. U.S. atty. No. Dist. Calif., San Francisco, 1981-82; counsel, sr. counsel to sr. litigation counsel Bank of Am. NT & SA, 1982-86. Lectr. FBI Acad., Quantico, Va., 1980, Internat. Bankers Assn. Calif., 1994, Calif. Bankers Assn., 1994, Cmty. Bankers No. Calif., 1994, 95; judge Golden Medallion Broadcast Media awards State Bar of Calif., 1985; judge pro tem Mcpl. Ct. City and County of San Francisco, 1989—; conciliator Peninsula Conflict Resolution Ctr.; panelist World Intellectual Property Orgn., Geneva; arbitrator internat. Commercial arbitration ctrs., Vancouver, Cairo, Singapore, Kuala Lumpur, India; CPR Panel of Disting. Neutrals; mem. panel Nat. Assn. for Dispute Resolution. Author: Alternative Dispute Resolution for Financial Institutions, 1995, revised, 1996, 97, 98; bd. editors Yale Law Jour., 1974-75; editor Litigation, jour. ABA litigation sect., 1978-81; mem. editl. adv. bd. Bancroft-Whitney, 1991-94; contbr. articles to profl. jours. Bd. dirs. Neighborhood Legal Assistance Found., San Francisco, 1985-87, Nob Hill Assn., San Francisco, 1985-93; bd. dirs., fin. com. St. Francis Found., San Francisco, 1993-94. 1st lt. inf., USAR, 1965-71. Recipient UPI Award for Newswriting, 1958; Harvard Coll. scholar, 1958-62, Fulbright scholar, 1962-63; Columbia U. Internat. fellow, 1964-65. Fellow Internat. Acad. Mediators, Am. Coll. Civil Trial Mediators, Hong Kong Inst. Arbitrators, Chartered Inst. Arbitrators (London); mem. ABA (corp. counsel com. 1986-96, alternative dispute resolution sect. 1994-98), Assn. Atty. Mediators (v.p. No. Calif. chpt. 1995), State Bar of Calif. (pub. affairs com. 1982-85, litigation sect. 1990-96), Bar Assn. of San Francisco (bench-bar media com. 1985-96, alternative dispute resolution com. 1994-98), Assn. Bus. Trial Lawyers No. Calif., Assn. of Former U.S. Attys. No. Dist. Calif., Am. Arbitration Assn. (mem. comml. arbitration panel, No. Calif. adv. coun., mediator Am. Arbitration Ctr. for Mediation), Nat. Assn. Dispute Resolution, The Mediation Soc. (chmn. bd., pres.), Profl. Atty. Mediators, Cmty. Bds. of San Francisco (conciliator), French-Am. C. of C., German-Am. C. of C. West U.S., Harvard Club of San Francisco (bd. dirs. 1986-94, pres. 1992-94), Yale Club of San Francisco (bd. dirs. 1989-94), Soc. Profls. in Dispute Resolution, Columbia U. Alumni Club of No. Calif. (exec. com. 1978-92). Alternative dispute resolution, Banking, General civil litigation. Office: Ste 3780 44 Montgomery St San Francisco CA 94104 Address: 2635 Etna St Berkeley CA 94704 E-mail: rms@robertmsmith.com

SMITH, ROBERT SHERLOCK, lawyer, educator; b. N.Y.C., Aug. 31, 1944; s. Robert and Janet W. (Welt) S.; m. Dian Goldston Smith, Aug. 31, 1969; children: Benjamin Eli, Emlen Matthew, Rosemary Friedman. BA, Stanford U., 1965; LLB, Columbia U., 1968. Bar: N.Y. 1968, U.S. Dist. Ct. (so. dist.) N.Y. 1969, U.S. Dist. Ct. (ea. dist.) N.Y. 1977, U.S. Ct. Appeals (2d cir.) 1970, U.S. Ct. Appeals (4th cir.) 1986, U.S. Ct. Appeals (1st cir.) 1988, U.S. Ct. Appeals (7th cir.) 1989, U.S. Ct. Appeals (6th cir.) 1995, U.S. Ct. Appeals (D.C. and 8th cirs.) 1997, U.S. Ct. Appeals (5th cir.) 1999, U.S. Tax Ct. 1974, U.S. Supreme Ct. 1979. Assoc. Paul, Weiss, Rifkind, Wharton & Garrison, N.Y.C., 1968-76, ptnr., 1976—. Vis. prof. Columbia Law Sch., N.Y.C., 1980-81, lectr. law, 1981-90. Mem. ABA (sect. litigation 1977—), Assn. Bar City N.Y. (com. fed. legis. 1981-84, com. on judiciary 1984-87, com. on bicentennial of U.S. Constitution 1988-91), Federalist Soc. N.Y. (pres. lawyers chpt. 1994—). Republican. Mem. Reformed Ch. Federal civil litigation, State civil litigation. Office: Paul Weiss Rifkind Wharton & Garrison 1285 Avenue of The Americas New York NY 10019-6028 E-mail: rsmith@paulweiss.com

SMITH, RONALD EHLBERT, lawyer, educator, referral-based distributor, public speaker, writer and motivator, real estate developer; b. Atlanta, Apr. 30, 1947; s. Frank Marion and Frances Jane (Canida) S.; m. Annemarie Krumholz, Dec. 26, 1969; children: Michele, Erika, Damian. BME, Stetson U., 1970; postgrad., Hochschule Fuer Musik, Frankfurt, Fed. Republic Germany, 1971-74; Masters in German Lit., Germany & Middlebury Coll., 1975; JD, Nova U., 1981. Bar: Fla. 1982, U.S. Dist. Ct. (mid. dist.) Fla. 1983, U.S. Ct. Appeals (11th cir.) 1990, Ga. 1994, U.S. Dist. Ct. (no. dist.) Ga. 1994. Asst. state atty. 10th Jud. Cir. Ct., Bartow, Fla., 1982-85; pvt. practice Lakeland, 1985-94, Atlanta, 1994—; of counsel Mark Boychuk & Assocs. and Law Offices of Lori Lero, 1998—. Supervising atty. Bridging the Gap Project, 2000—; rsch. asst. 10th Jud. Cir. Ct., Bartow, 1981-82; instr. Broward County C.C., Ft. Lauderdale, Fla., 1976-79, 91-94, pub. and pvt. schs., Broward County, Atlanta Schs., 1998—, Offenbach, Germany, 1971-78; instr. Polk C.C. and Police Acad., Winter Haven, Fla., 1981-94; adj. prof. English, Ga. State U., 1996—; adj. prof. law DeKalb Coll., 1997—; reader ETS GMAT, 1997—; part-time police instr. Police Acad., Forsyth, Ga., 1996—; counselor Jr. Achievement, 1997—, music instr. Atl. Pub. Schs., 1999—. Tchr., drama dir. Disciples I and II, United Meth. Ch., Lakeland, 1980-94, Glenn Meml. United Meth. Ch., Atlanta, 1994—, cand. to ministry, 2000—; Billy Graham counseling supr., 1994—;promoter Promise Keepers, 1995—; spkr., promoter ProNet, 1996—; min. music Scott Blvd. Bapt. Ch., Decatur, Ga., 1998, Gideon Internat., 1999—; candidate Ordained Ministry United Meth. Ch. Freedom Bridge fellow German Acad. Exch. Svc., Mainz, 1974-75. Mem. ABA, Christian Legal Soc., Lakeland Bar Assn., Am. Immigration Lawyers Assn. General civil litigation, Education and schools, Estate planning. E-mail: smith321@bellsouth.net

SMITH, R(ONALD) SCOTT, lawyer; b. Washington, June 30, 1947; s. Joseph Peter Smith and Roberta Ann (Bailey) George; m. Cheryle Rae Coffman, Nov. 15, 1974 (div. July 1977); m. Gloria Jean Haralson, Nov. 30, 1985. BJ, U. Mo., 1970, JD, 1973. Bar: Mo. 1973, U.S. Dist. Ct. (we. dist.) Mo. 1973, U.S. Ct. Appeals (10th cir.) 1990, U.S. Ct. Appeals (8th cir.) 1992, U.S. Dist. Ct. (ea. dist.) Mo. 1996. Field dir. The Mo. Bar, Jefferson City, 1973-75; law clk. to judge Mo. Ct. Appeals (we. dist.), 1975-76; ptnr. Shirkey, Norton & Smith, Kansas City, 1976-77, Jackson & Sherman, P.C. and predecessors, Kansas City, 1977-84, Birmingham & Furry, Kansas City, 1984, Birmingham, Furry & Smith, 1985-92, Birmingham, Furry, Smith & Stubbs, 1992-95, Furry & Smith, Kansas City, 1996—. Author: (with others) Automobile Accident Handbook, 1984, rev., 1986, Vexatious Refusal and Bad Faith, 1990, Insurance Claims, 1993; editor: The Rights & Responsibilities of Citizenship in a Free Society, 1974, Due Process of Law, 1974, News Headnotes, 1976-84, Young Lawyer, 1977-80; mem. editorial bd. Mo. Bar Jour., 1978-81; (TV series) legal script advisor Lex Singularis, 1973-75; (multimedia) producer, author Freedoms Lost, 1976; producer, playwright (musical-comedy play) Silly in Philly, 1987. Mem. ABA (mem. various coms.), Mo. Bar Assn. (dist. 12 chmn. 1979—, mem. various coms., Disting. Svc. award young lawyers sect. 1978, 79, 80), West Mo. Def. Lawyers Assn., Kansas City Met. Bar Assn. (pres. young lawyers sect. 1981-82, mem. various coms., Disting. Svc. award young lawyers sect. 1982, Leadership award sr. sect. 1985, First Ann. Pres. award sr. sect. 1987), Kansas City Claim Assn., Phi Delta Phi. Democrat. Roman Catholic. General civil litigation, Personal injury, Product liability. Home: 3411 Shady Bend Dr Independence MO 64052-2816 Office: 1600 Bryant Bldg 1102 Grand Blvd Kansas City MO 64106-2316 Fax: (816) 842-5600. E-mail: scottsmith@furrysmithlaw.com

SMITH, ROY PHILIP, judge; b. S.I., N.Y., Dec. 29, 1933; s. Philip Aloysius and Virginia (Collins) S.; m. Elizabeth Helen Wink, Jan. 23, 1965; children: Matthew P., Jean E. BA, St. Joseph's Coll., Yonkers, N.Y., 1956; JD, Fordham U., 1965. Bar: N.Y. Asst. reg. counsel FAA, N.Y.C., 1966-79; adminstrv. law judge U.S. Dept. Labor, Washington, 1979-83; adminstrv. appeals judge Benefits Rev. Bd., 1983—, chmn., chief adminstrv. appeals judge, 1988-90. Adj. prof. aviation law Dowling Coll., Oakdale, N.Y., 1972-79; adj. prof. transp. law Adelphi U., Garden City, N.Y., 1975-79; vis. prof. Georgetown U. Law Sch., 1989—. With U.S. Army, 1957-59. Mem. Assn. of Bar of City of N.Y. (sec.-treas. aeronautics com. 1978-79), Fed. Adminstrv. Law Judges Conf. (treas. 1983-84, mem. exec. com. 1982-83), Internat. Platform Assn., Friendly Sons of St. Patrick, Edgemoor Club, Georgetown U. Libr. Assocs. Avocation: tennis. Home: 6700 Pawtucket Rd Bethesda MD 20817-4836 Office: Benefits Rev Bd 200 Constitution Ave NW Washington DC 20210-0001 E-mail: smith-roy@d01.gov

SMITH, SCOTT ORMOND, lawyer; b. Altadena, Calif., Mar. 30, 1948; s. Donald Ormond and Jerry Ann (Shaw) S.; children— Victoria, Jeffrey Ormond, Meagan Ashley, Caitlin Brooke. BS, U. So. Calif., 1971; JD, Loyola U., L.A., 1974. Bar: Calif. 1974, U.S. Dist. Ct. (so., no., cen. and ea. dists.) Calif. 1975, U.S. Ct. Appeals (9th cir.) 1975, U.S. Supreme Ct. 1984. Assoc. Foonberg & Frandzel, Beverly Hills, Calif., 1974-77; ptnr. Nelsen & Smith, L.A. , 1977-80; ptnr. Morganstern, Mann & Smith, Beverly Hills, 1980-83; sr. ptnr. Smith & Smith, L.A., Calif., 1983-94; of counsel Buchalter, Nemer, Fields & Younger, 1994—. lectr. Rutter Group, Calif., 1982— , Continuing Edn. of Bar, Calif., 1983— . Mem. ABA, Calif. State Bar, L.A. County Bar (chair provisional and post-judgment remedies sect. 1997-98, exec. com., 1990—), Fin. Lawyers Conf. (bd. govs. 1982-86), Bankruptcy Study Group, Phi Alpha Delta, Beta Gamma Sigma. Republican. Presbyterian. Banking, Bankruptcy, Consumer commercial. Office: Buchalter Nemer Fields & Younger 601 S Figueroa St Fl 24 Los Angeles CA 90017-5704

SMITH, SELMA MOIDEL, lawyer, composer; b. Warren, Ohio, Apr. 3, 1919; d. Louis and Mary (Oyer) Moidel; 1 child, Mark Lee. Student UCLA, 1936-39, U. So. Calif. Law School, 1939-41; JD, Pacific Coast U., 1942. Bar: Calif. 1943, U.S. Dist. Ct. 1943, U.S. Supreme Ct. 1958. Gen. practice law; mem. firm Moidel, Moidel, Moidel & Smith, 1943—. Field dir. civilian adv. com. WAC, 1943-45; mem. nat. bd. Med. Coll. Pa. (formerly Womans's Med. Coll. Pa.) 1953—, mem. exec. bd. 1976-80, pres. 1980-82, chmn. past pres. com. 1990-92. Author: A Century of Achievement: The National Association of Women Lawyers, 1998, The First Women Members of the ABA, 1999; composer numerous works including Espressivo-Four Piano Pieces (orchestral premiere 1987, performance Nat. Mus. Women in the Arts 1989). Decorated La Orden del Merito Juan Pablo Duarte (Dominican Republic), 1956. Fellow Am. Bar Found., ABA (jr. bar conf. 1946-52, activities com. 1948-49); mem. State Bar Calif. (conf. com. on unauthorized practice of medicine 1964, Disting. Svc. award 1993), L.A. Bar Assn. (servicements legal aid com. 1944-45, psychopathic ct. com. 1948-53, Outstanding Svc. award 1993), L.A. Lawyers Club (pub. defenders com. 1951), Nat. Assn. Women Lawyers (chair com. unauthorized practice of law, social commn. UN, regional dir. western states, Hawaii 1949-51, jud. adminstrn. com. 1960, nat. chair world peace through law com. 1966-67, liaison to ABA Sr. Lawyers Divsn. 1996—, chair bd. elections 1997-98, centennial com. 1997-99, Lifetime Svc. award, 1999), League of Ams. (dir.), Inter-Am. Bar Assn., So. Calif. Women Lawyers Assn. (pres. 1947, 48), Women Lawyers Assn. L.A. (chair Law Day com. 1966, subject of oral hist. project 1986, hon. life mem., 1998), Coun. Bar Assns. L.A. County (charter sec. 1950), Calif. Bus. Womens Coun. (dir. 1951), L.A. Bus. Womens Coun. (pres. 1952), Calif. Pres. Coun. (1st v.p.), ABA Sr. Lawyers Divsn. (vice-chair editl. bd. Experience mag. 1997-99, chair 1999—, chair arts com. 1998-99, exec. coun. 1999—), Nat. Assn. Composers U.S.A. (dir. 1974-79, luncheon chair 1975), Nat. Fedn. Music Clubs (vice-chair Western region 1973-78), Calif. Fedn. Music Clubs (chair Am. Music 1971-75, conv. chair 1972), Docents L.A. Philharm. (v.p. 1973-83), chair Latin Am. cmty. rels., press and pub. rels. 1972-75, cons. coord. 1973-75), Euterpe Opera Club (v.p. 1974-75, chair auditions 1972, chair awards 1973-75), ASCAP, Iota Tau Tau (dean L.A. 1947, supreme treas. 1959-62), Plato Soc. of UCLA (Toga editor, 1990-93, sec. 1991-92, chmn. colloquium com. 1992-93, discussion leader UCLA Constitution Bicentennial Project, 1985-87, moderator UCLA extension lecture series 1990, Exceptional Leadership award 1994), Assn. Learning in Retirement Orgns. in West (pres. 1993-94, exec. com. 1994-95, Disting. Svc. award 1995), Calif. Supreme Ct. Hist. Soc. (bd. dir, 2001-). General practice. Home: 5272 Lindley Ave Encino CA 91316-3518

SMITH, SHARON LOUISE, lawyer, consultant; b. Williamsport, Pa., Apr. 21, 1949; d. Stuart Mallory and Phyllis Virginia (Hartzell) S. Student, Schiller Coll., Heidelberg, Fed. Republic Germany, 1969-70; AB, Grove City Coll., 1971; MA, Kent State U., 1973; JD, Temple U., 1978. Bar: Pa. 1978, U.S. Dist. Ct. (we. dist.) Pa. 1980, U.S. Ct. Appeals (3rd cir.) 1992. Assoc. Laurel Legal Services, Brookville, Pa., 1980-82; pvt. practice, 1982—. Cons. Prothonotary, Brookville, 1984-86. Mem. multidisciplinary team for child abuse Jefferson County Child Welfare Dept., Brookville, 1985; bd. dirs. Clarion-Jefferson Community Action, Brookville, 1982, Clearfield-Jefferson Drug and Alcohol Commn., DuBois, Pa., 1983-84. Mem. Pa. Bar Assn., Law Alumnae Assn. Temple U. Presbyterian. Avocations: swimming, reading. Bankruptcy, Probate, Real property. Home: 172 Franklin Ave Brookville PA 15825-1164 Office: 197 Main St Brookville PA 15825

SMITH, SHEILA MARIE, lawyer; b. Chgo. d. Donald Thomas and Catherine Ellen (Mariga) Morrison; m. Melvin Smith, Nov. 11, 1989. BSEE, Purdue U., 1981; JD, U. Cin., 1995. Bar: Ohio 1995, U.S. Dist. Ct. (so. dist.) Ohio 1996, U.S. Ct. Appeals (6th cir.) 1996, U.S. Supreme Ct., 1999. Mfg. engr., 1981-92; assoc. Freking & Betz, Cin., 1995-99, ptnr., 2000—. Spkr. in field. Named to Order of Coif U. Cin., 1995. Mem. ABA, Am. Trial Lawyers Assn., Nat. Employment Lawyers Assn., Ohio Employment Lawyers Assn., Cin. Employment Lawyers Assn., Ohio Bar Assn., Cin. Bar Assn. Avocations: golf, traveling, cooking. Civil rights, Federal civil litigation, Labor. Home: 3345 Legendary Trails Dr Cincinnati OH 45245-3074 Office: Freking & Betz 215 E 9th St Fl 5 Cincinnati OH 45202-2139 E-mail: ssmith@frekingandbetz.com

SMITH, STEPHEN EDWARD, lawyer; b. Boston, Aug. 5, 1950; s. Sydney and Minnie (Appel) S.; m. Eileen Beth O'Farrell, June 15, 1986; children: Nora, Bennett, Liliana. AB in Polit. Sci., Boston U., 1972; JD, Washington U., St. Louis, 1976. Bar: Ill. 1976, Mass. 1985, U.S. Dist. Ct. (no. dist.) Ill. 1977, U.S. Dist. Ct. (no. dist.) Ind. 1986, U.S. Dist. Ct. Mass. 1987, U.S. Dist. Ct. (ea. dist.) Wis. 1987, U.S. Ct. Appeals (7th cir.) 1981, U.S. Supreme Ct. 1998. Assoc., ptnr. Brown & Blumberg, Chgo., 1976-80; founding ptnr. Cantwell, Smith & Van Daele, 1980-84; ptnr. Gottlieb & Schwartz, 1984-85; of counsel Siemon, Larsen & Prudy, 1985-90; solo pracititioner, 1990-94; assoc. prof. clin. practice Ill. Inst. Tech. Chgo.-Kent Coll. law, 1994-95; of counsel Field & Golan, 1995—2001, Stephen Edward Smith & Assocs., Chgo., 2001—. Mediator Ctr. for Conflict Resolution, Chgo., 1992—; cmty. adv. coun. WBEZ, Chgo., 1985—; arbitrator NASD, Chgo., 1994—, Nat. Futures Assn.; mediator, arbitrator Duke U. Pvt. Adjudication Ctr.; mem. adj. faculty Northwestern U. Sch. Law, 2000—. Author: Update, ADR for Financial Institutions, 1996, 97. Past. bd. dirs., past pres. Jane Addams Ctr., Hull House Assn., Chgo. Fellow Chartered Inst. Arbitrators; mem. Am. Arbitration Assn. (comml. and internat. panels), Maritime Law Assn. U.S., Chgo. Internat. Dispute Resolution Assn. (dir.), Internat. Ct. Arbitration, London Ct. Internat. Arbitration (panel of neutrals), London Ct. Arbitration (panel of neutrals), Univ. Club Chgo., The Lawyer's Club Chgo. (sec.-treas. 1999-2000), Chgo. Lincoln Am. Inn. Ct., Internat. C. of C. (panel of neutrals). Federal civil litigation, General civil litigation, Private international. Office: Stephen Edward Smith & Assocs 55 E Monroe St Ste 3910 Chicago IL 60602

SMITH, STEPHEN MARK, lawyer; b. Newport News, Va., July 1, 1948; s. Joseph and Marian (Sturman) S.; m. Dawn Lee Williams, Dec. 10, 1978; children: Ryan David, Miles Stephen. BA in Psychology, William & Mary, 1971, JD, 1974. Bar: Va. 1974, N.Y. 1975, D.C. 1975, U.S. Supreme Ct., U.S. Ct. Appeals (2d, D.C., 4th cirs.). Lawyer Rothblatt, Rothblatt, et al., N.Y.C., 1974-76, Joseph Smith Ltd., Hampton, Va., 1976-99; founding mem. Waldo & Lyle, P.C. Bd. dirs. Enrenfried Techs. Mem. com. Va. Beach Dems., 1990—; bd. dirs., coord. Va. state Trial Lawyers Pub. Justice. Included in Best Lawyers in Am., 1997—. Mem. ATLA, Am. Bd. Trial Lawyers (diplomate), Am. Bd. Trial Advocates, Va. Trial Lawyers Assn. (bd. dirs. 1978—), Brain Injury Assn. Va. (bd. dirs. 1997—). Avocations: fishing, reading, boating, jogging, golf. Libel, Personal injury, Product liability. Office: Waldo & Lyle PC 301 W Freemason St Hampton VA 23661-3215

SMITH, STEVEN LEE, judge; b. San Antonio, Apr. 19, 1952; s. Bill Lee and Maxine Rose (Williams) S.; m. Rebecca Ann Brimmer, Aug. 5, 1978; children: William Christopher, Laura Charlotte. B in Music Edn. magna cum laude, Abilene Christian U., 1974; JD, U. Tex., 1977. Bar: Tex. 1977. U.S. Dist. Ct. (so. dist.) Tex. 1979, U.S. Dist. Ct. (we. dist.) Tex. 1980; cert. civil trial lawyer, Tex. Bd. Legal Specialization. Assoc. Dillon & Giesenschlag, Bryan, Tex., 1977-80, ptnr., 1980-84, Dillon, Lewis, Elmore & Smith, Bryan, 1985-88, Hoelscher, Lipsey, Elmore and Smith, College Station, Tex., 1988-94; asst. mcpl. judge City of College Station, 1988-91, presiding mcpl. judge, 1992-95; judge Brazos County Ct. at Law # 1, Bryan, 1995-98, 361st Dist. Ct., Bryan, 1999—. Chair Nat. Conf. Spl. Ct. Judges, 2001—. Chmn. Brazos Valley chpt. March of Dimes, 1983-84; Leadership Brazos Devel. Program, Bryan/Coll. Sta. C. of C., 1984-85; pres. Meml. Student Ctr. Opera and Performing Arts Soc., College Station, 1985-86; trustee Abilene Christian U., 2001—. Recipient Charles Plum Disting. Svc. award Tex. A&M U., 1986. Mem. ABA, Abilene Christian U. Alumni Bd., U. Tex. Law Sch. Alumni Assn. (dist. dir. 1986-89), U. Tex. Ex-Students Assn. Exec. Coun. (club rep. 1987-88), Optimists (pres. 1982-83). Mem. Ch. of Christ. Avocations: golf, flying. Home: 3840 Cedar Ridge Dr College Station TX 77845-6275 Office: 361st Dist Ct 300 E 26th St Ste 305 Bryan TX 77803-5361 E-mail: ssmith@co.brazos.tx.us

SMITH, STEVEN RAY, law educator; b. Spirit Lake, Iowa, July 8, 1946; s. Byrnard L. and Dorothy V. (Fischbeck) S.; m. Lera Baker, June 15, 1975. BA, Buena Vista Coll., 1968; JD, U. Iowa, 1971, MA, 1971. Bar: Iowa 1971, Ky. 1987, Ohio 1992. From asst. to assoc. dean Sch. Law U. Louisville, 1974-81, acting dean, 1974-75, 76, prof. law, 1971-88, assoc. in medicine Med. Sch., 1983-88; dep. dir/ Assn. Am. Law Schs., 1987-88; dean, prof. law Cleve. State U., 1988-96; pres., dean and prof. Calif. Western Sch. of Law, 1996—. Author: Law, Behavior and Mental Health: Policy and Practice, 1987; contbr. chpts. to books, articles to profl. jours. Trustee U. Louisville, 1980-82, SCRIBES, 1993—; chmn. faculty adv. com. Ky. Coun. Higher Edn., 1981-82; pres. Ky. Congress of Senate Faculty Leaders, 1982-84; bd. trustees Am. Bd. Profl. Psychology, 1994—. Recipient Grawemeyer award Innovative Teaching. Metroversity Consortium, 1983, Pres. award Cleve.-Marshall Law Alumni Assn., 1995. Fellow Ohio State Bar Found.; mem. ABA (stds. rev. com. 1991-95, govt. rels. com. 1993-95, joint commn. ABA/Assn. Am. Law Schs. financing of legal edn. 1993-94, 97-98, coun. sect. legal edn. and admission to the bar 1997—), APA (pub. mem. ethics com.), Am. Econs. Assn., Assn. Am. Law Schs. (chmn. librs. com., dep. dir. 1987-88, mem. accreditation com. 1993-96, chair accreditation com. 1994-96), Ohio State Bar Assn. (coun. of dels. 1992-96), Order of Coif, City Club of Cleve. (pres. 1994-95). Office: Calif Western Sch Law Office of Pres 225 Cedar St San Diego CA 92101-3046

SMITH, SUSAN KIMSEY, lawyer; b. Phoenix, Jan. 15, 1947; d. William Lewis and Margaret (Bowes) Kimsey; m. Alfred Jon Olsen, Apr. 15, 1979. Student, U. Ariz., 1965-66; BA, Principia Coll., 1969; MA, U. Va., 1970; JD, Ariz. State U., 1975. Bar: Ariz.; accredited estate planning law specialist, tax law specialist. Atty. trust dept. Valley Nat. Bank Ariz., Phoenix, 1976-77; assoc. Lane & Smith, Ltd., 1977-78; mem., pres. Olsen-Smith, Ltd., 1979—. Mem. Phoenix Tax Workshop, 1976—, Tax Study Group, 1979—, 401 Com., 1982—; chmn. taxation sect. State Bar Ariz., 1985-86, tax adv. commn.; lectr. in field. Author: Estate Planning Practice Manual, 1984; mem. editl. bd. Practical Tax Lawyer, 1985—; contbr. articles to profl. jours. Bd. dirs., gift tax adv. com. Ariz. Cmty. Found., chair legal adv. com.; bd. dirs., chair planning adv. com. Banner Health Found. Recipient J.P. Walker Am. History award, Principia Coll., 1969, Ethics award, State Bar Ariz., 1974. Fellow Am. Coll. Trust and Estate Counsel Regent (chair Ariz. 1992-97, chair bus. planning com.), Am. Coll. Tax Counsel; mem. ABA (chair com. econs. tax practice 1983-84, chair com. liaison, sect. econs. law. practice 1983—, selection com. appts. to U.S. Tax Ct., com. mem. sect. taxation 1976—, com. mem. sect. real property probate and trust law 1982—, chair taxation task force on family partnerships, editl. bd. Practical Tax Lawyer), Internat. Acad. Estate and Trust Law, State Bar Ariz. (chair taxation sect. 1985-86, tax adv. commn., cert. tax specialist, cert. estate and trust specialist), Maricopa County Bar Assn., Fed. Bar Assn. (vice-chair estate and gift taxation com., taxation coun. 1979-80), Valley Estate Planners (pres., elected first life time mem.), Ctrl. Ariz. Estate Planning Coun. (bd. dirs. 1986-88), The Group, Alpha Lambda Delta, Phi Alpha Eta. Republican. Estate planning, Probate, Estate taxation. Office: Olsen-Smith Ltd 301 E Virginia Ave Ste 3300 Phoenix AZ 85004-1218

SMITH, TEFFT WELDON, lawyer; b. Evanston, Ill., Nov. 18, 1946; s. Edward W. and Margery T. (Weldon) S.; m. Nancy Jo Smith, Feb. 25, 1967; children: Lara Andrea, Tefft Weldon II. BA, Brown U., 1968; JD, U. Chgo., 1971. Bar: Ill. 1971, U.S. Supreme Ct. 1977. Sr. litigation ptnr. Kirkland & Ellis, Chgo., 1971—, ptnr.-in-charge competition and antitrust practice group. Mem. adv. bd. Bur. Nat. Affairs Antitrust and Trade Regulation Reporter; instr. trial advocacy. Contbr. numerous articles on trial practice and antitrust issues to law jours. Mem. ABA (litigation sect., antitrust law sect.), Econ. Club., Univ. Club, Mid-Am. Club, Sea Pines Country Club (Hilton Head, S.C.). Avocations: squash, Ferraris, sculpture. Office: Kirkland & Ellis 200 E Randolph St Fl 54 Chicago IL 60601-6636 also: 655 15th St NW Washington DC 20005-5701

SMITH, THOMAS SHORE, lawyer; b. Rock Springs, Wyo., Dec. 7, 1924; s. Thomas and Anne E. (McTee) S.; m. Jacqueline Emily Krueger, May 25, 1952; children: Carolyn Jane, Karl Thomas, David Shore. BSBA, U. Wyo., 1950, JD, 1959. Bar: U.S. Dist. Ct. Wyo. 1960, U.S. Ct. Appeals (10th cir.) 1960, U.S. Tax Ct. 1969, U.S. Supreme Ct. 1971. Of counsel Smith, Stanfield & Scott, LLC, Laramie, Wyo., 1963-94, Brown, Nagel, Waters & Hiser, LLC, Laramie, 1994—. Atty. City of Laramie, 1963-86; instr. mcpl. law U. Wyo., 1987; dir. budget and fin. Govt. of Am. Samoa, 1954-56. Bd. dirs. Bur. Land Mgmt., Rawlins, Wyo., 1984-89, chmn. bd. dirs., 1991-95; bd. dirs. Ivinson Hosp. Found., 1994-95; bd. dirs. U. Wyo. Found., 1991-99, pres., 1994-95, bd. dirs. Bank of Laramie, 1998—. Francis Warren scholar, 1958. Mem Wyo. Bar Assn. (pres. 1984-85), Albany County Bar Assn., Western States Bar Conf. (pres. 1985-86), Elks. Republican. Episcopalian. Avocation: golf. Probate, Real property. Office: Brown Nagel Waters & Hiser LLC PO Box 971 515 E Ivinson Ave Laramie WY 82070-3157

SMITH, TURNER TALIAFERRO, JR. lawyer; b. Washington, Dec. 16, 1940; s. Turner Taliaferro and Lois (Fisk) S.; m. Christine H. Perdue; children: Turner T., III, John Webb Tyler. BA magna cum laude, Princeton U., 1962; LLB cum laude, Harvard U., 1968. Bar: Va. 1968, D.C. 1977. Ptnr. Hunton & Williams, Richmond, Va., 1975—; tchr. environ. law Washington and Lee U., 1978, Coll. William and Mary, 1979, 80. Mem. ABA (chmn. standing com. environ. law 1983, 84, 85, chmn. corp., banking and bus. law sect.'s com. on environ. controls 1973-80), Va. Bar Assn., Richmond Bar Assn., Internat. Bar Assn. Administrative and regulatory, Environmental, Legislative. Office: Hunton & Williams Ave Louise 106 1050 Brussels Belgium

SMITH, VALERIE A. lawyer; b. Orange, Calif., July 30, 1969; d. George Andrew III and Pamela Sue S. BA, Calif. State U., 1992; JD, Western State U., 1997. Bar: Calif., U.S. Dist. Ct. (ctrl. and so. dist.) Calif. Billing coord. Bryan Cave LLP, Irvine, Calif., 1994-98; assoc. Smith, Smith & Harter LLP, Santa Ana, 1998-99, Law Offices David E. Gentry, Santa Ana, 1999—. Mem. Girl Scouts USA. Mem. ABA, Calif. State Bar Assn. (cmty. outreach com. 1998-2001), Orange County Bar Assn., Robert A. Banyard Inn of Court. Avocations: reading, charity/volunteer work, theatre, music. General civil litigation, Family and matrimonial, Personal injury. Office: Grancell Lebovitz Stander Marx & Barnes PC 25 N 14th Street 460 San Jose CA 95112

SMITH, VINCENT MILTON, lawyer, designer, Feng Shui lecturer, consultant; b. Barbourville, Ky., Nov. 21, 1940; s. Virgil Milton and Louis (McGalliard) S.; 1 child, Jessica Todd. BA, Harvard U., 1962; LLB, Yale U., 1965. Bar: N.Y. 1966. Assoc. Breed, Abbott & Morgan, N.Y.C., 1965-70, Debevoise & Plimpton, N.Y.C., 1970-75, ptnr., 1975-95; CEO Lang, Winslow & Smith Co., Chatham, N.J., 1995-98; owner The VMS Feng Shui Design Co., 1998—. Vis. Feng Shui prof. Berea (Ky.) Coll., 1999, Williams Coll., Williamstown, Mass., 2001; mem. adv. bd. Chgo. Title Ins. Co., N.Y.C., 1979—; Feng Shui lectr. N.Y. Open Ctr., 1999-2001. Trustee Chatham Players, N.J., 1967-77, 87-91, Summit Friends Meeting, Chatham, 1973-99, N.J. Shakespeare Festival, Madison, 1975-80, Playwrights Theatre N.J., 1989-91. Mem. ABA, N.Y. State Bar Assn., Assn. of Bar of City of N.Y., Am. Land Title Assn., Urban Land Inst. Mem. Soc. of Friends. Clubs: Harvard, N.Y. Athletic. Landlord-tenant, Real property. Office: Debevoise & Plimpton 875 3rd Ave Fl 23 New York NY 10022-6225 E-mail: umsdesign@aol.com

SMITH, WALTER ERNEST, lawyer; b. Cin., Jan. 1, 1947; s. Walter F. and Kathleen M. (Vickers) S.; m. Healther Williamson, Mar. 3, 1979; children: Walter Todd, Kristan Lyn, Melanie Kathleen, Jennifer Erin. BS, Ohio State U., 1968; JD, Stetson U., 1971. Bar: Ohio 1971, Fla. 1971; cert. civil trial and bus. litigation law. Ptnr. Smith & Kircher, Cin., 1971-73, Davis & Smith, West Palm Beach, Fla., 1973-78, Meros & Smith PA, St. Petersburg, 1978—. With USAR, 1969-75. Mem. ABA, Ohio Bar Assn., Fla. Bar Assn., Palm Beach Bar Assn., St. Petersburg Bar Assn., Am. Assn. Trial Lawyers, Pinellas County Trial Lawyers. Democrat. Methodist. Family and matrimonial, Real property.

SMITH, WALTON NAPIER, lawyer; b. Macon, Ga., Feb. 26, 1942; s. Robert Monroe and Marion Rose (Napier) S.; m. Susan Rush Baum, Oct. 10, 1970; children: Rush Hendley, Berkeley Bosman. AB cum laude, Dartmouth Coll., 1964; JD, Harvard U., 1967. Bar: Ga. 1966, D.C. 1972, Ill. 1978, U.S. Supreme Ct. 1971. Counsel Nat. R.R. Passenger Corp., Washington, 1971-75; assoc. Lord, Bissell & Brook, Washington and Chgo., 1975-79, ptnr. Chgo. and Atlanta, 1980—. Bd. dirs. Brit. Am. Bus. Group. Mem. bd. Upper Chattahoochee Riverkeeper Fund. Served to capt. JACG, U.S. Army, 1964-71. Decorated Bronze Star, Army Commendation medal. Mem. ABA, Ill. Bar Assn., State Bar Ga., Nat. Assn. R.R. Trial Counsel, Union League Club (Chgo.), World Trade Club. Democrat. Episcopalian. Environmental, Insurance, Personal injury. Office: The Proseemium 1170 Peachtree St Ste 1900 Atlanta GA 30309 E-mail: wsmith@lordbissell.com

SMITH, WAYNE RICHARD, lawyer; b. Petoskey, Mich., Apr. 30, 1934; s. Wayne Anson and Frances Lynetta (Cooper) S.; m. Carrie J. Swanson, June 18, 1959; children: Stephen, Douglas (dec.), Rebecca. AB, U. Mich., 1956, JD, 1959. Bar: Mich. 1959. Asst. atty. gen. State of Mich., 1960-62; pros. atty. Emmet County (Mich.), 1963-68; dist. judge 90th Jud. Dist., Mich., 1969-72; city atty. City of Petoskey, 1976-98. Trustee North Central Mich. Coll., 1981-98, chmn., 1992-97; trustee/chmn. N. Ctrl. Mich. Coll. Found., 1999—; mem. No. Mich. Community Mental Health Bd., 1972-92, chmn., 1979-81. Mem. Emmet-Charlevoix Bar Assn. (pres. 1967), State Bar Mich., Mich. State Bar Found. Presbyterian. Land use and zoning (including planning), Probate, Real property. Home: PO Box 4677 Harbor Springs MI 49740-4677 Address: 365 E Main St PO Box 4677 Harbor Springs MI 49740-4677

SMITH, WENDY HOPE, lawyer; b. N.Y.C., Jan. 19, 1957; d. Morton and Doris Smith. AB, Smith Coll., 1978; JD, Boston U., 1981. Bar: N.J. 1981, U.S. Dist. Ct. 1981, U.S. Ct. Appeals (3d cir.), Supreme Ct. U.S. Law sec. to judge Superior Ct. N.J., Bergen County, 1981-82; assoc. firm Sellar, Richardson, Stuart & Chisholm, Roseland, N.J., 1982-89, ptnr., 1989-97, Sellar Richardson, P.C., 1997-2000, Marshall, Dennehey, Warner, Coleman & Goggin, Roseland, N.J., 2000—. Mem. adv. com. Inst. CLE, 1983-91. Mem. ABA, Am. Arbitration Assn., N.J. Bar Assn., Bergen County Bar Assn., Essex County Bar Assn., Trial Attys. N.J., Mensa, Smith Coll. Alumnae Assn. (fund rep. 1978-83). General civil litigation, Construction, Personal injury. Home: 401 Hancock Ct Edgewater NJ 07020-1627 Office: Marshall Dennehey Warner Coleman & Goggin 425 Eagle Rock Ave Ste 302 Roseland NJ 07068

SMITH, WILLIE TESREAU, JR. retired judge, lawyer; b. Sumter, S.C., Jan. 17, 1920; s. Willie T. and Mary (Moore) S. ; student Benedict Coll., 1937-40; AB, Johnson C. Smith U., 1947; LLB, S.C. State Coll., 1954, JD, 1976; m. Anna Marie Clark, June 9, 1955; 1 son, Willie Tesreau, III. Admitted to S.C. bar, 1954; began gen. practice, Greenville, 1954; past exec. dir. Legal Svcs. Agy. Greenville County, Inc.; state family ct. judge 13th Jud. Circuit S.C., 1977-91; ret. 1991. Past mem. adv. bd. Greenville Tech. Edn. Ctr. Adult Edn. Program and Para-Legal Program; mem. adv. bd. Greenville Tech. Coll. Found. Bd.; mem., past bd. visitors Presbyn. Coll., Clinton, S.C.; past bd. dirs. Greenville Urban League; past trustee Greenville County Sch. Dist.; past v.p. Peace Ctr. for Performing Arts. With AUS, 1942-45, USAF, 1949-52. Represented in Bell South African Am. History Calendar. Mem. Am., Nat. (jud. coun.), S.C., Greenville County bar assns., Southeastern Lawyers Assn., Nat. Coun. Juvenile and Family Ct. Judges, Am. Legion, Greater Greenville C. of C. (past dir.), Phillis Wheatley Assn. (dir.), NAACP, Omega Psi Phi, Delta Beta Boule, Sigma Pi Phi. Presbyterian (past chmn. bd. trustees Fairfield-McClelland Presbytery, past moderator Foothills Presbytery). Clubs: Masons, Shriners, Rotary. Home: 601 Jacobs Rd Greenville SC 29605-3318

SMITH, YOUNG MERRITT, JR. lawyer; b. Hickory, N.C., July 25, 1944; s. Young Merritt and Christine Ellen (White) S.; m. Louise Garner Price, Sept. 6, 1966 (div. Aug. 1974); 1 child, Patrick Adam; m. Charlie Mae Early, Nov. 19, 1977 (div. May 1985); m. Mary Gayle Jones, June 8, 1985; children: Mary Gaither, Jennifer Gayle. AB, U. N.C., 1966; JD, Duke U., 1969. Bar: N.C. 1969. Pres. The Litchfield Plantation Co., Pawleys Island, S.C., 1969-74, The Figure Eight Island Co., Wilmington, N.C., 1971-74; ptnr. Smith and Smith, Hickory, 1974-87; lawyer in pvt. practice, 1987—. Trustee Fund for Peace, N.Y.C., 1970-79, United Health Services N.C., Durham, 1971-73, N.C. Design Found., Raleigh, 1973-76. Mem. N.C. Bar Assn., Delta Kappa Epsilon. Democrat. Episcopalian. Real property. Office: Young M Smith Jr Atty PO Drawer 1948 225 4th St NW Ste 200 Hickory NC 28603 E-mail: ysmith@youngsmithlaw.com

SMITHSON, LOWELL LEE, lawyer; b. Kansas City, Mo., Apr. 29, 1930; s. Spurgeon Lee and Lena Louise (Ruddy) S.; m. Rosemary Carol Leitz, Jan. 30, 1960 (div. Sept. 1985); m. Phyllis Galley Westover, June 8, 1986; children: Carol Maria Louise, Katherine Frances Lee. AB in Polit. Sci., U. Mo., 1952, JD, 1954. Bar: Mo. 1954, U.S. Dist. Ct. (we. dist.) Mo. 1955, U.S. Supreme Ct. 1986. Ptnr. Smithson & Smithson, Kansas City, 1956-59; assoc. Spencer, Fane, Britt & Browne, 1959-64, ptnr., 1964—. Adj. prof. law U. Mo., Kansas City, 1982. Pres. Kansas City Mental Health Assn., 1963-65; mem. bd. pres. All Souls Unitarian Ch. Kansas City, 1965-67; chmn. com. select dean for law sch. U. Mo., 1983. Btry. Comdr. U.S. Army, 1954-56, Korea. Mem. Kansas City Bar Assn., Lawyers Assn. Kansas City, Assn. Trial Lawyers Am., Western Mo. Def. Lawyers Assn., Fed. Energy Bar Assn., Phi Beta Kappa, Phi Delta Phi. Democrat. Unitarian Ch. Avocations: skiing, reading, painting, swimming, canoeing. General civil litigation, Condemnation, Environmental. Home: 1215 W 65th St Kansas City MO 64113-1803 Office: Spencer Fane Britt & Browne 1000 Walnut 1400 Commerce Bank Bldg Kansas City MO 64106-2140 E-mail: lsmithson@spencerfane.com

SMOCK, TIMOTHY ROBERT, lawyer; b. Richmond, Ind., June 24, 1951; s. Robert Martin and Thelma Elizabeth (Cozad) S.; m. Martha Carolene Middleton, Apr. 4, 1992; children: Andrew Zoller, Alison Pierce. BA, Wittenberg U., 1973; JD cum laude, Ind. U., 1977. Bar: Ind. 1977, Ariz. 1979, U.S. Dist. Ct. (so. dist.) Ind. 1977, U.S. Dist. Ct. Ariz. 1979, U.S. Ct. Apeals (7th cir.) 1977, U.S. Ct. Appeals (9th cir.) 1979. Jud. clk. Ct. of Appeals of Ind., Indpls., 1977-79; assoc. Lewis and Roca, Phoenix, 1979-82; assoc./shareholder Gallagher & Kennedy, 1982-89; ptnr. Scult, French, Zwillinger & Smock, 1989-94, Smock and Weinberger, Phoenix, 1994-99, Richards and Smock, Phoenix, 1999—. Judge, pro tempore Maricopa County Superior Ct., Phoenix, 1989—; faculty, State Bar Course on Professionalism, Ariz. Supreme Ct./State Bar, Phoenix, 1992—; speaker, Continuing Legal Edn., Maricopa County and Ariz. State Bar, 1988—. Mem. ABA, Ariz. Bar Assn., Maricopa Bar Assn., Def. Rsch. Inst. General civil litigation, Insurance, Professional liability. Office: Richards and Smock 1202 E Missouri Ave Ste 150 Phoenix AZ 85014-2900 E-mail: Timothy.Smock@azbar.org

SMOLEV, TERENCE ELLIOT, lawyer, educator; b. Bklyn., Oct. 5, 1944; s. Lawrence and Shirley (Lebowitz) S.; m. Sherry Gale Rosen, Nov. 24, 1968 (div.); children: Cindy, Scott; m. Phyllis C. Rudko, Oct. 8, 1995. BBA, Hofstra U., 1966; JD, American U., 1969; LLM, NYU, 1974. Bar: N.Y. 1970. Acct. Peat Marwick & Mitchell, N.Y.C., 1969-70; dir. deferred giving Hofstra U., Hempstead, N.Y., 1971-74; editor Panel Publishers, Greenvale, 1970-71; ptnr. Naidich & Smolev, P.C., Bellmore, 1972-92; pvt. practice Terence E. Smolev, P.C., Mineola, 1992-2000; ptnr. Forchelli, Curto, Schwartz, Mineo, Carlino & Cohn LLP, 2000—, ptnr. in charge tax, trusts and estates, 2001—. Bd. trustees Hofstra U., 1992—; adj. prof. Hofstra U., Hempstead, N.Y., 1971—; dist. counsel North Merrick (N.Y.) UFSD, 1975-99. Author of book chpt. Mem. Nassau County, N.Y. Dem. Com., 1972-80, mem. judicial screening com., 1992—; mem. IRS Small Bus. Adv. Com., Washington D.C., 1975-77; bd. dirs. Arthritis Found. L.I., 1995-97, mem Israeli Bond Cabinet Long Island, 1996—; bd. dirs. L.I. chpt. Anti-Defamation League. Recipient George M. Estabrook award Hofstra U., 1991, Alumni Achievement award Hofstra U., 1993, Cmty. Svc. award Hebrew Acad. Nassau County, 1997; named Senator of Yr., Hofstra U., 1985, Alumnus of Yr., 1996. Mem. ABA, N.Y. State Bar Assn., Nassau County Bar Assn., N.Y. State Assn. Sch. Attys. (pres. 1984), Hofstra U. Alumni Senate (pres. 1987-89), Hofstra U. Club (bd. dirs. 1981-95). Avocations: photography, golf. Estate planning, Probate, Corporate taxation. Office: PO Box 31 330 Old Country Rd Ste 301 Mineola NY 11501 E-mail: tsmolev@fesmec.com

SMOLKER, GARY STEVEN, lawyer; b. L.A., Nov. 5, 1945; s. Paul and Shayndy Charolette (Sirott) S.; m. Alice Graham; children: Terra, Judy, Leah. BS, U. Calif., Berkeley, 1967; MS, Cornell U., 1968; JD cum laude, Loyola U., L.A., 1973. Bar: Calif. 1973, U.S. Dist. Ct. (ctrl. dist.) Calif. 1973, U.S. Tax Ct. 1973, U.S. Ct. Appeals (9th cir.) 1973, U.S. Supreme Ct. 1978, U.S. Dist. Ct. (so., ea. and no. dists.) Calif. 1981. Guest rschr. Lawrence Radiation Lab., U. Calif., 1967; tchg. fellow Sch. Chem. Engring., Cornell U.; mem. tech. staff Hughes Aircraft Co., Culver City, Calif., 1968-70; in advanced mktg. and tech. TRW, Redondo Beach, 1970-72; sole practice Beverly Hills, 1973-89, L.A., 1989—. Guest lectr. UCLA Extension, 1973-74, Loyola U. Law Sch., 1979; speaker, panelist in field; adv. Loyola U. Law Sch., 1973—. Columnist Heating Piping Air Conditioning Engring. Mag., 1999—; contbr. articles to profl. jours. Mem. Nat. Assn. Real Estate Editors, Calif. State Bar Assn., L.A. County Bar Assn., Beverly Hills Bar Assn. (sr. editor jour. 1978-79, contbg. editor jour. 1980-82, 86-90, editor-in-chief 1984-86, pub. Smolker Letter 1985—), B'nai B'rith (anti-defamation league). Jewish. Achievements include inventor self-destruct aluminium tungstic oxide films, electrolytic anticompromise process. Construction, Finance, Real property. Office: 4720 Lincoln Blvd Ste 280 Marina Del Rey CA 90292

SMOUSE, H(ERVEY) RUSSELL, lawyer; b. Oakland, Md., Aug. 13, 1932; s. Hervey Reed and Vernie (Rush) S.; m. Creta M. Staley, June 15, 1955; children: Kristin Anne, Randall Forsyth, Gregory Russell. AB, Princeton U., 1955; LLB, U. Md., 1958. Bar: Md. 1958, U.S. Tax Ct. 1979, U.S. Ct. Appeals (4th cir.) 1960, U.S. Supreme Ct. 1974. Atty., Atty. Gen.'s Honors Program, Dept. Justice, Washington, 1958-60, asst. U.S. atty. Dist. Md., 1960-62; assoc. Pierson and Pierson, Balt., 1962-64; atty. B.&O. R.R., Balt., 1964-66; mem. Pierson and Pierson, 1966-69; mem. Clapp, Somerville, Black & Honemann, Balt., 1969-74; Law Offices H. Russell Smouse, 1974-81; mem. Melnicove, Kaufman, Weiner & Smouse, P.A., Balt., 1981-89, chair litigation, 1985-89, Whiteford, Taylor & Preston, Balt., 1989-93, chair, litigation dept., 1989-93; head gen. litigation Law Offices Peter G. Angelos, 1993—; gen. counsel Balt. Orioles, 1993—; permanent mem. judicial conf. U.S. Ct. Appeals (4th cir.); v.p. Legal Aid Bur. Balt. City, 1972-73; bd. dirs. Md. Legal Svcs. Corp., 1987-93. Fellow Am. Coll. Trial Lawyers; mem. ABA, Md. State Bar Assn. (gov. 1981-83), Bar Assn. Balt. City (chmn. grievance com. 1969-70, chmn. judiciary com. and nominating com. 1980, mem. exec. com. 1969-70, 80, chmn. exec. com. lawyers' com. for ind. judiciary 1989-96), Nat. Assn. R.R. Trial Counsel (exec. com., v.p. ea. region 1986-92). Republican. Presbyterian. Federal civil litigation, State civil litigation, Criminal.

SMYTH, PAUL BURTON, lawyer; b. Phila., Aug. 15, 1949; s. Benjamin Burton and Florence Elizabeth (Tomlinson) S.; m. Denise Elaine Freeland, May 31, 1975. BA, Trinity Coll., 1971; JD, Boston Coll., 1974. Bar: Conn. 1974, D.C. 1975, U.S. Dist. Ct. D.C., 1980, U.S. Supreme Ct., 1985. With Dept. Interior, 1974—. Atty. Office of Hearings and Appeals, Arlington, Va., 1974-76, atty. Office of Solicitor, Washington, 1976-82, asst. solicitor for land use and realty, Washington, 1982-87; deputy assoc. solicitor for energy and resources, Washington, 1987-93, acting dir. Office of Hearings and Appeals, Arlington, 1993-94, dep. assoc. solicitor. for energy and resources, Washington, 1994-95, for land and water resources, 1995—; lectr. environ. law George Washington U. Law Sch., Washington, 1997—. Editor: Federal Reclamation and Related Laws Annotated, Reclamation Reform Act Compilation, 1982-88; contbr. articles to legal publs. Bd. dirs. EcoVoce, 1998—; trustee Rocky Mtn. Mineral Law Found., 1999—. Mem. ABA (coun. 1991-94, budget officer 1994-98, sec. natural resources, energy and environ. law, exec. editor Nat. Resources and the Environ. 1989-91). E-mail: paul. Office: Office of Solicitor Dept Interior 18th And C Sts NW Washington DC 20240-0001 E-mail: smyth@ios.doi.gov

SNAID, LEON JEFFREY, lawyer; b. Johannesburg, Republic of South Africa, Dec. 24, 1946; came to U.S., 1981; s. Mannie and Hene (Blume) S.; children: Jedd, Nicole. Diploma in Law, U. Witwatersrand, Johannesburg, 1969. Bar: Supreme Ct. Republic South Africa 1971, High Ct. of the Kingdom of Lesotho 1976, Calif. 1982, U.S. Dist. Ct. (so. and ctrl. dists.) Calif. 1982, U.S. Supreme Ct. 1999; cert. immigration law specialist, State Bar Calif. Bd. Legal Specialization. Assoc. Reeders, Teeger & Rosettenstein, Johannesburg, 1972; sole practice, 1973-76; ptnr. Snaid & Snaid, 1976-81; sole practice San Diego, 1982—. Lectr. legal edn. seminars, San Diego, 1984—. Author, pub. quar. newsletter Immigration and Internat. Law, The Newcomers Guide to Living in the U.S.A. Mem. ABA, Am. Immigration Lawyers Assn. (past chmn. continuing legal edn. San Diego chpt.), San Diego County Bar Assn. (past chmn. immigration com.). Lodge: Rotary. Immigration, naturalization, and customs, Private international. Home: 5060 Via Papel San Diego CA 92122-3923 Office: Ste # 211 2727 Camino Del Rio S San Diego CA 92108

SNAPP, ROY BAKER, lawyer; b. Strang, Okla., May 9, 1916; s. Harry Moore and Verda Mildred (Austin) S.; m. Dorothy Faye Loftis, Jan. 27, 1942; children: Deborah, Bryan Austin, Martha Lynn, Barbara, James. Lawyer. B.S. in Pub. Adminstrn, U. Mo., 1936; LL.B., Georgetown U., 1941, LL.M., 1942. With U.S. State Dept., 1941; spl. adviser comdg. gen. (Manhattan (Atomic Bomb) Project), 1946; dir. internat. affairs U.S. AEC, 1947, 1st sec., 1948-54, asst. to chmn., 1954-55, sr. staff mem. nat. security coun., 1953-55; v.p. atomic div. (Am. Machine & Foundry), 1957; v.p. Am. Machine & Foundry Co., Washington office, 1961. Bd. dirs. Electro-Nucleonics, Inc.; ptnr. Bechhoefer, Snapp and Trippe, 1966. Commd. ensign USNR 1942; assigned secretariat of U.S. Joint Chiefs of Staff and Combined (U.S.-Brit), Chiefs of Staff; naval mem. 1945; Intelligence Staff of Joint Cheifs Staff and Combined Chiefs Staff promoted to lt. comdr. 1945. Recipient D.S.M. AEC, 1955 Mem. Phi Gamma Mu, Delta Theta Phi. Baptist. Clubs: Univ. (Washington), Columbia Country (Washington). Home: 11446 Savannah Dr Fredericksburg VA 22407-9108

SNAPP, WILLIAM DORSEY, lawyer; b. Danville, Ill., Apr. 17, 1947; s. Eugene Gilbert and Thelma Lucille (Moles) S.; m. Teal Evans, May 30, 1970; 1 child, William Teal. AB, U. Ill., 1969, JD, 1976; postgrad., Ill. State U., 1971. Bar: Ill. 1976, Ga. 1994, U.S. Dist. Ct. (no. dist.) Ill. 1976, U.S. Dist. Ct. (no., mid. and so. dists.) Ga. 1994, U.S. Ct. Appeals (7th cir.) 1977, U.S. Ct. Appeals (6th cir.) 1983, U.S. Ct. Appeals (11th cir.) 1994, U.S. Supreme Ct. 1983. Assoc. Jenner and Block, Chgo., 1976-92, ptnr., 1983-92; regional atty. Atlanta Dist. Office U.S. EEO Commn., 1992-99; ADR coord., 1999—. Contbr. articles to profl. jours. Mem. ABA. Federal civil litigation, State civil litigation, Labor. Home: 2323 Deerfield Chase SE Conyers GA 30013-6307 E-mail: william.snapp@eeoc.gov

SNEAD, KATHLEEN MARIE, lawyer; b. Steubenville, Ohio, July 1, 1948; d. Donald Lee and Mary Alice (Hobright) O'Dell; m. John Jones Snead, Oct. 14, 1972; 1 child, Megan Marie. BA, Pa. State U., 1970; JD, U. Denver, 1979. Bar: Colo. 1979, U.S. Ct. Appeals (10th cir.) 1980, U.S. Supreme Ct. 1986. Field examiner NLRB, Pitts., 1970-72; freelance photographer Charleston, W.Va., 1973-74; labor relations examiner U.S. Dept. Labor, Denver, 1974-77, labor relations officer, 1978-79; staff atty. Denver & Rio Grande Western R.R., 1979-81, asst. gen. atty., 1981-84, gen. atty., 1984-92, Southern Pacific Lines, 1992-96, Union Pacific R.R., Denver, 1996-97; pvt. practice Golden, Colo., 1997—. Mem. ABA, Colo. Bar Assn. (adv. coun. environ. law sect.), Colo. Women's Bar Assn., Colo. R.R. Assn. (dir. 1982-84). Avocations: reading, swimming, biking, skating. General civil litigation, Environmental, Labor. Home: 233 S Devinney St Golden CO 80401-5316 E-mail: skaterlaw@aol.com

SNEED, JAMES LYNDE, lawyer; b. Tulsa, June 24, 1938; s. Earl and Cornelia (Lynde) S.; m. Jane Barnes, Sept. 5, 1959; children: David, Elizabeth, Thomas. AB cum laude, Harvard U., 1960; JD, U. Okla., 1963. Bar: Okla. 1963, U.S. Dist. Ct. (no. dist.) Okla. 1963. Ptnr. Conner, Winters, Randolph & Ballaine, Tulsa, 1962-70; chmn., pres., ptnr. Sneed, Lang, Adams & Barnett, 1970-86; pvt. practice, 1986—. Bd. dirs. Grand River Dam Authority, 1974-79; trustee Hillcrest Med. Ctr., Tulsa, 1974-92; active Salvation Army Bd., 1995—. Fellow Am. Bar Found., Okla. Bar Found. (pres. 1982—, chmn. 1985); mem. ABA, Okla. Bar Assn., Okla. Bar Assn., Tulsa County Bar Assn., Am. Judicature Soc., Summit Club, Tulsa Tennis Club (pres. 1978-81), Order of Coif, Phi Delta Phi. Democrat. Presbyterian. General corporate, Oil, gas, and mineral, Estate planning. Home: 1618 E 30th Pl Tulsa OK 74114-5308 Office: 309 Philtower 427 S Boston Ave Tulsa OK 74103-4141 E-mail: jlsneedlaw@sbcglobal.net

SNEED, JOSEPH TYREE, III, federal judge; b. Calvert, Tex., July 21, 1920; s. Harold Marvin and Cara (Weber) S.; m. Madelon Juergens, Mar. 15, 1944 (dec. Dec. 1998); children— Clara Hall, Cara Carleton, Joseph Tyree IV. BBA, Southwestern U., 1941; LLB, U. Tex., Austin, 1947; SJD, Harvard, 1958. Bar: Tex. bar 1948. Instr. bus. law U. Tex., Austin, 1947, asst. prof. law, 1947-51, asso. prof., 1951-54, prof., 1954-57, asst. dean, 1949-50; counsel Graves, Dougherty & Greenhill, Austin, 1954-56; prof. law Cornell U., 1957-62, Stanford Law Sch., 1962-71; dean Duke Law Sch., 1971-73; dep. atty. gen. U.S. justice dept., 1973; judge U.S. Ct. Appeals (9th cir.), San Francisco, 1973—, now sr. judge. Cons. estate and gift tax project Am. Law Inst., 1960-69 Author: The Configurations of Gross Income, 1967, Footprints on the Rocks of the Mountain, 1997; contbr. articles to profl. jours. Served with USAAF, 1942-46. Mem. ABA, State Bar Tex., Am. Law Inst., Order of Coif. Office: US Ct Appeals PO Box 193939 San Francisco CA 94119-3939

SNEED, SPENCER CRAIG, lawyer; b. Juneau, Alaska, Dec. 30, 1951; s. Gene Eric and Sarah Anne (McNeil) S.; m. Magna Cyd Coster, Sept. 19, 1981; children: Kenneth Craig, Joseph Bernard, Anne Irene. BA in Philosophy magna cum laude, Ariz. State U., 1975; JD, Willamette U., 1978. Bar: Alaska 1978. Assoc. Hartig, Rhodes, Norman, Mahoney & Edwards, Anchorage, 1978-82, ptnr., 1982-91, Bogle & Gates, 1991-99, Dosey & Whitney, 1999—. Mem. ABA, Alaska Bar Assn., Am. Bankruptcy Inst., Phi Kappa Phi. Banking, Bankruptcy, Consumer commercial. Home: 6731 Spectrum Cir Anchorage AK 99516-3726 E-mail: sneed.spencer@dorseylaw.com

SNEERINGER, STEPHEN GEDDES, lawyer; b. Lancaster, Ohio, Mar. 27, 1949; s, Stanley Carlylle and Mary Eleanor (Fry) S.; m. Kristine Karen Serfling, Oct. 6, 1974; children: Mary Rhonda, Robyn Kathleen. BA magna cum laude, Denison U., 1971; JD, Washington U., 1974. Bar: Mo. 1974. Sr. v.p. A.G. Edwards & Sons Inc., St. Louis, 1974—. Arbitrator N.Y. Stock Exchange, Nat. Assn. Securities Dealers, Nat. Futures Assn., Am. Arbitration Assn. Editor: Urban Law Ann., 1973-74; bd. editors Securities Arbitration Commentator. Am. Jurisprudence scholar, 1974. Mem. ABA (dispute resolution sect., arbitration com.), Mo. Bar Assn., Securities Industries Assn. (arbitration com.), Futures Industries Assn., Nat. Assn. Securities Dealers (mem. nat. arbitration and mediation com. 1992-94, 2001—), Securities Industry Conf. on Arbitration. Federal civil litigation, State civil litigation, Securities. Office: AG Edwards & Sons Inc 1 N Jefferson Ave Saint Louis MO 63103-2205

SNELL, BRUCE M., JR. state supreme court justice; b. Ida Grove, Iowa, Aug. 18, 1929; s. Bruce M. and Donna (Potter) S.; m. Anne Snell, Feb. 4, 1956; children: Rebecca, Brad. AB, Grinnell Coll., 1951; JD, U. Iowa, 1956. Bar: Iowa 1956, N.Y. 1958. Law clk. to presiding judge U.S. Dist. Ct. (no. dist.) Iowa, 1956-57; asst. atty. gen., 1961-65; judge Iowa Ct. Appeals, 1976-87; justice Iowa Supreme Ct., 1987—. Comments editor Iowa Law Rev. Mem. ABA, Iowa State Bar Assn., Am. Judicature Soc., Order of Coif. Methodist. Home: PO Box 192 Ida Grove IA 51445-0192 Office: Iowa Supreme Ct St Capitol Bldg Des Moines IA 50319-0001

SNIDER, JEROME GUY, lawyer; b. Mar. 14, 1950; s. Theodore Charles and Minnie Snider; m. Naomi S. Herman, Sept. 20, 1981; children: Benjamin Herman, Todd Nathaniel. AB, Rutgers U., 1972; JD, U. Pa., 1975. Bar: N.Y. 1976, U.S. Dist. Ct. (so. and ea. dists.) N.Y. 1976, U.S. Dist. Ct. (no. dist.) Calif. 1979, U.S. Dist. Ct. D.C. 1983, U.S. Ct. Appeals (6th cir.) 1984, U.S. Ct. Appeals (D.C. cir.) 1986, U.S. Supreme Ct. 1980. Law clk. to chief judge U.S. Dist. Ct. (so. dist.) N.Y., N.Y.C., NY, 1975—77; assoc. Davis Polk & Wardwell, 1977—82, ptnr. Washington, 1983—94, N.Y.C., 1994—. Mem.: ABA, Bar Assn. of the City of N.Y. Jewish. Federal civil litigation, State civil litigation. Office: Davis Polk & Wardwell 450 Lexington Ave New York NY 10017-3911

SNOW, CHARLES, lawyer, director; b. Bklyn., May 3, 1932; s. Irving S. and Bessie Siegel) S.; m. Deanna Friedman, Jan. 15, 1961; children: Lisa C., Amy M. BA, U. Vt., 1954; LLB, Bklyn. Law Sch., 1959. Bar: N.Y. 1959, U.S. Dist. Ct. (ea. and so. dists.) N.Y. 1961, U.S. Ct. Appeals (2d cir.) 1961, U.S. Supreme Ct. 1965. Dep. asst. atty. gen. N.Y. Dept. Law, N.Y.C., 1959-60; asst. U.S. atty. U.S. Dist. Ct. (ea. dist.) N.Y., Bklyn., 1960-61; asst. regional adminstr. SEC, N.Y.C., 1961-68; ptnr. Wofsey Certilman Hart Snow & Becker, P.C., 1968077, Snow Becker Krauss, P.C., N.Y.C., 1977—. Gen. counsel Securities Traders' Assn. N.Y.; bd. dirs. Walker Industries, Inc., Lake Mahopac, N.Y. Chmn. Harrison (N.Y.) Planning Bd., 1977-88. Mem. N.Y. State Bar Assn. (mem. bus. sect., com. on securities regulation), Securities Traders Assn. N.Y. (hon.). Republican. Jewish. Federal civil litigation, General corporate, Securities. Office: 605 3rd Ave New York NY 10158-0180 E-mail: csnow@sbklaw.com

SNOW, TOWER CHARLES, JR. lawyer; b. Boston, Oct. 28, 1947; s. Tower Charles and Margaret (Harper) S.; m. Belinda L. Snow. AB cum laude English, Dartmouth Coll., 1969; JD, U. Calif., Berkeley, 1973. Bar: Calif. 1973, U.S. Dist. Ct. (no. dist.) Calif. 1973, U.S. Ct. Appeals (9th cir.) 1973, U.S. Supreme Ct. 1976, U.S. Dist. Ct. (ea. dist.) Calif. 1979, U.S. Ct. Appeals (fed. cir.) 1980, U.S. Ct. Claims 1980, U.S. Ct. Appeals (2d cir.) 1987, N.Y. 1988, U.S. Dist. Ct. (ea. and so. dists.) N.Y. 1988, U.S. Dist. Ct. (ctrl. dist.) Calif. 1989, U.S. Dist. Ct. (no. dist.) Tex. 1995, U.S. Dist. Ct. (so. dist.) Calif. 1996, U.S. Dist. Ct. Ariz. 1996. Ptnr., chmn. litigation dept. Orrick, Herrington & Sutcliffe, San Francisco, 1973-89; ptnr. Shearman & Sterling, 1989-94; ptnr., chmn. securities litigation group, mem. policy com. Brobeck, Phleger & Harrison, LLP, 1995-97; chmn., CEO Brobeck, Phleger & Harrison, 1998—. Arbitrator Nat. Assn. Securities Dealers, Am. Stock Exch., N.Y. Stock Exch., Pacific Coast Stock Exch., Superior Ct. City and County San Francisco, Am. Arbitration Assn.; lectr. in field. Author numerous law handbooks and articles to prof. jours. Mem. San Francisco Mus. Soc., San Francisco Symphony, San Francisco Ballet, San Francisco Opera, Am. Conservatory Theatre. Named one of 100 Most Influential Lawyers in Am., Nat. Law Jour., 2000, one of 100 Most Influential Lawyers in Calif., Calif. Law and Bus., 2000. Mem. ABA (chmn. subcom. pub. offering litig. 1984-88, co-chair task force on securities arbitration 1988-89, vice chair securities litig. com. 1986-88), Continuing Edn. Bar (bus. law inst. planning com. 1986), Securities Industry Assn., Nat. Inst. Trial Advocacy, San Francisco Bar Assn. (pres. securities litig. sect. 1995). Democrat. Avocations: internat. travel, skiing, running, scuba diving, photography. Federal civil litigation, State civil litigation, Securities. Home: 177 Ridge Dr Napa CA 94558-9777 Office: Brobeck Phleger & Harrison LLP Spear St Tower One Market St San Francisco CA 94105 E-mail: tswow@brobeck.com

SNOWBARGER, VINCE, former congressman; b. Kankakee, Ill., Sept. 16, 1949; s. Willis Edward and Wahnona Ruth (Horger) S.; m. Carolyn Ruth McMahon, Mar. 25, 1972; children: Jeffrey Edward, Matthew David. BA in History, So. Nazarene U., 1971; MA in Polit. Sci., U. Ill., 1974; JD, U. Kans., 1977. Bar: Kans. 1977, U.S. Dist. Ct. Kans. 1977, Mo. 1987. Instr. Mid-Am. Nazarene Coll., Olathe, Kans., 1973-76; ptnr. Haskin, Hinkle, Slater & Snowbarger, 1977-84, Dietrich, Davis, Dicus et al, Olathe, 1984-88, Armstrong, Teasdale, Schafly & Davis, Overland Park, Kans., 1989-92; Holbrook, Heaven & Fay, P.C., Merriam, 1992-94; ptnr. Snowbarger & Veatch LLP, Olathe, 1994-96; mem. 105th Congress from 3rd Kans. dist., 1997-99; exec. dir. Kans. Assn. Am. Educators, 2000—. Mem. Kans. Legislature, Topeka, 1985-96; majority leader Ho. of Reps., 1993-96; mem. Olathe Planning Commn., 1982-84, Leadership Olalthe; divsn. chmn. United Way, Olathe, 1985-88, chmn. citizen rev. com., 1991-95. Mem. Olathe Area C. of C. (bd. dirs. 1984). Republican. Nazarene. Avocation: politics. Home: 1451 E Orleans Dr Olathe KS 66062-5728 E-mail: vincesnowbarger@netscape.net

SNOWISS, ALVIN L. lawyer; b. Lock Haven, Pa., June 16, 1930; s. Benjamin and Lillian (Kalin) S.; m. Jean Yarnell, Mar. 16, 1973. BA, U. Pa., Phila., 1952, JD, 1955; hon. alumnus, Pa. State U., 1998. Bar: Pa. 1956, U.S. Dist. Ct. (mid. dist.) Pa. 1958, U.S. Supreme Ct. 1972. Pvt. practice, Lock Haven, 1955-61; ptnr. Lugg & Snowiss, 1961-74, Lugg, Snowiss, Steinberg & Faulkner, Lock Haven, 1974-86, Snowiss, Steinberg Faulkner, and Hall LLP, Lock Haven, 1987—. Solicitor Clinton County, Lock Haven, 1964-72. Chmn. bd. Lock Haven Hosp. Found., 1986-92; pres. Lock Haven Hosp., 1982-86; bd. govs. Clinton County Cmty. Found., Lock Haven, 1970-97; chmn. adv. bd. Palmer Mus. Art, State College; v.p. bd. trustees Ross Libr., Lock Haven, 1963-86; mem. exec. com. Pa. Rep. Com., Harrisburg, 1974-80; state committeeman Clinton County Rep. Com., 1967-80. Fellow Am. Coll. Trust and Estate Counsel, Am. Bar Found., Pa. Bar Found. (founding, bd. dirs. 1984-95); mem. Pa. Bar Assn. (zone del. 1976-82, zone gov. 1983-86, treas. 1987-90), Clinton County Bar Assn. (pres. 1975-76), Kiwanis (pres. Lock Haven 1966-67). Republican. Avocations: art history, golf, historical research. E-makl. Estate planning, Probate, Real property. Home: 414 W Main St Lock Haven PA 17745-1107 Office: 333 N Vesper St Lock Haven PA 17745-1342 E-mail: ajsnow16@aol.com

SNYDER, ALLEN ROGER, lawyer; b. Washington, Jan. 26, 1946; s. Henry and Sylvia (Oxenburg) S.; m. Susan Port, Aug. 10, 1969; children: Joanna, Carolyn. BA with distinction, George Washington U., 1967; JD magna cum laude, Harvard U., 1971. Bar: D.C. 1973, U.S. Dist. Ct. D.C., Md., U.S. Ct. Appeals (D.C., 4th, 5th, 6th, 8th, 11th cirs.), U.S. Supreme Ct. Temp. assoc. Williams, Connolly & Califano, Washington, 1971; law clk. to assoc. justice J. Harlan U.S. Supreme Ct., 1971, law clk. to assoc. justice W. Rehnquist, 1972; assoc. Hogan & Hartson, Washington, 1972-78, ptnr., 1979—. Mem., then chmn. D.C. Cir. Commn. on Admissions and Grievances, 1984-90, D.C. Ct. Appeals Bd. Profl. Responsibility, 1978-84;mem. D.C. Cir. Adv. Com. on Procedures, 1986-92; mem. com. on pro se litigation U.S. Dist. Ct. Bd. dirs. Jewish Found. Group Homes, Rockville, Md., 1982-86. Served with USAR, 1968-74. Fellow Am. Acad. of Appellate Lawyers; mem. D.C. Bar Unified (chmn. steering com. div. cts., lawyers and adminstrn. justice 1974-77, long range planning com. 1976, bd. govs. 1977-78), Washington Coun. Lawyers (bd. dirs. 1976-91), Am. Psychiat. Assn. (exec. sec. com. jud. action 1974-77). Civil rights, Federal civil litigation, State civil litigation. Office: Hogan & Hartson 555 13th St NW Ste 800E Washington DC 20004-1161 E-mail: ARSnyder@HHLaw.com

SNYDER, ARTHUR KRESS, lawyer; b. L.A., Nov. 10, 1932; s. Arthur and Ella Ruth (Keck) S.; m. Mary Frances Neely, Mar. 5, 1953; children: Neely Arthur, Miles John; m. Michele Maggie Noval, May 14, 1973; 1 child, Erin-Marisol Michele; m. Delia Wu, Apr. 18, 1981. BA, Pepperdine U., 1953; JD, U. So. Calif., 1958; LLD, Union U., 1980. Bar: Calif. 1960, U.S. Supreme Ct. 1982. Sole practice, L.A., 1960-67; founder, pres. Arthur K. Snyder Law Corp., 1981-94; pres. Snyder & Assocs., Attys., 1994—. Pres. Marisol Corp., real estate and fgn. trade, 1978—; pres. real estate holdings Keck Investment Properties, 1990—; past instr. L.A. City Schs.; CFO Royal Star of Nev., Restaurateurs, 1999—. Mem. City Coun. L.A., 1967-85. Served to capt. USMC. Decorated La Tizona de El Cid Compeador (Spain), medal Legion of Honor (Mex.), Hwa Chao Zee You medal (Republic of China), numerous other commendations, medals, awards. Mem. ABA, ATLA, Los Angeles County Bar Assn., World Film Inst. (chmn. bd. dirs. 1997—), Calif. Bar Assn., L.A. County Bar Assn., Am. Judicature Soc., Masons. Baptist. Administrative and regulatory, State civil litigation, Real property. Office: 1000 W Sunset Blvd Ste 200 Los Angeles CA 90012-2105 E-mail: artsnyder@alumni.usc.edu

SNYDER, JEAN MACLEAN, lawyer; b. Chgo., Jan. 26, 1942; d. Norman Fitzroy and Jessie (Burns) Maclean; m. Joel Martin Snyder, Sept. 4, 1964; children: Jacob Samuel, Noah Scot. BA, U. Chgo., 1963, JD, 1979. Bar: Ill. 1979, U.S. Dist. Ct. (no. dist.) Ill. 1979, U.S. Ct. Appeals (7th cir.) 1981. Ptnr. D'Ancona & Pflaum, Chgo., 1979-92; prin. Law Office of Jean Maclean Snyder, 1993-97; trial counsel The MacArthur Justice Ctr. U. Chgo. Law Sch., 1997—. Contbr. articles to profl. jours. Mem.: ABA (mem. coun. on litigation sect. 1989—92, editor-in-chief Litigation mag. 1987—88, co-chair First Amendment and media litigation com. 1995—96, co-chair sect. litigation task force on gender, racial and ethnic bias 1998—2001, standing com. on strategic comms. 1996—2001), ACLU of Ill. (bd. dirs. 1996—99), Lawyers for the Creative Arts (bd. dirs. 1995—97). General civil litigation, Entertainment, Intellectual property. Office: The MacArthur Justic Ctr Univ of Chgo Law Sch 1111 E 60th St Chicago IL 60637-2776 E-mail: jean_snyder@law.uchicago.edu

SNYDER, JOHN GORVERS, lawyer; b. Boston, June 20, 1960; s. Philip Francis and Sylvia (Gorvers) S.; m. Hinda Mala Simon, July 8, 1984; children: Monica Paige, Kimberly Blaine. BA, Johns Hopkins U., 1982; JD, Cornell U., 1987. Bar: Mass. 1988, U.S. Dist. Ct. Mass. 1989. Ptnr. banking law, bus. law and corp. law dept. Craig & Macauley P.C., Boston, 1995-2000, assoc. banking law, bus. law and corp. law dept., 1987-94; v.p. acquisitions and devel. Simon Cos., LP, Braintree, Mass., 2000—. Lectr. New England Coll. Fin., 1994-2000. Active Combined Jewish Philanthropies, Boston, 1991—, Anti-Defamation League, Boston, 1993-94. Mem. Mass. Bar Assn., Boston Bar Assn., Phillips Exeter Acad. Alumni Assn., Phi Alpha Delta Internat., Omicron Delta Kappa (Johns Hopkins U. chpt., pres. 1981-82), Delta Upsilon (Johns Hopkins U. chpt.). Avocations: golf, tennis. Bankruptcy, Contracts commercial, General corporate. Home: 7 Laurus Ln Newton Center MA 02459-3138 Address: Simon Cos LP Attn: John G Snyder VP 10 Forbes Rd Braintree MA 02184-2605

SNYDER, PAUL, JR. lawyer; b. Hollywood, Calif., Jan. 18, 1943; s. Paul and Helen Jean (Trayan) S.; m. Kathy Jane Pope, Oct. 7, 1945 (div.); m. Martha Kate Frick, June 15, 1948; children: Jeffrey Randall, Suzanne Leigh. BA, U. Colo., 1965, JD, 1967. Bar: Colo. 1967. Assoc. Williams, Taussig & Trine, 1967-70; ptnr. Taussig, McCarthy & Snyder, 1970-73; of counsel Taussig & Cobb, 1974-75; pres. Snyder, Neuman & Enwall PC, 1978-81, Paul Snyder Jr. PC, Boulder, Colo., 1981-83; ptnr. Martin and Snyder, 1983-85, Brauchli-Snyder LLC, 1986-96; atty. Town of Westcliffe, 1997—; ptnr. Stevens & Snyder, 1998—. Faculty Nat. Inst. Trial Advocacy, 1982-94. Chmn. Boulder Growth Mgmt. Task Force, 1980-81. Mem. Colo. Bar Assn., Boulder Bar Assn. (Merit award 1993). General practice, Land use and zoning (including planning), Real property. Home: 4928 County Road 125 Westcliffe CO 81252-8600 Office: 4928 County Road 125 Westcliffe CO 81252-8600

SNYDER, ROBERT JOHN, lawyer; b. Phila., June 2, 1952; s. Robert John and Lilja (Anderson) S. BA cum laude, St. John's U., 1974; JD, U. N.D., 1977. Bar: N.D. 1977, Minn. 1977, U.S. Dist. Ct. N.D. 1977, U.S. Ct. Appeals (8th cir.) 1982, U.S. Supreme Ct. 1982. Ptnr. Coles & Snyder, Chartered, Bismarck, N.D., 1977-89, Wheler, Wolf, Bismarck, 1989-93, Snyder Coles Lawyers, Bismarck, 1993-99, Snyder Law Office, Bismarck, 1999—. Judge, Bismarck Teen Ct., 1999—; alt. bd. dirs. Legal Aid N.D., Bismarck, 1982-84. Vol. Bismarck United Way, 1979; active talking book S.D. State Program for Handicapped, Pierre, 1983-84. Named one of Outstanding Young Men of Am., 1979. Mem. ABA, Assn. Trial Lawyers A., N.D. Bar Assn. (com. revision o pattern jury instrns. 1981, revision code of profl. responsibility 1983-87), Internat. Platform Assn., Mensa, Intertel. Bismarck Jaycees (outstanding officer 1979, Outstanding Young Bismarcker 1985), Apple Creek Country Club, Elks, Ky. Cols. State civil litigation, Criminal, Personal injury. Office: Snyder Law Office PO Box 1321 Bismarck ND 58502-1321 E-mail: snyhunt@btigate.com

SNYDER, WILLARD BREIDENTHAL, lawyer; b. Kansas City, Kans., Dec. 18, 1940; s. N.E. and Ruth (Breidenthal) S.; m. Lieselotte Dieringer, Nov. 10, 1970 (dec. Nov. 1975); 1 child, Rolf; m. T.J. Sewall, May 17, 1996. BA, U. Kans., 1962, JD, 1965; postgrad., Hague Acad. Internat. Law, The Netherlands, 1965-66, U. Dijon, France, 1966; grad., Command and Gen. Staff Coll., Ft. Leavenworth, Kans., 1977. Bar: Kans. 1965, Mo. 1986, U.S. Tax Ct. 1977, U.S. Ct. Mil. Appeals 1981, U.S. Dist. Ct. Kans. 1965, U.S. Supreme Ct. 1977. Atty., Kansas City, 1970-80, 85—; trust officer, corp. trust officer Security Nat. Bank., 1980-83, corp. sec., 1983-85; pres. Real Estate Corp. Inc., Leawood, Kans., 1984—; adv. dir. United Mo. Bank, 1985-90. Bd. dirs. Blue Ridge Bank, mem. trust and investment com., 1991—; German Consul (H) for Kans., Western Mo., 1972—. Platte Woods (Mo.) City Coun., 1983-84; mem. exec. bd. dirs. regional coun. Boy Scouts Am.; bd. govs. Liberty Meml. Assn.; mem. nomination com. MacJannett Found., Talloires, France; chmn. Breidenthal-Snyder Found.; trustee St. Mary Coll.; mem. nominating and exec. com. Hoover Pres. Libr.; bd. dirs. Unicorn Theatre. Col. Kans. Army N.G.; col. USAR ret. Decorated Bundensverdienst Kreuz, 1982, BVK 1KL (Germany), 1992, Bundeswehr Kreuz (silver), 1987, Ge. Abn., Legion of Merit; KARNG medal of excellence; named to Hon. Order Ky. Cols., 1988; recipient Golden Honour badge German Vet. Orgn., Bavaria, 1988, Mil. Order of WW award, OCS Hall of Fame. Mem. Mo. Bar Assn., Kansas City Bar Assn., Kansas City Hosp. Attys., Mil. Order of World Wars (chpt. comdr. 1983-84, regional comdr. 1987-91, Patrick Henry award), Nat. Eagle Scout Assn. Avocations: scuba, hunting, Notgeld collections, cartridge collection. General corporate, Public international, Non-profit and tax-exempt organizations. Office: 8014 State Line Rd Ste 203 Shawnee Mission KS 66208-3712

SNYDERMAN, MARC IAN, lawyer; b. Phila., Apr. 5, 1972; s. Neil Robert and Carol Sue S. BA, Dickinson Coll., 1994; JD, Rutgers U., 1997. Bar: N.J. 1997, N.Y. 1998. Assoc. Ballon Stoll Bader & Nadler, P.A., N.Y.C., 1998-99; contract mgr. Insight Comms. Co., 1999—. Mem. ABA (bus. sect.), Assn. of the Bar of the City of N.Y., N.Y. State Bar Assn. Republican. Jewish. Avocations: sports, music, politics. Contracts commercial, General corporate, Securities. Home: 350 E 77th St Apt 2A New York NY 10021 Office: Insight Comm Company 810 Seventh Ave New York NY 10019

SNYDERMAN, PERRY JAMES, lawyer; b. Chgo., Oct. 9, 1932; s. Max and Frances (Kaplan) S.; m. Elaine Pomper, Aug. 14, 1955; children: Michelle, Sol, Robin. BS, Bradley U., 1954; JD, DePaul U., 1959. Sr. ptnr. Rudnick & Wolfe, Chgo., 1960—; pvt. practice gen. real estate; resort property time-sharing project adminstr.; lectr. in field; instr. Real Estate Securities and Syndication Inst. Contbr. articles to profl. publs. Pres. Jewish Community Ctrs. Chgo., 1980; mem. Urban Land Inst., 1980, Ill. Devel. Fin. Authority; chmn. Am. Resorts and Residential Devel. Assn.; trustee DePaul U. Bd. With U.S. Army, 1956-58. Mem. ABA, Ill. Bar Assn., Chgo. Bar Assn. (bd. mgrs.), Am. Coll. Real Estate Lawyers, Chgo. Coun. Lawyers. Real property. Home: 254 Hazel Ave Highland Park IL 60035-3337 Office: Rudnick & Wolfe 203 N La Salle St Ste 1800 Chicago IL 60601-1210

SOBEL, LIONEL STEVEN, law educator; b. Indpls., Feb. 20, 1946; s. Herbert and Vivienne (Simon) S.; m. Carol Marion Phillips, June 16, 1968; children— Lindsay Sara, Katherine Joanna. A.B., U. Calif.-Berkeley, 1966; J.D., UCLA, 1969. Bar: Calif. 1970, U.S. Dist. Ct. (cen. dist.) Calif. 1970, U.S. Ct. Appeals (9th cir.) 1974, U.S. Supreme Ct. 1983. Assoc. Loeb & Loeb, Los Angeles, 1969-73; sole practice, Los Angeles, 1973-77; ptnr. Freedman & Sobel, Beverly Hills, Calif., 1977-82; prof. law Loyola Law Sch., Los Angeles, 1982— ; editor, pub. Entertainment Law Reporter, Los Angeles, 1979— ; adj. prof. U. So. Calif., Los Angeles, 1974-78. Author: Professional Sports and the Law, 1977. Editor Entertainment Law Reporter, 1979— . Contbr. articles to profl. jours. Recipient Nathan Burkan award ASCAP, 1969. Mem. ABA, Los Angeles Copyright Soc. Democrat. Jewish. Office: Loyola Law Sch 1441 W Olympic Blvd Los Angeles CA 90015-3980 also: Entertainment Law Reporter Pub Co 2210 Wilshire Blvd # 311 Santa Monica CA 90403-5706

SOBERON, PRESENTACION ZABLAN, state bar administrator; b. Cabambangan, Bacolor, Pampanga, Philippines, Feb. 23, 1935; came to U.S., 1977; naturalized, 1984; d. Pioquinto Yalung and Lourdes (David) Zabian; m. Damaso Reyes Soberon, Apr. 2, 1961; children: Shirley, Sherman, Sidney, Sedwin. Office mgmt., stenography, typing cert., East Cen. Colls., Philippines, 1953; profl. sec. diploma, Internat. Corr. Schs., 1971; A in Mgmt. Supervision, Skyline and Diablo Coll., 1979, LaSalle Ext. U., 1980-82; AA, cert. in Mgmt. and Supervision, Diablo Valley Coll. With U.S. Fed. Svc. Naval Base, Subic Bay, Philippines, 22 yrs, clerical, stenography and secretarial postitions, 1955-73, adminstrv. asst., 1973-77; secretarial positions Mt. Zion Hosp. and Med. Ctr., San Francisco, 1977, City Hall, Oakland, Calif., 1978; with State Bar Calif., San Francisco, 1978-79; secretarial positions gen. counsel divsn. and state bar ct. divsn., adminstrv. asst. fin. and ops. divsn., 1979-81; office mgr. sects. and coms. dept., profl. and pub. svcs., 1981-83; appointment adminstr. office of bar rels., 1983-86; adminstr. state bar sects. bus. law sect., estate planning, trust and probate law sect., labor and employment law sect., office of bar rels., 1986-89; adminstr. antitrust and trade regulation law sect., labor and employment law sect., workers' compensation sect., edn. and meeting svcs., 1989-96; adminstr. criminal law sect., 1996—; labor and law employment law sect., 1996—; internat. law sect., 1996—; workers' compensation sect., 1996—; edn. and meeting svcs., 1996-98; ret., 1998. Disc jockey/announcer Philippine radio stas. DZYZ, DZOR and DWHL, 1966-77. Organizer Neighborhood Alert Program, South Catamaran Circle, Pittsburg, Calif., 1979-80. Recipient 13 commendation certs. and outstanding pers. monetary awards U.S. Fed. Svc., 1964-77, 20 Yr. U.S. Fed. Svc. pin and cert., 1975; Nat. 1st prize award for cmty. svc. and achievements Nat. Inner Wheel Clubs Philippines, 1975; several plaques and award certs. for cmty. and sch. activities and contbns. Olongapo City, Philippines. Mem. NAFE, Am. Soc. Assn. Execs., N.Y.C. Olongapo-Subic Bay Assn. No Calif. (Pittsburg rep. 1982-87, bus. mgr. 1988-89, 97-98, 99-2000, pub. rels. officer 1993-94), Castillejos Assn. of No. Calif., SRF Tigers No. Calif. Roman Catholic. Home: 207 South Catamaran Circle Pittsburg CA 94565 Office: State Bar of Calif 180 Howard St San Francisco CA 94105-1639

SOBLE, MARK RICHARD, lawyer; b. San Francisco, Dec. 25, 1964; BA with deptl. honors, Stanford U., 1985; JD, U. Mich., 1988. Bar: Calif. 1988, U.S. Dist. Ct. (cen. dist.) Calif. 1988, U.S. Dist. Ct. (ea. dist.) Calif. 1990. Law clk. to chief judge U.S. Dist. Ct. for S.D., Pierre, 1988-89; assoc. Lewis, D'Amato, Brisbois & Bisgaard, L.A., 1989-90; counsel enforcement div. Fair Polit. Practices Commn., Sacramento, 1990-96, sr. counsel, 1996—. Note editor U. Mich. Jour. Law Reform, 1987-88. Raymond K. Dykema scholar U. Mich. 1987. Mem. State Bar Calif., Sacramento County Bar Assn. (mng. editor Docket 1997, mem.-at-large bar coun. 1998-00). Office: Fair Polit Practices Commn 428 J St Ste 700 Sacramento CA 95814-2331

SOBOL, ALAN J. lawyer; b. Newark, Dec. 18, 1948; s. Max and Marjorie (Namorovsky) S.; m. Kathreen Miriam Campbell, June 2, 1984; 1 child, Laura Emily. B.A. with honors, U. Md., 1971; J.D., U. Akron, 1974. Bar: Ohio 1974, U.S. Ct. Appeals (2d cir.) 1975, U.S. Ct. Appeals (1st and 6th cirs.) 1976, U.S. Supreme Ct. 1978, D.C. 1978, Md. 1978, U.S. Ct. Appeals (4th cir.) 1979, U.S. Ct. Appeals (5th, 9th and 11th cirs.) 1982, U.S. Dist. Ct. D.C. 1983, U.S. Dist. Ct. Conn. 1986, Conn. 1988, U.S. Ct. Appeals (3d cir.) 1988. Trial atty. criminal div. U.S. Dept. Justice, Washington, 1974-79, spl. asst. U.S. atty., Alexandria, Va., 1979-80, Key West, Fla., 1980, San Francisco, 1980-81, trial atty. gen. litigation criminal div., Washington, 1980-82; assoc. gen. counsel Nat. RR Passenger Corp., Washington, 1982-86; assoc. Tyler, Cooper & Alcorn, New Haven, 1986—. Case & Comments editor Akron Law Rev., 1972-74. Recipient U.S. Atty. Gen.'s Honor Law Grad. award U.S. Dept. Justice, 1974. Mem. ABA (litigation sect. 1982—), D.C. Bar Assn. (litigation sect. 1982—), Phi Alpha Delta, Phi Sigma Alpha, Phi Sigma Delta (house master 1969-70). Federal civil litigation, Contracts commercial, Labor. Home: 606 Tamarack Rd Cheshire CT 06410-3228 Office: Tyler Cooper & Alcorn 205 Church St New Haven CT 06510-1805

SODEN, RICHARD ALLAN, lawyer; b. Feb. 16, 1945; s. Hamilton David and Clara Elaine (Seale) S.; m. Marcia LaMonte Mitchell, June 7, 1969; children: Matthew Hamilton, Mark Mitchell. AB, Hamilton Coll., 1967; JD, Boston U., 1970. Bar: Mass. 1970. Law clk. to judge U.S. Ct. Appeals (6th cir.), 1970-71; assoc. firm Goodwin, Procter & Hoar LLP, Boston, 1971-79, ptnr., 1979—. Instr. Law Sch. Boston Coll., Chestnut Hill, Mass., 1973-74. Mem. South End Project Area Com.; hon. dir. United South End Settlements, pres., 1977-79; chmn. Boston Mcpl. Rsch. Bur.; pres. Boston Minuteman coun. Boy Scouts Am.; trustee Judge Baker Children's Ctr., chmn., 1994-96, pres., 1992-94; trustee New Eng. Aquarium, Boston U.; bd. visitors Boston U. Goldman Sch. Grad. Dentistry; mem. bd. overseers WGBH; mem. Mass. Minority Bus. Devel. Commn.; mem. Adv. Task Force on Securities Regulation; mem. Adv. Com. on Legal Edn.; steering com. Lawyers Com. for Civil Rights under Law, chmn., 1992-94. Mem. ABA (chmn. standing com. on bar svcs. and activities), Nat. Bar Assn., Mass. Bar Assn. (past vice chmn. bus. law coun. 1990-91), Boston Bar Assn. (pres. 1994-95), Mass. Black Lawyers Assn. (pres. 1980-81). General corporate, Finance, Securities. Home: 42 Gray St Boston MA 02116-6210 Office: Goodwin Procter & Hoar LLP Exchange Pl Boston MA 02109-2803

SODERQUIST, LARRY DEAN, lawyer, educator, consultant, writer; b. Ypsilanti, Mich., July 20, 1944; s. Hugo E. and Emma A. (Johanson) S.; m. Ann Mangelsdorf, June 15, 1968; children: Hans, Lars. BS, Ea. Mich. U., 1966; JD, Harvard U., 1969. Bar: N.Y. 1971, Tenn. 1981. Assoc. Milbank, Tweed, Hadley & McCloy, N.Y.C., 1971-76; assoc. prof. law U. Notre Dame, South Bend, Ind., 1976-80, prof., 1980-81; vis. prof. law Vanderbilt U. Law Sch., Nashville, 1980-81, prof., 1981—. Dir. corp. and securities law inst. 1993—; of counsel Dinsmore & Shohl LLP; spl. master U.S. Dist. Ct. (no. dist.) Ohio, 1977; vis. prof. law Harvard U. Law Sch., Cambridge, Mass., 1999. Author: Corporations, 1979, 5th edit., 2001, Understanding the Securities Laws, 3d edit., 1993, Securities Law, 1998, Securities Regulation, 4th edit., 1999, Corporate Law and Practice, 2d edit., 1999,

Law of Federal Estate and Gift Taxation: Code Commentary, 1978, Analysis, 1980, Investor's Rights Handbook, 1993; (novel) The Labcoat, 1998; contbr. articles to profl. jours. Capt. U.S. Army, 1969-71. Decorated Army Commendation medal. Mem. ABA, Am. Law Inst. Presbyterian. Home: 2000 Grand Ave Ste 801 Nashville TN 37212 Office: Vanderbilt U Sch Law 131 21st Ave S Nashville TN 37203-1120

SOFFAR, WILLIAM DOUGLAS, lawyer; b. Houston, Sept. 8, 1944; s. Benjamin and Esther Goldy (Garfinkel) S.; m. Nancy Elise Axelrod, Mar. 29, 1969 (div. Sept. 1989), m. Gail Shinbaum, Jan. 16, 2000; children: Pamela Beth, Stephanie Michelle, Jill Denise. BA, U. Houston, 1966, JD, 1969. Bar: Tex. 1969, U.S. Dist. Ct. (so. dist.) Tex. 1970, U.S. Ct. Appeals (5th cir.) 1974, U.S. Supreme Ct. 1974; cert. mediator in civil law and family law. Atty. examiner U.S. Interstate Commerce Commn., Washington, 1969-70; atty. Law Office of Adolph Uzick, Houston, 1970-72, Walsh & Soffar, Houston, 1972-73; lawyer, sole practice Law Offices of William D. Soffar, 1973-74; ptnr. Soffar & Levit, 1974—. Family law and civil mediator, basic mediation and family mediation trainer Atty.-Mediator's Inst. Bd. dirs. Miller Theater Adv. Coun., Houston, 1985-90, Zina Garrison Found., Houston, 1989-91. Mem. Houston Bar Assn. (bd. dirs., family law sect. mem. 1989-90), Jewish Cmty. Ctr. (health club com. 1971—), Jewish Family Svc. (bd. dirs. 1970-71), Phi Delta Phi. Jewish. Avocations: travel, reading, raquetball. Family and matrimonial, General practice, Personal injury. Office: Soffar & Levit 6575 West Loop S Ste 630 Bellaire TX 77401-3604

SOGAARD, KLAUS, lawyer; b. Aalborg, Denmark, Oct. 17, 1955; m: Elisabeth Rask Jorgensen, May 30, 1987; children: Christian, Henrik. JD, Aarhus, Denmark, 1980; LLM, U. Pacific, Sacramento, CA, 1985. Mem. Danish Bar. Partner Gorrissen Federspiel Kierkegaard, Copenhagen, Denmark, 1980-2000. Banking, Mergers and acquisitions, Securities. Office: Gorrissen Federspiel Kierkegaard HC Andersens Blvd 12 1553 V Copenhagen Denmark Fax: 45 33414133. E-mail: ks@gfklaw.dk

SOGG, WILTON SHERMAN, lawyer; b. Cleve., May 28, 1935; s. Paul P. and Julia (Cahn) S.; m. Saralee Frances Krow, Aug. 12, 1962 (div. July 1975); 1 child, Stephanie; m. Linda Rocker Lehman, Dec. 22, 1979 (div. Dec. 1990); m. Nancy Rosenfield Walsh, June 2, 1991. AB, Dartmouth Coll., 1956; JD, Harvard U., 1959; postgrad., London Grad. Sch. Bus. Studies, 1974-76. Bar: (Ohio) 60, (Fla) 70, (U.S. Tax Ct.) 61, (U.S. Supreme Ct.) 69. Assoc. Gottfried, Ginsberg, Guren & Merritt, 1960-63, ptnr., 1963-70, Guren, Merritt, Feibel, Sogg & Cohen, Cleve., 1970-84; of counsel Hahn, Loeser, Freedheim, Dean and Wellman, 1984-85; ptnr. Hahn Loeser & Parks LLP, 1986-2000; of counsel McCarthy, Lebit, Crystal & Haiman Co., 2001—. Trustee, pres. Cleve. Jewish News; adj. prof. Cleve. State Law Sch., 1960—; lectr. Harvard U. Law Sch., 1978-80. Author: (with Howard M. Rossen) new and rev. vols. of Smith's Review Legal Gems series, 1969—; editor: Harvard Law Rev.; contbr. articles to profl. jours. Trustee Jewish Cmty. Fedn. of Cleve., 1966-72; bd. overseers Cleveland Marshall Coll. Law, Cleve. State U., 1969—, vis. com. Coll. Bus. Adminstrn., 1996-00; mem. U.S. and State of Ohio Holocaust commns. Fulbright fellow U. London, 1959-60. Mem. Ohio Bar Assn., Fla. Bar Assn., Germany Philatelic Soc., Oakwood Club, Union Club, Chagrin Valley Hunt, Phi Beta Kappa. General corporate, Estate planning, Taxation, general. Home: PO Box 278 Gates Mills OH 44040-0278 Office: McCarthy Lebit Crystal & Haiman 1800 Midland Bldg 101 W Prospect Ave Cleveland OH 44115-1088 E-mail: wss@mccarthylebit.com

SOIFER, AVIAM, educator, former university dean; b. Worcester, Mass., Mar. 18, 1948; married; 2 children. BA cum laude, Yale U., 1969, MA in Urban Studies, JD, Yale U., 1972. Bar: Conn. 1974, U.S. Dist. Ct. Conn. 1974, U.S. Supreme Ct. 1994. Law clk. to Judge Jon O. Newman U.S. Dist. Ct. Conn., 1972-73; asst. prof. U. Conn. Sch. Law, 1976-77, assoc. prof., 1977-78, prof., 1978-80, Boston U. Sch. Law, 1980-93, 98—; dean Boston Coll. Law Sch., 1993-98. Vis. prof. Boston U. Sch. Law, 1979-80. Author: Law the the Company We Keep, 1995; contbr. numerous articles to profl. jours. Vice chair Supreme Jud. Ct. Mass. Task Force on Jud. Edn., 1996—; mem. steering com. 1st Cir. Task Force on Gender, Race and Ethnicity, 1995-99; bd. trustees New Eng. Med. Ctr., 1997—. Harvard Program in Law and Humanities fellow, 1976-77; Kellog Nat. fellow, 1981-84. Mem. ABA (commn. on coll. and univ. legal studies 1996—0. Office: Boston Coll Law Sch 885 Centre St Newton Center MA 02459-1148

SOKAL, ALLEN MARCEL, lawyer; b. Phila., Dec. 17, 1946; s. Michael Rudolf and Olga (Pories) S.; m. Judith Ann Berkowitz, May 25, 1968; children— Michelle Paula, Shira Hermine. B.S. in Chem. Engring., U. Pa., 1968; J.D., Georgetown U., 1972. Bar: Va. 1973, U.S. Patent and Trademark Office 1973, D.C. 1974, U.S. Dist. Ct. (D.C. dist.) 1978, U.S. Ct. Appeals (fed. cir.) 1982, U.S. Supreme Ct. 1987. Patent examiner U.S. Patent Office, Washington, 1968-73; assoc. Sughrue, Rothwell Mion, Zinn & Macpeak, Washington, 1973-74; tech. adviser, law clk. U.S. Ct. Customs and Patent Appeals, Washington, 1974-76; assoc. Finnegan, Henderson, Farabow, Garrett & Dunner, 1976-82, ptnr., 1982— . Contbr. articles to profl. jours. Recipient spl. achievement award U.S. Patent Office, 1970, 71, 72. Mem. D.C. Bar (vice chmn. patent, trademark and copyright div. 1983-84, chmn. 1984-85), Am. Patent Law Assn. (chmn. current ct. cases subcom. of chem. practice com. 1979-81), Assn. Former Ct. Customs and Patent Appeals Law Clks. and Tech. Advisors (sec. 1980), ABA, Bar Assn. D.C., Va. State Bar, Tau Beta Pi, Phi Lambda Upsilon. Democrat. Jewish. Intellectual property, Patent, Trademark and copyright. Home: 10317 Gainsborough Rd Rockville MD 20854-4041 Office: Finnegan Henderson Farabow Garrett & Dunner 1300 I St NW Ste 700 Washington DC 20005-3314

SOKOL, LARRY NIDES, lawyer, educator; b. Dayton, Ohio, Sept. 28, 1946; s. Boris Franklin and Kathryn (Konowitch) S.; m. Beverly Butler, Aug. 3, 1975; children: Addie Teller, Maxwell Philip. BA, U. Pa., 1968; JD, Case Western Res. U., 1971. Bar: Oreg. 1972, U.S. Dist Ct. Oreg. 1972, U.S. Ct. Appeals (9th cir.) 1973, U.S. Supreme Ct. 1980. Law clk. chief judge Oreg. Ct. Appeals, Salem, 1971-72; pvt. practice Portland, Oreg., 1972—; prof. law Lewis and Clark Law Sch. Adj. prof. law sch. environ. litigation Lewis & Clark U., 1984— Commr. planning City of Lake Oswego, Oreg., 1981-84. Sgt. USAR, 1968-74. Mem. Oreg. State Bar Assn. (chmn. litigation sect. 1983, disciplinary rev. bd. 1982-85), Oreg. Trial Lawyers Assn. Democrat. Jewish. Avocations: running, swimming, squash, model trains, scuba diving. Environmental, Personal injury. Office: 735 SW 1st Ave Portland OR 97204-3326

SOKOLOV, RICHARD SAUL, real estate company executive; b. Phila., Dec. 7, 1949; s. Morris and Estelle Rita (Steinberg) S.; m. Susan Barbara Saltzman, Aug. 13, 1972; children: Lisa, Anne, Kate. BA, Pa. State U., 1971; JD, Georgetown U., 1974. Assoc. Weinberg & Green, Balt., 1974-80, ptnr., 1980-82; v.p., gen. counsel The Edward J. DeBartolo Corp., Youngstown, Ohio, 1982-86, sr. v.p. devel., gen. coun., 1986-94; pres., CEO DeBartolo Realty Corp., 1994-96; pres., COO Simon DeBartolo Group, Indpls., 1996-98; pres, COO Simon Property Group, 1998—. Mem. investment com. Jewish Fedn., Youngstown, 1992—; trustee U. Wis.-Madison Ctr. for Urban Land Econs. Rsch., Youngstown/Mahoning Valley United Way. Alumni fellow Pa. State U., 2000. Mem. Internat. Coun. Shopping Ctrs. (trustee 1994—, chmn. 1998-99), Urban Land Inst. (assoc.). Office: Simon Property Group 115 W Washington St Ste 1465 Indianapolis IN 46204-3464

SOKOLOW, LLOYD BRUCE, lawyer, psychotherapist; b. N.Y.C., Nov. 3, 1949; s. Edwin Jay and Harriet (Corman) S.; m. Christina Carol Smolinski, Jan. 27, 1979; children: Joshua, Jessica. BA, U. Buffalo, 1971, MS, 1974, JD, 1978, PhD, 1979. Bar: U.S. Dist. Ct. (we. dist.) N.Y. 1979, Conn. 1985, U.S. Dist. Ct. Conn. 1986. Rsch. scientist Rsch. Inst. on Alcoholism, Buffalo, 1976-80; legal cons. N.Y. Gov.'s Task Force on Drinking and Driving, Albany, 1979-82; pvt. practice Schenectady, N.Y., 1980-2001; counsel, exec. dir. Conifer Park, Scotia, 1981-83; counsel, dir. substance abuse svcs. Inst. of Living, Hartford, Conn., 1984-86; founder, exec. dir. Lifestart Health Svcs., 1986—. Atty. Town of Knox, N.Y., 1980-92. Bd. dirs. Schenectady Community Svc. Bd., 1982-89, pres. 1989; dir. addictions State of Md., 1988-89; mem. Surrogate Decision Making Commn., 1990-2001, N.Y. Commn. on Quality of Care; counsel Apogee, Inc., 1996-99. Regent scholar NY State, 1967; Univ. fellow U. Buffalo, 1973, Baldy Law fellow, 1979. Mem. APA. Family and matrimonial, Health, Real property. Home: 2183 Grand Blvd Niskayuna NY 12309-5843 Office: 1356 Union St Schenectady NY 12308-3018 E-mail: 1pilot@aol.com

SOLAN, LAWRENCE MICHAEL, lawyer; b. N.Y.C., May 7, 1952; s. Harold Allen and Shirley (Smith) S.; m. Anita Lois Rush, Mar. 27, 1982; children: Renata, David. BA, Brandeis U., 1974; PhD, U. Mass., 1978; JD, Harvard U., 1982. Bar: N.J. 1982, N.Y. 1984. Law clk. to Hon. Pollock Supreme Ct. N.J., Morristown, 1982-83; assoc. Orans, Elsen & Lupert, N.Y.C., 1983-89, ptnr., 1989-96; assoc. prof. law Bklyn. Law Sch., 1996-2000, prof. law, 2000—. Vis. assoc. prof. Princeton U., 1999-2000; bd. dirs. Internat. Acad. Law and Mental Health. Author: The Language of Judges, 1993, Pronominal Reference, 1983. Mem. Assn. of Bar of City of N.Y., Phi Beta Kappa. Home: 163 Ralston Ave South Orange NJ 07079-2344 Office: Bklyn Law Sch 250 Joralemon St Brooklyn NY 11201-3700

SOLANO, CARL ANTHONY, lawyer; b. Pittston, Pa., Mar. 26, 1951; s. Nick D. and Catherine A. (Occhiato) S; m. Nancy M. Solano, 1989; children: Melanie A., Carla Nicole. BS magna cum laude, U. Scranton, 1973; JD cum laude, Villanova U., 1976. Bar: Pa. 1976, U.S. Dist. Ct. (ea. dist.) Pa. 1978, U.S. Ct. Appeals (3rd cir.) 1980, U.S. Ct. Appeals (5th cir.) 1981, U.S. Supreme Ct. 1982, U.S. Ct. Appeals (9th cir.) 1986, U.S. Dist. Ct. (mid. dist.) Pa. 1988, U.S. Ct. Appeals (6th cir.) 1988, U.S. Ct. Appeals (Fed. cir.) 1989, U.S. Ct. Appeals (7th cir.) 1996. Law clerk Hon. Alfred L. Luongo U.S. Dist. Ct., Ea. Dist. Pa., Phila., 1976-78; assoc. Schnader, Harrison, Segal & Lewis, Phila., 1978-84, ptnr., 1985—. adj. prof. Villanova U. Sch. Law, 1999. Mem. ABA, Am. Law Inst., Pa. Bar Assn. (statutory law com. 1980-95), Phila. Bar Assn., St. Thomas More Soc., Justinian Soc., Order of Coif, Pi Gamma Mu. Roman Catholic. Appellate, Communications, Libel. Home: 5 Barrister Ct Haverford PA 19041-1137 Office: Schnader Harrison Segal & Lewis LLP 1600 Market St Ste 3600 Philadelphia PA 19103-7287

SOLANO, HENRY L. lawyer; m. Janine Solano; children: Mateo, Amalia, Guadalupe. BS in Mech. Engring., U. Denver; JD, U. Colo.; LLD (hon.), U. Denver. Asst. atty. gen. Human Resources divsn. Colo. Dept. Law, 1977-82; asst. U.S. atty. Dist. Colo., 1982-87; U.S. atty. for Colo. U.S. Dept. Justice, Denver, 1994-98; solicitor U.S. Dept. Labor, Washington, 1998-2001; ptnr. LeBoeuf, Lamb, Greene & MacRae L.L.P., Denver, 2001—. Exec. dir. Colo. Dept. Instns., 1987-91, Colo. Dept. Regulatory Agys., 1987; acting exec. dir. Colo. Dept. Corrections, 1989-90; chair Cabinet Coun. on Families and Children, 1990-91; mem. adv. com. U.S. Atty. Gen., 1994-95; lectr. Kennedy Sch. Govt. Bd. dirs. Nat. Latino Children's Inst., Mex.Am. Legal Def. Edn. Fund, Denver Housing Authority, Denver Women's Commn., Colo. Dept. Social Svcs., Colo. Transit Constrn. Authority, Regional Transit Dist. , Labor, Pension, profit-sharing, and employee benefits, Legislative. Office: LeBoeuf Lamb Greene & MacRae 633 17th St Ste 2000 Denver CO 80202

SOLBERG, NORMAN ROBERT, lawyer; b. Toledo, Aug. 28, 1939; s. Archie Norman and Margaret Jane (Olsen) S.; m. Megumi; children: Eric Norman, Anne Olsen, Robert Charles Kenneth. BA, Columbia Coll., 1961; LLB, Columbia U., 1964; postgrad., Parker Sch. Law, 1969. Bar: N.Y. 1964, Mass. 1973, Mo. 1978, Ill. 1984, Japan 1992. Assoc. firm Wickes, Riddell, Bloomer, Jacobi & McGuire, N.Y.C., 1964-69; sr. atty. Gullette Co., Boston, 1969-75; asst. internat. counsel Monsanto Co., St. Louis, 1975-79; sr. staff counsel Household Internat., Inc., Prospect Heights, Ill., 1979-87; v.p., gen. counsel Alberto-Culver Co., Melrose Park, 1987-89; atty. pvt. practice, 1989—. Pvt. practice Solberg Internat. Law Office, Osaka, Japan, 1992—. Mem. ABA (chmn. law dept. mgmt., orgns. and profl. matters, com. corp. counsel 1983-93, chmn. Asia-Pacific law, internat. bus. law com. 1992-93, sect. bus. law), Osaka Bar Assn. Republican. Lutheran. General corporate, Private international, Mergers and acquisitions. Office: Maison D'Or Michino Ste 901 2-31 Kanzakicho Chuo-ku Osaka 540-0016 Japan Fax: 81-6-767-5198. E-mail: solberg@gaiben.com

SOLBERG, THOMAS ALLAN, retired lawyer; b. Parkers Prairie, Minn., Mar. 23, 1933; s. Francis A. and Gladys K. Solberg; m. Alla H. Swanton, June 27, 1981. BBA in Fin., U. Miami, 1956; JD, U. Mich., 1959. Bar: N.Y. 1959, U.S. Dist. Ct. (we. dist.) N.Y. 1959, Mich. 1959, Fla. 1975. Assoc. Harter, Secrest & Emery, Rochester, N.Y., 1959-68, ptnr. NY, 1968—98; ret., 1998. Lectr. Am. Coll. Contbr. articles to legal and profl. publs. Bd. dirs. Rochester Rehab. Ctr. Served with USAFR, 1959-65. Mem. Fla. Bar, Monroe Golf Club. General corporate, Estate planning, Estate taxation.

SOLBERT, PETER OMAR ABERNATHY, lawyer; b. Copenhagen, Mar. 9, 1919; (parents Am. citizens); s. Oscar N. and Elizabeth (Abernathy) S.; m. Deborah Kirk, Sept. 8, 1945. BA, Yale U., 1941; JD, Harvard U., 1948. Bar: N.Y. 1949. Assoc. Davis Polk & Wardwell, N.Y.C., 1948-57, ptnr., 1957-89, sr. counsel, 1989—. Dep. asst. sec. for internat. security affairs U.S. Dept. Def., Washington, 1963-65. Bd. dirs. Ctr. Am. Archaeology, Archaeol. Conservancy, Am. Assn. Internat. Commn. Jurists. Lt. comdr. USNR, 1941-45. Mem. ABA, Am. Fgn. Law Assn., Am. Soc. Internat. Law, Am. Assn. of Internat. Commn. Jurists (bd. dirs.), Internat. Bar Assn., Internat. Law Assn., Union Internat. des Advocats, Assn. of Bar of City of N.Y. Banking, General corporate, Private international. Home: 416 W Neck Rd Huntington NY 11743-1625 Office: Davis Polk & Wardwell 450 Lexington Ave Fl 31 New York NY 10017-3982

SOLERUD, HANS GUNNAR, lawyer; b. Strangnas, Sweden, Aug. 7, 1938; s. Sven Emanuel and Elsa Sofia S.; m. Anita Berit Else-Marie Gustafsson, Sept. 13, 1938. LLM, U. Uppsala, Sweden, 1963. Asst. judge Sollentuna & Farentuna Dist. Ct., Stockholm, 1963-66; sec. The Stockholm C. of C., 1966-68; assoc. Wetter & Swartling, Stockholm, 1968-72; in-house co. atty. AB SKF, Gothenburg, Sweden, 1972-74; ptnr. Carl Swartling, Stockholm, 1974-85; justice Supreme Ct., 1986-97; mem. Law Coun., 1991-93; ptnr. Gernandt & Danielsson, 1997—. Deputy chmn. The Arbitration Inst. Stockholm C. of C., 1986-93, The Securities Coun., Stockholm, 1987-93, The Disciplinary Com. Stockholm Stock Exch., 1993—; chmn. The Info. Practices Com. Swedish Pharm. Industry, Stockholm, 1992-99, Bonus Presskopia, Stockholm, 1996—. Mem. Swedish Bar Assn. (deputy bd. 1985, 99). Antitrust, Alternative dispute resolution, General corporate. Home: Granrotsvagen 9 S-182 46 Enebyberg Sweden Office: Gernandt & Danielsson Nybrogatan 11 S-114 87 Stockholm Sweden Fax: 4686626101. E-mail: hans-gunnar.solerud@gda.se

SOLET, MAXWELL DAVID, lawyer; b. Washington, May 15, 1948; s. Leo and Pearl (Rose) S.; m. Joanne Marie Tolksdorf, Sept. 27, 1970; children: David Marc, Paul Jacob. AB, Harvard U., 1970, JD, 1974. Bar: Mass. 1974, U.S. Tax Ct. 1976, U.S. Ct. Claims 1976, U.S. Supreme Ct. 1976. Assoc. Gaston Snow & Ely Bartlett, Boston, 1974-79, Mintz, Levin, Cohn, Ferris, Glovsky & Popeo, P.C., Boston, 1979-82, ptnr., 1982—. Mem. ABA, Mass. Bar Assn., Boston Bar Assn. (chmn. tax sect. 1987-89), Nat. Assn. Bond Lawyers (mem. steering com. bond atty.'s workshop 1992-95). Taxation, general, State and local taxation. Home: 15 Berkeley St Cambridge MA 02138-3409 Office: Mintz Levin Cohn Ferris Glovsky & Popeo PC One Financial Ctr Boston MA 02111 E-mail: msolet@mintz.com

SOLIS, CARLOS, lawyer; b. Managua, Nicaragua, May 15, 1945; came to U.S., 1952; s. Carlos and Luisa (Serrano) S. BA, U. San Francisco, 1967, JD, 1969. Bar: Calif. 1970, U.S. Dist. Ct. (cen. and no. dists.) Calif. 1970, U.S. Ct. Appeals (9th cir.) 1970, U.S. Dist. Ct. (ea. dist.) Calif. 1972, U.S. Dist. Ct. (so. dist.) Calif. 1973, U.S. Supreme Ct. 1973. Assoc. Kindel & Anderson, Los Angeles, 1976-76, ptnr., 1976-96, Heller Ehrman White & McAuliffe LLP, 1996—. Exec. legal counsel, bd. dirs. internat. student ctr. UCLA, 1976-86, exec. v.p., 1981-86; instr. atty. asst. program UCLA, 1977-79; bd. advisors Los Angeles Internat. Trade Devel. Corp., 1981-87. Assoc. editor U. San Francisco Law Rev., 1968-69; contbr. articles to profl. jours. Bd. dirs. ARC, L.A., 1978-93, 95—, chmn. audit com., 1985-88, bd. advisors, 1993—; bd. dirs. March of Dimes, L.A., 1982-87, L.A. Pub. Theater Found., 1978-81, Young Musicians Found., 1979-80, Boys and Girls Club East L.A., 1986-89; bd. dirs. Am. Diabetes Assn., L.A., 1986-93, chmn., 1989-91, bd. dirs. Calif., 1988-93, chmn., 1992-93, mem. nat. minority initiative task force, 1986-92, bd. dirs. Nat., 1993-95; vice chmn. bd. L.A. United Way, 1982-83, bd. dirs., 1980—, corp. bd. dirs., 1982-96, treas., 1989-93; pres. L.A. Open Golf Found., 1979-80. Recipient Alumni award U. San Francisco, 1969, Province award Phi Delta Phi, 1969. Mem. Los Angeles Jr. Chamber (pres., chmn. bd. dirs. 1980-81, Most Improved com. award 1975, Dir. of Yr. award 1977, Outstanding Bus. Leader award 1980), Assocs. Los Angeles C. of C., Los Angeles Area C. of C. (bd. dirs. 1979-80), U. San Francisco Alumni Assn. (pres. San Gabriel Valley chpt. 1976-80), Latin Am. Ctr. Assocs. (pres. 1980-82, bd. advisors 1980-88), Alpha Sigmu Nu, Phi Delta Phi. Bankruptcy, General civil litigation, Contracts commercial. Home: 201 La Vereda Rd Pasadena CA 91105-1227 Office: Heller Ehrman White & McAuliffe LLP 601 S Figueroa St 40th FL Los Angeles CA 90017-5758 E-mail: csolis@hewn.com

SOLIS, CARLOS EDUARDO, lawyer; b. Fort Worth, Tex., Sept. 14, 1972; s. Jose Luis and Laura Elena S.; m. Theresa C. Solis, Aug. 23, 1997. BBA, U. Tex., 1994; JD, U. Houston, 1997. Bar: Tex., U.S. Dist. Ct. (so. dist.) Tex. Assoc. Meredith, Donnell & Abernathy, Corpus Christi, Tex., 1997, Lindow & Treat, San Antonio, 1997—. Assoc. editor Houston Jour. of International Law, 1996-97. Mem. San Antonio Bar Assn., San Antonio Young Lawyers Assn., Tex. Young Lawyers Assn. Roman Catholic. State civil litigation, Insurance, Personal injury. Office: Lindow & Treat 112 E Pecan Ste 2700 San Antonio TX 78205

SOLIS, LINO A. lawyer, real estate consultant; b. Trujillo, Colon, Honduras, July 22, 1963; came to U.S., 1969; s. Lino and Avelina S.; m. Ginger T. Haynes, Aug. 22, 1992; 1 child, Grant Richard. BA, Howard U., 1993; JD, N.Y. Law Sch., 1996. Bar: N.Y. 1998, Conn. 1998. Dir. bus. and legal affairs The Mecca Group, LLC, N.Y.C., 1998—. Real estate cons. Trea Estates and Enterprises, Inc., N.Y.C., 1998—. Mem. Assn. of the Bar of the City of N.Y., N.Y. County Lawyers Assn., N.Y. State Bar Assn., Conn. Bar Assn. Avocations: reading, traveling. General corporate, Entertainment, Real property. Home: 220 Congress St #4F Brooklyn NY 11201

SOLL, HERBERT D. attorney general of Northern Mariana Islands; b. 1936; BS, U. Denver, 1958, LLB, 1960. Dir. Peace Corps , Rio de Janeiro, Brazil, 1967-70; chief pub. defender Alaska, 1971-75; trust territory pub. defender, 1975-79; dir. criminal prosecution Alaska, 1986-90; dir. Peace Corps, Sao Tome, 1990-93; judge Superior Ct., 1979-86; atty. gen. No. Mariana Islands, Saipan, 2000—. Office: Office Atty Gen PO Box 10007 Adminstrn Bldg Saipan MP 96950 E-mail: acsoll@gtepacifica.net

SOLO, GAIL DIANNE, lawyer; b. Sacramento, Calif., Aug. 29, 1950; d. Myron B. and Betty (Codron) S.; children: Rebecca Joy, Michaela Amy. AB, UCLA, 1972, JD, 1975. Bar: Calif. 1975, U.S. Dist. Ct. (cen. dist.) Calif. 1976, U.S. Dist. Ct. (no. dist.) Calif. 1976. Aide to Senator Robbins, Calif. State Senate, Sacramento, 1975; assoc. McKay & Byrne, Los Angeles, 1976-78, Joseph Shalant Law Corp., Los Angeles, 1978-79; prin. Solo & Baron, Los Angeles, 1979-87; of counsel McKay, Byrne, Graham & Van Dam, Los Angeles, 1987—; co-founder Women's Legal Clinic, Los Angeles, 1979—, Attys. Against Discrimination, Los Angeles, 1981—. Mem. United Jewish Welfare Fund, 1976—, Los Angeles World Affairs Council, 1980—, mem. Am. Jewish Congress Commn. on Law and Social Action; supervising atty. First African Meth. Episcopal-Temple Isaiah Law Project, 1995—. Recipient Outstanding Service award Women's Legal Clinic, 1979. Mem. Am. Judicature Soc., Affiliated Network Exec. Women, Women Lawyers Assn. Los Angeles, Los Angeles County Bar Assn., Consumer Attys. Assn. Los Angeles, Beverly Hills Bar Assn. (women and law com.), NOW. Democrat. Jewish. Labor, Personal injury. Office: McKay Byrne Graham & Van Dam 3250 Wilshire Blvd Ste 603 Los Angeles CA 90010-1578

SOLOMON, ANDREW P. lawyer; b. Newark, 1953; BA, Brown U., 1975; JD, Harvard U., 1984. Bar: N.Y. 1985. With firm Sullivan & Cromwell, N.Y.C. Corporate taxation, Taxation, general. Office: Sullivan & Cromwell 125 Broad St New York NY 10004-2489

SOLOMON, FREDERIC, lawyer; b. Fort Valley, Ga., Aug. 1, 1911; s. Aaron Moses and Mayme (Wice) S.; m. Anita Ostrin, July 4, 1954; children— Andrew Mark, Laurie Ann. B.S. in Physics summa cum laude, U. Ga., 1933, J.D. with honors, 1933. Bar: Ga. 1933, D.C. 1949, U.S. Supreme Ct. 1938. Assoc. Powell, Frazer, Goldstein & Murphy, Atlanta, 1933-34; with Fed. Res. Bd., Washington, 1934-76; spl. counsel Colton and Boykin, Washington, 1976— ; cons. Bur. Budget, Washington, 1947. Contbr. chpts. to books, articles to profl. jours. Served to maj. USMC, 1942-45, col. USMCR. Mem. ABA (chmn. banking com., adminstrv. law sect. 1979-82, vice chmn. internat. and comparative adminstrv. law com. 1984-88), Fed. Bar Assn., Am. Econ. Assn., Phi Beta Kappa, Phi Kappa Phi. Jewish. Club: Gridiron, Sphinx, Woodmont. Home: 7517 Holiday Ter Bethesda MD 20817-6611 Office: Colton & Boykin Ste 600 1025 Thomas Jefferson St NW # 0 Washington DC 20007-5201

SOLOMON, LEWIS DAVID, law educator; b. N.Y.C., Aug. 25, 1941; s. Milton A. and Ruth (Lewis) S.; m. Janet Stern, Mar. 28, 1971; 1 son, Michael Stern. BA, Cornell U., 1963; JD, Yale U., 1966. Bar: N.Y. 1969. Law clk. U.S. Dist. Ct., Wilmington, Del., 1966-67; assoc. Colton, Weissberg, Hartnick & Yamin, N.Y.C., 1968-73; assoc. prof. law U. Mo.-Kansas City Law Sch., 1973-77; prof. law George Washington U. Nat. Law Ctr., Washington, 1977—. Author: Federal Income Taxation: Problems and Materials, 1979; Trusts and Estates: A Basic Course: Problems, Planning and Policy, 1981; Corporations: Law and Policy, Materials and Problems, 1982, Corporate Acquisitions, Mergers and Divestitures, 1983, Tax Planning Strategies, 1985, Taxation of Investments, 1987, 2nd edit., 1994, Problems Cases and Materials on Federal Income Taxation, 1987, Corporations: Law and Policy, Materials and Problems, 4th rev. edit. 1998, Federal Taxation of Estates, Trusts and Gifts: Cases, Problems and

Materials, 1989, Trusts and Estates: Cases, Problems and Materials, 1989, Corporations: Explanations and Examples, 1990, Corporate Finance and Governance, revised edit., 1996, Business Workout Strategies: Tax and Legal Aspects, 1992, Asset Protection Strategies: Tax and Legal Aspects, 1993, Business Contracts: Forms and Tax Analysis, 2nd. edit., 1994, Estate Planning: Complete Guide and Workbook, 1994, Law of Estates, Trusts and Gifts, 1996, Asset Protection Strategies: Tax and Legal Aspects, 2d edit., 2001, others. Carnegie Endowment for Internat. Peace grantee, 1976. Mem. ABA, Phi Beta Kappa. Home: 3720 Alton Pl NW Washington DC 20016-2206 Office: George Washington U Nat Law Ctr 720 20th St NW Washington DC 20052 E-mail: lsolomon@main.nlc.qwu.edu

SOLOMON, MARK RAYMOND, lawyer, educator; b. Pitts., Aug. 23, 1945; s. Louis Isadore and Fern Rhea (Josselson) S. BA, Ohio State U., 1967; MEd, Cleve. State U., 1971; LLM in Taxation, Georgetown U., 1976. Bar: Ohio, Mich., U.S. Dist. Ct. (ea. dist.) Mich., U.S. Ct. Appeals (6th cir.), U.S. Tax Ct., U.S. Ct. Fed. Claims. Tax law specialist corp. tax br. Nat. Office of IRS, 1973-75; assoc. Butzel, Long, Gust Klein & Van Zile, Detroit, 1976-78; dir., v.p. Shatzman & Solomon, P.C., Southfield, Mich., 1978-81; prof., chmn. tax/bus. law dept., dir. MS in Taxation Program Walsh Coll., Troy, 1981—; of counsel Meyer, Kirk, Snyder & Lynch, PLLC, Bloomfield Hills, 1981—. Adj. prof. law U. Detroit, 1977-81. Editor: Cases and Materials on Consolidated Tax Returns, 1978, Cases and Materials on the Application of Legal Principles and Authorities to Federal Tax Law, 1990. Mem. Mich. Bar Assn., Kiwanis (bd. dirs.), Phi Eta Sigma. Avocation: bridge (life master). Estate planning, Corporate taxation, Taxation, general. Home: 2109 Golfview Dr Apt 102 Troy MI 48084-3926 Office: Meyer Kirk Snyder & Lynch PLLC 100 W Long Lake Rd Ste 100 Bloomfield Hills MI 48304-2773 also: Walsh Coll 3838 Livernois Rd Troy MI 48083-5066 E-mail: msolomon@walshcol.edu

SOLOMON, RANDALL LEE, lawyer; b. Dayton, Ohio, June 8, 1948; BA summa cum laude, Wright State U., 1970; JD, Case Western Res. U., 1973. Bar: Ohio 1973, U.S. Dist. Ct. (no. dist.) Ohio 1973, U.S. Ct. Appeals (6th cir.) 1973, U.S. Ct. Appeals (fed. cir.) 1988. Ptnr. Baker & Hostetler, Cleve. Speaker in field. Fellow Am. Coll. Trial Lawyers; mem. ABA (mem. litigation, tort and ins. practice sects., mem. toxic and hazardous substances and environ. law coms.), Ohio State Bar Assn., Cleve. Bar Assn. (chair litigation sect. 1991-92), Nat. Inst. Trial Advocacy (mem. nat. session 1978), Def. Rsch. Inst., Anthony J. Celebrezze Inn. of Ct. (master). General civil litigation, Construction, Environmental. Office: Baker & Hostetler 3200 Nat City Ctr 1900 E 9th St Ste 3200 Cleveland OH 44114-3475 E-mail: rsolomon@bakerlaw.com

SOLOMON, ROBERT H. lawyer; b. Bklyn., Aug. 23, 1958; s. Murray and Mildred (Teger) S.; m. Felicia Irene Smith, June 30, 1985; children: Zachary, Alexander. BS in Econ cum laude, U. Pa., 1979; JD, Duke U., 1982. Bar: N.Y. 1983, U.S. Supreme Ct., U.S. Ct. Internat. Trade, U.S. Dist. Ct. (ea. & so. dists.) N.Y. Assoc. LeBeouf Lamb Leiby & MacRae, N.Y.C., 1982-84, Wofsey Certilman Haft et al, N.Y.C., 1984-87, Zimmer Victor Schwartz et al, N.Y.C., 1987-89; prin. Solomon & Assocs. PLLC, Long Beach, N.Y., 1989—. Arbitrator N.Y. Dist. Ct., Hempstead, 1989—. Trustee Long Beach Bdn. Edn., 1995; pres. Lido Home Civic Assn. David Siegal scholar Duke U., 1980-82, Regents scholar, 1980. Mem. ABA, N.Y. State Bar Assn., Bar Assn. of N.Y.C., Nassau County Bar Assn., Long Beach Lawyers Assn. (pres. 1995-2000), Wharton Club. Avocation: tennis. General civil litigation, Contracts commercial, Finance. Office: 24 E Park Ave Long Beach NY 11561-3504 E-mail: Pennduke@aol.com

SOLOMON, RODNEY JEFF, lawyer; b. Hamilton, Ohio, Apr. 14, 1949; s. Julius Franklin and Justine Paula (Rodney) S.; m. Nancy Griesemer, Oct. 17, 1976; children: Julia, Justin. BA, Amherst Coll., 1971; MPA, Harvard U., 1976, JD, 1979. Bar: Mass. 1979, D.C. 1979, U.S. Dist. Ct. Mass. 1988. Legis. asst. Office of sen. Robert Taft Jr., Washington, 1971-76; legal asst. Cambridge-Somerville Legal Svcs., Cambridge, Mass., 1977-78; cons. Mayor's Office Cmty. Devel., Chelsea, 1977-78; assoc. Caplar & Bok, Boston, 1978; spl. counsel Mass. Housing Fin. Agy., 1979-80; acting asst. adminstr. planning and redevel. Boston Housing Authority, 1980-81, spl. counsel to receiver, dir. spl. projects, 1980-83, from acting gen. counsel to gen. counsel, 1983-92; from dep. exec. dir. to acting exec. dir. Housing Authority City of Atlanta, 1992-94; dir. spl. actions Office Pub. and Indian Housing/U.S. Dept. HUD, Washington, 1994-96, sr. dir. policy and legislation, 1996-99; dep. asst. sec. for policy, program and legis. initiatives U.S. Dept. HUD, 1999—. Mem. staff distressed properties com. Coun. Large Pub. Housing Authorities, Washington, 1990-94; mem. Housing Working Group, Pres.'s Commn. on Model State Drug Laws, 1992. Author reports, legislation in field. Bd. dirs. Midnight Basketball League of Atlanta, Inc. Recipient Friend of Coun. of Large Pub. Housing Authorities award (nat. legis.), 1991, Proclamation by Mayor of City of Boston of "Rod Solomon Day", June 18, 1992; citations for svc. to Boston's Pub. Housing Residents, Mass. Senate and Ho. of Reps., 1992; recognition of assistance provided on Housing and Community Devel. Act of 1992, U.S. Senate Banking, Housing and Urban Affairs Com., 1992, Coun. of Large Pub. HousingAuthorities, 1999, others. Mem. Mass. Bar Assn., D.C. Bar. Office: US Dept Housing Urban Devel 451 7th St SW Washington DC 20410-0001

SOLOMON, STEPHEN L. lawyer; b. N.Y.C., Aug. 15, 1942; s. Sam and Ruth (Goldblum) S.; m. Regina Fisher, Aug. 14, 1969; children: Todd, Lisa. AB, Columbia Coll., 1964; LLB, NYU, 1967. Bar: N.Y. 1967, U.S. Dist. Ct. (so. and ea. dists.) 1969, U.S. Ct. Customs 1970, U.S. Supreme Ct. 1975. Assoc. Burns, Jackson, Summit, N.Y.C., 1969-74; ptnr. Miller, Singer, Michaelson & Raives, 1974-79; ptnr., pres. Jarblum, Solomon & Fornari, PC, 1979-97; ptnr. Rubin Baum LLP, 1997—. Contbr. articles to profl. jours. Active Com. on Philanthropic Orgns., N.Y.C., 1980-83; bd. dirs. Emanu-El Midtown YM/YWHA, N.Y.C., 1979-85, Columbia Coll. Alumni Assn., 1995—. Mem. Assn. Bar City of N.Y. Democrat. General corporate, Real property, Non-profit and tax-exempt organizations. Home: 40 Fifth Ave New York NY 10011-8843 Office: Rubin Baum LLP 30 Rockefeller Plz Fl 29 New York NY 10112-0093

SOLOWAY, DANIEL MARK, lawyer; b. Buffalo, Jan. 21, 1959; s. Sol Murray and Shirley (Prashker) S.; m. Natalie Ann-Marie Chin, June 10, 1989; children: Rachel Ann, Rebecca Leigh. BA cum laude, SUNY, Buffalo, 1982; JD with honors, Fla. State U., 1985. Bar: Fla. 1985, U.S. Dist. Ct. (no. dist.) Fla. 1985, (mid. dist.) Fla. 1995, (so. dist.) Ala. 1986, U.S. Ct. Appeals (11th cir.) 1985, U.S. Supreme Ct. 1989; bd. cert. in civil trial law, Fla.; cert. Nat. Bd. Trial Advocacy, 1998, civil ct. mediator, 2000. Law clk. Circuit Judge, Tallahassee, 1983-84, Douglass, Davey, Cooper & Coppins, Tallahassee, 1984-85; ptnr. McKenzie & Soloway, Pensacola, Fla., 1985-98; pvt. practice Daniel M. Soloway, P.A., 1998—. Author: Criminal Justice: An Analysis Toward Reform, 1981; contbr. articles to profl. jours.; editor Escambia-Santa Rosa Bar Assn. newsletter, 1989-90, Dry Shoes, Fla. Bar Jour., 1992. Profl. adv. bd. N.W. Fla. Epilepsy Soc., Pensacola, 1989—; speaker on AIDS, State of Fla. Dept. HRS, 1988—; active Escambia County Human Rels. Commn., 1996-98. Recipient Pro Bono Svc. award Escambia-Santa Rosa Bar, 1989-90, Pro Bono Svc. Pres.'s award Fla. Bar, 1990. Mem. Million Dollar Advocates Forum (diplomat), ABA, Assn. Trial Lawyers Am., Escambia-Santa Rosa Bar Assn. (editor newsletter 1989-90), Acad. Fla. Trial Lawyers (speaker 1993—), Nat. Orgn. Social Security Claimants Reps.. Democrat. Jewish. Avocation: writing. Civil rights, General civil litigation, Personal injury. Office: 901 Scenic Hwy Pensacola FL 32503-6866

SOMACH, RICHARD BRENT, lawyer; b. Allentown, Pa., Mar. 29, 1950; s. Lawrence and Lillian R. (Siegelbaum) S.; m. Lynda Weiss, June 8, 1980; children: Samantha Hetti, Jennifer Leigh. BA, Lehigh U., 1971; JD, Hofstra U., 1974. Bar: Pa. 1974, U.S. Dist. Ct. (ea. and mid. dists.) Pa. 1975, U.S. Supreme Ct. 1978. Law clk. Lehigh County Ct. Common Pleas, Allentown, 1974-75; pvt. practice, 1975-80; ptnr. Somach & VanGilder, 1980-98, Somach & Wester, Allentown, 1998—. Solicitor Lehigh County Sheriff's Office, Allentown, 1976-84, 96—, asst. solicitor, 1995—. Mem. Pa. Bar Assn., Lehigh County Bar Assn. (bd. dirs. 1979-94, pres. 1992). Contracts commercial, General practice, Real property. Home: 951 Robin Hood Dr Allentown PA 18103-2938 Office: Somach & Wester Law Offices 1132 W Hamilton St Allentown PA 18101-1025

SOMER, STANLEY JEROME, lawyer; b. N.Y.C., Oct. 29, 1943; s. David Meyer and Rose (Bleifeld) S.; children: Penny Lynn, Andrew Michael; m. Batia Lebhar, Sept. 13, 1987. BBA in Acctg., Hofstra U., 1966; JD, New York Law Sch., 1969. Bar: N.Y. 1970, U.S. Dist. Ct. (ea. and so. dists.) N.Y. 1972, U.S. Tax Ct. 1983. Assoc. Halpin, Keough & St. John, N.Y.C., 1970-71, Bodenstein & Gumson, N.Y.C., 1971-73; counsel Heatherwood Comm., Hauppauge, N.Y., 1973-74; ptnr. Somer & Wand, P.C., Commack and Smithtown, 1974-88, Somer, Wand & Farrell, Commack and Smithtown, 1989-90; sole practice, 1990-98; ptnr. Somer & Heller LLP, Commack, 1999—. Lectr. N.Y. Law Sch., N.Y.C., 1970-73, Income Property Cons., Huntington, N.Y., 1976-85. Commiteeman Suffolk Reps., East Northport, N.Y., 1978. Mem. N.Y. State Bar Assn., Suffolk Bar Assn., Comm. Assoc. Inst., L.I. Builders Inst. Lodge: Lions (pres. East Northport chpt. 1977-78). General practice, Landlord-tenant, Real property. Office: Somer & Heller LLP 2171 Jericho Tpke Ste 350 Commack NY 11725-2947

SOMER-GREIF, PENNY LYNN, lawyer; b. New Hyde Park, N.Y., Mar. 30, 1970; d. Stanley Jerome and Janice Somer; m. Brian Scott Greif. BS, SUNY, Binghamton, 1992; JD, Am. U., 1995. Bar: N.J. 1996, N.Y. 1996, D.C., 2001. Atty.-advisor U.S. SEC, Washington, 1995-2000; assoc. Arnold & Porter, 2000—. Avocations: dancing, reading, exercise. Office: 555 Twelfth NW Washington DC 20004-1206 E-mail: penny@greif.net

SOMERS, CLIFFORD LOUIS, lawyer; b. Portland, Maine, Dec. 27, 1940; s. Norman Louis and Adeline Wilhemina (Witzke) Somers; m. Jennie Sierra Somers; children from previous marriage: Alan Mark, Penelope Lee. BA, U. Fla., Gainsville, 1965, JD, 1967. Bar: Fla 1967, US Ct Mil Appeals 1968, US Dist Ct (mid dist) Fla 1972, cert.: (civil trial lawyer), (mediator). Ptnr. Burton, Somers & Reynolds, Tampa, 1975-77, Miller, McKendree & Somers, Tampa, 1977-85, Miller, McKendree & Somers, Tampa, 1985-89, Somers and Morgan, Tampa, 1989-91, Somers and Assocs., Tampa, 1991-99, Barr, Murman, Tonelli, Slother & Sleet, Tampa, 1999—. Instr law Univ Fla, Gainesville, 1967; secy, treas Chester H Ferguson-Morris S White Inn, Am Inns Ct, 1987—89, pres-elect, 1989—90, pres, 1990—91. Contbr. articles to profl jours. With U.S. Army, 1961—64, Vietnam, capt JAG U.S. Army, 1968—72, mil judge JAG U.S. Army, 1971—72. Mem.: Fla Bar Asn (chmn procedure rules comt 1991—92), Def Research Inst (chmn 2d dist area west coast 1985—95), Am Bd Trial Attys (vpres Tampa chpt 1990—91), Am Legion (comdr Post 278 1975), Brandon Vets Post and Park. Avocations: writing, aerobics, weight lifting. State civil litigation, Insurance, Personal injury. Home: 2517 S Ysabella St Tampa FL 33629 Office: Barr Murman Tonelli Slother & Sleet Ste 1700 201 E Kennedy Blvd Tampa FL 33602-5829 E-mail: csomers@barrmurman.com

SOMERS, FRED LEONARD, JR. lawyer; b. Orange, N.J., July 5, 1936; AB, U. Va., 1958, LLB, 1961. Bar: Va. 1961, Mo. 1963, Ga. 1967, U.S. Tax Ct. 1971, U.S. Supreme Ct. 1978. CEO Fred L. Somers JR., PC, Atlanta, 1970—. Mem. Citizens Adv. Park Com., DeKalb County, Ga., 1969, Citizens Bond Commn. DeKalb County, 1970; chmn. DeKalb County Charter Commn., 1970; vice chmn. DeKalb County Planning Commn., 1971-77; chmn., trustee Callanwolde Found., 1971-83; chmn. Oglethorpe Housing Devel. Authority, De Kalb County, 1974; bd. dirs., pres. Nat. Club Assn., 1982-2000. Author: The Written Management Contract: Comfort for the Club and the Manager, 1987, More About Private Club Buyouts, 1986, Sources of Revenue for Clubs, 1989, Creative Funding for Capital Needs, 1989, A Prolegomenon to a Right of Private Association, 1988, Model Bylaws for the Private Club, 1996, Model Club Rules, 1998, HOw to Effectively Select a Club Operating Entity, 1990, After Portland, What Next?, 1990, Golf Course Development, 1991, Model Golf Rules--A Guide for Clubs, 1998, Changing Your Operating Entity, 1992, Let's G Equity!, 1992, Open or Closed Door?, 1994, Golf Course Liability and Exposures: A Primer for Private Clubs, 1995, Pivot or Perish, 1996, Grass vs. Members: Should Spikeless Shoes be Optional or Mandatory?, 1996, How to Structure a Redeemable Equity Certificate Program, 2000, Private Club Facility Access Issues, 2001. Mem. ABA, Atlanta Bar Assn. Computer, General corporate, Real property. Home: 1015 Oakpointe Pl Atlanta GA 30338-2621 Office: 2 Ravinia Dr Atlanta GA 30346-2104 E-mail: somersf@abanet.org

SOMERS, KRISTINA ELIZABETH, lawyer; b. Derby, Conn., June 6, 1970; d. Robert Milton Somers and Hiroko Akita. BA, Yale U., 1992; JD, Boston Coll., 1995. Bar: Wis. 1995. Law clk. State of Conn.—Legal Rsch., New Haven, 1995-96, Milw. County, Milw., 1997; assoc. Resnick & Assocs., 1997, Michael Best & Friedrich LLP, Milw., 1997—. Office: Michael Best & Friedrich LLP 100 E Wisconsin Ave Ste 3300 Milwaukee WI 53202-4108 Fax: 414-277-0656. E-mail: kesomers@mbf-law.com

SOMERWITZ, HERBERT SAUL, lawyer; b. Bklyn., May 2, 1941; s. Sidney and Esther (Seidenberg) S.; m. Mary Pauline Hubbuch, Sept. 28, 1968; children: Jennifer, Caren, Erica. BA, NYU, 1962, LLB, 1965, LLM, 1966. Bar: N.Y. 1966, U.S. Dist. Ct. (so. dist.) N.Y. 1969, U.S. Ct. Appeals (2d cir.) 1969. Assoc. Miller & Summit, N.Y.C., 1968-70; atty. Port Authority of N.Y. and N.J., 1970-78, asst. chief contract divsn., 1978-93, chief contracts divsn., 1993—. Author: The Peruvian Land Registration System, 1967. Vol. Peace Corps., Lima, Peru, 1966-68. Mem. N.Y. County Lawyers Assn. Home: 9 Arbor Dr Ho Ho Kus NJ 07423-1603 Office: Port Authority of NY and NJ One World Trade Ctr New York NY 10048 E-mail: hsomerwi@panynj.gov

SOMMERFELD, DAVID WILLIAM, lawyer, educator; b. Detroit, Jan. 21, 1942; s. Henry Anthony and Hilda (Diffley) S.; m. Anne Marlaine Toth, June 27, 1964; children: Catherine, David Jr., Michael, Caroline. BS, U. Detroit, 1963; JD, Detroit Coll., 1967. Trust officer Nat. Bank Detroit, 1963-68; tax supr. Ernst & Ernst, Detroit, 1968-73; ptnr. Monaghan, Campbell, LoPrete & McDonald, 1973-77; prof. Detroit Coll., 1977-86; ptnr. Butzel Long, Detroit, 1987—. Lectr. Ind. Soc. CPAs, Indpls., 1980-93, Ohio Soc. CPAs, Columbus, 1987, W.Va. Soc. CPAs, Charleston, 1983-86, 91. Editor Mich. Probate and Trust Law Jour., 1981-83. Named one of Best Lawyers in Am. Woodward/White Inc., 1999-2001. Fellow Am. Coll. of Trust and Estate Counsel; mem. Mich. Bar Assn., Detroit Bar Assn., Am. Inst. CPA's, Mich. Assn. CPA's, Forest Lake Country Club, Detroit Athletic Club. Roman Catholic. Avocations: bowling, spectator sports, gardening. Estate planning, Estate taxation. Office: Butzel Long Ste 200 100 Bloomfield Hills Pkwy Bloomfield Hills MI 48304

SOMMERS, WILLIAM JOHN, JR. lawyer; b. New Orleans, Jan. 1, 1950; s. William John and Frances (Laurie) S.; m. Donna Marie Berthelot, May 22, 1971; children— Tara, Todd. B.A., Loyola U., New Orleans, 1972, J.D., 1975. Bar: La. 1975, U.S. Dist. Ct. (ea. dist.) La. 1976, U.S. Dist. Ct. (mid. dist.) La. 1979, U.S. Dist. Ct. (we. dist.) La. 1981, U.S. Ct. Appeals (5th cir.) 1981, U.S. Ct. Appeals (11th cir.) 1981. Law clk. U.S. Dist. Ct., New Orleans, 1975-77; assoc. firm Christovich & Kearney, New Orleans, 1977-80; counsel Exxon Co. U.S.A., New Orleans, 1980— . Casenote editor Loyola Law Rev., 1975; contbr. articles to profl. publs. Mem. ABA, La. Assn. Def. Counsel. Republican. Roman Catholic. Admiralty, Federal civil litigation, Oil, gas, and mineral. Office: Exxon Co USA PO Box 60626 New Orleans LA 70160-0626

SONDE, THEODORE IRWIN, lawyer; b. N.Y.C., Jan. 7, 1940; s. Martin and Anne (Greenbaum) S.; m. Susan Kolisch, Sept. 10, 1964; children: Andrea Martine, David Ian. BA, CCNY, 1961; LLB, NYU, 1964; LLM, Georgetown U., 1967. Bar: N.Y. 1964, D.C. 1978, U.S. Supreme Ct. With SEC, Washington, 1964-80, asst. gen. counsel Office Gen. Counsel, 1970-74, assoc. dir. divsn. enforcement, 1974-80; dir. Office Enforcement, FERC, 1980-81, mem. Cole, Corette & Abrutyn, 1982-90, Dechert, Price & Rhodes, 1990—. Adj. prof. Georgetown U. Law Sch. 1977-95, George Washington U. Nat. Law Ctr., 1976-82. Contbr. articles to law jours. Federal civil litigation, Securities. Office: Dechert Price & Rhoads 1175 I St NW Washington DC 20005-3913 E-mail: tsonde@dechert.com

SONDERBY, SUSAN PIERSON, federal judge; b. Chgo., May 15, 1947; d. George W. and Shirley L. (Eckstrom) Pierson; m. James A. De Witt, June 14, 1975 (dec. 1978); m. Peter R. Sonderby, Apr. 7, 1990. AA, Joliet (Ill.) Jr. Coll., 1967; BA, U. Ill., 1969; JD, John Marshall Law Sch., 1973. Bar: Ill. 1973, U.S. Dist. Ct. (cen. and so. dists.) Ill. 1978, U.S. Dist. Ct. (no. dist.) Ill. 1984, U.S. Ct. Appeals (7th Cir.) 1984. Assoc. O'Brien, Garrison, Berard, Kusta and De Witt, Joliet, 1973-75, ptnr., 1975-77; asst. atty. gen. consumer protection div., litigation sect. Office of the Atty. Gen., Chgo., 1977-78, asst. atty. gen., chief consumer protection divsn. Springfield, Ill., 1978-83; U.S. trustee for no. dist. Ill. Chgo., 1983-86; judge U.S. Bankruptcy Ct. (no. dist.) Ill., 1986-98, chief fed. bankruptcy judge, 1998—. Adj. faculty De Paul U. Coll. Law, Chgo., 1986; spl. asst. atty. gen., 1972-78; past mem. U.S. Trustee adv. com., consumer adv. coun. Fed. Res. Bd.; past sec. of State Fraudulent I.D. com., Dept. of Ins. Task Force on Improper Claims Practices; former chair pers. rev. bd., mem. task force race and gender bias U.S. Dist. Ct.; jud. conf. planning com. 7th Cir. Jud. Conf.; former mem. Civil Justice Reform Act Adv. Com., Ct. Security com. Mem. Fourth Presbyn. Ch., Art Inst. Chgo.; past mem. Westminster Presbyn. Ch., Chgo. Coun. of Fgn. Rels.; past bd. dirs. Land of Lincoln Coun. Girl Scouts U.S.; past mem. individual guarantors com. Goodman Theatre, Chgo.; past chair clubs and orgns. Sangamon County United Way Capital campaign; past bd. dirs., chair house rules com. and legal subcom. Lake Point Tower; past mem. Family Svc. Ctr., Aid to Retarded Citizens, Henson Robinson Zoo. Fellow Am. Coll. Bankruptcy (circuit admissions com.); mem. Nat. Conf. Bankruptcy Judges (legis. outreach com.), Am. Bankruptcy Inst., Comml. Law League Am. (exec. coun. bankruptcy and insolvency sect., bankrupcty com., past vice chmn. U.S. Trustee Rev. com., edn. com.), 7th Cir. Bar Assn. (former treas.), Fed. Bar Assn. (hon.), Lawyers Club Chgo. (hon.), Nordic Law Club, John Marshall Law Sch. Alumni Assn. (bd. dirs.), Abraham Lincoln Marovitz Inn of Ct. (master, former pres.). Avocations: travel, flying, interior decorating. Office: US Bankruptcy Ct 219 S Dearborn St Ste 638 Chicago IL 60604-1702

SONDOCK, RUBY KLESS, retired judge; b. Apr. 26, 1926; d. Herman Lewis and Celia (Juran) Kless; m. Melvin Adolph Sondock, Apr. 22, 1944; children: Marcia Cohen, Sandra Marcus. AA, Cottey Coll., Nevada, Mo., 1944; BS, U. Houston, 1959, LLB, 1961. Bar: Tex. 1961, U.S. Supreme Ct. 1977. Pvt. practice, Houston, 1961-73, 89—; judge Harris County Ct. Domestic Rels. (312th Dist.), 1973-77, 234th Jud. Dist. Ct., Houston, 1977-82, 83-89; justice Tex. Supreme Ct., Austin, 1982; of counsel Weil Gotshal and Manges, 1989-93, Houston Ctr., 1993—. Mem. ABA, Tex. Bar Assn., Houston Bar Assn., Houston Assn. Women Lawyers, Order of Barons, Phi Theta Phi, Kappa Beta Pi, Phi Kappa Phi, Alpha Epsilon Pi. Address: 550 Westcott #220 Houston TX 77007

SONEGO, IAN G. assistant attorney general; b. Louisville, May 27, 1954; s. Angelo and Zella Mae (Causey) S. BA in Polit. Sci. with high honors, U. Louisville, 1976, JD, 1979. Bar: Ky. 1979, U.S. Dist Ct. (ea. dist.) Ky. 1980, U.S. Dist. Ct. (we. dist.) Ky. 1989, U.S. Ct. Appeals (6th cir.) 1989, U.S. Supreme Ct. 1990. Asst. atty. Office Commonwealth's Atty. Pike County, Pikeville, Ky., 1980, sr. asst. atty., 1988-89; assoc. John Paul Runyon Law Firm, 1981-87; asst. atty. gen. Office Atty. Gen., Frankfort, Ky., 1989—. Lectr. criminal law Ky. Bar Assn., Jenny Wiley Park, 1981, Ky. Prosecutors Confs., 1989, 93; mem. Atty. Gen.'s task force child sexual abuse, 1992-94, Nat. Conf. on Domestic Violence, 1996. Contbg. editor Ky. Prosecuter Newsletter, 1991—. Recipient Kesslman award, U. Louisville, 1975, Bd. trustee award, 1979, Outstanding Prosecutor award, Ky. Atty., Award Outstanding Advocacy, Assn. Govt. Attys. in Capital Litigation, 2001. Mem.: Ky. Commonwealth's Attys. Assn. (hon.; lectr. 1987, 90, chmn. com. ethics 1984—86, bd. dirs. 1983—85, Spl. award 1987). Office: Office Atty Gen Criminal Appellate Divsn 1024 Capital Center Dr Frankfort KY 40601-8204 E-mail: isonego@law.state.ky.us

SONG, BING, lawyer, researcher; b. Changsha, Hunan, China, May 23, 1966; d. Lun Xiao Song and Jing Yun Xue; m. Daniel Albert Bell, May 22, 1964; 1 child, Julien Bell. BA in Law, Beijing U., 1988; MLitt in Internat. Rels., Oxford U., 1991; LLM in Trade Regulation, NYU, 1996. Bar: N.Y. 1996. Rsch. fellow in Chinese law E. Asian Polit. Economy, Singapore, 1991-94; project mgr., grantee Beijing Office Ford Found., 1996-97; assoc. Baker & McKenzie, Hong Kong, 1997-99, Milbank Tweed Hadley & McCloy LLP, Hong Kong, 1999—. Founder, dir. One Country Two Sys. Law Ctr., Hong Kong, 2000—. Editor: U.S. and German Judicial Systems and Processes, 1998, Justice and Economic Development: Distinguished Lecturers Series in Law, 1998; contbr. articles to profl. jours. Mem. N.Y. Bar Assn., Asia Soc., Ctr. E. Asian Studies (hon.). Avocations: swimming, traveling, singing, food. Mergers and acquisitions, Securities.

SONG ONG, ROXANNE KAY, lawyer, judge; b. Phoenix; d. Joe Henry and Sue (Tang) Song; m. Richard H. Ong, Nov. 25, 1978; children: Jocelyn, Bradley. BA, Ariz. State U., 1975; JD, U. Ariz., 1978. Bar: Ariz. 1979, U.S. Dist. Ct. Ariz. 1979, U.S. Ct. Appeals (9th cir.) 1986, U.S. Supreme Ct. 1992. Pvt. practice, Phoenix, 1979, 85—; asst. city prosecutor Phoenix City Prosecutor's Office, 1979-82; asst. city prosecutor, asst. city atty. Scottsdale (Ariz.) City Atty.'s Office, 1982-85; pro tempore judge Scottsdale City Ct., 1986-89; assoc. city judge City of Scottsdale, 1989-91; mcpl. ct. judge City of Phoenix, 1991-2001; asst. presiding judge The Phoenix Mcpl. Ct., 2001—. Mem. Ariz. Supreme Ct.'s Commn. on Minorities, adv. com. on Judicial Ethics; vice chair of Ariz. Supreme Ct. Com. on Judicial Edn. and Tng. Former mem. community adv. bd. Sta. KAET-TV, Tempe, Ariz; mem. First Chinese Bapt. Ch., Scottsdale Leadership Class V, Valley Leadership Class XV; mem. exec. bd. Ariz. So. Bapt. Conv.; co-leader Ariz. Cactus Pine troop Girl Scouts/Brownies; former mem. parent adv. bd. Paradise Valley/Scottsdale YMCA; bd. dirs. Ariz. Bapt. Children's Svcs., Inst. Cultural Diversity; mem. commn. on minorities, adv. com. on jud. ethics, vice chair com. on jud. edn. and tng., Ariz. Supreme Ct. Recipient Law Related to Edn. award Ariz. Bar Found., 1999; named among 100 Outstanding Women and Minorities, Maricopa County Bar Assn. and Ariz. State Bar. Mem. ABA, Maricopa County Bar Assn., Christian Legal Soc., Ariz. Women Lawyers Assn., Am. Judges Assn., Nat. Assn. Women Judges, Ariz. Magistrates Assn., Ariz. Cts. Assn., U. Ariz. Law Coll. Assn., Phi Delta Phi, Phi Kappa Phi, Alpha Lambda Delta, Kappa Delta Phi, Pi Lambda Theta. Republican. Avocations: music, sports. E-mila. Criminal, Immigration, naturalization, and customs. Office: Phoenix Mcpl Ct 300 W Washington St # 607 Phoenix AZ 85003-2103 E-mail: roxann.songong@azbar.org

SORENSEN, HARVEY R. lawyer; b. Chgo., Nov. 3, 1947; s. Harvey T. and Jean Louise (Cline) S.; m. Emily Smith, May 31, 1969 (div. May 1980); children: Abigail, Jeanne, Cornelia; m. Stephanie Sorensen, Dec. 31, 1980; 1 child, Tyler. BA, Beloit Coll., 1969; MSBA, Boston U., 1972; JD cum laude, Northwestern U., 1974. Bar: Wis. 1974, U.S. DISt. Ct. (ea. dist.) Wis. 1974, U.S. Dist. Ct. Kans., U.S. Tax Ct., 1975. Tax acct. Arthur, Young & Co., Chgo., 1974; assoc. Whyte & Hirschboeck, Milw., 1974-75; asst. adj. prof. Wichita (Kans.) State U. Sch. Bus., 1979; ptnr. Foulston & Siefkin, Wichita, 1975—. Trustee, vice chmn. Kans. Pub. Telecom. Svc., 1978-97, chmn., 1997-99; chmn. Wichita Downtown Devel. Corp., 1996—, City of Wichita Self Supporting Mcpl. Improvement Dist., 2001—; project bus. cons. Jr. Achievement, 1978-93; trustee Wichita Symphony Soc., 1986-96, Wichita Collegiate Sch., 1994—, Wichita Sedgewick County Hist. Mus., 1986-89, Wichita Arts Coun., 1979-82, Goodwill Industries/Easter Seals of Kans. Area, 2001—; commr. City of Eastborough, Kans., 1991-93; bd. cmty. advisors KMUW, 1981-82; treas. St. James Episcopal Ch., 1996-99. With U.S. Army, 1970-72. Fellow Am. Coll. Tax Counsel; mem. ABA, Wichita Bar Assn., Kans. Bar Assn. (past sect., v.p., pres. tax. sect. 1984-88), Attys. for Family Held Enterprises, Wichita Area C. of C. (bd. dirs. 2000—), Rotary. Republican. Episcopalian. Corporate taxation, Estate taxation, Taxation, general. Home: 13 Colonial Ct Wichita KS 67207-1056 Office: Foulston & Siefkin 700 Nations Bank Fin Ctr Wichita KS 67202-2207

SORETT, STEPHEN MICHAEL, lawyer, educator; b. Newark, May 2, 1949; s. Louis and Felice (Hoch) S.; m. Karen Ann Maris, Mar. 17, 1978. BA, Yale U., 1971; JD, George Washington U., 1976. Bar: Md. 1976, D.C. 1977, U.S. Dist. Ct. D.C. 1977, U.S. Claims Ct. 1977, U.S. Supreme Ct. 1979. Atty., advisor GAO, Washington, 1976-80; sr. atty. EPA, 1980-83; mgr. govt. contracts and grants, nat. coord. privatization & infrastructure svcs. Touche Ross & Co., 1983-86; dep. gen. counsel AAI Corp., Balt., 1986-90, dir., legal and asst. sec., 1991-93; v.p. contracts, asst. gen. counsel ICF Internat., Inc., 1993-94; dir. govt. contracts program Nat. Law Ctr./George Washington U., Washington, 1994-95; dir. govt. contract svcs. Grant Thornton LLP, 1995-2000; counsel Reed Smith LLP, Washington, 2000—. V.p. Privatization Coun., N.Y.C., 1984—; professorial lectr. Am. U. Kogod Sch. Bus., 1982-85. Author: (with others) Federal Grant Law, 1979, Privatization, 1988; editor (newsletter) Forum, 1982-83; contbr. articles to profl. jours. Treas. Greater Colesville Citizens Assn., Silver Spring, Md., 1982-84. Mem. ABA (chmn. fed. grants and contracts com. 1981-82, vice-chmn. environ. values com. 1985-92, vice-chmn. R & D com. 1988-92, vice-chmn. privatization and outsourcing com. 1996—), Fed. Bar Assn. (chmn. fed. grants com. 1982-88, bd. dirs. D.C. chpt. 1982-86, Disting. Svc. award 1983), Nat. Security Indsl. Assn. (environ. steering com. 1990—, procurement policy com. 1991—), Yale Club (Washington). General corporate, Environmental, Government contracts and claims. Home: 11512 W Hill Dr Rockville MD 20852-3749 Office: Reed Smith LLP 11th Fl 1301 K St NW East Tower Washington DC 20005 E-mail: kam1@erols.com, ssorett@reedsmith.com

SORKIN, LAURENCE TRUMAN, lawyer; b. Bklyn., Oct. 20, 1942; s. Sidney and Lilly (Kowensky) S.; m. Joan Carol Ross, June 25, 1972; children: Andrew Ross, Suzanne Ross. AB summa cum laude, Brown U., 1964; LLB, Yale U., 1967; LLM, London Sch. Econs./Polit. Sci., 1968. Law clk. to Judge J. Joseph Smith U.S. Ct. Appeals (2d cir.), 1968-69; assoc. Cahill Gordon & Reindel, N.Y.C., 1969-75, ptnr., 1975—. Vis. lectr. Yale U., 1972, 73; lectr. various profl. orgns.; rsch. asst. to Lester and Bindman for book Race and Law in Great Britain, 1972. Contbr. to State Antitrust Law (Lifland), 1984; author: (with Lifland, Sorkin and Van Cise) Understanding the Antitrust Laws, 1986. Bd. dirs. Legal Aid Soc., N.Y.C., 1988-94, N.Y. Lawyers for Pub. Interest, 1990-93. Fulbright scholar, 1967-68. Mem. ABA (antitrust law sect. 1978—), N.Y. State Bar Assn. (antitrust sect., chmn. com. on legislation 1978-79, sect. sec. 1979-80, chmn. com. on mergers 1987-89, chmn. Clayton Act com. 1989-94, exec. com. 1989-94, comml. and fed. litigation sect. chmn. com. antitrust 1996-98), Assn. Bar City N.Y. (mem. com. trade regulation 1974-77, 95-98, com. on electric funds transfer 1979-80), Yale Law Sch. Assn. (exec. com. 2000—), Phi Beta Kappa. Administrative and regulatory, Antitrust, Federal civil litigation. Office: Cahill Gordon & Reindel 80 Pine St Fl 17 New York NY 10005-1790 E-mail: lsorkin@cahill.com

SORKIN, SAUL, lawyer; b. N.Y.C., June 24, 1925; s. Samuel and Paulene Sorkin; m. Ellen Weinberg, June 24, 1956; children: David J., Richard E., John E. BA, Bklyn. Coll., 1948; JD, Harvard U., 1951. Bar: N.Y., U.S. Dist. Ct. (so. and ea. dists.) N.Y., U.S. Ct. Appeals (2d cir.), U.S. Supreme Ct. Spl. atty., atty. gen. N.Y. State Dept. Law, N.Y.C., 1991-93; assoc. Newman, Aronsen & Newmann, 1993-94; pvt. practice; ptnr. Kroll & Trouct; of counsel Furman & Del Corp., Great Neck, N.Y. Sgt. U.S. Army, 1993-96. Office: Furman and Del Corp PC 11 Grace Ave Great Neck NY

SOROKIN, ETHEL SILVER, lawyer; b. Hartford, Conn., 1928; d. Jacob M. and Jennie (Klein) Silver; m. Milton Sorokin, June 25, 1950; children: Rachel B., Sharon L., Leo T. BA, Vassar Coll., 1950; LLB with honors, U. Conn., 1953. Bar: Conn. 1953, U.S. Dist. Ct. Conn. 1955, U.S. Ct. Appeals (2d cir.), U.S. Supreme Ct. 1960. Assoc. Levine & Katz, Hartford, Conn., 1953-56; ptnr. Sorokin & Sorokin, 1956-89, Sorokin, Gross & Hyde PC, Hartford, 1989-93, of counsel, 1994—. Lectr. law., advisor law rev. U. Conn., 1955-58, 61-66; sec. Conn. Jud. Rev. Council, 1978-92; spkr. in field. Editor-in-chief U. Conn. Law Rev., 1953; mem. editl. bd. Conn. Bar Jour., 1951-56; contbr. articles to profl. jours. Trustee U. Conn. Law Found., Hartford, 1976-92, pres., 1978-79; dir. treas. Ctr. for First Amendment Rights, Inc., 1993-96, pres., 1996—. Mem. ABA (media law com., 1st amendment com.), Conn. Bar Assn. (family law sect., chmn. legis. com. 1984-87, chmn. UMPA study com. 1986, media-law com. 1992—). Office: Pullman & Conley LLC 90 Statehouse Sq Hartford CT 06103

SORRELL, WILLIAM H. state attorney general; b. Burlington, Vt., Mar. 9, 1947; s. Marshal Thomas and Esther Sorrell; m. Mary Alice McKenzie; children: McKenzie, Thomas. AB, U. Notre Dame, 1970; JD, Cornell U., 1974. Dep. state's atty. Chittenden County State of Vt., 1975-77, state's atty. Chittenden County, 1977-78, 89-92; ptnr. McNeil, Murray & Sorrell, 1978-89, sec. adminstrn., 1992-97; atty. gen. State of Vt., 1997—. Pres. United Cerebral Palsy Vt.; sec. Vt. Coalition Handicapped; bd. dirs. Winooski Valley Pk. Dist. Office: Office Atty Gen 109 State St Montpelier VT 05609-0001

SORRELS, RANDALL OWEN, lawyer; b. Va., Dec. 11, 1962; s. Charles Vernon and Marjorie Elaine (Jones) S.; m. Cheryl Ann Casas, June 29, 1985; children: Ashley Michelle, Stephanie Leigh, Darby Nicole, Garrett Ryan. BA in Polit. Sci.and Speech Comm. magna cum laude, Houston Bapt. U., 1984; JD magna cum laude, South Tex. Coll. Law, 1987. Bar: Tex. 1987, U.S. Dist. Ct. (so. dist.) Tex.; bd. cert. in civil trial law and personal injury trial law tex. Bd. Legal Specialization. Assoc. Fulbright & Jaworski, Houston, 1987-90; ptnr. Abraham, Watkins, Nichols, Sorrels, Matthews & Friend, 1990—. Contbr. articles to profl. jours. Fellow Tex. Bar Found. (trustee 1997-2000, sustaining life), Houston Bar Found. , Tex. Bar Found. (sustaining life); mem. ABA, Houston Bar Assn. (v.p. 2000-2001, dir. 1998-2000), Houston Trial Lawyers Found. (pres. 2000-2001), Houston Trial Lawyers Assn. (pres. 1999-2000), Houston Lawyer's Referal Svc. (pres. 2000-2001), State Bar Tex. (dir. 1994-97), Tex. Trial Lawyers Assn. (dir. 1994—), Houston Trial Lawyers Found. (dir. 1998—), Houston Trial Lawyers Assn. (v.p. 1996-98, dir. 1993-96), Am. Bd. Trial Advs. (1997—), Nat. Bd. Trial Advs., Coll. State Bar Tex., Coll. State Bar Tex., Houston Trial Lawyers Found., Houston Bar Assn., Tex. Young Lawyers Assn., Houston Young Lawyers Assn., Assn. Civil Trial and Appellate Specialists, Am. Trial Lawyers Assn., Million Dollar Advs. Forum, Tex. Assn. Def. Counsel (former mem.), Am. Inns of Ct. Insurance, Personal injury, Product liability. Home: 311 Terrace Dr Houston TX 77007-5046 Office: Abraham Watkins Nichols Sorrels Matthews & Friend 800 Commerce St Houston TX 77002-1776

SOSLAND, KARL Z. lawyer; b. Springfield, Mass., Apr. 3, 1933; s. Saul and Bessie (Shub) S.; m. June L. Sosland, Mar. 31, 1975; children: Daniel, Cynthia, Jayne, Rachel, Elizabeth. BA, U. Conn., 1955; LLB, Columbia U., 1959. Bar: N.J. 1960. Assoc. Robert Gruen, Hackensack, N.J., 1960-64, Gruen & Sosland, Hackensack, 1964-65, Scangarella and Sosland, Pompton Plains, 1965-70; pvt. practice Pompton Plains, Paramus, 1970-97, Hackensack, 1997—. Atty. Bd. Adjustment Norwood (N.J.), 1965-74; mcpl. atty. Pequannock Twp., N.J., 1971-80; judge Mcpl. Ct. Pompton Lakes, 1976-78. Active Fairlawn (N.J.) Bd. Edn., 1964-66; pres. Kinnelon (N.J.) Bd. Edn., 1971. Mem. ABA, N.J. Bar Assn., Morris County Bar Assn., Bergen City Bar Assn. State civil litigation, Contracts commercial, Real property. Home: 11 Tecumseh Trl Oakland NJ 07436-2802 Office: Continental Plz 19 Main St Hackensack NJ 07601-7023 E-mail: ksosland@aol.com

SOSMAN, MARTHA B. judge; BA Middlebury Coll, JD U. Mich. Assoc. Foley, Hoag & Eliot, Boston, 1979—84; with U.S. Atty.'s Office, 1984—89; founding ptnr. Kern, Sosman, Hagerty, Roach & Carpenter, 1989—93; apptd. judge Superior Ct., Concord, Mass., 1993; assoc. justice Mass. Supreme Jud. Ct., 2000—. Office: Mass Supreme Jud Ct New Ct House Pemberton Sq Boston MA 02108*

SOSNOV, AMY W(IENER), lawyer; b. Atlantic City; d. Noel J. and Edith C. Wiener; m. Steven R. Sosnov, Aug. 9, 1969; children: Jonathan, Elizabeth. BS, Temple U., 1970; JD, Villanova U., 1973. Bar: Pa 1973. Ptnr. Sosnov & Sosnov, Norristown, Pa., 1973—. Pres. Nat. Coun. Jewish Women, Phila., 1983—, U.M. Meals on Wheels, 1975-76, Wilson Arts Ctr., 1995-99; bd. dirs. Freedom Valley Girl Scouts, 1997-99; pres. Martin S. Wilson, Jr. Ctr. of the Arts, Inc. Recipient Legion of Honor, Chapel of Four Chaplains, Phila., 1978; named Contemporary Women of Honor, Ency. Brit., 1983. Mem. ABA, N.J. Bar Assn., Nat. Assn. Women Lawyers, Pa. Bar Assn., Montgomery County Bar Assn., Hadassah/Kadimah (pres. King of Prussia, Pa. 1980-82). Family and matrimonial, Probate, Non-profit and tax-exempt organizations, Estate planning. Office: Sosnov & Sosnov 540 Swede St Norristown PA 19401-4807 also: 47 N Tallahassee Ave Atlantic City NJ 08401-3333

SOSSAMAN, WILLIAM LYNWOOD, lawyer; b. High Point, N.C., May 30, 1947; s. Robert Allison and Elizabeth Bryce (Hethcox) S.; m. Sandra Clare Ward, June 9, 1973; children: Joana Leslie, David Lynwood. AB, Davidson Coll., 1969; JD, Vanderbilt U., 1972. Bar: Fla. 1972, U.S. Ct. Mil. Appeals 1973, U.S. Dist. Ct. (mid. dist.) Fla. 1977, Tenn. 1978, U.S. Dist. Ct. (we. dist.) Tenn. 1979, U.S. Dist. Ct. (no. dist.) Miss. 1979, U.S. Dist. Ct. (ea. and we. dists.) Ark, 1980, U.S. Dist. Ct. (mid. dist.) Tenn. 1985, U.S. Dist. Ct. (ea. dist.) Mich. 1988, U.S. Ct. Appeals (6th and 8th cirs.) 1989, U.S. Ct. Appeals (11th cir.) 1991. Mktg. resch. analyst First Tenn. Bank, Memphis, 1967-70; assoc. Alley, Rock & Dinkel, Tampa, Orlando and Miami, Fla., 1972-73, Rock & Brown, Orlando, 1976-77, Young & Perl, Memphis, 1978-88; ptnr. Allen, Scruggs, Sossaman, & Thompson, 1988—. Asst. county atty. Shelby County Govt., Memphis, 1978-79; asst. city atty. City of Memphis, 1978-79. Author: Preventing Lawsuits for Wrongful Termination, 1995. N.Am. regional sec. Project Ams., Davidson, N.C., 1967-69. Capt. U.S. Army, 1973-76. Named Hon. City Councilman City of Memphis, 1982. Mem. ABA (labor and employment sect., litigation sect., EEO com.), Fla. Bar (labor and employment law sect.), Mgmt. Counsel Roundtable (chmn. 1986-87), Def. Rsch. Inst. (employment law com.), Tenn. Bar Assn. (labor law sect.), Memphis Bar Assn., The Justice Network (bd. dirs. 1990-93), Poplar Pike Arts Guild (bd. dirs. 1998—). Presbyterian. Federal civil litigation, Labor. Home: 8411 Beaverwood Dr Germantown TN 38138-7641 Office: Allen Scruggs Sossaman & Thompson Brinkley Plz Ste 650 80 Monroe Ave Memphis TN 38103-2481 E-mail: wls@asstlaw.com

SOSTARICH, MARK EDWARD, lawyer; b. Milw., Apr. 10, 1953; s. Edward Michael and Sophia (Hibler) S.; m. Karen Sue Baranek, June 12, 1976; children: Samantha Nicole, Alex Edward. BA with distinction, U. Wis., 1975, JD cum laude, 1978. Bar: Wis. 1978, U.S. Dist. Ct. (ea. and we. dists.) Wis. 1978, U.S. Ct. Appeals (7th cir.) 1988. Assoc. Godfrey & Kahn, Milw., 1978-84, ptnr., 1984-96, Petrie & Stocking SC, Milw., 1997—. Editor-in-chief U. Wis. Law Rev., 1978, mem., 1977. Mem. bd. visitors U. Wis., Madison, 1983-88; commr. South Milwaukee (Wis.) Housing Authority, 1985-86; mem. South Milwaukee Fire and Police Commn., 1986-92, sec., 1987-91, pres., 1991-92; mem. Wis. Elections Bd., 1987-95, vice chmn., 1990, chmn., 1991; chmn. Dem. Party of Wis., 1995-97; mem. platform and resolutions com. Wis. Dem. Com., 1984-86, chmn., 1986-2000, mem. exec. com., mem. adminstrv. com., 1986—, 1st vice chmn., 1993; mem. Assn. State Dem. Chairs, 1995-97; mem. Dem. Nat. Com., 1993, 1995-97; chmn. Milwaukee County Dem. Party, 1986-97, v.p., 2001—; mem., usher, high sch. Sun. sch. tchr., chmn. organ fundraising com. Trinity Luth. Ch., South Milwaukee. Mem. ABA, Wis. Bar Assn., Milw. Bar Assn., Seventh Cir. Ct. Appeals Bar Assn. Avocations: state and local politics, collecting contemporary art. Federal civil litigation, State civil litigation, Criminal. Home: 1785 Tamarack St South Milwaukee WI 53172-1048 Office: Petrie & Stocking SC 111 E Wisconsin Ave #1500 Milwaukee WI 53202

SOTOMAYOR, SONIA, judge; b. N.Y.C., June 25, 1954; d. Juan Luis and Celina (Baez) S.; m. Kevin Edward Noonan, Aug. 14, 1976 (div. 1983). AB, Princeton (N.J.) U., 1976; JD, Yale U., 1979. Bar: N.Y. 1980, U.S. Dist. Ct. (ea. and so. dists.) N.Y. 1984. Asst. dist. atty. Office of Dist. Atty. County of N.Y., N.Y.C., 1979-84; assoc., ptnr. Pavia & Harcourt, 1984-92; fed. judge U.S. Dist. Ct. (so. dist.) N.Y., 1992-98; cir. judge U.S. Ct. Appeals (2nd Cir.), 1998—. Editor Yale U. Law Rev., 1979. Bd. dirs. P.R. Legal Def. and Edn. Fund, N.Y.C., 1980-92, State of N.Y. Mortgage Agy., N.Y.C., 1987-92, N.Y.C. Campaign Fin. Bd., 1988-92; mem. State Adv. Panel on Inter-Group Rels., N.Y.C., 1990-91. Mem. Phi Beta Kappa. Office: US Courthouse 40 Foley SqRm 410 New York NY 10007-1502*

SOULE, ROBERT GROVE, lawyer; b. Boston, Jan. 12, 1958; s. Augustus W. and Mary R. Soule; m. Maura Kelley, Aug. 21, 1982; children: Courtney K., Katherine W., Zachary A. BA, Harvard U., 1979; JD, Suffolk U., 1983. Bar: Mass. 1983, U.S. Dist. Ct. Mass. 1983. Of counsel First Am. Title Ins. Co., Boston, 1982-85, asst. regional counsel, 1985-87; New Eng. states counsel Minn. Title Ins. Co., 1987-89; N.E. regional counsel Old Republic Title Ins. Co., 1989-93; mgr. nat. divsn. Lawyers Title Ins. Corp. (LandAmerica), 1993—. Contbr. articles to profl. jours., chpts. to books. Mem. Am. Land Title Assn., New Eng. Land Title Assn. (bd. dirs. 1996—, pres. 1999—), Mass. Conveyancers Assn. (title standards com. 1987—, exec. com. 1989-92), Mass. Bar Assn. Real property. Office: LandAmerica One Washington Mall Boston MA 02108-2804 Fax: 617-619-4848. E-mail: rsoule@landam.com

SOUTENDIJK, DIRK RUTGER, lawyer, corporate executive; b. Amsterdam, Netherlands, Apr. 13, 1938; came to U.S., 1946, naturalized, 1965; s. Louis Rutger Willem and Hermina C. (Schoonman) S.; m. Mary Tremaine, Dec. 22, 1961; children— Dirk Willem, Gregory Louis. B.A., Yale U., 1960; J.D., Columbia U., 1963. Bar: N.Y. 1966, Pa. 1975. Assoc., Shearman & Sterling, N.Y.C., 1963-68; laywer Westinghouse Electric Co., Pitts., 1968-77; gen. counsel Union Camp Corp., Wayne, N.J., 1977— , v.p. 1978— , sec. 1978— . Bd. dirs. Mid-Atlantic Legal Found., Phila., 1978— . Mem. ABA, Assn. of Bar of City of N.Y. Republican. Congregationalist. Club: Union League (N.Y.C.). Home: 52 Briarcliff Rd Mountain Lakes NJ 07046-1306 Office: Union Camp Corp 6400 Poplar Ave Memphis TN 38197-0100

SOUTER, DAVID HACKETT, United States supreme court justice; b. Melrose, Mass., Sept. 17, 1939; s. Joseph Alexander and Helen Adams (Hackett) S. BA, Harvard U., 1961, LLB, 1966; Rhodes scholar, Oxford U., 1961-63, MA, 1989. Bar: N.H. Assoc. firm Orr & Reno, Concord, 1966-68; asst. atty. gen. N.H., 1968-71; dep. atty. gen., 1971-76; atty. gen., 1976-78; assoc. justice Superior Ct. N.H., 1978-83, N.H. Supreme Ct., 1983-90; judge U.S. Ct. Appeals (1st cir.) N.H., 1990; assoc. justice U.S. Supreme Ct., Washington, 1990—. Trustee Concord Hosp., 1973-85, pres. bd. trustees, 1978-84; bd. overseers Dartmouth Med. Sch., 1981-87. Mem. N.H. Bar Assn., N.H. Hist. Soc. (v.p. 1980-85, trustee 1976-85), Phi Beta Kappa. Republican. Episcopalian.*

SOUTER, SYDNEY SCULL, lawyer; b. Trenton, N.J., June 17, 1931; s. Sydney H. and Josephine (Scull) S.; children: Gifford MacLeod, Julia Elizabeth, Matthew Thomas, Jeffrey James, Michael Andrew. BA, Yale U., 1954, JD, 1959. Bar: Conn. 1959, N.J. 1960. Assoc. Minton, Dinsmore & Bohlinger, Trenton, 1960-62, McCarthy, Bascik & Hicks, Princeton, N.J., 1963-64; ptnr. Baggit, Souter & Stonaker, 1965-66; sr. ptnr. Souter, Scozzari & Steffens, 1966-69, Souter & Kettell, Princeton, 1970-75, Souter & Steffens, Princeton, 1977-80, Souter & Selecky, Princeton, 1980-82, Souter & Morrow, Princeton, 1983-91, Souter and Voliva, Princeton, 1991—. Bd. dirs. Ewing Bank & Trust Co. (counsel 1962-70); pres. The Hamilton Bank (counsel 1971-77). Mcpl. Judge Montgomery Twp., Somerset County, N.J., 1966-68, East Windsor Twp., Mercer County, N.J., 1971-73, Princeton Twp., Mercer County, 1981-89; asst. counsel County of Mercer, Trenton, 1990-91, dep. counsel, 1991-96, 2001—; counsel Mercer County Park Commn., 1996—; state committeeman Rep. Party, 2001—. Mem. ABA, N.J. State Bar Assn., Mercer County Bar Assn., Princeton Bar Assn., Rotary Club Princeton (pres. 1990-91), Kiwanis Club (pres. Princeton 1968). Presbyterian. Administrative and regulatory, General civil litigation, Real property. Office: Souter and Voliva 40 Nassau St Princeton NJ 08542-4522

SOUTHERN, ROBERT ALLEN, lawyer; b. Independence, Mo., July 17, 1930; s. James Allen and Josephine (Ragland) S.; m. Cynthia Agnes Drews, May 17, 1952; children: David D., William A., James M., Kathryn S. O'Brien. B.S. in Polit. Sci., Northwestern U., 1952, LL.B., 1954. Bar: Ill. 1955. Assoc. Mayer, Brown & Platt, Chgo., 1954-64, ptnr., 1965-96, mng. ptnr., 1978-91, L.A., 1991-96; CEO So. Assocs., Gurnee, Ill., 1997—. Editor in chief Northwestern U. Law Rev., 1953-54. Trustee, v.p., gen. counsel LaRabida Children's Hosp. and Rsch. Ctr., Chgo., 1974-89; trustee Kenilworth (Ill.) Union Ch., 1980-88; pres. Joseph Sears Sch. Bd., 1977-79; trustee Rush-Presbyn.-St. Luke's Med. Ctr., 1983-91, life trustee, 1991—; bd. dirs. Boys and Girls Clubs Chgo., 1986-91; governing mem. Orchestral Assn. Chgo., 1988-93. With U.S. Army, 1955-57. Mem. ABA, Chgo. Bar Assn., Lawyers Club Chgo., Order of Coif, Indian Hill Club, Chgo. Club. Banking, General corporate, Securities. Office: 7600 Bittersweet Dr Gurnee IL 60031-5110 E-mail: southern@wwa.com

SOUTHWORTH, WILLIAM WALTER, lawyer, title insurance company executive; b. Cleve., Feb. 23, 1942; s. William A. and Ruth (Able) S.; m. Gaye B. Flanagan, June 15, 1968; children: Julie K., William J. AB, Rutgers U., 1964; JD, Boston U., 1967. Bar: Mass. 1967, U.S. Dist. Ct. Mass. 1972. Assoc. Keith, Reed and Wheatley, Brockton, Mass., 1972-74; title atty. Lawyers Title Ins. Corp., Boston, 1974-78; v.p., mgr., counsel Title USA Ins. Corp. N.Y., 1978-89; v.p. Security Title & Guaranty Co., 1989-93; asst. v.p. Fidelity Nat. Title Ins. Co. N.Y., 1993—. Co-author: Crocker's Notes on Common Forms, 2000. Chmn. Heart Sunday, Am. Heart Assn., Brockton, 1975; bd. dirs. Brockton Symphony Orch., 1976-79; trustee, treas. Prelude Concert Series, Scituate, Mass., 1984. Capt. AUS, 1968-72. Mem. Boston Bar Assn. (co-chmn. real estate legis. com. 1996-2000, chair 2000), Mass. Conveyancers Assn., New Eng. Land Title Assn. (pres. 1983-84), Scituate Tennis Club. Real property. Home: 31 Lotus Ave Scituate MA 02066-2638 Office: Fidelity Nat Title Ins Co N Y 133 Federal St Boston MA 02110-1703 E-mail: wsouthworth@fnf.com

SOUTTER, THOMAS DOUGLAS, retired lawyer; b. N.Y.C., Nov. 1, 1934; s. Thomas G. and Hildreth H. (Callanan) S.; m. Virginia Hovenden; children: Alexander D., Christopher A., Hadley H. BA, U. Va., 1955, LL.B., 1962; postgrad., Advanced Mgmt. Program, Harvard U., 1980. Bar: N.Y. 1962, R.I. 1969. Atty. Breed, Abbott & Morgan, N.Y.C., 1962-68; with Textron Inc., Providence, 1968-95, gen. counsel, 1970-95, v.p., 1971-80, sr. v.p., 1980-85, exec. v.p., gen. counsel, 1985-95; cons., 1995-97. Mem. adv. bd. Internat. and Comparative Law Ctr., 1975-95; mem. Assn. Gen. Counsel; bd. dirs. Avco Fin. Svcs., Inc., 1985-95, Paul Revere Corp. 1993-95; trustee New England Legal Found. Nat. chmn. ann. giving campaign U. Va. Law Sch., 1992-94, mem. exec. com. campaign, 1995-2000; former trustee Providence Preservation Soc., Providence Performing Arts Ctr.; mem. U. Va. Arts and Scis. Alumni Coun.; mem. Narragansett coun. Boy Scouts Am. Lt. USNR, 1955-59. Mem. ABA, N.Y. State Bar Assn., R.I. Bar Assn., Internat. Bar Assn. Antitrust, General corporate, Private international. Office: 2 White Birch Ln Barrington RI 02806-4932 E-mail: tdsout@aol.com

SOYSTER, MARGARET BLAIR, lawyer; b. Washington, Aug. 5, 1951; d. Peter and Eliza (Shumaker) S. AB magna cum laude, Smith Coll., 1973; JD, U. Va., 1976. Bar: N.Y. 1977, U.S. Dist. Ct. (so. and ea. dists.) N.Y. 1977, U.S. Ct. Appeals (2nd cir.) 1979, U.S. Supreme Ct. 1981, U.S. Ct. Appeals (4th cir.) 1982, U.S. ct. Appeals (11th cir.) 1987, U.S. Ct. Appeals (7th cir.) 1991, U.S. Ct. Appeals (3d cir.) 1992. Assoc. Rogers & Wells, N.Y.C., 1976-84, ptnr., 1984-99, Clifford Chance Rogers & Wells LLP, N.Y.C., 2000—. Mem. ABA, Assn. of Bar of City of N.Y., Nat. Assn. Coll. and Univ. Attys., Phi Beta Kappa. Federal civil litigation, Labor, Libel. Office: Clifford Chance Rogers & Wells LLP 200 Park Ave Ste 5200 New York NY 10166-0005

SPACE, THEODORE MAXWELL, lawyer; b. Binghamton, N.Y., Apr. 3, 1938; s. Maxwell Evans and Dorothy Marie (Boone) S.; m. Susan Shultz, Aug. 18, 1962 (div. Apr. 1979); children: William Schuyler, Susanna; m. Martha Collins, Apr. 6, 1991. AB, Harvard U., 1960; LLB, Yale U., 1966. Bar: Conn., 1966, U.S. Dist. Ct. Conn. 1966, U.S. Supreme Ct. 1970, U.S. Tax Ct. 1989, U.S. Ct. Appeals (2nd cir.) 1967, U.S. Ct. Appeals (6th cir.) 1992, U.S. Ct. Appeals (11th cir.) 1994, U.S. Dist. Ct. (ea. dist.) Mich. 1997. Assoc. Shipman & Goodwin LLP, Hartford, Conn., 1966-71, ptnr., 1971—, mng. ptnr., 1984-87, adminstv. ptnr., 1988-91. Mem. Bloomfield (Conn.) Bd. Edn., 1973-85, chmn., 1975-85; treas. Citizens Scholarship Found., Bloomfield, 1971-73, bd. dirs., 1973-91; mem. Bloomfield Human Rels. Commn., 1973-75; mem. Bloomfield Town Dem. Com., 1976-83; corporator Hartford Pub. Libr., 1976—; trustee Conn. Hist. Soc., 1997—, mem. libr. com., 1990—, chair, 1993-2000; chmn. fin. com., coun. mem. Unitarian Soc. Hartford, 1988-91. Lt. (j.g.) USN, 1960-63. Mem. ABA, Conn. Bar Assn. (mem. exec. com. adminstrv. law sect. 1980—), Hartford County Bar Assn., Am. Law Inst., Am. Health Lawyers Assn., Conn. Health Lawyers Assn., Swift's Inn, Hartford Club. Democrat. Unitarian Universalist. Avocations: reading, classical music. Administrative and regulatory, General civil litigation, Health. Home: 59 Prospect St Bloomfield CT 06002-3038 Office: Shipman & Goodwin LLP One American Row Hartford CT 06103-2833

SPAEDER, ROGER CAMPBELL, lawyer; b. Cleve., Dec. 20, 1943; s. Fred N. and Luceil (Campbell) S.; m. Frances DeSales Sutherland, Sept. 7, 1968; chidlren: Michael, Matthew. BS, Bowling Green U., 1965; JD with honors, George Washington U., 1970. Bar: D.C. 1971, U.S. Dist. Ct. D.C. 1971, U.S. Ct. Appeals (D.C. cir.) 1971, U.S. Ct. Claims 1979, U.S. Dist. Ct. Md. 1984, U.S. Ct. Appeals (2d and 4th cirs.) 1985, U.S. Supreme Ct. 1976. Asst. U.S. atty. D.C., Washington, 1971-76; ptnr. Zuckerman, Spaeder, Goldstein, Taylor & Kolker, 1976—. Faculty Atty. Gen. Advocacy Inst., 1974-76, Nat. Inst. Trial Adv., 1978-79; adj. faculty Georgetown U. Law Ctr., 1979-80, Am. U. Ctr. Adminstrn. Justice, 1976-79; lectr. D.C. Bar Continuing Legal Edn. Programs, 1980—; Cardozo Prize judge Yale Law Sch., 1992; master Edward Bennett Williams Inn of Ct., 1996—; mem. D.C. Cir. Jud. Conf., 1991. Contbr. articles to profl. jours. and chpts. to books. Recipient Spl. Achievement award Dept. Justice, 1971. Mem. ATLA, ABA (co-chair com. on complex crimes litigation 1989-92, divsn. co-dir. sect. litigation 1992—), Bar Assn. D.C. (lectr. Criminal Practice Inst. 1977-80), D.C. Bar (com. criminal jury instrns. 1972, divsn. cts. lawyers, adminstrn. of justice 1976-78; adv. com. continuing legal edn. 1986), Def. Rsch. Inst., Assn. Plaintiffs' Trial Attys., Nat. Assn. Criminal Def. Lawyers, Omicron Delta Kappa. Federal civil litigation, Criminal. Home: 7624 Georgetown Pike Mc Lean VA 22102-1412 Office: Zuckerman Spaeder Goldstein Taylor & Kolker 1201 Connecticut Ave NW Fl 12 Washington DC 20036-2605

SPAETH, NICHOLAS JOHN, lawyer, former state attorney general; b. Mahnomen, Minn., Jan. 27, 1950; AB, Stanford U., 1972, JD, 1977; BA, Oxford U., Eng., 1974. Bar: Minn. 1979, U.S. Dist. Ct. (Minn.) 1979, U.S. Ct. Appeals (8th cir.) 1979, N.D. 1980, U.S. Dist. Ct. (N.D.) 1980, U.S. Supreme Ct. 1984. Law clk. U.S. Ct. Appeals (8th cir.), Fargo, N.D., 1977-78; law clk. to Justice Byron White U.S. Supreme Ct., Washington, 1978-79; pvt. practice, 1979-84; atty. gen. State of N.D., Bismarck, 1984-93; ptnr. Dorsey & Whitney, Fargo, 1993-99, Oppenheimer, Wolff & Donnelly, Mpls., 1999, Cooley Godward, Palo Alto, 1999—. Adj. prof. law U. Minn., 1980-83. Rhodes scholar, 1972-74. Democrat. Roman Catholic. Criminal. Office: Employers Reins Corp 5200 Metcalf Overland Park KS 66201

SPAHN, GARY JOSEPH, lawyer; b. N.Y.C., July 23, 1949; s. Harry G. and Mary (Hopkins) S.; m. Lois Luttinger, Aug. 9, 1975; children: Gary J. Jr., Lori J. BA, L.I. U., 1971, MA, 1976; JD, U. Richmond, 1975. Bar: Va. 1975, U.S. Ct. Appeals (4th cir.) 1975, U.S. Supreme Ct. 1980. Law clk. to Hon. Judge Dortch U.S. Dist. Ct. (ea. dist.) Va., Richmond, 1975-77; from assoc. to ptnr. Mays & Valentine, 1977—, now ptnr., past chmn. products liability and ins. sect. Lectr. in field, 1980—; mem. judicial conf. U.S. Ct. Appeals (4th cir.). Co-author: Virginia Law of Products Liability, 1990. Pres. Southhampton Citizens Assn., Richmond, 1982-85; bd. dirs. Southhampton Recreation Assn., Richmond. 1983, Chesterfield County Crime Solvers, 1997—; mem. coun. Southside Montessori Sch., Richmond, 1983-85. With USAF, 1967-73. Mem. ABA (litigation and tort and ins. sects.), Internat. Assn. Def. Counsel, Am. Assn. Ins. Attys., Assoc. Def. Trial Attys., Def. Rsch. Inst., Va. Assn. Def. Attys., Va. Mfrs. Assn., Products Liability Adv. Counsel, Va. Power Boat (commodore). Avocations: boating, basketball, racquetball. General civil litigation, Insurance, Personal injury. Office: Troutman Sanders Mays & Valentine PO Box 1122 1111 E Main St Richmond VA 23219-3531

SPAIN, H. DANIEL, lawyer; b. Pasadena, Tex., Nov. 27, 1950; s. Harry Willard and Janet Lessie Spain; m. Glenna Dianne Brittain, Dec. 27, 1975; children: Summer, Sara. BBA in Fin., U. Tex., 1973; JD, U. Houston, 1976. Bar: Tex. 1977, U.S. Supreme Ct. 1981, Colo. 1992, U.S. Dist. Ct. (ea., so., we. and no. dists.) Tex., U.S. Dist. Ct. (ea. dist.) Okla., U.S. Ct. Appeals (5th cir.); bd. cert. civil trial law Nat. Bd. Trial Advs.; bd. cert. Tex. Bd. Legal Specialization. Asst. gen. atty. So. Pacific Transp., Houston, 1977-80; atty. Thompson & Spain, 1981-86, Womble & Spain, Houston, 1987-99, Spain & Hastings, Houston, 1999—. Fellow Houston Bar Found.; mem. Maritime Law Assn. U.S. (assoc.), Def. Rsch. Inst., Nat. Assn. R.R. Trial Counsel, Tex. Assn. R.R. Trial Counsel, State Bar Tex., Houston Bar Assn. Baptist. Avocations: church work, golf. General civil litigation, Personal injury, Product liability. Office: Spain & Hastings 909 Fannin St Ste 2350 Houston TX 77010-1027

SPAIN, RICHARD COLBY, lawyer; b. Evanston, Ill., Nov. 17, 1950; s. Richard Francis and Anne Louise (Brinckerhoff) S.; m. Nancy Lynn Mavec, Aug. 3, 1974; children: Catherine Day, Sarah Colby. BA cum laude, Lawrence U., 1972; JD, Case Western Reserve U., 1975; LLM in taxation, John Marshall Law Sch., 1985. Bar: Ohio 1975, Ill. 1982, U.S. Dist. Ct. (no. dist.) Ohio 1977, U.S. Dist. Ct. (no. dist.) Ill. 1982, Mass. 1996. Ptnr. Spain & Spain, Cleve., 1975-82, Whitted & Spain, PC, Chgo., 1985-89, Spain, Spain & Varnet PC, Chgo., Northborough, Mass., 1989—; assoc. Canel Whitted & Aronson, Chgo., 1982-85. Dir., sec. Stone Perforating Co., Chgo., 1988—, Chgo. EDM, Inc., Chgo., Wheeling, Ill., 1994—. Contbr. articles to profl. jours. Treas. ARC Ill., 1993—; dir. Chgo. Youth Symphony Orch., 1983—. Mem. Chikaming Country Club (dir. 1992-94), The Winter Club Lake Forest, The Carlton Club (Chgo.). Estate planning, Probate, Estate taxation. Home: 1320 N State Pkwy Chicago IL 60610-2118 Office: Spain Spain & Varnet PC 33 N Dearborn St Ste 2220 Chicago IL 60602-3118 E-mail: rspain@spainspainvarnet.com

SPAIN, THOMAS B. retired state supreme court justice; Justice Ky. Supreme Ct, Frankfort, 1991-95; ret., 1995; of counsel Whitfield & Calvert, P.S.C. Office: Whitfield & Calvert PSC PO Box 656 29 E Center St Madisonville KY 42431-2037

SPALDING, ANDREW FREEMAN, lawyer; b. Toledo, June 24, 1951; s. Dean and Shirley Louise (Maitland) S.; m. Adele Taylor, May 17, 1980; children: Amy Louise, Adam Freeman, Audrey Wade, Abigail Maitland. BA, U. Calif., Berkeley, 1973; JD, So. Meth. U., 1977. Bar: Tex. 1977, U.S. Dist. Ct. (so., ea. and we. dists.) Tex. 1978, U.S. Ct. Appeals (5th cir.) 1978; bd. cert. civil trial law, personal injury trial law. Assoc. Bracewell & Patterson, Houston, 1977-84, ptnr., 1985—. Notes and comments editor Southwestern Law Jour., Dallas, 1976-77. Fellow Tex Bar Found., Houston Bar Found.; mem. State Bar Tex., Houston Bar Assn., Tex. Assn. Def. Counsel, Def. Rsch. Inst., Knights Momus, Krewe Maximilian, Pan Tex. Assembly, Houston Country Club. Federal civil litigation, General civil litigation, State civil litigation. Office: Bracewell & Patterson 2900 S Tower Pennzoil Pla 711 Louisiana St Ste 2900 Houston TX 77002-2781 E-mail: aspalding@bracepatt.com

SPALDING, CATHERINE, lawyer; b. Lebanon, Ky. d. Hugh C. and Bernadette (Hill) S. BS in Biology, Spalding U., Louisville, 1970; JD, U. Louisville, 1983. Bar: Ky., U.S. Ct. Appeals (6th cir.), Ct. Vets. Appeals, Fed. Dist. Ct. Pvt. practice law, Louisville, 1983—; asst. county atty. Jefferson County, 1993-2000, family court's parents' atty., 2000—. Editor newsletter Ky. Bar Assn. Family Law Sect.; editor book supplement: Kentucky Family Law, 1990. Past bd. dirs. LWV, Portland Mus. Louisville. Mem. ABA, Ky. Bar Assn. (chairperson family law sect. 1990-91, spkr., moderator seminars), Louisville Bar Assn. (chairperson social security sect. 1992-93), AAUW (past bd. dirs.), DAR (past bd. dirs.) Optimist Club (past bd. dirs.), LWV (past bd. dirs.). Avocation: snow skiing. Family and matrimonial, Juvenile, Personal injury. Home: 1917 Trevilian Way Louisville KY 40205-2139 Office: Ste 3 325 W Ormsby Ave Louisville KY 40203-2907 Fax: 502-634-4488. E-mail: cslaw@kih.net

SPALLONE, JEANNE FIELD, retired state judge; b. N.Y.C., Jan. 18, 1928; d. Charles William and Flora (Kopp) Field; m. Daniel Francis Spallone, June 4, 1950; children: Janne Field Spallone, Niel Francis Spallone, James Field Spallone. BS, U. Conn., 1950. News and feature writer, reporter Middletown (Conn.) Press, 1952-53, 59-65; adminstrv. asst. to amb. Hon. Chester Bowles, Essex, Conn., 1953-56; mem. Conn. State Legislature, Hartford, 1959-61; columnist op-ed Middletown Press, 1993-96; judge of probate State of Conn., Dept. Judiciary, Dist. of Deep River, Hartford, 1979-95. Contbr. articles to jours., books, newspapers. Trustee, historian Deep River Hist. Soc., 1976-94; chmn. bd. dirs. Winthrop Cemetery Assn., 1978—. Mem. Conn. Order Women Legislators, Soroptimists (pres. local chpt. 1982-84), Block Island (R.I.) club (pres. 1982-84). Democrat. Avocations: family history, travel. Home and Office: 6 Westbrook Rd Deep River CT 06417-1504

SPANBOCK, MAURICE SAMUEL, lawyer; b. N.Y.C., Jan. 6, 1924; s. Benjamin and Belle (Ward) S.; m. Marion Rita Heyman, Nov. 21, 1954; children: Jonathan H., Betsy W. BA, Columbia U., N.Y.C., 1944; LLB, Harvard U., 1950. Bar: N.Y. 1950. Assoc. Goldstone and Wolff, N.Y.C., 1950-52; ptnr. Carro and Spanbock (name changed to Carro, Spanbock, Kaster et al), 1952-94; of counsel Kleinberg Kaplan Wolff & Cohen, 1994—. Trustee Carnegie Coun. on Ethics and Internat. Affairs, N.Y.C., 1980-86, 93-2000, chmn. bd., 1987-92; hon. pres. Lincoln Square Synagogue, N.Y.C.; sec. Ohr Torah Stone Instns. Israel. Cpl. AUS, 1943-46, ETO. Mem. ABA (chmn. com. on taxation, patent, trademark and copyright law sect. 1979-81), Assn. of Bar of City of N.Y. (com. on copyright 1965-67, art law com. 1977-80, 86-88), Fed. Bar Coun., Nat. Panel Arbitrators, Am. Abitration Assn., Practising Law Inst. (panel on copyrights, 1979). Jewish. General corporate, Entertainment, Estate planning. Home: 88 Central Park W New York NY 10023-5209 Office: Kleinberg Kaplan Wolff & Cohen 551 5th Ave Fl 18 New York NY 10176-1800

SPARACINO, JOANN, lawyer, trade and investment consultant; b. Passaic, N.J., Feb. 25, 1956; d. Carlo and Lillian Ida (Thinschmidt) S.; 1 child, Jason Alexander Leshner. BA cum laude, NYU, 1978; JD, U. Miami, 1989. Bar: Fla. 1989. Contract atty. pvt. firms, Miami and Washington, 1989-94; pres., gen. counsel Alexis Internat., Inc., Washington, 1994—. Cons., spkr. SADC Ambs. Workshop on Trade and Investment, Washington, 1998; participant meetings on the devel. of the African Growth and Opportunity Act, Washington, 1994-99; del. U.S. Presdl. Mission to the African-African Am. Summit, Harare, Zimbabwe, 1997; cons. White House Roundtables on Trade and Investment in Africa, Washington, 1998. Contbr. articles to profl. jours. Recipient scholarship NYU, 1977. Mem. ABA (co-chair subcom. on African trade and investment 1994-98), Fla. Bar. Avocations: world cultures, international travel, raising awareness about African issues and U.S.-Africa interests. Home: 5415 Connecticut Ave NW Apt 406 Washington DC 20015-2743 Office: Alexis Internat Inc 1730 K St NW Ste 304 Washington DC 20006-3839 E-mail: jsparacino@alexisint.com

SPARKES, JAMES EDWARD, lawyer; b. Syracuse, N.Y., Oct. 29, 1948; s. Edward William and Kathryn Claire (MacDonald) S.; m. Karen M. Kelley, June 28, 1975; children: Matthew Kelley, Bryan Kelley. BA, Coll. Holy Cross, 1971; MA, Nelson A. Rockefeller Coll. Pub. Affairs and Policy, SUNY-Albany, 1974; JD cum laude, Syracuse U., 1976. Bar: N.Y. 1977, U.S. Dist. Ct. (no. dist.) N.Y. 1977, U.S. Tax Ct. 1977, U.S. Supreme Ct. 1986. Dep. dir. ct. adminstrn. N.Y. State Office Ct. Adminstrn., Rochester, 1972-73; asst. dist. atty. Onondaga County, Syracuse, 1977-79; assoc. Hancock & Estabrook, Syracuse, 1979-83, ptnr., 1983—; instr. polit. sci. Adirondack Community Coll., Glens Falls, N.Y., 1973-74. Youth racing coach, instr. Toggenburg Ski Sch., U.S. Eastern Amateur Ski Assn., 1972—, Profl. Ski Instrs. Am., 1985—; advisor Explorers div. Boy Scouts Am., Syracuse, 1977-80. Mem. ABA, N.Y. State Bar Assn., Assn. Trial Lawyers Am., Onondaga County Bar Assn., Am. Arbitration Assn. (comml. arbitration panel 1983—), N.Y. State Trial Lawyers Assn. Democrat. Roman Catholic. Clubs: Cavalry (Manlius, N.Y.); Bellevue Country (Syracuse). Avocation: skiing. General corporate, Land use and zoning (including planning), Real property. Home: 237 Whitestone Cir Syracuse NY 13215-1575 Office: Hancock & Estabrook 1400 One Mony Plz Syracuse NY 13202

SPARKMAN, STEVEN LEONARD, lawyer; b. Sarasota, Fla., May 30, 1947; s. Simeon Clarence and Ursula (Wahlstrom) S.; m. Terry Jeanne Gibbs, Aug. 23, 1969; children: Joanna Jeanne, Kevin Leonard. BA, Fla. State U., 1969, JD, 1972. Bar: Fla. 1972, U.S. Dist. Ct. (mid. dist.) Fla. 1974, U.S. Ct. Appeals (5th cir.) 1975. Legal rsch. asst. Office Gen. Counsel, Fla. Dept. Revenue, Tallahassee, 1971; legis. intern com. on community affairs Fla. Ho. of Reps., 1971-72; jud. rsch. aide Fla. 2d Dist. Ct. Appeals, Lakeland, 1972-73; asst. county atty. Hillsborough County, Tampa, Fla., 1973-75; assoc. Carlton, Fields, Ward, Emmanuel, Smith & Cutler, P.A., 1975-80, sr. atty., 1980-2001; pvt. practice Plant City, Fla., 2001—. Mem. bd. visitors Fla. State U. Coll. Law, 1994-00. Sec., bd. dirs. Bapt. Towers Plant City, Inc., 1981-84; deacon 1st Bapt. Ch., Plant City, 1980—. 1st lt. USAFR, 1973. Mem. Fla. Bar Assn. (exec. coun. local govt. law sect. 1978-79), Hillsborough County Bar Assn., Plant City Bar Assn., Tampa Kiwanis (bd. dirs. 1980-82, 96-98, Layman of Yr. 1984, 89), Tampa Kiwanis Found. (bd. dirs. 1997-2000). Democrat. Land use and zoning (including planning), Real property, Estate planning. Office: Steven L Sparkman PA 212 N Collins St Plant City FL 33566 E-mail: sls@sparklaw.com

SPARKS, BILLY SCHLEY, lawyer; b. Marshall, Mo., Mar. 1, 1923; s. John and Clarinda (Schley) S.; m. Dorothy O. Stone, May 14, 1946; children: Stephen Stone, Susan Lee Sparks Raben Taylor, John David. AB, Harvard U., 1945, LLB, 1949. Bar: Mo. 1949. Ptnr. Langworthy, Matz & Linde, Kansas City, Mo., 1949-62, Linde, Thomason, Fairchild, Langworthy, Kohn & Van Dyke, Kansas City, 1962-91; ret., 1991. Mem. Mission (Kans.) Planning Coun., 1954-63; treas. Johnson County (Kans.) Dem. Ctrl. Com., 1958-64; candidate for rep. 10th Dist., Kans., 1956, 3d Dist., 1962; mem. Dist. 100 Sch. Bd., 1964-68, pres., 1967-69; mem. Dist. 512 Sch. Bd., 1969-73, pres., 1971-72; del. Dem. Nat. Conv., 1964; ; mem. Kans. Civil Svc. Commn., 1975-90. Lt. USAAF, 1944-46. Mem. ABA, Mo. Bar Assn., Kansas City Bar Assn., Law Assn. Kansas City, Harvard Law Sch. Assn. Mo. (past dir.), Nat. Assn. Sch. Bds. (mem. legis. com. 1968-73), St. Andrews Soc., Harvard Club (v.p. 1953-54), The Kansas City (Mo.) Club, Milburn Golf and Country Club, Am. Legion, Kansas City C. of C. (legis. com. 1956-82), Mem. Christian Ch. Federal civil litigation, State civil litigation, General practice. Home and Office: 8517 W 90th Ter Shawnee Mission KS 66212-3053

SPARKS, JOHN EDWARD, lawyer; b. Rochester, Ind., July 3, 1930; s. Russell Leo and Pauline Anna (Whittenberger) S.; m. Margaret Joan Snyder, Sept. 4, 1954; children: Thomas Edward, William Russell, Kathryn Chapman McCarthy. A.B., Ind. U., 1952; LL.B., U. Calif., Berkeley, 1957; postgrad., London Sch. Econs., 1957-58. Bar: Calif. 1958. Assoc. Brobeck, Phleger & Harrison, San Francisco, 1958-66, ptnr., 1967-95, of counsel, 1996—. Adj. prof. law U. San Francisco, 1967-69; pres. Legal Aid Soc. San Francisco, 1978-79, dir., 1971-81. Editor U. Calif. Law Rev., 1956-57. Served to 1st lt. Q.M.C. U.S. Army, 1952-54, Korea. Recipient Wheeler Oak Meritorious award U. Calif., Berkeley, 1986. Fellow Am. Bar Found., Am. Coll. Trial Lawyers; mem. State Bar Calif., Bar Assn. San Francisco (bd. dirs. 1974-75), ABA, Am. Judicature Soc., Boalt Hall Alumni Assn. (pres. 1983-84), Pacific Union Club (San Francisco), Democrat. Administrative and regulatory, General civil litigation, State civil litigation. Office: Brobeck Phleger & Harrison Spear St Tower 1 Market Plz Fl 31 San Francisco CA 94105-1100 E-mail: jsparks@brobeck.com

SPARKS, ROBERT RONOLD, JR. lawyer; b. Bklyn., Dec. 4, 1946; s. Robert Ronold Sr. and Marjorie Anne (Boehm) S. BA, Va. Mil. Inst., 1969; JD, U. Va., 1972. Bar: U.S. Dist. Ct. (D.C. cir.) 1979, U.S. Dist. Ct. (ea. dist.) Va. 1979, U.S. Ct. Appeals (2d cir.) 1986, U.S. Ct. Appeals (D.C. cir.) 1975, Va. 1972, U.S. Ct. Appeals (4th cir.) 1982, U.S. Ct. Mil. Appeals 1976, U.S. Tax Ct. 1978, U.S. Supreme Ct. 1981, U.S. Dist. Ct. Md. 1993. From assoc. to ptnr. Sedam & Herge, McLean, Va., 1977-85; ptnr. Herge, Sparks & Christopher, 1985—. Mem. Bd. Regents James Monroe Law Office Mus. and Meml. Library, Fredericksburg, Va., 1983-86. Mem. Fairfax County Redevel. and Housing Authority, Fairfax, 1981-82; commr. Fairfax County Indsl. Devel. Authority, 1980-81, Fairfax County Planning Commn., 1983-89. Lt. USNR, 1972-77, Philippines. Mem. Va. Bar Assn., D.C. Bar Assn., Rotary (treas., bd. dirs. 1978-80). Roman Catholic. General civil litigation, Constitutional. Home: 6448 Spring Ter Falls Church VA 22042-3141 Office: Herge Sparks Christopher 6862 Elm St Ste 360 Mc Lean VA 22101-3867

SPARKS, SAM, federal judge; b. 1939; BA, U. Tex., 1961, LLB, 1963. Aide Rep. Homer Thornberry, 1963; law clk. to Hon. Homer Thornberry U.S. Dist. Ct. (we. dist.) Tex., 1963-65; assoc. to ptnr., shareholder Hardie, Grambling, Sims & Galatzan (and successor firms), El Paso, Tex., 1965-91; dist. judge U.S. Dist. Ct. (we. dist.) Tex., 1991—. Fellow Am. Coll. Trial Lawyers, Tex. Bar Found. (life); mem. Am. Bd. Trial Advocates (advocate), State Bar Tex. Office: US Dist Ct Judge 200 W 8th St Ste 100 Austin TX 78701-2333

SPARKS, THOMAS E., JR. lawyer; b. Little Rock, Jan. 11, 1942; children: Thomas Gunnar, Erik Richard, Andrew Pal. BS, Washington and Lee U., 1963; JD, U. Ark., 1968; LLM, Harvard U., 1970. Bar: Ark. 1968, Calif. 1970. Assoc. Pillsbury Madison & Sutro, San Francisco, 1970-76; ptnr. Pillsbury, Madison & Sutro, 1977-84, Baker & McKenzie, San Francisco, 1984-87, Pillsbury Madison & Sutro, San Francisco, 1987-2000, Pillsbury Winthrop, San Francisco, 2001—. Trustee Grace Cathedral, San Francisco. 1st lt. U.S. Army, 1965. Mem. ABA, Calif. Bar Assn., Olympic Club (San Francisco), Calif. Tennis Club (pres. 2000). Securities. Office: Pillsbury Winthrop 50 Fremont St San Francisco CA 94105-2230

SPARKS, WILLIAM JAMES ASHLEY, lawyer, educator; b. Victoria, B.C., Can., Jan. 27, 1949; BA, U. Victoria, 1970; JD, Duke U., 1973. Bar: N.Y. 1974, Fla. 1992, U.S. Dist. Ct. (so. and ea. dists.) N.Y. 1974, U.S. Ct. Appeals (2d cir.) 1974, N.J. 1989, U.S. Dist. Ct. N.J. 1989. Assoc. Dewey, Ballantine, Bushby, Palmer & Wood, N.Y.C., 1973-78; counsel Olin Corp., Stamford, Conn., 1979-89; sr. litigation counsel W.R. Grace & Co., N.Y.C., 1989—. Adj. prof. Pace U. Sch of Law, White Plains, N.Y., 1984-91. Mem. ABA, N.Y. State Bar Assn., Internat. Assn. Def. Counsel, ACCA, Assn. Bar City N.Y. Home: 1370 Clark St Merrick NY 11566 Office: 5400 Broken Sound Blvd Boca Raton FL 33487 E-mail: william.sparks@grace.com

SPARROW, ROBERT E. lawyer; b. N.Y.C., Feb. 26, 1935; s. Sidney G. and Dorothy (Boardman) S.; m. Marcia Galler, Apr. 14, 1957; children: Laurie Joy, David Gregory. BA, Columbia U., 1955, JD, 1957. Bar: N.Y. 1957, U.S. Dist. Ct. (ea. and so. dists.) N.Y. 1961, U.S. Supreme Ct. 1962. Ptnr. firm. Sparrow, Singer & Schreiber, N.Y.C., 1957—. Mem. com. on character and fitness, appellate divsn. N.Y. Supreme Ct., 1992—. Pres. Eastern Queens Dem. Club, N.Y., 1971, Pub. Sch. 188 PTA, Queens, 1971. Served as sgt. USAR, 1957-63. Mem. Queens Criminal Cts. Bar Assn. (pres. 1971-72), Queens County Bar Assn. (vice chmn. criminal cts. com. 1973-76). Democrat. Jewish. Lodges: K.P., B'nai B'rith, Elks. Criminal, General practice, Personal injury. Home: 21749 Stewart Rd Flushing NY 11364-3538 Office: Sparrow Singer & Schreiber 12510 Queens Blvd Kew Gardens NY 11415-1519

SPATH, GREGG ANTHONY, lawyer; b. New Rochelle, N.Y., Nov. 13, 1952; s. Richard Dennis and Renee (Turtletaub) S.; m. Lois Lang, Mar. 18, 1979; 1 child, Emma Lang. Student, Coll. William and Mary, 1970-72; BA in English, U. Rochester, 1974; JD, New Eng. Sch. Law, 1977; LLM in Trade Regulation, NYU, 1979. Bar: N.Y. 1978, U.S. Supreme Ct. 1984, Pa. 1990. Spl. legal counsel Western Electric Co., N.Y.C., 1978-81; atty. St. Regis Paper Co., 1981-82; asst. gen. counsel, sec. patent com. United Mchts. and Mfrs., Inc., 1982-87; corp. counsel Adidas USA, Inc., Warren, N.J., 1987-88; exec. v.p., corp. counsel Hy-Art Industries, Inc., Kingston, Pa., 1988-90; sec., treas., gen. counsel Regency Mfg. Co., Inc., Wilkes-Barre, 1990-93, Renee Mfg. Co., Inc., Exeter, 1993-95; corp. counsel real estate Nextel Comm., Inc., Reston, Va., 1996-99, corp. counsel intellectual property/licensing, 2000; of counsel Swidler, Berlin, Shereff, Friedman, LLP, Washington, 2000—. Contbr. New Eng. Law Rev., 1976, tech. editor, 1976-77. Mem. ABA (sects. of antitrust, patent, trademark and copyright law, comms. law). Avocations: fundraising, sports, music, theatre, cinema. Contracts commercial, Intellectual property, Real property. Office: Swidler Berlin Shereff Friedman LLP 3000 K St NW Washington DC 20007 E-mail: gaspath@swidlaw.com

SPATT, ARTHUR DONALD, federal judge; b. 1925; Student, Ohio State U., 1943-44, 46-47; LLB, Bklyn. Law Sch., 1949. Assoc. Davidson & Davidson, N.Y.C., 1949, Lane, Winard, Robinson & Schorr, N.Y.C., 1950, Alfred S. Julien, N.Y.C., 1950-52, Florea & Florea, N.Y.C., 1953; pvt. practice, 1953-67, Spatt & Bauman, 1967-78; justice 10th judicial cir. N.Y. State Supreme Ct., 1979-82; adminstrv. judge Nassau County, 1982-86; assoc. justice appellate div. Second Judicial Dept., 1986-89; dist. judge U.S. Dist. Ct. (ea. dist.) N.Y., Bklyn., 1989-90, Uniondale, N.Y., 1990-2000, Central Islip, 2000—. Active Jewish War Vets.; With USN, 1944. Mem. ABA, Assn. Supreme Ct. Justices State of N.Y., Bar Assn. Nassau County, Jewish Lawyers Assn. Nassau County, Bklyn. Law Rev. Assn., Long Beach Lawyers Assn., Theodore Roosevelt Am. Inn of Ct., Master of the Bench. Office: Long Island Courthouse 1024 Federal Plaza Central Islip NY 11722-4445

SPEAKER, SUSAN JANE, lawyer; b. Dallas, Dec. 25, 1946; d. William R. and Jane E. (Aldrich) Turner; m. David C. Speaker, Dec. 21, 1968; children: David Allen, Melissa. BA, U. Ark., 1970, JD, 1985. Bar: Okla. 1985, U.S. Dist. Ct. (no., ea. and we. dists.) Okla. 1985. Assoc. Hall, Estill, Hardwick, Gable, Golden & Nelson, P.C., Tulsa, 1985-91; atty. Resolution Trust Corp., 1991-92; shareholder Speaker & Matthews, P.C., 1992-96; atty. Comml. Fin. Svcs., Inc., Tulsa, 1996-99; dir. properties and concessions Dollar Rent A Car Systems, Inc., 1999—. Editor U. Ark. Law Rev., 1983-85. Mem. ABA, ATLA, Okla. Bar Assn., Tulsa Bar Assn., Tulsa Title and Probate Lawyers Assn., Phi Beta Kappa, Delta Theta Phi. General corporate, Landlord-tenant, Real property.

SPEAR, H(ENRY) DYKE N(EWCOME), JR. lawyer; b. New London, Conn., Feb. 26, 1935; s. Henry D. N. and Helene (Vining) S.; m. Karla A. Dalley, Sept. 9, 1995. BA, Trinity Coll., Hartford, Conn., 1958; JD, U. Conn., 1960. Bar: Conn. 1960. Pvt. practice matrimonial law, Hartford, 1961—. Mem. Conn. Bar Assn., Hartford County Bar Assn. Republican. Methodist. Family and matrimonial. Office: 10 Trumbull St Hartford CT 06103-2404 E-mail: dykespear@home.com

SPEARS, LARRY JONELL, lawyer; b. Webb, Miss., Jan. 10, 1953; s. John Spears and Lillian Belle Embrey; m. Treycè L. Gaston, Jan. 14, 1989;children: Lyndzè Rae, Joshua Lawrence. BS, U. Ill., 1976, JD, 1979; MS, So. Ill. U., 1990. Bar: Ill. 1980. Asst. atty gen. Ill. Atty. Gen.'s Office, Murphysboro, 1980-84; asst. pub. defender Jackson County Pub. Defender's Office, 1985; lectr. Crime Study Ctr., Carbondale, Ill., 1985; sole practice, 1985-86; asst. state's atty. Peoria (Ill.) State's Atty. Office, 1986-90, Sangamon County State's Atty. Office, Springfield, Ill., 1990-94.

Cons. Minority Contractors Assn., Carbondale, 1985; mem. Inmate Advocacy Group, Murphysboro, 1985-86; lectr. Sangamon State U., Springfield, 1990-96. Elijah P. Lovejoy scholar, 1972. Mem. Ill. State Bar Assn., McLean County Bar Assn., Adminstrn. of Justice Assn. (treas. 1984-85), Am. Soc. Criminology (discussant 1984-85), Midwest Criminal Justice Assn., Am. Judicature Soc., LWV, Sphinx Club (Carbondale), Phi Alpha Delta (treas. 1979), Alpha Phi Sigma. Republican. Baptist. Avocations: golf, fishing, songwriting, tennis, volleyball. Home: 1603 E Oakland Ave Bloomington IL 61701-5617 Office: Ill State U Student's Legal Svcs Normal IL 61761 E-mail: ljspear@mail.ilstu.edu

SPEARS, ROBERT FIELDS, lawyer; b. Tulsa, Aug. 1, 1943; s. James Ward and Berneice (Fields) S.; m. Jacquelyn Castle, May 10, 1961; children: Jeff, Sally. BBA, Tex. Tech. U., 1965; JD, U. Tex., 1968. Bar: Tex. 1968. Assoc. Rain, Harrell, Emery, Young & Doke, Dallas, 1968-73, ptnr., 1974-87, Locke Purnell Rain Harrell, Dallas, 1987-91; gen. counsel Fin. Industries Corp., Austin, Tex., 1991-96; gen. counsel, sec. Lone Star Techn. Inc., Dallas, 1996—. Pres. Sr. Citizens of Greater Dallas, 1988. Mem. ABA, Tex. Bar Assn., Dallas Bar Assn., Dallas Country Club, Phi Delta Phi. Republican. Baptist. Avocation: tennis. General corporate, Mergers and acquisitions, Securities. Office: Lone Star Technologies Inc PO Box 803546 Dallas TX 75380-3546

SPEARS, RONALD DEAN, lawyer; b. Michigan City, Ind., July 30, 1951; s. Lonnie and Frances Ellen (Benad) S.; m. Annette Jean Greffe, Dec. 22, 1973; 1 child, Donald Dean. BA, U. Ill., 1974; JD, So. Ill. U., 1977. Bar: Ill. 1977, U.S. Dist. Ct. (ctrl. and so. dists.) Ill. 1977, U.S. Ct. Appeals (7th cir.) 1977, U.S. Supreme Ct. 1983. Law clk. U.S. Dist. Ct., Springfield, Ill., 1977-79; ptnr. Miley, Meyer, Austin, Spears & Romano, P.C., Taylorville, 1985-93; judge Ill. Cir. Ct., 4th Jud. Cir., 1993—. Atty. City of Taylorville, 1981; atty. YMCA, 1986-89, pres., 1987. Col. (JAGC) Ill. Army N.G. Mem. ABA, Ill. State Bar Assn. (bd. govs. 1997—), Christian County Bar Assn. (pres. 1987), So. Ill. U. Law Sch. Alumni Assn. (pres. 1984), Lincoln-Douglas Am. Inn of Ct., Optimists (pres. 1986, lt. gov. 1986-87), Toastmasters (pres. 1988). Federal civil litigation, State civil litigation, Personal injury. Home: 3501 Lake Dr Taylorville IL 62568-8930 Office: Illinois Circuit Court 4th Jud Cir Rm 316 Christian County Courthouse Taylorville IL 62568-2245 Fax: (217) 824-5023. E-mail: jspears@chipsnet.com

SPECTER, HOWARD ALAN, lawyer; b. Pitts., Dec. 1, 1939; s. Ben and Ethel (Gorn) S.; m. Elaine Spatz, Jan. 1, 1986. BA, U. Pitts., 1961, JD, 1964. Bar: Pa. 1964, U.S. Ct. Appeals (3d cir.) 1973, U.S. SUpreme Ct. 1974, U.S. Ct. Appeals (5th, 6th and 9th cirs.) 1976, U.S. Ct. Appeals (11th cir.) 1981, U.S. Ct. Appeals (10th cir.) 1983. Assoc. Litman, Litman & Harris, Pitts., 1964-67; ptnr. Litman, Litman, Harris & Specter, P.A., 1967-82; pvt. practice, 1982—. Mem. faculty, chmn. Nat. Coll. Advocacy, 1977-83. Contbr. articles to legal publs. Fellow Roscoe Pound-Am. Trial Lawyers Assn. (trustee); mem. ABA (bus. torts com. litigation sect. 1975, subcom. on multidist. litigation antitrust law sect. 1975), Am. Bd. Trial Advocates, Assn. Trial Lawyers Am. (chmn. comml. litigation sect. 1976-77, sec. 1979-80, pres. 1982-83), Pa. Trial Lawyers Assn., Pa. Bar Assn., Acad. Trial Lawyers Allegheny County (pres. 1989-90), Tex. Trial Lawyers Assn., Acad. Fla. Trial Lawyers, Belli Soc. (pres. 1983-84). Democrat. Jewish. Federal civil litigation, Personal injury, Product liability. Office: Koppers Building Fl 26 Pittsburgh PA 15219-1826 also: 272 Chestnut St Meadville PA 16335-3205

SPECTER, RICHARD BRUCE, lawyer; b. Phila., Sept. 6, 1952; s. Jacob E. and Marilyn B. (Kron) S.; m. Jill Ossenfort, May 30, 1981; children: Lauren Elizabeth, Lindsey Anne, Allison Lee. BA cum laude, Washington U., St. Louis, 1974; JD, George Washington U., 1977. Bar: Mo. 1977, U.S. Dist. Ct. (ea. and we. dists.) Mo. 1977, U.S. Ct. Appeals (8th cir.) 1977, Ill. 1978, Pa. 1978, U.S. Dist. Ct. (ea. dist.) Ill. 1979, U.S. Ct. Appeals (7th cir.) 1979, Calif. 1984, U.S. Dist. Ct. (cen. dist.) Calif. 1985, U.S. Ct. Appeals (9th cir.) 1986, U.S. Dist. Ct. (so. dist.) Calif. 1987, U.S. Dist. Ct. (no. dist.) Calif. 1988, U.S. Supreme Ct. 1999. Assoc. Coburn, Croft, Shepherd, Herzog & Putzell, St. Louis, 1977-79; ptnr. Herzog, Kral, Burroughs & Specter, 1979-82; exec. v.p. Uniqey Internat., Santa Ana, Calif., 1982-84; pvt. practice law L.A. and Irvine, 1984-87; ptnr. Corbett & Steelman, Irvine, 1987—. Instr. Nat. Law Ctr. George Washington U. 1975. Mem. ABA, Ill. Bar Assn., Mo. Bar Assn., Pa. Bar Assn., Calif. Bar Assn. Jewish. State civil litigation, Entertainment, Sports. Home: 37 Bull Run Irvine CA 92620-2510 Office: 18200 Von Karman Ave Ste 200 Irvine CA 92612-1086 E-mail: rspecter@corbsteel.com

SPECTOR, BRIAN FRED, lawyer; b. Bklyn., Aug. 24, 1952; s. Harry and Mildred S.; m. Meryl Joy Linder, June 22, 1975; children: Randi Jill, Andrew Jay. BA in Polit. Sci. cum laude, Syracuse U., 1974; JD magna cum laude, U. Miami (Fla.), 1978. Bar: Fla. 1978, U.S. Dist. Ct. (so. and mid. dists) Fla. 1978, U.S. Ct. Appeals (5th cir.) 1978, U.S. Ct. Appeals (11th cir.) 1981, U.S. Supreme Ct. 1985. Jud. clk. to Hon. Bryan Simpson U.S. Ct. Appeals (5th cir.), Jacksonville, Fla., 1978-79; instr. U. Miami, 1980-81, adj. faculty, 1985. Contbr. articles to profl. jours.; former comments editor U. Miami Law Rev.; bd. editors So. Dist. Digest, 1982-87, chmn. 1984-85. Mem. ABA (bus. law sect. litigation sect., patent trademark and copyright law sect.), Fla. Bar Assn. (trial lawyers sect. bus. law sect., bus. litigation com. subcom. for standard jury instrns. in comml. cases, civil procedure rules com.), Am. Judicature Soc., Fed. Bar Assn., Dade County Bar Assn., Acad. Fla. Trial Lawyers (amicus curiae com.), Wig and Robe, Bar and Gavel, Omicron Delta Kappa. Federal civil litigation, State civil litigation, Intellectual property. Office: 201 S Biscayne Blvd Ste 1100 Miami FL 33131-4327 E-mail: bspector@knsacs.com

SPECTOR, DAVID M. lawyer; b. Rock Island, Ill., Dec. 20, 1946; s. Louis and Ruth (Vinikour) S.; m. Laraine Fingold, Jan. 15, 1972; children: Rachel, Laurence. BA, Northwestern U., 1968; JD magna cum laude, U. Mich., 1971. Bar: Ill. 1971, U.S. Dist. Ct. (no. dist.) Ill. 1971, U.S. Ct. Appeals (7th cir.) 1977, U.S. Ct. Appeals (4th cir.) 1984, U.S. Dist. Ct. (cen. dist.) Ill. 1984. Clk. Ill. Supreme Ct., Chgo., 1971-72; ptnr., assoc. Isham, Lincoln & Beale, 1972-87; ptnr. Mayer, Brown & Platt, 1987-97, Hopkins & Sutter, Chgo., 1997-2001, Schiff, Hardin & Waite, Chgo., 2001—. Chmn. ABA Nat. Inst. on Ins. Co. Insolvency, Boston, 1986; co-chmn. ABA Nat. Inst. on Internat. Reins.: Collections and Insolvency, N.Y., 1988; chmn. ABA Nat. Inst. on Life Ins. Co. Insolvency, Chgo., 1993; spkr. in field. Editor: Law and Practice of Insurance Company Insolvency, 1986, Law and Practice of Life Insurer Insolvency, 1993; co-editor: Law and Practice of International Reinsurance Collections and Insolvency, 1988; contbr. articles to profl. jours. Mem. ABA (chair Nat. Inst. on Life Insurer Insolvency 1993), Chgo. Bar Assn., Lawyer's Club of Chgo. Federal civil litigation, Insurance. Home: 2100 N Lincoln Park W Chicago IL 60614-4648 Office: Schiff Hardin & Waite 6600 Sears Tower Chicago IL 60606 E-mail: dspector@schiffhardin.com

SPECTOR, MARTIN WOLF, lawyer, business executive; b. Phila., 1938; BA, Pa. State U., 1959; JD, U. Pa., 1962. Bar: Pa. 1962. Judge U.S. Dist. Ct., until 1967; asst. gen. counsel ARA Services, Phila., assoc. gen. counsel, 1969-76, v.p., 1976-83, gen. counsel, 1983—, formerly sr. v.p.; exec. v.p. ARAMARK, 1985—. Served to lt. USN, 1953-56. Office: ARAMARK 1101 Market St Ste 45 Philadelphia PA 19107-2988*

SPECTOR, PHILLIP LOUIS, lawyer; b. L.A., July 15, 1950; s. Everett L. Spector and Rebecca (Horn) Newman; m. Carole Sue Lebbin, May 11, 1980; children: Adam, David. Student, U. Birmingham, Eng., 1970-71; BA with highest honors, U. Calif., Santa Barbara, 1972; M in Pub. Policy, JD magna cum laude, Harvard U., 1976. Bar: Calif. 1976, D.C. 1978, U.S. Ct. Appeals (D.C. cir.) 1983, U.S. Supreme Ct. 1983, U.S. Dist. Ct. D.C. 1985. Law clk. U.S. Ct. Appeals (2d cir.), Brattleboro, Vt., 1976-77; law clk. to U.S. Supreme Ct., Washington, 1977-78; assoc. asst. to Pres. U.S., 1978-80; assoc. Verner, Liipfert, Bernhard & McPherson, 1980-83; ptnr. Goldberg & Spector, 1983-92, Paul, Weiss, Rifkind, Wharton & Garrison, Washington, 1992-98; mng. ptnr., mem. mgmt. com., 1998—. Cons. U.S. exec. br. Close-Up Found., Alexandria, Va., 1980—. Co-author: Communications Law and Practice, 1995, Communications and Techology Alliances: Business and Legal Issues, 1996; mem. bd. editors Multimedia & Internet Strategist; contbr. articles to profl. jours. Mem. Coun. on Fgn. Rels., N.Y.C., 1980-85; moot ct. judge Nat. Assn. Attys. Gen., Washington, 1987—; adviser Dem. caucus U.S. Ho. Reps., Washington, 1981-83; speechwriter, podium prodr. Dem. Nat. Convs., N.Y.C., 1980, Phila., 1982, San Francisco, 1984, Atlanta, 1988, N.Y.C., 1992, Chgo., 1996, L.A., 2000. Recipient Disting. Achievement in Pub. Svc. Medal U. Calif., Santa Barbara, 1981, Close-Up Found. awards Via Satellite Mag., Vol. Recognition award Nat. Assn. Attys. Gen., 1993; named Leading Satellite Specialist in Washington, European Counsel, 2000. Mem. ABA (former chair internat. comm. law com.), Fed. Communications Bar Assn., Bethesda Country Club, Wintergreen Ptnrs., Phi Beta Kappa. Jewish. Communications, Computer, Private international. Office: Paul Weiss Rifkind Wharton & Garrison 1615 L St NW Ste 1300 Washington DC 20036-5694 E-mail: pspector@paulweiss.com

SPEER, JOHN ELMER, paralegal, reporter, counselor; b. Conrad, Mont., Mar. 19, 1956; s. Elmer Constant and Mildred Saphronia (LaBelle) S.; m. Sharron D. Knotts, May 23, 1982 (div. Mar. 1986); 1 child, Jeremy Keith; 1 foster child, Casey; m. Adah C. Corbett, May 10, 2000; stepchildren: Jody, Jay, Jill, Jessica. Paralegal assoc., Coll. of Great Falls, Mont., 1994; BS in paralegal studies, U. of Great Falls, Mont., 1999. Bar: Mont. 1996; cert. scuba diver. Farmer, Valier, Mont., 1956-73; janitor Shelby (Mont.) pub. schs., 1974-75; freelance news reporter Sta. KSEN, Shelby, 1980—, various TV stas., newspapers, Great Falls, 1980-90; office cleaner Parkdale Housing Authority, 1990-95; freelance paralegal, 1993—; law clk., paralegal Mont. State Dist. Judge Thomas McKittrick, 1993. Rschr. line-up identification appeal binder to U.S. Supreme Ct., 1993; trial assistance atty. Chas. Joslyn, spring 1996. Contbr. victim-witness assistance program operating manual, 1992. Counselor and adv. Victim-Witness Assistance Svcs., Great Falls, 1991-93. Mem. Mont. Big Sky Paralegal Assn., Am. Counseling Assn., Brain Injury Assn. of Mont. (chpt. v.p. 1997). Jehovah's Witness. Avocations: hiking, fishing, cooking, travel, swimming. Address: PO Box 206 Great Falls MT 59403-0206

SPELFOGEL, EVAN J. lawyer, educator; b. Boston, Jan. 28, 1936; s. Morris R. and Helen S. (Steinberg) S.; m. Beverly Kolenberg; children: Scott, Douglas, Karen. AB, Harvard U., 1956; JD, Columbia U., 1959. Bar: Mass. 1959, N.Y. 1964, U.S. Supreme Ct. 1969. Atty. Office of Solicitor, U.S. Dept. Labor, Washington, Boston, 1959-60, NLRB, Boston, N.Y.C., 1960-64; assoc. Simpson, Thacher & Bartlett, N.Y.C., 1964-69, Dewey, Ballantine, N.Y.C., 1969-77; ptnr. Fellner, Rovins & Gallay, 1977-80, Summit, Rovins & Feldesman, N.Y.C., 1981-91, Epstein Becker and Green, P.C., N.Y.C., 1991—. Adj. prof. law Baruch Coll., CCNY. Bd. editors Developing Labor Law: The Board, The Courts and the National Labor Relations Act, also co-editor-in-chief Supplements; bd. sr. editors Employee Benefits Law; contbr. articles to profl. jours. Fellow Coll. Labor and Employment Lawyers; mem. ABA (sect. on labor and employment law, exec. coun. 1978-86, co-editor sect. newsletter 1976-92, editl. bd. The Labor Lawyer 1996—, mem. ho. dels. 1987-90, sect. dispute resolution 1992—), FBA (coun. on labor law), N.Y. State Bar Assn. (chmn. labor and employment law sect. 1977-78, exec. coun. 1975—, ho. dels. 1978-79, com. on profl. discipline 1987-90), Assn. of Bar of City of N.Y. (labor com. 1968-71, 87-90, employee benefits com. 1992-96), Indsl. Resl. Rsch. Assn. (sec. N.Y. chpt. 1999-2000, pres. 2000-01), Am. Arbitration Assn. (nat. panel labor arbitrators), Harvard Varsity Club, Phi Alpha Delta. Labor. Home: 17 Parkside Dr Great Neck NY 11021-1042 Office: 250 Park Ave New York NY 10177-0001 E-mail: espelfog@ebglaw.com

SPELFOGEL, SCOTT DAVID, lawyer; b. Boston, Nov. 27, 1960; s. Evan. J. and Beverly (Kolenberg) S. BS, Boston U., 1982; JD, Syracuse U., 1985; LLM, Boston U., 1990. Bar: Mass. 1985, N.Y. 1986, U.S. Dist. Ct. (no. dist.) N.Y. 1986, U.S. Dist. Ct. Mass. 1987; lic. real estate broker, Mass., 1987. Assoc. Jeffrey M. McCrone, P.C., Syracuse, N.Y., 1985-87, Tatarian Law Offices, Boston, 1987-88; asst. gen. counsel The Berkshire Group, 1988-90, v.p., asst. gen. counsel, 1990-96, v.p., gen. counsel, 1996, sr. v.p., gen. counsel, 1997—. Mem. ABA, Am. Corp. Counsel Assn., Boston Bar Assn., N.Y. Bar Assn., Mass. Bar Assn. General civil litigation, General corporate, Real property. Home: 27 Sentry Hill Rd Sharon MA 02067-1521 Office: The Berkshire Group 1 Beacon St Ste 1500 Boston MA 02108-3116

SPELLACY, JOHN FREDERICK, lawyer; b. Steubenville, Ohio, Mar. 24, 1930; s. Joseph Roland and Thelma Fay (Stone) S.; m. Martha Jane Manning June 18, 1955; children— Joseph, James, John, Lawrence. Ph.B., Loyola Coll. Balt., 1952; LL.D., U. Miami (Fla.) 1958. Bar: Fla. 1960, U.S. Dist. Ct. (so. dist.) Fla. 1961. Ptnr., Kirsch & Spellacym Fort Lauderdale, Fla., 1958-69, DiGiulian, Spellacy, Ft. Lauderdale, 1969-83, Spellacy & McFann, Ft. Lauderdale, 1983— ; municipal judge City of Plantation, Fla., 1971-75. Mem. City Council, Plantation, 1962-71. Served to capt. USMC, 1952-54. Fellow Fla. Trial Lawyers Assn.; mem. Am. Arbitration Assn., ABA, Fed. Bar Assn., Fla. Bar, Assn. Trial Lawyers Am., Am. Judicature Soc., Broward County Mcpl. Judges Assn. (pres. 1974-75), Broward County. Trial Lawyers Assn. (pres. 1978-79). Democrat. Roman Catholic. Club: Civitan (v.p. Plantation 1965-70). Lodge: Elks. Insurance, Personal injury. Home: 7200 SW 8th Ave Apt 128 Gainesville FL 32607-1887 Office: Spellacy & McFann 888 SE 3rd Ave Fort Lauderdale FL 33316-1173

SPELLMAN, THOMAS JOSEPH, JR. lawyer; b. Glen Cove, N.Y., Nov. 11, 1938; s. Thomas J. and Martha H. (Erwin) S.; m. Margaret Mary Barth, June 23, 1962; children: Thomas Joseph, Kevin M., Maura N. BS, Fordham U., 1960, JD, 1965. Bar: N.Y. 1966, U.S. Dist. Ct. (so. and ea. dist.) N.Y. 1968, U.S. Ct. Appeals (2nd cir.) 1980, U.S. Supreme Ct. 1981. Staff atty. Allstate Ins. Co., N.Y.C., 1966-69; trial atty. Hartford Ins. Co., Hauppauge, N.Y., 1969-71; ptnr. Wheller & Spellman, Farmingville, 1971-76, Devitt, Spellman, Barrett, Callahan & Kenney, LLP, Smithtown, 1976—. Mem. grievance com. 10th Jud. Dist., Westbury, N.Y., 1984-92. Trustee Acad. St. Joseph, Brentwood, N.Y., 2000—. Capt. USAR, 1960-68. Fellow: Am. Bar Found., N.Y. Bar Found.; mem.: Suffolk County Bar Assn. (bd. dirs., sec.-treas. v.p. 1982—, pres. 1992—93), N.Y. Bar State Bar Assn. (ho. of dels. 1989—, nominating com. 1992—93, v.p. 1996—98), Swordfish Club. Westhampton Beach, N.Y. (bd. dirs., sec. 2000—). General civil litigation, Insurance, Personal injury. Home: 8 Highwoods Ct Saint James NY 11780-9610 Office: Devitt Spellman et al 50 Route 111 Ste 314 Smithtown NY 11787-3700

SPELTS, RICHARD JOHN, lawyer; b. Yuma, Colo., July 29, 1939; s. Richard Clark and Barbara Eve (Pletcher) S.; children: Melinda, Meghan, Richard John Jr.; m. Gayle Merves, Nov. 14, 1992. BS cum laude, U. Colo., 1961, JD, 1964. Bar: Colo. 1964, U.S. Dist. Ct. Colo. 1964, U.S. Supreme Ct. 1968, U.S. Ct. Appeals (10th cir.) 1970, U.S. Dist. Ct. (ea. dist.) Mich. 1986. With Ford Motor Internat., Cologne, Germany, 1964-65; legis. counsel to U.S. Senator, 89th and 90th Congresses, 1967-68; minority counsel U.S. Senate Subcom., 90th and 91st Congresses, 1968-70; asst. U.S. atty., 1st asst. U.S. atty. Fed. Dist. of Colo., 1970-77; pvt. practice Denver, 1977-89; risk mgr. sheriff's dept. Jefferson County, Golden, Colo., 1990-91. Owner Video Prodn. for Lawyers, 1991—. Selected for Leadership Denver, 1977; recipient cert. for outstanding contbns. in drug law enforcement U.S. Drug Enforcement Adminstrn., 1977, spl. commendation for criminal prosecution U.S. Dept. Justice, 1973, spl. commendation for civil prosecution U.S. Dept. Justice, 1976. Mem. Fed. Bar Assn. (chmn. govt. torts seminar 1980), Colo. Bar Assn. (bd. govs. 1976-78), Denver Bar Assn., Colo. Trial Lawyers Assn., Denver Law Club, Order of Coif. Republican. Methodist. Home and Office: 9671 Brook Hill Ct Littleton CO 80124-5431 Fax: (303) 662-9957

SPENCE, GERALD LEONARD, lawyer, writer; b. Laramie, Wyo., Jan. 8, 1929; s. Gerald M. and Esther Sophie (Pfleeger) S.; m. Anna Wilson, June 20, 1947; children: Kip, Kerry, Kent, Katy; m. LaNelle Hampton Peterson, Nov. 18, 1969. BSL, U. Wyo., 1949, LLB, 1952, LLD (hon.), 1990. Bar: Wyo. 1952, U.S. Ct. Claims 1952, U.S. Supreme Ct. 1982. Sole practice, Riverton, Wyo., 1952-54; county and pros. atty. Fremont County, 1954-62; ptnr. various law firms, Riverton and Casper, 1962-78; sr. ptnr. Spence, Moriarity & Schuster, Jackson, 1978—. Lectr. legal orgns. and law schs. Author: (with others) Gunning for Justice, 1982, Of Murder and Madness, 1983, Trial by Fire, 1986, With Justice for None, 1989, From Freedom to Slavery, 1993, How To Argue and Win Every Time, 1995, The Making of a Country Lawyer, 1996, O.J.: The Last Word, 1997, Give Me Liberty, 1998, A Boy's Summer, 2000, Gerry Spence's Wyoming: The Landscapes, 2000, Half Moon and Empty Stars, 2001. Mem. ABA, Wyo. Bar Assn., Wyo. Trial Lawyers Assn., Assn. Trial Lawyers Am., Nat. Assn. Criminal Def. Lawyers Criminal, Personal injury, Product liability. Office: Spence Moriarity & Schuster PO Box 548 Jackson WY 83001-0548

SPENCE, HOWARD TEE DEVON, judge, arbitrator, lawyer, consultant, insurance executive, government official; b. Corinth, Miss., Sept. 29, 1949; s. T. P. and Dorothy M.S.; m. Diane Earl Williams, Feb. 26, 1977 (div. June 1986); children: Derek, Tina, Steven. BA, Mich. State U., 1970, M in Criminal Justice Adminstrn., 1975, M in Labor-Indsl. Relations, 1981, MBA, 1983; JD, U. Mich., 1976, M in Pub. Adminstrn., 1977. Bar: Mich. 1976, U.S. Dist. Ct. (ea. dist.) Mich. 1976, U.S. Ct. Appeals (6th cir.) 1976, U.S. Supreme Ct. 1980, U.S. Dist. Ct. (we. dist.) Mich. 1986; cert. ins. examiner. Counselor State Prison of So. Mich., Jackson, 1971-76; personnel adminstr. Mich. Dept. Commerce, Lansing, 1976-77; asst. dir. Mich. Pub. Service Commn., 1977-78; dep. ins. commr. Mich. Ins. Bur., 1978-92; ptnr., cons. Spence & Assocs., 1983—; adminstrv. law judge State of Mich., 1992—. Arbitrator U.S. Dist. Ct. (we. dist.) Mich., Grand Rapids, 1986, Mich. Employment Rels. Commn., 1992—; adj. law prof. Thomas M. Cooley Law Sch., Lansing, 1977-80; adj. instr. Nat. Jud. Coll., Reno, 1993-98; presenter in field. Author short stories. Sec., v.p. Ingham County Housing Commn., Okemos, Mich., 1985-90; bd. dirs. Econ. Devel. Corp. City of Lansing, 1981-85. Mem.: NAACP (life), ABA (editor in chief NCALJ newsletter 1998—), Mich. Bar Assn. (legal edn. com.), Nat. Bar Assn., Assn. BlackJudges Mich., Mich. Assn. Adminstrv. Law Judges (pres. 1998), Nat. Conf. Adminstrv. Law Judges, Nat.Conf. Adminsgtrv. Law Judges, Black Lawyers Assn., Wolverine Bar Assn., Black Lawyers Assn., Ins. Regulatory Examiners Soc. (bd. dirs., nat. pres. 1990—91), Blue Key, Alpha Pi Alpha, Kappa Delta Lambda (pres., chmn. bd. dirs., adminstr. Project Alpha, Edn. Found. Inc.). Mem. Ch. of Christ. Club: Renaissance, Economic (Detroit). Avocations: tennis, racquetball, camping, dancing. Home: 1637 Willow Creek Dr Lansing MI 48917-9643 E-mail: htspence@spence-associates.com

SPENCER, DAVID JAMES, lawyer; b. Altadena, Calif., June 23, 1943; s. Dorcy James and Dorothy Estelle (Pingry) S.; m. Donna Rae Blair, Aug. 22, 1965; children: Daniel, Matthew. BA, Rocky Mountain Coll., 1965; JD, Yale U., 1968. Bar: Minn. 1968, U.S. Dist. Ct. Minn. 1968, U.S. Ct. Appeals (8th cir.) 1970. Mem. firm Briggs and Morgan, P.A., Mpls. and St. Paul, 1968—. Contbg. author 10 William Mitchell Law Rev., 1984; contbr. articles to profl. jours. Trustee Rocky Mountain Coll., Billings, Mont., 1980—; bd. dirs. Reentry Svcs., Inc., 1993—, River Valley Arts Coun., 1996—, Stillwater Area Arts Ctr. Alliance, 1998—, Homeward Bound, Inc., 1999—; pres., bd. dirs. St. Croix Friends of Arts, Stillwater, Minn., 1981-84; bd. dirs. Valley Chamber Chorale, Stillwater, 1989-92; v.p. Minn. Jaycees, St. Paul, 1974; elder Presbyn. Ch. Recipient Silver Key St. Paul Jaycees, 1974; Disting. Svc. award Rocky Mountain Coll., 1981, Outstanding Svc. award, 1988, Disting. Achievement award, 1992. Fellow Am. Coll. Real Estate Lawyers; mem. ABA, Minn. Bar Assn., Hennepin County Bar Assn., Stillwater Country Club, Stillwater Sunrise Rotary Club (bd. dirs. 1997-99). Presbyterian. Avocations: trout fishing, golf, singing. Condemnation, Landlord-tenant, Real property. Home: 10135 Waterfront Dr Woodbury MN 55129 Office: Briggs & Morgan 2200 First Nat Bank Bldg 332 Minnesota St Ste W2200 Saint Paul MN 55101-1396 E-mail: dspencer@Briggs.com

SPENCER, GEORGE HENRY, lawyer; b. Vienna; s. Frank Henry and Lillian (Godin) S.; m. Joan Betty Spencer, Sept. 16, 1956 (dec.); children: Lucy, Margaret, Robert, Nancy; m. Mollie Cole Sabol, Oct. 31, 1987; stepchildren: Jeanne, Marta. BE, Yale U., 1948; JD, Cornell U., 1952. Bar: D.C., N.Y. Examiner U.S. Patent Office, 1952-54; sole practice N.Y.C., Washington, 1954-62; ptnr. Spencer & Frank, Washington, 1962-98, Venable, Washington, 1998—. Master of bench Prettyman-Leventhal Am. Inn of Ct.; lectr. World Trade Inst. Served to capt. JAGC, U.S. Army, 1956-62. Mem. ABA, Am. Patent Law Assn., Lawyer-Pilots Bar Assn., Am. Arbitration Assn. (panel of arbitrators), Cosmos Club (Washington). Avocations: aviation, music, German and French language studies, poetry. Patent, Trademark and copyright. Home: 1102 Flor Ln Mc Lean VA 22102-1737 Office: Venable Attys at Law 1201 New York Ave NW Ste 1000 Washington DC 20005-3917 E-mail: specole@aol.com, ghspencer@venable.com

SPENCER, JOHN RICHARD, lawyer, business executive; b. Kansas City, Mo., Apr. 11, 1940; s. Paul Ripley and Teressa (Wagner) S.; B.B.A., U. Tex., 1964, LL.B., 1965; m. Joyce Ann Rhodenbaugh, Dec. 19, 1961; children— Stephen Myles, Kelly Lynn. Admitted to Tex. bar, 1965, Alaska bar, 1971, U.S. Supreme Ct. bar; assoc. Jarrard Cammack & Assos., Pasadena, Tex., 1965-66; post judge adv. Ft. Richardson, Alaska, 1967-70; city atty. City of Anchorage, 1971-75, exec. mgr., chief exec. officer municipality utilities, 1977-81; regional adminstr. EPA, Seattle, 1981-83; sr. v.p. Riedel Internat., Portland, Oreg., 1983— ; pres. Reidel Environ Services Co., 1984— ; v.p., gen. counsel RCA Alascom, Anchorage, 1975-77; pres. Anchorage Tire Center; trustee Alaska Elec. Health and Welfare and Pension Trust; past chmn. fed. regional council Seattle Fed. Exec. Bd. Former vice pres. Anchorage Retarded Childrens Assn.; former pres. Rehab. Industries Anchorage; former mem. Anchorage Police and Fire Retirement Bd.; chmn. energy com. Alaska Mcpl. League; former treas. Susitna Power Now, Inc.; chmn. bd. Olympics '92, Inc.; former state chmn. U.S. Olympic Com. Served with AUS, 1966-67; maj. Res. Decorated Army Commendation medal, Legion of Merit. Mem. Fed. (pres. Alaska chpt.), Am., Alaska, Tex. bar assns., Republican. Presbyterian. Clubs: Rotary, Newport Yacht, Anchorage Racquet. Contbr. articles to profl. jours. Home: 5048 Foothills Dr Apt A Lake Oswego OR 97034-4109 Office: PO Box 3320 Portland OR 97208-3320

SPENCER, ROBIN GRAHAM NELSON, lawyer; b. Wallasey, Cheshire, England, 1958; s. Peter Nelson and June Graham Linnet S.; m. Candida Trench Morison, May 19, 1990; children: Samuel, Freya, Zanna. BA with honors, Cambridge U., Eng., 1980, MA, 1984. Bar: Supreme Ct. Judicature Eng. and Wales. Prin. Her Majesty's Custom and Excise, London, 1983-86; assoc. Durrant Piesse, 1987, Applery, Spurling & Kempe, Hamilton, Bermuda, 1987-89, Lovells, London, 1990-94, ptnr., 1994—. Profumo scholar Inner Temple, 1981. Mem. R3, Internat. Assn. Ins. Receivers. Bankruptcy, Contracts commercial, Insurance. Office: Lovells 65 Holborn Viaduct London EC1A 2DY England Office Fax: 0207 296 2001. E-mail: robin.spencer@lovells.com

SPENCER, ROGER KEITH, lawyer; b. N.Y.C., July 2, 1946; s. Martin and Ruth Edith (Weiss) S.; children: William Cary, Elizabeth Ann, Freda Rose, Samuel Jacob, Lily Helene. BS, U. Mich., 1968; JD, Northwestern U., 1976. Bar: Ariz. 1976, U.S. Dist. Ct. Ariz. 1976, U.S. Ct. Appeals (9th cir.) 1976, U.S. Supreme Ct. 1983; cert. real property law Ariz. State Bar; lic. real property specialist. Mem. Shell & Wilmer, Phoenix, 1976-83; ptnr. Winston & Strawn, 1983-89, Quarles, Brady, Streich, Lang LLP, Phoenix, 1989—. Lectr. numerous real estate law seminars. Contbr. articles to profl. jours. Mem. Pheonix Men's Symphony Guild, 1977-78, Fiesta Bowl Com., 1989—; bd. dirs. Men's Arts Coun. Phoenix Art Mus., 1983—, Fiesta Bowl Com., 1988—; ptnr. Valley Partnership, 1988—; mem. Superbowl com., 1990—; active Gov. Strategic Partnership for Econ. Devel., 1993—. Capt. USAF, 1968-73. Mem. ABA (sect. corp., banking and bus. law, sect. real property, probate and trust law), State Bar Ariz., Maricopa County Bar Assn., U. Mich. Alumni Assn., Northwestern U. Alumni Assn., Phoenix Club, Rotary 100. Banking, Contracts commercial, Real property. Office: Quarles Brady Streich Lang LLP Two North Central Ave Phoenix AZ 85004

SPENCER, WILLIAM THOMAS, lawyer; b. Detroit, Oct. 18, 1950; s. Leo Joseph and Dorothy F. (Flynn) S.; m. Mary F. Twardochleb, July 23, 1983. B.A., U. Mich., 1973; J.D. cum laude, Wayne State U., 1976. Bar: Mich. 1976, U.S. Dist. Ct. (ea. dist.) Mich. 1978, U.S. Ct. Appeals (6th cir.) 1978. Staff atty. Legal Services Eastern Mich., Bay City, 1976-77; staff atty. Dietrich & Cassavaugh, Detroit, 1978-85; prin. William T. Spencer, P.C., 1985—. Active Friends Belle Isle. Mem. ABA, State Bar Mich., Assn. Trial Lawyers Am., Mich. Trial Lawyers Assn., U. Mich. Alumni Assn. Roman Catholic. Clubs: Motor City Striders (Detroit), Redford Roadrunners (Mich.), Les Amis Du Vin (Detroit), Mich. United Conservation (Lansing), Sierra. State civil litigation, Personal injury, Workers' compensation. Home: 20006 Longridge Ct Northville MI 48167-2905 Office: 3327 Cadillac Tower Detroit MI 48226

SPER, JANE, lawyer; b. N.Y.C., June 23, 1955; d. Roy and Rose (Heringman) S.; m. Thomas Gilbert Rosenthal, June 17, 1979 (div. Aug. 1997); children: Amy Katharine, Elizabeth Claire. BA in Polit. Sci. magna cum laude, U. Pa., 1976; JD, George Washington U., 1979. Bar: Va., 1979. Assoc. May, Miller & Parsons, Richmond, Va., 1979-81, Christian, Cocke & Dolbeare, Richmond, 1983-85, Staples, Greenberg, Minardi & Kessler, Richmond, 1985-86, Mays & Valentine, Richmond, 1986-90, Hirschler, Fleischer, Weinberg, Cox & Allen, Richmond, 1997—. Bd. dirs. Theatre IV, 1980-94, pres., 1984-86; bd. dirs. Daily Planet, 1992-98, treas., 1995-98; bd. dirs. YWCA, 1984-92, pres., 1989-91, mem. adv. coun., 1993—, chair, 1999-00; bd. dirs. Jewish Cmty. Ctr. Richmond, 1982-86, 91-96, trustee profit sharing plan and trust, 1985-97; bd. dirs. Met. Interfaith Assembly, 1992-94; bd. dirs. Jewish Cmty. Fedn. Richmond, 1986-87, chair jewish career women's network, 1984-87; mem. adv. coun. MetroTEEN, 1994-96, bd. trustees Congregation Beth Ahabah Museum and Archives, 1992-96, adv. bd. Richmond Gay Community Foundation, 2000—. Mem. Met. Richmond Women's Bar Assn. (mem. exec. com. 1985-89, pres. 1987-88, chair jud. nominations com. 1985-86), Va. Women Attys. Assn. (bd. dirs. 1983-86), U. Pa. Alumni Club Richmond (bd. dirs. 1986-92, chair secondary sch. com. 1980—, Ben Franklin award for disting. svc. to univ. and cmty. 1987), Richmond Bar Assn., Crew Network (Nat. Delegate 2000—). Avocations: tennis, film, travel, reading, golf. Office: Hirschler Fleischer Weinberg Cox & Allen PO Box 500 701 E Byrd St Richmond VA 23218-0500

SPERLING, ALLAN GEORGE, lawyer; b. N.Y.C., Dec. 10, 1942; s. Saul and Gertrude (Lober) S.; m. Susan Kelz, 1965 (div. 1999); children: Matthew Laurence, Stuart Kelz, Jane Kendra; m. Ferne Goldberg, 2001. Bar: N.Y. 1969, U.S. Ct. Appeals (2d cir.) 1975. Law clk. to presiding justice U.S. Dist Ct., New Haven, 1967-68; assoc. Cleary, Gottlieb, Steen & Hamilton, N.Y.C., 1968-75, ptnr., 1976—. Editor Yale Law Jour. Bd. dirs. Vol. Lawyers for the Arts, 1998—, Merce Cunningham Dance Found., N.Y.C., 1985-98, 2000—, chmn. bd., 1992-98; chmn. bd. Rye (N.Y.) Arts Ctr. Inc., 1985-88, bd. dirs., 1990-94; bd. dirs. Friends of the Neuberger Mus. of Art, Purchase, N.Y., 1989—, chmn. bd., 1997-2000. Mem. ABA, N.Y. State Bar Assn., Order of Coif, Phi Beta Kappa. General corporate, Finance, Securities. Home: 2 Fifth Ave New York NY 10011 Office: Cleary Gottlieb Steen & Hamilton 1 Liberty Plz Fl 43 New York NY 10006-1470

SPERLING, SHELDON J. prosecutor; BA Northeastern State Coll., JD U. Tulsa. Pvt. practice, Tulsa, 1979—82; asst. dist. atty. Okla. Dist. Atty.'s Office, 1983—85; asst. U.S. atty. Ea. Dist. Okla. U.S. Dept. Justice, 1985—2001, U.S. atty., 2001—. Office: 1200 W Okmulgee St Muskogee OK 74401*

SPERO, KEITH ERWIN, lawyer, educator; b. Cleve., Aug. 21, 1933; s. Milton D. and Yetta (Silverstein) S.; m. Carol Kohn, July 4, 1957 (div. 1974); children: Alana, Scott, Susan; m. Karen Weaver, Dec. 28, 1975. BA, Western Res. U., 1954, LLB, 1956. Bar: Ohio 1956. Assoc. Sindell, Sindell & Bourne, Cleve., 1956-57, Sindell, Sindell, Bourne, Markus, Cleve., 1960-64; ptnr. Sindell, Sindell, Bourne, Markus, Stern & Spero, 1964-74, Spero & Rosenfield, Cleve., 1974-76, Spero, Rosenfeld & Bourne, LPA, Cleve., 1977-79, Spero & Rosenfield Co. LPA, 1979—. Tchr. bus. law U. Md. overseas div., Eng., 1958-59; lectr. Case-Western Res. U., 1965-69; instr.; nat. panel arbitrators Am. Arbitration Assn. Author: The Spero Divorce Folio, 1966, Hospital Libaiblity for Acts of Professional Negligence, 1979. Trustee Western Res. Hist. Soc., 1984—2000, exec. com., 1992—2000; v.p., chmn. libr. display and collections com. Western Res. Hist. Soc, 1992—95, chmn. history mus. com., 1995—99; commodore Dugway Creek Yacht Club, 1985—87; bd. dirs. Vail Valley Inst., 2000—. 1st lt. UAGC USAF, 1957—60, capt. Res. USAF, 1960—70. Fellow Am. Acad. Matrimonial Lawyers; mem. ABA, Ohio Bar Assn., Cleve. Bar Assn., Cuyahoga County Bar Assn., Ohio Acad. Trial Lawyers (pres. 1970-71), Assn. Trial Lawyers Am. (state committeeman 1971-75, bd. govs. 1975-79, sec. family law litigation sect. 1975-76, vice-chmn. 1976-77, chmn. 1977-79), Am. Bd. Trial Advs., Order of Coif, Masons, Phi Beta Kappa, Zeta Beta Tau, Tau Epsilon Rho. Jewish. (trustee, v.p. congregation 1972-78). State civil litigation, Family and matrimonial, Personal injury. Office: 440 Leader Bldg E 6th and Superior Cleveland OH 44114-1214 E-mail: keith@vail.net

SPERO, MORTON BERTRAM, retired lawyer; b. N.Y.C., Dec. 6, 1920; s. Adolph and Julia (Strasburger) S.; m. Louise Thacker, May 1, 1943; children: Donald S., Carol S. Flynn. BA, U. Va., 1942, LLB, 1946. Bar: Va. 1946, U.S. Supreme Ct. 1961. Mem. legal staff NLRB, Washington, 1946-48; sole practice Petersburg, Va., 1948-70; sr. ptnr. Spero & Levinson, 1970-75, Spero & Diehl, Petersburg, 1975-85; sole practice, 1985-2001; retired, 2001. Chmn. The Community Bank, Petersburg, 1976-79, dir., 1976-91. Chmn. United Fund Drive, 1960, bd. dirs., 1999—; pres. Dist. IV Petersburg Coun. Social Welfare, Southside Sheltered Workshop, 1965, pres. Congregation B'rith Achim, 1973. Served to lt. USNR, 1943-45. Recipient Outstanding Mem. award Petersburg chpt. B'nai B'rith, 1966; Svc. to Law Enforcement award Petersburg Police Dept., 1965. Fellow Am. Acad. Matrimonial Lawyers; mem. Va. Bar Assn., Petersburg Bar Assn. (pres. 1981-82), Va. State Bar (coun. 1981-84, chmn. criminal law sect. 1972, chmn. family law sect. 1979, bd. dirs. litigation sect. 1983-86, Lifetime Achievement award for family law sect. 1995), Va. Trial Lawyers Assn. (v.p. 1972), Civitan Club (hon.), Rotary, Elks (exalted ruler 1968). Democrat. Jewish. State civil litigation, Criminal, Family and matrimonial. Home and Office: 9706 Bunker Ct Petersburg VA 23805-9125 Fax: 804-733-0157

SPEVAK, ERIC SCOTT, lawyer; b. Syracuse, N.Y., Feb. 28, 1959; s. Mannie and Sylvia Spevak. BA, Hobart Coll., 1981; JD, Villanova U., 1984. Bar: Pa. 1984, N.J. 1984. Assoc. Archer & Greiner, P.C., Haddenfield, N.J., 1984-86; ptnr. Gerstein, Cohen & Spevak, 1986-90, Adinolfi & Spevak, P.A., Cherry Hill, 1990—. Instr. Inst. for Continuing Legal Education, N.J., 1995—. Contbr. articles to profl. jours. Mem. N.J. State Family Law Assn., (exec. com. 1995), South Jersey Family Inns of Ct. (v.p. 1997—), Camden County Bar Assn. (trustee 1988-92, chmn. family law com. 1989-94, co-chair 1999, 2000). Avocations: soccer coach, baseball coach, basketball official. Family and matrimonial. Office: Adinolfi and Spevak PA 70 Tanner St Haddonfield NJ 08033-2419

SPEYER, DEBRA GAIL, lawyer; b. N.Y.C., Jan. 8, 1959; d. Frank R. and Lynn (Lederer) S.; m. Bruce H. Levin, Mar. 30, 1986. BBA, Hofstra U., Hempstead, N.Y., 1980, JD, 1984, MBA, 1988. Bar: N.Y. 1986, Pa. 1986, Conn. 1986, Fla. 1988, D.C. 1988. Atty., v.p. Thomson McKinnon Securities, N.Y.C., 1984-87; pvt. practice North Miami, Fla., 1987-88; atty. Nat. Assn. Securities Dealers, Phila., 1988-90; pvt. practice, 1990—. Arbitrator NASD, N.Y. Stock Exch.; lectr. Phila. Bar Assn., 1996—, course planner; cons. Phila. Corp. for the Aging. Dir. Nat. Cong. Syn Youth, Merrick, N.Y., 1983-86; pres. A.F.S.I., 1988-90, bd. dirs., 1990—; bd. dirs. Heart to Heart, 1993—, Judicare Sr. Citizen Project, 1998—; pres. AMIT, 1994-98. Named One of Best Lawyers in Phila. Phila. Mag. Mem. ABA, N.Y. State Bar Assn., Conn. Bar Assn., Pa. Bar Assn., Phila. Bar Assn. (co-chair elder law com. 1997—), Am. Trial Lawyers Assn., D.C. Bar Assn., Fla. Bar Assn., Phi Alpha Delta (treas. 1982-83). Avocations: golf, art. Estate planning, Probate, Securities. Office: The Lendell Bldg 232 S 3rd St Philadelphia PA 19106-3811 E-mail: debra@speyerlaw.com

SPICER, S(AMUEL) GARY, lawyer, writer; b. Dickson, Tenn., Jan. 8, 1942; s. Clark and E. Maybelle (Hogin) S.; m. Katherine M. Stettner, May 12, 1972; children: Victoria, S. Gary Jr., Matthew, Katy, Mark, David. BA, Adrian Coll., 1964; MBA, Wayne State U., 1965; JD, Detroit Coll. Law, 1969. Bar: Mich. 1969, Tenn. 1969. With pers. dept. GM Truck & Coach, Detroit, 1964-66; with trust dept. Nat. Bank Detroit, 1966-69; acct. Price Waterhouse & Co., Detroit, 1969-71; propr. Law Firm of S. Gary Spicer, 1971—. Author: Surviving Success, 1990. Co-chmn. endowment com. Adrian (Mich.) Coll., 1982-94, Don and Dolly Smith Found., Detroit, 1981—; trustee Pam Lewis Found, 1995—, Don Baylor Found., 1995—, Detroit Tigers Players Home Clubhouse Scholarship Fund; performing arts com. Detroit Pub. Schs.; elder, treas., Fort St. Presbyn. Ch. With USAR, 1965-71. Recipient Young Alumni Achievement award Adrian Coll. Alumni Assn., 1987; named to Athletic Hall of Fame, Adrian Coll., 1996. Mem. Detroit Athletic Club, Detroit Club. Avocations: Russian literature, squash, fitness running. General corporate, Entertainment, Sports.

SPIEGEL, EDNA Z. lawyer; b. N.Y.C., 27 Oct. m. Rubin E. Spiegel; children: Linda F. Spiegel Duboff, Joyce I., Bennett L. BS, NYU, 1948, MA, 1949; JD, Seton Hall U., 1986. Bar: N.J. 1988, U.S. Dist. Ct. N.J. 1988, U.S. Supreme Ct. 1993; lic. asst. prin., lic. prin. N.Y.C. Bd. Edn. Substitute tchr. music N.Y.C. Bd. Edn., 1950-52, tchr. music, 1952-81; pvt. legal practice River Edge, N.J., 1990—. Atty. River Edge Environ. Protection Commn., 1987—96; with cmty. outreach on advance directives Holy Name Hosp., Teaneck, NJ, 1994—97; trustee Bergen County Legal Svcs., Hackensack, 1999—; lawyer law day Divsn. Human Svcs. Bergen County, 1988—. Mem. Nat. Acad. Elder Law Attys. (charter mem. N.J. chpt.), N.J. Women Lawyers' Assn., N.J. State Bar Assn. (charter, elder law sect.), Bergen County Bar Assn. (charter, elder law com.), Women Lawyers in Bergen County, Hadassah/The Womens Zionist Orgn. of Am. (River Dell chpt., v.p. programs 1978-80, 96—, chmn. Am. affairs 1979—, Woman of the Yr. 1996, Nat. Leadership award 1997). Avocations: gardening, painting, cooking, swimming, collectibles. Estate planning, Probate, Elder Law. Office: 25 Wayne Ave River Edge NJ 07661-1809 E-mail: ezsesq@aol.com

SPIEGEL, H. JAY, lawyer; b. Cleve., July 7, 1952; s. Martin and Thea (Lange) S. BS, Cornell U., 1974; JD, George Mason U., 1981. Bar: Va. 1981, U.S. Patent Office 1982, U.S. Ct. Appeals (fed. cir.) 1982, U.S. Dist. Ct. (ea. dist.) Va. 1982, U.S. Supreme Ct. 1984, D.C. 1986. Primary and asst. examiner U.S. Patent and Trademark Office, Arlington, Va., 1974-82; assoc. Sherman & Shalloway, Alexandria, 1982-88, of counsel, 1988; pvt. practice., 1988-96; pvt. practice, Mt. Vernon, Va., 1996—. Owner, pres. Premium Products, Inc., Alexandria, 1984—, Jumpstart. Patentee sporting goods and jewelry; inventor Toe-Tal Tee and Ground Zero Tee football tees, PENTA five panel football. Mem.: ATLA, Am. Intellectual Property Law Assn., Licensing Exec. Soc. Avocations: boating, travel. Entertainment, Patent, Trademark and copyright. Office: H Jay Spiegel & Assocs PC PO Box 444 Mount Vernon VA 22121-0444 E-mail: jayspiegel@aol.com

SPIEGEL, HART HUNTER, retired lawyer; b. Safford, Ariz, Aug. 30, 1918; s. Jacob B. and Margaret (Hunter) S.; m. Genevieve Willson, Feb. 12, 1946; children: John Willson, Claire Margaret Spiegel Brian, Jennifer Emily Spiegel Grellman. BA, Yale U., 1940, LLB, 1946. Bar: Calif. 1946, D.C. 1960. Assoc. Brobeck, Phleger & Harrison, San Francisco, 1947-55, ptnr., 1955-90. Chief counsel IRS, Washington, 1959-61, mem. adv. group to commr., 1975. Served to lt. USMC, 1942-46, PTO. Mem. ABA (coun. mem. tax sect. 1966-68), Am. Law Inst., Bar Assn. San Francisco (pres. 1983), Pacific Union Club, Berkeley Tennis Club (pres. 1964-65). Corporate taxation, State and local taxation. Home: 3647 Washington St San Francisco CA 94118-1832 Office: Brobeck Phleger & Harrison 1 Market Pla Spear St Tower San Francisco CA 94105

SPIEGEL, JERROLD BRUCE, lawyer; b. N.Y.C., Apr. 11, 1949; s. Seymour S. and Estelle (Minsky) S.; m. Helene Susan Cohen, Mar. 3, 1972; children: Dana Sean, Amy Barrett, Evan Tyler. BS, Queens Coll., 1970; JD cum laude, NYU, 1973. Bar: N.Y. 1974. Assoc. Austrian, Lance & Stewart, N.Y.C., 1973-75, Gordon Hurwitz Butowsky Baker Weitzen & Shalov, N.Y.C., 1975-79; ptnr. Shapiro Spiegel Garfunkel & Driggin, 1979-86, Frankfurt Garbus Kurnit Klein & Selz P.C., N.Y.C., 1986—. Editor Ann. Survey Am. Law, 1972-73, Mem. ABA (corp. law sect.), Order of the Coif, Omicron Delta Epsilon. Computer, General corporate, Intellectual property. Office: Frankfurt Garbus Kurnit Klein & Selz PC 488 Madison Ave Fl 9 New York NY 10022-5754

SPIEGEL, LINDA F. lawyer; b. Bronx, N.Y., Mar. 13, 1953; d. Rubin E. and Edna (Zucker) S.; m. Paul Duboff, June 12, 1983; 1 child, Joshua Michael. AB, Barnard Coll., Columbia U., 1974; JD, Boston U., 1978. Bar: N.J. 1978, U.S. Dist. Ct. N.J. 1978, N.Y. 1980, U.S. Dist. Ct. (so. and ea. dists.) N.Y. 1980, U.S. Supreme Ct. 1982. Tax editor Prentice Hall, Englewood, N.J., 1978; pvt. practice, Hackensack, 1978-83, 88—; assoc. Friedman, Carney & Wilson, Newark, 1983-84; pvt. practice New Milford, N.J., 1984-85; assoc. LaFianza and Strull, Hackensack, 1985-87, ptnr., 1987-88. Instr. Inst. Legal Asst. and Paralegal Tng., Mahwah, N.J., 1978-81; co-vice chair Bergen County Youth Svcs. Commn., 2001. Spkr. Boy Scouts Am., Bergen, N.J., 1980; mem. atty.-acct. divsn. United Jewish Cmty., River Edge, N.J., 1978—; trustee Women's Am. Orgn. Rehab. through Tng., 1987-88; chmn. Jean Robertson Women Lawyers Scholarship Found., Inc., 1987-94. Mem. ABA, Am. Arbitration Assn. (comml. and constrn. arbitrator 1989—), N.J. Women Lawyers Assn., N.J. State Bar Assn., Bergen County Bar Assn. (trustee 1989-94, editor-in-chief Bergen Barrister 1991-94), Women Lawyers in Bergen County (pres. 1987-89), B'nai Brith. Democrat. Avocations: theater, tennis, swimming, square and country dancing. Alternative dispute resolution, General civil litigation, Family and matrimonial. Office: 79 Main St Ste 1 Hackensack NJ 07601-7126 E-mail: lfsesq@aol.com

SPIEGEL, S. ARTHUR, federal judge; b. Cin., Oct. 24, 1920; s. Arthur Major and Hazel (Wise) S.; m. Louise Wachman, Oct. 31, 1945; children: Thomas, Arthur Major II, Andrew, Roger Daniel. BA, U. Cin., 1942, postgrad., 1949; LLB, Harvard U., 1948. Assoc. Kasfir & Chalfie, Cin., 1948-52; assoc. Benedict, Bartlett & Shepard, 1952-53, Gould & Gould, Cin., 1953-54; ptnr. Gould & Spiegel, 1954-59; assoc. Cohen, Baron, Druffel & Hogan, 1960; ptnr. Cohen, Todd, Kite & Spiegel, 1961-80; judge U.S. Dist Ct. Ohio, 1980—; sr. status, 1995—. Served to capt. USMC, 1942-46 Mem. ABA, FBA, Ohio Bar Assn., Cin. Bar Assn., Cin. Lawyers Club. Democrat. Jewish. Office: US Dist Ct 838 US Courthouse 5th Walnut St Cincinnati OH 45202

SPIEGELBERG, FRANK DAVID, lawyer; b. Washington, Aug. 21, 1948; s. Joseph H. and Ruth (May) S.; m. Linda Rae Gordesky, June 28, 1970; children: Adam Jay, Kimberly Joy. BA, Kent State U., 1970; JD, Duke U., 1973. Bar: Md. 1973, Tex. 1977, Okla. 1978, U.S. Ct. Mil. Appeals 1974, U.S. Dist. Ct. (no. dist.) Okla. 1978, U.S. Ct. Appeals (10th cir.) 1978, U.S. Dist. Ct. (we. dist.) Okla. 1985, U.S. Supreme Ct. 1985. Assoc. Dukes, Troese, Mann & Wilson, Landover, Md., 1973; litigation atty. Cities Service Co., Tulsa, 1978-82, sr. litigation atty., 1982; atty. Apache Corp., Tulsa, 1982-86; of counsel Boesche, McDermott & Eskridge, Tulsa, 1986-87, ptnr., 1988—. Pres. Burning Tree Homeowners Assn., Tulsa, 1981-85, bd. dirs. 1981-85, 87-88; mem. Union Sch. Bd., Tulsa, 1989—. Served as capt. USAF, 1974-77. Recipient Air Force Commendation medal, 1977, cert. of Appreciation for seminar, Okla. Assn. Def. Counsel, 1982. Mem. Okla. Bar Assn., Tex. Bar Assn., Tulsa County Bar, Tulsa County Bar Assn., Assn. Trial Lawyers Am., Kent State U. Alumni Assn., Duke U. Alumni Assn., Sigma Phi Epsilon Alumni Assn. State civil litigation, General corporate, Oil, gas, and mineral. Home: 9032 E 67th St Tulsa OK 74133-2207 Office: Boesche McDermott & Eskridge 800 Oneok Plaza 100 W 5th St Tulsa OK 74103-4240

SPIELMAN, KIM MORGAN, lawyer, educator; b. Ft. Wayne, Ind., Jan. 1, 1953; s. George Homer and Mary Ruth (Steininger) S.; m. Susan Kay Altekruse, Apr. 15, 1972; children: Matthew Ryan, Nathan Daniel. BS, Ind. U., 1982, MPA, 1984; JD with high distinction, Ohio No. U., 1986. Bar: Ind. 1987, U.S. Dist. Ct. (no. and so. dists.) Ind. 1987, U.S. Ct. Appeals (7th cir.) 1990. Officer Ft. Wayne Police Dept., 1975-84; assoc. Barnes & Thornburg, Ft. Wayne, 1986-91; assoc. prof. Ind. U., 1988—; chief counsel Allen County Prosecutor's Office, 1991-92; with Beers, Mallers, Backs & Salin, 1992-95; gen. counsel Hercules Machinery Corp., 1995-98, Blackburn & Green, Ft. Wayne, 1999—. Instr. Ft. Wayne Police Acad. Del. Ind. State Rep. Conv., Indpls., 1982, 84, 92, 94, 96, 98; bd. dirs. Jr. Achievement of No. Ind.; ward chmn. Mayor's Police/Cmty. Rels. Task Force, 1997-98; pres. Safety and Security Svcs., LLC; judge pro tem, Allen County Superior Ct.; mem. Bd. Public Safety, City Ft. Wayne, 1998-2000. Mem. ABA, ATLA, Ind. Bar Assn., Allen County Bar Assn., Greater Ft. Wayne C. of C. Republican. Lutheran. Home: 3222 Sudbury Pl Fort Wayne IN 46815-6224 Office: 3344 Mallard Cove Ln Fort Wayne IN 46804-2884 E-mail: kspielman@blackburn-green.com

SPIES, FRANK STADLER, lawyer; b. Adrian, Mich., Aug. 7, 1939; s. Charles F. and Lucille M. (Stadler) S.; m. Lynette K. Wells, July 25, 1964; children: Anne, Jane, Charles. BBA, U. Mich., 1961, LLB, 1964. Bar: Mich. 1964, U.S. Dist. Ct. (we. dist.) Mich. 1964, U.S. Ct. Appeals (6th cir.) 1971. Assoc. Schmidt, Smith, Howlett & Halliday, Grand Rapids, Mich., 1964-66; asst. city atty. City of Grand Rapids, 1966-69, U.S. Dept. Justice, Grand Rapids, 1969-77; U.S. atty. Western Dist. Mich., 1974-77; pvt. practice, 1977-81, 84-97; assoc. Kaufman, Payton & Kallas, 1981-84, Bensinger, Cotant, Menkes & Aardema, Grand Rapids, 1997—. Instr. bus. law Davenport Coll., Grand Rapids, 1967-68, Grand Valley State U., Grand Rapids, 1978-79. Recipient Dirs. Honor award U.S. Secret Svc., 1977. Mem. ABA, Grand Rapids Bar Assn., Nat. Assn. Former U.S. Attys., Grand Rapids East Rotary, Republican. Presbyterian. Insurance, Personal injury, Product liability. Home: 2122 Tenway Dr SE Grand Rapids MI 49506-4526 Office: 983 Spaulding Ave SE Grand Rapids MI 49546-3700 E-mail: fspies@bcma.net

SPIES, LEON FRED, lawyer; b. Blue Grass, Iowa, Oct. 8, 1950; s. Fred William and Alma Lois (Lineburg) S.; m. Janet Rae Peterson, July 15, 1979; children: Caitlin, Allison. BBA with distinction, U. Iowa, 1972, JD with distinction, 1975. Bar: Iowa 1975, U.S. Dist. Ct. (no. and so. dists.) Iowa 1975, U.S. Ct. Appeals 1975, U.S. Supreme Ct. 1987. Assoc. Heintz & Mellon, Iowa City, 1975-76; ptnr. Mellon & Spies, 1976—. Magistrate jud. dept. State of Iowa, 1978-83; instr. trial advocacy U. Iowa Coll. Law, 1996—. Bd. chmn. Johnson County Red Cross, Iowa City, 1982-84; bd. dirs. Big Bros./ Big Sisters, Johnson County, Iowa, 1985-89. Fellow Iowa Acad. Trial Lawyers; mem. ABA, ATLA, Iowa Bar Assn., Assn. Trial Lawyers Iowa, Am. Judicature Soc., Am. Inns of Ct. (master, pres. Dean Mason Ladd Inn 1995-96). Democrat. Methodist. State civil litigation, Criminal, Personal injury. Home: 2349 Kent Ct NE Iowa City IA 52240-9633 Office: Mellon & Spies 102 S Clinton St Iowa City IA 52240-4024

SPIKE, MICHELE KAHN, lawyer; b. Paterson, N.J., Oct. 1, 1951; d. Nathan and Clara (Spinella) Kahn; m. John Thomas Spike, May 26, 1973; 1 child, Nicholas Nathan. BA summa cum laude, Conn. Coll., 1973; JD cum laude, Boston U., 1976. Bar: N.Y. 1977, U.S. Dist. Ct. (so. and ea. dists.) N.Y. 1977. Assoc. Hale, Russell & Gray, N.Y.C., 1976-82; sole practice, N.Y.C., 1982-86; with Dolgenos, Newman & Cronin, N.Y.C., 1986-89. Editor: (exhbn. catalogue) Italian Still Life Paintings, 1983, Baroque Portraiture in Italy, 1984. Mem. ABA, Bar Assn. City N.Y., Phi Beta Kappa. General corporate, Real property, Art. Home: 152 Engle St Tenafly NJ 07670-2704

SPILLANE, DENNIS KEVIN, lawyer; b. N.Y.C., Sept. 15, 1953; s. Denis Joseph and Mary Kate (Sullivan) S. BA magna cum laude, Manhattan Coll., 1974; JD, N.Y. Law Sch., 1978; MS in Taxation, Pace U., 1986, post-masters cert. in bus., 1992. Bar: N.Y. 1979, U.S. Dist. Ct. (ea. and so. dists.) N.Y. 1979, U.S. Tax Ct. 1986, D.C. 1988, U.S. Ct. Appeals (2d cir.) 1988, U.S. Supreme Ct. 1988, Conn. 1989. Asst. dist. atty. Borough of Bronx, N.Y.C., 1978-85; prin. atty. N.Y. State Tax Dept., 1985-87; supervising atty. Office of Profl. Discipline, N.Y. State Edn. Dept., 1987—. Prof. law and taxation Pace U., 1987—. Contbr. articles to profl. jours. Mem. Conn. Bar Assn, N.Y. State Bar Assn., D.C. Bar Assn. Conservative. Roman Catholic. Office: NY State Edn Dept 475 Park Ave S Frnt 3 New York NY 10016-6901

SPILLIAS, KENNETH GEORGE, lawyer; b. Steubenville, Ohio, Nov. 8, 1949; s. George and Angeline (Bouyoucas) S.; m. Monica Mary Saumweber, May 10, 1975; children: Geoffrey David, Alicia Anne, Stephanie Marie. BA, Pa. State U., 1971; JD magna cum laude, U. Pitts., 1974. Bar: Pa. 1974, Fla. 1978, U.S. Supreme Ct. 1978, U.S. Ct. Appeals

(2d, 3d, 4th, 5th, 6th cirs.) 1975, (11th cir.) 1981, U.S. Dist. Ct. (mid. dist.) Fla. 1979, U.S. Dist. Ct. (so. dist.) Fla. 1978; cert. cir. ct. mediator. Trial atty. U.S. Dept. Justice, Washington, 1974-76; asst. dist. atty. Dist. Atty. of Allegheny County, Pitts., 1976-78; asst. atty. gen. Fla. Dept. Legal Affairs, West Palm Beach, Fla., 1978-79; ptnr. Spillias & Mitchell, 1979-82, Considine & Spillias, West Palm Beach, 1982-83, Schneider, Maxwell, Spillias et al, West Palm Beach, 1984-86, Wolf, Block, Schorr et al, West Palm Beach, 1986-88, Shapiro & Bregman, West Palm Beach, 1988-91; of counsel Greenberg, Traurig et al, 1991; pvt. practice, 1991-97; ptnr. Lewis, Longman & Walker, P.A., 1997—. Instr. bus. law Coll. of the Palm Beaches, West Palm Beach, 1980-81; CLE lectr. Palm Beach County Bar Assn., 1983—. County commr. Bd. County Commrs., Palm Beach County, 1982-86; co-founder, mem. Children's Svcs. Coun., Palm Beach County, 1986-91; steering com. Fla. Atlantic U. Inst. of Govt., Boca Raton, 1983-94; bd. dirs. The Literacy Coalition of P.B.C., West Palm Beach, 1990-2000, health and human svcs. Fla. Dist. IX, 1995-98, Ctr. for Family Svc., West Palm Beach, 1992-96, Palm Beach County Coun. of Arts, 1987-1988, West Palm Beach Planning Bd., 1997—; mem. policy coun. Fla. Inst. Govt., Tallahassee, 1985-86; fund raising chmn. United Cerebral Palsey Telethon, West Palm Beach, 1984-85; judge Palm Beach Post Pathfinders Awards, 1992-98. Recipient Cmty. Svc. award Downtown Civitan Club, West Palm Beach, 1983, Man of the Day award United Cerebral Palsey, 1986, Spl. Honoree award Palm Beach County Child Advocacy Bd., 1986, Children's Trust award Exch. Club/Dick Webber Ctr. for Prevention Child Abuse, 1991, Up and Comers Award in Law, South Fla. Bus. Jour./Price Waterhouse, 1988, Achievement award Nat. Assn. Counties, 1986; named to Outstanding Young Men of Am., U.S. Jaycees, 1975, 84. Mem. ABA, Palm Beach County Bar Assn. (appellate practice com. 1990—), Am. Hellenic Ednl. Progressive Assn. Fla. Bar Assn. (pres. 2001-2002, appellate advocacy and city, county and local govt. sects.), Order of Coif, Kiwanis. Avocations: sports, writing, theater, reading, music. Appellate, General civil litigation, Municipal (including bonds). Home: 147 Gregory Rd West Palm Beach FL 33405-5029 Office: Ste 1000 1700 Palm Beach Lakes Blvd West Palm Beach FL 33401-2006

SPINA, ANTHONY FERDINAND, lawyer; b. Chgo., Aug. 15, 1937; s. John Dominic and Nancy Maria (Ponzio) S.; m. Anita Phyllis De Orio, Jan. 28, 1961; children: Nancy M. Spina Okal, John D., Catherine M. Spina Samatas, Maria J. Spina Samatas, Felicia M. BS in Social Sci., Loyola U., Chgo., 1959; JD, DePaul U., 1962. Bar: Ill. 1962. Assoc. Epton, Scott, McCarthy & Bohling, Chgo., 1962-64; pvt. practice Elmwood Park, Ill., 1964-71; pres. Anthony & Spina, PC, 1971-84, Spina, McGuire & Okal, PC, Elmwood Park, 1985—. Codifier Rosemont Village Ordinances, 1971, Elmwood Park Bldg. Code, 1975, Leyden Twp. Codified Ordinances, 1987. Mem. Elmwood Pk. Bldg. Code Planning Commn. Bd. Appeals; bd. dirs. Sheridan Carrol Charitable Works Fund, 1996—; atty. Leyden Twp., Ill., 1969—89, Village of Rosemont, 1971; counsel for Pres. and dir. Cook County Twp. Ofcls. Ill., 1975—96; counsel for exec. dir. Ill. State Assn. Twp. Ofcls., 1975—96; counsel Elmwood Park Village Bd., 1967—89, Norwood Park St. Lighting Dist., 1988—, various Cook County Twps. including DuPage, 1980—82, Maine, 1981—97, Norwood Park, 1982—, Wayne, 1982—84, Berwyn Twp., 1997—99, Hanover Twp., 1997, Cook County Hwy. Commrs. Traffic Fine Litigation, 1974—96, 1999—2001, Hanover Twp. Mental Health Bd., 1991—, Glen Edens Assn., 1994—99, Berwyn Twp. Mental Health Bd., 1997—. Recipient Lacodaire medal, Deans Key Loyola U., Loyola U. Housing awards, 1965, 71, 76; Appreciation award Cook County Twp. Ofcls., av rating Martindale-Hubbel. Mem. ABA, Ill. Bar Assn., Chgo. Bar Assn., West Suburban Bar Assn. Cook County (past chmn. unauthorized practice law sect.), Am. Judicature Soc., Justinian Soc. Lawyers, Ill. State Twp. Attys. Assn. (past v.p., pres. 1982-86, dir. 1996-99, dir. emeritus 1999—), Nat. Inst. Town and Twp. Attys. (past v.p., pres. 1993-95, Ill. del.), Montclare/Leyden C. of C., Edgebrook C. of C. (past bd. dirs.), Nat. Assn. Italian Am. Lawyers, Joint Civic Com. Chgo. (exec. com.), World Bocce Assn. (dir.), St. Rocco Soc. Simbario, KC (scribe, trustee, past Grand Knight, bldg. corp. dir. 1967-99), Calabresi in Am. Orgn. (bd. dirs. 1991—), Fra Noi Ethnic Publ. (dir. 1995—), Blue Key, Delta Theta Phi, Tau Kappa Epsilon, Pi Gamma Mu. Roman Catholic. State civil litigation, Estate planning, General practice. Office: 7610 W North Ave Elmwood Park IL 60707-4100 E-mail: spinalaw@aol.com

SPINA, FRANCIS X. judge; m. Sally O'Donnell; 2 children. BA, Amherst Coll.; JD, Boston Coll. Prosecutor, Berkshire County, Mass., 1979—83; pvt. law practice Pittsfield, 1983—93; judge Mass. Superior Ct., 1993-97, Appeals Ct., Pittsfield, 1997-99; assoc. justice Mass. Supreme Jud. Ct., Boston, 1999—. Office: Mass Supreme Ct New Ct House Pemberton Sq Boston MA 02108*

SPIOTTO, JAMES ERNEST, lawyer; b. Chgo., Nov. 25, 1946; s. Michael Angelo and Vinnetta Catherine (Henninger) S.; m. Ann Elizabeth Humphreys, Dec. 23, 1972; children: Michael Thomas, Mary Catherine, Joan Elizabeth, Kathryn Ann. AB, St. Mary's of the Lake, 1968; JD, U. Chgo., 1972. Bar: Ill. 1972, U.S. Dist. Ct. (no. dist.) Ill. 1973, U.S. Ct. Appeals (3rd and 7th cir.) 1974, U.S. Supreme Ct. 1978, U.S. Ct. Appeals (9th cir.) 1984, U.S. Dist. Ct. (so. dist.) Calif. 1984. Exclusionary rule study-project dir. Law Enforcement Assistance Agy. Grant, Chgo., 1972; law clk. to presiding justice U.S. Dist. Ct., 1972-74; assoc. Chapman and Cutler, 1974-80, ptnr., 1980—. Chmn. program on defaulted bonds and bankruptcy Practising Law Inst., 1982—, chmn program on troubled debt financing, 1987— Author: Defaulted Securities, 1990; contbr. numerous articles to profl. jours. With USAR, 1969-75. Mem. Assn. Bond Lawyers, Soc. Mcpl. Analysts, Law Club of City of Chgo., Union League, Econs. Club Chgo. Roman Catholic. Bankruptcy, Federal civil litigation, Municipal (including bonds). Office: Chapman and Cutler 111 W Monroe St Ste 1700 Chicago IL 60603-4006

SPITZ, HUGO MAX, lawyer; b. Richmond, Va., Aug. 17, 1927; s. Jacob Gustav and Clara (Herzfeld) S.; m. Barbara Steinberg, June 22, 1952; children: Jack Gray, Jill Ann Levy, Sally Spitz. AA, U. Fla., 1948, BLaws, 1951, JD, 1967. Bar: Fla. 1951, S.C. 1955, U.S. Dist. Ct. (so. dist.) Fla. 1951, U.S. Dist. Ct. (ea. dist.) S.C. 1956, U.S. Ct. Appeals (4th cir.) 1957. Asst. atty. gen. State of Fla., Tallahassee, 1951; assoc. Williams, Salomon & Katz, Miami, Fla., 1951-54, Steinberg & Levkoff, Charleston, S.C., 1954-57; sr. ptnr. The Steinberg Law Firm L.L.P., 1957-2001. Lectr. S.C. Trial Lawyers Assn., Columbia, 1958—, S.C. U. Sch. Law, Columbia, 1975, S.C. Bar Assn., 1955—; assoc. mcpl. judge Charleston, 1972-74, mcpl. judge, 1974-76; commr. Charleston County Substance Abuse Commn., 1976-79; bd. govs. S.C. Patient's Compensation Fund, Columbia, 1978-97; adv. mem., atty. S.C. Legis. Coun. for Worker's Compensation; chmn. bd. dirs. Franklin C. Fetter Health Ctr., Charleston, 1977-78; mem. S.C. Appellate Def. Commn., 1985-86; founding sponsor Civil Justice Found., 1986—; bd. pres. Charleston Jewish Fedn., 1990-91, pres., 1991-92. Pres. Synagogue Emanu-El, 1969-71. With USN, 1945-46. Awarded Order of Silver Crescent, Gov. S.C., 2001. Fellow S.C. Bar Assn., U. S.C. Ednl. Found.; mem. ABA, Civil Justice Found., S.C. Law Inst., S.C. Trial Lawyers Assn. (founder and pres. 1985-86), S.C. Claimants' Attys. for Worker's Compensation (Hon. life bd. mem., exec. com. 1986, Order of Silver Crescent award 2001), S.C. Worker's Compensation Ednl. Assn. (bd. dirs. 1978-98), S.C. Law Inst., Am. Judicature Soc., Trial Lawyers Am. (mem. pres. council 1986-87, stalwart 2001), Nat. Rehab. Assn., Nat. Orgn. Social Security Claimants' Reps. S.C. Bar (chmn. trial and appellate sect. 1982-83, ho. of dels. 1984-85), So. Assn. Workmen's Compensation Adminstrs., Nat. Inst. for Trial Advocacy (com. chmn. 1985), Hebrew Benevolent Soc. (life, pres. 1974-75), Jewish Cmty. Ctr. (Charleston) (v.p. 1972-74), Hebrew Orphan Soc. (life, pres. 2000-01), B'nai B'rith, Elks (life). Democrat. State civil litigation, Personal injury, Workers' compensation. Home: 337 Confederate Cir Charleston SC 29407-7430 E-mail: hspitz@home.com

SPITZBERG, IRVING JOSEPH, JR. lawyer, corporate executive; b. Little Rock, Feb. 9, 1942; s. Irving Joseph and Marie Bettye (Seeman) S.; m. Roberta Frances Alprin, Aug. 21, 1966 (div. 1988); children— Edward Storm, David Adam; m. Virginia V. Thorndike, Dec. 24, 1988. B.A., Columbia U., 1964; B.Phil., Oxford U., 1966; J.D., Yale U., 1969. Bar: Calif. 1969, D.C. 1985, Va. 1995. Asst. prof. Pitzer Coll., Claremont, Calif., 1969-71; fellow Inst. Current World Affairs, N.Y.C., 1971-74; vis. lectr. Brown U., Providence, 1973; assoc prof. SUNY, Buffalo, 1974-80, dean of coll., 1974-78; gen. sec. AAUP, Washington, 1980-84; exec. dir. Coun. for Liberal Learning of Assn. Am. Colls., 1985-89; pres. The Knowledge Co., Fairfax, Va., 1985-2001; ptnr. Spitzberg & Drew, Washington, 1990-92; of counsel Spirer & Goldberg, 1993—; pvt. practice, 1993—. Coord. Alvan Ikoku Coll., Nigeria, 1979-80; cons. Bd. Adult Edn., Kenya, 1973-74, Philander Smith Coll., Little Rock, 1978-80; co-dir. nat. study on campus life for Carnegie Found. for Advancement Teaching, 1989-90. Author and editor: Exchange of Expertise, 1978, Universities and the New International Order, 1979, Universities and the International Exchange of Knowledge, 1980; author: Campus Programs on Leadership, 1986, Racial Politics in Little Rock, 1987; co-author: (with Berdahl and Moodie), Quality and Access in Higher Education, 1991, (with Virginia Thorndike) Creating Community on College Campuses, 1992. Founder Coalition for Ednl. Excellence, Western N.Y., 1978-80; founding mem. Alliance for Leadership Devel., Washington, 1985; counsel GASP, Pomona, Calif., 1969-71; Dem. Committeeman, Erie County, N.Y., 1978-80; founding pres. Internat. Found. for St. Catherine's Coll., Oxford, 1986-91; founder Coun. for Liberal Learning; mem. Ethical Culture Soc. Nat. winner Westinghouse Sci. Talent Search, 1960; Kellett scholar Trustees of Columbia U., 1964-66. Mem. Am. Immigration Lawyers Assn., Nat. Acad. Elder Law Attys., Assn. Study Higher Edn., Washington Ethical Soc., Columbia Club, Yale Club (Washington). Jewish. Avocations: kids, the Internet. Estate planning, Immigration, naturalization, and customs, Probate. E-mail: 1js@aol.com

SPITZER, ELIOT, state attorney general; m. Silda Spitzer; 3 children. Grad., Princeton U., 1981; JD, Harvard U., 1984. Clk. U.S. Judge Robert W. Sweet; assoc. Paul, Weiss, Rifkind, Wharton & Garrison, Skadden Arps Slate Meagher & Flom; ptnr. Constantine & Ptnrs., N.Y.C.; asst. dist. atty. State of N.Y., Manhattan, 1986-92, atty. gen. Albany, 1999—. Analyst, commentator on nat. news programs including NBC's Today Show, CNN's Burden of Proof, CNBC, Court TV. Editor Harvard Law Rev.; contbr. articles in leading newspapers and legal jours. Founder Ctr. for Cmty. Interest; trustee Montifiore Med. Ctr. Office: NY State Attorney General Attn Peter Drago The Capitol Albany NY 12224-0341 also: 120 Broadway New York NY 10271-0002*

SPITZER, HUGH D. lawyer; b. Seattle, Feb. 14, 1949; s. George Frederick and Dorothy Lea (Davidson) S.; m. Ann Scales, Oct. 14, 1983; children: Johanna Spitzer, Claudia Spitzer, Jenny Spitzer. BA, Yale U., 1970; JD, U. Wash., 1974; LLM, U. Calif., 1982. Bar: Wash. 1974, U.S. Dist/ Ct. (ea. and we. dists.) Wash. 1975, U.S. Ct. Appeals (9th and D.C. cirs.) 1975, U.S. Supreme Ct. 1980. Program analyst N.Y.C. Health and Hosp. Corp., 1970-71; labor lawyer Hafer, Cassidy & Price, Seattle, 1974-76; legis. asst. Seattle City Coun., 1976-77; legal counsel to mayor City of Seattle, 1977-81; mcpl. bond lawyer Foster Pepper & Shefelman, PLLC, Seattle, 1982—. Affiliate prof. sch. law U. Wash. Contbr. articles to profl. jours. Vice chair Puget Sound Water Quality Authority Wash. State, 1989-96; chair Seattle Law Income Housing Levy Oversight com., 1988-96; chair Wash. State Affordable Housing Adv. Bd., 2000—. Mem. Nat. Assn. Bond Lawyers, Pub. Legal Edn. Working Group, Am. Judicature Soc. (mem. exec. com. Coun. on Pub. Legal Edn.). Democrat. Avocations: piano, hiking, skiing. Municipal (including bonds). Office: Foster Pepper & Shefelman PLLC 1111 3rd Ave Bldg Ste 3400 Seattle WA 98101-3292 E-mail: spith@foster.com

SPITZER, MATTHEW LAURENCE, law educator, dean; b. L.A., June 23, 1952; s. William George and Jeanette Dorothy (Navsky) S.; m. Jean Fuksman, July 8, 1973; 1 child, Amanda Elizabeth. BA in Math., UCLA, 1973; JD, U. So. Calif., 1977; PhD in Social Scis., Calif. Inst. Tech., 1979. Assoc. Nossaman, Guthner, Knox & Elliott, L.A., 1977-79; asst. prof. Northwestern U., Chgo., 1979-81; William T. Dalessi prof. law U. So. Calif., L.A., 1987-2000, from assoc. prof. to prof., 1984—, dir. law and rational choice programs, 1990-2000, dir. Comms. Law and Policy Ctr., 1998—2000; prof. law and social scis. Calif. Inst. Tech., Pasadena, 1992-2000; dean, Carl Mason Franklin prof. law U. So. Calif., L.A., 2000—. Vis. prof. law U. Chgo., 1996, Stanford (Calif.) U., 1997; mem. organizing com. Telecoms. Policy Rsch. Conf., Washington, 1991-94. Author: Seven Dirty Words and Six Other Stories, 1986; co-author: (with T. Hazlett) Public Policy Toward Cable Television, 1997. Recipient (shared with Elizabeth Hoffman) Ronald H. Coase prize U. Chgo., 1986. Mem. Am. Law and Econs. Assn. (bd. dirs. 1997-2000). Avocations: paperweight collecting, audiophile. Office: U So Calif Law Sch Los Angeles CA 90089-0071*

SPITZER, VLAD GERARD, lawyer; b. Bucharest, Romania, Mar. 3, 1956; came to U.S., 1963; s. Adrian and Carole Spitzer; m. Denise J. Borenstein, July 9, 1989; 1 child, Max Oliver. BA with honors, NYU, 1978; JD, Yeshiva U., 1981. Bar: N.Y. 1988, Conn. 1995, U.S. Dist. Ct. (so. and ea. dists.) N.Y. 1988, U.S. Dist. Ct. Conn. 1996, U.S. Ct. Appeals (2d cir.) 1994, U.S. Supreme Ct. 1995. Asst. dist. atty. Dist. Atty.'s Office of King's County, Bklyn., 1981-83; ptnr. Goldbergh & Spitzer LLC, N.Y.C., 1988-95, Stamford, Conn., 1995—. Adv. bd. Nat. Employee Rights Inst., Cin., 1997—; founding mem. Conn. Employee Rights Inst., Stamford, Conn., 1997; coop. atty. ACLU, N.Y. Civil Liberties Union; judge Wagner Nat. Lab. and Employment Law Moot Ct., N.Y. Law Sch., 1996-98. Belkin scholar, 1981. Mem. ATLA (labor and employment sect. 1996—), Assn. of the Bar of the City of N.Y., Nat. Employment Lawyers Assn., Conn. Bar Assn. (labor and employment sect. 1996—, employee benefits com. 1996—), Nat. Employee Rights Inst., Stamford-Norwalk Regional Bar Assn., Stamford Rotary Club. Civil rights, General practice, Labor. Office: Spitzer Sundheim & Brey LLC 350 Bedford St Ste 401 Stamford CT 06901-1741

SPITZLI, DONALD HAWKES, JR. lawyer; b. Newark, Mar. 19, 1934; s. Donald Hawkes and Beatrice (Banister) S.; children: Donald Hawkes III, Peter Gilbert, Seth Armstrong. A.B., Dartmouth Coll., 1956; LL.B., U. Va., 1963. Bar: Va. 1963. Assoc. Willcox, Savage, Lawrence, Dickson & Spindle, Norfolk, Va., 1964-67, 68-70, ptnr., 1971-77; atty. Eastman Kodak Co., Rochester, N.Y., 1967-68; pres. Marine Hydraulics Internat., Inc., Chesapeake, Va., 1978-80; sole practice Virginia Beach, 1980—. Owner Chieftain Motor Inn, Hanover, N.H., 1980-87. Comdr. USNR, 1956-70. Episcopalian. Bankruptcy, Family and matrimonial, General practice. Office: 281 Independence Blvd Ste 605 Virginia Beach VA 23462-2975 E-mail: airbuzzard24@aol.com

SPIVACK, EDITH IRENE, lawyer; b. Apr. 19, 1910; d. Harry A. and Ethel Y. (Mantell) Spivack; m. Bernard H. Goldstein, Dec. 22, 1933; children: Rita Goldstein Christopher, Amy Goldstein Bass. BA, Barnard Coll., 1929; LLB, Columbia U., 1932; Doctorate (hon.) , St. John's U. Bar: N.Y. 1933, U.S. Dist. Ct. (so. dist.) N.Y. 1949, U.S. Dist. Ct. (ea. dist.) Pa. 1973, U.S. Ct. Appeals 1950, U.S. Ct. Appeals 1975, U.S. Supreme Ct. 1969. Assoc. asst. Corp. Counsel's Office, City of N.Y., 1934—76, exec. asst., 1976—95, exec. asst. emeritus, 1995—. Spl. master appellate divsn. 1st Dept., 1991, mem. com. on character and fitness, 1995—. Active Planned Parenthood, Legal Aid Soc.; rep. to alumni coun., past bd. dir. Columbia Law Sch. Recipient Pub. Svc. award, Fund for City of N.Y., 1975, Columbia award for Conspicuous Svc., 1975, Outstanding Pub. Svc., NIMLO, 1976, Disting. Svc. award, Mayor Koch, 1981, Disting. Alumnae award, Barnard Coll, 1984, Disting. and Dedicated Corp. Counsel Svc. award, 1986. Fellow: N.Y. Bar Found. (Cmty. Svc. award); mem.: N.Y. State Bar Assn. (judiciary com., del., status of women in cts. com., Fifty-yr. Lawyer award 1984, 60 yr. dedicated svc. award), Am. Bar Found., N.Y. County Lawyers Assn. (bd. dirs., fin. com., women's rights com., judiciary com., mem. com. on coms., Edith Irene Spivack award Named after her, William Nelson Cromwell award 1976), Assn. Bar City N.Y. (cts. and mem. com., judiciary com.), N.Y. County Lawyers Found., Am. Judicature Soc., Columbia U. Law Sch. Alumni Assn. (medal for excellence com., Outstanding Woman award in No. Hempstead), Princeton Club (N.Y.C.). Democrat. Jewish. Bankruptcy, Condemnation, Real property. Home: 21 Colonial Rd Port Washington NY 11050-4307 Office: Office Corp Counsel 100 Church St New York NY 10007-2601

SPIVEY, BROADUS AUTRY, lawyer; b. Lakeview, Tex., Oct. 7, 1936; s. Claude Clifton and Mary Eddith (Stafford) S.; m. Ruth Ann King, Aug. 1, 1956; children: Danny C., Marci M. Diploma, Clarendon Jr. Coll., 1956; BA in Govt., U. Tex., 1960, JD, 1962. Bar: Tex. 1962, U.S. Dist. Ct. (no., so., we. and ea. dists.) Tex., U.S. Ct. Appeals (5th cir.) 1971, U.S. Ct. Claims (11th cir.) 1979, U.S. Supreme Ct. 1973, UTE Indian Tribal Ct. 1997; cert. in personal injury trial law Tex. Bd. Legal Specialization. Asst. county atty. Lubbock County, Lubbock, Tex., 1962-64; ptnr. West, Spivey & Brackett, 1964-65; assoc. Huff & Bowers, 1965-70; sole practitioner, 1970-71; ptnr. Gibbins & Spivey, Austin, Tex., 1971-76; sr. ptnr. Spivey & Ainsworth and predecessor firms, 1976—. Author: The Trial of Contested Paternity Cases, 1977; co-author: Texas Pattern Jury Charges, vol. 3, 1982; contbr. articles to profl. jours. Fellow Internat. Soc. Barristers, Internat. Acad. Trial Lawyers (bd. dirs. 1993—, editor law rev. The Advocate), Am. Coll. Trial Lawyers; mem. Travis County Bar Assn., Capital Area Trial Lawyers Assn. (pres. 1977-79), State Bar Tex. (chmn. tort and compensation sect. 1976-77, Supreme Ct. adv. com. 1984-90, pres. 2001-), Fed. Bar Assn., Tex. Bar Found., Am. Bd. Trial Advocates, Lawyer Pilots Bar Assn., Tex. Trial Lawyers Assn. (pres. 1981-82), Assn. Trial Lawyers Am. (cert., bd. govs. 1982-85), Trial Lawyers Pub. Justice (bd. dirs. 1982-93, treas. 1989-90), Delta Theta Phi (Outstanding Alumnus award, 1973, 1978). Democrat. Methodist. Avocations: skiing, piloting, reading, woodworking. Aviation, General civil litigation, Personal injury. Home: 4013 Sierra Dr Austin TX 78731-3913 Office: Spivey Grigg Kelly Knisely 48 East Ave Austin TX 78701-4317*

SPIZZ, HARVEY WARREN, lawyer; b. Bklyn., Apr. 7, 1943; s. Conrad and Sara (Fagin) S.; m. Valerie Holder, Mar. 22, 1969; children— Hayley, Erica. A.B., Columbia U., 1964; J.D., U. Miami, 1967. Bar: Fla. 1967, N.Y. 1968, U.S. Dist. Ct. (ea. and so. dist.) N.Y. 1970, U.S. Ct. Appeals (2d cir.) 1970, U.S. Supreme Ct. 1974. Counsel SBA, Washington, 1967-68; sr. staff atty. Cals & Bronx Legal Services, N.Y.C., 1968-71; exec. dir. Clinic, Hofstra Law Sch., Hempstead, N.Y., 1971-73, prof., exec. dir. Law Sch., 1973-76; ptnr. Spizz & Cooper, Mineola, N.Y., 1976— . Bd. dirs. Community Organ. for Parents and Youth, Gt. Neck, N.Y., 1983— , Community Action Legal Services, N.Y.C., 1974-76, Bronx Legal Services, 1973-76; vol. counsel CLASP, Gt. Neck, N.Y. Mem. Nassau County Bar Assn. Democrat. Jewish. Federal civil litigation, State civil litigation, General practice. Home: 41 Devon Rd Great Neck NY 11023-1660 Office: Spizz and Cooper 114 Old Country Rd Mineola NY 11501-4400

SPOLAN, HARMON SAMUEL, lawyer; b. Phila., Dec. 12, 1935; s. Jay and Edythe (Greenberg) S.; m. Betty Jane Evnitz, Mar. 30, 1958; children: Michael, Suzanne. AB, Temple U., 1957, LLB, 1959; postgrad., Oxford U., 1966. Bar: Pa. 1960. Ptnr. Ravetz & Shuchman, Phila., 1960-68, Blair & Co., N.Y.C., 1968-72; v.p. Butcher & Singer, Phila., 1972-74; pres. Capital First Corp., 1974-75, State Nat. Bank, Rockville, Md., 1975-78, Jefferson Bank, Phila., 1978-99; pres., bd. dirs. JeffBanks, Inc., 1986-99; sr. mem. Cozen O'Connor, 1999—. Lectr. law U. Pa., Phila., 1964-68. Author: Federal Aids to Financing, 1970; contbr. articles to profl. jours. Former chmn. bd. Huntingdon Hosp., Willow Grove, Pa., 1982-89; bd. dirs. YMHA, Phila., 1978—; bd. dirs. Anti-Defamation League, 1982. Named Man of Yr., Nat. Assn. Women Bus. Owners, 1978, Disting. Alumnus, Central H.S., 1975. Mem. ABA, Phila. Bar Assn. Democrat. Jewish. Banking, General corporate, Finance. Office: 1900 Market St Philadelphia PA 19103-3527 E-mail: hspolan@cozen.com

SPONZILLI, EDWARD GEORGE, lawyer, history educator; b. Newark, Mar. 30, 1948; s. Edward James and Dorothy Maria (Murillo) S. BA in History with high honors, Rutgers U., 1971, JD, 1975; summer diploma Cath. Inst. of Paris, 1971; MA, Columbia U., 1972. Bar: N.J. 1975, U.S. Dist. Ct. N.J. 1975, U.S. Ct. Appeals (3d cir.) 1976, U.S. Supreme Ct. 1979, U.S. Ct. Appeals (D.C. cir.) 1979, N.Y. 1981. Law clk. to chief judge U.S. Dist. Ct. N.J., Newark, 1975-77; assoc. Pitney, Hardin & Kipp, Morristown, N.J., 1975-81, Dunn, Pashman, Sponzilli, Swick & Finnerty (formerly Cummins, Dunn & Pashman), Hackensack, N.J., 1982—, ptnr., 1984-94; ptnr. Norris, McLaughlin & Marcus, Pa., 1994—; co-adj. prof. Rutgers U., New Brunswick, N.J., 1980-81, 94, 98; mcpl. pros. Rutgers U., 1981—; counsel Judo of N.J. Inc., Cranford, 1983—; mem. 1975 Rutgers Jessup Internat. Law Moot Ct. Team; judge law sch. moot ct. competition Seton Hall, 1977-79, 81, 84, 86; coach Rutgers Coll. Mock Trial Team, 1994-97. Active Rutgers U. Found., 1987—. Recipient Nancy Higgenson Dorr award Rutgers U., 1971, Disting. Svc. award Animals Need You-Kindness Corp., N.J., 1981; Henry Rutgers scholar. Mem. ABA (trial practice com. of litigation sect.), N.J. State Bar Assn., Fed. Bar Assn., Assn. Fed. Bar N.J., Assn. Trial Lawyers Am., N.J. Trial Lawyers Assn., Trial Attys. N.J. (trustee 1987—), Bergen County Bar Assn., Essex County Bar Assn., Middlesex County Bar Assn., Am. Hist. Assn., So. Hist. Assn., Orgn. Am. Historians, Civil War History Assn., Rutgers U. Law Sch. Alumni Assn. (exec. counsel, nominating com. 1982, program dir. 1982, alumni fedn. rep.), "Scarlet R" Round Table Alumni Assn., Columbia Grad. Faculties Alumni Assn., Phi Beta Kappa, Kappa Sigma (dist. grand master, 1986—, alumnus advisor 1978—, trustee Gamma Upsilon chpt., sec. 1978-79, v.p. 1979-82, pres. 1982-86, 94—, chair 1995-97), Phi Alpha Delta. Federal civil litigation, State civil litigation, Labor. Home: 37 Brookside Ave Caldwell NJ 07006-5603 Office: Norris McLaughlin & Marcus PA 721 Rt 202-206 PO Box 1018 Somerville NJ 08876-1018

SPOONHOUR, JAMES MICHAEL, lawyer; b. San Antonio, Mar. 24, 1946; s. Robert W. and Marie C. (Schulze) S.; m. Terri Walker; children: Taylor, Erin, Whitney, Michael. BA, U. Nebr., 1968, MA, 1970; JD, Georgetown U., 1974. Bar: Fla. 1974, U.S. Dist. Ct. (mid. dist.) Fla. 1974. Assoc. Lowndes, Piersol, Drosdick & Doster, Orlando, Fla., 1974-76; asst. prof. law Loyola U., New Orleans, 1976-77; ptnr. Lowndes, Drosdick, Doster, Kantor & Reed, P.A., Orlando, 1977—. Lectr. on eminent domain and property taxes. Contbr. to profl. publs. Bd. dirs. Vis. Nurse Assn., Orlando, 1979-89, Croquet Found. Am., 2001—; chmn. sch. bd. The First Acad., Orlando, 1986-89. With USAF, 1970-72. Mem. ABA, Assn. Trial Lawyers Am., Fla. Bar, Orange County Bar Assn. Republican. General civil litigation, Condemnation, State and local taxation. Office: Lowndes Drosdick Doster Kantor & Reed PA 215 N Eola Dr Orlando FL 32801-2095 E-mail: james.spoonhour@lowndes-law.com

SPOTSWOOD, ROBERT KEELING, lawyer; b. Balt., July 11, 1952; s. William Syson and Helen Marie (Fairchild) S.; m. Ashley Hayward Wiltshire, Aug. 19, 1978; children: Robert Keeling, Mary Hayward. BS with highest distinction in Applied Math., U. Va., 1974, JD, 1977. Bar: Ala. 1977, U.S. Dist. Ct. (no. dist.) Ala. 1979, U.S. Dist. Ct. (so. dist.) Ala. 1980, U.S. Ct. Appeals (5th cir.) 1979, U.S. Ct. Appeals (11th cir.) 1981, U.S. Dist. Ct. (mid. dist.) Ala. 1986, U.S. Supreme Ct. 1987. Ptnr. Bradley, Arant, Rose & White, Birmingham, Ala., 1977—. Mem. Birmingham Bar Assn., ABA. Club: Mountain Brook. Federal civil litigation, General civil litigation, Labor. Home: 3865 Cove Dr Birmingham AL 35213-3801 Office: Bradley Arant Rose & White PO Box 830709 Birmingham AL 35283-0709

SPRANSY, JOSEPH WILLIAM, corporate lawyer; b. Durham, N.C., July 17, 1946; s. George Brower and Marion Elizabeth (Dibble) S.; m. Lillian Drew Darden, Aug. 8, 1970; children: Katherine Leigh, Joseph William II. AB in Math., King Coll., Bristol, Tenn., 1968; JD, U. N.C., 1973. Bar: Ala. 1973, U.S. Dist. Ct. (no. dist.) Ala. 1973, U.S. Ct. Appeals (5th cir.) 1976, U.S. Supreme Ct. 1980, U.S. Ct. Appeals (11th cir.) 1981. Math. tchr. Castlewood (Va.) High Sch., 1968-70; program dir. Camp Monroe, Laurel Hill, N.C., 1968-70; assoc. Bradley, Arant, Rose & White, Birmingham, Ala., 1973-79; corp. counsel U.S. Pipe and Foundry Co., 1979-99, v.p., 1999—. Moderator Birmingham Presbytery, Presbyn. Ch. USA, 1987—, vice moderator, 1986—; elder Mountain Brook Presbyn. Ch., 1982-84, 1986-88, 91-94, 98-2000. Mem. ABA, Ala. State Bar Assn. (chair labor and employment sect. 1992-93, chair bus. law sect. 1999-2000), Birmingham Bar Assn., Assn. Corp. Counsel in Am. (bd. dirs. Ala. chpt. 1985—), U. N.C. Alumni Assn. (pres. Ala. chpt. 1983-84), Phi Alpha Delta. Club: Birmingham Sailing. Avocations: woodworking, sailing, running. Antitrust, General corporate, Labor. Home: 4000 Hunters Ln Birmingham AL 35243-5820 Office: US Pipe and Foundry Co 3300 1st Ave N Birmingham AL 35222-1200 E-mail: jspransy@uspipe.com

SPRINGER, CHARLES EDWARD, retired state supreme court chief justice; b. Reno, Feb. 20, 1928; s. Edwin and Rose Mary Cecelia (Kelly) S.; m. Jacqueline Sirkegian, Mar. 17, 1951; 1 dau., Kelli Ann. BA, U. Nev., Reno, 1950; LLB, Georgetown U., 1953; LLM, U. Va., 1984; student Grad. Program for Am. Judges, Oriel Coll., Oxford (Eng.), 1984. Bar: Nev. 1953, U.S. Dist. Ct. Nev. 1953, D.C. 1954, U.S. Supreme Ct. 1962. Pvt. practice law, Reno, 1953-80; atty. gen. State of Nev., 1962, legis. legal adv. to gov., 1958-62; legis. bill drafter Nev. Legislature, 1955-57; mem. faculty Nat. Coll. Juvenile Justice, Reno, 1978—; juvenile master 2d Jud. Dist. Nev., 1973-80; justice Nev. Suprem Ct., Carson City, 1981—; vice-chief justice Nev. Supreme Ct., 1987, chief justice, 1998-99, ret., 1999. Mem. Jud. Selection Commn., 1981, 98, Nev. Supreme Ct. Gender Bias Task Force, 1981—; trustee Nat. Coun. Juvenile and Family Ct. Judges, 1983—; mem. faculty McGeorge Sch. Law, U. Nev., Reno, 1982—; mem. Nev. Commn. for Women, 1991-95. With AUS, 1945-47. Recipient Outstanding Contbn. to Juvenile Justice award Nat. Coun. Juvenile and Family Ct. Judges, 1989, Midby-Byron Disting. Leadership award U. Nev., 1988. Mem. ABA, Am. Judicature Soc., Am. Trial Lawyers Assn., Phi Kappa Phi. Office: Nev Supreme Ct Capitol Complex 201 S Carson St Carson City NV 89701-4702

SPRINGER, ERIC WINSTON, lawyer; b. N.Y.C., May 17, 1929; s. Owen Winston and Maida Christina (Stewart) S.; m. Cecile Marie Kennedy, Oct. 25, 1958; children: Brian, Christina. AB, Rutgers U., 1950; LLB, NYU, 1953. Bar: N.Y. 1953, Pa. 1975, U.S. Dist. Ct. (we. dist.) Pa. 1978. Law clk. to justice N.Y. State Supreme Ct., 1955-56; research assoc. U. Pitts., 1956-58, asst. prof. law, 1958-64, assoc. prof. law, 1965-68; dir. compliance EEOC, 1967; v.p., dir. Publs. Aspen Systems Corp., Pitts., 1968-71; ptnr. Horty, Springer & Mattern, Pitts., 1971-82, exec. v.p., 1982— ; dir. Duquesne Light Co., Pitts. Author: Group Practice and the Law, 1969. Editor Nursing and the Law, 1970; Automated Medical Records and the Law, 1971; contbg. editor monthly newsletter Action-Kit for Hosp. Law, 1973— . Bd. dirs. Presbyn. Univ. Hosp., Pitts., 1966—, Cath. Health Corp., Omaha, 1988—, Hosp. Utilization Project., Pitts., 1975-86; mem. Pitts. Commn. on Human Relations, 1963-68, chmn., 1964-68. Fellow Am. Coll. Healthcare Execs. (hon.), Am. Pub. Health Assn.; mem. ABA, Nat. Bar Assn., Allegany County Bar Assn., Am. Acad. Hosp. Attys. (charter), Order of Coif. Democrat. Health. Office: Horty Springer & Mattern PC 4614 5th Ave Pittsburgh PA 15213-3663

SPRINGER, JEFFREY ALAN, lawyer; b. Denver, Feb. 26, 1950; s. Stanley and Sylvia (Miner) S.; m. Amy Mandel, Nov. 11 1995; children: Cydney Erin, Samantha Libby, Jackson Stanley, Harrison Louis. AB, Princeton U., 1972; JD, U. Colo., 1975. Bar: Colo. 1975, U.S. Dist. Ct. Colo. 1975, U.S. Ct. Appeals (10th cir.) 1975, U.S. Supreme Ct. 1978, U.S. Ct. Appeals (8th cir.) 1986. Assoc. Gerash & Springer, Denver, 1975-79; sole practice, 1979-81; pres. Springer and Steinberg, P.C., 1981—. Mem. com. on mcpl. ct. rules Supreme Ct. Colo., 1985-86; mem. standing criminal justice act com. U.S. Dist. Ct., 1994-96. Mem. ABA, Assn. Trial Lawyers Am., Colo. Trial Lawyers Assn. (bd. dirs. 1988-90), Colo. Criminal Def. Bar (bd. dirs. 1985-86, 87-88, pres. 1988-89). Criminal, Personal injury. Office: 1600 Broadway Ste 1950 Denver CO 80202-4920 E-mail: jspringer@uswest.net

SPRINGER, PAUL DAVID, lawyer, motion picture company executive; b. N.Y.C., Apr. 27, 1942; s. William W. and Alma (Markowitz) S.; m. Mariann Frankfurt, Aug. 16, 1964; children: Robert, William. BA, U. Bridgeport, 1963; JD, Bklyn. Law Sch., 1967. Bar: N.Y. 1968, U.S. Dist. Ct. (so. and ea. dists.) N.Y. 1968, U.S. Ct. Appeals (2d cir.) 1970, U.S. Supreme Ct. 1973, Calif. 1989. Assoc. Johnson & Tannenbaum, N.Y.C., 1968-70; assoc. counsel Columbia Pictures, 1970, Paramount Pictures, N.Y.C., 1970-79, v.p., theatrical distbn. counsel, 1979-85, sr. v.p., chief resident counsel East Coast, 1985-87, sr. v.p., asst. gen. counsel L.A., 1987—. Bar: N.Y. 1968, U.S. Dist. Ct. (so. and ea. dists.) N.Y. 1968, U.S. Ct. Appeals (2d cir.) 1970, U.S. Supreme Ct. 1973, Calif. 1989. Trustee West Cunningham Park Civic Assn., Fresh Meadows, N.Y., 1978—. Mem. ABA, Assn. of Bar of City of N.Y., L.A. Copyright Soc., Acad. Motion Picture Arts and Scis., Motion Picture Pioneers. Antitrust, Federal civil litigation, General corporate. E-mail: paul_springer@paramount.com

SPRITZER, RALPH SIMON, lawyer, educator; b. N.Y.C., Apr. 27, 1917; s. Harry and Stella (Theuman) S.; m. Lorraine Nelson, Dec. 23, 1950; children: Ronald, Pamela. B.S., Columbia U., 1937, LL.B., 1940. Bar: N.Y. bar 1941, U.S. Supreme Ct. bar 1950. Atty. Office Alien Property, Dept. Justice, 1946-51; anti-trust div. Dept. Justice, 1951-54, Office Solicitor Gen., 1954-61; gen. counsel FPC, 1961-62; 1st asst. to solicitor gen. U.S., 1962-68; prof. law U. Pa., Phila., 1968-86, Ariz. State U., Tempe, 1986—; gen. counsel AAUP, 1983-84. Adj. prof. law George Wasington U., 1967; cons. Adminstrv. Conf. U.S., Ford Found., Pa. Gov.'s Justice Commn. Served with AUS, 1941-46. Recipient Superior Service award Dept. Justice, 1960; Tom C. Clark award Fed. Bar. Assn., 1968 Mem. Am. Law Inst. Home: 1024 E Gemini Dr Tempe AZ 85283-3004 Office: Ariz State Univ Coll Law Tempe AZ 85287

SPRIZZO, JOHN EMILIO, federal judge; b. Bklyn., Dec. 23, 1934; s. Vincent James and Esther Nancy (Filosa) S.; children— Ann Esther, Johna Emily Sprizzo Bolka, Matthew John. BA summa cum laude, St. John's U., Jamaica, N.Y., 1956; LLB summa cum laude, St. John's U., 1959. Bar: N.Y. 1960. Atty. U.S. Dept. Justice, 1959-63; asst. U.S. atty. so. dist. N.Y. Dept. Justice, N.Y.C., 1963-68, chief appellate atty., 1965-66, asst. chief criminal div., 1966-68; assoc. prof. Fordham U. Law Sch., 1968-72; ptnr. Curtis, Mallet-Prevost, 1972-81; dist. judge U.S. Dist. Ct. (so. dist.) N.Y., 1981—. Cons. Nat. Com. for Reform of Criminal Laws, N.Y.C., 1971-72; mem. Knapp Commn., 1971-72; assoc. atty. Com. of Ct. on Judiciary, N.Y.C., 1971-72 Co-contbr. articles to profl. law revs. Mem. ABA, D.C. Bar Assn., Assn. of Bar of City of N.Y. Office: US Dist Ct US Courthouse Foley Sq New York NY 10007-1501

SPROWLS, PAUL ALAN, lawyer; b. Louisville, Dec. 27, 1951; s. Paul Harris and Nelle (Oldacre) S.; m. Ellen Virginia Culpepper, Apr. 11, 1981. BA, Tulane U., 1973, JD, 1976. Bar: Fla. 1977, La. 1981, Colo. 1988, U.S. Dist. Ct. (we. dist.) La. 1981, U.S. Ct. Appeals (5th and 11th cirs.) 1981, U.S. Supreme Ct. 1984. Spl. agt. FBI, Washington, 1977-81; assoc. Coleman, Dutrey & Thomson, New Orleans, 1981; asst. U.S. atty. Dept. Justice, Lafayette, La., 1981-83, Tallahassee, 1983—. Evaluation staff Dept. Justice, Washington, 1983-89. Pres. Foxcroft Civic Assn., Tallahassee, 1987—, Rosehill Homeowners Assn., 1994-99. Served with USNR, 1985—. Mem. ABA, Am. Judicature Soc. Republican. Avocations: tennis, golf, sailing. Office: US Courthouse 111 N Adams St Tallahassee FL 32301

SPRUNG, ARNOLD, lawyer; b. N.Y.C., Apr. 18, 1926; s. David L. and Anna (Stork) S.; m. Audrey Ann Caire; children: Louise, John, Thomas, Doran, D'Wayne. AB, Darmuth Coll., 1947; JD, Columbia U., 1950. Bar: N.Y. 1950, U.S. Dist. Ct. (so. dist.) N.Y. 1950, U.S. Patent Office 1952, U.S. Dist. Ct. (we. dist.) N.Y. 1954, U.S. Ct. Appeals (2d cir.) 1958, U.S. Ct. Customs and Patent Appeals 1958, U.S. Dist. Ct. (ea. dist.) N.Y. 1962, U.S. Dist. Ct. (no. dist.) Tex. 1971, U.S. Supreme Ct. 1971, and others. Sr. ptnr. Sprung, Kramer, Schaefer & Briscoe, Westchester, N.Y., 1950—. Lt. USN, 1943-46, PTO. Mem. ABA, N.Y. Intellectual Property Assn. Avocations: skiing, wind surfing, racquetball, biking, tennis. Intellectual property, Patent, Trademark and copyright. E-mail: asprung@aol.com

SPRY, DONALD FRANCIS, II, lawyer; b. Bethlehem, Pa., Nov. 17, 1947; s. Donald Francis and Carol Annette (Bolger) S.; m. Mary Frances, June 20, 1981; stepchildren: Michael Matlaga, Michelle Fehnel. BA, Moravian Coll., 1969; JD, U. Pitts., 1972. Bar: Pa. 1972, U.S. Dist. Ct. (ea. dist.) Pa. 1975. Assoc. Law Offices of Edmund P. Turtzo, Bangor, Pa., 1973-76; ptnr. Turtzo, Spry, Powlette & Sbrocchi, P.C., 1976-83, Turtzo, Spry, Powlette, Sbrocchi & Faul, P.C., Bangor and Stroudsburg, Pa., 1983-90, Turtzo, Spry, Sbrocchi, Faul & LaBarre, P.C., Bangor and Stroudsburg, 1990-2000, King, Spry, Herman, Freund & Faul, LLC, Allentown, Stroudsburg, Bangor, 2001—. Capt. USAR 1979-80. Mem. ABA (family law sect.), Pa. Bar Assn. (family law sect. edn. law com., zone del. Ho. of Dels.), Northampton County Bar Assn. (family law com.), North County Bar Assn. (pres.-elect 1989, pres. 1990), Pa. Sch. Bds. Assn., Nat Sch. Bds. Assn., ACLU, Edn. Law Assn., Pomfret Club. Republican. Methodist. Capt. USAR, 1979-80. Mem. ABA (family law sect.), Pa. Bar Assn. (family law sect. edn. law com., zone del. Ho. of Dels.), Northampton County Bar Assn. (family law com.), North County Bar Assn. (pres.-elect 1989, pres. 1990), Pa. Sch. Bds. Assn., Nat. Sch. Bds. Assn., ACLU, Edn. Law Assn., Pomfret Club. Republican. Methodist. Education and schools, Family and matrimonial. Office: King Spry Herman Freund & Faul LLC 109 Broadway Bangor PA 18013-2505 also: 930 N 9th St Stroudsburg PA 18360-1208 also: 110-112 N 6th St Allentown PA 18105

SPURGEON, EDWARD DUTCHER, law educator, foundation administrator; b. Newton, N.J., June 2, 1939; s. Dorsett Larew and Mary (Dutcher) S.; m. Carol Jean Forbes, June 17, 1963; children: Michael Larew, Stephen Edward. AB, Princeton U., 1961; LLB, Stanford U., 1964; LLM in Taxation, NYU, 1968. Bar: Calif. 1965. Assoc. atty. Stammer McKnight et al, Fresno, Calif., 1964-67, Paul Hastings Janofsky and Walker, L.A., 1968-70, ptnr., 1971-80; prof. law U. Utah, Salt Lake City, 1980-90, Wm. H. Leary prof. law and policy, 1990-93, assoc. dean acad. affairs Coll. Law, 1982-83, dean Coll. Law, 1983-90; dean Sch. Law U. Ga., Athens, 1993-98, prof., 1993—; ptnr. Moyle & Draper, Salt Lake City, 2000—. Vis. prof. law Univ. Coll. London, fall 1990, Stanford U. Law Sch., spring 1991; ex-officio mem. Utah State Bar Commn., 1984-90. Co-author: Federal Taxation of Trusts, Grantors and Beneficiaries, 1st edit., 1978, 2d edit., 1989, 3d edit., 1997. Mem. Utah Gov.'s Task Force Officers and Dirs. Liability Ins., 1985-87, Utah Dist. Ct. Reorgn. Commn., 1986-87, Justice in 21st Century Commn., Utah, 1989-91; bd. visitors, exec. com. Stanford U. Law Sch., 1988-93; pres., dir. Albert and Elaine Borchard Found., 1983—; exec. dir. Ctr. on Law and Aging, 1998—; dir. Nat. Sr. Citizens Law Ctr., 1999—. Mem. ABA (Commn. on Legal Problems of the Elderly 1991-95, spl. advisor 1995—), Am. Bar Found. Office: U of Ga Law School Athens GA 30602

SPURGEON, ROBERTA KAYE, lawyer; b. Genoa, Ohio, Sept. 2, 1938; d. Donald Howard and Audrey June (Schimmel) B. BS, U. Cin., 1963; MS, Yale U., 1965; JD, U. Calif., Berkeley, 1976. Bar: Ohio 1977, U.S. Dist. Ct. (no. dist.) Ohio 1977, U.S. Ct. Appeals (6th cir.) 1982. Staff nurse Vis. Nurse Svc., Toledo, 1960-61, VA Hosp., Cin., 1963; instr. Boston U. Sch. Nursing, 1965-67; asst. prof. Boston Coll. Sch. Nursing, Chestnut Hills, Mass., 1967-71; dept. chmn., asst. prof. Yale U. Sch. Nursing, New Haven, 1971-73; pvt. practice Cleve., 1976—. Contbr. articles to profl. jours. Active Greater Cleve. Growth Assn., 1981—; del. 8th dist. Jud. Conf., 1988, 89. Mem. Ohio State Bar Assn., Cleve. Bar Assn. Unitarian. Avocations: cooking, gardening, computing. Federal civil litigation, State civil litigation, General practice. Office: 55 Public Sq Ste 1575 Cleveland OH 44113-1971

SQUADRON, HOWARD MAURICE, lawyer; b. N.Y.C., Sept. 5, 1926; s. Jack H. and Sarah (Shereshevsky) S.; m. Lorraine Vlosky, Oct. 25, 1953 (dec. Oct. 1967); children: William, Richard, Diane; m. Anne Helen Strickland, June 6, 1972; children: Seth, Daniel. AB, CCNY, 1946; LLD, Columbia U., 1947. Bar: N.Y. 1948, U.S. Dist. Ct. (so. and ea. dists.) N.Y. 1950. Bigelow teaching fellow U. Chgo., 1947-48; assoc. Stroock, Stroock & Lavan, 1948-50, Phillips, Nizer, Benjamin & Krim, 1952-54; counsel Am. Jewish Congress, 1950-52; sr. ptnr. Squadron, Alter & Weinrib (and predecessor), N.Y.C., 1954-64, Squadron & Plesent, N.Y.C., 1965-70, Squadron Ellenoff Plesent & Sheinfeld and predecessors, N.Y.C., 1970—. Assoc. prof. CUNY; founder Howard M. Squadron Program in Law, Media and Society at Benjamin N. Cardozo Law Sch. of Yeshiva U. Editor: Columbia Law Rev, 1946-47. Active Am. Jewish Congress, 1950—, sr. v.p., 1976—78, pres., 1978—84; chmn. Conf. Presidents Maj. Am. Jewish Orgns., 1980—82; trustee Soc. Advancement Judaism; chmn. emeritus City Ctr. Fifty-fifth St. Theatre Found., N.Y.C. Capt. JAGC USAR, 1948—62. Recipient Disting. Service award CCNY, 1973 Mem. ABA, Assn. of Bar of City of N.Y., N.Y. State Bar Assn., Century Assn. Democrat. Club: Century Assn. General practice. Office: Squadron Ellenoff Plesent & Sheinfeld 551 5th Ave Fl 22 New York NY 10176-0049

SQUIRE, BRUCE M. lawyer; b. Phoenix, July 27, 1956; s. Donald R. and Martha (Thomas) S.; m. Susan L. Wiebke, May 31, 1980; children: Jessica, Adam. BS with honors, No. Ariz. U., 1978; JD, Ariz. State U., 1981. Bar: Ariz., 1981, U.S. Dist. Ct. Ariz. 1981, U.S. Tax. Ct. 1982; cert. specialist personal injury and wrongful death litigation State Bar of Ariz. Of counsel Brown, Arenofsky & Squire, Mesa, Ariz., 1981—. Contbr. articles to profl. jours.; co-host: (radio talk show) The Law and You, 1995-96. Vol. Vol. Lawyers Program, Phoenix, 1986—. Mem. Ariz. Trial Lawyers Assn. (sustaining), Maricopa City Bar Assn., E. Valley Bar Assn. (pres. 1986-87). State civil litigation, Personal injury. Office: Brown Arenofsky & Squire 1745 S Alma School Rd Ste 130 Mesa AZ 85210-3055 E-mail: bruce@baslawfirm.com

SQUIRE, WALTER CHARLES, lawyer; b. N.Y.C., Aug. 5, 1945; s. Sidney and Helen (Friedman) S.; m. Sara Jane Abamson; children: Harrison, Russell, Zachary, Andrew. BA, Yale U., 1967; JD, Columbia U., 1971. Bar: N.Y. 1971, U.S. Dist. Ct. (so. and ea. dists.) N.Y. 1975, U.S. Ct. Appeals (2d cir.) 1974, U.S. Supreme Ct. 1977. Ptnr. Jones Hirsch Connors & Bull P.C., N.Y.C., 1986-98, Jacobson, Mermelstein & Squire, LLP, N.Y.C., 1998—; prin. Squire & Co., LLC, 1998—. Bd. govs. Arthritis Found. N.Y., Inc., 1993-99; bd. dirs. MedicAlert Found., N.Y., 1990-99. Mem. ABA, N.Y. State Bar Assn., Assn. of Bar of City of N.Y., Internat. Bar Assn., Licensing Execs. Soc., Chartered Inst. Arbitrators (London), Am. Arbitration Assn. (arbitrator 1975-2000, mediator 1993—), Am. Acad. Hosp. Attys., Risk Ins. Mgmt. Soc. (lectr. 1983-84), AIDA Reinsurance & Ins. Arbitration Soc. (cert.). General corporate, Insurance, Trademark and copyright. Office: Jacobson Mermelstein et al 52 Vanderbilt Ave New York NY 10017-3808

SQUIRES, JOHN HENRY, judge; b. Oct. 21, 1946; married; five children. AB cum laude, U. Ill., 1968, JD, 1971. Bar: Ill. 1971, U.S. Dist. Ct. (cen. dist.) Ill. 1972, U.S. Tax Ct. 1978. Assoc. Brown, Hay & Stephens, Springfield, Ill., 1971-76, ptnr., 1977-87; judge U.S. Bankruptcy Ct. No. Dist. Ill. ea. divsn., 1988—. Trustee in bankruptcy, 1984-87; adj. prof. law John Marshall Law Sch., Chgo., 1994, DePaul U., Chgo., 1995-96; lectr. Am. Bankruptcy Inst., Sangamon County Bar Assn., Winnebago County Bar Assn., Chgo. Bar Assn., Ill. Inst. CLE, Comml. Law League Am., DuPage County (Ill.) Bar Assn. Mem. Nat. Conf. Bankruptcy Judges, Am. Bankruptcy Inst., Fed. Bar Assn., Chgo.-Lincoln Am. Inn of Ct., Am. Bus. Club, Union League Club Chgo. Office: US Bankruptcy Ct No Dist Ill Ea Div 219 S Dearborn St #656 Chicago IL 60604-1702

SQUIRES, WILLIAM RANDOLPH, III, lawyer; b. Providence, Sept. 6, 1947; s. William Randolph and Mary Louise (Gress) S.; m. Elisabeth Dale McAnulty, June 23, 1984; children: Shannon, William R. IV, Mayre Elisabeth, James Robert. BA in Econs., Stanford U., 1969; JD, U. Tex., 1972. Bar: Wash. 1973, U.S. Dist. Ct. (we. dist.) Wash. 1973, U.S. Dist. Ct. (ea. dist.) Wash. 1976, U.S. Ct. Appeals (9th cir.) 1976, U.S. Supreme Ct. 1976, U.S. Ct. Fed. Claims 1982. Assoc. Oles, Morrison, Rinker, Stanislaw & Ashbaugh, Seattle, 1973-78; ptnr., chmn. litig. group Davis Wright Tremaine, 1978-97; mem. Summit Law Group, 1997—. Fellow Am. Coll. Trial Lawyers; mem. ABA, Internat. Bar Assn., Wash. State Bar Assn., King County Bar Assn., Wash. Athletic Club, Rainier Club (Seattle). Episcopalian. Federal civil litigation, Construction, Labor. Home: 5554 NE Penrith Rd Seattle WA 98105-2845 Office: Summit Law Group 1505 Westlake Ave N Ste 300 Seattle WA 98109-6211 E-mail: randys@summitlaw.com

STAAB, MICHAEL JOSEPH, lawyer; b. Hays, Kans., Oct. 12, 1955; s. Robert Joseph and Beatrice Agnes (Schenk) S.; m. Kathy Lee Brock, Jan. 11, 1986; children: Colton Brock, Matthew Michael. BA magna cum laude, Ft. Hays State U., 1978; JD, Drake U., 1981; LLM in Health Law, DePaul U., 1993. Bar: Idaho 1981, U.S. Dist. Ct. Idaho 1981, Utah 1986, U.S. Dist. Ct. Utah 1986, Ill. 1990, U.S. Dist. Ct. (no. dist.) Ill. 1990. Assoc. Quane, Smith, Howard and Hull, Boise, Idaho, 1981-83, Meuleman & Miller, Boise, 1983; pvt. practice, 1983-85; ptnr. Biele, Haslam & Hatch, Salt Lake City, 1985-89, Parsons, Behle & Latimer, Salt Lake City, 1989-90; assoc. Steinberg, Polacek & Goodman, Chgo., 1990-93, Ruff, Weldenaar and Reidy, Ltd., Chgo., 1994-96; ptnr. Gardner, Carton and Douglas, 1996—. Mem. Chgo. adv. bd. Drake U., 1996—. Contbr. articles to legal publs. Bd. dirs. Winnetka Village Caucus, 1992-94, Big Bros./Big Sisters, Salt Lake City, 1985-89, Utah Head Injury Assn., Salt Lake City, 1988-90, Pediat. Brain Injury Assn., Salt Lake City, 1988-90. Mem. ABA, Ill. Bar Assn., Chgo. Bar Assn., Nat. Health Lawyers Assn., Nat. Order of Barristers, Order of Omega, K.C., Phi Kappa Phi, Phi Alpha Theta, Phi Eta Sigma. Roman Catholic. Avocations: bicycling, reading, basketball, baseball, antiques. Health. Home: 173 De Windt Rd Winnetka IL 60093-3708 Office: 321 N Clark St Chicago IL 60610-4714 E-mail: mstaab@gcd.com

STABLER, LEWIS VASTINE, JR. lawyer; b. Greenville, Ala., Nov. 5, 1936; s. Lewis Vastine and Dorothy Daisy Stabler; m. Monteray Scott, Sept. 5, 1958; children: Dorothy Monteray Scott, Andrew Vastine, Monteray Scott Smith, Margaret Langston. BA, Vanderbilt U., 1958; JD with distinction, U. Mich., 1961. Bar: Ala. 1961. Assoc. Cabaniss & Johnston, Birmingham, Ala., 1961-67; assoc. prof. law U. Ala., 1967-70; ptnr. Cabaniss, Johnston, Gardner, Dumas & O'Neal (and predecessor firms), Birmingham, 1970-91, Walston, Stabler, Wells, Anderson and Bains, Birmingham, 1991-97; pvt. practice, 1997—. Mem. com. of 100 Candler Sch. Theology, Emory U. Bd. editors: Mich. Law Rev, 1960-61. Fellow Am. Bar Found. (life); mem. Am. Law Inst., Ala. Law Inst. (mem. council, dir. 1968-70), ABA, Ala. Bar Assn., Birmingham Bar Assn., Am. Judicature Soc., Am. Assn. Railroad Trial Counsel, Order of Coif. Methodist (cert. lay speaker). Clubs: Country of Birmingham, Rotary. Antitrust, Federal civil litigation, State civil litigation. Home: 3538 Victoria Rd Birmingham AL 35223-1404 Office: PO Box 53-1161 Birmingham AL 35253-1161

STACEY, JAMES ALLEN, retired judge; b. Norwalk, Ohio, Dec. 26, 1925; s. James Calvin and Glenna (Cleveland) S.; m. Marlyn Frederick, Aug. 21, 1948; children: James A., Libble M. Romigh, Lorrie Stacey Singler, David F., CamAllison Shenigo, Tricia Stacey Berger. Student, Bucknell U., 1943-44, Ohio Wesleyan U., 1944, 46, 47, U. N.C., 1944-45; JD, Cleveland-Marshall Law Sch., 1951. Bar: Ohio 1952, U.S. Dist. Ct. (no. dist.) Ohio 1955. Ptnr. McGory & Stacey, Sandusky, Ohio, 1954-56; assoc. Steinemann & Zieher, 1956-60; ptnr. Work, Stacey & Moyer, 1960-67; judge Sandusky Mcpl. Ct., 1967-95, ret., 1995. Mem. Ohio State Traffic Law Com., 1969-95, chmn., 1978-82. Mem. Erie-Ottawa Mental Health Bd., 1968-87; mem. Ex-Offenders for Help Bd., 1975-81; bd. dirs. Camp Fire Girls, 1956-60, L.E.A.D.S., 1984-86, Sandusky C. of C., 1984-86. Served with USNR, 1943-46. Mem. Ohio State Bar Assn., Ohio Mcpl. Judges Assn. (exec. bd. 1970-80), Am. Judicature Soc., Am. Judges Assn., Erie County Bar Assn., Amvets, Sandusky Exch. Club (bd. dirs. 1999—), Elks, Eagles Club, Italian-Am. Beneficial Club. Republican. Presbyterian. Home: 1407 Julianne Cir Sandusky OH 44870-7032

STACK, BEATRIZ DE GREIFF, lawyer; b. Medellin, Antioquia, Colombia, Feb. 3, 1939; came to U.S., 1967; d. Luis and Carolina (González) de Greiff; m. Norman L. Stack Jr., Dec. 18, 1972; children: Carolina M., Ingrid C. BS, Sch. Sacred Heart, Medellin, 1956; LLD, U. Pontificia Bolivariana, Medellin, 1961; cert. of attendance, Inst. Internat. Studies, Geneva, Switzerland, 1965; M in Comparative Law, George Washington U., 1974. Bar: Medellin 1963, Pa. 1983, Va. 1992. Trademarks examiner U.S. Patent and Trademark Office, Arlington, Va., 1977-78; legal rschr. Land and Natural Resources divsn. U.S. Dept. Justice, Washington, 1980-86; legal officer Food and Agr. Orgn., UN, Rome, 1986-89; legal counsel Pan Am. Health Orgn. Staff Assn., Washington, 1989-92; pvt. practice Mc Lean, Va., 1992—. City judge Caldas, Antioquia, 1989-92; city atty. City of Medellin, 1963; head polit. sci. inst. Antioquia State U., Medellin, 1965; instr. in lang. Peace Corps Vols., Mex., 1968; asst. exec. sec. Interam. Commn. Women, OAS, Washington, 1970; stats. asst. Pan Am. Health Orgn., Washington; cons. Inst. Internat. Law and Econ. Devel., Washington, 1974; ct. interpreter U.S. Magistrate Ct. Alexandria, Va.; legal cons. Mozambique, 1992. Sec. Cath. Daus. Am., Arlington, 1985-86; pres. Colombian Cultural Forum, 1991-94. Mem. Alumna Spanish Sacred Heart (v.p. 1990). Democrat. Roman Catholic. Appellate, Federal civil litigation, Estate planning. E-mail: degreiffst@aol.com

STACK, CHARLES RICKMAN, lawyer; b. Boston, Sept. 26, 1935; s. John Joseph and Caroline Bernadett (Rickman) S.; m. Barbara Alice Levine, Oct. 12, 1963; children— Caroline K., Kevin C., Constance K. BSBA, U. Fla. 1957, JD, 1960; diplomate Nat. Bd. Trial Advocacy; cert. Fla. Bd. Trial Certification. Bar: Fla. 1960, U.S. dist. ct. (so. dist.) Fla. 1960. Assoc. Macfarlane, Ferguson, Allison & Kelly, Tampa, Fla., 1960-62; ptnr. High, Stack, Lazenby, Bender, Palahach & Lacasa, Miami, Fla., 1962— , sr. ptnr. 1968— ; mem., sec. U.S. Dist. Ct. Peer Rev. commn., 1983— ; instr. bus. law U. South Fla. 1960-62; instr. comml. law Am. Inst. Banking, Tampa, 1960-62. Contbr. numerous articles to profl. jours. Chmn. Fla. Jud. Nominations Commn. for 11th Cir., 1970-76; Dade County campaign chmn. Reubin Askew for Gov., 1970, Steve Clark for Mayor, 1972; mem. Fla. Constn. Revision Com., 1968; chmn. Fla. Corp. Income Tax Com., 1972; mem. Fla. Dem. Conv. Com., 1972; mem. City of Miami Downtown Devel. Authority, 1979-82. Mem. ABA, ATLA, Am. Bd. Trial Advocacy, Fla. Bar Assn., Lawyers for Pub. Justice, Acad. Fla. Trial Lawyers, Tex. Trial Lawyers, Dade County Trial Lawyers, Com. of 100, Dade County Bar Assn., Brevard County Bar Assn., Million Dollar Advs. Forum, Univ. Club (Miami). Democrat. Episcopalian. Federal civil litigation, State civil litigation, Personal injury. Home: 2655 S Le Jeune Rd Ste 1108 Coral Gables FL 33134-5802 Office: 2655 S Le Jeune Rd Ste 1108 Coral Gables FL 33134-5802

STACK, DANIEL, lawyer, financial consultant; b. July 29, 1928; s. Charles and Gertrude (Heller) Stack; m. Jane MArcia Gordon, Apr. 08, 1953; children: Joan, Gordon. BA cum laude, Bklyn. Coll., 1949; LLB, Columbia U., 1952; LLM, Georgetown U., 1955. Bar: N.Y. 1956. Project adminstr. Am. Overseas Fin. Corp., 1957—58; asst. counsel. ABC-TV, N.Y.C., NY, 1959—60; gen. counsel IFC Securities Corp., 1961—63; exec. asst. to sr. v.p. N.Y. Stock Exch., 1963—64; sec. pension com. Consol. Foods Corp., Chgo., 1967—69; v.p. legal Seaway Multi Corp. Ltd., Toronto, Canada, 1969—72; v.p. mergers and acquisitions Acklands Ltd., 1972—74; sr. v.p., sec., counsel Greenwich Svs. Bank., N.Y.C., 1978—81; sole prctice, 1982—85; ptnr. Brennen and Stack, 1986—96; cons. venture capital, corp. fin., med. edn., health care, mining, and oil, 1982—. Pres. Bus. and Fin. Resources, Inc., 1982—84; adj. faculty NYU; officer and dir. various pub. cos.; bd. adv. Sch. of Bus., St. John's U.; chmn. sect. on mergers and acquisitions North Am. Soc. for Corp. Planning; lectr., guest spkr. on mergers and acquisitions Fac. of Mgmt. Studies, Univ. Toronto, 1974, SUNY, Buffalo, 1976; gen. counsel Greater N.Y. Safety Coun., 1980—. Info. officer U.S. Naval Acad., 1972—; mem. Congl. mil svc. acads. nominations com. and Civil Svc. intern selection com., 1978—. Lt. j.g. USNR, 1952—55, Capt. USNR, 1983, ret. Decorated Joint Svc. Commendation medal, Naval Order of US; scholar, N.Y. Regents, 1945—49. Mem.: ABA, N.Y. State Bar Assn., N.Y. County Lawyer's Assn. (chmn. law com.), Ramapo Rep. Org. Republican. General corporate, Mergers and acquisitions, Securities. Home: 8 Linda Dr Suffern NY 10901-3004

STACK, JANE MARCIA, lawyer; b. Bklyn., Aug. 11, 1928; m. Daniel Stack, Apr. 18, 1953; children: Joan, Gordon. Student, Ohio U., 1945-47; BA, NYU, 1949; JD, N.Y. Law Sch., 1983. Bar: N.Y., 1984; U.S. Dist. Ct. (ea. and so. dists.) N.Y. 1988. Assoc. Shannon, Flaherty, Purchase, N.Y., 1984-85, Schwall & Becker, New City, 1985-87; pvt. practice Suffern, 1987-90; sr. atty. N.Y. State Div. Human Rights, N.Y.C., 1990—. Vice-pres. Montebello (N.Y.) Civic Assn., 1988—. Republican. Administrative and regulatory, Civil rights, Labor. Home: 8 Linda Dr Suffern NY 10901-3004 Office: NY State Div Human Rights 1 Fordham Plz Bronx NY 10458-5871

STACKABLE, FREDERICK LAWRENCE, lawyer; b. Howell, Mich., Dec. 4, 1935; s. Lawrence Peter and Dorothea R. (Kiney) S. BA, Mich. State U., 1959; JD, Wayne State U., 1962. Bar: Mich. 1962, U.S. Dist. Ct. (ea. and we. dists.) Mich. 1964; U.S. Supreme Ct. 1968. Commr., Ingham County Cir. Ct. V.p. Mich. Assn. Cir. Ct. Commrs., 1963, pres., 1967-70; 18th dist. rep. Ingham County Bd. Suprs.; mem. Com. on Mich. Law Revision Comm.; state rep. 58th House Dist., 1971, 72, 73, 74. County del. Rep. Party, Ingham County, Mich., 1969-70, state del., Mich., 1971-74; Lansing city atty., 1975. Recipient Disting. Alumni award Wayne State U. Sch. Law, Detroit, 1987. Mem. Mich. Bar Assn., Ingham County Bar Assn., Nat. Conf. Commrs. Uniform State Laws, Mich. Trail Riders Assn. (dir., past pres.), Mich. Internat. Snowmobile Assn., Sportsman's Alliance Mich., Cycle Conservation Club, Am. Judicature Soc. Avocations: horseback riding, snowmobiling, skiing, traveling. General civil litigation, Personal injury, Probate. Office: 300 N Grand Ave Lansing MI 48933-1214

STACY, DON MATTHEW, lawyer; b. Bluefield, W.Va., Dec. 7, 1954; s. Fred T. and Emma J. (Holey) S.; m. Nancy Jane Lusk, Mar. 20, 1982. BA in Econs., W.Va. U., 1975, JD, 1979. Bar: W.Va. 1979. Atty. United Mine Workers Am., Beckley, W.Va., 1979-81; ptnr. Stacy and Shunute Attys. at Law, Mt. Hope, 1981-82; pvt. practice Beckley, 1982—. Sec. Citizens So. Bank, Beckley, 1995—. Named one of Best Lawyers in Am., 1998-2002. Mem. ATLA, W.Va. State Bar Assn., Raleigh County Bar Assn., W.Va. Trial Lawyers Assn. Pension, profit-sharing, and employee benefits, Personal injury, Workers' compensation. Office: 600 Neville St Ste 200 Beckley WV 25801-5352

STADLER, JAMES ROBERT, lawyer; b. Anderson, S.C., June 1, 1964; s. Robert Edgar and Dorothy Ann (Rhoads) S.; m. Laura Ann Rankin, Oct. 28, 1989. AB summa cum laude, Albion (Mich.) Coll., 1986; JD cum laude, U. Notre Dame, South Bend, Ind., 1989. Bar: Mich. 1989, U.S. Dist. Ct. (we. dist.) Mich. 1989, U.S. Dist. Ct. (ea. dist.) Wis., 1996, U.S. Dist. Ct. (ea. dist.) Mich. 1999, U.S. Dist. Ct. (no. dist.) N.Y. 1999, U.S. Ct. Appeals (7th cir.) 1995. Ptnr. Varnum, Riddering, Schmidt & Howlett LLP, Grand Rapids, Mich., 1989—. Contbr. articles to profl. jours. Sec. IRRA West Mich. Mem. ABA, Mich. Bar Assn., Grand Rapids Bar Assn., Phi Beta Kappa. Avocation: travel. Labor, Workers' compensation. Office: Varnum Riddering Schmidt & Howlett LLP PO Box 352 Grand Rapids MI 49501-0352

STADNICAR, JOSEPH WILLIAM, lawyer; b. Corpus Christi, Tex., Oct. 30, 1963; s. Edward and Carrie Louise (Garris) S.; m. Susan Marie Bitzel, Apr. 25, 1992. BBA, John Carroll U., 1986; MBA, Ohio State U., 1989, JD, 1990. Bar: Ohio 1990. Assoc. Gerald E. Schlafman Co., Fairborn, Ohio, 1991-95; pvt. practice Beavercreek, 1995-97. Asst. prosecuting atty. City of Fairborn, 1990-95; prosecuting atty. City of Beavercreek, 1990-2001; assoc. Hammond & Stier Law Office, Beavercreek, 1996-98, ptnr. Hammond, Stier and Stadnicar, 1998—. Trustee Greene County Domestic Violence Project, Inc., Xenia, Ohio, 1995—; trustee, Am. Heart Assn., Miami Valley, Ohio, 1996—; trustee Fairborn Area 2005: Shared vision Corp. Mem. ABA, Ohio Bar Assn., Greene County Bar Assn., Rotary, Beavercreek C. of C., Fairborn C. of C. Avocations: fishing, camping. General civil litigation, Contracts commercial, Personal injury. Office: 3834 Dayton Xenia Rd Beavercreek OH 45432-2833 E-mail: stadnicar@aol.com

STAGEBERG, ROGER V. lawyer; B of Math. with distinction, U. Minn., 1963, JD cum laude, 1966. Assoc. Mackall, Crounse & Moore, Mpls., 1966-70, ptnr., 1970-86; shareholder and officer Lommen, Nelson, Cole & Stageberg, P.A., 1986—. Co-chmn. joint legal svcs. funding com. Minn. Supreme Ct., 1995-96. Mem. U. Minn. Law Rev. Bd. dirs. Mpls. Legal Aid Soc., 1970—, treas., 1973, pres., 1977, dir. of fund, 1980—, chmn. of fund, 1998-2000; chmn. bd. trustees Colonial Ch. of Edina, 1975, chmn. congregation, 1976, pres. found., 1978; officer, trustee Mpls. Found, 1983-88. Mem. Minn. State Bar Assn. (numerous offices and coms., pres. 1994), Hennepin County Bar Assn. (chmn. securities law sect. 1979, chmn. attys. referral svc. com. 1980, sec. 1980, treas. 1981, pres. 1983), Order of Coif. General corporate, Mergers and acquisitions, Securities. Office: Lommen Nelson Cole & Stageberg PA 1800 IDS Center 80 S 8th St Minneapolis MN 55402-2100 E-mail: roger@lommen.com

STAGG, CLYDE LAWRENCE, lawyer; b. St. Petersburg, Fla., May 22, 1935; s. Milton Gurr and Clyda Montese (Lawrence) S.; m. Betsy Barron, Aug. 22, 1959; children: Sharon, Brian, Lauren, Stephen. BSJ, U. Fla., 1956, LLB, 1959. Bar: Fla. 1959, U.S. Dist. Ct. (mid. dist.) Fla. 1959, U.S. Ct. Appeals (5th cir.) 1969, U.S. Supreme Ct. 1971, U.S. Ct. Appeals (11th cir.) 1987. Assoc. Shackleford, Farrior, Tampa, Fla., 1959-60; asst. solicitor Hillsborough County Solicitor's Office, 1960-61; chief asst. state atty. State Atty.'s Office, 1963-64, asst. state atty., 1961-63; ptnr. Whitaker, Mann & Stagg, Knight, Jones & Whitaker, Tampa, 1965-67, Holland & Knight, Tampa, 1968-74, 80-86, Stichter, Stagg, Hoyt, et al, Tampa, 1974-79, Stagg, Hardy, Ferguson, Murnaghan & Mathews P.A., Tampa, 1986-93, Akerman, Senterfitt & Eidson P.A., Tampa, 1993—. Bd. dirs. Fla. Lawyers Mut. Ins. Co. Mem., sec. Hillsborough Area Regional Transit Authority, Tampa, 1979-85; mem., sec., vice chmn., chmn. Tampa Sports Authority, 1985-89; bd. dirs. United Way Greater Tampa, Inc., 1988-91; bd. dirs. Fla. Blood Svcs. Inc., Tampa, 1989—, sec., 1999—; spl. counsel to U.S. Senator Bob Graham, 1988; commr., nat. conf. of commrs. Uniform State Laws, 1997—. Mem. ABA, Am. Bar Found., Fla. Bar (bd. govs. 1974-75), Hillsborough County Bar Assn. (pres. 1970-71, Outstanding Lawyer award 1998), Fla. Bar Found., Am. Bd. Trial Advocates, Greater Tampa C. of C. (bd. dirs. 1988-91), Am. Inn Ct. (master emeritus of bench). Alternative dispute resolution, General civil litigation, Product liability. Home: 3303 W San Nicholas St Tampa FL 33629-7034 Office: Akerman Senterfitt & Eidson PA PO Box 3273 Tampa FL 33601-3273

STAGG, TOM, federal judge; b. Shreveport, La., Jan. 19, 1923; s. Thomas Eaton and Beulah (Meyer) S.; m. Margaret Mary O'Brien, Aug. 21, 1946; children: Julie, Margaret Mary. B.A., La. State U., 1943, J.D., 1949. Bar: La. 1949. With firm Hargrove, Guyton, Van Hook & Hargrove, Shreveport, 1949-53; pvt. practice law, 1953-58; sr. ptnr. firm Stagg, Cady & Beard, 1958-74; judge U.S. Dist. Ct. (we. dist.) La., 1974-84, 91-92, chief judge, 1984-90, sr. judge, 1992—. Pres. Abe Meyer Corp., 1960-74, Stagg Investments, Inc., 1964-74; mng. partner Pierremont Mall Shopping Center, 1963-74; v.p. King Hardware Co., 1955-74; Mem. Shreveport Airport Authority, 1967-73, chmn., 1970-73; chmn. Gov.'s Tidelands Adv. Council, 1969-70; del. La. Constl. Conv., 1973-74; chmn. rules com., com. on exec. dept.; mem. Gov.'s Adv. Com on Offshore Revenues, 1972-74 Active Republican party, 1950-74, del. convs., 1956, 60, 64, 68, 72; mem. Nat. Com. for La., 1964-72, mem. exec. com., 1964-68; Pres. Shreveport Jr. C. of C., 1955-56; v.p. La. Jr. C. of C., 1956-57. Served to capt., inf. AUS, 1943-46, ETO. Decorated Bronze Star, Purple Heart with oak leaf cluster, Combat Inf. badge. Mem. Am., La., Shreveport bar assns. Office: US Dist Ct 300 Fannin St Ste 4100 Shreveport LA 71101-3123

STAHL, MADONNA, retired judge; b. Robinson, Ill., Sept. 26, 1928; d. Lawrence Joy and Inez Lucille (Kennedy) S.; children: Khushro Ghandhi, Rustom Ghandhi, Behram Ghandhi. BS, U. Ill., 1950; JD, Albany Law Sch., 1973. Bar: N.Y. 1974, U.S. Dist. Ct. (no. dist.) N.Y. 1974, U.S. Ct. Appeals (2nd cir.) 1975, U.S. Supreme Ct. 1978. Atty. trainee N.Y. State Dept. Commerce, Albany, 1973-74; atty. Legal Aid Soc., 1974-76; ptnr. Powers, Stahl & Somers (and predecessor firms), 1976-89; part-time judge Albany City Ct., 1984-89, full-time judge, 1990-97; ret., 1997. Mem. com. on character and fitness N.Y. State Supreme Ct. A.D. 3d Dept., Albany, 1980-86; jud. hearing officer State of N.Y., 1997-2000. Lobbyist Com. for Progressive Legislation, Schenectady, 1968-70. Mem. N.Y. State Bar Assn., Women's Bar Assn. State N.Y. (Capital dist. pres. 1983-84). Democrat. Unitarian. E-mail: judge_stahl@yahoo.com

STAHL, NORMAN H. federal judge; b. Manchester, N.H., 1931; BA, Tufts U., 1952; LLB, Harvard U., 1955. Law clk. to Hon. John V. Spalding Mass. Supreme Ct., 1955-56; assoc. Devine, Millimet, Stahl & Branch, Manchester, N.H., 1956-59, ptnr., 1959-90; dist. judge U.S. Dist. Ct. (N.H. dist.), 1990-92; cir. judge U.S. Ct. Appeals (1st cir.), Concord, N.H., 1992—. Del. to Rep. Nat. Conv., 1988. Mem. N.H. Bar Assn. Office: US Courthouse Ste 8730 1 Courthouse Way Boston MA 02210

STAHL, ROY HOWARD, lawyer; b. Phila., May 7, 1952; s. Howard Charles and Elizabeth (Seitz) S.; m. Corinne Jarrett, Apr. 22, 1978; children: Benjamin Bradley, Alexander Roy. BA, Pa. State U., 1974; JD, Villanova Sch. Law, 1977. Bar: Pa. 1977. Asst. gen. counsel Gilbert Assocs., Inc., Reading, Pa., 1977-82; dir. group legal svcs. Phila. Svcs. Group, Bryn Mawr, Pa., 1982-84; corp. counsel Phila. Suburban Corp., Bryn Mawr, 1984-85, v.p. adminstrn., corp. counsel Phila. Sub. Corp., 1985-88, v.p., gen. counsel, 1988-91; sr. v.p., gen. counsel, 1991—. Pres. Ashbridge Homeowners Assn., Downingtown, Pa., 1984; pres. Glen Craig Homeowners Assn., 1991. Fellow Harry J. Loman Ins. Rsch. Found., 1977. Mem. ABA, Montgomery County Bar Assn., Del. County Bar Assn., Phila. Bar Assn., Pa. Bar Assn. Contracts commercial, Computer, Public utilities. Office: Phila Suburban Corp 762 W Lancaster Ave Bryn Mawr PA 19010-3402

STAKELY, CHARLES AVERETT, lawyer; b. Montgomery, Ala., June 2, 1935; s. Charles A. and Harriotte (Johnston) S.; children: Charles, Ben, Frank, Harry. Student, U. Ala., 1953-55, JD, 1960; student, U. Ariz., 1955-57. Bar: Ala. 1960, U.S. Dist. Ct. (mid. dist.) Ala., U.S. Ct. Apeals (5th cir.), U.S. Ct. Appeals (11th cir.), U.S. Tax Ct. Assoc. Rushton, Stakely, Johnston & Garrett, Montgomery, 1960-65, ptnr., 1965—, sr. ptnr. Instr. Jones Law Sch., Montgomery. Contbr. articles to profl. jours. Chmn. bd. Montgomery YMCA, Montgomery Park and Recreation Dept.; mem. Ala. Securities Commn.; founding mem. Ala. Constl. Commn.; chmn. bd. dirs. Ala. Shakespeare Festival, Montgomery Symphony Orch. Assn. Named Man of Yr. City of Montgomery, 1975; recipient Disting. Svc. award, Jaycees, 1972. Mem. ABA, Ala. Bar Assn., Am. Coll. Trial Lawyers (state chmn. 1994-96), Montgomery County Bar Assn., Ala. Def. Lawyers Assn., Internat. Assn. Ins. Counsel, Am. Soc. Hosp. Attys. Baptist. General practice, Insurance. Office: Rushton Stakely Johnston & Garrett PO Box 270 Montgomery AL 36101-0270

STAKER, ROBERT JACKSON, federal judge; b. Kermit, W.Va., Feb. 14, 1925; s. Frederick George and Nada (Frazier) S.; m. Sue Blankenship Poore, July 16, 1955; 1 child, Donald Seth; 1 stepson, John Timothy Poore. Student, Marshall U., Huntington, W.Va., W.Va. U., Morgantown, U. Ky., Lexington; LL.B, W.Va. U., 1952. Bar: W.Va. 1952. Practiced in, Williamson, 1952-68; judge Mingo County Circuit Ct., 1969-79; U.S. dist. judge So. Dist. W.Va., Huntington, 1979-95, sr. U.S. dist. judge, 1995—. Served with USN, 1943-46. Democrat. Presbyterian. E-mail: robert_staker@wvsd.uscourts.gov

STALEY, CHARLES RALLS, lawyer; b. Watseka, Ill., Mar. 14, 1938; s. Charles Weed and Vivien Elfrieda (Ralls) S.; m. Renate Maria Henze, Sept. 15, 1962; children: Christine, Heather, Charles. AB, Harvard U., 1960; JD, U. Chgo., 1963. Bar: Ill. 1963, U.S. Dist. Ct. (no. dist.) Ill. 1963. Assoc. Wilson & McIlvaine, Chgo., 1963-72, ptnr., 1972-86, Schiff Hardin & Waite, Chgo., 1986—. Mem. bd. Evanston-Skokie Sch. Dist. No. 65, Ill., 1978-85, pres., 1979-83, bd. dirs., McGaw YMCA Evanston, 1993—. Recipient Outstanding Contbn. to City award City of Evanston, 1981, Outstanding Contbn. to Sch. Bd. award Dist. 65 Bd. Edn., 1983. Mem. ABA, Chgo. Bar Assn. Clubs: Rotary (Chgo.), Evanston Golf, Metropolitan, Legal, Law (Chgo.). Contracts commercial, Landlord-tenant, Real property. Home: 2206 Lincoln St Evanston IL 60201-2202 Office: Schiff Hardin & Waite 7200 Sears Tower Chicago IL 60606

STALEY, JOHN FREDRIC, lawyer; b. Sidney, Ohio, Sept. 26, 1943; s. Harry Virgil and Fredericka May (McMillin) S.; m. Sue Ann Bolin, June 11, 1966; children: Ian McMillin, Erik Bolin. AB in History, Fresno State Coll., 1965; postgrad., Calif. State U., Hayward, 1967-68; JD, U. Calif., San Francisco, 1972. Bar: Calif. 1972. Ptnr. Staley, Jobson & Wetherell, Pleasanton, Calif., 1972—. Lectr. U. Calif. Hastings Coll. Law, San Francisco, 1973-74; founding mem. Bank of Livermore (now U.S. Bank); del. U.S.-China Joint Conf. on Law, Beijing, 1987. Mem. Livermore City Coun., 1975-82, vice mayor, 1978-82; bd. dirs. Alameda County Tng. and Employment Bd., Alameda-Contra Costa Emergency Med. Svcs. Agy., Valley Vol. Ctr. With M.I., U.S. Army, 1966-67. Fellow Am. Acad. Matrimonial Lawyers; mem. ABA, Calif. State Bar, Alameda Bar Assn., Amador Valley Bar Assn., Calif. Assn. Cert. Fmaily Law Specialists (pres. 1988-89, Hall of Fame award 1994), Hastings Coll. Law Alumni Assn. (bd. dirs.). Family and matrimonial, Real property. Office: Staley Jobson & Wetherell Ste 310 5775 Stoneridge Mall Rd Pleasanton CA 94588-2838

STALEY, JOSEPH HARDIN, JR. lawyer; b. Tyler, Tex., May 23, 1937; s. Joseph Hardin and Mildred Lucille (Wilkerson) S.; m. Linda Luan Best, June 20, 1959; children: Joe H. III, Stefanie Staley Rice, LuAnne Staley Hobbs. BA, Yale U., 1959; LLB, U. Tex., 1964. Bar: Tex. 1964, U.S. Dist. Ct. (no. dist., so. dist., we. dist.) Tex., U.S. Ct. Appeals (5th cir.), U.S. Tax Ct., U.S. Supreme Ct. Assoc. Locke, Purnell, Boren, Laney & Neely, Dallas, 1964-68; minority counsel U.S. Senate Banking and Currency Com., Washington, 1968-70; ptnr. Locke Purnell Rain Harrell, Dallas, 1970-99; pvt. practice, 1999—. Mem. grievance com. State Bar Tex., Dalls, 1977-86, bd. dirs., Austin, 1983-86. Candidate U.S. Congress, 13th Dist. Tex., 1970; nat. adv. coun. U.S. Small Bus. Adminstrn., Washington, 1972-78; bd. dirs. Yale Club Dallas, 1972—, Dallas Soc. for Crippled Children, 1980-85, Dallas Area Red Cross, 1984—, FOCAS, 1985-89, Met. Dallas YMCA, 1986-91; mem. Tex. Constitution Revision Com., Dallas, 1974; regent Midwestern State U., Wichita Falls, Tex., 1989-94; bd. dirs. John Tower Ctr. Polit. Studies, So. Meth. U., 1996—. Fellow Tex. Bar Found.; mem. Salesmanship Club Dallas, The Links N.Y., Dallas Country Club (bd. govs.), Dallas Petroleum Club, Preston Trail Golf Club. Republican. Methodist. Avocations: golf, fishing, hunting. Administrative and regulatory, Condemnation, Transportation. Home: 4445 Rheims Pl Dallas TX 75205-3626 Office: Pvt Practice Joe H Staley 5949 Sherry Ln Dallas TX 75225

STALL, RICHARD J., JR. lawyer; b. Covington, Ky., July 5, 1941; BS with distinction, Purdue U., Lafayette, Ind., 1963; JD, Stanford U., Calif., 1966. Bar: Calif., U.S. Supreme Ct., U.S. Dist. Ct. (ctrl. dist.), U.S. Ct. Appeals (9th cir.). Assoc. Lawler, Felix & Hall (now Arter & Hadden), L.A., 1966-70; ptnr. pvt. practice, 1971-93, Stall, Astor & Goldstein, L.A., 1994—. Contbg. author: Insurance Journal. Mem.: ABA, Am. Arbitration Assn., Assn. Bus. Trial Lawyers, Beverly Hills Bar Assn. (real estate sect.), Calif. State Bar Assn. (real estate sect.), L.A. County Bar Assn., Nat. Assn. Railroad Trial Counsel, Santa Monica Bar Assn., Culver-Marina Bar Assn. (past pres., dir.), Lion's Club (past pres.), Sigma Chi (Delta Delta Chpt. past pres.), Tau Beta Pi. Office: Stall Astor & Goldstein Ste 200 10507 W Pico Blvd Los Angeles CA 90064-2319 Fax: 310-470-3673. E-mail: rstall@picolaw.com

STALLARD, WAYNE MINOR, lawyer; b. Onaga, Kans., Aug. 23, 1927; s. Minor Regan and Lydia Faye (Randall) S.; m. Wanda Sue Bacon, Aug. 22, 1948; children: Deborah Sue, Carol Jean, Bruce Wayne (dec.). BS, Kans. State Tchrs. Coll., Emporia, 1949; JD, Washburn U., 1952. Bar: Kans. 1952. Pvt. practice, Onaga, 1952—. Atty. Cmty. Hosp. Dist. No. 1, Pottawatomie, Jackson and Nemaha Counties, Kans., 1955—; Pottawatomie County atty., 1955-59; city atty. Onaga, 1953-79; atty Unified Sch. Dist. 322, Pottawatomie County, Kans., 1966-83; bd. dirs. North Ctrl. Kans. Guidance Ctr., Manhattan, 1974-78; lawyer 2d dist. jud. nominating commn., 1980—; atty. Rural Water Dist. No. 3, Pottawatomie County, Kans., 1974—, Rural Water Dist. No. 4, Pottawatomie County, 1995—; chmn. Pottawatomie County Econ. Devel. Com., 1986-92, atty., 1992—. Fund dir. chmn. Pottawatomie County chpt. Nat. Found. for Infantile Paralysis, 1953-54. Sgt. AUS, 1946-47. Mem. ABA, Kans. Bar Assn., Pottawatomie County Bar Assn., Am. Judicature Soc., City Attys. Assn. Kans. (dir. 1963-66), Onaga C. of C., Masons, Shriners, Order Ea. Star, Gamma Mu, Kappa Delta Pi, Delta Theta Phi, Sigma Tau Gamma. Mem. United Ch. of Christ. Probate, Real property, Taxation, general. Home: 720 High St Onaga KS 66521 Office: 307 Leonard St Onaga KS 66521-9734

STALLINGS, RONALD DENIS, lawyer; b. Evansville, Ind., Feb. 22, 1943; s. Denis and Gertrude (Tong) S.; m. Vicki Lee Chandler, Aug. 21, 1965; children: Courtnay, Claire, Ryan. B in Indsl. Engring., Ga. Inst. Tech., 1965; LLB, U. Va., 1968. Bar: Ga. 1968. Assoc. Powell, Goldstein, Frazer & Murphy LLP, Atlanta, 1968-75, ptnr., 1976-2000, co-counsel, 2001—; sr. v.p., gen. counsel, corp. sec. Reliance Trust Co., 2001—. Co-author: Georgia Corporate Forms, 1988. Mem. ABA, Ga. Bar Assn., Atlanta Bar Assn., Nat. Assn. Bond Lawyers, Am. Soc. Corp. Secs., Phoenix Soc. Atlanta (trustee 1987-93). Roman Catholic. Banking, General corporate, Finance. Home: 4601 Polo Ln NW Atlanta GA 30339-5345 Office: Reliance Trust Co Ste 900 3384 Peachtree Rd NE Atlanta GA 30326-1106 E-mail: rstallings@relico.com

STALNAKER, LANCE KUEBLER, lawyer; b. Tampa, Fla., Jan. 2, 1948; s. Leo Jr. and June Esther Stalnaker. BS in Journalism, U. Fla., 1970, JD, 1973. Bar: Fla. 1973, U.S. Dist. Ct. (mid. dist.) Fla. 1974, U.S. Ct. Appeals (5th cir.) 1974, U.S. Ct. Appeals (11th cir.) 1981. Ptnr. Stalnaker & Stalnaker, Tampa, 1973-75; pvt. practice, 1975-83, 91—; staff atty. Legal Aid Bur. of Hillsborough County, 1983-85, interim exec. dir., atty., 1985-86, exec. dir., atty., 1986-90. Asst. cir. ct. commr. 13th Jud. Cir., Tampa, 1981-82. Pres. St. John's Luth. Ch., 1997-99, mem. bd. dirs., 1999—; mem. steering com. Pregnancy Care Ctr. Ministries, Tampa, 1999—. Capt. U.S. Army Res. to 1978. Mem. Hillsborough County Bar Assn. (family law sect.), Fla. Bar (family law sect.). Family and matrimonial, Probate. Office: 1319 W Fletcher Ave Tampa FL 33612-3310

STALNAKER, TIM, lawyer; b. Columbus, Ohio, Oct. 12, 1948; s. Armand Carl and Rachel (Pickett) S. BA, Oberlin Coll., 1970; JD, U. Mich., 1973. Bar: Mo. 1973, U.S. Dist. Ct. (ea. dist.) Mo. 1973, U.S. Ct. Appeals (8th cir.) 1974. Assoc. firm Lewis & Rice, St. Louis, 1973-82, ptnr., 1982-87; ptnr. Gallop, Johnson & Neuman, St. Louis, 1987-91, Harris Dowell, Fisher, Harris & Stalnaker, 1991—. Mem. ABA, St. Louis Bar Assn., Mo. Bar Assn. Federal civil litigation, Labor, Pension, profit-sharing, and employee benefits. Office: Harris Dowell Fisher Harris & Stalnaker 15400 S Outer 40 Ste 202 Chesterfield MO 63017-2063

STAMM, CHARLES H. lawyer; Exec. v.p., gen. counsel Tchrs. Ins. & Annuity Assn., N.Y.C. Office: Tchrs Ins & Annuity Assn 730 3rd Ave New York NY 10017-3206

STAMPS, THOMAS PATY, lawyer, consultant; b. Mineola, N.Y., May 10, 1952; s. George Moreland and Helen Leone (Paty) S.; children: Katherine Camilla, George Belk, Elizabeth Margaret, Carley Lynn, Walker Paty; m. Diana Lynn Whittaker, Dec. 11, 1993. BA, U. Ill., 1973; postgrad., Emory U., 1975-76; JD, Wake Forest U., 1979. Bar: Ga. 1979, N.C. 1979.

Pers. dir. Norman Jaspan, N.Y.C., 1973-74; assoc. Macey & Zusmann, Atlanta, 1979-81; prin. Zusmann, Small, Stamps & White PC, 1981-85; mem. Strategic Capital Am., L.L.C., 1998—. Ptnr. Destin Enterprises, Atlanta, 1983-85. Author: Study of a Student, 1973, History of Coca-Cola, 1976; asst. editor Ga. Jour. So. Legal History, 1991-94. Atty. Vol. Lawyers for Arts, Atlanta, 1981—94, Atlanta Vol. Lawyers Found.; active High Mus. Art, 1986—, Atlanta Hist. Soc., Atlanta Bot. Gardens, Atlanta Symphony Orch., Ga. Trust Hist. Preservation, Ind.; sec. Friends of Woodrow Wilson, 1988—, chmn. dinner, 1990—; trustee Ga. Legal History Found., 1989—; pres. N. Springs H.S. Touchdown Club, 2000—01; founding dir. Sandy Springs Youth Basketball Program, 1999—2000; mem. Dem. Party Ga., Atlanta, 1983—; mem. Bench and Bar Com. State Bar Ga., 1996—; chmn. Summer Law Inst., Atlanta, 1981—85; panel mem. U.S. Bankruptcy Trustees No. Dist. Ga., 1982—92. Named to Honorable Order of Ky. Colonels; recipient Svc. award Inst. Continuing Legal Edn., Athens, Ga., 1981, 86. Fellow Ga. Bar Found.; mem. Atlanta Bar Assn. (com. chmn. 1981-85, bd. dirs. litigation sect. 2001—, mem. jud. selection com. 2001—, chmn. history com. 2001—), N.C. Bar Assn., Lawyers Club, North Springs H.S. Touchdown Club (pres. 2000—), Phi Alpha Delta (justice, Atlanta 1982-83, emeritus 1983). Office: 7715 Jett Ferry Rd Atlanta GA 30350-5419

STANDISH, WILLIAM LLOYD, judge; b. Pitts., Feb. 16, 1930; s. William Lloyd and Eleanor (McCargo) S.; m. Marguerite Oliver, June 12, 1963; children: Baird M., N. Graham, James H., Constance S. BA, Yale U., 1953; LLB, U. Va., 1956. Bar: Pa. 1957, U.S. Supreme Ct. 1967. Assoc. Reed, Smith, Shaw & McClay, Pitts., 1957-63; ptnr., 1963-80; judge Ct. Common Pleas Allegheny County (Pa.), 1980-87, U.S. Dist. Ct. (we. dist.) Pa., 1987—. Solicitor Edgeworth Borough Sch. Dist., 1963-66. Bd. dirs. Sewickley (Pa.) Cmty. Ctr., 1981-83, Staunton Farms Found., mem., 1984—, trustee, 1984-92; corporator Sewickley Cemetery, 1971-87; trustee Mary and Alexander Laughlin Children's Ctr., 1972-90, Leukemia Soc. Am., 1978-80, We. Pa. chpt., 1972-80, We. Pa. Sch. Deaf, 1983—, YMCA of Sewickley, 1996—; bd. dirs. Pitts. Theol. Sem., 2001—. Recipient Pres. award Leukemia Soc. Am., 1980. Mem. ABA, Pa. Bar Assn., Allegheny County Bar Assn., Am. Judicature Soc., Acad. Trial Lawyers Allegheny County (treas. 1977-78, bd. dirs. 1979-80), Am. Inn of Ct. (Pitts. chpt. 1993—). E-mail: Judge William. Office: US Dist Ct 605 US Post Office Ct House 700 Grant St Pittsburgh PA 15219-1906 E-mail: Standish@pawd.uscourts.gov

STANHAUS, JAMES STEVEN, lawyer; b. Evergreen Park, Ill., Oct. 22, 1945; s. Wilfrid Xavier and Mary (Komanecky) S.; m. Naomi Evelyn Miller, June 27, 1971; 1 child, Heather. AB magna cum laude, Georgetown U., 1966; JD magna cum laude, Harvard U., 1970. Bar: Ill. 1970, U.S. Dist. Ct. (no. dist.) Ill. 1970. Assoc. Mayer, Brown & Platt, Chgo., 1971-76, ptnr., 1977—. Mem. ABA, Ill. Bar Assn., Chgo. Bar Assn., Chgo. Council Lawyers, Chgo. Estate Planning Council, Phi Beta Kappa. Club: River (Chgo.). Avocations: computers, tennis, racquetball. Estate planning, Probate, Personal income taxation. Office: Mayer Brown & Platt 190 S La Salle St Ste 3100 Chicago IL 60603-3441 E-mail: jstanhaus@mayerbrown.com

STANISCI, THOMAS WILLIAM, lawyer; b. Bkln., Nov. 16, 1928; s. Vito and Angela Marie (Martino) S.; m. Catherine Ellen Cullen, June 4, 1955; children: Thomas, Marianne, Ellen, William, Peter. BA, St. John's Coll. Men, 1949, JD, 1953, postgrad., 1954. Bar: N.Y. 1953, U.S. Dist. Ct. (so. and ea. dists.) N.Y. 1956, U.S. Supreme Ct., 1981; diplomate Am. Bd. Profl. Liability Attys. (trustee). Assoc. Diblasi Marasco & Simone, White Plains, N.Y., 1954-60; mem. Simone Brant & Stanisci, 1960-66, Shayne Dachs Stanisci & Harwood, Mineola, N.Y., 1966-83; sr. mem. Shayne Dachs Stanisci Corker & Sauer, 1983—. Lectr. Practising Law Inst., 1975-79; instr., lectr. Am. Mgmt. Assn., 1976-77, N.Y. State Bar Assn., 1993, 94; guest lectr. Adelphi U., Hofstra U., 1975-79; guest speaker, panelist network and local TV programs. Contbr. articles in field. With U.S. Army, 1950-52. Mem. Am. Arbitration Assn., Am. Bd. Trial Advs., Nassau Suffolk Trial Lawyers Assn. (bd. dirs. 1978-90, treas. 1991, sec. 1992, vice chmn. 1993-94, chmn. 1995-96), Nassau County Bar Assn. (bd. dirs. 1993-96, lectr. acad. law), Columbian Lawyers. State civil litigation, Insurance, Personal injury.

STANKEE, GLEN ALLEN, lawyer; b. Clinton, Iowa, Sept. 27, 1953; s. Glen Earl and Marilyn Jean (Clark) S.; m. Carol Ann Prowe, Feb. 19, 1984. BSBA, Drake U., 1975; MBA, Mich. State U., 1977; JD, U. Detroit, 1979; LLM in Taxation, U. Miami, 1983. Bar: Mich. 1980, U.S. Dist. Ct. (ea. dist.) Mich. 1980, U.S. Ct. Appeals (6th cir.) 1980, U.S. Tax Ct. 1980, Fla. 1981, U.S. Ct. Appeals (11th cir.) 1981, U.S. Dist. Ct. (so. dist.) Fla. 1982, U.S. Dist. Ct. (mid. dist.) 1984, U.S. Supreme Ct. 1987; CPA, Fla. Assoc. Raymond & Dillon P.C., Detroit, 1980-81, West Palm Beach, Fla., 1981-85, prin., 1985-86, Ft. Lauderdale, 1987-93; ptnr. Ruden, McClosky, Smith, Schuster & Russell, P.A., 1993—. Contbr. articles to profl. jours. Mem. ABA, Fed. Bar Assn., Fla. Bar Assn., Mich. Bar Assn., Am. Inst. CPA's, Fla. Inst. CPA's, Palm Beach County Bar Assn., South Fla. Republican. Avocation: golf. Federal civil litigation, Corporate taxation, State and local taxation. Office: Ruden McClosky Smith Schuster & Russell PA PO Box 1900 Fort Lauderdale FL 33302-1900 E-mail: GAS@ruden.com

STANLEY, BRIAN JORDAN, corporate lawyer; b. Duncan, Okla., Sept. 10, 1954; s. Elmer E. and Betty Sue Stanley; m. Ruth Anne Lynn Stanley, Apr. 6, 1979 (div. Mar. 1989); children: Lindsey Jordan, Brent Alan; m. Francine Michelle La Valle, Oct. 18, 1996. BA in Polit. Sci., U. Okla., 1979; JD with honors, Oklahoma City U., 1985. Bar: Okla. 1985, U.S. Dist. Ct. (we. dist.) Okla. 1985. Sports writer The Norman (Okla.) Transcript, 1979-80; oil and gas landman Milt McCullough, Oklahoma City, 1980-81; trust officer Liberty Nat. Bank & Trust, 1981-83; atty. Michael P. Rogalin, 1985-86, William H. Mattoon, Norman, 1986-87, Fed. Deposit Ins. Corp., Oklahoma City, 1987, Reed, Shadid & Pipes, Oklahoma City, 1987-88, Mosburg, Sears, Kunzman & Bollinger, Oklahoma City, 1988; v.p., corp. gen. counsel The Hefner Co., Inc., 1989—. Bd. dirs. The Hefner Co., Inc.; trustee Dr. Brent Hisey Irrevocable Trust, Oklahoma City, 1998—. Contbr. articles to profl. jours. Mem. ABA, Okla. Bar Assn. Republican. Episcopalian. Avocations: Italian language, theology, politics. General corporate, Oil, gas, and mineral, Real property. Office: The Hefner Co Inc PO Box 2177 Oklahoma City OK 73101-2177 E-mail: vito1954@hotmail.com

STANLEY, BRUCE MCLAREN, SR. lawyer; b. Cleve., May 13, 1948; s. Willard Cyrus and Isabel (Anderson) S.; m. Pamela Soderholm, June 23, 1984; children: Bruce McLaren, Willard Charles. BA with high honors, Coll. William and Mary, 1970; JD, U. Va., 1974. Bar: Fla. 1974, U.S. Dist. Ct. (so. dist.) Fla. 1974, U.S. Dist. Ct. (mid. dist. Fla., U.S. Ct. Appeals (5th cir.) 1975, U.S. Ct. Appeals (11th cir.) 1982, U.S. Supreme Ct. 1978; diplomate Nat. Bd. Trial Advocacy. Assoc. Bradford, Williams, McKay, Kimbrell, Hamann & Jennings, Miami, Fla., 1974-79; ptnr. Blackwell, Walker, Gray, Powers, Flick & Hoehl, 1979-85, Henderson, Franklin, Starnes & Holt, Ft. Myers, Fla., 1985—, shareholder, 1989—. Mem. ABA, Fla. Bar Assn. (cert. in trial civil law 1984), Dade County Bar Assn. (bd. dirs. 1982-85), Lee County Bar Assn., Internat. Assn. Def. Counsel. Avocation: commercial pilot. Federal civil litigation, State civil litigation, Personal injury. Home: 2506 Mcgregor Blvd Fort Myers FL 33901-5828 Office: Henderson Franklin Starnes & Holt PO Box 280 Fort Myers FL 33902-0280 E-mail: bruce.stanley@henlaw.com

STANLEY, IAN G. lawyer; b. Eng., Apr. 25, 1957; MA, U. Cambridge (Eng.), 1980. Bar: solicitor Eng., Wales 1984. Ptnr. Allen & Overy, London, 1990—. General corporate, Insurance, Mergers and acquisitions. Office: Allen & Overy One New Change London EC4M 9QQ England

STANLEY, KEITH EUGENE, lawyer; b. Syracuse, N.Y., Mar. 15, 1951; s. Eugene Ridgway and Margeret Alice (Lake) S. BS, Mich. State U., 1973; JD, U. Mich., 1981. Bar: D.C. 1981. Atty. Office of Chief Counsel, IRS, Washington, 1981—. Avocation: photography. Office: IRS Office of Chief Counsel Corp:Br4 1111 Constitution Ave NW Washington DC 20224-0001 E-mail: kestan@kestan.com

STANLEY, WILLIAM MARTIN, lawyer; b. Milton, Fla., July 21, 1967; s. William Martin Sr. and Diane (Davies) S.; m. Lorraine Haire, Dec. 17, 1994. BA, Hampden-Sydney Coll., 1989; JD, D.C. Sch. law, 1994. Bar: Va. 1994, U.S. Dist. Ct. (we. and ea. dists.) Va. 1995, U.S. Ct. Appeals (4th cir.),1994. Assoc. atty. Davis & Assocs., Fairfax, Va., 1994-96, Cohen, Gettings, Dunham & Davis, Arlington, 1996-98; ptnr. Davis & Stanley, LLC, Fairfax, 1998—. Bd. dirs. The Paralegal Inst., Fairfax, 1991—, prof., 1991—; bd. dirs. Cambridge Sta. Assn., Farifax, 1996—. Mem. Fairfax City Rep. Com., 1996—. Mem. ATLA, Va. Trial Lawyers Assn., Fed. Bar Assn., Va. State Bar Assn. Methodist. Avocations: golf, fishing. General civil litigation, Criminal, General practice. Office: Davis & Stanley LLC 9502A Lee Hwy Fairfax VA 22031-2303

STANSELL, LELAND EDWIN, JR. lawyer, mediator, educator; b. Central, S.C., July 13, 1934; s. Leland Edwin and Hettie Katherine (Hollis) S.; children: James Leland, Susan. BS, Fla. So. Coll., 1957; LLB, U. Miami, Fla., 1961, JD, 1968. Bar: Fla. 1961; cert. civil mediator Fla. Supreme Ct., U.S. Dist. Ct. Fla. Assoc. Wicker & Smith, Miami, 1961-62, ptnr., 1962-75; pvt. practice, 1975-99, Leland E. Stansell, Jr., P.A., 1995—. Chmn. Appellate Jud. Nominating Com., Dade County (Fla.), 1983-87; mem. adv. com. Am. Arbitration Assn., 1975-90. Served with U.S. Army, 1957. Mem. ABA (ho. of dels. 1982-86), Fla. Bar (bd. govs. 1966-70, 70-80), Dade County Bar Assn. (dir. 1969-72, exec. com. 1974-75, pres. 1975-76), U. Miami Law Alumni Assn. (dir., officer, pres. 1968-69), Fla. Criminal Def. Attys. Assn. (treas. 1964-66), Am. Judicature Soc., Am. Bd. Trial Advs., Internat. Assn. Def. Counsel, Fla. Acad. Profl. Mediators, Fedn. Ins. Counsel, Miami Beach Rod and Reel Club (pres.), Coral Reef Yacht Club, Bankers Club, Ocean Reef Yacht Club, Delta Theta Phi (pres. Miami alumni chpt. 1966, regional dir. 1968. General civil litigation, Insurance, Personal injury. Office: 19 W Flagler St Miami FL 33130-4400

STANTON, ELIZABETH MCCOOL, lawyer; b. Lansdale, Pa., Apr. 12, 1947; d. Leo J. and Helen M. (Gillooly) McCool; m. Robert J. Stanton, June 13, 1970; children: Jonathan R., James Alfred. BBA, Drexel U., 1969; JD magna cum laude, U. Houston, 1979. Bar: Tex. 1979, U.S. Dist. Ct. (so. dist.) Tex. 1980, Ohio 1982, U.S. Dist. Ct. (so. dist.) Ohio 1983, U.S. Ct. Appeals (6th cir.) 1986, (3d cir.) 1992, U.S. Supreme Ct. 1990. Assoc. Friedman & Chaffin, Houston, 1979-80, Law Offices of Elaine Brady, Houston, 1980-81, Moots, Cope & Weinberger Co., L.P.A., Columbus, Ohio, 1981-86; prin. Moots, Cope and Kizer Co. L.P.A., 1986-89, Moots, Cope, Stanton and Kizer, P.A., Columbus, 1989-91, Moots, Cope & Stanton Co., L.P.A., Columbus, 1991-98, Moots, Cope, Stanton & Carter, Co., L.P.A., Columbus, 1998-2000; sole practice, 2000; ptnr. Chester, Willcox & Saxbe LLP, 2000—. Mem. Ohio Supreme Ct./Ohio State Bar Assn. Task Force on Gender Fairness in the Legal Profession, 1991-93. Drexel Bd. Trustees scholar, 1965-67, Internat. Ladies Garment Workers Union scholar, 1965-69. Mem. ABA, State Bar Tex., Ohio Bar Assn. (vice-chair govt. edn. and constrn. law com. 2001-), Columbus Bar Assn. (chair Labor Law Com. 1996-98), Nat. Assn. Women Lawyers (Ohio Reps. 1995—), Ohio Women's Bar Assn. (founding mem., bd. trustees 1994-97), Women Lawyers Franklin County (treas. 1989-90, bd. dirs. 1990-92), St. Thomas More Soc., Phi Kappa Phi, Beta Gamma Sigma. Democrat. Roman Catholic. Administrative and regulatory, Education and schools, Labor. Address: Chester Willcox & Saxbe LLP 17 South High St Ste 900 Columbus OH 43215-3413 E-mail: estanton@cwslaw.com

STANTON, GEORGE PATRICK, JR. lawyer; b. Fairmont, W.Va., Nov. 21, 1933; s. George Patrick and Wilma Roberta (Everson) S.; m. Shirley Jean Champ, Sept. 3, 1956; children: George Patrick, Edward Scott. BS in Bus. Adminstrn., Fairmont Coll., 1956; MBA in Fin., U. Dayton, 1969; JD, U. Balt., 1977. Bar: Md. 1978, U.s. Dist. Ct. Md. 1978, W.Va. 1979, U.S. Dist. Ct. (so. dist.) W.Va. 1979, U.S. Dist. Ct. (no. dist.) W.Va. 1980, U.S. Ct. Appeals (4th cir.) 1985. Auditor 1st Nat. Bank Fairmont, 1955-61; asst. cashier S.C. Nat. Bank, Columbia, 1961-64; sr. sys. analyst Chase Manhattan Bank, N.Y.C., 1964-65; asst. v.p. Winters Nat. Bank, Dayton, Ohio, 1965-69, Md. Nat. Bank, Balt., 1969-74; v.p. Equitable Trust Co., 1974-79; gen. ptnr. Stanton & Stanton Attys. at Law, Fairmont, 1979—. Staff sect. leader, mem. faculty Sch. for Bank Adminstrn. U. Wis.-Madison, 1978-89. Treas. Montaineer Area coun. Boy Scouts Am., Fairmont, 1982-90; pres. Three Rivers Coal Festival, Inc., Fairmont, 1984-85, pres., 1985-86, bd. dirs., 1982-86; pres. Appalachian Coal Festival, 1985-86, bd. dirs., 1985—; mem. adv. bd. Inst. for Living, Fairmont, 1983-85; pres. Firemans' CSC, Fairmont, W.Va., 1992-96. Mem. ABA, ATLA, Comml. Law League Am., W.Va. Bar Assn. (Kaufman award 1997), Marion County Bar Assn., Md. Bar Assn., W.Va. Trial Lawyers Assn., Marion County C. of C. (bd. dirs. 1983—), Fairmont State Coll. Alumni Assn. (bd. dirs. 1982—, pres. 1992-94), Fairmont Field Club, Rotary, Masons. Consumer commercial, Personal injury, Real property. Home: 2 W Hills Dr Fairmont WV 26554-5015 Office: Stanton & Stanton PO Box 968 WesBanco Bldg Ste 707 Fairmont WV 26555-0968

STANTON, LOUIS LEE, federal judge; b. N.Y.C., Oct. 1, 1927; s. Louis Lee and Helen Parsons (La Fétra) S.; m. Berit Eleonora Rask; children: L. Lee, Susan Helen Benedict, Gordon R., Fredrik S. BA, Yale U., 1950; JD, U. Va., 1955. Assoc. Davis Polk Wardwell Sunderland & Kiendl, N.Y.C., 1955-66, Carter, Ledyard & Milburn, N.Y.C., 1966-67, ptnr., 1967-85; sr. judge U.S. Dist. Ct. (so. dist.) N.Y., 1985—. Served to 1st lt. USMCR, 1950-52. Fellow Am. Coll. Trial Lawyers, N.Y. Bar Found.; mem. Va. Bar Assn.

STANTON, PATRICK MICHAEL, lawyer; b. Phila., Sept. 8, 1947; s. Edward Joseph and Helen Marie (Coghlan) S.; m. Kathleen Ann Fama, Aug. 22, 1970; children: Cheryl Marie, Susan Elizabeth. BS in History, St. Joseph's U., 1969; JD, U. Va., 1972; MBA, Fairleigh Dickinson, 1984. Bar: Ohio 1972, U.S. Dist. Ct. (so. dist.) Ohio 1972, N.J. 1982, U.S. Dist. Ct. N.J. 1982, N.Y. 1984. Assoc. Taft, Stettinius & Hollister, Cin., 1972-80; labor counsel Union Camp Corp., Wayne, N.J., 1980-83; dir. labor rels., equal employment oppurtunity programs W.R. Grace & Co., N.Y.C., 1983-86; of counsel Shanley & Fisher, P.C., Morristown, N.J., 1986-89, ptnr., chmn. labor and employment group, 1989-95; dir. Stanton, Hughes, Diana, Cerra, Mariani & Margello, P.C., 1995—. Adj. prof. bus. law Fairleigh Dickinson Univ.; pres. Sidney Reitman employment law Am. Inn. Ct., 1997-2001. Pres., bd. dirs. N.Y. State Adv. Coun. on Employment Law, Inc., N.Y.C., 1985-86. DuPont scholar U. Va., 1970. Mem. ABA, N.J. State Bar Assn. (exec. com. labor employment law sect. 1989—, rec. sec. 1995-97, treas. 1997-99, 2d vice chair 1999-2001, 1st vice chair 2001—), Phi Alpha Theta, Delta Mu Delta. Roman Catholic. Labor. Home: 292 Forest Ave Glen Ridge NJ 07028-1808 Office: Stanton Hughes Diana Cerra Mariani & Margello PC 10 Madison Ave Ste 402 Morristown NJ 07960-7303 Fax: 973-656-1611. E-mail: pstanton@stantonhughes.com

STANTON, ROGER D. lawyer; b. Oct. 4, 1938; s. George W. and Helen V. (Peterson) S.; m. Judith L. Duncan, Jan. 27, 1962; children: Jeffrey B., Brady D., Todd A. AB, U. Kans., 1960, JD, 1963. Bar: Kans. 1963, U.S. Dist. Ct. Kans. 1963, U.S. Ct. Appeals (10th cir.) 1972, U.S. Supreme Ct. 1973. Assoc. Stanley, Schroeder, Weeks, Thomas & Lysaught, Kansas City, 1968-72, Weeks, Thomas & Lysaught, Kansas City, 1969-80, also bd. dirs., chmn. exec. com., 1981-82, Stinson, Mag & Fizzell, Kansas City, 1983-96, chmn. products practice group, also bd. dirs., 1993-95; ptnr. Berkowitz, Feldmiller, Stanton, Brandt, Williams & Shaw, Prairie Village, Kans., 1997—. Chmn. bd. editors Jour. Kans. Bar Assn., 1975-83; contbr. articles to profl. jours. Active Boy Scouts Am., 1973-79; pres. YMCA Youth Football Club, 1980-82; co-chmn. Civil Justice Reform Act com. Dist. of Kans., 1991-95; bd. dirs. Kans. Appleseed Found., 2000—. Fellow Am. Coll. Trial Lawyers (state chmn. 1984-86); mem. Internat. Assn. Def. Counsel, Exec. com., 1994-99 East Kansas/West Miss. Chpt., Am. Bd. Trial Adv., Def. Rsch. Inst. (state co-chmn. 1979-90, Exceptionl Performance award 1979), Kans. Bar Assn. (Pres.'s award 1982), Johnson County Bar Found. (pres., trustee), Chmn. Bench/Bar Com. of Johnson Co. Bar Assn., Kans. Assn. Def. Counsel (pres. 1977-78), Kans. Inn. Ct., U. Kans. Sch. Law Alumni Assn. (bd. dirs. 1972-75). Federal civil litigation, Health, Securities. Office: Berkowitz Feldmiller Stanton Brandt Williams & Stueve 4121 W 83rd St Ste 227 Prairie Village KS 66208

STAPLES, LYLE NEWTON, lawyer; b. Radford, Va., Feb. 16, 1945; s. Lester Lyle and Velma Jean (King) S.; m. Christie Mercedes Carr, Feb. 1, 1971; children: Scott Andrew, John Randolph, Brian Matthew, Melissa Ann. BA, U. Md., 1967, JD, 1972; LLM in Taxation, Georgetown U., 1977. Bar: Md. 1973, U.S. Supreme Ct. 1978, U.S. Tax Ct. 1981, U.S. Dist. Ct. Md. 1981, U.S. Ct. Appeals (4th cir.) 1981. Tax law specialist IRS, Washington, 1972-77; assoc. Hessey & Hessey, Balt., 1978-82, Rosenstock, Burgee & Welty, Frederick, Md., 1982-84; sole practice Hampstead, 1984-91; mem. firm Johnson, Parker & Hess, Westminster, 1991-96; pvt. practice, 1996—. Vis. asst. prof. Towson (Md.) State U., 1981-82. Treas., bd. dirs. Literacy Coun. of Carroll County, Inc., 1993-98. Served with U.S. Army, 1968-69, Vietnam. Mem. ABA, Md. Bar Assn., Fin. Planning Assn., Carroll County C. of C. Democrat. Methodist. General corporate, Estate planning, Taxation, general. Home: 813 Clearview Ave Hampstead MD 21074-2325 Office: 56 W Main St Westminster MD 21157-4844

STAPLETON, JAMES FRANCIS, lawyer; b. Bridgeport, Conn., June 30, 1932; s. James M. and Lucy V. (Moran) S.; m. Margaret M. Daly, July 13, 1957; children: James F., Mark T., Paul and Kathleen. BSS, Fairfield U., 1954; LLB, Boston Coll., 1957; LLM, Georgetown U., 1958. Bar: Conn. 1957, U.S. Dist. Ct. (ea. and so. dists.) N.Y. 1979, U.S. Ct. Appeals (2d cir.) 1966, U.S. Dist. Ct. Conn. 1961, Mass. 1957, U.S. Supreme Ct. 1965, U.S. Ct. Appeals (D.C. cir.) 1958. Atty., Appellate Sect., Antitrust Divsn. U.S. Dept. Justice, 1957-58; assoc., ptnr. Marsh, Day & Calhoun, Bridgeport, 1958-73; city atty. City of Bridgeport, 1971-73; legis. counsel Conn. Bankers Assn., 1971-73; judge Conn. Superior Ct., 1973-78; chmn. Criminal Justice Commn. State of Conn., 1991-95; ptnr. Day, Berry & Howard, Stamford, Conn., 1978—. Mem. Bridgeport Bd. Edn., 1960-69. Fellow Am. Bar Found., Am. Coll. Trial Lawyers (chmn. state com. 1994-96, regent 1996-2000); mem. ABA, Am. Bd. Trial Advocates, Conn. Bar Assn. (bd. govs., ho. of dels., v.p., pres.), Fed. Bar Coun. Found. for 2d Circuit (v.p.), Bridgeport Bar Assn., Stamford-Darien Bar Assn. Alternative dispute resolution, General civil litigation. Home: 225 Winton Rd Fairfield CT 06430-3858 Office: Day Berry & Howard One Canterbury Green Stamford CT 06901 E-mail: jfstapleton@dbh.com

STAPLETON, JOHN OWEN, lawyer; b. Montgomery, Ala., July 24, 1951; s. Max O. Stapleton and Margaret (Lois) Gardner; m. Andrea Carol White, Apr. 1973 (div. June 1975); 1 child, Stefanie Michele; m. Nancy Jean Corbett, Sept. 20, 1980 (div. Apr. 2001); 1 child, Kellie Nichole. BS, U. Montevallo, 1976; JD, Samford U., 1980. Bar: Fla. 1981, U.S. Dist. Ct. (no. dist.) Fla. 1981, U.S. Ct. Appeals (11th cir.) 1982, U.S. Ct. Appeals (Fed. cir.) 1985, U.S. Dist. Ct. (mid. and so. dist.) Fla. 1993, U.S. Supreme Ct. 1999; bd. cert. in city, county and local govt. law, Fla. Assoc. Shimek & Sutherland PA, Pensacola, Fla., 1981-83; pvt. practice, 1984-91; asst. county atty. Escambia County, Fla., 1992-93; asst. county atty. labor and employment divsn. Broward County, 1993—. Guardian ad litem program 1st Jud. Cir., 1984-88. Democrat. Avocations: fishing, woodworking, boardgaming, reading, WWII ETO info. Office: Office of County Atty Broward County Govt Ctr 115 S Andrews Ave Ste 423 Fort Lauderdale FL 33301-1801 E-mail: jstapleton@broward.org

STAPLETON, LARRICK B. lawyer; b. Parkersburg, W.Va., Jan. 2, 1936; s. Robert Reese and Rae L. (Wooley) S.; children: Rebecca Mason, Ainsley Marquit, Jenny Baker. BA in Econs., U. W.Va., 1957, JD, 1960. Bar: W.Va. 1960, U.S. Ct. Appeals (4th cir.) 1960, Pa. 1963, N.J., 1985, U.S. Dist. Ct. (ea. dist.) Pa. 1963, N.J., 1985, U.S. Ct. Appeals (3d cir.) 1963. Law clk. U.S. Ct. Appeals (4th cir.), Richmond, Va., 1960-61; assoc. Ballard, Spahr, Phila., 1961-63; spl. counsel Pa. Dept. Justice, Counsel Bur. Corps., Harrisburg, 1964-72; prof. corp. law Temple U., Phila., 1972-76; ptnr. Fell & Spalding, Phila., 1963-70, 82-86; chief counsel Pa. Racing Commn., Harrisburg, 1974-78; sec., dir. Sci. Dynamics, Cherry Hill, N.J., Telvue Corp.; with Envimed Svcs., Inc., Communications Security Corp. Editor W.Va. Law Rev., 1957-60. Contbr. articles to legal jours. Appellate counsel ACLU, Phila., 1970— ; assoc. counsel Phila. Republican Com., 1965-70, Phila. Democratic Com., 1973-80. Mem. ABA, W.Va. Bar Assn., Pa. Bar Assn., Pa. Soc., Delta Sigma Rho. Federal civil litigation, General corporate, Securities. Home: 812 Wickfield Rd Wynnewood PA 19096-1611 Office: Larrick B Stapleton Esq 812 Wickfield Rd Wynnewood PA 19096-1611

STAPLETON, WALTER KING, federal judge; b. Cuthbert, Ga., June 2, 1934; s. Theodore Newton and Elizabeth Grantland (King) S.; m. Georgianna Duross Stapleton; children: Russell K., Theodore N., Teryl J. B.A., Princeton, 1956; LL.B., Harvard, 1959; LL.M., U. Va., 1984. Bar: Del. Assoc. mem. firm Morris, Nichols, Arsht & Tunnell, Wilmington, Del., 1959-65; dep. atty. gen. State of Del., 1963; partner Morris, Nichols, Arsht & Tunnell, 1966-70; judge U.S. Dist. Ct. Del., Wilmington, 1970-85, chief judge, 1983-85; judge U.S. Ct. Appeals (3d cir.), 1985—. Dep. atty. gen., Del., 1964; mem. Jud. Conf. U.S., 1984-85. Bd. dirs. Am. Bapt. Chs., U.S.A., 1978. Baptist. Office: US Ct Appeals 844 N King St Wilmington DE 19801-3519

STARCHER, LARRY VICTOR, state supreme court justice; b. Rocksdale, W.Va., Sept. 25, 1942; AB cum laude, W.Va. U., 1964, JD, 1967. Bar: W.Va. 1967. Former judge and chief judge W.Va. Ct. (17th jud. cir.), 1977-96; now justice W.Va. Supreme Ct. Appeals, 1997—. Pvt. practice, Morgantown, 1976—; dir. North Ctrl. W.Va. Legal Aid Soc., 1969-76; former instr. law, pub. adminstrn., and history W.Va. U.; contract adminstr. W.Va. U., 1966-67, asst. to v.p., 1967-69. Editor W.Va. Law Rev.; contbr. articles to profl. jours. Mem. City Coun. Morgantown, 1971-72; former mem. Young Dems. Fellow Harvard U., summer 1978. Mem. Am. Correctional Assn., W.Va. Jud. Assn., W.Va. State Bar, Monongalia County Bar Assn., Beta Theta Pi, Phi Delta Phi, Phi Alpha Theta, Pi Sigma Alpha. Avocations: carpentry, gardening, skiing. Office: Supreme Ct Appeals State Capital Rm E 307 Charleston WV 25305*

STARING, GRAYDON SHAW, lawyer; b. Deansboro, N.Y., Apr. 9, 1923; s. William Luther and Eleanor Mary (Shaw) S.; m. Joyce Lydia Allum-Poon, Sept. 1, 1949; children: Diana Hilary Agnes, Christopher Paul Norman. AB, Hamilton Coll., 1947; JD, U. Calif., Berkeley, 1951. Bar: Calif. 1952, U.S. Supreme Ct. 1958. Atty. Office Gen. Counsel, Navy Dept., San Francisco, 1952-53; atty. admiralty and shipping sect. U.S.

Dept. Justice, 1953-60; assoc. Lillick & Charles (now Nixon Peabody), 1960-64, ptnr., 1965-95, of counsel, 1995—. Titulary mem. Internat. Maritime Com.; bd. dirs. Marine Exchange at San Francisco, 1984-88, pres. 1986-88; instr. pub. speaking Hamilton Coll., 1947-48; adj. prof. Hastings Coll. Law, 1996-97, Boalt Hall, U. Calif., 1999. Author: Law of Reinsurance, 1993; assoc. editor Am. Maritime Cases, 1966-92, editor, 1992—; contbr. articles to legal jours. Mem. San Francisco Lawyers Com. for Urban Affairs, 1972-90; bd. dirs. Legal Aid Soc., San Francisco, 1974-90, v.p., 1975-80, pres., 1980-82. With USN, 1943-46, comdr. USNR. Fellow Am. Bar Found., Am. Coll. Trial Lawyers; mem. ABA (chmn. maritime ins. com. 1975-76, mem. standing com. admiralty law 1976-82, 86-90, chmn. 1990, ho. dels. 1986-90), FBA (pres. San Francisco chpt. 1968), Bar Assn. San Francisco (sec. 1972, treas. 1973), Calif. Acad. Appellate Lawyers, Maritime Law Assn. U.S. (exec. com. 1977-88, v.p. 1980-84, pres. 1984-86), Brit. Ins. Law Assn., Brit.-Am. C. of C. (bd. dirs. 1987-2001), World Trade Club San Francisco, Tulane Admiralty Inst. (permanent adv. bd.), Assocs. Maritime Mus. Libr. (dir. 1990—, pres. 1992-94). Admiralty, General civil litigation, Insurance. Office: 2 Embarcadero Ctr Ste 2700 San Francisco CA 94111-3900 E-mail: gstaring@lillick.com, Starlaw@aol.com

STARK, ALBERT MAXWELL, lawyer; b. Trenton, N.J., May 3, 1939; m. Ellen Stark, Nov. 20, 1966; children: Jared, Rachel. BA, Darmouth Coll., Hanover, N.H., 1960; LLD, U. Pa., Phila., 1963. Bar: N.J. 1964. Asst. to gov. of N.J., 1964; asst. atty. City of Trenton, 1965-66; asst. prosecutor Mercer County, N.J., 1967-68. Host radio programs Lawline, WHWH, 1985-95, In the Pub. Interest, WIMG, 1996. Recipient Humanitarian award Thomas A. Edison State Coll., 2000, award Trial Attys. of N.J., 2000. Mem. ABA, N.J. Bar Assn., Mercer County Bar Assn., Mercer County C. of C. (Citizen of Yr. 1994), Rotary Internat. (Fred Harris fellow 1996). Avocations: writing, tennis, skiing. Office: Stark & Stark 993 Lenox Dr Ste 301 Lawrenceville NJ 08648-2316

STARK, LISA KAY, lawyer; b. Appleton, Wis., Mar. 15, 1957; d. Roy Harry and Lorna Mae S.; m. Mark W. Kalish, Oct. 2, 1982 (div. Nov. 1988); 1 child, Michael S. Kalish; m. Thomas J. Misfeldt, July 2, 1990. BA, U. Wis., 1979, JD, 1982. Bar: Wis. 1982. Assoc. Misfeldt & Olson, Eau Claire, Wis., 1982-85; ptnr. Misfeldt, Olson & Stark, 1985-89, Misfeldt, Stark, Richie & Wickstrom, Eau Claire, 1989-98, Misfeldt, Stark, Richie, Wickstrom & Wachs, Eau Claire, 1998-2000; judge Eau Claire County Circuit Ct., 2000—. Ct. commr. Eau Claire County, 1991—. Bd. dirs. Eau Claire Regional Arts Ctr., 1989-95, United Way, Eau Claire, 1997—; mem. various coms. City of Eau Claire Comprehensive Plan and Loan Fund, 1992—. Mem. State Bar Wis. (family law sect., mem. standing com. on profl. ethics), Civil Trial Counsel Wis. (dir. 1993-98), Eau Claire Area C. of C. (bd. dirs., past chair). Congregationalist. Home: 1184 Bittersweet Rd Eau Claire WI 54701-5602 Office: Eau Claire County Courthouse 721 Oxford Ave Eau Claire WI 54703

STARK, MICHAEL LEE, lawyer, educator; b. Watseka, Ill., Apr. 29, 1936; s. Lee J. and Enid Lucille (Pickett) S.; m. Mary Elizabeth Campbell, Aug. 29, 1958; children— Robert C., Charles H., David M. B.B.A., Miami U., Oxford, Ohio, 1958; J.D., U. Ind., 1961. Bar: Ind. 1961, Ohio 1967. Trust officer A.M. Fletcher Nat. Bank, and Trust, Indpls., 1961-66; v.p. First Nat. Bank, Akron, Ohio, 1966-69; assoc. Roetzel & Andress, Akron, 1969-70, ptnr., from 1970, mng. ptnr., from 1980; now ptnr. Stark & Knoll, Akron; adj. prof. taxation U. Akron, 1981— ; lectr. Ohio Continuing Legal Edn. V.p. United Way, Akron, 1970-75. Fellow Am. Coll. Probate Lawyers; mem. ABA, Akron Estate Planning Assn., (past pres.), Ohio Bar Assn. (council dels. 1980-88), Akron Pension Council, Akron Probate Ct. Commn. (pres. 1975), Phi Beta Kappa, Beta Alpha Psi, Omicron Delta Kappa. Republican. Mem. Disciples of Christ Ch. Clubs: Portage, Firestone (Akron). Pension, profit-sharing, and employee benefits, Probate, Corporate taxation. Office: Stark & Knoll 76 S Main St Akron OH 44308-1812

STARKE, HAROLD E., JR. lawyer; b. Richmond, Va., Aug. 1, 1944; BA, Randolph-Macon Coll., 1967; JD, U. Richmond, 1971; LLM in Taxation, NYU, 1973. Bar: Va. 1971, D.C. 1981. Mem. Troutman Sanders Mays & Valentine, LLP, Richmond. Editor U. Richmond Law Rev., 1970-71. Bd. trustees Randolph-Macon Coll., 1983-85, 95-97, 99—. Fellow Am. Coll. Tax Counsel; mem. ABA (taxation, bus. law, real property, probate and trust law sects), Va. State Bar (chmn. taxation sect. 1985-86), D.C. Bar, Richmond Estate Planning Coun., Randolph-Macon Estate Planning Coun. (chmn. 1985—), McNeill Honor Soc., Phi Delta Phi. General corporate, Estate planning, Taxation, general. Office: Troutman Sanders Mays & Valentine LLP Bank of Am Center PO Box 1122 Richmond VA 23218-1122

STARKEY, CAROL A. lawyer, prosecutor; b. Wheatridge, Colo., Dec. 6, 1961; d. Gerald H. Starkey and Angela M. Scavello. Student, Colo. Coll., 1983; BA, U. Colo., 1984; JD, Suffolk U., 1988. Bar: Mass., U.S. Dist. Ct. Mass. Assoc. Law Offices of Edward Fegues, Boston, 1988-89; asst. dist. atty. Bristol County Dist. Atty.'s Office, New Bedford, Mass., 1989-93; asst. atty. gen. Office of Atty. Gen., Boston, 1993-95, chief asst. for econ. crimes divsn. criminal bur., 1995—. Mem. Supreme Jud. Ct. Com. on Lawyer Advt., Boston, 1997-99; spkr. in field. Ward del. Voting Ward # 3, Boston, 1998. Mem. Mass. Bar Assn. (mem. com. on legislature proposals related to criminal law 1999). Avocations: reading, cooking, sailing. Office: Office Atty Gen 1 Ashburton Pl Rm 2010 Boston MA 02108-1518

STARKMAN, GARY LEE, lawyer; b. Chgo., Sept. 2, 1946; s. Oscar and Sara (Ordman) S. AB, U. Ill., 1968; JD cum laude, Northwestern U., 1971. Bar: Ill. 1971, U.S. Dist. Ct. (no. dist.) Ill. 1972, U.S. Ct. Appeals (7th cir.) 1972, U.S. Supreme Ct. 1974, Trial Bar U.S. Dist. Ct. (no. dist.) Ill. 1982, U.S. Ct. Appeals (3d cir.) 1984, U.S. Ct. Appeals (D.C. cir.) 1984. Asst. U.S. Atty. No. Dist. Ill., 1971-75; gen. counsel, dir. rsch. Citizens for Thompson Campaign Com., 1975-77; counsel to Gov. of Ill., 1977-81; ptnr. Ross & Hardies, Chgo., 1990—; admissions com. U.S. Dist. Ct. (no. dist.) Ill., 1982-90. Co-author: (textbook) Cases and Comments on Criminal Procedure, 1974, 5th edit., 1998; contbr. articles to profl. jours.; reviewer in field. Chmn. state agys. divsn. Jewish United Fund Met. Chgo., 1978-81; chmn. Ill. Racing Bd., 1991-96; bd. dirs. Internat. Assn. Racing Commn., 1992-94; cmty. adv. bd. Jr. League Chgo., 1979-83. Recipient John Marshall award for appellate litigation Atty. Gen. U.S., 1974, Nat. Svc. award Tau Epsilon Phi, 1968; named one of Ten Outstanding Young Citizens, Chgo. Jr. C. of C., 1978. Mem. ABA (litigation sect.), Chgo. Bar Assn. (constl. law com.), Decalogue Soc., Northwestern U. Law Alumni Assn. Federal civil litigation, State civil litigation, Criminal. Office: Ross & Hardies 150 N Michigan Ave Ste 2500 Chicago IL 60601-7567 E-mail: gary.starkman@rosshardies.com

STARKOFF, ALAN GARY, lawyer; b. Cleve., May 31, 1950; s. Harvey Herbert Starkoff and Honey Beverly (Stein) Simmons; children— Brandon Mitchell, Brooke Erin; m. Kathleen Klingbiel, Jan. 9, 1982; 1 child, William K. B.S., Ohio State U., 1972; J.D., Cleve. State U., 1975. Bar: Ohio 1975, Fla. 1975, Pa. 1981, U.S. Dist. Ct. (no. dist.) Ohio 1975, U.S. Supreme Ct. 1979. Assoc. Starkoff & Gallagher, Cleve., 1975-78; ptnr. Starkoff & Starkoff, Cleve. 1978-84; prin. Gaines & Stern Co. L.P.A., Cleve., 1984-98; prin. Schuttenstein Zox and Dunn, Columbus, Ohio, 1999—; dir. Stanspec Corp., Cleve. 1981— . Councilman City of University Heights, Ohio, 1980-81; vice chmn. Charter Rev. Commn., University Heights, 1979; mem. Cuyahoga County Republican Orgn., Cleve. 1980-81. Mem. ABA, Columbus Bar Assn., Fla. Bar Assn., Ohio State Bar Assn., Pa. Bar Assn., Assn. Trial Lawyers Am., Cleve. Trial Lawyers Assn. State civil litigation, General corporate, Personal injury. Home: 4387 Tarrytown Ct New Albany OH 43054-9679 Office: Schottenstein Zox & Dunn 41 S High St Columbus OH 43215-6101

STARNES, OSCAR EDWIN, JR. lawyer; b. Raleigh, N.C., May 3, 1924; s. Oscar and Marion (Fletcher) S.; m. Lida Martin, July 8, 1978; children by previous marriage: Oscar Edwin, Amy Elizabeth, Jane Marion. BS, Davidson Coll., 1947; LLB, U. N.C., 1950. Bar: N.C. 1950. Mem. Van Winkle, Buck, Wall, Starnes & Davis and predecessor firm, Asheville, N.C., 1950—, pres., 1973—. Corp. counsel City of Asheville, 1958-67; town atty. Town of Biltmore Forest, 1981—. Served with U.S. Army, 1943-46. Decorated Purple Heart. Fellow Am. Coll. Trial Lawyers (state chmn. 1979-80); mem. ABA, N.C. Bar Assn (mem. gen. practice hall of fame 1992, chair sr. lawyers divsn. 1993-94), Buncombe County Bar Assn. (pres. 1972-73), Assn. N.C. Def. Lawyers (bd. dirs. 1981-84). Avocations: travel, tennis, water sports. General practice, Insurance, Land use and zoning (including planning). Office: Van Winkle Buck Wall Starnes & Davis PA 11 N Market St Ste 300 Asheville NC 28801-2932 E-mail: ostarn@vanwinklelawfirm.com

STARR, ISIDORE, law educator; b. Bklyn., Nov. 24, 1911; BA, CCNY, 1932; LLB, St. John's U., Jamaica, N.Y., 1936; MA, Columbia U., 1939; JSD, Bklyn. Law Sch., 1942; PhD, New Sch. Social Rsch., 1957. Bar: N.Y. 1937. Tchr. various high schs., N.Y.C., 1934-61; from assoc. prof. to prof. edn. Queen's Coll., 1961-75, prof. emeritus, 1975—. Dir. Inst. on Law-Related Edn., Lincoln-Filene Ctr., Tufts U., 1963; dir. Law Studies Inst., N.Y.C., 1974; adv. on Our Living Bill of Rights Film Series (6 films) Ency. Brit. Ednl. Corp.; mem. Ariz. Ctr. for Law-Related Edn.; mem. coun. on pub. legal edn. State of Wash., 2001—; cons. in field. Author: The Lost Generation of Prince Edward COunty, 1968, The Gideon Case, 1968, The Feiner Case, 1968, The Mapp Case, 1968, The Supreme Court and Contemporary Issues, 1968, Human Rights in the United States, 1969, The American Judicial System, 1972, The Idea of Liberty, 1978, Justice: Due Process of Law, 1981; co-editor Living American Documents, 1971. Bd. dirs. Phi Alpha Delta Juvenile Justice Program, 1981—. 1st lt. U.S. Army, 1943-46. John Hay fellow, 1952-53; recipient Outstanding Citizen award Philip Morris Cos., 1992. Mem. ABA (hon. chair adv. commn. on Youth Edn. for Citizenship, Isidore Starr award for Spl. Achievment in Law Studies, Leon Jaworski award 1989), Am. Judicature Soc., Am. Soc. Legal History, Am. Legal Studies Assn., Nat. Coun. Social Studies (past pres.), Washington Coun. Pub. Legal Edn., Phi Beta Kappa, Phi Alpha Delta (cert. of appreciation 1981). Address: 12501 Greenwood Ave N Apt C110 Seattle WA 98133-8000

STARR, IVAR MILES, lawyer; b. N.Y.C., Sept. 19, 1950; s. Charles S. Scholnicoff and Rosalie (Paletz) Starr. AA, Nassau Community Coll., 1970; BA, Queens Coll., 1972; JD, U. Miami, 1980. Bar: Fla. 1981, U.S. Dist. Ct. (so. dist.) Fla. 1981, N.Y. 1988. Rep. securities sales Aetna Variable Life Ins. Co., Garden City, N.Y., 1973-75; freelance real estate broker New Fairfield, Conn., 1973-79; assoc. Law Offices of Peter Lopez, Miami, Fla., 1981-82, Mills & London P.A., Miami, 1982; pvt. practice, 1982—. Lectr. Dade County (Fla.) Consumer Advs. Office, 1984-87; instr. paralegal courses Briarcliffe Coll., 1991. Candidate judge Dade County Ct., 1988. Recipient Outstanding Svc. award Miami Beach Bd. Realtors, 1986, 87, 88, 91, 92. Mem. The Fla. Bar (vol. bar liaison com. 1993-96), Miami Beach Bar Assn. (bd. dirs. 1984—, treas. 1991, v.p. 1993, pres.-elect 1995, pres. 1996, immediate past pres. 1997), Miami Beach C. of C. (lectr. 1985-89), Better Bus. Bur. South Fla. (arbitrator 1984—, Cert. of Appreciation 1985), Queens Coll. Alumni in South Fla. (chmn. 1986-96), Internat. Toastmasters (so. divsn. gov. dist. 47 1993-94, Able Toastmaster Bronze 1992, Able Toastmaster Silver 1993, dist. 47 pub. rels. officer 1997-98, Dist. 47 Enthusiasm award 1993-94, Disting. Toastmaster 1994, 99, Advanced Toastmaster gold and Competent Leader 1997, Advanced Toastmaster Silver and Advanced Leader 1999, Disting. Toastmaster, 1999, Competent Toastmaster 2000). Avocations: boating, swimming, music. State civil litigation, General practice, Real property. Home: 7705 Abbott Ave Apt 504 Miami FL 33141-2389 Office: 350 Lincoln Rd Ste 407 Miami FL 33139-3155

STARRETT, FREDERICK KENT, lawyer; b. Lincoln, Nebr., May 23, 1947; s. Clyde Frederick and Helen Virginia (Meyers) S.; m. Linda Lee Jensen, Jan. 19, 1969; children: Courtney, Kathryn, Scott. BA, U. Nebr., 1969; JD, Creighton U., 1976. Bar: Nebr. 1976, Kans. 1977, U.S. Dist. Ct. Nebr. 1976, Mo. 1987, U.S. Dist. Ct. Kans. 1977, U.S. Ct. Appeals (8th and 10th cirs.) 1983, U.S. Dist. Ct. (we. dist.) Mo. 1987, U.S. Supreme Ct. 1993. Pvt. practice law, Great Bend, Kans., 1976-77, Topeka, 1977-86; ptnr. Miller, Bash & Starrett, P.C., Kansas City, Mo., 1986-90, Lathrop Norquist & Miller, 1990-91, Lathrop and Norquist, Overland Park, Kans., 1991-95, Lathrop & Gage L.C., Overland Park, 1996—. Jud. nominating commr. 10th Jud. Dist., 2000—. Lt (j.g.) USNR, 1969-72. Mem. ABA, Kans. Bar Assn. (pres. litigation sect. 1985-86), Am. Bd. Trial Advs. (pres. Kansas chpt. 1997), Def. Rsch. Inst., (state rep. Kans. 1998-2001), Mo. Orgn. Def. Lawyers, Civitan Club (pres. 1985-86, Disting. Pres. award 1985-86). Democrat. Presbyterian. Avocations: aviation, scuba diving. Federal civil litigation, State civil litigation, Personal injury. Office: Lathrop & Gage LC 1050/40 Corporate Woods 9401 Indian Creek Pkwy Overland Park KS 66210-2005 E-mail: fstarrett@lathropgage.com

STARRS, ELIZABETH ANNE, lawyer; b. Detroit, Jan. 1, 1954; d. John Richard and Mabel Angeline (Gilchrist) S. BA, U. Mich., 1975; JD, Suffolk U., 1980. Bar: Mass. 1980, Colo. 1983, U.S. Dist. Ct. Mass. 1980, U.S. Ct. Appeals (1st. cir.) 1980, Colo. 1983, U.S. Dist. Ct. Colo. 1983, U.S. Ct. Appeals (10th cir.) 1983. Assoc. Denner & Benjoya P.C., Boston, 1980-83, Kennedy & Christopher P.C., Denver, 1983-86, ptnr., 1986—, pres., mng. ptnr., 1994-2000. Mem. jud. nominating commn. 2d Jud. Dist., Colo., 2000-06. Troop leader Girl Scouts U.S., Denver, 1984-85; pres. Colo. Women's Bar Assn. Found., 1992-94. Fellow Am. Coll. Trial Advs., Colo. Bar Found.; mem. ATLA, FBA, Colo. Bar Assn. (litigation coun. 1989-96, chair 1993-94, profl. liability chair 1991-93), Denver Bar Assn. (pres.-elect 2001—), Colo. Women's Bar Assn. (bd. dirs. 1984-85, v.p. 1989-90), U.S. Dist. Ct. Colo. (com. conduct 1997—), Am. Bd. Trial Advs., Def. Rsch. Inst., Faculty of Fed. Advs. Roman Catholic. Federal civil litigation, State civil litigation, Professional liability. Office: Kennedy & Christopher PC 1660 Wynkoop St Ste 900 Denver CO 80202-1197

STARRS, JAMES EDWARD, law and forensics educator, consultant; b. Bklyn., July 30, 1930; s. George Thomas and Mildred Agatha (Dobbins) S.; m. Barbara Alice Smyth, Sept. 6, 1954; children: Mary Alice, Monica, James, Charles, Liam, Barbara, Siobhan, Gregory. BA, LLB, St. John's U., Bklyn., 1958; LLM, NYU, 1959. Bar: N.Y. 1958, D.C. 1966, U.S. Ct. Mil. Appeals 1959, U.S. Dist. Ct. (so. and ea. dists.) N.Y. 1960. Assoc. Lawless & Lynch, N.Y.C., 1958; tchg. fellow Rutgers U., Newark, 1959-60; asst. prof. law DePaul U., Chgo., 1960-64; assoc. prof. law George Washington U., Washington, 1964-67, prof. law, 1967—, prof. forensic scis., 1975—. Cons. Nat. Commn. Reform Fed. Criminal Laws, Washington, 1968, Cellmark Diagnostics, Germantown, Md., 1987—, Time-Life Books, 1993; participant re-evaluation sci. evidence and trial of Bruno Richard Hauptmann for Lindbergh murder, 1983; participant reporting sci. re-analysis of firearms evidence in Sacco and Vanzetti trial, 1986; project dir. Alfred G. Packer Victims Exhumation Project, 1989, A Blaze of Bullets: A Sci. Investigation into the Deaths of Senator Huey Long and Dr. Carl Austin Weiss, 1991, Meriwether Lewis Exhumation Project, 1992—, Frank R. Olson Exhumation Project, 1994, Jesse W. James Exhumation Project, 1995, Samuel Washington-Harewood Excavations, 1999, The Boston Strangler Re-Investigation, 2000, The Exhumation of Carl E. Willis, Sr., 2001; Snider lectr. U. Toronto, 1999, Boston Strangler Re-Investigation, 2000. Author: (with Moenssens and Inbau) Scientific Evidence in Criminal Cases, 1986; (with Moenssens, Inbau and Henderson) Scientific Evidence in Civil and Criminal Cases, 1995; editor: The Noiseless Tenor, 1982; co-editor: (review) Scientific Sleuthing, 1976—; mem. editl. bd. Jour. Forensic Sci., 1980-98, Encyclopedia of Forensic Sciences; contbr. articles to profl. jours. Sgt. U.S. Army, 1950-53, Korea. Recipient Vidocq Soc. award, 1993; Ford Found. fellow, 1963; vis. scholar in residence USMC, 1984. Fellow Am. Acad. Forensic Sci. (chmn. jurisprudence sect. 1984, 94, 95, bd. dirs. 1986-89, 98-2001, Jurisprudence Sect. award 1988, Disting. fellow 1996); mem. ABA (emeritus), Mid-Atlantic Assn. Forensic Sci., Assn. Trial Lawyers Am., Internat. Soc. Forensic Sci. (chmn. jurisprudence sect. 1988), Internat. Assn. for Identification (co-chmn. historic cases sect. 1998—). Roman Catholic. Home: 8602 Clydesdale Rd Springfield VA 22151-1301 Office: George Washington U Nat Law Ctr 720 20th St NW Washington DC 20006-4306 E-mail: jstarrs@main.nlc.gwu.edu

STATHIS, NICHOLAS JOHN, lawyer; b. Calchi, Greece, Feb. 27, 1924; Republican. s. John and Sylvia (Koutsonouris) S. Student, Columbia U., 1942-43, 44-48, AB, 1946, JD, 1948. Bar: N.Y. 1949. Assoc. James Maxwell Fassett, N.Y.C., 1948-50; asst. counsel to spl. com. to investigate organized crime in interstate commerce U.S. Senate, Washington, 1951; trial atty. Fidelity & Casualty Co., N.Y.C., 1952; law sec. to Harold R. Medina Judge U.S. Ct. Appeals (2d cir.), 1952-54; spl. dep. atty. gen. N.Y. State Election Frauds Bur., Dept. Law, 1956; assoc. Watson, Leavenworth, Kelton & Taggart, N.Y.C., 1954-60, ptnr., 1961-81, Hopgood, Calimafde, Kalil, Blaustein & Judlowe, N.Y.C., 1981-84, Botein, Hays & Sklar, N.Y.C., 1984-89; of counsel White & Case, 1989-93; corp. coun., dir. intellectual property Aphton Corp., 1993—. Lectr. Practising Law Inst., 1968-69. Contbr. articles to profl. jours. on trademarks. Pres., exec. dir., chmn., bd. dirs. Found. Classic Theatre and Acad., 1973—; bd. dirs. Concert Artists Guild, 1974-91, Pirandello Soc., 1976—, Bklyn. Philharm. Orch., 1986-91, Orpheon, Inc., 1986-98, Friends of Young Musicians, 1998—. With AUS, 1943-44. Mem. ABA, Assn. of Bar of City of N.Y., N.Y. State Bar Assn., Fed. Bar Coun., Am. Intellectual Property Law Assn., N.Y. Intellectual Property Law Assn. Republican. Greek Orthodox. Federal civil litigation, Patent, Trademark and copyright. Home: 1885 John F Kennedy Blvd Jersey City NJ 07305-2113 Office: 515 Madison Ave Ste 725 New York NY 10022-5403

STATKUS, JEROME FRANCIS, lawyer; b. Hammond, Ind., June 13, 1942; s. Albert William and Helen Ann (Vaicunas) S.; children: Wesley Albert, Nicholas Jerome. BA, So. Ill. U., 1964; JD, U. Louisville, 1968; MA, U. Wyo., 1974. Bar: Wyo. 1971, U.S. Dist. Ct. Wyo. 1971, Wis. 1989, D.C. 1977, U.S. Ct. Claims 1973, U.S. Supreme Ct. 1974, U.S. Ct. Appeals (10th cir.) 1973, U.S. Ct. Appeals (7th cir.) 1992. Law clk. U.S. Dist. Ct., So. Dist. Ill., Peoria, 1968-69; asst. atty. gen. State of Wyo., Cheyenne, 1971-75; legis. asst. to U.S. Senator Clifford Hansen Washington, 1975-76; asst. U.S. atty. U.S. Dept. Justice, Dist. of Wyo., 1976-77; sole practice Cheyenne, 1978-79; assoc. Horisky, Bagley & Hickey, 1979-81; ptnr. Rooney, Bagley, Hickey Evans & Stratkus, 1981-88; exec. dir. Wyo. State Bar, 1988-89; trustee Village of Germantown, Wis., 1991-93; office share Ladewig and Rechlicz, 1990-93; pvt. practice Douglas, Wyo., 1993-96; asst. pub. defender State of Wyo., 1993-96. Pres. Ret. Sr. Vol. Program, Cheyenne, 1982-83; treas. Pathfinder (drug rehab.), Cheyenne, 1982-85; bar commr. 1st Jud. Dist., 1985-87; mem. Future Milw., 1991; chair Waukesha County Devel. Disability Adv. Coun., 1996—; mem. Washington County Econ. Devel. Com. Served with USNR, 1969-70. Mem. Wyo. Bar Assn., D.C. Bar Assn., Wis. State Bar Assn., Wyo. Trial Lawyers Assn. (bd. dirs. 1984-85), KC, VFW. Republican. Roman Catholic. Criminal, General practice. Home: PO Box 14 Germantown WI 53022-0014 Office: W156N 11340 Pilgrim Rd Germantown WI 53022

STATLAND, EDWARD MORRIS, lawyer; b. Washington, Aug. 20, 1932; s. Harry and Rebecca (Berman) S.; m. Pearl Axelrod, June 1, 1958; children: Stuart J., Carole B. AB, George Washington U., 1954, JD with honors, 1959. Bar: D.C. 1959, Md. 1959. Asst. corp. counsel D.C., Washington, 1960-62; assoc. Miller, Brown & Gildenhorn, 1962-70; ptnr. Brown, Gildenhorn & Statland, 1970-75; sr. ptnr. Statland & Zaslav, 1975-83; ptnr. Statland, Nerenberg, Nassau, Buckley & Squires, 1984-90, Statland & Buckley, P.C., Washington, 1990—. Pres., bd. dirs. Hebrew Home of Greater Washington, D.C. Served with U.S. Army, 1954-56. Mem. ABA, Md. State Bar Assn., Montgomery County Bar Assn., D.C. Bar Assn. (panel mem.), Am. Arbitration Assn., Nat. Assn. Securities Dealers, Assn. Plaintiffs Trial Attys., Am. Judicature Soc. General civil litigation, Family and matrimonial, Personal injury. Home: 4515 Willard Ave Chevy Chase MD 20815 Office: 1823 L St NW Washington DC 20036

STAUBER, RONALD JOSEPH, lawyer; b. Toledo, Nov. 8, 1940; s. Frederick I. and Anna R. (Kline) S.; m. Doreen Lynn Toll, Aug. 19, 1967 (div.); children: Brandon, Deborah. BBA, U. Toledo, 1962; JD, Ohio State U., 1965. Bar: Calif. 1967, U.S. Dist. Ct. (cen. and ea. dists.) Calif. 1967, U.S. Supreme Ct. 1972. Corp. counsel Div. Corps., Dept. Investments State of Calif., L.A., 1965-67; ptnr. Blacker & Stauber, Beverly Hills, Calif., 1967-77, Ronald J. Stauber, Inc., Beverly Hills and L.A., 1978-86, 88—, Stauber & Gersh, Beverly Hills and Washington, 1986-87. Bd. dirs. Willys Asset Mgmt., Inc., Meridian Enterprises, Inc. Served in USNG. Mem. Beverly Hills Bar Assn. (corp. com., real estate com.), L.A. Bar Assn. (bus. and corp. sect., judge pro tem Mcpl. Ct.), ABA (corps., banking and bus. law sects.), Calif. State Bar Assn. (real property sect.). Democrat. Jewish. General corporate, Real property. Office: 1880 Century Park E Ste 300 Los Angeles CA 90067-1611 E-mail: ronstauber@stauber.com

STAUBITZ, ARTHUR FREDERICK, lawyer, healthcare products company executive; b. Omaha, Mar. 14, 1939; s. Herbert Frederick Staubitz and Barbara Eileen (Dallas) Alderson; m. Linda Medora Miller, Aug. 18, 1962; children: Michael, Melissa, Peter. AB cum laude, Wesleyan U., Middletown, Conn., 1961; JD cum laude, U. Pa., 1964. Bar: Ill. 1964, U.S. Dist. Ct. (no. dist.) Ill. 1964, U.S. Ct. Appeals (7th cir.) 1964, Pa. 1972. Assoc. Sidley & Austin, Chgo., 1964-71; sr. internat. atty., asst. gen. counsel, dir. Japanese ops. Sperry Univac, Blue Bell, Pa., 1971-78; from asst. to assoc. to dep. gen. counsel Baxter Internat. Inc., Deerfield, Ill., 1978-85, v.p., dep. gen. counsel, 1985-90; v.p. Baxter Diagnostics, 1990-91; sr. v.p., sec., gen. counsel Amgen, Inc., Thousand Oaks, Calif., 1991-92; v.p., gen. mgr. Ventures Group Baxter World Trade Corp., Deerfield, Ill., 1992-93; v.p., sec., gen. counsel Baxter Internat. Inc., 1993, sr. v.p., gen. counsel, 1993-97, sr. v.p. portfolio strategy, 1997-98. Bd. dirs. Aastrom Bioscis., Inc. Mem. Planning Commn., Springfield Twp., Montgomery County, Pa., 1973-74, mem. Zoning Hearing Bd., 1974-78; bd. dirs. Twp. H.S. Dist. 113, Deerfield and Highland Park, Ill., 1983-91, pres., 1989-91; trustee Food and Drug Law Inst., 1991-92, 93-96, Carthage Coll., Kenosha, Wis., 1996—, exec. com., 1999—; bd. dirs. Music of the Baroque, 1994-2001, vice-chmn. Mem. ABA. Episcopalian. Antitrust, General corporate, Private international. Home: 232 Deerfield Rd Deerfield IL 60015-4412 also: 6251 E Placita Aspecto Tucson AZ 85750 E-mail: staubitz@msn.com

STAUFFER, ERIC P. lawyer; b. Tucson, Feb. 1, 1948; s. Robert D. and Jeanne E. (Catlin) S.; m. Jane F. Snyder, Aug. 2, 1969; children: Curtis Austen, Marcus Elias, Laura Afton. BA, U. South Fla., 1969; JD, Yale U., 1972. Bar: Ariz. 1972, Maine 1974, D.C. 1979. Spl. asst. to gov., fed. state coord. State of Maine, 1973-75; Maine alt. to New England Regional Commn., 1973-75; gen. counsel Maine State Housing Auth., 1976-77; adminstrv. asst. to chmn. Dem. Nat. Com., 1977-78; mem. Preti, Flaherty, Beliveau Pachios & Haley, LLC, Portland, Maine, 1978—. Bd. dirs. Jr.

Achievement Maine, Inc., 1995-98; pres. Goodwill Industries No. New Eng., 1981-82, bd. dirs., 1979-93, 99—. Mem. Am. Health Lawyers Assn., Maine State Bar Assn., Ariz. State Bar, D.C. Bar, Maine Real Estate Devel. Assn. (bd. dirs. 1991—, Pub. Svc. award 1992). Contracts commercial, Computer, Mergers and acquisitions. Office: Preti Flaherty Beliveau Pachios & Haley LLC PO Box 9546 One City Ctr Portland ME 04112-9546 E-mail: estauffe@preti.com

STAUFFER, RONALD EUGENE, lawyer; b. Hempstead, N.Y., Jan. 22, 1949; s. Hiram Eugene and Florence Marie (Hintz) S.; m. Vicki Lynn Hartman, June 12, 1973; children: Eric Alan, Craig Aaron, Darren Adam. SB, MIT, 1970; JD magna cum laude, Harvard U., 1973. Bar: D.C. 1973, U.S. Ct. Mil. Appeals 1976, U.S. Tax Ct. 1979. Ptnr. Hogan & Hartson, Washington, 1977-87, Sonnenschein Nath & Rosenthal, Washington, 1988—. Contbr. articles to profl. publs. Capt. U.S. Army, 1970-77. Mem. ABA (chair TIPS Employee Benefits Com. 1977—), D.C. Bar Assn., Tau Beta Pi, Sigma Gamma Tau. Avocations: running, water skiing. Pension, profit-sharing, and employee benefits, Corporate taxation. Home: 10207 Woodvale Pond Dr Fairfax Station VA 22039-1658 Office: Sonnenschein Nath & Rosenthal 1301 K St NW Ste 600 Washington DC 20005-3317

STAVINS, RICHARD LEE, lawyer; b. Urbana, Ill., Sept. 26, 1943; s. Sidney and Joan (Shaul) S.; m. Karen Kessler, June 18, 1967; children: Eric, Randi. BS, Northwestern U., 1965, JD, 1968. Bar: Ill. 1968, U.S. Dist. Ct. (no. dist.) Ill. 1969, U.S. Ct. Appeals (7th cir.) 1969. U.S. Supreme Ct. 1972. Assoc. Dorfman, DeKoven & Cohen, Chgo., 1968-70, Blumenthal & Schwartz, Chgo., 1970-76; ptnr. Blumenthal & Stavins, 1976-81, Keith & Greenblatt, Chgo., 1981-82, Greenblatt Yusim & Stavins, Chgo., 1982-85; assoc. Robbins, Salomon & Patt, 1985-86, ptnr., 1986—. Ford Found. fellow, 1967. Federal civil litigation, General civil litigation, State civil litigation. Home: 155 N Harbor Dr Chicago IL 60601-7364 Office: Robbins Salomon & Patt 25 E Washington St Chicago IL 60602-1708

STAYIN, RANDOLPH JOHN, lawyer; b. Cin., Oct. 30, 1942; s. Jack and Viola (Tomin) S.; children: Gregory S., Todd R., Elizabeth J. BA, Dartmouth Coll., 1964; JD, U. Cin., 1967. Bar: Ohio 1967, U.S. Dist. Ct. (so. dist.) Ohio 1968, U.S. Dist. Ct. D.C. 1977, U.S. Ct. Appeals (6th cir.) 1968, U.S. Ct. Appeals (fed. cir.) 1986, U.S. Supreme Ct. 1974, U.S. Ct. Appeals (D.C. cir.) 1976, U.S. Ct. Internat. Trade, 1985. Assoc. Frost & Jacobs, Cin., 1967-72; exec. asst., dir. of legislation U.S. Sen. Robert Taft, Jr., Washington, 1973-74, chief of staff, 1975-76; assoc. Taft, Stettinius & Hollister, 1977, ptnr., 1978-88, Barnes & Thornburg, Washington, 1988—. Mem. adv. coun. U.S. and FGN. Comml. Svc., U.S. Dept. Commerce. Chmn., mem. numerous coms., chmn., worker campaigns for local politicians Rep. Party state and local orgns.; mem. Citizens to Save WCET-TV, 1967-72, Fine Arts Fund, 1970-72, Cancer Soc., 1970-72; chmn. agy. rels. com. Hamilton County Mental Health and Mental Retardation Bd., 1969-71, vice chmn., 1971, chmn., 1971-72; v.p. Recreation Commn., City of Cin., 1970-72; mem. funds mgmt. com. Westwood 1st Presbyn. Ch., 1968, v.p., 1969, pres., 1970, trustee, 1970, elder, 1971-72; bd. dirs. Evans Mill Pond Owners Assn., v.p., 1986, pres., 1987; chmn. Washington Nat. Cathedral Fund Com., mem. devel. com. Mem. ABA (sect. on internat. law and practice, vice chmn. com. on nat. legislation 1977-79, internat. sect., anti-trust sect.), Am. Soc. Assn. Execs. (legal sect., internat. sect.), Internat. Bar Assn., D.C. Bar Assn. (com. on internat. law). Avocations: theater, tennis, skiing, travel, reading. Administrative and regulatory, Private international, Legislative. Office: Barnes & Thornburg 1401 I St NW Ste 800 Washington DC 20005-2225

STEADMAN, JOHN MONTAGUE, appellate court judge; b. Honolulu, Aug. 8, 1930; s. Alva Edgar and Martha (Cooke) S.; m. Alison Storer Lunt, Apr. 8, 1961; children— Catharine N., Juliette M., Eric C. Grad., Phillips Acad., Andover, Mass., 1948; BA summa cum laude, Yale U., 1952; LLB magna cum laude, Harvard U., 1955. Bar: D.C. 1955, Calif. 1956, U.S. Supreme Ct. 1964, Hawaii 1977. Assoc. Pillsbury, Madison & Sutro, San Francisco, 1956-63; atty. Dept. Justice, 1963-64; dep. under sec. army for internat. affairs, 1964-65; spl. asst. to sec. and dep. sec. def. Dept. Def., 1965-68; gen. counsel Dept. Air Force, 1968-70; vis. prof. law U. Pa. Law Sch., 1970-72; prof. law Georgetown U. Law Ctr., Washington, 1972-85, assoc. dean, 1979-84; assoc. judge D.C. Ct. Appeals, 1985—. Instr. Lincoln Law Sch., San Francisco, 1961-62, San Francisco Law Sch., 1962-63; vis. prof. U. Mich. Sch. Law, 1976, U. Hawaii Sch. Law, 1977; of counsel firm Pillsbury, Madison & Sutro, Washington, 1979-85 Editor: Harvard Law Rev, 1953-55. Sinclair-Kennedy Traveling fellow, 1955-56 Mem. Am. Law Inst., Cosmos Club, Phi Beta Kappa, Delta Sigma Rho, Zeta Psi. Episcopalian. Home: 2960 Newark St NW Washington DC 20008-3338 Office: DC Ct Appeals 500 Indiana Ave NW Washington DC 20001-2131 E-mail: steadman@dcca.state.dc.us

STEARNS, FRANK WARREN, lawyer; b. Washington, July 20, 1949; s. Robert Maynard and Ermyntrude (Vaiden) S.; m. Judith Anne Ketcheson, Sept. 7, 1974; children: Frank W. Jr., Brian S., Joe G. BA, Washington & Lee, 1971; JD with honors, George Washington U., 1974. Bar: Washington DC 1975, Va. 1980, U.S. Supreme Ct. 1980, U.S. Dist. Ct. DC 1975, U.S. Ct. Appeals (DC cir.) 1975, U.S. Ct. Appeals (4th cir.) 1985. Law clk. Superior Ct. D.C., Washington, 1974-75; asst. corp. counsel Office of the Corp. Counsel, 1975-79; asst. county atty. County Atty's Office, Fairfax County, Va., 1979-80; mng. ptnr. Wilkes Artis P.C., Fairfax, 1984-2001; ptnr. Venable, Baetjer & Howard, LLP, McLean, 2001—. Bd. dirs. No. Va. Bldg. Industry Assn., 1987-94; trustee Greater Washington Bd. Trade, 1987—; chmn. tech. adv. com. NVBIA, Loudoun, Va., 1986-90. Coun. Excellence in Govt., Washington, 1989—98; Commr. Arlington County Econ. Devel. Commn., Arlington, Va., 1987—91. Mem. Barristers, Counsellors. Avocations: tennis, golf. Construction, Land use and zoning (including planning), Real property. Office: Ste 400 2010 Corporate Ridge Mc Lean VA 22102-7847 E-mail: fwstearns@venable.com

STEARNS, RICHARD GAYLORE, judge; b. L.A., June 27, 1944; s. Gaylore Rhodes and Jeannetta Viola (Hofheinz) S.; m. Patricia Ann McElligott, Dec. 21, 1975. BA, Stanford U., 1968; MLitt, Oxford U., Eng., 1971; JD, Harvard U., 1976. Bar: Mass. Dep. campaign mgr. McGovern for Pres., Washington, 1970-72; spl. asst. U.S. Senate, 1972-73; asst. dist. atty. Norfolk County, Dedham, 1976-79, 80-82; del. dir. Kennedy for Pres., Washington, 1979-80; asst. U.S. atty. U.S. Dept. Justice, Boston, 1982-90; assoc. justice Superior Ct. Mass., 1990-94; U.S. dist. judge U.S. Dist. Ct. Mass., 1994—. Author: Massachusetts Criminal Law: A Prosecutor's Guide, 21st edit., 2001. Mem. jud. conf. com. on federal-state jurisdiction, mem. mass torts working group; trustee Vincent Meml. Hosp., Boston. Rhodes scholar, 1968. Mem. ABA, Mass. Bar Assn., Phi Beta Kappa. Office: US Courthouse 1 Courthouse Way Ste 7130 Boston MA 02210-3009

STEARNS, SUSAN TRACEY, lighting design company executive, lawyer; b. Seattle, Oct. 28, 1957; d. Arthur Thomas and Roberta Jane (Arrowood) S.; m. Ross Alan De Alessi, Aug. 11, 1990; 1 child, Chase Arthur. AA, Stephens Coll., 1977, BA, 1979; JD, U. Wash., Seattle, 1990. Bar: Calif. 1990, U.S. Ct. Appeals (9th cir.) 1990, U.S. Dist. Ct. (no. dist.) Calif 1990, U.S. Dist. Ct. (we. dist.) Wash. 1991, Wash. 1991. TV news prodr. KOMO, Seattle, 1980-86; atty. Brobeck, Phleger & Harrison, San Francisco, 1990-92; pres. Ross De Alessi Lighting Design, Seattle, 1993—. Author periodicals in field. Alumnae Assn. Coun. Stephens Coll., Columbia, Mo., 1995—. Named Nat. Order of Barristers U. Washington, Seattle, 1990. Mem. ABA (mem. state labor and employment law subcom.), Wash. State Bar Assn. (mem. bench-bar-press com.), State Bar Calif., King County Bar Assn., Bar Assn.San Francisco, Wash. Athletic Club. Avocations: travel, dance. Office: Ross De Alessi Lighting Design 2815 2nd Ave Ste 280 Seattle WA 98121-3217

STEBBINS, HENRY BLANCHARD, lawyer; b. Hartford, Conn., June 14, 1951; s. Herbert Bellows and Katherine (Reynolds) S.; m. Alison Finney, May 30, 1976; children: Duncan Finney, Martha Reynolds, H. Benjamin. BA cum laude, U. N.H., 1973; JD, Boston U., 1976. Bar: N.H. 1976, U.S. Dist. Ct. N.H. 1976. Assoc. Sheenan, Phinney, Bass & Green, Manchester, N.H., 1976-80, ptnr., 1980-97, mgmt. com., 1994-97; sr. ptnr. Stebbins Lazos & Van Der Beken, N.H., 1997—. Trustee Manchester Boys and Girls Club, 1983—; chmn. Vocat. Partnership Found., 1986-91; bd. dirs. Brookside Ch. Nursery Sch., 1984-90, Leadership N.H., 1994-95; bd. dirs. United Way Greater Manchester, 1986-95, chmn., 1990-92; mem. N.H. Rep. State com., N.H. Rep. Fin. Com., N.H. Legal Counsel, Dole for Pres. Campaign; mem. fin. com. George W. Bush Presdl. Campaign. Mem. ABA, N.H. Bar Assn., Manchester Bar Assn. (pres. 1982-83), Assn. Bank Holding Cos. (lawyers div. 1985-93), Greater Manchester C. of C. (mem. exec. com. 2000—, legal counsel 1999—), Rissa Club. Banking, Construction, Real property. Office: 66 Hanover St Manchester NH 03101-2230

STEEL, JOHN MURRAY, lawyer; b. Los Angeles, Dec. 14, 1945; s. John Murray and Jo Ellen (Collins) S.; children: Jacob C., Sara B.; m. Rebecca Maria Hunt, June 10, 1989; children: Britta J., Cerise O. B.A. in Polit. Sci., Stanford U., 1967; J.D., U. Wash., 1970. Bar: Wash. 1970, U.S. Dist. Ct. (we. dist.) Wash. 1970, U.S. Tax Ct. 1974, U.S. Ct. Appeals (9th cir.) 1970. Assoc. Garvey, Schubert, Adams & Barer, Seattle, 1970-73, ptnr., 1974-88; ptnr. Riddell Williams, Bullitt & Walkinshaw, 1988-2000, Gray Cary Ware & Freidenrich, Seattle, 2000-. Bd. editors Wash. Law Rev., 1969-70. Mem. ABA, Seattle-King County Bar Assn., Wash. State Bar Assn. (bus. law sect., exec. com. 1988-2001, mem. securities com., chair 1991-92, corp. act. com. 1990—, co-chair 1993-2001), Order of Coif. Club: Wash. Athletic (Seattle). General corporate, Securities. Office: Gray Cary Ware & Freidenrich 999 Third Ave Ste 4000 Seattle WA 98104-4033 Business E-Mail: jstee@graycary.com

STEELE, ANITA MARTIN (MARGARET ANNE MARTIN), law librarian, legal educator; b. Haines City, Fla., Dec. 30, 1927; d. Emmett Edward and Esther Majulia (Phifer) Martin; m. Thomas Dinsmore Steele, June 10, 1947 (div. 1969); children: Linda Frances, Roger Dinsmore, Thomas Garrick, Carolyn Ann; m. James E. Beaver, Mar. 1980. BA, Radcliffe Coll., 1948; J.D., U. Va., 1971; M.Law Librarianship, U. Wash., 1972. Asst. prof. law U. Puget Sound, Tacoma, 1972-74, assoc. prof. law, 1974-79, prof. law, 1979—, dir. law library, 1972-94; prof. law, dir. law libr. Seattle U., Tacoma, 1994—. Author: (book) Martin and Carmichael Descendants in Georgia, 1811-1994, 1994; contbr. articles to profl. jours.; mem. editorial adv. bds. various law book pubs., 1980—. Treas., Congl. Campaign Orgn., Tacoma, 1978, 80; mem. adv. bd. Clover Park Vocat.-Tech. Sch., Tacoma, 1980-82. Mem. Am. Assn. Law Libraries, Internat. Assn. Law Libraries, Am. Soc. Internat. Law. Republican. Home: 4434 Pheasant Ridge Rd Apt 303 Roanoke VA 24014-5280 Office: Seattle U Sch Law 950 Broadway Tacoma WA 98402-4405

STEELE, DWIGHT CLEVELAND, lawyer; b. Alameda, Calif., Jan. 23, 1914; s. Isaac Celveland Steele and Mirah Dinsmore Jackson; m. Alberta Evelyn Hill, Oct. 19, 1940; children: Diane Smith, Marilyn Steele. AB, U. Calif., Berkeley, 1935, LLB, JSD, 1939. Bar: Calif. 1939. V.p., mgr. Distributors Assn. of San Francisco, 1941-46; pres. Hawaii Employers Coun., Honolulu, 1946-59; pres., gen. counsel Lumber and Mill Employers Assn., Oakland, Calif., 1961-76, League to Save Lake Tahoe, 1976-78, 89—; chmn. citizens adv. com. Bay Conservation and Devel. Co., San Francisco, 1997—; chmn. Citizens for Eastshore State Park, Calif., 1986—; v.p. Save San Francisco Bay Assn., Berkeley, 1988-91. Dir. Spirit of Stockholm Found., Nairobi, Kenya, 1975-89, Planning and Conservation Found., Sacramento, 1975-91, Eugene O'Neill Found., Walnut Creek, Calif., 1976-81, Tahoe Baikal Inst., 1991—; chmn. Heart Fund Drive, Hawaii, 1959; advisor Legis. Land Use Task Force, Sacramento, 1975-77. Mem. ABA, Hawaii Bar Assn. Democrat. Avocations: skiing, travel. Environmental, Labor. Home: PO Box 696 Tahoe City CA 96145-0696 Office: 1212 Rossmoor Pkwy Walnut Creek CA 94595-2501 Fax: 925-933-1711

STEELE, ERIC HENRY, lawyer; b. Chgo., Mar. 5, 1941; s. Henry Bernard and Ivy (Newman) S.; m. Talmage Mullen, Oct. 17, 1970; children: Margaret Ivy, Henry Donnan. AB, Yale U., 1963; JD, Harvard U., 1967; postgrad., Northwestern U., 1991. Bar: Ill. 1967. Assoc. Aaron, Aaron, Schimberg & Hess, Chgo., 1967-70, Sonnenschein, Carlin, Nath & Rosenthal, Chgo., 1970-72; sr. rsch. atty., project dir. Am. Bar Found., 1972-86; v.p., dir. planning R & D Merchandise Mart Properties, Inc., 1986-90; prin. cons. Steele Cons. Group and Steele, Scharbach Assoc. LLC, 1991—. Rsch. fellow Ctr. Study Criminal Justice, U. Chgo. Law Sch., 1973-75. Contbr. articles to profl. jours. Dir. MAP 2000 study Met. Housing and Planning Coun., Chgo., 1980-82. Mem. ABA, Chgo. Bar Assn., Inspired Partnerships (bd. dirs., sec. bd.), Phi Beta Kappa. E-mail: esteele@ssa-lawtech.com

STEELE, ROBERT MICHAEL, lawyer; b. Arlington, Va., Aug. 23, 1956; s. John Wesley and Mary Eleanor Steele; m. Betty Gail Koppelman, May 23, 1981; 1 child, Robin Leslie. BA in History summa cum laude, Furman U., 1978; JD, Vanderbilt U., 1981. Bar: Fla. 1981, U.S. Dist. Ct. (mid. and so. dists.) Fla. 1981, R.I. 1988, Tenn. 1994. Formerly assoc. Carlton, Fields, Ward, Emmanuel, Smith & Cutler, Tampa, Fla., 1981-87; ptnr. Tillinghast Collins & Graham, Providence and Boston, 1987-93, Baker, Donelson, Bearman & Caldwell, P.C., Nashville and Washington, 1993—. Articles editor Vanderbilt U. Law Rev.; contbr. articles to profl. jours. Trustee Elliott Cheatham Scholarship Fund, Vanderbilt Law Sch., Nashville, 1981—. Recipient Endel History medal Furman U., 1978. Mem. ABA (natural resources energy and environ. law sect., bus. law sect., real property law sect.), Fla. Bar Assn., Tenn. Bar Assn. (environ. law sect.), R.I. Bar Assn., Order of Coif, Phi Beta Kappa. Environmental. Office: Baker Donelson et al 211 Commerce St Ste 1000 Nashville TN 37201 E-mail: rsteele@bdbc.com

STEELE, RODNEY REDFEARN, judge; b. Selma, Ala., May 22, 1930; s. C. Parker and Miriam Lera (Redfearn) S.; m. Frances Marion Blair, Aug. 1, 1964; children: Marion Scott, Claudia Redfearn, Parker Blair. AB, U. Ala., 1950, MA, 1951; LLB, U. Mich., 1954. Bar: Ala. 1954, U.S. Dist. Ct. (mid. dist.) Ala. 1959, U.S. Ct. Appeals (5th cir., now 11th cir.) 1981. Law clk. Ala. Ct. Appeals, 1956-57; assoc. Knabe & Nachman, Montgomery, Ala., 1957-61; asst. U.S. atty. Dept. Justice, 1961-66; staff atty. So. Bell T&T Co., Atlanta, 1966-67; judge U.S. Bankruptcy Ct., Mid. dist. Ala., Montgomery, 1967—, chief judge, 1985-99; ret., 1999—. Served with U.S. Army, 1954-56, Korea. Mem. ABA, Ala. State Bar, Montgomery County Bar Assn. Democrat. Episcopalian. Home: 1227 Magnolia Curv Montgomery AL 36106-2136

STEELMAN, FRANK (SITLEY), lawyer; b. Watsonville, Calif., June 6, 1936; s. Frank S. Sr. and Blossom J. (Daugherty) S.; m. Diane Elaine Duke, June 27, 1960; children: Susan Butler, Robin Thurmond, Joan Bentley, David, Carol Pina. BA, Baylor U., 1958, LLB, 1962. Spl. agt. IRS, Houston, 1962-64, atty. for estate tax, 1964-68; trust officer First City Nat. Bank, 1968-71; sr. v.p., trust officer First Bank & Trust, Bryan, Tex., 1971-73; assoc. Goode, Skrivanek & Steelman, College Station, 1973-74; pvt. practice Bryan, 1974—. Vis. lectr. Tex. A&M U., College Station, 1974-75; mcpl. judge City of Bryan, 1986-88. Bd. dirs. Bryan Devel. Found., 1994-97; mem. Bryan Zoning Bd. Adjustments, 1992-94; pres. Brazos Valley Estate Planning Coun., 1973-74, Am. Heart Assn., 1975-76; deacon, mem. ch. choir, Sunday sch. tchr. So. Bapt. Ch.; v.p. bd. dirs. Bryan Bus. Coun., 1998-99. Mem. Rotary (bd. dirs. Bryan club 1973-74). Avocations: walking, golf. Bankruptcy, Family and matrimonial, Probate. Office: 1810 Greenfield Plz Bryan TX 77802-3492 E-mail: fssteelman@aol.com

STEEN, JOHN THOMAS, JR. lawyer; b. San Antonio, Dec. 27, 1949; s. John Thomas and Nell (Donnell) S.; m. Ida Louise Clement, May 12, 1979; children: John T. III, Ida Louise Larkin, James Higbie Clememt. AB cum laude, Princeton U., 1971; JD, U. Tex., 1974. Bar: Tex. 1974, U.S. Dist. Ct. (we. dist.) Tex. 1976, U.S. Ct. Appeals (5th cir.) 1989. Assoc. Matthews & Branscomb, San Antonio, 1977-82; ptnr. Soules, Cliffe & Reed, 1982-83; sr. v.p., gen. counsel, dir. Commerce Savs. Assn., 1983-88; pvt. practice, 1988—. Trustee San Antonio Acad., 1976-81, 87-93, chmn. bd., 1989-91; adv. coun. San Antonio Acad., 1991—; v.p. Bexar County Easter Seal Soc., San Antonio, 1976-77; trustee, vice-chmn. San Antonio C.C. Dist., 1977-82; bd. dirs. Tex. Easter Seal Soc., Dallas, 1977-80, San Antonio Rsch. and Planning Coun., 1978-81, Cmty. Guidance Ctr., 1983-84, Accord Med. Found., 1987-92; vice-chmn. Leadership San Antonio, 1978-79; dir. Fiesta San Antonio Commn., 1982-83, 93-96, 98—; commr. Bexar County, San Antonio, 1982, Tex. Commn. on Economy and Efficiency in State Govt., 1985-89; adv. bd. Coliseum, 1985-91, chmn. bd. 1990-91; pres. San Antonio Performing Arts Assn., 1984-85; bd. trustees World Affairs Coun. San Antonio, 1982—, chmn. bd., 1984-86; trustee United Way, San Antonio, 1985-92, Tex. Cavaliers Charitable Found., 1994-97, Austin Coll., 1996—; adv. bd. U. Tex., San Antonio, 1987—; active Pan-Tex. Assembly, 1985—; commr. Tex. Alcoholic Beverage Commn., 1998—; exec. com. Rep. Eagles, 2000—. 1st lt. USAR. Named Chevalier Confrérie de Chevaliers du Tastevin, Sous-Commanderie de So. Tex., 1994—. Fellow San Antonio Bar Found., Tex. Bar Found. (life); mem. Tex. Bar Assn., San Antonio Acad. Alumni Assn. (pres. 1976-77), Ivy Club (Princeton, N.J.), San Antonio German Club (pres. 1982-83), Order of Alamo, Tex. Cavaliers (bd. dirs. 1989-92, 94-97, comdr. 1994-95, King Antonio LXXIV 1996-97, Kings coun. 1997—), San Antonio Country Club (bd. govs. 1990-93, v.p. 1992-93), Argyle Club, Conopus Club (bd. dirs. 1989-90), Princeton Club San Antonio and South Tex. (pres. 1980-81), Maclean Soc. Princeton U., Chevalier, Confrèrie des Chevaliers du Tastevin, Sous-Commanderie de Southern Tex., Phi Delta Phi. Republican. General corporate, Real property. Home: 601 Garraty Rd San Antonio TX 78209-6148 Office: 300 Convent St Ste 2440 San Antonio TX 78205-3710

STEER, RICHARD LANE, lawyer; b. Bklyn., July 20, 1949; s. Irving and Sheila Peggy (Rothman) S.; m. Carole Marcia Liebman, Aug. 20, 1972; children: Stephanie Jill, Adam Benjamin. BA, Alfred U., 1971; JD cum laude, New Eng. Sch. Law, 1974; cert. in EEO, Cornell U., 1978. Bar: N.Y. 1975, U.S. Dist. Ct. (so. dist.) N.Y. 1975, U.S. Dist. Ct. (ea. dist.) N.Y. 1975, U.S. Ct. Appeals (2d cir.) 1977, U.S. Supreme Ct. 1980. Asst. corp. counsel City of Yonkers, N.Y., 1975-78; assoc. Stein, Davidoff & Malito, N.Y.C., 1978-80; sr. labor assoc. Epstein, Becker, Borsody & Green, P.C., N.Y.C., 1980-84; counsel Stein, Davidoff & Malito, N.Y.C., 1984-87, ptnr., 1987-89; ptnr. Davidoff & Malito, 1989—; lead trial counsel Yonkers Police Dept., U.S. Dist. Ct. (so. dist.) N.Y., 1984-86; adj. prof. law Pace U., 1984—; lectr. Profl. Ins. Agts. N.Y. Capt. JAGC, USAR, 1979-80. Recipient Am. Jurisprudence award Lawyers Coop., 1972-73. Mem. Am. Arbitration Assn. (lectr.), ABA, N.Y. State Bar Assn. (lectr. annual meeting 1986), Fed. Bar Coun., Adminstrv. Mgmt. Soc. (lectr.), Ins. Wholesalers Assn., CPCU (Long Island, Buffalp chpts.), Indsl. Rels. Rsch. Assn. (lectr. 1984), N.Y. State Pub. Employer Labor Rels. Assn., Def. Rsch. Inst., Westchester County Bar Assn., Yonkers Lawyers Assn., Blue Key, Delta Theta Phi. Democrat. Jewish. Bankruptcy, Federal civil litigation, Labor. Home: 147 Edgars Ln Hastings On Hudson NY 10706-1107

STEFANON, ANTHONY, lawyer; b. Bellefonte, Pa., Sept. 6, 1949; s. Severino and Dorothy (Albright) S.; m. Elizabeth Jo Windsor, Nov. 22, 1969; children: Dyon, Justin. BS in Aerospace Engring., Pa. State U., 1971; JD, Dickinson U., 1977. Bar: Pa. 1977, U.S. Dist. Ct. (mid. dist.) Pa. 1977, U.S. Ct. Appeals (3rd cir.) 1991. Assoc. Myers & Potteiger, Harrisburg, Pa., 1977-79; ptnr. Myers, Potteiger & Stefanon, 1979-82; assoc. Thomas & Thomas, 1982-85; ptnr. Stefanon & Lappas, 1985-88; pvt. practice, 1988—. Mem. Assn. of Trial Lawyers of Am., Pa. Trial Lawyers Assn., Pa. Bar Assn., Dauphin County Bar Assn. Avocations: pvt. aircraft pilot, squash, soccer, auto restorations. General civil litigation, Personal injury, Product liability. Office: 407 N Front St Harrisburg PA 17101-1221

STEFFEN, THOMAS LEE, former state supreme court justice, lawyer; b. Tremonton, Utah, July 9, 1930; s. Conrad Richard and Jewel (McGuire) S.; m. LaVona Ericksen, Mar. 20, 1953; children— Elizabeth, Catherine, Conrad, John, Jennifer Student, U. So. Calif., 1955-56; BS, U. Utah, 1957; JD with honors, George Washington U., 1964; LLM, U. Va., 1988. Bar: Nev. 1965, U.S. Dist. Ct. Nev. 1965, U.S. Tax Ct. 1966, U.S. Ct. Appeals 1967, U.S. Supreme Ct. 1977. Contracts negotiator U.S. Bur. Naval Weapons, Washington, 1961-64; private practice Las Vegas, 1965-82; justice Supreme Ct. Nev., Carson City, 1982-94, chief justice, 1995-97, ret., 1997, chmn. code of jud. conduct study com., 1991; of counsel Hutchison & Steffen, Las Vegas, also Provo, Utah, 1997—. Vice chmn. Nev. State Jud. Edn. Coun., 1983-84; chmn. Nev. State-Fed. Jud. Coun., 1986-91, mem., 1986-93. Mem. editorial staff George Washington U. Law Rev., 1963-64; contbr. articles to legal jours. Bd. dirs. So. Nev. chpt. NCCJ, 1974-75; mem. exec. bd. Boulder Dam Area coun. Boy Scouts Am., 1979-83; bd. visitors Brigham Young U., 1985-89. Recipient merit citation Utah State U., 1983 Mem. Nev. Bar Assn. (former chmn. So. Nev. med.-legal screening panel), Nev. Trial Lawyers Assn. (former dir.) Republican. Mem. LDS Ch. Avocations: reading, spectator sports. Office: Lakes Business Park 8831 W Sahara Ave Las Vegas NV 89117-5865 also: 481 E Normandy Dr Provo UT 84604-5963 E-mail: Tlsrcjnset@aol.com

STEGER, WILLIAM MERRITT, federal judge; b. Dallas, Aug. 22, 1920; s. Merritt and Lottie (Reese) S.; m. Ann Hollandsworth, Feb. 14, 1948; 1 son, Merritt Reed (dec.). Student, Baylor U., 1938-41; LL.B., So. Meth. U., 1950. Bar: Tex. 1951. Pvt. practice, Longview, 1951-53; apptd. U.S. dist. atty. Eastern Dist. Tex., 1953-59; mem. firm Wilson, Miller, Spivey & Steger, Tyler, Tex., 1959-70; U.S. dist. judge Ea. Dist. Tex. U.S. Dist. Ct. (ea. dist.) Tex., 1970—, sr. judge, 1988—. Republican candidate for gov. of Tex., 1960; for U.S. Ho. of Reps., 1962; mem. Tex. State Republican Exec. Com., 1966-69; chmn. Tex. State Republican Party, 1969-70. Pilot with ranks 2d lt. to capt. USAAF, 1942-47. Mem. ABA, State Bar Tex., Masons (32 degree, Shriner). Home: 801 Meadowcreek Dr Tyler TX 75703-3524 Office: US Courthouse PO Box 1109 Tyler TX 75710-1109

STEIGMAN, ERNEST R. lawyer; b. N.Y.C., Oct. 9, 1940; s. Philip and Esther (Aaronson) S.; m. Harriet G. Chaiet, May 30, 1964; children: Richard, Allison. BBA, CCNY, 1963; LLB, NYU, 1965. Bar: N.Y. 1965, U.S. Dist. Ct. (so. and ea. dists) N.Y. 1967, U.S. Supreme Ct. 1971. Assoc. Gair, Gair & Conason, N.Y.C., 1965-73, ptnr., 1973-90, Gair, Gair, Conason, Steigman & Mackauf, 1990—. Mem. Nassau County Bar Assn., N.Y. State Trial Lawyers' Assn. Trial Lawyers Am., N.Y. State Bar Assn., Order of Coif. State civil litigation, Insurance, Personal injury. Office: Gair Gair Conason 80 Pine St Fl 34 New York NY 10005-1768

STEIN, ALLAN MARK, lawyer; b. Montreal, Quebec, Can., Oct. 18, 1951; came to U.S., 1977; s. Boris and Beatrice (Fishman) S. B in Commerce, Sir George Williams, 1972; BA, Loyola, Montreal, 1973; B in Civil Law, McGill U., 1976, LLB, 1977; JD, Nova U., 1979. Bar: Fla. 1979, U.S. Dist. Ct. (so. dist.) Fla. 1979, U.S. Ct. Appeals (5th cir.) 1980, U.S. Ct. Appeals (11th cir.) 1983, U.S. Dist. Ct. Ariz. 1993. Assoc. Law Offices of Paul Landy Beiley, Miami, Fla., 1980, Heitner & Rosenfeld, Miami, 1980-85, Rosenfeld & Stein, Miami, 1985-90, Rosenfeld, Stein & Sugarman, Miami, 1990-94, Rosenfeld & Stein P.A., Miami, 1994—. Mem. North Dade Bar Assn. (bd. dirs. 1985-90). Republican. Jewish. Avocation: photography, HISTORY. Bankruptcy, Consumer commercial, Contracts commercial. Office: 18260 NE 19th Ave Ste 202 Miami FL 33162-1632

STEIN, DANIEL ALAN, public interest lawyer; b. Washington, Mar. 9, 1955; s. Edward Seymour and Ann Rose Stein; m. Sharon McCloe, Oct. 18, 1986; children: Claire, Corrieanne. BA, Ind. U., 1977; JD, Cath. U. Am., 1984. Bar: D.C. 1984, U.S. Dist. Ct. D.C. 1985, U.S. Ct. Appeals (D.C. cir.) 1987, U.S. Tax Ct. 1987. Profl. staff mem. select com. on narcotics abuse and control U.S. Ho. of Reps., Washington, 1977-81; pvt. practice, 1984-89; exec. dir. Immigration Reform Law Inst., 1986-88, Fedn. for Am. Immigration Reform, Washington, 1982-86, 89—. Mem. adv. bd. Social Contract periodical, Petosky, Mich., 1990—. Mem. Capitol Hill Club, Nat. Press Club. Republican. Avocations: trombone, American history, western civilization, jazz, antique books. Office: Fedn for Am Immigration Reform 1666 Connecticut Ave NW Ste 400 Washington DC 20009-1039

STEIN, ELEANOR BANKOFF, judge; b. N.Y.C., Jan. 24, 1923; d. Jacob and Sarah (Rashkin) Bankoff; m. Frank S. Stein, May 27, 1947; children: Robert B., Joan Jenkins, William M. Student, Barnard Coll., 1940-42; BS in Econs., Columbia U., 1944; LLB, NYU, 1949; grad. Ind. Jud. Coll., 1986. Bar: N.Y. 1950, Ind. 1976, U.S. Supreme Ct. 1980. Atty. Hillis & Button, Kokomo, Ind., 1975-76, Paul Hillis, Kokomo, 1976-78, Bayliff, Harrigan, Kokomo, 1978-80; judge Howard County Ct., Kokomo, 1981-89; ret., 1989; co-juvenile referee Howard County Juvenile Ct., 1976-78. Mem. Republican Women's Assn. Kokomo, 1980—; bd. dirs. Howard County Legal Aid Soc., 1976-80; dir. Howard County Ct. Alcohol and Drug Svcs. Program, 1982-89; bd. advisors St. Joseph Hosp., Kokomo, 1979—; bd. dirs. Kokomo Human Rels. Commn., 1967-70, Howard County Children's Ctr., 1993—. Mem. law rev. bd. NYU Law Rev., 1947-48. Mem. Am. Judicature Soc., Ind. Jud. Assn., Nat. Assn. Women Judges, ABA (apptd. Ind. del. jud. adminstrn. div. 1987), Ind. Bar Assn., Howard County Bar Assn. Jewish. Clubs: Kokomo Country, Altrusa. Home: 3204 Tally Ho Dr Kokomo IN 46902-3985

STEIN, GARY S. state supreme court justice; b. Newark, June 13, 1933; s. Morris J. and Mollie (Goldfarb) S.; married, July 1, 1956; children— Jill, Carrie, Michael, Terri, Jo; m. Et Tilchin, July 1, 1956 A.B., Duke U., 1954, LL.B. with distinction, 1956; D.H.L. (hon.), N.J. Inst. Tech., 1985. Bar: D.C. 1956, Ohio 1957, N.Y. 1958, N.J. 1963. Research asst. U.S. Senate AntiTrust and Monopoly Subcom., Washington, 1955; assoc. Kramer, Marx, Greenlee & Backus, N.Y.C., 1956-65; sole practice Paramus, N.J., 1966-72; ptnr. Stein & Kurland, Esquires, 1972-82; dir. Gov.'s Office of Policy and Planning, Trenton, 1982-85; assoc. justice Supreme Ct. N.J., Hackensack, 1985—. Mcpl. atty., Paramus, 1967-71; counsel N.J. Election Law Revision Commn., 1970; atty. Bd. Adjustment, Teaneck, N.J., 1973-82 Mem. editorial bd. Duke Law Jour., 1954-56, assoc. editor, 1955-56. Mem. Dist. Ethics Com. for Bergen County, N.J., 1977-80, chmn. 1981. Served with U.S. Army, 1957-58, 61-62 Mem. ABA, N.J. State Bar Assn. (com. on state legislation 1973-79, chmn. 1973-76, jud. selection com. 1976-81, Constl. amendment com. 1977-79, court modernization com. 1976-79), Bergen County Bar Assn., Order of Coif. Jewish. Avocation: tennis. Office: NJ Supreme Ct 25 Main St Hackensack NJ 07601-7015

STEIN, JOHN C. lawyer; b. Flint, Mich., May 8, 1939; s. Joseph Aloyosius and Gertrude (Carlin) S.; m. Dorothea Ruel, Nov. 20, 1965; children: John Jr., Christian, Peter, Thea. BA, U. San Francisco, 1963; JD, U. Calif. Hastings, San Francisco, 1966; cert., Mil. Justice Sch., Newport, R.I., 1968. Bar: Calif. 1966, U.S. Dist. Ct. (no., ctrl. and so. dists.) Calif. 1969. Dep. city atty. City of San Francisco, Office of City Atty., 1969-71; with The Boccardo Law Firm, San Francisco, 1971-81, mng. ptnr. San Jose, Calif., 1981-99. Judge pro tem San Francisco County Superior Ct., 1978—, Santa Clara County Superior Ct., 1981—; lectr. U. Santa Clara Law Sch., 1985—, Hastings Coll. of Law, U. C. San Francisco. Bd. dirs. Katherine Delmar Burke Sch. Girls, San Francisco, 1988-92, Planning Orgn. for The Richmond, San Francisco, 1985-88. Capt. USMC, 1966-69. Fellow Am. Coll. Trial Lawyers; mem. ATLA, Consumer Attys. of Calif., Am. Bd. Trial Advocates. Democrat. Roman Catholic. Avocations: golf, skiing, SCUBA diving. Personal injury. Office: Boccardo Law Firm 111 W Saint John St Ste 1100 San Jose CA 95113-1107

STEIN, LAWRENCE A. lawyer; b. Balt., Mar. 18, 1965; s. Hersh and Ellen (Hart) S.; m. Diane Wells, June 23, 1991; children: Joshua A., Julie E. AB, U. Chgo., 1988; JD, No. Ill. U., 1993. Bar: Ill. 1993, U.S. Dist. Ct. (no. dist.) Ill. 1993, U.S. Ct. Appeals (7th cir.) 1993, Md. 1994, U.S. Dist. Ct. Md. 1994, U.S. Supreme Ct. 1997. Shareholder Huck, Bouma, Martin, Jones & Bradshaw, Wheaton, Ill., 1993—. Advisor Prairie State Legal Svcs., Carol Stream, Ill., 1993—. Commr. Glen Ellyn (Ill.) Architecture Review Commn., 1994-97. Recipient Am. jurisprudence award for excellence in appellate advocacy Lawyers Coop., 1991. Mem.: ABA, DuPage County Bar Assn., Ill. State Bar Assn., Am. Inns Ct., Phi Delta Phi. Republican. Jewish. Appellate, Banking, Probate. Home: 69 Ott Ave Glen Ellyn IL 60137-5632 Office: Huck Bouma Martin Jones & Bradshaw 1755 S Naperville Rd Ste 200 Wheaton IL 60187-8144 E-mail: lstein@huckbouma.com

STEIN, MILTON MICHAEL, lawyer; b. N.Y.C., Sept. 18, 1936; s. Isidore and Sadie (Lefkowitz) S.; m. Jacqueline Martin, June 17, 1962; children: April, Alicia. AB, Columbia U., 1958, LLB, 1961. Bar: N.Y. 1962, Pa. 1971, U.S. Supreme Ct. 1971. Asst. dist. atty. N.Y. County, 1962-67; sr. counsel Nat. Commn. for Reform of Fed. Criminal Law, Washington, 1967-70; asst. dist. atty., chief of appeals City of Phila., 1970-73; asst. dir. Nat. Wire Tapping Commn., Washington, 1973-75; dir. D.C. Law Revision, 1975-77; spl. asst. HUD, 1977-79; asst. gen. counsel U.S. Commodity Futures Trading Commn., 1979-83; v.p. N.Y. Futures Exch., N.Y.C., 1983-89, N.Y. Stock Exch., N.Y.C., 1989—. Mem. ABA, N.Y. State Bar Assn., Assn. of Bar of City of N.Y. Democrat. Jewish. Administrative and regulatory, Securities. Home: Hudson House PO Box 286 Ardsley On Hudson NY 10503-0286 E-mail: m.stein@nyse.com

STEIN, ROBERT ALLEN, legal association executive, law educator; b. Mpls., Sept. 16, 1938; s. Lawrence E. and Agnes T. (Brynildson) S.; m. Sandra H. Stein; children: Linda Stein Routh, Laura Stein Conrad, Karin Stein O'Boyle. BS in Law, U. Minn., 1960, JD summa cum laude, 1961; LLD (hon.), Uppsala U., Sweden, 1993. Bar: Wis. 1961, Minn. 1967. Assoc. Foley, Sammond & Lardner, Milw., 1961-64; prof. U. Minn. Law Sch., Mpls., 1964-77; assoc. dean U. Minn., 1976-77, v.p. adminstrn. and planning, 1978-80; dean U. Minn. Law Sch., 1979-94; faculty rep. men's intercollegiate athletics U. Minn., 1981-94; of counsel Mullin, Weinberg & Daly, PA, Mpls., 1970-80, Gray, Plant, Mooty, Mooty & Bennett, Mpls., 1980-94; exec. dir., COO ABA, Chgo., 1994—. Vis. prof. UCLA, 1969-70, U. Chgo., 1975-76; commr. Uniform State Laws Commn. Minn., 1973—; v.p. Nat. Uniform Laws Com., 1991-93, exec. comm., 1991—, sec., 1997—; acad. fellow Am. Coll. Trusts and Estates Counsel, 1975—; vis. scholar Am. Bar Found., Chgo., 1975-76; trustee Gt. No. Iron Ore Properties, 1982—, Uniform Laws Found., 1992—; advisor Restatement of Law Second, Property, 1977—, Restatement of Law Trusts (Prudent Investor Rule), 1989-90, Restatement of Law Third, Trusts, 1993—; chmn. bd. dirs. Ednl. Credit Mgmt. Corp., 1993—; bd. dirs. Fiduciary Counselling Inc. Author: Stein on Probate, 1976, 3d edit., 1995, How to Study Law and Take Law Exams, 1996, Estate Planning Under the Tax Reform Act of 1976, 2d edit, 1978, In Pursuit of Excellence: A History of the University of Minnesota Law School, 1980, contbr. articles to profl. jours. Founding bd. dirs. Park Ridge Ctr., 1985-95; co-chair Gov.'s Task Force on Ctr. for Treatment of Torture Victims, 1985, bd. dirs., 1985-87. Fellow Am. Bar Found (bd. dirs. 1987-94), Am. Coll. Tax Counsel; mem. ABA (coun. sect. of legal edn. and admission to bar 1986-91, vice chairperson 1991-92, chair-elect 1992-93, chair 1993-94), Internat. Acad. Estate and Trust Law (academician), Am. Judicature Soc. (bd. dirs. 1984-88), Am. Law Inst. (coun. mem. 1987—, exec. com. 1993—), Minn. Bar Assn. (bd. govs. 1979-94, exec. coun., probate and trust law sect. 1973-77), Hennepin County Bar Assn. Home: 990 N Lake Shore Dr Apt 7A Chicago IL 60611-1342 Office: American Bar Assn 750 N Lake Shore Dr Chicago IL 60611-4497

STEIN, STEPHEN WILLIAM, lawyer; b. N.Y.C., Apr. 12, 1937; s. Melvin S. and Cornelia (Jacobowitz) S.; m. Judith N., Jan. 22, 1966. AB, Princeton U., 1959; LLB, Columbia U., 1962; LLM, NYU, 1963. Bar: N.Y. 1962, Fla. 1962. Assoc. White & Case, N.Y.C., 1963-67; atty. advisor U.S. Agy. Internat. Devel., Washington, 1967-69, regional legal advisor Mission to India New Delhi, 1969-71, asst. gen. counsel Washington, 1971-73; assoc. ptnr. Delson & Gordon, N.Y.C., 1973-87; ptnr. Kelley Drye & Warren, 1987—. Mem. U.S. exec. com. Indonesian Trade, Tourism & Investment Promotion Program, 1990-92; mem. U.S.-Indonesia Trade & Investment Adv. Com., 1989-92; vis. instr. internat. Devel. Law Inst., 1993; lectr. Internat. Law Inst., Washington, 1984, 85; spkr. in field. Mem. ABA (mem. sect. internat. law, co-chair African law com. 1999—), Internat. Bar Assn. (mem. sect. energy resources law, sect. bus. law, mem. various coms.), Assn. Bar of City of N.Y. (mem. com. project fin. 1997—, mem. com. Asian affairs 1992—, former mem. others), Am. Indonesian C. of C. (bd. dirs. 1986—, pres. 1989-96). Oil, gas, and mineral, Finance, Private international. Home: 320 Central Park W New York NY 10025-7659 Office: Kelley Drye & Warren 101 Park Ave Fl 30 New York NY 10178-0062 E-mail: sstein@kelleydrye.com

STEINBACH, HAROLD I. lawyer; b. Bronx, N.Y., Aug. 31, 1956; s. Aaron and Phyllis (Feldfeber) S.; m. Beryl Joy Schwartz, Mar. 14, 1982; children: Sarah Brandl, Rachel Beth, Avi Michael. BA, SUNY, Binghamton, 1978; JD, NYU, 1981. Bar: N.Y. 1982, N.J. 1983, U.S. Dist. Ct. (so. dist.) N.Y. 1982. Assoc. Flemming, Zulack & Williamson, N.Y.C., 1981-83; assoc., then ptnr. Kleinberg, Kaplan, Wolff & Cohen, P.C., 1983-2000; ptnr. Parker Duryee Rosoff & Haft, PC, 2000—. Trustee Jewish Braille Inst. Am., Inc., 1992—. Mem. N.Y. State Bar Assn. (bus. law and property law sects.), Phi Beta Kappa. Jewish. General corporate, Real property. Home: 665 Ogden Ave Teaneck NJ 07666-2203 Office: Parker Duryee Rosoff and Haft PC 529 Fifth Ave New York NY 10017 Fax: 212-972-9487. E-mail: hsteinbach@parkerduryee.com

STEINBAUM, ROBERT S. publisher, lawyer; b. Englewood, N.J., Oct. 13, 1951; s. Paul S. and Esther R. (Rosenberg) S.; m. Rosemary Konner, May 26, 1982; children: Marshall, Elliot. BA, Yale U., 1973; JD, Georgetown U., 1976. Bar: D.C. 1976, N.J. 1980, N.Y. 1982. Atty. Cole & Groner P.C., Washington, 1976-79; asst. U.S. atty. U.S. Atty.'s Office, Newark, 1979-84; atty. Scarpone & Edelson, 1984-87; publ. N.J. Law Jour., 1987—. Trustee N.J. Jewish News, Whippany, 1990-95, 96—. Trustee N.J. Jewish News, Whippany, 1990-95, 96—, treas., 2000—; trustee Blood Ctr. N.J., East Orange, N.J., 1987-93, Leadership N.J., 1990, Leadership Newark, 1997—. Office: NJ Law Jour PO Box 20081 238 Mulberry St Newark NJ 07101-6081 E-mail: rsteinbaum@amlaw.com

STEINBERG, HOWARD ELI, lawyer, holding company executive, public official; b. N.Y.C., Nov. 19, 1944; s. Herman and Anne Rudel (Sinnreich) S.; m. Judith Ann Schucart, Jan. 28, 1968; children: Henry Robert, Kathryn Jill. AB, U. Pa., 1965; JD, Georgetown U., 1969. Bar: N.Y. 1970, U.S. Dist. Ct. (so. and ea. dists.) N.Y. 1973, U.S. Ct. Appeals (2d cir.) 1976. Assoc. Dewey, Ballantine, Bushby, Palmer & Wood, N.Y.C., 1969-76, ptnr., 1977-83; exec. v.p., gen. counsel Reliance Group Holdings, Inc., 1983-2000, exec. v.p., chief corp. ops., 2000—01; exec. v.p., gen. counsel Prudential Securities Inc., 2001—. Chmn. N.Y. State Thruway Authority, 1996-99; dep. chmn. L.I. Power Authority, 1999—. Editor Georgetown Law Jour., 1968-69. Bd. dir. Puerto Rican Legal Def. and Edn. Fund. Inc., 1993-95, Sheltering Arms Childrens Svc., 1997—; bd. regents Georgetown U., 1999—; bd. overseers U. Pa. Sch. Arts and Scis., 1989—. Capt. JAGC, USAR, 1972-74. Mem. ABA, N.Y. State Bar Assn., Assn. of Bar of City of N.Y. (com. on securities regulation 1984-87, com. on corp. law 1987-90, com. on fed. legis. 1990-93, chair ad hoc com. on Senate Confirmation Process 1991-92), Univ. Club. Jewish. General corporate, Securities. Office: Prudential Securities Inc One Seaport Plaza New York NY 10292

STEINBERG, JEROME LEONARD, lawyer; b. N.Y.C., Sept. 1, 1930; s. Frank and Minnie (Bender) S.; m. Sandra Sutter, Dec. 18, 1954; children— Robert Bruce, Marc Scott. B.B.A., CCNY, 1952; J.D., Bklyn. Law Sch., 1955. Bar: N.Y. 1955, U.S. Dist. Ct. (ea. and so. dists.) N.Y. 1957. Sole practice, N.Y.C. 1955-60; atty. N.Y.C. Housing Authority, 1960-65; law sec. Civil Ct. City of N.Y., Bklyn., 1965-70, judge, 1970-80; ptnr. Fein & Steinberg, Bklyn., 1980— ; lectr. in field. Bd. dirs. Peoples Regular Democratic Club, 1965-70, Seneca Regular Dem. Club, 1980— ; mem. N.Y. Commn. on Problems of Deaf, N.Y., 1968-70. Jewish. Lodge: K.P. General practice, Insurance, Personal injury. Home: 16625 Powells Cove Blvd Apt 1E Beechhurst NY 11357-1505 Office: 50 Court St Brooklyn NY 11201-4859

STEINBERG, JONATHAN ROBERT, judge; b. Phila., Jan. 3, 1939; s. Sigmund Hopkins and Hortense B. (Gottlieb) S.; m. Rochelle Helene Schwarts, May 30, 1963; children: Andrew Joshua, Amy Judith. BA, Cornell U., 1960; LLB cum laude, U. Pa., 1963. Bar: D.C. 1963, U.S. Ct. Appeals (D.C. cir.) 1964. Law clk. to judge U.S. Ct. Appeals (D.C. cir.), 1963-64; atty. advisor, then dep. gen. counsel Peace Corps, Washington, 1964-69; com. on labor and pub. welfare, counsel subcom. vets. affair U.S. Senate, 1969-71, counsel subcom. on R.R. retirement, 1971-73, counsel spl. subcom. on human resources, 1972-77, chief counsel com. on vets affairs., 1977-81, minority chief counsel and staff dir. com. on vets. affairs, 1981-87, chief counsel and staff dir. com. on vets. affairs, 1987-90; assoc. judge U.S. Ct. of Appeals for Vets. Claims, 1990—. Contbr. to legal jours. Bd. dirs. Bethany West Recreation Assn., Bethany Beach, Dels., 1973-84, 86-90. Mem. ABA, D.C. Bar Assn., Order of Coif. Democrat. Jewish. Office: US Ct of Appeals for Vets Claims 625 Indiana Ave NW Ste 900 Washington DC 20004-2917

STEINBERG, MARK ROBERT, lawyer; b. Chgo., Aug. 23, 1945; s. Matthew and Irma (Polacek) S.; m. Marjorie Anne Scott, Sept. 3, 1966; 1 child, Matthew Martin. BA, Carleton Coll., 1966; MA, Stanford U., 1968; JD cum laude, Northwestern U., 1972. Bar: Calif. 1972, U.S. Dist. Ct. (cen. dist.) Calif. 1973, U.S. Dist. Ct. (no., ea. and so. dists.) Calif. 1980, U.S. Ct. Appeals (3d cir.) 1981, U.S. Ct. Appeals (9th cir) 1983, U.S. Ct. Appeals (fed. cir.) 1991. Ptnr. O'Melveny & Myers, L.A., 1980-93, 97—; counselor to legal adviser U.S. Dept. of State, Washington, 1993-94; dir. exec. office for nat. security, assoc. dep. atty. gen. U.S. Dept. Justice, 1994-95; spl. rep. for persons missing and detained in the former Yugoslavia U.S. Dept. State, Bosnia-Herzegovina, 1996-97. Sr. policy advisor Internat. Commn. on Missing Persons (Cyrus Vance, chmn.), 1996-97. Articles editor Northwestern U. Law Rev., 1971-72. Trustee Carleton Coll., 1990-94; bd. dirs. Legal Aid Found., L.A., 1990-93; bd. dirs. Town Hall of L.A.; dep. gen. counsel Ind. Commn. on L.A. Police Dept., 1991; mem. U.S. Presdl. Transition Team, Dept. Justice, 1992-93; chmn. L.A. City Atty. Transition Team, 2001. Mem. Coun. on FFgn. Rels., Carleton Coll. Alumni Assn. (pres. 1988-90). Office: O'Melveny & Myers 400 S Hope St Los Angeles CA 90071-2899

STEINBERG, MORTON M. lawyer; b. Chgo., Feb. 13, 1945; m. Miriam C. Bernstein, Aug. 25, 1974; children: Adam Michael, Shira Judith. AB with honors, U. Ill., 1967; JD, Northwestern U., 1971. Bar: Ill. 1971, DC 1994, Colo. 1995, U.S. Dist. Ct. (no. dist.) Ill. 1971, U.S. Dist. Ct. Colo. 1998, U.S. Ct. Appeals (7th cir.) 1971, U.S. Supreme Ct. 1974. Assoc. Caffarelli & Wiczer, Chgo., 1971-73, Arnstein, Gluck, Lehr, Barron & Milligan, Chgo., 1974-76, ptnr., 1977-86, Piper, Marbury, Rudnick & Wolfe and predecessor, 1986—. Speaker in field. Sr. editor Jour. Criminal Law and Criminology, Northwestern U., 1969-71. Chmn. Chgo. region Leaders Tng. Fellowship, 1962-63; bd. dirs. Camp Ramah in Wis., Inc., Chgo., 1974—, sr. v.p., 1992-94, pres. 1994—; bd. dirs., v.p. Camp Ramah in Wis. Endowment Corp., 1993—; bd. dirs. North Suburban Synagogue Beth-El, Highland Park, Ill, 1978—, corp. sec., 1983-87, pres. 1989-91, chmn. bd. trustees, 1991-93, trustee, 1991—; mem. Nat. Ramah Commn., 1987—, v.p., 1994—; bd. dirs. Found. Conservative Judaism in Israel, 1985-90; Midwest region bd. dirs. United Synagogue of Conservative Judaism, 1989-91, 94—; mem. editor's cir. Jewish Forward Newspaper, 1997-2000; trustee Am. Jewish Hist. Soc., 1998—; charter mem. U.S. Holocaust Meml. Mus., 1992; pro bono counsel Frank Lloyd Wright Preservation Trust, Oak Park, Ill., 1996—. Served with USAR, 1969-75. Recipient Youth Leadership award Nat. Fedn. Jewish Men's Clubs, N.Y.C., 1963; cert. of merit U.S. Dist. Ct. Fed. Defender Program, Chgo., 1969. Mem. ABA, Internat. Wine Law Assn., D.C. Br, Std. Club, Ill. State Bar Assn., Chgo. Bar Assn. Jewish. Contracts commercial, General corporate, Real property. Home: 1320 Lincoln Ave S Highland Park IL 60035-3459 Office: Piper Marbury Rudnick & Wolfe Ste 1800 203 N La Salle St Chicago IL 60601-1225 E-mail: morton.steinberg@piperrudnick.com

STEINDLER, WALTER G. retired lawyer; b. N.Y.C., Dec. 2, 1927; s. Mortimer B. and Ray (Feingold) S.; m. Carol A. Halpin, June 28, 1969; children: Michael, Morty, Melissa, Amy, Ellen. BA, Queens Coll., 1950; JD, NYU, 1953. Bar: N.Y. 1953, U.S. Supreme Ct. 1965, U.S. Dist. Ct. (ea. dist.) N.Y. 1972, U.S. Dist. Ct. (so. dist.) 1974, U.S. Ct. Appeals (2d cir.) 1974. Ptnr. Borden Skidell Fleck & Steindler, Jamaica, N.Y., 1955-62; pvt. practice law Babylon, 1962-67; town atty. Town of Babylon, 1967-69; asst. county atty. Suffolk County, N.Y., 1970-71; ptnr. Sarisohn, Carner, Steindler, Lebow, Braun & Castrovinci, Commack, 1976-93; ret., 1993. Capt., judge adv. 2d area command N.Y. Guard, N.Y.C., 1965-70; guardian ad litem 20th Jud. Cir. Lee County, Fla., 1995-98. With U.S. Army, 1946-47. Mem. Free Sons Israel (pres. 1953), Masons. State civil litigation, Family and matrimonial. Office: 350 Veterans Memorial Hwy Commack NY 11725-4330

STEINER, DAVID MILLER, lawyer; b. Phoenix, Apr. 9, 1958; s. Paul Miller and Nan (Adamson) S. BA, Columbia U., 1980; MALD, Tufts U., 1985; JD, Cornell U., 1988; M of Internat. and Pub. Affairs, Columbia U., 1989; LLM in Taxation, NYU, 1993. Bar: N.Y. 1988. English tchr. Peace Corps, Tahoua, Niger, 1980-82; law clk. to Judge Jane Restani U.S. Ct. Internat. Trade, N.Y.C., 1989-91; law clk. to Judge Reynaldo Garza U.S. Ct. Appeals (5th cir.), Brownsville, Tex., 1991-92; assoc. Wasserman, Schneider and Babb, 1993-95; with N.Y.C. Law Dept. Office of the Corp. Counsel, 1995—. Mem. ABA, Assn. Bar City N.Y. (state and local tax com.), N.Y. County Lawyers Assn. (com. on taxation), Fgn. Policy Assn., Apollo Cir.-Met. Mus. Art, Univ. Club, Columbia Club. Avocations: ballroom dancing, backgammon, running. Home: 4 W 109th St Apt 2A New York NY 10025-2673 Office: NYC Law Dept Office of Corp Counsel 100 Church St New York NY 10007-2601 E-mail: sirius_001@yahoo.com

STEINER, GEOFFREY BLAKE, lawyer; b. El Paso, Tex., Aug. 28, 1952; s. LeRoy Marshall Steiner and Rosemary (Thurman) Milligan; m. Maria del Rosario Serrano, Dec. 24, 1975 (div. Jan. 1988); children: Karen Alexandra, Xavier Oliver; m. Rosemarie Sylvia Erb, May 5, 1990; 1 child, Geoffrey Blake Jr. AB, Washington U., St. Louis, 1978; JD, Samford U., 1981. Bar: Fla. 1983, U.S. Dist. Ct. (mid. dist.) Fla. 1983, U.S. Ct. Appeals (11th cir.) 1985. Asst. pub. defender Office Pub. Defender, 13th Jud. Cir., Tampa, Fla., 1982-84; assoc. Hamilton & Douglas, P.A., 1984-86, Mulholland and Anderson, Tampa, 1986-87, Limberopolous, Steiner & Cardillo, Tampa, 1987-89; pres. Geoffrey B. Steiner & Assocs., P.A., 1989—. Co-author: Florida Rules of Juvenile Procedure Annotated, 1982. Mem. Fla. Bar (bd. cert. civil trial lawyer Bd. of Specialization and Certification), Hillsborough County Bar Assn., Assn. Trial Lawyers Am., Acad. Fla. Trial Lawyers, Fla. Assn. Criminal Defense Lawyers, Hunter's Green Country Club, Masons (32d degree), Shriners, Delta Theta Phi, Beta Theta Pi. Methodist. Avocations: golf, tennis. General civil litigation, Criminal, Personal injury. Office: 2529 W Busch Blvd Ste 100 Tampa FL 33618-4546

STEINER, HENRY JACOB, law and human rights educator; b. Mt. Vernon, N.Y., June 14, 1930; s. Meier and Bluma (Henigson) S.; m. Pamela Pomerance, Aug. 1, 1982; stepchildren: Duff, Jacoba. BA magna cum laude, Harvard U., 1951, MA, LLB magna cum laude, Harvard U., 1955. Bar: N.Y. 1956, Mass. 1963. Law clk. to Hon. John M. Harlan U.S. Supreme Ct., 1957-58; assoc. Sullivan and Cromwell, N.Y.C., 1958-62; asst. prof. sch. law Harvard U., Cambridge, Mass., 1962-65, prof., 1965—, Jeremiah Smith Jr. prof. law, 1986—. Founder, dir. law sch. Human Rights Program, 1984—; prof. Harvard Law Sch., chmn. univ. com. on human rights studies, 1992—; vis. prof. CEPED, Rio de Janeiro, Brazil, 1968-69; bd. dirs. U. Middle East project, 1996-99, chair bd. dirs., 2000—; vis. prof. Yale U., New Haven, 1972-73, Stanford U., 1965; cons. AID, 1962-64, Ford Found., 1966-69. Co-author: (textbook) Transnational Legal Problems, 4th edit., 1994, Tort and Accident Law, 2d edit., 1989, International Human Rights in Context: Law, Politics, Morals, 2d edit., 2000; author: Moral Argument and Social Vision in the Courts, 1987, Diverse Partners: Non-Governmental Organizations in the Human Rights Movement, 1991; former devels. editor Harvard Law Rev.; contbr. articles to profl. jours. Office: Harvard U Law Sch Cambridge MA 02138

STEINGASS, SUSAN R. lawyer; b. Cambridge, Mass., Dec. 18, 1941; BA in English Lit., Denison U., 1963; MA in English Lit. with honors, Northwestern U., 1965; JD with honors, U. Wis., 1976. Bar: Wis. 1976, U.S. Dist. Ct. Wis. 1976. Instr. dept. English La. State U., 1965-66, Calif. State Coll., L.A., 1966-68, U. Wis., Stevens Point, 1968-72; law clk. Hon. Nathan S. Heffernan Wis. Supreme Ct., 1976-77; ptnr. Stafford, Rosenbaum, Reiser and Hansen, 1977-85; judge Dane County Cir. Ct., Wis., 1985-93; ptnr. Habush, Habush & Rottier, S.C., Madison, 1993—. Lectr. civil procedure, environ. law, evidence, trial advocacy Law Sch., U. Wis., 1981—; instr. Nat. Inst. for Trial Advocacy, 1987—, Nat. Jud. Coll., 1993—. Note and comment editor Wis. Law Rev., 1974-76; co-editor: Wisconsin Civil Procedure Before Trial, 1994, The Wisconsin Rules of Evidence: A Courtroom Handbook, 1998—. Chairperson Wis. Equal Justice Task Force, 1989-91. Named Wis. Trial Judge of Yr. Am. Bd. Trial Advocates, 1992. Fellow Wis. Bar Found.; mem. ATLA, ABA (ho. dels. 2000—), Am. Bar Found., Am. Law Inst., Am. Adjudicature Soc. (bd. dirs., v.p.), Wis. Bar Assn. (pres. 1998-99), Wis. Law Alumni Assn. (bd. dirs., v.p.), Wis. Acad. Trial Lawyers, Wis. Equal Justice Fund (pres.), Dane County Bar Assn., Order of the Coif. Personal injury. Office: Habush Habush Davis & Rottier SC 150 E Gilman St Ste 2000 Madison WI 53703-1481 E-mail: ssteinga@habush.com

STEINHAUER, GILLIAN, lawyer; b. Aylesbury, Bucks, Eng., Oct. 6, 1938; d. Eric Frederick and Maisie Kathleen (Yeates) Pearson; m. Bruce William Steinhauer, Jan. 2, 1960; children: Alison (Humphrey) Eric, John, Elspeth. AB cum laude, Bryn Mawr (Pa.) Coll., 1959; JD cum laude, U. Mich., 1976. Bar: Mich. 1976, Mass. 1992, Tenn. 1998, U.S. Dist. Ct. (ea. dist.) Mich. 1976, U.S. Ct. Appeals (6th cir.) 1982. From assoc. to sr. ptnr. Miller, Canfield, Paddock & Stone, Detroit, 1976-92; dir. Commonwealth of Mass. Workers' Compensation Litigation Unit, Boston, 1992—. Chancellor Cath. Ch. St. Paul, Detroit, 1976-83, 91; pres. bd. trustees Cath. Cmty. Svcs. Inc., 1989-92; bd. dirs. Spaulding for Children, 1991-92, Davenport House, 1992-96, chair 1995-96, mem. Vestry St. Michael's Ch., Marblehead, Mass., 1994-97. Mem. Mich. State Bar Found. (life), Fed. Jud. Conf. 6th Cir. (life). Home: 505 Tennessee St #417 Memphis TN 38103

STEINHORN, IRWIN HARRY, lawyer, educator, corporate executive; b. Dallas, Aug. 13, 1940; s. Raymond and Libby L. (Miller) S.; m. Linda Kay Shoshone, Nov. 30, 1968; 1 child, Leslie Robin. BBA, U. Tex., 1961, LLB, 1964. Bar: Tex. 1964, U.S. Dist. Ct. (no. dist.) Tex. 1965, Okla. 1970, U.S. Dist. Ct. (we. dist.) Okla. 1972. Assoc. Oster & Kaufman, Dallas, 1964-67; ptnr. Parness, McQuire & Lewis, 1967-70; sr. v.p., gen. counsel LSB Industries, Inc., Oklahoma City, 1970-87; v.p., gen. counsel USPCI, Inc., 1987-88; ptnr. Hastie & Steinhorn, 1988-95; mem., officer, dir. Conner & Winters, 1995—. Adj. prof. law Oklahoma City U. Sch. Law, 1979—; lectr. in field. Mem. adv. com. Okla. Securities Commn., 1986—; mem. exec. adv. bd. Oklahoma City U. Sch. Law, 2000—; bd. dirs. Okla. Venture Forum, 2000—. Served to capt. USAR, 1964-70. Mem. ABA, Tex. Bar Assn., Okla. Bar Assn. (bus. assn. sect., sec.ptreas. 1986-87, chmn. 1988-89), Com. to Revise Okla. Bus. Corp. Act, Oklahoma City Golf and Country Club, Rotary, Phi Alpha Delta. Republican. Jewish. General corporate, Environmental, Securities. Home: 1932 NW 18th Oklahoma City OK 73116 Office: Conner & Winters One Leadership Sq 211 N Robinson Ave Ste 1700 Oklahoma City OK 73102-7136 E-mail: isteinhorn@cwlaw.com

STEINMAN, JOAN ELLEN, lawyer, educator; b. Bklyn., June 19, 1947; d. Jack and Edith Ruth (Shapiro) S.; m. Douglass Watts Cassel, Jr., June 1, 1974 (div. July 1986); children: Jennifer Lynn, Amanda Hilary. Student, U. Birmingham, Eng., 1968; AB with high distinction, U. Rochester, 1969; JD cum laude, Harvard U., 1973. Bar: Ill. 1973. Assoc. Schiff, Hardin & Waite, Chgo., 1973-77; asst. prof. law Chgo.-Kent Coll. Law Ill. Inst. Tech., 1977-82, assoc. prof., 1982-86, prof., 1986-98, Disting. prof., 1998—, interim dean, 1990-91. Cons. in atty. promotions Met. Dist. Greater Chgo., 1981, 85. Contbr. articles to law jours. Coop. atty. ACLU Ill., Chgo., 1974, Leadership Coun. for Met. Open Cmtys., Chgo., 1975, Better Bus. Bur. Met. Chgo., 1987; apptd. bd. arbitrators Nat. Assn. Security Dealers, 1989—2000; apptd. to Ill. Gov.'s Grievence Panel, 1987; bd. dirs. Pro Bono Advocates, 1995—99. Recipient Julia Beveridge award Ill. Inst. Tech., 1996, Ralph L. Brill award Chgo. Kent Coll. Law, 1997; Norman and Edna Frehling scholar Chgo.-Kent Coll. Law, 1989-93. Mem. ABA, Am. Law Inst. (advisor Fed. Jud. Code Revision project 1996-2001, complex litigation project 1990-93, restatement of the law, third, torts, products liability 1993; cons. group transnat. rules of civil procedure 2000), Am. Assn. Law Schs. (exec. com. civil procedure sect. 1998-99), Soc. Am. Law Tchrs., Chgo. Coun. Lawyers (fed. cts. com.), AAUW (legal advocacy network 1987-2000), Chgo.-Lincoln Am. Inn. of Ct. (master 1991), Order of Coif, Phi Beta Kappa. Democrat. Jewish. Office: Chgo Kent Coll Law 565 W Adams St Chicago IL 60661-3613

STELL, CAMILLE STUCKEY, paralegal, educator; b. Smithfield, N.C., Mar. 6, 1962; d. Harvey L. Jr. and Priscella W. Stuckey; m. C. Robert Stell, Jr., Aug. 6, 1983. BA, Meredith Coll., Raleigh, N.C., 1984. Cert. legal asst. Litigation paralegal Young Moore Henderson & Alvis, Raleigh, 1984-94; risk mgmt. and claims paralegal Lawyers Mut. Liability Ins. Co. N.C., Cary, 1994—; paralegal educator Legal Assts. program Meredith Coll., Raleigh, 1988—. Mem. paralegal editl. bd. Legal Asst. Today mag., 1996—. Democrat. Baptist. Avocations: reading, writing. Office: Lawyers Mut Liability Ins 8000 Weston Pkwy Ste 340 Cary NC 27513-2123

STELTZLEN, JANELLE HICKS, lawyer; b. Atlanta, Sept. 18, 1937; d. William Duard and Mary Evelyn (Embrey) Hicks; divorced; children: Gerald William III, Christa Diane. BS, Okla. State U., 1958; MS, Kans. State U., 1961; JD, U. Tulsa, 1981. Bar: Okla. 1981, U.S. Dist. Ct. (no., ea. and we. dists.) Okla. 1981, U.S. Tax Ct. 1982, U.S. Ct. Claims 1982, U.S. Ct. Appeals (10th cir.) 1983, U.S. Ct. Appeals (Fed. cir.) 1984, U.S. Supreme Ct. 1986; lic. real estate broker. Pvt. practice, Tulsa, 1981-97; 2d dep. legal Tulsa County Clk., 1997-2000. Lectr. Coll. of DuPage, Glen Ellyn, Ill., 1976, Tulsa Jr. Coll., 1981-88; dietitian, Tulsa; res. dep. for Tulsa County Sheriff's Office. Christian counselor 1st United Meth. Ch., Tulsa, 1986—, coord. legal counseling ministry, 1985—, lay pastor, 1987—; mem. Tulsa County Bd. Equalization and Excise Tax Bd., 1989-90; mem. Leadership Tulsa XX, 1993—; recipient of Leadership Tulsa Paragon award, 1996; bd. dirs. Sister Cities Tulsa/San Luis Potosi, 1988—, South Peoria Neighborhood Connection Found., 1991—, pres., 1995-96; active Tulsa County Tax Oversight Com., 1994—, Tulsa Home Rule Charter Com., 1994—. Recipient Okla. Sr. Olympics medal. Mem. Okla. Bar Assn., Tulsa County Bar Assn., Vol. Lawyers Assn. (bd. dirs.), Am. Dietetic Assn., Tulsa Dist. Dietetic Assn., Kiwanis Internat., Mensa, DAR, Delta Zeta. Republican. Avocations: swimming, scuba diving, jogging, bicycling, reading, painting, needlework, photography. Family and matrimonial, Probate, Real property. Home: 6636 S Jamestown Pl Tulsa OK 74136-2615

STENBERG, DONALD B. state attorney general; b. David City, Nebr., Sept. 30, 1948; s. Eugene A. and Alice (Kasal) S.; m. Susan K. Hoegemeyer, June 9, 1971; children: Julie A., Donald B. Jr., Joseph L., Abby E. BA, U. Nebr., 1970; MBA, JD cum laude, Harvard U., 1974. Bar: Nebr. 1974, U.S. Dist. Ct. Nebr. 1974, U.S. Ct. Appeals (fed. cir.) 1984, U.S. Ct. Claims 1989, U.S. Ct. Appeals (8th cir.) 1989, U.S. Supreme Ct., 1991. Assoc. Barlow, Watson & Johnson, Lincoln, Nebr., 1974-75; ptnr. Stenberg and Stenberg, 1976-78; legal counsel Gov. of Nebr., 1979-82; sr. prin. Erickson & Sederstrom, 1983-85; pvt. practice law, 1985-90; atty. gen. State of Nebr., 1991—. Mem. Phi Beta Kappa. Republican. Office: Office of Atty Gen 2115 State Capitol Lincoln NE 68509-8000

STENDER, NEAL A. lawyer; BA, U. Calif., 1982; JD, Stanford Law Sch., Calif., 1989. Bar: Calif. 1990. China rep. Fuqua World Trade Corp., Beijing, 1980-81, China office mgr., 1983-86; assoc. Morrison & Foerster, San Francisco, 1990-93; second cons. Lee & Ko, Seoul, 1992-93; assoc. Allen & Overy, Hong Kong, 1993-96, ptnr., 1996-98, Dorsey & Whitney, Hong Kong, 1998-2001. Contbr. articles to profl. mags. including Hong Kong Staff mag., 1994, China Law Briefing mag., 1995, China-Britain Trade Rev. mag., 1999, House Counsel mag., 2000, China-Britain Trade Rev. mag., 2000; contbr. to book chpt. Mem. Law Soc. Hong Kong (spl. adminstrv. region China 1999). General practice, Intellectual property, Private international. Office: Dorsey & Whitney Ste 3008 1 Pacific Pl 88 Queensway Hong Kong China Fax: (852)2524-3000. E-mail: stender.neal@dorseylaw.com

STENEHJEM, WAYNE KEVIN, state attorney general, lawyer; b. Mohall, N.D., Feb. 5, 1953; s. Martin Edward and Marguerite Mae (McMaster) S.; m. Tama Lou Smith, June 16, 1978 (div. Apr. 1984); 1 child, Andrew; m. Beth D. Bakke, June 30, 1995. AA, Bismarck (N.D.) Jr. Coll., 1972; BA, U. N.D., 1974, JD, 1977. Bar: N.D. 1977. Ptnr. Kuchera & Stenehjem, Grand Forks, N.D., 1977-2000; spl. asst. atty. gen. State of N.D., 1983-87; mem. N.D. Ho. Reps. , 1976-80, N.D. State Senate, 1980-2000, pres. pro tempore, 1998-99; atty. gen. State of N.D., 2000—. Chmn. Senate Com. on Social Svcs., 1985-86, Senate Com. on Judiciary, Interim Legis. Judiciary Com., 1995-2000, Legis. Coun., 1995-2000; mem. Nat. Conf. Commrs. on Uniform State Laws, 1995—; mem. Gov.'s Com. on Juvenile Justice. Chmn. Dist. 42 Reps., Grand Forks, 1986-88; bd. dirs. N.D. Spl. Olympics, 1985-89, Christus Rex Luth. Ch., pres., 1985-86. Named Champion of People's Right to Know, Sigma Delta Chi, 1979, Outstanding Young Man of N.D., Grand Forks Jaycees, 1985, N.D. Friend of Psychology, N.D. Psychol. Assn., 1990; recipient Excellence in County Govt. award N.D. Assn. Counties, 1991, Legis. Svc. award State Bar Assn. N.D., 1995. Mem. N.D. State Bar Assn. (Legis. Svc. award), Grand Forks County Bar Assn. Home: 1216 Crestview Ln Bismarck ND 58501 Office: Office of the Atty Gen State Capitol Bldg 600 E Boulevard Ave Bismarck ND 58505*

STENMARK, ANNA ROMELL, lawyer; b. Pitea, Sweden, June 1, 1962; d. Jan and Marianne Romell Lundberg; m. Mikael Stenmark, July 22; children: Jacob, Beatrice. LLM, U. Uppsala, Sweden, 1988, U. Notre Dame, 1991. Law clk. Dist. Attys. Office, Vasteras, Sweden, 1988, Dist. Ct., Vasteras, 1989-92; lawyer Adminstrv. Ct. of Appeal, Sundsvall, Sweden, 1993, Dist. ADM Ct., Gavle, Sweden, 1994, ADM Ct. of Appeal, Sundisall, Sweden, 1994-96; tax mgr. PriceWaterhouse Coopers, Stockholm, 1996-98; assoc. Advokat Firman Lindahl, Uppsala, Sweden, 1998-2000, ptnr. Sweden, 2001—. Consumer commercial, Taxation, general. Office: Advokat Firm Lindahl Kungsgat 17-19 PO Box 1203 75152 Uppsala Sweden E-mail: anna.romell.stenmark@lindahl.se

STENSVAAG, JOHN-MARK, legal educator, lawyer; b. Mpls., July 1, 1947; s. John Monrad and Hannah (Mehus) S.; m. Nancy Kay Strommen, June 19, 1970; children: Eric Paul, Nellie Marlene, Rebecca Gayle, Kirsten Elizabeth, Jonathan Michael. BA, Augsburg Coll., Mpls., 1969; JD, Harvard U., 1974. Bar: Minn. 1974, U.S. Dist. Ct. Minn. 1977, U.S. Ct. Appeals (D.C. cir.) 1978. Law clk. U.S. Ct. Appeals (8th cir.), Duluth, Minn., 1974-75, U.S. Dist. Ct. Minn., Mpls., 1975-76; spl. asst. atty. gen. Minn. Pollution Control Agy., Roseville, 1976-79; asst. prof. law Vanderbilt U., Nashville, 1979-83, assoc. prof., 1983-87, prof., 1987-88. Vis. prof. law U. Iowa, Iowa City, 1987-88, prof., 1988—. Author: Hazardous Waste Law and Practice, vol. 1, 1986, vol. 2, 1989, Clean Air Act: Law and Practice, vol. 1, 1991, vol. 2, 1993, Materials on Environmental Law, 1999; contbr. articles to legal publs. Danforth Grad. fellow, 1969-73. Lutheran. Home: 4 Heather Dr Iowa City IA 52245-3227 Office: U Iowa Coll Law Iowa City IA 52242 E-mail: J-Stensvaag@uiowa.edu

STENZEL, PAULETTE LYNN, business law educator, lawyer; b. Ypsilanti, Mich., July 9, 1951; d. Paul and Juanita Ilene (Harrison) S.; m. John C. Scherbarth, Aug. 26, 1978. BA, Albion Coll., 1972; JD, Wayne State U., 1979. Bar: Mich. 1979. Tchr. French and Spanish Albion (Mich.) Schs., 1972-74, Gaylord (Mich.) Schs., 1974-76; staff atty. S.E. Mich. Legal Svcs., Adrian and Jackson, Mich., 1979-81; sole practice Southfield, 1981-82; asst. prof. bus. law Mich. State U., East Lansing, 1982-87, assoc. prof. bus. law, 1987-94, prof. bus. law, 1994—. Mem. ABA, Mich. Bar Assn., Acad. Internat. Bus., Acad. Legal Studies in Bus., Mid-West Bus. Law Assn., Mich. Scholars in Coll. Tchg., Tri-State Bus. Law Assn., Mortar Bd., Phi Beta Kappa. Office: Mich State U 315 Eppley Ctr East Lansing MI 48824-1121 E-mail: stenzel@msu.edu

STEPHAN, GEORGE PETER, lawyer, international business consultant; b. Milw., July 15, 1933; s. Peter George and Aphrodite (Moisakos) S.; m. Gesella Arolene Hofmeister, Nov. 5, 1955; children: Peter, Christopher, Paul, Cynthia. BS, U. Wis., 1954, LLB, 1958; M in Comparative Law, U. Chgo., 1960. Bar: Wis. 1958, N.Y. 1962. Assoc. Shearman & Sterling, N.Y.C., 1961-69; sec. Kollmorgen Corp., Simsbury, Conn., 1969-72, v.p., sec. gen. counsel, 1972-82, exec. v.p. Stamford, 1982-84, vice chmn., 1984-90, chmn., 1991—, also bd. dirs. Bd. dirs. Barr Labs., Inc., Sartorius Sports, Ltd. Contbr. articles to profl. jours. Trustee Hartwick Coll., 1977-87, 88—; bd. advisors Hartwick Humanities in Mgmt. Inst., 1987—. 1st lt., U.S. Army, 1955-57. Fellow Ford Found., 1958-60; Fulbright fgn. scholar, 1959-60. Mem. ABA. Greek Orthodox. Avocations: tennis, skiing, woodworking, reading, traveling. Home: 132 Westmont St West Hartford CT 06117-2926 Office: Stonington Group Inc 118 Ridgewood Rd Glastonbury CT 06033-3639

STEPHAN, KENNETH C. state supreme court justice; b. Omaha, Oct. 8, 1946; m. Sharon Ross, Apr. 19, 1969; children: Alissa Potocnik, Karen Borchert, Charles. BA, U. Nebr., 1968, JD with high distinction, 1972. Bar: Nebr. Former pvt. practice atty., 1973-97; judge Nebr. Supreme Ct., Lincoln, 1997—. With U.S. Army, 1969—71. Mem.: Nebr State Bar Asn (former chmn young lawyers sect, former mem house delegs), Lincoln Bar Asn (former trustee), Am Col Trial Lawyers (jud fellow). Office: Nebr Supreme Ct State Capitol Bldg Rm 2211 PO Box 98910 Lincoln NE 68509-8910 E-mail: kstephan@nsc.state.ne.us

STEPHEN, JOHN ERLE, lawyer, consultant; b. Eagle Lake, Tex., Sept. 24, 1918; s. John Earnest and Vida Thrall (Klein) S.; m. Gloria Yzaguirre, May 16, 1942; children: Vida Leslie Stephen Renzi, John Lauro Kurt. JD, U. Tex., 1941; postdoctoral, Northwestern U., 1942, U.S. Naval Acad. Postgrad. Sch., Annapolis, 1944; cert. in internat. law, U.S. Naval War Coll., Newport, R.I., 1945; cert. in advanced internat. law, U.S. Naval War Coll., 1967. Bar: Tex. 1946, U.S. Ct. Appeals (D.C. cir.) 1949, U.S. Tax Ct. 1953, U.S. Supreme Ct. 1955, U.S. Dist. Ct. D.C. 1956, U.S. Ct. Appeals (2nd cir.) 1959, U.S. Ct. Appeals (7th cir.) 1964, U.S. Dist. Ct. (so. dist.) N.Y. 1964, U.S. Dist. Ct. (so. dist.) Fla. 1969, D.C. 1972, U.S. Dist. Ct. (no. dist.) Ill. 1974, U.S. Dist. Ct. (we. dist.) Wash. 1975, Mich. 1981, U.S. Dist. Ct. (we. dist.) Mich. 1981, U.S. Dist. Ct. (so. dist.) Tex. 1981. Gen. mgr., corp. counsel Sta. KOPY, Houston, 1946; gen. atty., exec. asst. to pres. Tex. Star Broadcasting Co. and affiliated cos., 1947-50; ptnr. Hofheinz & Stephen, 1950-57; sr. v.p., gen. counsel TV Broadcasting Co., Tex. Radio Corp., Gulf Coast Network, 1953-57; spl. counsel, exec. asst. Mayor, City of Houston, 1953-57; spl. counsel Houston C. of C., 1953-56; sr. v.p., gen. counsel Air Transp. Assn. Am., Washington, 1958-70; v.p., gen. counsel Amway Corp. and affiliated cos., Ada, Mich., 1971-82; counsellor, cons. Austin, Tex., 1983—. Chief protocol City of Houston, 1953-56; advisor Consulates Gen. of Mex., San Antonio, Houston, New Orleans, Washington, 1956-66; atty. Gen. Creighton W. Abrams, Comdr. U.S. Mil. Assistance Command, Vietnam, Saigon/Washington, 1970-71; mem. adv. bd. Jour. of Air Law and Commerce, 1966-72; vis. lectr. Harvard Bus. Sch., Pacific Agribus. Conf., The Southwestern Legal Found., Inter-Am. Law Conf., Inst. Aerospace Law; apptd. by Pres. of U.S. legal advisor, del. U.S. Diplomatic Dels. to Internat. Treaty Confs., Paris, London, Rome, Tokyo, Madrid, Bermuda, Guadalajara, Dakar, 1961-71, Internat. Air-Rte. Dels. to U.K., France, Spain, Portugal, Belgium, The Netherlands, Japan, Rep. of Korea, Mex., Australia, Argentina, Soviet Union, and Brazil, 1960-70; legal advisor, del. U.S. dels. to UN Specialized Orgns., Montreal, Geneva, 1964-71; U.S. rep. Internat. Conf. on Aircraft Disturbance, London, 1966; hon. faculty mem., vis. lectr. sch. of law, sch. of bus., U. Miami, 1968—; accredited corr. UN, Rep. and Dem. Nat. Convs.; exec. officer USNR Pub. Affairs Co. 8-7, 1950-57. Author, editor, media prodr. Comm. and transp. group chief Harris County/Houston CD, 1952-56; chmn. legal com. Nat. Aircraft Noise Abatement Coun., Washington; mem. adv. bd. Houston Mus. Fine Arts, 1953-57; bd. dirs. Contemporary Arts Assn., 1952-57; mem. exec. com. Tex. Transp. Inst., 1964-72; conferee Global Strategy Conf., Naval War Coll., 1958. Comdr. USNR, 1941-46, PTO; mem. staff Supreme Allied Command, NATO. Recipient Jesse L. Lasky award RKO Pictures-CBS, Hollywood, Calif., 1939, H.J. Lutcher Stark prize U. Tex., 1938, 39, Walter Mack award PepsiCo, U. Tex., 1941, Best U.S. Pub. Svc. Broadcasts award CCNY, 1946, First-FM (West) award Frequency Modulation Assn., Houston, 1947, Tex. State Network award mobile coverage Nat. Presdl. Convs., Phila., 1948, Chgo., 1952, Trusonic Wireless Microphone award Acad. Motion Picture Arts & Scis., Beverly Hills, 1951, Frank White award, Mutual Broadcasting Sys., N.Y., 1953, H.M.S. Sheffield citation Brit. Royal Navy U.S. Cruise, 1954, C.R. Smith Aviation Devel. award, Am. Airlines, N.Y., 1955, KLM Royal Dutch Airlines award, Washington, 1956, Capt. Eddie Rickenbacker Air Transport Advancement award Eastern Air Lines, N.Y., 1956, Padre Alvarez award Boys Town Chorale World Tour, Canavati Industries, Monterrey, 1957, Allied Rod & Gun Club Triple Crown trophy, Gander, Nfld., 1958, Iron Duke award No. Va. Lit. Soc., Arlington, 1962, President's Outstanding commendation, U.S. Naval War Coll., Newport, 1967, IBM Corp. Exec. Computer Concepts prize, San Jose, Calif., 1976, M.Y. ENTERPRISE award Peter Island, Brit. V.I., 1978, Glacier Bay award M.V. MALIBU, Sitka, Alaska, 1980. Mem. ABA (past chmn., mem. coun. sect. pub. utility, comms. and transp. law, standing com. on aero. law), The Am. Law Inst. (advisor Restatement (2d) of Torts), World Peace Through Law Ctr. Geneva (past chmn. internat. aviation law com.), The Fed. Bar Assn. (exec. com. transp. coun., comms. coun.), The D.C. Bar, State Bar Tex. (50 Yr. Meritorious Practice award 1996), State Bar Mich., Fed. Comms. Bar Assn., Assn. ICC Practitioners, Am. Judicature Soc., Washington Fgn. Law Soc. (vis. lectr. 1967-68), USS St. Paul Assn. (hon.), Japanese Air Law Soc. (hon. mem. 1966—), Venezuelan Air and Space Law Soc. (hon.), SOVEDAE (hon. Caracas), USS St. Paul Assn., USS Pres. Adams Assn., Naval Submarine League, Naval War Coll. Found., Internat. Club (Washington), Explorers Club (Washington), Houston Polo Club, Lake Shore Club (Chgo.), Nat. Aviation Club (Washington), Saddle and Cycle Club (Chgo.), Breakfast Club (Houston), Execs. Club (Houston), Order Ky. Cols. (amb.), Ark. Travelers, Tex. Navy Adm., Flying Col., Quintana Roo Safari, Phi Eta Sigma, Delta Sigma Rho (pres Tex. chpt. 1940). Home: 6904 Ligustrum Cv Austin TX 78750-8352 E-mail: magnusmedia@aol.com

STEPHENS, HAROLD (HOLMAN STEPHENS), lawyer; b. Enterprise, Ala., Nov. 29, 1954; s. Holman Harrison and Louise (Bass) S. BA, U. Ala., 1976, JD, 1980. Bar: Ala. 1980, U.S. Dist. Ct. (no. dist.) Ala. 1980, U.S. Ct. Appeals (11th cir.) 1981, U.S. Supreme Ct. 1994. Asst. U.S. atty. U.S. Dist. Ct. (no. dist.) Ala., Birmingham, 1980-82; assoc. Lanier, Shaver & Herring, Huntsville, Ala., 1982-84, ptnr., 1985-88, Lanier, Ford, Shaver & Payne PC, Huntsville, 1988-98, Bradley Arant Rose & White LLP, Huntsville, 1998—. Lectr. U. Ala., Huntsville, 1982-86, So. Jr. Coll., Huntsville, 1984-86. Bd. dirs. Huntsville-Madison County Mental Health Ctr., 1983-89, 91-97, pres. 1987-88; bd. dirs. Big Bros./Big Sisters of N. Ala., Huntsville, 1983-87, Friends of Pub. Radio, Huntsville, 1984-86; bd. dirs. Girls, Inc., 1998—, pres., 2000-01. Mem. ABA, Trial Attys. Am., Ala. Bar Assn. (chmn. litigation sect. 1998-99), Huntsville-Madison (Ala.) County bar Assn. (v.p. young lawyers div. 1986-87, pres. 1987-88). Baptist. Avocations: tennis, golf, hiking. Federal civil litigation, State civil litigation, Insurance. Home: 1502 Locust Cir SE Huntsville AL 35801-2005 Office: Bradley Arant Rose & White LLC 200 Clinton Ave W Ste 900 Huntsville AL 35801-4900 Fax: 256-517-5200. E-mail: hstephens@barw.com

STEPHENS, RICHARD H. prosecutor; Adj. prof. SMU Sch. of Law & Cox Sch. of Bus.; asst. dist. atty. under Henry Wade; military judge US Navy; private practice Dallas; US Atty., 1993, Northern Dist. , Tex. Office: US Attorney 1100 Commerce St 3rd Fl Dallas TX 75242-1699*

STEPHENS, ROBERT F. former state supreme court chief justice; b. Covington, Ky., Aug. 16, 1927; Student, Ind. U.; LL.B., U. Ky., 1951. Bar: Ky. 1951. Asst. atty., Fayette County, Ky., 1964-69; judge, 1969-75; atty. gen. Ky. Frankfort, 1976-79; justice Supreme Ct. Ky., 1979-99, chief justice, 1982-98; sec. Ky. Justice Cabinet, 1999—. Pres. Conf. of chief justices, 1992-93; chmn. Nat. Ctr. for State Ct., 1992-93. Staff: Ky. Law Jour. Bd. dirs. Nat. Assn. Counties, 1973-75; 1st pres. Ky. Assn. Counties; 1st chmn. Bluegrass Area Devel. Dist.; chmn. Ky. Heart Assn. Fund Drive, 1976-78. Served with USN, World War II. Named Outstanding Judge of Ky., Ky. Bar Assn., 1986, Outstanding County Judge, 1972; recipient Herbert Harley award Am. Judicature Soc; inducted into U. Ky. Coll. of Law Hall of Fame, 1996. Mem. Warren Burger Soc., Nat. Ctr. for State Cts., Order of Coif. Democrat. Office: Ky Justice Cabinet 403 Wapping St Frankfort KY 40601-2638

STEPHENS, R(OBERT) GARY, lawyer; b. Lindsay, Okla., Sept. 21, 1942; s. William Denno and Leta Mildred (Jones) S.; m. Lurinda Lou Osborne; children: Trent Delno, Skyler Wynne. Student U. Okla., 1960-62, U. Houston, 1968-72; JD, South Tex. Coll., 1975. Bar: Tex. 1975, U.S. Dist. Ct. (so. dist.) Tex. 1976, (ea. dist.) Tex. 1976, (no. dist.) Tex. 1984, U.S. Ct. Appeals (5th cir.) 1979, U.S. Supreme Ct. 1984. Assoc. Kronzer, Abraham & Watkins, Houston, 1975-81; ptnr. R. Gary Stephens, P.C., Houston, 1981-84, Stephens & Garner, P.C., Houston, 1985-88, Stephens & Clark, Sugarland, Tex., 1988—; chmn. bd. dirs. Hobby Comm Bank, 1987—; adj. prof. South Tex. Coll. of Law, Houston, 1980—. Trustee Terrace Meth. Ch., Houston, 1981-85. Served with USAF, 1963-67. Mem. Am. Trial Lawyers Assn., Tex. Trial Lawyers Assn. (bd. dirs. 1986—, chmn. fundraising com. 1988-89), Houston Trial Lawyers Assn., ABA (vice chmn. products liability com. 1979-84). Club: Barton Creek Country Club (Austin). Federal civil litigation, State civil litigation, Personal injury. Home: 8332 Merlin Dr Houston TX 77055-4833 Office: 520 Post Oak Blvd Ste 600 Houston TX 77027-9479 also: 1301 S Capital Of Texas Hwy Austin TX 78746-6513

STEPHENS, WILLIAM THEODORE, lawyer, business executive; b. Balt., Mar. 31, 1922; s. William A. and Mildred (Griffin) S.; m. Arlene Alice Lesti, June 2, 1958; children: William Theodore Jr., Renée Adena. Grad., Balt. City Coll., 1941; student, U. Md., 1946-47; AB, JD, George Washington U., 1950, postgrad., 1951. Bar: D.C. 1951, Md. 1950, Va. 1959. Assoc. J.L. Green, Washington, 1950-51; with J.M. Cooper, 1952-54; sr. ptnr. Stephens Law Firm, 1955—. Gen. counsel Exotech, Inc., Gaithersburg, Md.; prin. owner BARBCO, Inc., Va., Fairfax Raquet Club; gen. counsel various nat. corps. and assns. Author: Rental Contracts - Contracts for the Rental of Personal Property, 2000. 1st lt. AUS, 1941-45. Mem. ABA, D.C. Bar Assn. (sect. taxation 1959—, sect. corps, banking and bus. law 1960—), Bar Assn. D.C. (sec. taxation 1959-68), XVI Corps Assn. (pres. 1967), Commonwealth Club, Univ. Club, Capitol Hill Club, Army-Navy Country Club, Regency Sport and Health Club, Jockey Club, LaCosta Country Club, Racquet Club Internat., Kappa Alpha (preceptor, ct. of honor, James Ward Wood Province 1988-91), Delta Theta Phi. Administrative and regulatory, General corporate, Legislative. Home: 1800 Old Meadow Rd Mc Lean VA 22102-1819 Address: PO Box 2569 Rancho Santa Fe CA 92067-2569 also: 881 Ocean Dr Key Biscayne FL 33149-2609 Office: PO Box 1096 Mc Lean VA 22101-1096 E-mail: slfwts@aol.com

STEPHENSON, ALAN CLEMENTS, lawyer; b. Wilmington, N.C., Nov. 7, 1944; s. Abram Clements and Ruth (Smith) S.; m. Sherri Jean Miller, Dec. 19, 1970; children: Edward Taylor, Anne Baldwin. AB in Hist., U. N.C., 1967; JD, U. Va., 1970. Bar: N.Y. 1971. Assoc. Cravath, Swaine & Moore, N.Y.C., 1970-78, ptnr., 1978-88; mng. dir. Wasserstein, Perella and Co. Inc., 1988-92; ptnr. Cravath, Swaine & Moore, 1992—. Mem. external adv. bd. undergrad. honors program U. N.C., 1998—. Bd. trustes Poly Prep Country Day Sch., N.Y.C., 2000—. Morehead scholar John M. Moorehead Found., 1963. Mem. N.Y. State Bar Assn., Assn. of Bar of City of N.Y., The Brook Club, The Links Club, Tuxedo Club, Union Club, Phi Beta Kappa. General corporate, Securities. Home: 1107 5th Ave New York NY 10128-0145 Office: Cravath Swaine & Moore 825 8th Ave Fl 38 New York NY 10019-7475

STEPHENSON, MASON WILLIAMS, lawyer; b. Atlanta, May 29, 1946; s. Donald Grier and Katherine Mason (Williams) S.; m. Linda Frances Partee, June 13, 1970; children: Andrew Mason, Walter Martin. AB cum laude, Davidson Coll., 1968; JD, U. Chgo., 1971. Bar: Ga. 1971, U.S. Dist. Ct. (no. dist.) Ga. 1985. Assoc. Alston, Miller & Gaines, Atlanta, 1971-76, ptnr., 1976-77, Trotter, Bondurant, Griffin, Miller & Hishon, Atlanta, 1977-82, Bondurant, Miller, Hishon & Stephenson, Atlanta, 1982-85, King & Spalding, Atlanta, 1985—. Mem. fin. com. Atlanta Olympic Organizing Com., 1988-90. Mem. ABA (sect. bus. law, real property, probate and trust sect.), Am. Coll. Real Estate Lawyers, State Bar Ga. (exec. com., real property law sect. 1989-97, chair intangible rec. tax com. 1994-97), Atlanta Bar Assn. (chair real estate sect. 1981-82), Causeway Club, Capital City Club, Phi Beta Kappa, Phi Delta Phi. Avocations: sailing, skiing, jogging. Real property. Office: King & Spalding 191 Peachtree St NE Ste 4900 Atlanta GA 30303-1740

STEPHENSON, RICHARD ISMERT, lawyer; b. Augusta, Kans., Oct. 13, 1937; s. Paul Noble and Dorothy May (Ismert) S.; m. Mary Lynn Bryden, July 2, 1967 (div. 1973); 1 child, Richard William; m. Linda Cox, Apr. 5, 1976. BA, U. Kans., 1958; JD, U. Mich., 1965. Bar: Kans. 1965, U.S. Dist. Ct. Kans. 1965, U.S. Ct. Appeals (10th cir.) 1965. Assoc. Fleeson, Gooing, Coulson & Kitch, Wichita, Kans., 1965-72, ptnr., 1973-95; gen. counsel RAGE Inc. and Affiliated Cos., 1995—. Lt. (j.g.) USNR, 1959-62. Recipient Hilden Gibson award U. Kans., 1958. Mem. ABA (forum on franchising), Def. Rsch. Inst., Internat. Assn. Def. Counsel, Kans. Bar Assn., Wichita Bar Assn., Wichita Country Club, Pi Sigma Alpha, Beta Theta Pi. Avocations: golf, fishing. General corporate. Home: 9203 Killarney Wichita KS 67206-4027 Office: RAGE Inc 1313 N Webb Rd Ste 200 Wichita KS 67206-4077

STEPHENSON, ROSCOE BOLAR, JR. state supreme court justice; b. Covington, Va., Feb. 22, 1922; A.B., Washington and Lee U., 1943, J.D., 1947, LL.D. (hon.), 1983. Bar: Va. 1947. Ptnr. Stephenson & Stephenson, Covington, 1947-52; commonwealth's atty. Alleghany County, Va., 1952-64; ptnr. Stephenson, Kostel, Watson, Carson and Snyder, Covington, 1964-73; judge 25th Jud. Cir. Ct. Commonwealth Va., 1973-81; justice Va. Supreme Ct., Richmond, 1981-97, sr. justice, 1997—. Recipient Covington Citizen of Yr. award, 1973, Outstanding Alumni award Covington H.S., 1973, Disting. Alumnus award Washington and Lee U., 1997. Fellow Am. Coll. Trial Lawyers; mem. Va. State Bar (council 1969-73), Va. Bar Assn., Va. Trial Lawyers Assn., Order of Coif, Omicron Delta Kappa. Home: North Ridge Hot Springs VA 24445 Office: Va Supreme Ct 214 W Main St PO Box 198 Covington VA 24426-0198 also: Va Supreme Court Supreme Court Bldg 100 N 9th St Richmond VA 23219-2335

STEPTOE, MARY LOU, lawyer; b. Washington, July 15, 1949; d. Philip Pendleton and Irene (Hellen) S.; m. Peter E. Carson, Sept. 1986; children: Elizabeth Maud, Julia Grace. BA, Occidental Coll., 1971; JD, U. Va., 1974. Bar: Va., 1974, Supreme Ct., 1987, D.C. 1996. Staff atty., Bur. of Competition FTC, Washington, 1974-79, atty. advisor to commr., 1979-86, exec. asst. to chmn., 1988-89, assoc. dir., Bur. of Competition, 1989-90, dep. dir., 1990-92, acting dir., 1992-95, dep. dir., 1995-96; ptnr. Skadden Arps Slate Meagher & Flom LLP.

STERLING, ERIC EDWARD, lawyer, legal policy advocate; b. N.Y.C., Oct. 25, 1949; s. Bowen and Helen (Champnella) S.; m. June S. Beittel, Oct. 1996; 1 child, Maya Rebecca. BA, Haverford Coll., 1973; JD, Villanova (Pa.) U., 1976. Bar: Pa. 1976, U.S. Supreme Ct. 1980. Asst. pub. defender Del. County, Media, Pa., 1976-79; asst. counsel sub. on criminal justice U.S. Ho. Reps., Washington, 1979-81, counsel subcom. on crime, 1981-89; pres. The Criminal Justice Policy Found., 1989—. Cons. Dem., Rep. and Libertarian Party orgns. and candidates, 1982—; cons. The Brookings Instn., 1990, Office of Pers. Mgmt., 1990, GAO, 1992, Nat. News Media, 1989—; lectr. Am. U. Sch. Pub. Affairs, Washington, 1984-86, U. Colo. Conf. on World Affairs, 1990-99, others. Founder, dir. Nat. Drug Strategy Network, 1989-2000; mem. D.C. Mayor's Adv. Com. on Drug Abuse, 1990; mem. steering com. D.C. Safe Streets Project, 1990-91; bd. dirs. Families Against Mandatory Minimums Found., 1991—, Forfeiture Endangers Am. Rights, 1993-95, William Penn House, 1992-98; mem. Vol. Com. of Lawyers, 1995—. Recipient Cert. of Appreciation, U.S. Bur. Alcohol, Tobacco and Firearms, 1982, U.S. Postal Inspection Svc., 1988, Justice Gerald LeDain award for achievement in law Drug Policy Found., 1999. Mem. ABA (individual rights and responsibility sect.), APHA, Am. Soc. Criminology, Nat. Assn. Criminal Def. Lawyers. Mem. Soc. of Friends. Avocations: swimming, bicycling, hiking. Office: The Criminal Justice Policy Found 1225 Eye St NW Ste 500 Washington DC 20005-3914 E-mail: esterling@cjpf.org

STERLING, HAROLD G. lawyer, real estate developer, bank executive; b. Bklyn., Jan. 23, 1925; s. Philip and Rosalind (Mendel) S.; m. Elaine Ruth Druckman, June 28, 1953; children: Robin Patricia, Brian Richard. BA, NYU, 1950; JD, Yale U., 1954. Bar: N.Y. 1956, N.J. 1955, U.S. Dist. Ct. (so. dist.) N.Y. 1956. Assoc. Lum, Fairlie & Foster, Newark, 1954-56, 57-58, Gordon, Brady, Caffrey & Keller, N.Y.C., 1957; asst. gen. counsel Tishman Realty & Constrn., N.Y.C., 1958-62; v.p., gen. counsel Met. Structures, N.Y.C. and Balt., 1962-63; chmn. bd., gen. counsel Sutton Constrn. Co., Clifton, N.J., 1964—; bd. dirs., exec. com. Berkeley Fed. Savs., Millburn, N.J., 1975-85; chmn. bd. dirs. Berkeley Fin. Corp., Milburn, 1983-86; pres, chief exec. officer Berkeley Realty Group Millburn, 1983-87; counsel Wilentz, Goldman & Spitzer, Woodbridge, N.J., 1987—; lectr. real estate and devel. Soc. Indsl. Realtors, N.J. Mortgage Bankers Assn., N.J. Home Builders Assn., Inst. Continuing Legal Edn., Exec. Enterprises. Trustee Temple B'nai Abraham, Livingston, 1965-80, Newark Beth Israel Med. Ctr., 1974-88, Bd. Mem. Inst., 1989—, Hosp. Ctr. of Oranges, 1990—; cons. West Orange (N.J.) Bd. Edn. With Signal Corps, U.S. Army, 1943-48, ETO. Mem. ABA, Phi Alpha Delta. Club: Green Brook Country (West Caldwell, N.J.). Construction, Real property. Home: 31 Glenview Rd South Orange NJ 07079-1003 Office: Wilentz Goldman & Spitzer 90 Woodbridge Ctr Dr Ste 901 Woodbridge NJ 07095-1146

STERN, CARL LEONARD, former news correspondent, federal official; b. N.Y.C., Aug. 7, 1937; s. Hugo and Frances (Taft) S.; m. Joy Elizabeth Nathan, Nov. 27, 1960; children: Lawrence, Theodore. A.B., Columbia U., 1958, M.S., 1959; J.D., Cleve. State U., 1966, J.D. (hon.), 1975, New Eng. Coll. Law, 1977. Bar: Ohio 1966, D.C. 1968, U.S. Supreme Ct. 1969. Law corr. NBC News, Washington, 1967-93; dir. Office of Pub. Affairs U.S. Dept. Justice, 1993-96; Shapiro Prof. of Media and Pub. Affairs George Washington U., 1996—. Lectr. Nat. Jud. Coll.; adj. prof. George Washington U., Stanford U. Editorial bd.: The Dist. Lawyer. Mem. Dept. Transp. Task Force on Assistance to Families in Aviation Disasters, 1997; mem. nat. adv. coun. Cleveland-Marshall Law Sch. Recipient Peabody award, 1974, Emmy award, 1974, Gavel award, 1969, 74, Headliner Club award, 1991, Edmond J. Randloph award U.S. Dept. Justice. Mem. ABA (vice chmn. criminal justice sect. com. on criminal justice and the media, gov., forum com. on communications law, working group intelligence requirements and criminal code reform, standing com. on strategic comms.), AFTRA (nat. exec. bd. 1984-86, first v.p. Washington, Balt. chpt. 1985-87). Home: 2956 Davenport St NW Washington DC 20008 Office: George Washington U #400 805 21st St NW Washington DC 20052 E-mail: cstern@gwu.edu

STERN, DONALD KENNETH, former prosecutor; BA, Hobart Coll., 1966; JD, Georgetown U., 1969; LLM, U. Pa., 1973. Intern Dist. Atty.'s Office, Mineola, N.Y., 1967, Citizen's Adv. Ctr., Washington, 1968; staff atty. Defender Assn. Phila., Cmty. Legal Svcs., Phila., 1969-71; adj. prof. law, supervising atty. Boston Coll. Law Sch., Boston Coll. Legal Assistance Bur., 1971-73, asst. prof. law, dir. clin. programs, supervising atty., 1973-75; asst. atty. gen., dir. atty. gen. clin. program, Mass. Atty. Gen.'s Office, Boston Coll. Law Sch., 1975-77, asst. prof. law, dir. atty. gen. clin. program, spl. asst. atty. gen., 1977-78, asst. atty. gen., dir. atty. gen. clin. program, 1978-79; chief govt. bur. Mass. Atty. Gen.'s Office, 1979-82; assoc. Hale and Dorr, Boston, 1982-85, jr. ptnr., 1985-87, sr. ptnr., 1987, 91-93, of counsel, 1990-91; chief legal counsel to Gov. Mass., 1987-90; U.S. atty. Dist. Mass., 1993—2001. Office: Bingham Dana LLP Federal St Boston MA 02210-1726 E-mail: dkstern@bingham.com

STERN, DORON DANIEL, lawyer; b. Jerusalem, Israel, Feb. 18, 1958; s. Gideon Karl and Tamar S.; m. Anat Shamgar, Aug. 18, 1982; children: Gad, Tamar. LLB, Hebrew U., 1983. Fgn. atty. Willkie Farr & Gallagher, N.Y.C., 1983-86; assoc. Yossi Avraham & Co., Tel Aviv, 1986-87; assoc., ptnr. Y. Raveh & Co., Israel, 1987-94; founder, ptnr. Tulehinsky Stern & Co., Israel, 1995—. Judge in disciplinary ct. Israel Bar, 2000—; dir. IBecha, 1999-2001; panelist IVC and UC confs., 1999—; advisor Jerusalem Ventere Ptnr., 1999—. Mem. Natir Acting Sch., Jerusalem, Tenuot Dance, Nature Preservation. Sgt. Elite Commando Unit, IDF, 1976-96. Mem. Israeli Bar Assn. Avocations: hiking, music, literature, photography. Environmental, Finance, Mergers and acquisitions. Office: Tulchinsky Stern & Co 22 Kanjei Nesharm 984 GM Jerusalem Israel Fax: 972-2-6513133. E-mail: jer@tslaw.co.il

STERN, ELIZABETH ESPIN, lawyer; b. Prince Georges County, Md., June 21, 1961; d. Cesar A. and M. Cecilia (Salvador) E.; m. Michael L. Stern, May 16, 1992; 1 child, Alexander. BA magna cum laude, U. Va., 1983, JD, 1986. Bar: Va. 1986, U.S. Dist. Ct. (ea. dist.) Va., D.C. 1988. Ptnr. comml. immigration Shaw, Pittman, Potts & Trowbridge, Washington, 1986—. Moderator Counsel Connects Immigration Discussion Group. Mem. editorial bd. Bus Law Inc., 1987—; editor-in-chief Free-Market Cuba Bus. Jour; contbg. writer Tech. Law Notes, 1987—, The Changing Workplace, 1991—. Past chair young lawyers sect. Vol. Bar Assn. D.C. Recipient Martin Preis award Vol. Bar Assn. D.C., 1992. Mem. NAFE, Am. Immigration Lawyers Assn., Va. Bar Assn., D.C. Bar Assn. (internat. sec. 1986—, del. to ABA, chair young lawyers sect. 1992-93, Young Lawyer of Yr. 1994), Immigration Tech. Assn. Am. Republican. Avocation: journalism. Immigration, naturalization, and customs, Labor. Home: 8529 Century Oak Ct Fairfax Station VA 22039-3343 Office: Shaw Pittman Potts & Trowbridge 2300 N St NW Fl 5 Washington DC 20037-1172

STERN, GERALD MANN, lawyer; b. Chgo., Apr. 5, 1937; s. Lloyd and Fannye (Wener) S.; m. Linda Stone, Dec. 20, 1969; children: Eric, Jesse, Maia. B.S. in Econs., U. Pa., 1958; LL.B. cum laude, Harvard, 1961. Bar: D.C. 1961, Calif. 1991, U.S. Supreme Ct. 1971. Trial atty. civil rights div. U.S. Dept. Justice, 1961-64; assoc. firm Arnold & Porter, Washington, 1964-68, ptnr., 1969-76; founding ptnr. Rogovin, Stern & Huge, Washington, 1976-81; exec. v.p., sr. gen. counsel Occidental Petroleum Corp., 1981-82, L.A., 1982-92; spl. counsel fin. instn. fraud and health care fraud U.S. Dept. Justice, Washington, 1993-95; ind. legal cons. pvt. practice, 1995—; cons. Antitrust divsn. U.S. Dept. Justice, 1998—. Author: The Buffalo Creek Disaster, 1976; co-author: Southern Justice, 1965, Outside the Law, 1997. Trustee Facing History and Ourselves, 1996—. Mem. ABA. Home and Office: 3322 Newark St NW Washington DC 20008-3330 Fax: 202-364-2595. E-mail: GMS37@aol.com

STERN, HERBERT JAY, lawyer; b. N.Y.C., Nov. 8, 1936; s. Samuel and Sophie (Berkowitz) S.; children: Jason Andrew and Jordan Ezekiel (twins), Samuel Abraham, Sarah Kathrine. B.A., Hobart Coll., 1958; J.D. (Ford Found. scholar), U. Chgo., 1961; LL.D. (hon.), Seton Hall Law Sch., 1973, Hobart Coll., 1974; L.H.D. (hon.), Newark State Coll., 1973; D.C.L. (hon.), Bloomfield Coll., 1973; Litt.D. (hon.), Montclair State Coll., 1973. Bar: N.Y. 1961, N.J. 1971. Asst. dist. atty., New York County, 1962-65; trial atty. organized crime and racketeering sect. Dept. of Justice, 1965-69; chief asst. U.S. atty. Dist. of N.J., Newark, 1969-70, U.S. atty., 1971-74, U.S. dist. judge, 1974-87; ptnr. Stern, Greenberg & Kilcullen, Roseland, N.J., 1990—. Adv. com. U. Chgo. Law Sch. Author: Judgment in Berlin, 1984 (Valley Forge award Freedoms Found. 1984, Torch of Learning award Am. Friends of Hebrew U. 1987), Trying Cases to Win, Vol. I, 1991, Vol. II, 1992, Vol. III, 1993, Vol. IV, 1995; co-author: Trying Cases to Win, Anatomy of A Trial, 1999, Trying Cases to Win: Evidence Weapons for Winning, 2000; subject of book Tiger in the Court, 1973. Trustee Hobart and William Smith Colls. Named One of America's 10 Outstanding Young Men U.S. Jr. C. of C., 1971; Swartzer scholar U. Chgo. Law Sch., 1985; recipient Dean's Club award U. Akron Sch. Law, 1986, medal of excellence Hobart Coll., 1990, Citizen's award N.J. Acad. Medicine, 1997. Fellow ABA, Am. Law Inst. (Clarence Darrow award), Internat. Platform Assn.; mem. ABA, N.J. Bar Assn., Fed. Bar Assn. (past pres. Newark chpt., recipient William J. Brennan, Jr. award 1987), Essex County Bar Assn., Am. Judicature Soc., Phi Alpha Delta. Achievements include being subject of book Tiger in the Court, 1973. Office: 75 Livingston Ave Roseland NJ 07068-3701

STERN, JOHN JULES, lawyer; b. Paterson, N.J., Apr. 15, 1955; s. Howard and Muriel (Lubowitt) S.; m. Joyce Levine; children: Julianne Lauren, David Charles; stepchildren: Robert Malcomnson, Aaron Malcomnson, Jarred Malcomnson. Student, Northwestern U., 1972-73; BA, Brandeis U., 1976; M in Pub. Adminstrn., JD, U. So. Calif., 1979. Bar: Calif. 1979, U.S. Dist. Ct. (cen. dist.) Calif. 1979, U.S. Ct. Appeals (9th cir.) 1979, N.J. 1980, U.S. Dist. Ct. N.J. 1980, U.S. Ct. Appeals (3d cir.) 1982, U.S. Supreme Ct. 1997, U.S. Ct. Claims; cert. civil trial atty. Supreme Ct. N.J., 2000. Law sec. to chancery judge N.J. Superior Ct., Paterson, 1979-80; assoc. Stern, Steiger, Croland, Tanenbaum & Schielke, Paramus, N.J., 1980-83, ptnr., 1983-95; atty. Planning Bd., Montvale, 1989-93, Borough of Montvale, 1993-99; ptnr. Forman Stern P.C., Paramus, 1995-97; sr. ptnr. Stern Berenbroick, P.A., N.J., 1997-2001, Williams, Caliri, Miller, Otley & Stern, P.C., Wayne, 2001—. Lectr. land use and planning Nat. Bus. Inst., 1999—. Contbr. articles to profl. jours. Mem. ABA (jud. adminstrn. div., antitrust div. 1979—), N.J. Bar Assn., Calif. Bar Assn., Trial Attys. N.J. (trustee 1987-89), N.Y. Acad. Scis., Passaic County Bar Assn. (chmn. equity jurisprudence com. 1984—, chmn. com. civil and constl. rights 1984—), Bergen County Bar Assn., Morris County Bar Assn., Am. Judicature Soc. Democrat. Jewish. Avocations: sailing, soccer, golf. Antitrust, Federal civil litigation, State civil litigation.

STERN, PETER R. lawyer; b. East Orange, N.J., Nov. 2, 1947; s. Ralph and Jacqueline Rene (Piot) S. BA, Columbia U., 1969, JD, 1972. Bar: N.Y. 1973, U.S. Dist. Ct. (so. and ea. dists.) 1973, U.S. Ct. Appeals (2d cir.) 1975, U.S. Ct. Appeals (3d cir.) 1995, U.S. Ct. Appeals (D.C. cir.) 2001, U.S. Supreme Ct. 1979. Law clk. to judge U.S. Dist. Ct., N.Y.C., 1972-74; assoc. Winthrop, Stimson, Putnam & Roberts, 1974-80; founding ptnr. Berger, Steingut, Weiner, Fox & Stern, 1980-85; ptnr. Berger & Steingut, 1986-90, Berger Steingut Tarnoff & Stern, N.Y.C., 1990-93, Berger, Steingut & Stern, N.Y.C., 1993-94, Berger, Stern & Webb, LLP, N.Y.C., 1994—. Bd. dirs. Kitchen Ctr., N.Y.C., 1978-90; bd. advisors Franklin Furnace, 1984-97; law adv. coun. Internat. Found. for Art Rsch., 1988—. Bd. dirs. Vol. Lawyers for Arts, 1995—, chmn. 1999—. Mem. ABA, N.Y.C. Bar Assn., Fed. Bar Coun., N.Y. State Bar. Federal civil litigation, State civil litigation, General practice. Office: 900 3rd Ave New York NY 10022-4728 E-mail: pstern@bswny.com

STERN, RALPH DAVID, lawyer; b. Longview, Tex., June 20, 1943; children: Eric, Justin. AB, Bucknell U., 1963; JD, U. Chgo., 1966. Bar: D.C. 1967, Ill. 1967, Calif. 1970, U.S. Supreme Ct. 1970. Law clk. Ill. Appellate Ct., Chgo., 1966-67; assoc. Ressman & Tishler, 1968-70; exec. asst. Orange County Bd. Suprs., Santa Ana, Calif., 1970-71; gen. counsel San Diego City Schs., 1971-83; ptnr. Whitmore, Kay & Stevens, Palo Alto, Calif., 1983-88, Stern & Keebler, San Mateo, 1988-90; gen. counsel Schs. Legal Counsel, Hayward, 1990—. Chmn. Nat. Coun. Sch. Attys., 1982-83; pres. Leagal Aid Soc. San Diego, 1976-79, Nat. Orgn. on Legal Problems of Edn., 1981-82. Editor: Law and the School Principal, 1978; contbr. articles to profl. jours. Mem. exec. bd., county membership chair Boy Scouts Am., San Diego, 1979-81; vice chmn. Laurels for Leaders, San Diego, 1980-83; mem. ednl. adminstrn. adv. com. U. San Diego, 1981-86.; mem. adv. com. West's Ednl. Law Reporter, 1981-85. Named Outstanding Young Citizen, San Diego Jaycees, 1977. Office: Schs Legal Counsel 313 W Winton Ave Rm 372 Hayward CA 94544-1136

STERN, SHIRLEY, lawyer, author; b. Bklyn., Aug. 16, 1929; d. Bernard and Bessie (Tasgal) Gartenstein; m. Leonard W. Stern, Dec. 24, 1949; children: Erwin Samuel, Elana Debra, Gil Avram. BA, CUNY, 1950, MA, 1956; JD, St. John's U., 1982. Bar: N.Y. 1983. Freelance writer, New Hyde Park, N.Y., 1972—; sole practice, New Hyde Park, 1983—. Author: Exploring Jewish History, 1979; Exploring Jewish Wisdom, 1980; Exploring Jewish Holidays, 1981; Exploring the Prayerbook, 1982; Exploring the Torah, 1984. Mem. Nassau County Bar Assn. Democrat. Jewish. Office: 26 Birchwood Dr New Hyde Park NY 11040-3744

STERNMAN, JOEL W. lawyer; b. N.Y.C., Oct. 20, 1943; s. Abraham and Sarah (Simon) S.; children: Mark S., Cheryl A.; m. Barbara E. Shiers, March 31, 1985; children: Matthew S., Julia S. AB, Dartmouth Coll., 1965; LLB, Yale U., 1968. Bar: N.Y. 1970, U.S. Dist. Ct. (so. and ea. dists.) N.Y. 1971, U.S. Ct. Appeals (2d cir.) 1972, U.S. Supreme Ct. 1984, U.S. Ct. Appeals (6th cir.) 1985, U.S. Ct. Appeals (9th cir.) 1994, U.S. Tax Ct. 1996, U.S. Dist. Ct. (ea. dist.) Mich. 1997. Law clk. to judge U.S. Dist. Ct., New Haven, 1968-69; assoc. Rosenman Colin Freund Lewis & Cohen, N.Y.C., 1969-77; ptnr. Rosenman & Colin LLP, 1977—. Editor Yale Law Jour., New Haven, 1966-68. Mem. Phi Beta Kappa. Federal civil litigation, General civil litigation, State civil litigation. Office: Rosenman & Colin LLP 575 Madison Ave New York NY 10022-2585 E-mail: jwsternman@rosenman.com

STERNS, PATRICIA MARGARET, lawyer, consultant; b. Phoenix, Jan. 30, 1952; d. Lawrence Page and Mildred Dorothy (Barabas) S. BA, Ariz. State U., 1974; JD, U. Ariz., 1977. Bar: Ariz. 1978, U.S. Dist. Ct. Ariz. 1978, U.S. Supreme Ct. 1986. With Sterns and Tennen, Phoenix, 1978—. Judge pro tempore Superior Ct. Ariz., County of Maricopa, 1983-99; mem. Domestic Rels. Study Com., 1984-86, judge Jessup Internat. Moot Ct. Competition and semi-finals rounds, 1984—, regional rounds, 1981—; cons. internat. law; lectr. Am. Grad. Sch. Internat. Mgmt., 1982, Princeton U. Space Mfg. Facilities Conf., 1979; participant Internat. Astronautical Fedn., 1978—. Contbr. articles to profl. publs.; mem. Ariz. Law Rev. Fellow Ariz. Bar Found.; mem. AIAA, ABA (family law, internat. law sects., aerospace law com.), Am. Soc. Internat. Law (space law sect.), Maricopa County Bar Assn. (family law sect.), Internat. Inst. Space Law (bd. dirs., sec. bd. dirs. U.S. membership), Internat. Bar Assn., Internat. Acad. Astronautics, Internat. Astronautical Fedn., Ariz. Bar Assn., Profl. Rodeo Cowboys Assn. (assoc.), Am. Quarter Horse Assn., U. Club Phoenix (1990-99). Family and matrimonial, Private international. Office: 849 N 3rd Ave Phoenix AZ 85003-1408 Fax: (602) 253-7767

STERNSTEIN, ALLAN J. lawyer; b. Chgo., June 7, 1948; s. Milton and Celia (Kaganove) S.; m. Miriam A. Dolgin, July 12, 1970 (div. July 1981); children— Jeffery A., Amy R.; m. Beverly A. Cook, Feb. 8, 1986; children: Cheryl L., Julia S. B.S., U. Ill., 1970; M.S., U. Mich., 1972; J.D., Loyola U., 1977. Bar: Ill. 1977, U.S. Dist. Ct. (no. dist.) Ill. 1977, U.S. Dist. Ct. (no. dist.) Ohio 1977, U.S. Dist. Ct. (ea. dist) Mich. 1986, U.S. Dist. Ct. (we. dist.) Mich. 1990, U.S. Ct. Customs and Patent Appeals 1978, U.S. Ct. Appeals (7th cir.) 1979, U.S. Ct. Appeals (Fed. cir.) 1982. Patent agent Sunbeam Corp., Oak Brook, Ill., 1972-76; ptnr. Neuman, Williams, Anderson & Olson, Chgo., 1976-84; div. patent counsel Abbott Labs., North Chgo., Ill., 1984-87; ptnr. Brinks Hofer Gilson & Lione, Chgo., 1987—, mng. ptnr., 1996-99; adj. prof. of law John Marshall Law Sch., 1989-90, DePaul Univ., 1990-92, Univ. Ill., 1992—; lectr. Nat. Sci. and Tech. Devel. Agy. Chunlangkon U., Bangkok, Thailand, 1994; arbitrator Cir. Ct. Cook County, Ill., 1996—. Co-author: Designing an Effective Intellectual Property Compliance Program; contbr. article to profl. jour. Legal advisor Legal Aid Soc., Chgo., 1974-76, Pub. Defender's Office, Chgo., 1974. Teaching fellow U. Mich., 1971-72; research grantee U. Mich., U.S. Air Force, 1971-72. Mem. ABA, Chgo. Bar Assn., Patent Law Assn. of Chgo. (com. chmn. 1982), Am. Intellectual Property Law Assn., Licensing Execs. Soc., Tau Beta Pi, Sigma Tau, Sigma Gamma Tau, Phi Eta Sigma. Jewish. Federal civil litigation, Patent, Trademark and copyright. Office: Brinks Hofer Gilson & Lione Ste 3600 455 N Cityfront Plaza Dr Chicago IL 60611-5599

STERRETT, SAMUEL BLACK, lawyer, former judge; b. Washington, Dec. 17, 1922; s. Henry Hatch Dent and Helen (Black) S.; m. Jeane McBride, Aug. 27, 1949; children: Samuel Black, Robin Dent, Douglas McBride. Student, St. Albans Sch., 1933-41; grad., U.S. Mcht. Marine Acad., 1945; BA, Amherst Coll., 1947; LLB, U. Va., 1950; LLM in Taxation, NYU, 1959. Bar: D.C. 1951, Va. 1950. Atty. Alvord & Alvord, Washington, 1950-56; trial atty. Office Regional Counsel, Internal Revenue Service, N.Y.C., 1956-60; ptnr. Sullivan, Shea & Kenney, Washington, 1960-68; municipal cons. to office vice pres. U.S., 1965-68; judge U.S. Tax Ct., 1968-88, chief judge, 1985-88; ptnr. Myerson, Kuhn & Sterrett, Washington, 1988-89; of counsel Vinson & Elkins, 1990—. Bd. mgrs. Chevy Chase Village, 1970-74, chmn., 1972-74; 1st v.p. bd. trustees, mem. exec. com. Washington Hosp. Center, 1969-79, chmn. bd. trustees, 1979-84, mem. bd. trustees, 1999—; chmn. bd. trustees Washington Healthcare Corp., 1982-87; chmn. bd. trustees Medlantic Healthcare Group, 1987-89; mem. audit com. Medstar Health, 1990—; mem. Washington Cathedral, 1973-81, 99—, mem. fin. com., 1998—, chmn., 1999—; mem. governing bd. St. Albans Sch., 1977-81; trustee Louise Home, 1979-89. Served with AUS, 1943; Served with U.S. Mcht. Marine, 1943-46. Fellow Am. Bar Found.; mem. ABA, D.C. Bar Assn., Am. Coll. Tax Counsel, Soc. of the Cincinnati, Coun. for Future, Am. Inns. of Ct., Chevy Chase Club (bd. govs. 1979-84, pres. 1984), Met. Club, Lawyers Club, Alibi Club, Alfalfa Club, Ch. of N.Y. Club, Beta Theta Pi. Episcopalian. Office: Vinson & Elkins 1455 Pennsylvania Ave NW Fl 7 Washington DC 20004-1013

STETSON, CATHERINE BAKER, lawyer, lobbyist; b. N.Y.C., Dec. 3, 1948; d. Chandler Alton and Betty Jean Stetson; m. Bradley S. Root, May 30, 1985 (div. June 1992). BA, Vassar Coll., Poughkeepsie, N.Y., 1971; MA, Brown U., Providence, 1972; PhD, U. N.Mex., 1977, JD, 1981. Bar: N.Mex., 1981, U.S. Supreme Ct., U.S. Ct. Appeals (10th cir.), U.S. Dist. Ct. N.Mex., U.S. Ct. Claims, Pueblo of Laguna Tribal Ct., Pueblo of Zuni Tribal Ct, Pueblo of Santa Clara Tribal Ct. Instr. Nat. Coll., Albuquerque, 1976-77, 82-85; assoc. Ussery & Parrish, P.A., 1982-86; mng. ptnr. Gover, Stetson & Williams, P.C., 1986-97; pres. Stetson Law Offices, P.C., 1997—; v.p. Legi X Co., 1997—. Dir. Fed. Home Loan Bank Dallas. Contbr. articles to profl. jours. Bd. regents Mus. N.Mex., 1990-96; N.Mex. co-chair Clinton/Gore '96; mem. Clinton Gore Nat. Fin. Bd., 1995-96; bd. dirs. Dem. Nat. Com. Fin., 19996-97; N.Mex. chair DNC Women's Leadershp Forum, 1996; mem. state ctrl. com. N.Mex. Dem. Party, 1991-97; mem. exec. com. N.Mex. Fair Housing and Rental Task Force, 1992-96; dir Bien Mur Indian Arts and Crafts Ctr., Sandia, 1992-97, chair, 1992-96. Mem. ABA (vice chair environ. quality com. 1991-97, vice chair Native Am. natural resources com. 1997—), State Bar N.Mex. (law practice mgmt. com. 1989-91, dir. Indian Law sect. 1987-91, chair 1989-90, disciplinary bd. hearing officer 1993—. Office: 1305 Rio Grande Blvd NW Albuquerque NM 87104-2696

STETTER, ROGER ALAN, lawyer; b. N.Y.C., Mar. 12, 1947; s. William Adolphe, Jr. and Dorothy Shirley (Adler) S.; m. Barbara Jean Hensley, Dec. 25, 1974; children: David O'Neill, John Roger. B.S. in Indsl. and Labor Relations, Cornell U., 1968; J.D., U. Va., 1971. Bar: Va. 1971, N.Y. 1978, La. 1982. Atty. Legal Aid Soc., Roanoke, Va., 1971-72; asst. prof. law La. State U., Baton Rouge, 1972-76; litigation assoc. Mudge Rose Guthrie Alexander & Ferdon, N.Y.C., 1977-82; ptnr. Lemle & Kelleher, L.L.P. (and predecessor firms, New Orleans, 1983—; dir., vis. asst. prof. criminal def. unit U. Tenn. Legal Clinic, Knoxville, 1975-76; adj. assoc. prof. Benjamin N. Cardozo Sch. Law, N.Y.C., 1978-81. Editor in chief La. Environmental Handbook, (Lawyers Co-op 1995), La. Appellate Practice Handbook (Lawyers Co-op 1986), Manual of Recent Devels. in the Law (La. Bar Assn. 1985), Environ. Newsletter (La. Bar Assn. 1992—); contbr. articles to legal jours. Bd. dirs. Community Service Ctr., Inc., New Orleans, 1983-89; Legal Aid Bur. of New Orleans, 1985—. Mem. Am. Law Inst., La. Bar Assn., Va. Bar Assn., New Orleans Bar Assn., Assn. Bar City N.Y., U. Va. Alumni Assn. La. Democrat. Antitrust, Federal civil litigation, Environmental. Home: 4429 Baronne St New Orleans LA 70115-4803 Office: Lemle & Kelleher LLP 601 Poydras St New Orleans LA 70130-6029

STEUER, RICHARD MARC, lawyer; b. Bklyn., June 19, 1948; s. Harold and Gertrude (Vengar) S.; m. Audrey P. Forchheimer, Sept. 9, 1973; children: Hilary, Jeremy. BA, Hofstra U., 1970; JD, Columbia U., 1973. Bar: N.Y. 1974, U.S. Dist. Ct. (ea. and so. dists.) N.Y. 1974, U.S. Ct. Appeals (2d cir.) 1974, U.S. Supreme Ct. 1979, U.S. Dist. Ct. (no. dist.) N.Y. 1984, U.S. Dist. Ct. (we. dist.) N.Y. 1997, U.S. Ct. Appeals (3d cir.) 1987, U.S. Ct. Appeals (5th cir.) 1995. Ptnr. Kaye Scholer LLP, N.Y.C., 1973—, chair antitrust practice group, 1996—. Adj. assoc. prof. law NYU, 1985; lectr. in field; neutral evaluator U.S. Dist. Ct. Ea. Dist., N.Y, 1994-96. Author: A Guide to Marketing Law: Law and Business Inc., 1986; contbr. articles to profl. jours. Fellow: Am. Bar Found. (others); mem.: ABA (lectr. 1969, lectr. 1978, chmn. monograph com. refusals to deal and exclusive distributorships 1983, editl. bd. antitrust devel. vol. 1984—86, lectr. 1985, vice-chmn. program com. 1988—91, lectr. 1989, chmn. spring meeting program com. 1991—92, Sherman Act sect. 1 com. 1991—93, coun. sect. antitrust law 1993—96, chmn. publs. com. 1996—98, lectr. 1997, lectr. 1998, editl. chmn. Antitrust mag. 1998—2001, lectr. 1999, coun. sect. antitrust law 2001—, lectr. 2000), Assn. Bar City N.Y. (lectr. 1983—99, chmn. antitrust and trade regulation 1995—98, antitrust and trade regulation, internat. trade, lectures and CLE coms). Antitrust, General civil litigation, Trademark and copyright. Office: Kaye Scholer LLP 425 Park Ave New York NY 10022-3506 E-mail: rsteuer@kayescholer.com

STEVENS, AMY W. lawyer; b. Nashville, Nov. 8, 1968; d. Arthur Robert and Judith Ann Welhoelter; m. Richard Donald Stevens, July 25, 1997. BA, Colgate U., 1991; JD, Pepperdine U., Malibu, Calif., 1996. Bar: Tenn. 1996. Sole practitioner, Nashville, 1996-99; atty. Gladstone, Doherty & Assocs., PLLC, 1999—. Patriot League scholar athlete, 1991. Mem. ABA (intellectual property sect., entertainment and sports law sect.), Tenn. Bar Assn., Nashville Bar Assn., Lawyers Assn. for Women. Avocation: volleyball. Office: Gladstone Doherty & Assocs PLLC 49 Music Sq W Ste 300 Nashville TN 37203-3230 E-mail: Astevens@edge.net

STEVENS, C. GLENN, judge; b. Rockford, Ill., Oct. 29, 1941; s. Robert W. and Mary Louise (Shaughnessy) S.; m. Suzanne Ruth Corkery, July 4, 1967; children: Robert W., Angela M. BS, St. Louis U., 1964, JD, 1966. Bar: Ill. 1966, Mo. 1966, U.S. Dist. Ct. (so. dist.) Ill. 1966, U.S. Dist. Ct. (ea. dist.) Ill. 1968. Law clk. to judge U.S. Dist. Ct. (so. dist.) Ill., Springfield, Ill., 1966-67; instr. St. Louis U., 1967-68; assoc. Pope & Driemeyer, Belleville, Ill., 1967-74, ptnr., 1974-77; judge State of Ill., 1977—. Bd. editors St. Louis U. Law Rev., 1965-66. Arbitrator Am. Arbitration Assn., St. Clair County, Ill, 1970-77. With U.S. Army, 1958-66. Mem. Mo. Bar Assn., Ill. Judges Assn., Am. Judges Assn., Ill. State Bar Assn., St. Clair County Bar Assn., East St. Louis Bar Assn., Phi Delta Phi (pres. Murphy Inn 1965-66). Democrat. Roman Catholic. Avocations: antique cars, soccer coach. Office: Saint Clair County Courthouse Public Sq Belleville IL 62220

STEVENS, CAPRI R. lawyer; b. Phila., May 13, 1974; d. Philip J. and Davida B. Stevens. BBA, Temple U., 1994; JD, Villanova Univ., 1997. Bar: Pa. 1997, N.J. 1997. Law clk. to Judge Kafrissen Common Pleas Ct., Phila., 1997-98; assoc. Margolis Edelstein, 1998-99, Reger & Rizzo, Phila., 1999—. Mem. ATLA, ABA, Pa. Bar Assn., Phila. Bar Assn. Avocation: competitive equestrian horse show jumping. Insurance. Office: Parkview Tower Ste 250 1150 First Ave King Of Prussia PA 19406

STEVENS, CLARK VALENTINE, lawyer; b. Detroit, Nov. 28, 1933; s. Valentine W. and Florence Mary (Potrykus) S.; m. Kathleen Rose Tobosky, Sept. 1, 1956; children: Mark, Glenn. B.S. in Acctg., U. Detroit, 1958; J.D., Wayne State U., 1967. C.P.A., Mich.; bar: Mich. 1967. Auditor, City of Detroit, 1958-60, IRS, 1960-65; tax mgr. Ernst & Ernst, 1965-69; mem. firm Regan & Stevens, 1969— ; sec., dir. Mich. Rivet Corp., Warren, 1974—; bd. dirs. Tuff Machine Co., Warren, Mich. Mem. Mich. Bar Assn., Mich. Assn. C.P.A.s. Republican. Roman Catholic. Club: Grosse Pointe Yacht. General corporate, Estate planning, Corporate taxation. Office: Stevens & Howe PLC 23409 Jefferson Ave Ste 104 Saint Clair Shores MI 48080-3449

STEVENS, DAVID BOYETTE, law educator; b. Augusta, Ga., Aug. 31, 1923; s. Henry Boyette and Floreid Elizabeth (Miller) S.; m. Willa King Horner, July 18, 1942; children: David Boyette, Caroline Elizabeth, Paul King. BS in Bus., U. N.C., 1949, JD, 1951; LLM, Duke U., 1956. Bar: N.C. 1951, U.S. Ct. Mil. Appeals 1965, U.S. Supreme Ct. 1967. Commd. 2d lt. U.S. Army Air Force, 1944; advanced through grades to col. USAF, 1968; asst. prof. internat. law U.S. Air Force Acad., Colorado Springs, Colo., 1959-63; judge adv., acting dir. U.S. Air Force Judiciary, Washington, 1963-70; ret., 1970; asst. prof. bus. East Carolina U., Greenville, N.C., 1970-74, prof., 1984—, dir. EEO Office, 1974-81, univ. atty., 1970—. Divsn. chmn. United Fund Svc., East Carolina U., 1972; mem. Greenville Bd. Adjustments, 1983—. Recipient Meritorious Achievement award USAF, 1970, Outstanding Svc. award East Carolina U. Law Soc., 1978. Mem. Fed. Bar Assn., N.C. Bar Assn., Pitt County Bar Assn., Nat. Assn. Coll. and Univ. Attys., Kiwanis (pres. Greenville 1976-77, lt. gov. 1979-80, Disting. Lit. Gov. ward 1981), Delta Theta Phi. Democrat. Baptist. Home: 221 Churchill Dr Greenville NC 27858-8947

STEVENS, HERBERT FRANCIS, lawyer, law educator; b. Phila., Nov. 19, 1948; s. Herbert F. and Lois Marie (Kenna) S.; m. Jane Pickard, 1994; children: Sarah, Ben. SB, MIT, 1970; JD, Catholic U. Am., 1974; ML in Tax, Georgetown U, 1983. Bar: D.C., 1975; U.S. Supreme Ct., 1980. Law clk Md. Ct. of Spl. Appeals, 1974-75; with Morgan, Lewis & Bockius, Washington, 1975-78, Lane & Edson, P.C., Washington, 1979-89, Kelley Drye & Warren, Washington, 1989-93, Nixon Peabody LLP, Washington, 1993—; adj. prof. Georgetown U. Law Ctr., 1983-98. Spkr. nat. confs., seminars, TV Editor: Real Estate Aspects of the 1984 Tax Law, 1984; author: Real Estate Taxation: A Practitioner's Guide, 1986, Developer's Guide to Low Income Housing Tax Credit, 4th edit., 2000. Bd. dirs. Ctr. for Mental Health, Inc., 1987-2000 (exec. com.); bd. dirs. Nat. Fund for U.S. Botanic Garden, 1992—, exec. com. Mem. ABA, D.C. Bar Assn. Democrat. Presbyterian. Real property, Securities, Taxation, general. Home: 8301 Hackamore Dr Potomac MD 20854-3877 Office: Nixon Peabody LLP 401 9th St NW Washington DC 20004-2128 E-mail: hstevens@nixonpeabody.com

STEVENS, JOHN PAUL, United States supreme court justice; b. Chgo., Apr. 20, 1920; s. Ernest James and Elizabeth (Street) S.; m. Elizabeth Jane Sheeren, June 7, 1942; children: John Joseph, Kathryn Stevens Jedlicka, Elizabeth Jane Stevens Sesemann, Susan Roberta Stevens Mullen; m. Maryan Mulholland, Dec. 1979. A.B., U. Chgo., 1941; J.D. magna cum laude, Northwestern U., 1947. Bar: Ill. 1949. Practiced in, Chgo.; law clk. to U.S. Supreme Ct. Justice Wiley Rutledge, 1947-48; assoc. firm Poppenhusen, Johnston, Thompson & Raymond, 1949-52; asso. counsel sub-com. on study monopoly power, com. on judiciary U.S. Ho. of Reps., 1951; ptnr. firm Rothschild, Stevens, Barry & Myers, 1952-70; U.S. circuit judge, 1970-75; assoc. justice U.S. Supreme Ct., 1975—. Lectr. anti-trust law Northwestern U. Sch. Law,, 1952-54, U. Chgo. Law Sch., 1955-58; mem. Atty. Gen.'s Nat. Com. to Study Anti-Trust Laws, 1953-55. Served with USNR, 1942-45. Decorated Bronze Star Mem. Chgo. Bar Assn. (2d v.p. 1970), Am., Ill., Fed. bar assns., Am. Law Inst., Order of Coif, Phi Beta Kappa, Psi Upsilon, Phi Delta Phi. Office: US Supreme Ct Supreme Court Bldg One 1st St NE Washington DC 20543*

STEVENS, PAUL LAWRENCE, lawyer; b. Glen Ridge, N.J., Aug. 18, 1947; s. Mead Ferrin and Mary Nealtha (Cherry) S.; m. Cathy Lee Danskin, Sept. 13, 1969; children: Todd Benjamin, Laura Catherine. BA, U. N.H., 1969; JD cum laude, Dickinson Sch. of Law, 1975. Bar: Pa. 1975, U.S. Dist. Ct. (ea. and mid. dists.) Pa. 1975, U.S. Ct. Appeals (3d cir.) 1979, U.S. Supreme Ct. 1980. Law clk. to pres. judge Pa. Superior Ct., Carlisle, 1975-76; ptnr. Sweet, Stevens, Tucker & Katz, Doylestown, Pa., 1985—. Editor Dickinson Law Rev., 1975. Bd. govs. Dickinson Sch. Law, 2001—. Served to 1st lt. U.S. Army, 1969-82. Mem. ABA (Spl. Achievement award 1983), Pa. Bar Assn. (bd. govs. 1981-84, chmn. ho. of dels. 1987-89, pres. 1994-95), Bucks County Bar Assn. (bd. dirs. 1978-80), Pa. Sch. Bd. Solicitors' Assn. (v.p. 1985-87, pres. 1987-88). Republican. Avocations: photography, skiing. Education and schools, Labor. Home: 56 Sandywood Dr Doylestown PA 18901-2942 Office: 116 E Court St Doylestown PA 18901-4321

STEVENS, PAUL SCHOTT, lawyer; b. New Orleans, Nov. 19, 1952; s. Miles Gordon and Rosemary Louise (Schott) S.; m. Joyce Lynn Pilz, Aug. 18, 1979; Paul Schott Jr., Alexander Holmes, Andrew Colby, Carl Bernard. BA magna cum laude, Yale U., 1974; JD, U. Va., 1978. Bar: D.C. 1979, U.S. Dist. Ct. D.C. 1979, U.S. Ct. Appeals (D.C. cir.) 1979, U.S. Ct. Appeals (fed. cir.) 1983, U.S. Supreme Ct. 1982. Assoc., prin. Dickstein, Shapiro & Morin, Washington, 1978-85, ptnr., 1989-93; dep. dir., gen. counsel Pres.'s Blue Ribbon Commn. on Def. Mgmt., 1985-86; legal adviser NSC, 1987, exec. sec., 1987-89; spl. asst. to Pres. for nat. security affairs The White House, 1987-89; exec. asst. to Sec. of Defense, 1989; sr. v.p., gen. counsel Investment Co. Inst., 1993-97; sr. v.p., gen. counsel Mut. Funds and Internat. Enterprise, Charles Schwab & Co., Inc., San Francisco, 1997-99; ptnr. Dechert, Washington, 1999—. Lectr. law Washington Coll. Law, Am. U., Washington, 1980-83; trustee M.G. Stevens Corp., New Orleans, 1978—; mem. quality of markets com. NASDAQ Stock Market, Inc., 1997, mem. investment cos. com. NASD Regulation, Inc., 1999; mem. adv. bd. Ctr. Banking & Fin. Law, Boston U., 1996—. Chmn. bd. dirs. Student Conservation Assn., Charlestown, N.H., 1986-87, bd. dirs., 1985-91, 94-96, sec., gen. counsel, 1991-93. Recipient medal for disting. pub. svc. Dept. Def., 1989; Bates fellow Yale U., 1973, Scholar of House, 1973-74; Rotary Internat. Found. grad. fellow, 1978, U.S.-Japan Leadership fellow Japan Soc., 1989-90, assoc. fellow Saybrook Coll., Yale U., 1993—. Mem. ABA (chmn. standing com. law and nat. security 1995-98), Fed. Bar Assn., D.c. Bar Assn., Internat. Bar Assn., Coun. Fgn. Rels., Met. Club, Yale Club, Elizabethan Club, Cosmos Club. Republican. Roman Catholic. Office: Dechert 1775 Eye St NW Washington DC 20006-2402 E-mail: paul.stevens@dechert.com

STEVENS, THOMAS CHARLES, lawyer; b. Auburn, N.Y., Oct. 17, 1949; s. Alice (Kerlin) S.; m. Christine Eleanor Brown, June 2, 1973; children: Erin, Leigh, Timothy. BA, SUNY, Albany, 1971; JD, Duke U., 1974. Bar: Ohio 1974. Mng. ptnr. Thompson, Hine & Flory, Cleve., 1991-96; vice-chmn., chief adminstrv. officer, sec. KeyCorp., 1996—. Trustee Greater Cleve. Growth Assn., 1993-96, Greater Cleve. Roundtable, 1993—, Playhouse Sq. Found., 1998—; active Leadership Cleve., 1992-93, Young Audiences, 1999—, 1999 United Way Campaign. Mem. ABA, Cleve. Bar Assn., Am. Soc. Corp. Secs., Nisi Prius. Banking, General corporate, Securities. Office: KeyCorp 127 Public Sq Cleveland OH 44114-1306 E-mail: thomas_stevens@keybank.com

STEVENSON, ADLAI EWING, III, lawyer, former senator; b. Chgo., Oct. 10, 1930; s. Adlai Ewing and Ellen (Borden) S.; m. Nancy L. Anderson, June 25, 1955; children: Adlai Ewing IV, Lucy W., Katherine R., Warwick L. Grad., Milton Acad., 1948; A.B., Harvard U., 1952, LL.B., 1957. Bar: Ill. 1957, D.C. 1977. Law clk. Ill. Supreme Ct., 1957-58; assoc. Mayer, Brown & Platt, Chgo., 1958-66, ptnr., 1966-67, 81-83, of counsel, 1983-91; treas. State of Ill., 1967-70; U.S. senator from Ill., 1970-81; chmn. SC&M Internat. Ltd., Chgo., 1991-95, pres., 1995-98, chmn. of bd., 1998—. Mem. Ill. Ho. of Reps., 1965-67; Dem. candidate for gov. of Ill., 1982, 86. Capt. USMCR, 1952-54. Private international. Office: 20 N Clark St Ste 750 Chicago IL 60602

STEVENSON, DEYDRA, court administrator; b. Abilene, Tex., Mar. 29, 1955; d. Clarence Elliott (dec. Jan. 2000) and Sue Frances Elliott; m. Bobby Ray Stevenson, Feb. 22, 1974 (dec. June 1999); children: Scott De'Wayne, Pamela Nicole. Grad. H.S., Abilene. Cert. ct. adminstr. level I and II. Switchboard operator City of Abilene Police Dept., 1979; dep. ct. clk. City of Abilene Mcpl. Ct., 1979-98, ct. adminstr., 1998—. Active United Way of Abilene; mem. com. City of Abilene-Women in History Program. Tex/ Teem Ct. Assn. Mem. Tex. Mcpl. Ct. Clk. Assn. (presenter 1992-99) Tex. Ct. Clk. Assn. (edn. com. West Tex. chpt. 1997-99), Tex. Mcpl. Ct. Assn. (bd. dirs. 2000). Pentecostal. Avocations: walking, movies, church activities, family activities. Office: Abilene Mcpl Ct 555 Walnut St Abilene TX 79601-5254 also: City of Abilene PO Box 60 Abilene TX 79604-0060 E-mail: Stevensd@Abelinetx.com

STEVENSON, JAMES RICHARD, radiologist, lawyer; b. Ft. Dodge, Iowa, May 30, 1937; s. Lester Lawrence and Esther Irene (Johnson) S.; m. Sara Jean Hayman, Sept. 4, 1958; children: Bradford Allen, Tiffany Ann, Jill Renee, Trevor Ashley. BS, U. N.Mex., 1959, JD, 1987; MD, U. Colo., 1963. Diplomate Am. Bd. Radiology, Am. Bd. Nuc. Medicine, Am. Bd. Legal Medicine, 1989: Bar: N.Mex. 1987, U.S. Dist. Ct. N.Mex. 1988. Intern U.S. Gen. Hosp., Tripler, Honolulu, 1963-64, resident radiology Brook, San Antonio, 1964-67; radiologist, ptnr. Van Atta Labs., Albuquerque, 1970-88, Radiology Assocs. of Albuquerque, 1988—, pres., 1994-96. Radiologist, ptnr. Civerolo, Hansen & Wolf, Albuquerque, 1988-89; adj. asst. prof. radiology U. N.Mex., 1970-71; pres. med. staff AT & SF Meml. Hosp., 1979-80, chief of staff, 1980-81, trustee, 1981-83. Author: District Attorney manual, 1987. Participant breast screening Am. Cancer Soc., Albuquerque, 1987-88; dir. profl. divsn. United Way, Albuquerque, 1975. Maj. U.S. Army, 1963-70, Vietnam; col. M.C. USAR, 1988—. Decorated Bronze Star; Allergy fellow, 1960; Med.-Legal Tort scholar, 1987. Fellow Am. Coll. Radiology (councilor 1980-86, mem. med. legal com. 1990-96), Am. Coll. Legal Medicine, Am. Coll. Nuc. Medicine, Am. Coll. Nuc. Physicians, Radiology Assn. Albuquerque; mem. AMA (Physicians' Recognition award 1969—), Am. Soc. Law & Medicine, Am. Arbitration Assn., Albuquerque Bar Assn., Soc. Nuc. Medicine (v.p. Rocky Mountain chpt. 1975-76), Am. Inst. Ultrasound in Medicine, N.Am. Radiol. Soc. (chmn. med. legal com. 1992-95), N.Mex. Radiol. Soc. (pres. 1978-79), N.Mex. Med. Soc. (chmn. grievance com.), Albuquerque-Bernalillo County Med. Soc. (scholar 1959), Nat. Assn. Health Lawyers, ABA (antitrust sect. 1986—), N.Mex. State Bar, Albuquerque Bar Assn., Sigma Chi, Albuquerque Country Club, Elks, Masons, Shriners. Republican. Methodist. Home: 3333 Santa Clara Ave SE Albuquerque NM 87106-1530 Office: Medical Arts Imaging Ctr A6 Med Arts Sq 801 Encino Pl NE Albuquerque NM 87102-2612

STEVENSON, ROBIN HOWARD, lawyer; b. Marlborough, Mass., Nov. 9, 1961; s. Gerald Howard and Rosemary Pearl Stevenson; m. René Collette Cone, Dec. 19, 1987; children: Victoria Collette. BA, U. South Fla., 1986; JD, U. Fla., 1992. Bar: Fla. 1993, U.S. Dist. Ct. (mid. dist.) Fla. 1994. Asst. pub. defender Pub. Defender's Office 10th Jud. Cir./Fla., Sebring, 1994; assoc. Weaver and Assocs., Lake Wales, Fla., 1994-98; sole practitioner Bartow, 1998—. Capt. U.S. Army Res., 1991—. Mem. Polk County Trial Lawyers Assn., Polk County Criminal Def. Lawyers Assn., Rex Quality Corp. Homeowners Assn. (pres. 1995-98), Kiwanis Club. Methodist. Avocations: weightlifting, running, fishing, reading, coin collecting. Appellate, General civil litigation, Criminal. Office: 1640 N Park Ave Bartow FL 33830-3105

STEWARD, JAMES BRIAN, lawyer, pharmacist; b. Cleve., Mar. 25, 1946; s. Louis Fred and Helen Elaine (Goodwin) S.; m. Betty Kay Krans, Dec. 14, 1968; children: Christina Lynn, Brian Michael. BS in Pharmacy, Ferris State Coll., 1969; JD, U. Mich., 1973. Bar: Mich. 1973, U.S. Dist. Ct. (we. dist.) Mich. 1979, U.S. Cir. Ct. (6th Cir.) 1980, U.S. Supreme Ct. 1986. Pharmacist Revco Pharmacies, Grand Rapids, Mich., 1969-70, Coll. Pharmacy, Ypsilanti, 1970-73; assoc. Bridges & Collins, Negaunee, 1973-80; ptnr. Steward, Peterson, Sheridan & Nancarrow, Ishpeming, 1980-94, Steward & Sheridan, Ishpeming, 1995—. Mem., chmn. Negaunee Commn. on Aging, 1974-86; mem., chmn., sec. Marquette County Commn. on Aging, 1976-82; trustee, v.p., pres. Negaunee Bd. Edn., 1984-88, 91-95; mem., chmn., adv. bd. trustee Greater Ishpeming Area Cmty. Fund, 1995—; mem. combined ad hoc com. Marquette County Commn. on Aging, 1996; bd. mem. Noguemanon Trails Network, 2000—. Mem. Nat. Acad. Elder Law Attys., Mich. Bar Assn. (mem. awards com. 1996—), Marquette County Bar Assn. (sec.- treas., v.p., pres.), Am. Soc. for Pharmacy Law, Nat. Acad. Elder Law Attys., Noguemanon Trails Network (mem. bd. 2000—), Greater Ishpeming Cross County Ski Club, Superiorland Cross Country Ski Club, Wawonowin Country Club, Phi Delta Chi, Rho Chi. Avocations: cross country ski racing, downhill and water skiing, running, biking, classic cars. General corporate, Probate, Real property. Office: 205 S Main St Ishpeming MI 49849-2018

STEWARD, MARTIN JOHN, lawyer; b. Chelsea, Mass., Dec. 21, 1945; s. John L. and Catherine Marie (Geraghty) S.; m. Connie M. Huber, June 29, 1968; children— Patrick J., Catherine R. Student U. Madrid, 1964; B.A., Coll. St. Thomas, St. Paul, 1968; J.D., William Mitchell Coll. Law, St. Paul, 1972. Bar: Minn. 1972, U.S. Dist. Ct. Minn. 1972. Clk., assoc. Jardine, Logan & O'Brien, St. Paul, 1969-72; atty., staff judge adv. U.S. Air Force, Duluth, Minn., 1973; assoc. Muir & Wieneke, Rochester, Minn., 1973-76; pres. Steward, Perry, Mahler & Bird, P.A., Rochester, 1976-87; v.p., dir. Stewardship, Inc., Rochester, 1981-86. Pres., bd. dirs. Rochester Art Ctr., 1976-82; bd. dirs., conv. chmn. Olmsted County Democratic Farm Labor Party, 1976-87 ; chmn. attys. div. United Way, Rochester, 1983-84; mem. support com. Rochester Meth. Hosp., 1978-84 . Mem. ABA, Trial Lawyers Assn. Am., Minn. Trial Lawyers Assn. (com. mem. 1984), Olmsted County Bar Assn. (bd. dirs. 1984-86). Roman Catholic. Clubs: University (Rochester) (bd. dirs. 1983-87); Decathalon (Mpls.). State civil litigation, Personal injury, Workers' compensation. Office: McLeod & Mahoney PO Box 1343 125 High St Boston MA 02104

STEWART, ALLAN FORBES, lawyer; b. Kansas City, Kans., Nov. 14, 1947; s. Ernest William and Elizabeth Jeannette (Forbes) S. BA, U. Mo., St. Louis, 1969; JD, St. Louis U., 1972. Bar: Mo. 1972, Ill. 1979, Md. 1986, U.S. Dist. Ct. (we. dist.) Mo. 1973, U.S. Dist. Ct. (ea. dist.) Mo. 1978, U.S. Dist. Ct. (so. dist.) Ill. 1978, U.S. Ct. Appeals (8th cir.) 1975, U.S. Supreme Ct. 1976. Staff atty. Legal Aid Soc., Clayton, Mo., 1972-76; ptnr. Braun, Newman, Stewart, 1976-81, Braun & Stewart, Clayton, 1981-82; pres. Braun, Stewart & Anderson, Inc. and predecessor firms, 1982-97; ptnr. Beach, Burcke, Helfers, Mittleman & Stewart, St. Louis, 1997-99; prin. Beach, Stewart, Heggie, Mittleman LLC, 1999—. Contbr. chpts. to books. With Army N.G., 1970-76. Fellow am. Acad. Matrimonial Lawyers, Am. Acad. Adoption Attys.; mem. Mo. Bar Assn. (chmn. juvenile sect. 1982—, Pres. award 1983), St. Louis County Bar Assn. (chmn. family law sect. 1979-81). Family and matrimonial, Juvenile, Pension, profit-sharing, and employee benefits. Home: 1077 Jackson Ave Saint Louis MO 63130-2226 Office: 222 S Central Ave Ste 900 Saint Louis MO 63105-3575

STEWART, CARL E. federal judge; b. 1950; BA magna cum laude, Dillard U., 1971; JD, Loyola U., New Orleans, 1974. Atty. Piper & Brown, Shreveport, La., 1977-78; staff atty. La. Atty. Gen. Office, 1978-79; asst. U.S. atty. Office U.S. Atty. (we. dist.) La., 1979-83; prin. Stewart & Dixon, 1983-85; spl. asst. dist. atty., asst. prosecutor City of Shreveport, 1983-85; judge La. Dist. Ct., 1985-91, La. Ct. Appeals (2d cir.), 1991-94, U.S. Ct. Appeals (5th cir.), 1994—. Adj. instr. dept. mgmt. and mktg. La. State U., Shreveport, 1982-85. Mem. chancellor's adv. bd. La. State U., Shreveport, 1983-89, chmn., 1988-89; mem. black achievers program steering com. YMCA, 1990. Capt. JAGC, 1974-77, Tex. Mem. Nat. Bar Assn., Am. Inns. of Ct. (Harry Booth chpt. Shreveport), Black Lawyers Assn. Shreveport-Bossier, La. Conf. Ct. Appeal Judges, La. State Bar Assn. (bench/bar liaison com.), Omega Psi Phi (Rho Omega chpt.). Office: US Ct Appeals 5th Cir 300 Fannin St Ste 2299 Shreveport LA 71101-3124

STEWART, DAVID PENTLAND, lawyer, educator; b. Milw., Dec. 24, 1943; s. James Pentland and Frederica (Stockwell) S.; children from previous marriage: Jason, Jonathan; m. Jennifer Kilmer, June 21, 1986; children: Daniel, Mary Elizabeth. AB, Princeton U., 1966; JD, MA, Yale U., 1971; LLM, N.Y.U., 1975. Bar: N.Y. 1972, U.S. Dist. Ct. (ea. and so. dists.) N.Y. 1973, U.S. Ct. Appeals (2d cir.) 1973, D.C. 1976. Assoc. Donovan, Leisure, Newton & Irvine, N.Y.C., 1971-76; atty. adviser, office of legal adviser U.S. Dept. State, Washington, 1976-82, asst. legal adviser, 1982—. Adj. prof. law Georgetown U., Washington, 1984—, Am. U., Washington, 1985-86, Johns Hopkins U. Sch. Advanced Internat. Studies, 2000—; vis. lectr. Sch. Law U. Va., 1993-96, Nat. Law Ctr., George Washington U., 1993—. Contbr. articles to profl. jours.; also editorial adv. bds. Mem. dean's adv. coun. internat. law Am. U., 1984-88. Served to maj. USAR, 1970-87. Mem. ABA, Fed. Bar Assn., Am. Soc. Internat. Law, Internat. Law Assn. (adv. coun. procedural aspects internat. law inst.). Office: US Dept State Office Legal Adviser Washington DC 20520-6310 E-mail: stewartdp@ms.state.gov

STEWART, JAMES MALCOLM, lawyer; b. Aberdeen, Wash., May 8, 1915; s. Malcolm M. and Ethel Lucille (Hinman) S.; m. Dorothy Vera Gilardi, Sept. 16, 1945; children: Barbara Jane, Robert Bruce, William James. BA, U. Wash., 1939, JD, 1941. Bar: Wash., 1941, U.S. Dist. Ct. (we. dist.) Wash., 1948, U.S. Supreme Ct., 1998. Dep. prosecuting atty. Grays Harbor County, Wash., 1945-48; pvt. practice Montesano, 1952-99. Pres., dir. Gray Harbor Coll. Found., Aberdeen, 1955-95; bd. dirs. St. Joseph Hosp., Aberdeen, 1972-87; organizer Gray Harbor Cmty. Found., Aberdeen, 1993; scout leader Boy Scouts Am. Lt. USNR, 1942-45, PTO, admirality officer, 1945-46, lt. comdr., 1950-52, Korea, ret. Decorated 16 Battle Stars, 2 Silver Stars, Gold Star. Mem. Am. Judicature Soc., Wash.

State Bar Assn. (50 Yr. award, 1991), Gray Harbor Bar Assn. (pres. 1953), Aberdeen Pioneers Assn. (pres., dir. 1948-98), Lions (Melvin Jones award 1997), Elks, Sigma Nu, Phi Delta Phi. Republican. Episcopalian. Avocations: tree farming, hiking, horseback riding, tennis. General corporate, Estate planning, General practice. Home: 711 3rd St N # D Montesano WA 98563-1625

STEWART, JEFFREY B. lawyer; b. Chgo., Feb. 6, 1952; s. Bruce A. and Harriet B. Stewart. AB magna cum laude (R. Choate scholar), Dartmouth Coll., 1974; JD, Emory U., 1978. Bar: Ga. 1978, U.S. Dist. Ct. (no. dist.) Ga., U.S. Ct. Appeals (5th and 11th dists.). Ptnr., chair corp. dept. Arnall Golden & Gregory, Atlanta, 1978. Mem. editl. bd. Emory Law Jour., 1977-78. Mem. ABA, State Bar Ga. Health, Mergers and acquisitions, Securities. Home: 5280 N Powers Ferry Rd Atlanta GA 30327 Office: Arnall Golden & Gregory 1201 W Peachtree St NW Ste 2800 Atlanta GA 30309-3454

STEWART, JOSEPH GRIER, lawyer; b. Tuscaloosa, Ala., July 24, 1941; s. Jesse Grier and Kyle Vann (Pruett) S.; m. Linda Louise Hogue, Mar. 2, 1963; children: Joseph Grier Jr., Robert Byars, James Vann. BS, U. Ala., Tuscaloosa, 1963, LLB, 1966. Bar: Ala. 1966, U.S. Dist. Ct. (no. dist.) Ala. 1968, U.S. Dist. Ct. (middle Dist.of Ala.), 1996, U.S. Tax Court. Ptnr. Burr & Forman LLP, Birmingham, Ala., 1968—. Mem. ABA, Ala. State Bar, Birmingham Bar Assn. (chmn. com. 1989-90), Ala. Law Inst., Kiwanis, Birmingham Tip Off Club (pres. 1988-89). Methodist. Avocation: tennis. Contracts commercial, General corporate, Mergers and acquisitions. Office: Burr & Forman LLP 3100 S Trust Tower 420 20th St N Birmingham AL 35203-5200

STEWART, JUDITH A. judge, former prosecutor; U.S. atty. So. Dist. Ind., Indpls., 1993-2000; judge, Brown County Indiana State Court, Nashville, 2000—. Office: Brown County Circuit Court Court House Nashville IN 47448*

STEWART, MICHAEL B. lawyer, mechanical and aerospace engineer; b. Royal Oak, Mich., Nov. 5, 1963; s. Colin M. and Jacqueline P. Stewart; m. Katherine Hewitt, May 1987; children: Elizabeth and Caitlin. BSME, BA in English, U. Mich, 1987, MS in Aerospace Engring., 1988, JD, 1991. Assoc. Dykema Gossett PLLC, Bloomfield Hills, Mich., 1991-96; mnging. ptnr. Rader, Fishman & Grauer PLLC, 1996—. Contbr. articles to profl. jours. Named 40 Under 40 Honoree Crain's Detroit Bus., 1998. Mem. ABA, Intellectual Property Law Assn., Mich. Patent Law Assn., Mich. Bar Assn., Oakland County Bar Assn. (chmn. continuing legal edn. subcom. for IP com. 1998), Optimists (bd. dirs. 1993-97), Delta Theta Phi (dean., bd. govs., Detroit alumni senate). Avocations: cycling, woodworking. Computer, Intellectual property, Patent. Office: Rader Fishman & Grauer PLLC 39533 Woodward Ave Ste 140 Bloomfield Hills MI 48304-5098 E-mail: mbs@raderfishman.com

STEWART, PAMELA L. lawyer; b. Bogalusa, La., Mar. 13, 1953; d. James Adrian and Patricia Lynn (Wood) Lloyd; m. Steven Bernard Stewart, Aug. 31, 1974 (div. July 1980); 1 child, Christopher. BA, U. New Orleans, 1986; JD, U. Houston, 1990. Intern La. Supreme Ct., New Orleans, 1984, Councilman Bryan Wagner, New Orleans, 1984-85; legal asst. Clann, Bell & Murphy, Houston, 1988-89, Tejas Gas Corp., Houston, 1989-90; atty. Law Offices of Pamela L. Stewart, Katy, Tex., 1991—. Bd. dirs. Alliance for Good Govt., New Orleans, 1983-84, Attention Deficit Hyperactivity Disorder Assn. Tex., 1989-90; vol. Houston Vol. Lawyers Program, Houston, 1992—; mem. Planned Giving Coun.; bd. dirs. West Lane Place Civic Assn., sec., 2001—; mem. com. Lawyers Against Waste, Habitat for Humanity. Innsbruck scholar, U. New Orleans, 1985. Fellow Inst. Politics; mem. ABA, Tax Freedom Inst., Nat. Assn. Consumer Bankruptcy Attys., Nat. Assn. Elder Law Attys., Am. Networking Trust Planning Attys., Houston Bar Assn., Nat. Assn. of Chpt. 13 Trustees (assoc.), Katy Bar Assn. (3d v.p. 1997-98), Houston Assn. Debtors Attys. (pres. 1996-98), Upper Kirby Dist. Optimist Club (v.p. 2000-01, pres. 2001—), Planned Giving Coun., Feng Shui Guild, Feng Shui Basics (pres.). Methodist. Avocations: music, cooking, swimming, politics. Estate planning, Probate, Personal income taxation. Home: 3326 Midlane St Houston TX 77027-5614 Office: 4265 San Felipe St Ste 1100 Houston TX 77027-2998 E-mail: PLSatty@swbell.net

STEWART, RICHARD BURLESON, lawyer, educator; b. Cleve., Feb. 12, 1940; s. Richard Siegfreid and Ruth Dysert (Staten) S.; m. Alice Peck Fales, May 13, 1967; children: William, Paul, Elizabeth; m. Jane Laura Bloom, Sept. 20, 1992; children: Emily, Ian. AB, Yale U., 1961; MA (Rhodes scholar), Oxford (Eng.) U., 1963; LLB, Harvard U., 1966; D (hon.), Erasmus U., Rotterdam, 1993. Bar: D.C. 1968, U.S. Supreme Ct 1971. Law clk. to Justice Potter Stewart, U.S. Supreme Ct., 1966-67; assoc. Covington & Burling, Washington, 1967-71; asst. prof. law Harvard U., 1971-75, prof., 1975-82, Byrne prof. adminstrv. law, 1982-89, assoc. dean, 1984-86; asst. atty. gen. environment and natural resources div. Dept. Justice, Washington, 1989-91; prof. law NYU Law Sch., 1992-94, Emily Kempin prof. law, 1994—; of counsel Sidley & Austin, 1992—. Spl. counsel U.S. Senate Watergate Com., 1974; vis. prof. law U. Calif., Berkeley Law Sch., 1979-80, U. Chgo. Law Sch., 1986-87, Georgetown U., 1991-92, European U. Inst., 1995; dir. Ctr. Environ. and Land Use Law, Health Effects Inst.; mem. adv. bd. Environ. Def. Author: (with P. Menell) Environmental Law and Policy, 1994, (with S. Breyer, C. Soustein and M. Spitzer) Administrative Law and Regulation, 1979, 4th edit., 1999, (with E. Rehbinder) Integration Through Law: Environmental Protection Policy, 1985, paper edit., 1987; editor: (with R. Revesz) Analyzing Superfund: Economics, Science, and Law, 1995, Markets v. Environment?, 1995. Fellow Am. Acad. Arts and Scis.; mem. ABA, Am. Law Inst. Office: NYU Law Sch 40 Washington Sq S New York NY 10012-1099 E-mail: stewartr@juris.law.nyu.edu

STEWART, RICHARD WILLIAMS, lawyer; b. Harrisburg, Pa., Aug. 21, 1948; s. Alexander H. and M. Winifred (Williams) S.; m. Mary A. Simmonds, June 7, 1975; 1 child, Anne W. AB cum laude, Franklin and Marshall Coll., 1970; JD, Duke U., 1973. Bar: Pa. 1973, U.S. Dist. Ct. (mid. dist.) Pa. 1975, U.S. Tax Ct. 1984. Assoc. Stone & Sajer, New Cumberland, Pa., 1973-77; ptnr. Stone, Sajer & Stewart, 1977-87, Johnson, Duffie, Stewart & Weidner, Lemoyne, Pa., 1987—. V.p. Secured Land Transfers, Inc., Camp Hill, Pa., 1985-2000, pres., 2000—; solicitor West Shore Sch. Dist., Lemoyne, Pa., 1977-93, No. York County Sch. Dist., Dillsburg, Pa., 1984—, Camp Hill Sch. Dist., 1986—, Fairview Twp., 1987-98; v.p. Cedar Cliff Abstract Agy., 1980-87. Chmn. Cumberland County Rep. Com., 1981-84; mem. Rep. State Com. Pa., 1990—. Mem. ABA, Pa. Bar Assn., Cumberland County Bar Assn., Supreme Ct. of Pa. (disciplinary bd. mem. 1998—), Ctrl. Pa. Estate Planning Coun. (bd. dirs. 1983-85), Pa. Sch. Solicitors Assn. (pres. 1995), Rotary (bd. dirs. West Shore). Presbyterian. Consumer commercial, Probate. Home: 1811 Warren St New Cumberland PA 17070-1148 Office: 301 Market St Lemoyne PA 17043-1628

STEWART, ROBERT CAMPBELL, lawyer; b. Phila., Dec. 8, 1936; s. Harold Leroy and Cecilia Eleanor (Finn) S.; m. Mary Elizabeth Pisula, Sept. 1, 1978; children: David Patrick, Margaret Colleen, Richard Michael, Cowles A. BA, U. Md., 1961; JD, George Washington U., 1966. Bar: Md. 1966, D.C. 1989. Mental health info. svc. officer N.Y. State Supreme Ct., N.Y.C., 1966-68; asst. states atty. Balt., 1968-71; spl. atty. Buffalo Strike Force, 1971-73, atty. in charge, 1973-78, Newark Strike Force, 1978-94; supervisory asst. U.S. Atty., 1994; ret., 1994. Vis. lectr. Nat. Coll. Dist. Attys., Houston, 1973—; Am. law expert East European Law Reform Cons. Firm, 1996-99; cons. in field. Author: Identification and Investigation of Organized Criminal Activity, 1980. Sgt. USMC, 1957-58. Mem. Nat. Dist. Attys. Assn. Address: Newark Strike Force 220 St Paul St 970 Broad St Westfield NJ 07090

STEYER, HUME RICHMOND, lawyer; b. N.Y.C., Dec. 25, 1953; s. Roy Henry and Margaret (Fahr) S.; m. Nanahya C. Santana, Sept. 23, 1989; children: Ian A., Isabella P. BA, U. Pa., 1975; JD, Harvard U., 1978. Bar: N.Y. 1979. Assoc. Hughes Hubbard & Reed, N.Y.C., 1978-86, Morris & McVeigh, N.Y.C., 1986-91, ptnr., 1991-97, Seward & Kissel LLP, N.Y.C., 1997—. Bd. nat. advisors Mus. Am. Folk Art, N.Y.C., 1984—, Sharonsteel Found., 1988—, Open Space Inst., 1996—, North County Sch., 1996—, Am. Fedn. for Aging Rsch., 1995—. Mem. ABA, N.Y. State Bar Assn., Assn. of Bar of City of N.Y. (com. on trusts, estates and surrogate's cts.). Democrat. Clubs: University (N.Y.C.), Shinnecock Hills Country (Southampton, N.Y.), Tuxedo (N.Y.). Estate planning, Private international, Probate. Home: 24 Tower Hill Loop Tuxedo Park NY 10987-4061 Office: Seward & Kissel LLP 1 Battery Park Plz New York NY 10004 E-mail: steyer@sewkis.com

STICK, MICHAEL ALAN, lawyer; b. Elizabeth City, N.C., June 2, 1954; s. David and Phyllis (Stapells) S.; m. Debra Joan Braselton, May 22, 1993. BA, Davidson Coll., 1976; JD, U. N.C., 1981. Bar: Ill. 1981, U.S. Dist. Ct. (no. dist.) Ill. 1982, U.S. Ct. Appeals (7th cir.) 1983, U.S. Ct. Appeals (8th cir.) 1986. Assoc. Jenner & Block, Chgo., 1981-84, Butler, Rubin, Newcomer, Saltarelli & Boyd, Chgo., 1984-87; ptnr. Butler, Rubin, Saltarelli & Boyd, 1988—. Co-author: Environmental Law Handbook, 1988, Environmental Law in Illinois, 1993; mem. staff U. N.C. Law Rev., 1979-80. Chmn. spl. gifts divsn. United Way Crusade of Mercy, Chgo., 1993-94. Me. ABA, Chgo. Bar Assn. Democrat. Methodist. Avocations: travel, skiing, art. General civil litigation, Environmental. Home: 616 E Hickory St Hinsdale IL 60521-2413 Office: Butler Rubin Saltarelli & Boyd Three First Nat Pla # 1800 Chicago IL 60602

STIEFEL, LINDA SHIELDS, lawyer; b. Syracuse, N.Y., Nov. 14, 1948; d. Harold F. and Ellen (Brown) Shields; m. John L. Stiefel, Sept. 20, 1969; 1 child, John L. BS, Tusculum Coll., 1988; JD, Akron Sch. Law, 1991. Bar: Ohio 1992, D.C. 1993, N.Y. 1998, U.S. Dist. Ct. (no. dist.) Ohio 1993, U.S. Supreme Ct. 1997. Judicial law clk. Stark County Common Pleas, Canton, Ohio, 1991-94; pvt. practice Louisville, 1992-97, Cape Vincent, N.Y., 1998—. Active Ohio Dem. Nat. Com., Columbus, Stark County Dem. Party, Canton, Ohio, 1991-97; trustee, mem. exec. com. Am. Handweaving Mus. Mem. ABA, NOW, N.Y. State Bar Assn., Jefferson County Bar Assn. Methodist. Appellate, Family and matrimonial, Probate. Home and Office: 596 West Broadway Cape Vincent NY 13618

STIEGLITZ, ALBERT BLACKWELL, lawyer; b. Warrenton, Va., May 21, 1936; s. Valentine Henry and Mary (Blackwell) S.; m. Rosemary Jeanne Dommerich, Nov. 11, 1971; children— Albert Blackwell Jr., John Dommerich. Student U. Fla., 1954-1955; B.A., U. Miami, 1958, LL.B., 1964. Bar: Fla. 1964, U.S. Dist. Ct. (so. dist.) Fla. 1964, U.S. Ct. Appeals (5th and 11th cirs.) 1964. Ptnr. Fowler, White, Burnett, Hurley, Banick and Strickroot, Miami, Fla., 1969— . Served to 1st lt. USAF, 1958-61. Mem. ABA, Fla. Bar Assn., Internat. Assn. Ins. Counsel (exec. com. 1981-84), Dade County Def. Bar Assn. (pres. 1978-79), Delta Theta Phi. Republican. Episcopalian. Clubs: Riviera Country (Coral Gables); Com. of 100, Bath (Miami Beach, Fla.); University, Bankers (Miami). Lodge: Rotary. Federal civil litigation, State civil litigation, Personal injury. Office: Fowler White Burnett Hurley et al City Nat Bank Building Fl 5 Miami FL 33130

STIEHL, WILLIAM D. federal judge; b. 1925; m. Celeste M. Sullivan; children: William D., Susan M. Student, U. N.C., 1943-45; LLB, St. Louis U., 1949. Pvt. practice, 1952-78; ptnrs. Stiehl & Hess, 1978-81; ptnr. Stiehl & Stiehl, 1982-86; judge, former chief judge U.S. District Court, (so. dist.) Ill., East Saint Louis, 1986—. Spl. asst. atty. gen. State of Ill., 1970-73. Mem. bd. Belleville Twp. High Sch. and Jr. Coll., 1949-50, 54-56, pres., 1956-57, Clair County, Ill., county civil atty., 1956-60. Mem. Ill. State Bar Assn., St. Clair County Bar Assn. Office: US Dist Ct 750 Missouri Ave East Saint Louis IL 62201-2954

STIER, EDWIN H. lawyer; b. Newark, Nov. 2, 1939. B.A., Rutgers U., 1961, LL.B., 1964. Bar: N.J. 1965, U.S. Supreme Ct. 1979. Asst. U.S. atty. Fed. Ct., Newark, 1965-69; chief criminal div. U.S. Atty.'s Office, Newark, 1967-69; asst. atty. gen., dir. criminal justice State of N.J., Trenton, 1969-82; ptnr. Kirsten, Friedman & Cherin, Newark, 1982— . Author: White Collar Crime, 1981. Environmental. Office: Trucking Employees 707 Summit Ave Union City NJ 07087-3463

STILES, KEVIN PATRICK, lawyer, banker; b. Bklyn., Sept. 3, 1949; s. Edward F. and Catherine T. (Bennett) S.; m. Elaine P. Slavin, Dec. 22, 1973; children: Lauren Elaine, Matthew Slavin. BA, Holy Cross Coll., 1971; JD, Georgetown U., 1974. Bar: D.C. 1974, R.I. 1976, U.S. Dist. Ct. R.I. 1976. Trust rep. Riggs Nat. Bank, Washington, 1974-76; trust bus. devel. officer Old Stone Bank, Providence, 1976-78; assoc. firm Nolan & Dailey, Coventry, R.I., 1976-78; asst. v.p. R.I. Hosp. Trust Nat. Bank, Providence, 1980-82, v.p., 1982-84, sr. v.p., 1984-89; dir. mktg. securities div. Bank of Boston, 1989, chief fiduciary officer, 1990—. Pres., Agassiz Beach Assn., Newport, R.I., 1982-83; bd. dirs. Newport Music Festival, 1982—, R.I. Estate Planning Coun., 1983—, pres. 1989-90; chmn. deferred giving R.I. chpt. ARC, 1983—; trustee Newport County Mental Health Assn. Trust, 1984; mem. fin. com. St. Mary's Roman Cath. Ch., Newport, 1984—. Mem. ABA, D.C. Bar Assn., R.I. Bar Assn. (probate and trust com. 1980—), Newport County Bar Assn., Holy Cross Club (Providence), Georgetown Univ. Club. Estate planning, Probate. Office: Bank of Boston PO Box 1959 MS 01-07-05 Boston MA 02106

STILES, MARY ANN, lawyer, author, lobbyist; b. Tampa, Fla., Nov. 16, 1944; d. Ralph A. and Bonnie (Smith) S.; m. Barry Smith. AA, Hills Community Coll., 1973; BS, Fla. State U., 1975; JD, Antioch Sch. Law, 1978. Bar: Fla. 1978. Legis. analyst Fla. Ho. of Reps., Tallahassee, 1973-74, 74-75; intern U.S. Senate, Washington, 1977; v.p., gen. counsel Associated Industries Fla., Tallahassee, 1978-81, gen. counsel, 1981-84, spl. counsel, 1986-97; assoc. Deschler, Reed & Crichfield, Boca Raton, Fla., 1980-81; founding ptnr. Stiles, Taylor, & Grace, P.A., Boca Raton, Tampa, Orlando, Talahassee, and Miami, 1982—, shareholder, dir. Tampa; gen. counsel Associated Industries Ins. Co., Inc., 1996—, Associated Industries Fla., Inc., 1997—, Associated Industries Ins. Svcs., Inc., 1997—. Shareholder, dir. Six Stars Devel. Co. of Fla., Inc. Platnum Bank; br. chair Employers 1st Trust, Inc.; shareholder, pres. 42nd St., The Bistro; mem. Workers' Compensation Task Force, 2000-01. Author: Workers' Copmensation Law Handbook, 1980-94 edit. Bd. dirs., sec. Hillsborough C.C. Found., Tampa, 1985-87, 94-96; bd. dirs. Hillsborough Area Regional Transit Authority, Tampa, 1986-89, Boys and Girls Club of Tampa, 1986—; The Spring, 1992-93, What's My Chance, 1992-94; mem. Gov.'s Oversite Bd. on Workers' Compensation, 1989-90, Workers' Compensation Rules Com., Fla. Bar, 1990-95, 2000—, Workers' Compensation Exec. Counsel Fla. Bar, 1990-95, Jud. Nominating Commn. for Workers' Compensation Cts., 1990-93, trustee Hillsborough Cmty. Coll., 1994-99, vice-chair, 1995-96, chair, 1996-97; bd. dirs. Seminole Boosters, Inc., Fla. State U., 1996—. Mem. ABA, Fla. Bar Assn., Hillsborough County Bar Assn., Hillsborough Assn. Women Lawyers, Fla. Assn. Women Lawyers, Fla. Women's Alliance, Hillsborough County Seminole Boosters (past pres.). Democrat. Baptist. Club: Tiger Bay (Tampa, past pres., sec.) Avocations: boating, reading. Administrative and regulatory, Insurance, Workers' compensation. Office: 315 S Plant Ave Tampa FL 33606-2325 also: 111 N Orange Ave Ste 850 Orlando FL 32801-2338 also: 317 N Calhoun St Tallahassee FL 32301-7605 also: PO Box 310397 Miami FL 33231-0397

STILES, MICHAEL, prosecutor; Atty. U.S. Dept. Justice, Phila., 1993—. Office: US Attys Office 615 Chestnut St Fl 1250 Philadelphia PA 19106-4404

STILL, CHARLES HENRY, lawyer; b. Lubbock, Tex., Sept. 22, 1942; s. Charles Alphonso and Henri Sue S.; m. Frances Eugenia Odell, Apr. 29, 1967; children: Charles Henry Jr., Kathryn Elizabeth. BBA in Acctg., Tex. Tech. U., 1965; JD with honors, U. Tex., 1968. Bar: Tex. 1968. Assoc. Fulbright & Jaworski, Houston, 1968-75, ptnr., 1975—, head corp. dept., 1984-99, mem. exec. com., 1992-99. Speaker numerous confs. and meetings; bd. dirs. Oyo Geospace Corp., TrueTime Inc. Comment editor Tex. Law Rev., 1967-68. Bd. dirs. Alley Theatre, Houston, 1980-81, St. Luke's Episcopal Hosp., Houston, 1991—, Free Enterprise Inst., Houston, 1993—; mem. vestry Christ Ch. Cathedral, Houston, 1981-84, sr. warden, 1983, chancellor, 1986—. Fellow Am. Bar Found., Tex. Bar Found., Houston Bar Found.; mem. ABA (bus. law sect. 1968—, corp. laws com. 1983-89, fed. regulation of securities com. 1976—, subcom. on proxy statements and tender offers 1979—, com. on legal opinions 1989—, adminstrv. law sect. 1981—, law firms com. 1990—, chmn. 1998—, ethics 2000 task force 1999—, multiple disciplinary practice task force 1998—), Am. Law Inst., State Bar Tex. (chmn. bus. law sect. 1984-85, mem. coun. 1982-86, chmn. securities law com. 1981-83, com. on corp. laws 1985—, legislation in pub. interest com. 1983-84), Forest Club, Petroleum Club, Order of Coif, Phi Delta Phi, Phi Kappa Phi, Gamma Phi Beta, Beta Alpha Psi, Phi Delta Theta, Phi Eta Sigma. Avocations: hunting, reading, photography. General corporate, Mergers and acquisitions, Securities. Home: 3734 Locke Ln Houston TX 77027-4006 Office: Fulbright & Jaworski 1301 Mckinney St Ste 5100 Houston TX 77010-3095

STILLER, JENNIFER ANNE, lawyer; b. Washington, May 4, 1948; d. Ralph Sophian and Joy (Dancis) S. AB in Econs. and History, U. Mich., 1970; JD, NYU, 1973. Bar: Pa. 1973, U.S. Dist. Ct. (mid. dist.) Pa. 1977, U.S. Supreme Ct. 1978, Ill. 1979, U.S. Dist. Ct. (no. dist.) Ill. 1979, U.S. Dist. Ct. (ea. dist.) Pa. 1983, U.S. Ct. Appeals (3rd cir.) 1983, U.S. Ct. Appeals (D.C. cir.), 1996. Dep. atty. gen. Pa. Dept. Justice, Harrisburg, 1973-75, Pa. Dept. Health, Harrisburg, 1975-78; sr. staff atty. Am. Hosp. Assn., Chgo., 1978-80, mgr., dept. fed. law, 1980-81; gen. counsel Ill. Health Fin. Authority, 1981-82; sr. assoc. Berriman & Schwartz, King of Prussia, Pa., 1983-85, Wolf, Block, Schorr & Solis-Cohen, Phila., 1985-88, Montgomery, McCracken, Walker & Rhoads, LLP, Phila., 1988-90; ptnr. Montgomery, McCracken, Walker & Rhoads, 1990-2000, chair health law group, 1991-2000; sr. counsel Tenet Healthcare Corp., 2000-2001; pvt. practice Haverford, Pa., 2001—. Contbr. health law articles to profl. jours. Mem. ABA (gov. com. Health Law Forum 1994-95), Am. Health Lawyers Assn. (bd. dirs. 1997—), Forum of Exec. Women, Pa. Soc. Healthcare Attys. (pres. 1995). Avocations: gardening, bicycling, hiking, music. Health. Office: Law Office Jennifer A Stiller 625 Haydock Ln Haverford PA 19041-1207 E-mail: jennifer.stiller@tenethealth.com

STILLMAN, ELINOR HADLEY, retired lawyer; b. Kansas City, Mo., Oct. 12, 1938; d. Hugh Gordon and Freda (Brooks) Hadley; m. Richard C. Stillman, June 25, 1965 (div. Apr. 1975). BA, U. Kans., 1960; MA, Yale U., 1961; JD, George Washington U., 1972. Bar: D.C. 1973, U.S. Ct. Appeals (10th cir.) 1975, U.S. Ct. Appeals (9th cir.) 1976, U.S. Ct. Appeals (2d cir.) 1976, U.S. Ct. Appeals (5th cir.) 1983, U.S. Ct. Appeals (4th cir.) 1985, U.S. Supreme Ct. 1976. Lectr. in English CUNY, 1963-65; asst. editor Stanford (Calif.) U. Press., 1967-69; law clk. to judge U.S. Dist. Ct. D.C., Washington, 1972-73; appellate atty. NLRB, 1973-78; asst. to solicitor gen. U.S. Dept. Justice, 1978-82; supr. appellate atty. NLRB, 1982-86, chief counsel to mem. bd., 1986-88, 94-00, chief counsel to chmn. bd., 1988-94; ret., 2000. Mem. ABA, D.C. Bar Assn., Order of Coif, Phi Beta Kappa. Democrat.

STIMMEL, TODD RICHARD, lawyer, business executive; b. Freeport, N.Y., Jan. 20, 1954; s. Leonard E. and Lorraine Joyce (Greenfield) S.; m. Andrea Jane Katz, Aug. 20, 1978; children: Samantha, Harrison. BA, Columbia U., 1976; JD, Harvard U., 1979. Bar: N.Y. 1980. Assoc. Cravath Swaine & Moore, N.Y.C., 1979-83, O'Sullivan Graev & Karabell, N.Y.C., 1983-85, ptnr., 1985-93; CEO Napp Co., 1993-2000; chmn. Stage III Techs., 2000—. Mem. Phi Beta Kappa. Club: Harvard. Avocation: sports. General corporate, Securities. Home: 201 E 87th St Apt 27J New York NY 10128-3206 Address: NAPPCO 570 Lexington Ave Fl 22 New York NY 10022-6837 E-mail: trstimmel@aol.com

STINCHFIELD, JOHN EDWARD, lawyer; b. Alameda, Calif., July 31, 1947; s. John Eastwood and Pauline Finch (Acker) S.; m. Niall O'Melia, May 15, 1976; children: John Ryan, Noel O'Neil. BA, Wesleyan U., Middletown, Conn., 1969; JD, U. Calif., 1973. Bar: Calif. 1974, D.C. 1980. Atty. advisor Divsn. Corp. Fin. U.S. SEC, 1974-76, Divsn. Investment Mgmt. SEC, 1976-77; atty., advisor Bur. of Competition U.S. FTC, 1977-79; corp. counsel, sec. The Donohoe Cos., Inc., Washington, 1979—, also bd. dirs. Bd. dirs. Fed. Ctr. Plaza Corp. Bd. dirs. Christmas in April of Washington, D.C., Inc. Mem. ABA, D.C. Bar Assn., State Bar Calif., Columbia Country Club (Chevy Chase, Md.), Tenley Sport and Health Club. Construction, Pension, profit-sharing, and employee benefits, Real property. E-mail: johns@donohoe.com

STINEHART, ROGER RAY, lawyer; b. Toledo, Jan. 27, 1945; s. Forrest William and Nettie May (Twyman) S.; m. Martha Jean Goodnight, Sept. 19, 1970; children: Amanda Jean, Brian Scott. BS, Bowling Green (Ohio) State U., 1968; JD, Ohio State U., 1972. Bar: Ohio 1972. Fin. analyst Gen. Electric, Detroit, 1968-69; assoc. Gingher & Christensen, Columbus, Ohio, 1972-76, ptnr., 1976-80; sr. v.p., gen. counsel, sec. G.D. Ritzy's, Inc., 1983-85; ptnr. Jones, Day, Reavis & Pogue, 1980-83, 85—. Adj. prof. law Capital U., Columbus, 1976-79; mem. adv. com. Ohio securities divsn. Dept. Commerce, Columbus, 1979—; fellow Columbus Bar Found., 1992—; adv. bd. The Entrepreneurship Inst., 1992-95. Contbr. Ohio State U. Coll. Law Jour., 1970-72. Gen. counsel, trustee Internat. Assn. Rsch. on Leukemia and Related Diseases, 1975—; v.p., trustee Hospice of Columbus, 1978-80; trustee Cen. Ohio chpt. Leukemia Soc. of Am., Columbus, 1983-93, v.p., 1985-87; trustee Ohio Cancer Rsch. Assocs., Columbus, 1983—, v.p., 1990—. With USMCR, 1963-68. Mem. ABA (bus. law com., franchise law com.), Ohio State Bar Assn. (corp. law com., franchise law com.), Columbus Bar Assn. (securities law com., chmn. 1981-83, bus. law com., franchise law com.), Rotary Club (Columbus), Sigma Tau Delta, Beta Gamma Sigma. General corporate, Mergers and acquisitions, Securities. Home: 2155 Waltham Rd Columbus OH 43221-4149 Office: Jones Day Reavis & Pogue 1900 Huntington Ctr Columbus OH 43215-6103

STINNETT, MARK ALLAN, lawyer; b. Jackson, Miss., Sept. 15, 1955; s. Allan J. and Joan (Mouser) S.; m. Carol Fowler, Sept. 5, 1992; children: Michelle, Michael. BA in Polit. Sci. with honors, Tex. Tech U., 1977; JD with honors, U. Tex., 1980. Bar: Tex. 1980, U.S. Dist. Ct. (no. and ea. dists.) Tex. 1981, U.S. Ct. Appeals (5th cir.) 1993. Founding ptnr., mng. ptnr. Stinnett Thiebaud & Remington L.L.P., Dallas, 2000—; shareholder Cowles & Thompson, 1996-2000. Mem. Philmont Ranch com. Boy Scouts Am. Mem. ABA, Am. Bd. Trial Advocates, Am. Inns of Ct., Am. Coll. Legal Medicine, Am. Health Lawyers Assn., State Bar of Tex., Dallas Bar

Assn., Tex. Assn. Def. Counsel, Dallas Assn. Def. Counsel, Def. Rsch. Inst., Inns Ct. (barrister Dallas chpt. 1988-91), Tex. Ctr. Legal Ethics and Professionalism, Nat. Eagle Scout Assn., Philmont Staff Assn. (pres. 1994-98). Avocations: backpacking, softball, military history. General civil litigation, Personal injury, Product liability. Home: 5541 Mallard Trce Frisco TX 75034-5058 Office: Stinnett Thiebaud & Remington LLP 1445 Ross Ave Ste 4800 Dallas TX 75202-2702 E-mail: mstinnett@strlaw.net

STINNETT, TERRANCE LLOYD, lawyer; b. Oakland, Calif., July 22, 1940; s. Lloyd Monroe and Gertrude (Hyman) S. BS, Stanford U., 1962; JD magna cum laude, U. Santa Clara, 1969. Bar: Calif. 1970, U.S. Dist. Ct. (no. dist.) Calif. 1970, U.S. Dist. Ct. (ea. ctrl. and so. dists) Calif. 1975, U.S. Ct. Appeals (9th cir.) 1970, U.S. Supreme Ct. 1975. Law clk. to judge Calif. Ct. Appeals, San Francisco, 1969-70; assoc. Hyman, Rhodes & Aylward, Fremont, Calif., 1970-71, Glicksberg, Kushner & Goldberg, San Francisco, 1972-77; mem. Goldberg, Stinnett Meyers & Davis, 1977—. Bd. dirs. Fremont Bancorp, Fremont Bank, vice-chmn. bd., 1998-2000. Mem. ABA, Bar Assn. San Francisco (chmn. bench bar liaison com. for U.S. Bankruptcy Ct., No. Dist. of Calif. 1997). Republican. Roman Catholic. Bankruptcy. Home: 131 Alamo Hills Ct Alamo CA 94507-2243 Office: Goldberg Stinnett Meyers & Davis 44 Montgomery St Ste 2900 San Francisco CA 94104-4803 E-mail: tstinnett@gsmdlaw.com

STINSON, DONNA HOLSHOUSER, lawyer; b. Urbana, Ill., Dec. 6, 1949; d. Don Franklin and Marion (Stankus) Holshouser; m. William Ide Stinson, May 11, 1974; children— Eric Owen, Lillian Elizabeth. B.A., U. Ill.-Chgo., 1969; J.D., Duke U., 1974. Bar: Fla. 1974. Asst. atty. gen. Fla. Atty. Gen.'s Office, Tallahassee, 1974-76; assoc. law firm Daniel S. Dearing, Tallahassee, 1976-78; dist. counsel Dept. Health and Rehab. Service, Tallahassee, 1978-79, gen. counsel, 1979-82; ptnr. Moyle, Flanigan, Katz, Fitzgerald & Sheehan, Tallahassee, 1982— . Mem. ABA, Nat. Health Lawyers Assn., Am. Assn. Hosp. Attys. Democrat. Administrative and regulatory, Health. Home: 330 N 12th St Quincy FL 32351-1575 Office: Moyle Flanigan Katz Fitzgerald & Sheehan 118 N Gadsden St Tallahassee FL 32301-1508

STINSON, STEVEN ARTHUR, lawyer; b. Rochester, Ind., Dec. 14, 1946; s. Dean King and Lavonna Jeannette (Bailey) S.; m. Sherry Elizabeth Overton, Mar. 23, 1968; children: Nathaniel Overton, Stephanie Noelle. BA, Vanderbilt U., 1969, JD, 1972; MALS, U. Mich., 1977; LLM in Air and Space Law, McGill U., 1982. Bar: Ind. 1972, Fla. 1972, Tenn. 1995, U.S. Dist. Ct. (so. dist.) Fla. 1979, U.S. Dist. Ct. (mid. dist.) Fla. 1982, U.S. Dist. Ct. (mid. dist.) Tenn. 1995, U.S. Ct. Appeals (5th and 11th cirs.) 1981, U.S. Ct. Appeals (6t cir.) 1995, U.S. Ct. Mil. Appeals 1991, U.S. Supreme Ct. 1976. Sole practice, Rochester, 1973-76; prosecutor 41st Jud. Cir., 1975-76; assoc. Walton, Lantaff, Schroeder & Carson, West Palm Beach, Fla., 1985-86; mem. Jordan & Stinson, P.A., 1986-91, Davis, Colbath, Isaacs & Stinson P.A., West Palm Beach, 1992; assoc. Metzger, Sonnenborn & Rutter, P.A., 1992-94; sole practice Murfreesboro, Tenn., 1995-2000; of counsel Gunster, Yoakley & Stewart, P.A., West Palm Beach, 2000—. Contbr. articles to profl. publs. Legal Counsel, bd. dirs. Palm Beach County Republican Exec. Com., 1984-88, 93-94; bd. dirs. United Way Palm Beach Conty, Inc., 1987-94, Legal Aid Soc. Palm Beach County, 1989-94, Leadership Palm Beach County; pres. Palm Beach Nat. Civic Assn., Lake Worth, Fla., 1987-88; alt. del. Rep. Nat. Conv., 1984. Lt. col. USAR, ret. Named Jaycee of Yr., Rochester Jaycees, 1973. Mem. ABA, Fla. Bar, Palm Beach County Bar Assn. (pres. 1989-90, pres. young lawyers sect. 1983-84), bd. dirs. 1984-86, treas., 1986-87, sec. 1987-88, pres. 1989-90), Tenn. Bar Assn., Rutherford County Bar Assn. (treas. 1997, sec. 1998, v.p. 1999, pres. 2000), Soc. Chartered Property and Casualty Underwriters (sec. Gold Coast chpt. 1991-92, v.p. 1992-93, pres. 1993-94, sec. Mid-Tenn. chpt. 1998-99, treas. 1999-2000), Masons, Shriners, Elks, Moose, Kiwanis (bd. dirs. West Palm Beach 1981-83, lt. gov. Div. 1 East 1999-2000). Federal civil litigation, General civil litigation, State civil litigation. Office: Gunster Yoakley & Stewart 777 S Flagler Dr Ste 500 E West Palm Beach FL 33401-6194 E-mail: sstinson@gunster.com

STITH, JOHN STEPHEN, lawyer; b. Cin., Apr. 15, 1939; s. David Clyde and Dorothy Mae S.; m. Carolyn Liles, June 24, 1961; children: Stephen Liles, Laura Elizabeth, Sarah Anne. AB cum laude, Princeton U., 1961; JD summa cum laude, U. Cin., 1964. Bar: Ohio 1964. Assoc. Frost & Jacobs, Cin., 1964-70, ptnr., 1970-2000; mem. Frost Brown Todd LLC, 2000—. Instr. U. Cin. Coll. Law, Chase Coll. Law, No. Ky.; mem. com. on professionalism Supreme Ct. Ohio, 1993-95, 97—, chmn., 1999—. Trustee Cin. Mus. Natural History, 1980-89, 99-2001; bd. dirs. Dan Beard coun. Boy Scouts Am., 1982—; bd. dirs. Greater Cin. Found., 1996—, chmn., 2001—. Recipient William A. Mitchell award Community Chest Cin., 1980. Mem. ABA, Ohio State Bar Assn. (constl. rev. com.), Ohio Met. Bar Assns. (pres.), Cin. Bar Assn. (pres.), Greater Cin. C. of C. (gen. counsel). Presbyterian. Clubs: Cin. Country, Queen City (Cin.); Queen City Anglers. General corporate, Private international, Securities. Office: Frost Brown Todd 2200 PNC Ctr 201 E 5th St Ste 2500 Cincinnati OH 45202-4182 E-mail: jsstith@fuse.net, jstith@fbtlaw.com

STITH, LAURA DENVIR, judge; b. St. Louis, Oct. 30, 1953; BA magna cum laude, Tufts U., 1975; JD magna cum laude, Georgetown U., 1978. Law clk. to Hon. Robert E. Seiler, Mo. Supreme Ct., 1978—79; assoc. Shook, Hardy & Bacon, Kansas City, Mo., 1979—84, ptnr., 1984—94; judge. Mo. Ct. Appeals (we. dist.), 1994—2001; judge Supreme Ct. Mo., 2001—. Office: PO Box 150 Jefferson City MO 65102*

STOCK, STUART CHASE, lawyer; b. St. Louis, July 19, 1946; s. Sheldon Harry and Muriel Cecile (Lovejoy) S.; m. Judith Ann Stewart, July 18, 1970; 1 child, Frederick Chase. BS with highest distinction, Purdue U., 1968; JD magna cum laude, Harvard U., 1971. Bar: Mo. 1971, Ind. 1973, D.C. 1974. Law clk. to Chief Judge Henry J. Friendly U.S. Ct. Appeals 2d cir., New York, 1971-72; law clk. to Justice Thurgood Marshall U.S. Supreme Ct., Washington, 1972-73; assoc. Covington & Burling, 1974-78, ptnr., 1978—. Lectr. law U. Va., Charlottesville, 1987-90. Mem. Am. Law Inst. Antitrust, Banking, Mergers and acquisitions. Office: Covington & Burling PO Box 7566 1201 Pennsylvania Ave NW Washington DC 20044

STOCKARD, JANET LOUISE, lawyer; b. Beaumont, Tex., July 22, 1948; d. Louise (Land) S. BS with honors, U. Tex., 1970, JD, 1973. Bar: Tex. 1973. Pvt. practice, Austin, Tex., 1973—. Vol. dep. registrar for voter registration Lake Travis Elem. Sch.; supporter Women's Advocacy Project, Rape Crisis Center; mem. City of Austin Parks and Recreation Bd., 1977-79; adv. com. mem. Lake Travis, 1996-97. Named one of Most Noteworthy Austinites of Yr., Austin Homes and Gardens mag., 1983, Best Atty., '96, Austin Chronicle Readers. Roman Catholic. Criminal.

STOCKBURGER, JEAN DAWSON, lawyer; b. Scottsboro, Ala., Feb. 4, 1936; d. Joseph Mathis Scott and Mary Frances (Alley) Dawson; m. John Calvin Stockburger, Mar. 23, 1963; children: John Scott, Mary Staci, Christopher Sean. Student, Gulf Park Coll., 1954-55; BA, Auburn U., 1958; M in Social Work, Tulane U., 1962; JD, U. Ark., Little Rock, 1979. Bar: Ark. 1979, U.S. Dist. Ct. (ea. dist.) Ark. 1980. Assoc. Mitchell, Williams, Selig, Gates & Woodyard and predecessor, Little Rock, 1979-85, ptnr., 1985-94, of counsel, 1994—. Bd. dirs., sec. Cen. Ark. Estate Planning Council, Little Rock, 1984-85, 2d v.p., 1985-86; pres. Cen. Ark. Estate Council, 1987-88. Assoc. editor U. Ark. Law Rev., 1978-79. Bd. dirs. Sr. Citizens Activities Today, Little Rock, 1983-88, treas., 1986-88; bd. dirs. Vol. Orgn. for Ctrl. Ark. Legal Svcs., 1986-91, sec., 1987-88, chmn., 1989-91, H.I.R.E. Inc., 1994—; sec. Little Rock Cmty. Mental Health Ctr., 1994-96, v.p., 1996-99, pres., 1999—. Mem. ABA, Ark. Bar Assn. (chmn. probate and trust law sect. 1986-88), Pulaski County Bar Assn. (bd. dirs. 1994-97), Am. Coll. Trust and Estate Counsel. Democrat. Methodist. Estate planning, Probate. Office: Mitchell Williams Selig Gates & Woodyard 425 W Capitol Ave Ste 1800 Little Rock AR 72201-3525

STOCKMEYER, NORMAN OTTO, JR. law educator, consultant; b. Detroit, May 24, 1938; s. Norman O. and Lillian R. (Hitchman) S.; m. Marcia E. Rudman, Oct. 1, 1966; children: Claire, Kathleen, Mary Frances. AB, Obelin Coll., 1960; JD, U. Mich., 1963. Bar: MIch. 1963, U.S. Ct. Appeals (6th cir.) 1964, U.S. Supreme Ct. 1974. Legis. grad. fellow Mich. State U., 1963; legal counsel Senate Judiciary Com., Mich. Legislature, 1964; law clk. Mich. Ct. Appeals, 1965, commr., 1966-68, rsch. dir., 1969-76; assoc. prof. law Thomas M. Cooley Law Sch., 1977-78, prof., 1978—. Vis. prof. Mercer U. Sch. Law, 1986, Calif. Western Sch. Law, 1993; lectr. Mich. Judicial Inst., 1995. Editor Mich. Law of Damages, 1989; contbr. numerous articles to state and nat. legal jours. Named one of 88 Greats, Lansing State Jour., 1988. Fellow Am. Bar Found. (life); mem. ABA (chmn. Mich. membership 1972-73, ho. of dels. 1988-92, editl. bd. Compleat Lawyer 1990-99), Nat. Conf. Bar Founds. (trustee 1985-90, sec. 1988-89), Mich. State Bar Found. (pres. 1982-85, trustee 1971-92), State Bar Mich. (chmn. Young Lawyers sect. 1971-72, rep. assembly 1972-79, bd. commrs. 1985-93), Ingham County Bar Assn. (bd. dirs. 1981-85), Mich. Assn. Professions (bd. dirs. 1981-84, Profl. of Yr. 1988), Thomas M. Cooley Legal Authors Soc. (pres. 1982-83), Scribes (bd. dirs. 1994—), Delta Theta Phi (dean Christiancy Senate 1962, Outstanding Prof. 1984). Address: PO Box 13038 Lansing MI 48901-3038 E-mail: stockmen@cooley.edu

STOCKSTILL, CHARLES JAMES, lawyer, engineer; b. Bogalusa, La., Aug. 5, 1929; s. Charles Thomas And Eleanor Estelle (Foxworth) S.; m. Lois Elaine Hendrickson, May 15, 1973; 1 child, James Thomas. B.S.M.E., La. State U., 1954; J.D., St. Mary's U., 1968; LL.M. in Internat. Law, NYU, 1972. Bar: Tex. 1968, D.C. 1972, Va. 1981. Commd. 2d lt. U.S. Air Force, 1952, advanced through grades to capt., 1964; outside plant engr. So. Bell Telephone Co., Lake Charles, La., 1955-59; mech. engr. San Antonio Air Material Area, 1964-69; commd. maj. U.S. Army, 1969, advanced through grades to lt. col., 1978; judge adv. 1969-81; ret. 1981; contract adminstr. Washington Met. Area Transit Authority, 1981-82; adminstr. test and evaluation U.S. Navy, Arlington, Va., 1982— . Fellow AIAA (assoc.); mem. Inter-Am. Bar Assn., Am. Soc. Internat. Law, Tex. Bar Assn., Va. Bar Assn., D.C. Bar Assn. Democrat. Methodist. Lodges: Masons, Shriners. Home: 604 Kearney Ct SW Vienna VA 22180-6426

STODDARD, GLENN MCDONALD, lawyer; b. Washington, Feb. 18, 1958; s. Charles Hatch and Patricia (Coulter) S.; m. Sharon Lynn Stake, Aug. 22, 1981; children: Patrick M., Chloe F. BS, U. Wis., Stevens Point, 1980; MS, U. Wis., Madison, 1984, JD, 1994. Bar: Wis. 1995, U.S. Dist. Ct. (ea. and we. dists.) Wis. 1995. Assoc. code adminstr. Washburn County, Shell Lake, Wis., 1980-81; assoc. planner Manitowoc County, 1981-82; legis. aide Wis. Legis., Madison, 1983-85; asst. dir. Gov.'s Commn. on Agr., 1985; exec. dir. Wis. Land Cons. Assn., 1985-89; dir. govt. affairs Wis. Farmers Union, Chippewa Falls, 1989-92; law clk. U. Wis. Legal Asst. Program, Madison, summer 1993, Wis. Dept. Justice, Madison, summer 1994; ptnr./shareholder Garvey & Stoddard, S.C., 1995-99. Author: Essentials of Forestry, 4th edit., 1987. Chmn. Wis. Environ. Decade, Inc., Madison, 1991-92. Named Outstanding Citizen Adv., Ctr. for Pub. Rep., Madison, 1991. Mem. ATLA, ABA, State Bar Wis., Wis. Acad. Trial Lawyers. Avocations: outdoor recreation, karate, Tai Chi, reading. General civil litigation, Environmental, Labor. Office: Garvey & Stoddard SC 634 W Main St Ste 101 Madison WI 53703-2687

STOFFREGEN, PHILIP EUGENE, lawyer; b. Greeley, Colo., Dec. 10, 1947; s. Jack Elwin and Betty Jean (Bowman) S.; m. Margaret Ann Snyder, Feb. 2, 1969; 1 child. BA, U. Iowa, 1969, MS, 1970, MA, 1972, JD, 1977. Bar: Iowa 1977, U.S. Dist. Ct. (so. and no. dists.) Iowa 1977, U.S. Ct. Appeals (8th cir.) 1978, D.C. Appeals 1980, U.S. Supreme Ct. 1981. Assoc. Belin, Harris, Helmick & Heartney, Des Moines, 1977-81, ptnr., 1981-82; gen. counsel Iowa Commerce Commn., Des Moines, 1983-85; ptnr. Brick, Seckington, Bowers, Swartz & Gentry, Des Moines, 1985-88, Dickinson, Mackaman, Tyler & Hagen, 1988—; asst. prof. indsl. engring. Iowa State U., 1982-83. Author: Telecom. Deregulation: A State-by-State Analysis of Legislation, 1988, 89, 90. Bd. dirs. Regional Health Outreach Enterprises and Regional Health Svcs., 1984—, chmn. 1992—. Mem. Order of Coif. Communications, Public utilities, FERC practice. Home: 4150 Greenwood Dr Des Moines IA 50312-2826 Office: Dickinson Makaman Tyler & Hagen 1600 Hub Tower Des Moines IA 50309-3944 E-mail: pstoffre@dickinsonlaw.com

STOHR, DONALD J. federal judge; b. Sedalia, Mo., Mar. 9, 1934; s. Julius Leo and Margaret Elizabeth (McGaw) S.; m. Mary Ann Kuhlman, July 31, 1957 children: Elizabeth M., Anne M., Jane C., Sara M., Ellen R. BS, St. Louis U., 1956, JD, 1958. Bar: Mo. 1958, U.S. Dist. Ct. (ea. dist.) Mo. 1958, U.S. Ct. Appeals (8th cir.) 1966, U.S. Supreme Ct. 1969. Assoc. Hocker Goodwin & MacGreevy, St. Louis, 1958-63, 66-69; asst. counselor St. Louis County, 1963-65, counselor, 1965-66; U.S. atty. Ea. Dist. Mo., St. Louis, 1973-76; ptnr. Thompson & Mitchell, 1969-73, 76-92; judge U.S. Dist. Ct. (ea. dist.) Mo., 1992—. Mem. ABA, Mo. Bar Assn., Am. Judicature Soc., St. Louis Met. Bar Assn. Office: US Court & Custom House 1114 Market St Rm 813 Saint Louis MO 63101-2034

STOKES, ARCH YOW, lawyer, writer; b. Atlanta, Sept. 2, 1946; s. Mack B. and Rose Stokes; m. Maggie Mead; children: Jennifer Jean, Austin Christopher, Susannah Rose, Travis, Emmarose. BA, Emory U., 1967, JD, 1970. Bar: Ga. 1970, U.S. Dist. Ct. (no. dist.) Ga. 1970, U.S. Ct. Appeals (5th cir.) Ga. 1970, U.S. Ct. Mil. Appeals 1971, U.S. Ct. Appeals (9th cir.) Ga. 1980, (2d cir.) Ga. 1990, U.S. Supreme Ct. 1981, U.S. Dist. Ct. (no. dist.) Calif. 1981, U.S. Ct. Appeals (11th cir.) Calif. 1982, U.S. Ct. Appeals (7th cir.) Calif. 1986, U.S. Ct. Appeals (1st cir.) Calif. 1992, U.S. Ct. Appeals (8th cir.) Calif. 1991, U.S. Dist. Ct. (no. dist.) N.Y. 1991, U.S. Dist. Ct. (ea. dist.) Mich. 1986. Ptnr. Stokes Lazarus & Carmichael, Atlanta, 1972-92, Stokes & Murphy, Atlanta, 1992—, San Diego, Pitts., Dallas, 1992—, Las Vegas. Author: The Wage & Hour Handbook, 1978, rev. edit., 2000, The Equal Employment Opportunity Handbook, 1979, The Collective Bargaining Handbook, 1981. Founding mem. adv. bd. William F. Harrah Hotel Coll., U. Nev., Las Vegas, also vis. spkr.; vis. spkr. Cornell U., Johnson and Wales U., U. Houston, Ga. State U. Recipient Hal Holbrook award Internat. Platform Assn., 1990. Mem. ABA, ATLA, Union Internat. des Avocats, Internat. Soc. Hospitality Cons., Confrérie de la Chaîne des Rôtissuers, Am. Hotel and Motel Assn. General civil litigation, Labor. Office: Stokes & Murphy 3593 Hemphill St College Park GA 30337-0468

STOKES, JAMES CHRISTOPHER, lawyer; b. Orange, N.J., Mar. 19, 1944; s. James Christopher and Margaret Mary (Groome) S.; m. Eileen Marie Brosnan, Sept. 7, 1968; children: Erin Margaret, Michael Colin, Courtney Dorothy. AB, Holy Cross Coll., 1966; JD, Boston Coll., 1975. Bar: Hawaii 1975, U.S. Ct. Appeals (1st and 9th cirs.) 1976, Mass. 1977, U.S. Ct. Internat. Trade 1988. Officer USMC, 1966-72; assoc. Carlsmith, Carlsmith, Wichman & Case, Honolulu, 1975-76, Bingham, Dana & Gould (now Bingham Dana LLP), Boston, 1976-82, ptnr. London, 1980-84, Boston, 1982—. Contbr. articles to profl. jours. Active personnel bd. Town of Wellesley, Mass., 1984-89, chmn. bd., 1988-89, town moderator, 1992-97. Capt. USMC, 1966-72, Vietnam. Mem. Hawaii Bar Assn., Mass. Bar Assn., Internat. Bar Assn., Boston Bar Assn., Traveller's Club (London), Union Club (Boston), Wellesley Club (bd. dirs.), German-Am. Bus. Club (Boston) (bd. dirs.). Roman Catholic. General corporate, Finance, Private international. Office: Bingham Dana LLP 150 Federal St Boston MA 02110-1713 E-mail: jcstokes@bingham.com

STOKES, JAMES SEWELL, lawyer; b. Englewood, N.J., Jan. 24, 1944; s. James Sewell III and Doris Mackey (Smith) S.; m. Esther Moger, Aug. 19, 1967; children: Jessica Neale, Elizabeth Sewell BA, Davidson (N.C.) Coll., 1966; LLB, Yale U., 1969. Bar: Ga. 1969. Asst. to gen. counsel Office Gen. Counsel of the Army, Washington, 1969-72; assoc. Alston, Miller & Gaines, Atlanta, 1972-77; ptnr. Alston & Bird (previously Alston, Miller & Gaines), 1977—, chmn. environ. group, 1987-96, 98—, chmn. bus. devel. com., 1983-85, 93-94, 96—; mem. ptnr.'s com. Alston & Bird, 1995-98; chmn., 1998. Speaker on environ. matters to various seminars and meetings; mem. Gov.'s Environ. Adv. Coun., 1991—, chmn., 1997-99; chmn. Gov.'s Conf. on Pollution Prevention and the Environment, 1997. Contbr. articles to profl. jours. Co-chmn. Spotlight on Ga. Artists V, 1986; mem. City of Atlanta Zoning Rev. Bd., 1978-85, chmn., 1984-85; bd. dirs. Brookwood Hills Civic Assn., 1975-77, pres., 1977; bd. dirs. Nexus Contemporary Arts Ctr., Atlanta, 1987-92, vice chmn. capital campaign, 1989, chmn. nominating com., 1988, chmn. fundraising com., 1987-88; bd. dirs. Butler St. YMCA N.W. br., 1973-75, Dynamo Swim Club, 1988-91, Arts Festival Atlanta, 1994-98; trustee Inst. Continuing Legal Edn., Athens, 1980-81, Trinity Sch., Atlanta, 1988, 97—, Charles Loridans Found., 1994—; mem. session Trinity Presbyn. Ch., 1986-89, 97—, clk. of session, 1988-89, chmn. cmty. concerns com., 1987-88, chmn. pers. com., 1989-90, 99—, chmn. assoc. pastor search com., 1991-92; bd. dirs. The Hambidge Ctr., 2000—; bd. dirs. Park Pride, 1992; bd. dirs. Ga. C. of C., 1998—, chmn. environ. com., 1987-92, environ. legal counsel, 1981-87; mem. spl. program Leadership Atlanta, 1979-80, Leadership Ga., 1985; mem. Ga. bd. advisors Trust for Pub. Land, 1990-95. Capt. U.S. Army, 1969-72. Decorated D.S.M.; recipient Spl. award Atlanta chpt. AIA, 1988, Mayor Andrew Young, 1985. Mem. ABA (natural resources sect.), State Bar Ga. (chmn. environ. law sect. 1979-82), Atlanta Bar Assn., City of Atlanta Hist. Preservation (policy steering com. 1989), Ga. C. of C. (bd. dirs. 1998—), Atlanta C. of C. (water resources task force 1982-87, solid waste task force 1989, air quality task force 1993-97, environ. affairs com. 1998—), Ga. Indsl. Developers Assn. (hazardous waste com. 1983-84), Phi Beta Kappa, Omicron Delta Kappa. Avocations: swimming, bird watching, community activities. Environmental, Land use and zoning (including planning). Home: 129 Palisades Rd NE Atlanta GA 30309-1532 Office: Alston & Bird One Atlantic Ctr 1201 W Peachtree St LLP Atlanta GA 30309-3424

STOKES, SIMON JEREMY, lawyer; b. Blackpool, England; m. Sarah-Lee Burrows, 1993; 1 child, Hannah. BA, Oxford U., England, 1986; MS, MIT, 1988; LLM, U. Wales, Cardiff, 1997; MA, Oxford U., 1990. Clk. Bristows Cooke & Carpmael, London, England, 1990-92; asst. solicitor McKenna & Co., 1992-94, Manches & Co., Oxford, England, 1994-96; assoc. Allen & Overy, London, 1996-99; ptnr. Tarlo Lyons, 1999—. Club counsel MIT Club Gt. Brit., London, 2000. Contbr. articles to profl. jours. Tech. & Policy Program scholar, MIT, 1986. Mem. City London Solicitors, Freeman. Anglican. Avocations: art, architecture. Communications, Computer, Intellectual property. Office: Tarlo Lyons Solicitors 33 St Johns Ln London EC1M 4DB England Fax: 020 7 814 9421. E-mail: simon.stokes@tarlolyons.com

STOKHOLM, JON ULRIK, lawyer; b. Frederiksberg, Denmark, Apr. 23, 1951; s. Toke and Birgit (Jespersen) Stokholm; m. Birte Jorgensen. Law degree, U. Copenhagen, 1975; postgrad., Stanford U., 1991. Bar: Supreme Ct. Denmark 1983. Asst. atty., assoc. Kammeradvokaturen, Copenhagen, Denmark, 1975-80; assoc. Niels Th. Kjøbye & Co., Denmark, 1980-83; ptnr., 1984-85, Poulsen, Westergaard, Cadovius, Stokholm, 1985-90, Lind & Cadovius, Copenhagen, Denmark, 1990—. Chmn. Adv. Com. on Tax Matters, 1989-97. Author: The Danish Stamp Act, 1994. Mem. Danish Bar and Law Soc. (mem. coun. 1991-97, pres. 1999—). Administrative and regulatory, Admiralty, Contracts commercial. Home: Soløsevej 17 DK-2820 Gentofte Denmark Office: Lind & Cadovius Østergade 38 DK-1100 Copenhagen K Denmark Home Fax: 45 39 65 74 30; Office Fax: 45 33 33 81 01. E-mail: js@lindcad.dk

STOKKE, DIANE REES, lawyer; b. Kansas City, Mo., Jan. 29, 1951; d. William James and Marybeth (Smith) Rees; m. Larry Ernst Stokke, June 9, 1973; children: Michelle, Megan, Carly. AB magna cum laude, Gonzaga U., 1972; JD with high honors, U. Wash., 1976. Bar: Wash. 1976, U.S. Dist. Ct. (ea. dist.) Wash. 1976, U.S. Dist. Ct. (we. dist.) Wash. 1976, U.S. Ct. Appeals (9th cir.) 1980. Assoc. Preston, Thorgrimson, Ellis & Holman, Seattle, 1976-83; ptnr. Preston, Gates & Ellis LLP, 1983—. Atty. Seattle Ctr. Found., 1977-83. Trustee Seattle Infant Devel. Ctr., 1984-86, Fremont Pub. Assn., 1994-2001. Gonzaga U. scholar, 1968. Mem. ABA, Wash. State Bar Assn. (spl. dist. counsel 1985-88), Seattle-King County Bar Assn., Wash. Women Lawyers, Order of Coif. Roman Catholic. Contracts commercial, General corporate, Real property. Office: Preston Gates & Ellis LLP 5000 Columbia Seafirst Ctr 701 5th Ave Ste 5000 Seattle WA 98104-7078 E-mail: dianes@prestongates.com

STOLL, NEAL RICHARD, lawyer; b. Phila., Nov. 7, 1948; s. Mervin Stoll and Goldie Louise (Serody) Stoll Wilf; m. Linda G. Seligman, May 25, 1972; children: Meredith Anne, Alexis Blythe. BA in History with distinction, Pa. State U., 1970; JD, Fordham U., 1973. Bar: N.Y. 1974, U.S. Dist. Ct. (ea. dist.) N.Y. 1974, U.S. Ct. Appeals (2d cir.) 1974, U.S. Ct. Appeals (11th cir.) 1982, U.S. Dist. Ct. (ea. dist.) Mich. 1983, U.S. Dist. Ct. (so. dist.) N.Y. 1974, U.S. Supreme Ct. 1986. Assoc. Skadden, Arps, Slate, Meagher & Flom, LLP, N.Y.C., 1973-81, mem., 1981—. Lectr. Practicing Law-Inst., N.Y.C. Author: (with others) Aquisitions Under the Hart Scott Rodino Antitrust Improvements Act, 1980; contbr. articles to profl. pubs. Mem. Assn. Bar City of N.Y. (mem. trade regulation com. 1983-85), ABA, N.Y. State Bar Assn. Democrat. Antitrust, Federal civil litigation. Office: Skadden Arps Slate Four Times Sq New York NY 10036-6522 E-mail: nstoll@skadden.com

STOLL, RICHARD G(ILES), lawyer; b. Phila., Oct. 2, 1946; s. Richard Giles and Mary Margaret (Zeigler) S.; m. Susan Jane Nicewonger, June 15, 1968; children: Richard Giles III, Christian Hayes. BA magna cum laude, Westminster Coll., 1968; JD, Georgetown U., 1971. Bar: D.C. 1971, U.S. Dist. Ct. D.C. 1971, U.S. Ct. Appeals D.C. 1971, U.S. Ct. Appeals (4th cir.) 1977. Assoc. Arent, Fox, Kintner, Plotkin & Kahn, Washington, 1971-73; atty. Office of Gen. Counsel EPA, 1973-77, asst. gen. counsel, 1977-81; dep. gen. counsel Chem. Mfrs. Assn., 1981-84; ptnr. Freedman, Levy, Kroll & Simonds, 1984-2001, Foley & Lardner, Washington, 2001—. Instr. environ. law and policy U. Va., Charlottesville, 1981-90. Co-author: Handbook on Environmental Law, 1987, 88, 89, 91, Practical Guide to Environment Law, 1987; contbr. articles to profl. jours.; moderator, panelist legal ednl. TV broadcasts and tapes ABA and Am. Law Inst. Elder Georgetown Presbyn. Ch. Capt., USAR, 1968-76. Recipient Alumni Achievement award Westminster Coll., 1998. Mem. ABA (sect. environment, energy and resources; chmn. water quality com. 1980-82, hazardous waste com. 1983-85, coun. mem. 1985-88, sect. chmn. 1990-91), Washington Golf and Country Club, Cosmos Club. Avocations: piano, golf, music composition. Administrative and regulatory, Environmental. Office: Foley & Lardner 3000 K St NW Washington DC 20007 E-mail: rstoll@foleylaw.com

STOLPMAN, THOMAS GERARD, lawyer; b. Cleve., June 2, 1949; s. Joseph Eugene and Katherine Ann (Berry) S.; m. Marilyn Heise, Aug. 17, 1974; children: Jennifer, Peter. BA, UCLA, 1972; JD, Los Angeles, 1976. Bar: Calif. 1976, U.S. Dist. Ct. (ctrl. dist.) Calif. 1976, U.S. Dist. Ct (ea. dist.) Calif. 1985, U.S. Dist. Ct. (so. dist.) Calif. 1995, U.S. Ct. Appeals (9th cir.) 1993, U.S. Supreme Ct. 1994. Ptnr. Stolpman Krissman Elber & Silver LLP, Long Beach, Calif., 1976—. Editor The Forum, 1978-84; editor-in-chief The Advocate, 1984-87; contbr. articles to profl. jours. Bd. dirs. Miraleste Recreation and Park Dist., Rancho Palos Verdes, Calif., 1982-96. Named Trial Lawyer of Yr. So. Calif., Verdictum Juris, 1984. Fellow Am. Coll. Trial Lawyers, Internat. Acad. Trial Lawyers; mem. ATLA, State Bar of Calif. (bd. govs. 1993-97, chair com. client rels. and assistance 1994-95, v.p. 1995-96, pres. 1996-97, chmn. com. on courts and legis. 1995-96), L.A. Trial Lawyers Assn. (bd. govs. 1979-93, pres. 1989), Calif. Trial Lawyers Assn. (bd. govs. 1987-90, exec. com. 1989-90, 2001, fin. sec. 2001), L.A. County Bar Assn. (bd. trustees 1986-87, exec. com. litigation sect. 1990-94), Am. Bd. Trial Advocates, Nat. Bd. Trial Advocacy (cert.), South Bar Bar Assn., Long Beach Bar Assn. Democrat. Roman Catholic. Admiralty, Federal civil litigation, Personal injury. Office: Stoplman Krissman Elber & Silver LLP PO Box 22609 111 W Ocean Blvd Fl 19 Long Beach CA 90801-5609 E-mail: stolpman@stolpman.com

STOLZBERG, MICHAEL MEYER, lawyer; b. N.Y.C., Jan. 31, 1914; s. Max and Betty (Herzberg) S.; m. Maely Danielle, Apr. 12, 1942 (div. June 1946); m. Sylvia R. Robyns, Oct. 6, 1946; children— Karen G., Eric M. B.B.A., CCNY, 1936; LL.B., Columbia U., 1936. Bar: N.Y. 1936, Calif. 1946. Mem. firm Stolzberg & Keller, N.Y.C., 1937-42; referee Unemployment Ins. Appeals Bd., Los Angeles, 1946-49; judge Workers Compensation Appeals Bd., Los Angeles, 1949-67; mem. firm Stolzberg & Spencer, Los Angeles, 1967— ; of counsel Oliver, Sloan, Vargas, Lindvig & Matthew, Los Angeles, 1983— ; adj. prof. S.W. U. Law Sch., Los Angeles, 1950-58. Mem. Los Angeles County Democratic Central Com., 1958-66. Served to capt. U.S. Army, 1942-46, CBI. Mem. Calif. Applicants Attys. Assn., Pasadena Bar Assn., Los Angeles County Bar Assn. Democrat. Workers' compensation. Home: 1540 Arroyo View Dr Pasadena CA 91103-1903

STONE, ALAN ABRAHAM, law and psychiatry educator, psychiatrist; b. 1929; AB, Harvard U., 1950; MD, Yale U., 1955. Lectr. Harvard U., 1966-72, asst. prof. psychiatry, 1966-69, assoc. prof., 1969-72, prof. law, psychiatry, 1972—, Touroff-Glueck prof. law, psychiatry, 1982—. Adv. com. project mentally Ill Am. Bar Found., 1967-71; com. revision criminal code Mass. Gov., 1968-72; com. menhtally disabled ABA, 1973-77; chmn. Mass. Com. Psychosurgery, 1974-75; Tanner lectr. Stanford U., 1982; mem. Justice Panel on Waco, 1993. Author: (with Onque) Longitudinal Studies of Child Behavior, 1961, Mental Health and Law: A System in Transition, 1975, Law, Psychiatry and Morality: Essays and Analysis, 1984; editor: (with Sue Stone) Abnormal Personality Through Literature, 1966. Capt. M.C., U.S. Army, 1959-61. Recipient Manfred S. Guttmacher award, Isaac Ray award, 1982; Ctr. Advanced Study Behavioral Sci. fellow Stanford U., 1980-81. Mem. Am. Psychiat. Assn. (trustee, v.p., pres., chmn. com. jud. action 1974-79), Group Advancement Psychiatry. Office: Harvard U Law Sch 1575 Massachusetts Ave Cambridge MA 02138-2801

STONE, ANDREW GROVER, lawyer; b. L.A., Oct. 2, 1942; s. Frank B. and Meryl (Pickering) S.; divorced; 1 child, John Blair. BA, Yale U., 1965; JD, U. Mich., 1969. Bar: D.C. 1970, U.S. Dist. Ct. D.C. 1970, U.S. Ct. Appeals (D.C. cir.) 1972, Mass. 1981. Assoc. Rogers & Wells, Washington, 1969-71; atty. Bur. Competition, FTC, 1971-80; antitrust counsel Digital Equipment Corp., Maynard, Mass., 1980-83, mgr. N.E. law group, 1983-86, mgr. headquarters sales law group, 1986-88; asst. general counsel U.S. (acting), 1987, 88; corp counsel Washington, 1988-90; corp. counsel, pub. sect. mktg. Thinking Machines Corp., Cambridge, Mass., 1990-91, corp. counsel, 1992-95; pvt. practice on-site legal svcs. Marblehead, 1995—. Corp. mem. Tenacre Country Day Sch., Wellesley, Mass., 1981-88. Mem. ABA (bus. law sect.), Mass. Bar Assn. (internat. law steering com. 1993-94), Boston Bar Assn. (membership com. 1998-2000, chair corp. counsel com. 1995-98, gen. counsel forum 1995—), Am. Arbitration Assn. (comml. arbitrator), New Eng. Corp. Counsel Assn., Assn. Ind. Gen. Counsel. Contracts commercial, Computer, Government contracts and claims.

STONE, DAVID PHILIP, lawyer; b. N.Y.C., Sept. 11, 1944; s. Robert and Laura Stone; m. Arlene R. Stone, June 11, 1966; children: Aaron J., Rachel E. AB, Columbia U., 1967; JD, Harvard U., 1970. Bar: N.Y. 1971. Assoc. Cahill, Gordon & Reindel, N.Y.C., 1970-74, Baer & McGoldrick, N.Y.C., 1974-76, Weil, Gotshal & Manges, L.L.P., N.Y.C., 1976-79, ptnr., 1979—. Private international, Mergers and acquisitions, Securities. Office: Weil Gotshal & Manges LLP 767 5th Ave Fl Concl New York NY 10153-0119

STONE, EDWARD HERMAN, lawyer; b. July 20, 1939; s. Sidney and Ruth Stone; m. Pamela G. Gray (dec. 1990); children: Andrew, Matthew; m. Elaine Ornitz, Dec. 22, 1995. BS in Acctg., U. Ill., 1961; JD, John Marshall Law Sch., 1967. Bar: Ill. 1967, Calif. 1970; cert. specialist Calif. probate, estate planning, and trust law. With IRS, 1963-71; assoc. Eilers, Baranger, Myers & Smith, 1971-72; pvt. practice Newport Beach, Calif., 1972-2001; mem. Davis, Samuelson, Goldberg & Blakely (formerly Cohen, Stokke & Davis), Santa Ana, 1984-88; pvt. practice, 1988-89; ptnr. Edward H. Stone A Law Corp., 1990—. Instr. income and estate taxes Western States U. Sch. Law, 1971-72, mem. CEB Joint Adv. Com., Estating Planning subcom.; judge pro tem, jud. arbitrator Orange County Superior Ct.; moderator, spkr. on probate and trust litigation, Orange county, 1999, 2001; mediator for IRS ADR for tax cases in appeals, 2000—; moderator, spkr. Calif. Trust Probat Litigation CEB, 1999-2001. Contbr. articles to profl. jours. Bd. dirs. Eastbluff Homeowners Comty. Assn., Newport Beach, 1980-82, pres., 1981-82; pres. Jewish Family Svcs. Orange County, 1975; v.p., bd. dirs. Orange County Jewish Fedn. of Orange County, 1985-88; bd. dirs. Heritage Points Orange County, 1992-95. Mem. Orange County Bar Assn. (vice-chmn. estate planning probate and trust law sect. 1976-77, chmn. sect. 1977-78, chairperson ADR com. 1996, instr. Probate Clinic 1980, spkr. in substansive law; dir. 1977-82, chmn. Profl. Ednl. Coun. 1980-82, past chmn. profl. edn. coun., chmn. Orange County Bar del. of real property and probate sect. for state bar conv. 1992—), Phi Alpha Delta (pres. alumni chpt. 1975-76). General corporate, Estate planning, Probate.

STONE, F. L. PETER, lawyer; b. Wilmington, Del., Feb. 24, 1935; s. Linton and Lorinda (Hamlin) S.; m. Therese Louise Hannon, Apr. 7, 1969; 1 child, Lisa Judith. AB, Dartmouth Coll, 1957; LLB, Harvard U., 1960. Bar: Del. Supreme Ct. 1960, U.S. Ct. Appeals (3d cir.) 1964, U.S. Supreme Ct. 1965, U.S. Ct. Appeals (fed. cir.) 1983. Assoc. Connolly, Bove & Lodge, Wilmington, 1960-64; dep. atty. gen. State of Del., 1965-66; atty. Del. Gen. Assembly, Dover, 1967-68; counsel Gov. Del., 1969; U.S. atty. Dist. of Del., Wilmington, 1969-72; ptnr. Connolly, Bove, Lodge, & Hutz, 1972-97; counsel Trzuskowski, Kipp, Kelleher & Pearce, 1997-98, 2001—; dep. atty. gen., counsel to ins. dept. State of Del., 1998-2001. Mem. Del. Agy. to Reduce Crime, 1969-72, Del. Organized Crime Commn., 1970-72, State Drug Abuse Coun., 1990-93, State Judicial Nominating Commn., 1991-93, State Coun. Corrections, 1992-99; co-founder, adj. prof. criminal justice progra, West Chester (Pa.) U., 1975-79; chmn. Gov.'s Harness Racing Investigation Com., 1977, Del. Jai Alai Commn., 1977-78, Del. Govs. Corrections Task Force, 1986-88. Contbr. articles to profl. jours. Chmn. UN Day, Del., 1989; mem. Del. Gov.'s Task Force on Prison Security, 1994—95; trustee Leukemia Soc. Am., N.Y.C., 1972—74, Marywood Coll., Scranton, Pa., 1974—79, Ursuline Acad., Wilmington, 1974—80; bd. dirs. Boys and Girls Club Del., 1997—, Seamen's Ctr., Port of Wilmington, 2001—; Rep. candidate for atty. gen. Del., 1990; mem. Rep. exec. com. Wilmington region, 1991—2000; chmn. re-election campaign Del. Ins. Commr., 1996. Mem. Port of Wilmington Maritime Soc. (bd. dirs., chair 1998-2000), Wilmington Country Club, Lincoln Club Del. (pres. 1994), Wilmington Rotary (bd. dirs. 1995-97), Nat. Assn. Former U.S. Attys. (bd. dirs. 1995-98). Roman Catholic. Avocations: hiking/mountaineering, tennis, golf, music. General civil litigation, General corporate, Administrative and regulatory. Office: Box 429 1020 N Bancroft Pky Wilmington DE 19899

STONE, GEOFFREY RICHARD, law educator, lawyer; b. Nov. 20, 1946; s. Robert R. and Shirley (Weliky) S.; m. Nancy Spector, Oct. 8, 1977; children: Julie, Mollie. BS, U. Pa., 1968; JD, U. Chgo., 1971. Bar: N.Y. 1972. Law clk. to Hon. J.S. Kelly Wright U.S. Ct. Appeals (D.C. cir.), 1971-72; law clk. to Hon. William J. Brennan, Jr. U.S. Supreme Ct., 1972-73; asst. prof. U. Chgo., 1973-77, assoc. prof., 1977-79, prof., 1979-84, Harry Kalven Jr. disting. svc. prof., 1984-93, dean Law Sch., 1987-93, provost, 1994—. Author: Constitutional Law, 1986, 4th edit., 2001, The Bill of Rights in the Modern State, 1992, The First Amendment, 1999, Eternally Vigilent: Free Speech in the Modern Era, 2001; editor The Supreme Ct. Rev., 1991—; contbr. articles to profl. jours. Bd. dirs. Ill. divsn. ACLU, 1978-84; bd. advisors Pub. Svc. Challenge, 1989; bd. govs. Argonne Nat. Lab., 1994—. Fellow AAAS; mem. Chgo. Coun. Lawyers (bd. govs. 1976-77), Assn. Am. Law Schs. (exec. com. 1990-93), Legal Aid Soc. (bd. dirs. 1988), Order of Coif. Office: U Chgo 5801 S Ellis Ave Chicago IL 60637-5418

STONE, KATHLEEN GALE, criminal justice educator, researcher, consultant; b. Birmingham, Eng., May 9, 1943; came to U.S., 1970; d. Eric Harold and Gertrude Alice (Taylor) Johnson; m. Christopher Stephen Lange, July 11, 1964 (div. Nov. 1971); 1 child, Tamara Alice Merry; m. Sheldon Leslie Stone, Nov. 24, 1971. children— Rosalinda Dawn, Adam Douglas. B.A. in Econs. 1st class with honors, U. Manchester (Eng.), 1965, M.A. in Econs. with distinction, 1967, Ph.D., 1976. Research asst. U. Manchester, 1969-70; instr. anthropology SUNY,-Geneseo, 1970-72; vis. lectr. George Peabody Coll., 1974-76; program coordinator women's studies Vanderbilt U., 1976-77; asst. prof. sociology Tenn. State U., 1979; asst. prof. Wells Coll., Aurora, N.Y., 1980-82; lectr. sociology Elmira Coll., N.Y., 1982— , asst. prof. criminal justice, 1982— . Vol., Tompkins County Info. and Referral, N.Y., 1982-83. Mem. Am. Anthrop. Assn., S.E. Women's Studies Assns. (conf. organizer), Acad. Criminal Justice Scis. Quaker. Office: Elmira Coll Dept Criminal Justice Elmira NY 14901

STONE, RICHARD JAMES, lawyer; b. Apr. 30, 1945; s. Milton M. and Ruth Jean (Manaster) S.; m. Lee Lawrence, Sept. 1, 1979; children: Robert Allyn, Katherine Jenney, Grant Lawrence. BA in Econs., U. Chgo., 1967; JD, UCLA, 1970. Bar: Calif. 1971, Oreg. 1994, D.C., 2000. Assoc. O'Melveny & Myers, L.A., 1971-77; dep. asst. gen. counsel U.S. Dept. Def., Washington, 1978-79; asst. to sec. U.S. Dept. Energy, 1979-80; counsel Sidley & Austin, L.A., 1981, ptnr., 1982-88; ptnr., head litigation dept. Milbank, Tweed, Hadley & McCloy, 1988-94; mng. ptnr. Zelle & Larson, LLP, 1994-97; counsel Ball Janik LLP, Portland, Oreg., 1998—. Gen. counsel and staff dir. Study of L.A. Civil Disturbance for Bd. Police Commrs., 1992; adj. prof. law Lewis and Clark Northwestern Sch. Law, 1998-99; lawyer rep. 9th Cir. Jud. Conf., 1998-99. Editor-in-chief: UCLA Law Rev., 1970. Mem. Pub. Sector Task Force, Calif., State Senate Select Com. on Long Range Policy Planning, 1985-86, U.S. del. Micronesian Polit. Status Negotiations, 1978-79; mem. adv. panel Coun. Energy Resource Tribes, 1981-85; mem. vestry St. Aidan's Episcopal Ch., 1990-93, 97-98, sr. warden, 1998; dir. Legal Aid Found. L.A., 1991-99, officer, 1994-98, pres., 1997-98; dir. Portland City United Soccer Club, 1999-2000. Recipient Amos Alonzo Stagg medal and Howell Murray Alumni medal U. Chgo., 1967; honoree Nat. Conf. Black Mayors, 1980; recipient spl. citation for outstanding performance Sec. Dept. Energy, 1981. Fellow Am. Bar Found.; mem. ABA, FBA, Calif. Bar Assn., Oreg. Bar Assn., L.A. County Bar Assn. (trustee 1986-88), Assn. Bus. Trial Lawyers, Multnomah County Bar Assn., Phi Gamma Delta. Antitrust, Federal civil litigation, State civil litigation. Home: 3675 NW Gordon St Portland OR 97210-1285 Office: Ball Janik LLP 101 SW Main St Portland OR 97204-3228 E-mail: rstone@bjllp.com

STONE, SAMUEL BECKNER, lawyer; b. Martinsville, Va., Feb. 4, 1934; s. Paul Raymond and Mildred (Beckner) S.; m. Shirley Ann Gregory, June 18, 1955; children: Paul Gregory, Daniel Taylor. BSEE, Va. Polytech. Inst. & State U., 1955; JD, George Wash. U., 1960. Bar: Md. 1960, Calif. 1963, Patent and Trademark Office. Patent examiner, 1955-58; patent adv. Naval Ordinance Lab., Silver Spring, Md., 1958-59; assoc. Thomas & Crickenberger, Washington, 1959-61, Beckman Instruments Inc., Fullerton, Calif., 1961-65, Lyon & Lyon, L.A., 1965-72, ptnr., 1972, mng. ptnr. Irvine, Calif., 1982-2000. Judge Disneyland Com. Svc. Awards, Anaheim, Calif., 1987. Mem. Orange County Bar Assn. (bd. dirs. 1988-91, travel seminar chair 1986-92), Orange County Patent Law Assn. (pres. 1987, bd. exec. com. 1987-90), Calif. Bar Assn. (intellectual property sect. bd. 1987-90), Am. Arbitration Assn. (intellectual property panel neutral arbitrators 1997-2000), Am. Electronics Assn. (lawyers com. 1988-99, co-chair 1996-97), Orange County Venture Group (dir. 1985-99, pres. 1996-97), Rams Booster Club (dir. 1984-90), Pacific Club (mem. legal adv. com., chair 1989-92, bd. dirs. 1999—). Republican. Avocations: tennis, water-skiing, music. Intellectual property, Patent, Trademark and copyright. Home: 1612 Antigua Way Newport Beach CA 92660-4344 Office: Lyon & Lyon 1900 Main St Fl 6 Irvine CA 92614-7317 E-mail: sbstone@lyonlyon.com

STONE, SHELDON, lawyer; b. Jersey City, June 16, 1947; s. Leonard and Claire (Orlean) S.; m. Esther Curland, Dec. 19, 1970; children: Lesley-Anne, Jaime. BA, Rutgers U., 1969; JD, Seton Hall U., 1972. Bar: N.J. 1972, U.S. Dist. Ct. N.J. 1972, N.Y. 1980. Ptnr. Stone & Stone, Teaneck, N.J., 1972—. Tchr. New Milford (N.J.) Bd. Edn., 1974-76; counsel, cons. Richard Nader Entertainment, Inc.; investigator Atty. Ethics Com., Bergen County, N.J., 1984; settlement referee Superior Ct., Bergen County, 1984-97; lectr. Eastern Bergen Multiple Listing System, Bergen County, periodically. Mem. ABA, N.J. Bar Assn., Bergen County Bar Assn., Major League Baseball Players Assn. (approved player rep.), Nat. Collegiate Athletic Assn. (approved player rep.). Lodge: Lions (v.p.). Contracts commercial, General corporate, Real property. Home: 135 Birchwood Rd Old Tappan NJ 07675-6810 Office: Stone & Stone 517 Cedar Ln Teaneck NJ 07666-1710

STONE, VICTOR J. law educator; b. Chgo., Mar. 11, 1921; s. Maurice Albert and Ida (Baskin) S.; m. Susan Abby Cane, July 14, 1951; children: Mary Jessica, Jennifer Abby, Andrew Hugh William. AB, Oberlin Coll., 1942; JD, Columbia U., 1948; LLD, Oberlin Coll., 1983. Bar: N.Y. 1949, Ill. 1950. Assoc. Columbia U., N.Y.C., 1948-49, Sonnenschein, Chgo., 1949-53; rsch. assoc. U. Chgo., 1953-55; asst. prof. law U. Ill., Champaign, 1955-57, assoc. prof. law, 1957-59, prof. law, 1959-91, prof. law emeritus, 1991—, assoc. v.p. acad. affairs, 1975-78. Mem. jud. adv. coun. State Ill., 1959-61; mem. com. jury instrns. Ill. Supreme Ct., 1963-79, reporter, 1973-79; mem. Ill. State Appellate Defender Commn., 1973-83, vice-chmn., 1973-77, 79-83; bd. dirs. Champaign County Ct.-Apptd. Spl. Advocate Program, 1995-99, pres., 1998-99. Co-editor: Ill. Pattern Jury Instructions, 1965, 71, 77; Civil Liberties and Civil Rights, 1977. Trustee Oberlin Coll., 1982-97, AAUP Found., 1983-90. Lt. USNR, 1942-46. Ford Found. fellow, 1962-63. Fellow Ill. Bar Found. (charter 1986—); mem. ABA, CASA (bd. dirs. 1994-98, pres. 1998-99), Ill. Bar Assn. (chmn. individual rights and responsibilities 1971-72, mem. coun. civil practice and procedure 1978-82), Chgo. Bar Assn., AAUP (gen. counsel 1978-80, pres. 1982-84 , pres. Ill. conf. 1968-70, pres. Ill. chpt. 1964-65, mem. coun. 1982-90), ACLU (bd. dirs. Ill. div. 1986-96, exec. com. 1991-96), Am. Bar Found. (life 1986), State Univs. Annitants Assn. (pres. 1994-95, mem. state exec. com. 1995-97). Office: U Ill Coll Law 504 E Pennsylvania Ave Champaign IL 61820-6909 E-mail: v-stone@uiuc.edu

STOOPS, DANIEL J. lawyer; b. Wichita, Kans., May 27, 1934; s. Elmer F. and Margaret J. (Pickrell) S.; m. Kathryn Ann Piepmeier, Aug. 28, 1954; children: Sharon, Janet. BA, Washburn U., 1956, JD, 1958. Bar: Kans. 1958, Ariz. 1959, U.S. Dist. Ct. Kans. 1958, U.S. Dist. Ct. Ariz. 1960, U.S. Ct. Appeals (9th cir.) 1975, U.S. Supreme Ct. 1971. Assoc. Wilson, Compton, & Wilson, Flagstaff, Ariz., 1959-64; ptnr. Wilson, Compton & Stoops, 1964-67, Mangum, Wall & Stoops, Flagstaff, 1967-77, Mangum, Wall, Stoops & Warden, Flagstaff, 1977—. Editor Washburn Law Rev., 1958. Pres. Flagstaff Festival of the Arts, 1988-89, Flagstaff Sch. Bd., 1961-73, Ariz. Sch. Bd. Assn., 1971 Fellow Ariz. Bar Found., Am. Bar Found., Am. Coll. Trial Lawyers (state chmn. 1984-85), Internat. Soc. Barristers; mem. Ariz. Bar Assn. (pres. 1980-81), Masons. Republican. Methodist. Avocations: golf, political and historical reading and research. General civil litigation, Insurance, Personal injury. Office: Mangum Wall Stoops & Warden 100 N Elden St Flagstaff AZ 86001-5295 E-mail: mswattys@aol.com

STORER, MARYRUTH, law librarian; b. Portland, Oreg., July 26, 1953; d. Joseph William and Carol Virginia (Pearson) Storer; m. David Bruce Bailey, 1981; children: Sarah, Allison. BA in History, Portland State U., 1974; JD, U. Oreg., 1977; M in Law Librarianship, U. Wash., 1978. Bar: Oreg. 1978. Assoc. law libr. U. Tenn., Knoxville, 1978-79; law libr. O'Melveny & Myers, L.A., 1979-88; dir. Orange County Pub. Law Libr., Santa Ana, Calif., 1988—. Mem. Am. Assn. Law Librs. (exec. bd. 1999—), So. Calif. Assn. Law Librs. (pres. 1986-87), Coun. Calif. County Law Librs. (sec.-treas. 1990-94, pres. 1994-96), Arroyo Seco Libr. Network (chair 2000—). Democrat. Episcopalian. Office: Orange County Public Law Library 515 N Flower St Santa Ana CA 92703-2304

STORER, THOMAS PERRY, lawyer; b. Washington, July 14, 1944; s. Morris Brewster and Gretchen Geuder (Schneider) S.; m. Julia Manganip Owek, Dec. 22, 1966; children: Lingbawan Frederick, Allinnawa Elizabeth, Gessingga Nathaniel. BA in Math., Harvard U., 1965, JD, 1979; MPA, Woodrow Wilson Sch. Pub. and Internat. Affairs, 1969. Bar: Mass. 1979, U.S. Dist. Ct. Mass. 1979. Program officer U.S. Peace Corps, Kuala Lumpur, Malaysia, 1969-72; analyst, unit chief Bur. of Budget State of Ill., Springfield, 1972-74; dep. dir. Ill. Dept. Pub. Aid, 1974-76; cons. Mass. Medicaid Program, Boston, 1976-79; assoc. Goodwin, Procter & Hoar, 1979-87, ptnr., 1987—. Vol. U.S. Peace Corps, Bontoc, Mountain Prov., Philippines, 1965-67; elder Newton (Mass.) Presbyn. Ch., Mass., 1987-98. Mem. ABA, Mass. Bar Assn. Avocations: music, computers. Computer, General corporate, Intellectual property. Home: 22 Hobart Rd Newton Centre MA 02459-1313 Office: Goodwin Procter & Hoar LLP Exchange Pl Boston MA 02109-2803 E-mail: tpstorer@ix.netcom.com, tstorer@gph.com

STOREY, LEE A. lawyer; b. Ypsilanti, Mich., Nov. 28, 1959; d. Henry Perry Herold and Elsie Lorraine (Long) Wolf; m. William Storey; children: Jason Michael, Jenifer Lorraine. Student, U. Mich., 1977-79; BA, UCLA, 1982, MA, 1984; JD, U. Calif., Berkeley, 1987. Bar: Ariz. 1988, U.S. Dist. Ct. 1990. Circulations mgr. Inst. Archaeology UCLA, 1980-84; rsch. asst. John Muir Inst., Napa, Calif., 1985, Am. Indian Resources Inst., Oakland, 1985; assoc. editor Ecology Law Quarterly U. Calif., Berkeley, 1985-86; assoc. Evans, Kitchel & Jenckes, Phoenix, 1987-89, Gallagher & Kennedy, Phoenix, 1989-90, Meyer, Hendricks, Victor, Osborn & Maledon, Phoenix, 1991-95; ptnr. Meyer Hendricks Bivens & Moyes P.A., 1995-99; prin. ptnr. Moyes Storey, Ltd., 1999—. Guest lectr. water transfers Hydrological Soc. Symposium, Phoenix, 1989, environ. studies Ariz. State U., Tempe, 1990, water quality Soc. Mining Engrs., Denver, 1991, water transfers Wind River Assocs., Denver, 1991-92, Phoenix, 1992, Central Ariz. Project Utilization, Am. Water Resources Assn. Symposium, Tucson, 1992, Colo. River Basin Tribes, Coun. Energy Resource Tribes, Tucson, 1993, Indian Sovereignty, U.S. Dept. Interior, Bureau Reclamation, Phoenix, 1993; Indian Econ. Devel. Fed. Indian Bar Albuquerque, 1994, Water Rights, Ariz. Judicial Conf., Ariz. State Bar, Tucson, 1994, National Land Coun. sem., Water Rights, Rico Rico, Ariz., 1995, Ariz. Water Law, 2000; chair Ambs. for Change, 1996—; adj. prof. Indian water rights Sch. Law Ariz. State U., 1992, 97, mem. adv. com. on Indian law program Coll. of Law, 1999—. Co-author: Leasing Indian Water: Choices in Colorado River Basin, 1988; contbr. articles to profl. jours.; mem. Calif. Law Rev. U. Calif. Berkeley, 1985-87. Landlord tenant clinics Vols. Lawyers Program, Phoenix, 1988-89; mem. Ariz. Ctr. for Law-Related Edn., Ariz. Bar Found., Drug Awareness Program for Schs., 1990; chmn. bd. Ambs. for Change, 1996—. Scholar UCLA, 1980-84; recipient Am. Jurisprudence award Lawyers Coop., 1986. Mem. ABA, Ariz. State Bar Assn. (mem. com. on minorities and women in law 1993-97, chair-elect Indian law sect. 1997-98, chair 1998—, asst. editor Environ. and Natural Resources newsletter 1990-94, editor Indian law sect. Arrow newsletter 1996—), Ariz. Women Lawyers Assn., Maricopa County Bar Assn. Environmental, Native American, Real property. Office: Moyes Storey 3003 N Central Ave Ste 1250 Phoenix AZ 85012-2923

STORMER, NANCY ROSE, lawyer; b. Traverse City, Mich., Mar. 7, 1950; d. Benjamin Voice and Frances Rose (Gold) S.; m. Michael Charles Bagge, Aug. 1, 1985; children: Sean, Kiernan. AA, Harriman (N.Y.) Coll., 1973; BA magna cum laude, Marist Coll., 1977; JD, Antioch Sch. Law, 1981. Bar: N.Y. 1983, U.S. Dist. Ct. (no. dist.) N.Y. 1983, U.S. Supreme Ct. 1989. Staff atty. Legal Aid Soc. Mid N.Y., Utica, 1983-95, sr. atty., 1990-95; atty. in pvt. practice, 1995—. Bd. dirs. Sister City Project, Utica, 1986-90, Salvation Army, Utica, 1988-89; mem. adv. coun. office for aging Oneida County Office for Aging, Utica, 1993-96; co-chairperson adv. coun. Hispanos Unidos, Utica, 1994. Named Profl. Woman of Yr. YWCA of Mohawk Valley, 1999. Mem. N.Y. State Bar Assn., Oneida County Bar Assn., Nat. Health Lawyers. Avocations: travel, reading, crafts. Home: 1314 Rutger St Utica NY 13501-2526 Office: Adirondack Bank Bldg 185 Genesee St Ste 1519 Utica NY 13501-2102

STORMS, CLIFFORD BEEKMAN, lawyer; b. Mount Vernon, N.Y., July 18, 1932; s. Harold Beekman and Gene (Pertak) S.; m. Barbara H. Grave, 1955 (div. 1975); m. Valeria N. Parker, July 12, 1975; children: Catherine Storms Fischer, Clifford Beekman. BA magna cum laude, Amherst Coll., 1954; LLB, Yale U., 1957. Bar: N.Y. 1957. Assoc. Breed, Abbott & Morgan, N.Y.C., 1957-64; with CPC Internat., Inc., Englewood Cliffs, N.J., 1964-97, v.p. legal affairs, 1973-75, v.p., gen. counsel, 1975-88, sr. v.p., gen. counsel, 1988-97, atty. alternate dispute resolution, corp. dir., 1997—; pvt. practice Greenwich, Conn., 1997—. Bd. dirs. Corn Products Internat., Inc., Atlantic Legal Found.; mem. Conn. Alternate Dispute Resolution panel Ctr. for Pub. Resources. Trustee emeritus Food and Drug Law Inst. Mem. ABA (com. of corp. gen. counsel), Am. Arbitration Assn. (panel arbitrators large complex case program), Assn. Gen. Counsel (pres. 1992-94), Assn. Bar City N.Y. (sec., com. on corp. law depts. 1979-81), Indian Harbor Yacht Club, Yale Law Sch. Assn. (exec. com.), Phi Beta Kappa. Alternative dispute resolution, General corporate. Home: 19 Burying Hill Rd Greenwich CT 06831-2604 Office: Ste 100 Two Sound View Dr Greenwich CT 06830 E-mail: cbstorms@aol.com

STORTI, PHILIP CRAIG, lawyer; b. San Francisco, Apr. 13, 1946; s. Peter Paul and Ada Marie (Ripley) S.; m. Tanya Ann Hepworth, Apr. 29, 1972; children— Tyler James, John Peter, Jeffrey Frank. B.S. in Econs. cum laude, U. Idaho, 1968; J.D. with highest honors, Hastings Coll., San

Francisco, 1971. Bar: Calif. 1972, Idaho 1972, U.S. Dist. Ct. Idaho 1972, U.S. Dist. Ct. Calif. 1972, U.S. Supreme Ct. 1980, U.S. Ct. Mil. Appeals 1973. Law clk. Idaho Supreme Ct., Boise, 1971-72; assoc. Hawley Troxell Ennis and Hawley, Boise, 1975-78, ptnr., 1979— ; mem. standing com. appellate rules Idaho Supreme Ct., 1983— . Comment editor Hastings Law Jour., 1970-71. Bd. dirs. Boys Clubs Am., Boise, 1980-83. Served to capt. USMC, 1972-75. Recipient Disting. Service award Idaho Supreme Ct. 1972. Mem. Idaho Law Found. (mem. bd. dirs. 1990—), U. Iowa Found. (mem. bd. dirs. 1989—), Idaho State Bar Assn. (bar exam. com. 1979-83), Boise Bar Assn. (nominating com.), U. Idaho Alumni Assn. Club: Hillcrest Country (Boise). Antitrust, Construction, Labor. Home: 3614 Trail Cir Boise ID 83704-4563 Office: Hawley Troxell Ennis and Hawley 999 Main St Ste 701 Boise ID 83702-9000

STOTLER, ALICEMARIE HUBER, judge; b. Alhambra, Calif., May 29, 1942; d. James R. and Loretta M. Huber; m. James Allen Stotler, Sept. 11, 1971. BA, U. So. Calif., 1964, JD, 1967. Bar: Calif. 1967, U.S. Dist. Ct. (no. dist.) Calif. 1967, U.S. Dist. Ct. (cen. dist.) Calif. 1973, U.S. Supreme Ct. 1976; cert. criminal law specialist. Dep. Orange County Dist. Attys. Office, 1967-73; mem. Stotler & Stotler, Santa Ana, Calif., 1973-76, 83-84; judge Orange County Mcpl. Ct., 1976-78, Orange County Superior Ct., 1978-83, U.S. Dist. Ct. (cen. dist.) Calif., L.A., 1984—. Assoc. dean Calif. Trial Judges Coll., 1982; lectr., panelist, numerous orgns.; standing com. on rules of practice and procedure U.S. Jud. Conf., 1991—, chair, 1993-98; mem. exec. com. 9th Cir. Jud. Conf., 1989-93, Fed. State Jud. Coun., 1989-98, jury com., 1990-92, planning com. for Nat. Conf. on Fed.-State Jud. Relationships, Orlando, 1991-92, planning com. for We. Regional Conf. on State-Fed. Jud. Relationships, Stevens, Wash., 1992-93; chair dist. ct. symposium and jury utilization Ctrl. Dist. Calif., 1985, chair atty. liaison, 1989-90, chair U.S. Constn. Bicentennial com., 1986-91, chair magistrate judge com., 1992-93; mem. State Adv. Group on Juvenile Justice and Delinquency Prevention, 1983-84, Bd. Legal Specializations Criminal Law Adv. Commn., 1983-84, victim/witness adv. com. Office Criminal Justice Planning, 1980-83, U. So. Calif. Bd. Councilors, 1993—; active team in tng. Leukemia Soc. Am., 1993, 95, 97, 2000; legion lex bd. dirs. U. So. Calif. Sch. Law Support Group, 1981-83. Winner Hale Moot Ct. Competition, State of Calif., 1967; named Judge of Yr., Orange County Trial Lawyers Assn., 1978, Most Outstanding Judge, Orange County Bus. Litigation Sect., 1990; recipient Franklin G. West award Orange County Bar Assn., 1985. Mem. ABA (jud. adminstrn. divsn. and litigation sect. 1984—, nat. conf. fed. trial judges com. on legis. affairs 1990-91), Am. Law Inst., Am. Judicature Soc., Fed. Judges Assn. (bd. dirs. 1989-92), Nat. Assn. Women Judges, U.S. Supreme Ct. Hist. Soc., Ninth Cir. Dist. Judges Assn., Calif. Supreme Ct. Hist. Soc., Orange County Bar Assn. (mem. numerous com.s, Franklin G. West award 1984), Calif. Judges Assn. (mem. com. on jud. coll. 1978-80, com. on civil law and procedure 1980-82, Dean's coll. curriculum commn. 1981), Calif. Judges Found. Office: Ronald Reagan Fed Bldg & Courthouse 411 W 4th St Santa Ana CA 92701-4500

STOTTER, LAWRENCE HENRY, lawyer; b. Cleve., Sept. 24, 1929; s. Oscar and Bertha (Lieb) S.; m. Ruth Rapoport, June 30, 1957; children: Daniel, Jennifer, Steven. BBA, Ohio State U., 1956, LLB, 1958, JD, 1967. Bar: Calif. 1960, U.S. Supreme Ct. 1973, U.S. Tax Ct. 1976. Pvt. practice, San Francisco, 1963—; ptnr. Stotter and Coats, 1981-97; sole practitioner, 1997—; mem. faculty Nat. Judicial Coll.; mem. Calif. Family Law Adv. Commn., 1979-80. Editor in chief: Am. Bar Family Advocate mag, 1977-82; TV appearances on Phil Donahue Show, Good Morning America. Pres. Tamalpais Conservation Club, Marin County, Calif.; U.S. State Dept. del. Hague Conf. Pvt. Internat. Law, 1979-80; legal adv. White House Conf. on Families, 1980— . Served with AUS, 1950-53. Mem. ABA (past chmn. family law sect.), Am. Acad. Matrimonial Lawyers (past nat. v.p.), Calif. State Bar (past chmn. family law sect.), San Francisco Bar Assn. (past chmn. family law sect.), Calif. Trial Lawyers Assn. (past chmn. family law sect.) Family and matrimonial. Home: 2244 Vistazo St E Belvedere Tiburon CA 94920-1970 Office: 1255 Columbus Ave # 200 San Francisco CA 94133-1326 E-mail: lhstotter@aol.com

STOUP, ARTHUR HARRY, lawyer; b. Kansas City, Mo., Aug. 30, 1925; s. Isadore and Dorothy (Rankle) S.; m. Kathryn Jolliff, July 30, 1948; children: David C., Daniel P., Rebecca Ann, Deborah E. Student, Kansas City Jr. Coll., Mo. 1942-43; BA, U. Kansas City, 1950; JD, U. Mo., Kansas City, 1950. Bar: Mo. 1950, D.C. 1979, U.S. Dist. Ct. (we. dist.) Mo., U.S. Dist. Ct. Kans., U.S. Dist. Ct. Ariz. Pvt. practice law, Kansas City, 1950—. Chmn. U.S. Jud. Merit Selection Com. for Western Dist. Mo., 1981. Chmn. com. to rev. continuing edn. U. Mo., 1978—79; mem. dean search com. U. Mo. Law Sch., Kansas City, 1994—95; trustee U. Mo.-Kansas City Law Found., 1972—, pres., 1979—82; trustee U. Mo., 1979—2001, hon. trustee, 2001—. With USNR, 1942—45. Recipient Alumni Achievement award, U. Mo., Kansas City, 1975, Law Found. Svc. award, U. Mo.-Kansas City Law Found., 1987. Fellow Internat. Soc. Barristers (state mem. chmn.), Am. Bar Found. (life mem.); mem. ABA (ho. dels. 1976-80), Kansas City Met. Bar Assn. (pres. 1966-67, Dean of Trial Bar award 1991), Mo. Bar (bd. govs. 1967-76, v.p. 1972-73, pres. elect 1973-74, pres. 1974-75), Lawyers Assn. Kansas City Mo., Mo. Assn. Trial Attys. (sustaining), Assn. Trial Lawyers Am. (sustaining), So. Conf. Bar Pres.'s (life), Mobar Research Inc. (pres. 1978-86), Phi Alpha Delta Alumni (justice Kansas City area alumni 1955-56). Lodges: Optimists (pres. Ward Pkwy. 1961-62, lt. gov. Mo. dist. internat. 1963-64), Sertoma, B'nai B'rith Federal civil litigation, General civil litigation, Personal injury. Home: 9002 Western Hills Dr Kansas City MO 64114-3566 Office: Palace Bldg Ste 250 1150 Grand Blvd Kansas City MO 64106-2317 Fax: 816-474-0714

STOUT, LOWELL, lawyer; b. Tamaha, Okla., July 23, 1928; s. Charles W. and Rosetta (Easley) S.; m. Liliane Josue, Nov. 29, 1952; children: Georgianna, Mark Lowell. Student, Northeastern State Coll., Tahlequah, Okla., 1946-49, U. Okla., 1949-51; LLB, U. N.Mex., 1952. Bar: N.Mex. 1952. Ptnr. Easley, Quinn & Stout, Hobbs, N.Mex., 1954-58, Girand & Stout, Hobbs, 1958-60; pvt. practice, 1960-80; ptnr. Stout & Stout, 1980—. With U.S. Army, 1952-54. Perenially listed in Best Lawyers in America. Fellow Am. Coll. Trial Lawyers; mem. Assn. Trial Lawyers Am., State Bar N.Mex., N.Mex. Trial Lawyers Assn., Lea County Bar Assn. General civil litigation, Personal injury, Workers' compensation. Home: 218 W Lea St Hobbs NM 88240-5110 Office: Stout & Stout PO Box 716 Hobbs NM 88241-0716

STOVALL, CARLA JO, state attorney general; b. Hardner, Kans., Mar. 18, 1957; d. Carl E. and Juanita Jo (Ford) S. BA, Pittsburg (Kans.) State U., 1979; JD, U. Kans., 1982. Bar: Kans. 1982, U.S. Dist. Ct. Kans. 1982. Pvt. practice, Pittsburg, 1982-85; atty. Crawford County, 1984-88; gov. Kans. Parole Bd., Topeka, 1988-94; atty. gen. State of Kansas, 1995—. Lectr. law Pittsburg State U. 1982-84; pres. Gilston Internat. Mktg., Inc., 1988—. Bd. dirs., sec. Pittsburg Family YMCA, 1983-88. Mem. ABA, Kans. Bar Assn., Crawford County Bar Assn. (sec. 1984-85, v.p. 1985-86, pres. 1986-87), Kans. County and Dist. Attys. Assn., Nat. Coll. Dist. Attys., Pittsburg State U. Alumni Assn. (bd. dirs. 1983-88), Pittsburg Area C. of C. (bd. dirs. 1983-85, Leadership Pitts. 1984), Bus. and Profl. Women Assn. (Young Careerist 1984), Kans. Assn. Commerce and Industry (Leadership Kans. 1983), AAUW (bd. dirs. 1983-87). Republican. Methodist. Avocations: travel, photography, tennis. Home: 3561 SW Mission Ave Topeka KS 66614-3637 Office: Atty Gen Office Meml Hall 120 SW 10th Ave Fl 2 Topeka KS 66612-1597*

STOVER, DAVID FRANK, lawyer; b. Phila., May 15, 1941; s. Emory Frank and Beatrice Norah (Spinelli) S. A.B., Princeton U., 1962; J.D., U. Pa., 1965. Bar: D.C. 1966, U.S. Ct. Appeals (D.C. cir.) 1968, U.S. Ct. Appeals (9th cir.) 1969, U.S. Ct. Appeals (4th cir.) 1972. Atty. FPC, Washington, 1965-71, Tally & Tally, Washington, 1972-75; asst. gen. counsel Postal Rate Commn., Washington, 1975-79, gen. counsel, 1979-92, regulatory cons. 1992—. Author: (with Bierman, Lamont, Nelson) Geothermal Energy in the Western United States, 1978. Mem. Fed. Bar Assn. Episcopalian. Home and Office: 2970 S Columbus St # 1-B Arlington VA 22206-1450

STOVER, STEPHAN WALLACE, lawyer, state agency administrator; b. Columbus, Ohio, Nov. 3, 1946; s. Wilmer Wallace and Virginia Carol (Harmon) S.; m. Mary Garvin, Mar. 15, 1969; children— Elizabeth Harmon, Daniel Garvin. B.S. in Edn., Ohio State U., 1969, M.S. in Edn. Adminstrn., 1971; J.D. Washington U., St. Louis, 1974. Bar: Ohio 1975. Tchr. social studies Columbus South High Sch., 1969-72; atty. examiner Ohio Indsl. Commn., 1975; staff atty. Ohio Legis. Service Commn., Columbus, 1975-77; asst. dir. Ohio Ethics Commn., Columbus, 1977-81, exec. dir., 1981-86; adminstrv. dir. Ohio Supreme Ct., 1987—. mem. council on Govtl. Ethics Laws Steering Com., 1985-87, sec., 1986, chmn. 1987. Mem. Columbus Mus. of Art, pres. jr. council, 1979-80, chmn. membership council, 1980-82; active First Community Ch.; bd. dirs. Conf. State Ct. Adminstrn., 1995—. Served to capt. USAR, 1977. Recipient Am. Jurisprudence Prize Washington U., 1974, Jack L. Garden Humanitarian award, 1974, COGEL award Coun. Govtl. Ethics Laws, 1991. Mem. Ohio Bar Assn., Columbus Bar Assn., Conf. State Ct. Adminstrs., Nat. Assn. Ct. Mgmt. Ohio State U. Pres.'s Club, Ohio State U. Alumni Assn., Phi Kappa Tau (bd. govs. 1970-80). Clubs: Athletic Club of Columbus. Home: 2140 Lane Rd Columbus OH 43220-3012 Office: 30 E Broad St Fl 3 Columbus OH 43215-3414

STOWE, CHARLES ROBINSON BEECHER, management consultant, educator, lawyer; b. Seattle, July 18, 1949; s. David Beecher and Edith Beecher (Andrade) S.; m. Laura Everett, Mar. 9, 1985. BA, Vanderbilt U., 1971; MBA, U. Dallas, 1975; JD, U. Houston, 1982; PhD, U. Warsaw, Poland, 1998. Bar: Tex. 1982, U.S. Dist. Ct. (so. dist.) Tex. 1984, U.S. Tax Ct. 1984. Acct. exec. Engleman Co., Dallas, 1974-75; instr. Richland Coll., 1976; acct. Adthur Andersen & Co., 1976-78; part-time pub. rels. cons.; dir. Productive Capital Assocs., 1975-81; pres. Stowe & Co., Dallas, 1978—; from asst. to prof. dept. gen. bus. and fin. Coll. Bus. Adminstrn., Sam Houston State U., 1982—, dir. Office Internat. Programs, 1997-2001. Dir. Office Free Enterprise and Entrepreneurship, 1983-86, Office Internat. programs, 2001—; adminstrv. intern asst. to pres., spring, 1985. Author: Bankruptcy I Micro-Mash Inc., 1989, rev. edit., 1995, The Implications of Foreign Financial Instutions on Poland's Emerging Entrepreneurial Economy, 1999; co-author: CPA rev.; co-editor: Lnowledge Cafe for Intellect Product and Intellectual Entrepreneurship, 2001; editor Houston Jour. Internat. Law, 1981-82; contbr. articles to profl. jours. Trustee Stowe-Day Found., 1979-80; mem. nat. adv. bd. Young Am.'s Found., 1979—; vol. faculty State Bar Tex. Profl. Devel. Program, 1988—; vol., mediator Dispute Resolution Ctr. Montgomery County; mediator so. dist. U.S. Dist. Ct. Tex. 1993; teach chief U.S. Mil. liaison Rep. Poland, 1994; pub. affairs officer George C. Marshall European Ctr. Security Studies, 1997. With USNR, 1971-74; capt. Res. Recipient Freedoms Found. award, Navy Achievement medal, Gold Star, Def. Meritorious Svc. medal with oak leaf cluster, Navy Meritorious Svc. award; Summer fellow Tex. Coordinating Bd., 1988, Prince-Babson fellow Entrepreneurship Symposium, 1991. Mem. ABA, Am. Arbitration Assn., State Bar Tex. (vol. faculty profl. devel. program 1988-90, vice chair profl. efficiency and econ. rsch. com. 1993, chair law office mgmt. com. 1993-94), Walker County Bar Assn. (pres. 1987-88), Pub. Rels. Soc. Am., Tex. Assn. Realtors, U.S. Navy League, Naval Res. Assn., Res. Officers Assn., Dallas Vanderbilt Club (pres. 1977-78). Office: PO Box 2144 Huntsville TX 77341-2144

STRACENER, CAROL ELIZABETH, lawyer; b. Baton Rouge, Mar. 28, 1951; d. Nealon and Mary Helen (Langlois) S.; m. John Joseph Nicholson, June 2, 1973; 1 child, Courtney Elizabeth. BS, La. State U., 1973; JD, So. U., 1977. Bar: La., U.S. Dist. Ct. (mid. dist.) La. 1985.Sole practioner, Baton Rouge, 1978— . Mem. La. Bar Assn., East Baton Rouge Bar Assn., La. Assn. for Women Attys., Am. Judicature Soc., Alpha Xi Delta (L.A. chpt.), Am., Bus. Women's Assn. (LaCapitale chpt.). Republican. Methodist. Fax: 225-767-1977. E-mail: cstracen@aol.com. Family and matrimonial, General practice, Probate. Home: 15000 Highland Rd Baton Rouge LA 70810-5523 Office: Carol E Stracener Atty 8888 Bluebonnet Blvd Baton Rouge LA 70810

STRACHAN, NELL B. lawyer; b. Portland, Oreg., Feb. 1, 1941; d. Louis and Agnes (Clarke) Berelson; m. Peter D. Ward, Feb. 19, 1982; children— Sarah, Margaret, Jane; stepchildren— Anne, Amy Ward. B.A., Whitman Coll., Wash., 1962; J.D., U. Md., 1974. Bar: Md. 1974, U.S. Dist. Ct. Md. 1974, U.S. Ct. Appeals (4th cir.) 1976. Assoc., Venable, Baetjer & Howard, Balt., 1974-81, ptnr., 1982— . Chmn. task force Balt Sch. System, 1983; chmn. Balt. City Commn. on Women, 1984— ; mem. Md. central com. Democratic Party, 1983— . Mem. ABA (assoc. editor Litigation pub. of litigation sect. 1977-83), Md. Bar Assn. (founding mem. litigation council 1978-82, chmn. judicial eval. com. 1987-91, vice chair judicial adminstrn. sect. 1990—). Club: Wranglers Law (Balt.). Federal civil litigation, State civil litigation, Education and schools. Home: 108 Longwood Rd Baltimore MD 21210-2120 Office: Venable Baetjer & Howard 1800 Mercantile Bank & Trust Blg 2 Hopkins Plz Ste 2100 Baltimore MD 21201-2982

STRADER, TIMOTHY RICHARDS, lawyer; b. Portland, Oreg., Jan. 17, 1956; s. Charles J. and Carol Jane (Dwyer) S.; m. Lisa M.K. Bartholomew, May 21, 1988; children: Kelly Meehan, Erin Dwyer. BBA in Mgmt., U. Notre Dame, 1978; JD, Willamette U., Salem, Oreg., 1981; LLM in Taxation, U. Fla., Gainesville, 1982. Bar: Oreg. 1981. Assoc. McEwen, Hanna, Gisvold & Rankin, Portland, 1982-85, Bullivant, Houser, Bailey, Hanna, Portland, 1985-87, Hanna, Urbgkeit, Jensen, et al., Portland, 1987-88, Hanna, Murphy, Jensen, Holloway, Portland, 1988-89; mem. Hanna, Kerns & Strader, P.C., 1989—. Mem. editorial bd. State Bar Estate Planning Newsletter, 1987—. Mem. alumni bd. Jesuit H.S., Portland, 1982-94, trustee, 1993-99; bd. dirs. Valley Cath. Sch., Beaverton, 1989-95; mem. Estate Planning Coun., Portland, 1990—, bd. dirs., 2000—. Mem. ABA, Multnomah Bar Assn., Multnomah Athletic Club, Waverley Country Club. Estate planning, Probate, Corporate taxation. Office: Hanna Kerns & Strader 1300 SW 6th Ave Ste 300 Portland OR 97201-3461 E-mail: TRStrader@aol.com

STRADLEY, RICHARD LEE, lawyer; b. Chula Vista, Calif., Sept. 10, 1951; s. George R. and Betty J. (Laughman) S.; m. Christine A. Crofts, Sept. 7, 1991; 1 child, Samuel Richard. BA, Coll. Santa Fe, 1972; JD, U. Mich., 1975. Bar: Miss. 1975, U.S. Dist. Ct. (no. dist.) Miss. 1975, U.S. Dist. Ct. Mont. 1980, U.S. Ct. Appeals (5th and 9th cirs.) 1980, U.S. Dist. Ct. (so. dist.) Miss. 1981, U.S. Ct. Appeals (10th and 11th cirs.) 1981, U.S. Tax Ct. 1981, U.S. Surpeme Ct. 1981, Mont. 1982, U.S. Dist. Ct. (we. dist.) Tenn. 1982, U.S. Dist. Ct. (no. dist.) Tex. 1984, Oreg. 1985, U.S. Dist. Ct. Oreg. 1986, U.S. Dist. Ct. Nebr. 1986, Wyo. 1994. Sole practice, 1975—; staff atty. East Miss. Legal Svcs., Forest, 1979. Mem. Christian Legal Soc. Avocations: chess, computers, woodworking. E-mail: richard. Federal civil litigation, Probate, Estate taxation. Office: PO Box 2541 Cody WY 82414-2541 E-mail: l.stradley@bigfoot.com

STRAIN, JAMES ARTHUR, lawyer; b. Alexandria, La., Oct. 11, 1944; s. William Joseph and Louise (Moore) S.; m. Cheryl Sue Williamson, Aug. 19, 1967; children: William Joseph, Gordon Richard, Elizabeth Parks. BS in Econs., Ind. U., 1966, JD, 1969. Bar: Ind. 1969, U.S. Dist. Ct. (so. dist.) Ind. 1969, U.S. Ct. Appeals (7th cir.) 1972, U.S. Supreme Ct. 1975, U.S. Ct. Appeals (5th cir.) 1978. Instr. Law Sch. Ind. U., Indpls., 1969-70; law clk. to Hon. John S. Hastings 7th Cir. Ct. Appeals, Chgo., 1970-71; assoc. Cahill, Gordon & Reindel, N.Y.C., 1971-72; law clk. to Hon. William H. Rehnquist U.S. Supreme Ct., Washington, 1972-73; assoc. Barnes, Hickam, Pantzer & Boyd, Indpls., 1973-75; ptnr. Barnes, Hickam, Pantzer & Boyd (name changed to Barnes & Thornburg), 1976-96, Sommer & Barnard, PC, Indpls., 1996—. Adj. asst. prof. law Ind. U. Sch. Law, 1986-92. Mem., bd. dirs. The Penrod Soc., Indpls., 1976—, Indpls. Symphonic Choir, 1988-91, Festival Music Soc., Indpls., 1990-96. Mem. 7th Cir. Bar Assn. (meetings chmn. Ind. chpt. 1979-88, portraits 1988-89, bd. govs. 1989—, 1st v.p. 1995, pres. 1996). Avocations: photography, music. General corporate, Mergers and acquisitions, Securities. Office: Sommer & Barnard PC 4000 Bank One Tower 111 Monument Cir Ste 4000 Indianapolis IN 46204-5198 E-mail: strain@sommerbarnard.com

STRAND, ROGER GORDON, federal judge; b. Peekskill, N.Y., Apr. 28, 1934; s. Ernest Gordon Strand and Lisabeth Laurine (Phin) Steinmetz; m. Joan Williams, Nov. 25, 1961. AB, Hamilton Coll., 1955; LLB, Cornell U., 1961; grad., Nat. Coll. State Trial Judges, 1968. Bar: Ariz. 1961, U.S. Dist. Ct. Ariz. 1961, U.S. Supreme Ct. 1980. Assoc. Fennemore, Craig, Allen & McClennen, Phoenix, 1961-67; judge Ariz. Superior Ct., 1967-85, U.S. Dist. Ct. Ariz., Phoenix, 1985—. Assoc. presiding judge Ariz. Superior Ct., 1971-85; lectr. Nat. Jud. Coll., Reno, 1978-87; mem. jud. conf. U.S. com. on automation and tech. Past pres. cen. Ariz. chpt. Arthritis Found. Lt. USN, 1955-61. Mem. ABA, Ariz. Bar Assn., Maricopa County Bar Assn., Nat. Conf. Fed. Trial Judges, Phi Delta Phi, Aircraft Owners and Pilots Assn. Lodge: Rotary. Avocations: computer applications, golf, fishing. Home: 5825 N 3rd Ave Phoenix AZ 85013-1537 Office: Sandra Day O'Connor US Courthouse SPC 57 401 W Washington Phoenix AZ 85003-2156

STRASBAUGH, WAYNE RALPH, lawyer; b. Lancaster, Pa., July 20, 1948; s. Wayne Veily and Jane Irene (Marzolf) S.; m. Carol Lynne Taylor, June 8, 1974; children: Susan, Wayne T., Elizabeth. AB, Bowdoin Coll., 1970; AM, Harvard U., 1971, PhD, 1976, JD, 1979. Bar: Ohio 1979, Pa. 1983, U.S. Tax Ct. 1980, U.S. Ct. Fed. Claims 1980, U.S. Ct. Appeals (fed. cir.) 1982, U.S. Dist. Ct. (no. dist.) Ohio 1979, U.S. Dist. Ct. (ea. dist.) Pa. 1983. Assoc. Jones Day Reavis & Pogue, Cleve., 1979-82, Morgan Lewis & Bockius, Phila., 1982-84, Ballard Spahr Andrews & Ingersoll, LLP, Phila., 1984-88, ptnr., 1988—, chmn. tax group, 2001—. Mem. ABA (tax sect., chmn. com. 1992-94), Phila. Bar Assn. (tax sect., chmn. fed. tax com. 1992, coun. mem. 1995, sec.-treas. 1996, vice-chmn. 1997-98, chmn. 1999-2000). Episcopalian. Mergers and acquisitions, Corporate taxation, Taxation, general. Office: Ballard Spahr Andrews & Ingersoll LLP 1735 Market St Ste 5100 Philadelphia PA 19103-7599 E-mail: strasbaugh@ballardspahr.com

STRATAKIS, CHRIST, lawyer; b. Chios, Greece, June 6, 1928; s. John and Sophie S.; m. Mary C. Skinitis, Oct. 25, 1959; children: Sophia, John, Irene. BS in Econs., Drexel U., 1951; JD, NYU, 1955. Bar: N.Y. 1956, U.S. Dist. Ct. (so. and ea. dists.) 1957, U.S. Ct. Appeals (2d cir.) 1958, U.S. Ct. Customs 1965, U.S. Supreme Ct. 1970. Gen. counsel Nat. Shipping & Trading Corp., N.Y.C., 1955-59; with Poles, Tublin, Patestides & Stratakis, 1960-61, ptnr., 1961-62, sr. ptnr., 1962—. Chmn. adv. coun. Ctr. Byzantine and Modern Greek Studies/Queens Coll., Flushing, N.Y., 1990—; treas., vice-chmn., bd. dirs. Drexel U., 1990-96, 98—; cons., lectr. in field. Contbr. articles to profl. jours. Chmn. sch. bd. Sch. of the Transfiguration, Corona, N.Y., 1967-78; adv. coun. N.Y. dist. SBA, 1971-73; archon nat. coun. Order of St. Andrew the Apostle; chmn., legal com. Archdiocesan Coun. Greek Orthodox Archdiocese Am., 1998-2000. Decorated knight Holy Sepulchre of Jerusalem; recipient St. Pauls award Greek Orthodox Archdiocese N.Am. and S.Am., 1976, Laymans award, 1991, medal of honor Govt. of Greece, 1974. Mem. ABA, Maritime Law Assn. U.S., United Chios Socs. Am. (supreme legal advisor 1960-82), Whitehall Club (N.Y.C.), Douglaston Club (N.Y.), Greek-Am. Dem. of Queens Club (chmn. law com. 1960-74), Sigma Rho, Phi Alpha Delta. Greek Orthodox. Admiralty, Contracts commercial, General corporate. Office: 5th Floor 46 Trinity Pl Fl 5 New York NY 10006-2207

STRATTON, EVELYN LUNDBERG, state supreme court justice; b. Bangkok, Feb. 25, 1953; came to U.S., 1971 (parents Am. citizens); d. Elmer John and Corrine Sylvia (Henricksen) Sahlberg; children: Luke Andrew, Tyler John; m. Jack A. Lundberg. Student, LeTourneau Coll., Longview, Tex., 1971-74; AA, U. Fla., 1973; BA, U. Akron, 1976; JD, Ohio State U., 1978. Bar: Ohio 1979, U.S. Dist. Ct. (so. dist.) Ohio 1979, U.S. Ct. Appeals (6th cir.) 1983. Assoc. Hamilton, Kramer, Myers & Cheek, Columbus, 1979-85; ptnr. Wesp, Osterkamp & Stratton, 1985-88; judge Franklin County Ct. Common Pleas, 1989-96; justice Ohio State Supreme Ct., 1996—. Vis. prof. Nat. Jud. Coll., 1997—; spkr. legal seminars. Contbr. articles to profl. jours. Trustee Ohio affiliate Nat. Soc. to Prevent Blindness, 1989—, bd. dirs., trustee Columbus Coun. World Affairs, 1990-99, chmn. bd. dirs., 1999—; bd. dirs., trustee Dave Thomas Adoption Found., 1996—, ArChSafe Found., 1997—; mem. women's bd. Zephyrus League Cen. Ohio Lung Assn., 1989—; mem. Alliance Women Cmty. Corrections, 1993—. Recipient Gold Key award LeTourneau Coll., Gainesville, Fla., 1974, Svc. commendation Ohio Ho. of Reps., 1984, Scholar of Life award St. Joseph's Orphanage, 1998. Mem. ABA, ATLA, Columbus Bar Assn. (bd. govs. 1984-88, 90—, lectr.), Ohio Bar Assn. (jud. adminstrv. and legal reform com., coun. dels. 1992-96, Ohio Cmty. Corrections Orgn. (trustee 1995—), Columbus Bar Found. (trustee 1986-91, officer, sec. 1986-87, v.p. 1987-88), Am. Inns of Ct., Women Lawyers Franklin County, Phi Alpha Delta (pres. 1982-83). Office: Supreme Ct Ohio 30 E Broad St Fl 3 Columbus OH 43266-3414*

STRATTON, WALTER LOVE, lawyer; b. Greenwich, Conn., Sept. 21, 1926; s. John McKee and June (Love) S.; children: John, Michael, Peter (dec.), Lucinda; m. DeAnna Weinheimer, Oct. 1, 1994. Student, Williams Coll., 1943; A.B., Yale U., 1948; LL.B., Harvard U., 1951. Bar: N.Y. 1952. Assoc. Casey, Lane & Mittendorf, N.Y.C., 1951-53; assoc. Donovan, Leisure, Newton & Irvine, N.Y.C., 1956-63, ptnr., 1963-84, Gibson, Dunn & Crutcher, 1984-93, Andrews & Kurth, N.Y.C., 1993-95, of counsel, 1996—. Asst. U.S. atty. So. Dist. N.Y., N.Y.C., 1953-56; lectr. Practising Law Inst. Served with USNR, 1945-46. Fellow Am. Coll. Trial Lawyers; mem. ABA, Fed. Bar Coun., N.Y. State Bar Assn., Indian Harbor Yacht Club, Colo. Arlberg Club. Clubs: Indian Harbor Yacht, Colo. Arlberg, Yale (N.Y.C.). Home: 434 Round Hill Rd Greenwich CT 06831-2639 Office: Andrews & Kurth 805 3rd Ave New York NY 10022-7513 E-mail: walterstratton@andrews-kurth.com

STRAUB, CHESTER JOHN, judge; b. Bklyn., May 12, 1937; s. Chester and Ann (Majewski) S.; m. Patricia Morrissey; children: Chester, Michael, Christopher, Robert. AB, St. Peter's Coll., 1958; JD, U. Va., 1961. Bar: N.Y. State 1962, U.S. Dist. Ct. (so. and ea. dists.) N.Y. 1963, U.S. Ct. Appeals (2d cir.) 1967, U.S. Supreme Ct. 1978. Assoc. Willkie Farr & Gallagher, N.Y.C., 1963-71, ptnr., 1971-98; mem. N.Y. State Assembly, 1967-72, N.Y. State Senate, 1973-75, Dem. Nat. Com., 1976-80; Judge U.S. Ct. Appeals (2nd cir.), 1998—. Former mediator U.S. Dist. Ct. (so. dist.) N.Y. and neutral evaluator U.S. Dist. Ct. (ea. dist.) N.Y.; chmn. N.Y. State statewide jud. screening com., 1988-94, first dept. jud. screening

com., 1983-94; mem. Senator Moynihan's jud. selection com., 1976-98. Mem. Cardinal's Com. of Laity for Cath. Charities N.Y.; trustee Lenox Hill Hosp., With U.S. Army, 1961-63. Mem. Am. Bar Assn., N.Y. State Bar Assn., Assn. of Bar of City of N.Y.C., Kosciuszko Found. Office: US Ct Appeals Second Circuit 500 Pearl St New York NY 10007-1316

STRAUCH, JOHN L. lawyer; b. Pitts., Apr. 16, 1939; s. Paul L. and Delilah M. (Madison) S.; m. Gail Lorraine Kohn, Dec. 5, 1991; children: Paul L., John M., Lisa E. BA summa cum laude, U. Pitts., 1960; JD magna cum laude, NYU Sch. Law, 1963. Law clk. to Judge Sterry Waterman U.S. Ct. Appeals (2d cir.), St. Johnsbury, Vt., 1963-64; assoc. Jones, Day, Reavis & Pogue, Cleve., 1964-70, ptnr., 1970—, mem. adv. com., partnership com., chmn. litigation group. Mem. Statutory Com. on Selecting Bankruptcy Judges, Cleve., 1985-88; mem. lawyers com. Nat. Ctr. for State Cts. Editor-in-chief: NYU Law Rev., 1962-63; contbr. chpt. to book. Pres., trustee Cleve. Task Force on Violent Crimes, 1985-88; trustee Legal Aid Soc., Cleve., 1978, Cleve. Greater Growth Assn., 1985-86, Citizens Mental Health Assembly, 1989-90, lawyers com. Nat. Ctr. for State Cts., 1989—. Fellow Am. Coll. Trial Lawyers (life); mem. ABA, Ohio Bar Assn., Cleve. Bar Assn. (trustee 1980-83, pres. 1985-86), Fed. Bar Assn. (trustee Cleve. chpt. 1978-79, v.p. Cleve. chpt. 1979-80), Sixth Fed. Jud. Conf. (life), Ohio Eighth Jud. Conf. (life), Order of Coif, Inns of Ct., Oakmont Country Club, The Country Club, Kiawah Island Club, Phi Beta Kappa. Federal civil litigation, State civil litigation. Home: 28149 N Woodland Rd Cleveland OH 44124-4522 Office: Jones Day Reavis & Pogue N Point 901 Lakeside Ave E Cleveland OH 44114-1190

STRAUGHN, ROBERT OSCAR, III, lawyer; b. Vallejo, Calif., Nov. 1, 1942; s. Robert Oscar Jr. and Phyllis Ruth (Main) S.; m. Mavis Marie Ann Turpeinen, May 25, 1975; 1 child, Megan Marie. BS, U. Minn., 1965, MSCE, 1971; JD cum laude, William Mitchell Coll. Law, 1976. Bar: Minn. 1976, U.S. Dist. Ct. Minn. 1979. Staff engr. Arctic Health Research Ctr., Fairbanks, Alaska, 1967-70; sr. design engr. Ellison-Pihlstrom, Inc., St. Paul, 1971-77; asst. atty. City of St. Paul, 1977-79; counsel, v.p. legal Oxford Properties, Inc., Mpls., 1979-84; ptnr. O'Connor & Hannan, 1984-90; v.p. McGrann Shea Anderson Carnival Straughn & Lamb, 1990—. Del. St. Anthony Park Cmty. Coun., 1986—92, 1999—2001, chair, 1987—90; del. Univ. Ave. Corridor Initiative, 1999—2001; bd. dirs. Ramsey County Hist. Soc., St. Paul, 1986—92, sec., 1991—92; mem. adv. com. Ramsey County Regional R.R. Authority, 1988—91; bd. dirs. Univ. United, 1994—2000, 2001—, v.p., 1995—96, pres., 1996—97. Mem. ABA, Minn. Bar Assn., Hennepin County Bar Assn., Christian Legal Soc. (adv. bd. 1988-91, bd. dirs. Minn. chpt. 1991—), Midway C. of C. (bd. dirs. 1990-94, v.p. 1991-92, pres. 1992-93), St. Paul Area C. of C. (bd. dirs. 1992-93), Bldg. Owners and Mgrs. Assn., Assn. Pub. Justice, Chi Epsilon. Presbyterian. Environmental, Land use and zoning (including planning), Real property. Home: 2200 Hoyt Ave W Saint Paul MN 55119-3033 Office: McGrann Shea Anderson Carnival 2600 US Bancorp Ctr 800 Nicollet Mall Minneapolis MN 55402-7035 E-mail: ros@mcgrannshea.com

STRAUSER, ROBERT WAYNE, lawyer; b. Little Rock, Aug. 28, 1943; s. Christopher Columbus and Opal (Orr) S.; m. Atha Maxine Tubbs, June 26, 1971 (div. 1991); children: Robert Benjamin, Ann Kathleen; m. Terri D. Seales, Oct. 17, 1998. BA, Davidson (N.C.) Coll., 1965; postgrad., Vanderbilt U., Nashville, 1965-66; LLB, U. Tex., 1968. Bar: Tex. 1968, U.S. Ct. Mil. Appeals 1971. Staff atty. Tex. Legis. Coun., Austin, 1969-71; counsel Jud. Com., Tex. Ho. of Reps., 1971-73; chief counsel Jud. Com., Tex. Constl. Conv., 1974; exec. v.p. and legis. counsel Tex. Assn. Taxpayers, 1974-85; assoc. Baker & Botts, 1985-87, ptnr., 1988—. Assoc. editor Tex. Internat. Law Jour., 1968. Mem. Tex. Ho. Speakers Econ. Devel. Com., Austin, 1986-87; assoc. dir. McDonald Obs. Bd. Visitors, 1988—; mem. adv. bd. Sch. of Social Work, U. Tex. Lyceum Assn., 1980-81, 84-88; mem. bd. dirs. Tex. Assn. Bus. and C. of C.; mem. Dean's Roundtable, U. Tex. Law Sch.; bd. dirs. Austin Symphony Orch. Soc., 1985—, v.p., 1993-94, nominating com., 1998. Capt. USNR, ret. Named Rising Star of Tex., Tex. Bus. Mag., 1983. Fellow Tex. Bar Found.; mem. State Bar of Tex. (coun. mem. tax sect.), Tex. Assn. Bus. and C. of C.s (bd. dirs. 1999), Travis County Bar Assn., Headliners Club (Austin). Administrative and regulatory, Legislative. Home: 3312 Gilbert St Austin TX 78703-2102 Office: Baker & Botts 1600 San Jacinto Blvd Austin TX 78701

STRAUSS, CATHERINE B. lawyer; b. San Francisco, June 11, 1947; d. John Lawrence and Betty (Rosenblatt) Blumlein; m. Jerome Frank Strauss III, June 21, 1970; children: Jordan Lawrence, Elizabeth Johanna. AB, Brown U., 1969; MSS, Bryn Mawr Coll., 1973; JD, Temple U., 1976. Bar: Pa. 1976, U.S. Dist. Ct. (ea. dist.) Pa. 1981. Assoc. Drinker, Biddle & Reath, Phila., 1976-79; asst. counsel Penn Mut., 1979-83, dir. acquisitions, 1983-85, asst. v.p. sales, 1985-87, v.p. human resources, 1987-96; sr. v.p. human resources Harleysville (Pa.) Ins. Cos., 1996—. Chmn. bd. trustees Womens Law Project, Phila., 1989—; bd. dirs. Family Svc. Phils., 1978—85, Career Alternatives, Jenkintown, Pa., 1984—85; trustee United Way, Phila., 1982—2000, officer, 1992—94, exec. com., 1992—95, chair human resources com., 2000—; active Loma Human Resources Coun., 1990—96; mem. Center in the Park, 2001—. Mem.: NAII (human resources com. 1996—), Assn. for Blind. Contracts commercial, General corporate, Insurance. Office: Harleysville Ins Cos 355 Maple Ave Harleysville PA 19438-2297 E-mail: cstrauss@harleysvillegroup.com

STRAUSS, ELLEN LOUISE FELDMAN, lawyer; b. Worcester, Mass. d. William and Miriam (Jagodnik) Feldman; m. Douglas A. Strauss (div. May 1977). BA, Western Conn. State Coll., 1978; JD, Franklin Pierce Law Ctr., 1981. Bar: Conn. 1983, U.S. Dist. Ct., Conn., 1983, U.S. Dist. Ct., so. dist., N.Y., 1991, ea. dist., 1991. Self-employed Ellen L.F. Strauss, Esq., Weston, Conn., 1983—. Bd. dirs. Human Lactation Ctr., Fairfield, Conn., 1987—, Efficacy, Hartford, Conn., 1997—. Contbr. columns to local newspapers. Founder, mem. Keep Weston Rural, Conn., 1984—. Mem. Am. Trial Lawyers Assn., Conn. Trial Lawyers Assn. Avocation: travel. Family and matrimonial, Juvenile, Personal injury. Office: Ellen LF Strauss Esq 88 Ladder Hill Rd N Weston CT 06883-1107 E-mail: ELFS88LAW@aol.com

STRAUSS, GARY JOSEPH, lawyer; b. N.Y.C., July 6, 1953; s. Stanley Vinson and Frieda (Fischoff) S. BA magna cum laude, City Coll. of N.Y., 1974; JD, NYU, 1977. Bar: N.Y. 1978, Fla. 1980. Assoc. Finley, Kumble, Wagner, Heine & Underberg, N.Y.C., 1977-79; ptnr. Phillips, Nizer, Benjamin, Krim & Ballon, 1979-87, Gaston & Snow, N.Y.C., 1987-88; pvt. practice, 1988—. Mem. ABA (chmn. N.Y. com. current literature and real property law 1977), Fla. Bar Assn., N.Y. State Bar Assn. Real property. Home: 57 W 38th St Fl 9 New York NY 10018-5500

STRAUSS, PETER L(ESTER), law educator; b. N.Y.C., Feb. 26, 1940; s. Simon D. and Elaine Ruth (Mandle) S.; m. Joanna Burnstine, Oct. 1, 1964; children: Benjamin, Bethany. AB magna cum laude, Harvard U., 1961; LLB magna cum laude, Yale U., 1964. Bar: D.C. 1965, U.S. Supreme Ct. 1968. Law clk. U.S. Ct. Appeals D.C. Cir., 1964-65, U.S. Supreme Ct., 1965-66; lectr. Halle Selassie U. Sch. Law, Addis Ababa, Ethiopia, 1966-68; asst. to solicitor gen. Dept. Justice, Washington, 1968-71; assoc. prof. law Columbia U., 1971-74, prof., 1974—, Betts prof., 1985—, vice-dean, 1996. Gen. counsel NRC, 1975-77, Adminstrv. Conf. U.S., 1984-95; Byrne vis. prof. Sch. Law Harvard U., Cambridge, Mass., 1994. Adv. bd. Lexis Electronic Author's Press, 1995-99; editor: Administrative Law Abstracts, 1997—; author: (with Abba Paulos translator) Fetha Negast: The Law of the Kings, 1968; (with others) Administrative Law Cases and Comments, 1995, supplement 1999, Introduction to Administrative Justice in the United States, 1989; (with Paul Verkuil) Administrative Law Problems, 1983; contbr. articles to profl. jours. Recipient John Marshall prize Dept. Justice, 1970, Disting. Svc. award NRC, 1977. Mem. ABA (chair sect. administrv. law and regulatory practice 1992-93, Disting. Scholarship award 1988), Am. Law Inst. Office: Columbia U Law Sch 435 W 116th St New York NY 10027-7201

STRAUSS, ROBERT DAVID, lawyer; b. Cambridge, Mass., Oct. 20, 1951; s. Walter Adolf and Lilo (Teutsch) S.; m. Deborah Mackall, Feb. 15, 1986 (div. Dec. 1998); 1 child, Benjamin Walter. BA, Emory U., 1973, JD, 1976. Bar: Ga. 1976. Assoc. Gambrell & Russell, Atlanta, 1976-81; ptnr. Smith, Gambrell & Russell, 1981-89, Trotter Smith & Jacobs, Atlanta, 1989-92, Troutman Sanders, Atlanta, 1992—. Contbr. articles to profl. jours. Mem. ABA (chmn. leasing subcom. 1988-94, uniform comml. code com.), State Bar of Ga., Equipment Leasing Assn. Am. Aviation, Contracts commercial, Finance. Home: Apt 3415 1401 W Paces Ferry Rd NE Atlanta GA 30327-2455 Office: Troutman Sanders 5200 Bank of Am Plz 600 Peachtree St NE Atlanta GA 30308-2216 E-mail: bo.strauss@troutmansanders.com

STRAUSS, WILLIAM VICTOR, lawyer; b. Cin., July 5, 1942; s. William Victor and Elsa (Lovitt) S.; m. Linda Leopold, Nov. 9, 1969; children: Nancy T., Katherine S. AB cum laude, Harvard U., 1964; JD, U. Pa., 1967. Bar: Ohio 1967. Pres. Security Title and Guaranty Agy., Inc., Cin., 1982—, Strauss & Troy, Cin., 1995—. Trustee Cin. Psychoanalytic Inst., 1990—, Cin. Contemporary Arts Ctr., 1997—. Mem. ABA, Nat. Assn. Office and Indsl. Parks, Ohio State Bar Assn., Cin. Bar Assn., Ohio Land Title Assn. Contracts commercial, Estate planning, Real property. Home: 40 Walnut Ave Wyoming OH 45215-4350 Office: Strauss & Troy Fed Res Bldg 150 E 4th St Fl 4 Cincinnati OH 45202-4018

STRAW, LAWRENCE JOSEPH, JR. lawyer; b. Phila., Dec. 22, 1945; s. Lawrence Joseph and Margaret (Wise) S.; m. Linda Carol McClain, Jan. 27, 1973; 1 child, Stacie Victoria. AB, Boston Coll., 1967; JD, U. So. Calif., 1970. Bar: Calif. 1971, U.S. Dist. Ct. (cen. dist.) Calif. 1971, U.S. Supreme Ct. 1977, U.S. Dist. Ct. (ea. and no. dists.) Calif. 1983, U.S. Ct. Appeals (9th cir.) 1983, U.S. Dist. Ct. (so. dist.) Calif. 1992. Atty. Mobil Oil Corp., L.A., 1970-72; assoc. dir. exec. office of pres. Office Econ. Opportunity, Washington, 1973; atty. Mobil Oil Corp., L.A., 1974-82; ptnr. Smaltz & Neelley, 1982-85, Straw & Gilmartin, Santa Monica, Calif., 1985-97, Straw & Gough, L.A., 1997—. Lectr. Calif. Air Resources Bd. Air Pollution Enforcement Symposium, 1983—. Contbg. author: California Environmental Law and Land Use Practice. Mem. edn. appeal bd. U.S. Dept.Edn., Washington, 1986-90; candidate Calif. Atty. Gen., 1986; chmn. L.A. County Tax Assessor's Adv. Com., L.A., 1987-90. Mem. State Bar of Calif., Federalist Soc., Conservative Caucus Inc. (treas. 1975—), Calif. Yacht Club. Republican. Roman Catholic. Avocation: yacht racing. Federal civil litigation, State civil litigation, Environmental. Office: Straw & Gough 12304 Santa Monica Blvd Ste 300 Los Angeles CA 90025-2593 E-mail: ijs@smoglaw.com

STRAYHORN, RALPH NICHOLS, JR. lawyer; b. Durham, N.C., Feb. 16, 1923; s. Ralph Nichols and Annie Jane (Cooper) S.; m. Donleen Carol MacDonald, Sept. 10, 1949; children: Carol Strayhorn Rose, Ralph Nichols III BSBA, U. N.C., 1947, LLB, JD, 1950. Bar: N.C. 1950, U.S. Dist. Ct. (mid. and ea. dists.) N.C. 1950, U.S. Ct. Appeals (4th cir.) 1950. Assoc. Victor S. Bryant, Sr., Durham, 1950-55; ptnr. Bryant, Lipton, Strayhorn & Bryant, 1956-62; sr. ptnr. Newson, Graham, Strayhorn & Hedrick, 1962-78; gen. counsel Wachovia Corp./Wachovia Bank and Trust Co., NA, Winston-Salem, N.C., 1978-88; of counsel Kilpatrick Stockton, 1988—. Legal adv. com. to N.Y. Stock Exch., 1986-89; adv. dir. Wachovia Bank and Trust Co., Durham, 1973-78; mem. N.C. Gen. Assembly, 1959-61; bd. of visitors U. N.C., Wake Forest U. Law Sch. Chmn. bd. 1st Fed. Savs. & Loan Assn., Durham, 1976-78. Lt. comdr. USNR, 1943-46. Fellow Am. Coll. Trial Lawyers, Am. Bar Found., Internat. Assn. Def. Counsel; mem. ABA, N.C. Bar Assn. (pres. 1971-72), Newcomen Soc. U.S., 4th Jud. Conf., Old Town Club (Winston-Salem). Episcopalian. Banking, Contracts commercial. Office: Kilpatrick Stockton 1001 W 4th St Winston Salem NC 27101-2410

STRAZZELLA, JAMES ANTHONY, law educator, lawyer; b. Hanover, Pa., May 18, 1939; s. Anthony F. and Teresa Ann Strazzella; m. Judith A. Coppola, Oct. 9, 1965; children: Jill M., Steven A., Tracy Ann, Michael P. AB, Villanova U., 1961; JD, U. Pa., 1964. Bar: Pa. 1964, D.C., 1965, U.S. Dist. Ct. (ea. and mid. dists.) Pa. 1969, U.S. Ct. Appeals (3rd cir.) 1964, U.S. Ct. Appeals (D.C. cir.) 1965, U.S. Ct. Appeals (4th cir.) 1983, U.S. Supreme Ct. 1969. Law clk. to Hon. Samuel Roberts Pa. Supreme Ct., 1964-65; asst. U.S. atty. D.C., 1965-69; vice dean, asst. prof. law U. Pa., Phila., 1969-73; faculty Temple U., 1973—; James G. Schmidt chair in law, 1989—; acting dean, 1987-89. Chief counsel Kent State investigation Pres.'s Commn. Campus Unrest, 1970; chmn. Atty. Gen.'s Task Force on Family Violence, Pa., 1985-89; mem., chmn. justice ops. Mayor's Criminal Justice Coordinating Commn., Phila., 1983-85; Pa. Joint Coun. Criminal Justice, 1979-82; mem. Com. to Study Pa.'s Unified Jud. Sys., 1980-82; Jud. Coun. Pa., 1972-82; chmn. criminal procedural rules com. Pa. Supreme Ct., 1972-85; mem. task force on prison overcrowding, 1983-85, rsch. adv. com., 1988, Pa. Commn. on Crime and Delinquency; chmn. U.S. Magistrate Judge Merit Selection Com., 1991, mem., 1989, 90, 91; co-chair Mayor's Transition Task Force on Pub. Safety, Phila., 1992; designate D.C. Com. on Adminstrn. of Justice Under Emergency Conditions, 1968; del. D.C. Jud. Conf., 1985, 95. Contbr. articles to profl. jours. and books. Mem. adv. bd. dirs., past pres. A Better Chance in Lower Merion; dir. Hist. Fire Mus., Phila., 1978—; bd. dirs. Lower Merion Hist. Soc., 1998—2000, Neighborhood Civic Assn., Bala-Cynwyd, Pa., 1984—87, Smith Meml. Playground in Fairmount Pk., 1997—, Coun. Legal Edn. Opportunity Bd., 1997—; bd. trustees Bala Cynwyd Pub. Libr., 1999—. Recipient award for disting. tchg. Linback Found., 1983, Advancement of Justice award Pa. Atty. Gen., 1989, Disting. Pub. Svc. award Assn. State and County Detectives, 1989, Spl. Merit award Pa. Assn. Police Chiefs, 1989, significant contbn. to legal scholarship and edn. Beccaria award Phila. Bar Assn. and Nat. IAB Assn., 1995. Fellow: Am. Bar Found.; mem.: ABA (faculty appellate judges seminars 1975—, various coms., acad. advisor appellate judges edn. com. 1993—, reporter task force on federalization criminal law 1998—99), Am. Law Inst., FBA (Phila. crim. law com. adv. bd. 1988—93, chmn. nat. criminal law com. 1991—92), Pa. Bar Assn. (commn. profl. stds. 1981—84, chmn. criminal law sect. 1986—88, Merit award 1987), Phila. Bar Assn. (criminal justice sect., appellate cts. com.), St. Thomas More Soc. (pres. 1985—86, past dir. Phila. area, St. Thomas More award 1996), Order of the Coif (exec. bd. U. Pa.). Roman Catholic. Home and Office: 100 Maple Ave Bala Cynwyd PA 19004-3017 Office: Temple U Law Sch 1719 N Broad St Philadelphia PA 19122-6002

STRECK, FREDERICK LOUIS, III, lawyer; b. St. Louis, Nov. 6, 1960; s. Frederick Louis Jr. and Joan Kathrine (Faerber) S.; m. Michelle Renee Harding; children: Frederick IV, Robert Harding, Joseph Walter, Samuel Franklin. BBA, Tex. Christian U., 1983; JD, St. Mary's U., 1986. Bar: Tex. 1986, U.S. Dist. Ct. (no. dist.) Tex. 1987, U.S. Ct. Appeals (5th cir.) 1987; bd. cert. in personal injury trial law, civil trial advocacy; diplomate Am. Bd. of Trial Advocacy. Atty. Kugle, Stewart, Dent & Frederick, Ft. Worth, 1986-89, The Dent Law Firm, 1990—. State del. Dem. Party, Tex., 1988. Fellow Tex. State Bar Coll.; mem. ABA, ATLA, Am. Coll. Barristers (sr. counsel), Tex. Trial Lawyers Assn., Million Dollar Adv. Forum, Am. Coll. Barristers (sr. counsel). Democrat. Roman Catholic. Avocations: wine collecting, golf, fishing, scuba diving. Federal civil litigation, Personal injury, Workers' compensation. Office: The Dent Law Firm 1120 Penn St Fort Worth TX 76102-3417 Fax: 817-332-5809. E-mail: fstreck3@yahoo.com

STRECKER, DAVID EUGENE, lawyer; b. Carthage, Mo., Nov. 29, 1950; s. Eugene Albert and Erma Freida (Wood) S.; m. Katherine Ann Pugh; children: Charles David, Carrie Christina. BA, Westminster Coll., 1972; JD, Cornell U., 1975, M in Indsl. Labor Rels., 1976. Bar: N.Y. 1976, Okla. 1981, U.S. Dist. Ct. (no. dist.) N.Y. 1976, U.S. Dist. Ct. (ea. dist.) Okla. 1984, U.S. Dist. Ct. (we. dist.) Okla. 2000, U.S. Dist. Ct. (we. and ea. dists.) Ark. 2000, U.S. Ct. Appeals (no. dist.) Okla. 1981, U.S. Ct. Appeals (10th cir.) 1982, U.S. Ct. Appeals (6th cir.) 1990, U.S. Supreme Ct. 1991. Assoc. Conner & Winters, Tulsa, 1980-85, ptnr., 1985-91, Shipley, Inhofe & Strecker, Tulsa, 1991-95, Strecker & Assocs. P.C., Tulsa, 1995—. Instr. paralegal program Tulsa Jr. Coll., 1985—, mem. adv. com., 1986-91; mem. Cornell Secondary Schs. Com., Tulsa, 1985—; adj. instr. labor rels. Okla. State U., 1995—; master Am. Inns of Ct. Bd. dirs., v.p. Tulsa Sr. Svcs., 1988-91; mem. pers. com. Philbrook Art Mus. Capt. JAGC, U.S. Army, 1976-80. Mem. ABA, Okla. Bar Assn. (chmn. labor sect. 1990-91), Tulsa County Bar Assn. (continuing legal edn. com. 1981—), Soc. for Human Resource Mgmt., Tulsa Area Human Resources Assn. (gen. counsel 1989—, v.p. 1994-98, bd. dirs. family and children's svcs. 2000—), Kappa Alpha. Democrat. Episcopalian. Avocations: jogging, golf. Federal civil litigation, Labor, Workers' compensation. Home: 5112 E 107th St Tulsa OK 74137-7238 Office: Midcontinent Tower 401 S Boston Ste 2150 Tulsa OK 74103-4009 E-mail: sandk@juno.com

STREET, ERICA CATHERINE, lawyer; b. Lansing, Mich., July 5, 1958; d. Cassius English and Helen Joanna (Hoesman) S.; m. Robert John Pratte, Oct. 20, 1984; 1 child, Chelsea Nicole Pratte. BA, Hillsdale Coll., 1979; JD, U. Mich., 1981. Bar: Minn. 1982, U.S. Dist. Ct. Minn. 1982, U.S. Ct. Appeals (8th cir.) 1983. Assoc. Best & Flanagan, Mpls., 1981-85; sr. counsel Fingerhut Corp., Minnetonka, Minn., 1985-89, Target Stores, Mpls., 1989-97, asst. gen. counsel, 1997-99; pres. Dayton Hudson Brands Inc., 1999-2000, Target Brands, Inc., Mpls., 2000—. Entertainment, Intellectual property, Trademark and copyright. Office: Target Brands Inc 33 S 6th St Minneapolis MN 55402-3601 E-mail: erica.street@target.com

STREICHER, JAMES FRANKLIN, lawyer; b. Ashtabula, Ohio, Dec. 6, 1940; s. Carl Jacob and Helen Marie (Dugan) S.; m. Sandra JoAnn Jennings, May 22, 1940; children: Cheryl Ann, Gregory Scott, Kerry Marie. BA, Ohio State U., 1962; JD, Case Western Res. U., 1966. Bar: Ohio 1966, U.S. Dist. Ct. (no. dist.) Ohio 1966. Assoc. Calfee, Halter & Griswold, Cleve., 1966-71, ptnr., 1972—. Bd. dirs. The Mariner Group Inc., Ft. Myers, Fla., Spectra-Tech Inc., Stamford, Conn., Mid Am. Consulting; mem. Divsn. Securities Adv. Bd., State of Ohio; lectr. Case Western Res. U., Cleve. State U.; mem. pvt. sector com. John Carroll U. Trustee Achievement Ctr. for Children, Western Reserve Hist. Soc., Make-A-Wish Found. Endowment. Mem. ABA, Fed. Bar Assn., Ohio State Bar Assn., Assn. for Corp. Growth, Ohio Venture Assn., Greater Cleve. Bar Assn. (founding chmn. corp., banking, bus. law sect.), Ohio State U. Alumni Assn., Case Western Res. U. Alumni Assn., Newcomen Soc., Bluecoats Club (Cleve.), Mayfield Country (bd. dirs. 1985-89), Tavern Club, Union Club, Hunting Valley Gun Club, The Pepper Pike Club, Beta Theta Pi, Phi Delta Phi. Roman Catholic. Republican. Securities. Home: 50 Windrush Dr Chagrin Falls OH 44022-6841 Fax: 216-241-0816. E-mail: j.streich@calfee.com

STREICKER, JAMES RICHARD, lawyer; b. Chgo., Nov. 9, 1944; s. Seymour and De Vera (Wolfson) S.; m. Mary Stowell, Mar. 11, 1989; children: David, Sarah. AB, Miami U., 1966; JD, U. Ill., 1969. Bar: Ill. 1969, U.S. Dist. Ct. (no. dist.) Ill. 1970, U.S. Ct. Appeals (7th cir.) 1971, U.S. Supreme Ct. 1980, U.S. Dist. Ct. (ea. dist.) Wis., (no. dist.) Ind. 1986. Asst. atty. gen. State of Ill., 1970-71, asst. appellate def., 1971-75; dep. appellate def. First Dist. Ill., 1975; asst. U.S. atty. No. Dist. Ill., 1975-80; chief criminal receiving and appellate div. U.S. Attys. Office, Ill., 1979-80; ptnr. Cotsirilos, Tighe & Streicker, Chgo., 1980—. Instr. Trial Adv. John Marshall Law Sch., 1979-80, U.S. Atty. Gens. Adv. Inst. 1978-80, Nat. Inst. for Trial Adv. 1981—; lectr. Ill. Inst. Continuing Legal Edn., Sentencing, New Techniques and Attitudes, 1986, Healthcare Fraud and Abuse Seminar, 1998, Fed. Bar Assn., 1990. Mem. ABA, Nat. Assn. Criminal Def. Lawyers, Am. Coll. Trial Lawyers, Am. Bd. Criminal Lawyers, Ill. State Bar Assn., Chgo. Bar Assn. Antitrust, General civil litigation, Criminal.

STREICKER, RICHARD DANIEL, lawyer, record company executive; b. Chgo., Aug. 1, 1952; s. Ned Charles and Dolores May (Tronsky) S. BA, U. Mich., 1974; JD, Harvard U., 1978. Bar: Ill. 1978, U.S. Dist. Ct. (no. dist.) Ill. 1979, Calif. 1980, U.S. Dist. Ct. (cen. dist.) Calif. 1981, Oreg. 1988, N.Y. 1994. Assoc. Mayer, Brown & Platt, Chgo., 1978-79, Mitchell, Silberberg & Knupp, Los Angeles, 1980-81; sr. v.p. legal and bus. affairs Warner Bros. Records Inc., N.Y.C., 1982—. Mem. Ill. Bar Assn., Calif. Bar Assn., Oreg. State Bar, N.Y. State Bar. Avocations: literature, music. Entertainment. Office: Warner Bros Records Inc 75 Rockefeller Plz New York NY 10019-6908

STREIT, MICHAEL J. judge; b. Sheldon, Iowa; 1 child. BA, U. Iowa, 1972; grad., U. San Diego Sch. Law, 1975. Cert.: (U.S. Ct. Appeals) 1996. Asst. atty. Lucas County, atty.; dist. ct. judge, 1983; Supreme Ct. justice Iowa State Supreme Ct., 2001—. Mem.: Supreme Ct. Edn. Adv. Com., Judges Assn. Edn. Com., Iowa Jud. Inst., Supreme Ct. Jud. Tech. Com., Blackstone Inn of Ct. Office: State House Des Moines IA 50319*

STRENSKI, ROBERT FRANCIS, lawyer; b. Chgo., Oct. 10, 1947; s. Bernard F. and Harriet L. (Prokopiak) S. BS, U. Ill., 1969; JD, Washington U., St. Louis, 1973; postgrad., U. Colo., 1975. Bar: Mo. 1973, Colo. 1974. Acct. Motorola, Inc., Chgo., 1970, City and County of Denver, 1973-74, asst. city atty., 1974—. Precinct committeeman Denver Dem. Com., 1976-78, dist. fin. chmn., 1977-78; arbitrator Better Bus. Bur., Denver, 1977—; mediator Ctr. for Dispute Resolution, Denver, 1980 Mem. Colo. Bar Assn., Denver Bar Assn., Nat. Inst. Mcpl. Law Officers (ethics com. 1985-88), Am. Arbitration Assn. (arbitrator). Democrat. Roman Catholic. Home: 410 Pearl St Denver CO 80203-3808 Office: Law Dept City & County Denver 353 City And County Bldg Denver CO 80202 E-mail: strenrf@ci.denver.co.us

STRICKLAND, ANNETTE WEBB, lawyer; b. Kinston, N.C., Oct. 29, 1965; d. Davis Speight and Helen Edwards Webb; m. Robert J. Strickland, May 17, 1997. BS in Criminal Justice, N.C. Wesleyan Coll., 1991; JD, N.C. Ctrl. U., 1997. Bar: N.C. 1997. Paralegal Cranfill, Sumner & Hartzog, Raleigh, N.C., 1986-97; assoc. Wallace, Morris & Barwick, Kinston, 1997—. Mem. ABA, N.C. Bar Assn., N.C. Assn. Women Attys. Criminal, Family and matrimonial, General practice. Office: Wallace Morris & Barwick 131 S Queen St Kinston NC 28501

STRICKLAND, TOM, former prosecutor; married; three children. Bachelor's degree, La. State U., 1974; JD, U. Tex., 1977. Chief policy adv. to Gov. Dick Lamm, 1982-84; sr. ptnr. Brownstein, Hyatt, Farber, and Strickland, 1999; U.S. atty. Colo. dist. U.S. Dept. Justice, 1999—2001. Dem. candidate U.S. Sen., 1996. Office: 1961 Stout St Ste 1200 Denver CO 80294-1200*

STRICKLAND, WILTON L. lawyer; b. Ft. Myers, July 1, 1942; s. Lorenzo Strickland and Mary Voncille Singletary; m. Barbara Hathaway Lahna (div. July 1984); children: Amy Beth Strickland-Quattlebaum, Wilton Hathaway Strickland. BA, U. Fla., 1964; JD, Stetson U., 1969. Bar: Fla. 1969, U.S. Dist. Ct. (so. dist.) Fla. 1969, Trial Bar (so. dist.) Fla. 1983, U.S. Dist. Ct. (mid. dist.) Fla. 1988, U.S. Ct. Appeals (5th cir.) 1978, U.S. Ct. Appeals (11th cir.) 1981, U.S. Supreme Ct. 1977. Ptnr. Howell, Kirby, Montgomery et al, Ft. Lauderdale, Fla., 1969-73, Ferrero, Middlebrooks &

Houston, Ft. Lauderdale, 1974-77, Ferrero, Middlebrooks & Strickland, Ft. Lauderdale, 1977-91, Strickland & Seidule, Ft. Lauderdale, 1991-98; pvt. practice Wilton L. Strickland, P.A., 1998—. Chmn. bd. Hospice Care Broward County, Inc.; bd. dirs. Salvation Army Broward County; mem. Helping Abandoned and Dependent Youth. Mem. ABA, ATLA, Fla. Bar (mem. ethics com.), Acad. Fla. Trial Lawyers (dir. 1980-84), Broward County Trial Lawyers Assn. (past pres. 1981), Broward County Bar Assn., Am. Bd. Trial Advs. (founder Broward County chpt.), Million Dollar Advocates Forum, The Bar Register of Preeminent Lawyers, Phi Alpha Delta (former pres. Brewer chpt.). Democrat. Presbyterian. Avocations: winter skiing, reading, hiking, boating, white water rafting. General civil litigation, Personal injury, Product liability. Home: 2897 NE 25th St Fort Lauderdale FL 33305-1722 Office: # 303 1401 E Broward Blvd Ste 303 Fort Lauderdale FL 33301-2100

STRIDIRON, IVER ALLISON, attorney general; m. Priscilla Blyden; 4 children. BA Lincoln U., 1969; JD, Howard U., 1974. Atty. U.S. Nuclear Regulatory Commn., U.S. Commn. on Civil Rights, Washington, 1974—77; pvt. practice St. Thomas, 1977—99; mem. V.I. Legis., 1981—83, 1985—89; atty. gen. V.I., 1999—. Office: Dept Justice 48B-50C Kronprindsens Gade GERS Bldg 2nd fl Charlotte Amalie VI 00802*

STRIEFSKY, LINDA A(NN), lawyer; b. Carbondale, Pa., Apr. 27, 1952; d. Leo James and Antoinette Marie (Carachilo) S.; m. James Richard Carlson, Nov. 3, 1984; children: David Carlson, Paul Carlson, Daniel Carlson. BA summa cum laude, Marywood Coll., 1974; JD, Georgetown U., 1977. Bar: Ohio 1977. Assoc. Thompson Hine LLP (formerly Thompson, Hine & Flory), Cleve., 1977-85, ptnr., 1985—. Loaned exec. United Way N.E. Ohio, Cleve., 1978; trustee Cleve. Pub. Radio. Mem. ABA (real estate fin. com. 1980-87, vice chmn. leader liability com. 1993-97, mem. non-traditional real estate fin. com. 1987—), Am. Bar Found., Am. Coll. Real Estate Lawyers (bd. govs. 1994-98, treas. 1999), Internat. Coun. Shopping Ctrs., Nat. Assn. Office and Indsl. Parks, Urban Land Inst. (chmn. Cleve. dist. coun. 1996-2000), Cleve. Real Estate Women, Ohio Bar Assn. (bd. govs. real property sect. 1985-97), Greater Cleve. Bar Assn. (chmn. bar applicants com. 1983-84, exec. coun. young lawyers sect. 1982-85, chmn. 1984-85, mem. exec. coun. real property sect. 1980-84, Merit Svc. award 1983, 85), Pi Gamma Mu. Democrat. Roman Catholic. Contracts commercial, Construction, Real property. Home: 2222 Delamere Dr Cleveland OH 44106-3204 Office: Thompson Hine LLP 3900 Key Ctr 127 Public Square Cleveland OH 44114-1216 E-mail: linda.striefsky@thompsonhine.com

STRIMBU, VICTOR, JR. lawyer; b. New Philadelphia, Ohio, Nov. 25, 1932; s. Victor and Veda (Stancu) S.; m. Kathryn May Schrote, Apr. 9, 1955 (dec. 1995); children: Victor Paul, Michael, Julie, Sue; m. Marjorie Bichsel, Oct. 23, 1999. BA, Heidelberg Coll., 1954; postgrad., Western Res. U., 1956-57; JD, COlumbia U., 1960. Bar: Ohio 1960, U.S. Supreme Ct. 1972. With Baker & Hostetler LLP, Cleve., 1960—, ptnr., 1970—. Bd. dirs. North Coast Health Ministry; mem. Bay Village (Ohio) Bd. Edn., 1976-84, pres., 1978-82; mem. indsl. rels. adv. com. Cleve. State U., 1979—, chmn., 1982, 98; mem. Bay Village Planning Commn., 1967-69; life mem. Ohio PTA; mem. Greater Cleve. Growth Assn.; trustee New Cleve. Campaign, 1987—, North Coast Health Ministry, 1989—, Heidelberg Coll., 1996—; mem. indsl. rels. adv. com. Cleve. State U., 1979—, chmn., 1982, vice chmn., 1998. With AUS, 1955-56. Mem. ABA, Ohio Bar Assn., Greater Cleve. Bar Assn., Ohio Newspaper Assn. (minority affairs com. 1987—), Ct. of Nisi Prius Club, Cleve. Athletic Club, The Club at Soc. Ctr. Republican. Presbyterian. Labor. Office: Baker & Hostetler LLP 3200 National City Ctr 1900 E 9th St Ste 3200 Cleveland OH 44114-3475

STRINGER, EDWARD CHARLES, state supreme court justice; b. St. Paul, Feb. 13, 1935; s. Philip and Anne (Driscoll) S.; m. Mary Lucille Lange, June 19, 1957 (div. Mar. 1991); children: Philip, Lucille, Charles, Carolyn; m. Virginia L. Ward, Sept. 10, 1993. BA, Amherst Coll., 1957; LLD, U. Minn., 1960. Bar: Minn. Ptnr. Stringer, Donnelly & Sharood, St. Paul, 1960-69, Briggs & Morgan, St. Paul, 1969-79; sr. v.p., gen. counsel Pillsbury Co., Mpls., 1980-82, exec. v.p., gen. counsel, 1982-83, exec. v.p., gen. counsel, chief adminstrv. officer, 1983-89; gen. counsel U.S. Dept. Edn., Washington, 1989-91; chief of staff Minn. Gov. Arne H. Carlson, 1992-94; assoc. justice Minn. Supreme Ct., St. Paul, 1994—. Mem. ABA, Minn. State Bar Assn., Ramsey County Bar Assn. (sec. 1977-80), Order of Coif, Mpls. Club. Congregationalist. Home: 712 Linwood Ave Saint Paul MN 55105-3513 Office: Minn Judicial Center 25 Constitution Ave Saint Paul MN 55155-1500

STRODE, JOSEPH ARLIN, lawyer; b. DeWitt, Ark., Mar. 5, 1946; s. Thomas Joseph and Nora (Richardson) S.; m. Carolyn Taylor, Feb. 9, 1969; children: Tanya Briana, William Joseph. BSEE with honors, U. Ark., 1969; JD, So. Meth. U., 1972. Bar: Ark. 1972. Design engr. Tex. Instruments Inc., Dallas, 1969-70; patent agent Tex. Instruments, 1970—72; assoc. Bridges, Young, Matthews, Drake, Pine Bluff, Ark., 1972-74, ptnr., 1975—. Chmn. Pine Bluff Airport Commn., 1993; bd. dirs. United Way Jefferson County, Pine Bluff, 1975-77, campaign chmn., 1983, pres., 1986, exec. com., 1983-87; bd. dirs. Leadership Pine Bluff, 1983-85. Mem. Ark. Bar Assn., Jefferson County Bar Assn. (pres. 1995), Pine Bluff C. of C. (dir. 1981, 84, 94, 97), Ark. Wildlife Fed. (dir. 1979-81), Jefferson County Wildlife Assn. (dir. 1973-80, pres. 1974-76), Kiwanis (lt. gov. Mo.-Ark. divsn. 1983-84, chmn. lt. govs. 1983-84), Order of Coif, Tau Beta Pi, Eta Kappa Nu. Banking, Contracts commercial, Intellectual property. Home: 7600 Jay Lynn Ln Pine Bluff AR 71603-9387 Office: 315 E 8th Ave Pine Bluff AR 71601-5005 E-mail: joestrode@bridgesplc.com

STROEBEL, JOHN STEPHEN, lawyer; b. May 17, 1951; s. Paul George and Patricia (Smith) S.; m. Denise Mary McGee, Sept. 16, 1978; children— Jonathan Paul, James Philip, Jennifer Patricia. B.A., Hamilton Coll., 1973; J.D., Cornell U., 1976. Bar: Pa. 1976, U.S. Dist. Ct. (ea. dist.) Pa. 1976. Assoc. Dechert Price & Rhoads, Phila., 1976-78; asst. legal counsel Rohm & Haas Co., Phila., 1976-78, asst. gen. counsel, 1978-85, assoc. gen. counsel 1985—; dir. The Philadelphia Singers, Music Group of Phila. Mem. Phi Beta Kappa. Republican. Episcopalian. Antitrust, General corporate. Home: 1021 Beaumont Rd Berwyn PA 19312-2007 Office: Rohm & Haas Co Independence Mall W Philadelphia PA 19105

STROM, J. PRESTON, JR. lawyer; b. May 21, 1959; s. Grace and J.P. Sr. S.; m. Donna Savoca, Oct. 5, 1985; children: Margaret, Caroline. BA, U. S.C., 1981, JD, 1984. Bar: S.C. 1984, U.S. Dist. Ct. S.C., 1984, U.S. Ct. Appeals (4th cir.) 1984. Asst. solicitor 5th Jud. Cir., S.C., 1985-86; ptnr. Leventis, Strom & Wicker, 1986-88, Harpootlian & Strom, 1988-90, Bolt, Popowski, McCulloch & Strom, 1990-93; acting U.S. atty. Office U.S. Atty., S.C., 1993, U.S. atty., 1993-96; atty. Strom Law Firm, LLC, Columbia, 1996—. Chmn. Law Enforcement Coord. Com.; chmn. juvenile justice and child support enforcement subcom. U.S. Dept. Justice; active Atty. Gen. Adv. Com. Mem. S.C. Bar, S.C. Trial Lawyers Assn., Richland County Bar Assn. (chmn. criminal law sect.). General civil litigation, Criminal. Office: Strom & Young LLP 1201 Hampton St Ste 3A Columbia SC 29201-2865

STROM, LYLE ELMER, federal judge; b. Omaha, Jan. 6, 1925; s. Elmer T. and Eda (Hanisch) S.; m. Regina Ann Kelly, July 31, 1950; children: Mary Bess, Susan Frances (dec.), Amy Claire, Cassie A., David Kelly, Margaret Mary, Bryan Thomas. Student, U. Nebr., 1946-47; AB, Creighton U., 1950, JD cum laude, 1953. Bar: Nebr. 1953. Assoc. Fitzgerald, Brown, Leahy, Strom, Schorr & Barmettler and predecessor firm, Omaha, 1953-60, ptnr., 1960-63, gen. trial ptnr., 1963-85; judge U.S. Dist. Ct. Nebr., 1985-87, chief judge, 1987-94, sr. judge, 1995—. Adj. prof. law Creighton U., 1959-95, clinical prof., 1996—; mem. com. pattern jury instrns. and practice and proc. Nebr. Supreme Ct., 1965-91; spl. legal counsel Omaha Charter Rev. Commn., 1973; chair gender fairness task force U.S. Ct. Appeals (8th cir.), 1993-97. Exec. com Covered Wagon Coun. Boy Scouts Am., 1953-57, bd. trustees and exec. com. Mid-Am. Coun., 1988—; chmn. bd. trustees Marian H.S., 1969-71; mem. pres. coun. Creighton U., 1990—. Ensign USNR and with U.S. Maritime Svc., 1943-46. Fellow Am. Coll. Trial Lawyers, Internat. Acad. Trial Lawyers; mem. Nebr. Bar Assn. (ho. of dels. 1978-81, exec. coun. 1981-87, pres. 1989-90), Nebr. Bar Found. (bd. trustees 1998—), Omaha Bar Assn. (pres. 1980-81), Am. Judicature Soc., Midwestern Assn. Amateur Athletic Union (pres. 1976-78), Rotary (pres. 1993-94), Alpha Sigma Nu (pres. alumni chpt. 1970-71). Republican. Roman Catholic. Office: US Dist Ct Roman Hruska Courthouse 111 S 18th Plz Ste 3190 Omaha NE 68102

STROM, MICHAEL A. lawyer; b. Chgo., Dec. 14, 1952; s. David H. and Sylvia (Abelson) S.; m. Sherry Sinett, May 29, 1977; children: Eric M., Shayna D. BA, U. Ill., 1974; JD, Boston U., 1977. Bar: Ill. 1977, U.S. Dist. Ct. (no. dist.) Ill. 1977. Assoc. Schaffenegger, Watson & Peterson, Chgo., 1978-85; ptnr., 1985-95; ptnr. Brydges, Riseborough, Peterson, Franke & Morris, Chgo., 1995-96; assoc. French, Kezelis & Kominiarek, Chgo., 1996—. Mem. Ill. State Bar Assn., Chgo. Bar Assn., Trial Lawyers Club Chgo., Ill. Assn. Def. Trial Counsel, Chgo. Coalition for Law Related Edn. (instr. 1984—). Jewish. Federal civil litigation, State civil litigation, Personal injury. Office: French Kezelis & Kominiarek 33 N Dearborn St Ste 700 Chicago IL 60602-3104

STROM, MILTON GARY, lawyer; b. Rochester, N.Y., Dec. 5, 1942; s. Harold and Dolly (Isaacson) S.; m. Barbara A. Simon, Jan. 18, 1975; children: Carolyn, Michael, Jonathan. BS in Econ., U. Pa., 1964; JD, Cornell U., 1967. Bar: N.Y. 1968, U.S. Dist. Ct. (W. dist.) N.Y. 1968, U.S. Ct. Claims 1969, U.S. Ct. Mil. Appeals 1969, U.S. Ct. Appeals (D.C. cir.) 1970, U.S. Supreme Ct. 1972, U.S. Dist. Ct. (so. dist.) N.Y. 1975. Atty. SEC, Washington, 1968-71; assoc. Skadden, Arps, Slate, Meagher & Flom, N.Y.C., 1971-76, ptnr., 1977—. Served with USCGR, 1967-73. Mem. ABA, N.Y. State Bar Assn. (corp. law sect.), Assn. of Bar of City of N.Y., Internat. Bar Assn. Republican. Jewish. Club: Beach Point. Avocations: tennis, skiing, golf. E-mail: m. General corporate, Securities. Office: Skadden Arps Slate Meagher & Flom 4 Times Sq Fl 24 New York NY 10036-6595 E-mail: strom@skadden.com

STROMBERG, JEAN WILBUR GLEASON, lawyer; b. St. Louis, Oct. 31, 1943; d. Ray Lyman and Martha (Bugbee) W.; m. Gerald Kermit Gleason, Aug. 28, 1966 (div. 1987); children: C. Blake, Peter Wilbur; m. Kurt Stromberg, Jan. 3, 1993; 1 child, Kristoffer Stromberg. BA, Wellesley Coll., 1965; LLB cum laude, Harvard U., 1968. Bar: Calif. 1969, D.C. 1978. Assoc. Brobeck, Phleger & Harrison, San Francisco, 1969-72; spl. counsel to dir. div. corp. fin. SEC, Washington, 1972-76, assoc. dir. div. investment mgmt., 1976-78; of counsel Fulbright & Jaworski, 1978-80, ptnr., 1980-96; dir. fin. instns. and market issues GAO, 1996-97; cons., 1997—. Mem. adv. panel on legal issues GAO, 1992-96, NASD select com. on Nasdaq, 1994-96; trustee AARP Investment Program and AARP Scudder Mut. Funds, 1997-2000; dir. Scudder Mutual Funds, 2000—. Dir. William and Flora Hewlett Found., 2000—. Mem. ABA (chmn. subcom. on securities and banks, corp. laws com., bus. sect. 1982-93), D.C. Bar Assn. (chmn. steering com. bus. sect. 1982-84), FBA (chair exec. coun., securities com. 1993-95), Am. Bar Retirement Assn. (bd. dirs. 1986-90, 94-96), Phi Beta Kappa. General corporate, Securities. Home and Office: 3816 Military Rd NW Washington DC 20015-2704

STROMME, GARY L. law librarian; b. Willmar, Minn., July 8, 1939; s. William A. and Edla A. (Soderberg) S.; m. Suzanne Readman, July 21, 1990. BA, Pacific Luth. U., 1965; BLS, U. B.C., Vancouver, Can., 1967; JD, U. Calif., San Francisco, 1973. Bar: Calif. 1973, U.S. Supreme Ct. 1977. Serials libr. U. Minn. St. Paul. Campus Libr., 1967-69; asst. libr. McCutchen, Doyle, Brown and Enerson, San Francisco, 1970-71, Graham & James, San Francisco, 1971-73, ind. contracting atty., 1973-74; law libr. Pacific Gas and Electric Co., 1974-95; cons., 1995—. Lectr. in field. Author: An Introduction to the use of the Law Library, 1974, 76, Basic Legal Research Techniques, 1979. With USAF, 1959-63. Mem. ABA (chmn. libr. com. of sect. econs. of law practice 1978-82), Am. Assn. Law Librs. (chmn. com. on indexing of legal periodicals 1986-88), Western Pacific Assn. Law Librs., No. Calif. Assn. Law Librs., Pvt. Law Librs., Corp. Law Librs. Home: 6106 Ocean View Dr Oakland CA 94618-1841 E-mail: stromme@aimnet.com

STRØMME, VIDAR, lawyer; b. Lyngdal , Norway, Nov. 17, 1958; Candidate of Jurisprudence, U. Oslo (Norway), 1983. Bar: Supreme Ct. Norway 1992. Police prosecutor, Follo, Norway, 1983-85; assoc. judge Ålesund, Norway, 1985-87; dist. atty. D Molde, Norway, 1987-88; legal counsellor Sunnmørsbanken, Norway, 1988-89; atty. gen. civil affairs Oslo, 1989-93; ptnr. Law Firm Schjødt, 1993—. Communications, Entertainment, Libel. Office: Advokatfirmaet Schjødt Dronning Mauds GT 11 Postboks 2444 0201 Oslo Norway

STRONE, MICHAEL JONATHAN, lawyer; b. N.Y.C., Feb. 26, 1953; s. Bernard William and Judith Semem (Sogg) S.; m. Andrea Nan Acker, Jan. 27, 1979; children: Noah Gregory, Joshua Samuel. BA cum laude, Colby Coll., 1974; JD, Fordham Law Sch., 1978. Bar: N.J. 1978, N.Y. 1979, Conn. 1988, U.S. Ct. Appeals (2d and 3d cirs.) 1979, U.S. Dist. Ct. (so. and ea. dists.) N.Y. 1979, U.S. Dist. Ct. N.J. 1979). Assoc. Ratheim Hoffman et al, N.Y.C., 1978-80, Boetin Hays et al, N.Y.C., 1980-84; v.p., assoc. gen. counsel, asst. sec. GE Investment Corp., Stamford, Conn., 1984-2000; v.p., gen. counsel real estate GE Asset Mgmt. Inc., 2000—. Bd. dirs. N.Y. chpt. Juvenile Diabetes Found., N.Y.C., 1981-89, vice chmn., 1981-88; mem. fin. com. Juvenile Diabetes Found. Internat., 1981-86; asst. prin. bassist Westchester Symphony Orch., Scarsdale, N.Y., 1982-2000, pres., 1982-87, chmn. bd., 1982-90, exec. mng. dir., 1990-93; vice chmn. ann. dinner NCCJ, 1987; bd. dirs. Parkinson's Disease Soc. Am., 1989-96, chmn. merger com., 1991-96; bd. dirs. Parkinson's Action Network, 1994-98; trustee Jewish Cmty. Ctr. of Harrison, 1996—, mem. ritual com., 1996—, chmn., 2000—, chmn. alt. svcs. com., lay cantor, 1997—; chmn. county United Way Campaign, 1999, bd. dirs. Harrison Little League, 2001— Mem. ABA (chmn. pension plan investments 1989-91, chmn. asset mgmt. 1992-94, 95-97, significant legis. coms. 1985-92, chmn. subcom. on joint ventures 1988-90), Am. Coll. Real Estate Lawyers (com. professionalism 1994—, v. chmn. 1999-2000), Am. Polit. Items Collectors, The Corp. Bar Assn., Nat. Assn. Real Estate Investment Mgrs. (sr. legal officers adv. com. 1993—, ann. forum chair 1997), Colby Coll. Alumni Coun. (nominating com. 1994-97), Fordham Law Alumni Assn., The Internat. Netsuke Soc., Jewish Geneal. Soc. Republican. General corporate, Pension, profit-sharing, and employee benefits, Real property. Home: 10 Genesee Trail Harrison NY 10528-1802 Office: Gen Electric Asset Mgmt Inc 3003 Summer St Stamford CT 06905-4316 E-mail: michael.strone@corporate.ge.com

STRONG, GEORGE GORDON, JR. litigation and management consultant; b. Toledo, Apr. 19, 1947; s. George Gordon and Jean Boyd (McDougall) S.; m. Annsley Palmer Chapman, Nov. 30, 1974; children: George III, Courtney, Meredith, Alexis. BA, Yale U., 1969; MBA, Harvard U., 1971; JD, U. San Diego, 1974. Bar: Calif. 1974, U.S. Dist. Ct. (cen. dist.) Calif. 1974; CPA, Calif., Hawaii, cert. mgmt. cons. Contr. Vitredent Corp., Beverly Hills, Calif., 1974-76; sr. mgr. Price Waterhouse, L.A., 1976-82, ptnr., 1987-93, mng. ptnr. west region dispute analysis and corp. recovery, 1993-98, mem. policy bd., bd. dirs., 1995-98, combination bd., 1997-98; bd. ptnrs., prin Pricewaterhouse Coopers LLP, 1998-2001; global oversight bd. Pricewaterhouse Coopers, 1998-2001; exec. v.p., COO Internat. Customs Service, Long Beach, Calif., 1982-84; CFO Uniform Software Systems, Santa Monica, 1984-85; exec. v.p., COO Cipherlink Corp., 1986; pres. Woodleigh Lane, Inc., Flintridge, Calif., 1985-87. Treas. L.A. SPCA; bd. dirs. So. Calif. Humane Soc. Mem. ABA, AICPA, Calif. State Bar, Calif. Soc. CPAs, Andover Abbott Alumni So. Calif. (bd. dirs.), Inst. Mgmt. Cons., Harvard Bus. Sch. Alumni Assn. (bd. dirs. 1996-99), Harvard Bus. Sch. Assn. So. Calif. (chmn. bd. trustees scholarship fund 1992—, pres. 1988-89, dir. 1996-99, 2001—), Harvard Club N.Y., Yale Club N.Y., Lincoln Club, Calif. Club, Jonathan Club, Flint Canyon Tennis Club, Olympic Club, Annandale Golf Club, Coral Beach and Tennis Club, Mid Ocean Golf Club, Royal Bermuda Yacht Club, Valley Hunt Club. Republican. Presbyterian. Avocations: golf, tennis, bridge. Federal civil litigation, State civil litigation, Computer. Home: 5455 Castle Knoll Rd La Canada Flintridge CA 91011-1319 Office: 400 S Hope St Ste 2200 Los Angeles CA 90071-2823 E-mail: george.strong@us.pwcglobal.com

STROTHER, JAY D. legal editor; b. Wichita, Kans., May 31, 1967; m. Cynthia L. Mehnert, Sept. 7, 1991; children: Garrett, Claire. BA, U. Tulsa, 1989. Editor U.S. Jr. C. of C., Tulsa, 1990-93, Assn. Legal Adminstrs., Vernon Hills, Ill., 1993—; editor-in-chief Legal Mgmt. Mag. Author: ALA News. Mem. Am. Soc. Assn. Execs., Soc. Nat. Assn. Publs. (bd. dirs. Chgo. chpt.), Internat. Assn. Bus. Communicators (bd. dirs., suburban v.p. 1994-95), Am. Soc. Bus. Press Editors. Office: Assn Legal Adminstrs 175 E Hawthorn Pkwy Vernon Hills IL 60061-1463 E-mail: jstrother@alanet.org

STROTHER, LANE HOWARD, lawyer; b. Altus, Okla., Mar. 26, 1945; s. Lynn H. and Elwanda (Melton) S.; m. Judith L. Cook, Dec. 17, 1966; children: Jodi L., Megan K., Mica J. BA, Ouachita Bapt. U., 1968; MEd, U. Ark., 1970, JD, 1979. Bar: Ark. 1979, U.S. Dist. Ct. (we. and ea. dists.) Ark. 1979, Mo. 1987. Gen. agt. Res. Life Ins. Co., Dallas, 1968-70; assoc. dir. devel. Ouachita Bapt. U., Arkadelphia, Ark., 1971-76; agt. Northwestern Nat. Life Ins. Co., Little Rock, 1976-79; ptnr. Osmon, Wilber & Strother, Mountain Home, Ark., 1979-81, Strother Firm, Mountain Home, 1981—. Cons. Our Way, Little Rock, 1976-77; bd. dirs. Ark. Bapt. Newsmagazine, 1981-86, 87-93. Bd. dirs. Ind. Coll. Fund Ark.; sec. Ouachita Bapt. U. Devel. Council, Arkadelphia, 1979-83. Served to 1st lt. U.S. Army, 1970-71. Named one of Outstanding Young Men of Am., 1971. Mem. ABA, Ark. Bar Assn., Baxter County Bar Assn. (pres. 1987-88). Democrat. Baptist. Lodge: Rotary. Avocation: tennis. Consumer commercial, Estate planning, General practice. Home: 940 E 4th St Mountain Home AR 72653-4112 Office: 1 Cedar Sq PO Box 1600 Mountain Home AR 72654-1600 E-mail: Strother@mtnhome.com

STROTHER, ROBIN DALE, lawyer; b. Albuquerque, June 18, 1951; s. Ralph Lawrence and Ruth Lillian (Balfour) S.; m. Nancy Anne Blackwood, Jan. 4, 1975; children— Shane Blackwood, Tracy Dawn. Student U.S. Mil. Acad., 1969-71; B.A., U. Tex., 1973; J.D., U. N.Mex., 1976. Bar: N.Mex. 1976, U.S. Dist. Ct. N.Mex. 1976, U.S. Ct. Appeals (10th cir.) 1976. Assoc., Shaffer, Butt, Jones & Thornton, Albuquerque, 1976-78, Tansey, Rosebrough, Roberts & Gerding, Farmington, N.Mex., 1978— . Bd. dirs. Am. Lung Assn. N.Mex., Albuquerque, 1980— . Mem. San Juan County Bar Assn. (pres. 1984—), State Bar Assn. N.Mex. (v.p. Young Lawyers Div. 1978), U. N.Mex. Alumni Assn. (pres. San Juan County chpt. 1984—), Pi Sigma Alpha. Democrat. Baptist. General civil litigation, Personal injury, Workers' compensation. Office: Tansey Rosebrough Gerding & Strother PO Box 129 Farmington NM 87499-0129

STROUD, ROBERT EDWARD, lawyer; b. Chester, S.C., July 24, 1934; s. Coy Franklin and Leila (Caldwell) S.; m. Katherine C. Stroud, Apr. 8, 1961; children: Robert Gordon, Margaret Lathan. AB, Washington and Lee U., 1956, LLB, 1958. Bar: Va. 1959, U.S. Ct. Appeals (4th cir.) 1967, U.S. Tax Ct. 1959. Assoc. McGuire, Woods, Battle & Boothe LLP, Charlottesville, Va., 1959-64; ptnr. McGuire Woods, LLP, 1964—, mem. exec. com., 1978-89. Lectr. math. Washington and Lee U., 1957-59; lectr. bus. tax Grad. Bus. Sch., U. Va., Charlottesville, 1969-87, lectr. corp. taxation law sch., 1985-91; lectr. to legal edn. insts., lectr. in corp. law Washington and Lee Law Sch., Lexington Va., 1984. Co-author: Buying, Selling and Merging Businesses, 1975; editor-in-chief Washington and Lee Law Rev., 1959; editor: Advising Small Business Clients, Vol. 1, 1978, 4th edit., 1994, Vol. 2, 1980, 3d edit., 1990; contbr. articles to profl. jours. Pres. Charlottesville Housing Found., 1968-73; mem. mgmt. coun. Montreat Conf. Ct., N.C., 1974-77; trustee Presbyn. Found., 1972-73, Union Theol. Sem., Va., 1983-91; bd. dirs. Presbyn. Outlook Found., 1974—, pres., 1985-88; mem. governing coun. Presbyn. Synod of the Virginias, 1973-78, moderator of coun., 1977-78, moderator of Synod, 1977-78; trustee, v.p. Va. Tax Found., 1984-95; adv. bd. Westminster Orgn. Concert Series, 1989-93; bd. dirs. Shannon Found. for Excellence in Pub. Edn., Charlottesville, 1996—; adv. bd. Ashlawn-Highland Summer Festival, 1989—, pres., 1994-2000; gov. coun. Presbyn. Presbytery of the James, 1993-96, moderator of coun., 1995-96; moderator of presbytery, 1997. Capt. inf. U.S. Army, 1958, with res. 1958-70. Fellow Am. Bar Found., Va. Law Found.; mem. ABA, Va. State Bar, Va. Bar Assn., Nat. Tax Inst., Am. Judicature Soc., Washington and Lee Law Sch. Assn. (governing coun. 1974-80, pres. 1979-80), Redland Club, Bull and Bear Club, Phi Delta Sigma, Omicron Delta Kappa, Phi Delta Phi. Democrat. General corporate, Mergers and acquisitions, Corporate taxation. Home: 345 Terrell Ct Charlottesville VA 22901-2171 Office: McGuire Woods LLP PO Box 1288 Charlottesville VA 22902-1288 E-mail: rstroud@mcguirewoods.com

STROUGO, ROBERT ISAAC, lawyer; b. N.Y.C., May 23, 1943; s. Victor and Mary Strougo; m. Barbara Lieb, June 27, 1976; children: Debra, David. BA, CCNY, 1965; JD, N.Y. Law Sch., 1970. Bar: N.Y. 1971, U.S. Dist. Ct. (so. and ea. dists.) N.Y. 1975. Pvt. practice, N.Y.C., 1971—; owner NYC Realty; also investment and fin. adviser; arbitrator Civil Ct. of N.Y. Active Rep. Nat. Com.; mem. Nat. Rep. Senatorial Com., Rep. Campaign Coun. Recipient certs. of recognition Nat. Rep. Congl. Com.; honoree Eisenhower Commn. Rep. Nat. Com., 1997. Mem. ABA, Kings County Bar Assn., N.Y. State Legis. Com., Nat. Defenders Assn., N.Y. State Com. on Trial Cts., Bklyn. Bar Assn., Am. Judges Assn., Am. Arbitration Assn. (arbitrator civil ct.), Am. Registry of Arbitrators. E-mial. General practice, Real property, Securities. Home: 305 E 86th St # 17ne New York NY 10028-4702 Office: 21 E 40th St Ste 1800 New York NY 10016-0501 E-mail: strougo@aol.com, atty.nyc@aol.com

STROUP, STANLEY STEPHENSON, lawyer, educator; b. Los Angeles, Mar. 7, 1944; s. Francis Edwin and Marjory (Weimer) S.; m. Sylvia Douglass, June 15, 1968; children: Stacie, Stephen, Sarah. A.B., U. Ill., 1966; J.D., U. Mich., 1969. Bar: Ill. 1969, Calif. 1981, Minn. 1984. Atty. First Nat. Bank Chgo., 1969-78, asst. gen. counsel, 1978-80, v.p., 1980; sr. v.p., chief legal officer Bank of Calif., San Francisco, 1980-84; sr. v.p., gen. counsel Norwest Corp., Mpls., 1984-93, exec. v.p., gen. counsel, 1993-98, Wells Fargo & Co., San Francisco, 1998—. Mem. adj. faculty Coll. Law, William Mitchell Coll., St. Paul, 1985-98; mem. Regulatory Affairs Coun., Bank Adminstrn. Inst., 1996—. Bd. dirs. San Francisco Zool. Soc., 2000—, Legal Aid Soc. San Francisco, 1999—. Mem. ABA, Ill. Bar Assn., State Bar Calif., Minn. Bar Assn., Bar Assn. San Francisco (bd. dirs. 2000—), Fin. Svcs. Roundtable. Banking, Contracts commercial. Office: Wells Fargo & Co 633 Folsom St San Francisco CA 94107-3600 E-mail: stroupss@wellsfargo.com

STROYD, ARTHUR HEISTER, lawyer; b. Pitts., Sept. 5, 1945; 1 child, Elizabeth. AB, Kenyon Coll., 1967; JD, U. Pitts., 1972. Bar: Pa. 1972, U.S. Dist. Ct. (we. dist.) Pa. 1972, U.S. Ct. Appeals (3d cir.) 1972. Law clk. to judge U.S. Ct. Appeals (3d cir.), Phila., 1972-75; mng. ptnr. Allegheny region Reed, Smith, LLP, Pitts., 1975—. Mem. Nat. Adv. Council on Child Nutrition, U.S. Dept. Agriculture, 1984-85. Treas. Mt. Lebanon Zoning Hearing Bd., 1978-81; pres. bd. dirs. Mt. Lebanon Sch. dist., 1981-87; solicitor Allegheny County Rep. Com., 1988-95; pres. bd. dirs. Ctr. for Theatre Arts, Pitts., 1984-93; grad. Leadership Pitts., 1991-92; chair bd. dirs. Mt. Lebanon Hosp. Authority, 1993—; coun. U. Pitts. Cancer Inst., 1993—; mem. alumni coun. Kenyon Coll., 1996-2000; bd. dirs. Edn. Policy and Issues Ctr., 2000—. Lt. USNR, 1969-71. Mem. ABA, Pa. Bar Assn., Allegheny County Bar Assn. (bd. govs., past chair civil litigation sect., past chmn. judiciary com.), Acad. Trial Lawyers (treas., bd. govs.), Duquesne Club, Western Pa. Hist. Soc. (bd. dirs. 1999—). Episcopalian. Avocations: skiing. Federal civil litigation, State civil litigation, Construction. Office: Reed Smith LLP 435 6th Ave Ste 2 Pittsburgh PA 15219-1886 E-mail: astroyd@reedsmith.com

STRUIF, L. JAMES, lawyer; b. Alton, Ill., Sept. 18, 1931; s. Leo John and Clara Lillie (Bauer) S.; m. Shirley Ann Spatz, Mar. 24, 1965; children: Scott B., Jamie Lynn, Susan Marie, Jeffrey James. BS, Northwestern U., 1953; JD, U. Ill., Champaign, 1960. Bar: Ill. 1960, U.S. Dist. Ct. (so. Dist.) Ill. 1960. Gen. counsel So. Ill. U., 1960-64; pvt. practice Struif Law Offices, Alton, Ill., 1964—. Lectr. So. Ill. U., Edwardsville, 1960-65. Author: Guide to Law for Laymen, 1987, Field Guide to 150 Prairie Plants of S.W. Ill., 1989. Scoutmaster Boy Scouts Am., Alton, 1966-69; active civil rights worker, Miss., 1964; trustee The James and Anne Nelson Found. With USN, submarines 1953-57, Pacific. Recipient Chmns. award Madison County Urban League, 1989, Blazing Star award The Nature Inst., 1990. Mem. Assn. Trial Lawyers Am., Ill. Trial Lawyers Assn., Ill. Bar Assn. Democrat. Mem. United Ch. of Christ. Avocations: nature, gardening, science, piano. Bankruptcy, Estate planning, Probate. Office: The Struif Law Offices 2900 Adams Pkwy Alton IL 62002-4857

STRULL, JAMES RICHARD, lawyer; b. N.Y.C., Oct. 31, 1946; s. Abraham Arthur and Beverly Ann (Lamot) S.; m. Catherine Koziel, Sept. 25, 1983. B.B.A., Coll. Ins. N.Y.C., 1971; J.D., N.Y. Law Sch., 1974. Bar: N.J. 1974, U.S. Dist. Ct. N.J. 1974, N.Y. 1980, U.S. Supreme Ct. 1983, U.S. Tax Ct. 1986. Ins. broker Strull Garber Corp., N.Y.C., 1967-74; assoc. Ludmer & Slaff, Wood Ridge, N.J., 1974; ptnr. Ludmer, Slaff & Strull, Wood Ridge, 1975-78; with Ludmer & Strull, Wood Ridge, 1978-81; ptnr. La Fianza, Strull & Marshall, Hackensack, N.J., 1981—; staff atty., bd. advisers Fin. Road Maps, Inc., Clifton, N.J., 1983— . Bd. dirs. Bergen County Catholic Youth Orgn., Paramus, 1978-80; mem. Greater N.J. Estate Planning Council, 1984— . Lodge: Lions (pres. 1979). General corporate, Probate, Real property. Office: LaFianza and Strull Continental Plaza III 433 Hackensack Ave Hackensack NJ 07601

STRUTHERS, MARGO S. lawyer; BA, Carleton Coll., 1972; JD cum laude, U. Minn., 1976. Atty., shareholder Moss & Barnett, P.A. and predecessor firms, Mpls., 1976-93; ptnr. Oppenheimer Wolff & Donnelly, LLP, 1993—. Mem. Am. Health Lawyers Assn., Minn. State Bar Assn (bus. law sect., former chair nonprofit com., former chair and former mem. governing coun. health law sect.). Health. Office: Oppenheimer Wolff & Donnelly LLP Plaza VII 45 S 7th St Ste 3300 Minneapolis MN 55402-1614 E-mail: mstruthers@oppenheimer.com

STRUTIN, KENNARD REGAN, lawyer, educator, legal information consultant; b. Bklyn., Dec. 1, 1961; s. Fred and Estelle (Brodzansky) S. BA summa cum laude, St. John's U., Jamaica, N.Y., 1981; JD, Temple U. Sch. Law, Phila., 1984; MLS, St. John's U., 1994. Bar: N.Y. 1986, U.S. Dist. Ct. (ea. and so. dists.) N.Y. 1990, U.S. Dist. Ct. (no. and we. dists.) N.Y. 1991, U.S. Ct. Appeals (2d cir.) 1990, U.S. Ct. Appeals (fed. cir.) 1991, U.S. Tax Ct. 1991, U.S. Ct. Mil. Appeals 1991, U.S. Supreme Ct. 1990. Atty. pvt. practice, West Hempstead, N.Y., 1986; trial atty. Nassau County Legal Aid Soc., Hempstead, 1987-88, Orange County Legal Aid Soc., Goshen, 1988-90; atty. pvt. practice, West Hempstead, 1990-91; staff atty. N.Y. State Defenders Assn., Albany, 1991-93; adj. asst. prof. St. John's U., Jamaica, 1993-96; small claims tax assessment hearing officer Supreme Ct., Nassau, Suffolk, 1993-96; law libr. Syracuse U. Coll. Law, 1996-98; legal info. cons., 1998—. Spkr. lawyer in classroom Nassau County Bar Assn., Mineola, N.Y., 1987-94; spkr. pre-release program Correctional Facilities, Lower Hudson Valley, N.Y., 1989-94. Author: ALI-ABA's Checklist Manual on Representing Criminal Defendants, 1998; co-author: (computer-assisted, interactive instrnl. program) Legal Research Methodology; contbr. articles to profl. jours. Recipient Orange County Exec. Recognition award, 1990, 93, 2nd place winner libr. divsn. Donald Trautman Ctr. for Computer-Assisted Legal Instrn. Lesson Writing Competition, 1996-97. Mem. Beta Phi Mu.

STRUVE, GUY MILLER, lawyer; b. Wilmington, Del., Jan. 5, 1943; s. William Scott and Elizabeth Bliss (Miller) S.; m. Marcia Mayo Hill, Sept. 20, 1986; children: Andrew Hardenbrook, Catherine Tolstoy, Frank Leroy Hill, Guy Miller, Beverly Marcia Wise Hill (dec.), Elena Wise Struve-Hill. AB summa cum laude, Yale U., 1963; LLB magna cum laude, Harvard U., 1966. Bar: N.Y. 1967, D.C. 1986, U.S. Dist. Ct. (so. dist.) N.Y. 1970, U.S. Dist. Ct. (ea. dist.) N.Y. 1973, U.S. Dist. Ct. (no. dist.) Calif. 1979, U.S. Dist. Ct. D.C. 1987, U.S. Dist. Ct. (no. dist.) N.Y. 2000, U.S. Ct. Appeals (2d cir.) 1969, U.S. Ct. Appeals (D.C. cir.) 1973, U.S. Ct. Appeals (8th cir.) 1976, U.S. Ct. Appeals (9th cir.) 1979, U.S. Supreme Ct. 1971, U.S. Dist. Ct. (we. dist.) N.Y. 1991. Law clk. Hon. J. Edward Lumbard, Chief Judge United States Ct. Appeals for 2d Circuit, 1966-67; assoc. Davis Polk & Wardwell, N.Y.C., 1967-72, ptnr., 1973—, Ind. Counsel's Office, 1987-94. Mem. ABA, N.Y. State Bar Assn., Assn. of Bar of City of N.Y. (chmn. com. antitrust and trade regulation, 1983-86, chmn. com. fed. cts. 1998-2001), Am. Law Inst. Antitrust, General civil litigation. Home: 116 E 63rd St New York NY 10021-7325 Office: Davis Polk & Wardwell 450 Lexington Ave Fl 31 New York NY 10017-3982

STUART, ALICE MELISSA, lawyer; b. N.Y.C., Apr. 7, 1957; d. John Marberger and Marjorie Louise (Browne) S. BA, Ohio State U., 1977; JD, U. Chgo., 1980; LLM, NYU, 1982. Bar: N.Y. 1981, Ohio 1982, N.Y. 1982, Fla. 1994, U.S. Dist. Ct. (so. dist.) Ohio, 1983, U.S. Dist. Ct. (so. and ea. dists.) N.Y. 1985. Assoc. Schwartz, Shapiro, Kelm & Warren, Columbus, Ohio, 1982-84, Paul, Weiss, Rifkind, Wharton & Garrison, N.Y.C., 1984-85, Kassel, Neuwirth & Geiger, N.Y.C., 1985-86, Phillips, Nizer, Benjamin, Krim & Ballon, N.Y.C., 1987-97; pvt. practice, 1997-98; atty. LeBoeuf, Lamb, Greene & MacRae, 1998—. Adj. prof. So. Coll., Orlando, Fla., 1997-98. Surrogate Speakers' Bur. Reagan-Bush Campaign, N.Y.C., 1984; mem. Lawyers for Bush-Quayle Campaign, N.Y.C., 1988. Mem. ABA, N.Y. State Bar Assn., Winston Churchill Meml. Library Soc., Jr. League, Phi Beta Kappa, Phi Kappa Phi, Alpha Lambda Delta. Republican. General corporate, Finance, Securities. Office: LeBoeuf Lamb Greene & MacRae 125 W 55th St New York NY 10019-5369

STUART, GLEN R(AYMOND), lawyer; b. Kimpese, Congo, Mar. 4, 1959; came to U.S., 1960; s. Charles H. and Jeannette B. (Spinney) S.; m. Susan K. Sharpless, May 26, 1984; children: Jennifer Jacqueline, David Charles, Andrew William. BA, Franklin and Marshall Coll., 1981; JD, U. Va., 1984. Bar: Pa. 1984, U.S. Dist. Ct. (ea. dist.) Pa. 1984, U.S. Dist. Ct. (mid. dist.) Pa. 1986, U.S. Ct. Appeals (3rd cir.) 1988, U.S. Supreme Ct. 1997. Ptnr. Morgan, Lewis & Bockius, LLP, Phila., 1984—. Mem. ABA, Pa. Bar Assn., Phila. Bar Assn., Order of Coif. Democrat. Baptist. Avocations: soccer, golf, softball, tennis, running. Federal civil litigation, Environmental, Public utilities. Home: 21 Harvey Ln Malvern PA 19355-2907 Office: Morgan Lewis & Bockius LLP 1701 Market St Philadelphia PA 19103-2903 Fax: (215) 963-5299. E-mail: gstuart@morganlewis.com

STUART, HAROLD CUTLIFF, lawyer, business executive; b. Oklahoma City, July 4, 1912; s. Royal Cutliff and Alice (Bramlitt) S.; m. Joan Skelly, June 6, 1938 (dec. 1994); children: Randi Stuart Wightman, Jon Rolf; m. Frances Langford, Nov. 18, 1994. J.D., U. Va., 1936. Bar: Okla. 1936, D.C. 1952. Ptnr. Stuart, Biolchini, Turner & Givray, Tulsa; judge Common Pleas Ct., 1941-42; asst. sec. U.S. Air Force, 1949-51; chmn. bd. 1st Stuart Corp., radio, oil, real estate and investments, Tulsa; dir. Lowrance Electronics, Inc. Spl. cons. to sec. Air Force, 1961-63; mem. Okla. Hwy. Commn., 1959-63; bd. dirs. Great Empire Broadcasting Inc., Wichita, Kans. Trustee emeritus Lovelace Found., Albuquerque; trustee N.Am. Wildlife Fedn; mem. Nat. Eagle Scout Coun. Boy Scouts Am., Disting. Eagle Scout; past pres. Air Force Acad. Found., chmn. bd. Served from 1st lt. to col. USAAF, 1942-46, ETO. Decorated Bronze Star (U.S.) and 6 battle stars; comdr. Order of St. Olav; King Haakon 7th Victory medal; medal of Liberation (Norway); Croix de Guerre (Luxembourg); named to Okla. Aviation and Space Hall of Fame, Okla. Hall of Fame Mem. Am., Okla., D.C. bar assns., Air Force Assn. (dir., nat. pres., chmn. bd. 1951-52), Tulsa C. of C., Tulsa Headliner, Falcon Found. (vice chmn.), Ducks Unltd. (trustee), Delta Kappa Epsilon. Democrat. Clubs: Southern Hills Country, The Boston (Tulsa); Burning Tree (Washington), Willoughby Golf, The Amb. (Stuart, Fla.) General corporate, Legislative, Military. Home: PO Box 96 2460 Palmer St Jensen Beach FL 34958-0096 also: 4590 E 29th St Tulsa OK 74114-6208

STUART, LYN (JACQUELYN L. STUART), judge; b. Sept. 23, 1955; m. George Stuart; children: Tucker, Shepard, Kelly. BA in Sociology and Edn., Auburn U., 1977; JD, U. Ala., 1980. Asst. atty. gen. State of Ala.; exec. asst. to commr. and spl. asst. atty. gen. Ala. Dept. Corrections; asst. dist. atty. Baldwin County; dist. judge, 1988—97; judge Ala. Cir. Ct., 1997—2000; justice Ala. Supreme Ct., 2001—. Republican. Office: 300 Dexter Ave Rm 3-215 Montgomery AL 36104-3741*

STUART, PAMELA BRUCE, lawyer; b. N.Y.C., Feb. 13, 1949; d. J. Raymond and Marion Grace (Cotins) S. AB with distinction, Mt. Holyoke Coll., 1970; JD cum laude, U. Mich., 1973. Bar: N.Y. 1974, D.C. 1975, U.S. Dist. Ct. D.C. 1979, U.S. Ct. Appeals (D.C. cir.) 1980, U.S. Supreme Ct. 1980, U.S. Dist. Ct. Md. 1989, Md. 1992, Va. 1993, U.S. Ct. Appeals (4th cir.) 1993, Fla. 1994, U.S. Dist. Ct. (ea. dist.) Va. 1994, U.S. Dist. Ct. (no. dist.) N.Y. 1996, U.S. Dist. Ct. (so. dist.) Fla. 1998, U.S. Dist. Ct. (so. dist.) N.Y. 1999, U.S. Dist. Ct. (ea. dist.) N.Y. 1999, U.S. Dist. Ct. (mid. dist.) Fla. 2001. Trial atty., deputy asst. dir. Bur. of Consumer Protection, FTC, Washington, 1973-79; asst. U.S. atty. U.S. Atty's Office, 1979-85; sr. trial atty. Office of Internat. Affairs, U.S. Dept. Justice, 1985-87; atty. Ross, Dixon & Masback, 1987-89; mem. Lobel, Novins, Lamont & Flug, 1989-92; pvt. practice, 1992—. Instr. Nat. Inst. for Trial Advocacy, Atty. Gen.'s Advocacy Inst., Legal Edn. Inst., Fed. Practice Inst.; mem. Jud. Conf. D.C., 1985-88, 91-98; mem. Jud. Conf., D.C. Cir., 1996, 98, 2000; assoc. mem. Consular Corps Washington; legal analyst CNN, MSNBC, Fox News, other TV networks. Author: The Federal Trade Commission, 1991; contbr. articles to profl. jours. Bd. dirs. Anacostia Econ. Devel. Corp., 1993—, Anacostia Holding Co., Inc., Anacostia Mgmt. Co., Inc., 1997—. Mem. ABA (mem. internat. criminal law com., chmn., 1993-96, chmn. fed. crim rules subcom. white collar crime com. sect. criminal justice 1997-99), Bar Assn. D.C. (bd. dirs. 1995—), Asst. U.S. Attys. Assn. D.C. (exec. coun. 1993-99, pres. 1998-99), Assn. Trial Lawyers Am., Women's Bar Assn. D.C., Fla. Bar (mem. exec. coun. real property probate and trust law sect. 1999—), Alumnae Assn. Mt. Holyoke Coll. (bd. dirs. 1986-89, 92-95, Alumnae medal of honor 1990), Edward Bennett Williams Inn of Ct. (master of bench), Fed. City Club (bd. govs. 1992—), Cosmos Club. Avocations: writing, interior design, investments, piano. Federal civil litigation, Criminal, Private international. Home: 5115 Yuma St NW Washington DC 20016-4336 Office: The Stuart Bldg 1750 N Street NW Washington DC 20036 also: 111 Johns Island Dr Apt 7 Vero Beach FL 32963-3274 E-mail: pamstuart@aol.com

STUART, PETER FRED, lawyer; b. Savona, N.Y., June 23, 1939; s. Chester M. and Gertrude (Manning) S.; m. Karin Sandal, May 30, 1964; children: Peter Christopher, Sandal Clay, Grant Alan. AB, Dartmouth Coll., 1961; JD, Dickinson Sch. Law, 1969. Bar: Conn. 1970, U.S. Ct. Appeals (2d cir.) 1974, U.S. Ct. Mil. Appeals 1974, U.S. Supreme Ct. 1974. Commd. ensign USN, 1961, advanced through ranks to commdr., 1979, resigned, 1981; staff atty. Conn. Gen. Life Ins. Co., Hartford, 1969-72; shareholder O'Brien, Shafner, Bartinik, Stuart & Kelly P.C., Groton, Conn., 1972—. Corporator New Eng. Savings Bank, New London, Conn., 1979-86. City councilor Town of Groton, 1974-78. Mem. Ct. Corps. Com. (exec. com. mem.). Lodge: Rotary (local pres. 1982-83). Avocation: gardening. Consumer commercial, General corporate, General practice. Office: PO Box 929 475 Bridge St Groton CT 06340-3723

STUART, ROBERT ALLAN, JR. lawyer; b. Sept. 8, 1948; s. Robert Allan and Elizabeth (Pexton) Stuart; m. Kirsten Christianson, June 16, 1973 (div. Mar. 1975); children: Elizabeth Corinne, Christopher Todd; m. Margaret Anne Griffith, Apr. 09, 1977. BA, Bowdoin Coll., 1970; JD, U. Ill., 1973. Bar: Ill. 1973, U.S. dist. Ct. (so. dist.) Ill. 1973, U.S. Supreme Ct. 1980, U.S. Tax Ct. 1981. Assoc. Brown Hay & Stephens, Springfield, Ill., 1973—78, ptnr., 1979—. Pres. Sangamon County Hist. Soc., 1983; council mem. exec. bd. Abraham Lincoln Coun. Boy Scouts Am., 1986, pres., 1991—92; bd. dir. Goodwill Industries, Springfield, Ill., 1983—92; chmn. spl. gifts Springfield YMCA capital fund drive, 1986, bd. dir., 1989—92; chmn. fund raising Sangamon County unit Am. Heart Assn., 1984; chmn. United Way Found. Sangamon County, 1999—2000; chmn. United Way Campaign, 1996; bd. dir. Nat. Recreation Found.; bd. trustees Ill. State Mus. Soc., Meml. Med. Ctr. Found., 2001—; vice chmn. Springfield C. of C., 2001—; trustee 1st Presbyn. Ch., Springfield, 1987—90, elder. Fellow: Am. Coll. Trust Estate Coun.; mem.: ABA, Ill. Bar Assn. (estate planning coun. 1981—87, chmn. 1986—87), St. Louis Bar Assn. Sangamon Valley Estate Planning Council (bd. dir. 1982—83), Chgo. Bar Assn., Abraham Lincoln Assn., Nat. Eagle Scout Assn. (chmn. Abraham Lincoln coun. 1984), Rotary (dist. gov. 1985—86, zone inst. chmn. 1987, zone inst. chmn. 1997, 33rd degree AASR), Masons, Shriners. Estate planning, Probate, Estate taxation. Home: 610 Williams Blvd Springfield IL 62704-2802 Office: 205 S 5th St Springfield IL 62701-1406

STUART, WALTER BYNUM, IV, lawyer; b. Grosse Tete, La., Nov. 23, 1946; s. Walter Bynum III and Rita (Kleinpeter) S.; m. Lettice Lee Binnings, May 18, 1968; children: Courtney Lyon, Walter Burke V. Student, Fordham U., 1964-65; BA, Tulane U., 1968, JD, 1973. Bar: La. 1973, U.S. Dist. Ct. (ea. and we. dists.) La. 1974, U.S. Tax Ct. 1974, U.S. Supreme Ct. 1981, U.S. Dist. Ct. (so. dist.) Colo. 1987, U.S. Dist. Ct. (so. dist.) Tex. 1989. Ptnr. Stone, Pigman, Walther, Wittman and Hutchinson, New Orleans, 1973-78, Singer Hutner Levine Seeman and Stuart, New Orleans, 1978-81, Gordon, Arata, McCollam and Stuart, New Orleans, 1981-88, Vinson & Elkins, Houston, 1988—. Instr. Tulane U. Law Sch., 1978-82; mem. faculty Banking Sch. of the South; bd. dirs. Inst. Politics; mem. adv. bd. City Atty.'s Office, New Orleans, 1978-79. Bd. dirs., gen. counsel Houston Grand Opera, 1992—. Mem. ABA, La. Bar Assn., Tex. Assn. Bank Counsel (pres. 1994-95), La. Bankers Assn. (chmn. bank counsel com.). Banking, Federal civil litigation, Contracts commercial. Office: Vinson & Elkins 2500 First City Tower 1001 Fannin St Ste 3300 Houston TX 77002-6706 E-mail: wstuart@velaw.com

STUART, WILLIAM CORWIN, federal judge; b. Knoxville, Iowa, Apr. 28, 1920; s. George Corwin and Edith (Abram) S.; m. Mary Elgin Cleaver, Oct. 20, 1946; children: William Corwin II, Robert Cullen, Melanie Rae, Valerie Jo. BA, State U. Iowa, 1941, JD, 1942. Bar: Iowa 1942. Pvt. practice, Chariton, 1946-62; city atty., 1947-49; mem. Iowa Senate from, Lucas-Wayne Counties, 1951-61; justice Supreme Ct. Iowa, 1962-71; judge U.S. Dist. Ct., So. Dist. of Iowa, Des Moines, 1971-86, sr. judge, 1986—. With USNR, 1943-45. Recipient Outstanding Svc. award Iowa Acad. Trial lawyer, 1987, Iowa Trial Lawyers Assn., 1988, Spl. award Iowa State Bar Assn., 1987, Disting. Alumni, U. Iowa Coll. Law, 1987. Mem. ABA, Iowa Bar Assn., Am. Legion, All For Iowa, Order of Coif, Omicron Delta Kappa, Phi Kappa Psi, Phi Delta Phi. Presbyterian. Club: Mason (Shriner). Home: 216 S Grand St Chariton IA 50049-2139

STUCK, HAVEN LAURENCE, lawyer; b. Aberdeen, S.D., Nov. 6, 1946; s. Laurence Henry and Vera Fern (Haven) S.; m. Terri Lynn Wall, Mar. 17, 1984. B.S., S.D. State U., 1968, M.S., 1972; J.D., U. S.D., 1975. Bar: S.D. 1975, U.S. Dist. Ct. S.D. 1975. Shareholder, mem. Lynn, Jackson, Shultz & Lebrun, Rapid City, S.D., 1975— . Pres. Central States Fair, Rapid City, 1981; pres. Pennington County Fire Adv. Bd., Rapid City, 1980. Served to 1st lt. U.S. Army, 1968-70. Mem. ABA (v.p. agrl. law com. 1979-84, v.p. comml. law com. 1985—). Democrat. Lutheran. Club: Cosmopolitan (pres. 1984-85). General civil litigation, Contracts commercial. Home: Route 1 RR 1 Box 1160 Rapid City SD 57702-9706

STUCKY, SCOTT WALLACE, lawyer; b. Hutchinson, Kans., Jan. 11, 1948; s. Joe Edward and Emma Clara (Graber) S.; m. Jean Elsie Seibert, Aug. 18, 1973; children: Mary-Clare, Joseph. BA summa cum laude, Wichita State U., 1970; JD, Harvard U., 1973; MA, Trinity U., 1980; LLM with high honors, George Washington U., 1983; postgrad., Nat. War Coll., 1993. Bar: Kans. 1973, U.S. Dist. Ct. Kans. 1973, U.S. Ct. Appeals (10th cir.) 1973, U.S. Ct. Mil. Appeals 1974, U.S. Supreme Ct. 1976, D.C. 1979, U.S. Ct. Appeals (D.C. cir.) 1979. Assoc. Ginsburg, Feldman & Bress, Washington, 1978-82; chief docketing and svc. br. Nuclear Regulatory Commn., 1982-83; legis. counsel U.S. Air Force USAF, 1983-96, gen. counsel sen. com. on armed svcs., 1996—. Lectr. bus. law Maria Regina Coll., Syracuse, N.Y., 1977; congrl. fellow Office Senator John Warner, 1986; res. judge adv. USAF Res., Washington, 1982—; col. Appellate Mil. Judge, USAF Ct. Criminal Appeals, 1991-95, 97-98; sr. reservist USAF Judiciary, 1995-97, Air Res. Personnel Ctr., 1998-99, Air Force Legal Svcs. Agy., 1999—. Contbr. articles to profl. jours. Capt. USAF, 1973-78. Decorated Air Force Meritorious Svc. medal with two oak leaf cluster. Mem. Fed. Bar Assn., Judge Advs. Assn. (bd. dirs. 1984-88), Res. Officers Assn., Wichita State U. Alumni Assn. (pres. chpt. 1981-86, nat. bd. dirs. 1986-92), Adoption Svc. Info. Agy. (bd. dirs. 1998—), Army and Navy Club (Washington), Mil. Order of Loyal Legion U.S. (state comdr. and recorder 1984-92, nat. treas. 1987-89, nat. vice comdr. 1989-93, nat. comdr.-in-chief 1993-95), Sons of Union Vets Civil War (chpt. vice-comdr 1986-88), Phi Delta Phi, Phi Alpha Theta, Phi Kappa Phi, Omicron Delta Kappa, Sigma Phi Epsilon. Republican. Episcopalian. Home: 11004 Homeplace Ln Potomac MD 20854-1406 Office: Sen Armed Svcs Com 228 Senate Office Bldg Washington DC 20510-0001

STUEVER, FRED RAY, lawyer; b. East Saint Louis, Ill., Aug. 13, 1945; s. Fred Francis and Marcella (Strake) S. B.A., U. Ill., Champaign, 1967; J.D., U. Miami, 1972. Bar: Fla. 1972. Staff atty. Ryder System, Inc., Miami, Fla., 1973-79, div. counsel, 1979-81, sr. div. counsel, 1981-83, asst. gen. counsel, 1983— . Served with U.S. Army, 1969-71. Mem. ABA, Fla. Bar, Corp. Counsel Assn. Dade County, Am. Soc. Corp. Secs. Democrat. Roman Catholic. Contracts commercial, General corporate. Office: Ryder System Inc 3600 NW 82nd Ave Miami FL 33166-6623

STUHLDREHER, GEORGE WILLIAM, lawyer; b. Mansfield, Ohio, Nov. 20, 1923; s. George Henry and Clara Sophia (Gabel) S.; m. Fay McClurg, Jan. 7, 1956 (div.); children: Karen Louise, Diane Marie; m. Norah Constance Burran, July 1, 1978. Student, Kans. State Coll., 1943-44, U. Detroit, 1946-47; BA, Ohio State U., 1948, JD summa cum laude, 1951. Bar: Ohio 1951, U.S. Dist. Ct. (no. dist.) Ohio 1953, U.S. Ct. Appeals (6th cir.) 1955, U.S. Supreme Ct. 1979; diplomate Am. Bd. Profl. Liability Attys. Atty., ptnr. Gallagher, Sharp, Fulton & Norman and predecessor firms, Cleve., 1951—. Dir. Bulkley Bldg. Co., Cleve.; bd. govs. Am. Bd. Profl. Liability Attys., 1991—. Editor-in-chief Ohio State Law Jour., 1951. Mem. Citizens League Cleve. Served to cpl. U.S. Army, 1943-46. Mem. ABA, Am. Judicature Soc., Internat. Assn. Def. Counsel, Def. Rsch. Inst., Ohio Bar Assn., Ohio Assn. Civil Trial Attys., Cleve. Bar Assn., Cleve. Assn. Civil Trial Attys. (pres. 1973), Phi Sigma Kappa, Phi Delta Phi, Order of Coif. Federal civil litigation, State civil litigation, Professional liability. Home: 6 Edgewater Sq Cleveland OH 44107-1808 Office: Gallagher Sharp Fulton & Norman Gallagher Sharp Fulton & Norman 630 Bulkley Bldg Cleveland OH 44115

STUKENBERG, MICHAEL WESLEY, lawyer; b. Freeport, Ill., Feb. 22, 1951; s. Wesley W. and Nancy Jack (Baker) S.; m. Amanda Reed Eggert, July 21, 1973; children: Sarah Reed, William Robinson. BA, Princeton U., 1973; JD, Vanderbilt U., 1976. Bar: Tex. 1977, U.S. Tax Ct. 1977, U.S. Dist. Ct. (so. dist.) Tex. 1982. Assoc. firm Matthews & Branscomb, Corpus Christi, Tex., 1976-81, shareholder, 1981—. Gov. Art Mus. South Tex., Copus Christi, 1990-96; dir., pres. Corpus Christi Estate Planning Coun., 1989-98; trustee, chair bd. trustees YMCA Corpus Christi, 1997-. Fellow Am. Coll. Trust and Estate Counsel; mem. ABA, Tex. Bar Assn. (tax sect.), Tex. Acad. of Probate and Trust Lawyers, Coll. of State Bar of Tex. Episcopalian. Clubs: Corpus Christi Yacht, Causeway (Southwest Harbor, Maine). Estate planning, Estate taxation, Taxation, general. Home: 3502 Aransas St Corpus Christi TX 78411-1302 E-mail: mstukenberg@mattbran.com

STULL, GORDON BRUCE, lawyer; b. Dighton, Kans., Aug. 3, 1945; s. Eldon W. and Mildred M. (Zink); m. Carol Joyce Hampton, Aug. 1, 1973; children: Megen, Colby, Braden, Benton. BA, Ft. Hays U., 1967; JD, U. Kans., 1975. Bar: Kans. 1975. Assoc. Morris, Laing et al, Wichita, Kans., 1975-76; ptnr. Hampton, Hampton, Stull et al, Pratt, 1976-81; exec. v.p., gen. counsel Tex. Energies, Inc., 1981-83; pres. Wheatstate Oilfield Svcs., Inc., 1983-84, Gordon B. Stull Atty. PA, Pratt, 1984-93; mem. Stull & Rein LLC, 1993—. Counselor Pratt County, 1985—. County coord. Nancy Landon Kassebaum Senate Campaign, Pratt County, 1980; elder Pratt Presbyn. Ch., 1978-81. Sgt. U.S. Army, 1968-71. Mem. ABA, Kans. Bar Assn. (oil and gas sect., pres.-elect 1989—, bd. editors Oil and Gas Handbook, Merit award for coord. agr. law seminar 1980), Kans. Trial Lawyers Assn., Pratt County Bar Assn. (pres. 1980, 86), Jaycees (Disting. Svc. award 1980), Lions (pres. 1989), Elks (jud. advisor 1976—). General civil litigation, Oil, gas, and mineral, General practice. Home: 40353 NE 10th St Pratt KS 67124-9801 Office: 1320 E 1st St Pratt KS 67124-2064

STUMBO, JANET LYNN, state supreme court justice; b. Prestonsburg, Ky. d. Charles and Doris Stanley S.; m. Ned Pillersdorf; children: Sarah, Nancee, Samantha. BA, Morehead State U., 1976; JD, U. Ky., 1980. Bar: Ky. 1980, W. Va. 1982. Staff atty. to Judge Harris S. Howard Ky. Ct. Appeals, 1980-82; asst. county atty. Floyd County, 1982-85; ptnr. Turner, Hall & Stumbo, P.S.C., 1982-88; prosecutor Floyd Dist. Ct. and Juvenile Ct.; ptnr. Stumbo, DeRossett & Pillersdorf, 1989; judge Ct. Appeals, Ky., 1989-93, Supreme Ct. of Ky., 1993—. Named to Morehead State U.

Alumni Assn. Hall of Fame, 1990, U. Ky. Coll. Law Alumni Hall of Fame, 1999; recipient Justice award Ky. Women Advocates, 1991, Outstanding Just award Ky. Women Advocates, 1995, Bull's Eye award Women in State Govt. Network, 1995. Office: Ky Supreme Ct Capitol Bldg Rm 226 700 Capitol Ave Frankfort KY 40601-3410 also: 311 N Arnold Ave Ste 502 Prestonsburg KY 41653-1279

STUMER, MARK BRADLEY, lawyer, restaurateur, business consultant; b. N.Y.C., May 31, 1969; s. Nathan and Roberta Adele (Klau) S. LLB, SUNY, Albany, 1991; JD, N.Y. Law Sch., 1995. Bar: N.Y. 1995, U.S. Dist. Ct. (ea. and so. dists.) N.Y., 1995. Pres. Marker Entertainment, Inc., 1992-95, Mark B. Stumer & Assoc., P.C., N.Y.C., 1995—; owner Tja! Restaurant, 1999—; pres. Soho Consulting Group, 1996—. Contbr. articles to profl. jours. including Nat. Restaurant Assn., Restaurant Law, The Legal Monitor, and The Restaurateur; pub. Restaurant Law newsletter, Restaurant and Bar Law newsletter, , Entertainment Law & Fin., Bus. Lawyer. Mem. ABA, N.Y. State Bar Assn. (former chmn. copyright sect. student divsn. 1993-94), Nat. Assn. Trial Lawyers, Nat. Employment Lawyers Assn. (N.Y. chpt.), Young Entreprenuers Orgn., Nat. Restaurant Assn., N.Y. State Restaurant Assn., N.Y. County Lawyers Assn. Office: Mark B Stumer & Assocs PC 101 5th Ave New York NY 10003-1008 E-mail: mark@newyorklawfirm.org

STUMPF, FELIX FRANKLIN, law educator; b. Boston, Feb. 10, 1918; s. Karl Heinrich and Annette (Schreyer) S.; m. Martha Wickland, May 29, 1948; m. Betty-Jo Danielson, Aug. 5, 1959; children: Eric, Kenneth, Kirk, Mark, Paul. AB magna cum laude, Harvard U., 1938, LLB, 1941. Bar: Mass. 1941, Calif. 1946, Nev. 1975, U.S. Dist. Ct. (no. dist.) Calif. 1946, U.S. Dist. Ct. Nev. 1981, U.S. Ct. Appeals (9th cir.) 1948, U.S. Supreme Ct. 1967. Assoc. Hale & Dorr, Boston, 1941-42, McCutchen, Thomas, Matthews, Griffiths & Greene, San Francisco, 1946-50, Livingston, Leeker & Feldman, San Francisco, 1950-53; adminstr. Calif. Continuing Edn. Bar/U. Calif. Extension, Berkeley, 1953-70; staff atty. U.S. Dist. Ct. No. Dist. Calif., San Francisco, 1971-73; acad. dir. Nat. Jud. Coll. U. Nev., Reno, 1973-84, jud. rsch. cons., 1988—; prof. Old Coll. Nev. Sch. Law, 1984-85, dean, 1985—88. Of counsel White Law, chartered, Reno, 1988—. Contbr. articles to profl. jours. Trustee Washoe Legal Svcs. 1st lt. AC, U.S. Army, 1942-46. Recipient First Harrison Tweed award Assn. Continuing Legal Edn. Adminstrs., 1969, Francis Raule award, 2000. Mem. ABA, Nev. Bar Assn., Washoe County Bar Assn., Am. Judicature Soc., Nev. Bar Found. (past trustee), Am. Law Inst., Am. Bar Assn., Com. on Continuing Prof. Edu. Democrat. Home: 4205 Slide Mountain Dr Reno NV 89511-6529 Office: U Nev Nat Judicial Coll Reno NV 89503 also: White Law Chartered Reno NV 89503 E-mail: stumpf@judges.org

STUMPF, LARRY ALLEN, lawyer; b. Dayton, Ohio, Jan. 11, 1947; s. Joseph Theodore and Daisy Evelyn (Means) S.; B.S. in Bus. Adminstrn., Northwestern U., 1969; J.D., NYU, 1973. Bar: N.Y. 1973, Fla. 1979, U.S. Dist. Ct. (all dists.) N.Y. 1973, U.S. Dist. Ct. (all dist.) Fla. 1979, U.S. Ct. Appeals (2d cir.) 1974, U.S. Ct. Appeals (5th cir.) 1979, U.S. Ct. Appeals (11th cir.) 1982, U.S. Ct. Appeals (D.C. cir.) 1978, U.S. Supreme Ct. 1976. Assoc. Shearman & Stirling, N.Y.C., 1973-75; assoc., ptnr. Goldstein, Goldman, Kessler & Underberg, Rochester, N.Y., Miami, Fla., 1975-84; ptnr. Finley, Kumble, Wanger, Heine, Underberg, Manley & Casey, Miami, Fla., 1984-88; ptnr., Rubin, Baum, Levin, Freidman, Constant & Bilzin, Miami, Fla., 1988—. Town justice, Macedon, N.Y., 1980-81. Mem. ABA, Fed. Bar Assn., Assn. Trial Lawyers Am., N.Y. State Bar Assn., Assn. Bar City N.Y. Democrat. Jewish. Banking, Federal civil litigation, Contracts commercial. Home: 14261 SW 16th St Fort Lauderdale FL 33325-5908 Office: Rubin Baum Levin Freidman Constant & Bilzin 2500 First Union Financial Ctr Miami FL 33131-2313

STUNTEBECK, CLINTON A. lawyer; b. Hibbing, Minn., May 25, 1938; s. Robert F. and S. Mary Stuntebeck; m. Mary Joan Carmody; children: Robin, M. Alison, Susan, John, William. BA in Psychology, U. Minn., 1960; LLB, U. Maine, 1968. Bar: Pa. 1969, U.S. Dist. Ct. (ea. dist.) Pa. 1969. Ptnr., chmn. corp. fin. and securities, mem. exec. com. Schnader, Harrison, Segal & Lewis, Phila. Bd. dirs. Markel Corp., Greater Phila. First Partnership for Econ. Devel.; lectr. corp. and securities law. Contbr. articles to profl. jours. Pres. Radnor (Pa.) Twp. Bd. Commn., 1981-83, 92-99; bd. visitors U. Maine Sch. Law; trustee Cabrini Coll.; bd. dirs. Am. Heart Assn. Capt. USAF, 1960-68. Mem. ABA, Am. Law Inst., Pa. Bar Assn., Phila. Bar Assn., Securities Industry Assn. (law and compliance com.), U. Maine Law Alumni Assn. (pres. 1974-76), Union League Phila., Phila. Country Club, Sunday Breakfast Club, Corinthian Yacht Club. Avocations: sailing, skiing, golf, tennis. Finance, Mergers and acquisitions, Securities. Office: Schnader Harrison Segal 1600 Market St Ste 3600 Philadelphia PA 19103-7287 E-mail: cstuntebeck@schnader.com

STURM, WILLIAM CHARLES, lawyer; b. Milw., Aug. 4, 1941; s. Charles William and Helen Ann (Niesen) S.; m. Kay F. Sturm, June 10, 1967; children: Patricia, Elizabeth, Katherine, William, Susan. B.S. in Bus. Adminstrn., Marquette U., 1963; J.D., 1966. Bar: Wis. 1966, U.S. Dist. Ct. (ea. dist.) Wis. 1966, U.S. Supreme Ct. 1980. Sole practice, Milw., 1966-78; ptnr. Rausch, Hamell, Ehrle & Sturm, S.C., 1978-81, Rausch, Hamell, Ehrle, Sturm & Blom, Milw., 1981-83, Rausch, Hamell, Ehrle & Sturm, 1983-95, Rausch, Hamell, Sturm & Israel S.C., 1995-98, Rausch, Sturm, Israel & Hornik, S.C., 1999—. Asst. prof. Marquette U., 1982-91; lectr. U. Wis., Milw., 1991-97, sr. lectr. 1997—. Contbr. articles to profl. jours. Mem. adv. bd. Pallotine Order, 1985—. Recipient Editors award Wis. Med. Credit Assn., 1980. Mem. ABA, Wis. Bar Assn., Comml. Law League Am. (exec. council midwestern dist. 1981-83, 86-88, chmn. state membership com. 1981-88, nat. nominating council 1984-86, 1988-89, sec., 2d v.p. midwestern dist. 1989-90, 1st v.p. midwestern dist. 1990-91, chmn. 1991-92, nat. bd. govs. 1997-99, pres.-elect 2000-2001, pres. 2001—), Nat. Spkrs. Assn., Am. Bus. Law Assn., Midwest Bus. Law Assn. (sec. 1988-89, v.p. 1989-90, pres. 1990-91), Wis. Profl. Speakers Assn., Healthcare Fin. Mgmt. Assn., Beta Alpha Psi (faculty v.p. Psi chpt. 1985-88, Eta Theta chpt. 1992-99), Midwest Bus. And Health Assn. (v.p. procs. 1987-88, v.p. program 1988-89, pres. 1989-90). Clubs: Westmoor Country (Milw.); Kiwanis (pres. 1979, lt. gov. div. 5, 1980) (Wauwatosa, Wis.). Bankruptcy, Consumer commercial. Office: 1233 N Mayfair Rd Milwaukee WI 53226-3255 E-mail: wsturm@wiscollect.com

STURMAN, PHILIP, lawyer; b. Charleston, S.C., Aug. 18, 1944; s. Coleman Harry and Ruth (Silverman) S.; m. Faith Waxman July 6, 1968; children— David Coleman, Dena Ilana. B.A., Fla. Atlantic U., 1966; J.D., U. Balt., 1972. Bar: Md. 1972, U.S. Ct. Appeals (D.C. cir.) 1974, U.S. Dist. Ct. D.C. 1975, U.S. Supreme Ct. 1976. Munday, Sturman & Everton, P.A., Towson, Md. Served with USN, 1966-68. Mem. ABA, Md. Bar Assn., Balt. City Bar Assn., D.C. Unified Bar Assn., Def. Research Inst. Federal civil litigation, State civil litigation, Insurance. Home: 1615 Park Ave # 4 Baltimore MD 21217-4306

STUTT, JOHN BARRY, lawyer; b. Phila., Feb. 1, 1948; m. Dena Lieberman; children: Timothy, Margaret. BBA, U. Wis., 1971, MBA, 1973, JD, 1974. Bar: Wis. 1974, Mo. 1974. Asst. counsel Mo. Dept. Revenue, Jefferson City, 1974-75; asst. gen. counsel Mo. Hwy. Dept., 1975-77; assoc. Stewart, Peyton, Crawford & Crawford, Racine, Wis., 1978-83; ptnr. Stewart, Peyton, Crawford, Crawford & Stutt, 1983—. Mem. Wis. Bar Assn. (sec., bd. dirs. young lawyers div. 1983, environ. law com. 1985—), Acad. Trial Lawyers, Jaycees (pres. Racine). Banking, Personal injury, Real property. Home: 4820 Alcyn Dr Racine WI 53402-2508 Office: 840 Lake Ave Racine WI 53403-1566 E-mail: stutt@execpc.com

STUTZMAN, THOMAS CHASE, SR. lawyer; b. Portland, Oreg., Aug. 1, 1950; s. Leon H. and Mary L. (Chase) S.; m. Wendy Jeanne Craig, June 6, 1976; children: Sarah Ann, Thomas Chase Jr. BA with high honors, U. Calif., Santa Barbara, 1972; JD cum laude, Santa Clara U., 1975. Bar: Calif. 1976; cert. family law specialist. Pvt. practice, San Jose, Calif., 1976-79; pres., sec., CFO Thomas Chase Stutzman, PC, 1979—. Legal counsel DMJ Pro Care, Inc., Sparacino's Foods, Tax Firm, Inc., United Charities, Marina Assocs. Inc., E.M.I. Oil Filtration Systems, Inc., Creative Pacifica, Inc., Am. First Tech., Excel-Law Video, Inc., First Am. Real Estate Financing Co., Hoffman Industries, Inc., Info. Scan Tech., Inc., PRD Construction Mgmt. Svcs., Marine Biogenic Pharm. USA, Inc., Mi Pueblo Mt. View, Inc., others; instr. San Jose State U., 1977-78. Bd. dirs. Santa Cruz Campfire, 1978-80, Happy Hollow Park, 1978-80, 83-86, Pacific Neighbors, pres., 1991-92. Mem. Calif. Bar Assn., Santa Clara County Bar Assn. (chmn. environ. law com. 1976-78, exec. com. family law), Assn. Cert. Law Specialists, San Jose Jaycees (Dir. of Yr. 1976-77), Rotary, Lions (dir. 1979-81, 2d v.p. 1982-83, 1st v.p. 1983-84, pres. 1984-85), Scottish Rite, Masons, Phi Beta Kappa. Congregationalist. State civil litigation, Family and matrimonial, Real property. Office: 1625 The Alameda Ste 626 San Jose CA 95126-2207 E-mail: stutzman@tomstutzman.com

STYER, JANE M. computer consultant; b. Bethlehem, Pa., Apr. 14, 1957; d. LeRoy V. and Pauline M. (Diehl) S. Assoc in Gen. Edn., NCACC, 1977, Assoc in Applied Sci., 1979; BS in Computer Sci., St. Francis de Sales Coll., 1985, cert. profl. legal sec., 1986. PC technician A+ cert. 1997. Legal sec., asst. Lower Saucon Police Dept.; asst. to treas., bookkeeper Lehigh Valley Motor Club, Allentown, Pa.; real estate and probate paralegal, office mgr. various attys., Lehigh & Delaware Valleys, 1976-82; title ins. agt., owner, mgr. Abstractors' Svcs., Bingen, 1982—; quality control theory checker, tax preparer H & R Block, 1992—. Mem. NAFE, Nat. Assn. Legal Secs. (Continuing Legal Edn. Recognition award 1988), Lehigh-Northampton Counties (chmn. continuing legal edn. com. 1984-88, seminar chmn. 1985-88), Pa. Assn. Notaries, Single Sq. Dancers U.S.A. (nat. sec. 1986-87), Bachelors and Bachelorettes, Internat. (sec. Mid-Atlantic region 1980-84). Avocations: camping, square and round dancing, horseback riding. Office: Abstractors' Svcs 3228 Bingen Rd Bethlehem PA 18015-5707 E-mail: JMStyer@juno.com

STYKA, RONALD JOSEPH, lawyer; b. Detroit, Oct. 29, 1946; s. Joseph Richard and Julia (Misiak) S.; m. Georgina Felicia Buttigieg, May 28, 1971; children— R. Jason, George P., Joseph R. II, James A. AB, U. Detroit, 1968; JD, U. Mich., 1971. Bar: Mich. 1971, U.S. Dist. Ct. (ea. and we. dist.) Mich. 1972, U.S. Ct. Appeals (6th cir.). Asst. atty. gen., asst. in charge comty. health divsn. Mich. Dept. Atty. Gen., Lansing, 1971— . Pres., Briarwood Homeowners Assn., Okemos, Mich., 1980-83; mem. bd. edn. Okemos Pub. Schs., 1990—, pres., 1994-96 ; chief YMCA Indian Guides, Okemos, 1984. Mem. Assn. Asst. Atty. Gens. Mich. (founding mem., pres. 1976), Cath. Lawyers Guild (founding mem. Lansing Diocese, pres. 1998-99), KC (founding mem. Okemos chpt., grand knight 1998-2000). Democrat. Roman Catholic. E-mail: stykar@ag.state.mi.us. Office: Dept Atty Gen 4th Fl One Michigan Ave Bldg Lansing MI 48909

SUBAK, JOHN THOMAS, lawyer; b. Trebic, Czechoslovakia, Apr. 19, 1929; came to U.S., 1941, naturalized, 1946; s. William John and Gerda Maria (Subakova) S.; m. Mary Corcoran, June 4, 1955; children: Jane Kennedy, Kate, Thomas, Michael. BA summa cum laude, Yale U., 1950, LLB, 1956. Bar: Pa. 1956. From assoc. to ptnr. Dechert, Price & Rhoads, Phila., 1956-76, v.p., gen. counsel, dir., 1976-77; group v.p., gen. counsel, dir. Rohm and Haas Co., 1977-93; counsel Dechert Price & Rhoads, 1994—. Bd. dirs. Newport Corp. Editor: The Bus. Lawyer, 1982-83. Bd. dirs. Am. Cancer Soc., 1982-95; trustee Smith Coll. Lt. (j.g.) USN, 1950-53. Mem. ABA (chmn. corp. and bus. law sect. 1984-85), Am. Law Inst. (coun. mem.), Defender Assn. of Phila. (v.p., bd. dirs. 1982-95), Merion Cricket Club, Lemon Bay Club. Democrat. Roman Catholic. General corporate. Office: Dechert Price & Rhoads 4000 Bell Atlantic Tower Philadelphia PA 19102-2793 E-mail: johnsubak@aol.com

SUBIN, FLORENCE, retired lawyer; b. N.Y.C., June 5, 1935; d. George and Beatrice (Rodam) Kroser; m. Bert W. Subin, June 6, 1953 (dec.); children: Glen D., Beth Subin Ambler. BA, Herbert H. Lehman Coll., 1972; JD magna cum laude, Bklyn. Law Sch., 1975. Bar: N.Y. 1976, U.S. Dist. Ct. (so. and ea. dists.) N.Y. 1976. Pvt. practice, N.Y.C. and Scarsdale, N.Y., 1976-99; retired. Trustee Bklyn. Law Sch., 1998—. Mem. Assn. Trial Lawyers City of N.Y. (bd. dirs. 1982-86), Met. Women's Bar Assn. (pres. 1979-81, bd. dirs. 1981—), Bronx Women's Bar Assn. (pres. 1983-85), Bklyn. Law Sch. Alumni Assn. (pres. 1992-94), Phi Beta Kappa. Personal injury, Probate.

SUFLAS, STEVEN WILLIAM, lawyer; b. Camden, N.J., Oct. 7, 1951; s. William V. and Dorothy (Stafre) S.; m. Rochelle B. Volin, Apr. 15, 1978; children: Allison, Rebecca, Whitney. BA, Davidson Coll., 1973; JD with honors, U. N.C., 1976. Bar: N.J. 1976, Pa. 1978, U.S. Dist. Ct. N.J., U.S. Ct. Appeals (3d cir.). Field atty. NLRB, Phila., 1976-80; assoc. Archer & Greiner P.C., Haddonfield, N.J., 1980-86, ptnr., 1986—. Fellow Coll. of Labor and Employment Lawyers; mem. ABA, Pa. Bar Assn., Phila. Bar Assn., N.J. Bar Assn. (exec. com. labor and employment law sect. 1985—, officer 1993—, chmn. 1999-2001), Order of Coif, Omicron Delta Kappa. Labor. Office: Archer & Greiner PC 1 Centennial Sq Haddonfield NJ 08033-2328

SUGARMAN, ROBERT ALAN, lawyer; b. Hartford, Conn., May 31, 1947; s. Sidney M. and Sylvia (Shear) S.; children: Lauren, James. BA, George Washington U., 1969; JD, U. Va., 1972. Bar: Fla. 1972, U.S. Dist. Ct. (so. dist.) Fla. 1972, U.S. Dist. Ct. (ctrl. dist.) Fla. 1973, U.S. Ct. Appeals (D.C. cir.) 1973, U.S. Tax Ct. 1976, U.S. Dist. Ct. (no. dist.) Fla. 1981, U.S. Ct. Appeals (11th cir.) 1981, U.S. Supreme Ct. 1978. Ptnr. Kaplan, Sicking, Hessen, Sugarman et al, P.A., Miami and Ft. Lauderdale, Fla., 1972-85, Sugarman & Susskind, P.A., Miami and Ft. Lauderdale, 1985—. Spl. prof. Fla. Internat. U., Miami, 1976-80; gen. counsel Fla. AFL-CIO, Tallahassee, 1980-85; mem. adv. bd. AFL-CIO Lawyers Coordinating Com., Washington, 1983-87. Bd. dirs. Temple Sinai of North Dade, North Miami Beach, Fla., v.p., 1987-92, Michael-Ann Russell Jewish Cmty. Ctr., North Miami Beach. Fellow Coll. Labor & Employment Lawyers; mem. ABA (labor law sect.), Nat. Assn. Pub. Pension Plan Attys., Fla. Bar Assn. (exec. bd. labor and employment law sect.), Internat. Found. Employee Benefit Plans, Israel Bonds Labor Adv. Bd. Democrat. Labor, Pension, profit-sharing, and employee benefits. Office: Sugarman & Susskind PA Ste 750 2801 Ponce De Leon Blvd Coral Gables FL 33134-6920 E-mail: sugarman@sugarmansusskind.com

SUGARMAN, ROBERT P. lawyer; b. Passaic, N.J., Aug. 29, 1949; s. Meyer and Sylvia (Schwartz) S.; m. Louise Aufiero, June 29, 1980; children: Lauren, Jason. BA, Rutgers Coll., 1971; JD, Columbia U., 1975. Bar: N.Y. and N.J. 1976, U.S. Dist. Ct. (so. dist.) N.Y. 1976, U.S. Dist. Ct. (ea. dist.) N.Y. 1977, U.S. Ct. Appeals (2d cir.) 1992. Assoc. Paul, Weiss, Rifkind, Wharton & Garrison, N.Y.C., 1975-79, Milberg Weiss Bershad Hynes & Lerach, N.Y.C., 1979-82, ptnr., 1983-99, Office Robert Sugarman, Uniondale, N.Y., 2000—. Federal civil litigation, General civil litigation, Securities. Office: Ste 400 50 Charles Lindberg Blvd Uniondale NY 11553

SUGG, REED WALLER, lawyer; b. Morganfield, Ky., Dec. 1, 1952; s. Matt Waller and Iris (Omer) S. BA, Furman U., 1975; JD, Vanderbilt U., 1978. Bar: Mo. 1978, Ill. 1979, U.S. Ct. Appeals (8th, 9th and 7th cirs.), U.S. Dist. Ct. (ea. dist.) Mo., U.S. Dist. Ct. (so. dist.) Ill. Atty. Coburn, Croft, Shepherd & Herzog, St. Louis, 1978-79, Shepherd, Sandberg & Phoenix, St. Louis, 1979-90, Sandberg, Phoenix & von Gontard, St. Louis, 1990—. Mem. ABA, Bar Assn. Met. St. Louis, Christian Legal Soc., Lawyers Assn. St. Louis, Aviation Ins. Assn., Lawyer-Pilots Bar Assn., Phi Beta Kappa. Republican. Presbyterian. Clubs: Mo. Athletic, Westborough Country (St. Louis). Avocations: basketball, golf, tennis, reading. Federal civil litigation, State civil litigation, Personal injury. Home: 12825 Brighton Woods Dr Saint Louis MO 63131-1413 Office: Sandberg Phoenix & von Gontard 1 City Ctr Ste 1500 Saint Louis MO 63101-1880

SUHR, PAUL AUGUSTINE, lawyer; b. Sonwunri, Chonbuk, Korea, Jan. 20, 1940; came to U.S. 1966; s. Chong-ju and Oksuk (Pang) So; m. Angeline M. Kang Suhr; 1 child, Christopher. BA, Campbell Coll., Buies Creek, N.C., 1968; MA, U. N.C., Greensboro, 1970; MS, U. N.C., Chapel Hill, 1975; JD, N.C. Cen. U., 1988. Bar: N.C. 1989, U.S. Dist. Ct. (ea. and mid. dist.) N.C. 1989, U.S. Ct. Appeals D.C. 1990, U.S. Ct. Appeals (4th cir.) 1992. Bibliographer N.C. Div. of State Libr., Raleigh, 1975-78; dir. Pender County Pub. Libr., Burgaw, N.C., 1978-80; libr. Tob. Lit. Svc., N.C. State U., Raleigh, 1980-85; pvt. practice law Law Offices of Paul A. Suhr, PLLC, Raleigh and Fayetteville, N.C., 1989—. Author short stories and novelettes various lit. mags., jours. and revs. Mem. Human Resources and Human Rels. Adv. Commn., City of Raleigh, 1990-95, chmn., 1994-95. N.C. Humanities Com. grantee, 1979-80; recipient Presdl. award President of Korea, 1992. Mem. ABA, ATLA, Am. Immigration Lawyers Assn., N.C. Bar Assn., N.C. Trial Lawyers Assn., Wake County Bar Assn. (bd. dirs. 1996-97), D.C. Bar Assn. Democrat. Roman Catholic. Avocations: gardening, fishing, writing. Criminal, Immigration, naturalization, and customs, Personal injury. Office: 1110 Navaho Dr Ste 502 Raleigh NC 27609-7322 E-mail: paulsuhr@bellsouth.net

SUHRHEINRICH, RICHARD FRED, federal judge; b. 1936; BS, Wayne State U., 1960; JD cum laude, Detroit Coll. Law, 1963, LLM, 1992, U. Va., 1990. Bar: Mich. Assoc. Moll, Desenberg, Purdy, Glover & Bayer, 1963-67; asst. prosecutor Macomb County, 1967; ptnr. Rogensues, Richard & Suhrheinrich, 1967; assoc. Moll, Desenberg, Purdy, Glover & Bayer, 1967-68; ptnr. Kitch, Suhrheinrich, Saurbier & Drutchas, 1968-84; judge U.S. Dist. Ct. (ea. dist.) Mich., Detroit, 1984-90, U.S. Ct. Appeals (6th Cir.), Lansing, 1990—. Mem. State Bar Mich., Ingham County Bar Assn. Office: US Ct Appeals 6th Cir USPO & Fed Bldg 315 W Allegan St Rm 241 Lansing MI 48933-1514*

SUKO, LONNY RAY, judge; b. Spokane, Wash., Oct. 12, 1943; s. Ray R. and Leila B. (Snyder) S.; m. Marcia A. Michaelsen, Aug. 26, 1967; children: Jolynn R., David M. BA, Wash. State U., 1965; JD, U. Idaho, 1968. Bar: Wash. 1968, U.S. Dist. Ct. (ea. dist.) Wash. 1969, U.S. Dist. Ct. (we. dist.) Wash. 1978, U.S. Ct. Appeals (9th cir.) 1978. Law clk. U.S. Dist. Ct. Ea. Dist. Wash., 1968-69; assoc. Lyon, Beaulaurier & Aaron, Yakima, Wash., 1969-72; ptnr. Lyon, Beaulaurier, Weigand, Suko & Gustafson, Yakima, 1972-91, Lyon, Weigand, Suko & Gustafson, P.S., 1991-95; U.S. magistrate judge, Yakima, 1971-91, 95—. Mem. Phi Beta Kappa, Phi Kappa Phi. Office: PO Box 2726 Yakima WA 98907-2726

SUKONECK, IRA DAVID, lawyer; b. Newark, Jan. 20, 1947; s. Edward and Mae (Rosenkrantz) S.; m. Vicki Sherman, Oct. 29, 1972; children: Marc, Randi. BS in Pharmacy, Northeastern U., 1969; JD, Suffolk U., 1972. Bar: Mass. 1972, N.J. 1973, U.S. Dist. Ct. N.J. 1973, U.S. Supreme Ct. 1978; cert. workers compensation law atty. Assoc. Cohn & Lifland, Saddlebrook, N.J., 1972-73; assoc. ptnr. Braff, Harris & Sukoneck, Livingston, 1973—. Mem. ABA, N.J. Bar Assn., Assn. Trial Lawyers Am., Am. Inns of Ct., N.J. Workers Compensation Def. Assn. Personal injury, Real property, Workers' compensation. Office: Braff Harris Sukoneck Wortman Harris Sukoneck 570 W Mount Pleasant Ave Ste 18 Livingston NJ 07039-1688 E-mail: isukoneck@bhs-law.com

SULAK, TIMOTHY MARTIN, lawyer; b. Waco, Tex., Nov. 29, 1952; s. Albin R. and Josephine S. Sulak; m. Gail Garrett, Aug. 18, 1952. BA with honors, U. Tex., Austin, 1975, JD, 1978. Cert. personal injury trial lawyer. Asst. county atty. Travis County, Austin, 1978-79, asst. dist. atty., 1979-80; mem. firm Morris, Craven & Sulak, 1980—. Mem. Commn. for Lawyer Discipline, 2000—, vice chair, 2000—. Master: Am. Inns of Ct.; fellow: Tex. Bar Found. (bd. trustees 2000—, sec., treas. 2000—01, chair-elect 2001—), Austin Young Lawyers Assn. Found. (life; founding); mem.: ABA, ATLA, Nat. Conf. Bar Pres., Coll. State Bar Tex., Tex. Trial Lawyers Assn. (dir. 1993—), Capital Area Trial Lawyers (exec com. 1991), Tex. Ctr. Legal Ethics and Professionalism, Trial Lawyers Pub. Justice Found., Travis County Bar Assn. (fee dispute com., chair 1989, bd. dirs. 1990, comptr. 1991, treas. 1992, sec. 1993, pres.-elect 1994, pres. 1995), State Bar Tex. (dir. 1997—2000, exec. com. 1998—2000, presdl. citation 1999, Outstanding Third Yr. dir. award 2000). Personal injury, Product liability. Home: 3605 Windsor Rd Austin TX 78703-1508 Office: Morris Craven & Sulak 3307 Northland Dr Ste 234 Austin TX 78731-4942

SULLIVAN, BARRY, lawyer; b. Newburyport, Mass., Jan. 11, 1949; s. George Arnold and Dorothy Bennett (Furbush) S.; m. Winnifred Mary Fallers, June 14, 1975; children: George Arnold, Lloyd Ashton. AB cum laude, Middlebury Coll., 1970; JD, U. Chgo., 1974. Bar: (Mass.) 1975, (Ill.) 1975, Va.: 1995, bar: (U.S. Dist. Ct. (no. dist.) Ill.) 1976, (U.S. Ct. Appeals (7th cir.)) 1976, U.S. Ct. Appeals (10th cir.) : 1977, bar: (U.S. Supreme Ct.) 1978, (U.S. Ct. Appeals (11th cir.)) 1986, (U.S. Ct. Appeals (5th and 9th cirs.)) 1987, (U.S. Ct. Appeals (fed. cir.)) 1993, (U.S. Ct. Appeals (D.C. cir.)) 1994, (U.S. Ct. Appeals (4th cir.)) 1997. Law clk. to judge John Minor Wisdom U.S. Ct. Appeals (5th cir.), New Orleans, 1974-75; assoc. Jenner & Block, Chgo., 1975-80; asst. to solicitor gen. of U.S. U.S. Dept. of Justice, Washington, 1980-81; ptnr. Jenner & Block, Chgo., 1981-94, 2001—; prof. law Washington and Lee U., Lexington, Va., 1994-2001, dean, 1994-99, v.p., 1998-99; Fulbright prof. U. Warsaw, Poland, 2000; lectr. in law U. Chgo., 2001—. Vis. fellow Queen Mary and Westfield Coll., U. London, 2001; spl. asst. atty. gen. State of Ill., 1989-90; lectr. in law Loyola U., Chgo., 1978-79; adj. prof. law Northwestern U., Chgo., 1990-92, 93-94, vis. prof., 1992-93; Jessica Swift Meml. lectr. in constnl. law Middlebury Coll., 1991. Assoc. editor U. Chgo. Law Rev., 1973-74; contbr. articles to profl. jours. Trustee Cath. Theol. Union at Chgo., 1993—; mem. vis. com. Irving B. Harris Grad. Sch. Public Policy Studies U., Chgo., 2001—; mem. vis. com. U. Chgo. Divinity Sch., 1987—2001; mem. adv. panel Fulbright Sr. Specialist Program, 2001—. Yeats Soc. scholar, 1968; Woodrow Wilson fellow, Woodrow Wilson Found., 1970. Mem. ABA (chmn. coord. com. on AIDS 1988-94, mem. standing com. on amicus curiae briefs 1990-97, mem. coun. of sect. of individual rights and responsibilities 1993-98, mem. sect. of legal edn. com. on law sch. adminstrn. 1994-98, chair sect. legal edn. com. on professionalism 1999-2000), Va. Bar Assn., Va. State Bar (chair sect. on edn. of lawyers 1998-99), Bar Assn. 7th Fed. Cir. (vice chmn. adminstrv. justice com. 1985-86), Am. Law Inst., Lawyers Club Chgo., Phi Beta Kappa. Democrat. Roman Catholic. Appellate, Federal civil litigation. Home: 5555 S Everett Apt A1-2 Chicago IL 60637 Office: Jenner & Block One IBM Plz Chicago IL 60611 E-mail: bsullivan@jenner.com

SULLIVAN, BRENDAN V., JR. lawyer; b. Providence, Mar. 11, 1942; AB, Georgetown U., 1964, JD, 1967. Bar: R.I. 1967, D.C. 1970, U.S. Dist. Ct. D.C. 1970, U.S. Ct. Appeals (D.C. cir.) 1970, U.S. Supreme Ct. 1972, U.S. Dist. Ct. Md. 1974, U.S. Ct. Appeals (4th cir.) 1981, U.S. Ct. Appeals (3d cir.) 1979, U.S. Ct. Appeals (6th cir.) 1991, U.S. Ct. Appeals (9th cir.) 1996, U.S. Ct. Fed. Claims 1998. Mem. Williams & Connolly, Washington. Lectr. Practicing Law Inst., 1981—, Md. Inst. for Continuing Profl. Edn. of

Lawyers, Inc., 1979—, D.C. Criminal Practice Inst., 1975-81. Author: Grand Jury Proceedings, 1981, Techniques for Dealing with Pending Criminal Charges or Criminal Investigations, 1983, White Collar Criminal Practice Grand Jury, 1985. Fellow Am. Coll. Trial Lawyers; mem. ABA, R.I. Bar Assn., D.C. Bar. Office: Williams & Connolly 725 12th St NW Washington DC 20005-5901

SULLIVAN, CHARLES, JR. lawyer; b. Beaumont, Tex., Oct. 20, 1943; BS, Lamar U., 1967; JD, U. Houston, 1973. Bar: Tex. 1973. Mem. Fulbright & Jaworski L.L.P., Houston. Mem. ABA, State Bar Tex., Houston Bar Assn. Environmental. Office: Fulbright & Jaworski LLP 1301 Mckinney St Ste 5100 Houston TX 77010-3031 E-mail: csullivan@fulbright.com

SULLIVAN, DANIEL FREDERICK, lawyer; b. Mason City, Iowa, Nov. 14, 1925; s. Daniel Frederick and Adeline (Kobbe) S.; m. Patricia Mendes Da Costa, July 10, 1945 (div. Oct. 1967); children— Catherine Mary Weybright, Terrance Elizabeth, Daniel Frederick, Christopher John; m. Susan Templeton, Aug. 14, 1981. B.A., U. Iowa, 1951; J.D., U. Wash., 1955. Bar: Wash. 1955, U.S. Dist. Ct. (we. and ea. dists.) Wash. 1956, U.S. Ct. Appeals (9th cir.) 1959, U.S. Supreme Ct. 1978. Assoc., Daniel F. Sullivan & Assocs., Seattle, 1955— . Served to capt. U.S. Army, 1945-53, ETO, Korea. Fellow Am. Bd. Trial Advocates, Am. Bd. Profl. Liability Attys.; mem. Am. Trial Lawyers Assn. (bd. govs. 1977—), Trial Lawyers for Pub. Justice (pres. 1983), Western Trial Lawyers Assn. (pres. 1979), Wash. State Trial Lawyers Assn. (pres. 1975, Trial Lawyer of Yr. 1975, 84). Democrat. Roman Catholic. Clubs: Ingelwood Country, Harbor (Seattle). Federal civil litigation, State civil litigation, Personal injury. Home: 423 Lake Washington Blvd Seattle WA 98122-6441 Office: Law Offices of Daniel F Sullivan & Assocs Howe St Fl 10 Seattle WA 98109-2524

SULLIVAN, E. THOMAS, dean; b. Amboy, Ill., Dec. 4, 1948; s. Edward McDonald and Mary Lorraine (Murphy) S.; m. Susan A. Sullivan, Oct. 2, 1971. BA, Drake U., 1970; JD, Ind. U., Indpls., 1973. Bar: Ind. 1973, Fla. 1974, D.C. 1975, Mo. 1980. Law clk. to Judge Joe Eaton, U.S. Dist. Ct. for So. Dist. Fla., Miami, 1973-75; trial atty. U.S. Dept. Justice, Washington, 1975-77; sr. assoc. Donovan, Leisure, Newton & Irvine, 1977-79; prof. law U. Mo., Columbia, 1979-84; assoc. dean, prof. Washington U., St. Louis, 1984-89; dean U. Ariz. Coll. Law, Tucson, 1989-95; William S. Pattee prof. law, dean U. Minn. Law Sch., Mpls., 1995—. Fellow Am. Bar Found.; mem. Am. Law Inst., Am. Econ. Assn. Home: 180 Bank St SE Minneapolis MN 55414-1042 Office: U Minn Law Sch Walter F Mondale Hall Office 381 229 19th Ave S Minneapolis MN 55455*

SULLIVAN, EDWARD JOSEPH, lawyer, educator; b. Bklyn., Apr. 24, 1945; s. Edward Joseph and Bridget (Duffy) S.; m. Patte Hancock, Aug. 7, 1982; children: Amy Brase, Molly Elsasser, Mary Christine. BA, St. John's U., 1966; JD, Willamette U., 1969; MA, cert. Urban Studies, Portland State U., 1974; LLM, Univ. Coll., London, 1978; diploma in law, Univ. Coll., Oxford, 1984; MA, U. Durham, 1999. Bar: Oreg. 1969, D.C. 1978, U.S. Dist. Ct. Oreg. 1970, U.S. Ct. Appeals (9th cir.) 1970, U.S. Supreme Ct. 1972. Counsel Washington County, Hillsboro, Oreg., 1969-75; legal counsel Gov. of Oreg., Salem, 1975-77; ptnr. O'Donnell, Sullivan & Ramis, Portland, Oreg., 1978-84, Sullivan, Josselson, Roberts, Johnson & Kloos, Portland, Salem and Eugene, 1984-86, Mitchell, Lang & Smith, Portland, 1986-90, Preston Gates & Ellis, Portland, 1990—. Bd. dirs., pres. Oreg. Law Inst. Contbr. numerous articles to profl. jours. Chmn. Capitol Planning Commn., Salem, 1975-77, 78-81. Mem. ABA (local govt. sect., com. on planning and zoning, adminstrv. law sect.) Oreg. State Bar Assn., D.C. Bar Assn., Wash. State Bar Assn., Am. Judicature Soc., Am. Polit. Sci. Assn. Democrat. Roman Catholic. Administrative and regulatory, Land use and zoning (including planning). Office: Preston Gates & Ellis 222 SW Columbia Ste 1400 Portland OR 97201-6632 Business E-Mail: esulliva@prestongates.com

SULLIVAN, EDWARD LAWRENCE, lawyer; b. Boston, May 8, 1955; s. Edward L. and Dorothy L. (Gregory) S.; m. Susan M. Griffin, Dec. 2, 1983; children: Erica A., Brittany M. BA in Polit. Sci., St. Anselm Coll., 1977; JD, St. Louis U., 1980. Bar: Mo. 1980, Mass. 1981, Ill. 1981, D.C. 1986. Atty., Ill. divsn. Peabody Coal Co., Fairview Heights, 1980-85; legis. counsel Peabody Holding Co., Washington, 1985-88; dir., legal and pub. affairs, western divsn. Peabody Coal Co., Flagstaff, Ariz., 1988-90; sr. counsel Peabody Holding Co., St. Louis, 1990-94; gen. counsel Powder River Coal Co., Gillette, Wyo., 1994-95; gen. counsel, western region Peabody Holding Co., St. Louis, 1995—. Industry rep. royalty policy com. U.S. Dept. Interior, Washington, 1995—. Mem. Bar Assn. Met. St. Louis. Administrative and regulatory, Contracts commercial, Natural resources. Office: Peabody Holding Co Inc 701 Market St Ste 700 Saint Louis MO 63101-1895

SULLIVAN, EUGENE JOHN, lawyer; b. Chestertown, Md., May 13, 1946; s. Eugene John and Dorothy Ann (Douglas) S.; m. Maryann Hill. BA with high honors, U. Md., 1969; JD, Columbia U., 1972. Bar: N.Y. 1973, Pa. 1980, U.S. Dist. Ct. (so. and ea. dists.) N.Y. 1973, U.S. Ct. Appeals (2d cir.) 1975, N.J. 1976, U.S. Supreme Ct. 1976, U.S. Ct. Appeals (3d cir.) 1976, U.S. Dist. Ct. N.J. 1976, U.S. Ct. Appeals (D.C. cir.) 1977, U.S. Ct. Claims 1978, U.S. Ct. Customs and Patent Appeals 1978. Assoc. Kirlin, Campbell & Keating, N.Y.C., 1972-75; dep. atty. gen. div. law N.J. Dept. Law and Pub. Safety, Trenton, 1976-81, asst. atty. gen., 1981-89; ptnr. Peckar & Abramson, 1989—; mem. com. on civil model jury charges N.J. Supreme Ct., 1983-89, com. on civil case mgmt. and procedure, 1983. Author, editor: Division of Law Litigation Manual, 1983; contbr. articles to profl. jours. With USN, 1964-67. Mem. ABA (sec. litigation, sect. anti-trust law, sect. pub. contract law), N.J. Bar Assn., Pa. Bar Assn., Columbia Law Sch. Alumni Assn., Phi Beta Kappa, Phi Kappa Phi, Phi Eta Sigma, Phi Alpha Theta. Roman Catholic. Home: 42 Silvers Ln Plainsboro NJ 08536-1116 Office: 70 Grand Ave River Edge NJ 07661-1935

SULLIVAN, EUGENE RAYMOND, federal judge; b. St. Louis, Aug. 2, 1941; s. Raymond Vincent and Rosemary (Kiely) S.; m. Lis Urup Johansen, June 18, 1966; children— Kim, Eugene II. BS, U.S. Mil. Acad., 1964; JD, Georgetown U., 1971. Bar: Mo. 1972, D.C. 1972. Law clk. to judge U.S. Ct. Appeals (8th cir.), St. Louis, 1971-72; assoc. Patton Boggs & Blow, Washington, 1972-74; asst. spl. counsel The White House, 1974; trial counsel U.S. Dept. of Justice, 1974-82; dep. gen. counsel U.S. Air Force, 1982-84, gen. counsel, 1984-86; gov. Wake Island, 1984-86; judge U.S. Ct. Appeals (Armed Forces), Washington, 1986-90, 95—, chief judge, 1990-95. Mem. Fed. Commn. To Study Honor Code at West Point, 1989-90. Trustee U.S. Mil. Acad., 1989—. With US Army, 1964-69. Decorated Bronze Star, Air medal, airborne badge, ranger badge, others. Republican. Roman Catholic. Home: 6307 Massachusetts Ave Bethesda MD 20816-1139 Office: US Ct Appeals (Armed Forces) 450 E St NW Washington DC 20442-0001

SULLIVAN, FRANK, JR. state supreme court justice; b. Mar. 21, 1950; s. Frank E. and Colette (Cleary) S.; m. Cheryl Gibson, June 14, 1972; children: Denis M., Douglas S., Thomas R. AB cum laude, Dartmouth Coll., 1972; JD magna cum laude, Ind. U., 1982; LLM, U. Va., 2001. Bar: Ind. 1982. Mem. staff Office of U.S. Rep. John Brademas, 1974-79, dir. staff, 1975-78; with Barnes & Thornburg, Indpls., 1982-89; budget dir. State of Ind., 1989-92; exec. asst. Office of Gov. Evan Bayh, 1993; assoc. justice Ind. Supreme Ct., 1993—. Mem. ABA, Ind. State Bar Assn., Indpls. Bar Assn. Home: 6153 N Olney St Indianapolis IN 46220-5166 Office: State House Rm 321 Indianapolis IN 46204-2728

SULLIVAN, FREDERICK LAWRENCE, lawyer; b. Holyoke, Mass., Oct. 11, 1937; s. Frederick L. and Helen (Fitzgerald) S.; m. Judith Ann Boldvay, Feb. 13, 1965; children: Mark, Meghan. BS, Manhattan Coll., 1959; JD, Fordham U., 1965. Bar: N.Y. 1966, U.S. Dist. Ct. (ea. and so. dist.) N.Y. 1972, Mass. 1973, U.S. Dist. Ct. Mass. 1972, U.S. Ct. Appeals (2nd cir.) 1972. Labor atty. Allied Stores Corp., N.Y.C., 1965-69; assoc. Jackson, Lewis, Schnitzler & Krupman, 1969-72, Marshall & Marshall, Springfield, Mass., 1972-76; ptnr. Sullivan & Hayes, 1976—. Cons. Employee Rels., Inc., Springfield, 1977—. Co-author book: Massachusetts Non-Profit Organizations, 1992; contbr. articles to profl. jours. Pres. bd. dirs. Children's Mus., Holyoke, Mass., 1988-92; bd. dirs. United Way, Holyoke, 1987-92, Springfield Symphony, 1989-94; pres., chmn. St. Patrick's Parade Com., Holyoke, 1985-92. Mem. ABA, Mass. Bar Assn. (employment law coun. rep.). Labor. Office: Sullivan & Hayes 1 Monarch Pl Ste 1200 Springfield MA 01144-1200

SULLIVAN, JAMES A., III, lawyer; b. Chgo., Feb. 26, 1941; s. James A. and Helen A. Sullivan; m. Kathleen Gundel, May 23, 1970; children: James A., Shannon S. BA, St. Joseph Coll., Rensselaer, Ind., 1963; JD, U. Detroit, 1966. Bar: Mich. 1967, U.S. Dist. Ct. (ea. dist.) Mich. 1967, U.S. Ct. Appeals (6th cir.) 1974, U.S. Supreme Ct. 1974. Law clk. Ct. Appeals Mich., 1966-67; assoc. Vandeveer, Garzia, Tonkin, Kerr & Heaphy PC, Detroit, 1967-73, ptnr., 1972-99. Instr. Mich. State Bar Legal Edn. Program, 1967-70. Active United Found. Mem. ABA, State Bar Mich., Detroit Bar Assn., Am. Judicature Soc., Am. Arbitration Assn., Grosse Pointe Yacht Club, Elks (past exalted ruler). Roman Catholic. Federal civil litigation, State civil litigation, Personal injury. Office: PO Box 65 Saint Clair Shores MI 48080 E-mail: james_sullivan_1999@yahoo.com

SULLIVAN, JOHN CORNELIUS, JR. lawyer; b. Erie, Pa., Oct. 23, 1927; s. John Cornelius and Catherine J. (Carney) S.; m. Helen E. Kennedy, Feb. 3, 1951; children: John III, Timi Ann, Michael, Elizabeth. BA in Econs., Allegheny Coll., 1953; LLB, Dickinson Sch. Law, 1959. Bar: Pa. 1960, U.S. Supreme Ct. 1976. Sales rep. IBM Corp., 1953-56; mem. firm Nissley, Clecker & Fearen, Harrisburg, Pa., 1959-63; ptnr. Nauman, Smith, Shissler & Hall, 1964—. Asst. city solicitor City of Harrisburg, 1964-68, city solicitor, 1968-70; gen. counsel Harrisburg Redevel. Authority, 1964-68, Harrisburg Mcpl. Authority, 1964-87; solicitor Silver-Spring Twp., 1970-81; dir. accounts and fin. City of Harrisburg, 1963; mem. Pa. House of Reps., 1963-64. Assoc. editor Dickinson Law Rev., 1958-59; editor Dauphin County Reporter, 1961-63. Chmn. bd. dirs. Harrisburg Pub. Library, 1965-73; bd. dirs., sec. Harrisburg Hosp.; bd. dirs. Harrisburg Hosp. Found., 1975-89. Mem. ABA, Pa. Bar Assn., Dauphin County Bar Assn. (past. dir.), The Pa. Soc. (N.Y.C.), Phi Gamma Delta. Contracts commercial, Estate planning, Libel. Home: 107 Sample Bridge Rd Mechanicsburg PA 17050-1940 Office: 200 N 3rd St Fl D18 Harrisburg PA 17101-1518

SULLIVAN, KATHLEEN MARIE, dean, law educator; BA, Cornell U., 1976, Oxford (Eng.) U., 1978; JD, Harvard U., 1981. Law clk. Hon. James L. Oakes U.S. Ct. Appeals (2d cir.), 1981-82; pvt. practice, 1982-84; asst. prof. Harvard U., Cambridge, Mass., 1984-89, prof., 1989-93, Stanford (Calif.) U., 1993—, Paradise fellow, 1995-96, Stanley Morrison prof., 1996—, dean, Richard E. Lang prof., 1999—. Vis. prov. U. So. Calif. Law Ctr., 1991, Stanford U., 1992; lectr., commentator on constnl. law. Co-editor: (with Gerald Gunther) Constitutional Law, 13th edit., 1997. Named one of 50 Top Women Lawyers Nat. Law Jour., 1998; recipient John Bingham Hurlbut award for excellence in tchg. Stanford U., 1996. Fellow Am. Acad. Arts and Scis. Office: Stanford U Law Sch Bldg Lawsh 559 Nathan Abbott Way Stanford CA 94305-8610*

SULLIVAN, KEVIN PATRICK, lawyer; b. Waterbury, Conn., June 9, 1953; s. John Holian Sullivan and Frances (McGrath) Coon; m. Peggy Hardy, June 13, 1975 (div. Jan. 1985); m. Jarnine Welker, Feb. 15, 1985; children: S. Craig Lemmon, Michael Scott Lemmon, Lindsay Michelle Lemmon. BS in Polit. Sci., BS in Police Sci. cum laude, Weber State Coll., 1979; JD, Pepperdine U., 1982. Bar: Utah 1982, U.S. Dist. Ct. Utah 1982, U.S. Ct. Appeals (10th cir.) 1986, U.S. Supreme Ct. 1986. Assoc. Farr, Kaufman & Hamilton, Ogden, Utah, 1982-87; ptnr. Farr, Kaufman, Hamilton, Sulivan, Gorman & Perkins, 1987-91, Farr, Kaufman, Sullivan, Gorman & Perkins, Ogden, 1991—. Judge pro tem Utah 2d Cir. Ct.; city prosecutor of South Ogden, 1990-92. Mem. Eccles Community Art Ctr., Victim's Rights Com. of 2d Jud. Dist. Mem. ABA (criminal justice sect., litigation sect., justice and edn. fund lawyers' coun.), ACLU, ATLA, Utah Bar Assn. (criminal law, young lawyer, litigation sects., unauthorized practice law com.), Utah Trial Lawyers Assn., Utah Assn. Criminal Def. Lawyers, Weber County Bar Assn. (criminal law sect., pres.-elect 1993, pres. 1994), Weber County Pub. Defenders Assn. (assoc. dir. 1987), Weber State Coll. Alumni Assn., Amicus Pepperdine, Elks, Kiwanis, Phi Kappa Phi. Mem. LDS Ch. Avocations: skiing, golf, tennis, fishing. E-mail: kpsWutahlinx.com. State civil litigation, Criminal, Personal injury. Home: 2731 E 6425 S Ogden UT 84403-5461 Office: Farr Kaufman Sullivan Gorman & Perkins 205 26th St Ste 34 Ogden UT 84401-3109

SULLIVAN, LAWRENCE MATTHEW, lawyer; b. Wilmington, Del., Sept. 5, 1937. AB in Philosophy, King's Coll., 1959; LLB, Cath. U. Am., 1964. Bar: U.S. Supreme Ct., Del. 1965, U.S. Dist. Ct. Del. 1966. Pvt. practice, 1965—; asst. county atty., New Castle County, 1966-67; register of wills, New Castle County, 1966-70; pub. defender, State of Del., 1970—; instr. bus. and real estate law, Wilmington Coll., 1969-78, Del. Tech. and Community Coll., 1978-80, Del. State Coll., 1980-82, Brandywine Coll; vice chmn. and mem. various coms. Criminal Justice Coun. Del.; mem. Del. Supreme Ct.'s Planning and Long Range Ct.'s Planning Coms., Del. Supreme Ct. Commn. on Del. Cts. 2000, Del. Agy. to Reduce Crime, Gov.'s Crime Reduction Task Force, Sentencing Accountability Commn., various other coms. Co-author: Delaware Fundamentals of Real Estate, University of Delaware Press, 1980. Sec. Rep. City Com; pres. Active Young Reps. of Wilmington; vice chmn. Young Rep. Nat. Fedn; vice chmn. Moot Ct. Bd. Govs, 1963-64; pres. Student Bar Assn., 1963-64. With U.S. Army, Del. Nat. Guard. Named Del.'s Outstanding Young Rep. of Yr., 1965, Wilmington's Young Man of Yr., 1966, one of Outstanding Young Men of Am., 1968. Mem. ABA, Am. Arbitration Assn., Assn. Trial Lawyers Am., Del. Bar Assn., Del. Trial Lawyers Assn., New Castle County Officials Assns. (pres. 1968-70), Phi Alpha Delta. General practice. Office: Sullivan & Bartley 1010 Concord Ave # 201 Wilmington DE 19802-3367

SULLIVAN, MARK FRANCIS, lawyer, b. Oakland, Calif., May 28, 1947; s. Peter Jeremiah and Lillian Marie (Filippa) S.; m. Millicent Anne Meunier, Sept. 22, 1973; children— Patrick Mark, Matthew Francis, Mark Francis, Thomas John, John David. A.B. summa cum laude, Georgetown U., 1969; J.D. cum laude, U. Mich. 1972. Bar: Mich. 1972, N.Y. 1973, Hawaii 1973. U.S. Dist. Ct. (we. dist.) Mich. 1978, U.S. Ct. Appeals (6th cir.) 1980, U.S. Ct. Mil. Appeals 1973, U.S. Ct. Appeals (D.C. cir.) 1980, Calif. 1983, N.C. 1984, U.S. Dist. Ct. (no. and so. dists.) Calif. 1984, U.S. Ct. Appeals (9th cir.) 1984. Litigation atty. Landman, Hathaway, Latimer, Clink & Robb, Muskegon, Mich., 1977-79; sr. atty. Gen. Telephone Co. of Mich., Muskegon, 1979-82; sr. atty. Gen. Telephone Co. of S.E. Durham, N.C., 1982-84; litigation atty. Gen. Telephone Calif., Santa Monica, Calif., 1984-85, Thousand Oaks, 1985-87; v.p., gen. counsel GTE Airfone Inc., Oak Brook, Ill., 1987-89; litigation atty. GTE Tel. Ops. West Area, Thousand Oaks, Calif., 1989-91; assoc. gen. counsel litigation GTE Calf. Inc., Thousand Oaks, 1991-2000; law lectr., part-time instr. Muskegon Bus. Coll., Mich. 1977-81; cons. Hawaiian Telephone Co., Honolulu, 1982-83; prof. law So. Calif. Inst. Law, Ventura, Calif., 1990-92. Pub. speaker Mich. Right to Life com., Muskegon, 1981; sustaining mem. Rep. Nat. Com., Washington, 1980—2001; alumni interviewer alumni admissions program Georgetown U., Durham, 1983-84. Capt. JAGC, USNR, 1972-2001. Mem. Calif. Bar Assn., L.A. County Bar Assn., Ventura County Bar Assn., Mich. Bar Assn., Hawaii State Bar, N.C. Bar Assn., Navy-Marine Corps. Judge Advs. Assn., Aircraft Owners and Pilots Assn., Phi Beta Kappa. Roman Catholic. Avocation: aviation. Federal civil litigation, State civil litigation, Labor. Home: 1686 Margate Pl Westlake Village CA 91361-1521 Office: Sullivan Sottle & Taketa LLP Attys Ste 205 31351 Via Colinas Westlake Village CA 91362 E-mail: msullivan@sstlawfirm.com

SULLIVAN, MICHAEL J. prosecutor; b. Oct. 3, 1954; m. Terry Sullivan, 1975; children: Joseph, Kelly, Allyson, James. Grad., Boston Coll., 1979; JD, Suffolk U., 1983. Assoc. Bolles and Pritchard, 1983—90; ptnr. McGovern and Sullivan, 1990—95; dist. atty. Plymouth County, Mass., 1995—2001; U.S. atty. Dist. of Mass., 2001—; mem. Mass. Ho. Reps., 1991—95. Rep. dist. 7 Mass. Ho. of Reps., 1990—, mem. ways and means, post audit and oversight and steering and policy coms., spl. com. on edn. reform. Office: US Attys Office US Courthouse Ste 9200 1 Courthouse Way Boston MA 02210*

SULLIVAN, MICHELLE CORNEJO, lawyer; b. St. Louis, June 29, 1958; m. Dennis Keith Sullivan, May 18, 1985. BS, U. Calif., Berkeley, 1980; JD, U. Santa Clara, 1983. Bar: Calif., 1984; U.S. Dist. Ct. (no. dist.) Calif., 1984, (so. dist.) Calif., 1985; cert. family law specialist. Legal dept. Four-Phase Computers, Cupertino, Calif., 1984; asst. dist. atty. San Benito County, Hollister, 1984-85; assoc. Walters & Ward, Rancho Bernardo, 1986-87, Law Offices of Rebecca Prater, Carlsbad, 1987-88; pvt. practice Escondido & San Diego, 1988—. Pres. Women in Networking, San Diego, 1987; western horse show judge Calif. State Horseman's Assn., 1985; adv. com. San Diego Regional Conf. on Women, trustee, 1993-95. Law Faculty scholar U. Santa Clara, 1982-83. Mem. ABA, State Bar Assn., San Diego County Bar Assn. (cert. specialist), Bar Assn. No. San Diego County (chair family law sect. 1996-98, cert. specialist), Escondido Rotary Main Club, Rancho Bernardo C. of C. (amb. 1986-87), San Diego Trial Lawyers Assn. (family law sect.), Lawyers Club (v.p. 1988-89). Avocations: western horseback riding, golf, sailing, scuba diving. Alternative dispute resolution, Estate planning, Family and matrimonial. Office: 16486 Bernardo Center Dr San Diego CA 92128-2518 E-mail: mcslaw@pacbell.net

SULLIVAN, MORTIMER ALLEN, JR. lawyer; b. Buffalo, Sept. 19, 1930; s. Mortimer Allen Sr. and Gertrude (Hinkley) S.; m. Maryanne Calella, Nov. 20, 1965; children: Mark Allen, Michael John. BA, U. Buffalo, 1954. Bar: N.Y. 1964, U.S. Dist. Ct. (we. dist.) N.Y. 1966, U.S. Dist. Ct. (no. dist.) N.Y. 1967, U.S. Supreme Ct. 1970. Counsel liability claims Interstate Motor Freight System, Grand Rapids, Mich., 1964-82. V.p. J.P.M. Sullivan, Inc., Elmira, N.Y., 1959-67; govt. appeal agt. U.S. Selective Service System, 1967-71; dep. sci. div. Erie County (N.Y.) Sheriff's Office, 1971—, lt., 1986—. Inventor (with others) in field; creator, dir. video depiction JudiVision, 1969; composer High Flight, 1983. Chmn. com. on Constn. and Canons Episcopal Diocese of Western N.Y., 1975-96; bd. dirs. Erie County Law Enforcement Found., Inc., 1987—; bd. dirs. Orchard Park (N.Y.) Symphony Orch., 1975-97, v.p., 1977-79, 91-94. With USAF, 1954-57; spl. agt. Air Force Office of Spl. Investigations, 1972-87, col. res. ret. Decorated Legion of Merit. Mem. Erie County Bar Assn. (chmn. law and tech. com., 1970-81), Transp. Lawyers Assn., Kappa Alpha Soc. Republican. Clubs: Saturn (Buffalo); Wanakah (N.Y.) Country. Avocation: aviation. General practice. Home: 19 Knob Hill Rd Orchard Park NY 14127-3917 Office: 88 S Davis St PO Box 1003 Orchard Park NY 14127-8003 E-mail: masulaw@aol.com

SULLIVAN, PATRICK JAMES, lawyer; b. Orange, Calif., Sept. 17, 1943; s. Leo Charles Sullivan and Virginia (Wohosky) Souza; m. Pamela Pressler, Aug. 17, 1974; children: Shannon, Erin. BA, U. So. Calif., 1965; JD, Loyola U., Los Angeles, 1974. Bar: Calif. 1974, U.S. Ct. Appeals (9th cir.) 1978, U.S. Supreme Ct. 1979, U.S. Ct. Appeals (3rd cir.) 1983, U.S. Tax Ct. 1986, U.S. Ct. Appeals (2d and 8th cirs.) 1989. Trial atty. U.S. Dept. Justice, Washington, 1974-75; ptnr. Sullivan, Jones & Archer, San Diego and San Francisco, 1975-83, Hewitt, Sullivan & Marshall, San Diego, 1983-87, King & Ballow, 1987-90, Sullivan & Hirsch, San Diego, 1990—; arbitrator San Diego Superior Ct., 1979-83; lectr. U. Calif. Securities Regulations Inst., 1985; chmn. Am. Law Inst. Anti-trust Conf., 1988, 91; mem. faculty Hastings Ctr. For Trial and Appelate Advocacy, 1989-92, Calif. Continuing Edn. of Bar, 1989—. Served to 1st lt. U.S. Army, 1966-69; Vietnam. Decorated Bronze Star. Fellow Am. Bar Found.; mem. ABA (litigation and antitrust sects., ho. dels.), Am. Law Inst., Am. Judiciary Soc., Nat. Inst. Trial Adv. (faculty 1986—), ABOTA, Am. Inn Ct. Republican. Roman Catholic. Lodge: Rotary (Newhall, Calif.). Antitrust, Federal civil litigation, Securities. Home: 325 Whitewood Pl Encinitas CA 92024-3137 Office: 401 W A St Ste 2300 San Diego CA 92101-7915

SULLIVAN, PETER THOMAS, III, lawyer; b. Jersey City, Aug. 6, 1950; s. Peter T. Jr. and Daisy (Stallard) S.; m. Brenda J. Stanley, July 1, 1972 (div. 1980); children: Patrick, Margaret McGaw-Sullivan. BA, So. Ill. U., 1972; JD, DePaul U., 1976. Bar: Ill. 1976, U.S. Dist. Ct. (no. dist.) Ill. 1976, U.S. Ct. Appeals (7th ci.) 1982. Assoc. Thomas, Kostantacos & Traum, Rockford, Ill., 1976-77; atty. Pub. Defender's Office, 1977-82; ptnr. Sreenan, Cain & Sullivan, 1982-89; pvt. practice Pete Sullivan & Assocs., 1989—. Mem. Assn. Trial Lawyers Am., Ill. Bar Assn., Ill. Trial Lawyers Assn. Democrat. Roman Catholic. Personal injury, Product liability, Workers' compensation. Office: Pete Sullivan & Assoc PC 134 N Main St Rockford IL 61101-1169

SULLIVAN, ROBERT EMMET, JR. lawyer; b. Detroit, Oct. 2, 1955; s. Robert Emmet Sr. and Gloria Marie (Lamb) S. BA in Polit. Sci. and Sociology, Wayne State U., 1977; M Urban Planning, U. Mich., 1979; JD, U. Detroit, 1983; postgrad., Oxford (Eng.) U., 1981. Bar: Mich. 1984, U.S. Dist. Ct. (we. dist.) Mich. 1984, U.S. Dist. Ct. (ea. dist.) Mich. 1984, U.S. Ct. Appeals (6th cir.) 1984, U.S. Ct. Appeal (D.C. cir.) 1984, U.S. Tax Ct. 1984, D.C. 1985, U.S. Supreme Ct. 1987. Planning commr. City of Detroit, 1982-85; shareholder Sullivan, Ward, Bone, Tyler & Asher, P.C., Detroit, 1984—. Bd. dirs. Internat. Inst. of Met. Detroit. Contbr. articles to profl. jours. Active St. Scholastica Parish Ch., North Rosedale Park Civic Assn., Detroit Hist. Soc. Moffitt scholar, 1982, 83. Mem. AIA, Detroit Bar Assn., Mich. Soc. Planning Ofcls., Am. Inst. Cert. Planners. Roman Catholic. General civil litigation, Constitutional, Land use and zoning (including planning). Home: 7464 Wilshire West Bloomfield MI 48322-2875 Office: Sullivan Ward Bone Tyler & Asher 25800 Northwestern Hwy Southfield MI 48075-1000 E-mail: rsullivanjr@swbta.com

SULLIVAN, THOMAS MICHAEL, lawyer; b. Jan. 18, 1943; s. John Cavanaugh and Eileen (O'Leary) Sullivan; m. Patricia Jane, Aug. 19, 1966. BA, Western Mich. U., 1965; JD cum laude, Wayne State U., 1968. Bar: Mich. 1968, U.S. Dist. Ct. (ea. dist.) Mich. 1968, U.S. Tax Ct. 1969, U.S. Ct. Appeals (6th cir.) 1974. Mem. firm Moorman Profl. Corp., Detroit, 1968—, pres., 1987—. Adj. faculty U. Detroit Mercy Law Sch., 1973—81; bd. dir. Vista Maria, Dearborn, Mich., pres., 1991—96. Bd. dir. Boys Hope Girls Hope, Detroit, 1999—. Mem.: ABA, State Bar Mich., Detroit Bar Assn., Detroit Athletic Club, Bayview Yacht Club (Detroit). Roman Catholic. State civil litigation, General corporate, Labor. Home: 49752 Keycove Chesterfield MI 48047-4307 Office: Berry Moorman Profl Corp 600 Woodbridge Detroit MI 48226-4302

SULLIVAN, WARREN GERALD, business executive, lawyer; b. Chgo., Sept. 8, 1923; s. Gerald Joseph and Marie (Fairrington) S.; m. Helen Ruth Young, Aug. 21, 1948 (div.); children: Janet M., Douglas W., William C.; m. Helen Louise Curtis. BA, U. Ill., Urbana, 1947; JD, Northwestern U., 1950. Bar: Ill. 1950, Conn. 1971, Mo. 1981, U.S. Ct. Appeals (7th cir.) 1955, U.S. Ct. Appeals (DC cir.) 1964, U.S. Ct. Appeals (6th cir.) 1966, U.S. Ct. Appeals (2nd cir.) 1974, U.S. Supreme Ct. 1968. Atty Ill. Dept. Revenue, Chgo., 1950-52; from assoc. to ptnr. Naphin, Sullivan & Banta and predecessors, 1952-69; v.p. personnel Avco Corp., Greenwich, Conn., 1969-75; v.p. indsl. rels. Gen. Dynamics Corp., St. Louis, 1975-84; mgmt. cons., 1984—. Author: Contbr. Articles to Profl. Jours. Bd. dirs. YMCA Greater St. Louis. 1st lt. Mil. Intelligence Svc., 1942-45; mil. govt. USAR, 1949-54. Fellow Col.. Labor and Employment Lawyers; mem. ABA, Conn. Bar Assn., Mo. Bar Assn., Bellerive Country (Creve Coeur, Mo.), Delta Tau Delta, Phi Delta Phi. Labor. Office: 410 N Newstead Ave Apt 11S Saint Louis MO 63108-2641 E-mail: wgsulli@attglobal.net

SULLIVAN, WILLIAM FRANCIS, lawyer; b. Boston, June 15, 1957; s. William Henry and Susan (White) S.; m. Mary Lou Hutchinson, June 13, 1982; children: William H., Conor R., Brennan M. BA, U. Notre Dame, 1979; JD, Boston Coll., 1982. Bar: Mass. 1982, U.S. Dist. Ct. Mass. 1984, U.S. Ct. Appeals (1st cir.) 1997. Asst. dist. atty. Norfolk County, Dedham, Mass., 1983-84; assoc. Barry, Masterson, Sullivan & Largey, Quincy, 1985-87; ptnr. Barry, Sullivan & Largey, 1988-90, Sullivan & Largey, Quincy, 1990—. Coach, referee Canton (Mass.) Youth Soccer, 1984—; bd. dirs. Com. for Immigrants and Refugees; elected del. Mass. Dem. Conv., 1990; fellow Mass. Bar Found. Mem. ABA, Nat. Assn. Criminal Def. Attys., Mass. Assn. Criminal Def. Attys., Mass. Bar Assn. (bd. dirs.), Norfolk County Bar Assn. (pres. 2000-01), Quincy Bar Assn., Mass. Acad. Trial Attys. Democrat. Roman Catholic. Club: Notre Dame Monogram (South Bend, Ind.). Criminal, General practice, Personal injury. Home: 29 Kings Rd Canton MA 02021-1725 Office: Sullivan & Largey 277 Newport Ave Wollaston MA 02170-1736 E-mail: sullnd@aol.com, wsullivan@lawyers.com

SULLIVAN, WILLIAM J. state supreme court justice; Student, St. Thomas Sem., 1958-59; BA in Polit. Sci., Providence Coll., 1962; B in Civil Law, Coll. William and Mary, 1965, JD, 1970. Judge Conn. Superior Ct., 1978-97, Conn. Appellate Ct., 1997-99; assoc. justice Conn. Supreme Ct., 1999-2001; chief justice, 2001—. Office: Conn Supreme Ct Supreme Ct Bldg 231 Capitol Ave Hartford CT 06106-1548

SULLIVAN-SCHWEBKE, KAREN JANE, lawyer; b. Spokane, Wash., Feb. 25, 1955; d. John and Helen (Bartlett) Sullivan; m. Ethan K. Schwebke, Apr. 18, 1987; children: Noah, Eli. BA, U. Wash., 1978, MBA, JD, 1987. Exec. asst. to corp. controller Pay'n Save Corp., Seattle, 1980-83; tchg. asst. U. Wash. Coll. Bus., 1984-85; law clk. Bogle & Gates Law Firm, 1985, PACCAR, Inc., Bellevue, Wash., 1986, U. Wash. Law Sch., Seattle, 1987; dir. Boys and Girls Club Puget Sound, Everett, Wash., 1988-90; legal counsel Fla. State Human Rights Commn., 1995-97; exec. dir. Benton and Franklin Counties Wash. State Family Policy Coun., Kennewick, 1997-99; exec. dir., legal coun., CFO Mid-Columbia Regional Symphony and Ballet, Richland, Wash., 1999—. Chair City of Kennewick Civil Svc. Commn., 2000—; mem. chamber Leadership Tri-Cities Class 2001; bd. dirs. Women Helping Women Fund. Mem. NOW, Kappa Delta, U. Wash. Alumnae Assn. (dist. gov.), Rotary, DOVIA. Democrat. Avocations: reading, painting, interior decorating, gardening. Home: 2001 S Newport St Kennewick WA 99337-7811 E-mail: schweet4@msn.com

SULLIVANT, WESLEY BENTON, lawyer; b. Denton, Tex., Aug. 7, 1969; s. William Benton and Elizabeth Sullivant. BA, Midwestern State U., 1992; JD, St. Mary's U., San Antonio, 1996. Bar: Tex. 1997. Assoc. Sullivant, Sullivant & Meurer, L.L.P., Gainesville, Tex., 1997—. Bd. dirs. Frank Buck Zool. Soc., Gainesville, 1997—. Recipient cert. of merit Gainesville Police Dept. 1996. Mem. ABA, Tex. Bar Assn., Tex. Trial Lawyers Assn., Cooke County Bar Assn. (treas. 1998—), Masons (32d degree). Democrat. Avocations: hunting, shooting, water sports. Criminal, Family and matrimonial, Personal injury. Office: Sullivant Sullivant & Meurer PO Box 1517 209 S Dixon St Gainesville TX 76241

SULLY, IRA BENNETT, lawyer; b. Columbus, Ohio, June 3, 1947; s. Bernie and Helen Mildred (Koen) S.; m. Nancy Lee Pryor, Oct. 2, 1983. BA cum laude, Ohio State U., 1969, JD summa cum laude, 1974. Bar: Ohio 1974, U.S. Dist. Ct. (so. dist.) Ohio 1974. Assoc. Schottenstein, Garel, Swedlow & Zox, Columbus, 1974-78; atty. Borden, Inc., 1978-80; sole practice, 1980—. Instr. Real Estate Law Columbus Tech. Inst., 1983-88; title ins. agt. Sycamore Title Agy., Columbus, 1983— . Bd. dirs. Rsch. Franklin County Celeste for Gov., Columbus, 1978; asst. treas. Pamela Conrad for City Coun., Columbus, 1979; treas. Leland for State Rep., Columbus, 1982, 84, Leland for City Atty., Columbus, 1985; active Ohio Dem. Bldg. Com., 1995-98; commentator Sta. WOSU, Columbus, 1980; trustee Ohio State U. Undergrad. Student Govt. Alumni Soc., 1997—, pres., 2000—. Mem. ABA, Ohio Bar Assn., Columbus Bar Assn., Agonis Club (Columbus). Democrat. Jewish. Avocations: running, coin collecting. Contracts commercial, Probate, Real property. Home: 200 Reinhard Ave Columbus OH 43206-2616 Office: 844 S Front St Columbus OH 43206-2543

SULTANIK, JEFFREY TED, lawyer; b. N.Y.C., July 26, 1954; s. Solomon and Anna (Tiger) S.; m. Judith Ann Clyman, Nov. 14, 1981; children: Evan A., Sara A. BA cum laude, U. Pa., Phila., 1976; JD, Hofstra U., 1979. Bar: Pa. 1979, Fla. 1980, U.S. Dist. Ct. (ea. dist.) Pa., U.S. Ct. Appeals (3d cir.). Ptnr. Fox, Rothschild, O'Brien & Frankel, L.L.P., Lansdale, Pa., 1979-81; solicitor Upper Merion Sch. Dist., 1995—. Solicitor Boyertown (Pa.) Area Sch. Dist., 1981—, Perkiomen Valley Sch. Dist., Rahns, Pa., 1983—, North Montco Vocat.-Tech. Sch., Lansdale, 1981—, Souderton (Pa.) Area Sch. Dist., 1989—, Wallingford-Swarthmore Sch. Dist., 1999—; spl. counsel Penn Delco Sch. Dist., Aston, Pa., Coun. Rock Sch. Dist., Newtown, Pa., 1998, Kennett Consolidated Sch. Dist., 1999—, Colonial Sch. Dist., 1996—, Owen J. Roberts Sch. Dist., 1999—, Wissahickon Sch. Dist., 1999—, Norristown Sch. Dist., 1999—, Marple Newtown Sch. Dist., 2000—; spl. counsel Owen J. Roberts Sch. Dist., 1999—; co-chair pers. com., mktg./admissions com., sec. bd. trustees Germantown Acad., Ft. Washington, Pa., 1991—; presenter in field. Regular columnist Your School and the Law, 1992. Mem. Nat. Sch. Bds. Assn., 2001. Mem. Nat. Assn. Sch. and Coll. Attys., Nat. Sch. Bds. Assn., Pa. Sch. Bds. Assn., Inc., Pa. Assn. Sch. Bus. Ofcls. (cert. of appreciation 1991), Pa. Bar Assn. (labor and edn. sects.), Montgomery County Bar Assn. (mcpl. law com. 1983—), Lehigh U. Law Forums, Assn. Del. Valley Ind. Schs. Republican. Jewish. Avocations: automobiles, travel. Education and schools, Labor, Municipal (including bonds). Home: 2056 Spring Valley Rd Lansdale PA 19446-5114 Office: Fox Rothschild O'Brien & Frankel LLP 1250 S Broad St Ste 1000 Lansdale PA 19446-5343 E-mail: jsultanik@frof.com

SUMIDA, GERALD AQUINAS, lawyer; b. Hilo, Hawaii, June 19, 1944; s. Sadamy and Kimiyo (Miyahara) S. AB summa cum laude, Princeton U., 1966; JD, Yale U., 1969. Bar: Hawaii 1970, U.S. Dist. Ct. Hawaii 1970, U.S. Ct. Appeals (9th cir.) 1970, U.S. Supreme Ct. 1981. Rsch. assoc. Ctr. Internat. Studies, Princeton U., 1969; assoc. Carlsmith, Ball, Honolulu, 1970-76, ptnr., 1976-99; gen. counsel Asian Devel. Bank, 1999—. Mem. cameras in courtroom evaluation com. Hawaii Supreme Ct., 1984-86. Co-author: (with others) Legal, Instutional and Financial Aspects of An Inter-Island Electrical Transmission Cable, 1984, Alternative Approaches to the Legal, Instutional and Financial Aspects of Developing an Inter-Island, Electrical Transmission Cable System, 1986; editor Hawaii Bar News, 1972-73; contbr. chpts. to books. Mem. sci. and statis. com. Western Pacific Fishery Mgmt. Coun., 1979-99; mem. study group on law of armed conflict and the law of the sea Comdr. in Chief Pacific, USN, 1979-82; chmn. Pacific and Asian Affairs Coun. Hawaii, 1991, pres., 1982-91, bd. govs., 1976-96; bd. govs. ARC, 1994-2000, mem. exec. com., 1996-2000, chmn. human resources com., 1996-2000, chmn. Hawaii chpt., 1983-99, bd. dirs., 1983-99, vice chmn., 1990; chmn. Hawaii C. of C., 1997-98, bd. dirs., 1990-99; vice chmn. Honolulu Com. Fgn. Rels., 1983—; pres., dir., founding mem. Hawaii Ocean Law Assn., 1978—; mem. Hawaii Adv. Group for Law of Sea Inst., 1977-85; pres. Hawaii Inst. Continuing Legal Edn., 1979-83, dir., 1976-87; pres., founding mem. Hawaii Coun. Legal Edn. Youth, 1980-83, dir., 1983-88; chmn. Hawaii Commn. Yr. 2000, 1976-79; mem. Honolulu Cmty. Media Coun., 1976-99, exec. com., 1976-84, legal coun., 1979-83; bd. dirs. Hawaii Imin Centennial Corp., 1983-90, Hawaii Pub. Radio, 1983-88, Legal Aid Soc. Hawaii, 1984; founding gov., exec. v.p., chmn. rules and procedures Ctr. Internat. Comml. Dispute Resolution, 1987—; exec. com. Pacific Aerospace Mus., 1991—; exec. com. Pacific Islands Assn., 1988—; exec. com. Asia-Pacific Ctr. Res. Internat. Bus. Disputes, 1991-95; mem. Coun. Asia-Pacific Dispute Rsch. Ctrs., 1991-95; bd. dirs. U.S. C. of C., 1998—; mem. Pacific Basin Econ. Coun., 1993—; mem. mgmt. com. PBEC-U.S. Nat. Com., 1994-99. Recipient cert. of appreciation Gov. of Hawaii, 1979, resolutions of appreciation Hawaii Senate and Ho. of Reps., 1979; grantee Japan Found., 1979. Mem. ABA, Hawaii Bar Assn. (pres. young lawyers sect. 1974, v.p. 1984), Japan-Hawaii Lawyers Assn., Am. Soc. Internat. Law, Internat. Bar Assn., Am. Judicature Soc., Inter-Pacific Bar Assn., Internat. Law Assn., Plaza Club (Honolulu), Colonial Club (Princeton). Democrat. Administrative and regulatory, General corporate, Private international. Office: Office Gen Coun Asian Devel Bank 6 ADB Ave 0401 Metro Manila Mandaluyong The Philippines also: Gen Coun Asian Devel Bank PO Box 789 0980 Manila The Philippines E-mail: gsumida@adb.org

SUMIDA, KEVIN P.H. lawyer; b. Honolulu, Feb. 14, 1954; s. William H. and Dorothy A. (Iwamoto) S. BA in Philosphy, Case Western Res. U., 1976; JD, U. Pa., 1979. Bar: Hawaii 1979, U.S. Ct. Appeals (9th cir.) 1981. Assoc. Fong & Miho, Honolulu, 1979-81; law clk. to hon. judge Harold M. Fong U.S. Dist. Ct., 1981-82; assoc. Matsui & Chung, 1982-89; ptnr. Matsui Chung Sumida & Tsuchiyama, 1989—. Bd. dirs., officer Farrington Alumni and Community Found., Honolulu, 1980—. Mem. ABA (litigation sect., tort and ins. practice sect.), Hawaii Bar Assn. Avocation: music. General civil litigation, Insurance, Personal injury. Office: Matsui Chung Sumida & Tsuchiyama 737 Bishop St Ste 1400 Honolulu HI 96813-3205

SUMMERS, CLYDE WILSON, law educator; b. Grass Range, Mont., Nov. 21, 1918; s. Carl Douglas and Anna Lois (Yontz) S.; m. Evelyn Marie Wahlgren, Aug. 30, 1947; children: Mark, Erica, Craig, Lisa. BS, U. Ill., 1939, JD, 1942, LLD, 1998; LLM, Columbia U., 1946, JSD, 1952; LL.D., U. Leuven, Belgium, 1967, U. Stockholm, 1978, U. Ill., 1998. Bar: N.Y. 1951. Mem. law faculty U. Toledo, 1942-49, U. Buffalo, 1949-56; prof. law Yale U., New Haven, 1956-66, Garver prof. law, 1966-75; Jefferson B. Fordham prof. law U. Pa., 1975-90, prof. emeritus, 1990—. Hearing examiner Conn. Commn. on Civil Rights, 1963-71 Co-author: Labor Cases and Material, 1968, 2d edit., 1982, Rights of Union Members, 1979, Legal Protection for the Individual Employee, 1989, 2d edit., 1995; co-editor: Labor Relations and the Law, 1953, Employment Relations and the Law, 1959, Comparative Labor Law Jour., 1984-97. Chmn. Gov.'s Com. on Improper Union Mgmt. Practices N.Y. State, 1957-58; chmn. Conn. Adv. Council on Unemployment Ins. and Employment Service, 1960-72; mem. Conn. Labor Relations Bd., 1966-70, Conn. Bd. Mediation and Arbitration, 1964-72. Guggenheim fellow, 1955-56; Ford fellow, 1963-64; German-Marshall fellow, 1977-78; NEH fellow, 1977-78, Fullbright fellow, 1984-85. Mem. Nat. Acad. Arbitrators (nat. chmn.), Internat. Soc. Labor Law and Social Legislation. Congregationalist. Home: 753 N 26th St Philadelphia PA 19130-2429 Office: U Pa Sch Law 3400 Chestnut St Philadelphia PA 19104-6204 E-mail: csummers@law.upenn.edu

SUMMERS, HARDY, state supreme court justice; b. Muskogee, Okla., July 15, 1933; s. Cleon A. and Fern H. Summers; m. Marilyn, Mar. 16, 1963; children: Julia Clare, Andrew Murray. BA, U. Okla., 1955, LLB, 1957. Asst. county atty. Muskogee County, 1960-62; pvt. practice law Muskogee, 1962-76; dist. judge 15th dist. Okla. Dist. Ct., 1976-85; justice Okla. Supreme Ct., Oklahoma City, 1985-99, chief justice, 1999-2000. Sec. Muskogee County Election Bd., 1965-72. Capt. JAGC, USAF, 1957-62. Mem. ABA, Okla. Bar Assn., Okla. Jud. Conf. (pres. 1984). Avocations: outdoor sports, music. Office: Okla Supreme Ct Rm 202 State Capital Bldg Oklahoma City OK 73105

SUMMERS, PAUL, state attorney general; b. Somerville, Tenn., Mar. 28, 1950; BS, Miss. State U.; JD, U. Tenn. Dist. atty. gen. 25th Jud. Dist., Somerville, Tenn., 1982-90; judge Ct. of Criminal Appeals, Nashville, 1990-99; atty. gen. State of tenn., 1999—. Adj. prof. law U. Memphis; former adj. faculty Cumberland U.; pres. elect, Tenn. Dist. Atty.'s Gen. Conf.; mem. Ct. Criminal Appeals, 1990-99; lectr. in field. Former mem. Tenn. Sentencing Commn.; col. Tenn. Army N.G. With USAF. Mem. Tenn. Bar Assn. (former gov.), Tenn. Dist. Attys. Gen. Conf. (pres.). Avocations: racquetball, rollerblading, karate (black belt). Office: Office of the Attorney General 500 Charlotte Ave Nashville TN 37243-1401*

SUMMERS, THOMAS CAREY, lawyer; b. Frederick, Md., Feb. 9, 1956; s. Harold Thomas and Doris Jean (Culler) S.; m. Robin Ann Stalnaker, May 12, 1990; children: Kristin, Heather, Lindsay. BA, Dickinson Coll., 1978; JD, U. Balt., 1981. Bar: Md. 1981, U.S. Dist. Ct. Md. 1981, D.C. 1986. Assoc. Ellin & Baker, Balt., 1979-89, Peter G. Angelos, Balt., 1989—. Adj. prof. law U. Balt. Sch. of Law. Mem. ABA, Md. State Bar Assn., Md. Trial Lawyers Assn. Democrat. Lutheran. Avocation: golf. State civil litigation, Personal injury, Professional liability. Office: Law Offices of P G Angelos One Charles Ctr Baltimore MD 21201

SUMMERS-POWELL, ALAN, lawyer; BA, Yale Coll., 1985; JD, U. Pa., 1988. Bar: N.Y. 1989, N.J. 1989, U.S. Dist. Ct. (dist.) N.J. 1989, D.C. 1990, Fla. 1993, U.S. Dist. Ct. (mid. dist.) Fla. 1996, U.S. Ct. Appeals (11th cir.) 1996, U.S. Tax Ct. 1997, U.S. Dist. Ct. (so. dist.) Fla. 2001. Pvt. practice, Palm Harbor, Fla. Chmn. David Leasing and Devel., Inc. Bankruptcy, Consumer commercial, Probate. Office: PO Box 6043 Palm Harbor FL 34684-0643

SUMNER, JAMES DUPRE, JR. lawyer, educator; b. Spartanburg, S.C., Nov. 30, 1919; s. James DuPre and Frances Grace (Harris) S.; m. Evvie Lucille Beach, Apr. 1, 1945 (dec.); children: Chery Erline (Mrs. Horacek), James DuPre III; m. Doris Kaiser Malloy, Oct. 20, 1972; children: John L. Malloy III, Mary Margaret Malloy, Kenneth S. Malloy, James M. Malloy. AB, Wofford Coll., 1941; LLB, U. Va., 1949; LLM, Yale U., 1952, JSD, 1955. Bar: Va. 1948, Calif. 1957. Practice law, Los Angeles, 1957—; instr. law U. S.C., 1949-52; assoc. prof. UCLA, 1952-55, prof., 1955—. Distinguished vis. prof. Instituto Luigi Sturzo, Rome, 1959; vis. prof. U. Tex., 1962, U. So. Calif., 1971; lectr. Calif. Bar Rev. Co-author: An Anatomy of Legal Education; contbr. articles to profl. jours. Lt. col. inf. AUS, 1941-46, ETO. Decorated Silver Star, Purple Heart with oak leaf cluster. Mem.: Calif. Bar Assn., Va. Bar Assn., Westwood Village Bar Assn. (pres.), Rotary (pres. Westwood Village chpt.), Bel Air Assn. (bd. dirs.), L.A. Country Club, Westwood Village Sertome Club (pres.), Sertoma (pres.), Braemar Country Club. Republican. Methodist. Home: 10513 Rocca Pl Los Angeles CA 90077-2904

SUNDAR, VIJENDRA, lawyer educator; b. Nausori, Rewa, Fiji Islands, Oct. 27, 1940; came to U.S., 1966; s. Bisu R. and Pran Pati Sundar; m. Lynette Sue Schmid, June 13, 1987; children: Jesse Christopher Mikaele, Eric Lynn Kalani, Christina Elizabeth Ululani. BBA in Mktg., U. Hawaii, 1976; JD, Antioch U., 1979. Bar: U.S. Ct. Mil. Appeals 1983, Omaha Tribal Ct. 1983, U.S. Trust Ter. of Pacific 1983. Co-owner, mgr. Rewa Ice & Aerated Water Factory, Rewa Lodge & Cafe, Nausori, Fiji Islands, 1962-67; coord., instr. Pacific and Asia Linguistics Inst., Honolulu, 1968, Univ. Hawaii, Peace Corps Ctrs., 1968-98; paralegal Puget Sound Legal Asst. Found., Tacoma, 1975-76; atty., rschr. Inst. for Law and Rsch., Washington, 1980-81; atty. Legal Aid Soc., Inc., Omaha, 1982-84, Multnomah County Legal Aid Svcs., Inc., Portland, Oreg., 1984-85; instr. Platt Coll., Jefferson City, Mo., 1986-88; acting dir., vis. asst. prof. Columbia Coll., Columbia, 1989; acad. & legal cons., 1990-92; owner, operator, businessman Fairview Motel, Kemmerer, Wyo., 1996—. Town councillor Nausori (Fiji Islands) Town Coun., 1965-68; bd. dirs. Improvement Means People Allied for Change Together, Omaha, 1983-84; commn. mem. com. welfare of farm workers, 1985; parliamentarian, bd. dirs. Am. Indian Ctr., Omaha, 1983-84. Reginald Heber Smith Ctmty. Lawyer fellow Howard Univ., 1984-85. Mem. ABA. Avocations: swimming, fishing, traveling, cooking, acting. Address: PO Box 367 Kemmerer WY 83101-0367

SUNDERMEYER, MICHAEL S. lawyer; b. Kansas City, Mo., Feb. 8, 1951; s. Edgar W. and Ruth (Shobe) S.; m. Susan Talarico; children: Kim Marie, Mark Shobe. BA, U. Kans., 1973; JD, U. Va., 1976. Bar: D.C., Md., Va., U.S. Dist. Ct. D.C., U.S. Dist. Ct. Md., U.S. Dist. Ct. (ea. dist.) Va., U.S. Dist. Ct. (no. dist.) Okla., U.S. Ct. Appeals (D.C. cir.), U.S. Ct. Appeals (4th cir.), U.S. Ct. Appeals (5th cir.), U.S. Ct. Appeals (3d cir.). Law clk. to Hon. John Minor Wisdom U.S. Ct. Appeals (5th cir.), New Orleans, 1976-77; law clk. to Hon. Harry A. Blackmun U.S. Supreme Ct., Washington, 1977-78; assoc. Williams & Connolly, 1978-84, ptnr., 1985—. Editor-in-chief Va. Law Rev., 1975-76. Mem. ABA. Administrative and regulatory, Federal civil litigation, Professional liability. Office: Williams & Connolly 725 12th St NW Washington DC 20005-5901 E-mail: msundermeyer@wc.com

SUOJANEN, WAYNE WILLIAM, lawyer; b. Salem, Oreg., July 5, 1950; BA, Northwestern U., 1972; SM, MIT, 1974, PhD, 1977; JD, U. Pa., 1980. Bar: Pa. 1980, Calif. 1997. Ptnr. Hoyle, Morris & Kerr, Phila., 1989-97, Kasdan, Simonds & Epstein, LLP, Irvine, Calif., 2001—. Joseph Scanlon fellow MIT, 1974-75. Mem. ABA, State Bar of Calif., Phila. Bar Assn., Orange County Bar Assn., Am. Concrete Inst. Construction, Product liability, Toxic tort. Home: 11 Morning Vw Irvine CA 92612-3716 Office: Kasdan Simonds Et Al 2600 Michelson Dr Fl 10 Irvine CA 92612-1550 E-mail: wsuojanen@kasdansimonds.com

SUPINO, ANTHONY MARTIN, lawyer; b. Weehawken, N.J., Oct. 1, 1962; s. Anthony Edward and Gloria (DeBari) S. BA, Rutgers U., 1984, postgrad., 1984-85, JD, 1988. Bar: N.J. 1988, U.S. Dist. Ct. N.J. 1988, N.Y. 1989, U.S. Dist. Ct. (so. dist.) N.Y. 1990, U.S. Ct. Appeals (3d cir.) 1991. Law sec. to the Hon. Marie L. Garibaldi Supreme Ct. of N.J., Jersey City, 1988-89; litigation assoc. Cravath, Swaine & Moore, N.Y.C., 1989-92; spl. litigation assoc. Chadbourne & Parke, 1992-93; ptnr. Arkin, Schaffer & Supino, 1994-96; pvt. practice Supino, Jacobs & Rudy, N.Y.C., West Orange, N.J., 1996—. Community organizer Human Serve Fund, New Brunswick, N.J., 1984. Democrat. Avocations: coin collecting, sports, weightlifting. Antitrust, Criminal, Securities. Home: 30 Quimby Pl West Orange NJ 07052-5208 Office: Anthony M Supino & Assocs 475 5th Ave New York NY 10017-6220

SUREAU, FRANÇIS MAURICE, lawyer; b. Paris, Sept. 19, 1957; s. Claude Guy and Jeannine (Murset) S.; m. Ayyam Wassef, May 24, 1994; children: Maryam, Victoire. Student, Inst. D'Etudes Politiques, 1978, Ecole Nat. D'Adminstrn., Paris, 1981. Mem. Conseil D'Etat, Paris, 1981-95; atty. Paris Bar, 1995—; lawyer Davrois Villey et Assocs., Paris. Author: La Corruption du Siecle, 1988, L'Infortune, 1990 (prix Acad. Française 1991), Le Sphinx de Darwin, 1996 (prix Goncourt de la Nouvelle 1996), Lambert Pacha, 1998. Home: 134 rue de Grenelle 78007 Paris France Office: Dacrois Villey et Assocs 69 Ave Victor Hugo 75116 Paris France Fax: 01 45 01 91 68. E-mail: fsureau@devroisvilley.paris.barreau.fr

SUSKO, CAROL LYNNE, lawyer, accountant; b. Washington, Dec. 5, 1955; d. Frank and Helen Louise (Davis) S. BS in Econs. and Acctg., George Mason U., 1979; JD, Cath. U., 1982; LLM in Taxation, Georgetown U., 1992. Bar: Pa. 1989, D.C. 1990; CPA, Va., Md. Tax acct. Reznick Fedder & Silverman, P.C., Bethesda, Md., 1984-85; sr. tax acct. Pannell Kerr Forster, Alexandria, Va., 1985; tax specialist Coopers & Lybrand, Washington, 1985-87; supervisory tax sr. Frank & Co., McLean, Va., 1987-88; mem. editl. staff Tax Notes Mag., Arlington, 1989-90; adj. faculty Am. U., Washington, 1989—; tax atty. Marriott Corp., 1993-94; sr. tax mgr. Host Marriott Inc., 1994-99, KPMG LLP, McLean, Va., 1999—. Mem. ABA, AICPAs, Va. Soc. CPAs, D.C. Soc. CPAs, D.C. Bar Assn. Corporate taxation, Taxation, general, State and local taxation. Office: KPMG LLP Ste 3064 1660 International Dr Mc Lean VA 22102-4832 E-mail: csusko@kpmg.com

SUSMAN, MORTON LEE, lawyer; b. Aug. 6, 1934; m. Nina Meyers, May 1, 1958; 1 child, Mark Lee. BBA, So. Meth. U., 1956, JD, 1958. Bar: Tex. 1958, U.S. Dist. Ct. (so. dist.) Tex. 1961, U.S. Ct. Appeals (5th cir.) 1961, U.S. Supreme Ct. 1961, U.S. Ct. Appeals (11th cir) 1981, D.C. 1988, U.S. Ct. Appeals (D.C. cir.) 1988, N.Y. 1990, Colo. 1996. Asst. U.S. atty., Houston, 1961-64; 1st asst. U.S. atty., 1965-66; U.S. atty., 1966-69; ptnr. Weil, Gotshal & Manges and predecessor firm Susman & Kessler, Houston, 1969-97; ret., 1998. Lt. USNR, 1958-61. Fellow Am. Coll. Trial Lawyers, Tex. Bar Found.; mem. ABA, FBA (dir., Younger Fed. Lawyer award 1968), Tex. Bar Assn. Democrat. Alternative dispute resolution, Federal civil litigation, State civil litigation. Home: 1000 Uptown Park Blvd Houston TX 77056-3247

SUSSE, SANDRA SLONE, lawyer; b. Medford, Ma., June 1, 1943; d. James Robert and Georgie Coffin (Bradshaw) Slone; m. Peter Susse, May 10, 1969 (div. May 1993); 1 child, Toby. BA, U. Mass., 1981; JD, Vt. Law Sch., 1986. Bar: Mass. 1986, U.S. Dist. Ct. Mass. 1988, U.S. Ct. Appeals (1st cir.) 1995. Staff atty. Western Mass. Legal Svcs., Springfield, 1986—. Mem. ABA, Women's Bar Assn. Mass. Avocations: hiking, German literature, films, skating. Address: Western Mass Legal Serv 127 State St Fl 4 Springfield MA 01103-1905 E-mail: ssusse@wmls.org

SUSSMAN, ALEXANDER RALPH, lawyer; b. Bronx, N.Y., Sept. 24, 1946; s. Herman R. and Claire (Blumenson) S.; m. Edna Rubin, Mar. 24, 1973; children: Jason, Carl, Matthew, Eric. AB cum laude, Princeton U., 1968; JD, Yale U., 1972. Bar: N.Y. 1973, U.S. Dist. Ct. (so. and ea. dists) N.Y. 1974, U.S. Ct. Appeals (2d, 3d, 5th, 6th, 8th and 10th cirs.) 1983, U.S. Supreme Ct. Law clk. to justice U.S. Dist. Ct., N.Y.C., 1972-73; assoc. Cravath, Swaine & Moore, 1974-76, Fried, Frank, Harris, Shriver & Jacobson, N.Y.C., 1977-79, ptnr., 1979—. Author: (with A. Fleischer, Jr.) Responses to Takeover Bids, 2000, Takeover Defense, 2 vols., 2000; editor Yale Law Jour., 1971-72. Mem. N.Y. Lawyers for Pub. Interest, 1983—, mem. exec. com., bd. dirs., 1983—; bd. dirs., mem. exec. com. Legal Aid Soc., 1987-93. Fulbright scholar U. Bordeaux, 1969. Mem. ABA, Am. Law Inst., N.Y. State Bar Assn., Assn. of Bar of City of N.Y. (fed. cts. com.

1984-87, jud. com. 1987-90, chmn. legal assistance com. 1988-91, Marden lectr. com. 1991-94, chmn. mergers and acquisitions com. 1995-99). General civil litigation, Mergers and acquisitions, Securities. Home: 20 Oak Ln Scarsdale NY 10583-1627 Office: Fried Frank Harris Shriver & Jacobson 1 New York Plz Fl 25 New York NY 10004-1980

SUSSMAN, MARK RICHARD, lawyer; b. Bklyn., Feb. 4, 1952; s. Vincent E. and Rhoda (Urowsky) S.; m. Lisa Rosner, June 8, 1975; children: Corey, Randi, Samuel. BS in Civil Engring., Tufts U., 1974; JD, U. Pa., 1977. Bar: Pa. 1977, D.C. 1980, Conn. 1981. Trial atty. land and natural resources div. U.S. Dept. Justice, Washington, 1977-81; assoc. Murtha, Cullina, Richter & Pinney, Hartford, Conn., 1981-86, ptnr., 1987—; chmn. environ. dept. Murtha Cullina LLP, Hartford, Conn., 1990—. Gov.'s blue ribbon panel to evaluate environtl. permit programs, 1996. Chmn. conservation commn. Windsor, Conn., 1984-2000; mem. Conn. Hazardous Waste Mgmt. Service Recycling Task Force, 1986, Legis. Task Force on Environ. Permitting, 1992, Conn. State Implementation Plan Revision Adv. Com., 1984—. Mem. ABA (natural resources sect.), Conn. Bar Assn. (chmn. conservation and environ. quality sect. 1984-87, faculty continuing legal edn.), Conn. Bus. and Industry Assn. (steering com. environ. policies coun. 1990-93, 98—) Tau Beta Pi. Federal civil litigation, State civil litigation, Environmental. Home: 62 Timothy Ter Windsor CT 06095-1652 Office: Murtha Cullina LLP City Pl 185 Asylum St Ste 29 Hartford CT 06103-3469

SUTCLIFFE, ERIC, lawyer; b. Calif., Jan. 10, 1909; s. Thomas and Annie (Beare) S.; m. Joan Basché, Aug. 7, 1937; children: Victoria, Marcia, Thomas; m. Marie C. Paige, Nov. 1, 1975. AB, U. Calif., Berkeley, 1929, LLB, 1932. Bar: Calif. 1932. Mem. firm Orrick, Herrington & Sutcliffe, San Francisco, 1943-85, mng. ptnr., 1947-78. Trustee, treas., v.p. San Francisco Law Libr., 1974-88; founding fellow The Oakland Mus. of Calif.; bd. dirs. Merritt Peralta Found., 1988; past bd. dirs. Hong Kong Bank of Calif., Friends of U. Calif. Bot. Garden, sec. Fellow Am. Bar Found (life); mem. ABA (chmn state regulation securities com. 1960-65), San Francisco Bar Assn. (chmn. corp. law com., 1964-65), San Francisco C. of C. (past treas., dir.), State Bar Calif., Pacific Union Club, Bohemian Club, Phi Gamma Delta, Phi Delta Phi, Order of Coif. Home: 260 King Ave Oakland CA 94610-1231 Office: Old Fed Reserve Bank Bldg 400 Sansome St San Francisco CA 94111-3304

SUTER, BEN, lawyer; b. Sacramento, Dec. 14, 1954; s. Alexander Frederick and Anne Ida (De Bergen) S.; m. Lizanne Bouchard, Dec. 23, 1979; children: Tycho Benjamin, Hadley Theadora, Miles Kepler, Rex Sebastian. BA in Philosophy, U. Calif., Santa Barbara, 1978; JD, U. Calif., San Francisco, 1982. Bar: Calif. 1982, U.S. Dist. Ct. (cen., ea., no. and so. dists.) Calif. 1982, Ariz. 1983, Hawaii 1984, U.S. Dist. Ct. Ariz. 1990, U.S. Supreme Ct. 1987. Assoc. Keesal, Young & Logan, San Francisco and Long Beach, Calif., 1982-87, ptnr., 1987—. Federal civil litigation, Real property, Securities. Office: Keesal Young & Logan 4 Embarcadero Ctr San Francisco CA 94111-4106

SUTHERLAND, LOWELL FRANCIS, lawyer; b. Lincoln, Nebr., Dec. 17, 1939; s. Lowell Williams and Doris Genevieve (Peterson) S.; m. Virginia Kay Edwards, Aug. 29, 1992. AB, San Diego State Coll., 1962; LLB, Hastings Coll. Law, 1965; children: Scott Thorpe, Mark James, Sandra Doris. With Cooper, White & Cooper, attys., San Francisco, 1963-66; admitted to Calif. bar, 1966; with Wien & Thorpe, attys., El Centro, 1966-67; ptnr. Wien, Thorpe & Sutherland, El Centro, 1967-74, Wien, Thorpe, Sutherland & Stamper, 1973-74, Sutherland, Stamper & Feingold, 1974-77, Sutherland & Gerber, 1977—, Sutherland & Sutherland. Mem. ABA, Calif. Bar Assn., Imperial County Bar Assn. (Recognition of Experience awards), San Diego (named Outstanding Trial Lawyer April 1981, Oct. 1983, Trial Lawyer of Yr. 1982), Trial Lawyers Assns., Thurston Soc., Nat. Bd. Trial Advs. (diplomate), Am. Bd. Trial Advocates (assoc.), Theta Chi. Mem. editorial staff Hastings Law Jour., 1964-65. Condemnation, Insurance, Personal injury. Home: 1853 Sunset Rd El Centro CA 92243-3518 Office: 300 S Imperial Ave Ste 7 El Centro CA 92243-3149

SUTHERS, JOHN WILLIAM, prosecutor; b. Denver, Oct. 18, 1951; s. William Dupont and Marguerite A. (Ryan) S.; m. Janet Gill, May 21, 1976; children: Alison, Catherine. BA in Govt. magna cum laude, U. Notre Dame, 1974; JD, U. Colo., 1977. Bar: Colo. 1977, U.S. Dist. Ct. Colo. 1977, U.S. Ct. Appeals (10th cir.) 1979. Dep. dist. atty. 4th jud. dist. State of Colo., Colorado Springs, 1977-79; chief dep. dist. atty. 4th jud. dist. State of Colo. , 1979-81; assoc. Sparks, Dix, Enoch, 1981-82; ptnr. Sparks, Dix, Enoch, Suthers & Winslow, 1982-89; dist. atty. 4th Jud. Dist., 1989—97; sr. counsel Sparks, Dix, 1997—99; exec. dir. Colo. Dept. Corrections, 1999—2001; U.S. atty. U.S. Atty.'s Office Colo. Dist., 2001—. Mem. adv. bd. Sec. of state, Denver, 1983-89; Colo. commr. Uniform State laws, 1993—. Author: Fraud and Deceit, 1982, How to Liquidate a Lemon, 1983. Pres., chmn. bd. dirs. Community Corrections of Pikes Peak Region Inc., 1984-87; El Paso County Rep. Ctrl. com., Colorado Springs, 1985—, Colo. State Rep. Ctrl. com., 1989—; bd. dirs. Crimestoppers, Inc., Colorado Springs, 1985-88, Colo. Dist. Atty.'s Coun. (exec. com. 1992—, pres. 1994-95, treas. 1993). Zimmerman Found. scholar, 1970-74. Mem. Colo. Bar Assn. (com. chmn.), El Paso County Bar Assn. (pres. 1990-91), Notre Dame Colorado Springs (pres. 1983-84). Roman Catholic. Avocations: tennis, baseball cards. Home: 3040 Electra Dr Colorado Springs CO 80906-1089 Office: US Atty 1225 17th St Ste 700 Denver CO 80202*

SUTPHIN, WILLIAM TAYLOR, lawyer; s. William Halstead and Catharine (Bonner) S.; m. Alissa L. Kramer, June 21, 1958. AB in History, Princeton U., 1957; LLB, U. Pa., 1960. Bar: N.J. 1960; U.S. Ct. Appeals (3d cir.) 1964, U.S. Supreme Ct. 1965. Assoc. Stryker, Tams & Dill, Newark, 1960-67, ptnr., 1967-73; sole practice Princeton, N.J., 1973—. Coadj. faculty mem. Rutgers U. Govt. Svcs. Tng. Program, 1973—; assoc. counsel N.J. Planning Ofcls., 1975—. Mem. Princeton Twp. Planning Bd., 1967-72, Regional Planning Bd. Princeton, 1970-74; atty. Green Brook Twp. Planning Bd., 1972-2001, Millstone Twp. Bd. Adjustment, 1978-98, Del. Twp. Bd. Adjustment, 1982—, Princeton Borough Bd. Adjustment, 1983—; committeeman Twp. Princeton, 1973-75, police commr., 1974-75; treas. Youth Employment Svc. Princeton Inc., 1981-84. Served with U.S. Army, 1953-56, capt. JAGC Ret. Mem. N.J. Bar Assn. (chmn. ins. com. 1979-81), Princeton Bar Assn. (pres. 1981-82), N.J. Inst. Mcpl. Attys. General civil litigation, Land use and zoning (including planning), Probate. Home: 501 Jefferson Rd Princeton NJ 08540-3418 Office: Law Offices of William T Sutphin 34 Chambers St Princeton NJ 08542-3700 E-mail: william.t.sutphin@verizon.net

SUTTER, LAURENCE BRENER, lawyer; b. N.Y.C., Feb. 5, 1944; s. Meyer and Beatrice Sutter; m. Betty A. Satterwhite, June 9, 1979. AB, Columbia Coll., 1965; JD, N.Y.U., 1976. Bar: N.Y. 1977, U.S. Dist. Ct. (so. and ea. dists.) N.Y. 1977. Assoc. Shea & Gould, N.Y.C., 1976-80, Meyer, Suozzi, English & Klein P.C., Mineola, N.Y., 1980-82; assoc. counsel publs. Gen. Media Internat., Inc., N.Y.C., 1982-96, sr. v.p., gen. counsel, 1997—. With N.Y. Army N.G., 1966-72. Mem. Assn. of Bar of City of N.Y. (mem. com. on civil rights 1986-89, mem. com. on comm. and media law 1989-92, mem. com. on copyright and lit. property 1994-97), First Amendment Lawyers Assn., Nat. Arts Club, Orient (N.Y.) Yacht Club (dir. 1997-2000, sec. 2000-2001). Democrat. Jewish. Avocations: music, sailing. Communications. Office: Gen Media Comm Inc 11 Penn Plz 12th Fl New York NY 10001-2006

SUTTERFIELD, JAMES RAY, lawyer; Bar: La. 1967, U.S. Dist. Ct. (ea. dist.) La. 1967, U.S. Ct. Appeals (5th cir.) 1967, U.S. Dist. Ct. (mid. dist.) La. 1971, D.C. 1977, U.S. Supreme Ct. 1977, U.S. Dist. Ct. (we. dist.) La. 1982, U.S. Dist. Ct. (ea. dist.) Tex. 1985, Tex. 1993. Assoc. Law Offices Walter F. Marcus, New Orleans, 1967, Huddleston & Davis, New Orleans, 1968-70, ptnr., 1970-72, Sutterfield & Vickery, New Orleans, 1973-82, Carmouche, Gray & Hoffman, New Orleans, 1982-89; sr. dir. Hoffman Sutterfield Ensenat A.P.L.C., 1989-97; sr. ptnr. Sutterfield & Webb LLC, 1997—. Faculty mem. 10th diving accident and hyperbaric oxygen treatment course Duke U.; del. Undersea and Hyperbaric Med. Soc. Nat. Oceanographic and Almospheric Adminstrn.; speaker in field. Author: (with others) Commercial Damages, 1989; mem. editl. bd. Hull Claims Analysis; contbr. articles to profl. jours. Mem. ABA (chmn. excess surplus lines and reins. com.), La. Bar Assn., 5th Cir. Bar Assn., D.C. Bar Assn., La. Assn. Def. Counsel, Internat. Assn. Def. Counsel (chmn. maritime and energy law com., class action and multiparty litigation com.), Maritime Law Assn. U.S. (chmn. marine product liability com.), Def. Rsch. Inst. Admiralty, Insurance. Office: Sutterfield & Webb 650 Poydras St Fl 27 New Orleans LA 70130-6101 E-mail: jsutterfield@swslaw.com

SUTTLE, DORWIN WALLACE, federal judge; b. Knox County, Ind., July 16, 1906; s. William Sherman and Nancy Cordelia (Hungate) S.; m. Anne Elizabeth Barrett, Feb. 1, 1939 (dec.); children: Stephen Hungate, Nancy Joanna Suttle Walker (dec.); m. Lucile Cram Whitecotton, Aug. 21, 1956; stepchildren: Fred and Frank Whitecotton. JD, U. Tex., 1928. Bar: Tex., U.S. Supreme Ct. 1960. Practiced law, Uvalde, Tex., 1928-64; U.S. dist. judge Western Dist. Tex., 1964-2000, ret., 2000. Democrat. Methodist. Fax: 210-472-6572

SUTTLE, STEPHEN HUNGATE, lawyer; b. Uvalde, Tex., Mar. 17, 1940; s. Dorwin Wallace and Ann Elizabeth (Barrett) S.; m. Rosemary Williams Davison, Aug. 3, 1963; children: Michael Barrett, David Paull, John Stewart. BA, Washington and Lee U., 1962; LLB, U. Tex., 1965. Bar: Tex. 1965, U.S. Dist. Ct. (no. and we. dists.) Tex. 1965, U.S. Ct. Appeals (5th cir.) 1967, U.S. Supreme Ct. 1970. Law clk. to Hon. Leo Brewster U.S. Dist. Ct. (no. dist.) Tex., Ft. Worth, 1965-67; ptnr. McMahon, Surovik, Suttle, Buhrmann, Hicks & Gill, P.C., Abilene, Tex., 1970—. Pres. Abilene Boys Clubs, Inc., 1975-76; bd. dirs. Abilene Cmty. Theater, 1979-80, Abilene Fine Arts Mus., 1977-78. Fellow: Am. Coll. Trial Lawyers, Am. Bd. Trial Advocates, Tex. Bar Found., State Bar Tex. (dir. 1999—2002); mem.: Assn. Def. Trial Attys., Tex. Assn. Def. Counsel, Def. Rsch. Inst., Tex. Young Lawyers Assn. (chmn. bd. dirs. 1976), Am. Judicature Soc. (bd. dirs. 1981—84), Abilene Bar Assn. (pres. 1987—88), Tex. Bar Assn., ABA (chmn. young lawyers sect. award of merit 1976), Abilene Country Club. Democrat. Episcopalian. Federal civil litigation, State civil litigation. Home: 1405 Woodland Trl Abilene TX 79605-4705 Office: McMahon Surovik Suttle Buhrmann Hicks & Gill PC PO Box 3679 Abilene TX 79604-3679 E-mail: ssuttle@mcmahonlawtx.com

SUTTON, JOHN EWING, lawyer; b. San Angelo, Oct. 7, 1950; s. John F. Jr. and Nancy (Ewing) S.; 1 son, Joshua Ewing; 1 stepson, Michael Brandon Ducote. BBA, U. Tex., 1973, JD, 1976. Bar: Tex. 1976, U.S. Tax Ct. 1977, U.S. Ct. Claims 1977, U.S. Ct. Appeals (5th cir.) 1978, U.S. Dist. Ct. (we. dist.) Tex. 1979, U.S. Supreme Ct. 1980; CPA, Tex. Tax specialist Peat, Marwick, Mitchell & Co., CPAs, Dallas, 1976-77; ptnr. Shannon, Porter, Johnson, Sutton and Greendyke Attys. at Law, San Angelo, Tex., 1977-87; judge 119th Dist. Ct. of Tex., 1987-99; pvt. practice Law Offices of John E. Sutton, 1999—. Treas. Good Shepherd Episcopal Ch., San Angelo, 1979-81; co-chmn. profl. divsn. United Way, San Angelo, 1980-82; trustee Angelo State U. Found., 1987-99, pres., 1988-91, 95-97, v.p., 1992-94, 98-99, sec.-treas., 1991-92. Fellow Tex. Bar Found.; mem. ABA, Tex. Bar Assn., Tex. Criminal Def. Lawyers Assn., Tom Green County Bar Assn. (sec.-treas. young lawyers 1977-78), AICPAs, Tex. Soc. CPAs (bd. dirs. 1980-87, pres. San Angelo chpt. 1980-81, mem. state exec. com. 1981-82, 86-87, state sec. 1986-87, chmn. profl. ethics com. 1985-86, Young CPA of Yr. 1984-85), Concho Valley Estate Planning Coun. (v.p. 1979-80, also dir.). State civil litigation, Criminal. Office: Law Office of John E Sutton 117 S Irving St San Angelo TX 76903-6419

SUTTON, JOHN F., JR. law educator, dean, lawyer; b. Alpine, Tex., Jan. 26, 1918; s. John F. and Pauline Irene (Elam) S.; m. Nancy Ewing, June 1, 1940; children: Joan Sutton Parr, John Ewing. J.D., U. Tex., 1941. Bar: Tex. 1941, U.S. Dist. Ct. (we. dist.) Tex. 1947, U.S. Ct. Appeals (5th cir.) 1951, U.S. Supreme Ct. 1960. Assoc. Brooks, Napier, Brown & Matthews, San Antonio, 1941-42; spl. agt. FBI, Washington, 1942-45; assoc. Matthews, Nowlin, Macfarlane & Barrett, San Antonio, 1945-48; ptnr. Kerr, Gayer & Sutton, San Angelo, Tex., 1948-50, Sutton, Steib & Barr, San Angelo, 1951-57; prof. U. Tex.-Austin, 1957-65, William Stamps Farish prof., 1965-84, A.W. Walker centennial chair, 1984-88, emeritus, 1988—, dean Sch. Law, 1979-84. Editor: (with Wellborn) Materials on Evidence, 8th edit., 1996, (with Dzienkowski) Cases and Materials on Professional Responsibility of Lawyers, 1989, (with Schuwerk) Guideline to the Texas Disciplinary Rules of Professional Conduct, 1990; contbr. articles to profl. jours. Served to 1st lt. JAGC USAR, 1948-54. Fellow Am. Bar Found. (life), Tex. Bar Found. (life); mem. ABA (com. on ethics 1970-76), State Bar Tex. (com. on rules of profl. conduct, com. adminstrn. rules of evidence), Philos. Soc. Tex., Order of Coif, U. Tex. Club, Phi Delta Phi, San Angelo Country Club, North Austin Rotary (pres. 1969). Presbyterian. Home: 3830 Sunset Dr San Angelo TX 76904-5956 Office: U Tex Sch Law 727 E Dean Keeton St Austin TX 78705-3224

SUTTON, SAMUEL J. lawyer, educator, engineer; b. Chgo., July 21, 1941; s. Samuel J. and Elaine (Blossom) S.; m. Anne V. Sutton, Aug. 28, 1965; children: Paige, Jean, Leah, Jepson. BA in History and Philosophy, U. Ariz., 1964, BSEE, 1967; JD, George Washington U., 1969. Bar: Ariz. 1969, D.C. 1970, U.S. Ct. Appeals (fed. cir.) 1983. Patent atty. Gen. Electric Co., Washington, Phoenix, 1967-70; ptnr. Cahill, Sutton & Thomas, Phoenix, 1970-95, of counsel, 1995—. Prof. law Ariz. State U., Tempe, 1975—; expert witness Fed. Dist. Cts., 1983—; trial cons. to numerous lawyers, 1972—; arbitrator Am. Arbitration Assn., Phoenix, 1971—. Author: Patent Preparation, 1976, Intellectual Property, 1978, Art Law, 1988, Law, Science and Technology, 1991, Licensing Intangible Property, 1994, Commercial Torts, 1995, Patent Litigation, 1996; pub. sculptures installed at Tanner Sq., Phoenix, Tucson Art Inst., Mobil Corp., Mesa, Ariz., Cox Devel. Co., Tempe, Ariz., Downtown Phoenix, Desert Bot. Garden, Phoenix, Gateway Ctr., Phoenix, Sedona Sculpture Garden, Construct Gallery, Phoenix. Chmn. air pollution hearing bd. City of Phoenix, Maracopa County, 1970-85. Recipient Patent prize Patent Resources Group, 1979, Publ. award IEEE, 1967, Genematus award U. Ariz., 1964, Disting. Achievement award Ariz. State U., 1980, Construct Sculpture prize, 1989. Avocation: large scale steel sculpture. Intellectual property, Patent, Trademark and copyright. Office: Cahill Sutton & Thomas PO Box 32694 Phoenix AZ 85016-4791 E-mail: sam.sutton@asu.edu

SUTTON, WILLIAM DWIGHT, lawyer; b. Butler, Pa., Oct. 22, 1916; s. James S. Sutton and Ada Elizabeth Emrick; m. Mary Ella Newsome, Dec. 4, 1943; children: Ann, Melissa. BA, Washington & Jefferson, 1938; JD, U. Mich., 1941. Bar: Pa. 1946, U.S. Ct. Appeals (3d cir.) 1946, U.S. Supreme Ct. 1946. Assoc. atty. Donovan, Leisure, Newton & Irvine, N.Y.C., 1941-42; ptnr. Thorp Reed & Armstrong, Pitts., 1952-90, sr. ptnr., 1991—. Major U.S. Army, 1942-46, PTO. Decorated Bronze Star, 1944. Mem. ABA, Pa. Bar Assn., Allegheny County Bar Assn. General corporate, Private international, Probate. Home: 605 Scenic View Dr Pittsburgh PA 15241-3999 Office: Thorp Reed & Armstrong 20 Stanwix St Fl 9 Pittsburgh PA 15222-4802

SVAB, STEPHEN, lawyer; b. Cleve., Oct. 28, 1954; s. Bert and Elizabeth (Biro) S. BA in English, John Carroll U., 1976; MA in Journalism, Penn State U., 1978; JD in Law, Case Western Reserve U., 1982. Bar: Ohio 1983, U.S. Dist. Ct. (no. dist.) Ohio 1983. Segment producer Nightwatch CBS News, Washington, 1984-88; assignment editor USA Today On TV, Rossyln, Va., 1989; chief news media divsn. Office of Pub. Affairs FCC, Washington, 1990-94, sr. atty. video svcs. divsn. Mass Media Bur, 1994—. Mem. Young Benefactors of Smithsonian Instn., Washington, 1993, Women's Mus. of the Arts, Washington, 1994. Mem. ABA, Ohio State Bar Assn., Fed. Comm. Bar Assn., N.Y. Rd. Runners Club. Roman Catholic. Avocations: weight training, biking, tennis, reading, marathon running. Office: FCC 445 12th St SW Washington DC 20554-0001 E-mail: ssvab@fcc.gov

SVENGALIS, KENDALL FRAYNE, law librarian; b. Gary, Ind., May 16, 1947; s. Frank Anthony and Alvida Linnea (Matheus) S.; children: Hillary Linnea, Andrew Kendall; m. Ellen Christine Haffling, June 16, 2001. BA, Purdue U., 1970, MA, 1973; MLS, U. R.I., 1975. Reference librarian Roger Williams Coll., Bristol, R.I., 1975, Providence (R.I.) Coll., 1975-77; asst. law librarian R.I. State Law Library, Providence, 1976-82, state law librarian, 1982—. Adj. prof. libr. and info. studies U. R.I., 1987—. Author: The Legal Information Buyer's Guide and Reference Manual, 1996 (Best Legal Reference Book of 1996), 97-98, 98-99, 2000, 2001; editor: The Criv Sheet, 1988-94; contbr. articles to profl. jours. Chmn. jud. branch United Way Com. R.I., 1980. Recipient AALL Joseph L. Andrews Bibliographical awd. Mem. Am. Assn Law Librs. (state, ct. and county libr. spl. interest sect., recipient Connie E. Bolden significant publ. award 1993, 99, bd. dirs. 1986-88, 96-99), Law Librs. New Eng. (treas. 1983-85, v.p. 1985-86, pres. 1986-87), Com. on Rels. with Info. Vendors (editor 1988-94), New Eng. Law Libr. Consortium (v.p. 1990-92, pres. 1992-94). Republican. Lutheran. Home: 204 Wyassup Rd North Stonington CT 06359 Office: RI State Law Libr Frank Licht Jud Complex 250 Benefit St Providence RI 02903-2719 E-mail: ksven@ids.net, rilawpress@ids.net

SWACKER, FRANK WARREN, lawyer; b. N.Y.C., May 18, 1922; m. Irene Maloney Michael; children: Carolyn, Frances, Michele, Ruth. BA, Union Coll., Schnectady, 1947; JD, U. Va., 1949; LLM in Internat. Law, NYU, 1961. Bar: Va. 1948, N.Y. 1950, Ohio 1962, Wis. 1969, D.C. 1977, Fla. 1991, U.S. Ct. Internat. Trade 1978, U.S. Supreme Ct. 1952. Pvt. practice, N.Y.C., 1949-54, 64-68, Washington, 1977-84, Clearwater, Fla., 1984-89, St. Petersburg, 1994—; atty. Caltex Petroleum Corp., N.Y.C., 1955-60, Marathon Oil Co., Ohio, 1961-63; internat. counsel Allis-Chalmers Corp., Milw., 1968-78; sr. mem. Swacker & Assocs., P.C., Springfield, Va., 1980=84, chmn., pres. firm, sr. mem. Largo, Fla., 1989-93; dir. ATM CardPay, 1993-94; vice chmn. Lasergate Sys., Inc., 1995-99. Spl. asst. dep. atty. gen. State of N.Y., 1950; govtl. adviser U.S., P.I., Algeria; lectr. Ohio No. U., 1962, N.Y. World Trade Inst., 1976; adj. prof. Stetson U. Coll. Law, St. Petersburg, Fla., 1996-2000, LLM internat. adv. coun., 1997—. Author: Business International Guide for Going Global, 1999; co-author: World Trade Without Barriers: World Trade Organization and Dispute Resolution, 1995, vol. 2, 1996; co-editor, contbr. Bus. and Legal Aspects of Latin American Trade and Investment, 1977, Reference Manual on Doing Business with Latin America, 1979; contbr. articles to legal jours. Mem. internat. bus. adv. bd. U. So. Fla., 1993-94. Lt. (j.g.) USN, 1943-46, WWII. Mem. ABA (lectr. 1978, internat. comml. arbitration com. 1991—), Nat. Law Inst., Am. Arbitration Assn. (panel experts), World Intellectual Property Orgn. (arbitration panel). General corporate, Private international. E-mail: integra10@aol.com

SWAIN, LAURA TAYLOR, judge; b. Bklyn., Nov. 21, 1958; d. Justus E. and Madeline V. (Allgood) Taylor; m. Andrew J. Swain, Oct. 12, 1991. AB, Harvard U., 1979, JD, 1982. Bar: Mass. 1982, N.Y. 1983, U.S. Dist. Ct. (so. and ea. dists.) N.Y. 1983. Law clk to chief judge U.S. Dist. Ct. (so. dist.) N.Y., 1982-83; assoc. Debevoise & Plimpton, N.Y.C., 1983-95, counsel, 1995-96; U.S. bankruptcy judge U.S. Bankruptcy Ct., Bklyn., 1996-2000; U.S. dist. judge U.S. Dist. Ct. (so. dist.) N.Y., N.Y.C., 2000—. Mem. N.Y. State Bd. Law Examiners, Albany, 1986-96; mem. multistate bar exam. com. Nat. Conf. Bar Examiners, 1987-99, mem. testing, R&D devel. com., 1990-94, mem. long range planning com., 1994-96; cons. N.Y. Profl. Edn. Project, 1995-96. Co-contbr. articles on employee benefits, employee stock ownership plans, acctg. and bankruptcy to profl. publs.; contbg. author: New York Insurance Law, 1991. Trustee Diocese of N.Y. (Episcopal), 1991-92; mem. Dessoff Choirs, N.Y.C., 1984-92; bd. dirs. Episcopal Charities, Inc., 1996—, Coalition Consumer Bankruptcy Debtor Edn., 1998—. Mem. ABA, Assn. of Bar of City of N.Y., Met. Black Bar Assn., N.Y. State Bar Assn., Nat. Conf. Bankruptcy Judges, Nat. Assn. Women Judges. Episcopalian. Avocation: music. Federal civil litigation, Labor, Pension, profit-sharing, and employee benefits. Office: US Dist Ct So Dist NY 40 Foley Sq New York NY 10007

SWAIN, W. TIMOTHY, lawyer; b. Benton, Ill., Aug. 20, 1909; s. Theodore Paul and Malinda Gertrude (Jones) S.; m. Katherine Altorfer, Oct. 3, 1936; children— Nancy Swain Crawford, Timothy II, Cynthia Swain Davis. A.B., U. Ill., 1931, J.D., 1933. Bar: Ill. 1934, of counsel Swain Hartshorn & Scott, Ill. Trustee U. Ill., 1955-75; mem. council legal advisors Republican Nat. Com., 1983-89. Recipient Disting. Service award U. Ill. Alumni Assn. Fellow Am. Bar Found.; mem. Ill. Bar Found. (pres. 1958-59, bd. dirs. 1958-82), Peoria County Bar Assn. (pres. 1954-55), Ill. Bar Assn. (chmn. corp. com. 1946, bd. govs. 1952-55, 62, pres. 1958-59), ABA (ho. of dels. 1958-64, chmn. bar activities sect. 1962, law list com. 1963-69, del. to jud. adminstr. div. lawyers conf. 1980-81, sec. lawyers div. 1981-83), Bar Assn. 7th Fed. Cir. (bd. dirs. 1977-83), world Peace through Law Ctr. (planning com. 1977), Am. Judicature Soc., Soc. Trial Lawyers of Ill., Scribes. Baptist. Clubs: Creve Coeur (past bd. dirs.), Country of Peoria. Home: 7412 N Edgewild Dr Peoria IL 61614-2116 Office: Swain Hartshorn & Scott 1806 Assoc Bank Plz Peoria IL 61602

SWAN, ALAN CHARLES, law educator; b. Kalimpong, West Bengal, India, Dec. 29, 1933; came to U.S., 1945; s. Charles Lundeen and Kathleen Vivian (Doucette) S.; m. Mary Joe Smith, Aug. 28, 1954; children— Kathleen Jeanette, Amalie Christine, Alan Charles. B.A., Albion Coll., 1954; J.D., U. Chgo., 1957. Bar: N.Y. 1958. Assoc. Milbank, Tweed, Hadley & McCloy, N.Y.C., 1957-61; asst. gen. counsel AID, Washington, 1961-66; asst. v.p. U. Chgo., professorial lectr. Grad. Sch. Bus., 1966-72; prof. law U. Miami, Coral Gables, Fla., 1972— ; mem. Nat. Lawyers Com. for Soviet Jewry, 1971-80. Author: The Regulation of International Business and Economic Relations, 2d edit., 1997; contbr. articles to profl. jours. Trustee Plymouth Congregational Ch., Miami, 1998-2001; mem. Miami Com. on Fgn. Relations, 1976— . Mem. Am. Law Inst, ABA, Am. Soc. Internat. Law, Internat. Law Assn., Fla. Bar Assn. Democrat. Home: 14901 SW 82nd Ave Miami FL 33158-1906 Office: U Miami Sch Law Coral Gables FL 33124

SWAN, GEORGE STEVEN, law educator; b. St. Louis; BA, Ohio State U., 1970; JD, U. Notre Dame, 1974; LLM, U. Toronto, 1976, SJD, 1983. Bar: Ohio 1974, U.S. Dist. Ct. (so. dist.) Ohio 1975, U.S. Supreme Ct. 1987, U.S. Ct. Appeals (6th and 11th cirs.) 1993, U.S. Ct. Appeals (10th cir.) 1994, D.C. 1997, Ga. 1997, U.S. Dist. Ct. (no. dist.) Ga. 1997, Fla. 1997, Minn. 1998, Nebr. 1998, N.D. 1998, U.S. Ct. Appeals (7th cir.) 1998, La. 1999, Mass. 1999; ChFC, CLU, CFP; registered investment advisor. Sec. of state, N.C., 1990; asst. atty. gen. State of Ohio, Columbus, 1974-75; jud. clk. Supreme Ct. Ohio, 1976-78; asst. prof. Del. Law Sch., Wilmington, 1980-83, assoc. prof., 1983-84; prof. law St. Thomas U. Law Sch., Miami, Fla., 1984-88; jud. clk. U.S. Ct. Appeals (7th cir.), Chgo., 1988-89; assoc. prof. N.C. Agrl. & Tech. State U., Greensboro, 1989—. Vis. prof.

John Marshall Law Sch., Atlanta, 1996-97, 2000-01. Contbr. articles to law jours. Mem. Ohio State Bar Assn., D.C. Bar, State Bar Ga., Fla. Bar, Mass. Bar Assn., Nebr. State Bar Assn., La. State Bar Assn., N.D. State Bar Assn., Soc. of Fin. Svc. Profls., Fin. Planning Assn., Am. Polit. Sci. Assn. Office: Merrick Hall 1601 E Market St Greensboro NC 27411

SWAN, MICHAEL ROBERT, lawyer; b. Passaic, N.J., Oct. 8, 1957; s. Harry A. and Marilyn P. S.; m. Katherine L. Goldman, May 24, 1982. BA in English cum laude, Montclair State Coll., 1979; JD with honors, U. Tex., 1982. Bar: N.Mex. 1982, U.S. Dist. Ct. N.Mex. 1982, Tex. 1984, U.S. Dist. Ct. (no. dist.) Tex. 1984, U.S. Ct. Appeals (5th cir.) 1985. Assoc. Poole, Tinnin & Martin, Albuquerque, 1982-84, Lippe & Lay, Dallas, 1984-85, Brice & Mankoff, Dallas, 1985-89; shareholder Choate & Lilly, 1989-90; atty. FDIC, Dallas, 1990—. Founder & pres. Basenji Rescue and Transport, Inc., 1997—. Cert. arbitrator Better Bus. Bur., Dallas, 1985—, 90. Mem. Phi Delta Phi, Phi Kappa Phi. Avocations: dog rescue. Administrative and regulatory, Banking, Federal civil litigation. Home: 8299 Middle Essex Cove Cordova TN 38016-5140

SWAN, PETER NACHANT, law educator, legal advisor; b. Seattle, Sept. 17, 1936; s. John William and Virginia Louise (Nachant) S.; m. Joyce Nelson, Apr. 20, 1968; children— Kimberly, Matthew, Channing. B.S., Stanford U., 1958, J.D., 1961. Bar: Calif. 1962, U.S. Dist. Ct. (no. dist.) Calif. 1962, U.S. Supreme Ct. 1966, Oreg. 1979. Assoc. Lillick, McHose & Charles, San Francisco, 1962-70; assoc. prof. law U. Oreg., Eugene, 1970-74, prof., 1974— , asst. to pres. for legal affairs, 1980— . Author: Legal Aspects of the Transportation and Receipt of Liquified Natural Gas, 1975; Ocean Oil and Gas & The Law, 1979. Contbr. articles to profl. jours. Mem. Tau Beta Phi. Office: U Oreg Sch Law Eugene OR 97403

SWANN, BARBARA, lawyer; b. N.Y., Sept. 15, 1950; d. George Arthur. BA summa cum laude, Montclair State U., 1988; JD, Rutgers Law, 1992. Bar: N.J. 1992, D.C. 1994, N.Y. 1995, U.S. Dist. Ct. N.J. 1992, U.S. Ct. Appeals (3rd cir.) 1994, U.S. Dist. Ct. N.Y. 1996, Calif. 2000. Correspondent The Associate Press, Newark, 1974-80; reporter, bureau chief The Hudson Dispatch, Union City, 1973-80; editorial page editor The Paterson (N.J.) News, 1980-81; v.p., acct. supr. Gerald Freeman, Inc., Clifton, N.J., 1981-86; pres. LePore Assoc., Inc., West Caldwell, 1986-89; law clk. to Hon. Robert N. Wilentz N.J. Supreme Ct., 1992-93; law clk. to Hon. Leonard I. Garth U.S. Ct. Appeals (3rd cir.), 1993-94; assoc. Cahill, Gordon & Reindel, N.Y., 1994-97; liaison Republic of Ga. ABA Cen. and East European Law Initiative, 1997-98, media law specialist, 1998-2000; exec. dir. Internat. Sr. Lawyers Project, N.Y.C., 2000—. Editor-in-chief: Rutgers Computer & Technology Law Jour., 1991-92. Founding trustee Ctr. for Children's Advocacy, Riverdale, N.J. 1994—. Mem. ABA, Assn. of the Bar of the City of New York, N.J. State Bar Assn., N.Y. County Lawyers' Assn. Am. Inn of Ct., D.C. Bar Assn., State Bar Calif. General civil litigation, Constitutional, Libel. E-mail: swann2002@email.msn.com

SWANN, RICHARD ROCKWELL, lawyer, banker; b. Orlando, Fla., May 7, 1940; s. Pervie P. and Maesther (Mears) S.; m. Doris Orr (dec. Oct. 1983); children— Dorothy Orr, Christian Mears, Campbell Thornal, Doris Reed. A.B., Duke U., 1961, J.D., 1963. Bar: Fla. 1963. Mem. Swann & Haddock, Orlando, 1963— ; chmn. bd. First Fidelity Savs. & Loan, Orlando, Am. Pioneer Savs. Bank, Orlando, Am. Pioneer, Inc., Orlando; dir. Overseas Pvt. Investment Corp., Washington, 1977-82; bd. govs. Overseas Investment Reins., 1978-82. Mem. ABA, Orange County Bar Assn., Fla. Bar Assn. Democrat. Office: Swann and Haddock 1 duPont Ctr 411 E Jackson St # 4986 Orlando FL 32801-2855

SWANSON, ARTHUR DEAN, lawyer; b. Onida, S.D., Apr. 19, 1934; s. Obert W. and Mary I. (Barnum) S.; m. Paula Swanson, Aug. 22, 1965 (div. Feb. 1984); children: Shelby, Dean, Sherry; m. Ann Swanson, Aug. 21, 1989. BA, Wash. State U., 1956; JD, U. Wash., 1963. Bar: Wash. 1963. Dep. prosecutor King County, Seattle, 1964-65; ct. commr. Renton and Issaquah Dist. Cts., Wash., 1966-68; pvt. practice law Renton, 1965—. Lectr. various orgns.; former counsel Wash. State Law Enforcement Assn., Wash. State Dep. Sheriff's Assn. Served with Fin. Corps, U.S. Army, 1956-58. Named one of Best Lawyers Am., 1991-92, 93-94, 95-96, 97-98, 99-2000, 2001—. Fellow Am. Coll. Trial Lawyers; mem. Wash. State Bar Assn. (past sec. trial sect.), Seattle-King County Bar Assn. (bd. trustees 1977-80), Assn. Trial Lawyers Am., Wash. State Trial Lawyers Assn. (past pres.), Am. Bd. Trial Advs. (bd. dirs., pres. Wash. state chpt. 1995-96), Damage Attys. Roundtable (pres. 1998-99). Democrat. Avocation: tennis. State civil litigation, Insurance, Personal injury. Office: 4512 Talbot Rd S Renton WA 98055-6216 E-mail: adswanson@aol.com

SWANSON, CHARLES WALTER, lawyer; b. Bluefield, W.Va., Mar. 6, 1954; s. Don B. and Ann (Hughes) S.; m. Linda Susan Doak, Aug. 12, 1978 (div.); m. Pamela Lynn Reeves, Dec. 10, 1988. BA, Pfeiffer Coll., 1976; JD, U. Tenn., 1979. Bar: Tenn. 1979, U.S. Dist. Ct. (ea. dist.) Tenn. 1979, U.S. Ct. Appeals (6th cir.) 1983. Spl. judge juvenile ct. Knoxville (Tenn.) County, 1979-81; asst. city atty. City of Knoxville, 1981-84; assoc. Pryor, Flynn, Priest & Harber, Knoxville, 1984—. Atty. city council Knoxville, 1985—. Mem. ABA, Tenn. Bar Assn., Knoxville Bar Assn., Tenn. Trial Lawyers Assn., Knoxville Barristers (exec. com.). Democrat. Methodist. Avocations: softball, tennis, golf, hiking. General practice, Personal injury. Office: Sheppeard & Swanson 616 W Hill Ave Knoxville TN 37902-2703 E-mail: cswanson@shepswan.com

SWANSON, ROBERT LEE, lawyer; b. Fond du Lac, Wis., July 15, 1942; s. Walfred S. and Edna F. (Kamp) S.; m. Mary Ruth Francis, Aug. 19, 1967; children: Leigh Alexandra, Mitchell Pearson. BS, U. Wis., 1964; JD, Valparaiso U., 1970; LLM, Boston U., 1979. Bar: Wis. 1970, U.S. Dist. Ct. (ea. dist.) Wis. 1970, U.S. Dist. Ct. (we. dist.) Wis. 1974, U.S. Tax Ct. 1981, U.S. Dist. Ct. (cen.) Ill. 1988, Okla. 1999, U.S. Ct. Appeals (7th cir.) 1999. Atty. Kasdorf, Dahl, Lewis & Swietlik, Milw., 1970-73; atty., ptnr. Wartman, Wartman & Swanson, Ashland, Wis., 1973-80; city atty. City of Ashland, 1976-80; atty., ptnr. DeMark, Kolbe & Brodek, Racine, 1980-95; ptnr. Hartig, Bjelajac, Swanson & Koenen, 1995-99; contract atty. Okla. Indigent Def. System, Lincoln County, 2000—. Lectr. civil rights and discrimination laws, 1980—; lectr. bus. law Cardinal Strich U., 1996-99, U. Wis.-Parkside, 1997-99; contractor Okla. Indigent Def. Sys.,Lincoln County, 2000—, participating atty. Alliance Defense Fund 2000—. Columnist (legal) Burlington Std. Press, 1991-95, Wis. Restaurant Assn. Mag., 1986. Vice comdr. USCG Aux. Bayfield (Wis.) Flotilla, 1975-81; v.p., bd. dirs. Meml. Med. Ctr., Ashland, 1975-80; chmn. Ashland County Rep. Party, 1976-79; vol. atty. ACLU Wis., 1975-90. 1st lt. U.S. Army, 1964-66. Named one of Outstanding Young Men of Am., Jaycees, 1978; recipient Disting. Achievement in Art and Sci. of Advocacy award Internat. Acad. Trial Lawyers, 1970. Mem. Racine County Bar Assn. (bd. dirs. 1986-89), Wis. Acad. Trial Lawyers, Def. Rsch. Inst., Am. Hockey Assn. U.S. (coach, referee 1983-90), Am. Legion. Avocations: softball, volleyball, hockey. General civil litigation, General corporate, General practice. Home: RR 1 Box 478 Stroud OK 74079-9723 E-mail: rswanson@brightok.net

SWANSON, VICTORIA CLARE HELDMAN, lawyer; b. Aug. 28, 1949; d. Paul F. and Anne F. (Thomas) Schmitz; m. Louis M. Heldman, Sept. 21, 1971 (div. 1973); m. John Askins, Feb. 28, 1975 (div. 1977); m. Thomas C. Swanson, Feb. 13, 1988. BA in journalism with distinction, Ohio State U., 1972; JD, U. Detroit, 1975. Bar: Mich. 1975, Colo. 1984, U.S. Dist. Ct. (ea. and we. dists.) Mich. 1975, U.S. Ct. Appeals (6th cir.) 1977, U.S. Ct. Appeals (3d cir.) 1980, U.S. Supreme Ct. 1983, U.S. Ct. Appeals (10th cir.) 1984, U.S. Ct. Appeals (5th cir.) 1989, cert.: NBTA (civil trial advocate) 1994. Assoc. Lopatin, Miller, Bindes & Freedman, Detroit, 1973—76; ptnr. Schaden, Swanson & Lampert, 1977—90, Sears, Anderson & Swanson, P.C., Colorado Springs, Colo., 1991—96, Sears & Swanson, Colorado Springs, 1997—. Adj. prof. U. Detroit Sch. Law, 1982. Author (with Richard F. Schaden): (non-fiction) Product Design Liability, 1982; author: (with others) Women Trial Lawyers: How They Succeed in Practice and in the Courtroom, 1986; author: (chpt.) Anatomy of a Personal Injury Lawsuit, 1992; author: (and editor) (handbook) Colorado Auto Litigators Handbook, 1995, Colorado Courtroom Handbook, 1998. Mem.: Mich. Bar Assn., Colo. Bar Assn., Assn. Trial Lawyers Am., Colo. Trial Lawyers Assn. (past pres.), Mich. Trial Lawyers Assn. General civil litigation, Federal civil litigation, Personal injury. Office: Sears & Swanson 2 N Cascade Ave Colorado Springs CO 80903-1631

SWANSON, WALLACE MARTIN, lawyer, investor; b. Fergus Falls, Minn., Aug. 22, 1941; s. Marvin Walter and Mary Louise (Lindsey) S.; children: Kristen Lindsey, Eric Munger. B.A. with honors, U. Minn., 1962; LL.B. with honors, So. Methodist U., 1965. Bar: Tex. 1965. Assoc. Coke & Coke, Dallas, 1965-70; ptnr. firm Johnson & Swanson, 1970-88; prin. Wallace M. Swanson, P.C., Rice, 1988—; chmn., CEO Ace Cash Express Inc., Irving, 1987-88, State St. Capital Corp., 1990—. Served with USNR, 1960-65. Mem. Tex. Bar Found., State Bar Tex. (securities com. 1972-86, chmn. 1978-80, coun. bus. law sect. 1980-86), Crescent Club. Methodist. General corporate, Mergers and acquisitions, Real property. Address: 6234 FM 879 Ennis TX 75119

SWART, MICHAEL, lawyer; b. Aug. 7, 1941; s. Joseph and Loretta (Rose) S.; m. Mary McConnell, Apr. 12, 1969; children: Mary E., Katherine E., Emily R. AB, Georgetown U., 1963; JD, SUNY, 1967. Bar: N.Y. 1976, U.S. Dist. Ct. (we. dist.) N.Y. 1970. Ptnr. Jaekle, Fleischmann & Mugel, Buffalo, 1969-79; gen. counsel Goldome Bank, 1979-84; ptnr. Phillips, Lytle, Hitchcock, Blaine & Huber, 1982-92; v.p., gen. counsel MDS Matrix Inc., 1992-2000; v.p., sr. trust officer HSBC Bank, 2000—. Bd. chmn. Vis. Nurse Assn. Buffalo, 1981-84; bd. dirs. Shea's O'Connell Presrva tion Guild, Ltd., Opera Sacre; vol. Lawyers for the Arts, Pub. TV Fundraising Com.; Republican committeeman, 1971— ; bd. dirs., pres. Buffalo Ballet Theatre, Inc., Hospice of Buffalo; chmn. adv. bd. Sisters of St. Joseph; mem. Diocesan Commn. on Peace and Justice. Served to capt. U.S. Army, 1967-69. Mem. ABA, N.Y. State Bar Assn., Erie County Bar Assn. (treas., chmn. banking law com.), Nat. Assn. Mut. Savs. Banks, Savs. Banks Assn. N.Y. State (banking law com.), Am. Legion (officer). Roman Catholic. Clubs: Buffalo Canoe (Point Abino, Ont., Can.); Saturn (Buffalo). Banking, General corporate. Address: 19 Granger Pl Buffalo NY 14222-1227 Office: HSBC Bank Blaine & Huber 2300 HSBC Center Buffalo NY 14203-2887

SWARTZ, CHARLES ROBERT, lawyer; b. Norfolk, Va., Jan. 28, 1944; BA, U. Va., 1965; JD, U. Ga., 1968. Bar: Va. 1968. Ptnr. McGuireWoods LLP, Richmond, Va., 1969—. Fellow Am. Coll. Real Estate Lawyers; mem. Internat. Assn. Attys. and Execs. in Corp. Real Estate. Real property. Office: McGuireWoods LLP 1 James Ctr 901 E Cary St Richmond VA 23219-4057 E-mail: cswartz@mcguirewoods.com

SWARTZ, MELVIN JAY, lawyer, writer; b. Boston, July 21, 1930; s. Jack M. and Rose (Rosenberg) S.; children: Julianne, Jonathan Samuel. BA, Syracuse U., 1953; LLB, Boston U., 1957. Bar: N.Y. 1959, Ariz. 1961. Assoc. Alfred S. Julian, N.Y.C., 1957-59; ptnr. Finks & Swartz, Youngtown, Sun City, Phoenix, 1961-70, Swartz & Jeckel, P.C., Sun City, Youngtown, Scottsdale, 1971-82; exec. v.p. APPPRO, Inc. Author: Don't Die Broke, A Guide to Secure Retirement, 1974, rev. edit., 2000, (book and cassettes) Keep What You Own, 1989, rev. edit., 2000, Retire Without Fear, 1995; columnist News-Sun, Sun City, 1979-83; author column Swartz on Aging. Bd. dirs. Valley of the Sun Sch. for Retarded Children, 1975-79. Mem. ABA, Ariz. Bar Assn., N.Y. Bar Assn., Maricopa County Bar Assn., Scottsdale Bar Assn., Ctrl. Ariz. Estate Planning Coun., Masons (Phoenix). Jewish. Estate planning, Probate, Estate taxation. Office: 3416 N 44th St Unit 22 Phoenix AZ 85018-6044 E-mail: swartzmj@worldnet.att.net

SWARTZBAUGH, MARC L. lawyer; b. Urbana, Ohio, Jan. 3, 1937; s. Merrill L. and Lillian K. (Hill) S.; m. Marjory Anne Emhardt, Aug. 16, 1958; children: Marc Charles, Kathleen Marie, Laura Kay. BA magna cum laude, Wittenberg Coll., 1958; LLB magna cum laude, U. Pa., 1961. Bar: Ohio 1961, U.S. Dist. Ct. (no. dist.) Ohio 1962, U.S. Claims Ct. 1991, U.S. Ct. Appeals (6th cir.) 1970, U.S. Ct. Appeals (3d cir.) 1985, U.S. Ct. Appeals (Fed. cir.) 1995, U.S. Supreme Ct. 1973. Law clk. to judge U.S. Ct. Appeals (3d cir.), Phila., 1961-62; assoc. Jones, Day, Reavis & Pogue, Cleve., 1962-69, ptnr., 1970-98; ret., 1998; cons., 1998—. Note editor U. Pa. Law Rev., 1960-61. Co-chmn. Suburban Citizens for Open Housing, Shaker Heights, Ohio, 1966; v.p. Lomond Assn., Shaker Heights, 1965-68; trustee The Dance Ctr., Cleve., 1980-83; amb. People to People Internat., 1986; chmn. legal divsn. Cleve. campaign United Negro Coll. Fund, 1989-96. Mem. ABA (litigation sect., sr. lawyers divsn.), Fed. Bar Assn., Ohio Bar Assn., Cleve. Bar Assn., Order of Coif, Beta Theta Pi. Democrat. Avocations: poetry, painting, music, skiing, squash, photography. Federal civil litigation, State civil litigation. Office: Jones Day Reavis & Pogue N Point 901 Lakeside Ave E Cleveland OH 44114-1190

SWEARER, WILLIAM BROOKS, lawyer; b. Hays, Kans. Grad., Princeton U., 1951; law degree, U. Kans., 1955. Bar: Kans. 1955. Pvt. practice, Hutchinson, Kans., 1955—; ptnr. Martindell, Swearer & Shaffer, LLP, 1955—. Mem. Kans. Bd. Discipline for Attys., 1979-92, chmn., 1987-92. With U.S. Army, 1952-53, Korea. Mem. ABA (ho. of dels. 1995-2000), Am. Bar Found. (state chair 1998—), Kans. Bar Assn. (pres. 1992-93, various offices, mem. coms.), Kans. Assn. Sch. Attys. (pres. 1989-90), Reno County Bar Assn. General corporate, Education and schools, Probate. Office: PO Box 1907 Hutchinson KS 67504-1907 E-mail: wbs@martindell-law.com

SWEDA, EDWARD LEON, JR. lawyer; b. Boston, Dec. 31, 1955; s. Edward Leon and Lucy (Daniszewski) S. BA, Boston Coll., 1977; JD, Suffolk Law Sch., Boston, 1980. Pvt. practice, Boston, 1981—. Lobbyist Group Against Smoking Pollution, Boston, 1980-93. Vol. Common Cause, Boston, 1977-83. Recipient Appreciation award, Am. Lung Assn. Mass., Boston, 1989. Democrat. Roman Catholic. Criminal, Labor, Legislative. Home: 172 Boston St Dorchester MA 02125-1142 Office: GASP Kenmore Sta PO Box 15463 Boston MA 02215-0008 E-mail: esweda@lynx.nev.edu

SWEENEY, ASHER WILLIAM, state supreme court justice; b. Canfield, Ohio, Dec. 11, 1920; s. Walter William and Jessie Joan (Kidd) S.; m. Bertha M. Englert, May 21, 1945; children: Randall W., Ronald R., Garland A., Karen M. Student, Youngstown U., 1939-42; LL.B., Duke U., 1948. Bar: Ohio 1949. Practiced law, Youngstown, Ohio, 1949-51; judge adv. gen. Dept. Def., Washington, 1951-65; chief Fed. Contracting Agy., Cin., 1965-68; corp. law, 1968-77; justice Ohio Supreme Ct., Columbus, 1977—. Democratic candidate for Sec. of State Ohio, 1958. Served with U.S. Army, 1942-46; col. Res. 1951-68. Decorated Legion of Merit, Bronze Star; named to Army Hall of Fame Ft. Benning, Ga., 1981 Mem. Ohio Bar Assn., Phi Delta Phi. Democrat. Home: 6690 Drake Rd Cincinnati OH 45243-2706 Office: Ohio Supreme Ct 30 E Broad St Fl 3D Columbus OH 43215-3414

SWEENEY, DAVID BRIAN, lawyer; b. Seattle, June 23, 1941; s. Hubert Lee and Ann Louise (Harmon) S.; m. Janice Kay Goins, June 18, 1983; children: Stuart, Jennifer, Ann, Katharine. BA Magna cum laude, Yale U., 1963; LLB, Harvard U., 1967. Bar: Wash. 1968, U.S. Dist. Ct. (we. dist.) Wash. 1968, U.S. Ct. Appeals (9th cir.) 1968. Assoc. Roberts, Shefelman, Lawrence, Gay and Moch, Seattle, 1968-75; ptnr. Roberts, Shefelman, Lawrence, Gay & Moch (then Robert & Shefelman, then Foster, Pepper & Shefelman), 1976—. Mem. Seattle-King County Bar Assn., Wash. State Bar Assn., ABA, Estate Planning Council of Seattle. Republican. Presbyterian. Clubs: College, Harbor. Estate planning, Probate, Real property. Home: 17506 SE 46th St Bellevue WA 98006-6527 Office: Foster Pepper & Shefelman 1111 3rd Ave Fl 34 Seattle WA 98101-3292 E-mail: sweed@foster.com

SWEENEY, DEIDRE ANN, lawyer; b. Hackensack, N.J., Mar. 17, 1953; d. Thomas Joseph and Robin (Thwaites) S. AB cum laude, Mt. Holyoke Coll., 1975; JD, Fordham U., 1978. Assoc. Curtis, Mallet-Prevost, Colt & Mosle, N.Y.C., 1978-84, Eaton & Van Winkle, N.Y.C., 1984-86; ptnr. Jacobs, Persinger & Parker, 1986—. Adj. instr. Adelphi U., N.Y.C., 1982-86. Class agt. Mt. Holyoke Coll. Alumni Fund, South Hadley, Mass., 1975-80; chmn. nominating com. Mt. Holyoke Class of 1975, 1990-94; mem. Archdiocese N.Y. Bequests and Planned Gifts Com., 1988-97; mem. Hi-Five Scholarship com. CUNY, 2000—. Mem. Assn. of Bar of City of N.Y. (uniform state laws com. 1982-85). Democrat. Roman Catholic. Estate planning, Probate, Estate taxation.

SWEENEY, EMILY MARGARET, prosecutor; b. Cleve., May 2, 1948; d. Mark Elliot and Neydra (Ginsburg) Mirsky; m. Patrick Anthony Sweeney, Dec. 30, 1983; 1 child, Margaret Anne. BA, Case Western Res. U., 1970; JD, Cleve. Marshall Coll. Law, 1981. Bar: Ohio 1981. Tchr. English Cleve. Pub. Schs., 1970; plant mgr. Union Gospel Press Pub. Co., Cleve., 1971-73; publ. specialist Cleve. State U., 1973-82; asst. U.S. atty. Dept. Justice, Cleve., 1982—; now U.S. atty., 1993—. Precinct committeeman Woodmere, Ohio, 1978; mem. Atty. Gen.'s Adv. Com. U.S. Attys., 1993-96, 98-99, chmn. office mgmt. and budget subcom., 1993—, mem. asset forfeiture, civil issues, controlled substances and drug demand reduction, LECC/victim witness subcoms., 1993—; chmn. law enforcement coord. com. No. Dist. Ohio, 1993—. Recipient Eddy award for graphic design, 1977, Spl Achievement award U.S. Dept. Justice, 1985. Mem. Fed. Bar Assn. Democrat. Office: US Atty's Office 1800 Bank One Ctr 600 Superior Ave E Ste 1800 Cleveland OH 44114-2600*

SWEENEY, EVERETT JOHN, lawyer; b. Thomas, Okla., Mar. 22, 1945; s. John and Lucille (Wright) S. m. Sherryl M. Sweeney, Sept. 27, 1964; children: John Chad, Andrea Rachelle. BS, Southwestern State Coll., 1967; JD, U. Okla. 1970. Bar: Okla. 1970, U.S. Dist. Ct. (we. dist.) Okla. 1970, U.S. Ct. Apl.s (10th cir.) 1970, U.S. Supreme Ct. 1982. Instr., Southwestern State Coll., Weatherford, Okla., 1970-72; counsel Am. Fidelity Assurance Co., Oklahoma City, 1972-74; assoc. Robert G. Grove, Oklahoma City, 1974-76; legal asst. Supreme Ct. Okla., Oklahoma City, 1976-77; assoc. Miskovsky & Sullivan, Oklahoma City, 1977-78; sole practice, Norman, Okla., 1978—. Mem. Cleveland County Bar Assn., Oklahoma County Bar Assn., Okla. Trial Lawyers Assn., Assn. Trial Lawyers Am. Democrat. Baptist. Insurance, Libel, Personal injury. Home: 2641 Brentwood Dr Norman OK 73069-5062 Office: Sweeney & Franklin 303 S Peters Ave Norman OK 73069-6024

SWEENEY, FRANCIS E. state supreme court justice; b. Jan. 26, 1934; married; 4 children. BSBA, Xavier U., 1956; JD, Cleve.-Marshall Law Sch., 1963. Profl. football player Ottawa Rough Riders, Ont., Can., 1956-58; mem. legal dept. Allstate Ins. Co., Cleve., 1958-63; asst. prosecuting atty. Cuyahoga County, 1963-70; judge Cuyahoga County Ct. of Common Pleas, 1970-88; judge (8th cir.) U.S. Ct. Appeals, 1988-92; justice Ohio Supreme Ct., Columbus, 1992—. With U.S. Army, 1957-58. Recipient Legion of Honor award Xavier U., 1956, Outstanding Jud. Svc. award Ohio Supreme Ct., 1972-85, Alumnus of Yr. award Xavier U., 1977. Office: Ohio Supreme Ct 30 E Broad St Fl 3 Columbus OH 43266-0001*

SWEENEY, JOHN LAWRENCE, lawyer; b. Staten Island, N.Y., Jan. 5, 1962; s. Lawrence Patrick and Lauretta (Kronen) S.; m. Karen Anne Hrebenak, Aug. 26, 1988; children: Conor, Lauren, Devin, Pearse. BA, Yale U., 1984; JD magna cum laude, Seton Hall U., 1990; LLM in Taxation, NYU, 1993. Bar: N.J. 1990, U.S. Dist. Ct. N.J. 1990, N.Y. 1991, U.S. Tax Ct. 1995. Assoc. Connell, Foley & Geiser, Roseland, N.J., 1990-92, Lampf, Lipkind, Prupis & Pettegrew, West Orange, 1992-93; atty. pvt. practice, Morristown, 1993-2000; pntr. Sweeney & Flanagan, LLC, 2001—. Editor, Peapack-Gladstone Gazette, 2000—. Interview supr. Yale Alumni Schs. Com., 1991—; charter mem. Seton Hall Prep Hall of Fame Com., 1984-94. Mem. N.J. Bar Assn., N.Y. Bar Assn., Morris County Bar Assn., Yale Club Ctrl. N.J. (trustee 1991-94, 1997—, sec. 1997-99, pres. 1999—), New Providence Lions Club Internat., KC (fin. sec. 2000—). Estate planning, Probate, Taxation, general. Home: 14 Farm Cottage Rd Gladstone NJ 07934-2007 Office: 51 Dumont Pl Morristown NJ 07960-4125 E-mail: sweenlaw@aol.com

SWEENEY, NEAL JAMES, lawyer; b. Paterson, N.J., Nov. 1, 1957; s. Bernard Thomas and Mary Agnes (Keneally) S.; m. Mary Elizabeth Finocchiaro, Oct. 27, 1984; children: Daniel Fulton, Clare Kenneally, Moira Ann. BA in History and Polit Sci., Rutgers U., 1979; JD, George Washington U., 1982. Bar: Ga. 1982, U.S. Dist. Ct. (no. dist.) Ga. 1982, U.S. Dist. Ct. (no. dist.) Tex. 1982, U.S. Claims Ct. 1984, U.S. Ct. Appeals (5th cir.) 1987. Assoc. Smith, Currie & Hancock, Atlanta, 1982-87, ptnr., 1988-98; pntr. Kilpatrick Stockton LLP, 1998—. Co-author: Construction Business Handbook, 1985, Holding Subcontractors to Their Bids, 1986, Subcontractor Default, 1987, The New AIA Design and Construction Documents, 1988, Proving and Pricing Claims, 1995, Fifty State Construction Lien and Bond Law, 1992, Who Pays For Defective Design?, 1997; editor: Construction Subcontracting, 1991, Common Sense Construction Law, 1997; editor Wiley Construction Law Update, 1992—; notes editor G.W.U.J. Internat. Law and Econs., 1981-82. Mem. ABA (pub. contract law sect., forum com. on constrn. industry), Atlanta Bar Assn., Am. Arbitration Assn. (panel of arbitrators), Water Environment Fedn. (editl. adv. bd. 1994-97). Roman Catholic. Federal civil litigation, Construction, Government contracts and claims. Home: 3834 Vermont Rd NE Atlanta GA 30319-1211 Office: Kilpatrick Stockton LLP 1100 Peachtree St NE Ste 2800 Atlanta GA 30309-4530

SWEENEY, THOMAS FREDERICK, lawyer; b. Detroit, Feb. 10, 1943; s. Harold Eugene and Marion Genevieve (Lunz) S.; m. Susan Carol Horn, Dec. 27, 1968; children: Sarah Elizabeth, Neal Thomas. AB, U. Mich., 1965, JD, 1968. Bar: Mich. 1968, U.S. Dist. Ct. (ea. dist.) Mich, 1968, U.S. Tax Ct. 1979, U.S. Supreme Ct. 1985. Assoc. Fischer, Franklin, Ford, Simon & Hogg, Detroit, 1969-73, ptnr., 1974-85, Houghton, Potter, Sweeney & Brenner, Detroit, 1986-95; mem. Clark Hill, Birmingham, Mich., 1995—, mem. exec. com., 1999—. Spkr. Inst. CLE. Contbr. articles to legal jours. Bd. dirs. Cmty. House Assn., 1990-98, pres. 1993-95; mem. Birmingham (Mich.) Charter Rev. Commn., 1977; trustee Baldwin Pub. Libr., Birmingham, 1981—. Mem. ABA, Oakland County Bar Assn. (chmn. taxation com. 1988-89), Forest Hills Swim Club (pres. 1985-87). Roman Catholic. Probate, Estate taxation, Taxation, general. Home: 1493 Buckingham Ave Birmingham MI 48009-5866 Office: Clark Hill 255 S Old Woodward Ave Ste 301 Birmingham MI 48009-6182 E-mail: tsweeney@clarkhill.com

SWEET, LOWELL ELWIN, lawyer, writer; b. Flint, Mich., Aug. 10, 1931; s. Leslie E. and Donna Mabel (Latta) S.; m. Mary Ellen Ebben, Aug. 29, 1953; children: Lawrence Edward, Diane Marie, Sara Anne. BA in Psychology, Wayne State U., 1953; LLB, U. Wis., 1955. Bar: Wis. 1955, U.S. Dist. Ct. (ea. dist.) Wis. 1955, U.S. Dist. Ct. (no. dist.) Ill. 1958. Ptnr. Morrissy, Morrisy, Sweet & Race and predecessor firms, Elkhorn, Wis.,

1957-70; ptnr., pres. Sweet & Reddy, 1970-01. Instr. gen. practice sect. U. Wis. Law Sch., 1978, 79, 86, 90; lectr. real estate law Wis. Bar, Gateway Tech., Carthage Coll. Inst., 1974—. Author: Phased Condominiums for Matthew Bender, 1992; co-editor: Condominiuim Law Handbook, 1981, 93; mem. editl. bd. Workbook for Wis. Estate Planners, 1990. Mem. Walworth County Rep. com.; sect. Wis. Jt. Survey Commn. on Debt Mgmt. With CIC, U.S. Army, 1955-57. Named Outstanding Young Man of Am., Elkhorn Jaycees, 1966; recipient citation for svc. in drafting Wis. Condominium Law, Wis. Legislature, 1978. Fellow ABA, Wis. Law Found.; mem. Wis. Bar Assn. (gov. 1972-75, 91-93, 99-01), Walworth County Bar Assn., Am. Judicature Soc., The Best Lawyers in Am., Am. Coll. Real Estate Lawyers, Kiwanis, Lions, Moose, KC. General corporate, Probate, Real property. Home: 830 Hazel Ridge Rd #1103 Elkhorn WI 53121-1624 Office: Law Office of Lowell E Sweet SC 114 N Church St Elkhorn WI 53121-1202

SWEET, ROBERT WORKMAN, federal judge; b. Yonkers, N.Y., Oct. 15, 1922; s. James Allen and Delia (Workman) S.; m. Adele Hall, May 12, 1973; children by previous marriage— Robert, Deborah, Ames, Eliza. B.A., Yale U., 1944, LL.B., 1948. Bar: N.Y. 1949. Asso. firm Simpson, Thacher & Bartlett, 1948-53; asst. U.S. atty. So. Dist. N.Y., 1953-55; asso. firm Casey, Lane & Mittendorf, 1955-65, partner, 1957-65; counsel Interdepartmental Task Force on Youth and Juvenile Delinquency, 1958-78; dep. mayor City of N.Y., 1966-69; partner firm Skadden, Arps, Slate, Meagher & Flom, N.Y.C., 1970-77; mem. hearing office N.Y.C. Transit Authority, 1975-77; U.S. dist. judge So. Dist. N.Y., N.Y.C., 1978—. Participant USIA Rule of Law Program in Albania, 1991; observer Albanian elections, 1992. Pres. Community Service Soc., 1961-78; trustee Sch. Mgmt. Urban Policy, 1970— , Taft Sch.; vestryman St. Georges Epis. Ch., 1958-63. Served to lt. (j.g.) USNR, 1943-46. Recipient Alumni citation of merit Taft Sch., 1985, various other awards, citations for service as dept mayor N.Y.C. Mem. ABA, Assn. of Bar of City of N.Y., N.Y. Law Inst., N.Y. County Lawyers Assn., State Bar Assn., Am. Legion (comdr. Willard Straight Post) Clubs: Quaker Hill Country, Century Assn., Merchants, Indian Harbor Yacht, Mid City Rep.

SWENDIMAN, ALAN ROBERT, lawyer; b. Arlington, Va., Apr. 5, 1947; s. Robert Charles and Jessie (Birse) S.; m. Kathleen Shea, Oct. 8, 1977; children: Shelley Christine, Robert Alan. AB in Polit. Sci., U. N.C., 1969; JD, Georgetown U., 1973. Bar: Md. 1973, D.C. 1974, U.S. Dist. Ct. D.C. 1974, U.S. Dist. Ct. Md. 1974, U.S. Ct. Appeals (D.C. cir.) 1974, U.S. Ct. Appeals (4th cir.) 1974, U.S. Supreme Ct. 1980. Law clk. to chief judge U.S. Dist. Ct. Md., 1973-74; ptnr. Jackson & Campbell, Washington, 1974-92, 93—, mng. ptnr., 1989-90; gen. counsel Fed. Labor Rels. Authority, 1992-93. Edn. appeal bd. Dept. Edn., 1982—90; gen. counsel Legal Svcs. Corp., Washington, 1983—84; adj. prof. George Mason Law Sch., 1988—91; mem. White House Presdl. Personnel, 1989. Gen. counsel Nat. Capital Cmty. Found.; past chmn. bd. Columbia Lighthouse for the Blind; chmn. bd. Boy Scouts NCAC, Jr. Achievement; dep. site coord. inaugural Md. Reagan-Bush Campaign, 1985; elder Presbyn. Ch., Kensington, Md.; bd. trustees Goodwill Industries. Mem. D.C. Bar Assn., Md. Bar Assn., Montgomery County Bar Assn., Jud. Conf. D.C. Cir., Greater Washington Bd. Trade, Nat. Assn. Corp. Dirs., U. N.C. Alumni Assn., Barristers Club, Counsellors Club, Rotary, Phi Beta Kappa, Phi Eta Sigma. Non-profit and tax-exempt organizations, Estate planning, Probate. Office: Jackson & Campbell PC 1120 20th St NW Ste 300S Washington DC 20036-3437 E-mail: aswendiman@jackscamp.com

SWERDLOFF, DAVID ALAN, lawyer; b. Buffalo, Sept. 19, 1948; s. John and Joan (Harris) S.; m. Shelley Ann Taylor, Oct. 6, 1974; children: Joan Taylor, Laura Taylor, Carolyn Taylor. AB, Brown U., 1970; MS, Northwestern U., 1974; JD, U. Conn., 1979. Bar: Conn. 1979, U.S. Dist. Ct. Conn. 1981. Assoc. Day, Berry & Howard, Hartford, Conn., 1979-83, Stamford, 1983-86, ptnr., 1986—. Sec., bd. dirs. Teen Life Ctr. Inc., Stamford, 1984-89. Bd. dirs. Vol. Ctr., Stamford, 1991-97, Sr. Svcs. of Stamford, 1998—, Stamford Mus. and Nature Ctr., 2000—. Mem. ABA, Conn. Bar Assn. (exec. com. sect. on corps. and other bus. ogrns. 1988—), Stamford Region Bar Assn. (chmn. bus. law com. 1989-91, treas. 1994-95, sec. 1995-96, v.p. 1996-98, pres. 1998-99). Contracts commercial, General corporate. Home: 87 Alexandra Dr Stamford CT 06903-1731 Office: Day Berry & Howard 1 Canterbury Grn Ste 7 Stamford CT 06901-2047 E-mail: dswerdloff@dbh.com

SWERDLOFF, ILEEN POLLOCK, lawyer; b. Bronx, N.Y., July 15, 1945; d. Seymour Pollock and Selma (Goldin) Feinstein; m. Mark Harris Swerdloff, Dec. 24, 1967; 1 child, Jonathan Edward. BA, SUNY, 1967; JD, Western New Eng. Sch. of Law, 1978. Bar: Conn. 1979, U.S. Dist. Ct. Conn. 1981, U.S. Supreme Ct. 1985. Mng. ptnr. Swerdloff & Swerdloff, West Hartford, Conn., 1980—. Sec. Chrysalis Ctr., Hartford, Conn., 1988-91, pres., 1991-92. Mem. Am. Bar Assn., Conn. Bar Assn., Hartford County Bar Assn., Hartford Assn. Women Attys. Jewish. Avocations: knitting, aerobics. Consumer commercial, Family and matrimonial, General practice. Home: 9 Beacon Heath Farmington CT 06032-1524 Office: Swerdloff & Swerdloff 61 S Main St West Hartford CT 06107-2486

SWERDLOFF, MARK HARRIS, lawyer; b. Buffalo, Sept. 7, 1945; s. John and Joan (Harris) S.; m. Ileen Pollock, Dec. 24, 1967; 1 child, Jonathan Edward. BA, SUNY, Buffalo, 1967; JD, U. Conn., 1975. Bar: Conn. 1975, U.S. Dist. Ct. Conn. 1975, U.S. Ct. Appeals (2d cir.) 1983, U.S. Supreme Ct. 1985, Fla. 1977. Assoc. Wilson, Asbel & Channin, Hartford, Conn., 1975-78; ptnr. Swerdloff & Swerdloff, West Hartford, 1978—. Pres. Arpus Enterprises, Old Saybrook Conn., 1993—; trial fact finder Superior Ct., Hartford, 1990—; arbitrator Dispute Resolution Inst., Hartford, 1990—. Mem. ABA, Conn. Bar Assn., Conn. Trial Lawyers Assn. Democrat. Jewish. Avocations: photography, travel, cooking. General civil litigation, Family and matrimonial, Personal injury. Home: 9 Beacon Heath Farmington CT 06032-1524 Office: Swerdloff & Swerdloff 61 S Main St West Hartford CT 06107-2486 E-mail: mhsips@mindspring.com

SWERLING, JACK BRUCE, lawyer; b. N.Y.C., May 30, 1946; s. Benjamin Fidel and Jeanette (Fidler) S.; m. Erika Andrea Helfer, Jan. 17, 1970; children: Bryan, Stephanie. BA, Clemson U., 1968; JD, U. S.C., 1973. Bar: S.C. 1973, U.S. Dist. Ct. S.C. 1973, U.S. Ct. Appeals (4th cir.) 1974, U.S. Supreme Ct. 1978. Ptnr. Law Firm of Isadore Lourie, Columbia, S.C., 1973-83, Swerling, Harpootlian & McCulloch, Columbia, 1983-92; pvt. practice, 1992—. Mem. Pre-Trial Intervention Adv. Com., 1980-82; mem. adv. com. Child Victim Ct. Notebook divsn. Pub. Safety Programs, 1987; mem. S.C. Bd. Law Examiners, 1987-92, S.C. Bd. Grievances and Discipline, 1994-97; adj. prof. U. S.C. Sch. Law, Columbia, 1986—; clin. prof. dept. Neuropsychiatry Sch. Medicine, 1988—; mem. S.C. Supreme Ct. com. on model criminal jury instructions, chmn. bule ribbon task force criminal docketing com. Author: South Carolina Criminal Trial Notebook, 1991; co-author: Criminal Trial Advocacy; contbr. articles to profl. jours. Co-pres. Jewish Cmty. Ctr., Columbia, 1977. Fellow Am. Coll. Trial Lawyers, Am. Acad. Appellate Lawyers, Am. Bd. Criminal Lawyers, S.C. Bar Found.; mem. ABA, ATLA, Am. Judicature Soc., Nat. Assn. Criminal Def. Lawyers, S.C. Trial Lawyers Assn. (chmn. criminal law sect. 1979-82), S.C. Bar Assn. (chmn. criminal law sect. 1985-86), Richland County Bar Assn. (chmn. criminal law sect. 1988-89). Democrat. Jewish. Avocation: shooting sporting clays. Criminal. Office: 1720 Main St Ste 301 Columbia SC 29201-2850

SWETNAM, DANIEL RICHARD, lawyer; b. Columbus, Ohio, Dec. 22, 1957; s. Joseph Neri and Audrey Marguerite (Mason) S.; m. Jeannette Deanna Dean, June 7, 1980; children: Jeremiah Daniel, Laura Janelle, Andrew Michael. BA, Ohio State U., 1979; JD, U. Cin., 1982. Bar: Ohio 1982, U.S. Dist. Ct. (so. dist.) Ohio 1982, U.S. Ct. Appeals (6th cir.) 1986, U.S. Supreme Ct. 1986. Assoc. Schwartz, Warren & Ramirez, Columbus, 1982-88, ptnr., 1989-96; prin. Schottenstein, Zox & Dunn, 1997—. Deacon Grace Brethren Ch., Worthington, Ohio, 1989—; mem. Grace Brethren Christian Schs. Commn., 1993-98. Mem. ABA, Ohio State Bar Assn., Columbus Bar Assn., Comml. Law League Am., Order of Coif. Republican. Avocations: golf, tennis. Bankruptcy, General civil litigation. Home: 2178 Stowmont Ct Dublin OH 43016-9563 Office: Schottenstein Zox & Dunn 41 S High St Columbus OH 43215-6101

SWIBEL, STEVEN WARREN, lawyer; b. Chgo., July 18, 1946; s. Morris Howard and Gloria S.; m. Leslie S.; children: Deborah, Laura. BS, MIT, 1968; JD, Harvard U., 1971. Bar: Ill. 1971, U.S. Dist. Ct. (no. dist.) Ill. 1971, U.S. Tax Ct. 1973, U.S. Ct. Appeals (7th cir.) 1981. Assoc. Sonnenschein Carlin Nath & Rosenthal, Chgo., 1971-78, ptnr., 1978-84, Rudnick & Wolfe, 1984-93, Schwartz, Cooper, Greenberger, Krauss Chartered, Chgo., 1993—. Adj. prof. taxation Ill. Inst. Tech. Kent Coll. Law, Chgo., 1989—; lectr. in field; contbr. articles to profl. jours. Ednl. counselor MIT, 1979—; bd. dirs. MIT Alumni Fund, 1992-95, Ragdale Found., 1987-00, treas, 1987-92; bd. dirs. Kids In Danger, 1998—. Recipient Lobdell Disting. Svc. award MIT Alumni Assn., 1989. Mem. ABA (com. partnerships sect. taxation), Ill. Bar Assn., Chgo. Bar Assn. (fed. taxation com., exec. subcom. 1984—, chmn. subcom. on real estate and partnerships 1986-87, vice-chmn. 1988-89, chmn. 1990), Met. Club, MIT Club (dir. Chgo. chpt. 1980-91, 96—, sec. 1980-87, pres. 1987-89), Sigma Xi, Tau Beta Pi, Eta Kappa Nu. General corporate, Corporate taxation, Personal income taxation. Office: Schwartz Cooper Greenberger & Krauss Chartered 180 N La Salle St Ste 2700 Chicago IL 60601-2757 E-mail: swibel@alum.mit.edu

SWIFT, AUBREY EARL, lawyer, petroleum engineer; b. Tulsa, Sept. 21, 1933; s. Virgil and Edith (Jackson) S.; m. Modell Paulding, Oct. 5, 1951 (div.); children: Terry Earl, Vannessa Suzanne; m. Glenda Kay Arnce, Apr. 8, 1978 (div.); 1 son, Nickolas Gorman. BS in Petroleum Engring., U. Okla., 1955; JD, S. Tex. Coll. Law, 1968; MBA, Pepperdine U., 1988. Bar: Tex. 1968, U.S. Supreme Ct. 1977. Petroleum engr. Humble Oil Co. div. Exxon, Houston, 1955-62; v.p. Mich.-Wis. Pipe Line, Houston, 1962-79, Am. Natural Gas Prodn., Houston, 1962-79; pres., chmn., chief exec. officer Swift Energy Co., Houston, 1979— ; cons. Northwest Ala. Gas Dist., Hamilton, 1979—. Served to 1st lt. U.S. Army, 1956-57. Mem. Tex. Soc. Profl. Engrs., Soc. Petroleum Engrs. AIME, Order of Lytae, Tau Beta Pi. Presbyterian. General corporate, Oil, gas, and mineral.

SWIFT, JOHN GOULDING, lawyer; b. Lake Charles, La., Nov. 12, 1955; s. Goulding William Jr. and Betty Jane (Richardson) S.; m. Jan Lynette Whitehead. BS, La. State U., 1977, JD, 1980. Bar: La. 1980, U.S. Dist. Ct. (we. dist.) La. 1982, U.S. Ct. Appeals (5th cir.) 1983, U.S. Dist. Ct. (mid. dist.) La. 1985, U.S. Dist. Ct. (ea. dist.) Tex. 1986, U.S. Dist. Ct. (ea. dist.) La. 1986, U.S. Ct. Appeals (4th cir.) 1992, U.S. Supreme Ct. 1997. Law clk. to presiding justice U.S. Dist. Ct. (we. dist.) La., Lake Charles, 1980-81; assoc. Davidson, Meaux, Sonnier, McElligott & Swift, Lafayette, La., 1981-85, ptnr., 1985-89, sr. ptnr., 1990—2001; ptnr. Swift & Rhoades L.L.P., 2001—. Mem. Gulf Coast Conservation Assn.; bd. dirs. Hidden Hills Cmty., Inc., 1987-93, pres., 1989-93; bd. dirs. Lafayette Parish unit Am. Cancer Soc., 1992-99, pres., 1996-97, bd. dirs. La. divsn., 1995-96; youth dir., mem. adminstrv. bd. Meth. Ch., 1992-93, chair staff-parish rels. com., 1996, mem. adminstrv. bd., 1996, 98, 99, trustee, 1996-98, chair, 1998. Mem. ABA, La. Bar Assn. (com. to study permanent disarmanent, ho. of dels. 1996—), La. Def. Counsel, La. Bar Found. (bd. dirs. 1997—, sec., treas. 2000—), Assn. Def. Trial Attys., Lafayette Parish Bar Assn. (bd. dirs. 1988-95, pres. 1993-94), 15th Jud. Dist. Bar Assn. (pres. 1993-94), La. State U. Alumni Fedn., Ducks Unltd., Kiwanis (Acadiana chpt. 1989-95), Acadiana Inns of Ct. Republican. Avocations: running, fishing, hunting. General civil litigation, Insurance, Product liability. Home: 105 Oakwater Dr Lafayette LA 70503-2227 Office: Swift & Rhoades LLP PO Box 53107 Lafayette LA 70505 E-mail: jswift@swiftrhoades.com

SWIFT, STEPHEN CHRISTOPHER, lawyer; b. N.Y.C., Jan. 7, 1954; s. James Stephen and Rhoda Emma Jean (Howd) S. AA, Lansing C.C., 1980; BA, Mich. State U., 1983; JD, Wayne State U., 1988. Bar: Mich. 1988, Hawaii 1989, D.C. 1991, Va. 1995, Md. 1998, U.S. Dist. Ct. D.C. 1997, U.S. Dist. Ct. Md. 1998, U.S. Dist. Ct. (ea. and we. dists.) Va. 1995, U.S. Dist. Ct. Hawaii 1989, U.S. Ct. Fed. Claims 1990, U.S. Ct. Internat. Trade 2000, U.S. Bankruptcy Ct. (ea. and we. dists.) Va. 1995, U.S. Tax Ct. 1997, U.S. Ct. Appeals (fed., D.C., 9th cirs.) 1990, U.S. Ct. Appeals (4th cir.) 1995, U.S. Supreme Ct. 1992; registered patent atty. 1994. Pvt. practice, Honolulu, Hawaii, 1989-94, Arlington, Va., 1995—. Mem. ABA, Fed. Bar Assn., Fed. Cir. Bar Assn., Am. Intellectual Property Law Assn. Intellectual property, Patent, Trademark and copyright. Office: Swift Law Office 2231 Crystal Dr Ste 500 Arlington VA 22202-3736 Fax: 703-418-1895. E-mail: steve@swift-law.com

SWIFT, STEPHEN JENSEN, federal judge; b. Salt Lake City, Sept. 7, 1943; s. Edward A. and Maurine (Jensen) S.; m. Lorraine Burnell Facer, Aug. 4, 1972; children: Carter, Stephanie, Spencer, Meredith, Hunter. BS, Brigham Young U., 1967; JD, George Washington U., 1970. Trial atty. U.S. Dept. Justice, Washington, 1970-74; asst. U.S. atty. U.S. Atty.'s Office, San Francisco, 1974-77; v.p., sr. tax counsel Bank Am. N.T. & S.A., 1977-83; judge U.S. Tax Ct., Washington, 1983—. Adj. prof. Golden Gate U., San Francisco, 1976-83, U. Balt., 1987—. Mem. ABA, Calif. Bar Assn., D.C. Bar Assn. Office: US Tax Ct 400 2nd St NW Washington DC 20217-0002

SWITZER, FREDERICK MICHAEL, III, lawyer, arbitrator, mediator; b. St. Louis, Sept. 7, 1933; s. Frederick Michael Jr. and Viola Marie (Bardenheier) S.; m. Suzanne Elizabeth Reichardt, Aug. 28, 1970. BA cum laude, U. Notre Dame, 1956; JD, Washington U., 1959, LLM, 1972. Bar: Mo. 1959, U.S. Ct. Mil. Appeals 1960, U.S. Supreme Ct. 1962, U.S. Dist. Ct. (ea. dist.) Mo. 1993, U.S. Tax Ct. 1974, U.S. Ct. Appeals (8th cir.) 1978, U.S. Dist. Ct. (we. dist.) Mo. 1992, U.S. Ct. Appeals (4th cir.) 1994. Assoc. Switzer, Barnes & Toney, St. Louis, 1963-65, ptnr., 1965-75, Fordyce & Mayne, St. Louis, 1975-87, Coburn Croft, St. Louis, 1987-92, Danna, McKitrick, P.C., St. Louis, 1992—. Dir. Bardenheier Wine Co., St. Louis, 1983-85; instr. St. Louis Univ., 1971-72. Pres., dir. St. Louis Industry Adv. Group, 1971-90; dir. St. Louis Abbey Sch. Soc., 1975—; mem. employee benefits adv. com. City of Ladue (Mo.), 1980—, St. Louis Indsl. Rsch. Assn., 1991—; secr., dir. Citizens for Mo.'s Children, St. Louis, 1986-91; adv. bd. Am. Youth Found., St. Louis, 1989—, pres. Friends of Am. Youth Found., 2000—. Capt. USNR, 1959-63. Recipient Mitchell award for playwriting, Univ. Notre Dame, 1959. Mem. ABA (labor employment section, equal employment opportunity law com., immigration law com., litig. section, gen. practice section), Assn. Atty. Mediators, Mo. Bar Assn. (labor law com., chmn. mil. law com. 1969-71, bar jour. com.), St. Louis Bar Assn. (labor law com.), Assn. Trial Lawyers Am., Strathalbyn Farms Club (past dir., past asst. secr.), Phi Delta Phi. Republican. Roman Catholic. Avocations: sailing, equestrian, tennis. Alternative dispute resolution, General civil litigation, Labor. Office: Danna McKitrick PC 150 N Meramec Ave Fl 4 Saint Louis MO 63105-3779 E-mail: fswitzer@dmfirm.com

SWOPE, RICHARD MCALLISTER, retired lawyer; b. West Chester, Pa., Apr. 19, 1940; s. Charles Seigel and Edna McPherson (McAllister) S.; m. Karen Diane Glass, Aug. 24, 1963 (div. 1972). BS in Edn., Bucknell U., 1962; LLB cum laude, Washington and Lee U., 1968. Bar: Va. 1968. Ret., 1998. Instr. Nat. Inst. Trial Advocacy, 1982-86. Mem. Virginia Beach Beautification Commn.; bd. dirs. Virginia Beach Orchestral Assn., 1982-88; v.p., bd. dirs. Swope Found., West Chester, Pa., 1961—; v.p. Swope Scholarship Found. Capt. USMC, 1962-65. Mem. Va. Assn. Def. Attys. (bd. dirs. 1975-78, 88-90), Va. State Bar Assn., Norfolk/Portsmouth Bar Assn., Virginia Beach Bar Assn., Virginia Beach C. of C., Rotary (pres. 1982, Paul Harris fellow). Avocation: golf. Civil rights, General civil litigation, Insurance. Home: 936 Poquoson Cir Virginia Beach VA 23452-4646 Office: 936 Poquoson Cir Virginia Beach VA 23452-4646

SWYGERT, MICHAEL I(RVEN), legal educator; b. Hammond, Ind., Nov. 20, 1939; s. Luther Merrit and Mildren (Kercher) S.; m. Dianne Margaret Jeffrey, Sept. 2, 1961; children— Jeffrey Michael, Gregory Robert. Student Carleton Coll., 1958-60; A.B. cum laude, Valparaiso U., 1965, J.D. summa cum laude, 1967; LL.M., Yale U., 1968. Bar: Ill. 1967, U.S. Dist. Ct. (no. dist.) Ill. 1969, U.S. Ct. Appeals (7th cir.) 1971, U.S. Ct. Appeals (D.C. cir.) 1971. Assoc. Hopkins, Sutter, Owen, Mulroy, Wentz & Davis, Chgo., 1968-70; asst. prof., asst. dean Sch. Law Valparaiso (Ind.) U., 1969-72; prof. law DePaul U., Chgo., 1972-80, Stetson U., St. Petersburg, Fla., 1980— ; vis. prof. law Cambridge U., Eng., 1986-87, Emory U., Atlanta, 1988-89; mediator, conciliator Ind. Employment Relations Bd., Indpls., 1974— , hearing officer, 1974-79; lectr. Sch. Pub. Affairs, Ind. U., Gary, 1974-78. Co-author, editor Maximizing the Law School Experience, 1983; co-author The Legal Handbook of Business Transactions, 1987. Contbg. author Creditor Rights, 1974. Vol. atty. Ch. Fedn. Chgo., 1968-70. Recipient Homer and Dolly Hand Award for Excellence in Rsch., 1988. Mem. ABA, Am. Law Inst., Soc. Profls. in Dispute Resolution, Chgo. Bar Assn., Ill. Bar Assn., Am. Arbitration Assn. (arbitrator), Phi Alpha Delta. Presbyterian. Home: 2600 70th Ave S Saint Petersburg FL 33712-5639 Office: 1301 61st Ave N Saint Petersburg FL 33703-1042

SYKES, DIANE S. state supreme court justice; b. Milw. children: Jay, Alexander. B, Northwestern U., 1980; JD, Marquette U., 1984. Reporter Milw. Jour.; law clk. to Hon. Terence T. Evans; assoc. Whyte & Hirschboeck S.C.; judge Milw. County Ct., 1992, Wis. Supreme Ct., Madison, 1999—. Office: Wis Supreme Ct PO Box 1688 Madison WI 53702*

SYLVER, PETER T. lawyer; b. Queens, N.Y., Oct. 25, 1968; s. Alebis R. and Dolores M. Sylver. BS, John Jay Coll., 1994; JD, Hofstra U., 1997. Law clk. to Judge C. Blacksheer U.S. Dist. Ct. (so. dist.) N.Y., 1997-98; assoc. Kramer, Levin, Naftalis & Frankel, LLP, N.Y.C., 1998—. Author: Native Son: A Critique, 1993 (award 1993). Counsel Hale House, N.Y.C., 1998. Mem. Nat. Bar Assn., N.Y. State Bar Assn., Assn. of Bar of City of N.Y. Bankruptcy, General corporate. Office: Kramer Levin Naftalis & Frankel LLP 919 3d Ave New York NY 10022

SYLVESTER, TORREY ALDEN, lawyer; b. Waterville, Maine, Nov. 10, 1936; s. Fred A. and Erma R. (Allen) S.; m. Jennifer O. Fusedale, Mar. 2, 1963; children: Steven, Samuel, Susannah, Linda. BA, U. Maine, 1959, LLB, 1970. Bar: Maine 1970, U.S. Dist. Ct. Maine, 1970. Assoc. Rudman Rudman & Carter, Bangor, Maine, 1970-73; ptnr. Barnes & Sylvester, Houlton, Maine, 1973-86, sole practice, 1986—. Served with USNR, 1959-64, to capt. USN, 1965-86. Mem. Assn. Trial Lawyers Am., Maine Trial Lawyers Assn., U. Maine Alumni Assn. (chmn. nat. fund drive 1978-80). Republican. Baptist. Lodges: Rotary, Masons. Avocations: walking, writing, golf, barbershop quartet singing., skiing. General civil litigation, Personal injury, Workers' compensation. Office: 64 Main St Houlton ME 04730-2119

SYVERUD, KENT DOUGLAS, dean; b. Rochester, N.Y., Oct. 23, 1956; s. Warren Lukken and Janet (Thatcher) S.l; m. Ruth Chi-Fen Chen, May 22, 1982; children: Steven, Brian, David. BSFS, Georgetown U., 1977; JD, U. Mich., 1981, MA, 1983. Bar: D.C. 1982, Mich. 1993. Law clk. to Judge Oberdorfer U.S. Dist. Ct. D.C., Washington, 1983-84; law clk. Justice O'Connor Supreme Ct. U.S., 1984-85; assoc. Wilmer, Cutler & Pickering, 1985-97; exec. sec. Mich. Law Revision Commn., Lansing, 1993-95; prof. U. Mich. Law Sch., Ann Arbor, 1987-97; dean, Garner Anthony prof. Vanderbilt U. Law Sch., Nashville, 1997—. Chair exec. com. Inst. for Continuing Legal Edn., Ann Arbor, 1995-97. Mem. Am. Law Inst., Law and Soc. Assn. Office: Vanderbilt Law Sch 21st Ave S Nashville TN 37240-0001*

SZABO, ELIZABETH MARYANN, lawyer; b. Passaic, N.J. d. William Guy and Stasia (Siejwa) S. BA cum laude, Wilson Coll., 1976; JD, N.Y.U., 1986. Bar: N.J. 1988, U.S. Dist. Ct. N.J. 1988, Pa. 1988, N.Y. 1991, U.S. Dist. Ct. (ea. dist.) N.Y. 1991, U.S. Dist. Ct. (so. dist.) N.Y. 1991, U.S. Supreme Ct. 1994. Asst. dir. Multistate Legal Studies, N.Y.C., 1986-90; pvt. practice, 1991—. Arbitrator Small Claims Ct., Civil Ct. City of N.Y., 1997—; columnist Immigration Law, Asenta Newspaper, 1997—, Weekly Bengalee, 1994-96, India Horizons, 1995. Fundraiser Campaign for Coun. Woman Jenny Lim, N.Y.C., 1997. Mem. Nat. Lawyers Guild (exec. com. 1996-98, sec. N.Y. chpt. 1996-99, lectr. immigration law), N.Y. County Lawyers Assn. (consumer bankruptcy com. 1994-98, immigration com. 1994-98, Pro Bono award 1994, 95), N.Y. State Bar Assn. (public interest com. 1995-97), Small Claims Arbitrators Assn., Fed. Bar Assn. Democrat. Episcopalian. Avocations: photography, poetry, painting, acting. Office: 401 Broadway Ste 605 New York NY 10013-3005

SZALKOWSKI, CHARLES CONRAD, lawyer; b. Amarillo, Tex., Apr. 14, 1948; s. Chester Casimer and Virginia Lee Szalkowski; m. Jane Howe, Dec. 28, 1971; children: Jennifer Lee, Stephen Claude. BA, BS in Acctg., Rice U., 1971; MBA, JD, Harvard U., 1975. Bar: Tex. 1975. Assoc. Baker Botts L.L.P., Houston, 1975-82, ptnr., 1983—. Speaker in field. Chmn. ann. fund campaign Rice U., Houston, 1991-93, chmn. Fund Coun., 1995-96; chmn. adminstrv. bd. St. Luke's United Meth. Ch., Houston, 1994, chmn. bd. trustees, 1997; vice chmn. DePelchin Children's Ctr., Houston, 1998—; bd. dirs. Meth. Children's Home, Waco, MIT Enterprise Forum of Tex., Houston. Mem. ABA (fed. regulation of securities com.), Am. Law Inst., State Bar Tex. (chmn. bus. law sect. 1991-92), Houston Bar Assn. (chmn., corp. counsel sect. 1989-90), Harvard Law Sch. Assn. Tex. (pres. 1983-84), Tex. Bus. Law Found. (bd. dirs., exec. com. 1988—, chmn. 1998-2000), Assn. Rice U. Alumni (bd. dirs. 1999—, chmn. various coms. 1981-86), Assn. for Corp. Growth (bd. dirs., Houston chpt.), Houston Philos. Soc. General corporate, Mergers and acquisitions, Securities. Office: Baker Botts LLP 1 Shell Plz 910 Louisiana St Ste 3000 Houston TX 77002-4991

SZALLER, JAMES FRANCIS, lawyer; b. Cleve., Jan. 22, 1945; s. Frank Paul and Ellen Grace (O'Malley) S.; m. Roberta Mae Curtin, Oct. 23, 1967 (div. Aug. 1975); m. Charlene Nancy Smith, Apr. 28, 1984. AA, Cuyahoga Community Coll., 1967; BA, Cleve. State U., 1970, JD cum laude, 1975. Bar: Ohio 1975, U.S. Dist. Ct. (no. dist.) Ohio 1975, U.S. Supreme Ct. 1982, U.S. Ct. Appeals (6th cir.) 1983, U.S. Ct. Appeals (4th cir.) 1986. Assoc. Metzenbaum, Gaines & Stern, Cleve., 1975-79; sr. ptnr. Brown & Szaller Co., L.P.A., 1979—. Lectr. law Cleve. State U., 1977-81. Mem. editorial bd. Cleve. State U. Law Rev., 1973-75.; contbr. articles to profl. jours. Mem. Ohio State Bar Assn., Greater Cleve. Bar Assn., Cleve. Acad.

Trial Lawyers, Ohio Acad. Trial Lawyers (Disting. Svc. award 1996), Assn. Trial Lawyers Am., Nat. Coll. Advocacy (advocate). Democrat. Roman Catholic. Avocations: gourmet cooking, automobile racing. General civil litigation, Personal injury. Office: Brown & Szaller Co LPA 14222 Madison Ave Cleveland OH 44107-4510 E-mail: szaller@lawandhelp.com

SZECSODI, ZSOLT, lawyer, consultant; b. Kecskemét, Hungary; s. György and Györgyné Szecsödi. Degree in law, U. Budapest, 1998, postgrad., 2000—, U. Tours, France, 1999. Legal intern ABA CEELI program, Budapest, 1997-98; assoc. Burai-Kovács & Ptnrs., mem. Andersenlegal, 1998—. Mem. Budapest Bar Assn. General corporate, Labor, Real property. Office: Burai-Kovács & Ptnrs Váci ut 35 1134 Budapest Hungary Fax: 36-1-451-7179. E-mail: zsolt.szecsodi@hu.andersenlegal.com

SZUCH, CLYDE ANDREW, lawyer; b. Bluefield, W.Va., Nov. 22, 1930; s. Nicholas and Aranka (Rubin) S.; m. Rosalie Hirschman Wulfson, Sept. 5, 1954; children: Peter Alan, Richard Coleman. BA, Rutgers, 1952; LLB, Harvard U., 1955. Bar: N.J. 1955, U.S. Dist. Ct. N.J. 1955, U.S. Ct. Appeals (3rd cir.) 1958, U.S. Supreme Ct. 1962. Law clk. to assoc. justice William J. Brennan Jr. U.S. Supreme Ct., Washington, 1956-57; asst. U.S. atty. U.S. Attys. Office, Newark, 1957-58; assoc. Pitney, Hardin & Kipp, 1958-62; ptnr. Pitney, Hardin, Kipp & Szuch, Morristown, N.J., 1962-2000, of counsel, 2001—. Mem. panel Ctr. for Pub. Resources, N.J.; bd. dirs. Vt. Rlwy. Inc., Clarendon & Pittsford R.R. Co., Burlington, Vt., Brennan Ctr. for Justice; panelist AAA Large Complex Cases. Gov. N.J. region Nat. Conf. for Comty. and Justice. Fellow Am. Bar Found.; mem. ABA, Am. Law Inst., N.J. State Bar Assn., Morris County Bar Assn., Essex County Bar Assn., Fed. Bar Assn. (N.J. chpt.), N.J. C. of C. (bd. dirs.), Nat. Legal Aid Defender Assn., Hist. Soc. U.S. Ct. Appeals for 3d Cir. Federal civil litigation, General civil litigation, State civil litigation. Office: Pitney Hardin Kipp & Szuch PO Box 1945 Morristown NJ 07962-1945

SZWALBENEST, BENEDYKT JAN, lawyer; b. Poland, June 13, 1955; s. Sidney and Janina (Bleishtif) S.; m. Shelley Joy Leibel, Nov. 8, 1981. BBA, Temple U., 1978, JD, 1981. Law clk. Fed. Deposit Ins. Corp., Washington, 1980; law clk. to presiding justice U.S. Dist. Ct. (ea. dist.) Pa., Phila., 1980-81; staff atty., regulatory specialist Fidelcor, Inc. and Fidelity Bank, 1981-86; regulations specialist sr. regulatory staff Fed. Res. Bank of N.Y., N.Y.C., 1986-89; s.v.p. regulatory compliance, sec. Custodial Trust Co. subs. Bear Stearns, Princeton, 1990—; mng. dir. Bear Stearns & Co., Inc., 1998—. Author: Federal Bank Regulation, 1980. Mem. Commonwealth of Pa. Post-secondary Edn. Planning Commn., Harrisburg, 1977-79; trustee Pop Warners Little Scholars, Phila., 1981-86. Recipient E. Gerald Corrigan Pres.'s Award for Excellence, 1988. Mem. ABA (nat. sec., treas. law student div. 1980-81, Silver Key award 1980, Gold Key award 1981), Am. Judicature Soc., Am. Bankers Assn. (cert. compliance specialist, lectr. 1984—), Temple U. Sch. Bus. Alumni Assn. (sec. 1982-84, v.p. 1984-86, pres. 1986-88, bd. dirs. gen. alumni assn. 1986-88), Tau Epsilon Rho, Omicron Delta Epsilon. Avocations: baseball, tennis, skiing. Administrative and regulatory, Banking, Securities. Home: 1504 Brookfield Rd Yardley PA 19067-3930 Office: Custodial Trust Co 101 Carnegie Ctr Princeton NJ 08540-6231

TA, TAI VAN, lawyer, researcher; b. Ninh Binh, Vietnam, Apr. 16, 1938; came to U.S., 1975; s. Duong Van and Loan thi (Pham) T.; m. Lien-Nhu Tran, Oct. 26, 1967; children: Becky, John, Khuong Virginia, Dora. LLB, U. Saigon, Vietnam, 1960; MA, U. Va., 1964, PhD, 1965; LLM, Harvard U., 1985. Bar: Mass. 1986, U.S. Dist. Ct. Mass. 1987. Prof. U. Saigon Law Sch., 1965-75, Nat. Sch. Adminstrn., 1965-75; ptnr. Tang thi Thanh Trai & Ta Van Tai, 1968-75; legal rschr. Reed Smith Shaw & McClay, Pitts., 1975; rsch. assoc. Harvard U. Law Sch., Cambridge, Mass., 1975—, adj. lectr., 1998—; pvt. practice, Brookline, 1986—; rsch. scholar NYU Law Sch., N.Y.C., 1990-94. Cons. Milbank Tweed Hadley & McCloy, N.Y.C., 1979, Shearman & Sterling, N.Y.C., 1979, Paul Weiss Rifkind Wharton and Garrison, N.Y.C., 1989, 90. Co-author: The Laws of Southeast Asia, 1986, The Le Code: Law in Traditional Vietnam, 1987, Investment Law in Vietnam, 1990; author: Vietnamese Tradition of Human Rights, 1988; contbr. articles to profl. jours. Commr. Mass. Govs. Asian-Am. Coun., 1992—. Fulbright scholar 1960-62; grantee Asia Found., 1972, Ford Found., 1975-76, Aspen Inst. 1993. Avocations: piano, swimming, foreign languages. Criminal, General practice, Private international. Home: 145 Naples Rd Brookline MA 02446-5748 Office: Harvard U Law Sch Pound 423 1563 Massachusetts Ave Cambridge MA 02138-2903

TAALMAN, JURI E. lawyer; b. Tartu, Estonia, Nov. 1, 1940; s. Aarne and Linda (Kutt) T.; m. Tania J. Taalman, June 1, 1944; children: Laura, Linda, Alina. BS in Math., U. Chgo.; JD, U. Conn. Bar: Conn. 1969, U.S. Dist. Ct. Conn. 1971, U.S. Supreme Ct. 1975, U.S. Ct. Appeals (2d cir.) 1996. Assoc., dir. Brown, Jacobson, Jewett & Laudone, P.C., Norwich, Conn., 1972-82; ptnr. Taalman & Phillips, Norwichtown, 1982-92; ABA liaison Republic of Estonia, 1993-94; lectr. law U. Tartu, 1994-95; USIA prof. in residence Supreme Ct. of Estonia, 1994-95; founder Estonian Law Ctr.; v.p. Parallax Group Internat., Glastonbury, Conn., 1996—. State civil litigation, General practice, Personal injury. Home: Cemetery Rd RR 1 Baltic CT 06330-9801 Office: Parallax Group Internat PO Box 1241 Glastonbury CT 06023-1241 E-mail: taalmans@aol.com

TABAK, MORRIS, lawyer; b. Warsaw, Poland, July 23, 1944; came to U.S. 1953, naturalized, 1957; s. Joseph Irving and Zina T. (Basista) T.; m. Karen Elaine Tomber, Aug. 31, 1969; children: Adam Jason, Jessica Lee, Joshua Paul. BS, Ind. U., 1970, JD magna cum laude, 1972. Bar: Ind. 1972, Tex. 1984. Assoc. Talesnick & Kleiman, Indpls., 1972-73; ptnr. Kilroy & Tabak, Indpls., 1973-74, Stivers & Tabak, Indpls., 1974-77; labor relations rep. Coastal Corp., Houston, 1978-82; atty., Alameda Corp., Houston, 1982-84; mem. Brochstein & Slobin, Houston, 1984-87; ptnr. F. Shaw & Assocs., Houston, 1987—. Bd. dirs. Beth El, Stafford, Tex., 1981— . Served with U.S. Spl. Forces, 1965-67, Vietnam. Named Ky. Col., 1982. Mem. Ind. Bar Assn., Harris Bar Assn., Tex. Bar Assn., Ft. Bend Bar Assn., Beta Gamma Sigma. Jewish. Clubs: Houston City, Sweetwater Country. Federal civil litigation, State civil litigation, Labor. Office: F Shaw & Assocs 6161 Savoy Dr Ste 1000 Houston TX 77036-3316

TABLER, BRYAN G. lawyer; b. Louisville, Jan. 12, 1943; s. Norman Gardner and Sarah Marie (Grant) T.; m. Susan Y. Beidler, Dec. 28, 1968 (div. June 1987); children: Justin Elizabeth, Gillian Gardner; m. Karen Sue Strome, July 24, 1987. AB, Princeton U., 1969; JD, Yale U., 1972. Bar: Ind. 1972, U.S. Dist. Ct. (so. dist.) Ind. 1972, U.S. Dist. Ct. (no. dist.) Ind. 1976, U.S. Ct. Appeals (7th cir.) 1976, U.S. Supreme Ct. 1976. Assoc. Barnes & Thornburg, Indpls., 1972-79, ptnr., chmn. environ. law dept., 1979-94; v.p., gen. counsel, sec. IPALCO Enterprises, Inc., 1994—; sr. v.p., gen. coun., sec. Indpls. Power & Light Co., 1994—. Mem. exec. com. Environ. Quality Control, Inc., Indpls., 1985-97. Mem. Indpls. Mus. of Art, 1972—; bd. dirs. Indpls. Symphony Orch., 1995—. 1st lt. U.S. Army, 1964-68, Vietnam. Mem. ABA, Ind. Bar Assn., Bar Assn. of the 7th Cir., Indpls. Bar Assn. Avocation: golf. Federal civil litigation, General corporate, Environmental. Home: 137 Willowgate Dr Indianapolis IN 46260-1471 Office: Indpls Power & Light Co One Monument PO Box 1595 Indianapolis IN 46206-1595

TACHA, DEANELL REECE, federal judge; b. Jan. 26, 1946; BA, U. Kans., 1968; JD, U. Mich., 1971. Spl. asst. to U.S. Sec. of Labor, Washington, 1971-72; assoc. Hogan & Hartson, 1973, Thomas J. Pitner, Concordia, Kans., 1973-74; dir. Douglas County Legal Aid Clinic, Lawrence, 1974-77; assoc. prof. law U. Kans., 1974-77, prof., 1977-85, assoc. dean, 1977-79, assoc. vice chancellor, 1979-81, vice chancellor, 1981-85; judge U.S. Ct. Appeals (10th cir.), Denver, 1985—; U.S. sentencing commr., 1994-98; chief judge U.S. Ct. Appeals (10th cir.), Denver, 2001—. Office: US Ct Appeals 10th Cir 643 Massachusetts St Ste301 Lawrence KS 66044-2292

TACHNA, RUTH C. lawyer, educator; b. N.Y.C. d. Max and Rose (Rosenblatt) T.; m. Paul Bauman (dec.); children: Leslie Bauman Levy, Lionel. BA, Cornell U., 1935; LLB cum laude, Bklyn. Law Sch., 1937. Bar: N.Y. 1938, Calif. 1978, U.S. Dist. Ct. (so. dist.) N.Y. 1966, U.S. Ct. Appeals (2d cir.) 1966, U.S. Supreme Ct. 1956. Founding atty. Legal Aid, Westchester, N.Y., 1960-64; sr. ptnr., of counsel Tachna & Krassner, White Plains, 1964—. Prof. law Northrop U. Sch. Law, L.A., 1977-85. Group mng. editor Matthew Bendor, N.Y.C., 1968-77. Staff atty., founder Legal Aid for Srs., Santa Monica, Calif., 1980-83. Mem. Calif. Bar Assn., L.A. County Bar Assn. General practice. Office: 7-11 B Way White Plains NY 10601 E-mail: tachnac@aol.com

TAFF, EARL WAYNE, lawyer; b. Princeton, Mo., Nov. 1, 1949; s. James Walter and Margaret Louise (Ragan) T.; m. Mary Kathryn Bedsworth, Dec. 1, 1967; children— David Wayne, Kathy, Angela Margaret. BA with distinction, U. Mo.-Kansas City, 1976, J.D. with distinction, 1976. Bar: Mo. 1977, U.S. Dist. Ct. (we. dist.) Mo. 1977, U.S. Ct. Appeals (8th cir.) 1978. Assoc. Morris & Foust, Kansas City, Mo., 1976-80; assoc., shareholder, dir. Sherman, Wickens, Lysaught & Speck, Kansas City, 1981— ; counsel Citizens Rally Against Pollution, Independence, Mo., 1983— ; frequent lectr. on products liability. Contbr. articles to DRI Products Liability Course Book, others. Mem. citizens adv. com. Fort Osage Sch. Dist., Independence, 1984. Served with USMC, 1967-71. Univ. scholar U. Mo.-Kansas City, 1975, 76. Mem. Def. Research Inst. (vice chmn. products liability com. 1985-88, chmn. 1988—), Assn. Trial Lawyers Am., ABA, Internat. Assn. Def. Counsels, Mo. Bar Assn., Kansas City Bar Assn., Am. Bd. Trial Advs., Mo. Orgn. Def. Lawyers, West Mo. Def. Lawyers Assn., Order of Bench and Robe, Omicron Delta Kappa. Republican. Federal civil litigation, State civil litigation, Insurance. Home: RR 2 Box 831 Independence MO 64050-9614 Office: Sherman Wickens Lysaught & Speck PC PO Box 26530 Kansas City MO 64196-6530

TAFT, NATHANIEL BELMONT, lawyer; b. Tarrytown, N.Y., Aug. 12, 1919; s. Louis Eugene and Etta Minnie (Spivak) Topp; m. Norma Rosalind Pike, May 22, 1943 (dec. Dec. 1997); children: Charles Eliot, Stephen Pike. BS in Econs., Fordham U., 1940; JD, Harvard U., 1948. Bar: N.Y. 1949. Asst. to gen. counsel N.Y. State Ins. Dept., Albany, 1948-50; law dept. N.Y. Life Ins. Co., N.Y.C., 1951-65, group dept., 1965-84, ret. as group v.p., 1984; sole practice law White Plains, N.Y., 1985—. Lectr., author on healthcare reform, 1992—. Contbr. articles to profl. jours.; author monographs on group ins. regulation. Bd. dirs. Westchester Philharmonic, 1991—, v.p., gen. counsel, 1999-2001, pres., 2001—. Mem. ABA, N.Y. State Bar Assn., Nat. Assn. Physicians (sec.-treas. 1991—). Republican. Jewish. Avocations: golf, writing. Administrative and regulatory, Insurance, Pension, profit-sharing, and employee benefits. Home and Office: 16 Sparrow Cir White Plains NY 10605-4624 E-mail: nat@nattaftlaw.com

TAFT, PERRY HAZARD, lawyer, retired; b. L.A., Jan. 23, 1915; s. Milton and Sarah Taft; m. Callie S. Taft, Aug. 15, 1968; children by previous marriage: Stephen D., Sally L., Sheila R. Student, U. Calif., Berkeley, 1932-35; AB, UCLA, 1936; LLB, George Washington U., 1940. Bar: Calif. 1940. Spl. atty. Antitrust Divsn. U.S. Dept. Justice, L.A., 1941-42; dep. atty. gen. State of Calif., San Francisco, 1943-44; regional rep. Coun. State Govts., 1944-45; regional dir. govt. affairs Trans World Airlines, L.A., 1945-57; Pacific coast mgr. Am. Ins. Assn., San Francisco, 1948-66; gen. counsel Assn. Calif. Ins. Cos., Sacramento, 1967-73; asst. city atty. City of Stockton, Calif., 1973-79; pres. Perry H. Taft, P.C., Stockton, 1979-85; arbitrator Surps Line Assn., Calif., 1965-98. Contbr. articles to profl. jours. Bd. dirs. Stockton East Water Dist., 1979-83, pres., 1981-83; mem. San Joaquin County Water Adv. Com., 1982-85. Mem. State Bar of Calif., Elkhorn Country Club, Psi Upsilon. General corporate, Legislative. Home: 8615 Stonewood Dr Stockton CA 95209-2656

TAGGART, THOMAS MICHAEL, lawyer; b. Sioux City, Iowa, Feb. 22, 1937; s. Palmer Robert and Lois Allette (Sedgwick) T.; m. Dolores Cecilia Baroway Renfro, Jan. 4, 1963; children: Thomas Michael Jr., Theodore Christopher; m. Mary Ann Gribben, Feb. 7, 1976. BA, Dartmouth Coll., 1959; JD, Harvard U., 1965. Bar: Ohio 1965, U.S. Dist. Ct. (so. dist.) Ohio 1967, U.S. Dist. Ct. (no. dist.) Ohio 1981, U.S. Supreme Ct. 1997. Ptnr. Vorys, Sater, Seymour & Pease, Columbus, Ohio, 1965—. Lectr. Ohio Legal Ctr. Inst., Ohio Mfrs. Assn., Capital U. Ctr. for Spl. and Continuing Legal Edn. Capt. USMC, 1959-63. Mem. ABA, Ohio Bar Assn. (bd. govs. 1991-99, liability ins. com. 1996-97, 99-00, pres. 1997-98, trustee Found. 1996-98, 2000—, chair commn. on jud. evaluations 2000, Ohio Bar medal 1999), Columbus Bar Assn. (bd. govs., pres. 1989-90), Ohio Assn. Civil Trial Attys., Am. Arbitration Assn., Columbus Area C. of C. Methodist. General civil litigation, State civil litigation, Workers' compensation. Home: 145 Stanbery Ave Columbus OH 43209-1465 Office: Vorys Sater Seymour & Pease 52 E Gay St Columbus OH 43215-3161

TÄHTINEN, JYRKI JUHANI, lawyer; b. Helsinki, Finland, Nov. 16, 1961; s. Reijo Kalervo and Pirkko Liisa Tähtinen; m. Merja Kristiina Hipari; children: Oona, Oliver, Olivia. LLM, U. Helsinki, 1985; MBA, Helsinki Sch. Econs., 1989. Legal counsel City of Helsinki, 1983-87; assoc. Attys. at Law Pello & Pakarinen, Helsinki, 1987-90, Attys. at Law Borenius & Kemppinen, Helsinki, 1990-91, ptnr., 1991—. Finance, Mergers and acquisitions, Securities. Home: Jatasalmentie 12A 00830 Helsinki Finland Office: Borenius & Kemppinen Ltd Yrjönkatu 13A 00120 Helsinki Finland Office Fax: 358 9 6153 3494. E-mail: jyrki.tahtinen@borenius.fi

TAIT, JOHN REID, lawyer; b. Toledo, Apr. 7, 1946; s. Paul Reid and Lucy Richardson (Rudderow) T.; m. Christina Ruth Bjornstad, Mar. 12, 1972; children: Gretchen, Mary. BA, Columbia U., 1968; JD, Vanderbilt U., 1974. Bar: Idaho 1974, U.S. Dist. Ct. Idaho 1974, U.S. Ct. Appeals (9th cir.) U.S. Supreme Ct., Nez Perce Tribal Ct. Assoc. Keeton & Tait, Lewiston, Idaho, 1974-76, ptnr., 1976-86, 89—, Keeton, Tait & Petrie, Lewiston, 1986-88. Chmn. bd. No. Rockies Action Group, Helena, Mont., 1985-86, bd. dirs., 1981-88; mem. Lewiston Hist. Preservation Commn., 1975-94, chmn., 1988-94; bd. dirs. Idaho Legal Aid Svcs., Boise, 1975-99, Idaho Housing Agy., Boise, 1984-91, St. Joseph Regional Med. Ctr. Found., Inc., 1989-94, Lewiston Ind. Found. for Edn., Inc., 1996—; Dem. precinct committeeman, 1976-86, state committeeman, 1977-94, 2000—; del. Dem. Nat. Conv., 1980, 84; regional coord. Idaho State Dem. Party, 1996-99; treas. Larry LaRocco for Congress, 1990, 92. With U.S. Army, 1968-71. Recipient Pro Bono Svc. award Idaho State Bar, 1988, Cmty. Recognition award Lewiston Intergovtl. Coun., 1992, Spl. Recognition award Idaho Legal Aid Svcs., 1993. Mem. ABA, ATLA, Idaho Trial Lawyers Assn. (regional dir. 1976-77, 86-88, 97—), Clearwater Bar Assn. (sec. 1974-76, pres. 1984-86), Consumer Attys. Calif., Workplace Injury Litigation Group. State civil litigation, General practice, Workers' compensation. Office: Keeton & Tait PO Drawer E 312 Miller St Lewiston ID 83501-1944 Fax: 208-746-0962. E-mail: lewlawus@lewiston.com

TAKASUGI, ROBERT MITSUHIRO, federal judge; b. Tacoma, Sept. 12, 1930; s. Hidesaburo and Kayo (Otsuki) T.; m. Dorothy O. Takasugi; children: Jon Robert, Lesli Mari. BS, UCLA, 1953; LLB, JD, U. So. Calif., 1959. Bar: Calif. bar 1960. Practiced law, Los Angeles, 1960-73; judge East Los Angeles Municipal Ct., 1973-75, adminstrv. judge, 1974, presiding judge, 1975; judge Superior Ct., County of Los Angeles, 1975-76; U.S. dist. judge U.S. Dist. Ct. (cen. dist.) Calif., 1976—. Nat. legal counsel Japanese Am. Citizens League; guest lectr. law seminars Harvard U. Law Sch. Careers Symposium; commencement spkr.; mem. Legion Lex U. So. Calif. Law Ctr.; mem. Civil Justice Reform Act and Alt. Dispute Resolution Com., mem. Adv. Com. on Codes of Conduct of the Jud. Conf. of the U.S., 1987-92, Code of Conduct of Judges. Mem. editorial bd. U. So. Calif. Law Rev., 1959; contbr. articles to profl. jours. Calif. adv. com. Western Regional Office, U.S. Commn. on Civil Rights, 1983-85; chmn. blue ribbon com. for selection of chancellor L.A. C.C. With U.S. Army, 1953-55. Harry J. Bauer scholar, 1959; recipient U.S. Mil. Man of Yr. award for Far East Theater U.S. Army, 1954, Jud. Excellence award Criminal Cts. Bar Assn., cert. of merit Japanese-Am. Bar Assn., Lifetime Achievement award, 2000, Disting. Svc. award Asian Pacific Ctr. and Pacific Clinics, 1994, Freedom award Sertoma, 1995, Pub. Svc. award Asian Pacific Am. Legal Ctr. So. Calif., 1995, Trailblazer award So. Calif. region NAPABA, 1995, Spl. award Mex.-Am. Bar Assn., 1996, Spirit of Excellence award ABA, 1998, Pub. Svc. award Japanese Am. Citizens League, 1999; named Judge of Yr. Century City Bar Assn., 1995. Mem. U. So. Calif. Law Alumni Assn. (dir.). Office: US Dist Ct 312 N Spring St Los Angeles CA 90012-4701

TALBERT, HUGH MATHIS, lawyer; b. Kennett, Mo., Dec. 3, 1937; s. Clifford Roscoe and Katharyn (Hoy) T.; m. Carol Sullivan, June 1, 1962 (div. Feb. 1968); m. Carol Ann Frederick, July 18, 1973; children: Katharyn Hoy, William Hugh, Geoffrey Richard. AB, Washington U., St. Louis, 1959, LlB, 1962. Bar: Mo. 1962, U.S. Dist. Ct. (ea. dist.) Mo. 1965, Ill. 1965, U.S. Dist. Ct. (so. dist.) Ill. 1966, U.S. Ct. Appeals (7th cir.) 1971. Assoc. Strubinger, Tudor, Tombrink and Wion, St. Louis, 1962-65, Wiseman, Hallett, Mosele and Shaikewitz, Alton, Ill., 1965-67; ptnr. Chapman and Talbert, Granite City, 1967-73; pres. Talbert & Assocs., PC, Alton, 1974—. Asst. adj. prof. Trial Advocacy St. Louis U. Law Sch., 1992—. Mem. ABA, Assn. Trial Lawyers Am., Ill. State Bar Assn., Ill. Trial Lawyers Assn. (bd. mgrs. 1978-87), The Mo. Bar Assn., Mo. Assn. Trial Lawyers, Madison County Bar Assn., Maritime Law Assn. of the U.S., Acad. of Rail Labor Attys., Million Dollar Advs. Forum. Democrat. Methodist. Avocations: landscaping, hiking and mountaineering, sailing. Admiralty, Personal injury, Product liability. Home: 1750 Liberty St Alton IL 62002-4514 Office: Talbert & Assocs PC PO Box 800 630 E Broadway Alton IL 62002-6308 E-mail: talbert@piasanet.com

TALESNICK, STANLEY, lawyer; b. Indpls., June 4, 1927; s. Louis and Rose (Galerman) T.; m. Joan Goldstone, Mar. 16, 1952 (div. Feb. 1967); children: Jill Wilkins, Jane Talesnick, Kay Gilmore; m. Claudia Jean Ferrell, Nov. 28, 1969 (dec.). AB, Ind. U., 1948, LLB, 1950, JD, 1967. Bar: Ind. 1950, U.S. Dist. Ct. (no. and so. dists.) Ind. 1950, U.S. Dist. Ct. (ea. dist.) Wis. 1991, U.S. Ct. Appeals (7th cir.) 1961, U.S. Supreme Ct. 1980; cert. bus. bankruptcy law Am. Bd. Cert. Ptnr. Dulberger, Talesnick, Claycombe & Bagal, Indpls., 1952-57, Bagal & Talesnick, Indpls., 1957-67, Talesnick & Kleiman, Indpls., 1967-74, Dann Pecar Newman Talesnick & Kleiman, Indpls., 1974-94; bankruptcy and creditor's rights counsel Leagre, Chandler & Millard, 1995-1999; of counsel Ancel & Dunlap, LLP, —, 2000—. Asst. city atty. City of Indpls., 1959-67; instr. bus. law Butler U., Indpls., 1981-82. Chmn. Ind. bd. NCCJ, 1974-76; v.p. Jewish Fedn. Greater Indpls., 1985-89, pres. 1989-91; bd. dirs. Coun. Jewish Fedns. (now United Jewish Cmtys.), 1986-90; treas. Indpls. Hebrew Congregation, 1967-70; v.p. Indpls. Hebrew Congregation Found., 1992-96. With USN, 1945-46, USNR. Disting. fellow Ind. Bar Assn.; recipient Liebert I. Mossler Cmty. Svc. award outstanding & enduring vol. svcs. Jewish Fedn. Greater Indpls. Inc., 1997. Fellow Comml. Law Found.; mem. Ind. State Bar Assn. (ho. of dels. 1985—), Indpls. Bar Assn. (v.p. 1989-90, chmn. comml. and bankruptcy sect. 1985, bd. mgrs. 1994-96), Lawyers Assn. Indpls., Comml. Law League Am., Am. Bankruptcy Inst., B'nai Brith (local pres. 1957-58). Democrat. Jewish. Banking, Bankruptcy, Contracts commercial. Home: 140 Olde Mill Cir S Dr Indianapolis IN 46260 Fax: 317-263-3871. E-mail: st@ancel.net

TALIAFERRO, HENRY BEAUFORD, JR. lawyer; b. Shawnee, Okla., Jan. 12, 1932; s. Henry Beauford Sr. and Laudys L. (Anthony) T.; m. Janet Stewart Myers, Nov. 23, 1955 (div. Feb. 1985); children: Sarah Stewart T. deLeon, Henry B. III, William N.; m. Patricia Ann Calloway, May 16, 1987. BA, U. Okla., 1954, JD, 1956. Bar: Okla. 1956, U.S. Supreme Ct. 1966, D.C. 1969, U.S. Claims Ct. 1970. Assoc. Monnet, Hayes & Bullis, Oklahoma CIty, 1956-59, ptnr., 1959-66; exec. dir. O.E.O. legal svcs. program Oklahoma County, 1966-67; dir. congl. rels., acting exec. dir. Pres.'s Nat. Adv. Commn. on Civil Disorders, Washington, 1967-68; assoc. solicitor for Indian Affairs Dept. of the Interior, 1968-69; pvt. practice, 1969-70; ptnr. Casey, Lane & Mittendorf, 1970-80; exec. v.p., gen. counsel The GHK Cos., Oklahoma City, 1980-83; of counsel Kerr, Irvine & Rhodes, 1987—. Cons. Gas Pipeline Acquisitions & Mgmt., Oklahoma City, 1983-87; mem. Interstate Oil and Gas Compact Commn., 1980—, Okla. Commn. on Nat. Gas Policy, 1991-99, Okla. Energy Resources Bd., 1994—, vice-chair, 1996-97, chair, 1997-99. Author: (with others) Report of Presidents National Advisory Commission on Civil Disorders, 1968; contbr. articles to profl. jours. Candidate 5th dist. U.S. Ho. of Reps., Okla., 1966; mem. planning commn. Fairfax County, Va., 1973, platform com. Dem. Nat. Conv., San Francisco, 1984. Mem. ABA, Okla. Bar Assn., D.C. Bar Assn., Met. Club (Washington), Oklahoma City Golf and Country Club. Democrat. Episcopalian. Avocations: fishing, golf. Office: Kerr Irvine Rhodes & Ables 201 Robert S Kerr Ave Ste 600 Oklahoma City OK 73102-4267

TALLACKSON, JEFFREY STEPHEN, lawyer; b. Washington, May 10, 1943; s. John Robert and Betty Marcelle (Crockett) T.; m. Christine Ann Johnson, Aug. 10, 1974. BA, Yale U., 1965; LLB, Columbia U., 1968. Bar: N.Y. 1968. Law clk. to judge U.S. Dist. Ct. (so. dist.) N.Y., N.Y.C., 1968-70; assoc. Milbank, Tweed, Hadley & McCloy, 1970-78, ptnr., 1979-87; exec. v.p., gen. counsel, sec. Am. Savs. Bank, White Plains, N.Y., 1987-92; ptnr. Lowy & Tallackson, N.Y.C., 1993-96; pvt. practice, 1996-2000; assoc. Brauner, Baron, Rosenzweig & Klein, L.L.P., 2000—. Mem. exec. com. N.Y. Law Inst., N.Y.C., 1980-87; bd. dirs., exec. v.p., gen. counsel, sec. Riverhead Savs. Bank., 1988-92; chmn. com. on banking law and regulation Community Banking Assn. N.Y. State, 1990-92; sec. banking law com. of the Assn. of Bar of City of N.Y., 1997-2000. Mem. ABA, N.Y. State Bar Assn., Assn. Bar City N.Y. Democrat. E-mail: (office) (home). Banking, General corporate, General practice. Home: 77 W 24th St Apt 21E New York NY 10010-3226 Office: Brauner Baron Rosenzweig & Klein LLP 61 Broadway New York NY 10006-2794 E-mail: jtallackson@braunerbaron.com, jtallack@ix.netcom.com

TALLERICO, THOMAS JOSEPH, lawyer; b. Detroit, Oct. 24, 1946; s. Joseph Louis and Irene Marie (Srock) T.; m. Ellen Marie Donnelly, May 12, 1973; children— Brian Thomas, Anne Elizabeth. B.A. cum laude, Sacred Heart Sem., 1968; J.D. cum laude, U. Mich., 1973. Bar: Mich. 1974, D.C. 1976. Atty.-adviser Dept. State, Washington, 1973-76; assoc. Jaffe, Snider, Raitt & Heuer, Detroit, 1976-81, ptnr.; now mem. Howard & Howard Attys. PC; spl. asst. atty. gen. Mich., 1983— . Trustee Met. Detroit Youth Found., 1983— . Mem. ABA, Detroit Bar Assn., Oakland County Bar Assn. Club: Detroit Athletic. Antitrust, Federal civil litigation, State civil litigation. Office: Howard & Howard Attys PC 1400 N Woodward Ave Ste 250 Bloomfield Hills MI 48304-2876

TALLEY, MICHAEL FRANK, lawyer; b. Chesterfield, S.C., Aug. 14, 1945; s. Frank and Rosena A. Talley; m. Dianne Wright, May 24, 1980; children: Michanna, Michael. BA, S.C. State U., 1966; MA, Howard U., 1971, JD, 1976. Bar: S.C. 1976, U.S. Dist. Ct. S.C. 1976, U.S. Ct. Appeals (4th cir.) 1976, U.S. Ct. Appeals (11th cir.) 1994. French instr. S.C. State U., Orangeburg, 1970-71, Tenn. State U., Nashville, 1971-73; staff atty. Presdl. Clemency Bd., White House, Washington, 1975; atty. Bishop Law Firm, Greenville, S.C., 1976-77, Talley, Green & Lewis, Greenville, 1977-87, Talley Law Firm, Greenville, 1987—. French lab. instr. Howard U., Washington, 1973-76. Bd. dirs. Legal Svcs. for Western S.C., Greenville, 1978-82. Earl Warren Legal fellowship NAACP Legal Def. Fund, 1973-76; recipient Cert. of Appreciation S.C. Bar Pro Bono Program, 1991. Mem. S.C. Bar Assn., Nat. Bar Assn., Greenville C. of C., Kappa Alpha Psi. Avocations: fishing, traveling, swimming, reading. Criminal, General practice, Personal injury. Home: 208 Boling Rd Greenville SC 29611-7604 Office: Talley Law Firm 206 Green Ave Greenville SC 29601-3436

TALLEY, RICHARD BATES, lawyer; b. Oklahoma City, Mar. 19, 1947; s. Olin Jack and Betty Lee (Bates) T.; m. Joan Walker, Sept. 15, 1992; children from a previous marriage: Richard Bates Jr., Samuel Logan, Bradley Dale, Rachel Alexandra. BBA, Okla. U., 1969, JD, 1972. Bar: Okla. 1972, U.S. Dist. Ct. (we. dist.) Okla. 1972, U.S. Ct. Appeals (10th cir.) 1973, U.S. Dist. Ct. (no. dist.) Tex. 1987, U.S. Tax Ct. 1987.; CPA, Okla. Atty. Talley, Crowder & Gallagher, Norman, Okla., 1995. Bd. dirs. Bacchus Enterprises, Inc., Norman, The Top of the Center, Inc. Pres. Cleveland Co. YMCA. Mem. ABA, Okla. Bar Found., Okla. Bar Assn., Okla. Trial Lawyers Assn., Okla. Soc. CPAs, Cleve. County Bar Assn., Soc. CPAs. Democrat. Methodist. Avocations: clock collecting, motorcycling, golf, boating. General civil litigation, Contracts commercial, General corporate. Home: 1819 Joe Taylor Cir Norman OK 73072-6650 Office: Talley Crowder & Gallagher 219 E Main St Norman OK 73069-1304 E-mail: rtalley@mmcable.com

TALLMAN, RICHARD C. federal judge, lawyer; b. Oakland, Calif., Mar. 3, 1953; s. Kenneth A. and Jean M. (Kemppe) T.; m. Cynthia Ostolaza, Nov. 14, 1981. BSC, U. Santa Clara, 1975; JD, Northwestern U., 1978. Bar: Calif. 1978, Wash. 1979, U.S. Dist. Ct. (no. dist.) Calif. 1979, U.S. Dist. Ct. (we. dist.) Wash. 1979, U.S. Ct. Appeals (9th cir.) 1979, U.S. Dist. Ct. Hawaii 1986, U.S. Supreme Ct. 1997, U.S. Dist. Ct. (ea. dist.) Wash. 1998. Law clk to Hon. Morrell E. Sharp U.S. Dist. Ct. (we. dist.) Wash., Seattle, 1978-79; trial atty. U.S. Dept. Justice, Washington, 1979-80; asst. U.S. atty. (we. dist.) Wash., Seattle, 1980-83; ptnr. Schweppe, Krug & Tausend, PS, 1983-89; mem. Bogle & Gates, PLLC, 1990-99; ptnr. Tallman & Severin, LLP, 1999-2000; apptd. U.S. cir. judge U.S. Ct. Appeals (9th cir.), 2000—. Chmn. western dist. Wash. Lawyer Reps. to Ninth Cir. Jud. Conf., 1996-97. Instr. Nat. Park Svc. Seasonal Ranger Acad., Everett and Mt. Vernon, Wash., 1983-93; chmn. Edmonds C.C. Found., Lynnwood, Wash., 1990-92; gen. counsel Seattle-King County Crime Stoppers, 1987-99; mem. exec. bd. Chief Seattle coun. Boy Scouts Am., 1997—. Mem. ABA, FBA (trustee 1992-93, v.p. 1994, pres. 1995), Seattle-King County Bar Assn., Rainier Club, Wash. Athletic Club. Avocations: hunting, hiking, fishing. Office: Park Place Bldg 1200 Sixth Avenue 21st FL Seattle WA 98101-3123

TALMADGE, PHILIP ALBERT, former state supreme court justice, former state senator; b. Seattle, Apr. 23, 1952; s. Judson H., Jr. and Jeanne C. T.; m. Darlene L. Nelson, Sept. 6, 1970; children: Adam, Matthew, Jessica, Jonathan, Annemarie. BA magna cum laude, Yale U., 1973; JD, U. Wash., 1976. Bar: Wash. 1976. Assoc. Karr Tuttle Campbell, 1976-89; pres. Talmadge & Cutler, P.S., 1989-95; senator State of Wash., 1979-94; justice Supreme Ct. Wash., 1995-2001. Chair Senate Judiciary Com., 1981, 83-87, Senate Health and Human Svcs. Com., 1992-95, Wash. Senate, 1978-94, ways and means com., children and family svc. com., edn. com. Fellow Am. Assn. Appellate Lawyers; mem. King County Bar Assn., Wash. State Bar Assn.. Author: The Nixon Doctrine and the Reaction of Three Asian Nations, 1973; editor Law Rev., U. Washl., 1975-76; contbr. articles to profl. jours.

TALMO, RONALD VICTOR, lawyer, law educator; b. Wilmington, Del., May 16, 1951; s. Victor Rinaldo and Jessie (Rash) T.; m. Corinne J. Richardson, June 29, 1991; 1 child, Ellery. B.A. in Sociology, U. Del., 1974; J.D., Pepperdine U., 1977. Bar: Calif. 1977, U.S. Dist. Ct. (cen. dist.) Calif. 1977. Sole practice, Santa Ana, Calif., 1977-82; ptnr. firm Wallin, Roseman & Talmo, Tustin, Calif., 1982-85; prof. law, Western State U., Fullerton, Calif., 1979— . Contbr. articles to law revs. Legal dir. Orange County chp. ACLU, Costa Mesa, Calif., 1978-82. Recipient Civil Rights award ACLU, 1984. Mem. Orange County Bar Assn. (mem. faculty coll. trial advocacy 1984-88). Democrat. Civil rights, Criminal. Office: Western State U Coll of Law 1111 N State College Blvd Fullerton CA 92831-3000

TALT, ALAN R. lawyer; b. Stockton, Calif., June 17, 1929; s. Daniel Henry and Josephine (LeSaffre) T.; m. Marjorie Schutte, Sept. 12, 1953; children: Bradley Alan, Stephen Scott, Mark Kevin, Karen Talt Beardsley. BA, U. Calif., Berkeley, 1951, JD, 1954. Bar: Calif. 1955, U.S. Dist. Ct. (no. and so. dists.) Calif. 1955, U.S. Ct. Appeal (9th cir.) 1955. Law clk. to the chief judge U.S. Ct. Appeal (9th cir.), San Francisco, 1954-55; pvt. practice, L.A. and Pasadena, Calif., 1955—. Gen. counsel Kirkhill Rubber Co., Brea, Calif., 1988—; gen. counsel, bd. dirs. KAPCO, Brea, 1985—; gen. counsel Caine, Farber & Gordon, Pasadena, 1986—. Asst. editor: Williston Casebook Contract Law, 1953. Pres. San Gabriel Valley Learning Soc., Pasadena, 1976-77; nat. v.p. Newman Clubs Am., 1949-50. Samuel Bell-McKee fellow, 1948; U. Calif. Berkeley Alumni scholar, 1947. Mem. Calif. State Bar, Jonathan Club, Valley Club (pres.), Ironwood Country Club. Avocations: fly fishing, philately. General corporate, Estate planning, Real property. Home: 1375 St Albans Rd San Marino CA 91108-1860 Office: 790 E Colorado Blvd Ste 710 Pasadena CA 91101-2190 E-mail: artaltlaw@aol.com

TAMMELLEO, A. DAVID, lawyer, editor, publisher; b. Providence, Aug. 9, 1935; s. Anthony and Kathleen (Gilleran) T.; m. Marylouise Kenney, Aug. 8, 1964; children: David A., Kathy. BA cum laude, Providence Coll., 1957; JD cum laude, Boston Coll., 1961. Bar: R.I. 1962, U.S. Dist. Ct. R.I., U.S. Ct. Appeals (1st cir.), U.S. Supreme Ct. Spl. investigative legal counsel State of R.I., Providence, 1961-69; sr. ptnr. A. David Tammelleo & Assocs., 1962—; chief trial counsel Monti & Monti, 1969-78; chief legal counsel Dept. Employment Security State of R.I., 1978-82; pub. Medica Press Inc., 1984—, editor-in-chief, 1984—. Lectr. on hosp., med. and nursing law through U.S., 1984—; legal cons. Med. Econs. mag., 1984—. Editor: Nursing Law's Regan Report, 1984—; Hospital Law's Regan Report, 1984—, Medal Law's Regan Report, 1984—; mem. editl. bd. RN mag., 1984-94; contbg. editor RN Jour., 1984—; columnist Legally Speaking, Advice of Counsel, 1984—; contbr. articles to legal jours. Atty., mem. biomed. ethics comm. Diocese of Providence, 1984—. Fellow R.I. Bar Found. (editl. bd. R.I. Bar jour. 1975-90, R.I. Bar Assn. (med.-legal com., joint com. with R.I. Med. Soc.); mem. ABA, Am. Judicature Assn., Am. Acad. Hosp. Attys., Nat. Health Lawyers Assn., R.I. Bar Assn., Cath. Health Assn., New Eng. Conf. Cath. Health Assn., Boston Coll. Law Sch. Deans Coun., Boston Coll. Law Sch. Alumni Assn. Avocations: sailing, tennis, jogging, astronomy, aeronautics. General practice, Health, Personal injury. Office: 10 Dorrance St Ste 500 Providence RI 02903-2018 E-mail: Adtlaw@aol.com

TAMULONIS, FRANK LOUIS, JR. lawyer; b. Pottsville, Pa., Sept. 26, 1946; s. Frank Louis Sr. and Cecelia Florence (Hoffman) T.; m. Jane Alice Troutman, June 26, 1976; children: Kathryn Lydia, Frank Louis III. AB, Cornell U., 1968; JD, Villanova Law Sch., 1971. Bar: Pa. 1971, U.S. Supreme Ct. 1975, U.S. Ct. Appeals (3d cir.) 1981. Law clk. to dist. judge U.S. Dist. Ct. (ea. dist.), Phila., 1971-74; assoc. Kassab, Cherry & Archbold, Media, Pa., 1974-76, Zimmerman, Lieberman & Derenzo, Pottsville, 1976—. Contbr. articles to profl. jours. Mem. Am. Trial Lawyers Assn., Def. Research Inst., Pa. Def. Inst., Inst. Pa. Trial Lawyers Assn., Pa. Bar Assn., Schuylkill County Bar Assn. Republican. Roman Catholic. State civil litigation, Personal injury, Workers' compensation. Office: Zimmerman Lieberman & Derenzo PO Box 238 111 E Market St Pottsville PA 17901-2914

TANAKA, J(EANNIE) E. lawyer; b. L.A., Jan. 21, 1942; d. Togo William and Jean M. Tanaka. BA, Internat. Christian U., Tokyo, 1966; MSW, UCLA, 1968; JD, Washington Coll., 1984. Bar: Calif. 1984, U.S. Dist. Ct. (cen., no. dists.) Calif. 1985, U.S. Ct. Appeals (9th cir.) 1985, D.C. 1987. Instr. Aoyama Gakuin, Meiji Gakuin, Sophia U., Tokyo, 1968-75; with program devel. Encyclopedia Britannica Inst., 1976-78; instr. Honda, Mitsubishi, Ricoh Corps., 1975-80; with editorial dept. Simul Internat.; assoc. Seki and Jarvis, L.A., 1984-86, Jones, Day, Reavis & Pogue, L.A., 1986-87, Fulbright, Jaworsky and Reavis, McGrath, L.A., 1987-89; asst. counsel Unocal, 1989-91; pvt. practice, 1991—; counsel Calif. Dept. Corps., 1993—. Active Japan-Am. Soc., L.A., 1984-95, Japanese-Am. Citizens League, L.A., 1981, 92—, Japanese Am. Cultural and Cmty. Ctr., 1986-89; vol. Asian Pacific Am. Legal Ctr. So. Calif., 1985-86. Mem. Japanese-Am. Bar Assn., Mensa. Democrat. Mem. Foursquare Meth. Ch. Avocations: Japanese language, Chinese language, U.S.-Far East relations, martial arts. Administrative and regulatory, General corporate, Securities. Address: 13204 Summertime Ln Culver City CA 90230

TANENBAUM, GERALD STEPHEN, lawyer; b. Phila., Dec. 12, 1945; s. Harold Jack and Matilda (Fleischman) T.; m. Gretchen Jonas; children: Jennifer, Rebecca. AB, U. N.C., 1967; JD, U. Ga., 1970. Bar: Ga. 1970, N.Y. 1971, U.S. Dist. Ct. (so. dist.) N.Y. 1974, U.S. Ct. Appeals (2d cir.) 1974. Assoc. Cahill Gordon & Reindel, N.Y.C., 1970-78, ptnr., 1978—. General corporate, Mergers and acquisitions, Securities. Office: Cahill Gordon & Reindel 80 Pine St Fl 17 New York NY 10005-1790 Business E-Mail: gtanenbaum@cahill.com

TANENBAUM, JAY HARVEY, lawyer; b. N.Y.C., Nov. 17, 1933; s. Leo Aaron and Regina (Stein) T.; m. Linda Goldman, May 28, 1961; children: Susan Hillary, Steven Eric. BA, Hobart and William Smith Colls., 1954; LLB, Union U., 1957, JD, 1961. Bar: N.Y. 1957, U.S. Dist. Ct. (so. dist.) N.Y. 1961, U.S. Supreme Ct. 1967. Internat. trader Associated Metals and Minerals Corp., N.Y.C., 1960-64; pvt. practice, 1964—. Corp. counsel Internat. Gate Corp., Gen. Gate Corp. Mem. N.Y. State Bar Assn., N.Y. Trial Lawyers Assn., Bronx County Bar Assn. Jewish. Club: St. James (London), Le Club (N.Y.). FERC practice, Family and matrimonial, Personal injury.

TANENBAUM, RICHARD HUGH, lawyer; b. Washington, July 10, 1947; s. Joseph M. and Shirley (Levin) T.; m. Cindy Marks, Mar. 22, 1996; children: Brian J., Drew S. BS, Bradley U., 1969; JD, Cath. U. Am. Sch. Law, 1974. Bar: Md. 1974, D.C. 1975, U.S. Ct. Claims 1975, U.S. Ct. Appeals (D.C. cir.) 1975, U.S. Ct. Appeals (4th cir.) 1982, U.S. Tax Ct. 1982, U.S. Supreme Ct. 1982. Consumer edn. developer, tchr. Peoria (Ill.) Pub. Sch. System, 1969-71; legal asst. Pay Bd., Exec. Office of Pres., Washington, 1971-72; acct. Alexander Grant & Co., 1972; assoc. Jones, Day, Reavis & Pogue, 1973-78; ptnr. Lerch, Early & Brewer, Bethesda, Md., 1978-85; atty. pvt. practice, 1985—. Mng. editor Cath. U. Law Rev., Washington, 1974. Recipient Superior Performance award Exec. Office of Pres., Washington, 1972. Mem. ABA, Montgomery County Bar Assn., D.C. Bar Assn., Bethesda-Chevy Chase C. of C. (bd. dirs. 1980-83), Bethesda Country Club, Rotary (charter mem., bd. dirs. 1980—). Contracts commercial, General corporate, Real property. Office: Ste 775 N 7315 Wisconsin Ave Bethesda MD 20814-3202 E-mail: RHT775N@aol.com

TANGEN, JON PAUL, laywer; b. Quincy, Mass., Apr. 7, 1944; s. George Henry and Bertha Marie (Backius) T.; m. Valerie Ann Clayton, June 27, 1964; children: Nathaniel Clayton, Kristoffer Willis, Thomasine Deyo. BA, Washington and Jefferson Coll., Pa., 1966; LLB, U. Va., 1969; LLM, George Washington U., 1976. Bar: Va. 1969, Alaska 1975, U.S. Dist. Ct. Alaska 1975, U.S. Ct. Appeals (9th cir.) 1977. Atty.-advisor Office Gen. Counsel, U.S. Dept. Commerce, Washington, 1973-75; mem. Robertson, Monagle, Eastaugh & Bradley, Juneau, Alaska, 1975-86; pvt. practice, Juneau, 1986—. Served to capt. U.S. Army, 1969-73. Mem. ABA, Va. Bar Assn., Alaska Bar Assn., Alaska State C. of C. (chmn. bd. dirs. 1983-84), Alaska Miners Assn. (pres. 1978-80), Rocky Mountain Mining Found., N.W. Mining Assn. (trustee 1979-80), Rotary, Masons. Republican. Episcopalian. Oil, gas, and mineral, Environmental, Insurance. Office: PO Box 21808 Juneau AK 99802-1808

TANICK, MARSHALL HOWARD, lawyer, law educator; b. Mpls., May 9, 1947; s. Jack and Esther (Kohn) T.; m. Cathy E. Gorlin, Feb. 20, 1982; children: Lauren, Ross. BA, U. Minn., 1969; JD, Stanford U., 1973. Bar: Calif. 1973, Minn. 1974. Law clk. to presiding justice U.S. Dist. Ct., Mpls., 1973-74; assoc. Robins, Davis & Lyons, 1974-76; ptnr. Tanick & Heins, P.A., 1976-89, Mansfield & Tanick, Mpls., 1989—. Prof. constrn., real estate and media law U. Minn., Mpls., 1983—, Hamline U., St. Paul, 1982—; prof. constl. law William Mitchell Coll. Law, 1994. Editor: Hennepin Lawyer, Bench, Bar and Litigation mag.; contbr. articles to mags. Avocation: writing. Federal civil litigation, State civil litigation, Communications. Home: 1230 Angelo Dr Minneapolis MN 55422-4710 Office: Mansfield & Tanick 900 2nd Ave S Ste 1560 Minneapolis MN 55402-3383

TANIGUCHI, YASUHEI, law educator; b. Kyoto, Japan, Dec. 26, 1934; s. Tomohei and Mihoko T.; m. Akiko Shimada Apr. 2, 1961; children: Yasushi, Tomoko. LLB, Kyoto U., Japan, 1957; LLM, U. Calif., Berkeley, 1963; JSD, Cornell U., Ithaca, NY, 1964. certified Full Jurist, Legal Training and Research Inst. of Supreme Court of Japan. Prof. of law Kyoto U., Kyoto, Japan, 1959-98, Teikyo U., Tokyo, Japan, 1998-2000, Tokyo Keizai U., Tokyo, Japan, 2000—. Vis. prof. of law U. Michigan, Ann Arbor, 1976-77, Harvard U., Cambridge, 1993, New York U., 1995-97; of counsel Matsuo & Kosugi, 1998—; council mem. Internat. Council for Commercial Arbitration, 1990—. Author: (book) Insolrency Law, 1976, Civil Procedure, 1987, Procedure and Procedural Justice, 1995. Pres. Kyoto Labor Relations Commn., 1985-92; mem. Law Revision Commn., Ministry of Justice of Japan, 1983-97, Appellate Body, World Trade Org., Genevea, 2000—. Mem. Japan Civil Procedure Assn. (pres. 1992-95), Internat. Assn. of Preocedural Law (v.p. 1994—), Internat. Law Assn., Chartered Inst. Aritrators. Avocations: music, skiing. Office: Matsuo & Kosugi 7-14-16 Ginza Chuo-ku 104-0061 Tokyo Japan Fax: 03-3542-9330. E-mail: tanigy@mknet.chuo.tolyo.jp

TANKOOS, SANDRA MAXINE, court reporting services executive; b. Bklyn., Nov. 12, 1936; d. Samuel J. and Ethel (Seltzer) Rich; m. Kenneth Robert Tankoos, Mar. 17, 1957; children: Robert Ian, Gary Russell, Jenine Sheryl. AA, Stenotype Inst., 1957; BA, Queens Coll., 1969; MA, C.W. Post Coll., 1973. Cert. stenotype reporter, 1959. Ct. reporter free lance, N.Y.C., 1957-70; tchr. Spanish various high schs., L.I., 1970-76; pres. Tankoos Reporting, N.Y.C., 1976—, Ar-Ti Recording, Mineola, N.Y., 1977—. Contbr. articles to profl. jours. Past pres., bd. dirs. Temple Sinai, Roslyn Hts., N.Y., 1989-91, Am. Jewish Acad., West Hempstead, 1984-94, LWV, Roslyn, 1969-75, NOW, Nassau County, 1975-77, bd. dirs. Religious Action Ctr., Washington, 1995—, ARZA, 1997—. Mem. N.Y. State Shorthand Reporters Assn. (bd. dirs. 1998—). Avocations: writing, piano. Home: 77 Shepherd Ln Roslyn Heights NY 11577-2508 Office: Ar-Ti Recording Inc 142 Willis Ave Mineola NY 11501-2613 also: Tankoos Reporting Co 305 Madison Ave New York NY 10165

TANNENBAUM, BERNARD, lawyer; b. N.Y.C., July 14, 1928; s. Jacob and Lillian (Jupiter) T.; m. Elinor Fried, June 3, 1950; children: Jody, Ilene, Carol, Jeffrey. BA in Edn., NYU, 1950, JD, 1953; MA (hon.), Internat. U. Comm., 1974. Bar: N.Y. 1954, D.C. 1980, U.s. Dist. Ct. (so. and ea. dists.) N.Y. 1961, U.S. Ct. Claims 1964, U.S. Supreme Ct. 1964. Assoc. Halperin, Natanson, Shivitz & Scholar, N.Y.C., 1952-54; sole practice Mineola, N.Y., 1954-60, N.Y.C., 1969-87; ptnr. Fried, Beck, Tannenbaum & Field, 1960-69; counsel Meltzer, Lippe, Goldstein & Wolf, Mineola, 1987—. Spl. counsel U.S. Senate Subcom. on Juvenile Delinquency, Washington, 1965-70, subcom. on Panama Canal U.S. Ho. of Reps., Washington, 1970-71, com. on mcht. marine and fisheries U.S. Ho. of Reps., 1977-80; arbitrator Am. Arbitration Assn., N.Y.C., 1965— , Small Claims Divsn. Civil Ct., N.Y.C., 1975—. Contbr. NYU Law Rev., editor, pub., The Democratic Forum, 1960-73; bd. dirs., trstee, chmn. Daytop Village Inc., N.Y.C., 1983—; bd. advisors Assn. Children with Retarded Mental Devel., N.Y.C., 1984-86. Contracts commercial, Legislative, Real property. Office: 190 Willis Ave Mineola NY 11501-2693 E-mail: Tanbern@aol.com

TANNENWALD, PETER, lawyer; b. Washington, Apr. 8, 1943; s. Judge Theodore and Selma (Peterfreund) T.; m. Carol B. Baum, May 25, 1969; 1 child, Jonathan Mark. AB, Brown U., 1964; LLB, Harvard U., 1967. Bar: U.S. Dist. Ct. D.C. 1968, U.S. Ct. Appeals (D.C. cir.) 1968, U.S. Supreme Ct. 1972. Assoc. Arent, Fox, Kintner, Plotkin & Kahn, Washington, 1967-74, ptnr., 1975-94; v.p. Irwin, Campbell & Tannenwald, P.C., 1995—. Columnist The LPTV Report, 1988-92. Mem. cmty. coun. Sta. WAMU-FM, Washington, 1986-93, 94-97; dir. Brown Broadcasting Svc., Inc., Providence, 1970—; chmn. maj. law firms divsn. Nat. Capital Area affiliate United Way, 1977-79. Mem. Harvard Law Sch. Assn. D.C. (pres. 1979-80), Harvard Law Sch. Assn. (sec. 1982-84). Avocations: electronics, photography. Communications. Office: Irwin Campbell Tannenwald PC 1730 Rhode Island Ave NW Washington DC 20036-3101

TANNER, DEE BOSHARD, retired lawyer; b. Provo, Utah, Jan. 16, 1913; s. Myron Clark and Marie (Boshard) T.; m. Jane Barwick, Dec. 26, 1936 (div. Aug. 1962); children: Barry, Diane McDowell; m. Reeta Walker, Dec. 6, 1981. BA, U. Utah, 1935; LLB, Pacific Coast U., 1940; postgrad., Harvard U., 1936, Loyola U., L.A., 1937. Bar: Calif. 1943, U.S. Dist. Ct. (so. dist.) Calif. 1944, U.S. Ct. Appeals (9th cir.) 1947, ICC 1964, U.S. Dist. Ct. (ea. dist.) Calif. 1969, U.S. Supreme Ct. 1971. Assoc. Spray, Davis & Gould, L.A., 1943-44; pvt. practice, 1944; assoc. Tanner and Sievers, 1944-47, Tanner and Thornton, L.A., 1947-54, Tanner, Hanson, Meyers, L.A., 1954-64; ptnr. Tanner and Van Dyke, 1964-65, Gallagher and Tanner, L.A., 1965-70; pvt. practice Pasadena, Calif., 1970-95; retired, 1995. Mem. L.A. Bar Assn., World Affairs Assn., Harvard Law Sch. Assn., Lawyers' Club L.A. Federal civil litigation. Home and Office: 1720 Lombardy Rd Pasadena CA 91106-4127 E-mail: rpltd@aol.com

TANNER, ERIC BENSON, lawyer; b. St. Louis, Aug. 27, 1949; s. Robert H. and Delores (Benson) T.; m. Rosalind Grace Tanner, June 23, 1978; children: Jacob, Adam. BA, U. Mo., Columbia, 1971; JD, U. Mo., Kansas City, 1975; cert., Coll. Fin. Planning, Denver, 1988. Bar: Mo. 1975. Instr. paralegal program Avila Coll., Kansas City, 1982-84; staff atty. Legal Aid Western Mo., 1975-83; pvt. practice, 1983-86; asst. v.p. trust dept. United Mo. Bank, NA, 1986-90; staff atty. Shook, Hardy & Bacon, 1990-93; v.p. trust dept., sr. trust atty. Commerce Bank, N.A., 1993—. CLE lectr. on estate planning topics to various bar assns. and univs., 1975—. Contbr. articles to law jours. Mem. planned giving com. Nat. Kidney Found., Kans. and Kansas City met. area, 1995-97; vol. Habitat for Humanity, 1997, 99; bd. dirs. Prime Health, 1980-86. Mem. ABA, Mo. Bar Assn., Kansas City Met. Bar Assn., Lawyers Assn. Kansas City, Kansas City Corp. Fiduciaries Assn. (pres. 1997), Estate Planning Soc. Kansas City. Estate planning, Probate, Estate taxation. Office: Commerce Bank NA 1000 Walnut St Ste 800 Kansas City MO 64106-2160

TANNER, GORDON OWEN, lawyer; b. Mobile, Ala., Oct. 28, 1948; s. Cecil Owen and Mae Jewel (Brannan) T.; m. Jane Ellen Watson, July 31, 1971; children: Brooke Elizabeth, Lindsey Ford, Hampton Lovejoy. BA, U. Ala., 1970; JD, Vanderbilt U., 1972. Bar: Tenn. 1973, Ala. 1977, U.S. Dist. Ct. (so. dist.) Ala. 1977, U.S. Tax Ct. 1978, U.S. Ct. Mil. Appeals 1973, U.S. Ct. Appeals (5th and 11th cirs.) 1980, D.C. 1997. Assoc. McDermott, Slepian, Windom & Reed, Mobile, 1977-80, ptnr., 1980-84, mng. atty., 1981-86; ptnr. Sirote, Permutt, McDermott, Slepian, Friend, Friedman Held &, 1986-89, Sirote & Permutt, P.C., 1989-97; gen. counsel Air ForceCtr. for Housing Excellence, Brooks AFB, Tex., 1997—. Sec., dir. Bay Title Ins. Co., Mobile, 1978-88. Bd. dirs. Cmty. Concert Assn. of Mobile, 1982, Hist. Mobile Devel. Commn., 1988-93, Dumas-Wesley Cmty. Ctr., 1990-97, The Dauphin Way Found., 1988-97, Mobile AIDS Support Svc., 1993-96, Mobile United, 1993-97, Leadership Mobile, 1992, The Presdl. Owners, 1998—, Fed. City Performing Arts Assn., 1998-2000, Arts San Antonio!, 2000—, The Univ. Club of Washington, 2000—, Alamo Bus. Coun., 2000—, St. Mark's Epis. Ch., 2000—; mem. planning coun. United Way of Southwest Ala., 1992-97. Lt. col. USAF, 1973-94, col. 1995—, to maj. USAFR, 1983. Named Outstanding Reservist of Yr. Strategic Air Command, 1989. Mem. ABA, Ala. State Bar, Mobile Bar Assn., Eastern Shore C. of C. (bd. dirs.), Mobile Area C. of C., Tenn. Bar Assn., Southeastern Admiralty Law Inst., Jubilee Jaycees (bd. dirs. 1978-80), Bayside Acad. (bd. dirs. 1982-88), Bayside Found. (bd. dirs. 1986-90), Econ. Rev. Coun. Democrat. Methodist. Lodge: Eastern Shore Sertoma (bd. dirs. 1977-90, Most Outstanding Mem. 1980) (Daphne, Ala.). Avocation: sailing. Banking, Federal civil litigation, Contracts commercial. Home: PO Box 90662 San Antonio TX 78209-9088 Office: Air Force Ctr Housing Excellence 8004 Arnold Dr Brooks AFB TX 78235

TANNON, JAY MIDDLETON, lawyer; b. Augusta, Ga., Feb. 24, 1956; m. Elizabeth M. Gabhart; 1 child, Katherine. BA, U. N.C., 1978; JD, U. Va., 1982; MBA, U. Louisville, 1983. Bar: Ky. 1982. Ptnr. Brown, Todd & Heyburn, Louisville, 1982-2000; exec. committee Frost, Brown, & Todd LLC, 2000—; chmn. Kentucky WorldTrade Ctr., 1999—. Chmn., founder Comml. Dispute Resolution Inc., Louisville, 1986—. Contbg. author Ky. Bus. Orgns.; contbr. articles to profl. jours. Bd. dirs. U. Louisville Sch. Bus., 1985—, Independent Industries, Inc. 1988—; mem. Louisville Venture Forum, Japan-Am. Soc. Ky. Hearst Found. scholarship, 1974, Johnston scholar U. N.C., 1976, Phillips scholar U. N.C., 1977, du Pont scholar U. Va., 1979. Mem. ABA, Internat. Bar Assn., Ky. Bar Assn., Louisville Bar Assn., b.d dirs., Vivao plc, Bd. Advisors, Evermore Investments LLC. Alternative dispute resolution, General corporate, Mergers and acquisitions. Office: Frost Brown & Todd LLC 400 W Market St Ste 3200 Louisville KY 40202-3363 E-mail: jrannon@fbtlaw.com

TANOUS, JAMES JOSEPH, lawyer; b. Olean, N.Y., Sept. 11, 1947; s. Michael F. and Philomena M. (Eade) T.; m. Constance M. Griffin, Nov. 27, 1982; children: James M., Michele P. BA, St. Bonaventure U., 1969; JD, U. Va., 1972. Bar: N.Y. 1973, U.S. Dist. Ct. (we. dist.) 1973, U.S. Ct. Appeals (2d cir.) 1973. Ptnr. Jaeckle Fleischmann & Mugel, LLP, Buffalo, 1973—. Served to capt. USAR, 1971-79 Mem. ABA, N.Y. State Bar Assn. General corporate, Securities. Home: 1885 Woodard Rd Elma NY 14059-9366 Office: Jaeckle Fleischmann & Mugel LLP 12 Fountain Plz Buffalo NY 14202-2292 E-mail: jtanous@jaeckle.com

TANZER, JACOB, former justice Oregon Supreme Court; b. Longview, Wash., Feb. 13, 1935; s. Joseph S. and Fannie B. (Rosenfeld) T.; BA, U. Oreg., 1956, LLB, 1959; m. Elaine Rhine; children: Joshua, Jessica, Rachel, Elan. Bar: Oreg. 1959. Pvt. practice with firm Granata & Tanzer, Portland, 1959-62; trial atty., organized crime and racketeering sect., then civil rights divsn. U.S. Justice Dept., Washington, 1962-64; dep. dist. atty. Multnomah County, Portland, 1964-69; solicitor gen. Oreg. Justice Dept., Salem, 1969-71; dir. Oreg. Dept. Human Resources, Salem, 1971-73; judge Oreg. Ct. Appeals, Salem, 1973-80; justice Oreg. Supreme Ct., Salem, 1981-83; ptnr., of counsel Ball, Janik & Novack, Portland, 1983—. Alternative dispute resolution, General civil litigation. Office: One Main Place Suite 1100 101 SW Main Portland OR 97204

TAPLEY, JAMES LEROY, retired lawyer, railway corporation executive; b. Greenville, Miss., July 10, 1923; s. Lester Leroy and Lillian (Clark) T.; m. Priscilla Moore, Sept. 9, 1950. AB, U. N.C., 1947, JD with honors, 1950. Bar: N.C. 1951, D.C. 1962. With So. Ry. Co., Washington, 1953-83, gen. solicitor, 1967-74, asst. v.p. law, 1974-75, v.p. law, 1975-83; v.p. Washington counsel Norfolk So. Corp., Washington, 1983-87; ret., 1987. Mem. Phi Beta Kappa, Kappa Sigma. Clubs: Chevy Chase. Administrative and regulatory, Antitrust, General corporate.

TARASI, LOUIS MICHAEL, JR. lawyer; b. Cheswick, Pa., Sept. 9, 1931; s. Louis Michael and Ruth Elizabeth (Records) T.; m. Patricia Ruth Finley, June 19, 1954; children: Susan, Louis Michael III, Elizabeth, Brian, Patricia, Matthew. BA, Miami U., Ohio, 1954; JD, U. Pa., 1959. Bar: Pa. 1960, U.S. Dist. Ct. (we. dist.) Pa. 1960, U.S. Ct. Appeals (3d cir.) 1964, U.S. Supreme Ct. 1969, U.S. Dist. Ct. (we. dist.) Tex. 1988, U.S. Ct. Appeals (5th cir.) 1989, U.S. Ct. Appeals (4th cir.) 1994, U.S. Ct. Fed. Claims 1987, U.S. Dist. Ct. Colo. 1998; cert. civil trial adv. Nat. Bd. Trial Advocacy. Assoc., owner Burgwin, Ruffin, Perry & Pohl, Pitts., 1960-68; ptnr. Conte, Courtney & Tarasi, Beaver County, Pa., 1968-78, Tarasi & Tighe, Pitts., 1978-82, Tarasi & Johnson, P.C., Pitts., 1982-95, Tarasi & Assocs., P.C., Pitts., 1995-99, The Tarasi Lawfirm, P.C., Pitts., 1997-2001, Tarasi, Tarasi & Fishman, P.C., Pitts., 2001—. Mem. parish coun. St. James Ch., Sewickley, Pa.; mem. Sewickley Borough Allegheny Coun., 1978-1982. With U.S. Army, 1954-56. Fellow Internat. Soc. Barristers; mem. Assn. Trial Lawyers Am. (gov., rep.), Pa. Trial Lawyers Assn. (pres. 1979-80), Acad. Trial Lawyers Allegheny County, Allegheny County Bar Assn., Pa. Bar Assn., West Pa. Trial Lawyers Assn. (pres. 1975), St. Thomas More Soc. (award 1991), Melvin Belli Soc. Democrat. Roman Catholic. Avocations: reading, golf, lecturing. General civil litigation, Personal injury, Toxic tort. Home: 1 Way Hollow Rd Sewickley PA 15143-1192 Office: Tarasi Tarasi & Fishman 510 3d Ave Pittsburgh PA 15219-2107

TARAVELLA, CHRISTOPHER ANTHONY, lawyer; b. Pueblo, Colo., Sept. 19, 1951; s. Frank Louis and Ann Jean T.; m. Kathleen; children: Nicholas M., John L. BS in Engring. Mechanics, USAF Acad., 1973; JD, U. Colo., 1976; postgrad., Harvard U., 1996. Bar: Iowa 1976, Colo. 1976, U.S. Ct. Mil. Appeals 1976, U.S. Dist. Ct. Colo. 1976, Fla. 1977, U.S. Supreme Ct. 1982, U.S. Ct. Appeals (fed. cir.) 1983, D.C. 1984, U.S. Claims Ct. 1984, Mich. 1985. Commd. 2nd lt. USAF, 1973, legal intern Staff Judge Adv. Denver, 1973-76, advanced through grades to lt. col. Hurlburt Field, Fla., 1976-78, asst. staff judge adv. Zaragoza, Spain, 1978-81, chief cir. trial counsel Washington, 1981-83; chief Constitutional Torts Br. Civil Litigation, 1983-85; resigned USAF, 1985; asst. gen. counsel Chrysler Motors Corp., Highland Park, Mich., 1985-90; asst. gen. counsel comml. affairs, chief patent counsel Chrysler Corp., Auburn Hills, 1990-96; v.p., gen. counsel Chrysler Fin. Co. LLC, Southfield, 1997—. Mem. governing com. Conf. on Consumer Fin. Law. Staff Judge Adv. USAFR, 927 Air Refueling Group, Selfridge Air NG Base, Mich., 1985-94. Mem. Am. Fin. Svcs. Assn. (bd. dirs.). General civil litigation, Patent, Trademark and copyright. Office: Chrysler Fin Co LLC CIMS 465-25-02 27777 Franklin Rd Southfield MI 48034-2337 Business E-Mail: cat8@daimlerchrysler.com

TARCHI, ENRICO MARIA, lawyer; b. Pescara, Italy, Sept. 3, 1965; s. Sergio and Ziggiotto (Lina) T. Law degree, Teramo, Italy, 1990. Trainee Cappuccilli Law Firm, Pescara, Italy, 1990-92; assoc. lawyer Tarchi & Fimiani Law Firm, Italy, 1992-95; assoc. Vassalli Law Firm, Nilan, Italy, 1995-99; asst. Norton Rose, London, 2000—. Fgn. lawyer Coudert Bros., N.Y.C., 1997. Avocations: tennis, skiing, golf. Contracts commercial, Finance, Intellectual property. Office: Norton Rose via Visconti DiModrone 21 20122 Milan Italy E-mail: tarchi@ustouroke.com

TARLAVSKI, ROMAN, lawyer; b. Riga, Latvia, USSR, Dec. 24, 1965; arrived in The Netherlands, 1979; s. Yuri and Mila (Ortenberg) T.; m. Monique Gerbrandine Remslag, June 12, 1998. Law degree, U. Amsterdam, 1992; corp. law specialist, Grotius Acad., Nygmegen, The Netherlands, 1997. Bar: Amsterdam. Lawyer Andersen Legal, Amstelveen, 1993—. Lectr. in field. Named Talented and Promising Young Lawyer Quote Profls., 2000. Mem. Amsterdam-St. Petersburg Young Bar Assn. (chmn. training project 1996-97), Amsterdam Young Bar Assn. Contracts commercial, General corporate, Mergers and acquisitions. Office: Andersen Legal Prof WM Keesomlaan 8 1183 DJ Amstelveen The Netherlands Fax: 31208808747. E-mail: roman.tarlavski@nl.andersenlegal.com

TARNACKI, DUANE L. lawyer; b. Detroit, Dec. 21, 1953; s. Leo A. and Dorothy O. (Roginski) T.; m. Sheila Rimmel, July 28, 1994. BA in Psychology with high distinction and high honors, U. Mich., 1976; MBA with honors, JD cum laude, U. Notre Dame, 1980. Bar: Mich. 1980, U.S. Dist. Ct. (so. dist.) Mich., 1980. Ptnr., mem. Clark Hill P.L.C., Detroit, 1980—. Sec. Ctr. for Creative Studies, 1991-96; bd. dirs. Stratford Shakespearean Festival of Am., sec., 1991—; bd. dirs. Detroit Hist. Soc., Juvenile Diabetes Found. Met. Detroit chpt., 1990-95, Acct. Aid Soc., 1990-96; gen. counsel Econ. Club of Detroit, 1995—; vice chmn., exec. com. Planned Giving Roundtable of S.E. Mich., 1992-98. Author: Establishing a Charitable Foundation in Michigan, 1986, 3d edit., 1999, The Responsibilities of Service: A Guide for Directors of Nonprofit Organizations in Michigan, 1997, 99; co-author: The Michigan Community Foundation Legal Reference, 1993, 2d edit., 1996; assoc. editor Notre Dame Lawyer, 1977-80. Mem. increasing philanthropy and govt. rels. coms., Coun. Mich. Founds., planned giving com., Karmanos Cancer Inst., 1991-94; bd. dirs. Mich Supreme Court Hist. Soc. Inc., 1988-96; mem. legal adv. subcom. to comty. found. com. Coun. on Founds., IRS Exempt Orgns. Liaison Group; trustee Thompson-McCully Found., The Futures Found. Fellow Mich. State Bar Found.; mem. ABA (nonprofit corps. com., bus. law sect., real property, probate and trust law and tax sects.), Detroit Regional C. of C. (bus. contbns. com.), Mich. Bar Assn. (nonprofit corp. com., bus. law sect., probate and estate planning law and tax sects.), Econ Club. Roman Catholic. Estate planning, Non-profit and tax-exempt organizations. Home: 39824 Woodside Dr N Northville MI 48167-3429 Office: 500 Woodward Ave Ste 3500 Detroit MI 48226-3485

TARNOFF, JEROME, lawyer; b. June 22, 1931; s. Meyer and Anne (Soshnick) T.; children: Marcy Jane, Margery Lynne; m. Nancy Radin, 1990. AB, Syracuse U., 1952; JD, Columbia U., 1957. Bar: N.Y. 1957, U.S. Dist. Ct. (so. and ea. dists.) N.Y. 1960, U.S. Ct. Appeals (2d cir.) 1961. Ptnr. Sheldon and Tarnoff, N.Y.C., 1957-78, Feldesman, D'Atri, Tarnoff & Lubitz, N.Y.C., 1978, Baskin and Sears, P.C., N.Y.C., 1979-84, Baskin & Steingut P.C., 1984-85, Berger & Steingut, 1986-92, Morrison, Cohen, Singer & Weinstein, LLP, 1993—. Contbr. article to legal jour. Chmn. policy com. N.Y. Dem. Party, 1975-78, vice chmn. N.Y. County, 1978—, mem. nat. com., 1980-88; mem. Cmty. Planning Bd. #8, 1966-75; bd. dirs. Grand St. Settlement, 1973—, Assoc. Y's of N.Y., 1972-88. With U.S. Army, 1952-54. Recipient Disting. Svc. award NAACP, 1975, Cert. Achievement, El Diario-La Prensa, 1977. Mem. ABA, N.Y. State Bar Assn., Assn. of Bar of City of N.Y., N.T. County Lawyers, Am. Arbitration Assn. (nat. panel arbitrators), Phi Alpha Delta, Sunningdale Country Club (Scarsdale, N.Y.), Harmonie Club (N.Y.C.), Audubon, Masons. Jewish. General civil litigation, Family and matrimonial, Municipal (including bonds). Office: Morrison Cohen Singer & Weinstein 750 Lexington Ave New York NY 10022-1200 E-mail: jtarnoff@mcsw.com

TARONJI, JAIME, JR. lawyer; b. N.Y.C., Nov. 20, 1944; s. Jaime and Ruth T.; m. Mary Taronji, May 16, 1970; children: Ian A., Mark N., Nicole V. BA, George Washington U., 1972; JD, Georgetown U., 1976. Bar: Va. 1977. Asst. to dep. staff dir. U.S. Commn. on Civil Rights, Washington, 1972-76; trial atty. FTC, 1976-79; antitrust counsel Westinghouse Electric Corp., Pitts., 1979-81; group legal counsel Dana Corp., Toledo, 1982-88; v.p., gen. counsel, asst. sec. Packaging Corp. Am. subs. Tenneco, Evanston, Ill., 1988-95; law v.p. NCR Corp., Dayton, 1996-99; v.p., gen. counsel, sec. Dayton Superior Corp., 1999—. Author: The 1970 Census Undercount of Spanish Speaking Persons, 1974; editor: Puerto Ricans in the U.S., 1976. Capt. M.I., U.S. Army, 1965-70, Vietnam. Mem. ABA (antitrust sect.). Democrat. Roman Catholic. Antitrust, General corporate, Mergers and acquisitions. Home: 5 Grandon Rd Dayton OH 45419-2548 Office: Ste 130 7777 Washington Village Dr Dayton OH 45459-3976 E-mail: jimtaronji@daytonsuperior.com

TARPY, THOMAS MICHAEL, lawyer; b. Columbus, Ohio, Jan. 4, 1945; s. Thomas Michael and Catherine G. (Sharshal) T.; m. Mary Patricia Canna, Sept. 9, 1967; children: Joshua Michael, Megan Patricia, Thomas Canna, John Patrick. AB, John Carroll U., 1966; JD, Ohio State U., 1969. Bar: Ohio 1969, U.S. Dist. Ct. (so. dist.) Ohio 1972, U.S. Dist. Ct. (no. dist.) Ohio 1974, U.S. Ct. Appeals (6th cir.) 1982, U.S. Supreme Ct. 1997. Assoc. Vorys, Sater, Seymour & Pease LLP, Columbus, 1969-76, ptnr., 1977-85, 87—; v.p. Liebert Corp., 1985-87. Chmn. Columbus Graphics Commn., 1980; mem. Columbus Area Leadership Program, 1975. With U.S. Army, 1969-75. Fellow Coll. Labor and Employment Lawyers; mem. ABA, Ohio Bar Assn., Columbus Bar Assn. General corporate, Labor, Pension, profit-sharing, and employee benefits. Office: Vorys Sater Seymour & Pease LLP PO Box 1008 52 E Gay St Columbus OH 43215-3161

TASHIMA, ATSUSHI WALLACE, federal judge; b. Santa Maria, Calif., June 24, 1934; s. Yasutaro and Aya (Sasaki) T.; m. Nora Kiyo Inadomi, Jan. 27, 1957; children: Catherine Y., Christopher I., Jonathan I. AB in Polit. Sci., UCLA, 1958; LLB, Harvard U., 1961. Bar: Calif. 1962. Dep. atty. gen. State of Calif., 1962-67; atty. Spreckels Sugar divsn. Amstar Corp., 1968-72, v.p., gen. atty., 1972-77; ptnr. Morrison & Foerster, L.A., 1977-80; judge U.S. Dist. Ct. (ctrl. dist.) Calif., 1980-96, U.S. Ct. Appeals (9th cir.), Pasadena, Calif., 1996—. Mem. Calif. Com. Bar Examiners, 1978-80 With USMC, 1953-55. Mem. ABA, State Bar Calif., Los Angeles County Bar Assn. Democrat. Office: US Ct Appeals PO Box 91510 125 S Grand Ave Pasadena CA 91105-1652*

TASKER, JOSEPH, lawyer, educator; b. Tulsa, May 6, 1950; s. Joseph and Kathryn Lucille (Ahlstrom) T.; m. Constance Lee Sontheimer, May 28, 1971; children: Joseph III, Kathryn Holly. BA, U. Okla., 1972; JD, George Washington U., 1975. Bar: D.C. 1975, U.S. Dist. Ct. D.C. 1981, U.S. Ct. Appeals (D.C. cir.) 1981, U.S. Ct. Internat. Trade 1981, U.S. Ct. Appeals (fed. cir.) 1984. Staff atty. Bur. of Competition FTC, Washington, 1975-79, asst. to dir., 1979-81; assoc. Bishop, Cook, Purcell & Reynolds, 1981-85, ptnr., 1986-90; v.p., assoc. gen. counsel, govt. affairs Compaq Computer Corp., 1990-99. Lectr. in sociology George Washington U., 1974, 77, lectr. George Washington U. Law Sch., 1982. Mem. ABA, D.C. Bar Assn., Order of Coif, Phi Beta Kappa. Democrat. Antitrust, Federal civil litigation, Private international.

TASKER, MOLLY JEAN, lawyer; b. Cumberland, Md., Feb. 13, 1945; d. Samuel Paul Tasker and Peggy Evelyn Purinton; m. Richard Mark Curtis, June 7, 1985. AA, Santa Fe Jr. Coll., 1968; BA, Fla. Atlantic U., 1970; JD, Fla. State U., 1973. Bar: Fla. 1973, U.S. Supreme Ct. 1992, U.S. Dist. Ct. (mid. dist.) Fla. 1997. Atty., advisor CIA, Washington, 1974-82, asst. gen. counsel, 1983-95, chair publs. rev. bd., 1993-95; ptnr. Tasker & Stephens, PA, Indian Harbour Beach, Fla., 1996—. Bd. dirs. Brevard County Emergency Med. Svc. Found., Melbourne, Fla., Cmty. Housing Initiative, Melbourne; guest lectr. Fla. So. Coll., Lakeland, 1997-01. Exec. sec. Brevard County (Fla.) Juvenile Justice Coun., 1997—; vice-chair Brevard County Dem. Exec. Com., 1997-98; chair govtl. affairs com. C. of C., Melbourne, 1998-99. Recipient Spl. Recognition award Brevard County Legal Aid, Inc., Fla., 1997, 2000; Fulbright Travel grant Fla. State U. Ctr. for Slavic and East European Studies, 1972. Mem. AAUW, LWV, Phi Alpha Delta, Phi Gamma Nu. Lutheran. Avocations: photography, reading, tennis, boating. Public international, Land use and zoning (including planning), Legislative. Home: 4050 Carolwood Dr Melbourne FL 32934-7179 Office: 244 E Eau Gallie Blvd Satellite Beach FL 32937-4874

TATE, DAVID KIRK, lawyer; b. Detroit, Apr. 20, 1939; s. Andrew Golden and Izona (Kirk) T.; divorced; children— De Marcus David Holland, Lisa Arlayne. BS in Math., Mich. State U., 1963; JD, U. Detroit, 1973. Bar: Mich. 1973, U.S. Dist. Ct. (ea. dist.) Mich. 1973, U.S. Tax Ct. 1973. Assoc., Patmon, Young & Kirk, P.C., Detroit, 1973-76; staff atty. Detroit Edison Co., 1976-77; asst. counsel R.J. Reynolds Industries, Inc., Winston-Salem, N.C., 1977-79; assoc. counsel R.J. Reynolds Tobacco Co., Winston-Salem, 1979-82, counsel corp. and comml., 1982-86, sr. counsel, 1986—, asst. sec., 1984; dir. Legal Svcs. of N.C., Raleigh, 1983-88; negotiator, author numerous multi-million dollar contracts. Bd. dirs. Dearborn Med. Ctr., Mich., 1975-77; mem. U.S. Selective Svc. Appeals Bd., Middle dist. N.C., 1982; mem. coll./industry cluster St. Augustine's Coll., Raleigh, 1983; bd. dirs. N.C. Vietnam Vets Leadership Program, Inc., 1985-90, vice chmn. bd., 1989-90. Capt. inf. U.S. Army, 1963-68; Vietnam. Decorated Bronze Star, Air medal. Mem. ABA (contracts com. 1984-86, chmn. steering com. div. #5, forum on constrn. industry 1988-92), State Bar Mich., N.C. Bar Assn. (bd. govs. 1988-91), Forsyth County Bar Assn., Alpha Phi Alpha (chpt. pres. 1961-63). Democrat. Mem. First Bapt. Ch. (bd. deacons, pastoral rels. com. 1988-91). Contracts commercial, Construction, Landlord-tenant. Home: 2736 Woodlore Trl Winston Salem NC 27103-6546 Office: RJ Reynolds Tobacco Co 401 N Main St Winston Salem NC 27101-3804

TATE, STONEWALL SHEPHERD, lawyer; b. Memphis, Dec. 19, 1917; m. Janet Graf; children: Adele Shepherd, Shepherd Davis, Janet Reid Walker. BA, Southwestern at Memphis (now Rhodes Coll.), 1939; JD, U. Va., 1942; LLD (hon.), Samford U., 1979, Suffolk U., 1982, Capital U., 1989, Rhodes Coll., 1993. Bar: Va. 1941, Tenn. 1942. Chmn. bd. Martin, Tate, Morrow & Marston, P.C. (and predecessor firms), Memphis, 1947—. Chmn. pres.'s coun. Rhodes Coll., 1995-96, sec. bd. trustees, 1967-77, 80-84. Pres. Episcopal Churchmen of Tenn., 1961-62; sec. standing com. Episcopal Diocese of Tenn., 1969-71; pres. Chickasaw Coun. Boy Scouts Am., 1967-78. With USNR, 1942-46; comdr. USNR; ret. Decorated Order of Cloud Banner (China); recipient Silver Beaver award Boy Scouts Am., 1963, Disting. Eagle Scout award, 1980, Disting. Svc. medal Rhodes Coll., 1978, Disting. Alumni award, 1991, Lawyers' Lawyer award Memphis Bar Assn., 1990; Memphis Rotary Club Civic Recognition award, 1983; Paul Harris fellow, 1985. Fellow Am. Bar Found., Am. Coll. Trust and Estate Counsel, Internat. Acad. Estate and Trust Law, Coll. Law Practice Mgmt. (hon.), Tenn. Bar Found., Memphis and Shelby County Bar Found.; mem. ABA (chmn. standing com. on profl. discipline 1973-76, chmn. standing com. on scope and correlation of work 1977, chmn. task force on lawyer advt. 1977, pres. ABA 1978-79, chmn. standing com. on lawyer competence 1986-92, mem. coun. sr. lawyers divsn. 1997-2001), Am. Judicature Soc. (past bd. dirs.), Am. Law Inst., Lawyer-Pilots Bar Assn., Tenn. Bar Assn. (pres. 1963-64), Memphis and Shelby County Bar Assn. (pres. 1959-60), Nat. Conf. Bar Pres. (pres. 1972-73, Alumnus of Yr. 1996), U.S. 6th Cir. Jud. Conf. (life), U. Va. Law Sch. Alumni Assn. (mem. exec. coun. 1974-77), Rhodes Coll. Alumni Assn. (pres. 1951-53), Rotary (pres. 1982-83, bd. dirs. 1974, 80-84, 89-90), Raven Soc., Order of Coif, Phi Beta Kappa, Omicron Delta Kappa, Phi Delta Phi, Sigma Alpha Epsilon (highest effort award N.Y.C. Alumni Assn. 1979). General corporate, Estate planning, Probate. Office: Martin Tate Morrow & Marston PC Falls Bldg 22 N Front St Ste 1100 Memphis TN 38103-1182 E-mail: sstate@martintate.com

TATEL, DAVID STEPHEN, federal judge; b. Washington, Mar. 16, 1942; s. Howard Edwin and Molly (Abramowitz) T.; m. Edith Sara Bassichis, Aug. 29, 1965; children: Rebecca, Stephanie, Joshua, Emily. BA, U. Mich., 1963; JD, U. Chgo., 1966. Bar: Ill 1966. Instr. U. Mich., Ann Arbor, 1966-67; assoc. Sidley & Austin, Chgo. and Washington, 1967-69, 70-72; dir. Chgo. Lawyer's Com., 1969-70, Nat. Lawyers Commn. for Civil Rights Under Law, Washington, 1972-74; dir. Office for Civil Rights HEW, 1977-79; assoc., ptnr. Hogan & Hartson, 1974-77, ptnr., 1979-94; cir. judge U.S. Ct. Appeals (D.C. cir.), 1994—. Lectr. Stanford U. Law Sch., 1991-92; co-chmn. Nat. Lawyers Com. for Civil Rights Under Law, Washington, 1989-91; chmn., bd. dirs. Spencer Found., Chgo., 1990-97. Bd. dirs. Carnegie Found. for Advancement in Tchg., Stanford, Calif., 1997—. Office: US Ct Appeals 333 Constitution Ave NW 3818 US Courthouse Washington DC 20001-2802

TATEOKA, REID, lawyer; b. Salt Lake City, Jan. 11, 1954; s. Matt M. and Ida S. (Shimizu) T.; m. Shauna Reid, June 3, 1977; children: Jacob Reid, Elizabeth Ann, John Robinson. BA, U. Utah, 1978; JD, Brigham Young U., 1981. Bar: Utah 1981, U.S. Dist. Ct. (cen. dist.) Utah 1981, U.S. Ct. Appeals (10th cir.) 1986. Assoc. McKay, Burton, Thurman & Condie, Salt Lake City, 1981-85; ptnr., shareholder, dir. McKay, Burton & Thurman, 1985-89, pres., 1989—. Lectr. on problem collections in Utah, 1988, 90. Treas. Japanese Am. Citizens League, Salt Lake City, 1983, 88-90, pres., 1991-96, bd. dirs., 1997—; active Salt Lake coun. Boy Scouts Am. Mem. Am. Inns of Cts., Phi Delta Phi (provincial pres. 1984—). Mem. LDS Ch. Avocations: skiing, golf, fishing. General civil litigation, Construction. Office: McKay Burton & Thurman Gateway Tower East Ste 600 Salt Lake City UT 84133 E-mail: reid@mbt-law.com

TAUB, ELI IRWIN, family court judge; b. N.Y.C., July 6, 1938; s. Max and Belle (Slutsky) T.; m. Nancy Denise Bell, May 15, 1983; 1 child, Jennifer. BA, Bklyn. Coll., 1960; JD, NYU, 1963. Bar: N.Y. 1964, U.S. Dist. Ct. (no. dist.) N.Y. 1979. Ptnr. Silverman, Silverman & Taub, Schenectady, N.Y., 1971-77; pres. Eli I. Taub, P.C., 1978-2001; judge Schenectady County (N.Y.) Family Ct., 2001—. Arbitrator Am. Arbitration Assn., N.Y. Employment Rels. Bd., 1966-2001; N.Y. State Pub. Employers Rels. Bd.; hearing officer, paralegal adv. com. Schenectady County C.C. Chmn. trustees Joseph Egan Supreme Ct. Library, Schenectady, 1980, 81, 84; pres. Schenectady County Republican Club, 1985-86; v.p. Jewish Fedn. Schenectady, 1983-86; mem. surrogate decision making com. N.Y. State Commn. on Quality of Care for the Mentally Disabled, to 2001; bd. dirs. Jewish Cmty. Ctr., Jewish Family Svcs. United Jewish Fedn. of N.E. N.Y., to 2001; advocate Nat. Coll. of Advocacy. Recipient Vol. of Yr. award Jewish Family Svcs., 1998, Humanitarian of Yr. award Alcohol and Substance Abuse Coun., 2001. Mem. ATLA, Am. Arbitration Assn., Nat. Orgn. of Social Security Claimant Reps., Indsl. Rels. Rsch. Assn., N.Y. State Bar Assn., N.Y. State Trial Lawyers Assn., Schenectady County Bar Assn., Capital Dist. Trial Lawyers Assn., Injured Workers Bar Assn., B'nai B'rith (pres. 1976-77, spl. award 1982, youth svcs. award 1985). Family and matrimonial, Personal injury, Workers' compensation. Home: 105 N Ferry St Schenectady NY 12305-1610 Office: 620 State St Schenectady NY 12305 Fax: 518-393-0719

TAUB, LINDA MARSHA, lawyer; b. N.Y.C., Dec. 14, 1943; d. Harry Mark and Estelle Pearl (Weinberg) Lewin; m. David Stephen Taub, June 23, 1964; children: Andrew Scott, Marc Douglas, Joshua M. BA in History, L.I. U., 1975; JD, Hofstra U., 1983. Bar: N.Y. 1984, U.S. Dist. Ct. (ea. dist.) N.Y. 1984, U.S. Dist. Ct. (so. dist.) N.Y. 1986, U.S. Supreme Ct. 1991, U.S. Ct. Appeals (2d cir.) 1995. Assoc. Weinstein & Dezorett, Garden City, N.Y., 1983-84, Semon & Mondshein, Jericho, 1985-91, ptnr. Woodbury, 1991—. Asst. sec. DaMart Enterprises, Inc., Syosset, N.Y., 1987—. Chmn. Hillel, Hofstra U., Hempstead, N.Y., 1997—. Mem. ABA, N.Y. State Bar Assn., Nassau County Bar Assn., Nassau County Women's Bar Assn. (chair jud. diversity com. 1996-97, bd. dirs. 1997—). General civil litigation, Family and matrimonial, Real property. Office: Semon & Mondshein 7600 Jericho Tpke Ste 200 Woodbury NY 11797-1732

TAUB, STEPHEN RICHARD, lawyer; b. N.Y.C., Oct. 5, 1944; s. Irving Robert and Sylvia T.; m. Alyson Zoe Winter, Dec. 23, 1968. BA, Queens Coll., 1965; JD, NYU, 1968. Bar: N.Y. 1969, U.S. Dist. Ct. (ea. and so. dists.) N.Y. 1970, U.S. Ct. Appeals (2nd cir.) 1971, U.S. Supreme Ct. 1972. Asst. dist. atty., bur. chief Kings County Dist. Attys. Office, Bklyn., 1970-77; pvt. practice Garden City, N.Y., 1977-96; ptnr. Ostrow and Taub, LLP, from 1996, Schlissel, Ostrow, Karabatos, Poepplein & Taub, PLLC, Mineola, N.Y. Matrimonial case neutral evaluator Nassau County Supreme Ct., Mineola, 1997—. Village Justice Village Kensington, Great Neck, N.Y., 1986-98; Acting Village Justice Village Old Brookville, N.Y., 1998—. Fellow Am. Acad. Matrimonial Lawyers; mem. ABA, N.Y. Family Law Am. Inn of Ct. (master), N.Y. State Bar Assn., N.Y. State Magistrates Assn., Nassau County Bar Assn., Nassau County Magistrates Assn. (pres. 1993-94). Avocation: tennis. Office: Schissel Ostrow Et Al 190 Willis Ave Mineola NY 11501

TAUB, THEODORE CALVIN, lawyer; b. Springfield, Mass., Jan. 1, 1935; s. Samuel and Sara Lee (Daum) T.; m. Roberta Mae Ginsburg, Aug. 23, 1959; children: Tracy, Andrew, Adam. AB, Duke U., 1956; JD, U. Fla., 1960. Bar: Fla., 1960, U.S. Supreme Ct. Atty. Shumaker, Loop & Kendrick, Tampa. Asst. city atty. City of Tampa, 1963-67; city atty. City of Temple Terrace, Fla., 1974—; panelist in field. Contbr. articles to profl. jours. Chmn. Tampa-Hillsborough (Fla.) County Exp. Authority, 1974-84; mem. Hillsborough County Charter Commn., 1966-69, Local Govt. Mgmt. Efficiency Com., 1979, State of Fla. Environ. Efficiency Study Commn., 1986-88; founder Tampa Bay Performing Arts Ctr. Fellow: Am. Bar Found; mem. ABA (chmn. real property litigation com. 1981-86, chmn. com. on housing and urban environ. 1989-91), Am. Coll. Real Estate Lawyers (bd. govs.), Am. Land Title Assn. (lenders' counsel group), Fla. Bar Assn. (bd. cert. real estate lawyer), Fla. Jaycees (pres.), Tau Epsilon Phi. Democrat. Jewish. General civil litigation, Land use and zoning (including planning), Real property. Home: 4937 Lyford Cay Rd Tampa FL 33629-4828 Office: Bank of Am 101 E Kennedy Blvd Ste 2800 Tampa FL 33602-5869 E-mail: ttaub@broadandcassel.com

TAUBENFELD, HARRY SAMUEL, lawyer; b. Bklyn., June 27, 1929; s. Marcus Isaac and Anna (Engelhard) T.; m. Florence Spatz, June 17, 1956; children: Anne Gail Weisbrod, Stephen Marshall. BA, Bklyn. Coll., 1951; JD, Columbia U., 1954. Bar: N.Y. 1955, U.S. Supreme Ct. 1965, U.S. Dist. Ct. (so. and ea. dists.) N.Y. 1976. Assoc. Benjamin H. Schor, Bklyn., 1955-58; ptnr. Zuckerbrod & Taubenfeld, Cedarhurst (N.Y.), N.Y.C., 1958—; bd. dirs. Cornerstone Real Estate Income Trust, 1993—, Next Generation Mktg., Inc., 1996-99. Village atty. Village of Cedarhurst, 1977-88, trustee, 1989-2001; mem. bd. Downtown Cedarhurst Bus. Improvement Dist., 1993; legis. chmn., counsel Nassau County Village Ofcls., 1979-86, v.p., 1991-93, pres., 1993-94, mem. exec. com., 1989-99, chmn.

intergovtl. liaison com., 1991-93; mem. legis. com. N.Y. State Conf. Mayors, 1979-87, 92-93; mem. exec. bd. Tri-County Village Ofcls., 1991-95, pres., 1993-94; arbitrator Am. Arbitration Assn. Dist. Ct. Nassau County, 1980—, Assessment Rev. Panel, Supreme Ct., Nassau County, 1981—; mem. Constl. Bicentennial Com., 1987-89; hon. trustee Cong. Beth Shalom, Lawrence, N.Y., 1990-2001; nat. bd. dirs. Zionist Orgn. Am. Assoc. chmn. Am. Zionist Fedn., 1985-87; pres. Herut Zionists Am., 1977-79; v.p. Hartman YMHA, 1983-87; del. World Zionist Congress, 1977, 82, 87; mem. Zionist Gen. Coun., 1977-83; bd. govs. Jewish Agy., 1983-92; mem. exec. com. World Zionist Orgn., 1983-92; trustee United Jewish Appeal, 1986-91; bd. dirs. United Israel Appeal, 1986-91; hon. vice chmn., bd. dirs. Jewish Nat. Fund, 1987-89; nat. bd. dirs. Am. for a Safe Israel; hon. pres. World Coun. Herut Hatzoa, Jerusalem, Internat. Bd. Youthtown of Israel. Recipient Centenial award Jabotinsky Found. 1981, Betar Youth award World Betar 1982, award Internat. League for Repatriation of Russian Jews 1977, Youth Towns of Israel Leadership award 1973, Israel Bonds Leadership award 1976, Life Time Achievement award Israel Bonds 1991, Defender of Jerusalem award 1991, Israel Bonds Menachem Begin Leadership award, 1999. Mem. Internat. Assn. Jewish Lawyers and Jurists, Jewish War Vets., B'nai B'rith, Nordau Circle Club, Zionist Orgn. of Am., Beth El Synagogue, New Rochelle, N.Y. Contracts commercial, Municipal (including bonds), Real property. Home: 21 N Chatsworth Ave Larchmont NY 10538 Office: PO Box 488 575 Chestnut St Cedarhurst NY 11516-2223

TAURMAN, JOHN DAVID, lawyer; b. Charleston, W.Va., May 22, 1946; s. Ralph and Mikanna Elizabeth (Clark) T.; m. Donna Jill Naroff, June 13, 1981; children: Devon Elliott, Kyra Justine, Quinn Juliet. BA magna cum laude, Duke U., 1968; JD cum laude, Harvard U., 1971. Bar: D.C. 1971, U.S. Supreme Ct. 1981, Tex. 1984, U.S. Ct. Appeals (D.C., 3d, 5th 9th and 10th cirs.), U.S. Dist. Ct. D.C., U.S. Dist. Ct. (so. and no. dists.) Tex., U.S. Ct. Fed. Claims. Assoc. Covington & Burling, Washington, 1971-78, Vinson & Elkins, Washington, 1979-82, ptnr. Houston, 1982-90, Washington, 1990—. Lectr. State Bar Inst. Tex., 1983. Editor Harvard Law Rev., 1969-71. Mem. ABA, State Bar Tex., D.C. Bar Assn., Phi Beta Kappa. Antitrust, Federal civil litigation. Office: Vinson & Elkins Willard Office Bldg 1455 Pennsylvania Ave NW Fl 7 Washington DC 20004-1013 E-mail: jtaurman@velaw.com

TAURO, JOSEPH LOUIS, federal judge; b. Winchester, Mass., Sept. 26, 1931; s. G. Joseph and Helen Maria (Petrossi) T.; m. Elizabeth Mary Quinlan, Feb. 7, 1959 (dec. 1978); children— Joseph L., Elizabeth H., Christopher M.; m. Ann Lefavour Jones, July 12, 1980. AB, Brown U., 1953; LLB, Cornell U., 1956; JD (hon.), U. Mass., 1985, Suffolk U., 1986, Northeastern U., 1990, New Eng. Sch. Law, 1992, Boston U., 1997, Brown U., 1998. Bar: Mass. 1956, D.C. 1960. Assoc. Tauro & Tauro, Lynn, Mass., 1958-59; asst. U.S. atty. Dept. Justice, Boston, 1959-60; ptnr. Jaffee & Tauro, Boston and Lynn, Mass., 1960-71; chief legal counsel Gov. of Mass., Boston, 1965-68; U.S. atty. Dept. Justice, 1972; judge U.S. Dist. Ct., 1972—; chief judge U.S. Dist. Ct., Mass., 1992-99. Mem. exec. com. Cornell Law Assn., Ithaca, N.Y., 1968-71; mem. adv. coun. Cornell Law Sch., Ithaca, 1975-80; vis. prof. law Boston U. Law Sch., 1977—; mem. Jud. Conf. U.S., 1994-97, mem. com. on operation of jury sys., 1979-86, mem. adv. com. on codes of conduct, 1988-94. Trustee Brown U., 1978—, Mass. Gen. Hosp., Boston, 1968-72, Children's Hosp. Med. Ctr., Boston, 1979-94. 1st lt. U.S. Army, 1956-58. Recipient Disting. Alumnus award Cornell U. Law Sch., 1992, Brown Bear award Brown U., 1993; named one of 10 Outstanding Young Men, Greater Boston Jaycees, 1966. Fellow Am. Bar Found.; mem. Mass. Bar Assn., Boston Bar Assn. (coun. 1968-71), D.C. Bar Assn., Boston Yacht Club (Marblehead, Mass.). Republican. Roman Catholic. Avocations: sports; reading; music; films; theater. Office: 1 Courthouse Way Ste 7110 Boston MA 02210-3009

TAUSEND, FREDRIC CUTNER, lawyer, university dean; b. N.Y.C., July 6, 1933; s. Stanley and Louise (Cutner) T.; m. Sandra Adkisson, Apr. 26, 1962 (div. Sept. 1976); children— Jessica, Rachel; m. Marilyn Lewis, Jan. 20, 1979. A.B. magna cum laude, Harvard U., 1954, LL.B., 1957. Bar: U.S. Dist. Ct. (we. dist.) Wash., U.S. Ct. Appeals (9th cir.), U.S. Supreme Ct. Asst. gen. atty., div. antitrust and consumer protection State of Wash., Seattle, 1963-64; assoc. Schweppe, Krug, & Tausend, Seattle, 1958-62, 65, ptnr., 1966-80, 85-90; dean Sch. Law, U. Puget Sound, Tacoma, 1980-86; ptnr. Preston, Gates & Ellis, Seattle, 1990—. Chmn. King County Bd. Adjustment, Seattle, 1967, Seattle Crime Prevention Adv. Commn., 1971-74 Served with U.S. Army, 1957-58. Fellow Am. Bar Found., Am. Coll. Trial Lawyers; mem. Wash. State Bar Assn. (chmn. antitrust div. 1981-82), ABA. Democrat. Jewish. Clubs: Harvard (N.Y.C.); Wash. Athletic (Seattle). Federal civil litigation, State civil litigation. Office: 5000 Columbia Ctr 701 5th Ave Seattle WA 98104-7097

TAVROW, RICHARD LAWRENCE, lawyer, corporate executive; b. Syracuse, N.Y., Feb. 3, 1935; s. Harry and Ida Mary (Hodess) T.; m. Barbara J. Silver, Mar. 22, 1972; children— Joshua Michael, Sara Hallie. A.B. magna cum laude, Harvard U., 1957, LL.B., 1960, LL.M., 1961; postgrad., U. Copenhagen, 1961-62, U. Luxembourg, 1962. Bar: N.Y. bar 1961, U.S. Supreme Ct. bar 1969, Calif. bar 1978. Atty. W.R. Grace & Co., N.Y.C., 1962-66; asst. chief counsel Gen. Dynamics Corp., 1966-68; chief counsel office of fgn. direct investments U.S. Dept. Commerce, Washington, 1969-71; ptnr. Schaeffer, Dale, Vogel & Tavrow, N.Y.C., 1971-75; v.p., sec., gen. counsel Prudential Lines, Inc., 1975-78, also bd. dirs.; v.p., sec., gen. counsel Am. Pres. Lines, Ltd., Oakland, Calif., 1978-80, sr. v.p., sec., gen. counsel, 1980-91, also bd. dirs.; sr. v.p., sec., gen. counsel Am. Pres. Cos., Ltd., 1983-91, also bd. dirs. Calif.; sr. ptnr. Law Offices of R.L. Tavrow, 1991—; chmn., pres., CEO Diabetes Healthcare & Life Enhancement Ltd., 1998—. Instr. Harvard Coll., 1959-61; lectr. Am. Mgmt. Assn., Practising Law Inst., other assns. Recipient Silver Medal award Dept. Commerce, 1970; Fulbright scholar, 1961-62 Mem. ABA, State Bar Calif., Internat. Bar Assn., Am. Soc. Internat. Law, Am. Corp. Counsel Assn., Am. Soc. Corp. Secs. Inc., Harvard Law Sch. Assn., Navy League, Harvard Club (N.Y.C.). Administrative and regulatory, General corporate, Transportation.

TAYLOR, ALLAN BERT, lawyer; b. Cin., June 28, 1948; s. H Ralph and Henrietta Irene (Medalia) Taylor; m. Sally Ann Silverstein, June 06, 1971; children: Rachel Elizabeth, Karen Ruth. AB, Harvard U., 1970, M in Pub. Policy, JD, Harvard U., 1975. Bar: Conn 1975, US Ct Appeals (DC cir) 1977, US Dist Ct (so dist) NY 1979, US Ct Appeals (2d cir) 1979, US Supreme Ct 1979, US Ct Appeals (1st and 10th cirs) 1991. Law clk. to J. Skelly Wright D.C. Cir., Washington, 1975-76; law clk. to Thurgood Marshall U.S. Supreme Ct., 1976-77; assoc. Day, Berry & Howard, Hartford, Conn., 1977-83, ptnr., 1983—. Overseer Bushnell Meml Hall Corp, Hartford, 1992—. Bd dirs Hartford Infant Action Project, 1990—, pres, 1999; elected mem Hartford City Coun, 1981—87, Hartford Bd Educ, 1989—93, vpres, 1991—93; mem Conn State Bd Educ, Hartford, 1994—; chmn charter revision communications City of Hartford, 1999—2000; bd dirs Conn Asn Bds Educ, Hartford, 1989—93, Hartford Stage Co, 1993—2001. Mem.: ABA, Conn Bar Asn, Hartford Bar Asn, Phi Beta Kappa. Democrat. Jewish. Avocations: astronomy, reading. Federal civil litigation, Insurance, Public utilities. Home: 238 Whitney St Hartford CT 06105-2270 Office: Day Berry & Howard City Place Hartford CT 06103 E-mail: abtaylor@dbh.com

TAYLOR, AMYSUE, lawyer, nurse; b. Columbus, Ohio, Nov. 1, 1954; m. Richard Taylor, Aug. 1, 1980; children: Richie, Kip. BSN, U. Cin., 1977; MS, Ohio State U., 1979; JD, Capital U., 1983; diploma, Nat. Inst. Trial Advocacy, 1987. Bar: Ohio 1983, U.S. Dist. Ct. (so. dist) Ohio, U.S. Ct. Appeals (6th cir.) 1983. Assoc. Zacks Luper Wolinete, Columbus, 1983-84, Jacobson Maynard Tuschman & Kalur, Columbus, 1984-88, Michael F. Colley Co. LPA, Columbus, 1989-93; pvt. practice, 1993—. Co-author: Operative Obstetrics, 1995. Investigative rev. bd. com. Park Med. Ctr./Ohio State U. East, Columbus, 1990-2000. Mem. Am. Trial Lawyers Assn., Ohio Trial Lawyers, Columbus Bar Assn. (chair dr./lawyer com. 1991-94), Franklin County Trial Lawyers. General civil litigation, Personal injury, Professional liability. Office: 505 S High St Columbus OH 43215-5601 Fax: 614-224-9599. E-mail: hhtaylor@pol.net

TAYLOR, ANNA DIGGS, judge; b. Washington, Dec. 9, 1932; d. Virginius Douglass and Hazel (Bramlette) Johnston; m. S. Martin Taylor, May 22, 1976; children: Douglass Johnston Diggs, Carla Cecile Diggs. BA, Barnard Coll., 1954; LLB, Yale U., 1957. Bar: D.C. 1957, Mich. 1961. Atty. Office Solicitor, Dept. Labor, W, 1957-60; asst. prosecutor Wayne County, Mich., 1961-62; asst. U.S. atty. Eastern Dist. of Mich., 1966; ptnr. Zwerdling, Maurer, Diggs & Papp, Detroit, 1970-75; asst. corp. counsel City of Detroit, 1975-79; U.S. dist. judge Eastern Dist. Mich. Detroit, 1979—. Hon. chair, trustee United Way Cmty. Found., S.E. Mich., Detroit Inst. Arts; co-chair, vol. Leadership Coun.; trustee Henry Ford Health Sys., Cmty. Found. for S.E. Mich. Mem. Fed. Bar Assn., State Bar Mich., Wolverine Bar Assn. (v.p.), Yale Law Assn. Episcopalian. Office: US Dist Ct 740 US Courthouse 231 W Lafayette Blvd Detroit MI 48226-2700

TAYLOR, CARROLL STRIBLING, lawyer; b. Port Chester, N.Y., Jan. 14, 1944; s. William H. Jr. and Anna P. (Stribling) T.; m. Nancy S. Tyson, Apr. 7, 1968; children: Heather, Kimberly, Tori, Tiffany, Tacy. AB, Yale U., 1965; JD, U. Calif., Berkeley, 1968. Bar: Hawaii 1969, Calif. 1969, U.S. Dist. Ct. Hawaii 1969, U.S. Dist. Ct. (cen. dist.) Calif. 1975, U.S. Ct. Appeals (9th cir.) 1975. Rschr. Legis. Reference Bur., Honolulu, 1968-70; reporter Jud. Coun. Probate Code Revision Project, 1970-71; assoc. Chun, Kerr & Dodd, 1971-75; ptnr. Hamilton & Taylor, 1975-80; officer, dir. Char, Hamilton, Taylor & Thom, 1980-82, Carroll S. Taylor Atty. at Law, A Law Corp., Honolulu, 1982-86; ptnr. Taylor & Leong, 1986-91, Taylor, Leong & Chee, Honolulu, 1991—. Adj. prof. Richardson Sch. Law U. Hawaii, Honolulu, 1981-86, 88-90, 97; mem. Disciplinary bd. of Supreme Ct. of Hawaii, 1994—, vice chair, 1997-99, chair, 2000—; dir. Am. Nat. Lawyers Ins. Reciprocal, 1997-2000; mem., bd. dirs. Hanahauoli Sch., 1992-97. Fellow Am. Coll. Trust and Estate Counsel; mem. ABA, Calif. Bar Assn., Hawaii State Bar Assn., Hawaii Inst. Continuing Legal Edn. (pres. 1986-88), Pla. Club (Honolulu). Episcopalian. State civil litigation, Probate, Estate planning. Home: 46-429 Hololio St Kaneohe HI 96744-4225 Office: 737 Bishop St Ste 2060 Honolulu HI 96813-3214 E-mail: ctaylor@hawaii.rr.com

TAYLOR, CLIFFORD WOODWORTH, state supreme court justice; b. Delaware, Ohio, Nov. 9, 1942; s. Alexander E. and Carolyn (Clifford) T.; m. Lucille Taylor; 2 children. BA, U. Mich., 1964; JD, George Washington U., 1967. Asst. prosecuting atty. Ingham County, 1971-72; ptnr. Denfield, Timmer & Taylor, 1972-92; judge Mich. Ct. of Appeals, 1992-97, Supreme Ct. Justice, 1997—. Mem. standing com. on professionalism Mich. State Bar, 1992. Bd. dirs. Mich. Dyslexia Inst., 1991—, Friends of the Gov.'s Residence, 1991—; mem. St. Thomas Aquinas Ch. With USN, 1967-71. Fellow Mich. State Bar Found.; mem. Mich. Supreme Ct. Hist. Soc., Federalist Soc., Cath. Lawyers Guild, State Bar. Home: 9760 Sunny Point Dr Laingsburg MI 48848 Office: Mich Supreme Ct PO Box 300052 Lansing MI 48909

TAYLOR, DAVID BROOKE, lawyer, banker; b. Salt Lake City, Oct. 14, 1942; s. Lee Neff and June Taylor; m. Carolyn Kaufholz, May 29, 1965; children: Stewart, Allison. BA, U. Utah, 1964; JD, Columbia U., 1967. Bar: N.Y. 1967, N.C. 1995. Ptnr. Wickes, Riddell, Bloomer, Jacobi & McGuire, N.Y.C., 1967-79, Morgan, Lewis & Bockius, N.Y.C., 1979-89; banker, lawyer Chase Manhattan Bank, N.A., 1989-92; pres. Geoenertec Corp., 1992-93; ptnr. Fennebresque, Clark, Swindall & Hay, Charlotte, N.C., 1994-98, McGuire & Woods, LLP, Charlotte, 1999—. Mem. ABA, N.Y. State Bar Assn., N.C. Bar Assn. Banking, General corporate, Finance. Home: 3815 Beresford Rd Charlotte NC 28211-3713 Office: McGuire & Woods LLP 100 N Tryon St Ste 2900 Charlotte NC 28202-4022

TAYLOR, FREDERICK WILLIAM, JR. (FRITZ TAYLOR), lawyer; b. Cleve., Oct. 21, 1933; s. Frederick William Sr. and Marguerite Elizabeth (Kistler) T.; m. Mary Phyllis Osborne, June 1, 1985. BA in History, U. Fla., 1957; MA in Near East Studies, U. Mich., 1959; JD cum laude, NYU, 1967. Bar: N.Y. 1968, Calif. 1969, U.S. Dist. Ct. (cen. dist.) Calif. 1969. Govt. rels. rep. Arabian Am. Oil Co., Dhahran, Saudi Arabia, 1959-63, oil supply coord. N.Y.C., 1963-68, sr. counsel Dhahran, 1969-71, gen. mgr. govt. rels. orgn., 1971-74, v.p. indsl. rels., 1974-78; assoc. O'Melveny & Myers, L.A., 1968-69; ptnr. Burt & Taylor, Marblehead, Mass., 1978-80; pres., chief exec. officer Nat. Med. Enterprises Internat. Group, L.A., 1980-82; counsel Chadbourne, Parke & Afridi, United Arab Emirates, 1982-84; ptnr. Sidley & Austin, Cairo, 1984-87, Singapore, 1987-93; spl. counsel Heller Ehrman White & McAuliffe, L.A. and Singapore, 1993-95; legal advisor, corp. counsel law divsn. Lucent Techs. Internat. Inc., Riyadh, Saudi Arabia, 1995—. Contbr. articles to profl. jours. Mem. ABA, Calif. Bar Assn., Order of Coif, Singapore Cricket Club, Tanglin Club, Chanqi Sailing Club, Singapore Am. Club, Dirab Golf Club. Contracts commercial, General corporate, Private international. Home: 9875 E Shadowlake Ct Claremore OK 74017-1444 Office: Lucent Techs Int Inc PO Box 4945 Khurais Rd Riyadh 11412 Saudi Arabia

TAYLOR, GRACE ELIZABETH WOODALL (BETTY TAYLOR), law educator, law library administrator; b. Butler, N.J., June 14, 1926; d. Frank E. and Grace (Carlyon) Woodall; m. Edwin S. Taylor, Feb. 4, 1951 (dec.); children: Carol Lynn Taylor Crespo, Nancy Ann Filer. AB, Fla. State U., 1949, MA, 1950; JD, U. Fla., 1962. Instr. asst. librarian U. Fla., 1950-56; asst. law librarian Univ. Libraries, U. Fla., 1956-62; dir. Legal Info. Ctr., 1962—, prof. law, 1976—; Clarence J. TeSelle prof. of law U. Fla., 1994—. Trustee Nat. Ctr. for Automated Rsch., N.Y.C., 1978-96; past chmn. joint com. on LAWNET, Am. Assn. Law Librs., Am. Assn. Law Schs. and ABA, 1978—; cons. to law librs., 1975—; mem. adv. com. N.E. Regional Data Ctr., U. Fla., 1990—. Co-author: American Law Publications, 1986, 21st Century: Technology's Impact, 1988, Law in the Digital Age: The Challenge of Research in Legal Information Centers, 1996, also articles. Recipient 1st Disting. Alumni award Fla. State U. Libr. Sch., 1983, 2d Marya Langer/C.Q. award law and polit. sci. sect. ACRL and Congl. Quar., 1997; Lewis Scholar Fla. Legislature, 1947-50; grantee NEH, 1981-82, Coun. Libr. Resources, 1984-86; Dist. Svc. award, Florida Library Assn., 2000. Mem.: ABA (Law Libr. Congress facilities com. 1991—97), Am. Assn. Law Librs. (exec. bd. 1981—84, Marian Gould Gallagher Disting. Svc. award 1997, Aspen Law and Bus. Rsch. grant 1997), Am. Assn. Law Schs. (accreditation com. 1978—81), OCLC Users Coun. (pres. 1983—86), Phi Beta Kappa (v.p. U. Fla. chpt. 1994—95, pres. 1995—96), Beta Phi Mu. Democrat. Methodist. Avocations: computers, genealogy, crafts, gardening, grandchildren. Office: U Fla Legal Info Ctr Gainesville FL 32611 E-mail: Taylor@law.ufl.edu

TAYLOR, JERRY F(RANCIS), lawyer; b. Memphis, Oct. 2, 1934; s. Rex Brewster and Naomi (Robertson) T.; m. Jo(dy) Evelyn Katz, Mar. 5, 1971; 1 child, Deborah Pagan. BS, Memphis State U., 1956; JD, U. Tenn., 1963. Bar: U.S. Dist. Ct. Tenn. (we., mid. and ea. dists.) 1965, U.S. Dist. Ct. Miss. (mid. dist.) 1963, U.S. Ct. Appeals (6th cir.) 1970. Assoc. Krivcher & Cox, Memphis, 1963-65; sr. ptnr. Holt, Batchelor, Taylor & Spicer, 1965-80, Wilkes, McCullough & Taylor, Memphis, 1980-89, Taylor, Halliburton, Ledbetter & Caldwell, Memphis, 1989—. Pres. Second Chance Inc., 1988— Fundraiser United Way Memphis, 1982; bd. dirs. Jeff Steinberg Ministries, 1983—, Outreach to Youth, Inc., 1983—; pres., trustee Cen. Ch., Inc., 1988—. Served to capt. USAF, 1957-60. Law Sch. scholar Memphis-Shelby County Bar Assn., 1961. Mem. ABA, ATLA (state committeeman 1968), Tenn. Bar Assn., Memphis-Shelby County Bar Assn., Tenn. Trial Lawyers Assn. (bd. govs. 1984-89), Am. Bd. Trial Advocates (nat. bd. dirs. 1989—, advocate 1985—, sec. Tenn. chpt. 1985-86, pres.-elect Tenn. chpt. 1987-88, pres. 1988—), Am. Inns Ct. (founder, master Leo Beaman chpt. 1995—), Lawyers Involved in Tenn. (trustee 1983-89), Masons, Shriners. Personal injury. Home: 109 N Main St Apt 1101 Memphis TN 38103-5019 Office: Taylor Halliburton Ledbetter & Caldwell 44 N 2nd St Ste 200 Memphis TN 38103-2270

TAYLOR, JOB, III, lawyer; b. N.Y.C., Feb. 18, 1942; s. Job II and Anne Harrison (Flinchbaugh) T.; m. Mary C. August, Oct. 24, 1964 (div. 1978); children: Whitney August, Job IV; m. Sally Lawson, May 31, 1980; 1 child, Alexandra Anne. BA, Washington & Jefferson Coll., 1964; JD, Coll. William and Mary, 1971. Bar: N.Y. 1972, U.S. Dist. Ct. (no., so. ea. and we. dists.) N.Y. 1973, U.S. Ct. Appeals (2d cir.) 1973, U.S. Ct. Claims 1974, U.S. Tax Ct. 1974, U.S. Supreme Ct. 1975, U.S. Ct. Appeals (9th cir.) 1976, U.S. Ct. Mil. Appeals 1977, U.S. Ct. Appeals (D.C. and 10th cirs.) 1977, D.C. 1981, U.S. Ct. Internat. Trade 1981, U.S. Ct. Appeals (fed. cir.) 1982, U.S. Dist. Ct. (no. dist.) Calif. 1983, U.S. Ct. Appeals (6th cir.) U.S. Dist. Ct., 1987, U.S. Ct. Appeals (3d cir.) 1990, U.S. Dist. Ct. Conn. 1996. Ptnr. Olwine, Connelly, Chase, O'Donnell & Weyher, N.Y.C., 1971-85, Latham & Watkins, N.Y.C., 1985—. Served to lt. USN, 1964-68. Mem. ABA, Assn. Bar City N.Y., La Confrerie des Chevaliers du Tastevin, Racquet and Tennis Club, Wee Burn Country Club (Darien, Conn.), New Canaan Country Club.. Republican. Episcopalian. Avocations: squash, tennis, golf, reading. Antitrust, Federal civil litigation, Computer. Office: Latham & Watkins 885 3rd Ave Fl 9 New York NY 10022-4834

TAYLOR, JOE CLINTON, judge; b. Durant, Okla., Mar. 28, 1942; s. Luther Clinton and Virena (Parker) T.; m. Margaret Pearl Byers, June 8, 1963; children: Marna Joanne, Leah Alison, Jocelyn Camille. Student, Southeastern State Coll., 1960-62; BA, Okla. State U., 1965; JD, U. Okla., 1968. Bar: Okla. 1968. Pvt. practice, Norman, Okla., 1968-69; apptd. spl. dist. judge Durant, 1969-72; assoc. dist. judge Bryan County, Okla., 1972-76; dist. judge, chief judge 19th Dist. Ct., 1976-93; presiding judge Southeastern Okla. Jud. Adminstrv. Dist., 1984-92, Choctaw Tribal Ct., 1979-83; pres. Okla. Jud. Conf., 1987-88; chmn. Assembly Presiding Judges, 1989-90; presiding judge trial div. Okla. Ct. on the Judiciary, 1991-93; Okla. Ct. of Tax Rev., 1992—; judge Okla. Ct. of Civil Appeals, Tulsa, 1993—. Chmn. bd. dirs. Durant Youth Svcs., 1976-93; bd. dirs. Bryan County Youth Svcs., Inc., 1971-93. Lt. Col. USAR. Mem. Lions, Phi Sigma Epsilon, Delta Theta Phi. Mem. Ch. of Christ. Home: PO Box 329 Durant OK 74702-0329 Office: Ct Civil Appeals 601 State Bldg 440 S Houston Ave Tulsa OK 74127-8922 E-mail: joe.taylor@oscn.net

TAYLOR, JOEL SANFORD, lawyer; b. Hazleton, Pa., Oct. 8, 1942; s. Robert Joseph and Alice Josephine (Sanford) T.; m. Donna Rae Caron, Mar. 26, 1967; children: Jason, Adam, Jeremy. BA, Swarthmore Coll., 1965; LLB, Columbia U., 1968. Bar: N.Y. 1969, U.S. Dist. Ct. (so. and ea. dists.) N.Y. 1970, U.S. Ct. Appeals (2d cir.) 1970, Ohio 1973, U.S. Dist. Ct. (no. dist.) Ohio 1974, U.S. Supreme Ct. 1974, U.S. Dist. Ct. (so. dist.) Ohio 1975, U.S. Ct. Appeals (6th cir.) 1975, U.S. Dist. Ct. (ea. dist.) Ky. 1979. Law clk. hon. Constance B. Motley U.S. Dist. Ct., N.Y.C., 1968-69; assoc. Paul, Weiss, Rifkind, Wharton & Garrison, 1969-72; exec. asst. Ohio Office of Budget & Mgmt., Columbus, Ohio, 1972-74; asst. atty. gen. Ohio Atty. Gen., 1974-83, chief counsel, 1983-91; ptnr. Dinsmore & Shohl, 1991-2000; fin. dir. City of Columbus, 2000—. Pres. Ohio Sundry Claims Bd., Columbus, 1972-74, Ohio State Controlling Bd., Columbus, 1973-74; mem., bd. trustees Ohio State Tchrs. Retirement System, Columbus, 1986-91. Mem. Govt. Fin. Officers Assn., Columbia Law Alumni Assn., Ohio Sierra Club, Nat. Wildlife Fedn., Nature Conservany. Administrative and regulatory, General civil litigation, Environmental. Office: City Hall 90 W Broad St Columbus OH 43215-9000 E-mail: jstaylor@cmhmetro.net

TAYLOR, JOHN CHESTNUT, III, lawyer; b. N.Y.C., Jan. 7, 1928; s. John Chestnut and Jean Elizabeth (Willis) T.; m. Dolores Yvonne Sunstrom, Nov. 17, 1950; children: Jane Willis, John Sunstrom, Anne Holliday. B.A., Princeton U., 1947; LL.B., Yale U., 1950. Bar: N.Y. 1950, D.C. 1972. Assoc. Paul, Weiss, Rifkind, Wharton & Garrison, N.Y.C., 1950, 52-60, ptnr., 1961-85, 87-91, of counsel, 1986-87, 92—; exec. v.p., dir. AEA Investors Inc., 1985-86, pres., 1986-87. Bd. dirs. AFS Intercultural Programs, Inc., N.Y.C., 1972-80, trustee, 1973-79, chmn., 1975-79; trustee Carnegie Corp. N.Y., N.Y.C., 1975-84, chmn., 1979-84; trustee, mem. exec. com. Devereux Found., 1992—, vice chmn., 1994—. Served to capt. JAGC, AUS, 1950-52. Mem. Assn. of Bar of City of N.Y., Order of Coif, Phi Beta Kappa, Phi Delta Phi. Democrat. Home: 1 Hammock View Ln Savannah GA 31411-2603 Office: Paul Weiss Rifkind Wharton & Garrison 1285 Avenue Of The Americas New York NY 10019-6064 E-mail: budsunny@aol.com

TAYLOR, JOHN DAVID, lawyer; b. Long Beach, Calif., Jan. 10, 1933; s. Edwin Wright and Jean Anne (Thomas) T.; children: Jean Anne, Anne Catherine. BS, U. Calif.-Berkeley, 1954, JD, 1959. Bar: Calif. 1960. Assoc. Taylor Kupfer Summers & Rhodes (and predecessor firms), L.A., 1960-64, ptnr., 1964—. Assoc. editor Calif. Law Rev., 1958-59. Pres. Legal Aid Found. Los Angeles County, 1973-74. Served to 1st lt. USAF, 1954-56. Fellow Am. Coll. Probate Counsel (life), Am. Bar Found.; mem. Los Angeles County Bar Assn. (pres. 1978-79), Los Angeles County Bar Found. (pres. 1985-86), Order of Coif, Phi Beta Kappa, Beta Gamma Sigma. Club: Chancery (pres. 1988-89). Estate planning, Probate, Estate taxation. Office: 301 E Colorado Blvd Suite 407 Pasadena CA 91101

TAYLOR, KERNS BOWMAN, retired administative law judge, lawyer; b. Austin, Tex., June 27, 1920; s. Q.C. and Marian (Kerns) T.; m. Nora W. Smith, Feb. 29, 1992. JD, U. Tex., 1948. Bar: Tex. 1948. Assoc. Taylor & Chandler, Austin, 1948-52; spl. asst. U.S. atty. Dept. Justice, 1953; ptnr. Cain & Taylor, Liberty, Tex., 1953-59; asst. atty. gen. State Atty. Gen., Austin, 1965-72; U.S. adminstrv. law judge HHS Social Security Adminstrn., Houston, 1973-99; ret., 1999. Served to capt. Q.M.C., AUS, 1940-45, to col. JAGC, USAR, 1965-70. Mem. Houston Fed. Bar Assn. (pres. 1978-79), Houston Ret. Officers Assn. (pres. 1979), Am. Legion (comdr. 1963), Capital City Kiwanis (pres. 1968-69). Home: 1733 W Sam Houston Pky S Houston TX 77042-2971 Office: Office Hearings and Appeals Social Security Adminstrn 6800 W South Ste 300 Bellaire TX 77401-4522

TAYLOR, LELAND BARIDON, lawyer; b. Poughkeepsie, N.Y., July 5, 1920; s. Alexander J. and Elsie Jane (Van Wyck) T.; m. Rosemary Olcott Coon, June 24, 1945; children: Barry Eugene, Craig Cameron, Mark Alexander, Meg Olcott Taylor Casey. BS, Syracuse U., 1942, JD, 1948. Bar: N.Y. 1948, U.S. Dist. Ct. (no. dist.) N.Y. 1954, U.S. Supreme Ct. 1958. Ptnr. Fitzgerald, Taylor, Pomeroy & Armstrong and predecessor, Cortland, N.Y., 1948-2000; of counsel Pomeroy, Armstrong, Baranello & Casullo, 2000—. Judge City of Cortland, 1952-57; bd. dirs. First Nat. Bank of Dryden, Monroe Abstract & Title Corp. Trustee Cortland Free Libr., 1950—; bd. dirs. Coll. Devel. Found., Cortland, 1960-2000. With Supply Corps., USNR, 1942-45. Named Cortland County Jr. C. of C. Young Man of Yr., 1952, N.Y. State Young Man of Yr., 1953, N.Y. State Jaycees, 1953, Syracuse U. Letterman of Distinction, 1977. Fellow N.Y. Bar Found., Am. Bar Found.; mem. ABA, N.Y. State Bar Assn. (v.p. 1974-76, sec. 1976-79, chmn. fin. com. 1979-84), Cortland County Bar Assn., Rotary (Paul Harris fellow), Masons, Auto of Syracuse Club. Presbyterian. Real property, Estate taxation. Address: 16 Tompkins St Cortland NY 13045-2541

TAYLOR, MARVIN EDWARD, JR. lawyer; b. Smithfield, N.C., Oct. 15, 1937; s. Marvin Edward and Ellen Borden Broadhurst T.; m. Karin Gunilla Guggenheim, Nov. 29, 1969; 1 child, Karin Elizabeth Guggenheim. AB, U. N.C., 1960, JD with honors, 1965. Bar: N.Y. 1966, N.C. 1968, U.S. Dist. Ct. (ea. dist.) N.C. 1973, U.S. Ct. Appeals (4th cir.) 1974, Calif. 1976. Assoc. Nixon Mudge Rose Guthrie Alexander & Mitchell, N.Y.C., 1965-67, Sanford Cannon Adams & McCullough, Raleigh, N.C., 1967-71; atty. pvt. practice, 1972-75, 1984—; corp. counsel Memorex Corp., Santa Clara, Calif., 1975-80; atty. pvt. practice, Hickory, N.C., 1983. Dept. counsel GE Co., Hickory, N.C., 1980-82. Dir. Parents' Assn. N.C. State U., Raleigh, 1989-93, Coun. Entrepreneurial Devel, Research Triangle Park, N.C., 1985-88, chmn. pub. com., 1985-88; participant N.C. Ctr. Nonprofits Pro Bono Program, Raleigh, 1994—. With USAF, 1960-62. Mem. N.C. Bar Assn. (com. comml. banking & bus. law 1970-75, subcom. securities regulation 1972-75, bus. law sect. coun. 1982-85, 85-90, internat. law com. 1990-92, internat. law & practice sect. coun. 1992-95, pub. info. com. 1995—), Swedish-Am. C. of C. N.C. (co-founder, dir., sec./treas. 1998—), N.C. Law Rev. Staff, 1964 (rsch. editor 1965), Order of Coif. Democrat. Episcopalian. Avocations: skiing, photography, reading. Contracts commercial, General corporate, Private international. Office: 119 SW Maynard Rd Cary NC 27511-4472

TAYLOR, RAYMOND MASON, lawyer, former government official, educator; b. Washington, Jan. 1, 1933; s. Thaddeus Raymond and Mary Ada (Mason) T.; m. Rachel High; 1 dau., Elizabeth Lee Taylor Garber (Mrs. Kenneth Richard Garber). AB, U. N.C.-Chapel Hill, 1955, JD, 1960. Cert. law librarian Am. Assn. Law Libraries, 1968. Bar: N.C. 1960, U.S. Dist. Ct. (ea. dist.) N.C. 1960, U.S. Supreme Ct. 1970, U.S. Ct. Appeals (4th, 5th, 6th, 7th, 8th and 9th cirs.) 1977, U.S. Ct. Internat. Trade 1978, U.S. Ct. Appeals (11th cir.) 1981, U.S. Ct. Appeals (D.C. cir.) 1983, U.S. Ct. Mil. Appeals 1983. Staff reporter Washington (N.C.) Daily News, 1952, 54; adminstrv. asst. CD, Winston-Salem and Forsyth County, N.C., 1955; adminstrv. intern City of Winston-Salem, 1958; research asst. justice N.C. Supreme Ct., Raleigh, 1960-61; assoc. Gardner, Connor & Lee, Wilson, N.C., 1961-64; adj. instr. bus. law Atlantic Christian Coll. (now Barton Coll.), 1962-63, adj. prof., 1963-64; marshal, librarian N.C. Supreme Ct., 1964-77; sole practice Raleigh, N.C., 1977-81, 83—. Asst. U.S. atty., chief of appellate sect. Eastern Dist. N.C., 1981-82; supt. documents of US, asst. pub. printer of U.S., assoc. gen. counsel U.S. GPO, Washington, 1982-83; ptnr. Hall, Hill, O'Donnell, Taylor, Manning & Shearon, 1985-87; vis. lectr. econs. and bus. law N.C. State U., Raleigh, 1967-85; project dir. Fed. Jud. Ctr. Study of Fed. Ct. Libraries, 1976-77; dir. N.C. Law Research Facilities Study, 1970; chmn. State and Ct. Law Libraries of the U.S. and Can., 1973-74; mem. Info. Industry Council to Pub. Printer of U.S., 1981-83. Chmn. Parents' Day Campbell U., 1979, chmn. Parents Fund, 1981-82; mem. Wake County Libr. Commn., 1979-81. Served with CIC, U.S. Army, 1955-57. Recipient N.C. Soc. County and Local Historians award, 1955, Tar Heel of Week, 1971, award of Excellence Soc. Tech. Communication, 1976. Mem. N.C. Bar Assn., Nat. Acad. Elder Law Attys. (state coord. 1991-95), Sons of Confederate Vets., Order Golden Fleece (pres. 1958-59), Rotary (pres. 1992-93, Paul Harris fellow 1992, Holoman Disting. Svc. award West Raleigh club 1997), Pi Sigma Alpha, Phi Delta Phi, Omicron Delta Kappa, N.C. Supreme Ct Hist. Soc. (trustee, 1999-). General practice, Estate planning, Probate. Home: 3073 Granville Dr Raleigh NC 27609-6917 Office: 225 Hillsborough St Ste 280 Raleigh NC 27603-5948

TAYLOR, RICHARD POWELL, lawyer; b. Phila., Sept. 13, 1928; s. Earl Howard and Helen Moore (Martin) T.; m. Barbara Jo Anne Harris, Dec. 19, 1959; 1 child, Douglas Howard. BA, U. Va., 1950, JD, 1952. Bar: Va. 1952, D.C. 1956. Law clk. U.S. Ct. Appeals for 4th Circuit, 1951-52; assoc. Steptoe & Johnson LLP, Washington, 1956-61, ptnr., 1962—, chmn. transp. dept., 1978—; sec., corp. counsel Slick Corp., 1963-69, asst. sec., 1969-72, also bd. dirs., 1965-68; sec., corp. counsel Slick Indsl. Co., 1963-72; sec., bd. dirs. Slick Indsl. Co. Can. Ltd, 1966-72. Bd. dirs. Intercontinental Forwarders, Inc., 1969-72. Mem. Save the Children 50th Anniversary Com., 1982; gen. counsel Am. Opera Scholarship Soc., 1974—; mem. lawyer's com. Washington Performing Arts Soc., 1982—; mem. adv. com. Rock Creek Found. Mental Health, 1982—; mem. nat. adv. bd. DAR, 1980-83, chmn., 1983—; mem. men's com. Project Hope Ball, 1980—; nat. vice chmn. for fin. Reagan for Pres., 1979-80; mem. exec. fin. com. 1981 Presdl. Inauguration; mem. President's Adv. Com. for Arts, 1982—, Rep. Nat. Com., 1983—; Md. fin. chmn. Reagan-Bush '84, Bush-Quayle '88. Served to lt (j.g.), Air Intelligence USNR, 1952-56. Mem. ABA (co-chmn. aviation com. 1964-76, chmn. 1976-77), Fed. Bar Assn., D.C. Bar Assn., Va. Bar Assn., Fed. Energy Bar Assn., Am. Judicature Soc., Assn. Transp. Practitioners, Internat. Platform Assn., Raven Soc., Order of Coif, Univ. Club, Capital Hill Club, Nat. Aviation Club, Aero Club, Congl. Country Club (Washington), Potomac (Md.) Polo Club. Episcopalian. Administrative and regulatory, General corporate, Transportation. Home: 14914 Spring Meadows Dr Germantown MD 20874-3444 Office: 1330 Connecticut Ave NW Washington DC 20036-1704 E-mail: rtaylor@steptoe.com

TAYLOR, ROBERT LEE, lawyer, former judge; b. North Wildwood, N.J., Sept. 6, 1947; s. Louis Edward and Elizabeth (Zuccato) T.; m. Julie Ann Adams, Apr. 28, 1979; children: Tracy, Jennifer, Kathryn, Robyn. BS, James Madison U., 1969; JD, Washington and Lee U., 1974. Bar: N.J. 1974, U.S. Dist. Ct. N.J. 1974, U.S. Ct. Appeals (3d cir.) 1982, U.S. Supreme Ct. 1991. Assoc. George M. James, Wildwood, 1974-78; ptnr. Way, Way, Goodkin & Taylor, 1978-81, Way, Way, & Taylor, Wildwood, 1981-82; pvt. practice law Stone Harbor, N.J., 1982—; judge Mid. Twp. Mcpl. Ct., 1984-89. Organizer, dir. First so. State Bank, Avalon, N.J.; mem. dist. 1 ethics com. N.J. Supreme Ct., 1994-96; solicitor Lower Twp., N.J., 1994-96; diplomate N.J. Mcpl. Law. Advisor Law Explorers Boy Scouts Am., 1981, exec. bd. so. N.J. coun., 1995—; chmn. Cape May County Dem. Com., 1996-98. With U.S. Army, 1969-71. Mem. ABA, N.J. Bar Assn. (gen. coun. 1978-82), Cape May County Bar Assn. (pres. 1980-81), Cape May County Mcpl. Judges Assn. (treas. 1987-89), N.J. Jud. Conf. (del. 1978-82), Am. Legion, DAV (life), Delta Theta Phi. Democrat. Roman Catholic. Avocations: skiing, tennis, golf. General civil litigation, General practice, Real property. Office: 9712 3rd Ave # 4 Stone Harbor NJ 08247-1931 E-mail: rltaylor@pro-usa.net

TAYLOR, ROBERT P. lawyer; b. Douglas, Ariz., May 6, 1939; s. Paul Burton and Mary Ruth (Hart) T.; m. Sybil Ann Cappelletti, May 30, 1963 (div. Apr. 1974); children: David Scott, Nicole; m. Anne Dale Kaiser, Sept. 21, 1991. BSEE, U. Ariz., 1961; JD, Georgetown U., 1969. Bar: U.S. Ct. Appeals (9th circ.) 1969, U.S. Ct. Appeals (1st, 2d, 3d, 6th, and Fed. circs.), U.S. Supreme Ct., 1975. Elec. engr. Motorola Corp., Phoenix, 1961, Bell & Howell, Pasadena, Calif., 1964-65; examiner U.S. Patent Office, Washington, 1966-69; atty. Pillsbury Madison & Sutro, San Francisco, 1969-96, Howrey, Simon, Arnold & White, LLP, Menlo Park, Calif., 1996—. Mem. adv. commn. Patent Law Reform, Washington, 1990-92; mem. adv. bd. Litigation Risk Analysis, Palo Alto, Calif., 1985—. Contbr. articles to profl. jours. Dir. Ind. Colls. of No. Calif., San Francisco, 1982-96, officer, 1988-96. Fellow Am. Coll. Trial Lawyers; mem. ABA (chair sect. antitrust 1991-92), Am. Law Inst. Avocations: bicycling, cooking, hiking. Office: Howrey Simon Arnold & White LLP 301 Ravenswood Ave Menlo Park CA 94025-3434

TAYLOR, ROGER DALE, lawyer; b. Booneville, Ark., Apr. 6, 1950; s. Carl Edward and Amanda (Wilkins) T.; m. Elizabeth Payne, Feb. 20, 1988; children: Zachary, Grace, Greta, Wilkins. BSEE, U. Ark., 1972; JD with honors, George Washington U., 1980. Bar: D.C. 1980, Tex., 1981, Ga., 1996. Assoc. Vinson & Elkins, Houston, 1981-83, Busby, Rehm & Leonard, Washington, 1983-85, Finnegan, Henderson, Washington, 1985-90, ptnr. Tokyo, 1990-92, Washington, 1992-96, Atlanta, 1997—, Alston & Bird, Atlanta, 1996-97. Adj. prof. Law Sch. Cath. U. Am., Washington, 1992-95. Mem. Am. Intellectual Property Assn., Atlanta Soc. Clubs, Licensing Execs. Soc. (chmn. Japan com. 1994—), World Trade Ctr. Atlanta, Order of the Coif, Tau Beta Phi, Etta Kappa Nu. Office: Finnegan Henderson 3200 Suntrust Plz 303 Peachtree St NE Atlanta GA 30308-3201

TAYLOR, ROGER LEE, lawyer; b. Canton, Ill., Apr. 6, 1941; s. Ivan and Pauline Helen (Mehr) T.; m. E. Anne Zweifel, June 13, 1964. BA, Knox Coll., 1963; JD cum laude, Northwestern U., 1971. Bar: Ill. 1971, U.S. Dist. Ct. (no. dist.) Ill. 1971, U.S. Dist. Ct. (no. dist.) Tex. 1975, U.S. Ct. Appeals (7th cir.) 1972, U.S. Ct. Appeals (5th and 11th cirs.) 1981, U.S. Supreme Ct. 1975. Assoc. Kirkland & Ellis, Chgo., 1971-78, ptnr., 1978—. Trustee Knox Coll., interim pres. 2001. Mem. ABA, Chgo. Coun. Lawyers, Friends of the Parks (bd. dirs.), Order of Coif, Univ. Club, Mid-Am. Club Chgo., Soangetaha Country Club (Galesburg, Ill.). Federal civil litigation, Labor. Office: Kirkland & Ellis 200 E Randolph St Fl 60 Chicago IL 60601-6606

TAYLOR, VAUGHAN EDWARD, lawyer, educator; b. Portland, Maine, Oct. 3, 1947; s. Henry Landes and Elinor (Paine) T. BA cum laude, Dartmouth Coll., 1969; JD, U. Va., 1972. Bar: Maine 1972, Va. 1972, U.S. Ct. Mil. Appeals 1976, U.S. Supreme Ct. 1976, N.C. 1982. Commd. def. counsel U.S. Army, 1972, advanced through grades to maj., 1974; assoc. prof. U.S. Army JAG Sch., Charlottesville, Va., 1977-80; sr. ptnr. Taylor, Horbaly & Black Attys. Mil. Law, Jacksonville, N.C., 1981—. Sr. instr., maj. U.S. Army Res. JAG Sch., Charlottesville, 1980-89. Contbr. articles to profl. jours. Recipient Army Commendation medal West Germany, Meritorious Svc. medal. Mem. ABA, Am. Assn. Trial Lawyers. Administrative and regulatory, Criminal, Military. Office: Atty at Mil Law 825 Gum Branch Rd Ste 117 Jacksonville NC 28540-6268

TAYLOR, WALTER WALLACE, retired lawyer; b. Newton, Iowa, Sept. 18, 1925; s. Carrol W. and Eva (Greenly) T.; m. Mavis A. Harvey, Oct. 9, 1948; children: Joshua Michael (dec. 1980), Kevin Eileen, Kristin Lisa, Jeremy Walter, Margaret Jane, Melissa E., Amy M. AA, Yuba Coll., 1948, AB, 1950; MA, U. Calif., 1955; JD, McGeorge Coll. Law, 1962. Adminstrv. analyst USAF, Sacramento, 1951-53; personnel, research analyst Calif. Personnel Bd., 1954-56; civil svc., personnel analyst, chief counsel, gen. mgr. Calif. Employees Assn., 1956-75; staff counsel, chief profl. standards Calif. Commn. Tchr. Credentialing, 1975-88, ret., 1988. Staff counsel State Office Real Estate appraiser Licensing and Certification, 1992-94, ret.; tchr. discipline civil service, personnel cons. Author: Know Your Rights, 1963-64. Served USCGR, 1943-46. Mem. Calif. State Bar, Am., Sacramento County Bar Assns. Democrat. Home e-mail: walt. Home: 4572 Fair Oaks Blvd Sacramento CA 95864-5336 E-mail: taylor@quiknet.com

TAYLOR, WILLARD B. lawyer; b. N.Y.C., 1940; BA, Yale U., 1962, LLB, 1965. Bar: N.Y. 1966. With firm Sullivan & Cromwell, N.Y.C. Adj. faculty NYU Law Sch. Trustee North European Oil Royalty Trust. Mem. N.Y. State Bar Assn. (chair tax sect. 1983-84), Am. Law Inst. Office: Sullivan & Cromwell 125 Broad St Fl 28 New York NY 10004-2489

TAYLOR, WILLIAM JAMES (ZAK TAYLOR), lawyer; b. Milw., Jan. 26, 1948; s. William Elmer and Elizabeth Emily (Lupinski) T.; m. Marlou Belyea, Sept. 20, 1975; children: Danielle Belyea, James Zachary Belyea. BA in Econs., Yale U., 1970; JD, Harvard U., 1976. Bar: Calif. 1976, U.S. Dist. Ct. (cen. dist.) Calif. 1976, U.S. Dist. Ct. (no. dist.) Calif. 1977, U.S. Ct. Appeals (9th cir.) 1977, U.S. Dist. Ct. (ea. dist.) Calif. 1980, U.S. Supreme Ct. 1980, U.S. Tax Ct. 1988. Law clk. to hon. Shirley M. Hufstedler U.S. Ct. Appeals (9th cir.), L.A., 1976-77; assoc. Broebeck, Phleger & Harrison, San Francisco, 1977-83; ptnr. Broebeck, Phleger and Harrison, 1983-95; shareholder Taylor & Jenkins, P.C., Oakland, Calif., 1995-96, Chilvers & Taylor, P.C., Oakland, 1996-99; of counsel Brobeck, Phleger & Harrison, LLP, San Francisco, 2000—. Bd. dirs. Berkeley (Calif.) Law Found., 1988-91, Legal Svcs. for Children (recipient Jean Waldman Child Advocacy award, San Francisco 1988), 1983-89; co-chmn. Attys. Task Force for Children, San Francisco, 1983-89. Editor-in-chief Harvard Civil Rights, Civil Liberties Law Rev., 1976; bd. editors No. Dist. Calif. Digest, 1978-83; co-author: California Antitrust Law, 1991; contbg. editor: Calif. Bus. Law Reporter, 1995-96, Antitrust Law Developments, 1997. With U.S. Army, 1970-73. Mem. ABA, Bar Assn. San Francisco (bd. dirs. 1986-87, chair antitrust sect. 1987, chair fed. cts. sect. 1995-97), Am. Bus. Trial Lawyers Assn., Nat. Health Lawyers Assn., Calif. Soc. Healthcare Attorneys, Barristers of San Francisco (bd. dirs. 1980-82, v.p. 1982-83). Democrat. Antitrust, General civil litigation, Health. Office: Brobeck Phleger & Harrison LLP 1 Market Spear Tower San Francisco CA 94105-1420 E-mail: wtaylor@brobeck.com, wta9786011@cs.com

TAYLOR, WILLIAM WOODRUFF, III, lawyer; b. Richmond, Va., July 30, 1944; s. William Woodruff Jr. and Ida (Winstead) T.; m. Susan Broadhurst, Sept. 29, 1984; children: Katherine Lowell, Matthew Gordon. AB, U. N.C., 1966; LLB, Yale U., 1969. Bar: N.C. 1969, D.C. 1970, U.S. Ct. Appeals (2nd, 4th, 5th and 11th cirs.), U.S. Supreme Ct. Law clk. to judge U.S. Dist. Ct. Del., Wilmington, 1969-70; staff atty. Pub. Defender Service, Washington, 1970-75; assoc. Ginsburg, Feldman and Bress, 1975-78; ptnr. Zuckerman, Spaeder, Goldstein, Taylor & Kolker L.L.P., 1978—. Instr. dept. forensic sci. George Washington U., Washington, 1973-74; adj. prof. Columbus Sch. Law, Cath. U. Am., Washington, 1973-76; mem. D.C. Commn. on Jud. Disabilities and Tenure, 1978-83, chmn., 1979-83; vis. prof. U. N.C. Law Sch., fall 1991. Fellow Am. Coll. Trial Lawyers; mem. ABA (criminal justice sect., vice chmn. for govtl. affairs 1989-92, chair criminal justice sect. 1996-97), Nat. Inst. for Trial Advocacy (faculty 1978—, chmn. pub. defender svc. assn. 1984-89). Episcopalian. Avocations: fly fishing, tennis. Federal civil litigation, General civil litigation, Criminal. Office: Zuckerman Spaeder Goldstein Taylor & Kolker LLP 1201 Connecticut Ave NW Washington DC 20036-2638

TEARE, JOHN RICHARD, JR. lawyer; b. Phila., Sept. 23, 1954; divorced; 1 child, John III; m. Gale Angela Waters, June 5, 1982; children: Angela, Stephanie. BS in Criminal Justice summa cum laude, Wilmington Coll., 1987; JD cum laude, U. Richmond, 1990. Bar: W.Va. 1990, U.S. Dist. Ct. (so. dist.) W.Va. 1990, U.S. Dist. Ct. (no. dist.) W.Va. 1996, U.S. Ct. Appeals (4th cir.) 1991. Sec. guard U. Del., Newark, 1973-76; police officer City of Dover (Del.), 1976-85; summer assoc. Hirschler Fleischer Weinberg Cox & Allen, Richmond, 1989; ptnr. Bowles Rice McDavid Graff & Love, PLLC, Charleston, W.Va., 1990—; mem. exec. com., 2000—. Counsel Charleston Police Civil Svc. Commn.; instr. Charleston Regional Police Acad., 1999. Cub scout leader Boy Scouts Am., Felton, Del., 1984-88, asst. scoutmaster, Richmond, 1988-89, Charleston, 1991-98; chmn. pub. safety commn. Greater Charleston C. of C., 1991; sec. United Meth. Men, 1993; dir. Charleston Leadership Coun. on Pub. Safety, 1993-97, chmn. police dept. resource task force, 1994-97; dir./sec. Kanawha County Pub. Safety Coun., 2000—. Mem. ABA, W.Va. Bar Assn., Kanawha County Bar Assn., Def. Rsch. Inst. (state liaison to govtl. liability com./bus. litigation com.), Def. Trial Counsel W.Va., Nat. Manufactured Housing Atty. Network, Fraternal Order of Police, Nat. Eagle Scout Assn., McNeill Law Assn., Greater Charleston C. of C., Delta Epsilon Rho. United Methodist. Avocations: camping, fishing, stamp collecting. Civil rights, General civil litigation, Labor. Home: 1565 Virginia St E Charleston WV 25311-2416 Office: Bowles Rice McDavid Graff & Love PLLC PO Box 1386 Charleston WV 25325-1386 E-mail: jteare@bowlesrice.com

TECLAFF, LUDWIK ANDRZEJ, law educator, consultant, author, lawyer; b. Czestochowa, Poland, Nov. 14, 1918; came to U.S., 1952, naturalized, 1958; s. Emil and Helena (Tarnowska) T.; m. Eileen Johnson, May 30, 1952. Mag Iuris, Oxford (Eng.) U., 1944; MS, Columbia U., 1955; LLM, NYU, 1961, JSD, 1965. Attaché Polish Fgn. Ministry, London, 1943-46; consul in Ireland, Polish Govt. in London, 1946-52; student libr. Columbia U. Sch. Libr. Sci., 1953-54; libr. Bklyn. Pub. Libr., 1954-59; rsch. librar. Fordham U. Sch. Law, 1959-62, asst. prof. law, 1962-65, assoc. prof. law, 1965-68, prof. 1968-89, prof. emeritus, 1989—, dir. law libr., 1962-86; cons. in field. With Polish Army, 1940-43, France, Eng. Recipient Clyde Eagleton award in internat. law NYU, 1965. Mem. Am. Soc. Internat. Law, Internat. Law Assn., Am. Law Librs. Assn., Internat. Coun. Environ. Law, Internat. Water Law Assn. Roman Catholic. Author: The River Basin in History and Law, 1967; Abstraction and Use of Water, 1972; Legal and Institutional Responses to Growing Water Demand, 1978; Economic Roots of Oppression, 1984, Water Law in Historical Perspective, 1985; editor: (with Albert E Utton) International Environmental Law, 1974, Water in a Developing World, 1978, International Groundwater Law, 1981, Transboundary Resources Law, 1987; contbr. articles on water law, law of the sea and environ. law to law jours. Office: Fordham U Sch Law 140 W 62nd St New York NY 10023-7407

TEE, VIRGINIA, lawyer; b. Damariscotta, Maine, Aug. 7, 1956; d. Lawrence Edward and Rosamond (Stetson) Tee; m. David A. Danaee, Oct. 29, 1982; children: Christina Nicole Danaee, Erica Michelle Danaee. BA in English, Fla. State U., 1978; JD, U. Puget Sound, 1992. Bar: Fla. 1992, Wash. 1994. Corp. counsel AT&T Wireless Svcs., Inc., Redmond, Wash., 1993-99; asst. gen. counsel drugstore.com,inc., Bellevue, 1999—. Mem. editl. adv. bd. Wash. State Bar News, 1996-98; mem. MCLE Bd., 1998—, chair, 2000-01. Mem. Wash. State Bar Assn., Fla. State Bar Assn. Office: drugstore.com 13920 SE Eastgate Way Bellevue WA 98005-4440

TEGENKAMP, GARY ELTON, lawyer; b. Dayton, Ohio, Nov. 27, 1946; s. Elmer Robert and Dorothy Ann (Hummerich) T.; m. June Evelyn Barber, Aug. 2, 1969; children: Emily Stratton, Andrew Elton. BA in Polit. Sci., U. South Fla., 1969; JD, Coll. William and Mary, 1972. Bar: Va. 1972, U.S. Dist. Ct. (we. and ea. dists.) Va. 1972, U.S. Ct. Appeals (4th cir.) 1973. Law clk. to presiding judge U.S. Dist. Ct. (we. dist.) Va., U.S. Ct. Appeals (4th cir.), Abingdon, Va., 1972-73; assoc. Hunter, Fox & Trabue, Roanoke, 1973-77; ptnr. Fox, Wooten and Hart P.C., 1977-90, Wooten & Hart, P.C., Roanoke, Va., 1991-95; asst. city atty. Office of Roanoke City Atty., 1995—. Active United Way, Roanoke Valley, 1976; legal advisor Roanoke Jaycees, 1976-77. Mem. Va. Bar Assn. (constrn. and environ. sects.), Va. Assn. Def. Attys., Roanoke Bar Assn. (chmn. com. CLE 1983-86, 6th dist. ethics com. 1988-91), Local Govt. Attys. Va. United Methodist. Avocations: coin collecting, youth sports programs. Federal civil litigation, State civil litigation, Municipal (including bonds). Home: 2524 Stanley Ave SE Roanoke VA 24014-3332 Office: Office Roanoke City Atty 464 Municipal Bldg 215 Church Ave SW Roanoke VA 24011-1517

TEIMAN, RICHARD B. lawyer; b. Bklyn., May 19, 1938; AB, Princeton U., 1959; LLB, Harvard U., 1962. Bar: N.Y. 1963. Ptnr. Winston & Strawn and predecessor Cole and Deitz, N.Y.C., 1968—. Trustee Citizens Budget Commn., 1993—. Mem. Assn. Bar City N.Y. (com. Admiralty 1975-78, 87, chair 1988-91), Maritime Law Assn. (com. Maritime Financing 1980—, chmn. subcom. Recodification U.S. Ship Mortgage Act 1986-91, chmn. subcom. U.S. Coastguard, Citizenship and Related Matters 1988-94), Phi Beta Kappa. Admiralty, Contracts commercial, General corporate. Home: 5 Pryer Ln Larchmont NY 10538-4012 Office: Winston & Strawn 200 Park Ave Rm 4100 New York NY 10166-0005 E-mail: rteiman@winston.com

TEITELBAUM, LEE E. dean, law educator; b. New Orleans, Nov. 4, 1941; BA magna cum laude, Harvard Coll., 1963; LLB, Harvard U., 1966; LLM, Northwestern U., 1968. Bar: Ill. Staff atty. Chgo. Lawyer Project, 1966-68; asst. prof. law U. N.D., 1968-70; assoc. prof. law SUNY, Buffalo, 1970-73; vis. assoc. prof. law U. N.Mex. Law Sch., 1972, assoc. prof. law, 1973-74, prof. law, 1974-87; prof. law, dir. Ctr. for the Study of Legal Policy Relating to Children Ind. U. Law Sch., 1980-81, vis. prof., 1987, U. Utah Coll. Law, 1985, prof. law, 1986-90, assoc. dean acad. affairs, 1987-90, acting dean, 1988, dean, 1990-98, Alfred C. Emery prof. law, 1994-99; Allan R. Tessler dean and prof. of law Cornell Law Sch., 1999—. Fellow legal history program U. Wis., Madison, 1984; mem. test audit subcom., bd. trustees Law Sch. Admissions Coun.; bd. mem. Law and Soc. Assn. Author: (with A. Gough) Beyond Control: Status Offenders in the Juvenile Court, 1977 (with W.V. Stapleton) In Defense of Youth: The Role of Counsel in American Juvenile Courts, 1972; contbr. articles to profl. jours.; bd. editors Law & Soc. Rev., 1982-87, Law & Policy, Jour. Legal Edn., 1990-92. Fellow ABA (reporter ABA-IJA project on standards for juvenile justices, standards relating to the role of counsel for pvt. parties 1979); mem. Law & Soc. Assn. (bd. trustees 1977-80), Utah Minority Bar Assn. (award), Assn. Am. Law Schs. (exec. com.). Office: Cornell U Law School Myron Taylor Hall Ithaca NY 14853-4901*

TEITELBAUM, STEVEN USHER, lawyer; b. Chgo., Nov. 29, 1945; s. Jerome H. and Marion Judith (Berlin) T.; m. Cathy Ann Rosenblatt, Mar. 11, 1984. A.B., boston U., 1967; J.D., Union U., 1975. Bar: N.Y. 1976, U.S. Dist. Ct. (no. dist.) N.Y. 1976, U.S. Supreme Ct. 1980, U.S. Ct. Appeals (2d cir.) 1993; cert. arbitrator. Sr. atty. N.Y. State Dept. Health, Albany, 1976-79; counsel N.Y. State Office Bus. Permits, 1979-83; sole practice, 1983-95; dep. commr., gen. counsel N.Y. State Dept. Taxation and Fin., 1995-99; pvt. practice Albany, 1999—. Staff judge advocate U.S. Army Res. Watervliet Arsenal, N.Y., 1978-84. Author: Streamlining the Regulatory Procedures of the Department of Agriculture, 1982. Active Found. Bd. Ctr. for Disabled, Empire State Performing Arts Ctr., treas.; treas. bd. trustees Albany Acad. for Girls. Served with U.S. Army, 1968-69. Mem. Am. Arbitration Assn. (com. on pub. health 1976-80, faculty on adminstrv. law 1980, com. on adminstrv. law 1980-84, 93-95, labor and employment sect., taxation sect. exec. com. 1985—). Clubs: Fort Orange (Albany), Country Club Troy (N.Y.). Administrative and regulatory, Taxation, general, State and local taxation. Home: 17 Carstead Dr Slingerlands NY 12159-9266 Office: 111 Washington Ave Ste 206 Albany NY 12210 E-mail: yrt@prodigy.net

TEKLITS, JOSEPH ANTHONY, lawyer; b. Belleville, Ill., July 18, 1952; s. Frank Anthony and Mary (Bodish) T.; m. Deborah Ann Keevill, June 1, 1974; children: Jessica, Joseph, Michael. BA, Coll. St. Francis de Sales, Allentown, Pa., 1974; JD, U. Notre Dame, 1977. Bar: Ind. 1977, U.S. Dist. Ct. (so. and no. dists.) Ind. 1977, Pa. 1988, Pa. 1988, U.S. Dist. Ct. (ea. dist.) Pa. 1988, U.S. Ct. Appeals (3d cir.) 1988, U.S. Dist. Ct. (ea. dist.) Mich. 1989, U.S. Ct. Appeals (6th cir.) 1990, U.S. Ct. Appeals (11th cir.) 1993, U.S. Supreme Ct. 1995, U.S. Dist. Ct. Colo. 1999. Legal counsel CTS Corp., Elkhart, Ind., 1977-80; mng. labor counsel Sperry Corp. (name now Unisys Corp.), Blue Bell, Pa., 1980-87; asst. gen. counsel Unisys Corp., 1987-95, assoc. gen. counsel, 1995—. Mem. mgmt. com. Equal Employment Opportunity Law. Mem. ABA (EEO com. labor and employment law and litigation sects.), Delta Epsilon Sigma. Republican. Roman Catholic. Administrative and regulatory, Federal civil litigation, Labor. Office: Unisys Corp Hdqrs PO Box 500 Blue Bell PA 19424-0001

TELEPAS, GEORGE PETER, retired lawyer; b. Kingston, N.Y., Nov. 20, 1935; s. Peter G. and Grace Telepas; m. Regina Tisiker, Sept. 6, 1969 (div.); m. Patricia Kilstofte, Apr. 30, 1995. BS, U. Fla., 1960; JD, U. Miami, 1965. Bar: Fla. 1965, Colo. 1986. Assoc. Preddy, Haddad, Kutner & Hardy, 1966-67, Williams & Jabara, 1967-68; pvt. practice Miami, Fla., 1968-98. Mem. citizens bd. U. Miami. With USMC, 1954-56. Mem. ATLA, ABA, Fla. Bar Assn., Colo. Bar Assn., Dade County Bar Assn., Fla. Trial Lawyers Assn., Dade County Trial Lawyers Assn., Delta Theta Phi, Sigma Nu. Personal injury. Address: 13320 Marsh Landing Palm Beach Gardens FL 33418

TELESCA, MICHAEL ANTHONY, federal judge; b. Rochester, N.Y., Nov. 25, 1929; s. Michael Angelo and Agatha (Locurcio) T.; m. Ethel E. Hibbard, June 5, 1953; children: Michele, Stephen. AB, U. Rochester, 1952; JD, U. Buffalo, 1955. Bar: N.Y. 1957, U.S. Dist. Ct. (we. dist.) N.Y. 1958, U.S. Ct. Appeals (2nd cir.) 1960, U.S. Supreme Ct. 1967. Ptnr. Lamb, Webster, Walz, Telesca, Rochester, N.Y., 1957-73; surrogate ct. judge Monroe County, 1973-82; judge U.S. Dist. Ct. (we. dist.) N.Y., Rochester, 1982—, chief judge, 1989-95. Apptd. to Alien Terrorist Removal Ct. by Chief Justice Rehnquist, U.S. Supreme Ct., 1996; bd. dirs. Fed. Jud. Ctr. Bd. govs. Genesee Hosp., Rochester; mem. adv. bd. Assn. for Retarded Citizens, Al Sigl Ctr., Rochester. Served to 1st lt. USMC, 1955-57. Recipient Civic medal Rochester C. of C., 1983, Hutchinson medal U. Rochester, 1990. Mem. ABA, Am. Judicature Soc., Am. Inns. of Ct. (founder, pres. Rochester chpt.), Justinian Soc. Jurists, N.Y. State Bar Assn., Monroe County Bar Assn. Republican. Roman Catholic. Office: US Dist Ct 272 US Courthouse 100 State St Ste 212 Rochester NY 14614-1309

TELGENHOF, ALLEN RAY, lawyer; b. Flint, Mich., Jan. 31, 1964; s. Gerald H. and Bernice Kay Telgenhof; m. Judy Michele Campbell, Sept. 5, 1986; children: Tyler, Allyson, Will, Luke. BA, Mich. State U., 1987; JD cum laude, Thomas M. Cooley Law Sch., 1989. Bar: Mich. 1989, U.S. Dist. Ct. (ea. dist.) Mich. 1992, U.S. Ct. Appeals (6th cir.) 1992, U.S. Dist. Ct. (we. dist.) Mich. 1997. Legis. analyst Mich. Ho. of Reps., Lansing, 1989; assoc. Hicks & Schmidlin, P.C., Flint, 1990-93; pvt. practice law Clio, Mich., 1993-94; ptnr. Pointner, Joseph, Corcoran & Telgenhof, P.C., Charlevoix, 1994-98, Joseph, Corcoran & Telgenhof, P.C., Charlevoix, 1998-2000, Joseph, Corcoran, Telgenhof & Snyder, P.C., Charlevoix, 2000—. Advisor Clio H.S. Law Club, 1992-94; founder, pres. Clio Area Edn. Found., 1992-94; presenter in field. Trustee Clio Bd. Edn., 1992-94, Charlevoix Bd. Edn., 1995—, pres., 1997—; commr. City of Charlevoix Planning Commn., 1995-96. Named Alumnus of Yr. Clio H.S., 1999. Mem. ABA, Charlevoix-Emmet Bar Assn. Democrat. Avocations: sports, sailing, family activities. General civil litigation, Criminal, Securities. Office: Joseph Corcoran Et Al PO Box 490 203 Mason St Charlevoix MI 49720-1337 Fax: 231-547-3014. E-mail: atelgenhof@chartermi.net

TELLERIA, ANTHONY F. lawyer; b. June 6, 1938; s. Carolos E. and Melida (Amador) Telleria; m. Dolores A. Rockney, Nov. 03, 1962; children: Matthew J., Andrea F. LLB, Southwestern U., 1964. Bar: Calif. 1964. Pvt. practice, L.A., 1964—71; sr. ptnr. Telleria, Townley & Doran, 1971—75; pvt. practice, 1975—. Mem.: Calif. Trial Lawyers Assn., L.A. County Bar Assn., Am. Arbitration Assn. (L.A. adv. coun. accident claims com.), Consumer Attys. Assn. of L.A. State civil litigation, Criminal, Personal injury. Home: 1615 Rose Ave San Marino CA 91108-3001 Office: 150 E Colorado Blvd Ste 206 Pasadena CA 91105-3722

TEMKO, STANLEY LEONARD, lawyer; b. N.Y.C., Jan. 4, 1920; s. Emanuel and Betty (Alderman) T.; m. Francine Marie Salzman, Mar. 4, 1944 (dec. Dec. 1998); children: Richard J., Edward J., William D. AB, Columbia U., 1940, LLB, 1943. Bar: N.Y. 1943, D.C. 1951. Practice in, N.Y.C., 1943, 46-47; law clk. Mr. Justice Wiley Rutledge, U.S. Supreme Ct., Washington, 1947-48; legal counsel Econ. Coop. Adminstrn., 1948-49; assoc. Covington & Burling, Washington, 1949-55, ptnr., 1955-90, sr. counsel, 1990—. Editor-in-chief: Columbia Law Rev, 1942-43. Trustee Beauvoir Sch., 1963-69; trustee Columbia U., 1980-91, trustee emeritus, 1991—, mem. bd. visitors Sch. Law, 1961-98, mem. emeritus, 1999—; mem. bd. govs. St. Albans Sch., 1967-73, chmn., 1971-73. 2nd lt. U.S. Army, 1943-46. Decorated Bronze Star; recipient medal for conspicuous alumni svc. Columbia U., 1979. Fellow Am. Bar Found. (chmn. rsch. com. 1970-72); mem. ABA, Am. Law Inst., D.C. Bar Assn., Columbia U. Sch. Law Alumni Assn. (pres. 1982-84), Met. Club, Nat. Press Club, Phi Beta Kappa. Administrative and regulatory, Antitrust, Health. Home: 4811 Dexter Ter NW Washington DC 20007-1020 Office: Covington & Burling 1201 Pennsylvania Ave NW Washington DC 20004-2401 E-mail: stemko@cov.com

TEMPLE, L. PETER, lawyer; b. Chgo., Mar. 24, 1948; s. John Albert and Helene (Psiharis) T.; m. Susan Schneider, Sept. 4, 1971; children— Peter J., Benjamin L., Emily K. B.A., Haverford Coll., 1970; J.D., Boston U., 1973. Bar: Pa. 1973. Gen. counsel State Dept. Mental Health, Concord, N.H., 1972-73; assoc. Larmore & Scarlett, Kennett Square, Pa., 1973-75; mng. ptnr. Larmore, Scarlett, Myers & Temple, Kennett Square, 1975— ; dir. Elmwood Savs. Bank, Kennett Square, Abstracting Co. Chester County, West Chester, Pa. Mem. Chester County Bar Assn. (bd. dirs. 1981-83, chmn. jud. qualifications com. 1980-81), ABA, Pa. Bar Assn. Probate, Real property, Estate taxation. Home: 709 E Baltimore Pike Kennett Square PA 19348-2429 Office: Larmore Scarlett Myers & Temple PO Box 384 Kennett Square PA 19348-0384

TENNEN, LESLIE IRWIN, lawyer, consultant; b. Toronto, Aug. 26, 1952; came to U.S., 1961; s. Edward and Elsie (Liberbaum) T. BA with distinction, U. Ariz., 1973, JD, 1976; Mount Scopus, Hebrew U., Jerusalem, 1975. Bar: Ariz. 1977, U.S. Dist. Ct. Ariz. 1979. Sole practice, Tucson, 1977-79; ptnr. Sterns and Tennen, Phoenix and Tucson, 1979—. Cons. internat. law and aerospace activities; lectr. univs., colls. and law schs.; mem. Ariz. Space Commn., 1994-2000, also profl. aviation and aerospace congresses and seminars in N.Am., Europe, Asia, S.Am., Australia; judge Jessup Internat. Moot Court Competition, 1982, 83, 85, 92; dir., treas. Assn. U.S. Mems. Internat. Inst. Space Law; com. mem. U. Belarusian Culture Internat. Orgn. Contbr. Ariz. Law Rev., 1975-76; contbr. articles to profl. jours. Precinct committeeman State Dem. Conv., 1972-73. Received highest score Ariz. Bar Exam., Feb. 1977. Mem. AIAA (sr.), Ariz. Bar Found., Internat. Eurasian Acad. Scis., Internat. Inst. Space Law, Internat. Acad. Astronautics, Am. Soc. Internat. Law, Soc. Aerospace Communicators Inc., Internat. Law Assn., Planetary Soc., Fedn. Aerospace Socs. in Tucson (exec. bd.). General civil litigation, Contracts commercial, Private international. Office: 849 N 3rd Ave Phoenix AZ 85003-1408 E-mail: LTennen@astrolaw.com

TENUTA, LUIGIA, lawyer; b. Madison, Wis., June 4, 1954; d. Eugene P. and Nancy (Gardner) T. AB in Internat. Studies with honors, Miami U., Oxford, Ohio, 1976; JD, Capital U., 1981; postgrad., Pontifical Coll. Josephinum, 1987-88. Bar: Ohio 1981. With internat. mktg. dept. Dresser Industries, Columbus, Ohio, 1976-80, analyst strategic planning, 1980, mgr. internat bus. planning Stratford, Conn., 1981; pvt. practice law Columbus, 1981—. Former mem. devel. com. Miami U. Mem. Ohio Bar Assn., Columbus Bar Assn. Roman Catholic. General civil litigation, General practice. Office: 6400 Riverside Dr Dublin OH 43017-5197

TEPPER, R(OBERT) BRUCE, JR. lawyer; b. Long Branch, N.J., Apr. 1, 1949; s. Robert Bruce and Elaine (Ogus) T.; m. Belinda Wilkins, Nov. 26, 1971; children: Laura Katherine, Jacob Wilkins. AB in HIstory, Dartmouth Coll., 1971; JD cum laude, MA in Urban Affairs, St. Louis U., 1976. Bar: Mo. 1976, Calif. 1977, Ill. 1978, U.S. Ct. Appeals (7th cir.) 1978, (8th cir.) 1976, (9th cir.) 1978, U.S. Dist. Ct. (ctrl., no. and so. dists.) Calif. 1978. Asst. gen. counsel St. Louis Redevel. Authority, 1976-77; assoc. Goldstein & Price, St. Louis, 1977-78, Loo, Merideth & McMillan, L.A., 1978-82; sole practice, 1982-84; sr. prin., CFO Kane, Ballmer and Berkman, 1984—. Litigation counsel to San Diego, Santa Barbara, Huntington Beach, Anaheim, Culver City, Lynwood, Norwalk, Redondo Beach, Oceanside, Ontario, Oxnard, Pasadena, Moreno Valley, Grover Beach, Glendale and Hawthorne, Calif.; spl. counsel redevel. agy. City L.A.; judge pro tempore Los Angeles County Mcpl. Ct., 1983— ; grader State Bar Calif., 1980-84; lectr. in land use and environ. issues. Assoc. editor St. Louis U. Law Jour., 1974-76; mem. editl. bd. L.A. Lawyer; contbr. articles to legal jours. Mem. ABA, Los Angeles County Bar Assn. (com. on jud. evaluations), Assn. Bus. Trial Lawyers., So. Calif. Dartmouth Club (bd. dirs. 1980-83), L.A. Athletic. Republican. Jewish. State civil litigation, Environmental, Land use and zoning (including planning). Home: 10966 Wrightwood Ln Studio City CA 91604-3957 Office: Kane Ballmer & Berkman 515 S Figueroa St Ste 1850 Los Angeles CA 90071-3335 E-mail: TAPatKBB@aol.com

TERK, GLENN THOMAS, lawyer; b. Feb. 27, 1949; s. Raymond Arthur and Marguerite Ida (Nichols) T.; m. Mary Ann Michaud, Sept. 25, 1982. BSME, Clarkson Coll. Tech., 1971; JD, U. Conn., 1976. Bar: Conn. 1976, U.S. Dist. Ct. Conn. 1976. Engr. Combustion Engring. Co., Windsor, Conn., 1971-76; assoc. Francis, Kroopnick & O'Neil, Hartford, 1976-78; ptnr. Brignole & Terk, 1993-95; pvt. practice, 1995—. Mem. Dem. Town Com., Windsor, 1978-79, Windsor Inland Wetlands Commn., 1978-79, Rep. Town com., Wethersfield, 1997—; chmn. Trinity United Meth. Ch. adminstrv. bd., Windsor, 1982-83, finance chmn. 1997—. Mem. Conn. Bar Assn. (lawyers and cmty. subcom. 1981-85, real property exec. com. 1994—, comml. law com. 1994—). Contracts commercial, General practice, Real property. Home: 445 Old Reservoir Rd Wethersfield CT 06109-3956 Office: 81 Wolcott Hill Rd Wethersfield CT 06109-1242 E-mail: Gterk@cs.com

TERMINI, ROSEANN BRIDGET, lawyer, educator; b. Phila., Feb. 2, 1953; d. Vincent James and Bridget (Marano) T. BS magna cum laude, Drexel U., 1975; MEd, Temple U., 1979, JD, 1985, grad. in food and pharmacy law, 1998. Bar: Pa. 1985, U.S. Dist. Ct. (ea. dist.) Pa. 1985, D.C. 1986. Jud. clk. Superior Ct. of Pa., Allentown, 1985-86; atty. Pa. Power & Light Co., 1986-87; corp. counsel food and drug law Lemmon Co., Sellersville, Pa., 1987-88; sr. dep. atty. bur. consumer protection plain lang. law Office of Atty. Gen., Harrisburg, 1988-96; prof. Villanova U. Sch. Law, 1996-2000; prof. food and drug law Temple U. Sch. Pharmacy, 1998—. Contbr. articles to profl. jours., law revs.; spkr. continuing legal edn.-plain lang. laws, environ. conf.; adj. prof. Widener U. Sch. Law, 1993—, Dickinson Sch. Law. Author: Food, Drug and Medical Device Law: Topics and Cases, 2001; contbr. articles to profl. jours, law revs.; spkr. environ. conf. Active in Sr. Citizens Project Outreach, Hospice, 1986—; mem. St. Thomas More Law Bd. Mem. ABA (various coms.), Bar Assn. D.C., Pa. Bar Assn. (ethics, exceptional children and environ. sects., Plain English award 1999), Temple U. Law Alumni Assn., Drexel U. Alumni Assn., Omicron Nu, Phi Alpha Delta. Avocations: tap dancing, hiking, cross-country skiing. E-mail: rtermini@attorney.com

TERNUS, MARSHA K. state supreme court justice; b. Vinton, Iowa, May 30, 1951; BA, U. Iowa, 1972; JD, Drake U., 1977. Bar: Iowa. 1977, Ariz. 1984. With Bradshaw, Fowler, Proctor & Fairgrave, Des Moines, 1977-93; justice Iowa Supreme Ct., 1993—. Editor-in-chief Drake Law Rev., 1976-77. Mem. Polk County Bar Assn. (pres. 1984-85), Phi Beta Kappa, Order of Coif. Office: Iowa Supreme Ct State Capital Bldg Des Moines IA 50319-0001*

TERP, THOMAS THOMSEN, lawyer; b. Fountain Hill, Pa., Aug. 12, 1947; s. Norman T. and Josephine (Uhran) T.; m. Pamela Robinson; children: Stephanie, Brian, Adam; step-children: Taylor Mefford, Grace Mefford. BA, Albion (Mich.) Coll., 1969; JD, Coll. of William and Mary, 1973. Bar: Ohio 1973, U.S. Dist. Ct. (so. dist.) Ohio 1973, U.S. Ct. Appeals (6th cir.) 1973, U.S. Supreme Ct. 1979. Assoc. Taft, Stettinius & Hollister, Cin., 1973-80, ptnr., 1981—. Bd. dirs. Starflo Corp., Orangeburg, S.C., Attorneys' Liability Assurance Soc., Ltd., Hamilton, Bermuda, ALAS, Inc., Chgo. Editor-in-chief William & Mary Law Rev., 1972-73; mem. bd. editors Jour. of Environ. Hazards, 1988—, Environ. Law Jour. of Ohio, 1989—. Mem. Cin. Athletic Club, Coldstream Country Club, Epworth Assembly (Ludington, Mich.), Lincoln Hills Golf Club (Ludington), Queen City Club. Avocations: tennis, golf, travel. General civil litigation, Environmental. Office: 1800 Firstar Tower 425 Walnut St Cincinnati OH 45202 E-mail: terp@taftlaw.com

TERRA, SHARON ECKER, lawyer; b. Pitts., Jan. 12, 1959; d. James and Carole Dombro Ecker; m. Edward George Terra, Feb. 8, 1987. BA, Rollins Coll., 1980; JD, Nova Law Sch., 1988. Bar: Fla. 1988, U.S. Dist. Ct. (so. dist.) Fla. 1989, Pa. 1990, U.S. Dist. Ct. (we. dist.) Pa. 1990. Staff acct. Arthur Andersen & Co., Miami, 1980-81; fin. officer Embraer Aircraft Corp., Ft. Lauderdale, Fla., 1981-82; pvt. practice Hollywood, 1988-90, Pitts., 1990—. Mem. ABA, AICPA's, Allegheny County Bar Assn., Am. Trial Lawyers Assn. Republican. Criminal, General practice, Personal injury. Home: 1057 Old Orchard Dr Gibsonia PA 15044-6081 Office: Ecker Ecker & Ecker 1116 Frick Building Pittsburgh PA 15219-6165

TERRELL, G. IRVIN, lawyer; b. Houston, Sept. 28, 1946; s. George I. and Adella (Weichert) T.; m. Karen Steenberg, Jan. 8, 1984; 1 child, Katharine. BA, U. Tex., 1968, JD, 1972. Bar: Tex., U.S. Supreme Ct., U.S. Ct. Appeals (3d and 5th cirs.), U.S. Dist. Ct. (so., no. and ea. dists.) Tex., U.S. Dist. Ct. (we. dist.) Pa. Assoc. Baker & Botts, Houston, 1972-79, ptnr., 1980—. Mem. ABA, Houston Bar Assn., Internat. Soc. Barristers. Federal civil litigation, General civil litigation, State civil litigation. E-mail: irv.terrell@bakerbotts.com

TERRELL, JAMES DANIEL, lawyer; b. Kansas City, Oct. 22, 1956; s. D. Ronald and Bobbie L. (Graham) T.; m. Lori J. McAlister, May 31, 1980; children: Justin Daniel, Christopher James, Alexander Graham. BS, Ctrl. Mo. State U., 1979; JD, U. Mo., 1982. Bar: Mo. 1982, U.S. Dist. Ct. (we. dist.) 1982, U.S. Dist. Ct. (ea. dist.) Mo. 1984. Assoc. Wasinger, Parham & Morthland, Hannibal, Mo., 1982-87; ptnr. Wasinger, Parham, Morthland Terrell & Wasinger, 1987—. Bd. dirs. Marion County Svcs. for the Developmentally Disabled, Hannibal, 1989—. Mem.: Mo. Bar Assn. (family law sect.), 10th Jud. ir. Bar Assn. (pres. 2001—), U. Mo. Alumni Assn. (life)), Phi Delta Phi. General civil litigation, Family and matrimonial, Insurance. Office: Wasinger Parham Morthland Terrell & Wasinger 2801 Saint Marys Ave Hannibal MO 63401-3775

TERRY, DAVID WILLIAM, lawyer; b. Temple, Tex., May 21, 1958; s. Victor Lewis and Jon Gayle (Kirschner) T.; m. Katherine Ellen Noll, Dec. 5, 1987; children: Nicholas William, John Benjamin. BA, Colo. Coll., 1981; JD, South Tex. Coll. Law, 1985. Bar: Tex. 1986, U.S. Dist. Ct. (no. and ea. dists.) Tex. Briefing atty. U.S. Ct. Appeals (4th cir.), San Antonio, 1986-87; pvt. practice Dallas, 1987—. Exec. editor South Tex. Law Rev., 1985. Pres. East Dallas Cppr. Parish, 1992. Mem. Tex. Trial Lawyers Assn. (bd. dirs. 1992—), Am. Assn. Portrait Artists, Dallas Trial Lawyers Assn. (bd. dirs. 1994—), ATLA, Coll. State Bar Tex. (pro bono coll.). Democrat. Methodist. Avocations: oil painting, portraits and landscapes. Personal injury, Product liability. Office: 12221 Merit Dr Ste 1650 Dallas TX 75251-3102 E-mail: davidterry@davidterry.com

TERRY, FREDERICK ARTHUR, JR. lawyer; b. Buffalo, May 24, 1932; s. Frederick Arthur and Agnes Elizabeth (Tranter) T.; m. Barbara Anderson. BA, Williams Coll., 1953; LLB, Columbia U., 1956. Bar: N.Y. 1957, U.S. Dist. Ct. (so., no. and ea. dists.) N.Y., U.S. Ct. Appeals (2d cir.), U.S. Tax Ct., U.S. Supreme Ct. Law clk. U.S. Ct. Appeals (2nd cir.), 1956-57; assoc. Sullivan & Cromwell, N.Y.C., 1957-65, ptnr., 1965-99, sr. counsel, 2000—. Bd. dirs. Eisenhower Fellowships, Natural Resources Def. Coun., Weinman Found.; sec., mem. bd. McIntosh Found.; trustee, chmn. com. on trust and estate gift plans Rockefeller U.; trustee Harold K. Hochschild Found.; chmn. Flagler Found. Mem. ABA, N.Y. State Bar Assn., Assn. of Bar of City of N.Y., Century Assn., River Club, Union Club, India House, Doubles, Maidstone Club (East Hampton, N.Y.), Lyford Cay Club (Bahamas), The Bathing Corp. (Southampton, N.Y.). Office: Sullivan & Cromwell 125 Broad St Fl 25 New York NY 10004-2400

TERRY, JACK CHATTERSON, lawyer; b. Monett, Mo., Nov. 23, 1919; s. Jacob E. and Florence V. (Chatterson) T.; m. Susan W. Terry, June 7, 1941; children: Susan L. Terry Galewaler, Philip C. BA in History and Govt., U. Mo., Kansas City, 1949, JD, 1952. Bar: Mo. 1952, U.S. Supreme Ct. 1961. Sole practice, Independence, Mo., 1952—. Mem. Mo. Legislature, 1955-56; legis. liaison officer Jackson County (Mo.), 1967-68; atty. Inter-City Fire Protection Dist., 1955-74; city atty. City of Blue Summit (Mo.), 1971-76; atty. Jackson County (Mo.) Bd. Election Commrs., 1974—. Pres. Independence Good Govt. League, 1961-63, Jackson County League Better Govt., 1962-66. Served as officer USAAF, 1941-46, PTO. Decorated Purple Heart, Air medal. Mem. ABA, Mo. Bar Assn., Kansas City Bar Assn., Inter-City Kiwanis (pres. 1967), Masons, Shriners. Democrat. Mem. Christian Ch. (Disciples of Christ). Family and matrimonial, Personal injury, Workers' compensation. Home: 614 Bellevista Dr Independence MO 64055-1746 Office: 554 S Ash St PO Box 7800 Independence MO 64053

TERRY, JOHN ALFRED, state supreme court judge; b. Utica, N.Y., May 6, 1933; s. Robert Samuel and Julia Berenice (Collins) T. B.A. magna cum laude, Yale U., 1954; J.D., Georgetown U., 1960. Bar: D.C. 1960. Asst. U.S. atty. for D.C., 1962-67; staff atty. Nat. Commn. Reform of Fed. Criminal Laws, Washington, 1967-68; pvt. practice law, 1968-69; chief appellate div. U.S. Atty.'s Office for D.C., 1969-82; judge D.C. Ct. Appeals, 1982—. Mem. D.C. Bar (bd. govs. 1977-82), ABA, Phi Beta Kappa Office: DC Ct Appeals 500 Indiana Ave NW Washington DC 20001-2138

TERRY, JOHN HART, retired utility company executive, congressman; b. Syracuse, N.Y., Nov. 14, 1924; s. Frank and Saydee (Hart) T.; m. Catherine Jean Taylor Phelan, Apr. 15, 1950; children: Catherine Jean (Mrs. Richard Thompson), Lynn Marie (Mrs. Robert Tacher), Susan Louise (Mrs. Stanley Germain), Mary Carole (Mrs. Stephen Brady). B.A., U. Notre Dame, 1945; J.D., Syracuse U., 1948. Bar: N.Y. bar 1950, D.C. bar 1972. Asst. to partner Smith & Sovik, 1948-59; asst. sec. to Gov. State of N.Y., 1959-61; sr. partner firm Smith, Sovik, Terry, Kendrick, McAuliffe & Schwarzer, 1961-73; sr. v.p., gen. counsel, sec. Niagara Mohawk Power Corp., Syracuse, 1973-87; counsel Hiscock & Barclay, 1987-94; atty. in pvt. practice, 1994-99; ret., 2000. Mem. N.Y. State Assembly, 1962-70, 92d Congress from 34th N.Y. Dist., 1971-73; presdl. elector, 1972. State chmn. United Services Orgn., 1964-73; past pres. John Timothy Smith Found.; Founder, dir. Bishop Foery Found., Inc.; dir. St. Joseph's Hosp. Council; past pres. Lourdes Camp; bd. dirs. N.Y. State Traffic Council; past nat. bd. dirs. Am. Cancer Soc.; mem. adv. council Syracuse U. Sch. Mgmt.; past pres. Cath. Youth Orgn.; bd. dirs. Syracuse Community Baseball Club. Served to 1st lt. AUS, 1943-46. Decorated Purple Heart, Bronze Star; named Man of Year Syracuse Jr. C. of C., 1958, Man of Yr. N.Y. State Jr. C. of C., 1959, Young Man of Yr. U. Notre Dame Club Cen. N.Y., 1959; recipient U. Notre Dame Exemplar award, 1997, Rev. Theodore Hesborgh Alumni award, 1997. Mem. ABA (utility law sect.), N.Y. State Bar Assn. (chmn. com. on public utility law), Onondaga County Bar Assn. (chmn. membership and legis. coms.), D.C. Bar Assn., County Officers Assn., Citizens Found., U. Notre Dame, Syracuse U. law assns., Am. Legion, VFW, DAV, 40 and 8, Mil. Order of Purple Heart, Bellevue Country Club, Capitol Hill Club (Washington), Vero Beach Country Club. Roman Catholic.

TERRY, JOSEPH RAY, JR. lawyer; b. Vicksburg, Miss., Aug. 10, 1938; s. Joseph Ray Sr. and Alma Blanche (Smith) T.; m. Louise Caroline Beland, July 17, 1965; children: Kathleen A., Marie L., Bernard R. JD, Loyola U., 1965. Bar: D.C. 1966, Miss. 1968, U.S. Ct. Appeals (5th cir.) 1971, Ga. 1973, U.S. Dist. Ct. (no. and so. dists.) Ga. 1973, U.S. Ct. Appeals (D.C. cir.) 1973, U.S. Supreme Ct. 1973, U.S. Ct. Appeals (8th cir.) 1974, U.S. Dist. Ct. (we. dist.) Tenn. 1983, U.S. Ct. Appeals (6th cir.) 1989; cert. mediator. Trial atty. civil rights div. U.S. Dept. Justice, Washington, 1966-69; assoc. regional counsel U.S. Dept. HUD, Atlanta, 1969-70; ptnr. Crosland, Myer, Rindskopf & Terry, 1974-76; regional counsel EEOC, 1970-73, supr. trial atty. Litigation Cen., 1976-79, regional atty. Memphis, 1979-96, dep. gen. counsel Washington, 1996-99, cons., lectr., mediator, 1999—. Part-time asst. atty. City of Atlanta, 1975-76; cons. NLRB, Memphis, 1981-82; adj. prof. law Emory U., 1971-75; vis. prof. law St. Louis U., 1973-74, William C. Wefel disting. vis. prof. law, 1998—; acting program dir. EEOC, Washington, 1983, acting dist. dir., Memphis, 1984-85; bd. dirs. Fed. Credit Union, 1984-91; mem. adv. com. to U.S. Dist. Ct. for western dist. Tenn., 1990-93, chmn. case mgmt. subcom., 1991-98; mem. faculty Southwestern Legal Found., Dallas, spring 1998; cons. equal employment, 1999—; cert. gen. civil mediator Supreme Ct. Tenn., 2000. Author: (jour.) Eliminating the Plaintiff's Attorney in Equal Employment Litigation: A Shakespearean Tragedy, Labor Lawyer, 1989, Memphis and Race, The Commercial Appeal, 1987. Cons. Alaska Human Rights Commn., Anchorage, 1981; bd. dirs. Nat. Kidney Found. of West Tenn., Memphis, pres., 1984-85; bd. dirs. United Meth. Neighborhood Ctr., 1985-88; bd. dirs. St. Patrick's Parish Coun., Memphis, pres., 1986-88; mem. Leadership Memphis, 1988-99; bd. dirs. Place of Grace Ministries, Carlisle, Pa., 1997—. Named Honor Law Graduate U.S. Atty. Gen., 1965. Mem. ABA (EEOC liaison com. 1987-89), Fed. Bar Assn. (bd. dirs. 1988-89, v.p. West Tenn. chpt. 1991-92, pres. 1993-94, nat. coun. 1996-99, named Younger Fed. Lawyer of Yr. 1973), Supreme Ct. Hist. Soc., St. Thomas More Lawyers Guild, Salvation Army (bd. dirs. 1995-96). Roman Catholic. Avocations: tennis, golf, skiing, hiking, reading. Home: 1560 Harbert Ave Memphis TN 38104-5033

TERRY, T(AYLOR) RANKIN, JR. lawyer; b. Louisville, Sept. 17, 1946; s. T. Rankin Sr. and C. Ruth (Ochs) T.; m. Kristine Ann Luther, May 24, 1969; 1 child, Taylor Rankin III. BSME, U. Ky., 1968; JD, Washington U., 1971; LLM in Taxation, U. Fla., 1976. Bar: Fla. 1971, Ky. 1971. Assoc. Boehl, Stopher, Graves & Deindoerfer, Louisville and Paducah, Ky., 1971-72; from assoc. to ptnr. Roberts, Watson et al, Ft. Myers, Fla., 1972-77; ptnr. Terry, Adams & Corbin, 1977-81, Terry & Terry, Ft. Myers, 1981—. Mem. NSPE, Fla. Engring. Soc., Ky. Bar Assn., Fla. Bar (ethics com. 1976-78, civil rules com., drafting subcom. 1981—). Democrat. Presbyterian. General civil litigation, Personal injury, Taxation, general. Office: Terry & Terry 2121 Mcgregor Blvd Fort Myers FL 33901-3411 E-mail: tterry8063@aol.com

TERSCHAN, FRANK ROBERT, lawyer; b. Dec. 25, 1949; s. Frank Joseph and Margaret Anna (Heidt) T.; m. Barbara Elizabeth Keily, Dec. 28, 1974; 1 child, Frank Martin. BA, Syracuse U., 1972; JD, U. Wis., 1975. Bar: Wis. 1976, U.S. Dist. Ct. (ea. and we. dists.) Wis. 1976, U.S. Ct. Appeals (7th cir.) 1979, U.S. Ct. Appeals (10th cir.) 1989, U.S. Supreme Ct. 1982. From assoc. to ptnr. Frisch, Dudek & Slattery Ltd., Milw., 1975-88; ptnr. Slattery and Hausman Ltd., 1988-94, Terschan & Steinle

Ltd., Milw., 1994-96, Terschan, Steinle & Ness, Milw., 1996—. Treas., sec. Ville du Park Homeowners Assn., Mequon, Wis., 1985-86; cub scout packmaster pack 3844 Boy Scouts Am., 1989-90, asst. scoutmaster Troop 865, 1991-93. Mem. ABA, Am. Bd. Trial Advocates, Wis. Bar Assn., Milw. Bar Assn., Assn. Trial Lawyers Am., Wis. Acad. of Trial Lawyers (bd. dirs. 1996—), 7th Cir. Bar Assn., Order of Coif. Republican. Lutheran. Avocations: swimming, coin collecting, reading, outdoor activities. Federal civil litigation, General civil litigation, Personal injury. Home: 10143 N Lake Shore Dr Mequon WI 53092-6109 Office: 2600 N Mayfair Rd Ste 700 Milwaukee WI 53226-1314 E-mail: terstein@execpc.com

TERTERIAN, GEORGE, lawyer; b. Beirut, Lebanon, Jan. 30, 1966; s. Ohannes Terterian and Sirvart Kelian. BA, Wayne State U., 1988, JD, 1991. Bar: Calif. 1994, U.S. Dist. Ct. (ctrl. dist.) Calif. 1994. Pvt. practice, Encino, Calif., 1995—. Mem. ABA, ATLA, CAAC, Consumer Attys. Assn. of L.A., Kessab Ednl. Assn. (bd. dirs.), Phi Alpha Theta. Democrat. Avocations: travel, cooking, studying history, athletics. General civil litigation, Personal injury. Office: Penthouse 16133 Ventura Blvd Ph A Encino CA 91436-2447

TESCH, TAMARA DIANNE, lawyer; b. Rapid City, S.D., June 25, 1973; d. Wayne Edwin and Goldia Dianne Block; m. Dan Ray Tesch; 1 child, Abigail. BS in Med. Tech., U. S.D., 1995; JD, De Paul U., 1998. Bar: Minn., 1998, S.D., 2000; cert. med. technologist. Co-owner Block Masonry, Inc., Rapid City, 1988—; processor, closer Bank Am., Bloomington, Minn., 1998—; pvt. practice lawyer Rosemount, 1998—; pvt. prac. lawyer Affiliates, 2000—; stewardship and compliance officer Planned Giving, 2000—01. Mem.: ABA, Minn. State Bar Assn. (mock trial coach, 1998, 99), S.D. Bar Assn. (mock trial coach 1998—2000), Dakota County Bar Assn. Avocations: reading, walking. Home: 14200 Belfast Ct Rosemount MN 55068-4963 E-mail: tdtesch@stthomas.edu

TESSENSOHN, JOHN ALVIN, lawyer, author, playwright; b. Singapore, Oct. 28, 1967; s. Edward Anthony and Magdalene Theresa (Lioe) T; m. Junko Inagaki. LLB with honors, Nat. U. Singapore, 1992; LLM with honors, Fordham U., 1998. Advocate and solicitor Supreme Ct. of Singapore, 1993. Assoc. in litig. Abraham Low & Ptnrs., Singapore, 1992-94; intellectual property counsel Shusaku Yamamoto Patent Law Offices, Osaka, Japan, 1994—; pvt. practice N.Y., 1999—. Mem. editl. bd. I.P. Asia, 1995—, Trademark World, 1999—, Patent World, 1999—; country corr. European Intellectual Property Rev., 1996—; author: (plays) The Breasts of Tiresias, Too Glam One, A Cup of Coffee, So Glam One, Mission of the Coming Day, 1988-94; columnist Singapore Internet Cmty., 1997; mem. adv. bd. World INtellectual Property Report, 1998, World Licensing Law Report, 1999; contbr. articles to profl. jours. Resident playwright Gung-Ho Theater Ensemble, Singapore, 1988-94. Recipient Outstanding Contbn. to the Arts award Victoria Jr. Coll., Singapore, 1986, Presdl. citation for Nat. Vol.'s Month, Pres. Republic of Singapore, 1991. Mem. Law Soc. of Singapore, Internat. Trademark Assn., Osaka Internat. Lawyers Assn, N.Y. State Bar Assoc. (counselor, atty.-at-law). Roman Catholic. Avocations: drama, travel, writing, swimming, film. Office: Shusaku Yamamoto 1-2-27 Shiromi Chuo-ku Osaka 540-6015 Japan

TESSIER, DENNIS MEDWARD, paralegal, lecturer, legal advisor, consultant; b. Royal Oak, Mich., Sept. 20, 1956; s. Medward James and Marilyn (Pitsos) T.; m. Michelle Terri Zeichick, July 28, 1990; 1 child, Brian Jae. Cert. paralegal, U. West L.A., 1987, cert. atty. practice, 1990; cert. in epidemiology, U.S. CDC, 1991. Reprodn. analyst Burroughs Corp., Detroit, 1975-76; mixologist Holiday Inn, Inc., Belair, Calif., 1977-83; spl. asst. office of the gen. counsel U.S. Jud. Intelligence Agy., Pacific Sta., L.A., 1981—; mixologist R.W. Grace Inc., Marina Del Rey, Calif., 1984-86; paralegal O'Melveny & Myers, L.A., 1986, Haight, Brown & Bonesteel, Santa Monica, Calif., 1987-93, Helsell & Fetterman, Seattle, 1993-94, Nintendo of Am. Inc., Redmond, Wash., 1994-96, Tousley Brain PLLC, Seattle, 1996-98, Preston Gates & Ellis, Seattle, 1998—. Family law cons. Helping Svcs., L.A., 1990-93, L.A. Clinic, 1990; rschr. Tessier & Assocs. Rsch., Topanga Canyon, Calif., 1983—; with Starlight Found., Redmond, Wash., 1993—. Author: Beauty in Motion, 1983, Champerty and Barratry, 1998. Creek Rat Esquire, 1999; contbr. articles to profl. jours. Mem. ABA (sci. and tech. law, jud. adminstrn. sects.), ATLA, Soc. Epidemiology Rsch., Assn. Investigative Scis., Judges Advs. (JAG) Assn., U.S. Nat. Acad. Scis. Academe Industry Program (spkr. CLE), Am. Legion. Democrat. Lutheran. Avocations: music, arts. Home: 21100 Pioneer Way Edmonds WA 98026-6947 Office: Preston Gates & Ellis 701 Fifth Avete 5600 Seattle WA 98104 E-mail: dtessier@justice.com, dennist@prestongates.com

TESTA, RICHARD JOSEPH, lawyer; b. Marlboro, Mass., Apr. 21, 1939; s. Joseph N. and Jeannette (Clement) T.; children: Jo-Anne, Richard J. Jr., Nancy, Susan, Karen. AB, Assumption Coll., 1959; LLB, Harvard U., 1962. Bar: Mass. 1962. Chmn. Testa, Hurwitz & Thibeault, Boston, 1973—. Mem. ABA. Roman Catholic. General civil litigation, General corporate. Office: Testa Hurwitz & Thibeault High St Tower 125 High St Boston MA 02110-2725 E-mail: testa@tht.com

TETI, LOUIS N. lawyer; b. Bryn Mawr, Pa., May 29, 1950; BA, Dickinson Coll., 1972; JD, Temple U., 1976, LLM in Tax., 1981. Bar: Pa. 1976. Ptnr. MacElree Harvey, Ltd., West Chester and Exton, Pa. Mem. disciplinary bd. Surpeme Ct. Pa., 2000—. Fellow Am. Coll. Trust and Estate Counsel; mem. ABA (ho. dels. 1985-91, 99—), Pa. Bar Assn. (chmn. young lawyers divsn. 1982-83, bd. govs. 1982-85, 91-94, 97-2001, pres. 1999-2000), Chester County Bar Assn. (sec. 1979-82, 86-88, v.p. 1989, pres.-elect 1990, pres. 1991, chair young lawyers sect. 1977, bd. dirs. 1977-92), Chester County Estate Planning Coun. (pres. 1988-89). Banking, Real property, Taxation, general. Office: MacElree Harvey Ltd 740 Springdale Dr Ste 110 Exton PA 19341-2865 Fax: 610 524 9857. E-mail: lteti@macelree.com

TETTLEBAUM, HARVEY M. lawyer; m. Ann Safier; children: Marianne, Benjamin. AB, Dartmouth Coll., 1964; JD, AM in History, Washington U. Sch. Law, 1968. Asst. dean Washington U. Sch. Law, 1969-77; asst. atty. gne., chief counsel Consumer Protection and Anti-Trust Div., 1970-77; pvt. practice Jefferson City, Mo., 1977-90; mem., chmn. health law practice group Husch & Eppenberger, LLC, 1990—. Contbr. articles to profl. jours. Treas. Mo. Rep. State Com., 1976—; v.p. Moniteau County R-1 Sch. Dist. Bd., 1991-95, pres., 1995-96; mem. Calif. R-1 Sch. Bd., 1990-96, v.p., 1993-95, pres., 1995-96. [e]m. Am. Health Lawyers Assn. (bd. dirs. 1993-99, co-chair long-term care and the law program 1993-2001, chair 2001—, chair long-term care and law program 2001—, chair long term care substantive law com. 1997-2001), Mo. Bar Assn. (health and hosp. law com., chmn. adminstrv. law com., vice chair delivery of legal svc. com., Mo. statewide legal svc. com.), Am. Health Care Assn. (legal subcom. 1994—). Administrative and regulatory, Health. Home: 56295 Little Moniteau Rd California MO 65018-3069 Office: Husch & Eppenberger LLC Monroe House Ste 300 235 E High St PO Box 1251 Jefferson City MO 65102-1251

TETZLAFF, CHARLES ROBERT, prosecutor; b. Oct. 15, 1938; s. Donald H. and Harriet (Ranney) T.; m. Joan Seugling, July 1, 1962; children: Julie Lynn Mulrow, Carl Lawrence. BA, U. Vt., 1960; LLB, Boston U., 1963; LLM, NYU, 1964. Bar: Vt. 1964, U.S. Supreme Ct. 1970. Judge advocate USAF, 1965-68; dep. state's atty. Chittenden County, Vt., 1968-70; ptnr. Latham, Eastman, Schweyer and Tetzlaff, 1969-93; U.S. atty. dist. Vt. Office U.S. Atty., Burlington, 1993—. Trustee Vt. Legal Aid, 1976-78; chair Dist. 4 Environ. Commn., 1979-83, Gov. Sentencing Study Commn., 1985-86; active Vt. Bd. Bar Examiners, 1980-84, State Police Adv. Commn., 1985-86, Gov. Bail Amendment Task Force. Capt. USAF, 1965-68. Mem. ABA, Vt. Bar Assn., Chittenden County Bar Assn. Office: US Attys Office PO Box 570 11 Elmwood Ave Burlington VT 05402

TETZLAFF, THEODORE R. lawyer; b. Saukville, Wis., Feb. 27, 1944; AB magna cum laude, Princeton U., 1966; LLB, Yale U., 1969. Bar: Ind. 1969, D.C. 1969, Ill. 1974. Legis. asst. to Congressman John Brademas, 1970; exec. dir. Nat. Conf. Police Community Rels., 1970-71; acting dir. U.S. Office Legal Svcs., Office Econ. Opportunity, Washington, 1972-73; counsel, Com. Judiciary U.S. Ho. of Reps., 1974; v.p., legal and external affairs Cummins Engine Co., 1980-82; gen. coun. Tenneco, Inc., Greenwich, Conn., 1992-99, C.T.; ptnr. Jenner & Block, Chgo., 1976-80, 82—. Bd. dirs. Continental Materials Corp., Chgo. Pres. Chgo. area Found. Legal Svcs., 1983—; commr. Pub. Bldg. Commn. Chgo., 1990—. Reginald Heber Smith fellow, 1969-70. Mem. ABA (chair sect. litigation 1991-92), Ill. State Bar Assn., Ind. State Bar Assn., D.C. Bar. Office: Jenner & Block 1 E Ibm Plz Fl 4200 Chicago IL 60611-7600

TEVRIZIAN, DICKRAN M., JR. federal judge; b. Los Angeles, Aug. 4, 1940; s. Dickran and Rose Tevrizian; m. Geraldine Tevrizian, Aug. 22, 1964; children: Allyson Tracy, Leslie Sara. BS, U. So. Calif., 1962, JD, 1965. Tax acct. Arthur Andersen and Co., Los Angeles, 1965-66; atty., ptnr. Kirtland and Packard, 1966-72; judge Los Angeles Mcpl. Ct., 1972-78, State of Calif. Superior Ct., Los Angeles, 1978-82; ptnr. Manatt, Phelps, Rothenberg & Tunney, 1982-85, Lewis, D'Amato, Brisbois & Bisgaard, Los Angeles, 1985-86; judge U.S. Dist. Ct., 1986—. Adv. dir. sch. pub. policy U. Calif., L.A. Adv. dir. UCLA Sch. Pub. Policy. Named Trial Judge of the Yr., Calif. Trial Lawyers Assn., 1987, L.A. County Bar Assn., 1994-95; recipient Peter the Great Gold Medal of Honor Russian Acad. Natural Scis., 1998, Ellis Island Medal of Honor award, 1999. Mem. Calif. Trial Lawyer's Assn. (trial judge of yr. 1987), L.A. County Bar Assn. (trial judge of yr. 1994-95), Malibu Bar Assn. (fed. ct. trial judge of yr. 1998). Office: US Dist Ct Royal Federal Bldg 255 E Temple St Los Angeles CA 90012-3332

TEWES, R. SCOTT, lawyer; b. Chgo., Mar. 23, 1956; s. Raymond Henry and Vivian Marie Tewes; m. Marcia Anne King, June 5, 1981; children: Benjamin Scott, Matthew Philip, Madeline Anne Marie, Carrie Elizabeth. BS, Bob Jones U., 1978, MS, 1980; JD, U. S.C., 1983. Bar: S.C. 1983, D.C. 1985, Ga. 1987, U.S. Supreme Ct. Assoc. Brown & Hagins, Greenville, S.C., 1983-86; law clk. to Hon. Jean Galloway Bissell U.S. Ct. Appeals Fed. Cir., Washington, 1986-87; assoc., ptnr. Kilpatrick Stockton, Atlanta, 1987—. Articles editor S.C. Law Rev., 1982-83; contbr. articles to profl. jours. Active Greenville (S.C.) County Alcohol and Drug Abuse Commn., 1985-86; trustee Killian Hill Baptist Ch., Lilburn, Ga., 1994-2000. Mem. S.C. Bar (practice and procedure com., bar ethics adv. com. 1985-86), Am. Intellectual Property Law Assn., Fed. Cir. Bar Assn., Christian Legal Soc., Federalist Soc., Lic. Execs. Soc., Order of Barristers. Avocations: running, biking, skiing. Federal civil litigation, Constitutional, Patent. Office: Kilpatrick Stockton 1100 Peachtree St NE Ste 2800 Atlanta GA 30309-4530 E-mail: stewes@kilpatrickstockton.com

TEYKL, JAMES STEPHEN, lawyer; b. Houston, Dec. 21, 1954; s. Irvin Frank and Marjorie Doris (Johnston) T.; m. Mary Beth Crowson, Apr. 30, 1983. BA, U. Ill., 1977; JD, Northwestern U., 1980. Bar: Ill. 1980, U.S. Dist. Ct. (no. dist.) Ill. 1980, U.S. Ct. Appeals (7th cir.) 1981. Assoc. Anthony Scariano & Assocs., P.C., Chicago Heights, Ill., 1980-81; ptnr. Greenberg & Teykl, P.C., Homewood, 1981-91; sole practice Crete, 1991—. Guest lectr. law Thornton Community Coll., South Holland, Ill., 1982—. Trustee, Ill. C.C. Dist. 515, Chicago Heights, 1983-89; mem. Taxpayers Adv. Bd., Chgo, 1983. Mem. Ill. Bar Assn. Episcopalian. Consumer commercial, General corporate, Probate. Home: 3417 Huntley Ter Crete IL 60417-1393 Office: Law Offices James S Teykl PC PO Box 283 Crete IL 60417-0283

THACKERAY, JONATHAN E. lawyer; b. Athens, Ohio, July 30, 1936; s. Joseph Eugene and Betty Rutherford (Boright) T.; m. Sandra Ann McMahon; children: Jennifer, Sara, Amy, Jonathan. A.B. cum laude, Harvard U., 1958, J.D., 1961. Bar: Ohio 1961, U.S. Dist. Ct. (no. dist.) Ohio 1961, U.S. Supreme Ct. 1972, U.S. Ct. Appeals (6th cir.) 1973, U.S. Ct. Appeals (9th cir.) 1982, N.Y. 1993. Assoc. Vorys, Sater, Seymour & Pease, Columbus, Ohio, 1961, Baker & Hostetler, Cleve., 1965-72, ptnr., 1973-93; v.p., gen. counsel The Hearst Corp., N.Y.C., 1993—. Served to lt. USNR, 1961-65. Mem. ABA, Ohio Bar Assn., Cleve. Bar Assn., Am. Law Inst. Antitrust, Federal civil litigation, Communications. Office: The Hearst Corp 959 8th Ave New York NY 10019-3795

THADDEUS, ALOYSIUS PETER, JR. lawyer; b. Galveston, Tex., Jan. 11, 1954; s. Aloysius Peter and Marhta Ann (Cox) T.; m. Anne Arundel Locker; B.A., St. Edwards U., 1976; J.D., 1982. Bar: Tex. 1982, U.S. Dist. Ct. (so. dist.) Tex. 1983. Briefing atty. Tex. Ct. Criminal Appeals, 1982-83; assoc. Judin, Barron & Seljos, McAllen, Tex., 1983-87, Law Office of Ramon Garcia, 1987—. Mem. State Bar Tex., ABA, Hidalgo County Bar Assn. (bd. dirs. 1986-87), Tex. Young Lawyers Assn. (bd. dirs. 1987—), Hidalgo County Young Lawyers Assn., Tex. Trial Lawyers Assn., Am. Trial Lawyers Assn. Democrat. Roman Catholic. State civil litigation, Personal injury, Workers' compensation. Office: 100 E Savannah Ave Ste 400 Mcallen TX 78503-1237

THALACKER, ARBIE ROBERT, lawyer, director; b. Marquette, Mich., Apr. 17, 1935; s. Arbie Otto and Jeanne (Emmett) T.; m. Rita Annette Skaaren, Sept. 11, 1956 (div. July 1992); children: Marc Emmett, Christopher Paul, Robert Skaaren; m. Deborah B. Garrett, Jan. 10, 1998. AB, Princeton U., 1957; JD, U. Mich., 1960. Bar: N.Y. 1961, U.S. Ct. Appeals (2d cir.) 1962. Assoc. Shearman & Sterling, N.Y.C., 1960-68, ptnr., 1968—. Dir. Detrex Corp., Detroit, 1981—, chmn. bd., 1993-96. Leader Rep. Dist. Com., 1966-68; v.p., trustee Greenwich Village Soc. for Hist. Preservation; trustee Naropa Univ.; bd. dirs. Meredith Monk House Found., Shambhala Internat. Mem. ABA, N.Y. Bar Assn., Assn. Bar City N.Y. (securities regulatory commn. 1975-78), Wine and Food Soc. (bd. dirs. 1976-78, 85-93, 94—), Chevaliers du Tastevin, Commanderie de Bordeaux, Siwanoy Country Club (bd. govs. 1976-79), Derby Club, Links Club, Verbank Hunting and Fishing Club. Private international, Mergers and acquisitions, Securities. Home: 17 Commerce St New York NY 10014-3763 Office: Shearman & Sterling 599 Lexington Ave Fl C2 New York NY 10022-6069

THALER, PAUL SANDERS, lawyer, mediator; b. Washington, May 4, 1961; s. Martin S. Thaler and Barbara (Friedman) Mishkin; m. Melinda Ann Frostic, Oct. 12, 1991; children: Rachel Leigh, Daniel Martin. AB, Vassar Coll., 1983; JD, Georgetown U., 1987. Bar: Md. 1987, D.C. 1988, U.S. Ct. Appeals (D.C. and 4th cirs.) 1988, U.S. Dist. Ct. Md. 1988, U.S. Ct. Appeals (fed. cir.) 1989, U.S. Dist. Ct. D.C. 1989, U.S. Ct. Internat. Trade 1990, U.S. Supreme Ct. 1992. Assoc. Cooter & Gell, Washington, 1987-93; ptnr. The Robinson Law Firm, 1993-96, Thaler Liebeler Machado & Rasmussen, LLP, 1996—; guest lectr. negotiations mediation George Washington U. Law Sch., 1996—. Adj. prof. Kogod Sch. Bus., Am. U. Bus. Ethics, Bus. Law, 1999—. Treas. Montgomery Highlands Estates Homeowners Assn., Silver Spring, Md., 1990-99; mediator Superior Ct. of D.C., 1991—; mem. adv. com. Vassar Coll. Fund, 1996-99; trustee Nat. Child Rsch. Ctr., Washington, 1998-2001. Mem. ABA (sect. dispute resolution, vice chmn. ethics 1994-98), D.C. Bar Assn., Md. Bar Assn., Soc. Profls. in Dispute Resolution, Acad. Family Mediators. Alternative dispute resolution, General civil litigation, General practice. Home: 9429 Locust Hill Rd Bethesda MD 20814-3939 Office: Thaler Liebeler Machado & Rasmussen LLP Ste 200 1919 Pennsylvania Ave NW Washington DC 20006

THARP, JAMES WILSON, lawyer; b. Hoisington, Kans., Nov. 22, 1942; s. James Alfred and Jeanette B. (Wilson) Tharp Adams; children: Jennifer, Juliana, Damien. AB, U. Kans., 1965, JD, 1968. Bar: Kans. 1968, U.S. Dist. Ct. Kans. 1968, Ohio 1969, U.S. Ct. Appeals (10th cir.) 1969, U.S. Dist. Ct. (so. dist.) 1970, U.S. Ct. Appeals (6th cir.) 1974, Hawaii 1977, U.S. Dist. Ct. Hawaii 1977, U.S. Ct. Appeals (9th cir.) 1977, U.S. Supreme Ct. 1978, No. Mariana Islands 1978, U.S. Dist. Ct. No. Mariana Islands 1978, U.N. Trust Territory Pacific Islands, 1978, Rep. of Marshall Island, 1983. Asst. atty. gen State of Ohio, 1969-70; gen. counsel Ohio Dept. Edn., 1970-72; pvt. practice Columbus, Ohio, 1972-74; counsel FHA, Columbus and L.A., 1974-76; area counsel HUD, 1976-79; pvt. practice law, Honolulu, 1979—; real estate broker Hawaii, 1980—. Adminstrv. hearing officer State of Hawaii, 1984—; arbitrator Hawaii Judiciary, 1987—; bd. dirs., chief academic advisor Pacific Western U. Dir., v.p. Hawaii Literacy, Inc., 1988-91; dir. Hawaii State Theatre Coun., 1988-93. Lever Brothers scholar, Scholarship Hall scholar, 1960-61. Mem. SAG, Hawaii Bar Assn. (rep. Gov.'s Coun. for Literacy 1987-91), Kansas Club Hawaii (gov. 1983-84), Masons. Avocations: reading, acting. Consumer commercial, General corporate, Real property. Office: 1210 Auahi St Ste 104 Honolulu HI 96814-4922

THARP, TONNA K. lawyer; b. Sedalia, Mo., Apr. 9, 1972; d. Paul Leon and Judith Kay Tharp. BS in Comms., U. Mo., Columbia, 1994; JD, U. Mo., Kansas City, 1997. Bar: Mo., Kans., U.S. Dist. Ct. (we. dist.) Mo., U.S. Dist. Ct. Kans. Assoc. Dunn Keller Gillespie Johnson & Latz, L.C., Kansas City, Mo., 1997—. Spkr. on equine law. Contbr. articles to equine publs. Mem. Am. Quarter Horse Assn. (3d pl. in world championship 1994), Mo. Quarter Horse Assn., Mo. Equine Coun. Avocation: national level competition at quarter horse shows. Banking, Contracts commercial, Equine law. Office: Dunn Keller Gillespie Johnston & Latz LC 800 W 47th St Ste 406 Kansas City MO 64112

THAU, WILLIAM ALBERT, JR. lawyer; b. St. Louis, June 22, 1940; s. William Albert and Irene Elizabeth (Mundy) T.; m. Jane Hancock, Sept. 7, 1961; children: William Albert, Caroline Jane, Jennifer Elizabeth. BS in Indsl. Mgmt., Ga. Inst. Tech., 1962; JD, U. Tex., 1965. Bar: Tex. 1965. Ptnr., head of real estate sect. Jenkens & Gilchrist, Dallas, 1965—. Chmn. real estate developer/builder symposium S.W. Legal Found, 1975-79; bd. dirs. Southwestern Film Archives, So. Meth. U.; lectr. Practicing Law Inst. Author: Negotiating the Purchase and Sale of Real Estate, 1975; editor Tex. State Bar Assn. Newsletter on Real Estate, Probate and Trust Law, 1978-81; contbr. articles to Real Estate Rev., 1983—. Bd. dirs. St. Philips Sch., Dallas, 1988, So. Meth. U.; trustee Dallas Can. Acad., 1987-88. Mem. ABA, Tex. State Bar Assn. (chmn. real estate, probate, trust law sect.), Am. Coll. Real Estate Lawyers. Republican. Contracts commercial, Construction, Real property. Office: Jenkens & Gilchrist 1445 Ross Ave Ste 3200 Dallas TX 75202-2785

THAXTON, MARVIN DELL, lawyer; b. Electra, Tex., June 1, 1925; s. Montgomery Dell and Ida (Scheurer) T.; m. Carolyn Moore Alexander, Aug. 30, 1949; children: Rebecca Thaxton Henderson, Gail Thaxton Fogleman, Marvin D. Jr. JD, U. Ark., 1949. Bar: Ark. 1949, U.S. Dist. Ct. (ea. dist.) Ark. 1952, U.S. Dist. Ct. (we. dist.) Ark. 1978, U.S. Dist. Ct. (we. dist.) Okla., U.S. Supreme Ct. 1987. Prin. Thaxton Furniture Co., Newport, Ark., 1949-50; ptnr. Thaxton, Hout & Howard, Attys., 1950-97; retired, 1997. Spl. assoc. justice Ark. Supreme Ct., 1978, 84; examiner Ark. State Bd. Law Examiners, 1968-73, chmn. 1973. Pres. Newport Sch. Dist. Bd. Edn., 1964; past pres. Ea. Ark. Young Men's Clubs; adult leader Newport area Boy Scouts Am., 1949-94; bd. dirs. Newport Hosp. and Clinic Inc., 2000. Officer U.S. Mcht. Marine, 1945-46, PTO. Fellow Ark. Bar Found.; mem. ABA, Ark. Bar Assn. (honor cert. 1973), Newport C. of C. (pres. 1956, bd. dirs. 1997-2000), Newport Rotary Club (past pres., Paul Harris fellow 1990), Sigma Chi. Democrat. Methodist. Avocations: hunting, fishing, boating. General corporate, General practice, Real property. Home: 12 Lakeside Ln Newport AR 72112-3914 E-mail: mdtjd@ipa.net

THEBERGE, NORMAN BARTLETT, educator, lawyer; b. Norfolk, Va., Dec. 1, 1946; s. Norman Bartlett and Marjorie Delight (Malbon) T.; m. Louis Cobb Dibrell, Sept. 9, 1978; children— Mary Knight, Susan Dibrell. B.S. in Biology, Coll. William and Mary, 1969; J.D., Marshall-Wythe Law Sch., Williamsburg, Va., 1973; LL.M., U. Miami, Coral Gables, Fla., 1974. Bar: Va. 1974. prof. Coll. William & Mary, 1985—, acting assoc. dean Sch. Marine Sci., 1984-85, chmn. marine resource mgmt. subfaculty, 1976-86, chmn. dept. ocean and coastal law; lectr. Marshall Wythe Law Sch., 1974-83; asst. prof. dept. marine sci. U. Va., Gloucester Point, 1974-76; sr. marine scientist Va. Inst. Marine Sci., Gloucester Point, 1983-84; cons. Office of Tech. Assessment, Dept. Energy, U.S. Fish and Wildlife Service, other state and fed. agys.; mem. adv. bd. Inst. Law and Pub. Health Protection, Arlington, Va., 1984—. Contbr. numerous articles to profl. publs. Mem. ABA, Va. Bar Assn., AAUP. Presbyterian. Office: Va Inst Marine Sci Gloucester Point VA 23062

THEISEN, HENRY WILLIAM, lawyer; b. N.Y.C., Feb. 21, 1939; s. Charles and Jennie J. (Callahan) T.; m. Kathleen Anne Brennan, Jan. 23, 1966 (div. Oct. 1992); children: Gordon H., Anne, Maureen R., William R.; m. Deborah S. Lynch, June 11, 1994. BBA, Manhattan Coll., 1961; JD, Fordham U., 1966. Bar: N.Y. 1967, U.S. Dist. Ct. (no. dist.) N.Y. 1968, U.S. Ct. Appeals (2d cir.) 1971, U.S. Supreme Ct. 1974. Acct. Patterson & Ridgway, CPAs, N.Y.C., 1961-64; ptnr. Adams, Theisen & May, Ithaca, N.Y., 1967—; prosecutor City of Ithaca, 1969; estate tax atty. N.Y. State, Albany, 1976-90; county atty. Tompkins County, Ithaca, 1994—. Examining counsel Ticor Title Guaranty Co., Monroe Title Ins. Corp.; corp. sec., bd. dirs. Paleontol. Rsch. Instn., Ithaca; lectr. wills and trusts adult edn. program Bd. Coop. Ednl. Svcs., Tompkins County, N.Y., 1995-99. Author: (fin. and estate planning) Financial and Estate Planning Records, 1996. Pres. Ithaca Cmty. Music Sch., 1970; bd. reps. Tompkins County, Ithaca, 1976-81; bd. dirs. Tompkins Cmty. Hosp., 1980-83, Ctr. for Arts at Ithaca, Inc. (Hangar Theatre), 1989-92, Suicide Prevention Found. Tompkins County, 1996—; race dir. Finger Lakes Marathon, 1992-96; bd. dirs. Spl. Children's Ctr., 1969-74, pres., 1973-74; bd. dirs. Tompkins County SPCA, 1973-76, pres., 1976; chmn. task force orgn. Ithaca Pub. Edn. Initiative Inc., 1995-96; panel mem. Jud. Candidate Rating Panel, Binghamton, N.Y., 1993-94; candidate Supreme Ct. Justice, N.Y., 1992 Mem. Tompkins County Bar Assn. (pres. 1990), Tompkins County C. of C. (pres. 1993), Estate Planning Coun. Tompkins County (co-founder, pres. 1985), Ithaca Rotary Club. Democrat. Roman Catholic. Avocations: watercolor painting, long distance running. Municipal (including bonds), Probate, Real property. Office: Adams Theisen & May 301 The Clinton House 103 W Seneca St Ste 304 Ithaca NY 14850-4191 E-mail: atm@clarityconnect.com Deceased.

THEUT, C. PETER, lawyer; b. Center Line, Mich., July 24, 1938; s. Clarence William and Anna Marie (Martens) T.; m. Judith Fern Trombley, Aug. 4, 1962; children: Elizabeth Anne, Kristin Claire, Peter Christopher, Sarah Nicole. BA, U. Mich., 1960, LLB, 1963. Bar: Calif. 1964, Mich. 1964, U.S. Dist. Ct. (no. dist.) Ohio 1968, U.S. Dist. Ct. (ea. dist.) Mich. 1968. Assoc. Overton, Lyman & Prince, L.A., 1963-67; ptnr. Foster, Meadows and Ballard, Detroit, 1968-72, Theut & Schellig, Mt. Clemens, Mich., 1972-80, Hill, Lewis, Mt. Clemens, 1980-88, Butzel, Long, Detroit, 1988—. Stockbroker; chmn. Butzel Long Global Trade Group. Mem. ABA

(internat. law sect., TIPS admiralty com.), Mich. State Bar Assn., Detroit Bar Assn., Macomb County Bar Assn., Calif. Bar Assn., Maritime Law Assn. (past chmn. recreational boating com.), Nat. Marine Bankers Assn. (gen. counsel), Mich. Boating Industry Assn. (gen. counsel) Lex Mundi, North Star Sail Club. Republican. Admiralty, Contracts commercial, Private international. Home: 38554 Hidden Ln Clinton Township MI 48036-1826 E-mail: theut@butzel.com

THIBEAULT, GEORGE WALTER, lawyer; b. Cambridge, Mass., Sept. 21, 1941; s. George Walter and Josephine (Maraggia) T.; m. Antoinette Miller, June 30, 1963; children: Robin M., Holly Ann. BS, Northeastern U., 1964; MBA, Boston Coll., 1966, JD, 1969. Bar: Mass. 1969. Assoc. Gaston & Snow, Boston, 1969-73; ptnr. Testa, Hurwitz & Thibeault, 1973—. Mem. ABA, Mass. Bar Assn., Am. Arbitration Assn. General corporate, Private international, Securities. Home: 181 Caterina Hts Concord MA 01742-4773 Office: Testa Hurwitz & Thibeault High St Tower 125 High St 22d Fl Boston MA 02110-2704 E-mail: thibeault@tht.com

THIBODEAU, THOMAS RAYMOND, lawyer; b. St.Paul, Feb. 5, 1942; m. Mollie Nan Mylor, Sept. 24, 1966; 1 child, Matthew Raymond. BA in Polit. Sci. cum laude, U. St. Thomas, St. Paul, 1964; JD, U. Minn., 1967. Bar: Minn. 1967, U.S. Dist. Ct. Minn. 1967, U.S. Ct. Appeals (8th cir.) 1970, U.S. Supreme Ct. 1982, Wis. 1983, U.S. Dist. Ct. Wis. 1983, N.D. 2000, U.S. Dist. Ct. N.D., 2000; solicitor Supreme Ct. Eng. and Wales, 1996; cert. civil trial specialist Nat. Bd. Trial Advocacy. Ptnr. Johnson, Killen & Thibodeau, Duluth, Minn., 1967-2000, Thibodeau, Johnson & Feriancek PLLP, Duluth, 2000—. Pres. Legal Aid Service N.E. Minn., Inc., 1969-74; mem. civil justice reform act adv. com. U.S. Dist. Ct. Minn. Mem. revision Civil Jury Instruction Guide IV, 1997—. Chmn. Duluth City Charter Commn., 1976-78; vol. atty. St. Louis County Heritage and Arts Ctr., Duluth, 1980-87; pres. bd. trustees Marshall Sch., 1990-92. Recipient Disting. Alumni award U. St. Thomas, 1985. Fellow Internat. Soc. Barristers, Am. Coll. Trial Lawyers; mem. Am. Bd. Trial Advs. (advocate), Minn. Bar Assn. (chmn. specialization com. 1974-78, co-chmn. revision Civil Injury Instrn. Guide III com. 1982-85, 96-99), Minn. Def. Lawyers Assn. (pres. 1988-89), Acad. Cert. Trial Lawyers of Minn. (pres. elect 1993, pres. 1994-95), Internat. Assn. Def. Counsel, Assn. Def. Trial Attys. Avocations: hunting, skiing, scuba diving and other water sports, reading. Federal civil litigation, State civil litigation, Personal injury. Office: Thibodeau Johnson & Feriancek PLLP 800 Lonsdale 302 W Superior St Duluth MN 55802-1802

THIEL, CLARK T. lawyer, architect; b. San Diego, Aug. 30, 1963; s. John D. and Marilyn M. Thiel; m. Pamela J. Lee, May 28, 1995.; 1 child, Kaelli Nikelle. BS, U. Wis., 1984, MArch, 1988; JD, U. Calif., Davis, 1997. Bar: Calif. 1997, U.S. Dist. Ct. (no. and ctrl. dists.) Calif. 1997. Atty. Long & Levitt LLP, San Francisco; project arch., mgr. WAT&G, Honolulu; designer Thompson & Rose, Cambridge, Mass.; arch. HNTB, Inc., Boston. Editor-in-chief U. Calif. Law Review, 1996-97; contbr. articles to profl. jours. Nathan Burkan Meml. award ASCAP, 1996. Mem. ABA, AIA, Nat. Coun. Archtl. Registration Bds. Construction, Intellectual property. Office: Long & Levitt LLP 101 California St San Francisco CA 94111

THIELE, HERBERT WILLIAM ALBERT, lawyer; b. Gananoque, Ont., Can., Apr. 14, 1953; s. Herbert and Bertha (Shields) T.; m. Kathi M. Brown, May 29, 1982; children: Herbert R. R., Eric W. R., Brian A. J., Kelly M. M., Kevin M. H., Karl S. H. BA, U. Notre Dame, 1975; JD, U. Fla., 1978. Bar: Fla. 1978, U.S. Dist. Ct. (so. dist. trial and gen. bars) Fla. 1979, U.S. Ct. Appeals (5th and 11th cirs.) 1981, U.S. Supreme Ct. 1982, U.S. Tax Ct. 1983, U.S. Dist. Ct. (no. dist.) Fla. 1991. Assoc. Law Offices of Roger G. Saberson, Delray Beach, Fla., 1979-81; asst. city atty. City of Delray Beach, 1979-81, city atty., 1981-90; county atty. Leon County, Tallahassee, 1990—. Bd. dirs. Delray Beach Mcpl. Employees Credit Union, 1985-88. Recipient award of recognition Stetson U. Law Rev., 1989, Ralph A. Marsicano award for Local Govt. Law, Fla. Bar, 1991. Mem. ABA (vice-chmn. urban, state and local govt. com. of gen. practice sect. 1991-95, mem. labor and employment law, litigation, govt. lawyers, gen. practice and trial practice com. sects.), ATLA, FBA, Fla. Bar (exec. coun. sect. 1986-87, sec./treas. 1987-88, chmn.-elect 1988-89, chmn., 1989-90, immediate past chmn. 1990-91, ex-officio officer 1991—, trial, real property, gen. practice and labor and employment law sects., bar com. on individual rights and responsibilities 1986-90, long-range planning com. 1991-93, continuing legal edn. com. 1998-99, Paul S. Buchman award in local govt. law 2000), Tallahassee Bar Assn., Fla. Mcpl. Attys. Assn. (steering com. 1985-86, bd. dirs. 1980-89, sec./treas. 1989-90, Fla. Mcpl. Atty. of Yr. 1987), Fla. Assn. Police Attys., Nat. Inst. Mcpl. Law Officers (pers. and labor law com., trial practices and litigation com., legal advocacy com., 11th cir. rep. 1989-90), Am. Soc. for Pub. Adminstrn., Fla. Pub. Employer Labor Rels. Assn., Fla. Assn. County Attys. (chmn. coun. county attys. 1990-91, bd. dirs. 1991-93, treas. 1993, sec. 1993-94, v.p. 1994-95, pres. 1995-96, chmn. 1996-97, bd. dirs. 1997—, Recognition award 1994, Ethics in Govt. award 1998, 2001). Republican. Avocations: music, sports, philately. Home: 318 Milestone Dr Tallahassee FL 32312-3574 Office: Office of Leon County Atty Leon County Courthouse Tallahassee FL 32301

THIEROLF, RICHARD BURTON, JR. lawyer; b. Medford, Oreg., Oct. 27, 1948; s. Richard Burton Sr. and Helen Dorothy (Rivolta) T. BA, Columbia U., N.Y.C., 1970; JD, U. Oreg., 1976. Bar: Oreg. 1976, U.S. Dist. Ct. Oreg. 1976, U.S. Ct. Appeals (9th cir.) 1977, U.S. Dist. Ct. (no. dist.) Calif. 1980, U.S. Supreme Ct. 1993, U.S. Ct. Fed. Claims 1993. Staff atty. Orgn. of the Forgotten Am., Inc., Klamath Falls, Oreg., 1976-77, exec. dir., 1977-79; ptnr. Jacobson, Thierolf & Dickey, P.C., Medford, 1980—. Mem. City of Medford Planning Commn., 1990-92; mem. Jackson County Planning Commn., 2001—; mem. Medford Sch. Dist. 549-C Budget Com., 1991-92, chmn., 1991. Mem. ABA, Fed. Bar Assn., Oreg. State Bar (local profl. responsibility com. 1987-89, mem. fed. practice and procedure com. 1994-97, sec. 1995-97, jud. adminstrn. com. 1998-2001, low income legal svcs. com. 1990-93, ho. of dels. 1999-2000), Jackson County Bar Assn. (sec. 1988), So. Oreg. Estate Planning Coun. (bd. dirs.2001—). Episcopalian. Avocation: violin. Federal civil litigation, General practice, Native American. Home: 234 Ridge Rd Ashland OR 97520-2829 Office: Jacobson Thierolf & Dickey PC Two N Oakdale Ave Medford OR 97501 E-mail: dthierolf@jacobsonthierolfdickey.com

THIES, RICHARD LEON, lawyer, director; b. Nov. 7, 1931; s. Arnold C. Thies and Wilma J. (Pattison) Player; m. Marilyn Lucille Webber, June 15, 1954; children: David, Nancy, Susan, John, Anne. BA, U. Ill., 1953; JD, 1955. Bar: Ill. 1955, U.S. Dist. Ct. (ea. dist.) Ill. 1958, U.S. Supreme Ct. 1986. Instr. engring. law U. Ill., Urbaba, 1955-56; ptnr. Webber & Thies, P.C., 1958—. Past mem. Urbana Prk Dist. Bd.; bd. dirs., past mem. Nat. Acad. Arts, Champaign-Urbana Urban League; past bd. dirs., past pres. Salvation Army, Champaign County. Served as 1st lt. USAF, 1956-58. Fellow Am. Bar Found (chair 1993-94), Ill. State Bar Found.; mem. ABA (ho. of dels. 1984-2002, bd. gov. 1988-91, exec. com. 1990-91, Am. Bar Retirement Assn. Bd. 1992-2000), Am. Law Inst. Ill. Bar Assn. (various offices, pres. 1986-87), Champaign County Bar Assn. (v.p.), Urbana C. of C. (pres.), Urbana Country Club, Kiwanis (pres. Champaign-Urbana). Democrat. Presbyterian. General practice. Office: Webber & Thies PC 202 Lincoln Sq PO Box 189 Urbana IL 61803-0189 E-mail: rthies@webberthies.com

THIESSEN, BRIAN DAVID, lawyer; b. Grass Valley, Calif.; s. John J. and Ellen Emily Agnes (Larsen) T.; m. Carolyn Owen, June 16, 1962; children: Robert, Erica, Bill. AB, Duke U., 1960; postgrad. SUNY, Plattsburg, 1961-62; JD, Hastings Coll. Law, 1967. Bar: Calif. 1967, U.S. Dist. Ct. (no., so., ea. and we. dists.) Calif. 1967, U.S. Ct. Appeals (9th cir.) 1968, U.S. Supreme Ct., 1982. With Kaiser Industies, 1964-67; founder Mt. Diablo Courthouse Alternatives Program, 1990—; prof. John F. Kennedy U., Orinda, Calif., 1977-79; sec., dir. 1st Western Savs. and Loan Assn.; judge pro tem various mcpl. and superior cts., Contra Costa County, Calif., 1975—; ct.-appointed arbitrator Contra Costa Superior Ct., Martinez, Calif., 1980—. Mem. governing bd. East Bay Community Found., 1973-79; chmn. San Ramon Valley Planning Com., 1973; pres. Mt. Diablo council Boy Scouts Am., Walnut Creek, Calif., 1986-87; scoutmaster Boy Scouts Am., Alamo, 1986-89; mem. Diablo Valley Found. for Aging; mem. Alamo Park and Recreation Commn., 1984-88, chmn., 1986-87. Served to capt. USAF, 1960-63. Cert. family law specialist. Named San Ramon Valley Citizen of Yr. Valley Pioneer newspaper, 1973; recipient Silver Beaver award Boy Scouts Am., 1989. Mem. Am. Bar Assn., Internat. Bar Assn., Trial Lawyers Am., State Bar Assn. (hearing referee 1980—), Am. Arbitration Assn., Contra Costa County Bar Assn. (past pres.), Calif. Trial Lawyers, Hastings Coll. of Law Alumni Assn. (mem. bd. govs., v.p.), Rotary (bd. dirs. 1986—, pres. 1991—, named Alamo Citizen of Yr. 1987), Lions, Jaycees (past pres.). Republican. Congregationalist. General civil litigation, Family and matrimonial, Real property. Home: 100 Los Balcones Alamo CA 94507-2035 Office: 3201 Danville Blvd Ste 295 Alamo CA 94507-1978

THIGPEN, RICHARD ELTON, JR. lawyer; b. Washington, Dec. 29, 1930; s. Richard Elton and Dorothy (Dotger) T.; m. Nancy H. Shand, Dec. 15, 1951; children: Susan B., Richard M. AB, Duke U., 1951; LLB, U. N.C., 1956. Bar: N.C., 1956, U.S. Ct. Appeals (4th cir.) 1960, U.S. Ct. Appeals (5th cir.) 1960, U.S. Ct. Appeals (10th cir.) 1974, U.S. Tax Ct. 1958, U.S. Ct. Claims 1978. Lawyer FTC, Washington, 1956-58, Thigpen & Hines, Charlotte, N.C., 1958-84, Moore & Van Allen, Charlotte, 1984-88, Poyner & Spruill, Charlotte, 1988-93; gen. counsel Richardson Sports, 1994-98. Dir. Charlotte-Mecklenburg YMCA, 1964-88, Heineman Med. Rsch. Ctr., Charlotte, 1970—, Charlotte C. of C., 1982-85. Lt. USNR, 1951-53. Fellow Am. Bar Found., Am. Coll. Tax Counsel (regent 1989-95, vice chmn. 1992, chmn. 1993-94); mem. ABA, N.C. State Bar, N.C. Bar Assn. (pres. 1988-89, chmn. tax sect. 1976-80), Sports Lawyers Assn. (bd. dirs. 1995—). Avocation: golf, travel. Sports, Taxation, general, State and local taxation. Office: 1045 Providence Rd Ste 200 Charlotte NC 28207-2568

THISSELL, CHARLES WILLIAM, lawyer; b. Sioux Falls, S.D., Nov. 23, 1931; s. Oscar H. and Bernice Grace Janet (Olbertson) T.; m. Leila Amoret Rossner; Jan. 24, 1959; children— Amoret Gates, William Richards. B.A., Augustana Coll., Sioux Falls, 1953; J.D., U. Calif.-Berkeley, 1959. Bar: Calif. 1960, U.S. Dist. Ct. (no. and ea. dists.) Calif. 1960, Ct. Appeals (9th cir.) 1966, U.S. Claims Ct. 1974, U.S. Ct. Appeals (D.C., 5th cirs.) 1985, U.S. Supreme Ct. 1985. Cert.in trial advocacy Nat. Bd. Trial Advocacy. Trial counsel Calif. Dept. Transp. San Francisco, 1959-66; asst. gen. counsel law dept. Pacific Gas and Electric Co., San Francisco, 1966-91; ptnr. Morris, Taylor & Hill (formerly Morris, Taylor, Hays & Higaki), San Francisco, 1991-93; pvt. practice law, 1993—; instr. San Francisco Law Sch., 1962-63; arbitrator Superior Cts. San Francisco and Marin County, 1979—. Vice chmn. Marin County Rep. Cen. Com., 1983-84; pres. Marin County Rep. Coun., 1981-82; chancellor, vestry mem. St. Luke's Episcopal Ch., San Francisco, 1979-82. Lt. (j.g.) USNR, 1953-56; comdr., Ret. Mem. ABA, San Francisco Bar Assn. (chmn. trial lawyers sect. 1974). Clubs: Commonwealth of Calif. (chmn. environ. energy sect. 1981-83), Marines Meml. Federal civil litigation, State civil litigation, Condemnation. Home and Office: Charles William Thissell Atty at Law PO Box 9 Kiln MS 39556-0009

THOGERSEN, KAI, lawyer; b. Oslo, Norway; married. Candidate in Jurisprudence, U. Oslo, 1987. Bar: Norway. Legal adviser Oslo Tax Office, 1987-88; assoc. judge Skien (Norway) and Porsgrunn City Ct., 1988-89; assoc. Thommessen Krefting Greve Lund, Oslo, 1989-96, ptnr., 1996—. Mem. Norwegian Bar Assn. General corporate, Mergers and acquisitions, IT and Telecomms. Office: Thommessen Krefting Greve Lund AS PO Box 1484 N-0116 Oslo Norway E-mail: kai.thogersen@tkgl.no

THOMAS, ANN VAN WYNEN, law educator; b. The Netherlands, May 27, 1919; came to U.S., 1921, naturalized, 1926; d. Cornelius and Cora Jacoba (Daansen) Van Wynen; m. A.J. Thomas Jr., Sept. 10, 1948. AB with distinction, U. Rochester, 1940; JD, U. Tex., 1943; post doctoral degree, So. Meth. U., 1952. U.S. fgn. svc. officer, Johannesburg, South Africa, London, The Hague, The Netherlands, 1943-47; rsch. atty. Southwestern Legal Found., Sch. Law So. Meth. U., Dallas, 1952-67; asst. prof. polit. sci. So. Meth. U. Sch. Law, 1968-73, assoc. prof., 1973-76, prof., 1976-85, prof. emeritus, 1985—. Author: Communism versus International Law, 1953, (with A.J. Thomas Jr.) International Treaties, 1950, Non-Intervention—The Law and its Import in the Americas, 1956, OAS: The Organization of American States, 1962, International Legal Aspects of Civil War in Spain, 1936-1939, 1967, Legal Limitations on Chemical and Biological Weapons, 1970, The Concept of Aggression, 1972, Presidential War Making Power: Constitutional and International Law Aspects, 1981, An International Rule of Law—Problems and Prospects, 1974. Chmn. time capsule com. Grayson County Commn. on Tex. Sesquicentennial, 1986-88; co-chmn. Grayson County Commn. on Bicentennial U.S. Constn., 1988-93; co-chmn. com. Grayson County Sesquicentennial, 1994-97; co-chmn. Grayson County Commn. on the Millenium, 1997—. Recipient Am. medal Nat. DAR Soc., 1992. Mem. Tex. Bar Assn., Am. Soc. Internat. Law, Grayson County Bar Assn. Home: Spaniel Hall 374 Coffee Cir Pottsboro TX 75076-3164

THOMAS, ARCHIBALD JOHNS, III, lawyer; b. Jacksonville, Fla., Apr. 27, 1952; s. Archibald Johns and Jean (Snodgrass) T.; m. Martha Ann Marconi, Sept. 1, 1973. BA, U. So. Fla., 1973; JD, Stetson U., 1977. Bar: Fla. 1977, U.S. Dist. Ct. (mid. dist.) Fla. 1977, U.S. Ct. Appeals (11th cir.) 1981, U.S. Supreme Ct. 1981, U.S. Claims Ct. 1990; cert. labor and employment law, Fla. Law clk. to U.S. magistrate U.S. Dist. Ct., Tampa, Fla., 1977-78; 1st asst. fed. pub. defender U.S. dist. Ct., Jacksonville, 1978-84; sr. ptnr. Thomas & Skinner, P.A., 1984-89; pvt. practice, 1990—. Mem. ATLA (employment rights sect.), Fla. Bar Assn. (pres. 1982-83), NACDL, Nat. Employment Lawyers Assn. (co-chmn. Fla. chpt. 1992), Fla. Nat. Employment Lawyers Assn. (v.p. 1999—, pres.-elect, 2001), Jacksonville Bar Assn. Democrat. Avocation: sailing. Labor. Home: 708 Mccollum Cir Neptune Beach FL 32266-3789 Office: Riverplace Tower Ste 1640 Jacksonville FL 32207 E-mail: archibald@job-rights.com

THOMAS, CLARENCE, United States supreme court justice; b. Savannah, Ga., June 23, 1948; BA, Holy Cross Coll., 1971; JD, Yale U., 1974. Bar: Mo. Asst. atty. gen. State of Mo., Jefferson City, 1974-77; atty. Monsanto Co., St. Louis, 1977-79; legis. asst. to Sen. John C. Danforth, Washington, 1979-81; asst. sec. for civil rights Dept. Edn., 1981-82; chmn. U.S. EEOC, 1982-90; judge U.S. Ct. Appeals, 1990-91; assoc. justice U.S. Supreme Ct., 1991—. Office: US Supreme Court Supreme Ct Bldg 1 First St NE Washington DC 20543-0001*

THOMAS, DUKE WINSTON, lawyer; b. Scuddy, Ky., Jan. 25, 1937; s. William E. and Grace T.; m. Jill Staples, Oct. 24, 1964; children: Deborah L., William E. II, Judith A. BSBA, Ohio State U., 1959, JD, 1964. Bar: Ohio 1964, U.S. Dist. Ct. Ohio 1966, U.S. Ct. Appeals (3d cir.) 1971, U.S. Ct. Appeals (6th cir.) 1972, U.S. Supreme Ct. 1973, U.S. Ct. Appeals (7th cir.) 1979. Ptnr. Vorys, Sater, Seymour and Pease, LLP, Columbus, Ohio, 1964—. Bd. dirs. Ohio Bar Liability Ins. Co., Frontstep, Inc. Fellow Internat. Soc. Barristers, Am. Coll. Trial Lawyers (chmn. Ohio joint select com. on jud. compensation 1987), Am. Bar Found. (life), Ohio Bar Found., Columbus Bar Found.; mem. ABA (ho. of dels. 1985—, state del. 1989-95, bd. govs. 1995-98), Ohio Bar Assn. (pres. 1985), Columbus Bar Assn. (pres. 1978), Pres.'s Club Ohio State U., The Golf Club, Worthington Hills Country Club, Columbus Athletic Club. Federal civil litigation, General civil litigation, State civil litigation. Home: 2090 Sheringham Rd Columbus OH 43220-4358 Office: Vorys Sater Seymour & Pease LLP PO Box 1008 52 E Gay St Columbus OH 43215-3161 E-mail: dwthomas@vssp.com

THOMAS, ELLA COOPER, lawyer; b. Ft. Totten, N.Y. d. Avery John and Ona Caroline (Gibson) C.; m. Robert Edward Lee Thomas, Nov. 22, 1938 (dec. Jan. 1985); 1 child, Robert Edward Lee Jr. Student, Vassar Coll., 1932-34, U. Hawaii, 1934-35, George Washington U., 1935-36, JD, 1940. Bar: U.S. Dist. Ct. D.C. 1942, U.S. Ct. Appeals (D.C. cir.) 1943, U.S. Supreme Ct. 1947, U.S. Tax Ct. 1973. Secret maps custodian U.S. Dist. Engrs., Honolulu, 1941-42; contbg. editor Labor Rels. Reporter, Washington, 1942; assoc. Smith, Ristig & Smith, 1942-45; law libr. George Washington Law Sch., 1946-53; reporter of decisions U.S. Tax Ct., 1953-75. Author: Law of Libel and Slander, 1949. Mem. Inter-Am. Bar Assn. (coun. mem. 1973-99), D.C. Bar Assn. Avocations: physical fitness, crostics, Mote Marine Lab. vol. computer. Home: 1700 3rd Ave W Apt 118 Bradenton FL 34205

THOMAS, EUGENE C. lawyer; b. Idaho Falls, Idaho, Feb. 8, 1931; s. C.E. Thomas; m. Jody Raber; children: Michael E., Stephen R. A.B., Columbia U., 1952, J.D., 1954, LLD (hon.) Univ. Idaho, 1986, LLD (hon.), Coll. of Idaho, 1987. Bar: Idaho, 1954, U.S. Dist. Ct. Idaho 1957, US Ct. Appeals (9th cir.) 1958, U.S. Supreme Ct. 1970. Pros. atty. Ada County, Boise, Idaho, 1955-57; founding ptnr. Moffatt, Thomas, Barrett, Rock & Fields, Boise, 19578—; bd. dirs. Shore Lodge, Inc., McCall, Idaho, Nelson-Ball Paper Products, Inc., Longview, Wash., Peregrine Industries, Inc., Boise. Bd. editors ABA Jour., 1980-87. Bd. dirs. St. Luke's Regional Med. Ctr. and Mountain States Tumor Inst., Boise, 1963— , pres., chmn. bd. 1972-79; trustee Coll. of Idaho, 1980—, mem. exec. com., 1982—; trustee Associated Taxpayers of Idaho, 1983—, chmn., 1988-90. trustee Boise Futures Found., 1973—, bd. dirs., 1981—, bd. dirs. Univ./Community Health Scis. Assn., 1981—; chmn. Mayor's Select Com. on Downtown Devel., 1982-83. Named Exec. of Yr., Boise chpt. Nat. Secs. Assn., 1978, John Price lectr. 1987 ann. conf. Nat. Coll. Dist. Attys.; recipient disting. svc. award Idaho Pros. Attys., 1985, disting. svc. award Chgo. Vol. Legal Svc. Found., 1986. Fellow Internat. Acad. Trial Lawyers, Am. Bar Found. (trustee 1980-82, 86-87), Am. Law Inst.; mem. ABA (ho. of dels. 1971— , chmn. ho. of dels. 1980-82, bd. govs. 1980-82, pres. 1986-87, chmn. spl. com. on internat. affairs 1987-88), Idaho State Bar (pres. 1971-72, disting. lawyer award 1980, 86), Def. Research Inst. (state chmn. Pacific region 1978—), Idaho Assn. Def. Counsel (trustee 1966-69, pres. 1967-68), Internat. Assn. Ins. Counsel, Am. Bd. Trial Advocates, Fourth Dist. Bar Assn. (pres. 1962-63), Internat. Bar Assn. (chmn. biennial conf., governing coun. 1985-86), Conference of Pres. Union Internat. des Avocats (pres.), Nat. Conf. Bar Pres. (trustee 1974-76), Law Soc. Eng. and Wales (hon.), La Barra Mexicana (hon.), New Zealand Law Soc. (hon.), Can. Bar Assn. (hon.), Integrated Bar of the Philippines (hon.), Rocky Mountain Oil and Gas Assn. (chmn. Idaho legal com. 1978—). Clubs: Arid (dir. 1977-79), Hillcrest Country (bd. dirs. 1969-72) (Boise). General civil litigation, General corporate, Legislative. Office: Moffatt Thomas Barrett Rock & Fields PO Box 829 Boise ID 83701-0829

THOMAS, FREDERICK BRADLEY, lawyer; b. Evanston, Ill., Aug. 13, 1949; s. Frederick Bradley and Katherine Kidder (Bingham) T.; m. Elizabeth Maxwell, Oct. 25, 1975; children: Bradley Bingham, Stephens Maxwell, Rosa Macaulay. AB, Dartmouth Coll., 1971; JD, U. Chgo., 1974. Bar: Ill. 1974. Law clk. to hon. judge John C. Godbold U.S. Ct. Appeals (5th cir.), Montgomery, Ala., 1974-75; assoc. Mayer, Brown & Platt, Chgo., 1975-80, ptnr., 1981—. Bd. dirs. St. Gregory Episcopal Sch., 1989—; bd. trustees La Rabida Children's Hosp., 1990—. Mem. ABA, Chgo. Council Lawyers. Republican. Episcopalian. Computer, General corporate, Mergers and acquisitions. Office: Mayer Brown & Platt 190 S La Salle St Ste 3100 Chicago IL 60603-3441 E-mail: fthomas@mayerbrown.com

THOMAS, GLORIA, lawyer, nurse, state program administrator; AAN, Phoenix Coll., 1966; BSN, Marquette U., 1977; JD, U. Wis., 1984. Bar: Wis.; RN. Staff nurse, charge nurse Doctors Hosp., Phoenix, 1966-72; head nurse Mt. Sinai Hosp., Milw., 1972-75; nursing supr. St. Anthony's Hosp., 1975-77; staff nurse Meriter Hosp., Madison, Wis.; acting nurse cons. Wis. DRL, 1986-87; asst. chief nursing Wis. Dept. Corrections, 1990-93, legal-adminstrv. rules coord., 1993-96, dir. office program audit and evaluation, 1996-2000; asst. legal counsel, 2000—. Cons. health care auditor Am. Correctional Assn. Trustee, Sunday sch. tchr. Mt. Zion Bapt. Ch., Madison. Mem. ABA, Wis. Bar Assn., Am. Correctional Assn., Sigma Theta Tau. Office: PO Box 7925 3099 E Washington Ave Madison WI 53707-7925 E-mail: gloria.thomas@doc.state.wi.us

THOMAS, GREGG DARROW, lawyer; b. Jacksonville, Fla., July 31, 1951; BA magna cum laude, Vanderbilt U., 1972; JD with honors, U. Fla., 1976. Bar: Fla. 1976, D.C. 1978. Law clk. U.S. Dist. Ct. (mid. dist.) Fla., 1976-79; mem. Holland & Knight, Tampa, Fla., 1979-; ptnr., 1983-. Exec. editor U. Fla. Law Rev., 1975-76. Bd. dirs. Vol. Lawyer's Resource Ctr., 1990-95; trustee Tampa Mus. of Art, 1993—, vice chmn., 1998, chair, 1999-2001. Mem. ABA (mem. forum com. comm. law 1983—), Am. Judicature Soc., Fla. Bar (co-chair Fla. bar media and comm. com. 1987-88, mem. grievance com. 1988, chmn. 1989-91), Fla. Bar Found. (mem. legal assistance to poor com. 1988-91), Hillsborough Bar Assn., D.C. Bar, Phi Beta Kappa. Constitutional, Intellectual property, Libel. Office: Holland & Knight PO Box 1288 400 N Ashley Dr Ste 2300 Tampa FL 33602-4322 E-mail: gthomas@khlaw.com

THOMAS, JAMES JOSEPH, II, lawyer; b. Allentown, Pa., May 17, 1951; s. James Joseph and Charlene Marie (Beiter) T. B.A., Coll. William and Mary, 1973, J.D., 1976. Bar: Ga. 1976, U.S. Dist. Ct. (no. dist.) Ga. 1976, U.S. Ct. Appeals (5th, 10th, 11th cirs.) 1976. Assoc. Long & Aldridge, Atlanta, 1976-81, ptnr., 1982— , mng. ptnr., 1984. Editor-in-chief William and Mary Law Rev., 1975-76. Mem. Ga. State Bar Com. on Proflessionalism in Law Schs., 1988. Recipient Weber Diploma for top law student, William and Mary Law Sch., 1976. Mem. Atlanta Council Younger Lawyers (chmn. juvenile ct. com. 1983-84), ABA, Assn. Trial Lawyers Am., Ga. Trial Lawyers Assn., Atlanta Bar Assn. Clubs: Lawyers, Atlanta City (Atlanta). Federal civil litigation, State civil litigation. Office: Long Aldridge & Norman 1 Peachtree Ctr Ste 5300 303 W Peachtree St NW Atlanta GA 30308-3503

THOMAS, JEREMIAH LINDSAY, III, lawyer; b. Wilmington, Del., June 20, 1946; s. Jeremiah Lindsay Jr. and Dorothy Eleanor (Conway) T.; m. Clara Ewing Ruthrauff, Oct. 17, 1981; children: Catherine Ewing, Lindsay Barlow. BA, U. Va., 1968, JD, 1972. Bar: N.Y. 1973. Assoc. Simpson Thacher & Bartlett, N.Y.C., 1972-79, ptnr., 1979—. Mem.: ABA, N.Y. State Bar Assn., Assn. Bar of City of N.Y., Met. Golf Assn. (legal counsel 1984—, exec. com. 1992—98, dir. Found. 1992—98). General corporate, Securities. Office: Simpson Thacher & Bartlett 425 Lexington Ave Fl 15 New York NY 10017-3954 E-mail: jthomas@stblaw.com

THOMAS, JOSEPH WINAND, lawyer; b. New Orleans, Aug. 2, 1940; s. Gerald Henry and Edith Louise (Winand) T.; m. Claudette Condoll, Aug. 2, 1960 (div. Nov. 1985); children: Jeffery J., Anthony W.; m. Shawn B. Watkins, May 26, 1986 (div. June 1989); children: Adelle, Anne; m. Sandra J. Green, May 17, 1992; children: Winand, Elizabeth, Alice, Shepard, Julia.

BS, Loyola U., Chgo., 1967; JD, Loyola U., New Orleans, 1973; MBA, Tulane U., 1984. Bar: La. 1973, U.S. Dist. Ct. (ea. dist.) La. 1973, U.S. Ct. Appeals (5th cir.) 1973, U.S. Supreme Ct. 1976, D.C. 1980. Staff atty. New Orleans Legal Assistance Corp., 1973-74; asst. atty. gen. State of La., 1974-80; pvt. practice New Orleans, 1980—. Pres., bd. dirs. New Orleans Legal Assistance Corp. Active NAACP, New Orleans, 1987-89; bd. dirs. Urban League, New Orleans. Mem. ABA, Louis Martinet Legal Soc., New Orleans Bar Assn., La. Bar Assn. Democrat. Roman Catholic. General civil litigation, State civil litigation, Personal injury. Office: 2 Canal St New Orleans LA 70130-1408 E-mail: jthomas@jwtlaw.com

THOMAS, LOWELL SHUMWAY, JR. lawyer; b. Phila., Aug. 9, 1931; s. Lowell Shumway and Josephine (McVey) T.; m. Judith Evans, Aug. 27, 1955; children: Megan E., Heather McVey, Lowell S., Taylor G. BA, Dartmouth Coll., 1953; JD, U. Pa., 1960. Bar: Pa. 1961, U.S. Tax Ct. 1961, U.S. Dist. Ct. (ea. dist.) Pa. 1961, U.S. Ct. Appeals (3d cir.) 1961. Assoc. Duane, Morris & Heckscher, Phila., 1960-64, Saul, Ewing, Remick & Saul, Phila., 1965-68, ptnr., 1968-96, of counsel, 1997—. Bd. dirs. Boardwalk Securities Corp., Peter Lumber Co., Chestnut Hill Acad., Phila., 1978-86; bd. dirs. Southeastern Pa. ARC, 1975-82, chmn., 1983-86, bd. govs., 1989-95; trustee Beaver Coll. 1987-2000, emeritus trustee, 2001—, chmn., 1989-903. Author: Taxation of Marriage, Separation and Divorce, 1986. Trustee Barra Found., 1999—. Lt. USN, 1953-57. Fellow Am. Coll. Tax Counsel; mem. ABA, Pa. Bar Assn., Phila. Bar Assn., Phila. Bar Found. (trustee 1980-83), Am. Law Inst., Suunybrook Golf Club. Republican. Episcopalian. Pension, profit-sharing, and employee benefits, Corporate taxation, Personal income taxation. Office: Saul Ewing Remick & Saul 3800 Centre Sq W Philadelphia PA 19102 E-mail: LST8012@acadia.net

THOMAS, RITCHIE TUCKER, lawyer; b. Cleve., Aug. 12, 1936; '; s. Myron F. and Marjorie (Ritchie) T.; m. Elizabeth Blackwell Hanes Main, Jan. 1, 1994. BA, Cornell U., 1959; JD, Case-Western Res. U., 1964. Bar: Ohio 1964, U.S. Dist. Ct. (no. dist.) Ohio 1964, U.S. Ct. Appeals (D.C. cir.) 1971, U.S. Ct. Appeals (fed. cir.) 1973, U.S. Ct. Fed. Claims 1973, U.S. Ct. Internat. Trade 1976, U.S. Ct. Appeals (9th cir.) 1985. Assoc. office of gen. counsel U.S. Tariff Commn., Washington, 1964-67; assoc. Squire, Sanders & Dempsey, Cleve., 1967-69, Cox, Langford & Brown, Washington, 1969-74; ptnr. Squire, Sanders & Dempsey, 1974—. Mem. exec. com. Meridian House Internat., Washington, 1977-94; Washington rep. Am. C. of C. in Germany, 1984—; v.p. bd. dirs. Belgian Am. Assn., 1989—. Assoc. editor Western Res. U. Law Rev., 1964; columnist Commerce Germany; contbr. articles to profl. jours. Mem. Waring Prize Com., Western Res. Acad., 1996—. Recipient various book award West Pub. Co., 1964. Mem. Fed. Bar Assn., D.C. Bar Assn., Order of Coif. Administrative and regulatory, General corporate, Private international. Home: 6700 Bradley Blvd Bethesda MD 20817-3045 Office: Squire Sanders & Dempsey 1201 Pennsylvania Ave NW PO Box 407 Washington DC 20044-0407 E-mail: rtthomas@ssd.com

THOMAS, ROBERT PAIGE, lawyer; b. Columbus, Ohio, July 31, 1941; s. Charles Marion and Elsie (Cavanaugh) T.; children: Paige Cason, Park Cavanaugh. B.A., Vanderbilt U., 1963, M.A., 1965, J.D., 1970. Bar: Tenn. 1970, U.S. Dist. Ct. (mid. dist.) Tenn. 1970, U.S. Ct. Appeals (6th cir.) 1977. Assoc. Boult, Cummings, Conners & Berry, Nashville, 1970-74, ptnr., 1974—, mng. ptnr., 1977-84. chmn. Tenn. Dem. Party; Mem. Bill Clinton's Nat. Fin. Com.; fin. chmn. Sen. Jim Sasser. Mem. ABA, Tenn. Bar Assn., Nashville Bar Assn. Democrat. Episcopalian. Clubs: Yale of N.Y.C.; Belle Meade Country, Cumberland, Nashville City. Labor, Real property, Government relations. Office: PO Box 198062 Nashville TN 37219-8062

THOMAS, ROBERT R. judge; b. Rochester, N.Y., Aug. 7, 1952; m. Maggie Thomas; 3 children. BA in govt., U. Notre Dame, 1974; JD, Loyola U., 1981. Cir. ct. judge DuPage County, 1988, acting chief judge, 1989—94; judge Appellate Ct. Second Dist., 1994—2000; Supreme Ct. justice Ill. State Supreme Ct., 2000—. Mem.: DuPage County Bar Assn., Acad. All-Am. Hall of Fame (life) NCAA Silver Ann. Award 1999). Office: Bldg A Rm 207A 1776 S Naperville Rd Wheaton IL 60187*

THOMAS, ROBERT WESTON, lawyer; b. May 11, 1950; s. Fillmore and Brunhilde (Schmidt) Thomas; m. Mary Ellen Meyers, Aug. 23, 1975; children: M. Ryan, Colleen A., Emily M. BA, Albion Coll., 1971; JD, Wayne State U., 1975. Bar: Mich. 1975, U.S. Dist. Ct. (ea. and we. dists.) Mich. 1976. V.p., sec. Fillmore Thomas & Co., Inc., Lapeer, 1971—87; law clk. Mich. Ct. Appeals, Lansing, 1975—76; sole practice Lapeer, 1976—83; mem. Thomas & Hable, 1983—86; bd. dir., treas. Fillmore Thomas & Co., Inc., 1983—93; sole practice, 1986—99; v.p., gen. mgr., sec. Fillmore Thomas & Co., Inc., 1988—99, pres., sec., 1999—. Mem. Citizens Adv. Coun., Oakdale Ctr., 1978—79. Mem.: ABA, State Bar Mich., Lapeer County Bar Assn. (sec. 1978—86, pres. 1986—87, treas. 1987—90), Lapeer Rotary (treas. 1984—97, pres. 1998—99, rotary internat. dist. 6330 dist. gov.-elect 2001—), Lapeer County Players (treas. 1983—86). Episcopalian. Consumer commercial. Home: 310 Hickory Ln Lapeer MI 48446-1341 Office: 350 County Center St Lapeer MI 48446-2500

THOMAS, SIDNEY R. federal judge; b. Bozeman, Mont., Aug. 14, 1953; m. Martha Sheehy. BA in Speech-Comm., Mont. State U., 1975, JD cum laude, 1978; D (hon.), Rocky Mountain Coll., 1998. Bar: Mont. 1978, U.S. Dist. Ct. Mont. 1978, U.S. Ct. Appeals (9th cir.) 1980, U.S. Dist. Ct. (9th cir.) 1980, U.S. Ct. Fed. Claims 1986, U.S. Supreme Ct. 1994. Shareholder Moulton, Bellimgham, Longo and Mather, P.C., Billings, 1978-96; judge U.S. Ct. Appeals 9th Cir., 1996—. Adj. instr. Rocky Mountain Coll., Billings, 1982-95. Contbr. articles to profl. jours. Recipient Gov.'s award for pub. svc., 1978, Outstanding Faculty award Rocky Mountain Coll., 1988. Mem. ABA, State Bar Mont., Yellowstone County Bar Assn. Office: US Ct Appeals Ninth Circuit PO Box 31478 Billings MT 59107-1478*

THOMAS, STEPHEN PAUL, lawyer; b. Bloomington, Ill., July 30, 1938; s. Owen Wilson and Mary Katherine (Paulsen) T.; m. Marieanne Sauer, Dec. 7, 1963 (dec. June 1984); 1 child, Catherine Marie; m. Marcia Aldrich Toomey, May 28, 1988; 1 child, Ellen Antonia. BA, U. Ill., 1959; LLB, Harvard U., 1962. Bar: Ill. 1962. Vol. Peace Corps, Malawi, Africa, 1963-65; assoc. Sidley & Austin, Chgo., 1965-70, ptnr., 1970-2000. Lectr. on law Malawi Inst. Pub. Adminstrn., 1963-65. Pres. Hyde Park-Kenwood Cmty. Conf., Chgo., 1988-90; trustee Chgo. Acad. for Arts, 1991—, chmn., 1992-97; bd. dirs. Union League Civic and Arts Found., Chgo., 1999—. Recipient Paul Cornell award Hyde Park Hist. Soc., 1981. Mem. ABA, Chgo. Bar Assn., Chgo. Fedn. of Musicians, Lawyers Club of Chgo., Union League Club Chgo., Chgo. Literary Club. Democrat. Roman Catholic. Avocation: jazz piano playing. General corporate, Private international, Securities. Home: 5740 S Harper Ave Chicago IL 60637-1841 Office: care Sidley & Austin 55 W Monroe St Chicago IL 60603-5001 E-mail: sthomas@sidley.com

THOMAS, STEVEN ALLEN, lawyer; b. Birmingham, Ala., Mar. 19, 1951; s. Reginald Allen and Billie Ruth (Brewer) T.; m. Rebecca Phillips, Aug. 1972; children: Jennifer Ruth, Matthew Allen. AS, Walker Coll., Jasper, Ala., 1971; BA, U. Ala., Tuscaloosa, 1973; JD, Samford U., Birmingham, Ala., 1976. Bar: Ala. 1977, U.S. Dist. Ct. (no. dist.) Ala. 1986. Law clk. Circuit Ct. Walker Co., Jasper, 1978-83; lawyer Beaird, Thomas, Higgins, 1983-91; ptv. practice, 1991—. Judge Mcpl. Ct., Carbon Hill, Ala., 1983—, Nauvoo, Ala., 1985-88, Arley, Ala., 1991—, Oakman, Ala., 1997—. Legal counsel Ala. Jaycees, Clanton, 1986-88; pres. Ala. Mining Mus., Dora, 1989—; treas. Jasper Band Boosters, 1993-95; advisor Explorers, 1991-98; bd. dirs. Assn. Ala. Fairs, Inc., 1998—, 1st v.p. 2000, pres. 2001. Named Jaycee of Yr., Jasper Jaycees, 1983, 84, Officer of Yr., 1984, 88. Mem. ABA, Ala. Bar Assn., Walker County Bar Assn. (pres. 1990-91), East Walker C. of C. (pres. 1992-94), Phi Alpha Delta. Methodist. Avocations: fishing, reading, swimming, boating, spectator sports. Family and matrimonial, Personal injury, Probate. Home: 1401 9th Ave W Jasper AL 35501-4538 Office: PO Box 1951 Jasper AL 35502-1951 E-mail: sterenjd76@aol.com

THOMAS, THORP, lawyer; b. Alexander, Ark., Sept. 15, 1923; s. Howard Norman and Letitia Helen (Miller) T.; m. Kermit Maurice Toombs (dec. Feb. 1998); children: Victoria, Helen, Deborah, Thorp Jr., Terry; m. Marie Elaine Underwood, July 22, 1999. Student, Little Rock Jr. Coll., 1945; JD, U. Ark., 1950. Bar: Ark., U.S. Ct. Appeals (8th cir.) Ark., U.S. Supreme Ct. Claims examiner Fidelity & Casualty Co. N.Y., Little Rock, 1950-53; asst. atty. gen. Atty. Gen.'s Office, 1953-63; pvt. practice law, 1963—. Chmn. planning commn., Alexander, Ark., 1980—. Mem. ABA, Ark. Bar Assn., Masons. Democrat. Methodist. Avocations: music, art, aviation. Home: 8310 Louwanda Dr Little Rock AR 72205-1666 E-mail: tmthomas@arkansas.net

THOMAS, WAYNE LEE, lawyer; b. Sept. 22, 1945; s. Willard McSwain and June Frances (Jones) T.; m. Patricia H. Thomas, Mar. 16, 1968; children: Brigitte Elisabeth Williams, Kate Adelaide. BA, U. Fla., 1967, JD cum laude, 1971. Bar: Fla. 1971, U.S. Supreme Ct. 1975, U.S. Ct. Appeals (5th cir.) 1975, U.S. Ct. Appeals (11th cir.) 1981, U.S. Ct. Claims 1976, U.S. Dist. Ct. (mid. dist.) Fla. 1973, U.S. Dist. Ct. (so. dist. trial bar) Fla. 1975; cert. mediator and arbitrator. Law clk. U.S. Dist. Ct. (mid. dist.) Fla., 1971-73; assoc. Trenam, Simmons, Kemker, Scharf, Barkin, Frye & O'Neill, PA, Tampa, 1973-77, ptnr., 1978-81; founder, pres. McKay & Thomas, PA, 1981-89; ptnr. Carlton, Fields, Ward, Emmanuel, Smith & Cutler, PA, 1989-95; pvt. practice Tampa, 1995—. Mem. ABA, Fla. Bar (chmn. sect. gen. practice 1981-83, mem. ethics com., vice chmn. unauthorized practice law com. 1994-98, vice chmn. fed. practice com. 1995-96, chmn. 1996-97, mem. bd. bar examiners 1986-91, chmn. 1990-91, chmn. unauthorized practice law com. 13A 1998-2001), Nat. Conf. Bar Examiners (multistate profl. responsibility exam. policy com. 1994—), Hillsborough County Bar Assn. (chmn. grievance com. 1985-86), Order of Coif, Fla. Blue Key, Phi Kappa Phi, Omicron Delta Kappa. Democrat. Alternative dispute resolution, Federal civil litigation, State civil litigation. Office: 707 N Franklin St Fl 10 Tampa FL 33602-4430 E-mail: wayne.lee@verizon.net

THOMAS, WILLIAM GRIFFITH, lawyer; b. Washington, Nov. 1, 1939; s. Henry Phineas and Margaret Wilson (Carr) T.; m. Suzanne Campbell Foster, June 7, 1960. Student, Williams Coll., 1957-59, Richmond Coll., 1960; JD, U. Richmond, 1963. Bar: Va. 1963. Ptnr. Reed Smith LLP, Falls Church, Va., 1999—. Pres. Va. Electric and Power Co., Richmond. Sec. Va. Dem. Com., 1968-70, chmn., 1970-72. Mem. ABA, Va. State Bar Assn., Alexandria Bar Assn., Am. Law Inst., Am. Coll. Real Estate Lawyers. Contracts commercial, Legislative, Real property. Home: 4783 Herring Creek Rd Aylett VA 23009 Office: Reed Smith LLP 3110 Fairview Park Dr Ste 1400 Falls Church VA 22042-4503 E-mail: wthomas@reedsmith.com

THOMAS, WILLIAM HERMAN, JR. lawyer; b. Waynesville, Mo., Apr. 2, 1947; s. William Herman and Norma Lee (Lacey) T.; m. Barbara Lee Killian, Aug. 22, 1970; children— Margaret, Julia, Caroline. B.S. in Mgmt., MIT, 1969; J.D., U. Mo.-Columbia, 1972. Bar: Mo. 1973, U.S. Dist. Ct. (ea. and we. dists.) Mo. 1974. Ptnr. firm Moore & Thomas, Rolla, Mo., 1974, firm Routh, Thomas & Birdsong, Rolla, 1975-83; pres. firm Thomas, Birdsong, Clayton & Haslag, P.C., Rolla, 1983— . Contbr. to Mo. Law Rev., 1972. Pres., bd. dirs. Rolla Cerebral Palsy Sch., 1980-81; bd. dirs. Rolla Area Sheltered Workshop, 1979-80, Rolla Sch. Dist., 1980-84. Recipient Disting. Service award Rolla Jaycees, 1979. Mem. ABA, South Central Bar Assn. (pres. 1974-75), Phelps County Bar Assn. (pres. 1975-76), Mo. Bar Assn. Democrat. Lodge: Kiwanis. State civil litigation, General corporate, Probate. Home: 1015 Ironhorse Rd Rolla MO 65401-4740 Office: Thomas Birdsong Clayton & Haslag PO Box 248 Rolla MO 65402-0248 also: 200 N Lynn St Waynesville MO 65583-2540

THOMAS, WILLIAM SCOTT, lawyer; b. Joliet, Ill., Aug. 16, 1949; AB, Stanford U., 1971; JD, U. Calif., Hastings, 1974; LLM in Taxation, Golden Gate U., 1981. Bar: Calif. 1975, U.S. Dist. Ct. (no. dist.) Calif. 1975, U.S. Tax Ct. 1982. Tax editor Internat. Bur. Fiscal Documentation, Amsterdam, Holland, 1974-75; tax atty. Chevron Corp., San Francisco, 1975-77; from assoc. to ptnr. Brobeck, Phleger & Harrison, 1978—. Bd. dirs. Value Line Inc., N.Y.C. Mem. ABA (taxation sect.), Calif. Bar Assn. (exec. com. taxation sect. 1984-89, chmn. 1987-88). E-mail. Probate, Personal income taxation, State and local taxation. Office: Brobeck Phleger & Harrison 1 Market Plz Ste 341 San Francisco CA 94105-1420 E-mail: wthomas@brobeck.com

THOMASCH, ROGER PAUL, lawyer; b. N.Y.C., Nov. 7, 1942; s. Gordon J. and Margaret (Molloy) T.; children: Laura Leigh, Paul Butler. BA, Coll. William and Mary, 1964; LLB, Duke U., 1967. Bar: Conn. 1967, Colo. 1974. Assoc. atty. Cummings & Lockwood, Stamford, Conn., 1967-70; trial atty. U.S. Dept. Justice, Washington, 1970-73; ptnr. Roath & Brega, Denver, 1975-87; mng. ptnr. Denver office of Ballard, Spahr, Andrews & Ingersoll LLP, 1987—. Vis. assoc. prof. of law Drake U. Sch. Law, Des Moines, 1973-74; frequent lectr. in field, U.S. and Can.; adj. faculty mem. U. Denver Coll. Law, 1976-80. Recipient Leland Forrest Outstanding Prof. award, Drake U. Sch. Law, 1973. Fellow Am. Coll. of Trial Lawyers, Colo. Bar Found.; mem. ABA, Colo. Bar Assn., Denver Country Club, Univ. Club. Antitrust, Federal civil litigation, State civil litigation. Office: Ballard Spahr Andrews & Ingersoll LLP 1225 17th St Ste 2300 Denver CO 80202-5535 E-mail: Thomasch@BallardSpahr.com

THOME, DENNIS WESLEY, lawyer; b. Yakima, Wash., Feb. 1, 1939; s. Walter John and Vareta Lucille (Voris) T.; m. Penelope Lee Freeman, Aug. 27, 1961; children: Christopher, Geoffrey. BSBA, U. Denver, 1961, JD, 1967. Bar: Colo. 1967, U.S. Dist. Ct. Colo. 1967, Calif. 1971, U.S. Dist. Ct. (cen. dist.) Calif. 1971, U.S. Supreme Ct. 1971, U.S. Ct. Appeals (9th cir.) 1972. Assoc. Pehr & Newman, Westminster, Colo., 1967-69, Juggert, VaVerka & Wayman, Costa Mesa, Calif., 1975-77; house counsel Wycliffe Bible Translators, Inc., Huntington Beach, 1969-73; pvt. practice Newport Beach, 1973-75, Denver, 1977—. Bd. dirs. First Fruit, Inc., Newport Beach, MOPS Internat., Inc., Denver, Reach Internat., Inc., Denver; mem. Centennial Estate Planning Coun., 1977—. Treas. Gibson for Mayor Com., Denver, 1967; bd. dirs. Christian Eye Ministry, Inc., San Diego, 1983-91, World Eye Care, Inc., 1990-91, Christian Legal Soc. Metro Denver, Inc., 1994-98; chmn. Arvada (Colo.) Covenant Ch., 1993-94; bd. dirs., sec. Wycliffe Bible Translators, Inc., Huntington Beach, Calif., 1977-83. Mem. Colo. Bar Assn. (Bill of Rights com. 1977-90, 92—), State Bar Calif., Omicron Delta Kappa. Avocations: city league volleyball. Estate planning, Non-profit and tax-exempt organizations, Probate. Office: 7515 W 17th Ave Ste C Lakewood CO 80215-3302

THOMPSON, ALVIN W. judge; b. 1953; BA, Princeton U., 1975; JD, Yale U., 1978. With Robinson & Cole, Hartford, Conn., 1978-94; dist. judge U.S. Dist. Ct., 1994—. Mem. ABA, Conn. Bar Assn., Hartford County Bar Assn. Office: US Dist Ct 450 Main St Rm 240 Hartford CT 06103-3022

THOMPSON, ANNE, court administrator; b. Tulsa, Mar. 27, 1942; d. L.R. and Mary Ann Scott (Kilgore) Funston; children: Andrea, Jeffrey. BA, Okla. Bapt. U., 1964; MA, U. Ctrl. Okla., 1986. Adminstr. Dept. Corrections, Oklahoma City, 1979-86; ct. adminstr. City of Tulsa, 1986—. Mem. Leadership Tulsa, 1991. Fellow Inst. Ct. Mgmt., Nat. Ctr. for State Cts.; mem. Nat. Assn. Ct. Mgmt. (bd. dirs. 1997-99), Okla. Ct. Clks. Assn. (pres. 1996-97). Office: City of Tulsa 600 Civic Ctr Tulsa OK 74103-3829

THOMPSON, DAVID F. lawyer; b. Chgo., Oct. 19, 1942; s. Charles F. and Helen (Enright) T.; m. Monica McAleer, Dec. 15, 1973; children—Megan, Kristin. B.S., Loyola U., Chgo., 1965, M.S. in Indsl. Relations, 1966; J.D., Northwestern U., 1969. Bar: Ill. 1970, U.S. Dist. Ct. (no. dist.) Ill. 1970. Assoc., McDermott, Will & Emery, Chgo., 1969-72; asst. v.p. First Nat. Bank of Chgo., 1972-77; ptnr. Daleiden, Thompson & Tremaine, Ltd. and predecessors, Chgo., 1977— . Mem. ABA, Ill. State Bar Assn. General corporate, General practice, Pension, profit-sharing, and employee benefits. Office: 333 N Michigan Ave Chicago IL 60601-3901

THOMPSON, DAVID RENWICK, federal judge; b. 1930; BS in Bus., U. So. Calif., 1952, LLB, 1955. Pvt. practice law with Thompson & Thompson (and predecessor firms), 1957-85; judge U.S. Ct. Appeals (9th cir.), 1985-98, sr. judge, 1998—. Served with USN, 1955-57. Mem. ABA, San Diego County Bar Assn., Am. Bd. Trial Lawyers (sec. San Diego chpt. 1983, v.p. 1984, pres. 1985). Office: US Ct Appeals 940 Front StRm 2193 San Diego CA 92101-8919*

THOMPSON, GORDON, JR. federal judge; b. San Diego, Dec. 28, 1929; s. Gordon and Garnet (Meese) T.; m. Jean Peters, Mar. 17, 1951; children— John M., Peter Renwick, Gordon III. Grad., U. So. Calif., 1951, Southwestern U. Sch. Law, Los Angeles, 1956. Bar: Calif. 1956. With Dist. Atty.'s Office, County of San Diego, 1957-60; partner firm Thompson & Thompson, San Diego, 1960-70; U.S. dist. judge So. Dist. Calif., 1970—, chief judge, 1984-91, sr. judge, 1994—. Mem. ABA, Am. Bd. Trial Advocates, San Diego County Bar Assn. (v.p. 1970), San Diego Yacht Club, Delta Chi. Office: US Dist Ct 940 Front St San Diego CA 92101-8994

THOMPSON, HOLLEY MARKER, lawyer, marketing professional; b. Jamestown, N.Y., Jan. 30, 1947; d. Burdette James and Mary (Novitske) Marker; children: Jennifer Kristen Simos, Kendra Elise Blair, Jennifer Lynn, Stephanie Lynn; m. Lawrence D. Thompson. AAS, Jamestown C.C., 1966; BS, Ohio U., 1969; MA, W.Va. U., 1974, JD, 1980. Bar: W.Va. 1980, U.S. Dist. Ct. (so. dist.) W.Va. 1980, Pa. 1982, U.S. Dist. Ct. (we. dist.) Pa. 1982. Tchr. math. various pub. schs., Santa Ana (Calif.), Lakewood (N.Y.) and Morgantown (W.Va.), 1970-77; atty. for students W.Va. U., Morgantown, 1980; assoc. libr., lectr. W.Va. U. Coll. Law, 1980-83; assoc., libr. Jackson, Kelly, Holt & O'Farrell, Charleston, W.Va., 1983-86; cons. Hildebrandt, Inc., Somerville, N.J., 1986-94; v.p. mktg., assn. markets profl. rels. Lexis-Nexis, Dayton, Ohio, 1994—. Spkr. in field. Contbr. articles to profl. jours. Mem. ABA, Spl. Libr. Assn., Am. Assn. Law Libs., N.J. Assn. Law Libs., Legal Mktg. Assn., Phi Delta Phi. Office: Lexis-Nexis 9443 Springboro Pike Miamisburg OH 45342 E-mail: holley.thompson@lexis-nexis.com

THOMPSON, JAMES LEE, lawyer; b. L.I., N.Y., Sept. 9, 1941; s. Robert Luther and Marjorie Emma (Jones) T.; m. Diana Dill Stevenson, June 29, 1963; children: James C., Thomas J. BA, Yale U., 1963; JD, U. Va., 1966. Bar: Va. 1966, Md. 1966, U.S. Ct. Mil. Appeals 1968, U.S. Dist. Ct. Md. 1972, U.S. Supreme Ct. 1978. Ptnr. Miller & Canby, Rockville, Md., 1970—, head litigation, 1975—. Mem. jud. conf. U.S. Ct. Appeals (4th cir.). Mem. Thousand Acres Assn., Deep Creek Lake, Md., 1985-87. Capt. JAGC, USMC, 1966-70. Decorated D.S.M. Fellow Am. Coll. Trial Lawyers; mem. ABA, Md. State Bar Assn. (bd. govs. 1975, 78, 79, 83, 89, 94, sec. 1995, pres. 1999-00), Montgomery County Bar Assn. (pres. 1987-88, Cert. of Merit 1985), Nat. Conf. Bar Pres., Md. Bar Found., Montgomery County Bar Found. (pres. 1988-89), Loophole Club (pres. 1978-79), Phi Delta Phi. Democrat. Episcopalian. Avocations: sailing, skiing, tennis, golf, gardening. State civil litigation, General practice. Home: 419 Russell Ave Apt 110 Gaithersburg MD 20877-2836 Office: Miller & Canby 200 Monroe St Ste B Rockville MD 20850-4423

THOMPSON, JAMES ROBERT, JR. lawyer, former governor; b. Chgo., May 8, 1936; s. James Robert and Agnes Josephine (Swanson) T.; m. Jayne Carr, 1976; 1 child, Samantha Jayne. Student, U. Ill., Chgo., 1953-55, Washington U., St. Louis, 1955-56; J.D., Northwestern U., 1959. Bar: Ill. 1959, U.S. Supreme Ct. 1964. Asst. state's atty., Cook County, Ill., 1959-64; assoc. prof. law Northwestern U. Law Sch., 1964-69; asst. atty. gen. State of Ill., 1969-70; chief criminal div., 1969; chief dept. law enforcement and pub. protection, 1969-70; 1st asst. U.S. atty. No. Dist. Ill., 1970-71, U.S. atty., 1971-75; counsel firm Winston & Strawn, Chgo., 1975-77, ptnr., chmn. exec. com., 1991—; gov. Ill., 1977-91. Chmn. Pres.' Intelligence Oversight Bd., 1989—93; adv. bd. Fed. Emergency Mgmt. Agy., 1991—93; bd. govs. Chgo. Bd. Trade; bd. dirs. FMC Corp., FMC Techs., Inc., Jefferson Smurfit Group, PLC, Prime Retail Inc., Hollinger Internat., Inc., Prime Group Realty Trust, Navigant Consulting Inc., Maximus, Inc., Chgo. Mus. Contemporary Art, Lyric Opera Chgo., Econ. Club Chgo., Civic Com., Comml. Club Chgo., Execs. Club Chgo. Co-author: Cases and Comments on Criminal Justice, 2 vols, 1968, 74, Criminal Law and Its Adminstration, 1970, 74. Chmn. Ill. Math. and Sci. Acad. Found.; chmn. Rep. Gov's. Assn., 1982, Nat. Gov.'s Assn., Midwest Gov.'s Assn., Coun. Gt. Lakes Gov's., 1985. Mem. ABA, Ill. Bar Assn., Chgo. Bar Assn. Republican. Office: Winston & Strawn 35 W Wacker Dr Ste 4200 Chicago IL 60601-1695

THOMPSON, JAMES WILLIAM, lawyer; b. Dallas, Oct. 22, 1936; s. John Charles and Frances (Van Slyke) T.; m. Marie Hertz, June 26, 1965 (dec. 1995); children: Elizabeth, Margaret, John; m. Linda Ball Dozier, May 2, 1998. BS, U. Mont., 1958, JD, 1962. Bar: Mont. 1962; CPA, Mont. Acct. Arthur Young & Co., N.Y.C., summer 1959; instr. bus. adminstrn. Ea. Mont. Coll., Billings, 1959-60, U. Mont., Missoula, 1960-61; assoc. Cooke, Moulton, Bellingham & Longo, Billings, 1962-64, James R. Felt, Billings, 1964-65; asst. atty. City of Billings, 1963-64, atty., 1964-66; ptnr. Felt, Speare & Thompson, Billings, 1966-72, McNamer, Thompson & Cashmore, 1973-86, McNamer & Thompson Law Firm PC, 1986-89, McNamer, Thompson, Werner & Stanley, P.C., 1990-93, McNamer Thompson Law Firm PC, 1993-98, Wright Tolliver Guthals Law Firm PC, 1999—. Bd. dirs. Associated Employers of Mont., Inc., 1989-98; mem. adv. coun. Sch. Fine Arts, U. Mont., 1997-2001. Mem. Billings Zoning Commn., 1966-69; v.p. Billings Cmty. Action Program (now Dist. 7 Human Resources Devel. Coun.), 1968-70, pres., 1970-75, trustee, 1975—; mem. Yellowstone County Legal Svcs. Bd., 1969-70; City-County Air Pollution Control Bd., 1969-70; pres. Billings Symphony Soc., 1970-71; bd. dirs. Billings Studio Theatre, 1967-73, United Way Billings, 1973-81, Mont. Inst. Arts Found., 1986-89, Downtown Billings Assn., 1986-90, Billings Area Bus. Incubator, Inc., 1991-94, Found. of Mont. State U., Billings, 1992-98, Mont. Parks Assn., 1997—, Rimrock Opera Co., 1998—; mem. Diocesan exec. coun., 1972-75; mem. Billings Transit Commn., 1971-73; mem. City Devel. Agy., 1972-73. Mem. ABA, Am. Acad. Estate Planning Attys., Nat. Acad. Elder Law Attys., State Bar Mont., Yellowstone County Bar Assn. (bd. dirs. 1983-87, pres. 1985-86), C. of C., Elks, Kiwanis (pres. Yellowstone chpt. 1974-75), Sigma Chi (pres. Billings alumni assn. 1963-65). Episcopalian. Estate planning, Probate, Estate taxation. Home: 123 Lewis Ave Billings MT 59101-6034 Office: 10 N 27th St PO Box 1977 Billings MT 59103-1977 E-mail: JWTLDT@aol.com

THOMPSON, JOEL ERIK, lawyer; b. Summit, N.J., Sept. 15, 1940; s. Maurice Eugene and Charlotte Ruth (Harrington) T.; m. Bonnie Gay Ransa, June 15, 1963 (div. Dec. 1980); m. Deborah Ann Korp, Dec. 24, 1980 (div. Jan. 1987); children: Janice Santiesteban, Amber. Student, Va. Poly. Inst., 1958, Carnegie Inst. Tech., 1960-61; BSME cum laude, Newark Coll. Engring., 1966; JD, Seton Hall, 1970. Bar: N.J. 1970, Ariz. 1975, U.S. Tax Ct. 1972, U.S. Ct. Claims 1972, U.S. Customs Ct., 1972, U.S. Ct. Mil. Appeals, 1972, U.S. Ct. Customs and Patent Appeals 1972, U.S. Dist. Ct. N.J. 1970, Ariz. 1975, U.S. Ct. Appeals (9th cir.) 1975, U.S. Supreme Ct. 1975; cert. specialist criminal law Ariz. Bd. Legal Specialization; lic. profl. engr., N.J. Sr. technician Bell Tel. Labs., Inc., Murray Hill, N.J., 1965-67, patent agent, 1967-70, staff atty., 1970-73; sr. trial atty. N.J. Pub. Defender's Office, Elizabeth, N.J., 1973-74; assoc. Cahill, Sutton and Thomas, Phoenix, 1974-76; trial lawyer Maricopa County Pub. Defender's Office, 1976-80; trial lawyer, criminal law specialist Henry J. Florence, Ltd., 1980-86; pvt. practice, 1987—. Judge Superior Ct. Ariz., Phoenix, 1987-95; instr. Phoenix Regional Police Acad., 1976-80, Glendale C.C., 1977, Ariz. State U. Sch. of Law, 1978, Am. Inst., 1990; pres., CEO Eagle Master Corp., Phoenix, 1995—; pres. Joel Erik Thompson, Ltd., Phoenix, 1987—; bd. dirs. Am. Loans, Inc., San Diego, 1999-; presenter in field. Contbr. articles to profl. jours. Mem. planning com. Camelback East Village, Phoenix, 1992-98, chmn., 1993-96; mayor's select com., Phoenix, 1997, blue ribbon com. Maricopa Assn. Govs., 1996-97. Mem. Ariz. Bar Assn., Nat. Assn. Criminal Def. Lawyers, Ariz. Attys. Criminal Justice (charter), Ariz. Assn. Pvt. Investigators (hon.), Internat. Assn. Identification (hon.), Tau Beta Pi, Pi Tau Sigma. Criminal, Land use and zoning (including planning). Office: 3104 E Camelback Rd # 521 Phoenix AZ 85016-4502 E-mail: joel.thompson@azbar.org

THOMPSON, LORAN TYSON, lawyer; b. N.Y.C., Dec. 23, 1947; s. Kenneth Webster and Mary (Tyson) T.; m. Meera Eleanora Agarwal, Apr. 2, 1976. BA magna cum laude, Amherst Coll., 1969; MA, Harvard U., 1970, JD, 1976. Bar: N.Y. 1977, U.S. Tax Ct. 1977. Assoc. Breed, Abbott & Morgan, N.Y.C., 1976-83, ptnr., 1983-93, Whitman Breed Abbott & Morgan LLP, N.Y.C., 1993-2000, Winston & Strawn, N.Y.C., 2000—. Mem. ABA, N.Y. State Bar Assn. (exec. com., tax sect. 1991-98, co-chmn. com. on nonqualified employee benefits 1991-95, co-chmn. com. on qualified plans 1995-98), Assn. Bar of City of N.Y., Phi Beta Kappa. Pension, profit-sharing, and employee benefits, Corporate taxation, Taxation, general. Home: 79 W 12th St Apt 12G New York NY 10011-8510 Office: Winston & Strawn 200 Park Ave New York NY 10166-4193 E-mail: lthompso@winston.com

THOMPSON, MARTTIE LOUIS, lawyer; b. Meridian, Miss., July 5, 1930; s. Samuel L. and Rosie (Young) T.; m. Cornelia Gaines, Apr. 2, 1966; 1 child, Sandra M. Ruffin. BS, U. Toledo, 1954; postgrad., St. John's U., 1955-57, Columbia U., 1977. Bar: N.Y. 1963, D.C. 1980, U.S. Dist. Ct. (so. and ea. dists.) N.Y. 1966, U.S. Ct. Appeals (2d cir.) 1966, U.S. Supreme Ct. 1971. Atty. Wolf, Popper, Ross, Wolf and Jones, N.Y.C., 1963-65; assoc. William C. Chance, Jr., 1965-66; house counsel Ft. Greene Cmty. Corp., Bklyn., 1966-68; mng. atty. MFY Legal Svcs., Inc., N.Y.C., 1968-70. Gen. counsel and exec. dir. Cmty. Action, N.Y.C., 1971-77; regional dir. Legal Svcs. Corp., Phila., 1977-84; adj. prof. Seton Hall Law Ctr., 1979-80; chmn. Nat. Employment Law Project. Contbr. articles to profl. jours. Pres., Stockton Civic Assn., 1978; mem. East Orange Planning Bd. and Citizens Union, 1976; bd. dirs. Nat. Legal Aid and Defenders Assn., 1980. Sgt. USAF

THOMPSON, MICHAEL, lawyer; b. Des Moines, Aug. 2, 1951; s. Harold L. and Carolyn Annette (Yacinich) T.; m. Barbara Ann Haafke, Oct. 29, 1977 (div. Oct. 1984). BA, U. No. Iowa, 1973; MA, U. Iowa, 1976, JD, 1975. Bar: Iowa 1976, N.Y. 1978, Mo. 1980, Tex. 1994, Ill. 1999, U.S. Ct. Appeals (2d cir.) 1980, U.S. Ct. Appeals (7th cir.) 1982, U.S. Ct. Appeals (D.C. cir.) 1982, U.S. Ct. Appeals (fed. cir.) 1987, U.S. Ct. Internat. Trade 1987, U.S. Supreme Ct. 1984. Asst. atty. gen. Iowa Dept. Justice, Des Moines, 1976; economist Iowa Commerce Commn., 1976-77; spl. asst. N.Y. Pub. Svc. Commn., Albany, 1977-80; commerce counsel Mo. Pacific R.R., St. Louis, 1980-83; atty. Southwestern Bell Corp., 1983-95; sr. atty. internat. SBC Comms., Inc., San Antonio, 1995-97, gen. atty. internat., 1997-2000; pvt. practice Evanston, Ill., 2000—. Adj. instr. corp. fin. Drake U., Des Moines, 1977. Mem. ABA, Chgo. Yacht Club, Houston Yacht Club, Am. Alpine Club, Grolier Club, Phi Alpha Delta. Republican. Contracts commercial, Intellectual property, Private international. Office: 1555 Sherman Ave Ste 362 Evanston IL 60201 Fax: 847-733-1807. E-mail: thompsonlawchicago@earthlink.net

THOMPSON, ORVAL NATHAN, lawyer; b. Shedd, Oreg., Nov. 29, 1914; s. Otto M. and Laura L. (Halverson) T.; m. Barbara B. Webb, Oct. 15, 1939 (div. 1957); m. Jessie Mila Jackson, Nov. 24, 1958 (dec. 1983); children: Kathleen Persons, Richard, Marion Wells; m. Bonnie Aufranc, Aug. 9, 1987. BS, U. Oreg., 1935, JD, 1937; LLM, Northwestern U., 1939. Bar: Oreg. 1937, U.S. Ct. Appeals (9th cir.) 1949, U.S. Supreme Ct. 1945. Practiced, Albany, Oreg., 1938—, of counsel Weatherford, Thompson, Quick & Ashenfelter, P.C., 1972—; dir. Citizens Valley Bank, 1956-86, Key Bank Oreg., 1986-89; sec. Oreg. Metall. Corp., 1955-97, dir., 1987-94. Mem. Oreg. Ho. of Reps., 1941-42; mem. Oreg. Senate, 1947-50; legal advisor to gov. Oreg., 1957-58. Lt. USNR, 1942-46. Mem. ABA, Oreg. Bar Assn., Linn County Bar Assn. (past pres.), Albany Area C. of C., Masons, Springhill Country Club, Elks, Phi Beta Kappa. Democrat. Presbyterian. General corporate, Estate planning, Probate. Home: 9310 Stonebridge Dr College Station TX 77845-9332 Office: Weatherford Thompson et al 130 W 1st Ave PO Box 667 Albany OR 97321-0219

THOMPSON, PAMELA MARY, lawyer; b. Newcastle, England, July 2, 1956; d. Arthur and Marjorie Thompson. BA with honors, Oxford U., 1975. Trainee solicitor Bischoft & Co., London, 1980-82, solicitor, 1982-87, ptnr., 1987-99, Eversheds, London, 1999—. Mem. Women's Solicitor Group. Avocations: reading, cinema, wine. Office: Eversheds Senator Ho 85 Queen Victoria St London EC4V 4J1 England Office Fax: 020 7919 4919. E-mail: Thompspm@eversheds.com

THOMPSON, PAUL MICHAEL, lawyer; b. Dubuque, Iowa, Aug. 30, 1935; s. Frank W. and Genevieve (Cassutt) T.; m. Mary Jacqueline McManus, Jan. 30, 1960; children: Anne, Tricia, Paul, Tim, Jim. B.A. magna cum laude, Loras Coll., 1957; LL.B., Georgetown U., 1959. Bar: Iowa 1959, D.C. 1959, Va. 1966. Atty. appellate ct. br. NLRB, Washington, 1962-66; assoc. Hunton & Williams, Richmond, Va., 1966-71, ptnr., 1971—. Adj. prof. The T.C. Williams Sch. Law, U. Richmond. Served with JAGC, USAF, 1960-62. Mem. ABA, Va. State Bar, Va. Bar Assn., Internat. Bar Assn., Commonwealth Club. Roman Catholic. Federal civil litigation, Labor. Office: Hunton & Williams 951 E Byrd St Riverfront Pla E Tower Richmond VA 23219-4074 E-mail: pthompson@hunton.com

THOMPSON, PETER RULE, lawyer; b. Cleve., Apr. 26, 1943; s. Allen Paul and Phyllis Gwendolyn (Clark) T.; m. Pamela Stufflebeme, Aug. 12, 1967; children— Christina, Peter Rule Jr. B.A., So. Meth. U., 1965, J.D., 1968. Bar: Tex. 1968, U.S. Dist. Ct. (no. dist.) Tex. 1972, U.S. Ct. Appeals (5th cir.) 1972, U.S. Supreme Ct. 1973. Asst. city atty. City of Dallas, 1970-74; sr. atty. Enserch Corp., Dallas, 1974-79; gen. atty. Dorchester Gas Corp., Dallas, 1979-82, gen counsel, chief legal officer, 1982—; pvt. practice, Dallas, 1985—. Mem. Dallas Bar Assn., ABA. Presbyterian. Clubs: Brookhaven Country. General civil litigation, General corporate, Labor. Office: 5025 Arapaho Rd Ste 400 Dallas TX 75248-4656

THOMPSON, RALPH GORDON, federal judge; b. Oklahoma City, Dec. 15, 1934; s. Lee Bennett and Elaine (Bizzell) T.; m. Barbara Irene Hencke, Sept. 5, 1964; children: Lisa, Elaine, Maria. BBA, U. Okla., 1956, JD, 1961. Bar: Okla. 1961. Ptnr. Thompson, Thompson, Harbour & Selph (and predecessors), Oklahoma City, 1961-75; judge U.S. Dist. Ct. for Western Dist. Okla., 1975—; chief judge U.S. Dist. Ct. (we. dist.) Okla., 1986-93. Mem. Okla. Ho. of Reps., 1966-70, asst. minority floor leader, 1969-70; spl. justice Supreme Ct. Okla., 1970-71; tchr. Harvard Law Sch. Trial Advocacy Workshop, 1981—; apptd. by chief justice of U.S. to U.S. Fgn. Intelligence Surveillance Ct., 1990-97; elected to jud. conf. of the U.S., 1997; apptd. to Edward J. Devitt Disting. Svc. Justice award selection com., 1997-99; apptd. by chief justice of U.S. to exec. com. of Jud. Conf. of the U.S., 1998-2000; coord. Long Range Planning for Fed. Judiciary, 1999-2000. Co-author: Bryce Harlow: Mr. Integrity, Bob Burke and Ralph G. Thompson, 2000. Rep. nominee for lt. gov., Okla., 1970; chmn. bd. ARC, Oklahoma City, 1970-72; chmn., pres. Okla. Young Lawyers Conf., 1965; mem. bd. visitors U. Okla., 1975-78. Lt. USAF, 1957-60, col. Res., ret. Decorated Legion of Merit; named Oklahoma City's Outstanding Young Man, Oklahoma City Jaycees, 1967, Outstanding Fed. Trial Judge, Okla Trial Lawyers Assn., 1980; recipient Regents Alumni award U. Okla., 1990, Disting. Svc. award, 1993, Jour. Record award for Disting. Svc., 2001; inducted Okla. Hall of Fame, 1995; nominee Pulitzer Prize, 2000. Fellow Am. Bar Found.; mem. ABA, Fed. Bar Assn., Okla. Bar Assn. (chmn. sect. internat. law and gen. practice 1974-75), Oklahoma County Bar Assn. (Jud. Svc. award 1988), Jud. Conf. U.S. (com. on ct. adminstrn. 1981-89, com. on fed.-state jurisdiction 1988-91), U.S. Dist. Judges Assn. 10th Cir. (pres. 1992-94), Rotary (hon.), Order of Coif, Am. Inns of Ct. (pres. XXIII 1995-96), Phi Beta Kappa (pres. chpt. 1985-86, Phi Beta Kappa of Yr. 1991), Beta Theta Pi, Phi Alpha Delta. Episcopalian. Office: US Dist Ct 200 NW 4th St Oklahoma City OK 73102-3027

THOMPSON, RONALD EDWARD, lawyer; b. Bremerton, Wash., May 24, 1931; s. Melville Herbert and Clara Mildred (Griggs) T.; m. Marilyn Christine Woods, Dec. 15, 1956; children: Donald Jeffery, Karen, Susan, Nancy, Sally, Claire BA, U. Wash., 1953, JD, 1958. Bar: Wash. 1959. Asst. city atty. City of Tacoma, 1960-61; pres. firm Thompson, Krilich, LaPorte, West & Lockner, P.S., Tacoma, 1961-99. Judge pro tem Mcpl. Ct., City of Tacoma, Pierce County Dist., 1972—, Pierce County Superior Ct., 1972—. Chmn. housing and social welfare com. City of Tacoma, 1965-69; mem. Tacoma Bd. Adjustment, 1967-71, chmn., 1968; mem. Tacoma Com. Future Devel., 1961-64, Tacoma Planning Commn., 1971-72; bd. dirs., pres. Mcpl. League Tacoma; bd. dirs. Pres. Tacoma Rescue Mission, Tacoma Pierce County Cancer Soc., Tacoma-Pierce County Heart Assn., Tacoma Grand Cinema, Tacoma-Pierce County Coun. for Arts, Econ. Devel. Coun. Puget Sound, Tacoma Youth Symphony, Kleiner Group Home, Tacoma C.C. Found., Pierce County Econ. Devel. Corp., Wash. Transp. Policy Inst.; Coalition to Keep Wash. Moving, precinct committeeman Rep. party, 1969-73. With AUS, 1953-55; col. Res. Recipient Internat. Cmty. Svc. award Optimist Club, 1970, Patriotism award Am. Fedn. Police, 1974, citation for cmty. svc. HUD, 1974, Disting. Citizen award Mcpl. League Tacoma-Pierce County, 1985; named Lawyer of the Yr. Pierce County Legal Secs. Assn., 1992. Mem. ATLA, Am. Arbitration Assn. (panel of arbitrators), ABA, Wash. State Bar Assn., Tacoma-Pierce County Bar Assn. (sec. 1964, pres. 1979, mem. cts. and judiciary com. 1981-82), Wash. State Trial Lawyers Assn., Tacoma-Pierce County C. of C. (bd. dirs., exec. com., v.p., chmn.), Downtown Tacoma Assn. (com. chmn., bd. dirs. exec. com., chmn.), Variety Club (Seattle), Lawn Tennis Club, Tacoma Club, Optimist (Tacoma, internat. pres. 1973-74), Phi Delta Phi, Sigma Nu. Roman Catholic. General civil litigation, Personal injury, Real property. Home: 3101 E Bay Dr NW Gig Harbor WA 98335-7610 Office: Atty Law PO Box 1189 7525 Pioneer Way Ste 101 Gig Harbor WA 98335-1165 E-mail: retpllc@att.net

THOMPSON, SHARON ANDREA, lawyer; b. New Bedford, Mass., May 31, 1948; d. Russell Edwin and Elma (Andreasen) T. BS, Mich. State U., 1970; JD, Antioch Sch. Law, 1976. Bar: N.C. 1976, U.S. Dist. Ct. (ea. and mid. dists.) N.C. 1976. Ptnr. Mailman & Thompson, Raleigh, N.C., 1976-79; prin. Thompson & McAllaster, P.A., Durham, N.C., 1979-89; ptnr. Thompson & Burgess, Durham, 1989—; adminstrv. hearing officer N.C. Dept. Human Resources, 1981-86. Mem. Durham Human Rels. Commn., 1979-82. Mem. N.C. Bar Assn., Durham County Bar Assn., N.C. Acad. Trial Lawyers, N.C. Assn. Women Attys. (bd. dirs. 1979-81, 83-85); elected to N.C. Ho. of Reps., 1987-89, re-elected, 1989-90. Civil rights, Family and matrimonial, Labor. Home: 1809 Glendale Ave Durham NC 27701-1323 Office: Thompson & Burgess PO Box 2164 Durham NC 27702-2164

THOMPSON, T. JAY, lawyer; b. Ponca City, Okla., Aug. 10, 1947; s Lurtis Howard and Frances (Wood) T. BS U. Okla., 1969, JD Washington U., St. Louis, 1972; LLM in Labor Law, George Washington U., 1976; LLM in Internat. Law U. Cambridge (Eng.), 1979. Bar: Okla. 1972, D.C. 1976, U.S. Ct. Appeals (D.C. cir.) 1976, U.S. Supreme Ct. 1976, U.S. Dist. Ct. D.C. 1976, U.S. Dist. Ct. (no. dist.) Tex. 1987, Colo. 1979, U.S. Ct. Appeals (10th cir.) 1979, U.S. Dist. Ct. (no., ea. and we. dists.) Okla. 1983, U.S. Dist. Ct. (so. dist.) Tex. 1984, U.S. Ct. Appeals (8th cir.) 1984, Tex. 1986, U.S. Ct. Appeals (7th and 5th cirs.) 1986, N.Y. 1994, U.S. Dist. Ct. (so. dist.) 1994, U.S. Ct. Appeals (2d cir.) 1994. Assoc. Holland & Hart, Denver, 1979-82, dir. Nichols, Wolfe, Stamper, Nally & Fallis, Inc., Tulsa, 1982-86, assoc. gen. counsel Burlington No. R.R. Co., Ft. Worth, Tex., 1986-87, assoc. Akin, Gump, Strauss, Hauer & Feld, Washington, 1987-91, staff v.p., deputy gen. coun. Continental Airlines, Inc., 1991-93, sr. attorney AT&T Corp., 1993—. Contbr. articles to legal jours. Capt. USAF, 1972-78. Decorated USAF Commendation medal; Alfred P. Sloan Merit scholar Knox Coll., 1966. Mem. ABA, Okla. Bar Assn., D.C. Bar, Tex. Bar Assn., N.Y. State Bar Assn., Pi Mu Epsilon. Labor, Federal civil litigation, Civil Rights. Civil rights, Federal civil litigation, Labor. Office: AT&T Corp PO Box 1995 Liberty Corner NJ 07938-1995

THOMPSON, TERENCE WILLIAM, lawyer; b. Moberly, Mo., July 3, 1952; s. Donald Gene and Carolyn (Stringer) T.; m. Caryn Elizabeth Hildebrand, Aug. 30, 1975; children: Cory Elizabeth, Christopher William, Tyler Madison. BA in Govt. with honors and high distinction, U. Ariz., 1974; JD, Harvard U., 1977. Bar: Ariz. 1977, U.S. Dist. Ct. Ariz. 1977, U.S. Tax Ct. 1979. Assoc. Brown & Bain P.A., Phoenix, 1977-83, ptnr., 1983-92, Gallagher and Kennedy, P.A., Phoenix, 1992—. Legis. aide Rep. Richard Burgess, Ariz. Ho. of Reps., 1974; mem. bus. adv. bd. Citibank Ariz. (formerly Great Western Bank & Trust, Phoenix), 1985-86. Mem. staff Harvard Law Record, 1974-75; rsch. editor Harvard Internat. Law Jour. ,1976; lead author, editor-in-chief: Arizona Corporate Practice, 1996; contbr. articles to profl. jours. Mem. Phoenix Mayor's Youth Adv. Bd. 1968-70, Phoenix Internat.; active 20-30 Club, 1978-81, sec. 1978-80, Valley Leadership, Phoenix, 1983-84, citizens task force future financing needs City of Phoenix, 1985-86; exec. coun. Boys and Girls Clubs of Met. Phoenix, 1990-2000, sr. coun. 2000—; bd. dirs. Phoenix Bach Choir, 1992-94; deacon Shepherd of Hills Congl. Ch., Phoenix, 1984-85; pres. Maricopa County Young Dems., 1982-83, Ariz. Young Dems., 1983-84, sec. 1981-82, v.p. 1982-83; exec. dir. Young Dems. Am., 1985, exec. com. 1983-85; others. Fellow Ariz. Bar Found.; mem. State Bar Ariz. (vice chmn. internt. law sect. 1978, sec. securities law sect. 1990-91, vice chmn. sect. 1991-92, chmn.-elect 1992-93, chmn. 1993-94, exec. coun. 1988-96, sec. bus. law sect. 1992-93, vice chmn. 1993-94, chmn. 1994-95, exec. coun. 1996-98), Nat. Assn. Bond Lawyers, Nat. Health Lawyers, Greater Phoenix Black C. of C. (bd. dirs. 1999-2001), Blue Key, Phi Beta Kappa, Phi Kappa Phi, Phi Eta Sigma. General corporate, Health, Securities. Home: 202 W Lawrence Rd Phoenix AZ 85013-1226 Office: Gallagher & Kennedy PA 2575 E Camelback Rd Phoenix AZ 85016-9225

THOMS, DAVID MOORE, lawyer; b. N.Y.C., Apr. 28, 1948; s. Theodore Clark and Elizabeth Augusta (Moore) T.; m. Susan Rebecca Stuckey, Dec. 16, 1972. BA, Kalamazoo Coll., 1970; M in Urban Planning, Wayne State U., 1975, LLM in Taxation, 1988; JD, U. Detroit, 1979. Bar: Mich. 1980, N.Y. 1995. Planner City of Detroit, 1971-75; atty. Rockwell and Kotz, P.C., Detroit, 1980-87; pvt. practice David M. Thoms & Assocs., P.C., 1987—. Adj. assoc. prof. Madonna U., 1993—; presenter NYU Tax Inst. Editor Case and Comment U. of Detroit Law Rev., 1978-79. Mem. program com. Fin. and Estate Planning Coun. Detroit, 1980—; mem. adv. bd., chmn. nominating com., mem. exec. com. Met. Detroit Salvation Army, 1980—, sec.-treas., vice chmn., 1994-95, chmn., 1995-96; bd. dirs. bylaws and property com., mem. nominating com., devel. com., exec. com. Mich. chpt. ARC; bd. dirs. L'Alliance Française de Grosse Pointe, French Festival of Detroit, Inc., 1986-89, 91-94, pres.; bd. dirs. Fedn. of Alliances Françaises, 1989-95, 97—, also past treas., v.p., chmn. fin. com., pres., 2000-01; trustee Detroit Symphony Orch. Hall, Inc., dir., 1996-97; trustee Kalamazoo Coll., 1993-97, dir., exec. com., 1995-97; dir. vis. com. European art DIA, 1995-97. Decorated Officier dans l'Ordre des Palmes Academiques; recipient Prix Charbonnier; Burton scholar U. Detroit, 1979. Mem. ABA (chmn. subcom. on probate and estate planning, mem. charitable trust com.), Fed. Bar Assn., Oakland County Bar Assn., Detroit Bar Assn., State Bar Mich., N.Y. Bar Assn., Bar Assn. of City of N.Y., Am. Planning Assn. (Mich. chpt.), Detroit Athletic Club, Renaissance Club, The Grosse Pointe Club. Mem. United Church of Christ. Avocations: tennis, architectural history, music, travel, art history. General corporate, Estate planning, Corporate taxation. Office: 400 Renaissance Ctr Ste 950 Detroit MI 48243-1678 E-mail: thoms@ameritech.net

THOMS, JEANNINE AUMOND, lawyer; b. Chgo. d. Emmett Patrick and Margaret (Gallet) Aumond; m. Richard W. Thoms; children: Catherine Thoms, Alison Thoms. AA, McHenry County Coll., 1979; BA, No. Ill. U., 1981; JD, Ill. Inst. Tech., 1984. Bar: Ill. 1984, U.S. Dist. Ct. (no. dist.) Ill. 1984, U.S. Ct. Appeals (7th cir.) 1985. Assoc. Foss Schuman Drake & Barnard, Chgo., 1984-86, Zukowski Rogers Flood & McArdle, Crystal Lake and Chgo., 1986-92, ptnr., 1992—. Arbitrator 19th Jud. Ct. Ill., 1991—. Mem. Women's Adv. Coun. to Gov., State of Ill.; mem. McHenry County Mental Health Bd., 1991-98, v.p., 1993-94, pres., 1995-98. Mem. ABA, LWV, Ill. State Bar Assn. (coun. trust and estates sect. 2000—, dist. scholarship com. 2001), Chgo. Bar Assn., McHenry County Bar Assn., Am. Trial Lawyers Assn., Acad. Family Mediators (cert.), Women's Network, Phi Alpha Delta. Estate planning, Municipal (including bonds), Probate. Office: Zukowski Rogers Flood & McArdle 50 N Virginia St Crystal Lake IL 60014-4126 also: 100 S Wacker Dr Chicago IL 60606-4006

THOMSON, BASIL HENRY, JR. lawyer, university general counsel; b. Amarillo, Tex., Jan. 17, 1945; m. Margaret Shepard, May 4, 1985; children: Christopher, Matthew, Robert. BBA, Baylor U., 1968, JD, 1973. Bar: Tex. 1974, U.S. Ct. Mil. Appeals 1974, U.S. Supreme Ct. 1977, U.S. Dist. Ct. (we. dist.) Tex. 1988, U.S. Ct. Appeals (fed. cir.) 1990. Oil title analyst Hunt Oil Co., Dallas, 1971-73; atty., advisor Regulations and Adminstrv. Law div. Office of Chief Counsel USCG, Washington, 1973-77; dir. estate planning devel. dept. Baylor U., Waco, Tex., 1977-80, gen. counsel, 1980—. Adj. prof. law Baylor U.; lobbyist legis. Ind. Higher Edn., 71st Session of Tex. Legislature; mem. legis. com. Gov.'s Task Force on Drug Abuse; dir. govtl. relations Baylor U.; speaker at meetings of coll. and univ. adminstrs.; assisted in drafting legis. for Texan's War on Drugs Tex. Legislature; mem. legal adv. com. United Educators Ins. Risk Retention Group, 1994-96; mem. legal svcs. rev. panel Nat. Assn. Ind. Colls. and Univs., 1997—, 2d v.p., 2001—, Nat. Assn. Coll. and Univ. Attys. Active Heart O'Tex. coun. Boy Scouts Am.; bd. dirs. Longhorn Coun. on Alcoholism and Drug Abuse, 1987-91; mem. bd. adjustment City of Woodway. Recipient Pres.'s award Ind. Colls. and Univs. of Tex., 1994, Dist. award of merit Boy Scouts Am. Fellow Coll. State Bar Tex.; mem. ABA, FBA, Nat. Assn. Coll. and Univ. Attys. (fin., nominations and elections coms. 1994-95, bd. dirs. 1988-91), Tex. Bar Assn., Waco Bar Assn., McLennan County Bar Assn., Owners Assn. of Sugar Creek, Inc. (bd. dirs. 1995-2000). Baptist. Avocations: backpacking, running, environmental concerns. Home: 100 Sugar Creek Pl Waco TX 76712-3410 Office: Baylor U PO Box 97034 Waco TX 76798-7034 E-mail: Basil_Thompson@Baylor.edu

THOMSON, GEORGE RONALD, lawyer, educator; b. Wadsworth, Ohio, Aug. 25, 1959; s. John Alan and Elizabeth (Galbraith) T. BA summa cum laude, Miami U., Oxford, Ohio, 1982, MA summa cum laude, 1983; JD with honors, Ohio State U., 1986. Bar: Ill. 1986, U.S. Dist. Ct. (no. dist.) Ill. 1986. Teaching fellow Miami U., 1982-83; dir. speech activities Ohio State U., Columbus, 1983-86; assoc. Peterson, Ross, Schloerb & Seidel, Chgo., 1986-87, Lord, Bissell & Brook, Chgo., 1987-94; asst. corp. counsel employment litig. divsn. City of Chgo., 1994—. Adj. prof. dept. comm. De Paul U., Chgo., 1988-90; presenter in field. Contbr. articles to profl. jours. Fundraiser Chgo. Hist. Soc., Steppenwolf Theater Co., AIDS Legal Counsel Chgo., Smithsonian Instn., Washington, 1988-90, U.S. Tennis Assn., 1990—; bd. dirs. Metro Sports Assn., 1992-94, Gerber-Hart Libr. and Archives, 1993-95, Gay and Lesbian Tennis Alliance Am., 1993-95, Team Chgo., 1994-96; mem. coord. coun. Nat. Gay and Lesbian History Month; mem. Lawyer's Com. for Ill Human Rights; dir. Chgo. Internat. Charity Tennis Classic, 1993, 94, 95, 98. Recipient Spl. Commendation Ohio Ho. of Reps., 1984, 85, Nat. Forensics Assn. award, 1982. Mem. ABA, Chgo. Bar Assn., Lesbian and Gay Bar Assn., Speech Comm. Assn. Am., Mortar Bd., Phi Beta Kappa, Phi Kappa Phi, Omicron Delta Kappa, Delta Sigma Rho-Tau Kappa Alpha, Phi Alpha Delta. Presbyterian. Avocations: tennis, flute, antiques, folk arts and crafts, reading, travel. General civil litigation, Environmental, Insurance. Home: 2835 N Pine Grove Ave Unit 2S Chicago IL 60657-6109 Office: City of Chgo Dept of Law 30 N La Salle St Ste 1020 Chicago IL 60602-2503

THOREN-PEDEN, DEBORAH SUZANNE, lawyer; b. Rockford, Ill., Mar. 28, 1958; d. Robert Roy and Marguerite Natalie (Geoghegan) Thoren; m. Steven E. Peden, Aug. 10, 1985. BA in Philosophy, Polit. Sci./Psychology, U. Mich., 1978; JD, U. So. Calif., 1982. Bar: Calif. 1982. Assoc. Bushkin, Gaines & Gaims, L.A., 1982-84, Rutan & Tucker, Costa Mesa, Calif., 1984-86; sr. counsel First Interstate Bancorp, L.A., 1986-96; ptnr. Pillsbury Winthrop LLP, 1996-2001; asst. gen. counsel CarsDirect-.com; gen. counsel CD1 Financial.com; gen. counsel, sr. v.p., chief privacy officer PayMyBills.Com, 2000. Lectr. on e-commerce, privacy Bank Secrecy Act and Ethics. Supervising editor U. So. Calif. Entertainment Law Jour., 1982-83, Entertainment Publishing and the Arts Handbook, 1983-84; contbr. articles to profl. jours. Mem. ABA (past vice-chmn. compliance exec. com., money laundering task force, privacy task force, co chmn. BSA staff commentary com.), Calif. Bankers Assn. (regulatory compliance com., co-chmn. regulatory compliance conf., past ex-officio mem. state govt. rels. com., co-vice chmn., vice-chmn., Regulatory Compliance Profl. award 1997, Frandzel award for outside counsel 2001, award 2001), Calif. State Bar Assn. (chmn., consumer fin. com.). Avocations: riding, travel, reading, skiing. Banking, Labor. Office: Pillsbury Winthrop LLP Ste 2800 725 S Figueroa St Los Angeles CA 90017-5443

THORNBURG, LACY HERMAN, federal judge; b. Charlotte, N.C., Dec. 20, 1929; s. Jesse Lafayette and Sarah Ann (Ziegler) T.; m. Dorothy Todd, Sept. 6, 1953; children— Sara Thornburg Evans, Lacy Eugene, Jesse Todd, Alan Ziegler. A.A., Mars Hill Coll., 1950; B.A., U. N.C., 1951, J.D., 1954. Bar: U.S. Dist. Ct. (we. dist.) N.C. Practiced law, Webster, N.C., 1954-67; superior ct. judge State of N.C., 1967-83, atty. gen, 1985-92; emergency judge N.C. Superior Ct., Webster, 1993-94; mem. Nat. Indian Gaming Commn., 1994-95; judge U.S. Dist. Ct. for N.C., Asheville, 1995—. Mem. staff Congressman Taylor, Sylva, N.C., 1960, Congressman

David Hall, Sylva, 1959-60; mem. N.C. Ho. of Reps., 1961-65; mem. N.C. Cts. Commn., N.C. Criminal Code Commn., Capital Planning Commn., Raleigh. Chmn. Jackson County Bd. of Health, Sylva, 1965-84; commr. Tryon Palace, New Bern, N.C. Served with U.S. Army, 1947-48. Mem. Lions, Masons, Shriners. Democrat. Avocations: fly fishing, skeet shooting. Office: US Dist Ct 241 US Courthouse 100 Otis St Asheville NC 28801-2611

THORNBURGH, DICK (RICHARD L. THORNBURGH), lawyer, former United Nations official, former United States attorney general, former governor; b. Pitts., July 16, 1932; s. Charles Garland and Alice (Sanborn) T.; m. Virginia Walton Judson, Oct. 12, 1963; children: John, David, Peter, William. B in Engring., Yale, 1954; LLB, U. Pitts., 1957; hon. degrees, from 30 colls. and univs. Bar: Pa. 1958, U.S. Supreme Ct. 1965, D.C. 1998. Atty. Kirkpatrick & Lockhart, Pitts., 1959-69, 77-79, 87-88, 91-92, 94—; U.S. atty. for Western Pa., 1969-75; U.S. asst. atty. gen. Dept. Justice, Washington, 1975-77; gov. State of Pa., Harrisburg, 1979-87; dir. Inst. Politics John F. Kennedy Sch. Govt., Harvard U., 1987-88; U.S. atty. gen. Washington, 1988-91; under-sec.-gen. for adminstrn. and mgmt. UN, N.Y.C., 1992-93. Del. Pa. Constl. Conv., 1967-68; chmn. State Sci. and Technology Inst.; vice chair World Com. on Disability; bd. dirs. Elan Corp. plc, Nat. Mus. Indsl. History. Mem. Coun. Fgn. Rels., Am. Law Inst.; trustee Urban Inst. Fellow Am. Bar Found.; mem. Am. Judicature Soc. Republican. Office: Kirkpatrick & Lockhart LLP 1800 Massachusetts Ave NW Washington DC 20036-1800

THORNLOW, CAROLYN, law firm administrator, consultant; b. Kew Gardens, N.Y., May 25, 1954; 1 child, Johanna Louise Ramm. BBA magna cum laude, Baruch Coll., 1982. Gen. mgr. Richard A. Ramm Assocs., Levittown, N.Y., 1972-78; adminstr. Tunstead Schechter & Torre, N.Y.C., 1978-82, Cowan Liebowitz & Latman, P.C., N.Y.C., 1982-84, Rosenberg & Estis, P.C., N.Y.C., 1984-85; contr. Finkelstein, Borah, Schwartz, Altschuler & Goldstein, P.C., 1986-92; pres. Concinnity Svcs., Hastings, N.Y., 1984—. Instr. introduction to law office mgmt. seminars Assn. Legal Adminstrs., N.Y.C., 1984. Editor: The ABA Guide to Professional Managers in the Law Office, 1996; contbr. numerous articles to profl. jours. Mem. ABA (bd. dirs. law practice mgmt. div. 2000—), N.Y. Assn. Legal Adminstrs. (v.p. 1982-83), Internat. Assn. Legal Adminstrs. (asst. regional v.p. 1983-84, regional v.p. 1984-85), Nat. Soc. Tax Profls. (cert. tax profl.), Am. Mgmt. Assn., Inst. Cert. Profl. Mgrs. (cert.), ABA, Inst. Cert. Mgmt. Accts., Mensa, Beta Gamma Sigma, Sigma Iota Epsilon. Home and Office: 445 Broadway Hastings On Hudson NY 10706 E-mail: cthornlow@concinnityservices.com, lawbucks@aol.com, CRTinNY@aol.com

THORNTON, D. WHITNEY, II, lawyer; b. Miami, Fla., Oct. 17, 1946; s. Dade Whitney and Hilda (Bryan) T.; m. Jane Collis, Nov. 27, 1971; children: Bryan Whitney, Elizabeth Jane, Virginia Anne. BA, Washington and Lee U., 1968, JD cum laude, 1970. Bar: Va. 1970, D.C. 1976, U.S. Ct. Appeals (4th cir.) 1978, U.S. Supreme Ct. 1980, Calif. 1987, U.S. Ct. Appeals (9th cir.) 1987. Atty. Naval Air Sys. Command, Dept. Navy, Washington, 1970-73; asst. counsel to comptr. Dept. Navy, 1973-74, asst. to gen. counsel, 1974-76; assoc. Sullivan & Beauregard, Washington, 1976-77, ptnr., 1977-81, Bowman, Conner, Touhey & Thornton, Washington, 1981-83; pres. Continental Maritime Industries, Inc., San Francisco, 1983-87; ptnr. Dempsey, Bastianelli, Brown & Touhey, 1987-91, Seyfarth Shaw, San Francisco, 1992—. Contbr. articles to profl. jours. Mem. ABA (pub. contract law sect., chmn. suspension and debarment com. 1977), FBA (vice chmn. govt. contracts coun., Disting. Svc. award 1981), Washington Golf and Country Club (Arlington, Va.), Blackhawk Country Club (Danville, Calif.). Republican. Methodist. Construction, Government contracts and claims, General civil litigation. Office: Seyfarth Shaw 101 California St Ste 2900 San Francisco CA 94111-5858 E-mail: wthornton@sf.seyfarth.com

THORNTON, EDWARD ROBERT, JR. lawyer; b. Manchester, N.H., July 27, 1939; s. Edward Robert and Rita Marie (Kirby) T.; m. Jeanie Cameron Raymond, Aug. 21, 1965 (div. June 1980); m. Kathleen Elizabeth Herod, Aug. 28, 1981; children: Kara, Tara, Meaghan, Maura, Shaunna. AB, Dartmouth Coll., 1961; JD, U. Maine, 1965. Bar: N.H. 1965, U.S. Dist. Ct. N.H. 1965, U.S. Tax Ct. 1977, U.S. Supreme Ct. 1977. Ptnr. Thornton & Thornton, P.A., Manchester, 1965—; spl. justice Derry Dist. Ct. 1987—, instr. bus. law Mt. St. Mary's Coll., Hooksett, N.H., 1966-67. State parliamentarian N.H. Jaycees, 1969; merit badge counselor Boy Scouts Am., Manchester, 1965—; fund raiser Cath. Charities of N.H., Manchester, 1965—; bd. dirs. Greater Manchester chpt. Nat. Coun. on Alcoholism, 1981—, Farnum Ctr. Rehab. Ctr, 1985—; participant People's Law Sch., 1989; mem. adv. bd. substance abuse program Manchester High Sch. West, 1987—. Mem. ABA (com. on small firms 1980—, subcom. on assocs. 1980—, com. on part-time and spl. justices, subcom. computers in small firms 1982—, sect. on jud. adminstrn.), N.H. Bar Assn. (participant various programs, mem. Hillsborough County case monitoring com. 1983—, com. on profl. continuity 1981—, com. coop. with cts. 1983—, lawyers asst. com. 1986—, pres. Pro Bono Lawyer of Yr. 1986, pres. Spl. Achievement award 1988), Manchester Bar Assn. (dist. ct. system improvement com. 1978-79, Hillsborough County Law Libr. com. 1983-84), Assn. Trial Lawyers Am. (state del. 1985—), N.H. Trial Lawyers Assn. (founding mem., treas. 1977-78, bd. govs. 1977—, pres. 1983-84, various coms. 1977—, mem. of the decade 1988), N.H. Conveyancers Coun., N.H. Dist. and Mcpl. Ct. Judges Assn., Am. Judges Assn. State civil litigation, Personal injury, Real property. Office: Thornton & Thornton PA 771 Chestnut St Manchester NH 03104-3011

THORNTON, MICHAEL PAUL, lawyer; b. Lexington, Ky., May 13, 1948; s. Paul Alfred and Wilma Elsa (Hasekoester) T.; m. Deborah Phillips Davis, July 7, 1979; children— Barrett Parker, Katherine Davis. A.B., Dartmouth Coll., 1972; J.D., Vanderbilt U., 1975. Bar: N.H. 1975, U.S. Dist. Ct. N.H. 1975, Maine 1979, U.S. Dist. Ct. Maine 1979, Mass. 1982, U.S. Dist. Ct. Mass. 1982, U.S. Ct. Claims 1980. Assoc. Burns, Bryant, Hinchey, Cox & Shea, Dover, N.H., 1975-78; ptnr. Mulvey & Thornton, Portsmouth, N.H., 1978-80, Thornton & Early, Boston, 1980— . Served with USMC, 1966-68, Vietnam. Mem. ABA, Assn. Trial Lawyers Am. Democrat. Federal civil litigation, Environmental. Home: 1 Devonshire Pl Apt 2006 Boston MA 02109-3514 Office: Thornton & Early 200 Portland St Boston MA 02114-1722

THORNTON, RAY, state supreme court justice, former congressman; b. Conway, AR, July 16, 1928; s. R.H. and Wilma (Stephens) T.; m. Betty Jo Mann, Jan. 27, 1956; children: Nancy, Mary Jo, Stephanie. B.A., Yale, 1950; J.D., U. Ark., 1956. Bar: Ark. 1956, U.S. Supreme Ct 1956. Pvt. practice in, Sheridan and Little Rock, 1956-70; atty. gen. Ark., 1971-73; mem. 93d-95th Congresses from 4th Ark. dist.; exec. dir. Quachita Bapt. U./Henderson State U. Joint Ednl. Consortium, Arkadelphia, Ark., 1979-80; pres. Ark. State U., Jonesboro and Beebe, 1980-84, U. Ark. System, Fayetteville, Little Rock, Pine Bluff, Monticello, 1984-89; mem. 102nd-104th Congresses from 2d Ark. dist., 1991-96; assoc. justice Ark. Supreme Ct., 1997—. Chmn. Ark. Bd. Law Examiners, 1967-70; Del. 7th Ark. Constl. Conv., 1969-70 Chmn. pres.'s devel. council Harding Coll., Searcy, Ark., 1971-73. Served with USN, 1951-54, Korea. Mem. AAAS (chmn. com. on sci., engring. and public policy 1980). Office: PO Box 826 Little Rock AR 72203-0826

THORNTON, ROBERT FLOYD, lawyer; b. Willard, Ohio, Jan. 27, 1932; s. Martin Floyd and Rosemary (Boehringer) T.; m. Joan Shanefelter, June 28, 1952; children— Rebecca, Kathryn, Alec, Andrew, Aaron. B.B.A., Ohio State U., 1955; LL.B., 1958. Bar: Ohio 1958, U.S. Dist. Ct. (no. dist.) Ohio 1966, U.S. Ct. Appeals (6th cir.) 1969. Ptnr. firm Thornton, Thornton & Harwood, Willard, Ohio, 1958— ; law dir. City of Willard, 1960-68. Mem. bd. edn. Willard City Sch. Dist., 1971-79. Served to 1st lt. U.S. Army, 1955-57. Mem. Huron County Bar Assn. (pres. 1984), Ohio State Bar Assn. (del. 1978-82), Ohio Acad. Trial Lawyers (pres. 1975-76), Ohio State Bar Found., Order of Coif. Roman Catholic. Lodge: Elks. State civil litigation, General practice, Personal injury. Home: 46 Hillcrest Dr Willard OH 44890-1609 Office: Thornton Thornton & Harwood 111 Myrtle Ave Willard OH 44890-1424

THORPE, NORMAN RALPH, lawyer, automobile company executive, retired air force officer; b. Carlinville, Ill., Oct. 17, 1934; s. Edwin Everett and Imogene Midas (Hayes) T.; m. Elaine Frances Pritzman, Nov. 1, 1968; children: Sarah Elizabeth, Carrie Rebecca. AB in Econs., U. Ill., 1956, JD, 1958; LLM in Pub. Internat. Law, George Washington U., 1967. Bar: Ill. 1958, Mich. 1988, U.S. Supreme. Ct. 1969. Commd. 2d lt. USAF, 1956, advanced through grades to brig. gen., 1983; legal advisor U.S. Embassy, Manila, 1969-72; chief internat. law hdqrs. USAF, Washington, 1972-77; staff judge adv. 21st Air Force, McGuire AFB, N.J., 1977-80, USAF Europe, Ramstein AB, Fed. Republic Germany, 1980-84; comdr. Air Force Contract Law Ctr., Wright-Patterson AFB, Ohio, 1984-88, ret., 1988; mem. legal staff, group counsel GM Def. and Power Products Gen. Motors Corp., Detroit, 1988—. Member adv. group Dept. of Def. Blue Ribbon Com. on Code of Conduct, 1975; USAF del. Internat. Aero. and Astronautical Fedn., Budapest, 1983; adj. prof. U. Dayton Sch. Law, 1986-87; partnership counsel U.S. Advanced Battery Consortium, Legal Advisor U.S. Coun. Automotive Rsch., Chrysler Corp., Ford Motor Co., GM, 1990—. Contbr. articles to profl. jours. Staff mem. Commn. on Police Policies and Procedures, Dayton, 1986; trustee Dayton Philharm. Orch., 1987-88. Recipient Disting. Svc. medal Legion of Merit. Mem. ABA (chmn. com. internat. law sect. 1977-80, coun. mem. pub. contract law sect. 1986-88, chmn. com. pub. contract law sect. 1988-95, chair-elect pub. contract law sect. 2000-01, vice chair 1999-2000, chair-elect 2000-01, chair 2001-02), Air Force Assn., Dayton Coun. on World Affairs, Army/Navy Club, Detroit Econ. Club. Republican. Avocations: music, piano, gardening. Contracts commercial, Government contracts and claims, Private international. Home: 498 Abbey Rd Birmingham MI 48009-5618 Office: Gen Motors Corp Legal Staff 300 Renaissance Ctr Detroit MI

THORSON, ANDREW H. lawyer; b. Muskegon, Mich., Dec. 28, 1966; married, Aug. 21, 1993. BA, Mich. State U., 1989; LLM, Kyoto (Japan) U., 1998; JD, Boston U., 1993. Bar: Mich. 1993, Calif. 1998; cert. fgn. lawyer, Japan. Assoc. Dickinson Wright PLLC, Detroit, 1993-95; fgn. legal trainee Ohebashi Law Offices, Osaka, Japan, 1996-97; assoc. Graham & James LLP, L.A., 1998-2000; sr. assoc. Dorsey & Whitney LLP, Minato-ku, Tokyo, 2000—. Contbr. articles to law jours. Monbusho fellow Ministry Edn., Japan, 1995-98 General corporate, Private international, Mergers and acquisitions. Office: Dorsey & Whitney LLP 4-3-1 Toranomon Minato-ku Tokyo 105-6016 Japan

THORSON, STEVEN GREG, lawyer; b. Van Nuys, Calif., Feb. 7, 1948; s. Robert G. and Ruth C. T.; m. Patricia Lynn LaPointe, Aug. 3, 1974; 1 child, Kai Johannes. BA, St. Olaf Coll., 1977; JD, Hamline U., 1980. Bar: Minn. 1980, U.S. Dist. Ct. Minn. 1980, U.S. Tax Ct. 1980, U.S. Ct. Appeals (8th cir.) 1980. Pres. Thorson & Berg, Maple Grove, Minn., 1990-99; with Barna, Guzy & Steffen, Ltd. Attys. at Law, Mpls., 1999—. Lectr. continuing legal edn., 1986—; apptd. to Minn. State Bar Assn. Commn. on Unauthorized Practice of Law, 1990-92; atty. for Columbus Twp. (Anoka County), 1981-96; mem. residential real estate com. Minn. State Bar Assn., 1992—. Mem. ch. coun. Peace Luth. Ch. Named One of Minn. Top Lawyers, Mpls/St. Paul mag., 1998, 2000, 01. Mem. ABA, Minn. State Bar Assn. (real property coun., chair publs. com. 2001—), Hennepin County Bar Assn. (chmn. purchase agreement com. 1986-88), Anoka County Bar Assn. (pres. real estate sect. 1988). Avocations; alpine and nordic skiing. Land use and zoning (including planning), Municipal (including bonds), Real property. Home: 12071 Norway St NW Minneapolis MN 55448-2243 Office: 400 Northtown Fin Plz 200 Coon Rapids Blvd NW Ste 400 Minneapolis MN 55433-5894 E-mail: sthorson@bgslaw.com

THOYER, JUDITH REINHARDT, lawyer; b. Mt. Vernon, N.Y., July 29, 1940; d. Edgar Allen and Florence (Mayer) Reinhardt; m. Michael E. Thoyer, June 30, 1963; children: Erinn Thoyer Rhodes, Michael John. AB with honors, U. Mich., 1961; LLB summa cum laude, Columbia U., 1965. Bar: N.Y. 1966, D.C. 1984. Law libr. U. Ghana, Accra, Africa, 1963-64; assoc. Paul, Weiss, Rifkind, Wharton & Garrison, N.Y.C., 1966-75, ptnr., 1975—. Mem. TriBar Opinion Com., 1995—. Bd. visitors Law Sch. Columbia U., N.Y.C., 1991—; bd. dirs. Women's Action Alliance, N.Y.C., 1975-89, pro bono counsel, 1975-97; mem. Women's Coun. Dem. Senatorial, campaign com., 1993-97; organizing com. Alumnae Columbia Law Sch., 1996—. Mem. N.Y. County Lawyers Assn. (mem. securities and exchs. com. 1976-98), Assn. of Bar of City of N.Y. (mem. securities regulation com. 1976-79, mem. recruitment of lawyers com. 1980-82, mem. spl. com. on mergers, acquisitions and corp. control contests 1996—). Home: 1115 5th Ave Apt 3B New York NY 10128-0100 Office: Paul Weiss Rifkind Et Al 1285 Ave of Americas New York NY 10019-6028

THRAILKILL, DANIEL B. lawyer; b. Sept. 21, 1957; BSBA, U. Ark., 1979; JD, Univ. Ark., 1981. Bar: Ark. 1982, Tex. 1988, U.S. Dist. Ct. (eas. and we. dists.) Ark. 1982, U.S. Dist. Ct. (ea. dist.) Okla. 1995, U.S. Ct. Appeals (8th cir.) 1983, U.S. Supreme Ct. 1985. Ptnr. Page, Thrailkill & McDaniel, P.A., Mena, Ark., 1981—. Assoc. prof., lectr. rich Mountain C.C.; assoc. justice Ark. Supreme Ct., 1996—; city atty. Cities of Mena and Hatfield. Mem.: ATLA, ABA, Ark. Bar Assn. (bd. govs., tenured del.), Ark. Trial Lawyers Assn., Lions Club, Phi Alpha Delta. Methodist. General practice, Personal injury, Real property. Home: 200 Craig St Mena AR 71953-2427 Office: Page Thrailkill & McDaniel 311 DeQueen St Courthouse Sq W Mena AR 71953

THRASHER, LOUIS MICHAEL, lawyer; b. Jamestown, N.Y., Mar. 9, 1938; s. James W. Thrasher and Elizabeth E. Brill; divorced; children— Lisa M., Christopher M. A.B., Alfred U., 1960; J.D., U. Cin., 1967; M.P.A., Harvard U., 1974. Bar: Ohio, 1967, U.S. Supreme Ct. 1978, Nebr. 1981. Trial atty. U.S. Dept. Justice, Washington, 1967-70, dir. west coast field office civil rights div., Los Angeles 1970-71, dep. chief voting section, Washington, 1971-72, assoc. dir. office instns., 1972-74, dir. office spl. litigation, 1974-78, spl. counsel litigation, 1978-80; chief criminal div. U.S. Atty's. Office, San Francisco, 1980-81; ptnr. Mattson, Ricketts, et al, Lincoln, Nebr., 1981— . Bd. editors Law Rev. U. Cin., 1966-67. Served to 1st lt. U.S. Army, 1961-63. Recipient Atty. Gen's. Spl. Achievement award U.S. Dept. Justice, 1980. Mem. ABA, Nebr. Bar. Assn., Lincoln Bar Assn., Assn. Trial Lawyers Am., Nebr. Trial Lawyers Assn., U.S. Supreme Ct. Hist. Soc., Order of Coif. Federal civil litigation, State civil litigation. Office: Mattson Ricketts et al 1401 S 1st St Lincoln NE 68502-1902

THROWER, RANDOLPH WILLIAM, lawyer; b. Tampa, Fla., Sept. 5, 1913; s. Benjamin Key and Ora (Hammond) T.; m. Margaret Munroe, Feb. 2, 1939; children: Margaret (Mrs. W. Thomas MacCary), Patricia (Mrs. John R. Barmeyer), Laura (Mrs. David T. Harris, Jr.), Randolph William, Mary (Mrs. George B. Wickham). Grad., Ga. Mil. Acad., 1930; BPh, Emory U., 1934, J.D., 1936. Bar: Ga. bar 1935, D.C. bar 1953. Partner Sutherland, Asbill & Brennan, Atlanta, Washington, 1947-69, 71—. Commr. internal revenue, 1969-71; Lectr. bar, legal meetings; spl. agt. FBI, 1942-43; mem. Arthur Andersen & Co. Bd. of Rev., 1974-80, Nat. Council on Organized Crime, mem. exec. com., 1970-71 Past pres. Ga., Met. Atlanta mental health assns.; chmn. City of Atlanta Bd. Ethics 1981-93; past trustee Emory U., Clark Coll.; past chmn., trustee Wesleyan Coll.; bd. govs. Woodward Acad.; past chmn. bd. visitors Emory U. Served as capt. USMCR, 1944-45. Mem. Atlanta Legal Aid Soc. (past pres.), Emory U. Alumni Assn. (past pres.), ABA (chmn. spl. com. on survey local needs 1971-78, past chmn. sect. taxation, mem. ho. of dels. 1964-66, 74-89), Ga. Bar Assn., Atlanta Bar Assn. (past pres.), Am. Bar Found. (dir. 1980-88, pres. 1986-88, medal 1993), Am. Law Inst., Atlanta Lawyers Club (past pres.), U.S. Claims Ct. Bar Assn. (pres. 1987-88), Phi Delta Phi. Republican. Methodist. Clubs: Commerce (Atlanta), Capital City (Atlanta), Piedmont Driving (Atlanta); Metropolitan (Washington). Estate planning, Estate taxation, Taxation, general. Home: 2240 Woodward Way NW Atlanta GA 30305-4043 Office: Sutherland Asbill & Brennan Ste 2300 999 Peachtree St NE Atlanta GA 30309 E-mail: rwthrower@sablaw.com

THURMAN, ANDREW EDWARD, lawyer; b. Raleigh, N.C., May 11, 1954; s. William Gentry and Peggy Lou (Brown) T.; m. Patricia Thurman, May 19, 1979 (dec. 1989); children: Gentry Brown, Harrison Beauchamp, Andrew Guilford; m. Tracy Fletcher, Nov. 16, 1991; 1 child, Spencer Lee. BA, Columbia U., 1976; JD, Coll. William and Mary, 1979; MPH, U. Okla., 1984. Bar: Va. 1979, Okla. 1980, U.S. Ct. Appeals (10th cir.) 1981, U.S. Supreme Ct. 1985, Pa. 1988. Staff atty. Dept. of Human Services, Oklahoma City, 1979-80; counsel State of Okla. Teaching Hosps., 1980-84; mem. Miller, Dollarhide, Dawson & Shaw, 1984-87; ptnr. Berkman, Ruslander, Pohl, Lieber & Engel, Pitts., 1988-89; of counsel Buchanan Ingersoll, 1989; sr. v.p. and gen. counsel Forbes Health System, 1989-96; sr. counsel Allegheny Health Edn. & Rsch. Found., 1997-98; dep. gen. counsel Allegheny U. Hosps. West, 1998-99; asst. gen. counsel W. Penn. Allegheny Health Sys., 1999—; assoc. prof. Carneige-Mellon U., 2000—. Pres. Council of Neighborhood Assns., Oklahoma City, 1984, Lincoln Terr. Neighborhood Assn., Oklahoma City, 1984; trustee Rader Trust, Oklahoma City, 1980—; treas. Bd. dirs. State Okla. Tchg. Hosps. Found., Oklahoma City, 1984-87, Newman Meml. Hosp., 1983-87, Willowview Hosp., Spencer, Okla., 1985-87, Allegheny U. Med. Ctrs., 1997—, AUMC/Cannonsburg Ambulance Svc., 1997—, Allegheny U. Hosps. West, 1998—, Diversified Health Group, 1998-99, Allegheny Med. Practices Network, 1999—, Allegheny Speciality Practice Network, 1999—; chair HCWP Ethics Task Force, 1993-2000. Fellow Am. Health Lawyers Assn.; mem. St. Anthony Hall Club of N.Y.C. (pres. 1976), Rivers Club. Democrat. Presbyterian. Avocation: reading detective novels. Health. Home: 106 Richmond Dr Pittsburgh PA 15215-1039 Office: Allegheny Gen Hosp 320 E North Ave Pittsburgh PA 15212-4756 E-mail: athurman@wpahs.org, andy@thurmans.net

THURMOND, GEORGE MURAT, judge; b. Del Rio, Tex., Oct. 22, 1930; s. Roger H. and Day (Hamilton) T.; m. Elsiejean Davis, June 27, 1959; children: Carolyn Day, Georganna, Sarah Gail. BA, U. of the South, 1952; JD, U. Tex., 1955. Bar: Tex. 1955. Ptnr. Montague & Thurmond, Del Rio, 1955-69; judge Tex. Dist. Ct. (63rd dist.), 1970-2000, sr. judge, 2000—. Presiding judge 6th Adminstrv. Region, Del Rio, 1983-87; chmn. jud. sect. State Bar Tex., 1988-89. Editor: U. Tex. Law Review, 1955. Rep. Tex. Ho. of Reps., 1955-58. Mem. ABA, Tex. Bar Assn. Democrat. Episcopalian. Avocations: jogging, traditional jazz, model railroading. Office: 243 W Strickland St Del Rio TX 78840-5729 E-mail: gmthur@delrio.com

THURMOND, GERALD PITTMAN, lawyer; b. Madison, Ga., Aug. 20, 1936; s. Gilbert Duard and Viola Elnora (Pittman) T.; m. Ann Sexton, May 21, 1960; children: Gerald Pittman, William R., Susan A. BBA, U. Ga., 1958, JD cum laude, 1964; LLM in Taxation, Georgetown U., 1981. Bar: Ga. 1963, Pa. 1970, D.C. 1976, U.S. Dist. (no. dist.) Ga., U.S. Dist. Ct. (we. dist.) Pa., U.S. Ct. Appeals (5th dist.), Tex. 1988. Atty. Troutman, Sams, Schroder & Lockerman, Atlanta, 1964-68; staff atty., gen. counsel Gulf Oil Corp., Pitts., 1963-73, asst. to chmn. bd., pres. and exec. v.p.'s, 1973, adminstrv. v.p., 1974-75, Washington counsel, 1975-83, sr. counsel, 1983-85, corp. asst. sec., corp. affairs, Chevron Corp., 1985-87, asst. gen. counsel natural gas, 1987-91. Gulf Oil Co.; assoc. gen. counsel, Chevron Products Co., 1992— employee chmn. United Fund of Houston, 1975. Served to 1st lt. AUS, 1958-60. Mem. ABA, D.C. Bar Assn., Ga. State Bar, Tex. State Bar, Allegheny County Bar Assn., Ga. State Soc. (bd. dirs.), Houston C. of C., U.S. C. of C. (coun.l on antitrust policy), NAM (com. on corp. governance and competition, com. on regulatory reform), Met. Racquet Club, Phi Kappa Phi. Episcopalian. Home: 1 E Broad Oaks Dr Houston TX 77056-1201 Office: 1301 Mckinney St Ste 2200 Houston TX 77010-3031

THURSWELL, GERALD ELLIOTT, lawyer; b. Detroit, Feb. 4, 1944; s. Harry and Lilyan (Zeitlin) T.; m. Lynn Satovsky, Sept. 17, 1967 (div. Aug. 1978); children: Jennifer, Lawrence; m. Judith Linda Bendix, Sept. 2, 1978 (div. May 1999); chldren: Jeremy, Lindsey. LLB with distinction, Wayne State U., 1967. Bar: Mich. 1968, N.Y. 1984, D.C. 1985, Colo. 1990, Ill. 1992, U.S. Dist. Ct. (ea. dist.) Mich. 1968, U.S. Ct. Appeals (7th cir.) 1968, U.S. Supreme Ct. 1994. Student asst. to U.S. Atty. Eas. Dist. Mich., Detroit, 1966; assoc. Zwerdling, Miller, Klimist & Maurer, 1967-68; st. prnt. The Thurswell Law Firm, Southfield, Mich. Arbitrator Am. Arbitration Assn., Detroit, 1969—; mediator Wayne County Cir. Ct., Mich., 1983—, Oakland County Cir. Ct. Mich., 1984—, also facilitator, 1991; twp. atty. Royal Oak Twp., Mich., 1982—; lectr. Oakland County Bar Assn. People's Law Sch., 1988. Pres. Powder Horn Estates Subdivsn. Assn., West Bloomfield, Mich., 1975, United Fund, West Bloomfield, 1976. Arthur F. Lederly scholar Wayne State U. Law Sch., 1965; Wayne State U. Law Sch. grad. profl. scholar, 1965, 66. Mem. ATLA (treas. Detroit met. chpt. 1986-87, v.p. 1989-90, pres. 1991-93), Mich. Bar Assn. (investigator/arbitrator grievance bd., atty. discipline bd., chmn. hearing panel), Mich. Trial Lawyers Assn. (legis. com. on govtl. immunity 1984), Detroit Bar Assn. (lawyer referral com., panel pub. adv. com. jud. candidates), Oakland County Bar Assn., Skyline Club (Southfield). State civil litigation, Personal injury. Office: The Thurswell Law Firm 1000 Town Ctr Ste 500 Southfield MI 48075-1221

THYNESS, ERIK, lawyer; b. Oslo, Norway, May 30, 1961; s, Paul and Ellen Marie Thyness; m. Ingunn Almas, Dec. 30, 1989; children: Cathinka, Christian, Carl. Cand. jur., U. Oslo, 1987. Bar: Norway 1989. Inhouse counsel Norsk Hydro ASA, Oslo, 1988-93; assoc. judge Soer-Gudbrandsal Dist. Ct., Lillehammer, Norway, 1989-90; gen. counsel Hafslund Nycomed ASA, Oslo, 1993-96; ptnr. Wirsholm Mellbye & Bech, 1996—. Contbg. author: Cross-Border Mergers in Europe, 1989; contbg. author: Mergers and Acquisitions, 1998. Lt. col. Norwegian Army, 1980—. Mem. Norwegian Bar Assn. Mergers and acquisitions, Securities, Corporate taxation. Office: Wiersholm Mellbye & Bech Ruseloekkvein 26 Oslo 0251 Norway Fax: 47 21 02 10 01. E-mail: erik.thyness@wiersholm.no

TIBBLE, DOUGLAS CLAIR, lawyer; b. Joliet, Ill., May 26, 1952; BA, DePaul U., 1974; JD, Syracuse U., 1977, MPA, 1978. Bar: Ill., U.S. Dist. Ct. (no. dist.) Ill., U.S. Ct. Appeals (7th cir.), U.S. Supreme Ct. Ptnr. McBride, Baker & Coles, Oakbrook Terrace, Ill., 1996—. Mem. ABA, DuPage County Bar Assn., Chgo. Bar Assn. General civil litigation, Contracts commercial, Construction. Office: McBride Baker & Coles 1 Mid America Plz Ste 1000 Oakbrook Terrace IL 60181-4710 E-mail: tibble@mbc.com

TICE, DOUGLAS OSCAR, JR. federal bankruptcy judge; b. Lexington, N.C., May 2, 1933; s. Douglas Oscar Sr. and Lila Clayton (Wright) T.; m. Janet N. Capps, Feb. 28, 1959 (div. Sept. 1976); children: Douglas Oscar III, Janet E.; m. Martha Murdoch Edwards, June 8, 1996. BS, U. N.C., 1955, JD, 1957. Bar: N.C. 1957, U.S. Ct. Appeals (4th cir.) 1964, Va. 1970, U.S. Dist. ct. (ea. dist.) Va. 1976, U.S. Bankruptcy Ct. (ea. dist.) Va. 1976. Exec. sec. N.C. Jud. Coun., Raleigh, 1958-59; assoc. Baucom & Adams, 1959-61; trial atty. Office Dist. Coun., IRS, Richmond, Va., 1961-70; corp. atty. Carlton Industries, Inc., 1970-75; ptnr. Hubard, Tice, Marchant &

Samuels, P.C., 1975-87; judge U.S. Bankruptcy Ct. (ea. dist.), Richmond, Norfolk, Alexandria, Va., 1987-99, chief judge, 1999—. Co-author: Monument & Boulevard, Richmond's Grand Avenues, 1996; contbr. articles to profl. jours. Vice pres. Richmond Pub. Forum, 1976-80, com. chmn. Richmond Forum, Inc., 1986-2001; past pres. Richmond Civil War Roundtable, mem., 1965—; bd. dirs. Epilepsy Assn. Va., Inc., 1976-87. Capt. USAR, 1957-66. Mem. ABA, Va. Bar Assn., City of Richmond Bar Assn., Am. Bankruptcy Inst., Nat. Conf. Bankruptcy Judges, So. Hist. Assn., Va. Hist. Soc., Old Dominion Sertoma (pres. Richmond chpt. 1967). Home: 2037 W Grace St Richmond VA 23220-2003 Office: US Bankruptcy Ct 1100 E Main St Ste 341 Richmond VA 23219-3538 E-mail: home:dotice@aol.com, bus.douglas_tice@vaeb.uscourts.gov

TICE, LAURIE DIETRICH, lawyer; b. Houston, Apr. 9, 1959; d. Donald Vernon and June (Reagan) Dietrich; m. Michael Dean Tice, Feb. 25, 1984 (div. May 1991); children: Rachel Michele, Rebekah Leigh. ABA approved, Southwestern Paralegal Inst., Houston, 1989; BA in History with highest honors, U. Tex., El Paso, 1994; JD, U. Tex., 1997. Bar: Tex. 1997. Legal sec. Gant & Juarez, Carlsbad, N.Mex., 1979-80; dep. clk. 5th Jud. Dist. Ct. N.Mex., 1980-82; legal asst. Hinkle, Cox, Eaton, Coffield & Hensley, Roswell, N.Mex., 1982-86, Kemp, Smith, Duncan & Hammond, El Paso, Tex., 1986-92; assoc. McGinnis, Lochridge & Kilgore L.L.P., Austin, 1997-99, Rogers & Whitley, L.L.P., Austin, 1999—. Elder, chair resource and planning com., Univ. Presbyn. Ch., Austin, 2000-; mem. UPC Hard Knox Tennis Team. Franklin Myers Endowed Presdl. scholar, 1994-95, Judge Wilson Cohen Endowed Presdl. scholar, 1995-96, Israel Dreeben Endowed Meml. scholar, 1995-96. Mem. ABA, Tex. Bar Assn., Travis County Bar Assn. (dir. real estate sect.), Travis County Women Lawyers Assn. (membership com., dir., treas. 2001-02), Austin Young Lawyers Assn., Golden Key, Mortar Board (pres.), Beta Sigma Phi (rec. sec. 1984-85), Alpha Lambda Delta, Phi Alpha Theta (pres., sec.), Alpha Chi. Democrat. General corporate, Real property. Home: 4404 Travis Country Cir Apt A2 Austin TX 78735-6601 E-mail: ltice@rwllp.com

TICHENOR, JAMES LEE, lawyer, writer, filmmaker; b. Phila., Feb. 8, 1943; s. LeGrand L. and Elizabeth L. (Panetta) T.; m. Ellen Harriet Wertheim, 1968 (div. 1976); children: Dylan M., Aaron A.; m. Nancy Louise Keller, Dec. 2, 1976; children: James E., Diane E. BA, Antioch Coll., 1976; JD, Rutgers U., 1984. Bar: Pa. 1984. Pres. Cinetel Film Prodns., Phila., 1978-83; pvt. practice in law, 1984-86; atty., advisor U.S. Dept. Housing and Urban Devel., 1986-91, assoc. field counsel, 1991—. Vol. lawyer Phila. Vol. Lawyers for Arts, 1984-87; founding mem. Baha'i Justice Soc., 1986-88. Editor (film) Boreal Forest, 1979 (Alberta Film Festival award 1979). Chmn. Spiritual Assembly of Baha'is of Phila., 1968-94, 2000—. With U.S. Army, 1964-66. Recipient Hammer award, Nat. Performance Rev. Fair Housing Processing Procedures, 1998. Mem. Wapiti Archers. Avocations: canoeing, archery, genealogy. Office: US Dept Housing and Urban Devel Office Counsel 100 Penn Sq E Fl 11 Philadelphia PA 19107-3322

TICKNER, ELLEN MINDY, lawyer; b. Phila., May 30, 1951; d. Arnold Charles Tickner and Priscilla Frances (Wertlieb) Klomparens. B.S., Northwestern U., 1973; postgrad. U. Miami, Coral Gables, Fla., 1973-74; J.D., DePaul U., 1976. Bar: Ill. 1977, Mich. 1977, U.S. Dist. Ct. (ea. dist.) Mich. 1979, U.S. Ct. Appeals (6th cir.) 1986, U.S. Dist. Ct. (no. dist.) Calif. 1989. Legal research and writing instr. U. Detroit Sch. Law, 1976-77; staff atty. Juvenile Defender Office, Detroit, 1977-79; litigation atty. U. Mich. Inst. Gerontology, Ann Arbor, 1980; clin. instr. law U. Mich. Law Sch., Ann Arbor, 1980-82, clin. asst. prof. law, 1982-83; assoc. Raymond, Rupp, Wienberg, Stone & Zuckerman, P.C., Troy, Mich., 1984-87, assoc. Miller, Canfield, Paddock & Stone, Detroit, 1987—. Bd. dirs. Family Law Project, Ann Arbor, 1980-83, Mich. chpt. Nat. Com. for Prevention of Child Abuse, Lansing, 1980-82. Contbr. articles to legal jours. Mem. Women Lawyers Assn. of Mich. (bd. dirs. 1981-82), 13th Nat. Conf. Women and the Law (steering com. 1981-82), ABA (litigation, real property, probate and trust law sects.), Oakland County Bar Assn. (vice chmn. continuing legal edn. com. 1986-88, chair 1988-90), State Bar Mich. (standing com. on mandatory continuing legal edn. 1989—), Detroit Bar Assn. General civil litigation, Computer, Securities. Office: Miller Canfield Paddock & Stone 150 W Jefferson Ave Ste 2500 Detroit MI 48226-4416

TIDWELL, WILLIAM C., III, lawyer; b. Haleyville, Ala., May 21, 1946; s. William C. and Lera (Jones) T.; m. Gloria Myrick, Jan. 24, 1970. BSChemE, U. Ala., 1969, JD, 1972. Bar: La. 1972, Ala. 1972, U.S. Dist. Ct. (so. dist.) Ala. 1976, U.S. Ct. Appeals (5th cir.) 1972, (11th cir.) 1981, U.S. Supreme Ct. 1979, U.S. Dist. Ct. (mid. dist.) Ala. 1982, U.S. Dist. Ct. (no. dist.) Ala. 1986, U.S. Dist. Ct. (ea. dist.) La. 1989. Assoc. firm Kullman, Lang, Inman & Bee, New Orleans, 1972-75; ptnr. firm Hand, Arendall, Bedsole, Greaves & Johnston, Mobile, Ala., 1975—; speaker Ala. Continuing Legal Edn. of Bar, Tuscaloosa, Ala.; mem. planning com. Multi-State Labor and Employment Law Seminar, 1987—. Mem. equal employment opportunity com. Def. Research Inst., 1979—; mem. com. on devel. of law Nat. Labor Relations Act, 1982—. Mem. Ala. State Bar (chmn. labor law sect. 1986-87), Fed. Bar Assn. (pres. Mobile chpt. 1986-88), Mobile C. of C., Mobile Country Club, Athelstan Club. Methodist. Administrative and regulatory, Labor. Home: 169 S Georgia Ave Mobile AL 36604-2311 Office: Hand Arendall Bedsole Greaves & & Johnston 2800 1st Ave Mobile AL 36617-1754

TIERNEY, KEVIN JOSEPH, lawyer; b. Lowell, Mass., Dec. 13, 1951; s. Joseph Francis and Esther Rowena T. BS cum laude, Bowdoin Coll., 1973; JD, U. Maine, 1976. Bar: Maine 1976. Atty. Union Mutual Life Ins. Co., Portland, Maine, 1976-80, asst. counsel, 1980, 2d v.p., counsel, 1980-84, 2d v.p., counsel, corp. sec., 1984-86, UNUM Corp., Portland, 1986-89, v.p., corp. counsel, sec., 1989-91, gen. counsel, sr. v.p., sec., 1991-99. Bd. dirs. Pine Tree Alcoholism Treatment Ctr., Maine, 1977-84, So. Regional Alcoholism and Drug Abuse Coun., Maine, 1982-85; mem. radiation therapy tech. adv. com. So. Me. Vocat. Tech. Inst., 1985; trustee Portland Symphony Orch., 1990-99. Mem. Am. Soc. Corp. Secs., Am. Corp. Counsel Assn., Maine State Bar Assn., Cumberland County (Maine) Bar Assn., Assn. of Life Ins. Counsel. General corporate, Insurance, Mergers and acquisitions.

TIERNEY, MICHAEL EDWARD, lawyer; b. N.Y., July 16, 1948; s. Michael Francis and Margaret Mary (Creamer) T.; m. Alicia Mary Boldt, June 6, 1981; children: Colin, Madeleine. BA, St. Louis U., 1970, MBA, JD, St. Louis U., 1978. Bar: Mo. Assoc., law clk. Wayne L. Millsap, PC, St. Louis, 1977-80; staff atty. Interco. Inc., 1980-83; textile divsn. counsel Chromalloy Am. Corp., 1984-87; v.p., sec. P.N. Hirsch & Co., 1983-84; sr. counsel, asst. sec. Jefferson Smurfit Corp., 1987-92, v.p., gen. counsel, sec., 1993-99, Kinexus Corp., St. Louis, 1999—. Adv. bd. St. Louis Area Food Bank, 1980—. U.S. Army Security Agy., 1970-73. Mem. Racquet Club St. Louis, Old Warson Country Club. Republican. Roman Catholic. Avocations: sailing, squash. General corporate, Mergers and acquisitions, Securities. Home: 10 Twin Springs Ln Saint Louis MO 63124-1139 Address: Kinexus Corp 18500 Edison Ave Chesterfield MO 63005-3629

TIFFANY, JOSEPH RAYMOND, II, lawyer; b. Dayton, Ohio, Feb. 5, 1949; s. Forrest Fraser and Margaret Watson (Clark) T.; m. Terri Robbins, Dec. 1, 1984. AB magna cum laude, Harvard U., 1971; MS in Internat. Relations, London Sch. Econs., 1972; JD, U. Calif., Berkeley, 1975. Bar: U.S. Dist. Ct. (no. dist.) 1975, U.S. Dist. Ct. (ea. dist.) 1977, U.S. Ct. Appeals (9th cir.) 1982. Assoc. Pillsbury, Madison & Sutro, San Francisco, 1975-82, ptnr., 1983-2001, Pillsbury Winthrop LLP, San Francisco, 2001—. Mem. ABA (antitrust, intellectual property, litigation sects.), Calif. Bar Assn., Harvard Club. Federal civil litigation, State civil litigation, Libel. Office: Pillsbury Winthrop LLP 2550 Hanover St Palo Alto CA 94304-1115 E-mail: jtiffany@pillsburywinthrop.com

TIFFORD, ARTHUR W. lawyer; b. Bklyn., July 7, 1943; s. Herman and Dorothy (Kessler) T.; m. Barbara J. Sinreich, Aug. 15, 1965; children: Melissa Beth, Alexandra Lynn. BA, CUNY, 1965; JD, Bklyn. Law Sch., 1967. Bar: N.Y. 1967, Fla. 1967, U.S. Dist. Ct. (so. dist.) Fla. 1968, U.S. Ct. Mil. Appeals 1968, U.S. Ct. Appeals (5th cir.) 1971, U.S. Dist. Ct. (mid. dist.) Fla. 1979, U.S. Ct. Appeals (10th cir.) 1979, U.S. Ct. Appeals (1st cir.) 1982, U.S. Ct. Appeals (9th cir.) 1982, U.S. Ct. Appeals (11th cir.) 1981, U.S. Ct. Appeals (fed. cir.) 1985, U.S. Ct. Appeals (4th cir.) 1998, U.S. Claims Ct. 1985, U.S. Tax Ct. 1988. Rschr., mgr. clk. Cravath, Swaine & Moore, N.Y.C., 1967; asst. U.S. atty. U.S. Dept. Justice (so. dist. Fla.), Miami, 1971-72; pvt. practice, 1972—. With USMC, 1968-71, USMCR, 1971-92, ret. col. Mem. ABA, Am. Trial Lawyers Asns., Fla. Trial Lawyers Assn., Nat. Assn. Criminal Def. Lawyers, N.Y. Bar Assn., Fla. Bar Assn., Marine Corps Res. Officers Assn. (pres. Greater Miami chpt. 1978-79, 81-82, 84-85, nat. bd. dirs. 1987-89). Democrat. Avocations: writing, photography, parachuting, scuba diving, running. Home: 9980 SW 128th St Miami FL 33176-5632 Office: 1385 NW 15th St Miami FL 33125-1621 Fax: 305-325-1825. E-mail: tiffordlaw@aol.com

TIGANI, BRUCE WILLIAM, lawyer; b. Wilmington, Del., May 10, 1956; s. J. Vincent Jr. and Josephine C. (DeAngelis) T.; m. Janice Rowe, Sept. 25, 1982; children: Jessica Lynne, Bruce William Jr. Student, Georgetown U., 1974-75; BBS, U. Del., 1978; JD, Villanova U., 1981. Bar: Del. 1981, Pa. 1982, U.S. Dist. Ct. Del. 1982, U.S. Dist. Ct. (ea. dist.) Pa. 1982, U.S. Tax Ct. 1982. Assoc. Lord & Mulligan, Media, Pa., 1981-84, resident atty. Wilmington, 1984-87, ptnr., 1987-88; mng. ptnr. Werb, Tigani, Hood & Sullivan, 1988-99, Tigani & Hood LLP, Wilmington, 2000—. Del. to IRS, Mid. Altantic Regional liason. Mem. lay adv. bd. The Little Sisters of Poor; active Rep. Com. of State Del. Mem. ABA, Del. State Bar Assn. (chmn. tax sect. 1991-92, real estate sect., chair trusts and estates sect. 1997-98, lectr. bus. and tax seminars), Wilmington Tax Group (chmn. 1994-95), Del. State C. of C. (commerce tax com.), Estate Planning Coun. Del., Inc. (bd. dirs. 1993-95), Concord Country Club, Univ. and Whist Club Wilmington, Blue and Gold Club. Avocations: golf, softball. Estate planning, Real property, Taxation, general. Office: Tigani & Hood LLP PO Box 1471 1801 Mellon Bank Ctr 919 Market St Wilmington DE 19899-1471 E-mail: btigani@TiganihoodLaw.com

TIGHE, MARIA THERESA, project manager; b. Huntington, N.Y., Apr. 26, 1972; d. Thomas Richard and Theresa (Matarazzo) T. BS with honors, St. John's U., 1994; MBA in Gen. Mgmt., Dowling Coll.; cert. in e-bus. mgmt., NYU. Project mgr. Weil, Gotshal & Manges LLP, N.Y.C., 1994—. Cheerleader Arena Football, Albany, N.Y., 1992; active campaigns Rep. Party, Smithtown, N.Y., 1994—; Notary Pub., Assn. for Children for Inforcement of Support (ACES). student advisor Sage Jr. Coll., Albany, 1992; lobbyist Child Support Enforcement, Wash. Mem. Internat. Soc. Poets, Golden Key Honor Soc., Am. Bar Assn. Women Rainmakers, Nu Epsilon Delta. Avocations: writing poems, exercising. Office: Weil Gotshal & Manges LLP 767 5th Ave Fl Conc1 New York NY 10153-0119

TIKOSH, MARK AXENTE, lawyer; b. Arad, Banat, Romania, Aug. 17, 1955; came to U.S., 1981; s. Axente and Elena Ticosh; m. Mary Victoria Rotarescu, Sept. 10, 1979. BBA in Acctg. summa cum laude, Calif. State U., Fullerton, 1989; JD, U. of the Pacific, 1992, LLM, 1993. Bar: Calif. 1993. Acct., auditor II Orange County Probation Dept., 1984-88; pvt. practice Sacramento, 1993-94, Long Beach, 1994—. Cons. U. Banat Acad. Found., Timisoara, Romania, 1997—, mem. CATO Inst. Editor The Transnational Lawyer, 1991. Scholarship McGeorge Legal Edn. Endowment Found., 1989-90, Dana Found., 1992-93. Mem. Calif. State Bar Assn. (estate planning trust and probate law sect.), L.A. County Bar Assn. (litigation sect.), Cato Inst., Beta Gamma Sigma. Republican. Avocations: travel, history, philosophy. Appellate, Private international, Probate. Office: 800 E Ocean Blvd Ste 100 Long Beach CA 90802-5463

TILEWICK, ROBERT, lawyer; b. N.Y.C., Jan. 16, 1956; s. David and Helen (Fogel) T.; m. Susan Dara Tilewick; children: Naomi Seana, Benjamin Solomon. BA, Columbia U., 1977; JD, Temple U., 1985. Bar: N.Y. 1986, Ct. 1993, U.S. Dist. Ct. (so. and ea. dists.) N.Y. 1988, U.S. Ct. Appeals (2d cir.) 1989, U.S. Dist. Ct. Conn. 1991. Systems analyst, cons. Personnelmetrics, Inc., N.Y.C., 1977-80, 81-82; assoc. Cravath, Swaine & Moore, 1985-87, Paul, Weiss, Rifkind, Wharton & Garrison, N.Y.C., 1987-91, 96-97, Wiggin & Dana, New Haven, 1991-96, Kalow, Springut & Bressler, N.Y.C., 1997-99, Graham & James, N.Y.C., 1999—. Co-designer race timing system for N.Y.C. Marathon, 1977-82. NIH grantee Marine Biol. Lab., Woods Hole, Mass, 1980. Mem. ABA, N.Y.C. Bar Assn., Conn. Bar Assn., New Haven Bar Assn., Supreme Ct. Hist. Soc. Avocation: music. Federal civil litigation, General civil litigation. Office: 885 3rd Ave New York NY 10022-4834

TILLEY, NORWOOD CARLTON, JR. federal judge; b. Rock Hill, S.C., 1943; s. Norwood Carlton and Rebecca (Westbrook) T. BA, Wake Forest U., 1966, JD, 1969. Bar: N.C. 1969, U.S. Dist. Ct. (middle dist.) N.C. 1971. Law clk. to Hon. Eugene A Gordon, U.S. Dist. Judge Middle Dist. N.C., 1969-71; asst. U.S. atty. Mid. Dist. N.C., Greensboro, 1971-73, U.S. atty., 1974-77, U.S. dist. judge Durham, 1988—; ptnr. Osteen, Adams, Tilley & Walker, Greensboro, 1977-88. Instr. Wake Forest U. Sch. Law, 1980. Office: US Dist Ct PO Box 3443 Greensboro NC 27402-3443

TILLMAN, MASSIE MONROE, mediator, retired federal judge; b. Corpus Christi, Tex., Aug. 15, 1937; s. Clarence and Artie Lee (Stewart) T.; m. Karen Wright, July 2, 1993; children: Jeffrey Monroe, Holly. BBA, Baylor U., 1959, LLB, 1961. Bar: Tex. 1961, U.S. Dist. Ct. (no. dist.) Tex. 1961, U.S. Ct. Appeals (5th cir.) 1969, U.S. Supreme Ct. 1969; bd. cert. Personal Injury Trial Law, Tex. Ptnr. Herrick & Tillman, Ft. Worth, 1961-66; pvt. practice, 1966-70, 79-87; ptnr. Brown, Herman et al, 1970-78, Street, Swift et al, Ft. Worth, 1978-79; U.S. bankruptcy judge Ft. Worth divsn. No. Dist. Tex., 1987-2001; mediator, 2001—. Author: Tillman's Trial Guide, 1970; comments editor, case notes editor; mem. editl. bd. Baylor Law Rev., 1960-61. Mem. Ft. Worth Symphony League. Fellow Am. Bd. Trial Advocates, Tex. Bar Found.; mem. Ft. Worth/Tarrant County Bar (bd. dirs. 1969-70, v.p. 1970-71), Trial Attys.'s of Am., Nat. Conf. of Bankruptcy Judges, Am. Bankruptcy Inst., Tex. Trial Lawyers Assn. Republican. Baptist. Avocations: competition shotgun shooting, quail hunting. Address: PO Box 20213 Fort Worth TX 76102

TILLMAN, MICHAEL GERARD, lawyer; b. Ft. Wayne, Ind., Oct. 26, 1951; s. Robert Burl and Theresa Ellen (Till) T.; m. Joan Catharine McTigue, Dec. 19, 1981; children: Leah McTigue, Claire Tillman. BA, Harvard U., 1974; JD, U. Fla., 1984. Bar: Fla. 1985. Shareholder Scruggs & Carmichael, P.A., Gainesville, Fla., 1985-94, Coffey, Tillman, Kalishman & Owens, P.A., Gainesville, 1994-97, Wealth Strategies Collaborative, Gainesville, 1997-98, Tillman Rogers Tansey, Gainesville, 1998-99; pvt. practice, 1999—. Legal com. Arica Inst., N.Y.C., 1992-96; fellow, faculty mem. Inst., Global Ctr. for Wealth Strategies Planning. Pres. Gainesville Estate Planning Coun., Gainesville Cmty. Found. Mem. Fla. Bar (real property and probate sect. 1990—, mem. estate and trust tax com.), Nat. Network of Estate Planning Attys. Buddhist. Avocations: teaching T'ai Chi Chuan, swimming, triathlons. Estate planning. Home: 4457 SW 84th Pl Gainesville FL 32608 Office: Michael Tillman PA 5346 SW 91st Ter Gainesville FL 32608-7124

TILSE, CHRISTIAN, lawyer; b. Gummersbach, Germany, Jan. 9, 1947; s. Gunther and Eva Tilse; m. Ina Messerschmidt, June 13, 1980; children: Carsten, Axel, Justus, Felix. Dr. jur., Freiburg Univ., 1968. Asst. Münchener Rückversicherung AG, Munich, 1977; pvt. practice Dortmund, Germany, 1978—. Mem. Rotary. With Germany Army, 1966-68. Office: Menold & Aulinger Kleppingstr 9-11 Dortmund 44135 Germany Office Fax: 0231 958584951. E-mail: christian.tilse@menold-aulinger.de

TIMBERG, SIGMUND, retired lawyer; b. Antwerp, Belgium, Mar. 5, 1911; came to U.S., 1916, naturalized, 1921; s. Arnold and Rose (Mahler) T.; m. Eleanor Ernst, Sept. 22, 1940; children: Thomas Arnold, Bernard Mahler, Rosamund and Richard Ernst (twins). A.B., A.M., Columbia U., 1930, LL.B., 1933. Bar: N.Y. 1935, U.S. Supreme Ct. 1940, D.C. 1954. Sr. atty., solicitors' office Dept. Agr., 1933-35, chief, soil conservation sect., 1935-38; staff mem. Temporary Nat. Econ. Com., 1938-39; sr. atty. SEC, 1938-42; chief, property relations and indsl. orgn. div., reoccupation br. Bd. Econ. Warfare and Fgn. Econ. Adminstrn., 1942-44; spl. asst. to atty. gen., antitrust div. Dept. Justice, 1944-45, chief judgments and judgment enforcement sect., 1946-52; sec. UN Com. on Restrictive Bus. Practices, 1952-53; cons. UN, 1953-55, 62-64; pvt. law practice, 1954-88. Prof. law Georgetown U. Law School, 1952-54; faculty Parker Sch. Comparative Law, Columbia U., 1967-80; spl. counsel Senate Mil. Affairs Subcom. on Surplus Property Legislation, 1944; mem. Mission for Econ. Affairs, Am. Embassy, London, 1945; del. Anglo-Am. Telecommunications Conf., Bermuda, 1945, Geneva Copyright Conf., 1952; cons. Senate Patents Subcom., 1961, UN Patents Study, 1962-64, OAS, 1970; mem. adv. com. on fed. policy on indsl. innovation, patent and info. policy sub com., 1978-79, adv. com. on internat. investment, tech. and devel., 1979-85. Contbr. articles on antitrust, intellectual property and internat. law to legal periodicals. Mem. ABA, D.C. Bar Assn., Internat. Bar Assn., Internat. Law Assn., Am. Soc. Internat. Law, Washington Fgn. Law Soc., Am. Law Inst., Assn. Bar City N.Y., Copyright Soc. Am., Cosmos Club (Washington), Philosophy Club (Washington). Antitrust, Private international, Trademark and copyright. Home: 3519 Porter St NW Washington DC 20016-3177

TIMBERLAKE, MARSHALL, lawyer; b. Birmingham, Ala., July 25, 1939; s. Landon and Mary (Perry) T.; m. Rebecca Ann Griffin, Aug. 22, 1987; children: Sumner Timberlake Starling, Jane Ellison. BA, Washington and Lee U., 1961; JD, U. Ala., 1970. Bar: Ala. 1970, Ala. Supreme Ct. 1970, U.S. Dist. Ct. (no., so. and mid. dists.) Ala. 1970, U.S. Supreme Ct. 1976, U.S. Ct. Appeals (11th and 5th cirs.) 1981, U.S. Ct. Appeals (D.C. cir.) 1991. Assoc. Balch & Bingham Law Firm, Birmingham, 1970-76, ptnr., 1976—. Pres. Legal Aid Soc., Birmingham, 1980-81; chmn. Ala. Supreme Ct. Commn. on Dispute Resolution, 1994-96, commr., 1996—; trustee Ala. Dispute Resolution Found., 1995—, vice chmn., 1997—. Pres. Ala. Alcohol and Drug Abuse Coun., 1994-95, dir., 1989—; v.p. Assn. Atty. Mediators, 1994-97; co-chair Gov.'s Task Force on State Agy. Alternative Dispute Resolution, 1998—; bd. dirs. Partnership Assistance to the Homeless, 1998—, chmn. endowment fund com., 1999—. Capt. U.S. Army, 1962-66, Vietnam. Recipient Ann. award Dispute Resolution Inst., 1998; hon. fellow State Agy. ADR Program, 2001. Fellow Ala. Law Found.; mem. ABA, Ala. State Bar (chmn. corp. banking and bus. law sect. 1981-82, chmn. state bar task force on alternative dispute resolution 1992-94, State Bar Merit award 1995, co-chmn. state bar com. on ADR 1996-97, mem. state bar task force on jud. selection 1996-98), Birmingham Bar Assn. (mem. and co-chmn. grievance com. 1972-74, chmn. ethics com. 1975-76, chmn. unauthorized practice of law com. 1976-77, chmn. spl. projects com. 1994-95, co-chmn. com. on jud. and legal reform 1996-97, chmn. com. on jud. and legal reform 1997-98), Am. Arbitration Assn. (state adv. com.), Ala. Acad. Atty. Mediators (co-founder), Redstone Club (bd. govs. 1977 -78), Rotary (Birmingham chpt., chmn. civic club found. 1984), Beaux Arts Krewe, Mountain Brook Club. Republican. Presbyterian. Avocations: tennis, thoroughbred racing, photography. General civil litigation, Environmental, Public utilities. Office: Balch & Bingham 1901 6th Ave N Birmingham AL 35203-2618 Home: 3349 Brookwood Rd Birmingham AL 35223-2020

TIMCHAK, LOUIS JOHN, JR. lawyer, real estate executive; b. Johnstown, Pa., June 7, 1940; s. Louis John and Edna Ann Timchak; m. Susan Truesdale Mueller; children: Louis John, Alexander Mueller, Christopher Truesdale. AB, Georgetown U., 1962; JD, U. Pitts., 1965. Bar: Pa. 1965, D.C. 1966, Fla. 1970, N.Y. 1973, Ga. 1980; lic. real estate broker, N.Y., Fla. Sole practice, Johnstown, 1968-69; real estate atty. Marriott Corp., Washington, 1969-73; assoc. Finley, Kumble, Wagner, Heine & Underberg, N.Y.C., 1973-74; v.p., corp. counsel Phipps Land Co., Atlanta, 1974-76; regional v.p. IDR Mgmt., Inc., 1976-79; real estate cons. Boothe Fin. Corp., 1980; v.p., gen. counsel The Bankers Land Co., Palm Beach Gardens, Fla., 1980-83; v.p., mgr. corp. devel. Merrill Lynch Realty Inc., Stamford, Conn., 1983-84; Scott, Royce, Harris & Bryan, Palm Beach, Fla., 1984-85; sr. v.p. Turner Devel. Corp., North Palm Beach, 1985-86; pres., dir. Turner Real Estate Group Inc., 1986-88; sole practice, 1988-97, 99—; pres. Timchak Real Estate Group II, Inc., 1988-97; v.p., gen. counsel, sec. Jumbo Sports, Inc., Tampa, Fla., 1997-99. Bd. advisors Proudfoot Cons. Co., West Palm Beach, 2000—. Founding dir., past pres. Palm Beach County Devel. Bd., bd. dirs., 1984-86; bd. dirs. Palm Beach County chpt. Am. Heart Assn., 1983-91, sec., 1984, 1st v.p., 1985, pres., 1987, chmn. bd. dirs., 1988-90; mem. Leadership Palm Beach County. Served to lt. JAGC, USNR, 1965-68, Vietnam. Mem. ABA, D.C. Bar Assn., Hillsborough County Bar Assn., Urban Land Inst., Nat. Assn. Corp. Real Estate Execs., North Palm Beach County C. of C. (bd. dirs. 1981-83, 84—, treas. 1983, v.p. 1985). Club: City Tavern (Washington). Office: 18810 Place Antibes Lutz FL 33549

TIMLIN, ROBERT J. judge; b. 1932; BA cum laude, Georgetown U., 1954, JD, 1959, LLM, 1964. Atty. Douglas, Obear and Campbell, 1960-61, Law Offices of A.L. Wheeler, 1961; with criminal divsn. U.S. Dept. Justice, 1961-64; atty. U.S. Atty. Office (ctrl. dist.) Calif., 1964-66, Hennigan, Ryneal and Butterwick, 1966-67; city atty. City of Corona, Calif., 1967-70; prin. Law Office of Robert J. Timlin, 1970-71, 75-76; ptnr. Hunt, Palladino and Timlin, 1971-74, Timlin and Coffin, 1974-75; judge Mcpl. Ct., Riverside, Calif., 1976-80, Calif. Superior Ct., Riverside, 1980-90; assoc. justice Calif. Ct. Appeals, 1990-94; judge U.S. Dist. Ct. (ctrl. dist.) Calif., L.A., 1994—. Part-time U.S. Magistrate judge Ctrl. Dist. Calif., 1970-74. Served U.S. Army, 1955-57. Mem. ABA, Calif. Judges Assn., Phi Alpha Delta. Office: US Dist Ct Central District of Calif Eastern Divsn 3470 12th St Riverside CA 92501

TIMMER, BARBARA, United States Senate official, lawyer; b. Holland, Mich., Dec. 13, 1946; d. John Norman and Barbara Dee (Folensbee) T. BA, Hope Coll., Holland, Mich., 1969; JD, U. Mich., 1975. Bar: Mich. 1975, U.S. Supreme Ct., 1995. Assoc. McCrosky, Libner, VanLeuven, Muskegon, Mich., 1975-78; apptd. to Mich. Women Commn. by Gov., 1976-79; staff counsel subcom. commerce, consumer & monetary affairs Ho. Govt. Ops. Com., U.S. Ho. of Reps., 1979-82, 85-86; exec. v.p. NOW, 1982-84; legis. asst. to Rep. Geraldine Ferraro, 1984; atty. Office Gen. Counsel Fed. Home Loan Bank Bd., 1986-89; gen. counsel Com. on Banking, Fin. and Urban affairs U.S. Ho. of Reps., Washington, 1989-92; asst. gen. counsel, dir. govt. affairs ITT Corp., 1992-96; ptnr. Alliance Capitol, 1994—; sr. v.p., dir. govt. rels. Home Savs. of Am., Irwindale, Calif., 1996-99; ptnr. Manatt, Phelps & Phillips, Washington, 1999—; gen. counsel MyPrimeTime, Inc.,

San Francisco, 2000-01; asst. sec. U.S. Senate, 2001—. Editor: Compliance With Lobbying Laws and Gift Rule Guide, 1996. Recipient Affordable Housing award Nat. Assn. Real Estate Brokers, 1990, Acad. of Women Achievers, YWCA, 1993. Mem. ABA (bus. law sect., electronic fin. svcs. subcom.), FBA (chair, exec. coun. banking law com., Exchequer Club, bd. dirs. Women in Housing and Fin., 1992-94, gen. counsel 1994-98), Supreme Ct. Bar Assn., Supreme Ct. Hist. Soc., Mich. Bar Assn., Bar of Dist. Columbia. Episcopalian. Address: PO Box 21777 Washington DC 20009-9777 E-mail: btimmerdc@earthlink.net

TIMMINS, EDWARD PATRICK, lawyer; b. Denver, June 8, 1955; s. M. Edward and Elizabeth Jean (Imhoff) T.; m. Mary Joanne Deziel, Dec. 27, 1985; children: Edward Patrick Jr., Joan Deziel. BA with honors, Harvard U., 1977; JD magna cum laude, U. Mich., 1980. Bar: Colo. 1981, U.S. Ct. Appeals (D.C. and 9th cirs.) 1982, U.S. Dist. Ct. Colo. 1984, U.S. Ct. Appeals (10th cir.) 1984. Law clk. to cir. justice U.S. Ct. Appeals (7th cir.), Chgo., 1980-81; trial atty. U.S. Dept. Justice, Washington, 1981-84; asst. U.S. atty. Denver, 1984-88; dir. Otten, Johnson, Robinson, Neff & Ragonetti P.C., 1985-96; pres. Timmins & Assocs., LLC, 1996—. Sr. editor U. Mich. Law Rev., 1979-80. Bd. dirs., vice chair Colo. Easter Seals; bd. dirs., chair Denver Pub. Schs. Found.; bd. dirs., chmn. career exploring com. Boy Scouts Am.; bd. dirs. March of Dimes, Am. Ireland Fund. Harvard Nat. scholar, 1976. Mem. ABA, Colo. Bar Assn. (exec. coun. jud. sect.), Denver Bar Assn., Order of Coif, Friends of Harvard Rowing. Avocations: skiing, tennis, squash. Antitrust, General civil litigation, Labor. Office: Timmins & Assocs LLC 1625 Broadway Ste 300 Denver CO 80202-4739

TIMMONS, PETER JOHN, lawyer; b. Madison, Wis., Jan. 23, 1954; s. Donald Ralph and Mary Jean (Boyd) T.; m. Michele Lynn Spolar, Dec. 17, 1977; children: Megan Ann, Andrew Peter. BA summa cum laude, Hamline U., 1976; JD, U. Minn., 1979. Bar: Minn. 1979, U.S. Dist. Ct. Minn. 1979, U.S. Ct. Appeals (8th cir.) 1979. Assoc. Bruce Douglas & Assocs., Mpls., 1979-80, Cousineau, McGuire et al, Mpls., 1980-82; ptnr. Moss & Barnett, 1982-91, Sokol, Rudquist & Timmons, Mpls., 1991-93, Sokol and Timmons, Mpls., 1994-96; sole practitioner, 1996—. Bd. dirs. Lawyers Credit Union, Mpls., pres. 1986-87. Asst. scoutmaster Boy Scouts Am., Mpls., 1980-82, 96—, cubmaster cub scout pack, Mpls., 1993-94; campaigner Dem. Farmer Labor candidates, Mpls., 1980—, chmn. local precinct, 1986-88, caucus convenor, 1988. Mem. Minn. Bar Assn., Hennepin County Bar Assn., Minn. Trial Lawyers Assn., Minn. Assn. Criminal Def. Lawyers, Phi Beta Kappa, Pi Gamma Mu. Avocations: reading, politics, biking, golf. State civil litigation, Criminal, Personal injury. Home: 5035 Lyndale Ave S Minneapolis MN 55419-1215 Office: 2000 Wells Fargo Plaza 7900 Xerexs Ave S Minneapolis MN 55431 E-mail: pjtimmons@juno.com

TINAGLIA, MICHAEL LEE, lawyer; b. Chgo., Dec. 21, 1952; s. Michael Leo and Josephine (Esposito) T.; m. Lucia Yolando Guzzo, Oct. 14, 1978; children: Laura, Lisa, Elena. BA, Northwestern U., 1974; JD, DePaul U., 1977. Bar: Ill. 1977, U.S. Dist. Ct. (no. dist.) Ill. 1978, U.S. Dist. Ct. (ea. dist.) Wis. 1986. Assoc. Arnold & Kadjan, Chgo., 1977-79; ptnr. Leader & Tinaglia, 1979-86; assoc. Laser, Schostok, Kolman & Frank, 1987-92; prin. Law Office of Michael Lee Tinaglia Ltd., 1992-93, 2000—; equity ptnr. DiMonte & Lizak, Park Ridge, Ill., 1994-99. V.p., corp. counsel Tiara Med. Sys., Inc., Oak Forest, Ill. Contbr. articles to profl. jours. Alderman City Coun., Park Ridge, 1997—, mem. pub. safety com., 1997—, mem. procedures and regulations com. Mem. Ill. Bar Assn., Chgo. Bar Assn. Roman Catholic. Avocations: skiing, guitar. General civil litigation, Labor, Pension, profit-sharing, and employee benefits. Office: Law Offices of Michael Lee Tinaglia 161 N Clark St Ste 2550 Chicago IL 60601-3246

TINDALL, ROBERT EMMETT, lawyer, educator; b. N.Y.C., Jan. 2, 1934; s. Robert E. and Alice (McGonigle) T.; children: Robert Emmett IV, Elizabeth. BS in Marine Engring., SUNY, 1955; postgrad., Georgetown U. Law Sch., 1960-61; LLB, U. Ariz., 1963; LLM, NYU, 1967; PhD, City U., London, 1975. Bar: Ariz. 1963. Mgmt. trainee GE, Schenectady, N.Y., Lynn, Mass., Glens Falls, N.Y., 1955-56, 58-60; law clk. Haight, Gardner, Poor and Havens, N.Y.C., 1961; prin., mem. Robert Emmett Tindall & Assocs., Tucson, 1963—; assoc. prof. mgmt. U. Ariz., 1969—. Vis. prof. Grad. Sch. of Law, Soochow U., China, 1972, Grad. Bus. Ctr., London, 1974, NYU, 1991—; dir. MBA program U. Ariz., Tucson, 1975-81, dir. entrepreneurship program, 1984-86; investment cons. Kingdom of Saudi Arabia, 1981—; lectr. USIA, Eng., India, Mid. East, 1974; lectr. bus. orgn. and regulatory laws Southwestern Legal Found., Acad. Am. and Internat. Law, 1976-80. Actor cmty. theatres, Schenectady, 1955-56, Harrisburg, Pa., 1957-58, Tucson, 1961-71; appeared in films Rage, 1971, Showdown at OK Corral, 1971, Lost Horizon, 1972; appeared in TV programs Gunsmoke, 1972, Petrocelli, 1974; author: Multinational Enterprises, 1975; contbr. articles on domestic and internat. bus. to profl. jours. Served to lt. USN, 1956-58. Fellow Ford Found., 1965-67; grantee Asia Found., 1972-73. Mem. Strategic Mgmt. Soc., State Bar of Ariz., Acad. Internat. Bus., Screen Actors Guild, Honourable Soc. of Mid. Temple (London), Phi Delta Phi, Beta Gamma Sigma, Assn. Corp. Growth, Royal Overseas League (London). General corporate, General practice, Private international. Home: PO Box 42196 Tucson AZ 85733-2196 Office: Coll Bus & Public Adminstrn U Ariz Dept Mgmt & Policy Tucson AZ 85721-0001

TINDOL, MELTON CHAD, lawyer; b. Enterprise, Ala., June 5, 1972; s. Jackey and Susan Creel Tindol; m. Julie Brooke Oliver, Dec. 28, 1991; children: Rebecca Brooke, Kaitlin Von. BA, U. Ala., Tuscaloosa, 1994; JD, Yale U., 1997. Bar: Ala. 1997. Law clk. Hon. J. Albritton U.S. Dist. Ct., Montgomery, Ala., 1997-98; assoc. Maynard, Cooper & Gale, 1998—. Mem. Autauga County Rep. Club, Prattville, Ala., 1998—. Mem. Federalist Soc. (treas. 1995-96), Phi Beta Kappa. Baptist. Avocations: reading, guitar, politics. Federal civil litigation, State civil litigation, Constitutional. Home: 1839 Seasons Dr Prattville AL 36104 Office: Maynard Cooper & Gale 201 Monroe St Ste 1940 Montgomery AL 36104

TIPPING, HARRY A. lawyer; b. Bainbridge, Md., Nov. 2, 1944; s. William Richard and Ann Marie (Kelly) T.; m. Kathleen Ann Palmer, July 12, 1969; 1 child, Christopher A. B.A., Gannon U., 1966; J.D., U. Akron, 1970. Bar: Ohio. Asst. law dir. City of Akron, Ohio, 1971-72, chief asst. law dir., 1972-74; ptnr. Gillen, Miller & Tipping, Akron, 1974-77, Roderick, Myers & Linton, Akron, 1977-87; prin., COO Harry A. Tipping Co. L.P.A., Akron, 1987—. Mem. Fairlawn Charter Rev. Commn., 1990—; chmn. bd. Assessment Equalization for the City of Fairlawn, 1989, 90, 97; chmn. Bd. of Tax Appeals, City of Fairlawn, Ohio, 1979-81, mem. merger com., 1980-82. With USCGR, 1966-72. Mem. ABA, Am. Bd. Trial Advocates (advocate), Akron Bar Assn., Ohio Bar Assn., Def. Rsch. Inst., Am. Arbitration Assn., Fedn. Ins. & Corp. Counsel. Republican. Roman Catholic. Clubs: Fairlawn Country (Ohio), Catawaba Island (Ohio), Firestone County (Akron, Ohio). Federal civil litigation, State civil litigation, Labor. Office: 1 Cascade Plz Ste 2200 Akron OH 44308-1135

TISCI, MICHAEL ANTHONY, lawyer; b. Chgo., June 1, 1960; s. Anthony Phillip and Bonnie (Lou) T. BA, U. Tex., Austin, 1981; JD, U. Tulsa, 1984. Bar: Okla. 1985, Ariz. 1991, U.S. Dist. Ct. (we. dist.) Okla., U.S. Dist. Ct. ARiz., U.S. Ct. Appeals 9th and 10th cirs.). Sr. atty. FDIC, San Francisco, 1985-94; assoc. Womble, Carlyle, Sandride & Rice, Winston-Salem, N.C., 1994-96; assoc. gen. counsel, sr. v.p. Branch Banking and Trust Co., 1996—. Contbr. articles to profl. jours. Mem. ABA, ATLA. Avocations, travel, Chinese history.

TISDALE, DOUGLAS MICHAEL, lawyer; b. Detroit, May 3, 1949; s. Charles Walker and Violet Lucille (Battani) T.; m. Patricia Claire Brennan, Dec. 29, 1972; children: Douglas Michael Jr., Sara Elizabeth, Margaret Patricia, Victoria Claire. BA in Psychology with honors, U. Mich., 1971, JD, 1975. Bar: Colo. 1975, U.S. Dist. Ct. Colo. 1975, U.S. Ct. Appeals (10th cir.) 1976, U.S. Supreme Ct. 1979. Law clk. to chief judge U.S. Dist. Ct. Colo., Denver, 1975-76; ptnr. Brownstein Hyatt Farber & Strickland, P.C., 1976-92; shareholder Popham, Haik, Schnobrich & Kaufman, Ltd., 1992-97, dir., 1995-97; ptnr. Baker & Hostetler LLP, Denver, 1997—. Dir. Vail Valley Med. Ctr., 1990—; chmn. bd. dirs. Eagle Health Care Ctr., Inc., 2001—. City councilman Cherry Hills Village, Colo., 2000—. Bankruptcy, Federal civil litigation, Real property. Home: 4662 S Elizabeth Ct Cherry Hills Village CO 80110-7106 Office: Baker & Hostetler LLP 11th Fl 303 E 17th Ave Fl 11 Denver CO 80203-1264

TITLEY, LARRY J. lawyer; b. Tecumseh, Mich., Dec. 9, 1943; s. Leroy H. and Julia B. (Ruesink) T.; m. Julia Margaret Neukom, May 23, 1970; children: Sarah Catherine, John Neukom. BA, U. Mich., 1965, JD, 1972. Bar: Va. 1973, Mich. 1973. Assoc. Hunton & Williams, Richmond, Va., 1972-73, Varnum, Riddering, Schmidt & Howlett, Grand Rapids, Mich., 1973—. Trustee Friends Pub. Mus., 1985—94; bd. dirs. Pub. Mus. Found., 1988—97, pres., 1992—95; bd. dirs. Camp Optimist YMCA, 1993—98, Peninsular Club, 1994—, pres., 1997. Mem. ABA, Mich. Bar Assn., Grand Rapids Bar Assn. General corporate, Pension, profit-sharing, and employee benefits. Home: 520 Roundtree Dr NE Ada MI 49301-9707 Office: Varnum Riddering Schmidt & Howlett Bridgewater Pl PO Box 352 Grand Rapids MI 49501-0352 E-mail: ljtitley@vrsh.com

TITONE, VITO JOSEPH, state supreme court justice; b. Bklyn., July 5, 1929; s. Vito and Elena (Ruisi) T.; m. Margaret Anne Viola, Dec. 30, 1956; children: Stephen, Matthew, Elena Titone Hill, Elizabeth. BA, NYU, 1951; JD, St. John's U., 1956, LL.D., 1984. Bar: N.Y. 1957, U.S. Dist. Ct. (ea. and so. dists.) N.Y., 1962, U.S. Supreme Ct. 1964, U.S. Ct. Appeals N.Y. 1985. Ptnr. Maltese & Titone, N.Y.C., 1957-65, Maltese, Titone & Anastasi, N.Y.C., 1965-68; assoc. counsel to pres. pro tem N.Y. State Senate, 1965; justice N.Y. State Supreme Ct, N.Y.C., 1969-75; assoc. justice appellate div. 2d dept., 1975-85; judge N.Y. State Ct. Appeals, Albany, 1985—; of counsel Mintz & Gold LLP, N.Y.C., 1998—. Adj. prof. Coll. S.I., CUNY, 1969-72, St. John's U., Jamaica, N.Y., 1969-85. Bd. editors N.Y. Law Jour., 1999; contbr. articles to law jour. Bd. govs. Daytop Village Inc., N.Y.C.; bd. dirs. Boy Scouts Am.; bd. trustees The Am. Parkinson Disease Assn. With U.S. Army, 1951-53, to col. N.Y. State Guard. Named Citizen of Yr. Daytop Village, N.Y.C., 1969, Disting. Citizen Wagner Coll., S.I., 1983, Outstanding Contbr. Camelot Substance Abuse Network, 1983; recipient citation of merit S.I. Salvation Army Adv. Bd., 1983, Rapollo award Columbian Lawyers Assn., 1983, Disting. Judiciary award Cath. Lawyers Guild Diocese of Bklyn., 1991, Disting. Svc. award N.Y. State Lawyers Assn., Justice William Brennan award N.Y. Assn. Criminal Def. Lawyers, 1993, Life Achievement award N.Y. Conf. Italian Am. State Legislators, 1994, Ellis Island Medal of Honor, 1997, gold medal Bklyn. Bar Assn., 1997. Mem. ABA, N.Y. State Bar Assn., Richmond County Bar Assn., Supreme Ct. Justice Assn., VFW, Am. Legion (past comdr.), Charles C. Pinckney Tribute Def. Assn. of N.Y., Justinian Soc., K.C. Roman Catholic. Office: Mintz and Gold LLP 444 Park Ave S New York NY 10016-7321

TITTSWORTH, CLAYTON (MAGNESS), lawyer; b. Tampa, Fla., Nov. 8, 1920; Student, U. Tampa, 1939-42; LLB, Stetson Law Sch., 1951. Bar: Fla. 1951; cert. cir. mediator. Ptnr. Tittsworth & Tittsworth, Tampa, 1951-65, Brandon, Fla., 1964-73, pvt. practice, 1973-83, Tittsworth and Curry, PA, Brandon, 1983-87, 1987—. Mem. ABA, Fla. Bar Assn. State civil litigation, Probate, Real property. Office: 1021 Hollyberry Ct Brandon FL 33511-7657 E-mail: cmt20@msn.com

TITUS, BRUCE EARL, lawyer; b. N.Y.C., June 5, 1942; BA, Coll. William and Mary, 1964, JD, 1971. Bar: Va. 1971, D.C. 1972, Md. 1984. Asst. dir. torts br., civil divsn. U.S. Dept. Justice, 1971-82; mem. Jones, Waldo, Holbrook and McDonough, Washington; ptnr. Venable, Baetjer and Howard, LLP, McLean, Va., 1986-976; prin. Rees, Broome & Diaz P.C., Vienna, 1997—. Exec. editor William & Mary Law Review, 1970-71. Mem. ABA, Va. State Bar, D.C. Bar, Fairfax Bar Assn. (pres. 1999-2000), Md. State Bar, Phi Delta Phi, Omicron Delta Kappa. Alternative dispute resolution, General civil litigation, Construction. Office: Rees Broome & Diaz PC 9th Fl 8133 Leesburg Pike Vienna VA 22182-2706

TITUS, JON ALAN, lawyer; b. Milw., Oct. 6, 1955; s. Mary (Irwin) Stephenson; m. Laura Jean Newman, Sept. 5, 1982; children: Katherine, Derek. BA, U. Ariz., 1977; JD, Ariz. State U., 1980. Bar: Ariz. 1980, U.S. Dist. Ct. Ariz. 1980; cert. real estate specialist. Pres. Titus, Brueckner & Berry, P.C., Scottsdale, Ariz., 1980—. Mem. Ariz. Kidney Found., 1984—, pres., 1991-92. Recipient Alumni Achievement award Ariz. State U., 1996. Mem. Ariz. Bar Assn. (chmn. securities regulation sect. 1986-87), Maricopa County Bar Assn., Scottsdale Bar Assn. (dir. 1993-95). Antitrust, Real property, Securities. Office: Titus Brueckner & Berry PC 7373 N Scottsdale Rd Ste 252B Scottsdale AZ 85253-3513

TITUS, VICTOR ALLEN, lawyer; b. Nevada, Mo., Sept. 2, 1956; s. Charles Allen and Viola Mae (Cliffman) T.; m. Laraine Carol Cook, Oct. 13, 1974 (div. Feb. 1982); 1 child, Matthew; m. Deborah Diane Carpenter, Apr. 10, 1984; 1 child, Jacquelynn. BS, BA, Ctrl. Mo. State U., 1978; JD, U. Mo., 1981. Bar: N.Mex. 1981, U.S. Dist. Ct. N.Mex. 1981, Mo. 1982, U.S. Ct. Appeals (10th cir. 1983), U.S. Supreme Ct. 1986, Colo. 1989, Ariz. 1995. Lawyer Jay L. Faurot, P.C., Farmington, N.Mex., 1981-83; ptnr. Faurot & Titus, P.C., 1983-85; lawyer, sole proprietor Victor A. Titus, P.C., 1985—. Arbitrator in civil disputes Alternative Dispute Resolution-Arbitration; liquor lic. hearing officer City of Farmington, 1989-94. Contbr. articles to profl. jours. Adult Behind Youth, Boys & Girls Club, Farmington, 1987—; mem. hosp. adv. bd. San Juan Regional Med. Ctr., Farmington, 1988-93. Recipient San Juan County Disting. Svc. award N.Mex. Bar Assn., 1984; named one of Best Lawyers in Am., 1995-96, 97—. Mem. Assn. Trial Lawyers of Am., N.Mex. Trial Lawyers (bd. dirs. 1983—, pres. 1993-94), State Bar of N.Mex. (disciplinary bd. 1997—, specialization com. 1992-98, legal advt. com. 1990), San Juan County Bar Assn. (pres. 1984), Nat. Assn. Criminal Def. Lawyers (life), Colo. Trial Lawyers. Democrat. Avocation: sports. E-mial. Criminal, Personal injury, Workers' compensation. Home: 5760 Pinehurst Farmington NM 87402-5078 Office: Victor A Titus PC 2021 E 20th St Farmington NM 87401-2516 E-mail: titusmurphy@cyberport.com

TJOFLAT, GERALD BARD, federal judge; b. Pitts., Dec. 6, 1929; s. Gerald Benjamin and Sarita (Romero-Hermoso) T.; m. Sarah Marie Pfohl, July 27, 1957 (dec.); children: Gerald Bard, Marie Elizabeth; m. Marcia Penman Parker, Feb. 21, 1998. Student, U. Va., 1947-50, U. Cin., 1950-52; LL.B., Duke U., 1957; D.C.L. (hon.), Jacksonville U., 1978; LLD (hon.), William Mitchell Coll. Law, 1993. Bar: Fla. 1957. Individual practice law, Jacksonville, Fla., 1957-68; judge 4th Jud. Cir. Ct. Fla., 1968-70, U.S. Dist. Ct. for Middle Dist. Fla., Jacksonville, 1970-75, U.S. Ct. Appeals, 5th Cir., Jacksonville, 1975-81, U.S. Ct. Appeals, 11th Cir., Jacksonville, 1996—, chief judge, 1989-96. Mem. Adv. Corrections Coun. U.S., 1975—87, Jud. Conf. of U.S., 1989—, Fed. Jud. Ct. Com. on Sentencing, Probation an dPretrial Svcs., 1988—90; mem. coun. adminstrn. probation system Jud. Conf. of U.S., 1972—87, chmn., 1978—87; U.S. del. 6th and 7th UN Congress for Prevention of Crime and Treatment of Offenders. Hon. life mem., bd. visitors Duke U. Law Sch., 2000; pres. North Fla. coun. Boy Scouts Am., 1976—85, chmn., 1985—90; trustee Jacksonville Marine Inst., 1976—90, Episc. H.S., Jacksonville, 1975—90; mem. vestry St. Johns Cathedral, 1969—71, 1973—75, 1977—79, 1981—83, 1985—87, 1993, 1995—96, sr. warden, 1975, 1983, 1987, 1991, 1992. Recipient Merit award Duke U., 1990, Fordham-Stein prize, 1996. Mem. ABA, Fla. Bar Assn., Am. Law Inst., Am. Judicature Soc. Episcopalian. Office: US Ct Appeals US Courthouse PO Box 960 311 W Monroe St Rm 539 Jacksonville FL 32201

TOAL, JEAN HOEFER, state supreme court justice; b. Columbia, S.C., Aug. 11, 1943; d. Herbert W. and Lilla (Farrell) Hoefer; m. William Thomas Toal; children: Jean Hoefer Eisen, Lilla Patrick. BA in Philosophy, Agnes Scott Coll., 1965; JD, U. S.C., 1968; LHD (hon.), Coll. Charleston, 1991; LLD (hon.), Columbia Coll., 1992, The Citadel, 1999, Francis Marion U., 1999. Bar: S.C. Assoc. Haynsworth, Perry, Bryant, Marion & Johnstone, 1968-70; ptnr. Belser, Baker, Barwick, Ravenel, Toal & Bender, Columbia, 1970-88; assoc. justice S.C. Supreme Ct., 1988-00, chief justice, 2000—. Mem. S.C. Human Affairs Commn., 1972-74; mem. S.C. Ho. of Reps., 1975-88, chmn. house rules com., constitutional laws subcom. house judiciary com.; mem. parish coun. and lector St. Joseph's Cath. Ch.; chair S.C. Juvenile Justice Task Force, 1992-94; chair S.C. Rhodes Scholar Selection Com., 1994. Mng. editor S.C. Law Rev., 1967-68. Bd. visitors Clemson U., 1978; trustee Columbia Mus. Art; bd. trustees Agnes Scott Coll., 1996—. Named Legislator of Yr. Greenville News, Woman of Yr., U. S.C.; recipient Disting. Svc. award S.C. Mcpl. Assn., Univ. Notre Dame award, 1991, Algernon Sydney Sullivan award U. S.C., 1991. Mem. John Belton O'Neill Inn of Ct., Phi Beta Kappa, Mortar Bd., Order of the Coif. Office: Supreme Ct SC PO Box 12456 Columbia SC 29211-2456

TOBACK, ARTHUR MALCOLM, lawyer; b. N.Y.C., Dec. 18, 1944; s. Cecil and Lisa (Saltzman) T.; m. Patricia Anne Kruse, May 30, 1969; children— Sharon Tova, Sonya Celena, Lia Shoshana. B.A., U. Pa., 1966; J.D., Georgetown U., 1969; Bar: D.C. 1969, N.Y. 1973; U.S. Ct. Appeals (2nd cir.), U.S. Dist. Ct. (so. dist.) N.Y. U.S. Dist. Ct. (ea. dist.) N.Y. U.S. Supreme Ct. 1975, U.S. Tax Ct. 1982. Appellate atty. ICC, Washington, 1969-71; enforcement atty. EPA, N.Y.C., 1971-72; assoc. Kaye, Scholer, Fierman, Hays & Handler, N.Y.C., 1972-78; co-founder, sr. ptnr. Horwitz, Toback & Hyman, N.Y.C., 1978— . Contbg. editor: Georgetown Law Jour., 1968-69. Bd. dirs., mem. exec. com. Sutton Pl. Synagogue, N.Y.C., 1978— ; bd. dirs. Tonetta Lake Park Assn., Brewster, N.Y., 1981— . Mem. Assn. of Bar of City of New York, Democrat. Federal civil litigation, State civil litigation, Contracts commercial. Home: 320 E 25th St New York NY 10010-3140 Office: Horwitz Toback & Hyman 1114 Avenue Of The Americas New York NY 10036-7703

TOBER, STEPHEN LLOYD, lawyer; b. Boston, May 27, 1949; s. Benjamin Arthur Tober and Lee (Hymoff) Fruman; m. Susan V. Schwartz, Dec. 22, 1973; children: Cary, Jamie. Grad., Syracuse U., 1971, JD, 1974. Bar: N.H. 1974, U.S. Dist. Ct. N.H. 1974, U.S. Supreme Ct. 1978, N.Y. 1981. Assoc. Flynn, McGuirk & Blanchard, Portsmouth, N.H., 1974-79; sole practice, 1979-81; ptnr. Aeschliman & Tober, 1981-91; prin. Tober Law Offices, P.A., 1992—. Lectr. Franklin Pierce Law Ctr., Concord, N.H., 1978-80. Contbr. articles to law jours. Mem. Portsmouth Charter Commn., 1976, Portsmouth Planning Bd., 1977-81; del. N.H. Constl. Conv., Concord, 1984; city councilman, Portsmouth, 1977-81. Fellow ABA (chair credentials and admissions com. ho. dels.), Am. Bar Found., N.H. Bar Assn. (pres. 1988-89, chair com. to redraft code of profl. responsibility, Disting. Svc. award, 1986, 94); mem. ATLA (gov. 1980-86), N.H. Trial Lawyers Assn. (pres. 1977), New Eng. Bar Assn. (bd. dirs. 1988-91), N.H. Bd. Bar Examiners. Democrat. Jewish. Avocations: reading, tennis. State civil litigation, General practice, Personal injury. Home: 55 T J Gamester Ave Portsmouth NH 03801-5871 Office: Tober Law Offices PA PO Box 1377 Portsmouth NH 03802-1377 E-mail: toberlaw@nh.ultranet.com

TOBIN, BENTLEY, lawyer; b. Bklyn., N.Y., Feb. 8, 1924; s. Nathan H. and Mildred E. (Aronoff) T.; m. Nancy Gurvitz, Sept. 13, 1947; children— Patricia E., Mitchell H.; m. 2d, Beverly Ann Mucciarone, Feb. 17, 1979. B.S., CCNY, 1943; LL.B., Harvard U., 1948. Bar: N.Y. 1948, Mass. 1951, R.I. 1952. Atty. N.Y.C. Housing Authority, 1948-49; ptnr. Titiev, Greenman & Tobin, Boston, 1949-52; sr. ptnr. Tobin & Silverstein, Inc., Providence, 1952-84; ptnr. Hinckley, Allen, Tobin & Silverstein, 1984-87, Hinckley, Allen, Comen, 1987-92, Hinckley, Allen & Snyder, 1992—; chmn. bd. Landmark Health Systems, Inc. Served in USAR, 1943-46. Mem. ABA, R.I. Bar Assn., Woonsocket Bar Assn. Contracts commercial, Probate, Real property. Office: Hinckley Allen Snyder 1500 Fleet Ctr Providence RI 02903-2319 Also: Landmark Health Systems Inc 115 Cass Ave Woonsocket RI 02895-4705

TOBIN, BRUCE HOWARD, lawyer; b. Detroit, July 17, 1955; s. Marshall Edward and Rhoda Maureen (Milman) T.; m. Kathleen Tobin; children: Benjamin Stewart, Jenna Rose, Lainie Nicole. BA in Social Sci., Mich. State U., 1978; JD, Detroit Coll. Law, 1982; LLM in Taxation, NYU, 1983. Bar: Mich. 1982, Fla. 1982, Nebr. 1983, U.S. Dist. Ct. (ea. dist.) Mich. 1982, U.S. Tax Ct. 1983. Assoc. Kutak, Rock & Campbell, Omaha, 1983-85; ptnr. Lebow & Tobin P.L.L.C., West Bloomfield, Mich., 1985—. Pres. West Bloomfield Sch. Bd. Mem. ABA, Fla. Bar Assn., Mich. Bar Assn. (tax com. 1985—), Nebr. Bar Assn. Jewish. Real property, Corporate taxation, Estate taxation. Office: Lebow & Tobin PLLC 7001 Orchard Lake Rd Ste 312 West Bloomfield MI 48322-3607 Fax: (248) 851 4303. E-mail: btobin@lebowardtobin.com

TOBIN, JAMES MICHAEL, lawyer; b. Santa Monica, Calif., Sept. 27, 1948; s. James Joseph and Glada Marie (Meisner) T.; m. Kathleen Marie Espy, Sept. 14, 1985. BA with honors, U. Calif., Riverside, 1970; JD, Georgetown U., 1974. Bar: Calif. 1974, Mich. 1987. From atty. to gen. atty. So. Pacific Co., San Francisco, 1975-82; v.p. regulatory affairs So. Pacific Communications Co., Washington, 1982-83; v.p., gen. counsel Lexitel Corp., 1983-85; v.p., gen. counsel, sec. ALC Communications Corp., Birmingham, Mich., 1985-87, sr. v.p., gen. counsel, sec., 1987-88; of counsel Morrison & Foerster, San Francisco, 1988-90, ptnr., 1990—. Mem. ABA, Calif. Bar Assn., Mich. Bar Assn., Fed. Communications Bar Assn. Republican. Unitarian. Avocations: carpentry, travel. Administrative and regulatory, Communications, General corporate. Home: 3134 Baker St San Francisco CA 94123-1805 Office: Morrison & Foerster 425 Market St Ste 3100 San Francisco CA 94105-2482 E-mail: jtobin@mofo.com

TOBISMAN, STUART PAUL, lawyer; b. Detroit, June 5, 1942; s. Nathan and Beverly (Porvin) T.; m. Karen Sue Tobisman, Aug. 8, 1965; children: Cynthia Elaine, Neal Jay. BA, UCLA, 1966; JD, U. Calif., Berkeley, 1969. Bar: Calif. 1969. Assoc. O'Melveny & Myers, L.A., 1969-77, ptnr., 1977—. Dir. Burton G. Bettingen Corp. Contbr. articles to profl. jours. Trustee L.A. County Bar Assn., 1983-84. With USN, 1961-63. Fellow Am. Coll. Trust and Estate Counsel; mem. Phi Beta Kappa, Order of Coif. Office: O'Melveny & Myers LLP 1999 Avenue Of The Stars Los Angeles CA 90067-6035

TOCK, JOSEPH, lawyer; b. Cleve., Aug. 22, 1954; s. Julius Joseph and Marianna Yvonne (Carracio) T.; m. Celia Jane Shubert. BA, Kent State U., 1979; JD, Case Western Res. U., 1983. Bar: Ohio, 1983, U.S. Ct. Mil. Appeals, 1983, Colo. 1988, Guam 1995. Commd. 1st lt. USAF, 1983, advanced through grades to lt. col., 2001, asst. staff judge advocate, chief civil law Kans., 1983-84, Yokota Air Base, Japan, 1984-85, area def. counsel 7th cir. Japan, 1985-87, dep. staff judge advocate, chief mil. justice Kelly AFB, Tex., 1987-88; dep. county atty. El Paso County, Colo., 1989-90; pvt. practice Colorado Springs, 1990-91; staff atty. Guam Legal Svcs. Corp., 1991-92; asst. atty. gen. White Collar unit Prosecution Divsn., Agana, Guam, Guam, 1992-95, 1st asst. to chief prosecutor Guam,

1994-96; asst. atty. gen. Solicitor's Divsn., Guam, 1996-97; lead atty. for drug unit Prosecution Divsn., Guam, 1997-2001, chief criminal prosecutor, chief labor law Andersen AFB, Guam, 2001—. Dep. staff judge advocate Peterson AFB, Colo., 1990-91, Andersen AFB, Guam, 1991—; instr. family law Pikes Peak C.C., 1990-91; lectr. Continental Security Divsn., San Antonio, 1987-88, NCO prep course, Kelly AFB, Tex., 1987-88, Profl. Mil. Edn. Ctr., Yokota Air Base, 1984-87. Mem. Internat. Legal Soc. Japan, Am. Legion. Roman Catholic. Avocations: golf, handball, sailing, scuba. Office: Atty Gen Prosecution Divsn 36 ABW/JA Unit 14003 Box 28 APO AP GU 96910 Address: 1037 Rota Dr Yigo GU 96929 E-mail: tockj@hotmail.com

TODD, ALBERT CRESWELL, III, lawyer; b. Greenwood, S.C., June 17, 1950; s. Albert Creswell and Marjorie (Byrd) T.; m. Deborah Moore, July 22, 1972; children: Andrew, Anna, David, John. BS in Indsl. Mgmt., Clemson U., 1972; JD, U. S.C., 1975; LLM in Estate Planning, U. Miami, 1976. Bar: S.C. 1975, U.S. Tax Ct. 1976, U.S. Ct. Appeals (4th cir.) 1976; cert. specialist in estate planning, probate and trust law. Pvt. practice, Columbia, S.C., 1976-78; assoc. Robert P. Wilkins, 1976-79; ptnr. Todd & Johnson, LLP, 1978—. Instr. advanced estate planning The Am. Coll., 1980-81; lectr. in field; mem. adv. bd. Branch-Bank & Trust Co., Columbia. Editl. asst. Drafting Wills and Trust Agreements in South Carolina, 1976; author: (booklets) A Diagrammatic Guide to Estate Planning, 2001, An Overview of Estate Settlement in South Carolina, 1997. Bd. dirs. Children's Hosp. at Richland Meml., HisAcres, Forest Lake Ednl. Found., chmn., 1988-89; tchr. Bethel Bible Series St. Martins-in-the-Fields Episcopal Ch., Columbia, 1983-87; adv. bd. Columbia Internat. U., 1985—; bd. dirs., sec.-treas. Episc. Ministry to the Aging, 1985-86; adv. bd. Estate Planning and Probate Specialization Cert., 1987-90, chmn., 1989-90. Fellow Am. Coll. Trust and Estate Counsel; mem. ABA (real property, probate, and trust law sect.), S.C. Bar Assn. (chmn. estate planning, probate and trust law sect. 1981-82, lectr. 1975—), Richland City Bar Assn. (chmn. estate planning, probate and trust sect. 1979-80), Internat. Assn. of Fin. Planners (pres. Columbia chpt. 1985-86), Phi Delta Phi. Episcopalian. Estate planning, Probate, Estate taxation. Office: Todd & Johnson LLP 609 Sims Ave PO Box 11262 Columbia SC 29211 E-mail: altodd@toddandjohnson.com

TODD, ERICA WEYER, lawyer; b. Beacon Falls, Conn., Sept. 22, 1967; d. Richard Burton and Elizabeth Jane (Weyer) T. BA in Biology, U. Bridgeport, 1989, JD, 1992; postgrad., Quinnipiac U. Bar: Conn. 1992, U.S. Dist. Ct. Conn. 1993, U.S. Supreme Ct., 1998; bd. cert. trial atty. Ptnr. Trotta, Trotta and Trotta, New Haven, 1993—. Admissions counselor Quinnipiac Coll. Sch. of Law, Hamden, 1992-93. Mem. ABA, Conn. Bar Assn. (exec. com. Young Lawyers divsn. 1993-99), New Haven Bar Assn. (exec. com. Young Lawyers Assn. 1994—), Def. Rsch. Inst., Assn. Trial Lawyers of Am., Ct. Trial Lawyers Assn., Conn. Def. Lawyers, Quinnipiac Coll. Sch. Law Alumni Assn. (pres. 2000—, Alumni award for Svc. 1994). Democrat. Roman Catholic. Avocation: golf. General civil litigation, Insurance, Personal injury. Home: 551 Skokorat Rd Beacon Falls CT 06403-1457 Office: Trotta Trotta & Trotta 195 Church St Eighth Fl PO Box 802 New Haven CT 06503-0802 E-mail: etodd@trottalaw.com

TODD, JAMES DALE, federal judge; b. Scotts Hill, Tenn., May 20, 1943; s. James P. and Jeanette Grace (Duck) T.; m. Jeanie M. Todd, June 26, 1965; 2 children. BS, Lambuth Coll., 1965; M Combined Scis., U. Miss., 1968; JD, Memphis State U., 1972. Bar: Tenn. 1972, U.S. Dist. Ct. (we. dist.) Tenn. 1972, U.S. Ct. Appeals (6th cir.) 1973, U.S. Supreme Ct. 1975. Tchr. sci., chmn. sci. dept. Lyman High Sch., Longwood, Fla., 1965-68, Memphis U. Sch., 1968-72; ptnr. Waldrop, Farmer, Todd & Breen, P.A., 1972-83; cir. judge div. II 26th Jud. Dist., Jackson, Tenn., 1983-85; judge U.S. Dist. Ct. (we. dist.) Tenn., 1985-2001, chief judge, 2001—. Named Alumnus of Yr. Lambuth Coll. Alumni Assn., 1985. Fellow Tenn. Bar Found.; mem. Fed. Judges Assn. (bd. dirs. 1998—), Fed. Bar Assn., Jackson Madison County Bar Assn. (pres. 1978-79), Dist. Judges Assn. of 6th Cir. (pres. 2000-2001). Methodist. Office: US Dist Ct 111 S Highland Ave Jackson TN 38301-6107

TODD, JOHN JOSEPH, lawyer; b. St. Paul, Mar. 16, 1927; s. John Alfred and Martha Agnes (Jagoe) T.; m. Dolores Jean Shanahan, Sept. 9, 1950; children: Richard M., Jane E., John P. Student, St. Thomas Coll., 1944, 46-47; B.Sci. and Law, U. Minn., 1949, LL.B., 1950. Bar: Minn. bar 1951. Practice in, South St. Paul, Minn., 1951-72; partner Thuet and Todd, 1953-72; asso. justice Minn. Supreme Ct., St. Paul, 1972-85; sole practice West St. Paul, 1985-92; of counsel Brenner & Glassman Ltd., Mpls., 1992-99, Orme & Assoc., Eagan, Minn., 1999—. Served with USNR, 1945-46. Mem. state bar assns., VFW. Home: 6689 Argenta Trl W Inver Grove Heights MN 55077-2208 Office: Orme & Associates 3140 Neil Armstrong Blvd Eagan MN 55121-2273 E-mail: jtodd@ormelaw.com, jjbtodd@aol.com

TODD, STEPHEN MAX, lawyer; b. Kansas City, Mo., Oct. 22, 1941; s. Louis O. and A. Maxine (Mittag); m. Carlene Harre; children: Stephanie A., Louis P. BA, Kans. State U., 1963; JD, U. Kans., 1966. Bar: Kans. 1966, U.S. Dist. Ct. Kans. 1966, U.S. Ct. Appeals (10th cir.) 1967, U.S. Supreme Ct. 1971, Mo. 1973. Assoc. Schroeder, Heeney, Groff & Spies, Topeka, 1966-72; office counsel Chgo. Title Ins. Co., Kansas City, 1973-78, regional counsel, 1978—. Author: Missouri Foreclosures of Deeds of Trust, 1983, 4th edit. 2001; contbr., editor books. Mem. Kans. Bar Assn., Mo. Bar (chmn. property law com. 1990-92), Am. Coll. Real Estate Lawyers, Kiwanis (pres. Topeka Downtown Club 1971-72, lt. gov. Mo.-Ark. dist. 1976-77, pres. Kansas City South Platte Club 1979-80), Phi Delta Phi. Insurance, Real property. Home: 5519 N Woodhaven Ln Kansas City MO 64152-4319 Office: Chgo Title Ins Co PO Box 26370 Kansas City MO 64196-6370 E-mail: todds@ctt.com, stoddinkc@kc.rr.com

TOFTNESS, CECIL GILLMAN, lawyer, consultant; b. Glasgow, Mont., Sept. 13, 1920; s. Anton Bernt and Nettie (Pedersen) T.; m. Chloe Catherine Vincent, Sept. 8, 1951. AA, San Diego Jr. Coll., 1943; student, Purdue U., Northwestern U.; BS, UCLA, 1947; JD cum laude, Southwestern U., 1953. Bar: Calif. 1954, U.S. Dist. Ct. (so. dist.) Calif. 1954, U.S. Tax Ct. 1974, U.S. Supreme Ct. 1979. Pvt. rpactice, palos Verdes Estates, Calif., 1954—. Chmn. bd., pres., bd. dirs. Fishermen & Mchts. Bank, San Pedro, Calif., 1963-67; v.p., bd. dirs. Palos Verdes Estates Bd. Realtors, 1964-65; participant Soc. Expdn. through the Northwest Passaage. Chmn. capital campaign fund Richstone Charity, Hawthorne, Calif., 1983; commencement spkr. Glasgow H.S., 1981. Served to lt. (j.g.) USN, 1938-46, ETO, PTO, commdg. officer USS Ptarmigan, 1941-45. Decorated Bronze Star; mem. Physicians for Prevention of Nuclear War which received Nobel Peace prize, 1987; named Man of Yr., Glasgow, 1984. Mem. South Bay Bar Assn., Southwestern Law Sch. Alumni Assn. (class rep. 1980—), Themis Soc.-Southwestern Law Sch., Schumacher Founders Cir.-Southwestern Law Sch. (charter), Kiwanis (sec.-treas. 1955-83, v.p., pres., bd. dirs.), Masons, KT. Democrat. Lutheran. Estate planning, Probate, Estate taxation. Home: 2229 Via Acalones Palos Verdes Peninsula CA 90274-1646 Office: 2516 Via Tejon Palos Verdes Estates CA 90274-6802 E-mail: cgtoftness@aol.com

TOGNARELLI, RICHARD LEE, lawyer; b. Collinsville, Ill., Aug. 12, 1949; s. Albert John and Rosalie Frances (Brogliatto) T.; m. Gail Marie Culliton, June 11, 1971; children: Michael Anthony, Matthew Paul. AB, St. Louis U., 1971, JD, 1974. Bar: Ill. 1975, U.S. Dist. Ct. (so. dist.) Ill. 1975, U.S. Dist. Ct. (ea. dist.) Ill. 1975, U.S. Ct. Appeals (7th cir.) 1976. Clk., then assoc. firm Dunham, Boman, Leskera & Churchill, East St. Louis, Ill., 1973-78; ptnr. Cadagin, Cain & Tognarelli, Collinsville, 1978-84; ptnr. firm Tognarelli & Mattea, Collinsville, 1984-91, Tognarelli & Levo, P.C., Collinsville, 1992—. Pres. parish coun. Sts. Peter and Paul Roman Cath. Ch., Collinsville, 1988—. Named One of Outstanding Young Men of Am., Collinsville Jaycees, 1981, also recipient Disting. Svc. award, 1984. Mem. ABA (sect. of econs. of law practice com. on lawyer rels. with pub. 1986-87, vice-chair crim. justice com. sec. gen. practice 1990-93, vice-chmn. criminal law com. gen. practice sect. 1990—), Ill. Trail Lawyers Assn. (membership com.), Ill. State Bar Assn. (chmn. jud. adv. polls com. 1986-87, membership and bar activities 1988-93, com. pub. rels.), Collinsville C. of C. (chmn. ambs. 1984-87, v.p. orgn. affairs 1986-88, pres. 1988-90), Rotary (pres. Collinsville 1983-84), KC, Phi Beta Kappa. Democrat. General practice, Personal injury, Probate. Home: 303 Chesapeake Ln Collinsville IL 62234-4374 Office: Tognarelli & Levo PC PO Box 68 Collinsville IL 62234-0068

TOLINS, ROGER ALAN, lawyer; b. Bklyn., Jan. 25, 1936; s. Albert and Claire (Rothstein) T.; m. Doris Levine, May 15, 1960; children: Fran, Jonathan. AB with distinction, Dartmouth Coll., 1956; LLB, NYU, 1959, LLM in Taxation, 1961. Bar: N.Y. 1959. Assoc. Brennan, London & Buttenwieser, N.Y.C., 1961-67; ptnr. Goldfeld, Charak, Tolins & Lowenfels, 1967-74, Tolins & Lowenfels, N.Y.C., 1975—. Guest lectr. in securities law Seton Hall U. Sch. Law, 1989—. With U.S. Army, 1959-60. Mem. ABA (sect. on taxation), N.Y. State Bar Assn. Administrative and regulatory, General corporate, Corporate taxation.

TOLL, PERRY MARK, lawyer, educator; b. Kansas City, Mo., Oct. 28, 1945; s. Mark Irving and Ruth (Parker) T.; m. Mary Anne Shottenkirk, Aug. 26, 1967; children: Andrea Lynne, Hillary Anne. BS in Polit. Sci. and Econs., U. Kans., 1967, JD, 1970. Bar: Mo. 1970 1970, U.S. Dist. Ct. (we. dist.) Mo. 1970, U.S. Tax. Ct. 1979, U.S. Supreme Ct. 1979. With Shughart, Thomson & Kilroy P.C., Kansas City, 1970—, pres., 1995—, chmn. bus. dept., 1999—. Asst. prof. deferred compensation U. Mo., Kansas City, 1979-83; bd. dirs., pres. Heart of Am. Tax Inst., Kansas City, 1975-87. Mem., chmn. Prairie Village (Kans.) Bd. Zoning Appeals, 1977-95. Mem. ABA, Mo. Bar Assn., Nat. Health Lawyers Assn., Am. Agr. Law Assn., Mo. Merchants and Mfrs. Assn., Greater Kansas City Med. Mgrs. Assn., Lawyers Assn. Kansas City, East Kans. Estate Planning Coun. (bd. dirs., pres.), Phi Kappa Tau (bd. dirs. Beta Theta chpt.). Estate planning, Health, Pension, profit-sharing, and employee benefits. Office: Shughart Thomson & Kilroy 12 Wyandotte Plz 120 W 12th St Ste 1500 Kansas City MO 64105-1929

TOLL, SEYMOUR I. lawyer, writer, educator; b. Phila., Feb. 19, 1925; s. Louis David and Rose (Eisenstein) T.; m. Jean Marie Barth, June 25, 1951; children: Emily Barth, Elizabeth Terry, Martha Anne, Constance Nora Frances. BAmagna cum laude, Yale U., 1948, LLB, 1951. Bar: N.Y. 1953, U.S. Dist. Ct. (ea. dist.) Pa. 1955, Pa. 1956, U.S. Ct. Appeals (3d cir.) 1956, U.S. Dist. Ct. (so. dist.) N.Y. 1958, U.S. Supreme Ct. 1958, U.S. Ct. Appeals (5th cir.) 1970. Law clk. U.S. Dist. Ct. (so. dist.), N.Y.C., 1951-52; from assoc. to ptnr. Richter, Lord, Toll & Cavanaugh, Phila., 1955-65, 69; sole practice, 1965-68, 69-74; ptnr. Toll, Ebby, Langer & Marvin, 1975-2001; of counsel Marvin, Larsson, Henkin & Scheuritzel, 2001—. Vis. lectr. U. Pa. Law Sch., 1978-86. Author: Zoned American, 1969, A Judge Uncommon, 1993 (Athenaeum Literary award 1995); jour. editor: The Retainer, 1972-73, A Court's Heritage, 1984-88; jour. assoc. editor: The Shingle, 1970-78, editor, 1979-80; contbr. numerous articles to profl. jours. Pres. Phila. Citizen's Coun. on City Planning, 1967-69; pub. dir., mem. exec. com. Phila. Housing Devel. Corp., 1967-72; bd. dirs. The Libr. Co. Phila. (pres. 1992-98). Grantee Am. Philos. Soc., 1968. Mem. ABA, Pa. Bar Assn., Phila. Bar Assn. (Fidelity Bank award 1984), Am. Coll. Trial Lawyers, 3d Cir. Jud. Conf. (permanent del.), Jr. Legal Club, Phi Beta Kappa. Democrat. Jewish. Clubs: The Franklin Inn (pres. 1981-84), Yale (Phila.). Avocations: music, sailing, travel. Antitrust, Federal civil litigation, Libel. Home: 453 Conshohocken State Rd Bala Cynwyd PA 19004-2642 Office: Marvin Larsson Henkin & Scheuritzel Centre Sq West Ste #3510 1500 Market St Philadelphia PA 19102 E-mail: stoll@marvinlarsson.com

TOLLEY, EDWARD DONALD, lawyer; b. San Antonio, Jan. 31, 1950; s. Lyle Oren and Mary Theresa Tolley; m. Beth Dekle Tolley; 1 child, Edward Spencer. BBA, U. Ga., 1971, MBA, 1974, JD, 1975. Bar: Ga. 1975, U.S. Dist. Ct. (5th cir.) 1976, U.S. Supreme Ct. 1978, U.S. Ct. Appeals (11th cir.) 1981. Ptnr. Cook, Noell, Tolley Bates and Michael and predecessor firms, Athens, Ga., 1975—. Lectr. various colls., univs., civic and profl. groups. Mem. Family Counseling Assn. of Athens, Inc., mem. Gov.'s Commn. on Criminal Sanctions and Correctional Facilities, 1988-90; past bd. dirs. Am. Cancer Soc.; pres. Clarke County Bd. Edn., 1992-93. Recipient award for cmty. svc. Chief Justice Ga. Supreme Ct., 2000. Fellow Ga. Bar Found., Am. Bd. Criminal Lawyers (bd. dirs. 1987, pres. 1996); mem. Fed. Bar Assn. (sec. 1983, treas. 1985, pres. Macon chpt. 1997-98), Ste Bar Ga. (chmn. law office and econ. com., bd. govs. 1985—, formal adv. opinion bd.), Ga. Trial Lawyers (v.p.), Ga. Assn. Criminal Def. Lawyers (pres. 1985, Indigent Def. award 1983, 88), Athens Bar Assn. (past pres.), Am. Judicature Soc., Order of Barristers (Cmty. Svc. award Chief Justice Ga. Supreme Ct., 2000). General civil litigation, Criminal, Personal injury. Office: Cook Noell et al 304 E Washington St Athens GA 30601-2751

TOMAIN, JOSEPH PATRICK, dean, law educator; b. Long Branch, N.J., Sept. 3, 1948; s. Joseph Pasquale and Bernice M. (Krzan) T.; m. Kathleen Corcione, Aug. 1, 1971; children: Joseph Anthony, John Fiore. AB, U. Notre Dame, 1970; JD, George Washington U., 1974. Bar: N.J., Iowa. Assoc. Giordano & Halleran, Middletown, N.J., 1974-76; from asst. to prof. law Drake U. Sch. Law, Des Moines, 1976-83; prof. law U. Cin. Coll. Law, 1983—, acting dean, 1989-90, dean, 1990—, Nippert prof. law, 1990—. Vis. prof. law U. Tex. Sch. Law, Austin, 1986-87. Author: Energy Law in a Nutshell, 1981, Nuclear Power Transformation, 1987; co-author: Energy Decision Making, 1983, Energy Law and Policy, 1989, Energy and Natural Resources Law, 1992, Regulatory Law and Policy, 1993, 2d edit., 1998, Energy, The Environment and the Global Economy, 2000. Bd. trustees Ctr. for Chem. Addictions Treatment, Cin., Vol. Lawyers for Poor, Cin.; mem. steering com. BLAC/CBA Round Table, Cin.; chair KnowledgeWorks Found. Served with USAR, 1970-76. Mem. ABA, Am. Law Inst., Ohio State Bar Assn. (del.), Cin. Bar Assn. (bd. trustees). Roman Catholic. E-mail: joseph. Home: 3009 Springer Ave Cincinnati OH 45208-2440 Office: U Cin Coll Law Office Dean PO Box 210040 Cincinnati OH 45221-0040 E-mail: tomain@law.uc.edu

TOMAO, PETER JOSEPH, lawyer; b. Bklyn., Feb. 11, 1951; s. Joseph Louis Marie A. T.; m. Kathryn Carter Reed, Oct. 15, 1978. BA, St. John's U., Queen's, N.Y., 1973; JD, Columbia U., 1976. Bar: N.Y. 1977, D.C. 1980, U.S. Dist. Ct. D.C.,1980, U.S. Ct. Appeals (2d cir.), 1983, U.S. Dist. Ct. (ea. dist.) N.Y. 1985, U.S. Dist. Ct. (so. dist.) N.Y. 1997. Trial atty. antitrust div. U.S. Dept. Justice, Washington, 1976-82; asst. U.S. atty. U.S. Dist. Ct. (ea. dist.) N.Y., Bklyn., Uniondale, and Garden City, N.Y., 1982-97; ptnr. Del Gadio & Tomao, Uniondale, 1997-99; pvt. practice Garden City, 1999—. Mem. Nassau County Bar Assn. (fed. cts. chmn. 1996-97, 99-2001), N.Y. Bar Assn., Theodore Roosevelt Am. Inn of Ct. (pres. 1996-97). Office: 226 Seventh St Ste 302 Garden City NY 11530-1666 E-mail: ptomao@justice.com

TOMAR, RICHARD THOMAS, lawyer; b. Camden, N.J., Mar. 4, 1945; s. William and Bette (Brown) T.; children: Lindsay, Leanne Meryl, Daniel Gregory. AB, Columbia Coll., 1967; JD, U. Pa., 1970. Bar: D.C. 1971, N.J. 1971, Md. 1976. Pvt. practice, Washington, 1971-73; ptnr. Philipson, Mallios & Tomar, P.C., 1973-89, Margolius, Mallios, Davis, Rider & Tomar, LLP, Washington, 1989—. Mem. D.C. Trial Lawyers Assn. (bd. dirs. 1980-89). Federal civil litigation. Office: Margolius Mallios Davis Rider & Tomar LLP 1828 L St NW Ste 500 Washington DC 20036-5127 E-mail: rtomar@mmdrt.com

TOMAR, WILLIAM, lawyer; b. Camden, N.J., Oct. 10, 1916; s. Morris and Katie (Sadinsky) T.; m. Bette Brown, Nov. 28, 1942; children: Richard T., Dean Jonathon. LLB cum laude, Rutgers U., 1939. Bar: N.J. 1940, U.S. Ct. Appeals (3d cir.) 1953, U.S. Supreme Ct. 1953, Fla. 1975, D.C. 1978. Sr. ptnr. Tomar, O'Brien, Kaplan, Jacobi & Graziano, Haddonfield, N.J., 1958—. Mem. faculty Ctr. Trial and Appellate Advocacy, Hastings Coll. Law, U. Calif., 1971-86, Nat. Coll. Advocacy, Harvard U. Law Sch., 1973-75. Mem. UN Speakers Bur., UNICEF, 1960—; mem. adv. bd. Salvation Army, 1967-84, Inst. Med. Rsch., 1967—, N.J. Capital Punishment Study Commn., 1972-73, Touro Law Sch., 1981; mem. adv. bd. N.J. Student Assistance Bd., 1987-98, vice chmn., 1992-98; bd. dirs. South Jersey Assn. Performing Arts, Haddonfield Symphony Soc., 1985—; bd. dirs., pres. 1992-99; mem. exec. bd. So. N.J. Coun. Boy Scouts Am., 1985—, pres. 1992—, Disting. Citizen award, 2001; vice chmn., mem. bd. trustees Cooper Hosp., Univ. Med. Ctr. 1979-97, bd. mem. emeritus 1998; mem. planning com. World Peace Through Law Ctr., 1970—; trustee Cooper Med. Ctr., 1979—. Recipient Disting. Alumni award Rutgers U. Sch. Law, 1996, Neighbor of Yr. award N.J. chpt. ARC, 1999; honored at Juvile Diabetes Found. South Jersey ann. gala, 2000. Fellow Am. Coll. Trial Lawyers; mem. ABA, Assn. Trial Lawyers Am. (assoc. editor jour. 1962-68, gov. 1963-64, nat. parliamentarian 1964-70, nat. exec. com. 1964-70, chmn. seminars 1965 lectr. student adv. program 1968—), World Jurist Assn. (founding mem. 1974—), N.J. Bar Assn. (fee arbitration com. 1972-74, 75-77), Trial Lawyers of N.J. (cert. by Supreme Ct. of N.J. as civil trial atty, Trial Bar award 1977), N.J. Workers Compensation Assn. (trustee 1958-83), N.Y. Trial Attys. Assn., Phila. Trial Lawyers Assn., Camden County Bar Found. (bd. trustees 1986—), Camden County Bar Assn., (com. on rels. of bench and bar 1964—, adult edn. com. 1975—). General civil litigation, Environmental, Personal injury. Office: 20 Brace Rd Cherry Hill NJ 08034-2634

TOMASULO, VIRGINIA MERRILLS, retired lawyer; b. Belleville, Ill., Feb. 10, 1919; d. Frederick Emerson and Mary Eckert (Turner) Merrills; m. Nicholas Angelo Tomasulo, Sept. 30, 1952 (dec. May 1986); m. Harrison I. Anthes, Mar. 5, 1988. BA, Wellesley Coll., 1940; LLB (now JD), Washington U., St. Louis, 1943. Bar: Mo. 1942, U.S. Ct. Appeals (D.C. cir.) 1958, Mich. 1974, U.S. Dist. Ct. (ea. dist) Mo. 1943, U.S. Supreme Ct. 1954, U.S. Tax Ct. 1974, U.S. Ct. Appeals (6th cir.) 1976. Atty. Dept. of Agr., St. Louis and Washington, 1943-48; Office of Solicitor, Chief Counsel's Office IRS, Washington and Detroit, 1949-75; assoc. Baker & Hostetler, Washington, 1977-82, ptnr., 1982-89, of counsel, 1989, ret., 1989. Sec. S.W. Day Care Assn., Washington, 1971-73. Mem. ABA, Mo. Bar, Fed. Bar, Village on the Green Residents Assn. (chair health care com., mem. fin. com.), Wellesley Club (Ctrl. Fla.). Episcopalian. Corporate taxation, Personal income taxation, Tax-exempt organizations. Home: 570 Village Pl Apt 300 Longwood FL 32779-6037

TOMICH, LILLIAN, lawyer; b. L.A. d. Peter S. and Yovanka P. (Ivanovic) T. AA, Pasadena City Coll., 1954; BA in Polit. Sci., UCLA, 1956, cert. secondary tchg., 1957, MA, 1958; JD, U. So. Calif., 1961. Bar: Calif., U.S. Ct. Appeals (9th Cir.) 1978. Sole practice, 1961-66; house counsel Mfrs. Bank, L.A., 1966; assoc. Hurley, Shaw & Tomich, San Marino, Calif., 1968-76, Driscoll & Tomich, San Marino, 1976—. Dir. Continental Culture Specialists Inc., Glendale, Calif. Trustee St. Sava Serbian Orthodox Ch., San Gabriel, Calif. Recipient Episcopal Gramata award Serbian Orthodox Met. of Midwestern Am., 1993, Episcopal Gramata award Serbian Orthodox Bishop of Western Am., 1996; Charles Fletcher Scott fellow, 1957; U. So. Calif. Law Sch. scholar, 1958. Mem. ABA, Calif. Bar Assn., Los Angeles County Bar Assn., Women Lawyers Assn., San Marino C. of C., UCLA Alumni Assn., Town Hall and World Affairs Coun., Order Mast and Dagger, Iota Tau Tau, Alpha Gamma Sigma, Pi Kappa Delta. General civil litigation, General corporate, Probate. Office: 2460 Huntington Dr San Marino CA 91108-2643

TOMITA, SUSAN K. lawyer; b. Wailuku Maui, Hawaii, Jan. 10, 1954; d. Kazuo Tomita and Helen E.V. Ing; 1 child, Anthony. BA, Stanford U., 1976; JD, U. Santa Clara, 1979. Staff atty. Nat. Indian Youth Coun., Albuquerque, 1979-80; assoc. Luebben, Hughes & Kelly, 1980-83; ptnr. Luebben, Hughes & Tomita, 1983-88; shareholder Tomita & Simpson, P.C., 1988—. Chair elder law sect. N.Mex. State Bar, Albuquerque, 1995-96, chair Indian law sect., 1988-89, mem. com. on legal svcs. to disabled, 1993—. Author: The Handbook for Guardians and Conservators: A Practical Guide to New Mexico Law, 1997, Alternatives to Guardianships and Conservatorships, 1997. Bd. dirs. Alzheimer's Assn., Albuquerque, 1996—, Legal Aid Soc. Albuquerque, 1985-87, Indian Pueblo Legal Svcs., Santa Ana, N.Mex., 1981-83. Mem. Nat. Acad. Elder Law Attys., N.Mex. Estate Planning Coun. Democrat. Presbyterian. Avocations: bicycling, reading. Estate planning, Probate, Estate taxation. Office: Tomita & Simpson PC 4263 Montgomery Blvd NE Ste 210 Albuquerque NM 87109-6708

TOMLINSON, HERBERT WESTON, lawyer; b. Upland, Pa., Feb. 11, 1930; s. Herbert Elmer and Hilda Josephine (Schlosbon) T.; m. Mary Jean Litwhiler, Oct. 27, 1961. BS, Pa. State U., 1952, postgrad., 1956-57; JD, Dickinson Sch. Law, 1960; postgrad., Temple U. Law Sch., 1969-73; BA with highest distinction, Pa. State U., 1994. Bar: Pa. 1961, U.S. Supreme Ct. 1968; lic. pilot. Law clk., pres. Delaware County Bar Assn., 1960-61; assoc. DeFuria Larkin Defuria, Chester, Pa., 1960-62, Hodge & Balderston, Chester, 1962-65, Edward McLaughlin, Chester, 1965-67; exec. dir. Legal Svcs. Program, Deleware County, 1967-69; atty. pvt. practice, Media, Pa., 1969—; sr. staff atty. Delaware County Pub. Defender's Office, 1969—. Prof. bus. law Pa. State U., 1969-75, Widener U., 1971-76, 78-80, Delaware County C.C., 1971-75; arbitrator Am. Arbitration Assn. Actor in TV commercials, 1998—. Legal counsel Disabled Vets Am.; county dir. Delaware County March of Dimes, 1966-71; rep. candidate U.S. Ho. Reps., 1976; rep. committeeman, 1966—, treas. 168th Legis. Dist., 1975-81; chmn. Media Rep. Com., 1975-76, Media Borough Auditor, 1975-79; nat. dir. Jaycees, 1965-66. Capt. USMCR, 1952-56. Named Outstanding Young Men Am. U.S. Jaycees, 1966. Mem. AAUP, ABA, Am. Assn. Trial Lawyers, Nat. Assn. Securities Dealers, Am. Arbitration Assn., Pa. Bar Assn., Pa. Trial Lawyers Assn., Delaware County Bar Assn., Delaware County Real Estate Bd., Delaware County Med. Soc. (dir. pub. health fund 1967—), Aircraft Owners and Pilots Assn., Kiwanis, Masons, Shriners, Rotary, Phi Tehta Kappa (past pres.), Phi Kappa Phi, Alpha Sigma Lambda), Screen Actors Guild. Republican. Presbyterian. Family and matrimonial, Personal injury, Probate. Home: 103 Kershaw Rd Wallingford PA 19086-6311 Office: 8 W Front St Media PA 19063-3306 E-mail: westontomlinson@msn.com

TOMLINSON, MARGARET LYNCH, lawyer; b. Cleve., June 21, 1929; d. John Joseph and Margaret (Stevenson) Lynch; m. Alexander C. Tomlinson. AB, Smith Coll., 1950; JD, N.Y. Law Sch., 1963. Bar: N.Y. 1963, D.C. 1971, U.S Ct. Appeals (D.C. cir.) 1971. Staff officer Dept. of State, 1950-55; U.S. Del. UN Gen. Assembly, N.Y.C., 1964-68; asst. legal adviser U.S. Mission to the UN, 1963-69; asst. to Sen. Claiborne Pell, Washington, 1969-71; sr. adviser U.S. Del. to the Law of the Sea Conf.,

1972-78; ptnr. Dickey, Roadman & Dickey, Washington, 1978-82; cons. office gen. counsel CIA, 1987-93. Cons. Law of the Sea; bd. dirs. Coun. Ocean Law, Washington, 1984—, vice-chmn., 1994—; U.S. del. spl. session UN Gen. Assembly, 1994. Contbr. articles to profl. jours. Mem. ABA (internat. law sect., chmn. law of the sea com.), Am. Soc. Internat. Law, Internat. Law Assn., D.C. Bar Assn., Nat. Press Club, Sulgrave Club. Public international. Home: 3314 P St NW Washington DC 20007-2701

TOMLINSON, WARREN LEON, lawyer; b. Denver, Apr. 2, 1930; s. Leslie Aultimer and Esther (Hasler) T.; m. Lois Elaine Retallack, Aug. 8, 1953 (div. 1987); children: Stephanie Lynn, Brett Louis; m. Linda Jane Beville, May 17, 1989. BA, U. Denver, 1951; JD, NYU, 1954. Bar: Colo. 1954, U.S. Dist. Ct. Colo., U.S. Ct. Appeals (10th cir.) 1958, U.S. Supreme Ct.. 1960. Assoc. Holland & Hart, Denver, 1958-63, ptnr., 1963-95, mediator, arbitrator, 1995—. Contbr. numerous articles to profl. jours. Lt. U.S. Army, 1954-58. Fellow Coll. Labor and Employment Lawyers; mem. ABA (chmn. law practice mgmt. sect. 1988-89, charter fellow Coll. of Law Practice Mgmt. 1994). Republican. Episcopalian. Avocations: skiing, white-water rafting. General civil litigation, Construction, Labor. Home: 5017 Main Gore Dr S Apt 4 Vail CO 81657-5426 Office: Holland & Hart 555 17th St Ste 2900 Denver CO 80202-3979 E-mail: wltvail@aol.com

TOMLJANOVICH, ESTHER M. state supreme court justice; b. Galt, Iowa, Nov. 1, 1931; d. Chester William and Thelma L. (Brooks) Moellering; m. William S. Tomljanovich, Dec. 26, 1957; 1 child, William Brooks. AA, Itasca Jr. Coll., 1951; BSL, St. Paul Coll. Law, 1953, LLB, 1955. Bar: Minn. 1955, U.S. Dist. Ct. Minn. 1958. Asst. revisor of statutes State of Minn., St. Paul, 1957-66, revisor of statutes, 1974-77, dist. ct. judge Stillwater, 1977-90; assoc. justice Minn. Supreme Ct., St. Paul, 1990-98. Mem. adv. bd. women offenders Minn. Dept. Corrections, 1999—; mem. leadership com. So. Minn. Legal Svcs. Corp., 1999—. Former mem. North St. Paul Bd. Edn., Maplewood Bd. Edn., Lake Elmo Planning Commn; bd. trustees William Mitchell Coll. Law, 1995—, Legal Rights Ctr., pres., bd. dirs., 1999), Southern Minn. Legal Services Corp., Itasca Community Coll. Found, bd. dir. 1996—; pres., bd. dirs. Medica Health Ins. Co. Recipient Centennial 2000 award William Mitchell Coll; named one of One Hundred Who Made a Difference William Mitchell Coll. Law Mem. Minn. State Bar Assn., Bus. and Profl. Women's Assn. St. Paul (former pres.), Minn. Women Laywers (founding mem.). Office: Supreme Ct MN 423 Minnesota Judicial Center 25 Constitution Ave Saint Paul MN 55155-1500

TOMPERT, JAMES EMIL, lawyer; b. Battle Creek, Mich., July 21, 1954; s. James Russell and Marjorie Mary (Storkan) T. BA, Duke U., 1976; JD, U. Mich., 1981. Bar: D.C. 1981, Md. 1985, Va. 1986. Legis. asst. to congressman U.S. Ho. of Rep., Washington, 1977-78; assoc. Baker & Hostetler, 1981-84, Cooter & Gell, Washington, 1984-86, ptnr., 1987-94, Cooter Mangold Tompert & Wayson LLC, Washington, 1995—. Mem. Arts Club Washington, 1989—, Univ. Club of Washington, 1997—. Mem. ABA, D.C. Bar Assn. Federal civil litigation, General civil litigation, State civil litigation. Office: Cooter Mangold Tompert & Wayson LLC 5301 Wisconsin Ave NW Washington DC 20015-2015 E-mail: jtompert@cootermangold.com

TOMPKINS, JOSEPH BUFORD, JR. lawyer; b. Roanoke, Va., Apr. 4, 1950; s. Joseph Buford and Rebvecca Louise (Johnston) T.; m. Nancy Powell Wilson, Feb. 6, 1993; children: Edward Graves, Claiborne Frobes; 1 stepchild, Clayton Tate Wilson. BA in Politics summa cum laude, Washington and Lee U., 1971; M Pub. Policy, JD, Harvard U., 1975. Bar: Va. 1975, U.S. Ct. Appeals (D.C. cir.), U.S. Ct. Appeals (5th cir.), 1977, U.S. Supreme Ct. 1977, U.S. Dist. Ct. D.C. 1982, U.S. Ct. Appeals (11th cir.) 1982, U.S. Ct. Appeals (3d cir.) 1983, U.S. Ct. Appeals (6th cir.) 1985, U.S. Ct. Appeals (7th cir.) 1991, U.S. Ct. Appeals (4th cir.) 1993. Assoc. Sidley & Austin (now Sidley Austin Brown & Wood), Washington, 1975-79, ptnr., 1982—; assoc. dir. Office Policy and Mgmt. Analysis criminal divsn. U.S. Dept. Justice, 1979-80, dep. chief fraud sect. criminal divsn., 1980-82. Contbr. articles to legal publs. Mem. Va. Bd. Health Professions, Richmond, 1984-92, vice chmn., 1984-86, chmn., 1986-88, 90-91. Mem. ABA (white collar crime com. criminal justice sect. 1980—, chmn. task foce on computer crime 1982-92), FBA, Va. Bar Assn., D.C. Bar Assn., Phi Beta Kappa, Federal civil litigation, State civil litigation, Criminal. Home: 8146 Wellington Rd Alexandria VA 22308-1214 Office: Sidley Austin Brown & Wood 1501 K St NW 8th Fl Washington DC 20005 Fax: 202-736-8711. E-mail: jtompkins@sidley.com

TOMPKINS, RAYMOND EDGAR, lawyer; b. Oklahoma City, July 13, 1934; s. Charles Edgar and Eva Mae (Hodges) T.; m. Sue Anne Sharpe, June 10, 1963; children: Matthew Stephen, Christopher T., Katherine Anne. BS, Okla. State U., 1956; JD, U. Okla., 1963. Bar: Okla. 1963, U.S. Dist. Ct. (no. dist.) Okla. 1963, U.S. Dist. Ct. (we. dist.) Okla. 1964, U.S. Ct. Appeals (10th cir.) 1965, U.S. Supreme Ct. 1968, U.S. dist. Ct. (ea. dist.) Okla. 1969, U.S. Ct. Appeals (9th cir.) 1981, U.S. Ct. Appeals (4th cir.) 1986. Adminstrv. asst. U.S. Congress, 1966-68; ptnr. Linn & Helms, Oklahoma City, 1980-90, Daughery, Bradford, Haught & Tompkins, P.C., Oklahoma City, 1990-94; shareholder Conner & Winters, P.C., 1994—. Mediator and arbitrator Nat. Assn. Securities Dealers. Past chmn. bd. trustees Okla. Ann. Methodist Conf., St. Luke's United Meth. Ch.; past chmn. adminstrv. bd.; mem. Okla. Bur. Investigation Commn., past chmn.; past gen. counsel Rep. State com., Interstate Oil Compact. Maj. USAR. Recipient award of Honor Oklahoma City Bi-Centennial Commn., 1976. Fellow Am. Coll. Civil Trial Mediators; master William S. Holliway Am. Inns of Ct. (emeritus, pres.), Robert J. Turner Am. Inn of Ct. (pres.); mem. ABA, Okla. County Bar Assn. (Pres.'s award 1988), Okla. Bar Assn. (chmn. bench and bar com. 1995-97, chmn.-elect ADR sect., Law Day award), Am. Arbitration Assn. (mediator/arbitrator), NASD (mediator, arbitrator), Am. Judicature Soc., Assn. Atty.-Mediators (past pres. Okla. chpt., nat. dir. and sec., Nat. President's award 2000), Blue Key, Lions (pres. Oklahoma City chpt.). General civil litigation. Home: 329 NW 40th St Oklahoma City OK 73118-8419 Office: 211 N Robinson Ave Ste 1700 Oklahoma City OK 73102-7136

TONA, THOMAS, lawyer; b. Flushing, N.Y., July 30, 1968; s. Thomas Peter and Lorraine T. BA, Hofstra U., 1990, JD, 1993. Bar: N.Y. 1994, U.S. Dist. Ct. (so. and ea. dists.) 1994. Assoc. Generosa & Carusona, P.C., Mineola, N.Y., 1993-94, Deutsch & Schneider, Queens, 1994-95, Cartier, Hogan, Sullivan, Bernstein & Auerbach, Patchogue, 1996—. Advisor Hofstra U. Sch. of Law Moot Ct., Hempstead, N.Y., 1993; judge Pace Law Sch. Moot Ct., Westchester, N.Y., 1996. Mem. ABA, N.Y. State Bar Assn., Suffolk County Bar Assn., Nat. Inst. for Trial Advocacy (cert.), Sons of Italy. Roman Catholic. State civil litigation, Insurance, Personal injury. Office: Cartier Hogan Sullivan Bernstein & Auerbah 77 Medford Ave Patchogue NY 11772-1230

TONDEL, LAWRENCE CHAPMAN, lawyer; b. N.Y.C., Apr. 9, 1946; s. Lyman Mark and Jean (Basch) T.; m. Sharyn A. Smith, Aug. 3, 1974; children: Michael Lawrence, Kathryn Chapman. Student, The Lawrenceville Sch., 1964; AB, Wesleyan U., 1968; JD, U. Mich., 1971. N.Y. 1972. Assoc. Brown & Wood LLP, N.Y.C., 1971-79, ptnr., 1980-97, sr. ptnr., 1997-2001; ptnr. Sidley Austin Brown & Wood LLP, 2001—. Chmn. Internat. Bus. Comm. Ann. Internat. Forum on Offshore Funds, 1993-2000. Trustee Elisabeth Morrow Sch., Englewood, N.J., 1988-93; mem. Washington U. St. Louis Exec. Com. Parents Coun., 2000-2001. Mem. ABA, Am. Law Inst., Am. Bar Found., Assn. Bar City N.Y. Republican. Episcopalian. Contracts commercial, Finance, Securities. E-mail: ltondel@sidley.com

TONE, PHILIP WILLIS, retired lawyer, former federal judge; b. Chgo., Apr. 9, 1923; s. Elmer James and Frances (Willis) T.; m. Gretchen Altfillisch, Mar. 10, 1945; children: Michael P., Jeffrey R., Susan A. BA, U. Iowa, 1943, JD, 1948. Bar: Iowa 1948, Ill. 1950, D.C. 1950. Law clk. Justice Wiley B. Rutledge, Supreme Ct. U.S., Washington, 1948-49; assoc. firm Covington & Burling, 1949-50; assoc., ptnr. firm Jenner & Block, Chgo., 1950-72, 80-97; judge U.S. Dist. Ct., 1972-74, U.S. Ct. Appeals (7th cir.), Chgo., 1974-80; spl. counsel Nat. Commn. on Causes and Prevention of Violence, 1968-69, U.S. Senate subcom. to investigate individuals representing interests of fgn. govts., 1980. Chmn. Ill. Supreme Ct. Rules Com., 1968-71, sec., 1963-68; mem. Com. on Jud. Br. of Jud. Conf. of U.S., 1987-91; gen. counsel U.S. Golf Assn., 1988-92; mem. Fed. Jud. Fellows Commn., 1986-92; chmn. Fed. Jud. Ctr. Found. Contbr. articles to legal periodicals. With AUS, 1943-46. Grad. fellow Law Sch. Yale U., 1948. Fellow Am. Coll. Trial Lawyers (regent 1984-87, pres. 1988-89); mem. ABA, Am. Bar Found., Am. Law Inst., Ill. Bar Assn. (bd. govs. 1960-64), Chgo. Bar Assn. (bd. mgrs. 1966-69), Am. Judicature Soc., Law Club Chgo. (pres. 1979-80), Legal Club Chgo. Antitrust, Federal civil litigation, General civil litigation.

TONELLO, MATTEO, lawyer; b. Mirano, Venezia, Italy, Sept. 18, 1971; JD, U. Bologna, Italy, 1994; LLM, Harvard Law Sch., 1997; PhD, Scuola Superiore Sant'Anna, Pisa, Italy, 1998. Bar: N.Y., 1998, Italian Bar, 1998. Assoc. Davis, Polk & Wardwell, N.Y.C., 1998—. Vis. scholar Yale Law Sch., New Haven, Conn., 1997. Author: (book) The Abuse of Limited Liability of Business Corporation, 1999; contbr. articles to profl. jours. and publs. Recipient Felice Gianani award Italian Bank Assn., 1996. Office: Davis Polk & Wardwell 450 Lexington Ave New York NY 10003

TONSING, MICHAEL JOHN, lawyer, educator, arbitrator; b. Los Angeles, May 10, 1943; s. John Maurice and Mary Ellen (McMahon) T.; m. Cecilia Ann Degnan, Jan. 29, 1966; children— Catherine, Michael, Jr. B.A., St. Mary's Coll., 1965; M.A., Claremont Grad. Sch., 1970; J.D., U. San Francisco, 1975. Bar: Calif. 1976, U.S. Dist. Ct. (no. dist.) Calif. 1976, U.S. Supreme Ct. 1981, U.S. Ct. Mil. Appeals 1982, U.S. Ct. Appeals (9th cir.) 1982. Sole practice, Walnut Creek, Calif., 1976-77; adminstrv. law judge Pub. Employment Relations Bd., San Francisco, 1977-80; jud. fellow U.S. Supreme Ct., Washington, 1980-81; asst. U.S. atty. Dept. Justice, San Francisco, 1981-84; assoc. O'Gara & McGuire, San Francisco, 1984-85; ptnr. Pierucci & Tonsing, Oakland, Calif., 1985-88; prin. Tonsing Law Offices Oakland and San Mateo, Calif., 1988-94, Littler Mendelson, San Francisco, 1994-99; cons. Employment Law Tng., 1997—; adj. prof. St. Mary's Coll. Paralegal Program, Moraga, Calif., 1977—, also dir.; chair bd. Calif. Admin. Law Coll., Sacramento, 1978-80. Vol. San Francisco Bay council Girl Scouts U.S., Oakland, 1966—: scoutmaster Piedmont (Calif.) Council Boy Scouts Am., 1987-91; dir. San Francisco chpt. Nat. Found. for Ilietis and Colitis, 1988-94; trustee Dunsmuir House & Gardens, Inc., 1988-94. Weaver fellow Claremont Grad. Sch., Calif., 1966; recipient Tom C. Clark award U.S. Supreme Ct., Washington, 1981. Mem. ABA, Fed. Bar Assn. (pres. San Francisco chpt. 1985-86, nat. v.p. for 9th cir., 1986-90, editor The Federal Lawyer 1995—), Am. Arbitration Assn. (labor arbitrator 1979—), Bar Assn. San Francisco, Alameda County Bar Assn., U. San Francisco Law Sch. Alumni Assn. (pres. 1992-93, bd. govs. 1986-95), Lakeview Club, Claremont Country. Republican. Roman Catholic. Federal civil litigation, Education and schools, Labor. Office: Employment Law Tng Inc 650 California St Fl 20 San Francisco CA 94108-2702

TOOBIN, JEFFREY ROSS, writer, legal analyst; b. N.Y.C., May 21, 1960; s. Jerome and Marlene Sanders T.; m. Amy Bennett McIntosh, May 31, 1986; children: Ellen Frances, Adam Jerome. AB, Harvard U., 1982, JD, 1986. Bar: N.Y. 1987. Law clerk Hon. J. Edward Lumbard, N.Y.C., 1986-87; assoc. counsel Indep. Counsel Lawrence Walsh, Washington, 1987-89; asst. U.S. Atty. Ea. Dist. N.Y., Bklyn., 1990-93; legal analyst ABC News, N.Y.C., 1996—; staff writer The New Yorker, 1993—. Author: Opening Arguments: A Young Lawyer's First Case-United States v. Oliver North, 1991, The Run of His Life: The People v. O.J. Simpson, 1996, A Vast Conspiracy: The Real Story of the Sex Scandal that Nearly Brought Down a President, 2000, Too Close To Call: The Thirty Six Day Battle To Decide the 2000 Election, 2001; contbr. articles to The New Yorker. Office: The New Yorker 4 Times Sq New York NY 10036-6592

TOOHEY, BRIAN FREDERICK, lawyer; b. Niagara Falls, N.Y., Dec. 14, 1944; s. Matthew and Marilyn (Hoag) T.; m. Mary Elizabeth Monihan; children: Maureen Elizabeth, Matthew Sheridan, Margaret Monihan, Mary Catherine, Elizabeth Warner. BS, Niagara U., 1966; JD, Cornell U., 1969. Bar: N.Y. 1969, N.Mex. 1978, Ohio 1980. Ptnr. Cohen, Swados, Wright, Hanifin & Bradford, Buffalo, 1973-77; pvt. practice Santa Fe, 1977-79; of counsel Jones, Day, Reavis & Pogue, Cleve., 1979-80, ptnr., 1981—. Mem. Citizens League Greater Cleve., 1982—. Lt. JAG Corps, USNR, 1970-73. Mem. ABA, N.Y. State Bar Assn., State Bar N.Mex., Ohio State Bar Assn., Greater Cleve. Bar Assn. Roman Catholic. Federal civil litigation, Insurance. Home: 25 Pepper Creek Dr Cleveland OH 44124-5279 Office: Jones Day Reavis & Pogue N Point 901 Lakeside Ave E Cleveland OH 44114-1190 E-mail: bftoohey@jonesday.com

TOOHEY, JAMES KEVIN, lawyer; b. Evanston, Ill., July 16, 1944; s. John Joseph and Ruth Regina (Cassidy) T.; m. Julie Marie Crane, Nov. 1, 1969 (div. Aug. 1977); children: Julie Colleen, Jeanne Christine; m. Anne Margaret Boettingheimer, May 28, 1983; children: James Robert, Kevin John, Casey Anne. BBA, U. Notre Dame, 1966; JD, Northwestern U., 1969. BAr: Ill. 1969, U.S. Dist. Ct. (no. dist.) Ill. 1971, U.S. Dist. Ct. (ctrl. dist.) Ill. 1991, U.S. Ct. Appeals (7th cir.) 1973, U.S. Ct. Appeals (8th cir.) 1975, U.S. Supreme Ct. 1988. Assoc. Taylor, Miller, Magner, Sprowl & Hutchings, Chgo., 1970-71; asst. U.S. Atty. Office U.S. Atty., 1971-74; assoc. Ross, Hardies, O'Keefe, Babcock & Parsons, 1974-77; ptnr. Ross & Hardies, 1978—. Mem. St. Mary of the Wood Parish Coun., 1999—. Mem. Ill. State Bar Assn., Soc. Trial Lawyers, Assn. Advancement of Automotive Medicine, Ill. Assn. Def. Attys., Trial Lawyers Club Chgo., Edgebrook Sauganash Athletic Assn. (bd. dirs., commr. 1993-96; softball, baseball, and basketball coach). Federal civil litigation, State civil litigation, Product liability. Office: Ross & Hardies 150 N Michigan Ave Ste 2500 Chicago IL 60601-7567 E-mail: james.toohey@rosshardies.com

TOOLE, BRUCE RYAN, reired lawyer; b. Missoula, Mont., June 21, 1924; s. John Howard and Marjorie Lee (Ross) T.; m. Loris Knoll, Sept. 29, 1951; children: Marjorie, Ryan, Allan. JD, U. Mont., 1949. Bar: Mont., U.S. Ct. Appeals (9th & Fed. cirs.), U.S. Supreme Ct., U.S. Claims Ct. Sole practice, Missoula, 1950; dep. county atty. Missoula County, 1951; ptnr. Crowley Law Firm, Billings, Mont., 1951-92, of counsel, 1992—; ret. Editor Mont. Lawyer, 1979-83. Mem. Mont. Com. for Humanities, Missoula; v.p. Billings Preservation Soc.; precinctman Yellowstone County Reps. With U.S. Army, 1944-45, ETO. Fellowship grantee NEH, Harvard U., 1980. Fellow Am. Coll. Trial Lawyers, Am. Bar Found.; mem. Am. Bd. Trial Advs., State Bar Mont. (pres. 1977-78), Yellowstone County Bar (pres. 1973, chmn. com. on mediation 1992), Internat. Assn. Def. Counsel. Avocations: politics, history, photography, metal work. Alternative dispute resolution, General civil litigation. Home: 3019 Glacier Dr Billings MT 59102-0711 Office: Crowley Law Firm 490 N 31st St Ste 500 Billings MT 59101-1288 E-mail: crowley@crowleylaw.com

TOOLE, JOHN HARPER, lawyer; b. Johnson City, N.Y., Apr. 4, 1941; s. Edward Joseph and Anne (Junius) T.; m. Lamar Sparkman, May 30, 1969; children: John Carter, Lucy Bland. BS, U. Va., 1963; JD, Washington Coll. of Law, 1971. Bar: Va. 1971, D.C. 1972. From assoc. to ptnr. Lewis, Mitchell & Moore, Tysons Corner, Va., 1971-77; ptnr. Watt, Tieder, Killian, Toole & Hoffar, 1978-82; ptnr., of counsel McGuire, Woods, Battle & Boothe, 1983-90, ptnr. McClean, Va., 1990-99; assoc. Cooley Godward LLP, Reston, 2000—. 1st. Lt. U.S. Army, 1963-66. Mem. ABA, Va. State Bar, Va. Bar Assn., D.C. Bar Assn. Banking, Contracts commercial, Real property. Office: Cooley Godward LLP 11951 Freedom Dr Reston VA 20190-5601 Fax: 703 456-8100. E-mail: jtoole@cooley.com

TOOMAJIAN, WILLIAM MARTIN, lawyer; b. Troy, N.Y., Sept. 26, 1943; s. Leo R. and Elizabeth (Gundrum) T.; children: Andrew, Philip. AB, Hamilton Coll., 1965; JD, U. Mich., 1968; LLM, N.Y.U., 1975. Bar: N.Y. 1968, Ohio 1978. Mem. firm Cadwalader, Wickersham & Taft, N.Y.C., 1971-77, Baker & Hostetler, Cleve., 1977—. Served to lt. USCG, 1968-71. Mem. ABA, Ohio Bar Assn., Cleve. Bar Assn., Cleve. Tax Club. Contracts commercial, Corporate taxation, Personal income taxation. Home: 3582 Lytle Rd Cleveland OH 44122-4908 Office: Baker & Hostetler 3200 National City Ctr 1900 E 9th St Ste 3200 Cleveland OH 44114-3475

TOOMEY, RICHARD ANDREW, JR. lawyer; b. Portsmouth, N.H., Oct. 21, 1944; s. Richard Andrew and Elizabeth Neal (Rylander) T.; m. Jeanne Zurmuhlen. BA, U. N.H., 1966; JD, NYU, 1969. Bar: N.Y. 1969, Mass. 1989. Atty. VISTA, Mpls., 1969-71; assoc. Carter, Ledyard & Milburn, N.Y.C., 1971-77; v.p., sr. assoc. counsel Chase Manhattan Bank, 1977-89; gen. coun. Shawmut Bank NA, Boston, 1989-94; dep. gen. coun. Shawmut Nat. Corp., 1995; group sr. counsel Fleet Fin. Group, 1996-2000; gen. counsel Fleet Bank NA, 1996-2000; asst. gen. counsel Sovereign Bank, 2000—. Mem. Boston Bar Assn., Assn. of Bar of the City of N.Y. Banking, Finance, Securities. E-mail: rtoomey@sovereignbank.com

TOONE, THOMAS LEE, lawyer; b. Kermit, Tex., Oct. 28, 1947; s. Herbert Hoover and Kathlyn (Collins) T.; m. Jane Elizabeth McCaslin, July 23, 1993; children: Thomas Lee Jr., John Kevin. BA in Zoology and Pre-Med, U. Tex., 1970, JD, 1973. Bar: Tex. 1973, Ariz. 1976, U.S. Dist. Ct. Ariz. 1976, U.S. Ct. Appeals (9th cir.) 1981, U.S. Supreme Ct. 1982; cert. specialist personal injury and wrongful death, PADI Open Water; lic. pilot, airplane single engine land. State senate legal counsel Tex. State Senate, Austin, Tex., 1970-73; elections atty. Tex. Sec. State, 1973-75; judge adv. USNG Res., 1973-76; trial atty. Beer & Toone, P.C., Phoenix, 1975—. Mem. faculty Nat. Inst. Trial Adv., Crash Survival Investigation Advanced Course; judge pro tempore Maricopa County Superior Ct. 1st lt. USNG, 1970-76. Fellow Ariz. Bar Found.; mem. ABA, Maricopa County Bar Assn. (sec., bd. dirs./treas., pres. elect, pres. 1995—), Am. Bd. Trial Advs. (assoc. mem., sec. 1998—, pres.-elect), Nat. Transp. Safety Bd. Bar Assn. (founding mem.), Ariz. Assn. Def. Counsel, Lawyer-Pilots Bar Assn., Def. Rsch. Inst., Internat. Assn. Def. Counsel. Avocations: rodeo events, snowskiing, tennis, jogging, hiking. Aviation, Insurance, Personal injury. Office: Beer Toone & Sheedy PC 76 E Mitchell Dr Phoenix AZ 85012-2330

TOOTHAKER-WALKER, STEPHANIE JEAN, lawyer; b. Ft. Lauderdale, Fla., Aug. 3, 1968; d. Stephen W. Toothaker and Nancy W. Gregoire; m. John A. Walker, Mar. 6, 1999. BA in Polit. Sci., U. Fla., 1991, JD, 1997. Staff aide U.S. Senator Bob Graham, Tallahassee, 1991, campaign rsch. dir., 1992, spl. projects coord. Washington, 1993-94; atty. Greenberg Traurig, Miami, Fla., 1998-99, Ruden McClosky et al, Ft. Lauderdale, 1999—. Mem. ABA, Dade County Bar Assn., U. Fla. Law Alumni Assn. Democrat. Roman Catholic. Office: Ruden McClosky et al 200 E Broward Blvd Fort Lauderdale FL 33301-1963

TOOTHMAN, JOHN WILLIAM, lawyer; b. Bryn Mawr, Pa., Dec. 6, 1954; s. Nolan Ernest Toothman and Caroline Nell Reed Pawl; m. Elizabeth McGee; 1 child, William. BS ChemE with honors, U. Va., 1977, MS ChemE, 1979; JD cum laude, Harvard U., 1981. Bar: D.C. 1981, Va. 1987, U.S. Dist. Ct. (ea. dist.) Va. 1987, U.S. Ct. Fed. Claims 1987, U.S. Ct. Appeals (4th and fed. cir.) 1987, U.S. Supreme Ct. 1987, Md. 1990, U.S. Dist. Ct. Md. 1990, U.S. Bankruptcy Ct. (ea. dist.) Va. 1994, U.S. Dist. Ct. Colo. 1998. Assoc. Howrey & Simon, Washington, 1981-83, Akin, Gump, Strauss et al, Washington, 1983-84; trial atty. civil div. U.S. Dept. Justice, 1984-86; assoc. John Grad & Assocs., Alexandria, Va., 1986-88; ptnr. Grad, Toothman, Logan & Chabot, P.C., 1988-89, Shulman, Rogers, Gandal, Pordy & Ecker, P.A., Alexandria, 1989-93; founder The Devil's Advocate & The Toothman Law Firm, P.C., 1993—. Guest lectr. George Washington U. Law Sch., 1988; lectr. in field; founder LitWatch, 1999. Author: (with Douglas Danner) Danner & Toothman Trial Practice Checklists, 1989, 2d edit., 2001; contbr. articles to profl. jours. NSF fellow, 1977. Mem. ABA (Ross Essay award 1995), Am. Corp. Counsel Assn., Sigma Xi, Tau Beta Pi. Federal civil litigation, General civil litigation, Contracts commercial. Address: 300 N Lee St Ste 450 Alexandria VA 22314-2640 E-mail: jtoothman@litwatch.com

TOPELIUS, KATHLEEN ELLIS, lawyer; b. July 15, 1948; BA, U. Conn., 1970; postgrad., U. Md., 1971-74; JD, Cath. U. Am., 1978. Bar: D.C. 1978, U.S. Supreme Ct. 1988. Atty. office of gen. counsel Fed. Home Loan Bank Bd., 1978-80; ptnr. Morgan, Lewis & Bockius, Washington, 1985-93, Bryan Cave, Washington, 1993—. Recipient Alpha award Fed. Home Loan Bank Bds., 1979. Office: Bryan Cave 700 13th St NW Fl 7 Washington DC 20005-5921

TOPOL, ALLAN JERRY, lawyer, author; b. Pitts., June 16, 1941; s. Morry and Selma (Weisman) T.; m. Barbara Rubenstein, July 27, 1963; children— David, Rebecca, Deborah, Daniella. B.S. in Chemistry, Carnegie-Mellon U., 1962; LL.B., Yale U., 1965. Bar: U.S. Dist. Ct. D.C. 1966, U.S. Ct. Appeals (D.C. cir.) 1966, U.S. Supreme Ct. 1968. Assoc. Covington & Burling, Washington, 1965-73, ptnr., 1973— . Author: The Fourth of July War, 1978; A Woman of Valor, 1980. Contbr. articles to profl. jours. and newspapers. Environmental. Office: Covington & Burling PO Box 7566 1201 Pennsylvania Ave NW Washington DC 20004-2401

TOPOL, ROBIN APRIL LEVITT, lawyer; b. N.Y.C., 02 Apr. d. Anatole Roy and Phyllis Patricia (Redman) Levitt; m. Clifford Miles Topol, Oct. 23, 1982. Student, Stanford U., Eng., 1974; BA, Barnard Coll., 1976; JD, NYU, 1979; postgrad. exec. mgmt. program, Yale U., 1987. Bar: N.Y. 1980, Fla. 1981. Ptnr. real estate dept., comml. real estate and leasing Kurzman & Eisenberg, White Plains, N.Y., 1996—. Trustee alumni bd. dirs. Yale U. Sch. Mgmt., 1987-88. Mem. ABA (vice chmn. real property com. 1986-90), N.Y. County Bar Assn. (real estate com. 1986-96), Women's Bar Assn. (chmn. real estate com. 1980-96). Avocations: tennis, golf, running. Real property. Office: Kurzman & Eisenberg 1 N Broadway White Plains NY 10601-2310

TOPP, SUSAN HLYWA, lawyer; b. Detroit, Oct. 9, 1956; d. Michael Leo and Lucy Stella (Rusak) Hlywa; m. Robert Elwin Topp, July 25, 1985; children: Matthew, Sarah, Michael and Jamie (triplets). BS in Edn. cum laude, Ctrl. Mich. U., 1978; JD cum laude, Wayne State U., Detroit, 1991. Bar: Mich. 1992, U.S. Dist. Ct. (ea. dist.) Mich. 1992. Conservation officer Mich. Dept. Natural Resources, Pontiac, 1980-88, environ. conservation officer Livonia, 1988-93; pvt. practice Gaylord, Mich., 1993; ptnr. Rolinski & Topp, PLC, 1993; assoc. Plunkett & Cooney, PC, 1995—. Adj. faculty Audubon Internat. Active Rocky Mountain Mineral Law Found., Urban Land Inst. Recipient Am. Jurisprudence award Wayne State U., 1987, Trial Advocacy award, 1988. Mem. ABA (nat. resources and environ. law com.), AAUW, Mich. State Bar Assn. (environ. law sect. coun. mem. 1999), Mich. C. of C. Roman Catholic. Avocations: backpacking, skiing, scuba diving, back-country camping, canoeing. Oil, gas, and mineral, Environmental, Real property. Office: Plunkett & Cooney PC 123 W Main St Gaylord MI 49735-1397 E-mail: toppsu@plunkettlaw.com

TOPPER, ROBERT CARLTON, lawyer; b. Tuscaloosa, Ala., May 23, 1949; s. Robert Carlton and Marguerite (Ekdahl) T.; m. Linda L. Stranathan, Apr. 12, 1980. B.A., So. Meth. U., 1970; J.D., 1973. Bar: Tex. 1973. Vice-pres. Am. Title Co. Dallas, 1975-80, v.p., 1983-90; comml. title officer United Title Co., 1990-92; Dallas br. counsel, title prodn. mgr., chief title officer Lawyers Title Ins. Corp., 1992-93; v.p. Dallas-Fidelity Nat. Title Agy., 1993-96; ptnr. Tennant & Topper, 1993-95; pvt. practice law, 1995-97; underwriting counsel Commonwealth Land Title Ins. Co., 1997—; judge Dallas County Probate Ct., 1981-82; master Mental Illness Ct., Dallas, 1983. Vice pres. Dallas County Young Republicans, 1978-79; dir. Dallas County North Rep. Club, 1995-96; parliamentarian Dallas County Rep. Assembly, 1984-87, v.p., 1985-86, bd. dirs. Mem. Dallas Bar Assn. Congregationalist. Probate, Real property. Office: Commonwealth Land Title Ins Co 12201 Merit Dr Ste 450 Dallas TX 75251-3115

TORGERSON, LARRY KEITH, lawyer; b. Albert Lea, Minn., Aug. 25, 1935; s. Fritz G. and Lu (Hillman) T. BA, Drake U., 1958, MA, 1960, LLB, 1963, JD, 1968; MA, Iowa U., 1962; cert., The Hague Acad. Internat. Law, The Netherlands, 1965, 69; LLM, U. Minn., 1969, Columbia U., 1971, U. Mo., 1976; PMD, Harvard U., 1973; EdM, 1974. Bar: Minn. 1964, U.S. Dist. Ct. Minn. 1964, Wis. 1970, Iowa 1970, U.S. Dist. Ct. (no. dist.) Iowa 1971, U.S. Tax Ct. 1971, U.S. Supreme Ct. 1972, U.S. Dist. Ct. (ea. dist.) Wis. 1981, U.S. Ct. Appeals (8th cir.) 1981. Asst. corp. counsel 1st Bank Stock Corp. (88 Banks), Mpls., 1963-67, 1st Svc. Corp. (27 ins. agys., computer subs.), Mpls., 1965-67; v.p., trust officer Nat. City Bank, 1967-69; sr. mem. Torgerson Law Firm, Northwood, Iowa, 1969-87; trustee, gen. counsel Torgerson Farms, 19677—, Redbirch Farms, Kensett, Iowa, 1987—, Sunburst Farms, Grafton, 1987—, Gold Dust Farms, Bolan, 1988—, Torgerson Grain Storage, Bolan, 1988—, Indian Summer Farms, Bolan, 1991—, Sunset Farms, Bolan, 1992—, Sunrise Farms, Grafton, 1994—. CEO, gen. counsel Internat. Investments, Mpls., 1983-96, Trans-oceanic, Mpls., 1987-96, Torgerson Capital, Northwood, 1996—, Torgerson Investments, Northwood, 1984—, Torgerson Properties, Northwood, 1987—, Torgerson Ranches, Sundance, Wyo., 1998—, Hawaiian Investments Unltd., Maui, Hawaii, 1998—, Internat. Investments Unltd., San Pedro, Belize, 1999—. Recipient All-Am. Journalism award Thomas Arkle Clark Outstanding Achievement award, 1958, Dennis E. Brumfield Outstanding Achievement award, 1958, Johnny B. Guy Outstanding Leadership award, 1958; named to Outstanding Young Men of Am., U.S. Jaycees; Hagen scholar, Honor scholar. Mem. ABA, Am. Judicature Soc., Iowa Bar Assn., Minn. Bar Assn., Wis. Bar Assn., Hennepin County Bar Assn., Mensa, Drake Student-Faculty Coun., Drake Student Alumni Coun. (chmn.), Jaycees, Harvard Bus. Sch. Study (pres., exec. com., univ. editor in chief), Psi Chi, Circle K (pres. local chpt.), Phi Alpha Delta, Omicron Delta Kappa (pres. local chpt.), Pi Kappa Delta (pres. local chpt.), Alpha Tau Omega (pres. local chpt., Silver Bullet Outstanding Leadership award, 1965, 66), Pi Delta Epsilon (founder, chpt. pres.), Alpha Kappa Delta, Alpha Scholastic Hon. (U. editor-in-chief), Harvard Bus. Sch. Exec. Com. (U. editor-in-chief). Lutheran. General corporate, Real property, Taxation, general.

TORKILDSON, RAYMOND MAYNARD, lawyer; b. Lake City, S.D., Nov. 19, 1917; s. Gustav Adolph and Agnes (Opitz) T.; m. Sharman Elizbeth Vaughn, Sept. 8, 1956; children: Stephen, Thomas. S.B., U. S.D., 1946; J.D., Harvard U., 1948. Bar: Calif. 1949, Hawaii 1950. Assoc. James P. Blaisdell, Honolulu, 1949-52; ptnr. Moore, Torkildson & Rice and successors, 1955-64; exec. v.p. Hawaii Employers Council, 1964-67; ptnr. Torkildson, Katz, Fonseca, Jaffe, Moore & Hetherington and predecessors, 1967-72; sr. ptnr., 1972-92; of counsel, 1993—. Mem. mgmt. com. Armed Forces YMCA, Honolulu, 1971; treas. Hawaii Republican Com. 1977-83. Served with U.S. Army, 1941-46; lt. col. Res. ret. Mem. ABA, Hawaii Bar Assn. Roman Catholic. Clubs: Oahu Country, Pacific (Honolulu). Labor.

TORMEY, JAMES ROLAND, JR. lawyer; b. San Jose, Calif., May 27, 1935; s. James Roland and Hope (Allario) T.; m. Mary Patricia O'Donnell, Oct. 16, 1957 (div. Oct. 1982); children— Anne, Erin, Christopher, Gregory, Marc; m. Mary Elizabeth Fenn, Feb. 28, 1985. Student San Jose State U., 1953-56; J.D., Santa Clara U., 1960. Bar: Calif. 1961, U.S. Supreme Ct. 1976. Sole practice, Burlingame and San Mateo, Calif., 1961-80; sr. ptnr. Tormey & Roesch, San Mateo, 1980—; dir. Borel Bank & Trust Co., San Mateo, audit co. chmn., 1985-96. Contbr. articles to state, nat. and local trustees' publs. Trustee, San Mateo County Community Coll. Dist., 1971-95; nominee Calif. Senate, 1974; mem., former pres. San Mateo County Congress of Elected Ofcls., Redwood City, Calif., 1977-84; mem. Govtl. Research Council, Redwood City, 1977-90; bd. dirs. Republican Central Com., 1975-78. Served to capt. JAGC, U.S. Army, 1957-65. Recipient Disting. Service award San Mateo Jr. C. of C., 1969. Mem. Calif. State Bar Assn. (hearing referee), Calif. Trial Lawyers, San Mateo County Bar Assn. (treas., dir.), San Mateo County Barrister's Club (dir. 1963-68, former pres.). Club: Bombay Bicycle Riding (dir. 1975-78, 84-86, pres. 1978) (Burlingame). Lodge: Elks. Banking, Contracts commercial, Real property. Office: Tormey & Roesch 520 S El Camino Real Ste 520 San Mateo CA 94402-1718

TORNSTROM, ROBERT ERNEST, lawyer, oil company executive; b. St. Paul, Jan. 17, 1946; s. Clifford H. and Janet (Hale) T.; m. Betty Jane Hermann, Aug. 5, 1978; children: Carter, Gunnar, Katherine. BA, U. Colo., 1968, JD, 1974; diploma grad. sch. mgmt. exec. program, UCLA, 1990. Bar: Colo. 1974, U.S. Dist. Ct. Colo. 1974, Calif. 1975, U.S. Dist. Ct. (cen. dist.) Calif. 1975. Atty. Union Oil Co. of Calif., L.A., 1974-76, counsel internat. div., 1977-78, regional counsel Singapore, 1976-77; sr. atty. Occidental Internat. Exploration and Prodn. Co., Bakersfield, Calif., 1978-81, mng. counsel, 1981-85, v.p., assoc. gen. counsel, 1985-88, v.p., regional ops. mgr., 1988-91; pres. Occidental Argentina, Buenos Aires, 1991-93, Occidental of Russia, Moscow, 1993-94; dir. comml. negotiations Occidental Internat., 1994-96; chmn. of bd. Sullivan Petroleum Co., 1997—. Bd. dirs., chmn. bd. Parmaneft Joint Venture, Vanyogannef JV, Moscow; bd. dirs. Calif. Land and Cattle Co., King City, 602 Operating Corp.; exec. bd. Cmty. House, Bakersfield; legal cons. Island Creek Coal Co., Lexington, Ky. Capt. U.S. Army, 1968-71, Vietnam. Decorated Bronze Star. Mem. Am. Soc. Internat. Law, Am. Corp. Counsel Assn., Soc. Mayflower Descendants, Moscow Country Club, Stockdale Country Club. Republican. Episcopalian. Avocations: skiing, tennis, golf, riding, collecting classic automobiles. General corporate, Oil, gas, and mineral, Private international. Home: 310 Mount Lowe Dr Bakersfield CA 93309-2468 Office: 1508 18th St Ste 222 Bakersfield CA 93301

TORO, AMALIA MARIA, lawyer; b. Hartford, Conn., Nov. 6, 1920; d. Frederick and Maria (Casale) T. BA, U. Conn., 1942; JD, Yale U., 1944. Bar: Conn. 1944. Assoc. Wiggin & Dana, New Haven, 1944-46; atty., dir., chief elections div. Office Sec. of State, Conn., 1946-75; judge Ct. Common Pleas State of Conn., 1975; pvt. practice Hartford, Conn., 1975—. Alt. pub. mem. Conn. Bd. Mediation and Arbitration, 1996—. Former mem. Ford Found Com. on Voting and Election Systems; mem. State Employees' Retirement Commn., 1956-75, past vice-chmn; apptd. mem. Conn. Elections Enforcement Commn., 2000—. Recipient AMITA award in law, 1970, Humanitarian award Columbus Day Celebration Com., 1986. Mem. Greater Hartford Bus. and Profl. Women (pres. 1989-91, Woman of the Yr. award 1969), Conn. Bar Assn. (Merit award 1973), Conn. Assn. Mcpl. Attys. (past pres.), Greater Hartford U. Conn. Alumni Assn. (past pres.) Estate planning, Personal injury, Probate. Office: 234 Pearl St Hartford CT 06103-2113

TORPEY, SCOTT RAYMOND, lawyer; b. Detroit, July 4, 1955; s. Raymond George and Carmela Rose (Aquaro) T. BA in English, Wayne State U., 1978; JD, U. Detroit, 1982. Bar: Mich. 1984, D.C. 1985, N.Y. 1990, Ill. 1990, Calif. 1991, U.S. Dist. Ct. (ea. and we. dist.) Mich., U.S. Dist. Ct. (so., we., no. and ea. dists.) N.Y. 1990, U.S. Dist. Ct. (no., cen. and so. dists.) Ill. 1990, U.S. Dist. Ct. (D.C. dist.) 1989, U.S. Dist. Ct. (cen., so., no. and ea. dists.) Calif., 1991, U.S. Tax Ct., U.S. Ct. Appeals (D.C., fed., 2d, 6th, 7th and 9th cirs.), U.S. Supreme Ct. 1988. Ligitation ptnr. Jaffe, Raitt, Heuer and Weiss, PC, Detroit, 2000—; assoc. Long & Levit, San Francisco, 1982-83, Keating, Canham & Wells, Detroit, 1983-85; ligitation ptnr. Kohl, Secrest, Wardle, Lynch, Clark & Hampton, Farmington Hills, Mich., 1985-2000. Editor Tax Law Jour., 1981, Corp., Fin. and Bus. Law Jour., 1982. Mem. ABA, Fed. Bar Assn., Lawyer-Pilots Bar Assn., Bar Assn. San Francisco, Mich. State Bar Assn. (chmn. aviation torts com. of aviation law sect. 1992—). Republican. Avocations: sports, music, sports cars. Aviation, General civil litigation, Product liability. Office: Jaffe Raitt Heuer & Weiss 1 Woodward Ave Ste 2400 Detroit MI 48226

TORRES, ERNEST C. federal judge; b. 1941; AB, Dartmouth Coll., 1963; JD, Duke U., 1968. Assoc. Hinckley, Allen, Salisbury & Parsons, 1968-74; ptnr. Saunders & Torres, 1974-80; assoc. justice R.I. Superior Ct., 1980-85; asst. v.p. Aetna Life and Casualty, 1985-86; ptnr. Tillinghast, Collins & Graham, 1986-87; chief judge U.S. Dist. Ct. R.I., Providence, 1988—. Pres. East Greenwich (R.I.) Town Coun., 1972-74; state rep. R.I. Ho. of Reps., 1975-80, dep. minority leader, 1977-80. Recipient Disting. Svc. award Jaycees, 1974; named Man of Yr., Prince Henry Soc. R.I., 1988, Prince Henry Soc. Mass., 1995; Alfred P. Sloan scholar Dartmouth Coll. Mem. ABA, ATLA, FBA, R.I. Bar Assn., Jaycees (Dist. Svc. award 1974), Prince Henry Soc. of R.I., Prince Henry Soc. of Mass. Office: US Dist Ct J O Pastore Fed Bldg Rm 363 Providence RI 02903

TORREY, CLAUDIA OLIVIA, lawyer; b. Nashville, June 10, 1958; d. Claude Adolphus and Rubye Mayette (Prigmore) T. BA in Econ., Syracuse U., 1980; JD, N.Y. Law Sch., 1985. Bar: N.Y. State 1988. Legal intern Costello, Cooney & Fearon, Syracuse, N.Y., 1979; legal clk. First Am. Corp., Nashville, 1981; legal asst. James I. Meyerson, N.Y.C., 1982-85; jud. law clk. N.Y. State Supreme Ct., 1985; interim project supr., legal asst. CUNY Ctrl. Office, 1985-86; legal analyst Rosenman & Colin Law Firm, N.Y.C., 1986-87; asst. counsel N.Y. State Legis., Albany, 1988-90; atty., cons. pvt. practice, Nashville, Cookeville, Tenn., 1991—. Bd. mem. Children's Corner Day Care Ctr., Albany, N.Y., 1989-90. Author column Health Law Jour. of N.Y. State Bar Assn., 1996—. Ch. rep. FOCUS exec. coun. Westminster Presbyn. Ch., Albany, 1990; v.p. dormitory coun., flr. rep. Syracuse U., 1977-79. Mem. ABA (young lawyers divsn. liaison to ABA forum on health law 1994-96), Internat. Platform Assn., N.Y. State Bar Assn. (chmn. health law sect. study group on health info., privacy and confidentiality 1998-99), Alpha Kappa Alpha. Avocations: singing, reading, harp, travel, art. Education and schools, General practice, Health. Home and Office: PO Box 150234 Nashville TN 37215-0234 E-mail: jewel3@prodigy.net

TORRUELLA, JUAN R. federal judge; b. 1933; BS in Bus. and Fin., U. Pa., 1954; LLB, Boston U., 1957; LLM, U. Va., 1984; MPA, U. P.R., 1984; LLD, St. John's U., 1995. Judge U.S. Dist. Ct. P.R., San Juan, 1974-82, chief judge, 1982-84; judge U.S. Ct. Appeals (1st cir.), 1984-94, 2001—, chief judge, 1994-2001. Former mem. jud. conf. com. on the Adminstrn. of the Fed. Magistrate Sys; mem. jud. conf. exec. com. on Internat. Jud. Reform. Mem. ABA, Fed. Bar Assn., Assn. Labor Rels. Practitioners P.R. and V.I., D.C. Bar Assn., P.R. Bar Assn.*

TORSHEN, JEROME HAROLD, lawyer; b. Chgo., Nov. 27, 1929; s. Jack and Lillian (Futterman) T.; m. Kay Pomerance, June 19, 1966; children: Jonathan, Jacqueline. BS, Northwestern U., 1951; JD, Harvard U., 1955. Bar: Ill. 1955, U.S. Dist. Ct. (no. dist.) Ill. 1955, U.S. Ct. Appeals (7th cir.) 1958, (8th cir.) 1961, (9th and D.C. cirs.) 1972, U.S. Supreme Ct. 1972. Assoc. Clausen, Hirsh & Miller, Chgo., 1955-62; pres. Jerome H. Torshen, Ltd., 1963-87, Torshen, Schoenfield & Spreyer, Ltd., Chgo., 1987-94, Torshen, Spreyer, Ltd., Chgo., 1994, Torshen, Spreyer & Garmisa, Ltd., Chgo., 1994-97, Torshen, Spreyer, Garmisa & Slobig, Ltd., Chgo., 1997—. Spl. asst. atty. gen. Ill., 1965-70; assoc. counsel Spl. Commn. Ill. Supreme Ct., 1969; counsel Ill. Legis. Redistricting Commn., 1971-72; spl. state's atty. Cook County, Ill., 1979-81, 83-86; spl. counsel Met. San. Dist. Greater Chgo., 1977-81, 84-88. Contbr. articles to profl. jours. Counsel Cook County Dem. Cen. Com., Chgo., 1982-87; bd. dirs. Jewish Family and Community Svc., Parents' Coun. Washington U., St. Louis, 1988-92; mem. collectors' group Mus. Contemporary Art; sustaining fellow Art Inst. Chgo. Served with U.S. Army, 1951-52. Recipient Torch of Learning award Am. Friends of Hebrew U., 1985, Outstanding Civic Duty award, Union League Club of Chgo., 1967. Fellow Am. Coll. Trial Lawyers; mem. ABA, Chgo. Bar Assn. (commn. on jud. evaluation 1986-90), Bar Assn. 7th Cir. Appellate Lawyers Assn. (founder, pres. 1976-77), Decalogue Soc., Standard Club, Sixty Club of Chgo., Union League Club of Chgo., Lawyers Club Chgo. Federal civil litigation, State civil litigation, Insurance. Office: 105 W Adams St Ste 3200 Chicago IL 60603-4109 E-mail: law@torshen.com

TOSCANO, OSCAR ERNESTO, lawyer; b. Ecuador, Jan. 24, 1951; s. Hugo and Maruja (Lopez) T.; children: Marina, Tracy, Oscar Emerson, Jacob, Nicole, David. BA, UCLA, 1975; JD, Loyola U., L.A., 1978. Bar: Calif. 1978, U.S. Dist. Ct. (9th dist.) Calif. 1978. Pvt. practice, Glendale, 1978—. Mem. Assn. Consumer Attys. of L.A., Consumer Attys. of Calif., Los Angeles County Bar, Mex.-Am. Bar Assn., State Bar Calif., Glendale Bar Assn., Hispanic Alumni Scholarship Found. Avocations: tennis, chess, trial work. Criminal, Family and matrimonial, Insurance. Office: 625 W Broadway Glendale CA 91204-1058

TOUBY, KATHLEEN ANITA, lawyer; b. Miami Beach, Feb. 20, 1943; d. Harry and Kathleen Rebecca (Hamper) T.; m. Joseph Thomas Woodward; children: Mark Andrew, Judson David Touby. BS in Nursing, U. Fla., 1965, MRC in Rehab. Counseling, 1967; JD with honors, Nova U., 1977. Bar: Fla. 1978, D.C. 1978. Counselor Jewish Vocat. Svc., Chgo., 1967-68; rehab. counselor Fla. Dept. Vocat. Rehab., Miami, 1968-70; spl. asst., asst. U.S. atty. U.S. Dept. Justice, 1978-80; assoc. Pyszka & Kessler, P.A., 1980-83; ptnr. Touby & Smith, P.A., 1983-89, Touby, Smith, DeMahy & Drake, P.A., Miami, 1989-94, Touby & Woodward, P.A., Miami, 1994—. Chmn. adv. exec. bd. Paralegal Edn. program Barry U., 1986-87; lectr. Food and Drug Law Inst., 1987-89, 91; lectr. environ. law Exec. Enterprises, 1987-88; lectr. trial techniques, Hispanic Nat. Bar Assn., St. Thomas Law Sch.; adj. prof. product liability Can. Govt., U.S. Trade and Mktg. Dept., 1989-95. Co-author: The Environmental Litigation Deskbook, 1989; contbr. chpts. to books, articles to profl. jours. Mem. ABA, Am. Inns of Ct. (pres. 1998-99, pres.-elect St. Thomas Law Sch. chpt. 1997-98, pres. 1998-99), Dade County Bar Assn. (legal aid, pub. svcs. com. 1988), Fed. Bar Assn. (bd. dirs. 1989—, v.p. 1991-92, pres.-elect So. Fla. chpt. 1992-93, pres. 1993-94), Phi Delta Phi (province pres. 1982-85, bd. dirs. 1985-87). Roman Catholic. General civil litigation, Insurance, Personal injury. Home: 450 Sabal Palm Rd Miami FL 33137-3352 Office: Touby & Woodward PA 250 Bird Rd Ste 308 Miami FL 33146-1424

TOUBY, RICHARD, lawyer; b. Sioux City, Iowa, Nov. 17, 1924; s. Louis and Rebecca (Keck) T.; m. Marion Lascher, Aug. 6, 1949; children: Jill Diane, Kim Paula. LLB, U. Miami, 1948; LLM, Duke U., 1950. Bar: Fla. 1948. Faculty U. Miami, Coral Gables, Fla., 1948-63; mem. 8th Air Force Meml. Assn., 305 Bomb Group (H) Assn., 1994—. 1st Lt. USAF, 1943-45. Contracts commercial, General corporate, General practice. Office: 19 W Flagler St Ste 907 Miami FL 33130-4407

TOUCHY, DEBORAH K.P. lawyer, accountant; b. Pasadena, Tex., Dec. 9, 1957; d. Donald Carl and Bobbie Jo (Jackson) Putzka; m. Harry Roy Touchy, Jr., Feb. 23, 1980. BBA, Baylor U., 1979; JD, U. Houston, 1988. Bar: Tex. 1989; CPA, Tex.; cert. in estate planning and probate law Tex. Bd. Legal Specialization. Sr. mgr. tax KMPG Peat Marwick, Houston, 1980-86; assoc. Fizer Beck Webster & Bentley, 1989-90; pvt. practice law, 1990—; chmn. spl. events Jr. League Houston, 1997-98. Editor Houston Law Rev., 1988-89. Chmn. ticket sales incentives Chi Omega, Houston, 1985; active ticket sales Mus. Fine Arts, Houston, 1984; facilities chmn. Woodland Trails West Civic Orgn., Houston, 1982-83; pres. Women Attys. in Tax & Probate, 1994-95; active St.John's Sch., 1999—. Recipient Outstanding Alumi award Beta Alpha Psi, 1997. Mem. ABA (estate-probate sect. 1989—, vice chmn. commn. property com. 1994—), AICPA (taxation sect., estate and gift tax com. 1992-95, 1998—), Tex. Soc. CPAs (bd. dirs. 1995—, chmn. tax inst. com. 1996-97, estate planning com. 1990-94, 96—), Houston Chpt. CPAs (chmn. taxpayer edn. 1985-86, chmn. membership com. 1992-93, v.p. 1993-94, 96-97, chmn. tax forums 1994-95, long range planning com. 1995-96, chmn. leadership devel. 1997-98, treas. 1998-99, chmn. ann. charity event 1999-2000, bd. dirs. 1999-2000, pres. 2001—), Houston Bar Assn. (estate-probate sect. 1989—), State Bar Tex. (estate-probate sect. 1989—, mem. elder law com. 1991-97), Houston Estate and Fin. Forum, Baylor U. Women's Assn. (treas. 1993-94, chmn. fin. com. 1994-95, parliamentarian 1995-96, sec. 1996-97, pres. 1997-98, chmn. audit com. 1999-2000), Chief Justice-Advocates, Tex. Bd. Legal Specializations (cert. estate planning, probate law 1994), Order of Coif, Omicron Delta Kappa, Phi Delta Phi, Beta Alpha Psi (Outstanding Alumni 1997). Estate planning, Probate, Taxation, general. Office: PO Box 130122 Houston TX 77219-0122

TOUMEY, DONALD JOSEPH, lawyer; BA, Williams Coll., 1978; JD, Yale U., 1981. Bar: N.Y. 1982, D.C. 1985, U.S. Supreme Ct. 1986. Law clk. to judge U.S. Ct Appeals (2d cir.), N.Y.C., 1981-82; spl. asst. to gen. counsel U.S. Dept. Treasury, Washington, 1982-85; assoc. Sullivan & Cromwell, N.Y.C., 1985-90; ptnr., 1990—. Republican. Banking, Mergers and acquisitions, Securities. Office: Sullivan & Cromwell 125 Broad St New York NY 10004-2489

TOUREK, STEVEN CHARLES, lawyer; b. Evanston, Ill., Apr. 28, 1948; s. Charles Frank, Jr. and Gertrude Jean (Steiner) T.; children: Peter S., Samuel C., Olivia, Charles. BA, Dartmouth Coll., 1970; MA, Cambridge U., 1974, LLB, 1975; postgrad. in law, Yale U., 1970-71. Bar: Minn. 1976, Wis. 1981, U.S. Dist. Ct. Minn. 1976, U.S. Dist. Ct. (we. dist.) Wis. 1982, U.S. Ct. Appeals (8th cir.) 1981, U.S. Dist. Ct. (ea. dist.) 1988, U.S. Ct. Internat. Trade 1988. Asst. dean Dartmouth Coll., Hanover, N.H., 1971-72; assoc. Oppenheimer, Wolff, Foster, Shepard & Donnelly, St. Paul, 1975-79; ptnr. Winthrop & Weinstine, 1979—. Rufus Choate scholar Dartmouth Coll., 1966-70; Reynolds fellow, 1973-74; fellow Hattie M. Strong Found., 1972-73. Mem. ABA, Minn. Bar Assn., Wis. Bar Assn., Minn. Trial Lawyers Assn., Assn. Trial Lawyers Am. Antitrust, Federal civil litigation, State civil litigation. Office: Winthrop & Weinstine 3200 Dain Rauscher Pla 60 S 6th St Minneapolis MN 55402-4400 E-mail: stourek@winthrop.com

TOUSLEY, RUSSELL FREDERICK, lawyer; b. New Haven, Nov. 19, 1938; s. Russell F. and Della (Ermer) T.; m. Sarah Morford, July 23, 1963; children: Ellen Elizabeth, Kenneth Morford. BA cum laude, Yale Coll., 1960; JD, U. Wash., 1967. Bar: Wash. 1967. Assoc. Davis Wright, Seattle, 1967-69; v.p. Safecare Co., Inc., 1969-78, Winmar Co., Inc., Seattle, 1977-78; ptnr. Tousley Brain Stephens PLLC, 1978—. Trustee Seattle Opera Assn., 1980—, pres., chmn. bd., 1985-87; trustee Seattle Chamber Music Festival, 1990-93; moderator Plymouth Congl. Ch., Seattle, 1975-77, 83-85, trustee, 1969-93, adminstrn., property and fin. bd., 1999—. Lt. (j.g.) USN, 1960-64. Mem. ABA, Wash. State Bar Assn., Seattle-King County Bar Assn., Internat. Coun. Shopping Ctrs. (assoc.), Rainier Club, Seattle Tennis Club, Rotary. Avocations: opera, reading, collecting mint U.S. regular issue stamps. Finance, Private international, Real property. Office: Tousley Brain PLLC Key Tower 56th Flr 700 5th Ave Ste 5600 Seattle WA 98104-5056 E-mail: rftousley@tousley.com

TOWERY, CURTIS KENT, lawyer; b. Hugoton, Kans., Jan. 29, 1954; s. Clyde D. and Jo June (Curtis) T. BA, Trinity U., 1976; JD, U. Okla., 1979; LLM in Taxation, Boston U., 1989. Mem. Curtis & Blanton, Pauls Valley, Okla., 1980-81; lawyer land and legal dept. Trigg Drilling Co., Oklahoma City, 1981-82; adminstrv. law judge Okla. Corp. Commn., 1982-85; counsel Curtis & Blanton, Pauls Valley, 1985-88; adminstrv. law judge Okla. Dept. Mines, Oklahoma City, 1985-88, assoc. gen. counsel, 1989-92; contracts and purchasing adminstr., atty. Okla. Turnpike Authority, 1992-93; asst. gen. counsel Okla. Corp. Commn., 1993-97; spl. judge City of Oklahoma City, 1997—2000; adminstrv. law judge Okla. Dept. of Labor, 1998; v.p., trust officer Bank One Trust, Oklahoma City, 1998-2000; mgr. Cherokee Capital Holdings, 2000—. Bd. dirs. First Nat. Bank Pauls Valley, 1983-88. Assoc. bd. Okla. Mus. Art, 1985-88, Okla. Symphony Orch., 1987-92; assoc. bd. Ballet Okla., 1987-92, sec., 1990-91, v.p., 1988-89; mem. Oklahoma City Estate Planning Coun., Ruth Bader Ginsburg Am. Inn of Ct., 1999—. Mem. ABA, Tex. Bar Assn., Okla. Bar Assn., Faculty House, Rotary, Elks, Phi Alpha Delta, Sigma Nu. Democrat. Presbyterian. Avocations: flying, golf, traveling, investment analysis. Oil, gas, and mineral, Probate, Estate taxation. Home: PO Box 14891 Oklahoma City OK 73113-0891 Office: 1200 NW 63d St Ste 200 Oklahoma City OK 73116

TOWERY, JAMES E. lawyer; b. Los Alamos, N.Mex., July 12, 1948; s. Lawson E. and Irma (Van Apeldorn) T.; m. Kathryn K. Meier, July 20, 1991; 1 child, Mark J. BA, Princeton U., 1973; JD, Emory U., 1976. Assoc. Morgan Beauzay Hammer, San Jose, Calif., 1977-79; ptnr. Morgan & Towery, 1979-89; assoc. Hoge Fenton Jones & Appel, 1989-90, ptnr., 1990—. Chmn. bd. trustees Alexian Bros. Hosp., San Jose, Calif., 1995-98. Mem. ABA (ho. of dels. 1989-98, standing com. client protection 1996—, chair 1998-00), State Bar Calif. (v.p. and chair discipline com. 1994-95, bd. govs. 1992-96, pres. 1995-96, presiding arbitrator, fee arbitration program 1990-92), Santa Clara County Bar Assn. (counsel 1984-85, treas. 1987, pres. 1989). Health, Personal injury, Professional liability. Office: Hoge Fenton Jones 60 S Market St San Jose CA 95113-2351

TOWNSEND, BRIAN DOUGLAS, paralegal; b. Tokyo, Sept. 22, 1961; s. Thomas and Juanita Evora (Sanford) T.; m. Gloria Ann Wigfall, Aug. 23, 1986; children: Brian D. Jr., Brianna A. BA in Criminology, U. Md., 1983. Legal aide Kirkland & Ellis, Washington, 1984-85; legal asst. to mng. clk. Cadwalader, Wickersham & Taft, 1985-87; paralegal specialist, Office of Chief Counsel U.S. Dept. Transp. Maritime Adminstrn., 1987-90, U.S. Dept. Treasury, IRS, Washington, 1990-92; litigation support specialist U.S. Dept. Justice, Tax Divsn., 1992-93; paralegal specialist Resolution Trust Corp., 1993-95, FDIC, Washington, 1996-98, U.S. Dept. Treasury, OIG, Washington, 1998-99; program specialist FOIA/PA U.S. Dept. Treasury, OFAC, 1999-2000; mgmt. analyst U.S. Dept. Agr., 2000—. Avocations: bowling, fishing, swimming, chess, football. Office: US Dept Agr 1400 Independence Ave SW Washington DC 20250-9884 E-mail: briandouglastownsend@yahoo.com, brian.townsend@usda.gov

TOWNSEND, EARL C., JR. lawyer, writer; b. Indpls., Nov. 9, 1914; s. Earl Cunningham and Besse (Kuhn) T.; m. Emily Macnab, Apr. 3, 1947 (dec. Mar. 1988); children: Starr, Vicki M., Julia E. (Mrs. Edward Goodrich Dunn Jr.), Earl Cunningham III, Clyde G. Student, De Pauw U., 1932-34; AB, U. Mich., 1936, JD, 1939. Bar: Ind. 1939, Mich. 1973, U.S. Supreme Ct. 1973, U.S. Ct. Appeals (4th, 5th, 6th, 7th cirs.), U.S. Dist. Ct. (no. and so. dists.) Ind., U.S. Dist. Ct. (dist.) Va., U.S. Dist. Ct. (ea. dist.) Mich. Sr. ptnr. Townsend & Townsend, Indpls., 1941-64, Townsend, Hovde &

Townsend, Indpls., 1964-84, Townsend & Townsend, Indpls., 1984—. Dep. prosecutor, Marion County, Ind., 1942-44; radio-TV announcer WIRE, WFBM, WFBM-TV, Indpls., 1940-53, 1st TV announcer Indpls. 500 mile race, 1949, 50; Big Ten basketball referee, 1940-47; lectr. trial tactics U. Notre Dame, Ind. U., U. Mich., 1968-79; chmn. faculty seminar on personal injury trials Ind. U. Sch. Law, U. Notre Dame Sch. Law, Valparaiso Sch. Law, 1981; mem. Com. to Revise Ind. Supreme Ct. Pattern Jury Instrns., 1975-83; lectr. Trial Lawyers 30 Yrs. Inst., 1986; counsel atty gen., 1988-92. Author: Birdstones of the North American Indian, 1959; editor: Am. Assn. Trial Lawyers Am. Jour., 1964-88; contbr. articles to legal and archeol. jours.; composer (waltz) Moon of Halloween. Trustee Cathedral High Sch., Indpls., Eiteljorg Mus. Am. Indian and Western Art, Cale J. Holder Scholarship Found. Ind. U. Law Sch.; life trustee, bd. dirs., mem. fin. and bldg. coms. Indpls. Mus. Art; life trustee Ind. State Mus.; founder, dir. Meridian St. Found.; mem. dean's coun. Ind. U.; founder, life fellow Roscoe Pound/Am. Trial Lawyers Found., Harvard U.; fellow Meth. Hosp. Found. Recipient Ind. Univ. Writers Conf. award, 1960, Hanson H. Anderson medal of honor Arsenal Tech. Schs., Indpls., 1971; named to Coun. Sagamores of Wabash, 1969; Rector scholar, 1934, Ind. Basketball Hall of Fame; hon. chief Black River-Swan Creek Saginaw-Chippewa Indian tribe. Fellow Internat. Acad. Trial Lawyers, Internat. Soc. Barristers, Ind. Bar Found. (life trustee, disting. fellow award); mem. ASCAP, ABA (com. on trial techniques 1964-76, aviation and space 1977—), Assn. Trial Lawyers Am. (v.p.), Ind. State Bar Assn. (Golden Career award 1989), Indpls. Bar Found. (disting. charter 1986), Ind. Trial Lawyers Assn. (pres. 1965, pres. Coll. Fellows 1984-90, Lifetime Achievement award 1992), Am. Bd. Trial Advs. (diplomate, pres. Ind. chpt. 1980-86), Am. Arbitration Assn. (nat. arbitrators panel), Am. Judicature Soc., State Bar of Mich. (Champion of Justice award 1989), Roscommon County Bar Assn., 34th Jud. Cir. Bar Assn., Bar Assn. 7th Fed. Cir. (bd. govs. 1966-68), Mich. Trial Lawyers Assn., Soc. Mayflower Descendants (gov. 1947-49), Ind. Hist. Soc., Marion County/Indpls. Hist. Soc. (bd. dirs.), U. Mich. Pres. Club, U. Mich. Victors Club (founder, charter mem.), Trowel and Brush Soc. (hon.), Genuine Indian Relic Soc. (founder, pres., chmn. frauds com.), The Players Club, Key Biscayne Yacht Club, Columbia Club, Masons (33 degree), Shriners, Delta Kappa Epsilon, Phi Kappa Phi. Republican. Methodist. Avocations: art, Indian relics. Aviation, Federal civil litigation, State civil litigation. Home: 5008 N Meridian St Indianapolis IN 46208-2624

TOWNSEND, EDWIN CLAY, lawyer; b. Parsons, Tenn., Nov. 22, 1924; s. Mahlon Nathaniel Emma Annie (Odle) T.; m. Marjorie Lucille Duncan, Sept. 10, 1950; children: Edwin Townsend Jr., Karin Davis. Student, Union U., Jackson, Tenn., 1942-43, 1946; LLB, Cumberland U., Lebanon, Tenn., 1947, BA, 1948; JD, Stamford U., Birmingham, Ala., 1969. Bar: Tenn. 1947, U.S. Dist. Ct. Tenn. 1949. Ptnr. Townsend & Townsend, Parsons. Del. 1977 Tenn. Ltd. Const. Conv., 1977; mem. Bd. Profl. Responsibility of Supreme Ct. Tenn., Nashville, 1982-88. Trustee Lambuth Coll., Jackson, 1980-92; bd. dirs. Meth. Found., Memphis, 1980-86; bd. dirs. Tenn. River Four County Port Authority, Parsons, 1980—, chmn., 1980-81, 85-86. With USN, 1943-45, PTO. Decorated Purple Heart. Mem. ABA, Tenn. Bar Assn. (bd. govs., com. on adminstrn. justice, ho. of dels.), Tenn. Bar Found., Vets. of Fgn. Wars, Am. Disabled Vets., Am. Legion. Democrat. Methodist. Lodges: Lions (local pres. 1952-53, 66-67, dist. gov. 1961-62, bd. dirs. West Tenn. Lions Found. 1982-86), Elks. General corporate, Personal injury, Probate. Office: Townsend & Townsend 121 Tennessee Ave S Parsons TN 38363-2521

TOWNSEND, JOACHIM RUDIGER (JACK TOWNSEND), lawyer; b. Worpswede, Germany, Dec. 18, 1941; came to U.S., 1948, naturalized, 1960; s. Richard L. (stepfather) and Annamarie (Jaster) T.; m. Diane Kathleen Smith, May 26, 1984. B.A., U. Md., 1969; J.D. with honors, George Washington U., 1973. Bar: D.C. 1973, Va. 1975. Analyst Dept. Treasury, Washington, 1969-72; clk. Dept. Justice, Washington, 1973; assoc. counsel Naval Air Systems Command, Dept. Navy, Washington, 1974-85; counsel Spares and Competition Program, Naval Supply Systems Command, 1985— . Served with USN, 1961-65. Mem. Fed. Bar Assn. Roman Catholic. Home: 5315 Montgomery St Springfield VA 22151-3850 Office: Naval Supply Systems Command Office Of Counsel Washington DC 20361

TOWNSEND, JOHN MICHAEL, lawyer; b. West Point, N.Y., Mar. 21, 1947; s. John D. and Vera (Nachman) T.; m. Frances M. Fragos, Oct. 8, 1994; children, James E., Patrick M. BA, Yale U., 1968, JD, 1971. Bar: N.Y. 1972, U.S. Dist. Ct. (so. and ea. dists.) N.Y. 1975, U.S. Ct. Appeals (2nd cir.) 1975, U.S. Supreme Ct. 1975, U.S. Ct. Appeals (8th cir.) 1982, U.S. Ct. Appeals (7th and 10th cirs.) 1986, D.C. 1990, U.S. Dist. Ct. D.C. 1990, U.S. Ct. Appeals (D.C. cir.) 1990, U.S. Ct. Appeals (4th cir.) 1991, U.S. Ct. Appeals (fed. cir.) 2000, U.S. Ct. Fed. Claims, 2000. Assoc. Hughes Hubbard & Reed, LLP, N.Y.C., 1971-73, 75-80, ptnr., 1980—; assoc. Hughes Hubbard & Reed, Paris, 1973-74. Bd. dirs., exec. com., chair arbitration law com. Am. Arbitration Assn.; trustee U.S. Coun. Internat. Bus. Editl. bd. ADR Currents. 1st lt. USAR, 1971-75. Mem. ABA, Am. Law Inst., Internat. Bar Assn., Assn. Bar City N.Y., Union Internat. des Avocats, Univ. Club, Yale Club (N.Y.C.). Democrat. Episcopalian. Antitrust, Alternative dispute resolution, Private international. Office: Hughes Hubbard & Reed LLP 1775 I St NW Washington DC 20006-2401 Fax: (202) 721-4646. E-mail: townsend@hugheshubbard.com

TOWNSEND, PETER LEE, lawyer; b. Glendale, Calif., July 21, 1926; s. Craig and Georgia (Barhyte) T.; m. Irma Mathilde Greisberger, Aug. 12, 1947; children— Ingrid P., Russell T., Dorothy Poole. J.D. summa cum laude, McGeorge Coll. Law, 1958. Bar: Calif. 1959, U.S. Supreme Ct. 1982. Dep. dist. atty., Stockton, Calif., 1959-60; litigation counsel Western Title Ins. Co. of San Francisco, 1960-68; counsel Townsend Law Offices, 1969— . Served to capt., inf., U.S. Army, 1944-54. Republican. Clubs: Marin County Bar, San Rafael Yacht.

TOWNSEND, WILLIAM JACKSON, lawyer; b. June 4, 1932; s. Robert Glenn and Lois Juanita (Jackson) T. BS, Wake Forest U., 1954; student, U. Ky., 1957, U. Louisville, 1958; JD, U. N.C., 1960. Lawyer; b. Grayson, Ky., June 4, 1932; s. Robert Glenn and Lois Juanita (Jackson) T. BS, Wake Forest U., 1954; Student U. Ky., 1957, U. Louisville, 1958, U. N.C., 1960. Bar: N.C. 1965. Claims adjuster State Farm Ins. Co., 1963; sole practice, Fayetteville, N.C., 1965—; pub. adminstr. Robeson County, N.C., 1966; dir., treas. Colonial Foods, Inc., St. Paul, N.C., 1959—; tax atty. City of Lumberton, 1966-67 . Served as 1st lt. U.S. Army, 1954-56. Mem. N.C. Bar Assn., N.C. State Bar, Cumberland County Bar Assn., N.C. Bar Assn., Scabbard and Blade (pres.), Delta Theta Phi. Presbyterian. Club: Kiwanis (treas. Fayetteville 1973-82). General corporate, Family and matrimonial, Personal injury. Office: PO Box 584 2109 Elvira St Apt 806 Fayetteville NC 28302

TOWNSLEY, TODD ALAN, lawyer; b. Bloomington, Ind., Mar. 25, 1966; s. Kenneth Raymond and Wilma Irene Townsley; m. Elizabeth Anne Arrington, Feb. 13, 1993; children: Justin Morales, Lex Alan. BA, Ind. U., 1988; JD, Harvard U., 1991. Bar: U.S. Dist. Ct. (mid. dist.) La. 1992. Assoc. Cox, Cox, Townsley & Fowler, Lakes Charles, La., 1991-94; ptnr. The Townsley Law Firm, 1995—. Editor Harvard Jour. Law and Pub. Policy, 1990-91. Coach Little League Baseball, Lake Charles, La., 1994—. Mem. ATLA, La. Trial Lawyers Assn., S.W. La. Bar Assn. Methodist. Personal injury. Office: The Townsley Law Firm 3102 Enterprise Blvd Lake Charles LA 70601-8722

TRACHSEL, WILLIAM HENRY, corporate lawyer; b. El Paso, Tex., Apr. 20, 1943; BS in Aerospace Engring., U. Fla., 1965; JD, U. Conn., 1971. Bar: Conn. 1971. With United Tech. Corp., Hartford, Conn., 1965-93, v.p., sec. and dep. gen. counsel, 1993-98, sr. v.p., gen. counsel, sec., 1998—. Mem. ABA, Am. Corp. Counsel Assn. Office: United Tech Corp Bldg Hartford CT 06101 E-mail: trachswh@corphq.utc.com

TRACHTMAN, JERRY H. lawyer; b. Phila., Aug. 10, 1945; BSEE, Pa. State U., 1967; JD, U. Fla., 1976. Bar: Fla. 1976, U.S. Dist. Ct. (mid. dist.) Fla. 1978, U.S. Supreme Ct. 1980, U.S. Ct. Appeals (11th cir.) 1989; cert. aviation law. Elec. engr. N.Am. Aviation, Columbus, Ohio, 1967-68, Apollo spacecraft systems engr. Kennedy Space Ctr., Fla., 1968-71; Skylab project engr. Martin Marietta, 1971-74; pvt. practice Satellite Beach, Fla., 1976-80; atty., mng. ptnr. Trachtman, Henderson and Futchko, P.A., Melbourne, 1980—. Adj. prof. aviation law Fla. Inst. Tech., Melbourne, 1983-90; mem. adv. bd. Kaiser Coll., Melbourne, 1994—. Pres. Jewish Fedn. Brevard County, 2000—, bd. dirs. 1996—. Recipient Apollo achievement award NASA. Mem. ATLA, Fla. Bar Assn. (chmn. aviation law com. 1995-96, vice chmn. 1993-95), Lawyer-Pilots Bar Assn., NTSB Bar Assn. (founder 1984—), Acad. Fla. Trial Lawyers. Aviation, State civil litigation, Personal injury. Office: Ste #300 1735 W Hibiscus Blvd Melbourne FL 32901-2616 E-mail: jerryht@aviation-law.cc

TRACT, MARC MITCHELL, lawyer; b. N.Y.C., Sept. 20, 1959; s. Harold Michael and Natalie Ann (Meyerowitz) T.; m. Sharon Beth Widrow; children: Melissa Hope, Harrison Michael, Sarah Michelle. BA in Biology, Ithaca Coll., 1981; JD, Pepperdine U., 1984. Bar: N.Y. 1985, N.J. 1985, D.C. 1986. Assoc. Kroll & Tract, N.Y.C., 1985-90, ptnr., 1990-94, Rosenman & Colin LLP, N.Y.C., 1994—. Bd. dirs. Sorema N.Am. Reinsurance Co., N.Y.C., Navigators Group Inc., N.Y.C., MAPFRE Reinsurance Corp., San Francisco, C.A., AXA Nordstern Art Ins. Corp., N.Y.C., Fortress Ins. Co., Rosemont, Ill., N.Y.C., Forethought Life Ins. C. N.Y., Rochester. Bd. dirs. Italian Acad. Found. Decorated Order of Merit of Savoy. Mem. ABA, Assn. of Bar of City of N.Y., N.Y. State Bar Assn., N.J. State Bar Assn., N.Y. County Lawyers Assn., Am. Coun. Germany, Old Westbury Golf and Country Club, Met. Club, Econ. Club N.Y. Republican. General corporate, Insurance, Mergers and acquisitions. Office: Rosenman & Colin LLP 575 Madison Ave Fl 11 New York NY 10022-2511

TRACTENBERG, CRAIG R. lawyer; b. Phila., Dec. 5, 1956; s. Jerome and Diane (Epstein) T.; m. Anna P. McDonald, June 9, 1981; children: David, Jeremy. BA, La Salle Coll., Phila., 1979; JD, Temple U., 1981. Bar: Pa. 1981, N.J. 1983, U.S. Dist. Ct. (ea. dist.) Pa. 1981, U.S. Dist. Ct. N.J. 1983, U.S. Ct. Appeals (2d cir.) 1983, U.S. Ct. Appeals (3rd cir.) 1990, U.S. Supreme Ct. 1987. Assoc. Abraham, Pressman & Bauer, P.C., Phila., 1981-87, ptnr., 1987-97; shareholder Buchanan Ingersoll, Profl. Corp., 1998—. Bd. dirs. Rita's Water Ice Franchising, Inc.; judge pro tem Phila. Ct. Common Pleas. Contbg. editor Franchise Law Quar., Franchise Law Digest, U. Mich. Jour. Law Rev., Franchise Update, Sum., 1991; contbr. articles to law jours. and profl. publs. Trustee Har Zion Temple, Penn Valley, Pa., 1988—, Friends of ALS, 1989. Mem. ABA (faculty forum com. on franchising 1989), Pa. Bar Assn. (chmn. com. on franchising), Phila. Bar Assn., N.J. Bar Assn. (com. on fundraising), Internat. Franchise Assn., Rotary (pres. Bryn Mawr, Pa. chpt. 1989), Republican. Avocations: running, golf, electronics. Bankruptcy, Contracts commercial, Franchising. Home: 249 Ithan Creek Rd Villanova PA 19085-1339 Office: Buchanan Ingersoll Profl Corp 1835 Market St 14th Fl Philadelphia PA 19103-2985

TRACY, J. DAVID, lawyer, educator; b. Ft. Worth, Jan. 1, 1946; s. Dennis Ford and Virginia Eloise (Hall) T.; m. Jeral Ann Wilson, June 3, 1967; children: Bradley Wilson, Jennifer Diann. BA with honors, U. Tex., 1968, JD, 1970; LLM, So. Meth. U., 1971. Bar: Tex. 1971, U.S. Tax Ct. 1971, U.S. Ct. Appeals (5th cir.) 1976, U.S. Supreme Ct. 1978; cert. in estate planning, probate and tax law Tex. Bd. Legal Specialization. Ptnr. Cantey & Hanger, LLP, Ft. Worth. Bd. dirs. Ft. Worth Conv. and Vis. Bur., sec., 1987-89; adj. prof. advanced corp. taxation So. Meth. U., 1975-77; lectr. continuing legal edn.; council mem. real estate, probate and trust law sect. State Bar Tex., 1983-87; newsletter editor 1987-89, chmn., 1991-92; mem. Coll. State Bar Tex., tax law adv. commn. Tex. Bd. Legal Specialization, 1987-2000, chair, 1999-2000. Contbr. articles to law jours. Mem. adv. bd. dirs. Tarrant County Conv. Ctr., 1983-89, chmn., 1986-87. Named Outstanding Young Lawyer of Tarrant County, Tarrant County Young Lawyers Assn., 1982. Fellow Am. Coll. Trust and Estate Counsel, Tex. Bar Found., Tarrant County Bar Found.; mem. ABA, Ft. Worth Club, Colonial Country Club, Phi Delta Phi. Presbyterian. Estate planning, Pension, profit-sharing, and employee benefits, Taxation, general. Office: 801 Cherry St Ste 2100 Fort Worth TX 76102-6821 E-mail: dtracy@canteyhanger.com

TRAGER, DAVID G. federal judge; b. Mt. Vernon, N.Y., Dec. 23, 1937; s. Sol and Clara (Friedman) T.; m. Roberta E. Weisbrod, May 2, 1972; children: Mara Emet, Josiah Samuel, Naomi Gabrielle. B.A., Columbia Coll., 1959; LL.B., Harvard U., 1962. Bar: N.Y. Assoc. Berman & Frost, 1963-65, Butler, Jablow & Geller, 1965-67; asst. corp. counsel Appeals Div. City of N.Y., 1967; law clk. Judge Kenneth B. Keating, N.Y. State Ct. Appeals, 1968-69; asst. U.S. atty. chief, appeals div., 1970-72; U.S. atty. Ea. Dist. N.Y., Bklyn., 1974-78; prof. Bklyn. Law Sch., 1972-94, dean, 1983-94; judge U.S. Dist. Ct. (ea. dist.) N.Y., Bklyn., 1994—. Chmn. Mayor's Com. on Judiciary, 1982-89, N.Y. State Temp. Commn. on Investigation, 1983-90. Mem. N.Y.C. Charter Rev. Commn., 1986-89. With USAR, 1962-65, USNR, 1965-69. Mem. ABA, N.Y. State Bar Assn., Assn. Bar City N.Y., Fed. Bar Council (pres. 1986-88), Am. Law Inst., Am. Judicature Soc. Office: US Courthouse 225 Cadman Plz E Brooklyn NY 11201-1818

TRAGER, MICHAEL DAVID, lawyer; b. N.Y.C., Feb. 15, 1959; s. Philip and Ina (Shulkin) T.; m. Mariella Gonzalez, Sept. 12, 1987; children: Nicholas, Alexander. BA, Wesleyan U., Middletown, Conn., 1981; JD, Boston U., 1985. Bar: Mass. 1985, Conn. 1986, Fla. 1988, D.C. 1989. Staff atty. enforcement divsn. Securities & Exchange Com., Washington, 1985-87; assoc. Morgan, Lewis & Bockius, Miami, Fla., 1987-88; participating assoc. Fulbright & Jaworski, Washington, 1989-92; ptnr. Trager & Trager, 1992-93; of counsel Fulbright & Jaworski, 1993-94, ptnr., 1995—, co-head securities litigation and enforcement. Bd. dirs. Jewish Nat. Fund-Mid-Atlantic Region, 1993-97; officer Horace Mann PTA, 1997-99. Mem. ABA (bus. law sect. fed. regulation securities com. and civil litigation and SEC enforcement matters subcom., litigation sect. securities litigation com. and SEC enforcement subcom., class action and derivative litigation com. and securities litigation subcom., task force on SEC's insider trading and selective disclosure rules), Assn. SEC Alumni, Securities Industry Assn. (legal and compliance divsn.), D.C. Bar (corp., fin. and securities law sect. corp. counsel and planning group for broker-dealer programs 1992-94, broker-dealer regulation com., task force on SEC's proposed insider trading and selective disclosure rules), Mass. Bar, Fla. Bar., Conn. Bar., Bond Market Assn. (litigation adv. com.). Administrative and regulatory, Federal civil litigation, Securities. Office: Fulbright & Jaworski 801 Pennsylvania Ave NW Fl 3-5 Washington DC 20004-2623

TRAGOS, GEORGE EURIPEDES, lawyer; b. Chgo., July 15, 1949; s. Euripedes G. and Eugene G. (Gatziolis) T.; m. Donna Marie Thalassites, Nov. 18, 1978; children: Louise, Gina, Peter. BA, Fla. State U., 1971, JD, 1974. Bar: Fla., U.S. Dist. Ct. (mid., so. dists.) Fla., U.S. Dist. Ct. (we. dist.) Tenn., U.S. Ct. Appeals (5th, 11th cirs.). Legis. aide Fla. Ho. of Reps., 1972-73; tax analyst tax and fin. com., 1973-74; chief, felony asst. states atty. State of Fla., Clearwater, 1974-78; partner firm Case, Kimpton, Tragos & Burke, P.A., Clearwater Beach, 1978-83; chief criminal div. U.S. Atty.'s Office for Middle Dist. Fla., Tampa, 1983-85; lead trial asst. Pres. Organized Crime Drug Enforcement Task Force, 1985; sole practice Clearwater, 1985—. Contbr. articles to profl. jours. and frequent lectr. Mem. Clearwater Bar (pres. 1994), Fla. Bar Assn. (chmn. fed. practice com. 1986, chmn. criminal law sect. 2000, chmn. bar evidence com. 1990), Fla. Assn. Criminal Def. Lawyers (pres. 1991), Fla. State U. Alumni Assn. Law Sch. (bd. dirs.), Tampa Bay Fed. Bar Assn. (v.p. 1989), Clearwater Beach Jaycees (pres. 1979), Fla. U. Gold Key Club (pres. 1972), Ahepa. Democrat. Mem. Greek Orthodox Ch. Avocations: boating, tennis. Office: 600 Cleveland St Ste 700 Clearwater FL 33755-4158 E-mail: greeklaw@verizon.net

TRAHAIR, ANDREW JAMES, lawyer; b. Sydney, Australia, Sept. 7, 1963; s. Nicholas Snowden and Salley Marie Trahair; m. Nan Kathleen Dunham, Nov. 10, 1995; children: Esme, Linus. BCom./LLB, U. New South Wales, Australia, 1986. Bar: New South Wales 1987, Eng. and Wales 1991. Ptnr. Allen & Overy, London, 1994-97, Clayton Utz, Sydney, 1998-2000, Allen & Overy, Singapore, 2001—. Banking, General corporate, Finance. Office: Allen & Overy Singapore 1 Robinson Rd #18-00 AIA Tr Singapore 048542 Singapore Fax: 65-435 7474. E-mail: andrew.trahair@allenovery.com

TRAICOFF, SANDRA M. lawyer; b. O'Neill, Nebr., Aug. 31, 1944; d. Theodore Edwin and Ella Pauline (Fuhrer) Rustemeyer; m. Chris J. Traicoff, Feb. 17, 1973. BA in Polit. Sci. and Asian Studies, U. Kans., 1967; MA in L.S., U. Ill., 1970; JD, DePaul U., 1978. Bar: Ill. 1978, Mich. 1990. Asst. reference and documents libr. U. Ill. Law Libr., Urbana, 1970-73; assoc. libr., head pub. svcs. DePaul U. Law Libr., Chgo., 1973-77; loan rev. officer Comml. Nat. Bank of Peoria (Ill.), 1978-82; corp. sec. Midwest Fin. Group, Inc., Peoria, 1982-86; v.p., sec. and gen. counsel Midwest Fin. Group, Inc., 1986-89; atty. Howard & Howard Attys. P.C., Peoria, 1989—; lectr., cons. Comml. Nat. Mgmt. Cons. Co., Peoria, 1979-82; lectr. Grad. Sch. Libr. Scis., U. Chgo., 1975-77. Bd. dirs. Heart of Ill. Big Bros./Big Sisters, Peoria, 1981-86, pres. bd., 1981-82; bd. dirs., mem. coms. YWCA, Peoria, 1981-92, bd. dirs. 1986-92, v.p., 1987-89, pres. bd., 1989-91. Regents scholar U. Colo., Boulder, 1962, Univ. Fellow U. Ill., Urbana, 1968. Mem. ABA, Ill. Bar Assn., Mich. Bar Assn., Peoria County Bar Assn., Beta Phi Mu. Home: 912 W Shoreline Ct Dunlap IL 61525-9541 Office: Howard & Howard 321 Liberty St Peoria IL 61602-1403

TRAN, JULIE HOAN, lawyer; b. Dalat, Vietnam, May 25, 1970; came to U.S., 1975; d. My Ich and Ngu Thi Tran. BA in English, Baylor U., 1992; JD, Cornell Law Sch., 1995, postgrad. Bar: Tex. 1996, N.Y. 1996. Assoc. Akin, Gump, Strauss, Hauer & Feld, LLP, Houston, 1995-99, N.Y.C., 1999-2000; gen. counsel Bluefly, Inc., 2000—. Co-chmn., lectr. Conference on Creating and Structuring Internat. Joint Ventures, 1999; mem. Firm Hiring Com., 1998-99. Gen. editor Jour. of Pub. Law and Policy, 1994-95. Mem. ABA, N.Y. Bar Assn., Phi Delta Phi. General corporate, Private international, Mergers and acquisitions. Office: Bluefly Inc 9th Fl 42 W 39th St New York NY 10018 E-mail: julie@bluefly.com

TRANCHINA, FRANK PETER, JR. lawyer; b. New Orleans, July 18, 1953; s. Frank P. and Effie (Volpe) T.; m. Susan Kendrick, Sept. 28, 1995. BA, Loyola U., New Orleans, 1976, JD, 1979. Bar: La. 1979, U.S. Ct. Appeals (5th cir.) 1981, Calif. 1994. Assoc. Law Offices Guy W. Olano, Jr., Kenner, La., 1979-86, Satterlee, Mestayer & Freeman, New Orleans, 1986-88; ptnr. Tranchina & Martinez, A.P.L.C., 1988-98, Tranchina & Assocs., New Orleans, 1998—. Lectr. in field, 1989—; asst. grader for civil code I, La. Bar Exam., 1989-97. Contbr. articles to legal jours. Fellow Am. Acad. Matrimonial Lawyers (bd. cert. family law specialist La.); mem. ABA (trial techniques com. family law sect., law practice mgmt. com.), La. State Bar (chmn. CLE family law sect. 1989-90, treas. 1990, vice chmn. 1991-92, chmn. 1992-94), New Orleans Bar Assn., Toastmasters (pres. Metairie, La. 1981-84), Jefferson Parish Bar Assn. (chmn. CLE 1989-90, 91-92 domestic rels. sect.). Family and matrimonial. Home: 51 Cardinal Ln Mandeville LA 70471-6758

TRAPP, JAMES MCCREERY, lawyer; b. Macomb, Ill., Aug. 11, 1934; BA, Knox Coll., 1956; JD, U. Mich., 1961. Bar: Ill. 1961. Ptnr. McDermott, Will & Emery, Chgo., 1961-98, sr. counsel, 1998—. Chmn. Ill. Inst. Continuing Legal Edn., 1978-79, bd. dirs., 1980-86, pres., 1984-85. Fellow Am. Coll. Trust and Estate Counsel (Ill. chmn. 1980-83, nat. regent 1983—, treas. 1989-90, sec. 1990-91, v.p. 1991-92, pres.-elect 1992-93, pres. 1993-94, exec. com. 1986-94), Am. Bar Found., Ill. Bar Found.; mem. ABA, Ill. State Bar Assn., Chgo. Bar Assn. (chair trust law com. 1972-73, com. on coms. 1972-74), Internat. Acad. Estate and Trust Law, Am. Law Inst. (pres.), Chgo. Estate Planning Coun. Office: McDermott Will & Emery 227 W Monroe St Ste 3100 Chicago IL 60606-5096

TRAPP, MARY JANE, lawyer; b. Columbus, Ohio, July 6, 1956; AB cum laude, Mount Holyoke Coll., 1978; JD, Case Western Reserve U., 1981. Bar: Ohio 1981, U.S. Supreme Ct. 1987. Ptnr. Apicella and Trapp, Cleve. Commr. Supreme Ct. Ohio Bd. Commrs. on Unauthorized Practice of Law, 1986—89; mem. Supreme Ct. Rules adv. com., 1997—. Fellow: Am. Bar Found., Ohio State Bar Found.; mem.: ABA, Ohio State Bar Assn. (pres. 2001—), Ohio Acad. Trial Lawyers, Cuyahoga County Bar Assn. (trustee 1986—93, trustee 1999—), Cleve. Bar Assn. (trustee 1995—98). Personal injury, Family and matrimonial, Professional liability. Office: Apicella and Trapp 1200 Bond Ct Bldg 1300 E 9th St Ste 1200 Cleveland OH 44114-1503*

TRAUB, RICHARD KENNETH, lawyer; b. Lakewood, N.J., Aug. 4, 1950; s. Harold W. and Muriel N. (Zurlin) T.; m. Barbara Lynn Wright, July 9, 1972; children: Russell S., Melissa L. BBA, U. Miami, Coral Gables, Fla., 1972, JD cum laude, 1975. Bar: Fla. 1975, N.Y. 1976, N.J. 1976, U.S. Dist. Ct. N.J. 1976, U.S. Supreme Ct. 1979, U.S. Dist. Ct. (ea. & so. dists.) N.Y. 1981. Ptnr. Wilson, Elser, Moskowitz, Edelman & Dicker, N.Y.C., 1975-95, Traub Eglin Lieberman Straus, Hawthorne, N.Y., 1996—. Ptnr. Time for Patty Stables, N.J., 1992—; officer, dir. X-Ray Duplications, Inc., N.J.; ptnr., founder Fractured Greetings, N.J.; mem., lectr. Fedn. Ins. and Corp. Counsel, 1993—, mem. admissions com., industry cooperation ins. coverage and alt. dispute resolution coms.; lectr. Inst. for Internat. Rsch., Washington, 1988, Engring. News Record Constrn. Claims Conf., 1991. Author: Legal and Professional Aspects of Construction Management, 1990, The Year 2000 and Potential Liabilities and Otherwise, 1999, Litigating Year 2000 Cases, Chapter 8, Insurance Coverage, 1999, Practical Environmental Forensics--Process and Case Histories, 2000; contbr. articles to profl. jours. Bd. dirs. Pop Warner Football Assn., Holmdel, N.J., 1989—. Mem. ABA (forum com. on constrn. industry 1989, tort and ins. practice sect. 1985—, computer litigation sect.), N.Y. State Bar Assn., N.J. Bar Assn., Fla. Bar Assn., Fedn. Ins. and Corp. Counsel (spkr. The Millenium Bug ins. coverage sect., vice chair ins. coverage and Y2K sects., chair tech. and e-commerce sect., vice chair tech. com., editor The Roster), Def. Rsch. Inst. Construction, Environmental, Insurance. Office: Traub Eglin Lieberman Straus Mid-Westchester Exec Park Three Skyline Dr Hawthorne NY 10532 also: 505 Main St Hackensack NJ 07601-5900 E-mail: rtraub@tels.com

TRAUBE, VICTORIA GILBERT, lawyer; b. L.A., Sept. 3, 1946; d. Shepard and Mildred (Gilbert) T. BA, Radcliffe Coll., 1968; MA, Harvard U., 1970; JD, U. Pa., 1974. Bar: N.Y. 1975, U.S. Dist. Ct. (so. dist.) N.Y. 1975, U.S. Ct. Appeals (2d cir.) 1975. Assoc. Paul, Weiss, Rifkind, Wharton & Garrison, N.Y.C., 1974-81; from assoc. counsel to dir. bus. affairs Home Box Office Inc., 1981-85; counsel Stults & Marshall, 1985-86; v.p. bus. affairs Reeves Entertainment Group, L.A., 1986-87,

Internat. Creative Mgmt., N.Y.C., 1987-95; sr. v.p., gen. counsel Rodgers & Hammerstein Orgn., 1995—. Adj. prof. Cardozo Law Sch., N.Y.C., 1986. Mem. Assn. of Bar of City of N.Y. (chair entertainment law com. 1998-2000). General corporate, Entertainment. Office: Rodgers & Hammerstein Orgn 1065 Ave of Americas New York NY 10018 E-mail: vtraube@rnh.com

TRAUTH, JOSEPH LOUIS, JR. lawyer; b. Cin., Apr. 22, 1945; s. Joseph L. and Margaret (Walter) T.; m. Barbara Widmeyer, July 4, 1970; children: Jennifer, Joseph III, Jonathan, Braden, Maria. BS in Econs., Xavier U., 1967; JD, U. Cin., 1973. Bar: Ohio 1973, U.S. Dist. Ct. (so. dist.) Ohio 1973, U.S. Ct. Appeals (6th cir.) 1973, U.S. Supreme Ct. 1988, Ky. 2000. Ptnr. Keating, Muething & Klekamp, PLL, Cin., 1973-80, Keating, Muething & Klekamp, Cin., 1980—. Speaker real estate law, 1974—. Contbr. articles to real estate publs. Mem. Rep. Leadership Coun., Cin., 1987—, Parish Coun., Cin., 1990. Mem. Cin. Bar Assn. (grievance com., real estate com., negligence com.). Roman Catholic. Avocations: running, tennis, reading. General civil litigation, Land use and zoning (including planning), Real property. Office: Keating Muething & Klekamp 1800 Provident Tower 1 E 4th St Ste 1400 Cincinnati OH 45202-3717 E-mail: jtrauth@kmklaw.com

TRAUTMAN, HERMAN LOUIS, lawyer, educator; b. Columbus, Ind., Sept. 26, 1911; s. Theodore H. and Emma (Guckenberger) T.; m. Marian Lucille Green, Sept. 1, 1940; children: Stephen M., Pamela C.; LLB with distinction Ind. U., 1937, BA, 1946, JD with distinction, 1946; postgrad., NYU, 1953, Ford Found. faculty fellow, Harvard U., 1954-55. Bar: Ind. 1937, U.S. Tax Ct., U.S. Ct. Appeals (6th cir.) Tenn. Sole practice, Evansville, Ind., 1937-43; pres. Crescent Coal Co., Evansville, 1941-43; prof. law U. Ala. Tuscaloosa, 1946-49; prof. law Vanderbilt U., 1949—, prof. law emeritus, 1977; NYU vis. prof., 1955, U. Mich., Ann Arbor, 1963-64; ptnr. Trautman & Trautman, Nashville, 1976-85; sole practice, Nashville, 1986—. Served to lt. comdr. USN, 1943-46. Mem. ABA, Am. Law Inst., Tenn. Bar Assn., Nashville Bar Assn., Nat. Conf. Jud. Adminstrs., Estate Planning Coun., Order of Coif, Phi Gamma Delta, Belle Meade Club, Univ. Club, Kiwanis. Methodist. Probate, Estate taxation, Taxation, general. Address: PO Box 150862 Nashville TN 37215-0862

TRAUTMAN, WILLIAM ELLSWORTH, lawyer; b. San Francisco, Nov. 27, 1940; s. Gerald H. and Doris Joy (Tucker) T.; m. Dorothy Williamson, June 17, 1962; children: Darcey, Torey. AB, U. Calif., Berkeley, 1962, LLB, 1965. Bar: Calif. U.S. Supreme Ct., Calif. Dist. Ct., U.S. Ct. Appeals (9th and fed. cirs.). Assoc. Chickering & Gregory, San Francisco, 1965-71, ptnr., 1972-81, Brobeck, Phleger & Harrison, San Francisco, 1981—, mng. ptnr., 1992-96, litigation dept. chair, 1984-91. Pres. Oakland (Calif.) Mus. Assn., 1981-83; mem. profl. ethics com. State Bar Calif., 1974-77. Fellow Am. Coll. Trial Lawyers; mem. Legal Aid Soc. (bd. dirs. 1982-93, pres. 1985-88), Bar Assn. San Francisco (bd. dirs. 1972-73), Calif. Barristers (bd. dirs., v.p.), Barrister's Club of San Francisco (v.p. 1973), Boalt Hall Alumni Assn. (bd. dirs. 1993-99, pres. 1997-98), U. Calif.-Berkeley Found. (bd. trustees 1998-2001). Antitrust, General civil litigation, Insurance. Office: Brobeck Phleger & Harrison 1 Market St San Francisco CA 94105-1420 E-mail: wtrautman@brobeck.com

TRAVIS, JAY A., III, lawyer; b. McComb, Miss., June 8, 1940; s. John A. and Katharine (Brennan) T., Jr.; m. Judith Thompson, Sept. 8, 1965; children: Kathy, John E., William. BBA, U. Miss., 1962, JD, 1965. Bar: Miss. 1965, U.S. Dist. Ct. (so. dist.) Miss. 1967, U.S. Ct. Appeals (5th cir.) 1970. Assoc. Thompson, Alexander & Crews, Jackson, Miss., 1967-69; ptnr. Butler, Snow, O'Mara, Stevens & Cannada, 1969—. Chmn. Miss. Law Inst., 1974; pres. Estate Planning Coun. Miss., 1975-76. Mem. vestry, cathedral warden St. Andrew's Episc. Ch., 1983-87. Capt. JAGC, USAR, 1965-73. Fellow Am. Coll. of Trust & Estate Counsel (bd. of regents, 1994-2000, state chmn. 1987-92), Am. Bar Found.; mem. ABA (fellow young lawyers sect.), Miss. State Bar (pres. young lawyers sect. 1975-76), Miss. Bar Assn. (chmn. estates and trusts sect. 1987-88), Hinds County Bar Assn. (pres. 1988-89), Univ. Club, River Hills Club, Phi Delta Phi. General corporate, Estate planning, Probate. Office: PO Box 22567 Jackson MS 39225-2567 E-mail: MMatzka@sandw.com

TRAXLER, WILLIAM BYRD, JR. federal judge; b. Greenville, S.C., May 1, 1948; s. William Byrd and Bettie (Wooten) T.; m. Patricia Alford, Aug. 21, 1972; children: William Byrd III, James McCall. BA, Davidson Coll., 1970; JD, U. S.C., 1973. Assoc. William Byrd Traxler, Greenville, 1973-75; asst. solicitor 13th Jud. Ct., 1975-78, dep. solicitor, 1978-81, solicitor, 1981-85, resident cir. judge, 1985-92; U.S. Dist. judge Dist. of S.C., 1992-98; judge U.S. Ct. of Appeals (4th cir.), 1998—. Recipient Outstanding Svc. award Solicitors Assn., S.C., 1987, Leadership award Probation, Parole & Pardon Svcs., S.C., 1990. Office: PO Box 10127 Greenville SC 29603-0127

TRAYLOR, CHET D. state supreme court justice; b. Columbia, La., Oct. 12, 1945; s. John Hardy and Bernice (Bogan) T.; children: Mary Therese, Leigh Ann, Anna Marie. BA in Govt., N.E. La. State U., 1969; JD, Loyola U., 1974. Bar: La. Judge 5th Jud. Dist. Ct., Franklin, Richland and West Carroll Parishes, La., 1985-97; assoc. justice La. Supreme Ct., 1997—. Past legal advisor La. State Police; past investigator La. Dept. Justice; asst. dist. atty., Franklin Parish, 1975-76. Founding bd. mem. Winnsboro Econ. Devel. Found.; mem. Rocky Mountain Conservation Fund. With U.S. Army. Mem. ABA, La. Bar Assn., La. Dist. Judges Assn., NRA (life), Franklin Parish Mental Health Assn. (past bd. dirs.), Winnsboro Lions Club (past bd. dirs.), Greenwings (founder John Adams chpt.). Methodist. Office: Supreme Ct 301 Loyola Ave New Orleans LA 70112-1814*

TRAYLOR, ROBERT ARTHUR, lawyer; b. Syracuse, N.Y., Jan. 15, 1949; s. Robert Arthur and Julia Elizabeth (McNulty) T.; m. Bonita Lynn Schmidt, Nov. 26, 1977. BS, LeMoyne Coll., 1970; JD cum laude, Syracuse U., 1975. Bar: N.Y., U.S. Dist. Ct. (no. dist.) N.Y., U.S. Tax Ct. Assoc. Love, Balducci & Scaccia, Syracuse, N.Y., 1976-77; estate tax atty. IRS, 1977-81; assoc. Scaccia Law Firm, 1981—. Contbr. articles to profl. jours. Of counsel St. Ann Sch., Syracuse, 1981—, mem. coordinating com. Vision 2000 1994—, mem. bd., 1998—. With U.S. Army, 1970-72. Mem. ABA, Onondaga County Bar Assn. (vol. lawyer program 1993—, Vol. Lawyer of Month 1994), World Wildlife Fedn. Republican. Roman Catholic. Avocations: motorsports, military history, Catholic education. General civil litigation, Probate, Real property. Home: 112 Knowland Dr Liverpool NY 13090-3130 Office: Scaccia Law Firm State Tower Bldg Ste 402 Syracuse NY 13202-1798

TRAYNOR, JOHN MICHAEL, lawyer; b. Oakland, Calif., Oct. 25, 1934; s. Roger J. and Madeleine (Lackmann) T.; m. Shirley Williams, Feb. 11, 1956; children: Kathleen Traynor Millard, Elizabeth Traynor Fowler, Thomas. BA, U. Calif., Berkeley, 1955; JD, Harvard U., 1960. Bar: Calif. 1961, U.S. Supreme Ct. 1966. Dep. atty. gen. State of Calif., San Francisco, 1961-63; spl. counsel Calif. Senate Com. on Local Govt., Sacramento, 1963; assoc. firm Cooley Godward, LLP, San Francisco, 1963-69, ptnr., 1969—. Adviser 3d Restatement of Unfair Competition, 1988-95, 3d Restatement of Torts; Products Liability, 1992-97, Apportionment, 1994-99, 1988 Revs. 2d Restatement of Conflict of Laws, 3rd Restatement of Restitution and Unjust Punishment, 1997-; lectr. U. Calif. Boalt Hall Sch. Law, Berkeley, 1982-89, 1996-98; chmn. EarthJustice Legal Def. Fund (formerly Sierra Club Legal Defense Fund), 1989-91, pres. 1991-92, trustee, 1974-96. Mem. bd. overseers Inst. for Civil Justice The RAND Corp., 1991-97; bd. dirs. Environ. Law Inst., 1991-97, 00—, Sierra Legal Def. Fund (Can.), 1990-96. Served to 1st lt. USMC, 1955-57. Fellow AAAS, Am. Bar Found. (life); mem. Am. Law Inst. (coun. 1985—, pres. 2000—), Bar Assn. San Francisco (pres. 1973). Federal civil litigation, State civil litigation, Intellectual property. Home: 3131 Eton Ave Berkeley CA 94705-2713 Office: Cooley Godward LLP 1 Maritime Plz Ste 2000 San Francisco CA 94111-3510 E-mail: traynormt@cooley.com

TRCA, RANDY ERNEST, lawyer; b. Mason City, Iowa, Mar. 29, 1957; s. Ernest Edward and Emily (Hrubes) T. BS, N.W. Mo. State U., 1978; JD, U. Iowa, 1981, MBA, 1982. Bar: Iowa 1981, U.S. Dist. Ct. (no. and so. dists.) Iowa 1982. Pvt. practice law, Iowa City, 1982—. Mem. edn. com. Iowa City C. of C., 1982-88. Mem. Iowa State Bar Assn. Democrat. Roman Catholic. Avocations: golfing, skiing, jogging, travel, culture. Bankruptcy, Family and matrimonial, Personal injury. Home: 1915 Muscatine Ave Iowa City IA 52240-6409 Office: 1232 E Burlington St Iowa City IA 52240-3212 E-mail: rtlawfirm@prodigy.net

TREACY, GERALD BERNARD, JR. lawyer; b. Newark, July 29, 1951; s. Gerald B. Sr. and Mabel L. (Nesbitt) T.; m. Joyce M. Biazzo, Apr. 6, 1974. BA summa cum laude, Rider Coll., 1973; JD, UCLA, 1981. Bar: Calif. 1981, Wash. 1982, D.C. 1995. Tchr. English Arthur L. Johnson Regional High Sch., Clark, N.J., 1973-77; assoc. Gibson, Dunn & Crutcher, L.A., 1981-82; ptnr. Perkins Coie, Bellevue, Wash., 1982-94, McGuire Woods Battle & Boothe, McLean, Va. and Bellevue, Va., 1994-96, Egger, Betts, Austin, Treacy, Bellevue, Wash., 1996-98; mem. Treacy Law Group, 1998—; of counsel Montgomery Purdue Blankenship and Austin, Seattle, 2000—. Chmn. bd. dirs. estate planning adv. bd. U. Wash., Seattle, 1990-92; presenter TV Seminar, Where There's a Will, PBS affiliate. Author: Washington Guardianship Law, Administration and Litigation, 1988, supplemented, 1991, 2d edit., 1992, supplemented, 1993, Supporting Organizations, 1996. Mem. endowment fund com. United Way, Seattle, 1987-89, exec. com. Washington Planned Giving Coun., 1993-94, 96-98; bd. dirs., mem. adv. bd. ARC, Seattle, 1985-89, Arthritis Gift, 1987-89, Seattle Symphony, 1992, Seattle U., 1996. Mem. Eastside King County Estate Planning Coun., Order of Coif. Avocations: photography, hiking, ethnic and classical music, poetry, host/writer Gilbert & Sullivan radio show. Estate planning, Probate, Estate taxation. Office: 11201 SE 8th St Ste 170 Bellevue WA 98004

TREACY, VINCENT EDWARD, lawyer; b. Mass., Jan. 30, 1942; AB, Boston Coll., 1964; JD with honors, George Washington U., 1971. Bar: Va. 1972, D.C. 1973, Md. 1999; U.S. Supreme Ct. 1976. Atty. Fed. Labor Rels. Coun., Washington, 1971-73; legis. atty. Am. law divsn. Congrl. Rsch. Svc., Libr. Congress, 1973-98; sole practitioner, 1998—. Legis. cons. Romanian Legal Analysis and Legis. Drafting Conf., Senate and Chamber Duputies Romania, Bucharest, 1996. Mem. law rev. staff George Washington Law Rev., 1970. Mem. ABA, George Washington Law Alumni Assn. (pres. Capitol Hill chpt. 1986-87), Order of Coif. Entertainment, Labor, Pension, profit-sharing, and employee benefits.

TREADWAY, JAMES CURRAN CORBETT, lawyer, investment company executive, former government official; b. Anderson, S.C., May 21, 1943; s. James C. and Maxine (Hall) T.; m. Susan Pepper Davis, Sept. 6, 1969; children: Elizabeth Pepper Hall, Caroline Worrell Harper Corbett. AB summa cum laude, Rollins Coll., 1964; JD summa cum laude, Washington and Lee U., 1967. Bar: Ga. 1967, Mass. 1968, D.C. 1970. Assoc. Candler, Cox, McClain & Andrews, Atlanta, 1967-68, Gadsby & Hannah, Boston and Washington, 1968-72; ptnr. Dickstein, Shapiro & Morin, Washington, 1972-82; commr. SEC, 1982-85; ptnr. Baker & Botts, 1985-87; exec. v.p., chmn. dept. merchant banking, exec. com. Paine Webber Group Inc., N.Y.C., 1987—. Chmn. Nat. Commn. on Fraudulent Fin. Reporting, 1985-87; chmn. bd. dirs. Washington & Lee U. Sch. Law, 1992-94; spl. expert adviser, witness various U.S. congl. coms.; lectr. in field. Editor-in-chief Wash. & Lee U. Law review, 1966-67. Recipient Wildman Medal Am. Acctg. Assn., 1989. Mem. Mass. Bar Assn., Ga. Bar Assn., D.C. Bar Assn., Chevy Chase (Md.) Club, Bedford (N.Y.) Golf and Tennis Club, City Tavern Club, Met. Club, Univ. Club (Washington), Verbank Hunting and Fishing Club (Uniondale N.Y.; dir. 1995—), Order of Coif, Phi Beta Kappa, Omicron Delta Kappa. Republican. Roman Catholic. Home: Laurel Ledge RD 4 Croton Lake Rd Bedford Corners NY 10549 Office: PaineWebber Group Inc 1285 Ave of Americas New York NY 10019-6028

TRECEK, TIMOTHY SCOTT, lawyer; b. Racine, Wis., Sept. 26, 1968; s. Robert Thomas and Mona Marie Trecek; m. Karyn Marie Kwiatkowski, Aug. 27, 1994; children: Gabrielle Grace, Danielle Terese. BS in Polit. Sci., Marquette U., 1990, JD, 1993. Bar: Wis. 1993, U.S. Dist. Ct. (ea. dist.) Wis. 1993. Atty. Kasdorf, Lewis & Swietlik, Milw., 1993-95, Habush, Habush, Davis & Rottier, Milw., 1995—. Mem. ABA, Wis. Acad. of Trial Lawyers (com. mem. bd. attys. profl. responsibility), Wis. State Bar Assn., Assn. of Trial Lawyers of Am. Roman Catholic. Avocations: golfing, family. General civil litigation, Personal injury. Office: Habush Habush & Rottier 777 E Wisconsin Ave 2300 Milwaukee WI 53202-5381 E-mail: ttrecek@habush.com

TREES, PHILIP HUGH, lawyer; b. Greenfield, Ind., Mar. 23, 1953; s. Philip Lee and Lauretta May (Cummins) T.; m. Debra J. Tapanes, June 21, 1975 (div. May 1981); m. Diane Heller D'Amico, May 28, 1982; child, Philip Thomas, Andrew Thomas Trees. BA, Fla. State U., 1974, JD with honors, 1977. Bar: Fla. 1978, U.S. Dist. Ct. (mid. dist.) Fla. 1978, U.S. Tax Ct. 1978, U.S. Ct. Appeals (5th and 11th cirs.) 1978, U.S. Supreme Ct. 1978. Assoc. Gray, Harris & Robinson, P.A., Orlando, Fla., 1977-81; ptnr. Gray, Harris & Robinson, P.A., Orlando, 1981—; bd. dirs. Goodwill Industries of Cen. Fla. Mem. exec. com. Task Force to Revitalize South Orange Blossom Trail, Orlando; mem. Orlando Crime Commn.; grad. Leadership Orlando program, 1985. Recipient Price Waterhouse and Orlando Bus. Jour. Up and Comers award in Law, 1989. Mem. ABA, Fla. Bar Assn., Orange County Bar Assn. (chmn. news media and pub. relations com. 1982-84, chmn. law and edn. com. 1984-87, Outstanding Chmn. award 1982-86, treas.), Am. Judicature Soc., Fla. C. of C. (edn. com.). Clubs: University (Orlando); Sabal Point Country (Longwood, Fla.). Federal civil litigation, State civil litigation, Consumer commercial. Office: 111 S Maitland Ave Maitland FL 32751-5647

TREMAYNE, ERIC FLORY, lawyer; b. Washington, Nov. 29, 1945; s. Bertram William and Frances (Lewis) T.; m. Barbara Ann Williams, Sept. 18, 1982. B.A., Westminster Coll., 1967; J.D., Washington U., St. Louis, 1973. Bar: Mo. 1973, U.S. Dist. Ct. (ea. and we. dists.) Mo., 1973. Assoc. Tremayne, Lay, Carr, Bauer, Clayton, Mo., 1973-77, ptnr., 1978—; prosecuting atty. City of Wildwood (Mo.), 1996-2000; dir. Option Computer Corp., St. Louis. St. Louis. Campaign aide Citizens for Kit Bond, St. Louis, 1972; bd. dirs. YMCA of the Ozarks. Served to sp. 4 U.S. Army, 1968-70. Mem. St. Louis County Bar Assn. (Outstanding Young Lawyer, 1981, pres. 1983-84), Bar Assn. Met. St. Louis. Republican. Anglican. Clubs: St. Louis Beta Theta Pi (v.p. 1978-90), Sports Car Club Am. (instr. 1979—). Federal civil litigation, State civil litigation, General corporate. Home: 433 Eatherton Valley Rd Wildwood MO 63005-4103 Office: Tremayne Lay Bauer Coleman & Grady LLP 7777 Bonhomme Ave Ste 1600 Clayton MO 63105-1911

TRENCHER, WILLIAM MANNES, lawyer; b. Bklyn., Mar. 9, 1947; s. B. Bernard and Lillian (F.) T.; m. Susan, June 20, 1970; children— Emily, Julie, Daniel. BA, Am. U., 1969, JD, 1972. Bar: Va. 1973, D.C., Md. Adminstr. Am. U. Law Inst., Washington, 1972-75, dir. Moot Ct. program; assoc. rsch. sci. Am. Inst. for Rsch., Washington, 1975-80; atty. Adminstrv. Office of U.S. Cts., Washington, 1980-88; trial atty. tax divsn. Dept. Justice, Washington, 1988-90; prin., founding ptnr. Steffan & Trencher, P.C., Fairfax, Va., 1990-92; counsel Bayh, Connaughton & Malone, P.C., Washington, 1992-95; gen. consel Commerce Funding Corp., Vienna, Va., 1995-98; chief counsel U.S. Internat. Trade Commn. Fellow Am. U. Law Inst.; mem. Legal Aid Soc. Banking. Home: 9723 St Andrews Dr Fairfax VA 22030-1856 Office: USITC 500 E St NW Washington DC 20436-0003

TRENT, JOHN THOMAS, JR. lawyer; b. Hammond, Ind., Mar. 11, 1954; s. John Thomas and Sally (Ritter) T.; m. Laura Marie Nelson, Aug. 5, 1978; children: Lauren, Valerie, Alex. AB, Wabash Coll., 1976; JD, Vanderbilt U., 1979. Bar: Tenn. 1979, U.S. Dist. Ct. (mid. dist.) Tenn. Mng. dir. Boult, Cummings, Conners & Berry P.L.C., Nashville, 1979—. Spkr., panelist real estate and other groups. Chmn. adminstrv. bd. and other coms. and offices West End United Meth. Ch., Nashville, 1983—99; bd. dirs. Cumberland Sci. Mus., 1997—, Jr. Achievement Middle Tenn. Fellow Nashville Bar; mem. ABA, Nat. Assn. Indsl. and Office Parks (past bd. dirs. Nashville chpt.), Tenn. Bar Assn., Nashville Bar Assn., Nat. Assn. Bond Lawyers, Assn. Attys. and Execs. in Corp. Real Estate. Appellate, Municipal (including bonds), Real property. Office: Boult Cummings Connors & Berry PLC 414 Union St Ste 1600 Nashville TN 37219-1744

TREUSCH, PAUL ELLSWORTH, law educator, lawyer; b. Chgo. m. Phyllis Freedman, 1941; 1 child, Karen Treusch Lord. PhB, U. Chgo., 1932; JD cum laude, 1935. Bar: Ill. 1935, D.C. 1945, Mass. 1974, U.S. SUpreme Ct. 1939. Ovt. practice, Chgo., 1935-37; mem. law faculty La. State. U., Baton Rouge, 1937-38; atty. Office of Chief Counsel IRS, Washington, 1938-70; mem. excess profits tax coun., 1948-51; asst. chief counsel litigation, 1951-70; adj. prof. law Howard U., Washington, 1965-70; prof., 1970-73, 76-79; prof. emeritus, 1979—. Professorial lectr. law George Washington U., 1966-73; prof. law Boston U., 1973 -76, prof. emeritus, 1976—; head Washington office Winston Strawn, Washington, 1970-73; prof. Southwestern U., L.A., 1979—; lectr. Zhongshan U. Law Dept., 1991—, Hong Kong U. and City U. Law Schs., 1991—. Co-author: treatise: Tax Exempt Charitable Organizations, 1978, 83, 88. Bd. dirs., legal counsel Burgundy Farm Country Day Sch.; bd. dirs. Washington Inst. Mental Hygiene. Mem. Fed. Bar Assn. (nat. pres. 1969-70, nat. coun.), Fed. Bar Found (dir.), ABA (life; exempt orgn. and internat. law coms.), Am. Law Inst. (life). Clubs: Cosmos (Washington); Nat. Press (Washington), Nat. Lawyers; Los Angeles Athletic. Office: Southwestern U Sch Law 675 S Westmoreland Ave Los Angeles CA 90005-3905 Fax: 213-383-1688

TREVENA, JOHN HARRY, lawyer; b. Dunedin, Fla., Dec. 28, 1961; s. Ernest Lewis and Lenora Geraldine (Adelson) T.; m. Susan Lee Corris, Nov. 23, 1988; 1 child, Samuel Alan. BA in criminal justice, Univ. S. Fla., 1982; Fla. Police standards, Pinellas Police Acad., 1982; JD, Stetson Univ., 1985. Bar: Fla., U.S. Dist. Ct. (mid. dist.) Fla. 1986; bd. cert. criminal trial lawyer, Fla. Pvt. practice, Largo, Fla. Editorial bd. Fla. Bar Jour., Fla. Bar News, 1990-93. Mem. Clearwater and Am. Bar Assn., Fla. Bar Assn., Fla. Assn. Criminal Def. Lawyers, Pinellas County Trial Lawyers Assn., Pinellas County Criminal Def. Lawyers Assn., Nat. Assn. Criminal Def. Lawyers, Am. Judicature Soc., Tampa Bay Cath. Lawyers Guild, Inc. Roman Catholic. Democrat. Civil rights, Criminal. Home: 423 Buttonwood Ln Largo FL 33770-4060 Office: 801 W Bay Dr Ste 509 Largo FL 33770-3220 E-mail: trevenalaw@aol.com

TREVETT, THOMAS NEIL, lawyer; b. Rochester, N.Y., Mar. 14, 1942; S. Frank E. and Andrea (Kuhn) T.; m. Margaret H. Hepburn, July 29, 1967; children; Monica, Millicent, Thomas. BS, St. John Fisher Coll., 1964; JD, Albany Law Sch., 1967. Bar: N.Y. 1967, U.S. Dist. Ct. (we. dist.) N.Y. 1968. Assoc. Thomas J. Meagher, Rochester, 1967-68, Trevett, Lenweaver, Salzer, and predecessor Gough, Skipworth, Summers, Eves & Trevett, Rochester, 1968—; pres. Trevett, Lenweaver, Salzer, and predecessor Gough, Skipworth, 1985-89. N.Y. estate tax atty., 1974-92. State Dem. committeeman; bd. dirs. Genesee region March Dimes, Rochester Area Multiple Sclerosis Soc., chmn. bd., 1992-94; chmn. bd. trustees McQuaid Jesuit N.S., 1997. Mem. ABA, N.Y. State Bar Assn., (ho. of dels. 1981, chmn. Ins. Negligence and Compensation Law sect. 1989-90, John E. Leach award, 1996), Monroe County Bar Assn. (trustee 1996—, pres. 1999—), Def. Rsch. Inst., Fedn. Ins. Corp. Counsel, Wayne County Bar. Assn. (pres. 1978-79). Roman Catholic. E-mai. Estate planning, Personal injury, Real property. Office: 700 Reynolds Arc Rochester NY 14614-1803 also: 2003 Main St 2003 Ridge Rd Ontario NY 14519 E-mail: ttrevett@trevettetal.com

TRICARICO, JOSEPH ARCHANGELO, lawyer; b. N.Y.C., May 6, 1940; s. Nicholas and Frances Tricarico; m. Mildred Grandi, Feb. 12, 1972; 1 child, Nicholas. BS, St. Johns U., 1963, JD, 1967. V.p. trust counsel U.S. Trust Co. N.Y., N.Y.C., 1973—. Author: Generation-Skipping Transfers: A Primer, 1984. Pro bono arbitrator small claims ct. Civil Ct. of City of N.Y., S.I., 1981—; trustee Eger Health Care Ctr., S.I., 1990—. Mem. ABA (com. bus. law 1990—, vice chair com. generation-skipping transfers 1993—, com. taxation 1984—), Am. Corp. Counsel Assn. (com. securities litigation 1991—, com. environ. law 1992—), N.Y. Bankers Assn. (spl. counsel trust legis. and regulatory com. 1991—), N.Y. Bar Assn., New York County Lawyers Assn. (com. on legis. 1989—), Am. Judges Assn. (hon. judge 1985—). Bankruptcy, Probate, Securities. Office: US Trust Co NY 114 W 47th St New York NY 10036-1510 E-mail: jtricarico@ustrust.com

TRIENENS, HOWARD JOSEPH, lawyer; b. Chgo., Sept. 13, 1923; s. Joseph Herman and Myrtle (Wilsberg) T.; m. Paula Miller, Aug. 27, 1946; children: John, Thomas, Nancy. BS, Northwestern U., 1945; JD, 1949. Bar: Ill. 1949, N.Y. 1980, U.S. Dist. Ct. (no. dist.) Ill. 1949, U.S. Dist. Ct. (so. and ea. dists.) N.Y. 1980, U.S. Ct. Appeals (2d, 3d, 7th, 8th, 10th, 11th and D.C. cirs.), U.S. Supreme Ct. 1954. Assoc. firm Sidley, Austin, Burgess & Harper, Chgo., 1949-50; law clk. to Chief Justice Vinson, 1950-52; assoc. Sidley, Austin, Burgess & Smith, Chgo., 1952-56; ptnr. Sidley Austin Brown & Wood, 1956—; v.p., gen. counsel AT&T, 1980-86. Trustee Northwestern U., 1967—. With USAAF, 1943-46. Mem. ABA, Ill. Bar Assn., Chgo. Bar Assn., N.Y. State Bar Assn., Am. Coll. Trial Lawyers, Lawyers Club (Chgo.), Chgo. Club, Casino Club (Chgo.), Mid-Day Club, Skokie Country Club, Shoreacres Club, Glen View Club (Golf, Ill.), Met. Club (Washington), Old Elm Club, Sigma Chi. Democrat. Administrative and regulatory, Antitrust, Appellate. Home: 690 Longwood Ave Glencoe IL 60022-1761 Office: Sidley Austin Brown & Wood Bank One Plz 10 S Dearborn Chicago IL 60603-2003 E-mail: htrienens@sidley.com

TRIEWEILER, TERRY NICHOLAS, state supreme court justice; b. Dubuque, Iowa, Mar. 21, 1948; s. George Nicholas and Anne Marie (Oastern) T.; m. Carol M. Jacobson, Aug. 11, 1972; children: Kathryn Anne, Christina Marie, Anna Theresa. BA, Drake U., 1970, JD, 1972. Bar: Iowa 1973, Wash. 1973, U.S. Dist. Ct. (so. dist.) Iowa 1973, U.S. Dist. Ct. (we. dist.) Wash. 1973, Mont. 1975, U.S. Dist. Ct. Mont. 1977. Staff atty. Polk County Legal Services, Des Moines, 1973; assoc. Hullin, Roberts, Mines, Fite & Riveland, Seattle, 1973-75, Morrison & Hedman, Whitefish, Mont., 1975-77; sole practice, Whitefish; justice Mont. Supreme Ct., Helena, 1991—; lectr. U. Mont. Law Sch., 1981—; mem. com. to amend civil proc. rules Mont. Supreme Ct., Helena, 1984, commn. to draft pattern jury instrns., 1985; mem. Gov.'s Adv. Com. on Amendment to Work Compensation Act, adv. com. Mont. Work Compensation Ct. Mem. ABA, Mont. Bar Assn. (pres. 1986-87), Wash. Bar Assn., Iowa Bar Assn., Assn. Trial Lawyers Am., Mont. Trial Lawyers Assn. (dir., pres.). Democrat. Roman Catholic. Home: 1079 Woodbridge Dr Helena MT 59601-5477 Office: Mont Supreme Ct 215 N Sanders St Rm 410 PO Box 203001 Helena MT 59620-3001*

TRIMBLE, JAMES T., JR. federal judge; b. Bunkie, La., Sept. 13, 1932; s. James T. Sr. and Mabel (McNabb) T.; m. Murel Elise Biles, Aug. 18, 1956; children: Elise, Mary Olive Beacham, Martha McNabb Elliott Rumsey, Sarah Trimble Moritz. Student, U. La., Lafayette, 1950-52; BA in Law, La. State U., 1955, JD, 1956. Bar: La. 1956. With Gist, Murchison & Gist (now Gist, Methvin, Hughes & Munsterman), 1959-78, Trimble, Percy, Smith, Wilson, Foote, Walker & Honeycutt, 1979-86; U.S. magistrate U.S. Dist. Ct. (we. dist.) La., 1986-91, judge, 1991—. Lt. USAF, 1956-59. Mem. Fed. Judges Assn., Southwest La. Bar Assn., La. Bar Assn., La. Bar Found. Avocations: jogging, gardening, tennis. Office: 611 Broad St Ste 237 Lake Charles LA 70601-4380

TRIMBLE, SANDRA ELLINGSON, lawyer; b. Buffalo, May 10, 1952; d. Andrew C. and Edna E. Ellingson; children: Samuel James, Stephen Joseph. BA with highest distinction, Colo. State U., 1974; MEd, Sul Ross State U., 1977; JD cum laude, Georgetown U., 1989. Bar: Md. 1989, D.C. 1990. Contract specialist USAF, Pope AFB, N.C., 1979-81; purchasing rep. Damson Oil Corp., Houston, 1982-86; summer assoc. Fried Frank Harris Shriver & Jacobson, Washington, 1988; law clk. Sullivan & Cromwell, 1988-89; assoc. Cleary Gottlieb Steen & Hamilton, 1989-97; of counsel Orrick Herrington & Sutcliffe LLP, 1997—. Assoc. notes editor Georgetown Law Jour., 1988-89. Recipient Disting. Achievement in Advocacy award Internat. Acad. Trial Lawyers, 1989; Nat. Merit scholar, 1970; law fellow Georgetown U. Law Ctr., 1987-88. Mem. ABA, Phi Beta Kappa. General corporate, Finance, Securities. Office: Orrick Herrington & Sutcliffe LLP 3050 K St NW Ste 200 Washington DC 20007-5135 E-mail: strimble@orrick.com

TRIMBLE, STEPHEN ASBURY, lawyer; b. Washington, July 25, 1933; s. South, Jr. and Elaine (Lazaro) T.; m. Mary Ellen Lynagh, Aug. 8, 1964. A.B. in Polit. Sci., U. N.C., 1955; LL.B., Georgetown U., 1961. Bar: D.C. 1961, U.S. Ct. Appeals (D.C. cir.) 1961, U.S. Supreme Ct. 1965, U.S. Ct. Claims 1979. Dep. clk. U.S. Dist. Ct. D.C., 1958-60, law clk. to fed. judge, 1960-62; asst. corp. counsel D.C., 1962; assoc. Hamilton & Hamilton, Washington, 1962-64, ptnr., 1964—. Mem. Sentencing Guidelines Commn. D.C. Superior Ct., 1984-92. Contbr. articles to publs.; lectr. in field. Sec. John Carroll Soc., Washington, 1965-77, bd. govs., 1979-83; mem. adv. bd. Salvation Army, Washington, 1982-91; trustee Maret Sch., Washington, 1976-84, v.p., 1981-84. 1st lt. USMC, 1955-58. Fellow Am. Coll. Trial Lawyers (D.C. chmn. 1981-82), Am. Bar Found. (grievance com. U.S. Dist. Ct. D.C. 1978-83, chmn. 1981-83, counseling panel U.S. Dist. Ct. D.C. 1990-94, chmn. 1990-94); mem. ABA (ho. of dels. 1975-77), Bar Assn. D.C. (pres. 1976-77, dir. 1971-73, sec. 1973-75), D.C. Bar (dir. 1978-81), Nat. Assn. R.R. Trial Counsel (pres. 1977-78, dir. 1970—, Disting. Svc. award 1995), Nat. Conf. Bar Pres., The Counsellors (Washington, pres. 1972-73), D.C. Def. Lawyers (v.p. 1974), The Barristers (sec. 1971, pres. 1981), Def. Rsch. Inst., Nat. Assn. Coll. and Univ. Attys., D.C. Council for Ct. Excellence (dir. 1983-92, exec. com. 1984-86), Jud. Conf. D.C. Cir., Jud. Conf. D.C. Cts., Chevy Chase Club (bd. govs. 1982-87, pres. 1986-87), Lawyers Club Washington (pres. 1991), Met. Club, Kiwanis (v.p. local chpt. 1985-86, pres. 1986-87). Roman Catholic. Federal civil litigation, State civil litigation, Personal injury. Office: Hamilton & Hamilton Ste 1100 1775 Pennsylvania Ave Washington DC 20006-4605 E-mail: sat@hamiltonlaw.com

TRIMMIER, CHARLES STEPHEN, JR. lawyer; b. Chgo., June 25, 1943; s. Charles Stephen and Lucille E. (Anderson) T.; m. Rae Wade Trimmier, Aug. 19, 1966; children: Charles Stephen, Hallie Wade. BA, U. Ala., Tuscaloosa, 1965, JD, 1968. Bar: Ala. 1968. From assoc. to ptnr. Rives, Peterson, Pettus and Conway, Birmingham, Ala., 1968-77; pres. TrimmierLaw Firm, Birmingham and Mobile, Boca Raton, Fla., 1977—. Gen. counsel Nat. Assn. State Chartered Credit Union Suprs., Ala. Credit Union League, Fla. Credit Union League, La. Credit Union League. Editor-in-chief: Ala. Law Rev., 1968. Mem. ABA (bus. and banking law sect., credit union com.), Ala. Bar Assn., Birmingham Bar Assn., Comml. Law League, Ala. Law Inst., Shades Valley Rotary, Shades Valley Jaycees (sec. 1973). Episcopalian. E-mial. Contracts commercial, General corporate, Private international. Home: 3819 River View Cir Birmingham AL 35243-4801 Office: Trimmier Law Firm PO Box 1885 Birmingham AL 35201-1885 E-mail: steve@trimmier.com

TRINDER, RACHEL BANDELE, lawyer; b. Ibadan, Nigeria, Feb. 21, 1955; came to U.S., 1977; d. Victor William John and Margaret (Almond) T. BA with honors, Oxford U., 1977, MA, 1994; LLM, U. Va., 1978. Bar: D.C. 1979, U.S. Dist. Ct. 1979, U.S. Ct. Appeals (D.C. cir.) 1980, U.S. Supreme Ct. 1986. Assoc. Zuckert, Scott & Rasenberger, LLP, Washington, 1978-85, ptnr., 1985—. V.p. aviation spl. interest chpt. Transp. Rsch. Forum, 1988-90, exec. v.p., 1990-91, gen. counsel, 1989-91; mem. bd. advisors 3d Ann. Symposium on Law and Outer Space, 1991, program dir., mem. bd. advisors, 4th Ann., 1991-92. Contbr. articles to legal jours. Bd. govs. Internat. Student House, 1986-93, mem. exec. com., asst. treas., 1987-88, mem. bd. advisors, 1993-97. Fellow English Speaking Union, 1977. Mem. ABA, FBA (chair space law com. 1990-94, chair internat. law sect. 1994-96), Internat. Bar Assn., Fed. Bar Assn., Internat. Inst. Space Law (life), Internat. Aviation Women's Assn. (dir.-at-large 1996-98), Internat. Inst. Air and Space Law (bd. govs., exec. com. 1992—), Internat. Aviation Club (bd. govs. 1984-86, pres. 1986), Aero Club (bd. govs. 1993—, pres. 2000), Nat. Aeronautic Assn. (bd. govs. 2000—). Aviation, Federal civil litigation, General corporate. Home: 1266 Dartmouth Ct Alexandria VA 22314-4784 Office: Zuckert Scott & Rasenberger LLP 888 17th St NW Washington DC 20006-3939 E-mail: rbtrinder@zsrlaw.com

TRIO, EDWARD ALAN, lawyer, accountant; b. Newark, N.J., Dec. 29, 1952; s. Edward B. and Dorothy J. (Salvia) T.; m. Patricia Ann Sherwood, June 19, 1982; children: Edward Joseph, Michael John. B.B.A., U. Notre Dame, 1974; J.D., Hamline U., St. Paul, 1977; LL.M. in Taxation with honors, Chgo.-Kent Coll. Law, 1984. Bar: Ill. 1977, U.S. Dist. Ct. (no. dist.) Ill. 1977, U.S. Tax Ct. 1979, U.S. Supreme Ct. 1984. C.P.A. Staff auditor Donald E. Bark, C.P.A., Arlington Heights, Ill., 1972-77; assoc. Graf & Gulbrandsen, Morton Grove, Ill., 1977-80; ptnr. Schneider, Graf & Trio, Morton Grove, 1980-82; tax specialist Deloitte Haskins & Sells, Chgo., 1982-85; assoc. Gould & Ratner, Chgo., 1985-90, ptnr., 1991—. Mem. ABA, AICPA, Ill. State Bar Assn., Chgo. Bar Assn., KC. Roman Catholic. Estate planning, Probate, Personal income taxation. Home: 909 N Derbyshire Ave Arlington Heights IL 60004-5776 Office: Gould & Ratner 222 N La Salle St Ste 800 Chicago IL 60601-1086

TRIPP, KAREN BRYANT, lawyer; b. Rocky Mount, N.C., Sept. 2, 1955; d. Bryant and Katherine Rebecca (Watkins) Tripp; m. Robert Mark Burleson, June 25, 1977 (div. 1997); 1 child, Hamilton Chase Tripp Barnett. BA, U. N.C., 1976; JD, U. Ala., 1981. Bar: Tex. 1981, U.S. Dist. Ct. (so. dist.) Tex. 1982, U.S, Ct. Appeals (fed. cir.) 1983, U.S. Dist. Ct. (ea. dist.) Tex. 1991, U.S. Supreme Ct. 1994, U.S. Dist. Ct. (no. dist.) Tex. 1998, U.S. Ct. Appeals (5th and 9th cirs.) 2000, U.S. Ct. Appeals (3d cir.) 2001. Law clk. Tucker, Gray & Espy, Tuscaloosa, Ala., 1978-81; law clk. to presiding justice Ala. Supreme Ct., Montgomery, summer 1980; atty. Exxon Prodn. Rsch. Co., Houston, 1981-86, coord. tech. transfer, 1986-87; assoc. Arnold, white and Durkee, 1988-93, shareholder, 1994-98, Winstead, Sechrest & Minick, Attys. at Law, Houston, 1998; pres. Blake Barnett & Co., 1996—; pvt. practice, 1999—. Creator, program planner, master of ceremonies 1st and 2d intellectual property law confs. for women corp. counsels. Editor Intellectual Property Law Rev., 1995-2001; contbr. articles to profl. jours. Chair U. Houston Fall CLE Inst. on Intellectual Property, 2000. Mem. ABA (intellectual property law sect., ethics com. 1992-96), Houston Bar Assn. (interprofl. rels. com. 1988-90), Houston Intellectual Property Law Assn. (outstanding inventor com. 1982-84, chmn. 1994-95, sec. 1987-88, treas. 1991-92, bd. dirs. 1992-94, 98-2000, nominations com. 1993, 96, chmn. fall CLE Inst. 2000), Tex. Bar Assn. (antitrust law com. 1984-85, chmn. internat. law com. intellectual property law sect. 1987-88, internat. transfer tech. com. 1983-84), Tex. Exec. Women, Women's Fin. Exch., Am. Intellectual Property Lawyers Assn. (patent law com. 1995), Women in Tech. (founder), Lil Eli's Club (founder), Phi Alpha Delta. Republican. Episcopalian. Intellectual property, Patent, Trademark and copyright. Office: 1100 Louisiana St Ste 2690 Houston TX 77002-5216 E-mail: ktripp@tripplaw.com

TRIPP, NORMAN DENSMORE, lawyer; b. Binghamton, N.Y., Apr. 11, 1938; s. Merritt Frederick and Eleonore Graves (Satterley) T.; m. Jane Grace Mighton, June 15, 1962; children: Jennifer, Norman, Christine, Michael. BA, U. Miami, 1962; JD magna cum laude, Cleve. State U., 1967. Bar: Ohio, Fla. Chmn. Tripp Scott P.A., Fort Lauderdale, Fla.; gen. counsel Cert. Tours (Delta Dream Vacations). Past mem. bd. adjustment City of Fort Lauderdale; past chair Ft. Lauderdale Downtown Devel. Authority; mem. South Fla. Annenberg Challenge, Broward County; mem. City of Ft. Lauderdale Downtown Devel. Bd.; past bd. trustees, vice chmn. State of Fla. C.C. System; past trustee U. Miami, Coral Gables, Fla; vice chmn., trustee Fla. Atlantic U. Mem. Am. Soc. Travel Agts., ABA, Broward County Bar Assn., Fla. Bar Assn., Ocean Reef Club (Key Largo), Fort Lauderdale Yacht Club, Grande Oaks Golf Club. Contracts commercial, Insurance, Real property. Office: Tripp Scott PA PO Box 14245 Fort Lauderdale FL 33302-4245

TRISTANO, SANDRA, lawyer; b. Aug. 30, 1951; d. Elias and Shirley (wood) Snitzer; m. Michael Eugene Tristano, Sept. 29, 1979. BA, Cornell U., 1973; JD, Washington U., St. Louis, 1977. Bar: Ill. 1977, U.S. Dist. Ct. (cen. dist.) Ill. 1977. Staff atty. Ill. Dept. Pub. Aid, Springfield, 1977-80; gen. counsel Ill. Dept. Energy and natural Resources, 1980-90, Pace Suburban Bus Svc., 1992-2000; bd. mem. Ill. Labor Rels. Bd., 2000—. Pro bono vol. Vols. for Justice, Springfield, 1983—; chmn. ABA Pub. Transp. Com., 1997-99. Mem. ABA, Ill. Bar Assn. Home: 1438 Crown Ln Glenview IL 60025-1227

TROCANO, RUSSELL PETER, lawyer; b. Hackensack, N.J., Sept. 7, 1963; s. Rosario Mario and Barbara Ann (Costa) T. BA, Seton Hall U., 1984; JD, Fordham U., 1987, LLM, 1992. Bar: N.J. 1987, N.Y. 1988. Law clk. to presiding justice County of Middlesex, New Brunswick, N.J., 1987-88; assoc. Sellar Richardson Law Firm, Newark and Roseland, 1988, Morgan Melhuish Monaghan Law Firm, Livingston, 1988-89; prin., owner Russell P. Trocano, Ridgewood, 1989—. Mem. San Guisseppe Societa de Santa Croce de Camerina, Paterson, N.J., 1989—. Fordham U. scholar, 1987. Mem. ABA, N.J. Bar Assn., N.Y. State Bar Assn., Bergen County Bar Assn., Passaic County Bar Assn., Brehon Law Soc., Arthur T. Vanderbilt Inn of Cts., Phi Alpha Theta. Roman Catholic. Avocations: mineral collecting, travel, reading. Bankruptcy, Consumer commercial, General practice. Home: 60 S Maple Ave Ridgewood NJ 07450-4542 Office: 7 E Ridgewood Ave Ridgewood NJ 07450-3807

TROFFKIN, HOWARD JULIAN, lawyer, diversified company executive; b. Port Chester, N.Y., Jan. 30, 1937; s. Irving and Frieda Troffkin; m. Rhea Dorothy, May 12, 1963; children: Stephen, Barbara. BS in Chemistry, St. Lawrence U., 1959; postgrad., Columbia U., 1959-60; JD, Georgetown U., 1970. Bar: Va. 1971, D.C. 1972. Rsch. chemist Am. Cyanamid Co., 1961-66, legal trainee, 1966-67, patent agt., 1967-71; assoc. Pennie, Edmonds, Morton, Taylor & Adams, Washington, 1971-77; patent atty. W.R. Grace & Co., Columbia, Md., 1977-86, sr. patent counsel, 1987-98; pvt. practice, 1998—. Patentee in chemistry field. Mem. Willerburn Civic Assn., 1971-75. Served with AUS, 1960-61. Mem. ABA, Va. Bar Assn., D.C. Bar Assn., Washington Patent Lawyers Assn., Md. Patent Law Assn. (pres. 1981-83), Am. Intellectual Property Law Assn., Am. Chem. Soc., Concrete Corrosion Inhibitors Assn. (sec./counsel). Jewish. Avocations: woodcrafting, travel. Intellectual property, Patent, Trademark and copyright. Home and Office: 7808 Ivymount Ter Potomac MD 20854-3218 E-mail: Troffkin@aol.com

TROOBOFF, PETER DENNIS, lawyer; b. Balt., June 22, 1942; s. Benjamin M. and Rebecca C. (Cohen) T.; m. Rhoda Morss, Aug. 10, 1969; children: Hannah, Abigail. BA cum laude, Columbia U., 1964; LLB cum laude, Harvard U., 1967; LLM, London Sch. Econs., 1968; diploma cum laude, Hague (Netherlands) Acad. Internat. Law, 1968. Bar: N.Y. 1968, D.C. 1970. Rsch. assoc., Harvard U. Law Sch., 1968-69; asst. to exec. editor for The Advocates, Sta. WGBH-TV, Boston, 1969; assoc. Covington & Burling, Washington, 1969-75, ptnr., 1975—; lectr., dir. seminars The Hague Acad. Internat. Law, 1972, 82, lectr., 1986, mem. curatorium, 1991—; lectr. The Hague Acad. External Programn Beijing, 1987, Harare, 1993, internat. orgns. U. Va. Sch. Law, 1973; head U.S. del. 3d Inter-Am. Specialized Conf. Pvt. Internat. Law, La Paz, Bolivia, 1984; mem. U.S. del. Hague Conf. private internat. law, 1993, 96, 97—; mem. sec. of state adv. com. private internat. law, 1990—. Frank Knox Meml. fellow. Mem. Coun. Fgn. Rels., Am. Law Inst., Am. Soc. Internat. Law (pres. 1990-92, bd. editors Am. Jour. of Internat. Law 1980-92, 94—), Internat. Law Assn., Washington Inst. Fgn. Affairs. Club: Cosmos, City (Washington). Contbr. chpts., articles to profl. publs.; editor: Law and Responsibility in Warfare-The Vietnam Experience, 1975. General corporate, Private international, Public international. Office: Covington & Burling PO Box 7566 1201 Pennsylvania Ave NW Washington DC 20044

TROST, EILEEN BANNON, lawyer; b. Teaneck, N.J., Jan. 9, 1951; d. William Eugene and Marie Thelma (Finlayson) Bannon; m. Lawrence Peter Trost Jr., Aug. 27, 1977; children: Lawrence Peter III, William Patrick, Timothy Alexander. BA with great distinction, Shimer Coll., 1972; JD cum laude, U. Minn., 1976. Bar: Ill. 1976, U.S. Dist. Ct. (no. dist.) Ill. 1976, Minn. 1978, U.S. Tax Ct. 1978, U.S. Supreme Ct. 1981. Assoc. McDermott, Will & Emery, Chgo., 1976-82, ptnr., 1982-93; v.p. No. Trust Bank Ariz. N.A., Phoenix, 1993-95; ptnr. Sonnenschein Nath & Rosenthal, Chgo., 1995—. Mem. Am. Coll. Trust and Estate Coun., Minn. Bar Assn., Internat. Acad. Estate and Trust Law, Chgo. Estate Planning Coun. Roman Catholic. Estate planning, Probate, Estate taxation. Office: Sonnenschein Nath & Rosenthal 8000 Sears Tower Chicago IL 60606 E-mail: etrost@sonnenschein.com

TROTT, STEPHEN SPANGLER, federal judge, musician; b. Glen Ridge, N.J., Dec. 12, 1939; s. David Herman and Virginia (Spangler) T.; children: Christina, Shelley; m. Carol C. BA, Wesleyan U., 1962; LLB, Harvard U., 1965; LLD (hon.), Santa Clara U., 1992. Bar: Calif. 1966, U.S. Dist. Ct. (cen. dist.) Calif. 1966, U.S. Ct. Appeals (9th cir.) 1983, U.S. Supreme Ct. 1984. Guitarist, mem. The Highwaymen, 1958—; dep. dist. atty. Los Angeles County Dist. Atty.'s Office, Los Angeles, 1966-75, chief dep. dist. atty., 1975-79; U.S. dist. atty. Central Dist. Calif., Los Angeles, 1981-83; asst. atty. gen. criminal div. Dept. Justice, Washington, 1983-86; mem. faculty Nat. Coll. Dist. Attys., Houston, 1973—; chmn. central dist. Calif. Law Enforcement Coordinating Com., 1981-83; coordinator Los Angeles-Nev. Drug Enforcement Task Force, 1982-83; assoc. atty. gen. Justice Dept., Washington, 1986-88; chmn. U.S. Interpol, 1986-88; judge U.S. Ct. of Appeals 9th Cir., Boise, Idaho, 1988—. Trustee Wesleyan U., 1984-87; bd. dirs., pres. children's Home Soc., Idaho, 1990—; pres., bd. dirs. Boise Philharm. Assn., 1995—, v.p., 1997-99, pres., 1999—. Recipient Gold record as singer-guitarist for Michael Row the Boat Ashore, 1961, Disting. Faculty award Nat. Coll. Dist. Attys., 1977 Mem. Am. Coll. Trial Lawyers, Wilderness Fly Fishers Club (pres. 1975-77), Brentwood Racing Pigeon Club (pres. 1977-82), Idaho Racing Pigeon Assn., Magic Castle, Internat. Brotherhood Magicians, Idaho Classic Guitar Soc. (founder, pres. 1989—). Republican. Office: US Ct Appeals 9th Cir 667 US Courthouse 550 W Fort St Boise ID 83724-0101

TROTT, WILLIAM MACNIDER, lawyer; b. Raleigh, N.C., July 30, 1946; s. Graham Foard and Cornelia (McKimmon) T.; m. Holly Wooten, Oct. 17, 1970 (div.); children: Hollister Wooten, James McKimmon; m. Jean Little, Aug. 11, 1984; children: Elizabeth Yost, William MacNider. AB, U. N.C., 1968, JD, 1971; LLM with highest honors, George Washington U., 1971. Bar: N.C. 1971, U.S. Dist. Ct. (ea., mid. and we. dists.) N.C. 1975, U.S. Supreme Ct. 1975. Assoc. Young, Moore and Henderson, Raleigh, 1975-78; ptnr., mem. Young, Moore & Henderson, 1978—. Mem. N.C. Law Rev., 1969-71; lectr., author N.C. Bar Assn., 1984, 85, 87, Am. Law Firm Assn., 1999, 2000, Lorman Ednl. Svcs., 2000, 2001. Pres. Capital Area Soccer League, Raleigh, 1984-85; bd. dirs. N.C. Tennis Assn., Greensboro, 1987-94, N.C. Tennis Found., 1994—, v.p. ; mem. Wake County Pks. and Recreation Commn., Raleigh, 1988-97, vice chmn., then chmn.; mem. sch. health adv. commn. Wake County Bd. Edn., 1997-99; sec., v.p. Raleigh Tennis Found., 1996—. Lt. JAGC, USNR, 1971-75. Morehead scholar U. N.C., 1964-68, Wettach scholar U. N.C. Law Sch., 1968-71; state tennis age group doubles champion, 1963, 64, 98. Mem. ABA, N.C. Bar Assn., Wake County Bar Assn., Execs. Club. Episcopalian. Insurance, Labor, Legislative. Office: Young Moore & Henderson PO Box 31627 Raleigh NC 27622-1627

TROTTA, FRANK P., JR. lawyer; BA, SUNY, Albany; JD, Union U., Albany; LLM, NYU; MBA, Columbia U. Bar: N.Y. U.S. Dist. Ct. (no. and we. dists.) N.Y., U.S. Ct. Mil. Appeals, U.S. Dist. Ct. (so. and ea. dists.) N.Y., U.S. Ct. Internat. Trade, U.S. Tax Ct., U.S. Supreme Ct., U.S. Ct. Appeals (D.C. cir.), U.S. Ct. Customs and Patent Appeals, D.C., Conn., Pa. Assoc. Weil, Gotshal & Manges, N.Y.C.; pvt. practice Washington, N.Y.C., New Rochelle, Greenwich, Conn. Former mem. bd. govs. Fund for Justice and Edn., ABA; mem. faculty Practicing Law Inst.; governing mem. Nat. Jud. Coll., Am. Bar Endowment, ABRA Pension Fund; chmn. bd. advisors Columbia U. Grad. Sch. Bus., Inst. for Non-for-Profit Mgmt. Chmn. New Rochelle Rep. Party; mem., bd. dirs. Boys Town of Italy. Legislative.

TROTTER, THOMAS ROBERT, lawyer; b. Akron, Ohio, Apr. 11, 1949; s. Fred and Josephine (Daley) T. BA, Ohio U., 1971; JD, Tulane U., 1975. Bar: Ohio 1975, D.C. 2000, U.S. Dist. Ct. (no. dist.) Ohio 1975. Assoc. Squire, Sanders & Dempsey, Cleve., 1975-80; mem. Buckingham, Doolittle & Burroughs, Akron, 1980—. Chair taxation and legis. com. Akron Regional Devel. Bd., 1988-95. Trustee Akron Symphony Orch., 1984-93, Cascade CDC, Inc., Akron, 1983—, Akron-Summit Solid Waste Mgmt. Authority, 1994-97; trustee Weathervane Cmty. Playhouse, 1996—, pres., 1999-2001. Mem. ABA, Ohio Bar Assn. (chair local govt. law com.), Akron Bar Assn., Nat. Assn. Bond Lawyers, Sigma Alpha Epsilon. Democrat. Contracts commercial, Municipal (including bonds), Securities. Home: 589 Avalon Akron OH 44320-2048 Office: Buckingham Doolittle & Burroughs PO Box 1500 50 S Main St Akron OH 44308-1828 E-mail: ttrotter@bdblaw.com

TROUT, LINDA COPPLE, state supreme court chief justice; b. Tokyo, Sept. 1, 1951; BA, U. Idaho, 1973, JD, 1977; LLD (hon.), Albertson Coll. Idaho, 1999. Bar: Idaho 1977. Judge magistrate divsn. Idaho Dist. Ct. (2d jud. divsn.), 1983-90, dist. judge, 1991-92, acting trial ct. adminstr., 1987-91; justice Idaho Supreme Ct., 1992—, chief justice, 1997—. Instr. coll. law U. Idaho, 1983, 88. Mem. Idaho State Bar Assn., Clearwater Bar Assn. (pres. 1980-81).*

TROUTMAN, CHARLES HENRY, III, lawyer; b. Wooster, Ohio, Mar. 25, 1944; s. Charles Henry and Lois Margaret (Dickason) T. BA, Wheaton Coll., 1966; JD, Am. U., 1969; M in Comparative Law, So. Meth. U., 1970. Bar: Ill. 1969, D.C. 1969, Guam 1973, U.S. Ct. Appeals (9th cir.) 1973, Trust Territory Pacific Islands, 1973, U.S. Supreme Ct. 1976, Commonwealth of No. Mariana Islands 1978. Asst. atty. gen., Guam, 1970-74; assoc. Cronin, Trotman & Assocs., Guam, 1974-75; atty. gen., Guam, 1975-77; counsel Dept. Edn., Guam, 1977-78; compiler of laws Govt. of Guam, Agana, 1978—, acting atty. gen., 1987; mem. counsel Commn. on Self-Determination, Guam, 1987—. Mem. ABA, Fed. Bar Assn. (sec. local chpt.), Am. Soc. Internat. Law, Christian Legal Soc., Guam Bar Assn. Presbyterian. E-mail: troutman@hotmail.com. Home: PO Box 455 Agana GU 96932-0455 Office: Judicial Ctr 2-2 OOE 120 W OBrien Dr Hagatra GU 96910

TROUTMAN, E. MAC, federal judge; b. Greenwood Township, Pa., Jan. 7, 1915; s. Emmett Theodore and Kathryn (Holman) T.; m. Margaret Petrick, Nov. 23, 1944; children— Jane A., Jean K. A.B., Dickinson Coll., 1934, LL.B., 1936. Bar: Pa. 1937. With Phila. and Reading Coal and Iron Co., 1937-58, gen. counsel, 1954-58; gen. atty. Phila. and Reading Corp., 1958-67; gen. counsel Reading Anthracite Co., 1958-61, Reserve Carbon Corp., 1961-66, So. Carbon Corp., 1966-67; solicitor Blue Mountain Sch. Dist., 1963-67, Blue Mountain Area Sch. Authority, 1963-67, Orwigsburg Municipal Authority, 1966-67, Am. Bank and Trust Co., Reading and Pottsville, Pa., 1957-67; exec. sec., gen. counsel Pa. Self-Insurers Assn., 1962-67; U.S. judge Eastern Dist. Pa., from 1967, sr. judge, 1982-98; retired, 1998. Bd. dirs. Greater Pottsville Indsl. Devel. Corp., 1963-67, Pa. C. of C., 1955-65, Greater Pottsville Area C. of C., 1961-64, Orwigsburg Community Meml. Assn., 1950-66, Schuylkill County Soc. Crippled Children, 1945-67; v.p., dir. Pottsville Hosp. and Warne Clinic, 1960-67. Served with AUS, World War II. Mem. ABA, Pa. Bar Assn., Schuylkill County Bar Assn. (vice chancellor 1955-57, chmn. jud. vacancies and unauthorized practice coms. 1960, chmn. medico-legal com. 1963-65) Lutheran (pres. coun. 1961—). Home: Kimmel's Rd Orwigsburg PA 17961

TROY, JOSEPH FREED, lawyer; b. Wilkes-Barre, Pa., Aug. 16, 1938; s. Sergei and Shirley Jean T.; m. Brigitta Ann Balos, June 9, 1962; children: Darcy Kendall, Austin Remy. BA, Yale U., 1960; LLB, Harvard U., 1963. Bar: Calif. 1964, D.C. 1979. Assoc. Hindin, McKittrick & Marsh, Beverly Hills, Calif., 1964-68, ptnr., 1968-70; pres. Troy & Gould, Los Angeles, 1970—; lectr. Calif. Continuing Edn. of Bar, 1972-80, 94; dir. Amerigon Inc., 1993-96, Movie Gallery, Inc., 1994—, Digital Video Systems, Inc., 1996-98, Argoquest, Inc., 2000-2001. Author: Let's Go: A Student Guide to Europe, 1962, Accountability of Corporate Management, 1979; co-author: Protecting Corporate Officers and Directors from Liability, 1994, Advising and Defending Corporate Directors and Officers, 1998. Pres. L.A. Chamber Orch. Soc., 1968-75, chmn. bd. dirs., 1975-78, vice chmn. bd. dirs., 1978-81; bd. dirs. L.A. Opera, 1972-2001, mem. exec. com., 1987-99; hon. consul of Tunisia, L.A., 1984-88; chmn. Internat. Festival Soc.; bd. dirs. Brentwood Pk. Property Owners Assn., 1988-2001. Reid Hall fellow U. Paris, 1958 Mem. ABA, Calif. State Bar Assn. (chmn. task force on complex litigation 1997-99), D.C. Bar Assn., L.A. County Bar Assn. (chmn. bus. and corp. law sect. 1977-78), French Am. C. of C. U.S. (exec. v.p. 1983-85), French Am. C. of C. L.A. (chmn. 1982-84), Wine and Food Soc. So. Calif. Inc. (bd. dirs.), Beach Club, Calif. Club. Office: 1801 Century Park E Ste 1600 Los Angeles CA 90067-2318 E-mail: jftroy@troygould.com

TRUE, ROY JOE, lawyer; b. Shreveport, La., Feb. 20, 1938; s. Collins B. and Lula Mae (Cady) T.; m. Patsy Jean Hudsmith, Aug. 29, 1959; children: Andrea Alane, Alyssa Anne, Ashley Alisbeth. Student, Centenary Coll., 1957; BS, Tex. Christian U., 1961; LLB, So. Meth. U., 1963, postgrad., 1968-69. Bar: Tex. 1963. Pvt. practice, Dallas, 1963—; pres. Invesco

Internat. Corp., 1969-70, True & Shackelford and predecessors, 1975—. Bus. adviser, counselor Mickey Mantle, 1969-95; dir. The Mickey Mantle Found., 1995-98. Mem. editl. bd. Southwestern Law Jour, 1962-63. Served with AUS, 1956. Mem. ABA, Dallas Bar Assn., Tex. Assn. Bank Counsel, Phi Alpha Delta. Banking, Contracts commercial, General corporate. Home: 5601 Ursula Ln Dallas TX 75229-6429 Office: 5420 LBJ Fwy Dallas TX 75240-6222

TRUEHEART, HARRY PARKER, III, lawyer; b. Rochester, N.Y., Mar. 27, 1944; s. Harry Parker and Bertha (Hendryx) T.; m. Karen Ellingson, June 26, 1965; children: Eric Parker, Kathryn Marie. BA, JD, Harvard U. Bar: N.Y. 1970, Fla. 1975. Assoc. Nixon, Hargrave, Devans & Doyle LLP (now Nixon Peabody LLP), Rochester, 1969-77, ptnr., 1977—, spkr. fed. ct. practice, 1979-83, mng. ptnr., 1995—. Arbitrator, mediator Ctr. Pub. Resources, Inst. Dispute Resolution, Am. Arbitration Assn. Co-author: Federal Civil Practice; contbr. chpt. to book; contbr. articles on fed. ct. litigation, microfilm records, profl. liability in connection with use of computers to profl. jours. Trustee Sta. WXXI Broadcasting, The Greater Rochester Metro C. of C.; bd. dirs. High Tech. of Rochester, Inc., Park Ridge Found. Fellow N.Y. Bar Found., The Chartered Inst. Arbitrators, The Coll. Law Practice Mgmt.; mem. ABA, N.Y. State Bar Assn. (chair comml. and fed. litig. sect. 1992-93, house of del.), Monroe County Bar Assn., Fed. Bar Coun. (v.p.), Am. Arbitration Assn. Federal civil litigation, State civil litigation, Contracts commercial. Office: Nixon Peabody LLP Clinton Sq Rochester NY 14604 also: Nixon Peabody LLP 437 Madison Ave New York NY 10022-7001 E-mail: htrueheart@nixonpeabody.com

TRUETT, HAROLD JOSEPH, III (TIM TRUETT), lawyer; b. Alameda, Calif., Feb. 13, 1946; s. Harold Joseph and Lois Lucille (Mellin) T.; 1 child, Harold Joseph IV; m. Anna V. Billante, Oct. 1, 1983 (dec. June 2000); 1 child, James S. Carstensen. BA, U. San Francisco, 1968, JD, 1975. Bar: Calif. 1975, Hawaii 1987, U.S. Dist. Ct. (ea., so., no., and cen. dists.) Calif. 1976, Hawaii 1987, U.S. Ct. Appeals (9th cir.) 1980, U.S. Supreme Ct. 1988, U.S. Ct. Fed. Claims, 1995. Assoc. Hoberg, Finger et al, San Francisco, 1975-78, Bledsoe, Smith et al, San Francisco, 1979-80, Abramson & Bianco, San Francisco, 1980-83; mem. Ingram & Truett, San Rafael, 1983-90; prin. Law Office of H.J. Tim Truett, San Francisco, 1991-93, Winchell & Truett, San Francisco, 1994—. Lectr. trial practice Am. Coll. Legal Medicine, 1989-90, Calif. Continuing Edn. of the Bar. Bd. dirs. Shining Star Found. 1991—, pres., 2001—, Marin County, Calif.; mem. Marin Dem. Coun., San Rafael, 1983-90. Lt., aviator USN, 1967-74. Mem. ABA, Hawaii Bar Assn., Calif. Bar Assn. (com. for adminstrn. of justice, conf. of dels.), San Francisco Bar Assn., San Francisco Trial Lawyers Assn., Lawyers Pilots Assn. Roman Catholic. State civil litigation, Personal injury, Product liability, Aviation, Professional liability. Home: 48 Valley Rd San Anselmo CA 94960 E-mail: hjtimtruett@home.com

TRUJILLO, LORENZO A. lawyer, educator; b. Denver, Aug. 10, 1951; s. Filbert G. and Marie O. Trujillo; m. Ellen Alires; children: Javier Antonio, Lorenzo Feliciano, Kristina Alires. BA, U. Colo., 1972, MA, 1974, postgrad.; EdD, U. San Francisco, 1979; JD, U. Colo., 1993. Bar: Colo. 1994, U.S. Dist. Ct. Colo. 1994, U.S. Ct. Appeals (10th cir.) 1994, U.S. Supreme Ct. 1999; cert. edn. tchr., prin., supt., Colo. Exec. assoc. Inter-Am. Rsch. Assocs., Rosslyn, Va., 1980-82; exec. dir. humanities Jefferson County Pub. Schs., Golden, Colo., 1982-89; pvt. practice edn. cons. Lakewood, 1989-93; gen. corp. counsel Am. Achievement Schs., Inc., 1994-96; atty. Frie, Arndt & Trujillo Law Firm, Arvada, 1994-96, ptnr., 1995-97; dist. hearing officer, dir. of instrn. Adams County Sch. Dist. 14, 1999—, dir. human resources, 1998-99, dist. attendance officer/legal counsel, prin. H.S., 1999—. Co-chair Mellon fellowships The Coll. Bd., N.Y.C., 1987-93; cons. U.S.I.A. Fulbright Tchr. Exch. Program, Washington, 1987-93; editl. advisor Harcourt, Brace, Jovanovich Pub., Orlando, Fla., 1988-93; mem. Colo. Supreme Ct. Multicultural Commn., 1996-98, 99—; mem. Colo. Supreme Ct. Families in the Cts. Commn., 2001—. Contbr. numerous articles to profl. jours. Mem. panel of arbitrators Am. Arbitration Assn., 1994. Recipient Legal Aid Clinic Acad. award Colo. Bar Assn., 1993, Pro Bono award, 1993, Loyola U. Acad. award, 1993, Gov.'s award for excellence in the arts State of Colo., 1996. Mem. Colo. chpt. Am. Assn. Tchrs. of Spanish and Portuguese (pres. 1985-88), Am. Immigration Lawyers Assn., Nat. Sch. Bds. Coun. Sch. Attys., Nat. Assn. Judiciary Interpreters and Translators, Colo. Bar Assn. (probate and trust sect., grievance policy com. 1995-97, ethics com. 1995-96), U. San Francisco Alumni Assn. (founder, pres. 1987-90), Phi Delta Kappa (chair internat. edn. com. 1988-89), Phi Alpha Delta. Avocation: violinist. Education and schools, Estate planning, General practice. Office: Adams County Sch Dist 14 6500 E 72d Ave Commerce City CO 80022-2380

TRUMBULL, TERRY ALAN, energy and environmental consultant, lawyer; b. Berkeley, Calif., Nov. 5, 1945; s. Larry Edward and Emily Josephine (Grote) T.; m. Patricia Jane Vogel, Aug. 24, 1968; children: Eryn, Morgann. BA, U. Calif., Davis, 1967; JD, Georgetown U., 1970; LLM, George Washington U., 1973. Bar: Calif. 1973, D.C., 1971. Mem. legal staff Dept. Interior, Washington, 1970; sr. staff Inst. Pub. Adminstrn., Washington, 1970-71; legal adviser to dept. asst. adminstr. planning and evaluation EPA, Washington, 1972-73; legis. and regulatory counsel Gen. Electric Co., San Jose, Calif., 1973-78; ptnr. Atkinson, Farasyn, Smith, Sherer and Trumbull, Mountain View, Calif., 1978-79; dep. town atty., Town of Woodside; chmn. Calif. Waste Mgmt. Bd., Sacramento, full time 1979-84, part time 1984-85; pres. Edarra, Inc., Palo Alto, Calif., 1983—; environ. law instr. dept. environ. studies San Jose State U., 1998— . Mem. Nat. Commn. on Resource Conservation and Recovery, 1981— ; mem. Hazardous Waste Mgmt. Council, 1982-84. Mem. Santa Clara County Planning Commn., 1976-79, 96—, chmn., 1979; chmn. Calif. Planning Roundtable, 1980-81; mem. Santa Clara County Energy Task Force, Santa Clara County Environ. Task Force. Mem. Calif. Bar Assn., Calif. County Planning Commrs. Assn. (chmn. air quality com. 1976-79), Calif. Geothermal Energy Coordinating Council, Assn. State Solid Waste Ofcls. (chmn. solid waste com., bd. dirs. 1979-84). Democrat. Environmental, Legislative, Municipal (including bonds). Office: 1011 Lincoln Ave Palo Alto CA 94301-3046

TRYBAN, ESTHER ELIZABETH, lawyer; b. Chgo., Aug. 14, 1958; d. Chester Joseph and Lottie Elizabeth (Napora) T. AAS with honors, Elgin (Ill.) C.C., 1977, AS with honors, 1982; BS with honors, Roosevelt U., Chgo., 1986; JD, U. Chgo., 1989. Bar: Ill. 1989, U.S. Dist. Ct. (no. dist.) Ill. 1989, U.S. Ct. Appeals (7th cir.) 1990, U.S. Supreme Ct., 1996. Supr. adminstrv. svcs. law dept. Motorola, Inc., Schaumburg, Ill., 1977-86; staff law clk. U.S. Bankruptcy Ct., No. Dist. Ill., Chgo., 1989-90; asst. corp. counsel City of Chgo., 1990—. Mem. ABA, Nat. Lawyers Guild, Assn. Former Bankruptcy Law Clks, Ill. State Bar Assn., Chgo. Bar Assn. (chair govt. svc. com. 1996-97). Roman Catholic. Avocations: reading, football, traveling. Office: City Chgo Dept Law 30 N Lasalle St Ste 900 Chicago IL 60602-2503

TSAI, JACLYN YU-LING, lawyer; b. Taichung, Taiwan, Republic of China, Aug. 22, 1955; d. Hsi-Yu Tsai and Bi-Yuin Chen; m: Chung-Teh Lee; children: James, Joseph. Graduate, Sch. Law, Nat. Taiwan U., China, 1977-78, LLB, 1977. Bar: Taiwan, 1984. Judge I-Lan, Chang-Hwa, Taoyuan & ShinLin District Cts., Taipei, Taiwan, 1982-91; gen. counsel IBM, Taiwan, 1991-98; ptnr. Lee, Tsai & Partners, Taiwan, 1998—. Author: Legal Guide to Multimedia, 1998; contbr. articles to profl. jours. Mem. Inter-Pacific Bar Assn., Asian Patent Attys. Assn. Avocations: reading, music, art, swimming, climbing. Intellectual property, Mergers and acquisitions, Securities. Office: Lee Tsai & Ptnrs 5A 218 Tun Hwa S Rd Soc 2 106 Taipei Taiwan China Fax: 886-2 2378-5781. E-mail: jaclyntsai@leetsai.com.tw

TSCHINKEL, ANDREW JOSEPH, JR. law librarian; b. Catskill, N.Y., Aug. 8, 1952; s. Andrew Joseph and Marie Frances (O'Connor) T.; m. Frances K. Quigley, Nov. 4, 1989. BA summa cum laude, St. John's Coll., Jamaica, N.Y., 1975, MLS, 1977; MBA, Fordham U., 1983. Grad. asst. div. libr. sci. St. John's U., Jamaica, 1975-77, asst. law libr., 1977-79, adj. law librarian, 1983-87; head librarian Christ the King High Sch., Middle Village, N.Y., 1979-80; sr. law librarian Bklyn. Supreme Ct., 1980-81; prin. law librarian N.Y. Supreme Ct., Jamaica, 1981—. Recipient Pub. Svc. award Queens Borough Pres. and N.Y. Tel. Co., 1986; named Alumnus of Yr. Grad. Sch. Arts & Scis. Divsn. Libr. & Info. Sci. St. John's U., 1993. Mem. Am. Assn. Law Librs., Law Libr. Assn. Greater N.Y., Elks, Beta Phi Mu. Republican. Office: NY Supreme Ct Libr 88-11 Sutphin Blvd Jamaica NY 11435-3716

TSE, CHARLES YUNG CHANG, drug company executive; b. Shanghai, China, Mar. 22, 1926; s. Kung Chao and Say Ying (Chen) T.; m. Vivian Chang, Apr. 25, 1955; 1 dau., Roberta. BA in Econs, St. John's U., Shanghai, 1949; MS in Acctg, U. Ill., 1950; JD, N.Y. Law Sch., 1990. Asst. to controller Am. Internat. Group, N.Y.C., 1950-54, asst. mgr. Singapore-Malaysia, 1955-57; with Warner-Lambert Co., Morris Plains, N.J., 1957-86, area mgr. S.E. Asia, 1966-68, regional dir. S.E. Asia, 1968-69, v.p. Australasia, 1970-71, pres. Western Hemisphere Group, 1971-72, pres. Pan Am. Mgmt. Center, 1972-76, pres. European Mgmt. Center, 1976-78, pres. Internat. Group, 1979-86, sr. v.p. corp., 1980-83, exec. v.p. corp., 1984-85, vice chmn., 1985-86. Dir. Foster Wheeler Corp., Livingston, N.J., 1984-98, Superior Telecom., Inc., 1996—, Com. of 100; mem. faculty bus. adminstrn. dept. Fairleigh Dickinson U., 1961-64; pres. Cancer Rsch. Inst., Inc., N.Y.C., 1991-92. Bd. visitors CCNY, 1974-78; trustee Morristown Meml. Hosp. (N.J.), 1982-86; bd. dirs. Bus. Council for Internat. Understanding, 1984-87. Mem. NAM (dir. 1984-86), Assn. of the Bar of the City of N.Y. (mem. Asian affairs com. 1991—). Office: 300 Park Ave Fl 17 New York NY 10022-7402

TSISMENAKIS, GEORGIA, lawyer, tax accountant; BS, Bklyn. Coll.; MBA, Pace U.; JD, Fordham U. Bar: N.Y. 1995; CPA, N.Y. Pvt. practice, Bklyn. Eastern Orthodox. Avocations: golf, tennis, aviation travel. Office: 2086 E 19th St Brooklyn NY 11229-3902

TUBMAN, WILLIAM CHARLES, lawyer; b. N.Y.C., Mar. 16, 1932; s. William Thomas and Ellen Veronica (Griffin) T.; m. Dorothy Rita Krug, Aug. 15, 1964; children: William Charles Jr., Thomas Davison, Matthew Griffin. BS, Fordham U., 1953, JD, 1960; postdoctoral, NYU Sch. Law, 1960-61. Bar: N.Y. 1960, U.S. Ct. Appeals (2d cir.) 1966, U.S. Supreme Ct. 1967, U.S. Ct. Customs and Patent Appeals 1971. Auditor Peat, Marwick Mitchell & Co., N.Y.C., 1956-60; sr. counsel Kennecott Corp., 1960-82, Phelps Dodge Corp., N.Y.C., 1982-85, sec., 1985-95, v.p., 1987-95; pres. Phelps Dodge Found., Phoenix, 1988-95. Author: Legal Status of Minerals Beyond the Continental Shelf, 1966. Mem. scholarship adv. coun. U. Ariz., 1990-92; active Big Bros., Inc., N.Y.C., 1963-73; trustee Phoenix Art Mus., 1989-94; bd. dirs. St. Joseph Hosp. Found., 1994—, chmn., 1994-95; bd. dirs. The Phoenix Symphony, 1994-95. Recipient Disting. Svc. cert. Big Brothers Inc., 1968. Mem. ABA, N.Y. State Bar Assn., Maricopa County Bar Assn. Democrat. Roman Catholic. Antitrust, General corporate, Securities. E-mail: 110061.1604@compuserve.com

TUCKER, BOWEN HAYWARD, lawyer; b. Providence, Apr. 13, 1938; s. Stuart Hayward and Ardelle Chase (Drabble) T.; m. Jan Louise Brown, Aug. 26, 1961; children: Stefan Kendric Slade, Catherine Kendra Gordon. AB in Math., Brown U., 1959; JD, U. Mich., 1962. Bar: R.I. 1963, Ill. 1967, U.S. Supreme Ct. 1970. Assoc. Hinckley & Allen, Providence, 1962-66; sr. atty. Caterpillar, Inc., Peoria, Ill., 1966-72; counsel FMC Corp., Chgo., 1972-82, sr. litigation counsel, 1982-95, assoc. gen. counsel, 1995-2000; v.p. eLaw Forum, 2000—. Chmn. legal process task force Chgo. Residential Sch. Study Com., 1973-74, mem. Commn. on Children, 1983-85, Ill. Com. on Rights of Minors, 1974-77, Com. on Youth and the Law, 1977-79; mem. White House Conf. on Children, ednl. svcs. subcom., 1979-80; chairperson Youth Employment Task Force, 1982-83; mem. citizens com. on Juvenile Ct. (Cook County), 1978-94, chmn. detention subcom., 1982-92; mem. econ. effects adv. com. Rand Inst. Civil Justice, 1990-92; bd. dirs. Voices Ill. Children, 1998—. 1st lt. U.S. Army, 1962-69. Mem. ABA, Am. Law Inst., Ill. State Bar Assn., R.I. Bar Assn., Chgo. (chmn. com. on juvenile law, 1976-77), Chgo. Lincoln Inn of Ct. (sec., treas. 1996-98), Constrn. Industry Mfrs. Assn. (exec. com. of Lawyers' Coun. 1972, 75-79, vice chmn. 1977, chmn. 1978-79), Mfrs. Alliance (products liability coun. 1974-95, vice chmn. 1981-83, chmn. 1983-85), Product Liability Adv. Coun. (bd. dirs. 1986-2000, exec. com. 1990-97, vice chmn. 1991-93, chmn. 1993-95), ALCU (bd. dirs. Ill. divsn. 1970-79, exec. com. 1973-79, sec. 1975-77), Am. Arbitration Assn. (mem. panel of arbitrators 1985-96), Phi Alpha Delta, Brown Univ. of Chgo. Club (nat. alumni schs. program 1973-85, v.p. 1980-81, pres. 1981-86), Lawyers Club of Chgo. General civil litigation, Juvenile, Product liability. Home: 107 W Noyes St Arlington Heights IL 60005-3747 Office: 200 E Randolph St Ste 6700 Chicago IL 60601-6436 E-mail: btucker@elawforum.com, btucker@iname.com

TUCKER, EDWIN WALLACE, law educator; b. N.Y.C., Feb. 25, 1927; s. Benjamin and May Tucker; m. Gladys Lipschutz, Sept. 14, 1952; children: Sherwin M., Pamela A. BA, NYU, 1948; LLB, Harvard U., 1951; LLM, N.Y. Law Sch., 1963, JSD, 1964; MA, Trinity Coll., Hartford, Conn., 1967. Bar: N.Y. 1955, U.S. Dist. Ct. (ea. and so. dists.) N.Y. 1958, U.S. Ct. Appeals (2d cir.) 1958, U.S. Supreme Ct. 1960. Pvt. practice, N.Y.C., 1955-63; Disting. Alumni prof. and prof. bus. law U. Conn., Storrs, 1963—, mem. bd. editors occasional paper and monograph series, 1966-70. Author: Adjudication of Social Issues, 1971, 2d edit., 1977, Legal Regulation of the Environment, 1972, Administrative Agencies, Regulation of Enterprise, and Individual Liberties, 1975, CPA Law Review, 1985; co-author: The Legal and Ethical Environment of Business, 1992; book rev. editor Am. Bus. Law Jour., 1964-65, adv. editor, 1974—; co-editor Am. Bus. Jour., 1965-73; mem. editl. bd. Am. Jour. Small Bus., 1979-86; editor Jour. Legal Studies Edn., 1983-85, editor-in-chief, 1985-87, adv. editor, 1987—; mem. bd. editors North Atlantic Regional Bus. Law Rev., 1984—. With USAF, 1951-55. Recipient medal of excellence Am. Bus. Law Assn., 1979. Mem. Acad. Legal Studies in Bus., North Atlantic Regional Bus. Law Assn. Home: 11 Eastwood Rd Storrs Mansfield CT 06268-2401

TUCKER, MARCUS OTHELLO, judge; b. Santa Monica, Calif., Nov. 12, 1934; s. Marcus Othello Sr. and Essie Louvonia (McLendon) T.; m. Indira Hale, May 29, 1965; 1 child, Angelique. BA, U. So. Calif., 1956; JD, Howard U., 1960; MA in Criminal Justice, Chapman U., 1997; BS in Liberal Arts, Regents Coll., SUNY, 1999. Bar: Calif. 1962, U.S. Dist. Ct. (cen. dist.) Calif. 1962, U.S. Ct. Appeals (9th cir.) 1965, U.S. Ct. Internat. Trade 1970, U.S. Supreme Ct. 1971. Pvt. practice, Santa Monica, 1962-63, 67-74; dep. atty. City of Santa Monica, 1963-65; asst. atty. U.S. Dist. Ct. (Cen. Dist.) Calif., 1965-67; commr. L.A. Superior Ct., 1974-76; judge mcpl. ct. Long Beach (Calif.) Jud. Dist., 1976-85; judge superior ct. L.A. Jud. Dist., 1985—; supervising judge L.A. County Dependency Ct. L.A. Superior Ct., 1991-92, presiding judge Juvenile divsn., 1993-94. Asst. prof. law Pacific U., Long Beach, 1984, 86; justice pro tem U.S. Ct. Appeals (2nd cir.), 1981; mem. exec. com. Superior Ct. of L.A. County, 1995-96. Mem. editl. staff Howard U. Law Sch. Jour., 1959-60. Pres. Community Rehab. Industries Found., Long Beach, 1983-86, Legal Aid Found., L.A., 1976-77; bd. dirs. Long Beach coun. Boy Scouts Am., 1978-92. With U.S. Army, 1960-66. Named Judge of Yr. Juvenile Cts. Bar Assn., 1986, Disting. Jurist Long Beach Trial Trauma Coun., 1987, Honoree in Law Handy Community Ctr., L.A., 1987, Bernard S. Jefferson Jurist of Yr. John M. Langston Bar Assn. Black Lawyers, 1990, Judge of Yr. Long Beach Bar Assn., 1993, Judge of Yr., First Ann. Adoption Cong., 1997, Jurist of Yr., Juvenile Cts. Bar Assn., 1997, Daniel O'Connell award Irish-Am. Bar Assn., 1999; recipient award for Law-Related Edn. Constl. Rights Found./L.A. County Bar Assn., 1992, commendation L.A. County Bd. Suprs., 1994. Fellow Internat. Acad. Trial Judges; mem. ABA, Calif. Judges Assn. (chmn. juvenile law com. 1986-87), Langston Bar Assn. (pres. bd. dirs. 1972, 73), Calif. Assn. Black Lawyers, Santa Monica Bay Dist. Bar Assn. (treas. 1969-71), Am. Inns of Ct., Selden Soc. Avocations: comparative law, traveling. Office: 415 W Ocean Blvd Dept 245 Long Beach CA 90802-4512

TUCKER, ROBERT HENRY, lawyer; b. N.Y.C., Dec. 5, 1937; s. Al and Sylvia G. (Hoffman) T.; m. Linda B. Klein, July 4, 1963; children: Daniel Jay, Julie Carol, Ruth Leslie. BA, Queens Coll., 1958; JD, Georgetown U., 1961. Bar: N.Y. 1962, U.S Dist. Ct. (ea. and so. dists.) N.Y. 1964, U.S. Ct. Appeals (2d cir.) 1966, U.S. Supreme Ct. 1967. Assoc. Spitzbart & Hertan, Huntington, N.Y., 1962-63, Silverstein, Balin, Pares & Soloway, New Hyde Park, N.Y., 1963-64; pvt. practice law, Forest Hills, N.Y., 1964-72; ptnr. Weiss, Tucker, Topper, Melville, N.Y., 1972-80; pvt. practice law, Melville, 1980-83, 85-88, Smithtown, N.Y., 1989—; ptnr. Tucker & Lacher, Melville, 1983-85, past pres. Pres. exec. bd. L.I. Regional Bd. Anti-Defamation League, Great Neck, N.Y.; mem. nat. law com. Anti-Defamation League of B'nai B'rith, N.Y.C. With U.S. Army, 1961-63. Mem. Assn. Trial Lawyers Am., N.Y. State Trial Lawyers Assn., Comml. Law League Am., N.Y. State Bar Assn., Suffolk County Bar Assn. (chmn. com. banking, corporate and bus. law 1982-84), Suffolk Acad. Law (merit recognition 1984). Democrat. Jewish. Lodge: B'nai B'rith (bd. govs. dist. 1). State civil litigation, Consumer commercial, Family and matrimonial. Home: 62 Mcculloch Dr Dix Hills NY 11746-8329

TUCKER, WATSON BILLOPP, lawyer; b. Dobbs Ferry, N.Y., Nov. 16, 1940; s. Watson Billopp and Mary (Prema) T.; children: Robin, Craig, Christopher, Alexander, John. BS, Northwestern U., Evanston, Ill., 1962; JD magna cum laude, Northwestern U., 1965. Bar: Ill. 1965, U.S. Dist. Ct. (no. dist.) Ill. 1966, U.S. Supreme Ct. 1971, U.S. Dist. Ct. (no. dist.) N.Y. 1976, U.S. Ct. Appeals (2d, 3d, 5th, 6th, 7th, and 9th cirs.). Ptnr. Mayer, Brown & Platt, Chgo., 1972-99, Smith Tucker & Brown, DeKalb, Ill., 1999—. Trial lawyer Aon Corp., Chgo. Fellow Am. Coll. Trial Lawyers. Antitrust, General civil litigation, Securities. Office: Smith Tucker & Brown 115 N 1st St Dekalb IL 60115-3201 E-mail: wbtucker@smithtuckerbrown.com

TUCKER, WILLIAM E. lawyer, consultant; b. Okla., Sept. 2, 1937; s. Owen and Dixie (Stiles) T.; m. Nancy L. Henkins, Nov. 25, 1956; children: Desiree, Gayle. BS, S.D. Sch. Mines and Tech., 1956; JD, Okla. U., 1962. Bar: Okla. 1962, Colo. 1962. With legal dept. J.M. Huber Corp. and Marathon Oil Co., Denver, Tulsa, 1962-65; asst. atty. gen. Colo., 1965-74; ptnr. Tucker & Brown, Denver, 1974-80, Washington, 1982-2000, McLean, Va., 2001—. Mem. U.S. del. to West Germany, 1969; host of del. rep. nat. conv. Japanese Diet Mems., 1972; spl. commn. rep. UN, 1977-81; counsel White House, 1980-81; mem. civil justice model legis. com. Am. Legis. Exch. Coun., 1986; chief parliamentarian White House Conf. Small Bus., 1986; internat. observing team to Phillipine elections, 1986; lectr. Charles U., Prague, Czech Republic, 1993; lectr. internat. trade Georgetown U., Washington, 1993; cons. presdl. transition Korean Govt., 1988; mem. dels. of govt. and bus. leaders to Taiwan, Korea, Japan, Australia, Singapore, Korea, Hong Kong, Moscow, 1986-87; panelist Kenan Inst., 1991, Mt. St. Mary's Coll., 1992; lectr. in field. Contbr. articles to profl. jours. Chmn. drafting com. Am. Tort Reform Assn., 1986-87; active polit. campaigns; officer, bd. dirs. The Fund for Am. Studies; bd. dirs. Air Force Acad. Found., Inc., Netherland-Am. AMity Trust, Internat. Exch. Coun., Hungarian-U.S. Bus. Coun., U.S.O. World, People to People Internat., 1999—, chmn. internat. liaison com., 2000—; co-founder, pres. Czech and Slovac Am. Amity Assn., 1991; U.S. del., Moscow, 1988; observing team Republic of China elections, 1989; advisor polit. strategy for elections Hungarian Smallholders Party, 1990; active U.S.A.-ROC Econ. Coun.; past state chmn., nat. gen. counsel Young Reps.; past bd. dirs. Am. Coun. Young Polit. Leaders; chmn. organizing com. Dutch-Am. Heritage Day, 1991-97; co-chmn. internat. rels. com. U.S. Olympic Com., 1997—; vice-chmn. Friends of Slovakia, 2001—. 2d lt. C.E., U.S. Army, 1958. 2d lt. CE U.S. Army, 1958. Recipient Hungarian Presdl. citation, Presdl. medal, 2000, Disting. Alumni award S.D. Sch. Mines and Tech., 2000. Mem. World Affairs Coun., Washington Golf & Country Club. Methodist. Administrative and regulatory, Oil, gas, and mineral. E-mail: tuckintl@radix.net

TUCKER, WILLIAM P. lawyer, writer; b. Kingston, N.Y., Jan. 26, 1932; s. Philip and Mary (McGowan) T.; m. Dolores F. Beaudoin, June 10, 1961; children: Andrew M., Thomas B., Mary A. BA with honors, Hunter Coll., 1958; JD with honors, St. John's U., 1962. Bar: N.Y. 1962, U.S. Dist. Ct. (ea. dist.) N.Y. 1963, Fla. 1980. Assoc. Mendes & Mount, N.Y.C., 1962-63; ptnr. Cullen and Dykman, Bklyn. and Garden City, N.Y., 1963-98, Golden, Wexler & Sarnese, Garden City/Purchase/S.I., 1998-2001; pvt. practice, 2001—. Former gen. counsel Broadway Nat. Bank, Wartburg Luth. Svcs., Luth. Ctr. for the Aging, Martin Luther Ter. Apts., Inc., Interfaith Med. Ctr., Roosevelt Savs. Bank, Olympian Bank, GreenPoint Bank, Ridgewood Savs. Bank, Atlantic Liberty Savs., F.A., Bethpage Fed. Credit Union, Mcpl. Credit Union, Lincoln Savs. Bank, Bklyn. Savs. Bank, Met. Savs. Bank, Crossland Savs. Bank, Bushwick Savs. Bank, Anchor Savs. Bank; former spl. counsel OCI Mortgage Corp., Bklyn C. of C., Downtown Bklyn. Bus. Assn., Bank of N.Y., Chase Manhattan Bank, Fleet Bank, Kraft Credit Union, Apple Bank for Savs., Barclays Bank of N.Y.; chmn. bd. dirs. Broadway Nat. Bank. Author: DP-or Billy and Jerry in the Promised Land, 1996, Moving Home Plate, 1999, Excalibur. Past mem. Selective Svc. Bd.; past pres. St. Vincent Ferrer Home Sch. Assn.; del. Diocesan Union Holy Name Socs.; mem. coun. St. Johns's U.; mem. coun. of regents St. Francis Coll., Bklyn.; bd. dirs. Faith Home Found., St. Josephs Coll. Mem. Am. Coll. Real Estate Lawyers, N.Y. State Bar Assn., Fla. Bar Assn., Savs. Banks Lawyers Assn. Bklyn., N.Y. Land Title Assn., Suffolk County Bar Assn., Savs. Bank Assn. N.Y. State (law com.), Bklyn. Mcpl. Club (pres.), Knight of Malta. Avocations: co-owner Salem Keizer Volcanoes N.W. League baseball team, Norwich Navigators Ea. League baseball team; v.p. N.W. Profl. Baseball League; bd. dirs. Bklyn. Sportsplex Inc. Banking, General practice, Real property. Home: 23 Bunker Hill Dr Huntington NY 11743-5705 Office: 202 East Main St Ste 303 Huntington NY 11743 E-mail: wptucker@att.net

TUCK-RICHMOND, DOLETTA SUE, prosecutor; b. Hugo, Okla., June 18, 1966; d. Benny Doyle and Tommie Marie (Cousins) T.; m. Lyle Richmond, Sept. 30, 1995; 1 child, Rachelle Jay Marie. AS, Murray State Coll., Tishomingo, Okla., 1986; BS magna cum laude, S.E. Okla. State U., 1988; JD with highest honors, U. Okla., 1991. Bar: Okla. 1991, U.S. Dist. Ct. (we., ea., and no. dists.), U.S. Ct. Appeals (10th cir.). Summer assoc. Andrews Davis, Oklahoma City, 1989-90; instr. in legal rsch, writing and oral advocacy U. Okla., Norman, 1989-91; assoc. Crowe & Dunlevy, Oklahoma City, 1991-93, Tulsa, Okla., 1993-94; pvt. practice Antlers, 1994; exempt orgn. specialist IRS, Oklahoma City, 1994-95; asst. atty. gen. State of Okla., 1995—; asst. U.S. atty. U.S. Atty's. Office (we. dist.) Okla., 1999—. Author: Joint Defense Agreements Can It Help Your Client, 1998, King For a Day: An Overview of Federal and State Qui Jam Provisions, 1999; contbg. author, editor: Oklahoma Environmental Law Practitioner's Handbook, 1992. Firm com. mem., participant Harvest Food Dr., Oklahoma City, 1991; chairperson Okla. Young Lawyers Rape Victims Assistance Com., 1992-94; bd. dirs. Okla. County Young Lawyers Divsn., 1993; participant, vol. Legal Aide of Western Okla., 1991. Named Miss Murray State Coll., Student Senate Pres., Tishomingo, Okla., 1986-86, Order of Coif U. Okla., Norman, Okla., 1991, Okla. Law Review U. Okla., Norman,

1991. Mem. FBA, Okla. Bar Assn. (bd. dirs., young lawyers divsn. 1993-95, mock trial com. 1994-95, liaison mental health com. 1994-95), Am. Agrl. Law Assn., Phi Delta Phi, Phi Kappa Phi (Spl. Act award for U.S. Atty. 1996, 97). Democrat. Baptist. Avocations: tennis, reading, writing, knitting, sports events. Home: 1624 SW 128th Pl Oklahoma City OK 73170-5018 Office: US Atty's Office Western Dist of Okla 210 Park Ave Ste 400 Oklahoma City OK 73102-5628

TUFARO, RICHARD CHASE, lawyer; b. N.Y.C., July 9, 1944; s. Frank P. and Stephania A. (Maida) T.; m. Helen M. Tufaro, June 25, 1977; children: Mary C., Edward F., Paul R., Cynthia M. AB magna cum laude, Dartmouth Coll., 1965; LLB cum laude, Harvard U., 1968. Bar: N.Y. 1969, D.C. 1992, Md. 1994; U.S. Dist. Ct. (so. dist.) N.Y. 1973, U.S. Dist. Ct. (ea. dist.) N.Y. 1978, U.S. Dist Ct. (D.C. dist.), 1994; U.S. Dist. Ct. (Md. dist.), 1996, U.S. Ct. Apls. (2d cir.) 1973, (5th cir.) 1976, (9th cir.) 1979, (6th cir.) 1980, (4th cir.), 1995; U.S. Ct. Claims, 1985, U.S. Ct. Appeals (3d cir.) 1990, U.S. Ct. Appeals (D.C. cir.) 1992; U.S. Sup. Ct., 1975. Law clk. Appellate-Div. N.Y. State, N.Y.C., 1970-71, assoc. Milbank, Tweed, Hadley & McCloy, N.Y.C., 1971-72, adminstrv. asst. White House Domestic Coun., Washington, 1972-73, assoc. Milbank, Tweed, Hadley & McCloy, N.Y.C., 1973-77, ptnr. 1978—. Served to capt. U.S. Army, 1968-70. Decorated Bronze Star with oak leaf cluster. Mem. ABA, Am. Mgmt. Assn., Phi Beta Kappa. Federal civil litigation, State civil litigation, Contracts commercial. Home: 7109 Heathwood Ct Bethesda MD 20817-2915 Office: 1825 I St NW Ste 1100 Washington DC 20006-5417

TUKE, ROBERT DUDLEY, lawyer, educator; b. Rochester, N.Y., Dec. 5, 1947; s. Theodore Robert and Doris Jean (Smith) T.; m. Susan Devereux Cummins, June 21, 1969; children: Andrew, Sarah. BA with distinction, U. Va., 1969; JD, Vanderbilt U., 1976. Bar: Tenn. 1976, U.S. Dist. Ct. (mid. dist.) Tenn. 1976, U.S. Ct. Appeals (6th cir.) 1976, U.S. Ct. Appeals (4th cir.) 1978, U.S. Ct. Appeals (fed. cir.) 1993, U.S. Supreme Ct. 1986, U.S. Ct. Internat. Trade 1993. Assoc. Farris, Warfield & Kanaday, Nashville, 1976-79, ptnr., 1980-94, Tuke Yopp & Sweeney, Nashville, 1994-99, Doramus Trauger & Ney, Nashville, 2000—. Adj. prof. law Vanderbilt U. Law Sch., Nashville; faculty PLI, 1995—; mem. AMA Drs.' Adv. Network. Author: (with others) Tennessee Practice, 1992—; editor Vanderbilt Law Rev.; contbr. articles to profl. jours. Mem. Tenn. Adoption Law Study Commn., 1993-96, Metro CATV Com. Capt. USMC, 1969-73. Decorated Cross of Gallantry; Patrick Wilson Merit scholar. Mem. ABA, Nat. Health Law Assn., Nat. Assn. Bond Lawyers, Am. Acad. Adoption Attys., Tenn. Bar Assn., Nashville Bar Assn., Order of Coif. Democrat. Episcopalian. Avocations: rowing, running, cycling, hiking, travel. General corporate, Health, Securities. Office: 222 4th Ave N Nashville TN 37219-2115 E-mail: rtuke@dtnlaw.com

TULCHIN, DAVID BRUCE, lawyer; b. N.Y.C., Dec. 2, 1947; s. Philip Tulchin and Mary (Weiner) Black; m. Nora Barrett, Aug. 20, 1972; children: Rachel, Daniel, Laura. BA, U. Rochester, 1970; JD, Harvard U., 1973. Bar: N.Y. 1974, U.S. Dist. Ct. (so. & ea. dists.) N.Y. 1975, U.S. Ct. Appeals (2d cir.) 1975, U.S. Supreme Ct. 1977, U.S. Ct. Appeals (5th cir.) 1978, U.S. Ct. Appeals (1st & 6th cirs.) 1984, U.S. Dist. Ct. (no. dist.) Ohio 1984, U.S. Ct. Appeals (3d, 4th & Fed. cirs.) 1988, U.S. Ct. Appeals (7th cir.) 1991, U.S. Dist. Ct. (we. dist.) N.Y., 1996. Law clk. to Judge Frederick V.P. Bryan U.S. Dist. Ct. So. Dist. N.Y., 1973-75; assoc. Sullivan & Cromwell, 1975-82, ptnr., 1982—. Mem. ABA, Assn. Bar of City of N.Y., Fed. Bar Coun., N.Y. State Bar Assn., Fed. Cir. Bar Assn. General civil litigation. Office: Sullivan & Cromwell 125 Broad St Fl 28 New York NY 10004-2489

TULLY, RICHARD T. C. lawyer, petroleum landman; b. Alliance, Nebr., Apr. 9, 1949; s. Thomas Bernard and Anna (Tully) Coupens; m. Deborah Elaine Williams, May 26, 1974 (div. 1977); m. Cecilia R. Buchanan, Feb. 16, 1980; children— Tanya Elizabeth, Rikki Allison, Anna Marie. B.A., N.Mex. State U., 1971; J.D., U. N.Mex., 1974. Bar: N.Mex. 1975, U.S. Dist. Ct. N.Mex. 1977, U.S. Ct. Appeals (10th cir.) 1978, U.S. Supreme Ct. 1982. Assoc. firm Darden, Sage & Darden, Las Cruces, N.M., 1974; landman El Paso Natural Gas Co., El Paso, 1974-76; gen. counsel, landman Dugan Prodn. Corp., Farmington, N.M., 1976-79; v.p. James B. Cooney, P.A., Farmington, N.Mex., 1979-81; sole practice, Farmington, 1981— ; dir. Aztec Energy Corp., 1982; v.p., dir. Southwest Mud & Chem. Co., Farmington, 1982— . Mem. steering com. New Mexicans for Jobs & Energy, 1979-81; treas. Morgan for Senate Com., 1984; Morgan for Gov. com., 1986. Mem. ABA, State Bar N.M. (dir. natural resources sect. 1987—, chair 1989), Assn. Trial Lawyers Am., Am. Assn. Petroleum Landmen, Am. Petroleum Inst., Ind. Producers Assn., N.Mex. C. of C., Desk & Derrick (adv., bd. dirs. 1977-79), Delta Theta Phi. Republican. Presbyterian. Clubs: San Juan Country, N.Mex. Amigos. Lodge: Elks. FERC practice, Oil, gas, and mineral, Estate planning. Home: 6012 Bayhill Dr Farmington NM 87402-5044 Office: 111 N Orchard Ave Farmington NM 87401-6208

TUMOLO, MICHAEL L. corporate lawyer; V.p., counsel Toys 'R' Us, Paramus, N.J., 1981—. Office: Toys R Us 461 From Rd Paramus NJ 07652-3524 E-mail: tumolom@toysrus.com

TUNE, JAMES FULCHER, lawyer; b. Danville, Va., May 13, 1942; s. William Orrin and Susan Agnes (Fulcher) T.; m. Katherine Del Mickey, Aug. 2, 1969; children: Katherine Winslow, Jeffrey Bricker. BA, U. Va., 1964; MA, Stanford U., 1970, JD, 1974. Bar: Wash. 1974, U.S. Dist. Ct. (we. dist.) Wash. 1974. Assoc. Bogle & Gates, Seattle, 1974-79, ptnr., 1980-99, head comml./banking dept., 1985-93, mng. ptnr., 1986-93, chmn., 1994-99; ptnr. Dorsey & Whitney LLP, 1999-2001, Stoel Rives LLP, Seattle, 2001—. Bd. dirs. BIEC Internat. Inc., Vancouver, Wash., BHP Steel Ams. Inc., Long Beach, Calif., Keynetics Inc., Boise, Idaho, Nichirei U.S.A., Inc., Seattle, Tengu Co., Santa Fe Springs, Calif.; chmn. Seattle-King City Econ. Devel. Coun., 1992. Chmn. Seattle Repertory Theatre, 1995; vice chmn. Corp. Coun. for the Arts, 2001. Lt. USN, 1964-69, Vietnam. Woodrow Wilson fellow, 1964, Danforth Found. fellow, 1964. Mem. ABA, Wash. State Bar Assn. (lectr. CLE 1976, 78, 84, 99), Seattle C. of C. (vice chmn. City Budget Task Force 1980-82), Ranier Club, Seattle Tennis Club, Phi Beta Kappa. Presbyterian. Banking, Contracts commercial, General corporate. Office: Stoel Rives LLP 600 University St Ste 3600 Seattle WA 98101-3197 E-mail: jftune@stoel.com

TUNGATE, JAMES LESTER, lawyer; b. Sept. 27, 1947; s. Ernest O. Jr. and Diantha (Woltz) T.; m. Susan Sumner, Aug. 25, 1973; children: Edward Ernest, James Aaron. BS, Ill. Wesleyan U., 1969; MA, Northwestern U.-Ill., 1970, PhD, 1972; JD, U. Ill.-Urbana, 1979; hon. DHL, London Sch. (Eng.), 1972. Bar: Ill. 1979, U.S. Supreme Ct. 1985. Spl. instr. Northwestern U., Evanston, Ill., 1971; prof., chmn. Loyola U., New Orleans, 1971-76; state dir. News Election Svc., 1972-74; dir. Inst. Religious Communications, 1974-76; asst. to state's atty. Iroquois County, Watseka, Ill., 1978; ptnr. Tungate & Tungate, 1979-98; pres. Tungate Law Offices, Ltd., 1998—. Media cons. Inst. Politics, New Orleans, 1973-76; legal cons., lectr. Iroquois Mental Health Ctr., Watseka, 1980— ; lectr. law Kankakee Community Coll., Ill., 1982; instr. law, Purdue U., 2000; dir. Iroquois Mental Health Ctr., 1980— ; chmn. Iroquois County chpt. ARC, 1982-84, 85— ; dir. Iroquois Republican Council, 1983— . Author: Romantic Images in Popular Songs, 1972; Readings in Broadcast law, 1975. Recipient Internat. Radio and TV Found. award; Harnow scholar U. Ill., 1976. Mem. Ill. Bar Assn., Iroquois County Bar Assn. (Law Day chmn., pres. 1998—), Chgo. Bar Assn., Pi Alpha Delta. Lodges: Masons (master 1982-83), Scottish Rite (most wise master 1997-98, 33-degree 1999), Mohammed Shrine. Republican. Methodist. Banking, General practice, Probate. Home: 146 W Hislop Dr Cissna Park IL 60924-8718 Office: Tungate Law Offices 744 E Walnut St PO Box 337 Watseka IL 60970-0337

TUOHEY, CONRAD GRAVIER, lawyer; b. N.Y.C., Dec. 27, 1933; s. James L. and Rose (Gravier) T.; BA, George Washington U., 1957; JD, U. Mich., 1960; m. Judith Octavia Jeeves, July 7, 1956; children: Octavia Jeeves, Heather Gravier, Meighan Judith, Caragh Rose. Admitted to Calif. bar, 1962, N.Y. bar, 1980, D.C. bar, 1980; sr. mem. firm Tuohey & Prasse; dir. Fed. Home Loan Bank, San Francisco, 1980-83; legal cons., counsel Calif. State Senate, 1981— ; counsel Senate Select Com. on the Pacific Rim, 1986-87. Mem. citizens adv. bd. Orange County Transit Com., 1966-68; pres. Calif. Alliance Partners for Progress, 1969-72, Friends of Calif. State U. at Fullerton, 1969-71; mem. InterAm. bd. Partners Alliance for Progress, 1969-72, nat. bd. dirs., 1970-72. Served with AUS, 1951-54. Decorated Combat Infantryman's Badge, Korean Service medal with 3 battle stars; named Outstanding Young Man of Yr., Fullerton Jr. C. of C., 1967. Mem. State Bar Calif., ABA (internat., corp., banking and bus. law sects.), Los Angeles Bar Assn., Orange County Bar Assn. chmn. environ. law sect.), D.C. Bar Assn., N.Y. Bar Assn., Kent Inn of Phi Delta Phi, Phi Sigma Kappa. Home: 24762 Red Lodge Pl Laguna Beach CA 92653-5832 Office: 26071 Merit Cir Ste 107 Laguna Hills CA 92653-7016

TUOHEY, MARK HENRY, III, lawyer; b. Rochester, N.Y., Sept. 27, 1946; s. Mark Henry T.; m. Martha; children: Brendan, Sean, Devin. BA in History, St. Bonaventure U., 1968; JD, Fordham U., 1973. Bar: D.C. 1973, U.S. Supreme Ct. 1980, U.S. Ct. Appeals (D.C. cir.) 1974, U.S. Dist. Ct. D.C. 1974, N.Y. 1984. Asst. U.S. atty. U.S. Atty.'s Office, Washington, 1973-77; spl. trial counsel U.S. Dept. Justice, 1977-79; spl. counsel to U.S. Atty. Gen., 1979; ptnr. Vinson & Elkins; dep. ind. counsel Whitewater Investigation, 1994-95; spl. counsel D.C. City Coun. Investigation of Met. Police Dept., 1998. Served to 1st lt. U.S. Army, 1970-71. Fellow Am. Coll. Trial Lawyers, Am. Law Inst., Am. Bar Found. (bd. dirs. 1980-85); mem. ABA (litigation sect. coun. 1980-90, chair standing com. on continuing edn. of bar, chair 1980-85, Am. Law Inst./ABA com. on continuing profl. edn. 1983—), D.C. Bar (pres. 1993-94, bd. govs. 1988-94), D.C. Bar Found. (chair 1998—), Jud. Conf. U.S. Ct. Appeals (D.C. cir.), Wm. Bryant Inn of Ct. (master). Federal civil litigation, Criminal, Government contracts and claims. Home: 1655 Kalmia Rd NW Washington DC 20012-1125 Office: Vinson & Elkins The Willard Office Bldg 1455 Pennsylvania Ave NW Fl 7 Washington DC 20004-1013 E-mail: mtouhey@velaw.com

TUPITZA, THOMAS ANTON, lawyer; b. Erie, Pa., Nov. 7, 1957; s. John and Geraldine Elizabeth (Girard) T.; m. Carol Jean Laird, Sept. 13, 1986; 1 child, Adam Victor. BA, Westminster Coll., Pa., 1979; JD, Harvard U., 1982. Bar: Pa. 1982, U.S. Dist. Ct. (we. dist.) Pa. 1982, U.S. Ct. Appeals (3d cir.) 1984. With Knox McLaughlin Gornall & Sennett, P.C., Erie, 1982—, ptnr., 1990—. Bd. dirs. Erie Summer Festival of Arts, 1983-94, Erie County Hist. Soc., 1992-98, pres., 1996-98, Erie City Mission, 1993—; Warner Theatre Preservation Trust, 1994—, Northwestern Legal Svcs., 1994—, pres., 1997-2000, Am. Bapt. Chs. Pa. and Del., 1984-96, pres., 1993-94, Inter-Ch. Ministries of Erie County, 1991-96, pres., 1993-95, Penn Attys. Title Ins. Co., 2000—, Erie Area Convention and Vistors Ctr Bureau, 2001-; fund distbn. chair United Way of Erie County, 1989; trustee Westminster Coll., 1998—; Chapel of the Four Chaplains, 1997—; trustee Colgate Rochester Crozer Div. Sch., 1997—, Discovery Square, Inc., 1996—, Corporator Hamot Health Found., 2001-. Mem. ABA, Nat. Assn. Bond Lawyers, Am. Health Lawyers Assn., Pa. Soc. Health Care Attys., Pa. Bar Assn., Erie County Bar Assn., Pa. Assn. Bond Lawyers (bd. dirs. 1994—), Erie Club, Theta Chi. Health, Municipal (including bonds), Real property. Office: Knox McLaughlin Gornall & Sennett PC 120 W 10th St Erie PA 16501-1410 E-mail: ttupitaz@kmgslaw.com

TURANO, DAVID A. lawyer; b. Ashtabula, Ohio, Sept. 9, 1946; s. Egidio A. and Mary Agnes (Bartko) T.; m. Karen J. Emmel, Aug. 29, 1970; children: Aaron, Thad, Bethen, Kyle. BS, Kent State U., 1968; JD, Ohio State U., 1971. Bar: Ohio 1971. Staff atty. The Pub. Utilities Commn. Ohio, Columbus, 1971-72; assoc., then ptnr. George, Greek, King, McMahon and Mcconnaughey, 1972-79; ptnr. Baker & Hostetler, 1979-96, Harris, Carter, Mahota, Turano & Mazza, Columbus, 1996-97, Harris, Turano & Mazza, Columbus, 1997—. Mem. ABA, Ohio State Bar Assn., Columbus Bar Assn., Transp. Lawyers Assn. Roman Catholic. Transportation. Office: Harris Turano & Mazza 941 Chatham Ln Ste 201 Columbus OH 43221-2416

TURBIN, RICHARD, lawyer; b. N.Y.C., Dec. 25, 1944; s. William and Ruth (Fiedler) T.; m. Rai Saint Chu-Turbin, June 12, 1976; children: Laurel Mei, Derek Andrew. BA magna cum laude, Cornell U., 1966; JD, Harvard U., 1969. Bar: Hawaii 1971, U.S. Dist. Ct. Hawaii 1971. Asst. atty. gen., Western Samoa, Apia, 1969-70; dep. pub. defender Pub. Defender's Office, Honolulu, 1970-74; dir. Legal Aid Soc. Hawaii, Kaneohe, 1974-75; sr. atty., pres. Law Offices Richard Turbin, Honolulu, 1975—. Legal counsel Hawaii Crime Commn., 1980-81. Co-author: Pacific; author: Medical Malpractice, Handling Emergency Medical Cases, 1991; editor Harvard Civil Rights-Civil Liberties Law Rev., 1969. Legal counsel Dem. Party, Honolulu County, 1981-82; elected Neighborhood Bd., 1985, elected chair, 1990-97; bd. dirs. Hawaii chpt. ACLU, 1974-78, East-West Ctr. grantee, 1971, 72. Mem. ATLA, ABA (chair internat. torts and ins. law and practice com., mem. governing coun., chair tort and ins. practice sect. 1999-2000, chair-elect 1998-99), Hawaii Bar Assn., Hawaii Trial Lawyers Assn. (bd. govs.), Hawaii Jaycees (legal counsel 1981-82), Chinese Jaycees Honolulu (legal counsel 1980-81), Honolulu Tennis League (undefeated player 1983), Hawaii Harlequin Rugby Club (sec., legal counsel 1978-82), Pacific Club, Outrigger Canoe Club. Jewish. State civil litigation, Personal injury, Workers' compensation. Home: 4817 Kahala Ave Honolulu HI 96816-5231

TURCOTTE, JOHN ARTHUR, JR. lawyer; b. Lowell, Mass., Mar. 27, 1950; s. John A. and Dorothy J. (Gillette) T.; m. Mary Catherine Willett, Nov. 12, 1976; 1 dau., Sarah Hamilton. B.S., Boston Coll., 1972; J.D., St. Louis U., 1976. Bar: Mo. 1977, U.S. Dist. Ct. (ea. dist.) Mo. 1979; U.S. Ct. Appeals (8th cir.) 1981. Law clk. to presiding justice Mo. Ct. Appeals (ea. dist.), St. Louis, 1976-78; assoc. Lashly, Caruthers, Baer & Hamel, St. Louis, 1978-81, ptnr., 1981-83; ptnr. Diekemper, Hammond, Shiners, Turcotte & Larrew, St. Louis, 1983—. Fellow Am. Acad. Matrimonial Lawyers; mem. ABA, Assn. Trial Lawyers Am., Mo. Assn. Trial Attys., Bar Assn. Met. St. Louis (chmn. com. on cts., Merit award 1983). Democrat. Roman Catholic. Family and matrimonial. Home: 139 Wildwood Ln Saint Louis MO 63122-5135 Office: Diekemper Hammond Shinners Turcotte & Larrew 7730 Carondelet Ave Ste 200 Saint Louis MO 63105-3326

TURETSKY, AARON, lawyer; b. Bklyn., Mar. 23, 1951; s. Victor and Edith (Levine) T.; m. Edna M. Real, July 21, 1990; children: Persephone Fatima, Aaron Jr. BA summa cum laude, Hunter Coll., N.Y.C., 1979; JD magna cum laude, N.Y. Law Sch., 1986. Bar: N.J. 1986, U.S. Dist. Ct. N.J. 1986, N.Y. 1987, U.S. Dist. Ct. (so. and ea. dists.) N.Y. 1987, U.S. Dist. Ct. (no. dist.) N.Y. 1988. Appellate law rsch. asst. appellate div. 2d dept. Supreme Ct. State of N.Y., 1986-87; atty. North Country Legal Svcs., Inc., Plattsburgh, N.Y., 1987-89; assoc. Holcombe & Bruno, 1989-90; pvt. practice, Keeseville, N.Y., 1990—. Law guardian Essex County Family Ct., 1990—; impartial hearing officer for children with disabilites, 1996—. Chmn. Essex County, N.Y. Conservative Com., 1990—; N.Y. St. Conservative Party N.E. regional vice. chmn., 1992—; eucharistic min. Cath. Community, Keeseville, N.Y. Mem. N.Y. State Bar Assn., Clinton County Bar Assn., Essex County Bar Assn., Elks, KC, Phi Beta Kappa. Roman Catholic. Education and schools, Family and matrimonial, General practice. Office: PO Box 367 Keeseville NY 12944-0367

TURK, JAMES CLINTON, federal judge; b. Roanoke, Va., May 3, 1923; s. James Alexander and Geneva (Richardson) T.; m. Barbara Duncan, Aug. 21, 1954; children— Ramona Leah, James Clinton, Robert Malcolm Duncan, Mary Elizabeth, David Michael. A.B., Roanoke Coll., 1949; L.L.B., Washington and Lee U., 1952. Bar: Va. bar 1952. Assoc. Dalton & Poff, Radford, Va., 1952-53; ptnr. Dalton, Poff & Turk, 1953-72; U.S. senator from Va., 1959-72; judge U.S. Dist. Ct. (we. dist.) Va., Roanoke, 1972-73, chief judge, 1973—. Dir. 1st & Mchts. Nat. Bank of Radford Mem. Va. Senate, from 1959, minority leader.; Trustee Radford Community Hosp., 1959— . Served with AUS, 1943-46. Mem. Order of Coif, Phi Beta Kappa, Omicron Delta Kappa. Baptist (deacon). Home: 1002 Walker Dr Radford VA 24141-3018 Office: US Dist Ct 246 Franklin Rd SW # 220 Roanoke VA 24011-2214 Fax: (540) 857-5123

TURK, JAMES CLINTON, JR. lawyer; b. Radford, Va., Oct. 27, 1956; s. James Clinton and Barbara (Duncan) T.; m. Allison Blanding, Oct. 16, 1993; children: Lindsey Leigh, Katherine Alexandra, Alana Rae. BA in Econs., Roanoke Coll., 1979; JD, Samford U., 1984. Bar: Va. 1984, U.S. Dist. Ct. (ea. and we. dists.) Va. 1984, U.S. Bankruptcy Ct. 1985, U.S. Ct. Appeals (4th cir.) 1985, U.S. Supreme Ct. 1988; cert. specialist in civil and criminal trial advocacy Nat. Bd. Trial Advocacy. Ptnr. Stone, Harrison & Turk, Radford, 1985—. Adj. prof. criminal justice dept. Radford U. Sec. Radford Rep. Com., 1984—; fundraising chmn. Am. Heart Assn., Radford, 1986—; bd. dirs. New River Valley Workshop, Inc., v.p., 1990-92, pres., 1992-93; bd. dirs. new River C.C. Ednl. Found.; apptd. chmn. and dir. Va. Student Assistance Authorities by Gov. George Allen, 1994—; escheator City of Radford and Pulaski County; rep. western dist. CJA Panel Attys., Va.; mem. 4th Cir. Jud. Conf. Mem. ATLA (sustaining, fellow Coll. of Advocacy), ABA, Am. Bd. Trial Advs., Am. Coll. Barristers, Am. Bd. Profl. Liability Attys., Va. Bar Assn. (civil litigation sect. coun. 1991—, criminal litigation sect. coun. 1994—), Nat. Assn. Criminal Def. Lawyers (life; death penalty com. and indigent def. com.), Va. Trial Lawyers Assn., Jaycees, Rotary. Republican. Roman Catholic. Avocations: weightlifting, skiing, travel, flying, scuba diving. State civil litigation, Criminal, Personal injury. Home: 460 Quailwood Dr Blacksburg VA 24060-6724 Office: Stone Harrison Turk PC PO Box 2968 Radford VA 24143-2968

TURLEY, J. WILLIAM, lawyer; b. Van Nuys, Calif., Jan. 11, 1948; s. Billy Brown and Kathryn Ann (Kuniak) T.; children: Timothy Jay, Damon Andrew. BA, U. Mo., 1970, JD, 1974. Bar: Mo. 1974, U.S. Dist. Ct. (we. dist.) Mo. 1974. Stockholder Wesner, Turley & Kempton, Inc., Sedalia, Mo., 1975-84; ptnr. Carnahan, Carnahan & Turley, Rolla, Mo., 1984-87, Robinson, Turley, Turley & White, 1987-89; ptnr. Williams, Robinson, Turley, Crump & White, 1989—; atty. City of Sedalia, 1976; pros. atty. Pettis County, Sedalia, 1976; Author: Trial Handbook for Missouri Lawyers, 1984; contbr. articles to profl. jours. Chmn. Sedalia Dem. Com., 1982; v.p. Mo. Lawyer's Trust Acct. Found., 1990. Mem. Mo. Bar Assn. (bd. govs. 1986—, exec. com. 1989-90), Assn. Trial Lawyers Am. (bd. govs. 1985-89), Mo. Assn. Trial Attys. (pres. 1985), Jaycees, Scribes, Moose. Democrat. Roman Catholic. Federal civil litigation, State civil litigation, Personal injury. Home: 2626 Huntleigh Pl Jefferson City MO 65109-1123 Office: Williams Robinson Turley Crump & White PO Box 47 Rolla MO 65402-0047

TURLEY, ROBERT JOE, lawyer; b. Mt. Sterling, Ky., Dec. 6, 1926; s. R. Joe and Mavis Clare (Sternberg) T.; m. Mary Lynn Sanders, Dec. 17, 1948 (dv.); children: Leighton Turley Isaacs, Lynn Turley McComas, R. Joe, Mavis Lee Turley Scully. Student, Berea Coll., 1944-45, St. Mary's Coll., Calif., 1945-46; LLB, U. Ky., 1949. Bar: Ky. 1949, U.S. Dist. Ct. (ea. dist.) Ky. 1950, U.S. Supreme Ct. 1959. Ptnr. Mooney & Turley and successor firms, Lexington, Ky., 1949-84, Turley & Moore, Lexington, 1984-89, of counsel, 1989-93. Chmn. Fed. Jud. Selection Commn. Ky., 1985-89; gen counsel Shriners Hosps. for Children, 1976-77, trustee, 1981-90, emeritus trustee, 1990—. Author: The Choices Are Yours, 1997, The Bridge of Faith, 2000; contbr. articles to legal jours. With USNR, 1944-46. Diplomate Nat. Bd. Trial Advocacy, 1980. Fellow Am. Coll. Trial Lawyers, Ky. Bar Found. (life); mem. Ky. Bar Assn. (sr. counselor, Outstanding Lawyer award 2001), St. Ives Jour. Club, Champions Trace Golf Club, Masons, Shriners. Home: 111 Woodland Ave Lexington KY 40502-6415

TURNAGE, FRED DOUGLAS, lawyer; b. Ayden, N.C., Sept. 24, 1920; s. Fred C. and Lou (Johnson) T.; m. Margaret Futrell, Aug. 21, 1943 (div. Nov. 1980); children: Betty Lou Griffith, Douglas C.; m. Elizabeth Louisa Turnage, Jan. 23, 1981. Grad. Naval Sch. on Far Eastern Civil Affairs, Princeton U., 1945; LLB, Wake Forest U., 1948, LLD, 1970. Bar: N.C. 1948, U.S. Supreme Ct. 1953, U.S. Dist. Ct. D.C. 1965, U.S. Ct. Appeals (D.C. cir.) 1967, U.S. Ct. Appeals (4th and 7th cirs.) 1979. Trial atty. antitrust div. U.S. Dept. Justice, Kansas City, Mo., 1948-51, sr. trial atty. antitrust div. Washington, 1951-65, spl. asst. to atty. gen., 1965; sr. ptnr. Cleary, Gottlieb, Steen & Hamilton, 1968—. Lectr. continuing legal edn. courses, 1973-77. Contbr. articles to profl. jours. Bd. Visitors Wake Forest U. Sch. Law, Winston-Salem, N.C., 1980—. Served to 1st lt. AUS, 1942-46. Recipient Disting. Service in Law citation Wake Forest U., 1979. Mem. ABA (antitrust and litigation sects.), Fed. Bar Assn., Adv. Bd. Antitrust Bulletin, Wake Forest U. Alumni Assn. (pres. 1977), Nat. Lawyers Clubs. Methodist. Avocations: fishing, golf, writing. Antitrust, Federal civil litigation, Criminal. Home: 02 Fifth Ave Kitty Hawk NC 27949 Office: 2000 Pennsylvania Ave NW Washington DC 20006-1812

TURNAGE, JEAN ALLEN, retired state supreme court chief justice; b. St. Ignatius, Mont., Mar. 10, 1926; JD, Mont. State U., 1951; D Laws and Letters (non.), U. Mont., 1995. Bar: Mont. 1951, U.S. Supreme Ct. 1963. Formerly ptnr. Turnage, McNeil & Mercer, Polson, Mont.; formerly Mont. State senator from 13th Dist.; pres. Mont. State Senate, 1981-83; chief justice Supreme Ct. Mont., 1985-2001. Mem. Mont. State Bar Assn., Nat. Conf. Chief Justices (past pres.), Nat. Ctr. State Courts (past chair). Office: Turnage O'Neill & Mercer PO Box 460 Polson MT 59860

TURNBULL, H. RUTHERFORD, III, law educator, lawyer; b. N.Y.C., Sept. 22, 1937; s. Henry R. and Ruth (White) T.; m. Mary M. Slingluff, Apr. 4, 1964 (div. 1972); m. Ann Patterson, Mar. 23, 1974; children: Jay, Amy, Katherine. Grad., The Kent (Conn.) Sch., 1955; BA, Johns Hopkins U., 1959; LLB with hon., U. Md., 1964; LLM, Harvard U., 1969. Bar: Md., N.C. Law clerk to Hon. Emory H. Niles Supreme Bench Balt. City, 1959-60; law clerk to Hon. Roszel C. Thomsen U.S. Dist. Ct. Md., 1962-63; assoc. Piper & Marbury, Balt., 1964-67; prof. Inst. Govt. U. N.C., Chapel Hill, 1969-80, U. Kans., Lawrence, 1980—. Prof. spl. edn., courtesy prof. law U. Kans. Editor-in-chief Md. Law Review. Cons., author, lectr., co-dir. Beach Ctr. on Families and Disability, U. Kans.; pres. Full Citizenship Inc., Lawrence, 1987-93; spl. staff-fellow U.S. Senate subcom. on disability policy, Washington, 1987-88; bd. dirs. Camphill Assn. N.Am., Inc., 1985-87; trustee Judge David L. Bazelon Ctr. Mental Health Law, 1993-2000, chmn., 1999—. With U.S. Army, 1960-65. Recipient Nat. Leadership award Nat. Assn. Pvt. Residential Resources, 1988, Nat. Leadership award Internat. Coun. for Exceptional Children, 1996, Nat. Leadership award Am. Assn. on Mental Retardation, 1997, Century award Nat. Trust for Hist. Preservation in Mental Retardation, 1999; named Nat. Educator of Yr., ARC, 1982; Public Policy fellow Joseph P. Kennedy, Jr. Found., 1987-88. Fellow Am. Assn. on Mental Retardation

(pres. 1985-86, bd. dirs. 1980-86); mem. ABA (chmn. disability law commn. 1991-95), U.S.A. As sn. for Retarded Citizens (sec. and dir. 1981-83), Assn. for Persons with Severe Handicaps (treas. 1988, bd. dirs. 1987-90), Nat. Assn. Rehab. Rsch. and Tng. Ctrs. (chair govt. affairs com. 1990-93), Internat. Assn. Scientific Study of Mental Deficiency, Internat. League of Assns. for Persons with Mental Handicaps, Johns Hopkins U. Alumni Assn. (prs. N.C. chpt. 1977-79). Democrat. Episcopalian. Home: 1636 Alvamar Dr Lawrence KS 66047-1714 Office: U Kans 3111 Haworth Hall 1200 Sunnyside Ave Lawrence KS 66045-7534 E-mail: Rud@ku.edu

TURNBULL, REGINALD HARRISON, lawyer; b. Springfield, Mo., Nov. 3, 1946; s. John Howard and Margaret Maurine Turnbull; m. Anita K. Propst, Dec. 18, 1972; children: Bryce C., Kyle D., Ryan H. BA, N.W. Mo. State U., 1972; JD, U. Mo., Kansas City, 1976. Bar: Mo. 1976, U.S. Dist. Ct. (we dist.) Mo. 1976. Law clk. Jackson County Cir. Ct., Kansas City, Mo., 1976-77; asst. atty. gen. Mo. Atty. Gen., Jefferson City, 1977-81; dep. dir. for human resources Mo. Dept. of Mental Health, 1981-91; assoc. atty. Waltz & Jordan, Mo., 1991-96; shareholder, atty. Riner Turnbull and Walker P.C., 1996-99, Turnbull Law Office, P.C., Jefferson City. Pres. Jefferson City Parks and Recreation Commn., 1984-90, Jefferson City Parents and Tchrs. Orgn., 1994-96; scoutmaster Troop 1, Jefferson City, 1991-94. Mem. Jefferson City Breakfast Rotary Club, Nat. Acad. of Elder Law Attys. (chmn. trusts spl. interest group, bd. dirs. Mo. chpt.), Mo. Bar Assn. (probate trust, elder law), Nat. Orgn. of Social Security Claimant's Reps. Bankruptcy, Estate planning, Family and matrimonial. Home: 135 Forest Hill Ave Jefferson City MO 65109-0963 Office: Turnbull Law Office PC 200 E High St Jefferson City MO 65101-3207 Fax: 573-635-6584. E-mail: ribull@aol.com

TURNER, BENNIE L. b. West Point, Miss., Aug. 21, 1948; s. Robert and Ether (Hunter) T.; m. Edna Walker, Apr. 29, 1971; children— Angela, Carolyn, Leta. A.S., Mary Holmes Coll., 1968; B.A., Miss. State U., 1971; J.D., U. Miss., 1974. Bar: Miss. 1974, Miss. Supreme Ct. 1974, U.S. Dist. Ct. (no. dist.) Miss. 1974, U.S. Ct. Appeals (5th cir.) 1975. City prosecutor, West Point, Miss., 1977-79; county atty., Clay County, West Point, Miss., 1979— ; ptnr. law firm Walker & Turner, West Point, Miss., 1975— ; chmn. bd. dirs. North Miss. Rural Legal Service, Inc., Oxford, Miss., 1983—; mem. Miss. Senate from 16th dist., Jackson, 1992— ; mem. Miss. Bd. Bar Admissions, 1985— . Mem., Miss. Bar Complaints Com., Jackson, 1980-83. Chmn., Gov.'s Fleeing Felon Com., 1982; mem. Tenn-Tom Waterway Authority, 1980— , treas., 1985; mem. Sen. Stennis' Re-election Com., 1982. Named Outstanding Citizen, Clay County chpt. NAACP, 1983. Fellow Miss. Bar Found., mem. Magnolia Bar Assn., Assn. Trial Lawyers Am. Mem. African Methodist Episcopal Ch. Club: West Point Swim Assn. (pres. 1983-84). Home: RR 6 Box 113 West Point MS 39773-9665 Office: PO Box 1500 West Point MS 39773-1500

TURNER, CATRIN, lawyer; b. London; LLB with honors, Victoria U. Manchester, England, 1986. Trainee then asst. Campbell Park, 1987-91; asst. then ptnr. Davies Arosid Casper, London, 1991-99; ptnr. H2O (Henry Hepuoth Orgn.), 1999—. Fellow Royal Soc. Arts, England, 2000. Mem. Inst. Trademark Attys. (assoc.), Soc. Computer Law, Pharm. Tradesmarks Group. Avocations: carpentry, travel. Communications, Computer, Intellectual property. Home and Office: 5 John St London WC2N 2HH England Fax: 020 75397201. E-mail: catrinturner@h2o-law.com

TURNER, CHARLES CARRE, association executive; b. Clarksburg, W.Va., May 20, 1944; s. Joseph Archer and Mary Donovan T.; m. Deborah Andrews, Jan. 28, 1968; children— Brian Curtis, David Carre, Michael Andrews. B.A., St. Lawrence U., 1966; J.D., U. Denver, 1971. Bar: Colo. 1971. Adminstrv. asst. U. Denver, 1971-72, dir. continuing legal edn., 1972-75, asst. dean, 1975-80; exec. dir. Colo./Denver Bar Assns., 1980— . Editor Ann. Survey of Colo. Law, 1978—. Committeeman Denver Democratic Party, 1972-80; elder Central Presbyterian Ch., Denver, 1982-85. Served to 1st lt. U.S. Army, 1966-68. Mem. Denver Law Club (treas. 1980-81), Nat. Assn. Bar Execs. (exec. com.), Alzheimer's Assn. Colo. (adv. bd.), Law Club, Skyline Club. Office: Colo Bar Assn 1900 Grant St Ste 950 Denver CO 80203-4348

TURNER, DAVID ELDRIDGE, lawyer; b. Washington, Jan. 16, 1947; s. Olan Eldridge and Bernice Adele (Bothwell) T.; m. Lauren Turner-Hudson; children: Matthew David, Elizabeth Kristine, Jacob Michael. BS, Pa. State U., 1969; JD cum laude, Temple U., 1974. Bar: Pa. 1974, U.S. Dist. Ct. (ea. and mid. dists.) Pa. 1974, U.S. Ct. Appeals (3d cir.) 1983, U.S. Supreme Ct. 1985. With Liberty Mut. Ins. Co., Allentown, Pa., 1969-71; ptnr. Rhoda, Stoudt & Bradley, Reading, 1974-80, Kozloff, Diener, Turner & Payne P.C., Wyomissing, 1980-84; pres. Bingaman, Hess, Coblentz & Bell, P.C., Reading, 1985—. Instr. Pa. State U., Berks County, 1974-80; jud. appointee Berks County Ct. of Common Pleas, Reading, 1982-83. Supr. Robeson Twp. Bd. Suprs., Berks County, Pa., 1980-82. Mem. ABA, Pa. Bar Assn., Berks County Bar Assn., Pa. Trial Lawyers Assn., Pa. Def. Inst., Endlich Law Club, Mensa. Avocations: sculpture, rock climbing. Federal civil litigation, State civil litigation, Insurance. Office: Bingaman Hess Coblentz & Bell Treeview Corp Ctr Ste 100 2 Meridian Dr Wyomissing PA 19610 E-mail: deturner@bhcb.com

TURNER, DONALD ALLEN, lawyer; b. Cleve., Aug. 14, 1938; s. Louis O. and Harriet B. (Keizer) T.; m. Amy Glicksberg, Dec. 16, 1962 (div. Oct. 1980); children— Matthew, Kelli; m. Vikki Holley, Sept. 30, 1984 (div. 1989); m. Diane Fraunhoffer, 1992 (div. 1994); m. Renata Olgate, 1997. B. Metall. Engring., Ohio State U., 1963; J.D., Detroit Coll. Law, 1967. Bar: Mich. 1967, U.S. Dist. Ct. (ea. dist.) Mich. 1967. Ptnr., Turner & Schaden, Detroit, 1967-69, Nelson, Gracey, Turner, Detroit, 1969-72; pres. Turner & Turner, P.C., Southfield, Mich., 1972-91. Served with USNR, 1956-58. Mem. Assn. Trial Lawyers Am., Mich. Trial Lawyers Assn., State Bar Mich., Southfield Bar Assn., Oakland County Bar Assn. Jewish. Civil rights, Federal civil litigation, Personal injury. Home: 3923 Maple Hill St E West Bloomfield MI 48323-1742 Office: Turner & Turner PC 26000 W 12 Mile Rd Southfield MI 48034-1783

TURNER, E. DEANE, lawyer; b. Auburn, N.Y., Aug. 4, 1928; s. Alfred Edward and Bertha (Deane) T. AB summa cum laude, Princeton U., 1950; LLB cum laude, Harvard U., 1953. Bar: N.Y. 1953. Assoc. Dewey Ballantine, LLP and predecessor firms, N.Y.C., 1953-63, ptnr., 1963—, of counsel, 1991—. Treas. Harvard Law Sch. Assn., N.Y.C., 1964-83; elder, trustee Brick Presbyn. Ch., N.Y.C., 1976—, pres. bd. trustees, 1988-90; trustee Presbytery N.Y.C., 1993-98, pres. bd. trustees, 1995-98; com. to adminstr. James N. Jarvie Endowment, 1993-2000. Fellow Am. Coll. Investment Counsel (emeritus); mem. Union Club, John's Island Club, Phi Beta Kappa. Republican. General corporate, Finance. Home: 1120 5th Ave New York NY 10128-0144 also: 381 Llwyds Ln Johns Island Vero Beach FL 32963 Office: Dewey Ballantine LLP 1301 Avenue Of The Americas New York NY 10019-6022

TURNER, GEORGE MASON, lawyer; b. Butte, Mont., Sept. 2, 1935; s. William Dale and Bernice (Ownby) T.; m. Angela Gloria Aparicio, Oct. 14, 1995; children: Esther, Lesley, Allyson, Aarin, Alexander. BS in Polit. Sci., Brigham Young U., 1959, MS in Polit. Sci., 1960; JD, UCLA, 1968. Bar: Calif. 1969, U.S. Dist. Ct. Calif. 1969, U.S. Supreme Ct. 1976, U.S. Ct. Claims 1981, U.S. Tax Ct. 1981. Assoc. Munns & Kofford, Pasadena, Calif., 1969-72; ptnr. Turner & Smart, 1972-85, The Law Offices of George M. Turner, Pasadena, 1985—; pvt. practice, 1972—. Instr. estate tax law Am. Coll. Bryn Mawr, Pa., 1976; monitor Continuing Edn. of Bar, Calif., 1985. Author: Revocable Trusts, 1983, 4th edit., 1998, Irrevocable Trusts, 1985, 3d edit., 1997, Trust Administration and Fiduciary Responsibility, 2d edit., 2000, Revocable Trusts-The Centerpiece of Estate Planning, 1998. V.p. San Gabriel Valley Boy Scouts Am., Pasadena, 1976-78; pres. San Gabriel Valley Estate Planning Co., Pasadena, 1979-80; bd. dirs., chmn. bd. Calif. Family Study Ctr., North Hollywood, 1975-92, Ettie Lee Homes, Los Angeles, 1984-90. Recipient Silver Beaver award Boy Scout Am., 1979. Mem. ABA, Calif. Bar Assn., Los Angeles Bar Assn., Pi Sigma Alpha. Republican. Mormon. Avocation: photography. Estate planning, Probate, Estate taxation.

TURNER, HUGH JOSEPH, JR. lawyer; b. Paterson, N.J., Oct. 5, 1945; s. Hugh Joseph and Louise (Sullivan) T.; m. Charlene Chiappetta, Feb. 11, 1983. BS, Boston U., 1967; JD, U. Miami, Coral Gables, Fla., 1975. Bar: Fla. 1975, U.S. Dist. Ct. (so., no. and mid. dists.) Fla. 1975, U.S. Ct. Appeals (11th cir.) 1981, U.S. Supreme Ct. 1984. Tchr. Browne & Nichols, Cambridge, Mass., 1968-72; ptnr. Smathers & Thompson, Miami, Fla., 1981-87, Kelley Drye & Warren, Miami, 1987-93, English, McCaughan & O'Bryan, Ft. Lauderdale, 1993—. Chmn. Fla. Bar internat. law sect., 1988-89. Contbg. author book on internat. dispute resolution Fla. Bar, 1989; contbr. articles to profl. jours. Bd. dirs. Japan Soc. South Fla., Miami, 1989-97; mem. Sea Ranch Lakes Village Coun., 1997-2000; mayor Sea Ranch Lakes, 2000—. Mem. ABA, Def. Rsch. Inst. Avocation: running. General civil litigation, Private international, Product liability. Office: English McCaughan O'Bryan 100 NE 3rd Ave Ste 1100 Fort Lauderdale FL 33301-1144

TURNER, JAMES THOMAS, judge; b. Clifton Forge, Va., Mar. 12, 1938; s. James Thomas and Ruth (Greene) T.; m. Patricia Sue Renfrow, July 8, 1962; 1 child, James Thomas. BA, Wake Forest Coll., 1960; JD, U. Va., 1965. Bar: Va. 1965, U.S. Ct. Appeals (4th and fed. cirs.), U.S. Supreme Ct. Assoc. Williams, Worrell, Kelly & Greer, Norfolk, Va., 1965, ptnr., 1971-79; U.S. magistrate U.S. Dist. Ct. (ea. dist.) Va., 1979-87; judge U.S. Ct. Fed. Claims, 1987—. Mem. ABA, Fed. Bar Assn., Va. Bar Assn., Norfolk and Portsmouth Bar Assn. (sec. 1975-79). Office: US Ct Fed Claims 717 Madison Pl NW Washington DC 20005-1011

TURNER, LAURENCE H. lawyer, engineer; b. N.Y.C., Nov. 29, 1949; s. Sidney and Sylvia Turner. B in Mech. Engring., Pratt Inst., N.Y., 1973; MBA, Baruch Coll., 1977; JD, Bklyn. Law Sch., 1996. Bar: N.Y. 1997; lic. profl. engr., N.Y., N.J. Adminstrv. engr. N.Y.C. Dept. Environ. Protection, Elmhurst, N.Y., 1984—. Avocations: water skiing, travel. Home: 99-72 66 Rd #5V Rego Park NY 11374-4442

TURNER, LESTER NATHAN, lawyer, international trade consultant; b. Colmar, Ky., July 11, 1933; s. Clifford G. and Minnie G. (Ensor) T.; m. Sandra B. Ward, July 3, 1976; children: Kimberly L., Michele M., Renee S., Mark L., Jeffrey S., Derek Kyle. BS, Lincoln Meml. U., 1955; JD, U. Mich., 1959. Bar: Mich. 1960, U.S. Dist. Ct. (ea. and we. dist.) Mich., U.S. Ct. Appeals (6th cir.), U.S. Supreme Ct. 1982. Law clk. to presiding justice, research atty. Mich. Supreme Ct., Lansing, 1960-62; ptnr. Sinas, Dramis, Brake & Turner, 1960-78; sole law practice, bus. law, internat. cons. primarily in Mid. East Countries with emphasis on Palestine Nat. Authority, Lansing, Harbor Springs, Mich., 1978—; prin., CEO Palestinian Tourism Co. Ltd., Palestinian Co. Transp. Ltd., North Bay Ltd. Mem. std. jury instrn. com. Mich. Supreme Ct., Lansing, 1963-73; cons. higher commn. investment and fin. Palestinian Pres., 1997—. Mem. Mich. State Bar Assn., Mich. Trial Lawyers Assn. (bd. dirs. 1963-74, vice pres. 1974). Methodist. General civil litigation, Education and schools, General practice. Office: PO Box 499 Harbor Springs MI 49740-0499 E-mail: Lntlaw@chartermi.net

TURNER, MARK MCDOUGALL, lawyer; b. Carlisle, Eng., Sept. 3, 1956; BA, Oxford U., 1979. Bar: solicitor, 1983. Ptnr. Denton Hall, London, 1988-95, Garrett & Co., London, 1995-97, Herbert Smith, London, 1998—. Author: Butterworth's Ency. of Competition Law, 1993, International Technology Transfers, 1995. Fellow Royal Soc. Arts; mem. United Oxford and Cambridge Univ. Club. Communications, Computer, E-business. Office: Herbert Smith Exchange House, Primrose St London EC2A 2HS England

TURNER, SHAWN DENNIS, lawyer; b. Salt Lake City, Apr. 19, 1959; s. Gerald Lewis and Cynthia Sue Turner; m. Pamela M. Morgan, May 31, 1985; children: Erin K., Jessica L. BS, U. Utah, 1984; MBA, Cornell U., 1986; JD, Brigham Young U., 1990. Bar: Utah 1990, U.S. Dist. Ct. Utah 1992, U.S. Ct. Appeals (10th cir.) 1992, U.S. Tax Ct. 1992, U.S. Ct. Claims 1993. Law clk. Utah Atty. Gen.'s Office, Salt Lake City, 1988-89; assoc. McKay Burton & Thurman, 1990-91; shareholder Brown, Larson, Jenkins & Halliday, 1991-96; ptnr. Larson, Turner, Fairbanks & Dalby, L.C., 1996—. Tax cons. Deloitte Haskins & Sells, Salt Lake City, 1986-87; agt. Attys. Title, Salt Lake City, 1996—; mem. Advantage Title Co., Salt Lake City, 1997—. Mem. Utah State Bar Assn. (tax sect., litig. sect., estate planning sect.), U.S. Chess Fed. Appellate, General civil litigation, Taxation, general. Office: Larson Turner Fairbanks & Dolby L C 4516 S 700 E Ste 100 Salt Lake City UT 84107-8319

TURNER, TOM, writer, editor; b. Oakland, Calif., 1942; m. Mary Jorgensen; children: Bret and Kathryn (twins). BA in Polit. Sci., U. Calif., 1965. Vol. Peace Corps, Turkey, 1965-67; grant analyst Head Start, 1968; editor, adminstrv. asst. Sierra Club, 1968-69; various positions including exec. dir. Friends of the Earth, 1969-86, also editor Not Man Apart; staff writer, dir. publs., sr. editor Earthjustice, 1986—. Author: Wild By Law: the Sierra Club Legal Defense Fund and the Places It Has Saved, 1990, Sierra Club: 100 Years of Protecting Nature, 1991; contbr. to The Ency. of the Environment, 1994, also chpts. to books; contbr. articles to Sierra, Defenders, Wilderness, San Francisco Chronicle, San Francisco Examiner, L.A. Times, Oakland Tribune,Washington Post, Mother Earth News, Outside, others. Office: Earthjustice 180 Montgomery St Ste 1400 San Francisco CA 94104-4236 E-mail: tturner@earthjustice.org

TURNHEIM, JOY KAREN, lawyer; b. Jersey City, Apr. 21, 1965; d. Palmer and Gloria Grace (Freer) T. AB, Dartmouth Coll., 1985; JD, Northwestern U., 1988; MBA with distinction, DePaul U., 1993; MPhil, NYU, 1997. Bar: Ill. 1988, U.S. Dist. Ct. (no. dist.) Ill. 1988. Law clk. to Hon. Sophia H. Hall Ill. Circuit Ct., Chgo., 1988-89; assoc. Nathanson & Wray, 1989-90, Horvath & Wigoda, Chgo., 1990; pvt. practice Law Offices Joy K. Turnheim, 1991—; exec. dir. Chenny Troupe, Chgo., 1993. Adj. prof. Columbia Coll., 1992-94; chpt. atty. Assn. Women in Metals Industry, 1989-91. Treas. Presbyn. Women in 4th Ch., Chgo., 1989-94; chmn. Silver Apple Ball, Chgo., 1990; moderator Kairos Fellowship, Chgo., 1990-92; deacon 4th Presbyn. Ch., 1992-95; mem. Jr. League Chgo., 1992—; chair Project CON!CERN, 1995—; founding mem., women's bd. Community Support Svcs., 1992-95; mem. Friends of Red Cross, 1990-94. Mem. ABA, Ill. State Bar Assn., Chgo. Bar Assn., Chgo. Soc. Clubs, Am. Inns of Ct. (Wigmore chpt.). Avocations: tennis, skiing, golf.

TURO, RON, lawyer; b. Fort Wayne, Ind., Apr. 2, 1955; s. John B. and Joan L. (Gluntz) T.; m. Claire Teresa Fetterman T., May 24, 1980; children: Andrew Jacob, Patricia Erin, Dominic Earl. BA in History with honors, Pa. State U., 1978; JD, Dickinson Sch. Law, 1981. Bar: Pa. 1981, U.S. Dist. (mid. dist.) Pa. 1982, U.S. Supreme Ct. 1987, U.S. Ct. Appeals (3d cir.) 1989. Ast. pub. defender Cumberland County, Carlisle, Pa., 1981-84; ptnr. Griffie & Turo, 1984-89; pvt. practice, 1989—. Lectr. Dickinson Sch. Law, 1996—, Weidener U. Sch. Law, 2000, adj. prof., 2001—. Founder Cumberland County Police Recognition Dinner, Carlisle, Pa., 1985—; mem. Nat. Cath. Com. on Scouting, 1988—; chmn. Region III, Pa., N.J., 1993-95, parliamentarian and legal coun., 1991—, advisor religious act, 1998-2000; bd. dirs. AHEDD, Inc., 1993-94, vice chmn. 1994-95, chmn., 1995—; trustee David E. Baker Scholarship Trust, 1997—; bd. dirs. Pa. Assn. for the Blind, 1998—, exec. search com., 1999-2000. Recipient St. George Emblem Boy Scouts Am., 1983, Eagle Scout 1969, Golden AAD Emblem, 1989. Mem. Nat. Lawyer's Assn., Nat. Assn. Criminal Def. Lawyers, Pa. Bar Assn., Pa. Assn. Criminal Def. Lawyers, Solicitor's Assn., Pa. Boroughs, Pa. Twp. Assns., Cumberland County Bar Assn. (social chmn. 1985-98, pub. rels. com. 1998—, bench-bar com. 1998—, membership chmn. 2000—), St. Thomas More Soc. (v.p. 1996-98, treas. 1998—), Mensa (local sec. 1990-92, editor 1992-95, ombudsman 2000—), KC (pres. Capital area chpt. 1989, Knight of Yr. 1981, grand knight 1985-87, 93-95, fin. sec. 1996—, dist. dep. 1998—). Republican. Roman Catholic. Avocations: scuba diving, travel. General civil litigation, Criminal. Office: 28 S Pitt St Carlisle PA 17013-3211 E-mail: RonTuro@TuroLaw.com

TUROFF, JACK NEWTON, lawyer; b. Cleve., Dec. 8, 1933; s. Herman and Jean Y. (Pearlman) T.; m. Carole R., Aug. 19, 1961; children: Hyleri, Raechel, Elana, Avril. BSBA, Ohio State U., 1955, JD, 1960. Bar: Ohio 1970, U.S. Dist. Ct. (no. dist.) Ohio 1961, U.S. Supreme Ct. 1969. Asst. atty. gen. State of Ohio, 1960-62; sole practice Cleve., 1960-62; assoc. Dudnik, Komito, Nurenberg, Plevin, Dempsey & Jacobson Assn., 1963-64; ptnr. Turoff & Turoff, 1965-81, 82—. Ptnr. Koplow, Pomerantz, Turoff & Turoff Co., L.P.A., Cleve., 1981-82; cons. and lectr. in field of bus. Bd. dirs., sec. Jewish Children Group Homes, 1962-78; mem. Dem. Exec. Com., 1963-79; state steering rep. Senator Henry Jackson Presdl. campaign, 1980; active Dem. county congl. campaigns; chmn. bd. Neighborhood Counseling Svc., 1980—; bd. dirs. West Side Community Mental Health Cr., 1982-88, Belle Found., 1995—; bd. trustees Belle Found., 1995. With USAF, 1956-59, USAFR, 1959-70. Recipient Svc. award Big Bros. Am., 1975, Outstanding Svc. award Neighborhood Counseling Svc., 1983. Mem. ATLA, Ohio State Bar Assn., Greater Cleve. Bar Assn., Cuyahoga County Bar Assn., Ohio Harness Horsemen's Assn (bd. dirs. 1983-89). KP. General civil litigation, General practice, Personal injury. Office: Turoff and Turoff 727 National City Bank Bldg 629 Euclid Ave Cleveland OH 44114-3003

TURRENTINE, HOWARD BOYD, federal judge; b. Escondido, Calif., Jan. 22, 1914; s. Howard and Veda Lillian (Maxfield) T.; m. Virginia Jacobsen, May 13, 1965 (dec.); children: Howard Robert, Terry Beverly; m. Marlene Lipsey, Nov. 1, 1991. AB, San Diego State Coll., 1936; LLB, U. So. Calif., 1939. Bar: Calif. 1939. Practiced in, San Diego, 1939-68; judge Superior Ct. County of San Diego, 1968-70, U.S. Dist. Ct. (so. dist.) Calif., Calif., sr. judge, 1970—. Served with USNR, 1941-45. Mem. ABA, Fed. Bar Assn., Am. Judicature Soc. Office: US Dist Ct 940 Front St San Diego CA 92101-8994

TUSCHMAN, JAMES MARSHALL, lawyer; b. Nov. 28, 1941; s. Chester and Harriet (Harris) T.; m. Ina S. Cheloff, Sept. 2, 1967; children: Chad Michael, Jon Stephen, Sari Anne. BS in Bus., Miami U., Oxford, Ohio, 1963; JD, Ohio State U., 1966. Bar: Ohio 1966, U.S. Ct. Appeals (6th and 7th cirs.), U.S. Supreme Ct. Assoc. Shumaker, Loop & Kendrick, Toledo, 1966-84, ptnr., 1970-84; co-founder, chmn. ops. com. Jacobson Maynard Tuschman & Kalur, 1985-97; COO Ohio Ferrous Group Omnisource Corp., 1998-99; dir. bus. devel. Northern Ohio Group, 1999—. Chmn. bd., sec. Tuschman Steel Co., Toledo, 1969-76, Toledo Steel Supply Co., 1969-86; vice-chmn. bd. Kripke Tuschman Industries, Inc., 1977-85; ptnr. Starr Ave. Co., Toledo, 1969-86. Chmn. bd. trustees U. Toledo; past trustee, chmn. fin. com., past treas. Maumee Valley Country Day Sch.; past trustee, v.p., treas. Temple B'nai Israel, 1984-88. Fellow Internat. Soc. Barristers; mem. Am. Bd. Trial Advocates, Ohio Bar Assn., Toledo Bar Assn., Toledo Club, Inverness Country Club, Zeta Beta Tau, Phi Delta Phi. Insurance, Personal injury. Home: 2579 Olde Brookside Rd Toledo OH 43615-2233 Office: Omnisource Corp 5130 N Detroit Ave Toledo OH 43612-3515 E-mail: jtuschman@omnisource.com

TUTHILL, JAMES PEIRCE, lawyer; b. Montclair, N.J., July 3, 1947; s. Oliver Wills and Virginia (Austin) T.; m. Wendy Booth, Feb. 28, 1970. B.A., Rockford Coll., Ill., 1969; J.D., Northwestern U., 1972. Bar: Ill. 1972, U.S. Ct. Appeals (7th cir.) 1980, Wis. 1981, Calif. 1984. Ptnr. firm Schuyler, Ballard and Cowen, Chgo., 1972-80; atty. Bucyrus-Erie Co., South Milwaukee, Wis., 1980-83, corp. atty. subs. co. Western Gear Corp., Lynwood, Calif., 1983-85; sr. atty. Pac Tel Mobile Access subs. Pacific Telesis Group, Costa Mesa, Calif., 1985— . Mem. fin. com. City of Delafield, Wis., 1982-83. Mem. Chgo. Bar Assn. (chmn. health and hosp. law com. young lawyers sect. 1977-79). Club: Chicago. State civil litigation, Contracts commercial, General corporate. Home: 3407 Stagecoach Dr Lafayette CA 94549-1817 Office: Pacific Bell 140 New Montgomery St Ste Bsmt San Francisco CA 94105-3705

TWARDY, STANLEY ALBERT, JR. lawyer; b. Trenton, N.J., Sept. 13, 1951; s. Stanley Albert Twardy and Dorothy M. Stonaker. BS with honors, Trinity Coll., 1973; JD, U. Va., 1976; LLM, Georgetown U., 1980. Bar: Conn. 1976, D.C. 1978, U.S. Supreme Ct. 1979, U.S. Ct. Appeals (2d cir.) 1984. Assoc. Whitman & Ransom, Greenwich, Conn., 1976-77; counsel com. on small bus. U.S. Senate, 1977-79, counsel to Senator Lowell Weicker Jr., 1979-80; ptnr. Silver, Golub & Sandak, Stamford, Conn., 1980-85; U.S. atty. Dist. of Conn., 1985-91; chief of staff Office of Gov. Lowell Weicker, Conn., 1991-93; ptnr. Day, Berry & Howard, Stamford, 1993—. Mem. nat. alumni exec. com. Trinity Coll., 1985—90, mem. athletic adv. com., 1992—, 1996—; chmn. City of Stamford Police Chief Selection Panel, 1993—94; mem. area adv. com. U. Conn. at Stamford, 1993—96; mem. strategic planning mgmt. com. U. Conn., 1993—95; Mem. vestry St. John's Episc. Ch., Stamford, 1983—86; bd. dirs. Drugs Don't Work!, 1989—93, 1994—2000, chmn. program com., 1989—91; bd. dirs. Spl. Olympics World Summer Games Organizing Com., Inc., 1993—95, Rehab. Ctr., 1993—, Stamford Health Found., 1995—. Mem. ABA, Conn. Bar Assn., Assn. Trial Lawyers Am., Conn. Trial Lawyers Assn., Phi Beta Kappa. Federal civil litigation, Constitutional, Criminal. E-mail: satwardy@dbh.com

TWEED, DOUGLAS STEVEN, lawyer; b. Cherry Point, N.C., Nov. 17, 1948; s. McDonald Douglass and Mary (Mullis) Tweed; m. Christie Moses, May 26, 1973; children— Jennifer, Jessica. B.A., Duke U., 1970, J.D., Vanderbilt U., 1973; jud. cert. Army Judges Course, Charlottesville, Va., 1977. Bar: Tenn. 1973, U.S. Ct. Mil. Appeals, 1974, U.S. Dist. Ct. (ea. dist.) Tenn. 1978, U.S. Ct. Appeals (6th cir.) 1984. Assoc. firm Hunter, Smith & Davis, Kingsport, Tenn., 1978-81, ptnr., 1981—. Served to capt. JAGC, USMC, 1973-78. Mem. staff Vanderbilt U Law Rev., 1972-73. Actor community theaters, Kingsport, 1980—; bd. dirs. Kingsport Fine Arts Ctr., Kingsport Tomorrow. Recipient Am. Jurisprudence award 1971. Mem. ABA, Def. Research Inst., Kingsport Bar Assn., Tenn. Bar Assn. Methodist. Federal civil litigation, Health, Employment. Office: Hunter Smith & Davis 1212 N Eastman Rd Kingsport TN 37664-3146

TWIETMEYER, DON HENRY, lawyer; b. Rochester, N.Y., June 4, 1954; s. Frederick Herman and Norma Frances (Porter) T.; m. Victoria Lynne Engleman, July 1, 1989; children: Laura Elizabeth, Jill Ann Cafarelli, Anthony R. Cafarelli. BA in Polit. Sci., Econs. with honors, SUNY, Buffalo, 1976; JD, Union U., 1979; LLM in Taxation, U. Miami, 1980; MBA in Acctg., Rochester Inst. Tech., 1983. Bar: N.Y. 1980, Fla. 1980, U.S. Ct. Cl. (we. dist.) N.Y. 1980, U.S. Dist. Ct. (so. dist.) Fla. 1980, U.S. Tax Ct. 1980, U.S. Ct. Appeals (5th and 11th cirs.) 1981, U.S. Supreme Ct. 1994, U.S. Bankruptcy Ct. 1994; CPA, N.Y. Tax acct. Davie, Kaplan & Braverman, Rochester, 1980-82; assoc. DeHond-Stowe Law Office, 1982-84, Lacy, Katzen, Ryen & Mittleman, Rochester, 1984-87;

mng. atty. DeHond Law Office, 1987-91, prin., 1991-92; assoc. Fix, Spindelman, Brovitz, Turk, Himelein & Shukoff, 1992-98; of counsel Saperston & Day, P.C., 1998—. Lectr. estate and gift taxes Found. Acctg. Edn., 1987-96. Author: Review and Update for Experienced Practitioners: Fiduciary, Estate and Gift Taxation, 1987-96. V.p. coun. Hope Luth. Ch., 1989-91, active meml. fund com., 1990-91, chmn. bldg. use com., 1990-91; chmn. missions and social concerns com. Bethlehem Luth. Ch., 1992-2000, mem. ch. coun., 1993-95, pres. ch. coun., 1994-95, deacon, 1994-95; mem. orgn. com. Luth. Charities Rochester Region, 1993-95, pres., dir., 1995-2000, adv. bd. dirs., 2000—; dir. Prevention Ptnrs., Inc., 1997—, pres., 2000—, fin. com., 1997—; mem. planned and deferred giving com. The Genesee Hosp. Found., 1998-2000. Mem. ABA (tax sect., entertainment and sports industries forum) Fla. Bar Assn. (tax sect., out of state practitioners divsn., real property, probate and trust sect.), N.Y. State Bar Assn. (tax sect., entertainment and sports law sect, trusts and estates sect.), Monroe County Bar Assn. (tax sect. and trusts and estates sect., exec. coun. 1996—, sec. 2000-01, chair 2001—, elder law com., intellectual property law com.), N.Y. State Soc. CPAs, Am. Assn. Atty.-CPAs, Estate Planning Coun. Rochester (exec. coun. 2000—), Rotary (internat. svc. com. 1994—, Rotary Internat. Found. com. 1994—, chairperson com. 1996—, Rochester Rotary Golf Tournament com. 1995-2000, planned giving com. 1997—), Phi Beta Kappa, Phi Alpha Delta, Omicron Delta Epsilon, Phi Eta Sima. Republican. Lutheran. Avocations: golf, tennis, skiing, philately. Entertainment, Estate planning, Taxation, general. Office: 2000 HSBC Plz Rochester NY 14604 Fax: (716) 325-5458. E-mail: dtwietmeyer@saperstonday.com

TWIG, JACK See BRANCH, JOHN WELLS

TWILLEY, JOSHUA MARION, lawyer; b. Dover, Del., Mar. 23, 1928; s. Joshua Marion and Alice Hunn (Dunn) T.; m. Rebecca Jane Buchanan, Dec. 27, 1952; children: Stephanie, Jeffrey, Linda Edgar, Joshua; m. Rosemary Miller, Dec. 1, 1972. BA cum laude, Harvard U., 1950, JD, 1953. Bar: Del. 1953, U.S. Dist. Ct. Del. 1960, U.S. Supreme Ct. 1976. Pvt. practice, Dover, 1955-72; sr. ptnr. Twilley, Jones & Feliceangeli, 1972-88, Twilley, Street & Brayerman, Dover, 1988-95, Twilley & Street, Dover, 1995—. Pres. Del. Indsl. Enterprises, Inc.; chmn. Incorporating Svcs. Ltd., Del. Incorporating Svcs. Ltd.; bd. dirs. 1st Nat. Bank Wyo.; sec. Sunshine Builders, Inc. mem. Del. Pub. Svc. Commn., 1975—, vice chmn. 1995—; pres. Kent County Levy Ct., 1970-75. Mem. exec. com. Del. Dem. Com., 1970-93; pres. Elizabeth Murphey Sch., 1957—. With U.S. Army, 1953-55. Mem ABA, Del. Bar Assn., Kent County Bar Assn. Democrat. Lutheran. Avocations: gardening, landscape architecture. Banking, Probate, Real property. Home: 124 Meadow Glen Dr Dover DE 19901-5544 Office: 426 S State St Dover DE 19901-6724 E-mail: rtwilley@erols.com

TWISS, ROBERT MANNING, prosecutor; b. Worcester, Mass., Aug. 2, 1948; s. Robert Sullivan Jr. and Marion (Manning) T.; m. Joan Marie Callahan, Aug. 4, 1979. BA, U. Mass., 1970; JD, U. San Francisco, 1975; MA in Criminal Justice, Wichita State U., 1979; LLM, Georgetown U., 1981. Bar: Mass. 1976, Calif., 1988, U.S. Ct. Appeals Armed Forces 1976, U.S. Dist. Ct. Mass. 1976, U.S. Ct. Appeals (1st cir.) 1976, U.S. Ct. Appeals (5th cir.) 1986, U.S. Ct. Appeals (9th cir.) 1988, U.S. Dist. Ct. (ea. and cen. dist.) Calif. 1989. Atty. office chief counsel IRS, Washington, 1980-86; trial atty. criminal div. U.S. Dept. Justice, 1986-87, asst. U.S. atty. Sacramento, 1987-93, 94—, chief organized crime and narcotics, 1991-92, 1st asst. U.S. atty., 1992-93, U.S. atty., 1993, exec. assst. U.S. atty., 1994. Contbr. articles to profl. jours. Capt. JAGC, U.S. Army, 1976-80 Named to McAuliffe Honor Soc. U. San Francisco, 1975; recipient Markham award Office Chief Counsel IRS, Washington, 1985. Avocation: athletics. Office: Office US Atty 501 I St 10th Fl Sacramento CA 95814-7306

TWITCHELL, E(RVIN) EUGENE, lawyer; b. Salt Lake City, Mar. 4, 1932; s. Irvin A. and E. Alberta (Davis) T.; m. Joyce A. Newey, Aug. 9, 1957 (div. May 1989); children: Robert R., Lauren E., David J., Michael S.; m. Linda Sue Wilson, 1991; children: Bonnie Wilson, Jimmy Wilson, Benjamin Wilson, Stefanie Wilson. Student, Brigham Young U., 1954-55; BA, Calif. State U., Long Beach, 1959; JD, UCLA, 1966. Bar: Mich. 1977, U.S. Dist. Ct. (ea. dist.) Mich., U.S. Supreme Ct. 1987. Contract adminstr. Rockwell No. Am. Aviation, Seal Beach, Calif., 1966-68; sr. contracts adminstr. McDonnell Douglas Corp., Long Beach, 1968-73; in-house counsel Albert C. Martin & Assocs., L.A., 1973-77; instr. bus. law Golden West Coll., Huntington Beach, 1973-74; corp. counsel, corp. sec. Barton Malow Co., Southfield, Mich., 1977-97, ret., 1997. Mem. Detroit EEO Forum, 1983-87; arbitrating and cons., 1997—. Editl. cartoonist Eufaula Tribune, 2001—. Pres. Corona (Calif.) Musical Theater, 1975-76; dist. chmn. Boy Scouts of Am.-North Trails, Oakland County, Mich., 1978-80; treas. Barton Malow PAC, Southfield, 1983-97. Sgt. USAF, 1950-52. Mem. ABA, Mich. Bar Assn., Am. Arbitration Assn. (arbitrator Detroit, Ala., Ga., and Fla. areas 1985-97, arbitrator Ala.-Ga. area 1997—), Am. Corp. Counsel Assn. (v.p., dir. 1983-97). Republican. Mem. LDS Ch. Avocations: cartooning, painting, karate, music, theatre, writing. Alternative dispute resolution, Construction, Labor. Home and office: 142 Gammage Rd Eufaula AL 36027-5874 E-mail: twitchell@mindspring.com

TWOMEY, THOMAS A., JR. lawyer, educator; b. N.Y.C., Dec. 8, 1945; s. Thomas A. and Mary (Maloney) T.; m. Judith Hope Twomey, Dec. 15, 1979; stepchildren: Erling Hope, Nisse Hope. BA, Manhattan Coll., 1967; postgrad., U.Va., 1967-68; JD, Columbia U., 1970. Bar: N.Y. 1972, U.S. Tax Ct. 1974. Asst. town atty. Town of Southampton N.Y., 1973-74; spl. asst. dist. atty. Suffolk County, N.Y., 1973-74; pvt. practice law Riverhead, 1974-75; ptnr. Hubbard & Twomey, 1976-79, Twomey, Latham, Shea & Kelley, Riverhead, 1980—. Chair N.Y. State East End Econ. and Environ. Task Force, 1993; mem. deans coun. Stonybrook Sch. Medicine, 1991—; adj. prof. environ. law Southampton Coll., 1977-78. Bd. dirs. East End Arts Coun., Riverhead, 1983, Guild Hall East Hampton, 1993—; bd. dirs. East Hampton Libr., 1994—, pres., 1998—; trustee L.I. Power Authority, 1989-94; town historian, Town of East Hampton, 1999, vice chair East Hampton Town 350th Anniversary com., 1998, editor East Hampton Histor. Collection; historian N.Y. State Dem. Com., 2000-01; chair East Hampton 350th lecture series, 1998. Recipient Environ. award, U.S. EPA, 1980. Mem. ABA, Suffolk County Bar Assn., State Energy Coun., N.Y. State Fresh Water Wetlands Appeals Bd. Democrat. State civil litigation, Estate planning, Real property. Home: PO Box 398 Riverhead NY 11901-0203 Office: Twomey Latham Shea & Kelley 33 W 2nd St Riverhead NY 11901-2701

TYACK, THOMAS MICHAEL, lawyer; b. Columbus, Ohio, June 20, 1940; s. George E. and E. Naomi (Ballard) T.; m. Patricia J. Clark, Sept. 7, 1969; children: Jonathan, Jeffrey, James, Justin. BA cum laude, Ohio State U., Columbus, 1962, Jd, 1965. Bar: Ohio 1965, U.S. Ct. Appeals (6th cir.) 1970, U.S. Supreme Ct. 1970, U.S. Dist. Ct. (so. dist.) Ohio 1972. Ptnr. Tyack, Scott & Colley, Columbus, 1965-79, Tyack Scott & Wiseman, Columbus, 1979-81; prin. Thomas M. Tyack Assocs. Co., L.P.A., 1981-90; ptnr. Tyack & Blackmore Co., L.P.A., 1991-94; pres. Tyack, Blackmore & Liston Co. LPA, 1994—. Bar examiner Ohio supreme Ct., 1975-80; lectr., legal asst. program Capital U., Ohio, 1977-90. Fellow Am. Coll. Trial Lawyers; mem. ABA, Ohio Bar Assn., Columbus Bar Assn., Franklin Ct. and Trial Lawyers, Assn. Trial Lawyers Am., Ohio Acad. Trial Lawyers, Ohio Acad. Trial Lawyers, Ohio Acad. Criminal Def. Lawyers, NDCDL. Republican. Methodist. Criminal, Family and matrimonial, Personal injury. Office: 536 S High St Columbus OH 43215-5605

TYLER, JOHN EDWARD, III, lawyer; b. Kansas City, Mo. BA, U. Notre Dame, 1986, JD, 1989. From assoc. to ptnr. Lathrop & Gage L.C., Kansas City, 1989-99; gen. counsel, sec. Ewing Marion Kauffman Found., 1999—. Adj. prof. Rockhurst U., Kansas City, 2000—. Contbr. articles to profl. jours. Pres. Genesis Sch., Kansas City, 1995-96, 96-97; pres. Archbishop O'Hara H.S., Kansas City, 1994-95, 95-96, 96-97; chair tax increment fin. commn. city of Raytown, Mo., 1997-99; bd. dirs. Ctr. for Mgmt. Assistance, Kansas City, pres., 1999, 2000, 2001. Named Man of Yr. Leukemia Soc., Kansas City, 1998, Bernie Hoffman award for cmty. svc. Cmty. Svc. Awards Found., 1997. Mem. ABA, Mo. Bar Assn. (Thomas D. Cochran award for cmty. svc. 1995), Kans. Bar Assn., Kansas City Metro. Bar Assn. (young lawyer of yr. 1998). Intellectual property, Labor, Non-profit and tax-exempt organizations. Home: 2420 SW Wintercreek Ct Lees Summit MO 64081-4085 Office: Ewing Marion Kauffman Found 4801 Rockhill Rd Kansas City MO 64110-2046

TYLER, MARVIN LEE, lawyer; b. Lander, Wyo., Jan. 28, 1955; s. Kenneth G. and Dorothy J. (DeWester) T.; m. Debra A. Taylor, July 26, 1975; children— Christopher Lindsey, Kara Janelle. A.A., Western Wyo. Community Coll., 1976; B.S., U. Wyo., 1977, J.D., 1981. Bar: Wyo. 1981. Assoc., Venta & Bath, Rock Springs, Wyo., 1981-83; ptnr. Bath & Tyler, Rock Springs, 1983— ; mcpl. judge Superior Mcpl. Ct., Wyo., 1981-84; dist. ct. commr. 3d Jud. Dist. Ct., Sweetwater County, Wyo., 1983— ; county ct. commr. Sweetwater County Ct., 1983— ; instr. Western Wyo. Community Coll., Rock Springs, 1981— . Bd. dirs. Vol. Info. and Referral Service, Rock Springs, 1981-84. Mem. ABA, Assn. Trial Lawyers Am., Wyo. Trial Lawyers Assn., Comml. Law League, Sweetwater County Bar Assn. Democrat. Methodist. Lodge: Elks. Office: Bath & Tyler 548 Broadway Rock Springs WY 82901

TYLER, PEGGY LYNNE BAILEY, lawyer; b. Seattle, Oct. 15, 1948; d. John Thomas and Doris Mae (Lindgren) Bailey; m. Tom Kenneth Newton, May 25, 1975 (div. 1980); m. Allan Gregory Lambert, Aug. 3, 1980 (div. May 1996); m. Charles Kevin Tyler, Sept. 12, 1997; children: Eli Raven, Joshua Alec. BA in Psychology, Beloit Coll., 1970; MS in Counseling Psychology, Ill. Inst. Tech., 1973; JD, Syracuse (N.Y.) U., 1978. Bar: D.C. 1983. Mental health specialist Ill. Dept. Mental Health, Chgo., 1971-72; mem. rsch. faculty Cornell U., Ithaca, N.Y., 1973-75; assoc. O'Connor, Sovocool, Pfann and Greenburg, 1978, Dacy, Richin & Meyers, Silver Springs, Md., 1979-81; ins. adminstr. Nat. Assn. Broadcasters, Washington, 1981-86, dir. ins. programs, 1986-90; assoc. Architect of the Capitol, 1990—. Co-author, editor: Broadcaster's Property and Liability Insurance Buying Guide, 1989. Bd. dirs. Hartford-Thayer Condominium Assn., 1994—, pres., 1995-96, sec., 1996-2000, treas., 2000—. Mem. D.C. Bar Assn. (mem. steering com. of arts entertainment, sports law sect. 1989-90, sect. editor newsletter 1989-90). Democrat. Jewish. Avocations: antiques, gourmet cooking, ballet. Office: Architect of the Capitol Office of Employment Counsel Rm H2-202 Ford House Office Bldg Washington DC 20515-0001 E-mail: ptyler@aoc.gov

TYSON, LAURA LANZA, lawyer; b. L.A., Sept. 29, 1971; d. Anthony Matthew and Laura Rimer Lanza; m. Michael Jay Tyson, Aug. 10, 1991. BS in Econs., McNeese State U., 1993; JD, U. Houston, 1997. Assoc. Winstead Sechrest & Minick PC, Houston, 1997-98, Baker Botts LLP, Houston, 1998—. Mem. Travis County Bar Assn. General corporate, Securities. Home: 2704 Fall Creek Estates Dr Spicewood TX 78669 Office: Baker Botts LLP 1600 San Jacinto Ctr 98 San Jacinto Blvd Austin TX 78701

TZANGAS, GEORGE JOHN, lawyer; b. Canton, Ohio, Oct. 1, 1930; s. John M. and Mary (Christian) T.; student Kent State U., 1948-50; BSC, Ohio U., 1952; J.D. (Univ. scholar), Washington and Lee U., 1956; m. Venus Mouskondis, Aug. 31, 1952; children: Marianne Tzangas Weiss, John Daniel, Byron George. Office mgr. Minerva (Ohio) plant U.S. Ceramic Tile Co., 1956-58; admitted to Ohio bar, 1957, U.S. Supreme Ct., 1979; sr. partner Tzangas, Plakas & Mannos, Canton, 1957—; dir. numerous cos. Bd. dirs. numerous charitable corps.; co-founder, pres. World Wide Orthodox Renewal for Christ, Inc., Canton; trustee Canton Scholarship Found.; mem. world missions com., spiritual renewal com. Greek Orthodox Ch. of N.Am. and S.Am.; mem. Bishop's Council, Pitts. Diocese, Greek Orthodox Ch. Mem. Fed. Bar Assn., Am., Ohio State, Stark County bar assns., Ohio Acad. Trial Lawyers, Assn. Trial Lawyers, Assn. Trial Lawyers Am., Am. Arbitration Assn. (panel 1977), Civil Justice Found., Am. Bankruptcy Inst., Comml. Law League Am., Christian Legal Soc., Canton Assn. Chs. (bd. dirs.), Phi Alpha Delta. Greek Orthodox. Author: Secrets of Life, 1971; (as John Christian) Have You Talked to Him?, 1974, Junkyard Princess, 1982. Federal civil litigation, Environmental, Land use and zoning (including planning). Office: 454 Citizens Savs Bldg Canton OH 44702

UBALDI, MICHAEL VINCENT, lawyer; b. Stockton, Calif., May 2, 1948; s. Ben Raymond and Audrey Grace (Smalley) U.; m. Terryanne Ubaldi (div. Apr. 1990); children: Jennifer N., Justin M.; m. Linda A. Ubaldi, Feb. 14, 1991. BA, Calif. State U., Sacramento, 1971; JD, U. Calif., San Francisco, 1974. Bar: Calif. 1974. Assoc. Bullen, McKone & McKinley, Sacramento, 1974-81; ptnr. Duncan, Ball, Evans & Ubaldi, 1981—. Bd. dirs. Sutter Hosps. Found., Sacramento, 1985-92, Make-A-Wish Found., Sacramento, 1990-98, Mercy Hosps. Found., Sacramento, 1993—; mem. bus. adv. bd. Sch. Bus. Calif. State U., Sacramento, 1999—. Mem. No. Calif. Assn. Def. Counsel (bd. dirs. 1998—). Avocations: golf, art, travel. Personal injury. Office: Duncan Ball Evans & Ubaldi 641 Fulton Ave Fl 2D Sacramento CA 95825-4800

UCHE, JACK-OSIMIRI, law educator; b. Rumuodogo, Nigeria, Sept. 14, 1960; m. Ngozi Osimiri; 3 children. LLM, Queen Mary Coll., London, 1984; B of Law, Nigerian Law Sch., Lagos, 1985. Projects tutor, rsch. coord. Abia State U., Uturu, 1988-94; head dpet. pvt. law U. Ado-Ekiti, 1998-2000; dean daculty law Ebonyl State U., Abakaliki, 2000—. Author: Modern Law of Landlord & Tenant in Nigeria, 1994, Fundamentals of Insurance Law in Nigeria, 1999, Nigerian Law of Landed Property; co-author: (chpts.) Nature of Standard Rents and its far Reacing Implication, 1996, Prsonnel, Supervision and Independence, 1996, Introduction to Law of Landed Property, 1999, Introduction to Easements & Profits and Mortgages, 1999; contbr. articles to profl. jours., newspapers. Rivers State Govt. Spl. Merit scholar, 1980-83; Lawrence Artwell London grantee, 1982-83. Fellow Soc. Advanced Legal Studies, Soc. Pub. Tchrs. Law; mem. Nigerian Bar Assn., Chartered Inst. Taxation Nigeria, Nigerian Assn. Law Tchrs., Internat. Bar Assn., Civil Liberties Orgn., Commonwealth Assn. Legal Edn. London, Acad. Staff Union Univs., Nigeria Environ. Law Soc., Hon. Soc. Inner Temples London. Avocations: reading, Christian music, football, travel. Address: 7 Ikwerre/Nanka St PO Box 5767 Port Harcourt Nigeria E-mail: osimiri@ph.nipost.com.ng

UCHTMANN, DONALD LOUIS, lawyer, law educator; b. East St. Louis, Ill., Sept. 18, 1946. BA in Agrl. Sci., U. Ill., 1968; MA in Econ. Devel., U. Leeds, Eng., 1972; JD, Cleve. State U., 1974. Bar: Ohio 1974, Ill. 1975. Asst. prof. U. Ill., Urbana, 1974-79, assoc. prof., 1979-82, prof. agrl. law, 1982—, vice chair U. Ill. senate, 1986-87, acting head dept. agrl. econs., 1987-88, dir. coop. extension svc., assoc. dean, 1988-95; legis. asst. Congressman Edward Madigan, Washington, 1982; participant internat. agrl. law programs. Author: (textbook) Agricultural Law: Principles and Cases; contbr. articles to profl. jours. Lt. USCGR, 1968-71. Fellow for internat. understanding Rotary Internat., Leeds, Eng., 1971. Bd. trustees Nat. 4-H Coun., 1994-95. Mem. Am. Agrl. Law Assn. (pres. 1981-82), Ill. Bar Assn., Rotary, Omicron Delta Kappa, Alpha Zeta, Gamma Sigma Delta. Office: U Ill 335 Mumford Hall 1301 W Gregory Dr Urbana IL 61801-9015

UDALL, THOMAS (TOM UDALL), congressman; b. Tucson, May 18, 1948; s. Stewart and Lee Udall; m. Jill Z. Cooper; 1 child, Amanda Cooper. BA, Prescott Coll., 1970; LLB, Cambridge U., Eng., 1975; JD, U. N.Mex., 1977. Law clk. to Hon. Oliver Seth U.S. Ct. Appeals (10th cir.), Santa Fe, 1977-78; asst. U.S. atty. U.S. Atty.'s Office, 1978-81; pvt. practice Santa Fe, 1981-83; chief counsel N.Mex. Health & Environ. Dept., 1983-84; ptnr. Miller, Stratvert, Togerson & Schlenker, P.A., Albuquerque, 1985-90; atty. gen. State of N.Mex., 1991-98; mem. 106th Congress from NM 3rd dist., 1999—, mem. small bus. com., mem. resources com., mem. vets.' affairs com. Past pres. Rio Chama Preservation Trust; mem. N.Mex. Environ. Improvement Bd., 1986—87; bd. dirs. La Compania de Teatro de Albuquerque, Santa Fe Chamber Music Festival, Law Fund. Mem. Nat. Assn. Attys. Gen. (pres. 1996), Kiwanis. Democrat. Office: US Ho Reps 502 Cannon HOB Washington DC 20515-0001 E-mail: tom.udall@mail.house.gov

UDASHEN, ROBERT NATHAN, lawyer; b. Amarillo, Tex., June 10, 1953; s. Leo Joe and Esther K. (Klugsberg) U.; m. Dale Lynn Sandgarten, Aug. 15, 1976. BA with high honors, U. Tex., 1974, JD, 1977. Bar: Tex. 1977, U.S. Ct. Appeals (5th cir.) 1978, U.S. Dist. Ct. (no. and so. dists.) Tex. 1978, U.S. Ct. Appeals (11th cir.) 1981, U.S. Supreme Ct. 1981, U.S. Dist. Ct. (ea. dist.) Tex. 1989, U.S. Dist. Ct. (we. dist.) Tex. 1991. Staff atty. Staff Counsel for Inmates, Huntsville, Tex., 1977-79; assoc., ptnr. Crowder, Mattox & Udashen, Dallas, 1979-85; ptnr. Udashen & Goldstucker, 1985-87; pvt. practice, 1987-94; ptnr. Milner, Lobel, Goranson, Sorrels, Udashen & Wells, Dallas, 1995-2000, Milner, Goranson, Sorrels, Udashen & Wells, Dallas, 2000—. Bd. dirs. Open, Inc., Dallas; instr. trial advocacy Sch. Law So. Meth. U., 1993-95; adj. prof. criminal procedure Sch. Law So. Meth. U., 1998-99, 2001. Contbr. articles to profl. jours. Adv. bd. Coalition for Safer Dallas, 1994. Mem. State Bar Tex. (penal code com. 1992-93), Nat. Assn. Criminal Def. Lawyers, Tex. Criminal Def. Lawyers Assn., Dallas Criminal Def. Lawyers Assn. Criminal. Office: Milner Goranson Sorrels Udashen & Wells 2515 Mckinney Ave Ste 1500 Dallas TX 75201-7604 E-mail: rudashen@att.net

UDELL, RICHARD, lawyer; b. Bklyn., Dec. 27, 1932; s. Alvin and Gertrude (Langsam) U.; m. Marguerite Hartshorne, July 3, 1955; m. children: Benjamin Alan, Edward H. BA, Reed Coll., 1955; LLB, U. Pa., 1958. Bar: N.Y. 1958, Fla. 1984. Pvt. practice, N.Y.C., 1959-65; counsel RCA Records, 1965-69; assoc. firm Machat & Kronfeld, 1969-71; counsel Famous Music Corp., 1971-72, Random House, Inc. subs. RCA, N.Y.C., 1972-75; gen. counsel Simon & Schuster, Inc. subs. Gulf & Western Industries, Inc., 1975-77; adminstrv. v.p., chief counsel Harcourt Brace Jovanovich, Inc., 1977-92; v.p., gen. counsel The McGraw Hill Sch. Pub. Co. unit McGraw-Hill Cos., Inc., 1992—. Mem. Bar Assn. City N.Y., Orange County Bar Assn., Fla. Bar Assn. Jewish. General corporate, Libel, Trademark and copyright. Office: McGraw-Hill Sch Pub Co 2 Penn Plz New York NY 10121-0101

UEHLEIN, E(DWARD) CARL, JR. lawyer; b. Boston, May 7, 1941; s. Edward Carl and Elizabeth (Thatcher) U.; m. Judith Taylor, June 16, 1962; children: Christine, Sara. Student, Bowdoin Coll., Brunswick, Maine, 1958-59; BA, Swarthmore Coll., 1962; LLB, Boston Coll., 1965. Bar: Mass. 1965, D.C. 1968. Atty. Nat. Labor Relations Bd., Atlanta, 1965-68; assoc. Morgan, Lewis & Bockius, Washington, 1968-71; exec. asst. to sec. U.S. Dept. Labor, 1971-73; ptnr. Morgan Lewis & Bockius, 1973—. Sec.-treas. Carlou Corp., Wilmington, Del., 1969-71. Fellow Ford Found., 1961. Mem. ABA, FBA, D.C. Bar Assn., Belle Haven Country Club, Ballybunion Golf Club, Royal Dornoch Golf Club. Republican. Avocations: travel, golf, reading. Labor. Office: Morgan Lewis & Bockius 1800 M St NW Washington DC 20036-5802 E-mail: ecuehlein@morganlewis.com

UEHLINGER, GERARD PAUL, lawyer; b. N.Y.C., July 30, 1949; s. Gerard Paul and Dorothy (Karthaus) U.; m. Julianne McGiffert, June 3, 1972; children— Kevin Gerard, Gregory James, Elizabeth Ann. A.B., Princeton U., 1971; J.D., U. Md., 1975. Bar: Md. 1975, U.S. Dist. Ct. Md. 1976, U.S. Ct. Appeals (4th cir.) 1979. Law clk. Ct. Appeals Md., 1975-76; assoc. Piper & Marbury, Balt., 1976-79, Gordon, Feinblatt et al, Balt., 1979-81, Law Office of Jerome Blum, Balt., 1981-83, Lentz, Hooper, Jacobs & Blevins, Balt., 1983-88. Chmn. Balt. City Foster Care Rev. Bd., East Region 1, 1980-86; mem. State Foster Care Rev. Bd., 1983-86; bd. of trustees Fellowship of Lights, Inc., 1985-88; pres. Md. Friends of Foster Children Found., Inc., 1987—; counsel several charitable religious and social orgns.. Mem. ABA, Md. State Bar Assn., Bar Assn. Balt. City (exec. com. young lawyers 1981-83, exec. com. 1982-83). Democrat. Roman Catholic. General civil litigation, Personal injury, Workers' compensation. Home: 504 Anneslie Rd Baltimore MD 21212-2009 Office: 1401 Munsey Bldg 7 N Calvert St Baltimore MD 21202-1940

UFBERG, MURRAY, lawyer; b. Danville, Pa., July 30, 1943; s. Alfred Eugene and Leah (Abrams) U.; m. Margery Ann Fishman, June 29, 1969; children: Aaron, Joshua, Rachel. BA, Bucknell U., 1964; JD, Duquesne U., 1968. Bar: Pa. 1969, U.s. Dist. Ct. (mid. dist.) Pa. Assoc. Rosenn, Jenkins & Greenwald, Wilkes-Barre, Pa., 1969-74; ptnr. Rosenn, Jenkins & Greenwald, L.L.P., 1974—. Chair Greater Wilkes-Barre Partnership, Inc., bd. dirs.; mem. legal com. Pa. Savs. Leagues, Inc. Chmn. United Way Wyo. Valley Gen. Campaign, Wilkes-Barre, 1990, bd. dirs. 1992-99; past pres. Ohav Zedek Synagogue, Wilkes-Barre, 1986-88, Jewish Cmty. Ctr. Wyoming Valley, 1982-83, Seligman J. Strauss Lodge/B'nai B'rith, Wilkes-Barre, 1970-74; bd. dirs., chmn. cmty. rels. coun. Jewish Cmty. Bd., 1993-97, 2000—; chmn. Jewish Cmty. Bd. of Wyoming Valley, 1997—, pres. Jewish Fedn. Greater Wilkes-Barre; mem. Coll. Misericordia; mem. Luzerne County adv. com. Pa. Economy League; mem. Pres. Adv. Coun. Keystone Coll.; chmn. Greater Wilkes-Barre Partnership, 2001—. Recipient Disting. Svc. award Wilkes-Barre Jaycees, 1979. Mem. ABA, Pa. Bar Assn., Luzerne County Bar Assn. (chmn. cmty. rels. com. 1997—), Wilkes-Barre Law and Libr. Assn., Duquesne U. Law Alumni Assn. (bd. govs.). Jewish. Avocations: sports, recreational reading. Contracts commercial, General corporate, Real property. Home: 644 Charles Ave Kingston PA 18704 Office: Rosenn Jenkins & Greenwald 15 S Franklin St Wilkes Barre PA 18711-0075 also: 120 E Broad St Hazleton PA 18201 also: 120 Wyoming Ave Scranton PA 18503 E-mail: mufberg@rfjlaw.com

UFFELMAN, JOHN EDWARD, lawyer; b. Portland, Oreg., Apr. 28, 1948; s. Edward Beebe and Margaret Mary (Mayer) U.; m. Patricia Ann Buck, June 24, 1972; 4 children. B.A., Gonzaga U., 1970; J.D., U. Oreg., 1973. Bar: Oreg. 1973, U.S. Dist. Ct. Oreg. 1974. Atty. Brink Moore Brink & Peterson, Hillsboro, Oreg. Trustee Mayer Found., Portland, Oreg., 1973-80, N.W. Outward Bound, Pacific Crest Outward Bound, Portland, 1978— . Republican. Roman Catholic. Lodges: Kiwanis, Elks. State civil litigation, Personal injury, Workers' compensation. Office: Brink Moore Brink & Peterson 163 SE 2nd Ave Hillsboro OR 97123-4026

UFFORD, CHARLES WILBUR, JR. lawyer; b. Princeton, N.J., July 8, 1931; m. Isabel Letitia Wheeler, May 20, 1961; children: Eleanor Morris Ufford Léger, Catherine Latourette Ufford-Chase, Alison Wistar Ufford Salem. BA cum laude (Francis H. Burr scholar), Harvard U., 1953, LLB, 1959; postgrad. (Lionel de Jersey Harvard studentship), Cambridge U., Eng., 1953-54. Bar: N.Y. 1961, U.S. Tax Ct. 1963. Assoc. Riggs, Ferris & Geer, N.Y.C., 1959-61; from assoc. to ptnr. Jackson, Nash, Brophy, Barringer & Brooks, 1961-78; ptnr. Skadden, Arps, Slate, Meagher & Flom, N.Y.C., 1978-92, of counsel, 1993-96. Contbr. articles to legal jours. Trustee Nat. Squash Racquets Edni. Found., N.Y.C., 1972-81; mem. Princeton monthly Meeting, Soc. of Friends, clk., 1986-88, 99; mem. exec. com. Friends Com. on Nat. Legislation, 1997-98; dir. Pennswood Village,

1998—. Nat. Intercollegiate Squash Racquets champion, 1952-53; mem. NCAA All-Am. Soccer lst team, 1952. Fellow Am. Coll. Trust and Estate Counsel (transfer tax study com. 1990-93); mem. ABA, N.Y. Bar Assn. (chmn. trusts and estates law sect. 1984), Assn. Bar City N.Y., N.Y. State Office of Ct. Adminstrn. (Surrogates Ct. Adv. Com., 1994-96), U.S. Squash Racquets Assn. (hon. life; trustee endowment fund 1984-96), Internat. Lawn Tennis Club U.S.A. (dir. 1982—). Office: 150 Mercer St Princeton NJ 08540-6827 E-mail: cuffordl@aol.com

UGHETTA, WILLIAM CASPER, lawyer, manufacturing company executive; b. N.Y.C., Feb. 8, 1933; s. Casper and Frieda (Bohland) U.; m. Mary L. Lusk, Aug. 10, 1957; children: William C., Robert L., Edward F., Mark R. AB, Princeton U, 1954; LLB, Harvard U., 1959. Bar: N.Y. 1959. Assoc. Shearman & Sterling, N.Y.C., 1959-67; asst. sec. Corning Glass Works, N.Y., 1968-70, sec., counsel, 1971-72, v.p., gen. counsel, 1972-82, sr. v.p., gen. counsel, 1983-98. Bd. dirs. Chemung Canal Trust Co., Covance Inc. Bd. dirs. Steuben Area coun. Boy Scouts Am.; officer Corning Glass Works Found.; trustee Corning C.C. Lt. (j.g.) USN, 1954-56. Mem. Assn. of Bar of City of N.Y., ABA, N.Y. State Bar Assn., Am. Corp. Counsel Assn. (trustee 1982-85), Princeton Club (N.Y.C.), Univ. Club (N.Y.C.), Corning Country Club. General corporate. Home: 13 North Rd Corning NY 14830-3235

UHERBELAU, JUDY, lawyer, state legislator; b. Masury, Ohio, Aug. 1, 1938; d. Richard C. and Audrey Bean Harriff; children: Angela J., Rebecca A. Nursing diploma, White Cross Hosp. Sch. Nursing, 1959; BS in Polit. Sci. and Econs., Ball State U., 1978; JD, UCLA, 1981. Bar: Calif. 1981, Oreg. 1982, U.S. Ct. Appeals (9th cir.), U.S. Ct. Claims, U.S. Dist. Ct. Oreg.; RN, Calif. Nurse, nurse instr. various hosps. and health care ctrs., 1961-73; atty. Thomas C. Howser, P.C., Ashland, Oreg., 1981—; state rep. Oreg. Ho. of Reps., Salem, 1994—2001. Bd. dirs. AIDS Task Force, 1985-87, Ashland Cmty. Hosp., 1989-96, treas., 1991-94; mem. adv. bd. Ashland H.S. Health and Support Ctr., 1990-94; mem. Jackson County Budget Com., 1991-94; bd. dirs. Cmty. Dispute Resolution Ctr., 1993-97; electoral supr. Bosnia, The Orgn. for Security and Cooperation in Europe, 1996, 97. Recipient Appreciation award MADD, 1998, Commendation award ACLU, 1998, Nancy Peterson Meml. award Rogue Valley Women's Polit. Caucus, 1999, Lindeman award Area Health Edn. Ctr. S.W. Oreg., 1999, State award for excellence Am. Acad. Nurse Practitioners, 1999; named Legislator of the Yr., Oreg. Hunter's Assn., 1995, Woman of Distinction, Soroptomists Internat., 1998, Legislator of Yr., Oreg. Nurses Assn., 1999. Mem. Oreg. State Bar (mem. law related edn. com. 1986-89, chair law related edn. com. 1988-89, mem. ethics com. 1992-95, chair ethics com. 1994-95, mem. practice and procedure com. 1995-98, jud. com. 2000-, House of Dels. 2000-, disciplinary trial bd. 2001-). Home: PO Box 640 Ashland OR 97520-0307 Office: 607 Siskiyou Blvd Ashland OR 97520-2139 also: PO Box 640 Ashland OR 97520-1825

UHL, CHRISTOPHER MARTIN, lawyer; b. Balt., Feb. 21, 1958; s. Robert Henry and Marie Antoinette (Carosella) U.; m. Gael Anna Evangelista, Feb. 16, 1991; children: Christopher Martin Uhl, Grace Molinari Uhl. BS in Acctg., Northeastern U., 1989, MBA, 1991; JD, New Eng. Sch. Law, 1992. Bar: Mass. 1993, N.Y. 1993, U.S. Dist. Ct. Mass. 1993, D.C. 1994, Maine 1994, U.S. Dist. Ct. D.C. 1994, U.S. Dist. Maine 1994, Conn. 1995, U.S. Supreme Ct., 1998, U.S. Dist. Ct. (ea. and so. dists.) N.Y. 1999, U.S. Dist. Ct. Conn. 1999, U.S. Ct. Appeals (1st cir.) 2000. Fingerprint technician FBI, Washington, 1976-79; project mgr. various constrn. cos., Balt., 1979-87, Admiral Constrn. Co., Boston, 1987-91; asst. dist. atty. Worcester (Mass.) Dist. Atty.'s Office, 1992-96; prin. Christopher Uhl, Attorney at Law, Worcester, 1997—. Prof. Becker Coll., Worcester, 1993-97. Bd. dirs. Am. Cancer Soc., Boston, 1990-96; ward coord. Reelect Dist. Atty. Campaign, Worcester, 1994; elected mem. Southborough Rep. Town Com., Southborough Housing Authority, Northborough/Southborough Regional Sch. Com. Named Hon. Mem. Rep. State Com. Republican. Roman Catholic. Roman Catholic. Office: 5 State St Worcester MA 01609-2893 Fax: (508) 797-4210. E-mail: attorney@uhllaw.com

ULLMAN, JAMES A. lawyer; b. Buffalo, Dec. 14, 1946; s. Robert A. and Sonya A. Ullman; m. Vivian E. Klein, Sept. 5, 1970; children: Alysa, Andrew, Lindsay. BA, U. Mich., 1968; JD, SUNY, Buffalo, 1971. Bar: N.Y 1972, Ariz. 1972, U.S. Dist. Ct. Ariz., U.S. Dist. Ct. (we. dist.) N.Y., U.S. Supreme Ct. 1984. Ptnr. Dagett & Ullman, Phoenix, 1973-76; sole practice, 1976-87, 93-98; ptnr. Eaton Dodge & Lazarus, 1987-89, Heron Burchette et al., Phoenix, Washington, 1988-90, Jennings Strouss & Salmon, Phoenix, 1990-93; sr. mem. O'Connor, Cavanagh, Anderson, Killingsworth & Beshears, 1998—. Instr. Maricopa C.C., Phoenix, 1996; adj. prof. law Western Internat. U., Phoenix, 1996-97. Contbr. articles to profl. jours. Chmn., mem. State C.C. Bd., 1990-97; pres., mem. State Bd. Edn., Ariz., 1991-97. Mem. Edn. Law Assn. (past pres.). Avocations: gourmet cooking, travel. Education and schools, Franchising, Trademark and copyright. Office: Greenberg Traurig 1 E Camelback Rd Ste 1100 Phoenix AZ 85012-1656

ULRICH, PAUL GRAHAM, lawyer, writer, editor; b. Spokane, Wash., Nov. 29, 1938; s. Donald Gunn and Kathryn (Vandercook) U.; m. Kathleen Nelson Smith, July 30, 1982; children: Kathleen Elizabeth Pennington, Marilee Rae McCracken, Michael Graham Ulrich. BA with high honors, U. Mont., 1961; JD, Stanford U., 1964. Bar: Calif. 1965, Ariz. 1966, U.S. Supreme Ct. 1969, U.S. Ct. Appeals (9th cir.) 1965. Law clk. judge U.S. Ct. Appeals, 9th Circuit, San Francisco, 1964-65; assoc. Lewis and Roca, Phoenix, 1965-70, ptnr., 1970-85; pres. Paul G. Ulrich P.C., 1985-92, Ulrich, Thompson & Kessler, P.C., Phoenix, 1992-94, Ulrich & Kessler, P.C., Phoenix, 1994-95, Ulrich, Kessler & Anger, P.C., Phoenix, 1995-2000, Ulrich & Anger, P.C., Phoenix, 2000—; owner Pathway Enterprises, 1985-91. Judge pro tem divsn. 1, Ariz. Ct. Appeals, Phoenix, 1986; instr. Thunderbird Grad. Sch. Internat. Mgmt., 1968-69, Ariz. State U. Coll. Law, 1970-73, 78, Scottsdale C.C., 1975-77, also continuing legal edn. seminars. Author and pub.: Applying Management and Motivation Concepts to Law Offices, 1985; editor: Arizona Appellate Handbook, 1978-2000, Working With Legal Assistants, 1980, 81, Future Directions for Law Office Management, 1982, People in the Law Office, 1985-86; co-author, pub.: Arizona Healthcare Professional Liability Handbook, 1992, supplement, 1994, Arizona Healthcare Professional Liability Defense Manual, 1995, Arizona Healthcare Professional Liability Update Newsletter, 1992-99; co-author, editor: Federal Appellate Practice: Ninth Circuit, 1994, 2d edit., 1999, supp. 2001; contbg. editor Law Office Econs. and Mgmt., 1984-97, Life, Law and the Pursuit of Balance, 1996, 2d edit., 1997. Mem. Ariz. Supreme Ct. Task Force on Ct. Orgn. and Adminstrn., 1988-89; mem. com. on appellate cts. Ariz. Supreme Ct., 1990-91; bd. visitors Stanford U. Law Sch., 1974-77; adv. com. legal assisting program Phoenix Coll., 1985-95; atty. rep. 9th Cir. Jud. Conf., 1997-2000. With U.S. Army, 1956. Recipient continuing legal edn. award State Bar Ariz., 1978, 86, 90, Harrison Tweed spl. merit award Am. Law Inst./ABA, 1987. Fellow Ariz. Bar Found. (founding 1985—); mem. ABA (chmn. selection and utilization of staff pers. com., econs. of law sect. 1979-81, mem. standing com. legal assts. 1982-86, co-chmn. joint project on appellate handbooks 1983-85, co-chmn. fed. appellate handbook project 1985-88, chmn. com. on liaison with non-lawyers orgns. Econs. of Law Practice sect. 1985-86), Am. Acad. Appellate Lawyers, Am. Law Inst. (life), Am. Judicature Soc. (Spl. Merit citation 1987), Ariz. Bar Assn. (chmn. econs. of law practice com. 1980-81, co-chmn. lower ct. improvement com. 1982-85, co-chmn. Ariz. appellate handbook project 1976-2000), Coll. Law Practice Mgmt., Maricopa County Bar Assn. (bd. dirs. 1994-96), Calif. Bar Assn., Phi Kappa Phi, Phi Alpha Delta, Sigma Phi Epsilon. Democrat. Appellate, Federal civil litigation, State civil litigation. Home: 2529 E Lupine Ave Phoenix AZ 85028-1823 Office: Ste 250 3707 N 7th St Phoenix AZ 85014-5057 E-mail: ulanpc@aol.com

ULRICH, THEODORE ALBERT, lawyer; b. Spokane, Wash., Jan. 1, 1943; s. Herbert Roy and Martha (Hoffman) Ulrich; m. Nancy Allison, May 30, 1966; children: Donald Wayne, Frederick Albert. BS cum laude, U.S. Mcht. Marine Acad., 1965; JD cum laude, Fordham U., 1970; LLM, NYU, 1974. Bar: N.Y. 1971, U.S. Ct. Appeals (2nd cir.) 1971, U.S. Supreme Ct. 1974, U.S. Ct. Claims 1977, U.S. Customs Ct. 1978, U.S. Ct. Internat. Trade 1981, U.S. Ct. Appeals (5th cir.) 1988, U.S. Ct. Appeals (D.C. cir.) 1992, Colo. 1993, U.S. Ct. Appeals (10 cir.) 1994. Mng. clk. U.S. Dept. Justice, N.Y.C., 1968-69, law clk. to federal dist. judge, 1969-70; assoc. Cadwalader, Wickersham & Taft, 1970-80, ptnr., 1980-94, Popham, Haik, Schnobrich & Kaufman, Ltd., Denver, 1994-96; sole practice law, 1996—. Co-author: Encyclopedia of International Commercial Litigation, 1991, Arbitration of Construction Contracts, V, 1991; contbg. author: Marine Engineering Economics and Cost Analysis, 1995; author, editor Fordham Law Rev., 1969. Leader Boy Scouts Am., Nassau County, N.Y., 1984-94, Denver, 1994—. Capt. USCGR, 1965-86. Mem. ABA, Colo. Bar, Denver Bar, Maritime Law Assn., Am. Soc. Internat. Law, Soc. Naval Architects and Marine Engrs., U.S. Naval Inst., Am. Arbitration Assn. Federal civil litigation, Contracts commercial, Private international. Home and Office: 4300 E 6th Ave Denver CO 80220-4940 E-mail: tnulrich@gte.net

UMEBAYASHI, CLYDE SATORU, lawyer; b. Honolulu, Sept. 2, 1947; s. Robert S. and Dorothy C. Umebayashi; m. Cheryl J. Much, June 27, 1975. BBA in Travel Industry Mgmt., U. Hawaii, 1969, JD, 1980. Spl. dept. atty. gen. Labor and Indsl. Rels. Appeals Bd., Honolulu, 1980-81; atty., dir., shareholder Kessner, Duca, Umebayashi, Bain & Matsunaga, 1981—. Commr. Hawaii Criminal Justice Commn. Bd. dirs. Wesley Found., Honolulu, 1993-97. Mem. Hawaii State Bar Assn. Personal injury, Real property, Workers' compensation. Office: Kessner Duca Umebayashi Bain & Matsunaga 220 S King St Fl 19 Honolulu HI 96813-4526

UMMER, JAMES WALTER, lawyer; b. Pitts., July 16, 1945; s. Walter B. and Rose P. (Gerhardt) U.; m. Janet Sue Young, Dec. 21, 1968; children: James Bradley, Benjamin F. BA, Thiel Coll., 1967; JD, Duke U., 1972. Bar: Pa. 1972. Trust officer Pitts. Nat. Bank, 1972-75; tax atty., shareholder Buchanan Ingersoll P.C., Pitts., 1975-92; prin. Hirtle, Callaghan & Co., 1992-93; shareholder Babst, Calland, Clements and Zomnir, 1993-99; ptnr. Reed, Smith, Shaw & McClay, 2000—. Golf course cons., Orlando, Fla. Trustee Thiel Coll., Greenville, Pa., 1984—, The Childrens' Inst., Pitts., 1984—; mem. bd. visitors Duke U. Div. Sch., 1999—. Fellow Am. Coll. Probate Counsel; mem. Estate Planning Coun. Western Pa. (pres. 1986-87), Tax Club (Pitts.), Duquesne Club, Rolling Rock Club, Oakmont Country Club. Republican. Presbyterian. Estate planning, Probate, Taxation, general. Home: 200 Woodland Farms Rd Pittsburgh PA 15238-2024 Office: Reed Smith LLP 435 6th Ave Ste 8 Pittsburgh PA 15219-1809

UNDERBERG, MARK ALAN, lawyer; b. Niagara Falls, N.Y., July 9, 1955; s. Alan Jack and Joyce Love (Wisbaum) U.; m. Diane Englander, Mar. 22, 1986; children: Andrew Englander, James Englander. BA, Cornell U., 1977, JD, 1981. Bar: N.Y. 1981. Law clk. to chief judge U.S. Ct. Appeals (3d cir.), Wilmington, Del., 1981-82; assoc. Debevoise & Plimpton, N.Y.C., 1982-87; mng. dir., dep. gen. counsel Henley Group, Inc., 1987-90, mng. dir., gen. counsel, 1990-92; v.p., gen. counsel Abex Inc., Hampton, N.H., 1992-95. V.p., gen. counsel Fisher Sci. Internat. Inc., Hampton, N.H., 1991-97, cons. 1997-98; counsel Paul, Weiss, Rifkind, Wharton & Garrison, N.Y.C., 1998-99, ptnr., 2000—. Editor-in-chief Cornell Law Rev., 1980-81. Mem. ABA, Assn. of Bar of City of N.Y., Genesee Valley Club, University Club. General corporate, Securities. Office: Paul Weiss Rifkind Wharton & Garrison Rm 200 1285 Avenue Of The Americas New York NY 10019-6065

UNDERWOOD, RICHARD HARVEY, law educator; b. Columbus, Ohio, Dec. 18, 1948; s. John Michael and Dorothy Ann (Orwick) U.; children: Nathan Alain, Stephanie. BS, Ohio State U., 1969, JD, 1976. Bar: Ohio 1976, U.S. Dist. Ct. (so. dist.) Ohio 1976, U.S. Ct. Appeals (6th cir.) 1976. Law clk. U.S. Dist. Ct. (so. dist.) Ohio, Cin., 1976-78; assoc. firm Vorys, Sater, Seymour & Pease, Columbus, Ohio, 1978-80; assoc. prof. law U. Ky., Lexington, 1980—. Contbr. articles to profl. jours. Served to capt. U.S. Army, 1969-73; Vietnam. Recipient Sanford D. Levy Meml. award N.Y. State Bar Assn., 1983, Duncan Faculty award U. Ky., 1984. Mem. Ky. Bar Assn. (chmn. ethics, unauthorized practice and model rules com. 1984—). Office: Coll Law U Ky Lexington KY 40506-0001

UNGAR, LAWRENCE BERYL, lawyer; b. Bklyn., Aug. 23, 1930; s. Eugene J. and Sophia L. (Eidman) U.; m. Pauline J. Hamburger, June 21, 1953; children— Pamela Lynn, Robert William. B.S. in Econs., U. Pa., 1953; J.D., NYU, 1962. Bar: N.Y. 1962. Systems engr. IBM, Armonk, N.Y., 1957-62, atty. 1965-88; assoc. Cravath, Swaine & Moore, N.Y.C., 1962-65; mng. litigation atty. Proskauer Rose Goetz & Mendelsohn, N.Y.C., 1989-95; mng. counsel Legal Authorities Network L.L.C., 1995-97, cons., 1997—. Served to lt. USN, 1953-57. Mem. Order of Coif, Beta Gamma Sigma. Antitrust, General corporate. Office: 11 Beverly Pl Larchmont NY 10538-2601

UNGARETTI, RICHARD ANTHONY, lawyer; b. Chgo., May 25, 1942; s. Dino Carl and Antoinette (Calvetti) U.; children: Joy A., Paul R. BS, DePaul U., 1964, JD, 1970. Bar: Ill. 1970, U.S. Dist. Ct. (no. dist.) Ill. 1970, U.S. Supreme Ct. 1980. Assoc. Kirkland & Ellis, Chgo., 1970-74; ptnr. Ungaretti & Harris, 1974—. Mem. adv. coun. DePaul Coll. Law, Chgo., 1988. Mem. ABA, Chgo. Bar Assn., Ill. State Bar Assn., Internat. Coun. Shopping Ctrs., Am. Coll. Real Estate Lawyers, Justinian Soc., Urban Land Inst. (assoc.), Lamda Alpha Avocations: golf, fishing, hunting. Land use and zoning (including planning), Landlord-tenant, Real property. Office: Ungaretti & Harris 3500 Three First Nat Plz Chicago IL 60602 E-mail: raungaretti@uhlaw.com

UNGARO-BENAGES, URSULA MANCUSI, federal judge; b. Miami Beach, Fla., Jan. 29, 1951; d. Ludivico Mancusi-Ungaro and Ursula Berliner; m. Michael A. Benages, Mar., 1988. Student, Smith Coll., 1968-70; BA in English Lit., U. Miami, 1973; JD, U. Fla., 1975. Bar: Fla. 1975. Assoc. Frates, Floyd, Pearson et al, Miami, 1976-78, Blackwell, Walker, Gray et al, Miami, 1978-80, Finley, Kumble, Heine et al, Miami, 1980-85, Sparber, Shevin, Shapo et al, Miami, 1985-87; cir. judge State of Fla., 1987-92; U.S. dist. judge U.S. Dist. Ct., 1992—. Mem. Fla. Supreme Ct. Race & Ethnic & Racial Bias Study Commn., Fla., 1989-92, St. Thomas U. Inns of Ct., Miami, 1991-92; mem. jud. resources com. Jud. Coun. U.S.; chmn. ct. svcs. com. So. Dist. Fla., chmn. magistrate judge com. Bd. dirs. United Family & Children's Svcs., Miami, 1981-82; mem. City of Miami Task Force, 1991-92. Mem. ABA, Fed. Judges Assn., Fla. Assn. Women Lawyers, Dade County Bar Assn., Eugene Spellman Inns of Ct. U. Miami. Office: US Dist Ct 301 N Miami Ave Fl 11 Miami FL 33128-7702

UNGER, CHARLES JOSEPH, lawyer; b. Alexandria, Va., Oct. 30, 1955; s. Gerald Bertram and Bette (Bernstein) U. BA, Northwestern U., 1973-77; JD, U. Ill., 1977-80. Bar: Calif. 1981, U.S. Dist. Ct. (ctrl. dist.) Calif. 1991. Law clerk Flanagan, Booth, Santa Ana, Calif., 1980-81, assoc. atty., 1981-86; ptnr. Flanagan, Booth & Unger, 1986—. Instr., DUI Defense U. So. Calif., L.A., 1985-97; therapist Foothill Ctr. for Personal and Family Growth, 1997—. Columnist Glendale (Calif.) News Press. Psychology doctorate Am. Behavioral Studies Inst., Tustin, Calif., 1985-97. Mem. Glendale Bar Assn. (pres. 1996-97). Democrat. Jewish. Criminal. Office: Flanagan Booth & Unger 1156 N Brand Blvd Glendale CA 91202-2504

UNGER, GERE NATHAN, physician, lawyer; b. Monticello, N.Y., May 15, 1949; s. Jessie Aaron and Shirley (Rosenstein) U.; m. Alicen J. McGowan, July 21, 1990; children: Elijah, Breena, Ari, Sasha, Arlen. JD, Bernadean U., 1979; MD, Inst. Polytecnico, Mexico City, 1986; D Phys. Medicine, Met. U., Mexico City, 1987; postgrad., Boston U., 1993, Harvard Law Sch., 1994-96; LLM in Med. Law, U. Glasgow, 2001. Dipomate Am. Bd. Forensic Examiners, Am. Bd. Med. Legal Analysis in Medicine and Surgery, Am. Bd. Forensic Medicine, Am. Bd. Risk Mgmt. Med. dir. Vietnam Vets. Post-Traumatic Stress Disorder Program, 1988-90; emergency rm. physician, cons. in medicaid fraud Bronx (N.Y.)-Lebanon Hosp., 1990—; clin. legal medicine Paladin Profl. Group, P.A., Palm Beach, Fla., 1992-98; pres. Albany Law Jour. Co., Inc., 1998—; jurisconsult Office of Gere Unger, M.D., J.D., 1999—. Mediator, arbitrator World Bank, 2000—; mediator, arbitrator, negotiator World Intellectual Property Orgn., 1994; mem. peer rev. com. Nat. Inst. on Disability and Rehab. Rsch., Office Spl. Edn., U.S. Dept. Edn., 1993; mem. clin. ethics com. Inst. Medecine Legale et de Medecine Sociale, Strasbourg, France, 1994; mem. surg. critical care com. Am. Soc. Critical Care Medicine, 1992; N.Y. state capt. Am. Trial Lawyers Exch., 1992. Mem. editl. bd. Am. Bd. Forensic Examiners, 1993, Jour. Neurol. and Orthopaedic Medicine and Surgery, 1993. Commandant Broward County Marine Corps League, 1995—. With USMC, 1968-72. Diplomate Am. Bd. Disability Analysts; fellow Internat. Coll. Surgeons (mem. ethics com. 1994, mem. emergency response program Ea. region 1994), Am. Acad. Neurol. and Orthopaedic Surgeons, Am. Coll. Legal Medicine, Am. Coll. Forensic Examiners, Exec. Practice Mgmt.; mem. ABA, ATLA, FBA (health com., rep. ABA 1994, chmn. med. malpractice/tort com. and FBA liaison to AMA), Nat. Coll. Advocacy, Internat. Bar Assn., Am. Coll. Physician Execs. (chair forum on law and med. mgmt. 1995), Kennedy Inst. Ethics, Am. Soc. of Laser Medicine and Surgery, Nat. Assn. of Forensic Econs., Am. Bd. Disability Analysts, Internat. Royal Soc. of Medicine (London). Avocations: flying, boating. Office: 8 Elk St Ste 3 Albany NY 12207-1010 E-mail: jurismed@justicemail.com

UNGER, PETER VAN BUREN, lawyer; b. Cin., Nov. 15, 1957; s. Sherman Edward and Polly Van Buren (Taylor) U.; m. Laura Meth Simone, June 29, 1991; children: Simone Taylor, Natalie Van Buren. BA in History, Polit. Sci., Miami U., Oxford, Ohio, 1980; JD, U. Cin., 1983; LLM in Securities, Georgetown U., 1987. Bar: Ohio 1984, D.C. 1985, U.S. Supreme Ct. 1991. Law clk. chief judge U.S. Dist. Ct. (so. dist.) Fla., Ft. Lauderdale, 1983-85; atty. enforcement divsn. SEC, N.Y.C., 1986-88; assoc. Fulbright & Jaworski, Washington, 1988-89, participating assoc., 1990-94, ptnr., 1995—. Mem. ABA (bus. law sect., com. fed. regulation of securities, sub-com. on civil litigation and SEC enforcement matters 1989—, litigation sect. com. on securities litigation sub-com. on SEC enforcement practice 1990—), Securities Industry Assn. (compliance and legal divsn.), D.C. Bar Assn. (corp., fin. and securities law sect. steering com.). Securities. Home: 3308 N St NW Washington DC 20007-2807 Office: Fulbright & Jaworski LLP 801 Pennsylvania Ave NW Washington DC 20004-2615 E-mail: punger@fulbright.com

UNGLESBY, LEWIS O. lawyer; b. New Orleans, July 6, 1949; s. Lewis Huber and Mary Jane (Holloway) U.; m. Gail Hoy, Aug. 15, 1970; children: Lewis, Lance, Blake. BS, U. Miss., 1971; JD, La. State U., 1974. Bar: La. 1974, U.S. Dist. Ct. (ea., mid., and we dists.) La. 1974, U.S. Ct. Appeals (5th cir.) 1974, U.S. Supreme Ct. 1980; cert. criminal trial adv. Nat. Bd. Trial Advocacy. Ptnr. Unglesby Koch & Reynolds; mem. judge's benchbook com. La. Supreme Ct., 1982—. Spl. counsel La. State Senate, 1991-98, Gov. La., 1996-98; lectr. La. Assn. Criminal Def. Lawyers, 1987-91. Editor criminal law sect. La. Trial Lawyers Brief, 1988—. Fellow Am. Bd. Criminal Lawyers; mem. ABA, La. Bar Assn. (ho. of dels. 1979-87, lectr.), NACDL, ATLA (criminal law com. 1989-90), La. Trial Lawyers Assn. (chmn. criminal law sect. 1983-85, bd. govs. 1983-94, exec. com. 1991-2000, lectr.). Criminal, Personal injury. Home: 14415 Highland Rd Baton Rouge LA 70810-5312 Office: 246 Napoleon St Baton Rouge LA 70802-5937

UNIS, RICHARD L. judge; b. Portland, Oreg., June 11, 1928; BS, JD, U. Oreg. Bar: Oreg. 1954, U.S. Dist. Ct. Oreg. 1957, U.S. Ct. Appeals (9th cir.) 1960, U.S. Supreme Ct. 1965. Judge Portland Mcpl. Ct., 1968-71, Multnomah County Dist. Ct., 1972-76, presiding judge, 1972-74; former judge Oreg. Cir. Ct. 4th Judicial Dist., 1977-90; former sr. dep. city atty. City of Portland; assoc. justice Oreg. Supreme Ct., Portland, 1990-96; spl. master U.S. Dist. Ct. House, 1996—. Adj. prof. of local govt. law and evidence Lewis & Clark Coll. Northwestern Sch. Law, 1969-76, 77-96; spl. master supr. La.-Pacific Inner-Seal Siding nationwide class action litig.; faculty mem. The Nat. Judicial Coll., 1971-2000; former faculty mem. Am. Acad. Judicial Edn. Author: Procedure and Instructions in Traffic Court Cases, 1970, 101 Questions and Answers on Preliminary Hearings, 1974. Bd. dirs. Oreg. Free from Drug Abuse; mem. Oreg. Adv. Com. on Evidence Law Revision, chmn. subcom., 1974-79. Maj. USAFR, JAGC, ret. Recipient Meritorius Svc. award U. Oregon sch. Law, 1988; named Legal Citizen of Yr. Oreg. Law Related Edn., 1987; inducted into The Nat. Judicial Coll. Hall of Honor, 1988. Mem. Am. Judicature Soc. (bd. dirs. 1975, Herbert Harley Nat. award 1999), Am. Judges Assn., Multnomah Bar Found., Oregon Judicial Conf. (chmn. Oreg. Judicial Coll. 1973-80, legis. com. 1976—, exec. com. of judicial edn. com., judicial conduct com.), N.Am. Judges Assn. (tenure, selection and compensation judges com.), Dist. Ct. Judges of Oreg. (v.p., chmn. edn. com.), Nat. Conf. Spl. Ct. Judges (exec. com.), Oreg. State Bar (judicial adminstrn. com., sec. local govt. com., com. on continuing certification, uniform jury instrn. com., exec. com. criminal law sect., trial practice sect. standards and certification com., past chmn., among others), Oreg. Trial Lawyers Assn. (named Judge of Yr. 1984). Office: US Dist Ct House 1000 SW 3rd Ave Portland OR 97204-2930

UNPINGCO, JOHN WALTER SABLAN, federal judge; b. 1950; BA, St. Louis U., 1972; MBA, JD, NYU, 1976; LLM, Georgetown U., 1983. Bar: Guam 1977, D.C. 1983, Calif. 1992. Atty. Ferenz, Bramhall, Williams & Gruskin, Guam, 1976-77; atty. Office Staff Judge Advocate USAF, 1977-85, civilian atty., Office Staff Judge Advocate, 1985-87; counsel U.S. Naval Air Warfare Ctr., China Lake, Calif., 1987-92; fed. judge U.S. Dist. Ct. (Guam dist.), 1992—. Part-time instr. U. Md. Far East divsn., Yokota Air Base, Tokyo, 1983-87, European divsn., RAF Mildenhall, Suffolk, U.K., 1979-82, U. Guam, 1994-99. Pres. Guam Swim League, 2000; pres. parish coun. Our Lady of Hope Parish, 2000-. Mem. ABA, State Bar Calif., Guam Bar Assn., Internat. Legal Soc. Japan, D.C. Bar Assn., NWC Community Fed. Credit Union (bd. dirs. 1991-92). Office: US Dist Ct 4th Fl US Courthouse 520 W Soledad Ave Hagatna GU 96910

UPRIGHT, KIRBY GRANT, lawyer; b. South Canaan, Pa., Sept. 12, 1946; s. Lyle Lee and Ellen May (Kirby) U.; m. Joyce Ann Keyasko, Oct. 4, 1975; children: Chad, Scott. BS, Pa. State U., 1970; JD, U. Akron, 1973; LLM in Taxation, Temple U., 1977. Bar: Pa. 1973, U.S. Dist. Ct. (mid. dist.) Pa. 1978, U.S. Ct. Appeals (3d cir.) 1981, U.S. Tax Ct. 1979; CPA,

Pa. Staff acct. Peat, Marwick, Mitchell, Phila., 1973-77; assoc. Henkleman, Kreder, O'Connell & Brooks, Scranton, Pa., 1977-82; ptnr. Hanna, Young, Upright & Catina, Stroudsburg, 1982—. Paralegal instr., paralegal adv. bd. Pa. State U., Worthington Scranton Campus, Dunmore, Pa., 1978-82. With U.S. Army, 1964-67, Vietnam. Fellow Am. Coll. Trust and Estate Counsel; mem. Jaycees (bd. dirs. Scranton chpt. 1977-79), Pa. State U. Alumni Assn., Pocono Mountain Club (Stroudsburg, pres. 1982-85), Masons, Rotary. Estate planning, Probate, Estate taxation. Home: 53 Wyndham Hills Cresco PA 18326-0053 Office: Hanna Young Upright & Catina 300 Stroud Bldg Stroudsburg PA 18360-1602 E-mail: kupright@hyuc.com

URAM, GERALD ROBERT, lawyer; b. Newark, July 11, 1941; s. Arthur George and Mildred (Stein) U.; m. Melissa Gordon, May 27, 1995; children: Michael, Alison, Carolyn Gordon Lewis. BA, Dartmouth Coll., 1963; LLB, Yale U., 1967. Bar: N.Y. 1967. Assoc. Paul, Weiss, Rifkind, Wharton & Garrison, N.Y.C., 1967-74; v.p., corp. counsel Prudential Bldg. Maintenance Corp., 1974; ptnr. Davis & Gilbert, 1974—. Lectr. N.Y. Law Sch. Contbr. to profl. publs. Bd. dirs. St. Francis Friends of Poor, Inc. Mem. ABA, N.Y. State Bar Assn., Assn. Bar City of N.Y. Landlord-tenant, Real property. Office: 1740 Broadway Fl 3 New York NY 10019-4315

URBAN, DONALD WAYNE, lawyer; b. Belleville, Ill., Oct. 9, 1953; s. Andrew Anthony and Eileen Marie (Tibbitt) U.; m. Mary Beth Evans, June 9, 1979 (div. Oct. 1994); m. Georgianna Dowling, Feb. 2, 1995; 1 child, Andrew Jared. BA, So. Ill. U., 1976; JD, Washington U., 1979. Assoc. Sprague & Sprague, Belleville, 1979-96; ptnr. Sprague & Urban, 1996—. Author, lectr. Ill. Inst. for CLE, Springfield. Author: Blasting & Subsidence Illinois Institute for Continuing Legal Education Handbook, 1983, vol. 2, 1986, vol. 3, 1989. Pres. Looking Glass Playhouse, Lebanon, Ill., 1988-90, 95-97, 99-01; spokesman St. Clair County Bicentennial, Belleville, 1989. Mem. Gamma Theta Upsilon. Democrat. Avocation: community theatre. Bankruptcy, Estate planning, Personal injury. Home: 815 Belleville St Lebanon IL 62254-1312 Office: Sprague & Urban 26 E Washington St Belleville IL 62220-2101

URBINA, RICARDO MANUEL, judge; b. 1946; BA, Georgetown U., 1967, JD, 1970. Trial atty. Pub. Defender Svc. for D.C., 1970-72; prin. Urbina & Libby, Washington, 1972-73, Law Office of Ricardo M. Urbina, Washington, 1973-74; prof. law, dir. criminal justice program Howard U., 1974-81; assoc. judge D.C. Superior Ct., 1981-94; judge U.S. Dist. Ct. D.C., 1994—. Adj. prof. Antioch Sch. Law, 1976, Georgetown U. Law Ctr., Washington, 1982, George Washington U. Nat. Law Ctr., Washington, 1993—; instr. Nat. Inst. Trial Advocacy, 1976, 78; vis. instr. trial advocacy Howard Law Sch., 1996—. Recipient VIDA award lifetime recognition comty. svc.; All-Am. track and field NCAA 880 Champion, 1966; named Georgetown U. Athletic Hall of Fame. Mem. ABA, D.C. Hispanic Bar Assn., Nat. Bar Assn., Hispanic Nat. Bar Assn., Washington Bar Assn., D.C. Bar Assn., Women's Bar Assn., Fahy Inns of Ct. (emeritus), Counsellors of Washington D.C., Coun. for Ct. Excellence, Nat. Coun. La Raza, Phi Delta Phi. Office: US Dist Ct DC US Courthouse Rm 4311 333 Constitution Ave NW Washington DC 20001-2802

URBOM, WARREN KEITH, federal judge; b. Atlanta, Dec. 17, 1925; s. Clarence Andrew and Anna Myrl (Irelan) U.; m. Joyce Marie Crawford, Aug. 19, 1951; children: Kim Marie, Randall Crawford, Allison Lee, Joy Renee. AB with highest distinction, Nebr. Wesleyan U., 1950, LLD (hon.), 1984; JD with distinction, U. Mich., 1953. Bar: Nebr. 1953. Mem. firm Baylor, Evnen, Baylor, Urbom, & Curtiss, Lincoln, Nebr., 1953-70; judge U.S. Dist. Ct. Nebr., 1970—; chief judge U.S. Dist. Ct. Dist. Nebr., 1972-86, sr. judge, 1991—. Mem. com. on practice and procedure Nebr. Supreme Ct., 1965-95; mem. subcom. on fed. jurisdiction Jud. Conf. U.S., 1975-83; adj. instr. trial advocacy U. Nebr. Coll. Law, 1979-90; bd. dirs. Fed. Jud. Ctr., 1982-86; chmn. com. on orientation newly apptd. dist. judges Fed. Jud. Ctr., 1986-89; mem. 8th Cir. Com. on Model Criminal and Civil Jury Instrns., 1983—; mem. adv. com. on alternative sentences U.S. Sentencing Com., 1989-91. Contbr. articles to profl. jours. Trustee St. Paul Sch. Theology, Kansas City, Mo., 1986-89; active United Methodist Ch. (bd. mgrs., bd. global ministries 1972-76, gen. com. on status and role of women, 1988-96, gen. conf. 1972, 76, 80, 88, 92, 96, 2000); pres. Lincoln YMCA, 1965-67; bd. govs. Nebr. Wesleyan U., chmn. 1975-80. With AUS, 1944-46. Recipient Medal of Honor, Nebr. Wesleyan U. Alumni Assn., 1983. Fellow Am. Coll. Trial Lawyers; mem. ABA, Nebr. Bar Assn. (ho. of dels. 1966-70, Outstanding Legal Educator award 1990), Lincoln Bar Assn. (Liberty Bell award 1993, pres. 1968-69), Kiwanis (Disting. Svc. award 1993), Masons (33 deg.), Am. Inns of Ct. (Lewis F. Powell Jr. award for Professionalism and Ethics 1995). Methodist. Home: 4421 Ridgeview Dr Lincoln NE 68516-1516 Office: US Dist Ct 586 Fed Bldg 100 Centennial Mall N Lincoln NE 68508-3859

UROWSKY, RICHARD J. lawyer; b. N.Y.C., June 28, 1946; s. Jacob and Anne (Granick) U. BA, Yale U., 1967, JD, 1972; BPhil, Oxford U., Eng., 1970. Bar: N.Y. 1973, U.S. Dist. Ct. (so. dist.) N.Y. 1973, U.S. Ct. Appeals (2d cir.) 1973, U.S. Supreme Ct. 1977. Law clk. to Justice Reed U.S. Supreme Ct., Washington, 1972-73; assoc. Sullivan & Cromwell, N.Y.C., 1973-80, ptnr., 1980—. Mem. ABA, Assn. of the Bar of the City of N.Y., Fed. Bar Coun., N.Y. County Lawyers Assn., Yale Club, Links, Lyford Cay Club. Antitrust, Federal civil litigation, Securities. Office: Sullivan & Cromwell 125 Broad St New York NY 10004-2489 E-mail: urowsky@sullcrom.com

URSU, JOHN JOSEPH, lawyer; b. 1939; BA, U. Mich., 1962, JD, 1965. Bar: Mich. 1966, Ky. 1970, Minn. 1972. Trial atty. FTC, 1965-67; staff mem. Pres.'s Commn. on Civil Disorders, 1967; advisor to commr. FTC, 1968-69; legal counsel GE, 1969-72; divsn. atty. 3M, 1972-74, sr. atty., 1974-76, assoc. counsel, 1976-81, asst. gen. counsel, 1981-86, assoc. gen. counsel, 1986-90, dep. gen. counsel, 1990-92, gen. counsel, 1992-93, v.p. legal affairs & gen. counsel, 1993-96, sr. v.p. legal affairs and gen. counsel, 1997—. Adj. faculty William Mitchell Coll. Law, 1978-82. Antitrust, General corporate, Product liability. Office: 3M Gen Offices 3M Ctr Bldg 220-14W-07 Saint Paul MN 55144-1000

USSERY, ALBERT TRAVIS, lawyer, investment company executive; b. Gulfport, Miss., Mar. 12, 1928; s. Walter Travis and Rosamond (Sears) U.; m. Margaret Grosvenor Paine, Nov. 22, 1950; children: Margaret Rosamond, John Travis, Marilyn Ann, Meredith Lee. AB, Washington U., St. Louis, 1950; LLB, U. N.Mex., 1951, JD, 1968; LLM, Georgetown U., 1955. Bar: N.Mex. 1951. Ptnr. Gallagher and Ussery, Albuquerque, 1951-53, Threet, Ussery & Threet, Albuquerque, 1957-60; assoc. with Alfred H. McRae, Albuquerque, 1961-63; ptnr. McRae, Ussery, Mims, Ortega & Kitts, Albuquerque, 1964-65; chmn. Am. Bank Commerce, 1966-70, pres., 1967-70; ptnr. Ussery, Burciaga & Parrish, Albuquerque, 1969-79; pres. Ussery & Parrish, P.A., Albuquerque, 1980—; spl. counsel to Albuquerque on water law, 1956-66; chmn. Rio Grande Valley Bank, Albuquerque, 1972-83, Bank of S.W., 1980-83; lectr. mil. law U. N.Mex., 1956, instr. corp. fin., 1956-57, lectr. bus. law, 1960-61; bd. dirs. 1st City Investment Brokers, Inc., 1983-85, Lovelace Med. Systems and Techs., Inc., 1983-84. Chmn. water adv. com. Albuquerque Indsl. Devel. Svc., 1960-66; vice chmn. N.Mex. Coun. on Econ. Edn., 1969-74; mem. N.Mex. Regional Export Expansion Council, 1969-74, mem. Albuquerque Armed Forces Adv. Assn., 1977—. Trustee Village Los Ranchos de Albuquerque, 1970-72; chmn. adv. bd. Lovelace-Bataan Med. Ctr., 1976-78; trustee Lovelace Med. Found., 1978-96, vice chmn., 1988-96; trustee Lovelace Respiratory Rsch. Inst., 1996—, chmn., 1966—; bd. dirs. Goodwill Industries N.Mex., 1957-65, Albuquerque Travelers Assistance, 1956-66, Family Consultation Svc., 1961-64, Albuquerque Symphony Assn., 1964-68, Hispanic Culture Found., 1983-92, Lovelace Health Plan Inc., 1985-89; bd. dirs. N.Mex. Arthritis Found., 1969-74, pres., 1971. Mem. Am., Fed., Albuquerque (treas. 1957-60) bar assns., State Bar N.Mex., Estate Planning Coun. Albuquerque (pres. 1962), N.Mex. Zool. Soc. (dir., pres. 1977-78), Am. Legion (comdr. 1962-63), Lawyers Club. (pres. 1983-84). Lodge: Kiwanis (dir. 1957-60). Banking, General corporate, Real property. Home: 37 Chaco Loop Sandia Park NM 87047-8505 Office: Ussery & Parrish PA 200 Rio Grande Valley Bldg 501 Tijeras Ave NW Albuquerque NM 87102-3109

UTTER, ROBERT FRENCH, retired state supreme court justice; b. Seattle, June 19, 1930; s. John and Besse (French) U.; m. Elizabeth J. Stevenson, Dec. 28, 1953; children: Kimberly, Kirk, John. BS, U. Wash., 1952; LLB, 1954. Bar: Wash. 1954. Pros. atty., King County, Wash., 1955-57; individual practice law Seattle, 1957-59; ct. commr. King County Superior Ct., 1959-64, judge, 1964-69, Wash. State Ct. Appeals, 1969-71, Wash. State Supreme Ct., 1971-95, chief justice, 1979-81; ret., 1995; lectr. Ctrl. and Eastern European Legal Inst., Prague, Czech Republic, 2000, 01, dean faculty Czech Republic, 2001—. Lectr. in field, leader comparative law tour People's Republic of China, 1986, 87, 88, 91, USSR, 1989, Republic of South Africa, 1997, Ukraine, Hungarian and Czech Republic, 1998; adj. prof. constl. law U. Puget Sound, 1987, 88, 89, 90, 91, 92, 93, 94; cons. CEELI, 1991, 93—, USIA, 1992; visitor to Kazakhstan, Kyrgystan Judiciary, 1993, 94, 95, 96, Outer Mangolia, 1997; lectr. to Albanian Judiciary, 1994, 95, 2000, to Georgian Judiciary, 1999. Editor books on real property and appellate practice. Pres., founder Big Brother Assn., Seattle, 1955-67; pres., founder Job Therapy Inc., 1963-71; mem. exec. com. Conf. of Chief Justices, 1979-80, 81-86; pres. Thurston County Big Bros./Big Sisters, 1984; lectr. Soviet Acad. Moscow, 1991; USIA visitor to comment on jud. system, Latvia, 1992, Kazakstan, 1993-94; trustee Linfield Coll. Named Alumnus of Yr., Linfield Coll., 1973, Disting. Jud. Scholar, U. Ind., 1987, Judge of Yr., Wash. State Trial Lawyers, 1989, Outstanding Judge, Wash. State Bar Assn., 1990, Outstanding Judge, Seattle-King County Bar Assn., 1992, Conder-Faulkner lectr. U. Wash. Sch. Law, 1995, Disting. Alumnus Sch. Law U. Wash., 1995; recipient Henry Jackson Disting. Pub. Svc. award Nat. Wash. Sch. Law, 2000. Fellow Chartered Inst. Arbitrators; mem. ABA (commentator on proposed constns. of Albania, Bulgaria, Romania, Russia, Lithuania, Azerbaijan, Uzbekistan, Byelarus, Kazakhstan and Ukraine), Am. Judicature Soc. (sec. 1987—, chmn. bd. dirs., mem. exec. com., Herbert Harley award 1983, Justice award 1998), Order of Coif. Baptist.

VACCA, ANTHONY, lawyer; b. Graniteville, R.I., Sept. 28, 1925; s. Charles and Jennie V.; m. Rose Catherine, Ovt. 6, 1951; children: Frances Jane, Carolyn Mary. PhB, Providence Coll., 1948; JD, Northeastern U., 1951. Bar: R.I. 1951, U.S. Dist. Ct. R.I., 1952, U.S. Supreme Ct. 1979. Instr. U. R.I. Coll. Law, 1961-62; judge Probate Ct., Smithfield, R.I., 1969-77; atty. pvt. practice, 1977—. Del. R.I. Constitutional Conv., 1964-69; mem. Spl. Legis. Commn. Probate Judges, 1975; ration com. Town of Smithfield, 1961, charter commn., 1974, price stabilization bd., 1976. With USN, 1943-45. Fellow Am. Coll. Probate Coun.; mem. R.I. Bar Assn. (exec. com. 1967-68, chmn. com. continuing legal edn. 1970, mem. ho. of dels. 1974, treas. 1975-76, sec. 1976-77, com. superior ct. bench=bar 1983). Independent. Roman Catholic. Personal injury, Probate. Home: 43 Maplecrest Dr Greenville RI 02828-2912 Office: 596 Newport Ave Pawtucket RI 02861-3237

VACCO, DENNIS C. lawyer; b. Buffalo, Aug. 16, 1952; s. Carmen A. and Mildred V.; m. Kelly McIlroy; children: Alex, Connor. BA, Colgate U., 1974; JD, SUNY, Buffalo, 1978. Bar: N.Y. 1978, Fed. Ct. 1978, 82. Asst. dist. atty. Office of Erie County Dist. Atty., Buffalo, 1978-82, chief G.J. bureau, 1982-88; U.S. Atty. We. Dist. N.Y., 1988-93; atty. gen. State of New York, Albany, 1993-98; v.p. for govtl. affairs Waste Mgmt. Inc., 1998-99; pres. Waste Mgmt. N.Y. LLC, 1999—. Chmn. Atty. Gen.'s Environ. Subcom., Atty. Gen.'s Subcom. on Organized Crime and Violent Crime; mem. Nat. Environ. Enforcement Coun. Co-chair Erie County Community Commn. on Alcohol and Substance Abuse; bd. dirs. United Way of Erie County. Recipient Environ. Enforcement Leadership award Atty. Gen. Dept. of Justice, Washington, 1991. Mem. N.Y. State Bar Assn., Erie County Bar Assn., Nat. Dist. Attys. Assn., N.Y. State Dist. Attys. Assn., NCCJ, Hamburg Devel. Corp., 100 Club of Buffalo, U. Buffalo Law Alumni Assn. (bd. dirs.). Republican. Roman Catholic. Avocations: travel, sports.

VACHSS, ANDREW HENRY, lawyer, author, juvenile justice and child abuse consultant; b. N.Y.C., Oct. 19, 1942; s. Bernard and Geraldine (Mattus) V. BA, Case Western Res. U., 1965; JD magna cum laude, New Engl. Sch. Law, 1975. Bar: N.Y. 1976, U.S. Dist. Ct. (so. and ea. dists.) N.Y. 1976. Program rep. USPHS, Ohio, 1965-66; unit supr N.Y.C. Dept. Social Svcs., 1966-69; urban coord. Community Devel. Found., Norwalk, Conn., 1969-70; dir. Uptown Community Orgn., Chgo., 1970-71; dep. dir. Medfield (Mass.)-Norfolk Prison Project, 1971-72; dir. intensive treatment unit ANDROS II, Roslindale, Mass., 1972-73; project dir. Mass. Dept. Youth Svcs., Boston, 1972-73; dir. Juvenile Justice Planning Project, N.Y.C., 1975-85; pvt. practice, 1976—. Organizer, coord. Calumet (Ind.) Community Congress, 1970; bd. dirs. Libra Inc., Cambridge, Mass., Advocacy Assocs., N.Y. and N.J.; adj. prof. Coll. New Resources, N.Y.C., 1980-81; lectr. trainer, speaker to numerous orgns.; cons. on juvenile justice and child abuse to numerous orgns., 1971—. Author: The Life-Style Violent Juvenile: The Secure Treatment Approach, 1979, (novels) Flood, 1985, Strega, 1987, Blue Belle, 1988, Hard Candy, 1989, Blossom, 1990, Sacrifice, 1991, Shella, 1993, Another Chance To Get It Right, 1995, Down in the Zero, 1994, Footsteps of the Hawk, 1995, Batman: The Ultimate Evil, 1995, False Allegations, 1996, Safe House, 1998, Choice of Evil, 1999, Dead and Gone, 2000, Pain Management, 2001;(graphic novels) Predator: Race War, 1995, Hard Looks, 1996; (collected short stories) Born Bad, 1994, Everybody Pays, 1999, (audiobook) Proving It, 2001; editor-in-chief New Eng. Law Rev., 1974-75; contbg. editor Parade; contbr. articles to legal publs. Bd. of counselors Childtrauma Acad., Baylor Coll. of Medicine; mem. expert adv. panel on catastrophic child abuse N.Y. State Office of Mental Health. Recipient Grand Prix de Lit. Policiére, 1988, Falcon award Maltese Falcon Soc. Japan, 1988, Deutschen Krimi Preis, Die Jury des Bochumer Krimi Archivs, 1989, Raymond Chandler award Giuria a Noir Festival, 2000; Indsl. Area Found. Tng. Inst. fellow, 1970-71, John Hay Whitney Found. fellow, 1976-77. Mem. PEN, Writers Guild of Am. Juvenile. Office: Ste 2805 420 Lexington Ave New York NY 10170-2899

VACKETTA, CARL LEE, lawyer, educator; b. Danville, Ill., Aug. 3, 1941; s. Peter G. and Julia M. (Columbus) V. BS, U. Ill., 1963, JD, 1965. Bar: Ill. 1965, D.C. 1968, U.S.Dist. Ct. D.C. 1968, U.S. Ct. Fed. Claims 1968, U.S. Supreme Ct. 1970. Tax lawyer GM, Detroit, 1965-66; ptnr. Sellers, Conner & Cuneo, Washington, 1968-74, Pettit & Martin, Washington, 1974-95, Piper & Marbury, Washington, 1995-99, Piper Marbury Rudnick & Wolfe LLP, Washington, 1999—. Adj. prof. law Georgetown U., 1971—. Co-author: Government Contract Default Termination, 1991, 93, 95, 97, 99; co-editor Extraordinary Contractual Relief Reporter, 1974—. Capt. U.S. Army, 1966-68. Fellow ABA (sec. pub. contract law sect. 1978-79, coun. 1979-82, pub. contract law sect., editor in chief Pub. Contract Law Jour. 1994—), Nat. Contract Mgmt. Assn.; mem. Fed. Bar Assn., D.C. Bar Assn., Nat. Assn. Purchasing Mgrs., University Club (Washington). Roman Catholic. Contracts commercial, Government contracts and claims. Office: Piper Marbury Rudnick & Wolfe LLP 1200 19th St NW Fl 7 Washington DC 20036-2430 also: Piper Marbury Rudnick & Wolfe LLP 6225 Smith Ave Baltimore MD 21209-3600 E-mail: carl.vacketta@piperudnick.com

VADEN, FRANK SAMUEL, III, lawyer, engineer; b. San Antonio, Nov. 13, 1934; s. Frank Samuel Jr. and Helen Alyne (Roberts) V.; m. Caroline Chittenden Gerdes, Feb. 20, 1960; children; Christina Louise (Mrs. Eugene Linton), Olivia Anne (Mrs. Warren Augenstein), Cecilia Claire (Mrs. Scott Johnson). BSEE and BS in Indsl. Engring., Tex. A&M U., 1957; JD, So. Meth. U., 1963. Bar: Tex. 1963, U.S. Dist. Ct. (we. and so. dists.) Tex. 1963, U.S. Ct. Appeals (5th, 9th, 11th and Fed. cirs.) 1963, U.S. Supreme Ct. 1986; registered U.S. Patent and Trademark Office 1964. Assoc. Arnold & Roylance, Houston, 1963-66; ptnr. Arnold, White & Durkee, 1966-73, mng. ptnr., 1973-78; prin. Frank S. Vaden III, P.C., 1978-80; sr. ptnr. Vaden, Eickenroht & Thompson, L.L.P., 1980-98; ptnr. Felsman, Bradley, Vaden, Gunter & Dillon, L.L.P., 1999-2000; of counsel Bracewell & Patterson, L.L.P., 2001—. Lectr. in field. Author: Invention Protection for Practicing Engineers, 1971; contbr. numerous articles to profl. jours. Capt. S.C., U.S. Army, 1957-67. Fellow Tex. Bar Found. (sustaining), Houston Bar Found. (sustaining); mem. ABA (mem. standing com. on specialization 1993-96), Tex. Bar Assn. (chair intellectual property law sec. 1984-85), Houston Bar Assn., Am. Intellectual Property Law Assn., Houston Intellectual Property Law Assn. (pres. 1985-86), U.S. Trademark Assn., Licensing Exec. Soc. (chmn. Houston chpt. 1987-88). Republican. Episcopalian. E-mila. Intellectual property, Patent, Trademark and copyright. Office: Bracewell & Patterson LLP 711 Louisiana St Ste 2900 Houston TX 77002-2781 E-mail: fvaden@bracepatt.com

VAGTS, DETLEV FREDERICK, lawyer, educator; b. Washington, Feb. 13, 1929; s. Alfred and Miriam (Beard) V.; m. Dorothy Larkin, Dec. 11, 1954; children: Karen, Lydia. Grad., Taft Sch., 1945; AB, Harvard U., 1948, LLB, 1951. Bar: Mass. 1961. Assoc. Cahill, Gordon, Reindel & Ohl, N.Y.C., 1951-53, 56-59; asst. prof. law Harvard Law Sch., 1959-62, prof., 1962—, Eli Goldston prof., 1981-84, Bemis prof., 1984—, dir. internat. tax program, 1998-2000. Counselor internat. law dept. State, 1976-77 Author: (with others) Transnational Legal Problems, 1968, 4th edit., 1994, Basic Corporation Law, 1973, 3d edit., 1989, Transnational Business Problems, 2d edit., 1998; editor: (with others) Secured Transactions Under the Uniform Commercial Code, 1963-64; assoc. reporter: (with others) Restatement of Foreign Relations Law; book rev. editor Am. Jour. Internat. Law, 1986-93, co-editor-in-chief, 1993-98. 1st lt. USAF, 1953-56. Recipient Max Planck Rsch. award, 1991. Mem. ABA, Am. Soc. Internat. Law, Coun. Fgn. Rels., Phi Beta Kappa. Home: 29 Follen St Cambridge MA 02138-3502 Office: Sch Law Harvard U Cambridge MA 02138 E-mail: vagts@law.harvard.edu

VAJTAY, STEPHEN MICHAEL, JR. lawyer; b. New Brunswick, N.J., Mar. 18, 1958; s. Stephen Michael and Veronica Gizella (Fehèr) V.; m. Gabriella Katherine Soltèsz, Aug. 5, 1989; children: Stephen, Andrew, Gregory, Daniel. BA, Rutgers U., 1980; JD, Georgetown U., 1983; LLM, NYU, 1989. Bar: N.J. 1984, U.S. Tax Ct. 1985. Assoc. McCarter and English LLP, Newark, 1983-91; ptnr. McCarter and English, 1991—. Trustee Hungarian Scout Assn. in Exteris, Garfield, N.J., 1985—; trustee Partnership for a Drug-Free N.J., Inc., Montclair, 1993—; adj. prof. law Seton Hall U. Sch. Law, Newark, 1995—; spkr. at lectrs. and seminars, 1992—. Contbr. articles to profl. jours. Mem. Bd. of Adjustment, New Brunswick, N.J., 1993-98. Mem. ABA, N.J. Bar Assn. (chmn. tax sect. 2001—), Essex County Bar Assn., Phi Beta Kappa. Roman Catholic. Mergers and acquisitions, Corporate taxation, Taxation, general. Office: McCarter and English LLP Four Gateway Ctr 100 Mulberry St Newark NJ 07102 E-mail: SVAJTAY@MCCARTER.com

VAKERICS, THOMAS VINCENT, lawyer; b. Lorain, Ohio, Mar. 26, 1944; s. Paul Peter and Margaret Theresa (Dobos) V.; m. Kathryn Ida Rogers, Aug. 7,1965; children: Meredith Vakerics Ehler, Mitchell Thomas. BA, Bowling Green State U., 1965; JD with honors, George Washington U., 1968. Bar: U.S. Dist. Ct. D.C. 1968, U.S. Ct. Appeals (D.C. cir.) 1969, U.S. Supreme Ct. 1974, U.S. Ct. Internat. Trade 1982, U.S. Ct. Appeals (Fed. cir.) 1982. Antitrust trial atty. FTC, Washington, 1969-73; assoc. Gore, Cladouhos & Brashares, 1973-75; ptnr. O'Connor & Hannan, 1975-84, Bayh, Tabbert & Capehart, Washington, 1984-86, Morgan, Lewis & Bockius, Washington, 1986-88, Winthrop, Stimson, Putnam & Roberts, Washington, 1988-94, Perkins Coie, 1994—. Vis. prof. Nihon U., Tokyo, 1981-88. Author: Antitrust Basics, 1985, Antidumping, Countervailing Duty and Other Trade Actions, 1987; contbr. articles to profl. jours. Mem. ABA (vice chmn. internat. antitrust law com. sect. internat. law and practice 1992-95), Internat. Bar Assn., D.C. Bar Assn., Solar Energy Rsch. Inst. (editl. adv. bd. Solar Energy Law Reporter 1979-82), Order of Coif, Phi Delta Phi, Pi Sigma Alpha, Phi Alpha Delta, Sigma Chi. Democrat. Roman Catholic. Antitrust, Private international. Home: 12820 Tewksbury Dr Herndon VA 20171-2427 Office: Perkins Coie 607 14th St NW Ste 800 Washington DC 20005-2003 E-mail: vaket@perkinscoie.com

VALAT DE CÓRDOVA, THIERRY, lawyer; b. Carcassonne, Aude, France, Dec. 26, 1971; s. Jean-Louis and Hélène V.; m. Luz Marina Valat de Córdova, Dec. 14, 1997. BA in Math., U. Calif., Berkeley, 1994; JD, Harvard U., 1997. Bar: N.Y. Assoc. Afridi & Angell, N.Y.C., 1997—. Banking, Private international, Mergers and acquisitions. Home: 65 Atlantic Ave #5 Brooklyn NY Office: Afridi & Angell 230 Park Ave New York NY 10169-0005

VALDECANTOS, CLARENCE DARROW CUNAN, lawyer; b. Makati City, Philippines, Oct. 10, 1971; s. Renato Bartolome and Elisa Cunan V.; m. Ronette Macaraeg, Apr. 30, 1993; children: Clarisse Paulina, Renato Elijah Corinne. AB in Journalism, U. Philippines, Quezon City, 1993; LLB, San Beda Coll. Law, Manila, Philippines, 1997. Assoc. Larc & Asset Pub. Rels. Firm, Manila, Philippines, 1993; legal asst. Romero Lagman Valdecantos Arreza Law Office, Makati City, Philippines, 1989-91; assoc. Abello Conecpcion Regala & Cruz Law, Philippines, 1997—. Mem. Integrated Bar Philippines. General corporate, Labor, Sports. Office: Abello Concepcion Regala 122 Gamboa St Makati City 0770 The Philippines Fax: 8160119. E-mail: accralaw@philonline.com.ph

VALENCIANO, RANDAL GRANT BOLOSAN, lawyer; b. Waimea, Hawaii, Nov. 17, 1958; s. Placido Dias and Maria (Bolosan) V.; m. Debbie F.I.; children: Marisa Claire Ihara, Dreana Rae Ihara, Randon Grant Ihara. BS, U. Oreg., 1980; JD, U. Wash., 1983. Bar: Hawaii 1983. Dep. pub. def. State of Hawaii, 1983-84; dep. prosecutor County of Kauai, 1984-87; ptnr. Valenciano & Zenger, Lihue, 1989-91; pvt. practice, 1996—. Arbitrator 5th Jud. Cir. State of Hawaii, 1988-91; mem. Defender Coun. State of Hawaii, 1989-91. Lawyer, coach Waimea High Sch. Mock Trial Team, 1986-88; bd. dirs. Hawaii United Meth. Union, Honolulu, 1987-91. Mem. Hawaii State Bar Assn., Kauai Bar Assn. (v.p. 1988-89), Kauai County Coun. (vice chair 1990—). Democrat. Avocation: sports card collecting, bonsai plants. General civil litigation, Criminal, Family and matrimonial. Home: Pua Nani St Lihue HI 96766 Office: 3016 Umi St Ste 211A Lihue HI 96766-1346

VALENTE, PETER CHARLES, lawyer; b. N.Y.C., July 3, 1940; s. Francis Louis and Aurelia Emily (Cella) V.; m. Judith Kay Nemeroff, Feb. 19, 1966; children: Susan Lynn, David Marc. BA, Bowdoin Coll., 1962; LLB, Columbia U., 1966; LLM, NYU, 1971. Bar: N.Y. 1967. Assoc. Blank Rome Tenzer Greenblatt LLP, N.Y.C., 1967-73, ptnr., 1973—, also co-chair tax and fiduciary dept. Co-author column on wills, estates and surrogates's practice N.Y. Law Jour. Fellow Am. Coll. Trust and Estate Counsel; mem.

ABA, N.Y. State Bar Assn. (lectr. on wills, trusts and estates), Assn. of Bar of City of N.Y., N.Y. County Lawyers' Assn. (former bd. dirs. and chmn. com. on surrogates' ct., lectr. on wills, trusts and estates), Phi Beta Kappa. Estate planning, Probate, Estate taxation. Office: Blank Rome Tenzer Greenblatt LLP 405 Lexington Ave New York NY 10174-0002 E-mail: pvalente@blankrome.com

VALENTINE, GARRISON NORTON, lawyer; b. N.Y.C., Apr. 7, 1929; s. Alan Chester and Lucia Garrison (Norton) V.; m. Margaret Brown Weeks, Mar. 15, 1952 (div. 1983); children: Peter, Stewart, Norah, Elizabeth; m. Inge Carola Froelich, Sept. 17, 1983; 1 stepchild, Carolyn A. Read. BA, Yale U., 1950, LLB, 1964. Bar: Conn. 1964, U.S. Dist. Ct. Conn. 1964. Assoc. Hoppin, Carey & Powell, Hartford, Conn., 1964-70, ptnr., 1970-86; ptnr. Ladwig & Valentine, Mystic, Conn., 1986-88; ptnr., bd. dirs. Waller, Smith & Palmer, P.C., New London, Conn., 1988—; sec., bd. dirs. Conn. Attys. Title Co., Rocky Hill, 1974—. Bd. dirs., sec. Mystic Marinelife Aquarium, Conn., 1984-87; bd. dirs. Summer Music, Inc., New London, 1984—; bd. govs. Stonington (Conn.) Community Ctr., 1986—, pres., 1988—. Served to capt. USAF, 1952-61. Mem. ABA, Conn. Bar Assn., Hartford County Bar Assn., New London County Bar Assn. Republican. Episcopalian. Club: Wadawanuck. Land use and zoning (including planning), Probate, Real property. Office: Waller Smith & Palmer PC 12 Roosevelt Ave Mystic CT 06355-2809

VALENTINE, H. JEFFREY, legal association executive; b. Phila., Sept. 28, 1945; s. Joshua Morton and Olga W. (Wilson) V.; 1 child, Karyn. BS, St. Louis U., 1964, postgrad., 1966-68. Programmer, systems analyst Honeywell Electronic Data Processing, Wellesley Hills, Mass., 1964-66; account exec. Semiconductor div. Tex. Instruments, New Eng., 1966-68; New Eng. sales exec., Mid-Atlantic regional mgr. Electronic Instrumentation Co., 1968-70; pres. Nat. Free Lance Photographers Assn., Doylestown, Pa., 1970-89; pres., dir. Towne Print & Copy Ctrs. Inc.; v.p., exec. dir. Nat. Paralegal Assn., 1982—; pres. Paralegal Assocs., Inc., 1982—; chief operating officer Doylestown Parking Corp., 1977-88. Bd. dirs. Law Enforcement Supply Co., Solebury, Valtronics Supply Co., Towne Print & Copy Centers Inc., Solebury, Doylestown Stationery and Office Supply, Energy Mktg. Assocs., Inc., Solebury, Paralegal Placement Network; pres. Paralegal Pub. Corp., 1983-90; pub. Paralegal Jour.; pres. Valco Enterprises Inc., 1986—, Paralegal Employment Sys., Inc., 1988, Solebury Press, Inc., 1989—; ptnr. J&S Gen. Contractors, 1993—, J&S Landscaping Tree Svc., 1993—; owner Specialized Computer Consulting, 1992—. Author: Photographers Bookkeeping System, 1973, rev. edit., 1978, Photographers Pricing Guides, 1971, 72, 74, 75, Available Markets Director's - 4 Vols., 1973-77, National Model Sources Directory, Nat. Paralegal Salary and Employment Survey, 1985-86, 88, 90-92, 93-94; also articles, bulls. and pamphlets. Exec. sec. Doylestown Bus. Assn., 1972-78, pres., 1979, 83, v.p., 1981. Recipient Internat. Men of Achievement award, 1988; named Personalities of the Am., 1988. Mem. London Coll. Applied Scis., Nat. Fedn. Paralegal Assns., Photog. Industry Coun., Nat. Assn. Legal Assts., Am. Soc Assn. Execs., Soc. Assn. Mgrs., Nat. Fedn. Ind. Business (mem. action coun. com.), Nat. Parking Assn., Nat. Office Products Assn., Graphic Arts Assn. Delaware Valley, Nat. Assn. Federally Licensed Firearms Dealers, Nat. Compostition Assn., Internat. Platform Assn. Office: PO Box 406 Solebury PA 18963-0406

VALENZUELA, MANUEL ANTHONY, JR. lawyer; b. L.A., Dec. 4, 1955; s. Manuel and Artimesa B. (Ruiz) V.; m. Guadalupe Roa, Nov. 8, 1980; children: Manuel Anthony III, Nancy Christine. BA in Polit. Sci., UCLA, 1978; MPA, U. So. Calif., 1982; JD, Southwestern U., L.A., 1987. Bar: Calif. 1987, U.S. Dist. Ct. (cen. dist.) Calif. 1987, U.S. Ct. Appeals (9th cir.) 1988, U.S. Supreme Ct. 1991. Legis. analyst L.A. City Coun., 1981-88; legal extern ACLU, L.A., 1985; assoc. county counsel County of Los Angeles, 1988-89, sr. assoc county counsel, 1989-90, dep. county counsel, 1990-94, sr. dep. county counsel, 1994-98, prin. dep. county counsel, 1998—. Mem. L.A. County Bar Assn. (exec. com. govtl. law sect. 1990-91, 95-96, 96—, sec. govtl. law sect. 1991-92, 2d vice chair govtl. law sect. 1992-93, 1st vice chair govtl. law sect. 1993-94, chair govtl. law sect. 1994-95, bd. trustees 1995-96), Mexican Am. Bar Assn. (bd. dirs. 1990, 91), L.A. County Counsel Assn. (bd. dirs. 1989-99), UCLA Latino Alumni Assn. (founder, bd. dirs. 1989-90, scholarship com. 1995-99), Constnl. Rights Found. (mock trial competition 1997-99). Democrat. Roman Catholic. Avocations: tennis, backpacking, photography, reading. Home: 9647 Val St Temple City CA 91780-1438 Office: Office of County Counsel 648 Hall of Adminstrn 500 W Temple St Los Angeles CA 90012-2713 E-mail: MValenzuela@counsel.co.la.ca.us

VALERIO, MATTHEW F. lawyer; b. Lawrence, Mass., Sept. 28, 1963; s. Fred Ernest Jr. Valerio and Carole Elaine (Closson) Mimeault; m. Joanne F. Stockton, Aug. 6, 1988. BA, St. Michael's Coll., 1985; JD, Western New Eng. Coll., 1988. Bar: Mass. 1989, Vt. 1989, U.S. Dist. Ct. Mass. 1989, U.S. Dist. Ct. Vt. 1989, U.S. Ct. Appeals (2d cir.) 1998. Pvt. practice, Springfield, Mass., 1989; assoc. Abatiell & Wysolmerski, Rutland, Vt., 1989-94; ptnr. Abatiell & Valerio, 1994—2001; defender gen. State of Vt., 2001—. Adj. prof. Coll. St. Joseph, Rutland, 1993-99. Fin. chmn. Rutland County Rep. Com., 1991-93. Mem. ABA (young lawyers divsn. dist. rep. Vt., Maine 1994-96, Vt. state membership chair 1995—), New Eng. Bar Assn. (bd. mem. 1997—, pres. 1999-2000), Vt. Trial Lawyers Assn., Vt. Bar Assn. (treas., exec. com. young lawyers sect. 1990-92, chmn.-elect exec. com. 1992, chmn. 1993-94, bd. bar mgr. 1992—, pres.-elect 2000-01, pres. 2001—), Vt. Criminal Def. Lawyers Assn. (bd. dirs. 1993-96), Assn. Trial Lawyers Am., Kiwanis (bd. dirs. Rutland chpt. 1990-96, v.p. 1991-92, pres. 1993-94, pres. Rutland area mentor program 1994-96, disting. svc. award 1989-92, N.E. dis disting. pres. award 1993-94). Avocations: baseball, wrestling, blues. General civil litigation, Criminal, Personal injury. Office: Office Defender Gen 120 State St Montpelier VT 05620-3301*

VALLIANOS, CAROLE WAGNER, lawyer; b. Phila., Aug. 19, 1946; d. F. Leonard Wagner and Helen Rose Pikunas; m. Peter Denis Vallianos, June 22, 1963; children: Kelly, Denis, Jamie Vallianos-Healy. BA, Calif. State U., Fullerton, 1981; JD, Southwestern U., 1995. Bar: Calif. 1997. Nonprofit cons., Manhattan Beach, Calif., 1982—; atty. in pvt. practice, 1997—, El Segundo, Calif., 1997—. Non-profit cons. USIA, Turkey, 1997, Cyprus, 1997, Bosnia, 1998, India, 1999. Pres. LWV Calif., 1989-91; bd. mem. LWV U.S., 1992-98, LWV Edn. Fund U.S., 1992-98; active Calif. Jud. Coun. Com. on Pvt. Judging, 1989-91, Calif. Jud. Coun. com. on Race and Ethnic Bias in the Cts., 1991-96, Calif. Jud. Coun. Com. on Access and Fairness in the Cts., 1994-97, Calif. Jud. Coun. Task Force on Jury Sys. Improvements, 1998—; mem. Women Lawyers L.A. Jail Project; mem. adv. bd. U. Fla. Marion Brechner Citizen Access Project. Mem. LWV Beach Cities (former pres.), Am. Judicature Soc. (bd. dirs. 1996—, exec. com. 2001-), First Amendment Coalition Calif. (bd. dirs. 1995—), Coalition for Justice (v.p. 1993—), Benjamin Aranda Inn of Ct. Avocations: travel, political memorabilia, literature. Civil rights, Labor, Non-profit and tax-exempt organizations.

VALLIANT, JAMES STEVENS, lawyer; b. Glendale, Calif., Sept. 29, 1963; s. William Warren and Carol Dee (Heath) V.; m. Holly Lynne White. BA, NYU, 1984; JD, U. San Diego, 1989. Bar: Calif. 1989. Law instr. U. San Diego, 1988-89; dep. dist. atty. Dist. Atty.'s Office, San Diego, 1989—. Host talk show WJM Prodns., Hollywood, Calif., 1996. Contbr. articles in objectivism and early Christianity. Recipient Citation of Appreciation MADD, 1993. Office: Dist Attys Office 330 W Broadway San Diego CA 92101-3825

VALOIS, ROBERT ARTHUR, lawyer; b. N.Y.C., May 13, 1938; s. Frank Jacob and Harriet Frances (LaCroix) V.; m. Ruth Emilie Skacil, Dec. 23, 1961; children: Marguerite Jeannette, Robert Arthur Jr. BBA, U. Miami, 1962; JD, Wake Forest U., 1972. Bar: N.C. 1972, Fla. 1972, U.S. Ct. Appeals (4th cir.) 1973, U.S. Dist. Ct. (ea. and mid. dists.) 1974, U.S. Supreme Ct. 1975, U.S. Ct. Appeals (6th cir.) 1986. Field examiner NLRB, Winston-Salem, N.C., 1962-70; from assoc. to ptnr. Maupin, Taylor, Ellis & Adams, P.A., Raleigh, 1972—; chmn. labor and employment sect. Maupin, Taylor & Ellis, P.A., 1972-97, chmn. bd. dirs., pres., 1997—. Vice chmn. Legal Svcs. Corp., Washington, 1984-90, bd. dirs. Served with USN, 1956-59. Mem. Greater Raleigh C. of C. (chmn. fed. govt. com. 1991—). Democrat. Presbyterian. Labor. E-mail: rvalois@maupintaylor.com

VAMOS, FLORENCE M. lawyer; b. N.Y.C., 09 Apr. d. Joseph Calabro and Louise Marie Horvath; m. Joseph S. Vamos. BA magna cum laude, U.Minn., 1974; JD, William Mitchell Coll. Law, St. Paul, 1978. Bar: Ind. 1978, Mich. 1982, U.S. Dist. Ct. (so. dist.) Ind. 1978, U.S. Dist. Ct. (no. dist.) Ind. 1979, U.S. Dist. Ct. (so. dist.) Mich. 1981, U.S. Dist. Ct (ea. dist.) Mich. 1982. Pvt. practice, South Bend, Ind., 1978-90, Mishawaka, 1990-2000, Edwardsburg, Mich., 2001—. Mem. Ind. State Bar Assn., Mich. State Bar Assn., Cass County (Mich.) Bar Assn., St. Joseph County (Ind.) Bar Assn., Nat. Inst. Trial Advocacy. Family and matrimonial, General practice, Trademark and copyright.

VAN ALSTYNE, W. SCOTT, JR. lawyer, educator; b. East Syracuse, N.Y., Sept. 21, 1922; s. Walter Scott and Cecil Edna (Folmsbee) Van A.; m. Margaret Reed Hudson, June 23, 1949 (div.); children: Gretchen Anne, Hunter Scott; m. Marion Graham Walker, May 3, 1980. B.A., U. Buffalo, 1948; M.A., U. Wis., 1950, LL.B., 1953, S.J.D., 1954. Bar: Wis. 1953. Assoc. Shea & Hoyt, Milw., 1954-56; asst. prof. law U. Nebr., 1956-58; pvt. practice Madison, Wis., 1958-72; prof. law U. Fla., 1973-90, prof. emeritus, 1990—; lectr. law U. Wis., 1958-72; lectr. Cambridge-Warsaw Trade Program Cambridge U. (Eng.), 1976. Vis. prof. law Cornell U., 1977, U. Leiden, The Netherlands, 1988, 91; spl. lectr. U. Utrecht, The Netherlands, 1991; vis. prof. Wake Forest U., 1997; spl. counsel Gov. of Wis., 1966-70; bd. dirs. non-resident divsn. State Bar Wis., 1981-96, pres., 1988-90, bd. govs. 1988-90. Prin. author: Goals and Missions of Law Schools, 1990; contbr. articles to profl. jours. Mem. Gov.'s Commn. on edn., Wis., 1969-71; cons. Wis. Commn. on Legal Edn., 1995-96. Served with AUS, 1942-45, 61-62; col. Res., ret. Decorated Legion of Merit. Mem. SR (N.Y.), Holland Soc. (N.Y.), Madison (Wis.) Club, Ft. Rensselaer (N.Y.) Club, Netherland Club (N.Y.C.), Order of Coif, Phi Beta Kappa, Omicron Delta Kappa, Phi Delta Phi. Republican. Presbyterian. Office: U Fla Holland Law Ctr Gainesville FL 32611

VAN ANTWERPEN, FRANKLIN STUART, federal judge; b. Passaic, N.J., Oct. 23, 1941; s. Franklin John and Dorothy (Hoedemaker) Van A.; m. Kathleen Veronica O'Brien, Sept. 12, 1970; children: Joy, Franklin W., Virginia. BS in Engring. Physics, U. Maine, 1964; JD, Temple U., 1967; postgrad., Nat. Jud. Coll., 1980. Bar: Pa. 1969, U.S. Dist. Ct. (ea. dist.) Pa. 1971, U.S. Ct. Appeals (3d cir.) 1971, U.S. Supreme Ct. 1972. Corp. counsel Hazeltine, Corp., N.Y.C., 1967-70; chief counsel Northampton County Legal Aid Soc., Easton, Pa., 1970-71; assoc. Hemstreet & Smith, 1971-73; ptnr. Hemstreet & VanAntwerpen, 1973-79; judge Ct. Common Pleas of Northampton County, Pa., 1979-87, U.S. Dist. Ct. (ea. dist.) Pa., Phila., 1987—. Appointed to U.S. Sentencing Commn. Jud. Working Group, 1992-93; appointed to U.S. Jud. Conf. Com. on Defender Svcs., 1997, chmn. subcom. on fed. defender funding, 2000-01; trial judge U.S. vs. Scarfo, 1988-89; adj. prof. Northampton County Area C.C., 1976-81; solicitor Palmer Twp., 1971-79; gen. counsel Fairview Savs. and Loan Assn., Easton, 1973-79. Contbr. articles to Cardozo Law Rev. Recipient Booster award Bus. Indsl. and Profl. Assn., 1979, George Palmer award Palmer Twp., 1980, Man of Yr. award, 1981, Law Enforcement Commendation medal Nat. Soc. SAR, 1990, Disting. Alumni Achievement award Newark Acad., 2001; named an Alumnus Who Has Made a Difference in the World, U. Maine, 1991. Mem. ABA (com. on jud. edn.), Fed. Bar Assn. (hon.), Fed. Cir. Bar Assn., Pa. Bar Assn., Northampton County Bar Assn., Am. Judicature Soc., Fed. Judges Assn., Pomfret Club, Nat. Lawyers Club Washington, Union League Club, Pa. Soc. Club, Sigma Pi Sigma. Office: US Dist Ct Holmes Bldg 2nd and Ferry St Easton PA 18042

VANASKIE, THOMAS IGNATIUS, judge; b. Shamokin, Pa., Nov. 11, 1953; s. John Anthony and Delores (Wesoloski) V.; m. Dorothy Grace Williams, Aug. 12, 1978; children: Diane, Laura, Thomas. BA magna cum laude, Lycoming Coll., 1975; JD cum laude, Dickinson U., Carlisle, Pa., 1978. Bar: Pa. 1978, U.S. Dist. (mid. dist.) Pa. 1980, U.S. Ct. Appeals (3rd cir.) 1982, U.S. Supreme Ct. 1983. Law clk. to chief judge U.S. Dist. Ct. (mid. dist.) Pa., Scranton, 1978-80; assoc. Dilworth, Paxson, Kalish & Kauffman, 1980-85, ptnr., 1986-92; prin. mem. Elliott, Vanaskie & Riley, 1992-94; chief judge U.S. Dist. Ct. (mid. dist.) Pa., Scranton. Counsel Gov. Robert P. Casey Com., Harrisburg, Pa., 1987-92; mem. automation and tech. com. U.S. Cir. Ct. 3d cir., 1998, co-chair 3d cir. task force on info. resources, 1998—. Contbr. articles to profl. jours. Mem. Scranton Waste Mgmt. Com., 1989; trustee Scranton Prep. Sch., 1997—. Recipient James A. Finnegan award Finnegan Found. Mem. Judicature, Pa. Bar Assn., Fed. Judges Assn. (bd. dirs. 1998). Democrat. Avocations: golf, reading. Office: William J Nealon Fed Bldg & US Courthouse PO Box 913 235 N Washington Ave Scranton PA 18501

VANBEBBER, GEORGE THOMAS, federal judge; b. Troy, Kans., Oct. 21, 1931; s. Roy Vest and Anne (Wenner) V.; m. Alleen Sara Castellani. AB, U. Kans., 1953, LLB, 1955. Bar: Kans. 1955, U.S. Dist. Ct. Kans. 1955, U.S. Ct. Appeals (10th cir.) 1961. Pvt. practice, Troy, 1955-58, 1961-82; asst. U.S. atty. Topeka, Kansas City, Kans., 1958-61; county atty. Doniphan County, Troy, 1963-69; mem. Kans. House of Reps., 1973-75; chmn. Kans. Corp. Commn., Topeka, 1975-79; U.S. magistrate, 1982-89; judge U.S. Dist. Ct., Kansas City, Kans., 1989-95, chief judge, 1995-2001. Mem. ABA, Kas. Bar Assn. Episcopalian. Office: US Dist Ct 529 US Courthouse 500 State Ave Kansas City KS 66101-2403

VAN BOKKELEN, JOSEPH SCOTT, prosecutor; b. Chgo., June 7, 1943; s. Robert W. and W. Louise (Reynolds) Van B.; m. Sally Wardall Huey, Aug. 14, 1971; children— Brian, Kate. B.A., U. Ind., 1966, J.D., 1969. Bar: Ind. 1969, U.S. Dist. Ct. (so. dist.) Ind. 1969, U.S. Dist. Ct. (no. dist.) Ind. 1973, U.S. Ct. Appeals (7th cir.) 1973, U.S. Supreme Ct. 1973. Dep. atty. gen. State of Ind., Indpls., 1969-71, asst. atty. gen., 1971-72; asst. U.S. atty. No. Dist. Ind., Hammond, 1972-75; ptnr. Goldsmith, Goodman, Ball & Van Bokkelen, Highland, Ind., 1975— ; U.S. atty. No. Ind. Dist., 2001-. Recipient Outstanding Asst. U.S. Atty. award U.S. Dept. Justice, 1974. Mem. ABA, Fed. Bar Assn., Ind. Bar Assn., Criminal Def. Lawyers Assn. Home: 9013 Indianapolis Blvd Highland IN 46322-2502 Office: 1001 Main St Ste A Dyer IN 46311-1234*

VAN BROEKHOVEN, ROLLIN ADRIAN, federal judge; b. Dallas, June 3, 1940; s. Harold and Loraine (Chafer) Van B.; m. Diana Gullett, Oct. 6, 1962; children: Gretchen, Heidi. BS, Wheaton Coll., 1962; JD cum laude, Baylor U., 1968; LLM, George Washington U., 1975; DPhil, Oxford U., 1991, DLitt, 1993; DPS (hon.), Gordon Coll., 1997. Bar: Tex. 1968, U.S. Ct. Mil. Appeals 1970, U.S. Ct. Claims 1970, U.S. Supreme Ct. 1975. Commd. 2nd lt. U.S. Army, 1962, advanced through grades to maj., 1969; trial atty. Ft. Hood, Tex., 1968-70, Heidelberg, West Germany, 1970-71; gen. counsel U.S. Army Procurement Agy., Frankfurt, West Germany, 1971-74; asst. gen. counsel Dept. Army, Washington, 1975-77, resigned, 1977; dep. counsel NAVSUP, Dept. Navy, Washington, 1977-80; judge Armed Svcs. Bd. Contract Appeals, 1980—. Editor-in-chief Baylor Law Rev., 1968; contbg. author textbooks; contbr. articles to legal jours. Pres. PTA, Frankfurt, 1972-74; mem. Frankfurt Cmty. Adv. Coun., 1972-74; mem. Child Abuse Coun., Killeen, Tex., 1968-69; elder, chmn. Evang. Free Ch., Manassas, Va., 1980-84; bd. dirs. Trinity Sem., Deerfield, Ill., 1982-88; trustee Outreach, Inc., Grand Rapids, Mich., 1977-95; mem. gen. bd. Evang. Free Ch. of Am., 1982-88, mem. stds. com. Evans Coun. for Fin. Accountability, 1982—; bd. regents, bd. incorp mems Dallas Theol. Seminary, 1988—; chmn. stds. com., bd. dirs. Evang. Coun. Fin. Accountability, 1982—. Recipient Spl. Recognition award Mariano Galvez U., Guatemala, 1984; decorated in svc. Mem. ABA, FBA, Tex. Bar Assn., Contract Appeals Judges Assn. (bd. dirs.), Oxford Soc. Scholars (chmn.). Republican. Home: 8026 Whitting Dr Manassas VA 20112-4705

VAN BUREN, DAVID PAUL, criminal justice educator; b. Silver Springs, N.Y., Nov. 5, 1947; s. LaVerne Robert and Frances Elaine (Carney) Van B. BA magna cum laude, St. Bonaventure U., 1969; MA, SUNY, Albany, 1971, PhD with distinction, 1984. Instr. Genesee C.C., Batavia, N.Y., 1971-72; security coord. Albany Housing Authority, 1975-76; prof. dept. criminal justice U. Wis., Platteville, 1976—, chmn. dept., 1986—, assoc. vice chancellor and dean Sch. Grad. Studies, 2000—. Vis. scholar inst. criminology U. Cambridge, Eng., 1987-88; vis. scholar dept. criminal justice No. Ariz. U., 1997-98; cons. in field. Author: Rural Justice, 1984; asst. editor Jour. Rsch. in Crime and Delinquency, 1984-86; contbr. articles to profl. jours., chpts. to books. Dem. candidate for sheriff, Wyoming County (N.Y.), 1972, mem. U. Wis. Regents Task Force on Status of Women, 1979-81. Grad. rsch. fellow, U.S. Dept. Justice, 1969-71. Mem. Wis. Criminal Justice Edn. Ass.n (pres. 1982, 88-89), Am. Soc. Criminology, Acad. Criminal Justice Sci., Cambridge U. Law Soc. (life), Delta Epsilon Sigma. Democrat. Roman Catholic. Home: 205 Ellen St Platteville WI 53818-3616 Office: U Wis One Univ Plz 314 Brigham Hall Platteville WI 53818-3099 E-mail: vanburen@uwplatt.edu

VAN CAMP, BRIAN RALPH, judge; b. Halstead, Kans., Aug. 23, 1940; s. Ralph A. and Mary Margaret (Bragg) Van C.; m. Diane D. Miller, 1992; children: Megan M., Laurie E. AB, U. Calif., Berkeley, 1962, LLB, 1965. Bar: Calif. 1966. Dep. atty. gen., State Calif., 1965-67; agy. atty. Redevel. Agy., City of Sacramento, 1967-70; asst./acting sec. Bus. and Trans. Agy., State of Calif., 1970-71; commr. of corps. State of Calif., Sacramento, 1971-74; partner firm Diepenbrock, Wulff, Plant & Hannegan, 1975-77, Van Camp & Johnson, Sacramento, 1978-90; sr. ptnr. Downey, Brand, Seymour & Rohwer, 1990-97; judge Superior Ct., Sacramento County, 1997—. Lectr. Continuing Edn. Bar, Practicing Law Inst., Calif. CPA Soc. Contbr. articles to profl. jours. Mem. Rep. State Ctrl. Com. Calif., 1974-78; pres. Sacramento Area Commerce and Trade Orgn., 1986-87; mem. electoral coll. Presdl. Elector for State of Calif., 1976; mem. Calif. Health Facilities Fin. Authority, 1985-89; mem. Capital Area Devel. Authority, 1989-97, chmn., 1990-97; mem. Calif. Jud. Coun. Task Force on Quality of Justice, 1998-99; bd. dirs. Sacramento Symphony Assn., 1973-85, 92-94, Sacramento Symphony Found., 1993—, Sacramento Valley Venture Capital Forum, 1986-90, League to Save Lake Tahoe, 1988-95, Valley Vision, Inc., 1993-97; elder Fremont Presbyn. Ch., 1967—. Recipient Sumner-Mering Meml. award Sacramento U. of Calif. Alumni Assn., 1962, Thos. Jefferson award Am. Inst. Pub. Svc., 1994, Excellence in Achievement award Calif. Alumni Assn., 1997; named Outstanding Young Man of Yr., Sacramento Jaycees, 1970, Internat. Young Man of Yr., Active 20-30 Club Internat., 1973. Mem. Boalt Hall Alumni Assn. (bd. dirs. 1991-94), Lincoln Club Sacramento Valley (bd. dirs., pres. 1984-86), U. Calif Men's Club (pres. 1968), Sutter Club, Kanadhar Ski Club, Rotary Club Sacramento (pres. 1993-94, Paul Harris Fellow award 1995), Comstock Club (pres. 1976-77). Republican. Presbyterian. Office: 720 9th St Sacramento CA 95814-1302 E-mail: Vancamp@saccourt.com

VAN CAMPEN, ARNOUD CLEMENS, lawyer; b. Enschede, Netherlands, May 4, 1972; s. Joost and Ada (Veldhuis) Van C. LLB, Utrecht U., 1997; European Law Degree, Cambridge (Eng.) U., 1996. Bar: Amsterdam Dist. Ct. 1997. Atty.-at-law Schut & Grosheide, Amsterdam, 1997—. Author publ. in Dutch Fin. Times. Mem. Vereniging voor Effectenrecht. Banking, General civil litigation, Securities. Office: Schut & Grosheide Advocaten Van Boshuizenstraat 12 Amsterdam 0183 The Netherlands Fax: 0031-20-6464955. E-mail: a.vancampen@schutgrosheide.nl

VANCE, MICHAEL CHARLES, lawyer; b. Marshalltown, Iowa, May 31, 1951; s. Randall Scott and Irma Vance; m. Bonnie K. Becker, Jan. 1, 1995; children: Thomas Randall, Patrick Michael. BA in Polit. Sci. and Econs., U. Iowa, 1973, JD with distinction, 1976. Bar: Iowa 1976, U.S Dist. Ct. (so. dist.) Iowa 1976, U.S. Tax Ct. 1991. Sole practice, Mt. Pleasant, Iowa, 1976—. Atty. City of Wayland, Iowa, 1976—; instr. bus. law Iowa Wesleyan Coll., Mt. Pleasant, 1977-78; asst. county atty. Henry County, Mt. Pleasant, 1979-97, jud. magistrate, 1997—. Mem., bd. dirs. Community Mental Health of Henry, Louisa and Jefferson Counties, Mt. Pleasant, 1977-82; chairperson Henry County Dems., Mt. Pleasant, 1978-83; pres. Mt. Pleasant Sesquicentennial Assn., 1984-86, St. Alphonsus Ch. Parish Council (pres. 1983-85), Mt. Pleasant, 1985— (trustee). Mem. ABA, Iowa Bar Assn. (bd. govs. 1996—), Henry County Bar Assn. (sec.-treas. 1977-78, v.p. 1978-79, pres. 1979-80, 88-91), Iowa Trial Lawyers Assn., Iowa Conf. Bar Assn. Presidents (bd. dirs. 1979-81), Iowa Assn. Jud. Magistrates (bd. dirs. 1998—), Mt. Pleasant C. of C. (bd. dirs. 1991-93, named Citizen of Yr. 1985), Mt. Pleasant Jaycees (bd. dirs. 1978-83), Rotary, KC, Omicron Delta Kappa, Omicron Delta Epsilon. Roman Catholic. General civil litigation, General practice, Probate. Home: 2005 Bittersweet Cir Mount Pleasant IA 52641-8301 Office: PO Box 469 101 N Jefferson St Mount Pleasant IA 52641-2039

VANCE, ROBERT PATRICK, lawyer; b. Feb. 12, 1948; s. James Robert and Lucy Juanita (McMath) V.; m. Sarah Elizabeth Savoia, June 11, 1971; 1 child, Robert Patrick, Jr. BA with honors, La. State U., 1970, JD, 1975. Bar: La. 1975, U.S. Dist. Ct. (ea. dist.) La. 1975, U.S. Dist. Ct. (mid. dist.) La. 1978, U.S. Dist. Ct. (we. dist.) La. 1979, U.S. Ct. Appeals (5th cir.) 1975, U.S. Ct. Appeals (11th cir.) 1981, U.S. Supreme Ct. 1981. Assoc. Jones, Walker, Waechter, Poitevent, Carrere & Denegre, New Orleans, 1975-80, ptnr., 1980—, exec. com., 1991-95, 97—, mng. ptnr., 1994-95,99-2000. Contbr. articles to profl. jours. Fellow Am. Coll. Bankruptcy, Nat. Bankruptcy Conf.; mem. ABA (past chair bankruptcy litigation com.), Am. Law Inst., La. State Bar Assn. (past chair consumer and bankruptcy law sect., chmn. continuing legal edn. com.), New Orleans Bar Assn., La. Bankers Assn. (chmn. bank counsel com. 1992-93), Pi Sigma Alpha, Phi Beta Kappa (Faculty Group award), Phi Kappa Phi. Democrat. Roman Catholic. Banking, Bankruptcy, Federal civil litigation. Home: 1821 State St New Orleans LA 70118-6219 Office: Jones Walker Waechter Poitevent Carrere & Denegre 201 Saint Charles Ave Ste 5200 New Orleans LA 70170-5100 E-mail: pvance@joneswalker.com

VANCE, VICTORIA LYNNE, lawyer; b. Cleve., Jan. 23, 1958; d. Thaddeus Joseph and Athalene (O'Donnell) Potelicki; m. Richard Allen Vance, May 21, 1983; children: Bailey Claire, Robin Elise, Riley Erin. AB in Econs. summa cum laude, John Carroll U., 1979; JD cum laude, Cornell U., 1982. Bar: Ohio 1982, U.S. Dist. Ct. (no. dist.) Ohio 1982, U.S. Dist. Ct. (so. dist.) Ohio 1997. Ptnr. Arter & Hadden, Cleve., 1982—. Active St. Dominic Sch., Ch.; mem. fin. adv. bd. parent group Hathaway Brown Sch. Mem. ABA, Ohio State Bar Assn., Cuyahoga County Bar Assn. Club: Cornell (Northeastern Ohio). Roman Catholic. General civil litigation, Personal injury, Product liability. Home: 21261 Sydenham Rd Shaker Heights OH 44122-2933 Office: Arter & Hadden 1100 Huntington Bldg Cleveland OH 44115 E-mail: vvance@arterhadden.com

VAN CLEVE, WILLIAM MOORE, lawyer; b. Mar. 17, 1929; s. William T Van Cleve and Catherine (Baldwin) Moore Van Cleve; m. Georgia Hess Dunbar, June 27, 1953; children: Peter Dunbar, Robert Baldwin, Sarah Van Cleve Van Doren, Emory Basford. Grad., Phillips Acad., 1946; AB in Econs., Princeton U., 1950; JD, Washington U., St. Louis, 1953, LLD (hon.), 2001. Bar: Mo. 1953. Assoc. Dunbar and Gaddy, St. Louis, 1955-58; ptnr. Bryan Cave LLP (and predecessor firm), 1958-2000, chmn., 1993-94, sr. counsel., 2001—. Bd. dirs. Emerson Electric Co. Trustee Washington U., 1983—, vice chmn. bd. trustees, 1988-93, 95-2000, chmn., 1993-95, mem. exec. com., 1985—; pres. Eliot Soc., 1982-86; chmn. Law Sch. Nat. Coun., 1986-93; commr. St. Louis Sci. Ctr., 1993-2000, bd. trustees, 2001—; bd. dirs., Parents As Tchrs. Nat. Ctr., 1991—, pres., 1997-2000. Mem. ABA, Bar Assn. Met. St. Louis, Mound City Bar Assn., St. Louis County Bar Assn., Order of Coif (hon.). Democrat. Episcopalian. Clubs: Princeton (pres. 1974-75), Noonday (pres. 1985), St. Louis Country, Bogey (pres. 1990-91), Round Table (St. Louis) General corporate, Estate planning, Non-profit and tax-exempt organizations. Home: 8 Dromara Rd Saint Louis MO 63124-1816 Office: Bryan Cave LLP 211 N Broadway Fl 36 Saint Louis MO 63102-2750 E-mail: wmvancleve@bryancave.com

VAN DE KAMP, JOHN KALAR, lawyer; b. Pasadena, Calif., Feb. 7, 1936; s. Harry and Georgie (Kalar) Van de K.; m. Andrea Fisher, Mar. 11, 1978; 1 child, Diana. BA, Dartmouth Coll., 1956; JD, Stanford U., 1959. Bar: Calif. 1960. Asst. U.S. atty., L.A., 1960-66; U.S. atty., 1966-67; dep. dir. Exec. Office for U.S. Attys., Washington, 1967-68, dir., 1968-69; spl. asst. Pres.'s Commn. on Campus Unrest, 1970; fed. pub. defender L.A., 1971-75; dist. atty. Los Angeles County, 1975-83; atty. gen. State of Calif., 1983-91; ptnr. Dewey Ballantine, L.A., 1991-96, of counsel, 1996—; pres. Thoroughbred Owners, Calif., 1996—. Bd. dirs. United Airlines. Mem. Calif. Dist. Attys. Assn. (pres. 1975-83), Nat. Dist. Attys. Assn. (v.p. 1975-83), Peace Officers Assn. L.A. County (past pres.), Nat. Assn. Attys. Gen. (exec. com. 1983-91), Conf. Western Attys. Gen. (pres. 1986). Administrative and regulatory, General civil litigation, General practice. Office: Dewey Ballantine LLP 333 So Grand Ave Ste 2600 Los Angeles CA 90071-1530

VAN DEMARK, RUTH ELAINE, lawyer; b. Santa Fe, May 16, 1944; d. Robert Eugene and Bertha Marie (Thompson) Van D.; m. Leland Wilkinson, June 23, 1967; children: Anne Marie, Caroline Cook. AB, Vassar Coll., 1966; MTS, Harvard U., 1969; JD with honors, U. Conn., 1976; MDiv, Luth Sch. Theology, Chgo., 1999. Bar: Conn. 1976, Ill. 1977, U.S. Dist. Ct. Conn. 1976, U.S. Dist. Ct. (no. dist.) Ill., U.S. Ct. Appeals (7th cir.) 1984, U.S. Supreme Ct. 1983; ordained to ministry, Luth Ch., 1999. Instr. legal rsch. and writing Loyola U. Sch. Law, Chgo., 1976-79; assoc. Wildman, Harrold, Allen & Dixon, 1977-84, ptnr., 1985-94; prin. Law Offices of Ruth E. Van Demark, 1995—; pastor Wicker Park Luth. Ch., 1999—. Mem. rules com. Ill. Supreme Ct., 1999—, chair appellate rules subcom., 1996—; mem. dist. ct. fund adv. com. U.S. Dist. Ct. (no. dist.) Ill., 1997—. Assoc. editor Conn. Law Rev., 1975-76. Bd. dirs. Lutheran Soc. Svcs. Ill., 1998—, sec., 2000—; mem. adv. bd. Horizon Hospice, Chgo., 1978—, YWCA Battered Women's Shelter, Evanston, Ill., 1982-86; del.-at-large White House Conf. on Families, L.A., 1980; mem. alumni coun. Harvard Divinity Sch., 1988-91; vol. atty. Pro Bono Advocates Chgo., 1982-92, bd. dirs., 1993-99, chair devel. com., 1993; bd. dirs. Friends of Pro Bono Advocates Orgn., 1987-89, New Voice Prodns., 1984-86, Byrne Piven Theater Workshop, 1987-90, Luth. Social Svcs. Ill. (sec., 2000—), 1998—; founder, bd. dirs. Friends of Battered Women and Their Children, 1986-87; chair 175th Reunion Fund Harvard U. Div. Sch., 1992. Mem. ABA, Ill. Bar Assn., Conn. Bar Assn., Chgo. Bar Assn., Appellate Lawyers Assn. Ill. (bd. dirs. 1985-87, treas. 1989-90, sec. 1990-91, v.p. 1991-92, pres. 1992-93), Women's Bar Assn. Ill., Jr. League Evanston (chair State Pub. Affairs Com. 1987-88, Vol. of Yr. 1983-84), Chgo. Vassar Club (pres. 1979-81), Cosmopolitan Club (N.Y.C.). Appellate, Federal civil litigation, State civil litigation. Home: 2046 W Pierce Ave Chicago IL 60622-1946 Office: 225 W Washington St Ste 2200 Chicago IL 60606-3408 E-mail: revlaw@msn.com

VANDERBILT, ARTHUR T., II, lawyer; b. Summit, N.J., Feb. 20, 1950; s. William Runyon and Jean (White) V. BA, Wesleyan U., Middletown, Conn., 1972; JD, U. Va., 1975. Bar: N.J. 1975, U.S. Dist. Ct. N.J. 1975, U.S. Supreme Ct. 1978. Jud. clk. to presiding justice N.J. Superior Ct., 1975-76, dep. atty. gen., 1976-78, asst. counsel to gov., 1978-79; ptnr. Carella, Byrne, Bain & Gilfillan, Roseland, N.J., 1979—. Chmn. Supreme Ct. Ethics Com.; mem. Supreme Ct. Adv. Com. Profl. Ethics. Author: Changing Law 1976, Jersey Justice, 1978, Law School, 1981, Treasure Wreck, 1986, Fortune's Children, 1989 (Book of the Month Club, Readers Digest and fgn. edits.), New Jersey's Judicial Revolution, 1997, Golden Days, 1998 (fgn. edits.), Jersey Jurists, 1998, The Making of a Bestseller, 1999. Trustee Elizabeth (N.J.) Presbytery. Named to N.J. Literary Hall of Fame. Fellow: ABA Found.; mem.: ABA (Scribes award 1976), N.J. Bar Assn., Am. Judicature Soc., Nat. Assn. Bond Lawyers, The Authors Guild, Inc., Nat. Writers Union, N.J. Lit. Hall of Fame. Republican. Presbyterian. Avocation: writing. Administrative and regulatory, Municipal (including bonds), Public utilities. Office: Carella Byrne Bain & Gilfillan 6 Becker Farm Rd Roseland NJ 07068-1735

VAN DER HORST, JAN, laywer; b. Breda, The Netherlands, May 27, 1958; m. Marie-Louise Filippini. M of Laws, U. Utrecht (The Netherlands), 1982; English Law, City of London Poly., 1982. Rsch. asst. U. Utrecht, 1981-82; program officer UN Agys., Brazil, 1982-86; assoc. Houthoff, Amsterdam, 1987-94; ptnr. Houthoff Buruma, Rotterdam, The Netherlands, 1994—. Mem. Dutch Assn. Internat. Law, Dutch Comml. Law Assn., Dutch Securities Law Assn., I.B.A. (sect. energy and natural resources). General corporate, Oil, gas, and mineral, Mergers and acquisitions. Office: Houthoff Buruma Weena 355 3013 AL Rotterdam The Netherlands Fax: (31) 10 217 27 02. E-mail: jhorst@houthoff.nl

VANDER LAAN, MARK ALAN, lawyer; b. Akron, Ohio, Sept. 14, 1948; s. Robert H. and Isabel R. (Bishop) Vander L.; m. Barbara Ann Ryzenga, Aug. 25, 1970; children: Aaron, Matthew. AB, Hope Coll., 1970; JD, U. Mich., 1972. Bar: Ohio 1973, U.S. Dist. Ct. (so. dist.) Ohio 1973, U.S. Ct. Appeals (6th cir.) 1978, U.S. Supreme Ct. 1981. Assoc. Dinsmore, Shohl, Coates & Deupree, Cin., 1972-79; ptnr. Dinsmore & Shohl, 1979—. Chair litig. dept., 2001—, spl. counsel Ohio Atty. Gen.'s Office, 1983—; spl. prosecutor State of Ohio, 1985-94; city solicitor City of Blue Ash, Ohio, 1987—, City of Silverton, Ohio, 1999—; trustee Cin. So. Railway, 1994—, pres., 1999—; trustee, chair Grassroots Leadership Acad., 1997—. Mem. Cin. Human Rels. Commn., 1980-86; mem. Leadership Cin. Class XIII, 1989-90; trustee Legal Aid Soc. of Cin., 1981-94, pres., 1988-90. Mem. ABA, Ohio Bar Assn., Cin. Bar Assn. (ethics com. 1983—), Sixth Cir. Jud. Conf. (life), Potter Stewart Inn of Ct. (master), Queen City Club. General civil litigation, General corporate. Office: Dinsmore & Shohl 1900 Chemed Ct 255 E 5th St Cincinnati OH 45202-4700

VANDERLAAN, ROBERT D. lawyer; b. Grand Rapids, Mich., Aug. 22, 1952; s. Donald Gene and Elizabeth Jo (Stankiewicz) V.; m. Betty Jane Thomas, June 25, 1983. BA, U. Detroit, 1974, JD, 1977. Bar: Mich. 1977, U.S. Dist. Ct. (we. dist.) Mich. 1977, U.S. Ct. Appeals (3d cir.) 1983, U.S. Ct. Appeals (6th cir.) 1978, U.S. Supreme Ct. 1981. Ptnr., pres., dir. firm Mohney, Goodrich & Titta, P.C., Grand Rapids, Mich., 1977-86; ptnr. Miller, Canfield, Paddock and Stone, Grand Rapids, 1986—. Bd. dirs. St. John's Home, Grand Rapids, 1980-87, Mercy Respite Care Corp., Grand Rapids, 1980-83, Grand Rapids Cath. Secondary Sch. Bd. Edn., 1982-89, treas. 1985-88, pres. 1988-89, Nat. Kidney Found. of Mich., trustee, 1988—, exec. com., 1989—; bd. dirs. Citizens League Greater Grand Rapids, 1988—, sec., treas., 1992-93, v.p. 1993—. Named One of Outstanding Young Men of Am., 1985. Mem. Nat. Inst. Trial Advocacy (faculty 1982—), Grand Rapids Bar Assn. (sec. 1988-89), Fed. Bar Assn. (western dist. Mich. v.p. programs, 1992-93, sec. 1993-94, v.p. ops. 1994—), Grand Rapids Jaycees (dir. 1979-80, legal counsel 1978-79, 82-83, v.p. 1985-86, pres. 1986-87, chmn. bd. 1987-88, Disting. Svc. award 1984). Roman Catholic. Federal civil litigation, State civil litigation. Office: Miller Canfield Paddock 1200 Campau Sq Plz 99 Monroe Ave NW Grand Rapids MI 49503-2639

VAN DER WALDE, PAUL D. lawyer, entrepreneur; b. Boston, Aug. 22, 1966; s. Peter H. and Roberta L. Van Der Walde. BS in Bus., Ariz. State U., 1989; JD, Santa Clara U., 1993. Bar: Calif., Ariz., U.S. Dist. Ct. (no. dist.) Calif. Atty. Mitchell, Stock & Burrow, San Jose, Calif., 1991-93, Law Offices of Daniel Cornell, San Jose, 1993-94; ptnr. Cornell & Van Der Walde, Palo Alto, Calif., 1994-97, Van Der Walde & Assocs., Cupertino, 1997—; pres. Legal Connection, 1998—. Mem. exec. com. Santa Clara Legal Referral Svcs., San Jose, 1998-99; bd. govs. Legal Connection, 1998—. Mem. ATLA, Santa Clara County Bar Assn., Consumer Attys. Calif. Avocations: skiing, hiking, whitewater rafting, cooking, the finer things in life. General civil litigation. Office: Van Der Walde & Assocs 20370 Town Center Ln Ste 100 Cupertino CA 95014-3226

VANDEVER, WILLIAM DIRK, lawyer; b. Chgo., Aug. 1, 1949; s. Lester J. and Elizabeth J. V.; m. Kathi J. Zellmer, Aug. 26, 1983; children: Barton Dirk, Brooke Shelby. BS, U. Mo., Kansas City, 1971, JD with distinction, 1974. Bar: Mo. 1975, U.S. Dist. Ct. (we. dist.) Mo. 1975. Dir. Popham Law Firm, Kansas City, Mo., 1975—. Lectr. in field, Kansas City Mo., 1979—. Issue editor U. Mo.-Kansas City Law Rev., 1974. Fellow Am. Bd. Trial Advs. (Best Lawyers in Am.-tort law); mem. ABA, ATLA, Mo. Assn. Trial Attys., Kansas City Met. Bar Assn. (treas., sec., pres., elected to 16th Jud. Commn. 1988-94), Kansas City Bar Found. (treas. 1992, sec. 1994, pres. 1996-98, pres. award domestic violence 1999), Interest on Lawyer Trust Accts. of Mo. (bd. govs.), Kansas City Mem. Svcs. (pres. 1988—, commr. 16th jud. cir. selection com.), U. Mo. Kansas City Found. (fin. com. 1998), Phi Delta Phi, Beta Theta Pi. Avocations: tennis, skiing, running, reading. General civil litigation, Personal injury, Product liability. Home: 11380 W 121st Ter Shawnee Mission KS 66213-1978 Office: Popham Law Firm 1300 Commerce Trust Bldg Kansas City MO 64106

VANDEWALLE, GERALD WAYNE, state supreme court chief justice; b. Noonan, N.D., Aug. 15, 1933; s. Jules C. and Blanche Marie (Gits) VandeW. BSc, U. N.D., 1955, JD, 1958. Bar: N.D., U.S. Dist. Ct. N.D. 1959. Spl. asst. atty. gen. State of N.D., Bismarck, 1958-75, 1st asst. atty. gen., 1975-78; justice N.D. Supreme Ct., 1978-92, chief justice, 1993—. Mem. faculty Bismarck Jr. Coll., 1972-76; chairperson-elect, chair Nat. Ctr. for State Cts. Rsch. adv. coun.; mem. fed.-state jurisdiction com. Jud. Conf. of the U.S. Editor-in-chief N.D. Law Rev, 1957-58. Active Bismarck Meals on Wheels Recipient Sioux award U. N.D., 1992, Ednl. Law award N.D. Coun. Sch. Attys., 1987, Love Without Fear award Abused Adult Resource Ctr., 1995, N. Dakota State Bar Assoc. Dist. Service Award, 1998. Mem. ABA (past co-chair bar admissions com. 1991-99, mem. coun. sect. legal edn. and admissions, chairperson elect coun. sect. legal edn. and admissions), State Bar Assn. N.D., Burleigh County Bar Assn., Conf. of Chief Justices (pres., past bd. dirs. 1996-98, chair fed.-state tribal rels. com.), Am. Contract Bridge League, Order of Coif, N.D. Jud. Conf. (exec. com.), Elks, KC, Phi Eta Sigma, Beta Alpha Psi (Outstanding Alumnus award Zeta chpt. 1995), Beta Gamma Sigma, Phi Alpha Delta. Roman Catholic. Office: ND Supreme Ct State Capitol 600 E Boulevard Ave Bismarck ND 58505-0530 E-mail: gvandewalle@ndcourts.com

VANDIVIER, BLAIR ROBERT, lawyer; b. Rapid City, S.D., Dec. 24, 1955; s. Robert Eugene and Barbara Jean (Kidd) V.; m. Elizabeth Louise Watson, July 26, 1980; children: Jessica Elizabeth, Jennifer Louise. BS magna cum laude, Butler U., 1978; JD cum laude, Ind. U., 1981. Bar: Ind. 1981, U.S. Dist. Ct. (so. dist.) Ind. 1981, U.S. Tax Ct. 1985. Assoc. Henderson, Daily, Withrow, Johnson & Gross, Indpls., 1981-83; assoc., ptnr. Johnson, Gross, Densborn & Wright, 1983-85, of counsel, 1985-87; v.p., sec. Benchmark Products, Inc. (formerly Benchmark Chem. Corp.), 1985-91, pres., 1991—, also bd. dirs.; ptnr. Gross & Vandivier, 1987-89; of counsel Riley, Bennett & Egloff, 1990—; mgmt. rep. Pro Com, L.L.C., 1991—. V.p. Seleco Inc., Indpls., 1988-93, pres., 1993—. Mem. com. Conner Prairie Settlement Fund Dr., Indpls., 1983-85, Riley Run, 1987—; mem. regulatory study com. City of Indpls., 1993-98. Mem. ABA, Ind. Bar Assn., Indpls. Bar Assn (bd. dirs. young lawyers divsn. 1982-85), Am. Electroplaters and Surface Finisher's Soc. (chmn. nat. law com. 1986-97, pres. Indpls. br. 1989, bd. mgrs. 1997—, tech. conf. bd. 1991-97, chmn. surface finishers ann. tech. conf. and exhbn. 1994, chmn. surface finishers focus group 1994—, Tech. Conf. Bd. Recognition award 1996), Nat. Assn. Metal Finishers (bd. dirs. 1998—, exec. com. 1998—, sec./treas. 2000-01, v.p. 2001—), Metal Finishing Suppliers Assn. (spl. projects svcs. com., 1988-93, chmn. 1993—, chmn. hazardous materials br. 1991-93, trustee 1992-95, v.p. 1995-97, pres. 1997-99, past pres. 1999—), Highland Golf Club, Highland Country Club (chmn. ins. com. 1989-94, golf. com. 1992-94, bd. dirs. 1995-97, chmn. fin. com. 1996-97) Surface Finishing Industry Coun. (bd. dirs., sec. 1997-98, pres. 1999), Econ. Club Indpls., Metal Finishing Found. (pres. 1999), Delta Tau Delta (chmn. 1987-97, bd. dirs. Beta Zeta Found. 1986, Outstanding Alumnus Beta Zeta chpt. 1986). Republican. Episcopalian. Avocations: golf, reading. Contracts commercial, General corporate, Real property. Home: 8927 Woodacre Ln Indianapolis IN 46234-2848 Office: Benchmark Products Inc PO Box 68809 Indianapolis IN 46268-0809

VAN DYKE, JON MARKHAM, law educator; b. Washington, Apr. 29, 1943; s. Stuart Hope and Eleonora (Markham) Van D.; m. Sherry Phyllis Broder, Feb. 12, 1978; children: Jesse Bernard, Eric Gabriel, Michelle Tiare. BA, Yale U., 1964; JD, Harvard U., 1967. Bar: D.C. 1968, Calif. 1970, Hawaii 1976. Asst. prof. law Cath. U., Washington, 1967-69; law clk. Calif. Supreme Ct., San Fransisco, 1969-70; vis. fellow Ctr. for Study of Democratic Instns., Santa Barbara, Calif., 1970-71; assoc. prof. law U. Calif., San Fransisco, 1971-75, prof., 1975-76; prof. law U. Hawaii, Honolulu, 1976—, project dir. law of the sea Sea Grant Coll. Program, 1979-88, 90-92, assoc. dean, 1980-82. Rsch. assoc. Environ. and Policy Inst., East-West Ctr., Honolulu, 1982-84, adj. rsch. assoc., 1986-92; exec. bd. Law of the Sea Inst., Honolulu, 1982-88; dir. U. Hawaii Inst. for Peace, 1988-90. Author: North Vietnam's Strategy for Survival, 1982, Jury Selection Procedures: Our Uncertain Commitment to Representative Panels, 1977; editor: Consensus and Confrontation: The United States and the Law of the Sea Convention, 1985, International Navigation: Rocks and Shoals Ahead?, 1988, Freedom for the Seas in the 21st Century, 1993, Sharing the Resources of the South China Sea, 1997, International Law and Litigation in the U.S., 2000, Checklists on Searches adn Seizures in Public Schools, 2001. Mem. Reapportionment Commn., Honolulu, 1981-82, ACLU Litigation Com., Honolulu, 1986-87, Hawaii Bicentennial Commn. of U.S. Constitution, 1987. Named Outstanding Profl Hawaii Assn. Plaintiffs Attys., 1984, 93; recipient Presdl. Citation for Teaching Excellence, 1987. Mem. Am. Soc. Internat. Law, Hawaii State Bar Assn., Internat. Coun. Environ. Law. Home: 4191 Round Top Dr Honolulu HI 96822-5009 Office: U Hawaii Law Sch 2515 Dole St Honolulu HI 96822-2328 E-mail: jvandyke@hawaii.edu

VAN EEGHEN, CHRISTIAAN PIETER, lawyer; b. Amsterdam, Aug. 8, 1951; s. Christiaan Pieter and Margaretha Aafke (Langeveld) Van E.; m. Famke Hajonides Van Der Meulen, Oct. 4, 1975; children: Mei, Susanna, Henriette, Pieter. M of Law, Amsterdam U., 1978. Assoc. Van Doorne & Warendorf, Amsterdam, 1978-80, Clifford Turner/Clifford Chance Amsterdam, Amsterdam, 1980-88; ptnr. Bos Oosterbaan & Van Eeghen NL, 1988-90, Oosterbaan & Van Eeghen Advocaten, Amsterdam, 1990—. Subst. judge Haarlem (The Netherlands) Dist. Ct., 1988. Trustee Doopsgezinde Gemeente, Amsterdam, 1978, Anslo Hofje, Amsterdam, 1990. Mem. Netherlands Bar Assn. Avocations: mountaineering, sailing, art. Contracts commercial, Real property. Home: 327 Keizersgracht 1016 EE Amsterdam The Netherlands Office: 35 Koningslaan Amsterdam 1075 AB The Netherlands Fax: 0031206717446

VAN FLEET, G. NELSON, financial executive; b. Scranton, Pa., May 10, 1936; s. George N. and Loretta R. (Bachman) Van F.; B.S., Pa. State U., 1958; J.D., Georgetown U., 1966; m. Patricia Ann Thomas, June 15, 1958; children— Margaret Meredith, Thomas Allen, Elizabeth Allison. Admitted to D.C. bar, 1966, Pa. bar, 1968, Kans. bar, 1971; with SEC, Washington, 1961-68; atty. firm Ringe, Peet & Mason, Phila., 1968-70; v.p., gen. counsel Beacon Resources Corp., Wichita, Kans., 1970-72; pres. Amortibanc Investment Co., Inc., Wichita, 1972-81; v.p. fin. Drillers, Inc. Houston, 1981-84, pres., Petrotel Prodn., Inc., Wichita, Kans., 1985—. Served to lt. U.S. Navy, 1958-61. Mem. Am. Bar Assn. Home: 2808 Oriole St Wichita KS 67204-5343 Office: 650 Sutton Pl Wichita KS 67202

VAN FLEET, GEORGE ALLAN, lawyer; b. Monterey, Calif., Jan. 20, 1953; s. George Lawson and Wilma Ruth (Williams) Van F.; m. Laurie Elise Koch, July 20, 1975; children: Katia Elaine, Alexander Lawson. BA summa cum laude, Rice U., 1976; JD, Columbia U., 1977. Bar: Tex. 1978, U.S. Dist. Ct. (so. dist.) Tex. 1978, U.S. Dist. Ct. (we. dist.) Tex. 1987, U.S. Dist. Ct. (no. dist.) Tex, 1988, U.S. Dist. Ct. (ea. dist.) Tex. 1991, U.S. Tax Ct., 1984, U.S. Ct. Appeals (5th cir.) 1978, U.S. Ct. Appeals (11th cir.) 1981, U.S. Ct. Appeals (D.C. cir.) 1982, U.S. Ct. Appeals (fed. cir.) 1993, U.S. Supreme Ct. 1981. Law clk. U.S. Ct. Appeals (2d cir.), N.Y.C., 1977; assoc. Vinson & Elkins, Houston, 1977-84, ptnr., 1984—. Co-chmn. Antitrust Practice Group. Editor: Compliance Manuals for the New Antitrust Era, 1989, Annual Review of Antitrust Law Developments, 2000; co-author: Federal Civil Procedure Before Trial-Fifth Circuit, 1997, supplement, 1999, The Competition Laws of NAFTA, Canada, Mexico, and the United States, 1997, Business and Commercial Litigation in Federal Courts, 1998, American Legal Ethics Library, 1998, State Antitrust Practice and Statutes, 1999, Doing Business in Texas, 1999; contbr. articles to profl. jours. Bd. visitors Columbia U., 1992—; mem. City of Houston Ethics Com., 1992-98, chmn. 1995-98; dir. Tex. Appleseed Found., 1998—, vice-chmn., 1999—. Recipient Ordroneaux prize Columbia U., 1977; James Kent scholar Columbia U., 1974-77. Fellow Tex. Bar Found.; mem. ABA (com. chmn. 1987-95, mem. coun. 1996-99, com. chmn. 2000—), Houston Bar Assn. (sect. chair 1991-93), Tex.-Mex. Bar Assn. (chmn. 1998-2000), Phi Beta Kappa. Democrat. Jewish. Antitrust, General civil litigation, Professional liability. Home: 3430 S Parkwood Dr Houston TX 77021-1238 Office: Vinson & Elkins LLP 1001 Fannin St Ste 2300 Houston TX 77002-6760 E-mail: avanfleet@velaw.com

VAN GILDER, DEREK ROBERT, lawyer, engineer; b. San Antonio, Feb. 26, 1950; s. Robert Ellis and Genevieve Delphine (Hutter) Van G. Student, U.S. Mil. Acad., 1969-71; BS in Civil Enging., U. Tex., 1974, JD, 1981; MBA, U. Houston, 1976. Bar: Tex. 1981, U.S. Ct. Appeals (5th and 9th cirs.) 1982, Calif. 1982, U.S. Dist. Ct. (cen. dist.) Calif. 1982, U.S. Dist. Ct. (ea. and so. dists.) Tex. 1982, U.S. Dist. Ct. (we. dist.) Tex. 1983, U.S. Dist. Ct. (no. dist.) Tex. 1988, U.S. Supreme Ct. 1988, D.C. 1990, U.S. Patent/Trademark 1990. Engr. various engrng cos., Houston, Longview and Austin, Tex., 1974-81; assoc. Thelen, Marrin, Johnson & Bridges, Los Angeles, 1981-82, Bean & Manning, Houston, 1982-85; pvt. practice Van Gilder & Assocs., 1985-94, Law Office of Derek R. Van Gilder, Bastrop, Tex., 1995—. Instr. Houston C.C., 1981-82; life mem., committeeman Houston Livestock Show & Rodeo, 1991-2000. Bd. dirs. Children's Advocacy Ctr. of Bastrop County, treas. 1996-2001; chmn. Friends of Science Park-MD Anderson Sci. Park., Smithville. Mem. ABA, ASCE, NSPE, Bastrop C. of C., Bastrop County Bar Assn., Coll. State Bar Tex., Am. Arbitration Assn. (panel of arbitrators), Tex. Soc. Profl. Engrs., Rotary Club Bastrop County (v.p. 1996-97, pres.-elect 1997-98, pres. 1998-99, asst. dist. gov. 2000—). Republican. Roman Catholic. Avocations: racquetball, golf, Scuba diving, photography. General civil litigation, Construction, Patent. Office: 916 Main St Bastrop TX 78602-3810

VAN GRAAFEILAND, ELLSWORTH ALFRED, federal judge; b. Rochester, N.Y., May 11, 1915; s. Ivan and Elsie (Gohr) VanG.; m. Rosemary Vaeth, May 26, 1945; children— Gary, Suzanne, Joan, John, Anne. AB, U. Rochester, 1937; LLB, Cornell U., 1940. Bar: N.Y. 1940. Practiced in, Rochester; now sr. judge U.S. Ct. Appeals for 2d Cir. Fellow Am. Bar Found., N.Y. Bar Found.; mem. ABA (ho. dels. 1973-75), N.Y. State Bar Assn. (v.p. 1972-73, pres. 1973-74, chmn. negligence compensation and ins. sect. 1968-69), Monroe County Bar Assn. (past pres.), Am. Coll. Trial Lawyers., Masons, Kent Club, Oak Hill Country Club. Home: 1 Tiffany Ct Pittsford NY 14534-1067 Office: Fed Bldg 100 State St Ste 423 Rochester NY 14614-1309

VAN GRACK, STEVEN, lawyer; b. Memphis, Oct. 6, 1948; s. Irving and Edna (Schwartz) Van Grack; m. Gail Beverly Lang, Nov. 18, 1972 (div.); children: Adam, Ryan, Brandon; m. Susan M Freeland, May 21, 1993. BA, U. Md., 1970, JD, 1974. Bar: 1974 (Md), DC 1976, US Dist Ct Md 1976, US Dist Ct DC 1976, US Ct Appeals (4th cir) 1977, US Supreme Ct 1978. Law clk. to presiding justice Montgomery County Cir. Ct., Rockville, Md., 1974-75; assoc. Joseph Roesser Law Offices, Silver Springs, 1975-78; ptnr. Ebert & Bowytz, Washington, 1978-80; mng. ptnr. Van Grack, Axelson & Williamowsky, Rockville, 1980—. Instr, lectr Montgomery Col, Germantown, Md., 1983—85. Cubmaster packs 1343 and 1449 Boy Scouts Am; coach Rockville Baseball Asn; trustee Shady Grove Adventist Hosp Found; co-chmn Montgomery County March of Dimes WalkAmerica Comt, 1998—2000; campaign mgr Comt to Elect the Sitting Judges, Rockville, 1982; mayor City of Rockville, 1985—87; gen counsel Montgomery County Dem Cent Comt, Kensington, Md., 1978—82; Dem cand 8th Congl Dist Md, 1994; chmn Md Real Estate Comn, 2001—; bd dirs Washington Met Coun Govts. With USAR, 1970—71. Named one of Oustanding Young Men Am, Jaycees, 1978, 1981; recipient Fifth Ann Pro Bono Serv Award, Montgomery County Bar Found, 1998, Extraordinary Commitment to the Delivery of Legal Servs Award, 1999, Nancy Dworkin Award, Montgomery County Comn Children and Youth, 2001. Fellow: Md Bar Found; mem.: ABA, ATLA, Md Bar Asn, Md Trial Lawyers Asn, Montgomery County Bar Asn (Outstanding Comt Chair of the Yr Award 2001), Rockville CofC (bd dirs). Jewish. Avocations: running, swimming, exercising, coin collecting, political button collecting. State civil litigation, Criminal, Personal injury. Home: 808 Fordham St Rockville MD 20850-1018 Office: Van Grack Axelson & Williamowsky 110 N Washington St Fl 5 Rockville MD 20850-2223 E-mail: sug@vawlaw.com

VAN GRUNSVEN, PAUL ROBERT, lawyer; b. Green Bay, Wis., Mar. 11, 1961; s. David Edward and Carol Ann (Janssen) Van G. BS, Marquette U., 1983, JD, 1986; LLM in Health Law, De Paul U., 1995. Bar: Wis. 1986, U.S. Dist. Ct. (ea. dist.) Wis. 1986. Mem. Techmeier & Van Grunsven, S.C., Milw., 1986-89, shareholder, 1989-2001; chair health law dept. Kasdorf, Lewis & Swietlik, S.C., 2001—. Adj. prof. Marquette U. Law Sch., Milw., 1995—. Recipient Am. Jurisprudence award Lawyer's Coop. Pub. Co., 1986. Mem. ATLA, Wis. Trial Lawyers for Public Justice, Wis. Acad. Trial Lawyers (bd. dirs., co-editor The Verdict), Wis. Bar Assn., Milw. Bar Assn. (co-chair health law sect.). Roman Catholic. Avocations: golf, football, baseball, basketball. General civil litigation, Health, Personal injury. Office: Techmeier & Van Grunsven SC 411 E Wisconsin Ave Ste 1100 Milwaukee WI 53202-4464

VAN GUNDY, GREGORY FRANK, lawyer; b. Columbus, Ohio, Oct. 24, 1945; s. Paul Arden and Edna Marie (Sanders) Van G.; m. Lisa Tamara Langer. B.A., Ohio State U., Columbus, 1966, J.D., 1969. Bar: N.Y. bar 1971. Asso. atty. firm Willkie Farr & Gallagher, N.Y.C., 1970-74; v.p. legal, sec. Marsh & McLennan Cos., Inc., 1974-79, v.p., sec., gen. counsel, 1979-2000, sec., 2000—. Mem. ABA, Phi Beta Kappa. Roman Catholic. Club: University (N.Y.C.). General corporate. Home: 232 Fox Meadow Rd Scarsdale NY 10583-1640 Office: Marsh & McLennan Cos Inc 1166 Avenue Of The Americas New York NY 10036-2728

VAN HOOMISSEN, GEORGE ALBERT, state supreme court justice; b. Portland, Oreg., Mar. 7, 1930; s. Fred J. and Helen F. (Flanagan) Van H.; m. Ruth Madeleine Niedermeyer, June 4, 1960; children: Geroge T., Ruth Anne, Madeleine, Matthew. BBA, U. Portland, 1951; JD, Georgetown U., 1955, LLM in Labor Law, 1957; LLM in Jud. Adminstrn., U. Va., 1986. Bar: D.C. 1955, Oreg. 1956, Tex. 1971, U.S. Dist. Ct. Oreg. 1956, U.S. Ct. Mil. Appeals 1955, U.S. Ct. Customs and Patent Appeals 1955, U.S. Ct. Claims 1955, U.S. Ct. Appeals (9th cir.) 1956, U.S. Ct. Appeals (D.C. cir.) 1955, U.S. Supreme Ct. 1960. Law clk. for Chief Justice Harold J. Warner Oreg. Supreme Ct., 1955-56; Keigwin teaching fellow Georgetown Law Sch., 1956-57; dep. dist. atty. Multnomah County, Portland, 1957-59; pvt. practice, 1959-62; dist. atty. Multnomah County, 1962-71; dean nat. coll. dist. attys., prof. law U. Houston, 1971-73; judge Cir. Ct., Portland, 1973-81, Oreg. Ct. Appeals, Salem, 1981-88; justice Oreg. Supreme Ct., 1988—2001. Adj. prof. Northwestern Sch. Law, Portland, Willamette U. Sch. Law, Portland State U.; mem. faculty Am. Acad. Judicial Edn., Nat. Judicial Coll.; Keigwin Teaching fellow Georgetown U. Law Sch. Mem. Oreg. Ho. of Reps., Salem, 1959-62, chmn. house jud. com. With USMC, 1951-53; col. USMCR (ret.). Recipient Disting. Alumnus award U. Portland, 1972. Master Owen M. Panner Am. Inn of Ct.; mem. ABA, Oreg. State Bar, Tex. Bar Assn., Oreg. Law Inst. (bd. dirs.), Arlington Club, Multnomah Athletic Club, Univ. Club. Roman Catholic. E-mial. Office: Oreg Supreme Ct 2105 SW Elm St Portland OR 97201 E-mail: gavanhoomissen@qwest.net

VAN HOY, PHILIP MARSHALL, lawyer; b. Washington, Nov. 8, 1947; s. Joe Milton and Helen Virginia (Spangler) V.; m. Sylvia Kathryn Smith, Dec. 30, 1972; children: Marshall, Travis. AB, Duke U., 1970; JD, U. N.C., 1973. Bar: N.C. 1973, U.S. Dist. Ct. (ea., we. and mid. dists.) N.C. 1974, U.S. Ct. Appeals (4th cir.) 1974, U.S. Supreme Ct. 1978. Labor counsel Duke Power Co., Charlotte, N.C., 1973-80; assoc. Siegel, O'Connor & Kaunen, 1980-83; ptnr. Mullins & Van Hoy, 1983-89, Van Hoy, Rentlinger & Admas, Charlotte, 1989—. Mem. N.C. OSHA Rev. Bd., 1985-92, Mecklenburg County, N.C. Personnel Commn., 1985-92, N.C. Leadership Coun. Co-state chmn. Gardner for Lt. Gov., 1988, alt. del. Rep. Nat. Conv., Detroit, 1980; chmn. Mecklenbyrg County Young Rep. Com., 1979-93, vice chmn., 1980-83; active Duke U. Athletics Coun., 1999—. 1st lt. U.S. Army, 1973-81. Mem. N.C. Bar Assn. (councillor labor and employment law sect. 1985-88, chmn. EEOC com. 1983-92), N.C. State Bar, 4th Cir. Jud. Conf., Rotary, Charlotte Cotillion Club (pres. 1979-80), City Club, Myers Park Country Club (dir. 1994-96, 2000—). Republican. Methodist. Federal civil litigation, Labor. Home: 2615 Hampton Ave Charlotte NC 28207-2521 Office: Van Hoy Reutlinger & Adams 737 East Blvd Charlotte NC 28203-5113

VAN KERREBROOK, MARY ALICE, lawyer; b. Houston, Aug. 21, 1961; d. Richard Rene and Phyllis Law (Banks) Van K. BA in Econs., Northwestern U., 1983; JD, So. Meth. U., 1986. Bar: Tex. 1986, U.S. Dist. Ct. (so. dist.) Tex. 1987, U.S. Ct. Appeals (5th cir.) 1988, U.S. Dist. Ct. (ea. dist.) Tex. 1989, U.S. Supreme Ct. 2000. Assoc. Wilson, Cribbs, Goren & Flaum, P.C., Houston, 1986-94, shareholder, 1994—. Trustee Tex. Com. on Natural Resources, Dallas, 1988—; mem. exec. com. Galveston Bay Found., Webster, Tex., 1991-93; pres. Katy Prairie Conservancy, Houston, 1995—. Appellate, General civil litigation, State and local taxation. Office: Wilson Cribbs Goren & Flaum PC 2200 Lyric Ctr 440 Houston TX 77002-1624 E-mail: mvkerrebrook@wcgf.com

VAN KIRK, THOMAS L. lawyer; b. Pa., June 25, 1945; s. Theodore and Mary Jane (Young) Van K.; children: Thomas Jr., Christopher. BA, Bucknell U., 1967; JD cum laude, Dickinson U., 1970. Bar: Pa., U.S. Dist. Ct. (we. and ea. dists.) Pa. 1971, U.S. Ct. Appeals (3d cir.) 1972, U.S. Supreme Ct. 1976. Clk. Pa. Superior Ct., 1970-71; assoc. Buchanan Ingersoll, Pitts., 1971-77, ptnr., 1978—, chief oper. officer, 1985—. Bd. dirs. Buchanan Ingersoll P.C.; v.p. State Pa. Economy League; bd. dirs. Western Pa. Economy League, chair, 1998. Chmn. Allegheny County Heart Assn. Walk, 1992; chair Pitts. Downtown Partnership, 1995-97; bd. dirs. Capital divsn. Pa. Economy League, sec./treas., 1995; bd. dirs. Pitts. Cultural Trust, 1998, SPIRC Bd. Fellow Am. Bar Found.; mem. ABA, Allegheny County Bar Assn., Duquesne Club, Rivers Club, Racquet Club Phila., The Club at Nevillewood. Democrat. Lutheran. Antitrust, Federal civil litigation, Public international. Home: 1010 Osage Rd Pittsburgh PA 15243-1014 Office: Buchanan Ingersoll PC 301 Grant St Fl 20 Pittsburgh PA 15219-1410

VAN LEUVEN, ROBERT JOSEPH, lawyer; b. Detroit, Apr. 17, 1931; s. Joseph Francis and Olive (Stowell) Van L.; m. Merri Lee Van Leuven; children: Joseph Michael, Douglas Robert, Julie Margaret. Student, Albion Coll., 1949-51; BA with distinction, Wayne State U., 1953; JD, U. Mich., 1957. Bar: Mich. 1957. Since practiced in, Muskegon, Mich.; ptnr. Hathaway, Latimer, Clink & Robb, 1957-68, McCroskey, Libner & Van Leuven, 1968-81, Libner-Van Leuven, 1982-99; ret., 1999. Past mem. coun. negligence law sect. State Bar Mich. Bd. dirs. Muskegon Children's Home, 1965-75. Served with AUS, 1953-55. Fellow Mich. Bar Found., Mich. Trial Lawyers Assn., Am. Coll. Trial Lawyers; mem. Delta Sigma Phi, Muskegon Country Club. Home: 410 Ruddiman Dr # 4 Muskegon MI 49445-2795 Office: Libner-Van Leuven Comerica Bank Bldg 801 W Norton Ave 4th Fl Muskegon MI 49441

VAN NISPEN, CONSTANT J.J.C. lawyer, educator; b. Oudenbosch, Brabant, The Netherlands, Jan. 28, 1950; s. Constant. A.I.L. and Johanna A.M. (Dekkers) Van N.; m. Marianne L.E.E. Doon, Sept. 16, 1977; children: Louise, Constantijn. LLM, Leyden (The Netherlands) U., 1972, PhD, 1978. Assoc. De Brauw Linklaters, The Hague, The Netherlands, 1977-83, ptnr. The Netherlands, 1984—; prof. Free U., Amsterdam, 1993—. Author: Injunctions, 1978, Remedies, 1988, Industrial Property, 1989; editor: Law on Civil Procedure, 1996. Chmn. Liberal Party, Leidschedam, 1980-83. With Intendance, 1975-76. Intellectual property, Patent, Trademark and copyright. Home: Koekoeklaan 4 2261 EX Leidschendam The Netherlands Office: De Brauw Linklaters Zuid Hollandlaan 7 2596 AL The Hague The Netherlands

VAN NUYS, PETER, lawyer; b. N.Y.C., June 19, 1939; s. Francis and Anna (Chute) Van N.; m. Helena Kristina Iivonen Capoen, June 27, 1981; children: Alexandra Anna, Kristina Jenni. AB, Harvard U., 1961, JD, 1964; postgrad., Columbia U., 1968; LLM in Taxation, NYU, 1970. Bar: N.Y. 1965, U.S. Dist. Ct. (so. and ea. dists.) N.Y. 1968, U.S. Ct. Appeals (2d cir.) 1969, U.S. Tax Ct. 1975. Assoc. Kramer, Marx, Greenlee & Backus, N.Y.C., 1965-69, Hale & Russell, N.Y.C., 1969, ptnr., 1970-80; sole practice, 1980-82; ptnr. Van Nuys, Turley & Nelson, 1982-83, Van Nuys & Nelson, N.Y.C., 1983-85; sole practice, 1985-89; ptnr. Baker, Nelson & Williams, 1990-91, Becker, Glynn, Melamed & Muffley, N.Y.C., 1991—. Lectr. estate planning for families with handicapped mems., 1986—. Bd. dirs., treas. Les Botiques de Noel, 1982-84; bd. dirs., sec. Planned Lifetime Asst. Network of N.Y., Inc.; bd. dirs. Disabled and Alone/Life Svcs. for the Handicapped, Inc.; bd. dirs. Westchester ARC, 1994-2000. With N.g., 1964-65, to lt. comdr. U.S. Navy Res., 1965-75. Mem. ABA, N.Y. State Bar Assn., Assn. of Bar of City of N.Y. (mem. joint com. on legal referral svc. 1984-91, chmn. 1987-88, mem. com. on legal issues affecting the handicepped 1988-91), Harvard Club. Estate planning, Probate, Taxation, general. Office: 299 Park Ave New York NY 10171-0002 E-mail: pvannuys@beckerglynn.com

VAN OEVEREN, EDWARD LANIER, lawyer, biologist, physician; b. Washington, Apr. 12, 1954; BA with high distinction, U. Va., 1976; M.D., Med. Coll. Va., 1995; JD, U. Va., 1981; BS with distinction, George Mason U., 1983; MPH, Johns Hopkins U., 1998. Bar: Va. 1981, U.S. Dist. Ct. (ea. dist.) Va. 1988, U.S. Temporary Emergency Ct. Appeals 1989; lic. physician, Va.; bd. cert. pub. health & preventive medicine. Pvt. practice legal cons., Falls Church, Va., 1984-85; pvt. practice law, 1986-89; pvt. practice law and biology, 1989-95; intern Med. Coll. Va., 1996-97; resident in preventive medicine Johns Hopkins U., Balt., 1997-99; pvt. practice law, medicine and biology Falls Church, 1997—. Editor: Federal Special Court Litigation, 1982. Election officer Fairfax County (Va.) Electoral Bd., 1989-90, 94-2001. Capt. Va. Army NG, 1996-97; 1st lt. USAR, 1995-96, capt., 1997—. Mem. AMA, Va. State Bar Assn., George Mason U. Alumni Assn. (scholarship, awards, rules and policies coms. 1989-91), Alpha Chi. Avocation: photography. Aviation, Federal civil litigation, Personal injury. Home: 3304 Patrick Henry Dr Falls Church VA 22044-1514 E-mail: EVanOeveren@pol.net

VAN RY, BRADLEY OTTO, lawyer; b. Conway, Ark., Oct. 19, 1966; s. Otto Rhomas and Tennie Joy Nooner Van Ry; m. Julie Elizabeth Mace, May 27, 1988; children: Jessica Julie, Brandi Julie, Tyler Bradley. BS, U. Nev., 1992; JD, U. Ariz., 1997. Bar: Ariz. U.S. Dist. Ct. Ariz., U.S. Ct. Appeals (9th cir.) 1997. Pvt. practice, Safford, Ariz., 1997—. General civil litigation, Personal injury, Product liability. Office: Van Ry Law Office 420 W 9th St Safford AZ 85546

VAN SCHOONENBERG, ROBERT G. lawyer; b. Madison, Wis., Aug. 18, 1946; s. John W. and Ione (Henning) Schoonenberg. BA, Marquette U., 1968; MBA, U. Wis., 1972; JD, U. Mich., 1974. Bar: Calif. 1975, Fla. 1976. Atty. Gulf Oil Corp., Pitts., 1974-81; exec. v.p., gen. counsel, sec. Avery Dennison Corp., Pasadena, Calif., 1981—. Judge pro tem Pasadena Mcpl. Ct., 1987-89. Dir., v.p. fin. adminstrn. Am. Cancer Soc., San Gabriel Vally Unit, 1987—; v.p., treas., dir., v.p. investments Pasadena Symphony Assn.; bd. dirs. Pasadena Recreation and Parks Found., 1983-84; mem. Pasadena Citizens Task Force on Crime Control, 1983-84; dir. Boy Scouts, San Gabriel Valley Coun., dir. public coun.; bd. dirs. Verugo Hills Hosp. Found.; trustee Southwestern U. Sch. Law. Mem. ABA, Am. Corp. Counsel Assn. (bd. dirs.), Am. Soc. Corp. Secs. (bd. dirs., pres. Southern Calif. chpt.), L.A. County Bar Assn. (past chair, corp. law dept. sect.), Corp. Counsel Inst. (bd. govs.), Jonathon Club, Flint Canyon Tennis Club, The Calif. Club, Wis. Union. Clubs: Athletic (Pasadena); Wis. Union. General corporate, Intellectual property, Securities. Office: Avery Dennison Corp 150 N Orange Grove Blvd Pasadena CA 91103-3534

VAN SICKLE, BRUCE MARION, federal judge; b. Minot, N.D., Feb. 13, 1917; s. Guy Robin and Hilda Alice (Rosenquist) Van S.; m. Dorothy Alfreda Hermann, May 26, 1943; children: Susan Van Sickle Cooper, John Allan, Craig Bruce, David Max. BSL, JD, U. Minn., 1941. Bar: Minn. 1941, N.D. 1946. Pvt. practice law, Minot, 1947-71; judge U.S. Dist. Ct. N.D., 1971-85, sr. judge, 1985—. Mem. N.D. Ho. of Reps., 1957, 59. Served with USMCR, 1941-46. Mem. ABA, N.D. Bar Assn., N.W. Bar Assn., Ward County Bar Assn., Am. Trial Lawyers Assn., Am. Coll. Probate Counsel, Am. Judicature Soc., Bruce M. Van Sickle Inns of Ct., Masons, Shriners, Elks, Delta Theta Phi. Office: US Dist Ct US Courthouse Rm 428 PO Box 670 Bismarck ND 58502-0670

VAN SWEARINGEN, CYNTHIA, lawyer; b. Quincy, Mass., Mar. 11, 1935; d. Graham and E. Ruth (Mackenzie) Smith; m. Guy Van Swearingen III, July 15, 1960 (div. 1980); children— Andrea, Guy IV, Johanna, Graham. B.A., Smith Coll., 1957; J.D., John Marshall Law Sch., 1977. Bar: Ill. 1977, U.S. Dist. Ct. (no. dist.) Ill. 1977. Editor West Group, Deerfield, Ill., 1977— . Mem. Chgo. Bar Assn. Office: West Group 155 Pfingsten Rd Deerfield IL 60015 E-mail: cynthiavanswearingen@westgroup.com

VAN TATENHOVE, GREGORY F. prosecutor; JD, U. Ky. Aide to U.S. Senator Mitch McConnell, Ky.; law clerk 6th U.S. Cir. Ct. Appeals; trial atty. Justice Dept.; chief of staff to 2nd dist. U.S. rep. Ron Lewis; U.S. atty. ea. dist., 2001—. Office: 110 W Vine St Ste 400 Lexington KY 40507-1671 Office Fax: 859-233-2666*

VAN TINE, MATTHEW ERIC, lawyer; b. Tomahawk, Wis., June 21, 1958; s. Kenneth G. and Louise (Olson) Van T.; m. Rena Marie David, Apr. 30, 1988; 1 child, Kristen. AB cum laude, Harvard Coll., 1980; JD magna cum laude, Boston U., 1983. Bar: Ill. 1983, Mass. 1983, U.S. Dist. Ct. Mass. 1984, U.S. Dist. Ct. (no. dist.) Ill. 1986, Seventh Cir., 2001. Law clk. to Hon. Raymond J. Pettine U.S. Dist. Ct. R.I., Providence, 1983-84; assoc. Palmer & Dodge, Boston, 1984-85, Schiff, Hardin & Waite, Chgo., 1985-88; asst. corp. counsel City of Chgo., 1988-92; assoc. to ptnr. Saunders & Monroe, Chgo., 1993-99; of counsel Miller Faucher and Cafferty, 2000—. Exec. editor: Boston University Law Rev., 1982-83. Mem. ABA, Chgo. Bar Assn., Inns of Ct. General civil litigation, Government contracts and claims, Labor. Office: Miller Faucher and Cafferty 30 N Lasalle St Ste 3200 Chicago IL 60602-2506 E-mail: mvantine@millerfaucher.com

VAN VALKENBURG, EDGAR WALTER, lawyer; b. Seattle, Jan. 8, 1953; s. Edgar Walter and Margaret Catherine (McKenna) Van V.; m. Turid L. Owren, Sept. 29, 1990; children: Ingrid Catherine, Andrew Owren. BA, U. Wash., 1975; JD summa cum laude, Willamette Coll. of Law, 1978; LLM, Columbia U., 1984. Bar: Oreg. 1978, U.S. Dist. Ct. Oreg. 1979, U.S. Ct. Appeals (9th cir.) 1980. Law clk. to assoc. justice Oreg. Supreme Ct., Salem, 1978-79; assoc. Stoel, Rives, Boley, Fraser & Wyse, Portland, Oreg., 1979-82, 84-86; ptnr. Stoel Rives LLP, 1986—; instr. Columbia U., N.Y.C., 1982-84. Bd. dirs. Portland Oregon Sports Authority. Editor-in-chief: Williamette Law Jour. 1977-78. Bd. dirs., chmn. Multnomah County Legal Aid, 1997-98; bd. dirs. Oreg. Legal Aid, 1998—. Mem. ACLU (pres. Oreg. chpt. 1991-93), Oreg. State Bar (chmn. antitrust sect. 1989-90, mem. Ho. of Dels. 1996-98). Antitrust, General corporate, Intellectual property. Office: Stoel Rives LLP 900 SW 5th Ave Ste 2300 Portland OR 97204-1229 E-mail: wvanvalkenburg@stoel.com

VAN VOORHIS, THOMAS, lawyer; b. Great Falls, Mont., Feb. 24, 1930; s. George E. and Ruthe (Williams) V.; AA, U. Calif., 1955; LLB, JD, Hastings Coll. Law, 1959; m. Eleanor Cooper, Mar. 21, 1958; children: Kevin, Karen, Thomas. Admitted to Calif. bar, 1960; pres. Campbell & Van Voorhis, Walnut Creek, Calif., 1960-82; of counsel Van Voorhis & Skaggs, 1982-85; of counsel McCutchen, Brown, Doyle & Enersen, 1985—; judge pro tem Walnut Creek-Danville Municipal Ct., 1974-82; pres. Domino II Cattle Co., Walnut Creek, 1971-86; v.p. Blackhawk Devel. Co., Danville, Calif., 1972-75; corp. sec., dir. RWC Calif. Co., Danville, 1975-85, RWC Nev. Co., Reno; sec., dir. Woodhill Devel. Co., Danville, 1976-85; dir. First Security Savs. Bank. Pres. Rep. Assembly, Walnut Creek, 1964. Bd. dirs. Walnut Creek (Cal.) Action for Beauty Council, Pacific Vascular Found., 1986. Served with USAF, 1950-54. Mem. State Bar Calif., ABA (com. on devel. and mgmt. real estate 1975—), Contra Costa Bar Assn., Internat. Assn. Fin. Planning. Office: 1855 Olympic Blvd Walnut Creek CA 94596-5089

VAN WIJNGAARDEN, BERNA JOHANNA, lawyer; b. Rotterdam, The Netherlands, Jan. 31, 1962; d. Johannes Lucas and Corrie (Konings) Van W.; m. Michiel Bonarius, June 7, 1995. Degree in law, Erasmus U., Rotterdam, 1991. Assoc. Van Wijngaarden Law Office, Schiedam, 1991-93, Trenité Van Doorne, Rotterdam, 1993—. Contbr. articles to profl. jours. Office: Stadermann Luiten Advocaten Schouwburgplein 30-34 Rotterdam 3012 CL The Netherlands

VAN ZANDT, DAVID E. dean; b. Princeton, N.J., Feb. 17, 1953; m. Lisa A. Huestis; children: Caroline, Nicholas. AB summa cum laude, Princeton U., 1975; JD, Yale U., 1981; PhD in Sociology, U. London, 1985. Bar: Ill. Clk. to Hon. Pierre N. Leval U.S. Dist. Ct. (so. dist.) N.Y., 1981-82; clk. to Hon. Harry A. Blackmun U.S. Supreme Ct., Washington, 1982-83; atty. Davis, Polk & Wardwell, 1984-85; mem. faculty Northwestern U. Law Sch., Chgo., 1985—, dean, 1995—. Mem. planning com. Northwestern U. Corporate Counsel Inst., Northwestern U. Corp. Counsel Ctr. Author: Living in the Children of God, 1991; mng. editor Yale Law Jour., 1980-81; contbr. articles to profl. jours. Office: Northwestern U Sch Law Office of Dean 357 E Chicago Ave Chicago IL 60611-3059*

VAN ZILE, PHILIP TAYLOR, III, lawyer, educator; b. Detroit, Feb. 17, 1945; s. Philip Taylor II and Ruth (Butzel) Van Z.; m. Susan Jones, Sept. 12, 1981; children: Caroline Sage, Philip Taylor IV. BA, Oberlin Coll., 1968; MDiv, Union Theol. Sem., 1971; JD, Mich. State U., 1975. Bar: Mich. 1976, D.C. 1976, U.S. Dist. Ct. (ea. dist.) Mich. 1976, U.S. Ct. Appeals (6th cir.) 1976, U.S. Supreme Ct. 1977, Pa. 1981. Law clk. Mich. Ct. Appeals, Detroit, 1976-78, Mich. Supreme Ct., Detroit and Lansing, Mich., 1978-80; asst. corp. counsel Office of Corp. Counsel, Washington, 1980-87; assoc. Killian & Gephart, Harrisburg, Pa., 1987-89; prin. Law Office of Philip T. Van Zile, 1989-91; assoc. coun. Office Chief Coun. Pa. Dept. Conservation and Natural Resources, 1991—; assoc. realtor M.C. Walker Realty, Mechanicsburg, Pa., 1997—. Teaching fellow Detroit Coll. Law, 1976-80; teaching asst. Detroit Gen. Hosp., 1978-80; teaching assoc. Acad. Med. Arts and Bus., Harrisburg, 1990-91. Contbr. articles to profl. jours. Ordained elder Mechanicsburg Presbyn. Ch., 1995—, chmn. vol. ministries, 1995, chmn. peacemaking, 1996, chmn. staff, 1997—. Mem. ABA, Kenwood Club (Chevy Chase, Md.). Administrative and regulatory, Environmental, Government contracts and claims. Office: Pa Dept Conservation/Natural Resources Office Chief Counsel 400 Market St Harrisburg PA 17101-2301

VARAT, JONATHAN D. dean, law educator; b. 1945; BA, U. Pa., Phila., 1967, JD, 1972. Law clk. to judge Walter Mansfield U.S. Ct. Appeals (2d cir.), N.Y.C., 1972-73; law clk. to justice Byron White U.S. Supreme Ct., Washington, 1973-74; assoc. O'Melveny & Myers, Los Angeles, 1974-76; acting prof. UCLA, 1976-81, prof., 1981—, assoc. dean, 1982-83, 91-92; dean UCLA Sch. Law, 1998—. Office: UCLA Sch Law 405 Hilgard Ave Los Angeles CA 90095-9000*

VARDAMAN, JOHN WESLEY, lawyer; b. Montgomery, Ala., Apr. 22, 1940; s. John Wesley and Elizabeth (Merrill) V.; m. Marianne Fay, June 14, 1969; children: Thomas, Shannon, John Wesley III, Davis. BA, Washington & Lee U., 1962; JD, Harvard U., 1965. Bar: D.C. 1966, U.S. Dist. Ct. (D.C.) 1967, U.S. Supreme Ct. 1970. Law clk. to justice Hugo Black U.S. Supreme Ct., 1965-66; assoc. Wilmer, Cutler & Pickering, Washington, 1966-70; ptnr. Williams & Connolly, 1970—; gen. counsel U.S. Golf Assn., 1999—. Contbr. articles to profl. jours. Mem. ABA, Am. Coll. Trial Lawyers, Congl. Country Club (Bethesda, Md.). Baptist. Avocation: golf. Federal civil litigation, Criminal, Environmental. Office: Williams & Connolly 725 12th St NW Washington DC 20005-5901

VARELLAS, SANDRA MOTTE, judge; b. Anderson, S.C., Oct. 17, 1946; d. James E. and Helen Lucille (Gilliam) Motte; m. James John Varellas, July 3, 1971; children: James John III, David Todd. BA, Winthrop U., 1968; MA, U. Ky., 1970, JD, 1975. Bar: Ky. 1975, Fla. 1976, U.S. Dist. Ct. (ea. dist.) Ky. 1975, U.S. Ct. Appeals (6th cir.) 1976, U.S. Supreme Ct. 1978. Instr. Midway Coll., Ky., 1970-72; adj. prof. U. Ky. Coll. Law, Lexington, 1976-78; instr. dept. bus. adminstrn. U. Ky., 1976-78; ptnr. Varellas, Pratt & Cooley, 1975-93, Varellas & Pratt, Lexington, 1993-97, Varellas & Varellas, Lexington, 1998—. Fayette County judge exec., Ky., 1980—; hearing officer Ky. Natural Resources and Environ. Protection Cabinet, Frankfort, 1984-88. Committeewoman Ky. Young Dems., Frankfort, 1977-80; pres. Fayette County Young Dems., Lexington, 1977; bd. dirs. Ky. Dem. Women's Club, Frankfort, 1980-84, bd. dirs., Bluegrass Estate Planning Coun., 1995-98; grad. Leadership Lexington, 1981; chairwoman Profl. Women's Forum, Lexington, Ky., 1985-86, bd. dirs., 1984-87, Aequum award com., 1989-92; mem. devel. coun. Midway Coll., 1990-92; co-chair Gift Club Com., 1992. Named Outstanding Young Dem. Woman, Ky. Young Dems., Frankfort, 1977, Outstanding Former Young Dem., Ky. Young Dems., 1983. Mem. Ky. Bar Assn. (treas. young lawyers divsn. 1978-79, long range planning com. 1988-89), Fla. Bar, Fayette County Bar Assn. (treas. 1977-78, bd. govs. 1978-80), LWV (nominating com. 1984-85), Greater Lexington C. of C. (legis. affairs com. 1994-95, bd.d irs. coun. smaller enterprises 1992-95). Club: The Lexington Forum (bd. dirs. 1996-99), Lexington Philharm. Guild (bd. dirs. 1979-81, 86—), Nat. Assn. Women Bus. Owners (chmn. cmty. liaison/govtl. affairs com. 1992-93), Lexington Network (bd. dirs. and sec. 1994-98). Office: Varellas & Varellas 167 W Main St Ste 1310 Lexington KY 40507-1398

VARGO, ROBERT FRANK, lawyer; b. St. Louis, Oct. 21, 1948; s. Frank John and Hazel Emma (Brisch) V.; m. Alice Anne McClelland, Sept. 23, 1977. BA, U. South Fla., 1970; JD, St. Mary's U., 1975; postgrad., U. Miami, 1983-84. Bar: Ala. 1975, Tex. 1984, U.S. Dist. Ct. (so. dist.) Ala. 1977; cert. comml. real estate law. Sole practice, Atmore, Ala., 1975-77, Bay Minette, Ala., 1977-84; assoc. Kaufman, Becker, Clare & Padgett, San Antonio, 1984—; instr. Jefferson Davis Jr. Coll., Brewton, Ala., 1976; magistrate Escambia County Dist. Ct., Atmore, 1976-77. Contbr. articles to legal jours. Pres., campaign chmn. United Fund, Bay Minette, 1981-84. Recipient Am. Jurisprudence awards Lawyers Coop. Pub. Co., 1974-75; Phi Alpha Delta scholar, 1975. Mem. ABA, Ala. State Bar, State Bar Tex., John M. Harlan Soc. Republican. Presbyterian. Lodges: Lions (v.p., bd. dirs. Atmore chpt., 1976-77), Kiwanis (bd. dirs. Bay Minette chpt., 1977-82). Banking, General corporate, Real property. Home: 109 Dunhill Dr SW Huntsville AL 35824-1330

VARMA, RISHI ANAND, lawyer; b. Boston, Nov. 17, 1972; s. Surendra Kumar and Kamlesh Varma. BA, Georgetown U., 1994, JD, 1997. Bar: N.Y. 1998. Assoc. Rosenman & Colin LLP, N.Y.C., 1997—. Avocations: novels, golf, travel, music. Communications, General corporate, Entertainment. Office: Rosenman & Colin LLP 575 Madison Ave New York NY 10022

VARNER, CARLTON A. lawyer; b. Creston, Iowa, July 14, 1947; BA, U. Iowa, 1969; JD magna cum laude, U. Minn., 1972. Bar: Calif. 1972. Mng. ptnr. Sheppard Mullin Richter & Hampton, L.A., 1991-98. Author: The Microsoft Case, Exclusionary Innovation, 1998, California Antitrust Law, 1999; co-author: Antitrust Law Developments, 4th edit., 1998. Mem. ABA, L.A. County Bar Assn. (chmn. antitrust sect. 1993-94). Antitrust. Office: Sheppard Mullin Richter & Hampton LLP 333 S Hope St Fl 48 Los Angeles CA 90071-1406 Fax: 213-620-1398. E-mail: cvarner@smrh.com

VASQUEZ, GERARD MANUEL, lawyer, international business consultant; b. Wallingford, Eng., Dec. 16, 1960; LLB with honors, Univ. Coll., London, 1983, LLM, 1984. Trainee solicitor Messrs. Knocker & Foskett, Sevenoaks, Kent, Eng., 1984-88; trainee Eduardo Amor Martinez & Asociados, Mojacar, Almeria, Spain, 1988-91; asst. solicitor Michael Soul & Assocs., London, 1991-93; cons. Malaga, Spain, 1993-95, Madrid, Spain, 1995-2000; gen. mgr., coord., cons. Lexfide, 2000—. Co-author: International Personal Tax Planning Encyclopaedia, 2000; contbr. to Circulo de Dirigentes. Mem. Interat. Fiscal Assn. Avocations: internet, e-law. Computer, General corporate, Private international. Office: Lexfide C/Ortega y Gasset 34 1 oB Madrid 28006 Spain Fax: 34-91 5783166. E-mail: mail@spanishlegalnet.com

VASSALLO, JOHN A. lawyer; b. N.Y.C., Aug. 19, 1937; s. John and Gilda (Di Desidero) V.; divorced; children: John C., Elena, Edward F. AB, Columbia U., 1959, LLB, 1962. Bar: N.Y. 1963, U.S. Dist. Ct. (so. and ea. dists.) N.Y. 1964, U.S. Ct. Appeals (2nd cir.) 1965. Assoc. Saxe, Bacon & O'Shea, N.Y.C., 1962-68; ptnr. Barovick & Konecky, 1968-70, Kurtz & Vassallo, N.Y.C., 1970-78, Franklin, Weinrib, Rudell & Vassallo, N.Y.C., 1978—. Fellow Am. Acad. Matrimonial Attys. (bd. govs.); mem. N.Y. State Bar Assn., Am. Coll. Family Trial Laywers (diplomate), Friars Club. General civil litigation, Family and matrimonial. Home: 285 Central Park W New York NY 10024-3006 Office: Franklin Weinrib Rudell & Vassallo 488 Madison Ave New York NY 10022-5702

VASSIL, JOHN CHARLES, lawyer; b. Youngstown, Ohio, Mar. 3, 1930; s. Callias and Anastasia (Kyriakides) V.; m. Anita Devlin, Nov. 28, 1965; 1 son, Russell. BS in Chem. Engring., Carnegie Inst. Tech., 1952; JD, George Washington U., 1958. Bar: N.Y. 1960, U.S. Dist. Cts. (so. and ea. dists.) N.Y. 1961, U.S. Ct. Appeals (2d cir.) 1965, U.S. Ct. Appeals (fed. cir.) 1982, U.S. Supreme Ct. 1961. Patent examiner U.S. Patent Office, 1955-58; ptnr. Morgan & Finnegan, LLP, N.Y.C., 1961—. Lectr. in field. Served with C.E., U.S. Army, 1953-55. Mem. ABA, Assn. Bar City N.Y., N.Y. Patent Law Assn., Am. Patent Law Assn., Am. Arbitration Assn. Patent, Trademark and copyright. Home: 420 E 54th St # 36H New York NY 10022-5179 Office: 345 Park Ave New York NY 10154-0004 E-mail: jcvassil@morganfinnegan.com

VASTI, THOMAS FRANCIS, III, lawyer; b. Poughkeepsie, N.Y., Sept. 22, 1966; s. Thomas F. Jr. and Faith Vasti; m. Suzanne Hammond, Aug. 17, 1991; children: Annelise Nicole, Matthew Thomas. BA, U. Notre Dame, 1988; JD, U. St. John's, 1991. Bar: N.Y. 1992, Conn. 1992, U.S. Dist. Ct. (ea. dist.) N.Y. 1995, U.S. Supreme Ct. 2001. Law clk. Vasti & Rutberg Esq., Pleasant Valley, N.Y., 1988-91; assoc. Vasti & Sears, 1991-96; v.p., sr. atty. Vasti & Sears, P.C., 1996-2000; pres., sr. atty. Vasti & Vasti, P.C., N.Y., 2000—. Spkr. Landlord/Tenant Litigation Nat. Bus. Inst., 1995. Treas., head coach No. Dutchess Raiders Pop Warner, Millbrook, NY, 1991—2001; legal counsel Mid-Hudson Conf. Pop Warner Little Scholars, 2000—. Mem. ABA, ATLA, N.Y. State Bar Assn., N.Y. State Trial Lawyers Assn., Dutchess County Bar Assn., Pleasant Valley C. of C. (v.p., trustee 1992—), KC, Notre Dame Alumni Club (sec. mid. Hudson Valley 1997, 98, v.p. 1999—). Republican. Roman Catholic. Avocations: youth sports coaching, golf, hunting, fishing, trombone playing. General civil litigation, Family and matrimonial, Personal injury. Office: Vasti & Vasti PC 1733 Main St Rte 44 PO Box 656 Pleasant Valley NY 12569-0656

VATER, CHARLES J. lawyer; b. Pitts., Feb. 8, 1950; s. Joseph A. and Helen M. (Genellie) V.; m. Diane E. Vater, June 10, 1972; children: Allison D., Elizabeth A. BA, U. Notre Dame, 1971; JD, U. Pitts., 1975. Bar: Pa. 1975, U.S. Dist. Ct. (we. dist.) Pa. 1975, U.S. Ct. Appeals (3d cir.) 1979. Assoc. Tucker Arensberg, P.C., Pitts., 1975-80, ptnr., shareholder, 1980—. Contbr. articles to profl. jours. Mem. Allegheny County Bar Assn. (probate coun. 1988-98, 99-2000, treas. 2001), Estate Planning Coun. Pitts. (bd. dirs. 1988-90, 95-97, pres. 2001), Order of Coif, Phi Beta Kappa. Contracts commercial, Estate planning, Probate. Home: 1615 Trolist Dr Pittsburgh PA 15241-2650 Office: Tucker Arensberg 1 Ppg Pl Ste 1500 Pittsburgh PA 15222-5413 E-mail: cvater@tuckerlaw.com

VAUGHAN, EDWARD GIBSON, lawyer; b. Dallas, Nov. 22, 1948; s. S.J. III and Martha Gibson) V. BBA, U. Tex., 1971; cert., City of London Coll., 1970; JD, St. Mary's U., 1975. Bar: Tex. 1975. Assoc. Johnson & Jones, Austin, 1975-76; ptnr. Harris & Vaughan, Uvalde, Tex., 1976-79, Kessler, Kessler & Vaughan, Uvalde, 1979-94. Dir. First State Bank Uvalde, Security State Bank of Persall. Mem. ABA, Tex. and Southwestern Cattle Raisers (bd. dirs.), Uvalde C. of C. (bd. dirs. 1979-83), Tex. State C. of C. (bd. dirs. 1982-85), Tex. Lyceum Assn. (bd. dirs. 1980-85), Tex. Assn. Bank Counsel (bd. dirs. 1984-87), Southwestern Legal Found., State Bar Tex., Uvalde County Bar Assn. (pres. 1979-80), Kendall County Bar Assn., Tex. Water Found. (bd. dirs. 1998—). Banking, Oil, gas, and mineral, Real property. Office: 1588 S Main St Ste 200 Boerne TX 78006-2300

VAUGHAN, HERBERT WILEY, retired lawyer; b. Brookline, Mass., June 1, 1920; s. David D. and Elzie G. (Wiley) V.; m. Ann Graustein, June 28, 1941. Student, U. Chgo., 1937-38; BS cum laude, Harvard U., 1941, LLB, 1948. Bar: Mass. 1948. Assoc. Hale and Dorr, Boston, 1948-54, jr. ptnr., 1954-56, sr. ptnr., 1956-89, co-mng. ptnr., 1976-80, of counsel, 1990—. Mem. bd. dirs. and fin. com. Boston and Maine R.R., 1961-64. Mem. standing com. The Trustees of Reservations, 1986-98, chmn., 1988-92, sec., 1992-98, asst. sec., mem. adv. coun., 1998—; mem. bd. trustees Am. Friends New Coll. (Oxford U.); mem. adv. coun. James Madison Program in Am. Ideals and Instns., Princeton U. Fellow Am. Bar Found. (life); mem. ABA, Mass. Bar Assn., Boston Bar Assn., Am. Law Inst., Am. Coll. Real Estate Lawyers, Am. Coun. Trustees and Alumni (mem. alumni leadership coun.), Bay Club, Badminton and Tennis Club, Union Club (Boston), Boston Econ. Club, Longwood Cricket Club (Brookline). Real property. Office: Hale and Dorr LLP 60 State St Boston MA 02109-1816 E-mail: Herbert.Vaughan@haledorr.com

VAUGHAN, JAMES JOSEPH MICHAEL, lawyer; b. Mar. 19, 1942; s. James M. and Elizabeth (McDonnell) Vaughan; m. Jeanette Rae Gerber, Aug. 05, 1967; children: Karen, Adrianne, Jennifer. BS, U. Scranton, 1963; JD, Cath. U., 1966. Bar: U.S. Dist. Ct. Md. 1979, U.S. Ct. Appeals (D.C. cir.) 1972, U.S. Ct. Claims 1973, U.S. Supreme Ct. 1977. Assoc. Dukes, Troese, et al, Chevy Chase, Md., 1969—72; atty. Assn. Am. Law Schs., Washington, 1972—76; mem. firm Giordano, Bush, Villareale & Vaughan, Upper Marlboro, Md., 1976—. Mem.: Assn. Trial Lawyers Am., Bar Assn. D.C., D.C. Bar Assn., Md. Bar Assn., Prince George's County Bar Assn. Democrat. Roman Catholic. State civil litigation, Personal injury, Workers' compensation. Office: Giordano Bush Villareale & Vaughan PA PO Box 520 Upper Marlboro MD 20773-0520

VAUGHAN, MICHAEL RICHARD, lawyer; b. Chgo., Aug. 27, 1936; s. Michael Ambrose and Loretta M. (Parks) V.; m. Therese Marie Perri, Aug. 6, 1960; children: Charles Thomas, Susan Enger. Student, U. Ill., 1954-59; LLB, U. Wis., 1962. Bar: Wis. 1962. Chief atty. bill drafting sect. Wis. Legislature, Madison, 1962-68, dir. legis. attys., 1968-72; assoc. Murphy & Desmond, and predecessor, 1972-73, ptnr., 1974—. Mem. Commn. Uniform State Laws, 1966-72; cons. Nat. Commn. on Marihuana and Drug Abuse, 1971-73; dir. State Bar Govtl. and Adminstrv. Law Sect., 1971-78, State Bar Interprofl. and Bus. Rels. Com., 1976-89; lectr. CLE seminars. Contbr. articles to law jours. Warden and vestryman St. Dunstan's Episcopal Ch., 1973-78, 80-87; mem. Wis. Episcopal Conf., 1972-76. Mem.: ABA, State Bar Wis., Dane County Bar Assn., Madison Club, Nakoma Club, U. Wis. Law Sch. Bencher Soc., Delta Kappa Epsilon. Administrative and regulatory, Legislative. Home: 4714 Lafayette Dr Madison WI 53705-4865 Office: 2 E Mifflin St Ste 800 Madison WI 53703-4217

VAUGHN, NOEL WYANDT, lawyer; b. Chgo., Dec. 15, 1937; d. Owen Heaton and Harriet Christy (Smith) Wyandt; m. David Victor Koch, July 18, 1959 (div.); 1 child, John David; m. Charles George Vaughn, July 9, 1971. BA, DePauw U., 1959; MA, So. Ill. U., 1963; JD, U. Dayton, 1979. Bar: Ohio 1979, U.S. Dist. Ct. (so. dist.) Ohio 1979, U.S. Cir. Ct. (6th cir.) 1987. Lectr. Wright State U., Dayton, 1965-67; communications specialist Charles F. Kettering Found., 1968-71; tchr. English Miami Valley Sch., 1971-76; law clk. to judge Dayton Mcpl. Ct., 1978-79; coordinator Montgomery County Fair Housing Ctr., Dayton, 1979-81, 85-89; atty. Henley Vaughn Becker & Wald, 1981-90; pvt. practice Noel W. Vaughn Law Offices, 1990—. Chmn. Dayton Playhouse, Inc., 1981—92; pres. Freedom of Choice Miami Valley, 1980—83, 1986—87; mem. com. Battered Woman Project-YWCA, 1983—84; pres. Legal Aid Soc., 1983—84; chmn. Artemis House, Inc., 1985—88, bd. dirs., 1988—97, ACLU, 1982—86, Miami Valley Arts Coun., 1985—86, AIDS Found., 1988—90, Miami Valley Fair Housing Ctr., Inc., 1992—94, Human Race Theatre Co., Inc., 1995—2000, Housing Justice Fund, 1979—, Dayton Sister City Com., 2001—. Recipient Order of Barristers award U. Dayton, 1979. Mem.: ABA, Dayton Bar Assn. (chmn. delivery legal svcs. com. 1983—84, family law com. 1991—, chmn. juvenile law com. 2001—), Ohio FAIR Plan Underwriting Assn. (bd. govs. 1986—92). Family and matrimonial, General practice, Juvenile. Office: 1205 Talbott Tower 131 N Ludlow St Dayton OH 45402-1110

VAUGHN, ROBERT CANDLER, JR. lawyer; b. Winston-Salem, N.C., Sept. 6, 1931; s. Robert Candler and Douglas Ellen (Arthur) V.; m. Carolyn Hartford, May 2, 1959; children: Patricia Anne, Robert Candler III. BS in Bus. Adminstrn., U. N.C., 1953, JD, 1955. Bar: N.C. 1955, U.S. Dist. Ct. (mid. dist.) 1959, U.S. Tax Ct. 1981. Assoc. Petree, Stockton & Robinson and predecessor firms, Winston-Salem, 1959-65, ptnr., 1965-2000. Bd. dirs. So. Nat. Bank, and predecessor bank, Winston-Salem. Pres. United Way Forsyth County, Winston-Salem, 1970-71; chmn. Winston-Salem Coliseum Commn., Winston-Salem Conv. Ctr. Commn., 1974-78; bd. advs. U. N.C. Tax Inst., Chapel Hill; bd. dirs. Legal Services N.C., 1985-86, Leadership Winston-Salem, Winston-Salem Found.; chmn. Forsyth Med. Ctr. Found., 1999—. Served to lt. USN, 1955-58. Fellow Am. Bar Found., Am. Coll. Probate Counsel; mem. N.C. Bar Assn. (pres. 1985-86, bd. dirs.), U. N.C. Law Alumni Assn. (pres. 1974-75), Am. Coll. Tax Counsel, Old Town Club, Piedmont Club, Rotary. Democrat. Methodist. General corporate, Probate, Estate taxation. Home: 2575 Club Park Rd Winston Salem NC 27104-2009 Office: Vaughn Perkinson Ehlingern Moxley & Stogner PO Box 25715 Winston Salem NC 27114 E-mail: bob.vaughn@vpems.com

VAUGHN, ROBERT GENE, law educator; b. Chickasha, Okla., Mar. 10, 1944; s. Owen and Ola Mae (Davis) V.; m. Nancy Gaye Breeden, June 28, 1969; children: Amanda Joy, Abigail Jane, Carolyn Elizabeth. BA, U. Okla., 1966, JD, 1969; LLM, Harvard U., 1970. Bar: Okla. 1969, D.C. 1971. Assoc. atty. Pub. Interest Rsch. Group, Washington, 1970-72; asst. prof. law Am. U., 1972-74, assoc. prof., 1974-77, prof., 1977-82, A. Allen King scholar and prof. law, 1982—, acting dep. dean, 1984-85. Editl. cons. Prentice Hall. Author: The Spoiled System: A Call for Civil Service Reform, 1975, Principles of Civil Service Law, 1976, Conflict of Interest Regulation in the Federal Executive Branch, 1979, Merit Systems Protection Board: Rights and Remedies, 1984, South American Consumer Protection Laws, 1996, A Documentary Companion to A Civil Action, 1999, Freedom of Information, 2000. Recipient award for outstanding tchg. Washington Coll. Law, Am. U., United Meth. Ch. Bd. Higher Edn., 1983. Democrat. Methodist. Office: Am U Washington Coll Law 4801 Massachusetts Ave NW Washington DC 20016-8181 E-mail: vaughn@wcl.american.edu

VEACH, ROBERT RAYMOND, JR. lawyer; b. Charleston, S.C., Nov. 28, 1950; s. Robert Raymond and Evelyn Ardell (Vegter) V.; m. Lori Sue Erickson, May 27, 1989. Student, St. Olaf Coll., 1968-70; BS in Acctg., Ariz. State U., 1972; JD, So. Meth. U., 1975. Bar: Tex. 1975, Nebr. 1975, U.S. Dist. Ct. Nebr. 1975, U.S. Dist. Ct. (no. dist.) Tex. 1975, Temporary Emergency Ct. Appeals 1975. Acctg. instr. Sch. Bus. So. Meth. U., Dallas, 1973-74; law clk. to Hon. Joe E. Estes U.S. Dist. Ct. No. Dist. Tex.-Temp. Emergency Ct. Appeals, 1975-76; assoc. Locke Purnell Boren Laney & Neely, 1976-80; v.p. The Lomas & Nettleton Co., 1980-83, Rauscher Pierce Refsnes, Inc., Dallas, 1983-87; pres. RPR Mortgage Fin. Corp., 1985-87; sr. shareholder Locke Purnell Rain Harrell, 1987-97; exec. v.p. Precision Imaging Solutions, Inc., 1998—; pvt. practice, 1998—. Allied mem. N.Y. Stock Exch., 1985-87; lectr. securities and banking confs.; bd. dirs. pvt. corps.; trustee Correctional Properties Trust (NYSE-CPV), chmn. audit and finance com., 1998—. Author legal articles. Dir. North Tex. affiliate Am. Diabetes Assn., Dallas, 1978-81; mem. Gov.'s Task Force Wash. State Housing Commn., 1982-83. Mem. ABA, State Bar of Tex., Nebr. State Bar Assn., Fed. Bar Assn., Dallas Bar Assn. Republican. Methodist. Avocations: golf, antique Am. firearms. General corporate, Finance, Securities. Home: 4223 Brookview Dr Dallas TX 75220-3801 Office: 2911 Turtle Creek Blvd Ste 1240 Dallas TX 75219-6277

VEAL, REX R. lawyer; b. Lafayette, Ga., May 2, 1956; s. Boyd Herman and Barbara Ann (Sharp) V.; m. Vicky Elizabeth Wilkins, Dec. 13, 1980; children: Matthew Aaron and Richard Andrew (twins). BA, U. Tenn., 1978, JD, 1980. Bar: Tenn. 1981, U.S. Dist. Ct. (ea. dist.) Tenn. 1981, U.S. Ct. Appeals (10th cir.) 1981, U.S. Ct. Appeals (6th cir.) 1984, U.S. Ct. Appeals (4th cir.) 1987, Ga. 1991, U.S. Dist. Ct. (no. dist.) Ga. 1991, U.S. Ct. Appeals (11th cir.) 1991, D.C. 1993, U.S. Dist. Ct. D.C. 1993, U.S. Ct. Appeals (D.C. and fed. cir.) 1993. Assoc. Finkelstein, Kern, Steinberg & Cunningham, Knoxville, Tenn., 1980-83; atty. FDIC, 1983-84, sr. atty., 1984-88, counsel liquidation Washington, 1988-89, assoc. gen. counsel, 1989-90; spl. counsel Resolution Trust Corp., 1989-90; ptnr. Powell, Goldstein, Frazer & Murphy, Atlanta and Washington, 1990-99, Kilpatrick Stockton LLP, Atlanta, 1999—. Lectr. in field. Contbr. articles to profl. jours. Mem. ABA, Tenn. Bar Assn., Ga. Bar Assn., Atlanta Bar Assn. Avocations: hiking, golf, collecting books. Contracts commercial, Finance, Real property. Home: 6201 Blackberry Hl Norcross GA 30092-1375 Office: Kilpatrick Stockton 1100 Peachtree St NE Ste 2800 Atlanta GA 30309-4501 E-mail: rveal@kilpatrickstockton.com

VEASEY, EUGENE NORMAN, state supreme court chief justice; b. Wilmington, Del., Jan. 9, 1933; s. Eugene E. and Elizabeth B. (Norman) V.; m. Suzanne Johnson, Aug. 4, 1956; children: Andrew Scott, Dluglas Ross, E. Norman Jr., Marian Elizabeth. AB, Dartmouth Coll., 1954; LLB, U. Pa., 1957. Bar: Del. 158, U.S. Supreme Ct. 1963. Dep. atty. gen. State of Del., 1961-62; chief dep., 1962-63; ptnr. Richards, Layton & Finger, Wilmington, Del., 1963-92; chief justice Del. Supreme Ct., 1992—. Contbr. articles to profl. jours. Bd. advisors U. Pa. Inst. for Law and Econs. Capt. Del. Air N.G., 1957-63. Fellow Am. Bar Found., Am. Coll. Trial Lawyers, Am. Intellectual Property Law Assn.; mem. Del. Bd. Bar Examiners (chmn. 1973-80), Del. Bar Assn. (pres. 1982-83, chmn. corp. law com. 1969-74, chmn. rules com. Del. Supreme Ct. 1974-80), ABA (chair bus. law sect. 1994-95, chair spl. com. on ethics 2000 1997—), Am. Law Inst. (bd. dirs. conf. chief jusice 1994-96, chair professionalism com. 1994-98, 1st v.p. 1998, pres.-elect 1998-99, pres. 1999-00), Nat. Ctr. State Cts. (chair bd. dirs. 1999-00). Republican. Episcopalian. E-mial. Office: Del Supreme Ct PO Box 1997 Wilmington DE 19899-1997 E-mail: eveasey@state.de.us

VECCHIO, CESARE GIOVANNI, lawyer; b. Pavia, Italy, Apr. 1, 1962; s. Luciano and Itala (Vallazza) V.; m. Eugenia Gilardi; children: federico, Alessandro, Michele. LLB, Pavia U., 1985. Bar: Italy. With Studio Tremonti, 1985-90; assoc. Chiomenti Law Firm, Milan, Italy, 1990-92, Tremonto Law Firm, Milan, 1992-96; ptnr. Freshfields, 1997—. Author: Finance Guide, 1992. General corporate, Mergers and acquisitions, Securities. Office: Freshfields Via dei Gioudini 7 20121 Mialn Italy

VEEDER, PETER GREIG, lawyer; b. Pitts., Aug. 13, 1941; AB, Princeton U., 1963; JD, U. Pitts., 1966. Bar: Pa. 1966, D.C. 1976. Lawyer Thorp Reed & Armstrong, Pitts., 1970-99; of counsel Thorp, Reed & Armstrong LLP, 1999—. Environmental. Office: Thorp Reed & Armstrong LLP 1 Oxford Ctr 301 Grant St Fl 14 Pittsburgh PA 15219-1425

VEGA, BENJAMIN URBIZO, retired judge, television producer; b. La Ceiba, Honduras, Jan. 18, 1916; m. Janie Lou Smith, Oct. 12, 1989; AB, U. So. Calif., 1938, postgrad., 1939-40; LLB, Pacific Coast U. Law, 1941. Bar: Calif. 1947, U.S. Dist. Ct. (so. dist.) Calif. 1947, U.S. Supreme Ct. 1958. Assoc. Anderson, McPharlin & Connors, L.A., 1947-48, Newman & Newman, L.A., 1948-51; dep. dist. atty. County of L.A., 1951-66; judge L.A., County Mcpl. Ct., East L.A. Jud. Dist., 1966-86, retired, 1986; leader faculty seminar Calif. Jud. Coll. at Earl Warren Legal Inst., U. Calif-Berkeley, 1978. Mem. Calif. Gov.'s Adv. Com. on Children and Youth, 1968; del. Commn. of the Califs., 1978; bd. dirs. Los Angeles-Mexico City Sister City Com.; pres. Argentine Cultural Found., 1983. Recipient award for outstanding services from Mayor of L.A., 1973, City of Commerce, City of Montebello, Calif. Assembly, Southwestern Sch. Law, Disting. Pub. Service award Dist. Atty. L.A. Mem. Conf. Calif. Judges, Mcpl. Ct. Judges' Assn. (award for Outstanding Services), Beverly Hills Bar Assn., Navy League, L.A. County, Am. Judicature Soc., World Affairs Council, Rotary (hon.), Pi Sigma Alpha. Home: 101 California Ave Apt 1207 Santa Monica CA 90403-3525

VEGA, MATIAS ALFONSO, lawyer; b. Paris, Feb. 2, 1952; s. Matias Guillermo and Colette (Lafosse) V.; m. Carmella Margarita Kurczewski, Nov. 20, 1982; 1 child, Alexandra Lafosse. AB, Yale U., 1974; JD, Harvard U., 1977. Bar: N.Y. 1978, U.S. Dist. Ct. (so. and ea. dists.) N.Y. 1979, U.S. Supreme Ct. 1984, U.S. Ct. Appeals (6th and 9th cirs.) 1985, U.S. Dist. Ct. (no. dist.) Calif. 1985. Assoc. Curtis, Mallet-Prevost, Colt & Mosle, N.Y.C., 1977-85, ptnr., 1986—. Contbr. articles to profl. jours. Mem. ABA, Am. Soc. Internat. Law, N.Y. State Bar Assn. (chmn. com. Latin Am. law, internat. law and practice sect. 1987-90), Yale Club. Republican. Roman Catholic. Finance, Private international, Mergers and acquisitions. Home: 31 Gedney Way Chappaqua NY 10514-1402 Office: Curtis Mallet-Prevost Colt 101 Park Ave Fl 34 New York NY 10178-0061 E-mail: matvega@msn.com, mvega@cm-p.com

VELTRI, STEPHEN CHARLES, lawyer, educator; b. Pitts., Mar. 29, 1955; s. Gabriel Alfred and Helen Louise (McConegly) V.; m. Melody Jo Mazzei, May 19, 1984. BA summa cum laude, U. Pitts., 1977; JD cum laude, Georgetown U., 1981; LLM, Columbia U., 1986. Info. specialist Library of Congress, Washington, 1978-80; assoc. Berkman Ruslander, Pitts., 1981-85; prof. law Ohio No. U., Ada, 1986. Democrat. Roman Catholic. Contracts commercial. Home: 416 Baldwin Ave Findlay OH 45840-2208 Office: Ohio Northern U Pettit Coll Law Ada OH 45810 E-mail: s-veltri@onu.edu

VENERUSO, JAMES JOHN, lawyer; b. Bklyn., Feb. 4, 1951; s. Jack and Ann (Maugeri) V.; m. Lillian B. Curto, Aug. 16, 1975; children: Jacquelyn, James, Stephen. BA, Iona Coll., 1972; JD, Widener U., 1975. Bar: N.Y. 1976, U.S. Ct. Claims 1977, U.S. Supreme Ct. 1979, U.S. Dist. Ct. (so. dist.) N.Y. 1979, Fla. 1980. Assoc. Griffin, Kane, Letsen & Coogan, Yonkers, N.Y., 1975-81; mng. ptnr. Griffin, Letsen, Coogan & Veneruso, Bronxville, 1981-94, Griffin Coogan & Veneruso, P.C., Bronxville, 1994—. Gen. counsel Throggs Neck Extended Care Facility Family Coun. Assoc. editor Jour. Corp. Law, Widener Law Sch., 1973-74; bd. editors Pace Law Rev., 1979-80. Bd. dirs. Big Bros.-Big Sisters, Yonkers, 1978-79, 83-84. Mem. N.Y. State Bar Assn., Westchester County Bar Assn. (features editor 1983-85, chmn. banking com. 1993—), Yonkers Lawyers Assn. (sec. 1982-83, fin. sec. 1983-84), N.Y. State Bankers Assn. (legal com. 1988—), Heartsong Found. (dir., gen. counsel pro bono 1992—), Greyston Found. (bd. dirs. 1999—), Bronxville C. of C. (bd. dirs. 1990-93, legal counsel 1993-95), Generoso Pope Found. (gen. counsel), Family Svcs. Soc. (bd. dirs., gen. counsel pro bono 1991-95), N.Y. State Banking Assn. (legal adv. com. 1992—), N.Y. State Bar Assn. (condominium and coops. com. 1990—), Westchester 2000 (bd. mem. 1998—), John Marshall Hon. Soc., Delta Lambda Sigma (pres. 1973-74). Democrat. Roman Catholic. Banking, Contracts commercial, Real property. Home: 100 Dellwood Rd Bronxville NY 10708-2006 Office: Griffin Coogan & Veneruso PC 51 Pondfield Rd Bronxville NY 10708-3805 E-mail: jjv@gcvpc.com

VENNING, ROBERT STANLEY, lawyer; b. Boise, Idaho, July 24, 1943; s. William Lucas and Corey Elizabeth (Brown) V.; m. Sandra Macdonald, May 9, 1966 (div. 1976); 1 child, Rachel Elizabeth; m. Laura Siegel, Mar. 24, 1979; 1 child, Daniel Rockhill Siegel. AB, Harvard U., 1965; MA, U. Chgo., 1966; LLB, Yale U., 1970. Bar: Calif., U.S. Dist. Ct. (no. dist.) Calif., 1971, U.S. Dist. Ct. (cen. dist.) Calif. 1973, U.S. Ct. Appeals (9th cir.) 1977, U.S. Supreme Ct. 1977, U.S. Ct. Appeals (fed. cir.) 1986, U.S. Ct. Appeals (D.C. cir.) 1987. Assoc. Heller Ehrman White & McAuliffe, San Francisco, 1970-73, 73-76, ptnr., 1977—, mem. exec. com., 1991-94. Vis. lectr. U. Wash., Seattle, 1973, Boalt Hall Sch. Law, U. Calif., Berkeley, 1982-85, 89, Sch. Bus., Stanford U., 1986-87. Editor Yale Law Jour., 1969-70. Early neutral evaluator U.S. Dist. Ct. (no. dist.) Calif., 1987—; mem. Natural Resources Def. Coun. Fellow Am. Bar Found. (life); mem. ABA, San Francisco Bar Assn. (past chair judiciary com.), CPR Inst. for Dispute Resolution, Olympic Club. Federal civil litigation, General civil litigation, State civil litigation. Office: Heller White & McAuliffe 333 Bush St San Francisco CA 94104-2806

VENTO, JOHN SEBASTIAN, lawyer; b. Pitts., Apr. 23, 1949; s. John Joseph and Rose Ann (Bellante) V.; m. Jacqueline Lynnette Rex, Aug. 19, 1972. BA cum laude, U. Pitts., 1971; JD cum laude, Duquesne U., 1974; LLM, U. Mich., 1979. Bar: U.S. Ct. Appeals (3d cir.) 1974, U.S. Dist. Ct. (we. dist.) Pa. 1974, U.S. Ct. Mil. Appeals 1975, Pa. 1974, U.S. Supreme Ct. 1980, Fla. 1981, U.S. Ct. Appeals (5th and 11th cirs.) 1981, U.S. Dist. Ct. (mid. dist.) Fla. 1981, U.S. Dist. Ct. (so. dist.) Fla. 1986, U.S. Ct. Internat. Trade, 1986. Law clk. U.S. Dist. Ct. (we. dist.) Pa., 1971-72; asst. staff judge advocate U.S. Air Force, MacDill AFB, Fla., 1974-76, chief internat law div., Clark AFB, Philippines, 1976-78; asst. prof. law U.S. Air Force Acad., Colo., 1979-81; atty. Trenam, Kemker, Scharf, Barkin, Frye, O'Neill & Mullis, P.A., Tampa, Fla., 1981—. Assoc. editor: Duquesne Law Rev., 1973-74; co-author curriculum materials; contbr. articles to profl. jours. Bd. dirs. Hillsborough Community Mental Health Clinic, Tampa, 1984-89; Tampa Gasparilla Festival Krewe of Sant 'Yago, 1986—; pres., Tampa Kiwanis Found., 1984-85. Served to capt. USAF, 1974-81; col. USAFR, 1981—. Yale Law scholar; NEH fellow, 1980; Alcoa grantee, 1973-74. Mem. ABA (co-chair constrn. litigation com., 1993-96), Inter-Am. Bar Assn., Am. Arbitrations Assn. (comml. arbitrator, mem. governing bd. Mid Fla. region 1997-99), Am. Soc. Internat. Law, Fla. Bar Assn.,

Hillsborough County Bar Assn., Nat. Order of Barristers, U. Mich. 4th Dist. Alumni Clubs Council (pres. 1986-89, dist. dir. 1989-92), U. Mich. Alumni Club (bd. dirs. Tampa Bay area 1984—), Phi Alpha Delta, Alpha Epsilon Pi. Republican. Roman Catholic. Club: Saddlebrook Golf and Country. Lodge: Kiwanis. E-mail: jsvento@trenan.com. Federal civil litigation, State civil litigation, Private international. Office: Trenam Kemker Scharf Barkin Frye O'Neill & Mullis PC 2700 Barnett Plaza 101 E Kennedy Blvd Tampa FL 33602-5179

VENTO, M. THÉRÈSE, lawyer; b. N.Y.C., June 30, 1951; d. Anthony Joseph and Margaret (Stechert) V.; m. Peter Michael MacNamara, Dec. 23, 1977; children: David Miles, Elyse Anne. BS, U. Fla., 1974, JD, 1976. Bar: Fla. 1977, U.S. Dist. Ct. (so. and mid. dists.) Fla. 1982, U.S. Ct. Appeals (5th and 11th cirs.) 1981, U.S. Supreme Ct. 1985. Clk. to presiding justice U.S. Dist. Ct. (so. dist.) Fla., Miami, 1976-78; assoc. Mahoney, Hadlow & Adams, 1978-79, Shutts & Bowen, Miami, 1979-84, ptnr., 1985-95; founding ptnr. Gallwey Gillman Curtis Vento & Horn, P.A., 1995—. Trustee Miami Art Mus., 1988—, v.p., 1999—; trustee The Beacon Coun., 1995-97, Law Sch. Alumni Coun., U. Fla., 1994—. Fellow Am. Bar Found.; mem. Dade County Bar Assn. (dir. young lawyers sect. 1978-83, editor newsletter 1981-83), Fla. Assn. for Women Lawyers, Fla. Bar Assn. (bd. govs., young lawyers div. 1983-85, civil procedure rules com. 1983-90, exec. coun. trial lawyers sect. 1996—), The Miami Forum (v.p. 1987-88, bd. dirs. 1989-91, co-pres. 2001—). Federal civil litigation, General civil litigation, Libel. Home: 3908 Main Hwy Miami FL 33133-6513 Office: Gallwey Gillman Curtis Vento & Horn PA 200 SE 1st St Ste 1100 Miami FL 33131-1912 E-mail: TVento@GGCVH.com

VENTRELLI, ANITA MARIE, lawyer; b. Berwyn, Ill., Apr. 20, 1964; d. Jose M. and Anita Marie (Loycano) Bolaños. AB, U. Mich., 1986; JD, DePaul U., 1989. Bar: Ill. 1990. Ptnr. Schiller DuCanto & Fleck, Chgo., 1997—. Fellow Am. Acad. Matrimonial Lawyers; mem. ABA, Ill. Bar Assn. Roman Catholic. Avocations: running, piano. Family and matrimonial. Office: Schiller DuCanto & Fleck 200 N La Salle St Ste 2700 Chicago IL 60601-1098 E-mail: aventrelli@sdflaw.com

VENTRES, DANIEL BRAINERD, JR. lawyer; b. Washington, Dec. 2, 1930; s. Daniel Brainerd and Sarah Helen (Dunlap) V.; m. Sarah Stevenson, May 22, 1954 (div. 1978); children: Katherine Ventres Canipelli, William Brainerd; m. Judith Martin, Dec. 27, 1984. BA in Bus. Adminstrn. and Econs., Ohio Wesleyan U., 1952; JD, George Washington U., 1957. Bar: Minn. 1960, U.S. Dist. Ct. Minn. 1965, U.S. Supreme Ct. 1969, U.S. Ct. Mil. Appeals 1972, U.S. Ct. Appeals (8th cir.) 1989. Appraiser, legal asst. Redevel. Land Agy., Washington, 1955-56; procurement and legal staff The Martin Co., Denver, 1957-59, Mpls. Honeywell Co., 1959-60; ptnr. Carlsen, Greiner & Law, Mpls., 1960-84, MacIntosh & Commers, Mpls., 1984-86; of counsel Gray, Plant, Mooty, Mooty & Bennett, PA, 1986-94, Gislason, Dosland, Hunter & Malecki, PA, Minnetonka, Minn., 1994-95; pvt. practice Mpls., 1995—. Assoc. counsel Amateur Athletic Union, Indpls., 1974-80, U.S. Swimming, Colorado Springs, Colo., 1978-80; chmn. ad hoc com. on dispute resolution alternatives in family law Minn. Supreme Ct., Mpls., 1993-96; adj. prof. family law Hamline U. Law Sch., St. Paul, 1993; referee settlement conf. program Hennepin County Dist. Ct., Mpls., 1994—; lectr. Nat. Bus. Inst. Seminars, 1994. Mem. Ind. Sch. Dist. 274 Bd. Edn., Hopkins, Minn., 1965-72; chmn., legis. coord. Suburban Sch. Dist. Joint Bd., Hopkins, 1972; v.p. adminstrn. U.S. Swimming Com.; U.S. swimming ofcl. Olympic Games, PanAm. Games, Aquatic World Games; chmn., dir. Minn. AAU swimming, Minn. AAU, 1968-80. Officer USMC, 1952-54; col. USMCR, 1972-78. Mem. ABA, FBA (bd. dirs., v.p. Minn. chpt. 1961—, Minn. rep. alternat dispute resolution com. 1995-96, chmn. subcom. on alternate dispute reolution practices, procedures and processes Minn. chpt. 1996—), Am. Acad. Matrimonial Lawyers, Am. Arbitration Assn. (arbitrator, mediator, evaluator Mpls. 1995-98), Minn. Bar Assn. (cert. arbitrator, mediator and evaluator, lectr. CLE 1988-95), Hennepin County Bar Assn., Masons. Consumer commercial, Family and matrimonial, Real property. Office: 625 2d Ave S Ste 419 Minneapolis MN 55402

VENTRES, JUDITH MARTIN, lawyer; b. Ann Arbor, Mich., Feb. 10, 1943; d. D. Lawrence and Donna E. (Webb) Moran; children: Laura M. Buford, Paul M. Martin, A. Lindsay McGill; m. Daniel B. Ventres Jr., Dec. 27, 1984. BA, U. Mich., 1963; postgrad., U. Jean Moulin, Inst. du Droit, Lyon, France, 1981; JD, U. Minn., 1982. Bar: Minn. 1982, Fla. 1991, Colo. 1994, U.S. Tax Ct. 1989, U.S. Dist. Ct. Minn. 1989, U.S. Ct. Appeals (8th cir.) 1989. Tax supr., dir. fin. planning, asst. nat. dir. Coopers & Lybrand, Mpls., 1981-84; dir. fin. planning Investors Diversified Services subs. Am. Express, Mpls. and N.Y.C., 1984-85; sr. tax mgr., dir. fin. planning KPMG Peat Marwick Main & Co., Mpls., 1985-89; prin. Martin & Assocs., PA, 1989-2000, Gray Plant Mooty Mooty & Bennett, P.A., Mpls., 2000—. Faculty Minn. CLE, 1994; adv. bd. Nicollet/Ebenezer, 1996. Owner Alternatax, Inc. Mem. Mpls. C. of C. Campaign, Downtown Coun. Coms., Mpls., 1982-84, Metro Tax Planning Group, 1984-86, Mpls. Estate Planning Coun., 1985-99, Planned Giving Coun.; class chmn. fundraising campaign U. Minn. Law Sch., Mpls., 1985, 98; bd. dirs. Ensemble Capriccio, chmn. fundraising com., 1998—; usher Christ Presbyn. Ch., Edina, Minn., 1983—; mem. adv. coun. on planned giving ARC. Mem. ABA (task force on legal fin. planning), Minn. Bar Assn., Hennepin County Bar Assn., Fla. Bar Assn., Colo. Bar Assn., Minn. Soc. CPAs (instr. continuing legal edn. 1983-84, continuing profl. edn. 1982-86, individual, trust and estate provisions Tax Reform Act 1986, continuing legal edn. -estate planning 1994), Minn. Planned Giving Coun., Am. Assn. Ind. Investors (speaker), Am. Soc. CLUs, Minn. Soc. CLUs, Minn. Women Lawyers, Fla. Women Lawyers, Lex Alumnae, U. Mich. Alumni Assn. (coun. govs. 1989—, scholarship chmn.), U. Minn. Alumni Club (bd. dirs. 1996, coun. govs. 1988-96, pres., treas. mem. com.), Minn. World Trade Assn., Internat. Assn. Fin. Planners, Edina C. of C., Interlachen Club, Athletic Club, Lafayette Club, U. Minn. Alumni Assn. (mem. univ. issues com., nat. bd. dirs. 1996-99). Estate planning, Probate, Personal income taxation. Home: 1355 Vine Pl Mound MN 55364-9635 Office: Gray Plant Mooty Mooty & Bennett 3400 City Center 33 S 6th Minneapolis MN 55402

VERCAMMEN, KENNETH ALBERT, lawyer; b. Edison, N.J., Aug. 7, 1959; s. Albert Peter and Carol Ann (Rasche) V.; m. Cynthia Ann Bachenski, July 9, 1989. BS, U. Scranton, 1981; JD, U. Del., 1985. Bar: N.J., Pa. 1985, N.Y. 1986, D.C. 1987. Mng. atty., Metuchen, N.J., 1990—. Adj. prof. Middlesex County Coll., Edison, 1990-91. Contbr. articles to profl. jours. Mem. Am. Cancer Soc., Edison, 1989—; counselor Cen. Jersey Road Runners, 1987. Named a Top Young Profl. by Am. Cancer Soc., New Brunswick, 1988, 89. Mem. KC. Roman Catholic. Avocations: cross-country running, soccer. Contracts commercial, Criminal, Personal injury. Office: 407 Main St Metuchen NJ 08840-1850

VERHAAREN, HAROLD CARL, lawyer; b. Salt Lake City, Apr. 11, 1938; m. Cynthia Mary Hughes, Nov. 25, 1964; children: Scott Harold, Steven Robert, Jill, Brent Carl, Brian Hughes. JD, U. Utah, 1965. Bar: Utah 1965, U.S. Supreme Ct. 1978. Law clk. to chief justice Utah Supreme Ct., 1964-65; v.p., bd. dirs. Nielsen & Senior PC, Salt Lake City. Judge pro tem Small Claims Ct. Salt Lake County, 1978-85. Chmn. Mt. Olympus Planning Dist., 1971-85; active Boy Scouts Am., 1967-97. Recipient Silver Beaver award Boy Scouts Am. Mem. Utah Bar Assn., Salt Lake County Bar Assn., Am. Arbitration Assn. (panel of arbitrators), Delta Theta Phi, Phi Kappa Phi, Phi Eta Sigma. Mormon. State civil litigation, Contracts commercial, Construction. Office: 260 Parkview Plaza 60 E South Temple 11th Fl Salt Lake City UT 84111 E-mail: hcv@ns-law.com

VERING, JOHN ALBERT, lawyer; b. Marysville, Kans., Feb. 6, 1951; s. John Albert and Bernadine E. (Kieffer) V.; m. Ann E. Arman, June 28, 1980; children: Julia Ann, Catherine Ann, Mary Ann. BA summa cum laude, Harvard U., 1973; JD, U. Va., 1976. Bar: Mo. 1976, U.S. Dist. Ct. (we. dist.) Mo. 1976, U.S. Ct. Appeals (10th cir.), 1980, U.S. Ct. Appeals (4th cir.) 1987, Kans. 1990, U.S. Dist. Ct. Kans. 1990; arbitrator, mediator. Assoc. Dietrich, Davis, Dicus, Rowlands, Schmitt & Gorman, Kansas City, Mo., 1976-81, ptnr., 1982-2001. Editor: U. Va. Law Rev., 1974-76. Bd. dirs. Greater Kansas City YMCA Southwest Dist., 1987. Mem. Harvard Club (adv. bd., schs. com. Kansas City 1977-2001, v.p. 1981-82, 92-93, pres. 1994-96, mem. adv. bd. 1996-2001). Democrat. Roman Catholic. Federal civil litigation, State civil litigation, Labor. Home: 1210 W 68th Ter Kansas City MO 64113-1904 Office: Armstrong Teasdale LLP 2345 Grand Blvd Ste 2000 Kansas City MO 64108-2617 E-mail: jvering@armstrongteasdale.com

VERNAVA, ANTHONY MICHAEL, lawyer; b. N.Y.C., May 13, 1937; s. Michel Antonio Vernava and Ana Avellina Guerriero. BS, Georgetown U., 1959; JD, Harvard U., 1962; LLM, NYU, 1965; MA in L.Am. Studies/Internat. Fin., George Washington U., 1999. Bar: N.Y. 1962, U.S. Dist. Ct. (so. and ea. dists.) N.Y. 1963, U.S. Ct. Appeals (2nd cir.) 1963, Mich. 1965, U.S. Dist. Ct. (ea. dist.) Mich. 1966, U.S. Tax Ct. 1966, U.S. Supreme Ct. 1966, Ill. 1973. Atty. Reid & Priest, N.Y.C., 1962-63, IBM Corp., Armonk, N.Y., 1963-65; assoc. prof. Wayne State U., Detroit, 1965-68, prof., 1968-72; pvt. practice law Detroit and Chgo., 1972-75; prof. law So. Meth. U., Dallas, 1975-76; prof. law, consulting atty. U. Detroit Sch. Law, 1976-95; pvt. practice internat. cons. Fairfax, Va., 1995—. Arbitrator Mich. Employment Rels. Commn., Detroit, 1988-95. Contbr. articles to profl. jours. Mem. ABA, N.Y. State Bar. Avocations: international travel, pre-Colombian civilizations, boating, hiking. Private international, Securities, Corporate taxation. Office: PO Box 99 Oakton VA 22124-0099

VERNIERO, PETER G. state supreme court justice; married; 2 children. BA summa cum laude, Drew U., 1981; JD, Duke U., 1984. Law clk. to Justice Robert L. Clifford, 1984; with Pitney, Hardin, Kipp & Szuch, Morristown, N.J., 1985-87; dir. Herold & Haines P.A., Warren; chief counsel, chief of staff Gov. Christine Whitman, Trenton; atty. gen. State of N.J., 1996-99; assoc. justice N.J. Supreme Ct., 1999—. Adj. prof. bus. law County Coll. Morris, 1986. Exec. dir. Rep. State Com., 1989-90. Office: NJ Supreme Ct Hunterdon County Justice Ctr 65 Park Ave Flemington NJ 08822-0970*

VERNON, DARRYL MITCHELL, lawyer; b. N.Y.C., May 4, 1956; s. Leonard and Joyce (Davidson) V.; m. Lauren Lynn Bernstein, Aug. 21, 1982. BA in Math., Tufts U., 1978; JD, Yeshiva U., 1981. Bar: N.Y. 1982, U.S. Dist. Ct. (so. and ea. dists.) N.Y. 1982, U.S. Ct. Appeals (2d cir.) 1987. Assoc. Hochberg & Greenberg, N.Y.C., 1981-82; ptnr. Greenberg & Vernon, 1982-83, Law Offices of Darryl M. Vernon, N.Y.C., 1983—; pres., ptnr. Vernon & Ginsburg, LLP, 1989—. Contbr. articles to profl. jours. Samuel Belkin scholar Yeshiva U., 1979. Mem. ABA, ATLA

VERON, J. MICHAEL, lawyer, writer; b. Lake Charles, La., Aug. 24, 1950; s. Earl Ernest and Alverdy (Heyd) V.; m. Melinda Anne Guidry, Jan. 2, 1993; children: John Heyd, Katharine Leigh, Dylan Michael Earl. BA, Tulane U., 1972, JD, 1974; LLM, Harvard U., 1976. Bar: La. 1974, U.S. Dist. Ct. (we. dist.) La. 1977, U.S. Dist. Ct. (ea. dist.) La. 1979, U.S. Dist. Ct. (mid. dist.) La., 1983, U.S. Dist. Ct. (ea. dist.) Tex. 1992), U.S. Ct. Appeals (5th cir.) 1981, U.S. Ct. Appeals (fed. cir.) 1996, U.S. Tax Ct. 1988. Law clk. to presiding justice La. Supreme Ct., New Orleans, 1974-75; sole practice Lake Charles, 1976-78; ptnr. Scofield, Gerard, Veron, Singletary & Pohorelsky (formerly Scofield, Gerard, Veron, Hoskins & Soileau), 1978—. Instr. legal method and rsch. Boston U., 1975-76; lectr. environ. law McNeese State U., 1976-79; faculty Tulane Trial Adv. Inst., 1980; adj. prof. La. State U. Sch. Law, 1993—. Author: The Greatest Player Who Never Lived, 2000, The Greatest Course That Never Was, 2001; mem. bd. editors Tulane Law Rev., 1972-73, assoc. editor, 1973-74. Mem. athletic adv. com. Tulane U., 1983-86; pres. Krewe of Barataria, 1980-86; bd. dirs. Friends of Gov.'s Program for Gifted Children, Inc., 1985. Named to La. State U. Law Ctr. Hall of Fame, 1993. Mem. U.S. Golf Assn. (sectional affairs com.), La. Golf. Assn. (bd. dirs., pres. 1990), Order of Coif, Maritime Law Assn., Lake Charles Country Club (pres. 1986). Roman Catholic. Avocations: golf, gin rummy, athletics. Federal civil litigation, General civil litigation, State civil litigation. Home: 2945 Par Dr Lake Charles LA 70605-5925 Office: Scofield Gerard Veron Singletary & Pohorelsky 1114 Ryan St Lake Charles LA 70601-5252 E-mail: mveron@sgvsp.com

VERRILL, CHARLES OWEN, JR. lawyer; b. Biddeford, Maine, Sept. 30, 1937; s. Charles Owen and Elizabeth (Handy) V.; m. Mary Ann Blanchard, Aug. 13, 1960 (dec.); children: Martha Anne, Edward Blanchard, Ethan Christopher, Elizabeth Handy, Matthew Lawton, Peter Goldthwait; m. Diana Baber, Dec. 11, 1993. AB, Tufts U., 1959; LLB, Duke U., 1962. Bar: D.C. 1962. Assoc. Weaver & Glassie, 1962-64, Barco, Cook, Patton & Blow, 1964-66, ptnr., 1967, Patton, Boggs & Blow, 1967-84, Wiley, Rein & Fielding, Washington, 1984—. Adj. prof. internat. trade law Georgetown U. Law Ctr., Washington, 1978—, Charles Fahy Disting. adj. prof., 1993; vis. sr. lectr. internat. trade law Duke U. Law Sch., 1998—; conf. chmn. The Future of Internat. Steel Industry, Bellagio, Italy, 1984, U.S. Agenda for Uruguay Round, Airlie House, Warrenton, Va., 1986, Polish Joint Venture Law, Cracow, Poland, 1987, Internat. Steel Industry II, Bellagio, 1987, Bulgaria and the GATT, Washington, 1977; chair, spkr. Protection of Intellectual Property from Theft and Piracy Abroad Southwestern Legal Found. Fgn. Investment Symposium, 1995, chair, panel on NAFTA 2 1/2 Years Later, 1996. Local dir. Tufts U. Ann. Fund, 1965-69; mem. Duke Law Alumni Coun., 1972-75; trustee Internat. Law Inst., 1981—, chmn. bd. trustees, 1983-87; apptd. to roster of dispute settlement panelists World Trade Orgn., 1995, 97; chmn. adv. bd. Inst. for Advancement of Svc., 1997—; mem. adv. com. rules U.S. Ct. Internat. Trade, 1998—; chmn. D.C. Cable Television Adv. Com., 1999—; mem. bd. visitors Duke U. Law Sch., 2000—. Mem. ABA, Internat. Bar Assn., D.C. Bar Assn., Order of Coif, Theta Delta Chi, Phi Delta Phi, Met. Club (Washington), Chevy Chase Club (Md.), Tarratine Club (Dark Harbor, Maine). Private international. Home: 3000 Q St NW Washington DC 20007-3080 Office: 1776 K St NW Washington DC 20006-2304 E-mail: cverrill@wrf.com

VERRONE, PATRIC MILLER, lawyer, writer; b. Glendale, N.Y.C., Sept. 29, 1959; s. Pat and Edna (Miller) V.; m. Margaret Maiya Williams, 1989; children: Patric Carroll Williams, Marianne Emma Williams, Theodore Henry Williams. BA, Harvard U., 1981; JD, Boston Coll., 1984. Bar: Fla. 1984, Calif. 1988, U.S. Dist. Ct. (mid. dist.) Fla. 1984, U.S. Dist. Ct. (ctrl. dist.) Calif. 1995, U.S. Ct. Appeals (9th cir.) 1995. Assoc. Allen, Knudsen, Swartz, DeBoest, Rhoads & Edwards, Ft. Myers, Fla., 1984-86; writer The Tonight Show, Burbank, Calif., 1987-90. Adj. prof. Loyola Law Sch., L.A., 1998-2000. Dir., producer, writer The Civil War--The Lost Episode, 1991; writer The Larry Sanders Show, 1992-94, The Critic, 1993-95; producer, writer The Simpsons, 1994-95, Muppets Tonight!, 1995-97 (Emmy award Best Children's Program 1998), Pinky and the Brain, 1998, Futurama, 1998— (Environ. Media award 2000, Emmy nominee 1999, 2001); editor Harvard Lampoon, 1978-84, Boston Coll. Law Rev., 1983-84, Fla. Bar Jour., 1987-88, L.A. Lawyer, 1994—; issue editor: Ann. Entertainment Law Issue, 1995-2001; contbr. articles to profl. jours. including Elysian Fields Quar., Baseball and the American Legal Mind, White's Guide to Collecting Figures, Frank Sinatra: The Man, The Music, The Legend. Bd. dirs. Calif. Confedn. of Arts, 1994-98, Mus. Contemporary Art, 1994-95. Mem. ABA (vice-chair arts, entertainment and sports law com. 1995-96), Calif. Bar, Calif. Lawyers for Arts, L.A. County Bar Assn. (sec. barristers exec. com., chair artists and the law com., steering com. homeless shelter project, intellectual property and entertainment law sect., state appelate jud. evaluation com., legis. activity com.), Fla. Bar Assn., Writers Guild Am. West (exec. com. animation writers caucus, bd. dirs. 1999-2001, sec., treas., 2001-, membership com., fin. com., legis. support com., 2001 contract negotiating com.), Harvard Club Lee County (v.p. 1985-86), Harvard Club So. Calif. Republican. Roman Catholic. Avocation: baseball. Home and Office: PO Box 1428 Pacific Palisades CA 90272-1428

VERTEFEUILLE, CHRISTINE S. judge; b. New Britain, Conn., Dec. 10, 1950; BA in Polit. Sci., Trinity Coll., 1972; JD, U. Conn., 1975. Pvt. practice, 1975-89; judge Conn. Superior Ct., 1989-94; adminstrv. judge Waterbury Jud. Dist., 1994-99, complex litigation judge, 1999; judge Appellate Ct., 1999-2000; assoc. justice Conn. Supreme Ct., 2000—. Alternate mem. Waterbury and New Haven (Conn.) Grievance Panels, 1985-89; faculty Conn. Judges Inst., 1989-94; mem. Commn. to Study the Atty. Grievance Process Appellate Ct., 1999. Mem. The Cheshire Commn. on Hadicapped and Disabled, 1988-89. Recipient Jud. award Conn. Trial Lawyers Assn., 1995. Mem. Conn. Bar Assn. (mem. exec. com. real property 1988-89). Office: Supreme Ct Bldg 231 Capitol Ave Hartford CT 06106*

VERTICCHIO, RICK, lawyer; b. Litchfield, Ill., July 10, 1953; s. Paul C. and Marge (Lacy) V.; children: Gina Maria, Jonathan Barry, Juliana. BA with honors, Ill. Coll., Jacksonville, 1975; JD with honors, So. Ill. U., 1978. Bar: Ill. 1978, U.S. Dist. Ct. (cen. and so. dists.) Ill. 1980, U.S. Ct. Appeals (4th cir.) 1980. Mem. Verticchio & Verticchio, Gillespie, Ill., 1978—. Asst. pub. defender Macoupin County, 1980-86. Editor So. Ill. Law Jour. Recipient William Jennings Bryant award for polit. sci. Ill. Coll., 1975, C.J.S. award for legal scholarship, 1977, Order of Barrister for appellate advocacy, 1978. Democrat. Roman Catholic. Home: 17509 Ridge Dr Carlinville IL 62626 Office: Verticchio & Verticchio 100 E Chestnut St Gillespie IL 62033-1501

VESSEL, ROBERT LESLIE, lawyer; b. Chgo., Mar. 21, 1942; s. Louis Frank and Margaret Ruth (Barber) V.; m. Diane White, Oct. 12, 1966; m. Lise Vessel, Dec. 19, 1992. BA, U. Ill., 1964; JD, Seton Hall U., 1973; LLM in Taxation, U. Miami, Coral Gables, Fla., 1980. Bar: N.J. 1973, Fla. 1981, U.S. Dist. Ct. (so. and mid. dists.) Fla. 1981, U.S. Ct. Appeals (11th cir.) 1981; bd. cert. civil trial, Fla. Assoc. Bennett & Bennett P.A., East Orange, N.J., 1973-76; ptnr. Kantor & Vessel, P.A., Wayne, 1976-81; assoc. Haddad Josephs & Jack, P.A., Coral Gables, Fla., 1981-85; ptnr. Mitchell Alley Rywant & Vessel, Tampa, 1985-89, Moffitt & Vessel, P.A., Tampa, 1989-94, Vessel & Morales, P.A., Tampa, 1994-99. With USNR, 1964-66. Mem. Assn. Trial Lawyers Am., Nat. Inst. Trial Advocacy, Acad. Fla. Trial Lawyers, Hillsboro County Bar Assn. Avocation: sailing. Federal civil litigation, Personal injury. Office: Robert L Vessel PA 1100 W Kennedy Blvd Tampa FL 33606-1966 E-mail: veslaw@msn.com

VESTAL, ALLAN W. dean, law educator; BA, Yale U., 1976, JD, 1979. Tchr. in areas of partnership and corp. law, comml. law, and real estate Faculty of Washington and Lee U. Sch. Law , 1989—2000. Practiced law for ten yrs., Wis., Iowa. Publ. (treatise with Prof. Hillman and Dean Weidner) The Revised Uniform Partnership Act ;contbr. chapters to books, law rev. articles including Kansas Law Rev., Tulane Law Rev. Mem.: Am. Law Inst. Office: Coll Law U Ky Lexington KY 40506-0048*

VESTAL, JOSEPHINE BURNET, lawyer; b. Iowa City, June 13, 1949; d. Allen Delker and Dorothy (Walker) V. Student, Williams Coll., 1970; BA, Mt. Holyoke Coll., 1971; JD, U. Wash., 1974. Bar: Wash. 1974, U.S. Dist. Ct. (we. dist.) Wash. 1974, U.S. Ct. Appeals (9th cir.) 1984, U.S. Ct. Appeals (D.C. cir.) 1984, U.S. Dist. Ct. (ea. dist.) Wash. 1993. Ptnr. Selinker, Vestal, Klockars & Andersen, Seattle, 1974-80; assoc. Williams, Kastner & Gibbs, 1981-87; mem. Williams, Kastner & Gibbs, PLLC, 1988—. Mem. ABA (labor and employment sect.), Def. Rsch. Inst. (labor and employment sect.), Wash. State Bar Assn., King County Bar Assn. Federal civil litigation, State civil litigation, Labor. Office: Williams Kastner & Gibbs PO Box 21926 Seattle WA 98111-3926 E-mail: jvestal@wkg.com

VETTER, JOANNE REINIGER, paralegal; b. Rochester, N.Y., Aug. 19, 1947; d. Carl Gotlieb and Stella (Dmytriw) Reiniger; m. Ernest J. Vetter, Oct. 7, 1967 (dec. Jan. 1993); 1 child, John; stepchildren: Stephen, Anne Robb. BS in Bus. Adminstrn., U. Akron, 1981; Paralegal Cert., Hammel Coll., Akron, Ohio, 1988. Paralegal Richard P. Martin LPA, Stow, Ohio, 1990-91; Pvt. Atty. Involvement coord. for Summit, Portage and Medina counties Western Res. Legal Svcs., Akron, 1991—; inside salesperson Falls Lumber and Millwork Co., Cuyahoga Falls, Ohio, 2000—. Asst. state dir. Am. Inst. for Paralegal Studies, Walsh Coll., Canton, Ohio, 1993-94; mem. adv. bd. legal assisting program U. Akron, 1993—; mem. adv. bd. Hammel Coll., 1990-92. Recipient Liberty Bell award, Akron Bar Assn., 1992. Mem. ABA, Dirs. of Vols. in Am., Women in the Wind Motorcycle Club, Omicron Delta Kappa. Roman Catholic. Avocations: woodworking, gardening, motorcycle.

VETTORI, PAUL MARION, lawyer; b. Washington, Sept. 6, 1944; s. Mariano L. and Bessie (Southerd) V.; m. Judith Ann Gersack, June 19, 1965; children: Joseph, Damon, Jason, Justin. AB, U. Md., Coll. Park, 1967; JD, U. Md., Balt., 1970. Bar: Md. 1970, U.S. Dist. Ct. Md. 1970, U.S. Ct. Appeals (4th cir.) 1970. Assoc. Frank, Bernstein, Conaway & Goldman, Balt., 1971-74; asst. atty. gen. Md. Atty. Gen.'s Office, 1974-75; ptnr. Shapiro, Vettori & Olander, 1975-81, Frank, Bernstein, Conaway & Goldman, Balt., 1981-91, Kenny, Vettori & Robinson, P.A., Balt., 1992-97, White, Miller, Kenny & Vettori, LLP, Towson, Md., 1997—. Mem. ABA, Md. State Bar Assn., Balt. County Bar Assn., Howard County Bar Assn., Rotary (pres.). Avocation: sports. General civil litigation. Office: White Miller Kenny & Vettori LLP 300 Lafayette Bldg 40 W Chesapeake Ave Towson MD 21204-4803 E-mail: vettori@wmkv.com

VEVERKA, DONALD JOHN, lawyer; b. Chgo., July 20, 1935; s. John Edward and Irene Cecelia (Wasil) V.; m. Mary Almjeld, May 27, 1967; children: Tanya, Holly, Marc. BS, Loyola U., Chgo., 1957; JD, DePaul U., 1963. Bar: Ill. 1963, U.S. Dist. Ct. (no. dist.) Ill. 1963, U.S. Ct. Appeals (7th cir.) 1963, U.S. Supreme Ct. 1968. Asst. state's atty. civil appeals sect. Cook County State's Attys. Office, 1963-67; asst. atty. gen. appeals sect. Ill. Atty. Gen. Office, 1967-68; house counsel Kenilworth Ins. Co., 1968-69; ptnr. Bradshaw, Speranza, Veverka & Brumlik, 1969-72; spl. asst. atty. gen., 1970-72; ptnr. Speranza & Veverka, Chgo., 1972-73, 74-90, Veverka Rosen & Haugh, 1990—. Officer Henehan Donovan Isaacson Speranza & Veverka, Ltd., Chgo., 1973-74; bd. dirs., officer DePaul Law Coun., 1972-83; mem. Ill. Supreme Ct. Com. on Pattern Jury Instrns. Assoc., 1973-96, chmn., 1993-96. Author: How To Buy or Sell Your Home Without a Lawyer, 1982; also articles. Bd. dirs. LaGrange Cmty. Meml. Hosp., 1979-89, officer, 1982-85, pres., 1986-87; bd. dirs. West Suburban YMCA, 1981—, chmn., 1997-99; bd. dirs. Rich Port YMCA; trustee Village of LaGrange Park, Ill., 1981-95; mem. police bd. Village of LaGrange Park, 1979, 80, 2000—. 1st lt. U.S. Army, 1967-69; capt. Res. Mem. ABA (faculty mem. Nat. Inst. Appellate Advocacy 1980, Ill. chmn. young lawyers com. on jud. selection 1971-72), Ill. State Bar Assn. (mem. com. on corrections reform 1973, also past mem. spkrs. bur., young mems. conf.), Bar Assn. Seventh Fed. Cir. (Ill. chmn. meetings com. 1976),

DePaul Alumni Assn. (governing bd. 1975-82), Phi Alpha Delta, Blue Key, Rich Port YMCA Men's Club (dir. 1980—, chmn. 1998, 99), Chgo. Athletic Club. Roman Catholic. General corporate, Family and matrimonial, General practice. Home: 709 N Park Rd La Grange Park IL 60526-1428 Office: 180 N Michigan Ave Chicago IL 60601-7401

VICK, PAUL ASHTON, lawyer; b. Rochester, N.Y., Sept. 30, 1945; s. Robert A. and Dorothy Lou (Flanders) V.; m. Gail A. VanHouten, Dec. 17, 1966; children— Jennifer, Christopher, Benjamin. B.A., Kalamazoo Coll., 1967; M.Div., Colgate Rochester Div. Sch., 1971; postgrad. New Eng. Sch. Law, 1972-73; J.D., SUNY-Buffalo, 1975. Bar: N.Y. 1976, U.S. Dist. Ct. (we. dist.) N.Y. 1976. Dir. Southeast Area Coalition Family Counseling, Rochester, 1969-72; assoc. firm Sullivan, Peters, Burns and Holtzberg, Rochester, 1976-79; ptnr. firm Sullivan, Peters, Burns, Holtzberg & Stander, Rochester, 1980-81, firm Phillips, Lytle, Hitchcock, Blaine & Huber, Rochester, 1982— . Trustee Immanuel Bapt. Ch., Rochester, 1984— ; bd. dirs. Cameron Community Ministries, Rochester, 1983— , Alternatives for Battered Women, Rochester, 1981— . Mem. Monroe County Bar Assn. (exec. council estate and trust sect. 1983—). Democrat. Lodge: Masons. Estate planning, Family and matrimonial. Home: 55 Monteroy Rd Rochester NY 14618-1211 Office: Phillips Lytle Hitchcock Blaine & Huber 1400 First Federal Plz Rochester NY 14614-1981

VICTOR, MICHAEL GARY, lawyer, physician; b. Detroit, Sept. 20, 1945; s. Simon H. and Helen (Litsky) V.; children: Elise Nicole, Sara Lisabeth. Bar: Ill. 1980, U.S. Dist. Ct. (no. dist.) Ill. 1980, U.S. Ct. Appeals (7th cir.) 1981; diplomate Am. Bd. Legal Medicine. Pres. Advocate Adv. Assocs., Chgo., 1982-95; asst. prof. medicine Northwestern U. Med. Sch., 1982—; pvt. practice law Barrington, Ill., 1982—; lectr. U. Ill., Chgo., 1999—. Dir. emergency medicine Loretto Hosp., Chgo., 1980-85, chief. sect. of emergency medicine St. Josephs Hosp., Chgo., 1985-87; v.p. Med. Emergency Svcs. Assocs., Buffalo Grove, Ill., 1989; v.p. MESA Mgmt. Corp.; of counsel Bollinger, Ruberry & Garvey, Chgo. Author: Informed Consent, 1980; Brain Death, 1980; (with others) Due Process for Physicians, 1984, A Physicians Guide to the Illinios Living Will Act, The Choice is Ours!, 1989. Recipient Service awards Am. Coll. Emergency Medicine, 1973-83. Fellow Am. Coll. Legal Medicine (bd. govs. 1996-97, alt. del. to AMA House of Dels. 1996-97), Chgo. Acad. Legal Medicine; mem. Am. Coll. Emergency Physicians (pres. Ill. chpt. 1980, med.-legal-ins. council 1980-81, 83-84), ABA, Ill. State Bar Assn., Am. Soc. Law and Medicine, Chgo. Bar Assn. (med.-legal council 1981-83), AMA, Ill. State Med. Soc. (med.-legal council 1980-86, 88), Chgo. Med. Soc. Jewish. State civil litigation, Health. Home and Office: 153 Aberdour Ln Palatine IL 60067-8001 E-mail: mgv@merle.acns.nwu.edu

VICTOR, RICHARD STEVEN, lawyer; b. Detroit, Aug. 3, 1949; s. Simon H. and Helen (Litsky) V.; m. Denise L. Berman, Nov. 26, 1978; children: Daniel, Ronald, Sandra. Bar: Mich. 1975, U.S. Dist. Ct. (ea. dist.) Mich. 1975. Assoc. Law Offices of Albert Best, Detroit, 1975; ptnr. Best & Victor, Oak Park, Mich., 1976-80; sole practice, 1981-85; ptnr. Law Offices of Victor, Robbins and Bassett and predecessor firms, Birmingham, Mich., 1986-93, Victor and Robbins and predecessor firms, Birmingham, 1993-98, Bloomfield Hills, Mich., 1998-2000; pvt. practice Richard S. Victor, PLLC, 2000—. Instr. in family law Oakland U., Rochester, Mich., 1976—; bd. dirs. Agy. for Jewish Edn., 1990; legal advisor family law Sta. Ask the Lawyer WXYT radio. Author: (column) Legally Speaking, Stepfamily Bull., 1984—; author, genera editor: Michigan Practitioners Series: Family Law and Practice, 1997; tech. advisor Whose Mother Am I? Aaron Spelling Prodns./ABC Movies; bd. editors Mich. Lawyers Weekly newspaper, 2000. Mem. community adv. bd. Woodland Hills Med. Ctr., 1981—; v.p. Bloomfield (Mich.) Sq. Homeowners Assn., 1985—, pres. 1988; chmn. legis. com. Birmingham Schs. PTA, 1987—. Recipient Award of Meritorious Svc. to the Chldren of Am., Nat. Coun. of Juvenile and Family Ct. Judges, 1993, Child Advocate of Yr. award Chld Abuse and Neglect Coun., 1994, Disting. Svc. award Oakland County Bar Assn., 1994, Lifetime Achievement award State Bar Mich., 1999, Disting. Alumni Award Nat. Alumni Assn. of Mich. State U.-Detroit Coll. of Law, 2000. Fellow Mich. State Bar Found., Am. Acad. Matrimonial Lawyers (bd. mgrs. Mich. chpt. 1999—, com. chair); mem. ABA (guest lectr. sem. 1988, exec. com. on custody 1989—), Mich. Bar Assn. (treas. family law sect. 1987-88, sec. 1988-89, chmn. continuing legal edn. com. family law sect., 1986-90, corr. sec. 1988-89, chmn. elect 1989-90, chmn. family law sect. 1990-91, Appreciation award from family law sect. 1987-89, Lifetime Achievement award family law sect. 1999, co-founder SMILE), Oakland County Bar Assn. (chmn. lawyer's admission com. 1981, unauthorized practice of law 1982, oldtimer's night 1984-85, speakers bur. 1985), Family Law Coun. (chmn. legis. com.), Grandparent Rights Orgn. (founder, exec. dir. 1984—, newsletter editor), B'nai B'rith Barristers. Jewish. Avocation: playing piano. Family and matrimonial, Personal injury. Office: Law Offices of Richard S Victor PLLC 100 W Long Lake Rd Ste 250 Bloomfield Hills MI 48304-2721 E-mail: rsvlaw@aol.com

VICTORY, JEFFREY PAUL, state supreme court justice; b. Shreveport, La., Jan. 29, 1946; s. Thomas Edward and Esther (Horton) V.; m. Nancy Clark Victory, Jan. 20, 1973; children: Paul Bradford, William Peter, Christopher Thomas, Mary Katherine. BA in History and Govt., Centenary Coll., 1967; JD, Tulane U., 1971. Bar: La. 1971. Ptnr. Tucker, Jeter, Jackson & Victory, Shreveport, 1971-82; dist. ct. judge 1st Jud. Dist. Ct., 1982-90; appellate judge 2d Circuit Ct. of Appeal, 1991-95; assoc. justice Supreme Ct. La., 1995—. Bd. dirs. CODAC Drug Abuse, Shreveport; mem. La. Sentencing Commn. La. NG, 1969-75. Mem. ABA, Shreveport Bar Assn., La. Bar Assn. Republican. Baptist. Avocations: tennis, motorcycles, classic cars. Office: Supreme Ct 301 Loyola Ave New Orleans LA 70112-1814

VIDERMAN, LINDA JEAN, paralegal, corporate executive; b. Follansbee, W.Va., Dec. 4, 1957; d. Charles Richard and Louise Edith (LeBoeuf) Roberts; m. David Gerald Viderman Jr., Mar. 15, 1974; children: Jessica Renae, April Mae, Melinda Dawn. AS, W.Va. No. C.C., 1983; cert. income tax prep., H&R Block, Steubenville, Ohio, 1986. Cert. surg. tech., fin. counselor; lic. ins. agt. Food prep. pers. Bonanza Steak House, Weirton, W.Va., 1981-83; ward clk., food svcs. Weirton Med. Ctr., 1982-84; sec., treas. Mountaineer Security Systems, Inc., Wheeling, W.Va., 1983-96; owner, operator The Button Booth, Colliers, 1985—; paralegal, adminstr. Atty. Dominic J. Potts, Steubenville, Ohio, 1987-92; gen. ptnr., executrix Panhandle Homes, Wellsburg, W.Va., 1988-96; sec.-treas., executrix Panhandle Homes, Inc., 1996—; ins. agt. Milico, Mass. Indemnity, 1991-92, L&L Ins. Svcs., 1992-94; paralegal Atty. Fred Risovich II, Weirton, 1991-93; sec. The Hon. Fred Risovich II, Wheeling, 1993; paralegal atty. Christopher J. Paull, Wellsburg, W.Va., 1993—; owner Wellsburg Office Supply, 1993-94; owner, operator Viderman Child Care Svcs. Co., Wellsburg, 1997—; owner, dir. Viderman & Assocs., 1997—. Notary pub., 1991—. Contbr. articles to profl. jours.; author numerous poems. Chmn. safety com. Colliers (W.Va.) Primary PTA, 1985-87; mem., sec. LaLeche League, Steubenville, Ohio, 1978-80; vol. counselor W.Va. U. Fin. Counseling Svc., 1990—; IRS vol. Vol. Income Tax Assistance Program, 1991—. Mem. W.Va. Writers Assn., Legal Assts. of W.Va., Inc., Am. Affiliate of Nat. Assn. Legal Assts., W.Va. Trial Lawyers Assn., Wellsburg Art Assn., Brooke County Genealogical Soc., Phi Theta Kappa. Jehovah's Witness. Avocations: Christian ministry, home computing, camping, genealogy, home schooling. Home: RR2 Box 28 Wellsburg WV 26070-9500 Office: Panhandle Homes Inc RR 2 Box 27A Wellsburg WV 26070-9500 E-mail: lviderman@aol.com

VIE, GEORGE WILLIAM, III, lawyer; b. Tampa, Fla., Mar. 21, 1961; s. George William Jr. and Cheri Ann (Bass) V. BS magna cum laude, U. Houston, Clear Lake, Tex., 1985; JD, U. Tex., 1988. Bar: Tex. 1989, U.S. Dist. Ct. (so. dist.) Tex. 1990, U.S. Ct. Appeals (5th cir.) 1990, U.S. Mil. Ct. Appeals 1995, U.S. Supreme Ct. 1995; bd. cert. civil appellate law Tex. Bd. Legal Specialization. Legal asst. Bankston, Wright & Greenhill, Austin, Tex., 1985-89, atty., 1989-90; ptnr. Mills, Shirley, Eckel & Bassett, Galveston, Tex., 1990—. Spkr. in field. Contbr. articles to legal publs. Fellow Tex. Bar Found.; mem. FBA, State Bar Tex., Phi Kappa Phi, Sigma Phi Epsilon. Appellate, Civil rights, Constitutional. Office: Mills Shirley Eckel & Bassett 2228 Mechanic St Ste 400 Galveston TX 77550-1591 E-mail: gvie@millshirley.com

VIENER, JOHN D. lawyer; b. Richmond, Va., Oct. 18, 1939; s. Reuben and Thelma (Kurtz) V.; m. Karin Erika Bauer, Apr. 7, 1969; children: John D. Jr., Katherine Bauer Viener Riordan. BA, Yale U., 1961; JD, Harvard U., 1964. Bar: N.Y. State 1965, U.S. Supreme Ct. 1970, U.S. Dist. Ct. (so. dist.) N.Y. 1974, U.S. Tax Ct. 1975. Assoc. Satterlee, Warfield & Stephens, N.Y.C., 1964-69; sole practice, 1969-76; sr. ptnr. Christy & Viener, 1976-98, Salans, Hertzfeld, Heilbronn, Christy & Viener, N.Y.C., 1999-2000; prin. 1st Global Tech. Mgmt., LLC, 2000—. Dir. BFD Capital Inc., 2001—; founder, bd. dirs., gen. counsel Foxfire Fund, Inc., 1968—88; gen. counsel, bd. dirs. Landmark Communities, Inc., 1970—, Am. Continental Properties Group, 1978, NF&M Internat., Inc., 1976—, Singer Fund, Inc., 1979—, Immunotherapy, Inc., 1997—99, Tupper Broadcasting Group Cos., 1996—, Viener Found., 1991—; gen. counsel Nat. Cancer Found. Cancer Care, 1982—85, Troster, Singer & Co., 1970—77; bd. dirs. Gen. Financiere Immob. et Commer. S.A., 1985—89; spl. counsel fin. instns., investment banking and securities concerns; real estate and tax advisor. Bd. dirs. York Theatre Co., 1999—, The N.Y. Pops, 1999—. Mem. Meeker Brook Sporting Assn., Fairfield County Hounds, Manursing Island Club, Washington Club, Palm Beach Polo. Real property, Securities, Corporate taxation. also: 650 Park Avenue New York NY 10021 Office: Salans Hertzfeld Heilbronn Christy & Viener 620 5th Ave New York NY 10020-2402

VIERSEN, ARNOUD C. lawyer, judge; b. Batavia, Java, Indonesia, Nov. 1, 1949; s. Jacob C. Viersen and Hendrica C. De Ruijter; m. Petronella Kooiman, June 7, 1975; children: Harald, Eline. LLM Dutch Law, Rijksuniversiteit Groningen, 1971, LLM in Taxation, 1973. Assoc. Loyens & Volkmaars, Rotterdam, 1977-86; ptnr. Loyens & Loeff, Amsterdam, 1986—. Dep.-judge District Ct., Tax Sect., Hertogenbosch, 1996. 2d lt. Royal Dutch Navy, 1975-77. Mem. Internat. Fiscal Assn., Internat. Bar Assn., European-Am. Tax Inst. (adv. bd. 1988—). Mergers and acquisitions, Corporate taxation. Office: Loyens & Loeff PO Box 71170 NL1008BD Amsterdam The Netherlands Home: 11 Van Montfoortlaan NL2596SN The Hague The Netherlands E-mail: arnoud.viersen@loyensloeff.com

VIETOR, HAROLD DUANE, federal judge; b. Parkersburg, Iowa, Dec. 29, 1931; s. Harold Howard and Alma Johanna (Kreimeyer) V.; m. Dalia Artemisa Zamarripa Cadena, Mar. 24, 1973; children: Christine Elizabeth, John Richard, Greta Maria. BA, U. Iowa, 1955, JD, 1958. Bar: Iowa 1958. Law clk. U.S. Ct. Appeals 8th Circuit, 1958-59; ptnr. Bleakley Law Offices, Cedar Rapids, Iowa, 1959-65; judge Iowa Dist. Ct., 1965-79, chief judge, 1970-79; U.S. dist. judge U.S. Dist. Ct. for So. Dist. Iowa, Des Moines, 1979-96, chief judge, 1985-92, sr. U.S. dist. judge, 1997—. Lectr. at law schs., legal seminars U.S. and Japan. Contbr. articles to profl. jours. in U.S. and Japan. Served with USN, 1952-54. Mem. ABA, Iowa Bar Assn. (pres. jr. sect. 1966-67), Iowa Judges Assn. (pres. 1975-76), 8th Cir. Dist. Judges Assn. (pres. 1986-88). Office: US Dist Ct 221 US Courthouse 123 E Walnut St Des Moines IA 50309-2035

VIG, VERNON EDWARD, lawyer; b. St. Cloud, Minn., June 19, 1937; s. Edward Enoch and Salley Johanna (Johnson) V.; m. Susan Jane Rosenow, June 10, 1961; 1 child, Elizabeth Karen. BA, Carleton Coll., 1959; LLB, NYU, 1962, LLM, 1963; postdoctoral studies, Univ. Parias, Fac. de Droit, 1964. Bar: N.Y. 1962; avocat, Paris, 1992. Assoc. Cleary, Gottlieb, Steen & Hamilton, Paris, 1964, Donovan, Leisure, Newton & Irvine, N.Y.C. and Paris, 1965-72, ptnr., 1972-86, LeBoeuf, Lamb, Greene & MacRae, N.Y.C., 1986—. Sr. warden Grace Ch., Bklyn., 1986-2001. George F. Baker scholar, Fulbright scholar, 1963-64, Ford Found. scholar, 1963-64. Mem. ABA (internat. and antitrust sects.), N.Y. State Bar Assn. (chmn. antitrust sect. 1987-88), Assn. of Bar of City of N.Y., Internat. Bar Assn., Union Internat. des Avocats, Heights Casino (bklyn.), Merriewold Club (Forestburgh, N.Y., bd. dirs. 1985-91). Episcopalian. Antitrust, General corporate, Private international. Office: LeBoeuf Lamb Greene & MacRae 125 W 55th St New York NY 10019-5369 E-mail: vvig@llgm.com

VIGDOR, JUSTIN LEONARD, lawyer; b. N.Y.C., July 13, 1929; s. Irving Barton and Ida (Devins) V.; m. Louise Martin, Mar. 8, 1952; children: Robert, Jill Vigdor-Feldman, Lisa Vigdor-Peck, Wendy Vigdor-Hess. LLB magna cum laude, St. John's U., 1951; LLM, N.Y.U., 1952. Bar: N.Y. 1951, U.S. Supreme Ct 1951, Fla. 1975. Ptnr. Boylan, Brown, Code, Vigdor & Wilson LLP, Rochester, N.Y., 1958—. Bd. dirs.IEC Electronics Corp.; former mem. faculty Nazareth Coll.; mem. N.Y. Uniform Law Commn., Nat. Conf. Uniform Law Commrs. Contbr. articles to profl. jours. Bd. dirs. AAA Western/Central N.Y., Found. for Jewish Cmty., Ames Amzalac Meml. Trust; pres. AAA N.Y. State , Inc., Al Sigl Ptnrs. Foundn., also past pres.; chmn. N.Y. State IOLA Fund. Served with JAGC, AUS, 1952-54. Recipient Community Svc. award, 1960, award for Svc. to Community and Legal Profession, 1983, Disting. Svc. award N.Y. State Assn. County Clks., 1985. Fellow Am. Bar Found., N.Y. Bar Found. (Nathaniel award for cmty. svc. and profl. accomplishment); mem. Fla. Bar Assn., N.Y. State Bar Assn. (past pres. Ho. of Dels.), Monroe County Bar Assn. (past pres.), Estate Planning Coun., Am. Arbitration Assn. (nat. panel 1962—), N.Y. State C. of C. (Disting. Svc. award 1964), Irondequoit Country Club. Democrat. Jewish. General corporate, Real property, Securities. Home: 16 Tobey Woods Pittsford NY 14534-1824 Office: 2400 Chase Sq Rochester NY 14604 E-mail: jvigdor@boylanbrown.com, jvigdor@aol.com

VIGIL, DANIEL AGUSTIN, academic administrator; b. Denver, Feb. 13, 1947; s. Agustin and Rachel (Naranjo) V.; m. Claudia Cartier. BA in History, U. Colo., Denver, 1978, JD, 1982. Bar: Colo. 1982, U.S. Dist. Ct. Colo. 1983. Project mgr. Mathematics Policy Rsch., Denver, 1978; law clk. Denver Dist. Ct., 1982-83; ptnr. Vigil and Bley, Denver, 1983-85; asst. dean sch. law U. Colo., Boulder, 1983-89, assoc. dean sch. law, 1989—. Apptd. by chief justice of Colo. Supreme Ct. to serve on Colo. Supreme Ct. Ad Hoc Com. on miniority participation in legal profession, 1988-94; adj. prof. U. Colo. Sch. Law; mem. Gov. Colo. Lottery Commn., 1990-97; mem. Colo. Supreme Ct. Hearing Bd., 1998—. Editor (newsletter) Class Action, 1987-88; co-editor (ethics com. column) Colo. Lawyer, 1995-97. Bd. dirs. Legal Aid Soc. Met. Denver, 1986-99, chmn. bd. dirs., 1998-99; past v.p. Colo. Minority Scholarhip Consortium, pres. 1990-91; mem. Task Force on Community Race Rels., Boulder, 1989-94; past mem. jud. nomination rev. com. U.S. Senator Tim Wirth; chmn. bd. dirs. Colo. Legal Svcs., 2000-. Mem. Colo. Bar Assn. (mem. legal edn. and admissions com. 1989-94, chmn. 1989-91, bd. govs. 1991, 97—), Hispanic Nat. Bar Assn. (chmn. scholarship com. 1990-95), Colo Hispanic Bar Assn. (bd. dirs. 1985-89, pres. 1990), Denver Bar Assn. (joint com. on minorities in the legal profession), Boulder County Bar Assn. (ex-officio mem., trustee), Phi Delta Phi (faculty sponsor). Roman Catholic. Avocations: skiing, cosmology. Home: 828 3d Ave PO Box 518 Lyons CO 80540-0518 Office: U Colo Sch Law PO Box 401 Boulder CO 80303 E-mail: Daniel.Vigil@colorado.edu

VIGIL, DAVID CHARLES, lawyer; b. Bklyn., Jan. 29, 1944; s. Charles S. and Kathleen A. (Liebert) V. BA, U. Colo., 1966; JD, U. N.Mex., 1969. Bar: Colo. 1969, U.S. Dist. Ct. Colo. 1969, U.S. Ct. Appeals (10th cir.) 1969, U.S. Supreme Ct. 1974. Pvt. practice, Denver, 1969-80, 96—; ptnr. Vigil & Vigil, 1980-96; broker Perry & Butler Realty, 1996-97, Keller Williams Realty, Denver, 1997—. Bd. dirs. Archdiocesan Housing Commn. Inc., 1998—, Housing for All, 1999—. Grantee Nat. Inst. for Trial Advocacy, 1983. Mem. ABA, ATLA, Colo. Bar Assn. (mem. ethics com. 1973-79, legal fee arbitration com. 1980-92), Denver Bar Assn. (mem. jud. selection and benefits com. 1975-90, chmn. 1988-90), Am. Arbitration Assn. (comml. arbitrator 1993-95), Assn. Trial Lawyers Colo., Colo. Hispanic Bar Assn. (bd. dirs. 1986-89, treas. 1988), Cath. Lawyers guild, NITA Advs. Assn., Elks. Federal civil litigation, State civil litigation, Personal injury. E-mail: davidcvigil@msn.com

VIGNERI, JOSEPH WILLIAM, lawyer; b. Decatur, Ill., July 28, 1956; s. Joseph Paul and Thelma Lucille (Pettus) V.; m. Martha Suzanne Smith, May 19, 1984; children: Craig Ashley, Emily Carmela. BA in Polit. Sci., Millikin U., 1980; JD cum laude, St. Louis U., 1983. Bar: Ill. 1983, U.S. Dist. Ct. (ctrl. dist.) Ill. 1983, U.S. Supreme Ct. 1990. Assoc. Rosenberg, Rosenberg, Bickes, Johnson & Richardson, Decatur, 1983-86; ptnr. Brilley & Vigneri, 1986-88; pvt. practice, 1988-92; ptnr. Vigneri & Robinson, Ill., 1993-95; pvt. practice, 1995—; asst. pub. defender Macon County, Ill., 1999—. Past mem. job. svc. employer com. Ill. Dept. Employment Security. Past mem. profl. adv. com. Vis. Nurses Assn.; past bd. dirs., treas. Macon County Mental Health Assn. Mem. ABA (sect. real property, probate and trust law, com. spl. needs and tech. com., vice chmn. gen. practice com. 1991-92, family law subcom., editor newsletter), Ill. Bar Assn. (sec. individual rights sect. 1986, mem. bus. advice and fin. planning sect. coun. 1995-97), Decatur Bar Assn. (continuing legal edn. com. 1994-95, tech. com. 1996-97). Republican. Roman Catholic. Avocations: reading, travel, computers. Criminal. Home: 65 Ridge Lane Dr Decatur IL 62521-5456 Office: PO Box 857 136 W Washington St Decatur IL 62525-0857 also: 212 W Vine St Taylorville IL 62568-1957 E-mail: jvigneri@earthlink.net

VIKTORA, RICHARD EMIL, lawyer; b. Chgo., July 1, 1943; s. Emil J. and Lillian B. (Smatlak) V.; m. Anne Marie Kus, Feb. 20, 1971. BS, U. Ill., 1965; JD, John Marshall Law Sch., 1969. Bar: Ill. 1969, U.S. Dist. Ct. (no. dist.) Ill. 1969, U.S. Ct. Appeals (7th cir.) 1970, U.S. Supreme Ct. 1975, N.Y. 1981, U.S. Dist. Ct. (so. and ea. dists.) N.Y. 1983. Assoc. Menk, Johnson & Bishop, Chgo., 1969-73; litigation group counsel, regulatory counsel, asst. sec. G.D. Searle & Co., Skokie, Ill., 1973-80; asst. sec., dir. gen. svcs. Revlon, Inc.; asst. sec. Revlon Group, Inc., N.Y.C., 1980-92; gen. counsel Skidmore, Owings & Merrill LLP, 1992—. Lawyer; b. Chgo., July 1, 1943; s. Emil J. and Lillian B. (Smatlak) V.; m. Anne Marie Kus, Feb. 20, 1971. B.S., U. Ill., 1965; JD, John Marshall Law Sch., 1969. Bar: Ill. 1969, U.S. Dist. Ct. (no. dist.) Ill. 1969, U.S. Ct. Appeals (7th cir.) 1970, U.S. Supreme Ct. 1975, N.Y. 1981, U.S. Dist. Ct. (so. and ea. dists.) N.Y. 1983. Assoc. Menk, Johnson, & Bishop, Chgo., 1969-73; instr. John Marshall Law Sch., Chgo., 1970-73; litigation group counsel, regulatory counsel, asst. sec. G.D. Searle & Co., Skokie, Ill., 1973-80; asst. sec., dir. gen. svcs. Revlon, Inc., also asst. sec. Revlon Group, Inc., N.Y.C., 1980-92; gen. counsel Skidmore Owings & Merrill LLP, N.Y.C., 1992—. Zoning adminstr. Village of Bartlett (Ill.), 1974, chmn. Plan Commn., 1975, trustee, 1975-79. Mem. ABA, Ill. State Bar Assn., Chgo. Bar Assn., Def. Research Inst., Am. Corp. Counsel Assn., Assn. Trial Lawyers Am., Def. Assn. N.Y., Assn. of Bar of City of N.Y., Westchester-Fairfield Corp. Counsel Assn., Order of John Marshall Law Sch., Delta Theta Phi (scholar Key), Anvil Club (East Dundee, Ill.), Masons. Republican. Roman Catholic. Zoning adminstr. Village of Bartlett, Ill., 1974, chmn. Plan Commn., 1975, trustee, 1975-79. Mem. ABA, Ill. State Bar Assn., Chgo. Bar Assn., Def. Rsch. Inst., Am. Corp. Counsel Assn., Assn. Trial Lawyers Am., Def. Assn. N.Y., Assn. of Bar of City of N.Y., Westchester-Fairfield Corp. Counsel Assn., Order of John Marshall Law Sch., Delta Theta Phi (scholar Key), Anvil Club (East Dundee, Ill.), Masons. Republican. Roman Catholic. General civil litigation, Construction, General corporate. Home: 11 Saddle Hill Ln Stamford CT 06903-2309 Office: Skidmore Owings & Merrill LLP 14 Wall St New York NY 10005-2101 E-mail: richard.e.viktora@som.com

VILLA, JOHN KAZAR, lawyer; b. Ypsilanti, Mich., June 9, 1948; s. John Joseph and Susie (Hoogasian) V.; m. Ellen A. Edwards, June 3, 1990. AB, Duke U., 1970; JD, U. Mich., 1973. Bar: D.C. 1973. Trial atty. U.S. Dept. Justice, Washington, 1973-77; assoc. Williams & Connolly, 1977-81, ptnr., 1981—. Author: legal treatises. Federal civil litigation, Professional liability. Office: Williams & Connolly 725 12th St NW Washington DC 20005-5901

VILLACORAT, ANNA TERESA CRUZ, lawyer; b. Quezon City, Philippines, May 7, 1970; d. Hector Angeles and Tersita Cruz V. JD with honors, Ateneo Law Sch., Makati City, Philippines, 1995; LLM, NYU, 2001. Jr. assoc. Castillo Laman Tan Pantaleon & San Jose Law Office, Makati City, Philippines, 1996-2000. Ayala Found. scholar, Philippines, 2001. Mem. Phi Kappa Phi, Phi Gamma Mu. Banking, General corporate, Securities. Home: 425 W 44th St New York NY 10036-4402 E-mail: annavillacorta@lycos.com

VILLAVASO, STEPHEN DONALD, lawyer, urban planner; b. New Orleans, July 12, 1949; s. Donald Philip and Jacklyn (Tully) V.; m. Regina Smith, Apr. 17, 1971; children: Christine Regina, Stephen Warner. BS in Econs., U. New Orleans, 1971, M in Urban and Regional Planning, 1976; JD, Loyola U., New Orleans, 1981. Bar: La. 1982; recognized ct. expert in land use, planning and zoning. Urban and regional planner Barnard & Thomas, New Orleans, 1976-78; dir. analysis and planning Office of Mayor, City of New Orleans, 1978-81; counsel for planning and devel. Office of City Atty., City of New Orleans, 1983-84; dir. planning and environ. affairs Tecon Realty, New Orleans, 1981-83; v.p. for planning and project mgmt. Morphy, Makofsky, Mumphrey & Masson, 1984-89; bus. devel. mgr. Waste Mgmt., Inc., 1989-96; pres. Villavaso & Assocs., LLC, 1996—, Brownfields Redevel. Profls. LLC, New Orleans, 2000—. Bd. dirs. Regional Loan Corp.; guest lectr., adj. prof. Coll. of Urban and Pub. Affairs, U. New Orleans, 1976—; spl. instr. grad. studies in urban planning So. U. New Orleans, 1987—. Bd. dirs. New Orleans Traffic and Transp. Bur., 1981-86, Riverfront Awareness, New Orleans, 1984-86; bd. dirs. Vols. Am. Greater New Orleans, 1987-96, vice chmn., 1990, chmn. bd., 1992-95. With USN, 1971-74. Named one of Outstanding Young Men of Am., 1980, 82. Mem. ABA, Am. Inst. of Cert. Planners, Am. Planning Assn. (pres. La. div. 1980-84, disting. svc. award 1985), Urban Land Inst., La. Bar Assn., U. New Orleans Alumni Assn. (bd. dirs. 1990—), Phi Kappa Phi, Delta Sigma Pi (pres. 1971), Omicron Delta Kappa. Democrat. Roman Catholic. Avocations: philately, camping, travel. E-mail. Environmental, Land use and zoning (including planning). Home: 6304 Beauregard Ave New Orleans LA 70124-4502 E-mail: villavaso.assoc.llc@worldnet.att.net

VINAR, BENJAMIN, lawyer; b. Rock Island, Ill., Apr. 10, 1935; s. Isidore and Bessie (Shaman) V.; m. Rochelle Weinfeld, June 17, 1962; children: Jacqueline, Dov, Elana, Daniella. BA, U. Ill., 1957; LLB, NYU, 1960. Bar: N.Y. 1961, U.S. Dist. Ct. (so. dist.) N.Y. 1962, U.S. Ct. Appeals

(2nd cir.) 1964, U.S. Supreme Ct. 1966, U.S. Dist. Ct. (ea. dist.) N.Y. 1971. Assoc. Donovan, Leisure, Newton & Irvine, N.Y.C., 1961-71; pvt. practice, 1971-76, Garden City, N.Y. and N.Y.C., 1986—; ptnr. Siff & Newman, P.C., N.Y.C., 1976-86. Contbr. articles to profl. jours. Mem. nat. law com. Anti-Defamation League, N.Y.C., 1975-2000; pres. Queens Jewish Community Coun., N.Y.C., 1979-81, Young Israel of Queens Valley, N.Y.C., 1984-86; v.p. Nat. Coun. Young Israel, 1986-90, YM-YMHA of No. Queens, N.Y.C., 1989-91; bd. dirs. Met. Coun. on Jewish Poverty, N.Y.C., 1984-89. Mem. ABA, Nassau Bar Assn. (chair appellate practice com.), NYU Law Rev. Alumni Assn. (pres. 1981-83), Order of Coif, Phi Beta Kappa, Phi Kappa Phi. Democrat. Appellate, State civil litigation, Insurance. E-mail: bvinar@compuserve.com

VINCENT, ADRIAN ROGER, lawyer; b. Daggett, Mich., May 21, 1948; s. Adrian Donald and Dorothy (Heiden) V. BA, U. Mich., 1970; JD, Wayne State U., 1973. Bar: Mich. 1973, U.S. Dist. Ct. (we. dist.) Mich. 1974, U.S. Supreme Ct. 1979, U.S. Ct. Appeals (6th cir.) 1982, Ill. 1986. Ptnr. Anderson/Green/Vincent & Ingram P.C., Lansing, Mich., 1973-85; pvt. practice cons., Chgo., 1985-88; ptnr. McGinty, Brown, Jakubiak, Frankland, Hitch & Henderson, East Lansing, Mich., 1989—. Bd. dirs. Legal Aid Ctr. Mich., 1976-80, legal counsel Planned Parenthood Affilates of Mich., Lansing, 1984. Mem. ABA, Chgo. Bar Assn., State Bar Mich., Ingham County Bar Assn., Assn. Trial Lawyers Am., Ill. Bar Assn. State civil litigation, Insurance, Personal injury. Home: 601 Abbott Rd East Lansing MI 48823-3322

VINCENT, JOHN K. prosecutor; U.S. atty. ea. dist., Calif. Office: 501 I St Ste 10-100 Sacramento CA 95814-2322 Office Fax: 916-554-2900*

VINCENT, THOMAS PHILIP, lawyer; b. Greenfield, Mass., Mar. 22, 1951; s. Donald Wallace and Mary Lou (Lockhart) V. BA magna cum laude, U. Mass., 1974; JD, So. Meth. U., 1977. Bar: Tex. 1977, Mass. 1978, U.S. Dist. Ct. Mass. 1978, U.S. Ct. Appeals (1st cir.) 1978, U.S. Supreme Ct. 1986. Pvt. practice, Northampton, Mass., 1978-79; assoc. Fogel & Fogel, P.C., Northampton, 1979-81; ptnr. Vincent & Green, Northampton, 1981-86, Vincent, Green, Lipton & White, Northampton, 1986—. Named in resolution of commendation Western Mass. Legal Svcs., 1983-88. Mem. ABA, Hampshire County Bar Assn. (mem. probate ct. com. 1988-89), Mass. Bar Assn. (mem. lawyer referral svc. com. 1988-89), Mass. Acad. Trial Attys., Assn. Trial Lawyers Am., Northampton Lions (v.p. 1983-84, pres. 1984-85). Democrat. Methodist. State civil litigation, Criminal, Family and matrimonial. Office: Vincent Green Lipton & White 5 Hampton Ave # 210 Northampton MA 01060-3809

VINCENTI, MICHAEL BAXTER, lawyer; b. Balt., Dec. 28, 1950; s. Rudolph and Betty (Jones) V.; m. Patricia Lynn Bishopp, Apr. 14, 1984; children: Sarah, Elizabeth. BA, Johns Hopkins U., 1972; JD, NYU Sch. Law, 1975. Bar: Ill. 1975, Ky. 1979; cert. comml. investor, Ky. Assoc. Sonnenschein, Nath & Rosenthal, Chgo., 1975-79; from assoc. to ptnr. Wyatt, Tarrant & Combs, Louisville, 1979—. Guest instr. Jefferson Cmty. Coll., Louisville, 1988-98. Sec., gen. counsel Louisville Sci. Ctr., 1993—; dir., counsel bd. trustees Chance Sch., Louisville, 1995-98. Mem. ABA, Internat. Coun. Shopping Ctrs., Ill. Bar Assn., Am. Land Title Assn. (lender's counsel group), Am. Coll. Real Estate Lawyers, Am. Coll. Mortgage Attys., Ky. Bar Assn., Louisville Bar Assn., Rotary, Louisville Boat Club, Lex Mundi. Episcopalian. Avocations: squash, racquetball, tennis, travel, reading. Contracts commercial, Landlord-tenant, Real property. Office: Wyatt Tarrant & Combs 500 W Jefferson St Ste 2700 Louisville KY 40202-2898 Fax: 502-589-0309. E-mail: mvincenti@wyattfirm.com

VINCENTI, SHELDON ARNOLD, law educator, lawyer; b. Ogden, Utah, Sept. 4, 1938; s. Arnold Joseph and Mae (Burch) V.; children: Matthew Lewis, Amanda Jo. AB, Harvard U., 1960, JD, 1963. Bar: Utah 1963. Sole practice law, Ogden, 1966-67; ptnr. Lowe and Vincenti, Ogden, 1968-70; legis. asst. to U.S. Rep. Gunn McKay, Washington, 1971-72, adminstrv. asst., 1973; prof., assoc. dean U. of Idaho Coll. of Law, Moscow, Idaho, 1973-83, dean, prof. law, 1983-95, prof. law, 1995—. Home: 2480 W Twin Rd Moscow ID 83843-9114 Office: U Idaho Coll Law 6th & Rayburn St Moscow ID 83843

VINEGRAD, ALAN, prosecutor; Graduate Magna Cum Laude, U. Pa, 1980; JD, NYU, 1984. Staff acct. Price Waterhouse & Co.; clerk Honorable Leonard B. Sand, US Dist. Ct. for the Southern Dist. , NY; private practice Meister Leventhal & Slade; chief of general crimes US Atty. Office, Brooklyn, NY, chief of civil rights, deputy chief of Criminal Div., chief of the Criminal Div., chief asst. US Atty.; interim US Atty. US Atty. Office, Eastern Dist. , New York, 2001—. Adj. prof. New York Law Sch., 1996—; guest lectr. Brooklyn Law Sch., Cardoza Sch. Law, Fordham Law Sch., Hofstra Law Sch., New York U. Law Sch., Yale Law Sch., Dept. Justice's Office of Legal Edu. Recipient Atty. Gen. award for Distinguished Service, Stimson Medal for Outstanding Prosecutor, US Atty. Office for Eastern Dist. of NY. Office: US Attorney US Courthouse 147 Pierrepont St Brooklyn NY 11201 Fax: 718-254-6479*

VINES, WILLIAM DORSEY, lawyer; b. Kingsport, Tenn., May 28, 1942; s. William D. and Ozella Mae (Eastridge) V.; m. Norma Rene Cobb, Nov. 24, 1964 (div. Jan. 1980); children: David, Gregory, Derek; m. Dawn Marie Cioppa, Mar. 31, 1984; 1 child, Rachel. JD, U. Tenn., 1965. Bar: Tenn. 1966, U.S. Dist. Ct. (ea. dist.) Tenn. 1966, U.S. Ct. Appeals (6th cir.) 1967, U.S. Supreme Ct. 1972; cert. civil trial specialist commn. on Continuing Legal Edn. and Specialization of Tenn./Nat. Bd. Trial Advocates; cert. Rule 31 Mediator/Tenn. Supreme Ct. Atty., Knoxville, 1966-72; ptnr. Butler, Vines & Babb, 1972—. Fellow Tenn. Bar Found.; mem. Knoxville Bar Assn. (past. pres.), Am. Inns of Ct. (master of bench emeritus). Avocations: flying, skiing, trout fishing. Alternative dispute resolution, General civil litigation, Personal injury. Office: Butler Vines & Babb PO Box 2649 Knoxville TN 37901-2649 E-mail: Wvines@bvblaw.com

VINKEMULDER, H. YVONNE, retired lawyer; b. Grand Rapids, Mich., Aug. 21, 1930; d. Arthur and Frances (DeWitt) V. Student, Calvin Coll., 1948-50, Blodgett Hosp. Sch. Nursing, 1950-52; BA, Trinity Coll., 1956; JD, U. Miami, Coral Gables, Fla., 1983. Bar: Wis. 1983. Staff nurse Little Traverse Hosp., Petoskey, Mich., 1952-53, Swedish Covenant Hosp., Chgo., 1953-55; campus nurse Trinity Coll., 1955-57; head nurse Colo. Coll., Colorado Springs, 1957-61; sec. Inter-Varsity Christian Fellowship, Chgo., 1961-65, asst. to dir. devel. Chgo. and Madison, Wis., 1965-74, dir. devel. Madison, 1974-80, dir. planned giving, 1979-81, 90-96, gen. counsel, 1983-96; ret., 1996. Cons. in devel. various orgns., 1976-80; cons. not-for-profit orgn., 1990-2000; lectr. internat. law Fgn. Language Inst., Tianjin, China, 1989. Columnist The Branch, 1976-79; contbg. author: A Guide to Wisconsin Non Profit Corporations, 1990; contbr. articles to mags. Bd. dirs. Internat. Fellowship of Evang. Students, Inc., Boston, 1975-85, Schloss Mittersill Christian Conf. Inc., Madison, 1985-93, 94—, Family Rsch. Inst., Madison, 2000—; clk. Faith Bapt. Ch., Madison, 1985-95; mem. stds. com. Evang. Coun. Fin. Accountability, 1989-96; mem. steering com. Evang. Legal Forum, 1988-90, gen. bd. Buckeye Evang. Free Ch., 1999-2000, Door Creek Ch., 2000—; legal cons., religious orgns., 1999—. Mem. Wis. State Bar Assn. Mem. Evang. Free Ch. Home: 801 Acewood Blvd Madison WI 53714-3209 E-mail: vinkemulder@juno.com

VINSON, C. ROGER, federal judge; b. Cadiz, Ky., Feb. 19, 1940; BS, U.S. Naval Acad., 1962; JD, Vanderbilt U., 1971. Bar: Fla. 1971. Commd. ensign USN, 1962, advanced through grades to lt., 1963, naval aviator, until 1968, resigned, 1968; assoc. to ptnr. Beggs & Lane, Pensacola, Fla., 1971-83; judge U.S. Dist. Ct. (no. dist.) Fla., 1983—, chief judge, 1997—. Mem. Jud. Conf. Adv. Com. on Civil Rules, 1993-99; mem. 11th Cir. Pattern Instrn. Com. Contbr. articles to profl. jours. Divsn. chair, area chair United Way of Escambia County; bd. dirs. Pensacola Arts Coun., also treas.; mem. corp. bd. Bapt. Hosp. of Pensacola, 1977-82; co-founder, v.p., charter bd. dirs. Escambia County Epilepsy Soc.; trustee, sec., vice chair Fellows Meml. Fund Found.; trustee Fla. Bapt. Found., 1979-83; Sunday sch. tchr., bd. dires. First Bapt. Ch. of Pensacola. Recipient J. Nixon Daniel Leadership award, 1976, Rinehardt Holm Disting. Svc. award, 1976, Pensacola Action '76 Achievement award, 1976; Wilson Merit scholar, 1968-71. Mem. Am. Judicature Soc., Fla. Bar, Escambia-Santa Rosa Bar Assn., Soc. Bar of 1st Jud. Cir., N.W. Fla. Fed. Bar Assn. (co-founder), Rotary Club of Pensacola (bd. dirs. 1997—, pres. 1998-99), Panhandle Tiger Bay Club (co-founder, chrter bd. dirs.). Office: US Courthouse 5th fl 1 N Palafox St # 32501 Pensacola FL 32501-5665

VINSON, WILLIAM THEODORE, lawyer, diversified corporation executive; BS, USAF Acad., 1965; JD, UCLA, 1969. Bar: Calif. 1970. Judge advocate USAF, 1970-74; trial counsel Phillips Petroleum, San Mateo, Calif., 1974-75; atty. Lockheed Corp., Westlake Village, 1975-90, v.p. & sec., 1990-92, v.p., gen. couns., 92-95; v.p., chief counsel Lockheed Martin Corp., 1995-98; cons. Lockheed Corp., 1998; dir. Entex Govt. Svcs., Inc., 2001—. Bd. dirs. Westminster Free Clinic, 2001—. General corporate, Government contracts and claims, Private international. Office: 5560 E Napoleon Ave Oak Park CA 91377-4746

VIOLANTE, JOSEPH ANTHONY, lawyer; b. Jersey City, June 15, 1950; s. Carmine Joseph and Rosa (Cardillo) V.; m. Linda Lee Munn, July 5, 1972; children: Joseph Anthony II, Christy Anne, Gina Lee. Student, St. Peter's Coll., Jersey City, 1972-74; BA, U. N.Mex., 1975; JD, U. La Verne (Calif.), 1980. Bar: Calif. 1981, D.C. 1990, U.S. Dist. Ct. (cen. dist.) Calif. 1982, (6th dist.) Ohio 1992, U.S. Ct. Appeals (fed. cir.) 1990, U.S. Ct. Appeals (D.C. cir.) 1991, U.S. Ct. Vets. Appeals 1990. Sole practice, Thousand Oaks, Calif., 1981-85; atty., cons. Bd. Vet. Appeals, Washington, 1985-90; staff counsel DAV, 1990-92, legis. counsel, 1992-96, dep. nat. legis. dir., 1996-97, nat. legis. dir., 1997—. Mem. adv. com. Bowie Cable T.V., 1989-91, bd. dirs., 1992-94. Co-host cable TV show Vets. Forum, 1991-94. Asst. coach Am. Youth Soccer Orgn., Thousand Oaks, 1981-84, Little League, Thousand Oaks, 1981-84; del. John Glenn Calif. Dem. Presdl. Primary, Thousand Oaks, 1984; active campaign Combined Fed., Washington, 1985; mem. presdl. del. Prisoners of War/Missing in Action, Southeast Asia, 1996. With USMC, 1969-72. Mem. ABA (vice chmn. vets. benefit com. 1991-98), DAV (life, comdr. 1990-91), VFW (life, comdr. 1984-85), KC, Calif. Bar Assn., Fed. Cir. Bar Assn. (chmn. vets appeal com. 1992-96, co-chmn. legis. com. 1996—, nominating com. 2000, bd. govs. 2001—), FBA (at-large bd. mem., vets. com. 1991-92, contbg. writer Tommy), D.C. Bar Assn., Italian-Am. Bar Assn., Nat. Italian-Am. Found., Coun. of 2,000, Nat. Italian Am. Found. (nat. mentors program), Am. Legion, Italian Am. War Vets., Marine Corps League, 3d Marine Divsn. Assn. (life), 2d Bn. 4th Marine Assn. Democrat. Roman Catholic. Avocations: collecting coins, soccer, softball, reading. Administrative and regulatory, Government contracts and claims, Legislative. Home: 2515 Ann Arbor Ln Bowie MD 20716-1562 Office: DAV Nat Svc & Legis Hdqrs 807 Maine Ave SW Washington DC 20024-2410

VIRELLI, LOUIS JAMES, JR. lawyer; b. Phila., Nov. 4, 1948; s. Louis James and Elsie Antoinette (Colombo) V.; m. Barbara Ann Rotella, Aug. 22, 1970; children: Louis J. III, Christopher F. BE in Mech. Engring., Villanova U., 1970; JD, U. Tenn., 1972. Bar: Pa. 1973, U.S. Patent and Trademark Office, 1973, U.S. Ct. Customs and Patent Appeals 1974, U.S. Dist. Ct. (we. dist.) Pa. 1976, U.S. Dist. Ct. (ea. dist.) Pa. 1977, U.S. Ct. Appeals (9th cir.) 1980, U.S. Ct. Appeals (D.C. cir.) 1982, U.S. Supreme Ct. 1982. Patent atty. Sperry New Holland Co., New Holland, Pa., 1973-74; assoc. counsel Westinghouse Co., Pitts., 1974-76; assoc. Paul & Paul, Phila., 1976-80, ptnr., 1980-84; patent counsel Nat. Starch and Chem. Co., Bridgewater, N.J., 1984-88, asst. gen. counsel, intellectual property, 1988-92, gen. counsel, intellectual property, 1992-95; asst. gen. counsel Patents Unilever U.S., Inc., Edgewater, 1988-95; v.p. gen. patent counsel Unilever N.V., P.L.C., 1995-96, sr. v.p., gen. patent counsel, 1997—. Arbitrator U.S. Dist. Ct. (ea. dist.) Pa., Phila., 1982-84. Mem. ABA, N.J. Patent Law Assn., Phila. Patent Law Assn., Assn. Corp. Patent Counsel (treas.). General corporate, Patent, Trademark and copyright. Office: Unilever US Inc 45 River Rd Edgewater NJ 07020-1017 also: Unilever PLC Unilever House Blackfriars London England E-mail: louis.virelli@unilever.com

VISH, DONALD H. lawyer; b. Ft. Benning, Ga., Jan. 18, 1945; s. D.H. Jr. and Dorris (Parrish) V.; m. Catherine Hamilton, Aug. 20, 1966 (div. 1986); children: Donald Hamilton, Daphne Mershon Sullivan; m. Margaret A. Handmaker, July 16, 1991. BA in English, Bellarmine Coll., 1968; JD cum laude, U. Louisville, 1971. Bar: Ky. 1971, Fla. 1972, U.S. Ct. Appeals (6th cir.) 1974. Sec., gen. counsel Gen. Energy Corp., Lexington, Ky., 1978-83; ptnr. firm Wyatt, Tarrant & Combs, 1980-88, Frost & Jacobs, Lexington, 1988-89, Brown Todd & Heyburn, 1991-98; gen. cousnel Ky. Coal Producers' Self-Ins. Fund, 1992-98; sec., gen. counsel AIK Co., 2001—. Apptd. assoc. solicitor U.S. Dept. Interior, 1989-91; assoc. prof. Coll. of Law, U. Ky., Lexington, part-time 1977-80, adj. assoc. prof. mineral law, 1979-85. Contbr. to legal ency. American Law of Mining, 2d edit., 1984; co-editor, contbr. Coal Law and Regulation, 1983, Ky. Election Law, 1995. Trustee Sayre Sch., Lexington, 1980-88, chmn. bd., 1986-88; mem. Blue Grass coun. Boy Scouts Am., 1988-93; apptd. gov. Ky. Registry of Election Fin., 1991-93. Fellow Am. Bar Found.; mem. ABA (chmn. coal com., natural resources sect. 1987), Am. Bar Found. (life), Am. Law Inst., Ea. Mineral Law Found. (trustee 1979-91, exec. com. 1979-82, chmn. coal subcom. 1984-85), Am. Judicature Soc., Fla. Bar, Ky. Bar Assn. (ethics com. 1983-85 chair residency com. 1998—). General corporate, Environmental. Home: 6306 Shadow Wood Dr Prospect KY 40059-9626 Office: Parrent & Vish 700 Kentucky Home Life Bldg 239 S 5th St Louisville KY 40202-3213

VITALE, JAMES DREW, lawyer; b. Livingston, N.J., Mar. 14, 1967; s. Joseph Anthony and Elizabeth Kathryn Vitale. BA, Rutgers U., Newark, 1990; JD, Rutgers U., Camden, N.J., 1994. Bar: N.J. 1994, U.S. Dist. Ct. N.J. 1994, N.Y. 1995. Atty. Am. Internat. Group, N.Y.C., 1994-97; assoc. Rosenman & Colin, LLP, 1997-98; regulatory compliance counsel Zurich North Am., Schaumburg, Ill., 1998-2000, v.p., counsel, 2000—. Mem. home warranty task force Calif. Bur. Electronic and Appliance Repair, Sacramento, 1998-99. Mem. ABA. Democrat. Roman Catholic. Avocations: golf, martial arts, music. Administrative and regulatory, General corporate, Insurance. Office: Zurich North America 1400 American Ln Schaumburg IL 60196-5452 E-mail: james.vitale@zurichna.com

VITKOWSKY, VINCENT JOSEPH, lawyer; b. Newark, Oct. 3, 1955; s. Boniface and Rosemary (Ofack) V.; m. Mary Gunzburg, May 16, 1981 (div. 1997); children: Vincent Jr., Victoria; m. Pandora Strasler, Sept. 18, 1999. BA, Northwestern U., 1977; JD, Cornell U., 1980. Bar: N.Y. 1981. Assoc. Hart and Hume, N.Y.C., 1980-84, Kroll & Tract, N.Y.C., 1984-87; of counsel Nixon, Hargrave, Devans & Doyle, 1988-89; ptnr. Buchalter, Nemer, Fields & Younger, 1990-95, Edwards & Angell LLP, N.Y.C., 1996—. Mem. panel arbitration London Ct. Internat. Arbitration; lectr. in field. Contbr. articles to profl. jours. Mem. ABA (com. chmn.), Am. Arbitration Assn. (inernat. panel arbitrators), Internat. Bar Assn. (com. officer), Internat. Law Assn., London Ct. Internat. Arbitration (panel mem.), Assn. Bar City of N.Y., Cornell Club, Human Rights Watch, IBA Human Rights Inst. (officer, com. on interventions and trial observations), Lawyers Com. for Human Rights. Alternative dispute resolution, General civil litigation, Private international. Home: 422 E 72d St Apt 15E New York NY 10021 Office: Edwards & Angell LLP 750 Lexington Ave Fl 12 New York NY 10022-1253

VITTUM, DANIEL WEEKS, JR. lawyer; b. Lynch, Ky., Feb. 10, 1939; s. Daniel W. and Kathryn Margaret (Jones) V.; m. Stephanie Ann Empkie, Aug. 18, 1962 (div. July 1987); children: Daniel W., III, Stephen F.; m. Christine L. Jacobek, Nov. 17, 1990. BS, U. Ill., 1961; JD, U. Mich., 1964. Bar: Ill. 1964, U.S. Dist. Ct. (no. dist.) Ill. 1965, U.S. Supreme Ct. 1977, U.S. Ct. Appeals (7th cir.) 1976, U.S. Ct. Appeals (4th cir.) 1982, U.S. Ct. Appeals (9th cir.) 1978, U.S. Ct. Appeals (Fed. cir.) 1982, U.S. Ct. Appeals (6th cir.) 1992. Assoc. Kirkland & Ellis, Chgo., 1964-69, ptnr., 1970—. Bd. dirs., pres. Northwestern U. Settlement Assn.; mem. vis. com. U. Mich. Law Sch. Mem. ABA, Am. Intellectual Property Assn., Intellectual Property Law Assn. Chgo., Order of Coif, Phi Beta Kappa. Clubs: Mid-Am., East Bank (Chgo.), Chgo. Yacht Club. Federal civil litigation, Patent, Trademark and copyright. Office: Kirkland & Ellis 200 E Randolph St Fl 54 Chicago IL 60601-6636

VLADECK, JUDITH POMARLEN, lawyer; b. Norfolk, Va., Aug. 1, 1923; BA, Hunter Coll., 1945; JD, Columbia U., 1947. Bar: N.Y. 1947, U.S. Supreme Ct. 1962. Assoc. Conrad & Smith, N.Y.C., 1947-51; sole practice, 1951-57; mem. Vladeck, Elias, Vladeck & Engelhard P.C., 1957—; sr. ptnr. Vladeck, Waldman, Elias & Englehard, P.C. Bd. dirs. Group Health Ins., Inc., Am. Arbitration Assn.; adj. prof. Fordham Law Sch.; mem. Civil Justice Reform Act Adv. Group of So. Dist. of N.Y.; adv. coun. CPR Jud. Project. Mem. adv. bd. Inst. for Edn. and Rsch. on Women and Work, Cornell U.; bd. dirs. N.Y. Civil Liberties Union, 1963-68; bd. dirs., counsel Tamiment Inst., Inc.; bd. dirs. lawyers' coordinating com. AFL-CIO; bd. mem. Non-Traditional Employment for Women. Recipient Hunter Coll. Profl. Achievement award, 1992, Edith Spivack award, 1998, Women of Power and Influence award N.Y. NOW, 1998, ORT Jurisprudence award, 1996; elected to Hunter Coll. Hall of Fame, 1988; non-traditional employment for women named building Judith P. Vladeck Ctr. for Women, 1989. Fellow Am. Bar Found., Coll. of Labor and Employment Lawyers; mem. ABA (co-chmn. labor law and equal employment coms.), N.Y. State Bar Assn. (labor law com.), Assn. of Bar of City of N.Y., N.Y. County Lawyers Assn., Fed. Bar Assn., Women's Bar Assn., Am. Arbitration Assn. (panel of arbitrators), Columbia Law Sch. Alumni Assn. (bd. dirs.), Harlem Inst. Fashion (counsel, bd. dirs.). General civil litigation, Labor. Home: 115 Central Park W New York NY 10023-4153 Office: Vladeck Waldman Elias & Engelhard 1501 Broadway Ste 800 New York NY 10036-5560 E-mail: jvladeck@vladeck.com

VOCHT, MICHELLE ELISE, lawyer; b. Detroit, Sept. 27, 1956; BA with honors, U. Mich., 1978; JD, Wayne State U., 1981. Bar: Mich., U.S. Dist. Ct. (ea. and we. dist.) Mich., U.S. Ct. Appeals (6th cir.), 1981. V.p., treas. Roy, Shecter & Vocht PC, Detroit, Bloomfield Hills, Mich., 1981—. Pro bono teaching faculty Detroit chpt. Fed. Bar Assn.; mediator Mediation Tribunal Wayne County Cir. Ct., 1989—; pre-sentencing probation officer 48th Dist. Ct., 1989-90. Mem. com. for re-election Mich. Supreme Ct. Justice, 1986; mem. Rep. Assembly, Oak County, 1992-99—; exec. bd. Birmingham Women's Community Ctr., 1987-88; bd. dir. Community Adv. Bd.-Arbor Clin. Group, Inc., 1989-91; mem. drug and alcohol abuse spl. task force County of Oakland, 1989-90. Mem. Am. Inns of Ct. (barrister 1984-87), Mich. Trial Lawyers Assn., Women Lawyers Assn., Oakland Trial Lawyers Assn. (exec. bd. dirs. 1982-84, 88—, sec. 1990—, v.p. 1991-92, pres. 1992-95), Oakland County Bar Assn., State Bar Assn. Mich. (chmn. gen. practice sect. 1984-86, sec. 1982-83, vice chmn. 1983-84, mem. civil procedure com. 1982-84, assoc. mem. lawyers and judges assistance com. 1988-89, hearing and panelist atty. discipline bd. 1982—, labor and employment sect., health care sect., computer law sect., chair drafting com. 1995-97, com. on state trial ct. adminstrn. 1995-98, com. on profession 1997, state ct. adminstrn. commn., 1996—), Mich. Employment Law Assn., Interna. Platform Assn., Indsl. Rels. Rsch. Assn. Roman Catholic. Avocations: tennis, hiking, history, humanities, and sciences. Federal civil litigation, State civil litigation, Labor. Home: 901 N Adams Rd Birmingham MI 48009-5646 Office: Roy Shecter & Vocht PC 36700 Woodward Ave Ste 205 Bloomfield Hills MI 48304-0930 E-mail: vocht@rsmv.com

VOGEL, CEDRIC WAKELEE, lawyer; b. Cin., June 4, 1946; s. Cedric and Patricia (Woodruff) V. BA, Yale U., 1968; JD, Harvard U., 1971. Bar: Ohio 1972, Fla. 1973, U.S. Tax Ct. 1972, U.S. Supreme Ct. 1975. Ptnr. Vogel, Heis, Wenstrup & Cameron, Cin., 1972-96; sole practice, 1997—. Bd. dirs. Pro Srs., 1994—. Chmn. mem.'s com. Cin. Art Mus., 1987-88; chmn. auction Cin. Hist. Soc., 1985; local pres. English Speaking Union, 1979-81, nat. bd. dirs., 1981; chmn. Keep Cin. Beautiful, Inc., 1994-96; active Bravo! Cin. Ballet, 1989; chmn. Act II Nutcracker Ball, 1987-88; bd. dirs. Merc Libr., 1991-98; bd. dirs. Cin. Preservation Assn., 1990-93, Cin. Opera Guild, 1997-99; vice chmn. Children's Heart Assn. Reds Rally, 1989; bd. dirs. Cin. Country Day Sch., 1983, pres. Alumni Coun. and Ann. Fund, 1983. Mem. Cin. Bar Assn., Fla. Bar Assn., Harvard Law Sch. Assn. Cin. (pres. 1997-99, Heimlich Inst. (trustee 1987—), Yale Alumni Assn. (del. 1984-87), Cin. Yale Club (pres. 1980-81, 96-97), Cincinnatus, The Lawyers Club Cin. (pres. 1995), Harvard Club of Cin. (bd. dirs. 1996-98, pres. 1999-2000). Republican. Consumer commercial, General practice, Probate. Home: 2270 Madison Rd Cincinnati OH 45208-2659 Office: 817 Main St Ste 800 Cincinnati OH 45202-2183

VOGEL, HOWARD STANLEY, lawyer; b. N.Y.C., Jan. 21, 1934; s. Moe and Sylvia (Miller) V.; m. Judith Anne Gelb, June 30, 1962; 1 son, Michael S. BA, Bklyn. Coll., 1954; JD, Columbia U., 1957; LLM in Corp. Law, NYU, 1969. Bar: N.Y. 1957, U.S. Supreme Ct. 1964. Assoc. Whitman & Ransom, N.Y.C., 1961-66; with Texaco Inc., 1966-99, gen. atty., 1970-73, assoc. gen. counsel, 1973-81, gen. counsel Tex. Philanthropic Found. Inc., 1979-82; gen. counsel Jefferson Chem. Co. Texaco Chems. Can. Inc., 1973-82; assoc. gen. tax counsel, gen. mgr. adminstr. Texaco Inc., White Plains, N.Y., 1981-99; counsel Allegaert Berger & Vogel LLP, N.Y.C., 1999—. Gen. tax counsel Texaco Found. Inc., 1995-99; pres., dir. 169 E. 69th Corp., 1981— . Served to 1st lt. JAGC, U.S. Army, 1958-60. Mem. ABA, Aassn. Bar City N.Y., Fed. Bar Coun., Assn. Ex-Mems. of Squadron A., Princeton Club (N.Y.C.). General corporate, Securities, Corporate taxation. Home: 169 E 69th St Apt 9D New York NY 10021-5163 Office: 18th Fl 111 Broadway Fl 18 New York NY 10006-1901 E-mail: hvogel@abv.com

VOGEL, JOHN WALTER, lawyer; b. Dansville, N.Y., Sept. 19, 1948; s. Walter Earl and Betty (Elston) V.; m. Pamela Hill; children: Michael John, Jennifer Alexandra. BA, SUNY, Albany, 1970; JD, Syracuse U., 1976. Bar: N.Y. 1976, U.S. Dist. Ct. (we. dist.) N.Y. 1979, U.S. Tax Ct. 1980, U.S. Supreme Ct., 1980, U.S. Dist. Ct. (no. dist.) N.Y. 1985, U.S. Ct. Appeals (2d cir.) 1985. Assoc. Edward J. Degnan Law Offices, Caniesteo, N.Y., 1976-77; atty. N.Y. State Dept. Agrl. & Markets, Albany, 1977-78; sole practice law Dansville, 1978—. V.p., legal counsel Dansville Econ. Devel. Corp., 1983—; closing atty. Farmers Home Adminstrn., Dansville, 1982—. Dir. Livingston County (N.Y.) Drug Abuse Prevention Council, 1981-82. Served with U.S. Army, 1970-73. Mem. N.Y. State Bar Assn., Livingston

County Bar Assn. (sec., treas. 1980-82, v.p. 1984-85, pres. 1985-86), Assn. Trial Lawyers Am., N.Y. State Trial Lawyers Assn., Dansville C. of C. (bd. dirs. 1985—). Republican. Presbyterian. State civil litigation, General practice, Personal injury. Home: 261 Main St Dansville NY 14437-1111 Office: 125 Main St Dansville NY 14437-1611

VOGELL, CONNIE, paralegal; b. New Britain, Conn., Mar. 5, 1942; d. Edward George and Sophie Cecelia (Horosczyk) Jackamonis; m. Frederick Eugene Vogell, July 7, 1973; children: Heather, Alison. BA, U. Conn., Storrs, 1964. Cert. paralegal. Libr. United Techs., East Hartford, Conn., 1964-74; title searcher Gould Larson, Bennet Wells McDonnell, P.C., Essex, 1987-98; probate paralegal Suisman Shapiro, Wool, Brennan, Gray & Greenburg, P.C., New London, 1998—. Mem. Nat. Coll. Probate Judges, Conn. Probate Assembly, Conn. Bar Assn., Conn. Coun. on Adoption. Democrat. Avocations: painting, tennis. Home: 121 Old Salt Works Rd Westbrook CT 06498-2051

VOGELMAN, LAWRENCE ALLEN, law educator, lawyer; b. Bklyn., Feb. 24, 1949; s. Herman and Gertrude (Wohl) V.; m. Deborah Malka, Jan. 24, 1971 (div. Aug. 1980); m. Marcia Sikowitz, Mar. 3, 1985 (div. Nov. 1999). BA, Bklyn. Coll., 1970; JD, Bklyn. Law Sch., 1973. Bar: N.Y. 1974, U.S. Dist. Ct. (so. and ea. dists.) N.Y. 1975, U.S. Ct. Appeals (2d cir.) 1975, U.S. Ct. Appeals (3d cir.) 1983, U.S. Supreme Ct. 1983, N.H. 1994, U.S. Dist. Ct. N.H. 1994, U.S. Ct. Appeals (1st cir.) 2001. Trial atty. Legal Aid Soc., N.Y.C., 1973-77; assoc. appellate counsel Criminal Appeals Bur., 1977-78; clin. prof. law Yeshiva U. Benjamin N. Cardozo Sch. Law, 1979-93; dep. dir. N.H. Pub. Defender, Concord, N.H., 1993-97; coun. Shuchman, Krause-Elmslie, P.L.L.C., 1997—. Adj. prof. law Franklin Pierce Law Ctr., 1994-98; faculty Inst. for Criminal Def. Advocacy, 1995—; program dir. Max Freund Litigation Ctr., 1984—; team leader Emory U. Trial Techniques Program, Atlanta, 1981-89, N.J. region, Nat. Inst. Trial Advocacy, 1997—; faculty N.E. region, Nat. Inst. Trial Advocacy, 1985—, Tom C. Clark Ctr. for Advocacy, Hofstra U. Sch. Law, 1985—, Legal Aid Socs. Trial Advocacy Program, 1986-89, Widener U. Law Sch. Intensive Trial Program, 1987-91, U. San Francisco Intensive Trial Advocacy Program, 1991—; mem. indigent's assigned counsel panel, appellate div. First Dept., N.Y.C., 1979-94; crminal justice act panel U.S. Dist. Ct. (so. and ea. dists.) N.Y., 1985-94, dist. N.H., 1997—; adminstrv. law judge N.Y.C. Environ. Control Bd., 1980-81. Author, editor: Cases and Materials on Clinical Legal Education, 1979; editor revisions to Eyewitness Identification. Pres. bd. trustees Woodward Park Sch., 1990—94; bd. dirs., legal coun. N.H. Civil Liberties Union. Fellow Am. Bd. Criminal Lawyers; mem. Assn. of Bar of City of N.Y., Assn. of Legal Aid Attys. (exec. v.p. 1977-78, exec. com. 1984-86, bargaining com. chairperson 1974-79), Soc. Am. Law Tchrs., Assn. Trial Lawyers Am (exec. com. civil rights sect.), Nat. Assn. Criminal Def. Lawyers (bd. dirs.), N.H. Bar Assn. (ethics com. 1995—, dispute resolution com. 1999—, bd. law examiners 1999—), N.H. Assn. Criminal Def. Lawyers, N.Y. State Defenders Assn., Order of Barristers, Am. Inns of Ct. (master Daniel Webster Inn of Ct.), Fortune Soc. (exec. com., bd. dirs.). Democrat. Jewish. Achievements include notable cases such as: People vs. Joel Steinberg, represented co-defendant, Hedda Nussbaum in homicide death Lisa Steinberg; U.S. vs. Falvey, in which Irish Rep. Army supporters were acquitted of gun running because of knowledge and approval of CIA; Bell vs. Coughlin, which involved highly publicized homicide of 2 N.Y. police officers; People vs. Roche, which established agy. def. to drug sale in State of N.Y.'s highest ct.; U.S. vs. Joseph, which appealed convictions in Brinks case. Home: 22 Cedar Point Rd Durham NH 03824 Office: Shuchman & Krause-Elmslie PLLC PO Box 220 Exeter NH 03833-0220 E-mail: lav@sisna.com, larryvpd@aol.com

VOICU, DANIEL, lawyer; b. Bucharest, Romania, Oct. 17, 1969; s. Ioan and Doina V.; m. Rodica Viezure, May 22, 1993; 1 child. Student, Law Faculty, Bucharest, 1993; Cert. Bus. Law, Asser Inst., The Hague, The Netherlands, 1996. Assoc. Arent Fox, Bucharest, 1998—. Contracts commercial, General corporate, Real property. Office: Arent Fox 1 N Titulgreu BV BLA 7 8CA AR 16 7000 Bucharest Romania Fax: 004012118721. E-mail: voicud@arentfox.ro

VOIGHT, BARTON R. judge; BA, MA, JD, U. Wyo. Justice Wyo. Supreme Ct., 2001—. Office: 2301 Capitol Ave Cheyenne WY 82002*

VOIGHT, ELIZABETH ANNE, lawyer; b. Sapulpa, Okla., Aug. 6, 1944; d. Robert Guy and Garnetta Ruth (Bell) Voight; m. Bodo Barske, Feb. 22, 1985; children: Anne Katharine, Ruth Caroline. BA, U. Ark.-Fayetteville, 1967, MA, 1969; postgrad., U. Hamburg (W.Ger.), 1966-67; J.D., Georgetown U., 1978. Bar: N.Y. 1979, Munich 1997. Lectr. German Oral Roberts U., Tulsa, 1968-69; tchr. German D.C. pub. schs., 1971-73; instr. German Georgetown U., Washington, 1973-74, adminstrv. asst. to dean Sch. Fgn. Svc., 1974-77; law clk. Cole Corette & Abrutyn, Washington, 1977-78; atty. Alston & Bird LLP (formerly Walter, Conston, Alexander & Green, P.C.), N.Y.C., 1978-88, Alston & Bird, LLP, Munich, 1990—, CMS Hasche Sigle Eschenlohr Peltzer Schaefer, Munich, 1990—. Author: (with Dr. Martin Peltzer) German Commercial Code, German-English Text, 4th edit., 1999, German Law Pertaining to Limited Liability Companies, German-English Text, 4th edit., 2000; translator articles for profl. jours. Chmn. regional screening Am. Field Svc., N.Y.C., 1981-86; founding mem. Am. Berlin Opera Found. German Acad. Exchange Program fellow, 1966-67; adv. coun. Georgetown U. BMW Ctr. German and European Studies. Mem. Assn. Bar City N.Y., Munich Bar Assn., Internat. Fiscal Assn., Internat. Bar Assn., Am. C. of C. in Germany (Munich regional com.), Phi Beta Kappa, Kappa Kappa Gamma. Contracts commercial, General corporate, Mergers and acquisitions. E-mail: elizabeth.voight@cmslegal.de, voight@camelot.de

VOIGT, STEVEN RUSSELL, lawyer; b. Geneva, Dec. 29, 1952; s. James Leroy and Martha Anne (Erikson) V.; m. Barbara Jeane Molcyk, Apr. 23, 1983; children: Kelsey Marie, Katelyn Anne. BS, U. Nebr., 1975, JD, 1978. Bar: Nebr. 1978, U.S. Dist. Ct. Nebr. 1978, U.S. Tax Ct. 1980. Assoc. Nye, Hervert, Jorgensen & Watson, Kearney, Nebr., 1978-80; ptnr. Giese, Butler & Voigt, 1980-82, Butler & Voigt, Kearney, 1982-85, Butler, Voigt & Brewster, Kearney, 1985-97, Butler, Voigt & Stewart P.C., Kearney, 1997—. Bd. dirs. Western Nebr. Legal Svcs., Scottsbluff, pres. bd. 1997—; pub. defender County of Kearney, Minden, Nebr., 1982—; pres. Nebr. Lawyers Trust Account Found., Lincoln, 1986-90. Mem. ABA (exec. coun. young lawyers div. 1985-86), Assn. Trial Lawyers Am., Nebr. State Bar Assn. (vice chair judiciary com.), Nebr. Criminal Defense Atty's. Assn., Sertoma (pres. Kearney chpt. 1983-84), Kearney Country Club (pres. of bd. dirs. 1995), Masons, Shriners. Avocations: golf, bicycling. Consumer commercial, Criminal, Family and matrimonial. Home: 5207 Avenue G Pl Kearney NE 68847-8598 Office: Butler Voigt & Stewart PC 2202 Central Ave Ste 200 Kearney NE 68847-5359

VOITOVICH, SERGEI ADAMOVICH, lawyer; b. Rovno, USSR, July 6, 1959; s. Adam Micholaevich and Valentina Petrovna V.; m. Svetlana Ivanovna Ilyankova V., Jan. 25, 1981; 1 child, Alexandra. LLM, Kiev (USSR) U., 1981; PhD, European U. Inst. Florence, Italy, 1993. Asst. prof. Kiev (USSR) U., 1981-88; assoc. prof. Kiev (USSR) U. Law Sch., 1988-94; chief lawyer Businex, Kiev, USSR, 1988-89, ConBis, Kiev, 1991-93; ptnr. Grischanko & Ptnrs., Ukraine, 1993—. Mem. Kiev Bnr., Ukraine, 1994—, IBA, London, 1995—, C. of Ind. Fgn. Investment, Kiev, Ukraine, 1997—. Author: International Economic Organizations, 1994. Contbr. over 50 profl. pubs. Appellate, Communications, Mergers and acquisitions. Office: Law Firm Grrschenbo & Ptnrs Mechnileova 20 Kiev 01021 Ukraine E-mail: sac@lawyers.kiev.uq

VOJCANIN, SAVA ALEXANDER, lawyer; b. Oak Lawn, Ill., Oct. 15, 1964; s. Jovan and Lili (Yovanovich) V. Diplomate, Culver Mil. Acad., 1981; BA with distinction, DePauw U., 1985; JD, Washington U., 1988. Bar: Ill. 1988, U.S. Dist. Ct. (no. dist.) Ill. 1989, U.S. Dist. Ct. (no. dist.) Tex. 1996. Assoc. Schaffenegger, Watson & Peterson Ltd., Chgo., 1988-91, Clausen Miller P.C., Chgo., 1991-98, ptnr., 1999—. Editor: Law, Culture and Values, 1989. Mem. Mayor's Adv. Coun. on Immigrant and Refugee Affairs, Chgo., 1992-97; trustee St. Basil Orthodox Ch. of Lake Forest, 1997—, sec. bd. trustees, 1999—. Mem. Serbian Bar Assn. Am. (bd. dirs.), Chgo. Bar Assn. General civil litigation, Construction, Insurance. Office: Clausen Miller PC 10 S LaSalle St Chicago IL 60603-1098

VOLK, KENNETH HOHNE, lawyer; b. Hackensack, N.J., Nov. 8, 1922; s. Henry L. and Constance (Brady) V.; m. Joyce Geary, May 11, 1954; children: Christopher H., Cynthia. BS, U.S. Naval Acad., 1946; LLB, Yale U., 1953. Ptnr. Burlingham, Underwood, N.Y.C., 1955-92; of counsel McLane, Graf, Raulerson & Middleton, Portsmouth, N.H., 1992—. Speaker various symposia and confs. on maritime law. Assoc. editor Am. Maritime Cases; contbr. articles to profl. jours. Pres. Maritime Assocs., N.Y.C., 1967-68; chmn. bd. dirs. Seamen's House YMCA, N.Y.C., 1971-76; sec., bd. dirs. Seamen's Ch. Inst., N.Y.C., 1977-92; bd. dirs. Strawbery Banke Mus., Portsmouth, N.H.; mem. adv. bd. Tulane Admiralty Law Inst.. Fellow Am. Bar Found., Am. Coll. Trial Lawyers; mem. ABA, Assn. Bar of City of N.Y., Maritime Law Assn. U.S. (exec. com. 1977-80, pres. 1990-92), Comite Maritime Internat. (titulary mem.), Quaker Hill Country Club (pres. 1976-78). Republican. Espicopalian. Avocations: reading, hiking, fishing. Office: McLane Graf Raulerson 30 Penhallow St Portsmouth NH 03801-3816

VOLK, STEPHEN RICHARD, lawyer; b. Boston, Apr. 22, 1936; s. Ralph and Miriam (Rose) V.; m. Veronica J. Brown, June 19, 1959 (dec. Feb. 1989); children: Jeffrey A., Andrew M., Michael J.; m. Diane Kemelman, Apr. 22, 1990; 1 child, Anne. Student, Dartmouth Coll., 1957; JD, Harvard U., 1960. Bar: N.Y. 1961. Assoc. Sherman & Sterling, N.Y.C., 1960-68, ptnr., 1968—, dep. sr. ptnr., 1988-91, sr. ptnr., 1991—2001; vice chmn. Credit Suisse First Boston, 2001—; w. Bd. dirs. ContiGroup Cos. Inc. Bd. dirs. Consol. Edison, Inc., 1996; trustee Consol Edison Co. N.Y.C., Inc., 1998, Harvard Law Sch. Assn., N.Y.C., 1999; mem. dean's adv. bd. Harvard Law Sch., 1997. Fellow Am. Bar Found.; mem. ABA (com. on securities regulation 1974), Assn. Bar City N.Y., Coun. on Fgn. Rels., Univ. Club, Phi Beta Kappa. General corporate, Mergers and acquisitions. Office: 11 Madison Ave 27th Fl New York NY 10010-3629

VOLLMER, RICHARD WADE, federal judge; b. St. Louis, Mar. 7, 1926; s. Richard W. and Beatrice (Burke) V.; m. Marilyn S. Stikes, Sept. 17, 1949. Student, Springhill Coll., 1946-49; LLB, U. Ala., 1953. Bar: Ala. 1953, U.S. Dist. Ct. (so. dist.) Ala. 1956, U.S. Ct. Appeals (5th cir.) 1963, U.S. Ct. Appeals (11th cir.) 1983. Sr. judge U.S. Dist. Ct. (so. dist.) Ala., 1990—. Mem. Mobile Bar Assn. (pres. 1990), Rotary (Paul Harris fellow 1988). Roman Catholic.

VOLUCK, JEFFREY M. lawyer; b. Atlantic City, N.J., Sept. 14, 1943; s. Allan and Sylvia (Wallo) V.; m. Sonia Voluck, Dec. 18, 1968; children—Tammy, Justin. B.S., LaSalle Coll., 1966; J.D., U. Balt., 1974. Bar: Pa. 1975, U.S. Dist. Ct. (ea. dist.) Pa. 1975, U.S. Ct. Appeals (3d cir.) 1975, U.S. Dist. Ct. Md. 1980. Assoc., Robert F. Simone, Phila., 1975, Gross & Sklar, Phila., 1976; pres. Jeffrey M. Voluck, Phila., 1977— . Contbr. articles to profl. jours. Served with U.S. Army, 1966. Mem. ABA, Assn. Trial Lawyers Am., Pa. Bar Assn., Phila. Trial Lawyers Assn. Criminal, Personal injury. Office: 42 S 15th St Fl 17 Philadelphia PA 19102-2218

VOLZ, WILLIAM HARRY, law educator, administrator; b. Sandusky, Mich., Dec. 28, 1946; s. Harry Bender and Belva Geneva (Riehl) V. BA, Mich. State U., 1968; MA, U. Mich., 1972; MBA, Harvard U., 1978; JD, Wayne State U., 1975. Bar: mich. 1975. Atty. pvt. practice, Detroit, 1975-77; mgmt. analyst Office of Gen. Counsel, HEW, Woodlawn, Md., 1977; from asst. to assoc. prof. to prof. bus law Wayne State U., Detroit, 1978-85, interim dean sch. bus. adminstrn., 1985, interim chair acctg. dept., 1997-99, dean, 1986-95; dir. Ctr. for Legal Studies Wayne State U. Law Sch., 1996-97. Cons. Merrill Lynch, Pierce, Fenner & Smith, N.Y.C., 1980-93, City of Detroit Law Dept., 1982, Mich. Supreme Ct., Detroit, 1981; ptnr. Mich. CPA Rev., Southfield, 1983-85; expert witness in product liability, comml. law and bus. ethics; pres. Wedgewood Group. Author: Managing a Trial, 1982; contbr. articles to legal jours.; mem. editl. bds. of bus. and law jours. Internat. adv. bd. Inst. Mgmt., I. L'viv, Ukraine, Legal counsel Free Legal Aid Clinic, Inc., Detroitm 1976—, Shared Ministries, Detroit, 1981, Sino-Am. Tech. Exch. coun., China, 1982; chair advt. rev. panel BBB, Detroit, 1988-90; pres. Mich. Acad. Sci., Arts and Letters, 1995-96, 98-2000, bd. dirs.; pres. Common Ground, PlAYERS; bd. dirs. Greater Detroit Alliance Bus., Olde Custodian Fund. Recipient Disting. Faculty award Wayne State Sch. Bus. Adminstrn., 1982. Mem. ABA, Amateur Medicant Soc. (commissionaire 1981-85), Players, Golden Key, Detroit Athletic Club, Econ. Club Detroit, Harvard Bus. Sch. Club Detroitm Alpha Kappa Psi, Beta Alpha Psu. Mem. Reorganized LDS Ch. Home: 3846 Wedgewood Dr Bloomfield Hills MI 48301-3949 Office: Wayne State U Sch Bus Adminstrn Cass Ave Detroit MI 48202 E-mail: w.h.volz@wayne.edu

VON BERNUTH, CARL W. lawyer, diversified corporation executive; b. Feb. 2, 1944; BA, Yale U., 1966, LLB, 1969. Bar: N.Y. 1970, Pa. 1990. Corp. atty. White & Case, 1969-80; assoc. gen. counsel Union Pacific Corp., N.Y.C., 1980-83, dep. gen. counsel fin. and adminstrn., 1984-88, v.p., gen. counsel Bethlehem, Pa., 1988-91, sr. v.p., gen. counsel, 1991-97, sr. v.p., gen. counsel and sec. Omaha, 1997—. Mem. Am. Corp. Counsel Assn., Practicing Law Inst. General corporate, Securities. Office: Union Pacific Corp 1416 Dodge St Rm 1230 Omaha NE 68179-0001 E-mail: cwvonber@up.com

VON DER HEYDT, JAMES ARNOLD, federal judge; b. Miles City, Mont., July 15, 1919; s. Harry Karl and Alice S. (Arnold) von der H.; m. Verna E. Johnson, May 21, 1952. BA, Albion (Mich.) Coll., 1942; JD, Northwestern, 1951. Bar: Alaska 1951. Pvt. practice, Nome, 1953-59; judge superior ct. Juneau, Alaska, 1959-66; from judge to sr. judge U.S. Dist. Ct. Alaska, 1966—; U.S. commr. Nome, 1951—; U.S. atty. div. 2 Dist. Alaska, 1951-53; mem. Alaska Ho. of Reps., 1957-59. Author: Mother Sawtooth's Nome, 1990, Alaska, The Short and Long of It, 2000. Pres. Anchorage Fine Arts Mus. Assn. Recipient Disting. Alumni award Albion Coll., 1995. Mem. Alaska Bar Assn. (mem. bd. govs. 1955-59, pres. 1959-60), Am. Judicature Soc., Masons (32d degree), Shriners, Phi Delta Phi, Sigma Nu. Club: Mason (32 deg.), Shriner. Avocation: researching Arctic bird life, creative writing. Office: US Dist Ct 222 W 7th Ave Box 40 Anchorage AK 99513-7564

VON KALINOWSKI, JULIAN ONESIME, lawyer; b. St. Louis, May 19, 1916; s. Walter E. and Maybelle (Michaud) von K.; m. Penelope Jayne Dyer, June 29, 1980; children by previous marriage: Julian Onesime, Wendy Jean von Kalinowski. BA, Miss. Coll., 1937; JD with honors, U. Va., 1940. Bar: Va. 1940, Calif. 1946. Assoc. Gibson, Dunn and Crutcher, L.A., 1946-52, ptnr., 1953-85, mem. exec. com., 1962-82, adv. ptnr., 1985—; CEO, chmn. Litigation Scis., Inc., Culver City, Calif., 1991-94, chmn. emeritus Torrance, 1994-96, Dispute Dyamics, Inc., Torrance, 1996-2000. Instr. Columbia Law Sch., Parker Sch. Fgn. and Comparative Law, summer 1981; instr. antitrust law So. Meth. Sch. of Law, summer 1982-84, bd. visitors, 1982-85; v.p., bd. dirs., dir. W.M. Keck Found.; mem. faculty Practising Law Inst., 1971, 76, 78, 79, 80; instr. in spl. course on antitrust litigation Columbia U. Law Sch., N.Y.C., 1981; mem. lawyers dels. com. to 9th Cir. Jud. Conf., 1953-67; UN expert Mission to People's Republic China, 1982. Contbr. articles to legal jours.; author: Antitrust Laws and Trade Regulation, 1969, desk edit., 1981; gen. editor: World Law of Competition, 1978, Antitrust Counseling and Litigation Techniques, 1984; gen. editor emeritus Antitrust Report. With USN, 1941-46, capt. Res. ret. Fellow Am. Bar Found., Am. Coll. Trial Lawyers (chmn. complex litigation com. 1984-87); mem. ABA (ho. of dels. 1970, chmn. antitrust law sect. 1972-73), State Bar Calif. (Anti-Trust Lawyer of Yr. award 2000), L.A. Bar Assn., U. Va. Law Sch. Alumni Assn., Calif. Club, L.A. Country Club, La Jolla Beach and Tennis Club, Phi Kappa Psi, Phi Alpha Delta. Republican. Episcopalian. Antitrust, Federal civil litigation, General civil litigation. Home: 12320 Ridge Cir Los Angeles CA 90049-1151 E-mail: JOvonK@aol.com

VON MANDEL, MICHAEL JACQUES, lawyer; b. Yokohama, Japan, Oct. 20, 1941; came to the U.S., 1946; s. Michael Maximillan and Suzanne (Jacques) V.M.; m. Mary Denise Bienvenue, Dec. 22, 1984; 1 child, Michelle Denise. AB in Econs., Georgetown U., 1964; JD, Cath. U., 1968; LLM in Taxation, NYU, 1970. Bar: Washington 1969, Conn. 1969, U.S. Supreme Ct. 1972, Ill. 1976, U.S. Dist. Ct. (no. dist.) Ill. 1976, U.S. Dist. Ct. (no. dist.) Ill. 1976, U.S. Ct. Appeals (7th cir.) 1976, Fla. 1977. Trial atty. FTC, Washington, 1968-69; trial atty. tax divsn. U.S. Dept. Justice, 1970-76; pvt. practice Chgo., 1976-93; ptnr. Von Mandel & Von Mandel, 1994—. Adj. prof. grad. tax program DePaul U., Chgo., 1980-83. Contbr. chpts. to books. Mem. ABA (tax and litigation sects. 1976—), Chgo. Bar Assn. (fed. tax com. 1976—), Fed. Bar Assn. (bd. dirs. 1981-93), Seventh Cir Bar Assn., Union League Club. Roman Catholic. Taxation, general, Personal income taxation. Address: 79 W Monroe St Ste 1000 Chicago IL 60603-4901 E-mail: mvmtax@aol.com

VON MEHREN, ARTHUR TAYLOR, lawyer, educator; b. Albert Lea, Minn., Aug. 10, 1922; s. Sigurd Anders and Eulalia Marion (Anderson) von M.; m. Joan Elizabeth Moore, Oct. 11, 1947; children— George Moore, Peter Anders, Philip Taylor S.B., Harvard U., 1942, LL.B., 1945, Ph.D., 1946; Faculty of Law, U. Zurich, 1946-47; Faculte de Droit, U. Paris, 1948-49; Doctor iuris (h.c.) Katholieke, Eke U., Leuven, 1985; Doctor iuris (h.c.), U. Panteon-Assas (Paris II), 2000. Bar: Mass. 1950, U.S. Dist. Ct. Mass. 1980. Law clk. U.S. Ct. Appeals (1st cir.), 1945-46; asst. prof. law Harvard U., 1946-53, prof., 1953-76, Story prof., 1976-93, prof. emeritus, 1993—, dir. East Asian legal studies program, 1981-83; acting chief legislation br., legal div. Occupation Mil. Govt. U.S.,Germany, 1947-48, cons. legal div., 1949. Tchr. Salzburg Seminar in Am. Studies, summers 1953, 54; Fulbright research prof. U. Tokyo, Japan, 1956-57, Rome, Italy, 1968-69; cons. legal studies Ford Found., New Delhi, 1962-63; vis. prof. U. Frankfurt, summer 1967, City Univ. Hong Kong, 1995; Ford vis. prof. Inst. Advanced Legal Studies, U. London, 1976; assoc. prof. U. Paris, 1977; Goodhart prof. legal sci. U. Cambridge, 1983-84, fellow Downing Coll., 1983-84, hon. fellow, 1984—; fellow Wissenschaftskolleg zu Berlin, 1990-91. Author: The Civil Law System: An Introduction to the Comparative Study of Law, 1957, 2d edit. (with J. Gordley), 1977, Law in the United States: A General and Comparative View, 1988; co-author: The Law of Multistate Problems: Cases and Materials in the Conflict of Laws, 1965, Conflict of Laws: American, Comparative, International, 1998, International Commercial Arbitration, 1999; mem. editl. bd. Am. Jour. Comparative Law, 1952-86; contbr. articles to profl. jours.; editor: Law in Japan-The Legal Order in a Changing Soc., 1963; mem. editorial com. Internat. Ency. Comparative Law, 1969—. Mem. U.S. Del. Hague Conf. pvt. internat. law, 1966, 68, 76, 80, 85, 93, 96, 2001. Named to Order of the Rising Sun, golden rays Japanese Govt., 1989; Guggenheim fellow, 1968-69; inst. fellow Sackler Inst. Advanced Studies, 1986-87. Mem. ABA (Leonard J. Theberge Award for Pvt. Internat. Law 1997, Sect. of Internat. Law and Practice), Am. Acad. Arts and Scis., Internat. Acad. Comparative Law, Institut de Droit Internat., Japanese Am. Soc. Legal Studies, Am. Soc. Comparative Law (bd. dirs., former pres.), Am. Soc. Polit. and Legal Philosophy, Institut Grand-Duchal (corr.), Phi Beta Kappa. Office: Harvard Law Sch/ AR-231 1545 Massachusetts Ave Cambridge MA 02138-2903 E-mail: vonmehre@law.harvard.edu

VON PASSENHEIM, JOHN B. lawyer; b. Calif., Nov. 25, 1964; s. Burr Charles and Kathryn E. (Kirkland) Passenheim. BA in English with honors, U. Calif.-Santa Barbara, 1986; JD, U. Calif., Hastings, 1989. Bar: Calif. 1989, U.S. Dist. Ct. (so. dist.) Calif. 1991. Pvt. practice, San Diego, 1990—. Organizer Rock The Vote, San Diego, 1992; primary atty. Calif. Lawyers for the Arts, San Diego; panelist Ind. Music Seminar, 1992, 93, 94; mem. Surfrider Found. Nat. Adv. Bd., 1995—; gen. counsel Greyboy Records, Posh Boy Records, Alchemical, Inc. Contbg. staff DICTA mag., 1990-94; editor (legal column) It's the Law, 1990-93. Exec. counsel San Diego chpt. Surfrider Found., 1991-95; vol. atty. San Diego Vol. Lawyer Program, 1990-93. General civil litigation, Entertainment, General practice. Office: 4425 Bayard St Ste 240 San Diego CA 92109-4089

VON SAUERS, JOSEPH F. lawyer; b. N.Y.C. s. Joseph F. and Margaret von Sauers; m. June A. von Sauers. BEE, Manhattan Coll., 1980; MBA, Pepperdine U., 1987; JD, Southwestern U., 1991; LLM, Columbia U., 1995. Bar: Calif. 1992, D.C. 1993, Minn. 1993, Tex. 1993, Colo. 1994, U.S. Patent and Trademark Office. Contracts negotiator Hughes Aircraft Co., El Segundo, Calif., 1985-92; atty. Jones, Day, Reavis & Pogue, Dallas, 1992-94, Loeb & Loeb, LLP, L.A., 1995-97, Gray, Cary, Ware & Freidenrich, Palo Alto, Calif., 1997-98; dep. gen. coun. Roland Corp. U.S., L.A., 1998—. Active Calif. Lawyers for Arts, L.A., 1996; guest spkr. Loyola U., L.A., 1996. Contbr. articles to profl. jours. Mem. Am. Legion. Comdr. USNR. Recipient Kuwait Liberation medal Saudi Arabian/Kuwaiti Govts., 1992, 96; Wildman scholar Southwestern U., 1987-91. Mem. Naval Res. Assn., L.A. County Bar Assn. Avocations: sailing, golf, tennis. Contracts commercial, Entertainment, Intellectual property.

VON TEUFFEL, NIKOLAI, lawyer; b. Düsseldorf, Germany, May 25, 1954; s. Günther and Helga von Teuffel; m. Ursula Dietrich, Sept. 5, 1986; children: Antonia, Georgia. Degree in law, U. Munich, Germany, 1979, PhD in Law, 1983. Bar: Hamburg 1982. Pvt. practice, Hamburg, 1982—. Mem. German Bar Assn., German Maritime Assn., Hamburg Bar Assn. Admiralty, Contracts commercial, General corporate. Office: Kretschmar von Teuffel Leverkus Kleine Johannisstrasse 2-4 20457 Hamburg Germany

VON WALD, RICHARD B. corporate lawyer; V.p., gen. counsel, sec. Manville Corp., Denver. General corporate. Office: Manville Corp PO Box 5108 Denver CO 80217-5108

VON WALDOW, ARND N. lawyer; b. Moenchen-Gladbach, Germany, Mar. 15, 1957; came to U.S., 1966; s. Hans Eberhard and Brigitte H. (Schulze-Kadelbach) von W.; m. Esther R. Haguel, May 25, 1987; children: Rachel J., Danielle M. BA, Syracuse U., 1980; JD, U. Pitts., 1983. Bar: La. 1983, Pa. 1989. Assoc. Sessions & Fishman, New Orleans, 1983-90, Eckert, Seamans, Cherin & Mellott, Pitts., 1990-91; ptnr. Meyer, Darragh, Buckler, Bebenek & Eck, 1991-99, Reed, Smith, Shaw & McClay, Pitts., 1999—. Mem. Product Liability Adv. Coun., Chgo., 1991—. Mem. ABA, Def. Rsch. Inst., Phi Beta Kappa. Contracts commercial, Insurance, Product liability. Home: 1738 Hempstead Ln Pittsburgh PA 15241-1376 Office: Reed Smith Shaw & McClay 435 6th Ave Ste 2 Pittsburgh PA 15219-1886

VOORHEES, RICHARD LESLEY, federal judge; b. Syracuse, N.Y., June 5, 1941; s. Henry Austin and Catherine Adeline (Fait) V.; m. Barbara Holway Humphries, 1968; children: Martha Northrop, Steven Coerte. BA, Davidson Coll., 1963; JD, U. N.C., Chapel Hill, 1968. Bar: N.C. 1968, U.S. Dist. Ct. (we. dist.) N.C. 1969, U.S. Tax Ct. 1969, U.S. Ct. Appeals (4th cir.) 1978, U.S. Dist. Ct. (mid. dist.) N.C. 1981. Mem., ptnr. Garland, Alala, Bradley & Gray, Gastonia, N.C., 1968-80; pvt. practice, 1980-88; judge U.S. Dist. Ct., Charlotte, 1988—, chief judge, 1991-98. Mem. N.C. State Rep. Exec. Com., Gaston County Rep. Com., chmn., 1979-83, U.S. Jud. Conf. Com., 1993—, case mgmt. and ct. adminstrn. com., 4th Cir. Ct. Appeals Jud. Coun., 1992-93; chmn. Gaston County Bd. Elections, Gastonia, 1985-86; alt. del. Rep. Nat. Conv., Kansas City, Kans., 1976. 1st lt. U.S. Army, 1963-65, U.S. Army Res., 1963-69. Mem. N.C. Bar Assn., Fed. Judges Assn., Dist. Judges Assn. Avocation: boating. Office: US Dist Ct WDNC 195 Fed Bldg 401 W Trade St Charlotte NC 28202-1619

VORT, ROBERT A. lawyer; b. Newark, Sept. 24, 1943; s. Saul S. and Ruth J. (Jacobson) V.; m. Elizabeth Hornstein, June 25, 1968 (div. Nov. 1979); m. Marcelle Greenstein, Nov. 18, 1979 (div. Jan. 1991); children: Joel, Abigail, Rebeccah; m. Tina Kruh, Feb. 4, 1996; 1 child, Hannah. BS in Econs., U. Pa., 1965; JD, Columbia U., 1968. Bar: N.J. 1968, N.Y. 1970, U.S. Ct. Appeals (2d and 3d cirs. 1975), U.S. Ct. Appeals (9th cir.) 1980, U.S. Ct. Appeals (5th cir.) 1981, U.S. Ct. Appeals (fed. cir.) 1984, U.S. Dist. Ct. N.J. 1968, U.S. Dist. Ct. (so. and ea. dists.) N.Y. 1984, U.S. Supreme Ct. 1977. Law clk. to Hon. Theodore I. Botter Superior Ct. of N.J., 1968-69; assoc. Davis & Cox, 1969-71, Israel B. Greene, 1971-73; sole practitioner, 1973-82; ptnr. Balk, Goldberger, Seligsohn, O'Connor & Rhatican, 1982-84, Kirsten, Friedman & Cherin, 1986; pvt. practice, 1984-85, 87-88; ptnr. Goldberg, Mufson & Spar, West Orange, N.J., 1988-91; counsel Donald Friedman, 1991-92; pvt. practice Tenafly, N.J., 1997—; ptnr. Pearce, Vort & Fleisig LLC, Hackensack, 2001—. Mem. ABA (litigation sect., family law sect., legal econs. sect.), N.J. State Bar Assn. (appellate practice subcom.), Bergen County Bar Assn. Appellate, General civil litigation, Family and matrimonial. Office: Pearce Vort & Fleisig LLC Court Plaza North 25 Main St Hackensack NJ 07601 E-mail: rvort@vortlaw.com

VORYS, ARTHUR ISAIAH, lawyer; b. Columbus, Ohio, June 16, 1923; s. Webb Isaiah and Adeline (Werner) V.; m. Lucia Rogers, July 16, 1949 (div. 1980); children: Caroline S., Adeline Vorys Cranson, Lucy Vorys Noll, Webb I.; m. Ann Harris, Dec. 13, 1980. BA, Williams Coll., 1945; LLB, JD, Ohio State U., 1949. Bar: Ohio 1949. From assoc. to ptnr. Vorys, Sater, Seymour & Pease LLP, Columbus, 1949-82, sr. ptnr., 1982-93, of counsel, 1993—. Supt. ins. State of Ohio, 1957-59; bd. dirs Vorys Bros., Inc., others. Trustee, past pres. Children's Hosp., Greenlawn Cemetery Found.; trustee, former chmn. Ohio State U. Hosps.; regent Capital U.; del. Rep. Nat. Conv., 1968, 72. Lt. USMCR, World War II. Decorated Purple Heart. Fellow Ohio State Bar, Columbus Bar Assn.; mem. ABA, Am. Judicature Soc., Rocky Fork Headley Hunt Club, Rocky Fork Hunt and Country Club, Capital Club, Phi Delta Phi, Chi Psi. Home: 5826 Havens Corners Rd Columbus OH 43230-3142 Office: Vorys Sater Seymour & Pease LLP PO Box 1008 52 E Gay St Columbus OH 43216-1008

VOSBURG, BRUCE DAVID, lawyer; b. Omaha, June 17, 1943; s. Noble Perrin and Dena V. (Ferrari) V.; m. Susan Simpson, May 27, 1972; children: Margaret Amy, Wendy Christine, Bruce David. BA, U. Notre Dame, 1965; BSME, 1966; JD, Harvard U., 1969. Bar: Nebr. 1969, Ill. 1970, U.S. Supreme Ct. 1974. Law clk. U.S. Dist. Ct. Nebr., 1969-70; assoc. Kirkland & Ellis, Chgo., 1970-72; ptnr. Fitzgerald & Schorr, Omaha, 1972—. Author: Financing Small Businesses, 1981, Securities Law Practice, 1987, Securities Law-Going Public, 1989, Trade Secret Protection, 1994, Protecting Intellectual Property, 1998, Intellectual Property Law, 1998. Pres. Children's Crisis Ctr., 1984-85, bd. dirs., 1973-84; pres. Nebr. Tennis Assn., 1976-77; mem. Leadership Omaha, 1979; chmn. bd. dirs. City of Omaha Parks and Recreation, 1985-92; founding dir. Friends of the Parks, 1988; bd. dirs. Omaha Pub. Libr. Found., 1997—, pres., 1999—; bd. dirs. Western Heritage Mus., 1998—. Fellow Nebr. Bar Found.; mem. ABA, Nat. Assn. Bond Attys., Nebr. Bar Assn. (chmn. securities com.), Omaha Bar Assn. (exec. coun. 1983-86), Rotary (dir. 1993—), Mo. Valley Tennis Assn. (chmn. grievance com. 1978—), Am. Intellectual Property Lawyers Assn., Tau Beta Pi. Republican. Roman Catholic. General corporate, Intellectual property, Securities. Office: 1100 Woodmen Towers Omaha NE 68102

VOSS, BARRY VAUGHAN, lawyer; b. St. Paul, July 25, 1952; s. James Lee and Stella Marie (Stewart) V.; m. Marilyn Williams, Jan. 25, 1980; children: Rori, Tiffini, Aaron. BA, U. Minn., 1975; JD, Hamline U., 1978. Bar: Minn. 1978, U.S. Dist. Ct. Minn. 1980, U.S. Ct. Appeals (8th cir.) 1982. Pres. Voss and Hickman, P.A., Mpls., 1978—. Spkr. in field. Author: A Taste of Cold Steel, 1999. Bd. dirs. Ramsey County Corrections Adv. Bd., St. Paul, 1977-79, Eden House Program, 1998—. Recipient Most Well-Prepared award Minn. Lawyers Judges' Choice, 1991. Mem. Am. Trial Lawyers Assn. (fire loss com.), Minn. Assn. Criminal Def. Attys. (bd. dirs. 1992-96), Minn. Trial Lawyers Assn., Minn. State Bar Assn. (civil litigation and criminal law sects.), Hennepin County Bar Assn. Democrat. Lutheran. Avocations: public speaking, sports, reading. General civil litigation, Criminal, Entertainment. Office: Voss and Hickman PA 527 Marquette Ave Ste 2355 Minneapolis MN 55402-1323

VRANICAR, MICHAEL GREGORY, lawyer; b. Hammond, Ind., Mar. 11, 1961; s. Melvin G. and Maryann R. (Szarek) V.; m. Marianna C. Livas, May 28, 1994. BSEE, U. Ill., 1983; JD, U. San Diego, 1987. Bar: Calif. 1987, Ill. 1988. Engr. Gen. Dynamics, San Diego, 1983-88; judge advocate USMC, Okinawa, Japan, 1988-91; assoc. Stellato & Schwartz, Chgo., 1992-94; ptnr. Plesha & Vranicar, 1995—. Arbitrator Cook County Arbitration Bd., Chgo., 1994—; judge regional competition Nat. Moot Ct., Chgo., 1992. Mem. Marine Corps Scholarship Found., Chgo. Ball Com. Maj. USMC Res., 1996—. Mem. Chgo. Bar Assn., Okinawa Bench and Bar Assn., Am. Legion. Republican. Roman Catholic. General civil litigation, General corporate, General practice. Office: 10540 S Western Ave Ste 103 Chicago IL 60643-2529

VRATIL, JOHN LOGAN, state legislator, lawyer; b. Great Bend, Kans., Oct. 28, 1945; s. Frank and Althea (Shuss) V.; m. Kathy Hoefer, June 21, 1971 (div. Dec. 1985); m. Anne Whitfill, Mar. 7, 1986 (div. Dec. 1992); children: Alison, Andy, Ashley. BS in Edn., U. Kans., 1967; postgrad., U. Southampton, Eng., 1967-68; JD, U. Kans., 1971; postgrad., U. Exeter, Eng., 1972. Bar: Kans. 1971, U.S. Dist. Ct. Kans. 1971, U.S. Ct. Appeals (10th and 8th cirs.) 1975. From assoc. to ptnr. Bennett, Lytle, Wetzler & Winn, Prairie Village, Kans., 1972-83; with Lathrop & Gage, Overland Park, 1983—; mem. Kans. Senate from 11th dist., Topeka, 1999—. Contbr. articles to profl. jours. Mem. recreation commn. Prairie Village, 1982-83, mem. planning commn., 1983-84; v.p. Usher Mansion Hist. Found., Lawrence, Kans., 1990—. Mem. ABA, Kans. Bar Assn. (pres. 1995-96, gov. 1988-97), Kans. Bar Found. (trustee 1996-99), Johnson County Bar Assn. (pres. 1979), Kans. Sch. Attys. Assn. (pres. 1985), Overland Park C. of C. (bd. dirs. 1985-94, pres. 1988). Republican. Avocations: sports, hunting, reading. Office: Lathrop & Gage 10851 Mastin Blvd Ste 1000 Overland Park KS 66210-2007 Address: Kansas Senate State Capitol Rm 120-S Topeka KS 66612 E-mail: jvratil@lathropgage.com, vratil@senate.state.ks.us

VRATIL, KATHRYN HOEFER, federal judge; b. Manhattan, Kans., Apr. 21, 1949; d. John J. and Kathryn Ruth (Fryer) Hoefer; children: Alison K., John A., Ashley A. BA, U. Kans., 1971, JD, 1975; postgrad., Exeter U., 1971-72. Bar: Kans. 1975, Mo. 1978, U.S. Dist. Ct. Kans. 1975, U.S. Dist. Ct. (we. dist.) Mo. 1978, U.S. Dist. Ct. (ea. dist.) Mo. 1985, U.S. Ct. Appeals (8th cir.) 1978, U.S. Ct. Appeals (10th cir.) 1980, U.S. Ct. Appeals (11th dist.) 1983, U.S. Supreme Ct., 1995. Law clk. U.S. Dist. Ct., Kansas City, Kans., 1975-78; assoc. Lathrop Koontz & Norquist, Mo., 1978-83; ptnr. Lathrop & Norquist, 1984-92; judge City of Prairie Village, Kans., 1990-92. Bd. dirs. Kans. Legal Bd. Svcs., 1991-92. Bd. editors Kans. Law Rev., 1974-75, Jour. Kans. Bar Assn., 1992—. Mem. Kansas City Tomorrow (XIV); bd. trustees, shepherd-deacon Village Presbyn. Ch.; nat. adv. bd. U. Kans. Ctr. for Environ. Edn. and Tng., 1993-95; bd. dirs. Kans. Legal Svcs., 1991-92. Fellow Kans. Bar Foun., Am. Bar Found.; mem. ABA (edtl. bd. Judges Jour. 1996—), Am. Judicature Soc., Nat. Assn. Judges, Fed. Judges Assn., Kans. Bar Assn., Mo. Bar Assn., Kansas City Met. Area Bar Assn., Wyandotte County Bar Assn., Johnson County Bar Assn., Assn. Women Judges, Lawyers Assn. Kansas City, Supreme Ct. Hist. Soc., Kans. State Hist. Soc., U. Kans. Law Soc. (bd. govs. 1978-81), Kans. U. Alumni Assn. (mem. Kansas City chpt. alumni bd. 1990-92, nat. bd. dirs. 1991-96, bd. govs. Adams Alumni Ctr. 1992-95, mem. chancellor's club 1993—, mem. Williams ednl. fund 1993—, mem. Jayhawks for higher edn. 1993-95), Homestead Country Club Prairie Village (pres. 1985-86), Native Sons and Daus of Kans. (life), Rotary, Jr. League Wyandotte and Johnson Counties, Order of Coif, Kans. Inn of Ct. (master 1993—, pres. 1999-2000), Phi Kappa Phi. Republican. Presbyterian. Avocations: cycling, sailing. Office: 511 US Courthouse 500 State Ave Kansas City KS 66101-2403

VREE, ROGER ALLEN, lawyer; b. Chgo., Oct. 2, 1943; s. Louis Gerard and Ruby June (Boersma) V.; m. Lauren Trumbull Gartside, Mar. 29, 1969; children: Jonathan Todd, Matthew David. BA, Wheaton Coll., 1965; MA, Stanford U., 1966, JD, 1969. Bar: Ill. 1969, U.S. Dist. Ct. (no. dist.) Ill. 1969. Assoc. Sidley & Austin, Chgo., 1969-75, ptnr., 1975—. Mem.: ABA, Chgo. Bar Assn., Univ. Club (Chgo.). Construction, Landlord-tenant, Real property. Office: Sidley & Austin Bank One Plz 10 South Dearborn Chicago IL 60603-2000 E-mail: rvree@sidley.com

VRONSKAYA, ANNA ALEXANDROVNA, lawyer, researcher; b. Pomichna, Kirovograd, Ukraine; d. Alexander Apollinarievich and Olga Victorovna Vronskaya. LLM, Taras Shevchenko Nat. U., Kyiv, Ukraine, 1996. Inhouse legal counselor Ukraina Joint Stock Bank, Kyiv, 1994-96; atty. at law Vasil Kisil & Ptnrs., 1996—. Avocations: travel, reading. General corporate, Mergers and acquisitions, Securities. Office: Vasil Kisil & Ptnrs 5/60 Zhylianska St Ste 1-2 01033 Kyiv Ukraine Office Fax: 38 044 220 48 77. E-mail: vronskaya@vkp.kiev.ua

VUKELICH, JOHN EDWARD, lawyer; b. Virginia, Minn., June 5, 1948; s. John Edward and Marguerite Smith V.; m. Lisa Carlson, Mar. 25, 1994; 1 child, Nicholas John. AB, Brown U., 1970; JD cum laude, William Mitchell Coll., 1970. Bar: Minn. 1975, U.S. Dist. Ct. Minn. 1975, U.S. Ct. Appeals (8th cir.) 1975. Assoc., ptnr. Dudley & Smith, St. Paul, 1975-85; atty. pvt. practice, Eden Prairie, Minn., 1986-94; assoc. Schwebel, Goetz & Sieben, Mpls., 1994—. With U.S. Army, 1970-76. Mem. Am. Trial Lawyers Assn., Minn. Trial Lawyers Assn. Avocations: woodworking, hunting, hockey. Insurance, Personal injury. Home: 5751 Long Brake Cir S Edina MN 55439-2619

WACHSMUTH, ROBERT WILLIAM, lawyer; b. Crowell, Tex., Jan. 20, 1942; s. Frederick W. and Dorothy (McKown) W.; m. Karin Lynn Kusiak; children: Wendi Leigh, Ashley Beth Bass, Matthew McKown, Daniel Kusiak. BA, U. Tex., 1965, JD, 1966, grad. bus. sch., 1976. Bar: Tex. 1966, U.S. Dist. Ct. (we. dist.) Tex. 1970, U.S. Ct. Appeals (5th cir., 11 cir.) 1975, U.S. Supreme Ct. 1979, U.S. Dist. Ct. (so. dist.) Tex. 1987. Assoc. Foster, Lewis, Langley, Gardner and Banack, San Antonio, 1969-73; of counsel H.B. Zachry Co., 1973-79; ptnr. Johnson, Johnston, Bowlin, Wachsmuth and Vives, 1973-79, Kelfer, Coatney & Wachsmuth, San Antonio, 1979-81, Kelfer, Coatney, Wachsmuth & Saunders, San Antonio, 1981-83, Brock & Kelfer, P.C., San Antonio, 1983-88, Coatney & Wachsmuth, P.C., San Antonio, 1989-92, Gendry, Sprague & Wachsmuth, P.C., San Antonio, 1992-94, The Kleberg Law Firm, P.C., San Antonio, 1994—. Panel arbitrators Fed. Ct. Annexed Program, San Antonio, 1987—, Bexar County Arbitration Program, San Antonio, 1988; instr. San Antonio Jr. Coll., 1972-74; bd. cert./civil trial law Tex. Bd. Legal Specialization, 1981—; mem. faculty constrn. mgmt. and contrn. exec. program Tex. A&M U. Contbr. articles to profl. jours. Bd. dirs. Halfway House San Antonio, San Antonio and South Tex. br. Jr. Achievement, 1997—. Capt., mil. judge USMCR, 1966-69, Vietnam. Fellow Tex. Bar Found., Coll. of the State Bar; mem. ABA (vice chmn. comms. industry com. 1998-2001, mem. steering com. divsn. VIII constrn. law forum 1999—), Tex. State Bar Assn. (bd. dirs., treas., sec., vice chmn. constrn. law sect. 1989-92, chmn. 1992-93), Coll. of the State Bar, Am. Arbitration Assn. (panel of arbitrators, panel of mediators), San Antonio Bar Assn. (chmn. alternative dispute resolution com.), Fed. Bar Assn., Am. Subcontractors Assn. (gen. counsel San Antonio chpt. 1984-92), Assn. Gen. Contractors (gen. counsel San Antonio chpt. 1995—), Plaza Club (social com.), Masons, Scottish Rite, Shriners, Optimists (pres. 1977-78).Jr. Achieivement (San Antonio and So. Tex., dir. 1997—). Republican. Episcopalian. Avocations: hunting, skiing, spectator sports. Antitrust, General civil litigation, Construction. Office: The Kleberg Law Firm PC 112 E Pecan St Ste 1300 San Antonio TX 78205-1538 E-mail: rwachsmuth@kleberg.com

WADDELL, PHILLIP DEAN, lawyer; b. Covington, Ky., Nov. 14, 1948; s. Ewell Edward and Sarah Isobel (Dean) W.; m. Jill Annette Tolson, Aug. 23, 1975; children: Nathan Ewell, James Seth. BA, Centre Coll. Ky., 1971; JD, No. Ky. U., 1982. Bar: Ky. 1982, Ohio 1983, Tenn. 1986. V.p., mgr. escrow Eagle Savings Assn., Cin., 1973-83; v.p. Union Planters Nat. Bank, Memphis, 1983-84; sr. v.p., liason First Nat. Bank & Trust Co., Oklahoma City, 1984-86; sr. v.p., sec., gen. counsel First Mortgage Strategies Group, Inc., Memphis, 1986-92; atty. pvt. practice, 1992—. Mem. ABA, Am. Judicature Soc., Ky. Bar Assn., Tenn. Bar Assn. Republican. Presbyterian. Lodge: Kiwanis. Contracts commercial, General corporate, Real property. Home: 2095 Allenby Rd Memphis TN 38139-4343 Office: 3169 Professional Plz Ste 2 Germantown TN 38139

WADE, EDWIN LEE, author, lawyer; b. Yonkers, N.Y., Jan. 26, 1932; s. James and Helen Pierce (Kinne) W.; m. Nancy Lou Sells, Mar. 23, 1957; children: James Lee, Jeffrey K. BS, Columbia U., 1954; MA, U. Chgo., 1956; JD, Georgetown U., 1965. Bar: Ill. 1965. Fgn. svc. officer U.S. Dept. State, 1956-57; mktg. analyst Chrysler Internat., S.A., Switzerland, 1957-61; intelligence officer CIA, 1961-63; industry analyst U.S. Internat. Trade Commn., 1963-65; gen. atty. Universal Oil Products Co., Des Plaines, Ill., 1965-72; atty. Amsted Industries, Inc., Chgo., 1972-73; chief counsel dept. gen. svcs. State of Ill., Springfield, 1973-75; sr. atty. U.S. Gypsum Co., Chgo., 1975-84; gen. atty. USG Corp., 1985, corp. counsel, 1986, asst. gen. counsel, 1987, corp. sec., 1987-90, corp. sec., asst. gen. counsel, 1990-93; prin. Edwin L. Wade, 1993-95; instr. Roosevelt U., Chgo., 1995-96. Author: (books) Constitution 2000: A Federalist Proposal for the New Century, 2000, Talking Sense at Century's End: A Barbarous Time...Now What?, 2000; editor: Let's Talk Sense, A Pub. Affairs Newsletter, 1994-98. Fellow Chgo. Bar Assn. (life); mem. ABA, Ill. Bar Assn., Am. Philatelic Soc., Royal Philatelic Soc. Can. Constitutional, General corporate, Public international. Home: 434 Mary Ln Crystal Lake IL 60014-7257 Office: Let's Talk Sense Publishing Co PO Box 6716 Chicago IL 60680-6716 E-mail: edwade@mymailstation.com

WADLER, ARNOLD L. lawyer, retired; b. Bklyn., Aug. 15, 1943; s. Samuel and Anne (Lowenthal) W.; m. Elissa I. Devor, Sept. 17, 1967; children: Craig A., Todd J. BA, Bklyn. Coll., 1964; JD, NYU, 1967. Bar: N.Y. 1968, N.J. 1974. Asst. gen. counsel Metromedia, Inc., N.Y.C., 1968-82, assoc. gen. counsel L.A., 1982-85, v.p., gen. counsel Secaucus, N.J., 1985-86, sr. v.p., gen. counsel, sec. East Rutherford, 1986—2000, ret., 2000. Pres., S&A Restaurant Corp., East Rutherford, 1992; exec. v.p., gen. counsel, sec. Metromedia Internat. Group, Inc., 1995; exec. v.p., gen. counsel, sec. Micromedia Fiber Network Inc., 1997, Big City Radio, Inc., also bd. dirs. Mem. Zoning Bd. Adjustment, Marlboro Twp., N.J., 1980-82; exec. v.p. Marlboro Jewish Ctr., 1980-82. Mem. ABA, N.Y. Bar Assn., KP (asst. sec. 1961-63). General corporate. Office: Metromedia Co Met Exec Towers 1 Meadowlands Plz Fl 6 East Rutherford NJ 07073-2100

WAGGONER, JAMES CLYDE, lawyer; b. Nashville, May 7, 1946; s. Charles Franklin and Alpha (Noah) W.; m. Diane Dusenbery, Aug. 17, 1968; children: Benjamin, Elizabeth. BA, Reed Coll., 1968; JD, U. Oreg., 1974. Bar: Oreg. 1974, U.S. Dist. Ct. Oreg. 1975, U.S. Ct. Appeals (9th cir.) 1980, U.S. Tax Ct. 1979, U.S. Supreme Ct. 1979. Clerk to presiding justice Oreg. Supreme Ct., Salem, 1974-75; assoc. Martin, Bischoff & Templeton, Portland, Oreg., 1975-78, ptnr., 1978-82, Waggoner, Farleigh, Wada, Georgeff & Witt, Portland, 1982-89, Davis Wright Tremaine, Portland, 1990—. Contbr. articles to profl. jours. Fulbright scholar U. London, 1968-69. Mem. ABA, Oreg. Bar Assn., Multnomah Bar Assn., Reed Coll. Alumni Assn. (v.p. 1988, pres. 1989, bd. mgmt.) Alzheimers Assn. of Columbia-Willamette (v.p. 1992, pres. 1993), Order Coif, Phi Beta Kappa. Democrat. Avocations: wood turning, calligraphy. Bankruptcy, Consumer commercial, Real property. Office: Davis Wright Tremaine 1300 SW 5th Ave Ste 2300 Portland OR 97201-5682

WAGGONER, LAWRENCE WILLIAM, law educator; b. Sidney, Ohio, July 2, 1937; s. William J. and Gladys L. Waggoner; m. Lynne S. Applebaum, Aug. 27, 1963; children: Ellen, Diane. BBA, U. Cin., 1960; JD, U. Mich., 1963; PhD, Oxford (Eng.) U., 1966. Assoc. Cravath, Swaine & Moore, N.Y.C., 1963; prof. law U. Ill., Champaign, 1968-72, U. Mich., Ann Arbor, 1974-84, Lewis M. Simes prof. law, 1987—. Dir. rsch., chief reporter joint editorial bd. for Uniform Probate Code, 1986-94, dir. rsch., 1994—, joint editl. bd. uniform trust and estate acts; adviser restatement (2d) of property, 1987-90; reporter restatement (3d) of property, 1990—. Author: Estates in Land and Future Interests in a Nutshell, 1981, 2d edit., 1993, Federal Taxation of Gifts, Trusts, and Estates, 3d edit., 1997, Family Property Law: Wills, Trusts, and Future Interests, 1991. Served to capt., U.S. Army, 1966-68. Fulbright scholar Oxford U., 1963-65. Mem. Am. Law Inst., Am. Coll. Trust and Estates Counsel, Internat. Acad. Estate and Trust Law. Office: U Mich Law Sch 625 S State St Ann Arbor MI 48109-1215

WAGGONER, MICHAEL JAMES, law educator; b. Evanston, Ill., Sept. 21, 1942; s. Alva Madison and Martha W.; m. Cynthia Lynn Goff, Mar. 17, 1984; children: Julia Lauren, Thomas Charles. AB, Stanford U., 1964; LLB, Harvard U., 1967. Bar: D.C. 1968. Assoc. Wilmer, Cutler & Pickering, Washington, 1971-73; assoc. prof. law U. Colo., Boulder, 1973—, assoc. dean, 1998—. Served to capt. USAF, 1968-71. Home: 930 Crestmoor Dr Boulder CO 80303-3117 Office: U Colo Law Sch 401 UCB Boulder CO 80309-0401 E-mail: waggonem@spot.colorado.edu

WAGGONER, WILLIAM JOHNSON, lawyer; b. Salisbury, N.C., Oct. 13, 1928; s. James Martin and Julia (Johnson) W.; m. Martha Anne Garwood, Aug. 8, 1953; children: William Johnson, Ellen Christine, David Garwood. Student, Catawba Coll., 1945-46, 48; AB, U. N.C., 1951, LLB, 1954. Bar: N.C. 1954. Ptnr. Weinstein, Mullenburg, Waggoner & Bledsoe, Charlotte, N.C., 1954-57; asst. U.S. atty. Western Dist. N.C., 1957-59; ptnr. Weinstein, Waggoner & Sturgess, 1959-70, Waggoner, Hasty & Kratt, Charlotte, 1970-84, Waggoner, Hamrick, Hasty, Montieth, Kratt, Cobb & McDonnell, Charlotte, 1985-88, Waggoner, Hamrick, Hasty, Montieth & Kratt PLLC, Charlotte, 1989—. Gen. counsel Mecklenburg Rep. Exec. Com., 1963-73; deacon Luth. Ch.; chmn. Charlotte Bd. Adjustment, 1970-72; mem. N.C. Bd. Elections, 1973-77. With AUS, 1946-47. Recipient Disting. Alumni award Catawba Coll. Mem. ABA, FBA, Am. Judicature Soc., N.C. Bar Assn., Toastmasters (past pres.), Kappa Alpha. General corporate, Corporate taxation, Estate planning. Office: Waggoner Hamrick Hasty Monteith & Kratt PLLC Two First Union Ctr Ste 2750 Charlotte NC 28282 E-mail: wjwaggoner@yahoo.com

WAGNER, ANDREW PORTER, lawyer; b. Danville, Pa., 1956; BA in Econs., Bucknell U., 1978; MBA in Finance, U. Wis., 1982; JD, So. Meth. U., 1984, LLM in Taxation, 1990. Bar: Tex. 1984, U.S. Tax Ct. 1986, U.S. Supreme Ct. 1990, U.S. Dist. Ct. (no. dist.) Tex. 1991. Tax counsel Am. Airlines, Fort Worth, 1985-93, sr. tax counsel, 1993—. Bd. dirs. N.W. Dallas County Flood Control Dist., 1994—, Coppell (Tex.) Recreation Devel. Corp., 1996—, Carrollton-Farmer Sch. Dist., Ednl. Found. Carrollton, 1997—. Mem. ABA, AICPA. State and local taxation. Office: Am Airlines MD 5656 4333 Amon Carter Blvd Fort Worth TX 76155-2605

WAGNER, ANNICE MCBRYDE, judge; BA, law degree, Wayne State U. With Houston and Gardner; gen. counsel Nat. Capital Housing Authority; people's counsel D.C.; assoc. judge Superior Court D.C., 1977-90, D.C. Ct. Appeals, 1990—, now chief judge. Mem. teaching team, trial advocacy workshop Harvard U. Office: Dist of Columbia Court of Appeals 500 Indiana Ave NW Ste 6000 Washington DC 20001-2131*

WAGNER, ARTHUR WARD, JR. lawyer; b. Birmingham, Ala., Aug. 13, 1930; s. Arthur Ward and Lucille (Lockheart) W.; m. Ruth Shingler, May 11, 1957; children: Celia Wagner Minter, Julia Wagner Dolce, Helen Wagner McAfee. BSBA, U. Fla., 1954, JD, 1957. Bar: Fla. 1957, U.S. Dist. Ct. (so. dist.) Fla. 1957, U.S. Dist. Ct. (mid. dist.) Fla. 1975. Ptnr. Wagner & McAfee, P.A., West Palm Beach, Fla., 1959-2000; ret., 2000—. Lectr. in field. Author: Art of Advocacy: Jury Selection, 1981; co-author: Anatomy of Personal Injury Lawsuit I & II, 1968 and 1981. Mem. 15th Jud. Nominating Com., Palm Beach City, 1979—82, 4th Dist. Nominating Commn., Palm Beach City, 1982—86; mem. pres.'s coun. U. Fla.; vestry, chancellor Holy Trinity Parish; bd. dirs. U. Fla. Found., 1996—2001. Fellow Internat. Acad. Trial Lawyers, Am. Coll. Trial Lawyers, Internat. Soc. Barristers, Am. Bd. Trial Advs.; mem. Assn. Trial Lawyers Am. (pres. 1975-76, hon. life trustee Roscoe Pound Found.), So. Trial Lawyers Assn. (pres. 1991), U. Fla. Law Coll. Alumni (mem. bd. govs.). Democrat. Episcopalian. Administrative and regulatory, General civil litigation, Personal injury.

WAGNER, BRENDA CAROL, lawyer; b. Fayetteville, N.C., Apr. 18, 1951; d. David H. and Mollie C. W. BS, N.C. Ctrl. U., 1973, JD, 1976. Bar: N.C. 1977, D.C. 1979, Md. 1987, U.S. Dist. Ct. (mid. dist.) N.C. 1977, U.S. Dist. Ct. D.C. 1987, U.S. Dist. Ct. Md. 1991, U.S. Ct. Appeals (4th cir.) 1983. Hearing officer N.C. ABC Bd., Raleigh, 1978-79; rsch. dir. N.C. Dept. Adminstrn., 1979-80; asst. pub. defender N.C. Pub. Defender, 27A Jud. Dist., Gastonia, 1980-81; asst. corp. counsel D.C. Govt., Washington, 1986-87; hearing officer D.C. Dept. Pub. Housing, 1991-97, D.C. Housing Authority, 2000—. Commr. N.C. Property Tax Study Commn., Raleigh, 1981-82; mem. League Women Voters, Washington, 1996—; life mem. Urban League, Washington, 1996—; bd. dirs. Legal Svcs. Bd., Raleigh, 1978-80, United Way, Gastonia, 1980-81, Planning Bd., Rocky Mount, N.C., 1983-86. Mem. ABA, ATLA, Nat. Bar Assn., Women's Bar Assn. D.C. Office: Wagner & Assocs 733 15th St NW Ste 908 Washington DC 20005-2112

WAGNER, CHRISTOPHER ALLEN, lawyer; b. Cleve., June 25, 1975; s. John Carroll and Dorothy A. W.; m. Christine M., June 25, 1975; children: Bradley M., Alexis M. BA in Psychology, U. Dayton, 1972; MS in Urban Policy, Cleve. State U., 1975; JD, Capital U., 1980; LLM, Georgetown U., 1984. Bar: Ohio 1980, Ga. 1984. Atty. anti-trust divsn. U.S. Dept. Justice, Washington, 1980-84, Atlanta, 1984-88; internat. counsel Scientific-Atlanta, 1988-96; exec. dir. strategic internat. bus., 1996—. Home: 1175 Clifton Rd NE Atlanta GA 30307-1229

WAGNER, CURTIS LEE, JR. judge; b. Nov. 8, 1928; m. Jeanne E. Allen (dec.); children: Curtis L. III, Rex A. Student, Tenn. Poly. Inst., 1947-49; LLB, U. Tenn., 1951. Bar: Tenn. 1952. Assoc. Kramer, Dye, McNabb and Greenwood, Knoxville, Tenn., 1951-54; atty.-adv. gen. crimes and fraud sect. Criminal Divsn. Dept. Justice, Washington, 1954-56; trial atty. Dept. Justice, 1954-60; assigned to Ct. of Claims sect. Civil Divsn., 1956-60; spl. asst. comms., transp. and utilities JAG Dept. Army, 1960-64; chief Regulatory Law Divsn., 1964-74; adminstrv. law judge FERC, 1974-79, chief adminstrv. law judge, 1979—. Mem. civilian lawyer career com., 1960-74; chmn. JAG incentive awards com. 1960-74; mem. Army Staff Awards Bd., 1964-74, Army Environ. Policy Council, 1972-74. Dist. commr. Nat. Capital Area coun. Boy Scouts Am., 1967-69; mem. Bd. Govts. Watergate of Alexandria Condo, 1996—; commr. Alexandria Redevel. and Pub. Housing Commn., 1996-2000. Decorated Meritorious Civilian Svc. award, Exceptional Civilian Svc. award; recipient citation for outstanding performance Dept. Army, 1961-74, Scouter's Tng. award Boy Scouts Am., 1965, Scoutmaster's Key, 1966, Commr.'s Key, 1968, Commr.'s Arrowhead Honor, 1966, Silver Beaver award 1969. Mem. Order of Arrow, Soc. Profls. in Dispute Resolution, Annapolis Yacht (parliamentarian) Club. Methodist. Office: Fed Energy Regulatory Commn 888 1st St NE Washington DC 20426-0002 E-mail: curtis.wagner@ferc.fed.us

WAGNER, DARRYL WILLIAM, lawyer; b. Dixon, Ill., Jan. 14, 1943; s. Earl L. and Lois Mae W.; m. Susan A. Aldrich; children: Peter Alan, Nicholas William. BA, Northwestern U., 1965, JD, 1968. Bar: Ill. 1968, U.S. Dist. Ct. (no. dist.) Ill. 1969, U.S. Ct. Appeals (7th cir.) 1971, Calif. 1982. Sr. counsel Sidley Austin Brown & Wood, Chgo., 1969—. Dir. Housing Options for People to Excell, Inc., 1992-94, 96—. Co-author: Illinois Municipal Law: Subdivisions and Subdivisions in Controls, 1978, 81. Mem. ABA, Internat. Assn. Attys. and Execs. in Corp. Real Estate, Ill. State Bar Assn., Chgo. Bar Assn. Presbyn. Construction, Environmental, Real property. Home: 526 A San Ysdidro Rd Santa Barbara CA 93108 Office: Sidley Austin Brown & Wood 555 W 5th St Ste 4000 Los Angeles CA 90013-3000 E-mail: dwagner@sidley.com, wwagneresq@springmail.com

WAGNER, JAMES PEYTON, lawyer; b. McKinney, Tex., July 22, 1939; s. Otto James and Jane Peyton (Adams) W.; m. Patricia Anne Squires, June 16, 1962; children: Jarrod Shannon, Anne Paige, Leslie Lauren, James Russell. BA, Tex. Tech. U., Lubbock, 1961; LLB, So. Meth. U., 1964. Bar: Tex. 1964, U.S. Dist. Ct. (no. dist.) Tex. 1965, U.S. Ct. Appeals (3rd and 5th cirs.) 1996, U.S. Supreme Ct. 1996. Atty. United American Ins. Co., Dallas, 1969-70, Employer's Ins. of Wausau, Dallas, 1970-73, Crumley Murphy and Shrull, Ft. Worth, 1973-77, Fillmore & Camp, Ft. Worth, 1977-78, Penner, Jones, Keith & Wagner, Ft. Worth, 1978-80, The Wagner Law Firm, Ft. Worth, Dallas, 1964-69, 80-85;, 1997—; prin. Keith and Wagner, P.C., Ft. Worth, 1985-89; assoc. Brockermeyer & Assocs., 1989-90; ptnr. Fielding, Barrett & Taylor, 1990-97. Author, contbr. course book: State Bar of Texas Personal Injury and Workers Compensation Practice Skills, 1987, 89. Mem. ATLA, State Bar Tex., Tarrant County Bar Assn., Coll. of State Bar Tex., Brain Injury Assn. Baha'i World Faith. Avocations: oenology, music. Insurance, Personal injury, Product liability. Home: 4240 Sudith Ln Midlothian TX 76065-6332 Office: 514 E Belknap St Fort Worth TX 76102 E-mail: jpw@jpwagnerlaw.com

WAGNER, JOHN LEO, lawyer, former magistrate judge; b. Ithaca, N.Y., Mar. 12, 1954; s. Paul Francis and Doris Elizabeth (Hoffschneider) W.; m. Marilyn Modin, June 18, 1987. Student, U. Nebr., 1973-74; BA, U. Okla., 1976, JD, 1979. Bar: Okla. 1980, Calif. 1999, U.S. Dist. Ct. (we. dist.) Okla. 1980, U.S. Dist. Ct. (no. and ea. dists.) Okla. 1981, U.S. Dist. Ct. (mid. dist.) Calif. 2000, U.S. Ct. Appeals (10th cir.) 1982. Assoc. Franklin, Harmon & Satterfield Inc., Oklahoma City, 1980-82; ptnr. Franklin, Harmon & Satterfield, Inc., 1982; assoc. Kornfeld, Franklin & Phillips, 1982-85, ptnr., 1985; magistrate judge U.S. Dist. Ct. No. Dist. Okla., Tulsa, 1985-97; dir. Irell & Manella LLP Alt. Dispute Resolution Ctr., Newport Beach, Calif., 1997—. Pres. U. Okla. Coll. Law Assn., 1991-92. Fellow Am. Coll. Civil Trial Mediators, ABA, Internat. Acad. Mediators; mem. Fed. Magistrate Judge's Assn. (dir. 10th cir. 1987-89), 10th Cir. Edn. Com., Okla. Bar Assn., Council Oak Am. Inn of Cts. (pres. 1992-93), Jud. Conf. U.S. (com. ct. adminstrn. and case mgmt. 1992-97), CPR-Georgetown Commn. Ethics and Standards in ADR. Republican. Office: Irell & Manella LLP Alt Dispute Resolution Ctr 840 Newport Center Dr Ste 450 Newport Beach CA 92660-6321 E-mail: jwagner@irell.com, usmag1@home.com

WAGNER, LYNN EDWARD, lawyer; b. Mt. Holly, N.J., Feb. 10, 1941; s. Edward John and Alma Elizabeth (Mason) W.; m. Maureen Elizabeth Bach, May 25, 1973; children: Daniel Preston, Matthew Evan. BS, Drexel U., 1965; JD, Duke U., 1968. Bar: Mass. 1968, U.S. Dist. Ct. Mass. 1968, Fla. 1972, U.S. Dist. Ct. (mid. dist.) Fla. 1972, U.S. Ct. Appeals (5th cir.) 1972, U.S. Supreme Ct. 1972, Pa. 1975, U.S. Dist. Ct. (we. dist.) Pa. 1975, U.S. Ct. Appeals (4th cir.) 1977, U.S. Ct Appeals (11th cir.) 1978, U.S. Ct. Appeals (D.C. cir.) 1980, U.S. Ct. Appeals (3d cir.) 1985, U.S. Dist. Ct. (so. dist.) Fla. 1991, U.S. Dist. Ct. (no. dist.) Fla. 1992, U.S. Dist. Ct. (mid. dist.) Fla., U.S. Ct. Appeals (5th cir.); cert. arbitrator and mediator; cert. Fla. Dept. Ins., Nat. Arbitration Forum, U.S. Dept. Labor, U.S. Equal Employment Opportunity Commn. Assoc. Foley, Hoag & Elliot, Boston, 1968-70; asst. prof. law U. Fla., Gainesville, 1971-73; sr. trial atty. U.S. EEOC, Washington, 1973-74; ptnr. Berkman, Ruslander, Pohl, Lieber & Engel, Pitts., 1975-84, Kirkpatrick & Lockhart, Pitts., 1985-86, Rumberger, Kirk, Caldwell, Cabaniss, Burke & Wechsler, Orlando, 1986-91, Cabaniss, Burke & Wagner, Orlando, 1991-94, Baker & Hostetler, Orlando, 1995-97, Rumrell, Wagner & Costabel, Orlando, 1997—; gen. counsel North Star Media, Inc., 1997-99. Gen. counsel Impact Comm., Inc., 1989-95; bd. dirs. Fla. Legal Svcs., Inc., 1998—. With USAR, 1960-61. Scholarship recipient Sch. Law, Duke U., Durham, N.C., 1965-68. Mem.: ATLA, ABA (litig. sect., employment law sect., dispute resolution sect.), Mass. Bar Assn., Pa. Bar Assn. (labor sect., dispute resolution sect.), Fla. Bar Assn. (labor sect., fed. ct. practice sect., dispute resolution sect.), Am. Arbitration Assn. (arbitration & mediation panels for employment, securities and comml.), Nat. Arbitration Forum, Nat. Assn. Securities Dealers (arbitration and mediation panels for securities and employment), Fla. Acad. Profl. Mediators, Fla. Acad. Trial Lawyers, Am. Judicature Soc., Leading Am. Attys., Soc. for Profls. in Dispute Resolution. Avocations: fishing, boating, travel. General civil litigation, Alternative dispute resolution, Labor. Home: 526 Alokee Ct Lake Mary FL 32746-2218 Office: Rumrell Wagner & Costabel 2400 Maitland Ctr Pky 225 2180 North Park Ave Ste 318 Winter Park FL 32789 E-mail: lynnewagner@mindspring.com

WAGNER, THOMAS JOSEPH, lawyer, insurance company executive; b. Jackson, Mich., June 29, 1939; s. O. Walter and Dorothy Ann (Hollinger) W.; m. Judith Louise Bogardus, Jan. 15, 1961; children— Ann Louise, Mark Robert, Rachel Miriam. B.A., Earlham Coll., 1957; J.D., U. Chgo., 1965. Bar: Ill. 1968, U.S. Supreme Ct. 1975. Asst. to gov. State of Ill., Springfield, 1966-67, legal counsel, adminstrv. asst. to treas., 1967-70; adminstrv. asst. to U.S. senator Adlai E. Stevenson, Washington, 1970-77; sr. v.p. govt. affairs div. Am. Ins. Assn., Washington, 1977-80; staff v.p. Ina Corp., 1980-82; v.p., chief counsel Property Casualty Group, CIGNA Corp., Phila., 1982-86, v.p., assoc. gen. counsel, 1986-88, sr. v.p., corp. sec., 1988-91, exec. v.p., gen. counsel, 1992—; trustee Eisenhower Exchange Fellowships, Inc.; bd. dirs. Inst. Law and Econs., U. Penn. Past chmn. Phila. Crime Commn. Africa-Asia Pub. Svc. fellow Syracuse U., 1965-66. Mem. ABA (bus. law com.), Am. Corp. Counsel Assn., U.S.-Pacific Econ. Cooperation Coun. Insurance, Legislative. Office: Cigna Corp PO Box 7716 1 Liberty Place 55th Fl Philadelphia PA 19192-1550

WAGONER, ANNA MILLS, prosecutor; BA, Agnes Scott Coll.; JD, Wake Forest U. Assoc. Woddson, Linn, Sayers, Lawther, Short and Wagoner, 1985—87, ptnr., 1987—90; judge Rowan County Dist. Ct., 1990—2001; U.S. Atty. Mid. Dist. N.C. U.S. Dept. Justice, 2001—. Office: PO Box 1858 Greensboro NC 27402*

WAGONER, DAVID EVERETT, lawyer; b. Pottstown, Pa., May 16, 1928; s. Claude Brower and Mary Kathryn (Groff) W.; children: Paul R., Colin H., Elon D., Peter B., Dana F.; m. Jean Morton Saunders; children: Constance A., Jennifer L., Melissa J. BA, Yale U., 1950; LLB, U. Pa., 1953. Bar: D.C. 1953, Pa. 1953, Wash. 1953. Law clk. U.S. Ct. Appeals (3d cir.), Pa., 1955-56; law clk. U.S. Supreme Ct., Washington, 1956-57; ptnr. Perkins & Coie, Seattle, 1957-96. Panel mem. of arbitration forum worldwide including People's Republic of China, B.C. Internat. Comml. Arbitration Ctr., Hong Kong Internat. Arbitration Centre, Asian/Pacific Ctr. for Resolution of Internat. Bus. Disputes and the Ctr. for Internat. Dispute Resolution for Asian/Pacific Region. Mem. sch. com. Mcpl. League Seattle and King County, 1958— , chmn., 1962-65; mem. Seattle schs. citizens coms. on equal ednl. opportunity and adult vocat. edn., 1963-64; mem. Nat. Com. Support Pub. Schs.; mem. adv. com. on community colls., to 1965, legislature interim com. on edn., 1964-65; mem. community coll. adv. com. to state supt. pub. instrn., 1965; chmn. edn. com. Forward Thrust, 1968; mem. Univ. Congl. Ch. Council Seattle, 1968-70; bd. dirs. Met. YMCA Seattle, 1968; bd. dirs. Seattle Pub. Schs., 1965-73, v.p., 1966-67, 72-73, pres., 1968, 73; trustee Evergreen State Coll. Found., chmn. 1986-87, capitol campaign planning chmn.; trustee Pacific NW Ballet, v.p. 1986. Served to 1st lt. M.C., AUS, 1953-55 Fellow Am. Coll. Trial Lawyers (mem. ethics com., legal ethics com.), Chartered Inst. Arbitrators, Singapore Inst. Arbitrators; mem. ABA (chmn. standing com. fed. jud. imprisonment, chmn. appellate advocacy com., mem. commn. on separation of powers and jud. independence), Wash. State Bar Assn., Seattle-King County Bar Assn., Acad. Experts, Swiss Arbitration Assn., Comml. Bar Assn. London, Nat. Sch. Bds. Assn. (bd. dirs., chmn. coun. Big City bds. edn. 1971-72), English-Speaking Union (v.p. Seattle chpt. 1961-62), Chi Phi. Alternative dispute resolution. Home: 4215 E Blaine St Seattle WA 98112-3229 Office: Internat Arbitration Chambers US BankCtr 1420 5th Ave Fl 22 Seattle WA 98101-4087

WAHLEN, EDWIN ALFRED, lawyer; b. Gary, Ind., Mar. 12, 1919; s. Alfred and Ethel (Pearson) W.; m. Alice Elizabeth Condit, Apr. 24, 1943 (div. 1983); children: Edwin Alfred, Virginia Elizabeth, Martha Anne; m. Elizabeth L. Corey, Nov. 23, 1984. Student, U. Ala., 1936-38; A.B., U. Chgo., 1942, J.D., 1948. Bar: Ill. 1948. Practiced in, Chgo., 1948—; mem. firm Haight, Goldstein & Haight, 1948-55; ptnr. Goldstein & Wahlen, 1956-59, Arvey, Hodes, Costello & Burman (and predecessor), 1959-91, Wildman, Harrold, Allen & Dixon, 1992—. Author: Soldiers and Sailors Wills: A Proposal For Federal Legislation, 1948. Served to 2d lt. AUS, 1942-46. Decorated Silver Star medal, Bronze Star medal. Mem. ABA, Ill. Bar Assn., Chgo. Bar Assn., Order of Coif, Phi Beta Kappa, Phi Alpha Delta. Contracts commercial, General corporate, Real property. Home: 1250 Breckenridge Ct Lake Forest IL 60045-3875 Office: 225 W Wacker Dr Chicago IL 60606-1224

WAILAND, GEORGE, lawyer; b. Munich, Fed. Republic Germany, Mar. 14, 1947; came to U.S., 1951; s. Max and Bella (Grylak) W.; m. Adele M. Rosen, Aug. 20, 1972; children: J. Zachary, William J. BS, NYU, 1969, JD, 1972. Bar: N.Y. 1973, U.S. Supreme Ct. 1976, U.S. Dist. Ct. (so., ea. dists.) N.Y. 1973, U.S. Dist. Ct. (no. dist.) N.Y. 1981, U.S. Claims Ct. 1979, U.S. Tax Ct., 1979, U.S. Ct. Appeals (2d cir.) 1973, U.S. Ct. Appeals (fed. cir.) 1982, U.S. Ct. Appeals (4th cir. and 9th cir.) 1986, U.S. Ct. Appeals (7th cir.) 1987. Assoc. Cahill Gordon & Reindel, N.Y.C., 1972-80, ptnr., 1980—. John Norton Pomeroy scholar NYU, 1970. General civil litigation, Securities. Home: 1050 Park Ave New York NY 10028-1031 Office: Cahill Gordon & Reindel 80 Pine St Fl 17 New York NY 10005-1790

WAINESS, MARCIA WATSON, legal administration consultant; b. Bklyn., Dec. 17, 1949; d. Stanley and Seena (Klein) Watson. Student, UCLA, 1967-71, 80-81, UCLA Grad. Sch., 1987-88. Office mgr., paralegal Lewis, Marenstein & Kadar, L.A., 1977-81; office mgr. Rosenfeld, Meyer & Susman, Beverly Hills, Calif., 1981-83; adminstr. Rudin, Richman & Appel, 1983; dir. adminstrn. Kadison, Pfaelzer, L.A., 1983-87; exec. dir. Richards, Watson and Gershon, 1987-93; legal mgmt. cons. Wainess & Co., 1993-99; dir. law firm svcs. Dutch Franklin Bus. Svcs., Inc., 1999-2000; dir. client adv. svcs. Green Hasson & Janks LLP, L.A., 2000—. Faculty UCLA Legal Mgmt. & Adminstrn. Program, 1983, U. So. Calif. Paralegal Program, L.A., 1985; adv. bd. atty. asst. tng. program UCLA, 1984-88; adj. faculty U. West L.A. Sch. Paralegal Studies, 1997-98. Mem. ABA (chair Displaywrite Users Group 1986, legal tech. adv. coun. litig. support working group 1986-87), Inst. Mgmt. Consultants, L.A. County Bar Assn. (exec. com. law office mgmt. sect.), Assn. Legal Adminstrs. (mem. editl. adv. bd. 1998—, bd. dirs. 1990-92, asst. regional v.p. Calif. 1987-88, regional v.p. 1988-89, pres. Beverly Hills chpt. 1985-86, membership chair 1984-85, chair new adminstrn. sect. 1982-84, mktg. mgmt. sect. com. 1989-90, internat. conf. com.), Beverly Hills Bar Assn. (chair law practice mgmt. sect. 1998-2000, chair women in legal profession co. 2000—). Avocations: historic preservation, antiques, interior design. Office: 10990 Wilshire Blvd Fl 16 Los Angeles CA 90024-3929 E-mail: mwwainess@gujadvisors.com

WAINWRIGHT, GEORGE, judge; b. Wilson County, N.C., Dec. 10, 1943; s. George Sr. and Susan Wainwright; m. Carol McChesney; children: Kennon, Ashton. Undergrad. degree, U. N.C., 1966; JD, Wake Forest U., 1984. Agribus. and real estate positions, Wilson, 1966-81; with Wheatly, Wheatly, Nobles & Weeks, Beaufort, N.C., 1986-90; apptd. judge Dist. Ct., 1991; resident Superior Ct. judge for N.C. Jud. Dist. 3B, 1994; justice Supreme Ct. N.C., 1999—. With USCGR, 1966-72 Morehead scholar, 1966. Mem. N.C. Bar Assn., Lookout Rotary Club. Presbyterian. Office: Supreme Ct NC Justice Bldg PO Box 1841 Raleigh NC 27602-1841

WAISANEN, CHRISTINE M. lawyer, writer; b. Hancock, Mich., May 27, 1949; d. Frederick B. and Helen M. (Hill) W.; m. Robert John Katzenstein, Apr. 21, 1979; children: Jeffrey Hunt, Erick Hill. BA with honors, U. Mich., 1971; JD, U. Denver, 1975. Bar: Colo. 1975, D.C. 1978. Labor rels. atty. U.S. C. of C., Washington, 1976-79; govt. rels. specialist ICI Americas, Inc., Wilmington, Del., 1979-87; dir. cultural affairs City of Wilmington, 1987; founder, chief writer Hill, Katzenstein & Waisanen, 1988—. Chmn. Delaware State Coastal Zone Indsl. Control Bd., 1993—. Mem. Fed. Bar Assn., Jr. League of Wilmington (v.p. 1985-86), Women's Rep. Club of Wilmington (bd. dirs. 1988-93), U. Mich. Club of Del. (pres. 1999—). Republican. Presbyterian. Administrative and regulatory, Environmental, Land use and zoning (including planning). Home: 1609 Mt Salem Ln Wilmington DE 19806-1134

WAITT, ROBERT KENNETH, lawyer; b. Seattle, Apr. 25, 1931; s. Charles Kenneth and Willa E. (Ryan) W.; m. Diane Dallam, Dec. 7, 1933; children: Mark Robert, Julie Lynn Reid. Student, Wash. State Coll., 1949-50, 52-53; LLB, Gonzaga U., 1957, JD, 1967. Bar: Wash. 1957, U.S. Supreme Ct. Assoc. Morrissey, Hedrick & Dunham, Seattle, 1957-59; ptnr. Benson & Waitt, 1959-60; assoc. Walsh & Margolis, 1960-62; ptnr. Murray, Dunham & Waitt, 1962-81, Waitt, Johnson & Martens, Seattle, 1981-90, of counsel, 1990—. Judge King County Dist. Ct., Seattle, 1965-81, City of Issaquah Mcpl. Ct., 1961-81; chmn. City Issaquah Civil Service Commn., 1963-69; chmn. Gonzaga Law Council, Gonzaga U. Sch. Law, Spokane, Wash., 1983-85; regent Gonzaga U., 1982-88. With USMC, 1950-52. Mem. Wash. Bar Assn., Sahalee Country Club, Bermuda Dunes Country Club, Tradition Club. State civil litigation, Insurance, Professional liability. Home: 3815 E Lake Sammamish Shorelane SE Sammamish WA 98075 Office: 7400 Columbia Ctr Seattle WA 98104-7035

WAKEFIELD, SUSANNAH JANE, lawyer; b. N.Y.C., Oct. 23, 1970; d. Scott Lawrence and Patricia Diana W. BA with honors, Durham U., Eng., 1993; diploma in Law, Coll. of Law, London, 1994, diploma in Legal Practice, 1995. Solicitor Cameron McKenna, 1995-99; assoc. LeBoeuf Lamb Greene & MacRae, London, 1999-2000, N.Y.C., 2001—. Mem. Law Soc. Eng. and Wales. Avocations: tennis, field hockey. Insurance, Professional liability. Office: LeBoeuf Lamb Greene MacRae 12 W 55th St New York NY 10019-5389

WAKS, JAY WARREN, lawyer; b. Newark, Dec. 6, 1946; s. Isadore and Miriam Waks; m. Harriet S. Siedman, July 27, 1969; children: Jonathan Warren, Allison Lindsay. BS, Cornell U., 1968, JD, 1971. Bar: N.Y. 1972, U.S. Ct. Appeals (2d cir.) 1972, U.S. Dist. Ct. (no. dist.) N.Y. 1972, U.S. Dist. Ct. (so. & ea. dists.) N.Y. 1973, U.S. Ct. Appeals (3d cir.) 1983, U.S. Dist. Ct. D.C. 1985, U.S. Supreme Ct. 1991. Law clk. to Hon. Inzer B. Wyatt U.S. Dist. Ct. So. Dist. N.Y., 1971-72; assoc. Kaye, Scholer, Fierman, Hays & Handler, N.Y.C., 1972-80; ptnr. Kaye Scholer LLP, 1981—; chmn. labor and employment law practice/litigation Kaye, Scholer, Fierman, Hays & Handler, chmn. health care law practice group and ADR practice group, mem. E-commerce practice group and internat. practice group. Mem exec. com., bd. dirs., sec. to bd. dirs. Work in Am. Inst., Inc., Scarsdale, N.Y., 1989—; mem., chair faculty numerous employment and labor law confs., 1982—; co-chair Glasser Legal Works Inst. on Litigation/Resolution of Complex Employment Discrimination Class Actions, 2000; chair Ann. Employment Law and Litigation Conf., 1992-96; spkr. law jour. seminars Gen. Coun. Conf., 1988—, winter conf. Fed. Bar Coun., 1999; conf. spkr. Am. Employment Law Coun., Law Edn. Inst./Bur. Nat. Affairs Books Nat. Continuing Legal Edn. Conf., Vail, 1998—. Bus. Watch columnist Nat. Law Jour., 1990—; contbg. author numerous articles to profl. jours. Mem. employment disputes com. CPR Inst. for Dispute Resolution, 1988—, chair, 1991—; mem. coun. Cornell U., 2000—, nat. chmn. Cornell Law Sch. ann. fund, 2001—; chmn. 20th, 25th and 30th reunion campaigns Cornell Law Sch., Ithaca, N.Y., nat. co-chair Cornell Law Sch. dean's spl. leadership commn. Class of '68, major gifts com. 1998, devel. exec. com.; mem. law sch. adv. coun. and visiting com. Cornell Law Sch. Named among nation's best litigators in employment law, The Nat. Law Jour., 1992; named among best lawyers in N.Y. and among 7 best corporate side labor/employment lawyers, N.Y. Mag., 1995. Mem. ABA, State Bar Calif., N.Y. State Bar Assn. (co-chair employment alternative dispute resolution com. 1995-99, labor and employment law sect., exec. com.), Assn. Bar of City of N.Y. (chmn. labor and employment law com. 1990-93). Avocations: swimming, tennis, skiing, bicycling, rollerblading. Federal civil litigation, Labor. Office: Kaye Scholer LLP 425 Park Ave New York NY 10022-3506 E-mail: jwaks@kayescholer.com

WALCHER, ALAN ERNEST, lawyer; b. Chgo., Oct. 2, 1949; s. Chester R. and Dorothy E. (Kullgren) W.; children: Dustin Alan, Michael Alan, Christopher Ray. BS, U. Utah, 1971, cert. in internat. rels., 1971, JD, 1974. Bar: Utah 1974, U.S. Dist. Ct. Utah 1974, U.S. Ct. Appeals (10th cir.) 1977, Calif. 1979, U.S. Dist. Ct. (so. dist.) Calif. 1979, U.S. Ct. Appeals (9th cir.) 1983, U.S. Dist. Ct. (ea., no., and so. dists.) Calif. 1994. Sole practice, Salt Lake City, 1974-79; ptnr. Costello & Walcher, L.A., 1979-85, Walcher & Scheuer, 1985-88, Ford & Harrison, 1988-91, Epstein Becker & Green, 1991—; judge pro tem Los Angeles Mcpl. Ct., 1986-91; dir. Citronia, Inc., Los Angeles, 1979-81. Trial counsel Utah chpt. Common Cause, Salt Lake City, 1978-79. Robert Mukai scholar U. Utah, 1971. Mem. Soc. Bar and Gavel (v.p. 1975-77), ABA, Fed. Bar Assn., Los Angeles County Bar Assn., Century City Bar Assn., Assn. Bus. Trial Lawyers, Phi Delta Phi, Owl and Key. Federal civil litigation, State civil litigation, Government contracts and claims. Home: 17933 Sunburst St Northridge CA 91325-2848 Office: Epstein Becker & Green Ste 1650 Two Embarcadero Ctr San Francisco CA 94111-5994 E-mail: awalcher@ebglaw.com, alan1002@earthlink.net

WALD, BERNARD JOSEPH, lawyer; b. Bklyn., Sept. 14, 1932; s. Max and Ruth (Mencher) W.; m. Francine Joy Weintraub, Feb. 2, 1964; children— David Evan, Kevin Mitchell. B.B.A. magna cum laude, CCNY; J.D. cum laude, NYU, 1955. Bar: N.Y. 1955, U.S. Dist. Ct. (so. dist.) N.Y. 1960, U.S. Dist. Ct. (ea. dist.) N.Y. 1960, U.S. Ct. Appeals (2d cir.) 1960, U.S. Supreme Ct. 1971. Mem. Herzfeld & Rubin, P.C. and predecessor firms, N.Y.C., 1955— . Mem. ABA, N.Y. State Bar Assn., Assn. Bar City N.Y., N.Y. County Lawyers Assn. Contracts commercial, General corporate, Private international. Office: Herzfeld & Rubin PC 40 Wall St Ste 5400 New York NY 10005-2301

WALD, MICHAEL H. lawyer, educator; b. Oceanside, N.Y., Feb. 11, 1953; s. Morton Lee Wald and Janice (Weinberg) Berger; m. Jacqueline O. Wald, May 25, 1980; children: Daniel, Rachel. Student, London Sch. Econs., 1973-74; BS, BA, U. Pa., 1974; JD, Duke U., 1977. Bar: Va. 1978, N.Y. 1978, D.C. 1978, U.S. Dist. Ct. (so. and ea. dists.) N.Y. 1978, U.S. Ct. Appeals (D.C. and 4th cirs.) 1978, U.S. Tax Ct. 1978, Fla. 1979, U.S. Dist. Ct. D.C. 1979, U.S. Dist. Ct. (ea. and we. dists.) Va. 1979, Tex. 1980, U.S. Ct. Appeals (5th cir.) 1981, U.S. Dist. Ct. (we. dist.) Tex. 1981, U.S. Dist. Ct. (no. dist.) Tex. 1982, U.S. Dist. Ct. (ea. dist.) Tex. 1988, U.S. Supreme Ct. 1983. Staff atty. FTC, Washington, 1977-78; assoc. Dunaway, McCarthy & Dye, 1979; assoc. gen. counsel Datapoint Corp., San Antonio, 1980-82, TGI Friday's, Dallas, 1982-83; mng. ptnr. Wald & Campbell, 1983-92; of counsel Ungerman Hill, P.C., 1993-94; owner Wald and Assocs., Richardson, Tex., 1994—. Mediator Dallas Mediation Ctr., 1984; arbitrator Am. Arbitration Assn., Dallas, 1984-96. Columnist, The Legalizer, Richardson Daily News, 1986. Recipient Am. Jurisprudence award Lawyers Coop., 1975. Mem. ABA, Dallas Bar Assn., North Texas Estate Planning Coun. (bd. dirs.), Kiwanis. Lodge: Rotary. Office: 300 N Coit Rd Ste 215 Richardson TX 75080-5433

WALD, PATRICIA MCGOWAN, retired federal judge; b. Torrington, Conn., Sept. 16, 1928; d. Joseph F. and Margaret (O'Keefe) McGowan; m. Robert L. Wald, June 22, 1952; children— Sarah, Douglas, Johanna, Frederica, Thomas. BA, Conn. Coll., 1948; LLB, Yale U., 1951; HHD (hon.), Mt. Vernon Jr. Coll., 1980; LLD (hon.), George Washington Law Sch., 1983, CUNY, 1984, Notre Dame U., John Jay Sch. Criminal Justice, Mt. Holyoke Coll., 1985, Georgetown U., 1987, Villanova U. Law Sch., Amherst Coll., N.Y. Law Sch., 1988, Colgate U., 1989, Hofstra Law Sch., 1991, New Eng. Coll., 1991, Hoffstra U., 1991, Vermont Law Sch., 1995. Bar: D.C. 1952. Clk. to judge Jerome Frank U.S. Ct. Appeals, 1951-52; assoc. Arnold, Fortas & Porter, Washington, 1952-53; mem. D.C. Crime Commn., 1964-65; atty. Office of Criminal Justice, 1967-68, Neighborhood Legal Svc., Washington, 1968-70; co-dir. Ford Found. Project on Drug Abuse, 1970, Ctr. for Law and Social Policy, 1971-72, Mental Health Law Project, 1972-77; asst. atty. gen. for legis. affairs U.S. Dept. Justice, Washington, 1977-79; judge U.S. Ct. Appeals (D.C. cir.), 1979—, chief

judge, 1986-91; judge Internat. Criminal Tribunal for Former Yugoslavia, The Hague, The Netherlands, 1999—. Author: Law and Poverty, 1965; co-author: Bail in the United States, 1964, Dealing with Drug Abuse, 1973; contbr. articles on legal topics. Trustee Ford Found., 1972-77, Phillips Exeter Acad., 1975-77, Agnes Meyer Found., 1976-77, Conn. Coll., 1976-77; mem. Carnegie Council on Children, 1972-77. Mem. ABA-Ctrl. and Ea. European Law Inst. (exec. bd. 1994-99, bd. editors ABA Jour. 1978-86), Am. Law Inst. (coun. 1979—, exec. com. 1985-99, 2d v.p. 1988-93, 1st v.p. 1993-98), Am. Acad. Arts and Scis., Phi Beta Kappa. Office: ICTY 1 Churchilliplain 2517 JW The Hague The Netherlands

WALDECK, JOHN WALTER, JR. lawyer; b. Cleve., May 3, 1949; s. John Walter Sr. and Marjorie Ruth (Palenschat) W.; m. Cheryl Gene Cutter, Sept. 10, 1977; children: John III, Matthew, Rebecca. BS, John Carroll U., 1973; JD, Cleve. State U., 1977. Bar: Ohio 1977. Product applications chemist Synthetic Products Co., Cleve., 1969-76; assoc. Arter & Hadden, 1977-85, ptnr., 1986-88, Porter, Wright, Morris and Arthur, Cleve., 1988-90, ptnr. in charge, 1990-96; ptnr. Walter & Haverfield, 1996—. Bd. advisors Litigation Mgmt., Inc., 2000—. Chmn. Bainbridge Twp. Bd. Zoning Appeals, Chagrin Falls, Ohio, 1984-94; trustee Greater Cleve. chpt. Lupus Found. Am., 1978-91, sec., 1979-86; trustee LeBlond Housing Corp., Cleve., 1990-96, sec., 1996, Univ. Circle, Inc., 1993-97, Fairmount Ctr. for Performing and Fine Arts, Novelty, Ohio, 1993-96, sect., 1994-95; bd. dirs. Geauga County Mental Health Alcohol and Drug Addiction Svc. Bd., Chardon, Ohio, 1988-97, treas., 1991-93, vice-chmn., 1993-95, chmn., 1995-97; mem. bd. advisors Palliative Care Svcs., Cleve. Clinic Cancer Ctr., 1989-91. Mem. Ohio State Bar Assn. (real property sect. bd. govs. 1992), Greater Cleve. Bar Assn. (real property, corp. banking sect, co-chair real estate law inst. 1990, 95, 96). Roman Catholic. Avocations: beekeeping, gardening, jogging. General corporate, Finance, Real property. Home: 18814 Rivers Edge Dr W Chagrin Falls OH 44023-4968 Office: Walter & Haverfield 50 Public Square 1300 Terminal Tower Cleveland OH 44113 E-mail: jwaldeck@walterhav.com

WALDMAN, BART, lawyer; b. Stamford, Conn., Oct. 24, 1948; s. Murry Robert and Beatrice Carol (Goldstein) W.; m. Nancy Vivian Smith, Jan. 1, 1981; children: Marcy Nicole, Tracy Michelle. AB, Harvard U., 1970; JD, Georgetown U., 1978. Bar: Wash. 1978. Spl. asst. to pres. Assn. of Am. Med. Colls., Washington, 1971-78; ptnr. Perkins Coie, Seattle, 1978—. Trustee Mcpl. League of King County, 1995-98; sec. Puget Sound Sr. Baseball League, 1996-99. Mem. ABA, Wash. Bar Assn., Seattle-King County Bar Assn., Sports Lawyers Assn. Health, Labor, Sports. Office: Perkins Coie 1201 3rd Ave Fl 4800 Seattle WA 98101-3029 E-mail: wald@perkinscoie.com

WALDMAN, DANIEL M. lawyer; JD Georgetown U., 1971. Bar: NJ. Ptnr. Waldman & Moriarty, Red Bank, NJ. Mem.: NJ Bar Assn. (pres. 2001—), Monmouth Bar Assn. (former pres.), Assn. County Bar Pres. General civil litigation, Family and matrimonial, Criminal. Office: 212 Maple Ave Red Bank NJ 07701*

WALDO, JAMES CHANDLER, lawyer; b. Seattle, Oct. 23, 1948; s. Burton Chandler and Margaret (Hoar) W.; m. Sharon B. Barber; children: Sara K., William K., John J. Grad., Whitman Coll., 1970; JD, Willamette U., 1974. Bar: Wash. 1974, U.S. Ct. Appeals (9th cir.) 1976. Exec. asst. Dept. of Labor, Washington, 1974-76; asst. U.S. atty. Justice Dept., Seattle, 1976-79; of counsel ESTEP & LI, 1979-80; prin. Gordon, Thomas, Honeywell, Malanca, Peterson & Daheim, P.L.L.C., 1981—. Chmn. N.W. Renewable Resources Ctr., Seattle, 1984-97, Wash. State Energy Strategy Com., 1991-93; spl. counsel on Water for Gov., 2001—. Trustee Western Wash. U., Bellingham, 1981-93. Recipient Outstanding Alumnus of Yr. Whitman Coll., 1994, Dir.'s award Wash. Dept. Fisheries, 1986, Pres.'s award Assn. Wash. Bus., 1988, Outstanding Citizen award Western Assn. Fish & Wildlife Agys., 1987. Republican. FERC practice, Environmental, Government contracts and claims. Office: Gordon Thomas Honeywell Malanca Peterson & Daheim PLLC PO Box 1157 Tacoma WA 98401-1157 Address: PO Box 1157 Tacoma WA 98401-1157

WALDRON, KENNETH LYNN, lawyer; b. Cape Girardeau, Mo., Oct. 18, 1941; s. Leonard Vernal and Edna Marion (Baskerville) W.; children: Leonard, Matthew, Charles. Student, Westminster Coll., 1959-61; BS, U. Mo., 1963, JD, 1966. Bar: Mo. 1966, U.S. Dist. Ct. (ea. dist.) Mo. 1968, U.S. Ct. Appeals (8th cir.) 1971, U.S. Supreme Ct. 1975. Salesman Nat. Biscuit Co., various locations, 1963-66; assoc. Buerkle & Lowes, Jackson, Mo., 1966-71; ptnr. Waldron & Assocs., 1971-91. Pres., CEO Eagle Environ. Products, Inc.; pres. Quail Springs Farm and Kennels, Inc., Stonewall Enterprises, Inc. Served to capt. U.S. Army, 1966-68. Decorated 2 Legions of Merit; named one of Outstanding Young Men in Am., 1972, 74, 76. Mem. Mo. Bar Assn., Assn. Trial Lawyers Am., Mo. Assn. Trial Attys., Am. Soc. Law and Medicine, Nat. Inst. Mcpl. Law Officers, Jackson Jaycees (Mo. legal counsel 1972-74, disting. service award 1968, 74), Am. Legion, Rotary. Republican. Baptist. Avocations: tennis, golf, hunting, bird dog field trials, music (vocal & guitar), songwriting. General civil litigation, Personal injury. Home: PO Box 270 Jackson MO 63755-0270 Office: Waldron & Assocs PO Box 270 Jackson MO 63755-0270

WALES, GWYNNE HUNTINGTON, lawyer; b. Evanston, Ill., Apr. 18, 1933; s. Robert Willett and Solace (Huntington) W.; m. Janet McCobb, Feb. 8, 1957; children— Thomas Gwynne, Catherine Anne, Louise Carrie. A.B., Princeton U., 1954; J.D., Harvard U., 1961. Bar: N.Y. 1962. Assoc. White & Case, N.Y.C., 1961-69, ptnr., 1969-2000, resident ptnr., 1969-75, Ankara, Turkey, 1998-2000. Served with USN, 1954-58. Mem. ABA, N.Y. State Bar Assn., Am. Law Inst., Union Internat. des Avocats Club: Round Hill (Greenwich, Conn.). Private international, Corporate taxation, Personal income taxation. Home: 93 Mountain Lake Lake Wales FL 33853

WALES, ROSS ELLIOT, lawyer; b. Youngstown, Ohio, Oct. 17, 1947; s. Craig C. and Beverly (Bromley) W.; m. Juliana Fraser, Sept. 16, 1972; children: Dod Elliot, James Craig. AB, Princeton U., 1969; JD, U. Va., 1974. Bar: Ohio 1974, U.S. Dist. Ct. (so. dist.) Ohio 1974, U.S. Ct. Appeals (5th cir.) 1979. Assoc. Taft, Stettinius & Hollister, Cin., 1974-81, ptnr., 1981—. Pres. U.S. Swimming, Inc., Colorado Springs, 1979-84, U.S. Aquatic Sports, Inc., Colorado Springs, 1984-88, 94-98. Pres. Cin. Active to Support Edn., 1987-88; chmn. sch. tax levy campaign, Cin., 1987; trustee The Childrens Home Cin., 1987—, v.p., 1995-98, pres., 1998—; bd. sec. Cin. State Tech. and C.C., 1995-98, vice-chmn., 1998-2000, chair 2000—; pres. Cin. Arts Sch., Inc., 2000-01; sec. Greater Cin. Arts and Edn. Ctr., 1996—; mem. U.S. Anti-Doping Agy., Colo. Springs. Mem. ABA, Ohio Bar Assn., Cin. Bar Assn., Internat. Swimming Fedn. of Lausanne, Switzerland (sec. 1988-92, v.p. 1992-2000). Presbyterian. General corporate, Health, Private international. Office: 1800 Firstar Twr 425 Walnut St Cincinnati OH 45202-3923 E-mail: wales@taftlaw.com

WALINSKY, ADAM, lawyer, foundation administrator; b. N.Y.C., Jan. 10, 1937; s. Louis J. Wilinsky and Michele (Benson) Walinsky Wilt; m. Jane L. Rosenhirsch, Aug. 25, 1961; children: Peter, Cara. AB, Cornell U., 1957; LLB, Yale U., 1961. Bar: N.Y. 1962, U.S. Dist. Ct. (so. dist.) N.Y. 1971, U.S. Ct. Appeals (2d cir.)1971, U.S. Supreme Ct. 1982. Law clk. U.S. Ct. Appeals for 2d Circuit, N.Y.C., 1961-62; assoc. Winthrop, Stimson, Putnam & Roberts, 1962-63; atty. Dept. Justice, Washington, 1963-64; legis. asst. to Senator Robert F. Kennedy, 1964-68; ptnr. Kronish, Lieb, Weiner & Hellman, N.Y.C., 1971-94; pres. Ctr. for Rsch. on Instns. and Social Policy, 1994—. Chmn. N.Y. State Commn. of Investigation, 1978-81. Author: The New Police Corps, 1982; mem. Yale Law Jour., 1960-61; contbr. articles to profl. publs. Trustee Robert Kennedy Meml., 1969—; chmn. Nat. Com. for the Police Corps. With USMCR, 1958. Ford Found. fellow, 1968. Mem. Assn. Bar of the City of N.Y. Democrat. Jewish. Federal civil litigation, State civil litigation, General practice. Office: 1114 Avenue Of The Americas New York NY 10036-7703

WALKER, BETTY STEVENS, lawyer; b. N.Y.C., Feb. 3, 1943; d. Randolph Blakney and Anne (Stevens) Wood; m. Paul Thomas Walker, Aug. 27, 1942; children: Camarf, Tarik, Kumi. BA in Polit. Sci. and History, Spelman Coll., 1964; JD, Harvard U., 1967. Bar: U.S. Dist. Ct. (DC) 1981, U.S. Ct. Appeals (DC cir.) 1977, U.S. Supreme Ct. 1996. Coord. southern schs. Legal Def. and Ednl. Fund, N.Y.C., 1964; asst. prof. polit. sci. Shaw U., Raleigh, N.C., 1968-69, faculty fellow, 1969-70; corp. atty. Southern Railway Co., Washington, 1974-77; exec. asst. to adminstr. Farmers Home Adminstrn. USDA, 1977-81; assoc. Walker & Walker Assoc., P.C., 1981—. Democrat. Mem. African Meth. Ch. Personal injury. Office: Walker & Walker Assoc PC 2807 18th St NW Washington DC 20009-2205

WALKER, CLARENCE WESLEY, lawyer; b. Durham, N.C., July 19, 1931; s. Ernie Franklin and Mollie Elizabeth (Cole) W.; m. Ann-Heath Harris, June 5, 1954; children: Clare Ann, Wesley Gregg. A.B., Duke U., 1953, LL.B., 1955. Bar: N.C. 1955. Assoc. Mudge Stern Baldwin & Todd, 1955-59; ptnr. Kennedy, Covington, Loddell & Hickman, Charlotte, N.C., 1961—. Bd. dirs. Lawyers Mut. Liability Ins. Co., Legal Services Corp. N.C., Oakwood Homes Corp. Glendale Group, Ltd.; lectr. N.C. Bar Found. Continuing Legal Edn. Insts., N.C. Jud. Planning Com., 1978-79; pres. Pvt. Adjudication Found. Chmn. bd. mgrs. Charlotte Meml. Hosp. and Med. Ctr., 1981-87; trustee N.C. Ctrl. U., 1979-83; vice-chmn. Charlotte-Mecklenburg Hosp. Authority, 1988-99; adv. bd. Ctrl. Piedmont Paralegal Sch.; trustee Carolinas Healthcare Found., Charlotte Country Day Sch., 1977-81; state chmn. Nat. Found. March of Dimes, 1968-70; chmn. Charlotte Park and Recreation Commn., 1970-73; bd. dirs. Charlotte Symphony, 1965-71, Bethlehem Ctr., 1975-77, N.C. Recreators Found., 1973-75; adv. bd. Charlotte Children's Theatre, 1972; bd. dirs. Charlotte C. of C., 1970-72; bd. visitors Duke U. Law Sch.; dir., gen. campaign chmn. United Way Ctrl. Carolinas, 1985. Fellow Am. Bar Found.; mem. N.C. Bar Assn. (pres. 1978-79, gov. 1971-75), ABA (state del. 1980-89, assembly del., bd. govs. 1997-2000, chair audit com., 2000—) 26th Jud. Dist. Bar Assn., Mecklenburg Bar Found. (trustee), Am. Law Inst., Order of Coif, Phi Eta Sigma, Phi Beta Kappa. Democrat. Methodist. General corporate, Public utilities, Securities. Home: 1047 Ardsley Rd Charlotte NC 28207-1815 Office: Kennedy Covington Lobdell & Hickman Bank of Am Corp Ctr 100 N Tryon St Ste 4200 Charlotte NC 28202-4006

WALKER, CRAIG MICHAEL, lawyer; b. Vt., 1947; m. Patricia A. Magruder; two children. BA, Williams Coll., 1969; JD, Cornell U., 1972. Bar: N.Y. 1973, U.S. Dist. Ct. (so. dist.) N.Y. 1975, U.S. Ct. Appeals (2d cir) 1975, U.S. Supreme Ct 1976. Assoc. Alexander & Green, N.Y.C., 1972-80, ptnr., 1980-86, chmn. litigation dept., 1985-86; ptnr. Walter, Conston, Alexander & Green P.C., 1987-89, Rogers & Wells LLP, N.Y.C., 1990-99, Clifford Chance Rogers & Wells LLP, N.Y.C., 2000—. Contbr. author: New York Forms of Jury Instruction, 1992; contbr. articles to profl. jours. Fellow Am. Bar Found.; mem. ABA, N.Y. State Bar Assn., Def. Rsch. Inst., Fed. Bar Coun. Democrat. Antitrust, Securities, Technology.

WALKER, DANIEL, JR. lawyer; b. Chgo., Jan. 29, 1949; s. Daniel and Roberta Marie (Dowse) W.; m. Loretta Graffort, May 27, 1979; children: Krista D., Daniel P. B.A., Santa Clara U., 1971; J.D., Northwestern U., 1974. Bar: Ill. 1974, U.S. Dist. Ct. (no. dist.) Ill. 1974, U.S. Dist. Ct. (7th cir.). Assoc. Arvey, Hodes, Costello & Burman, Chgo., 1974-77; ptnr. Dan Walker Law Offices, Oak Brook, Ill., 1977-87, Doyle, Ryan & Brustin, Chgo., 1987-88; ptnr. Dan Walker & Assoc., Hinsdale, Ill., 1988-89; Cesario & Walker, 1989—. Bd. dirs. Midwest Epilepsy Assn., 1980-82; precinct committeeman Democratic Party, DuPage County, Ill., 1978-83. Roman Catholic. Family and matrimonial, General practice, Personal injury. Home: 701 Mulberry Ct Naperville IL 60540-6335 Office: Cesario & Walker 211 W Chicago Ave Apt 118 Hinsdale IL 60521-3357

WALKER, FRANCIS JOSEPH, lawyer; b. Aug. 5, 1922; s. John McSweeney and Sarah Veronica (Meechan) W.; m. Julia Corinne O'Brien, Jan. 27, 1951; children: Vincent Paul, Monica Irene Hylton, Jill Marie Nudell, John Michael, Michael Joseph, Thomas More. BA, St. Martin's Coll., 1947; JD, U. Wash., 1950. Bar: Wash. Asst. atty. gen. State of Wash., 1950-51; pvt. practice Olympia, Wash., 1951—. Gen. counsel Wash. Cath. Conf., 1967-76. Lt. (j.g.) USNR, 1943-46; PTO. Consumer commercial, Probate, Estate taxation. Home and Office: 2723 Hillside Dr SE Olympia WA 98501-3460 E-mail: FJWalker@QWest.net

WALKER, GEORGE KONTZ, law educator; b. Tuscaloosa, Ala., July 8, 1938; s. Joseph Henry and Catherine Louise (Indorf) W.; m. Phyllis Ann Sherman, July 30, 1966; children: Charles Edward, Mary Neel. BA, U. Ala., 1959; LLB, Vanderbilt U., 1966; AM, Duke U., 1968; LLM, U. Va., 1972; postgrad. (Sterling fellow), Law Sch. Yale U., 1975-76. Bar: Va. 1967, N.C. 1976. Law clk. U.S. Dist. Ct., Richmond, Va., 1966-67; assoc. Hunton, Williams, Gay, Powell & Gibson, 1967-70; pvt. practice Charlottesville, Va., 1970-71; asst. prof. Law Sch. Wake Forest U., Winston-Salem, N.C., 1972-73, assoc. prof. Law Sch., 1974-77, prof. Law Sch., 1977—, mem. bd. advisors Divinity Sch., 1991-94; Charles H. Stockton prof. internat. law U.S. Naval War Coll., 1992-93. Vis. prof. Marshall-Wythe Sch. Law, Coll. William and Mary, Williamsburg, Va., 1979-80, U. Ala. Law Sch., 1985; cons. Naval War Coll., 1976—, Nat. Def. Exec. Res., 1991—, Naval War Coll., Operational Law Adv. Bd., 1993—. Author: The Tanker War, 1980-88, 2000; contbr. articles to profl. jours. With USN, 1959-62, capt. USNR, ret. Woodrow Wilson fellow, 1962-63; recipient Joseph Branch Alumni Svc. award, Wake Forest, 1988; named Hon. Atty. Gen. N.C., 1986. Mem.: ABA, Va. Bar Assn., N.C. Bar Assn. (v.p. 1997—98), Am. Soc. Internat. Law (exec. coun. 1988—91), Internat. Law Assn., Am. Judicature Soc., Am. Law Inst., Maritime Law Assn., Order of Barristers (hon.)), Piedmont Club, Order of the Coif (hon.)), Phi Beta Kappa, Sigma Alpha Epsilon, Phi Delta Phi. Democrat. Episcopalian. Home: 3321 Pennington Ln Winston Salem NC 27106-5439 Office: Wake Forest U Sch Law PO Box 7206 Winston Salem NC 27109-7206

WALKER, GEORGE WILLIAM, lawyer; b. Boston, Apr. 22, 1929; s. George William and Mary A. (Moran) W.; divorced; children— Sylvie T., Kathryn L. Student U. N.H., 1951; LL.B. cum laude, Boston U., 1954. Bar: N.H. 1954, Mass. 1954, U.S. Ct. Mil. Appeals 1955, U.S. Supreme Ct. 1960. Sole practice, Wolfeboro, N.H., 1959-60; ptnr. Cooper, Hall & Walker, Wolfeboro, 1961-81, Walker & Varney, Wolfeboro, 1982— ; prosecutor Carroll County (N.H.), 1967-69; judge Wolfeboro Dist. Ct., 1973— ; mem. N.H. Jud. Council, 1971-86 , chmn., 1984; chmn. bd., dir. Kingswood Trust & Savs. Bank, Wolfeboro, 1973-84. Moderator Gov. Wentworth Regional Sch. Dist., Wolfeboro; trustee Huggins Hosp., Wolfeboro. With USAR, 1955-59; capt. JAGC. Mem. N.H. Trial Lawyers Assn. (pres. 1979), ABA, N.H. Bar Assn. (pres. county chpt. 1960), N.H. Judges Assn., Am. Judicature Soc. Republican. Personal injury, Probate, Real property. Office: Walker & Varney 12 N Main St Wolfeboro NH 03894-4309

WALKER, IRVING EDWARD, lawyer; b. Balt., Jan. 31, 1952; s. Bertram and Mildred (Shapiro) W.; children: Brandon Harris, Aaron Seth, Emily Celeste. BA, Duke U., 1973; JD, U. Md., 1978. Bar: Md. 1978, U.S. Dist. Ct. Md. 1978, U.S. Ct. Appeals (4th cir.) 1980, U.S. Supreme Ct. 1995, U.S. Ct. Appeals (3d cir.) 2001. Assoc. Frank, Bernstein, Conaway & Goldman, Balt., 1978-85, ptnr., 1986-91; prin. Miles & Stockbridge, 1991-2001; spl. counsel Saul Ewing LLP, 2001—. Chair Bankruptcy & Creditors Rights Group, 1991-2000. Contbg. author: Bankruptcy Deskbook, 1986. Bd. dirs. Jewish Community Ctr. Greater Balt., 1986-88, Temple Emanuel of Balt., Inc., 1996—. Mem. ABA, Md. Bar Assn., Bar Assn. Balt. City (chmn. bankruptcy and bus. law com. 1989-90), Am. Bankruptcy Inst., Bankruptcy Assn. Dist. Md. (pres. 1992-93, chmn. Balt. chpt. 1989-91), Order of Coif. Avocations: soccer, weightlifting. Bankruptcy, Federal civil litigation. Office: Saul Ewing LLP 100 S Charles St 15th Fl Baltimore MD 21201 E-mail: iwalker@saul.com

WALKER, JOHN LOCKWOOD, lawyer; b. Atlanta, Sept. 3, 1952; s. James William and Doris (Camp) W.; m. Caroline Asher Walker, Jan. 16, 1952; children: Ann Caroline, John Lockwood Jr., Elizabeth Davis, Lindsay Eleise. BA, Duke U., 1974, JD, 1977. Atty. legal div. bd. govs. FRS, Washington, 1977-79; assoc. Simpson Thacher & Bartlett, N.Y.C., 1979-84; ptnr. Simpson, Thacher & Bartlett, 1984—. Mem. Fin. Svcs. Vol. Corps (dir., pres.), Coun. on Fgn. Rels., Met. Club of Washington, Univ. Club (N.Y.C.), Chevy Chase (Md.) Club, Bedford (N.Y.) Golf and Tennis Club. Democrat. Episcopalian. Banking, Finance, Securities. Office: Simpson Thacher & Bartlett 425 Lexington Ave Fl 11 New York NY 10017-3954 E-mail: J-Walker@stblaw.com

WALKER, JOHN MERCER, JR. federal judge; b. N.Y.C., Dec. 26, 1940; s. John Mercer and Louise (Mead) W.; m. Cristy West, June 20, 1980 (div. Apr. 1983); m. Katharine Kirkland, Feb. 14, 1987. BA, Yale U., 1962; JD, U. Mich., 1966. Bar: N.Y. 1969, U.S. Dist. Ct. (so. dist.) N.Y. 1971, U.S. Ct. Appeals (2d cir.) 1972, U.S. Supreme Ct. 1977, U.S. Ct. Appeals (D.C. cir.) 1982. Maxwell Sch. Pub. Adminstrn. fellow, state counsel Republic of Botswana, Africa, 1966-68; assoc. Davis, Polk and Warwell, N.Y.C., 1969-70; asst. U.S. atty. U.S. Dist. Ct. (so. dist.) N.Y., 1971-75; assoc. to ptnr. Carter, Ledyard and Milburn, 1975-81; asst. sec. enforcement ops. Dept. Treasury, Washington, 1981-85; judge U.S. Dist. Ct. (so. dist.) N.Y., 1985-89, U.S. Ct. Appeals (2nd cir.), 1989—, chief judge, 2000—. Adj. prof. NYU Law Sch., 1995—; gen. counsel Nat. Coun. on Crime and Deliquency, N.Y.C., 1977-81; chmn. Fed. Law Enforcement Tng. Ctr., Washington, 1981-85; spl. counsel Adminstrv. Conf. U.S., Washington, 1986-92; mem. budget com. jud. conf. Inst. Jud. Adminstrn., 1992—, dir., 1992—. Del. Rep. Nat. Conv., Detroit, 1980. With USMCR, 1963-67. Recipient Alexander Hamilton award Sec. of Treas., Washington, 1985, Secret Service Honor award, 1985. Mem. ABA, D.C. Bar Assn., Assn. Bar City of N.Y., Fed. Judges Assn. (pres. 1993-95). Republican. Episcopalian. Office: US Cir Ct 157 Church St New Haven CT 06510-2100*

WALKER, JOHN SUMPTER , JR. lawyer; b. Richmond, Ark., Oct. 13, 1921; s. John Sumpter and Martha (Wilson) W.; m. Eljana M. duVall, Dec. 31, 1947; children: John Stephen, Barbara Monika Ann, Peter Mark Gregory. BA , Tulane U., 1942; MS, U. Denver, 1952, JD, 1960; diploma, Nat. Def. U., 1981. Bar: Colo. 1960, U.S. Dist. Ct. Colo. 1960, U.S. Supreme Ct. 1968, U.S. Ct. Appeals (10th cir.) 1960, U.S. Tax Ct. 1981. With Denver & Rio Grande Western R.R. Co., 1951-61, gen. solicitor, 1961-89; pres. Denver Union Terminal Rlwy. Co. Apptd. gen. counsel Moffat Tunnel Commn., 1991; life mem. Children's Diabetes Fund. With U.S. Army, 1942-46. Decorated Bronze Star. Mem.: Colo. Bar Assn., Arapahoe County Bar Assn., Alliance Francaise (life)), Order of St. Ives, U. Denver Chancellor's Soc., Cath. Lawyers Guild. Republican. Roman Catholic. General corporate.

WALKER, JONATHAN LEE, lawyer; b. Kalamazoo, Mar. 8, 1948; s. Harvey E. and Olivia M. (Estrada) W. BA, U. Mich., 1969; JD, Wayne State U., 1977. Bar: Mich. 1977, U.S. Dist. Ct. (we. dist.) Mich. 1989, U.S. Dist. Ct. (no. dist.) Ill. 1991, U.S. Dist. Ct. (ea. dist.) Mich. 1983, Colo. 1996, U.S. Dist. Ct. Colo. 1996, U.S. Ct. Appeals (10th cir.) 1996. Assoc. Moore, Barr & Kerwin, Detroit, 1977-79; ptnr. firm Barr & Walker, 1979-82; assoc. firm Richard M. Goodman, P.C., 1983-87; hearing officer Mich. Civil Rights Commn., 1983-86; pvt. practice, 1988-89, Birmingham, Mich., 1990-98; dep. pub. defender Office of State Pub. Defender, Colorado Springs, Colo., 1998—. Participant Detroit Bar Assn. Vol. Lawyer Program. Bd. dirs. Cmty. treatment Ctr.-Project Rehab., Detroit, 1983-89; mem. scholarship com. Latino en Marcha Scholarship Fund, Detroit, 1984; treas. youth assistance program Citizens Adv. Coun., 1987; bd. mem. State Domestic Violence Offenders' Mgmt. Bd., 2001—. Mem. ATLA, State Bar Mich. Found., Wayne County Mediation Tribunal (mediator), Am. Arbitration Assn. (arbitrator), Nat. Lawyers Guild (exec. bd. Detroit chpt. 1988-92, pres. Detroit chpt. 1988-90), Mich. Trial Lawyers Assn. (co-chair coalition com. 1988-90, exec. bd. 1988-96, co-chair pro bono com. 1991-96), State Bar Mich. (com. on underrepresented groups in law 1980-92, chmn. 1983-85, mem. com. jud. qualifications 1985-86, Latin Am. affairs coun. 1978-96), Colo. Criminal Def. Bar, Legal Aid and Def. Assn. (bd. dirs. 1990-95), Hispanic Bar Assn., Trial Lawyers for Pub. Justice (founder 1981, mem. amicus com. 1985-86, state capt. 1991-95), Ctr. for Auto Safety, Washtenaw County Bar Assn. Criminal. Office: 25 N Cascade Ave Ste 400 Colorado Springs CO 80903-1642 E-mail: jonathan.walker@state.co.us

WALKER, JORDAN CLYDE, SR. lawyer, real estate executive; b. Clearfield, Utah, July 18, 1927; s. Clarence Clyde and Verlina June (Jordan) W.; m. Viola Dale Stoner, Mar. 15, 1947 (div. Nov. 1964); children: Jordan Clyde Jr., Pamela Jean, Olivia June, Aaron Kim (dec.); m. Maxine M. Armstrong, Aug. 4, 1967; children: Karen Joann, Mark Allen, Leslie Susan. JD, McGeorge Sch. Law, Sacramento, 1975. Bar: Calif. 1976. Mgr. sales Gen. Foods Corp., Sacramento, 1949-58; sales rep. Smith-Klein & French, Sacramento, 1959-63; ind. real estate salesman and developer, Sacramento, 1963-75; ptnr. Walker & Crawford, Sacramento, 1976—; owner, mgr. Walker & Assocs., Sacramento, 1979—; v.p., sec. Jordan Devel. Co., Inc., Sacramento, 1975—. Rep. fundraiser, Sacramento, 1980-87. Served with USN, 1945-46, PTO. Mem. Phi Alpha Delta. Mormon. Club: Sutter (Sacramento). Avocations: fly fishing, horseback riding, duck hunting. Construction, Landlord-tenant, Real property.

WALKER, PAUL HOWARD, lawyer; b. Baldwyn, Miss., Feb. 10, 1923; s. Howard Earl and Frances Caroline (McElroy) W.; m. Gwendolyn Yvonne Loomis, June 17, 1950; children: Michael D., Melinda K. Student, E. Miss. Jr. Coll., 1940-41, La. State U., 1941-43, U. Mo., 1943-44; JD with honors, George Washington U., 1948; BA, George Washington U, 2000; LL.M., George Washington U., 1949; postgrad., Harvard U., 1975-82. Bar: D.C. 1948, Md. 1959, Mass. 1969. Atty.-editor U.S. Tax Ct., Washington, 1950-53; asst. gen. counsel Life Ins. Assn. Am. (now Am. Coun. of Life Ins.), 1953-68; tax counsel New Eng. Mut. Life Ins. Co., Boston, 1968-86. Mem. tax policy adv. bd. Taxation with Representation Fund, Washington, 1975; adv. coun. Hartford Inst. on Ins. Taxation, Conn., 1981-83.$D Contbr. articles to profl. jours.; mem. adv. bd. Estate Planning Mag., 1973-86, Compensation Planning Jour., 1973-86. Trustee New Eng. Coll., Henniker, N.H., 1978-90, trustee emeritus, 1990-2000; chancellor New Eng. Diocese Anglican Ch. in Am., 1981—. Served with AUS, 1943-45; to capt. USAFR, 1951-63. Decrated Silver Star. Mem. ABA, SAR (pres. Mass. Soc. 1981-83, nat. trustee 1983-85, chancellor gen. 1986-88, pres. gen. 1992-93), Soc. of the War of 1812 in Mass. (state pres. 1996-97), Hon. Order of Ky. Cols., Sons of Confederate Vets., Knights Templar (comdr. Boston Commandery No. 2 1997-98, named Knight Comdr. of Temple of Grand Encampment 1997), Masons. Republican. Pension, profit-sharing, and employee benefits, Corporate taxation, Estate taxation. Home and Office: 85A Seminary Ave Apt 347 Newton MA 02466-2648 E-mail: pwalker@lasell.edu

WALKER, RICHARD HENRY, lawyer; b. Wilmington, Del., Dec. 29, 1950; s. Henry H. and Mary L. (Meister) W. BA, Trinity Coll., 1972; JD, Temple U., 1975. Bar: Pa. 1976, U.S. Supreme Ct. 1977, N.Y. 1978, D.C. 1981. Law clk. to Hon. Collins J. Seitz U.S. Ct. Appeals (3rd cir.), Wilmington, Del., 1975-76; assoc., ptnr. Cadwalader, Wickersham & Taft, N.Y.C., 1976-91; regional dir. N.E. office U.S. SEC, 1991-95, gen. counsel Washington, 1996-98, dir. enforcement, 1998—. Fellow Am. Bar Found. Office: SEC 450 5th St NW Rm 8213 Washington DC 20549-0001

WALKER, ROSS PAUL, lawyer; b. Chgo., Sept. 10, 1934; s. Ross Carl and Lucille Marie (Hock) W.; m. Elisabeth Charlotte Stein, Dec. 21, 1961. A.B., Earlham Coll., 1957; J.D., U. Chgo., 1960. Bar: Ind. 1960, U.S. Dist. Ct. (so. dist.) Ind. 1962, U.S. Dist. Ct. (no. dist.) Ind. 1972, U.S. Ct. Appeals (7th cir.) 1972. Practice law, Indpls., 1962— ; ptnr. firm Walker & Grills (formerly Dewester, Hall & Walker) since 1963— ; referee juvenile div. Superior Ct. Marion County, Indpls., 1964— . Served with U.S. Army, 1960-62. Mem. Ind. Bar Assn. (chmn. labor law sect. 1980-81). Republican. Roman Catholic. Juvenile, Labor, Workers' compensation. Home: 10115 Indian Lake Dr Indianapolis IN 46236 Office: Walker & Grills 315 Circle Towers Bldg Indianapolis IN 46204

WALKER, SHONN WAYNE, lawyer; b. Decatur, Ala., Feb. 25, 1969; s. Howard Wayne Walker and Janna Wyronne Craft; m. Brandi Michelle Myers, Oct. 9, 1998; 1 child, Shonn Wayne, Jr. BS, U. Ala., 1991; JD, Birmingham Sch. of Law, 1997. Bar: Ala., 1997. Law clk. to presiding justice, Birmingham, Ala., 1991-94; asst. commr. of agr. State of Ala., Montgomery, 1994; campaign coord. Bob Riley for Congress, Ashland, Ala., 1996; candidate for Ala. legis. Dist. 11 Ho., Cullman and Morgan County, 1998; lawyer, pvt. practice Cullman, 1997—. Presiding justice BPOE, Cullman, 1998—; asst. commr. of agr. State of Ala., 1993. Mem. ABA, ATLA, others. Democrat. Avocations: basketball, paint ball, running, walking, cards.

WALKER, TIMOTHY BLAKE, lawyer, educator; b. Utica, N.Y., May 21, 1940; s. Harold Blake and Mary Alice (Corder) W.; m. Sandra Blake; children: Kimberlee Corder, Tyler Blake, Kelley Loren. AB magna cum laude, Princeton U., 1962; JD magna cum laude, U. Denver, 1967, MA in Sociology, 1969. Bar: Colo. 1968, Calif. 1969, Ind. 1971. Asst. prof. law U. Pacific, 1968-69; vis. assoc. prof. U. Toledo, 1969-70; assoc. prof. Indpls. Law Sch., Ind. U., 1970-71, U. Denver, 1971-75, prof., 1975-99; prof. emeritus, 1999—; dir. adminstrn. of justice program U. Denver, 1971-78; pvt. practice Denver, 1972-79; of counsel Robert T. Hinds, Jr. & Assocs. PC, Littleton, Colo., 1980-85; ptnr., of counsel Cox, Mustain-Wood, Walker & Schumacher, 1985—. Cons., lectr. in field; rsch. on lay representation in adminstrv. agys., Colo., 1975-76. Contbr. articles to profl. jours.; editor: Denver Law Jour., 1966-67; editor-in-chief: Family Law Quar., 1983-92. Mem. Ind. Child Support Commn., 1970-71; pres. Shawnee (Colo.) Water Consumers Assn., 1975-84, 93-95; del. Colo. Rep. Conv., 1978. Colo. Bar Assn. grant, 1975-76. Fellow: Am. Sociol. Assn., Am. Acad. Matrimonial Lawyers, Internat. Acad. Matrimonial Lawyers, Am. Bar Found.; mem.: ABA (vice chmn. child custody subcom., sec. Family Law sect. 1992—93, vice chmn., sec. 1993—94, chmn. elect family law sect. 1994—95, chmn. 1995—96, chmn. child custody task force 2000—, alimony, maintenance and support com. 2000—, family sect. del. ho. of dels. 2000—), Calif. Bar Assn., Colo. Bar Assn., Ind. Bar Assn., Colo Trial Lawyers Assn. Presbyterian. Home: 7329 Rochester Ct Castle Rock CO 80104-9281 Office: 1900 Olive St Denver CO 80220-1857 also: 6601 S University Blvd Littleton CO 80121-2913

WALKER, VAUGHN R. federal judge; b. Watseka, Ill., Feb. 27, 1944; s. Vaughn Rosenworth and Catharine (Miles) W. AB, U. Mich., 1966; JD, Stanford U., 1970. Intern economist SEC, Washington, 1966, 68; law clk. to the Hon. Robert J. Kelleher U.S. Dist. Ct. Calif., L.A., 1971-72; assoc. atty. Pillsbury Madison & Sutro, San Francisco, 1972-77, ptnr., 1978-90; judge U.S. Dist. Ct. (no. dist.) Calif., 1990—. Mem. Calif. Law Revision Commn., Palo Alto, 1986-89; bd. advisors Law and Econs. Ctr., George Mason U., 1999—. Dir. Jr. Achievement of Bay Area, San Francisco, 1979-83, St. Francis Found., San Francisco, 1991-97, 98—. Woodrow Wilson Found. fellow U. Calif., Berkeley, 1966-67. Fellow Am. Bar Found.; mem. ABA (jud. rep., antitrust sect. 1991-95), Lawyers' Club of San Francisco (pres. 1985-86), Assn. Bus. Trial Lawyers (dir. 1996-98), Am. Law Inst., Am. Saddlebred Horse Assn., San Francisco Mus. Modern Art, Bohemian Club, Olympic Club, Pacific-Union Club. Office: US Dist Ct 450 Golden Gate Ave San Francisco CA 94102-3482

WALKER, WALTER HERBERT, III, lawyer, writer; b. Quincy, Mass., Sept. 12, 1949; s. Walter H. Jr. and Irene M. (Horn) W.; m. Anne M. DiScuillo, June 17, 1982; children: Brett Daniel, Jeffrey St. John. BA, U. Pa., 1971; JD, U. Calif., San Francisco, 1974. Bar: Calif. 1974, Mass. 1981. Appellate atty. ICC, Washington, 1975-77; trial atty. Handler, Baker, Greene & Taylor, San Francisco, 1977-80; ptnr. Sterns and Walker and predecessor firm Sterns, Smith, Walker & Grell, 1981-88; ptnr. firm Walker & Durham, 1988—. Author: A Dime to Dance By, 1983 (Best 1st Novel by Calif. Author), The Two Dude Defense, 1985, Rules of The Knife Fight, 1986, The Immediate Prospect of Being Hanged, 1989, The Appearance of Impropriety, 1992. Mem. ATLA, Consumer Attys. of Calif., San Francisco Trial Lawyers Assn., Mystery Writers Am. Democrat. Club: Hastings Rugby. Insurance, Personal injury, Product liability. Home: 604 Seminary Dr Mill Valley CA 94941-3169 Office: 50 Francisco St Ste 160 San Francisco CA 94133-2108

WALKER, WOODROW WILSON, retired lawyer, cattle and timber farmer; b. Greenville, Mich., Feb. 19, 1919; s. Craig Walker and Mildred Chase; m. Janet K. Keiter, Oct. 7, 1950; children: Jonathan Woodrow, William Craig, Elaine Virginia. BA, U. Mich., 1943; LLB, Cath. U., 1950. Bar: D.C. 1950, U.S. Supreme Ct. 1958, Va. 1959. Operator family farm, 1937-39; dir. Libr. of Congress Fed. Credit Union, 1957-60; atty. Am. law div. legis. reference Libr. Congress, Washington, 1951-60; pvt. practice, Arlington, Va., 1960-2000. Counsel Calvary Found., Arlington, 1970-85, first pres., 1972; judge moot ct. George Mason Law Sch., 1986; owner-operator Walker Farm Front Royal, Va., 1972—. Co-author rsch. publs. for U.S. Govt.; featured in Washington Post. V.p. Jefferson Civic Assn., Arlington, 1955-61; pres. Nellie Custis PTA, Arlington, 1960-61; sec. Arlington County Bd. Equalization Real Estate Assessment, 1962, chmn. 1963; com. chmn. Arlington Troop 108 Boy Scouts Am., 1964-69; mem. Arlington County Pub. Utilities Commn., 1964-66, vice chmn., 1965-66; pres. Betschler Class Adult Sunday Sch., Calvary United Meth. Ch., Arlington, 1965. Served with U.S. Army, 1943-45, PTO. Cited for notable deed in conduct of his legal duties Washington Post, 1996. Mem. ABA, Arlington County Bar Assn., Va. Farm Bur., Va. Cattleman's Assn. Methodist. Democrat. Consumer commercial, Contracts commercial, General practice. Home and Office: 2822 Ft Scott Dr Arlington VA 22202-2307

WALKOWIAK, VINCENT STEVEN, lawyer; b. Apr. 22, 1946; s. Vincent Albert and Elizabeth (Modla) W.; m. Linda Kae Schweigert, Aug., 1968; children: Jenifer, Steven. BA, U. Ill., 1968, JD, 1971. Bar: Ill. 1971, Tex. 1981, U.S. Ct. Appeals (8th cir.) 1971, (5th cir.) 1982, U.S. Dist. Ct. (ea., we., so., and no. dists.) Tex. 1982. Assoc. Dorsey, Marquart, Windhorst, West & Halladay, Mpls., 1971-74; ptnr. Fulbright & Jaworski LLP, Houston, 1982—. Prof. Fla. State U., Tallahassee, 1974-76, So. Meth. U., Dallas, 1976-84. Editor: Uniform Product Liability Act, 1980, Trial of a Product Liability Case, vol. 1, 1981, vol. 2, 1982, Preparation and Presentation of Product Liability, 1983, Attorney Client Privilege in Civil Litigation, 1997. Federal civil litigation, State civil litigation, Product liability. Office: Fulbright & Jaworski LLP 2200 Ross Ave Ste 2800 Dallas TX 75201-2784 E-mail: vwalkowiak@fulbright.com

WALKUP, CHARLOTTE LLOYD, lawyer; b. N.Y.C., Apr. 28, 1910; d. Charles Henry and Helene Louise (Wheeler) Tuttle; m. David D. Lloyd, Oct. 19, 1940 (dec. Dec. 1962); children: Andrew M. Lloyd, Louisa Lloyd Hurley; m. Homer Allen Walkup, Feb. 4, 1967. AB, Vassar Coll., 1931; LLB, Columbia U., 1934. Bar: N.Y. 1935, U.S. Supreme Ct. 1939, U.S. Dist. Ct. D.C. 1953, Va. 1954. Asst. solicitor Dept. Interior, Washington, 1934-45; asst. gen. counsel UNRRA, Washington and London, 1945-48; assoc. and cons. firms Washington, 1953, 55, 60; atty., spl. asst. Office Treasury, 1961-65, asst. gen. counsel, 1965-73. Cons. Rogers & Wells, Washington, 1975-86. Editor Columbia Law Rev., 1933-34. Pres. Alexandria Cmty. Welfare Coun., 1950-52; bd. dirs. Alexandria Coun. Human Rels., 1958-60, New Hope Found., 1977. Recipient Meritorious Svc. award Dept. Treasury, 1970, Exceptional Svc. award, 1973, Career Svc. award Nat. Civil Svc. League, 1973; named Hon. fellow Harry S. Truman Libr. Inst. Mem. Columbia U. Alumni Assn., Phi Beta Kappa. Democrat. Episcopalian. Home: 4800 Fillmore Ave Apt 1251 Alexandria VA 22311-5077 E-mail: walkup@home.com

WALL, CATHERINE WYNNE, lawyer; b. Rome, 1968; m. Bart D. Wall; 1 child, Julia Marie. BEE, U. Dayton, 1991; JD cum laude, St. Louis U., 1994. Bar: Mo., 1994, Ill. 1995, U.S. Patent Office 1996. Atty. Polster, Lieder, Woodruff and Lucchesi, L.C., St. Louis, 1992—. Sponsor Cath. Charities Refugee Svcs., St. Louis, 1998—. Mem. ABA (intellectual property sect.), IEEE, Bar Assn. of Met. St. Louis (patent, copyright and trademark sect., atty. lawyer referral and info. svc. 1998—), Ill. State Bar Assn., Mo. Bar Assn., Eta Kappa Nu. Office: Polster Lieder Woodruff & Lucchesi LC 763 S New Ballas Rd Ste 230 Saint Louis MO 63141-8704

WALL, DONALD ARTHUR, lawyer; b. Lafayette, Ind., Mar. 17, 1946; s. Dwight Arthur and Myra Virginia (Peavey) W.; m. Cheryn Lynn Heinen, Aug. 29, 1970; children: Sarah Lynn, Michael Donald. BA, Butler U., 1968; JD, Northwestern U., 1971. Bar: Ohio 1971, U.S. Dist. Ct. (no. dist.) Ohio 1973, U.S. Supreme Ct. 1980, Ariz. 1982, U.S. Dist. Ct. (no. dist.) W.Va. 1982, U.S. Ct. Appeals (6th cir.) 1982, U.S. Dist. Ct. Ariz. 1983, U.S. Ct. Appeals (9th and 10th cirs.) 1984, U.S. Ct. Appeals (5th cir.) 1988. Assoc. Squire, Sanders & Dempsey, Cleve., 1971-80, ptnr., 1980-82, Phoenix, 1983—. Spkr. at profl. meetings; program moderator. Contbr. articles to profl. jours. Trustee Ch. of the Saviour Day Ctr., Cleveland Heights, 1979-82; mem. adminstrv. bd. Ch. of Saviour, Cleveland Heights, 1980-83; fin. com. Paradise Valley (Ariz.) United Meth. Ch., 1986-87; bd. dirs., divsn. commr. North Scottsdale (Ariz.) Little League, 1983-92; bd. dirs. Epilepsy Found. N.E. Ohio, 1976-82, pres., 1981-82; bd. dirs. N.E. Cmty. Basketball Assn., 1993-99; bd. visitors U. Ariz. Law Sch., 1996—; bd. mgrs. Scottsdale-Paradise Valley YMCA, 1999—. Mem. ABA (torts and ins. practice and litigation sect., past chmn. r.r. law com., litigation sect.), Def. Rsch. Inst., Ariz. Bar Assn. (labor and trial practice sects.), Maricopa County Bar Assn., Ariz. Assn. Def. Counsel. Methodist. Federal civil litigation, State civil litigation, Labor. Office: Squire Sanders & Dempsey LLP 40 N Central Ave Ste 2700 Phoenix AZ 85004-4498 E-mail: dwall@ssd.com

WALL, KENNETH E., JR. lawyer; b. Beaumont, Tex., Apr. 6, 1944; s. Kenneth E. and W. Geraldine (Peoples) W.; m. Marjorie Lee Hughes, Dec. 21, 1968; children— Barbara, Elizabeth, Kenneth. Grad. Lamar U., 1966, U. Tex.-Austin, 1969. Bar: Tex. 1969, U.S. Supreme Ct. 1979. Asst. city atty., Beaumont, 1969-73, city atty., 1973-84; with firm Olson & Olson, Houston, 1984— ; dir. Tex. Mcpl. League Ins. Trust, 1979-84, vice chmn., 1983-84; counsel S.E. Tex. Regional Planning Commn., 1974, 76. Active Boy Scouts Am., Girl Scouts U.S.A. Mem. Nat. Inst. Mcpl. Law Officers (chmn. com. on local govt. pers. 1979-81, 82-84), State Bar Tex., Tex. City Attys. Assn. (pres. 1982-83), Jefferson County Bar Assn. (dir. 1975-77), Houston Bar Assn., Phi Delta Phi. Methodist. E-mail: kwall@olson.and-olson.com Land use and zoning (including planning), Municipal (including bonds), State and local taxation. Office: 333 Clay St Houston TX 77002-4000

WALL, ROBERT ANTHONY, JR. lawyer; b. Hartford, Conn., Mar. 3, 1945; s. Robert Anthony and Eileen (Fitzgerald) W.; children: Andrea, Melanie, Victoria, Robert, Natalie; m. Diana M. Wall. BA, Georgetown U., Washington, 1968; JD, Am. U., Washington, 1973. Bar: Conn. 1974, U.S. Ct. Appeals (D.C. cir.) 1974, U.S. Dist. Ct. Conn. 1974, U.S. Supreme Ct. 1977. Ptnr. Wall, Wall & Frauenhofer, Torrington, Conn., 1974-87; pvt. practice, 1987—. Mem. State of Conn. Rep. Ctrl. Com., 1976-79. Mem. Conn. Trial Lawyers Assn. (bd. govs. 1984-86), Ct. Washington #67 Foresters of Am. (trustee 1988—). Roman Catholic. Personal injury. Home: 55 Quail Run Torrington CT 06790-2550 Office: 8 Church St Torrington CT 06790-5247 Fax: 860-496-0128. E-mail: wallgawrych@yahoo.com

WALLACE, DON, JR. law educator; b. Vienna, Austria, Apr. 23, 1932; s. Don and Julie (Baer) W. (parents Am. citizens); m. Daphne Mary Wickham, 1963; children: Alexandra Jane, Sarah Anne, Benjamin James. B.A. with high honors, Yale U., 1953; LL.B. cum laude, Harvard U., 1957. Bar: N.Y. 1957, D.C. 1978. Assoc. Fleischmann, Jaeckle, Stokes and Hitchcock, N.Y.C., 1959-60, Paul, Weiss, Rifkind, Wharton and Garrison, N.Y.C., 1957-58, 60-62; rsch. asst. to faculty mem. Harvard Law Sch., Cambridge, Mass., 1958-59; regional legal adv. Middle East AID, Dept. State, 1963-65, dep. asst. gen. counsel, 1965-66; assoc. prof. law Georgetown U. Law Ctr., Washington, 1966-71, prof., 1971—; chmn. Internat. Law Inst., 1969—. Cons. AID, 1966-70, UN Centre on Transnat. Corps., 1977-78; counsel Wald, Harkrader & Ross, Washington, 1978-86, Arnold & Porter, 1986-89, Shearman & Sterling, 1989-98, Morgan, Lewis & Bockius, 1998—; legal advisor State of Qatar, 1979-82; chmn. adv. com. on tech. and world trade Office of Tech. Assessment, U.S. Congress, 1976-79; mem. Sec. of State's Adv. Com. on Pvt. Internat. Law, 1979—; mem. U.S. del. UN Conf. on State Succession in Respect of Treaties, Vienna, 1978; mem. U.S. del. new internat. econ. order working group UN Commn. Internat. Trade Law, Vienna, 1981—; vis. com. Harvar dLaw Sch., 1996—; mem. panel of judges World Trade Orgn., 1996-2000. Co-author: Internat. Business and Economics: Law and Policy; author: International Regulation of Multinational Corporations, 1976, Dear Mr. President: The Needed Turnaround in America's International Economic Affairs, 1984; editor: A Lawyer's Guide to International Business Transactions, 1977-87; contbr. numerous articles on internat. trade and law to profl. jours., books revs. on law and bus. to profl. jours. Coord. Anne Arundel County (Md.) Dem. Nat. Com., 1972-79; sec. Chesapeake Found., 1972-73; nat. chmn. Law Profs. for Bush and Quayle, 1988, 92, for Dole and Kemp, 1996; v.p., bd. govs. UNIDROIT Found., Rome, 1997—.$Dat. co-chmn. Law Profs. for Fulbright fellow, 1967, Eisenhower Exch. fellow, 1976. Mem. ABA (chmn. sect. internat. law 1978-79), Ho. of Dels. 1982-84), Am. Law Inst., Internat. Law Assn., Shaybani Soc. of Internat. Law (v.p.), Ctrl. and Ea. European Law Initiative (mem. adv. bd.), Cosmos Club, Met. Club. Home: 2800 35th St NW Washington DC 20007-1411 Office: Georgetown U Law Ctr 600 New Jersey Ave NW Washington DC 20001-2022

WALLACE, ELAINE WENDY, lawyer; b. Worcester, Mass., Feb. 16, 1949; d. Louis S. and Ida (Zeiper) W. BA, Yeshiva U., 1971; JD, John F. Kennedy Sch. Law, 1976. Sole practice, Oakland, Calif. Civil rights, Government contracts and claims, Labor. Home: 2430 Palmetto St # 1 Oakland CA 94602-2923 Office: 2430 Palmetto St # 2 Oakland CA 94602-2923

WALLACE, FRANKLIN SHERWOOD, lawyer, director; b. Bklyn., Nov. 24, 1927; s. Abraham Charles and Jennie (Etkin) Wolowitz; m. Eleanor Ruth Pope, Aug. 23, 1953; children: Julia Diane, Charles Andrew. Student, U. Wis., 1943-45; BS cum laude, U.S. Mcht. Marine Acad., 1950; LLB, JD, U. Mich., 1953. Bar: Ill. 1954. Practice law, Rock Island, Ill.; ptnr. Winstein, Kavensky & Wallace. Asst. state's atty. Rock Island County, 1967-68; local counsel UAW at John Deere-J.I. Case Plants. Former bd. dirs. Tri City Jewish Ctr.; former trustee United Jewish Charities of Quad Cities; former bd. dirs. Blackhawk Coll. Found. Mem. ABA, Ill. Bar Assn. (chmn. jud. adv. polls com. 1979-84), Rock Island County Bar Assn., Am. Trial Lawyers Assn., Ill. Trial Lawyers Assn., Nat. Assn. Criminal Def. Lawyers, Ill. Appellate Lawyers Assn., Am. Judicature Soc., Blackhawk Coll. Found. Democrat. Jewish. General civil litigation, Family and matrimonial, Labor. Home: 3405 20th Street Ct Rock Island IL 61201-6201 Office: Rock Island Bank Bldg Rock Island IL 61201 E-mail: fnewallace@aol.com

WALLACE, HENRY JARED, JR. lawyer; b. Pitts., Oct. 26, 1943; s. Henry Jared and Jane (Bowman) Wallace. BA, Harvard U., 1965, JD, 1968. Bar: Pa. 1969, U.S. Ct. Appeals (3d cir.) 1972, U.S. Supreme Ct. 1973, U.S. Ct. Appeals (6th cir.) 1976. Assoc. Reed Smith Shaw & McClay, Pitts., 1968-75, ptnr., 1975-94; pvt. practice, 1995—. Served with U.S. Army, 1968-70. Mem. ABA, Duquesne Club, Fox Chapel Golf Club, Harvard-Yale-Princeton Club (Pitts.). Federal civil litigation, State civil litigation, Labor. Home and Office: 149 Ridgeview Dr New Kensington PA 15068-9389

WALLACE, HERBERT NORMAN, lawyer; b. Syracuse, N.Y., Oct. 19, 1937; s. Louis H. and Betty (Wagner) W.; m. Frances Adele Groobman, June 1, 1963 (div. Sept. 1976); children: Craig, Julie; m. Frances Mae Souza, Nov. 12, 1977; 1 child, John. BA, Davis & Elkins Coll., 1959; JD, Syracuse U., 1962. Bar: N.Y. 1962, U.S. Dist. Ct. (no. dist.) N.Y. 1962. Asst. atty. gen. State of N.Y., Albany, 1963-66, asst. atty. gen in charge of Poughkeepsie (N.Y.) office Poughkeepsie, 1966-79; counsel to banking com. N.Y. State Senate, Albany, 1979-84, counsel to Senator Rolison, asst. majority leader, 1984-88; sole practice Poughkeepsie, N.Y., 1979-86, 94—; ptnr. Wallace & Moore, 1986-94, Wallace and Wallace, 2000—. Mem. Poughkeepsie Rep. Com., 1977-91. Recipient Ellis Island medal of hon. NECO, 1997. Mem. N.Y. State Bar Assn., Dutchess County Bar Assn. Jewish. Condemnation, General practice, Real property. Home: 65 Cardinal Dr Poughkeepsie NY 12601-5703 Office: 299 Main St Poughkeepsie NY 12601-3144

WALLACE, J. CLIFFORD, federal judge; b. San Diego, Dec. 11, 1928; s. John Franklin and Lillie Isabel (Overing) W.; m. Virginia Lee Schlosser, 1957 (dec.); m. Elaine J. Barnes, Apr. 8, 1996 (dec.); m. Dixie Jenee Robison Zenger, Apr. 2, 2001. B.A., San Diego State U., 1952; LL.B., U. Calif., Berkeley, 1955. Bar: Calif. 1955. With firm Gray, Cary, Ames & Frye, San Diego, 1955-70; judge U.S. Dist. Ct. for So. Dist. Calif., 1970-72, U.S. Ct. Appeals for 9th Circuit , San Diego, 1972-96; chief circuit judge U.S. Ct. Appeals for 9th Circuit, 1991—96, sr. circuit judge, 1996—. Contrbr. articles to profl. jours. Served with USN, 1946-49. Mem. Am. Bd. Trial Advocates, Inst. Jud. Adminstrn. Mem. LDS Ch. (stake pres. San Diego East 1962-67, regional rep. 1967-74, 77-79). Office: US Ct Appeals 9th Cir 940 Front St Ste 4192 San Diego CA 92101-8918

WALLACE, JAMES WENDELL, lawyer; b. Clinton, Tenn., July 13, 1930; s. John Nelson and Rose Ella (Carden) W.; m. Jeanne Mary Ellen Newlin; children: Karen Wallace Young, Michael James. Student, Syracuse U., 1952-53; BS, U. Tenn., Knoxville, 1959; JD, U. Tenn., 1958. Bar: Calif. 1959, U.S. Dist. Ct. (ctrl. dist.) Calif. 1959, U.S. Ct. Appeals (9th cir.) 1977, U.S. Supreme Ct. 1964. Sec., legal counsel Guidance Tech., Inc., Santa Monica, Calif., 1958-65; sr. atty., asst. sec. Varian Assocs., Palo Alto, 1965-67; gen. counsel, asst. sec. Electronic Splty. Co., Pasadena, 1967-69; asst. gen. counsel, asst. sec. The Times Mirror Co., L.A., 1969-75, assoc. gen. counsel, asst. sec., 1976-85, assoc. gen. counsel, sec., 1985-89; dir., v.p., sec. Flintridge Asset Mgmt. Co., San Marino, Calif., 1990—. Mem. editl. bd. Tenn. Law Rev., 1956-58. Served with USAF, 1951-55. Mem. Jonathan Club, Phi Delta Phi, Phi Kappa Phi. General corporate, Finance, Probate. Home: 5822 Briartree Dr La Canada Flintridge CA 91011-1825

WALLACE, KEITH M. lawyer; b. Evansville, Ind., Apr. 2, 1956; s. B. Joe and M. Joyce (Nicolaides) W.; 1 child, Elizabeth Anne. BA in Psychology, Ind. U., 1978; JD, Valparaiso U., 1983. Bar: Ky. 1984, Ind. 1983, U.S. Dist. Ct. (so. dist.) Ind. 1983, U.S. Ct. Appeals (7th cir.) 1985, U.S. Supreme Ct., 1997. Comml. credit analyst Old Nat. Bank, Evansville, 1978-79; assoc. Cubbage & Thomason, Henderson, Ky., 1983-84, Perdue & Stigger, Evansville, 1984-86; ptnr. Jones & Wallace, 1987-90; fgn. expert Peking U. Law Dept., People's Republic China, 1990-91; ptnr. Wright, Evans & Daly, Evansville, 1991-95, Jones & Wallace, Evansville, 1996-2001; of counsel Bowers Harrison, 2001—. Asst. city atty., Evansville, 1984-90; hearing officer City of Evansville Dept. Code Enforcement, 1992-99. Steward Christian Fellowship Ch., Evansville, 1988-90; vol. Evansville Rescue Mission, 1987-92, Habitat for Humanity, 1992—; bd. dirs. Impact Ministries, 1992—; exec. dir. Families Thru Internat. Adoptions, Inc., 1995—. Recipient Sagamore of the Wabash award Gov. Frank O'Bannon, 1999, Disting. Hoosier award Gov. Evan Bayh, 1996. Mem. Am. Acad. Adoption Attys., Ind. Bar Assn., Ky. Bar Assn., Evansville Bar Assn., Christian Legal Soc., Evansville Runners Club. General corporate, Environmental, Real property. Office: PO Box 1287 Evansville IN 47708 Fax: (812) 464-3676. E-mail: kwallace@ftia.org

WALLACE, NORA ANN, lawyer; b. Phila., May 24, 1951; AB, Vassar Coll., 1973; JD cum laude, Harvard U., 1976. Bar: N.Y. 1977. Mem. Willkie Farr & Gallagher, N.Y.C. Trustee Bklyn. Acad. Music, Harvard Law Sch. Assn., BAM Endowment Trust; bd. dirs. Joseph Collins Found. Office: Willkie Farr & Gallagher 787 7th Ave New York NY 10019-6099

WALLACE, STEVEN CHARLES, judge; b. Lubbock, Tex., Jan. 19, 1953; s. Charles Andrew Wallace and Alice Hillene (McMillin) Stone; m. Kathleen Louise Merrill, Apr. 3, 1976; children: Christine Merrill, Zachary Charles, Steven Kyle. BA, Tex. Tech U., 1975, JD, 1979. Bar: Tex. 1979, U.S. Dist. Ct. (no. dist.) Tex. 1980, U.S. Ct. Appeals (5th cir.) 1981. Asst. county atty. Parker County, Weatherford, Tex., 1979-80; asst. dist. atty. Tarrant County, Ft. Worth, 1980-83; pvt. practice, 1983-90; judge Tarrant County Ct. at Law # 2, 1991—. Chmn. prosecution and adjudication subcom. Tarrant 2000 Task Force, 1987—. Trustee Am. Judges Found. Recipient Am. Jurisprudence award Bancroft Whitney Co., 1979. Fellow Coll. State Bar of Tex.; mem. Am. Judges Assn. (bd. govs.), State Bar Tex., Tarrant County Bar Assn., Ridotto Club, Ridglea Country Club, Phi Alpha Delta, Phi Alpha Theta. Avocations: golf, fishing, music, traveling, astronomy. Office: Tarrant County Ct at Law # 2 Tarrant County Courthouse 100 W Weatherford St 240-A Fort Worth TX 76196-0234

WALLACE, THOMAS ANDREW, lawyer; b. Sapulpa, Okla., Oct. 12, 1923; s. Thomas Hiram and Lucy Romig (Mauldin) W.; m. Geraldine Jones, July 22, 1946 (div. Jan. 1965); children: Pamela, Thomas Andrew, James Creekmore, William Stuart; m. Nelda Sharp, July 21, 1965. BS, Columbia U., 1951, JD, 1953. Bar: Okla. 1952. Sole practice, Oklahoma City; faculty lectr. O.B.A., Ctr. for Law and Edn. Served with USMC, 1942-46. Mem. Okla. Bar Assn. (Golden Gavel award 1984, subcom. Okla.

evidence code, supreme ct. com., uniform jury instrns. com. 1979-81, Okla. Bus. Corp. Act, civil procedure com. 1981-84, chmn. legis. com. 1984-87), Okla. Trial Lawyers Assn. (pres. 1976, Meritorious Service award 1976), Assn. Trial Lawyers Am., Calif. Trial Lawyers Assn. Democrat. Federal civil litigation, Condemnation, Personal injury. Home: 12808 Deerfield Cir Oklahoma City OK 73142-5133

WALLACE, VIRGINIA BARTON, retired lawyer; b. Butler, PA, Sept. 14, 1908; d. James Lowrie and Olive Louise (Roberts) Barton; m. Sillman Eugene Wallace, Aug. 23, 1947 (div. Feb. 1979). BA, Wellesley Coll., Mass., 1930; postgrad., U. Wyo., 1946-48; JD, U. Penn., 1950. Bar: Pa. 1950. Editor Bulletin Index Mag., Pitts., 1931-34; freelance journalist Pitts./Gettysburg, 1934-42; assoc. White and Williams, LLP, Phila., 1950-61, ptnr., 1961-80; ret., 1980. 1st Lt. WAC, 1942-45, PTO. Decorated three Bronze stars, U.S. Army Mem. ABA, Pa. Bar Assn., Phila. Bar Assn., AAUW, LWV, VFW. Episcopalian. Avocations: music, bridge, travel, history. Home: 255 Crosslands Dr Kennett Square PA 19348-2324 E-mail: vbwallace@mymailstation.com

WALLACH, ERIC JEAN, lawyer; b. N.Y.C., June 11, 1947; s. Milton Harold and Jacqueline (Goldschmidt) W.; m. Miriam Grunberger, Mar. 21, 1976; children: Katherine, Emily, Peter. BA, Harvard U., 1968, JD, 1972. Bar: N.Y. 1973, U.S. Dist. Ct. (so. and ea. dists.) N.Y. 1973, U.S. Dist. Ct. (no. dist.) N.Y. 1989, U.S. Ct. Appeals (2nd cir.) 1973, (3d cir.) 1996, U.S. Tax Ct. 1976. Assoc. Webster & Sheffield, N.Y.C., 1972-77, Rosenman & Colin, N.Y.C., 1977-80, ptnr., 1981-96, mem. mgmt. com., 1993-96, chmn. employment practice group, 1985-96; ptnr., chmn. employment practice group Kasowitz, Benson, Torres & Friedman LLP, 1996—. Presenter, chmn. CLE programs, Practising Law Inst., Cambridge Inst., others. Mem. editl. bd. You and the Law, 1992-96; contbr. articles to profl. jours. Sec.-treas. Art Dealers Assn. Am., Inc., N.Y.C., 1985-96; trustee C.G. Jung Found. for Analytical Psychology; trustee Am. Jewish World Svc., Inc., N.Y.C., 1989-97, chmn., 1995-97; dir. N.Y. Jr. Tennis League. Mem. Harvard Club N.Y.C. (admissions com. 1992-94), Sunningdale Country Club, Poughkeepsie Tennis Club. Democrat. Avocations: sports, travel, reading. General civil litigation, Labor. Home: 20 W 64th St New York NY 10023-7180 also: 16 Buttonwood Ln Rhinebeck NY 12572-3510 Office: Kasowitz Benson Torres & Friedman LLP 1301 Ave of Ams New York NY 10019 E-mail: ewallach@kasowitz.com

WALLACH, EVAN JONATHAN, judge, international law educator; b. Superior, Ariz., Nov. 11, 1949; s. Albert A. and Sara Florence (Rothaus) W. BA, U. Ariz., 1973; JD, U. Calif., Berkeley, 1976; LLB in Internat. Law, Cambridge (Eng.) U., 1981. Bar: Nev. 1977, U.S. Dist. Ct. Nev. 1977, U.S. Supreme Ct. 1984, D.C. 1987, U.S. Ct. Appeals (9th cir.) 1989. Assoc. Lionel, Sawyer & Collins, Las Vegas, 1976-82, ptnr., 1983-95; apptd. U.S. Ct. Internat. Trade, N.Y.C., 1995—. Gen. counsel, pub. policy advisor to U.S. Sen. Harry M. Reid, Washington, 1987-88; gen counsel Nev. State Press Assn. 1989-95; instr. internat. law U. Nev., Las Vegas, 1981-82; atty., adv. internat. affairs Office Judge Adv. Gen. The Pentagon, 1991; adj. prof. law of war N.Y. Law Sch., 1997—, Bklyn. Law Sch., 2001—. Sr. editor: Nevada Civil Practice Handbook, 1993, Legal Handbook for Nevada Reporters, 1994; contbr. articles to profl. jours. Gen. counsel Nev. Dem. Party, 1980-84, 88-90; coord. Nevadans for Mondale, 1983-84, Nevadans for Gore, 1987-88; del. Dem. Nat. Conv., San Francisco, 1984, alt., Atlanta, 1988; dtate dir. campaign in Nev. and Ariz. Gore for Pres., 1988. With U.S. Army, 1969-71, Vietnam; maj. U.S. Army N.G., 1989—. Decorated Bronze Star, Air medal, Meritorious Svc. medal, Nev. Medal of Merit. Mem. ABA (Liberty Bell award 1992), Phi Beta Kappa. Jewish. Public international, Libel, Pension, profit-sharing, and employee benefits. Office: US Ct of Internat Trade One Federal Plaza New York NY 10278-0001

WALLACH, STEVEN ERNST, lawyer, pilot; b. N.Y.C., Mar. 21, 1944; s. Eduard Herbert Wallach and Karin (Wassermann) Grunebaum; m. Stefany Gay Rosehill (div. Oct. 1990); children: Shelby Karin, Shawna Beth; m. Geri Joan Grieco, Nov. 21, 1992. BS, USAF Acad., 1965; MS summa cum laude, U. So. Calif., 1971; JD magna cum laude, Nova U., 1986. Bar: Fla. 1986, D.C. 1988, U.S. Dist. Ct. (so. dist.) Fla. 1987, U.S. Dist. Ct. (mid. dist.) Fla. 1989, U.S. Dist. Ct. Ariz. 1989; cert. airline transport pilot, 1969; bd. cert. aviation law, 1998. Systems analyst Hughes Aircraft Co., L.A., 1971-72; airline capt. Eastern Air Lines, Miami, 1972-91; atty. Barwick, Dillian & Lambert P.A., Miami Shores, Fla., 1987-96; atty., ptnr. Thornton Davis & Murray, P.A., Miami, 1996-98. Aviation mgmt. cons. PRC Speas, Lake Success, N.Y., 1977-83, TRAMCO, Cambridge, Mass., 1972-77, A.V. lawyer, 1997, Steven Wallach Assoc., 1998—. Trustee Karin Grunebaum Cancer Found., Cambridge, 1979—. Capt. USAF, 1965-70. Decorated DFC, 5 air medals. Avocation: flying. Aviation, Product liability. Home: 2600 S Ocean Blvd Apt 21-E Boca Raton FL 33432

WALLER, EDWARD MARTIN, JR. lawyer; b. Memphis, July 2, 1942; s. Edward Martin and Freda (Lazarov) W.; m. Laura Jayne Rhodes, June 18, 1982; children: Lauren, Jonathan, Melissa. BA, Columbia U., 1964; JD, U. Chgo., 1967. Bar: Fla. 1967. Assoc. Fowler, White, Gillen, Boggs, Villareal & Banker, P.A., Tampa, Fla., 1967-72, ptnr., 1972—. Mem. ABA (standing com. professionalism chmn. 1995-97, banking and fin. transactions com., litigation sect. 1978-82, co-chmn. 1983-87, coun. 1990-92, budget officer 1996-2000, litigation sect.), Fla. Bar Assn., Hillsborough County Bar Assn., Bay Area Legal Svcs. (bd. dirs. 1996—). Democrat. Jewish. Federal civil litigation, State civil litigation. Office: Fowler White Gillen Boggs Villareal & Banker PO Box 1438 Tampa FL 33601-1438

WALLER, JOHN HENRY, JR. state supreme court justice; b. Mullins, S.C., Oct. 31, 1937; s. John Henry and Elnita (Rabon) W.; m. Jane McLaurin Cooper, Nov. 16, 1963 (div.); children: John Henry III, Melissa McLaurin; m. Debra Ann Meares, May 9, 1981; children: Ryan Meares, Rand Ellis. AB in Psychology, Wofford Coll., 1959; LLB, JD, U. S.C., 1963. Mem. S.C. Ho. of Reps., 1967-77, S.C. Senate, 1977-80; judge S.C. Cir. Ct., 1980-94; assoc. justice S.C. Supreme Ct., 1994—. Mem. S.C. Cir. Ct. Adv. Com., 1981-94, chmn., 1991-94; mem. S.C. Jud. Std. Com., 1991-94, chmn., 1992-94. Capt. U.S. Army, 1959-60. Mem. Millins Rotary Club (1st pres.), Masons, Shriners. Avocations: woodworking, golf, water sports, snow skiing. Office: SC Supreme Ct 103 Main St PO Box 1059 Marion SC 29571-1059 also: SC Supreme Ct Supreme Court PO Box 11330 Columbia SC 29211-1330

WALLER, WILLIAM LOWE, JR. state supreme court justice; b. Miss., Feb. 9, 1952; s. Bill Sr. and Carroll (Overton) W.; m. Charlotte Brawner, Aug. 4, 1979; children: William, Jeannie, Clayton. Student, Delta State U.; BA in Bus., Miss. State U., 1974; JD, U. Miss., 1977; grad., U.S. Army War Coll. Bar: Miss. 1977. Ptnr. Waller and Waller, 1977-97; judge City of Jackson, Miss., 1995-96; justice Miss. Supreme Ct., Jackson, 1997—. Chmn. lawyer referral svc. Miss. State Bar, 1987-89; chmn. Miss. Pub. Defenders Task Force, 2000; mem. Study Commn. on the Miss. Jud. Sys.; panelist Miss. Pro Bon Svc. Tchr. Sunday sch. First Bapt. Ch., Jackson, Miss.; past gen. counsel Ctrl. Miss. chpt. Lupus Found. Am.; bd. dirs., chmn. Jackson Coun. Neighborhoods. With Miss. Nat. Guard. Mem. ABA, Miss. Bar Assn., Christian Legal Soc., Am. Legion, Miss. Nat. Guard Assn. (sec., chmn. legis. com., bd. dirs.). Office: PO Box 117 Jackson MS 39205-0117

WALLINGER, M(ELVIN) BRUCE, lawyer; b. Richmond, Va., Dec. 27, 1945; s. Melvin W. and Ellen Scott (Barnard) W.; m. Rosemary Moore Hynes, Aug. 8, 1970; children: Mary Moore, Ann Harrison, Carrie. BA, U. Va., 1968, JD, 1972. Bar: Va. 1972, U.S. Dist. Ct. (we. dist.) Va. 1972, U.S. Ct. Appeals (4th cir.) 1976, U.S. Supreme Ct. 1978, U.S. Dist. Ct. (ea. dist.) Va. 1986; cert. comml. and employment mediator and arbitrator. Assoc. Wharton, Aldhizer & Weaver, Harrisonburg, Va., 1972-76, ptnr., 1976-98, mng. ptnr., 1998—. Bd. dirs. Shrine Mont, Inc., Orkney Springs, Va.; trustee Stuart Hall Sch., Staunton, Va., Shenandoah County Libr. Foun., Edinburg, Va. Fellow ABA, Am. Coll. Trial Lawyers, Va. Law Found.; mem. Va. Bar Assn. (exec. com. 1996-99), Harrisonburg Bar Assn. (pres. 1984), Va. State Bar (pres. young lawyers conf. 1981-82, chmn. 6th dist. disciplinary com. 1988-89), Va. Assn. Def. Attys. (pres. 1989-90). Republican. Episcopalian. Avocations: biking, scuba diving. Alternative dispute resolution, General civil litigation, Labor. Office: Wharton Aldhizer & Weaver 100 S Mason St Harrisonburg VA 22801-4022

WALLIS, BEN ALTON, JR. lawyer; b. Llano County, Tex., Apr. 27, 1936; s. Ben A. and Jessie Ella (Longbotham) W.; children from previous marriage: Ben a. III, M. Jessica; m. Joan Mery, 1987. BBA, U. Tex., 1961, JD, 1971; postgrad., Law Sch. So. Meth. U. Bar: Tex. 1966, U.S. Dist. Ct. (no. dist.) Tex. 1971, U.S. Ct. Appeals D.C. 1974, U.S. Dist. Ct. D.C. 1975, U.S. Dist. Ct. (we. dist.) Tex. 1975, U.S. Dist. Ct. (no. dist.) Calif. 1983, U.S. Ct. Appeals (5th cir.) 1975, U.S. Ct. Appeals (8th cir.) 1980, U.S. Ct. Appeals (11th cir.) 1981, U.S. Dist. Ct. (ea. dist.) Wis. 1983, U.S. Supreme Ct. 1974. Pvt. practice, Llano, 1966-67, Dallas, 1971-73; investigator, prosecutor State Securities Bd. Tex., 1967-71; v.p. of devel. Club Corp. Am., Dallas, 1973; assoc. counsel impeachment task force U.S. Ho. of Reps. Com. on Judiciary, Washington, 1974; prin. Law Offices of Ben Wallis, P.C., San Antonio, 1974—. Chmn. Nat. Land Use Conf., 1979-81; mem. Gov.'s Areawide Planning Adv. Com., 1975-78; pres. Inst. Human Rights Rsch., 1979-2000. Mem. ATLA, FBA, Coll. of State Bar of Tex., State Bar Tex. (former chmn. agr. tax com.), D.C. Bar Assn., San Antonio Bar Assn., Delta Theta Phi, Delta Sigma Pi. Republican. Baptist. General civil litigation, Condemnation, General practice. Office: GPM South Tower 800 NW Loop 410 Ste 350 San Antonio TX 78216-5619 E-mail: wallis@txdirect.net

WALLIS, OLNEY GRAY, lawyer; b. Llano, Tex., July 27, 1940; s. Ben Alton and Jessie Ella (Longbotham) W.; m. Linda Lee Johnson, June 29, 1963; children: Anne, Brett. BA, U. Tex., 1962, JD, 1965. Bar: Tex. 1965, U.S. Dist. Ct. (so. dist.) Tex. 1966, U.S. Ct. Mil. Appeals 1968, U.S. Surpeme Ct. 1970, U.S. dist. Ct. (we. dist.) Tex. 1976, U.S. Ct. Appeals (5th cir.) 1977, U.S. Tax Ct. 1980, U.S. Ct. Appeals (10th cir.) 1981, U.S. Ct. Appeals (11th cir.) 1983, U.S. Dist. Ct. (no. dist.) Tex. 1985, U.S. Dist. Ct. (ea. and we. dists.) Ark. 1985, U.S. Ct. Appeals (8th cir.) 1985. Assoc. Brown & Cecil, Houston, 1965-66; asst. U.S. atty. Dept. Justice, 1971-74; mem. Jefferson, Wallis & Sherman, 1975-81, Wallis & Pruitt, Houston, 1981-87, Wallis and Short, Houston, 1987—. Instr. U. Md., Keflauik, Iceland, 1968-69; mem. faculty continuing legal edn. U. Houston, 1981-84. Capt. USAF, 1969-70. Decorated Air Force Commendation medal. Mem. Assn. Trial Lawyers Am., Am. Judicature Soc., Tex. Trial Lawyers Assn., Houston Bar Found., Phi Delta Phi, Phi Kappa Tau. Federal civil litigation, State civil litigation, Criminal. Office: Wallis & Short 4300 Scotland St Houston TX 77007-7328 E-mail: ogwlawyer@earthlink.net

WALLMAN, LESTER, lawyer; b. N.Y.C. LLB, Bklyn. Coll., 1951; LLM, NYU, 1954. Bar: N.Y. 1952. Ptnr. Wallman, Gasman & McKnight, N.Y.C., 1967—. Panelist on divorce law TV networks; mem. Mayor's adv. commn. cultural affairs, N.Y.C. Author: Complete Guide to Family Law; appeared as panelist on divorce laws Cupid, Couples and Contracts, Geraldo, Good Morning America, Today. Chmn. Cmty. Planning Bd., N.Y.C., 1981-83; mem. N.Y.C. Commn. on Korean War Meml; active N.Y.C. Adv. Commn. on Cultural Affairs, 1999—. With U.S. Army, 1949-51. Mem. N.Y. State Bar Assn. (chmn. com. on legis. family law sect. 1976—), Am. Acad. Matrimonial lawyers, Nat. Art Club. Family and matrimonial. Office: Empire State Bldg 350 5th Ave Ste 3000 New York NY 10118-3022

WALLS, GEORGE RODNEY, lawyer; b. New Orleans, Sept. 30, 1945; s. Preston Rodney and Bobbe Cleo (Sharp) W.; m. Nancy Ellen Smith, June 29, 1974; children: Scott Christian, Brian Cannon. BA, U. Md., 1967, JD, 1970. Bar: Md. 1971, D.C. 1971, U.S. Dist. Ct. D.C. 1971, U.S. Supreme Ct. 1977. Assoc. counsel GAC Fin. Inc., Allentown, Pa., 1970-73; sr. atty. Quality Inns Internat., Inc., Silver Spring, Md., 1973-76; gen. counsel, sec. Suburban Bancorp., Bethesda, 1976-86; sr. assoc. gen. counsel, corp. sec. Sovran Fin. Corp., Norfolk, Va., 1986-90; sr. assoc. gen. counsel C&S/Sovran, 1990-91; asst. gen. counsel NationsBank Corp./Bank of Am., Charlotte, N.C., 1991—. Mem. Md. Bar Assn., D.C. Bar Assn., N.C. Bar Assn., Am. Assn. Corp. Secs., Am. Corp. Counsel Assn. Presbyterian. Banking, General corporate. Home: 12425 Pine Valley Club Dr Charlotte NC 28277-4023 Office: Bank of Am NCI 002 29 01 101 S Tryon St Charlotte NC 28255-0001 E-mail: gwall@carolina.rr.com, george.walls@bankofamerica.com

WALMER, JAMES L. lawyer; b. Wabash, Ind., Oct. 18, 1948; s. Warren D. and Josephine (Clupper) W.; m. Carolyn Gwen Lackey, Apr. 23, 1977; children: Ryan, Christian, Jonathan, Geoffrey. BS, Ball State U., 1971; JD, U. Tulsa, 1973. Bar: Okla. 1974, Ind. 1974, U.S. Dist. Ct. (no. and ea. dists.) Okla. 1974, U.S. Dist. Ct. (so. dist.) Ind. 1974, U.S. Dist. Ct. (no. dist.) Ind. 1975. Sole practice, Warsaw, 1974—; dep. prosecutor Kosciusko County, 1976-96. Town atty. Winona Lake, Ind., 1976—, Pierceton, Ind., 1980—. Chmn. bd. dirs. Cardinal Ctr. Inc., Warsaw, 1978-84; mem. philanthropy com. Ball State U., Muncie, Ind., 1986—; pres. Lincoln PTO, 1989-90; co-pres. Harrison PTO, 1993-94; trustee First United Meth. Ch., 1992-94; dir. Ind. Prosecutors Child Support Alliance, 1994-96; bd. dirs. Warsaw Little League, 1994-98, coach, 1990-96, 98. Mem. ABA, Ind. Bar Assn. (chmn. surrogacy com. family law sect. 1987-88), Kosciusko County Bar Assn. (treas. 1979—), Okla. Bar Assn., Ind. Mcpl. Lawyers Assn. Republican. Methodist. Lodges: Optimists (v.p. 1979-80), Shriners, Masons. Family and matrimonial, General practice. Home: 1705 E Springhill Rd Warsaw IN 46580-1805 Office: PO Box 1056 Warsaw IN 46581-1056 E-mail: walmer@kconline.com

WALNER, ROBERT JOEL, lawyer; b. Chgo., Dec. 22, 1946; s. Wallace and Elsie W.; m. Charlene Walner; children: Marci, Lisa. BA, U. Ill., 1968; JD, De Paul U., 1972; M in Mgmt. with distinction, Northwestern U., 1991. Bar: Ill. 1972, U.S. Dist. Ct. (no. dist.) Ill. 1972, U.S. Ct. Appeals (7th cir.) 1972, Fla. 1973. Atty. SEC, Chgo., 1972-73; pvt. practice, 1973—; adminstrv. law judge Ill. Commerce Commn., 1973-76; atty. Allied Van Lines, Inc., Broadview, Ill., 1976-79; sr. v.p., gen. counsel, sec. The Balcor Co., Skokie, 1979-92; prin. fin. ops. Balcor Securities divsn. The Balcor Co., 1984-92, pres., 1989-92; of counsel Lawrence, Walner & Assocs., Ltd., Chgo., 1992-93; sr. v.p., gen. counsel, sec. Grubb & Ellis Co., Northbrook, Ill., 1994—. Mem. securities adv. com. to Ill. Sec. of State, 1984-94; mem. editl. bd. Real Estate Securities Jour., Real Estate Securities and Capital Markets; program chmn. Regulators and You seminar. Contbr. chpts. to books, articles on real estate and securities law to profl. jours.; assoc. editor De Paul U. Law Rev. Mem. Kellogg Career Devel. Com., 1992-94, Kellogg Bus. Adv. Com., 1992—; mem. enterprise forum MIT, 1992—, mem. exec. com., 1993-94. With USAR, 1968-73. Mem. ABA, Ill. Bar Assn., Chgo. Bar Assn., Am. Real Estate Com. (pres. com. 1985-90), Real Estate Syndication Com. (chmn. 1982-85), Ill. Inst. Continuing Legal Edn., N.Am. Securities Adminstrs. Assn. Inc. (industry adv. com. to real estate com., 1987-89), Real Estate Securities and Syndication Inst. of Nat. Assn. Realtors (chmn. regulatory and legis. com., 1984, 87, group v.p. 1987, exec. com. 1987-90, specialist, real estate investment, counselor of real estate), Nat. Real Estate Investment Forum (chmn. 1985, 88), Real Estate Investment Assn. (founder, exec. com. 1990-92), Kellogg Alumni Club (bd. dirs., event chmn. 1996-98, v.p., exec. com. 1998-99), Beta G amma Sigma. General civil litigation, General corporate, Securities.

WALPIN, GERALD, lawyer; b. N.Y.C., Sept. 1, 1931; s. Michael and Mary (Gordon) W.; m. Sheila Kainer, Apr. 13, 1957; children: Amanda Eve, Edward Andrew, Jennifer Hope BA, CCNY, 1952; LLB cum laude, Yale Law Sch., 1955. Bar: N.Y. 1955, U.S. Supreme Ct. 1965, U.S. Ct. Appeals (2d cir.) 1960, (6th cir.) 1969, (3d cir.) 1976, (8th cir.) 1982, (9th cir.) 1983, (llth cir.) 1983, (7th cir.) 1984, U.S. Ct. Claims 1984. Law clk. to Hon. E.J. Dimock U.S. Dist. Ct. (so. dist.) N.Y., N.Y.C.; law clk. to Hon. F.P. Bryan U.S. Dist. Judge (so. dist.) N.Y., 1955-57; asst. U.S. atty., chief spl. prosecutions U.S. Atty. Office, 1960-65; sr. ptnr. Rosenman & Colin and predecessor firm, 1965—, chmn. litigation dept., 1985-96. Adv. com. Fed. Ct. So. Dist. N.Y., 1991—; co-chmn. lawyers divsn. Anti-Defamation League, N.Y., 1994-97; bd. dirs. Ctr. for Individual Rights, 1997—. Editor Yale Law Jour., 1953-54, mng. editor, 1954-55; contbr. articles to profl. jours. Pres. Parker Jewish Inst. for Health Care and Rehab., New Hyde Park, N.Y., 1987-90, trustee, 1979—; bd. dirs. Fund for Modern Cts., N.Y.C., 1985-91; mem. law com. Am. Jewish Com., 1980—; mem. Com. for Free World, N.Y.C., 1983-91; trustee, mem. exec. com. United Jewish Appeal-Fedn. Jewish Philanthropies, N.Y.C., 1984-96; mem. Nassau County Crime Commn., 1970; pres. Kensington Civic Orgn., Gt. Neck, N.Y., 1972-73. Recipient Quality of Life award United Jewish Appeal Fedn., 1978, Human Rels. award Am. Jewish Com., 1982, Gift of Life award Jewish Inst. Geriatric Care, 1987, Learned Hand award Am. Jewish Com., 1990, Human Rels. award Anti-Defamation League, 1998. Mem. ABA, Assn. Bar City N.Y., Fed. Bar Coun. (chmn. modern cts. com. 1989, v.p. 1991-95, chmn. bench and bar liaison com. 1994-95, vice chmn. 1995-97, chmn. bd. dirs. 1997-99, pres.-elect 2000—), Federalist Soc. (chmn. litigation sect. 1996-99, mem. bd. visitors 1999—), Univ. Club, Yale Club. Republican. Jewish. General civil litigation, Criminal, Securities. Home: 875 Park Ave New York NY 10021-0341 Office: Rosenman & Colin 575 Madison Ave Fl 20 New York NY 10022-2511 E-mail: GWalpin@Rosenman.com

WALSH, DAVID GRAVES, lawyer; b. Madison, Wis., Jan. 7, 1943; s. John J. and Audrey B. Walsh; married; children: Michael, Katherine, Molly, John. BBA, U. Wis., 1965; JD, Harvard U., 1970. Bar: Wis. Law clk. Wis. Supreme Ct., Madison, 1970-71; ptnr. Walsh, Walsh, Sweeney & Whitney, 1971-86; ptnr.-in-charge Foley & Lardner, 1986—. Bd. dirs. Nat. Guardian Life, Madison, 1981—; lectr. U. Wis., Madison, 1974-75, 77-78. Chmn. State of Wis. Elections Bd., Madison, 1978. Lt. USN, 1965-67, Vietnam. Recipient Disting. Bus. Alumnus award U. Wis. Sch. Bus., 1997. Maple Bluff Country Club (Madison) (pres. 1987). Roman Catholic. Avocations: tennis, golf, fishing. Bankruptcy, Contracts commercial, Communications. Home: 41 Fuller Dr Madison WI 53704-5962 Office: Foley & Lardner PO Box 1497 Madison WI 53701-1497

WALSH, JAMES HAMILTON, lawyer; b. N.Y.C., N.Y., May 20, 1947; s. Edward James and Helen Smith (Hamilton) W.; m. Janice Ausherman, Aug. 3, 1967; children: Tracy, Courtney, Eric. BA in Psychology, Bridgewater Coll., 1968; JD, U. Va., 1975. Bar: Va. 1975, U.S. Dist. Ct. (ea. and we. dists.) Va. 1975, U.S. Ct. Appeals (4thc ir.) 1976, U.S. Supreme Ct. 1982. Assoc. McGuire, Woods, Battle & Boothe (and predecessor firms), Richmond, Va., 1975-82, ptnr., 1982—. Instr. Nat. Inst. Trial Adv.; adj. prof. U. Richmond, 1992, 93; spl. prosecutor U.S. Dist. Ct. (ea. dist.) Va., 1979, 84. Contbr. articles to profl. jours. Mem. bd. trustees Bridgewater (Va.) Coll., mem. exec. com.; mem. staff Va. Law Rev. With U.S. Army, 1969-72. Mem. ABA (mem. antitrust sect. health care com., litigation sect.), Va. State Bar (bd. govs. antitrust sect. 1984-90, chmn. 1986), Va. Bar Assn. (chmn. criminal law sect. 1997, 98), Richmond Bar Assn., Willow Oaks, Order Coif, Phi Delta Phi. Episcopalian. Antitrust, General civil litigation, Product liability. Home: 113 Adingham Ct Richmond VA 23229-7761 Office: McGuire Woods Battle & Boothe 1 James Ctr 910 E Cary St Richmond VA 23219-4004 E-mail: jwalsh@mcguirewoods.com

WALSH, JAMES JOSEPH, lawyer; b. New Orleans, June 21, 1948; s. Francis Michael and Violet (Young) W.; m. Priscilla Robson Ferris, Oct. 12, 1972; children: Caitlin Marian, Alison Robson. BA, La. State U., 1970, JD, 1975. Bar: La. 1975, Mich. 1977, U.S. Ct. Appeals (6th cir.) 1981, U.S. Supreme Ct. 1991. Law clk. Mich. Ct. Appeals, Detroit, 1975-77; assoc. Bodman, Longley & Dahling, 1977-84, ptnr., 1984—. Counsel Outdoor Advt. Assn. Mich. Editor: La. Law Rev., 1975. Named to Hall of Fame, La. State U. Law Sch., 1988. Mem. ABA, State Bar Mich., Washtenaw County Bar Assn., Ann Arbor Club, Detroit Athletic Club, Mich. C. of C., Jefferson City Buzzards. Avocations: fishing, gardening, carpentry. Appellate, Federal civil litigation, General civil litigation. Home: 8025 Mast Rd Dexter MI 48130-9301 Office: Bodman Longley & Dahling 110 Miller Ave Ste 300 Ann Arbor MI 48104-1339 E-mail: jwalsh@bodmanlongley.com

WALSH, J(OHN) B(RONSON), lawyer; b. Buffalo, Feb. 20, 1927; s. John A. and Alice (Condon) W.; m. Barbara Ashford, May 20, 1966 (dec. Feb. 2001); 1 child, Martha. AB, Canisius Coll., 1950; JD, Georgetown U., 1952. Bar: N.Y. 1953, U.S. Supreme Ct. 1958, U.S. Ct. Internat. Trade 1969, U.S. Ct. Customs and Patent Appeals 1973. Trial atty. Garvey & Conway, N.Y.C., 1953-54; vol. atty. Nativity Mission, 1953-54; ptnr. Jaeckle, Fleischmann, Kelly, Swart & Augspurger, Buffalo, 1955-60; pvt. practice, 1961-75; ptnr. Jaeckle, Fleischmann & Mugel, 1976-80; with Walsh & Cleary, P.C., 1980-84; pvt. practice, 1984—; spl. counsel Ecology and Environment, Inc., Lancaster, N.Y., 1989—. Trial counsel antitrust div. Dept. Justice, Washington, 1960-61; spl. counsel on disciplinary procedures N.Y. Supreme Ct., 1960-76; appointee legal disciplinary coordinating com. State of N.Y., 1971; legis. counsel, spl. counsel to mayor Buffalo, 1995—; counsel to sheriff Erie County, 1969-72; legis counsel Niagara Frontier Transp. Authority; cons. Norfolk So. R.R., Ecology and Environment on Govtl. Affairs; guest lectr. univs. and profl. groups. Author: (TV series) The Law and You (Freedom Found. award, ABA award, Internat. Police Assn. award). Past pres. Ashford Hollow Found. Visual and Performing Arts; past trustee Dollar Bills, Inc.; past co-producer Grand Island Playhouse and Players. With U.S. Army, 1945-46. Recipient Gold Key Buffalo Jr. C. of C., 1962, award Freedom Found., 1966. Fellow Am. Bar Found.; mem. ABA (del. internat. conf. Brussels 1963, Mexico City 1964, Lausanne, Switzerland 1964, Award of Merit com. 1961-70, sec., vice chair, chmn. sect. bar activities 1965-69, mem. ho. of dels. 1969-70, mem. crime prevention and control com. 1968-70, vice chair sr. lawyers divsn., com. legislation and adminstrn. regulations 1992—, vice chair sr. lawyers divsn. membership com. 1993-94), N.Y. Trial Lawyers Assn., Am. Immigration Lawyers Assn., Am. Judicature Soc., N.Y. State Bar Assn. (past exec. sec.), Erie County Bar Assn., Buffalo Bar Assn., Nat. Pub. Employer Labor Relations Assn., Capital Hill Club of Buffalo, Am. Assn. Airport Execs., N.Y. State Bus. Coun. (environ. law subcom., chmn. subcom.), Buffalo Irish Club (bd. dirs.), Buffalo Athletic Club (past bd. dirs., past v.p.), Buffalo Canoe Club, Buffalo Club, Ft. Orange of Albany Club, KC, Knights of Equity, Leoknights, Phi Delta Phi, Delta Gamma. Roman Catholic. Environmental, Immigration, naturalization, and customs, Legislative. Home: 95 North Dr Eggertsville NY 14226-4158 Office: 368 Pleasant View Dr Lancaster NY 14086-1316 also: 210 Ellicott Sq Bldg Buffalo NY 14203-2402 E-mail: jbwalsh@ene.com

WALSH, JOSEPH LEO, III, lawyer; b. St. Louis, Dec. 7, 1954; s. Joseph Leo and Joan Marie (Bocklage) W.; m. Eileen Rose Boland, June 11, 1982; children: Katie Rose, Joseph L. IV, Brian James, John Patrick, Mary Elizabeth. BS cum laude, Loras Coll., 1977; JD, St. Mary's U., 1984. Bar: Tex. 1984, U.S. Dist. Ct. (so. dist.) Tex. 1985, Mo. 1986, U.S. Dist. Ct. (ea. dist.) Mo. 1989, U.S. Ct. Appeals (8th cir.) 1989, U.S. Supreme Ct. 1991. Assoc. Chamberlain, Hrdlicka, White, Johnson & Williams, Houston, 1984-86; atty. Haley, Fredrickson & Walsh, St. Louis, 1986-88; assoc. Gray & Ritter, 1988-95; pvt. practice, 1995—; mcpl. judge Divsn. 21st Jud. Cir. Ct., 2000-01, City of Frontenac, Mo., 2000-2001. Pro bono legal clinic St. Patrick Ctr., 1991—, Holy Guardian Angel Settlement, 1995—; jud. clk. U.S. Dist. Ct. (we. dist.) Tex., 1984. Co-author: Missouri Bar CLE Treatise on Torts, 2d edit., 1990; sr. assoc. editor St. Mary's U. Sch. Law Jour., 1983-84. Active Holly Hills Neighborhood Assn., 1991-93; v.p. Our Lady of Pillar Men's Club, 1998, pres., 1999-2000. Recipient Torts and Evidence award Lawyers' Co-op Pub. Co., 1982; named to Nat. Order Barristers, 1984. Mem. Assn. Trial Lawyers Am., Mo. Assn. Trial Attys., Bar Assn. Met. St. Louis, Lawyers Assn. St. Louis, Phi Delta Phi (pres. 1984). Roman Catholic. General civil litigation, Personal injury, Product liability. Home and Office: 10469 White Bridge Ln Saint Louis MO 63141-8415 Office: 720 Olive St Ste 750 Saint Louis MO 63101-2330

WALSH, JOSEPH RICHARD, lawyer; b. Atlanta, May 10, 1951; s. Joseph Radamaker and Meta Lucille (Cole) W.; m. Elisabeth Clare Kane, July 27, 1980; children: Lindsay Carolyn, Dana Elisabeth, Cameron Marisa. B in Indsl. Engring., Ga. Inst. Tech., 1973; JD, U. Ga., 1976; ML in Taxation, Georgetown Law Ctr., 1984. Bar: Ga. 1976, Va. 1978, D.C. 1979, Calif. 1984, U.S. Ct. Appeals (4th cir.) 1978, U.S. Ct. Appeals (5th cir.) 1976, U.S. Ct. Appeals (9th cir.) 1984, U.S. Ct. Appeals (11th cir.) 1982, U.S. Dist. Ct. (no. dist.) Ga. 1976, U.S. Dist. Ct. (no. dist.) Calif. 1984, U.S. Tax Ct. 1983, U.S. Claims Ct. 1983. Indsl. engr. So. Ry. System, Atlanta, 1973-74; atty. ICC, Washington, 1977-78, atty., asst. rail merger coordinator, 1979-84; assoc. Fulbright & Jaworski, Washington, 1978-79; counsel Bank of Am. Nat. Assn., San Francisco, 1984-85, sr. counsel, 1985-1998, asst. genl. counsel, 1998—; counselor Athens Legal Aid and Defender Soc., Ga., 1976; instr. comml. law San Francisco Law U. San Fransisco. 1987-92. Contbg. author Federal Regulatory Process: Practice and Procedure, 1981. Campaign vol. Jimmy Carter Presdl. Campaign, New Hampshire, 1976. Recipient Spl. Achievement awards ICC, 1981, 82, 83, Chmn.'s Commendation award, ICC, 1982, Extraordinary award Bank Am., 1988; named Outstanding Young Men Am. U.S. Jaycees, 1982. Ga. Inst. Tech. nat. merit scholar 1969; NSF grantee 1972. Mem. D.C. Bar Assn., Ga. Bar Assn., ABA, Fed. Bar Assn., Va. Bar Assn., Calif. Bar Assn., San Francisco Bar Assn., San Francisco Leasing Lawyers Forum, Am. Inst. Indsl. Engrs., Sierra Club, Phi Kappa Phi, Tau Beta Pi, Alpha Pi Mu. Presbyterian. Club: Lawyers (San Francisco), Commonwealth Calif. Administrative and regulatory, Contracts commercial, Private international. Office: Bank of Am N.A. CA705-04-01 555 California St San Francisco CA 94137-0001 E-mail: joseph.r.walsh@bankofamerica.com

WALSH, LAWRENCE ADRIAN, lawyer; b. New Orleans, Mar. 7, 1955; s. Joseph Wayne and Lorraine Beverly (Mason) W.; m. Virginia Obriotti, Aug. 16, 1980; children: Katherine Nicole, Victoria Ashley. Student Tulane U., 1974-75; BA, St. Mary's U., 1976, JD, 1978. Bar: Tex. 1978, U.S. Dist. Ct. (so. dist.) Tex. 1979, U.S. Ct. Appeals (5th cir.) 1981, U.S. Supreme Ct. 1984. Sole practitioner, Brownsville, Tex.; cons., Mexican Consulate, Brownsville, 1983— Mem. ACLU, ABA, Tex. Bar Assn., Cameron County Bar Assn., Tex. Criminal Def. Lawyers Assn., Nat. Assn. Criminal Def. Lawyers. Democrat. Roman Catholic. E-mail: lwalsh4532@aol.com. General civil litigation, Criminal, Private international. Home: 444 Calle Retama Brownsville TX 78520-7418 Office: Lawrence A Walsh Law Offices 950 E Van Buren St Brownsville TX 78520-7199

WALSH, MILTON O'NEAL, lawyer; b. Memphis, June 17, 1941; s. J. Milton and Rebie (Willis) W.; m. Janet Parker; children: Susan, Neal. BS, La. State U., 1964, JD, 1971. Bar: La. 1971. Salesman Met. Ins. Co., Baton Rouge, 1963-65; claims adjustor Safeco Ins. Co., 1965-68; law clk. Franklin, Moore, Beychok & Cooper, 1968-71, assoc., 1971-73; ptnr. Franklin, Moore, Cooper & Walsh, 1973-74, Franklin, Moore & Walsh, Baton Rouge, 1974-90; prin. O'Neal Walsh and Assocs., 1990—. Chmn. rules com. Baton Rouge City Ct., 1975-76, liaison com. 19th Jud. Dist. Ct., 1977; instr. in bus. law La. State U., 1974. Mem. ABA (mem. products liability com. 1978-79), Baton Rouge Bar Assn., La. Bar Assn., La. Assn. Def. Counsel (bd. dirs. 1982-84, 96-97), Internat. Assn. Def. Counsel (mem. casualty ins. com. 1980-81, mem. faculty 14th ann. counsel trial acad. 1986), Def. Rsch. Inst. (state chmn. 1980-82, regional v.p. 1983-86, bd. dirs. 1986-89, 96-98, mem. arbitration com., mem. nat. nominating com. 2000, Scroll of Merit award 1981, 82), Am. Bd. Trial Advocates (L.A. chpt., treas. 2000-01, v.p. 2001—, faculty mem. Masters in Trail 2000), Assn. Def. Trial Attys. (state chmn. 1984—, S.W. mem. chmn. 1985-95, v.p./pres.-elect 1995-96, pres. 1996-97, mem. exec. coun. 1990-93), Sherwood Forest Country Club (bd. dirs. 1977-79, pres. 1979), Phi Delta Phi. General civil litigation, Insurance. Office: O'Neal Walsh & Assocs 501 Louisiana Ave Baton Rouge LA 70802-5921 E-mail: onealwalsh@onealwalsh.com

WALSH, ROBERT ANTHONY, lawyer; b. Boston, Aug. 26, 1938; s. Frank and Emily Angelica (Bissitt) W.; m. Angela Rosalie Barile, Aug. 3, 1966; children: Maria, Robert II, Amy. SB, MIT, 1960; MS, Fla. Inst. Tech., 1967; JD, Suffolk U., 1971. Bar: Mass. 1971, U.S. Dist. Ct. Mass. 1972, U.S. Patent Office 1972, Can. Patent Office 1973, Ill. 1976, U.S. Supreme Ct. 1976, U.S. Ct. Appeals (Fed. cir.) 1982, U.S. Ct. Mil. Appeals 1983, Vt. 1996; registered profl. engr., Mass. Engr. Saturn Boeing, Michaud, La., 1964-65; program analyst RCA, Cape Canaveral, Fla., 1965-68; patent trainee, engr. Avco Research Lab., Everett, Mass., 1968-72; patent atty. GTE Labs., Waltham, 1972-73; group patent counsel Bell & Howell Co., Chgo., 1973-78; patent counsel ITT E. Coast Patents, Nutley, N.J., 1978-80, patent counsel internat., 1980-82, sr. patent counsel internat., 1982-86; dir. internat. patents ITT Corp., N.Y.C., 1986-87; gen. patent counsel ITT Def. Tech. Corp., Nutley, 1987-89; chief patent counsel Allied-Signal Aerospace Co., Phoenix, 1989-94; atty. IBM Corp., Essex Junction, Vt., 1994—. Ednl. counselor admissions MIT, No. N.J., 1978-89, Ariz., 1989-94; with Office of Judge Adv. Gen., Washington. Col. USAF, 1960-92. (ret.) Mem. ABA (co-chmn. subcom. PTC sect. 105), Tri-State USAFR Lawyers Assn. (Meritorious Achievement award 1980), KC (fin. sec. Scottsdale, Ariz. 1993-95), Internat. Patent Club (pres. 1988-89), Am. Intellectual Property Law Assn., Aerospace Industry Assn. (chmn. Intellectual Property com.), Chgo. Patent Law Assn., N.J. Patent Law Assn., Ariz. Patent Law Assn. (bd. dirs.), Sigma Xi. Roman Catholic. Patent, Trademark and copyright. Home: 171 Yacht Haven Dr Shelburne VT 05482-7776 Office: Intellectual Property Law Dept 915 1000 River St Essex Junction VT 05452-4201

WALSH, ROBERT K. dean; AB, Providence Coll., 1964; JD, Harvard U., 1967. Bar: Calif. 1967, Ark. 1979. Assoc. McCatchen, Black, Verleger & Shea, L.A., 1967-70; asst. prof. Villanova (Pa.) U., 1970-71, assoc. prof., 1971-73, prof., 1973-76; ptnr. Friday, Eldredge & Clark, Little Rock, 1981-89; dean, prof. Wake Forest Sch. Law, Winston-Salem, N.C., 1989—. Mem. ABA (chair accreditation com. 1984-86, chair standards rev. com. sect. legal edn. 1991—), N.C. Bar Assn. (chair bar bench and law schs. com. 1990-92, v.p., bd. govs. 1994-95). Office: Wake Forest Sch Law Worrell Profl Ctr PO Box 7206 Winston Salem NC 27109-7206*

WALSH, SEAN M. lawyer, audio-video computer forensics consultant; b. N.Y.C., Dec. 26, 1947; s. John W. and Catherine M. Walsh; m. Christine Ann Kull, June 10, 1978; children: Kathleen, Sean, Stephen. BS, Fordham U., 1970, JD, 1973. Bar: N.Y. 1974. Chief, asst. dist. atty. Dist. Atty.'s Office, N.Y.C., 1973-96; pres. Walsh Assocs. Forensic Cons., Douglaston, N.Y., 1997—; dep. counsel Office of Inspector Gen. N.Y.C. SCA. Officer/dir. Law Enforcement Video Assocs., Ft. Worth, 1989-95, dep. counsel, Office Inspector General, NYC. Author: Video and the Law, 1979; inventor non-linear video wire tapping rec. sys. Vice-chmn. N.Y.C. Cmty. Planning Bd., 1986-98; pres. Queens (N.Y.) Civic Congress, 1996—, past pres./dir. Douglaston Civic Assn. Recipient Outstanding Cmty. Bd. Work, N.Y.C., 1973, Outstanding Svc. to N.Y. State Police, 1992, Van Zandt Cmty. Svc. award, 1999; named Marshall to Little Neck Douglaston Meml. Day Parade, 1990. Mem. Assn. Bar City N.Y. (Comm. com. 1983-85, Computer com. 1997-2000), High Tech. Crime Investigation Assn. (pres. local chpt. 1994-96, internat. pres. 2000-2001). Avocations: sailing, skiing, scuba diving. Home: PO Box 238 Douglaston NY 11363-0238

WALSH, THOMAS CHARLES, lawyer; b. Mpls., July 6, 1940; s. William G. and Kathryne M. Walsh; m. Joyce Williams, Sept. 7, 1968; children: Brian Christopher, Timothy Daniel, Laura Elizabeth. BS in Commerce magna cum laude, St. Louis U., 1962, LLB cum laude, 1964. Bar: Mo. 1964, U.S. Dist. Ct. (ea. dist.) Mo. 1964, U.S. Ct. Appeals (8th cir.) 1968, U.S. Supreme Ct. 1971, U.S. Ct. Appeals (6th cir.) 1972, U.S. Ct. Appeals (5th cir.) 1974, U.S. Ct. Appeals (D.C. cir.) 1980, U.S. Ct. Appeals (7th cir.) 1982, U.S. Ct. Appeals (9th cir.) 1987, U.S. Ct. Appeals (4th cir.) 1989, U.S. Ct. Appeals (11th and fed. cirs.) 1992, U.S. Ct. Appeals (2d and 10th cirs.) 1993. Jr. ptnr. Bryan, Cave, McPheeters & McRoberts, St. Louis, 1964-73; ptnr. Bryan, Cave LLP, 1974—, mem. exec. com., 1980-96. Mem. 8th Cir. Adv. Com., 1983-86. Bd. dirs. St. Louis Symphony Soc., 1983-95. With U.S. Army, 1965-66; lt. USNR, 1966-71. Fellow Am. Coll. Trial Lawyers; mem. ABA, Mo. Bar Assn., St. Louis Bar Assn., Am. Law Inst., Mo. Athletic Club, Bellerive Country Club. Roman Catholic. Federal civil litigation, State civil litigation, Appellate. Office: Bryan Cave LLP 1 Metropolitan Sq 211 N Broadway Saint Louis MO 63102-2733 E-mail: tcwalsh@bryancavellp.com

WALSH, WILLIAM ARTHUR, JR. lawyer; b. Washington, Mar. 17, 1949; children: Jesse Creighton, Patrick McKay. BS in Econs. and Fin., U. Md., 1972; JD, U. Richmond, 1977. Bar: Va. Ptnr., head real estate, fin. and devel. team Hunton & Williams, Richmond, Va., 1977—. Mem. adv. bd. for law rev. U. Richmond. Trustee, pres., bd. dirs. Va. Commonwealth U. Real Estate Found.; mem. Va. Commonwealth U. Real Estate Circle of Excellence. Mem. ABA, Va. Bar Assn., Richmond Bar Assn. Home: 4705 Leonard Pky Richmond VA 23226-1337 Office: Hunton & Williams Riverfront Pla East Tower 951 E Byrd St Richmond VA 23219-4074

WALSOM, ROGER BENHAM, lawyer; b. London, Mar. 2, 1953; s. William and Ivy Doris Walsom; m. Susan Christina Walsom. JD with honors, U. Southampton, 1977. Registered solicitor. Solicitor Slaughter & May, London, 1978-83, Ashurst Morris Crisp, London, 1983-86, assoc., 1986-88, ptnr., 1988—. Author: Insurance: Structuring Complex Transactions, 1999. Mem. Law Soc. Avocations: reading, cycling, food and drink. General corporate. Office: Ashurst Morris Crisp Broadwalk Ho 5 Appold St London EC2A 2HA England Fax: 0207.638.1112. E-mail: roger.walsom@ashurst.com

WALSTON, RODERICK EUGENE, state government official; b. Gooding, Idaho, Dec. 15, 1935; s. Loren R. and Iva M. (Boyer) W.; m. Margaret D. Grandey; children: Gregory Scott W., Valerie Lynne W. A.A., Boise Jr. Coll., 1956; B.A. cum laude, Columbia Coll., 1958; LL.B. scholar, Stanford U., 1961. Bar: Calif. 1961, U.S. Supreme Ct. 1973. Law clk to judge U.S. Ct. Appeals 9th Cir., 1961-62; dep. atty. gen State of Calif., San Francisco, 1963-91, head natural resources sect, 1969-91, chief asst. atty. gen. pub. rights div., 1991-99; spl. dep counsel Kings County, Calif., 1975-76; gen. counsel Metropolitan Water Dist. So. Calif., 2000—. Mem. environ. and natural resources adv. coun. Stanford (Calif.) Law Sch. Contbr. articles to profl. jours.; bd. editors: Stanford Law Rev., 1959-61, Western Natural Resources Litigation Digest, Calif. Water Law and Policy Reporter; spl. editor Jour. of the West. Co-chmn. Idaho campaign against Right-to-Work initiative, 1958; Calif. rep. Western States Water Coun., 1986—; environ. and natural resources adv. coun., Stanford Law Sch. Nat. Essay Contest winner Nat. Assn. Internat. Rels. Clubs, 1956, Stanford Law Rev. prize, 1961; recipient Best Brief award Nat. Assn. Attys. Gen., 1997; Astor Found. scholar, 1956-58. Mem. ABA (chmn. water resources com. 1988-90, vice chmn. and conf. chmn. 1985-88, 90—), Contra Costa County Bar Assn., U.S. Supreme Ct., Hist. Soc., Federalist Soc., World Affairs Coun. No. Calif. Office: Metro Water Dist 700 N Alameda St Los Angeles CA 90012

WALTER, MICHAEL CHARLES, lawyer; b. Oklahoma City, Nov. 25, 1956; s. Donald Wayne and Viola Helen (Heffelfinger) W. BA in Polit. Sci., BJ Editl. Journalism, U. Wash., 1980; JD, Seattle U., 1983. Bar: Wash. 1985, U.S. Dist. Ct. (9th cir. 1985). Ptnr. Keating, Bucklin & McCormack, Seattle, 1985—. Instr. Bellevue (Wash.) C.C., 1983—. FAX: 206-223-9423. Mem. ABA, Wash. State Bar Assn., Seattle-King County Bar Assn., Wash. Def. Trial Laywers Assn., Seattle Claims Adjustors Assn., Wash. Assn. Mcpl. Attys., Def. Rsch. Inst., Am. Planning Assn. Avocations: running, swimming, hiking, coin collecting, photography. State civil litigation, Land use and zoning (including planning), Municipal (including bonds). Home: 11920 27th Pl SW Burien WA 98146-2438 Office: Keating Bucklin & McCormack Inc PS Bank of Am Plaza 800 5th Ave Seattle WA 98104 Fax: 206- 223-9423. E-mail: mwalter@kbmlawyers.com

WALTER, MICHAEL JOSEPH, lawyer; b. N.Y.C., Mar. 2, 1943; s. Samuel Lewis and Hilda (Finn) W.; m. Carla James, Mar. 2, 1973; children— Kristen, Lindsay. BA, U. Bridgeport, Conn., 1964; JD, Bklyn. Law Sch., 1967. Bar: N.Y. 1968, Tex. 1976. County atty. Broome County, Binghamton, N.Y., 1971-72; assoc. Drazen, Carmien & Young, Binghamton, 1972-74; pvt. practice law, Binghamton, 1974-76, Houston, 1976-80; v.p., gen. counsel Meineke Discount Mufflers, Houston, 1980-82; sr. v.p. law Computerland Corp., Oakland, Calif., 1983-84; gen. counsel Entre Computer Ctrs., Inc., Vienna, Va., 1984-87, v.p. gen. counsel Corp. for Open System, McLeans, Va., 1987—. Assoc. editor Litigation Mag., Chgo., 1981— . Contbr. articles to various publs. With U.S. Army, 1968-70. Republican. Federal civil litigation, General corporate, Franchising. Office: Corp for Open Systems 1750 Old Meadoco Rd Mc Lean VA 22102

WALTERS, BETTE JEAN, lawyer; b. Norristown, Pa., Sept. 5, 1946; BA, U. Pitts., 1967; JD, Temple U., 1970, LLM in Taxation, 1974. Bar: Pa. 1970, U.S. Dist. Ct. (ea. dist.) Pa. 1971. Law clk., assoc. William R. Cooper, Lansdale, Pa., 1969-72; spl. asst. to pub. defender Montgomery County (Pa.), 1973; pvt. practice North Wales, Pa., 1972-73; assoc. counsel Alco Standard Corp., Valley Forge, 1973-79, group counsel mfg., 1979-83; v.p., gen. counsel, sec. Alco Industries, Inc., 1983—, also bd. dirs., 1983—. Mem. corp. sponsors com. Zool. Soc. of Phila. Mem. ABA, DAR, Pa. Bar Assn., Montgomery County Bar Assn., Am. Corp. Counsel Assn., Licensing Execs. Soc.. Republican. General corporate, Private international, Labor. Office: Alco Industries Inc PO Box 937 Valley Forge PA 19482-0937 E-mail: bjwalters@alcoind.com

WALTERS, BILL, state senator, lawyer; b. Paris, Apr. 17, 1943; s. Peter Louis and Elizabeth Cecelia (Wilhelm) W.; m. Joyce Leslie Garrett Moore, Jan. 9, 1964 (div. 1970); children: Jamie, Sherry Ann; m. Shirley Ann Dixon, Aug. 20, 1971; 1 child, Sandra. BS, U. Ark., 1966, JD, 1971. Bar: Ark. 1971, U.S. Dist. Ct. Ark. 1971. Asst. prosecuting atty. 12th Jud. Dist. Ark., Ft. Smith, 1971-74; pvt. practice Greenwood, Ark., 1975—; mem. Ark. Senate, Little Rock, 1982-2000. Bd. dirs., sec.-treas. Mineral Owners Collective Assn. Inc., Greenwood; v.p., bd. dirs. Sebastian County Abstract & Title Ins. Co., Greenwood and Ft. Smith, Ark.; mem. Ark. Real Estate Commn., Ark. Abstract and Title Commn. Committeeman Rep. Ctrl. Com. Ark., Ft. Smith, 1980; search pilot CAP, Ft. Smith. Decorated Silver Medal of Valor; recipient Cert. of Honor Justice for Crime's Victims, 1983. Mem. Ark. Bar Assn., South Sebastian County Bar Assn. (pres. 1991-94), Profl. Landmen's Assn. Roman Catholic. Home: PO Box 280 Greenwood AR 72936-0280 Office: 1405 W Center Greenwood AR 72936-3200 E-mail: waltlawb@ipa.net

WALTERS, CHRISTOPHER KENT, lawyer; b. Bryn Mawr, Pa., Oct. 10, 1942; s. Lester K. and Margaret (Becker) W.; m. Teri R. Simon, Nov. 23, 1980. AB, Princeton U., 1964; JD, U. Mich., 1967. Bar: Pa. 1967, U.S. Supreme Ct. 1980. Ptnr. Reed Smith Shaw & McClay, Phila., 1980—. Capt. U.S. Army, 1968-70, Vietnam. General civil litigation, Construction, Product liability. Office: Reed Smith Shaw & McClay 2500 One Liberty Pl Philadelphia PA 19103

WALTERS, JESSE RAYMOND, JR. state supreme court justice; b. Rexburg, Idaho, Dec. 26, 1938; s. Jesse Raymond and Thelma Rachael (Hodgson) W.; m. Harriet Payne, May 11, 1959; children: Craig T., Robyn, J. Scott. Student, Ricks Coll., 1957-58; BA in Polit. Sci., U. Idaho, 1961, JD, 1963; postgrad., U. Washington, 1962; LLM, U. Va., 1990. Bar: Idaho 1963; U.S. Dist. Ct. Idaho 1964, U.S. Ct. Appeals (9th cir.) 1970. Law clk. to chief justice Idaho Supreme Ct., 1963-64; solo practice Boise, Idaho, 1964-77; atty. Idaho senate, 1965; dist. judge 4th Jud. Dist., Idaho, 1977-82, adminstrv. dist. judge, 1981-82; chief judge Idaho Ct. Appeals, Boise, 1982-97. Chmn. magistrate's commn. 4th jud. dist.; chmn. Supreme Ct. mem. services; chmn. Criminal Pattern Jury Instrn. Com.; mem. Civil Pattern Jury Instrn. Com. Republican committeeman Boise, 1975-77; mem. Ada County Rep. Ctrl. Com., 1975-77. Mem. Idaho Bar Assn. (bankruptcy com.), Idaho Adminstrv. Judges Assn., ABA, Am. Judicature Soc. (dir.), Assn. Trial Lawyers Am., Idaho Trial Layers Assn., Coun. Chief Judges Ct. Appeals (pres. 1994-95), Boise Estate Planning Coun., Jaycees (nat. dir. 1969-70, pres. Boise chpt. 1966-67), Lions, Elks, Eagles. Mormon. Office: Supreme Ct Idaho PO Box 83720 Boise ID 83720-3720

WALTHER, DALE JAY, lawyer; b. Elko, Nev., Oct. 15, 1948; s. Harold V. and Beryl H. (Brand) W.; m. Kazue Mori, Sept. 25, 1975; children—Kent, Brian, Nolan, Lisa, Curtis, Katie. B.A., Northwestern U., 1972; postgrad., Notre Dame U. summer law program, Japan, 1974; J.D., Calif. Western Sch. Law, 1975. Bar: Alaska 1975. Assoc. Law Offices Murphy Clark, Anchorage, 1975-80; ptnr. Clark, Walther & Flanigan, Anchorage, 1980-93, ptnr. Walther & Flanigan, Anchorage, 1993— . Mem. Anchorage Bar Assn., Alaska Bar Assn., ABA, Order of Barristers, Am. Arbitration Assn., Phi Alpha Delta. Lodge: Elks. State civil litigation, Insurance, Personal injury. Home: PO Box 100428 Anchorage AK 99510-0428 Office: Walther & Flanigan 807 G St 1029 W 3rd Ave Ste 250 Anchorage AK 99501-1969

WALTON, DAN GIBSON, lawyer; b. Houston, Mar. 26, 1950; s. Dan Edward and Lucy Frances (Gibson) W.; m. Martha Sandlin, June 24, 1972; children: Cole Gibson, Emily Wyatt. BA with honors, U. Va., 1972; JD with honors, U. Tex., 1975. Bar: Tex. 1975, U.S. Dist. Ct. (so. dist.) Tex. 1977, U.S. Ct. Appeals (D.C. cir.) 1975, U.S. Ct. Appeals (5th cir.) 1981, U.S. Supreme Ct. 2001; bd. cert. in civil trial law and personal injury. Law clk. to hon. Malcolm R. Wilkey D.C. Ct. Appeals (D.C. cir.), 1975-76; assoc. Vinson & Elkins, Houston, 1976-82, ptnr., 1982—. Bd. dirs. The Meth. Health Care Sys., Houston. Bd. dirs. Meml. Pk. Conservancy, Houston, 2000—, Tex. Equal Access to Justice Found., 2000—, State Bar of Tex., 1999—, South Tex. Coll. Law, Houston, 1994—, Covenant House Tex., Houston, 1993—, Briarwood Sch./Brookwood Cmty., Houston, 1991—; trustee St. John's Sch., Houston, 1997—, Good Samaritan Found., 1998—; co-chancellor Tex. Ann. Conf., United Meth. Ch., Houston, 1996—; mem. admission commn. U.S. Dist. Cts. for So. Dist. Tex. Fellow Am. Bar Found., Tex. Bar Found., Houston Bar Found. (chair 1994), Houston Bar Assn. (pres. 1998-99), Garland Walker Am. Inn of Ct. (master), Am. Bd. Trial Advocates (assoc.), Internat. Soc. Barristers, Internat. Assn. Def. Counsel, Tex. Assn. Def. Counsel. Avocations: golf, skiing. General civil litigation, Construction, Professional liability. Home: 3203 Ella Lee Ln Houston TX 77019-5923 Office: Vinson & Elkins LLP 2300 First City Tower 1001 Fannin St Ste 3201 Houston TX 77002-6706

WALTON, EDMUND LEWIS, JR. lawyer; b. Salisbury, Md., Sept. 4, 1936; s. Edmund Lewis and Iris Tull (White) W.; m. Barbara Post, Sept. 18, 1965: children: Southy E., Kristen P. BA, Coll. William and Mary, 1961, JD (Godwin scholar), 1963. Bar: Va. 1963, U.S. Dist. Ct. (ea. dist.) Va. 1964, U.S. Supreme Ct. 1971, U.S. Dist Ct. (we. dist.) Va. 1972, U.S. Ct. Appeals (4th cir.) 1980. Grad. asst. Coll. William and Mary, 1961-62; assoc. Simmonds, Coleburn, Towner & Carman, Arlington, Fairfax, Va., 1963-68, ptnr., 1968-74, Putbrese and Walton, McLean, Va., 1975; pvt. practice, 1976-82; sr. ptnr. Walton and Adams P.C., 1983—. Judge pro tem Fairfax County Cir. Ct., 1977—; commr. in chancery, 1990-97, legis. com. Va. State Bar, 1974-76; bus. law sect. exec. com. 1983-88, sec. 1984-85, vice chmn. 1985-86, chmn. 1986-87. Editor William and Mary Law Sch. Rev. 1961-63. Bd. dirs. Home Run Acres Civic Assn. 1968-70, v.p. 1969-70; bd. dirs. McLean Citizens Assn., 1976-79, 1st v.p. 1977-78; bd. dirs., pres. Rocky Run Citizens Assn., 1973-74; bd. dirs. Langley Sch. Inc., 1975-77, treas. 1976-77; mem. Fairfax County Rep. Com., 1966-82, chmn. 1970-72; del. Rep. Nat. Conv. 1972; mem Va. Rep. Ctrl. Com. 1976-77, exec. com. 1976-77; chmn. Providence Dist. Rep. Com., 1968-70; mem. 10th Congl. Dist. Rep. Com. 1970-77, vice chmn. 1974-76, chmn. 1976-77, mem. 8th Congl. Dist. Rep. Com. 1967-70; v.p. Arlington County Young Reps., 1965-66, counsel Arlington County Rep. Com. 1965-66; bd. dirs. McLean Planning Com. 1975-79, chmn. 1976-77; bd. dirs. McLean Office Sq. Condominium Assn., 1979-83, pres. 1979-82; chmn. Tysons Corner Citizens Task Force 1977-78; mem. Fairfax County Coun. on Arts; bd. dirs. Fairfax YMCA 1974-75; bd. dirs. Friends of Turkey Run Farm, 1981—, counsel 1981—, mem. exec. com. 1981-83. With U.S. Army 1956-59. Named McLean (Va.) Bus. Citizen of Yr. 1996. Fellow ABA Found. (life), Va. Law Found. (dir. 1991-97, mem. com. on continuing legal edn. 1990-91, chmn. 1992-93); mem. ABA, Am. Law Inst., Va. Bar Assn. (spl. com. to study rules of ethics 1981-84, membership com. 1981-84, exec. com. 1982-88, chmn. 1984-85, pres.-elect 1985-86, pres. 1986-87), Va. Continuing Legal Edn. Bd. (chmn. 1995-98), Arlington County Bar Assn., Fairfax County Bar Assn. (cts. com. 1975-77, dir. 1976-77), McLean Bar Assn. (dir. 1978-79, 80-83, sec. 1978-79, pres. 1980-82), Va. Trial Lawyers Assn., Am. Judicature Soc., William and Mary Law Sch. Assn. (dir. 1970-76), Fairfax County C. of C. (dir. ex officio 1981-83), McLean C. of C. (bd. dirs. 1995-96, McLean Bus. and Profl. Assn. (dir. 1976-85, 89-90, pres. 1981-83), Washington Golf and Country Club, Daufuskie Island Club, Lowes Island Club, Phi Alpha Delta. Episcopalian. Banking, State civil litigation, General corporate. Home: 2032 Mayfair Mclean Ct Falls Church VA 22043-1760 Office: PO Drawer EE 6862 Elm St Ste 400 Mc Lean VA 22101-3869 E-mail: ewalton@walton-adams.com

WALTON, JON DAVID, lawyer; b. Clairton, Pa., Sept. 18, 1942; s. Thomas Edward and Matilda Lucy (Sunday) W.; m. Carol Jeanne Rowland, Sept. 15, 1964; children: David Edward, Diane Elizabeth. BS, Purdue U., 1964; JD, Valparaiso U., 1969. Bar: Pa. 1969. Atty. U.S. Steel Corp. (now USX Corp.), Pitts., 1969-73; asst. gen. counsel Harbison-Walker Refractories, 1973-75, gen. counsel, 1975-81, v.p., gen. counsel, 1981-83; regional gen. counsel Dresser Industries, Inc., 1983-86; gen. counsel, sec. Allegheny Ludlum Corp., 1986-90, v.p., gen. counsel, sec., 1990-96, Allegheny Techs. Inc., Pitts., 1996—, sr. v.p., gen. counsel, sec., 1997—. Trustee Westminster Coll., 1997—. Trustee Westminster Coll., 1997—; pres., bd. dirs. Music for Mt. Lebanon, 1996—; bd. dirs. Pitts. Youth Golf Found., 1991-98; clk. of session Southminster Presbyn. Ch., 1998—. Mem. ABA, Pa. Bar Assn., Allegheny County Bar Assn., Am. Soc. Corp. Secs. (former pres. regional group), Am. Corp. Counsel Assn., Am. Arbitration Assn. (panel arbitrators), Duquesne Club, Valley Brook Country Club, Rolling Rock Club. General corporate, Securities. Home: 137 Hoodridge Dr Pittsburgh PA 15228-1803 Office: Allegheny Technologies Inc 1000 Six PPG Pl Pittsburgh PA 15222-5479 E-mail: jwalton@alleghenytechnologies.com

WALTON, RODNEY EARL, lawyer; b. Corvallis, Oreg., Apr. 28, 1947; s. Ray Daniel Jr. and Carolyn Jane (Smith) W. BA, Coll. of Wooster, 1969; JD, Cornell U., 1976; postgrad., Fla. Internat. U., Miami, 1997—. Bar: Fla. 1976, U.S. Dist. Ct. (so. dist.) Fla. 1976, U.S. Dist. Ct. (mid. dist.) Fla. 1977, U.S. Supreme Ct. 1980, U.S. Ct. Appeals (11th cir.) 1981. Assoc. to jr. ptnr. Smathers & Thompson, Miami, Fla., 1976-87; ptnr. Kelley, Drye and Warren, 1987-93; atty. Heinrich Gordon Hargrove Weihe & James, P.A., Ft. Lauderdale, 1994-97; adj. instr. U.S. mil. history Fla. Internat. U., 2001. Sec. bd. dirs. Kings Creek Condominium Assn., Miami, 1984-89, treas., 1984, pres., 1990-91. 1st lt. U.S. Army, 1969-73, Vietnam. Decorated Bronze Star. Mem. ABA, Fla. Bar. Republican. Methodist. Avocations: travel, reading, tennis, history. Home: 7985 SW 86th St Apt 430 Miami FL 33143-7014 E-mail: RodneyEarlWalton@aol.com

WALTON, STANLEY ANTHONY, III, lawyer; b. Chgo., Dec. 10, 1939; s. Stanley Anthony and Emily Ann (Pouzar) W.; m. Karen Kayser, Aug. 10, 1963; children: Katherine, Anne, Alex. BA, Washington and Lee U., 1962, LLB, 1965. Bar: Ill. 1965, U.S. Dist. Ct. (no. dist.) Ill. 1966, U.S. Ct. Appeals (7th cir.) 1966. Ptnr. Winston & Strawn, Chgo., 1965-89, Sayfarth Shaw Fairweather, Chgo., 1989-96. Trustee Village of Hinsdale (Ill.), 1985-89; bd. dirs. Washington and Lee Law Sch., Lexington, Va., 1975-78, bd. dirs. univ. alumni, 1983-87, pres., 1986-87; bd. dirs. UNICEF, Chgo., 1983; pres. Hinsdale Hist. Soc., 1979-81, 2001—, St. Isaac Jogues PTA, 1980; sec. Hinsdale Cmty. Svc., 2000—; bd. dirs. Hinsdale Ctrl. Found., 2000—. Mem. Ill. State Bar Assn., Phi Alpha Delta, Hinsdale Golf Club. Republican. Roman Catholic. Home and Office: 6679 Snug Harbor Dr Willowbrook IL 60514-1826

WALTS, WILLIAM EDWARD, II, lawyer; b. Ft. Worth, Dec. 20, 1948; s. William Edward and Helen Frances (Lyles) W.; m. Mary Ellen Mesker, Dec. 20, 1975; children— Danielle Marie, Darci Ann. B.A., U. Tex., 1970, J.D., 1974. Bar: Tex. 1974, U.S. Dist. Ct. (no. dist.) Tex. 1976, U.S. Dist Ct. (ea. dist.) Tex. 1977, U.S. Ct. Appeals (5th cir.) 1981. Assoc. Strasburger & Price, Dallas, 1974-80, ptnr., 1981—; adv. dir. Harwood Pacific Corp., 1993-94. Dir. United Cerebral Palsy Met. Dallas, 1992-93. Mem. State Bar Tex. (mem. real property forms com. 1984-86), Dallas Bar Assn., North Dallas C. of C. Mem. Opportunity Dallas, 1984; deacon, officer, tchr. Park Cities Bapt. Ch., Dallas, 1978-93. Real property. Home: 7612 Arborgate St Dallas TX 75231-4838 Office: Strasburger & Price 901 Main St Ste 4300 Dallas TX 75202-3724

WALZER, JAMES HARVEY, lawyer, author; b. Neptune, N.J., Jan. 24, 1949; s. Elwood John and Mary Elizabeth (Harvey) W.; m. Gloria Jean Demkowski, May 29, 1971; children: Sara, Emily, Amanda, Adam. BA, Bowdoin Coll., 1972; JD, Cleve. State U., 1975. Bar: N.J. 1975, U.S. Dist. Ct. N.J. 1975. Pvt. practice, Newark, 1975-78, Livingston, N.J., 1978-81, Boonton, 1981—. Legal forms editor All-State Legal, a div. of All-State Internat., Inc., Cranford, N.J., 1978—96. Author: Employment, Agency, Service Agreements, 1986, Motor Vehicle Law and Practice--Forms, 1988, 2 vols., 2000, Civil Practice Forms, 5 vols., 1990, 8 vols., 5th edit., 1998; editor, author: Legal Forms, 7 vols., 1995-96. Mem. Manville (N.J.) Bd. Adjustment, 1976; bd. dirs. Somerset-Sussex Legal Svcs. Mem. ABA, N.J. Bar Assn., Morris County Bar Assn. Democrat. E-mai. Family and matrimonial, General practice, Real property. Home: 18 Magda Ln Hillsborough NJ 08844-4217 Office: 103 William St PO Box 675 Boonton NJ 07005-0675 E-mail: jhwalzer@aol.com

WAMPLER, ROBERT JOSEPH, lawyer; b. Greensboro, Ind., Mar. 3, 1936; s. Cruden V. and Mary L. (James) W.; m. Karen A. Wiggins, Feb. 19, 1977; children: Eric J., Kelly L., Michael J. AB, Yale U., 1959; JD, Ind. U., 1963. Bar: Ind. 1963, U.S. Dist. Ct. (so. dist.) Ind. 1963, U.S. Supreme Ct. 1966, U.S. Ct. Appeals (7th cir.) 1972. Assoc. Kightlinger & Gray, Indpls., 1963—, ptnr., 1968—, sr. ptnr., 1971—. Author handbook on product liability; co-author: Trial Advocacy in Indiana, 1989. Sec., bd. dirs. Ivy Ridge Civic Assn., Indpls., 1975—. Fellow Indpls. Bar Found.; mem. Indpls. Bar Assn. (chmn. litigation sect. 1987), Ind. Bar Assn., Def. Trial Counsel Ind., Masons, Order of Coif, Phi Delta Phi. Republican. Episcopalian. Alternative dispute resolution, General civil litigation, Professional liability. Home: 5939 Cape Cod Ct Indianapolis IN 46250-1845 Office: Kightlinger & Gray LLP 151 N Delaware St Ste 660 Indianapolis IN 46204-2574 E-mail: rwampler@k-glaw.com

WANDER, HERBERT STANTON, lawyer; b. Cin., Mar. 17, 1935; s. Louis Marvin and Pauline (Schuster) W.; m. Ruth Cele Fell, Aug. 7, 1960; children: Daniel Jerome, Susan Gail, Lois Marlene. AB, U. Mich., 1957; LLB, Yale U., 1960. Bar: Ohio 1960, Ill. 1960. Law clk. to judge U.S. Dist. Ct. (no. dist.) Ill., 1960-61; ptnr. Pope Ballard Shepard & Fowle, Chgo., 1961-78, Katten Muchin Zavis, Chgo., 1978—. Trustee Michael Reese Found., 1991—; bd. dirs. Tel. & Data Systems, Chgo.; mem. legal adv. com. to the bd. govs. N.Y. Stock Exch., 1989-92; mem. legal adv. bd. Nat. Assn. Securities Dealers, Inc., 1996-99. Editor: (jour.) Bus. Law Today, 1992-93; editor-in-chief: (jour.) The Bus. Lawyer, 1993-94; contbr. numerous articles to profl. jours. Bd. dirs. Jewish Fedn. Met. Chgo., 1972—, pres., 1981-83; bd. dirs. Jewish United Fund, 1972—, pres., 1981-83, chmn. pub. affairs com., 1984-87, gen. campaign chmn., 1993; former regional chmn. nat. young leadership cabinet United Jewish Appeal; vice-chmn. large city budgeting conf. Coun. Jewish Fedns., 1979-82, bd. dirs., 1980—, exec. com., 1983-84. Mem. ABA (sec. bus. law sect. 1992-93, vice-chair 1993-94, chair-elect 1994-95, chair 1995-96, apptd. to commn. on multidisciplinary practice 1998), Ill. State Bar Assn., Chgo. Bar Assn., Yale Law Sch. Assn. (exec. com. 1982-86), Std. Club, Econ. Club, Northmoor Country Club, Phi Beta Kappa. General corporate, Mergers and acquisitions, Securities. Home: 70 Prospect Ave Highland Park IL 60035-3329 Office: Katten Muchin Zavis 525 W Monroe St Ste 1600 Chicago IL 60661-3693 E-mail: hwander@kmz.com

WANDERMAN, SUSAN MAE, lawyer; b. N.Y.C., Mar. 12, 1947; d. Leo and Muriel D. Wanderman. AB, Wheaton Coll., Norton, Mass., 1967; JD, St. John's U., 1970; LLM, NYU, 1976. Bar: N.Y. 1971, U.S. Dist. Ct. (ea. and so. dists.) N.Y. 1972, U.S. Ct. Appeals (2d cir.) 1973, U.S. Supreme Ct. 1974. Asst. legal officer, legal dept. Chem. Bank, N.Y.C., 1972-75; 2d v.p. legal dept. Chase Manhattan Bank N.A., N.Y.C., 1975-82; asst. gen. counsel Citicorp Services, Inc., N.Y.C., 1982-84, v.p. Citibank, N.A., N.Y.C.. 1984—; instr. bus. law and law for the layman LaGuardia Community Coll., 1976-77; law day speaker Queens County Supreme Ct., 1979-83; mem. Community Bd. 6, Queens County, N.Y.C., 1987—. Contbr. articles to legal publs. Past vol. N.Y. State Bar Assn. Lawyers in the Classroom. Mem. ABA, N.Y. State Bar Assn., Queens County Bar Assn. Banking, Computer, Pension, profit-sharing, and employee benefits. Office: Citibank NA One Court Sq Long Island City NY 11120

WANG, ALBERT HUAI-EN, lawyer; b. Tainan, Taiwan, Feb. 21, 1967; s. Tien-Yu Wang and Shiu-Yin Chen. BA magna cum laude, MA magna cum laude, UCLA, 1990; JD, Cornell U., 1994. Bar: N.Y. 1995. Tax specialist KPMG Peat Marwick, L.A., 1990-91; tchr. asst. Cornell Law Sch., 1993; assoc. Willkie Farr & Gallagher, N.Y.C., 1994-99, Schulte Roth & Zabel LLP, N.Y.C., 1999—. Legal counsel, mem. adv. coun. Asian Am. Bus. Devel. Ctr., N.Y.C., 1999—. Dir. Chinese Am. Voters Assn. of Queens, Orgn. of Chinese Ams. (N.Y. chpt.). U. Calif. regent scholar, 1986-90, Alumni scholar UCLA, 1986, Departmental scholar, 1989. Mem. ABA, N.Y. State Bar Assn., Chinese Fin. Soc. (dir., legal counsel), Taiwan Merchant Assn. N.Y., China Inst., Asia Soc., Phi Beta Kappa, Phi Delta Phi, Omicron Delta Epsilon. Democrat. General corporate, Private international, Securities. Home: 138-10 Franklin Ave Apt 5N Flushing NY 11355-3305 Office: Schulte Roth & Zabel LLP 919 3d Ave New York NY 10022 Fax: (212) 593-5955. E-mail: albert.wang@srz.com

WANG, CHARLESTON CHENG-KUNG, lawyer, engineer; b. Tainan, Republic of China, Oct. 17, 1956; came to U.S., 1972; s. Shan-Cheng and I-Tsen (Cheng) W.; m. Shirley Liao, Mar. 14, 1981; children: Vivian, Arthur Rex. BS in Econs. and Chem. Engring., U. Del., 1977; MBA in Internat. Bus., Xavier U., 1979; JD, No. Ky. U., 1982; postgrad., U. Cin., 1989, No. Territory U. Darwin, Australia, 1999. Bar: Ohio 1982, U.S. Dist. Ct. (so. dist.) Ohio 1983, U.S. Dist. Ct. (ea. dist.) Ky. 1983, U.S. Ct. Appeals (6th cir.) 1983; diplomate Am. Bd. Indsl. Hygiene; cert. indsl. hygienist. Chem. engr. Procter & Gamble, Cin., 1979-81, NIOSH, Cin., 1981-84; mng. ptnr. Groeber & Wang, 1982-85; compliance officer U.S. Dept. Labor, 1985-88; v.p., gen. counsel Environ. Enterprises, Inc., 1988—. Adj. prof. No. Ky. U., 1983—, U. Cin., 1985—. Author: How to Manage Workplace Derived Hazards and Avoid Liability, 1987, OSHA Compliance & Management Handbook, 1991; assoc. editor No. Ky. Law Rev., 1980-82; contbr. articles to profl. jours. Mem. Am. Acad. Indsl. Hygiene, Am. Inst. Chem. Engrs., Am. Conf. Govt. Indsl. Hygienists, Chinese Am. Assn. Cin. (pres. 1987-88). Avocation: swimming. Home: 11321 Terwilligers Valley Ln Cincinnati OH 45249-2744 Office: Wanglaw Bldg 6924 Plainfield Rd Cincinnati OH 45236-3789

WANGER, OLIVER WINSTON, federal judge; b. L.A., Nov. 27, 1940; m. Lorrie A. Reinhart; children: Guy A., Christopher L., Andrew G., W. Derek, Oliver Winston II. Student, Colo. Sch. Mines, 1958-60; BS, U. So. Calif., 1963; LLB, U. Calif., Berkeley, 1966. Bar: Calif. 1967, U.S. Dist. Ct. (ea. dist.) Calif. 1969, U.S. Tax Ct. 1969, U.S. Dist. Ct. (cen. dist.) Calif. 1975, U.S. Dist. Ct. (so. dist.) Calif. 1977, U.S. Dist. Ct. (no. dist.) Calif. 1989, U.S. Ct. Appeals (9th cir.) 1989. Dep. dist. atty. Fresno (Calif.) County Dist. Atty., 1967-69; ptnr. Gallagher, Baker & Manock, Fresno, 1969-74; sr. ptnr. McCormick, Barstow, Sheppard, Wayte & Carruth, 1974-91; judge U.S. Dist. Ct. (ea. dist.) Calif., 1991—. Adj. prof. law Humphreys Coll. Law, Fresno, 1968-70. Fellow Am. Coll. Trial Lawyers, Internat. Acad. Trial Lawyers; mem. Am. Bd. Trial Advs. (pres. San Joaquin Valley chpt. 1987-89, nat. bd. dirs. 1989-91), Am. Bd. Profl. Liability Attys. (founder, diplomate), Calif. State Bar (mem. exec. com. litigation sect. 1989-92, mem. com. on fed. cts. 1989-90), San Joaquin Valley Am. Inn of Ct. (pres. 1992-93), Beta Gamma Sigma. Office: US Dist Ct 5104 US Courthouse 1130 O St Fresno CA 93721-2201

WANKE, RONALD LEE, lawyer, educator; b. Chgo., June 22, 1941; s. William F. and Lucille (Kleinwachter) W.; m. Rose Klonowski, Oct. 23, 1987. BSEE, Northwestern U., 1964; JD, DePaul U., 1968. Bar: Ill. 1968. Assoc. Wood, Dalton, Phillips, Mason & Rowe, Chgo., 1968-71, ptnr., 1971-84, Jenner & Block, Chgo., 1984--. Lectr. John Marshall Law Sch., Chgo., 1985-94; mem. adv. com. intellectual property program, U. Fla. Coll. Law. Co-author: (book chpt.) International Intellectual Property Law, 1997; contbr. articles to Software Law Jour., 1987, Internat. Legal Strategy, 1995. Mem. ABA, Computer Law Assn., Intellectual Property Law Assn. Chgo. (chmn. inventor svcs. com. 1976, chmn. fed. rules com. 1981). Computer, Patent, Trademark and copyright. Home: 1806 N Sedgwick St Chicago IL 60614-5306 Office: Jenner & Block 1 E Ibm Plz Fl 4000 Chicago IL 60611-7603

WARD, ANTHONY JOHN, lawyer; b. L.A., Sept. 25, 1931; s. John P. and Helen C. (Harris) W.; m. Marianne Edle von Graeve, Feb. 20, 1920 (div. 1977); 1 son. Mark Joachim; m. Julia Norby Credell, Nov. 4, 1978 (div. 1999). BA, U. So. Calif., 1953; LLB, U. Calif., Berkeley, 1956. Bar: Calif. 1957. Assoc. Ives, Kirwan & Dibble, L.A., 1958-61; ptnr. Marapese and Ward, Hawthorne, Calif., 1961-69; pvt. practice Torrance, 1969-76; ptnr. Ward, Gaunt & Credell, 1976—. Served to 1st lt. USAF, 1956-58. Mem. ABA, Blue Key, Calif. Trial Lawyers Assn., Lambda Chi Alpha. State civil litigation, Personal injury, Probate. Office: Pavilion A 21525 Hawthorne Blvd Torrance CA 90503-6600

WARD, DENITTA DAWN, lawyer; b. Gardner, Kans., Apr. 29, 1963; d. Gerald Dee Ascue and Patricia Diane (Henderson) Ray; m. Kent Alan Ward, July 6, 1991; children: Alexander Patrick, Olivia Caitlyn. BA, U. Kans., 1985; JD magna cum laude, Georgetown U., 1989. Bar: Md. 1989, U.S. Ct. Appeals (fed. cir.) 1990, D.C. 1991, U.S. Ct. Internat. Trade 1991. Rsch. asst. Georgetown U., Washington, 1988-89; jud. clk. U.S. Ct. Appeals for Fed. Cir., 1989-90; assoc. Donovan Leisure Rogovin Huge & Schiller, 1990-94; atty. Fed. Election Commn., 1994-96, Marriott Internat., Inc., 1996-98; sr. v.p., gen. counsel Boulderbiz, Inc., 1999—. Mng. editor Law and Policy in Internat. Bus., 1988-89. Mem. ABA, Ct. of Appeals for Fed. Cir. Bar Assn., Ct. of Appeals of Fed. Cir. Former Jud. Clks. Assn., Order of Coif, Omicron Delta Kappa, Pi Sigma Alpha. Avocations: travel, gardening. Federal civil litigation, Contracts commercial, Labor. Home: 6999 Firerock Ct Boulder CO 80301-3814

WARD, GEORGE EDWARD, lawyer, law educator; b. Saginaw, Mich., Feb. 14, 1941; s. George E. and Mary Margaret (Hackett) W.; m. Margaret L. Barbour, June 13, 1968; children: Mary, William, Teresa, Anne, Thomas. AB, U. Detroit, 1963; JD, U. Mich., Ann Arbor, 1966. Bar: Mich. 1967. Rsch. atty. Mich. Supreme Ct., Lansing, 1966-67; assoc. Butzel, Long, Gust, Klein & VanZile, Detroit, 1967-71; exec. dir. Detroit Charter Commn., 1971-72; ptnr. Burgoyne, Kaufman, Roche & Ward, Detroit, 1972-82; of counsel Milmet, Vecchio, Ward & Carnago, 1982-86; chief asst. pros. atty. Wayne County, 1986-2000; sole practice Detroit, 2000—. Adj. prof. Detroit Coll. Law U. Mich., Dearborn, 1970—; cons. Pitts. Charter Commn., 1973, Pontiac Charter Commn., 1981, Traverse City Charter Commn., 1984—85; county pub. adminstr. State of Mich., Detroit, 1973—86. Author: The Duties of Liberty, 1992, Cases and Materials on the Regulation of Business Franchises, 1997, Liberty and Law: Culture, Court, Consent of the Governed, 2001; contbr. articles to profl. jours. Mich. Law Revision Commn., 1971—73; bd. dirs. Cranbrook Peace Found., Bloomfield Hills, Mich.; chmn. bd. Growth Works, 1999—; co-chmn. Gubernatorial Inaugural Com., 1983; bd. dirs. Wayne County Cath. Soc. Svcs., 1995—, Wayne County Neighborhood Legal Svcs., 1995—, Wayne Ctr. Developmentally Disabled, 1995—, chmn. bd., 2001; mem. pres.'s cabinet U. Detroit, 1980—. Fellow: Mich. State Bar Found.; mem.: Inc. Soc. Irish-Am. Lawyers (pres. 2000), State Bar Mich. (bd. commrs. 1990—96, Rep. Assembly 1979—82), Detroit Bar Assn. (sec. young lawyers sect. 1969—70, chmn. criminal law com. 1988—90), I.C.L.E., U. Mich. Pres. Club, Scribes Club, Alpha Sigma Nu. Roman Catholic. Alternative dispute resolution, Appellate, Condemnation, General civil litigation, Municipal (including bonds), Legislative, Probate. Address: 1100 Buhl Bldg Detroit MI 48226 E-mail: geoedward@aol.com

WARD, HIRAM HAMILTON, federal judge; b. Thomasville, N.C., Apr. 29, 1923; s. O.L. and Margaret A. W.; m. Evelyn M. McDaniel, June 1, 1947; children: William McDaniel, James Randolph. Student, Wake Forest Coll., 1945-47; J.D., Wake Forest U., 1950, LLD (hon.), 1996. Bar: N.C. bar 1950. Practiced law, Denton, N.C., 1950-51; staff atty. Nat. Prodn. Authority, Washington, 1951-52; partner firm DeLapp, Ward & Hedrick, Lexington, N.C., 1952-72; U.S. dist. judge Mid. Dist. N.C., 1972—, chief judge, 1982-88, sr. judge, 1988—. Mem. com. on Codes of Conduct of Jud. Conf., U.S., 1990-95; mem. Fourth Cir. Jud. Coun., 1984-87. Contbr. legal opinions to Fed. Supplement, F.2d & F.R.D., 1972—. Bd. visitors Wake Forest U. Sch. Law, 1973— ; Mem. N.C. Bd. Elections, 1964-72; trustee Wingate Coll., 1969-72. Served with USAAF, 1940-45. Decorated Air medal, Purple Heart; recipient Liberty Bell award N.C. Bar Assn., 1994. Mem. ABA, N.C. Bar Assn., Am. Judicature Soc., N.C. State Bar, Masons, Lions, Phi Alpha Delta (hon. life). Republican. Baptist. Home: 188 Forest Park Dr Denton NC 27239-8013 Office: Hiram H Ward US Courthouse 246 Fed Bldg 251 N Main St Winston Salem NC 27101-3914

WARD, HORACE TALIAFERRO, federal judge; b. LaGrange, Ga., July 29, 1927; m. Ruth LeFlore (dec.); 1 son (dec.). AB, Morehouse Coll., 1949; MA, Atlanta U., 1950; JD, Northwestern U., 1959. Bar: Ga. 1960. Instr. polit. sci. Ark. A.M. and N. Coll., 1950-51, Ala. State Coll., 1951-53, 55-56; claims authorizer U.S. Social Security Adminstrn., 1959-60; assoc. firm Hollowell Ward Moore & Alexander (and successors), Atlanta, 1960-69; individual practice law, 1971-74; judge Civil Ct. of Fulton County, 1974-77, Fulton Superior Ct., 1977-79; U.S. Dist. Ct. judge No. Dist. Ga., Atlanta, 1979-93; sr. judge U.S. Dist. Ct. No. Dist. Ga., 1993—. Lectr. bus. and sch. law Atlanta U., 1965-70; dep. city atty., Atlanta, 1969-70, asst. county atty., Fulton County, 1971-74 Former Trustee Friendship Baptist Ch., Atlanta; mem. Ga. adv. com. U.S. Civil Rights Commn., 1963-65; assisting lawyer NAACP Legal Def. and Edn. Fund, Inc., 1960-70; mem. Jud. Selection Commn., Atlanta, 1972-74, Charter Commn., 1971-72; mem. Ga. Senate, 1964-74, jud. com., rules com., county and urban affairs com.; mem. State Democratic Exec. com., 1966-74; former bd. dirs. Atlanta Legal Aid Soc.; bd. dirs. Atlanta Urban League, Fed. Defender Program, No. Dist. Ga.; trustee Met. Atlanta Commn. on Crime and Delinquency, Atlanta U., Fledgling Found. Mem. Am. Bar Assn., Nat. Bar Assn. (chmn. jud. council 1978-79), State Bar Ga., Atlanta Bar Assn., Gate City Bar Assn. (pres. 1972-74), Atlanta Lawyers Club, Phi Beta Kappa, Alpha Phi Alpha, Phi Alpha Delta, Sigma Pi Phi. Office: US Dist Court 2388 US Courthouse 75 Spring St SW Atlanta GA 30303-3309

WARD, JOE HENRY, JR. retired lawyer; b. Childress, Tex., Apr. 18, 1930; s. Joe Henry and Helen Ida (Chastain) W.; m. Carlotta Agnes Abreu, Feb. 7, 1959; children: James, Robert, William, John. BS in Acctg., Tex. Christian U., 1952; JD, So. Meth. U., 1964. Bar: Tex. 1964, Va. 1972, D.C. 1974; CPA, Tex. Mgr. Alexander Grant & Co. CPA's, Dallas, 1956-64; atty. U.S. Treasury, 1965-68; tax counsel U.S. Senate Fin. Com., 1968-72; pvt. practice Washington, 1972-83; asst. gen. counsel, tax mgr. Epic Holdings, Ltd. and Crysopt Corp., 1983-87; pvt. practice Washington and Va., 1987-95; ret., 1995. Lt. USNR, 1952-56. Mem. ABA, AICPA, Am. Assn. Atty.-CPA's, Univ. Club. Home: 2639 Mann Ct Falls Church VA 22046-2721

WARD, RICHARD ALVORD, retired lawyer; b. San Bernardino, Calif., Oct. 21, 1922; s. John Stanley and Grace Lucile (Alvord) W.; m. Jean Ann Redick, Dec. 24, 1976; children: Normandie, Richard A., Heidi M. AB with distinction, George Washington U., 1961, JD with honors, 1965. Bar: Va. 1965, D.C. 1965, U.S. Supreme Ct. 1971. Pvt. practice, Washington, 1965-67; ptnr. Berliner and Ward, 1967-74; assoc. Rice, Carpenter & Carraway, 1974-76, ptnr., 1976-83; ret., 1985. With USMC, 1942-63. Decorated DFC Air medal. Mem. Order of Coif, Phi Delta Pi, Phi Sigma Kappa. Home: PO Box 566 Irvington VA 22480-0566 E-mail: raward@rivnet.net

WARD, ROBERT JOSEPH, federal judge; b. N.Y.C., Jan. 31, 1926; s. Joseph G. and Honor V. (Hess) W.; m. Florence C. Maisel, Apr. 15, 1951 (dec. Mar. 1994); children: Laura Alice, Carolyn; m. Renée J. Sokolow, May 28, 1995. SB, Harvard Coll., 1945, LLB, 1949. Bar: N.Y. 1949. Practiced in, N.Y.C., 1949-51, 61-72; asst. dist. atty. N.Y. County, 1951-55; asst. U.S. atty. So. Dist. N.Y., 1956-61; judge U.S. Dist. Ct. (so. dist.) N.Y., 1972-91, sr. judge, 1991—. With USNR, 1944-46. Mem. N.Y. State Bar Assn., Assn. of Bar of City of N.Y., Fed. Bar Coun. Office: US Dist Ct US Courthouse Foley Sq New York NY 10007-1501

WARD, THOMAS JEROME, lawyer; b. New Kensington, Pa., May 6, 1936; s. Richard Thomas and Renatha Ann (Hruscienski) W.; m. Lindley Ann Bennett, Aug. 20, 1960; children: Christine Lester, Janice Nolte, Thomas, James, Jeffrey, Matthew. BS, Duquesne U., 1958; JD, Villanova U., 1961. Tax atty. Westinghouse Electric Corp., Pitts., 1961-65; successively atty., sr. atty., asst. gen. atty. Rockwell Mfg. Co., 1965-71, mgr. corp. devel., 1971-73; v.p., gen. counsel, sec. Disston Inc., 1973-78; ptnr. Meyer, Darragh, Buckler, Bebenek & Eck, 1978-84; v.p. fin. and law, gen. counsel, sec. Dravo Corp., 1984-87, sr. v.p. fin. and adminstrn., 1987-88, exec. v.p., 1988-90; sr. atty. Buchanan Ingersoll. PC; dir. Buchanan Ingersoll (Europa), Frankfurt, Germany, 1990-91; sr. v.p., gen. counsel Federated Svcs. Co., Pitts., 1991-99; spl. counsel Pietragallo, Bosick & Gordon, 1999—. Editor Villanova Law Rev., 1960-61. Bd. dirs., past pres. Cath. Charities of Pitts.; past bd. advisors Duquesne U. Sch. Bus. and Adminstrn., Pitts.; mem. bd. dirs., past pres. Bethel Park Cmty. Found. Mem. ABA, Pa. Bar Assn., Allegheny County Bar Assn., Century Club Disting. Alumni Duquesne U. Democrat. Roman Catholic. Club: Duquesne. Office: 38th Fl 1 Oxford Ct Fl 38 Pittsburgh PA 15219-1407 E-mail: tjw@pbandg.com

WARDELL, JOHN WATSON, lawyer; b. Mt. Erie, Ill., Oct. 25, 1929; s. Charles R. and Rada (Travers) W.; m. Carol J. Gross, Aug. 6, 1955; (div. 1984); children: Michael, Amy, Laurie, Douglas. BA, U. Ill., 1950, JD, 1956. Bar: Ill. 1956, U.S. Dist. Ct. (no. dist.) Ill. 1967. Counsel law dept. Standard Oil Co. (Ind.), 1956-61, Motorola, Inc., Franklin Park, Ill., 1961-68; pvt. practice, 1968-69, 71-75, 96—; ptnr. Franz, Franz, Wardell & Lindberg 1969-70, Wardell & Ungvarsky, 1970-71, Wardell & Meinhardt 1973-74, Wardell & Johnson Ltd. and predecessor, Crystal Lake, Ill., 1976-88, Palmer & Wardell, Schaumburg, Ill., 1987-96; gen. counsel, dir. Matsuo Electronics Am. Inc.; dir. other corps. Mem. Gov.'s Adv. Council 1969-73; bd. dirs. North Barrington (Ill.) Area Assn., 1970-84; mem. Lake County (Ill.) Taxpayers Com., 1970-73. With M.C., U.S. Army, 1951-53. Mem. ABA, Ill. Bar Assn. (chmn. younger mems. conf. 1965-66, council gen. practice sect. 1971-75, task force on profl. publicity 1976-78, council internat. law sect. 1982-86), Chgo. Bar Assn. (internat. and fgn. law com. 1970-83), N.W. Suburban Bar Assn., U. Ill. Scholarship Soc., Turnberry Country Club, Order of Coif, Phi Beta Kappa, Phi Delta Phi, Phi Kappa Phi. Republican. Contbr. articles to profl. jours. General corporate, Private international, Probate. Office: 675 N North Ct Ste 490 Palatine IL 60067-8173

WARDEN, JOHN L. lawyer; b. Evansville, Ind., Sept. 22, 1941; s. Walter Wilson and Juanita (Veatch) W.; m. Phillis Ann Rodgers, Oct. 27, 1960; children: Anne W. Clark, John L., W. Carson. AB, Harvard U., 1962; LLB, U. Va., 1965. Bar: N.Y. 1966, U.S. Ct. Appeals (2d cir.) 1966, U.S. Dist. Ct. (so. and ea. dists.) N.Y. 1967, U.S. Ct. Appeals (10th cir.) 1971, U.S. Supreme Ct. 1972, U.S. Ct. Appeals (D.C. cir.) 1980. Assoc. Sullivan & Cromwell, N.Y.C., 1965-73, ptnr., 1973—. Pres. U. Va. Law Sch. Found.; trustee Am. Ballet Theatre. Editor-in-chief: Va. Law Rev., 1964-65. Fellow Am. Coll. Trial Lawyers; mem. ABA, Am. Law Inst., N.Y. State Bar Assn., Assn. Bar City N.Y., N.Y. County Lawyers Assn., Knickerbocker Club, Down Town Assn. Club, Doubles Club, Bedford Golf and Tennis Club, Lyford Cay Club. Republican. Episcopalian. Antitrust, General civil litigation, Mergers and acquisitions. Office: Sullivan & Cromwell 125 Broad St Fl 28 New York NY 10004-2489 E-mail: wardenj@sullcrom.com

WARDLAW, KIM A.M. federal judge; b. San Francisco, July 2, 1954; m. William M. Wardlaw Sr., Sept. 8, 1984. Student, Santa Clara U., 1972-73, Foothill C.C., Los Altos Hills, Calif., 1973-74; AB in Comm. summa cum laude, UCLA, 1976, JD with honors, 1979. Bar: Calif., U.S. Dist. Ct. (cen. dist.) Calif. 1979, U.S. Dist. Ct. (so. dist.) Calif. 1982, U.S. Dist. Ct. Nev. 1985, U.S. Dist. Ct. (no. dist.) Calif. 1992, U.S. Dist. Ct Mont. 1993, U.S. Dist. Ct. Minn. 1994, U.S. Dist. Ct. (no. dist.) Ala. 1994, U.S. Dist. Ct. (so. dist.) Miss. 1995, U.S. Supreme Ct. Law clk. U.S. Dist. Ct. Cen. Dist. Calif., 1979-80; assoc. O'Melveny and Myers, 1980-87, ptnr., 1987-95; circ. judge U.S. Dist. Ct. Calif., L.A., 1995-98; cir. judge U.S. Ct. Appeals (9th cir.), 1998—. Presdl. transition team Dept. Justice, Washington, 1993; mayoral transition Team City of L.A., 1995—; bd. govs., vice-chair UCLA Ctr. for Comm. Policy, 1994—; cons. in field. Co-author: The Encyclopedia of the American Constitution, 1986; contbr. articles to profl. jours. Pres. Women Lawyers Pub. Action Grant Found., 1986-87; del. Dem. Nat. Conv., 1992; founding mem. L.A. Chamber Orchestra, 1992—; active Legal Def. and Edn. Fund, Calif. Leadership Coun., 1993—, Blue Ribbon of L.A. Music Ctr., 1993—. Named one of Most Prominent Bus. Attys. in L.A. County, L.A. Bus. Jour., 1995; recipient Buddy award NOW, 1995. Mem. ABA, NOW, Mex.-Am. Bar Assn. L.A. County, Calif. Women Lawyers, Women Lawyers Assn. L.A., L.A. County Bar Assn. (trustee 1993-94), Assn. Bus. Trial Lawyers (gov. 1988—), Orgn. Women Execs., Downtown Women Ptnrs, Chancery Club, Breakfast Club, Hollywood Womens Polit. Com., City Club Bunker Hill, Phi Beta Kappa. Office: US Dist Ct 9th Cir 125 S Grand Ave Rm 400 Pasadena CA 91109*

WARE, GUILFORD DUDLEY, lawyer; b. Dunnsville, Va., Apr. 15, 1925; s. Catesby and Lila (Maddox) W.; m. Nancy Smith, Jan. 17, 1959 (dec. Dec. 1974); children: Elizabeth Latane, Guilford Dudley Jr., David Burwell; m. Gay Dantzler, Sept. 17, 1977. BS in Commerce, U. Va., 1949, LLB, 1952. Bar: Va. 1952, U.S. Dist. Ct. (ea. dist.) Va. 1952, U.S. Supreme Ct. 1956, U.S. Ct. Appeals (4th cir.) 1957. Ptnr. Crenshaw, Ware & Martin, P.L.C., Norfolk, Va. Pres. YMCA, Norfolk, 1966-67, The Va. Symphony Orch., Norfolk, 1967-68; bd. dirs. Va. Inst. Marine Sci. Found., 2001—. Lt. col. USAF, 1943-46. Mem. ABA, ATLA, Norfolk/Portsmouth Bar Assn. (pres. 1987-88), Maritime Law Assn., Southeast Admiralty Law Inst. (seminar chmn. 1983, 89, gen. chmn. 1985), Am. Judicature Soc., Norfolk Yacht and Country Club, Harbor Club (pres. 1994-96), The Whitehall Club, Norfolk German Club (pres., gen. chmn. 1985), Best Lawyers of Amer., Virginia State Bar, Virginia Bar Assn., Ctr. Applied Sci. & Tech. (bd. dirs.), Norfolk Dredging Co. (pres. 1970-98), I'Anson-Hoffman Amer. Inn of Court (pres., 1999—). Admiralty, General corporate, General practice. Home: 7457 St Francis Ln Norfolk VA 23505-1757 Office: Crenshaw Ware & Martin PLC 1200 Bank of Am Ctr Norfolk VA 23510 Fax: (757) 623-5735. E-mail: gware@cwm-law.com

WARMER, RICHARD CRAIG, lawyer; b. Los Angeles, Aug. 12, 1936; s. George A. and Marian L. (Paine) W.; children: Craig McEchron, Alexander Richard. AB, Occidental Coll., 1958; MA, Tufts U., 1959; LLB, NYU, 1962. Bar: Calif. 1963, D.C. 1976. Assoc. O'Melveny & Myers, LLP, Los Angeles, 1962-69, ptnr., 1970-75, mng. ptnr. Washington, 1976-92, mem. mgmt. com., 1986-92, with San Francisco, 1994—. Speaker in field. Contbr. articles to profl. jours. Trustee Law Ctr. Found. NYU, 1981-94; dir. Headland Ctr. for Arts, San Francisco Jazz Orgn. Mem. ABA, D.C. Bar, State Bar Calif., Order of Coif, Phi Beta Kappa, Cosmos Club. Administrative and regulatory, Antitrust, General civil litigation. Home: 2224 Green St San Francisco CA 94123-4710 Office: O'Melveny & Myers LLP Embarcadero Ctr W 275 Battery St San Francisco CA 94111-3305 E-mail: rwarmer@omm.com

WARNER, CHARLES COLLINS, lawyer; b. Cambridge, Mass., June 19, 1942; s. Hoyt Landon and Charlotte (Collins) W.; m. Elizabeth Denny, Aug. 24, 1964; children: Peter, Andrew, Elizabeth. BA, Yale U., 1964; JD cum laude, Ohio State U., 1970. Bar: Ohio 1970. Assoc. Porter, Wright, Morris & Arthur and predecessor, Columbus, 1970-76, ptnr., 1976—, also mgr. labor and employment law dept., 1988-92. Pres. Peace Corps Svc. Coun., Columbus, 1974-76, Old Worthington (Ohio) Assn., 1976-78, Alliance for Quality Edn., Worthington, 1987-89, Worthington Ednl. Found., 1994-96, Opera Columbus, 1999—; chmn. lawyers sect. United Way, Columbus, 1983-84; mem. alumni adv. coun. Ohio State U. Fellow Am. Bar Found., Ohio Bar Found., Columbus Bar Found., Coll. Labor and Employment Lawyers; mem. ABA (subcom. chmn. EEO com. 1986-89, co-chair 2000—, exec. com. Met. Bar Caucus 1992-94, chmn. state & local bar ADR com. 1995-98), Ohio State Bar Assn. (coun. of dels. 1993—, chmn. fed. cts. com. 1992-94), Ohio Met. Bar Assn. (pres. 1991-92), Columbus Bar Assn. (pres. 1991-92, bd. govs. 1982-87, 88-93), FBA, Ohio Assn. Civil Trial Attys. (exec. bd. 1988-97), Ohio State U. Law Alumni Assn. (pres. 1996-97), Nat. Coun. Ohio State U. Coll. Law (pres.-elect 2000—), Capital Club, Yale Club (pres. 1979-81). Avocations: clarinet, singing, tennis. Federal civil litigation, General civil litigation, Labor. Home: 145 E South St Columbus OH 43085-4129 Office: Porter Wright Morris & Arthur 41 S High St Ste 2800 Columbus OH 43215-6194 E-mail: cwarner@porterwright.com

WARNER, KARL K. prosecutor; BS, U.S. Mil. Acad.; JD, W.Va. U. Gen. counsel to 10th Mountain Div. U.S. Army, 1994—96; legal counsel to two chmn. Joint Chiefs of Staff, 1996—98; gen. counsel U.S. Spl. Operations Command, 1998—2001; U.S. atty. so. dist. W.Va. U.S. Dept. Justice, 2001—. Office: PO Box 1713 Charleston WV 25326*

WARNER, PAUL M. prosecutor; BA, Brigham Young U., 1973, JD, 1976, MPA, 1984. With Utah Atty. Gen.'s Office, 1991-98; U.S. atty. Utah dist. U.S. Dept. Justice, 1998—. Office: 185 S St Ste 400 Salt Lake City UT 84111*

WARNER, RONALD, lawyer; b. N.Y.C., Apr. 15, 1944; s. Harry and Lorraine (Goodrich) W.; B.A., Tulane U., 1965; J.D., N.Y. U., 1968; m. Michele Elen Dressler, Sept. 28, 1968; children: Stephen Harlan, Bradley Douglas. Bar: N.Y. 1969, Calif. 1972, D.C. 1978. Assoc. firm Debevoise & Plimpton, N.Y.C., 1968-72; assoc. Troy, Malin & Pottinger, Los Angeles, 1973-75, ptnr., 1975-80; founding ptnr. Prince, Littenberg & Warner, Los Angeles, 1980-81; former ptnr. Kindel & Anderson, Los Angeles; now ptnr. Thelen, Marrin, Johnson & Bridges, Los Angeles; dir. Dynamic Sciences, Inc., Los Angeles. Chmn., So. Calif. alumni admissions com. Tulane U. Mem. Assn. Bar City N.Y., Am. Bar Assn., Los Angeles County Bar Assn., So. Calif. Swimming Assn. (chmn. no. sect. 1983—). Editor N.Y. U. Law Rev., 1967-68. Office: Thelen Marrin Johnson & Bridges 333 S Grand Ave Ste 3400 Los Angeles CA 90071-1538

WARNOCK, WILLIAM REID, lawyer; b. Detroit, July 25, 1939; s. William G. and Margery E. (Ford) W.; m. Sandra L. Klarich, Dec. 27, 1961; children: Cheryl Lynn, Laura Ellen. BBA, U. Mich., 1961, JD with distinction, 1964. Bar: Ill. 1964, U.S. Dist. Ct. (no. dist.) Ill. 1965, U.S. Supreme Ct. 1972, Mich. 1995. With Ross & Hardies, Chgo., 1964-70; regional counsel U.S. Dept. HUD, 1970-73; ptnr. Roan & Grossman, 1973-82; sole practice, 1982-85; ptnr. Siegel & Warnock, 1985-91; of counsel Donovan & Olsen, 1991; pres. William R. Warnock P.C., LaGrange, Ill., 1992—. Cons. Ill. Dept. Bus. and Econ. Devel., Chgo., 1977-78, Ill. Housing Devel. Authority, Chgo., 1973-78, Council State Housing Financing Agys., Washington, 1975-78; past pres., chmn. Atty.'s Title Guaranty Fund, Inc., Chgo., 1986-88, also bd. dirs., 1976—. Author: (legal references) Land Use and Zoning, 1974-88, Ward on Title Examination, 1975, Illinois Real Property Service: Real Estate Exchanges, 1988, Environmental Law and the Real Estate Lawyer, 1989-90. Mem. Ill. State Bar Assn., Am. Coll. Real Estate Lawyers, DuPage Club. Republican. Methodist. Avocations: boating, woodworking. Land use and zoning (including planning), Real property. Home: 13556 Pleasant View Rd Three Rivers MI 49093-8406 Fax: 708-482-0977

WARREN, ALVIN CLIFFORD, JR. lawyer, educator; b. Daytona Beach, Fla., May 14, 1944; s. Alvin Clifford and Barbara (Barnes) W.; m. Judith Blatt, Aug. 20, 1966; children— Allison, Matthew. B.A., Yale U., 1966; J.D., U. Chgo., 1969. Bar: Conn. 1970, Pa. 1975. Prof. law U. Conn.-West Hartford, 1969-73, Duke U., Durham, N.C., 1973-74, U. Pa., Phila., 1974-79, Harvard U. Law Sch., Cambridge, Mass., 1979— . Mem. ABA (tax sect.). Contbr. articles to law jours. Office: Law Sch Harvard U Cambridge MA 02138

WARREN, ELIZABETH, law educator; BS, U. Houston, 1970; JD, Rutgers U., 1976. Robert Braucher vis. prof. law Harvard U., Cambridge, Mass., 1992-93, Leo Gottlieb prof. law, 1995—. Mem. Nat. Bankruptcy Rev. Commn. Contbr. articles to profl. jours. Named one of 50 Top Women Lawyers Nat. Law Jour., 1998. Mem. Am. Law Inst. (v.p.). Office: Harvard U Law Sch Hauser 200 Cambridge MA 02138

WARREN, J(OHN) MICHAEL, lawyer; b. Port of Spain, Trinidad and Tobago, Dec. 16, 1939; came to U.S., 1946; s. John Milton and Isma Thelma (Farmer) W.; m. JoAnn Darlene Westermeier, June 24, 1961; children: John Douglas, Denise Marie, Stephanie Ann Larsen, Lynne Catherine Thatcher. BA, Tchr.'s Cert., Ea. Mich. U., 1961; JD, U. Mich., 1964. Bar: Mich. 1965. Assoc. Foster, Campbell, Lindermer & McGurrin, Lansing, 1965-70; exec. com. ptnr. Foster, Lindermer, Swift & Collins, 1970-80, pres., 1974-80, Warren, Cameron, Faust & Asciutto, Okemos, Mich., 1981—. Bd. dirs. Maxco, Inc., Lansing, Camp, Inc., Jackson, Mich. Pres. Chief Okemos coun. Boy Scouts Am., Lansing, 1989-91; pres. Lansing Region Comty. Found., 1994. Named Man of Yr., Gaelic League of Lansing, 1979; recipient Silver Beaver award Boy Scouts Am., 1990, Whitney Young award, 1996. Mem. Lansing Regional C. of C. (pres. 1980, Tireless award 1980). Avocations: genealogy, golf, reading. Home: 2150 Heritage Ave Okemos MI 48864-3614 Office: Warren Cameron Faust & Asciutto PO Box 26067 Lansing MI 48909-6067 E-mail: mandSWARREN@cs.com

WARREN, JOSEPH ADDISON, III, law and history educator; b. Ft. Pierce, Fla., July 23, 1944; s. Joseph Addison and Donna Belle (Fenstermacher) W. BA, Mich. State U., 1966, MA, 1967, PhD, 1976; JD, Thomas M. Cooley Law Sch., 1980. Bar: Mich., 1981, U.S. Supreme Ct. 1985. Prof. history and humanities Lansing (Mich.) C.C., 1969—; pvt. practice law Lansing, 1981—; owner Center Point Press, 1998—. Lectr. continuing edn. Mich. State U., East Lansing, 1995—; pub., editor Faculty Advocate Mag., Lansing, 1981-98; dir. Ctr. for Inner Awareness, Inc., Lansing, 1992—; rschr. Ralph Nader's Task Force on Congress, Lansing, 1971-74; forensic photographer Forensic Photographic Svcs., Lansing, 1977—; mem. Gov.'s Adv. Com. on Mich. Meat Stds., Lansing, 1974; co-counsel Wygant V. Jackson vs. Bd. of Edn., 1985; mem. com. on legal edn. State Bar of Mich., Lansing, 1987-89, U.S. Supreme Ct. Author: The Origins of the American Presidency, 1976; contbr. numerous articles to profl. publs. Mem. Mich. Fed. Bar Assn., Mich. State Bar Assn., Am. Acad. of Religion Studies, World Assn. Vedic Studies, Ctr. for Study of the Presidency, Internat. Vedanta Scholars in Indian Civilization, Am. Legal Studies Assn. Avocations: mentoring students and beginning professionals, international travel. Home: 1012 N Washington Ave Lansing MI 48906-4839 Office: 1016 N Washington Lansing MI 48906-4839

WARREN, MARTIN HUGH, lawyer; b. Bideford, Devon, U.K., Feb. 12, 1961; LLB, Bristol, Avon, 1982. Solicitor, 1985. Trainee Osborne Clarke, 1983-85; solicitor Eversheds, 1986-88, assoc., 1988-89, ptnr., 1989—. Author: People Management. ABA, Am. Employment Law Coun., Reform Club. Labor. Office: Fitzalan Ho Fitzalan Rd Cardiff CF24 0EE England Fax: 01633 882417; 029 2046 4347. E-mail: martinwarren@eversheds.com

WARREN, ROBERT STEPHEN, lawyer; b. Pasadena, Calif., Dec. 9, 1931; s. Harry Ludwig and Maxine Winifred (Hopkins) W.; m. Betty Lou Soden, June 11, 1955 (dec. Sept. 1991); children: Kimberly Ann, Stephen Hopkins; m. Anna Marie Pretzel, Dec. 28, 1993. BA in Econs., U. Southern Calif., 1953, LLB, 1956. Bar: Calif. 1956, Del., U.S. Ct. Appeals (9th cir.), U.S. Dist. Ct. (ctrl. dist.) Calif., U.S. Ct. Mil. Appeals, U.S. Dist. Ct. (so. dist.) Calif., U.S. Dist. Ct. (ea. dist.) Calif., U.S. Dist. Ct. (no. dist.) Calif., U.S. Dist. Ct. Wyo., U.S. Dist. Ct. Colo., U.S. Dist. Ct. (ea. dist.) Wash., U.S. Supreme Ct. From assoc. to ptnr. Gibson, Dunn & Crutcher, L.A., 1956, 59—. Contbr. articles to profl. jours.; assoc. editor Southern Calif. Law Rev.; speaker in field. Mem., former chair bd. councilors U. So. Calif. Law Ctr.; past pres., exec. com. mem. Western Justice Ctr. Found. 1st lt. U.S. Army, 1957-59. Recipient Learned Hand award Am. Jewish Com., 1988,, Shattuck-Price award Los Angeles County Bar Assn., 1989, Joseph A. Ball award Brennan Ctr. for Justice/NYU, 1997, Trial Lawyer Hall of Fame award Calif. State Bar Assn., 1998. Mem. Am. Coll. Trial Lawyers, Assn. Bus. Trial Lawyers, Order of Coif, City Club on Bunker Hill, Phi Beta Kappa. Republican. Presbyterian. Avocations: hiking, reading, tennis. General civil litigation. Office: Gibson Dunn & Crutcher 333 S Grand Ave Ste 4400 Los Angeles CA 90071-3197 E-mail: rwarren@gibsondunn.com

WARREN, WILLIAM BRADFORD, lawyer; b. Boston, July 25, 1934; s. Minton Machado and Sarah Ripley (Robbins) W.; children: John Coolidge, Sarah W. Jaffe; m. Arete B. Swartz, Sept. 20, 1985. AB magna cum laude, Harvard U., 1956, LLB cum laude, 1959. Bar: N.Y. 1960. Assoc. Dewey Ballantine, N.Y.C., 1959-68; ptnr. Dewey Ballantine, LLP, 1968—. Lectr. Inst. Fed. Taxation, N.Y. U., So. Fed. Tax Inst., Practicing Law Inst. Pres. Cintas Found., N.Y.C.; bd. dirs. John Carter Brown Libr., Providence, R.I.; adv. bd. dirs. Met. Opera Assn., N.Y.C. Mem. Am. Law Inst., Am. Coll. Trust and Estate Counsel (former regent), Acad. Am. Poets (bd. dirs., treas.), Internat. Acad. Estate and Trust Law (former exec. com.), N.Y. State Bar Assn. (chmn. com. taxation of trust and estates sect. 1980-83), Assn. Bar City N.Y., Soc. Mayflower Descs., Harvard Club, Knickerbocker Club, Century Club, Grolier Club (past pres.). Home: 520 E 86th St New York NY 10028-7534 Office: Dewey Ballantine LLP 1301 Avenue Of The Americas New York NY 10019-6022

WARSHAUER, IRENE C. lawyer; b. N.Y.C., May 4, 1942; m. Alan M. Warshauer, Nov. 27, 1966; 1 child, Susan. BA with distinction, U. Mich., 1963; LLB cum laude, Columbia U., 1966. Bar: N.Y. 1966, U.S. Dsit. Ct. (so. and ea. dist.) N.Y. 1969, U.S. Ct. Appeals (2d cir.) 1969, U.S. Dist. Ct. (no. dist.) N.Y. 1980, U.S. Supreme Ct. 1972. With 1st Jud. Dept., N.Y. State Mental Health Info. Svc., 1966-68; assoc. Chadbourne Parke Whiteside & Wolff, 1968-75; mem. Anderson Kill & Olick, P.C., N.Y.C., 1975-99, Fried & Epstein, N.Y.C., 2000—. Mediator U.S. Dist. Ct. (so. dist.) N.Y., N.Y. State Supreme Ct.; lectr. Columbia Law Sch., Def. Rsch. Inst., Aspen Inst. Humanistic Studies, ABA, Rocky Mountain Mineral Law Found., CPR Inst. Dispute Resolution; arbitrator NASD EEOC, NYSE, Am. Arbitration Assn. Contbr. chpts. to books, articles to profl. jours. Mem. County Dem. Com., 1968—. Named to Hon. Order Ky. Cols. Mem. ABA, Assn. Bar City N.Y. (judiciary com. 1982-84, mem. ADR com. 2000—), N.Y. State Bar Assn. (chmn. subcom. mentally disabled and cmty. 1978-82). Avocations: gardening, cooking, birding, theatre. Insurance, Personal injury. Office: Fried & Epstein 1350 Broadway New York NY 10018-7702

WARTHEN, HARRY JUSTICE, III, lawyer; b. Richmond, Va., July 8, 1939; s. Harry Justice Jr. and Martha Winston (Alsop) W.; m. Sally Berkeley Trapnell, Sept. 7, 1968; children: Martha Alsop, William Trapnell. BA, U. Va., 1961, LLB, 1967. Bar: Va. 1967, U.S. Ct. Appeals (4th cir.) 1967, U.S. Dist. Ct. (ea. dist.) Va. 1969. Law clk. to judge U.S. Ct. Appeals (4th cir.), Richmond, Va., 1967-68; assoc. Hunton & Williams, 1968—. Lectr. U. Va. Law Sch., Charlottesville, 1975-77, in field. Trustee exec. com. Hist. Richmond Found., 1986-95, 96—, pres., 2000—; trustee Woodrow Wilson Birthplace and Mus., 1997—; dir. exec. com. Preservation Alliance of Va., 1991-97, pres., 1994-96; elder, trustee endowment fund Grace Covenant Presbyn. Ch.; moderator Hanover Presbytery, Presbyn. Ch. (USA), 1988. Lt. U.S. Army, 1962-64. Fellow Am. Coll. Trust and Estate Counsel, Va. Law Found.; mem. ABA, Richmond Bar Assn., Va. Bar Assn. (chmn. sect. on wills, trusts and estates 1981-89), Antiquarian Soc. Richmond (pres. 1977-78, 98-99), Country Club Va., Deep Run Hunt Club. Republican. Probate, Estate taxation. Home: 1319 Shallow Well Rd Manakin Sabot VA 23103-2305 Office: Hunton & Williams Riverfront Plz E Tower Richmond VA 23219 E-mail: hwarthen@hunton.com

WARWICK, KATHLEEN ANN, corporate lawyer; b. Phila., Aug. 3, 1934; d. William and Mae Warwick. AB, Vassar Coll., 1956; LLB, Columbia U., 1963. Bar: N.Y. 1963, U.S. Dist. Ct. (ea. and so. dists.) N.Y. 1965, U.S. Ct. Appeals (2d cir.) 1966, U.S. Supreme Ct. 1973, U.S. Ct. Appeals (6th cir.) 1982. Atty. SEC, N.Y.C., 1965-69; assoc. Cadwalader, Wickersham & Taft, 1969-75; corp. securities counsel Mobil Corp., 1975-87; pvt. practice, 1987; regional adminstr. SEC, 1987. Spkr. Am. Law Inst., ABA, Fed. Bar Coun., Harcourt Brace Jovanovich Pub., others. Mem. adv. bd. Securities Regulation & Law Report, Bur. Nat. Affairs, Inc.; bd. contbg. editors and advisors Securities Regulation Law Journal. Mem. ABA (vice chmn. fed. reg. securities com. 1986—, chmn. subcom. on members and mem. svcs., chmn. subcom. on reporting cos. under 1934 Act 1981-86, co-chmn. corp. counsel com. 1983-86, sect. coordinator for in-house counsel activities, numerous other coms., sects., exec. council, corp., banking and bus. law sect.), N.Y. State Bar Assn. (various coms.), Assn. of Bar of City of N.Y. (adminstrv. law com. 1977-80, securities regulation com. 1982-85, chmn. subcom. on issuer regulation and periodic reporting 1984-85, corp. law com. 1985—, chmn. subcom. on programs 1986-87), Am. Law Inst., Fed. Bar Assn. (securities law com.), Fed. Bar Coun. (securities com.), Columbia U. Law Sch. Alumni Assn. (bd. dirs.), Vassar Club (N.Y.C.), Georgetown Club. Republican. General corporate, Securities. Home: 11 E 75th St New York NY 10021-2639

WASHBURN, DAVID THACHER, lawyer; b. Claremont, N.H., May 2, 1930; s. Walter Henry and Josephine Emmeline (Dana) W.; m. Joycemarie Springer, June 10, 1957 (div. Dec. 1975); children: Margaret Dana, David Thacher Jr., Robert Springer, John Putnam. BA, U. Vt., 1952; JD, NYU, 1955. Bar: N.Y. 1956, D.C. 1970, U.S. Supreme Ct 1970. From assoc. to ptnr. Paul, Weiss, Rifkind, Wharton & Garrison, N.Y.C., 1955-95, of counsel, 1996—. Adj. prof. CUNY Law Sch., 1997-98. Trustee Rye Neck Bd. Edn., Mamaroneck, N.Y., 1971-73, Cambridge (Mass.) Coll., 1980-88, The Yard, N.Y.C., 1986-95, ARIA Found., Inc., Williston, Vt., 1991—; trustee, mem. exec. com. Rare Ctr. for Tropical Conservation, Phila., 1979-80; dir. Sanctuary for Families, Inc., N.Y.C., 1994—, mem. exec. com., treas. 1995-2000. Mem. ABA, N.Y. State Bar Assn., Assn. of Bar of City of N.Y., The Coffee House, Doubles, Westchester Country Club. General corporate, Mergers and acquisitions, Probate. Home: 10 W 66th St New York NY 10023-6206 Office: Paul Weiss Rifkind Wharton & Garrison Fl 2 1285 Avenue of the Americas New York NY 10019-6064 E-mail: dwashburn@paulweiss.com

WASHINGTON, DONALD W. prosecutor; BS, U.S. Mil. Acad.; JD, S. Tex. Coll. Law. Capt. U.S. Army, 1977—82; with Conoco Inc., 1982—96, div. counsel, gen. litigation atty., 1991—96; ptnr. Jeansonne and Redmondet, Lafayette, La., 1996—2001; U.S. atty. We. Dist. La. U.S. Dept. Justice, 2001—. Capt. USAR, 1982—90. Office: 300 Fannin St Ste 3201 Shreveport LA 71101*

WASHINGTON, ERIC T. state supreme court justice; Assoc. Fulbright and Jaworski, Houston; legis. dir., counsel Rep. Michael Andrews; spl. counsel corp. counsel, prin. dep. corp. counsel; ptnr. Hogan & Hartson, Washington, 1990-95; apptd. Superior Ct., 1995; judge D.C. Ct. Appeals, 1999—. Office: DC Ct Appeals 6th Fl 500 Indiana Ave NW Fl 6 Washington DC 20001-2138

WASHINGTON, KAYE, lawyer; b. Detroit, Apr. 11, 1951; d. William Taft and Virginia (Hall) Washington; m. Thomas B. Casey, July 6, 1971 (div. 1979); 1 child, Camilo Kareem. B.A., U. Mich., 1973; grad. student Hastings Coll. Law, 1978-79; J.D., U. Calif.-Berkeley, 1981. Bar: Calif. 1981, U.S. Dist. Ct. (no., ea. and cen. dists.). Assoc. Fenwick, Stone, Davis and West, Palo Alto, Calif., 1981— . Chmn. hist. com. Allen Temple Baptist Ch., Oakland, Calif., 1985. Mem. NAACP, State Bar Calif., ABA, Nat. Bar Assn., Charles Houston Bar Assn. Democrat. Home: PO Box 19187 Oakland CA 94619-0187 Office: Fenwick Stone Davis and West Palo Alto CA

WASKO, STEVEN E. lawyer; b. Chgo., May 10, 1954; s. Theodore J. and Beverly W.; m. Elaine L. Enger, Oct. 3, 1981 (div. Aug. 1996); 1 child, Christine; m. Deborah Wasko; stepchildren: Tara, Raef, Brooke and Christopher. B in Spl. Studies cum laude, Cornell Coll., 1976; JD cum laude, Kent U., 1979. Bar: Ill. 1979, U.S. Dist. Ct. (no. dist.) Ill. 1979. Assoc. atty. Blanshan & Summerfield, Park Ridge, Ill., 1979-81; ptnr. Summerfield & Wasko, 1981-86; sole practitioner Steven Wasko and Assocs., 1986-90, mng. ptnr., 1992-95; ptnr. Wasko & Michaels, 1990-91, Steponate & Wasko Ltd., Park Ridge and Chgo., 1995—. Dir. Kolan Corp., Park Ridge, 1988—. Great Books leader Field Sch. Dist., Park Ridge, 1997—. Avocations: jogging, watercolors and fine art. Family and matrimonial. Office: 1580 N Northwest Hwy Park Ridge IL 60068-1444

WASSERMAN, RICHARD LEO, lawyer; b. Balt., Aug. 6, 1948; s. Jack B. and Claire (Gutman) W.; m. Manuele Delbourgo, May 13, 1973; children: Alexander E., Lauren E. AB, Princeton U., 1970; JD, Columbia U., 1973. Bar: N.Y. 1975, Md. 1978, U.S. Dist. Ct. (so. and ea. dists.) N.Y. 1975, U.S. Dist. Ct. Md. 1978, U.S. Ct. Appeals (2d cir.) 1975, U.S. Ct. Appeals (4th cir.) 1979, U.S. Supreme Ct. 1982. Law clk. to hon. Roszel C. Thomsen U.S. Dist. Ct. Md., Balt., 1973-74; assoc. Proskauer Rose Goetz & Mendelsohn, N.Y.C., 1974-78, Venable, Baetjer & Howard, Balt., 1978-81, ptnr., 1982—, also bd. dirs. Fellow Am. Coll. Bankruptcy, Md. Bar Found.; mem. ABA (bus. bankruptcy com.), Md. Bar Assn. (sec. coun. bus. law sect. 1989-92), Bar Assn. Balt. City (chmn. banking, bankruptcy and bus. law com. 1987-88), Bankruptcy Bar Assn. Dist. Md. (bd. dirs. 1988—, pres. 1990-91), Assn. Bar City N.Y., Am. Bankruptcy Inst.,

Princeton U. Alumni Assn. Md. (bd. dirs. 1980-98, pres. 1985-87), Suburban Club Baltimore County (bd. govs. 1982-89, 94-98, 2d v.p. 1986-87, sec. 1987-88, pres.-elect 1994-95, pres. 1995-97). Democrat. Jewish. Avocations: tennis, golf, bridge. Banking, Bankruptcy, Contracts commercial. Office: Venable Baetjer & Howard LLP 1800 Mercantile Bank Bldg Baltimore MD 21201 E-mail: rlwasserman@venable.com

WASSERMAN, STEPHEN ALAN, lawyer; b. Cleve., Apr. 7, 1948; s. Myron Earl and Eve Ruth (Milstein) W.; m. Sandra Shulamith Moltz, Oct. 20, 1978. BA, U. Wis., 1970; JD, Northeastern U., Boston, 1978. Bar: Mass. 1978, U.S. Dist. Ct. Mass. 1978. Housing atty. Neighborhood Legal Svcs., Lynn, Mass., 1978-83; ptnr. Barmack, Boggs and Wasserman, 1983-91; pvt. practice Salem, Mass., 1991-97, 98—, Boston, 1997-98. Bd. dirs. North Shore Cmty. Action Program, Peabody, Mass., 1995—. Avocations: reading, baseball, jogging. Landlord-tenant, Personal injury, Toxic tort. Office: 32 Church St Salem MA 01970-3737 E-mail: Swass@Shore.net

WASSERMAN, WILLIAM PHILLIP, lawyer; b. Los Angeles, Sept. 13, 1945; s. Al and Ceil (Diamond) W.; married; children: Sam, George. BA, U. Calif., Berkeley, 1967; JD, U. Calif., 1970. Bar: Calif. 1971, U.S. Tax Ct. 1971. Ptnr. Ernst & Young LLP, Los Angeles, 1970—. Lectr. in field.; participant in numerous programs, confs., and workshops in field in field. Mem. Editorial adv. bd.: Real Estate Taxation: A Practitioner's Guide, 1984—, Federal Tax Annual: Real Estate, 1982; contbr. numerous articles to profl. jours. Mem. ABA (nat. chmn Tax Sect. com. on real estate problems 1985-87), State Bar Calif., Los Angeles County Bar Assn., Calif. Bd. Legal Specialization (cert. taxation law specialist). Taxation, general. Office: Ernst & Young LLP 725 S Figueroa St Los Angeles CA 90017-5524

WASSERSTROM, ELLEN, lawyer; b. Wilkes-Barre, Pa., May 15, 1971; d. Barry and Glenda W. BS, Tulane U., 1993; JD, George Washington U., 1996, LLM in Tax, 1997. Bar: Fla., 1996; U.S. Tax Ct., 1996. Law clerk U.S. Tax Ct., Washington, 1994-95, atty. advisor, 1996—. Office: US Tax Ct 400 2nd St NW # 410 Washington DC 20217-0002

WATANABE, ROY NOBORU, lawyer; b. Honolulu, July 23, 1947; s. Tadao I. and Clara Y. W. AB, Columbia Coll., 1969; JD, Columbia U., 1973. Bar: N.Y. 1974, U.S. Dist. Ct. (so. and ea. dists.) N.Y. 1976, U.S. Ct. Appeals (2d cir.) 1976. Honors program atty. Office of Labor Rels., Office of Mayor, N.Y.C., 1973-76; assoc. Frankle & Greenwald, 1976, Cohn, Glickstein, Lurie, Ostrin, Lubell & Lubell, N.Y.C., 1976-79; ptnr. Cohn, Glickstein & Lurie (formerly Cohn, Glickstein, Lurie, Ostrin, Lubell & Lubell, 1979-88, Spivak, Lipton, Watanabe, Spivak & Moss, 1989—. Guest lectr. labor law Boston Coll., 1982, Union U., 1983, 85, Mercer U., 1997-2001, NYU Law Sch., 1998; faculty Practicing Law Inst., N.Y.C., 1987; panelist, lectr. regional conf. N.Y. State Bar Assn. labor and employment law sect. and Nat. Labor Rels. Bd., N.Y.C., 1986; mem. adv. bd. Ctr. for Labor and Employment Law, NYU Sch. Law, 2000—; author, commentator 50th ann. labor conf. NYU, 1997; bd. dirs. AFL-CIO Lawyers Coord. Com. Contbg. author: NLRA Law and Practice, 1991. Cooperating atty. Asian Am. Legal Def. & Edn. Fund., N.Y.C., 1982—; mem. bd. dirs. lawyers coordinating com. AFL-CIO, 2000—. Nat. Def. Fgn. Language fellow, Columbia U., 1967. Mem. Assn. of Bar of City of N.Y. (labor and employment law com. 1980-83, 86-89, legal and edn. and admission to bar com. 1984-85), N.Y. State Bar Assn. (exec. com., co-chair practice before N.Y. State Labor Rels. Bd. and Nat. Labor Rels. Bd. com. 1989-93, labor arbitration com. 1983—, entertainment, arts and sports law sect. 1989—). Entertainment, Labor, Pension, profit-sharing, and employee benefits. Office: Spivak Lipton Et Al 1700 Broadway Fl 21 New York NY 10019-5905

WATERS, JOHN B. lawyer; b. Sevierville, Tenn., July 15, 1929; s. J. B. and Myrtle (Paine) W.; m. Patsy Temple, Apr. 8, 1953; children: John B., Cynthia Beth. BS, U. Tenn., 1952, JD, 1961; D in Environ. Sci. (hon.), Milligan Coll., 1993. Bar: Tenn. 1961, U.S. Dist. Ct. (ea. dist.) Tenn. 1961, U.S. Supreme Ct. 1969, U.S. Dist. Ct. D.C. 1970. Of counsel Long, Ragsdale & Waters, P.C., Knoxville, Tenn. Mem. hearing com. Bd. Profl. Responsibility Supreme Ct., 1974—80, 1995—2001, Fed. co-chmn. Appalachian Regional Commn., 1696—1971; chmn. Sevier County Indsl. Bd., Sevierville Libr. Found.; mem. Gov.'s Com. Econ. Devel.; Tenn. rep. to So. Growth Policies Bd., 1970—74; appointed dir. by Pres. Reagan, TVA, Knoxville, 1984, appointed chmn. bd. dirs. by Pres. Bush, 92; bd. dirs. Inst. Nuclear Power Ops., 1985—93; trustee East Tenn. Bapt. Hosp., Knoxville; mem. Tenn.-Tombigbee Waterway Authority, 1993—2000; bd. dirs. East Tenn. Found.; chmn. Leadership Sevier, 1996—2001. Lt. USN, 1952-55. Fellow Am. Bar Found.; mem. Tenn. Bar Assn. (pres. 1983-84), Sevier County Bar Assn. (past pres.). Republican. Baptist. Nuclear power, Government contracts and claims, Public utilities. Home: Waters Edge 405 Burridge Dr Sevierville TN 37862-3202 also: 119 Commerce St Sevierville TN 37862-3524

WATERSTON, TASS DEVER, lawyer; b. Dallas, Sept. 27, 1966; s. Tom Lee and Jean Ivy (Hollingsworth) W.; m. Laura Ann Lodewick, June 12, 1993. BA, U. Tex., 1988; MBA, Dallas Bapt. U., 1990; JD, So. Meth. U., 1997. Bar: Tex. 1997. Adminstrv. intern Fed. Bur. Prisons, Seagoville, Tex., 1990-91; instr. Northwood U., Cedar Hill, 1991-96; intern 13th Dist. Ct. Appeals, Corpus Christi, 1996; assoc. Pate and Dodson, L.L.P., Beaumont, 1997—. Del. Tex. Dem. Conv., Houston, 1992, mem. state nominations com., Ft. Worth, 1994. Mem. ABA, Christian Legal Soc., Jefferson County Bar Assn., Barristers, Delta Theta Phi. General civil litigation, Legislative, Personal injury. Office: Pate and Dodson LLP 470 Orleans Ste 1201 Beaumont TX 77701-3012

WATHEN, DANIEL EVERETT, state supreme court chief justice; b. Easton, Maine, Nov. 4, 1939; s. Joseph Jackson and Wilda Persis (Dow) W.; m. Judith Carol Foren, July 14, 1960; children: Julanne Carol, Daniel Arthur. AB, Ricker Coll., 1962; JD, U. Maine, 1965; LLM (hon.), U. Va. Law Sch., 1988. Bar: Maine 1965. Atty. Wathen & Wathen, Augusta, Maine, 1965-77; trial judge Superior Ct. Maine, 1977-81; appellate judge Supreme Jud. Ct. Maine, 1981-92, state chief justice, 1992—. E-mail: Daniel.Wathen@state.me.us

WATKIN, VIRGINIA GUILD, retired lawyer; b. Clinton, Mass., July 28, 1925; d. George Cheever and Dorothy Louise (Springer) Guild; m. Donald M. Watkin, June 22, 1946; children: Henry M., Mary Ellen, Edward G., Ann Kymry. BA, Wellesley Coll., 1946; LLB, Columbia U., 1949; LLD (hon.), Norwich U., 1986. Bar: N.Y. 1949, D.C. 1952, Mass. 1963, U.S. Ct. Appeals (D.C. cir.) 1952, U.S. Supreme Ct. 1954, U.S. Dist. Ct. Mass. 1968, U.S. Ct. Appeals (1st cir.) 1968, U.S. Ct. Appeals (9th cir.) 1976, U.S. Ct. Appeals (4th cir.) 1980, U.S. Ct. Fed. Claims 1983, U.S. Ct. Appeals (5th cir.) 1993. Assoc. Covington & Burling, Washington, 1952-58; assoc. counsel Mass. Crime Commn., 1963-64; from assoc. to ptnr. Herrick, Smith, Donald, Farley & Ketchum, Boston, 1966-74; ptnr. Covington & Burling, Washington, 1974-2000; ret., 2000. Bd. vis. Columbia U. Sch. Law; bd. overseers Wellesley Coll. Stone Ctr. for Develop. Svcs. and Studies, 1989—, Wellesley Coll. Ctr. for Rsch. on Women, 1990—. Author: Taxes and Tax Harmonization in the Central American Common Market, 1967; contbr. articles to profl. jours. Trustee Northfield (Mass.) Mt. Hermon Sch. Bd., 1978-83, Norwich U., Northfield, Vt., 1977-90, Wellesley Coll., 1989—. Mem. ABA, Am. Law Inst., D.C. Bar Assn. (pres. 1993—), Soc. Woman Geographers, Columbia Law Sch. Alumni Assn. (regional v.p.), Wellesley Coll. Alumnae Assn. (bd. dirs. 1985-88), Cosmos Club. Federal civil litigation. Home: 3001 Veazey Ter NW Washington DC 20008-5454 Office: Covington & Burling PO Box 7566 1201 Pennsylvania Ave NW Washington DC 20044-7566

WATKINS, CHARLES MORGAN, lawyer; b. Newport News, Va., Sept. 12, 1954; s. Walter Edmond and Joanne Kathryn (Halla) Watkins; m. Margie Elizabeth Valentine, July 16, 1983; children: Kathryn Grace, Mark Emerson, James Morgan. AB, Franklin & Marshall Coll., 1976; JD, Dickinson Sch. of Law, 1981. Bar: DC 1981, US Ct Claims 1983, US Ct Appeals (fed cir) 1987, US Tax Ct 1987. Atty. office of chief counsel IRS, Washington, 1981-85; mem. Webster, Chamberlain & Bean, 1986—. Instr in tax law Ch Law and Tax Report. Author: (book) Nondiscrimination Rules for Employee Benefit Plans, 1988; author: ((with others)) Issues for Exempt Organizations: A Guide for State Associations, 1987;contbr. articles to profl jours. Ruling elder McLean Presbyy Ch. Mem.: Christian Legal Soc, Christian Mgmt Asn. Republican. Avocations: camping, canoeing, hiking, tennis. Non-profit and tax-exempt organizations, Pension, profit-sharing, and employee benefits, Taxation, general. Office: Webster Chamberlain & Bean Ste 1000 1747 Pennsylvania Ave NW Washington DC 20006-4693 E-mail: cwatkins@wc-b.com

WATSON, FORREST ALBERT, JR. lawyer, bank executive; b. Atlanta, May 7, 1951; s. Forrest Albert and Virginia Doris (Ritch) W.; m. Marlys Wise, Oct. 16, 1982; children: Annaliese Marie Elizabeth, Forrest Albert Watson III. AB, Emory U., 1973; JD, U. Ga., 1975; postgrad., Mercer U., 1979-80. Bar: Ga. 1975, U.S. Dist. Ct. (mid. dist.) Ga. 1976, U.S. Tax Ct. 1976, U.S. Ct. Appeals (5th cir.) 1977, U.S. Supreme Ct. 1980; cert. data processor; CFP. Assoc. Banks, Smith & Lambdin, Barnesville, Ga., 1976-78; ptnr. Watson & Lindsey, 1978-82; v.p., gen. counsel United Bank Corp., 1981-91, chief ops. officer, 1990-2000, exec. v.p., gen. counsel, 1991-2000, mem., bd. dirs., exec. v.p., 1991; pres. United Bank Mortgage; exec. v.p., sr. trust officer United Bank, Griffin, Ga., 1995-98, exec. v.p., bd. dirs. Zebulon, 1998—. Pres. United Bank Mortgage, 1993-95; gen. counsel Lamar State Bank, Barnesville, 1976-84; judge Small Claims Ct., Lamar County, Ga., 1976, City Ct. of Milner, Ga., 1977; lectr. IBM, 1984-85; atty. City of Meansville, Ga., 1976, City of Milner, 1977; bd. dirs. United Bank Corp. Assoc. editor Ga. Jour. Internat. Law, 1975. Gen. counsel Lamar County Devel. Authority, Barnesville, 1977; bd. dirs. Legaline Inc., Atlanta, 1983-85. Mem. ABA, Ga. Bar Assn., Cir. Ct. Bar Assn., Griffin Cir. Bar Assn., Ga. Rural Health Assn. (trustee 1981-82), S.E. Bank Card Assn. (operating com. 1986-91), Assn. Cert. Fin. Planners, Assn. Inst. Cert. Computer Profls., Internat. Assn. Fin. Planners. Methodist. Avocations: art, antiques, travel. Banking. Home: PO Box 347 Zebulon GA 30295-0347 Office: United Bank Corp PO Box 1337 110 Griffin St Zebulon GA 30295

WATSON, GLENN ROBERT, lawyer; b. Okla., May 2, 1917; s. Albert Thomas and Ethel (Riddle) W.; m. Dorothy Ann Mosiman, Feb. 25, 1945; 1 dau., Carol Ann. Student, East Cen. State U., Okla., 1933-36; LL.B., Okla. U., 1939. Bar: Okla. 1939, Calif. 1946. Pvt. practice law, Okla., 1939-41; ptnr., pres. Richards, Watson & Gershon, Los Angeles, 1946—; city atty. Industry, Calif., 1958-65, 78-83, Commerce, 1960-61, Cerritos, 1956-64, Victorville, 1962-63, Carson, 1968-2000, Rosemead, 1960-76, Seal Beach, 1972-78, South El Monte, 1976-78, Avalon, 1976-80, Artesia, 1976-97. Served with USNR, 1942-46. Mem. ABA, Los Angeles County Bar Assn., Am. Judicature Soc., Lawyers Club of Los Angeles (past pres.), Los Angeles World Affairs Council, Internat. Cir., La Canada C. of C. (past pres.), Order of Coif, Phi Delta Phi, Delta Chi. General practice, Municipal (including bonds), Real property. Home: 522 Paulette Pl La Canada CA 91011 Office: Richards Watson & Gershon 333 S Hope St Los Angeles CA 90071-1406 E-mail: gwatson@rwglaw.com

WATSON, JACK CROZIER, retired state supreme court justice; b. Jonesville, La., Sept. 17, 1928; s. Jesse Crozier and Gladys Lucille (Talbot) W.; m. Henrietta Sue Carter, Dec. 26, 1958; children: Carter Crozier (dec.), Wells Talbot. BA, U. Southwestern La., 1949; JD, La. State U., 1956; completed with honor, Appellate Judges Seminar, N.Y. U., 1974, Sr. Appellate Judges Seminar, 1980. Bar: La. 1956. Atty. King, Anderson & Swift, Lake Charles, La., 1956-58; prosecutor City of Lake Charles, 1960; asst. dist. atty. Calcasieu Parish, La., 1961-64; ptnr. Watson & Watson, Lake Charles, 1961-64; judge 14th Jud. Dist., La., 1964-72; judge ad hoc Ct. Appeals, 1st Circuit, Baton Rouge, 1972-73; judge Ct. Appeals, 3rd Circuit, Lake Charles, 1973-79; assoc. justice La. Supreme Ct., New Orleans, 1979-96, ret., 1996. Faculty advisor Nat. Coll. State Judiciary, Reno, 1970, 73; adj. prof. law summer sch. program in Greece, Tulane U., 1988-2000; adj. prof. law So. U., Baton Rouge, 1998-99; del. NEH Seminar, 1976; La. del to Internat. Conf. Appellate Magistrates, The Philippines, 1977; mem. La. Jud. Coun., 1986-92. 1st lt. USAF, 1950-54. Mem. ABA, La. Bar Assn., S.W. La. Bar Assn. (pres. 1973), Law Inst. State of La., La. Coun. Juvenile Ct. Judges (pres. 1969-70), Am. Judicature Soc., S.W. La. Camellia Soc. (pres. 1973-74), Am. Legion (post comdr. 1963), Lake Charles Yacht Club (commodore 1974), Blue Key, Sigma Alpha Epsilon, Phi Delta Phi, Pi Kappa Delta. Democrat. Baptist.

WATSON, JOHN ALLEN, lawyer; b. Ft. Worth, Sept. 18, 1946; s. John and Mary (Barlow) W.; m. Patricia L. Clardy, Oct. 24, 1946; 1 child, Virginia E. BA, Rice U., 1968; JD, U. Tex., Austin, 1971. Bar: Tex. 1971. Assoc. Fulbright & Jaworski, Houston, 1971-78, ptnr., 1978—. Mem. ABA. General corporate, Finance, Securities. Office: Fulbright & Jaworski LLP 1301 McKinney St Ste 5100 Houston TX 77010-3031 E-mail: jwatson@fulbright.com

WATSON, RICHARD THOMAS, lawyer; b. Lakewood, Ohio, Aug. 21, 1933; s. Thomas Earl Watson and Sara Lucille (Whapham) Hadfield; m. Judith C. Briggs, Aug. 6, 1960; children: David, Andrew, Susan (dec.). AB, Harvard U., 1954, JD, 1960. Bar: Ohio 1960. Assoc. Spieth, Bell, McCurdy & Newell, Cleve., 1960, ptnr., 1965, mng. ptnr., 1987—. Bd. dirs. numerous corps. Chancellor Episcopal Diocese of Ohio, Cleve., 1986—; mem. Harvard U. com. on univ. resources, 1992—; bd. trustees Cleve. Mus. Art, 1991—; trustee Case Western Res. U., 1993—. Mem. Union Club Cleve. Office: Spieth Bell McCurdy & Newell 925 Euclid Ave Ste 2000 Cleveland OH 44115-1408 E-mail: richardtwatson@worldnet.att.net

WATSON, ROBERT FRANCIS, lawyer; b. Houston, Jan. 9, 1936; s. Louis Leon and Lora Elizabeth (Hodges) W.; m. Marietta Kiser, Nov. 24, 1961; children: Julia, Melissa, Rebecca. BA, Vanderbilt U., 1957; JD, U. Denver, 1959. Bar: Colo. 1959, U.S. Dist. Ct. (no. dist.) Tex. 1967, U.S. Supreme Ct. 1968, Tex. 1973, U.S. Ct. Appeals (5th cir.) 1973, U.S. Dist. Ct. (so. dist.) Tex. 1980, U.S. Ct. Appeals (11th cir.) 1981. Law clk. U.S. Dist. Ct. Colo., 1960-61; trial atty. SEC, Denver, 1961-67, asst. regional adminstr. Ft. Worth, 1967-72, regional adminstr., 1972-75; ptnr. Law, Snakard & Gambill, P.C., 1975-98, of counsel, 1998—; gen. counsel USPA&IRA (now First Command Fin. Svcs., Inc.), 1998—. Counsel City of Ft. Worth Police Investigation Commn., 1975; spl. counsel Office Atty. Gen. State Ariz., 1977-78. Contbr. articles to profl. jours. Mem. Ft. Worth Crime Commn., 1987-93. Honoree 27th Ann. Rocky Mountain State-Fed.-Provincial Securities Conf. Fellow: Colo. Bar Assn. (life), Tex. Bar Found., U. Denver Law Sch. Alumni Coun., Coll. of State Bar Tex., Tarrant County Bar Assn., Ft. Worth Club; mem.: ABA, Fed. Bar Assn., State Bar Tex. (life)), Tex. Bus. Law Found. (bd.dirs. 1988—93), Shady Oak Country Club (Ft. Worth), Phi Delta Phi. Republican. Presbyterian. Federal civil litigation, General corporate, Securities. Office: First Command 4100 S Hulen St Fort Worth TX 76109 also: Law Snakard & Gambill PC 801 Cherry St Ste 3300 Fort Worth TX 76102-3819 E-mail: rfwatson@firstcommand.com

WATSON, ROBERT JAMES, lawyer; b. Oceanside, N.Y., Mar. 30, 1955; s. Ralph Joseph and Mildred Adeline (Knapp) W.; children: Emily Allyn, Caroline Elisabeth. BA, Biscayne Coll., 1976; JD, U. Fla., 1979. Bar: Fla. 1979, U.S. Dist. Ct. (so. dist.) Fla. 1980, U.S. Dist. Ct. (no. dist.) Fla. 1981, U.S. Dist. Ct. (mid. dist.) Fla. 1982, U.S. Ct. Appeals (11th cir.) 1982. Asst. pub. defender Law Offices of Elton Schwarz, Ft. Pierce, Fla., 1979-81; ptnr. Wilkinson & Watson P.A., Stuart, 1981-86; pvt. practice, 1986-90; ptnr. Frierson & Watson, 1990—. Mem. Fla. Bar Assn., Nat. Assn. Criminal Def. Lawyers, Acad. Fla. Trial Lawyers, Martin Assn. Criminal Def. Lawyers, Fla. Assn. Criminal Def. Lawyers. Democrat. Roman Catholic. Avocation: golf, running, skiing. Civil rights, Criminal, Personal injury. Home: 9 Emarita Way Stuart FL 34996-6704 Office: Frierson & Watson 3601 SE Ocean Blvd Ste 004 Stuart FL 34996-6737

WATSON, ROBERTA CASPER, lawyer; b. Boise, Idaho, July 11, 1949; d. John Blaine and Joyce Lucile (Mercer) C.; m. Robert George Watson, July 22, 1972; 1 child, Rebecca Joyce. BA cum laude, U. Idaho, 1971; JD, Harvard U., 1974. Bar: Mass. 1974, U.S. Dist. Ct. Mass. 1975, U.S. Supreme Ct. 1979, U.S. Ct. Appeals (1st cir.) 1979, U.S. Tax Ct. 1979, Fla. 1985, U.S. Dist. Ct. (mid. dist.) Fla. 1985, U.S. Dist. Ct. (so. dist.) Fla. 1987. Assoc. Peabody & Brown, Boston, 1974-78, Mintz, Levin, Cohn, Ferris, Glovsky & Popeo, Boston, 1978-84; sr. dir. Wolper Ross & Co., Miami, 1983-85; assoc. Trenam, Kemker, Scharf, Barkin, Frye, O'Neill & Mullis, P.A., Tampa, Fla., 1985-87, ptnr., 1988—. Co-author: A Physician's Guide to Professional Corporations; co-editor-in-chief COBRA Adv. Newsletter, 1997-2000; contbr. articles to profl. jours. Pres. Performing Arts Ctr. Greater Framingham, Mass., 1983; bd. dirs., Northside Mental Health Ctr., 1987—, pres. 1999-2001; trustee Unitarian Universalist Found., Clearwater, Fla., 1986—; bd. dirs. dist. 6 Cmty. Health Purchasing Alliance, pers. com. chair, 1998-2000. Named Bd. Nem. of Yr., Fla. Cmty. Mental Health, 1994. Mem. ABA (chair employee benefit com. sect. taxation 1995-96, chair employee benefits interest group health law sect. 1998-2001), Am. Coll. Employee Benefits Counsel (charter), Fla. West Coast Employee Benefits Coun. (bd. dirs., treas. 1997-98, v.p. 1998-2001, pres. elect 2001-2002), Harvard Club (bd. dirs. West Coast Fla. chpt.), Tampa Club, Order Ea. Star. Democrat. Avocations: music, metaphysics, Lincoln historian, genealogy. Health, Pension, profit-sharing, and employee benefits. Home: 124 Adalia Ave Tampa FL 33606-3304 Office: Trenam Kemker et al 2700 Barnett Pla Tampa FL 33602 E-mail: rcwatson@trenam.com

WATSON, STACY L. lawyer; b. Melbourne, Fla., Aug. 13, 1968; d. E. Lynn and Nancy Rowe Watson. BA, U. Fla., 1990; JD, John Marshall Law Sch., Chgo., 1997. Bar: Fla. 1997. Assoc. McGuire, Woods, Battle & Boothe LLP, Jacksonville, Fla., 1997. Mem. Assn. Environ. Profls. (bd. dirs. N.E. Fla. chpt. 1998—), Jacksonville Bar Assn. (bd. dirs. young lawyers sect. 1998—). Administrative and regulatory, Environmental. Office: McGuire Woods Battle Boothe 50 N Laura St Ste 3300 Jacksonville FL 32202

WATSON, THOMAS C. lawyer; b. Poplar Bluff, Mo., Feb. 26, 1945; s. William C. and Dorothy E. (Whitson) W.; children: Thomas II, Nathan, Edward, Clay, Luke; m. Sharlene Wonders, Mar. 19, 1994. BS, U. Memphis, 1967, MEd, 1968; JD, Washington U., St. Louis, 1972. Bar: Mo. 1972, D.C. 1973. Assoc. Morgan, Lewis & Bockius, Washington, 1973-78, ptnr., 1978-79, Crowell & Moring, Washington, 1979-95, Watson & Renner, 1996—. Avocations: hiking, biking. computers, hunting wild fowl. General civil litigation, General corporate, Toxic tort. Office: Watson & Renner 1919 M St NW Ste 400 Washington DC 20036

WATSON, THOMAS RILEY, lawyer; b. Mendin, La., Mar. 11, 1947; s. Lawrence Middleton Watson and Barbara Hazel (Moffat) Root. BA in History, U. S.C., 1969; MA in Nat. Security Affairs, U.S. Naval Postgrad. Sch., 1975; JD, U. Maine, 1982. Bar: Maine 1982, U.S. Dist. Ct. Maine 1982. Commd. USN, 1969, advanced through grades to comdr., 1983; trans. USNR, 1979; assoc. McTeague, Higbee & Libner, Brunswick, Maine, 1982-85, ptnr., 1985-99, Watson & Mann, P.A., Bath, 1999—. Author: (play) Rules of Engagement, 1986; editor U. Maine Law Rev., 1981-82. Decorated Air medal. Mem. ABA, Maine Bar Assn., Assn. Trial Lawyers Am. Democrat. Avocation: acting and writing for the theater. Labor, Personal injury, Workers' compensation. Home: PO Box 686 Bath ME 04530-0686 Office: Watson & Mann PA Po Box 710 Bath ME 04530-0170 E-mail: trwatson@street-law.com

WATSON, THOMAS ROGER, lawyer; b. Concord, N.H., May 14, 1951; s. Roger Edward and Mary (Hannigan) W. BA in Polit. Sci. cum laude, U. N.H., 1973; JD, Franklin Pierce Law Ctr., 1978. Bar: N.H. 1978, U.S. Dist. Ct. N.H. 1978, U.S. Ct. Appeals (1st cir.) 1978, Maine 1982, U.S. Dist. Ct. Maine 1982, U.S. Supreme Ct. 1986. Ptnr. Tybursky & Watson, Portsmouth, N.H., 1979-86, Tybursky, Watson & Harman, Portsmouth, 1987-88, Taylor, Keane, Blanchard, Lyons & Watson, P.A., Portsmouth, 1988-94, Watson, Lyons, & Bosen, P.A., Portsmouth, 1994-99, Watson & Bosen, P.A., Portsmouth, 2000—. Del. N.H. Constl. Conv., Concord, 1974. Mem. Maritime Heritage Commn., 1986-95, City of Portsmouth Hist. Dist. Commn., 1992, City of Portsmouth Planning Bd., 1992-94; bd. dirs. N.H. Small Bus. Devel. Ctr., 1993-95, N.H. Main St. Ctr., 1998—, sec., 2001—; mem. adv. bd. Ballet New England, 1997—; bd. advisors N.H. Small Bus. Devel. Ctr., 1992-95; bd. trustees Strawberry Banke Mus., 2000—, sec., 2001—. Named Portsmouth Citizen of Yr., 1995. Mem. ABA, Assn. Trial Lawyers Am. (state del. 1996—, chair-elect 1997-98, chair 1998-99, exec. com. 1998-99, co-chair coordinating com. on state rels. 2000—, Outstanding State Del. 1997), N.H. Bar Assn. (bd. govs. 1985-90), N.H. Trial Lawyers Assn. (bd. govs. 1989—, sec. 1982-92, treas. 1993-94, pres. elect 1994-95, pres. 1995-96, chair legis. com. 1992-95, 96-2000, recipient Pres.'s award 1993, 97, Spl. Recognition award 2000), Rockingham County Bar Assn., Franklin Pierce Law Ctr. Alumni Assn. (pres. 1985-86), N.H. Bar Found. (bd. govs. 1987-90), Greater Portmouth C. of C. (bd. dirs. 1988-92, chmn. 1990-92), Portsmouth Hist. Soc. (trustee 1994—, pres. 1995-97), Portsmouth Atheneum (propr. 1991—). General civil litigation, Family and matrimonial, Personal injury. Office: Watson & Bosen PA PO Box 469 Portsmouth NH 03802-0469

WATT, JOSEPH MICHAEL, state supreme court justice; b. Austin, Tex., Mar. 8, 1947; BA in History, Tex. Tech U., 1969; JD, U. Tex., 1972. Bar: Tex. 1972, Okla. 1974. Pvt. practice, Altus, Okla., 1972-85; judge Dist. Trial Ct., 1985-91; gen. counsel to gov. State of Okla., Oklahoma City, 1991-92; justice Okla Supreme Ct., Okahoma City, 1992—. Office: Okla State Supreme Ct State Capitol Rm 240 Oklahoma City OK 73105 Fax: 405-521-6982*

WATTERS, EDWARD MCLAIN, III, lawyer; b. 1943; s. Edward McL. and Lucy F. (Disston) W.; m. Susan Secor, May 12, 1979; children: Jennifer Susan, Ann Elizabeth. BA cum laude, Yale U., 1965; JD cum laude, U. Pa., 1970. Bar: Pa. 1970. Ptnr. Pepper Hamilton LLP, Phila., 1977—. Lectr. programs on estate planning and will drafting Pa. Bar Inst. Bd. dirs. Children's Cruise and Playground Soc. Pa., Sanitarium Playgrounds of N.J., others. Lt. USNR, 1965-75; chair Decedents Estate Adv. Com. to Pa. Legislature's Joint Sate Govt. Commn. Fellow Am. Coll. Trust and Estate Counsel (com. state laws); mem. ABA, Phila. Bar Assn., Pa. Bar Assn. (past chmn. legis. com. probate sect.), Phila. Estate Planning Coun. (past pres.), Yale Club of Phila., Penn Club, Merion Golf Club. Probate, Estate taxation, Personal income taxation. Office: Pepper Hamilton LLP 1235 Westlakes Dr Ste 400 Berwyn PA 19312-2416 E-mail: watterse@pepperlaw.com

WATTERS, RICHARD DONALD, lawyer; b. Midland, Mich., May 3, 1951; s. Donald Wayne and Madalyn Bird (Tinetti) W.; m. Ann Elizabeth Hutchison, May 24, 1975; children: Kelly E., Nathan Paul. BS in Indsl. Engring., Bradley U., 1973; JD cum laude, St. Louis U., 1976. BAr: Mo. 1976, U.S. Dist. Ct. (we. and ea. dists.) Mo. 1976, Ill. 1977, U.S. Ct. Appeals (8th cir.) 1981. Assoc. Lashly & Baer, P.C., St. Louis, 1976-81, ptnr., 1981—, dept. chmn., 1989—. Instr. St. Louis U. Sch. Law, 1977-79. Chmn., pres. United Cerebral Palsy Assn. St. Louis, 1985-88; bd. dirs. Canterbury Enterprises, sheltered workshop, St. Louis, 1988-94, participant Leadershp St. Louis, 1988-89; ethics com. DePaul Health Ctr., 1990—. Mem. Am. Health Lawyers Assn., Mo. Soc. Hosp. Attys. (bd. dirs. 1988-94, pres. 1990-91), Mo. Bar Assn. (vice chmn. health and hosp. com. 1988-90), Bar Assn. Metro. St. Louis (co-chmn. med.-legal com.). Republican. Avocation: sailing. Administrative and regulatory, General corporate, Health. Office: Lashly & Baer PC 714 Locust St Saint Louis MO 63101-1699 E-mail: rdwatters@lashlybaer.com

WATTS, BARBARA GAYLE, law academic administrator; b. Covington, Ky., Oct. 18, 1946; d. William Samuel and LaVerne Barbara (Ziegler) W. BA, Purdue U., 1968; MEd, U. Cin., 1969, JD, 1978. Bar: Ohio 1978, U.S. Dist. Ct. (so. dist.) Ohio 1978. Residence dir. Ohio State U., Columbus, 1969-71, asst. dean students, 1971-75; assoc. Frost & Jacobs, Cin., 1978-81; asst. dean U. Cin. Coll. Law, 1981-84, assoc. dean, 1984—. Trustee Summerfair Inc., Cin., 1982-85; bd. dirs. Pro-Srs., 1995—, sec., 1998-2000; bd. trustees ProKids, 1999—; mem. Summerfair Cmty. Adv. Com. Recipient Disting. Alumni award Purdue U. Sch. Liberal Arts, 2001; Schleman fellow Purdue U., 1968, Castleberry fellow AAUW, 1977. Mem. ABA, Ohio State Bar Assn. (Nettie Cronise Lutes award Sect. on Women in the Profession 2000), Cin. Bar Assn. (trustee 1992-98, sec. 1993-94), Nat. Assn. Women in Edn., Order of Coif, Chi Omega. Democrat. Office: U Cin Coll Law Clifton & Calhoun Sts Cincinnati OH 45221-0001

WATTS, STEVEN RICHARD, lawyer; b. Toledo, Oct. 5, 1955; s. James Hupp and Lona Jane Katherine (Miller) W.; m. Marcia Ann Jackson, Mar. 6, 1982; children: Lauren Brooke, Madison Ann. BA in History, Ohio State U., 1978; JD summa cum laude, U. Dayton, 1981. Bar: Ohio 1981, U.S. Dist. Ct. (so. dist.) Ohio 1981. Assoc. Smith & Schnacke, Dayton, Ohio, 1981-84, Porter, Wright, Morris & Arthur, Dayton, 1984-89, ptnr., 1990, Chernesky, Heyman & Kress P.L.L., Dayton, 1990—. Mem. ABA, Ohio State Bar Assn., Dayton Bar Assn. Presbyterian. Avocation: golf. General corporate, Securities. Home: 1101 Viewpoint Dr Dayton OH 45459-1442 Office: Chernesky Heyman & Kress PLL 1100 Courthouse Pla SW Dayton OH 45402 E-mail: srw@chklaw.com

WAXMAN, SETH PAUL, lawyer; b. Hartford, Conn., Nov. 28, 1951; s. Felix H. and Frieda (Goodman) W.; m. Debra F. Goldberg, Mar. 20, 1977; children: Noah, Sarah, Ethan. AB summa cum laude, Harvard U., 1973; JD, Yale U., 1977. Bar: D.C. 1978, U.S. Dist. Ct. D.C., 1979, U.S. Ct. Appeals D.C Circuit, 1979, U.S. Supreme Ct. 1982, U.S. Ct. Appeals (1st cir.), 2000, (2d cir.), 1998, (3d cir.), 1983, (4th cir.), 1982, (5th cir.), 1997, (6th cir.), 1998, (7th cir.), 1998, (8th cir.), 1998, (9th cir.), 1989, (10th cir.), 1998, (11th cir.), 1989, U.S. Ct. Appeals Fed. Circuit, 1998. Law clk to Judge Gerhard A. Gesell, Washington, 1977-78; ptnr. Miller Cassidy Larroca & Lewin, 1978-94; assoc. dep. atty. gen. U.S. Dept. Justice, 1994-96, dep. solitor gen., 1996-97, acting dep. atty. gen., 1997, solicitor gen. of the U.S., 1997-2001; vis. prof. Georgetown U. Law Ctr., 2001; vis. fellow Harvard U. JFK Sch. Gov., 2001; partner Wilmer, Cutler & Pickering, 2001. Disting. vis. from practice Georgetown U Law Ctr., 2001—. Dir. Legal Affairs mag.; contbr. numerous articles to legal jours. Dir. Nat. Found. for Jewish Culture; dir. program com. Supreme Ct. Hist. Soc. Michael C. Rockefeller fellow Harvard U., 1973-74; recipient Cardozo award for civil rights Anti-Defamation League, 1987. Fellow Am. Bar Found.; mem. ABA (mem. standing com. on professionalism, Pro Bono Publico award 1988), Am. Acad. Appellate Attys., Jud. Conf. U.S., Harvard Alumni Assn. (mem. com. to visit Harvard Coll., dir.). Federal civil litigation, Constitutional, Criminal. E-mail: waxman@law.georgetown.edu

WAXMAN, SHELDON ROBERT, lawyer; b. Chgo., Apr. 22, 1941; s. Henri and Ann (Sokolsky) W.; m. Katherine Slamski, Aug. 23, 1979; children: Josiah, Zoe. BA, U. Ill., 1963; JD, DePaul U., 1965. Bar: Ill. 1965, U.S. Supreme Ct. 1976, Mich. 1985. Staff atty. Argonne (Ill.) Nat. Lab., 1968-71; asst. U.S. Atty., Chgo., 1971-74; owner firm Waxman Tax & Legal Network, Chgo. and South Haven, Mich., 1976—; pres. Indecon Bus. Cons. Network, Ltd. Owner Ind. Contractor Cons. Svcs. Author: In the Teeth of the Wind, 2001; editor-in-chief New Z Letter; contbr. articles to profl. jours. Founder Freedom Lawyers of Am., People for Simplified Tax Law, Nukes to the Sun. Civil rights, General civil litigation, Criminal. Office: PO Box 309 South Haven MI 49090-0309

WAXSE, DAVID JOHN, judge; b. Oswego, Kans., June 29, 1945; s. I. Joseph and Mary (Poole) W.; m. Linda Schilling (div.); children: Rachel, Ryan, Rebecca; m. Judy Pfannenstiel, May 29, 1982; 1 child, Elayna. BA, U. Kans., 1967; teaching cert., Columbia U., 1968, JD, 1971. Bar: Kans. 1971, U.S. Ct. Appeals (10th cir.) 1971, U.S. Supreme Ct. 1975, U.S. Ct. Appeals (8th Cir.) 1998. Dean of students Intermediate Sch. 88, N.Y.C., 1968-70; spl. edn. tchr. Peter Cooper Sch., 1970-71; assoc. Payne & Jones, Olathe, Kans., 1971-74, ptnr., 1974-84; of counsel Shook, Hardy & Bacon, Overland Park, 1984-86, ptnr., 1986-95; shareholder Shook, Hardy & Bacon P.C., 1993-95; ptnr. Shook, Hardy & Bacon L.L.P., Kans., 1995-99; shareholder Shook, Hardy & Bacon P.C., 1993-95, v.p., asst. gen. counsel, 1995-99; U.S. magistrate judge Kansas City, 1999—. Mcpl. judge City of Shawnee, Kans., 1974-80; atty. City of DeSoto, Kans., 1972-79; adj. prof. U. Kans. Sch. Law, Lawrence, 1981-82; mem. juv. code adv. com. Kans. Jud. Coun., 1979-83, guardianship adv. com., 1982-83, atty. fees adv. com., 1986-87; mem. Civil Justice Reform Act Adv. Com., U.S. Dist. Ct. for Dist. Kans., 1991-95; mem. Kans. Commn. on Jud. Qualifications, 1992-99, vice-chmn. 1994-97, chair, 1997-99; v.p. Kans. Legal Svcs., Inc., 1980-82, pres., 1985-87; bd. advisors Kans. Coll. Advocacy, 1979-80; bd. trustees, lawyers' com. Civil Rights Under Law, 1997-99. Author: (with others) Kansas Employment Law, 1985, Litigating Employment Law Cases, 1987, Kansas Employment Law Handbook, 1991, supplements, 1992, 95, Kansas Annual Survey, 1990—. Mem. Kan. Gov.'s Adv. Com. on Criminal Justice, 1974-77; mem. Kans. Justice Commn., 1997-99; gen. counsel Western Mo. Dist. ACLU, 1976-78, 86-97, v.p., 1983-86, nat. bd. dirs., 1979-86, 91-99, chmn. children's rights com., 1980-86; mem. AIDS Pol. Network, 1987-99, med. treatment issues com., 1991-96, constn. com., 1991-99; mem. med./tech. com. AIDS Coun. Greater Kans. City, 1986-98, ethics com. consortium Midwest Bioethics Ctr., 1990—; bd. dirs. Parents Anonymous Kans., 1978-83, pres., 1979; bd. dirs., mem. fin. com. Kans. Com. for Prevention Child Abuse, 1980-83. Fellow Am. Bar Found., Kans. Bar Found.; mem. ABA (chmn. children's rights com. and family law sects. 1985-86), Am. Judicature Soc. (bd. dirs. 1997—, adv. com. for ctr. for judicial conduct 1997—), Kans. Bar Assn. (chmn. legal aid com. 1978-83, bd. govs. 1988—, v.p. 1996-97, pres.-elect 1997-98, pres. 1998-99, Pres.' Outstanding Svc. award 1982), Kans. City Met. Bar Assn., Johnson County Bar Assn. (chmn. legal aid com. 1975-82, 92-96). Office: U S Courthouse 500 State Ave Rm 219 Kansas City KS 66101-2400 E-mail: judge_waxse@ksd.uscourts.gov

WAYNE, ROBERT ANDREW, lawyer; b. Newark, Oct. 4, 1938; s. David Michael and Charlotte (Chesler) W.; m. Charlotte Fainblatt, Aug. 14, 1969; children— Andrew Mark, Gary Howard, Deborah Jill. B.A., Princeton U., 1960; J.D., Columbia U. 1963. Bar: N.J. 1964, U.S. Dist. Ct. N.J. 1964, U.S. Dist. Ct. (ea. and so. dists.) N.Y. 1966, U.S. Ct. Apls. (3d cir.) 1967, N.Y. 1981, U.S. Ct. Apls. (2d cir.) 1984, U.S. Supreme Ct. 1984, U.S. Claims Ct., 1984, U.S. Tax Ct. 1984. Assoc., Shanley & Fisher, Newark, 1964-69, ptnr., 1969-71; ptnr. Robinson, St. John & Wayne, Newark, 1971—. Mem. Democratic County Com., Livingston, N.J., 1971-74. Served with AUS, 1963-69. Mem. ABA, N.J. Bar Assn., Essex County Bar Assn., Monmouth County Bar Assn., Fed. Bar Assn., Am. Coll. Real Estate Lawyers. Jewish. General civil litigation, Contracts commercial, Real property. Office: Robinson St John & Wayne 2 Penn Plz E Newark NJ 07105-2245

WAYNE, ROBERT JONATHAN, lawyer, educator; b. Fresno, Calif., Apr. 4, 1951; s. William W. and Blanche Wayne; m. Dorothy A. Madden, Oct. 23, 1981; children: Daniel, Julia. BS, U. Oreg., 1971; JD, UCLA, 1974. Bar: Calif. 1974, Wash. 1975, U.S. Dist. Ct. (we. dist.) Wash. 1975, U.S. Ct. Appeals (9th and D.C. cirs.) 1975, U.S. Supreme Ct. 1979. Law clk. U.S. Ct. Appeals (D.C. cir.), 1974-75; assoc. Perkins, Coie, Stone, Olsen & Williams, Seattle, 1975-76; dep. prosecutor King County Prosecutor's Office, 1976-78; pvt. practice, 1978—. Instr. trial advocacy U. Wash., Seattle, 1977—; instr. trial advocacy Nat. Inst. Trial Advocacy, Seattle, 1979—, asst. team leader, 1990, team leader, 1991-99, team leader nat. session, 1993, program dir. N.W. region, 1998—. Mem. ATLA, NACDL (life, chmn. lawyers assistance strike force 1993-94), Wash. State Trial Lawyers Assn. (chmn. tort sect. 1983-85), Wash. State Bar Assn. (chmn. criminal law sect. 1982-83, 86-87, exec. com. 1980-88), Seattle-King County Bar Assn. (jud. screening com. 1988-91), Wash. Assn. Criminal Def. Lawyers (founder, bd. govs. 1986-89, 99-2001, chmn. lawyers assistance strike force 1986-90, 91-93, chmn. ann. meeting 1989-90, 2001), Order of Coif, Order of Barristers. Avocations: skiing, flying. General civil litigation, Criminal, Personal injury. Office: 2110 N Pacific St Ste 100 Seattle WA 98103-9126 E-mail: bwayne@trialsnw.com

WAZ, JOSEPH WALTER, JR. government relations consultant, author; b. Meriden, Conn., Jan. 13, 1953; s. Joseph Walter and Rose Marie (Barillaro) W.; m. Ann Stookey, Sept. 25, 1981; 1 child, Joseph W. III. AB, Boston U., 1975; JD, U. Conn., 1978. Bar: Conn. 1978; D.C. 1979, U.S. Ct. Appeals D.C. 1980. Dep. dir. Telecommunications Research and Action Ctr., Washington, 1979-82; sr. assoc. govt. rels. Wexler, Reynolds, Harrison & Schule, Inc., 1983-86; gen. counsel Wexler, Reynolds, Fuller, Harrison & Schule, Inc., 1986-90, ptnr., 1989-90; sr. v.p. The Wexler Group, a unit of Hill and Knowlton, Inc., Washington, 1990-92, exec. v.p., 1993—; gen. counsel The Wexler Group, 1990—. Author (with S. Simon): Reverse The Charges, 1983 (Book of the Month Club pro bono selection 1983); editor Telematics jour., The Computer Lawyer; contbr. articles to communications trade publs. Polit. broadcasting advisor Californians for Recycling and Litter Clean-up, L.A., 1982, Dukakis for Pres. Campaign, Boston, 1987-88; comm. policy advisor Clinton/Gore campaign, 1992; founding trustee FCBA Found., treas., 1992-93; mem. Montgomery County Alcohol and Other Drug Abuse Adv. Commn., 1993—. Mem. ABA (steering com., electronic media div., forum com. on communications), D.C. Bar Assn., Fed. Communications Bar Assn. (chmn. CLE and legislation coms.). Democrat. Avocations: music, travel, team sports. Home: 46 Summit St Philadelphia PA 19118-2833 Office: The Wexler Group 1317 F St NW Ste 600 Washington DC 20004-1157

WEATHERHEAD, LESLIE R. lawyer; b. Tacoma, Sept. 28, 1956; s. A. Kingsley and Ingrid A. (Lien) W.; m. Anali C. Torrado, June 24, 1985; children: Spencer, Madeleine, Audrey. BA, U. Oreg., 1977; JD, U. Wash., 1980. Bar: Wash. 1980, Oreg. 1996, U.S. Ct. Appeals (9th cir.) 1981, U.S. Dist. Ct. (ea. dist.) Wash. 1984, U.S. Ct. Internat. Trade 1984, Hawaii 1987, U.S. Dist. Ct. (we. dist.) Wash. 1989, Idaho 1989, U.S. Dist. Ct. Idaho 1989, U.S. Supreme Ct. 1994, Colville Tribal Ct. 1993, U.S. Ct. Appeals (10th cir.) 1995, U.S. Ct. Fed. Claims 1995, U.S. Ct. Appeals (fed. cir.) 1999. Asst. terr. prosecutor Territory of Guam, Agana, 1980-83; spl. asst. U.S. Atty. Dist. of Guam and No. Marianas, 1982-83; atty. Witherspoon, Kelley, Davenport & Toole, Spokane, 1984—. Lawyer-rep. 9th cir. jud. conf., 1989-95, lawyer-rep. chmn., 1995, 9th cir. adv. bd., 2001—; adj. faculty Gonzaga U. Sch. of Law, 1994-95. Contbr. articles on Indian law, administrv. investigations and fed. jurisprudence to profl. jours. Bd. dirs. Spokane Opera Co., 1989-96, pres., 1992-94. Mem. ABA, Fed. Bar Assn. (pres. ea. dist. 1996-97), Hawaii Bar Assn., Idaho Bar Assn., Wash. State Bar Assn., Oreg. State Bar Assn. Avocations: sailing, scuba, skiing. Administrative and regulatory, Federal civil litigation, Criminal. Office: Witherspoon Kelley Davenport & Toole 428 W Riverside Ave Spokane WA 99201-0301

WEATHERUP, ROY GARFIELD, lawyer; b. Annapolis, Md., Apr. 20, 1947; s. Robert Alexander and Kathryn Crites (Hesser) W.; m. Wendy Gaines, Sept. 10, 1977; children: Jennifer, Christine. AB in Polit. Sci., Stanford U., 1968, JD, 1972. Bar: Calif. 1972, U.S. Dist. Ct. 1973, U.S. Ct. Appeals (9th cir.) 1975, U.S. Supreme Ct. 1980. Assoc. Haight, Brown & Bonesteel, Santa Monica, Santa Ana, L.A., 1972-78, ptnr., 1979—. Judge Moot Ct. UCLA, Loyola U., Pepperdine U.; arbitrator Am. Arbitration Assn.; mem. com. Book Approved Jury Instrns. L.A. Superior Ct. Mem. ABA, Calif. Acad. Appellate Lawyers, Los Angeles County Bar Assn., Town Hall Calif. Republican. Methodist. Appellate, State civil litigation, Insurance. Home: 17260 Rayen St Northridge CA 91325-2919 Office: Haight Brown & Bonesteel Ste 800 6080 Center Dr Los Angeles CA 90045 E-mail: weatherup@hbblaw.com

WEAVER, ELIZABETH A. state supreme court justice; b. New Orleans; d. Louis and Mary Weaver. BA, Newcomb Coll.; JD, Tulane U. Elem. tchr. Glen Lake Cmty. Sch., Maple City, Mich.; French tchr. Leelanau Sch., Glen Arbor; pvt. practice; law clk. Civil Dist. Ct., New Orleans; atty. Coleman, Dutrey & Thomson; atty., title specialist Chevron Oil Co.; probate and juvenile judge Leelanau County, Mich., 1975-86; judge Mich. Ct. of Appeals, 1987-94; justice Mich. Supreme Ct., Lansing, 1995—. Chief justice Mich. Supreme Ct., 1999-2000; instr. edn. dept. Ctr. Mich. U.; mem. Mich. Com. on Juvenile Justice, Nat. Conv. State Adv. Groups on Juvenile Justice for U.S.; chair Gov.'s Task Force on Children's Justice, Trial Ct. Assessment Commn., Office Juvenile Justice and Deliquency Prevention; jud. adv. bd. mem. Law and Orgnl. Econs. Ctr. U. Kans.; treas. Children's Charter of Cts. of Mich. Chairperson Western Mich. U. CLE Adv. Bd.; mem. steering com. Grand Traverse/Leelanau Commn. on Youth; mem. Glen Arbor Twp. Zoning Bd.; mem. chamber arts north Leelanau County; mem. citizen's adv. coun. Arnell Engstrom Children's Ctr.; mem. cmty. adv. com. Pathfinder Sch. Treaty Law Demonstration Project; active Grand Traverse/Leelanau Mental Health Found. Named one of five Outstanding Young Women in Mich., Mich. Jaycees, Jurist of Yr., Police Officers Assn. of Mich.; recipient Ea. award Warren Easton Hall of Fame. Fellow Mich. State Bar Found.; mem. ABA, Mich. Bar Assn. (chair CLE adv. bd., chair crime prevention ctr., chair juvenile law com.), Nat. Coun. Juvenile and Family Judges, La. Bar Assn., Grand Traverse County Bar Assn., Leelanau County Bar Assn., Antrim County Bar Assn., Delta Kappa Gamma (hon.). Office: Mich Supreme Ct 3300 Grandview Plz 10850 E Traverse Hwy Traverse City MI 49684-1364

WEAVER, MICHAEL JAMES, lawyer; b. Bakersfield, Calif., Feb. 11, 1946; s. Kenneth James and Elsa Hope (Rogers) W.; m. Valerie Scott, Sept. 2, 1966; children: Christopher James, Brett Michael, Karen Ashley. AB, Calif. State U., Long Beach, 1968; JD magna cum laude, U. San Diego, 1973. Bar: Calif., 1973, U.S. Dist. Ct. (so. dist.) Calif. 1973, U.S. Ct. Appeals (9th cir.) 1975, U.S. Supreme Ct. 1977. Law clk. to chief judge U.S. Dist. Ct. (so. dist.) Calif., San Diego, 1973-75; 1st v.p. Latham & Watkins. Judge pro tem San Diego Superior Ct.; master of the Bench of the Inn, Am. Inns of Ct., Louis M. Welch chpt.; lectr. Inn of Ct., San Diego, 1981—, Continuing Edn. of Bar, Calif., 1983—, Workshop for Judges U.S. Ct. Appeals (9th cir.), 1990; mem. task force on establishment of bus. cts. sys. Jud. Coun. Calif., 1996-97. Editor-in-chief: San Diego Law Rev., 1973; contbr. articles to profl. jours. Bd. dirs., pres. San Diego Kidney Found., 1985-90; bd. dirs. San Diego Aerospace Mus., 1985-97; trustee La Jolla (Calif.) Playhouse, 1990-91. lt. USNR, 1968-74. Fellow Am. Coll. Trial Lawyers; mem. San Diego Assn. Bus. Trial Lawyers (founding mem., bd. govs.), San Diego Def. Lawyers Assn. (dir.), Am. Arbitration Assn., 9th Cir. Jud. Conf. (del. 1987-90), Calif. Supreme Ct. Hist. Assn. (bd. dirs. 1998—), Safari Club Internat. (San Diego chpt.), San Diego Sportsmen's Club, Coronado Yacht Club. Republican. Presbyterian. Avocations: reading, family activities, flying, skiing. Federal civil litigation, General civil litigation, State civil litigation. Office: Latham & Watkins 701 B St Ste 2100 San Diego CA 92101-8197 E-mail: mike.weaver@lw.com

WEAVER, MOLLIE LITTLE, lawyer; b. Alma, Ga., Mar. 11; d. Alfred Ross and Annis Mae (Bowles) Little; m. Jack Delano Nelson, Sept. 12, 1953 (div. May 1970); 1 dau., Cynthia Ann; m. 2d, Hobart Ayres Weaver, June 10, 1970; stepchildren: Hobart Jr., Mary Essa, Robert. BA in History, U. Richmond, 1978; JD, Wake Forest U., 1981. Bar; N.C. 1982, Fla. 1983; Cert. profl. sec.; cert. adminstrv. mgr. Supr., Western Electric Co., Richmond, Va., 1952-75; cons., owner Cert. Mgmt. Assocs., Richmond, 1975-76; sole practice, Ft. Lauderdale, Fla., 1982-86, Emerald Isle, N.C., 1986-89, Richmond, 1989—. Author: Secretary's Reference Manual, 1973. Mem. adv. coun. to Bus. and Office Edn., Greensboro, N.C., 1970-73, adv. com. to bus. edn. Va. Commonwealth U., Richmond, 1977. Recipient Key to City of Winston-Salem, N.C., 1963; Epps award for scholarship, 1978. Mem. ABA, N.C. Bar Assn., Fla. Bar Assn., Word Processing Assn. (v.p., founder Richmond 1973-75), Adminstrv. Mgmt. Soc. (com. chmn. Richmond, 1973-75), Phi Beta Kappa, Eta Sigma Phi, Phi Alpha Theta. Republican. E-mail: legal311@aol.com. Home: 12301 Renwick Pl Glen Allen VA 23059-6959

WEAVER, PAUL DAVID, lawyer; b. Chgo., Feb. 15, 1943; s. Paul Stanley and Margaret Elizabeth (Wurster) W.; m. Carol Lynne Homan, July 1, 1978; children: Paul Tyson, Samuel Lincoln. AB, Yale U., 1965; JD, U. Mich., 1971. Bar: Mass. 1971, Ohio 1972. Mgr. west coast Big 3 Industries, Houston, 1965-68; assoc. Goodwin, Procter & Hoar, Boston, 1971-78; sec., gen. counsel Houghton Mifflin Co., 1979-88, sr. v.p., gen. counsel, 1989—. Mem. Beverly (Mass.) Hosp. Corp., 1978—; town counsel Town of Wenham, Mass., 1976—, moderator, 1987—. Mem. ABA, Mass. Bar Assn., Boston Bar Assn., Assn. Am. Publs. (chmn. lawyers com. 1985-86), Am. Soc. Corp. Secs., Mass. City Solicitors/Town Counsels Assn., Mass. Moderators Assn., Myopia Hunt Club (Hamilton, Mass.), Yale Club (N.Y.C.), Phi Delta Phi. Avocations: antiques, skiing. General corporate, General practice, Trademark and copyright. Home: 88 Walnut Rd Wenham MA 01984-1611 Office: Houghton Mifflin Co 222 Berkeley St Fl 5 Boston MA 02116-3748

WEAVER, RONALD LEE, lawyer; b. Winston-Salem, N.C., June 8, 1949; s. Robert Lee and Laura (Reich) W.; m. Jacquelyn Kay Witt, June 12, 1971; children: Lara Alison, Ronald Lee, Andrew Michael. AB, U. N.C.-Chapel Hill, 1971; JD cum laude, Harvard U., 1974. Bar: Fla. 1974. Mem. Stearns, Weaver, Miller, Weissler, Ahadeff, Sitterson. P.A., Tampa, Fla., 1979-81, Carlton, Fields, Ward, Emmanuel, Smith & Cutler, Tampa, 1999, Stearns Weaver Miller Weissler Alhadeff & Sitterson PA, Tampa. Author: Florida and Federal Banking, 1981; Commercial Real Estate Acquisition, 1983; presented over 200 seminars on real estate and real estate law. Bd. dirs. St. Joseph's Health Ctr., Inc.; chmn. Am. Heart Assn., Tampa, 1983, Deacons First Bapt. Ch. Tampa; bd. fellows U. Tampa (program chmn.); bd. dirs. Nat. Assn. of Indsl. and Office Paris (gov. affairs com. 1985, Pres. award Outstanding Svc. 1986), St. Joseph's Health Ctr., Inc. Clubs: University, Palma Ceia Country (Tampa). Mem. ABA (chmn. real estate matters subcom., real property section, chmn. real estate fin. subcom. comml. fin. svcs. com.), Hillsborough County Bar Assn. (program chmn. 1980), Tampa C. of C. (chmn. cultural affairs, bd. govs. 1983); bd. dirs. Nat. Assn. Corp. Real Estate Execs. (lectr.), Phi Beta Kappa, Phi Eta Sigma. Environmental, Land use and zoning (including planning). Home: 4303 W Beachway Dr Tampa FL 33609-4202 Office: Stearns Weaver Miller Weissler Alhadeff & Sitterson PA 401 E Jackson St Ste 2200 Tampa FL 33602-5251 E-mail: vweaver@swmwas.com

WEAVER, TIMOTHY ALLAN, lawyer; b. Elkhart, Ind., Nov. 30, 1948; s. Arthur and Joan Lucile (Yoder) W.; m. Catherine Anne Power, Nov. 23, 1974; children: Daniel Timothy, Christopher Matthew, David Colwell. AB, Brown U., 1971; JD, U. Ill., 1974. Bar: Ill. 1974, Wis. 1999, U.S. Dist. Ct. (no. dist.) Ill. 1975, U.S. Ct. Appeals (7th cir.) 1975, U.S. Dist. Ct. (no. dist. trial bar) Ill. 1982, U.S. Dist. Ct. (ea. dist.) Wis. 1999. Asst. pub. defender Cook County Pub. Defender, Chgo., 1974-75; trial atty. Chgo. Transit Authority, 1975-78; assoc. Philip E. Howard Ltd., Chgo., 1978, Pretzel & Stouffer, Chartered, Chgo., 1978-82, ptnr., 1982—. Editor: Medical Malpractice, 1989, 92, 96; contbr. chpts. to books. Mem. ABA, Ill. State Bar Assn., Ill. Assn. Def. Trial Counsel, State Bar of Wis., Civil Trial Counsel of Wis., The Lawyers Club of Chgo. General civil litigation, Personal injury, Product liability. Office: Pretzel & Stouffer One S Wacker Dr #2500 Chicago IL 60606 E-mail: tweaver@pretzel-stouffer.com

WEBB, DAN K. lawyer; b. Macomb, Ill., Sept. 5, 1945; s. Keith L. and Phyllis I. (Clow) W.; student Western Ill. U., 1963-66; J.D., Loyola U., 1970; m. Laura A. Buscemi, Mar. 15, 1973; children— Jeffrey, Maggie, Michael, Melanie. Bar: Ill. 1970. Chief spl. prosecutions div. U.S. Atty.'s Office, Chgo., 1970-76; ptnr. firm Cummins, Decker & Webb, Chgo., 1976-79; dir. Ill. Dept. Law Enforcement, Chgo., 1979-80; ptnr. Pierce, Webb, Lydon & Griffin, Chgo., 1980-81; U.S. atty., Chgo., 1981-84; ptnr. Winston & Strawn, Chgo., 1984— ; instr. John Marshall Law Sch., 1975— , Loyola U. Sch. Law, 1980— . Vice chmn. Met. Fair and Expn. Authority, 1978— ; bd. advisers Mercy Hosp. and Med. Ctr.; mem. Chgo. Council on Arson. Recipient spl. commendation award U.S. Justice Dept., 1975; named 1 of 10 Outstanding Young Chicagoans, Chgo. Jaycees, 1979. Mem. ABA, Ill. Bar Assn., Chgo. Bar Assn., Fed. Bar Assn., Legal Club Chgo., Execs. Club Chgo. Republican. General civil litigation, Criminal. Home: 15w151 87th St Burr Ridge IL 60521-6389 Office: Winston & Strawn 35 W Wacker Dr Ste 4200 Chicago IL 60601-1695

WEBB, JOHN, retired state supreme court justice; b. Rocky Mount, N.C., Sept. 18, 1926; s. William Devin and Ella (Johnson) W.; m. Martha Carolyn Harris, Sept. 13, 1958; children: Caroline Webb Smart, William Devin. Student, U. N.C., 1946-49; LLB, Columbia U., 1952. Judge Superior Ct., Wilson, N.C., 1971-77, N.C. Ct. Appeals, Raleigh, 1977-86; justice Supreme Ct. N.C., 1986-99; ptnr. Webb & Webb, N.C., 1998—. Served with USN, 1944-46. Mem. N.C. Bar Assn. Democrat. Baptist. Home: 808 Trinity Dr W Wilson NC 27893-2131 Office: Webb & Webb 19 W Hargett St Raleigh NC 27601-1391

WEBB, MICHAEL R. lawyer; b. Christchurch, New Zealand, Aug. 9, 1953; LLB, Victoria U. of Wellington, New Zealand, 1975. Barristr and solicitor High Ct. of New Zealand, 1976. Barrister, solicitor Brandons, Wellington, 1976-78, ptnr. Brookfield, Wellington, 1978-90, Simpson Grierson, Wellington, 1991-95; barrister Wellington/Auckland, New Zealand, 1995—. Chmn. Learning Media Ltd. (NZ), 1993-2000—; bd. dirs. Fulton Hogan Ltd., 1998-; mem. New Zeland Securities Commn., 1992—; dir. Tower Trust Group, 2001. Contbr. articles to legal jours. Mem. New Zealand Bar Assn., Arbitrators and Mediators Inst. New Zealand, New Zealand Law Soc. (legis. com. 2000), Internat. Law Assn. (mem. coun. New Zealand br.), Pacific Econ. Coop. Coun. (fin. markets devel. group). Administrative and regulatory, Banking, General corporate. Office: Level 3, The Annex, Axa Bldg, 41 Shortland St Auckland New Zealand E-mail: mw@michaelwebb.co.nz

WEBB, THOMAS IRWIN, JR. lawyer, director; b. Toledo, Sept. 16, 1948; s. Thomas Irwin and Marcia Davis (Winters) W.; m. Polly S. DeWitt, Oct. 11, 1986; 1 child, Elisabeth Hurst. BA, Williams Coll., 1970; postgrad., Boston U., 1970-71; JD, Case Western Res. U., 1973. Bar: Ohio. Assoc. Shumaker, Loop & Kendrick, Toledo, 1973-79, ptnr., 1979—, chmn. corp. law dept., 1992-94, mgmt. com., 1994-99. Dir. Calphalon Corp., 1990-98, Yark Automotive Group, Inc. Coun. mem. Village of Ottawa Hills, Ohio, 1979-85, adviser Ohio divsn. Securities, 1979-85, commr. of taxation, Village of Ottawa Hills, Ohio, 1999—; bd. dirs. Kiwanis Youth Found. of Toledo, 1982—, Toledo Area Regional Transit Authority, 1989-91, Arts Commn. Greater Toledo, 1993—, exec. com., 1994-99, v.p., 1994-96, pres., 1996-97; bd. dirs. Jr. Achievement of Northwestern Ohio, Inc., 1992—, Lourdes Coll. Found., 1995-01, Toledo Orch. Assn., 1999—, Med. Coll. Ohio, 2001—, Lourdes Coll., 2001—. Mem. ABA, Ohio Bar Assn. (corp. law com. 1989—), Toledo Bar Assn., Northwestern Ohio Alumni Assn. of Williams Coll. (pres. 1974-83), Toledo-Rowing Found. (trustee 1985-2001), Toledo Area C. of C. (trustee 1991-98, exec. com. 1993-98, fin. com. 1993—), Order of Coif, Crystal Downs Country Club, Toledo Country Club, The Toledo Club (trustee 1984-90, pres. 1987-90), Williams Club N.Y., Crystal Lake Yacht Club. Republican. Episcopalian. General corporate, Mergers and acquisitions, Securities. Office: Shumaker Loop & Kendrick 1000 Jackson St Toledo OH 43624-1573

WEBB ANDERSON, JOANN MARIE, lawyer, community advocate; b. St. Louis, Nov. 19, 1942; d. Jeff and Nancy Mae (Harris) Webb; m. Clifton Earl Anderson, Dec. 30, 1966; children: Ronald James Anderson, Nancy Delia Anderson. Student, U. Mo., Columbia and St. Louis, 1960-62; BA in History, St. Louis U., 1967, JD, 1978; grad., Ind. U., 1974-75. Bar: Mo. 1979, U.S. Dist. Ct. U.S. V.I. 1981, U.S. Dist. Ct. (ea. dist.) Mo. 1979, U.S. Ct. Appeals (8th cir.) 1979, U.S. Ct. Appeals (3d cir.) 1982. Staff atty. Legal Svcs. Ea. Mo., St. Louis, 1979-80; staff atty., mng. atty. Legal Svcs. V.I., Christiansted, Frederiksted, 1980-81; asst. atty. gen. Govt. of V.I., St. Croix, 1981-83; supervising atty. civil divsn. Dept. of Justice, Office of Atty. Gen., 1984-85, acting chief, supervising atty., 1985-87; exec.dir. Navy Relief Soc./Japan Aux., Yokusuka, 1988-89; sole practitioner St. Louis, 1997—. Music arranger, exec. dir. St. Croix Inspirational Singers, 1983-85. Bd. dirs. Archway Cmtys., Inc., St. Louis, 1998—, Child Ctr. of Our Lady, 2001—; polit. action com. Coalition of 100 Black Women, St. Louis, 1990; planning and focus group Hyde Park Neighbors/Trinity Sq., St. Louis, 1990—; cmty. adv. panel bd. Mallinkrodt Chemical Co., 1998—. Mem. Bar Assn. Met. St. Louis (econ. devel. com.), Jr. League of St. Louis, Caths. Against Capital Punishment, Blacks for Life/Mo. Right to Life, Lawyers for Life (bd. dirs. St. Louis chot.), Zeta Phi Beta. Roman Catholic. Avocations: neighborhood development, historical preservation, reading, grandparenting, international travel. Labor, Personal injury. Home: 1420 Bremen Ave Saint Louis MO 63107-2918 Office: 1428 Salisbury St Saint Louis MO 63107-2939 E-mail: justmo@att.net

WEBBER, CARL MADDRA, lawyer; b. Champaign, Ill., May 23, 1944; s. Charles Maddra and Lucille Ethelyn (Rankin) W.; m. Catherine Ann Johnson, June 21, 1975; children: Wendy Elizabeth, Christopher Maddra, Alexandra Sandeen. BS, Northwestern U., 1966; JD, U. Ill., 1973. Bar: Ill. 1974, U.S. Dist. Ct. (cen. dist.) Ill. 1974, U.S. Ct. Appeals (7th cir.) 1979. Pres. Webber & Thies PC, Urbana, Ill., 1974—. Adj. prof. Coll. Commerce U. Ill., 1987-90. Contbr. articles to profl. jours. Active Champaign County Jail Cts. Tech. Adv. Com., 1978-79, Downtown Devel. & Redevel. Commn., Urbana, 1978-79, U. Ill. Pres. Coun., 1984—; pres. Downtown Urbana Promotion Com., 1981-82; bd. dirs. Prairielands Coun. Boy Scouts Am., 1974—, v.p., 1979-82, pres., 1997-99; bd. dirs. U. Ill. Libr. Friends Bd., v.p., 1984-86, pres., 1986-88; bd. visitors U. Ill. Coll. Law, 1980—. Lt. USN, 1966-70. Recipient Appreciation award City of Urbana, 1980. Fellow Am. Bar Found., Ill. Bar Found.; mem. ABA, Urbana C. of C. (dir. 1978-81, 87-89, chmn. bd. 1989-90), Champaign County Bar Assn. (bd. dirs. 1980-83, pres. 1981-82), Ill. Bar Assn. (family law sect. coun. 1978-79, real estate sect. coun. 1983-87, co-chmn. contract drafting com. 1984-88), Rotary (dir. local club 1980-82). Contracts commercial, General corporate, Real property. Home: 2007 Bentbrook Dr Champaign IL 61822-9205 Office: Webber & Thies PC 202 Lincoln Square PO Box 189 Urbana IL 61801

WEBER, ALBAN, association executive, lawyer; b. Chgo., Jan. 29, 1915; s. Joseph A. and Anna (von Plachecki) W.; m. Margaret Kenny, Dec. 29, 1951; children: Alban III, Peggy Ann, Gloria, Brian. AB, Harvard U., 1935, JD, 1937; MA, Northwestern U., 1962; LLM, John Marshall Law sch., 1967. Bar: Ill. 1938, Mich. 1985, Fla. 1997, U.S. Supreme Ct. 1946. Ptnr. Weber & Weber, 1937-41; gen. counsel Fgn. Liquidation Commn., State Dept., 1946; trust officer Lake Shore Nat. Bank, Chgo., 1952-55; univ. counsel Northwestrn U., Evanston, Ill., 1955-70; pres. Fedn. Ind. Ill. Colls. and Univs., 1970-85; of counsel Schuyler, Roche & Zwirner, 1984-94; pres. Benjamin Franklin Fund, Inc., 1965-75, Northwestern U. Press, Inc., 1961-65; chmn. State Assn. Execs. Coun., 1981. Pres. N.E. Ill. coun. Boy Scouts Am., 1970-71, dist. chmn. Gulfstream coun., 1994-95; alderman City of Chgo., 1947-51. Comdr. USNR, 1941-45, rear adm., 1969-75. Recipient Silver Beaver award Boy Scouts Am., 1946, Meritorious Svc. award Loyola U., 1978, Edn. for Freedom award Roosevelt U., 1984. Mem. Nat. Assn. Coll. and Univ. Attys. (pres. 1962), Harvard Law Soc. Ill. (pres. 1984), Navy League (pres. Evanston coun. 1967-70), Univ. Risk Mgmt. Assn. (pres. 1965), Naval Order U.S. (nat. comdr. 1970-72), Law Club, Econs. Club, Harvard Club, Execs. Club, Chgo. Yacht Club, White Lake Yacht Club, Kiwanis (lt. gov., pres. Port St. Lucie club), St. Lucie River Power Squadron (comdr.), Anchor Line Yacht Club (commodore). Home: 1555 SE Sunshine Ave Port Saint Lucie FL 34952-6011 E-mail: StormyWeber1@aol.com

WEBER, FREDRIC ALAN, lawyer; b. Paterson, N.J., July 31, 1948; s. Frederick Edward and Alida (Hessels) W.; m. Mary Elizabeth Cook, June 18, 1983. BA in History, Rice U., 1970; JD, Yale U., 1976. Bar: Tex. 1976, U.S. Dist. Ct. (so. dist.) Tex. Assoc. Fulbright & Jaworski, Houston, 1976-80, participating assoc., 1980-83, ptnr., 1983—. Dir. Houston Symphony Soc., 1993—, v.p. devel., 2001—. Recipient Benjamin Scharps prize Yale Law Sch., 1976, Ambrose Gherini prize Yale Law Sch., 1976. Mem. ABA, Am. Coll. Bond Counsel, Nat. Assn. Bond Lawyers (bd. dirs. 1988-89, treas. 1989-90, pres.-elect 1991, pres. 1991-92), Houston Bar Assn. Finance, Municipal (including bonds), Securities. Office: Fulbright & Jaworski LLP 1301 Mckinney St Ste 5100 Houston TX 77010-3031 E-mail: fweber@fulbright.com

WEBER, HERMAN JACOB, federal judge; b. Lima, Ohio, May 20, 1927; s. Herman Jacob and Ada Minola (Esterly) W.; m. Barbara L. Rice, May 22, 1948; children: Clayton, Deborah. BA, Otterbein Coll., 1949; JD summa cum laude, Ohio State U., 1951. Bar: Ohio 1952, U.S. Dist. Ct. (so. dist.) Ohio 1954. Ptnr. Weber & Hogue, Fairborn, Ohio, 1952-61; judge Fairborn Mayor's Ct., 1956-58; acting judge Fairborn Mcpl. Ct., 1958-60; judge Greene County Common Pleas Ct., Xenia, Ohio, 1961-82, Ohio Ct. Appeals (2d dist.), Dayton, 1982-85, U.S. Dist. Ct. (so. dist.) Ohio, Cin., 1985—. Chmn. Sixth Cir. Dist. Judges Conf., 1988, Ohio Jud. Conf., Columbus, 1980-82; pres. Ohio Common Pleas Judges Assn., Columbus, 1975. Vice-mayor City of Fairborn, 1955-57, council mem., 1955-59. Served with USNR, 1945-46. Office: US Dist Ct 801 100 E 5th St Cincinnati OH 45202-3905

WEBER, JOHN WALTER, insurance company executive; b. Rochester, N.Y., Jan. 10, 1959; s. Donald J. and Patricia M. (Mangon) W.; m. Tracy Ann Sitler, Nov. 4, 1989. BS, U. Conn., 1984. Claims supr. Hartford Ins. Group, Southington, Conn., 1986-90; regional claims mgr. Housing Authority Risk Retention Group, Cheshire, 1990—. Mem. U. Conn. Alumni Assn. Avocations: running, reading, softball, cooking. E-mail: Jweber6@earthlink.net

WEBER, WALTER WINFIELD, JR. lawyer; b. Ramsey, N.J., Feb. 7, 1924; s. Walter W. and Mary Elizabeth (Collins) W.; m. Margaret Gardner Wilson, May 12, 1951; children: Ellen, Anne. B.S., Va. Mil. Inst., 1947; LL.B., Columbia U., 1950. Bar: N.J. 1949, N.Y. 1952, U.S. Supreme Ct. 1966. Assoc. Weber, Muth and Weber, Ramsey, N.J., 1949-52, ptnr., 1953-95, of counsel Poff & Bowman LLC, Ramsey, NJ, 1995-2001; dir. Citizens First Bancorp, Inc., Glen Rock, N.J., and subs., 1962-94; judge Upper Saddle River Mcpl. Ct., 1955-56. Mem. bd. of mgrs. Bergen Pines County Hosp., 1972-76, v.p., 1976. Served in U.S. Army, 1943-45. Mem. Bergen County Bar Assn., N.J. State Bar Assn. (chmn. pub. utility law sect. 1972-74), Antique and Classic Boat Soc. (dir. 1987-99). Republican. Dutch Reformed. Clubs: Arcola Country (Paramus, N.J.), Joe Jefferson (Saddle River, N.J.), Masons. Estate planning, Probate, Estate taxation. Address: 1 Cherry Ln Ramsey NJ 07446-1848

WEBER, WILLIAM RANDOLPH, lawyer; b. Columbia, Mo., Jan. 3, 1952; s. William Harry and Marie Antoinette (Fehlig) W.; m. Sondra Jean Gust, Aug. 12, 1972; children: Ashley Elizabeth, William Matthew, Stacey Pauline. BA, Vanderbilt U., 1974; JD, St. Louis U., 1977. Bar: Mo. 1977, Ill. 1978, U.S. Dist. Ct. (ea. dist.) Mo. 1978, U.S. Ct. Appeals (8th cir.) 1978. Ptnr. Thompson Coburn, St. Louis, 1977-99, Hazelwood & Weber LLC, St. Charles, Mo., 1999—. Adv. bd. chmn. Firstar Bank N.A.; staff St. Louis U. Law Jour., 1975-76. V.p. St. Charles County Y's Men, Mo., 1979-80; chmn. bd. adv. Salvation Army, St. Charles, 1980-83; chmn. St. Charles County Rep. Com., 1978-84; active Mo. State Rep. Com., Jefferson City, 1978-86, St. Charles County Counsellor, 1985-87, v.p., bd. govs., 1986-87; spl. counsel City of St. Peters, 1998—; bd. govs. Truman State U., 1981-87; bd. dirs. St. Charles C. of C., 1984-98, pres., 1997; regional panel White House Fellowship Commn., 1988-92; chmn. bd. dirs. March of Dimes Birth Defects Found., St. Louis; vice-chmn. St. Charles County Transit Authority, 1992-2000. Recipient Disting. Cmty. Svc. award St. Charles Jaycees, 1984. Mem. ABA (ho. of dels. 1987-89), Am. Soc. Hosp. Attys., Mo. Bar Assn. (rep. young lawyers sect. 1982-98), St. Charles County Bar ASsn. (pres. 1984), Ill. Bar Assn., Eagle Scout Assn. Roman Catholic. Health, Real property. Office: Hazelwood & Weber LLC 200 N Third St Saint Charles MO 63301 E-mail: wweber@hazelwoodweber.com

WEBSTER, DAVID MACPHERSON, lawyer; b. Chgo., June 22, 1950; s. Robert Fielden and Julia Ornendorff (Macpherson) W.; m. Lucia Maxwell Blair, Oct. 3, 1987; 1 child, Jessie Maxwell. BA magna cum laude with hons. in History, Williams Coll., 1972; JD, U. Va., 1975; DD (hon.), Seabury-Western Theol. Sem., 2000. Bar: Ill. 1975. Assoc. Winston & Strawn, Chgo., 1975-81, ptnr., 1981-87; White House fellow Washington, 1987-88; spl. asst. to dir. FBI, 1988-89; asst. gen. counsel for multilateral negotiations U.S. Arms Control and Disarmament Agy., 1989-94; v.p., gen. counsel A.T. Kearney, Inc., Chgo., 1994—. Mem. adv. com. on Ill. Bus. Corp. Act Ill. Sec. of State, Chgo., 1982-87. Bd. dirs. WBEZ Alliance, Inc., Chgo., 1996—, Ill. Soc. for Prevention of Blindness, Chgo., 1980-87, 97-99, pres. 1999—, Better Govt. Assn., Chgo., 1997-99; chair bd. trustees Seabury-Western Theol. Sem., Evanston, Ill., 1993-96, trustee, 1988-96; trustee Episc. Charities and Profl. Svcs., Chgo., 1980-87. Mem. Am. Hist. Assn. (assoc.), Orgn. Am. Historians (assoc.), Ill. State Hist. Soc. (life), Chgo. Hist. Soc., Manuscript Soc., Abraham Lincoln Assn., White House Fellows Assn., Mid-Day Club (Chgo.), Univ. Club Chgo., Chgo. Coun. Fgn. Rels., Law Club City of Chgo., Phi Beta Kappa Assn. Chgo. (exec. com. 1996-98). Episcopalian. Avocations: history, writing. Home: 596 Arbor Vitae Rd Winnetka IL 60093-2302 Office: AT Kearney Inc 222 W Adams St Ste 2393 Chicago IL 60606-5307 E-mail: david.webster@atkearney.com

WEBSTER, PETER BRIDGMAN, lawyer; b. Boston, Jan. 11, 1941; s. John Archibald and Mildred (Bridgman) W.; m. Elaine Gerber, Dec. 20, 1964; children: Amy Elizabeth, Peter Bridgman, Timothy James. AB, Bowdoin Coll., 1962; LLB, Cornell U., 1965. Bar: Maine 1965, U.S. Dist. Ct. Maine 1965. Assoc., then sr. ptnr. Verrill & Dana, Portland, Maine, 1965—. Mem. grievance commn. Maine Bd. Bar Overseers, Augusta, 1979-88, chmn., 1984-88, mem. 1986-94, chmn. 1990-92; adj. prof. law U. Maine, Portland, 1981; mem. Maine Commn. on Ethics and Govtl. Practices, 1991—, chair 1997—, chair Lawyers' Fund for Client Protection. Recipient Alumni Svc. award Bowdoin Coll., 1999. Banking, General corporate, Education and schools. Home: 185 W Main St Yarmouth ME 04096-8400 E-mail: pwebster@verrilldana.com

WEBSTER, PETER DAVID, judge; b. Framingham, Mass., Feb. 12, 1949; s. Waldo John and Helen Anne (Borovek) W.; m. Michele Page Hernandez, Jan. 13, 1989; 1 stepchild, Alana Perryman. BS, Georgetown U., 1971; JD, Duke U., 1974; LLM, U. Va., 1995. Bar: Fla. 1974, U.S. Dist. Ct. (mid. dist.) Fla. 1975, U.S. Ct. Appeals (5th cir.) 1975, U.S. Dist. Ct. (so. dist.) Fla. 1977, U.S. Dist. Ct. (no. dist.) Fla. 1978, U.S. Supreme Ct. 1978, U.S. Ct. Appeals (11th cir.) 1981. Law clk. U.S. Dist. Judge, Jacksonville, Fla., 1974-75; assoc. Bedell, Bedell, Dittmar, Smith & Zehmer, 1975-78; ptnr. Bedell, Bedell, Dittmar & Zehmer, 1978-85; cir. judge State Fla., 1986-91; judge Dist. Ct. of Appeal, First Dist., State of Fla., Tallahassee, 1991—. Master of bench Chester Bedell Am. Inn of Ct., 1988-91, Tallahassee Am. Inn of Ct., 1992—; chmn. com. on standard jury instrns. in civil cases, chmn. court reporter cert. planning com.; mem. com. on trial ct. info. sys.; com. on confidentiality of records of jud. br. Fla. Supreme Ct. Contbg. author: Sanctions: Rule 11 and Other Powers, 1986, Florida Criminal Rules and Practice Manual, 1990. Bd. dirs. Jacksonville Area Legal Aid, Inc., 1978-82, River Region Human Svcs., Inc., Jacksonville, 1986-88; mem. adv. bd. P.A.C.E. Ctr. for Girls, Inc., Jacksonville, 1986-91; com. mem. Shawnee dist. North Fla. coun. Boy Scouts Am., 1974-78; mem. delinquency task force Mayor's Commn. on Children and Youth, City of Jacksonville, 1988-91; officer, mem. exec. bd. Suwanee River Area coun. Boy Scouts, 1991-96. Mem. Fla. Conf. Appellate Judges, Jacksonville Bar Assn., Tallahassee Bar Assn., Phi Beta Kappa, Phi Alpha Theta, Phi Eta Sigma. Office: 1st Dist Ct Appeal 301 Martin Luther King Blvd Tallahassee FL 32399-1850

WEBSTER, ROBERT BYRON, lawyer; b. Mar. 9, 1932; s. Don B. and Glennie E. (Cole) W.; children: Anne Elizabeth, Allison Dee, Peter Hey, James Byron. BA, U. Mich., 1955; JD, 1957. Bar: Mich. 1958, U.S. Dist. Ct. (ea. dist.) Mich., 1958, U.S. Dist. Ct. (we. dist.) Mich. 1972, U.S. Ct. Appeals (6th cir.) 1958, U.S Supreme Ct. 1972. Law clk. U.S. Dist. Ct., 1957-59; assoc., ptnr. Hill, Lewis, Adams, Coodrich & Tait, 1959-73; judge Cit. Ct., Oakland County, 1973-84; chief judge, 1977; chmn. Hill, Lewis, Birmingham P.C., Mich., 1982—. Chmn. Supreme Ct. Com. to Revise Ct Rules, 1975-78; mem. Mich. Ct. Rule Adv. Com., 1984; chair, State Bar Appellate Task Force, 1993; trustee, chmn. Horizon Health Systems, 1983—; co-chair Legis. Commn. on Cts. in 21st Century, 1990. Chmn. Oakland Rep. Com., 1970-71, commr. Nat. Commn. on Uniform State Laws, 1995—; dir. Am. Jud. Soc.; trustee Family and Children Svcs. Oalnald County, 1976-84; mem. Oakland Cmty. mental Health Bd. 1971-73; trustee Henry Ford Health Sys., 1995—; mem. state officer's commn., 1998-2000. Served with USAF, 1951-53. Fellow Am. Bar Found., State Bar Mich. Found., Am. Coll. Trial lawyers; mem. ABA 9mem. ho. dels. 1990—), Am. Law Inst., Fed. bar Assn., State Bar Mich. (commr. 1982-90, v.p. 1987-88, pres. elect 1988-89, pres. 1989-90), Oakland Bar Assn. Republican. Unitarian. Federal civil litigation, State civil litigation. Office: 3d Fl 255 S Old Woodward Ave Birmingham MI 48009-6182

WECHSLER, MARY HEYRMAN, lawyer; b. Green Bay, Wis., Jan. 8, 1948; d. Donald Hubert and Helen (Polcyn) Heyrman; m. Roger Wechsler, Aug. 1971 (div. 1977); 1 child, Risa Heyrman; m. David Jay Sellinger, Aug. 15, 1981; 1 stepchild, Kirk Benjamin; 1 child, Michael Paul. Student, U. Chgo., 1966-67, 68-69; BA, U. Wash., 1971; JD cum laude, U. Puget Sound, 1979. Bar: Wash. 1979. Assoc. Law Offices Ann Johnson, Seattle, 1979-81; ptnr. Johnson, Wechsler, Thompson, 1981-83; pvt. practice, 1984-87; ptnr. Mussehl, Rosenberg et al, 1987-88, Wechsler, Becker, Erickson, Ross, Roubik & Edwards, Seattle, 1988—. Mem. Bd. of Ct. Edn., 1998-2001; bd. dirs. U. Wash. Law Sch. Child Advocacy Clinic, 1996-99; mem. Walsh Commn. on Jud. Selection, 1995-96; mem. Wash. State commn. on domestic rels., 1996-97, 99-2001; chair edn. com. Access to Justice Bd., 1996-99, pub. trust and confidence com., 2000-2001; presenter in field. Author: Family Law in Washington, 1987, rev. edit., 1988, Marriage and Separation, Divorce and Your Rights, 1994; contbr. articles to legal publs. Mem. Wash. State Ethics Adv. Com., 1992-95; bd. dirs. Seattle LWV, 1991-92. Fellow Am. Acad. Matrimonial Lawyers (sec.-treas. Wash. state chpt. 1996, profl. com. nat. 1996-97, v.p. 1997-98, pres. 1999-2000, nat. arbitration com. 1999-2000, nat. interdisciplinary com. 1999-2000, nat. admissions procedure com. 2000-01); mem. ABA (chmn. membership Wash. state 1987-88), Wash. State Bar Assn. (exec. com. family law sect. 1985-91, chair 1988-89, media project com. 2001, ct. improvement com. 1998-2000, legs. com. 1991-96, Outstanding Atty. of Yr. family law sect. 1988, comms. com. 1997-98, disciplinary hearing officer 1998—), Wash. Women Lawyers, King County Bar Assn. (legis. com. 1985-2000, vice-chair 1990-91, chair family law sect. 1986-87, chair domestic violence com. 1986-87, trustee 1988-90, policy planning com. 1991-92, 2d v.p. 1992-93, 1st v.p. 1993-94, pres. 1994-95, long-range planning com. 1998-99, awards com. 1997-99, Outstanding Atty. award 1999), Nat. Conf. of Bar Pres. (commn. com. 1994-95, long range planning com. 1998-99), King County Bar Found. (trustee 1997-2000), Am. Judicature Soc. (v.p. Washington chpt. 2000-2001). State civil litigation, Family and matrimonial. Office: Wechsler Becker Erickson Ross Roubik & Edwards 701 5th Ave Seattle WA 98104-7097

WEDDINGTON, SARAH RAGLE, lawyer, educator, speaker, writer; b. Abilene, Tex., Feb. 5, 1945; d. Herbert Doyle and Lena Catherine Ragle. BS magna cum laude, McMurry Coll., 1965, hon. doctorate, 1979; JD, U. Tex., 1967; hon. doctorate, Hamilton Coll., 1979, Southwestern U., 1989, Austin Coll., 1993, Nova Southeastern U., 1999. Bar: Tex. 1967, D.C. 1979, U.S. Dist. Ct. (we., no. and ea. dists.) Tex., U.S. Ct. Appeals (5th cir.), U.S. Supreme Ct. Pvt. practice law, Austin, 1967-77; gen. counsel Dept. Agr., Washington, 1977-78; spl. asst. to Pres., 1978-79; asst. to Pres., 1979-81; chmn. Interdepartmental Task Force on Women, 1978-81; mem. Pres.'s Commn. on Exec. Exchange, 1981; Carl Hatch prof. law and pub. adminstrn. U. N.Mex., Albuquerque, 1982-83; pvt. practice law Austin, Tex., 1985—; dir. Tex. Office State-Fed. Rels., Austin, Washington, 1983-85. Vis. prof. govt. Wheaton Coll., Norton, Mass., 1981-83; sr. lectr. Tex. Woman's U., Denton, 1981-90, 93, U. Tex., Austin, 1986—. Author: A Question of Choice, 1992; contbg. editor Glamour mag., 1981-83. Mem. Tex. Ho. of Reps., 1973-77. Recipient Woman of Yr. award Tex. Women's Polit. Caucus, 1973, Time Mag. Outstanding Young Am. Leaders, 1979, Leadership awards Ladies Home Jour., 1980, spl. recognition Esquire mag., 1984, Elizabeth (Betty) Boyer award Equity Action League, 1992, Woman Who Dares award Nat. Coun. Jewish Women, 1993, Woman of Distinction award Nat. Conf. for Coll. Women Student Leaders, 1993, Colby award for Pub. Svc. Sigma Kappa, 1996, Hummingbird award Leadership Am., 1998; named Lectr. of Yr. Nat. Assn. for Coll. Activities, 1990, Tex. Women's C. of C. Tex. Woman of Century, 1999, San Antonio Express News Face of Century, 1999, 2000, Speaking Out for Justice award AAUW Legal Advocacy Fund, 2001, Ally award Possible Woman Leadership Conf., 2001 ; named One of the Most Influential Lawyers of the 20th Century, Tex. Lawyer, 2000, Tallest Texan award Houston Chronicle, 2000. Mem. Tex. Bar Assn. Constitutional, Family and matrimonial, General practice. Office: The Weddington Ctr 709 W 14th St Austin TX 78701-1707 E-mail: sw@weddingtoncenter.com

WEDGLE, RICHARD JAY, lawyer; b. Denver, Dec. 2, 1951; s. Joseph M. and Lillian E. (Brown) W.; m. Susan R. Mason, Oct. 17, 1987. BA, U. Calif., Berkeley, 1974; JD, U. Denver, 1978. Bar: Colo. 1978, U.S. Dist. Ct. Colo. 1978, U.S. Ct. Appeals (10th cir.) 1980. Ptnr. Cox, Wedgle & Padmore, P.C., Denver, 1978-85, Barnes, Wedgle & Shpall, P.C., Denver, 1986-87, Wedgle and Shpall, P.C., Denver, 1987-98, Wedgle and Friedman, P.C., Denver, 1998-2000, Wedgle and Assocs., P.C., 2000—. Vol. coord. Dick Lamm for Gov., 1974, citizen adv. office, 1975; bd. dirs. Cherry Creek Improvement Assn., 1985-88. Mem. ABA, Colo. Bar Assn., Denver Bar Assn., Jewish Cmty. Ctr. Avocations: running, biking, gardening. Federal civil litigation, State civil litigation, Family and matrimonial. Home: 365 Marion St Denver CO 80218-3927 Office: Wedgle & Assocs PC 730 17th St Ste 230 Denver CO 80202-3546

WEDGWOOD, RUTH, law educator, international affairs expert; b. N.Y.C. d. Morris P. and Anne (Williams) Glushien; m. Josiah Francis Wedgwood; May 29, 1982; 1 child, Josiah Ruskin Wedgwood. BA magna cum laude, Harvard U., 1972; fellow, London Sch. Econs., 1972-73; JD, Yale U., 1976. Bar: D.C., N.Y., U.S. Supreme Ct. Law clk. to judge Henry Friendly U.S. Ct. Appeals (2d cir.), N.Y.C., 1976-77; law clk. to justice Harry Blackmun U.S. Supreme Ct., Washington, 1977-78; spl. asst. to asst. atty. gen. U.S. Dept. Justice, 1978-80; asst. U.S. atty. U.S. Dist. Ct. (so. dist.) N.Y., N.Y.C., 1980-86; prof. law Yale U., New Haven, 1986—, faculty fellow Inst. for Social and Policy Studies, 1989—; faculty fellow Berkeley Coll., Yale U., 1989—; faculty internat. security program Yale U., 1992—, faculty UN studies program, 1992—. Mem. Sec. of State's Adv. Com. Internat. Law, 1993—; dir., sr. fellow project internat. orgns. and law Coun. Fgn. Rels., 1994—; Charles Stockton prof. internat. law U.S. Naval War Coll., Newport, R.I., 1998-99; Edward Burling prof. internat. law and diplomacy Nitze Sch. Advanced Internat. Studies, Johns Hopkins U., Washington, 2001—; mem. Hart-Rudman Commn. on Nat. Security in 21st Century, Dept. Def. Adv. Commn., 1999-2001; mem. acad. adv. com. to spl. rep. of UN Sec.-Gen. for Children and Armed Conflict, 1999—; dir. studies Am. Soc. Internat. Law, 2000—; guest scholar U.S. Inst. of Peace, Washington, 2001—; dir. studies Hague Acad Internat. Law, 2002—. Exec. editor Yale Law Jour., 1975-76; author: The Revolutionary Martyrdom of Jonathan Robbins, 1990, The Use of Force in International Affairs, 1992, American National Interest and the United Nations, 1996, Toward an International Criminal Court?, 1999, After Dayton: Lessons of the Bosnian Peace Process, 1999; mem. bd. editors Yale Jour. Law and Humanities, 1988-98, Am. Jour. Internat. Law, 1998—, World Policy Jour. (New Sch. Social Rsch.), 2001-; contbr. articles to profl jours. and popular publs. including N.Y. Times, Washington Post, Christian Sci. Monitor, Internat. Herald Tribune, Washington Times, Fin. Times, L.A. Times, Fgn. Affairs; commentator for CNN, Fox. Nat. Pub. Radio, Pub Broadcasting Systems. Prin. rapporteur U.S. Atty. Gen.'s Guidelines on FBI Undercover Ops., Informant Use and Racketeering and Gen. Crime Investigations, 1980; bd. dirs. Lawyers Com. for Human Rights, N.Y.C., 1988-94; mem. policy adv. com. UN Assn. U.S.A., 1998—; bd. dirs. Lawyers Alliance for World Security, 1999—. Recipient Israel Peres prize, 1976, Disting. Contbn. to Internat. Law award N.Y. State Bar Assn., 2000; Ford Found. Rsch. grantee; Rockefeller Found. fellow. Mem. ABA, Am. Law Inst., Am. Soc. Internat. Law (exec. com. 1995-98), Internat. Law Assn. (v.p. 1994—,

program chmn. Am. br. 1992), Assn. Am. Law Sch. (chmn. sect. internat. law 1995-96), Assn. of the Bar of the City of N.Y. (arms control and internat. security affairs com., chmn. 1989-92, chmn. internat. affairs coun. 1992-95, exec. com. 1995-99), Union Internationale des Avocats, U.S.A. (chpt. bd. govs. 1993-98), Coun. on Fgn. Rels., Elizabethan Club, Mory's Assn., Yale Club (N.Y.C.), Lawn Club. Office: Yale U Sch Law PO Box 208215 New Haven CT 06520-8215 also: Coun on Fgn Rels 58 E 68th St New York NY 10021-5953 E-mail: ruth.wedgwood@yale.edu

WEDIG, REGINA SCOTTO, lawyer; b. Pensacola, Fla., July 30, 1955; d. Anthony P. and Janet (Treadway) Scotto; m. Eric M. Wedig. BA magna cum laude, Loyola U., 1977; MA, Tulane U., 1979; JD, La. State U., 1984. Bar: Tenn. 1984, U.S. Dist. Ct. (ea., mid. and we. dists.) Tenn. 1984, La. 1985, U.S. Dist. Ct. (ea., mid. and we. dists.) La. 1985, U.S. Ct. Appeals (5th cir.) 1985, U.S. Ct. Appeals (11th cir.) 1998. Assoc. Harkavy, Shainberg, Kosten, et al, Memphis, 1984-88, Bordelon, Hamlin & Theriot, New Orleans, 1988-94, ptnr., 1994—. Chmn. moot ct. bd. Paul M. Herbert Law Sch., La. State U., Baton Rouge, 1983-84. Editor: (newsletter) LSU-Coastal Law Newsletter, 1983-84; author: (law jour.) La. Bar Jour., 1996. Mem. La. Bar Assn., Tenn. Bar Assn., New Orleans Bar Assn. Contracts commercial, Probate, Real property. Office: Bordelon Hamlin & Theriot 701 S Peters St New Orleans LA 70130-1588

WEEKLEY, FREDERICK CLAY, JR. lawyer; b. San Antonio, Aug. 29, 1939; s. F. Clay and Topsy (Stevens) W.; m. Lynda Freeman; children: Amber Lee Carothers, Caroline Lee. BBA, Baylor U., 1962, JD, 1963; LLM, NYU, 1969. Bar: Tex. 1963. Ptnr. Bracewell & Patterson, Houston, 1974-90; trust counsel Bank One, Tex., N.A., 1990-98; ptnr. Shannon, Gracey, Ratliff & Miller, LLP, Ft. Worth, 1999—. Mem. coun. real property, probate and trust law sect., State Bar of Tex., 1987-90; mem. adminstrv. coun. trust divsn. Tex. Bankers Assn., 1992-95, chmn. legis. com., 1992-95. Editor: Texas Wills System, 1984. Mem. Commn. Probate Law Examiners, Tex. Bd. Legal Specialization, 1978-82. Fellow Am. Coll. Trust and Estate Counsel. General corporate, Probate. Home: 1821 Mossy Oak St Arlington TX 76012-5619 Office: 777 Main St Fort Worth TX 76102

WEEKS, ARTHUR ANDREW, lawyer, law educator; b. Hanceville, Ala., Dec. 2, 1914; s. A.A. and Anna S. (Seibert) W.; m. Carol P. Weeks; children: John David, Carol Christine, Nancy Anna. A.B., Samford U., 1936; LL.B., J.D., U. Ala., 1939; LL.M., Duke U., 1950; LL.D. (hon.), Widener U., 1980. Bar: Ala. 1939, Tenn. 1948. Sole practice, Birmingham, Ala., 1939-41, 1946-47, 1954-61; dean, prof. law Cumberland U. Sch. Law, 1947-54; dean, prof. Samford U., 1961-72, prof. law, 1972-74, Cumberland Sch. Law, Samford U., 1984—, Del. Sch. Law of Widener U., Wilmington, 1974-82, dean, 1974-80, interim dean, 1982-83, dean emeritus, prof., 1983—. Served to capt. AUS, 1941-46. Mem. ABA, Tenn. Bar Assn., Ala. Bar Assn., Birmingham Bar Assn., Del. Bar Assn. (assoc.), Phi Alpha Delta, Phi Kappa Phi, Delta Theta Phi Home: 1105 Water Edge Ct Birmingham AL 35244-1437

WEGENER, MARK DOUGLAS, lawyer; b. Nov. 1, 1948; s. Virgil Albert and Jean Frances (Wilke) W.; m. Donna Chait, May 28, 1972; children: Tara, David, Marisa. Ba cum laude, Cen. Coll., Pella, Iowa, 1970; JD, Rutgers U., 1973. Bar: D.C. 1974, U.S. Dist. Ct. D.C. 1974, U.S. Ct. Appeals (D.C. cir.) 1974. Assoc. Howrey & Simon, Washington, 1973-79; ptnr. Howry Simon Arnold & White, 1979—. Mem. ABA (anti-trust sect., litigation sect.), The Metropolitan Club, Stage Harbor Yacht Club. Antitrust, Federal civil litigation, Private international. Office: Howrey Simon Arnold & White LLP 1299 Pennsylvania Ave NW Washington DC 20004-2400 E-mail: wegenerm@howrey.com

WEGNER, JUDITH WELCH, law educator, dean; b. Hartford, Conn., Feb. 14, 1950; d. John Raymond and Ruth (Thulen) Welch; m. Warren W. Wegner, Oct. 13, 1972. BA with honors, U. Wis., 1972; JD, UCLA, 1976. Bar: Calif. 1976, D.C. 1977, N.C. 1988, U.S. Supreme Ct. 1980, U.S. Ct. Appeals. Law clk. to Judge Warren Ferguson, U.S. Dist. Ct. for So. Dist. Calif., L.A., 1976-77; atty. Office Legal Counsel and Land & Natural Resources Divsn. U.S. Dept. Justice, Washington, 1977-79; spl. asst. to sec. U.S. Dept. Edn., 1979-80; vis. assoc. prof. U. Iowa Coll. Law, Iowa City, 1981; asst. prof. U. N.C. Sch. Law, Chapel Hill, 1981-84, assoc. prof., 1984-88, prof., 1988—, assoc. dean, 1986-88, dean, 1989-99; sr. scholar Carnegie Found. for Advancement of Tchg., 1999—. Spkr. in field. Chief comment editor UCLA Law Rev., 1975-76; contbr. articles to legal publs. Mem. ABA (chmn. planning com. African Law Sch. Initiative 1994, co-chmn. planning com. 1994 mid-yr. deans meeting sect. on legal edn. and admission to bar), N.C. Assn. Women Attys. (Gweneth Davis award 1989), N.C. State Bar Assn., Assn. Am. Law Schs. (mem. exec. com. sect. on law & edn. 1985-88, mem. exec. com. sect. on local govt. law 1989-92, mem. accreditation com. 1986-88, chmn. 1989-91, program chmn. 1992 ann. meeting, program chmn. 1994 ann. meeting, mem. exec. com. 1992-96, pres. 1995), Soc. Am. Law Tchrs., Nat. League Cities (coun.-mentor program 1989-91), Women's Internat. Forum, Order of Coif (nat. exec. com. 1989-91), Phi Beta Kappa. Democrat. Office: U NC Sch Law Van Hecke Wettach Hall Campus Box 3380 Chapel Hill NC 27599-3380 E-mail: judith_wegner@unc.edu

WEHDE, ALBERT EDWARD, lawyer; b. Milw., Feb. 14, 1935; s. Albert Christian and Mary Hubbel (Dewey) W.; m. Joan M. Forney, Nov. 4, 1978; children: John C., Edward T. BS, Marquette U., 1956, JD, 1960. Bar: Wis. 1960, Calif. 1968. Atty. AEC, Albuquerque, 1963-66; counsel Lockheed Aircraft Co., Sunnyvale and Redlands, Calif., 1966-73; assoc. Schultz & Manfield, Palo Alto, 1973-74; sr. counsel FMC Corp., Santa Clara, 1974-95; atty. AEW Internat. Cons., 1995—. Bd. dirs. Tech. Fed. Credit Union, San Jose, Calif., chmn., 1994-96. Pres. Mountain View (Calif.) Babe Ruth League, 1976; trustee Mid-Peninsula Family Services Assn., Palo Alto, 1973-74. Served to capt. U.S. Army, 1960-63. Mem. ABA (chmn. region VII pub. contracts sect. 1977-81), Santa Clara County Bar Assn. (co-chmn. corp. counsel sect. 1983-84, mem. exec. com.), Am. Corp. Counsel Assn. (chpt. sec., pres. 1988, bd. dirs. 1983-93). Democrat. Roman Catholic. Avocations: gourmet cooking, music, sports. Government contracts and claims, Private international. Home: 1106 Lorne Way Sunnyvale CA 94087-5157

WEIDEMEYER, CARLETON LLOYD, lawyer; b. Hebbville, Md., June 12, 1933; BA in Polit. Sci., U. Md., 1958; JD, Stetson U., 1961. Bar: Fla. 1961, D.C. 1971, U.S. Dist. Ct. (mid. dist.) Fla. 1963, U.S. Ct. Appeals (5th cir.) 1967, U.S. Ct. Appeals (D.C. cir.) 1976, U.S. Supreme Ct. 1966, U.S. Ct. Appeals (11th cir.) 1982. Rsch. asst. Fla. 2d Dist. Ct. Appeals, 1961-65; ptnr. Kalle and Weidemeyer, St. Petersburg, Fla., 1965-68; asst. pub. defender 6th Jud. Cir., 1966-69, 81-83; ptnr. Wightman, Weidemeyer, Jones, Turnbull and Cobb, Clearwater, 1968-82; pres. Carleton L. Weidemeyer, P.A. Law Office, 1982—. Guest lectr. Stetson U., 1978-80; lectr. estate planning seminars; bd. dirs. 1st Nat. Bank and Trust Co., 1974-78, Fla. Bank of Commerce, 1973-77. Author: (handbook) Arbitration of Entertainment Claims, Baltimore County's Second District, The Emerging Thirties, 1990, Area History, Baltimore County, 1990, History of Musicians' Association of Clearwater, Local 729, AFM, 1999; editor Ad Lib mag., 1978-81; contbr. numerous articles to profl. jours. and geneal. pubs.; performer This Is Your Navy Radio Show, Memphis, 1951-52; leader Polka Dots, The Jazz Notes, 1976—; mem. St. Paul Ch. Orch., Fla. Hist. Soc., 1973—, Md. Hist. Soc., 1990—, Pinellas County Estate Planning Assn., 1997—; performer Clearwater Jazz Holiday, 1980, 81, co-chmn., 1981. Bd. advisors Musician Ins. Trust; trustee Francis G. Prasse Meml. Scholarship Trust, 1984—; mem. planned giving com. Upper Pinellas Assn. Retarded Citizens, 1996-2001; bd. trustees Tampa Bay Rsch. Inst., 2001—; adv. com. Fla. Sheriff Youth Ranches, 1997—; bd. dirs. Pinellas Ctr. for Visually Impaired, 1999-2000; bd. dirs. Watson Ctr. for the Blind, 2000—. Served with USN, 1951-54. Mem. SAR, Musicians Assn. Clearwater (pres. 1976-81), Fla.-Ga. Conf. Musicians (sec., treas. 1974-76), NRA, ABA (sr. bar sect.), Fed. Bar Assn., Fla. State Hist. Soc., Md. Hist. Soc., Greater St. Petersburg Musicians Assn., Clearwater Bar Assn. (probate divsn.), Am. Fedn. Musicians (internat. law com. pres. so. conf. musicians 1979-80), Nat. Geneal. Soc., Clearwater Genealogy Soc., Md. Geneal. Soc., Augustan Soc., Lancaster (Pa.) Geneal. Soc., Pinellas (Fla.) Geneal. Soc. (lectr. 1995—), Carroll County (Md.) Geneal. Soc., Balt. County Geneal. Soc., Lancaster Mennonite Hist. Soc., Navy Hurricane Hunters, Sons Union Vets. Civil War, Md. Hist. Soc., Catonsville (Md.) Hist. Soc., Am. Legion, German Am. Geneal. Assn., DAV Fleet Res., Masons, Scottish Rite (Tampa), Egypt Temple Shrine, Moose, Sertoma (bd. dirs. Clearwater chpt. 1984-96, v.p. 1989-92), Phi Delta Phi, Sigma Pi, Kappa Kappa Psi. Entertainment, Estate planning, General practice. Home: 2261 Belleair Rd Clearwater FL 33764-2761 Office: Legal Arts Bldg Ste 1 501 S Fort Harrison Ave Clearwater FL 33756-5317

WEIDMAN, CHARLES RAY, lawyer; b. Harrisburg, Pa., May 13, 1922; s. Charles Ray and Carrie Fay (Walker) W.; m. Alice Paine Walsh, Feb. 2, 1946; children: Charles S., Christopher R., William W. BS in Fgn. Service, Georgetown U., 1948, JB, 1950. Bar: Mass. 1976, U.S. Dist. Ct. Mass. 1976, U.S. Ct. Appeals (1st cir.) 1979, U.S. Supreme Ct. 1982. Indsl. relations dir. Underwood Corp., Bridgeport, Conn., 1950-57; account exec. John L. Schwab Assocs., Bridgeport, 1957-59; v.p., Eversharp, Inc., Milford, Conn., 1959-67, Rotron, Inc., Woodstock, N.Y., 1967-76; prin. Charles Ray Weidman Assocs., Chatham, Mass., 1976— ; arbitrator Am. Arbitration Assn., Boston, 1958-84. Contbr. articles to profl. jours. Chmn. Bd. Edn., Stratford, Conn., 1965-67; chmn. Republican Town Com., Chatham, 1984-88; moderator Town of Chatham, 1985-88. Served to sgt. USMC, 1942-46, PTO. Mem. Mass. Bar Assn., Boston Bar Assn., IEEE, Nat. Marine Electronics Assn. (exec. v.p. 1979-84), Phi Delta Phi. Episcopalian. Lodge: Rotary Internat. (Chatham) (sec. 1982-84). Federal civil litigation, State civil litigation, General practice. Home: 61 Hallett Ln Chatham MA 02633-2408 Office: 938 Main St Chatham MA 02633-1820

WEIGHT, MICHAEL ANTHONY, lawyer, former judge; b. Hilo, Hawaii, Jan. 5, 1940; s. Leslie A. and Grace B. (Brown) W.; m. Victoria Noel; children: Rachael R., Elizabeth G., Thomas P. BA in History, U. Rochester, 1961; LLB, Vanderbilt U., 1967. Bar: Hawaii 1967, U.S. Ct. Appeals (9th cir.) 1968, U.S. Supreme Ct. 1972. Pvt. practice, Honolulu, 1974-97; former judge Dist. Ct. (1st cir.) Hawaii; asst. fed. pub. defender Dists. of Hawaii and Guam, 1997—. Bd. dirs. Bishop Mus. Assn. 1st lt. USMC, 1961-63. Mem. Hawaii Bar Assn., Hawaii Assn. Criminal Def. Lawyers (pres. 1986). Criminal. Office: Fed Pub Defenders Office 300 Ala Moana Blvd Honolulu HI 96850-0001

WEIL, ANDREW L. lawyer; b. Pitts., July 19, 1920; s. Ferdinand T. and Allene (Guthman) W.; m. Margaret G. Thompson, Aug. 11, 1949; children: Wendy T., Peter A. AB cum laude, Princeton U., 1943; LLB, U. Pitts., 1948, JD, 1968. Bar: Pa. 1949, U.S. Ct. Appeals (3d cir.) 1955, U.S. Supreme Ct. 1965. Solicitor Twp. of O'Hara, Pa., 1956-64; spl. att. assty. gen. Commonwealth of Pa., Pitts., 1964-76; ptnr. Weil, Vatz & Weil, 1958-68, Cleland, Hurtt, Witt & Weil, 1975-79, Rose, Schmidt, Hasley & DiSalle, 1980—. Bd. dirs. Mary Hillman Jennings Found., 1970—. Served to lt. col. U.S. Army, 1943-46, ETO. Decorated Purple Heart, Bronze Star. Mem. ABA, Pa. Bar Assn., Allegheny County Bar Assn., Am. Counsel Assn. (pres. 1982-83), Assn. Mcpl. and Sch. Solitors, Pitts. Athletic Club, Fox Chapel Racquet Club. Republican. Presbyterian. Contracts commercial, Probate, Real property. Office: Rose Schmidt Hasley & DiSalle Oliver Building Bldg 900 Pittsburgh PA 15222-2393 E-mail: aweil@rshdlaw.com

WEIL, CASS SARGENT, lawyer; b. N.Y.C., Nov. 6, 1946; s. Theodore and Ruth Frances (Sargent) W. BA, SUNY, Stonybrook, 1968; JD cum laude, William Mitchell Coll. of Law, 1980. Bar: Minn. 1980, U.S. Dist. Ct. Minn. 1980, U.S. Ct. Appeals (8th cir.) 1980, Wis. 1984, U.S. Ct. Appeals (7th cir.) 1984; cert. bankruptcy law specialist, consumer and bus. Am. Bd. Certification. Assoc. J.R. Kotts & Assoc., Mpls., 1980-81, Wagner, Rutchick & Trojack, St. Paul, 1981-83; ptnr. Zohlmann & Weil, Wilmar, Minn., 1983, Peterson, Franke & Riach, P.A., St. Paul, 1983-91, O'Connor & Hannan, Mpls., 1991-94, Moss & Barnett, P.A., Mpls., 1994—. Editor: Minn. Legal Forms, Bankruptcy, 1983, 87, 91, 92, 93. Recepient Leading Am. Atty. award Am. Rsch. Corp., 1994, 96, 98, 2000, Minn. Top Lawyers Mpls. St. Paul Mag., 1998. Mem. Minn. Bar Assn. (vice chmn. bankruptcy sect. 1984-88, chairperson 1988-89), Wis. Bar Assn., Am. Bankruptcy Inst., Turnaround Mgmt. Assn., Comml. Law League Am., Order of Barristers. Democrat. Jewish. Bankruptcy, Consumer commercial, Contracts commercial. Office: Moss & Barnett PA 4800 Wells Fargo Ctr Minneapolis MN 55402 also: 90 S 7th St Ste 4800 Minneapolis MN 55402 E-mail: weilc@moss-barnett.com

WEIL, GARY RONALD, lawyer; b. N.Y.C., Oct. 1, 1953; s. Leopold and Margarete (Ofsijowitz) W. BS in Acctg., NYU, 1974; JD, NY Law Sch., 1978. Bar: N.Y. 1978, U.S. Dist. Ct. (so. dist.) N.Y. 1980. Asst. county atty. Westchester County Atty.'s Office, White Plains, N.Y., 1978-81; asst. dist. atty. Bronx (N.Y.) Dist. Atty.'s Office, 1981—, Spl. Narcotics Prosecutor's Office, N.Y.C., 1985-87. Mem. ABA, N.Y. State Bar Asn. Democrat. Jewish. Avocations: philately, photography. Office: Bronx Dist Attys Office 198 E 161st St Bronx NY 10451-3506 E-mail: geedubs@aol.com, weilg@bronxda.net

WEIL, PETER HENRY, lawyer; b. N.Y.C., Nov. 20, 1933; s. Frank L. and Henrietta Amelia (Simons) W.; m. Helen Fay Kolodkin, Dec. 18, 1960; children: Karen W. Markus, Frank L. BA cum laude, Princeton U., 1954; LLB cum laude, Harvard U., 1957. Bar: N.Y. 1957, U.S. Dist. Cts. (so. and ea. dists.) N.Y. 1972. Assoc. Weil, Gotshal & Manges, N.Y.C., 1958-62; from assoc. to ptnr. Kaye Scholer, 1962-95, ret., 1995. Lectr. SMU Inst. on Comml. Financing, 1985-94, Banking Law Inst., 1987-89. Author: Asset Based Lending: An Introductory Guide to Secured Financing, P.L.I., 1989, 3d edit., 1996. Fellow Am. Coll. of Commercial Fin. Lawyers; former chmn. N.Y. bd. overseers, former bd. govs. Hebrew Union Coll., Jewish Inst. Religion, Cin., N.Y.C., Los Angeles, Jerusalem. With U.S. Army 1957-58. Mem. Ringwood Golden Master Volleyball Team, U.S. Nat. Champions, 1983 Mem. ABA, Assn. of Bar of City of N.Y. (banking law com. 1975-78). Banking, Bankruptcy, Contracts commercial.

WEIL, ROBERT IRVING, lawyer, arbitrator, mediator, retired judge; b. N.Y.C., Apr. 6, 1922; s. Irving Julius and Esther (Aisenstein) W.; m. Carol Ethel Tannenbaum, Nov. 6, 1946 (div. 1953); children: David Irving, Timothy Robert; m. Dorothy Granet Kornhandler, Sept. 12, 1958. AB, UCLA, 1943; MS in Journalism, Columbia U., 1944; JD, U. So. Calif., L.A., 1951. Bar: Calif. 1951, U.S. Dist. Ct. (cen. dist.) Calif. 1951, U.S. Supreme Ct. 1961. Assoc. Pacht, Tannenbaum & Ross, L.A., 1951-54; ptnr. Tannenbaum, Steinberg & Shearer, Beverly Hills, Calif., 1954-58, Aaronson, Weil & Friedman, L.A., 1958-75; judge Calif. County Superior Ct., 1975-90; pvt. practice, 1990—. V.p. L.A. Police Commn., 1973-75; chmn. Calif. Ctr. for Jud. Edn. and Rsch., Emoryville, 1989-90; lectr., seminar leader Calif. Jud. Coll., Berkeley, 1981—, The Rutter Group, L.A., 1981—. Co-author: California Practice Guide: Civil Procedure Before Trial, 1983; contbr. articles to profl. jours. Mem. ABA, Am. Judges Assn., Calif. Judges Assn. (pres. 1985-86, v.p. 1993-94), Pres.'s award 1987, v.p. 1993, Edn. award 1997), L.A. County Bar Assn., L.A. Copyright Soc., Beverly Hills Bar Assn. Avocations: writing, reading, travel, theatre. Alternative dispute resolution. Home and Office: 2686 Claray Dr Los Angeles CA 90077-2017 E-mail: robertweil@worldnet.att.net

WEILAND, MARK BRADLEY, corporate lawyer; b. Hinsdale, Ill., June 15, 1956; s. William Sheplar and Dorothy (Costello) W.; m. Susan Jean Hill, Nov. 14, 1987; children: William, Abigail. BA, U. Ill. Champaign, 1978; JD, U. Chgo.-Kent Coll. Law, 1981. Asst. state's atty. Dupage Co., Ill., 1982-86; atty. William D. Lyman and Assocs., Oakbrook Terr., 1986-87; gen. counsel/v.p. and corporate sec. Profl. Svc. Industries, Inc., Lombard, 1987—. Chmn. Advocate's Assembly, Silver Spring, Md., 1993—, Lawyer's Roundtable. Mem. ABA, Ill. Bar Assn., Am. Soc. Testing and Materials (mem. com. D-18 1998—), Chgo. Bar Assn., Columbia Yacht Club. Republican. Roman Catholic. Avocations: fly fishing, boating, woodworking. Office: Profl Svc Industries Inc 510 E 22nd St Lombard IL 60148-6110 Fax: 630-691-1498. E-mail: mark.weiland@psiusa.com

WEILER, PAUL CRONIN, law educator; b. Port Arthur, Ont., Can., Jan. 28, 1939; s. G. Bernard and Marcella (Cronin) W.; m. Florrie Darwin, 1988; children: Virginia, John, Kathryn, Charles. BA with honors, U. Toronto, 1960, MA with honors, 1961; LLB, Osgoode Hall Law Sch., 1964; LLM, Harvard Law Sch., 1965; LLD, U. Victoria, 1981, U. Toronto, 2000. Bar: Ont. Prof. law Osgoode Hall Law Sch., 1965-72; chmn. Labour Rels. Bd. B.C., 1973-78; Mackenzie King prof. Can. studies Harvard Law Sch., 1978-80, prof. law, 1980—, Henry J. Friendly prof. law, 1993—, prof. law, 1993—. Chief counsel U.S. Commn. Future of Worker-Mgmt. Rels.; prin. legal investigator Harvard U. Med. Practice Study Group; impartial umpire AFL-CIO; chief reporter Am. Law Inst. Tort Reform Project; cons. to U.S. Commn. on Comprehensive Health Care (Pepper Commn.); spl. counsel Govt. of Ont. Rev. of Workers' Compensation, 1980-88; mem. pub. rev. bd. UAW, chief counsel Pres.' commn. Future Worker-Mgmt. Rels., 1993-94; panelist, U.S./Can. Free Trade Agreement Softwood Lumber Arbitration, 1992-93. Author: Labor Arbitration and Industrial Change, 1970, In the Last Resort: A Critical Study of the Supreme Court of Canada, 1974; (with others) Labor Relations Law in Canada, rev. edit., 1974; (with others) Studies in Sentencing in Canada, 1974, Reconcilable Differences: New Directions in Canadian Labour Law, 1980, Reforming Workers Compensation, 1980, MEGA Projects: The Collective Bargaining Dimensions, 1981, Protecting the Worker from Disability, 1983, Governing the Workplace: The Future of Labor and Employment Law, 1990, (with others) Patients, Doctors, and Lawyers: Medical Injury, Malpractice Litigation and Patient Compensation, 1990, Medical Malpractice on Trial, 1991, (with others) A Measure of Malpractice, 1992, Text, Cases, and Problems on Sports & the Law, 1993, 2d edit., 1998, Text, Cases, and Problems on Entertainment, Radio, and the Law, 1997, Leveling the Playing Field, 2000; contbr. articles to profl. jours. Mem. Nat. Acad. Arbitrators, Nat. Acad. Social Ins., Nat. Acad. Sci., Inst. Medicine. Roman Catholic. Club: Cambridge Tennis (Cambridge, Mass.). Office: Harvard U Law Sch 1525 Massachusetts Ave Cambridge MA 02138-2903 E-mail: pweiler@law.harvard.edu

WEILL, (LIGE) HARRY, SR. lawyer; b. Chattanooga, Sept. 12, 1916; s. David Robert Weill Sr. and Elsie Rose (Wertheimer) W.; m. Marcelle Baum, Dec. 10, 1947; children: Lige Harry Jr., Elsie Florence, Marcelle Audrey. BA, U. Va., 1936; JD, Harvard U., Cambridge, Mass., 1940; LLD, Harvard U., 1940. Bar: Tenn. 1948, U.S. Ct. Appeals (6th cir.) 1954, U.S. Tax Ct. 1976, U.S. Supreme Ct. 1983. Assoc. Frazier & Roberts, 1940, 1944-59; ptnr. Roberts & Weill, 1959-62; sr. ptnr. Weill & Weill, Chattanooga. Instr. contract law, McKenzie Coll.; founder Rossville (Ga.) Bank, 1963. Past pres. Mizpah congregation; bd. dirs. Girls Club Chattanooga; mem. Estate Planning Coun. Chattanooga; past pres. Jaycees Jr. C of C Chattanooga. Lt. U.S. Army, 1941-44, PTO. Named mem. of Thomas Jefferson Soc. of Alumni Univ. Va., 1986; scholar Univ. Va., 1932. Mem. ABA, Assn. Trial Lawyers Am., Am. Judicature Soc., Tenn. Bar Assn., Tenn. Trial Lawyers Assn., Chattanooga Bar Assn., B'Nai Brith Internat. Assn., Walden Club, Kiwanis Club, Am. Legion, Zeta Beta Tau. Avocations: gardening, skiing, walking. Personal injury, Probate, Estate taxation. E-mail: hweill@weillaw.com

WEIMER, PETER DWIGHT, mediator, lawyer, corporate executive; b. Grand Rapids, Mich., Oct. 14, 1938; s. Glen E. and Clarabel (Kauffman) W.; children: Melanie, Kim; m. Judith Anne Minor. BA, Bridgewater Coll., 1962; JD, Howard U., 1969. Cert. mediator Supreme Ct. Va. Assoc. counsel Loporto & Weimer Ltd., Manassas, Va., 1970-75; chief counsel Weimer & Cheatle Ltd., 1975-79, Peter D. Weimer, P.C., Manassas, 1979-83; pres., mediator Mediation Ltd., 1981—. Pres. Citation Properties, Inc., Manassas, 1971-93; pres. Preferred Rsch. of No. Va., Inc., 1985-89, Pro Rsch. Inc., 1989-93, Pro Mgmt., Inc., 1990—; cons. Continental Title & Escrow, Inc., 1992-96. Mem. Va. Mediation Network. Address: PO Box 1616 Manassas VA 20108-1616 E-mail: pjweimer@gte.net

WEIN, STEPHEN JOSHUA, lawyer; b. Bklyn., May 13, 1950; s. Max and Natalie (Messing) W.; m. Livia Monica Kahan, Jan 27, 1974; children: David Abraham, Matthew Jonathan. BA in Polit. Sci., Bklyn. Coll., 1972; JD, Stetson U., 1976. Bar: Fla. 1976, U.S. Dist. Ct. (mid. dist.) Fla. 1976, U.S. Ct. Appeals (D.C. cir.) 1979, U.S. Ct. Appeals (5th and 11th cirs.) 1981, U.S. Tax Ct. 1985, U.S. Supreme Ct. 1980. Assoc. Belcher & Fleece, St. Petersburg, Fla., 1976-78; pvt. practice, 1978-79; assoc. Battaglia, Ross, Hastings & Dicus, 1979-81, ptnr., shareholder, 1981-93, Battaglia, Ross, Dicus & Wein, P.A., 1993—. Bd. dirs., sec. Cong. Beth Chai, Seminole, Fla., 1978-84; bd. dirs. Pinellas County Jewish Day Sch., St. Petersburg, 1980-90, v.p., 1988, pres., 1989; bd. dirs. Jewish Fedn. of Pinellas County, 1989—, pres., 1991-93; trustee Menorah Manor Found., 1994—. Mem. ABA (exec. bd 1997-, secy. 1997-2000, treas. 2001-), ATLA, NACDL, Fla. Bar Assn. (criminal law and trial lawyers sects., fed. practice com., evidence code com.), St. Petersburg Bar Assn., Cardozo Soc. (pres. 1996-98). Federal civil litigation, State civil litigation, Criminal. Office: Battaglia Ross Dicus & Wein PO Box 41100 980 Tyrone Blvd N Saint Petersburg FL 33710-6382 E-mail: swein@brdwlaw.com

WEINBERG, JAY M. lawyer; b. Norfolk, Va., Aug. 4, 1932; m. Sondra Erlach, Mar. 6, 1955; 1 child, James L.; BA in English, U. Va., 1954; JD, U. Va., 1959; Ptnr. Hirschler, Fleischer, Weinberg, Cox & Allen, Richmond, Va., from 1959; vis. lectr. U. Va. Law Sch., 1960-65. 1st v.p. Jewish Community Fedn. of Richmond, 1980-86, pres., 1986—; pres. Jewish Community Ctr., Brotherhood of Congregation Beth Ahabah; regional v.p. Beth Sholom Home of Va., Inc., 1984—; pres. Congregation Beth Ahabah, 1978-79; trustee Nat. Jewish Welfare Bd., United Way of Greater Richmond, Beth Ahabah Mus. and Archives; trustee endowment fund Jewish Family Services; chmn. bd. Heritage Savs. & Loan Assn., Heritage Fin. Corp.; vice chmn. The Richmond Black Student Found., 1984—; bd. dirs. Revitalization Com. of Va. Commonwealth U., Judiac Culture Com. of Va. Commonwealth U., Rector's Club U. Richmond; assoc. mem. Nat. Trust Hist. Preservation. Served to capt. M.I. Corps, U.S. Army, 1957-59. Recipient William B. Thalhimer Young Leadership award, 1967, Man of Yr. award Congregation Beth Ahabah Brotherhood, 1982, Brotherhood Citation award NCCJ, 1985. Mem. ABA, Va. State Bar Assn., Va. Bar Assn., City of Richmond Bar Assn., Am. Coll. Real Estate Lawyers, Jefferson Lit. Soc. (pres. 1954), Supreme Ct. Hist. Soc., Phi Epsilon Pi, Phi Delta Phi. Clubs: Bull & Bear (organizer); Westwood Racquet. Contbr. articles to profl. jours.; mem. editorial staff Alexander's Fed. Tax Handbook, 1959-61. Office: Hirschler Fleischer Weinberg et al Main Street Centre 701 E Byrd St Richmond VA 23219-4528

WEINBERG, ROBERT LESTER, lawyer, law educator; b. N.Y.C., May 23, 1931; s. Abraham Matthew and Beatrice (Kohn) W.; m. Patricia Wendy Yates, Aug. 19, 1956; children: Susan Clare, David Hal, Jeremy Michael. BA, Yale U., 1953, LLB, 1960; PhD in Econs., London Sch. Econs., U. London, 1960. Bar: D.C. 1961, Conn. 1960, U.S. Supreme Ct. 1963, U.S.

Ct. Appeals (D.C. and 2d cirs.) 1961, U.S. Ct. Appeals (3d and 7th cirs.) 1965, U.S. Ct. Appeals (6th cir.) 1968, U.S. Ct. Appeals (9th cir.) 1976, U.S. Ct. Appeals (10th cir.) 1977, U.S. Ct. Appeals (5th cir.) 1978, U.S. Ct. Appeals (4th cir.) 1982. Assoc. Law Offices of Edward Bennett Williams and successor firms, 1960-66; founding ptnr. Williams & Connolly, 1967-96, ret., 1996; vis. lectr. U. Va. Sch. Law, Charlottesville, 1965—; adj. prof. U. Tex. Sch. Law, summer 1986; chmn. standing com. on pro bono matters D.C. Cir. Jud. Conf., 1980-96. Columnist No. Va. Sun, 1970s; contbr. articles to profl. jours. Pres. No. Va. Fair Housing, Inc., 1968-69; chmn. Arlington Pub. Utilities Commn. (Va.), 1968, Arlington County Dem. Com., 1969-71, 10th Congl. Dist. Dem. Com., No. Va., 1972-76; del. Dem. Nat. Conv., 1976; pres. Arlington County Civic Fedn., 1973-75; mem. governing coun. Am. Jewish Congress, 1984—; Dem. nominee for Congress, 10th Congl. Dist., 1988, 96. Served with U.S. Army, 1957-59. Recipient Outstanding Citizen of Yr. award Washington Evening Star and Arlington County Civic Fedn., 1975, Servant of Justice award Legal Aid Soc. of D.C., 1996. Mem. ABA (ho. of dels. 1977-82, 93-98), Bar Assn. D.C. (pres. 1994-95), Conn. Bar Assn., D.C. Bar (pres. 1977-79), D.C. Bar Found. (pres. 1988-89, 91-92), Internat. Assn. Jewish Lawyers & Jurors (bd. dirs., gen. sec. 1997—), Nat. Jewish Dem. Coun. (bd. dirs.). Federal civil litigation, Criminal. Home: 4 Quaintance Rd Sperryville VA 22740-2412 Office: 5171 37th Rd N Arlington VA 22207-1825

WEINBERG, SHELLEY ANN, lawyer; b. Newark, Mar. 17, 1955; d. Martin R. and Ruby Weinberg; m. Gary Kessel, Oct. 17, 1998. BFA, Syracuse U., 1977; JD, Touro Law Sch., Jacob D. Fuchsberg Law Ctr., 1987. Bar: N.J. 1988, U.S. Dist. Ct. N.J. 1988. Assoc. Larry A. Chamish, Esq., Newark, 1988-90, Wysoker, Glassner & Weingartner, New Brunswick, N.J., 1990, Nelinson, Roche & Carter, East Orange, 1991-92, Miller & Pincus, Esqs., Livingston, 1992-93; pvt. practice law, 1993—. Pub. Interest Law fellow Touro Law Sch., 1986. Mem. ATLA, N.J. State Bar Assn., Essex and Morris County Bar Assns. (workers compensation sect.), Nat. Orgn. Social Security Claimants Reps. Democrat. Avocations: fine art, travel, Spanish language. Civil rights, Pension, profit-sharing, and employee benefits, Workers' compensation. Office: 17 Academy St Ste 706 Newark NJ 07102-2905 also: Headqtrs Plaza North Tower 14th Flr Morristown NJ 07963 also: 535 N 7th St Newark NJ 07107-2423

WEINBERG, STEVEN JAY, lawyer; b. Casa Grande, Ariz., July 3, 1950; s. Jerry and Suzanne (Fabricant) W.; m. Stephanie Allison Lund, Aug. 10, 1975; 1 son, Joshua Noah. B.A., UCLA, 1972; J.D., Pepperdine U., 1975. Bar: Calif. 1975. U.S. Dist. Ct. (cen. and no. dists.) Calif. 1975, U.S. Dist. Ct. (so. dist.) Calif. 1977. Assoc. Popelka, Allard, McCowan & Jones, San Jose, Calif., 1976-77, Law Offices of Thomas T. Anderson, Indio, Calif., 1977-85; assoc. Anderson, Parkinson, Weinberg and Miller, Indio, Calif., 1977-85, ptnr., 86-88; sole practice, 19886; bd. govs. Calif. Trial Lawyers Polit. Action Com., 1981— ; mem. faculty Nat. Coll. Advocacy, Assn. Trial Lawyers Am., 1984. Fellow Belli Soc.; mem. Assn. Trial Lawyers Am. (co-chmn. motorcycle crash worthiness litigation group), Am. Bd. Trial Advs. (assoc.), Calif. Trial Lawyers Assn. (bd. govs. 1981-87, sec. 1984-88, cert. recognition of experience in field of personal injury 1979, editor Products Liability Forum 1984), Western Trial Lawyers Assn. (bd. govs. 1985). Democrat. Jewish. Personal injury. Home: 48-125 Alder Ln Palm Desert CA 92260-6652 Office: 74-900 Hiway III Ste 224 Indian Wells CA 92210

WEINBERGER, ALAN DAVID, lawyer, corporate executive; b. Washington, July 31, 1945; s. Theodore George and Shirley Sunshine (Gross) W.; m. Lauren Myra Kaminski, Dec. 2, 1979; children: Mark Henry, Benjamin Charles. BA, NYU, 1967, JD, 1970; LLM, Harvard U., 1973. Bar: N.Y. 1971, D.C. 1978, U.S. Supreme Ct. 1980. Assoc. White & Case, N.Y.C., 1970-72; founding law prof. Vt. Law Sch., South Royalton, 1973-75; atty. SEC and Fed. Home Loan Bank Bd., Washington, 1977-81; founder, chmn. bd. dirs., CEO The ASCII Group Inc., 1984—; founder, chmn. bd. dirs. Tech. Net, Inc., Bethesda, Md., 1995. Mem. adv. bd. Ashton Tate Inc., Torrance, Calif., 1986-87; sponsor, agt. All Union Fgn. Trade Acad., Acad. Nat. Economy of USSR in U.S.A., 1988-90; chmn. U.S. adv. bd. Moscow State U. of Commerce, 1992—; chmn. govt. affairs com. Computer Tech. Industry Assn., 1993-95; mem. U.S. adv. bd. U.S.-UK Fulbright Commn., 1999—. Author: White Paper to Reform Business Education in Russia, 1996; law rev. editor NYU Sch. Law, 1970. Named one of Top 25 Most Influential Execs. in Computer Industry, Computer Reseller News, 1988; recipient CEO of Yr. award Cyber Chanels, 1999; named eInnovator of Yr. Cyber Channels Assn., 2000. Mem. Nat. Orgn. on Disability (CEO coun.), D.C. Bar Assn., Order of Coif, Kenwood Country Club. Avocation: tennis. Computer, General corporate. Office: ASCII Group Inc 7101 Wisconsin Ave Bethesda MD 20814-4871

WEINBERGER, HAROLD PAUL, lawyer; b. N.Y.C., Mar. 12, 1947; s. Fred and Elaine (Schonfeld) W.; m. Toby Ann Strassman, Dec. 15, 1968; children: James David, Karen Ellen. BA, CCNY, 1967; JD, Columbia U., 1970. Bar: N.Y. 1971, U.S. Dist. Cts. (so., ea., and no. dists.) N.Y. 1972, U.s. Ct. Appeals (2d cir.) 1972. Law clk. to presiding justice U.S. Ct. Appeals (2d cir.), N.Y.C., 1970-71; assoc. Kramer Levin Naftalis Frankel LLP, 1971-77, ptnr., 1978—. Recipient John Ordronaux prize Columbia U. Law Sch., 1970. Mem. ABA (intellectual property law sect. 1999—), Assn. Bar City N.Y. (com. fed. legislation 1975-78, com. on products liability 1983-86, mem. com. on trademarks and unfair competition 1995-97). Democrat. Jewish. Federal civil litigation, State civil litigation, Intellectual property. Home: 336 Central Park W New York NY 10025-7111 Office: Kramer Levin Naftalis & Frankel LLP 919 3rd Ave New York NY 10022-3902 E-mail: hweinberger@kramerlevin.com

WEINBERGER, PETER HENRY, lawyer; b. Cleve., Nov. 15, 1950; s. Eric and Eva (Grant) W.; m. Laurie Ann Novak, Aug. 26, 1972; children: Kelly, Adam. AB in Psychology, Syracuse U., 1972; JD, Case Western Res. U., 1975. Bar: Ohio 1975, U.S. Ct. Appeals (6th cir.) 1975, U.S. Ct. Appeals (4th cir.) 1986, Pa. 1995, U.S. Supreme Ct. 1995. Ptnr. Kube & Weinberger, Cleve., 1975-88, Spangenberg, Shibley & Liber, Cleve., 1988—. Lectr. to bar assns., Case Western Res. U. Sch. Law. Contb. articles to legal jours. Chmn. Solon (Ohio) Cable TV Adv. Com., 1984-85; mem. Solon Civil Svc. Commn., 1985-87, vice chmn., 1986-87; bd. dirs. 1st Unitarian Ch. Cleve., pres., 1992-93. Mem. ABA, Ohio Bar Assn., Cleve. Bar Assn. (chmn. young lawyers sect. 1980-81, charter mem. coun. litigation sect. 1987—), Cuyahoga Bar Assn. (pres. 1991-92, chmn. grievance com. 1984-86, trustee 1987—, cert. of appreciation 1985, 89, outstanding svc. award 1986), Assn. Trial Lawyers Am., Ohio Acad. Trial Lawyers (trustee 1999—), Cleve. Acad. Trial Attys. (pres. 1984-85, spl. merit award 1985), 8th Dist. Jud. Conf. (charter mem. commn. on pre-trials), Cuyahoga Bar Found. (pres. 1998—), Am. Bd. of Trial Advs. (adv.). Democrat. Unitarian. Personal injury. Home: 34910 Forest Ln Cleveland OH 44139-1441 Office: Spangenberg Shibley & Liber 2400 National City Ctr Cleveland OH 44114 E-mail: phw@spanglaw.com

WEINBERGER, STEVEN, lawyer, educator; b. Bklyn., Apr. 13, 1953; s. Robert Ira and Elaine (Lichtenthal) W.; m. Maureen Susan Horan, Oct. 15, 1978 (div. 1998); children: John William, Matthew Lawrence; m. Maria DiBenedetto, Sept. 26, 1998. BA, SUNY, Binghamton, 1974; JD, U. Miami, 1977; MS, Hartford Grad. Ctr., 1989. Bar: N.Y. 1978, Conn. 1987, U.S. Dist. Ct. (no. dist.) N.Y. 1981, U.S. Dist. Ct. Conn. 1990. Legis. atty. N.Y. City Council, 1977-78; asst. atty. Westchester County, White Plains, N.Y., 1978-79; sr. asst. atty. Broome County, Binghamton, 1979-81, dep. personnel officer, 1981-82; from labor rels. specialist to chief employee svcs. bur. State of Conn., Hartford, 1982-95, dir. retirement and benefit svcs. divsn., 1995—. Adj. prof. Teikyo Post U., Waterbury, Conn., 1984—, Albertus Magnus Coll., New Haven, 2000—. Mem. N.Y. State Bar Assn. Democrat. Jewish. Office: State of Connecticut Retirement & Benefit Svcs 55 Elm St Hartford CT 06106-1746 E-mail: steve.weinberger@po.state.ct.us

WEINBLATT, SEYMOUR SOLOMON, lawyer; b. Bklyn., May 6, 1922; s. David and Lillian (Kantor) W.; m. Dorothy Robinovitz, Mar. 16, 1946 (div. May 1973); children: Jeffrey Howard, Jan Robin; m. Elizabeth Jean King Shelton, June 3, 1973; children: Eric H. Waser, Mark S. Waser (dec.). BA in Zoology, Ind. U., 1947; JD with honors, Rutgers U., 1950, postgrad., 1950-53. Bar: N.J. 1951, U.S. Dist. Ct. N.J. 1951, U.S. Supreme Ct. 1957, U.S. Ct. Appeals (3d cir.) 1975. Atty. City of Manville, N.J., 1962-64, atty. bd. edn., 1962-66; of counsel Joe E. Strauss, Flemington, 1984—. Mem. bd. edn. Twp. of Bethlehem, 1977-80, pres. bd. edn., 1979; mem. planning and zoning bd. Town of Juno Beach, Fla., 1998—, vice chmn. bd., 2001—. Mem. ABA, Hunterdon County (N.J.) Bar Assn., Am. Legion, Jewish War Vets. Jewish. Avocations: real estate, sports, journalism. Home: 911 Ocean Dr Apt 803 Juno Beach FL 33408-1700 Office: Joe E Strauss 63 Main St Ste 204 Flemington NJ 08822-1421 Fax: (561) 622-6767. E-mail: junoweinblatt@att.net

WEINER, CHARLES R. federal judge; b. Phila., June 27, 1922; s. Max and Bessie (Chairney) W.; m. Edna Gerber, Aug. 24, 1947; children: William, Carole, Harvey. Grad., U. Pa., 1947, M.A., 1967, Ph.D., 1972; LL.B., Temple U., 1950. Bar: Pa. bar 1951. Asst. dist. atty. Philadelphia County, 1952-53; mem. Pa. Senate from Phila. County, 1952-67, minority floor leader, 1959-60, 63-64, majority floor leader, 1961-62; U.S. dist. judge Eastern Dist. Pa., 1967—; now sr. judge. Mem. Phila. County Bd. Law Examiners, 1959— Mem. Pres.'s Adv. Commn. Inter-Govtl. Rels., Phila., Pub. Policy Com., Phila. Crime Prevention Assn., Big Bros. Assn.; mem. Pa. Bd. Arts and Scis.; trustee, exec. com. Fedn. Jewish Philanthropies of Phila., Allied Jewish Appeal of Phila.; bd. dirs. Mental Health Assn. of Pa., Phila. Psychiat. Ctr., Phila. Tribune Charities, Phila. Wharton Ctr. Parkside YMCA, Jewish Publ. Soc. Am., The Athenaeum, and others. Recipient Phila. Fellowship award; Founder's Day award Temple U.; Alumni award U. Pa.; Founder's award Berean Inst.; others. Mem. ABA, Pa. Bar Assn., Phila. Bar Assn., Am. Law Inst. Office: US District Ct 6613 US Courthouse Ind Mall W 601 Market St Philadelphia PA 19106-1713

WEINER, EARL DAVID, lawyer; b. Balt., Aug. 21, 1939; s. Jacob Joseph and Sophia Gertrude (Rachanow) W.; m. Gina Helen Priestley Ingoglia, Mar. 30, 1962; children: Melissa Danis Balmain, John Barlow. A.B., Dickinson Coll., 1960; LL.B., Yale U., 1968. Bar: N.Y. 1969. Assoc. Sullivan & Cromwell, N.Y.C., 1968-76, ptnr., 1976—. Adj. prof. Rutgers U. Sch. Law, 1987-88; bd. dirs. Solvay Techs. Inc., Hedwin Corp., The Acting Co., vice chair, 1992—, v.p., 1991-92. Gov. Bklyn. Heights Assn., 1980-87, pres., 1985-87, adv. com., 1987—; gov. The Heights Casino, 1979-84, pres., 1981-84; trustee Bklyn. Bot. Garden, 1985—, chmn. 1998—; trustee Green-Wood Cemetery, 1986—, Bklyn. Hosp. Ctr., 1998—; bd. advisors Dickinson Coll., Carlisle, Pa., 1986-90, chmn., 1988-90, trustee, 1988—, vice chmn. 1998—; mem. adv. com. East Rock Inst., 1988—. Lt. USN, 1961-65. Fellow Fgn. Policy Assn. (sr.); mem. ABA, N.Y. State Bar Assn., Assn. Bar City N.Y. General corporate, Private international. Office: Sullivan & Cromwell 125 Broad St Fl 28 New York NY 10004-2489

WEINER, KENNETH BRIAN, lawyer; b. N.Y.C., Oct. 13, 1954; s. Irwin I. and Elayne B. (Biffer) W.; m. Sandra Hong, Apr. 30, 2000. BSCE, Case Western Res. U., 1976; JD summa cum laude, N.Y. Law Sch., 1986. Bar: N.Y. 1986, Washington 1997; registered profl. engr., N.J. Quality control engr. Cosmic Constrn. Co., Newport News, Va., 1976-77; project engr., geotech. engr. Mueser Rutledge Cons. Engrs., N.Y.C., 1977-86; assoc. Olwine, Connelly, Chase, O'Donnel & Weyner, 1986-91, Ballard Spahr Andrews & Ingersoll LLP, Washington, 1992, Reid & Priest LLP, Washington, 1992-95, ptnr., 1996-98, Thelen Reid & Priest LLP, Washington, 1998—. Contbr. articles to profl. jours. Mem. Aircraft Owners and Pilots Assn., Mooney Aircraft Pilots Assn. Avocations: flying, skiing. Contracts commercial, Construction, Finance. Office: Thelen Reid & Priest LLP 701 Pennsylvania Ave NW Washington DC 20004-2608 E-mail: kweiner@thelenreid.com

WEINER, LAWRENCE, lawyer; b. Phila., Aug. 20, 1942; s. Robert A. and Goldie Weiner; m. Jane M. Coulthard, Feb. 28, 1976; 1 child, Kimberly. BS in Econs., U. Pa., 1964, JD, 1967. Bar: Pa. 1967, U.S. Dist. Ct. (ea. dist.) Pa. 1967, Fla. 1970, U.S. Dist. Ct. (so. dist.) Fla. 1976, U.S. Ct. Appeals (5th cir.) 1976, U.S. Tax Ct. 1984. Assoc., ptnr. Blank, Rome, Klaus & Comisky, Phila., 1967-71, 1975-77; ptnr. Weiner & Weisenfeld, P.A., Miami Beach, Fla., 1971-73, Pettigrew & Bailey, Miami, 1973-75; pres. Lawrence Weiner, P.A., 1977-83; ptnr. Spieler, Weiner & Spieler, P.A., 1983-89, Weiner & Cummings, P.A., Miami, 1989-94, Weiner, Cummings & Vittoria, Miami, 1994—. Lectr. Wharton Sch. U. Pa., Phila., 1968-70; instr. bus. law and acctg. Community Coll. Phila., 1967-70; lectr. estate planning various non-lawyer groups, Miami, 1972—. Mem. Fla. Bar (liaison non-lawyers groups 1980-87), Pa. Bar Assn., Phila. Bar Assn., Dade County Bar Assn. (chmn. ins. com. 1977-78, probate law com. 1992—). Democrat. Jewish. General corporate, Estate planning, Probate. Office: Weiner Cummings & Vittoria 1428 Brickell Ave Ste 400 Miami FL 33131-3436

WEINER, MARCIA MYRA, lawyer; b. Chgo., Apr. 12, 1934; d. Adolph Carl and Esther (Kahan) Spitzer; m. Bernard Karl Weiner, Sept. 15, 1952; children— Audrey Weiner Scheinberg, Jodi Weiner Groff, Karen Weiner Miller. B.A., St. Mary's U., San Antonio, 1965, J.D., 1970. Bar: Tex. 1971. Atty.-advisor HUD, San Antonio, 1971-84, chief counsel, San Antonio, 1984-97; elected justice of the peace, Precinct 2 Place, Bexar County, Texas, 2000—. Recipient Spl. Achievement awards HUD, 1972, 75, 77, Hub Federal Women's Program Award, Leigh Curry Award, Federal Women's Program Council Management Award, Outstanding Business Woman of the Year, 2000. Mem. ABA, Alamo Unit #2 of the American Legion Auxiliary, Tex. Bar Assn., Fed. Bar Assn., Bexar County Women's Bar Assn., San Antonio Bar Assn., Randolph Roadrunners, Texas Wanderers, Greyhound Pets of Am. Office: Justice Ct Precinct 2 6715 Bandera Rd San Antonio TX 78238

WEINER, SANFORD ALAN, lawyer; b. Houston, Aug. 21, 1946; s. Abe I. and Zelda C. (Caplan) W.; m. Leslie Eve Grenadier, Aug. 16, 1970; children: Edward, David, Evan, Rebecca. BA, U. Tex., 1968; JD, Harvard U., 1971. Bar: Tex. 1971. Ptnr. Vinson & Elkins, Ltd. Liability Partnership, Houston, 1971—. V.p. Am. Coll. Real Estate Lawyers. Mem. Houston Bar Assn., Tex. Bar Assn., Houston Real Estate Lawyers Council, Anglo-Am. Real Property Inst. Jewish. Banking, Finance, Real property. Office: Vinson & Elkins L L P 1001 Fannin St Ste 3300 Houston TX 77002-6706

WEINGARTEN, SAUL MYER, lawyer; b. Los Angeles, Dec. 19, 1921; s. Louis and Lillian Dorothy (Alter) W.; m. Miriam Ellen Moore, Jan. 21, 1949; children: David, Steven, Lawrence, Bruce. AA, Antelope Valley Coll., 1940; AB, UCLA, 1942; cert., Cornell U., 1943; JD, U. Southern Calif., 1949. Bar: Calif. 1950, U.S. Supreme Ct., 1960. Prin. Saul M. Weingarten Assocs., Seaside, Calif., 1954—. Atty. City of Gonzales, Calif., 1954-74, City of Seaside, 1955-70; gen. counsel Redevel. Agy., Seaside, 1955-76, Security Nat. Bank, Monterey, Calif., 1968-74; bd. dirs., exec. com. Frontier Bank, Cheyenne, Wyo., 1984-99; pres. Quaestor, Inc., 1991-98. Author: Practice Compendium, 1950; contbr. articles to profl. jours. Del. Internat. Union of Local Authorities, Brussels, Belgium, 1963, 73; candidate state legislature Dem. Com., Monterey County, 1958; counsel Monterey Peninsula Mus. of Art, Inc., 1972-80; gen. counsel Monterey County Symphony Assn., Carmel, Calif., 1974-98, Mountain Plains Edn. Project, Glasgow, Mont., 1975-81; chmn. fund raising ARC, Monterey, 1964; chmn., bd. dirs. fund raising United Way, Monterey, 1962-63; pres., bd. dirs. Alliance on Aging, Monterey, 1968-82; bd. dirs. Family Svc. Agy., Monterey, 1958-66, Monterey County Cultural Coun., 1986-94, Clark Found., 1982—; dir., mem. exec. com. Monterey Bay Performing Arts Ctr., 1990. Served to commdr. USN, 1942-46, 50-54, Korea. Grad. fellow Coro Found., 1949-50. Mem. Calif. Bar Assn., Monterey County Bar Assn., Monterey County Trial Lawyers Assn., Rotary (pres. 1970-71, 82-83), Commonwealth Club, Meadowbrook Club. Jewish. Avocations: travel. Family and matrimonial, General practice, Real property. Home: 4135 Crest Rd Pebble Beach CA 93953-3008 Office: Ste D 1123 Fremont Blvd Seaside CA 93955-5759 E-mail: lsm147@juno.com

WEINGER, STEVEN MURRAY, lawyer; b. Chgo., Feb. 7, 1954; s. Paul and Joan (Taxay) W.; children: Blake, Paige, Haley. BA, Hampshire Coll., 1975; JD, U. Chgo., 1978. Bar: Fla. 1979, Ill. 1979, U.S. Dist. Ct. (so. dist.) Fla. 1979, U.S. Ct. Appeals (5th cir.) 1980, U.S. Ct. Appeals (11th cir.) 1981, U.S. Supreme Ct. 1982, U.S. Dist. Ct. (mid. dist.) Fla. 1989. Mem. faculty U. Miami Sch. Law, Coral Gables, Fla., 1978-79; ptnr. Kurzban, Kurzban & Weinger, P.A., Miami, 1979—. Bd. dirs. Sunrise Cmty. for Mentally Retarded, Miami, United Cerebral Palsy Tallahassee, Inc., Palmer-Trinity Sch., Miami, GobleStage, Inc., 1999—. Recipient Chmn.'s award Sunrise Cmty. for Mentally Retarded, 1987; honoree United Cerebral Palsy in South Fla., 1995, Fla. Assn. Rehab. Facilities, 1996, United Cerebral Palsy Assn., 1997. Mem. ABA, Assn. Trial Lawyers Am., Fla. Assn. Trial Lawyers. Federal civil litigation, General civil litigation, Health. Office: Kurzban Kurzban & Weinger 2650 SW 27th Ave Fl 2D Miami FL 33133-3003 E-mail: swmiami@aol.com

WEINIG, RICHARD ARTHUR, lawyer; b. Durango, Colo., Mar. 23, 1940; s. Arthur John and Edna (Novella) W.; m. Barbara A. Westerlund, June 16, 1964. BA in Polit. Sci., Stanford U., 1962, postgrad. in Soviet Studies, 1962-65; JD, U. Calif., San Francisco, 1971. Bar: Alaska 1971, U.S. Dist. Ct. Alaska 1971, U.S. Ct. Appeals (9th cir.) 1978, U.S. Supreme Ct. 1979. Assoc. Burr, Pease & Kurtz, Anchorage, 1971-73, Greater Anchorage Area Borough, 1973-75, Municipality of Anchorage, 1975-82; ptnr. Pletcher & Slaybaugh, Anchorage, 1982-88, Pletcher, Weinig & Merriner, Anchorage, 1988-99. Mem. editl. bd. Hastings Law Jour. Active Stanford U. Young Republicans, 1961-65, Sierra Club, Mountaineering Club, Knik Canoyers and Kayakers of Alaska, Alaska Ctr. for Environ. Mem. ABA, Alaska Bar Assn., Anchorage Bar Assn., NRA. Republican. Presbyterian. Condemnation, Insurance, Personal injury. Office: Pletcher Weinig & Fisher 800 E Dimond Blvd Ste 3-620 Anchorage AK 99515-2045 Office Fax: 907-349-7758. E-mail: richard@akinsurancedefense.com

WEINKOPF, FRIEDRICH J. lawyer; b. Bautsch, Germany, Feb. 17, 1930; Referendar, U. Marburg, Germany, 1954; LLM, U. Pa., 1958; JD, Chgo.-Kent Coll. Law, 1967. Bar: Ill. 1967. Ptnr. Baker & McKenzie, Chgo. Office: Baker & McKenzie 1 Prudential Plz 130 E Randolph St Fl 3600 Chicago IL 60601-6315

WEINMAN, GLENN ALAN, lawyer; b. N.Y.C., Dec. 9, 1955; s. Seymour and Iris Rhoda (Bergman) W. BA in Polit. Sci., UCLA, 1978; JD, U. So. Calif., 1981. Bar: Calif. 1981. Assoc. counsel Mitsui Mfrs. Bank, L.A., 1981-83; assoc. McKenna, Conner & Cuneo, 1983-85, Stroock, Stroock & Lavan, L.A., 1985-87; sr. counsel Buchalter, Nemer, Fields & Younger, 1987-91; ptnr. Keck, Mahin & Cate, 1991-93; sr. v.p., gen. counsel Western Internat. Media Corp., 1993-96; v.p. gen. counsel and human resources, sec. Guess?, Inc., 1996-2000; also bd. dirs.; chief adminstrv. officer Competitive Knowledge, Inc., 2000; v.p., gen. counsel, sec. Luminent, Inc., Chatsworth, Calif., 2000-01; exec. v.p., COO InsoVery Svcs. Group, Woodland Hills, 2001—. Bd. dirs. Guess? Retail Inc., Guess? Licensing, Inc., Guess.com., Inc. Mem. ABA (corp. banking and bus. law sect., com. on savs. instns., com. on banking law corp. counsel sect.), Calif. Bar Assn. (bus. law sect., com. fin. instns. 1989-91, com. consumer svcs. 1991-94), L.A. County Bar Assn. (corp. legal depts. sect., bus. and corps. law sect., subcom. on fin. instns.), Calif. Fashion Assn. (exec. bd. 1997-2000), , Am. Apparel Mfrs. Assn. (govt. rels. com. 1997-2000), Legion Lex, U. So. Calif. Law Alumni Assn., Phi Alpha Delta. Avocation: tennis. Contracts commercial, General corporate, Finance. Office: 20550 Nordhoff St Chatsworth CA 91311 E-mail: gaweinman@aol.com

WEINREB, MICHAEL LEONARD, lawyer; b. Freeport, N.Y., June 14, 1955; s. Donald and Stephanie (Herman) W.; m. Sharon M. Stertz, May 20, 1982; 1 child, Jessica. BS, Syracuse U., 1976; JD, Miami U., 1979. Bar: Fla. 1979, N.Y. 1981. Sole practice, 1981—; ptnr. Weinreb, Weinreb & Weinreb, 1986—. Pres. Omni Abstract Corp., Babylon, N.Y., 1978—. Family and matrimonial, Personal injury, Real property. Office: 475 Sunrise Hwy West Babylon NY 11704-6017 E-mail: MLWeinreb@att.net

WEINRICH, JOHNATHAN EDWARD, lawyer; b. N.Y.C., Sept. 17, 1949; s. John Edward and Anne (Murray) W.; children: Joy Teresa, Johnathan Joseph; m. Evelyn; 1 child, Kristina Lynn. BA, SUNY, Binghamton, 1974; JD, Vt. Law Sch., 1977. Bar: N.Y. 1978, U.S. Dist. Ct. (ea. and so. dist.) N.Y. 1978, U.S. Tax Ct. 1981, U.S. Ct. Appeals (2d cir.) 1980. Sr. staff atty. Legal Aid Soc., N.Y.C., 1979-81; ptnr. Rutberg & Weinrich, 1981-83; prin., owner Johnathan E. Weinrich Law Firm, 1983—. Legis. counsel N.Y.C. Councilman Ralph Colon, 1987-92, N.Y.C. Councilman David Rosado, 1992-96, N.Y.C. Councilman Federico Perez, 1997-98, N.Y. State Senator David Rosado, 1997-2000; mem. Gov.'s Metro Task Force on Correctional Services, N.Y.C., 1984; trustee Vt. Law Sch., 1975-76. Editor Vt. Law Rev., 1976-77. Counsel Excise Bonds, 1990—, Local One Security Officers Union, 1998—. Recipient State of N.Y. Legis. Resolution #759, 1989, N.Y. Coun. Proclaimation, 1992, N.Y. State Senate Resolution, 2000. Mem. ABA, N.Y. State Trial Lawyers Assn., Assn. Trial Lawyers Am., Bklyn. Bar Assn., Kings County Criminal Bar Assn., Legal Aid Alumni Assn., N.Y. State Defenders Assn., N.Y. State Assn. Criminal Def. Attys. (charter 1987—), Royal Order of Scotland. Lodge: Masons. Democrat. Roman Catholic. Criminal, Labor, Legislative. Address: 100 Williams St 3rd Fl New York NY 10038

WEINSCHEL, ALAN JAY, lawyer; b. Bklyn., Feb. 9, 1946; m. Barbara Ellen Schure, Aug. 20, 1967; children: Lawrence, Adam, Naomi. BA, Bklyn. Coll., 1967; JD, NYU, 1969. Bar: N.Y. 1970, U.S. Dist. Ct. (so. and ea. dists.) N.Y. 1973, U.S. Ct. Appeals (2d cir.) 1979, U.S. Ct. Appeals (9th cir.) 1986, U.S. Ct. Appeals (3d cir.) 1993, U.S. Ct. Appeals (7th cir.) 1996. Assoc. Breed, Abbott & Morgan, N.Y.C., 1969-74, Weil, Gotshal & Manges, N.Y.C., 1974-78, ptnr., 1978—. Lectr. Practising Law Inst., Ohio Legal Ctr., Am. Mgmt. Assn., Law Jour. Seminars, Law and Bus. Seminars, Glasser Legalworks, Insight Seminars, Mfrs.' Alliance. Author: Antitrust Intellectual Property Handbook, 2000. Trustee N.Y. Inst. Tech., Old Westbury, N.Y., 1969-76, Temple Sinai, Roslyn, N.Y., 1981-87, 89-95. Capt. U.S. Army res., 1969-74. Mem. ABA (editl. bd. Antitrust Devels. 1981-87), N.Y. State Bar Assn. (chmn. antitrust sect. 1993-95), Assn. Bar of City of N.Y. Antitrust, General civil litigation, Intellectual property. Office: Weil Gotshal & Manges 767 5th Ave New York NY 10153-0119 E-mail: alan.weinschel@weil.com

WEINSTEIN, ALAN EDWARD, lawyer; b. Bklyn., Apr. 20, 1945; s. John and Matilda W.; m. Patti Kantor, Dec. 18, 1965; children: Steven R., David A. AA, U. Fla., 1964; BBA, U. Miami, Fla., 1965, JD cum laude, 1968. Bar: Fla. 1968, U.S. Dist. Ct. (so. dist.) Fla. 1968, U.S. Ct. Appeals (5th cir.) 1969, U.S. Supreme Ct. 1973, U.S. Ct. Appeals (4th & 11th cirs.) 1981. Assoc. Cohen & Hogan, Miami Beach, Fla., 1968-71; pvt. practice, 1972-81; sr. ptnr. Weinstein & Preira, 1981-92; prin. Law Offices of Alan E. Weinstein, Miami, 1992—. Lectr. in field. Mem. ABA (criminal and family law sect. 1968—, white collar crime commn. 1986—), Nat. Assn. Criminal Def. Lawyers, 1st Family Law Am. Inn of Court, Fla. Bar Assn. (criminal and family law sect. 1968—, ethics com. 1987-88, bench/bar com. 1988-89, grievance com. 1999—), Fla. Criminal Def. Attys. Assn. (pres. 1978-79), Fla. Assn. Criminal Def. Lawyers (treas. 1989-90), Miami Beach Bar Assn., Soc. Wig and Robe, Phi Kappa Phi. Avocations: marlin fishing, reading, travel. Criminal, Family and matrimonial. Office: 1801 West Ave Miami FL 33139-1431 E-mail: defense1@bellsouth.net

WEINSTEIN, ANDREW H. lawyer; b. Pitts., Oct. 5, 1943; s. Adolph J. and Meta I. (Schwartz) W.; m. Susan Balber, Aug. 11, 1968; children: Jodi L., Toby M., Jamie M. BSBA, Duquesne U., 1965; JD, U. Pitts., 1968; LLM in Tax Law, NYU, 1969. Bar: Pa. 1969, U.S. Tax Ct. 1969, Fla. 1970, U.S. Dist. Ct. (so. dist.) Fla., U.S. Ct. Fed. Claims. Trial atty. IRS, L.A., 1969-70, Miami, Fla., 1970-73; ptnr. Glass, Schultz, Weinstein & Moss, Coral Gables, 1973-80, Holland & Knight, Miami, 1980—. Contbr. articles to profl. jours. Bd. dirs. New World Symphony, Miami, Performing Arts Found., Zool. Soc. Fla. Fellow Am. Coll. Tax Counsel; mem. ABA (tax sect. com., chmn. subcom. 1981-87, chmn. CLE subcom., adminstrv. practice com.), The Fla. Bar Assn. Republican. Avocations: golf, swimming, travel. Corporate taxation, Estate taxation, Personal income taxation. Office: Holland & Knight 701 Brickell Ave Ste 3000 Miami FL 33131-2898

WEINSTEIN, ARTHUR GARY, lawyer; b. N.Y.C., May 11, 1946; s. Jacob and Ada (Ambutter) W.; m. Judith Marilyn Rothstein, Dec. 24, 1969; children: Stephen, Marc. BA, Bklyn. Coll., 1967; JD, U. Pa., 1970. Bar: N.Y. 1971, N.J. 1977, U.S. Dist. Ct. (so. dist.) N.Y. 1973, U.S. Dist. Ct. N.J. 1977, U.S. Ct. Appeals (2d cir.) 1972, U.S. Supreme Ct. 1973. Asst. dist. atty. New York County, 1970-74, 85-86; asst. counsel Office of Ct. Adminstrn., N.Y., 1974-76; spl. asst. atty. gen. Dep. Atty. Gen.'s Office, N.Y.C., 1976—, counsel, 1981-85, spl. counsel, 1989-95. Editor U. Pa. Law Sch. Yearbook Report, 1969-70. E-mail: j-weinstein@rocketmail.com

WEINSTEIN, DIANE GILBERT, federal judge; b. Rochester, N.Y., June 14, 1947; d. Myron Birne and Doris Isabelle (Robie) Gilbert; m. Dwight Douglas Sypolt; children: Andrew, David. BA, Smith Coll., Northampton, Mass., 1969; postgrad., Stanford U., 1977-78, Georgetown U., 1978; JD, Boston U., 1979. Bar: D.C. 1979, Mass. 1979. Law clk. to judge D.C. Ct. Appeals, Washington, 1979-80; assoc. Peabody, Lambert & Meyers, 1980-83; asst. gen. counsel Office of Mgmt. and Budget, 1983-86; dep. gen. counsel U.S. Dept. Edn., 1986-88, acting gen. counsel, 1988-89; legal counselor to V.P. of U.S., White House; counsel Pres.'s Competitiveness Coun., Washington, 1989-90; judge U.S. Ct. Fed. Claims, 1990—. Dir. Democracy Devel. Initiative Fed. Bar Assn. Recipient Young Lawyer's award Boston U. Law Sch., 1989. Mem. Fed. Am. Inn of Ct. (Master), Federalist Soc. Republican. Office: US Ct Fed Claims 717 Madison Pl NW Washington DC 20439-0002

WEINSTEIN, HARRIS, lawyer; b. Providence, May 10, 1935; s. Joseph and Gertrude (Rusitzky) W.; m. Rosa Grunberg, June 3, 1956; children: Teme Ring, Joshua, Jacob. BS in Math., MIT, 1956, MS in Math., 1958; LLB, Columbia U., 1961. Bar: D.C. 1962. Law clk. to judge William H. Hastie U.S. Ct. Appeals (3d cir.), Phila., 1961-62; with Covington & Burling, Washington, 1962-67, 69-90, 1993—; chief counsel Office of Thrift Supervision U.S. Dept. of Treasury, 1990-92; asst. to solicitor gen. U.S. Dept. Justice, 1967-69. Pub. mem. Adminstrv. Conf. of U.S., 1982-90; lectr. U. Va. Law Sch., 1996; mgmt. com. Undiscovered Mgrs., LLC, 1998—. V.p. Jewish Social Svc. Agy., 1995-98; mem. MIT Corp., 1989-95. Mem. Nat. Press Club. Banking, General civil litigation. Home: 7717 Georgetown Pike Mc Lean VA 22102-1411 Office: Covington & Burling PO Box 7566 1201 Pennsylvania Ave NW Washington DC 20004-2401

WEINSTEIN, JACK BERTRAND, federal judge; b. Wichita, Kans., Aug. 10, 1921; s. Harry Louis and Bessie Helen (Brodach) W.; m. Evelyn Horowitz, Oct. 10, 1946; children: Seth George, Michael David, Howard Lewis. BA, Bklyn. Coll., 1943; LLB, Columbia, 1948; LLD (hon.), Bklyn. Law Sch., Yeshiva U., Albany Law Sch., Hofstra Law Sch., L.I. U., Yale U. Bar: N.Y. 1949. Assoc. Columbia Law Sch., 1948-49; law clk. N.Y. Ct. Appeals Judge Stanly H. Fuld, 1949-50; ptnr. William Rosenfeld, N.Y.C., 1950-52; mem. faculty Columbia Law Sch., 1952-67, prof. law, 1956-67, adj. prof., 1967-97; U.S. judge (Eastern Dist. N.Y.), 1967-93, chief judge, 1980-88; sr. judge Ea. Dist. N.Y., 1993—. Vis. prof. U. Tex., 1957, U. Colo., 1961, Harvard U., 1982, Georgetown U., 1991, Bklyn. Law Sch., 1988-97, others; counsel N.Y. Joint Legis. Com. Motor Vehicle Problems, 1952-54, State Sen. Seymour Halpern, 1952-54; reporter adv. com. practice and procedure N.Y. State Temp. Commn. Cts., 1955-58; adv. com. practice N.Y. Judicial Conf., 1963-66; adv. com. rules of evidence U.S. Jud. Conf., 1965-75, mem. com. jurisdiction, 1969-75, mem., 1983-86; mem. 2d Cir. Jud. Coun., 1982-88, U.S. Jud. Conf., 1983-86, others in past. Author: (with Morgan and Maquire) Cases and Materials on Evidence, 4th edit, 1965, (with Maguire, Chadbourne and Mansfield, 5th edit.), 1971, 6th edit., 1975, (with Mansfield, Abrams and Berger), 9th edit., 1997, (with Rosenberg) Cases and Materials on Civil Procedure, 1961, rev. edit, (with Smit), 1971, (with Smit, Rosenberg and Korn), 1976, (with Korn and Miller) New York Civil Procedure, 9 vols., rev. edit, 1966, Manual of New York Civil Procedure, 1967, Basic Problems of State and Federal Evidence, 1976, (with Berger) Weinstein's Evidence, 7 vols., 1967, rev. edit., 1993, Revising Rule Making Procedures, 1977, A New York Constitution Meeting Today's Needs and Tomorrow's Challenges, 1967, Disaster, A Legal Allegory, 1988, (with Greenawalt) Readings for Seminar on Equality and Law, 1979, (with Murphy) Readings for Seminar in Individual Rights in a Mass Society, 1990-91, (with Berger) Readings for Seminar in Science and Law, (with Feinberg) Mass Torts, 1992, 94, Individual Justice in Mass Litigation, 1995. Chmn. N.Y. Dem. adv. com. on Constl. Conv., 1955; bd. dirs. N.Y. Civil Liberties Union, 1956-62, Cardozo Sch. Law, Conf. on Jewish Social Studies, 1980-88; nat. adv. bd. Am. Jewish Congress, 1960-67, CARE, 1985-90, Fedn. Jewish Philanthropies, 1985-94; chmn. lay bd. Riverside Hosp. Adolescent Drug Users, 1954-55. Lt. USNR, 1943-46. Mem. ABA, N.Y. State Bar Assn., Assn. of Bar of City of N.Y., Nassau County Bar Assn., Am. Law Inst., Soc. Pub. Tchrs. Law (Eng.), Am. Acad. Arts and Scis. Jewish. Office: US Dist Ct US Courthouse 225 Cadman Plz E Brooklyn NY 11201-1818

WEINSTEIN, WILLIAM JOSEPH, lawyer; b. Detroit, Dec. 9, 1917; s. Joseph and Bessie (Abromovitch) W.; m. Evelyn Ross, Apr. 5, 1942 (dec.); children: Patricia, Michael; m. Rose Sokolsky, Oct. 25, 1972. LLB, Wayne State U., 1940. Bar: Mich. 1940, U.S. Dist. Ct. (ea. and so. dists.) Mich. 1940, U.S. Ct. Appeals (6th cir.) 1951, U.S. Ct. Appeals (9th cir.) 1972. Ptnr. Charfoos, Gussin & Weinstein, Southfield, Mich., 1951-54, Charfoos, Gussin, Weinstein & Kroll, Detroit, 1955-59, Gussin, Weinstein & Kroll, P.C., Detroit, 1965-73, Weinstein, Kroll & Gordon, P.C., Detroit, 1973-85; pvt. practice Southfield, 1985-87, Bloomfield Hills, Mich., 1987—. Mem. std. jury instrn. com. Mich. Supreme Ct. 1965-72. Contbr. articles to legal jours. Maj. gen. USMCR, 1941-75. Decorated Bronze Star with Combat V, Legion of Merit (2), Purple Heart (2). Recipient Disting. Alumnus award Wayne State U. Law Sch., 1968. Mem. Mich. Bar Assn. (chmn. negligence sect. 1962-63), Am. Coll. Trial Lawyers, Internat. Acad. Trial Lawyers, USN League (nat. v.p. 1971-72), Tam-o-Shanter Club (Orchard Lake, Mich.), St. Andrews Country Club (Boca Raton, Fla.). Federal civil litigation, State civil litigation, Personal injury. Home and Office: 3922 Wabeek Lake Dr E Bloomfield Hills MI 48302-1261 E-mail: marinewein@aol.com

WEINSTOCK, BENJAMIN, lawyer; b. Bklyn., Mar. 16, 1953; s. Morris and Sara (Pinkiewicz) W.; m. Eileen Weinstock, Sept. 8, 1984; children: Daniel, Etan, Allon, Ariel. BA, Yeshiva U., 1975; JD, Bklyn. Law Sch., 1978. Bar: N.Y. 1979, U.S. Dist. Ct. (ea. and so. dists.) N.Y. 1980, U.S. Ct. Appeals (2d cir.) 1980, U.S. Supreme Ct. 1982. Assoc. Ruskin, Moscou et al, Mineola, N.Y., 1978-82, ptnr., 1982—. Dep. village atty. Village of Cedarhurst, 1989-94, trustee, 1994—. Mem. ABA, N.Y. State Bar Assn. (com. on title and transfer). Republican. Jewish. Contracts commercial, Computer, Real property. Home: 505 Arbuckle Ave Cedarhurst NY 11516-1334 Office: Ruskin Moscou et al 170 Old Country Rd Mineola NY 11501-4307

WEINSTOCK, LEONARD, lawyer; b. Bklyn., Aug. 18, 1935; s. Samuel Morris and Evelyn (Reiser) W.; m. Rita Lee Itkowitz, May 25, 1963; children: Gregg Douglas, Valerie Lisa, Tara Diane. BS, Bklyn. Coll., 1956; JD, St. John's U., Bklyn., 1959. Bar: N.Y. 1961, U.S. Supreme Ct. 1964, U.S. Ct. Appeals (2d cir.) 1963, U.S. Dist. Ct. (ea. and so. dists.) N.Y. 1963, U.S. Tax Ct. 1963. Assoc. Bernard Helfenstein law practice, Bklyn., 1962-63; supr. All State Ins. Co., 1963-64; atty. Hertz Corp., N.Y.C., 1964-65; ptnr. Nicholas & Weinstock, Flushing, N.Y., 1965-68; v.p., ptnr. Garbarini & Scher, P.C., N.Y.C., 1968—. Lectr. Practicing Law Inst., N.Y.C., 1975—; arbitrator Nassau County Dist. Ct., Mineola, N.Y., 1979—, U.S. Dist. Ct. (ea. dist.) N.Y. 1986—; mem. Med. Malpractice Mediation Panel, Mineola, 1978—. Legal counsel Massapequa Soccer Club, N.Y., 1981—; county committeeman Dem. Party, Massapequa Park, N.Y., 1979—. With U.S. Army, 1959-62. Mem. ABA, N.Y. State Bar Assn., Nassau County Bar Assn. (mem. med. jurisprudence ins. com. 1978), N.Y. Trial Lawyers Assn. Avocations: stamp collecting, softball, racquetball. Federal civil litigation, State civil litigation, Personal injury. Home: 38 Barstow Rd Great Neck NY 11021-2218 Office: Garbarini and Scher PC Fl 35 1114 Avenue of the Americas New York NY 10036-7703

WEIS, JOSEPH FRANCIS, JR. federal judge; b. Pitts., Mar. 12, 1923; s. Joseph Francis and Mary (Flaherty) W.; m. Margaret Horne, Dec. 27, 1958; children: Maureen, Joseph Francis, Christine. BA, Duquesne U., 1941-47; J.D., U. Pitts., 1950; LLD (hon.), Dickinson Coll., 1989. Bar: Pa. 1950. Individual practice law, Pitts., 1950-68; judge Ct. Common Pleas, Allegheny County, Pa., 1968-70, U.S. Dist. Ct. (we. dist.) Pa., 1970-73, U.S. Ct. Appeals (3d cir.), Pitts., 1973-99, sr. judge, 1999—. Lectr. trial procedures, 1965—; adj. prof. law U. Pitts., 1986—; chmn. Fed. Cts. Study Com., Jud. Conf. Com. on Experiment to Videotape Trial Proceedings within the 3rd Cir., Internat. Jud. Conf. the Joint Am.-Can. Appellate Judges Conf., Toronto, 1986, London, 1985, futurist subcom. bicentennial com. Ct. Common Pleas, Allegheny County, Pa., 1988; participant programs legal medicine, Rome, London; mem. Am.-Can. Legal Exchange, 1987. Contbr. articles to legal jours. Mem. Mental Health and Mental Retardation Bd., Allegheny County, 1970-73; mem. Leukemia Soc., 1970-73, Knights of Malta, Am. Legion, 4th Armored Div. Assn., Disabled Am. Vets., Cath. War Vets., Mil. Order of the World Wars; mem. bd. adminstrn. Cath. Diocese Pitts., 1971-83; trustee Forbes Hosp. System, Pitts., 1969-74. Capt. AUS, 1943-48. Decorated Bronze Star, Purple Heart with oak leaf cluster; recipient St. Thomas More award, 1971, Phillip Amram award, 1991, Edward J. Devitt Disting. Svc. to Justice award, 1993, History Makers award, 1997. Fellow Internat. Acad. Trial Lawyers (hon.), Am. Bar Found.; mem. ABA (chmn. appellate judges' conf. 1981-83), Pa. Bar Assn., Allegheny Bar Assn. (past v.p.), Acad. Trial Lawyers Allegheny County (past pres), Am. Judicature Soc., Jud. Conf. U.S. (chmn. civil rules com. 1986-87, com. on adminstrn. bankruptcy system 1983-87, subcom. on jud. improvements 1983-87, chmn. standing com. rules of practice and procedure 1988), Inst. Jud. Adminstrn., KC. Home: 225 Hillcrest Rd Pittsburgh PA 15238-2307 Office: US Ct Appeals US PO & Courthouse 7th & Grant St Rm 513 Pittsburgh PA 15219

WEISBERG, ADAM JON, lawyer; b. Cocoa Beach, Fla., June 5, 1963; s. Melvin H. Weisberg and Joan Julie (Carney) Vargo; m. Cheryl Lynn Scupp, June 25, 1994. BS in Bus. Econs., Rider Coll., 1985; JD, N.Y. Law Sch., 1988. Bar: N.Y. 1989, N.J. 1989, U.S. Dist. Ct. 1989, Fla. 1991. Law clk., asst. prosecutor Middlesex County Prosecutors Office, New Brunswick, N.J., 1988-90; workers' compensation atty. Levinson Axelrod Wheaton, Edison, 1990-91; trial atty. workers compensation Richard J. Simon, Esq., New Brunswick, 1991-92; pvt. practice lawyer, 1992—; pres. Asbury Music Co., Belmar, N.J. Mem. ABA, N.J. Bar Assn., Middlesex County Bar Assn., Monmouth County Bar Assn., Assn. Criminal Def. Lawyers. Avocations: fishing, surfing. Criminal, Personal injury, Workers' compensation. Office: Monmouth Exec Plz II 1300 Highway 35 Ste 201 Ocean NJ 07712-3531 also: 46 Bayard St New Brunswick NJ 08901-2152

WEISBERG, DAVID CHARLES, lawyer; b. N.Y.C., June 25, 1938; s. Leonard Joseph and Rae M. (Kimberg) W.; m. Linda Gail Kerman, Aug. 27, 1975; children: Leonard Jay, Risa Beth. AB, U. Mich., 1958; LLB, Harvard U., 1961. Bar: N.Y. 1962, U.S. Dist. Ct. (so. and ea. dists.) N.Y. 1965, U.S. Supreme Ct. 1970. Assoc. Dreyer & Traub, Bklyn., 1962, Lee Franklin, Mineola, N.Y., 1962-65; pvt. practice, Patchogue, 1965-67, 77-80; ptnr. Bass & Weisberg, 1967-77, Davidow, Davidow, Russo & Weisberg, Patchogue, 1981-82, Davidow, Davidow, Weisberg & Wismann, Patchogue, 1982-87, Davidow, Davidow & Wismann, Patchogue, 1988-92, Weisberg & Wismann, Patchogue, 1992-98; propr. The Lawyer's Equalizer, 2000—. Assoc. justice and justice Village of Patchogue, 1968-70, village atty., 1970-85; spl. asst. dist. atty. Suffolk County, Patchogue, 1970-85; assoc. estate tax atty., appraiser N.Y. State Dept. Taxation and Fin., Hauppauge, N.Y., 1975-85; lectr. estate tax Suffolk County Acad. Law, 1976-84, negligence law, 1994; cons. in field. Law chmn. Suffolk County Dem. Com., N.Y., 1975-85; bd. dirs. Temple Beth El of Patchogue. With USAR, 1961-62. Mem. ATLA, N.Y. State Bar Assn., Suffolk County Bar Assn., Nassau-Suffolk Trial Lawyers Sect., Lions (pres. Medford 1978-79, 2d v.p. 1984-85). Avocations: bicycling, skiing. Appellate, General civil litigation, Estate planning. E-mail: dcw@lawyersequalizer.com, dcw608@yahoo.com

WEISBERG, SETH DAVID, lawyer; b. Berkeley, Calif., Sept. 28, 1968; AB, AM, Harvard U., 1991; JD, Columbia U., 1997. Bar: Calif. 1997. Assoc. Irell & Manella LLP, L.A., 1997—. Mem. IEEE, Am. Phys. Soc. Avocation: bridge. Intellectual property. Office: Irell & Manella LLP 1800 Ave of Stars Los Angeles CA 90067-4212

WEISBERGER, JOSEPH ROBERT, state supreme court chief justice; b. Providence, Aug. 3, 1920; s. Samuel Joseph and Ann Elizabeth (Meighan) W.; m. Sylvia Blanche Pigeon, June 9, 1951; children: Joseph Robert, Paula Ann, Judith Marie. AB, Brown U., 1942; JD, Harvard U., 1949; LLD (hon.), R.I. Coll., Suffolk U., Mt. St. Joseph Coll.; DCL (hon.), Providence Coll.; DHL (hon.), Bryant Coll.; LLD (hon.), Roger Williams Coll., 1992; LLD (hon.), Brown U., 1992, Constantine U., 1997; LLD, So. New England Sch. Law, 1998; DHL (hon.), Salve Regina U., 2001. Bar: Mass. 1949, R.I. 1950. With Quinn & Quinn, Providence, 1951-56; solicitor Glocester, R.I., 1953-56; judge Superior Ct. R.I., Providence, 1956-72; presiding justice R.I. Superior Ct., 1972-78; justice R.I. Supreme Ct., 1978—, 1978—, chief justice, 1993-2001, retired chief justice, 2001—. Adj. prof. U. Nev., 1986—; mem. faculty Nat. Jud. Coll.; vis. lectr. Providence Coll., Suffolk Law Sch., Roger Williams Coll.; Chmn. New Eng. Regional Conf. Trial Judges, 1962, 63, 65; chmn. New Eng. Regional Commn. Disordered Offender, 1968-71, R.I. Com. Adoption on Rules Criminal Procedure, 1968-72, chmn. of R.I. Adv. Com. Corrections, 1973, Nat. Conf. State Trial Judges ABA, 1977-78; exec. com. Appelate Judges Conf. ABA, 1979—, vice chmn., 1983-85, chmn., 1985-86; bd. dirs. Nat. Ctr. for State Cts., 1975-81. Chmn. editorial bd. Judges Jour., 1973-75. Pres. R.I. Health Facilities Planning Coun., 1967-70; chmn. Gov. R.I. Coun. Mental Health, 1968-73; moderator Town of East Providence, 1954-56; mem. R.I. Senate, 1953-56, minority leader, 1955-56; vice chmn. bd. trustee R.I. Hosp., 1968-92, St. Joseph's Hosp., trustee, 1962—. Lt. comdr. USNR, 1941-46. Recipient Erwin Griswold award Nat. Jud. Coll., 1989; named to R.I. Hall of Fame; Paul Harris fellow Rotary Internat. Fellow Am. Bar Found.; mem. ABA (ho. of dels., task force on criminal justice stds. 1977-79, exec. com. appellate judges' conf. 1979-95), KC, R.I. Bar Assn., Am. Judges Assn. (gov.), Inst. Jud. Adminstrn., Am. Judicature Soc. (Herbert Harley award 1990), Am. Law Inst., Order of St. Gregory (knight comdr. with star 1989, Goodrich award for Svc. 1995), Phi Beta Kappa (past pres. Alpha chpt. Brown U.). Home: 60 Winthrop St Riverside RI 02915-2624 Office: RI Supreme Ct 250 Benefit St Ste 7 Providence RI 02903-2724 E-mail: jweisberger@courts.state.ri.us

WEISEMAN, JAC BURTON, lawyer; b. Plainfield, N.J., Aug. 27, 1934; s. Albert and Gertrude (Gartenberg) W.; m. Constance R. Ahrons, June 17, 1956 (div. 1966); children: Geri Lynn, Amy Beth; m. Susan Miller, Nov. 29, 1969; children: Jennifer, Craig Barrett. AB, Lafayette Coll., 1956; JD, Rutgers U., Camden, 1967. Bar: N.J. 1967, U.S. Dist. Ct. N.J. 1967, U.S. Supreme Ct. 1984; cert civil trial lawyer N.J. Supreme Ct. Clk., law sec., Superior Ct. Law and Appelate Div., 1967; assoc. Blume & Kalb, Newark, 1968-69; ptnr. Blume, Kalb & Weiseman, 1970-74; mem. Blume & Weiseman, Newark, 1974-80, Blume, Weiseman & Vazquez, P.C., 1980-82; pvt. practice, Newark, 1982-85; ptnr. Weiseman, Sherman & Mella, P.C., Mountainside, N.J., 1985-86, pres. Weiseman & Mella, P.A., 1986-88; pres. Weiseman, Mella & Ruotolo, P.A., 1988—; model jury charges Supreme Ct. Com., 1986—. Fellow Roscoe Pound Found.; sustaining mem., master Richard J. Hughes chpt. Inns of Ct., 1988—; mem. exec. com. Aquatic Safety Injury Group, Detroit, 1984—, treas. 1988—; mem. civil case mgmt. com. N.J. Supreme Ct., 1984; bd. trustees Temple Shotoni, 1984-86, exec. v.p. 1985. Mem. ABA, Assn. Trial Lawyers Am. (bd. govs., bd. dirs. 1980—, exec. 1st v.p. 1987-88), Assn. Trial Lawyers N.J., Assn. Trial Lawyers Middlesex County (pres. 1979, exec. bd., trustee 1980—), N.J. Bar Assn., N.Y. Trial Lawyers Assn., Pa. Trial Lawyers Assn., Essex County Bar Assn., Union County Bar Assn. Jewish. State civil litigation, Personal injury, Workers' compensation. Home: 23 Briarcliff Dr Scotch Plains NJ 07076-2314 Office: 1055 Us Highway 22 Mountainside NJ 07092-2805 also: Gateway Ctr Fl 16 Newark NJ 07102-4015

WEISENBURGER, THEODORE MAURICE, retired judge, poet, educator, writer; b. Tuttle, N.D., May 12, 1930; s. John and Emily (Rosenau) W.; children: Sam, Jennifer, Emily, Todd, Daniel, Dwight, Holly, Michael, Paul, Peter; m. Maylyne Chu, Sept. 19, 1985; 1 child, Irene. BA, U. N.D., 1952, LLB, 1956, JD, 1969; BFT, Am. Grad Sch. Internat. Mgmt., Phoenix, 1957. Bar: N.D. 1963, U.S. Dist. Ct. N.D. 1963. County judge, tchr. Bensen County, Minnewaukan, N.D., 1968-75, Walsh County, Grafton, 1975-87; trial judge Devils Lake Sioux, Ft. Totten, 1968-84, Turtle Mountain Chippewa, Belcourt, 1974-87; U.S. magistrate U.S. Dist. Ct., Minnewaukan, 1972-75; Justice of the Peace pro tem Maricopa County, Ariz., 1988-92; instr. Rio Salado C.C., 1992—. Tchr. in Ethiopia, 1958-59. Author: Poetry and Other Poems, 1991. 1st lt. U.S. Army, 1952-54. Recipient Humanitarian award U.S. Cath. Conf., 1978, 82, Right to Know award Sigma Delta Chi, 1980, Spirit of Am. award U.S. Conf. Bishops, 1982. Home: 4353 E Libby St Phoenix AZ 85032-1732 E-mail: tmw@qwest.net

WEISER, FRANK ALAN, lawyer; b. L.A., Dec. 12, 1953; s. Carl and Rose (Klein) W.; m. Susan Koenig, Aug. 12, 1983. BA, UCLA, 1976; JD, Southwestern U., L.A., 1979; LLM in Taxation, U. San Diego, 1986. Bar: Calif. 1979, U.S. Dist. Ct. (cen. dist.) Calif. 1981, U.S. Tax Ct. 1982, U.S. Ct. Appeals (9th cir.) 1982, U.S. Supreme Ct. 1987, U.S. Ct. Claims 1987, U.S. Ct. Mil. Appeals 1988, U.S. Ct. Appeals (fed. cir.) 1989, U.S. Ct. Internat. Trade 1989, U.S. Ct. Appeals Temporary Emergency Ct., 1989, U.S. Ct. Vets. Appeals 1990, U.S. Dist. Ct. (no. and so. dists.) Calif. 1993. Tax cons., advanced underwriter Transam. Occidental Life Ins. Co., L.A., 1979-80; assoc. Law Offices Herman English, 1980-81; atty., owner Frank A. Weiser-A Law Corp., L.A., 1981—. Judge pro tem L.A. County Mcpl. Ct., 1987—. Editor So. Calif. mag., 1987—; contbr. articles to profl. jours. Bd. suprs. Michael Antonovich Election Com., 1988; mem. World Affairs Coun., L.A.; mem. U.S. Ct. of Vets. Appeals, 1990; assoc. mem. Calif. Rep. Cen. Com. Recipient official resolutions from Calif. State Legislature, 1989, joint rules com. resolution for state assembly and sate senate, 1990, Calif. State Assembly and Senate, 1989, L.A. County Bd. of Suprs., 1989, City Coun. of L.A., 1987, Congressional Cert. of Appreciation; tribute to him placed into official Congl. record, 1989; Nat. Merit scholar, 1971. Mem. ABA (internat. labor com., arts control and disarmament com., internat. employment practices com., editorial advisor internat. law and practive sect. publs. com., internat. property, estate and trust com., fgn. investment in U.S. com.), Fed. Bar Assn. (internat. law com.), Inter-Am. Bar Assn., Am. Judicature Soc., Assn. Trial Lawyers Am., Calif. Trial Lawyers Assn., L.A. Trial Lawyers Assn., Internat. Bar Assn., World Affairs Coun. L.A., World Inst. Achievement, L.A. Athletic Club. Estate planning, Private international, Land use and zoning (including planning). Office: 3460 Wilshire Blvd Ste 903 Los Angeles CA 90010-2230

WEISER, MARTIN JAY, lawyer; b. N.Y.C., Mar. 20, 1943; s. Jack J. and Esther (Attias) w.; m. Pamela D. Morgan, Sept. 4, 1966; children: Nicole, Jennifer. BA, Temple U., 1964; JD, Bklyn. Law Sch., 1967; LLM, NYU, 1975. Cert. tchr., N.Y.; bar: N.Y. 1967; U.S. Dist. Ct. (ea. dist.) N.Y. 1975, U.S. Dist. Ct. (so. dist.) N.Y., 1990. Assoc. Newman & O'Malley, N.Y.C., 1967-69; ptnr., pres. Raiskin, Weiser & Donofrio, P.C., 1970—. Counsel Metro N.Y. Oldsmobile Dealers Assn., 1988. Bd. dirs. East Hills, N.Y. Assn., 1986-87; v.p. Rio Assn., 1988, bd. dirs., pres., 1988—. Mem. N.Y. County Lawyers Assn., Nassau Bar Assn., N.Y. State Trial Lawyers Assn., Assn. Trial Lawyers of Am., Car and Truck Leasing Assn. Am., Inst. for Safety Analysis, Nob Hill Club (v.p. 1985-86). General civil litigation, Insurance, Personal injury. Office: Weiser & Assocs PC 215 Lexington Ave New York NY 10016-6023

WEISFELD, SHELDON, lawyer; b. McAllen, Tex., Feb. 20, 1946; s. Morris and Pauline (Horwitz) W.; m. Eve F. Weisfeld, Jan. 23, 1994; 1 child, Raquel Paolina. BBA, U. Tex., 1967; postgrad., Nat. U. Mex., Mexico City, 1969; JD, U. Houston, 1970. Bar: Tex. 1971, U.S. Dist. Ct. (so. dist.) Tex. 1978, U.S. Dist. Ct. (we. dist.) Tex. 1995, U.S. Ct. Appeals (5th cir.) 1978, U.S. Ct. Appeals (11th cir.) 1981, U.S. Supreme Ct. 1982. Pvt. practice, Austin, Tex., 1973-77; pvt. practice law Brownsville, 1980—. Asst. fed. pub. defender U.S. Dist. Ct. (so. dist.) Tex., Brownsville, 1977-80. Mem. Nat. Assn. Criminal Def. Lawyers, Tex. Criminal Def. Lawyers (dir.), ABA, ACLU Tex. (bd. dirs.), Fed. Bar Assn., State Bar Tex., Cameron County (Tex.) Bar Assn., Hidalgo County (Tex.) Bar Assn., Rotary Club, B'nai B'rith. Democrat. Federal civil litigation, Criminal. Office: 855 E Harrison St Brownsville TX 78520-7173 Fax: 956-544-7446. E-mail: isweisfeld@aol.com

WEISGALL, JONATHAN MICHAEL, lawyer; b. Balt., Mar. 17, 1949; s. Hugo David and Nathalie (Shulman) W.; m. Ruth Macdonald, June 3, 1979; children: Alison, Andrew, Benjamin. BA, Columbia Coll., 1970; JD, Stanford U., 1973. Bar: D.C. 1974, N.Y. 1974, U.S. Supreme Ct. 1982, Marshall Islands 1983. Law clk. to judge U.S. Ct. Appeals (9th cir.), San

Francisco, 1973-74; assoc. Covington & Burling, Washington, 1974-79; from assoc. to ptnr. Ginsburg, Feldman, Weil & Bress, 1980-83; pvt. practice, 1983-99; v.p. Legis. and Regulatory Affairs MidAmerican Energy Holdings Co., 1995—. Adj. prof. Georgetown U. Law Ctr. Author: Operation Crossroads: The Atomic Tests at Bikini Atoll, 1994; exec. prodr. documentary film Radio Bikini. Chmn. bd. dirs. Ctr. for Energy Efficiency and Renewable Techs.; trustee Arena Stage, Washington; bd. dirs. Meet the Composer. Mem. Geothermal Energy Assn. (past v.p., bd. dirs., pres.), Phi Beta Kappa. Jewish. Federal civil litigation, Public international, Legislative. Home: 5309 Edgemoor Ln Bethesda MD 20814-1323 Office: Ste 300 1200 New Hampshire Ave NW Washington DC 20036-6812 E-mail: jweisgall@aol.com

WEISMAN, FRED, lawyer; b. Cleve., Oct. 19, 1926; s. Max David and Sally (Miller) W.; m. Lois Jane Kutler, June 14, 1953; children: Marcy A., Mark A., Mitchell A. BA, Case Western Res. U., 1948, LLB, 1951. Bar: Ohio 1951, U.S. Dist. Ct. (no. and ea. dists.) Ohio 1953, N.Y. 1983. Diplomate Nat. Bd. Trial Advocacy (Civil). Assoc. A.H. Dudnik, Cleve., 1951-61; sr. atty. Fred Weisman, 1961-73, Weisman, Goldberg & Weisman Co., L.P.A., Cleve., 1973—. Acting judge Shaker Heights Mcpl. Ct.; lectr. Case Western Res. U. Law Sch. and Law Medicine Ctr., Cleveland State Law Sch., 1970—; trustee Cleve. Law Library, 1975—; chmn. lawyers div. United Appeal, 1970; chmn. alumni fund Case Western Res. U. Law Sch., 1974-75, 86-87, pres. bd. trustees, 1975-76. Fellow Internat. Acad. Trial Lawyers; mem. N.Y. Trial Lawyers Assn., Am. Trial Lawyers Assn. (mem. faculty), Ill. Trial Lawyers Assn., Ohio State Bar Assn. (mem. council dels. 12th dist. 1968-70), Ohio Acad. Trial Attys. (trustee), Cuyahoga County Bar Assn. (pres. 1971-72), Cleve. Acad. Trial Attys. (pres. 1973-74), Cleve. Bar Assn., Soc. Benchers Case Western Res. U. Law Alumni. Federal civil litigation, State civil litigation, Personal injury. Home: 5150 Three Village Dr PHB-L Lyndhurst OH 44124 Office: 1600 Midland Bldg Cleveland OH 44115 Home Fax: 440-995-1928; Office Fax: 216-781-6747

WEISMAN, PAUL HOWARD, lawyer; b. Los Angeles, Oct. 14, 1957; s. Albert L. and Rose J. (Zimman) W.; m. Allison L. Minas, Oct. 19, 1985. BA cum laude, U. Calif., Davis, 1979; JD, Loyola U., Los Angeles, 1982. Bar: Calif. 1982. Tax atty. legis. and regulations div. office of chief counsel Dept. of Treasury IRS, Washington, 1982-83, tax atty. dist. counsel/office of chief counsel L.A., 1983-87; tax atty. Law Offices of Paul H. Weisman, 1987—. Registered players contract rep. Nat. Football League Players Assn. Co-author BNA Tax Mgmt. Portfolio 638 Federal Tax Collection Procedure, publs. in field. Participant vol. Income Tax Assistance, L.A., 1981-83. Mem. San Fernando Valley Bar Assn., Beverly Hills Bar Assn. (co-chmn. tax ct. prose program). Republican. Avocations: sports, running, art, music, politics. Estate planning, Sports, Personal income taxation.

WEISS, ALVIN, lawyer; b. N.Y.C., Aug. 13, 1929; m. Hannah Weiss, July 3, 1958; 1 child, Betsy. BA, Rutgers U., 1951, LLB, 1953; LLM, N.Y.U., 1959. Bar: N.J. 1955, U.S. Dist. Ct. N.J. 1955, U.S. Ct. Appeals (3d cir.) 1967. Assoc. Whittemore, Porter & Pollis and Pollis, Williams & Pappas, 1955-56; assoc. Riker, Emery & Danzig, 1957-62; ptnr. Riker, Danzig, Scherer, Hyland, & Perretti, Morristown, N.J., 1963-86; judge Superior Ct. N.J., 1987-99, of counsel, Bromber & Newman, 1988—; chmn. N.J. Supreme Ct. Bd. Trial Atty. Cert., 1979-86. Trustee, Rutgers U., 1978— . Served with U.S. Army, 1953-55. Fellow Am. Coll. Trial Lawyers, Am. Bar Found.; mem. ABA, N.J. State Bar Assn., Essex County Bar Assn. (sec. 1982-84, pres. 1985-86), Fed. Bar Assn., Trial Lawyers N.J. Jewish.

WEISS, CHRISTOPHER JOHN, lawyer; b. Oswego, N.Y., Sept. 1, 1952; s. Robert Leo and Flora Elizabeth Weiss; m. Corinne Fratt, Mar. 28, 1973; children: Allison Ardis, Natalie Elizabeth, Christine Corinne, Kathryn Creigh. BS, Fla. State U., 1970, JD, 1977. Bar: Fla. 1977, U.S. Dist. Ct. (mid. and so. dists.) Fla. 1977, U.S. Supreme Ct. Ptnr. Holland and Knight (and predecessor firm), Orlando, Fla., 1977—. Lectr., author various constrn. litigation issues, 1977—. Mem. Orlando Rep. Com., 1975—. Mem. Fla. Bar, Orange County Bar Assn. (constrn. com. 1987—), Am. Arbitration Assn. (nat. panelist 1982—), Assoc. Gen. Contractors, Assoc. Builders and Contractors, Constrn. Fin. Mgrs. Assn. Avocations: camping, fishing, reading. State civil litigation, Construction. Office: Holland & Knight PO Box 1526 Orlando FL 32802-1526

WEISS, HARLAN LEE, lawyer; b. Washington, Dec. 6, 1941; s. Richard Stanley and Ethel (Schulman) W.; m. Elaine Sharon Schooler, Feb. 14, 1971; children: Rachel Shayna, Brian Adam. BA, U. Md.-College Park, 1963; JD with honors, U. Md.-Balt., 1966. Bar: Md. 1967, D.C. 1967, U.S. Dist. Ct. Md. 1967, U.S. Dist. Ct. D.C. 1967, U.S. Ct. Appeals (D.C. cir.) 1968, U.S. Ct. Appeals (4th cir.) 1977, U.S. Supreme Ct. 1970. Law clk. Ct. Appeals of Md., 1966-67; assoc. Surrey & Morse and predecessors, Washington, 1967-72, Sachs, Greenebaum, Taylor, Washington, 1972-76, ptnr., 1976-90; mem. Kivitz & Liptz, LLC, Chevy Chase, Md., 1990. Mem. Jud. Conf. D.C., 1978-79; arbitrator Am. Arbitration Assn. Federal civil litigation, State civil litigation, Insurance. Home: 12017 Cheyenne Rd Gaithersburg MD 20878-2011 Office: 650 Barlow Bldg 5454 Wisconsin Ave Chevy Chase MD 20815-6901

WEISS, MARK ANSCHEL, lawyer; b. N.Y.C., NY, June 20, 1937; s. George and Ida (Galin) W.; m. Joan Roth, June 8, 1958; children: Rebecca, Sarabeth, Jonathan, Deborah. AB, Columbia U., 1958; LLB magna cum laude, Harvard U., 1961. Bar: N.Y. 1961, D.C. 1962, U.S. Supreme Ct. 1965. Assoc. Covington & Burling, Washington, 1961-66, 69-70, ptnr., 1970—; spl. asst. to Under Sec. Treasury Dept., 1966-68; spl. asst. to sec., 1968-69. Mem. editl. adv. bd. Electronic Banking Law and Commerce Report. Mem. ABA, D.C. Bar, Fed. Bar Assn. (chmn. banking law com.). Antitrust, Banking, Private international. Office: Covington & Burling 1201 Pennsylvania Ave NW Washington DC 20004-2401

WEISS, RHETT LOUIS, lawyer; b. Kyushu, Japan, May 22, 1961; came to U.S., 1961; s. Armand Berl and Judith (Bernstein) W.; m. Kristen Sue Krieger, Oct. 11, 1987; children: Aaron Bradford, Alexander Donald, Andrew Franklin, Alison Judith. BS in Mgmt. cum laude, Tulane U., 1983; JD, Coll. William and Mary, 1986; exec. internat. bus. cert., Georgetown U., 1996; postgrad., U. N.C., 2000. Bar: Va. 1986, D.C. 1993, N.Y. 1995, U.S. Ct. Appeals (4th cir.) 1986, U.S. Tax Ct. 1987, U.S. Dist. Ct. (we. dist.) Va. 1989, U.S. Bankruptcy Ct. (we. dist.) Va. 1989, U.S. Dist. Ct. (ea. dist.) Va. 1989, U.S. Bankruptcy Ct. (ea. dist.) Va. 1996. Chief ops. officer First Fed. Savs. Bank Shenandoah Valley, Front Royal, Va., 1990-92; sr. atty. Weil, Gotshal & Manges LLP, Washington, 1992-97; dir. strategic relocation/expansion svcs., mem. mgmt. com. Bus. Incentives Group, KPMG Peat Marwick LLP, McLean, Va., 1997-99; CEO, chmn. DEALTEK, Ltd., Winchester, 1999—; former prin., dir. Adamson, Crump, Sharp & Weiss, P.C., Front Royal. Bd. dirs. Pentathlon Corp., Winchester, Va., Assns. Internat. Inc., McLean, Va., Weiss Pub. Co., Inc., Richmond, Va.; asst. town atty., counsel to Front Royal Planning Commn., 1987-90. Author: Portfolio Transactions: The Anatomy of a Deal, 1994, The Basics of Successful Negotiating, 1994, The Negotiating Process: Optimizing Give and Take, 1995, 96, 97, Doing Global Business in a United States Foreign-Trade Zone, 1996, 97, Sales and Use Tax-Exempt Construction: An Innovative Economic Development Tool to Help Land the Deal, 1997, Facility Development, Expansion and Operations: The Major Tax and Related Cost Aspects, 1998, Doing a Deal in the U.S.: Incentives and the Project Negotiation Process, 1998, Business Expansion and Facility Development: Incentives and the Project Development Process, 1999, 2000, Working With Economic Developers, 2000; Web-Enabled Site Selection: Getting the Information You Need at Internet Speed, 2000, Economic Development in the Electronic Age, 2001. Bd. dirs. Blue Ridge Arts Coun., Inc., 1987-92, v.p., 1989-90, pres., 1990-91; bd. dirs. Front Royal Little Theatre, Inc., 1988-89, Front Royal Warren County Unit Am. Heart Assn., 1991-92, Lord Fairfax C.C. Ednl. Found., 1991-94, Build-A-Future Found., 1994-98, v.p., 1997-98; Shenrapawa dist. chmn. Shenandoah area coun. Boy Scouts Am., 1988-89, coun. treas., 1991-92, coun. bd. dirs., 1987-94; adv. com. Small Bus. Assistance Ctr., Lord Fairfax C.C.; mem. Seaton Elem. Sch. devel. team D.C. Pub. Schs. Ptnrs. In Edn. Program, 1994-96; soccer coach Southwestern Youth Assn., 1998—. Recipient Nat. Quality Dist. award Boy Scouts Am., 1988, 89, Statuette award, 1992. Fellow John Marshall Soc. of Va. Bar Assn.; mem. ABA, Am. Econ. Devel. Coun., Internat. Econ. Devel. Coun., D.C. Bar (vice chmn. comml. trans. com. 1994-96, vice chmn. real property trans. com. 1996-97, chmn. 1997-98, real estate, housing and land use sect.), Va. State Bar, N.Y. Bar, Va., N.C. and S.C. Econ. Developers Assn., So. Econ. Devel. Coun., Valley Estate Planning Coun. (bd. govs. 1989-92, pres. 1992), Front Royal-Warren County C. of C. (bd. dirs. 1989-92, pres. 1990-91), Country Club Fairfax (Va.), Delta Tau Delta (sec. 1980-81), Beta Gamma Sigma, Beta Alpha Psi. Avocations: cars, outdoors, travel, music, sports. General corporate, Finance, Real property. Home: 7419 Kincheloe Rd Clifton VA 20124-1831 Office: DEALTEK Ltd PO Box 4069 Winchester VA 22604 E-mail: rweiss@dealtek.com

WEISS, RONALD PHILLIP, lawyer; b. Springfield, Mass., Apr. 28, 1947; s. Kermit Paul and Fay Roslyn (Robinovitz) W.; m. Janet Faye Landon, June 15, 1969; children: Emily, Katherine. BA, Dartmouth Coll., 1968; JD, U. Pa., 1972. Bar: Mass. 1972, U.S. Dist. Ct. Mass. 1975, U.S. Tax Ct. 1979, U.S. Ct. Appeals 2000. Assoc. Bulkley, Richardson and Gelinas, Springfield, Mass., 1972-78; ptnr. Bulkley, Richardson and Gelinas, LLP, 1978—. Pres. Estate Planning Coun. Hampden County, 1979-81; trustee Mass. Continuing Legal Edn. Inc., 1978-81. Author: (with others) Drafting Wills and Trusts in Massachusetts, 1990, 92, 94; editor: (with others) Massachusetts Corporate Tax Manual, 1986. Trustee Springfield Symphony Orch., 1986—, v.p. 1988-89, pres. 1989-91, chmn. 1991-94; mem. bd. advisors U. Mass. Family Bus. Ctr., 1992—; counsel Cmty. Found. of Western Mass.; trustee Jewish Fedn. Greater Springfield, 1986-90; mem. appropriations com. Town of Longmeadow, Mass., 1990-96, chmn. 1991-92, 95-96. Mem. ABA, Mass. Bar Assn. (chmn. taxation sect. 1978-81, bd. dels. 1979-81), Mass. Bar Found., Hampden County Bar Assn., Rotary. General corporate, Estate planning, Mergers and acquisitions. Office: Bulkley Richardson and Gelinas LLP 1500 Main St Ste 2700 Springfield MA 01115-0001

WEISS, TERRI LYNN, lawyer; b. Oct. 9, 1957; AB, Georgetown U., 1978, JD, 1981. Bar: N.Y. 1982, U.S. Dist. Ct. (so. and ea. dists.) N.Y. 1982, U.S. Ct. Appeals (2nd cir.), 1982. Assoc. Morgan, Lewis & Bockius, N.Y.C., 1981-86, Rosenman & Colin, N.Y.C., 1986-90; ptnr. Marino & Weiss P.C., White Plains, N.Y., 1990—. Mem. editl. bd. Jour. Am. Acad. Matrimonial Lawyers; Matrimonial Strategist; contbr. articles to profl. jours.; lectr. profl. orgns. Neutral evaluator Matrimonial Alt. Dispute Resolution Program, N.Y. County, N.Y.C., 1997—; arbitrator Domestic Rels. Fee Dispute Resolution Program, White Plains, N.Y., 1996—, Nat. Assn. Securities Dealers, N.Y.C., 1989—; bd. of profl. med. conduct N.Y. State Office Profl. Med. Conduct, N.Y. State Bd. Health, N.Y.C., 1988-98. Fellow Am. Acad. Matrimonial Lawyers (amicus com. N.Y. chpt. 1994—), Internat. Acad. Matrimonial Lawyers; mem. N.Y. State Bar Assn. (exec. com. family law sect. 1996—), Westchester Women's Bar Assn. State civil litigation, Family and matrimonial. Office: Marino & Weiss PC 162 Grand St White Plains NY 10601-4803

WEISSBARD, SAMUEL HELD, lawyer; b. N.Y.C., Mar. 3, 1947; children: Andrew Joshua, David S. BA, Case Western Res. U., 1967; JD with highest honors, George Washington U., 1970. Bar: D.C. 1970, U.S. Supreme Ct. 1974, Calif. 1998. Assoc. Fried, Frank, Harris, Shriver & Kampelman, 1970-73, Arent, Fox, Kintner, Plotkin & Kahn, 1973-78; prin. Weissbard & Fields, P.C., 1978-83; shareholder, v.p. Wilkes, Artis, Hedrick & Lane, Washington, 1983-86; ptnr. Foley & Lardner, 1986-97, L.A., 1997-98, co-chair creditors' rights workout and bankruptcy group Washington, 1992-95; sr. counsel Cox, Castle & Nicholson, L.L.P., Newport Beach, Calif., 1998—. Editor in chief George Washington U. Law Rev., 1969-70. Bd. dirs. Luther Rice Soc., George Washington U., 1985-87, Atlanta Coll. Art, 1993, Nat. Learning Ctr., 1993-96, Georgetown Arts Commn. and gen. counsel 1995-96; Chmn. steering com. of Lawyer's Alliance for Nat. Learning Ctr. and Capital Children's Mus., 1989-90; mem. steering com. DC/NLC Don't Drop Out Campaign, 1992,93, bd. dirs., 1994-96; devel. com. Shelter for the Homeless, 1998-99. Recipient John Bell Larner medal, 1970. Mem. ABA, D.C. Bar, Georgetown Bus. and Profl. Assn. (bd. dirs. 1993-96, sec., gen. counsel 1993-97), Orange County Bus. Assn. (legis. com. 1998-99), Order of Coif. Office: Cox Castle Nicholson LLP Ste 600 19800 MacArthur Blvd Irvine CA 92612-2435

WEISSBERG-ORTIZ, JUDITH LEE, lawyer; b. Iowa City, Mar. 11, 1949; d. Albert Oppenheimer and Muriel Rachel (Waxman) Weissberg; m. Luis Ortiz-Franco, Nov. 26, 1983. BA with honors in Cmty. Studies, U. Calif., Santa Cruz, 1972; JD, U. Calif., Davis, 1977. Bar: Calif. 1977. Acting regional dir., regional atty., atty. Agrl. Rels. Bd., Calif., 1977-83; atty. United Farm Workers Am., 1983—; assoc. Garcia & Maryanski, L.A., 1984—. Cons. to Cesar Chevez, pres. United Farm Workers Am. AFL-CIO, Calif., 1983—; mediator Ctr. for Dispute Resolution, Santa Monica; mediator Ctr. Cmty. Mediation, 1988-2000, appellate practice, 1985—. Active United Farm Workers Union AFL-CI), 1970—, Campaign for Econ. Democracy, L.A., 1982-84. Mem. Nat. Lawyers Guild (exec. bd. 1982-84). Democrat. Jewish. Home: 2333 E Vanowen Ave Orange CA 92867-4418 Office: PO Box 4154 Orange CA 92863

WEISSENBERGER, HARRY GEORGE, lawyer; b. Berlin, Fed. Republic of Germany, Aug. 20, 1928; s. Georg Wilhelm and Gabriele Anna (Hochberg) W.; m. Margaret Looper, Dec. 23, 1950 (dec.); children: Carol Weissenberger Schlicht, Harry George Jr., Bruce Lee. Student, Swiss Inst. Tech., 1946-47; BEE, Ga. Tech. Inst., 1950; JD, Emory U., 1952; LLM, George Washington U., 1956. Bar: Ga. 1952, U.S. Dist. Ct. (no. dist.) Ga. 1952, U.S. Ct. Appeals (4th cir.) 1952, U.S. Supreme Ct. 1956, U.S. Ct. Customs and Patent Appeals 1956, Mo. 1957, U.S. Dist. Ct. (ea. dist.) Mo. 1957, U.S. Ct. Appeals (8th cir.) 1957, Mich. 1961, U.S. Dist. Ct. (we. dist.) Mich. 1961, U.S. Ct. Appeals (7th cir.) 1961, Calif. 1964, U.S. Dist. Ct. (no. and cen. dists.) Calif. 1964, U.S. Ct. Appeals (9th cir.) 1964, U.S. Dist. Ct. (ea. dist.) Calif. 1974, U.S. Dist. Ct. (we. dist.) Tex. 1976, U.S. Dist. ct. (so. dist.) Calif. 1982, U.S. Ct. Appeals (Fed. cir.) 1982. Examiner U.S. Patent Office, Washington, 1955-56; assoc. Bruninga & Sutherland, St. Louis, 1956-58, Sutherland, Polster & Taylor, St. Louis, 1958-59, Price & Heneveld, Grand Rapids, Mich., 1959-61, ptnr., 1961-63, Mellin, Hanscom & Hursh, San Francisco, 1963-67, Mellin, Hursh, Moore & Weissenberger, 1967-74, Phillips, Moore, Weissenberger, Lempio & Strabala, San Francisco, 1974-76, Phillips, Moore, Weissenberger, Lempio & Majestic, San Francisco, 1976-78, Newport Beach, Calif., 1978-81, Weissenberger & Peterson, Newport Beach, 1982-86, Laguna Hills, Calif., 1986-90, Weissenberger, Peterson, Uxa & Myers, Laguna Hills, 1990-93; pvt. practice atty., 1993-99; of counsel Stout, Uxa, Buyan & Mullins, Irvine, Calif., 1999—. Dir., gen. counsel Ctr. for Sutton Movement Writing, Inc., Newport Beach, Calif., 1983-93. Mem. Indsl. League Orange County, 1982-93. Served to 1st lt. USAF, 1953-55. Recipient Honored Citizen award Orange County Bd. Suprs., 1992. Mem. Calif. Bar Assn., Am. Intellectual Property Law Assn., Orange County Patent Law Assn. (pres. 1985), Am. Arbitration Assn., Rotary (chpt. bd. dirs. 1988-94, 98, pres. 1991-92, Rotarian of the Yr. award 1989). Republican. Presbyterian. Patent, Trademark and copyright. Office: Ste 300 4 Venture Irvine CA 92618-7384 E-mail: weisspat@aol.com

WEISSMAN, BARRY LEIGH, lawyer; b. Los Angeles, May 30, 1948; s. Sidney and Eleanor (Siegel) W.; m. Beverly Jean Blumenfeld, Sept. 12, 1982. BA, U. Calif.-Davis, 1970; JD, U. Santa Clara, 1973. Bar: Calif. Supreme Ct. 1973, U.S. Dist. Ct. (cen. dist.) Calif. 1976, U.S. Supreme Ct. 1977, U.S. Ct. Appeals (D.C. cir.) 1978, N.Y. Ct. Appeals 1992. Sole practice law, Beverly Hills, Calif., 1974-82; ptnr. Valentini, Fini, Ferraro, Gallavotti & Weissman, Brentwood, Calif., 1982-85; mng. ptnr. L.A. office Kroll & Tract, 1985-87; ptnr. Knapp, Petersen & Clarke, L.A., 1989-93; ptnr. Graham & James, L.A., Calif., 1994-2000, ptnr. Squire Sanders & Dempsey, L.A., Calif.; judge pro tem L.A. Mcpl. Ct., 1975-1979; arbitrator Am. Arbitration Assn.; examiner State Bar Calif., 1976-80; mem. adv. commn malpractice ins., Calif. State Senate. Mem. ABA (mem. spl. com. on prepaid legal services, co-chmn. editorial bd. gen. practice sect.'s publs.), Beverly Hills Bar Assn., Century City Bar Assn. (bd. govs., chmn., editor Century City Bar Jour.), Beverly Hills C. of C. (co-chmn. legal justice com.), Colorado River Assn., Western Los Angeles Regional C. of C. (dir., chmn. com. on energy prodn. and conservation). General corporate, General practice, Private international. Office: Graham & James 801 S Figueroa St Los Angeles CA 90017-2573

WEISSMAN, I. DONALD, lawyer; b. Maywood, Calif., Feb. 6, 1950; s. Herbert and Esther D. (Lunine) W.; m. Bonnie Jill Burns, May 3, 1980; children— Kimberleh Ariel, Russell Meir, Douglas Solomon. B.A., Calif. State U.-Northridge, 1972; J.D., Loyola U., 1975. Bar: Calif. 1975, U.S. Dist. Ct. (cen. dist.) Calif. 1976. With Morgan, Wenzel & McNicholas, L.A., 1975-79, Simke, Chodos, Silberfeld & Soll Inc., L.A., 1979-83, Pettler & Kantor, L.A., 1983, Staitman & Snyder, Encino, Calif., 1984-88, ptnr. Staitman, Snyder, Weissman & Tannenbaum, 1989— . Mem. ABA, San Fernando Bar Assn., L.A. County Bar Assn., L.A. Trial Lawyers Assn., Assn. Trial Lawyers Assn., B'nai Brith. Jewish. State civil litigation, Insurance, Personal injury. Office: Staitman Snyder Weissman & Tannenbaum 15760 Ventura Blvd Ste 601 Encino CA 91436-3000

WEISSMAN, JEFFREY MARK, lawyer; b. N.Y.C., Dec. 26, 1946; s. Samuel and Gertrude (Goldenberg) W.; m. Linda Claire Fleder, June 27, 1971; children— Karen, Erica. B.S., MIT, 1969, M.A., Harvard U., 1970; J.D., N.Y. U., 1974. Bar: N.Y. 1975, Fla. 1977, U.S. Dist. Ct. (so. and ea. dists.) N.Y. 1975, U.S. Dist. Ct. (so. dist.) Fla., 1977, U.S. Dist. Ct. (mid. dist.) Fla. 1979, U.S. Ct. Appeals (2d cir.) 1975, U.S. Ct. Appeals (5th cir.) 1977, U.S. Ct. Appeals (11th cir.) 1981, U.S. Supreme Ct. 1982, U.S. Dist. Ct. (no. dist.) Fla. 1985, U.S. Tax Ct. 1985. Tchr., coach, Brookline, Mass., 1970-71; assoc. Rogers & Wells, N.Y.C., 1974-77; assoc., then ptnr. Brown, Malman & Salmon, Miami, Fla., 1977-80; with Sparber, Shevin, Shapo & Heilbronner, P.A., Miami, 1980-88, Beasley, Olle and Downs, Miami, 1988, Cohen & Silver, 1988; pvt. practice Weissman, Dervishi, Shepherd, Borgo & Nordlund, P.A., 1989—. Counselor MIT Upward Bound, 1968-69; mem. staff appellate div. N.Y. State, 1st and 2d depts. coms. for ct. adminstrn., 1972-73; researcher Am. Bar Found., 1973-74. MIT, 1965-69; N.Y. State Regents scholar, 1965, GM scholar, 1966-69, Harvard U. scholar, 1969-70, Root-Tilden scholar, 1971-74. Federal civil litigation, State civil litigation. Home: 3650 N 36th Ave Apt 64 Hollywood FL 33021-2557 Office: Emerald Lake Corp Park 3109 Stirling Rd # 101 Fort Lauderdale FL 33312-6558

WEISSMAN, WILLIAM R. lawyer; b. N.Y.C., Aug. 16, 1940; s. Emanuel and Gertrude (Halpern) W.; m. Barbra Phylis Gershman; 1 child, Adam; stepchildren: Eric, Jace, Julie Greenman. BA, Columbia U., 1962, JD cum laude, 1965. Bar: N.Y. 1965, D.C. 1969, U.S. Dist Ct. (no. dist.) Tex. 1965, U.S. Dist. Ct. (so. and ea. dists.) N.Y. 1977, U.S. Ct. Appeals (5th cir.) 1966, U.S. Ct. Appeals (D.C. dir.) 1969, U.S. Ct. Appeals (9th cir.) 1973, U.S. Ct. Apeals (2d and 3d cirs.) 1974, U.S. Ct. Appeals (10th cir.) 1979, U.S. Ct. Appeals (11th cir.) 1981, U.S. Supreme Ct. 1968. News dir., progrm dir. WKCR-FM, N.Y.C., 1960-62; law clk. U.S. dist. judge, Dallas, 1965-66; trial atty. antitrust divsn. Dept. Justice, Washington, 1966-69; spl. asst. U.S. atty., 1967; assoc. Wald, Harkrader & Ross, 1969-72, ptnr., 1973-85, Piper & Marbury LLP, Washington, 1986-99, Piper Marbury Rudnick & Wolfe LLP, Washington, 2000—. Instr. D.C. Bar continuing legal edn. program Georgetown U. Law Sch., Washington, 1980-89; environ. regulation course Exec. Enterprises, Inc., 1985-95. Mem. editl. bd. Jour. Environ. Regulation, 1991-95, Environ. Regulation & Permitting, 1995-2000. Parliamentarian Arlington County Dem. Com., 1971-75; mem. Arlington (Va.) County Tenant-Landlord Commn., 1973-77, chmn. 1975-77. Mem. ABA, ASTM (E-50 com. environ. assessment 1996—, rec. sect., 1998-99, vice chmn. 2000—), Columbia U. Washington Club (bd. dirs. 1987-93). Jewish. Administrative and regulatory, Appellate, Environmental. Home: 3802 Lakeview Ter Falls Church VA 22041-1313 Office: Piper Marbury Rudnick & Wolfe LLP 1200 19th St NW Fl 7 Washington DC 20036-2430 E-mail: william.weissman@piperrudnick.com

WEIST, WILLIAM BERNARD, lawyer; b. Lafayette, Ind., Dec. 23, 1938; s. Bernard Francis and Frances Loretta (Doyle) W.; m. Rosemary Elaine Anderson, Apr. 30, 1963; children: Sean M., Cynthia A. BBA, U. Notre Dame, 1961; JD, U. Louisville, 1970. Bar: Ky. 1971, Ind. 1971, U.S. Dist. Ct. (no. and so. dists.) Ind. 1971. Bank examiner Fed. Res. Bank, St. Louis, 1966-67; Trust officer Citizens Fidelity Bank, Louisville, 1967-71; pvt. practice Fowler, Ind., 1971—. Bd. dirs. Benton Fin. Corp., Fowler, Fowler State Bank; pros. atty. 76th Jud. Cir., Benton County, Ind., 1975-98. Capt. USAF, 1961-65. Fellow Ind. Bar Found. (charter mem.),; mem. Ind. State Bar Assn., Ind. Prosecuting Attys. Assn. (pres. 1979), Ind. Prosecuting Attys. Coun. (chmn. 1989), Nat. Dist. Attys. Assn. (bd. dirs.), Columbia Club (Indpls.), Elks, KC. Avocations: golf, reading. Estate planning, General practice, Probate. Home: 1000 E 5th St Fowler IN 47944-1520 Office: Weist Bldg Grant Ave Fowler IN 47944-0101

WEITKAMP, FREDRICK JOHN, lawyer; b. L.A., Nov. 14, 1927; s. Robert M. and Joanna (Fox) W.; m. Betty Sue Stiller, June 9, 1972; children: John F., Robert D., Melinda S., Valerie A. AB, Occidental Coll., 1950; LLB, U. So. Calif., 1952. Bar: Calif. 1953. Practice law, L.A., 1953-92; exec. dir. Phi Alpha Delta Law Frat. Internat., L.A., 1953-92; sr. ptnr. Weitkamp & Weitkamp, Granada Hills, Calif., 1953—; chmn. bd. dirs. Bank Granada Hills, 1983—. With U.S. Army, 1946-47. Fellow Am. Coll. Trust & Estate Counsel; mem. ABA, Calif. Bar Assn., Los Angeles County Bar Assn., San Fernando Valley Bar Assn., Granada Hills C. of C. (pres. 1956-57, Man of Yr. 1956), Toastmasters, Masons, Optimists (pres. 1964). Republican. Lutheran. Lodges: Masons, Optimists. Probate. Office: Weitkamp & Weitkamp 10724 White Oak Ave Granada Hills CA 91344-4690

WEITZ, HARVEY, lawyer, educator; b. Bklyn., Aug. 16, 1933; AB, Bklyn. Coll.; JD, Bklyn. Law Sch. Bar: N.Y. 1954, U.S. Dist. Ct. (ea. and so. dists.) N.Y. 1956. Diplomate Am. Bd. Profl. Liability Attys. Ptnr. Schneider, Kleinick, Weitz, Damashek & Shoot, N.Y.C., 1966—; dean N.Y. State Trial Lawyers Inst.; adj. prof. Bklyn. Law Sch.; spl. master Supreme Ct., 1980-84. Author: A Compendium of the Art of Summation, Weitz on Automobile Litigation: The No-Fault Handbook; editor in chief Trial Lawyers Quar., 1972-80. Served with U.S. Army. Fellow Internat. Acad. Trial Lawyers, Internat. Soc. Barristers, Roscoe Pound Found.; mem. N.Y. State Trial Lawyers Assn. (bd. dirs.), Trial Lawyers for Pub. Justice (bd. dirs.), Am. Bd. Trial Advocates (nat. bd. mem.), ATLA (bd. govs. 1981-93, nat. sec. 1986-87), N.Y. State Trial Lawyers Assn. (pres. 1980-82), Bklyn. Law Sch. Alumni Assn. (bd. dirs.), Inner Circle of Advocates, Nat. Forensic Ctr. (mem. adv. panel), N.Y. State Bar (lectr.), Nat. Practice Inst. (lectr.), Assn. of the Bar, N.Y. County Lawyers Assn. (lectr.), N.Y.C. Trial Lawyers Assn. Personal injury. Office: Schneider Kleinick Weitz Damashek & Shoot 233 Broadway Fl 5 New York NY 10279-0050 E-mail: hweitz@lawyer1.com

WEITZMAN, MARC HERSCHEL, lawyer; b. Milw., Feb. 1, 1950; s. J. Leonard and Esther (Charne) W.; m. Natalyn Ann Gipstein, Oct. 5, 1980; children: Benjamin, Marissa, Laura, Emily. BA, U. Calif., Santa Barbara, 1972; JD, Western State U., 1976. Bar: Calif. 1978, U.S. Dist. Ct. (cen. dist.) Calif. 1979, U.S. Ct. Appeals (9th cir.) 1981, U.S. Supreme Ct. 1987. Atty. State Compensation Ins. Fund, Long Beach, Calif., 1979-82, State Farm Ins. Co., Costa Mesa, 1982-85; assoc. Grancell, Grancell & Marshall, Santa Ana, 1985-88; ptnr. Hertz & Weitzman, Huntington Beach, 1988-89; pvt. practice Seal Beach, 1989—. Judge pro tem State of Calif. Divsn. Indsl. Rels.-Divsn. Indsl. Accidents, Norwalk, 1986—, Long Beach, 1984—, Santa Ana, 1995—; cert. workers' compensation specialist Calif. Bd. Legal Specialization-State Bar Calif., 1988—; arbitrator State of Calif. Divsns. Indsl. Rels. and Indsl. Accident, 1991. Mem. L.A. County Bar Assn., Orange County Bar Assn., Orange County Workers' Compensation Def. Assn., So. Calif. Rehab. Exch., Long Beach Bar Assn. Workers' compensation. Office: 3010 Old Ranch Pkwy Ste 200 Seal Beach CA 90740-2750

WELBAUM, R(OME) EARL, lawyer; b. Miami, Feb. 4, 1932; s. Rome Lewis and Helen Louise (Richter) W.; m. Joan M. Tubridy, May 16, 1959; children: Karl Patrick, Michael Frederick, Carrie Kathleen. BBA, U. Miami, 1954, LLB, 1959. Bar: Fla. 1959, U.S. Dist. Ct. (so. dist.) Fla. 1959, U.S. Ct. Appeals (5th cir.) 1963, U.S. Ct. Appeals (11th cir.) 1983. Law clk. to presiding judge 3d Dist. Ct. Appeals Fla., 1959-61; assoc., then ptnr. Welbaum, Guernsey, Hignston, Greenleaf & Gregory, LLP, Miami, 1961—. Capt. USAFR, 1954-62. Mem. ABA (mem. fidelity and surety com. 1988-89), Fla. Bar Assn., Dade County Bar Assn. Federal civil litigation, State civil litigation, Insurance. Office: 901 Ponce De Leon Blvd Miami FL 33134-3073

WELBORN, REICH LEE, lawyer; b. Winston-Salem, N.C., Nov. 1, 1945; s. Bishop M. and Hazel (Weatherman) W.; m. Martha Huffstetler, Aug. 27, 1966; children: Judson Allen, Spencer Brooks. AB, U. N.C., 1968, JD with honors, 1971. Bar: N.C. 1971. Assoc. Moore & Van Allen, PLLC and predecessor Powe Porter & Alphin, P.A., Durham, N.C., 1971-76; ptnr. Moore & Van Allen and predecessor Powe Porter & Alphin, P.A., 1976—. V.p. Family Counseling Svc., Durham, 1978-79. Recipient Order of Long Leaf Pine award Gov. of N.C., 1981, Spl. Citation, 1983. Mem. ABA, N.C. Bar Assn., Durham County Bar Assn. (pres. 1989-90), N.C. State Bar, Croasdaile Club (pres. 1989-90), Sertoma (pres. Durham chpt. 1987-88), N.C. Jaycees (pres. 1981-82), Durham C. of C. (bd. dirs. 1992-93, 98). General corporate, Real property, Securities. Home: 7 Lanecrest Pl Durham NC 27705-1854 Office: Moore & Van Allen PLLC 2200 W Main St Ste 800 Durham NC 27705-4658 E-mail: welbornr@mvalaw.com

WELCH, CAROL MAE, lawyer; b. Oct. 23, 1947; d. Leonard John and LaVerna Helen (Ang) Nyberg; m. Donald Peter Welch, Nov. 23, 1968 (dec. Sept. 1976). BA in Spanish, Wheaton Coll., 1968; JD, U. Denver, 1976. Bar: Colo. 1977, U.S. Dist. Ct. Colo. 1977, U.S. Ct. Appeals (10th cir.) 1977, U.S. Supreme Ct. 1981. Tchr. State Hosp., Dixon, Ill., 1969, Polo Cmty. Schs., 1969-70; registrar Sch. Nursing Hosp. of U. Pa., Phila., 1970; assoc. Hall & Evans, Denver, 1977-81, ptnr., 1981-92, spec. counsel, 1993-94; mem. Miller & Welch, L.L.C., 1995—. Mem. Colo. Supreme Ct. Jury Inst., Denver, 1982—; vice chmn. com. on conduct U.S. Dist. Ct., Denver, 1982-83, chmn., 1983-84; lectr. in field. Past pres. Family Tree, Inc. Named to Order St. Ives, U. Denver Coll. Law, 1977. Mem. ABA, Am. Coll. Trial Lawyers (state com.), Internat. Soc. Barristers, Internat. Assn. Def. Counsel, Am. Bd. Trial Advs. (treas. Colo. chpt. 1991-92, pres. 1992-93), Colo. Def. Lawyers Assn. (treas. 1982-83, v.p. 1983-84, pres. 1984-85), Denver Bar Assn., Colo. Bar Assn. (mem. litigation sect. coun. 1987-90), Colo. Bar Found. (trustee 1992—, pres. 1995-97), Def. Rsch. Inst. (chmn. Colo. chpt. 1987-90, regional v.p. 1990-93, bd. dirs. 1993-96), William E. Doyle Inn, The Hundred Club. Federal civil litigation, State civil litigation, Product liability. Office: Miller & Welch LLC 730 17th St Ste 925 Denver CO 80202-3598

WELCH, DAVID WILLIAM, lawyer; b. St. Louis, Feb. 26, 1941; s. Claude LeRoy Welch and Mary Eleanor (Peggs) Penney; m. Candace Lee Capages, June 5, 1971; children: Joseph Peggs, Heather Elizabeth, Katherine Laura. BSBA, Washington U., St. Louis, 1963; JD, U. Tulsa, 1971. Bar: Okla. 1972, Mo. 1973, U.S. Dist. Ct. (we. dist.) Mo. 1973, U.S. Dist. Ct. (ea. dist.) Mo. 1974, U.S. Ct. Appeals (8th cir.) 1977, U.S. Ct. Appeals (7th cir.) 1991. Contract adminstr. McDonnell Aircraft Corp., St. Louis, 1965-66; bus. analyst Dun & Bradstreet Inc., Los Angeles, 1967-68; atty. U.S. Dept. Labor, Washington, 1972-73; ptnr. Moller Talent, Kuelthau & Welch, St. Louis, 1973-88, Lashly & Baer, St. Louis, 1988-96, Armstrong Teasdale LLP, St. Louis, 1996—. Author: (handbook) Missouri Employment Law, 1988; contbr. book chpts. Missouri Bar Employer-Employee Law, 1985, 87, 89, 92, 94, Missouri Discrimination Law, 1999; co-editor: Occupational Safety and Health Law, 1996. Mem. City of Creve Coeur Ethics Commn., 1987-88, Planning and Zoning Commn., 1988-96; bd. dirs. Camp Wyman, Eureka, Mo., 1982—, sec., 1987-88, 2nd v.p. 1988-89, 1st v.p. 1990-92, pres., 1992-94. Mem. ABA, Fed. Bar Assn., Mo. Bar Assn., Okla. Bar Assn., St. Louis Bar Assn., Kiwanis (bd. dirs. St. Louis 1979—, sec. 1982-83, 93-94, v.p. 1983-84, 88-90, 92-93, Man of Yr. award 1985). Democrat. Mem. Christian Ch. (Disciples of Christ). Avocations: travel, landscaping, music. Labor. Home: 536 N Mosley Rd Saint Louis MO 63141-7633 Office: Armstrong Teasdale 1 Metropolitan Sq Ste 2600 Saint Louis MO 63102-2740

WELCH, JOSEPH DANIEL, lawyer; b. University City, Mo., Feb. 1, 1952; s. Robert Joseph and Mary Virginia (Church) W.; m. Sharon Susan Filipek, Mar. 16, 1973; children: Eric Ryan, Christopher Joseph, Colin Andrew, Maria Nicole, Theresa Katherine. BA cum laude, St. Louis U., 1974, JD, 1977. Bar: Mo. 1977, U.S. Dist. Ct. (ea. and we. dists.) Mo. 1977, U.S. Ct. Appeals (8th cir.) 1984, U.S. Supreme Ct. 1994. Assoc. Ely & Cary, Hannibal, Mo., 1977-79; ptnr. Ely, Cary & Welch, 1979-82, Ely, Cary, Welch & Hickman, Hannibal, 1982-99, Cary, Welch & Hickman, L.L.P., Hannibal, 1999—. Mem. Mississippi River Pky. Commn., St. Paul, 1988-95, head Mo. del., 1988; prof. bus. law Hannibal-LaGrange Coll., 1993-98; mem. Nat. Heritage Corridor Commn., Washington, 1990-96; speaker various orgns. Editor: Year in Review-Bankruptcy, 1991-94, co-author, 1988-90; speaker various profl. orgns.; contbr. articles to profl. jours. Bd. dirs. Mark Twain Area Physician's Recruitment Assn., Hannibal, 1984-85, Hannibal Free Pub. Libr., 1980-82, Hannibal C. of C., 1978-80, Hannibal Parks and Recreation Dept., 2000—; pres. Hannibal Ctrl. Bus. Devel., Inc., 1982-85; mem. Mo. Right-to-Life, 1977—; community adv. bd. St. Elizabeth Hosp., 1985-86; Birthright of Hannibal, Inc., 1980—, Holy Family Sch. Bd., 1990-95. Acad. scholar St. Louis U., 1970-74; recognition for Significant Contribution to Bush Administrn., Dept. Interior, 1993. Mem. ATLA, Mo. Assn. Trial Lawyers., Mark Twain Astron. Soc. (co-founder), Nat. Network of Estate Planning Attys. Roman Catholic. Avocations: parenting, basketball, tennis, boating, creative writing. Banking, Bankruptcy, General practice. Home: 601 Country Club Dr Hannibal MO 63401-3033 Office: Cary Welch and Hickman LLP 1000 Center St Hannibal MO 63401-3449

WELCH, RICHARD LON See ABELL, RICHARD BENDER

WELCH, SHANNON LOIS KATHLEEN, lawyer; b. Webster, Tex., July 29, 1972; d. Ronald Lloyd and Carolyn Sue Welch. BBA, So. Meth. U., 1993; JD, U. Tex., 1997. Bar: Tex. 1997. Assoc. Cowles & Thompson, P.C., Dallas, 1997-98, Sullivan, Parker & Cook, L.L.C., Dallas, 1999—. Mem. ABA, Tex. State Bar, Dallas Bar Assn., Dallas Assn. Young Lawyers. General civil litigation, Personal injury, Product liability. Office: Sullivan Parker & Cook LLC Ste 1000 2911 Turtle Creek Blvd Dallas TX 75219

WELCH, THOMAS ANDREW, retired lawyer, arbitrator; b. Lincoln, Nebr., Dec. 22, 1936; s. Lawrence William and Edna Alberta (Tangeman) W.; m. Ann Reinecke, Sept. 12, 1959; children: Jonathan Thomas, Michael Andrew, Susan Jennifer. Student, Stanford U., 1955-56; BA, UCLA, 1959; JD, Harvard U., 1965. Bar: Calif. 1966, U.S. Dist. Ct. (no. dist.) 1966, U.S. Ct. Appeals (9th cir.) 1966, U.S. Supreme Ct. 1976. Assoc. Brobeck, Phleger & Harrison, San Francisco, 1965-71, ptnr., 1972-96; ret., 1996. Bd. dirs. Ctr. Internat. Dispute Resolution, Honolulu. Chmn. bd. dirs. Youth Law Ctr., San Francisco, 1990—. Lt. USNR, 1959-66. Mem. ABA, Calif. Bar Assn., Am. Law Inst., Am. Arbitration Assn. (large complex case panel of neutrals). Republican. Presbyterian. Club: World Trade (San Francisco). Alternative dispute resolution, State civil litigation. Home and Office: 449 S Clovercrest Lane San Ramon CA 94583-5505 E-mail: thomwelch@home.com

WELDON, C. MICHAEL, lawyer; b. Portsmouth, Va., Mar. 31, 1949; s. Claude E. and Garnett (Bernard) W.; m. Victoria Tesoro (div. 1975); 1 son, Christopher. B.S., U.S. Mil. Acad., 1971; J.D., Vanderbilt U., 1976. Bar: Ky. 1976, U.S. Dist. Ct. (we. dist.) 1979, U.S. Dist. Ct. (ea. dist.) Ky. 1982, U.S. Supreme Ct., 1985. Assoc. Collier, Arnett & Coleman, Elizabethtown, Ky., 1978-79, ptnr., 1980-81; assoc. Burnam & Thompson, P.S.C., Richmond, Ky., 1981— ; adj. prof. paralegal studies Eastern Ky. U., 1982-84. Served to capt. U.S. Army, 1971-76. Recipient Profl. Merit award ABA, 1976; Judge Paul W. Brosman award U.S. Ct. Mil. Appeals, 1976. Mem. Ky. Bar Assn, Am. Legion (dept. judge advocate Ky. chpt., 1986-88). Republican. Bankruptcy, State civil litigation, Contracts commercial. Home: RR 1 Box 350 Paint Lick KY 40461-9801 Office: Burnam & Thompson PO Box 726 Richmond KY 40476-0726

WELGE, JACK HERMAN, JR. lawyer; b. Austin, Tex., Sept. 12, 1951; s. Jack Herman and Regina Victoria (Hunger) W.; m. Frances Ava Roddy Avent, Dec. 23, 1977; children: Kirsten Frances Page Welge, Kathleen Ava Regina Welge. BA, U. Tex., 1974; JD, St. Mary's U., 1977. Bar: Tex. 1977, U.S. Dist. Ct. (ea. dist.) Tex. 1979, U.S. Dist. Ct. (no. dist.) Tex. 1982, U.S. Ct. Appeals (5th cir.) 1983, U.S. Supreme Ct., 1984; cert. family law Tex. Bd. Legal Specialization 1984. Asst. dist. atty. Gregg County Criminal Dist. Atty., Longview, Tex., 1978-79; assoc. Law Office of G. Brockett Irwin, 1979-81; judge Mcpl. Ct. of Record, 1979-81; ptnr. Adams & Sheppard, 1981-83; pvt. practice, 1983—. Of counsel East Tex. Assn. for Abused Families, Longview, 1985-90. Bd. dirs. Longview Mus. and Arts Ctr., 1991-94, East Tex. Coun. on Alcoholism and Drug Abuse, Longview, 1981-83, Longview Comty. Theater, 1979-82, East Tex. Assn. for Abused Families, Longview, 1983-85; bd. dirs. Salvation Army, 1994—, chmn. 1997; vestry Trinity Episcopal Ch., Longview, 1993-96; co-chair legal profl. divsn. Gregg Co. United Way, 1996-97. Mem. State Bar of Tex. (pro bono coll., contested custody case panel, protective case panel, Gregg County lawyers pro bono project, Outstanding Contbn. award 1990, Disting. Svc. award 1993, 95, Outstanding Pro Bono Atty. 1994, 97), N.E. Tex. Bar Assn., Rotary (pres. Longview club 1987-88, Paul Harris fellow 1982, 22 Yrs. Perfect Attendance 2000), Gregg County Bar Assn. (pres. 1983), Gregg County Family Law Coun., Tex. Acad. Family Law Specialists, East Tex. Knife and Fork Club (pres. 1983-84), Mason, Delta Theta Phi (dean 1977, Bickett Senate), Delta Upsilon (Tex. chpt. found. bd. 1974-78). General civil litigation, Family and matrimonial, Probate. Office: PO Box 3624 413-415 S Green St Longview TX 75601-7534 E-mail: welgjhjr@hotmail.com

WELLEN, ROBERT HOWARD, lawyer; b. Jersey City, Aug. 19, 1946; s. Abraham Louis and Helen Rose (Krieger) W.; m. Anita Fass, June 16, 1968; children: Elizabeth, Judith Maria. BA, Yale Coll., 1968; JD, Yale U., 1971; LLM in Taxation, Georgetown U., 1975. Bar: Conn. 1971, D.C. 1972, Colo. 1982. Assoc. Fulbright & Jaworski, Washington, 1975-76, participating assoc., 1976-79, ptnr., 1979-93, Ivins, Phillips & Barker, Washington, 1993—. Adj. prof. law Georgetown U. Law Ctr., 1982-85. Contbr. articles to legal publs. Served to lt. JAGC, USNR, 1971-75. Mem. ABA (past asst. sec., past chmn. com. on corp. tax, sect. taxation, past supr. editor sect. taxation newsletter), Fed. Bar Assn. (coun. taxation), Phi Beta Kappa. Jewish. Corporate taxation, Taxation, general. Office: Ivins Phillips & Barker 1700 Pennsylvania Ave NW Washington DC 20006-4704 E-mail: rwellen@ipbtax.com

WELLER, CHARLES DAVID, lawyer; b. Hartford, Conn., Oct. 19, 1944; s. Harry Deets and Betty Jane (Allenbaugh) W. BA, Yale U., 1966; JD, Case Western Res. U., 1973. Bar: Ohio 1973, U.S. Dist. Ct. (so. dist.) Ohio 1974, U.S. Dist. Ct. (no. dist.) Ohio 1976, U.S. Ct. Appeals (6th cir.) 1987, U.S. Ct. Appeals (4th cir.) 1994, U.S. Supreme Ct. 1978. Math tchr. U.S. Peace Corps, Johore Bahru, Malaysia, 1966-68, spl. asst. Washington, 1969, dep. dir. so. region Atlanta, 1969-70; asst. atty. gen. antitrust sect. Ohio Atty.'s Gen. Office, Columbus and Cleve., Ohio, 1973-82; of counsel Jones, Day, Reavis & Pogue, Cleve., 1982-94; ptnr. Baker & Hostetler LLP, 1994—. Trustee Health Action Coun., Cleve., 1982-95, Health Sys. Agy. of North, 1983-92, Cleve. Health Edn. Mus., 1991-97. Mem. ABA (antitrust sect. and forum com. on health law), Yale Alumni Assn. Cleve. (trustee). Antitrust, General civil litigation, Health. Home: 12521 Lake Shore Blvd Cleveland OH 44108-1134 Office: Baker and Hostetler LLP 3200 National City Ctr Cleveland OH 44114-3485

WELLER, PHILIP DOUGLAS, lawyer; b. Richmond, Ind., May 5, 1948; s. Lawrence E. and Barbara Jean (Hughes) W.; m. Kathryn Jean Deucker, Apr. 3, 1971; 1 child, Leigh Rachel. Student, Ohio U., 1966-67; BS, Bowling Green State U., 1970; JD, Bates Coll. Law, 1975. Bar: Tex. 1975. Assoc. Vinson & Elkins, Houston, 1975-79, ptnr. Houston, Dallas, N.Y.C., 1980—, Baker, Brown, Sharman, Wise & Stephens, Houston, 1979-80. Speechwriter. Mem. ABA, Am. Coll. Real Estate Lawyers, Tex. Bar Assn., Houston Bar Assn., Dallas Bar Assn., D.C. Bar Assn., Assn. Bar City N.Y. Contracts commercial, Real property. Office: Vinson & Elkins LLP 666 Fifth Ave 26th Fl New York NY 10103

WELLFORD, HARRY WALKER, federal judge; b. Memphis, Aug. 6, 1924; s. Harry Alexander and Roberta Thompson (Prothro) W.; m. Katherine E. Potts, Dec. 8, 1951; children: Harry Walker, James B. Buckner P., Katherine T., Allison R. Student, U. N.C., 1943-44; BA, Washington and Lee U., 1947; postgrad. in law, U. Mich., 1947-48; LLD, Vanderbilt U., 1950. Bar: Tenn. 1950. Atty. McCloy, Myar & Wellford, Memphis, 1950-60, McCloy, Wellford & Clark, Memphis, 1960-70; judge U.S. Dist. Ct., 1970-82, U.S. Ct. Appeals (6th cir.), Cin. and Memphis, 1982-92, sr. judge, 1992—. Mem. pres.' adv. coun. Rhodes Coll. Chair Senator Howard Baker campaigns, 1964-66; chair Tenn. Hist. Commn., Tenn. Constnl. Bicentennial Commn., 1987-88; mem. charter drafting com. City of Memphis, 1967, Tenn. Am. Revolution Bicentennial Commn., 1976, com. on Adminstrn. Fed. Magistrates Sys., Jud. Conf. Subcom. Adminstrn. of Criminal Law Probation; clk. session, commr. Gen. Assembly; elder Presbyn. Ch.; moderator Memphis Presbytery, 1994. Recipient Sam A. Myar award for svc. to profession and community Memphis State Law U., 1963. Mem. Phi Beta Kappa, Omega Delta Kappa. Office: US Ct Appeals Clifford Davis Federal Bldg 167 N Main St Ste 1116 Memphis TN 38103-1887 Fax: 901-495-1356

WELLFORD, HILL B., JR. lawyer; b. Tulsa, Okla., Apr. 30, 1942; AB, Davidson Coll., 1964; JD, U. N.C., 1967. Bar: Va. 1968. Ptnr. Hunton & Williams, Richmond, Va. Lectr. in field. Mem. ABA, Va. Bar Assn. (chmn. com. labor rels. and employment law 1977-87), Assn. Trial Lawyers Am., Phi Delta Phi. Office: Hunton & Williams Riverfront Plaza East Tower PO Box 1535 Richmond VA 23218-1535

WELLINGTON, CAROL STRONG, law librarian; b. Altadena, Calif., Jan. 30, 1948; d. Edward Walters and Elizabeth (Leonards) Strong; m. David Heath Wellington, May 27, 1978; 1 child, Edward Heath. BA, Lake Forest (Ill.) Coll., 1969; MLS, Simmons Coll., 1973. Libr. Hill & Barlow, Boston, 1973-88, Peabody & Arnold LLP, Boston, 1988—. Mem. Am. Assn. Law Librs., Assn. Boston Law Librs. (v.p. 1979-80, pres. 1980-81), Spl. Librs. Assn., Law Librs. New England, Maugus Club (dir. 1991—). Office: Peabody & Arnold LLP 50 Rowes Wharf Fl 7 Boston MA 02110-3339 E-mail: cwellington@peabodyarnold.com

WELLINGTON, HARRY HILLEL, lawyer, educator; b. New Haven, Aug. 13, 1926; s. Alex M. and Jean (Ripps) W.; m. Sheila Wacks, June 22, 1952; children: John, Thomas. AB, U. Pa., 1947; LLB, Harvard U., 1952; MA (hon.), Yale U., 1960. Bar: D.C. 1952. Law clk. to U.S. Judge Magruder, 1953-54, Supreme Ct. Justice Frankfurter, 1955-56; asst. prof. law Stanford U., 1954-56; mem. faculty Yale U., 1956—, prof. law, 1960—, Edward J. Phelps prof. law, 1967-83, dean Law Sch., 1975-85, Sterling prof. law, 1983-92, Sterling prof. emeritus law, 1992—, Harry H. Wellington prof. lectr., 1995—; pres., dean, prof. law N.Y. Law Sch., N.Y.C., 1992-2000, dean emeritus, prof., 2000—. Ford fellow London Sch. Econs., 1965; Guggenheim fellow; sr. fellow Brookings Instn., 1968-71; Rockefeller Found. fellow Bellagio Study and Conf. Ctr., 1984; faculty mem. Salzburg Seminar in Am. Studies, 1985; John M. Harlan disting. vis. prof. N.Y. Law Sch., 1985-86; review person ITT-SEC; moderator Asbestos-Wellington Group; cons. domestic and fgn. govtl. agys.; trustee N.Y. Law Sch.; bd. govs. Yale U. Press; mem. jud. panel, exec. com. Ctr. Public Resources Legal Program; Harry H. Wellington lectr., 1995—. Author: with Harold Shepherd) Contracts and Contract Remedies, 1957, Labor and the Legal Process, 1968, (with Clyde Summers) Labor Law, 1968, 2d edit., 1983, (with Ralph Winter) The Unions and the Cities, 1971, Interpreting the Constitution, 1990; contbr. articles to profl. jours. Mem. ABA, Bar Assn. Conn., Am. Law Inst., Am. Arbitration Assn., Am. Acad. Arts and Scis., Common Cause (nat governing bd.). Office: NY Law Sch 57 Worth St New York NY 10013-2959 also: Yale U Sch Law New Haven CT 06520

WELLINGTON, RALPH GLENN, lawyer; b. Three Rivers, Mich., June 18, 1946; s. Cleon G. and Gladys M. (Cole) W.; m. Margaret Brennan; children: Ralph Glenn II, Jeffrey Scott, Tyler Cahill. BA, Kalamazoo Coll., 1968; JD, U. Mich., 1970. Bar: Pa. 1971, U.S. Dist. Ct. (ea. dist.) Pa. 1971, U.S. Dist. Ct. (mid. dist.) Pa. 1976, U.S. Ct. Appeals (3d cir.) 1978, U.S. Ct. Appeals (6th cir.) 1985, U.S. Supreme Ct. 1987. Atty. Schnader Harrison Segal & Lewis, Phila., chmn., 1998—. Frequent lectr. on litigation and ethics in U.S.A. and abroad. Contbr. articles to profl. jours. Trustee Kalamazoo Coll., 1992—. Fellow Am. Coll. Trial Lawyers, Internat. Acad. Trial Lawyers; mem. ABA, Nat. Assn. R.R. Trial Counsel, Aviation Ins. Assn., Lawyer-Pilots Bar Assn., Phila. Bar Assn. (chair profl. responsibility com. 1988), Phila. Cricket Club. Lutheran. Avocations: squash, golf, jazz piano. General civil litigation, Securities, Transportation. Home: 604 W Hartwell Ln Philadelphia PA 19118-4114 Office: Schnader Harrison Segal & Lewis 1600 Market St Ste 3600 Philadelphia PA 19103-7287

WELLNITZ, CRAIG OTTO, lawyer, English language educator; b. Elwood, Ind., Dec. 5, 1946; s. Frank Otto and Jeanne (Albright) W.; m. Karen Sue Thomas, Apr. 13, 1974 (div. Sept. 1987); children: Jennifer Suzanne, Anne Katherine; m. Carol L. Hinesley, Jan. 23, 1988. BA, Purdue U., 1969; MA, Ind. U., 1972; JD, Ind. U.-Indpls., 1978. Bar: Ind. 1978, U.S. Dist. Ct. (so. dist.) Ind. 1978, U.S. Supreme Ct. 1983, U.S. Ct. Appeals (7th and Fed. cirs.) 1984, U.S. Dist. Ct. (no. dist.) 1990; registered mediator, Ind. Instr. Danville Jr. Coll., Ill., 1972-74, S.W. Mo. State U., Springfield, Mo., 1974-75; ptnr. Coates, Hatfield, Calkins & Wellnitz, Indpls., 1978-98; pub. defender criminal divsn. Marion Superior Ct., Marion County, 1979-88, master commr. criminal divsn., 1988-96, registered mediator, 1998—; ptnr. Coates, Hatfield & Wellnitz, Indpls., 1999—. Instr. U. Indpls., 1981-82; mem. adj. faculty dept. English Butler U., Indpls., 1982—; instr. English Ind. U.-Purdue U., Indpls., 1987-90; pres. Ind. Account Mgmt., Inspls., 1985-94; v.p. Carol Craig Assocs., Indpls., 1987—; lectr. in field. Co-author: Successful Judgment Collection in Indiana, 1996, Emerging Trends in Indiana Commercial Collections, 2001; columnist A Jury of Your Peers, 1984-86. Vice committeeman Indpls. Rep. precinct, 1978; chmn. fin. com. St. Luke's United Meth. Ch., 1985-87; sponsor Christian Children's Fund, 1990—; active Am. Mus. Natural History, Indpls. Zoo, Children's Mus. Indpls., The Royal Oak Found. Postgrad. study grantee S.W. Mo. State U., Springfield, 1975. Mem.: AAUP, MLA, Def. Rsch. Inst., Nat. Assn. Retail Collection Attys., Am. Collectors Assn., Internat. Assn. Comml. Collectors, Creditors Internat., Ind. Bar Assn., Ind. Trial Lawyers Assn., Smithsonian Assocs., Libr. Congress Assocs., Spkrs. U.S.A., Internat. Spkrs. Network., Broad Ripple Village Assn., Columbia Club, Rivera Club Indpls., Elks. State civil litigation, Consumer commercial, Personal injury. Office: One Indiana Sq Ste 2335 Indianapolis IN 46204-2012 E-mail: Indplslaw@aol.com

WELLON, ROBERT G. lawyer; b. Port Jervis, N.Y., Apr. 18, 1948; s. Frank Lewis and Alice (Stevens) W.; m. Jan Montgomery, Aug. 12, 1972; children: Robert F., Alice Wynn. AB, Emory U., 1970; JD, Stetson Coll. Law, 1974. Assoc. Turner, Turner & Turner, Atlanta, 1974-78; ptnr. Ridley, Wellon, Schwieger & Brazier, 1978-86; of counsel Wilson, Strickland & Benson, 1987—. Adj. prof. Atlanta Law Sch., 1981-94; adj. prof. law Emory U. Sch. of Law, 1995—. Gov.'s task force chmn. Atlanta 2000, 1978; exec. com., treas., 2nd v.p. Atlanta Easter Seals Soc., 1983-88; rep. Neighborhood Planning Unit, 1981-83; adminstrv. bd. Northside United Meth. Ch. Served with USAR, 1970-76. Recipient Judge Joe Morris award Stetson Coll. Law, St. Petersburg, 1974, Charles E. Watkins svc. award 1995). Mem. Fla. Bar, State Bar. of Ga. (professionalism com. 1994—), Atlanta Bar Assn. (bd. dirs. 1978-88, pres. 1986-87, bd. trustees CLE), Lawyers Club Atlanta, Old War Horse Lawyers Club, Charles Longstreet Weltner Family Law Inn of Ct. (pres. 1997-2001), Atlanta Found. for Psychoanalysis, Inc. (bd. dirs. 1994-, exec. com. 1997—). Methodist. State civil litigation, Family and matrimonial, Personal injury. Office: Ste 1800 Promenade II 1230 Peachtree St NE Atlanta GA 30309 E-mail: rgwlaw@earthlink.net

WELLS, ANDREW NORMAN, lawyer; b. Staten Island, N.Y., July 25, 1953; s. Ira Merton and Mildred (Katz) W.; m. Melanie Resnick, Aug. 29, 1982; children: Justine Amanda Miriam, Georgina Clare Felicity. BS in Psychology cum laude, Tulane U., 1974; JD cum laude, Cornell U., 1979. Bar: N.Y. 1980. Assoc. Shea & Gould, N.Y.C., 1979-87, ptnr., 1988-91; assoc. gen. counsel Deloitte & Touche LLP, 1991—. Mem. ABA, N.Y. State Bar Assn. General corporate, Mergers and acquisitions, Securities. Office: Deloitte & Touche LLP 1633 Broadway New York NY 10019-6708

WELLS, BENJAMIN GLADNEY, lawyer; b. St. Louis, Nov. 13, 1943; s. Benjamin Harris and Katherine Emma (Gladney) W.; m. Nancy Kathryn Harpster, June 7, 1967; children: Barbara Gladney, Benjamin Harpster. BA magna cum laude, Amherst (Mass.) Coll., 1965; JD cum laude, Harvard U., 1968. Bar: Ill. 1968, Tex. 1973, U.S. Tax Ct. 1973, U.S. Ct. Claims 1975, U.S. Ct. Appeals (5th cir.) 1981, U.S. Dist. Ct. (so. dist.) Tex. 1985, U.S. Dist. Ct. (we. dist.) Tex. 1993. Assoc. Kirkland & Ellis, Chgo., 1968-69; assoc. to ptnr. Baker Botts, L.L.P. (formerly Baker & Botts, L.L.P.), Houston, 1973—. Contbr. articles to profl. jours. Mem. planned giving com. St. John's Sch., Houston (chmn. 1987-98); Harvard Legal Aid Bureau, 1966-68. Capt. U.S. Army, 1969-72. Fellow Am. Coll. Tax

Counsel; mem. ABA (chair corp. tax com. sect. on taxation 2001—), Houston Tax Roundtable (pres. 1994-95), The Forest Club, The Houston Club, Phi Beta Kappa. Presbyterian. Corporate taxation, Taxation, general. Office: Baker Botts LLP One Shell Plaza 910 Louisiana St Ste 3330 Houston TX 77002-4916 E-mail: benjamin.wells@bakerbotts.com

WELLS, LESLEY B. judge; b. Muskegon, Mich., Oct. 6, 1937; d. James Franklin and Inez Simpson Wells; m. Charles F. Clarke, Nov. 13, 1998; children: Lauren Elizabeth, Caryn Alison, Anne Kristin, Thomas Eliot. BA, Chatham Coll., 1959; JD cum laude, Cleve. State U., 1974; cert., Nat. Jud. Coll., 1983, 85, 87, cert., 89. Bar: Ohio 1975, U.S. Dist. Ct. (no. dist.) Ohio 1975, U.S. Supreme Ct. 1989. Pvt. practice, Cleve., 1975; ptnr. Brooks & Moffet, 1975-79; dir., atty. ABAR Litigation Ctr., 1979-80; assoc. Schneider, Smeltz, Huston & Ranney, 1980-83; judge Ct. of Common Pleas, 1983-94, U.S. Dist. Ct. (no. dist.) Ohio 6th Cir., Cleve., 1994—. Adj. prof. law and urban policy Cleve. State U., 1979-82. Editor, author: Litigation Manual, 1980. Past pres. Cleve. Legal Aid Soc.; legal chmn. Nat. Women's Polit. Caucus, 1981-82; chmn. Gov.'s Task Force on Family Violence, Ohio, 1983-87; mem. biomed. ethics com. Case Western Res. U. Med. Sch., 1985-94; mem. N.W. Ordinance U.S. Constn. Commn., Ohio, 1986-88; master Burton Inn of Ct., 1989—, counselor, 1993, pres., 1998-99; trustee Rosemary Ctr., 1986-92, Miami U., 1988-92, Urban League Cleve., 1989-90, Chatham Coll., 1989-94. Recipient Superior Jud. award Supreme Ct. Ohio, 1983, J. Irwin award Womenspace, Ohio, 1984, award Womens City Club, 1985, Disting. Alumna award Chatham Coll., 1988, Alumni Civic Achievement award Cleve. State U., 1992, Golden Gavel award Ohio Judges Assn., 1994, Outstanding Alumni award Cleve. Marshall Law Alumni Assn., 1994, Greater Cleve. Achievement award YWCA, 1995. Mem. ABA (coun. litigation sect. 1996-99), Am. Law Inst., Ohio Bar Assn., Ohio Womens Bar Assn., Cleve. Bar Assn. (Merit Svc. award 1983), Cuyahoga County Bar Assn., Nat. Assn. Women Judges, Philos. Club Cleve. Office: 338 US Courthouse 201 Superior Ave E Cleveland OH 44114-1201

WELLS, PETER NATHANIEL, judge, lawyer; b. Ogdensburg, N.Y., May 13, 1938; s. John Harris and Mary Theresa (Houlihan) W.; m. Diana Barry Wells, Apr. 8, 1967; childen: Mary, Sarah, Matthew. BS in Polit. Sci., Manhattan Coll., 1960; LLB, Boston Coll., 1963. Bar: N.Y. 1963, U.S. Dist. Ct. (no. dist.) N.Y. 1967, U.S. Dist. Ct. (we. dist.) N.Y. 1971, U.S. Ct. Appeals (d cir.) 1974, U.S. Ct. Appeals (3d cir.) 1978, U.S. Supreme Ct. 1974. Asst. atty. gen. State of N.Y., 1964-68; assoc. Costello, Cooney & Fearon, Syracuse, N.Y., 1968-70, ptnr. 5, 1970-76, Williams, Micale & Wells, Syracuse, 1976-88, Mackenzie Smith Lewis, Michell & Hughes, Syracuse, 1988; surrogate ct. judge Onondaga County, 1989—. Mem. EPTL-SCPA Legis. adv. com. of N.Y. State. Editl. bd. Warren's Heaton on Surrogate Ct. Chmn. Dewitt Republican Com., 1976-87; town justice Dewitt, N.Y., 1987-88. Served with USAR, 1963-69. Mem. ABA, N.Y. State Bar Assn., Onondaga County Bar Assn., Def. Rsch. Inst., Upstate Trial Lawyers Assn., N.Y. State Surrogates Assn. (pres. 1999-2001), Cavalry Club, Manlius Club (N.Y.). Roman Catholic. Home: 100 Downing Rd Syracuse NY 13214-1503 Office: Surrogate Ct Chambers Onondaga County Courth Syracuse NY 13202

WELLS, ROBERT ALFRED, lawyer; b. Louisiana, Mo., Dec. 1, 1942; s. Harry Armstrong and Irene Jacobson W.; m. Binney Kitchel, Dec. 21, 1968; children: Hylah, Theodore. BA with honors, DePauw U., 1964; JD cum laude, U. Mich., 1967. Bar: N.Y. 1968, N.H. 1971, Mo. 1981, U.S. Tax Ct. 1973, U.S. Supreme Ct. 1976, U.S. Mil. Ct. Appeals 1978. Assoc. Dewey, Ballantine, Bushby, Palmer & Wood, N.Y.C., 1967-68, McLane, Graf, Raulerson & Middleton, Manchester, N.H., 1971—. Trustee Heritage Heights/Homewood, 1994—, Soc. for Protection of N.H. Forests, 1988—96, sec., 1995—96; trustee, treas. Children's Trust Fund; dir., clerk Office Pub. Guardian; dir., v.p. Concord Cmty. Music Sch.; active St. Andrew's Episc. Ch., Hopkinton, NH, 1971—, vestry mem., 1974—77, warden, 1979—85; trustee Protestant Episc. Ch. of N.H., 1985—; bd. dirs. Am. Lung Assn. of N.H., pres., 1980—81, sec., 1990—; bd. dirs. Am. Lung Assn., 1982—94, exec. com., 1987—, v.p., 1990; mem. Town of Hopkinton Planning Bd., 1977—79; co-chmn. Hopkinton Master Plan Revision Com., 1986—88; chmn. State Adv. Com. to the U.S. Civil Rights Commn., 1985—89; bd. dirs. Pat's Peak Ednl. Found., Inc., 1982—87, Youth Soccer Assn. Lt. USN, 1968—70. Mem. Am Coll. Trust & Estate Counsel, N.H. Bar Assn. (chmn. elderly legal devel. Program 1978-81, continuing legal education program 1981-85, fee dispute resolution com. 1986-88), Internat. Assn. of Fin. Planners (edn. com. 1985—), Phi Beta Kappa. Episcopalian. Administrative and regulatory, Estate planning, Probate. Office: PO Box 326 Manchester NH 03105-0326

WELLS, STEVEN WAYNE, lawyer; b. Ft. Walton Beach, Fla., Sept. 8, 1960; s. H. Wayne and Shirley A. W.; m. Lisa Stieler, May 20, 1983; Robert, James, Jessica. BA in Comm., Mich. State U., 1982; JD with distinction, Detroit Coll. of Law, 1985. Bar: Mich. Asst. prosecutor Oakland County, Pontiac, Mich., 1985-88; mng. ptnr. Schnelz, Bondy & Wells, PC, Troy, 1988-93; shareholder, mng. ptnr. Cross Wrock, PC, Detroit, 1993-99; prin. shareholder Schnelz, Wells, Monaghan & Wells PC, Birmingham, Mich., 1999—. Lectr., presenter in field. Contbr. articles to State Bar Jour. Pres. Bloomfield Village Bd. Fellow Mich. Bar Assn.; ABA, ATLA, Detroit Bar Assn., Mich. Trial Lawyers Assn., Nat. Dist. Attys. Assn. Avocations: golf, tennis, coaching youth baseball, soccer. General civil litigation, Labor, Land use and zoning (including planning). Address: 255 S Old Woodward Ave Ste 200 Birmingham MI 48009-6184

WELMAKER, FORREST NOLAN, lawyer; b. McKinney, Tex., Aug. 13, 1925; s. Felix E. and Forrest Love (Baker) W.; div.; children: Forrest Nolan Jr., Mary Elizabeth Welmaker Young, Byron Skillin. BBA, U. Tex., 1950, LLD, 1953. Bar: Tex. 1953, U.S. Dist. Ct. (so. and we. dists.) Tex. 1956, U.S. Ct. Appeals (5th cir.) 1956, U.S. Tax Ct. 1959, U.S. Supreme Ct. 1956. Pvt. practice, San Antonio, 1953—. Past bd. dirs., officer United Fund San Antonio, San Antonio chpt. ARC, Children Welfare Bur. San Antonio, San Antonio YMCA. Capt. USNR, 1943-46, PTO, 1950-52, Korea. Fellow Tex. Bar Found., San Antonio Bar Found.; mem. San Antonio Bar Assn. (past bd. dirs., v.p., pres.), Tex. Assn. Def. Counsel, San Antonio Res. Officer Assn., Tex. Bar Assn. (past bd. dirs.), San Antonio Pla. Club, San Antonio German Club. Episcopalian. Avocations: handball, boating. General civil litigation, General practice, Personal injury. Home: 114 W Brandon Dr San Antonio TX 78209-6404 E-mail: nwelmaker@ev1.net

WELSH, SIR ALFRED JOHN, lawyer, consultant; b. Louisville, May 10, 1947; s. Elvin Alfred and Carol (Kleymeyer) W.; m. Lee Mitchell, Aug. 1, 1970; children: Charles Kleymeyer, Kathryn Thomas. BA, Centre Coll., 1969; JD, U. Ky., 1972; LLM in Internat. Law cum laude, U. Brussels, 1973. Bar: Ky. 1972, U.S. Dist. Ct. (we. and ea. dists.) Ky. 1972, U.S. Ct. Appeals (6th cir.) 1972. Atty. Ky. Atty. Gen. Office, Frankfort, 1973-74; legis. counsel to congressman Ho. of Reps., Washington, 1974-77; mng. ptnr. Nicolas Welsh Brooks & Hayward, Louisville, 1977—, Boone Welsh Brooks and Hayward Internat. Law. Hon. counsel of Belgium, 1983—; econ. devel. advisor Kingdom of Belgium; mem. Ky. Econ. Adv. Coun.; pres. Transcontinental Trading Cons., Ltd.; participant in North African Mideast Econ. Summit Conf., Morocco, 1994; bd. dirs. Intervention Resources, Inc. Bd. dirs. Greater Louisville Swim Found., 1983-94, exec. com., 1994—; bd. dirs. Louisville com. Coun. Fgn. Rels., 1993—, also pres.; bd. dirs. Jefferson County Alcohol and Drug Abuse Found., Louisville, 1986—, Intervention Resource, Inc., Louisville, 1998—, Internet. Resolve; mem. econ. task force of Ky. Legis. Agts. Decorated knight Order of the Crown (Belgium). Mem. ABA (internat. law sect., commn. on impairment), ATLA, Ky. Bar Assn. (bd. dirs. 1981-82, pres. young lawyers divsn. 1981-82), Am. Judicature Soc., Louisville C. of C. Democrat. Presbyterian. Avocations: swimming, water polo, soccer. General corporate, Private international, Personal injury. Office: Barristers Hall 1009 S 4th St Louisville KY 40203-3207

WELSH, JOHN BERESFORD, JR. lawyer; b. Seattle, Feb. 16, 1940; s. John B. and Rowena Morgan (Custer) W. Student, U. Hawaii, 1960, Georgetown U., 1960; BA, U. Wash., 1962; LLB, 1965. Bar: Wash. 1965. Staff counsel Joint Com. on Govtl. Cooperation, 1965-66; asst. atty gen. Dept. Labor and Industries, 1966-67; atty. Legis Counsel; acting as counsel Pub. Health Com., Labor Com., Pub. Employees Collective Bargaining Com., Com. on State Instns. and Youth Devel., State of Wash., 1967-73; sr. counsel Wash. Ho. of Reps., Ho. Com. on Social and Health Svcs., Olympia, WA, 1973-86; atty., spkr. Ho. of Reps., 1973; counsel Ho. Com. Human Svcs., 1987-91, 93-95, Ho. Com. on Health Care, 1987—. Counsel Ho. Com. on Trade and Econ. Devel., 1995-98, Joint Select Com. on Nurse Delegation, 1995-98, Joint Select Com. on Oral Health, 1996. legal cons. Gov's. Planning Commn. Vocat. Rehab., 1968, Gov.'s Commn. on Youth Involvement, 1969; envoy from Gov. Wash. to investiture of Prince of Wales, London, 1969, fac. Nat. Conf. State Legislatures, Denver, 1977, New Orleans, 1977; fac. Coun. Licensure, Enforcement and Regulation, San Francisco, 1984, Orlando, Fla., 1985, Denver, 1986, Kansas City, Mo., 1987, Washington, 1988, Indpls., 1989, Seattle, 1990, Ft. Lauderdale, Fla., 1991, Albuquerque, 1992, Boston, 1994, San Antonio, 1995, Norfolk, 1997; steering com., 1986-90, legis. issues com., 1986-88, Coun. of State Govts. com. on suggested state legis., 1988-95, sub. com. scope and agenda, 1988-95; mem. Souvenir Napoleonien, Paris. Vol. Hampton Rds. U.S. Naval Mus., mem. gov's. state medal merit com., 1986—. Recipient Hon. prof. health adminstrn. Eastern Wash. Univ., 1982. Mem. Wash. Bar Assn., Govtl. Lawyers Assn., Nat. Health Lawyers Assn., Soc. des Amis du Musee de l'Armee, Paris, English Speaking Union, La Societe Napoleoienne (pres.), Medals Soc. Am., Sons of Union Veterans of the Civil War, Custer Battlefield Hist. & Mus. Assn., 8th Army Air Force Hist. Assn., Northwest Hist. Assn. (bd. dirs.), The Colonial Williamsburg Found., Napoleonic Alliance (bd. dirs.), Alliance Francaise (Seattle), Souvenir Napoleonienne (Paris), Friends of Willie & Joe, Phi Delta Phi. Office: Wash Ho Reps PO Box 40600 Olympia WA 98504-0600

WELSH, PAUL PATRICK, retired lawyer; b. L.I., Dec. 13, 1941; s. Howard P. and Kathryn W.; m. Linda Franz, May 25, 1968; children: Sarah L., Carolyn A. AB, U. Pa., 1963, LLB, 1966. Bar: Pa. 1966, U.S. Dist. Ct. (ea. dist.) Pa. 1966, U.S. Dist. Ct. Del. 1970, U.S. Ct. Appeals (3d cir.) 1967, Dela. 1968, U.S. Supreme Ct. 1972. Assoc. Morgan, Lewis & Bockius, Phila., 1966-67, Morris, Nichols, Arsht & Tunnell, Wilmington, Del., 1967-72, ptnr., 1972-99; candidate for Del. Senate, 2000. Lawyer; b. L.I., Dec. 13, 1941; s. Howard P. and Kathryn W.; m. Linda Franz, May 25, 1968; children— Sarah L., Carolyn A. A.B., U. Pa., 1963, LL.B., 1966. Bar: Pa. 1966, U.S. Dist. Ct. (ea. dist.) Pa. 1966, U.S. Dist. Ct. Del. 1970, U.S. Ct. Appeals (3d cir.) 1967, Dela. 1968, U.S. Supreme Ct. 1972. Assoc., Morgan, Lewis & Bockius, Phila., 1966-67; assoc. Morris, Nichols, Arsht & Tunnell, Wilmington, Del., 1967-72, ptnr., 1972— . Mem. Wilmington Republican City Com., 1975—. Mem. ABA, Del. Bar Assn. Republican. Unitarian. Clubs: Greenville Country, University and Whist, Rodney Square. Contbr. articles to profl. jours. Mem. ABA, Del. Bar Assn. Republican. Unitarian. Bankruptcy, Federal civil litigation, State civil litigation. Home: 319 Cox Rd Newark DE 19711-3023 E-mail: paulwelsh@dca.net

WELT, PHILIP STANLEY, lawyer, consultant; b. Freeport, N.Y., July 5, 1959; s. Morris and Rose (Offenberg) W.; m. Karen Teresa Gault, May 22, 1994. BBA summa cum laude, Hofstra U., 1983; MBA, Columbia U., 1988; JD cum laude, NYU, 1995. Bar: N.J. 1995, N.Y. 1995; U.S. Dist. Ct. N.J. 1995, U.S. Dist. Ct. (so. and ea. dists.) N.Y. 1996, U.S. Ct. Appeals (2d cir.), 1997, U.S. Ct. Appeals Armed Forces, 2000, U.S. Supreme Ct. 1999; CPA, N.Y. Sr. mgr. Deloitte & Touche, N.Y.C., 1983-92; assoc. Reboul MacMurray Hewitt Maynard & Kristol, 1993, Davis Polk & Wardwell, N.Y.C., 1994, 1996-2001; jud. clk. U.S. Dist. Ct. N.J., Newark, 1995-96; special asst. dist. atty. Kings Co., N.Y., 1999—; asst. gen. counsel Am. Group Internat., Inc., 2001—. Bd. dirs., treas. Pub. Interest Law Found., N.Y.C., 1993-94; guest spkr. Boy Scouts Am., Nassau County, 1984-91, Nat. Assn. Accts., N.Y./N.J., 1988-92, others. Sr. editor Columbia Jour. World Bus., 1986-88; sr. exec. editor Ann. Survey Am. Law, 1993-95; contbr. articles to profl. jours. Vol. income tax asst. Dept. Treasury, IRS, N.Y.C., 1981-87; vol. Variety-The Children's Charity, N.Y.C., 1985-87; advisor Friends of Jon Kaiman, Nassau County, 1995. Provost's scholar Hofstra U., 1981-83, Deloitt & Touche fellow Columbia U., 1986-88; recipient Appreciation cert. Dept. Treasury, IRS, 1981-87, Variety, 1985-87, Bovenaan Outstanding Cmty. Svc. award Hofstra U., 1983, Orison S. Marden Moot Ct. Advocacy award NYU Sch. Law, 1993, Seymore A. Levy meml. award, 1995. Mem. ABA, AICPA, N.Y. State Bar Assn., N.Y. State Soc. CPAs, Beta Alpha Psi, Beta Gamma Sigma. Avocations: golf, rock climbing, photography, philately, amateur radio. Communications, Finance, Public international. Home: 157 Mountain Wood Rd Stamford CT 06903-2107 Office: Am Internat Group Inc 70 Pine St New York NY 10270

WENDEL, JOHN FREDRIC, lawyer, professional sports consultant; b. Newark, Nov. 8, 1936; s. John J. and Margaret D. (Mortimer) W.; m. Barbara Vaughn Smith, Dec. 17, 1960 (dec. July 1978); children: David I., Stephen F.; m. Carlene M. Arnoldini, 1 child, Carlene Margaret. BA, U. Fla., 1958; JD, Stetson U., 1963. Bar: Fla. 1963, U.S. Dist. Ct (so. and mid. dists.) 1964, U.S. Ct. Appeals (5th, 9th, and 11th cirs.) 1964, U.S. Supreme Ct. 1968. Assoc. Troiano & Roberts, Lakeland, Fla., 1963-64, George C. Dayton, Dade City, 1964-65; sole practice John F. Wendel, Lakeland, 1965, 1970-73; ptnr. Wendel & Schott, 1965-70; ptnr., pres. Wendel & McArthur, P.A., 1973-75, Wendel & Chritton and Successor Firms, Lakeland, Fla., 1975—. Town atty. Town of St. Leo, Fla., 1964-78, town judge, 1968; asst. mcpl. judge Lakeland, Fla., 1966; county atty. Citrus County, Fla., 1976-81; vis. prof. law, dir. Nat. Sports Law Inst., Marquette U. Law Sch., Milw., 1989-90; adj. prof. law Marquette U. Law Sch., Milw., 1990-91, Stetson U. Coll. Law, 1992-93; adj. faculty mem. Fla. So. Coll., Lakeland, 1963-65; faculty mem. St. Leo Coll., 1963-73; del. 2d Internat. Conf. Ptnrs. for Alliance for Progress; mem. Fla. Columbia Alliance Coms. and Subco. Mem. editorial bd. Sports Law and Fin., 1992-98. Active ARC; assoc. mem. counsel Fla. Sports Adv. Coun. Served to 1st lt. USMC, 1957-59. Named one of Lakeland's Five Outstanding Young Men, Jaycees, 1967. Mem. Am. Arbitrators Assn. (arbitrator alternative dispute resolution to settle sports disputes), Sports Lawyers Assn. (pres. 1986-93, sec., v.p., bd. dirs. 1986—, pres. emeritus, Award of Excellence 1993), The Fla. Bar (exec. coun. entertainment, arts and sports law sect.), Lakeland Bar Assn., Canon Law Soc. Am., Fla. Assn. County Attys. (pres. 1981), Lakeland Yacht and Country Club, KC. Republican. Roman Catholic. Administrative and regulatory, General civil litigation, Sports. Office: Wendel Chritton & Parks 5300 S Florida Ave PO Box 5378 Lakeland FL 33807-5378

WENDER, IRA TENSARD, lawyer; b. Pitts., Jan. 5, 1927; s. Louis and Luba (Kibrick) W.; m. Phyllis M.Bellows, June 24, 1966; children: Justin B., Sarah T; children by previous marriage: Theodore M., Abigail A., John B. Swarthmore Coll., 1942-45; JD, U. Chgo., 1948; LLM, NYU, 1951. Atty. Lord, Day and Lord, N.Y.C., 1950-52, 54-59; asst. dir. internat. program in tax. Harvard U. Law Sch., 1952-54; lectr. N.Y. U. Sch. Law, N.Y.C., 1954-59; ptnr. Baker and McKenzie, Chgo., 1959-61; founding ptnr. N.Y.C. office, 1961-71; sr. ptnr. Wender, Murase & White, 1971-82; of counsel, 1982-86; chmn. C. Brewer and Co., Ltd., Honolulu, 1969-75; pres., CEO A. G. Becker Paribas Inc., 1978-82; chmn., CEO Sussex Securities Inc., 1983-85; of counsel Patterson, Belknap, Webb & Tyler, N.Y.C., 1986-87, ptnr., 1988-93; of counsel, 1994—. Chmn. Perry Ellis Internat., Inc., N.Y.C., 1994; bd. dirs. REFAC Tech. Devel. Corp., N.Y.C., Dime Bancorp, N.Y.C.; Deotexis Inc., Bermuda; bd. mgrs. Swarthmore Coll, 1978-89; pres., bd. mgrs. PARC Vendome Condominium, 1990-94; trustee Putnet (Vt.) Sch., 1985-92, 93—, vice chmn., 1998—; trustee Brearley Sch., N.Y.C., 1980-85. Author: (with E.R. Barlow) Foreign Investment and Taxation, 1995. Dir., treas. Fountain House, Inc., N.Y., 1998—; dir. Am. Near East Refuge Aid, Washington; mem. Coun. on Fgn. Rels. Mem. ABA, N.Y. State Bar Assn., Assn. of Bar of City of N.Y. Home: 115 E 67th St New York NY 10021-5951 Office: Patterson Belknap Webb & Tyler LLP Ste 2300 1133 Avenue Of The Americas Fl 22 New York NY 10036-6731

WENDT, JOHN ARTHUR FREDERIC, JR. lawyer; b. Cleve. s. John Arthur Frederic and Martha Ann (Hunter) W.; m. Marjorie Rickard Richardson, Oct. 2, 1962; children: Wendy Wendt Wood, Eric A., John A. F. III, Hilary H.; m. Dorothy Fay Nuttall, Dec. 29, 1976. AB with honors, U. Mich., 1942; JD, U. Colo., 1951. Bar: Colo. 1951, U.S. Dist. Ct. Colo. 1951, U.S. Ct. Appeals (10th cir.) 1957, U.S. Supreme Ct. 1971. Assoc. Tippit, Haskell & Welborn, Denver, 1953-58; ptnr. Wendt & Kistler, 1958-62, Wendt Law Offices, Aspen, Colo., 1971-81, Delta, 1985—; dist. atty. 9th Jud. Dist. Colo., 1965-69; judge Pitkin County, Colo., 1971-78; dist. atty. 7th Jud. Dist. Colo., 1981-85; judge Cedaredge, Colo., 1986—. Contract mediator, Colo. Judiciary, 1995—. Chmn. Delta County Planning Commn., 1991-94. Maj. U.S. Army, 1942-46, 51-53. Decorated Purple Heart (2), Silver Star, Bronze Star (2). Mem. Am. Arbitration Assn., Acad. Family Mediators, Colo. Bar Assn. (gov. 1965-71, 82,85, 87-96), Pitkin County Bar Assn. (pres. 1971-72), Delta County Bar Assn. (pres. 1986-89), 7th Jud. Dist. Bench-Bar Com., U.S. Equestrian Team (chmn. Colo. chpt. 1976-86), Masters of Fox Hounds Assn., M.F.H. Roaring Fork Hounds, U.S. Pony Clubs, Inc. (gov. 1996-2000), Phi Kappa Psi, Phi Delta Phi, Phi Beta Kappa. Republican. Episcopalian. State civil litigation, General corporate, Family and matrimonial. Home: Lenado Farm 2130 Spruce Ln Cedaredge CO 81413-9565 Office: PO Box 94 540 Main St Delta CO 81416-1834

WENNER, CHARLES RODERICK, lawyer; b. New Haven, Jan. 10, 1947; s. Charles Bellew and Joan Rhoda (Morrison) W.; m. Jovita C. Vergara, June 11, 1999; 1 child, Abigail Jessica. BS, Coll. Charleston, 1969; JD, U. Conn., 1973. Bar: Conn. 1974, D.C. 1977. Law clk. Conn. Superior Ct., Hartford, 1973-74; staff atty. SEC, Washington, 1974-76, spl. counsel to chmn., 1976-77; assoc. Fulbright & Jaworski, 1977-81, ptnr., 1981—. Lectr. law sch. Law U. Conn., 1973-74. Trustee Calvary United Meth. Ch., Arlington, Va., 1993-95, 97-98; counselor Gospel Mission of Washington, 1991—; bd. dirs. Operation Friendship Internat., Inc., Washington, 1993—. Recipient Am. Hist. award DAR, Charleston, 1969. Mem. ABA, D.C. Bar Assn. Methodist. Avocations: running. Securities. Home: Apt 105 1101 S Arlington Ridge Rd Arlington VA 22202-1922 Office: Fulbright & Jaworski 801 Pennsylvania Ave NW Fl 3-5 Washington DC 20004-2623

WENTWORTH, THEODORE SUMNER, lawyer; b. Bklyn., July 18, 1938; s. Theodore Sumner and Alice Ruth (Wortmann) W.; m. Sharon Linelle Arkush, 1965 (dec. 1987); children: Christina Linn, Kathrun Allison; m. Diana Webb von Welanetz, 1989; 1 stepchild, Lexi von Welanetz. AA, Am. River Coll., 1958; JD, U. Calif., Hastings, 1962. Bar: Calif. 1963, U.S. Dist. Ct. (no. and ctrl. dists.) Calif., U.S. Ct. Appeals (9th cir.), U.S. Supreme Ct.; cert. trial specialist; diplomate Nat. Bd. Trial Advocacy; assoc. Am. Bd. Trial Advocates. Assoc. Adams, Hunt & Martin, Santa Ana, Calif., 1963-66; ptnr. Hunt, Liljestrom & Wentworth, 1967-77; pres. Solabs Corp.; chmn. bd., exec. v.p. Plant Warehouse, Inc., Hawaii, 1974-82; prin. Law Offices of Wentworth, Paoli & Purdy, Newport Beach & Temecula, Calif.; judge pro tem Superior Ct. Attys. Panel Harbor Mcpl. Ct. Owner Eagles Ridge Ranch, Temecula, 1977—. Author: Build a Better Spouse Trap, 2001. Pres., bd. dirs. Santa Ana-Tustin Cmty. Chest, 1972; v.p., trustee South Orange County United Way, 1973-75; pres. Orange County Fedn. Funds, 1972-73; bd. dirs. Orange County Mental Health Assn. Mem. ABA, Am. Bd. Trial Advocates (assoc.), State Bar Calif., Orange County Bar Assn. (dir. 1972-76), Am. Trial Lawyers Assn., Calif. Trial Lawyers Assn. (bd. govs. 1968-70), Orange County Trial Lawyers Assn. (pres. 1967-68), Lawyer-Pilots Bar Assn., Aircraft Owners and Pilots Assn., Bahia Corinthian Yacht Club, Pacific Club, Newport. Achievements include research in vedic prins., natural law, quantum physics and mechanics. Personal injury, Product liability. Office: 4631 Teller Ave Ste 100 Newport Beach CA 92660-8105 also: 41530 Enterprise Cir S Temecula CA 92590-4816 E-mail: ocrawfirm@aol.com

WERBER, STEPHEN JAY, lawyer, educator; b. N.Y.C., Apr. 20, 1940; s. Murray H. and Teddie Werber; m. Mary Jo Weinberg (dec. June 1965); m. Joan C. Kirsh, May 30, 1968; children: David S., Lauren F. BA, Adelphi U., 1961; JD, Cornell U., 1964; LLM, NYU, 1970. Bar: N.Y. 1965, U.S. Dist. Ct (no. dist.) Ohio 1970, U.S. Supreme Ct. 1970, U.S. Dist. Ct. (so. dist.) Ohio 1980, U.S. Ct. Appeals (6th cir.) 1982. Atty. FCC, Washington, 1964-65; assoc. Sidney G. Hollander, N.Y.C., 1965-67, Herzfeld & Rubin, N.Y.C., 1967-70; asst. prof. law Cleve. State U., 1970-73, assoc. prof.law, 1973-76, prof. law, 1976—; of counsel Guren, Merritt, Feibel, Sogg & Cohen, 1979-84, Weston, Hurd, Fallon, Paisley & Howley, 1984-89, cons. spl. litigation, 1989—. Asst. dean Cleve. State U., 1973-74; sec., treas. Am. Inns of Ct. Harold H. Burton chpt., 1990-91, counsellor, 1991-92, pres., 1993-94; mem. Consultative Group for Restatement Torts: Products Liability. Contbr. numerous articles on product liability to profl jours. Former bd. dirs. NE Ohio Multiple Sclerosis Soc., Bur. Jewish Edn.; v.p. Temple Emanu-El, 1983-85; dir. continuing legal edn. programs Cleve.-Marshall Alumni Assn. Mem. ATLA, AAUP, ABA (litigation sect., com. on mfrs. liability), Fed. Bar Assn., Am. Arbitration Assn., N.Y. State Bar Assn., Ohio Bar Assn., Ohio Assn. Civil Trial Lawyers. Democrat. Avocations: bridge, golf. Home: 2560 Lafayette Dr Cleveland OH 44118-4608

WERDEGAR, KATHRYN MICKLE, state supreme court justice; b. San Francisco; d. Benjamin Christie and Kathryn Marie (Clark) Mickle; m. David Werdegar; children: Maurice Clark, Matthew Mickle. Student, Wellesley Coll., 1954-55; AB with honors, U. Calif., Berkeley, 1957; JD with highest distinction, George Washington U., 1962; JD, U. Calif., Berkeley, 1990. Bar: Calif. 1964, U.S. Dist. Ct. (no. dist.) Calif. 1964, U.S. Ct. Appeals (9th cir.) 1964, Calif. Supreme Ct. 1964. Legal asst. civil rights divsn. U.S. Dept. Justice, Washington, 1962-63; cons. Calif. Study Commn. on Mental Retardation, 1963-64; assoc. U. Calif. Ctr. for Study of Law and Soc., Berkeley, 1965-67; spl. cons. State Dept. Mental Hygiene, 1967-68; cons. Calif. Coll. Trial Judges, 1968-71; atty., head criminal divsn. Calif. Continuing Edn. of Bar, 1971-78; assoc. dean acad. and student affairs, assoc. prof. Sch. Law, U. San Francisco, 1978-81; sr. staff atty. Calif. 1st Dist. Ct. Appeal, 1981-85, Calif. Supreme Ct., 1985-91; assoc. justice Calif. 1st Dist. Ct. Appeal, 1991-94, Calif. Supreme Ct., San Francisco, 1994—. Regents' lectr. U. Calif., Berkeley, 2000. Author: Benchbook: Misdemeanor Procedure, 1971, Misdemeanor Procedure Benchbook, 1975, 83; contbr. California Continuing Education of the Bar books; editor: California Criminal Law Practice series, 1972, California Uninsured Motorist Practice, 1973, I California Civil Procedure Before Trial, 1977. Recipient Charles Glover award George Washington U., 1962, J. William Fulbright award for disting. pub. svc. George Washington U. Law Sch. Alumni Assn., 1996, excellence in achievement award, Calif.

Alumni Assn., 1996, Roger J. Traynor Appellate Justice of Yr. award, 1996, Justice of Yr. award Consumer Attys. of Calif., 1998, also 5 Am. Jurisprudence awards, 1960-62. Mem. Nat. Assn. Women Judges, Am. Law Inst., Calif. Judges Assn., Nev./Calif. Women Judges Assn., Order of the Coif. Office: Calif Supreme Court 350 McAllister St San Francisco CA 94102-4783

WERLE, MARK FRED, lawyer; b. N.Y.C., Jan. 22, 1964; s. Fred Carl and Trude Marie W.; m. Michelle Lynne Geiringer, Aug. 20, 1989; children: Melissa, Jocelyn. BA, Hofstra U., 1987, JD, 1989. Bar: N.Y. 1990, Conn. 1990, Vt. 1997. Atty. Jacobowitz, Spessard, Garfinkel & Lesman, N.Y.C., 1992-95; gen. counsel North Atlantic Utilities, Inc., Sea Cliff, N.Y., 1995-97; atty. Ryan Smith & Carbine, Rutland, Vt., 1997—. Mem. ABA, N.Y. State Bar Assn., Vt. Bar Assn., Vt. Hotel & Restaurant Assn., Rutland C. of C., Killington C. of C. Avocations: music, sports, computers, travel. FERC practice, Insurance, Product liability. Home: 285 Thundering Brook Rd Killington VT 05751-9512 Office: Ryan Smith & Carbine PO Box 310 Rutland VT 05702-0310

WERLEIN, EWING, JR. federal judge; b. Houston, Sept. 14, 1936; s. Ewing and Ruth (Storey) W.; m. Kay McGibbon Werlein, June 29, 1963; children: Ewing Kenneth, Emily Kay. BA, So. Meth. U., 1958; LLB, U. Tex., 1961. Bar: Tex. 1961, U.S. Dist. Ct. (so. dist.) Tex. 1965, U.S. Dist. Ct. (ea. dist.) Tex. 1990, U.S. Ct. Appeals (5th cir.) 1970, U.S. Ct. Appeals (10th cir.) 1980, U.S. Claims Ct. 1985, U.S. Tax Ct. 1985, U.S. Supreme Ct. 1983. Ptnr. Vinson & Elkins, Houston, 1964-92; dist. judge U.S. Dist. Ct. (so. dist.) Tex., 1992—. Trustee So. Meth. U., Dallas, 1976-92, Asbury Theol. Sem., Wilmore, Ky., 1989—; mem. gen. bd. pub. United Meth. Ch., Nashville, 1974-84, chmn., 1980-84, chancellor Tex. ann. conf., 1977—; mem. exec. com. World Meth. Counh., 1981-96, treas, 1991-93. Capt. USAF, 1961-64. Fellow Am. Coll. Trial Lawyers, 1984, Internat. Soc. Barristers, 1987; recipient Disting. Alumni award SMU Alumni Assn., 1994. Fellow Am. Bar Found., Tex. Bar Found., Houston Bar Found.; mem. State Bar Tex. (dir. 1990-93), Nat. Conf. Bar Pres., Houston Bar Assn. (pres. 1988-89), Houston C. of C. (life), SAR, Order of Coif, Petroleum Club, Houston Club, Phi Beta Kappa. Office: US Dist Ct Tex US Courthouse 515 Rusk St Ste 9136 Houston TX 77002-2605

WERNER, ROBERT L. lawyer, consultant; b. N.Y.C., Feb. 28, 1913; s. Abraham L. and Elsa (Ludwig) W.; m. Raye Davies, Oct. 13, 1945; children: William, John. AB, Yale U., 1933; LLB, Harvard U., 1936. Bar: N.Y. 1936, U.S. Supreme Ct. 1936, also various fed. cts. and adminstrv. agys. 1936. Spl. asst. to U.S. atty. So. Dist. N.Y., 1936, asst. U.S. atty, 1937-40, confidential asst., 1940-42; 1st asst. civil div. U.S. Dept. Justice, Washington, 1946-47; spl. asst. to atty. gen. U.S., 1946-47; mem. law dept. RCA, N.Y.C., 1947, v.p., gen. atty., 1951-62, exec. v.p., gen. atty., 1962-66, exec. v.p., gen. counsel, 1966-78, dir., 1963-79, cons., 1978-83. Mem. adv. bd. Internat. and Comparative Law Ctr. Southwestern Legal Found., Dallas, 1966—, treas., 1970-72, vice chmn., 1972-73, chmn. advisory bd., 1974-76, found. trustee 1976-88, hon. trustee 1988—; lectr. Conf. Bd., Practicing Law Inst., others; mem. nat. adv. council corp. law depts. Practising Law Inst., 1974-78; com. on restrictive bus. practices U.S. council Internat. C. of C., 1973-78; N.Y. Lawyers' Com. for Civil Rights under Law, 1972-78. Trustee Ithaca Coll., N.Y., 1968-88, hon. trustee, 1988—, chmn. bd., 1976-78; trustee Salisbury (Conn.) Sch., 1975-77, N.Y. Chiropractic Coll., 1986-89; bd. dirs. Midtown Arts Common at St. Peter's Ch., 1983-89. Capt. U.S. Army, 1942-44; to lt. col. USAAF, 1944-46, ETO. Recipient Disting. Service award Ithaca Coll., 1988. Fellow Am. Bar Found.; mem. Internat., Fed., Am., N.Y. State, City N.Y., FCC bar assns., IEEE (sr.), Am. Legion, Harvard Law Sch. Assn., Assn. Gen. Counsel (emeritus), U.S. Naval Inst., Internat. Law Assn. (Am. br.), Nat. Legal Aid and Defender Assn. (dir. 1974-79), Am. Judicature Soc., Newcomen Soc., N.Y. County Lawyers' Assn., Am. Soc. Internat. Law, Yale Club, Harvard Club N.Y., Nat. Lawyers Club, Army and Navy Club (Washington), Coral Beach Club (Bermuda). Home: 116 E 68th St New York NY 10021-5955

WERT, ROBERT CLIFTON, lawyer; b. Pleasantville, N.J., Jan. 8, 1944; s. Clifton Robert and Anna Louise (McLarren) W.; m. Grace Elizabeth Dunbar, Dec. 16, 1967; children: Andrew, Amy, Bethany, Laura. BS in Acctg., Temple U., 1965, JD, 1968; grad., JAG Sch., 1982, Command & Gen. Staff Coll., 1984, U.S. Army JFK Spl. Warfare Ctr, 1987. Bar: Pa. 1968, U.S. Dist. Ct. (ea. dist.) Pa. 1968, U.S. Ct. Mil. Appeals 1969, US. Supreme Ct. 1981. Commd. 2d lt. mil. police USAR, 1965, advanced through ranks to lt. col., 1984, ret., 1990; mil. judge U.S. Army, Okinawa, Japan, 1970-73, chief trial counsel Japan, 1973, staff judge adv. Valley Forge Army Hosp., 1973-74, chief trial counsel N.J., 1974-76, chief legal asst. and claims, 1976-77, ret., 1990; chief staff counsel Southeastern Penn Transp. Authority, Phila., 1977-78, acting chief counsel, 1978-80, gen. counsel, 1980-84, dept. gen. mgr., 1984-86; exec. dir. Blank Rome Comisky & McCauley, 1986—. Owner Insulco, King of Prussia, Pa., 1972-79; co-owner Master Page Inc., Malvern, Pa., 1985-93. Bd. dirs. Evang. Assn. for Promotion of Edn., St. David's, Pa., Ea. Coll., 1988—, Crime Prevention Assn. Charitable Giving, Phila., 1991—; bd. dirs. Crime Prevention Assn., Phila., 1988-2001, chair exec. com., 1992-94, 1998-2001, treas., 1994-96, v.p., 1997-98; pres. Charlestown Townwatch, 1980-2000; coord. Twp. Emergency, 1984-99; vice-chair bd. supr. Charlestown Twp., 1998-2000;mem. bd. trustees Great Valley Presbyn. Ch., 2001—; deacon, Sunday Sch. supt., mem. bldg. com., chmn. property com. Ch. of the Savior, Wayne, Pa.; bd. dirs., asst. treas. Adv. Meth. Ch., Phila. Decorated Meritorious Svc. medal, Army Achievement medal, Overseas Svc. medal, Nat. Def. Svc. medal, various Res. decorations; recipient Pa. Gov.'s award, 1989. Mem. Assn. of Legal Adminstrs., Phila. Bar Assn., Temple U. Law Alumni Assn. (exec. com. 1995-96), Masons. Avocation: woodworking. General corporate, Military, Transportation. Office: Blank Rome Comisky & McCauley LLP One Logan Sq Philadelphia PA 19103-6998 E-mail: wert@blankrome.com

WERTHEIM, JAY PHILIP, lawyer; b. Lexington, Mass., Jan. 19, 1952; s. Richard M. and Marion F. (Glazier) W.; m. Jeanette M. Alexander. BS, MA, Stanford U., 1974; MD, U. Calif., San Francisco, 1979. Bar: Calif. 1979, U.S. Ct. Appeals (9th cir.) 1979, U.S. Dist. Ct. (ea. and no. dists.) Calif. 1979. Cons. Bank of Am., San Francisco, 1974-75; fin. analyst Assoc. Freight Lines, Oakland, Calif., 1975-78; assoc. Dinkelspiel & Dinkelspiel, San Francisco, 1980-88, Perkins Coie, L.A., 1988-95; assoc. gen. counsel Baxter Healthcare Corp., Irvine, Calif., 1995-2000; v.p., assoc. gen. counsel Edwards Lifescis. Corp., 2000—. Instr. legal writing and rsch. U. Calif., San Francisco, 1983-85; judge pro tem Mcpl. Ct. of State of Calif. L.A. Judicial Dist., 1991. Mem. ABA, Assn. Data Processing Svc. Orgns. (mem. lawyers' com. 1982-86), Bar Assn. San Francisco (com. on arbitration of fee disputes), Stanford Alumni Assn. (pres., bd. dirs. San Francisco chpt. 1980-84), Am. Assn. Equipment Lessors, Am. Arbitration Assn. (arbitrator), L.A. County Bar Assn., Orange County Bar Assn., The Asia Soc., L.A. World Affairs Coun., Buchanan Flying Club (v.p. 1981-82). General corporate, Mergers and acquisitions, Securities. Office: Edwards Lifescis Corp One Edwards Way Irvine CA 92614-5627 E-mail: jay_wertheim@edwards.com

WERTHEIM, JERRY, lawyer; b. Ft. Sumner, N.Mex., Oct. 11, 1938; s. Max Wertheim and Helen Nanna; m. Mary Carole May, Aug. 20, 1960; children: Jerry Todd, John Vincent. BA with honors, U. N.Mex., 1960; LLB, Georgetown U., 1964. Bar: N.Mex. 1964, U.S. Supreme Ct. 1981, U.S. Dist. Ct. N.Mex. 1964, U.S. Ct. Appeals (10th cir.) 1965. Asst. atty. gen. N.Mex. Atty. Gen. Office, Santa Fe, 1964-65; ptnr. Jones, Snead, Wertheim, Wentworth & Jaramillo, P.A., 1965—, pres., 1986—. Mem. N.Mex Supreme Ct.'s Rules of Evidence Com., 1976-93, Rules of Civil Procedure Com., 1993-99. Recipient award for Outstanding Svc. to Judiciary, N.Mex. Supreme Ct., 1982. Mem. N.Mex. State Bar (chmn. adv. opinions com. 1968-76, Outstanding Svc. award 1971, 74, 83, 84), Bar Assn. for U.S. Dist. Ct. for Dist. of N.Mex. (pres. 1996—), Assn. Trial Lawyers Am., N.Mex. Trial Lawyers Assn., 1st Jud. Dist. Bar Assn., Am. Bd. Trial Advocates, Am. Law Inst. E-mail: jerry@thejonesfirm.com. Federal civil litigation, State civil litigation, Probate. Office: Jones Snead Wertheim Wentworth & Jaramillo PA PO Box 2228 215 Lincoln Ave Santa Fe NM 87501

WESBROOKS, PERRY, lawyer, consultant, arbitrator; b. Burkburnett, Tex., June 14, 1932; s. Marquis Perry and Grace (Barrett) W.; m. Shirley Miller, July 5, 1955; children: Lynn Elaine Sterling, Mark Doss. BBA, U. Tex., 1957, JD, 1959. Bar: Tex. 1959, U.S. Dist. Ct. (no. dist.) Tex. 1961, U.S. Dist. Ct. (we. dist.) Tex. 1989, U.S. Dist. Ct. (we. dist.) Okla. 1982, U.S. Ct. of Appeals (5th cir.) 1969, U.S. Ct. Appeals (8th cir.) 1975, U.S. Supreme Ct. 1970. Asst. county atty. Wichita County, Wichita Falls, Tex., 1959-60; ptnr. Schenk & Wesbrooks, Wichita Falls, 1961-79; pres. Wesbrooks-Yandell, Wichita Falls, 1979-80, The Wesbrooks Firm, P.C., d/b/a Westbrook & Rugeley, Wichita Falls, 1980-87, 90—, Wesbrooks Firm, P.C., 1987—. Chmn. Aviation Adv. Bd., Wichita Falls, 1970-71. With USN, 1951-55. Mem. ATLA, Tex. State Bar Assn., Phi Alpha Delta. Democrat. Methodist. Bankruptcy, Personal injury, Product liability. Office: Wesbrooks Firm PC 212 Loop 11 PO Box 3367 Wichita Falls TX 76301-0367

WESELY, EDWIN JOSEPH, lawyer; b. N.Y.C., May 16, 1929; s. Joseph and Elizabeth (Peles) W.; children: Marissa Celeste, Adrienne Lee; m. Marcy Brownson, Sept. 23, 1992. Ed., Deep Springs Coll., 1945-47; AB, Cornell U., 1949; JD, Columbia U., 1954. Bar: N.Y. 1954, D.C. 1985, U.S. Supreme Ct. 1960, others. Law clk. to judge U.S. Dist. Ct. (so. dist.) N.Y., 1954-55; asst. U.S. atty. So. Dist. N.Y., 1955-57; assoc. Winthrop, Stimson, Putnam & Roberts, N.Y.C., 1957-63, ptnr., 1964-2000; sr. counsel Pillsbury Winthrop LLP, 2001—. Spl. master numerous cases; chmn. spl. com. on effective discovery in civil cases U.S. Dist. Ct. (ea. dist.) N.Y., 1982-84, com. on civil caseflow, 1985-88, com. on civil litigation, 1988—, civil justice reform adv. group, 1990-95; mem. com. on pretrial phase civil cases Jud. Coun. 2d Cir., 1984-86, standing com. on improvement civil litigation, 1986-89; ex-officio Civil Justice Reform Act adv. group U.S. Dist. Ct. (so. dist.) N.Y.; pres. CARE, 1986-89, chmn., 1978-86, 89-90, internat. bd. dirs., 1981-90, pres., 1987-90; bd. dirs. Internat. Rescue Com.; bd. dirs., exec. com. Internat. Ctr. in N.Y., 1990—, chmn., 1998—. Trustee Deep Springs Coll., 1991-2000; vice-chair, 1998-2000. Decorated Order of Civil Merit (Republic of Korea); recipient World Humanitarian award Fgn. Press Assn., 1988, Commendation Bd. Judges U.S. Dist. Ct. (ea. dist.) N.Y., 1993. Fellow Am. Coll. Trial Lawyers; mem. ABA (spl. adv. com. on internat. activities 1990-93, litigation sect. chmn. com. on discovery 1977-78, spl. com. study discovery abuse 1977-82, chmn. task force on liaison with internat. profl. assns. on matters of mutual concern 1989-93, Civil Justice Reform Act task force 1991-93, task force on the state of the justice sys. 1993-95, fed. initiatives task force 1995-98, co-chmn. task force on fed. and local rules 1997-98), UN Assn. U.S.A. (bd. dirs. 1991—), Assn. of Bar of City of N.Y. (com. chmn., organized demostration observation panel), Coun. on Fgn. Rels., River Club. Banking, Federal civil litigation, State civil litigation. Office: Pillsbury Winthrop LLP One Battery Park Pla New York NY 10004-1490 E-mail: eweselye@pillsburywinthrop.com

WESLEY, HOWARD BARRY, lawyer; b. Murphysboro, Ill., Aug. 26, 1955; s. Samuel Howard and Billie Mae (Nehring) W.; m. Rebecca Anne Hartman, May 24, 1986. BA, So. Ill. U., 1976, JD, 1979; LLM in Tax, U. Fla., 1981. Bar: Ill. 1979, U.S. Tax Ct. 1980, U.S. Dist. Ct. (so. dist.) Ill. 1981. Assoc. Morris & Wesley, Lewistown, Ill., 1979-80; ptnr. Wesley & Erbes, Murphysboro, 1981-93; assoc. Barrett, Thomey, Broom & Hughes, Carbondale, 1994-97; ptnr. Barrett, Thomey, Morris Brown & Hughes, 1997—. Adj. prof. So. Ill. U., 1990, 97. Pres. Dem. Dist. Com. Tacksa County, 1988. Mem. Ill. State Bar Assn. Democrat. Lutheran. Avocation: fishing. Consumer commercial, Personal injury, Workers' compensation. Office: 100 N Illinois Ave Carbondale IL 62901-1450 E-mail: bwesley@btbhw.com

WESLEY, RICHARD C. state supreme court justice; b. Canandaigua, N.Y., Aug. 1, 1949; s. Charles and Beatrice W.; m. Kathryn Rice; 2 children. BA summa cum laude, SUNY, Albany, 1971; JD, Cornell U., 1974. Assoc. Harris, Beach & Wilcox, 1974-76; with Welch, Streb & Porter, 1976-77; ptnr. Streb, Porter, Meyer & Wesley, 1977-86; justice Supreme Ct. 7th Jud. Dist., 1986—; supervising judge Criminal Cts. 7th Jud. Dist., 1991; judge appellate div. Supreme Ct. 4th Dept., 1994—97; assoc. judge N.Y. Ct. Appeals, Albany, 1997—. Creator Felony Screening Program, 1993; lectr. in field; bd. trustees Ctr. Dispute Resolution, Pre-Trial Svcs. Corp. Editor: Cornell Law Rev. Asst. counsel to Assembly Rep. leader James L. Emery, 1979-1982; assemblyman N.Y. State 136th Assembly Dist., 1982-84, 84-86; chair Livingston County Alcohol and Drug Abuse Prevention Coun.; bd. trustees United Ch. Livonia, Chances and Changes, Charles Settlement House; bd. dirs. Myers' Found.; driver Livonia Vol. Ambulance. Named Legislator of Yr., Livingston-Wyoming Assn. Retarded Citizens, 1988; recipient Disting. SUNY Alumni award SUNY Alumni Assn., 1997. Fellow N.Y. State Bar Found.; mem. Livingston County Bar Assn. (sec.), Supreme Ct. Justices Assn. (pres. 7th jud. dist.). Office: NY Ct Appeals Livingston County Govt Ctr 6 Court St Geneseo NY 14454-1030*

WESSEL, PETER, lawyer; b. N.Y.C., N.Y., Feb. 2, 1952; s. Harry Nathan Jr. and Charlene (Freimuth) W.; married Vicki Brodsky Scheck; children: Daniel, Elizabeth, Justin Scheck, Matthew Scheck. BS, Syracuse U., 1974, MPA, JD, 1980. Bar: N.Y. 1981, U.S. Dist. Ct. (no., so., ea. and we. dists.) N.Y. 1981, Fla. 1984, U.S. Ct. Mil. Appeals, 1988, U.S. Ct. Appeals (2d cir.) 1988, U.S. Supreme Ct. 1988. Confidential law clk. to Hon. David F. Lee Jr. N.Y. Supreme Ct., 1980-82; sr. atty. criminal def. div. The Legal Aid Soc., N.Y.C., 1982-87; pvt. practice, 1987—. Notes and comments editor Syracuse Law Rev., 1979-80; contbr. articles to profl. jours. Robert M. Anderson award for Writing and Legal Scholarship, 1980, Neal Brewster scholar, 1977-78, Syracuse U. Coll. Law scholar 1978-79, Louis Waters Meml. scholar, 1979-80, Hiscock, Cowie, Bruce & Lee scholar, 1979-80; Martindale-Hubbell a-v rated. Mem. ABA, N.Y. State Bar Assn., Assn. of Bar of City of N.Y., Fla. Bar Assn., Nat. Assn. Criminal Def. Lawyers, N.Y. State Assn. Criminal Def. Lawyers, N.Y. State Defender Assn., N.Y. State Trial Lawyers Assn., N.Y. County Lawyers Assn., N.Y. Criminal Bar Assn. General civil litigation, Criminal, Personal injury.

WESSLING, ROBERT BRUCE, lawyer; b. Chgo., Oct. 8, 1937; s. Robert Euans and Marguerite (Rickert) W.; m. Judith Ann Hanson, Aug. 26, 1961; children: Katherine, Jennifer, Carolyn. BA, DePauw U., 1959; JD, U. Mich., 1962. Bar: U.S. Dist. Ct. (cen. dist.) Calif. 1963, U.S. Ct. Appeals (9th cir.) 1965. Assoc. Latham & Watkins, L.A., 1962-70, ptnr., 1970-94, of counsel, 1995—. Bd. govs. Fin. Lawyers Conf., Los Angeles, 1974-2000. Mem. World Affairs Coun., L.A., Town Hall, L.A.; trustee DePauw U. Mem. ABA, Los Angeles Bar Assn., Phi Beta Kappa, Phi Delta Phi, Phi Eta Sigma, Order of Coif. Democrat. Methodist. Avocations: tennis, travel. Banking, Contracts commercial, Real property. Office: 633 W 5th St Ste 4000 Los Angeles CA 90071-2005 E-mail: bbwessling@aol.com

WEST, CAROL CATHERINE, law educator; b. Phila., May 23, 1944; d. Scott G. and Helen (Young) West. BA, Miss. U. for Women, 1966; MLS, U. So. Miss., 1984; JD, U. Miss., 1970. Pub. svcs. law libr. U. Va., Charlottesville, 1966-67; catalog law libr. U. Miss., Oxford, 1967-70; legis. reference libr. Miss. Legislature, Jackson, 1970-75; law libr. Miss. Coll., 1975-94, prof. law, 1975-2001. Del. White House conf. Libr. and Info. Svcs., 1991; cons. to Parliament of Armenia, 1995, Parliament of Tanzania, 1997; mem. Miss. Task Force on Gender Fairness in the Cts.; mem. bd. commr. Miss. Libr. Comm., 1993-98. Mem. ABA, Miss. Bar Assn. (Suzie Blue Buchanan award 2001), Hinds County Bar (bd. dirs. 1994-96), Miss. Women Lawyers Assn. (bd. dirs. 1991-93), Miss. Libr. Assn., Miss. Women's Political Network (bd. dirs. 1998—). Methodist. Office: Miss Coll Law Sch 151 E Griffith St Jackson MS 39201-1302

WEST, JAMES JOSEPH, lawyer; b. Tarentum, Pa., Nov. 26, 1945; s. Samuel Elwood and Rose (McIntyre) W.; m. Kathleen Geslak, Aug. 19, 1967; children: Joseph Allen, Yvonne Michelle, KaiLynn Ann. BS in Econs., St. Vincent Coll., 1967; JD, Duquesne U., 1970. Bar: Pa. 1971, U.S. Dist. Ct. (we. dist.) Pa. 1971, U.S. Ct. Appeals (3d cir.) 1971, U.S. Dist. Ct. (mid. dist.) Pa., 1980. Law clk. to presiding justice U.S. Dist. Ct., Pa., 1970-74; asst. U.S. atty. chief appellate sect. U.S. Atty.'s Office, Pitts., 1974-79; dep. dir. criminal law Pa. Atty. Gen.'s Office, Harrisburg, 1979-82; 1st asst. U.S. atty. U.S. Dist. Ct. (mid. dist.) Pa., 1982-84, U.S. atty., 1984-93; assoc. Sprague & Sprague, Phila., 1993-95; pvt. practice Harrisburg, Pa., 1995—. Mem. Nat. Environ. Enforcement Council. Recipient Outstanding Performance award U.S. Dept. Justice, 1974-78, Commendation Gov. of Pa., 1981. Mem. Pa. Bar Assn., Allegheny County Bar Assn., Dauphin County Bar Assn. Republican. Roman Catholic. Home: 1222 Cardinal Way Rd Hummelstown PA 17036-8548 Office: James West 105 N Front St Harrisburg PA 17101-1483 E-mail: jwestlaw@aol.com

WEST, JOSEPH D. lawyer; b. Ashland, Pa., Apr. 18, 1949; BCE, Villanova U., 1971; JD, George Washington U., 1977. Bar: Va. 1977, D.C. 1977. Sr. ptnr. Arnold & Porter, Washington, 1993—. Mem. Order of Coif. Federal civil litigation, Construction, Government contracts and claims. Office: Arnold & Porter 555 12th St NW Washington DC 20004-1206 E-mail: Joseph_West@aporter.com

WEST, JOSEPH KING, judge; b. Yonkers, N.Y., Sept. 11, 1929; s. Ralph and Nellie (Brown) W.; m. Shirley Arvene Gray, July 3, 1954; children: Rebecca, Joseph K. BS, Howard U., Washington, 1952; JD, Bklyn. Law Sch., 1961. Bar: U.S. Supreme Ct. 1962, N.Y. 1962, U.S. Dist. Ct. (so. dist.) N.Y. 1974. Asst. corp. counsel City of Yonkers, N.Y., 1964-65; asst. dist. atty. Pros. Office, White Plains, 1965-82; city ct. judge Yonkers City Ct., 1983-84; county ct. judge Westchester Jud. Ct., White Plains, 1985-99; supervising judge Criminal Cts. 9th Jud. Dist. Dutchess, Orange, Putnam, Rockland and Westchester Counties, 1991-98; state supreme ct. justice State of New York, 1999—. Bd. dirs. St. Joseph's Med. Ctr.; adv. bd. Yonkers Big. Bros./Big Sisters. 1st lt. U.S. Army, 1952-56. Mem. Westchester County Bar Assn., Yonkers Lawyers Assn., Alpha Phi Alpha. Avocations: sports, walking, tennis, piano. Office: Westchester County Ct 111 Dr Martin Luther King Jr B White Plains NY 10601-2509

WEST, KENNETH EDWARD, lawyer; b. Phila., June 30, 1963; s. Edward Brown and Delores Ann (Brooks) W.; m. Cheryl Y. Tolerico; children: Jessie Marie, Brooks T., Jennifer Zevra. BS, Pa. State U., 1985; JD, Villanova U., 1988. Bar: Pa. 1988, U.S. Dist. Ct. (ea. dist.) Pa. 1990, U.S. Dist. Ct. N.J. 1988; lic. real estate agent, Pa. Assoc. Pachtman, Douglass & Assocs., Folsom, Pa., 1988-90; ptnr. Douglass, West & Riley, Drexel Hill, 1990-93, Douglass, West & Assocs., Drexel Hill, 1993—. Mem. bancruptcy conf. U.S. Dist. Ct. (ea. dist.) Pa. Mem. Pa. Trial Lawyers Assn., Del. County Bar Assn. Avocations: squash, raquetball. Bankruptcy, Personal injury, Real property. Office: Douglass West & Assocs 830 N Landsdowne Ave Drexel Hill PA 19026-1526 E-mail: kendwa@aol.com

WEST, LEE ROY, federal judge; b. Clayton, Okla., Nov. 26, 1929; s. Calvin and Nicie (Hill) W.; m. MaryAnn Ellis, Aug. 29, 1952; children: Kimberly Ellis, Jennifer Lee. B.A., U. Okla., 1952, J.D., 1956; LL.M. (Ford Found. fellow), Harvard U., 1963. Bar: Okla. 1956. Individual practice law, Ada, Okla., 1956-61, 63-65; faculty U. Okla. Coll. Law, 1961-62; Ford Found. fellow in law teaching Harvard U., Cambridge, Mass., 1962-63; judge 22d Jud. Dist. Okla., Ada, 1965-73; mem. CAB, Washington, 1973-78, acting chmn., 1977; practice law Tulsa, 1978-79; spl. justice Okla. Supreme Ct., 1965; judge U.S. Dist Ct. (we. dist.) Okla., 1979-94; sr. judge U.S. Dist. Ct. (we. dist.), Okla., 1994—. Editor: Okla. Law Rev. Served to capt. USMC, 1952-54. Recipient Humanitarian award Nat. Conf. Cmty. and Justice, 2000, Jud. Excellence award Okla. Bar Assn., 2000. Mem. U. Okla. Alumni Assn. (dir.), Phi Delta Phi (pres. 1956), Phi Eta Sigma, Order of Coif. Home: 6500 E Danforth Rd Edmond OK 73034-7601 Office: US Dist Ct 3001 US Courthouse 200 NW 4th St Oklahoma City OK 73102-3027

WEST, ROBERT GRADY, lawyer; b. Dallas, Aug. 13, 1947; s. Robert Sorrells and Thelma Grady W.; m. Marsha Lee Riegert, June 5, 1971; children: Kathryn Lee, Laura Elaine. BA, Midwestern State U., 1969; JD, U. Tex., 1972. Bar: Tex. 1972, U.S. Dist. Ct. (no. dist.) Tex. 1975, U.S. Dist. Ct. (ea. dist.) Tex. 1992, U.S. Ct. Appeals (5th cir.) 1976. Assoc. McGown, Godfrey, Decker, McMackin, Shipman & McClane, Ft. Worth, 1972-77, ptnr., 1977-88, Decker, McMackin & McClane, Ft. Worth, 1988-90, Decker, Jones, McMackin, McClane, Hall & Bates, Ft. Worth, 1990-93; assoc. Michener, Larimore, Swindle, Whitaker, et al, 1993-98, ptnr., 1999-2000, Whitaker, Chalk, Swindle & Sawyer, 2000—. Bd. regents Midwestern State U., Wichita Falls, Tex., 1992-98; dir. Grace Found., Dallas, 1990-92; mem. Tex. Ctr. Legal Ethics & Professionalism, 1994—, Leadership Ft. Worth, 1984. Mem. Am. Assn. Profl. Landmen, State Bar Tex., Tarrant County Bar Assn. Presbyterian. Avocations: travel, musical theatre, walking, volunteering. Non-profit and tax-exempt organizations, Probate, Real property. Office: Whitaker Chalk Swindle & Sawyer 3500 City Ctr Tower II 301 Commerce St Fort Worth TX 76102-4186 E-mail: rwest@whitakerchalk.com

WEST, STEPHEN KINGSBURY, lawyer, director; b. Pittsfield, Mass., Sept. 28, 1928; s. William Bradford and Ruth (Osteyee) W.; m. Ann Wick, Apr. 30, 1955; children: Timothy Wick, Lucy West Engebretson, Todd Kingsbury, Daniel Wick. B.A., Yale U., 1950; LL.B., Harvard U., 1953. Assoc. Sullivan & Cromwell, N.Y.C., 1957-64, ptnr., 1964-97, of counsel, 1997—. Bd. dirs. Pioneer Mut. Fund, Boston, AMVESCAP Plc, London, Swiss Helvetin Fund, Inc., Dresdner RCM Global Strategic Income Fund. Served to lst lt. inf. U.S. Army, 1953-56. Mem. ABA, N.Y. State Bar Assn., Assn. Bar City N.Y. Insurance, Securities, Mergers and acquisitions. Office: Sullivan & Cromwell 125 Broad St Fl 28 New York NY 10004-2489

WESTBROOK, JAMES EDWIN, lawyer, educator; b. Camden, Ark., Sept. 7, 1934; s. Loy Edwin and Helen Lucille (Bethea) W.; m. Elizabeth Kay Farris, Dec. 23, 1956; children: William Michael, Robert Bruce, Matthew David. BA with high honors, Hendrix Coll., 1956; JD with distinction, Duke U., 1959; LLM, Georgetown U., 1965. Bar: Ark. 1959, Okla. 1977, Mo. 1982. Assoc. Mehaffy, Smith & Williams, Little Rock, 1959-62; asst. counsel, subcom. of U.S. Senate Jud. Com., Washington, 1963; legis. asst. U.S. Senate, 1963-65; asst. prof. law U. Mo., Columbia, 1965-68, asst. dean, 1966-68, assoc. prof., 1968-70, prof., 1970-76, 80—, James S. Rollins prof. law, 1974-76, 80—, Earl F. Nelson prof. law, 1982-99, emeritus prof., 1999—, interim dean, 1981-82; dean U. Okla. Coll. Law, Norman, 1976-80. George Allen vis. prof. law, U. Richmond, 1987; vis. prof. law Duke U., 1988, Washington U., St. Louis, 1996, 2001; reporter Mid-Am. Assembly on Role of State in Urban Crisis, 1970; dir. Summer Internship Program in Local Govt., 1968; cons. various Mo. cities

on drafting home-rule charters; mem. Gov.'s Adv. Coun. on Local Govt. Law, 1967-68, Fed. Practice Com. U.S. Dist. Ct. (we. dist.) Mo., 1986-90; chmn. Columbia Charter Revision Commn., 1973-74; mem. spl. com. labor relations Mo. Dept. Labor and Indsl. Rels., 1975; mem. Task Force on Gender and Justice, Mo. Jud. Conf., 1990-93; mem. com. to rev. govtl. structure of Boone County, Mo., 1991. Author: (with L. Riskin) Dispute Resolution and Lawyers, 1987, supplement, 1993, 2d edit., 1997, abridged edit. of 2d edit., 1998; contbr. articles to profl. jours. Chair search com. for chancellor U. Mo., Columbia, 1992, chair search com. for provost, 1998. Mem. ABA, Nat. Acad. Arbitrators, Assn. Am. Law Schs. (chmn. local govt. law round table coun. 1972), Ctrl. States Law Sch. Assn. (pres. 1982-83), Mo. Bar Assn. (vice chmn. labor law com. 1986-87, chmn. 1987-88, Spurgeon Smithton award 1995), Order of Coif, Blue Key, Alpha Chi. Roman Catholic. Home: 3609 S Woods Edge Rd Columbia MO 65203-6606 Office: U Mo Sch Law Columbia MO 65211-0001

WESTER, RURIC HERSCHEL, JR. lawyer; b. Ruskin, Fla., Aug. 9, 1930; s. Ruric Herschel and Mabel Olivia (Curry) W.; m. Joan Hisae Momohira, Oct. 12, 1951; children— Mary, John William, George Warham, Ruric Herschel, Mark, Luke. B.A. cum laude in Polit. Sci., St. Mary's U., San Antonio, 1973; J.D., 1976. Bar: Tex. 1976. Enlisted U.S. Air Force, 1948, served to maj., ret., 1970; owner, operator Fujiya Japanese Restaurant, San Antonio, 1970— ; sole practice, Seguin, 1976-79; atty. Lippe & Wester, Seguin, 1979-84; asst. county atty. Guadalupe County, Tex., 1983-84; ptnr. Wester & Roush, Austin, 1984-85, Wester & Wester, Austin, 1985—; instr. polit. sci. St. Mary's U., San Antonio, 1978, bus. law Tex. Lutheran Coll., Seguin, 1980. County chmn. Guadalupe County Republican Party, 1980-84; mem. Seguin Planning Commn., 1983-84; del. Rep. State Conv., Tex., 1972-84, 88, Nat. Conv., 1984. Mem. Tex. Bar Assn. (chmn. dist. subcom. on admissions 1979-85), Conservation Soc. Sequin (bd. dirs. 1965-85), Phi Delta Phi, Pi Gamma Mu. Methodist. Lodges: Lions (bd. dirs. 1976-78), Masons. State civil litigation, General practice, Real property. Home: PO Box 161163 Austin TX 78716-1163 Office: 1101 S Capitol Tex Bldg H Austin TX 78746

WESTERHAUS, DOUGLAS BERNARD, lawyer; b. Marion, Kans., Jan. 11, 1951; s. Edwin Gerard and Bernadine (Ullman) W.; m. Susan Elizabeth Scott, Aug. 20, 1973 (div. Jan. 1979); m. Karen Sue Giersch, Sept. 20, 1980 (div. Aug. 1997); children: John Joseph, Jamie Lynn, Jeffrey Michael; m. Victoria Lee Ruhga, March, 1998. BSBA, Kans. U., 1973, JD, 1976. Bar: Kans. 1976, U.S. Dist. Kans. 1976, U.S. Supreme Ct. 1980. Assoc. Harper & Hornbaker, Junction City, Kans., 1976-78, ptnr., 1978-80; prin. Westerhaus Law Office, Marion, Kans., 1980-86; pres. Hydrogen Energy Corp., 1986-91, also bd. dirs.; staff atty. THORN Ams., Inc., dba Rent-A-Ctr., Wichita, Kans., 1991-95, chief counsel human resources, 1995-96, assoc. gen. counsel, 1996-97; dir. Field Human Resources, 1997-98; exec. v.p. Mr. Goodcents Franchise Sys., Inc., 1999—. Atty. City of Grandview Plaza, Kans. 1977-80, City of Lehigh, Kans. 1980-86, Marion County, 1981-85; gen. counsel The Hydrogen Energy Corp., Kansas City, Mo. 1984-86, Marion Die & Fixture, 1980-86. Bd. dirs. St. Luke's Hosp., Marion, 1985-86. Mem. ABA, Kans. Bar Assn. (chmn. Lawyer Referral Commn. 1979-84, Outstanding Service award 1984), Marion County Bar Assn. (pres. 1985), Sedgwick County Bar Assn. Republican. Roman Catholic. General corporate, Labor. Home: 12813 King St Overland Park KS 66213-4416

WESTERN, MARION WAYNE, lawyer; b. Deseret, Utah, May 4, 1936; s. Francis Marion and Myrtle Brunson Western; m. Kathleen Ricks, May 16, 1959 (dec. Aug. 1978); children: Ellen Western Camp, Marc F., Amy Western Meador, James R.; m. Delores Biggs, Jan. 19, 1985. BS in Chemistry, Utah State U., 1961; JD with honors, George Washington U., 1964. Bar: Calif. 1966, U.S. Ct. Appeals (9th cir.) 1966, Utah 1975, U.S. Ct. Appeals (fed. cir.) 1983, U.S. Patent and Trademark Office 1965. Examiner U.S. Patent Office, Washington, 1961-64; patent atty. Shell Oil Co., San Francisco, 1964-73, Criddle & Thorpe, Salt Lake City, 1973-75; ptnr. Criddle, Thorpe & Western, 1976-79, Criddle & Western, Salt Lake City, 1979-80, Thorpe, North & Western, Sandy, Utah, 1980—. Avocations: outdoors, fishing, photography, poetry, classical music. Alternative dispute resolution, Contracts commercial, Construction. Office: Thorpe North & Western 8180 S 700 E Sandy UT 84070-0562

WESTIN, RICHARD AXEL, law educator, lawyer, consultant; b. London, July 8, 1945; came to U.S., 1952; s. Gosta Victor and Muriel Yalden (Thomson) W.; m. Judith A. Parke,r Sept. 3, 1978; m. 2d, Elizabeth J. Cook, June 13, 1981. BA, Columbia U., 1967, MBA, 1968; JD, U. Pa., 1972. Bar: Calif. 1973, Vt. 1975, U.S. Dist. Ct. (no. dist.) Calif. 1972, U.S. Dist. Ct. Vt. 1975. Cons. World Bank, 1969-72; assoc. Dewey, Ballantine, Bushby, Palmer & Wood, N.Y.C., 1972-75; tax counsel Vt. Life Ins. Co., Montpelier, 1975-79; prof. law U. Houston Law Ctr. Cons., dir. Millenium Leasing Corp., Paradise Land and Cattle, Inc. Author: Tax Lexicon, 1984, Natural Resource Taxation, 1987, Federal Tax Planning, 1990; author: (with others) Tax Fraud and Money Laundering, Accounting Periods and Methods, 1993;contbr. articles to profl. jours. Mem. ABA (leader task force on liquidation/reins). Home: 3141 Warrenwood Wynd Lexington KY 40502-3578

WESTMAN, CARL EDWARD, lawyer; b. Youngstown, Ohio, Dec. 12, 1943; s. Carl H. and Mary Lillis (Powell) W.; m. Carolyn J., July 17, 1965; children: C. Forrest, Stephanie A. BBA, Sam Houston State U., 1966; JD, U. Miami, 1969, LLM in Taxation, 1972. Bar: Fla. 1969. Ptnr. Frost & Jacobs, 1983-93, Roetzel & Andress, 1993-98; mktg. ptnr. Steel, Hector & Davis, Naples, Fla., 1999—. Active S.W. Fla. coun. Boy Scouts Am. Eagle Bd. of Rev., 1987—; trustee David Lawrence Found. for Mental Health, Inc., 1976-86, chmn. 1985-86; trustee Pikeville Coll., 1993—, Naples Cmty. Hosp., 1992—, NCH Healthcare Sys. Inc., 1995—, chmn. profl. capabilities com. physician credentialing, 1998—, vice-chmn.; vice-chmn. Naples Cmty. Hosp.; past pres. bd. trustees, elder Moorings Presbyn. Ch.; chmn. S.W. Fla. Adv. Bd., Rosenstiel Sch. of Marine and Atmospheric Sci., U. Miami. Master lic. capt. USCG. Mem. ABA, Fla. Bar Assn. (exec. coun., cir. rep. real property, probate and trust law sect., probate law com., trust law com.), Collier County Bar Assn., Estate Planning Coun., Coral Reef Yacht Club, Useppa Island Club. Estate planning, General practice, Probate. Home: 1952 Crayton Rd Naples FL 34102-5070 Office: 5551 Ridgewood Dr Ste 101 Naples FL 34108-2718 E-mail: cwestman@steelhector.com

WESTON, MICHAEL C. lawyer; b. Asheville, N.C., Aug. 13, 1938; m. Mary Ann Damme; two children. AB in English, Brown U., 1960; JD, U. Mich., 1963. Bar: Mich. 1964, Ill. 1973. Assoc. Clark Hill, Detroit, 1963-68; from sec. to pres. corp. and indsl. consortium Econ. Devel. Corp. of Greater Detroit, 1969-73; chief staff atty. Northwestern U., Evanston, Ill., 1973-81, v.p. legal affairs, 1981-89; v.p. and gen. counsel, 1990-2001. Lectr. minority bus. devel. Inst. Continuing Legal Edn., conflicts of interest Nat. Coun. Univ. Rsch. Adminstrs. Contbr. articles to profl. jours. Chmn. Univ. Gallery Com., 1982-85; bd. dirs. Northwestern U. Press. Mem. ABA (sec. taxation, com. on exempt orgns., ho. of dels., lectr. Inst. on Minority Bus. Devel.), Chgo. Coun. Lawyers, Nat. Assn. Coll. and Univ. Attys. (lectr. fed. tax matters, outside activities faculty mems. univ.-cmty. rels., med. risk mgmt., bd. dirs. 1985-88, 92-97, pres. 1995-96). E-mail: m-weston@northwestern.edu

WESTPHAL, MARJORIE LORD, lawyer; b. Erie, Pa., July 24, 1940; d. Thomas and Dorothy (Hofft) Lord; m. David Melvin Zurn, Sept. 2, 1960 (div. Sept. 1970); children: Rena Zurn Fulweiler, Amelie Susan, Christopher F.; m. Lester Roy Westphal, May 26, 1971. Student, Brown U., 1958-60; BS, Gannon U., 1974; JD, Case Western Res. U., 1978. Bar: Ohio 1979. Assoc. Kohrman, Jackson, Weiss, Cleve., 1980-81; sole practice, 1981-92. Trustee Emma Willard Sch., Troy, N.Y., 1978-80; dir. Ohioans for Merit Selection of Judges, Cuyahoga County, 1979; mem. Vol. Lawyers for the Arts, Citizens League of Cleve., Women's City Club Found.; treas. Women's Community Fund, 1991-92, Desert Foothills Music Fest. Mem. ABA, Ohio Bar Assn., Cleve. Bar Assn., Cleve. Women's Bar Assn, Pi Gamma Mu. Club: Cleve. Skating, Desert Mountain. Avocations: reading, sailing, the arts. General corporate, Estate planning, Personal income taxation. E-mail: joriel@earthlink.net

WESTWOOD, JAMES NICHOLSON, lawyer; b. Portland, Oreg., Dec. 3, 1944; s. Frederick Alton and Catherine (Nicholson) W.; m. Janet Sue Butler, Feb. 23, 1980; children: Laura, David. BA, Portland State U., 1967; JD, Columbia U., 1974. Bar: Oreg. 1974, U.S. Dist. Ct. Oreg. 1974, U.S. Ct. Appeals (9th cir.) 1978, U.S. Supreme Ct. 1981, U.S. Ct. Appeals (fed. cir.) 1984, U.S. Ct. Appeals (D.C. cir.) 1997. Assoc. Miller, Anderson, Nash, Yerke & Wiener, Portland, 1974-76, 78-81; asst. to pres. Portland State U., 1976-78; ptnr. Miller, Nash, Wiener, Hager & Carlsen, Portland, 1981-99, Stoel Rives LLP, Portland, 1999—. Recipient Disting. Svc. award Portland State U. Found., 1984, Outstanding Alumni award Portland State U., 1992. Mem. ABA (chmn. forest resources com. 1987-89), Oreg. Bar Assn. (chmn. appellate practice sect. 1996-97), Am. Acad. Appellate Lawyers, Univ. Club (bd. govs. 1994), City Club (pres. 1991-92), Park Blocks Found. (pres. 1999—). Republican. Unitarian. Federal civil litigation, State civil litigation, Government contracts and claims. Home: 3121 NE Thompson St Portland OR 97212-4908 Office: Stoel Rivers LLP 900 SW 5th Ave Ste 2600 Portland OR 97204-1268 E-mail: jnwestwood@stoel.com

WETSCH, LAURA JOHNSON, lawyer; b. Fargo, N.D., Nov. 18, 1959; d. Ronald Lee Johnson and Jacqualene Lee (Goudie) Johnson Trefz; m. John Robert Wetsch, Aug. 29, 1981; children: Julie Elizabeth, Katherine Anne, John Michael. AA, Bismarck (N.D.) State Coll., 1980; BA, U. N.D., 1982, JD, 1985. Bar: N.D. 1985, N.C. 1992. Law clk. to Hon. Patrick A. Conmy, U.S. Dist. Ct. for N.D., Bismarck, 1985-88; pvt. practice, Langdon, N.D., 1988-91; assoc. Jordan Price Wall Gray Jones & Carlton, PLLC, Raleigh, N.C., 1992-99; dir., v.p. legal affairs Hytec Cons., Inc., Cary, 1999—; of counsel Joyce L. Davis & Assocs., Raleigh, 1999—. Instr. bus. and criminal law U. N.D.-Lake Region, Cavalier, 1990-91; instr. paralegal studies Ctrl. Carolina C.C., Sanford, N.C., 1991-92; instr. bus. law Wake Tech. C.C., Raleigh, 1992-93. Author, editor (pamphlet) Crime Survivors Handbook, 1996; editor N.D. Women Lawyers Assn. Newsletter, 1990-91; contbr. articles to profl. jours. Vol. mediator and arbitrator Burleigh County Housing Authority, Bismarck, 1986-88; concessions co-chmn. Sanderson H.S. Band Boosters, 1996-2000; curbside cons. in employment law, N.C. Ctr. for Nonprofits, 1998. Mem. Nat. Employment Lawyers Assn., N.C. Bar Assn. (citizen edn. com. young lawyers divsn. 1994-96, chmn. membership svcs. com. young lawyers divsn. 1996-97), N.C. Acad. Trial Lawyers, Wake County Bar Assn. (fee arbitration com. 2001—). Democrat. Roman Catholic. Civil rights, General civil litigation, Labor. Office: Joyce L Davis & Assocs Two Hannover Sq Ste 1730 Raleigh NC 27602-0709 E-mail: lwetsch@jldavis.com

WETZEL, VOLKER KNOPPKE, law educator; BA, Wayne State U., 1966; MA, Goethe U., Franfurt, Fed. Republic Germany, 1967; LLD, U. Wis.-Madison, 1971. Bar: Wis. 1971, U.S. Dist. Ct. Wis. 1971, U.S. Supreme Ct. 1971. Asst. prof. law U. Wis.-Madison, 1971-74; vis. prof. law Bielefeld U., Fed. Republic Germany, 1974-76; dir. criminal justice U. West Fla., Pensacola, 1976-77; assoc. prof. law Vt. Law Sch., Royalton, 1977-81; dir. jud. edn. Wis. Supreme Ct., Madison, 1981—; cons. German Ministry Justice, Bonn, 1977—. Author: Defense of Criminal Cases in Wisconsin, 1974. Co-editor: Wis. Jud. Benchbooks, 1982. Contbr. articles to profl. jours. Bd. dirs. Ctr. for Comparative Law and Social Scis., Madison, 1982—. Russell Sage fellow, 1967-69; NEH fellow, 1980. Mem. Nast. Assn. State Jud. Educators (pres. 1994-95), Wis. Bar Assn., Internat. Sociol. Assn., Sociology of Law Rsch. Com. Address: Dir Judicial Edn Wis Supreme Ct 408 S Page St Stoughton WI 53589-2168

WETZLER, MONTE EDWIN, lawyer; b. N.Y.C., May 7, 1936; s. Alvin and Sally (Epstein) W.; m. Sally Jane Elsas, Dec. 19, 1963; 1 child, Andrew Elsas. AB, Brown U., 1957; LLB, U. Va., 1960; LLM in Taxation, NYU, 1966. Bar: N.Y. 1960, Calif. 1979. Assoc. Regan Goldfarb Heller Wetzler & Quinn, N.Y.C., 1960-66, ptnr., 1966-73, mng. ptnr., 1973-81; sr. v.p., gen. counsel Damson Oil Corp., N.Y.C., 1981-86, exec. v.p., CFO, 1986-88; pres. B&D Equities Inc., 1986-88; ptnr. Breed, Abbott & Morgan, N.Y.C., 1988-93, mng. ptnr., 1992-93; ptnr., exec. com. Whitman Breed Abbott & Morgan, N.Y.C., 1993-96; ptnr. Brown Raysman, Millstein Felder & Stein, 1997—. Editor: Selected Problems in Securities Law, 1972, Joint Ventures and Privatization in Eastern Europe, 1991-92. Counsel, N.Y. State Senate Com. on Housing, N.Y.C. Recipient Svc. award Practicing Law Inst., N.Y.C., 1973. Mem. ABA, N.Y. State Bar Assn. (exec. com. bus. law sect. 1993-94, securities law com.), Bar Assn. City N.Y., Harmonie Club (gov. 1983-84, 86-88), N.Y. Yacht Club, Essex Yacht Club, Phi Delta Phi, Order of Coif. Republican. Jewish. General corporate, Mergers and acquisitions, Securities. Home: 8 River Road Dr Essex CT 06426-1377 Office: Brown Raysman Millstein 185 Asylum St Ste 3303 Hartford CT 06103-3412

WEXELBAUM, MICHAEL, lawyer; b. Bklyn., Aug. 12, 1946; s. Joseph and Beatrice (Skurnick) W.; m. Cynthia Debra Schorr, Apr. 15, 1973 (dec. 1984); children: Joshua David, Stephanie Faye; m. Joan Brenda Math, Aug. 21, 1994; stepchildren: Jonathan David Kaye, Matthew Lawrence Kaye, Julie Dana Kaye. BA in Econs., Bucknell U., 1968; JD, NYU, 1971. Bar: N.Y. 1972, U.S. Dist. Ct. (so. and ea. dists.) N.Y. 1973, U.S. Dist. Ct. (ea. dist.) Wis. 1998. Assoc. Sherman, Citron & Karasik, P.C., N.Y.C., 1972-80, ptnr., head litigation dept., 1980-2001; ptnr. litigation dept. Snow Becker Krauss P.C., 2001—. Arbitrator Nat. Arbitration Forum, 1999—. Arbitrator Am. Arbitration Assn. and Gen. Arbitration Coun. of Textile and Apparel Industries, N.Y.C., 1982—. Mem. Bankruptcy Lawyers Bar Assn., Lawyers Assn. Textile and Apparel Industries (bd. govs.), Am. Arbitration Assn. (arbitrator), Nat. Arbitration Forum (arbitrator). Democratic. Jewish. Avocations: tennis, skiing, biking, theatre. General civil litigation, Contracts commercial, General practice. Home: 85 Norrans Ridge Dr Ridgefield CT 06877-4237 Office: Snow Becker Krauss PC 605 Third Ave New York NY 10158-0125 Office Fax: 212-455-0455. E-mail: mwexelbaum@sbklaw.com

WEXLER, BARBARA LYNNE, lawyer; b. Boston, Feb. 14, 1952; d. Sidney Abraham and Sylvia Dorothy (Finkelstein) W. BS, U. Mass., 1973; JD, Suffolk U., 1977. Bar: Mass. 1977, U.S. Dist. Ct. Mass. 1978, D.C. 1980, U.S. Ct. Appeals (1st cir.) 1982. Asst. dist. atty. Norfolk County, Dedham, Mass., 1977-78; asst. regional counsel Dept. Pub. Welfare, New Bedford, 1978-80, asst. gen. counsel Boston, 1980-88, assoc. gen. counsel for revenue recovery, 1988-93; dep. gen. counsel Divsn. Med. Assistance, 1993—. Trustee Pond Ln. Condominium Trust, Arlington, Mass., 1984-87. Mem. Mass. Bar Assn., Women's Bar Assn., Mass. Lesbian and Gay Bar Assn. Democrat. Jewish. Avocations: quilting, reading. Home: 12 Pond Ln Apt 41 Arlington MA 02474-6640 Office: Divsn Med Assistance 600 Washington St Boston MA 02111

WHALE, MICHAEL JOHN, lawyer, consultant; b. Auckland, New Zealand, June 14, 1953; s. John Frederick and Sheila W.; m. Deborah Joan Alexander, Jan. 29, 1977; children: Andrew, Charlotte, Edward. BCom, Auckland U., 1974; LLB with honors, 1978. Ptnr. Phillips Fox Solicitors, New Zealand, 1981-98; cons., 1998-2000, Lowndes Assocs. Lawyers, New Zealand, 2000—. Bd. dirs. INSOL Internat., Eng., chmn.; lectr. (part-time) U. Auckland, 1999-2000; co-convenor insolvency com. New Zealand Law Soc./Inst. Chartered Accts., 1993—. Bd. trustees Mt. Carmel Sch., Auckland, 1991-93; consul-gen. (hon.) for Thailand, Auckland, 1995—. Fellow Inst. Chartered Accts. New Zealand, Chartered Inst. Corp. Mgmt. New Zealand Inc.; mem. New Zealand Law Soc., Northern Club. Avocations: jogging, badminton, theatre, opera, reading. Alternative dispute resolution, Bankruptcy, General corporate. Office: Lowndes Assocs Level 5 18 Shortland St Auckland New Zealand Fax: 373 3423. E-mail: mjwhale@xtra.co.nz, whale@lowndeslaw.com

WHALEN, LAURENCE J. federal judge; b. 1944; BA, Georgetown Coll., 1967; JD, Georgetown U., 1970, LLM in Taxation, 1971. Judge U.S. Tax Ct., Washington, 1987—; atty. Crowe & Dunlevy, Oklahoma City, Hamel & Park, Washington. Spl. asst. to Asst. Atty. Gen.; trial atty., tax div. U.S. Dept. Justice. With USAR, 1971. Mem. ABA (taxation, litigation and bus. law sects.), Fed. Bar Assn. Office: US Tax Ct 400 2nd St NW Washington DC 20217-0002

WHALEN, PAUL LEWELLIN, lawyer, educator, mediator; b. Lexington, Ky. s. Elza Boz and Barbara Jean (Lewellin) W.; m. Teena Gail Tanner, Jan. 26, 1985; children: Ashley, Lars, Lucy. BA, U. Ky.; JD, Northern Ky. U.; cert., Bonn U., Fed. Republic Germany, 1981; student, U.S. Army J.A.G. Sch., 1988; diploma, USAF Squadron Officers Sch., 1998. Bar: W.Va. 1984, U.S. Ct. Appeals (6th cir.) 1984, Ky. 1985, U.S. Ct. Appeals (4th cir.) 1985, Ohio 1993. Assoc. Geary Walker, Parkersburg, W.Va., 1984-85; prin. Paul L. Whalen, Ft. Thomas, Ky., 1985—; advisor Families with Children from China, 1998—; prof. Def. Acquisition U., WP AFB; prof. pub. contract law Air Force Inst. Tech., 1999-2000; atty. Dept. of Air Force, Office of Chief Trial Atty. Contract Law Ctr., Wright Patterson AFB, 1988—89; hearing officer, prosecutor Ky. Dept. Ednl. Profl. Stds. Bd., 1995—97; mem. arbitration panel No. Ky., 1997—, Montgomery County, Ohio, 1998—; hearing officer Ky. Dept. Edn. IDEA, 1999—2000. Mem. Leadership No. Ky., Ft. Thomas Bd. Edn., 1987—99, chmn., 1990—94; mem. Ky. Bd. Edn., 2000—, Ky. Commn. on Human Svcs.; pres. ch. coun. HOMC, 2000; mem. Campbell County Foster Care Rev. Bd., Newport, Ky., 1986; bd. dirs. Ky. Coun. Child Abuse, Inc. Com. for Kids; dir. Ky. Sch. Bd. Assn., 1993—98; mem. Air Force Bicycle Team Ride Across Iowa, 1997—2000. Recipient Commendation No. Ky. Legal Aid, 1986-2001. Fellow Commonwealth Inst. Leadership; mem. Fed. Bar Assn., No. Ky. Bar Assn., Optimist Club, Kiwanis Club, Phi Alpha Delta. Democrat. Methodist. Avocations: freelance writing, stamp collecting, politics, amateur radio, bicycling. Consumer commercial, Family and matrimonial, Government contracts and claims. Home: 113 Ridgeway Ave Fort Thomas KY 41075-1333 Office: PO Box 22 Fort Thomas KY 41075 E-mail: paul.whalen@dau.mil

WHALEN, WAYNE W. lawyer; b. Savanna, Ill., Aug. 22, 1939; s. Leo R. and Esther M. (Yackley) W.; m. Paula Wolff, Apr. 22, 1970; children: Amanda, Clementine, Antonia, Nathaniel. BS, U.S. Air Force Acad., 1961; JD, Northwestern U., 1967. Bar: Ill. 1967, U.S. Ct. Appeals (7th cir.) 1968, U.S. Supreme Ct. 1972. Commd. 1st lt. USAF, 1961, ret., 1964; assoc. Mayer, Brown & Platt, Chgo., 1967-74, ptnr., 1974, Skadden, Arps, Slate, Meagher & Flom (Ill.), Chgo., 1984—. Bd. dirs. Van Kampen Funds, Oak Brook, Ill. Author: Annotated Illinois Constitution, 1972. Del. 6th Ill. Constitutional Conv., 1969-70, chmn. style drafting and submission com. Named Outstanding Young Lawyer, Chgo. Bar Found., 1970. Mem. Chgo. Club. General corporate. Office: Skadden Arps Slate Meagher & Flom 333 W Wacker Dr Ste 2100 Chicago IL 60606-1220

WHARTON, JOHN MICHAEL, lawyer; b. Ames, Iowa, June 16, 1944; s. Michael M. and M. Myrna (Petersen) W.; m. Pamela M. Rafdal, June 28, 1986; children: Lisa Elaine, Kimberly. BS, Iowa State U., 1967; JD, Drake U., 1970. Bar: Iowa 1970, Fla. 1972, U.S. Dist. Ct. (no. and so. dists.) Iowa 1974, U.S. Ct. Appeals (8th cir.) 1975, U.S. Ct. Mil. Appeals 1971. With Peddicord, Wharton, Thune & Spencer, PC, Des Moines, 1974—. Mem. Iowa Bd. Law Examiners, Des Moines, 1983-90. Capt. JAGD, USAF, 1970-74. Recipient Disting. Svc. award Phi Alpha Delta, 1970. Mem. ABA, Iowa State Bar Assn., Iowa Acad. Trial Lawyers, Lawyer-Pilots Bar Assn., Def. Rsch. Inst., Iowa Def. Counsel Assn., Assn. Trial Lawyers Am., Des Moines Golf and Country Club. Republican. Presbyterian. Federal civil litigation, State civil litigation, Insurance. Office: Peddicord Wharton Thune & Spencer PC 405 6th Ave Ste 700 Des Moines IA 50309-2415

WHARTON, THOMAS H(EARD), JR. lawyer; b. Houston, Dec. 18, 1930; s. Thomas Heard and Laura (Wellhausen) W. B.A., Rice U., 1952; LL.B., U. Tex., 1955. Bar: Tex. 1955, U.S. Dist. Ct. (so. dist.) Tex. 1966, U.S. Ct. Appeals (5th cir.) 1972. Assoc. firm Vinson & Elkins, Houston, 1959-70, ptnr., 1970— . Co-author: How to Live and Die with Texas Probate, 1969; Texas Estate Administration, 1975. Served with USN, 1956-59. Fellow Am. Coll. Probate Counsel, Tex. Bar Found. (life); mem. ABA, Houston Bar Assn. Republican. Methodist. Clubs: Houston, Houston City, Governors, Met. Racquet (Houston). Probate, Estate taxation. Home: 2210 Welch St Houston TX 77019-5618 Office: Vinson & Elkins 3400 1st City Tower 1001 Fannin St Ste 3300 Houston TX 77002-6706

WHATLEY, JACQUELINE BELTRAM, lawyer; b. West Orange, N.J., Sept. 26, 1944; d. Quirino and Eliane (Gruet) Beltram; m. John W. Whatley, June 25, 1966 (dec. July 1998). BA, U. Tampa, 1966; JD, Stetson U., 1969. Bar: Fla. 1969, Alaska 1971; cert. real estate law splst. Assoc. Tucker, McEwen, Smith & Cofer, Tampa, Fla., 1969-71; pvt. practice Anchorage, 1971-73; ptnr. Gibbons, Tucker, Miller, Whatley & Stein, P.A., Tampa, 1973—; pres., 1981—. Bd. dirs. Travelers Aid Soc., 1982-94; trustee Humana Women's Hosp., Tampa, 1987-93, Keystone United Meth. Ch., 1986-89, 99—. Mem. ABA, Fla. Bar Assn. (real estaet cert. com. 1993-95), Alaska Bar Assn., Tenn. Walking Horse Breeders and Exhibitors Assn. (v.p. 1984-87, dir. Fla. 1981-87, 90-93, 97-99, adv. com. Tenn. Walking Horse Celebrateion 1994-97), Fla. Walking and Racking Horse Assn. (bd. dirs. 1988-89, pres. 1980-82), Athena Club (Tampa). Republican. Methodist. Contracts commercial, Real property. Home: PO Box 17595 Tampa FL 33682-7595 Office: 101 E Kennedy Blvd Ste 1000 Tampa FL 33602-5146 E-mail: whatley@gte.net

WHEALE, DUNCAN DOUGLAS, lawyer; b. Bridgeport, Conn., Apr. 14, 1947; s. Howard Douglas and Mary Elizabeth (Wallace) W.; m. Carolyn Ann Alexander, Sept. 7, 1974; children— Douglas Ryan, Patrick John. B.S., The Citadel, 1969; LL.B. magna cum laude, John Marshall Law Sch., 1976. Bar: Ga. 1976, U.S. Dist. Ct. (no., mid. and so. dists.) Ga., U.S. Ct. Appeals (5th and 11th cirs.). Ptnr. Fulcher Law Firm, Augusta, Ga., 1976— ; chmn. Augusta Ports Authority, 1983— . Commr. Ga.-Carolina council Boy Scouts Am., 1979-82. Served to 1st lt. U.S. Army, 1970-71. Mem. State Bar Ga., Assn. Trial Lawyers Am., Ga. Def. Lawyers, The Citadel Alumni Assn. (bd. dirs. 1981—). Episcopalian. Federal civil litigation, State civil litigation. Home: 3720 Inverness Way W Lake Augusta GA 30907 Office: Fulcher Law Firm 520 Greene St Augusta GA 30901-1404

WHEAT, JOHN NIXON, lawyer; b. Liberty, Tex., Dec. 15, 1952; s. Thomas Allen and Dora (Arrendell) W. BA, Tulane U., 1975; JD, St. Mary's U., San Antonio, 1977. Bar: Tex. 1978, U.S. Dist. Ct. (ea. dist.) Tex. 1978, U.S. Ct. Appeals (5th cir.) 1979. Law clk. U.S. Dist. Ct. Ea. Dist. Tex., Beaumont, 1978-79; pvt. practice The Wheat Firm, Liberty, Tex., 1979—. Vice chmn. Chambers-Liberty County Navigation Dist., 1994-99, chmn., 1999—; pres. chpt. 10 Sons of Republic of Tex.; bd. dirs. Express Theater, Houston, Sam Houston Libr. and Rsch. Ctr.-Tex. State Archive.

Mem. ABA, Tex. Bar Assn., Liberty-Chambers County Bar Assn., Houston Bar Assn., Tower Club of Beaumont, Magnolia Ridge County Club, Knights of Neches, Delta Theta Phi. Republican. Episcopalian. Avocations: ranching, hunting, riding, philosophy. Banking, Probate, Real property. Office: 1704 Cos Ave PO Box 10050 Liberty TX 77575-7550

WHEATLEY, CHARLES HENRY, III, lawyer, biomedical technology company executive; b. Balt., Aug. 11, 1932; s. Charles Henry Jr. and Rebecca W. (Cloud) W.; m. Charlotte Beryl Davis, June 11, 1955; children: Charles H. IV, Craig A., Cheryl L. W. Jackson. BA in Polit. Sci. with hons., Western Md. Coll., 1954; JD with hons., U. Md., 1959. Bar: Md. 1960, D.C. 1981, U.S. Supreme Ct. 1964. Tchr. Carroll County Pub. Schs., Westminster, Md., 1955-56; officer, judge advocate U.S. Army, 1957-62; law clk. assoc. judge William R. Horney Md. Ct. Appeals, Annapolis, 1959-60; pvt. practice Md. and Washington, 1960—; mem. Md. legislature Ho. of Dels., Annapolis, 1962-66; pres., COO Cell Works, Inc., Balt., 1997—. Real estate, ins. exec. AID Realty & Ins. Co., Balt., 1960—; adj. coll. instr. Western Md. coll., Westminster, 1963-65, Villa Julie Coll., 1980-86, Balt. Cmty. Col., 1966-72; mem. adv. bd. Fleet Bus. Sch., Annapolis, Md., 1986-2001, Balt. Cmty. Col., 1986—; chmn. bd., ceo Regional Mfg. Inst., Balt., 1993-96; nat. del. White House Conf. on Small Bus., Washington, 1985. Contbr., editor: (weekly newspaper) Maryland Teacher, 1974-77; guest News Makers program WJZ-TV, 1985; contbr. articles to profl. jours. Md. del. Md. State Constitutional Convention, Annapolis, 1967-68; councilman Balt. City Coun., 1971-74. 1st lt. JAG U.S. Army, 1957-62. Received Cell Works Co. Computerworld-Smithsonian Science Innovation laureate award, 1999. Mem. Md. Commn. Mfg. Competitiveness, Md. State Bar Assn., Dist. Columbia Bar. Assn., Md. State Tchrs. Assn. (exec. sec. 1974-77), Order of the Coif, Pi Gamma Mu. Democrat. Methodist. Avocations: education, music, writing, photography, health. General corporate, Health, Legislative. Office: Cell Works Inc 6200 Seaforth St Baltimore MD 21224-6506

WHEELAN, R(ICHELIEU) E(DWARD), lawyer; b. N.Y.C., July 10, 1945; s. Richard Fairfax and Margaret (Murray) W. BS, Springfield (Mass.) Coll., 1967; MS, Iona Coll., 1977; JD, Pace U., 1981. Bar: N.Y. 1982, Minn. 1983, Colo. 1989, Tex. 1990, U.S. Dist. Ct. (no dist.) Calif. 1982, (so. dist.) Tex. 1991, U.S. Internat. Trade 1982, U.S. Ct. Appeals (2d cir.) 1982, (9th cir.) 1983, (5th cir.) 1993, U.S. Supreme Ct. 1994, U.S. Tax Ct. 1998; bd. cert. criminal law, trial advocacy. Lt. of detectives White Plains (N.Y.) Police Dept., 1969-81; area counsel IBM, Armonk, N.Y., 1981-89; gen. counsel Kroll Assocs. (Asia), Hong Kong, 1989-91; pvt. practice, Houston, 1991—. Mem. ABA (mem. sentencing guidelines com.), Nat. Assn. Criminal Def. Lawyers (life mem., mem. death penalty com., champion adv. bd.), Coll. of State Bar Tex., Pro Bono Coll. StateBar Tex., Tex. Assn. Criminal Def. Lawyers, NY State Bar Assn., NY Co. Lawyers Assn. Criminal, Personal income taxation. Office: 440 Louisiana St Houston TX 77002-1639

WHEELER, ANNE MARIE, lawyer; b. Plainfield, N.J., Apr. 27, 1954; d. William Joseph and Joan Agnes (McCarthy) Stief; m. Gary Marvin Wheeler, Aug. 16, 1980; children: Gary, Stephen, Claire. BA, Cath. U., 1976; JD, George Washington U., 1980. Bar: D.C. 1981, Md. 1990, U.S. Dist. Ct. D.C. 1981, U.S. Ct. Appeals (D.C. cir.) 1981. Law clk. to presiding justices FERC, Washington, 1980-81; atty. Kimberly-Clark Corp., Arlington, Va., 1982-83; assoc. Onek, Klein & Farr, Washington, 1983-91; of counsel Crowell & Moring LLP, 1991—. Ward rep. Takoma Park (Md.) Traffic Com., 1984-86. Mem. ABA, D.C. Bar Assn., Women's Bar Assn. D.C., Phi Beta Kappa. Democrat. Roman Catholic. Health, Personal injury. Home: 14608 Cutstone Way Silver Spring MD 20905-7444 Office: Crowell & Moring LLP 1001 Pennsylvania Ave NW Washington DC 20004 E-mail: nwheeler@crowell.com

WHEELER, CHARLES VAWTER, lawyer; b. Fay, Okla., Nov. 12, 1920; s. Claude A. and Bertha (Cooke) W.; m. Maryjo Meacham, Jan. 23, 1943; children— Allison Ann, Meacham. Student Harding Coll., 1938-39; student U. Okla., 1939-43, LL.B., 1948; student U. Tex., 1947; LL.M., NYU, 1973. Bar: Okla., 1943. Atty., Southwestern Bell Telephone Co., Oklahoma City, 1948-53; mem. firm Cantrell, Carey & McCloud, Oklahoma City, 1953-58; with Cities Service Co., Tulsa, 1958-83, gen. counsel, 1969-83; counsel Gable & Gotwalls, Tulsa, 1983-89; adj. prof. U. Tulsa, 1989-92; pvt. practice, Tulsa, 1992—; asst. adj. gen. State of Okla., 1966-68. Served with AUS, 1943-47, 50-52. Decorated Legion of Merit. Mem. ABA, Okla. Bar Assn., N.Y. State Bar Assn., N.G. Assn., Delta Tau Delta, So. Hills Country Club. Democrat. Unitarian. Home: 2300 Riverside Dr Apt 181 Tulsa OK 74114-2400 Office: 2000 E 4th Pl Tulsa OK 74104-2202

WHEELER, JAMES JULIAN, lawyer; b. Independence, Mo., Mar. 20, 1921; s. Luther I. and Edith (Hesler) W.; m. Janet L. Esau, Apr. 28, 1951; children: Linnell Gretzinger, Robert W. LLB, U. Mo., 1948. Bar: Mo. 1948, U.S. Dist. Ct. (ea. dist.) Mo. 1956. Prosecuting atty. County of Chariton, Mo., 1950-54, probate judge, 1974-75; circuit judge 9th Judicial Circuit Court, 1976-82; sole practice Keytesville, 1948-74, 82—. Served as cpl. USMC, 1941-46, PTO. Mem. ABA, Mo. Bar Assn., Am. Judicature Soc., Assn. Trial Lawyers Am. Democrat. State civil litigation, Criminal, General practice. Home: 112 Kennedy Ave Keytesville MO 65261 Office: 304 Walnut St Keytesville MO 65261-1064

WHEELER, JOHN WATSON, lawyer; b. Murfreesboro, Tenn., Sept. 11, 1938; s. James William and Grace (Fann) W.; m. Dorothy Anita Pressgrove, Aug. 5, 1959; children: Jeffrey William, John Harold. BS in Journalism, U. Tenn., 1960, JD, 1968. Bar: Tenn. 1968, U.S. Dist. Ct. (ea. dist.) Tenn. 1968, U.S. Supreme Ct. 1974, U.S. Ct. Appeals (6th cir.) 1975. Editor The Covington (Tenn.) Leader, 1963-65; adminstrv. asst. to lab. dir. UT-AEC Rsch. Lab., Oak Ridge, Tenn., 1965-68; assoc. Hodges, Doughty & Carson, Knoxville, 1968-72, ptnr., 1972—. Mem. commn. to study Applellate Cts. in Tenn.; chair U.S. Magistrate Merit Selection Panel, Ea. Dist., Tenn., 1991; mem. Bankruptcy Judge Merit Selection Panel, Ea. Dist. Tenn., 1992-94; chmn. Hist. Soc., U.S. Dist. Ct. (ea. dist.) Tenn. Mem. organizing com. Tenn. Supreme Ct. Hist. Soc. Lt. U.S. Army, 1961-63, capt. Res. Fellow Am. Bar Found. (life, Tenn. chair 1999—), Tenn. Bar Found. (life); mem. ABA (ho. of dels. 1986-2000), Tenn. Bar Assn. (pres. 1989-90, bd. govs. 1981-91), Nat. Conf. Bar Pres., Am. Inns. of Ct. (master of bench, emeritus), Internat. Assn. Def. Counsel, So. Conf. Bar Pres., 6th Cir. Jud. Conf. (life), Fox Den Country Club. Republican. Lutheran. Avocations: golf, travel. General civil litigation, Insurance, Workers' compensation. Home: 12009 N Fox Den Dr Knoxville TN 37922-2540 Office: Hodges Doughty & Carson PO Box 869 Knoxville TN 37901-0869

WHEELER, MALCOLM EDWARD, lawyer, law educator; b. Berkeley, Calif., Nov. 29, 1944; s. Malcolm Ross and Frances Dolores (Kane) W.; m. Donna Marie Stambaugh, July 25, 1981; children: Jessica Ross, M. Connor. SB, MIT, 1966; JD, Stanford U., 1969. Bar: Calif. 1970, Colo. 1992, U.S. Dist. Ct (cen. dist.) Calif. 1970, U.S. Ct. Appeals (9th cir.) 1970, U.S. Ct. Appeals (10th cir.) 1973, U.S. Dist. Ct. (no., so., ea. and cen. dists.) Calif. 1975, U.S. Ct. Appeals (11th cir.) 1987, U.S. Ct. Appeals (D.C. cir.) 1987, U.S. Supreme Ct. 1976, U.S. Ct. Appeals (3d cir.) 1989, (4th cir.) 1992, (8th cir.) 1993, (5th cir.) 1995, (Fed. cir.) 1998. Assoc. Howard, Prim, Smith, Rice & Downs, San Francisco, 1969-71; assoc. prof. law U. Kans., Lawrence, 1971-74; assoc. Hughes Hubbard & Reed, Los Angeles, 1974-77, ptnr., 1977-81, 83-85, cons., 1981-83; ptnr. Skadden, Arps, Slate, Meagher & Flom, 1985-91; dir. Parcel, Mauro, Hultin & Spaanstra P.C., Denver, 1991-98, Wheeler Trigg & Kennedy, P.C., Denver, 1998—. Vis. prof. U. Iowa, 1978, prof., 1979; prof. U. Kans., Lawrence, 1981-83; chief counsel U.S. Senate Select Com. to Study Law Enforcement Undercover Activities, Washington, 1982-83. Mem. editorial bd. Jour. Products Liability, 1984—; bd. editors Fed. Litigation Guide Reporter, 1986—; contbr. articles to profl. jours. Mem. ABA, Calif. Bar Assn., Colo. Bar Assn., Am. Law Inst. Federal civil litigation, General civil litigation, Product liability. Home: 100 Humboldt St Denver CO 80218-3932

WHEELER, RAYMOND LOUIS, lawyer; b. Ft. Sill, Okla., Feb. 10, 1945; s. Raymond Louis and Dorothy Marie (Hutcherson) W.; m. Priscilla Wheeler, July 1, 1966 (div. 1982); children: Jennifer, Hilary; m. Cynthia Lee Jackson, July 14, 1984 (div. 1994); children: Matthew Raymond, Madeline Elizabeth; m. Freddie Kay Park, June 10, 1995. BA, U. Tex., 1967; JD, Harvard U., 1970. Bar: Calif. 1972, U.S. Dist. Ct. (no., cen., ea. dists.) Calif., U.S. Ct. Appeals (9th cir.), U.S. Supreme Ct. Law clk. to hon. Irving L. Goldberg U.S. Ct. Appeals 5th cir., 1970-71; assoc. Morrison & Foerster, San Francisco, 1971-76, ptnr., 1976-90, Palo Alto, Calif., 1990—. Chmn. labor and employment law dept. Morrison & Foerster, San Francisco, 1984-88, 92—; lectr. labor and EEO law. Exec. editor Harvard Law Rev., 1969-70; editor in chief The Developing Labor Law; mem. nat. adv. bd. Indsl. Rels. Law Jour., 1980—; contbr. articles to law jours. Fellow Coll. Labor and Employment Lawyers; mem. ABA (chmn. com. on law devel. under labor rels. act 1990-93, coun. mem. sect. labor and employment 1994—). Republican. Labor. Office: Morrison & Foerster 755 Page Mill Rd Palo Alto CA 94304-1018 E-mail: rwheeler@mofo.com

WHEELER, WILLIAM CHAMBERLAIN, JR. association administrator, lawyer; b. Bklyn., Feb. 25, 1945; s. William Chamberlain and Helen (Spencer) W. BA, Amherst Coll., 1967; JD, Vanderbilt U., 1970. Bar: Mich. 1979; cert. assn. exec. Assoc. dir. manuscript acquisition Prentice-Hall, Inc., Englewood Cliffs, N.J., 1971-75; asst. dir. dept. law and taxation NYU Sch. Continuing Edn., 1975-77; dir. office continuing legal edn. U. Detroit Sch. Law, 1977-79; sr. rsch. scientist Hwy. Safety Rsch. Inst. U. Mich., 1978-79; cons. Dept. Transp., Washington, 1979-82; exec. dir. Assn. Continuing Legal Edn. Adminstrs., 1983-86; dir. edn. Am. Soc. Safety Engrs., Des Plaines, Ill., 1986-92; exec. v.p. Chgo. Assn. Life Underwriters, 1995-98; prin., CEO ADA Exec. Search, Inc., Chgo., 2000—. Dir. continuing legal edn. courses and publs., nat. insts. ABA, Chgo., 1982-86. Mem. ABA, State Bar Mich. Assn., Chgo. Soc. Assn. Execs., Fed. Bar Assn., Am. Soc. Assn. Execs., Phi Delta Phi. Office: Am Soc Safety Engrs 3716 N Fremont St Chicago IL 60613-3912

WHERRY, EDWARD JOHN, JR. lawyer; b. Trenton, N.J., Dec. 6, 1942; s. Edward John and Rita Ann (Convery) W.; m. Margaret Sherlene Lang, Apr. 12, 1969; children: John, Christopher, Patricia. BS, Villanova U., 1964; JD, U. Fla., 1967. Bar: N.J. 1967, U.S. Supreme Ct. 1973; cert. civil and criminal trial atty. N.J. Supreme Ct. and Nat. Bd. Trial Advocacy. Ptnr. Voorhees, Bennett & Wherry, Pennington, N.J., 1982-90, of counsel, 1990—. Adj. prof. of law and co-dir. Intense Advocacy Program Sch. of Law Widener U., Wilmington, Del., 1983-90, vis. assoc. prof. law, 1990-92, assoc. prof. 1992-95; mem. faculty Nat. Inst. for Trial Advocacy, 1984—; team leader N.E. Regional Program, 1985—; founding dean U. Orlando Sch. Law, 1995-96. Mem. ABA, N.J. Bar Assn., Mercer County Bar Assn., N.J. Trial Lawyers Assn., Am. Arbitration Assn., Nat. Assn. of Criminal Def. Lawyers, N.J. Criminal Def. Lawyers Assn. Home: PO Box One South Orleans MA 02662 E-mail: jwherry@capecod.net

WHICHARD, WILLIS PADGETT, law educator, former state supreme court justice; b. Durham, N.C., May 24, 1940; s. Willis Guilford and Beulah (Padgett) W.; m. Leona Irene Paschal, June 4, 1961; children: Jennifer Diane, Ida Gilbert. AB, U. N.C., 1962, JD, 1965; LLM, U. Va., 1984, SJD, 1994. Bar: N.C. 1965. Law clk. N.C. Supreme Ct., Raleigh, 1965-66; ptnr. Powe, Porter, Alphin & Whichard, Durham, 1966-80; assoc. judge N.C. Ct. Appeals, Raleigh, 1980-86; assoc. justice N.C. Supreme Ct., 1986-98; dean and prof. law Campbell U. Instr. grad. sch. bus. adminstrn. Duke U., 1978; vis. lectr. U. N.C. Sch. Law, 1986-98. Contbr. articles to profl. jours. Rep. N.C. Ho. of Reps., Raleigh, 1970-74; senator N.C. Senate, 1974-80, chair numerous coms. and commns.; N.C. legis. rsch. commn., 1971-73, 75-77, land policy coun., 1975-79; bd. dirs. Sr. Citizens Coordinating Coun., 1972-74; chair local crusade Am. Cancer Soc., 1977, state crusade chair, 1980, chair pub. issues com., 1980-84; pres., bd. chmn. Downtown Durham Devel. Corp., 1980-84; bd. dirs. Durham County chpt. ARC, 1971-79; Durham county campaign dir. March of Dimes, 1968, 69, chmn., 1969-74, bd. dirs. Triangle chpt., 1974-79; bd. advisors Duke Hosp., 1982-85, U. N.C. Sch. Pub. Health, 1985-96, U. N.C. Sch. Social Work, 1989—; bd. visitors N.C. Ctrl. U. Sch. Law, 1987—; mem. law sch. dean search com. U. N.C., 1978-79, 88-89, self-study com., 1985-86; pres. N.C. Inst. Justice, 1984-94; bd. dirs. N.C. Ctr. Crime and Punishment, 1984-94. Staff sgt. N.C. Army NG, 1966-72. Recipient Disting. Service award Durham Jaycees, 1971, Outstanding Legis. award N.C. Acad. Trial Lawyers, 1975, Outstanding Youth Service award N.C. Juvenile Correctional Assn., 1975, Citizen of Yr., Eno Valley Civitan Club, Durham, 1982, Faith Active in Pub. Life award N.C. Council of Churches, 1983, Outstanding Appellate Judge award N.C. Acad. Trial Lawyers, 1983, inducted Durham High Sch. Hall of Fame, 1987. Mem. ABA, N.C. Bar Assn. (v.p 1983-84), Durham County Bar Assn., U. N.C. Law Alumni Assn. (pres. 1978-79, bd. dirs. 1979-82), Nat. Guard Assn. (judge advocate 1972-73, legis. com. 1974-76), Order of Golden Fleece, Order of Grail, Order of Old Well, Amphoterothen Soc., Order of Coif, Phi Alpha Theta, Phi Kappa Alpha. Democrat. Baptist. Clubs: Durham-Chapel Hill Torch (pres. 1984-85), Watauga (Raleigh, pres. 1994-95). Home: 5608 Woodberry Rd Durham NC 27707-5335 Office: Wiggins Sch Law Campbell Univ PO Box 158 Buies Creek NC 27506-0158 E-mail: Whichard@webster.campbell.edu, whichool@earthlink.net

WHINSTON, STEPHEN ALAN, lawyer; b. Stamford, Conn., Mar. 27, 1948; s. Alfred Leonard and Rose (Eisgrau) W.; m. Joan Lenett, June 4, 1978; children: Stephanie Portnoy, Brian Arasim, Joshua. BA, Colgate U., 1970; JD, Case Western Res. U., 1973. Bar: Pa. 1973, U.S. Dist. Ct. (ea. dist.) Pa. 1973, U.S. Ct. Appeals (3d cir.) 1973, U.S. Ct. Appeals (8th cir.) 1995. Trial atty. U.S. Dept. Justice, Washington, 1974-79, sr. trial atty., 1979-83; atty. Berger & Montague, P.C., Phila., 1983-85, shareholder, 1986—. Bd. dirs. Disabilities Law Project, Phila., 1989—, Jewish Fedn. Housing, Inc., Cherry Hill, N.J., 1994-96. Mem. Pa. Prison Soc. (bd. dirs.). Avocation: music. Civil rights, General civil litigation, Securities. Office: Berger & Montague PC 1622 Locust St Philadelphia PA 19103-6305 E-mail: saw@bm.net

WHIPPLE, DEAN, federal judge; b. 1938; BS, Drury Coll., 1961; postgrad., U. Tulsa, 1961-62; JD, postgrad., U. Mo., 1965. Pvt. practice, Lebanon, Mo., 1965-75; cir. judge div. II 26th Jud. Cir. Mo., 1975-87; judge U.S. Dist. Ct., Kansas City, Mo., 1987-2000, chief judge, 2000—. Prosecuting atty. Laclede County, Mo., 1967-71. Mem. Cen. United Meth. Ch., Kansas City. With Mo. N.G., 1956-61; USAR, 1961-66. Mem. Mo. Bar Assn. (mem. pub. info. com. 1971-72, mem. judiciary com. 1971-72, mem. bd. govs. 1975-87, mem. exec. com. 1983-84, 86-87, mem. planning com. for ann. meeting 1985, 87, chmn. 1986, mem. selection com. for Lon Hocker award 1986), Mo. Trial Judges Assn., 26th Jud. Bar Assn., Laclede County Bar Assn. (pres. 1968-69, 72-73), Kansas City Met. Bar Assn., Kansas City Inn of Ct. (instr. 1988-93), Mo. Hist. Soc., Phi Delta Phi. Office: US Courthouse 400 E 9th St Kansas City MO 64106-2607

WHIPPLE, ROBERT JENKS, lawyer; b. Worcester, Mass., June 16, 1912; s. Robert Lee and Mildred Dean (Jenks) W.; m. Eleanor G. Thayer, Jan. 12, 1946 (div. 1958); children— Jeffrey, Wendy; m. Anne Coghlan, Nov. 3, 1960; children— Michael, Ellen. B.A., Princeton U., 1934; LL.B., Harvard U., 1937; hon. LL.D., Central New Eng. Coll., 1983. Bar: Mass. 1937, U.S. Dist. Ct. Mass. 1948, U.S. Supreme Ct. 1969. Assoc. Ropes Gray Boyden & Perkins, Boston, 1937-41, Gage Hamilton & June, Worcester, 1946-48; ptnr. June Fletcher & Whipple, Worcester, 1948-72; dir. Fletcher Tilton & Whipple, P.C., Worcester, 1972-96, ret. 1997; v.p., gen. counsel Warren Pumps, Inc., Mass., 1953-72; dir. Shawmut Worcester County Bank, N.A., Worcester, 1974-88; asst. dist. atty. Office Dist. Atty., Worcester County, 1947. Served to maj. AUS, 1941-45. Fellow Am. Coll. Probate Counsel; mem. ABA, Mass. Bar Assn., Worcester County Bar Assn. Republican. Unitarian. Clubs: Tatnuck Country (pres. 1960-62); Worcester (pres. 1970-72). General corporate, Probate, Personal income taxation. Home: 84 Briarwood Cir Worcester MA 01606-1200 Office: Fletcher Tilton & Whipple PC 370 Main St Worcester MA 01608-1723

WHITAKER, BENJAMIN PALMER, JR. lawyer; b. Hartford, Conn., July 4, 1937; s. Benjamin Palmer and Helen Frances (Johnson) W.; m. Susan Ann McIlwaine, Oct. 6, 1962 (div. 1983); children— Jeanne Ann, Benjamin Palmer III, Scott Theodore; m. 2d Janet Elizabeth Langley, June 4, 1983. B.S., Princeton U., 1958; J.D., Albany Law Sch., 1961. Bar: N.Y. 1962, adminstrv. asst. U.S. Ho. of Reps., Washington, 1961-63; ptnr. Allen and O'Brien, Rochester, N.Y., 1966-83; gen. counsel Pub. Enterprises, Inc., Rochester, 1983-85; sole practice, 1985—; chmn. bd. dirs., chief exec. officer Irving Place Capital and Investment Corp., Rochester, N.Y. Served to capt. USAF, 1963-65. Democrat. General corporate, Probate, Real property. Home: 1111 Park Ave Rochester NY 14610-1738 Office: 30 W Broad St Old City Hall Suite 505 Rochester NY 14614

WHITAKER, GLENN VIRGIL, lawyer; b. Cin., July 23, 1947; s. Glenn M. and Doris (Handlon) W.; m. Jennifer Lynn Angus, Oct. 22, 1990. BA, Denison U., 1969; JD, George Washington U., 1972. Bar: Md. 1972, D.C. 1973, Ohio 1980. Law clk. to judge U.S. Dist. Ct., Balt., 1972-73; assoc. O'Donoghue and O'Donoghue, Washington, 1973-76; trial atty. civil div. U.S. Dept. Justice, 1976-78, spl. litigation counsel, 1978-80; ptnr. Graydon, Head & Ritchey, Cin., 1980-92, Vorys, Sater, Seymour & Pease, Cin., 1992—. Emeritus master of bench Potter Stewart Inn of Ct., Cin., 1985—; adj. prof. law Coll. Law U. Cin..; mem. Am. Bd. Trial Advocates. Fellow Am. Coll. Trial Lawyers; mem. ABA, Ohio Bar Assn., D.C. Bar Assn., Md. Bar Assn., Cin. Bar Assn. Avocations: hiking, exploring. General civil litigation, Criminal, Personal injury. Office: Vorys Sater Seymour & Pease 221 E 4th St Ste 2100 Cincinnati OH 45202-5133

WHITAKER, MARY FERNAN, lawyer; b. Kansas City, Mo., May 29, 1958; d. James Paul and Mildred Louise (Connor) Fernan; m. Mark Dwight Whitaker, May 28, 1983; children: Paul Connor, James Sullivan, Helen Foster. BSN, George Mason U., 1982, JD, 1987. Bar: Va. 1987, Pa. 1995; cert. swim coach, Md. cert. swim judge. Nurse George Washington Med. Ctr., Washington, 1980-82, Mt. Vernon Hosp., Alexandria, Va., 1982-84; atty. Legal Svcs. No. Va., Arlington, 1987, Office Rev. and Appeals, EEOC, Falls Church, Va., 1987-88; pvt. practice Annadale, 1988-93, Pottsville, Pa., 1993-95, Coopersburg, 1995-96, Solomons, Md., 1996—. Adj. faculty paralegal program No. Va. C.C., 1992; counselor, mem. legal com. My Sister's Pl., Washington, 1987-93; mem. pro bono panel Legal Svcs. No. Va., Falls Church, 1997—. Vol. ARC, Alexandria, 1987; vol. atty. Women's Legal Def. Fund, Washington, 1989-91, Legal Svcs. No. Va., 1997—; mem. Shelter Outreach Program, 1990-93; v.p. Ravensworth Bristow Civic assn., 1990-93; head makeup design for cmty. theatre troupe Camelot Players, 1990-91; tchr. 3d grade religious edn. St. Michael's Ch. Choir, 1991-92, tchr. 8th grade religious edn., 1992-93, choir, 1992-93; tchr. 7th grade religious edn. St. Joseph Ch., 1995-96; swimmer U.S. Masters, 1997, 98; cert. stroke and turn judge Md. Swimming, 1998—. U.S. Master Swimmer, 1997-98. Mem. Va. State Bar Assn., Fairfax Bar Assn., Phi Delta Phi. Roman Catholic. Avocations: bicycling, swimming. Home and Office: 7104 Marlan Dr Alexandria VA 22307

WHITAKER, RONALD STEPHEN, lawyer; b. Cleve., Oct. 26, 1957; s. Wilbert S. and Dolores J. Whitaker; m. Carolyn M. Conyers, Sept. 29, 1984; children: Christopher, Chelsea. BA, UCLA, 1980, JD, 1983. Bar: Calif. 1983, U.S. Dist. Ct. (cen. dist.) Calif., 1983, U.S. Dist. Ct. (so. dist.) Calif., 1984, U.S. Dist. Ct. (ea. dist.) Calif., 1993, U.S. Ct. Appeals (9th cir.) 1983. Assoc. Ritter, Winne & Rodriguez, L.A., 1983-86, Spray, Gould & Bowers, L.A., 1986-88, prin., 1988-91; shareholder, founding mem. Robinson, Dilando & Whitaker, 1991—. Mem. ABA, Am. Bd. Trial Advocates, Def. Rsch. Inst., L.A. County Bar Assn., Nat. Bar Assn., John M. Langston Bar Assn. Republican. Avocations: basketball, softball. General civil litigation, Insurance, Labor. Office: Robinson Dilando & Whitaker 800 Wilshire Blvd Ste 1100 Los Angeles CA 90017-2615 E-mail: rwhitaker@rdwlaw.com

WHITAKER, THOMAS PATRICK, lawyer; b. Washington, Sept. 22, 1944; s. Thomas J. and Mary K. (Finn) W.; m. Donna Mae Brenish, Feb. 16, 1974; children: Laura, Kevin. BA, George Washington U., 1966, MPA, 1973, JD, 1979; postgrad., Naval War Coll., 1984. Bar: Va. 1979. Staff asst. Adminstrn. Office of U.S. Cts., Washington, 1972-73, analyst, 1975-77; cons. Planning Research Corp., McLean, Va., 1973-75; mgmt. analyst CAB, Washington, 1977-82; program analyst Social Security Adminstrn., Falls Church, Va., 1982—. Served to lt. (j.g.) USNR, 1966-71, Vietnam, capt. with Res. 1983-97. Acting U.S. Naval Attache, Malaysia, 1992. Mem. U.S. Naval Inst., Naval Res. Assn., Res. Officers Assn. Home: 9817 Days Farm Dr Vienna VA 22182-7306 E-mail: twhitake@hotmail.com

WHITE, BARRY BENNETT, lawyer; b. Boston, Feb. 13, 1943; s. Harold and Rosalyn (Schneider) W.; m. Eleanor Greenberg; children: Joshua S., Adam J., Benjamin D. AB magna cum laude, Harvard U., 1964, JD magna cum laude, 1967. Bar: Mass. 1967, U.S. Dist. Ct. Mass. 1967, U.S. Ct. Appeals (1st cir.) 1967. Assoc. Foley Hoag & Eliot, Boston, 1969-74, ptnr., 1975—, mem. exec. com., 1981-92, 93—, chmn. exec. com., 1987-91, mng. ptnr., 1991-92, 93—, mem. exec. com., 1991-96, sec., 1992-93. Chmn. Lex Mundi, 1994. Editor Harvard Law Rev., 1965-67. Sec., gen. counsel, exec. com. Greater Boston C. of C., Initiative for Competitive Inner City; bd. dirs., exec. com. Mass. Assn. Mental Health, 1985—, pres., 1993-95; bd. dirs. Boston Mcpl. Rsch. Bur., Vol. Lawyers Project, 1987-93, Support Ctr. of Mass., 1988-95; mem. Jewish Family and Children's Svcs., Boston, 1979-87; bd. visitors Boston U. Grad. Sch. Dentistry, 1981—; bd. trustees Jewish Cmty. Rels. Coun., 1988-92; chmn. com. for Clinton/Gore New Eng. Lawyers, 1992-96; chmn. Tsongas for Pres. Com., 1991-98. With USPHS, 1967-69. Mem. ABA, Mass. Bar Assn., Boston Bar Assn., Internat. Bar Assn., Am. Acad. Hosp. Attys., Am. Hosp. Assn. (adj. task force on health planning 1982-84, contbg. editor hosp. law manual 1981-84), Harvard Club Boston, Badminton and Tennis Club. Democrat. General corporate, Health, Private international. Office: Foley Hoag & Eliot 1 Post Office Sq Ste 1700 Boston MA 02109-2175 E-mail: bbwhite@fhe.com

WHITE, CHERYL DENNEY, lawyer; b. Akron, Ohio, Aug. 23, 1949; d. Chester Vernon and Marjorie Jean (Kinsey) Denney; m. Christopher John White, May 22, 1976. BA, U. Mo., 1971; JD, U. Mo., Kansas City, 1976; MLT, Georgetown U., 1981. Bar: Mo. 1977, U.S. Tax Ct. 1978, D.C. 1979, U.S. Claims Ct. 1981. Trial atty. IRS, Washington, 1977-81; assoc. Dickstein, Shapiro & Morin, 1981-86, Kaye, Scholer, Fierman, Hays & Handler, N.Y.C., 1986-87; asst. gen. counsel Prudential Ins. Co. Am., Newark, 1987-2000, v.p., corp. counsel, 2001—. Mem. ABA, Mo. Bar Assn., D.C. Bar Assn., Women in Employee Benefits, Inc. (nat. exec. bd. 1986-87, pres. N.Y. chpt. 1987-88). E-mail: (office) (personal). Pension, profit-sharing, and employee benefits. Office: Prudential Ins Co Am 751 Broad St 13-Pla Newark NJ 07102 E-mail: cheryl2.white@prudential.com, denney.white@worldnet.att.net

WHITE, EDWARD ALFRED, lawyer; b. Elizabeth, N.J., Nov. 23, 1934; BS in Indsl. Engring., U. Mich., 1957, JD, 1963. Bar: Fla. 1963, U.S. Ct. Appeals (5th cir.) 1971, U.S. Ct. Appeals (11th cir.) 1981, U.S. Supreme Ct. 1976. Assoc. Jennings, Watts, Clarke & Hamilton, Jacksonville, Fla., 1963-66, ptnr., 1966-69, Wayman & White, Jacksonville, 1969-72; pvt. practice, 1972—. Mem. aviation law com. Fla. Bar, 1972-94, chmn., 1979-81, bd. govs., 1984-88, admiralty com., 1984—, chmn., 1990-91, chmn. pub. relations com., 1986-88, exec. coun. trial lawyers sect., 1986-91, chmn. admiralty cert. com., 1995-97. Fellow Am. Bar Found.; mem. ABA (vice chmn. admiralty law com. 1995—), Fla. Bar Assn. (bd. cert. civil trial lawyer, bd. cert. admiralty lawyer), Jacksonville Bar Assn. (chmn. legal ethics com. 1975-76, bd. govs. 1976-78, pres. 1979-80), Assn. Trial Lawyers Am. (sustaining mem. 1984—), Acad. Fla. Trial Lawyers (diplomate), Fla. Coun. Bar Assn. Pres.'s, Lawyer-Pilots Bar Assn., Am. Judicature Soc., Maritime Law Assn. (proctor in admiralty), Southeastern Admiralty Law Inst. (bd. dirs. 1982-084, chmn., pres. 1994). Admiralty, General civil litigation, Personal injury. Home: 1959 Largo Rd Jacksonville FL 32207-3926 Office: 901 Blackstone Bldg 233 E Bay St Jacksonville FL 32202-3452 Fax: 904-356-6508

WHITE, EDWARD GIBSON, II, lawyer; b. Lexington, Ky., Nov. 7, 1954; s. Russell Edwin White and Betty Lee White-Estabrook; m. Cynthia Ann Reisz, Mar. 10, 1979; children: Edward Gibson III, William Elliot, John Alexander, Albert Grahm. BA, U. Tenn., Chattanooga, 1980; JD, U. Tenn., Knoxville, 1983. Bar: Tenn. 1983, U.S. Dist. Ct. (ea. dist.) Tenn. 1984, U.S. Ct. Appeals (6th cir.) 1985. Assoc. Hodges, Doughty & Carson, Knoxville, 1983-87, ptnr., 1988—. Bd. dirs. Knoxville affiliate The Susan G. Komen Breast Cancer Found., Inc., Elizabeth R. Griffin Rsch. Found. Mem. ABA (litigation sect. 1985—), Tenn. Bar Assn. (interprofl. code com. 1989—, med./legal com. 1991—), Knoxville Bar Assn. (treas. 1995-96, continuing legal edn. com. 1985-86, 88-91, chmn. 1992-94, mem. naturalization com. 1985-87, bd. govs. 1993-94, pres. elect 1996, pres. 1997, Pres.'s award 1992), Tenn. Def. Lawyers Assn., Def. Rsch. Inst. (med./legal com. 1985—), Am. Bd. Trial Advocates, Knoxville Bar Found. (bd. dirs.), U. Tenn. Pres.'s Club, Univ. Club, Cherokee Country Club, Knoxville Racquet Club. Republican. Avocations: tennis, golf, boating, water sports, bird hunting. General civil litigation, Insurance, Personal injury. Office: Hodges Doughty & Carson 617 Main St # 869 Knoxville TN 37902-2602

WHITE, GEORGE EDWARD, law educator, lawyer; b. Northampton, Mass., Mar. 19, 1941; s. George LeRoy and Frances Dorothy (McCafferty) W.; m. Susan Valre Davis, Dec. 31, 1966; children: Alexandra V., Elisabeth McC. BA, Amherst Coll., 1963; MA, Yale U., 1964, PhD, 1967; JD, Harvard U., 1970. Bar: D.C. 1970, Va. 1975, U.S. Supreme Ct. 1973. Vis. scholar Am. Bar Found., 1970-71; law clk. to Chief Justice Warren U.S. Supreme Ct., 1971-72; asst. prof. law U. Va., 1972-74, assoc. prof., 1974-77, prof., 1977-86, John B. Minor prof. law and history, 1987-92, disting. univ. prof., John B. Minor prof. law and history, 1992—. Vis. prof. Marshall-Wythe Law Sch. spring 1988, N.Y. Law Sch., fall 1988. Author books, including: The American Judicial Tradition, 1976, 2d edit., 1988, Tort Law in America: An Intellectual History (gavel award ABA 1981), 1980, Earl Warren: A Public Life (gavel award ABA 1983), 1982, The Marshall Court and Cultural Change, 1988, 2d edit., 1991 (James Willard Hurst prize 1990), Justice Oliver Wendell Holmes: Law and the Inner Self, 1993 (gavel award ABA 1994, Scribes award, 1994, Littleton-Griswold prize 1994, Triennial Order of the Coif award 1996), Intervention and Detachment: Essays in Legal History and Jurisprudence, 1994; Creating the National Pastime: Baseball Transforms Itself, 1903-1953, 1996, The Constitution and The New Deal, 2000; editor Studies in Legal History, 1980-86, Delegate in Law, 1986-97. Mem. AAAS, Am. Law Inst., Am. Soc. Legal History (bd. dirs. 1978-81), Soc. Am. Historians. Office: Law Sch U Va Charlottesville VA 22903-1789 E-mail: gewhite@law5.law.virginia.edu

WHITE, HARRY EDWARD, JR. lawyer; b. Menominee, Mich., Apr. 26, 1939; s. Harry Edward and Verena Charlotte (Leisen) W.; m. Mary P.A. Sheaffer, June 7, 1980. BS in Fgn. Svc., Georgetown U., Washington, 1961; LLB, Columbia U., 1964. Bar: N.Y. 1965, U.S. Supreme Ct. 1970, U.S. Dist. Ct. (so. dist.) N.Y. 1979, U.S. Tax Ct. 1980. Assoc. Milbank, Tweed, Hadley & McCloy, N.Y.C., 1964-65, 67-73, ptnr., 1974—. Contbr. chpts. to books, articles to legal jours. Served with M.I., U.S. Army, 1965-66, Vietnam. Decorated Bronze Star. Mem. ABA, Internat. Bar Assn., N.Y. State Bar Assn. (chmn. taxation com. internat. law practice sect. 1987-90, co-chmn. exempt orgns. com. tax sect. 1987-88), Internat. Law Assn., Am. Soc. Internat. Law, Assn. Bar of City of N.Y., Internat. Fiscal Assn. Republican. Roman Catholic. Corporate taxation, Taxation, general, Personal income taxation. Home: 333 E 55th St New York NY 10022-8316 Office: Milbank Tweed Hadley & McCloy 1 Chase Manhattan Plz Fl 47 New York NY 10005-1413 E-mail: hwite@milbank.com

WHITE, HUGH VERNON, JR. lawyer; b. Suffolk, Va., July 24, 1933; s. Hugh Vernon and Mary Lois (Claud) W.; m. Mary Margaret Flowers, Nov. 25, 1961; children: Hunter, William, John. BS in Civil Engring., Va. Mil. Inst., 1954; LLB, Washington & Lee U., 1961. Bar: Va. 1961. Engr. E.I. DuPont de Nemours & Co., Parlin, N.J., 1954-55; exec. dir. Va. Legis. Study Comm., Richmond, Va., 1961-63; assoc. Hunton & Williams, 1963-69, ptnr., 1969-99, sr. counsel, 1999—. Bd. dirs. Chesapeake Corp., Richmond, Va. Mem. Richmond First, 1966—, pres., 1971; bd. trustees Va. Hist. Soc., 1997—, Randolph-Macon Woman's Coll., 1997—, YMCA of Greater Richmond, 1996—, chmn. 2000-01. Lt. USAF, 1955-58. Mem. ABA, Va. Bar Assn., Richmond Bar Assn., Phi Beta Kappa, Omicron Delta Kappa. Presbyterian. Clubs: Commonwealth, Country (Richmond). Home: 512 S Gaskins Rd Richmond VA 23233-5710 Office: Hunton & Williams Riverfront Plaza East Tower PO Box 1535 Richmond VA 23218-1535 E-mail: hwhite@hunton.com

WHITE, JAMES BOYD, law educator; b. Boston, July 28, 1938; s. Benjamin Vroom and Charlotte Green (Conover) W.; m. Mary Louise Fitch, Jan. 1, 1978; children: Emma Lillian, Henry Alfred; children by previous marriage: Catherine Conover, John Southworth. AB, Amherst Coll., 1960; AM, Harvard U., 1961, LLB, 1964. Assoc. Foley, Hoag & Eliot, Boston, 1964-67; asst. prof. law U. Colo., 1967-69, assoc. prof., 1969-73, prof., 1973-75; prof. law U. Chgo., 1975-83; Hart Wright prof. law and English U. Mich., Ann Arbor, 1983—. Vis. assoc. prof. Stanford U., 1972 Author: The Legal Imagination, 1973, (with Scarboro) Constitutional Criminal Procedure, 1976, When Words Lose Their Meaning, 1981, Heracles' Bow, 1985, Justice as Translation, 1990, "This Book of Starres", 1994, Acts of Hope, 1994, From Expectation to Experience, 1999, The Edge of Meaning, 2001. Sinclair Kennedy Traveling fellow, 1964-65; Nat. Endowment for Humanities fellow, 1979-80, 92; Guggenheim fellow, 1993; vis. scholar Phi Beta Kappa, 1997-98. Mem. AAAS, Am. Law Inst. Office: U Mich Law Sch 625 S State St Ann Arbor MI 48109-1215

WHITE, JAMES RICHARD, lawyer; b. McKinney, Tex., Jan. 22, 1948; s. James Ray and Maxine (Brown) W.; children: Nicole Olivia, Mandi Leigh, James Derek. BBA, So. Meth. U., 1969, MBA, 1970, JD, 1973, LLM, 1977. Bar: Tex. 1973, U.S. Tax Ct. 1975, U.S. Supreme Ct. 1989, U.S. Ct. Appeals (5th cir.) 1989); cert. Comml. Real Estate Law Tex. Bd. Legal Specialization. Assoc. Elliot, Meer, Vetter, Denton & Bates, Dallas, 1973-74, Atwell, Cain & Davenport, Dallas, 1974-75; atty. Sabine Corp., 1975-77; assoc. Brice & Barron, 1977-79; ptnr. Millard & Olson, 1979-82, Johnson & Swanson, Dallas, 1982-83, Winstead, Sechrest & Minick P.C., Dallas, 1983—, hiring ptnr., 1987-2001, exec. com., 2000-01. Mem. staff Southwestern Law Jour., Dallas, 1971-73; mem. So. Meth. U. Moot Ct. Bd., Order Barristers, Dallas, 1972-73; prof. North Lake Coll., Dallas, 1985; bd. dirs. Tex. Assn. Young Lawyers, Austin, 1980-82; sec. bd. dirs. Dallas Assn. Young Lawyers, 1976-80. Contbr. articles to profl. jours. Chmn. bd. dirs. Tex. Lawyers Credit Union, Austin, 1980-82; pres. North Tex. Premier Soccer Assn., Dallas, 1979-81; v.p. Lake Highlands Soccer Assn., 1995-96, pres., 1996—; mem. regional mobility task force Real Estate Coun., City of Dallas, 1991-92, mem. downtown revitalization com., 1995-97; mem. Dallas Indsl. Devel. Bd., 1992-93, Dallas Higher Edn. Authority Bd., 1994-96; spkr.'s bur. and accreditation divsn. World Cup USA '94. Mem. ABA (mem. title ins. and survey, mortgage loan origination and structure com., mortgage financing and opinion, non-traditional comml. real estate fin. coms.), Tex. Bar Assn. (cert. 1973, mem. mortgage loan opinion com.), Tex. Coll. Real Estate Attys., Coll. State Bar Tex. Methodist. Avocations: soccer, golf, skiing, racquetball. Banking, Finance, Real property. Home: 8003 Hundley Ct Dallas TX 75231-4728 Office: Winstead Sechrest & Minick 5400 Renaissance Tower 1201 Elm St Ste 5400 Dallas TX 75270-2199 E-mail: jrwhite@winstead.com

WHITE, JEFFERY HOWELL, lawyer; b. Tyler, Tex., Aug. 4, 1959; s. Bluford D. and Tempie R. (Tunnell) W.; m. Michael Anne Mackley, May 21, 1989; children: Kristin, Alex, Landry. BS in History, So. Ark. U., 1983; JD, Oklahoma City U., 1986. Bar: Tex. 1987. Assoc. Dean White, Canton, Tex., 1986-90; asst. dist. atty. Van Zandt Co., 1991-94; ptnr. Elliott Elliott & White, 1994-97; pvt. practice Tex., 1997—. Mem. Van Zandt County Bar Assn. (v.p. 1999-2000, pres. 2000—), Tex. Criminal Def. Lawyers Assn. (sustaining), Tex. State Bar (dist. 1-A grievance com. 1996—). Democrat. United Methodist. Avocations: golf, tennis, spectator sports. Criminal, Family and matrimonial, Juvenile. Home: Box 1200 Van TX 75790-1200 Office: 157 N Buffalo St Canton TX 75103-1353

WHITE, JILL CAROLYN, lawyer; b. Santa Barbara, Calif., Mar. 20, 1934; d. Douglas Cameron and Gladys Louise (Ashley) W.; m. Walter Otto Weyrauch, Mar. 17, 1973. BA, Occidental Coll., L.A., 1955; JD, U. Calif., Berkeley, 1972. Bar: Fla. 1974, Calif. 1975, D.C. 1981, U.S. Dist. Ct. (no. and mid. dists.) Fla., U.S. Ct. Appeals (5th and 11th cirs.), U.S. Supreme Ct. Staff mem. U.S. Dept. State, Am. Embassy, Rio de Janeiro, 1956-58; with psychol. rsch. units Inst. Human Devel., Inst. Personality Assessment and Rsch., U. Calif., Berkeley, 1961-68; adj. prof. criminal justice program U. Fla., Gainesville, Fla., 1976-78; pvt. practice immigration and nationality law, 1976—. Contbr. articles to profl. jours. Mem. ABA, Am. Immigration Lawyers Assn. (bd. dirs. Ctrl. Fla. chpt. 1985-94, 95-96, 97-2000, chmn. Ctrl. Fla. chpt. 1988-89, co-chmn. so. regional liaison com. 1990-92, nat. bd. dirs. 1988-89), Bar Assn. 8th Jud. Cir. Fla., Fla. Bar (immigration and nationality law cert. com. 1994-99, chmn. cert. com. 1997-98, cert. in immigration and nationality law 1995-2005), Gainesville Area C. of C., Gainesville Area Innovation Network, Altrusa. Democrat. Immigration, naturalization, and customs. Office: 2830 NW 41st St Ste C Gainesville FL 32606-6667 E-mail: jwhite@cgnv.net

WHITE, JOHN JOSEPH, III, lawyer; b. Darby, Pa., Nov. 23, 1948; s. John J. Jr. and Catherine (Lafferty) W.; m. Catherine M Staley, Dec. 9, 1983. BS, U. Scranton, 1970; MPA, Marywood U., 1977; JD, Loyola U., New Orleans, 1983. Bar: Pa. 1983, U.S. Dist. Ct. (ea. dist.) Pa. 1983, N.J. 1984, U.S. Ct. Appeals (3d cir.) 1983, U.S. Dist. Ct. N.J. 1984, U.S. Tax Ct. 1984, D.C. 1985, U.S. Supreme Ct. 1987. Exec. dir. Scranton (Pa.) Theatre Libre, Inc., 1973-77; pub. Libre Press Inc., Scranton, 1977-83; pvt. practice Phila., 1983—. Pres. eMercury, Inc., Lansdowne, Pa., 1987—; N.Am. agt. Palacky U. Med. Sch., Olomouc, Czech Republic, 1995-2001. Founder, pub. Metro Mag., 1977-83. Founder, Scranton Pub. Theatre, 1976; dir. Scranton Theatre Libre, Inc., 1973. Capt. USAF, 1970-73; col. Res., 1973-89, col. ANG, 1999—, ret. 2000. Mem. ABA, Pa. Trial Lawyers Assn., Phila. Bar Assn., Phila. Trial Lawyers Assn., Air Force Assn. (chpt. pres. 1975—), Phi Delta Phi Internat. Legal Frat. Democrat. Roman Catholic. Avocations: jogging, art collecting. General civil litigation, Private international, Personal injury. E-mail: lawfirmusa@aol.com

WHITE, KATHERINE PATRICIA, lawyer; b. N.Y.C., Feb. 1, 1948; d. Edward Christopher and Catherine Elizabeth (Walsh) W. BA in English, Molloy Coll., 1969; JD, St. John's U., 1971. Bar: N.Y. 1972, U.S. Dist. Ct. (ea. and so. dists.) N.Y., 1973, U.S. Supreme Ct. 1976. Atty. Western Electric Co., Inc., N.Y.C., 1971-79; sr. atty. AT&T Corp., 1979-96, chief regulatory counsel-New Eng., 1996-97, law and govt. affairs v.p., gen. atty.-New Eng., 1997—. Adj. prof. law N.Y. Law Sch., N.Y.C., 1987-88, Fordham U. Sch. Law, 1988-91; bd. dirs. First Security Benefit Life Ins. Co. N.Y. Vol. Sloan Kettering Inst., 1973, North Shore U. Hosp., 1975, various fed., state and local polit. campaigns; judge N.Y. State Bicentennial Writing Competition, N.Y.C., 1977-78; chmn. Com. to Elect Supreme Ct. Judge, N.Y.C., 1982. Mem. Am. Corp. Counsel Assn., N.Y. State Bar Assn. (bus. and banking law com. real estate law sect., corp. counsel sect.), Assn. Bar City N.Y. (adminstrv. law com. 1982-85, young lawyers com. 1976-79, judge nat. moot ct. competition 1979-91), Cath. Lawyers Guild for Diocese of Rockville Centre (pres. 1980-81), St. John's U. Sch. Law Alumni Assn. (pres. L.I. chpt. 1986-88), Women's Nat. Rep. Club (bd. govs. 1988-91), Met. Club. Avocations: racing sailboats, figure skating, golf, tennis. Administrative and regulatory, Contracts commercial, Public utilities. Home: 1035 5th Ave Apt 14D New York NY 10028-0135 Office: AT&T 32 Avenue Of The Americas New York NY 10013-2473

WHITE, KENNETH JAMES, lawyer; b. Bryan, Ohio, Apr. 16, 1948; s. James Foster and Doris E. (Hatfield) W.; m. Diane G. Frechette, Sept. 20, 1969; children: James Renald, David Kenneth. BS cum laude in Journalism, Bowling Green State U., 1970; JD cum laude, U. Toledo, 1974. Bar: Ohio 1974, U.S. Dist. Ct. (no. dist.) Ohio 1974, U.S. Ct. Appeals (6th cir.) 1983. Law clk. to pres. judge U.S. Dist. Ct., Toledo, Ohio, 1974-76; ptnr. Spengler, Nathanson, McCarthy & Durfee, Toledo; ptnr. Jacobson, Maynard, Tuschman & Kalur, 1985—. Articles editor U. Toledo Law Rev. 1973-74. Author: (with others) Appellate Practice, Ohio Legal Center Institute, 1981; bd. govs., treas. U. Toledo Coll. Law Alumni Assn. Mem. Ohio Bar Assn., Toledo Bar Assn., The Fornoff Soc. (charter mem.), Ct. Practice Inst. (diplomate 1978). Federal civil litigation, State civil litigation, Personal injury. Home: 468 Patriot Dr W Waterville OH 43566-1152 Office: Jacobson Maynard Tuschman & Kalur 333 N Summit St Ste 1600 Toledo OH 43604-2617

WHITE, LINDA DIANE, lawyer; b. N.Y.C., Apr. 1, 1952; d. Bernard and Elaine (Simons) Schwartz; m. Thomas M. White, Aug. 16, 1975; 1 child, Alexandra Nicole. AB, U. Pa., 1973; JD, Northwestern U., 1976. Bar: Ill. 1976. Assoc. Walsh, Case, Coale & Brown, Chgo., 1976-77, Greenberger & Kaufmann (merged into Katten, Muchin), Chgo., 1977-82, ptnr., 1982-85, Sonnenschein Nath & Rosenthal, Chgo., 1985—. Mem. ABA (real property fin. com., comml. leasing com., real property, probate and trust law sect. 1987—), Ill. Bar Assn., Chgo. Bar Assn., Practicing Law Inst. (chmn. program on negotiating comml. leases 1995-99, real estate law adv. com.). Contracts commercial, Landlord-tenant, Real property. Office: Sonnenschein Nath & Rosenthal 8000 Sears Tower 233 S Wacker Dr Ste 8000 Chicago IL 60606-6491 E-mail: lwhite@sonnenschein.com

WHITE, MARY JO, prosecutor; BS, Coll. William $ Mary; MS in Psychology, Columbia U., JD, 1974. Chief asst. U.S. atty. Ea. Dist. N.Y., Bklyn.; U.S. atty. So. Dist. N.Y., Manhattan, 1993—. Office: US Attys Office 1 Saint Andrews Plz New York NY 10007-1701*

WHITE, MICHAEL LEE, lawyer; b. Dilley, Tex., Mar. 27, 1953; s. Deryl and Ruby Alice (Gillis) W. BA, Tex. A&M U., 1975; JD, U. Houston, 1978. Bar: Tex. 1979. Briefing atty. 14th Ct. Appeals, Houston, 1979; contracts analyst Texaco Inc., 1979-80, legis. coord., 1980-82; mgr. state govt. rels. Pennzoil Co., 1982-85, mgr. employee comms., pub. affairs liaison, 1985-87, mgr. media comm., 1987-88; dir. govt. affairs Met. Transit Authority Harris County, 1988-90; v.p. C. of C. divsn. Greater Houston Partnership, 1990-94; legis. cons., mediator, Austin, Tex., 1994—. Fellow Houston Bar Found.; mem. ABA, State Bar Tex., Houston Bar Assn., Tex. Lyceum Assn. (bd. dirs., exec. com. 1984-89), Travis County Bar Assn. Avocations: golf, tennis, skiing, reading. Office: PO Box 1667 Austin TX 78767-1667

WHITE, NICHOLAS L. legal educator; b. 1925; AB, Ohio Wesleyan U., 1950; JD, U. Cin., 1956. Bar: Ohio 1956, Ind. 1971, Tenn. 1978. Assoc. Taft, Stettinius & Hollister, Cin., 1956-65, ptnr., 1965-70; asst. dean adminstrn. Ind. U., Bloomington, 1970-73, prof. law, 1970-77, assoc. dean, 1974-77; dean, prof. law Memphis State U., 1977-84; prof. law U. Memphis, 1985—. Vis. prof. McGeorge Sch. of Law, Sacramento, Calif., 1984-85; cons. EPA Water Planning Divsn., 1974-77, Nat. Commn. Water Quality, 1975. Served with USMC, 1943-46. Mem. Phi Beta Kappa, Order of Coif, Omicron Delta Kappa. Office: U Memphis School of Law Memphis TN 38152 E-mail: nlwhite@memphis.edu

WHITE, PAMELA JANICE, lawyer; b. Elizabeth, N.J., July 13, 1952; d. Emmet Talmadge and June (Howlett) W. BA, Mary Washington Coll., 1974; JD, Washington and Lee U., 1977. Bar: Md. 1977, U.S. Dist. Ct. Md. 1978, D.C. 1979, U.S. Dist. Ct. D.C. 1979, U.S. Ct. Appeals (4th cir.) 1979, U.S. Ct. Appeals (D.C. cir.) 1981, U.S. Ct. Claims 1981, U.S. Ct. Appeals (2d cir.) 1983, N.Y. 1983, U.S. Dist. Ct. (so. dist.) N.Y. 1983, U.S. Ct. Appeals (9th cir.) 1988, U.S. Supreme Ct. 1981. Assoc. Ober, Grimes & Shriver, Balt., 1977-84; ptnr. Ober, Kaler, Grimes & Shriver, 1985—. Chair Employment Group, 1994—; mem. Md. Bd. Law Examiners, 1986-94; mem. select com. on Gender Equality, 1989-2000, chair, 1997-99; fed. dist. ct. adv. group, Civil Justice Reform Act, 1990. Note and comment editor Washington and Lee Law Rev. 1976-77, Washington and Lee Law Council 1983-87, emeritus mem., 1988-97, pres. 1991-92. Mem. Fed. Ct. Bicentennial Com., 1988-90; vol. Profl. Gov.'s Drug-Free Workplace Initiative, 1990-93; bd. trustees Washington and Lee U., 1995—. Named Disting. Alumna, Washington and Lee U., 1994, Hon. mem. Order of the Coif, 1994, Disting. Alumna, Mary Washington Coll., 2001. Fellow Am. Bar Found., Md. Bar Found. (award for excellence in the advancement of profl. competence 1996, bd. dirs. 2000—); mem. ABA (chair-elect tort and ins. practice employer/employee rels. com. 1998-99, chair 1999-2000, del. 2000—), Balt. Bar Found., Fed. Bar Assn., N.Y. State Bar Assn., Md. Bar Assn. (coun. legal edn. sect. 1987-96, chmn. 1992-93, labor sect. coun. 1992-96, professionalism com. 1991—, chmn. 1994-97, bd. govs. 1993-95, 98—, exec. com. 1994-95, 99-2001, pres.-elect 2000-2001, pres. 2001—), task force on professionalism chair 1996-97), D.C. Bar Assn., Balt. City Bar Assn. (exec. coun. 1995-96, 1997-98), Women's Bar Assn. Md. (treas. 1986-87, v.p. 1987-88, pres.-elect 1988-89, pres. 1989-90, bd. dirs. 1984-86, Rita C. Davidson award 2000), Md. Assn. Def. Counsel, Md. Inst. Continuing Profl. Edn. Lawyers (exec. com. 2000—), Pro Bono Resource Ctr. (exec. com. 2000-). Presbyterian. Avocation: baseball. Federal civil litigation, Labor, State civil litigation. Office: Ober Kaler Grimes & Shriver 120 E Baltimore St Ste 800 Baltimore MD 21202-1643

WHITE, PATRICIA DENISE, dean, law educator; b. Syracuse, N.Y., July 8, 1949; d. Theodore C. and Kathleen (Cowles) Denise; m. Nicholas P. White, Feb. 20, 1971 (div. 1997); children: Olivia Lawrence, Alexander Cowles. BA, U. Mich., 1971, MA, JD, 1974. Bar: D.C. 1975, Mich. 1988, Utah 1995. Assoc. Steptoe & Johnson, Washington, 1975-76; vis. asst. prof. Coll. of Law U. Toledo, 1976-77; assoc. Caplin & Drysdale, Washington, 1977-79; asst. prof. Law Ctr. Georgetown U., 1979-84, assoc. prof. Law Ctr., 1985-88; vis. prof. Law Sch. U. Mich., Ann Arbor, 1988-94; prof. U. Utah, Salt Lake City, 1994-98; counsel Parson, Behle and Latimer, 1995-98; dean, prof. Ariz. State U. Coll. Law, 1999—. Counsel Bodman, Longley and Dahling, Detroit, Ann Arbor, 1990-95. Contbr. articles to profl. jours. Office: Ariz State U Coll Law McAllister & Orange Sts PO Box 877906 Tempe AZ 85287-7906

WHITE, ROBERT JOEL, lawyer; b. Chgo., Nov. 1, 1946; s. Melvin and Margaret (Hoffman) W.; m. Gail Janet Edenson, June 29, 1969 (div. Dec. 1982); m. Penelope K. Bloch, Dec. 22, 1985. BS in Accountancy, U. Ill., 1968; JD, U. Mich., 1972. Bar: Calif. 1972, N.Y. 1985, U.S. Dist. Ct. (cen., ea., so. dists.) Calif. 1972, U.S. Ct. Appeals (9th cir.) 1978, U.S. Ct. Appeals (5th cir.) 1983, U.S. Ct. Appeals (6th cir.) 1984, U.S. Supreme Ct. 1977. Staff auditor Haskin & Sells, Chgo., 1968-69; assoc. O'Melveny & Myers, L.A., 1972-79, ptnr., 1980-2001, chair reorgn. and restructuring dept., 1986—; CEO O'Melvey Cons. LLC, 2001—. Vis. lectr. U. Mich. Law Sch., Ann Arbor, 1986; lectr. Profl. Edn. Sys., Inc., Dallas, 1987, L.A., 1987, 89, Phoenix, 1990, Practicing Law Inst., San Francisco and N.Y.C., 1989-93, Southwestern Legal Found., Dalalas, 1991, UCLA Bankruptcy Inst., 1993, UCLA, 1993; mem. L.A. Productivity Commn., 1993-96. Contbr. articles to profl. jours. Active Constl. Rights Found., 1980—; active Am. Cancer Soc., 1989—, mem. L.A. bd. dirs., 1995—; mem. Nat. Bankruptcy Conf., exec. com., 1999—. Fellow Am. Coll. Brankruptcy; mem. ABA (litigation sect., mem. comml. law and bankruptcy com. 1972—), L.A. County Bar Assn. (comml. law and bankruptcy sect., chmn. fed. cts. com. 1981-82, exec. com. 1982—), Assn. Bus. Trial Lawyers (bd. govs. 1983-85), Fin. Lawyers Conf. (bd. govs. 1986—, pres. 1990-91), Am. Bankruptcy Inst. Avocations: skiing, running, U.S. history. Bankruptcy, General civil litigation. Office: O'Melveny & Myers 400 S Hope St Los Angeles CA 90071-2899

WHITE, RONNIE L. state supreme court justice; AA, St. Louis C.C., 1977; BA, St. Louis U., 1979; JD, U. Mo., Kansas City, 1983. Bar: Mo. Law intern Jackson County Prosecutors Office; legal asst. U.S. Def. Mapping Agy.; trial atty. Office of Pub. Defender; mem. Mo. Ho. of Reps., 1989-93; judge Mo. Ct. Appeals, 1994; spl. judge Mo. Supreme Ct., 1994-95, justice, 1994-95, assoc. justice, 1995—. Adj. faculty Washington U. Sch. Law, 1997—. Office: PO Box 150 Jefferson City MO 65102-0150*

WHITE, ROWAN MCMURRAY, lawyer; b. Belfast, Northern Ireland, Apr. 9, 1953; s. Basil Rowan and Maureen Allen (née McMurray) White; m. Pamela Joan née Mack, August 2, 1980; children: Jonathan. David, Victoria. MA, U. Cambridge, England, 1974. Solicitor: Supreme Ct. Judicature, N. Ireland, 1977. Asst. solicitor Crawford, Lockhart and Co., Belfast, Ireland, 1977-79, J. & A. Caruth & Bamber, Ballymena County Antrim, Ireland, 1979-81, ptnr. Ireland, 1980-83; asst. solicitor Norman Wilson & Co., Belfast, Ireland, 1983-85, ptnr. Ireland, 1985-96, Arthur Cox N. Ireland, Belfast, 1996—. Chmn. Ballymena & Antrim Solicitors Assn., 1982-83, The Belfast Solicitors Assn., 1991-92. Vice-pres. Old Campbellian Soc., Belfast, 2001. Mem. Roll Solicitors, Republic Ireland, Law Soc. Nothern Ireland, Law Soc. Ireland, Royal North Ireland Yacht Club. Avocations: walking, reading. Landlord-tenant, Real property. Office: Arthur Cox Stokes House 17/25 Courer Sq Bast BT1 6HD Belfast Northern Ireland Fax: 028 9023 3464. E-mail: rwhite@arthurcox.ie

WHITE, SHIRLEY FAYE, lawyer; b. San Jose, Costa Rica, Jan. 16, 1955; d. Ernest and Eunice F. White; children: Kari Melissa Gibbs, Julian Richard Gibbs. BS, CUNY, 1980; JD, Atlanta Law Sch., 1994. Bar: Ga. 1997, U.S. Dist. Ct. (no. dist.) Ga. 1997. Pvt. practice, Stone Mountain, Ga., 1997—. Mem. Am. Immigration Lawyers Assn., Hispanic Bar Assn., DeKalb Lawyers Assn. Democrat. Episcopalian. Office: 4820 Redan Rd Ste B Stone Mountain GA 30088

WHITE, WALTER HIAWATHA, JR. lawyer; b. Milw., Aug. 21, 1954; s. Walter H. and Winifred (Parker) W.; m. Sonja Athene Rein, Dec. 30, 1977. Student, Leningrad Pedagogical Inst., USSR, 1976; BA, Amherst Coll., 1977; JD, U. Calif., Berkeley, 1980. Bar: Wis. 1980, U.S. Dist. Ct. (ea. dist.) Wis. 1980, U.S. Ct. Appeals (7th cir.) 1980, U.S. Supreme Ct. 1983. Assoc. Michael, Best & Friedrich, Milw., 1980-88; commr. securities State of Wis., 1988-91; ptnr. Quarles & Brady, Milw., 1991-94; mng. dir. Steptoe & Johnson Internat., Moscow, 1994-99; ptnr. Bryan Cave, London, 1999—. Trustee Milw. Found., 1992—; vice chmn. dist. com. Bd. Attys. Profl. Responsibility, Milw., 1984-87; bd. dirs. Wis. Trust Found., Madison, Church Mut. Ins. Co., Merrill, Wis., Ctrl. Asian Am. Enterprise Fund. Editor Black Law Jour., 1978-80; mem. editorial bd. Barrister Mag.; contbr. articles to profl. jours. Mem. Cardinal Stritch Coll. Bus. Adv. Bd., Milw., 1982-85, health law com. Wis. Civil Liberties Union, Milw., 1985—, Gov.'s Adv. Bd. to Legal Services Corp., Madison, 1982-87; sec. Milw. Forum Inc., 1982—; pres. Milw. Urban League, 1985; bd. dirs. WUWM Pub. Radio Sta., Milw., 1983-86, Family Service Milw., Inc., 1987-89, Neighborhood House of Milw., Inc., 1987—. John Woodruff Simpson fellow, 1977; Named one of the 86 most interesting people in Milw., Milw. Mag., 1986. Mem. ABA (chair young lawyers div. 1989-90, commn. on opportunities for minorities in the profession, del. assn. Soviet lawyers, co-chair commonwealth of ind. states law com. of internat. law and practice sect. 1990-91), Nat. Bar Assn., Assn. Internat. des Jeunes Avocats, Milw. Bar Assn., Wis. Black Lawyers Assn. (bd. dirs. 1982-83), Milw. Young Lawyers Assn. (pres. 1984-85, pres.'s award 1985), Bd. Bar Examiners, Milw. Found. Avocations: Russian lit., rowing, squash. General corporate, Health, Private international. Office: Bryan Cave LLP 33 Cannon St London EC4M 5TE England

WHITE, WILLIAM EARLE, lawyer; b. Dinwiddie County, Va., Aug. 19, 1898; s. William Richard and Annie Eliza (Hone) W.; m. Marian Louise Molloy, Apr. 24, 1924; children— Marion White DiStanislao, William Earle Jr., Stephen Graham. B.A., Richmond Coll., 1917; student Law Sch. Am. Expeditionary Forces, Beaune, France, 1919, Harvard Law Sch., 1920. Bar: Va. 1920, U.S. Ct. Appeals (4th cir.) 1940, U.S. Supreme Ct. 1941. Ptnr. Lassiter & White, 1922-24, White Hamilton Wyche & Shell, Petersburg, Va., 1927— ; ret. dir. 1st & Mechants Nat. Bank, Commonwealth Natural Gas (now part of Columbia Gas). Chmn. Hosp. Authority City of Petersburg. Served to cpl. USMC, 1917-1919. Fellow Am. Coll. Trial Lawyers, Am. Bar Found., Am Coll. Probate Counsel; mem. Am. Judicature Soc., Petersburg C. of C. (past pres.), Petersburg Bar Assn., Va. State Bar (pres. 1963-64). Democrat. Baptist. Federal civil litigation, General corporate, Probate. Office: White Hamilton Wyche & Shell 20 E Tabb St Petersburg VA 23803-4541

WHITE, WILLIAM NELSON, lawyer; b. Balt., Sept. 8, 1938; s. Nelson Cardwell and Ellen Atwell (Zoller) W.; m. Mary Kathleen Bitzel, Sept. 2, 1960 (div. 1971); children: Craig William, Jeffrey Alan, Colin Christopher; m. Christine Lewin Hanna, July 8, 1978. LLB, U. Md., 1968, JD, 1969. Bar: Md. 1972, U.S. Ct. Appeals (4th cir.) 1975, U.S. Dist. Ct. Md. 1976, U.S. Supreme Ct. 1976. Asst. state's atty., Balt., 1972; assoc. Brooks & Turnbull, 1973-76; pvt. practice, 1977—. Counsel St. Andrews Soc. Balt., 1989—; counsel, bd. dirs. St. George's Soc. Former elder, pres. deacons, trustee Roland Park Presbyn. Ch.; former mem. worship, music and sacrament coun., former elder Second Presbyn. Ch. Mem. ABA, Md. Bar Assn., Baltimore County Bar Assn., U. Md. Alumni Assn. for Greater Balt. (pres. 1977), Supreme Ct. Hist. Soc. Avocations: history, philosophy, classical music, tennis, sailing. State civil litigation, Insurance, Personal injury. Office: 10 Oak Hampton Dr Lutherville Timonium MD 21093

WHITEHEAD, JAMES FRED, III, lawyer; b. Atlanta, July 3, 1946; s. James Fred Jr. and Jessie Mae (Turner) W.; m. Joanne Christina Mayo, June 21, 1969 (div. Feb. 1992); children: Matthew Nicholas, Rebecca Catherine; m. Nancy Karean Hatley, May 28, 1992; stepchildren: Brandon, Madison. AB with distinction, Stanford U., 1968; JD, U. Mich., 1975. Bar: Wash. 1975, U.S. Dist. Ct. (we. dist.) Wash. 1975, U.S. Ct. Appeals (9th cir.) 1975, U.S. Supreme Ct. 1976, U.S. Dist. Ct. (ea. dist.) Wash. 1994, Alaska 1995, U.S. Dist. Ct. Alaska 1995. Assoc. LeGros, Buchanan, Paul & Madden, Seattle, 1975-79; dir., officer LeGros, Buchanan, Paul & Whitehead, 1979-92; ptnr. McGee, Reno & Whitehead, 1993; of counsel Holmes Weddle & Barcott, 1993-97, shareholder, 1997—. Organizer, lectr. Pacific Northwest Admiralty Law Inst., Seattle, 1981—; chmn. Internat. Maritime Law Conf., Seattle, 1996. Assoc. editor Am. Maritime Cases, 1991—; contbr. articles to profl. jours. Mem. ABA, Maritime Law Assn. of U.S. (bd. dirs. 2000—). Avocations: tennis, golf, boating, birding. Admiralty, Insurance, Personal injury. Office: Holmes Weddle & Barcott Wells Fargo Center Ste 2600 Seattle WA 98104 E-mail: jwhitehe@sea.hwb-law.com

WHITEHEAD, JAMES MADISON, law librarian; b. Mobile, Ala., July 16, 1929; s. James Manikee and Fanny (Salmon) W.; m. Elena Hulings, June 11, 1955; children: James M.M., John Douglass, Kenneth Clark, Julia Harker. BA, U. Chgo., 1951; JD, Tulane U., 1959; MS, La. State U., 1963; PhD, U. Pitts., 1981. Bar: La. 1959. Acting head pub. svscs. La. State U., New Orleans, 1965; head sci. library U. Colo., Boulder, 1965-66; asst. prof. head dept. circulation Va. Poly. Inst., Blacksburg, 1967-70; adminstrv. asst. Va. Poly. Ins. and State U., 1970-71; asst. prof., assoc. prof., law librarian Coll. William and Mary, Williamsburg, Va., 1971-76; asst. prof. SUNY, Geneseo, 1978-80, Atlanta U., 1980-84; pvt. practice Stone Mountain, Ga., 1984-85; libr. IV U. Ga. Law Library, Athens, 1985-95; ret., 1995. Cons. ultra microfiche adv. group Ency. Britannica, Blacksburg, 1969. Author: Logos of Library and Information Science: Apperceptions on the Institutes of Bibematics with Commentaries on the General Humanistic Method and the Common Philosophy, 1981. Asst. cubmaster Webelos, leader Boy Scouts Am., Blacksburg, 1969-70, patrol dad, adviser, 1970-71. Cpl. USMC, 1952-54. Mem. La. Bar Assn., Masons, Beta Phi Mu. Republican. Christian Scientist. Avocations: fishing, dog and cat care, poetry and play writing, reading. Home: 104 Hurst St Williamsburg VA 23185-3305 E-mail: jimnickie@aol.com

WHITEHEAD, JOHN WAYNE, law educator, organization administrator, author; b. Pulaski, Tenn., July 14, 1946; s. John M. and Alatha (Wiser) W.; m. Virginia Carolyn Nichols, Aug. 26, 1967; children: Jayson Reau, Jonathan Mathew, Elisabeth Anne, Joel Christofer, Joshua Benjamen. BA, U. Ark., 1969, JD, 1974. Bar: Ark. 1974, U.S. Dist. Ct. (ea. and we. dists.) Ark. 1974, U.S. Supreme Ct. 1977, U.S. Ct. Appeals (9th cir.) 1980, Va. 1981, U.S. Ct. Appeals (7th cir.) 1981, U.S. Ct Appeals (4th and 5th cirs.). Spl. counsel Christian Legal Soc., Oak Park, Ill., 1977-78; assoc. Gibbs & Craze, Cleve., 1978-79; sole practice law Manassas, Va., 1979-82; pres. The Rutherford Inst., Charlottesville, 1982—, also bd. dirs. Frequent lectr. colls., law schs.; past adj. prof. O.W. Coburn Sch. Law. Author: Schools on Fire, 1980, The New Tyranny, 1982, The Second American Revolution, 1982, The Stealing of America, 1983, The Freedom of Religious Expression in Public High Schools, 1983, The End of Man, 1986, An American Dream, 1987, The Rights of Religious Persons in Public Education, 1991, Home Education: Rights and Reasons, 1993, Religious Apartheid, 1994, Slaying Dragons, 1999, Grasping For the Wind, 2001, others; writer, dir.: (video series) Grasping for the Wind (Silver World medal N.Y. Film Festival), 1998-99; contbr. articles to profl. jours., chpts. to books. 1st lt. U.S. Army, 1969-71. Named Christian Leader of Yr. Christian World Affairs Conf., Washington, 1986; recipient Bus. and Profl. award Religious Heritage Am., 1990, Hungarian Freedom medal, Budapest, 1991. Mem. ABA, Ark. Bar Assn., Va. Bar Assn. Office: The Rutherford Inst PO Box 7482 Charlottesville VA 22906-7482

WHITEHORN, JO-ANN H. lawyer; b. N.Y.C., Aug. 11, 1948; d. Jules and Blanche Whitehorn. BA in History, U. Pa., 1969; JD, Columbia U., 1972. Bar: N.Y. 1973, U.S. Dist. Ct. (so. and ea. dists.) N.Y. 1973, U.S. Ct. Appeals (2d cir.) 1975, U.S. Supreme Ct. 1976. Asst. counsel Office Gen. Counsel, N.Y. Life Ins. Co., N.Y.C., 1972-77; assoc. Wien, Malkin & Bettex, N.Y.C., 1977-82; dep. gen. counsel Battery Park City Authority, N.Y.C., 1982, N.Y. State Urban Devel. Corp., N.Y.C., 1982—. Assoc. mem. Real Estate Bd. N.Y. Mem. ABA (sect. real property, probate and trust law), N.Y. State Bar Assn. (real property law sect.), Assn. of Bar of City of N.Y. (com. on sex and law 1973-82, chmn. 1978-82, sec. 1973-74; mem. com. on mil. justice and mil. affairs 1980-81, com. on real property law 1982-85), N.Y. County Lawyers' Assn., Assn. Real Estate Women, Mortar Bd., Sphinx and Key.

WHITEHOUSE, SHELDON, attorney general, lawyer; b. N.Y.C., Oct. 20, 1955; s. Charles Sheldon and Mary (Rand) W.; m. Sandra Christine Thornton, Sept. 20, 1986; 2 children. BA, Yale U., 1978; JD, U. Va., 1982. Bar: W.Va. 1982, R.I. 1983, U.S. Dist. Ct. R.I. 1984, U.S. Supreme Ct. 1986, U.S. Ct. Appeals (1st cir.) 1984. Atty., Providence, 1983-84; spl. asst. atty. gen., 1985-89; chief regulatory unit, 1988-90; asst. atty. gen., 1989-90; exec. counsel Office of Gov., 1991, dir. gov. policy office, 1991-92; dir. Dept. Bus. Regulation, 1992-94; U.S. atty for dist. of R.I., 1994-98; atty. gen. State of R.I., 1999—.

WHITE-MAHAFFEY, VIRGINIA L. lawyer; b. N.Y.C., Feb. 23, 1958; d. Robert B. and Veronica M. White; m. David C. Mahaffey, Aug. 20, 1983; children: Edward, Juliette. BA, Niagara U., 1980; JD, Harvard U., 1983. Bar: D.C. 1983. Assoc. Steptoe & Johnson LLP, Washington, 1984-90, ptnr., 1991—. Roman Catholic. Appellate, General civil litigation, Insurance. Office: 1330 Connecticut Ave NW Washington DC 20036-1704

WHITEMAN, JOSEPH DAVID, retired lawyer, manufacturing company executive; b. Sioux Falls, S.D., Sept. 12, 1933; s. Samuel D. and Margaret (Wallace) W.; m. Mary Kelly, Dec. 29, 1962; children: Anne Margaret, Mary Ellen, Joseph David, Sarah Kelly, Jane. B.A., U. Mich., 1955, J.D., 1960. Bar: D.C. 1960, Ohio 1976. Assoc. Cox, Langford, Stoddard & Cutler, Washington, 1959-64; sec., gen. counsel Studebaker group Studebaker Worthington, Inc., N.Y.C., 1964-71; asst. gen. counsel. United Telecommunications, Inc., Kansas City, Mo., 1971-74; v.p., gen. counsel, sec. Weatherhead Co., Cleve., 1974-77, Parker Hannifin Corp., Cleve., 1977-98; ret., 1998. Immediate past chmn. bd. dirs. St. Lukes Med. Ctr. Served as lt. USNR, 1955-57. Mem. ABA, Beta Theta Pi, Phi Delta Phi. Republican. Roman Catholic. Home and Office: 2508 Robinson Springs Rd Stowe VT 05672

WHITEMAN, ROBERT GORDON, lawyer; b. N.Y.C., Feb. 12, 1951; s. Robert Joseph and Bettye Rollins (Durrence) W.; m. Cynthia Vail White, Dec. 30, 1978; children: Alexander St. Julian, Elizabeth Ravenel. BA, Alfred U., 1973; JD, Drake U., 1976. Bar: N.Y. 1977, D.C. 1978, U.S. Ct. Appeals (2d cir.) 1983, U.S. Dist. Ct. (ea. and so. dists.) N.Y. 1983. Middle East mgr. Brady Internat., Kuwait, 1977-79; assoc. Howard Davis, N.Y.C., 1979-80, Mirabel, Wortman & Freidel, Huntington, N.Y., 1980-84, Whiteman & Gorray, Westbury, N.Y., 1984—; atty. cons. Jaime Palmer, Palma de Mallorca, Spain, 1979—. Mem. ABA, N.Y. State Bar Assn., Suffolk County Bar Assn., Assn. Trial Lawyers Am., Nassau-Suffolk Trial Lawyers Assn., Def. Research Inst. Club: Westchester Country (Rye, N.Y.). Insurance, Private international, Personal injury. Office: Whiteman & Gorray 1600 Stewart Ave Westbury NY 11590-6696

WHITESIDE, DAVID POWERS, JR. lawyer; b. Tupelo, Miss., Jan. 1, 1950; s. David Powers and Delores Dean (Gerkin) W. m. Roseanna McCoy, June 2, 1972; children: David III, Lauren. BA, Samford U., 1972; cert. Exeter Coll., Oxford U., England, 1974; JD, Duke U., 1975; LLM, U. Ala.-Tuscaloosa, 1980. Bar: Ala. 1975, U.S. Dist. Ct. (no. dist.) Ala. 1975, U.S. Ct. Appeals (5th cir.) 1975, U.S. Ct. Appeals (11th cir.) 1981, U.S. Supreme Ct. 1978. Assoc. Johnston, Barton, Proctor et al., Birmingham, Ala., 1975-81, ptnr., 1981—; gen. counsel, Personnel Bd. Jefferson County, Birmingham, 1981-86; legal counsel Jefferson County Citizens Supervisory Commn., Birmingham, 1982-85; lectr. Ala. Jud. Coll., 1985. First. v.p. Birmingham Music Club, 1979-81; mem. Com. for a Better Ala., Birmingham, 1981-82. Recipient Mark Donahue Meml. award Ala. Sports Car Club, 1981-82; winner Palm Beach Hist. Races, 1984, Bahama Vintage Grand Prix, 1987, 89, Grand Bahama Grand Prix, 1990, Lola Cars Cup, Jefferson 500, 1992, Dunlop Cup, 1992; named SVRA Driver of Yr., 1989, Rolex Endurance Champion, 1993, 94. Mem. U.S. Ct. of Appeals Fifth Cir. Jud. Conf. (Host com. 1977, del. 1978), U.S. Ct. Appeals 11th Cir. Jud. Conf. (del. 1982, 86), U.S. Ct. Appeals 5th and 11th Cirs. Jud. Conf. (del. 1989), Newcomen Soc. N.Am., Omicron Delta Kappa. Episcopalian. Club: Mountain Brook. Lodge: Rotary. Civil rights, State civil litigation, Labor. Home: 2840 Overton Rd Birmingham AL 35223-2734 Office: Johnston Barton Proctor Swedlaw & Naff 2900 Amsouth Harbert Plz Birmingham AL 35203-2600

WHITESIDE, WILLIAM ANTHONY, JR. lawyer; b. Phila., Feb. 23, 1929; s. William Anthony and Ellen T. (Hensler) W.; m. Eileen Ann Ferrick, Feb. 27, 1954; children: William Anthony III, Michael P., Eileen A., Richard F., Christopher J., Mary P. BS, Notre Dame U., 1951; LLB, U. Pa., 1954. Bar: Pa. 1955. Assoc. Speiser, Satinsky, Gilliland & Packel, Phila., 1956-58, ptnr., 1958-61, Fox, Rothschild, O'Brien & Frankel, Phila., 1961—. Trustee Am. Coll. Mgmt. and Tech., Dubrovnik, Croatia; chmn. emeritus bd. trustees and exec. com., emeritus trustee, Rochester Inst. of Tech.; mem. pres. adv. coun. U. Notre Dame; bd. dirs. PAL, mem. exec. com.; emeritus trustee Germantown Acad., past pres. 1st lt. USAF, 1954-56. Named Man of Yr. Notre Dame club Phila, 1967. Mem. ABA, Pa. Bar Assn., Phila. Bar Assn., N.Y. Union League Club, Pyramid Club, Wissahickon Skating Club, Pa Soc. Republican. Roman Catholic. Private international, Labor, Pension, profit-sharing, and employee benefits. Home: 7808 Cobden Rd Laverock PA 19038-7256 also: 901 Gardens Plz Ocean City NJ 08226-4719 Office: Fox Rothschild O'Brien & Frankel 2000 Market St Ste 10 Philadelphia PA 19103-3231

WHITFORD, JOSEPH PETER, lawyer; b. N.Y.C., Apr. 30, 1950; BA, Union Coll., 1972; JD, Syracuse U., 1975; LLM in Taxation, George Washington U., 1978. Bar: N.Y. 1976, D.C. 1977, Wash. 1979. Staff atty. divsn. corp. fin. SEC, Washington, 1975-78; assoc. Foster Pepper & Shefelman, Seattle, 1978-83, mem., 1983—. Chmn. bd. dirs. MIT Forum on the Northwest, 1992-93. General corporate, Finance, Securities. Office: Foster Pepper & Shefelman PLLC 1111 3rd Ave Ste 3400 Seattle WA 98101-3299

WHITING, RICHARD ALBERT, lawyer; b. Cambridge, Mass., Dec. 2, 1922; s. Albert S. and Jessie (Coleman) W.; m. Marvelene Nash, Feb. 22, 1948 (div. 1984); children— Richard A. Jr., Stephen C., Jeffrey D., Gary S., Kimberly G.; m. Joanne Sherry, Oct. 14, 1984 AB, Dartmouth Coll., 1944; JD, Yale U., 1949. Bar: D.C. 1949. Assoc. Steptoe & Johnson, Washington, 1949-55, ptnr., 1956-86, of counsel, 1987—. Adj. prof. Vt. Law Sch., South Royalton, 1985-90; mem. exec. com. Yale Law Sch. Assn., New Haven, 1985-88; mem. adv. bd. The Antitrust Bull., N.Y.C., 1975-99. Contbr. articles to profl. jours. Trustee Colby-Sawyer Coll., 1987-97. 1st lt. U.S. Army, 1945-46. Mem. ABA (council mem. Antitrust Law sect. 1977-85, del. to Ho. Dels. 1982-83, chmn. 1984-85) Presbyterian. Home: PO Box 749 Grantham NH 03753-0749 Office: 1330 Connecticut Ave NW Washington DC 20036-1704

WHITING, STEPHEN CLYDE, lawyer; b. Arlington, Va., Mar. 20, 1952; s. Richard A. Whiting; m. Patrice Quinn, May 24, 1980; children: Kelsey, Daniel, Seth, Samuel. BA magna cum laude, Dartmouth Coll., 1974; JD, U. Va., 1978. Bar: Maine 1978, U.S. Dist. Ct. Maine 1978, U.S. Ct. Appeals (1st cir.) 1999. Ptnr. Douglas, Whiting, Denham & Rogers, Portland, Maine, 1978-98; founder The Whiting Law Firm, P.A., 1998—. Maine state dir. Am. Ctr. Law and Justice, 1998—. Co-author: Trying the Automobile Injury Case in Maine, 1993, Premises Liability: Preparation and Trial of a Difficult Case in Maine, 1994, Trying Soft Tissue Injury Cases in Maine, 1995, How to Litigate Your First Civil Trial in Maine, 2001. Mem. ATLA, Maine Bar Assn., Maine Trial Lawyers Assn., Phi Beta Kappa. General civil litigation, Insurance, Personal injury. Office: The Whiting Law Firm PA 75 Pearl St Ste 207 Portland ME 04101 E-mail: whitinglaw@rcn.com

WHITLEY, JOE DALLY, lawyer; b. Atlanta, Nov. 12, 1950; s. Thomas Youngie and Mary Jo (Dally) W.; m. Kathleen Pinion, Sept. 27, 1975; children: Lauren Jacqueline, Thomas McMillan. BA, U. Ga., 1972, JD, 1975. Bar: Ga. 1975, U.S. Supreme Ct. 1989. Assoc. Kelly, Denney, Pease & Allison, Columbus, Ga., 1975-78; asst. dist. atty. Chattahoochee Jud. Cir., 1978-79; assoc. Hirsch, Beil & Partin, P.C., 1979-81; U.S. atty. Dept. Justice, Macon, Ga., 1981-87, dep. asst. atty. gen., Criminal Div. Washington, 1987-88, dep. assoc. atty. gen., 1988-89, acting assoc. atty. gen., 1989; ptnr. Smith, Gambrell & Russell, Atlanta, 1989-90; U.S. atty. Dept. of Justice, 1990-93; ptnr. Kilpatrick Stockton, 1993-97, Alston & Bird, Atlanta, 1997—. Mem. atty. gen.'s adv. com. Dept. Justice, Washington, 1982-85; chmn. organized crime and violent crime subcom. Atty. Gen.'s Adv. Com., 1990-93, mem. investigative subcom., chmn. white collar crime subcom., 1993-99. Treas. Muscogee County Young Reps., Columbus, 1979-80. Mem. Ga. Bar Assn., Macon Bar Assn., Young Lawyers Club (pres. Columbus chpt. 1980-81), Lawyers Club of Atlanta. Republican. Presbyterian. Criminal. Office: Alston & Bird 1201 W Peachtree St NW Atlanta GA 30309-3424 E-mail: jwhitley@alston.com

WHITLOCK, WILLIE WALKER, lawyer; b. Mineral, Va., Nov. 16, 1925; s. Edward Jackson and Lottie Alma (Talley) W.; m. Eula Madeline Dymacek, July 15, 1950; children: John D., Jane Whitlock Sisk. BS in Bus., Coll. William and Mary, 1950; Grad. of Laws, Va. Coll. Law, 1953. Bar: Va. 1955, U.S. Dist. Ct. Va. 1957. Atty. Town of Mineral, 1965-97; county atty. County of Louisa, 1976-79; adv. bd. Jefferson Nat. Bank, Mineral, 1972-98. Chmn. Louisa County Dem. Com., Louisa, Va., 1978-82, 32d Legis. Dist. Va., 1978-82. Sgt. U.S. Army, 1945-47. Mem. Va. State Bar, Piedmont Bar Assn. (pres. 1976), Louisa County Bar Assn. (pres. 1968-2000), Am. Legion, Lions, Masons. Baptist. Home and Office: PO Box 130 Mineral VA 23117-0130

WHITMAN, JULES ISIDORÉ, lawyer; b. N.Y.C., Apr. 30, 1923; s. Louis and Jenny (Mednitzky) W.; m. Aileen Epstein Whitman; children: David, Douglas. BBA, CCNY, 1943; LLB, NYU, 1948, LLM in Taxation, 1950. Bar: N.Y. 1948, Pa. 1950. Assoc. Otto A. Samuels, N.Y.C., 1948-50; trial atty. IRS, Phila., 1950-56; sr. ptnr., head tax dept. Dilworth, Paxson, Kalish & Kauffman, Phila., 1956-91, mng. ptnr., 1969-91; of counsel, Dilworth, Paxton, Kalish & Kauffman, Phila., 1992—; dir. U. Pa. Tax Conf., Phila.; lectr. Villanova U. Law Sch., Pa., 1980-81, NYU. Contbr. articles to profl. jours. Pres. Phila. chpt. Am. Jewish Com., 1977-79, chmn. bd., 1980-81, nat. gov., N.Y.C., 1981-84; bd. dirs. Citizens Crime Commn., Phila., 1980-92; trustee Rodeph Shalom Synagogue, Phila., 1980-86. Recipient Human Relations award Am. Jewish Com., 1983. Mem. ABA, Fed. Bar Assn., Pa. Bar Assn., Phila. Bar Assn. Jewish. Club: Locust (Phila.). Corporate taxation, Personal income taxation. Office: Dilworth Paxson Kalish & Kauffman 3200 Mellon Bank ctr 1735 Market St Philadelphia PA 19103-7501

WHITMER, FREDERICK LEE, lawyer; b. Terre Haute, Ind., Nov. 5, 1947; s. Lee Arthur and Ella (Diekhoff) W.; m. Valeri Cade; children: Caitlin Margaret, Meghan Connors, Christian Frederick. BA, Wabash Coll., 1969; JD, Columbia U., 1973. Bar: N.Y. 1975, U.S. Dist. Ct. (so. dist.) N.Y. 1975, N.J. 1976, U.S. Dist. Ct. N.J. 1976, U.S. Ct. Appeals (3d cir.) 1977, U.S. Ct. Appeals (fed. cir.) 1983, U.S. Ct. Appeals (2d cir.) 1987, U.S. Supreme Ct. 1988, U.S. Ct. Appeals (7th cir.) 1994. Assoc. Kaye, Scholer, Fierman, Hays & Handler, N.Y.C., 1973-76, Pitney, Hardin & Kipp, Morristown, N.J., 1976-78; ptnr. Pitney, Hardin, Kipp & Szuch, 1979—. Mem. ABA, N.J. Bar Assn., Phi Beta Kappa. Republican. Episcopalian. Antitrust, Federal civil litigation, Trademark and copyright. Home: 190 Hurlbutt St Wilton CT 06897-2706 Office: Pitney Hardin Kipp & Szuch PO Box 1945 Morristown NJ 07962-1945 E-mail: fwhitmer@phks.com

WHITMORE, BRUCE G. lawyer; BA, Tufts U., 1966; JD, Harvard U., 1969. Bar: N.Y. 1970, Calif. 1973, Pa. 1979. Gen. atty. ARCO Transp. Co., 1985-86; assoc. gen. counsel corp. fin. ARCO, 1986-90; v.p., gen. counsel ARCO Chem. Co., 1990-94; sr. v.p., gen. counsel, corp. sec. Atlantic Richfield Co., L.A., 1995-2000. Mem. ABA. *

WHITNEY, DAVID, prosecutor; b. Alamosa, Colo., Apr. 25, 1942; s. Robert F. and Clarissa I. (Wilson) W.; m. Martha Green, Sept. 26, 1980; children from previous marriage: LeAnn Gonzalez, Christopher. AB in Philosophy, UCLA, 1968, JD, 1971, postgrad., 1971-72. Bar: Calif. 1972, U.S. Dist. Ct. (cen. dist.) Calif. 1973, U.S. Ct. Appeals (9th cir.) 1981, U.S. Supreme Ct. 1985. Dep. pub. defender, L.A., 1972-74; pvt. practice, 1974-78, San Bernardino, Calif., 1978-86; dep. dist. atty. Dist. Atty.'s Office, 1986—, death penalty coord., psychiat. issues coord., 1988—, lead atty. major crimes unit, 1996—. Expert witness, lectr. in field. Chmn. Fire Commn., Forest Falls, Calif., 1988-95. Mem. Calif. Dist. Attys. Assn. (mem. state death penalty com. 1995—), Forensic Mental Health Assn. Calif. (pub. policy com. 1996—), Criminal Cts. Bar Assn. (bd. dirs. 1982-84), County Bar Assn. (jud. evaluation com. 1987-89, co-chmn. 1988, bench/bar com. 1989, chmn. office mgmt. adv. com. 1995, domestic violence prosecutions com. 1995). Democrat. Office: Office of Dist Atty 316 Mountain Vw San Bernardino CA 92415-0001

WHITNEY, DOUGLAS E., SR. lawyer; b. Malden, Mass., May 1, 1939; s. Edgar Gordon and Jennie (Johnson) W.; m. Carol Annette Morre, July 31, 1965 (div. 1994); children: Douglas, Jr., James A., Charles B.; m. Helleke Nieterink, May 11, 1996. BChem. Engring., Cornell U., 1962; JD, Columbia U., 1965. Bar: N.Y. 1965, Mass. 1970, Del. 1973, U.S. Dist. Ct. (so. dist.) N.Y. 1966, U.S. Dist. Ct. Mass. 1969, U.S. Dist. Ct. Del. 1973, U.S. Ct. Appeals (fed., 1st, 2d and 3d cirs.), U.S. Supreme Ct. 1972. Patent agt. Mobil Oil Corp., N.Y.C., 1963-65; assoc. Davis, Hoxie, Faithfull & Hapgood, 1965-69; ptnr. Russell & Nields, Boston, 1969-72, Morris, Nichols, Arsht & Tunnell, Wilmington, Del., 1972—. Bd. dirs. U.S. Orienteering Fedn., St. Louis, 1981-84, Tech. Properties, Inc., Ft. Worth, 1992-2000. Mem. ABA, Am. Intellectual Property Assn., Del. Bar Assn. Democrat. Congregationalist. Federal civil litigation, State civil litigation, Intellectual property. Home: 10 Hickory Ln Chadds Ford PA 19317-9715 Office: PO Box 1347 1201 N Market St Wilmington DE 19899 E-mail: dewsr@worldnet.att.net, dwhitney@mnat.com

WHITNEY, ENOCH JONATHAN, lawyer; b. Jacksonville, Fla., Oct. 7, 1945; s. Enoch Johnson and Iris Ida (Sperber) W.; m. Diane Marie Dupuy, Aug. 29, 1968; children: Elizabeth, William, Edward. BA, Fla. State U., 1967, JD, 1970; grad., FBI Nat. Law Inst., 1989. Bar: Fla. 1970, U.S. Dist. Ct. (no. dist.) Fla. 1970 U.S. Dist. Ct. (mid. dist.) Fla. 1982, U.S. Dist. Ct. (so. dist.) Fla. 1989, U.S. Ct. Appeals (5th cir.) 1971, U.S. Ct. Appeals (11th cir.) 1981, U.S. Supreme Ct. 1974. Rsch. asst. Fla. 1st Dist. Ct.

Appeals, Tallahassee, 1971; asst. atty. gen. Fla. Dept. Legal Affairs, 1971-74; asst. gen. counsel Fla. Dept. Hwy. Safety & Motor Vehicles, 1974-79, gen. counsel, 1979-82, 86—. Gen. counsel Fla. Parole and Probation Commn., Tallahassee, 1982-85; instr. Fla. Hwy. Patrol Tng. Acad., Tallahassee, 1977-82, 86—. Named Able Toastmaster, Toastmasters Internat., 1977. Mem. ABA, Tallahassee Bar Assn. (ex officio dir. 1989-97), Fla. Govt. Bar Assn. (pres. 1977-78), Fla. Bar (bd. govs. 1989-97, charter mem. govt. law sect. 1991, appellate law sect. 1994, bd. cert. appellate lawyer 1994—, budget com. 1992-95, 96-99, appellate cert. com. 1998—, vice chair 2001—), Fla. Coun. Bar Assn. Pres. (life), Fla. State U. Alumni Assn. (life), Fla. Gov. Gen. Counsels Assn. (pres. 1998-99), Fla. Assn. Women Lawyers, Tallahassee Assn. Women Lawyers, Fla. Supreme Ct. Hist. Soc., Supreme Ct. U.S. Hist. Soc., Atty. Gen.'s Hist. Soc. Fla., Fla. Sheriff's Assn., Govs. Club, Capital Tiger Bay Club, Fla. Assn. Police Attys., Kiwanis (pres. Tallahassee 1984-85, lt. gov. Fla. dist. 1986-87). Democrat. Roman Catholic. Avocations: antique collecting, reading. Home: 5001 Vernon Rd Tallahassee FL 32311-4534 Office: Fla Dept Hwy Safety & Motor Vehicles 2900 Apalachee Pky Tallahassee FL 32399-6552 E-mail: whitney.jon@hsmv.state.fl.us

WHITNEY, RICHARD BUCKNER, lawyer; b. Corpus Christi, Tex., Mar. 1, 1948; s. Franklyn Loren and Betty Wolcott (Fish) Whitney; m. Chantal Marie Gindt, Aug. 18, 1972; children: Jennifer L, James R, Katherine E. BA in Polit. Sci., Union Coll., 1970; JD, Case Western Res. U., 1973. Bar: Ohio 1973, US Ct Appeals (6th cir) 1974, US Ct Appeals (3d cir) 1987, US Dist Ct (so dist) NY 2000. From assoc. to ptnr. Jones, Day, Reavis & Pogue, Cleve., 1973—. Mem.: ABA, Ohio Bar Asn, Cuyahoga County Bar Asn, Cleveland Bar Asn (mem grievance comt, mem unauthorized practice of law comt), Legal Aid Soc Cleveland (trustee), Am Inns Cts, Order of Coif. Roman Catholic. General civil litigation, Product liability, Appellate. Home: 2750 Southington Rd Shaker Heights OH 44120-1603 Office: Jones Day Reavis & Pogue 901 Lakeside Ave Cleveland OH 44114-1190 E-mail: rbwhitney@jonesday.com

WHITNEY, ROBERT MICHAEL, lawyer; b. Green Bay, Wis., Jan. 29, 1949; s. John Clarence and Helen (Mayer) W. Student, U. Wis., 1967-70, JD, 1974. Bar: Wis. 1974, U.S. Dist. Ct. (we. dist.) Wis. 1979, U.S. Ct. Appeals (7th cir.) 1980, U.S. Dist. Ct. (ea. dist.) Wis. 1984, U.S. Supreme Ct. 1990, U.S. Ct. Appeals (9th cir.) 1992. Legal counsel Wis. State Election Bd., Madison, 1976-78; ptnr. Walsh, Walsh, Sweeney & Whitney, S.C., 1979-86, Foley & Lardner, Madison, 1986-2000, Lawton & Cates SC, Madison, 2000—. Counsel Dane County Advocates for Battered Women; instr. torts I, U. Wis. Labor Sch., 1996; adj. prof. U. Wis. Law Sch., 1996-97. Contbr. articles to profl. jours. Bd. dirs. Community TV, Inc., Madison, 1984-87, Transitional/Homeless Shelters. Mem. Assn. Trial Lawyers Am., Wis. Acad. Trial Lawyers, Wis. Bar Assn., Dane County Bar Assn., Rugby Club of Madison. Federal civil litigation, State civil litigation, Personal injury. Office: Lawton & Cates 10 E Doty St Ste 400 Madison WI 53703-5103

WHITSON, LISH, lawyer; b. Washington, Oct. 13, 1942; s. I. Lish and Clytie B. (Collier) W.; m. Barbara Lee Sullivan, Sept. 16, 1965; children: L. Richard, Kimberly S. BA in Philosophy, Pa. State U., 1965; JD, U. Wash., 1972. Bar: Wash. 1973, U.S. Dist. Ct. (we. dist.) 1973, U.S. Dist. Ct. (ea. dist.) 1977, U.S. Supreme Ct. 1977. Assoc. Seattle-King County Pub. Defender Assn., 1972-76, Helsell, Fetterman, Martin, Todd & Hokanson, Seattle, 1976-81, ptnr., 1981-98; of counsel Badgley Mullins, 1998-2000, Lish Whitson PLLC, Seattle, 2000—. Bd. dirs., past chmn. Downtown Emergency Svc. Ctr., Seattle, 1981-97; bd. dirs. Allied Arts, 1988-96, pres., 1994-96; mem. Allied Arts Found., 1997—; trustee Seattle Youth Symphony Orch., bd. dirs., 1986-95; mem. alumni bd. U. Wash. Law Sch., 1993-2001, treas., 1997-99, pres., 1999-2001. Fellow Am. Bar Found., Am. Coll. Trial Lawyers; mem. ABA (young lawyers divsn. rep. to exec. coun. 1979, mem. standing com. on lawyer referral svc. 1990-96, chmn. 1992-96, commn. on women in the profn. 1998-2001), ATLA, Am. Bd. Trial Advocates (assoc.), Wash. State Bar Assn. (gov. 1995-98), King County Bar Found. (mem. pres. coun.), King County Bar Assn. (pro bono com. chmn. 1981-84, bd. dirs. 1988-91, young lawyers sect. 1977-79, chmn. 1979, Pro Bono Svc. award 1993, Atty. of Yr. 2000), Fed. Bar Assn., Am. Judicature Soc. (bd. dirs. 1981-86), Seattle Pub. Def. Assn. (bd. dirs. 1982-86), Wash. Athletic Club. General civil litigation, Personal injury, Product liability. Office: Lish Whitson Pllc Ste 3800 999 3d Ave Seattle WA 98104 E-mail: lwhitson@whitsonlaw.com

WHITTEN, C. G. lawyer; b. Abilene, Tex., Apr. 1, 1925; s. C.G. and Eugenia (St. Clair) W.; m. Alene Henley, Nov. 25, 1945; children: Julie, Jennifer, Blake; m. Carol Owen, Apr. 22, 1977. JD, U. Tex.-Austin, 1949. Bar: Tex. 1949, U.S. Dist. Ct. (no. dist.) Tex. 1950, U.S. Supreme Ct. 1955. Assoc. Grisham & King, Abilene, Tex., 1949-52; ptnr. Jameson & Whitten, 1952-54, Jameson, Whitten, Harrell & Wilcox, 1954-58, Whitten, Harrell, Erwin & Jameson, 1958-68, Whitten, Sprain, Wagner, Price & Edwards, 1968-79, Whitten, Haag, Cobb & Hacker, 1979-82; sr. ptnr. Whitten, Haag, Hacker, Hagin & Cutbirth, 1983-87; pres. Whitten, Hacker, Hagin, Anderson & Rucker, P.C., 1987-92; of counsel Whitten & Young, 1992—; gen. counsel Pittencrieff Comms., Inc., 1992-97, sr. v.p., dir., 1994-97; pres. Abilene Improvement Corp., 1994-2001. Mem. tax. increment funding dist., 1995—, mem. adv. coun. U. of Tex. Press, 1995-2001, chmn. 1998-2000. Mem. Abilene Ind. Sch. Dist. Bd. Edn., 1956-76, pres. 1972-76. General corporate. Office: PO Box 208 Abilene TX 79604-0208

WHITTERS, JAMES PAYTON, III, lawyer, university administrator; b. Boston, Oct. 23, 1939; s. James P. Jr. and Norene (Jones) W.; m. Elizabeth Robertson, July 19, 1969; children: James P. IV, Catharine A. BA in History, Trinity Coll., Hartford, Conn., 1962; JD, Boston Coll., 1969; postgrad, U. Mass., Boston. Bar: Mass. 1969, U.S. Dist. Ct. Mass. 1970, U.S. Ct. Appeals (1st cir.) 1972. Assoc. Ely, Bartlett, Brown & Proctor, Boston, 1969-74, Gaston Snow & Ely Bartlett, Boston, 1974-79, ptnr., 1979-88, Gaston & Snow, Boston, 1988-91; of counsel Peabody & Brown, 1991-95; dir. Office Career Devel., Suffolk U. Law Sch., 1995—, adj. prof. Am. legal history, 1997—. Bd. dirs., sec. Robertson Factories, Inc., Taunton, Mass., 1979—; v.p. Alkalol Co., Taunton, 1976-97, sr. v.p., 1997—; vis. tchr. Groton (Mass.) Sch., 1993-94; mem. Mass. Conflict Intervention Mediation Team, 1995—. Bd. dirs. New Eng. com. NAACP Legal Def. Fund, 1982—, Beacon Hill Nursery Sch., 1976-78, Mass. Appleseed Ctr. Law and Justice, 1997—; chmn. Mass. Outdoor Advt. Bd., Boston, 1975-81; vice chmn. Mass. Jud. Nominating Coun., Boston, 1983-87; trustee Trinity Coll., 1983-95; trustee, sec. Hurricane Island Outward Bound Sch., 1977-87; bd. dirs. Mass. affiliate Am. Heart Assn., 1979-98, chmn., 1989-91; bd. dirs. Greater Boston Legal Svcs., 1982-84, 93-99, Mass. Assn. Mediation Programs and Practitioners, 1993-98; founder Beacon Hill Seminars, 2000-2001, bd. dirs., 2001—. Lt. (j.g.) USN, 1962-65. Recipient Alumni Excellence award Trinity Coll., 1987. Mem. Boston Bar Assn., Mass. Bar Assn., ABA, The Country Club (Brookline, Mass.). Democrat. Unitarian. Avocations: reading history, mountain climbing & jogging. Home: 44 Mount Vernon St Boston MA 02108-1302

WHITTIER, MONTE RAY, lawyer; b. Pocatello, Idaho, June 28, 1955; s. Raymond Max and Marjorie Lucille (Pea) W.; m. Denise Womack, May 29, 1982; children: Jason Dennis, Sarah Michelle, Sadie Mckenzie. BS in Acctg., U. Utah, 1976; JD, U. Idaho, 1978. Bar: U.S. Dist. Ct. Idaho, 1979, U.S. Supreme Ct. 1985, U.S. Tax Ct. 1989, U.S. Ct. Appeals (9th cir.) 1991, Idaho, 1979. Ptnr., shareholder Whittier & Souza, Pocatello, 1979-89; shareholder, mng. atty. Whittier, Souza & Naftz, 1989-97; asst. gen. counsel Melaleuca, Inc., Idaho Falls, 1997—. Vol. Internat. Spl. Olympics, South Bend, Ind., 1987, Mpls., 1991; mem. Magistrate Commn. 6th Jud. Dist., Pocatello, 1989-91; bd. dirs. Bannock Baseball, Inc., 1996-97; v.p. Idaho Falls Am. Legion Baseball, 2000—. Mem. ATLA, Idaho Trial Lawyers Assn. (bd. dirs. 6th Jud. Dist. Pro Bono award 1994), Civitan (pres. Bannock chpt. 1983-84, bd. dirs. 1981-87, 92-93, lt. gov. Intermountain chpt. 1986-87, Outstanding Pres. award 1984, Outstanding Svc. award 1982-83, 86-88, 91). Avocations: bicycling, skiing, golfing, Spl. Olympics vol. activities. General civil litigation, General corporate, Personal injury. Office: Melaleuca Inc 3910 S Yellowstone Hwy Idaho Falls ID 83402-6003 E-mail: mwhittier@melaleuca.com

WHITTINGTON, THOMAS LEE, lawyer; b. Waukesha, Wis., July 14, 1943; s. Floyd Leon and Winifred Carol (McDonald) W.; m. Ashley J. Whittington; children: Erin Elizabeth, Hilary Ann. BA, Coll. of Wooster, 1965; JD, U. Mich., 1967. Bar: Trust Terr. of Pacific Islands 1967, Mich. 1969, Wash. 1974, U.S. Dist. Ct. (we. dist.) Wash. 1974. Vol. Peace Corps, Micronesia, 1967-69; staff asst. legis. office Dept. Interior, Washington, 1969-74; ptnr. Thomas, Whittington, Anderson, Bergan & Studebaker, Issaquah, Wash., 1974-200, Scottsdale, Ariz., 2000—. Contracts commercial, Family and matrimonial, Real property. Office: Thomas Whittington Anderson Bergan & Studebaker 27685 N 72d Way Scottsdale AZ 85255

WHITWORTH, J. BRYAN, JR. oil company executive, lawyer; b. Baton Rouge, Aug. 14, 1938; s. Jennings Bryan Sr. and Virginia Ann (Calvert) W.; m. Sue Alice Walters, July 15, 1961 (Jan. 1982); children: Catherine Ann, Elizabeth, Suzanne Virginia; m. Donna Axum, Mar. 1, 1984. BS Pre-Law, U. Ala., 1961, LLM, 1964. Assoc. Cabaniss, Johnston, Gardner & Clark, Birmingham, Ala., 1964-66; gen. AT&T, Washington and N.Y.C., 1966-71; atty. Phillips Petroleum Co., Bartlesville, Okla., 1971-77, sr. counsel, 1977-79, assoc. gen. counsel, 1979-81, v.p. govt. relations, 1981-95, sr. v.p., gen. counsel and govt. relations, 1995—. Bd. dirs. Salk Inst. Biotechnology/Industry Assn. Inc., San Diego; mem. policy devel com. Am. Petroleum Inst., Washington, 1982—, Gov.'s Task Force on Higher Edn. in Okla. and the Council for Reorgn. of State Govt., Oklahoma City, 1985-87; bd. dirs. First Nat. Bank & First Bancshares Inc., Bartlesville. Former editor-in-chief Ala. Law Rev., U. Ala. Mem. Okla. Bar Assn., N.Y. Bar Assn., D.C. Bar Assn., Bartlesville Area C. of C. (v.p., bd. dirs. 1985-87, pres. 1987-88). Lodge: Rotary. Office: Phillips Petroleum Co 18 Phillips Bldg 4th and Keeler Ave Bartlesville OK 74004

WHORISKEY, ROBERT DONALD, lawyer; b. Cambridge, Mass., May 9, 1929; s. John Joseph and Katherine Euphemia (MacDonald) W.; m. Martha Beebe Poutas, Apr. 16, 1966; children: Alexandra, Jonathan, Eliza. AB, Harvard U., 1952; JD, Boston Coll., 1958; LLM, NYU, 1960. Bar: Mass. 1958, N.Y. 1963, U.S. Tax Ct. 1961, U.S. Claims Ct. 1969, U.S. Dist. Ct. (so. dist.) N.Y. 1969, U.S. Ct. Customs 1971, U.S. Ct. Appeals (2d cir.) 1972, U.S. Ct. Appeals (3d cir.) 1983, U.S. Ct. Appeals (D.C. cir.) 1991, U.S. Supreme Ct. 1974. Sr. trial atty. Office Chief Counsel, IRS, N.Y.C., 1960-67; assoc. Curtis, Mallet-Prevost, Colt & Mosle, 1967-70, ptnr., 1970-2000, of counsel, 2001—, exec. com., 1978-82, chmn. tax dept., 1982-87. Bd. dirs. Internat. Tax Inst., v.p., lectr., 1980-84, chmn. bd., pres., lectr., 1985-87; lectr. Practicing Law Inst., World Trade Inst., Tax Execs. Inst., Am. Mgmt. Assn., Coun. for Internat. Tax Edn.; bd. dirs. Life Ins. Co. of Boston and N.Y., Inc. Author: Foreign Trusts, 1977, Annual Institute on International Taxation, 1966, 80, 81, (with Sidney Pine, Ralph Seligman) Tax and Business Benefits of the Bahamas, 1986; contbg. author: International Boycotts, CCH Federal Tax Service, 1988, CCH Smart Tax CD-ROM: Third Party Information, John Wiley and Sons, Inc.'s Transfer Pricing, 1993, Transfer Pricing Under IRC & 482: Overview and Planning, Part I, 1996, Accuracy Related Penalty Regulations for Transfer Pricing, Part II, 1997, Third Party Information, Part III, 1997, U.S. Taxation of International Operations, Warren, Gorham Lamont, 1998; mem. editl. adv. bd. Corp. Bus. Taxation Monthly, 2000—. Trustee, treas. Montessori Sch. Westchester, 1974-77; mem. bd. ethics Village of Larchmont, N.Y., 1988—. With U.S. Army, 1952-54. Mem. ABA (com. on alternative tax sys. tax sect. 1994—, com. on ct. procedure tax sec. 1997—), N.Y. State Bar Assn. (com. on practice and procedure tax sect. 1990—), Assn. of the Bar of the City of N.Y., Harvard Club, Larchmont Yacht Club. Democrat. Roman Catholic. Corporate taxation, Estate taxation, Taxation, general. Office: Curtis Mallet-Prevost Colt & Mosle 101 Park Ave 35th Fl New York NY 10178-0061 E-mail: rwhoriskey@cm-p.com

WHYTE, GEORGE KENNETH, JR. lawyer; b. Waukegan, Ill., Oct. 10, 1936; s. George K. and Ella Margaret (Osgood) W.; m. Ann B. Challoner, June 20, 1964; children: Mary, Douglas. AB in Polit. Sci., Duke U., 1958; LLB, U. Wis., 1965. Bar: Wis. 1965. Law clk. to chief justice Wis. Supreme Ct., Madison, 1965-66; assoc. Quarles & Brady, Milw., 1966-73, ptnr., 1973—. Lt. USN, 1958-62. Mem. ABA (employment law sect.), Wis. Bar Assn. (former chmn. labor and employment law sect.), Rotary (pres. elect 2001-02), The Town Club, Milw. Athletic Club, Milw. Country Club. Congregationalist. Labor, Employment litigation. Home: 1026 W Shaker Cir Mequon WI 53092-6034 Office: Quarles & Brady 411 E Wisconsin Ave Ste 2550 Milwaukee WI 53202-4497 E-mail: gkw@quarles.com

WHYTE, KIERAN BART, lawyer; b. Johannesburg, Republic of South Africa, May 17, 1958; s. Patrick and Mauis Ann (O'Leary) W.; m. Linda Anne Wilkinson; children: Brendan, Garrett, Declan, Kira. BA, LLB, H. Dip. Co. Law, Witwaterstand; MDP, UNISA, South Africa. Admitted Attorney of the High Court of South Africa. Articled clerk Deneys Reitz, Republic of South Africa, 1981-84, professional asst. Republic of South Africa, 1984-86; legal adviser Dorbyl Ltd., Republic of South Africa, 1986-87; corporate consultant Eskom, Republic of South Africa, 1987-93; dir. Edward Naman & Friedlad Inc., 1993-2000, Edward Naman & Friedlad (pty) Ltd., 2000—. Dir. Kescor (pty) Ltd., 1989-92, trustee Cross Roads Sch., 1998—, governor KES VII Sch., 2001—. Sub. Lt., SA Navy, 1977-79. Mem. INLA, Northern Province Law Soc., Old Edwardians. Avocation: road running. Office: Edward Nathan & Friedland Ltd 2 Maude Street 2146 Sandlon Gaunberg South Africa E-mail: How@eng.co.za

WHYTE, RONALD M. federal judge; b. 1942; BA in Math., Wesleyan U., 1964; JD, U. So. Calif., 1967. Bar: Calif. 1967, U.S. Dist. Ct. (no. dist.) Calif. 1967, U.S. Dist. Ct. (cen. dist.) Calif. 1968, U.S. Ct. Appeals (9th cir.) 1986. Assoc. Hoge, Fenton Jones & Appel, Inc., San Jose, Calif., 1971-77, mem., 1977-89; judge Superior Ct. State of Calif., 1989-92, U.S. Dist. Ct. (no. dist.) Calif., San Jose, 1992—. Judge pro-tempore Superior Ct. Calif., 1977-89; lectr. Calif. Continuing Edn. of Bar, Rutter Group, Santa Clara Bar Assn., State Bar Calif.; legal counsel Santa CLara County Bar Assn., 1986-89; mem. county select com. Criminal Conflicts Program, 1988. Bd. trustees Santa Clara County Bar Assn., 1978-79, 84-85. Lt. Judge Advocate Gen.'s Corps, USNR, 1968-71. Recipient Judge of Yr. award Santa Clara County Trial Lawyers Assn., 1992, Am. Jurisprudence award. Mem. Calif. Judges Assn., Assn. Bus. Trial Lawyers (bd. govs. 1991-93), Santa Clara Inn of Ct. (exec. com. 1993—), San Francisco Bay area Intellectual Property Inn of Ct. (exec. com. 1994—). Office: US Courthouse 280 S 1st St Rm 2112 San Jose CA 95113-3002

WIANT, SARAH KIRSTEN, law library administrator, educator; b. Waverly, Iowa, Nov. 20, 1946; d. James Allen and Eva (Jorgensen) W.; m. Robert E. Akins. BA, Western State Coll., 1968; MLS, U. North Tex., 1970; JD, Washington & Lee U., 1978. Asst. law libr. Tex. Tech. U., 1970-72, 020, Washington & Lee U., Lexington, Va., 1972—, dir., 1978—, asst. prof. law, 1978-83, assoc. prof. law, 1984-92, prof. law, 1993—. Participant Conf. on Fair Use, NII, 1995-98. Co-author: Copyright Handbook, 1984, Libraries and Copyright: A Guide to Copyright Law in the 1990s, 1994, Legal Research in the District of Columbia, Maryland, and Virginia, 1995, 2d edit., 2000; contbr. chpts. to books; mem. adv. bd. Westlaw, 1990-93. Mem. ABA (com. on librs. 1987-93), Am. Assn. Law Librs. (copyright office rep., Spl. Dist. Svc. award Southeastern chpt. 1997), Am. Law Sch. (chmn. sec. on librs. 1990-92, accreditation com. 1991-94), Spl. Librs. Assn. (chair copyright com. 1990-96, copyright com., 1990-93, exec. bd., 1981-84, John Cotton Dana award 1997, President's award, 2001), Maritime Law Assn., U.S. Trademark Assn. Office: Washington & Lee U Law Libr Lewis Hall Lexington VA 24450 E-mail: wiants@wlu.edu

WICH, DONALD ANTHONY, JR. lawyer; b. Apr. 13, 1947; s. Donald Anthony and Margaret Louise (Blatz) W. BA with honors, Notre Dame U., Ind., 1969; JD, Notre Dame U., 1972. Bar: Fla. 1972, U.S. Dist. Ct. (so. dist.) Fla. 1972, U.S. Ct. Appeals (5th and 11th cirs.) 1982, U.S. Supreme Ct. 1976; cert. civil trial lawyer, 1983. Assoc. VISTA, Miami, Fla., 1972-74; atty. Legal Svcs., 1973-75; adj. prof. law U. Miami, 1974-75; ptnr. Wich, Wich & wich, P.A., Ft. Lauderdale, Fla., 1992—. Pres., dir. Legal Aid of Broward, Ft. Lauderdale, 1976-82; mem. 17th Cir. Jud. Nominating Commn., 1998-02; spl. prosecutor, grievance chmn. The Fla Bar, 1982-90; chmn. UPL Standing Com., 2001— Treas. St. Thomas More Sch. of So. Fla., 1989—. Mem. ABA, ATLA, Am. Arbitration Assn., North Broward Bar Assn. (pres. 1983-84), Acad. Fla. Trial Lawyers Assn. (sustaining mem.), Broward County Trial Lawyers Assn. (pres. 1988-89, sustaining mem.), Broward Bar Assn. (chmn. legis. com. 1984-85, exec. com. 1986-92, 94-98, chmn. bench-bar com. 1993-94, chmn. clk.-bar com. 1993-95, mem. 1998-99, pres. 1997-98), Tex. Trial Lawyers Assn., N.Y. Trial Lawyers Assn., Pompano Beach C. of C. (pres. 1989-90, dir. 1984-87, 92-95, govtl. affairs chmn. 1983-84, art show chmn. 1984-85, seafood festival chmn. 1986-90), Notre Dame Frederick Sorin Soc., Rotary (bd. dirs. 1987-91), Woodhouse (bd. dirs. 1990-91). General civil litigation, Personal injury, Real property. Office: Wich Wich & Wich PA 2400 E Commercial Blvd Fort Lauderdale FL 33308-4030 E-mail: wich3@msn.com

WICHMAN, HERMAN LEE, III, lawyer, financial consultant; b. St. Louis, July 3, 1919; s. Herman Lee and Pearl (Wilson) W.; m. Betty Morse, Oct. 16, 1961 (div. 1982); children by previous marriage— Dwight Lloyd, Susan. B.S. in Bus. Adminstrn., Washington U., St. Louis, 1942, M.B.A., 1943, LL.B., 1942, J.D., 1945. Bar: Mo. 1941. Assoc. Buder & Buder, St. Louis, 1941-42; with McDonnell-Douglas Co., St. Louis, 1942-52, asst. sec., 1946-51, sec., 1951-52, v.p., gen. counsel, 1949-52; corp. fin. cons., Dallas, 1952-56; founder, pres. Wickfield, Inc., Dallas, 1956-59; founder, dir., chmn. bd. Union Fin. Corp. (name now Transohio Co.), Cleve., 1959-62; founder, exec. v.p., chmn. exec. com. Republic Nat. Corp., Cleve., 1962-65; pres. Wichman Assocs., Inc., corp. fin. cons. mergers and acquisitions, San Francisco, Los Angeles and Indian Wells, Calif., 1965—; dir. Platt-LePage Aircraft Corp., Phila., Rotary Research Corp., Phila.; chmn. legal com. Aerospace Industries, Washington. Vice chmn. campaign ARC, St. Louis, 1950, chmn., 1951; chmn. Greater Bay area Washington U. Alumni Council, San Francisco, 1967-68, chmn. fund campaign, 1968; chmn. bd. trustees Calvary Presbyn. Ch., San Francisco. Mem. ABA, Mo. Bar, St. Louis Bar Assn. (chmn. ethics com. 1940-50), Tex. Bar Assn., Dallas Bar Assn., Phi Delta Phi, Sigma Nu. Republican. Clubs: Olympic, Eldorado Country, Casa Dorada. Home: 75114 Concho Dr Indian Wells CA 92210-8315 Office: Wichman Assocs Inc 2035 Westwood Blvd Los Angeles CA 90025-6332

WICK, LAWRENCE SCOTT, lawyer; b. San Diego, Oct. 1, 1945; s. Kenneth Lawrence (dec.) and Lorrayne (Scott) W.; m. Beverly Ann DeRoss, Aug. 26, 1972 (div.); children: Ryan Scott, Andrew Taylor, Hayley Lauren. BA, Northwestern U., Evanston, Ill., 1967; JD, Columbia U., 1970. Atty. Leydig Voit & Mayer Ltd., Chgo., 1978-84, shareholder, 1984-98; equity ptnr. Wildman, Harrold, Allen & Dixon, 1998—; v.p., gen. counsel Lionheart Prodns., Ltd., 1995—, Purple Nurple Prodns. Ltd., 2001—. V.p., gen. counsel Purple Nurple Prodns. Ltd., 2001—. Contbr. articles to profl. jours. and encys. Bd. govs., lectr. Brand Names Edn. Found., 1994-95; exec. dir. Lefkowitz Internat. Trademark Moot Ct., 1994-95; bd. dirs. Tangley Oaks Homeowners Assn., 1997-2000, treas., 1998-99, pres., 1999-2000. Mem. ABA, Internat. Trademark Assn. (N.Y.), Internat. Trade Assn. (Chgo. chpt.), Assn. Internat. Protection de la Propriete Industrielle (Geneva), Copyright Soc. U.S. (N.Y.), Pharm. Trade Marks Group (London), Am. Film Inst. (L.A.), Chgo. Bar Assn. (mem. fin. com.). Republican. Presbyterian. Avocations: international travel, film, swimming, snorkeling, free diving. Federal civil litigation, Intellectual property, Trademark and copyright. Home: 317 Rothbury Ct Lake Bluff IL 60044-1927 Office: Wildman Harrold Allen and Dixon 225 W Wacker Dr Ste 3000 Chicago IL 60606-1229 E-mail: Wick@Wildmanharrold.com

WICKER, THOMAS CAREY, JR. judge; b. New Orleans, Aug. 1, 1923; s. Thomas Carey and Mary (Taylor) W.; children: Thomas Carey III, Catherine Anne; m. Jane Anne Trepanier, Dec. 29, 1995. BBA, Tulane U., 1944, LLB, 1949, JD, 1969. Bar: La. 1949. Law clk. La. Supreme Ct., New Orleans, 1949-50; asst. U.S. Atty., 1950-53; practiced in New Orleans, 1953-72; mem. firm Simon, Wicker & Wiedemann, 1953-67; partner firm Wicker, Wiedemann & Fransen, 1967-72; dist. judge Jefferson Parish (La.), 1972-85, judge, Court of Appeal 5th cir., 1985-98, mem. faculty Nat. Jud. Coll., 1979-93, Tulane U. Sch. Law, 1978-83. Past bd. visitors Tulane U.; bd. dirs. La. Jud. Coll.; past pres. Sugar Bowl. Author: (with others) Judicial Ethics, 1982, (with others) Modern Judicial Ethics, 1992; editor Tulane Law Review, 1949. Lt. (j.g.), USNR, 1944-46. Mem. ABA (jud. div. council), La. (chmn. jr. bar sect. 1958-59, gov. 1958, mem. ho. of dels. 1960-72), Jefferson Parish, bar assns., Tulane U. Alumni Assn. (past pres.), Am. Judicature Soc., La. Dist. Judges Assn. (past pres.), Order of Coif, Beta Gamma Sigma, Pi Kappa Alpha. Episcopalian. Clubs: Rotary (pres. 1971-72), Metairie (La.) Country. Avocations: golf, photography, military history. Home: 500 Rue Saint Ann Apt 127 Metairie LA 70005-4639

WICKERHAM, RICHARD DENNIS, lawyer; b. Plainfield, N.J., Oct. 9, 1950; s. Richard Frame and Margaret Theresa (Waldron) W.; m. Margaret Ann Music, June 29, 1989. BS in Fgn. Svc., Georgetown U., 1972; JD, Fordham U., 1975. Bar: N.Y. 1976, U.S. Dist. Ct. (no. dist.) N.Y. 1977. Pvt. practice atty., counsellor at law, Schenectady, N.Y., 1976—; law guardian, 1976-85; atty., Office of Aging County of Schenectady, N.Y., 1981—. Mem. com. on profl. stds., 3d jud. dept. Appellate divsn. N.Y. Supreme Ct., 1996—, vice chmn., 2000-01. Mem. St. Clare's Hosp. Found. Leadership, Schenectady, 1990—. Recipient Cert. of Appreciation and Merit, The Lawyers' Fund for Client Protection of the State of N.Y., Albany, 1994. Mem. Rotary Internat., Schenectady County C. of C. Roman Catholic. Avocations: rowing, salt water fishing. General civil litigation, Estate planning, Probate. Home: 484 Hutchinson Rd Scotia NY 12302-6515 Office: PO Box 1167 28 Jay St Schenectady NY 12305-1900

WICKLUND, DAVID WAYNE, lawyer; b. St. Paul, Aug. 7, 1949; s. Wayne Glenwood and Elna Katherine (Buresh) W.; m. Susan Marie Bubenko, Nov. 17, 1973; children: David Jr., Kurt, Edward. BA cum laude, Williams Coll., 1971; JD cum laude, U. Toledo, 1974. Bar: Ohio 1974. Assoc. Shumaker, Loop & Kendrick, Toledo, 1974-80, ptnr., 1981—. Adj. instr. law, U. Toledo, 1988. Editor-in-chief U. Toledo Law Rev. 1973-74. Mem. ABA, Ohio State Bar Assn. (emeritus mem. bd. govs. antitrust sect. 1994-2001), Toledo Bar Assn., U. Toledo Coll. of Law Alumni Assn. (pres. 1999-2000), Inverness Club, Toledo Club. Antitrust, Bankruptcy, General civil litigation. Office: Shumaker Loop & Kendrick N Courthouse Sq 1000 Jackson St Toledo OH 43624-1573 E-mail: dwicklund@slk-law.com

WIDDEL, JOHN EARL, JR. lawyer; b. Minot, N.D., Nov. 17, 1936; s. John Earl Sr. and Angela Victoria W.; m. Yvonne J. Haugen, Dec. 21, 1973; children: John P., James M., Susan N., Andrea K. B in Philosophy, BSBA, U. N.D., 1966, BSBA, 1971. Bar: N.D. 1971, U.S. Dist. Ct. N.D., 1971,

U.S. Ct. Appeals (8th cir.) 1989. Ptnr. Thorsen & Widdel, Grand Forks, N.D., 1971-97; shareholder Law Offices ND, PC. Mcpl. judge City of Grand Forks, 1972—; ct. magistrate Grand Forks County, 1975. Mem. N.D. Foster Parent Program, 1974-87, Nat. Conf. of Bar Pres.; mem. bd. dirs. YMCA, Grand Forks, 1982; dist. chmn. Boy Scouts Am., 1987-88; corp. mem. ALTRU Hosp. With U.S. Army, 1960-62. Mem. Am. Acad. Estate Planning Attys., State Bar Assn. N.D. (bd. govs. 1983-88, pres. 1986-87), Greater Grand Forks County Bar Assn. (pres. 1982), N.E. Cen. Jud. Dist. (pres. 1983), Grand Forks Cemetery Assn. (bd. dirs. 1984-96, pres. 1989-94), Grand Forks Hist. Soc. (pres. 1983), Grand Forks Jaycees, Antique Automobile Club Am. (nat. bd. dirs. 1984-2000, v.p. 1985-98, sec.-treas. 1989, pres. N.D . region 1977-78, 83-84), Sertoma (bd. dirs. 1994-99, pres. 1997-98, dist. gov. 2001), Elks (exalted ruler 1985-86), Masonic Bodies (Kem Temple Potentate 1995), Nat. Assn. Estate Planning Coun. (accredited estate planner, 1994), N.D. Mcpl. Judges Assn. (dir. 1993—). Roman Catholic. General practice, Probate, Real property. Home: Box 5624 Grand Forks ND 58206-5624 Office: Law Offices North Dakota PC PO Box 5624 Grand Forks ND 58206-5624

WIDENER, HIRAM EMORY, JR. federal judge; b. Abingdon, Va., Apr. 30, 1923; s. Hiram Emory and Nita Douglas (Peck) W.; children: Molly Berendt, Hiram Emory III. Student, Va. Poly. Inst., 1940-41; B.S., U.S. Naval Acad., 1944; LL.B., Washington and Lee U., 1953, LL.D., 1977. Bar: Va. 1951. Pvt. practice law, Bristol, Va., 1953-69; judge U.S. Dist. Ct. Western Dist. Va., Abingdon, 1969-71, chief judge, 1971-72; judge U.S. Ct. Appeals 4th Circuit, Abingdon, 1972—. U.S. commr. Western Dist. Va., 1963-66; mem. Va. Election Laws Study Commn., 1968-69 Chmn. Rep. party 9th Dist. Va., 1966-69; mem. Va. Rep. State Ctrl. Com., 1966-69, state exec. com., 1966-69. Served to lt. (j.g.) USN, 1944-49; to lt. USNR, 1951-52. Decorated Bronze Star with combat V. Mem. Am. Law Inst., Va. Bar Assn., Va. State Bar, Phi Alpha Delta. Republican. Presbyterian. Home and Office: 180 E Main St Rm 123 Abingdon VA 24210-2839

WIDING, CAROL SCHARFE, lawyer; b. South Orange, N.J., Dec. 18, 1941; d. Howard Carman and Marjorie (McConaghy) Scharfe; m. C. Jon Widing, July 2, 1966; 1 child, Daniel McClure. BA, Wellesley Coll., 1964; MEd, Harvard U., 1965; JD, Widener U., 1980. Bar: Del. 1981, Pa. 1981, U.S. Dist. Ct. Del. 1981, U.S. Ct. Appeals (3d. cir.) 1983, Conn. 1984. Tchr. elem. schs., Lexington, Mass. and Bryn Mawr, Pa., 1964-68; pvt. tutor Ibadan, Nigeria, 1965; tchr. Phila. Adult Basic Edn. Acad., 1970-72; dep. atty. gen. child protection services Del. Dept. Justice, Wilmington, 1981-83; staff atty. UAW Legal Services, Newark, 1983; assoc. Hebb & Gitlin, P.C., Hartford, Conn., 1985-86, Steinberg & Louden, Hartford, 1986-87, Law Offices of Bruce Louden, Hartford, 1987-89, Louden and Forzani, Hartford, 1989-92; sole practitioner Hartford and Avon, Conn., 1992—. V.p. program AAUW, Middletown, Del. 1974; chmn. pub. relations and fundraising Lower New Castle County Med. Ctr., Middletown, 1980; bd. dirs. Epis. Community Services, Phila., 1970-72, UN Children's Fund, 1970-72; dir. Conn. Coun. for Divorce Mediation, 1995-97, Mediated Divorce Svcs., 1993—. Mem. ABA, Pa. Bar Assn., Del. Bar Assn., Conn. Bar Assn., Hartford County Bar Assn., Hartford Assn. Women Attys., Jr. League (program chmn. 1970), Phila. Homemakers' Assn. (bd. dirs. 1970-72), Acad. Family Mediators (practitioner). Avocations: piano, gardening. Alternative dispute resolution, Family and matrimonial. Home: 47 Fox Holw Avon CT 06001-3693 Office: 33 E Main St Ste 4 Avon CT 06001-3805 E-mail: cwid@snet.net

WIDMAN, DOUGLAS JACK, lawyer; b. Neptune, N.J., Feb. 28, 1949; s. Leonard and Phyllis (Rose) W.; m. Jill Rosenblad; children: Phyllis, Jared Leonard, Sarah. BA in Polit. Sci. cum laude, Syracuse U., 1971, JD, 1973. Bar: N.J. 1973, U.S. Dist. Ct. N.J. 1973, U.S. Supreme Ct. 1979, D.C. 1981, N.Y. 1990. Legal planner Syracuse-Onondaga (N.Y.) County Planning Agy., 1971-73; law sec. to presiding judges N.J. Dist. Ct. and N.J. Superior Ct., 1973-74; dep. atty gen. State Enforcement Bur. Div. Criminal Justice, Trenton, N.J., 1974; ptnr. Widman, Cooney, Barrett & Pavluk, Oakhurst, 1976—. Assoc. editor Syracuse Jour. Internat. Law & Commerce. Syracuse U. Coll. Law scholar, 1971-73; Syracuse U. Grad. Research fellow, 1972. Mem. N.J. Bar Assn., Phi Alpha Delta, Alpha Phi Omega, Pi Sigma Alpha. Environmental, Insurance, Personal injury. Office: Widman Cooney Barrett & Pavluk 1803 Hwy 35 Oakhurst NJ 07755-2911

WIDMARK, STEFAN, lawyer; b. Lund, Sweden, Aug. 16, 1963; LLM, U. Lund, 1989. Clk. Göteborg's (Sweden) Dist. Ct., 1989-92; assoc. Mannheimer Swartling, Stockholm, 1992-94, 96-98, Danowsky & Ptnrs., Stockholm, 1994-96, Vinge, Stockholm, 1998-2000; ptnr., 2001—. Communications, Intellectual property. Office: Vinge Smålandsgatan 20 111 87 Stockholm Sweden Fax: 46 8 6143190. E-mail: stefan.widmark@vinge.se

WIDOR, AIMEE L. lawyer; b. Rochester, N.Y., Oct. 17, 1972; d. Henry and Marilyn Sterling Widor. BA, SUNY, Geneseo, 1994; JD, U. Pitts., 1997. Bar: N.Y. 1998, U.S. Dist. Ct. (we. and no. dists.) N.Y. Assoc. Phillips, Lytle, Hitchcock, Blaine & Huber LLP, Rochester, 1997—. Vol. Lawyers for Learning, Rochester, 1997—. Mem. N.Y. State Bar Assn., Monroe County Bar Assn., Greater Rochester Assn. for Women Attys., Am. Inns. Ct. Federal civil litigation. Office: Phillips Lytle Et Al 1400 1st Federal Plz Rochester NY 14614

WIEBUSCH, RICHARD VERNON, lawyer, author; b. Schenectady, N.Y., Dec. 4, 1946; s. Vernon Ralph and Marjorie (Hush) W.; m. Margaret Alice Meacham, May 6, 1967; children— Kimberley Ann, Alice Christina, Katrina Elizabeth. A.B., Dartmouth Coll., 1968; J.D., Cornell U., 1973. Bar: N.H. 1973, U.S. Dist. Ct. N.H. 1973, U.S. Ct. Appeals (1st cir.) 1976. Chief consumer protection div. N.H. Atty. Gen., Concord, 1973-76, chief div. legal counsel, 1976-77; assoc. firm Sheehan, Phinney, Bass & Green, Manchester, N.H., 1977-78, ptnr, 1979-85; U.S. atty. Dist. Ct. N.H., Concord, 1985-88; ptnr. Sulloway, Hollis & Soden, Concord, 1988—; adj. prof. Franklin Pierce Law Ctr., Concord, 1985. Author: New Hampshire Civil Practice and Procedure, 3 vols., 1984. Dist. enrollment dir. Dartmouth Coll., Concord, 1976-85; mem. Downtown Concord Revitalization Commn., 1978-79; commr. N.H. Ballot Law Commn., 1981-85; mem. adv. com. State Law Library, 1982-85; pres. N.H. Estate Planning Council, 1983-84. Mem. ABA, Merrimack County Bar Assn., N.H. Bar Assn., Am. Judicature Soc. Republican. Administrative and regulatory, General corporate, Commercial litigation. Home: 30 Wintergreen Way Chilmark MA 02535-2049 Office: Hale & Door The Numerica Bldg 1155 Elm St Manchester NH 03101-1508

WIECHMANN, ERIC WATT, lawyer; b. Schenectady, N.Y., June 12, 1948; s. Richard Jerdone and Ann (Watt) W.; m. Merrill Metzger, May 22, 1971. BA, Hamilton Coll., 1970; JD, Cornell U., 1974. Bar: Conn. 1975, U.S. Dist. Ct. (so. and ea. dists.) N.Y. 1975, U.S. Dist. Ct. Conn. 1975, U.S. Dist. Ct. D.C. 1981, U.S. Ct. Appeals (2nd cir.) 1975, U.S. Ct. Appeals (9th cir.) 1980, U.S. Ct. Appeals D.C. 1982, U.S. Ct. Appeals (5th cir.) 1986, U.S. Ct. Appeals (10th cir.) 1989, U.S. Supreme Ct. 1978. Assoc. Cummings & Lockwood, Stamford, Conn., 1974-82, ptnr., 1982—, mng. ptnr. Hartford office, bd. dirs. Hartford, 1996—. Spl. pretrial master U.S. Dist. Ct. Conn. 1984—; state atty. trial referee, 1986—, mem. evidence code oversight com.; civil task force, civil jury instrn. com. Conn. Superior Ct., 1996-2000, docket control com., 2001— Contbr. articles to profl. jours. Active Zoning Bd. Appeals, New Canaan, Conn., 1984-85; bd. dirs. Conn. Rivers coun. Boy Scouts Am., trustee, 2001—. Mem. ABA (vice-chmn. toxics and hazardous law com. TIPS sect.), Def. Rsch. Inst., Internat. Assn. Def. Counsel (mem. faculty Def. Trial Acad. 1996, chmn. toxic and hazardous substance com. 1998-99, chmn. CLE bd. 2000-01), Internat. Soc. Barristers, Conn. Bar Assn. (exec. com. antitrust sect. 1982—, ct. rules adv. com, chmn. 1991-93), Golf Club Avon. Republican. Episcopalian. Antitrust, General civil litigation, Product liability. Home: 10 Langley Park Farmington CT 06032-1541 E-mail: ewiech@yahoo.com, ewiech@cl-law.com

WIEDER, BRUCE TERRILL, lawyer, electrical engineer; b. Cleve., Dec. 9, 1955; s. Ira J. and Judith M. (Marx) W. BSEE, Cornell U., 1978; MBA, U. Tex., 1980, JD with honors, 1988. Bar: Tex. 1988, U.S. Dist. Ct. (we. dist.) Tex. 1989, U.S. Patent and Trademark Office 1989, U.S. Ct. Appeals (fed. cir.) 1990, D.C. 1991, U.S. Supreme Ct. 1992, U.S. Dist. Ct. (no. dist.) Tex. 1995, Va. 1997, U.S. Dist. Ct. (ea. dist.) Va. 1997. Engr. Motorola, Inc., Austin, Tex., 1979-85; assoc. Arnold, White & Durkee, 1988-90; law clk. U.S. Ct. Appeals (Fed. cir.), Washington, 1990-91; assoc. Burns, Doane, Swecker & Mathis, Alexandria, Va., 1991-97, ptnr., 1998—. Adj. prof. Georgetown U. Law Ctr., 1998—. Mem. IEEE, ABA, Am. Intellectual Property Law Assn., Alpha Phi Omega (life), Beta Gamma Sigma (life). Computer, Patent, Trademark and copyright. Office: Burns Doane Swecker & Mathis 1737 King St Ste 500 Alexandria VA 22314-2727

WIEGLEY, ROGER DOUGLAS, lawyer; b. Buffalo, Dec. 8, 1948; s. Richard John and Georgianna (Eggleston) W. BA, SUNY, Buffalo, 1970; JD magna cum laude, U. Wis., 1977. Bar: Wis. 1977, Hawaii 1978, N.Y. 1982, D.C. 1982, Calif. 1986. Spl. asst. U.S. atty. U.S. Justice Dept., Honolulu, 1978-81; spl. asst. to gen. counsel Dept. of the Navy, Washington, 1981-82; assoc. Sullivan & Cromwell, 1982-88; ptnr. Sidley & Austin, 1988-94, Winthrop, Stimson, Putnam & Roberts, Washington, 1994-98; dir. Credit Suisse First Boston, N.Y.C., 1999—. Arbitrator nat. panel Am. Arbitration Assn., 1988—. Co-author: Trade and Export Finance, 2d edit., 2000; contbr. numerous articles to profl. jours. Served with USN, 1973-82. Mem. Assn. of Bar City of N.Y. (chmn. banking law com. 2000—). General corporate, Finance, Mergers and acquisitions. Office: Credit Suisse First Boston 11 Madison Ave New York NY 10010-3629

WIENER, JACQUES LOEB, JR. federal judge; b. Shreveport, La., Oct. 2, 1934; s. Jacques L. and Betty (Eichenbaum) W.; m. Sandra Mills Feingerts; children: Patricia Wiener Shifke, Jacques L. III, Betty Ellen Wiener Spomer, Donald B. BA, Tulane U., 1956, JD, 1961. Bar: La. 1961, U.S. Dist. Ct. (we. dist.) La. 1961. Ptnr. Wiener, Weiss & Madison, Shreveport, 1961-90; judge U.S. Ct. Appeals (5th cir.), New Orleans, 1990—. Mem. coun. La. State Law Inst., 1963; master of the bench Am. Inn of Ct., 1990-98. Pres. United Way N.W. La., 1975, Shreveport Jewish Fedn., 1969-70. Fellow Am. Coll. Trust and Estates Counsel, Am. Bar Found., La. Bar Found.; academician Internat. Acad. Estate and Trust Law; mem. ABA, La. State Bar Assn., Shreveport Bar Assn. (pres. 1982), Am. Law Inst. Avocations: fly fishing, upland game bird hunting, photography, travel. Office: Court of Appeals Building 600 Camp St Rm 244 New Orleans LA 70130-3425

WIENER, RONALD MARTIN, lawyer; b. Phila., June 1, 1939; s. William V. and Sylvia Wiener; children: Carol Jan, Alan Mark. AB, U. Pa., 1961; JD magna cum laude, Harvard U., 1964. Bar: D.C. 1965, Pa. 1966. Law clk. U.S. Tax Ct., 1964-66; assoc. Wolf, Block, Schorr and Solis-Cohen, Phila., 1966-72, ptnr., 1972—. Mem. commr.'s adv. group IRS, 1992-93. Fellow Am. Coll. Tax Counsel (regent 3d cir. 1996—); mem. ABA, Pa. Bar Assn., Phila. Bar Assn. (chair tax sect. 1989-90). Corporate taxation, , Taxation, general. Office: Wolf Block Schorr and Solis-Cohen LLP 1650 Arch St 2d fl Philadelphia PA 19103-2678 E-mail: rwiener@wolfblock.com

WIER, RICHARD ROYAL, JR. lawyer, inventor; b. Wilmington, Del., May 19, 1941; s. Richard Royal and Anne (Kurtz) W.; m. Anne E. Edwards, Nov. 25, 1978; children— Melissa Royal, Emma Kurtz; children from previous marriage: Richard Royal, III, Mimi Poole. BA in English, Hamilton Coll., 1963; LLB, U. Pa., 1966; postgrad., Temple U., 1981-82. Bar: D.C. 1967, Del. 1967, Pa. 1980, U.S. Dist. Ct. Del., U.S. Ct. Appeals (3d cir.), U.S. Supreme Ct. Assoc. Connolly, Bove & Lodge, Wilmington, 1966-68; dep. atty. gen. State of Del., 1968-70; state prosecutor Del. Dept. Justice, 1970-74; atty. gen. State of Del., 1975-79; ptnr. Prickett, Jones, Elliott, Kristol & Schnee, 1979-92; pvt. practice, 1993—. Lectr. criminal and labor law various instns. Active United Way campaign, 1976, 77; mem. supervisory bd. Gov.'s Commn. on Criminal Justice; bd. dirs. Del. Coun. Crime and Justice, 1982-89; mem. adv. coun. Diabetes Control, 1990-92; dir. Project Assist, 1992-95, Commn. on Outreach, 1994—. Recipient Law Enforcement award Newark Police Dept., 1974; Law Enforcement Commendation medal Nat. Soc. SAR, 1976; Ideal Citizen award Am. Found. for Sci. Creative Intelligence, 1976; Commendation Del. Gen. Assembly Senate, 1976, 77, 80; named one of Top Labor/Employment Attys. in Del., Del. Today, 1999, 2000. Mem. ABA, Nat. Dist. Attys. Assn. (state dir.), Del. Bar Assn. (chmn. criminal law sect. 1987-91, co-chmn. on drug crisis 1993—, vice chmn. labor law sect. 1987-88, chmn. 1989-90), Pa. Bar Assn., D.C. Bar Assn., Nat. Assn. Attys. Gen. (hon. life, exec. com.), Soc. Attys. Gen. Execs. (emeritus), Am. Judicature Soc., Am. Del. Trial Lawyers Assn., Nat. Assn. Extradition Ofcls. (hon. life, regional v.p., exec. dir.), Italian Radio/TV Assn. (hon., Outstanding Achievement award), Internat. Platform Assn., Pi Delta Epsilon. Criminal, Labor, Personal injury. Office: 1220 N Market St Ste 600 Wilmington DE 19801-2598 E-mail: rwier@wierlaw.com

WIERSMA, DAVID CHARLES, lawyer; b. Lakewood, Ohio, May 11, 1947; s. Milton Edward and Violet (Tinker) W.; m. Martha Denning, June 14, 1969 (div. Sept. 1976); 1 son, Andrew David; m. Eileen Marguerite Novello, July 21, 1978 (div. 1984); 1 child, Holly Elizabeth. BA in Econs./Math., U. Pitts., 1969; JD cum laude, Cleveland Marshall Coll. Law, 1976. Bar: Ohio 1976, U.S. Dist. Ct. (no. dist.) Ohio 1977. Tchr. high sch. Lorain City Schs., Ohio, 1969-72; trust officer Lorain County Savs. & Trust Co., Elyria, Ohio, 1972-76; assoc. Cook and Batista Co. L.P.A., Lorain, 1976-81, ptnr., 1981—. Trustees Lorain County Law Library Assn., Elyria, 1982—, pres. bd. trustees, 1986; trustee St. Joseph Urgent Care Ctr., Elyria, 1983-87, sec.-treas. bd. trustees, 1985-86; trustee, pres. bd. trustees home health care adv. bd. St. Joseph Hosp. and Health Ctr., 1988—; trustee Firelands council Boy Scouts Am., Vermilion, Ohio, 1983-85, Goodwill Industries Lorain County, Ohio, 1988—, HospiCorp Inc., 1988—. Mem. Ohio State Bar Assn., Lorain County Bar Assn., Greater Cleve. Bar Assn., Greater Lorain C. of C., Am. Mensa. Democrat. Lutheran. Lodge: Rotary. Banking, Probate, Real property. Home: 338 Brunswick Dr Avon Lake OH 44012-2918 Office: Cook and Batista Co LPA 209 W 6th St Lorain OH 44052-1744

WIERZBOWSKI, KRZYSZTOF FRANCISZEK, lawyer; b. Zyrardow, Poland, Mar. 8, 1956; s. Mieczyslaw and Boguslawa W.; children: Lukasz, Maria, Anna Teresa; m. Agnieszka Gawrysiak, Aug. 19, 1995; 1 child: Magdalena. ML, Warsaw U., 1979, postgrad., 1983. Qualified as judge, 1982; bar: Warsaw 1986. Trainee Zespol Adwokacki nr 19, Warsaw, 1983-88; atty. Attys. Agy. IUS, Ltd., 1988-91; ptnr. Dickinson, Wright, Moon, Van Dusen & Freeman, 1991-96, Baker & McKenzie, Warsaw, 1996-97, Wierzbowski & Szubielska, Warsaw, 1997—. Contbr. articles to profl. jours. including Polish Market, Am. Investor, others. Mem. IBA, Warsaw Bar. Communications, General corporate. Office: Wierzbowski & Szubielska Nowogrodzka 68 02 014 Warsaw Poland Fax: 48 22 523 4755. E-mail: krzysztof.wierzbowski@pl.landwellglobal.com

WIESE, LARRY CLEVENGER, lawyer; b. Huntsville, Tex., May 30, 1949; s. Arthur Edward and Lola Irene (Clevenger) W.; m. Patricia Petty Barr, Aug. 12, 1972; 1 son, Hugh Clevenger. B.S., Sam Houston State U., 1971; J.D., Tex. Tech. U., 1974; M.B.A., George Washington U., 1978. Bar: Tex. 1974, U.S. Ct. Mil. Appeals 1975, U.S. Supreme Ct. 1976, U.S. Dist. Ct. (so. dist.) Tex. 1979, U.S. Dist. Ct. (ea. dist.) Tex. 1980, U.S. Ct. Appeals (5th cir.) 1982. Staff atty. Shell Oil Co., Houston, 1978-80; atty. Houston div. Marathon Oil Co., 1980-84, Marathon Internat. Oil Co., London, 1984-87; sr. counsel internat. E & P Marathon Oil Co., Houston, 1987—. Contbr. article to profl. jour. Lectr. Ea. Mineral Law Found.; precinct chmn. Mayor Kathy Whitmire campaign, Houston, 1982; mem. Western Harris County Republican Men's Club, 1980-84, Gulf Coast Council Fgn. Affairs, Galveston, 1980-84. Served to lt. comdr. USCG, 1974-78. Named one of Outstanding Young Men in Am., 1981. Mem. Tex. Bar Assn., Houston Bar Assn. (chmn. corp. counsel sect. 1983-84), Houston Young Lawyers Assn. (program chmn. 1982-83), Maritime Law Assn., Res. Officers Assn., Navy League. Lutheran. Club: Luth. Men. State civil litigation, General corporate, Oil, gas, and mineral. Office: Marathon Oil Co PO Box 3128 Houston TX 77253-3128

WIGELL, RAYMOND GEORGE, lawyer; b. Chgo., Apr. 18, 1949; s. Raymond Carl and Amanda D. (Santiago) W.; m. Barbara E. Buettner, June 28, 1980; children: Katherine, Elizabeth, Charles. BA, U. Ill., Chgo., 1971; JD, John Marshall Law Sch., 1975; LLM in Taxation, DePaul U., 1991. Bar: Ill. 1975, U.S. Dist. Ct. (no. dist.) Ill. 1975, U.S. Ct. Appeals (7th cir.) 1978, U.S. Supreme Ct. 1979, U.S. Tax Ct. 1987. Pvt. practice law Raymond G. Wigell, Chgo., 1975-77; trial atty. Cook County Pub. Defender, 1977-78; pres., owner, atty. Wigell & Assocs., Chicago Heights, Ill., 1978—. Instr. MacCormac Jr. Coll., Chgo., 1976-77; lectr. in bus. law Oakton C.C., Des Plaines, Ill., 1976-84; adj. prof. Govs. State U., University Park, Ill., 1984-92. Commn. chair inquiry bd. Atty. Registration Disciplinary Commn. Supreme Ct. Ill., Chgo., 1985-90, commn. chair hearing bd., 1990-95. With USN, 1971-77. Mem. U. Ill. Alumni Assn. (life mem.). Roman Catholic. Entertainment, General corporate, Criminal. Office: Wigell & Assocs Atty at Law 418 Dixie Hwy Chicago Heights IL 60411-1739 E-mail: wgllaw@aol.com

WIGGER, JARREL L. lawyer; b. Wiesbaden, Germany, May 12, 1963; s. Philip Lee and Ervinetta (Maxey) W.; m. Rose Marie Riley, Aug. 1, 1987; children: Amy Elizabeth, Jordan Lee. BA in English, The Citadel, 1985; JD, Wake Forest U., 1988. Bar: S.C. 1988, U.S. Dist. Ct. S.C. 1993, U.S. Ct. Mil. Appeals 1991, U.S. Supreme Ct. 1998. Student prosecutor Forsyth County Dist. Atty. Office, Winston-Salem, N.C., 1988; assoc. Drose, Davidson & Bennett, Charleston, S.C., 1992-94, jr. ptnr., 1995-98; ptnr. Davidson, Bennett & Wigger, 1999—. Real estate cons. Co-editor, author: U.S. Navy Mass Casualty Handbook, 1991; co-editor: Law School for Nonlawyers Handbook, 1995. Lt. USN, 1986-92. Mem. ABA, ATLA, S.C. Trial Lawyers Assn., S.C. Bar Assn., Charleston County Bar Assn., Claimant Assn. for Workers Compensation (bd. govs.), Assn. Citadel Men (life), Citadel Brigadier Found., Charleston Area Citadel Club, Citadel Old Timers Wrestling Club (pres. 1996—), Sigma Tau Delta. Avocations: running, guitar, wrestling, coaching. General civil litigation, Personal injury, Workers' compensation. Office: 8086 Rivers Ave North Charleston SC 29406

WIGHTMAN, ALEC, lawyer; b. Cleve., Jan. 23, 1951; s. John and Betty Jane (Follis) W.; m. Kathleen A. Little, June 19, 1976; children: Nora, Emily. BA, Duke U., 1972; JD, Ohio State U., 1975. Bar: Ohio 1975, U.S. Tax Ct. 1982, U.S. Ct. Appeals (6th cir.) 1983. Assoc. Krupman, Fromson & Henson, Columbus, Ohio, 1975-77; ptnr. Krupman, Fromson, Bownas & Wightman, 1978-82; assoc. Baker & Hostetler, 1982-83, ptnr., 1984—. Mem. ABA, Ohio Bar Assn., Columbus Bar Assn., Ohio Oil and Gas Assn., Nat. Health Lawyers Assn. Avocation: tennis. Bankruptcy, Oil, gas, and mineral, Health. Office: Baker & Hostetler 65 E State St Ste 2100 Columbus OH 43215-4260

WILCOX, DONALD ALAN, lawyer; b. Grantsburg, Wis., July 18, 1951; s. John Charles and Lois Margaret (Finch) W.; m. Rachel Ann Johnson, Dec. 28, 1973; children: Benjamin Ray, Joseph Charles (dec.), Sara Johanna. BS, USAF Acad., 1973; JD, Georgetown U., 1979. Bar: Minn. 1979. Commd. 2d lt. USAF, 1973, advanced through grades to capt., resigned, 1979; assoc Holmquist & Holmquist, Benson, Minn., 1979-81; ptnr. Holmquist & Wilcox, 1981-90; shareholder Wilcox, Erhardt & Spates, P.A., Benson, 1990-91; pvt. practice, 1991—. Gen. counsel Swift County-Benson Hosp., 1981—, Farmers Mut. Coop., Bellingham, Minn., 1986—, Agralite Coop., Benson, 1986—, Kandiyohi Electric Coop., 1995—; atty. City of Benson, 1985—; examiner of titles, Swift County, Benson, 1986—, Federated Tel. Coop., Chokio, Minn., 1988—; bd. dirs. State Bank Danvers. Mem. Benson Planning Commn., 1979—; pres. Our Redeemer's Luth. Ch., Benson, 1985-86, 93-94; pres., bd. dirs. Swift County Homes, Inc., Benson, 1984-92. Recipient Lawyers Coop. Pub. award Lawyers Coop. Pub. Co., 1979. Mem. Minn. Bar Assn., Twelfth Dist. Bar Assn. (pres. 1995-96), Benson C. of C. (bd. dirs. 1981-84), Kiwanis (treas. Benson 1982-84, pres. 1999-00). Avocations: reading, golf, skiing. Contracts commercial, Probate, Real property. Home: 604 13th St S Benson MN 56215-2017 Office: 1150 Wisconsin Ave Benson MN 56215-1841 E-mail: dwilcox@willmar.com

WILCOX, GREGORY B. lawyer; b. Des Moines, Sept. 22, 1954; s. Lawrence R. and Mary T. Wilcox; m. Melinda S. Vande Lune, Sept. 4, 1976; children: Andrew, Austin, Morgan. BBA, U. Iowa, 1976; JD, Drake U., 1982. Bar: Iowa, 1982. V.p. Wilcox Enterprises, Inc., West Des Moines, Iowa, 1976-79; atty. Nyemaster Law Firm, Des Moines, 1982—, shareholder, dir., 1987—. Mem. bd. couns. Drake U. Law Sch., 1990-96, chair admissions com., 1992-93, exec. com., 1992-93. Assoc. articles editor Drake Law Sch., 1981-82; contbr. articles to profl. jours. Dir. Iowa State Chpt. March Dimes, Des Moines, 1993—; dir., sec. Iowa Sports Found., Des Moines, 1996—. Mem. ABA, Iowa State Bar Assn. (chair forms com. 1988-91, chair profl. corp. com. 1993-95), Polk County Bar Assn., Order of the Coif. Office: Nyemaster Law Firm 700 Walnut St Ste 1600 Des Moines IA 50309-3899

WILCOX, JOHN CAVEN, lawyer, corporate consultant; b. N.Y.C., Nov. 12, 1942; s. Daniel A. and Jessie Alexandra (Caven) W.; m. Vanessa Guerrini-Maraldi, Sept. 30, 1983; children Daniel D.G., William G.M., Julia G.M. BA magna cum laude, Harvard U., 1964; MA, U. Calif., Berkeley, 1965; JD, Harvard U., 1968; LLM, NYU, 1981. Bar: N.Y. 1973. Account exec. Georgeson & Co. Inc., N.Y.C., 1973-79, mng. dir., 1979-90, chmn., 1990; trustee Family Dynamics, Inc., 1979-96, Georgeson Shareholder Comm., Inc., 1999—. Dir. ACTV, Inc., GSC Proxitalia S.p.A.; chair cross-border voting practices com. Internat. Corp. Governance Network. Trustee Woodrow Wilson Nat. Fellowship Found., 1996, vice chmn., 1996—; trustee Bennington Coll., 1998—. With U.S. Army, 1968-70, Vietnam. Woodrow Wilson fellow. Mem. ABA, NYSE (mem. shareholders comm. com. 1989-95), Am. Soc. Corp. Secs., Nat. Assn. Security Dealers (mem. issuer affairs com 1990—), Downtown Assn., Harvard Club (N.Y.C.), Phi Beta Kapa. Democrat. Home: 580 West End Ave New York NY 10024-1723 E-mail: jwilcox@georgeson.com

WILCOX, JON P. state supreme court justice; b. Berlin, Sept. 5, 1936; m. Jane Ann; children: Jeffrey, Jennifer. AB in Polit. Sci., Ripon Coll., 1958; JD, U. Wis., 1965. Pvt. practice Steele, Smyth, Klos and Flynn, LaCrosse, Wis., 1965-66, Hacker and Wilcox, Wautoma, 1966-69, Wilcox, Rudolph, Kubasta & Rathjen, Wautoma, 1969-79; elected judge Waushara County Cir. Ct., 1979-92; apptd. justice Wis. Supreme Ct., 1992-97, elected justice 10-yr. term, 1997. Commr. Family Ct., Waushara County, 1977-79; vice

chmn., chmn. Wis. Sentencing Commn., 1984-92; chief judge 6th Jud. Dist., 1985-92; mem. State-Fed. Jud. Coun., 1992-99, Jud. Coun. Wis., 1993-98; mem. Prison Overcrowding Task Force, 1988-90; mem. numerous coms. Wis. Judiciary; mem. faculty Wis. Jud. Coll., 1986-97; chmn. Wis. Chief Judges Com., 1990-92; co-chair comm. on judiciary as co-equal br. of govt. Wis. State Bar, 1995-97; lectr. in field. Contbr. (with others): Wisconsin News Reporters Legal Handbook: Wisconsin Courts and Court Procedures, 1987. Bd. visitors U. Wis. Law Sch, 1970-76. Lt. U.S. Army, 1959-61. Named Outstanding Jaycee Wautoma, 1974; recipient Disting. Alumni award Ripon Coll., 1993. Fellow Am. Bar Found.; mem. ABA (com. on continuing appellate edn.), Wis. Bar Assn. (bench bar com.), Wis. Law Found. (bd. dirs.), Tri-County Bar Assn., Dane County Bar Assn., Trout Unltd., Ruffed Grouse Soc., Ducks Unltd., Rotary, Phi Alpha Delta. Office: Supreme Court State Capitol PO Box 1688 Madison WI 53701-1688

WILCOX, MARK DEAN, lawyer; b. May 25, 1952; s. Fabian Joseph and Zeryle Lucille (Tase) W.; m. Catherine J. Wertjes, Mar. 12, 1983; children: Glenna Lynn, Joanna Tessie, Andrew Fabian Joseph. BBA, U. Notre Dame, 1973; JD, Northwestern U., 1976; postgrad., The Am. Coll., 1979, 92; ChFC, Am. Coll., 1992. Bar: Ill. 1976, U.S. Dist. Ct. (no. dist.) Ill. 1976, Trial Bar 1982, U.S. Ct. Appeals (7th cir.) 1987, U.S. Supreme Ct. 1989. Staff asst. Nat. Dist. Attys. Assn., Chgo., 1974-75; trial asst. Cook County States Atty., 1975; intern U.S. Atty. No. Dist. Ill., 1975-76; assoc. Lord, Bissell & Brook, 1976-85, ptnr., 1986—. Bd. mgrs. YMCA Met. Chgo., Internat. Spl. Olympics; trustee Trinity United Meth. Ch. Mem. ABA (tort and ins. practice sect.), Am. Soc. CLU and ChFC, Chgo. Bar Assn. (ins. law com.), Nat. Assn. Ins. and Fin. Advisors, Def. Rsch. Inst., Soc. Fin. Svc. Profls., Trial Lawyers Club Chgo., Notre Dame Nat. Monogram Club, Union League Club, Chgo. Lions Rugby Football Club, Beta Gamma Sigma. General civil litigation, Insurance, Professional liability. Office: Lord Bissell & Brook 115 S La Salle St Ste 3200 Chicago IL 60603-3902

WILD, NELSON HOPKINS, lawyer; b. Milw., July 16, 1933; s. Henry Goetseels and Virginia Douglas (Weller) W.; m. Joan Ruth Miles, Apr. 12, 1969; children: Mark, Eric. A.B., Princeton U., 1955; LL.B., U. Wis., 1961. Bar: Wis. 1962, Calif. 1967; cert. specialist in probate, estate planning and trust law State Bar of Calif. Research assoc. Wis. Legis. Council, Madison, 1955-56; assoc. Whyte, Hirschboeck, Minahan, Harding & Harland, Milw., 1961-67, Thelen, Marin, Johnson & Bridges, San Francisco, 1967-70; sole practice law, 1970—. Mem. State Bar Calif. Client Trust Fund Commn., 1983, mem. exec. com. conf. dels., 1985-88. Contbr. articles to legal jours. Bd. dirs. Neighborhood Legal Assistance Found., San Francisco, 1974-85, chmn. bd., 1978-81. Served with USAF, 1956-58. Mem. ABA, Calif. Bar Assn., San Francisco Bar Assn., Am. Bar Found., Lawyers of San Francisco Club (gov. 1975, treas. 1981, v.p. 1982, pres.-elect 1983, pres. 1984), Calif. Tennis Club (bd. dirs. 1995-97, pres. 1997). General corporate, Estate planning, Probate. Office: 332 Pine St Ste 710 San Francisco CA 94104-3230

WILD, ROBERT WARREN, lawyer; b. Syracuse, N.Y., Mar. 25, 1942; s. Robert Sumner and Evelyn I. (Yorman) W.; m. Elizabeth Trowbridge, Sept. 5, 1965; children: Robert Mason, Alexander Lewis, Elizabeth Anne. BS, MIT, 1964; JD, Cornell U., 1970. Bar: N.Y. 1971, D.C. 1973. Engr. Smithsonian Astrophysical Obs., Cambridge, Mass., 1965-67; atty., advisor U.S. Dept. Justice, Washington, 1970-72; law clk. to Hon. Justice William H. Rehnquist U.S. Supreme Ct., 1972-73; ptnr. Nixon Peabody LLP, Rochester, N.Y., 1973—. Mem. Monroe County Bar Assn. (trustee 1990-91, 92-94, treas. 1992-94, counsel 1994—). Labor, Pension, profit-sharing, and employee benefits, Taxation, general. Office: Nixon Peabody LLP Clinton Sq PO Box 31051 Rochester NY 14603-1051 E-mail: rwild@nixonpeabody.com

WILD, VICTOR ALLYN, lawyer, educator; b. Logansport, Ind., May 7, 1946; s. Clifford Otto and Mary E. (Helvey) W.; 1 child, Rachel. BS in Pub. Adminstrn., U.Ariz., 1968, JD, 1974. Bar: Ariz. 1975, U.S. Dist. Ct. Ariz. 1975, Mass. 1984, U.S. Dist. Ct. Mass. 1984, U.S. Ct. Appeals (1st cir.) 1985, U.S. Ct. Appeals (9th cir.). Chief escrow officer Lawyers Title Co., Denver, 1971-72, escrow officer Tucson, 1970-71; law clk. Pima County Atty., 1973-75, dep. county atty., 1975-81, chief criminal dep., 1981-84; asst. U.S. Atty. Dist. of Mass., Boston, 1984—. Civef gen. crimes unit U.S. Atty.'s Office, Boston, 1986-89; seminar instr. Mass. Continuing Legal Edn., Internat. Assn. Law Enforcement Investment Analysts, Dept. of Justice Office Internat. Affairs, Dept. of Labor, FBI, U.S. Postal Svc., Internat. Assn. Fin. Crims Investigators, Secret Svc., State Bar Ariz., Tucson and Phoenix, 1981-84; instr. U. Ariz., Tucson, 1981-84, Pima C.C., Tucson, 1981-84. Mem. editl. bd. Episcopal Times, Diocese of Mass., 1988—. Mem. vestry St. Michael's Episc. Ch., Marblehead, Mass., 1986-90, lay Eucharistic min., 1988—, parish warden, 1992-96; mem. Boston Ctr. for Internat. Visitors, 1989—; bd. dirs. Crime Resistors, Inc., Tucson, 1983, CODAC, Tucson, 1983, 88-Crime, Inc., Tucson, 1983, Marblehead Seaport Trust, 1987-89, Old ahd Historic Oversight Com., 1999-2000; chmn. Marblehead Capital Planning Commn., 1989—; bd. dirs. Marblehead Citizen Scholarship Found., 1997—, Marblehead Sch. Master Plan. Com., 2000—; mem. PhD rev. com. Law Policy and Soc. Northeastern U., 1991-92; bd. dirs. Davenport House Child Enrichment Ctr., Marblehead, 1986-89. With USAF, 1968-70. Recipient Commendation awards Dept. Labor, Dept. State, USCG, USIA, U.S. Postal Svc., Dept. Treasury, EOUSA Rev., Software Pub. Assn., Mass. Ins. Fraud Bur.; named Prosecutor of Yr., Office Insp. Gen., U.S. Dept. Labor, 1986, DOJ Spec. Achievement Award, 1993, 95, 96. Master Boston Inn of Ct.; mem. Ariz. Bar Assn., Mass. Bar Assn., Tau Kappa Epsilon, Delta Sigma Pi, Phi Kappa Delta. Office: US Attys Office Ste 9200 US Courthouse One Courthouse Way Boston MA 02210

WILDE, WILLIAM RICHARD, lawyer; b. Markesan, Wis., Mar. 1, 1953; s. Leslie Maurice and Elaine Margaret (Schweder) W.; m. Carolyn Margaret Zieman, July 17, 1981 (div. 1987); 1 child, Leah Marie; m. Barbara Joan Rohlf, Jan. 6, 1990. BA, U. Wis., Milw., 1975; JD, Marquette U., 1980. Bar: Wis. 1980, U.S. Dist. Ct. (ea. and we. dists.) Wis. 1980. Dist. atty. Green Lake County, Green Lake, Wis., 1980-83, corp.counsel, 1981; ptnr. Curtis, Wilde and Neal, Oshkosh, 1983-97, Wilde Law Offices, Oshkosh, 1997—. Mem. ATLA, Wis. Bar Assn., Wis. Acad. Trial Lawyers (Amicus Curiae Brief com. 1987-92, bd. dirs., assoc. editor The Verdict, treas. 1993, sec. 1994, v.p. 1995, pres.-elect 1996, pres. 1997), Winnebago County Bar Assn., Green Lake County Bar Assn. General civil litigation, Insurance, Personal injury. Office: Wilde Law Offices 1901 S Washburn PO Box 3422 Oshkosh WI 54903-3422 also: PO Box 282 Markesan WI 53946-0282 E-mail: wildelaw@expc.com

WILDER, JAMES SAMPSON, III, lawyer, judge; b. Knoxville, Tenn., Mar. 15, 1949; s. James Sampson and Florence Louise (Summers) W. BS, Lambuth Coll., Jackson, Tenn., 1971; JD, Memphis State U., 1974. Bar: Tenn. 1974, U.S. Dist. Ct. (we. dist.) Tenn. 1975, U.S. Supreme Ct. 1981, U.S. Ct. Appeals (6th cir.) 1982. Assoc. Lt. Gov. John S. Wilder, Somerville, Tenn., 1974-75, ptnr., 1975-76, Wilder, Wilder & Johnson, Somerville, 1976-83; pvt. practice James S. Wilder III, 1983-95; gen. sessions judge Fayette County, Tenn., 1985-90; assoc. Petkoff and Lancaster, Memphis, 1995—. Scoutmaster troop 95 Boy Scouts Am., Somerville, 1975-77, com. person, 1977—. Paul Harris fellow Rotary, Somerville, 1977. Mem. ABA, Assn. Trial Lawyers Am., Tenn. Bar Assn., Tenn. Trial Lawyers Assn. (dir. 1983-86), Fayette County C. of C. (dir. 1979—), Somerville Rotary (dir. 1976—, charter pres. 1976-78). Methodist. Avocations: hunting, fishing. Federal civil litigation, State civil litigation, Personal injury. Home: PO Box 187 Somerville TN 38068-0187 Office: 135 West Market St PO Box 187 Somerville TN 38068

WILDER, MICHAEL STEPHEN, insurance company executive; b. New Haven, Sept. 8, 1941; BA, Yale U., 1963; JD, Harvard U., 1966. Bar: Conn. 1966. Atty. Hartford (Conn.) Fire Ins. Co., 1967-69, asst. gen. counsel, 1969-71, assoc. gen. counsel, 1971-75, gen. coun., sec., 1975-87, sr. v.p., gen. counsel, sec., 1987-95; sr. v.p., gen. counsel The Hartford Fin. Svcs. Group, Inc., 1995—. Mem. ABA, Conn. Bar Assn. Office: Hartford Fin Svcs Group Inc Hartford Plz Hartford CT 06115

WILDER, ROLAND PERCIVAL, JR. lawyer; b. Malden, Mass., June 21, 1940; s. Roland Percival and Clarissa (Hunting) W.; m. Susan McAra Randell, Sept. 3, 1965; children: Roland Percival III, William Randell. BA, Washington and Jefferson Coll., 1963; JD, Vanderbilt U., 1966. Bar: D.C. 1967, U.S. Dist. Ct. D.C. 1967, U.S. Ct. Appeals (D.C. cir.) 1967, U.S. Supreme Ct. 1972, U.S. Ct. Appeals (4th, 5th and 6th cirs.) 1976, U.S. Ct. Appeals (8th and 9th cirs.) 1977, U.S. Ct. Appeals (2d cir.) 1978, U.S. Ct. Appeals (11th cir.) 1981, U.S. Dist. Ct. Md. 1994, U.S. Ct. Appeals (3d cir.) 1997, U.S. Dist. Ct. Colo. 1997, U.S. Dist. Ct. (ea. dist.) Mich. 1999. Atty. Office of Solicitor U.S. Dept. Labor, Washington, 1967-69; asst. counsel civil rights office of solicitor U.S. Dept. Labor, 1969-70, counsel civil rights office of solicitor, 1970-71; supr. atty. office gen. counsel NLRB, 1972-74; assoc. gen. counsel Internat. Brotherhood Teamsters, 1974-85; sr. mem. Baptiste & Wilder P.C., 1985—. Lectr. numerous continuing legal edn. programs various states, 1970—. Mng. editor Vanderbilt U. Law Rev., 1965-66; contbr. articles to profl. jours. V.p. Arlington (Va.) Cubs Youth Club, Inc., 1975-81; coach Fairfax (Va.) Hockey Club, 1979-83. Mem. ABA, D.C. Bar Assn., Assn. Trial Lawyers Am., Phi Delta Phi, Pi Sigma Alpha, Phi Alpha Theta, Roosevelt Soc., Joint Council Flight Attendant Unions (hon. flight attendant 1985). Democrat. Avocations: history, tennis, skiing. Federal civil litigation, Labor, Pension, profit-sharing, and employee benefits. Office: Baptiste & Wilder PC 1150 Connecticut Ave NW Ste 500 Washington DC 20036-4194 E-mail: rpwilderjr@bapwild.com

WILDEROTTER, JAMES ARTHUR, lawyer; b. Newark, July 25, 1944; s. Arthur Walter and Dorothy Theresa (King) W.; m. Cheryl Lynn Clifford; children: James, Kristin, Kathryn. BA, Georgetown U., 1966; JD, U. Ill., 1969. Bar: D.C. 1969, U.S. Supreme Ct. 1974. Assoc. Covington & Burling, Washington, 1969-71; spl. asst. to Under Sec. Commerce, 1971-73; exec. asst. to Sec. HUD, 1973-74; assoc. dept. atty. gen. U.S., 1974-75; assoc. counsel to Pres. U.S., 1975-76; gen. counsel U.S. Energy Research and Devel. Adminstrn., 1976-77; of counsel Morgan, Lewis & Bockius, 1977-78; ptnr. Jones, Day, Reavis & Pogue, 1978-91, 95—; v.p., gen. counsel Internat. Paper Co., Purchase, N.Y., 1991-94. Editor in chief: U. Ill. Law Rev., 1968-69. Gen. counsel rules com. Rep. Nat. Conv., 1980; sec. James S. Brady Presdl. Found., 1982-88; gen. counsel Nat. Sudden Infant Death Syndrome Found., 1986-90, sec. Sudden Infant Death Syndrome Alliance, 1990-93. With USN, 1962-68. Mem. ABA Republican. Roman Catholic. Administrative and regulatory, General corporate. Home: 518 Duke St Alexandria VA 22314-3738 Office: Jones Day Reavis and Pogue 51 Louisiana Ave NW Washington DC 20001-2113

WILDES, LEON, lawyer, educator; b. Scranton, Pa., Mar. 4, 1933; BA magna cum laude, Yeshiva U., 1954; JD, NYU, 1957, LLM, 1959. Bar: N.Y. 1958, U.S. Dist. Ct. (so. dist.) N.Y. 1960, U.S. Supreme Ct. 1961. Ptnr. Wildes, Weinberg, Grunblatt & Wildes, P.C., N.Y.C., 1960—; adj. prof. law Benjamin N. Cardozo Sch. Law, 1981—. Contbr. numerous articles to law revs. Mem. ABA, Assn. of Bar of City of N.Y. (com. immigration and nationality law 1975-78, 88-91, 95-98), Am. Immigration Lawyers Assn. (nat. pres. 1970-71, bd. govs. 1971—, co-chair ethics com. 1993—, editor Immigration and Nationality Law Symposium 1983). Criminal, Immigration, naturalization, and customs, Consular. Office: 515 Madison Ave New York NY 10022-5403

WILENSKY, SAUL, lawyer; b. Bklyn., Dec. 9, 1941; s. Morris and Pearl (Wagman) W.; m. Sandra J. Brunault, Nov. 11, 1979; 1 child, Margot. BA, Hunter Coll., 1963; LLB, St. John's U., Bklyn., 1966; LLM, NYU, 1976. Bar: N.Y. 1967, U.S. Dist. Ct. (ea. and so. dists.) N.Y. 1970, U.S. Supreme Ct. 1971, U.S. Ct. Appeals (2d cir.) 1973, U.S. Dist. Ct. (no. dist.) N.Y. 1974. Ptnr. Lester, Schwab, Katz & Dwyer, N.Y.C., 1966—. State civil litigation, Personal injury, Product liability. Office: Lester Schwab Katz & Dwyer 120 Broadway Fl 39 New York NY 10271-0002 E-mail: swilensky@lskdnylaw.com

WILEY, EDWIN PACKARD, retired lawyer; b. Chgo., Dec. 10, 1929; s. Edwin Garnet and Marjorie Chastina (Packard) W.; m. Barbara Jean Miller, May 21, 1949; children: Edwin Miller, Clayton Alexander, Stephen Packard. BA, U. Chgo., 1949, JD, 1952. Bar: Wis. 1952, Ill. 1952, U.S. Dist. Ct. (ea. dist.) Wis. 1953, U.S. Supreme Ct. 1978. Assoc. Foley & Lardner, Milw., 1952-60, ptnr., 1960-98; ret. Bd. dirs. Genetic Testing Inst., Inc., other corps. and founds. Co-author: Bank Holding Companies: A Practical Guide to Bank Acquisitions and Mergers, 1988, Wisconsin Uniform Commercial Code Handbook, 1971; author: Promotional Arrangements: Discrimination in Advertising and Promotional Allowances, 1976; editor in chief U. Chgo. Law Rev., 1952. Bd. dirs. Blood Ctr. of Southeastern Wis., pres., 1978-82; pres. Blood Ctr. Rsch. Found., Inc., 1983-87; v.p. Friends of Schlitz Audubon Ctr., Inc., 1975-87; active United Performing Arts Fund of Milw.; pres. Wis. Conservatory ofMusic, 1968-73; pres. First Unitarian Soc. Milw., 1961-63; v.p. Mid-Am. Ballet Co., 1971-73, Milw. Ballet Co., 1973-74; pres. Florentine Opera Co., 1983-86; bd. dirs. Milw. Symphony Orch., pres., 1993-95; bd. dirs. Milw. Pub. Mus., Inc., sec., 1992—; bd. dirs. Wis. History Found., v.p., 1998—; bd. dirs. Preserve Our Parks, Inc., 1999—. Mem. ABA, State Bar of Wis., Milw. Bar Assn., Am. Law Inst., Order of Coif, Univ. Club, Phi Beta Kappa (pres. Greater Milw. assn. 1962-63). Antitrust, Banking, Private international. Home: 929 N Astor St Unit 2101 Milwaukee WI 53202-3488

WILEY, RICHARD EMERSON, lawyer; b. Peoria, Ill., July 20, 1934; s. Joseph Henry and Jean W. (Farrell) W.; m. Elizabeth J. Edwards, Aug. 6, 1960; children: Douglas S., Pamela L. B.S. with distinction, Northwestern U., 1955, J.D., 1958; LLM, Georgetown U., 1962; LLD (hon.), Cath. U. of Am., 1998. Bar: Ill. 1958, D.C. 1972. Pvt. practice, Chgo., 1962-70; gen. counsel FCC, Washington, 1970-72, mem., 1972-74, chmn., 1974-77, chmn. FCC's adv. com. on advanced TV svc., 1987-96; mng. ptnr. Wiley, Rein & Fielding, 1983—. Prof. law John Marshall Law Sch., U. Chgo., 1963-70. Chmn. adv. bd. Inst. for Tele-Info., Columbia U., 1989—. Capt. AUS, 1959-62. Recipient Emmy award Nat. Acad. Arts, 1997, Medal of Honor, Electronic Industries Am., 1996. Fellow Am. Bar Found.; mem. ABA (mem. ho. of dels. 1969-71, 77-84, chmn. young lawyers sect., 1977-84, chmn. Forum com. on communications 1969, chmn. bd. editors ABA Jour. 1984-89, chmn. com. on scope and correlation of work 1989, chmn. adminstrv. law and regulatory practice 1993-94), Fed. Bar Assn. (pres. 1977), Fed. Communications Bar Assn. (pres. 1987), Ill. Bar Assn., Chgo. Bar Assn., Adminstrv. Conf. U.S. (coun., sr. fellow), Phi Delta Phi, Phi Delta Kappa. Methodist. Communications. Home: 3818 N Woodrow St Arlington VA 22207-4345 Office: Wiley Rein & Fielding 1776 K St NW Ste 1100 Washington DC 20006-2332 E-mail: rwiley@wrf.com

WILEY, S. DONALD, lawyer, food products company executive; married. BA Westminster Coll., 1950, LLB U. Pa., 1953. Sole practice, 1953-55; asst. dist. atty. Allegheny County , Pa., 1955-56, atty. HJ Heinz Co., Pitts., 1956; asst to corp. sec., 1962-64, gen. counsel, 1964-70, v.p., gen. counsel, 1970-72, sr. v.p., sec, gen. counsel, 1972—, also bd. dirs. With U.S. Army Air Corp, 1945-46. General corporate. Office: H J Heinz Co 600 Grant St Ste 6000 Pittsburgh PA 15219-2857

WILHELM, ROBERT OSCAR, lawyer, civil engineer, developer; b. Balt., July 7, 1918; s. Clarence Oscar and Agnes Virginia (Grimm) W.; m. Grace Sanborn Luckie, Apr. 4, 1959. BSCE, Ga. Tech. Inst., 1947, MSIM, 1948; JD, Stanford U., 1951. Bar: Calif. 1952, U.S. Supreme Ct. Mem. Wilhelm, Thompson, Wentholt and Gibbs, Redwood City, Calif., 1952—; gen. cousnel Bay Counties Gen. Contractors; pvt. practice civil engring., Redwood City, 1952. Pres. Bay Counties Builders Escrow, Inc., 1972-88. Author: The Manual of Procedures for the Construction Industry, 1971, Manual of Procedures and Form Book for Construction Industry, 9th edit., 1995, Construction Law for Contractors, Architects and Engineers; columnist Law and You in Daily Pacific Builder, 1955—. With C.E., AUS, 1942-46. Named to Wisdom Hall of Fame, 1999. Mem. Bay Counries Civil Engrs. (pres. 1957), Peninsula Builders Exch. (pres. 1958-71, dir.), Calif. State Builders Exch. (treas. 1971), Del Mesa Carmel Cmty. Assn. (bd. dirs. 1997-99), Masons, Odd Fellows, Eagles, Elks. Construction, Government contracts and claims. Home: 134 Del Mesa Carmel Carmel CA 93923-7950 Office: 702 Marshall St Ste 510 Redwood City CA 94063-1826

WILKEN, CLAUDIA, judge; b. Mpls., Aug. 17, 1949; BA with honors, Stanford U., 1971; JD, U. Calif., Berkeley, 1975. Bar: Calif. 1975, U.S. Dist. Ct. (no. dist.) Calif. 1975, U.S. Ct. Appeals (9th cir.) 1976, U.S. Supreme Ct. 1981. Asst. fed. pub. defender U.S. Dist. Ct. (no. dist.) Calif., San Francisco, 1975-78, U.S. magistrate judge, 1983-93, dist. judge, 1993—; ptnr. Wilken & Leverett, Berkeley, Calif., 1978-84. Adj. prof. U. Calif., Berkeley, 1978-84; prof. New Coll. Sch. Law, 1980-85; mem. jud. br. com. Jud. Conf. U.S.; past mem. edn. com. Fed. Jud. Ctr.; chair 9th cir. Magistrates Conf., 1987-88. Mem. ABA (mem. jud. adminstrn. divsn.), Alameda County Bar Assn. (judge's membership), Nat. Assn. Women Judges, Order of Coif, Phi Beta Kappa. Office: US Dist Ct No Dist 1301 Clay St # 2 Oakland CA 94612-5217

WILKERSON, JAMES NEILL, retired lawyer; b. Tyler, Tex., Dec. 17, 1939; s. Hubert Cecil and Vida (Alexander) W.; m. Cal Cantrell; children: Cody, Ike. AA, Tyler Jr. Coll., 1960; BBA, U. Tex., 1966, JD, 1968. Bar: Tex. 1968, U.S. Supreme Ct. 1973, U.S. Dist. Ct. (we. dist.) Tex. 1974. Pvt. practice, Georgetown and Mason, Tex., 1977-2001; ret., 2001. Instr. Cen. Tex. Coll., Copperaas Cove, Tex., 1973-74; asst prof. law U.S. Mil. Acad., West Point, N.Y., 1971-73; pres. C&N Bus. Developers, 19925. Pres. Beautify Georgetown Assn., 1977-80, 81-82; pres. U. Tex. Young Reps., 1964-65; co-chmn. Bush for Pres., 1988, Reagan-Bush campaign, 1980; mem. Williamson County Rep. Com., 1977-81; chmn. Hist. Preservation Com., 1979-85; trustee 1st United Meth. Ch., 19945, chmn. bd. trustees, 1996-99; vol. Mason Lions Club, Steady Steps After Sch. Homework Helper; substitute tchr. Mason Schs. Col. USAR, 19685, trial judge JAGC, 1975-91, appellate judge Army Ct. Mil. Rev., 1991-93. Decorated Legion of Merit, Bronze Star, Air medal. Mem. Tex. State Bar Coll., Williamson County Bar Assn., Sertoma (v.p. 1981-83, 87, sec. 1988-89, pres. 1992-93), Lions (pres. 1982-83), Vietnam War Vets. Estate planning, Probate. Address: PO Box 1807 Mason TX 76856-1807

WILKINS, JERRY L. lawyer, clergyman; b. Big Spring, Tex., June 1, 1936; s. Claude F. and Grace L. (Jones) W.; children by previous marriage: Gregory, Tammy, Scott, Brett; m. Valerie Ann Nuanez, Aug. 1, 1986. BA, Baylor U., 1958, LLB, 1960. Bar: Tex. 1960, U.S. Dist. Ct. (no. dist.) Tex. 1960, U.S. Ct. Appeals (5th cir.); ordained to ministry, 1977. Pvt. practice, Dallas, 1960—; capt. Air Am., Vietnam, 1967-68, Joint Church Aid, Biafra, 1969-70, TransInternat. Airlines, Oakland, Calif., 1977-79; gen. counsel First Tex. Petroleum, Dallas, 1982; owner Wooltex, Inc., Dallas, 1983—; owner, dir., legal counsel Intermountain Gas Inc., Dallas, 1983-84; legal counsel, dir. USA First (co-founder USA First Panama); co-founder Nederlandse Fin. Panama; founder, dir. Comanche Peak Reclamation Inc.; bd. dirs. Engineered Roof Cons., Continental Tex. Corp., Arlington, Landlord Rsch. Inc., Acklin Pain Rsch. Inst., Inc., Irving, Tex., Silver Leaf Metals Internat. Inc., Silver Leaf Mining Inc., Tex. Recycling Industries, Inc., Minerals Exploration Inc., Land Techs. Inc., Environ. Techs. Inc., Environ. Contractors Inc., Environ. Enterprises Inc., Desert Resources Inc.; founder, chmn. bd. dirs. Tex. Reclamation Industries, Inc.; founder Oxford Securities Funding Inc., Manchester Securieties Funding Inc., Cambridge Securities Funding Inc.; bd. dirs., v.p. for legal affairs, underwriter Lloyds U.S. Inc.; bd. dirs., co-founder R O A S , Inc., Maritime Internat., Inc., Maritime Oil Recovery, Inc., Moriah Oil Recovery Barges, Inc., Megas Homes Internat., Urex Internat., Landlord Rsch. Co., Inc.; mem. legal counsel, bd. dirs. U.S. Fiduciary Co. Inc., U.S. Fiduciary Trust Co. Inc.; bd. dirs., legal counsel Lloyds U.S. Corp., Lloyds Link Inc., Lloyds Am. Inc., Image Security Co., Inc., Manchester Funding, Inc.; founder Kenai Cold Storage Inc., Kenai Pure Water Co., Arctic Pure Water Co., Arctic Cold Storage Inc., Shiloh Inc., Receivers, Inc., Internat. Equity Founding, Inc., C3 Plus Inc., UBO Sonoma Fin., UBO Caribbean Funding, Capstone Corp., Prowler Fouler Inc., Pacific Atlantic Funding Inc., Atlantic Funding, Inc.; bd. dirs., CEO Celex Nev., Inc.; bd. dirs. Minerals Exploration, Inc., Land Tech., Inc., Environ. Techs., Inc., Environ. Enterprises, Inc., Desert Gold Resources, Inc., Environ. Contractors, Inc.; co-founder USA First; cons. in field. Author: Gods Prosperity, 1980; So You Think You Have Prayed, 1980, Gods Hand in my Life, America, The Land of Sheep for Slaughter, I.R.S., America's Gestapo; Editor numerous books; contbr. articles to profl. jours. Bd. dirs., pres. Beasley For Children Found. Inc., Dallas, 1978—; mem. Rep. Presdl. Task Force, Washington, 1984—, Rep. Senatorial Inner Circle; bd. dirs., pilot Wings for Christians, Dallas, 1976—, Wings for Christ, Waco, Tex., 1976—. Recipient Cert. of Appreciation Parachute Club of Am., 1966; cert. of record holder for high altitude sky diving State of Tex., 1966, 67; Cert. of Achievement, Tex. State Guard, 1968. Mem. ABA, Nat. Lawyers Assn., Plaintiff Trial Lawyers Assn., Internat. Platform Assn., Tex. Trial Attys. Assn., Assn. Trial Lawyers Am., Quiet Birdmen, Tex. Outdoor Writers Assn., NRA, Tex. Rifle Assn., Parachute Assn. Am., P51 Mustang Pilots Assn., Phi Alpha Delta, U.S. Parachute Club (Monterey, Calif.). Avocations: shooting, hunting, fishing, flying, sports. Achievements: atty. (2 Tex. landmark cases) securing custody of female child for stepfather against natural parents (set the precedent which is now the standard visitation regarding children in divorce cases in Tex.), securing outside jail work program for convicted man, others. Federal civil litigation, State civil litigation, Oil, gas, and mineral. Office: PO Box 59462 Dallas TX 75229-1462

WILKINS, MICHAEL JON, state supreme court justice; b. Murray, Utah, May 13, 1948; s. Jack L. and Mary June (Phillips) W.; m. Diane W. Wilkins, Nov. 9, 1967; children: Jennifer, Stephanie, Bradley J. BS, U. Utah, 1975, JD, 1976; LLM, U. Va., 2001. Bar: Utah 1977, U.S. Dist. Ct. Utah 1977, U.S. Ct. Appeals (10th cir.) 1987, U.S. Supreme Ct. 1986. Mng. ptnr. Wilkins, Oritt & Headman, Salt Lake City, 1989-94; judge Utah Ct. Appeals, 1994—2000; justice Utah Supreme Ct, 2000—, mem. jud. coun., 2000—. Mem. Gov.'s Adv. Com. on Corp., Salt Lake City, 1989-94; mem. Utah Supreme Ct. Complex Steering Com., 1993-94; mem. Judiciary Standing Com. on Tech., 1995-2000, chmn., 1995-2000; mem. Legis. Compensation Commn., 1994-95. Trustee Utah Law Related Edn. Project, Inc., Salt Lake City, 1991-95, chmn., 1992-94. 1st lt. U.S. Army, 1968-72. Mem. LDS Ch. Office: Utah Supreme Ct 450 S State St PO Box 140210 Salt Lake City UT 84114-0210

WILKINS, WILLIAM WALTER, JR. federal judge; b. Anderson, S.C., Mar. 29, 1942; s. William Walter and Evelyn Louise (Horton) W.; m. Carolyn Louise Adams, Aug. 15, 1964; children: Lauren, Lyn, Walt. BA, Davidson Coll., 1964; JD, U. S.C., 1967. Bar: S.C., 1967, U.S. Dist. Ct. S.C. 1967, U.S. Ct. Appeals (4th cir.) 1969, U.S. Supreme Ct. 1970. Law clk. to judge U.S. Ct. Appeals 4th Cir., 1969; legal asst. to U.S. Senator Strom Thurmond, 1970; ptnr. Wilkins & Wilkins, Greenville, S.C., 1971-75; solicitor 13th Jud. Cir., 1974-81; judge U.S. Dist. Ct., Greenville,

1981-86, U.S. Ct. Appeals (4th cir.), 1986—. Lectr. Greenville Tech. Coll., 1973-97; chmn. U.S. Sentencing Commn., 1985-94. Editor-in-chief S.C. Law Rev., 1967; contbr. articles to legal jours. Served with U.S. Army, 1967-69. Named Outstanding Grad. of Yr. U. S.C. Sch. Law, 1967 Mem. S.C. Bar Assn., Wig and Robe. Republican. Baptist. Office: US Cir Ct 4th Ct PO Box 10857 Greenville SC 29603-0857

WILKINSON, JAMES ALLAN, lawyer, healthcare executive; b. Cumberland, Md., Feb. 10, 1945; s. John Robinson and Dorothy Jane (Kelley) W.; m. Elizabeth Susanne Quinlan, Apr. 14, 1973; 1 child, Kathryn Barrett. BS in Fgn. Svc., Georgetown U., 1967; JD, Duquesne U., 1978. Bar: Pa., U.S. Dist. Ct. (we. dist.) Pa. Legis. analyst Office of Mgmt. and Budget, Washington, 1972-73; dep. exec. sec. Cost of Living Coun., 1973-74; sr. fin. analyst U.S. Steel Corp., Pitts., 1974-82; ptnr. Buchanan Ingersoll, 1982-88; exec. v.p., gen. counsel Meritcare, 1988—; sr. v.p. Culwell Health Inc., 1991—. Adj. prof. U. Pitts. Sch. Law, 1988-91. Author: Financing and Refinancing Under Prospective Payment, 1985, Family Caregivers' Guide Planning and Decision Making for the Elderly, 1998; contbr. articles to profl. jours. Chmn. Oversight Com. on Organ Transplantation, Pitts., 1986-2001; sec.-treas. bd. dirs. Pitts. Symphony Soc., 1986-98, exec. com. bd. dirs., 1999—; bd. dirs. Western Pa. Com. of Prevention of Child Abuse, 1987-90, Comprehensive Safety Compliance, 1988-91, Buchanan Ingersoll Profl. corp., 1988-90, Parental Stress Ctr., 1990-94; sec. Ross Mountain Club, 1995-98, 99—, v.p., 1999—; bd. dirs. Carnegie Inst., 1997—, Carnegie Mus. Natural History, 1997—, Andy Warhol Mus., 1998—, Soc. for Contemporary Crafts, 1999—, treas., 2000—. Mem. Am. Soc. Law and Medicine, Am. Health Lawyers Assn., Audobon Soc. Southwestern Pa. (treas. 1996-2000), Duquesne Club. Republican. Episcopalian. General corporate, Health, Mergers and acquisitions. Home: 1005 Elmhurst Rd Pittsburgh PA 15215-1819 Office: Meritcare Inc 625 Stanwix St Ste 1220 Pittsburgh PA 15222-1415 E-mail: wilkinso@bellatlantic.net

WILKINSON, JAMES HARVIE, III, federal judge; b. N.Y.C., Sept. 29, 1944; s. James Harvie and Letitia (Nelson) W.; m. Lossie Grist Noell, June 30, 1973; children: James Nelson, Porter Noell. BA, Yale U., 1963-67; JD, U. Va., 1972; JD (hon.), U. Richmond, 1997, U. S.C., 1998. Bar: Va. 1972. Law clk. to U.S. Supreme Ct. Justice Lewis F. Powell, Jr., Washington, 1972-73; asst. prof. law U. Va., 1973-75, assoc. prof., 1975-78; editor Norfolk (Va.) Virginian-Pilot, 1978-81; prof. law U. Va., 1981-82, 83-84; dep. asst. atty. gen. Civil Rights div. Dept. Justice, 1982-83; judge U.S. Ct. Appeals (4th cir.), 1984—, chief judge, 1996—. Author: Harry Byrd and the Changing Face of Virginia Politics, 1968, Serving Justice: A Supreme Court Clerk's View, 1974, From Brown to Bakke: The Supreme Court and School Integration, 1979, One Nation Indivisible: How Ethnic Separatism Threatens America, 1997. Bd. Visitors U. Va., 1970-73; Republican candidate for Congress from 3d Dist. V a., 1970; bd. dirs. Fed. Jud. Ctr., 1992-96. Served with U.S. Army, 1968-69. Mem. Va. State Bar, Va. Bar Assn., Am. Law Inst. Episcopalian. Home: 1713 Yorktown Dr Charlottesville VA 22901-3035 Office: US Ct Appeals 255 W Main St Ste 230 Charlottesville VA 22902-5058

WILKINSON, ROBERT WARREN, lawyer; b. Oak Ridge, Dec. 7, 1950; s. Michael Kennerly and Virginia (Sleap) W.; m. Patsy Ann McFall, Jan. 3, 1980; 1 son, Michael McFall. B.A. cum laude, Emory U., 1975; J.D., U. Tenn., 1975; LL.M. in Taxation, Georgetown U., 1978. Bar: Tenn. 1975, U.S. Tax Ct. 1977, U.S. Ct. Claims 1977, U.S. Supreme Ct. 1978, U.S. Dist. Ct. (ea. dist.) Tenn. 1980. Assoc. Buxton, Lain & Buxton, Oak Ridge, 1979-83; ptnr. Buxton, Layton, Webster & Wilkinson, Oak Ridge, 1983— ; city atty. City of Oakdale, Tenn., 1981— ; atty. Morgan County Sch. Bd., Tenn., 1982— . Officer Arts Council Oak Ridge, 1983; bd. dirs. Hope of Oak Ridge, 1982, Daniel Arthur Rehab. Ctr., Oak Ridge, 1984. Served to maj. U.S. Army, 1976-79. Mem. ABA, Tenn. Bar Assn., Anderson County Bar Assn. Lodge: Rotary. General practice, Probate, Taxation, general. Home: 100 Carson Ln Oak Ridge TN 37830-7626 Office: Buxton Layton Webster & Wilkinson 107B W Tennessee Ave Oak Ridge TN 37830-6519

WILKS, LARRY DEAN, lawyer; b. Columbia, S.C., Jan. 8, 1955; s. Ray Dean and Jean (Garrett) W.; m. Jan Elizabeth McIllwain, May 2,1981; children: John Ray, Adam Garrett. BS, U. Tenn., 1977, JD, 1980. Bar: Tenn. 1981, U.S. Dist. Ct. (mid. dist.) Tenn. 1981, U.S. Supreme Ct. 1986, U.S. Ct. Appeals (6th cir.) 1993, U.S. Dist. Ct. (we. dist.) Tenn. 1996. Assoc. Mayo & Norris, Nashville, 1981-82; sole practice Springfield, Tenn., 1982-84; ptnr. Walton, Jones & Wilks, 1984, Jones & Wilks, 1984-89; pvt. practice Springfield, Tenn., 1989—. Chmn. Dem. Orgn. Robertson County Tenn., 1986-93. Fellow Tenn. Bar Found.; mem. ABA, ATLA, Tenn. Bar Assn. (assoc. gen. counsel 1991-94, gen. counsel 1994-99, bd. profl. responsibility 1993-98, bd. govs. 1991—, young lawyers divsn. lifetime fellow, asst. treas. 1999-2000, treas. 2000—), Tenn. Assn. Criminal Def. Lawyers, Tenn. Trial Lawyers Assn., Robertson County Bar Assn. (pres. 1993-96), Nat. Assn. Criminal Def. Laywers, Tenn. Young Lawyers Conf. (bd. dirs. 1987, editor quar. newsletter 1987-88, Mid. Tenn. v.p. 1988-89, v.p. 1989-90, pres.-elect 1990-91, pres. 1991-92). Methodist. Criminal, Personal injury, Product liability. Office: 509 W Court Sq Springfield TN 37172-2413

WILL, JOSEPH HENRY MICHAEL, lawyer, retired military officer; b. Erie, Pa., Aug. 2, 1945; s. Joseph Henry and Mary Ann (Hilbert) W.; m. Margaret Cotter, July 13, 1968 (div. Apr. 1986); children: Joseph Henry Michael, Christopher Patrick; m. Dorothy M. Quitoriano, Oct. 17, 1986. BS, SUNY, Buffalo, 1967; MBA, U. Tenn., 1975; JD, SUNY, Buffalo, 1980. Bar: N.Y. 1981, Colo. 1987. Commd. USAF, 1967, advanced through grades to maj., asst. staff judge advocate Ill., 1980-82, Clark Air Base, Phillipines, 1982-85, Keesler AFB, Miss., 1985-87; atty. advisor Office of the Staff Judge Advocate, Fort Lee, Va., 1987—. Republican. Roman Catholic. Home: 4916 Stewart Ln Disputanta VA 23842-4740 E-mail: willm@lee.army.mil

WILLARD, GREGORY DALE, lawyer; b. Pittsfield, Ill., Feb. 8, 1954; s. Wesley Dale and Rosmary (Stark) W.; m. Ann Julia Grier, June 3, 1978; children: Michael, David, John. BA summa cum laude, Westminster Coll., Fulton, Mo., 1976; JD cum laude, U. Ill., 1979. Bar: Mo., U.S. Dist. Ct. (ea. dist.) Mo., U.S. Ct. Appeals (8th Cir.). Staff asst. to Pres. Exec. Office of the Pres. The White House, Washington, 1976-77; ptnr. Bryan Cave, St. Louis, 1979—. Co-chmn. bankruptcy com. Met. Bar Assn., St. Louis, 1983-84. Bd. Dirs. St. Louis Children's Hosp., 1985-89, Found. for Spl. Edn., 1990—, Congress Neurol. Surgeons, 1998—. Mem. Congress of Neurol. Surgeons, Noonday Club. Banking, Bankruptcy, Consumer commercial. Office: Bryan Cave 211 N Broadway Saint Louis MO 63102-2733

WILLARD, JAMES ROBERT, lawyer; b. Camdenton, Mo., Jan. 29, 1934; s. Timothy Detweiler and Thelma Irene (Chandler) W.; m. Elizabeth Hess Buffe, Aug. 1, 1963; children: Kathryn Chandler Payne, David Matthew, Elizabeth Anne Vanbeber, James Robert, Timothy Detweiler. BSBA, U. Mo., 1955, JD, 1960. Bar: Mo. 1960, Kans. 1999, U.S. Dist. Ct. (we. dist.) Mo. 1961, U.S. Ct. Appeals (8th cir.) 1962, U.S. Ct. Appeals (10th cir.) 1963, U.S. Ct. Appeals (D.C. cir.) 1967, U.S. Supreme Ct. 1967. Assoc. Spencer Fane Britt & Browne LLP, Kansas City, Mo., 1960-65, ptnr., 1966—. Asst. instr. indsl. mgmt. U. Mo., Columbia, 1958-60; professorial lectr. labor law U. Mo., Kansas City, 1967. Contbr. articles to profl. jours. Active Reapportionment Commn., Mo. Ho. of Reps., 1966, Jackson County Charter Commn., 1970; chmn. Kans. City Election Bd., 1989-93, Jackson County Rep. Com., 1966-70. 1st lt. USAF, 1955-57. Mem. ABA (labor law sect.), Mo. Bar Assn., Kansas City Metro Bar Assn., Order of Coif, Omicron Delta Kappa, Phi Delta Pi. Labor. Home: 600 W 113th St Kansas City MO 64114-5209 Office: Indian Creek Pkwy Ste 700 Ste 700 9401 Indian Creek Pkwy Overland Park KS 66210-2005

WILLE, HANS GEORG, lawyer; b. Oslo, Norway, Aug. 21, 1958; s. Hans Georg and Eva Wille; m. Betty Agathe Mowinckel-Amundsen; children: Birgithe, Caroline. CandJur, U. Oslo, 1985. Bar: Oslo 1994. Adminstr OECD, Paris, 1989-90; legal counselor, dir. Ministry of Fin., Oslo, 1986-92; assoc. Bugge, Arentz-Hansen & Rasmussen, 1992-96; ptnr. Andersen Legal Advokatfirma ANS, 1996—. Author: IFA National Report, Taxation of Demergers, 1995; contbg. author: (textbook) Taxation of Corporations, 1988, Enterprise, Company and Taxation, 1995; contbr. articles to profl. jours. Mergers and acquisitions, Corporate taxation, Energy. Office: Andersen Legal ANS Drammensveien 165 POB 228 Skoyen, Oslo 0213 Norway Fax: 47 2292 8904. E-mail: hans.georg.wille@no.andersenlegal.com

WILLETT, THOMAS EDWARD, lawyer; b. N.Y.C., Nov. 8, 1947; s. Oscar Edward and Alice (Fleming) W.; m. Marilyn Kenney, Dec. 28, 1969; children: Thomas Justin, Christopher Joseph. BS, USAF Acad., Colo., 1969; JD with distinction, Cornell U., 1972. Bar: N.Y. 1973, U.S. Ct. Claims 1973, U.S. Supreme Ct. 1977. Judge advocate USAF, Syracuse, N.Y., 1973-75, Kincheloe AFB, Mich., 1975-77, USAF Hdqs., Washington, 1977-79; assoc. Harris, Beach & Wilcox, Rochester, N.Y., 1979-84, ptnr., 1985—. Pres. Monroe County Legal Assistance Corp., Rochester, 1983-89. Capt. USAF, 1969-79. Mem. ABA, N.Y. State Bar Assn., Monroe County Bar Assn., Order of Coif. Banking, General corporate, Securities. Office: Harris Beach LLP Granite Bldg 130 Main St E Rochester NY 14604-1687 E-mail: twillett@harrisbeach.com

WILLEY, BENJAMIN TUCKER, JR. lawyer; b. Richmond, Va., Feb. 23, 1946; s. Benjamin Tucker and Virginia (Bradshaw) W.; m. Beverly Jane Buscanics, Jan. 21, 1984; children by previous marriage: Benjamin Tucker III, Theresa. BA, U. Tex.-Arlington, 1973; JD, Oklahoma City U., 1976. Bar: Okla. 1976, Tex. 1985, U.S. Dist. Ct. (we. dist.) Okla. 1976. Ptnr. Evans & Willey, Oklahoma City, 1976-80; sr. ptnr. Willey & Singer, Oklahoma City, 1980—; chmn. continuing legal edn. program-title exam. basics and oil and gas title exam. U. Tulsa, 1984. Coach North Oklahoma City Soccer Club, 1980-83. Served to capt. U.S. Army, 1966-72, Vietnam. Decorated Bronze Star medal. Mem. Okla. Bar Assn. (chmn. continuing legal edn. program-Indian land titles 1983, mem. faculty oil and gas continuing legal edn. program 1983), Phi Delta Phi. Episcopalian. State civil litigation, Oil, gas, and mineral, Real property. Home: PO Box 14875 Oklahoma City OK 73113-0875 Office: Willey & Singer 501 NW Expressway St Ste 525 Oklahoma City OK 73118-6037

WILLEY, CHARLES WAYNE, lawyer; b. Dillon, Mont., Oct. 7, 1932; s. Asa Charles and Elizabeth Ellen Willey; m. Helene D., July 21, 1962 (div.); children: Stephen Charles, Heather Helene, Brent David, Scott D.; m. Alexis W. Grant, Jan. 26, 1986. BS with honors, Mont. State U., 1954; JD with high honors, U. Mont., 1959. Bar: Mont. 1959, Calif. 1960, U.S. Ct. Claims 1975, U.S. Tax Ct. 1975, U.S. Ct. Appeals (9th cir.) 1959, U.S. Ct. Appeals (Fed. cir.) 1983, U.S. Supreme Ct. 1972. Law clk. to presiding judge U.S. Ct. Appeals (9th cir.), 1959-60; ptnr. Price, Postel & Parma, Santa Barbara, Calif., 1960-77; pvt. practice, 1977-97; shareholder Hollister & Brace, 1998-2001. Prof. law corp.; instr. Santa Barbara City Coll., 1961-63, U. Calif., Santa Barbara, 1963-64; lectr. Mont. Tax Inst., 1990, 92, Am. Agr. Law Assn., 1993, 96. Chief editor Mont. Law Rev., 1958-59. Pres. Legal Aid Found. Santa Barbara, 1970; mem. Laguna Blanca Sch. Bd., pres. 1980-81; v.p. Phoenix of Santa Barbara. Served to capt. USAF, 1954-56. Mem. Santa Barbara County Bar Assn. (pres. 1972-73), Phi Kappa Phi, Phi Eta Sigma, Phi Delta Phi. Republican. Episcopalian. Lodge: Kiwanis. Avocations: reading, writing, traveling. State civil litigation, Estate planning, Real property. Office: 1126 Santa Barbara St Santa Barbara CA 93101-2008

WILLEY, STEPHEN DOUGLAS, lawyer, accountant, estate planner; b. Mt. Pleasant, Iowa, Apr. 30, 1950; s. Charles David Willey and Sally Ann (Hall) Stringer; m. Martha Frances Wood, June 3, 1978; children: Stephen David, John Brandon, Mark Charles, Andrew Joseph (twins). Student, U.S. Mil. Acad., 1969-70; BBA, U. Tex., Arlington, 1973; JD, U. Tex., 1978. Bar: Tex. 1978, U.S. Dist. Ct. (no. dist.) Tex. 1983, U.S. Tax Ct. 1985, U.S. Ct. Claims, 1988; cert. estate planning and probate law Tex. Bd. Legal Specialization; CPA, Tex. Acct. Ernst & Ernst CPAs, Ft. Worth, 1972-74; atty. Hilgers, Watkins, Ledbetter & Hays, Austin, Tex., 1976-78; acct. Rolater, Ducote & Belew, CPAs, Dallas, 1978-79; assoc. Hill, Heard & Oneal, Attys., Arlington, Tex., 1979-81; pvt. practice, 1981—. Adj. prof. Blaw, Tex. Wesleyan U.; lectr. in field. Pres. bd. Boys Clubs Arlington; mem. Northwest Arlington Homeowners Assn., YMCA Indian Guides, Meth. Men's club, Ch. choir; chmn. dist. com. Boy Scouts of Am., 1990-93. Mem. AICPA, Tex. Soc. CPAs, Am. Assn. Atty. CPAs, Arlington Bar Assn., (dir. 1997—), Dallas Bar Assn. (tax sect. real property, probate and trust sect.), Tex. State Bar (tax sect. real estate probate and trust law sect.), Coll. State Bar of Tex., Tex. Acad. Probate Counsel, Tarrant County Bar Assn., Tarrant County Debtor's Bar, Tex. Acad. Probate and Trust Lawyers, Fin. Planning Assn., Nat. Assn. Estate Planning Couns. (accredited estate planner), Mid-Cities Assn. CPAs (dir. 1997—), Arlington C. of C., U. Tex. Alumni Assn. (dir. 1997—), Rotary. Estate planning, Pension, profit-sharing, and employee benefits, Estate taxation. Office: Whitaker Chalk et al 3500 City Center Tower II 301 Commerce St Ste 3500 Fort Worth TX 76102 Fax: 817-878-0501. E-mail: swilley@whitakerchalk.com

WILLIAMS, ANN CLAIRE, federal judge; b. 1949; m. David J. Stewart. BS, Wayne State U., 1970; MA, U. Mich., 1972; JD, U. Notre Dame, 1975. Law clk. to Hon. Robert A. Sprecher, 1975-76; asst. U.S. atty. U.S. Dist. Ct. (no. dist.) Ill., Chgo., 1976-85; faculty Nat. Inst. for Trial Advocacy, 1979—, also bd. dirs.; judge U.S. Dist. Ct. (no. dist.) Ill., 1985-99, U.S. Ct. Appeals (7th cir.), Chgo., 1999—. Chief Organized Crime Drug Enforcement Task Force for North Ctrl. Region, 1983-85; mem. ct. adminstrn. and case mgmt. com. Jud. Conf. U.S., 1990-97, chair, 1993-97. Sec. bd. trustees U. Notre Dame; founder Minority Legal Resources, Inc. Mem. FBA, Fed. Judges Assn., Ill. State Bar Assn., Ill. Jud. Coun., Cook County Bar Assn., Women's Bar Assn. Ill., Black Women's Lawyers Assn. Greater Chgo. Office: US Ct Appeals 7th Circuit 219 S Dearborn St Ste 2612 Chicago IL 60604-1803

WILLIAMS, AUDREY MARINA, lawyer; b. London, Jan. 16, 1965; d. Eric Earl and Zalina Binns; m. Kevin Alan Williams, Sept 9, 1989. LLB, U. Southampton, Eng., 1986. Ptnr. Eversheds, Cardiff, Wales, 1989—. Author: Harrassment at Work, 1999, Family Friendly Working, 2000. Mem. Inst. Personnel Devel. Labor. Office: Eversheds Fitzalan House Fitzalan Rd Cardiff CF24 0EE Wales

WILLIAMS, BETTY OUTHIER, lawyer; b. Woodward, Okla., Sept. 11, 1947; d. Robert E. and Ethel M. (Castiller) Outhier; children: Amanda J., Emily Rebecca. BA, Oklahoma City U., 1969; JD, Vanderbilt U., 1972. Bar: Okla. 1972, U.S. Dist. Ct. (no. dist.) Okla. 1972, U.S. Dist. Ct. (ea. dist.) Okla. 1973, (U.S. Ct. Appeals (10th cir.) 1973, U.S. Supreme Ct. 1980, U.S. Dist. Ct. (we. dist.) Okla. 1988. Atty. Reginal Heber Smith Cmty. Lawyer Fellowship, Tulsa, 1972-73; asst. U.S. atty. Muskogee, Okla., 1973-81; U.S. atty., 1981-82; ptnr. Robinson, Locke, Gage, Fite & Williams, 1982-96, Robinson, Gage & Williams, Muskogee, 1996-97, Gage & Williams, Muskogee, 1997—. Chair local rules com. U.S. Bankruptcy Ct. Ea. Dist., Okla., 1994, U.S. Dist. Ct. Ea. Dist. Okla., 1995; adj. settlement judge U.S. Dist. Ct. Ea. Dis. Okla., 1998—. Mem. editl. bd. Okla. Law Enforcement Ops. Bull., 1993-94; editor Okla. Bar Jour., 1996-2002. Pres. Bus. and Profl. Women, Muskogee, 1975-77, 83; pres., bd. dirs. YWCA, Muskogee, 1975-82; bd. dirs. Green County Mental Health, Muskogee, 1986-88, WISH, 1990—; trustee Frontier Heritage Found., 1990-98; chmn. bd. commrs. Muskogee Housing Authority; adminstrv. bd. chmn., St. Paul United Meth. Ch., Muskogee, 1999-2001; state exec. com. Internat. Order the Rainbow for Girls. Named One of Outstanding Young Career Women, Bus. and Profl. Women, 1974. Fellow: Okla. Bar Found. (trustee 1989—, v.p. 1994, pres. 1996, gov. 2000—); mem.: ABA, Okla. Bar Assn. (editl. bd. 1996—, bd. govs. 2000—), Muskogee County Bar Assn. (pres. 1984—85), Soroptomists (pres. 1986—88), Order Eastern Star (Hope chpt.), Gamma Phi Beta (alumnae pres. 1993—). Republican. Methodist. Bankruptcy, Federal civil litigation, State civil litigation. Home: 4326 Oklahoma St Muskogee OK 74401-2351 Office: Gage & Williams PO Box 87 Muskogee OK 74402-0087 E-mail: bow@azalea.net

WILLIAMS, CHARLES JUDSON, lawyer, writer; b. San Mateo, Calif., Nov. 23, 1930; s. John Augustus and Edith (Babcock) W.; children: Patrick, Victoria, Apphia. AB, U. Calif., Berkeley, 1952, LLB, 1955. Bar: Calif. 1955, U.S. Supreme Ct., 1970. Assoc. Kirkbride, Wilson, Harzfeld and Wallace, San Mateo County, Calif., 1956-59; sole practice Solano County, 1959-64, Martinez, 1964—, Benicia, 1981-88; city atty. Pleasant Hill, 1962-80, Yountville, 1965-68, Benicia, 1968-76, 80-82, Lafayette, Calif., 1968—, Moraga, 1974-92, Danville, 1982-88, Pittsburg, 1984-93, Orinda, 1985-97. Lectr. Calif. Continuing Edn. Bar 1964-65, U. Calif. Extension 1974-76, John F. Kennedy U. Sch. Law 1966-69; spl. counsel to various Calif. cities; legal advisor Alaska Legis. Council 1959-61; advisor Alaska sup. ct. 1960-61; advisor on revision Alaska statues 1960-62; atty. Pleasant Hill Redevel. Agy. 1978-82; sec., bd. dirs. Vintage Savs. & Loan Assn., Napa County, Calif., 1974-82; bd. dirs. 23d Agrl. Dist. Assn., Contra Costa County, 1968-70. Author: California Code Comments to West's Annotated California Codes, 3 vols., 1965, West' California Code Forms, Commercial, 2 vols., 1965, West's California Government Code Forms, 3 vols., 1971, Supplement to California Zoning Practice, 1978, 80, 82, 84, 85, 87, 89, 91, 94, 96, 98, 2000, 01; contbr. articles to legal jours. Mem. ABA, Calif. Bar Assn., Contra Costa County Bar Assn. Administrative and regulatory, State civil litigation. Office: 1330 Arnold Dr Ste 149 Martinez CA 94553-6538 E-mail: chaslaw@aol.com

WILLIAMS, CLAY RULE, lawyer; b. Milw., Sept. 25, 1935; s. George Laverne and Marguerite Mae (Rule) W.; m. Jeanne Lee Huber, Jan. 18, 1986; children: Gwynne, Amy, Daniel, Sarah. BA, Lawrence U., 1957; LLB, U. Mich., 1960. Bar: Wis. 1960, U.S. Dist. Ct. (ea. and we. dists.) Wis. 1964, U.S. Ct. Appeals (7th cir.) 1965, U.S. Ct. Mil. Appeals 1963, U.S. Supreme Ct. 1963. Assoc. Gibbs, Roper & Fifield, Milw., 1963-67; ptnr., shareholder Von Briesen, Purtell & Roper, S.C., 1967-99, of counsel, 1999—. Mem. Gov.'s Task Force Creation Bus. Ct., 1994-99; instr. profl. seminars. Author: Berry, Davis, Deguire and Williams, Wisconsin Business Corporation Law, 1992; contbr. articles to profl. jours. Active Shorewood (Wis.) Sch. Bd., 1976-79. Capt. USAF, Judge Adv. Corps., 1960-63. Fellow Wis. Bar Found.; mem. ABA (sect. antitrust law, corp. counseling com.), Wis. Bar Assn. (co-chmn. com. to revise corp. laws 1986-90, chmn. standing com. on bus. corp. law 1990-97, Pres.'s Award of Excellence 1990, 97), Milw. Bar Assn. (probate and real property sect., joint bench-bar com. Ct. Appeals, 1986-88, long-range planning com. 1987), 7th Cir. Bar Assn., Am. Law Inst., Assn. Bar City N.Y., Milw. Club, Univ. Club. Republican. Episcopalian. Avocations: hunting, fishing, skiing, reading. General civil litigation, General corporate, Securities. Office: von Briesen Purtell & Roper SC 735 N Water St Milwaukee WI 53202-4100 E-mail: cwilliam@vonbriesen.com

WILLIAMS, FRANK J. chief justice, historian, author; b. Providence, Aug. 24, 1940; s. Frank and Natalie L. (Corelli) W.; m. Virginia E. Miller, Aug. 24, 1966. BA, Boston U., 1962, JD, 1970; MS in Taxation, Bryant Coll., 1986; LHD, Lincoln Coll., 1987. Bar: R.I. 1970, U.S. Dist. Ct. R.I. 1970, U.S. Supreme Ct. 1976. Assoc. Tillinghast, Collins & Graham, Providence, 1970-75, Leonard Decof Ltd., Providence, 1976-78; law clk. Graham, Reid, Ewing & Stapleton, 1969; law clk., adminstrv. asst. R.I. Atty. Gen., 1967-68; pres. Frank J. Williams Ltd., attys.-at-law, 1978-95; assoc. justice R.I. Superior Ct., 1995-2001; chief justice Supreme Ct. R.I., 2001—. Judge of probate Town of Hopkinton (R.I.), 1978-82, 84-90, solicitor, 1978-82, 84-87; judge of probate Town of West Greenwich, R.I., 1984-86, 92-95, solicitor, 1984-92, asst. solicitor, 1992—; dep. judge of probate, 1987-92; solicitor Town of Coventry, R.I., 1972-74, 76-78, Town of Barrington, R.I., 1993-95, Town of Bristol, R.I., 1995, Town of South Kingstown, R.I., 1995; past spl. counsel Towns of Westerly, Bristol, Hopkinton, South Kingstown, City of Providence; atty. Town of Smithfield Sewer Authority, 1974-90; legis. counsel R.I. Retail Fedn., 1975-93, Credit Info. Bur., R.I. Mortgage Bankers Assn., 1992-95; adj. prof. Roger Williams Sch. of Law, 1997—; lectr. bus. and legal practice R.I. Sch. Design, Providence, 1976-80; mem. panel of arbitrators Am. Arbitration Assn., panel of mediators R.I. Superior Ct., 1993-95; mem. R.I. Bd. Bar Examiners, 1987-95, chair, 1995; chair R.I. Housing and Mortgage Fin. Corp., 1995, The Lincoln Forum, 1996—. Pres. Lincoln Group of Boston, 1976-88, Abraham Lincoln Assn. Springfield, Ill., 1986-95, Ulysses S. Grant Assn., 1990—; elected del. R.I. Constnl. Conv., 1986; elected town moderator Richmond, R.I., 1989, 92-95; dist; moderator Chaniho Regional Sch. Dist., 1994; bd. dirs. John E. Fogarty Found. for Persons with Mental Retardation, 1975—, South County Hosp., 1995—, Narraganset coun. Boy Scouts Am., 1969-80, 98-2001; chmn. Lincoln adv. com. Brown U.; mem. Lincoln prize adv. com. Gettysburg Coll. Capt. U.S. Army, 1962-67; Vietnam. Decorated Bronze Star, Republic of Vietnam Gallantry Cross with silver star, combat infantryman's badge, Air medal with 2 oak leaf clusters, Army Commendation medal. Memlow ATLA (jud.); mem. Am. Judges Assn., Nat. Assn. for Ct. Mgmt., Am. Law Inst., Conf. Chief Justices, R.I. Bar Assn. (ho. of dels. 1986-93, chmn. new lawyers adv. com. 1976-87, chmn. mcpl. law com. 1993), Am. Antiquarian Soc., Pi Sigma Alpha, Alpha Phi Sigma. Roman Catholic. Office: 1111 Main St Hope Valley RI 02832-1610

WILLIAMS, GLEN MORGAN, federal judge; b. Jonesville, Va., Feb. 17, 1920; s. Hughy May and Hattie Mae W.; m. Jane Slemp, Nov. 17, 1962; children: Susan, Judy, Rebecca, Melinda. A.B. magna cum laude, Milligan Coll., 1940; J.D., U. Va., 1948. Bar: Va. 1947. Pvt. practice law, Jonesville, 1948-76; judge U.S. Dist. Ct. (we. dist.) Va., 1976-88, sr. judge, 1988—; commonwealth's atty. Lee County, Va., 1948-51; mem. Va. Senate, 1953-55. Mem. editorial bd.: Va. Law Rev., 1946-47. Mem. Lee County Sch. Bd., 1972-76; trustee, elder First Christian Ch., Pennington Gap, Va.; trustee Milligan Coll., 1990—, Appalachian Sch. of Law, 1995—. Lt. USN, 1942-46, MTO. Recipient Citation of Merit Va. Def. Lawyers Assn., Oustanding Alumnus award Milligan Coll., 1980, Svc. to Region award Emory & Henry Coll., 1996. Mem. ABA, Va. State Bar (citation of merit), Va. Bar Assn. (citation of merit), Fed. Bar Assn., Va. Trial Lawyers Assn. (Meritorious Svc. award 1986, Disting. Svc. award), Am. Legion, 40 and 8. Clubs: Lions, Masons, Shriners. E-mila. Office: US Dist Ct Fed Bldg PO Box 339 Abingdon VA 24212-0339 E-mail: glenw@vawd.uscourts.gov

WILLIAMS, HENRY NEWTON, retired lawyer; b. Dickson, Tenn., May 14, 1917; s. H. Newton and Cora Ethel (Wynns) W.; m. LaVerna Pearl Wharton, July 12, 1944 (dec.); children: John Wharton, George Wynns. BS, Mid. Tenn. State U., 1937; MA, U. Tenn., 1938; PhD, U. Chgo., 1951; JD, Vanderbilt U., 1952; LLM, Columbia U., 1954. Bar: Tenn. 1953, U.S. Ct. Appeals (3d cir.) 1954, U.S. Ct. Appeals (9th and 10th cirs.) 1955, U.S.

Supreme Ct. 1956, U.S. Ct. Appeals (D.C. cir.) 1957, D.C. 1960. Asst. prof. polit. sci. Vanderbilt U., Nashville, 1946-53; assoc. prof. law Mercer U., Macon, Ga., 1954-56; atty. U.S. Dept. Justice, 1956-68, FTC, Washington, 1968-70; dep. gen. counsel Selective Svc. Sys., 1970-76, gen. counsel 1976-99. Contbr. articles to law and polit. sci. jours. Col. U.S. Army, 1942-46. J.P. Chamberlain fellow Columbia U. Law Sch., 1953-54, Edward Hilman fellow U. Chgo., 1939-40, Univ. fellow, 1938-39. Mem. Am. Law Inst., ABA, Fed. Bar Assn., Tenn. Bar Assn., D.C. Bar Assn., Assn. of Bar of City of N.Y. Episcopalian. Home: 11811 Judson Rd Silver Spring MD 20902-2054

WILLIAMS, HENRY WARD, JR. lawyer; b. Rochester, N.Y., Jan. 12, 1930; s. Henry Ward and Margaret Elizabeth (Simpson) W.; m. Christina M.; children: Edith Williams Linares, Margaret Williams Warren, Sarah Williams Farrand, Ann Williams Treacy, Elizabeth DeLancey, Victoria Maureen. AB, Dartmouth Coll., 1952; LLB, U.Va., 1958. Bar: N.Y. 1959, U.S. Dist. Ct. (we. dist.) N.Y. 1959, U.S. Dist. Ct. (so. dist.) Mich. 1982, U.S. Ct. Appeals (2d cir.) 1963, U.S. Tax Ct. 1960, U.S. Supreme Ct. 1968, D.C. 1978. Ptnr. Harris, Beach & Wilcox, Rochester, 1958-78, Robinson, Williams, Angeloff & Frank, Rochester, 1978-80, Weidman, Williams, Jordon, Angeloff & Frank, Rochester, 1980-82, The Williams Law Firm, Rochester, 1982—. Exec. editor Va. Law Rev., 1957-58. Chmn. Genesee Finger/Lakes Regional Planning Coun., 1973-89; majority leader Monroe County Legislature, 1967-73; mem. alumni coun. Dartmouth Coll., 1995-99; mem. no. 8020 Nat. Ski Patrol Sys. Lt. (j.g.) USN, 1952-55. Mem. ABA, N.Y. State Bar Assn., Monroe County Bar Assn. (trustee 1982-85), Rochester Yacht Club, Royal Can. Yacht Club, Lake Yacht Racing Assn. (pres. 1985-87, hon. pres. 1988-90), Royal Ocean Racing Club, Royal Nfld. Yacht Club, Raven Soc., Order of Coif, Omicron Delta Kappa. General practice. Office: The Williams Law Firm PO Box 8 Scottsville NY 14546-0008

WILLIAMS, HOWARD RUSSELL, lawyer, educator; b. Evansville, Ind., Sept. 26, 1915; s. Clyde Alfred and Grace (Preston) W.; m. Virginia Merle Thompson, Nov. 3, 1942 (dec. Dec. 2000); 1 son, Frederick S.T. AB, Washington U., St. Louis, 1937; LLB, Columbia U., 1940. Bar: N.Y. 1941. With firm Root, Clark, Buckner & Ballantine, N.Y.C., 1940-41; prof. law, asst. dean U. Tex. Law Sch., Austin, 1946-51; prof. law Columbia U. Law Sch., N.Y.C., 1951-63; Dwight prof. Columbia Law Sch., 1959-63; prof. law Stanford U., 1963-85, Stella W. and Ira S. Lillick prof., 1968-82, prof. emeritus, 1982, Robert E. Paradise prof. natural resources, 1983-85, prof. emeritus, 1985—. Oil and gas cons. President's Materials Policy Commn., 1951; mem. Calif. Law Revision Commn., 1971-79, vice chmn., 1976-77, chmn., 1978-79 Author or co-author: Cases on Property, 1954, Cases on Oil and Gas, 1956, 5th edit., 1987, Decedents' Estates and Trusts, 1968, Future Interests, 1970, Oil and Gas Law, 8 vols., 1959-64 (with ann. supplements/rev. 1964-95), abridged edit., 1973, Manual of Oil and Gas Terms, 1957, 11th edit., 2000. Bd. regents Berkeley Bapt. Divinity Sch., 1966-67; trustee Rocky Mountain Mineral Law Found., 1964-66, 68-85. With U.S. Army, 1941-46. Recipient Clyde O. Martz Tchg. award Rocky Mountain Mineral Law Found., 1994. Mem. Phi Beta Kappa. Democrat. Home: 360 Everett Ave Apt 4B Palo Alto CA 94301-1422 Office: Stanford U Sch Law Nathan Abbott Way Stanford CA 94305

WILLIAMS, J. BRYAN, lawyer; b. Detroit, July 23, 1947; s. Walter J. and Maureen June (Kay) W.; m. Jane Elizabeth Eisele, Aug. 24, 1974; children: Kyle Joseph, Ryan Patrick. AB, U. Notre Dame, 1969; JD, U. Mich., 1972. Bar: Mich. 1972, U.S. Dist. Ct. (ea. dist.) Mich. 1972. Atty. Dickinson, Wright, PLLC (and predecessor firm), Detroit, 1972—, CEO Bloomfield Hills, Mich., 1991-2000. Mem. ABA, Mich. Bar Assn., Detroit Bar Assn., Notre Dame Club of Detroit (pres. 1984), Oakland Hills Country Club, Nat. Club Assn. (bd. dirs., sec. 1995-97, treas. 1997-98, v.p. 1998—), Detroit Regional C. of C. (bd. dirs., vice chmn. 1998—), Econ. Club Detroit (bd. dirs. 1996-2001), Detroit Legal News Co. (bd. dirs.). Roman Catholic. Banking, General corporate. Home: 993 Suffield Ave Birmingham MI 48009-1242 Office: 38525 Woodward Ave Ste 2000 Bloomfield Hills MI 48304 E-mail: jwilliams@dickinson-wright.com

WILLIAMS, J. MAXWELL, lawyer, arbitrator and mediator; b. Spartanburg, S.C., Aug. 11, 1943; BA, Vanderbilt U., 1965; JD, U. Fla., 1971. Bar: Fla. 1971, Tenn. 1980, U.S. Dist. Ct. (mid. dist.) Fla. 1973, U.S. Dist. Ct. (so. dist.) Fla. 1972, U.S. Dist. Ct. (we. dist.) Tenn. 1984, U.S. Ct. Appeals (5th and 11th cirs.) 1974, U.S. Supreme Ct. 1974; cert. mediator, Fla., Tenn. Atty. Kimbrell & Hamaan, Miami, Fla., 1971-73, State of Fla., Tampa, 1974-75; county atty. Hillsborough County, 1976-79; chief group counsel, asst. sec. W.R. Grace & Co., Memphis, 1980-98; v.p., gen. counsel, gov. rels. officer Memphis Light, Gas and Water, 1998—. Steering com. Shelby County Rep. Party, Memphis, 1991-95. With USMCR. Named Vol. of Yr., Memphis Legal Svcs., 1992, one of Outstanding Young Men in Am., 1980. Mem. Nat. Assn. Security Dealers (mediator, arbitrator 1996—), Memphis Bar Assn. (chair alt. dispute resolution com. 1996-98), Am. Arbitration Assn. (West Tenn. adv. coun. 1995—, mediator, arbitrator 1994—), Rotary. Baptist. Avocations: swimming, tennis, travel, weight training. org. Alternative dispute resolution, Public utilities, Real property. Home: 7242 Neshoba Cir Germantown TN 38138-3749 Office: Memphis Light Gas and Water 220 S Main St Memphis TN 38103-3917 E-mail: jmwilliams@mlgw

WILLIAMS, J. VERNON, lawyer; b. Honolulu, Apr. 26, 1921; s. Urban and W. Amelia (Olson) W.; m. Malvina H. Hitchcock, Oct. 4, 1947 (dec. May 1970); children— Carl H., Karin, Frances E., Scott S.; m. Mary McLellan, Sept. 6, 1980. Student, Phillips Andover Acad., 1937-39; B.A. cum laude, Amherst Coll., 1943; LL.B., Yale, 1948. Bar: Wash. 1948. Assoc. Riddell, Riddell & Hemphill, 1948-50, ptnr., 1950-95; sr. prin. emeritus Riddell Williams, P.S., Seattle, 1996—. Sec., dir. Airborne Freight Corp., 1968-79, gen. counsel, 1968-96. Chmn. March of Dimes, Seattle, 1954-55; Mem. Mayor's City Charter Rev. Com., 1968-69; chmn. Seattle Bd. Park Commrs., 1966-68; co-chmn. parks and open space com. Forward Thrust, 1966-69; dir. bd. and commrs. br. Nat. Recreation and Parks Assn., 1968-69; chmn. Gov.'s adv. com. Social and Health Services, 1972-75; Bd. dirs. Seattle Met. YMCA, 1965— , pres., 1976-79; trustee Lakeside Sch., 1971-79; mem. alumni council Phillps Andover Acad., 1970-73, Yale Law Sch., 1969-77; chancellor St. Mark's Cathedral, Seattle, 1964-2000. Served with USAAF, 1943-45. Mem. Univ. Club, Seattle Tennis Club, Birnam Wood Golf Club. Aviation, General corporate, Real property. Home: 1100 38th Ave E Seattle WA 98112-4434 Office: 4500 1001 4th Ave Plz Seattle WA 98154-1065

WILLIAMS, JACKIE N. law educator, former prosecutor; b. Roosevelt, Okla., Oct. 4, 1943; s. David Coleman and Grace Pearl (Southard) W.; children: Douglas Kennedy, Eric Neil. BBA, Wichita State U., 1967; JD, Washburn U. Law Sch., 1971. Bar: Kans. 1971. Asst. atty. gen. Kans. Atty. Gen.'s Office, Topeka, 1971-73; asst. dist. atty. Wichita, 1973-77; adminstrv. asst. U.S. Congressman Dan Glickman, Washington, 1977; asst. U.S. atty. Wichita, 1977-96; U.S. atty. Kans., 1996—2001; sr. fellow, criminal justice prog School of Community Affairs, Wichita State Univ , Kans., 2001—. Office: Wichita State Univ School of Community Affairs 302 Lindquist Hall, Box 135 Wichita KS 67260 E-mail: jackie.williams@wichita.edu*

WILLIAMS, KAREN HASTIE, lawyer; b. Washington, Sept. 30, 1944; d. William Henry and Beryl (Lockhart) Hastie; m. Wesley S. Williams, Jr.; children: Amanda Pedersen, Wesley Hastie, Bailey Lockhart. Cert., U. Neuchatel, Switzerland, 1965; BA, Bates Coll., 1966; MA, Tufts U., 1967; JD, Cath. U. Am., 1973. Bar: D.C. 1973. Staff asst. internat. gov. relations dept. Mobil Oil Corp., N.Y.C., 1967-69; staff asst. com. Dist. Columbia U.S. Senate, 1970, chief counsel com. on the budget, 1977-80; law clk. to judge Spottswood Robinson III U.S. Ct. Appeals (D.C. Cir.), Washington, 1973-74; law clk. to assoc. justice Thurgood Marshall U.S. Supreme Ct., 1974-75; assoc. Fried, Frank, Harris, Shriver & Kampelman, 1975-77, 1975-77; adminstr. Office Mgmt. and Budget, 1980-81; of counsel Crowell & Moring, 1982, ptnr., 1982—. Bd. dirs. Chubb Corp., Gannett Co., Inc., Sun Trust-Mid Atlantic Co., Charles E. Smith Residential Realty, Washington Gas Light Co., Continental Airlines. Trustee Greater Washington Research Ctr., chair. Mem. ABA (pub. contract law sect., past chair), Nat. Bar Assn., Washington Bar Assn., Nat. Contract Mgmt. Assn., NAACP (legal def. fund, bd. dirs.). Office: Crowell & Moring Ste 1200W 1001 Pennsylvania Ave NW Washington DC 20004-2505

WILLIAMS, KAREN JOHNSON, federal judge; b. Orangeburg, S.C., Aug. 4, 1951; d. James G. Johnson and Marcia (Reynolds) Johnson Dantzler; m. Charles H. Williams, Dec. 27, 1968; children: Marian, Ashley, Charlie, David. BA, Columbia Coll., 1972; postgrad., U. S.C., 1973, JD cum laude, 1980. Bar: S.C. 1980, U.S. Dist. Ct. S.C. 1980, U.S. Ct. Appeals (4th cir.) 1981. Tchr. Irmo (S.C.) Mid. Sch., 1972-74, O-W High Sch., Orangeburg, 1974-76; assoc. Charles H. Williams P.A., 1980-92; circuit judge U.S. Ct. Appeals (4th cir.), 1992—. Mem. exec. bd. grievance commn. S.C. Supreme Ct., Columbia, 1983-92. Mem. child devel. bd. First Bapt. Ch., Orangeburg; bd. dirs. Orangeburg County Mental Retardation Bd., 1986-94, Orangeburg-Calhoun Hosp. Found.; bd. visitors Columbia Coll., 1988-92; dir. Reg. Med. Ctr. Hosp. Found., 1988-92; mem. adv. bd. Orangeburg-Calhoun Tech. Coll., 1987-92. Mem. ABA, Am. Judicature Soc., Fed. Judges Assn., S.C. Bar Assn., Orangeburg County Bar Assn. (co-chair Law Day 1981), S.C. Trial Lawyers Assn., Bus. and profl. Women Assn., Rotary, Order of Wig and Robe, Order of Coif. Home: 2503 Five Chop Rd Orangeburg SC 29115-8185 Office: US Court of Appeals 4th Circuit 1021 Middleton St Orangeburg SC 29115-4783*

WILLIAMS, MARCUS DOYLE, judge; b. Nashville, Oct. 24, 1952; s. John Freelander and Pansy (Doyle) W.; m. Carmen Myrie, May 21, 1983; children: Aaron Doyle, Adam Myrie. BA with honors, Fisk U., 1973; JD, Cath. U. of Am., 1977. Bar: Va. 1977, D.C. 1978. Asst. commonwealth's atty. County of Fairfax, Fairfax, Va., 1978-80, asst. county atty. Faifax, 1980-87; dist. ct. judge 19th Jud. Dist., 1987-90; judge 19th Jud. Cir., 1990—. Lectr. bus. legal studies George Mason U., Fairfax, 1980-95; instr. pvt. investigators North Va. Community Coll., Fairfax, 1979; mem. Fairfax Criminal Justice Adv. Bd., 1980-86; faculty advisor Nat. Jud. Coll., 1991, faculty, 1992—; Am. participant lectr. for USIA, 1990; lectr. George Mason U. Law Sch., 1987. Book reviewer for ABA Jour., 1981-84; contbr. articles to legal jours. Bd. visitors Cath. U. Law Sch., 1998—. Recipient cert. of appreciation for outstanding svc. Burke-Fairfax Jack & Jill, Cert. of Appreciation, Nat. Forum for Black Pub. Adminstrs. and Black Women United for Action, 1995; Thomas J. Watson Found. fellow, 1977, Otis Smith award BLSA of Cath. U. Law Sch. Mem. ABA (chair subcom. Victims of Crimes 1996-2000), Fairfax Bar Assn. (CLE com., vice chmn. 1986-87), Am. Bus. Law Assn., Am. Judges Assn., Phi Alpha Delta, Beta Kappa Chi, Omega Psi Phi. Methodist. Office: Cir Ct 4110 Chain Bridge Rd Fairfax VA 22030-4009

WILLIAMS, MARJORIE L. retired lawyer; b. La Grange, Tex., Sept. 1, 1924; d. John Alexander and Juanita Ray (Robson) Logan; m. Sydney Eugene Simpson, Feb. 1952 (div. Aug. 1956); 1 child, John Phillip Williams; m. Edward Theodore Williams, Sept. 8, 1956 (dec.); children: Lucia Leigh, Bruce Gilman. BA, U. Tex., 1945, MA, 1970, JD, 1984. Bar: Tex. Acct. exec. Merrill Lynch, Houston, 1950-51; World Wide Travel, Detroit, 1952-54; tchr. L.G.I.S.D., La Grange, Tex., 1956-80; atty. Tex. Legis. Coun., Austin, 1986-88, Carl Parker, Port Arthur, Tex., 1992-94. Cons. Dept. Agr., 1988. Editor: (books) Texas: Land & People, Fayette Co. Chmn. Fayette Co. Historical Com., Tex. State Historical Assn.; archivist Fayette Co. Archives, Leisure World Historical Soc., Laguna Hills, Calif., Daughters Am. Revolution. Recipient Women of Yr., La Grange City. Democrat. Episcopalian. Avocations: computer, reading, geneology. Home: 3391 Punta Alta Unit A Laguna Woods CA 92653-0217

WILLIAMS, MAUREEN SYLVIA, legal administration; b. Buenos Aires, Argentina, Jan. 2, 1947; d. George Ronald and Amalia (Santisteban y Santa Cruz) W.; m. Miguel Benito Contin; 1 child: Viviane. Barrister, U. Buenos Aires, 1970; LLM, U. London, United Kingdom, 1974; LLD cum laude, U. Buenos Aires, 1980; Dipl337me Specialsation, Sorbonne, Paris, 1971. Bar: Buenos Aires. Sr. ptnr. Etcheverry-Gregorini Clusellas, Buenos Aires; career scientist Conicet, 1975-99, superior career scientist, 2000—. Vis. prof. Tulane U., 2000—; vis. scholar, Oxford U., Cambridge U., UK, 1983—; chmn. Public Internat. Law, U. Buenos Aires, 1993. Author: Telecomunicaciones Por Satelites, 1980 (Diplome D'Honneur, first prize, 1980), Derecho Int'l Contemporáneo, 1990 (special mention, 1992), El Riesgo Ambiental y Su Regulación, 1998, (award, 2000). Highest Career Hierarchy, Nat. Council Scientific Rsch., Argentina, 2000. Mem. Exec. Council Internat. Law Assn. (London, permanent rapporteur, 1988—, author, co-editor Report 66th Conference, 1994), Royal Inst. Internat. Affairs (Paris), Internat. Acad. Astronautics (Paris). Avocations: tennis. Office: AV Figuerua Alcorta 2263 1425 Buenos Aires Argentina also: U Buenos Aires Fac de Derecho AV Figuerua Alcorta 2263 1425 Buenos Aires Argentina E-mail: maureenw@fibertel.com.ar

WILLIAMS, MICHAEL ANTHONY, lawyer; b. Mandan, N.D., Sept. 14, 1932; s. Melvin Douglas and Lucille Ann (Gavin) W.; m. Marjorie Ann Herrar, Aug. 25, 1962 (div. 1989); children: Ann Margaret, Douglas Raymond, David Michael; m. Dorothy Ruth Hand, 1989. B.A., Coll. of St. Thomas, 1954; LL.B., Harvard U., 1959. Bar: Colo. 1959, N.D. 1959, U.S. Dist. Ct. Colo. 1959, U.S. Ct. Appeals (10th cir.) 1959, U.S. Supreme Ct. 1967. Assoc. Sherman & Howard and predecessor Dawson, Nagel, Sherman & Howard, Denver, 1959-65, ptnr., 1965-91; pres. Williams, Youle & Koenigs, P.C., Denver, 1991—. Served as 1st lt. USAF, 1955-57. Mem. Am. Coll. Trial Lawyers, Am. Bd. Trial Advs., Colo. Bar Found., Am. Law Inst., ABA, Colo. Bar Assn., Denver Bar Assn., Arapahoe County Bar Assn. Federal civil litigation, State civil litigation. Office: Williams Youle & Koenigs PC 950 17th St Ste 2450 Denver CO 80202-2811

WILLIAMS, MICHAEL EDWARD, lawyer; b. Ft. Worth, Aug. 10, 1955; s. Jerrol Evans and Helen Louise (Hoffner) W.; m. Jackie Ann Gordinier, Dec. 30, 1978; children: Margaret Eileen, James Andrew. BA, U. Calif., Riverside, 1977; JD, U. San Diego, 1980. Bar: Calif. 1980, U.S. Dist. Ct. (so. dist.) Calif. 1980, U.S. Tax Ct. 1981, U.S. Dist. Ct. (ea. and cen. dists.) Calif. 1982, U.S. Dist. Ct. (no. dist.) Calif. 1985. Assoc. Jamison & McFadden, Solana Beach, Calif., 1980-86, Dorazio, Barnhorst & Bonar, San Diego, 1986; sole practice Encinitas, Calif., 1987—. Atty. pro bono Community Resource Ctr., Encinitas, Calif., 1984—; vice moderator San Diego Presbytery, Presbyn. Ch. U.S.A., 1998, moderator, 1999. Mem. Calif. State Bar Assn. (fee arbitrator 1992—), San Diego County Bar Assn. (client rels. com. 1990—, fee arbitration com. 1991—, ct. arbitrator). Democrat. Presbyterian. Bankruptcy, State civil litigation, Contracts commercial. Office: 4405 Manchester Ave Ste 206 Encinitas CA 92024-7902

WILLIAMS, MICHAEL PETER ANTHONY, lawyer; b. Bridgeport, Conn., Sept. 1, 1945; s. Francis P.A. and Elsie Millicent (Blight) W.; m. Ethel Anderson Hoffman, Apr. 18, 1970; children— Greyson P., Trevor H., Meredith S., Tristan àBeckett. A.B. in English, Boston U., 1968; J.D., Cumberland Law Sch., 1974. Bar: Conn. 1974, U.S. Dist. Ct. Conn. 1974, U.S. Ct. Appeals (2d cir.) 1979. Assoc., Marsh, Day & Calhoun, Bridgeport, 1974-79, ptnr., 1980— ; counsel Pinewood Lake Assn., Trumbull, Conn., 1982— ; spl. counsel (Freedom of Info.) Town of Easton, 1989—. Mem. Trumbull Town Council, 1981-83, Trumbull Bd. Edn., 1983—, chmn., 1986-88; bd. dirs. Coop. Ednl. Services, Norwalk, Conn., 1984-86 . Mem. ABA, Conn. Bar Assn., Bridgeport Bar Assn. Republican. Contracts commercial, Probate, Real property. Home: 90 Chalker Beach Rd Old Saybrook CT 06475-1734 Office: Marsh Day & Calhoun 2507 Post Rd Southport CT 06490-1259 also: 955 Main St Bridgeport CT 06604-4300

WILLIAMS, NEIL, JR. lawyer; b. Charlotte, N.C., Mar. 22, 1936; s. Lyman Neil and Thelma (Peterson) W.; m. Sue Sigmon, Aug. 23, 1958; children: Fred R., Susan S. AB, Duke U., 1958, JD, 1961. Bar: Ga. 1962, U.S. Dist. Ct. (no. dist.) Ga. 1977, U.S. Ct. Appeals (11th cir.) 1977. Assoc. Alston & Bird (and predecessor firm), Atlanta, 1961-65, ptnr., 1966-99, mng. ptnr., 1984-96; gen. counsel, global ptnr. Amvescap Plc, 1999—. Bd. dirs. Nat. Data Corp., Atlanta, Printpack, Inc., Atlanta, Nat. Svc. Industries, Atlanta. Chmn. bd. trustees Duke U., 1983-88, trustee, 1980-93; chmn. bd. trustees Vasser Woolley Found., Atlanta, 1975—, Leadership Atlanta, 1976-80; trustee Brevard Music Ctr., 1977-86, 91—, Presbyn. Ch. USA Found., Jeffersonville, Ind., 1983-90, Research Triangle Inst., 1983-88, The Duke Endowment, Charlotte, N.C., 1997—; bd. dirs. Atlanta Symphony Orch., 1970-76, 84-93, 95-98, pres., 1988-90; Woodruff Arts Ctr., 1987-98, 99—; bd. counsellors The Carter Ctr., Atlanta, 1987-96; Cen. Atlanta Progress, 1984-96; bd. dirs. Am. Symphony Orch. League, Washington, 1990-2000, chmn., 1995-99. Recipient Disting. Alumni award Duke U., 1991, Rhyne award, 1996. Mem. ABA, Am. Bar Found., State Bar Ga., Am. Law Inst., Atlanta C. of C. (bd. dirs. 1992-97, vice chmn. 1994-97), Piedmont Driving Club, Commerce Club (Atlanta), University Club (N.Y.C.), Phi Beta Kappa, Omicron Delta Kappa. E-mail: neil. Contracts commercial, General corporate, Securities. Home: 3 Nacoochee Pl NW Atlanta GA 30305-4164 Office: Amvescap Plc 1315 Peachtree St NE Atlanta GA 30309-3503 Address: AMVESCAP PLC General Counsel 1315 Peachtree St NE Ste 500 Atlanta GA 30309-3503 E-mail: williams@amvescap.com

WILLIAMS, QUINN PATRICK, lawyer; b. Evergreen Park, Ill., May 6, 1949; s. William Albert and Jeanne Marie (Quinlan) W.; m. Ingrid E. Haas; children: Michael Ryan, Mark Reed, Kelly Elizabeth. BBA, U. Wis., 1972; JD, U. Ariz., 1974. Bar: Ariz. 1975, N.Y. 1984, U.S. Dist. Ct. Ariz. 1976. V.p., sec., gen. counsel Combined Comm. Corp., Phoenix, 1975-80; sr. v.p. legal and adminstrn. Swensen's Inc., 1980-86; of counsel Winston & Strawn, 1985-87, ptnr., 1987-89, Snell & Wilmer, Phoenix, 1989—. Chmn. Ariz. Tech. Incubator, 1993-94, Ariz. Venture Capital Conf., 1993, 94; co-chmn. Gov.'s Small Bus. Advocate Exec. Coun., 1993—; chair, bd. dirs. Greater Phoenix Econ. Coun., 1996—, Scottsdale Partnership; vice chair Gov. Regulatory Coun., 1995-97; sec. GSPED High Tech. Cluster, 1993—. Served with USAR, 1967-73. Mem. ABA, State Bar Ariz., Maricopa County Bar Assn., N.Y. Bar Assn., Internat. Franchise Assn., Scottsdale C. of C. (bd. dirs.), Paradise Valley Country Club, Scottsdale Charros. Republican. Roman Catholic. General corporate, Franchising, Securities. Home: 6201 E Horseshoe Rd Paradise Valley AZ 85253 Office: Snell & Wilmer One Arizona Ctr Phoenix AZ 85004 E-mail: qwilliams@msn.com

WILLIAMS, REBECCA LYNN, lawyer, nurse; b. LaGrange, Ill., Jan. 24, 1959; d. Richard Fowler and Anita (Albro) W. BSN magna cum laude, Duke U., 1981; JD, Loyola U., 1986. Bar: Ill. 1986, U.S. Dist. Ct. (no. dist.) Ill. 1986. Nurse Children's Meml. Hosp., Chgo., 1981-84, St. Jude's Hosp., Vieux Fort, St. Lucia, 1983; assoc. McDermott, Will & Emery, Chgo., 1986-88, Winston & Strawn, Chgo., 1988-93; ptnr. Sonnenschein Nath & Rosenthal, 1993-98; of counsel Davis Wright Tremaine LLP, Seattle, 1998—. Contbr. articles to profl. jours. Patron various civic, environ., charitable and polit. groups. Mem. ABA, ANA, Am. Health Lawyers Assn. Avocations: scuba diving, reading, hiking, photography. Health. Office: Davis Wright Tremaine LLP 2600 Century Sq 1501 4th Ave Seattle WA 98101-1688 E-mail: beckywilliams@dwt.com

WILLIAMS, RICHARD LEROY, federal judge; b. Morrisville, Va., Apr. 6, 1923; s. Wilcie Edward and Minnie Mae (Brinkley) W.; m. Eugenia Kellogg, Sept. 11, 1948; children: Nancy Williams Davies, R. Gregory, Walter L., Gwendolyn Mason. LLB, U. Va., 1951. Bar: Va. 1951. Ptnr. McGuire, Woods & Battle and predecessor firms, 1951-72; judge Cir. Ct. City of Richmond, 1972-76; ptnr. McGuire, Woods & Battle, 1976-80; dist. judge U.S. Dist. Ct., Richmond, Va., 1980—, sr. judge, 1992—. 2d lt. Air Corps., U.S. Army, 1940-45. Fellow Am. Coll. Trial Lawyers; mem. Va. State Bar, Va. Bar Assn., Richmond Bar Assn. Office: US Dist Ct/Lewis F Powell Ste 305 1000 E Main St Richmond VA 23219-3525 E-mail: barbarakreuter@uaed.uscourts.gov

WILLIAMS, RICHARD NESBITT, lawyer, educator; b. Youngstown, Ohio, July 17, 1943; s. Preston A,. and Dorothy (Gordon) W.; m. Judith Mac Pherson, Aug. 5, 1967; children: Eric, Wendy, Amanda. BA, Denison U., 1965; JD, U. Akron, Ohio, 1969. Asst. city atty. City of Cuyahoga Falls, Ohio, 1969-73; assoc. counsel Northwestern U., Evanston, Ill., 1973—. Adj. prof. U. No. Fla., Jacksonville, 1980—. Co-author: Evidence Handbook, 1975, 80. Corp. counsel Village of Hoffman Estates, Ill., 1973—. Mem. ABA, Ill. State Bar Assn. Republican. Presbyterian. Home: 1976 Fairway Ct Hoffman Estates IL 60195-2941 Office: Village of Hoffman Estates 1900 Hassell Rd Hoffman Estates IL 60195-2302 E-mail: rnw1976@aol.com

WILLIAMS, RICHARD THOMAS, lawyer; b. Evergreen Park, Ill., Jan. 14, 1945; s. Raymond Theodore and Elizabeth Dorothy (Williams) W. AB with honors, Stanford U., 1967, MBA, JD, Stanford U., 1972. Bar: Calif. 1972, U.S. Supreme Ct. 1977. Assoc.,then ptnr. Kadison Pfaelzer Woodard Quinn & Rossi, L.A., 1972-87; ptnr. Whitman & Ransom, 1987-93, Whitman, Breed, Abbott & Morgan, L.A., 1993-2000, Holland & Knight, LLP, L.A., 2000—. Contbg. editor Oil and Gas Analyst, 1978-84. Mem. ABA, L.A. County Bar Assn. Administrative and regulatory, Federal civil litigation, State civil litigation. Office: Holland & Knight LLP 633 W 5th St Los Angeles CA 90071-2005

WILLIAMS, RITA TUCKER, lawyer; b. Atlanta, Jan. 26, 1950; d. Claude Edward and Lillian Bernice (Barber) Tucker; m. Raymond Williams, Jr., Jan. 1, 1973; children: Monet Danielle, Brandon Raynard, Blake Hassan. BA, Spelman Coll., 1972; MA, U. Mich., 1976; JD, Emory U., 1987. Bar: Ga. 1987. Tchr. pub. schs., Suisun, Calif., 1977-82; assoc. Alston & Bird, Atlanta, 1987-89, Bernard & Assocs., Decatur, Ga., 1989-90; prin. Williams & Assocs., 1990—. Instr. seminar Nat. Inst. Trial Advocacy, Emory U., Atlanta, spring 1992-95, tutor 1st yr. law students, 1996. Named Outstanding Alumna, Emory U. Law Sch., 1996. Mem. ABA, State Bar Ga. Assn., Ga. Trial Lawyers Assn., Omicron Delta Kappa. Democrat. Office: 220 Church St Decatur GA 30030-3328 E-mail: ritw@atlonline.com

WILLIAMS, ROBERT DANA, lawyer; b. Hyannis, Mass., Feb. 21, 1939; s. Harold Warren and Winifred Josephine (Shores) W.; m. Gaye Carol Gorringe, May 30, 1964 (div. 1974); children: Sarah Ann, Amy Alden; m. Barbara Ellen Bruce, Aug. 7, 1976; children: Dana Ariana Brix, Nathaniel Shepard. AB magna cum laude, Harvard U., 1961, LLB, 1964. Bar: Mass. 1965. Rsch. asst. Am. Law Inst., Cambridge, Mass., 1964-65; assoc. Warner & Stackpole, Boston, 1965-71, ptnr., 1971-85; of counsel Hinckley, Allen, Tobin & Silverstein, Boston, 1985-87; ptnr. Hinckley, Allen, Snyder & Comen, 1987-90, Wayne, Lazares & Chappell, Boston, 1990-95, Masterman, Culbert & Tully, LLP, Boston, 1995—. Firm rep. New Eng. Entrepreneurship Coun., Inc. Boston, 1986-89. Bd. govs., exec. com. Concord (Mass.) Mus., 1980-86, capital campaign steering com., 1990-92; bd. dirs. Found. of Mass. Eye and Ear Infirmary, Boston,

1980-91; trustee, sec. Guidance Camps, Inc., 1968-86; trustee Mass. Eye and Ear Infirmary, 1971-99, bd. mgrs., 1980-91, chmn. nominating com., 1984-91; dir., sec. Napoleonic Soc. of Am., Clearwater, Fla., 1985-95; bd. dirs. Psychomotor Inst., Inc., Cambridge, Mass., 1979-95. Mem. Orgn. Am. Historians, Am. Soc. Legal History (com. on documentary preservation 1980-88), Phi Beta Kappa. Congregationalist. Avocations: history, antiquarian books. General corporate, Mergers and acquisitions, Securities. Home: 41 Monument St Concord MA 01742-1841 Office: Masterman Culbert & Tully LLP One Lewis Wharf Boston MA 02110-3985 E-mail: rdw@mctlaw.com

WILLIAMS, ROGER COURTLAND, lawyer; b. Atlanta, June 11, 1944; s. Ralph Roger and Beatrice (Hill) W.; m. Jo Ann Davenport, June 9, 1968; children: Melissa, Kimberly, Courtland. BS, U. Ala., 1966, JD, 1969. Bar: Ala. 1969, U.S. Dist. Ct. (no. and mid. dists.) Ala. 1969, U.S. Supreme Ct. 1972. V.p. Williams, Williams & Williams, P.C., Tuscaloosa, Ala., 1969-90, pres., 1990—. Adj. prof. U. Ala. Sch. Law, 1999—. Mem. bd. trustees Tuscaloosa Acad., 1987—, pres., 1990-94; bd. dirs. Children's Hands On Mus., Tuscaloosa, 1986-97. 1st lt. U.S. Army, 1969-71. Mem. ABA, Ala. State Bar Assn. (vice chmn. ADR com. 1997-98), Assn. Trial Lawyers Am., Nat. Acad. Arbitrators, Am. Arbitration Assn., Jaycees (nat. assoc. legal counsel 1979-80, state pres. 1978-79, pres. Ala. Found. 1980-81, Internat. Senator), Toastmasters (pres. 1975), Kiwanis (bd. dirs. 1974, 90, v.p. 1995-98, pres. 1998-99), Indian Hills Country Club (bd. dirs. 1996—). Methodist. Alternative dispute resolution, General civil litigation, General practice. Office: Williams Williams & Williams PC PO Box 2690 Tuscaloosa AL 35403-2690

WILLIAMS, RONALD DOHERTY, lawyer; b. New Haven, Apr. 6, 1927; s. Richard Hugh and Ethel W. (Nelson) w.; m. Laura Costarelli, Aug. 25, 1951; children: Craig F., Ronald D., Ellen A., Jane E. BA, U. Va., 1951; LLB, 1954. Bar: Conn. 1954. Assoc. Pullman, Comley, Bradley & Reeves, Bridgeport, Conn., 1954-60; ptnr., 1960-88, Williams, Cooney & Sheehy, 1989—. Mem. Fed. Jud. Com., 1988-91, com. unauthorized practice law, 1988-94, com. to study rules civil practice & procedure, 1984-86; atty. state trial referee, 1984-90. Selectman Town of Easton (Conn.), 1975-85, justice of the peace, 1977—, town atty., 1985-2000; mem. Bridgeport Area Found., 1971-90, adv. com. U. Bridgeport Law Sch., 1982-92; mem. statewide grievance com., 1985-91, chmn., 1989-91; mem. exec. bd. Sch. Law Quinnipiac Coll., 1994—. Served with U.S. Army, 1945-46. Fellow Am. Coll. Trial Lawyers; mem. ABA, Am. Bd. Trial Advs., Conn. Bar Assn. (bd. govs. 1975-78), Bridgeport Bar Assn. (pres. 1975), Conn. Def. Lawyers Assn. (pres. 1984-85), Trial Attys. Am. Republican. Roman Catholic. State civil litigation, Insurance, Personal injury. Home: 14 Newman Dr Easton CT 06612-1915 Office: 1 Lafayette Cir Bridgeport CT 06604-6021 E-mail: WilCooShee@aol.com

WILLIAMS, ROSEMARY HELEN, paralegal; b. Knoxville, Tenn., June 12, 1956; d. J. Roger and Helen Rachel (Davis) W. BS in Horticulture, U. Tenn., 1978; Assoc. in Applied Sci. in Legal Asst., Cleveland (Tenn.) State C.C., 1993. Horticulturist Bryant's Garden Ctr., Cleveland, 1986-91, Varnell Nursery, Cleveland, 1991-93; paralegal Shumacker & Thompson P.C., Chattanooga, 1993—. Mem. legal asst. adv. com. Cleve. State C.C., 1997—, U. Tenn., Chatanooga, 1997—. Contbr. articles to Legal Asst. Today. Mem. Nat. Assn. Legal Assts. (cert.), Tenn. Paralegal Assn. Avocation: estate administration. Office: Shumacker & Thompson 701 Market St Ste 500 Chattanooga TN 37402-4800

WILLIAMS, SPENCER MORTIMER, federal judge; b. Reading, Mass., Feb. 24, 1922; s. Theodore Ryder and Anabel (Hutchison) W.; m. Kathryn Bramlage, Aug. 20, 1943; children: Carol Marcia (Mrs. James B. Garvey), Peter, Spencer, Clark, Janice, Diane (Mrs. Sean Quinn). AB, UCLA, 1943; postgrad., Hastings Coll. Law, 1946; JD, U. Calif., Berkeley, 1948. Bar: Calif. 1949, U.S. Supreme Ct. 1952. Assoc. Beresford & Adams, San Jose, Calif., 1949, Rankin, O'Neal, Center, Luckhardt, Bonney, Marlais & Lund, San Jose, Evans, Jackson & Kennedy, Sacramento; county counsel Santa Clara County, 1955-67; adminstr. Calif. Health and Welfare Agy., Sacramento, 1967-69; judge U.S. Dist. Ct. (no. dist.) Calif., San Francisco, from 1971, now sr. judge. County exec. pro tem, Santa Clara County; adminstr. Calif. Youth and Adult Corrections Agy., Sacramento; sec. Calif. Human Relations Agy., Sacramento, 1967-70 Chmn. San Jose Christmas Seals Drive, 1953, San Jose Muscular Dystrophy Drive, 1953, 54; team capt. fund raising drive San Jose YMCA, 1960; co-chmn. indsl. sect. fund raising drive Alexian Bros. Hosp., San Jose, 1964; team capt. fund raising drive San Jose Hosp.; mem. com. on youth and govt. YMCA, 1967-68; Candidate for Calif. Assembly, 1954, Calif. Atty. Gen., 1966, 70; Bd. dirs. San Jose Better Bus. Bur., 1955-66, Boys City Boys' Club, San Jose, 1965-67; pres. trustees Santa Clara County Law Library, 1955-66. Served with USNR, 1943-46; to lt. comdr. JAG Corps USNR, 1950-52, PTO. Named San Jose Man of Year, 1954 Mem. ABA, Calif. Bar Assn. (vice chmn. com. on publicly employed attys. 1962-63), Santa Clara County Bar Assn., Sacramento Bar Assn., Internat. Assn. Trial Judges (pres. 1995-96), Calif. Dist. Attys. Assn. (pres. 1963-64), Nat. Assn. County Civil Attys. (pres. 1963-64), 9th Cir. Dist. Judges Assn. (pres. 1981-83), Fed. Judges Assn. (pres. 1982-87), Kiwanis, Theta Delta Chi. Office: US Dist Ct 280 S 1st St Rm 5150 San Jose CA 95113-3002

WILLIAMS, STEPHEN FAIN, federal judge; b. N.Y.C., N.Y., Sept. 23, 1936; s. Charles Dickerman and Virginia (Fain) W.; m. Faith Morrow, June 11, 1966; children: Susan, Geoffrey Fain, Sarah Margot Nu, Timothy Dwight, Nicholas Morrow. B.A., Yale U., 1958; J.D., Harvard U., 1961. Bar: N.Y. 1962, Colo. 1977. Assoc. Debevoise, Plimpton, Lyons & Gates, N.Y.C., 1962-66; asst. U.S. atty. So. Dist. N.Y., 1966-69; asst. prof. law U. Colo., Boulder, 1969-77, prof., 1977-86; judge U.S. Ct. Appeals (D.C. cir.), Washington, 1986—. Vis. prof. UCLA, 1975-76; vis. prof., fellow in law and econs. U. Chgo., 1979-80; vis. William L. Hutchison prof. energy law So. Meth. U., 1983-84; cons. Adminstrv. Conf. U.S., 1974-76, FTC, 1983-85; mem. Boulder Area Growth Study Commn., 1972-73 Contbr. articles to law revs., mags. Served with U.S. Army, 1961-62. Mem. Am. Law Inst. Office: US Courthouse 3rd & Constitution Ave NW Washington DC 20001 E-mail: Stephen_F._Williams@cadc.uscourts.gov

WILLIAMS, THEODORE JOSEPH, JR. lawyer; b. Pitts., July 23, 1947; s. Theodore Joseph and Isabel (McAnulty) W.; m. Sherri Lynne Foust, July 4, 1970; children: Kelley Shields, Jonathan Stewart, Jordan Fuller. BA, Purdue U., 1969; JD, U. Tulsa, 1974. Bar: Ill. 1975, Colo. 1996, U.S. Ct. Appeals (7th cir.) 1975, U.S. Dist. Ct. (no., so. and cen. dists.) Ill. 1975, Mo. 1978, U.S. Ct. Appeals (8th cir.) 1978, U.S. Dist. Ct. (ea. and we. dists.) Mo. 1978, U.S. Supreme Ct. 1978, D.C. 1981, U.S. Ct. Appeals (D.C. cir.) 1988, U.S. Dist. Ct. D.C 1988, U.S. Ct. Mil. Appeals 1991, U.S. Ct. Appeals (10 cir.) 1996, U.S. Dist. Ct. (no. dist.) Ind. 2000. Asst. city prosecutor City of Tulsa, 1974; trial atty., law dept. Chgo. and North Western R.R., Chgo., 1975-78; assoc. Thompson and Mitchell, St. Louis, 1978-81, Shepherd, Sandberg & Phoenix, P.C., St. Louis, 1981-84, ptnr., 1984-88; ptnr., chmn. transp. law dept. Armstrong, Teasdale, Schlafly & Davis, 1988-2001; achr. Williams, Venker & Sanders, LLC, 2001—. State counsel for Mo. and Ill., Chgo. and North Western Transp. Co., 1981-95. Assoc. editor Law. Jour., U. Tulsa, 1974. Treas. sch. bd. Mary Queen of Peace Sch., Webster Groves, Mo., 1986, v.p., 1987. Lt. col. USAR, 1991—. Mem. ABA (vice chmn. rail and motor carrier law com., torts and ins. practice law sect. 1989-90, chair-elect 1990-91, chair 1991-92), Ill. Bar Assn., Mo. Bar Assn., Def. Rsch. Inst. (chair, railroad law commn. 1996), Nat. Assn. R.R. Trial Coun., We. Conf. Ry. Coun., Assn. ICC Practitioners, Maritime Law Assn., Internat. Assn. Def. Coun., Transp. Lawyers Assn., Assn. Transp. Practitioners, D.C. Bar Assn., Colo. Bar Assn. Republican. Roman Catholic. Personal injury, Product liability, Transportation. Office: Williams Venker Sanders LLC Ste 1600 10 S Broadway St Saint Louis MO 63102 E-mail: Twilliams@wvslaw.com

WILLIAMS, THOMAS RAYMOND, lawyer; b. Meridian, Miss., Aug. 26, 1940; BS, U. Ala., 1962, LLB, 1964. Bar: Ala. 1964, Tex. 1979, U.S. Supreme Ct. 1980, D.C. 1983. Ptnr. McDermott, Will & Emery, Washington. Mem. D.C. Bar Assn., Ala. State Bar Assn., State Bar Tex. E-mial. Administrative and regulatory, Federal civil litigation, Constitutional. Office: McDermott Will & Emery 600 13th St NW Fl 12 Washington DC 20005-3096 E-mail: rwilliams@mwe.com

WILLIAMS, WILLIAM JOHN, JR. lawyer; b. New Rochelle, N.Y., Feb. 6, 1937; s. William John and Jane (Gormley) W.; m. Barbara Reuter. BA, Holy Cross Coll., Worcester, Mass., 1958; LLB, NYU, 1961. Bar: N.Y. 1961. Practiced in, N.Y.C., 1962—; ptnr. firm Sullivan & Cromwell, 1969—. Trustee NYU Law Sch. Found., 1977—, Holy Cross Coll., 1988-96. Fellow Am. Bar Found.; mem. ABA, Am. Law Inst., N.Y. State Bar Assn., Assn. of Bar of City of N.Y., U.S. Golf Assn. (mem. exec. com. 1978-87, sec. 1980-81, v.p. 1982-85, pres. 1986-87). Democrat. Roman Catholic. General corporate, Private international, Securities. E-mail: williamsw@sullcrom.com

WILLIAMSON, DEBORAH DAYWOOD, lawyer; b. Greenville, S.C., Mar. 8, 1954; d. Narcief M. Daywood and Margaret Elizabeth (Guy) Robbins; m. George F. Williamson, Nov. 9, 1974; children: Christal Elizabeth, Victoria Whitney. BA, San Antonio Coll., 1973, S.W. Tex. U., 1974, U. Tex., El Paso, 1977; JD, U. Houston, 1981. Bar: Tex. 1982, U.S. Dist. Ct. (we. dist.) Tex. 1983, U.S. Dist. Ct. (so. dist.) Tex. 1986, U.S. Dist. Ct. (no. dist.) Tex. 1989, U.S. Dist. Ct. Ariz. 1991, U.S. Ct. Appeals (5th cir.) 1983. Atty. Cox & Smith Inc., San Antonio, 1982—. Author: (with others) Single Asset Real Estate Bankruptcies, 1996; columnist Am. Bankruptcy Inst. Jour., 1985—. Fellow Tex. Bar Found., Am. Coll. Bankruptcy, San Antonio Bar Found.; master Am. Inns of Ct., William Session; mem. Am. Bankruptcy Inst. (pres. 1998-99), San Antonio Bankruptcy Bar Assn. Bankruptcy. Office: Cox & Smith Inc 112 E Pecan St Ste 1800 San Antonio TX 78205-1521 E-mail: ddwillia@coxsmith.com

WILLIAMSON, EDWIN DARGAN, lawyer, former federal official; b. Florence, S.C., Sept. 23, 1939; s. Benjamin F. and Sara (Dargan) W.; m. Kathe Gates, July 12, 1969; children: Samuel Gates, Edwin Dargan Jr., Sara Elizabeth. BA cum laude, U. of the South, 1961, DCL (hon.), 1992; JD, NYU, 1964. Bar: N.Y. 1965, D.C. 1988. Assoc. Sullivan & Cromwell, N.Y.C., 1964-70, ptnr., 1971-76, London, 1976-79, N.Y.C., 1979-88, Washington, 1988-90, 93—; legal adviser U.S. Dept. State, 1990-93. Regent U. of the South, Sewanee, Tenn., 1981-87, chmn., 1985-87, coun. fgn. rels., 1995—; bd. dirs. Nat. Dance Inst., N.Y.C., 1984-88, Episcopal Ch. Found., N.Y.C., 1986-94; vestryman St. James Episcopal Ch., N.Y.C., 1984-88. Mem. U.S. Coun. Internat. Bus., Bus. and Industry Adv. Com. to OECD (vice chmn. com. on multinat. enterprise and investments 1993—, chmn. BIAC expert group on multilat agt. on investment 1996-99, vice-chmn. BIAC 1998—, mem. exec. com. USCIB 1999—), Internat. Rep. Inst. (rule of law adv. bd. 1993—), Racquet and Tennis Club (N.Y.C.), Met. Club. Republican. Private international, Public international, Securities. E-mail: williamsone@sullcrom.com

WILLIAMSON, MICHAEL GEORGE, lawyer; b. West Point, N.Y., Feb. 22, 1951; s. John and Alice (MacAniff) W.; m. Linda Ann Cappelli, June 27, 1980. Student U.S. Mil. Acad., 1969-71; B.S. magna cum laude, Duke U., 1973; J.D., Georgetown U., 1976. Bar: Fla. 1976, U.S. Dist. Ct. (mid. dist.) Fla. 1977, U.S. Dist. Ct. (so. dist.) Fla. 1981. Instr. legal research and writing Georgetown U. Law Ctr., Washington, 1975-76; assoc. Johnson, Motsinger, Trisman & Sharp, Orlando, Fla., 1976-78; assoc. Maguire, Voorhis & Wells, Orlando, 1978-82, ptnr., 1982— ; instr. bus. law Valencia Community Coll., Orange County, Fla., 1978-80; lectr. seminars. Editor: Internat. Jour. Georgetown Law Ctr., 1975-76. Contbr. articles to profl. publs. Mem. steering com. 1984 Nat. Conf. Bankruptcy Judges, Orlando, 1984; chmn. com. on middle dist. bankruptcy rules, 1985. Mem. Fla. Bar Assn. (UCC/Bankruptcy com. 1978— , chmn. 1986-87), Orange County Bar Assn. (corp. and bus. law sect. chmn. 1984-85, chmn. bankruptcy law com. 1983-84). Republican. Roman Catholic. Bankruptcy. Home: 757 Terra Pl Maitland FL 32751-4583 Office: Maguire Voorhis & Wells PA 2 S Orange Ave Orlando FL 32801-2606

WILLIAMSON, RONALD THOMAS, lawyer; b. Paterson, N.J., Nov. 12, 1948; s. Thomas Sim and Jessie Carnegie (Sandilands) W.; m. Nancy Anne Hough, June 13, 1982; children: Kate Elizabeth, Brad Francis Thomas. BA, Rutgers U., 1970; JD cum laude, Widener U., 1975. Bar: Pa. 1976, U.S. Dist. Ct. (ea. dist.) Pa. 1976, U.S. Supreme Ct. 1979, U.S. Ct. Appeals (3d cir.) 1980. Assoc. Modell, Pincus, Hahn and Reich, Phila., 1976-77; asst. dist. atty., chief of appeals County of Montgomery, Norristown, Pa., 1977-85; sr. dep. atty. gen. appeals and legal svcs. sect. Pa. Atty. Gen., Harrisburg, 1997—, 1997—. Instr. search and seizure Southeastern Tng. Ctr., Pa. State Police, Worcester, 1979-85; legal instr. Montgomery County C.C., Whitpain, Pa., 1984. Contbr. to profl. publs. Bd. dirs. Denbigh Group Foster Home, Bridgeport, Pa., 1979-83, pres., 1984; mem. Cen. Montgomery Optimist Club, Norristown, 1980-81. Mem. Pa. Bar Assn., Montgomery County Bar Assn. (chmn. appellate ct. practice com., bd. dirs.). Republican. Presbyterian. Avocations: tennis, squash, sailing, triathlon, reading. Office: Pa Office Atty Gen 2490 Blvd of the Generals Norristown PA 19403-5234 E-mail: rwilliamson@attorneygeneral.gov

WILLIAMSON, THOMAS W., JR. lawyer; b. Miami, Fla., July 22, 1950; s. Thomas W. Sr. and Elizabeth (Worthington) W. BA, Va. Mil. Inst., 1972; JD, U. Richmond, 1976. Bar: Va., U.S. Dist. Ct. (ea. and we. dists.) Va., U.S. Ct. Appeals (4th cir.). Assoc. Emanual Emroch & Assocs., Richmond, Va., 1976-82; ptnr. Emroch & Williamson, 1982-92, Williamson & Stoneburner, L.C., Richmond, 1992-94, Williamson & Levecchia, L.C., Richmond, 1994—. Served to capt. USAR. Fellow Am.Coll. Trial Lawyers, Internat. Acad. Trial Lawyers; mem. ABA, Assn. Trial Lawyers Am., Va. State Bar, Va. Trial Lawyers Assn. (pres. 1995-96), Richmond Bar Assn., Richmond Trial Lawyers Assn. (pres. 1986-87), John Marshall Inn of Ct. (pres. 1995-96). Federal civil litigation, State civil litigation, Personal injury. Office: Williamson & Lavecchia LC 6800 Paragon Pl Ste 233 Richmond VA 23230-1652

WILLIAMSON, WALTER, lawyer; b. N.Y.C., Apr. 23, 1939; s. Zarah and Leah (Golding) W.; m. Barbara Alice Fisher, Sept. 9, 1973; children—Douglas Fisher, Andrew Fisher. B.A., Cornell U., 1960; M.D., NYU, 1964; J.D., Columbia U., 1973. Bar: N.Y. 1974, U.S. Dist. Ct. (ea. and so. dists.) N.Y. 1974, U.S. Ct. Appeals (2d cir.) 1975, U.S. Supreme Ct. 1977. Intern Mt. Sinai Hosp., N.Y.C., 1964-65; resident Hillside Hosp., Queens, N.Y., 1965-66; resident Mt. Sinai Hosp., N.Y.C., 1968-70; ptnr. Williamson & Williamson, N.Y.C., 1974-78; prin. Williamson & Williamson, P.C., N.Y.C., 1978— . Served as capt. M.C., USAF, 1966-68. Editor Columbia Law Rev., 1972-73. Fellow Am. Coll. Legal Medicine; mem. ABA, N.Y. State Bar Assn., Assn. of Bar of City of N.Y. (com. on medicine and law 1975-78, com. on uniform state laws 1988—), N.Y. County Lawyers Assn., Phi Beta Kappa, Phi Kappa Phi. State civil litigation, Insurance, Personal injury. Home: 322 Central Park W New York NY 10025-7629 Office: Williamson & Williamson PC 305 Broadway Fl 14 New York NY 10007-1192

WILLIAMSON, WALTER BLAND, lawyer; b. Selma, Ala., Apr. 6, 1938; s. Walter Bland and Tina (Matheny) W.; children: Michael Davis, Amy Caroline; m. Dana Leigh Freiburger, Jan. 2, 1999. BS, Stetson U., 1959; JD, Emory U., 1963. Bar: Okla. 1969, Ga. 1963, U.S. Ct. Mil. Appeals 1963, U.S. Supreme Ct. 1969. Atty. Office Gen. Counsel Fed. Deposit Ins. Corp., Washington, 1967; atty. Office Stds. Policy U.S. Dept. Commerce, 1968-69; shareholder Pray, Walker, Jackman, Williamson & Marlar and predecessors, Tulsa, 1969—, pres., 1993-98. Steering com. conf. on nuclear power generation Nat. Energy Law and Policy Inst., 1981; adv. com. on natural gas allowables Okla. Corp. Commn., 1983, 88. Active Okla. Energy Resources Bd., 1992-95; trustee Grace and Franklin Bernsen Found., Philbrook Mus. Art; bd. dirs. Indian Nations Coun., Boy Scouts Am.; governing bd. Jasmine Moran Childrens Mus. Capt. U.S. Army, 1963-67. Mem. ABA (vice-chmn. natural gas mktg. and transp. com., natural resource sect. 1986-88, co-chmn. energy com. adminstrv. law and regulatory practice sect. 1998-2000), Okla. Bar Assn. (chmn. mineral law sect. 1982), Tulsa County Bar Assn. (chmn. mineral law sect. 1979), Ind. Petroleum Assn. Am. (regional v.p. 1991-95), Fed. Energy Bar Assn., Okla. Ind. Petroleum Assn. (chmn. legal com. 1979-83, gen. counsel 1983—, Mem. of Yr. 1987), Energy Advocates (coord. 1987-88, 91), Phi Delta Phi. Administrative and regulatory, General corporate, Oil, gas, and mineral. Home: 1228 E 19th St Tulsa OK 74120-7419 Office: 900 Oneok Plz Tulsa OK 74103 E-mail: wbw@praywalker.com

WILLIG, WILLIAM PAUL, lawyer; b. Schenectady, N.Y., Mar. 29, 1936; s. James R. and Mildred (Nock) W. AB in Liberal Arts, St. Michael's Coll., Winooski Park, Vt., 1958; JD, Union U., 1962. Bar: N.Y.; U.S. Ct. Appeals (2nd cir.); IRS. Ptnr., shareholder, v.p. and head litigation dept. Higgins, Roberts, Beyerl & Coan, P.C., Schenectady, 1962-91; lead atty. Schenectady (N.Y.) Internat., Inc. (formerly Schenectady Chems., Inc.), 1991—; sole practitioner Saratoga Springs, 1991—. Panelist on Med. malpractice and arbitration N.Y. Supreme Ct., Empire Mediation & Arbitration, Inc.; chmn. legislative hearings Capitol Dist., 1965; prof. environ. studies Union Coll., 1993-94, legal process course; instr. comml. law evening divsn. Am. Inst. Banking; former practice ct. judge Albany Law Sch., Union U. Candidate N.Y. Supreme Ct. 4th Jud. Dist., 1981; mem. zoning review com. Town of Ballston; legal counsel, player Ballston Lake Theatre Co., former Big Brother, Big Brothers of Schenectady; emergency personnel, lectr. Am. Red Cross; historian Gold Cup The Antique Boat Museum, Clayton, N.Y. Mem. N.Y. State Bar Assn. (trial lawyers sect., environ. law sect. com.), Federated Bar Assn., Med. Malpractice Panel of N.Y., Schenectady County Bar Assn. (program chmn. legal aid com., Courthouse Dedication 1981, inter-profl. com., spkrs. bur., atty. referral com. 1986-89, co-chmn. mock trial tournament com. 1991-92, v.p. 1991-92, pres. 1992-93, bd. dirs. past pres. com. 1994-95), Ballson Lake Improvement Assn., Saratoga County C. of C., Schenectady County C. of C., Schenectady Jaycees, Am. Cancer Soc. (Schenectady County unit, co-chmn. Annual Golf Day Crusade 1978-78, com. 1976-95), Lake George Assn., St. Michael's Coll. Alumni Assn., Union U. Albany Law Sch. Alumni Assn., Am. Power Boat Assn. (unltd. racing commn., co-chmn. hist. com.), Mohawk Golf Club (Schenectady), Eagle Creek Country Club (Naples, Fla.). Democrat. Avocations: antique and classic power boats, golf, skiing. State civil litigation, Environmental, Personal injury. Office: PO Box 1082 526 Maple Ave Saratoga Springs NY 12866-5509

WILLINGHAM, CLARK SUTTLES, lawyer; b. Houston, Nov. 29, 1944; s. Paul Suttles and Elsie Dell (Clark) W.; m. Jane Joyce Hitch, Aug. 16, 1969; children: Meredith Moores, James Barrett. BBA, Tex. Tech U., 1967; JD, So. Meth. U., 1971, LLM, 1984. Bar: Tex. 1971. Ptnr. Kasmir, Willingham & Krage, Dallas, 1972-86, Finley, Kumble et al, Dallas, 1986-87, Brice & Mankoff, Dallas, 1988-98, Moseley Martens, LLP, Dallas, 1999—. Contbr. articles to profl. jours. Exec. com. Dallas Summer Musicals, 1979-93, pres., 1994-95. Mem. ABA (chmn. agrl. com. tax sect. 1984-86), State Bar Tex. (chmn. agrl. tax com. 1985-87), Dallas Bar Assn., Am. Law Inst., Tex. Rangers Law Enforcement Assn.(bd. dirs. 2000—), Nat. Cattlemen's Beef Assn. (bd. dirs., pres. 1998), U.S. Meat Export Fedn. (exec. com. 1991-93), Beef Industry Coun. (exec. com. 1990-91, promotion chmn. 1992-94), Tex. Cattle Feeders Assn. (bd. dirs., pres. 1988), Tex. Bd. Vet. Med. Examiners (pres. 1994), Tex. Beef Coun. (bd. dirs., pres. 1989), Dallas Country Club. Republican. Episcopalian. Corporate taxation, Estate taxation, Personal income taxation. Home: 3824 Shenandoah St Dallas TX 75205-1702 Office: Moseley & Standerfer 3878 Oak Lawn Ave Ste 400 Dallas TX 75219-4469

WILLIS, BRUCE DONALD, judge; b. Mpls., Jan. 29, 1941; s. Donald Robert and Marie Evelyn (Edwards) W.; m. Elizabeth Ann Runsvold, July 17, 1971; children: Andrew John, Ellen Elizabeth. BA in English, Yale U., 1962; LLB, Harvard U., 1965. Bar: Minn., 1965, U.S. Dist. Ct. Minn. 1965, U.S. Ct. Fed. Claims 1989, U.S. Ct. Appeals (8th cir.) 1991, U.S. Supreme Ct. 1992. Assoc. Popham, Haik, Schnobrich & Kaufman, Ltd., Mpls., 1965-71, ptnr., 1971-95; judge Minn. Ct. Appeals, 1995—. Mem. adv. bd. Minn. Inst. Legal Edn., 1985—, mem. jud. adv. bd. for the Law and Organizational Econs. Ctr. of the Univ. of Kansas, 1997—. Contbr. articles to profl. jours. Del. Rep. Nat. convs., 1976, 88; vice chmn. Ind.-Rep. Party Minn., 1979-81; mem. State Ethical Practices Bd., 1990-95, sec. 1990-91, vice chmn. 1991-92, chmn., 1992-93; mem. Minn. Commn. on Jud. Selection, 1991-94; mem. Minn. Bd. Jud. Stds., 1997—; mem. adv. com. on rules of civil appellate procedure Minn. Supreme Ct., 1997—. Named one of 1990's Lawyers of Yr., Minn. Jour. Law and Politics, 1991, one of Minn.'s Best Trial Lawyers, Minn. Lawyer, 1991. Mem. ABA, Minn. Bar Assn. (professionalism com. 1998—), Rolling Green Country Club. Mem. United Ch. of Christ. Home: 2940 Walnut Grove Ln N Plymouth MN 55447-1567 Office: Minn Jud Ctr 25 Constitution Ave Saint Paul MN 55155-1500 E-mail: bruce.willis@courts.state.mn.us

WILLIS, DAWN LOUISE, paralegal, small business owner; b. Johnstown, Pa., Sept. 11, 1959; d. Kenneth William and Dawn Louise (Joseph) Hagins; m. Marc Anthony Ross, Nov. 30, 1984 (div.); m. Jerry Wayne Willis, Dec. 16, 1989 (div.). Grad. high sch., Sacramento, Calif. Legal sec. Wilcoxen & Callahan, Sacramento, 1979-87, paralegal asst., 1987-88; legal adminstr. Law Office Jack Vetter, 1989-99; owner, mgr. Your Girl Friday Secretarial and Legal Support Svcs., 1991—; legal asst. Foley & Lardner, 1999-2001; case mgr. Larry Lockshin, Esq. Law Corp., 2001—. Vol. ARC, 1985, Spl. Olympics, 1997—. Mem. Sacramento Legal Secs. Assn. Democrat. Lutheran. Avocations: water sports, camping, reading, cooking. Office: Larry Lockshin Esq Law Corp 701 University Ave Ste 100 Sacramento CA 95825-6756

WILLIS, JOHN ALEXANDER, lawyer; b. Queens, N.Y., Feb. 3, 1966; s. John Joseph Willis and Dorothy Elizabeth (Savides) White. BA, SUNY, Stony Brook, 1989; JD, Nova Southeastern Law Ctr., 1994. Bar: Fla. 1994, U.S. Ct. Appeals (11th cir.) 1994, N.Y. 1995, U.S. Dist. Ct. (so. dist.) Fla. 1995, U.S. Supreme Ct., 1999. Acct. coord. Met. Life Ins. Co., Hauppauge, N.Y., 1989-91; cert. legal intern Palm Beach County State's Atty Office, West Palm Beach, Fla., 1994; assoc. David & French, P.A., Boca Raton, 1994-2000, Baker & Zimmerman, P.A., Boca Raton, 2000—. Mem. ATLA, Acad. Fla. Trial Lawyers, South Palm Beach County Bar Assn. Avocations: golf, computers, softball. General civil litigation, Insurance, Personal injury. Office: Baker & Zimmerman PA 6100 Glades Rd Ste 301 Boca Raton FL 33434 E-mail: jawillis@aol.com

WILLIS, RUSSELL ANTHONY, III, lawyer; b. Peoria, Ill., June 2, 1953; s. Russell A. and Martha Lois (Wilson) W.; m. Debra R. Austrin, July 27, 1975; children: Sarah E. Austrin-Willis, Benjamin D. Austrin-Willis. BA in English with honors, Ind. U., 1975; MA, U. Chgo., 1976; JD, St. Louis U., 1979; LLM, Wash. U., 1987. Bar: Mo. 1979, U.S. Dist. Ct. (ea.

and we. dists.) Mo. 1979, U.S. Ct. Appeals (8th cir.) 1980, U.S. Tax. Ct. 1982. Pvt. practice, St. Louis, 1981, 83-84; assoc. Tremayne, Lay, Carr & Bauer, 1981-83; of counsel Wolff & Frankel, 1983-84; asst. trust counsel Mercantile Trust Co., 1984-85; assoc. Guilfoil, Petzall & Shoemake, 1985-87; pvt. practice, 1987-88; assoc. Rothman, Sokol, Adler & Barry, 1988-89; trust counsel Mercantile Trust Co., 1989-91; pvt. practice Creve Coeur, Mo., 1991—. Contbr. articles to profl. jours. Mem. Mo. Bar Assn. (various coms. and sects.), Bar Assn. Met. St. Louis (legis. com.). General corporate, Estate planning, Estate taxation. E-mail: rawillis3@juno.com

WILLMETH, ROGER EARL, lawyer; b. Atchison, Kans., Apr. 24, 1946; s. Marion Clair and Virginia Rosemary (Bryant) W.; m. Janice Hazel Matthews, Apr. 14, 1973; children: Jennifer Lynn, Melissa Anne. Student, No. Ill. U., 1964-65, DePaul U., 1965-67; JD, John Marshall Law Sch., Chgo., 1970. Bar: Ill. 1970, Guam 1979, U.S. Dist. Ct. Guam 1979, U.S. Dist. Ct. (cen. dist.) Ill. 1979, U.S. Ct. Mil. Appeals 1971, U.S. Ct. Appeals (9th cir.) 1978, U.S. Supreme Ct. 1979. Asst. atty. gen. Territory of Guam, Agana, 1977-79, State of Ill., Springfield, 1979-81; gen. atty. 375th Air Base Group USAF, Scott AFB, Ill., 1981-84, atty., adviser air force comm. command, 1984-91; assoc. gen. counsel dept. air force The Pentagon, Washington, 1991—. Spl. asst. U.S. atty. So. Dist. Ill., 1983-84. Author: Determining Whether Modifications Are With9n the Scope of the Contract 29 A.F.L. rev 93, 1988. Bd. dirs. Country Lake Estates Owners Assn.; adminstrv. bd. First United Meth. Ch., Collinsville. Ret. Col. USAFR JAGC. Legion of Merit, Meritorious Svc. medal with oak leaf cluster, Decorated Air Force Commendation medal, Air Force Achievement medal; recipient Excellence award for civil litigation Guam Atty. Gen., 1979; named Outstanding Civilian Atty. of Yr., Mil. Airlift Command, 1982, Air Force Civilian Meritorious Svc. medal, 1984, 91. Mem. Guam Bar Assn., U.S. Tennis Assn., St. Clair Tennis Club (O'Fallon, Ill.). Methodist. Office: SAF / GCQ 1740 Air Force Pentagon Washington DC 20330-1740 E-mail: roger.willmeth@pentagon.af.mil

WILLSON, PRENTISS, JR. lawyer; b. Durham, N.C., Sept. 20, 1943; s. Prentiss and Lucille (Giles) W. AB, Occidental Coll., 1965; JD, Harvard U., 1968. Bar: Calif. 1969, U.S. Dist. Ct. (no. dist.) Calif. 1971, U.S. Ct. Appeals (9th cir.) 1971, U.S. Tax Ct. 1971, U.S. Supreme Ct. 1975. Instr. law Miles Coll., Birmingham, Ala., 1968-70; ptnr. Morrison & Foerster, San Francisco, 1970-98, Ernst & Young, Walnut Creek, Calif., 1998—. Prof. Golden Gate U., 1971-84; lectr. Stanford U. Sch. Law, 1985-88. Contbr. articles to profl. jours. Mem. ABA, Calif. Bar Assn. Democrat. Corporate taxation, Personal income taxation, State and local taxation. Office: Ernst & Young 1331 N California Blvd Walnut Creek CA 94596 E-mail: prentiss.willson@ey.com

WILLY, THOMAS RALPH, lawyer; b. Phila., Sept. 30, 1943; s. Albert Ralph and Dorothy Rose (Driver) W.; m. Kay Harris, Jan. 12, 1968; children: Elyn Alexandria, Jon Charles. BA in History, U. Mo.-Kansas City, 1966, JD with distinction, 1974. Bar: Mo. 1974, U.S. Tax Ct. 1982. Assoc. Deacy & Deacy, Kansas City, 1974-75, Logan, Hentzen, Haitbrink & Moore, Kansas City, 1975; ptnr. Hentzen, Haitbrink & Moore, 1976-78, Hentzen, Moore & Willy, Kansas City, 1978-80, Moore & Willy Profl. Corp., Kansas City, 1980-87, pres., dir., 1987-94; shareholder, dir., v.p. Van Osdol, Magruder, Erickson & Redmond, P.C., 1994—. Cons. Ctr. for Mgmt. Assistance, Kansas City; presenter living will project, Midwest Bioethics Ctr. Pres. Kansas City Swiss Soc., 1989-91, bd. dirs. 1993-96; bd. dirs. Greater Kansas City People to People, 1995-98, 2000—; active Greater Kansas City Coun. Philanthropy, Mid-Am. Planned Giving Coun., Nat. Com. on Planned Giving, Friends of Art, Kansas City, Kansas City Consensus, Hist. Kansas City Found. Capt. USAF, 1966-70. Mem. ABA (sect. internat. law, sect. bus. law), Mo. Bar Assn., Lions (bd. dirs. Leawood 1986-88, 90-92, sec. 1988-90, v.p. 1996-97. General corporate, Estate planning, Non-profit and tax-exempt organizations. Home: 10314 Lee Blvd Shawnee Mission KS 66206-2629 Office: 2700 Commerce Tower 911 Main St Kansas City MO 64105-2009 E-mail: twilly@vomer.com

WILMOTH, WILLIAM DAVID, lawyer; b. Elkins, W.Va., July 11, 1950; s. Stark Amasa and Goldie (Johnson) W.; m. Rebecca Weaver, Aug. 21, 1971; children: Charles, Anne, Samuel, Peter. BS in Fin. cum laude, W.Va. U., 1972, JD, 1975. Bar: W.Va. 1975, U.S. Dist. Ct. (so. dist.) W.Va. 1975, U.S. Dist. Ct. (no. dist.) W.Va. 1976, U.S. Ct. Appeals (4th cir.) 1977, U.S. Supreme Ct. 1981, Pa. 1986. Law clk. to presiding judge U.S. Dist. Ct. (no. dist.) W.Va., Elkins, 1975-76; assoc. Bachmann, Hess, Bachmann & Garden, Wheeling, W.Va., 1976-77; asst. U.S. atty. U.S. Dept. Justice, 1977-80; ptnr. Schrader, Byrd, Byrum & Companion, 1980-93; U.S. atty. U.S. Dist. Ct. (no. dist.) W.Va., W.Va., 1993-99; ptnr. Steptoe & Johnson, 1999—. Past pres., chmn. bd. dirs. nat. trail coun. Boy Scouts Am., Wheeling; chmn. bd. dirs. Wheeling Nat. Heritage Area Corp., Wheeling YMCA, State Coll. Sys. W.Va., past chmn. Mem. ABA, Def. Research Inst., Def. Trial Counsel W.Va., Rotary Club Wheeling (past pres.). Democrat. Criminal, Health, Insurance. Home: RR 4 Box 106 Wheeling WV 26003-9314 Office: Steptoe & Johnson PO Box 150 Wheeling WV 26003-0020 E-mail: wilmotw@steptoe-johnson.com

WILNER, ALAN M. judge; b. Balt., Jan. 26, 1937; AB, Johns Hopkins U., 1958, MLA, 1966; JD, U. Md., 1962. Assoc. Sherbow, Shea & Doyle, Balt., 1962-65; asst. atty. gen. State of Md., 1965-68; assoc. Venable, Baetjer & Howard, Balt., 1968-71; asst., then chief legis. officer, govs. staff, 1971-77; assoc. judge Ct. of Spl. Appeals, 1977-90, chief judge, 1990-96; judge Ct. of Appeals, Md., 1996—. Adj. faculty U. Md. Sch. of Law, U. Balt. Sch. of Law; with Judicial Inst. Md., 1997—, chmn. bd. dirs., 1999—; mem. Md. Alternative Dispute Resolution Commn., 1998—. Mem. ABA, Md. Bar. Found., Md. State Bar Assn., Balt. County Bar Assn. Office: Md Ct of Appeals County Courts Bldg 401 Bosley Ave Towson MD 21204*

WILSING, HANS ULRICH, lawyer; b. Bonn, Germany, Nov. 22, 1961; s. Karl Heinrich and Ursula Gela W.; m. Beate Elisabeth, Aug. 21, 1995; children: Caroline, Robert. Referendarexam, U. Bonn, 1992. Bar: Cologne 1992. Asst. U. Bonn, 1989-91; clk. Bauschert Law Office, Cologne, 1990-92, Bruckhans Law Office, Düsseldorf, Germany, 1991. Co-author: Professional Partnerships, 1994; contbr. article to profl. jour. Obergefreiter S. Tank Divsn., 1980-82. Mem. German/U.S. Lawyers Assn., German Bar Assn. General corporate, Mergers and acquisitions, Securities. Home: Frankenstrasse 40 50858 Cologne NRW Germany Office: Linklater Oppenhoff & Naedles Hohennaufenring 62 50674 Cologne NRW Germany Fax: 2091435. E-mail: huw@oppenhoff-naedles.com

WILSON, BRUCE BRIGHTON, retired transportation executive, lawyer; b. Boston, Feb. 6, 1936; s. Robert Lee and Jane (Schlotterer) W.; m. Elizabeth Ann MacFarland, Dec. 31, 1958; children: Mabeth, Mary, Bruce Robert, Caroline Daly. AB, Princeton U., 1958; LLB, U. Pa., 1961. Bar: Pa. 1962. Assoc. Montgomery, McCracken, Walker & Rhoads, Phila., 1962-69; atty. U.S. Dept. Justice, Washington, 1969-79, dep. asst. atty. gen. antitrust div., 1971-76; spl. counsel Consol. Rail Corp., Phila., 1979-81, gen. counsel litigation and antitrust, 1981-82, v.p., gen. counsel, 1982-84, v.p. law, 1984-87, sr. v.p. law, 1987-97, sr. v.p. merger, 1997. Bd. dirs. Phila. Indsl. Devel. Corp.; mem. mgmt. com. Concord Resources Group, 1989-91. Chmn. Radnor Twp. Cable Comms. Coun., 1993-2000; mem. Radnor Twp. Ethics Commn., 2000—. Fellow Salzburg Seminar in Am. Studies (Austria), 1965; fellow Felz Inst. State and Local Govt., 1967 Mem. ABA, Phila. Bar Assn., Corinthian Yacht Club, Beach Club Cape May. Home: 224 Chamounix Rd Wayne PA 19087-3606 E-mail: bbwils24@erols.com

WILSON, CHARLES HAVEN, lawyer; b. Waltham, Mass., July 27, 1936; s. Charles Haven Sr. and Kathryn (Sullivan) W.; children: Kathryn Wilson Self, Charles H. Jr. AB in Govt. magna cum laude, Tufts U., 1958; MS in Journalism, Columbia U., 1959; JD, U. Calif., Berkeley, 1967. Bar: D.C. 1968, U.S. Supreme Ct. 1972. Sr. law clk. to Chief Justice Earl Warren, 1967-68; from assoc. to counsel Williams & Connolly, Washington, 1968-90; sr. counsel ACLU of Nat. Capital Area, 1992-98; sr. staff atty. Bazelon Ctr. for Mental Health Law, 1998-99. Adj. prof. constitutional law Georgetown U. Law Ctr., 1971, 72. With U.S. Army, 1959-62. Mem. ABA (litigation sect. coun. 1976-79, dir publs. 1975-90, founding editor jour. Litigation 1974, bd. editors ABA Jour. 1985-91), Order of Coif. Democrat. Roman Catholic. Avocation: reading. Civil rights, General civil litigation, Constitutional.

WILSON, CHARLES REGINALD, lawyer, former prosecutor; BS, JD, U. Notre Dame. Bar: Fla. 1979. Law clk. to Hon. Joseph W. Hatchett U.S. Ct. Appeal for 11th Cir.; county judge 13th Jud. Cir. of Fla., 1987-90; sole practitioner Fla., 1981-86; U.S. magistrate judge U.S. Dist. Ct. (mid. dist.) Fla., 1990-94; U.S. atty. Middle Dist. Fla., 1994-99; U.S. cir. judge 11th Cir. Ct. Appeals, Tampa, Fla., 1999—. Mem. Fla. Bar Assn. (bd. govs. young lawyers sect.), Hillsborough County Bar Assn. (pres. young lawyers sect., Most Productive Young Lawyer award 1990). Office: 11th Cir Ct Appeals 801 N Florida Ave Ste 14B Tampa FL 33602-3849*

WILSON, CLAUDE RAYMOND, JR. lawyer; b. Dallas, Feb. 22, 1933; s. Claude Raymond and Lottie (Watts) W.; m. Emilynn Wilson; children: Deidra Wilson Graves, Melissa Woodard Utley, Michele Woodard Dunn. BBA, So. Meth. U., 1954, JD, 1956. Bar: Tex. 1956; CPA, Calif., Tex. Assoc. firm Cervin & Melton, Dallas, 1956-58; atty. Tex. & Pacific R.R. Co., 1958-60; atty. office regional counsel IRS, San Francisco, 1960-63, sr. trial atty. office chief counsel Washington, 1963-65; ptnr. Wilson & White, Dallas, 1965-98, Vial, Hamilton, Koch & Knox LLP, Dallas, 1998—. Chmn., Dallas dist. dir. IRS Adv. Commn., 1990-91. Chmn. Dallas Hist. Soc., 2000-01. Mem. ABA, AICPA (coun. 1989-93, tax exec. com.), State Bar Tex., Dallas Bar Assn. (pres. sect. taxation 1969-70), Tex. Soc. CPAs (pres. 1989-90, pres. Dallas chpt. 1983-84), Greater Dallas C. of C. (chmn. appropriations and tax com. 1990-91), Montaigne Club, Dallas Petroleum Club, Masons, Shriners, Delta Sigma Phi, Delta Theta Phi. Republican. Episcopalian. Taxation, general, Personal income taxation, State and local taxation. Office: Vial Hamilton Koch & Knox 4400 Bank One Ctr 1717 Main St Dallas TX 75201-7388 E-mail: cwilson@vialaw.com

WILSON, DONALD KENNETH, JR. lawyer, publisher; b. Lancaster, Pa., Mar. 5, 1954; s. Donald Kenneth and Gloria (Payne) W.; m. Lauren Elaine O'Connor, Sept. 3, 1977; children: Donald, Tameka, Veronica, Matthew. BA, U. So. Calif., 1976; JD, N.Y. Law Sch., 1979. Bar: Calif. 1979, U.S. Ct. Appeals (9th cir.) 1979, U.S. Ct. Appeals (ea. dist.) Mich., 1996, U.S. Ct. Appeals, Colo. 1997. Ptnr. Law Office, L.A., 1987-92; pres., chief operating officer Quincy Jones Productions, 1983-86; assoc. Garey, Mason & Sloane, 1979-82; pres., CEO 4 Kids Music, 1989—, Dotevema Music, L.A., 1989—; of counsel Law Offices Johnnie L. Cochran Jr., 1992—. Producer: (video documentary) Frank Sinatra, 1984 (Vira award 1985, Grammy nomination 1985); contb. articles to newspapers. Trustee First African Meth. Episc. Ch., 1989-97; mem. NAACP, L.A., 1990. Recipient Citizenship award, Am. Legion, 1972; named Outstanding Young Men of Am., 1982, 83, Outstanding Contbr. to Community, Entertainment Civic Orgn., 1986. Avocations: tennis, reading, walking, fishing. Office: Law Offices Johnnie L Cochran Jr 4929 Wilshire Blvd Ste 1010 Los Angeles CA 90010-3825

WILSON, GARY DEAN, lawyer; b. Wichita, Kans., June 7, 1943; s. Glenn E. and Roe Zella (Mills) W.; m. Diane Kay Williams, Dec. 29, 1965; children: Mark R., Matthew C., Christopher G. BA, Stanford U., 1965, LLB, 1968. Bar: D.C. 1970, U.S. Dist. Ct. D.C. 1970, U.S. Ct. Appeals (D.C. cir.) 1972, U.S. Ct. Appeals (7th cir.) 1979, U.S. Ct. Appeals (2d cir.) 1983. Law clk. U.S. Ct. Appeals, 2d cir., N.Y.C., 1968-69, U.S. Supreme Ct., Washington, 1969-70; assoc. Wilmer, Cutler & Pickering, 1970-75, ptnr., 1976—. Acting prof. law Stanford (Calif.) Law Sch., 1981-82. Bd. visitors Stanford Law Sch., 1990-92, 2000—. Democrat. Alternative dispute resolution, General civil litigation, Intellectual property. Home: 4636 30th St NW Washington DC 20008-2127 Office: Wilmer Cutler & Pickering 2445 M St NW Ste 900 Washington DC 20037-1435 E-mail: gwilson@wilmer.com, dwilson1@erols.com

WILSON, HUGH STEVEN, lawyer; b. Paducah, Ky., Nov. 27, 1947; s. Hugh Gipson and Rebekah (Dunn) W.; m. Clare Maloney, Apr. 28, 1973; children: Morgan Elizabeth, Zachary Hunter, Samuel Gipson. BS, Ind. U., 1968; JD, U. Chgo., 1971; LLM, Harvard U., 1972. Bar: Calif. 1972, U.S. Dist. Ct. (cen. dist.) Calif. 1972, U.S. Dist. Ct. (so. dist.) Calif. 1973, U.S. Ct. Appeals (9th cir.) 1975, U.S. Dist. Ct. (no. dist.) Calif. 1977, U.S. Supreme Ct. 1978, U.S. Dist. Ct. (ea. dist.) 1980. Assoc. Latham & Watkins, L.A., 1972-78, ptnr., 1978—. Recipient Jerome N. Frank prize U. Chgo. Law Sch., 1971. Mem. Calif. Club, Coronado Yacht Club, Order of Coif. Republican. Avocations: lit., zoology. Federal civil litigation, General corporate, Mergers and acquisitions. E-mail: steve.wilson@lw.com

WILSON, JAMES CHARLES, JR. lawyer; b. Birmingham, Ala., Sept. 13, 1947; s. James C. and Angelina (Serio) W.; m. Ann Bullock, Mar. 1, 1975; children: Brent Trammell, Lucy Bullock. BA, Tulane U., 1969, JD, 1972; MBA, Samford U., 1995. Ptnr. Bradley, Arant, Rose & White, Birmingham, 1972-90, Lange, Simpson, Robinson & Somerville, Birmingham, 1990-93, Sirote & Permutt, P.C., Birmingham, 1993-96; v.p. and gen. counsel Shop-A-Snak Food Mart, Inc., 1996; pres. Lucent Holdings, Inc., Golden, Miss., 1997-98; ptnr. Baker, Johnston & Wilson LLP, Birmingham, Ala., 1999—. Adj. prof. internat. bus. transactions and internat. law U. Ala., Tuscaloosa, 1983-85, 89-96; internat. bus. transactions Cumberland Sch. Law, 1990-95, adj. prof. corp. fin., 2001—. Author: Alabama Business Corporation Law, 1980; co-author: Corporate Law for the Healthcare Provider: Organization, Operation, Merger and Bankruptcy, 1993, Alabama Business Corporation Law Guide, 1995. Adv. bd. Jr. League of Birmingham, 1984; bd. dirs. Ala. chpt. Am. Liver Found., 1993-97, sec., 1994-95; trustee The Altamont Sch., 1995-2001, v.p., 1996-98, pres., 1998-2000. With U.S. Army, 1972-76. Mem. ABA (sect. internat. law, tax and corp., banking and bus. law), Ala. Bar Assn., Birmingham Bar Assn. (chmn. pub. rels. com. 1990), Birmingham Golf Assn. (pres., v.p., treas. 1982-84). Lodge: Rotary (pres. Birmingham-Sunrise club 1986-87). General corporate, Private international, Securities. Office: 1 Independence Plz Ste 322 Birmingham AL 35209-2634

WILSON, JOHN PASLEY, law educator; b. Newark, Apr. 7, 1933; s. Richard Henry and Susan Agnes (Pasley) W.; m. Elizabeth Ann Reed, Sept. 10, 1955 (div.); children: David Cables, John Pasley, Cicely Reed. AB, Princeton U., 1955; LLB, Harvard U., 1962. Bar: N.J. 1962, Mass. 1963, U.S. Dist. Ct. N.J. 1962, U.S. Dist. Ct. Mass. 1963. Budget examiner Exec. Office of Pres., Bur. of the Budget, Washington, 1955-56; assoc. Riker, Danzig, Scherer & Brown, Newark, 1962-63; asst. dean Harvard U. Law Sch., Cambridge, Mass., 1963-67; assoc. dean Boston U. Law Sch., 1968-82; dean Golden Gate U. Sch. Law, San Francisco, 1982-88, prof., 1988—. Vis. prof. dept. health policy and mgmt. Harvard U., 1988; cons. Nat. Commn. for the Protection of Human Subjects of Biomed. and Behavioral Rsch.; mem. Mass. Gov's Commn. on Civil and Legal Rights of Developmentally Disabled; former chmn. adv. com. Ctr for Cmty. Legal Edn., San Francisco. Author: The Rights of Adolescents in the Mental Health System; contbr. chpts. to books, articles to profl. jours. Bd. dirs. Greater Boston Legal Svcs., Chewonki Found.; mem. Health Facilities Appeals Bd., Commonwealth of Mass.; assoc. mem. Dem. Town Com., Concord; chmn. Bd. Assessors, Concord; bd. overseers Boston Hosp. for Women, past chmn. med. affairs com.; past mem. instl. rev. bd. Calif. Pacific Hosp., San Francisco. Served to lt. (j.g.) USNR, 1956-59. NIMH grantee, 1973. Mem. Nat. Assn. Securities Dealers (arbitrator). Office: Golden Gate U Sch Law 536 Mission St San Francisco CA 94105-2967 E-mail: jwilson@ggu.edu, jwlsn@earthlink.net

WILSON, JOSEPH MORRIS, III, lawyer; b. Milw., July 26, 1945; s. Joseph Morris Jr. and Phyllis Elizabeth (Cresson) W.; children: Elizabeth J., Eric M.; m. Dixie Lee Brock, Mar. 23, 1984. BA, Calif. State U., Chico, 1967; MA, U. Washington, 1968; JD summa cum laude, Ohio State U., 1976. Bar: Alaska 1976, U.S. Dist. Ct. Alaska 1976, U.S. Ct. Appeals (9th cir.) 1986. Recruiter and vol. U.S. Peace Corps, Republic of Benin, 1969-73; legal intern U.S. Ho. of Reps., Washington, 1975; ptnr. Guess & Rudd P.C., Anchorage, 1976-88, chmn. comml. dept., 1981-82, ptnr. compensation com., 1982-84; mgr. Alaska taxes, sr. tax atty. BP Exploration Inc., Alaska, 1990-99. Bus. law instr. U. Alaska, Anchorage, 1977-78. Mem. Alaska Bar Assn., World Affairs Coun. Democrat. Avocations: music, sports, travel. General corporate, Corporate taxation, State and local taxation. Home and Office: 2556 Palmera Cir Las Vegas NV 89121-4016 E-mail: jsphwlsn@aol.com

WILSON, JULIA ANN YOTHER, lawyer; b. Dallas, Sept. 6, 1958; d. Julian White and Mary Ann (Estes) Yother; m. Eugene Richard Wilson, 1983. BA, East Ctrl. U., Ada, Okla., 1980; JD, U. Okla., 1983. Bar: Okla. 1990, Calif. 1993, D.C. 1995; U.S. Ct. Appeals (9th cir.) Calif. 1993, U.S. Supreme Ct. 1993, U.S. Dist. Ct. (ctrl. dist.) Calif. 1993, U.S. Dist. Ct. (we. dist.) Okla., 1997. Assoc. Law Office of George Rodda Jr., Newport Beach, Calif., 1984-96; sole practice law Oklahoma City, 1996-97; assoc. Coldiron, Wilson & Assocs., 1997—. Served to 1st lt. USAR, 1980-86. Mem. ABA, D.C. Bar Assn., Calif. Bar Assn., Oklahoma County Bar Assn., Okla. Bar Assn. (litigation sect.), Orange County Bar Assn. General civil litigation, General practice, Probate. Office: Coldiron Wilson & Assocs 1800 E Memorial Rd Ste 106 Oklahoma City OK 73131-1827

WILSON, KAREN WILKERSON, paralegal; b. Reidsville, N.C., June 28, 1957; d. William Henry and Jean Gloria (Tiller) W.; married. Student, N.C. State U., 1975-77, Western Carolina U., Cullowhee, N.C., 1978-80; diploma, Profl. Ctr. Paralegal Studies, Columbia, S.C., 1988. Paralegal Ken H. Lester, Esquire, Columbia, 1989—, Lester, Jones and Clabaugh and predecessor, Columbia. Spkr. Alumni Profl. Ctr. Paralegal Studies, Columbia, 1988-95. Mem. ATLA, S.C. Trial Lawyers Assn. (paralegal rep. 1993-96). Democrat. Methodist. Office: Lester Jones & Clabaugh 1716 Main St Columbia SC 29201-2820

WILSON, L(EONARD) H(ENRY), lawyer; b. Poplar Bluff, Mo., Nov. 12, 1950; s. Vencil Willard and Helen Jane (Scheerer) W.; m. Carolyn Elizabeth Nix, June 1, 1974; 1 child, Jack Louis. BS with highest honors, U. So. Miss., 1972, MS, 1973; JD, U. Mo., Kansas City, 1975; grad. Miss. Sch. Banking, U. Miss., 1981, Sch. of Banking of South, La. State U., 1986. Bar: Mo. 1976, U.S. Dist. Ct. (we. dist.) Mo. 1976, Miss. 1979, U.S. Dist. Ct. (so. dist.) Miss. 1979. Asst. dist. counsel U.S. Army C.E., Kansas City, Mo., 1976-78; gen. counsel Miss. Bankers Assn., Jackson, Miss., 1978—; lectr. Miss. Sch. Banking, Oxford, 1981—; speaker bank attys. com. sessions Miss. State Bar convs., Biloxi, 1982-87. Editor: Selected Mississippi Banking Laws, 1979, 80, 82, 84, 86, 88. Congl. intern U.S. Congress, Washington, 1972; mem., sec. Gov.'s Com. to Mitigate Flood Damage, Jackson, Miss., 1979; treas., organizer Miss. Bankers Assn. Polit. Action Com., Jackson, 1979—. U. So. Miss. grad. fellow, Hattiesburg, 1972-73. Mem. ABA, Mo. Bar Assn., Miss. State Bar (bank attys. com. 1982-83, 85-86), Hinds County Bar Assn., Phi Kappa Phi, Colonial Country Club, Phi Alpha Delta. Presbyterian. Home: 28B Ridgeway Dr Belden MS 38826-9731 Office: Miss Bankers Assn PO Box 37 640 N State St Jackson MS 39202-3303

WILSON, LEVON EDWARD, law educator, lawyer; b. Charlotte, N.C., Apr. 2, 1954; s. James A. and Thomasina Wilson. BSBA, Western Carolina U., 1976; JD, N.C. Ctrl. U., 1979. Bar: N.C. 1981, U.S. Dist. Ct. (mid. dist.) N.C. 1981, U.S. Tax Ct. 1981, U.S. Ct. Appeals (4th cir.) 1982, U.S. Supreme Ct. 1984; lic. real estate broker, N.C.; cert. mediator N.C. Alternative Dispute Resolution Commn., arbitrator BBB. Pvt. practice, Greensboro, N.C., 1981-85; asst. county atty. Guilford County, 1985-88; asst. prof. N.C. Agrl. & Tech. State U., 1988-91, Western Carolina U., Cullowhee, N.C., 1991-96, assoc. prof., head dept. bus. adminstrn., law and mktg., 1996—. Pres. Trade Brokers Cons.; legal counsel, bd. dirs. Rhodes Assocs., Inc., Greensboro, 1982—; legal counsel Guilford County Sheriff's Dept., Greensboro, 1985-88; bd. dirs. Webster Enterprises, Inc. Contbr. articles to profl. jours. Bd. dirs. Post Advocacy Detention Program; active mem. Prison Litigation Study Task Force, Adminstrn. Justice Study Com. Recipient Svc. award Blacks in Mgmt., 1980, Excellence in Tchg. award Jay I. Kneedler Found. of Western Carolina U., 1994-95; Student in Free Enterprise fellow. Mem. ABA, N.C. Bar Asns., Acad. Legal Studies in Bus., Southeastern Acad. Legal Studies in Bus. (former editor-in-chief Jour. of Legal Studies in Bus., mng. editor), N.C. Assn. Police Attys., N.C. Real Estate Eudcators Assn., So. Acad. Legal Studies in Bus., Phi Delta Phi, Beta Gamma Sigma. Democrat. Methodist. Home: PO Box 620 Cullowhee NC 28723-0620 Office: Western Carolina U Coll of Bus Cullowhee NC 28723 Personal E-mail: levonwilson@msn.com; Business E-Mail: lwilson@wcu.edu

WILSON, MABLE JEAN, paralegal; b. Pine Bluff, Ark. d. James Arthur and Ruthia Mae (Dansby) Watson; children: Dana Eileen, Dana Kent, Carlos Alexander Fuller. BS, cert. in paralegal studies, U. So. Calif., 1982-86. Dep. sheriff L.A. County, 1971-80; ind. paralegal Wilson's Divorce Clinic, L.A., 1980—. Participant Dist. Atty. Victim Witness Program, L.A., 1991; active Brotherhood Crusade, 1992; mem. adv. bd. West L.A. Coll.-Paralegal Studies. Recipient Merit award L.A. County Bar Assn., 1993, Merit cert. City of L.A., County of L.A., Calif. Senate, U.S. Congress, Gov. State of Calif. Mem. Assn. Family and Conciliation Cts., Folk Power Inc. (bd. dirs. 1993—), Alpha Svc. Co. (v.p. 1993—, profl. women's adv. bd., Women's Inner Circle of Achievement), adv. bd on Paralegal Studies, W. L.A. Coll. Avocations: interior decorating, making stained glass windows, ceramics, painting, writing poetry. Office: 3860 Crenshaw Blvd Ste 201 Los Angeles CA 90008-1816

WILSON, MICHAEL MOUREAU, lawyer, physician; b. Cheverly, Md., Dec. 30, 1952; s. Kenneth Moureau and Helen (Rice) Smith. BS, MIT, 1974; JD, Georgetown U., 1977, MD, 1986. Bar: D.C. 1977, N.Y. 1980, U.S. Dist. Ct. D.C. 1980, U.S. Dist. Ct. Md. 1992, U.S. Ct. Appeals (D.C. cir.) 1980, U.S. Supreme Ct. 1981. Law clk. Hon. John B. Hannum U.S. Dist. Ct., Phila., 1977-78; assoc. Cravath Swaine & Moore, N.Y.C., 1978-79; asst. to gen. counsel NSF, Washington, 1979-82; resident in psychiatry St. Elizabeth Hosp., 1986-89; pvt. practice med. malpractice litigation, 1989—. Notes editor Am. Criminal Law Rev., 1976-77. Mem. ABA, Assn. Trial Lawyers Am., D.C. Trial Lawyers Assn., Phi Beta Kappa. Personal injury. Office: 1700 K St NW Ste 1007 Washington DC 20006-3815 E-mail: wilson@wilsonlaw.com

WILSON, PAUL DENNIS, lawyer; b. Milw., Apr. 23, 1953; s. Robert D. and Dorothy (Fischer) W.; m. Mary B. Donchez, June 15, 1985. AB cum laude, Princeton U., 1975; JD cum laude, NYU, 1981. Bar: Mass. 1982, U.S. Dist. Ct. Mass. 1983, U.S. Ct. Appeals (1st cir.) 1983. Law clk. to judge U.S. Dist. Ct., Atlanta, 1981-82; assoc. Mintz, Levin, Cohn, Ferris,

Glovsky and Popeo, Boston, 1982-90, ptnr., 1990—. Adj. lectr. Boston U., 1985—. Mem. ABA, Mass. Bar. Assn., Boston Bar Assn., Order of Coif. Avocations: hiking, canoeing, skiing. Federal civil litigation, State civil litigation, Real property. Home: 62 Staniford St Auburndale MA 02466-1112 Office: Mintz et al One Fin Ctr Boston MA 02111

WILSON, PAUL HOLLIDAY, JR. lawyer; b. Schenectady, N.Y., Sept. 4, 1942; s. Paul H. and Sarah Elizabeth (MacLean) W.; m. Elaine Hawley Griffin, May 30, 1964; children: Hollace, Paul, Kirsten, Katherine. AB, Brown U., 1964; LLB, MBA, Columbia U., 1967. Bar: N.Y. 1967, U.S. Dist. Ct. (so. dist.) 1968. Law clk. U.S. Dist. Ct. (so. dist.) N.Y., N.Y.C., 1967-68; assoc. Debevoise & Plimpton, 1968-75, ptnr., 1976—, fin. ptnr., 1980-88, 91-93, 2001—, dep. presiding ptnr., 1993-98. Vice-chmn., trustee St. Michael's Montessori Sch., N.Y.C., 1977-79, chmn. bd. trustees, 1979-81. Mem. ABA, Assn. Bar City N.Y. (mem. commn. on securities regulations 1985-88). Club: Vineyard Haven Yacht (Mass.) (vice-commodore 1985, commodore 1986-87). Avocations: sailing, reading, music. General corporate, Mergers and acquisitions, Securities. Office: Debevoise & Plimpton 875 3rd Ave Fl 23 New York NY 10022-6225 E-mail: phwilson@debevoise.com

WILSON, RHYS THADDEUS, lawyer; b. Albany, Ga., May 9, 1955; s. Joseph Farr Jr. and Betty Ann (Wilkins) W.; m. Carolyn Reid Saffold, June 2, 1984. AB, Duke U., 1976; JD, U. Ga., 1979; LLM, Emory U., 1985. Bar: Ga. 1979. Pvt. practice law, Atlanta, 1979-89; sr. v.p., gen. counsel Monarch Capital Group, Inc., 1989-92, Jackson & Coker, Inc., Atlanta, 1992-93; pres. Jackson & Coker Locum Tenens, Inc., 1993-95; ptnr. Robins, Kaplan, Miller & Ciresi, 1995—. Spkr. continuing legal edn. seminars. Contbr. articles to profl. jours. Mem. ABA, Ga. Bar Assn. (chmn. internat. law sect. 1987-88, exec. com. corp. and banking law sect. 1987-89, editorial bd. Ga. State Bar Jour. 1986-89), Atlanta Bar Assn. (editor newsletter 1984-86, Outstanding Svc. award 1986), Assn. for Corp. Growth, Atlanta Network Alliance, The Exec. Com. TEC, Atlanta Venture Forum, Tech. Alliance Ga., Capital City Club, Internet Corp. for Assigned Names and Numbers. Episcopalian. General corporate, Mergers and acquisitions, Securities.

WILSON, RICHARD RANDOLPH, lawyer; b. Pasadena, Calif., Apr. 14, 1950; s. Robert James and Phyllis Jean (Blackman) W.; m. Catherine Goodhugh Stevens, Oct. 11, 1980; children: Thomas Randolph, Charles Stevens. BA cum laude, Yale U., 1971; JD, U. Wash., 1976. Bar: Wash. 1976, U.S. Dist. Ct. (we. dist.) Wash. 1976, U.S. Ct. Appeals (9th cir.) 1977. Assoc. Hillis, Phillips, Cairncross, Clark & Martin, Seattle, 1976-81, ptnr., 1981-84, Hillis, Cairncross, Clark & Martin, Seattle, 1984-87, Hillis Clark Martin & Peterson, Seattle, 1987—, mem. mgmt. com., 1991—. Bd. dirs. Quality Child Care Svcs., Inc., Seattle; pres. Plymouth Housing Group, Seattle, 1998—2000, trustee, 1994—2000; bd. dirs. Plymouth Housing Properties, Seattle, 2001—, Quality Child Care Svcs., Inc., Seattle, Plymouth Housing Properties, Seattle; pres. Plymouth Housing Group, Seattle, 1998—2000, trustee, 1994—2001; lectr. various bar assns., 1980—. Contbr. articles to profl. jours. Chmn. class agts. Yale U. Alumni Fund, New Haven, 1984—87, class agt., 1971—2001, mem. class coun., 1991—96, mem. Western Wash. exec. com. Yale capital campaign, 1992—97, vice chmn. leadership gifts com. Yale 25th reunion, 1995—96, 30th reunion, 2000—01; mem., vice chmn. Medina (Wash.) Planning Commn., 1990—92; trustee, performer Seattle Gilbert & Sullivan Soc., 1984—92; chmn. class agts. Yale U. Alumni Fund, New Haven, 1985—87, class agt., 1971—2001, mem. class coun., 1991—96, mem. Western Wash. exec. com. Yale capital campaign, 1992—97, vice chmn. leadership gifts com. Yale 25th reunion, 1995—96, 30th reunion, 2000—01; mem., vice chmn. Medina (Wash.) Planning Commn., 1990—92; chmn. capital campaign Plymouth Congl. Ch., Seattle, 1995, moderator, pres. ch. coun., 1998—2000; trustee, performer Gilbert & Sullivan Soc., 1984—91; chmn. capital campaign Plymouth Congrl. Ch., Seattle, 1995, moderator, pres. ch. coun., 1998—2000. Mem. ABA, Wash. State Bar Assn. (dir. environ. and land use law sect. 1985-88), Seattle-King County Bar Assn., Kingsley Trust Assn. (pres. 1996-98), Yale Assn. of Western Wash. Congregationalist. Avocations: acting, singing, rare book collecting. Environmental, Land use and zoning (including planning), Real property. Home: 2305 86th Ave NE Bellevue WA 98004-2416 Office: Hillis Clark Martin & Peterson 1221 2nd Ave Ste 500 Seattle WA 98101-2925

WILSON, ROBERT FOSTER, lawyer; b. Windsor, Colo., Apr. 6, 1926; s. Foster W. and Anne Lucille (Svedman) W.; m. Mary Elizabeth Clark, Mar. 4, 1951 (div. Feb. 1972); children: Robert F., Katharine A.; m. Sally Anne Nemec, June 8, 1982. BA in Econs., U. Iowa, 1950, JD, 1951. Bar: Iowa 1951, U.S. Dist. Ct. (no. and so. dists.) Iowa 1956, U.S. Ct. Appeals (8th cir.) 1967. Atty. FTC, Chgo., 1951-55; pvt. practice, Cedar Rapids, Iowa, 1955—. Pres. Lawyer Forms, Inc.; dir. Lawyers Forms, Inc.; mem. Iowa Reapportionment Com., 1968; del. to U.S. and Japan Bilateral Session on Legal and Econ. Rels. Conf., Tokyo, 1988, Moscow Conf. on Law and Bilateral Rels., Moscow, 1990; U.S. del. to Moscow Conf. on Legal and Econ. Rels., 1990. Mem. Iowa Ho. of Reps., 1959-60; pres. Linn County Day Care, Cedar Rapids, Iowa, 1968-70. Sgt. U.S. Army, 1944-46. Mem. ATLA, Am. Arbitration Assn. (panel arbitrators), Iowa Bar Assn., Iowa Trial Lawyers Assn., Linn County Bar Assn., Am. Legion (judge adv. 1970-75, 87-93), Cedar View Country Club, Elks, Eagles, Delta Theta Phi. Democrat. Personal injury, Probate, Workers' compensation. Home: 100 1st Ave NE Cedar Rapids IA 52401-1128 Office: 810 Dows Bldg Cedar Rapids IA 52403-7010 E-mail: RWilsonlaw@aol.com

WILSON, ROGER GOODWIN, lawyer; b. Evanston, Ill., Sept. 3, 1950; s. G. Turner Jr. and Lois (Shay) W.; m. Giovinella Gonthier, Mar. 7, 1975. AB, Dartmouth Coll., 1972; JD, Harvard U., 1975. Bar: Ill. 1975, U.S. Dist. Ct. (no. dist.) Ill. 1976, U.S. Ct. Appeals (7th cir.) 1977, U.S. Dist. Ct. (no. dist.) Ind. 1985. Assoc. Kirkland & Ellis, Chgo., 1975-81, ptnr., 1981-86; sr. v.p., gen. counsel, corp. sec. Blue Cross/Blue Shield, 1986—. Speaker Nat. Healthcare Inst., U. Mich., 1987-93, Am. Law Inst.-ABA Conf. on Mng. and Resolving Domestic and Internat. Bus. Disputes, N.Y.C., 1988, Washington, 1990; cert. health cons. program Purdue U., 1993-94, Inst. for Bus. Strategy Devel., Northwestern U., 1993-94, The Health Care Antitrust Forum, Chgo., 1995, Nat. Health Lawyers Assn Managed Care Law Inst., 1995, Nat. Health Lawyers Assn. Conf. on Tax Issues in Healthcare Orgns., 1996. Contbg. editor Health Care Fraud and Abuse Newsletter, 1998—. Advisor Constl. Rights Found., Chgo., 1982-87; mem. So. Poverty Law Ctr., Montgomery, Ala., 1981—. Mem. ABA, Nat. Health Lawyers Assn. (spkr. 1984), Legal Assistance Found. of Chgo. (bd. dirs. 1998—), Chgo. Coun. Lawyers (bd. govs. 1988-92), Coun. Chief Legal Officers (conf. bd. 1995—), Coun. Corp. Governance (conf. bd. 1998-00), Dartmouth Lawyers Assn., Legal Assistance Found. Chgo. (bd. dirs. 1998—), Sinfonietta (bd. dirs. 1987—), Univ. Club, Mid-Am. Club, Phi Beta Kappa. General corporate, Health, Insurance. Home: 330 N Jefferson Ct Unit2004 Chicago IL 60661 Office: Blue Cross/Blue Shield 225 N Michigan Ave Ste 200 Chicago IL 60601-7601 E-mail: roger.wilson@bcbsa.com

WILSON, THOMAS MATTHEW, III, lawyer; b. Ware, Mass., Feb. 22, 1936; s. Thomas Matthew Jr. and Ann Veronica (Shea) W.; m. Deborah Ord Lockhart, Feb. 10, 1962; children: Deborah Veronica, Leslie Lockhart, Thomas Matthew IV. BA, Brown U., 1958; JD, U. Md., 1971. Bar: Md. 1972, U.S. Ct. Appeals (4th cir.) 1976, U.S. Supreme Ct. 1977. Sales mgr. Mid-Ea. Box Mfg. Co., Balt., 1966-74; asst. atty. gen., chief antitrust divsn. State of Md., 1974-79; ptnr. Tydings & Rosenberg, LLP, 1979—. Author: Defending an Antitrust Action Brought by a State, 1987, The Spectre of Double Recovery in Antitrust Federalism, 1989; co-author: Reciprocity and the Private Plaintiff, 1972; mem. editl. adv. bd. Bur. of Nat. Affairs Antitrust and Trade Regulation Report, 1979—. Mem. ABA (sect. on antitrust law 1974—, chmn. state antitrust enforcement com. 1986-89, antitrust sect. coun. 1990-93, coord. com. on legal edn. 1993—), Md. Bar Assn. (antitrust subcom. 1975-78), Internat. Bar Assn. (sect. on bus. law, antitrust law and monopolies com. 1983—), Churchwarden's Chess Club. Republican. Antitrust, Appellate, Franchising. Home: Baobab Farm Hampstead MD 21074 Office: Tydings & Rosenberg LLP 100 E Pratt St Baltimore MD 21202-1009

WILSON, THOMAS WILLIAM, lawyer; b. Bklyn., Sept. 14, 1935; s. Matthew and Alice (McCrory) W.; m. Eileen Marie McGann, June 4, 1960; children— Jeanne Alice, Thomas William, David Matthew, A.B., Columbia U., 1957, LL.B., 1960. Bar: N.Y. 1962, U.S. Dist. Ct. (so. and ea. dists.) N.Y. 1962, D.C. 1972. Assoc. Mendes and Mount, N.Y.C., 1961-65, Haller & Small, N.Y.C., 1965-66; gen. counsel Prudential of Gt. Brit., N.Y.C., 1966-68; mng. ptnr. Wilson, Elser, Moskowitz, Edelman & Dicker, N.Y.C., 1968— . Contbr. articles to profl. jours. Served with U.S. Army, 1960-65. Mem. ABA, N.Y. State Bar Assn., Def. Research Inst. (editorial bd. profl. liability reporter). Insurance. Office: Wilson Elser Moskowitz Edelman & Dicker 150 E 42nd St New York NY 10017-5612

WILSON, VIRGIL JAMES, III, lawyer; b. San Jose, Calif., July 25, 1953; s. Virgil James Wilson Jr. and Phyllis Emily (Mothorn) Brasser; children: Gabriel James Hekili, Alexander Robert Kaimoku, Hayley Noelani, Maia E. Kailani. BA with honors, U. Calif., Santa Cruz, 1975; JD cum laude, U. Santa Clara, 1981. Bar: Calif. 1981, U.S. Dist. Ct. (no. dist.) Calif. 1981, Hawaii 1982, U.S. Dist. Ct. Hawaii 1982, U.S. Ct. Appeals (9th cir.) 1987, U.S. Supreme Ct. 1987, Oreg. 1990, U.S. Dist. Ct. Oreg. 1998, U.S. Ct. Fed. Claims 1999; lic. pvt. investigator, Hawaii. Atty. James Krueger P.C., Wailuku, Maui, 1981-83; resident counsel Sterns & Ingram, Honolulu, 1983-89; pvt. practice Kailua, Hawaii, 1989—; of counsel Law Offices of Ian L. Mattoch, 1993-96; assoc. Thorp, Purdy, Jewett, Urness & Wilkinson, P.C., Springfield, Oreg., 1998-99. Owner Wilson Investigations, Santa Cruz, 1978-81, Honolulu, 1981—. Mem. Hawaii Bar Assn., Calif. State Bar Assn., Oreg. Bar Assn. Avocation: profl. magician. General civil litigation, Personal injury, Product liability. Fax: 541-607-6565. E-mail: VJWILSONiii@msn.com

WILSON, WILLIAM BERRY, lawyer; b. Cape Girardeau, Mo., June 17, 1947; s. Charles F. and Anita (Bartlum) W.; m. Suzanne T. Wilson; children: Matthew James, Sarah Talbot. BA summa cum laude, Westminster Coll., 1969; JD, U. Mich., 1972. Bar: Fla. 1972, U.S. Dist. Ct. (mid. dist.) Fla. 1972, U.S. Ct. Appeals (11th cir.) 1972, U.S. Supreme Ct. 1976; bd. cert. Civil Trial Lawyer, 1983—. Ptnr. Maguire, Voorhis & Wells P.A., Orlando, Fla., 1977-98, mng. dir., 1982-84, pres., 1984-97, chmn., 1997-98; ptnr. Holland & Knight LLP, 1998—, dir., 1999—. Mem. exec. com. and trust com., bd. dirs. SunTrust Bank Ctrl. Fla. Bd. overseers Crummer Sch. Bus., Rollins Coll., 1994—; chmn. Fla. Residential Property & Casualty Joint Underwriting Assn., 1995—2000; mem. Fla. Fed. Jud. Nominating Commn., 2001—; bd. dirs. Econ. Devel. Authority, Orlando, 1992—97, chmn., 1994—95, subcom. chmn. Project 2000 Orlando, 1985—87; bd. dirs. Fla. Symphony, Orlando1985; Fla. TaxWatch, Inc., 1992—98; bd. dirs. U. Ctrl. Fla. Found., 1996—, Jr. Achievement, 1998—; trustee Orlando Mus. Art, 1993—, pres., 1997—99. Mem.: ABA, Fla. Bar Assn. (mem. exec. coun. trial lawyers sect. 1987—98, chmn. 1996—97, code and rules of evidence com. 1982—88, chmn. 1986—88), Orange County Bar Assn. (chmn. fed. and state practice sect. 1982—84, mem. jud. rels. com. 1984—, chmn. 1987—98, chmn. professionalism com. 1997—99), Am. Bd. Trial Advocacy, Def. Rsch. Inst., Greater Orlando C. of C. (bd. dirs., exec. com. 1997—), Orlando Regional C. of C. (bd. dirs. 1997—, vice chmn. tech. 1999—, chair-elect 2001—), Rotary (bd. dirs.), Country Club of Orlando (bd. dirs.), Citrus Club (bd. dirs. 1994—, chmn. 1998—). Republican. Presbyterian. Avocations: tennis, scuba diving. Federal civil litigation, State civil litigation, Construction. Office: Holland & Knight LLP PO Box 1526 200 S Orange Ave Ste 2600 Orlando FL 32801-3453 E-mail: bwilson@hklaw.com

WILSON, WILLIAM R., JR. judge; b. 1939; Student, U. Ark., 1957-58; BA, Hendrix Coll., 1962; JD, Vanderbilt U., 1965. Atty. Autrey & Goodson, Texarkana, Ark., 1965-66, Wright, Lindsey & Jennings, Little Rock, 1969-72, Wilson & Hodge, Little Rock, 1972-74; prin. William R. Wilson Jr., P.A., 1974-80, Wilson & Engstrom, Little Rock, 1980-83, Wilson, Engstrom & Vowell, Little Rock, 1984, Wilson, Engstrom, Corum & Dudley, Little Rock, 1984-93; judge U.S. Dist. Ct. (ea. dist.) Ark., 1993—. Chair Ark. Supreme Ct. Com. on Model Criminal Jury Instrns., 1978—; active Ark. Supreme Ct. Com. on Civil Practice, 1982—. Lt. USN, 1966-69. Named Disting. Alumnus, Hendrix Coll., 1993, Outstanding Lawyer, Pulaski County Bar Assn., 1993. Mem. ABA, ATLA, Am. Bd. Trial Advocates (Nat. Civil Justice award 1992), Am. Coll. Trial Lawyers, Internat. Acad. Trial Lawyers, Internat. Soc. Barristers, Ark. Bar Assn. (Outstanding Lawyer 1991), S.W. Ark. Bar Assn., Ark. Trial Lawyers Assn. (pres. 1982, Outstanding Trial Lawyer 1988-89), Pulaski County Bar Assn. (Outstanding Lawyer 1993). Office: US Dist Ct Ea Dist 600 W Capitol Ave Ste 423 Little Rock AR 72201-3320

WILSON-COKER, PATRICIA ANNE, lawyer, social service administrator, educator; b. Willimantic, Conn., Aug. 26, 1950; d. Bertram W. and Mary Evelyn (Spurlock) Wilson; m. Edward H. Coker (div. 1973). BA, U. Conn., 1977, MSW, JD, 1981. Bar: Conn. 1981. Asst. prof. social work, dir. Ctr. for Child Welfare Studies St. Joseph Coll., West Hartford, Conn., 1981-86, assoc. prof. social work, chair social work & child welfare, 1986-88; exec. asst. to commr., statewide dir. divsn. children protective svcs. Conn. Dept. Children and Youth Svcs., Hartford, 1988-91, mediation panelist, Juan F. consent decree, 1990-91; monitoring panelist dept. children and youth svcs. Fed. Dist. Ct., New Haven, 1991-92; dir. social svc. planning & interdisciplinary program devel. Dept. Social Svcs., Hartford, Conn., 1992-93, dir. adminstrv. hearings and appeals Middletown, 1993-95, regional administr. north ctrl. region, 1995-99, commr., 1999—. Instr. U. Conn., Storrs, summer 1977, social rsch. asst. philosophy dept., summer 1978; legal social work intern juvenile unit Hartford (Conn.) Legal Aid Soc., 1978-79, legal rschr. juvenile unit, summer 1979, legal rschr., fall 1979; instr. Ea. Conn. State U., Willimantic, spring 1980; cons. New Eng. Clin. Assocs., West Hartford, 1985-86, Office of Policy & Mgmt., State Conn., Hartford, 1988, Perisky and Daniels, Hartford, 1988; apptd. Juvenile Justice Adv. Com. to the Office of Policy and Mgmt., State Conn., 1983-89, Conn. Task Force on Family Violence, 1985-86, Criminal Sanctions Task Force, 1987, Child Support Task Force, 1987-88, Conn. Children's Commn., 1988-91; assoc. prof. St. Joseph Coll., West Hartford, 1981-88, So. Conn. State Coll., New Haven, 1990—; trustee ednl. policies St. Joseph Coll., 1980-97, chair, 1997; lectr. and presenter in field. Contbr. articles to profl. jours. Recipient Judge Thomas Gill award Conn. Children in Placement Program, 1991, Annual award Conn. Coun. on Adoption, 1991, Disting. Alumna award U. Conn., 2001; named Educator of Yr., Conn. Girl Scout Coun., 1987. Fellow Conn. Bar Found. Office: Dept Social Svcs 25 Sigourney St Hartford CT 06106-5001 E-mail: PWCoker@aol.com, wilson-coker@po.state.ct.us

WILTSE, JAMES BURDICK, lawyer; b. St. Paul, Nov. 7, 1927; s. Verne Hazen and Frances J. (Carlson) W.; m. Lois J. Ashton, July 4, 1945 (dec. May 1961); children— James Burdick, Lois J., Kathryn E., Douglas V.; m. Yvonne Amoroso, Mar. 31, 1972; children— Jamie Jo, Julie Loiuse. B.A., Calif. State U.-Los Angeles, 1962; J.D., Southwestern U., Los Angeles, 1969. Bar: Pa. 1972, D.C. 1980, U.S. Dist. Ct. (we. dist.) Pa. 1972, U.S. Ct. Appeals (3d cir.) 1974, U.S. Supreme Ct. 1977. Law library cons. West Pub. Co., St. Paul, 1969-81; sr. ptnr. Wiltse & Nene, Pitts., 1981-84; assoc. Zoffer, Wiltse, Hackney & Lestitian, Pitts., 1984— . Treas. campaign to elect common pleas judge, 1979, commonwealth ct. judge, 1983, state rep., 1984. Served with U.S. Army, 1946-47; PTO. Mem. Pa. Bar Assn., D.C. Bar Assn., Allegheny County Bar Assn. (bd. dirs. credit union 1984), Assn. Trial Lawyers Am., Pa. Trial Lawyers Assn. Republican. Presbyterian. Club: Amen Corner (Pitts). Home: 2366 Englewood Dr Pittsburgh PA 15241-3349 Office: 408 Grant Bldg 310 Grant St Pittsburgh PA 15219-2202

WILTSHIRE, WILLIAM HARRISON FLICK, lawyer; b. Martinsburg, W.Va., Dec. 29, 1930; s. Harrison Flick and Virginia Faulkner (White) W.; m. Edith Hayward, Nov. 13, 1954; children: Ashley Wiltshire Spotswood, Winn Wiltshire Crockard, William Harrison Flick Jr., Ashton Hayward. BA, Shepherd Coll., 1952; JD, U. Fla., 1960. Bar: Fla. 1960, U.S. Ct. Appeals (5th cir.) 1960, U.S. Dist. Ct. (no. dist.) Fla. 1960, U.S. Dist. Ct. (so. dist.) La. 1975, U.S. Dist. Ct. (so. dist.) Ala. 1978, U.S. Dist. Ct. (so. dist.) Fla. 1980, U.S. Ct. Appeals (11th cir.) 1982, U.S. Supreme Ct. 1987; cert. in civil trial Nat. Bd. Trial Advocacy and Fla. Bar Assn. With Jones & Harrell, Pensacola, Fla., 1960-62; ptnr. Harrell, Wiltshire, Stone, Swearingen, Wilson & Harrell and predecessor firms, 1962—. Pres. Bayou Tex. Assn., 1967-71; dir. Fiesta Five Flags, 1968-82, pres. 1976-77. Contbr. articles to profl. jours. and textbooks. Trustee, gen. counsel Naval Aviation Mus. Found., 1989—; trustee Episcopal Day Sch., 1965-69; bd. dirs. Pensacola Acad. Arts and Scis., 1970-75, pres. 1973-74; bd. dirs. Gul Goast Coun. Boy Scouts Am., 1982—. Served with USN, 1952-57. Fellow Am. Coll. Trial Lawyers, Nat. Bd. Trial Advocacy; mem. ABA, Fla. Bar Assn., Am. Trial Lawyers Assn., Acad. Fla. Trial Lawyers, State Bar Fla. (chmn. trial lawyers sect. 1973-74, chmn. appellate rules com. 1974-78), Def. Rsch. Inst., Am. Judicature Soc., Rotary Club. Republican. Admiralty, Federal civil litigation, Personal injury. Address: PO Box 1832 Pensacola FL 32598-1832 Fax: (850) 432-7727. E-mail: whfw@aol.com

WIMPFHEIMER, MICHAEL CLARK, lawyer; b. N.Y.C., July 9, 1944; s. Henry and Ruth (Rapp) W.; m. Susanne Rabner, June 11, 1968; children: Jan Steven, Barry Scott, Luba Rachel. BA, Columbia U., 1964; JD, Harvard U., 1967. Bar: N.Y. 1967, U.S. Dist. Ct. (ea. and so. dists.) N.Y. 1974, U.S. Ct. Appeals (2d cir.) 1974, U.S. Ct. Mil. Appeals 1979, U.S. Claims Ct., 1992. Ptnr. Wimpfheimer & Wimpfheimer, N.Y.C., 1970—. V.p. Union of Orthodox Jewish Congregations of Am., N.Y.C., 1978—. Comdr. JAGC USNR, ret. Mem. ABA, N.Y. State Bar Assn., Bronx County Bar Assn. Jewish. Estate planning, General practice, Real property. Home: 2756 Arlington Ave Riverdale Bronx NY 10463-4807 Office: Wimpfheimer & Wimpfheimer 330 W 58th St Ste 600 New York NY 10019-1818 Fax: 212-247-8196

WINCHELL, MICHAEL GEORGE, lawyer; b. Ardmore, Okla., Oct. 30, 1949; s. George Stockwell and Willis Marion (Woolery) W.; m. Donna Jean Winchell; children: Merridith Elaine, Candace Michelle. BBA, Cen. State U., 1974; JD, U. Okla., 1976. Bar: Okla. 1977. Assoc. Sokolsky & Becker, Oklahoma City, 1977; asst. regional counsel GSA, Ft. Worth, 1977-87; adminstrv. judge EEOC Commn., Dallas, 1987-88; counsel S.E. bases USMC, 1988-89; chief counsel John F. Kennedy Space Ctr., 1993-97, Johnson Space Ctr., 1997—. Pres. GSA employee's assn., 1982-84; chief KSC Inter-Tribal Coun., 1993-97. Named Meritorious Executive of the Federal Senior Executive Service, President Clinton, 2000. Mem. Fed. Bus. Assn. (pres. 1984-85), FBA (pres. Ft. Worth chpt. 1981-82, bd. dirs. younger lawyers' div. 1981-85, 2d v.p. 5th cir. 1982-83, v.p. 1983-84, sec. cir. officers 1983-84, dep. chmn. cir. officers 1984-85, chmn. rules com. 1985-86), Southeastern Cherokee Confederacy (chief Eagle Clan 1992-93). Office: Code AL NASA Johnson Space Ctr Houston TX 77058

WINCHESTER, JAMES R. judge; m. Susan Winchester; 1 child Davis. BA U. Okla, JD Oklahoma City U. Pvt. practice, Weatherford, Okla., Hinton; assoc. dist. judge Caddo County, 1983; dist. judge 6th Judicial Dist. Okla., 1983—97; U.S. adminstrv. law judge, 1997—2000; justice Supreme Ct. Okla., 2000—. Office: Okla Supreme Ct State Capitol Bldg Rm 244 1200 N Lincoln Blvd Oklahoma City OK 73105*

WINCHESTER, RICHARD LEE, JR. lawyer; b. Memphis, May 21, 1924; s. Cassius Lee and Harriet Haywood (Bond) W.; m. Bette Anne Thompson, July 15, 1944; children— Robin Ann, Richard Lee Jr., John Thompson. LL.B., U. Tenn., 1949, J.D., 1965. Bar: Tenn. 1949. Sr. ptnr. Winchester Law Firm, Memphis, 1972— ; Shelby County atty., 1961-64; city atty., Arlington, Tenn., 1966— ; gen. counsel, bd. chmn. Community Bancshares, Inc.; sec. Beachfront Condos, Inc., N.Fla. Chmn. Germantown Planning Commn., 1958-61; mem. Gov.'s Commn. on Human Relations, 1962-68; vice chmn., treas. Memphis and Shelby County Democratic Exec. Com., 1958-72; state exec. com., pres. Tenn. Young Democrats, 1960-61; del. state and nat. Dem. Convs., 1964-68; nat. elector from Tenn., 1960-72; pres., bd. dirs. Mid-South Fair Assn., ARC.; trustee U. Tenn., 1975-84, Episcopal Girls Home, Bowld Hosp.; pres. Episcopal Planning Commn. Served to capt. inf. AUS, 1942-46, PTO. Fellow Tenn. Bar Found.; mem. ABA (past del.), Tenn. Bar Assn. (past pres. jr. sect.), Memphis Bar Assn. (past pres.), Shelby County Bar Assn. (past pres. jr. sect.), Am. Judicature Soc., Nat. Assn. Legal Aid and Pub. Defenders, Am. Legion (past post comdr., past state vice comdr.), 40 and 8, VFW (past post vice comdr.), U. Tenn. Alumni Assn. (past bd. govs., 9th dist. rep.), Sigma Alpha Epsilon, Phi Eta Sigma, Phi Kappa Phi, Omicron Delta Kappa. Episcopalian. Club: Tennessee. Lodges: Masons, Shriners, Jesters, Kiwanis. Banking, Probate. Office: Winchester Law Firm 6060 Poplar Ave Ste 38119 Memphis TN 38119

WIND, JACK JAY, lawyer; b. Jersey City, May 28, 1952; s. Bernard Wind and Lillian (Landy) Luger; m. Lona Whitmarsh, May 6, 1982; children: Jaime Mullette, Jessica Lauren. BS, Cornell U., 1974; JD, Suffolk U., 1977. Bar: N.J. 1977, U.S. Dist. Ct. N.J. 1977, U.S. Ct. Appeals (3d cir.); cert. mediator, N.J. From assoc. to shareholder Marguiles, Wind, Herrington & Knopf and predecessor firms, Jersey City, 1977—. Adj. prof. Upsala Coll., Orange, N.J., 1986-87; sec. ethics com. Supreme Ct. N.J. Dist., 1989—. Mem. N.J. State Bar Assn., Hudson County Bar Assn. Jewish. Federal civil litigation, State civil litigation. Home: 5 Wilson Ln Madison NJ 07940-2509 Office: Margulies Wind Herrington & Knopf 15 Exchange Pl Ste 510 Jersey City NJ 07302 E-mail: jjw@mwhklaw.com

WINDER, DAVID KENT, federal judge; b. Salt Lake City, June 8, 1932; s. Edwin Kent and Alma Eliza (Cannon) W.; m. Pamela Martin, June 24, 1955; children: Ann, Kay, James. BA, U. Utah, 1955; LLB, Stanford U., 1958. Bar: Utah 1958, Calif. 1958. Assoc. firm Clyde, Mecham & Pratt, Salt Lake City, 1958-66; law clk. to chief justice Utah Supreme Ct., 1958-59; dep. county atty. Salt Lake County, 1959-63, chief dep. dist. atty., 1965-66; asst. U.S. atty. Salt Lake City, 1963-65; partner firm Strong & Hanni, 1966-77; judge U.S. Dist. Ct., 1977-79, 1979-93, chief judge, 1993-97, sr. judge, 1997—. Examiner Utah Bar Examiners, 1975-79, chmn., 1977-79; mem. jud. resources com. Served with USAF, 1951-52. Mem. Am. Bd. Trial Advocates, Utah State Bar (Judge of Yr. award 1978), Salt Lake County Bar Assn., Calif. State Bar. Democrat. Office: US Dist Ct 110 US Courthouse 350 S Main St Salt Lake City UT 84101-2106

WINDER, RICHARD EARNEST, legal foundation administrator, writer, consultant; b. Vernal, Utah, Sept. 23, 1950; s. William Wallace and Winnifred (Jenkins) W.; m. Janice Fay Walker, Apr. 19, 1975; children: Scott Christian, Eric John, Brian Geoffrey, Laura Jeanne, Amy Elizabeth. BA magna cum laude, Brigham Young U., 1974, JD cum laude, 1978; MBA with honors, U. Michigan, Flint, 1988. Bar: Utah 1978, U.S. Dist. Ct. Utah 1978, Mich. 1979, U.S. Dist. Ct. (ea. and we. dists.) Mich. 1979.

Tchg. asst., grad. instr. Brigham Young U., Provo, Utah, 1976-78; law clk. Willingham & Coté, E. Lansing, Mich., 1978-79, atty., 1979-87; exec. v.p. Mgmt. Leasing, Inc., Battle Creek, 1987-88, Mgmt. Options, Inc., Lansing, 1988-91; fin. mgr. Mich. State Bar Found., 1991-94, dep. dir., fin. mgr., 1994—. Panelist 9th Nat. Legis. Conf. Small Bus., San Antonio, 1987; adj. prof. Davenport Coll. Bus., Lansing, 1990-92, mgmt. adv. com., 1993-96; mem. founding steering com. Capital Quality Initiative, Lansing, 1992-96; liaison State Bar Mich. Long Range Planning Process, 1996-97; co-founder, rsch. prin. Quality Dynamics Rsch. Inst., Haslett, Mich., 1994-97; rsch. prin. Leadership Dynamics Rsch. Inst., Haslett, 1998—. Author: (with others) Value Sharing: Value Building, 1990, Corporate Orienteering, 1995; contbr., bd. editors: Summary of Utah Real Property Law, 1978. Vol. leader Boy Scouts Am., Chief Okemos Coun., Lansing, 1978—. Fellow Mich. State Bar Found.; mem. ABA, Am. Soc. Quality Control (chmn. Lansing-Jackson sect. 1994-95, spkr. and writer 1992—), Mich. Bar Assn., Utah Bar Assn., Lansing Regional C. of C. (small bus. coun., MBA task force Bus. and Edn. com. 1988-92, recipient Chmn.'s award 1992), Beta Gamma Sigma. Republican. Mem. LDS Ch. Avocations: writing, speaking, computer technology, research, teaching. Office: Mich State Bar Found 306 Townsend St Lansing MI 48933-2012

WINDLE, SARAH PENNYQUICK, lawyer; b. Boston, Aug. 2, 1969; AB, Columbia U., 1991, JD, 1997. Bar: N.Y. 1997. Fin. analyst Kidder, Peabody & Co., N.Y.C., 1991-92, Bear Stearns & Co., N.Y.C., 1992-94; assoc. Cahill Gordon & Reindel, 1997—. General civil litigation. Office: Cahill Gordon & Reindel 80 Pine St New York NY 10005

WINE, L. MARK, lawyer; b. Norfolk, Va., Apr. 16, 1945; s. Melvin Leon and Mildred Sylvia (Weiss) W.; m. Blanche Weintraub, June 8, 1969; children: Kim, Lara, Dana. BA with high honors, U. Va., 1967; JD, U. Chgo., 1970. Bar: D.C. 1970, U.S. Supreme Ct. 1977. Assoc. Kirkland & Ellis, Washington, 1970-72, ptnr., 1978—; trial atty. land and natural resources divsn. Dept. of Justice, 1972-78. Lawyer; b. Norfolk, Va., Apr. 16, 1945; s. Melvin Leon and Mildred Sylvia (Weiss) W.; m. Blanche Weintraub, June 8, 1969; children— Kim, Lara, Dana. B.A. with high honors, U. Va., 1967; J.D., U. Chgo., 1970. Bar: D.C. 1970, U.S. Supreme Ct. 1977. Assoc., Kirkland & Ellis, Washington, 1970-72; trial atty. land and natural resources div. Dept. of Justice, Washington, 1972-78; ptnr. Kirkland & Ellis, Washington, 1978— . Mem. ABA. Mem. ABA. E-mail: mark. Administrative and regulatory, Federal civil litigation, Environmental. Office: Kirkland & Ellis 655 15th St NW Ste 1200 Washington DC 20005-5793 E-mail: wine@dc.kirkland.com

WINE, MARK PHILIP, lawyer; b. Iowa City, Jan. 6, 1949; s. Donald Arthur and Mary Lepha (Schneider) W.; children: Kathryn Bouquet, Nicholas Cox, Meredith Kathryn. AB, Princeton U., 1971; JD, U. Iowa, 1974. Bar: Iowa 1974, Minn. 1976, Calif. 1997, U.S. Dist. Ct. Minn. 1976, U.S. Ct. Appeals (8th cir.) 1976, U.S. Supreme Ct. 1984, U.S. Ct. Appeals (4th cir.) 1985, U.S. Ct. Appeals (7th and Fed. cirs.) 1992, U.S. Ct. Appeals (9th cir.) 1997, U.S. Dist. Ct. (so., no. and ctrl. dists.) Calif. 1997. Law clk. to judge U.S. Ct. Appeals (8th cir.), St. Louis, 1974-76; ptnr. Oppenheimer Wolff & Donnelly LLP, Mpls., 1976—. Mem. ABA, Internat. Assn. Def. Counsel (chair spl. com. on intellectual property), Princeton Club of Southern Calif., Calif. Bar Assn., L.A. Bar Assn. Democrat. Avocations: cooking, reading, biking, golf. Federal civil litigation, State civil litigation, Intellectual property. Home: 2960 Neilson Way Unit 303 Santa Monica CA 90405-5373 Office: Oppenheimer Wolff & Donnelly LLP 2029 Century Park E Fl 38 Los Angeles CA 90067-2901 E-mail: mwine@oppenheimer.com

WINE-BANKS, JILL SUSAN, lawyer; b. Chgo., May 5, 1943; d. Bert S. and Sylvia Dawn (Simon) Wine; m. Ian David Volner, Aug. 21, 1965; m. Michael A. Banks, Jan. 12, 1980. BS, U. Ill., Champaign, Urbana, 1964; JD, Columbia U., 1968; LLD (hon.), Hood Coll., 1975. Bar: N.Y. 1969, U.S. Ct. Appeals (2d, 4th, 5th, 6th, 7th and 9th cirs.), U.S. Supreme Ct. 1974, D.C. 1976, Ill. 1980. Asst. press. and pub. rels. dir. Assembly of Captive European Nations, N.Y.C., 1965-66; trial atty. criminal divsn. organized crime & racketeering U.S. Dept. Justice, 1969-73; asst. spl. prosecutor Watergate Spl. Prosecutor's Office, 1973-75; lectr. law sem. in trial practice Columbia U. Sch. Law, N.Y.C., 1975-77; assoc. Fried, Frank, Harris, Shriver & Kampelman, Washington, 1975-77; gen. counsel Dept. Army, Pentagon, 1977-79; ptnr. Jenner & Block, Chgo., 1980-84; solicitor gen. State of Ill. Office of Atty. Gen., 1984-86, dep. atty. gen., 1986-87; exec. v.p., chief oper., officer ABA, Chgo., 1987-90; atty. pvt. practice, 1990-92; v.p., dir. transaction & govt. rels. group Motorola Internat. Network Ventures, 1992-97; v.p. Alliances, Maytag Corp., 1999-2001. Mem. EEC disting. vis. program European Parliament, 1987; chmn. bd. dirs. St. Petersburg Telecom., Russia, 1994-97, Omni Capital Ptnrs., Inc., 1994-97. Recipient Spl. Achievement award U.S. Dept. Justice, 1972, Meritorious award, 1973, Cert. Outstanding Svc., 1975; decorated Disting. Civilian Svc. Dept. Army, 1979; named Disting. Vis. to European Econ. Cmty. Mem. Internat. Women's Forum, The Chgo. Network, Econ. Club, Exec. Club (bd. dirs. 1999—). Address: 1724 Asbury Ave Evanston IL 60201 E-mail: jillwinebanks@earthlink.net

WINER, JONATHAN HERMAN, lawyer; b. Abington, Pa., Nov. 30, 1951; s. David Arthur and Janet Mae (Ratner) W.; m. Carolyn Doris Winters, Aug. 25, 1974; children: Steven Morris, Rachel Louise. AB, Dartmouth Coll., 1973; JD, NYU, 1976. Bar: N.Y. 1977, U.S. Dist. Ct. (we. dist.) N.Y. 1977, Vt. 1983. Assoc. Nixon, Hargrave, Devans & Doyle, Rochester, N.Y., 1976-83; corp. atty Green Mountain Power Corp., South Burlington, Vt., 1983-85, sr. atty, 1985-88, asst. gen. counsel, 1988-89; v.p., COO, Mountain Energy Inc., 1989-96, pres., 1997-2001; dir. enXco East Coast, Inc., South Burlington, 2001—. Chmn. Brighton (N.Y.) Dem. Com., 1982-83; pres. Temple Sinai, 1994-95. Mem. Vt. Bar Assn., Dartmouth Alumni Coun. (regional rep. 1986-89). Democrat. Jewish. Clubs: Dartmouth (Burlington, Vt.) (pres. 1984-95). General corporate, Finance, Public utilities. Home: 183 Van Patten Pky Burlington VT 05401-1126 Office: enXco East Coast Inc 1233 Shelburne Rd Ste E5 South Burlington VT 05403 Business E-Mail: jonathanw@enxco.com

WINER, STEPHEN I. lawyer; b. Mpls., Jan. 30, 1965; s. Edward Lewis and Sandra Paulette W.; m. Julie Ellen Falk, June 8, 1997. BA summa cum laude, U. Minn., 1987; JD cum laude, Northwestern U., 1990. Bar: Minn. 1987, Tex. 1994. Assoc. Dorsey & Whitney LLP, Mpls., 1990-93; asst. gen. counsel AIM Mgmt. Group Inc., Houston, 1993—. Mem. ABA, Order of Coif. Avocation: investments. Computer, General corporate, Securities. Office: AIM Mgmt Group Inc 11 E Greenway Plz Ste 100 Houston TX 77046-1100

WING, ADRIEN KATHERINE, law educator; b. Aug. 7, 1956; d. John Ellison and Katherine (Pruitt) Wing; children: Che-Cabral, Nolan Felipe. AB magna cum laude, Princeton U., 1978; MA, UCLA, 1979; JD, Stanford, 1982. Bar: N.Y. 1983, U.S. Dist. Ct. (so. and ea. dists.) N.Y. 1983, U.S. Ct. Appeals (5th and 9th cirs.). Assoc. Curtis, Mallet-Prevost, Colt & Mosle, N.Y.C., 1982-86, Rabinowitz, Boudin, Standard, Krinsky & Lieberman, 1986-87; assoc. prof. law U. Iowa, Iowa City, 1987-93, prof., 1993—, disting. prof. law, 2001—. Mem. alumni council Princeton U., 1983-85, 96-2000, trustee Class of '78 Alumni Found., 1984-87, 93—, v.p. Princeton Class of 1978 Alumni, 1993-98, trustee Princeton U. 1995; mem. bd. visitors Stanford Law Sch., 1993-96. Mem. bd. editors Am. J. Comp. Law, 1993—. Mem. Iowa Commn. on African Ams. in Prisons, 1999—. Mem. ABA (exec. com. young lawyers sect. 1985-87), Nat. Conf. Black Lawyers (UN rep., chmn. internat. affairs sect. 1982-95), Internat. Assn. Dem. Lawyers (UN rep. 1984-87), Am. Soc. Internat. Law (exec. coun. 1986-89, 96-99, exec. com. 1988-99, group chair S. Africa 1993-95, nom. com. 1991, 93, membership com. 1994-95), Am. Friends Svc. Com. (bd. dirs. Middle East 1998—), Black Alumni of Princeton U. (bd. dirs. 1982-87), Transafrica Scholars Forum Coun. (bd. dirs. 1993-95), Iowa City Foreign Rels. Coun. (bd. dirs. 1989-94), Iowa Peace Inst. (bd. dirs. 1993-95), Coun. on Fgn. Rels., Internat. Third World Legal Studies Assn. (bd. dirs. 1996—, nom. trustee Princeton com. 1997-2000), Am. Assn. of Law Schs. (minority sect. bd. 1996—). Democrat. Avocations: photography, jogging, writing, poetry. Office: U Iowa Sch Law Boyd Law Bldg Iowa City IA 52242 E-mail: adrien-wing@uiowa.edu

WING, JOHN RUSSELL, lawyer; b. Mt. Vernon, N.Y., Jan. 20, 1937; s. John R. and Elinore (Smith) W.; m. Mary Zeller, Aug. 24, 1963 (div. June 1975); children: Ethan Lincoln, Catherine Dorothy; m. Audrey Strauss, Aug. 12, 1979; children: Carlin Elinore, Matthew Lawrence. BA, Yale U., 1960; JD, U. Chgo., 1963. Bar: N.Y. 1964. Assoc. Sherman & Sterling, N.Y.C., 1963-66; asst. U.S. atty. So. Dist. N.Y., 1966-78; chief fraud unit U.S. Dist. Atty. So. Dist. N.Y., 1971-78; ptnr. Weil, Gotshal & Manges, N.Y.C., 1978—. Contbr. articles to profl. jours. Fellow Am. Coll. Trial Lawyers; mem. ABA (white collar crime com. criminal justice sect. 1978—, environ. task force com. 1983-85), Assn. Bar of City of N.Y. (criminal advocacy com. 1985-88), Fed. Bar Coun. (2d cir. cts. com. 1982-84), N.Y. Coun. Def. Lawyers (bd. dirs. 1986-90). Republican. Episcopalian. Avocation: sailing. Home: 52 Livingston St Brooklyn NY 11201-4813 Office: Weil Gotshal & Manges 767 5th Ave Fl Concl New York NY 10153-0119

WINGET, WALTER WINFIELD, lawyer; b. Peoria, Ill., Sept. 12, 1936; s. Walter W. Winget and Arabella (Robinson) Richardson; m. Alice B. Winget, Sept. 23, 1993; children: Marie, Marshall. AB cum laude, Princeton U., 1958; JD, U. Mich., 1961. Bar: R.I. 1962, Ill. 1962, U.S. Supreme Ct. 1971; cert. civil trial advocate Nat. Bd. Trial Advocacy. Assoc. Edwards & Angell, Providence, 1961-64; sole practice Peoria, 1964-77; ptnr. Winget & Kane, 1977-2000, of counsel, 2000—. Asst. pub. defender Peoria, 1969-70; bd. dirs. various corps. Atty., bd. dirs. Better Bus. Bur. Cen. Ill., Inc. 1973-92, chmn., 1979-81. Served to sgt. U.S. Army, 1961-62. Mem. Ill. Bar Assn., Ill. Trial Lawyers Assn., Peoria County Bar Assn. (pres. 1991-92), Rice Pond Preserve. Republican. Episcopalian. Club: Peoria Country. Avocations: competitive target shooting, big game and duck hunting. Federal civil litigation, State civil litigation, General corporate. Home: 6712 N Post Oak Rd Peoria IL 61615-2347 Office: Winget & Kane 416 Main St Ste 807 Peoria IL 61602-1177

WINKLER, ALLEN WARREN, lawyer, educator; b. Chgo., Dec. 11, 1954; s. Maurice A. and Florence (Klein) W.; m. Bett C. Gibson, Nov. 1, 1986. BS, No. Ill. U., 1977; JD, Tulane U., 1981. Bar: La. 1982, Ill. 1982, U.S. Dist. Ct. (ea. dist.) La. 1982, U.S. Dist. Ct. (mid. dist.) La. 1987. Atty. La. Legal Clinic, New Orleans, 1982-84; pvt. practice law, 1984-85; staff atty. Oak Tree Savs. Bank, S.S.B., 1985-87, sr. atty., asst. v.p., 1987-90; atty. FDIC/Resolution Trust Corp., Baton Rouge, 1991-92, sr. atty. Atlanta, 1992-95; sr. corp. counsel Fleet Fin., Inc., 1996-97; pres. Legal Ease Inc., 1996—; corp. counsel Prudential Bank, 1997; gen. counsel, v.p. NCS Mortgage Svcs., Norcross, Ga., 1998-2000, gen. counsel, 1999-2000; exec. v.p., COO Companion Servicing Co., LLC, 1999-2000; corp. counsel Provident Bank, Atlanta, 2000-2001; sr. atty., v.p. SunTrust Bank, 2001—. Mem. faculty Franklin Coll. Ct. Reporting, Metairie, La., 1981-88; cons., guest lectr. paralegal studies Tulane U., New Orleans, 1982-90; guest lectr. U. New Orleans, 1988-90. Vol. Hawkins for Judge campaign, New Orleans. Mem. La. Bar Assn., Ill. Bar Assn. Consumer commercial, Contracts commercial, Real property. Home: 4754 Forest Glen Court Marietta GA 30066 Office: SunTrust Bank 2950 SunTrust Plz 303 Peachtree St NE Atlanta GA 30308 E-mail: allen.winkler@suntrust.com

WINKLER, CHARLES HOWARD, lawyer, investment management company executive; b. N.Y.C., Aug. 4, 1954; s. Joseph Conrad and Geraldine Miriam (Borok) W.; m. Joni S. Taylor, Aug. 28, 1993. BBA with highest distinction, Emory U., 1976; JD, Northwestern U., 1979. Bar: Ill. 1979, U.S. Dist Ct (no. dist.) Ill. 1979. Assoc. Levenfeld & Kanter, Chgo., 1979-80, Kanter & Eisenberg, Chgo., 1980-84, ptnr., 1985-86, Neal Gerber & Eisenberg, Chgo., 1986-96; sr. mng. dir., COO Citadel Investment Group, LLC, 1996—; sr. mng. dir. Citadel Trading Group, 1996—, Aragon Investments Ltd., Chgo., 1996—. Bd. dirs. Kensington Global Strategies Fund, Ltd., Antaeus Internat. Investments, Ltd., Jackson Investment Fund Ltd., Citadel Investment Group (Europe) Ltd. Author: (with others) Basic Tax Shelters, 1982, Limited Liability Companies: The Entity of Choice, 1995; mng. editor Northwestern Jour. Internat. Law and Bus., 1979. Mem. ABA (mem. sect. on taxation), Beta Gamma Sigma. General corporate, Securities, Taxation, general. Home: 50 E Bellevue Pl Chicago IL 60611-1129 Office: Citadel Investment Group LLC 225 W Washington St Fl 9 Chicago IL 60606-2418

WINKLER, DANA JOHN, lawyer; b. Wichita, Kans., Jan. 2, 1944; s. Donald Emil and Hazel Claire (Schmitter) W.; m. Mary Ann Seiwert, Oct. 14, 1967; 1 child, Jonathan. BA, Wichita State U., 1967; JD, Washburn Law Sch., 1971. Staff writer Wichita (Kans.) Eagle & Beacon, 1961-67; ptnr. Davis, Bruce, Davis & Winkler, Wichita, 1972-77; asst. city atty. City of Wichita, 1977-99; dir. Wichita Mcpl. Fed. Credit Union, 1980—, pres., 1982, 99-2000, sec.-treas., 1994-98, v.p., 1998-99. Dir. Deaf and Hard of Hearing Counseling Svc., 1979-80. Vol. Sedgwick County United Way, Wichita, 1973-74; vice-chmn. Wichita Pub. Schs. Spl. Edn. Adv. Coun., 1987-89. 1st lt. U.S. Army, 1967-69. Mem. Kans. Bar Assn., Wichita Bar Assn., Masons. Republican. Roman Catholic. Home and Office: 1621 Harlan St Wichita KS 67212-1842 E-mail: djwinkler@aol.com

WINNING, J(OHN) PATRICK, lawyer; b. Murphysboro, Ill., Oct. 29, 1952; s. William T. Jr. and Lillian (Albers) W.; m. Jessica Anne Yoder, June 17, 1978 (div. July 1999); children: Erika Anne, Brian Patrick, Derek Matthew. AB with distinction, Mo. Bapt. Coll., 1974; JD, St. Louis U., 1979. Bar: Mo. 1979, U.S. Dist. Ct. (ea. dist.) Mo. 1979, U.S. Ct. Appeals (8th cir.) 1979, U.S. Dist. Ct. (so. dist.) Tex. 1985, U.S. Ct. Appeals (5th cir.) 1987, U.S. Dist. Ct. (we. dist.) Tex. 1988, Tex. 1989. Assoc. Chused, Strauss, Chorlins, Goldfarb, Bini & Kohn, St. Louis, 1979-81; assoc. counsel Mfrs. Hanover Fin. Services, Phila., 1981-83; corp. counsel Cessna Fin. Corp., Wichita, Kans., 1983-85; atty. Southwestern Bell Publs., Inc., St. Louis, 1985-90; pvt. practice, 1990-2000; pres. Butler Hill Investments, Inc., 1990-91; prin. Success Mgmt. Group, 1991-96, DPPC Mgmt. Group, St. Louis, 1996-97; v.p., gen. counsel Winning Equipment Co., Herculaneum, Mo., 2000-01; assoc. Vogler Law Firm, P.C., 2000—. Sec., bd. dirs. Winning Equipment Co.; asst. prof. bus. adminstn. Mo. Bapt. Coll., 1986-91. Treas. Concerned Citizens of Chesterfield, 1989-91; deacon, mem. fin. com. 1st Bapt. Ch., Ellisville, Mo., 1992-93, vice chmn. fin. com., 1993-94, chmn. fin. com., 1994-95, vice chmn. deacons, 1993-95, chmn. deacons, 1997-98, dir. Sunday sch., 1993-94; trustee, chmn. athletic com., 1992-97, 98-2000, chmn. by-laws com. Mo. Bapt. Coll., 1992-96, sec. presdl. search com., 1994, mem., exec. com. bd. trustees, 1994-97, 98-2000; mgr. St. Louis Flames Youth Baseball, 1992-95; mgr. St. Louis Thunder Youth Baseball, 1995-97; coach St. Clare Bulls Basketball Team, 1994-97, St. Louis Wolfpack Youth Baseball, 1997-98; asst. scoutmaster troop 313, merit badge counselor Boy Scouts Am., 1997—; Camporee staff New Horizons dist. Boy Scouts Am., 1998-2000, adult leader tng. staff, 1998—, camping com., 1998-2000, dist. roundtable staff, 1999—, chmn. membership com. New Horizons dist., 1999—. Named one of Outstanding Young Men of Am., 1987, Outstanding Alumnus, Mo. Bapt. Coll., 1987-88; named to Athletic Hall of Fame, Mo. Bapt. Coll., 1989; recipient Wood Badge Adult Leadership Tng. award Boy Scouts Am., 1998. Mem. Nat. Lawyers Assn., Eagle Scouts Assn., Met. St. Louis Bar Assn., Christian Legal Soc., Acad. Family Mediators, Assn. Family and Conciliation Cts., Mo. Bapt. Coll. Alumni Assn. (pres. 1980-81, 88-90), St. Louis Assn., Christian Attys., West County C. of C., Chesterfield C. of C. Republican. Southern Baptist. Avocations: coaching baseball and basketball, reading, camping. General corporate, Family and matrimonial, Real property. Home: 868 Gardenway Ballwin MO 63011 Office: 2129 Barrett Station Rd Ste 313 Saint Louis MO 63131-1606

WINSHIP, BLAINE H. lawyer; b. Ithaca, N.Y., Apr. 3, 1951; s. Hershell F. and June M. (Nickless) W.; m. Karin M. Byrne, Dec. 21, 1979. AB magna cum laude, Dartmouth Coll., 1973; JD, Cornell U., 1976. Bar: Ill. 1976, Fla. 1982. Assoc. Sonnenschein, Nath & Rosenthal, Chgo., 1976-82; ptnr. Winship & Byrne, Miami, Fla., 1983—. Contbg. author: ABA Criminal Antitrust Manual, 1982. Mem. bd. trustees StageWorks, Tampa, Fla., 1984-86, pres., 1986. Rufus Choate scholar Dartmouth Coll., 1972-73. Mem. Miami City Club, Fla. Bar Assn. (vice chmn., antitrust and trade regulation com., exec. com. bus. law sect.), Phi Beta Kappa. Antitrust, Federal civil litigation. Home: 1014 Hardee Rd Coral Gables FL 33146-3330 Office: Winship & Byrne 200 S Biscayne Blvd Ste 1870 Miami FL 33131-2329

WINSLOW, JOHN FRANKLIN, lawyer; b. Houston, Nov. 15, 1933; s. Franklin Jarnigan and Jane (Shipley) W. BA, U. Tex., 1957, LLB, 1960. Bar: Tex. 1959, D.C. 1961. Atty., Hispanic law div. Library Congress, Washington, 1965-68; counsel, com. on the judiciary Ho. of Reps., 1968-71; atty., editor Matthew Bender & Co., 1973-79; atty. FERC, 1979-84; sole practice, 1984—. Researcher Hispanic Law Research, Washington, 1979—. Author: Conglomerates Unlimited: The Failure of Regulation, 1974; editor: Fed. Power Service, 1974-79; contbr. articles to Washington Monthly, Nation, 1975—. Mem. Tex. Bar Assn., D.C. Bar Assn. Administrative and regulatory, Public international. E-mail: jfwinslow@aol.com

WINSLOW, JULIAN DALLAS, retired lawyer, historian, writer; b. Elizabeth City, N.C., Oct. 10, 1914; s. Joseph D. and Mary Anne (Cooper) W.; m. Jean Littell, Dec. 27, 1941; children: Julian Dallas, Mary P. Winslow Reddick, Helen L. BS in Commerce, U. N.C., 1935, JD, 1941; MA in History, U. Del., 1988. Bar: N.C. 1941, Del. 1949, U.S. Dist. Ct. Del. 1952, U.S. Ct. Appeals (3d cir.) 1982. Assoc. J.H. LeRoy Jr., Elizabeth City, 1941-42; pvt. practice, 1945-48, Wilmington, Del., 1949-89; ret., 1989; ptnr. Winslow Realty Co., 1974—. Solicitor Currituck County (N.C.) Ct. 1946-47; chief of enforcement heavy machinery and indsl. materials sect. Office Price Stablzn., Del. dist. 1952; arbitrator Am. Arbitration Assn. Author: Samuel Maxwell Harrington, A Pioneer Judge, 1994, Sussex Awakens to the Toot, 1999. Lt. USCG, 1942-45. Decorated Philippine Liberation medal. Mem. ABA (real estate, probate and trust, labor sects.), Del. State Bar Assn. (com. labor and employment law). Republican. Episcopalian.

WINSTEAD, GEORGE ALVIS, law librarian, biochemist, educator, consultant; b. Owensboro, Ky., Jan. 14, 1916; s. Robert Lee and Mary Oma (Dempsey) W.; m. Elisabeth Donelson Weaver, July 18, 1943. BS, We. Ky. U., 1938; MA, George Peabody Coll., 1940, MLS, 1957, MEd, 1958. Head chemistry and biology dept. Belmont Coll., Nashville, 1952-56; head chemistry dept. George Peabody Coll., Vanderbilt U., 1956-58; assoc. law librarian Vanderbilt U., 1958-76; dir. Tenn. State Supreme Ct. Law Libraries, 1976—. Law cons. Tenn. Youth Legis., Nashville, 1976—; cons. civic clubs, local cols., 1976—, Tenn. State Govt. Depts. Archives, Nashville, 1976—. Author: Tenn. State Law Library Progress Reports, 1975, Supreme Court Library Personnel Guide, 1981, Designing Future Law Libraries' Growth and Expansion, 1982, Problem Identification and Solutions in Law Libraries, Tenn. Supreme Courts, 1985; mem. editl. bd. A Dictionary of Chemical Equations, 1952—. Mem. Col. Tenn. Gov.'s staff, Nashville, 1978. With USAAF, 1943-46. Named to Gov.'s Staff of Ky. Cols., Lexington, 1988. Fellow Am. Inst. Chemists, SAR. Baptist. Avocations: camping, hiking, traveling, crafts, antique cars. Home: 3819 Gallatin Pike Nashville TN 37216-2609 Office: Tenn Supreme Ct Libr Nashville TN 37219

WINSTON, HAROLD RONALD, lawyer; b. Atlantic, Iowa, Feb. 7, 1932; s. Louis D. and Leta B. (Carter) W.; m. Carol J. Sundeen, June 11, 1955; children: Leslie Winston Yannetti, Lisa Winston Shaw, Laura Winston Moritz. BA, U. Iowa, 1954, JD, 1958. Bar: Iowa 1958, U.S. Dist. Ct. (no. and so. dists.) Iowa 1962, U.S. Tax Ct. 1962, U.S. Ct. Appeals (8th cir.) 1970, U.S. Supreme Ct. 1969. Trust officer United Home Bank & Trust Co., Mason City, Iowa, 1958-59; mem. Breese & Cornwell, 1960-62, Breese, Cornwell, Winston & Reuber, Mason City, 1963-73, Winston, Schroeder & Reuber, Mason City, 1974-79, Winston, Reuber, Swanson & Byrne, P.C., Mason City, 1980-92, Winston, Reuber & Byrne, Mason City, 1992-96, Winston & Byrne, P.C., Mason City, 1996—. Police judge, Mason City, 1961-73. Contbr. articles to profl. jours. Past pres. Family YMCA, Mason City, Cerro Gordo County Estate Planning Coun.; active local charitable orgns. Capt. USAF, 1955-57. Fellow Am. Coll. Trust and Estate Counsel, Am. Bar Found. (life), Iowa Bar Found. (life); mem. ABA, ATLA, Iowa Bar Assn. (gov., lectr. ann. meeting 1977-79), 2d Jud. Dist. Bar Assn. (lectr. meeting 1981-82), Cerro Gordo County Bar Assn. (past pres.), Am. Judicature Soc., Mason City Country Club, Kiwanis, Masons. Republican. Presbyterian. General corporate, General practice, Probate. Office: Winston & Byrne 119 2d St NW Mason City IA 50401-3105 E-mail: hwinston@netins.net

WINSTON, JUDITH ANN, lawyer; b. Atlantic City, Nov. 23, 1943; d. Edward Carlton and Margaret Ann (Goodman) Marianno; m. Michael Russell Winston, Aug. 10, 1963; children: Lisa Marie, Cynthia Eileen. BA magna cum laude, Howard U., Washington, 1966; JD, Georgetown U., 1977. Bar: DC 1977, US Supreme Ct. Dir. EEO project Coun. Great City Schs., Washington, 1971-74; legal asst. Lawyers Com. for Civil Rights Under Law, 1975-77; spl. asst. to dir. Office for Civil Rights, HEW, 1977-79; exec. asst., legal counsel to chair U.S. EEO Commn., 1979-80; asst. gen. counsel U.S. Dept. Edn., 1980-86; dep. dir. Lawyers Com. for Civil Rights Under Law, 1986-88; dep. dir. pub. policy Women's Legal Def. Fund, Washington, 1988-90, chair employment discrimination com., 1979-88, ednl. cons., 1974-77; asst. prof. law Washington Coll. Law of Am. U., 1990-93, assoc. prof. law, 1993-95, rsch. prof. law, 2001—; gen. counsel U.S. Dept. Edn., Washington, 1993-2001; exec. dir. Pres.'s Initiative on Race, 1997-98; undersec. U.S. Dept. Edn., 2000-01; research prof law Washington Col Law Am Univ, 2001—. Author: (book) Desegregating Schools in the Great Cities: Philadelphia, 1970, Chronicle of a Decade 1961-70, 1970, Desegregating Urban Schools: Educational Equality/Quality, 1970;contbr. articles to profl jours. Pres bd dirs Higher Achievement Program; bd dirs Partners for Dem Change, Nat Pub Radio, Sothern Educ Found. Named Woman Lawyer of the Yr, Women's Bar Asn, 1997; recipient Margaret Brent, Am Bar Asn Comn Women in the Profession, 1998. Fellow: ABA Found; mem.: ACLU, Fed Bar Asn, DC Bar Asn, Washington Coun Lawyers, Washington Bar Asn, Nat Bar Asn, Lawyers Comt Civil Rights Under Law, Links Inc, Phi Beta Kappa, Alpha Kappa Alpha, Delta Theta Phi. Democrat. Episcopalian. Home: 1371 Kalmia Rd NW Washington DC 20012-1444 Office: Dept Edn 400 Maryland Ave SW Washington DC 20202-0001

WINTER, RALPH KARL, JR. federal judge; b. Waterbury, Conn., July 30, 1935; married. BA, Yale U., 1957, JD, 1960; JD (hon.), Bklyn. Law Sch., N.Y. Law Sch. Bar: Conn. 1973. Research assoc., lectr. Yale U., 1962-64, asst. prof. to assoc. prof. law, 1967-78, William K. Townsend prof. law, 1978-82, adj. prof. law, 1982—; spl. cons. subcom. on separation of powers U.S. Senate Com. on Judiciary, 1968-72; sr. fellow Brookings Inst., 1968-70; adj. scholar Am. Enterprise Inst., 1972-82; judge U.S. Ct.

Appeals (2d cir.), New Haven, 1982-97, chief judge, 1997-2000. Vis. prof. law U. Chgo., 1966; mem. adv. com. civil rules Jud. Conf. U.S., 1987-92, chair adv. com. rules evidence, 1993-96, mem. exec. com., 1998-2000, chair exec. com., 1999-2000. Contbr. articles to profl. jours. Recipient award Conn. Law Rev., Learned Hand award for excellence in fed. jurisprudence Fed. Bar Coun. Office: Second Circuit US Courthouse 141 Church St New Haven CT 06510-2030

WINTERSHEIMER, DONALD CARL, state supreme court justice; b. Covington, Ky., Apr. 21, 1932; s. Carl E. and Marie A. (Kohl) W.; m. Alice T. Rabe, June 24, 1961; children: Mark D., Lisa Ann, Craig P., Amy T., Blaise Q. BA, Thomas More Coll., 1953; MA, Xavier U., 1956; JD, U. Cin., 1959; LHD (hon.), No. Ky. U., 1999. Bar: Ky. 1960, Ohio 1960. Pvt. practice, Covington, Ky., 1960-76; city solicitor City of Covington, 1962-76; judge Ky. Ct. Appeals, Frankfort, 1976-83; justice Ky. Supreme Ct., 1983—, chmn. criminal rules com., 1988-94, chmn. continuing jud. edn. com., 1983—, chmn. rules com., 1994—. Del. Foster Parent Rev. Bd., 1985—; mem. adv. bd. Sta. WNKU-FM, 1984-94, Am. Soc. Writers on Legal Subjects. Trustee Sta. WNKU-FM. Recipient Cmty. Svc. award Thomas More Coll., 1968; recipient Disting. Alumnus award Thomas More Coll., 1982, Disting. Alumni award Coll. Law/U.Cin., 1998; named Disting. Jurist Chase Coll. Law, 1983, Outstanding Jurist Phi Alpha Delta Law Frat., 1990. Mem. ABA, Am. Judicature Soc., Ky. Bar Assn., Ohio Bar Assn., Cin. Bar Assn., Inst. Jud. Adminstrn., Am. Inss of Ct. (founder Chase chpt.). Democrat. Roman Catholic. Home: 224 Adams Ave Covington KY 41014-1712 Office: Ky Supreme Ct Capitol Building Room 235 700 Capitol Ave Frankfort KY 40601-3410

WINTHROP, LAWRENCE FREDRICK, lawyer; b. Apr. 18, 1952; s. Murray and Vauneta (Cardwell) W. BA with honors, Whittier Coll., 1974; JD magna cum laude, Calif. Western Sch., 1977. Bar: Ariz. 1977, Calif. 1977, U.S. Dist. Ct. Ariz. 1977, U.S. Dist. Ct. (so. dist.) Calif. 1981, U.S. Ct. Appeals (9th cir.) 1981, U.S. Dist. Ct. (cen. dist.) Calif. 1983, U.S. Supreme Ct. 1983. Assoc. Snell and Wilmer, Phoenix, 1977-83, ptnr., 1984-93, Doyle, Winthrop, P.C., Phoenix, 1993—. Judge pro tem Maricopa County Superior Ct., 1987-97, Ariz. Ct. Appeals, 1992—; lectr. Ariz. personal injury law and practice and state and local tax law Tax Exec. Inst., Nat. Bus. Inst., Profl. Edn. Systems, Inc., Ariz. Trial Lawyers Assn., Maricopa County Bar Assn.; bd. dirs. Valley of the Sun Sch., 1989-97, chmn., 1994-96; mem. Vol. Lawyers Program, Phoenix, 1980—. Editor-in-chief: Calif. Western Law Rev., 1976-77. Fellow Ariz. Bar Found., Maricopa Bar Found.; mem. ABA, Calif. Bar Assn., Ariz. Bar Assn. (mem. com. on exam. 1995—), Ariz. Tax Rsch. Assn. (bd. dirs. 1989-93), Maricopa County Bar Assn., Ariz. Assn. Def. Counsel (bd. dirs., pres. 1988-89, chmn. med.-malpractice com. 1993-95), Aspen Valley Club, LaMancha Racquet Club. Republican. Methodist. Avocations: music, golf, tennis. General civil litigation, Personal injury. Home: 6031 N 2nd St Phoenix AZ 85012-1210 Office: Doyle and Winthrop PC 3300 N Central Ave Ste 1600 Phoenix AZ 85012 E-mail: lwinthrop@doylewinthrop.com

WINTHROP, SHERMAN, lawyer; b. Duluth, Minn., Feb. 3, 1931; s. George E. and Mary (Tesler) W.; m. Barbara Cowan, Dec. 16, 1956; children: Susan Winthrop Crist, Bradley T., Douglas A. BBA, U. Minn., 1952; JD, Harvard U., 1955. Bar: Minn. 1955, U.S. Dist. Ct. Minn. 1955, U.S. Tax Ct. Law clk. to chief justice Minn. Supreme Ct., St. Paul, 1955-56; ptnr. Oppenheimer, Wolff & Donnelly, 1956-79; shareholder Winthrop & Weinstine P.A., 1979—. Bd. dirs. Bremer Fin. Corp., St. Paul, Minn., Capital City Partnership; bd. dirs., sec. St. Paul Progress Corp. Mem. ABA, Minn. Bar Assn. (chair exec. coun., bus. law sect. 1992-93), Ramsey County Bar Assn. Avocations: tennis, travel, family. Banking, General corporate, Real property. Home: 1672 Pinehurst Ave Saint Paul MN 55116-2158 Office: Winthrop & Weinstine PA 3200 Minn World Trade Ctr 30 7th St E Saint Paul MN 55101-4914

WINTRODE, RALPH CHARLES, lawyer; b. Hollywood, Calif., Dec. 21, 1942; s. Ralph Osborne and Maureen (Kavanagh) W.; m. Leslie Ann O'Rourke, July 2, 1966 (div. Feb. 1994); children: R. Christopher, Patrick L., Ryan B. BS in Acctg., U. So. Calif., 1966, JD, 1967. Bar: Calif. 1967, N.Y. 1984, Japan 1989, Washington 1990. From assoc. to ptnr. to of counsel Gibson, Dunn & Crutcher, Tokyo, L.A., Newport Beach and Irvine, Calif., 1967—. Sec. Music Ctr. Los Angeles County, 1986-88; bd. dirs. Coro Found., L.A. County, 1986-87. Mem. Newport Harbor Club, Am. Club Tokyo. Avocations: sailboat racing, car racing, flying. General corporate, Mergers and acquisitions, Real property. Office: Gibson Dunn & Crutcher 4 Park Plz Ste 1400 Irvine CA 92614-8557 also: 333 S Grand Ave Ste 4400 Los Angeles CA 90071-1548

WINTROL, JOHN PATRICK, lawyer; b. Wichita, Kans., Feb. 13, 1941; s. Clarence Joseph and Margaret (Gill) W.; m. Janet Lee Mitchell; children: John Howard, Joanna Lee. BA cum laude, Rockhurst Coll., 1963; JD, Georgetown U., 1969. Bar. D.C. 1969, U.S. Ct. Appeals (4th, 5th, 11th and D.C. cirs.) 1981, U.S. Dist. Ct. Md. 1984. Law clk. to Hon. Howard Corcoran U.S. Dist. Ct., Washington, 1969-71; assoc. Howrey & Simon, 1971-77; mng. ptnr. Perito, Duerk & Pinco, 1978-85; ptnr. Finley Kumble, 1985-87, Laxalt, Washington, Perito & Dubuc, Washington, 1988-91, McDermott, Will & Emery, Washington, 1991—. Mem. jud. conf. U.S. Ct. Appeals (D.C. cir.). Vol. Peace Corps, Turkey, 1963-65; bd. trustees Holton Arms Sch. Mem. ABA. Roman Catholic. Federal civil litigation, Contracts commercial, Administrative and regulatory. Office: McDermott Will & Emery 600 13th St NW Washington DC 20005-3096 E-mail: jwintrol@mwe.com

WINZENREID, JAMES ERNEST, lawyer, entrepreneur; b. Wheeling, W.Va., June 9, 1951; s. Ernest Christian and Dorothy Emma (Wolf) W.; m. Rebecca Lee Rice, Aug. 11, 1979; children: Diana Lee, Lauren Rice. AB, W. Liberty State Coll., 1973; MBA, W.Va. U., 1979; JD, Duquesne U., 1987; LLM, Wayne State U., 1989. Bar: Pa. 1987, U.S. Dist. Ct. (we. dist.) Pa. 1987. Staff asst. Wheeling Pitts. Steel Corp., Wheeling, 1974-78, supr. indl. relations, 1978; mgr. profl. planning and devel. Copperweld Corp., Pitts., 1978-79, mgr. human resources Glassport, Pa., 1979-81, plant mgr., 1981-83, group mgr. human resources Pitts., 1984-85, market program mgr., 1986-87; with lab. and employment dept. Eckert, Seamans, Cherin & Mellott, 1986-87; corp. staff rep. Tecumseh (Mich.) Products Co., 1987-89; v.p. human resources devel. Lafarge (Va.) Corp., 1989-94; v.p. human resources western region Lafarge Constrn. Materials, Calgary, Alta., Can., 1994-96, Lafarge Can. Inc., Calgary, 1996-99; mgr. union rels. GE, Bloomington, Ind., 2000—. Mng. editor Juris mag., 1986. Bd. dirs. Wheeling Symphony Soc., 1977-86, Wheeling Jaycees, 1976-78; mem. adv. bd. Jr. Achievement Southwestern Pa., 1981-83. Named Outstanding Young Men Am. U.S. Jaycees, 1979. Mem. ABA, Pa. Bar Assn., Allegheny Bar Assn., Am. Soc. Human Resources Mgmt., Human Resource Planning Soc., Phi Alpha Delta. Republican. Lutheran. Avocations: golf, reading. Labor. Home: 4647 Fox Moor Ln Greenwood IN 46143-9279 Office: GE 301 N Curry Pike Bloomington IN 47404-2502

WINZER, P.J. lawyer; b. Shreveport, La., June 7, 1947; d. C.W. Winzer and Pearlene Hall Winzer Tobin. BA in Polit. Sci., So. U., Baton Rouge, 1968; JD, UCLA, 1971. Bar: Bar: Calif. 1972, U.S. Supreme Ct. 1986. Staff atty. Office of Gen. Counsel, U.S. HEW, Washington, 1971-80; asst. spl. counsel U.S. Office of Spl. Counsel Merit Systems Protection Bd., Dallas, 1980-82; regional dir. U.S. Merit Systems Protection Bd., Alexandria, Va., 1982—. Mem. Calif. Bar Assn., Fed. Cir. Bar Assn., Delta Sigma Theta. Office: US Merit System Protection 1800 Diagnol Rd Ste 205 Alexandria VA 22314-2840

WIRKEN, CHARLES WILLIAM, lawyer; b. Moline, Ill., Aug. 29, 1951; s. Walter William and Elizabeth Claire (Mallory) W.; children: Nicole, Michelle. BS, U. Ariz., 1972, JD, 1975. 010BAr: Ariz. 1975, U.S. Dist. Ct. Ariz. 1976, U.S. Ct. Appeals (9th cir.) 1980, U.S. Ct. Appeals (Fed. cir.) 1985, U.S. Supreme Ct. 1980. Assoc. Killian, Legg & Nicholas, Mesa, Ariz., 1975-79; ptnr. Killian, Nicholas, Fischer, Wirken, Cook & Pew, 1980-97, Gust Rosenfeld P.L.C., 1997—. Pres. Vol. Lawyers Project, Phoenix, 1981-83; judge pro tem Ariz. Ct. Appeals, 1985—, Maricopa County Superior Ct., 1986—; mem. civil study com. Maricopa County Superior Ct., 1984—; bd. dirs. Cmty. Legal Svcs., Phoenix, 1979-82. Exec. v.p. East Valley Partnership, Mesa, 1984; pres. Tri-City Cath. Social Svc., Mesa, 1983, 94; bd. dirs. East Valley Cultural Alliance, Mesa, 1984. Mem. ATLA, State Bar Ariz. (bd. govs. 1995—), Maricopa County Bar Assn. (bd. dirs. 1983-91, pres. 1989-90), East Valley Bar Assn. (pres. 1979-80), Mesa C. of C. (dir. 1980-83), Am. Arbitration Assn. (arbitrator), Rotary (bd. dirs. 1980-89, pres. 1987-88). Democrat. Roman Catholic. Appellate, General civil litigation, Franchising. Home: 1708 E Knoll St Mesa AZ 85203-2171 Office: Gust Rosenfeld PLC 201 N Central Ave Ste 3300 Phoenix AZ 85073-3300

WIRKEN, JAMES CHARLES, lawyer; b. Lansing, Mich., July 3, 1944; s. Frank and Mary (Brosnahan) W.; m. Mary Morse, June 12, 1971; children: Christopher, Erika, Kurt, Gretchen, Jeffrey, Matthew. BA in English, Rockhurst Coll., 1967; JD, St. Louis U., 1970. Bar: Mo. 1970, U.S. Dist. Ct. (we. dist.) Mo. 1970. Asst. prosecuter Jackson County, Kansas City, Mo., 1970-72; assoc. Morris, Larson, King, Stamper & Bold, 1972-75; dir. Spradley, Wirken, Reismeyer & King, 1976-88, Wirken & King, Kansas City, 1988-93; pres. The Wirken Group, 1993—. Adj. prof. law U. Mo., Kansas City, 1984-89, 2001—; founder, chmn. Lender Liability Group. Author: Managing a Practice and Avoiding Malpractice, 1983; co-author Missouri Civil Procedure Form Book, 1984; mem. editorial bd. Mo. Law Weekly, 1989—, Lender Liability News, 1990—, Emerging Trends and Theories of Lender Liability, 1991; host. Wirken on the Law, KMBZ Radio, 1998—. Mem. ABA (exec. coun.), Nat. Conf. Bar Pres. (coun. 1992-96), Nat. Caucus of Met. Bar Leaders (exec. coun., pres. 1988-94), Am. Trial Lawyers Assn., L.P. Gas Group (founder, chair 1986-90), Mo. Bar Assn. (bd. govs. 1977-78, chmn. econs. and methods practice com. 1982-84, quality and methods of practice com. 1989-91, vice chmn. young lawyers sect. 1976-78), Mo. Assn. Trial Attys. (bd. govs. 1983-85), Kansas City Met. Bar Assn. (pres. young lawyers sect. 1975, chair legal assistance com. 1977-78, chair tort law com. 1982, pres. 1990). Federal civil litigation, State civil litigation, Personal injury. Home: 47 W 53rd Kansas City MO 64112 Office: The Wirken Law Group PC 2600 Grand Blvd Ste 440 Kansas City MO 64108-4628

WISE, AARON NOAH, lawyer; b. Hartford, Conn., Feb. 14, 1940; s. Joseph J. and Ethel (Sklar) W.; m. Genevieve Ehrlich, Dec. 17. 1966; children: Haywood Martin, Paul Russell, Renee Alicia. AB, Boston U., 1962; JD, Boston Coll., 1965; LLM in Comparative/Internat. Law, NYU, 1971; certificat de Doctorat, d' Université en Droit, U. Paris Law Sch., 1970. Bar: N.Y., U.S. Dist. Ct. (so. dist.) N.Y. Internat. atty. Schering-Plough, Kenilworth, N.J., 1969-74; ptnr. Conboy Hewitt O'Brien & Boardman, N.Y.C., 1974-80, Wise Lerman & Katz P.C. (formerly Rosenbaum Wise Lerman & Katz), N.Y.C., 1981-95, Klepner & Cayea, N.Y.C., 1995-98, Brand, Cayea & Brand, LLC, 1998-2000, Siller Wilk LLP, N.Y.C., 2000—. Lectr. bus. and legal groups U.S., Europe, Latin Am. Author: International Sports Law and Business (Kluwer Law Internat., 1997, 3 vols.), Foreign Businessman's Guide to U.S. Law-Practice-Taxation; contbr. articles to pubs. in U.S. and Europe. Mem. ABA, N.Y. State Bar Assn. Avocations: multi-lingual including French, Spanish, Portuguese, Italian, Russian, Japanese and German. Contracts commercial, Private international, Sports. Home: 38 Cummings Cir West Orange NJ 07052-2264 Office: Siller Wilk LLP 747 3rd Ave New York NY 10017-2803 E-mail: awise@sillerwilk.com

WISE, NANCY JOAN, lawyer; b. Oak Park, Ill., Aug. 5, 1950; d. Robert S. and Grace Ann (Ackerman) W. B.S., Wittenberg U., 1973; J.D., U. of Dayton, 1977. Bar: Ill. 1977, U.S. Dist. Ct. (no. dist.) Ill. 1977. Atty., Ceco Corp., Oak Brook, Ill., 1977-84, asst. sec., 1977— ; atty. Ceco Industries, Inc., Oak Brook, 1984— , asst. sec., 1984— . Mem. ABA, Chgo. Bar Assn. General corporate. Office: Ceco Industries Inc 1400 Kensington Rd Hinsdale IL 60523-2106

WISE, VIRGINIA JO, law educator, librarian; b. Midland, Mich., Nov. 8, 1950; d. Lester Allen and Frances Irene (Schoch) W.; m. Frederick F. Schauer, May 25, 1985. B in Gen. Studies, U. Mich., 1973, MLS, 1975; JD, Wayne Satte U., 1977. Bar: Calif. 1977, Tex. 1979, U.S. Dist. Ct. (no. dist.) Calif. 1978. Acquisitions and serials clk. U. Mich. Law Libr., Ann Arbor, 1973-74; asst. libr. Miller, Canfield, Paddock & Stone, Detroit, 1975-77; reference libr. Tarlton Law Libr., U. Tex., Austin, 1978-79; assoc. law libr. Harvard U. Law Libr., Cambridge, Mass., 1979-82; assoc. prof. law, dir. law libr. Boston U. Sch. Law, 1982-85; lectr. ref. libr. U. Mich., 1986-87, sr. assoc. libr., 1987-88, asst. prof. libr. and info. studies, 1988-90; lectr. Harvard U. Law Sch., 1990—. Cons. Houghton Mifflin Pub. Co., Boston, 1985-86, UN Devel. Program, 1997-2000. Book rev. editor, Tex. Bar Jour., 1978-79. Mem. ALA, Am. Assn. Law Librs. (rep. spl. librs. assn. 1986-88), Law Librarians New Eng., Calif. State Bar Assn., Tex. State Bar Assn. Office: Harvard Law Sch 126 Areeda Hall Cambridge MA 02138 E-mail: wise@law.harvard.edu

WISE, WARREN ROBERTS, retired lawyer; b. Beaver City, Nebr., Oct. 8, 1929; s. Harold Edward and Doris Lorene (Roberts) W.; m. Marcia Hench, Oct. 14, 1961; children: Debra, David, Susan. BS, U. Nebr., 1950, LLB, 1953; LLM, Georgetown U., 1960. Atty. U.S. Dept. Justice Lands Div., Washington, 1955-61, U.S. Dept. Justice Tax Div., Washington, 1961-63; assoc. counsel Mass. Mut. Life Ins. Co., Springfield, 1963-67, asst. gen. counsel, 1967-72, 2d v.p., assoc. gen. counsel, 1972-74, v.p., assoc. gen. counsel, 1974-85, sr. v.p., assoc. gen. counsel, 1985-88, exec. v.p., gen. counsel, 1988-93; ret., 1993. Author: Business Insurance Agreements, 1970, 80, 91; editor; Massachusetts Life Insurance Law, 1980. Chmn. bd. East Coast Conf., Evang. Covenant Ch., 1987-89, chmn. pension bd., 1984-86, exec. bd., 1995—; bd. dirs. Mass. Family Inst., 1994-98, vol. policy analyst, 1994-98. Mem. ABA (chmn. life ins. law com. torts and ins. sect. 1992-93), Assn. Life Inst. Counsel (bd. dirs. 1987-92, pres. 1992-93), Longmeadow Country Club, Laurel Oak Country Club. Republican. Avocation: golf. Home: 7831 Allen Robertson Pl Sarasota FL 34240-8634*

WISEHEART, MALCOLM BOYD, JR. lawyer; b. Miami, Fla., Sept. 18, 1942; s. Malcolm B. and Dorothy E. (Allen) W.; m. Michele I. Romanens, Dec. 11, 1976. BA, Yale U., 1965; MA in English Jurisprudence, Cambridge U., 1973; JD with honors, U. Fla., 1970. Bar: Fla. 1970, Eng. and Wales 1970, Jamaica 1970, Trinidad and Tobago, 1971, D.C. 1980; barrister Gray's Inn of Ct., London. Assoc. Helliwell, Melrose & DeWolf, Miami, 1970-72; sr. ptnr. Malcolm B. Wiseheart, Jr., P.A., 1973-86, 87-01, Wiseheart & Joyce, P.A., Miami, 1986-88. Sec., gen. counsel Wiseheart Found.; spl. master Dade County Property Appraisal Adjustment Bd., 1977-90; pres. Fla. Law Inst., 1980-2001; trustee, mem. exec. com. Players State Theater, 1982-84; bd. dirs. Sta. WLRN Pub. Radio, 1982, Coun. Internat. Visitors; trustee Ransom Everglades Sch., 1995-97. Named Most Outstanding, U. Fla. Law Rev. Alumnus, 1981. Mem. Fla. Bar (chmn. grievance com. 1978-81), Dade County Bar Assn. (dir. 1971-74, 86-89, treas. 1974-75, sec. 1975-77), Order of Coif, Yale Club (Miami pres. 1976-77), United Oxford and Cambridge Univs. Club (London). State civil litigation, Landlord-tenant, Real property. Office: Wiseheart Bldg 2840 SW 3rd Ave Miami FL 33129-2317 E-mail: mbwjr@bellsouth.net

WISEMAN, ALAN M(ITCHELL), lawyer; b. Long Branch, N.J., July 6, 1944; s. Lincoln B. and Gertrude (Gorcey) W.; m. Paula Wiseman, July 8, 1965; children: Steven, David, Julie. BA, Johns Hopkins U., 1965; JD, Georgetown U., 1968. Bar: Md. 1968, Ill. 1970, D.C. 1973. Law clk. to Hon. William J. McWilliams, Md. Ct. Appeals, 1968-69; assoc. Schiff, Hardin & Waite, Chgo., 1970-74; ptnr. Howrey & Simon, Washington, 1976—. Editor Georgetown Law Jour., 1967-68. Mem. U.S. C. of C. (coun. on antitrust policy). Antitrust, Federal civil litigation, Legislative. Office: 1299 Pennsylvania Ave NW Washington DC 20004-2400 E-mail: wisemana@howrey.com

WISEMAN, THOMAS ANDERTON, JR. federal judge; b. Tullahoma, Tenn., Nov. 3, 1930; s. Thomas Anderton and Vera Seleta (Poe) W.; m. Emily Barbara Matlack, Mar. 30, 1957; children: Thomas Anderton III, Mary Alice, Sarah Emily. B.A., Vanderbilt U., 1952, LL.B., 1954; LLM, U. Va., 1990. Bar: Tenn. Pvt. practice, Tullahoma, 1956-63; ptnr. Haynes, Wiseman & Hull, Tullahoma and Winchester, Tenn., 1963-71; treas. State of Tenn., 1971-74; ptnr. Chambers & Wiseman, 1974-78; judge U.S. Dist. Ct. (mid. dist.) Tenn., Nashville, 1978—, chief judge, 1984-91, sr. judge, 1995—; rep. 6th cir. Jud. Conf. of the U.S., 1997—, chair dist. judges conf., 1998-99. Mem. Tenn. Ho. of Reps., 1964-68; adj. prof. law Vanderbilt U. Sch. Law. Asso. editor: Vanderbilt Law Rev, 1953-54. Democratic candidate for gov., Tenn., 1974; Chmn. Tenn. Heart Fund, 1973, Middle Tenn. Heart Fund, 1972. Served with U.S. Army, 1954-56. Fellow Tenn. Bar Found.; mem. Fed. Judges Assn. (bd. dirs. 1982-87, v.p. 1992-91, 87-91, 6th cir. rep. to jud. conf. U.S. 1996-2001), Masons (33 deg.), Shriners, Amateur Chefs Soc. Presbyterian. Office: US Dist Ct 777 US Courthouse 801 Broadway Nashville TN 37203-3816

WISHEK, MICHAEL BRADLEY, lawyer; b. Pasadena, Calif., June 25, 1959; s. Homer Cedric and Donna Jean (Arnold) W.; m. Shari Patrice Rubin, June 7, 1981 (div. Feb. 1986); m. Dorothea Jean Palo, Feb. 12, 1988; children: Kirstin Alyce, Lauren Ashley. BS in Polit. Sci and Philosophy, Claremont Men's Coll., 1981; JD, U. Calif., Davis, 1985. Bar: Calif. 1986, U.S. Dist. Ct. (ea. dist.) Calif. 1986. Assoc. Michael S. Sands, Inc., Sacramento, 1986-91; ptnr. Rothschild & Wishek, 1991-96, Rothschild, Wishek & Sands, Sacramento, 1996-2001. Mem. Milton L. Schwartz Am. Inn of Ct., 2000—; adj. instr. trial practice U. Calif., Sch. Law, Davis. Mem. ABA, Calif. Bar Assn., Sacramento County Bar Assn. (co-chmn. criminal law sect. 1988-90), Calif. Attys. for Criminal Justice. Democrat. Avocations: snow skiing, backpacking, sailing. Criminal. Office: 901 F St Ste 200 Sacramento CA 95814-0733

WISHINGRAD, JAY MARC, lawyer; b. Bklyn., Apr. 19, 1949; s. Irving Wishingrad and Phyllis (Leibowitz) Wishingrad Mendelson; m. Susan Leshe, Aug. 9, 1980; 1 child, Mara Ilana. BA, NYU, 1971; JD cum laude, SUNY-Buffalo, 1975. Bar: N.Y. 1976, U.S. Dist. Ct. (so. and ea. dists.) N.Y. 1977, U.S. Sup. Ct. 1979. Law clk. appellate div., 4th dept. N.Y. State Supreme Ct., Rochester, 1975-77; litigation assoc. Kaye, Scholer, Fierman, Hays & Handler, N.Y.C., 1977-84; litigation ptnr. Shapiro, Spiegel, Garfunkel & Driggin, N.Y.C., 1984-86, Frankfurt, Garbus, Klein & Selz, P.C., N.Y.C., 1986—; adj. instr. Benjamin N. Cardozo Sch. Law, Yeshiva U., N.Y.C., 1978-80. Contbr. book revs., articles to profl. jours.; comment editor, Buffalo Law Rev.; columnist New York Law Jour. Mem. N.Y. Lawyers Against The Death Penalty (founding mem.), Assn. of Bar of City of N.Y., Phi Beta Kappa. Federal civil litigation, General civil litigation, Constitutional. Office: McLaughlin & Stern Ballen & Ballen 122 E 42nd St Fl 43 New York NY 10168-4399

WIST, TARJA TUULIA, lawyer; b. Helsinki, Finland, Sept. 25, 1965; d. Pertti Matti-Juhani and Leena Sirkku (Raassina) Lassila; m. Kai Henrik Wist, July 7, 1990; children: Helena, Henrik. LLM, U. Helsinki, Finland, 1989. Assoc. Roschier-Holmberg & Waselius, Helsinki, 1989-97; ptnr. Waselius & Wist, 1997—. Sec. to Legis. Commn. for Securities Market Legislation, 1990-93. Co-author: International Securities Law, 1996, A Practitioner's Guide to Takeovers and Margers in the European Union, 1997, rev. edit., 2000. Mem. Finnish Bar Assn., Legal Soc. Finland, Internat. Bar Assn. Banking, Mergers and acquisitions, Securities. Office: Eteläesplanadi 24A 00130 Helsinki Finland Fax: 358.0.9.6689.5222. E-mail: ww@waselius-wist.fi

WITHERELL, DENNIS PATRICK, lawyer; b. Dec. 15, 1951; s. Thomas William and Kathryn Marie (Savage) Witherell; m. Suzanne Witherell; children: Natalie, Jay. AB with highest honors, U. Mich., 1973; JD summa cum laude, Ohio State U., 1977. Bar: Ohio, U.S. Dist. Ct. (no. dist.) Ohio, U.S. Ct. Appeals (6th cir.). Law clk. U.S. Ct. Appeals (6th cir.), Cin., 1977—78; assoc. Shumaker, Loop & Kendrick, Toledo, 1978—83, ptnr., 1983—. Mem. exec. bd. March of Dimes Birth Defects Found., N.W. Ohio chpt., Toledo, 1978—91, chmn., 1982—84; bd. trustees Kidney Found. of Northwest Ohio, 1988—94, pres., 1992—93; bd. trustee Life Connection of Ohio, 1991—, Vis. Nurse-Extra Care, 1994—99. Mem.: ABA, Am. Health Lawyers Assn., Ohio State Bar Assn. (chmn. health care law com. 1988—92), Toledo Bar Assn, Soc. of Ohiio Hosp. Attys., Nat. Multiple Sclerosis Soc. (bd. trustees Notrthwest Ohio chpt. 1999—). Roman Catholic. Administrative and regulatory, Health, Non-profit and tax-exempt organizations. Home: 2256 Densmore Dr Toledo OH 43606-3167 Office: Shumaker Loop & Kendrick 1000 Jackson St Toledo OH 43624-1573 E-mail: dwitherell@slk-law.com

WITHERS, CARL RAYMOND, lawyer; b. Reading, Pa., Jan. 26, 1924; s. Stuart Snable Withers and Edith Garman; m. Jenny Constance Cory, Sept. 2, 1950; children: Wren, Jill, Bradford. AB, Wittenberg U., 1950; JD, U. Mich., 1953. Bar: Ohio 1954. Pvt. practice, Cleve., 1954—. Former pres. mus. Shaker Hist. Soc., Shaker Heights, Ohio, 1970—; former trustee, treas. N.E. Inter Mus. Coun., Cleve., 1980—; exec. com. Cuyahoga County Rep. Party, Cleve., 1984-94, Fairmount Presbyn. Ch. (former deacon and trustee), Cleve. Soldiers' and Sailors' Monument bd. trustees and sec. Mem. Ohio State Bar Assn. (former coun. of dels. 1955), Cleve. Bar Assn., Am. Legion (Army-Navy Shaker post 54, former commander, adjutant), Gt. Lakes Curling Assn. (treas., pres. 1985-96), Cleve. Grays, Estate Planning Coun. of Cleve., Cleve. Rotary Club, Cleve. City Club, Cleve. Skating Club (former trustee), Shaker Heights Republican Club, Beta Theta Pi (former pres.), Delta Theta Phi. Republican. Presbyterian. Avocation: curling, genealogy, American lithographs. Home: 3419 Courtland Rd Pepper Pike OH 44122-4280 Office: Van Aken Withers & Webster 629 Euclid Ave Cleveland OH 44114-3003

WITHERS, W. WAYNE, lawyer; b. Enid, Okla., Nov. 4, 1940; s. Walter O. and Ruby (Mackey) W.; m. Patricia Ann Peppers, Dec. 12, 1974; children: Jennifer Lynn, Whitney Lee. BA, U. Okla., 1962; JD, Northwestern U., 1965. Bar: Okla. 1965, Mo. 1970, U.S. Ct. Appeals (8th cir.), 1972, U.S. Supreme Ct. 1972, U.S. Ct. Appeals (fed. cir.) 1984, U.S. Ct. Appeals (D.C. cir.) 1985, U.S. Ct. Claims, 1988. Staff atty. FTC, Washington, 1965-68; co. atty. Monsanto Co., St. Louis, 1968-78, asst. gen. counsel, 1978-85; gen. counsel Monsanto Agrl. Co., 1985-89, v.p., gen. counsel; sr. v.p., sec., gen. counsel Emerson Electric Co., 1989—. V.p. Internat. Food Biotech. Coun., Washington, 1989-90; bd. dirs. Internat. Life Scis. Inst., Washington, 1989-90. Contbr. articles to profl. jours. Mem. ABA (sec.

corp. law dept.), Am. Law Inst., Assn. Gen. Counsel, Bar Assn. Met. St. Louis, Indsl. Biotech. Assn. (chmn. law com.), Environ. Law Inst. (assoc.), Nat. Agrl. Chem. Assn. (chmn. law com. 1983-85), The Conf. Bd. Coun. for Gen. Counsel (vice chmn. 1992-99), MAPI Law Coun. Administrative and regulatory, General corporate, Environmental. Office: Emerson Electric Co 8100 W Florissant Ave Saint Louis MO 63136-1494

WITHERWAX, CHARLES HALSEY, lawyer, arbitrator, mediator; b. Schroon Lake, N.Y., July 24, 1934; s. Halsey Jerome and Elizabeth Daisy (Bingham) W.; m. Marianne Jehander, June 24, 1980. BS in Marine Transp., N.Y. State Maritime Coll., 1956; LLB, Union U., 1959. Bar: N.Y. 1962, U.S. Dist. Ct. (so. dist.) N.Y. 1962, U.S. Supreme Ct. 1968, Hawaii 1971, U.S. Dist. Ct. Hawaii 1971, U.S. Ct. Appeals (9th cir.) 1984, U.S. Tax Ct. 1984, Nev. 1991, D.C. 1993, U.S. Ct. Appeals (2d cir.) 1995. Assoc. prof. N.Y. State Maritime Coll., Fort Schuyler, N.Y., 1963-64; asst. v.p., bond claims atty. Chubb Ins. Group, N.Y.C., 1961-70; v.p., gen. counsel Hawaiian Ins. Group, Honolulu, 1970-74; ptnr. Davis, Witherwax, Playdon & Gerson, 1974-78; prin. atty. Witherwax, Pottenger & Nishioka, 1978-91; of counsel D'Amato & Lynch, N.Y.C., 1992—. Author: (manual) Hawaii Construction Law, Mechanics Liens and Bond Claims, 1985, co-author, 1987. Bronx county chmn. N.Y. State Conservative Party, 1962-67; state sec. N.Y. State Conservative Party, 1967-70. Lt. comdr. USNR, 1959-79. Mem. ABA (vice chair fidelity and surety com. 1978-83), Internat. Assn. Def. Counsel. Roman Catholic. Avocations: sailing, travel, golf. Office: D'Amato & Lynch 70 Pine St 37th Fl New York NY 10270-0002 E-mail: www.simpnas2@aol.com

WITKIN, ERIC DOUGLAS, lawyer; b. Trenton, N.J., May 14, 1948; s. Nathan and Norma Shirley (Stein) W.; m. Regina Ann Bilotta, June 8, 1980; children: Daniel Robert, Sarah Ann. AB magna cum laude, Columbia U., 1969; JD, Harvard U., 1972. Bar: N.Y. 1973, D.C. 1989, U.S. Dist. Ct. (so. and ea. dists.) N.Y. 1974, U.S. Ct. Appeals (2d and D.C. cirs.) 1974, U.S. Supreme Ct. 1977, U.S. Dist. Ct. D.C. 1989. Assoc. Poletti, Freidin, Prashker & Gartner, N.Y.C., 1972-80, ptnr., 1980-85; sr. atty. labor Kaye, Scholer, Fierman, Hays & Handler, 1985-88; of counsel Akin, Gump, Strauss, Hauer & Feld, Washington, 1988-90; counsel Benetar, Bernstein, Schair & Stein, N.Y.C., 1990-99; ptnr. Roberts & Finger, LLP, 1999-2001, Greble & Finger, LLP, N.Y.C., 2001, Brown, Raysman, Millstein, Felder, & Steiner LLP, N.Y.C., 2001—. Treas., founder Property Owners Against Unfair Taxation, N.Y.C., 1983-90; trustee Congregation Emanu-El of Westchester, 1996—. Lawrence Chamberlain scholar Columbia U., N.Y.C., 1968; recipient Alumni medal Alumni Fedn. Columbia U., 1982. Mem. ABA (labor and employment law sect.), N.Y. State Bar Assn. (labor and employment law sect., com. on equal employment opportunity law), Assn. of Bar of City of N.Y. (spl. com. on sex and law 1975-82, com. on labor and employment law 1982-85, 92-94), Westchester County Bar Assn., Columbia Coll. Alumni Assn. (pres. 1988-90, bd. dirs. 1974—, Robert Lincoln Carey prize, Alumni prize 1969, Lions award 1990), Alumni Fedn. Columbia U. (alumni trustee nominating com. 1990-97, pres. 1997-99), Am. Soc. Pers. Adminstrn. (contbr. monthly newsletter 1986-88), Soc. Human Resource Mgmt., Soc. Columbia Grads. (bd. dirs. 1994-97), Human Resources Assn. N.Y., Phi Beta Kappa. Club: Harvard (N.Y.C.). Avocations: piano, sailing. Federal civil litigation, State civil litigation, Labor. Home: 103 Wendover Rd Rye NY 10580-1939 Office: Brown Raysman Millstein Felder & Steiner 900 3rd Ave Fl 23 New York NY 10022 E-mail: ewitkin@brownraysman.com, ericwitkin@aol.com

WITMAN, LEONARD JOEL, lawyer; b. N.Y.C., Nov. 7, 1950; s. Seymour and Ruth W.; m. Mona Soled, Aug. 25, 1950; children: Rachel, Leah. BA, Rutgers Coll., 1972; JD, N.Y. Law Sch., 1975. Bar: N.J. 1975, U.S. Dist. Ct. N.J. 1975, U.S. Ct. Appeals (2d cir.) 1975, U.S. Dist. Ct. (so. and ea. dists.) N.Y., 1976, U.S. Tax Ct. 1976. Tax law specialist IRS, Newark, 1975-78; assoc. Lampf, Lipkind, West Orange, N.J, 1978-81; ptnr. Brach, Eichler, Rosenberg, Silver, Bernstein, Hammer & Gladstone, Roseland, N.J., 1981-89, Witman, Stadmauer & Michaels, P.A., Florham Park, 1990—. Adj. law prof. Seton Hall U., N.J., Rutgers U. Grad. Sch. Bus., 1996—. Author: Top Heavy Pension Plans, 1985; contbr. articles to profl. jours. Mem. ABA, N.J. Bar Assn., (chmn. employee benefit com. 1984-86, chmn. taxation sect. 1987-88), Essex County Bar Assn., Morris County Bar Assn. Jewish. Pension, profit-sharing, and employee benefits, Taxation, general. Home: 31 Conkling Rd Flanders NJ 07836-9106 Office: Witman Stadtmauer & Michaels 26 Columbia Tpke Florham Park NJ 07932-2213

WITMER, JOHN HARPER, JR. lawyer; b. Phila., May 5, 1940; s. John Harper and Jane Carolyn (Lentz) Witmer; m. Arlene Marie Rosipal, June 9, 1962; 1 dau., Tara Leah. BA, Pa. State U., 1962; JD, George Washington U., 1969. Bar: Md. 1969, D.C. 1970, Ill. 1979. Mgmt. analyst Nat. Security Agy., Ft. Meade, Md., 1963-66; mem. Sidley & Austin, Washington, 1969-78; sr. v.p., gen. counsel DEKALB Energy Co., 1978-95, DEKALB Genetics Corp., 1978-99; ret., 1999. Mem. Ill. State Bar Assn., Md. State Bar Assn., D.C. Bar Assn. General corporate. Home: 2575 Greenwood Acres Dr Dekalb IL 60115-4916

WITMEYER, JOHN JACOB, III, lawyer; b. New Orleans, Dec. 18, 1946; s. John J. and Thais Audrey (Dolese) W. BS, Tulane U., 1968; JD with distinction, Duke U., 1971. Bar: N.Y. Assoc. Mudge Rose Guthrie & Alexander, N.Y.C., 1971-76; ptnr. Ford Marrin Esposito & Wittmeyer (now Ford, Marrin, Esposito, Witmeyer & Gleser LLP), 1976—. Bd. trustees Gregorian U. Found., 1999—; adv. coun. Paul Tulane Coll., Tulane U., 1998—. Col. U.S. Army; ret. General civil litigation, General corporate. Office: Ford Marrin Esposito Witmeyer & Gleser LLP Wall St Plz New York NY 10005-1875

WITORT, JANET LEE, lawyer; b. Cedar Rapids, Iowa, Mar. 10, 1950; d. Charles Francis Svoboda and Phyllis Harriet (Wilber) Miller; m. Stephen Francis Witort, Oct. 27, 1979. Student, U. Colo., 1968-69, U. Iowa, 1971; BA, U. No. Colo., 1972; JD, Loyola U., 1979. Bar: Ill. 1979, U.S. Dist. Ct. (no. dist.) Ill. 1979, U.S. Dist. Ct. (no. dist.) Ill. 1979, U.S. Supreme Ct. 1987. Paralegal Fed. Nat. Mortgage Assn., Chgo., 1973-75, Sidley & Austin, Chgo., 1975-76; assoc. Frankel, McKay & Orlikoff, 1979-81; atty. Mut. Trust Life Ins. Co., Oak Brook, Ill., 1981-86; assoc. counsel, asst. sec. N.Am. Co. for Life and Health Ins., Chgo., 1986-88; sr. atty. AMA, 1988-89; gen. coun., sec. AMA Ins., 1989-91, v.p. gen. counsel, sec., 1991-93; asst. gen. counsel Prudential Ins. and Fin. Svcs., 1984-98; sr. counsel Allianz Life Ins. Co. of N.Am., 1998—. Author: (with others) The Legal Assistant-A Self Statement, 1974, (with others) Requirements and Limitations Imposed by Corporate Law, 1989, updated, 1992. Vol. Rep. Campaign, Chgo., 1974-76, 90-93, Children's Hosp. Guild, North Oaks, Minn., 1993—, v.p. 1994-95, pres. 1996; vol. Sci. Mus. Minn., St. Paul, 1994—; trustee Hindsdale Ill. Pub. Libr., 1987-93, v.p., 1991-93; bd. dirs. Suburban Libr. Sys., Burr Ridge, Ill., 1988-91, sec. 1990-91; bd. dirs. Children's Hosp. Assn., St. Paul, 1995-96; active Jr. League, St. Paul, 1997—, North Oaks (Minn.) Planning Comm., 2000—; del. Mo. State Rep. Conv., 2000. Mem. ABA, Am. Soc. Med. Assn. Coun., Ill. Bar Assn., Chgo. Assn. Paralegal Assts. (sec. 1973-74), Chgo. Bar Assn. (chair life & health ins. subcom. 1992-93), Womans Bar Assn. of Ill. (mem. ins. com. 1987-93), Ill. Paralegal Assn. (v.p. 1975-76), Nat. Fed. Paralegal Assns. (midwest reg. dir. 1975-76), Am. Corp. Counsel Assn. (membership com. 1988-90), Phi Alpha Delta, Student Bar Assn. (class rep. 1976-77). Republican. Avocations: golf, travel, skiing. General corporate, Insurance, Real property. Office: 1750 Hennepin Ave Minneapolis MN 55403-2115

WITT, CAROL A. lawyer; b. Fremont, Ohio, Nov. 27, 1947; Student, Bowling Green State U., 1965-68; BS, Suffolk U., 1973, JD cum laude, 1977. Bar: Mass. 1977, U.S. Dist. Ct. Mass. 1978, U.S. Dist. Ct. Vt., 1982, U.S. Tax Ct. 1978. Assoc. Louison & Cohen, P.C., Brockton, Mass., 1977-79; ptnr. Louison, Witt & Hensley, P.C., 1979-83; mng. ptnr. Louison & Witt, 1983-96, Law Office of Carol A. Witt, Nantucket, Mass., 1996—. Fellow Am. Acad. Matrimonial Lawyers; mem. ABA, Mass. Bar Assn. (civil litigation sect. coun. 1984-87, chair family law sect. coun. 1990-92), Nantucket County Bar Assn., Women's Bar Assn., Mass. Bar Found. (trustee 1995-96), Mass. Continuing Legal Edn. Inc. (trustee 1992-98). E-mial. State civil litigation, Family and matrimonial. Home: 14 S Mill St Nantucket MA 02554-0308 Office: PO Box 308 Nantucket MA 02554-0308 E-mail: witt@nantucket.net

WITT, JOHN WILLIAM, lawyer; b. Los Angeles, Aug. 30, 1932; s. John Udo and Alice (Westervelt) W.; m. Lenora Jane Ticknor, Sept. 1, 1961; children: John David, Stephanie Anne Witt Mills, William Westervelt. AB, U. So. Calif., 1954, JD, 1960. Bar: State Bar Calif. 1961, U.S. Dist. Ct. (ctrl. dist.) Calif. 1961, U.S. Dist. (so. dist.) Calif. 1967, U.S. Supreme Ct. 1969. Dep. city atty. City of San Diego, 1961-64, chief criminal dep. city atty., 1964-67, chief dep. city atty., 1967-69, city atty., 1969-96; spl. counsel Lounsbery Ferguson Altona & Peak, LLP, San Diego, 1996—. Contbr. articles to profl. jours. Bd. dirs. Boys and GirlsClubs San Diego, 1972—, pres., 1985-87; bd. dirs. St. Paul's Episcopal Home, Inc., San Diego, 1982-88, 97—; exec. bd. San Diego County Council Boy Scouts Am, 1970-81, chmn. leadership tng. com., 1970-73, Bicentennial chmn., 1974-76, chmn. Jamboree com., 1977; bd. dirs. San Diego Armed Svc. YMCA, 1997—, Boys & Girls Found. San Diego, 1998—, San Diego Mus. Man, 2000—; chair San Diego County Election Campaign Fin. Control Commn., 2001—. Served with USMC, 1954-57, col. res. ret. Recipient Golden Achievement award Boys and Girls Clubs San Diego, 1989; named Pub. Lawyer of Yr. San Diego County Bar Assn., 1986, Disting. Eagle Scout Boy Scouts Am., 1975. Mem. ABA (state and local govt. law sec., coun. mem. 1980-84, 85-89, 96-98, chair 1992-93, mem. ho. dels. 1993-96, Nelson award 1996), Internat. Mcpl. Law Officers Assn. (pres. 1985-86, trustee 1976-87, Outstanding Nat. Pub. Svc. award 1986), League Calif. Cities (bd. dirs. 1985-96), League Calif. Cities City Atty.'s Dept. (pres. 1976-77), Calif. Dist. Attys. Assn. (bd. dirs. 1980-82), Southwestern Legal Found. (adv. bd. mem. mcpl. legal studies ctr. 1981—), State Bar Calif. (exec. com. pub. law sect. 1980-83), San Diego County Bar Assn. (chair pub. lawyers com. 1997-98), San Diego Lions Club (trustee welfare found. 1983-87, 90-97, chair 1992-93, pres. 1990-91, Diocesan standing com. 1974-78, 82-86, Diocesan bd. dirs. 1998—, dep. to gen. conv. 1985-97), Phi Alpha Delta. Republican. Episcopalian. Avocations: writing, travel, sports. E-mail: jwwitt@home.com

WITT, WALTER FRANCIS, JR. lawyer; b. Richmond, Va., Feb. 18, 1933; s. Walter Francis and Evelyn Virginia (Riggleman) W.; m. Rosemary Winter, Sept. 5, 1964; children: Leslie Anne Millman, Walter Francis III. BS, U. Richmond, 1954, JD, 1966. Bar: Va. 1966, D.C. 1974. Assoc. Hunton and Williams, Richmond, 1966-74, ptnr., 1974—. Contbr. articles to profl. jours. 1st lt. U.S. Army, 1955-57. Mem. ABA (chmn. real property com. sect. gen. practice 1995-2000, Va. Bar Assn., Richmond Bar Assn., D.C. Bar Assn., Phi Beta Kappa, Phi Delta Phi. General corporate, General practice, Real property. Home: 8901 Tresco Rd Richmond VA 23229-7725 Office: Hunton & Williams Riverfront Plaza East Twr 451 E Byrd St Richmond VA 23218-1535

WITTELS, BARNABY CAESAR, lawyer, writer; b. Phila., Mar. 28, 1948; s. David G. and Beatrice Tanya (Graitcr) W.; m. Heidi Jo Linsk, Sept. 8, 1974 (div. Aug. 1997); children: Kate Sophie, William David; m. Mary M. Labaree, Sept. 20, 1998. BA cum laude, Temple U., 1970; MA in Pol. Sci., Boston U., 1972, JD, 1975. Bar: Pa. 1975, U.S. Dist. Ct. (ea. dist.) Pa. 1985, U.S. Ct. Appeals (2d, 3d and 4th cir.) 1986. Asst. defender Defender Assn. of Phila., 1975-80; law clk. to Hon. Stanley Kubacki Ct. Common Pleas Phila. County, 1980-84; ptnr. Wittels, Newman & Bornstein, Phila., 1980-82; assoc. LaCheen & Alva, 1982-86; ptnr. LaCheen & Assoc., 1986—. Contbr. column to newspapers. Chair Northwest Victim Svcs., Phila., 1981-84, mem. counsel, 1984-90, mem. bd. dirs., 1983-90, chair, 1997— (outstanding svc. & leadership 1990), founding mem.; com. man 21st Divsn. Dem. Party, Phila., 1985-90, various polit. and jud. campaigns, 1980—; baseball coach Chestnut Hill Fathers Club, 1985-98, commr. 1991-93, 92-98; mem. exec. com. Northwest Interfaith Movement, 1985-86. Mem. NACDL, Pa. Assn. Criminal Def. Lawyers, Phila. Bar Assn. (fee dispute com. 1996—, mem. com. to elect good judges 1987-88, Pa. Bar Assn., Phila. Bar Found. (Apothaker award 1983). Democratic. Jewish. Avocations: writing, baseball, football, reading, woodworking. Appellate, Federal civil litigation, Criminal. Office: LaCheen & Assoc 3100 Lewis Tower Bldg Philadelphia PA 19102 Fax: 215 735-4649. E-mail: barnabyw@aol.com

WITTEN, ROGER MICHAEL, lawyer; b. Atlantic City, N.J., Nov. 13, 1946; s. H. Davis and Miriam P. (Popkin) W.; m. Jill S. Judd, June 5, 1971; children— Wendy D., Katherine J. A.B., Dartmouth Coll., 1968; J.D., Harvard U., 1972. Bar: D.C. 1973, U.S. Supreme Ct. 1976, numerous other fed. cts. Law clk. to judge U.S. Ct. Appeals (4th cir.), Balt., 1972-73; asst. spl. prosecutor Watergate Spl. Prosecution Force, Washington, 1973-74; ptnr. Wilmer, Cutler & Pickering, Washington, 1975—; chmn. Litigation Group Counsel Common Cause, Washington, 1983—. Served with U.S. Army, 1968-74. Mem. ABA, D.C. Bar Assn. Administrative and regulatory, General civil litigation, Criminal. Office: Wilmer Cutler & Pickering 2445 M St NW Ste 500 Washington DC 20037-1487

WITTENBRINK, JEFFREY SCOTT, lawyer; b. Cairo, May 24, 1960; s. Howard Samuel and Cherie Ellen (Martin) W.; m. Tamara Inez Parker, Aug. 5, 1989; children: Charlotte Jane, Jeffrey Scott Jr. BA, La. State U., 1984, JD, 1987. Bar: La. 1988, U.S. Dist. Ct. (ea. and mid. dists.) La. 1988, U.S. Dist. Ct. (we. dist.) La. 1989, U.S. Ct. Appeals (5th cir.) 1989, U.S. Supreme Ct. 1996. Law clk. to Judge William H. Brown, 19th Jud. Dist. Ct., Baton Rouge, 1987-88; assoc. Roy, Kiesel, Aaron & Tucker, 1988-91, Winston G. DeCuir & Assocs., Baton Rouge, 1991-93; pvt. practice Wittenbrink Law Firm, 1993—. Arbitrator Baton Rouge City Ct., 1993—; instr. CPCU's, Baton Rouge, 1991, Office Emergency Planning State of La., 1993. Contbr. articles to Around the Bar legal newsletter, 1987—. Coach debate team Cath. H.S., Baton Rouge, 1987-91, mock trial team Baton Rouge H.S., 1989-93; treas. Ingleside United Meth. Ch., Baton Rouge, 1991-92, trustee, bd. dirs., 1991—, chair pastor-parish com., 1992-2000, lay leader, 2001; mem., lectr. La. Vol. Lawyers for Arts, Baton Rouge, 1988—; bd. dirs. La. Crafts Coun., Baton Rouge, 1990—. Mem. ABA, ATLA, La. Bar Assn., Baton Rouge Bar Assn. (mem. newsletter com. 1987—, vol. indigent panel 1992—, chair CLE 1992—, chmn. membership com. 1993, chair Law Expo com. 1998, Pres.'s award 1993, Triple Century award 2001), Dean Henry George McMahon Am. Inn of Ct. (barrister, reporter 1993-95), Cortana Kiwanis (bd. dirs. 1994-97, pres. 1998-99, Lt. Gov. 2001-2002, Kiwanis Internat., La.-Miss.-W.Tenn. Dist. Divn. 8-B). Avocations: photography, fencing, writing. General civil litigation, Family and matrimonial, Personal injury. Office: 533 Europe St Baton Rouge LA 70802-6408 E-mail: jwbrink@aol.com

WITTIG, RAYMOND SHAFFER, lawyer, technology management advisor; b. Allentown, Pa., Dec. 13, 1944; s. Raymond Battie and Alice (Shaffer) W.; m. Beth Glover, June 21, 1975; children: Meaghan G., Allison G. BA, Pa. State U., 1966, MEd, 1968; JD, Dickinson Sch. Law, 1974. Bar: Pa. 1974, U.S. Ct. Appeals (D.C. cir.) 1978. Rsch. psychologist Intext Corp., Scranton, Pa., 1968; minority counsel Small Bus. Com., U.S. Ho. Reps., Washington, 1975-84; pvt. practice, 1984-92; tech. mgmt. group leader Geo-Ctrs., Inc., Newton Ctr., Mass., 1992—. Capt. U.S. Army, 1969-71. Mem. AAAS, ABA, Nat. Order Barristers, Tech. Transfer Soc., Fed. Lab. Consortium. Administrative and regulatory, Government contracts and claims, Legislative. E-mail: wittigsall@aol.com

WITTLINGER, TIMOTHY DAVID, lawyer; b. Dayton, Ohio, Oct. 12, 1940; s. Charles Frederick and Dorothy Elizabeth (Golden) W.; m. Diane Cleo Dominy, May 20, 1967; children: Kristine Elizabeth, David Matthew. BS in Math., Purdue U., 1962; JD with distinction, U. Mich., 1965. Bar: Mich. 1966, U.S. Dist. Ct. (ea. dist.) Mich. 1966, U.S. Ct. Appeals (6th cir.) 1968, U.S. Supreme Ct. 1971. Assoc. Clark Hill (formerly Hill Lewis), Detroit, 1965-72, ptnr., 1973—, head litigation dept., 1976-91, gen. counsel, 1997—. Mem. profl. assistance com. U.S. Dist. Ct. (ea. dist.) Mich., 1981-82; mem. Mich. Supreme Ct. Com. to Evaluate Mediation Ct. Rule, 1997-98; author, lectr. Ctr. for Internat. Legal Studies, 1999—. Mem. ho. of deps. Episc. Ch., N.Y.C., 1979—; vice chmn. Robert Whitaker Sch. Theology, 1983-87; sec. bd. trustees Episc. Ch., Diocese of Mich., Detroit, 1983—, sec. conv. Episc. Diocese of Mich., 1990—, ch. atty., 1997—, mem., sec. Episc. nat. econ. justice implementation com., 1988-95, mem. Episc. nat. exec. coun., 1991-97, mem. nat. audit com.; mem. Nat. Standing Commn. on Ministry Devel., 2000—; active Nat. Episc. Jubilee Ministry Com., Nat. Episc. Coalition for Social Witness and Justice, Fifth Province Episc. Ecclesiastical Ct. Appeal; mem. nat. audit com. Episcopal Ch.; bd. dirs. Episc. Student Found., U. Mich., 1990-93, 2000—; chair Grubb Inst. Behavioral Studies Ltd., Washington, 1986—; bd. dirs. Birmingham Village Playhouse, 2000—. Mem. ABA, State Bar Mich., Nat. Bd. Trial Advocacy (cert.), Engring. Soc. Detroit. General civil litigation, Alternative dispute resolution, Professional liability. Home: 736 N Glenhurst Dr Birmingham MI 48009-1143 Office: Clark Hill 500 Woodward Ave Ste 3500 Detroit MI 48226-3435

WLADIS, MARK NEIL, lawyer; b. Elizabeth, N.J., May 18, 1964; s. George L. and Roberta W. (Wolgin) W.; m. Diane F. Wladis, Nov. 18, 1990; children: Jacqueline P., Harrison S. BA, Muhlenberg Coll., 1986; JD, Syracuse U., 1989, LLM in Taxation, 1993. Bar: N.Y. 1990, Fla. 1995, U.S. Dist. Ct. (no. dist.) N.Y. 1991, U.S. Tax Ct. 1992. Tax assoc. Coopers & Lybrand, Syracuse, N.Y., 1989-90; assoc. Nottingham, Engel, Gordon & Kerr, 1991-92; ptnr. Melvin & Melvin, LLP, 1993-99, Devorsetz Stinziano Gilberti Heintz & Smith, P.C., Syracuse, 2000—. Vice-chmn Trustee Onandaga C.C., 2001-; bd. dirs. Ctrl. N.Y. Lupus Soc., Syracuse, 1992-94, Jewish Fedn., Syracuse, 1996—. Mem. Lafayette Golf and Country Club (bd. dirs. 1994-95). E-mial. General corporate, Probate, Taxation, general. Office: Devorsetz Stinziano Gilberti Heintz & Smith PC 555 E Genesee St Syracuse NY 13202-2157 E-mail: mwladis12@msn.com

WOHL, JAMES PAUL, lawyer, educator, author; b. N.Y.C., Oct. 3, 1937; s. Joseph and Mae (Kreshover) W.; m. Sigrid Elenor Sletteland, June 6, 1969 (div. Feb. 1979); children— Frederic, Kristin, Jenifer. Student Princeton U., 1955-57; A.B., Stanford U., 1962, J.D., 1963. Bar: Calif. 1963, Hawaii 1964, N.Y. 1969. Assoc. Carlsmith, Carlsmith, Wichman & Case, Honolulu, 1963-68, Fried, Frank, Harris, Shriver & Jacobson, N.Y.C., 1968-70; pres. Hawaii Land Corp., Honolulu, 1970-78; prof. law Laverne San Fernando Law Ctr., Sepulveda, Calif., 1978— ; bd. dirs. Original N.Y. Seltzer Can., Ltd.; chmn. bd. European Original N.Y. Seltzer Ltd., 1986—. Author novels: The Nirvana Contracts, 1977; Talon, 1978; The Blind Trust Kills, 1979. Bd. dirs. Salvation Army, Hilo, Hawaii, 1964-67; pres. Hawaii Media Adv. Council, 1975-76. Mem. Mystery Writers Am., West Hollywood C. of C. (dir. 1983—). Clubs: Princeton (N.Y.C.); Hilo Yacht. Home: 21 Old Barrack Yard London SW1 England Office: Golderown House Saint Albans Mews London W218Y England

WOHLFORTH, ERIC EVANS, lawyer; b. N.Y.C., Apr. 17, 1932; s. Robert Martin and Mildred Campbell (Evans) W.; m. Caroline Penniman, Aug. 3, 1957; children: Eric Evans, Charles Penniman. AB, Princeton U., 1954; LLB, U. Va., 1957. Bar: N.Y. 1958, Alaska, 1967. Assoc. Hawkins, Delafield & Wood, N.Y.C., 1957-66; ptnr. McGrath & Wohlforth, Anchorage, 1966-70; commr. revenue State of Alaska, 1970-72; ptnr. McGrath, Wohlforth & Flint, 1972-74, Wohlforth & Flint, Anchorage, 1974-87, Wohlforth, Argetsinger, Johnson & Brecht, Anchorage, 1988-98, Wohlforth, Vassar, Johnson & Brecht, Anchorage, 1999—. Mem. Alaska Investment Adv. Com., 1973-80. Chancellor Episcopal Diocese of Alaska, 1972—; mem., trustee, vice-chair Alaska Permanent Fund Corp., 1995—, chmn., 1997-99. Mem. Alaska Bar Assn., Assn. of Bar of City of N.Y. Finance, Municipal (including bonds). Home: 7831 Ingram St Anchorage AK 99502-3965 Office: 900 W 5th Ave Ste 600 Anchorage AK 99501-2044

WOHLSCHLAEGER, FREDERICK GEORGE, lawyer; b. St. Louis, Jan. 3, 1951; s. Elmer H. and Rosalie (Gruet) W.; m. Mary L. Heck, Jan. 3, 1976; 1 child, Kathryn M. AB, Princeton U., 1973; JD, St. Louis U., 1976. Bar: Mo. 1976, Ohio 1980. Assoc. Rassieur, Long et al, St. Louis, 1976-77; atty. Monsanto Co., 1977-80, Std. Oil Co., Cleve., 1980-90; v.p. legal affairs Morton Internat., Chgo., 1990-97; sr. v.p., gen. counsel, sec. Hartmarx Corp., 1997-2000; sr. v.p., gen. counsel, sec., interim CFO Maytag Corp., 2000—. Bd. dirs. Inland Corp., Cleve., Mid-Valley Pipeline Co., Tulsa, Miami Valley Corp., Cleve. General corporate, Finance, Mergers and acquisitions.

WOJCIECHOWSKI, MARC JAMES, lawyer; b. Wiesbaden, Germany, June 1, 1965; came to U.S., 1969; s. William Alios and Theresa Lorraine W.; m. Mary Hood, Aug. 11, 1990. BS in Criminal Justice summa cum laude, Southwest Tex. State U., 1987; JD, U. Houston, 1990. Bar: Tex. 1990, U.S. Dist. Ct. (so. dist.) Tex. 1992, U.S. Ct. Appeals (5th cir.) 1998. Assoc. Weller, Wheelus & Green, Beaumont, Tex., 1990-91, Wetzel & Herron, LLP, The Woodlands, 1991-95; ptnr. Herron, Williamson & Wojciechowski, LLP, Houston, 1995-97; prin. Wojciechowski & Assocs., PC, 1998—. Mem. The Woodlands Cmty. Assn., 1991—. Recipient scholarship award Tex. Assn. Police Chiefs, 1985-86. Mem. Tex. Assn. Def. Counsel. Roman Catholic. Avocations: racquetball, weight lifting, jogging, travelling. General civil litigation, Contracts commercial, Insurance. Office: Wojciechowski & Assocs PC 2 Northpoint Dr Ste 450 Houston TX 77060-3227

WOLAVER, STEPHEN ARTHUR, lawyer; b. Springfield, Ill., Sept. 4, 1950; s. Lynn Ellsworth and Arah Dean Phyllis (Scheele) W.; m. Gayla Sue Howard, Feb. 28, 1987; children: Lindy Allison, Scott. BS, Miami U., Oxford, Ohio, 1972; JD, Valparaiso U., 1975. Bar: Ohio 1975, U.S. Dist. Ct. (so. dist.) Ohio 1976, U.S. Ct. Appeals (6th cir.) 1997, U.S. Tax Ct. 1990, U.S. Supreme Ct. 1979. Ptnr. Gill, Wolaver & Welch, Fairborn, Ohio, 1975-81; asst. pros. atty. Greene County (Ohio), Xenia, 1976—, chief trial counsel, 1989—; ptnr. Wolaver, Sheets & Lewis, Fairborn, 1981—. Instr. Fairborn Bd. Edn., 1978—; adj. prof. Clark Tech. Coll., 1979-85; instr. Greene County Law Enforcement Police Acad., 1988—; faculty Nat. Advocacy Ctr. U. So. Carolina, 2001; lectr., 1982—, mem. law enforcement adv. com., 1983-86; advisor Fairborn (Ohio) H.S. Mock Trial Team, 1987-96. Greene County campaign chmn. Gov. Rhodes re-election com., 1978, 86, Voinovich for U.S. Senate; mem. Greene County Rep. Ctrl. Com., 1978—; youth counselor Bethlehem Luth. Ch., Fairborn, 1980-96, head usher com. pres. Rona Village Homeowners Assn., 1981; pres. Greene County Rep. Club, 1999-2000. Named one of Outstanding Young Men Am., Jaycees, 1981, Greene County Legal Secs. Boss of Yr. award, 1985, Outstanding Asst. Prosecutor of Yr. award Ohio Pros. Attys. Assn., 1998.

Mem. Greene County Bar Assn. (sec./treas. 1997, v.p. 1998, pres. 2000), Ohio Bar Assn., Assn. Trial Lawyers Am., Nat. Dist. Attys. Assn., Miami U. Alumni Assn., Sertoma (pres. 1982-83), Delta Tau Delta. Criminal, Probate, Estate taxation. Home: 3792 Westwind Dr Dayton OH 45440-3500 Office: Wolaver Sheets & Lewis Attys 1 1/2 S Central Ave Fairborn OH 45324-4790

WOLF, ALAN STEVEN, lawyer; b. Jersey City, Jan. 5, 1955; s. Lester Joel and Beatrice (Spiegel) W.; m. Donna Snow Wolf, Aug. 31, 1980; children: Lauren, Bradley. BA, Dartmouth Coll., 1977; JD, Southwestern U., L.A., 1980. Bar: Calif. 1980, U.S. Dist. Ct. (no., so., ea. and cen. dists.) Calif. 1980. With Alvarado, Rus & McClellen, Orange, Calif., 1981-84; ptnr. Cameron Dreyfuss & Wolf, 1984-89; pres. Gordon & Wolf, Newport Beach, Calif., 1989-91, Wolf & Pfeifer, Newport Beach, 1991-97, Wolf & Richards, Newport Beach, 1997—. Pres., founding dir. Laguna Beach (Calif.) Pop Warner Football, 1995-99, sec., 1996; chief Indian Princess Tribe, Laguna Beach, 1993; charter bd. dirs. Irvine Swim League, 1985. Mem. U.S. Foreclosure Network (bd. dirs. 1990-95, Com. Mem. of Yr. 1994), Calif. Mortgage Bankers Assn. (chmn. legal issues com. 1994-95), Dartmouth Club (pres. Orange County club 1991); fellow Am. Coll. Mortgage Attys. Avocations: computers, Internet. Bankruptcy, Finance, Real property. Office: The Wolf Firm 18 Corporate Plaza Dr Newport Beach CA 92660-7901

WOLF, BRUCE, lawyer; b. Phila., Dec. 16, 1955; s. Charles and Mary (Saionz) W. BA, Temple U., 1977; JD, Drake U., 1981. Bar: Pa. 1981, U.S. Dist. Ct. (ea dist.) Pa. 1981, U.S. Ct. Appeals (3d cir.) 1981. Assoc. LaCheen & Alva, Phila., 1981-88; pvt. practice, 1989—. Mem. Fed. Criminal Justice Act Panel, Phila., 1998—. Committeeman Phila. Dem. Party 63rd ward, 1994-2000. Mem. Phila. Bar Assn., Pa. Assn. Criminal Def. Lawyers. Democrat. Jewish. Criminal, Family and matrimonial, General practice. Office: 612 S 6th St 1st Fl Philadelphia PA 19147-2108 Fax: (215) 922-2194. E-mail: bwolf.esq@erols.com

WOLF, CHRISTOPHER, lawyer; b. Washington, Feb. 8, 1954; s. Alexander Jr. and Miriam (Auerbach) W. Student, London Sch. Econs., 1974-75; AB cum laude, Bowdoin Coll, 1976; JD magna cum laude, Washington and Lee U., 1980. Bar: D.C. 1980, U.S. Dist. Ct. D.C. 1980, U.S. Dist. Ct. (ea. dist.) Wis. 1985, U.S. Ct. Claims, 1985, U.S. Ct. Appeals (fed. cir.), U.S. Supreme Ct., U.S. Ct. Internat. Trade. Law clk. to presiding justice U.S. Dist. Ct. D.C., Washington, 1980-82; assoc. Arnold & Porter, 1982-86, Ballard, Spahr, Andrews & Ingersoll, Washington, 1986-88, ptnr., 1988-89, Proskauer Rose LLP, Washington, 1989—. Chmn. bd. dirs. Anti-Defamation League; bd. dirs. Boys and Girls Clubs, Greater Washington, Nat. Symphony Orch., Washington, Friends Assisting Nat. Symphony Orch., Washington, 1986—. Mem. ABA (chmn. subcom. on legis., pretrial practice com., litigation sect.), Fed. Bar Assn., Am. Soc. Internat. Law, Washington Council Lawyers, Order of Coif. Democrat. Avocations: music, running. Antitrust, Civil rights, Federal civil litigation. Home: 4618 Charleston Ter NW Washington DC 20007-1911 Office: Proskauer Rose LLP 1233 20th St NW Washington DC 20036 E-mail: cwolf@proskauer.com

WOLF, DIANE R. law consultant; b. Cheyenne, Wyo., Mar. 16, 1954; d. Erving and Joyce Wolf. BA in Gen. Lit., U. Pa., 1976; MA in Early Childhood Edn., Columbia U., 1980; JD, Georgetown U., 1995. Dir. vols. Reagan-Bush '84 Nat. Campaign, N.Y.C., 1984; commr. U.S. Commn. on Fine Arts, Washington, 1985-90; originator Operation Desert Fax, 1990-91; intern to Chief Judge Abner J. Mikva U.S. Ct. Appeals (D.C. cir.), 1994. Cons. Sen. Alan Cranston, Washington, 1990-92, UN Sec. Gen. Boutros Boutros-Ghali, N.Y.C., 1996; mem. adv. bd. U.S. Capitol Preservation Commn., Washington, 1992—. Mem. Madison coun. acquisitions com. Libr. Congress, Washington, 1995—. Recipient award of appreciation Soc. U.S. Commemmorative Coins, 1987-88. Mem. ABA, Ctrl. States Numismatic Assn. (hon. life) Jewish. Home: 28 E 73rd St New York NY 10021-4143

WOLF, G. VAN VELSOR, JR. lawyer; b. Balt., Feb. 19, 1944; s. G. Van Velsor and Alice Roberts (Kimberly) W.; m. Ann Holmes Kavanagh, May 19, 1984; children: George Van Velsor III, Timothy Kavanagh (dec.), Christopher Kavanagh, Elisabeth Huxley. BA, Yale U., 1966; JD, Vanderbilt U., 1973. Bar: N.Y. 1974, U.S. Dist. Ct. (so. dist.) N.Y. 1974, U.S. Ct. Appeals (2d cir.) 1974, Ariz. 1982, U.S. Dist. Ct. Ariz. 1982, U.S. Ct. Appeals (9th cir.) 1982. Agrl. advisor U.S. Peace Corps., Tanzania and Kenya, 1966-70; assoc. Milbank, Tweed, Hadley & McCloy, N.Y.C., 1973-75; vis. lectr. law Airlangga U., Surabaya, Indonesia, 1975-76; editor-in-chief Environ. Law Reporter, Washington, 1976-81; assoc. Lewis & Roca, Phoenix, 1981-84, ptnr., 1984-91, Snell & Wilmer, Phoenix, 1991—. Vis. lectr. law U. Ariz., 1990, Vanderbilt U., 1991, U. Md., 1994, Ariz. State U., 1995; cons. Nat. Trust Hist. Preservation, Washington, 1981. Editor: Toxic Substances Control, 1980; editor in chief Environ. Law Reporter 1976-81; contbr. articles to profl. jours. Bd. dirs. Ariz. divsn. Am. Cancer Soc., 1985—96, sec., 1990—92, vice-chmn., 1992—94, chmn., 1994—96, bd. dirs. S.W. divsn., 1996—, chmn., 1996—98, nat. bd. dirs., 1999—; bd. dirs. Herberger Theater Ctr., 1998—, sec., 2001—; bd. dirs. Phoenix Little Theatre, 1983—90, chmn., 1986—88. Recipient St. George medal Am. Cancer Soc., 1998. Mem. ABA (vice-chmn. SONREEL commn. state and regional environ. coop. 1995-98, co-chmn. 1998-2000, vice-chmn. environ. audits task force 1998-99, vice-chmn. SONREEL ann. meeting planning com. 1998-99), Assn. of Bar of City of N.Y., Ariz. State Bar Assn. (coun. environ. & nat. res. law sect. 1988-93, chmn. 1991-92, CLE com. 1992-98, chmn. 1997-98), Maricopa County Bar Assn., Ariz. Acad., Union Club N.Y.C., Univ. Club Phoenix, Phoenix Country Club. Environmental, Legislative. Office: Snell & Wilmer 1 Arizona Ctr Phoenix AZ 85004-0001 E-mail: vwolf@swlaw.com

WOLF, GARY WICKERT, lawyer; b. Slinger, Wis., Apr. 19, 1938; s. Leonard A. and Cleo C. (Wickert) W.; m. Jacqueline Weltzin, Dec. 17, 1960; children: Gary, Jonathan. BBA, U. Minn., 1960, JD cum laude, 1963. Bar: N.Y. 1964, U.S. Ct. Appeals (2d cir.) 1969, U.S. Dist. Ct. (so. dist.) N.Y. 1969, U.S. Supreme Ct. 1971. Assoc. Cahill, Gordon & Reindel, N.Y.C., 1963-70, ptnr., 1970—. Bd. dirs. N.J. Resources Corp., N.J. Natural Gas Co. Mem. N.Y. State Bar Assn. (com. on securities regulation), Anglers Club (N.Y.C.), Downtown Assn. (N.Y.C.), Mashomack Fish and Game Club. General corporate, Finance, Mergers and acquisitions. Home: 35 Fieldstone Dr Basking Ridge NJ 07920-1605 Office: Cahill Gordon & Reindel 80 Pine St Fl 17 New York NY 10005-1790

WOLF, JEROME THOMAS, lawyer; b. Austin, Minn., June 13, 1937; s. William B. and Charlotte Elaine (Rosenstock) W.; m. Ellen L., Jan. 9, 1965; children: Margo Ann, Gregory Thomas. BA, Yale U., 1959; JD, Harvard U., 1962. Bar: Minn. 1962, Mo. 1966, Kans. 1984. Ptnr. Sonnerschein, Nath & Rosenthal, Kansas City, Mo., 1994—, mng. ptnr., mem. firm mgmt. com., 1994-2000, chmn. firm mktg. com., 1999—. Chmn. Jewish Cmty. Rels. Bur. Kansas City, 1973—79, 2001—; mem. CPR commn. on future of arbitration Best Lawyers in Am. Capt. JAGC U.S. Army, 1962—66. Mem.: Kansas City Bar Assn. (pres. 1979), Kansas City Bar Found. (founding, pres. 1979—80), Mo. Bar, ABA, Phi Beta Kappa. Democrat. Federal civil litigation, State civil litigation. Home: 2411 W 70th Ter Shawnee Mission KS 66208-2741 Office: 4520 Main St Ste 1000 Kansas City MO 64111 E-mail: jw@sonnerschein.com

WOLF, MARK LAWRENCE, federal judge; b. Boston, Nov. 23, 1946; s. Jason Harold and Beatrice (Meltzer) W.; m. Lynne Lichterman, Apr. 4, 1971; children: Jonathan, Matthew. BA cum laude, Yale U., 1968; JD cum laude, Harvard U., 1971; hon. degree, Boston Latin Sch., 1990. Bar: Mass. 1971, D.C. 1972, U.S. Supreme Ct. 1976. Assoc. Surrey, Karasik & Morse, Washington, 1971-74; spl. asst. to dep. atty. gen. U.S. Dept. Justice, 1974-75, spl. asst. to atty. gen., 1975-76, dep. U.S. atty. Boston, 1981-85; from assoc. to ptnr. Sullivan & Worcester, 1977-81; judge U.S. Dist. Ct. Mass., 1985—. Lectr. Harvard U. Law Sch., Cambridge, Mass., 1990—; adj. prof. Boston Coll. Law Sch., 1992. Bd. dirs. Albert Schweitzer Fellowship, Boston, 1974—, pres., 1989-97, chmn., 1997—; chmn. John William Ward Fellowship, Boston, 1986—. Recipient cert. appreciation U.S. Pres., 1975, Disting. Service award U.S. Atty. Gen., 1985. Mem. Boston Bar Assn. (council 1982-85), Am. Law Inst. Office: US Dist Ct 1 Courthouse Way Boston MA 02210-3002

WOLF, MARSHALL JAY, lawyer; b. Cleve., Nov. 20, 1941; s. Sol J. and Ruth (Shapiro) W.; m. Judith Shermer, Ja. 29, 1967; children: Randi Caryn Sussman, Robert Howard. BA, Miami U., 1964; JD, Case Western Reserve U., 1967. Bar: Ohio 1967, U.S. Dist. Ct. (no. dist.) Ohio 1969. Law clk. to Common Pleas Ct. Cuyahoga County, Ohio, 1967-69; assoc. Metzenbaum, Gaines, Finley & Stern, Cleve., 1969-75; ptnr., dir. Metzenbaum, Gaines & Stern, 1975-81, Schwarzwald, Robiner, Wolf & Rock, Cleve., 1981-88, Wolf & Akers, Cleve., 1988—. Chief U.S. del., 1st World Congress Family Law and Children's Rights, Sydney, Australia, 1993. Editor: (with others) Managing Clients & Cases, 1986; contbr. articles to profl. jours. Trustee, Temple on the Heights, Pepper Pike, Ohio, 1971-81; mem. Cuyahoga County Dem. Exec. Com., Cleve., 1972-76; pres. Univ. Hts. Dem. Com., 1974-76. Fellow Am. Acad. Matrimonial Lawyers (pres. Ohio chpt.), Internat. Acad. Matrimonial Lawyers; mem. ABA (family law sect. coun. 1984—, chair 1992-93, house dels. 2000—), Ohio Acad. Trial Lawyers (chmn. family law com. 1976-77, Disting. Svc. award 1977), Cuyahoga County Bar Assn. (chmn. family law sect. 1981-84). Family and matrimonial. Home: 3958 W Meadow Ln Cleveland OH 44122-4775 E-mail: mjwolf@sprintmail.com

WOLF, MARTIN EUGENE, lawyer, educator; b. Balt., Sept. 9, 1958; s. Eugene Bernard and Mary Anna (O'Neil) W.; m. Nancy Ann Reinsfelder, May 9, 1980; children: Matthew Adam, Allison Maria, Emily Elizabeth. BA, Johns Hopkins U., 1980; JD, U. Md., 1991. Bar: Md. 1991, U.S. Dist. Ct. Md. 1992, U.S. Ct. Appeals (4th cir.) 1992, U.S. Ct. Appeals (2d cir.) 1993, U.S. Ct. Appeals (3d cir.) 1998, U.S. Ct. Appeals (11th cir.) 2000, U.S. Ct. Fed. Claims 2001. Mgmt. trainee Giant Foods, Inc., Landover, Md., 1980-82, dept. mgr., 1982-83, ops. analyst, 1983-86, fin. coord., 1986-89; law clk. Piper & Marbury, LLP, Balt., 1989-91, assoc., 1991-96; prin. Law Office of Martin E. Wolf, Abingdon, Md., 1996-99; ptnr. Quinn, Gordon & Wolf Chartered, Towson, 2000—. Dir. Giant Food Fed. Credit Union, Landover, 1984-89; pres. Stalagmite Properties, Ltd., Abingdon, Md., 1995-96; tchg. asst. U. Md. Sch. Law, Balt., 1992-94, adj. prof., 1996—. Pres. bd. dirs. Chesapeake Search & Rescue Dog Assn., Inc., 2000—. Mem. ABA, Md. State Bar Assn., Harford County Bar Assn., Harford County Bar Found. (Vol. Svc. award 1992, 94). Democrat. Roman Catholic. Avocations: Lacrosse, hockey. Appellate, General civil litigation, Condemnation. Home: 11 Mitchell Dr Abingdon MD 21009-1628 E-mail: mwolf@auinnlaw.com

WOLF, MICHAEL JAY, lawyer; b. Buffalo, Feb. 12, 1955; s. Ernest and Vivienne Francis (Hotz) W.; m. Patricia Jeanne Mabry, 1988. BA with distinction, U. Wis., 1977; JD, Washington U., St. Louis, 1982. Bar: Mo. 1982, Tex. 1986. Exec. dir. Community Youth Services, Sun Prairie, Wis., 1976-79; staff mem. com. on post office and civil svc. U.S. Ho. of Reps., 1982; asst. counsel, nat. counsel Nat. Treasury Employees Union, Austin, Tex. and Washington, 1982-93; spl. asst. ot the dir., program mgr., commr., fed. mediator Fed. Mediation and Conciliation Svc., 1993—. Mediator Dispute Resolution Ctr., Austin, 1985-93, Farmers Home Adminstrn. Roster of Mediators, 1989-93; arbitrator Nat. Panel Consumer Arbitrators Better Bus. Bur., 1984-93, U.S. Dist. Ct. (we. dist.) Tex., 1989; arbitrator, mediator Tex. Dist. Cts., Austin, 1989; bd. dirs. Coll. of Tex. Mediators, Travis County Dispute Resolution Ctr., Conflict Prevention and Resolution Svcs.; cons. bus., labor, govt. and cmty. orgns.; chair Alamo Fed. Exec. Bd, Shared Neutrals Consortium, 2000—; mem. adv. com. on mediator credentialing and ethics Tex. Supreme Ct., 1996-99. Author: Involve Your Bar in ADR, 1988, Voter Participation Project, 1986, Health and Safety in the Workplace, 1988, Court-Annexed Arbitration, Working With the Judiciary, 1990, Settlement Week, 1990; co-author: (radio drama) Museum of Consumer Horrors, 1980, Teacher's Guide to Law-Related Education, 1982; contbr. articles to profl. jours. Exec. dir. High Sch. Law Project, St. Louis, 1980-82; active Corp. of Execs., SBA, 1987-93. Recipient Tribute to Outstanding Achievement award Star Countryman, 1978, Community Service award Rotary Club, 1979; grantee Wis. Council on Criminal Justice, 1977-78, United Way of Dane County, 1978-79 Mem. ABA (gen. practice sect., vice chair com. on alt. dispute resolution 1991—, young lawyers div., liaison to ABA standing com. on dispute resolution 1991-93, crime victim svcs. com. 1982-87, vice-chmn. 1986-87, vice chmn. affiliate outreach project subcom. 1986-87, exec. com. alternative dispute resolution 1982-91, vice-chmn. 1987-90, chmn. 1990-91, nat. confs. 1987-88, chmn. subgrant com. 1988-89, publs. 1987-90, citizenship edn. 1982-86, labor law com. 1985-87, 89-91), Mo. Bar Assn., St. Louis Bar Assn. (chmn. subcom. 1981), Soc. Fed. Labor Relations Profls, State Bar of Tex. (alt. dispute resolution sect. 1987—, chmn. subcom. on funding and legis. 1989-91, pub. policy com. 1991-92, adv. com. to Tex. senate interim com. on alternative dispute resolution 1991-93), Tex. Young Lawyers Assn. (alt. dispute resolution com. 1987-91), Travis County Bar Assn. (alt. dispute resolution com. and continuing legal edn. com. 1987-93, subcom. on arbitration selection and tng. 1989-91, subcom. on Settlement Week 1989-91, subcom. on mediator selection and tng. 1990-91, chmn. 1990), Austin Young Lawyers Assn. (task force on professionalism dispute resolution 1992-93), Alamo Area Mediators Assn., San Antonio Personnel Mgmt. Assn. Democrat. Jewish. Avocations: raquetball, guitar, music, travel, theater. Office: Fed Mediation and Conciliation Svc 10500 Hwy 281 N Ste 115 San Antonio TX 78216 E-mail: mjwolfsa@umpire.com

WOLF, RICHARD V. lawyer; b. Paris, 1962; DrIur, U. Vienna, 1985; LLM, Harvard U., 1986. 2d v.p. Chase Manhattan Bank, Austria, 1992-93; M&A mgr. Crédit Lyonnais, Austria, 1993-94; ptnr. Wolf Theiss & Ptnrs., Austria, 1994—. Served with Austrian Army, 1980-81. Fulbright scholar, 1985-86. Mem. Internat. Bar Assn. Banking, Mergers and acquisitions, Securities. Office: Wolf Theiss & Ptnrs Schubertring 6 A-1010 Vienna Austria

WOLF, WAYNE LOWELL, criminal justice educator, researcher; b. Evergreen Park, Ill., June 2, 1947; s. Joseph John and Vivian Irene (Knuth) W.; m. Claudia Ann Johnson, Nov. 26, 1977; children— Bret W., Kristy L., Stacey W. B.A., U.S. Fla., Tampa, 1967, M.A., 1970; M.A.P.A., Governors State U., University Park, Ill., 1976; Ed.D., No. Ill. U., 1982. Sgt. Hazel Crest Police Dept., Ill., 1973-76; prof. criminal justice Thornton Community Coll., South Holland, Ill., 1976— ; adj. prof. Webster U., St. Louis, 1977— , Columbia Coll., St. Louis, 1978— , Calumet Coll., Whiting, Ind., 1982— ; owner Wolf Cons. Ltd., South Holland, 1980— . Recipient Palmer award for excellence in current affairs. Author: The Gin Bottle Riot of 1968, 1975; From Clergyman to Professional: A History of American Law Enforcement. Editor: Readings in Crime and Delinquency, 1982. Precinct capt. Republican Party, Cook County, Ill., 1976-83. Mem. Fraternal Order Police, Kappa Delta Pi, Roman Catholic. Office: Thornton Community Coll 15800 State St South Holland IL 60473-1200

WOLFE, CAMERON WITHGOT, JR. lawyer; b. Oakland, Calif., July 7, 1939; s. Cameron W. and Jean (Brown) W.; m. Frances Evelyn Bishopric, Sept. 2, 1964; children: Brent Everett, Julie Frances, Karen Jean. AB, U. Calif., Berkeley, 1961, JD, 1964. Bar: Calif. 1965, U.S. Dist. Ct. (no. dist.) Calif. 1965, U.S. Ct. Appeals (9th cir.) 1965, U.S. Tax Ct. 1966, U.S. Ct. Claims 1977, U.S. Ct. Appeals (3d cir.) 1980, U.S. Supreme Ct. 1986. Assoc., then ptnr. Orrick, Herrington & Sutcliffe, San Francisco, 1964—. Bd. dirs. Crowley Maritime Corp.; mem. steering com. Western Pension Conf. Pres. League To Save Lake Tahoe, 1979, 80; chmn. League To Save Lake Tahoe Charitable Truste, 1966-91, Piedmont Ednl. Fund Campaign, 1982-83; pres. Piedmont Ednl. Found., 1986-90; bd. dirs. Yosemite Fund, 1993—. With U.S. Army, 1957; with USAR, 1957-65. Mem. ABA (taxation com.), Calif. State Bar, San Francisco Bar Assn., San Francisco Tax Club (pres. 1997-98), Pacific Union Club, Claremont Country Club (Oakland, Calif.), Order of Coif, Phi Beta Kapa. Pension, profit-sharing, and employee benefits, Corporate taxation. Home: 59 Lakeview Ave Piedmont CA 94611-3514 Office: Orrick Herrington & Sutcliffe 400 Sansome St San Francisco CA 94111-3143

WOLFE, DAVID LOUIS, lawyer; b. Kankakee, Ill., July 24, 1951; s. August Christian and Irma Marie (Nordmeyer) W.; m. Gail Lauret Fritz, Aug. 25, 1972; children: Laura Beth, Brian David, Kaitlin Ann. BS, U. Ill., 1973; JD, U. Mich., 1976. Bar: Ill. 1976, U.S. Dist. Ct. (no. dist.) Ill. 1976. Assoc., Gardner, Carton & Douglas, Chgo., 1976-82, ptnr., 1983—; lectr. estate planning Aid Assn. for Lutherans SMART Program, Chgo., 1980-84; lectr. Ill. Inst. Continuing Legal Edn., Chgo. Bar Assn., Lake Shore Nat. Bank, Ill. State Bar Assn. Contbr. articles to legal publs. Recipient Recognition award Ill. Inst. Continuing Legal Edn., 1981-84. Mem. ABA (sects. on taxation, corp. banking and bus. law 1981—, lectr.), NFL Players Assn. (cert. contract advisor 1983—), NCAA (cert. contract advisor), Chgo. Assn. Commerce and Industry (employee benefit subcom. 1983—), Ill. State Bar Assn. (employee benefits sect. council, 1986-95, recognition award 1983), Phi Kappa Phi, Beta Alpha Psi, Beta Gamma Sigma, Sigma Iota Lambda, Phi Eta Sigma. E-mail: dwolfe@gcd.com. General corporate, Pension, profit-sharing, and employee benefits, Corporate taxation. Office: Gardner Carton & Douglas 321 N Clark St Ste 3300 Chicago IL 60610-4720

WOLFE, DEBORAH ANN, lawyer; b. Detroit, May 4, 1955; d. Adam and Mary A. (Smyth) Wolfe; m. Lester D. McDonald, May 23, 1987; children: Molly, Thomas. Student, Ariz. State U., Tempe, 1973-76; BA in Polit. Sci., Bus., Tex. Christian U., Ft. Worth, 1977; postgrad., So. Meth. U., 1977-78; JD, U. San Diego, 1980; grad., Gerry Spence's Trial Lawyers Coll., 1999. Bar: Calif. 1981, Ariz. 1982. Sole practice, San Diego, 1981-83; ptnr. Kremer & Wolfe, 1983-86; assoc. D. Dwight Worden, Solana Beach, Calif., 1986-89; pvt. practice San Diego, 1989-91; owner Wolfe & McDonald, 1991-96; shareholder Nugent & Newnham, San Diego, 1996—. Instr. San Diego Inn of Ct. Evidence, 1988-95. Floutist San Diego City Guard Band, 1981-93, Grossmont Sinfonia, La Mesa, 1982-83, Classical/Chamber Music Quartet, San Diego, 1983-87, Foothills United Meth. Ch. band, 1997—; leader Girl Scouts. Named one of Lawyers of the Yr. Calif. Lawyer Mag., 1996. Mem. Assn. Trial Lawyers Am., Consumer Attys. Calif., Consumer Attys. San Diego (pres. 1996, Outstanding Trial Lawyer award 1996, 2000, Trial Lawyer of Yr. award 1996), Lawyers Club (San Diego), San Diego Trial Lawyers Assn. (Outstanding Trial Lawyers award 1987), Am. Inns of Ct. (master), Nat. Bd. Trial Advocates. Insurance, Personal injury, Professional liability. Office: Nugent & Newnham 1010 2nd Ave Ste 2200 San Diego CA 92101-4911

WOLFE, HARRIET MUNRETT, lawyer; b. Mt. Vernon, N.Y., Aug. 18, 1953; d. Lester John Francis Jr. and Olga Harriet (Miller) Munrett; m. Charles Briant Wolfe, Sept. 10, 1983. BA, U. Conn., 1975; postgrad., Oxford (Eng.) U., 1976; JD, Pepperdine U., 1978. Bar: Conn. 1979. Assoc. legal counsel, asst. sec. Citytrust, Bridgeport, Conn., 1979-90; v.p., sr. counsel, asst. sec. legal dept. Shawmut Bank Conn., N.A., Hartford, 1990-96, pvt. practice, 1996-97; sr. v.p., gen. counsel, sec. Webster Fin. Corp., Waterbury, Conn., 1997—. Govt. rels. com. Electronic Funds Transfer Assn., Washington, 1983—. Mem. ABA, Conn. Bar Assn. (mem. legis. com. banking law sect.), Conn. Bankers Assn. (trust legis.com.), Guilford Flotilla Coast Guard Aux., U.S. Sailing Assn., Phi Alpha Delta Internat. (Frank E. Gray award 1978, Shepherd chpt. Outstanding Student award 1977-78). Banking, General corporate, Securities. Home: 621 Northwood Dr Guilford CT 06437-1124 Office: Webster Fin Corp Webster Plaza Waterbury CT 06702 E-mail: hwolfe@websterbank.com

WOLFE, J. MATTHEW, lawyer; b. Pitts., Mar. 29, 1956; s. James Michael and Mary Evangeline (Andrews) W.; m. Deborah Ann Smith, Oct. 2, 1982; children: James M. Jr., Ross M. BA, U. Pa., 1978; JD, Villanova U., 1981. Bar: Pa. 1981, U.S. Dist. Ct. (ea. dist.) Pa. 1985, U.S. Ct. Appeals (3rd cir.) 1985, U.S. Supreme Ct., 1992, U.S. Dist. Ct. (we. dist.) Pa. 1997. Atty. Cmty. Legal Svcs., Phila., 1981-82; pvt. practice, 1981-82, 89-95, 97-99; asst. counsel Pa. Dept. of Transp., Phila, 1983-86; spl. prosecutor Pa., 1984-86; spl. asst. dist. atty. Berks County, Reading, 1984-86; dep. atty. gen. Commonwealth of Pa., Phila., 1986-89; spl. asst. dist. atty., 1991-92; chief counsel Pa. Dept. Law and Industry, 1995-97; atty. Law Offices of Alice Ballard, 1998—. Gen. counsel Univ. Bus. Machines, Inc., Upper Darby, Pa., 1989-95; instr. Pa. Bar Inst., Harrisburg, 1984; Pa. workers compensation rules com. Pa. Dept. Laor & Industry, 1995-97, Pa. Worker's Compensation Fraud task force, 1996-97. Assoc. editor The Docket newspaper, 1980-81; contbr. articles to The Univ. City Trumpet newspaper, 1981-95. Ward leader 27th Ward Rep. Com., Phila., 1979—; bd. dirs. University City Town Watch, 1983-85; mem. Spruce Hill Cmty. Assn., Phila., 1980—, bd. dirs., 1982-96, 99—; chmn. Univ. City Rep. Com., 1990-96; mem. Sch. Bd. Task Force on Scholastics and Sports, Phila., 1986, Cedar Park Neighbors, 1986—; mem. neighborhood adv. coun. 19th Police Dist., Phila., 1987-93; vice chmn. Woodland Dist. Phila. coun. Boy Scouts Am., 1989-91; Eucharistic min. St. Francis de Sales Parish, 2000—, catechist confraternity of Christian doctrine program, 1995—, lector. Mem. ABA, Pa. Bar Assn. (mem. com. legal ethics and profl. responsibility 1986-95), Phila. Bar Assn. (mem. com. labor and employment law, instr. 1995), West Phila. C. of C. (bd. dirs. 1989-95, gen. counsel 1993-95, 98—), Pi Sigma Alpha, Phi Delta Theta (editor Phi Oracle newsletter). Roman Catholic. Home: 4256 Regent Sq Philadelphia PA 19104-4439 Office: 1700 Lewis Tower 225 South 15th St Philadelphia PA 19102 E-mail: matthew@wolfe.org

WOLFE, JAMES RONALD, lawyer; b. Pitts., Dec. 10, 1932; s. James Thaddeus and Helen Matilda (Corey) W.; m. Anne Lisbeth Dahle Eriksen, May 28, 1960 (dec. 1996); children: Ronald, Christopher, Geoffrey; m. Patricia D. Yoder, Oct. 30, 1999. B.A. summa cum laude, Duquesne U., 1954, DHL (hon.), 1997; LL.B. cum laude, NYU, 1959. Bar: N.Y. 1959. Assoc. Simpson Thacher & Bartlett, N.Y.C., 1959-69, ptnr., 1969-95, counsel, 1996-99. Co-editor: West's McKinney's Forms, Uniform Commercial Code, 1965. Served to 1st lt. U.S. Army, 1955-57. Mem. Assn. Bar City N.Y. Roman Catholic. Home: 500 SE 5th Ave Apt 601 Boca Raton FL 33432-5510 Office: Simpson Thacher & Bartlett 425 Lexington Ave New York NY 10017-3954

WOLFE, JOHN LESLIE, lawyer; b. Cuyahoga Falls, Ohio, Dec. 6, 1926; s. Leslie George and Phyllis (Bond) W.; m. Barbara Lou Carle, Dec. 27, 1950 (div.); children: David, Karla. AB, U. Akron, 1950; JD, U. Mich., 1953. Bar: Ohio 1953, U.S. Dist. Ct. (no. dist.) Ohio 1955, U.S. Ct. Appeals (6th cir.) 1966, U.S. Supreme Ct. 1970. Sole practice, Akron, 1953-56; asst. pros. atty. Summit County, 1956-57; assoc. Hershey & Browne, 1957-61, ptnr., 1961-85, Wolfe, Williams & Abdenour, Akron, 1986-90; sole practice, 1991—. Asst. atty. gen. State of Ohio, 1971-74; adj.

prof. trial practice U. Akron, 1975-80; counsel Tri County Regional Planning Commn. of Portage, Summit and Medina Counties, 1960-74. Trustee Akron Law Libr., 1961—; past pres. Progress Through Preservation. Served with U.S. Army, 1945-47. Recipient Ohio Legal Ctr. Inst. award of merit, 1966. Mem.: ABA, ATLA, Ohio State Bar Assn., Akron Bar Assn., Ohio Acad. Trial Lawyers, Nat. Employment Lawyers Assn. General civil litigation, Pension, profit-sharing, and employee benefits, Insurance. Office: National City Center 1 Cascade Plz Ste 740 Akron OH 44308-1154

WOLFE, RICHARD BARRY MICHAEL, lawyer; b. N.Y.C., Dec. 25, 1932; s. Herman E. and Florence (Cohen) W.; m. Lilyan Aren, June 8, 1957; children— Brian, Stacey. BA, Alfred U. (N.Y.), 1954; JD, Bklyn. Law Sch., 1957; postgrad. Practicing Law Inst., N.Y.C. Bar: N.Y. 1960. Gen. counsel to Katz, Leidman, Grossman, Wolfe & Freund, N.Y.C., 1970— . Tchr. high sch. (nights) various Jersey Temples; lectr. various synagogues, N.Y., N.J. councilman Matawan Twp. (N.J.), 1974-78, Aberdeen Twp. (N.J.), 1984— . Editor county newspaper of Dem. Party, 1972-73. With USAR, 1959-65. Recipient U.S. Naval Base Care award, 1981, Kiwanis award, 1979. Mem. N.Y. Workers Compensation Bar Assn. (trustee), N.Y. County Bar Assn. (labor com. 1979), Assn. Bar City N.Y. (young lawyers com. 1973), ABA (young lawyers com. 1965), Assn. Trial Lawyers Am. (young lawyers com.), Elks. Jewish. Administrative and regulatory, Securities, Workers' compensation. Home: 1629 Starling Dr Sarasota FL 34231-9121 Office: 80 Wall St Ste 614 New York NY 10005-3601

WOLFE, ROBERT SHENKER, retired lawyer; b. Quanah, Tex., May 29, 1945; s. William Shenker and Hortense (Goldbas) Asher; m. Ellyn Helene Peska, Nov. 3, 1979. B.A., Hamilton Coll., 1967; postgrad. MIT, 1969-70; J.D., Boston U., 1970. Bar: N.Y. 1970, U.S. Dist. Ct. (no. and ea. dists.) N.Y. 1970, U.S. Ct. Appeals (1st cir.) 1970, Mass. 1971, U.S. Dist. Ct. Mass. 1971. Assoc. firm Kaplan, Latti & Flannery, Boston, 1970-73; prin. Sriberg, Berman & Wolfe, Boston, 1973-76; propr. Wolfe Assocs., Boston, 1976— ; trial counsel Ricklefs & Uehlein, Boston, 1976-85 ; pres., bd. dir. Meditor Systems, Inc., Boston; vis. prof. admiralty law Suffolk, Boston, 1972-73; pres. bd. dirs. Sports Mgmt. Internat. Inc., 1988. Bd. dirs. Alchemic Art Gallery, Ipswich River Watershed Assn.; mem. growth planning subcom. Manchester Planning Bd., 1986, mem. bd. health, 1987—; pro bono vol. environ. issues Lawyers Referral Svc., 1975— . pres., bd. dirs. Heritage Preservation, Inc., Boston, 1983— . Author: Power, Pollution and Pub. Policy, 1971. Mem. Assn. Trial Lawyers Am., Mass. Bar Assn., Univ. Club. Jewish. Admiralty, Insurance, Personal injury. Office: Wolfe Assocs PO Box 1424 Manchester MA 01944-0852

WOLFF, DEBORAH H(OROWITZ), lawyer; b. Phila., Apr. 6, 1940; d. Samuel and Anne (Manstein) Horowitz; m. Morris H. Wolff, May 15, 1966 (div.); children: Michelle Lynn, Lesley Anne; m. Walter Allan Levy, June 7, 1987. BS, U. Pa., 1962, MS, 1966; postgrad., Sophia U., Tokyo, 1968; JD, Villanova U., 1979, LLM, 1988. Tchr. Overbrook H.S., Phila., 1962-68; homebound tchr. Lower Merior Twp., Mongomery County, 1968-71; asst. dean U. Pa., Phila., 1975-76; law clk. Stassen, Kostos and Mason, 1977-78; assoc. Spencer, Sherr, Moses and Zuckerman, Norristown, Pa., 1980-81; ptnr. Wolff Assocs., Phila., 1981—. Lectr. law and estate planning, Phila., 1980—. Founder Take a Brother Program; bd. dirs. Germantown Jewish Ctr.; h.s. sponsor World Affairs Club, Phila., 1962-68; mem. exec. com., sec. bd. Crime Prevention Assn., Phila., treas., bd. dirs., 1965—; v.p. bd. dirs. U. Pa. Alumnae Bd., Phila., 1965—, pres. bd. dirs., 1993—, v.p. organized classes, bd. crime prevention; chmn. urban conf. Boys Club Am., 1987, treas., 1999; active Hahnaman Brain Tumor Rsch. Bd.; v.p., bd. dirs. Crime Prevention; treas. Assn. of Alumnae Bd. Recipient 3d Ann. Cmty. Svc. award Phila. Mayor's Com. for Women, 1984; named Pa. Heroine of Month, Ladies Home Jour., 1984. Mem. Lions (pres. Germantown Club 1997—). General corporate, Probate, Taxation, general. Home and Office: 422 W Mermaid Ln Philadelphia PA 19118-4204

WOLFF, ELROY HARRIS, lawyer; b. N.Y.C., May 20, 1935; s. Samuel and Rose Marian (Katz) W.; children: Ethan, Anna Louise. A.B., Columbia U., 1957, LL.B., 1963. Bar: N.Y. 1963, D.C. 1969. Assoc. Kaye, Scholer, Fierman, Hays & Handler, N.Y.C., 1963-65; atty.-adviser to commr. FTC, Washington, 1965-67; sr. trial atty. Dept. Transp., 1967-69; assoc. Leibman, Williams, Bennett, Baird & Minow, Washington, 1969-70, ptnr., 1970-72, Sidley & Austin, Washington, 1972-99, sr. counsel, 2000—. Mem. adv. com. on practice and procedure FTC, 1969-71; chmn. adv. com. on procedural reform CAB, 1975 Served to 1st lt. USAF, 1957-60. Mem. ABA (chmn. spring meeting program 1992-94, coun. 1995-98), Union Internationale des advocats (chmn. competition law com. 1994-98), Army and Navy Club. Administrative and regulatory, Antitrust, Federal civil litigation. Office: Sidley Austin Brown & Wood 1501 K St NW Washington DC 20005-1403 E-mail: ewolff@sidley.com

WOLFF, FLORIAN, lawyer; b. Bochum, Germany, July 1, 1968; married. Law Degree, J.W. Goethe U., Frankfurt, Germany, 1993. Trainee German Law Firm, Moscow, 1995; assoc. Rossbach & Fischer, Frankfurt, 1996-98, ptnr., 1998—. Co-editor: Fax and Business Law Guide, Germany, 2001-. Computer, General corporate, , Antitrust. Office: Rossbach & Fischer Schaumainkai 101-103 Frankfurt 60596 Germany Fax: (0049) 69 631571 99. E-mail: wolff@rolaw.de

WOLFF, FRANK PIERCE, JR. lawyer; b. St. Louis, Feb. 27, 1946; s. Frank P. and Beatrice (Stein) W.; m. Susan Scallet, May 11, 1984; children: Elizabeth McLane, Victoria Hancox. BA, Middlebury Coll., 1968; JD, U. Va., 1971. Bar: Mo. 1971, U.S. Ct. Appeals (5th cir.) 1974, U.S. Ct. Appeals (8th cir.) 1975, U.S. Supreme Ct. 1975. Ptnr. Lewis, Rice & Fingersh, St. Louis, 1971-90; ptnr., sect. leader, bus. and transactional counseling sect., mem. oper. group Bryan Cave LLP, 1990—. Bd. dirs. Wood Ceilings, Inc. Bd. dirs. Leadership St. Louis, 1985-88, Washington U. Child Guidance Clinic, St. Louis, 1976-79, Jewish Family and Children's Svc., St. Louis, 1981-83, John Burroughs Sch., 1995-2000, BJC Health Sys., Inc., 1998—, The Butterfly House, 2001—; gen. counsel Mo. Bot. Garden, St. Louis, 1981—, Mo. Hist. Soc., St. Louis, 1997—; spl. counsel Saint Louis Symphony Soc., 1989—; trustee St. Louis Children's Hosp., 1995—, chairperson mission vision and values com., 1996-97, mem. exec. com., 1997-99; co-chmn. Parks Task Force, 2004 Inc. . Capt. USAR, 1968-76. Mem. ABA, Mo. Bar Assn., Bar Assn. Met. St. Louis (chmn. corp. sect. 1984-85), Noonday Club, Westwood County Club (chmn. fin. com. 1989-91, treas. 1989-91, v.p. 1991-93, pres. 1993-95, exec. com. 1989-95). Antitrust, General corporate, Non-profit and tax-exempt organizations. Home: 17 Clerbrook Ln Saint Louis MO 63124-1202 Office: Bryan Cave 211 N Broadway Ste 3600 Saint Louis MO 63102-2733

WOLFF, KURT JAKOB, lawyer, director; b. Mannheim, Germany, Mar. 7, 1936; s. Ernest and Florence (Marx) W.; m. Sanda Lynn Dobrick, Dec. 28, 1958; children; Tracy Ellin, Brett Harris. AB, NYU, 1955; JD, U. Mich., 1958. Bar: N.Y. 1958, U.S. Supreme Ct. 1974, Hawaii 1985, Calif. 1988. Atty. pvt. practice, N.Y.C., 1958-2000; assoc. Hays, Sklar & HErzberg, 1958-60; sr. assoc. Nathan, Mannheimer, Asche, Winer & Friedman, 1960-65, Otterbourg, Steindler, Houston & Rosen, N.Y.C., 1965-68, sr. ptnr., 1968-70, dir., treas., 1970—, CEO, 1982-99, gen. counsel, 1999. Spl. master N.Y. Supreme Ct., 1977-85; vol. master U.S. Dist. Ct. (so. dist.) N.Y., 1978-82. Lectr., U. Mich. Law Sch.; mem. com. of visitors U. Mich. Law Sch., 1993—; spl. mediator Dept. Disciplinary Com. Appellate Divsn. First Judical Dept., 1991-99. Contbr. articles to profl. jours. Mem. ABA (chmn. ins. com. econs. sect. 1980-82, editor arbitratino newsletter, arbitration com. sect. litigation), N.Y. State Bar Assn. (lectr.), Am. Arbitration Assn. (arbitrator), N.Y.C. Bar Assn. (arbitration com. 197-83, state cts. of superior jurisdiction com. 1983-86, mem. com. legal edn. & admission to the bar 1991-94), Hawaii State Bar Assn., Calif. State Bar Assn., Gen. Arbitration Coun. Textile Industry N.Y.C., Fed. Bar Coun. Federal civil litigation, State civil litigation, Contracts commercial. Home: 4 Juniper Ct Armonk NY 10504-1356 also: 48-641 Torrito Ct Palm Desert CA 92260 also: John Hancock Bldg 175 E Delaware Pl Apt 6504 Chicago IL 60611-7731 Office: 230 Park Ave New York NY 10169-0005

WOLFF, MICHAEL A. state supreme court judge; Grad., Dartmouth Coll., 1967; JD, U. Minn., 1970. Lawyer Legal Svcs.; mem. faculty St. Louis U. Sch. Law, 1975-98; judge Mo. Supreme Ct., 1998—. Chief counsel to gov., 1993-94, spl. counsel, 1994-98. Co-author: Federal Jury Practice and Instructions. Chief counsel to Gov. St. Louis, 1993-94, spl. counsel, 1994-98. Office: Supreme Ct MO PO Box 150 Jefferson City MO 65102-0150*

WOLFF, PAUL MARTIN, lawyer; b. Kansas City, Mo., July 22, 1941; s. Joseph L. and Eleanor B. Wolff; m. Rhea S. Schwartz, Oct. 9, 1976. BA, U. Wis., 1963; LLB, Harvard U., 1966. Bar: D.C. 1968, U.S. Ct. Appeals (D.C. and 2d cir.) 1968, U.S. Supreme Ct. 1975, U.S. Ct. Appeals (10th and fed. cirs.) 1981, U.S. Ct. Appeals (8th cir.) 1982, U.S. Tax Ct. 1982, U.S. Ct. Claims 1984. Law clk. to Judge James R. Durfee U.S. Ct. Claims, Washington, 1966-67; assoc. Williams & Connolly, 1967-75, ptnr., 1976—. Adj. prof. Catholic U. Law Sch., 1970-73. Co-author: Forensic Sciences; contbr. articles to legal jours. Bd. dirs. Washington Coun. for Civil Rights Under Law, 1980-90, Renwick Alliance, Washington, 1987-93, Am. Jewish Com., Washington, 1988-92, Washington Legal Clinic for Homeless, 1988-99, Opportunities for Older Ams. Found., 1988-92, Washington Performing Arts Soc., 1990—, Emeritus Found., 1992-99; vice chmn. D.C. Pub. Charter Schs. Resource Ctr., 1999—; dir. D.C. Sports Commn., 1994-2000; dir. Com. Pub. Edn., 1994-99; trustee Fed. City Coun., bd. trustees, 1996—; dir. Am. U., Corcoran Mus. of Art, overseer, 1997—. Mem. Georgetown Club, Econ. Club Washington (dir.), Phi Beta Kappa. Democrat. Avocations: photography, gardening, fly fishing, sculpting. Banking, Federal civil litigation, General civil litigation. Home: 4770 Reservoir Rd NW Washington DC 20007-1905 also: Oak Ridge Warrenton VA 20186 Office: Williams & Connolly 725 12th St NW Washington DC 20005-5901 Fax: 202-434-5580. E-mail: pwolff@wc.com, dcpmw@aol.com

WOLFORD, RICHARD HOWARD, lawyer; b. Chgo., Aug. 12, 1922; s. Darwin H. and Lila (Ferguson) W.; m. Helen Moore, Feb. 13, 1943; children: Richard George, Felicia Jane, Peter Arlington. AB, Harvard U., 1944, JD, 1948. Bar: Calif. 1949. Law clk. U.S. Ct. Appeals 9th Cir., San Francisco, 1948-49; sr. ptnr. Gibson, Dunn & Crutcher, L.A., 1963-80, of counsel, 1981—. Mem. Calif. Law Revision Commn., L.A., 1968-70; adj. prof. law (antitrust) U. Hawaii Law Sch., 1983. Pres. L.A. Jr. Bar Assn., 1957-58. Mem. ABA, Hawaii State Bar Assn., L.A. County Bar Assn. (trustee 1957-58), L.A. Country Club. Home: 3101 Old Pecos Tr 661 Santa Fe NM 87505-9025

WOLFRAM, CHARLES WILLIAM, law educator; b. Cleve., Feb. 28, 1937; s. Carl P. and Dona M. (Minitch) W.; m. Nancy Russell Bass, Dec. 18, 1965; children: Catherine Dana, Peter Russell. AB, Notre Dame U., 1959; LLB, U. Tex., 1962. Bar: D.C. 1962, Minn. 1974. Assoc. Covington & Burling, Washington, 1962-64; mem. FAA Contract Appeals Panel, 1964-65; asst. prof. law U. Minn., 1965-67, assoc. prof., 1967-70, prof., 1970-81; prof. law Cornell U., Ithaca, N.Y., 1982-84, Charles Frank Reavis Sr. prof. law, 1984-99, Charles Frank Reavis Sr. prof. emeritus, 1999—. Assoc. dean acad. affairs Cornell U., Ithaca, 1986-90, interim dean, 1998-99; vis. prof. U. So. Calif. Law Center, 1976-77. Author: (with J. Morris Clark) Professional Responsibiltiy: Issues for Minnesota Attorneys, 1976, Modern Legal Ethics, 1986; contbr. chpts. to books, articles to profl. jours. Mem. Am. Law Inst. (chief reporter Restatement of Law Governing Lawyers 2000), Order of Coif. Democrat. Office: Cornell Law Sch 106 Myron Taylor Hall Ithaca NY 14853-4901 E-mail: charles-wolfram@postoffice.law.cornell.edu

WOLFSON, JEFFREY STEVEN, lawyer; b. Worcester, Mass., Jan. 9, 1954; s. Jack L. and Marcia (Paul) W.; m. Judy Rosen, Oct. 25, 1981. AB summa cum laude, Tufts U., 1976; JD, Yale U., 1979. Bar: Mass. 1979, U.S. Dist. Ct. Mass. 1980, U.S. Ct. Appeals (1st cir.) 1980. Assoc. Goulston & Storrs, P.C., Boston, 1979-86, ptnr., 1986—. Clk. Malden Mills Industries, Inc., Lawrence, Mass., 1981-90. Author: Practice Points for the Family Business Corporate Lawyer, 1996. Bd. dirs. Performers Ensemble, Inc., Boston, 1985-89; bd. advisors Northeastern U. Ctr. Family Bus., 1991—, chmn., 1995-99. Mem. ABA, Boston Bar Assn., Phi Beta Kappa. General corporate, Entertainment, General practice. Home: 140 Whitman Rd Needham MA 02492-1021 Office: Goulston & Storrs PC 400 Atlantic Ave Boston MA 02110-3333 E-mail: jwolfen@govlstonstorrs.com

WOLFSON, WARREN DAVID, lawyer, specialty retail store company executive; b. Syracuse, N.Y., Mar. 2, 1949; s. Isaiah Wolfson and Rosalind (Rothman) Gingold; separated; children: Scott E., Tara N., Lynn T. BSBA, Boston U., 1970; JD, Syracuse U., 1974. Bar: N.Y. 1975, U.S. Tax Ct. 1975, U.S. Ct. Claims 1975, U.S. Ct. Appeals (2d cir.) 1975. Assoc., Hancock & Estabrook, Syracuse, 1974-80; sec. Fay's Inc., Liverpool, N.Y., 1980—, gen. counsel, 1981—, v.p., 1983-89, sr. v.p., 1989—; bd. dirs. Syracuse Label Co., Inc; bd. dirs. Drug Quiz Show, Inc. Bd. dirs., sec., treas. Fay's Found., Liverpool, 1982—; mem. adv. coun. Inst. for Sensory Rsch., Syracuse U., 1991—; bd. dirs. Jewish Home of Ctrl. N.Y. Mem. ABA, Am. Corp. Counsel Assn., Nat. Assn. Chain Drug Stores (mem. govtl. affairs com.), Lafayette Country Club. General corporate, Mergers and acquisitions, Securities. Office: Fay's Inc 7245 Henry Clay Blvd Liverpool NY 13088-3523

WOLFSON, WILLIAM STEVEN, lawyer; b. Bronx, N.Y., Dec. 6, 1951; s. Irving and Harriet (Levine) W.; m. Barbara L Libensperger, Aug. 19, 1979. B.A. in English Lit., Temple U., 1973; J.D., Del. Law Sch., 1976. Bar: N.J. 1976, U.S. Dist. Ct. N.J. 1976, U.S. Ct. Appeals (3rd cir.) 1979, U.S. Tax Ct. 1981, U.S. Supreme Ct. 1986. Assoc., John E. Weinhofer, Flemington, N.J., 1976-78; sole practice, Flemington, 1978-81, 88—; ptnr. Wolfson & Knee, Flemington, 1981-88; mem. N.J. Supreme Ct. Com. on County Dist. Ct. Practice, 1980-82; adj. faculty real estate law Raritan Valley Coll. Mem. environ. commn. Raritan Twp. Environ. Commn., 1976-79; mem. exec. com. Hunterdar County Reps.; bd. dirs. Hunterdon County Legal Services, Flemington, 1978-83; mem. Hunterdon Central High Sch. Bd. Edn. Mem. Hunterdon County Bar Assn. (legis. chmn. 1979-81), Assn. Trial Lawyers Am., N.J. State Bar (governing council Young Lawyers div. 1981-83), N.J. Trial Lawyers Assn. Republican. Lodge: Flemington Lions (past pres.), Elks. Bankruptcy, Personal injury, Real property. Home: 12 Hackberry Pl Sun Ridge Flemington NJ 08822 Office: 1 Capner St Flemington NJ 08822-1341

WOLK, BRUCE ALAN, law educator; b. Bklyn., Mar. 2, 1946; s. Morton and Gertrude W.; m. Lois Gloria Krepliak, June 22, 1968; children: Adam, Daniel. BS, Antioch Coll., 1968; MS, Stanford U., 1972; JD, Harvard U., 1975. Bar: D.C. 1975. Assoc. Hogan & Hartson, Washington, 1975-78; prof. U. Calif. Sch. Law, Davis, 1978—, acting dean, 1990-91, dean, 1993-98. Danforth Found. fellow, 1970-74, NSF fellow, 1970-72, Fulbright sr. research fellow, 1985-86. Mem. ABA, Am. Law Inst. Office: Univ Cal Davis Sch Law King Hall 400 Mrak Hall Dr Davis CA 95616-5201

WOLLAN, EUGENE, lawyer; b. N.Y.C., Nov. 2, 1928; s. Isidor and Mollie (Elterman) W.; m. Jean B. Sack, June 6, 1954 (div. 1974); children— Eric G., Jennifer J.; m. Marjorie Cama, Nov. 25, 1977; stepchildren— Valerie M. Rosenwasser, Jon J. Rosenwasser. B.A. cum laude, Harvard U., 1948, J.D., 1950. Bar: N.Y., 1950, U.S. Dist. Ct. (so. and ea. dists.) N.Y. 1953. U.S. Ct. Appeals (2d cir.) 1955, U.S. Ct. Mil. Appeals 1951, U.S. Supreme Ct. 1960; cert. arbitrator. Assoc. Rein Mound & Cotton, N.Y.C., 1953-62, ptnr., 1963-87, Mound, Cotton & Wollan, 1987—. Served to col. USAR, 1951-81. Mem. Internat. Assn. Ins. Counsel, Defense Research Inst., Internat. Soc. Barristers, Assn. Internationale De Droit Des Assurances, N.Y.C. Bar Assn., N.Y. County Lawyers, Judge Advocates Assn., Aida Reins. and Ins. Arbitration Soc. Clubs: Harvard (N.Y.C.), Met. Opera Guild (N.Y.C.). Federal civil litigation, State civil litigation, Insurance. Home: 430 E 57th St New York NY 10022-3061 Office: Mound Cotton & Wollan One Battery Park Pla New York NY 10004

WOLLE, CHARLES ROBERT, federal judge; b. Sioux City, Iowa, Oct. 16, 1935; s. William Carl and Vivian (Down) W.; m. Kerstin Birgitta Wennerstrom, June 26, 1961; children: Karl Johan Knut, Erik Vernon, Thomas Dag, Aaron Charles. AB, Harvard U., 1959; JD, Iowa Law Sch., 1961. Bar: Iowa 1961. Assoc. Shull, Marshall & Marks, Sioux City, 1961-67, ptnr., 1968-80; judge Dist. Ct. Iowa, 1981-83; justice Iowa Supreme Ct., Sioux City and Des Moines, 1983-87; judge U.S. Dist. Ct. (so. dist.) Iowa, Des Moines, 1987-92, chief judge, 1992-99. Faculty Nat. Jud. Coll., Reno, 1983—. Editor Iowa Law Rev., 1960-61 Vice pres. bd. dirs. Sioux City Symphony, 1972-77; sec., bd. dirs. Morningside Coll., Sioux City, 1977-81 Fellow Am. Coll. Trial Lawyers; mem. ABA, Iowa Bar Assn., Sioux City C. of C. (bd. dirs. 1977-78) Avocations: sports, art, music, literature. Office e-mail: charles r. Office: US Dist Judge 130 US Courthouse 123 E Walnut St Des Moines IA 50309-2011 E-mail: wolle@iasd.uscourts.gov

WOLLEN, W. FOSTER, lawyer; b. Union City, N.J., Dec. 24, 1936; s. Ross and Grace (Foster) W.; m. Sheila M. Culkin, Oct. 3, 1964; children: W. Foster, John Ross, Evan, Gillian. AB, Holy Cross Coll., 1958; LLB, U. Va., 1961. Bar: N.Y. 1962, D.C. 1990. Assoc. Shearman & Sterling, N.Y.C., 1962-70, ptnr., 1970-90, mng. ptnr., Washington, 1990-94, sr. v.p., dir. and gen. counsel Bechtel Group, Inc., 1994—. Served with U.S. Army, 1961-62. Fellow Am. Coll. Trial Lawyers (N.Y. chmn. 1987-88); mem. ABA, Bar Assn. City of N.Y. Roman Catholic. Note editor U. Va. Law Rev. Federal civil litigation, State civil litigation. Office: Bechtel Group Inc 50 Beale St PO Box 193965 San Francisco CA 94119-3965

WOLLER, JAMES ALAN, lawyer; b. Adrian, Mich., Dec. 27, 1946; s. Robert Arthur and Florence Emma (Jacob) W.; m. Jill Ann Samis, Aug. 18, 1968 (div. Aug. 1978); 1 child, Emily Erin; m. Elizabeth Julia Frey, May 22, 1982 (div. Apr. 1999); m. Carol Pierini, Oct. 29, 1999. BA, U. Mich., 1969; JD, Columbia U., 1974. Bar: N.J. 1974, U.S. Dist. Ct. N.J. 1974, U.S. Tax Ct. 1976, U.S. Supreme Ct. 1995. Assoc. McCarter & English, Newark, 1974-79; v.p. Pfaltz & Woller, PA, Summit, N.J., 1979-86, pres., 1987—. Editor Columbia U. Human Rights Law Rev., 1973-74. Mem. ABA, N.J. Bar Assn., Union County Bar Assn., Summit Bar Assn. (pres. 1987-88), Downtown Club (trustee 1997-99, treas. 1999, v.p. 2000, pres. 2001), Raritan Yacht Club (fin. sec. Perth Amboy, N.J. 1988-89, treas. 1989-92, vice commodore 1993-94, commodore 1994-95), Columbia Law Sch. Assn. N.J. (trustee 1992-97, v.p. 1997—). Republican. Methodist. Avocation: sailing. Banking, General corporate, Real property. Home: 249 Hanover St Annapolis MD 21401 Office: Pfaltz & Woller PA 382 Springfield Ave Ste 217 Summit NJ 07901-2780 E-mail: jimwoller@aol.com

WOLLINS, DAVID HART, lawyer; b. N.Y.C., Nov. 1, 1952; s. Donald John Wollins and Constance Joy Graham; m. Leslie Bjerg Lilly, Apr. 1, 1989; children: Alexandra Bjerg Lilly W., David Hart Jr. BS in Fin. and Mktg., U. Pa., 1974; JD, New Eng. Sch. Law, 1978. Bar: N.Y. 1979, U.S. Dist. Ct. (ea. and so. dists.) N.Y. 1979, U.S. Dist. Ct. Colo. 1986, U.S. Dist. Ct. (ea. dist.) Calif. 1999 U.S. Ct. Appeals (10th cir.) 1986, U.S. Ct. Appeals (fed., D.C. and 2d cirs.) 1990, U.S. Ct. Appeals (9th cir.), 1992, U.S. Ct. Claims 1983, U.S. Supreme Ct. 1994. Pres. Nature's Way Recycling Co., Boston, 1974-75; summer assoc. Phillips, Nizer, Benjamin, Krim & Ballon, N.Y.C., 1976-78, assoc., 1978-86; of counsel Cortez and Friedman, P.C., Englewood, Colo., 1986-87; mem. firm, co-head litigation dept. Brenman, Raskin, Friedlob & Tenenbaum, P.C., Denver, 1987-91; shareholder, head litigation dept. McGeady Sisneros & Wollins, P.C., 1991-95; spl. counsel Jonathan J. Hellman & Assoc., P.C., Englewood, Colo., 1995-96; mng. ptnr. Wollins, Hellman & Green, Denver, 1996—. Pro bono atty., City N.Y., 1978-86. Author short stories and numerous poems. Mem. N.Y. Bar Assn., Colo. Bar Assn., Colo. Trial Lawyers Assn., Denver Bar Assn. Federal civil litigation, General civil litigation, Securities. Home: 311 Bannock St # A/C Denver CO 80223-1174 Office: Wollins Hellman & Green 720 S Colorado Blvd Ste 620S Denver CO 80246-1943 Fax: 303-758-8111. E-mail: dhwollins@cs.com

WOLLMAN, ROGER LELAND, judge; b. Frankfort, S.D., May 29, 1934; s. Edwin and Katherine Wollman; m. Diane Marie Schroeder, June 21, 1959; children: Steven James, John Mark, Thomas Roger. BA, Tabor Coll., Hillsboro, Kans., 1957; JD magna cum laude, U. S.D., 1962; LLM, Harvard U., 1964. Bar: S.D. 1964. Sole practice, Aberdeen, 1964-71; justice S.D. Supreme Ct., 1971-85, chief justice, 1978-82; judge U.S. Ct. Appeals (8th cir.), 1985—, chief judge, 1999—; states atty. Brown County, Aberdeen, 1967-71. Served with AUS, 1957-59. Office: US Ct Appeals US Courthouse & Fed Bldg 400 S Phillips Ave Rm 315 Sioux Falls SD 57104-6824*

WOLNITZEK, STEPHEN DALE, lawyer; b. Covington, Ky., Mar. 13, 1949; s. Frederick William Jr. and Mary Ruth (Meiners) W.; m. Katherine Anita Bishop, Dec. 15, 1972; children: Marcus Stephen, Justin Bishop. BA cum laude, U. Notre Dame, 1970; JD, U. Cin., 1974. Bar: Ky. 1975, U.S. Dist. Ct. (ea. dist.) Ky. 1976, U.S. Supreme Ct. 1978, U.S. Dist. ct. (we. dist.) Ky. 1981, U.S. Ct. Appeals (6th cir.) 1991. Dep. sheriff Kenton County, Covington, 1971-75; assoc. Taliaferro & Smith, 1975-80; ptnr. Taliaferro, Smith, Mann, Wolnitzek & Schachter, 1980-86; officer Smith, Wolnitzek, Schachter & Rowekamp P.S.C., 1986-96; pres. Wolnitzek, Rowekamp, Bender & Bonar, P.S.C., 1996-98, Wolnitzek, Rowekamp & Bonar, P.S.C., Covington, 1998—. Bd. dirs. Ky. Legal Svcs. Plan Inc., 1984-96; adj. prof. Samuel Chase Coll. Law, No. Ky. U., 1995-98; mem. Ky. Jud. Retirement and Removal Commn. (now Ky. Jud. Conduct Commn.), 1995—, chair, 1996— Mem. exec. com. Kenton County Boys-Girls Club, 1981—, sec., 1995, v.p., 1996, pres., 1997; mem. exec. com. Ky. Law Enforcement Coun., Frankfort, 1984-93, vice chmn., 1991-93, chair cert. com., 1986-93; mem. City Coun., Ft. Wright, Ky., 1984-85, mem. Bd. Adjustment, 1986-97, vice chair, 1995-97; pres. No. Ky. Comty. Ctr., Covington, 1985-86; mem. bd. visitors Chase Coll. Law, no. Ky. U., 1995-97; bd. dirs. Kenton Housing Inc., 1986—, sec., 1991-93, v.p., 1993-95, pres., 1995-97; trustee No. Ky. Youth Leadership Found., 1992—, exec. com. bd. dirs., 1992—, pres., 1996-2001; gen. chair diocesean annual appeal Diocese of Covington, Ky., 2001. Recipient Roy Taylor award No. Ky. Legal Aid Soc., 1985, Disting. Lawyer award No. Ky. Bar Assn., 1998; named Vol. of Yr., Community Chest United Appeal, Cin., 1986. Master: Samuel P. Chase Am. Inns of Ct.; fellow: Am. Bar Found., Ky. Bar Found. (charter life, bd. dirs. 1989—94, bd. dirs. 1995—2000), No. Ky. Bar Found. (charter life); mem.: Ky. Bar Assn. (bd. govs. 1984—96, chmn. ann. conv. 1986, chmn. ho. of dels. 1986, v.p. 1992—93, pres. 1994—95), Def. Rsch. Inst., U. Cin. Alumni Assn. (trustee, bd. dirs. 1999—), Fraternal Order Police (Ky. gen. counsel 1975—), Ky. Def. Counsel. (bd. dirs. 1982—86), Assn. Def. Trial Attys.,

Ky. Coun. Sch. Bd. Attys. (bd. dirs. 1981—87), Nat. Coun. Sch. Bd. Attys., Notre Dame Club Cin. Democrat. Roman Catholic. Avocations: sports, reading. State civil litigation, Education and schools, Insurance. Home: 1836 Beacon Hl Covington KY 41011-3684 Office: Wolnitzek Rowekamp & Bonar PSC 502 Greenup St PO Box 352 Covington KY 41012-0352 E-mail: wolnitfam@fuse.net

WOLSON, CRAIG ALAN, lawyer; b. Toledo, Feb. 20, 1949; s. Max A. and Elaine B. (Cohn) W.; m. Janis Nan Braun, July 30, 1972 (div. Mar. 1986); m. Ellen Carol Schulgasser, Oct. 26, 1986; children: Lindsey, Michael and Geoffrey (triplets). BA, U. Mich., 1971, JD, 1974. Bar: N.Y. 1975, U.S. Dist. Ct. (so. and ea. dists.) N.Y. 1975, U.S. Ct. Appeals (2d cir.) 1975, U.S. Supreme Ct. 1978. Assoc. Shearman & Sterling, N.Y.C., 1974-81; v.p., asst. gen. counsel Thomson McKinnon Securities Inc., 1981-85; v.p., sec., gen. counsel J.D. Mattus Co., Inc., Greenwich, Conn., 1985-88; also bd. dirs. J.D. Mattus Co., Inc. and affiliated cos.; v.p., asst. gen. counsel Chem. Bank, N.Y.C., 1988-95; of counsel Williams & Harris, 1995-96; ptnr. Williams & Harris LLP, 1996-97; counsel Brown & Wood L.L.P., 1997-98, Mayer, Brown & Platt, N.Y.C., 1999-2001; spl. counsel Schulte Roth & Zabel LLP, 2001—. Dep. clk. Lucas County Courthouse, Toledo, 1968-69, 71-72. Articles and administrv. editor U. Mich. Law Rev., 1973-74. Mem. ABA, N.Y. State Bar Assn., Assn. of Bar of City of N.Y. (securities regulation com. 1994-97, corp. law com. 1997-2000, project fin. com. 2000—), Corp. Bar. Assn. of Westchester and Fairfield, Phi Beta Kappa, Phi Eta Sigma, Pi Sigma Alpha. Avocations: reading, playing piano, fine dining, theater. General corporate, Securities. Home: 29 Punch Bowl Dr Westport CT 06880-2130 Office: Schulte Roth & Zabel LLP 919 Third Ave New York NY 10022

WOMACK, MARY PAULINE, lawyer; b. Chattanooga, Dec. 3, 1942; d. Lucille (Thomas) W. BS, U. Chattanooga, 1964; JD, Woodrow Wilson Coll. Law, 1984. Bar: Ga. 1988, U.S. Dist. Ct. (no. dist.) Ga. 1988. Pvt. practice, Atlanta, 1988—. DeKalb County Dems., 66th dist., regional com. State of Ga. Mem. Ga. Bar Assn., Sigma Delta Kappa (past regional v.p.). Criminal, Landlord-tenant, Personal injury. Home: 3445 Ashwood Ln Atlanta GA 30341-4534 Office: 100 Peachtree St NW Ste 1950 Atlanta GA 30303-1919

WONG, CHRISTOPHER WAI C. lawyer; b. Kuala Lumpur, Federal Territory, Malaysia, Feb. 3, 1967; s. Kon Min Wong and Sow Yoong Chan. LLB with honors, U. Sheffield (Eng.), 1990. Bar: solicitor Supreme Ct. Eng. and Wales 1993; adv., solicitor Supreme Ct. Singapore 1995; legal practitioner High Ct. New South Wales, Australia 2000. Trainee solicitor Denton Hall, London, 1991-93; pupil Khattar Wong & Ptnrs., Singapore, 1993-94; adv., solicitor Wong Partnership, 1995-97, Kelvin Chia Partnership, Singapore, 1997-98, Harry Elias Partnership, Singapore, 1998-99; solicitor Baker & McKenzie, Sydney, 1999-2000, Minter Ellison, Sydney, 2000—, liaison officer Asian Focus Group, 2001—. Coach mock trial U. Sydney, 2000; presenter in field. Contbr. articles to profl. jours. Vol. multicultural affairs U. Sydney, 2000; mem. bd. legal edn. Student CTTE, Singapore, 1994. Mem. Law Soc. Eng. and Wales, Law Soc. Singapore, Law Soc. New South Wales, Malaysian & Singaporean Students Soc. (pres. 1987). Avocations: reading, travel, gym, swimming, music. Bankruptcy, Consumer commercial, Construction. Office: Minter Ellison Aurora Pl 88 Phillip St Sydney NSW 2000 Australia Fax: 612 9921-8123. E-mail: chris.wong@minterellison.com

WOO, CHANG ROK, lawyer; b. Kyangju, South Korea, Feb. 14, 1953; m. Ho Goun Chung Woo; children: Hye Won, Jae Hyong, Jae Ha. LLB, Seoul Nat. U., Korea, 1974; LLM, U. Wash. Law Sch., U.S.A, 1983. Judge advocate Navy, Seoul, Korea, 1976-79; assoc. Kim & Chang, Korea, 1979-84, ptnr. Korea, 1984-92, Woo & Ptnrs., Seoul, Korea, 1992-97; mng. ptnr. Woo. Yun, Kang, Jeong & Han, Korea, 1997—. Fellow EWHA Womans U., Korea, 1997—, lectr. Judicial Training and Resh. Insts., the Supreme Court of Korea, 1995-99, Seoul Nat. U. Law Sch., 1995-99, vis. lawyer Coudert Bros., NY, 1984, jud. rsch. and Tng. Insts., Supreme Ct. of Korea, Seoul, 1970, vis. scholar U. Calif., Bodt Hall, 1983. Author: A Brief Survey of Korean Corporate Liquidation and Bankruptcy Law, 1980, Residency As the Base for Tax Jurisdiction, 1986, Deductibility of Illegal Expenses, 1997, Tax Issues Related to Merger and Acquisition, 1997. Mem. Korean Bar Assn., Internat. Bar Assn., Internat. Fiscal Assn. General corporate, Government contracts and claims, Estate taxation. Office: Textile Ctr 12 Fl 944-31 Daechi-dong 135-713 Kangnam-gu Seoul Republic of Korea Fax: 82 2-528-5228. E-mail: crwoo@wooyun.co.kr

WOO, VERNON YING-TSAI, lawyer, real estate developer, judge; b. Honolulu, Aug. 7, 1942; s. William Shu-Bin and Hilda Woo; children: Christopher Shu-Bin, Lia Gay. BA, U. Hawaii, 1964, MA, 1966; JD, Harvard U., 1969. Pres. Woo Kessner Duca & Maki, Honolulu, 1972-87; pvt. practice law, 1987—. Judge per diem Honolulu Dist. Family Ct., 1978-84, 95—. Bd. dirs. Boys and Girls Club of Honolulu,. 1985-95, pres., 1990-92. Mem. ABA, Hawaii Bar Assn., Honolulu Bd. Realtors. Real property. Home: 1221 Victoria St Apt 2403 Honolulu HI 96814-1454 Office: Harbor Ct 55 Merchant St Ste 1900 Honolulu HI 96813

WOOD, ALLISON LORRAINE, lawyer; b. N.Y.C., May 30, 1962; d. Walter C. and Joan T. Wood. BA, Pace U., 1984; JD, DePaul U., 1987; postgrad., Northwestern U. Bar: Ill. 1987, U.S. Dist. Ct. (no. dist.) Ill. 1989, Fed. Trial Bar 1990. Judicial extern U.S. Bankruptcy Ct., Chgo., 1987; pub. defender, Office of Pub. Defender Cook County, Ill., 1987-89; counsel Peoples Energy Corp., Chgo., 1989-93; ptnr. Albert, Whitehead, P.C., 1993—. Adj. prof. DePaul U. Coll. Law, 1992—; hearing bd. chair Atty. Registration Disciplinary Commn. Chmn. bd. dirs. Ctrs. for New Horizons, 2001—; mem. Target Hope-Mentor; spkr. We Care Role Model. Mem. ABA (products sect., columnist trial sect. newsletter), Ill. State Bar Assn., Chgo. Bar Assn., Cook County Bar Assn. (bd. dirs., treas. 1993-98), DePaul U. Coll. of Law Alumni Bd. Bankruptcy, General civil litigation, Consumer commercial. Office: Albert Whitehead PC Ten N Dearborn Ste 600 Chicago IL 60602

WOOD, DIANE PAMELA, judge; b. Plainfield, N.J., July 4, 1950; d. Kenneth Reed and Lucille (Padmore) Wood; m. Dennis James Hutchinson, Sept. 2, 1978 (div. May 1998); children: Kathryn, David, Jane. BA, U. Tex., 1971, JD, 1975. Bar: Tex. 1975, D.C. 1978, Ill. 1993. Law clk. U.S. Ct. Appeals (5th cir.), 1975-76, U.S. Supreme Ct., 1976-77; atty.-advisor U.S. Dept. State, Washington, 1977-78; assoc. law firm Covington & Burling, 1978-80; asst. prof. law Georgetown U. Law Ctr., 1980-81, U. Chgo., 1981-88, prof. law, 1988-95, assoc. dean, 1989-92, Harold J. and Marion F. Green prof. internat. legal studies, 1990-95, sr. lectr. in law, 1995—; spl. cons. antitrust divsn. internat. guide U.S. Dept. Justice, 1986-87, dep. asst. atty. gen. antitrust divsn., 1993-95; cir. judge U.S. Ct. Appeals (7th cir.), 1995—. Contbr. articles to profl. jours. Bd. dirs. Hyde Park-Kenwood Cmty. Health Ctr., 1983-85. Mem. Am. Soc. Internat. Law, Am. law Inst., Internat. Acad. Comparative Law, Phi Alpha Delta. Democrat.

WOOD, DONALD F. lawyer; b. Bonne Terre, Mo., July 25, 1944; BSBA, Washington U., 1966; JD, Harvard U., 1969. Bar: Tex. 1970. Mng. ptnr. Vinson & Elkins, L.L.P., Austin. Fellow Houston Bar Found. (chmn. 1991); mem. Beta Gamma Sigma, Omicron Delta Kappa. Taxation, general. Office: Vinson & Elkins LLP 600 Congress Ave Ste 2700 Austin TX 78701-3200 E-mail: dwood@velaw.com

WOOD, HARLINGTON, JR. federal judge; b. Springfield, Ill., Apr. 17, 1920; s. Harlington and Marie (Green) W. A.B., U. Ill., 1942, J.D., 1948. Bar: Ill. 1948. Practiced in, Springfield, 1948-69; U.S. atty. So. Dist. Ill., 1958-61; mem. firm Wood & Wood, 1961-69; assoc. dep. atty. gen. for U.S. attys. U.S. dept. Justice, 1969-70; assoc. dep. atty. gen. Justice Dept., Washington, 1970-72, asst. atty. gen. civil div., 1972-73; U.S. dist. judge So. Dist. Ill., Springfield, 1973-76; judge U.S. Ct. Appeals (7th cir.), 1976—. Adj. prof. Sch. Law, U. Ill., Champaign, 1993; disting. vis. prof. St. Louis U. Law Sch., 1996—. Chmn. Adminstrv. Office Oversight Com., 1988-90; mem. Long Range Planning Com., 1991-96. Office: US Ct Appeals PO Box 299 600 E Monroe St Springfield IL 62701-1626

WOOD, JAMES JERRY, lawyer; b. Rockford, Ala., Aug. 13, 1940; s. James Ronald and Ada Love Wood; m. Earline Luckie, Aug. 9, 1959; children: James Jerry, William Gregory, Diana Lynn. AB, Samford U., 1964, JD, 1969. Bar: Ala. 1969, U.S. Supreme Ct. 1976. Dir. legal affairs Med. Assn. State of Ala., Montgomery, 1969-70; asst. atty. gen. State of Ala., 1970-72; asst. U.S. atty. Middle Dist. Ala., 1972-76; pvt. practice, 1977-78; pres. Wood & Parnell, P.A., Montgomery, Ala., 1979-89; pvt. practice, 1990—. Gen. counsel Ala. Builders Self-Insurance Fund, Home Builders Assn. of Ala.; chmn. character and fitness com. Ala. State Bar, 1981-84, 86-89, chair task force on quality of life, 1990-92, chair task force on mem. svcs., 1994-96. Capt. USAR, 1974-79. Fellow Am. Bar Found.; mem. ABA (ho. of dels. 1990-98), Ala. ABA Fellows (state chmn.), FBA (pres. Montgomery chpt. 1974-75), Am. Nat. Inns of Ct., Am. Soc. Assn. Execs., Ala. Assn. Workers Compensation Group Self-Insured Funds (chmn.), Ala. Bar Assn., Montgomery Bar Assn., Ala. Def. Lawyers Assn., Ala. Law Inst., Ala. Coun. Assn. Execs. (pres. 2001), Def. Rsch. Inst., Rotary (pres. Montgomery Capital chpt. 1986-87, 96-97). Republican. Baptist. Construction, General corporate, Workers' compensation. Office: PO Box 241206 Montgomery AL 36124-1206 E-mail: jjwood@mindspring.com

WOOD, JOHN MARTIN, lawyer; b. Detroit, Mar. 29, 1944; s. John Francis and Margaret Kathleen (Lynch) W.; m. Judith Anne Messer; children: Timothy Peter, Meagan Anne. BA, Boston Coll., 1966; JD, Cath. U. Am., 1969. Bar: D.C. 1970, U.S. Dist. Ct. D.C. 1970, U.S. Ct. Appeals (D.C. cir., 3d cir., 4th cir.), U.S. Supreme Ct. 1973. Trial atty, tax divsn. Dept. Justice, Washington, 1969-73; assoc. Reed Smith LLP, 1973-80, ptnr., 1980—, mng. ptnr., 1989-95, dir. legal pers., 1995-98. Dir. adv. bd. Salvation Army, Va. and Met. Washington, Leadership Washington, 1993—. Mem. D.C. Bar, Econ. Club of Washington, Barristers Club (Washington), River Bend Golf and Country Club, The Currituck Club (N.C.), Phi Alpha Delta, Delta Sigma Pi. Administrative and regulatory, Banking, Federal civil litigation. Home: 9490 Oak Falls Ct Great Falls VA 22066-4143 Office: Reed Smith LLP 1301 K St NW Ste 1100E Washington DC 20005-3373 E-mail: jwood@reedsmith.com

WOOD, L. LIN, JR. lawyer; b. Raleigh, N.C., Oct. 19, 1952; s. Lucian Lincoln and Josephine (Currin) W.; m. Deborah Anne Jamison, July 25, 1987; children:, Elizabeth Ashley, Matthew Carlton. BA cum laude Mercer U., 1974, JD cum laude, 1977. Bar: Ga. 1977, U.S. Dist. Ct. (no. and mid. dist.) Ga. 1977, U.S. Ct. Appeals (5th cir.) 1977, U.S. Ct. Appeals (11th cir.) 1981. Assoc. f Jones, Cork, Miller & Benton, Macon, Ga., 1977-80, Freeman & Hawkins, Atlanta, 1980-83; ptnr. Wood & Grant, Atlanta, 1983— . Mem. staff Mercer Law Rev., 1975-77. Recipient Am. Jurisprudence award 1976, 77, U.S. Law Week award, 1977. Mem. ABA, Assn. Trial Lawyers Am., State Bar Ga., Atlanta Bar Assn., Lawyers Club Atlanta, Ga. Trial Lawyers Assn. Republican. Methodist. Club: Atlanta City. State civil litigation, Insurance, Personal injury. Home: 561 Dalrymple Rd NE Atlanta GA 30328-1323 Office: Wood & Grant 620 Carnegie Atlanta GA 30303-1027

WOOD, LEONARD JAMES, lawyer; b. Camden, N.J., Dec. 21, 1949; s. Leonard and Virginia (Ferraro) W.; m. Catherine Mary Dugan, June 29, 1979; children: Leonard James III, Tara Kathleen. BA, Manhattan Coll., 1972; JD, Rutgers U., 1976. Bar: N.J. 1976, U.S. Ct. Appeals (3d cir.) 1977, U.S. Supreme Ct. 1980. Law clk. to presiding judge Chancery div. Superior Ct. of N.J., Camden, 1976-77; ptnr. Console, Marmero, Li Volsi, Wood, Curcio, Berlin, 1977-89, Ferreri and Wood, Voorhees, 1989-95, Morelli & Rinaldi, 1995-97; sole practice, 1997-99; ptnr. Wade & Wood LLC, 2000—. Mem. ABA (family law sect.), N.J. State Bar Assn. (family law sect.), Camden County Bar Assn. Family and matrimonial, Personal injury, Real property. Office: 1250 Chews Landing Rd Laurel Springs NJ 08021-2816

WOOD, ROBERT CHARLES, lawyer, real estate developer; b. Chgo., Apr. 8, 1956; s. Roy Edward and Mildred Lucille (Jones) W.; m. Jennifer Jo Briggs, Oct. 1984; children: Jacqueline Jones, Reagan Keith. BA in History, BBA in Real Estate, So. Meth. U., 1979, JD, 1982. Bar: Tex. 1983. Appraiser McClellan-Massey, Dallas, 1977-79; researcher, acquisitions officer Amstar Fin. Corp., 1979-80; prin. Robert Wood Cons., 1981-98; ptnr. Welch & Wood Attys. and Y2K Cons., 1998-2000; pvt. practice, 1995—; real estate investor and developer, 1998—. Cons. Plan Mktg. Cos., 1983-84; pvt. practice law, Dallas, 1983-84; gen. counsel Diversified Benefits, Inc., Dallas, 1984-86; nat. accts. mgr. Lomas & Nettleton Real Estate Group, Dallas, 1987-88; sr. pension cons., prin. Eppler, Guerin &Turner, 1988-93; chmn. adv. coun. on devel. Medisend, 1991; nat. consulting coord. fin. advisors coun., v.p. Callan Assocs., San Francisco, 1994-95; atty. at law, 1995—. Author: Electionomics: How the Money Managers View the Election, 1992, After the Congress Vote: How the Managers See Things Now, 1993, Y2K--The Year 2000 Issue: How Y2K Affects the Markets, 1998; mem. So. Meth. U. Law Rev., 1981-82; contbr. articles to profl. publs. Bd. dirs. Dallas unit Am. Cancer Soc., 1982-87, mem. spl. events com., 1986-87, mem. crusade com., 1987-88, mem. medisend adv. com., 1988-94, chmn. corp. devel. bd., 1989—. Mem. Tex. Bar Assn., Phila. Bar Assn., Phi Gamma Delta. Avocations: skiing, tennis, bicycling. Finance, Pension, profit-sharing, and employee benefits, Securities. E-mail: rccwood@aol.com

WOOD, ROBERT WARREN, lawyer; b. Des Moines, July 5, 1955; s. Merle Warren and Cecily Ann (Sherk) W.; m. Beatrice Wood, Aug. 4, 1979; 1 child, Bryce Mercedes. Student, U. Sheffield, Eng., 1975-76; AB, Humboldt State U., 1976; JD, U. Chgo., 1979. Bar: Ariz. 1979, Calif. 1980, Wyo. 2000, N.Y. 1989, D.C. 1993, Mont. 1998, U.S Tax Ct. 1980, Wyo.; Roll of Solicitors of Eng. and Wales, 1998. Assoc. Jennings, Strouss, Phoenix, 1979-80, McCutchen, Doyle, San Francisco, 1980-82, Broad, Khourie, San Francisco, 1982-85, Steefel, Levitt & Weiss, San Francisco, 1985-87, ptnr., 1987-91, Bancroft & McAlister, San Francisco, 1991-93; prin. Robert W. Wood, P.C., 1993—. Instr. in law U. Calif. San Francisco, 1981-82. Author: Taxation of Corporate Liquidations: A Complete Planning Guide, 1987, 2nd edit., 1994, The Executive's Complete Guide to Business Taxes, 1989, Corporate Taxation: Complete Planning and Practice Guide, 1989, S Corporations, 1990, The Ultimate Tax Planning Guide for Growing Companies, 1991, Taxation of Damage Awards and Settlement Payments, 1991, 2nd edit., 1998, Tax Strategies in Hiring, Retaining and Terminating Employees, 1991, The Home Office Tax Guide, 1991; co-author: (with others) California Closely Held Corporations: Tax Planning and Practice Guide, 1987, Legal Guide to Independent Contractor Status, 3d edit., 2000; editor: California Small Busines Guide, 4 vols., 1998, Home Office Money & Tax Guide, 1992, Tax Aspects of Settlements and Judgements, 1993, 2d edit., 1998, cumulative supplement, 2000; editor-in-chief The M & A Tax Report; editor: Limited Liability Companies: Formation, Operation and Conversion, 1994, 2d edit., 2001, Limited Liability Partnerships: Formation, Operation and Taxation, 1996; mem. editl. bd. Real Estate Tax Digest, The Practical Accountant, Jour. Real Estate Taxation. Fellow Am. Coll. Tax Counsel; mem. Calif. Bd. Legal Specialization (cert. specialist taxation), Candian Bar Assn., Bohemian Club, Law Coun. Australia. Republican. Mergers and acquisitions, Corporate taxation, Personal income taxation. Office: 477 Pacific Ave # 300 San Francisco CA 94133-4614

WOOD, WILLARD MARK, lawyer; b. Traverse City, Mich., Nov. 30, 1942; s. William Mark and Ebba Forsman Wood; m. Sharon McDermott, June 19, 1965; children: Sean, Pat, Kelly, Ryan, Casey. BA, Santa Clara U., 1964; JD, U. So. Calif., 1967. Bar: Calif., D.C., U.S. Supreme Ct. Judge advocate USMC, Vietnam, 1969-70; ptnr. O'Melveny & Myers, L.A., 1971—. Capt. USMC, 1967-71, Vietnam. Roman Catholic. Aviation, General civil litigation, Insurance. Office: O'Melveny & Myers 400 S Hope St Ste 1321 Los Angeles CA 90071-2899 E-mail: mwood@omm.com

WOOD, WILLIAM MCBRAYER, lawyer; b. Greenville, S.C., Jan. 27, 1942; s. Oliver Gillan and Grace (McBrayer) W.; m. Nancy Cooper, 1973 (dec. 1993); children: Walter, Lewis; m. Jeanette Dobson Haney, June 25, 1994. BS in Acctg., U. S.C., 1964, JD cum laude, 1972; LLM in Estate Planning (scholar), U. Miami, 1980. Bar: S.C. 1972, Fla. 1979, D.C. 1973, U.S. Tax Ct. 1972, U.S. Ct. Claims 1972, U.S. Supreme Ct. 1977. Intern ct. of claims sect., tax divsn. U.S. Dept. Justice, 1971; law clk. to chief judge U.S. Ct. Claims, Washington, 1972-74; ptnr. firm Edwards Wood, Duggan & Reese, Greer and Greenville, 1974-78; asst. prof. law Cumberland Law Sch., Samford U., Birmingham, Ala., 1978-79; faculty Nat. Inst. Trial Advocacy: N.E. Regional Inst., 1979, 83-90, 95-97, Fla. Regional Inst., 1989; teaching team 5th intensive trial techniques course Hofstra U., 1983; assoc. then capital ptnr. firm Shutts & Bowen, Miami, 1980-85; sole practice, 1985—; also Rock Hill, S.C., 1994—; of counsel Griffin, Smith, Caldwell, Helder & Lee, Monroe, N.C., 2001—. Contbg. editor: The Lawyers PC; Fla. editor: Drafting Wills and Trust Agreements; substantive com. editor ABA: The Tax Lawyer, 1983—. Pres. Piedmont Heritage Found., Inc. 1975-78; del. State Rep. Conv., 1985, 87, 90; exec. committeeman Miami-Dade County Republicans, 1988-94, co-gen. counsel, 1990-91; apptd. Miami-Dade County Indsl. Devel. Authority, 1990-94; mem. vestry Episc. Ch., 1993-94. With USAF, 1965-69, Vietnam. Decorated Air Force Commendation medal; recipient Am. Jurisprudence award in real property and tax I, 1971; winner Grand prize So. Living Mag. travel photo contest, 1969. Mem. ABA (taxation sect., teaching law com., 1994—), Greer C. of C. (pres. 1977, Outstanding leadership award 1976), Greater Greenville C. of C. (dir. 1977), Order Wig and Robe, Estate Planning Council South Fla., Omicron Delta Kappa. Club: Bankers (bd. govs. 1989-94). Lodge: Masons, Rotary. Estate planning, Probate, Estate taxation. Office: 5345 Wilgrove Mint Hill Rd Charlotte NC 28227-3467

WOODALL, THOMAS A. judge; b. Meridian, Miss., July 14, 1950; m. Debbie Bogan, 1972; children: Scott, Matthew, Claire. BA in History, Millsaps Coll., 1972; JD, U. Va., 1975. With Rives and Peterson, Birmingham, Ala., 1975—91; ptnr. Woodall and Maddox, 1991—96; circuit judge Jefferson County, 1996—2001; assoc. justice Ala. Supreme Ct., 2001—. Mem. Ala. Pattern Jury Instrn.-Civil Com., 1985—2001, vice chmn., 1992—2001. Republican. Methodist. Office: 300 Dexter Ave Montgomery AL 36104-3741*

WOODALL, W. DALLAS, lawyer; b. Youngstown, Ohio, June 8, 1937; s. William L. and Roberta (Gibson) W.; m. Velma H. Szakacs, June 7, 1958; children: John M., Laura Love Woodall, Christine L. Scarmuzzi. BS in Edn. cum laude, Youngstown State U., 1964; JD, Ohio State U., 1967. Bar: Ohio 1967. Pvt. practice law, Warren, Ohio, 1967-68; assoc. Letson, Letson, Griffith and Kightlinger, 1971-90; pres. Letson, Griffith, Woodall, Lavelle & Rosenberg Co. LPA, 1995—. V.p. Western Reserve coun. Boy Scouts Am., 1978, exec. bd.; elder First Presbyn. Ch., Warren, 1959—, trustee, 1975-77, 78-80, chmn. bd. trustees, 1980, 84; trustee Warren Libr. Assn., 1986-97, pres. 1987-91; mem. Trumbull County Met. Parks Bd., 1987-90; pres. Mahoning-Shandango Valley Estate Planning Coun. 1994. Mem. Ohio State Bar Assn. (bd. govs. probate and trust law sect. 1987-97), Trumbull County Bar Assn. (pres. 1985-86), Buckeye Club (Warren), Rotary (bd. dirs. 1982-84, 88-91, pres. 1989-90, dist. gov. 1994-95). Republican. Estate planning, Probate, Real property. Home: 3204 Crescent Dr NE Warren OH 44483-6306 Office: Letson Griffith Woodall Lavelle & Rosenberg Co LPA PO Box 151 Warren OH 44482-0151 E-mail: lawfirm@lgwlr

WOODBURN, RALPH ROBERT, JR. lawyer; b. Haverhill, Mass., Nov. 3, 1946; s. Ralph Robert and Josephine Marie (McClure) W.; m. Janet M. Smith, Sept. 15, 1985. BA, Mich. State U., 1967; JD, Harvard U., 1972; LLM, Boston U., 1981. Bar: Mass. 1972, U.S. Tax Ct. 1987. Assoc. Bowers, Fortier & Lakin, Boston, 1972-76; from assoc. to ptnr. Haussermann, Davison & Shattuck, 1976-83; ptnr. Palmer & Dodge, 1983—. Tchr. Harvard Ctr. for Lifelong Learning, Cambridge, Mass., 1986-89; chmn. Wellesley Cable Access Bd., 1993-95. Contbr. articles to Boston Bar Jour. and Estate Planning. Treas. Exeter Assn. of New Eng., Boston, 1985-89, v.p., 1989-91, pres., 1991-93. Fellow Am. Coll. Trust and Estate Counsel; mem. ABA, Boston Bar Assn. (chmn. probate legislation 1983-93), Brae Burn Country Club (Newton, Mass.), Harvard Club of Boston, Boston Probate and Estate Planning Forum (program chair 1996-97, moderator 1997-98), Harvard Travellers Club. Estate planning, Probate, Estate taxation. Home: 25 Cypress Rd Wellesley MA 02481-2918 Office: Palmer & Dodge 1 Beacon St Boston MA 02108-3190 E-mail: rwoodburn@palmerdodge.com

WOODBURY, ROBERT CHARLES, lawyer; b. Sheridan, N.Y., July 7, 1929; s. Wendell F. and Lillian S. (Towne) W.; m. Martha Bayard Page, Jan. 25, 1958. BEE, Rensselaer Poly. Inst., 1950; JD, Cornell U., 1953. Bar: N.Y. 1954, U.S. Dist. Ct. (so. dist.) N.Y. 1965, U.S. Dist. Ct. (we. dist.) N.Y. 1979, U.S. Ct. Appeals (4th cir.) 1964, U.S. Ct. Claims 1961, U.S. Ct. Mil. Appeals 1956, U.S. Patent Office 1961; lic. profl. engr., N.Y. Project engr. Army reactors program U.S. Atomic Energy Commn., 1957-60; assoc. Reid & Priest, N.Y.C., 1962-70; pvt. practice Dunkirk, N.Y., 1971—; ptnr. Aular & Woodbury, 1973-81, Morten & Woodbury, Dunkirk, 1982-88. Gen. counsel N.Y. State Temp. Commn. Environ. Impact Major Pub. Utility Facilities, 1970-71; del. N.Y. 8th Jud. Dist. Rep. Jud. Nominating Conv., 1985—; chmn. bd. dirs. Woodbury Farms, Ltd., 1965-98, Woodbury Vineyards, 1968-91. Assoc. trustee Buffalo Gen. Hosp. Found., 1994-96; trustees coun. Buffalo Gen. Healthcare Sys., 1996-98, steering com. 1996-98; mem. trustees coun. Kaleida Health Sys., Buffalo, 1998-2001, Kaleida Health Cmty. Coun., 2001—; founding pres. Chautauqua County Arts Coun., 1971; town atty. Town of Sheridan, 1972-75; dist. counsel city sch. dist. City of Dunkirk, 1973-82; co-founder No. Chautauqua Indsl. Roundtable, 1979; co-chmn. Chmn.'s Club, Chautauqua County Rep. Com. 1988-98; chmn., pres., dir., counsel Historic Harbor Renaissance, Inc., 1999—. Lt. USN, 1954-57. Fellow N.Y. Bar Found.; mem. N.Y. State Bar Assn. (chmn. com. atomic energy law 1967-69, chmn. com. pub. utility law 1969-71, mem. action unit 5 regulatory reform N.Y. 1980-83), Bar Assn. No. Chautauqua (pres. 1979), Cornell Law Assn., Rensselaer Alumni Assn., Dunkirk C. of C. (pres. 1979), Mid-Day Club Buffalo, Chautauqua Yacht Club. Republican. Presbyterian. Avocations: skiing, wine, sailing. Contracts commercial, General corporate, Nuclear power. Home: 3300 S Roberts Rd Fredonia NY 14063-9418 Office: PO Box 800 87 E 4th St Dunkirk NY 14048-2225 E-mail: bobhere@netsync.net

WOODCOCK, JOHN ALDEN, lawyer; b. Bangor, Maine, July 6, 1950; s. John Alden Woodcock and Joan (Carlin) Nestler; m. Beverly Ann Newcombe, July 14, 1973; children: John A., Patrick C., Christopher C. AB, Bowdoin Coll., 1972; MA, U. London, 1973; JD, U. Maine, 1976. Bar: Maine 1976, U.S. Dist. Ct. Maine 1976. Assoc. Stearns, Finnegan & Needham, Bangor, 1976-80; asst. dist. atty. Penobscot County, 1977-78; ptnr. Mitchell & Stearns, 1980-91, Weatherbee, Woodcock, Burlock & Woodcock, Bangor, 1991—. Mem. alumni coun. Bowdoin Coll., Brunswick, Maine, 1992—, pres., 1995-96, trustee, 1996—; bd. dirs. Ea. Maine Med. Ctr., Bangor, 1980—, chmn, 1996—, Ea. Maine Healthcare, Bangor, 1989—. Master Ballou Inn of Ct.; fellow Maine Bar Found.; mem. ABA, Maine State Bar Assn., Penobscot County Bar Assn. General civil litigation, Insurance, Personal injury. Home: 110 Main Rd N Hampden ME 04444-1404 Office: Weatherbee Woodcock Burlock & Woodcock 136 Broadway Bangor ME 04401-5206

WOODHOUSE, GAY VANDERPOEL, state attorney general; b. Torrington, Wyo., Jan. 8, 1950; d. Wayne Gaylord and Sally (Rouse) Vanderpoel; m. Randy Woodhouse, Nov. 26, 1953; children: Dustin, Houston. BA with honors, U. Wyo., 1972, JD, 1977. Bar: Wyo. 1978, U.S. Dist. Ct. Wyo., U.S. Supreme Ct. Dir. student Legal Svcs., Laramie, Wyo., 1976-77; assoc. Donald Jones Law Offices, Torrington, 1977-78; asst. atty. gen. State of Wyo., Cheyenne, 1978-84, sr. asst. atty. gen., 1984-89, spl. U.S. atty., 1987-89, asst. U.S. atty., 1990-95, chief dept. atty. gen., 1995-98, atty. gen., 1998—. Chmn. bd. Pathfinder, 1987; bd. dirs. S.E. Wyo. Mental Health; chmn. Wyo. Tel. Consumer Panel, Casper, 1982-86; spl. projects cons. N.Am. Securities Adminstrs. Assn., 1987-89; advisor Cheyenne Halfway House, 1984-93; chmn. Wyo. Silent Witness Initiative Zero Domestic Violence by 2010, 1997; chmn. Wyo. Domestic Violence Elimination Coun., 1999-2001. Mem. Laramie County Bar Assn. Republican. Avocations: inline speed skating, stained glass. Office: 123 Capitol Bldg Cheyenne WY 82002-0001 E-mail: gwoodh@state.wy.us

WOODHOUSE, THOMAS EDWIN, lawyer; b. Cedar Rapids, IA, Apr. 30, 1940; s. Keith Wallace and Elinor Julia (Cherny) W.; m. Kiyoko Fujiie, May 29, 1965; children: Miya, Keith, Leighton. AB cum laude, Amherst Coll., 1962; JD, Harvard U., 1965. Bar: N.Y. 1966, U.S. Supreme Ct. 1969, Calif. 1975. Assoc. Chadbourne, Parke, Whiteside & Wolff, N.Y.C., 1965-68; atty./adviser AID, Washington, 1968-69; counsel Pvt. Investment Co. for Asia S.A., Tokyo, 1969-72; ptnr. Woodhouse Lee & Davis, Singapore, 1972-74; assoc. Graham & James, San Francisco, 1974-75; asst. gen. counsel Natomas Co., 1975-81; mem. Lasky, Haas, Cohler & Munter, 1982-90; trust adminstr. Ronald Family Trust A, 1989—, Gordon P. Getty Family Trust, 1994—; sole practice Berkeley, 1990—. Of counsel Wilson, Sonsini, Goodrich & Rosati, Palo Alto, Calif., 1992-95; instr. law faculty U. Singapore, 1972-74; CEO, Vallejo Investments, 1997—. chmn. Police Rev. Com. of Berkeley (Calif.), 1980-84; mem. Berkeley Police Res., 1986—; bd. dirs. Friends Assn. of Svcs. for Elderly, 1979-84; clk. fin. com. Am. Friends Svc. Com. of No. Calif., 1979-83; pres. Zyzzyva Inc., lit. quar., 1985-87. Trustee Freedom from Hunger, 1989-99, Coun. of Friends Bancroft Libr., 1997—, Dominican Sch. of Philosophy and Theology, 1998—. With U.S. Army, 1958. Fellow Am. Bar Found. (life); mem. Calif. Bar Assn., Assn. Internat. de Bibliophilie, Harvard Club, Univ. Club, Book Club Calif., Roxburghe Club, Travellers Club, Grolier Club, Faculty Club U. Calif.-Berkeley, Mira Vista Golf and Country Club. Republican. Roman Catholic. General corporate, Private international, Patent. Home and Office: 1800 San Antonio Ave Berkeley CA 94707-1618 E-mail: tew@wodehus.com

WOOD KAHARI, BRENDA MARIE, lawyer; b. Washington, Jan. 29, 1951; d. Sylvester and Laverne Morris; m. Muzanenhamo Eric Kahari, June 13, 1981; children; Brent, Morris. BA, U. Dayton, 1972; JD, Howard U., 1975; LLM, Georgetown U., 1982. Bar: Ohio 1975, D.C. 1977. Legal intern Dept. State/U.S. AID, Washington, 1974-75; assoc. atty. Squire, Sanders & Dempsey, Cleve., 1975-78; assoc. counsel Pepco, Washington, 1978-81; legal advisor Ministry of Justice, Harare, Zimbabwe, 1981-86; pvt. practice B.W. Kahari Law Office, Harare/Washington, 1986; office affil. Soble Internat. Law, 1996. Bd. dirs. Olmur Investments, Harare; trustee Zimbabwe Health Care Trust, 1996—; bd. dirs. Nat. Anglican Theol. Colls., Zimbabwe, 1996. Author, reporter and spkr. in field of trademarks. Fellow Chartered Inst. Arbitrators; mem. Ohio Bar Assn., D.C. Bar Assn., Law Soc. Zimbabwe. Contracts commercial, Intellectual property, Private international. Home: 96 Montgomery Rd Highlands Harare Zimbabwe Office: BW Kahari 38 Samora Machel Ave Harare Zimbabwe

WOODKE, ROBERT ALLEN, lawyer; b. Schaller, Iowa, Dec. 23, 1950; s. Everett Albert and Helen Marie (Breihan) W.; m. Jan Melanie Lawrence, Aug. 15, 1987 (div. 1997). BS, Iowa State U., 1973; JD, Creighton U., 1977. Bar: Iowa 1977, Minn. 1978, U.S. Dist. Ct. (no. dist.) Iowa 1977, U.S. Dist. Ct.Minn. 1980. Law clk. Minn. 5th Dist. Ct., Marshall, 1977-78; assoc. Powell Law Office, Bemidji, Minn., 1978-82; pvt. practice, 1982—. Cons. Mgmt. Tng. Inst., Bemidji, 1987-88. Contbg. author: Flying Solo: A Survival Guide for Solo Lawyers, 1984, 2d edit., 1994, Going to Trial, 1989, 2d edit. 1999, Personal Injury Handbook, 1991. Recipient Ann. Legal Svc. award N.W. Minn. Legal Svcs., Moorehead, 1987. Mem. ABA (coun. mem. sect. gen. practice 1994-98; co-editor-in-chief Legal Tech. and Practice Guide 1996-98, mem. editl. bd.), Minn. Trial Lawyers Assn., Minn. Bar Assn. (chair sect. of gen. practice 1990-92, chair GP solo and small firm sect. 2000—), Beltrami County Bar Assn. (pres. 1988-89), 15th Dist. Bar Assn. (treas. 1986-87, pres. 1997-98), Downtown Bus. and Profl. Assn., Bemidji C. of C., Jaycees (v.p. 1986-87), Lions Club (2d v.p. Bemidji chpt. 1987-88, 1st v.p. 1988—, pres. 1989—). Republican. Lutheran. General civil litigation, General practice, Personal injury. Office: Brouse Woodke & Meyer PLLP 312 America Ave NW Bemidji MN 56601-3121 E-mail: rawoodke@paulbunyan.net

WOODLAND, IRWIN FRANCIS, lawyer; b. New York, Sept. 2, 1922; s. John James and Mary (Hynes) W.; m. Sally Duffy, Sept. 23, 1954; children: Connie, J. Patrick, Stephen, Joseph, William, David, Duffy. BA, Columbia U., 1948; JD, Ohio State U., 1959. Bar: Calif. 1960, Wash., 1991, U.S. Dist. Ct. (cen. dist.) Calif. 1960, U.S. Dist. Ct. (no. dist.) Calif. 1962, U.S. Dist. Ct. (so. dist.) Calif. From assoc. to ptnr. Gibson, Dunn & Crutcher, L.A., 1959-88. Bd. dirs. Sunlaw Energy Corp., Vernon, Calif. With USAF, 1942-45, ETO. Mem. ABA, Calif. Bar Assn., L.A. Bar Assn., Wash. State Bar Assn., Phi Delta Phi, Jonathan Club. Roman Catholic. Antitrust, General civil litigation, FERC practice. Address: Gibson Dunn & Crutcher 333 S Grand Ave Ste 4400 Los Angeles CA 90071-1548

WOODLOCK, DOUGLAS PRESTON, judge; b. Hartford, Conn., Feb. 27, 1947; s. Preston and Kathryn (Ropp) W.; m. Patricia Mathilde Powers, Aug. 30, 1969; children: Pamela, Benjamin. BA, Yale U., 1969; JD, Georgetown U., 1975. Bar: Mass. 1975. Reporter Chgo. Sun-Times, 1969-73; staff mem. SEC, Washington, 1973-75; law clk. to Judge F.J. Murray U.S. Dist. Ct. Mass., Boston, 1975-76; assoc. Goodwin, Procter & Hoar, 1976-79, 83-84, ptnr., 1984-86; asst. U.S. atty., 1979-83; judge U.S. Dist. Ct., 1986—. Instr. Harvard U. Law Sch., 1980, 81; mem. U.S. Jud. Conf. Com. on Security Space and Facilities, 1987-95; chmn. New Boston Fed. Courthouse Bldg. Com., 1987-98. Articles editor Georgetown Law Jour., 1973-75; contbr. articles to profl. jours. Chmn. Commonwealth of Mass. Com. for Pub. Counsel Svcs., 1984-86, Town of Hamilton Bd. Appeals, 1978-79. Recipient Dir.'s award U.S. Dept. Justice, 1983, Thomas Jefferson award for Pub. Architecture, AIA, 1996. Mem. ABA, Mass. Bar Assn., Boston Bar Assn., Am. Law Inst., Am. Judicature Soc., Am. Bar Found., Fed. Judges Assn. (bd. dirs. 1996-01), Mass. Hist. Soc. Office: US Courthouse 1 Courthouse Way Ste 4110 Boston MA 02210-3006

WOODROW, RANDALL MARK, lawyer; b. Anniston, Ala., June 17, 1956; s. Herbert Milisam and Rose (Marshall) W.; m. Carolyn Ann Jackson, Jan. 7, 1977; children: Amanda Lauren, Emily Claire, Taylor Jackson, Douglas Cockrell. BA in Polit. Sci., Jacksonville (Ala.) State U., 1978; JD, Samford U., 1981. Bar: Ala. 1981. Law clk. to judge U.S. Dist. Ct. (no. dist.) Ala., 1981-82; ptnr. Doster & Woodrow, Anniston, Ala., 1990—. Asst. dist. atty. 7th Jud. Cir., Anniston, 1983; adj. prof. Jacksonville State U., 1985-86. Chmn. crusade Calhoun County Cancer Soc., Anniston, 1983; mem. adminstrv. bd. dirs. 1st United Meth. Ch., Anniston, 1984—; pres. Boys Clubs of Anniston, Inc., 1985; mem. Calhoun County Econ. Devel. Coun., 1995—; mem. Jacksonville (Ala.) Planning Commn., 1995—; mem. City of Jacksonville Bd. Edn., 1996—. Mem. ABA, Ala. Bar Assn., Calhoun County Bar Assn., Calhoun County C. of C. Federal civil litigation, State civil litigation, General corporate. Home: 509 6th St NE Jacksonville AL 36265-1617 Office: Doster & Woodrow PO Box 2286 Anniston AL 36202-2286

WOODRUFF, RANDALL LEE, lawyer; b. Anderson, Ind., July 31, 1954; s. Billy Max and Phyllis Joan (Helmick) W.; m. Lucetta Farnham, Aug. 15, 1976. BA, Ind. U., 1976, JD, 1985. Bar: Ind. 1985, U.S. Dist. Ct. (no. and so. dists.) Ind. 1985, U.S. Supreme Ct. 1989. Exec. dir Cmty. Justice Ctr., Anderson, 1979-85; assoc. Shearer, Schrock & Woodruff, 1985-87; pvt. practice, 1987-97, Woodruff Law Offices, P.C., 1997—. Bd. dirs. East Cen. Legal Svcs. Program, Anderson, 1986-89; trustee Chpt. 7 Bankruptcy Panel, So. Dist. Ind., 1991—. Bd. dirs. Offender Aid & Restoration of the U.S., 1988-93. Mem. Ind. Assn. Criminal Def. Lawyers, Ct. Appointed Spl. Advocates (bd. dirs. 1988), Madison County Bar Assn. (sec./treas. 1990, v.p. 1991, pres. 1992). Methodist. Criminal, General practice, Personal injury. Office: 109 E 9th St Anderson IN 46016-1509 E-mail: rlwtrustee@home.com, rlwoodruff@home.com

WOODRUM, CLIFTON A., III, lawyer, state legislator; b. Washington, July 23, 1938; s. Clifton A. Jr. and Margaret (Lanier) W.; m. Emily Abbitt, Aug. 10, 1963; children: Robert, Meredith W. Snowden, Anne. AB, U. N.C., 1961; LLB, U. Va., 1964. Bar: Va. 1964, U.S. Dist. Ct. (we. dist.) Va. 1964, U.S. Ct. Appeals (4th cir.) 1968, U.S. Supreme Ct. 1970. Assoc. Dodson, Pence & Coulter, Roanoke, Va., 1964-68; ptnr. Dodson, Pence, Viar, Woodrum & Mackey, 1968-95; counsel Dodson, Pence & Viar, 1995-98; mem. Va. Ho. of Dels., 1980—. Chmn. 6th Dist. Dem. Com., Va., 1972-76; mem. State Water Commn., 1981-2000, State Crime Commn., 1982-2000, chmn., 1995-98; chmn. Med. Malpractice Study, Va., 1984-85, Freedom of Info. Study, 1998-2000; mem. Electric Utility Restructing Com., 1997—, Freedom of Info. Adv. Coun., 2000—, chair. Mem. ABA, Va. Bar Assn., Roanoke Bar Assn. Episcopalian. Federal civil litigation, State civil litigation, General practice. Home: 2641 Cornwallis Ave SE Roanoke VA 24014-3339 Office: Clifton A Woodrum PO Box 990 Roanoke VA 24005-0990

WOODS, CHRISTOPHER JOHN, lawyer, solicitor; b. Eng., Feb. 17, 1957; s. William Ernest and Jean W.; m. Sarah Karen Preston, Sept. 1, 1990; children: Henry, James. BA in Law, Nottingham Trent, Eng., 1979. Bar: Eng. 1984, Hong Kong 1988, N.Y. 1999. Trainee solicitor Norton Rose, London, 1982-84; solicitor Clifford Chance, London and Hong Kong, 1984-90; solicitor, ptnr. Simmons & Simmons, Hong Kong and N.Y.C., 1990—. Co-author: Technology Transfer in the PRC, 1988. Mem. Internat. Trademark Assn. (com. 1990). Avocations: classic cars, mountain biking. Computer, Intellectual property, Trademark and copyright. Office: Simmons & Simmons 570 Lexington Ave New York NY 10022-6837

WOODS, DANIEL JAMES, lawyer; b. Bklyn., Nov. 12, 1952; s. James J. and Elinor (Masten) W.; m. Kathryn Anne Morris, Dec. 27, 1974; children: Meghan M., Alexandra K., Shauna E. AB cum laude, U. So. Calif., 1974, JD, 1977. Bar: Calif. 1977, U.S. Dist. Ct. (cen., ea., so., and no. dists.) Calif., U.S. ct Appeals (9th cir.) 1978, U.S. Supreme Ct. 1981. Law clk. to judge U.S. Dist. Ct. (ctrl. dist.), Calif., 1977-78; assoc. Brobeck, Phleger & Harrison, L.A., 1978-84, ptnr., 1984-96, White & Case LLP, 1996—. Vol. pro tem L.A. Mcpl. Ct., 1985—, L.A. Superior Ct., 1989—. Mem. ABA (jud. adminstrn. sect.), Maritime Law Assn., Assn. Trial Lawyers Am. (assoc.). Roman Catholic. Avocations: tennis, bicycling, travel. Appellate, Federal civil litigation, State civil litigation. Office: White & Case LLP 633 W 5th St Los Angeles CA 90071-2627 E-mail: dwoods@whitecase.com

WOODS, GEORGE EDWARD, judge; b. 1923; m. Janice Smith. Student, Ohio No. U., 1941-43, 46, Tex. A&M Coll., 1943, Ill. Inst. Tech., 1943; JD, Detroit Coll. Law, 1949. Sole practice, Pontiac, Mich., 1949-51; asst. pros. atty. Oakland County, 1951-52; chief asst. U.S. atty. Ea. Dist. Mich., 1953-60, U.S. atty., 1960-61; assoc. Honigman, Miller, Schwartz and Cohn, Detroit, 1961-62; sole practice, 1962-81; judge U.S. Bankruptcy Ct., 1981-83, U.S. Dist. Ct. (ea. dist.) Mich., Detroit, 1983-93, sr. judge, 1993—. Served with AUS, 1943-46. Fellow Internat. Acad. Trial Lawyers, Am. Coll. Trial Lawyers; mem. Fed. Bar Assn., State Bar Mich. Office: US Dist Ct 277 US Courthouse 231 W Lafayette Blvd Detroit MI 48226-2700

WOODS, HARRY ARTHUR, JR. lawyer; b. Hartford, Ark., Feb. 15, 1941; s. Harry Arthur and Viada (Young) W.; m. Carol Ann Meschter, Jan. 21, 1967; children: Harry Arthur III, Elizabeth Ann. BA in Econs., Okla. State U., 1963; JD, NYU, 1966. Bar: N.Y. 1966, Okla. 1970. Assoc. White & Case, N.Y.C., 1966-67, Crowe & Dunlevy, Oklahoma City, 1971-75, ptnr., 1975—. Councilman City of Edmond, 1975-79, mayor pro tem, 1977-79. Capt. JAGC U.S. Army, 1967-71. Mem. ABA, Am. Law Inst., Internat. Assn. Def. Counsel, Okla. Bar Assn. (bd. govs. 2001-03, Outstanding Svc. award 1982, Golden Gavel award 1998, Neil Bogan Professionalism award 1998), Ruth Bader Ginsburg Inn of Ct. (pres. 1998-2000), Okla. County Bar Assn. (bd. dirs. 2001—). Democrat. Methodist. Avocations: flying, jogging, bicycling, photography, rock climbing. Federal civil litigation, State civil litigation, Product liability. Office: Crowe & Dunlevy 1800 Mid-America Tower 20 N Broadway Ave Ste 1800 Oklahoma City OK 73102-8273

WOODS, HENRY, federal judge; b. Abbeville, Miss., Mar. 17, 1918; s. Joseph Neal and Mary Jett (Wooldridge) W.; m. Kathleen Mary McCaffrey, Jan. 1, 1943; children— Mary Sue, Thomas Henry, Eileen Anne, James Michael. B.A., U. Ark., 1938, J.D. cum laude, 1940. Bar: Ark. bar 1940. Spl. agt. FBI, 1941-46; mem. firm Alston & Woods, Texarkana, Ark., 1946-48; exec. sec. to Gov. Ark., 1949-53; mem. firm McMath, Leatherman & Woods, Little Rock, 1953-80; judge U.S. Dist. Ct. (ea. dist.) Ark., 1980-95, sr. judge, 1995—. Referee in bankruptcy U.S. Dist. Ct., Texarkana, 1947-48; spl. assoc. justice Ark. Supreme Ct., 1967-74, chmn. com. model jury instrns., 1973-80; chmn. bd. Ctr. Trial and Appellate Advocacy, Hastings Coll. Law, San Francisco, 1975-76; mem. joint conf. com. ABA-AMA, 1973-78, Ark. Constl. Revision Study Commn., 1967-68. Author treatise comparative fault.; Contbr. articles to legal jours. Pres. Young Democrats Ark., 1946-48; mem. Gubernatorial Com. Study Death Penalty, 1971-73. Mem. ABA, Ark. Bar Assn. (pres. 1972-73, Outstanding Lawyer award 1975), Pulaski County Bar Assn., Assn. Trial Lawyers Am. (gov. 1965-67), Ark. Trial Lawyers Assn. (pres. 1965-67), Internat. Acad. Trial Lawyers, Internat. Soc. Barristers, Am. Coll. Trial Lawyers, Am. Bd. Trial Advocates, Phi Alpha Delta. Methodist. Home: 42 Wingate Dr Little Rock AR 72205-2556 Office: US Dist Ct 600 W Capitol Ave Ste 360 Little Rock AR 72201-3323

WOODS, JAMES ROBERT, lawyer; b. San Francisco, Aug. 3, 1947; s. Robert H. and Grace (Snowhill) W.; m. Linda Stephens; children: Heather F., Adam Boyd. AB with honors, U. Calif., Berkeley, 1969; JD, U. Calif., Davis, 1972. Bar: Calif. 1972, N.Y. 1973, U.S. Dist. Ct. (so. & ea. dists.) N.Y. 1975, U.S. Ct. Appeals (2d cir.) 1975, U.S. Dist. Ct. (no. dist.) Calif. 1984. Ptnr. LeBoeuf, Lamb, Greene & MacRae L.L.P., San Francisco, 1983—. Co-author: California Insurance Law and Practice; contbr. articles to profl. jours. General corporate, Insurance. Office: LeBoeuf Lamb Greene & MacRae LLP 1 Embarcadero Ctr Ste 400 San Francisco CA 94111-3619

WOODS, LARRY DAVID, lawyer, educator; b. Martinsburg, WV, Sept. 10, 1944; s. Allen Noel and Loyce L. (Dillingham) W.; children— Rachel, Allen, Sarah. B.A., Emory U., 1966; J.D., Northwestern U., 1969. Bar: Tenn. 1969, Ga. 1970. Dir. litigation Atlanta Legal Aid Soc., Inc., 1969-71; assoc. dir. Atlanta Mcpl. Defender Project, 1970; ptnr. Woods & Woods, Nashville, 1971—; assoc. prof. Tenn. State U., 1972-84, prof., 1984— ; bd. dirs. Citizen's Bank; lectr. Taft Ins., 1974-79, Am. Criminology Soc., 1984; chmn. bd. Southeastern Inst. Paralegal Tng. Nat. bd. editors' Matthew Benders, 1984— . Del., Tenn. Democratic Conv., 1972, 76, 80. Mem. Tenn. Bar Assn. (ho. of dels. 1979-85), Ga. Bar Assn., ABA, Fed. Bar Assn., Tenn. Assn. Criminal Def. Lawyers (dir. 1975-78). Methodist. Author: (with Fowler) Crime and Investigation, 1967; Compulsory Service and the Alternatives, 1968; The Strategy of Intervention, 1969; Pollution: Problems and Proposals, 1970; Co-editor: Tools for the Ultimate Trial: Tennessee Death Penalty Practice and Procedure, 1985; mem. editl. bd. James Pub. Co., 1993-95, The Fed. Lawyer, 1994-95. Federal civil litigation, General corporate, General practice. Office: 631 2nd Ave S Ste 1-R Nashville TN 37210-2025

WOODS, RICHARD DALE, lawyer; b. Kansas City, Mo., May 20, 1950; s. Willard Dale and Betty Sue (Duncan) W.; m. Cecelia Ann Thompson, Aug. 11, 1973 (div. July 1996); children: Duncan Warren, Shannon Cecelia; m. Mary Linna Lash, June 6, 1999. BA, U. Kans., 1972; JD, U. Mo., 1975. Bar: Mo. 1975, Kans. 2000, U.S. Dist. Ct. (we. dist.) Mo. 1975, U.S. Tax Ct. 1999. Assoc. Shook, Hardy & Bacon L.L.P., Kansas City, Mo., 1975-79, ptnr., 1980-2000; shareholder Kirkland & Woods, P.C., Overland Park, Kans., 2001—. Gen. chmn. Estate Planning Symposium, Kansas City, 1985-86; chair Northland Coalition, 1993. Chmn. fin. com. North Woods Ch., Kansas City, 1986-88, 93-96; mem. sch. bd. N. Kansas City Sch. Dist., 1990-97, treas., 1992-97; mem. North Kansas City Ednl. Found., 1998—, pres., 1999-2001; mem. planned giving com. Truman Med. Ctr., 1992—, chmn., 1992-98; mem. Clay County Tax Increment Fin. Commn., 1990-99; bd. dirs. Heart of Am. Family Svcs., 1998—, sec., 2000—. Fellow Am. Coll. Trust and Estate Counsel; mem. ABA, Mo. Bar Assn., Kans. Bar Assn., Johnson County Bar Assn., Kansas City Met. Bar Assn., Lawyers Assn. Kans. City (sec., v.p., pres. young lawyers sect. 1981-84), Kans. City Estate Planning Soc. (bd. dirs. 1985-88, 93-95). Democrat. Estate planning, Probate, Real property. Office: Kirkland & Woods PC 6201 College Blvd Ste 250 Overland Park KS 66211 E-mail: rwoods@kcnet.com

WOODS, ROBERT EDWARD, lawyer; b. Albert Lea, Minn., Mar. 27, 1952; s. William Fabian and Maxine Elizabeth (Schmit) W.; m. Cynthia Anne Pratt, Dec. 26, 1975; children: Laura Marie Woods, Amy Elizabeth Woods. BA, U. Minn., 1974, JD, 1977; MBA, U. Pa., 1983. Bar: Minn. 1977, U.S. Dist. Ct. Minn. 1980, U.S. Ct. Appeals (8th cir.) 1980, Calif. 2000. Assoc. Moriarty & Janzen, Mpls., 1977-81, Berger & Montague, Phila., 1982-83, Briggs and Morgan, St. Paul and Mpls., 1983-84, ptnr., 1984-99; exec. v.p., gen. counsel InsWeb Corp., Redwood City, Calif., 1999-2000; gen. counsel BORN Corp., Mpls., 2000—. Adj. prof. William Mitchell Coll. Law, St. Paul, 1985; exec. com., bd. dirs. LEX MUNDI, Ltd., Houston, 1989-93, chmn. bd. 1991-92; bd. dirs. Midwest Asia Ctr., 1993-95, chmn. bd., 1994-95. Author (with others) Business Torts, 1989; sr. contbg. editor: Evidence in America: The Federal Rules in the States, 1987. Mem. ABA, Minn. State Bar Assn., State Bar of Calif., Hennepin County Bar Assn., Ramsey County Bar Assn. (chmn. corp., banking and bus. law sect. 1985-87), Assn. Trial Lawyers Am., Wharton Club of Minn., Phi Beta Kappa. Federal civil litigation, General civil litigation, Securities. Home: 28 N Deep Lake Rd North Oaks MN 55127-6506

WOODS, WILLIAM HUNT, lawyer; b. Toledo, May 30, 1946; s. William Stanley and Marie Hunt W.; m. Mary Catherine Clucus, Aug. 5, 1972; children: Rebecca Lucile, William Clucus. BS in Edn., Ohio State U., 1968, JD cum laude, 1973. Bar: Ohio 1973, U.S. Dist. Ct. (no. and so. dists.) Ohio 1974, U.S. Ct. Appeals (6th cir.) 1980. Tchr. Perrysburg (Ohio) Pub. Schs., 1968-70; atty. McNamara & McNamara, Columbus, Ohio, 1976. Contbr. articles to profl. jours. Pres. North Columbus Jaycees, 1979-80. Fellow Columbus Bar Found.; mem. ABA (vice chair fidelity & surety law com. 1986-91, 93-98), Ohio State Bar Assn., Columbus Bar Assn. Democrat. Presbyterian. Avocations: genealogy, Civic War history, auto racing, golf. General civil litigation, Insurance, Fidelity and surety. Office: McNamara & McNamara 88 E Broad St Ste 1250 Columbus OH 43215-3558

WOODSIDE, FRANK C., III, lawyer, educator, physician; b. Glen Ridge, N.J., Apr. 18, 1944; s. Frank C. and Dorothea (Poulin) W.; m. Julia K. Moses, Nov. 15, 1974; children: Patrick Michael, Christopher Ryan. BS, Ohio State U., 1966, JD, 1969; MD, U. Cin., 1973. Diplomate Am. Bd. Legal Medicine, Am. Bd. Forensic Medicine, Am. Bd. Profl. Liability Attys. Mem. Dinsmore & Shohl, Cin.; clin. prof. pediats.emeritus U. Cin., 1992—. Adj. prof. law U. Cin., 1973—. Editor: Drug Product Liability, 1985—. Fellow Am. Coll. Legal Medicine, Am. Coll. Forensic Examiners, Am. Soc. Hosp. Attys., Soc. Ohio Hosp. Attys.; mem. ABA, FBA, Ohio Bar Assn., Internat. Assn. Def. Counsel, Def. Rsch. Inst. (chmn. drug and med. svc. com. 1988-91), Cin. Bar Assn. Personal injury, Product liability, Professional liability. Office: Dinsmore & Shohl 1900 Chemed Ctr 255 E 5th St Cincinnati OH 45202-4700 E-mail: woodside@dinslaw.com

WOODWORTH, RAMSEY LLOYD, lawyer; b. Syracuse, N.Y., Dec. 26, 1941; s. Woodrow Lloyd and Helen (Ramsey) W.; m. Diane Elizabeth McMillion, June 12, 1971; children: Scott, Ashley, Jeffrey. AB, Brown U., 1964; LLM cum laude, Syracuse (N.Y.) U., 1967. Bar: N.Y. 1967, D.C. 1968, U.S. Ct. Appeals (D.C. cir.) 1968. Atty., advisor FCC, Washington, 1967-68; from assoc. to ptnr. Hedrick & Lane, 1968-82; prin. Wilkes, Artis, Hedrick & Lane, Chartered, 1982-99; of counsel Shook, Hardy & Bacon LLP, 1999—. Convenor Peace Luth. Ch., Alexandria, 1985-86; pres. Broadcast Pioneers Ednl. Fund, Inc., 1997—. Mem. Fed. Comm. Bar Assn. (exec. com. 1986-89, chair profl. responsibility com. 1984-86, treas. 1989-90, chmn. Fed. Commn. Bar Assn. Found. 1991-93, trustee 1991-94, Univ. Club Washington, Order of Coif. Avocation: swimming. Administrative and regulatory, Communications, Intellectual property. Office: Shook Hardy & Bacon LLP 600 14th St NW Ste 800 Washington DC 20005-2099 E-mail: rwoodworth@shb.com

WOODY, DONALD EUGENE, lawyer; b. Springfield, Mo., Mar. 10, 1948; s. Raymond D. and Elizabeth Ellen (Bushnell) W.; m. Ann Louise Ruhl, June 5, 1971; children: Marshall Wittmann, Catherine Elizabeth. BA in Polit. Sci. with honors, U. Mo., 1970, JD, 1973. Bar: Mo. 1973, U.S. Dist. Ct. (we. dist.) Mo. 1973, U.S. Ct. Appeals (8th cir.) 1973, U.S. Supreme Ct. 1987. Assoc. Neale, Newman & Bradshaw, Springfield, 1973-74; ptnr. Taylor, Stafford & Woody, 1974-82, Taylor, Stafford, Woody, Cowherd & Clithero, Springfield, 1983-93, Taylor, Stafford, Woody, Clithero & Fitzgerald, Springfield, 1993-2000; of counsel Hall, Ansley, Rodgers & Condry, P.C., 2001—. Editor U. Mo. Law Rev., 1973. Chmn. county campaign U.S. senator Thomas Eagleton, Springfield, 1980; committeeman Greene County Dem. Party, Springfield, 1984-86; cons.

Children's Home Mayors commn., Springfield, 1985. Mem. ABA, Springfield Metro Bar Assn. (sec. 1977-80, precedure com. 1986, bd. dirs. 1991-93, pres.-elect 1995, pres. 1996), Assn. Trial Lawyers Am., Springfield C. of C. (chmn. performing arts com. 1980-84), Order of Coif, Phi Delta Phi. Avocations: fishing, growing roses, bicycling, running. Federal civil litigation, State civil litigation, Personal injury. Home: 1421 S Ginger Blue Ave Springfield MO 65809-2260 Office: Hall Ansley Rodgers and Condry PC PO Box 4609 1370 E Primrose Ste A Springfield MO 65804 E-mail: dwoody@harcpc.com

WOOLDRIDGE, WILLIAM CHARLES, lawyer; b. Miami, Fla., Feb. 24, 1943; s. Clarence Edward and Easter Marguerite (Souders) W.; m. Joyce L. Norton, June 15, 1968; children: William Charles, John Michael. BA, Harvard U., 1965; LLB, U. Va., 1969. Bar: Va. 1969. Atty. Norfolk and Western Ry. Co., 1973-82; with Norfolk So. Corp., 1982-2000, v.p. dept. law, 1996-2000. Pres. John Marshall Found., Richmond, Va., 1992-94; pres. Norfolk Hist. Soc., 1995-96; chair Friends of Chrysler Mus. Hist. Houses, 1997-99; bd. dirs. Sta. WHRO (FM and TV), 1997-2000. Capt. JAGC, U.S. Army, 1969-73. Mem. Va. Bar Assn. Republican. Administrative and regulatory, Antitrust, General corporate.

WOOLF, GEOFFREY STEPHEN, lawyer; b. London, Oct. 13, 1946; s. Edward and Ruth W.; m. Josephine Kay Likerman, Feb. 14, 1985; children: Nicholas, Simon, Alexander. LLB, Kings Coll., London, 1967. Ptnr. Stephenson Harwood, London, 1975-99, SJ Berwin & Co., London, 1999—. Mem. Insolvency Lawyers Assn. Banking, Bankruptcy, Consumer commercial. Office: SJ Berwin & Co 222 Grays Inn Rd WC1X 8XF London England Fax: 0207533 2000. E-mail: geoffrey.woolf@sjberwin.com

WOOLF, JOHN PAUL, lawyer; b. Bloomington, Ind., Apr. 21, 1943; s. Frank Edward and Martha Ann (Barrett) W.; m. Mary L. Waller, aug. 20, 1967; children: Thomas, Matthew, David, Susan. BS in Bus., Kans. State U., 1965; JD, U. Kans., 1968; postgrad. Nat. Coll. Advocacy, Suffolk U., 1976. Bar: Kans. 1968, U.S. Ct. Appeals (10th cir.) 1968, U.S. Ct. Appeals (5th cir.) 1977. Ptnr. Martin, Porter, Pringle, Schell & Fair, Wichita, Kans., 1970-82, Martin, Pringle, Oliver, Triplett & Wallace, Wichita, 1982-85, Triplett, Woolf & Garretson, Wichita, 1985—. Bd. dirs. Big Bros. Sedgwick County, 1973-77, pres., 1976-77; bd. dirs. Big Bros./Big Sisters Sedgwick County, 1977—, Big Bros./Big Sisters Am., 1978-85, mem. exec. com., 1980-85, pres. Region IX, 1979-83; bd. dirs. Kans. Vietnam Vets. Leadership Program, 1982-90. Served to cap., U.S. Army, 1968-70. Decorated Bronze stars (2), Nat. Def. medal, USARV Vietnam medal. Mem. ABA, Kans. Bar Assn., Wichita Bar Assn., Assn. Trial Lawyers Am., Kans. Trial Lawyers Assn., Wichita Country Club (pres. 1998-2000). Republican. Congregationalist. Federal civil litigation, State civil litigation, Product liability. Address: Triplett Woolf Garretson 2959 N Rock Rd Ste 300 Wichita KS 67226-5100 E-mail: pwoolf@twgfirm.com

WOOSNAM, RICHARD EDWARD, venture capitalist, lawyer; b. Anderson, Ind., June 27, 1942; s. Richard Wendelland Ruth (Cleveland) W.; children: Cynthia S., Elizabeth C. BS, Ind. U., 1964, JD, 1967, MBA, 1968. Bar: Ind. 1967, U.S. Dist. Ct. (so. dist.) Ind. 1967. Instr. bus. law Ind. U., Bloomington, 1966-68; assoc. Ferguson, Ferguson & Lloyd, 1967-68; dep. pros. Monroe County, 1967-68; tax acct. Price Waterhouse, Phila., 1968-69; v.p., treas. Innovest Group, Inc., 1969-82, chmn., pres., 1983—. Guest lectr. Wharton Sch. Bus., U. Pa., Ind. U., Bloomington, 1975—; bd. dirs. Capital Mgmt. Corp., N.Y. Achievement, L.L.C., Innovest Talent Svcs., Inc., Command Equity Group, LLC, Bridges Learning Sys., Inc., World Affairs Coun. of Phila., Fairmount Park Conservancy, Phila. Hospitality, Inc., Ctr. for Entrepreneurship and Innovation; trustee Pa. Acad. Fine Arts. Bd. dirs. Walnut St. Theatre; mem. nat. adv. bd. Point Breeze Performing Arts Ctr. Mem. ABA, Ind. Bar Assn., Union League of Phila., Sunday Breakfast Club, The Pa Soc. Home: 1810 Spruce St Philadelphia PA 19103-6677 Office: 2000 Market St Ste 1400 Philadelphia PA 19103-3214

WORK, CHARLES ROBERT, lawyer; b. Glendale, Calif., June 21, 1940; s. Raymond P. and Minna M. (Fricke) W.; m. Linda S. Smith, Oct. 4, 1965 (div.); children: Matthew Keehn, Mary Lucila Landis, Benjamin Reed; m. Veronica A. Haggart, Apr., 1985, 1 child, Andrew Haggart. BA, Wesleyan U., 1962; JD, U. Chgo., 1965; LLM, Georgetown U., 1966. Bar: D.C. 1965, Utah 1965. Asst. U.S. atty. D.C., 1966-73; dep. adminstr. law enforcement assistance adminstrn., U.S. Dept. Justice, 1973-75; ptnr. Peabody, Lambert & Meyers, Washington, 1975-82, McDermott, Will & Emery, Washington, 1982—. Recipient Rockefeller Pub. Service award 1978. Mem. D.C. Bar (pres. 1976-77). Federal civil litigation, State civil litigation, Private international. Office: McDermott Will & Emery 600 13th St NW Fl 12-8 Washington DC 20005-3005

WORKMAN, H(ARLEY) ROSS, patent lawyer; b. Salt Lake City, Dec. 31, 1940; s. Harley E. and Lucille (Ramsey) W.; m. Katherine Meyers, Dec. 7, 1962; children: Teri, Christopher, Heidi, Ryan. BA in Chemistry, U. Utah, 1967, JD, 1970. Bar: Utah 1970, U.S. Dist. Ct. Utah 1970, U.S. Dist. Ct. (no. dist.) Calif. 1983, U.S. Dist. Ct. (ea. dist.) Ky. 1984, U.S. Ct. Customs and Patent Appeals 1971, U.S. Ct. Claims 1971, U.S. Ct. Appeals (5th and 10th cirs.) 1979, U.S. Ct. Appeals (11th cir.) 1981, U.S. Supreme Ct. 1980, U.S. Ct. Appeals (fed. cir.) 1982. Assoc. Fox, Edward & Gardiner, Salt Lake City, 1970-73, ptnr., 1973-84, also dir.; ptnr. Workman, Nydegger & Seeley, Salt Lake City, 1984—, also dir. Contbr. articles to profl. jours. Pres. World Trade Assn. of Utah, Salt Lake City, 1978-79; chmn. Granite Mental Health Citizen's Council, Salt Lake City, 1973-75; del. Republican State Conv., Salt Lake City; del. Rep. County Conv. Recipient Danforth cert. appreciation, 1959; cert. appreciation Boy Scouts Am., 1983. Mem. Am. Intellectual Property Law Assn. (chmn. fed. practice and procedures com. 1982-83, sec. 1983, chmn. continuing legal edn. com. 1984-85, bd. dirs. 1986-89, del. com. of experts on the harmonization of certain provisions in laws for the protection of inventions), ABA, Utah State Bar Assn., Copyright Soc. of U.S., World Intellectual Property Orgn. Mormon. Federal civil litigation, Patent, Trademark and copyright. Home: 4093 Powers Cir Salt Lake City UT 84124-3427 Office: Workman Nydegger & Seeley 60 E South Temple 1000 Eagle Gate Towers Salt Lake City UT 84111

WORLEY, JANE LUDWIG, lawyer; b. Reading, Pa., Sept. 4, 1917; d. Walter Schearer and Marion Grace (Johns) L.; m. Floyd Edwin Worley, Oct. 30, 1946 (dec. Jan. 1982); children: Laetitia Anne, Thomas Allen, Christopher Ludwig. AB, Bryn Mawr Coll., 1938; JD, Temple U., 1942. Bar: Pa. 1943, U.S. Dist. Ct. (ea. dist.) Pa. 1980, U.S. Supreme Ct. 1968. Assoc. Richardson Moss & Richardson, Reading, 1943-48; pvt. practice Wernersville, Pa., 1948—. V.p., bd. dirs. Worley Lumber Co. Inc., Wernersville, 1955—. Sec. Friends of Reading Mus., 1986-91; sec. Berks County chpt. ARC, 1986-87, v.p., 1987-91. Mem. ABA, Pa. Bar Assn., Berks County Bar Assn., DAR, Jr. League Reading. Republican. Mem. United Ch. of Christ. Avocations: antique and art collecting, travel. Family and matrimonial, General practice, Real property. Office: 6210 Penn Ave Wernersville PA 19565

WORLEY, ROBERT WILLIAM, JR. retired lawyer; b. Anderson, Ind., June 13, 1935; s. Robert William and Dorothy Mayhew (Hayler) W.; m. Diana Lynn Matthews, Aug. 22, 1959; children: Nathanael, Hope Hillegas. BS in Chem. Engring., Lehigh U., 1956; LLB, Harvard U., 1960. Bar: Conn. 1960, U.S. Supreme Ct. 1966, Fla. 1977. Assoc. then ptnr. Cummings & Lockwood, Stamford, Conn., 1960-91; gen. counsel Consol. Asset Recover Corp. sub. Chase Manhattan Corp., Bridgeport, 1991-94; v.p., asst. gen. counsel The Chase Manhattan Bank, N.Y.C., 1994-2001; ret., 2001. Mem. trustees com. on bequests and trusts Lehigh U., 1979—; mem. Conn. Legis. Task Force on Probate Court Sys., 1991-93; chmn. Greenwich Arts Coun., 1981-82; v.p., bd. dirs. Greenwich Choral Soc., 1962-77, 80, mem., 1960-95; bd. dirs. Greenwich Ctr. for Chamber Music, 1981-85, Greenwich Symphony, 1986-89; commr. Greenwich Housing Authority, 1972-77; past mem. Rep. Town Com. Greenwich; mem. bldg. com. for sr. ctr. Greenwich Bd. Selectman, 1980-81. Capt. JAGC, AUS, 1965. Mem. Conn. Bar Assn. (exec. com. probate sect. 1980), Harvard Club Boston. Christian Scientist. Banking, Estate planning, Probate. Home: PO Box 1055 Marion MA 02738-0019

WORRELL, STEWART PHILLIP, lawyer, trust executive; b. Montreal, Apr. 13, 1956; Chmn. The Libr. Trust, Montreal, 1999—. Charter mem. Mbanx, Toronto, 1998—. Author: (poetry) Children Dressed in Black, 1999. Mem. Fed. Bar Assn., InterAm. Bar Assn., Conseil de Roi, U.S. Ski Assn., Beaconsfield Yacht Club, Univ. Club. Avocations: skiing, sailing, chess, golf, photography.

WORTHINGTON, CAROLE YARD LYNCH, lawyer; b. Knoxville, Tenn., Aug. 29, 1951; d. Charles R. and Alma (Allred) Yard; m. Robert F. Worthington Jr., Sept. 14, 1996; 1 child, Allison Kathleen. BA, U. Tenn., 1972, JD, 1977. Bar: Tenn. 1977, Ga. 1982. Assoc. Thomas, Leitner, Mann, Warner & Owens, Chattanooga, 1977-78, Thomas, Mann & Gossett, Chattanooga, 1978-81, ptnr., v.p., 1981-86; ptnr. Grant, Konvalinka & Harrison, P.C., 1987-96, Carole Lynch Worthington, Atty. at Law, Knoxville, 1996—. Sec. Nat. Transp. Rsch. Ctr., Inc.; mem. U. Tenn. Alliance of Women Philanthropists. Author: Estate Planning Tennessee Practice, 1992; asst. editor Tenn. Law Rev., 1976-77. Vice chmn. allocations United Way of Chattanooga, 1985, pilot campaign, 1986; active Jr. League of Chattanooga, 1981-92; mem. alumnae adv. coun. U. Tenn. Coll. Law, 1983-92, dean's cir., 1989—; bd. dirs. Mental Health Assn. Chattanooga Inc., 1986-92, 1st v.p., 1988-89, sec., 1989-92; trustee St. Nicholas Sch., 1992-95, East Tenn. Opera Guild, 2001—. Recipient Alumni Leadership award U. Tenn. Coll. Law, 1988, 92. Fellow Am. Bar Found., Tenn. Bar Found., Chattanooga Bar Found.; mem. ABA (assembly del. 1991-97, 98-2001, com. on legal aid and indigent defendants 1994-95, select com. of house 1994-96, standing com. on charter and by laws 1999-2000, standing com. on credentials and admissions 1999-2000, standing com. on credentials and admissions 1999-2000, com. on client rels. 2000-2002), Chattanooga Bar Assn. (bd. govs. 1982-89, sec.-treas. 1985-86, pres. 1987-88), Tenn. Bar Assn. (vice chair comml. law, banking and bankruptcy 1988-90, unified bar study com. 1990-91, chair bar leadership conf. 1990, editl. bd. Tenn. Bar Jour. 1991-94, Tenn. Bar Assn. long range planning com. 1992-95, 97-99, bd. govs. 1994-96, chair long range planning com. 1995-96, future of bar com. 1998-2001), Ga. Bar Assn., Nat. Conf. Lawyers and Realtors (ABA del. 1990-92), Nat. Conf. Bar Pres.'s (exec. coun. 1989-92, treas. 1992-93, sec. 1993-94, pres.-elect 1994-95, pres. 1995-96), Tenn. Bd. Profl. Responsibility, Phi Alpha Delta. General corporate, Probate, Securities. Home: 7618 Cherokee Springs Way Knoxville TN 37919-9033 E-mail: carole@clw-law.com

WORTHINGTON, DANIEL GLEN, lawyer, educator; b. Rexbury, Idaho, Aug. 15, 1957; BA magna cum laude, Brigham Young U., 1982, MEd, 1986, EdD, JD cum laude, Brigham Young U., 1989. Bar: Utah 1990. Asst. to assoc. dean students Brigham Young U., 1986-88, cons., 1987-89, mgr. planned giving, tech. cons., 1989-90, adj. prof. law and edn., 1989—; asst. dean students Coll. Eastern Utah, 1985-86; assoc. dean, exec. dir. devel. Porterville Coll. Found., 1990-91; prin. Worthington & Assocs., Provo, Utah, 1991-93; mng. atty., ptnr. Walstad & Babcock; assoc. dean U. S.D. Sch. Law, 1994-95, exec. v.p. found., 1995—. Assoc. v.p., gen. counsel U. Ctrl. Fla. Found., Orlando; adj. faculty Masters of Tax Program, U. Ctrl. Fla., 1995-99; sr. cons. Fla. Hosp. and the U. S.D. Bus. Sch., 1997—; cons. Citigroup Trust Svcs., 1997—; sr. cons. Fla. Hosp., 1997-99, v.p. gen. counsel, 1999—. Editor-in-chief jour. Edn. & Law Perspectives, 1986-88, co-chair, exec. adv. bd., dir., 1988-91; contbr. articles to profl. jours. Exec. v.p. S.D. Planned Giving Coun., 1994—; nat. assembly del. Nat. Com. on Planned, 1994—; pres. Greater Orlando Planned Giving Round Table, 1999—; v.p., gen. counsel Fla. Hosp. Found., 1999—. With USAFR, 1982-88. Mem. Supreme Ct. Hist. Soc., Federalist Soc., Nat. Soc. Fund Raising Execs., Phi Kappa Phi. Alternative dispute resolution, General corporate, Probate. Address: 7853 Horse Ferry Rd Orlando FL 32835 E-mail: dan_worthington@mail.flhmis.net

WORTHINGTON, SANDRA BOULTON, lawyer; b. Phila., July 12, 1956; BA with high distinction, U. Va., 1978; JD, Temple U., 1983. Bar: Pa. 1983, U.S. Dist. Ct. (ea. dist.) Pa. 1984. Summer clk. Ct. of Common Pleas Montgomery County, Pa., summer 1981; legal intern Peruto, Ryan & Vitullo, Phila., 1982-83; assoc. Michael D. Fioretti Law Office, 1983-84; founding ptnr. Stocker & Worthington Law Office, Jenkintown, Pa., 1984—. Legal counsel Phila. Women's Squash Racquets Assn., 1985—. Mem. Pa. Trial Lawyers Assn., Phila. Trial Lawyers Assn., Pa. Bar Assn., Montgomery County Bar Assn. Avocations: small business consulting, squash, tennis. Consumer commercial, Family and matrimonial, Personal injury. Office: Stocker & Worthington Law Offices 820 Homestead Rd Jenkintown PA 19046-2840

WORTHY, K(ENNETH) MARTIN, retired lawyer; b. Dawson, Ga., Sept. 24, 1920; s. Kenneth Spencer and Jeffrie Pruett (Martin) W.; m. Eleanor Vreeland Blewett, Feb. 15, 1947 (dec. July 1981); children: Jeffrie Martin, William Blewett; m. Katherine Teasley Jackson, June 17, 1983. Student, The Citadel, 1937-39; BPh, Emory U., 1941, JD with honors, 1947; MBA cum laude, Harvard U., 1943. Bar: Ga. 1947, D.C. 1948. Assoc. Foley & Lardner (formerly Hopkins & Sutter and Hamel & Park), Washington, 1948-51, ptnr., 1952-69, 72-90, sr. counsel, 1991—; asst. gen. counsel Treasury Dept., 1969-72; chief counsel IRS, 1969-72. Dir. Beneficial Corp., 1977-96, emeritus, 1996-98; mem. Nat. Coun. Organized Crime, 1970-72; cons. Justice Dept., 1972-74. Author: (with John M. Appleman) Basic Estate Planning, 1957; contbr. articles to profl. jours. Del. Montgomery County Civic Fedn., 1951-61, D.C. Area Health and Welfare Coun., 1960-61; mem. coun. Emory U. Law Sch., 1976—, chmn., 1993-95; trustee Chelsea Sch., 1981—, St. John's Coll., Annapolis, Md. and Santa Fe, 1987-93, 95-2001, Sherman Found., Newport Beach, Calif., 1991—, Associated Marine Inst. Found., 1999—, Ga. Wilderness Insts., 1997—, St. Simons Island Libr. Found., 2000—, chmn., 2001—; chmn. dept. fin. Episcopal Diocese, Washington, 1969-70; fellow Aspen Inst., 1982-92. Capt. AUS, 1943-46, 1951-52. Recipient Army Commendation Ribbon, 1945, Treasury Exceptional Svc. award and medal, 1972, IRS Commrs. award, 1972, Disting. Alumnus award Emory U., 1992. Fellow Am. Bar Found., Am. Coll. Tax Counsel (bd. regents 1980-88, chmn. 1985-87), Atlantic Coun. (counselor 1989-99); mem. ABA (coun. taxation sect. 1965-69, 72-75, chmn. 1973-74, del. Nat. Conf. Lawyers and CPAs 1981-87, ho. of dels. 1983-89, chmn. audit com. 1985-90), Fed. Bar Assn. (nat. coun. 1969-72, 77-79), Ga. Bar Assn., D.C. Bar, Am. Law Inst., Nat. Tax Assn., Am. Tax Policy Inst. (trustee 1989-98), Rotary, Chevy Chase Club, Met. Club, Sea Island Club, Harvard Club N.Y.C., Phi Delta Theta, Phi Delta Phi, Omicron Delta Kappa. Home: PO Box 30264 189 W Gascoigne Sea Island GA 31561 Office: Foley & Lardner 888 16th St NW Fl 7 Washington DC 20006-4103 E-mail: kworthy@foleylaw.com, kmartinworthy@aol.com

WOUTAT, PAUL GUSTAV, lawyer; b. Grand Forks, N.D., Sept. 7, 1937; s. Philip H. and Helen L. (McIntosh) W.; m. Mary G. Peterka, June 17, 1967; children— Julie R., John B., Paula M. B.A., U. N.D., 1959; J.D., U. Mich., 1962. Bar: N.D. 1962, U.S. Dist. Ct. N.D. 1965, U.S. Ct. Appeals (8th cir.) 1973, Minn. 1978. Trust officer 1st Nat. Bank, Grand Forks, 1962-64; ptnr. Vaaler, Warcup, Woutat, Zimney & Foster, Grand Forks, 1965— ; bd. dirs., chmn. Agassiz Health Systems Agy., Grand Forks, 1976-77; bd. dirs., chmn. Med. Ctr. Rehab. Hosp., Grand Forks, 1978— ; bd. dirs. chmn. United Hosps., Grand Forks, 1979— ; mem. Home Rule Charter Commn., Grand Forks, 1970. Served with Army N.G., 1956-66. Mem. Am. Arbitration Assn. (panel arbitrators), N.D. Def. Lawyers Assn., State Bar Assn. N.D., Def. Research Inst. (spl. asst. atty. gen. 1987-90. Federal civil litigation, State civil litigation, Insurance. Home: HC 70 Box 446 Laporte MN 56461-9804 Address: Vaaler Law Firm PO Box 13417 Grand Forks ND 58208-3417

WOVSANIKER, ALAN, lawyer, educator; b. Newark, Mar. 19, 1953; s. Harold and Sally (Gooen) W.; m. Susan Orme, Aug. 23, 1987. AB, Brown U., 1974; JD, Harvard U., 1977. Bar: N.J. 1977. Law clk. to presiding judge U.S. Dist. Ct. N.J., Camden, 1977-78; ptnr. Lowenstein Sandler PC, Roseland, N.J., 1978—. Adj. prof. Seton Hall Law Sch., 1988-91, Rutgers U. Law Sch., 1989-95; chmn. dist. ethics com. Supreme Ct. Contbr. articles to profl. jours. Mem. exec. com. N.J. chpt. Anti-Defamation League. Mem. Essex County Bar Assn. (trustee 1996-99, chmn. banking law com. 1994-97, chmn. corp. law com. 1999—). Banking, Mergers and acquisitions, Securities. Office: Lowenstein Sandler PC 65 Livingston Ave Roseland NJ 07068-1791 E-mail: awovsaniker@lowenstein.com

WRAY, CECIL, JR. lawyer; b. Memphis, Nov. 19, 1934; s. Thomas Cecil and Margaret (Malone) W.; m. Gilda Gates, Sept. 11, 1964; children: Christopher A., Kathleen Wray Baughman. Student, U. Va., 1952-53; BA magna cum laude, Vanderbilt U., 1956; LLB, Yale U., 1959. Bar: Tenn. 1959, N.Y. 1961, U.S. Supreme Ct. 1964. Registered counseil juridique, France, 1978-82. Law clk. to justice Tom C. Clark U.S. Supreme Ct., Washington, 1959-60; assoc. Debevoise & Plimpton, N.Y.C., 1960-67, ptnr., 1968-96, of counsel, 1997-99, resident ptnr. Paris, 1976-79. Adj. prof. N.Y. Law Sch., 1997—. Co-author: Innovative Corporate Financing Techniques, 1986. Pres. Search & Care, Inc., N.Y.C., 1981-87, Episcopal Charities, N.Y.; vestryman St. James' Ch., N.Y.C., 1982-87, warden, 1988-94; trustee Fondation des Etats-Unis, Paris, 1976-79, Ch. Pension Fund; bd. dirs. East Side Comty. Ctr., Inc.; bd. fgn. parishes Episcopal Ch., 1995—; bd. dirs. Hudson Highlands Land Trust; commr. Adirondack Park Agy. Fellow Am. Coll. Investment Counsel (trustee 1981-86, pres. 1983-84); mem. ABA, Am. Law Inst., Assn. Bar City N.Y., Coun. Fgn. Rels., Ausable Club (St. Huberts, N.Y.), Union Club, Century Club, Order of Coif, Phi Beta Kappa. Episcopalian. General corporate. Home: 47 E 88th St New York NY 10128-1152 Office: Debevoise & Plimpton 875 3rd Ave Fl 23 New York NY 10022-6225

WRAY, ROBERT, lawyer; s. George and Ann (Moriarty) W.; m. Lila Keogh (dec.); children: Jennifer, Edward, Hillary. BS, Loyola U., 1957; JD, U. Mich., 1960. Bar: D.C., Ill. 1960. Assoc. Hopkins & Sutter, Chgo., 1964-69; gen. counsel Agy. for Internat. Devel., 1969-71; sr. counsel TRW, Inc., 1972-73, Export-Import Bank of the U.S., 1974-79; prin. Robert Wray Assocs., 1979-86; internat. ptnr. Pierson, Ball & Dowd, 1986-87; prin. Robert Wray Assocs., 1988—; spec. counsel Graham & James, 1988-97; ptnr. Holland & Knight, Washington, 1997—. Recipient medal of superior honor Dept. of State. Mem. ABA, Fed. Bar Assn., Am. Soc. Internat. Law, Internat. Bar Assn., Bretton Woods Com., Met. Club, Talbot Country Club, Annapolis Yacht Club. Aviation, Private international. Office: Holland & Knight 2099 Pennsylvania Ave NW Washington DC 20026

WRAY, THOMAS JEFFERSON, lawyer; b. Nashville, July 17, 1949; s. William Esker and Imogene (Cushman) W.; m. Susan Elizabeth Wells, Aug. 19, 1972; children: William Clark, Caroline Kell. BA, Emory U., 1971; JD, U. Va., 1974. Bar: Tex. 1974, U.S. Dist. Ct. (so., no. and ea. dists.) Tex. 1976, U.S. Ct. Appeals (5th and 11th cirs.) 1976, U.S. Supreme Ct. 1987. Assoc. Fulbright & Jaworski, L.L.P., Houston, 1974-82; ptnr. Fulbright & Jaworski, 1982—. Mem. ABA, Coll. Labor and Employment Lawyers, Houston Bar Assn., Houston Mgmt. Lawyers Forum (chmn. 1981-82), Briar Club, Phi Beta Kappa. Republican. Episcopalian. Civil rights, Federal civil litigation, Labor. Home: 3662 Ella Lee Ln Houston TX 77027-4105 Office: Fulbright & Jaworski 1301 Mckinney St Ste 5100 Houston TX 77010-3095 E-mail: tjwray@fulbright.com

WRIGHT, ALLISON MARSHALL, lawyer; b. Opelika, Ala., Feb. 18, 1969; d. Warren Berry and Dale (Hays) Marshall; m. Morris Jackson Wright, June 11, 1994. BS in Bus. Adminstrn., Auburn (Ala.) U., 1991; JD, Samford U., Birmingham, Ala., 1996. Bar: Ala. 1996. Jud. law clk. 10th Jud. Cir. Ala., Birmingham, 1996-98; assoc. Porter, Porter & Hassinger, 1998—. Mem. ABA, Ala. State Bar, Birmingham Bar Assn., Jr. League Birmingham. Episcopalian. Office: Porter Porter & Hassinger 215 21st St N Ste 1000 Birmingham AL 35210-1145

WRIGHT, ARTHUR MCINTOSH, lawyer, industrial products consultant; b. El Dorado, Kans., Dec. 9, 1930; s. Ray Arthur and Anna (McIntosh) W.; A.B., Grinnell Coll., 1952; LL.B., Harvard, 1958; m. Mary Alice Smaltz, June 23, 1956; children: David A., Steven E., Carolyn E. Bar: Mo. 1959, Ill. 1964. Assoc. Swanson, Midgley, Jones, Blackmar & Eager, Kansas City, Mo., 1958-64; corp. atty. Baxter Labs., Inc., Morton Grove, Ill., 1964-67; v.p., sec., counsel N.Am. Car Corp., Chgo., 1968-71; sec., corp. counsel Ceco Corp., Chgo., 1971-77; v.p., gen. counsel, sec. Ill. Tool Works Inc., Glenview, 1977-91. Mem. New Trier Twp. High Schs. Bd. Edn., 1977-85, pres., 1983-85; mem. bd. advisors Chgo. Vol. Legal Svcs. Found., 1982-90, chmn., 1984-86; mem. bd. dirs. The Desert Chorale, Santa Fe, N.M., 1992-94, Food For Santa Fe, 1995—. Served with U.S. Army, 1953-55. Mem. Ill. Bar Assn., Am. Judicature Soc., Sigma Delta Chi. Presbyterian. General corporate, Mergers and acquisitions.

WRIGHT, BLANDIN JAMES, lawyer; b. Detroit, Nov. 29, 1947; s. Robert Thomas and Jane Ellen (Blandin) W.; children: Steven Blandin, Martha Kay. BA, U. Mich., 1969; JD, Dickinson Law Sch., 1972; LLM in Taxation, NYU, 1973; MS in Taxation with honors, Am. U., 1992. Bar: Pa. 1973, Fla. 1976, U.S. Tax Ct. 1977, D.C. 1979, U.S. Supreme Ct. 1979, Va. 1984, N.Y. 1991; CPA, Tex., 1978, Va., 1985. Atty. Office Internat. Ops. Nat. Office IRS, Washington, 1973-76; tax dir. Intairdril Ltd., London, 1976-78; tax atty. Allied Chem. Corp., Houston, 1978-79; v.p., gen. counsel Assoc. Oiltools, Inc., London, 1979-82; v.p. taxes, gen. counsel J. Lauritzen (USA), Inc., Charlottesville, Va., 1982-85; sole practice, 1985-88; ptnr. Richmond & Fishburne, 1988-90, of counsel, 1990-91; tax counsel Mobil Oil Corp., N.Y.C., 1990, Fairfax, Va., 1990-95; vice chmn., gen. counsel Cruise Holdings, Ltd., Miami, 1996-97; pres. Maritime Capital Group, Inc., 1998—. Officer Pamaco Partnership Mgmt. Corp., Va., 1986-91, CRW Energy Corp., 1986-90, Transp. & Tourism Internat., Inc., 1986—, Hotsprings Assocs., Inc., 1989-91, MDM Hotels, Inc., 1992-95, Internat. Shipping & Resorts, Inc., 1992—, United Holdings Ltd., 1993—, Cruise and Resorts Internat., Inc., 1994—; bd. dirs. Blandin J. Wright, P.C., Internat. Hospitality, Inc., CRS Holdings, Inc. Contbr. articles to profl. jours. Coach Charlottesville Youth Soccer, Baseball and Basketball, 1984-89; coach London Youth Baseball, 1982. Mem. ABA, AICPA, Am. Arbitration Assn. (arbitrator 1985—), Tex. Soc. CPAs, Va. Soc. CPAs, Fairfax County Bar Assn., Farmington Country Club, Deering Bay Yacht and Country Club, Mensa, Beta Gamma Sigma. Roman Catholic. Oil, gas, and mineral, Mergers and acquisitions, Corporate taxation. Home: 4770 Biscayne Blvd Ph G Miami FL 33137-3251

WRIGHT, BRADLEY ABBOTT, lawyer; b. Des Moines, Nov. 24, 1964; s. James Bradley and Carolyn (Abbott) W.; m. Alisa Labut, Aug. 24, 1993; children: Hannah, Alexandra. BA, Miami U., Oxford, Ohio, 1987; JD, Ohio State U., 1990. Bar: Ohio 1990. Assoc. Roetzel & Andress, Akron, Ohio, 1990-97, ptnr., 1997—. Grad. Leadership Akron, 1998; active Big Bros. and Big Sisters, Inc., Akron, United Way of Summit County, Akron. Mem. Akron Bar Assn. (vice chmn./social chmn.), Transp. Lawyers Assn., Def. Rsch. Inst., Assn. for Transp. Law Logistics and Policy, Am. Trucking Assn., Nat. Assn. R.R. Trial Counsel. Insurance, Transportation. Home: 91 N Hayden Pkwy Hudson OH 44236-3157 Office: Roetzel & Andress 222 S Main St Akron OH 44308-1533 E-mail: bwright@ralaw.com

WRIGHT, BRIAN RICHARD, lawyer, banker; b. Oneonta, N.Y., Oct. 15, 1944; s. W. Clyde and Mildred E. (Williams) W.; m. Josephine A. Brienza, July 31, 1964; children— Brian R. Jr., Kelly Lynne. A.B., Princeton U., 1966; J.D., U. Fla., 1969. Bar: Fla. 1969, N.Y. 1971. Law clk. U.S. Dist. Ct., Miami, Fla., 1969-71; asst. dist. atty. Broome County Dist. Attys. Office, Binghamton, N.Y., 1971-73; ptnr. Kramer, Wales & McAvoy, Binghamton, 1973-83, Kramer, Wales & Wright, Binghamton, 1984— ; dir., chmn. Wilber Nat. Bank, Oneonta, N.Y. Bd. dirs. Vestal Jr. Baseball League, 1971-75, Vestal Little League, 1975-77, Vestal Babe Ruth, 1977-79, Vestal Youth Soccer, 1976-81; sec. bd. trustees Hartwick Coll., Oneonta, N.Y., 1985—; chmn. devel. com. Nat. Soccer Hall of Fame, Oneonta. Mem. ABA, N.Y. State Bar Assn., Broome County Bar Assn. Republican. Presbyterian. Office: Kramer Wales & Wright PO Box 1865 Binghamton NY 13902

WRIGHT, EUGENE ALLEN, federal judge; b. Seattle, Feb. 23, 1913; s. Elias Allen and Mary (Bailey) W.; m. Esther Ruth Ladley, Mar. 19, 1938; children: Gerald Allen, Meredith Ann Wright Morton. AB, U. Wash., 1935, JD, 1937; LLD, U. Puget Sound, 1984. Bar: Wash. 1937. Assoc. Wright & Wright, Seattle, 1937-54; judge Superior Ct. King County, 1954-66; v.p., sr. trust officer Pacific Nat. Bank Seattle, 1966-69; judge U.S. Ct. Appeals (9th cir.), Seattle, 1969—. Acting municipal judge, Seattle, 1948-52; mem. faculty Nat. Jud. Coll., 1964-72; lectr. Sch. Communications, U. Wash., 1965-66, U. Wash. Law Sch., 1952-74; lectr. appellate judges' seminars, 1973-76, Nat. Law Clks. Inst., La. State U., 1973; chmn. Wash. State Com. on Law and Justice, 1968-69; mem. com. on appellate rules Jud. Conf., 1978-85, mem. com. on courtroom photography, 1983-85, com. jud. ethics, 1984-92, com. Bicentennial of Constn., 1985-87. Author: (with others) The State Trial Judges Book, 1966; also articles; editor: Trial Judges Jour., 1963-66; contbr. articles to profl. jours. Chmn. bd. visitors U. Puget Sound Sch. Law, 1979-84; mem. bd. visitors U. Wash. Sch. Law, 1996; bd. dirs. Met. YMCA, Seattle, 1955-72; lay reader Episc Ch. Served to lt. col. USAR, 1941-46, col. Res., ret. Decorated Bronze Star, Combat Inf. badge; recipient Army Commendation medal, Disting. Service award U.S. Jr. C. of C., 1948, Disting. Service medal Am. Legion. Fellow Am. Bar Found.; mem. ABA (coun. div. jud. adminstrn. 1971-76), FBA (Disting. Jud. Svc. award 1984), Wash. Bar Assn. (award of merit 1983), Seattle-King County Bar Assn. (Spl. Disting. Svc. award 1984. William L. Dwyer Outstanding Jurist award 2001), Order of Coif, Wash. Athletic Club, Rainier Club, Masons (33 degree), Shriners, Delta Upsilon (Disting. Alumni Achievement award 1989), Phi Delta Phi. Office: US Ct Appeals 9th Cir 902 US Courthouse 1010 5th Ave Seattle WA 98104-1195

WRIGHT, FREDERICK LEWIS, II, lawyer; b. Roanoke, Va., Sept. 17, 1951; s. Frederick Lewis and Dorothy Marie (Trent) W.; m. Margaret Suzanne Rey, Oct. 16, 1982; children: Lauren Elizabeth, Emily Trent. BA, Ga. State U., 1978; JD, U. Ga., 1981. Bar: Ga. 1982, U.S. Dist. Ct. (no. dist.) Ga. 1984, U.S. Ct. Appeals (11th, 8th and 4th cirs.) 1984, U.S. Supreme Ct. 1990. Law clk. to presiding justice U.S. Ct. Appeals, Atlanta, 1981-82; ptnr. Smith, Currie and Hancock, 1982-96, Vaughn, Wright and Stearns, Atlanta, 1997—. Articles editor Ga. Law Rev., 1980-81. Mem. ABA (forum com. constrn. industry), Assn. Trial Lawyers Am., Fed. Bar Assn., Order of Coif. Methodist. General civil litigation, Construction, Environmental. E-mail: fwright@vws-attys.com

WRIGHT, J(AMES) LAWRENCE, lawyer; b. Portland, Oreg., Apr. 12, 1943; s. William A. and Esther M. (Nelson) W.; m. Mary Aileene Roche, June 29, 1968; children: Rachel, Jonathan, Christopher. BBA, Gonzaga U., 1966, JD, 1972; LLM, NYU, 1977. Bar: Wash. 1972, U.S. Ct. Mil. Appeals 1974, U.S. Tax Ct. 1976, U.S. Supreme Ct. 1976. Prin. Halverson & Applegate, P.S., Yakima, Wash., 1972-74, 77—, pres., 1998—. Mem. St. Elizabeth Hosp. Found., Yakima, 1986-89, Yakima Meml. Hosp. Found., 1990—; pres. fin. bd. St. Paul's Cathedral, Yakima, 1979—; mem. fin. coun. Diocese of Yakima, 1994—; v.p. Apple Tree Racing Assn., 1986-87; bd. dirs. Capital Theatre, Yakima, 1985-95. Capt. U.S. Army, 1966-68, 74-76. Mem. ABA, Wash. Bar Assn., Yakima County Bar Assn., Rotary. Roman Catholic. Avocations: tennis, golf. General corporate, Estate planning, Taxation, general. Office: Halverson & Applegate PS PO Box 22730 311 N 4th St Yakima WA 98901-2467

WRIGHT, JOHN F. state supreme court justice; BS, U. Nebr., 1967, JD, 1970. Atty. Wright & Simmons, 1970-84, Wright, Sorensen & Brower, 1984-91; mem., coord. Commn. on Post Secondary Edn., 1991-92; judge Nebr. Ct. Appeals, 1992-94; assoc. justice Nebr. Supreme Ct., 1994—. Chmn. bd. dirs. Panhandle Legal Svcs., 1970 Mem. Scottsbluff Bd. Edn., 1980-87, pres., 1984, 86. Served with U.S. Army, 1970, Nebr. N.G., 1970-76. Recipient Friend of Edn. award Scottsbluff Edn. Assn., 1992. Office: Nebr Supreme Ct 2207 State Capitol PO Box 98910 Lincoln NE 68509-8910

WRIGHT, MINTURN TATUM, III, lawyer; b. Phila., Aug. 7, 1925; s. Minturn T. and Anna (Moss) W.; m. Nonya R. Stevens, May 11, 1957; children: Minturn T., Richard S., Robert M., Marianne F. BA, Yale U., 1949; LLB, U. Pa., 1952. Bar: Pa. 1953, U.S. Ct. Appeals (3d cir.) 1953, U.S. Supreme Ct. 1962. Law clk. U.S. Ct. Appeals (3d cir.), 1952-53; assoc. Dechert, Price & Rhoads, Phila., 1953-61, ptnr., 1961-95, chmn., 1982-84. Bd. dirs. Phila. Contributionship, Vector Security Co. Inc., Cotiga Devel. Co., Penn Virginia Corp.; vis. prof. U. Pa. Law Sch., 1965-69, 93-97. Contbr. articles to profl. jours. Trustee Acad. Natural Scis. Phila., 1958—, chmn., 1976-81; trustee Hawk Mountain Sanctuary Assn., chmn. bd. dirs., 1992-97; trustee Rare Ctr., Pa. chpt. The Nature Conservancy, Exec. Svc. Corps.; trustee Marshall-Reynolds Found. Served with U.S. Army, 1943-46. Mem. ABA, Pa. Bar Assn., Phila. Bar Assn., Nat. Coal Lawyers Assn., Eastern Mineral Law Assn. (trustee), Phila. Club, Milldam Club. Episcopalian. Contracts commercial, Probate. Office: Dechert Price & Rhoads 4000 Bell Atlantic Tower 1717 Arch St Ste 4000 Philadelphia PA 19103-2793

WRIGHT, PAUL WILLIAM, lawyer, oil company executive; b. Jamestown, N.Y., July 7, 1944; s. Julian M. and Ruth (Blake) W.; m. Elizabeth O'Rourke Wright, Nov. 22, 1975; children: Jeffrey, Stephen. BS in Bus. Adminstrn., Georgetown U., 1966, JD, 1969. Bar: Va. 1969, D.C. 1972, Tex. 1973, La. 1985, U.S. Supreme Ct. 1972. Staff atty. Fed Power Commn., 1969-70; assoc. Wolf & Case, Washington, 1970-72; atty. Exxon Corp., Houston, 1973—, chief atty., 1986-92; sr. staff counsel Exxon Co. Internat. Bd. dirs. La. Pro Bono-Project, 1986-90. Mem. ABA, Tex. Bar Assn., La. Bar Assn., Va. Bar Assn., D.C. Bar Assn., La. Bar Found. (bd. dirs., sec., treas. 1986-87, v.p. 1987-89, pres. 1989-91). E-mial. Alternative dispute resolution, General civil litigation, Private international. Office: Exxon Mobil Corp PO Box 2180 Houston TX 77252-1347 E-mail: paul.w.wright@exxon.com, pwwright66@yahoo.com

WRIGHT, ROBERT JOSEPH, lawyer; b. Rome, Dec. 13, 1949; s. Arthur Arley and Maude T. (Lacey) W.; m. Donna Ruth Bishop, Feb. 18, 1972; children: Cynthia Ashley, Laura Christine. BA cum laude, Ga. State U., 1979; JD cum laude, U. Ga., 1983. Bar: GA. 1983, U.S. Dist. Ct. (no. dist.) Ga. 1983, U.S. Dist. Ct. (mid. dist.) Ga. 1985. Assoc. Craig & Gainer, Covington, Ga., 1983-84, Heard, Leverett & Adams, Elberton, 1984-86; gen. counsel Group Underwriters, Inc., 1987—. Editorial staff Ga. Jour. Internat. and Comparative Law, 1981-82 Mem. State Bar Ga. (sec. legal econs. sect. 1987-88, chmn. legal econs. sect. 1988-90), Order of the Coif, Masons, Phi Alpha Delta. Baptist. Insurance, Land use and zoning (including planning), Personal injury. Home: 1030 E Canyon Creek Ct Watkinsville GA 30677-1500

WRIGHT, ROBERT PAYTON, lawyer; b. Beaumont, Tex., Feb. 15, 1951; s. Vernon Gerald and Huberta Read (Nunn) W.; m. Sallie Chesnutt Smith, July 16, 1977; children: Payton Cullen, Elizabeth Risher. AB, Princeton U., 1972; JD, Columbia U., 1975. Bar: Tex. 1975. Ptnr. Baker Botts L.L.P., Houston, 1975—. Author: The Texas Homebuyer's Manual, 1986. Mem. Am. Coll. Real Estate Lawyers (bd. dirs. 2002—), State Bar Tex. (chmn. coun. real estate, probate, trust law sect. 1994-95), Houston Bar Assn. (chmn. real estate sect. 1989-90), Tex. Coll. Real Estate Lawyers, Houston Real Estate Lawyers Coun., Houston Club. Episcopalian. Environmental, Finance, Real property.

WRIGHT, ROBERT ROSS, III, law educator; b. Ft. Worth, Nov. 20, 1931; m. Susan Webber; children: Robert Ross IV, John, David, Robin. BA cum laude, U. Ark., 1953, JD, 1956; MA (grad. fellow), Duke U., 1954; SJD (law fellow), U. Wis., 1967. Bar: Ark. 1956, U.S. Supreme Ct. 1968, Okla. 1970. Instr. polit. sci. U. Ark., 1955-56; mem. firm Forrest City, Ark., 1956-58; ptnr. Norton, Norton & Wright, 1959; asst. gen. counsel, asst. sec. Crossett Co., Ark.; atty. Crossett div. Ga.-Pacific Corp., 1960-63; asst. sec. Pub. Utilities Co., Crossett, Triangle Bag Co., Covington, Ky., 1960-62; faculty U. Ark. Law Sch., 1963-70; asst. prof., dir. continuing legal edn. and research, then asst. dean U. Ark., Little Rock, 1965-66, prof. law, 1967-70; prof. U. Okla., 1970-77; dean U. Okla. Coll. Law; dir. U. Okla. Law Center, 1970-76; vis. prof. U. Ark., Little Rock, 1976-77; Donaghey Disting. prof. U. Ark, 1977-99, Donaghey disting. prof. emeritus, 1999—. Vis. disting. prof. U. Cin., 1983; vis. prof. law U. Iowa, 1969-70; vis. prof. U. Ark., Little Rock, 1976-77; Ark. commr. Nat. Conf. Commrs. Uniform State Laws, 1967-70; past chmn. Com. Uniform Eminent Domain Code; past mem. Com. Uniform Probate Code, Ark. Gov.'s Ins. Study Commn.; chmn. Gov. Commn. on Uniform Probate Code; chmn. task force joint devel. Hwy. Research Bd.; vice chmn. Okla. Jud. Council, 1970-72, chmn., 1972-75; chmn. Okla. Center Criminal Justice, 1971-76 Author: Arkansas Eminent Domain Digest, 1964, Arkansas Probate Practice System, 1965, The Law of Airspace, 1968, Emerging Concepts in the Law of Airspace, 1969, Cases and Materials on Land Use, 3d edit., 1982, supplement, 1987, 5th edit., 1997, Uniform Probate Code Practice Manual, 1972, Model Airspace Code, 1973, Land Use in a Nutshell, 1978, 4th edit., 2000, The Arkansas Form Book, 1979, 2d edit., 1988, Zoning Law in Arkansas: A Comparative Analysis, 1980, Old Seeds in the New Land: A History and Reminiscences of the Bar of Arkansas, 2001; contbr. articles to profl. jours. Mem. Little Rock Planning Commn., 1978-82, chmn., 1982. Named Ark. Man of Year Kappa Sigma, 1958. Fellow Am. Law Inst., Am. Coll. Trust and Estate Counsel (acad.); mem. ABA (past chmn., exec. coun. gen. practice, solo and small firm sect., former chmn. new pubs. editl. bd., sect. officers conf., ho. of dels. 1994-2000, standing com. fed. jud. improvements 1998—), Ark. Bar Assn. (exec. coun. 1985-88, ho. of dels., life mem., chmn. eminent domain code com., past mem. com. new bar ctr., past chmn. preceptorship com., exec. com. young laywers sect.), Okla. Bar Assn. (past vice-chmn. legal internship com., former vice-chmn. gen. practice sect.), Pulaski County Bar Assn., Ark. Bar Found., U. Wis. Alumni Assn., Duke U. Alumni Assn., U. Ark. Alumni Assn., Order of Coif, Phi Beta Kappa, Phi Alpha Delta, Omicron Delta Kappa. Episcopalian. Home: 249 Pleasant Valley Dr Little Rock AR 72212-3170 Office: U Ark Law Sch 1201 McMath St Little Rock AR 72202-5142

WRIGHT, ROBERT THOMAS, JR. lawyer; b. Detroit, Oct. 4, 1946; s. Robert Thomas and Jane Ellen (Blandin) W.; m. Diana Feltman, June 8, 1994; children: Sarah Allison, Jonathan Brian. BA in History and Polit. Sci., U. N.C., 1968; JD, Columbia U., 1974. Bar: Fla. 1974. Assoc. Paul & Thomson, Miami, Fla., 1974-77, Mershon, Sawyer, Johnston, Dunwoody & Cole, Miami, 1977-81, ptnr., 1981-95, Shutts & Bowen, Miami, 1995-98, Verner, Liipfert, Bernhard, McPherson & Hand, Miami, 1998—, also bd. dirs. 1st lt. U.S. Army, 1968-71. Mem. ABA, Fla. Bar, Dade County Bar Assn. Avocations: golf, rugby, African cichlids. Federal civil litigation, State civil litigation, Insurance. Home: 11095 SW 84th Ct Miami FL 33156-4311 Office: Verner Liipfert et al 200 S Biscayne Blvd Ste 3100 Miami FL 33131-5324 E-mail: rtwjr1@aol.com, rtwright@verner.com

WRIGHT, SCOTT OLIN, federal judge; b. Haigler, Nebr., Jan. 15, 1923; s. Jesse H. and Martha I. Wright; m. Shirley Frances Young, Aug. 25, 1972. Student, Central Coll., Fayette, Mo., 1940-42; LLB, U. Mo., Columbia, 1950. Bar: Mo. 1950. City atty., Columbia, 1951-53; pros. atty. Boone County, Mo., 1954-58; practice of law Columbia, 1958-79; U.S. dist. judge Western Dist. Mo., Kansas City, from 1979. Pres. Young Democrats Boone County, 1950, United Fund Columbia, 1965. Served with USN, 1942-43; as aviator USMC, 1943-46. Decorated Air medal. Mem. ABA, Am. Trial Lawyers Assn., Mo. Bar Assn., Mo. Trial Lawyers Assn., Boone County Bar Assn. Unitarian. Clubs: Rockhill Tennis, Woodside Racquet. Lodge: Rotary (pres. Columbia 1965). Office: Charles E Whitaker Courthouse 400 E 9th St Ste 8662 Kansas City MO 64106-2684

WRIGHT, SUSAN WEBBER, judge; b. Texarkana, Ark., Aug. 22, 1948; d. Thomas Edward and Betty Jane (Gary) Webber; m. Robert Ross Wright, III, May 21, 1983; 1 child, Robin Elizabeth. BA, Randolph-Macon Woman's Coll., 1970; MPA, U. Ark., 1972, JD with high honors, 1975. Bar: Ark. 1975. Law clk. U.S. Ct. Appeals 8th Cir., 1975-76; asst. prof. law U. Ark., Little Rock, 1976-78, assoc. prof., 1978-83, prof., 1983-90, asst. dean, 1976-78; dist. judge U.S. Dist. Ct. (ea. dist.) Ark., 1990—, chief judge, 1998—. Vis. assoc. prof. Ohio State U., Columbus, 1981, La. State U., Baton Rouge, 1982-83; mem. adv. com. U.S. Ct. Appeals 8th Circuit, St. Louis, 1983-88. Author: (with R. Wright) Land Use in a Nutshell, 1978, 2d edit., 1985; editor-in-chief Ark. Law Rev., 1975; contbr. articles to profl. jours. Mem. ABA, Am. Judicature Soc., Ark. Bar Assn., Pulaski County Bar Assn., Am. Law Inst., Ark. Assn. Women Lawyers (v.p. 1977-78), Ark. Women's Forum. Episcopalian. Office: US District Court 600 W Capitol Ave Ste 520 Little Rock AR 72201-3329

WROBLE, ARTHUR GERARD, judge; b. Taylor, Pa., Jan. 21, 1948; s. Arthur S. and Sophia P. Wroble; m. Mary Ellen Sheehan, Nov. 19, 1977; children: Sophia Ann, Sarah Jean, Stacey Margaret. BSBA with honors, U. fla., 1970, MBA, 1971, JD, 1973. Bar: Fla. 1973, U.S. Ct. Appeals (5th cir.) 1974, U.S. Ct. Appeals (11th cir.) 1981, U.S. Dist. Ct. (so. dist.) Fla. 1974, U.S. Dist. Ct. (mid. dist.) 1982, U.S. Dist. Ct. (no. dist.) Fla. 1986, U.S. Army Ct. Mil. Rev. 1989, U.S. Ct. Mil. Appeals 1990, U.S. Supreme Ct. 1976. Ptnr. Burns, Middleton, Farrell & Faust (now Steel, Hector, Davis, Burns & Middleton), Palm Beach, Fla., 1973-82, Wolf, Block, Schorr & Solis, Cohen, Phila. & West Palm Beach, 1982-87, Scott, Royce, Harris & Bryan, P.A., Palm Beach, 1987-89, Grantham and Wroble, P.A., Lake Worth, 1989-92; prin. Arthur G. Wroble, P.A., West Palm Beach, 1992-2000; cir. judge 15th Jud. Ct. Fla., Palm Beach, 2000—. Mem. 15th Jud. Cir. Ct. Nominating Commn., 1979-83; mem. U. Fla. Law Ctr. Council, 1981-84, U.S. Magistrate Merit Selection Panel, so. dist. Fla., 1987; mem. adv. bd. alternative sentencing program Palm Beach County Pub. Defender's Office; adj. instr. bus. law Coll. of Boca Raton (now Lynn U.), 1988. Contbr. to profl. jours. Bd. dirs. Palm Glades Girl Scout Coun., 1996—. Served to lt. col. JAG, USAR. Named Eagle Scout, Boy Scouts Am., 1962. Mem. ABA, Fla. Bar (bd. govs. young lawyers sect. 1979-83, bd. govs. 1985-89), Palm Beach County Bar Assn. (pres. young lawyers sect. 1978-79, bd. dirs. 1978-81, sec.-treas. 1981-83, pres. 1984-85), Fla. Bar Found. (bd. dirs. 1990-93), Fla. Assn. Women Lawyers, Fla. Coun. Bar Assn. Pres. (bd. dirs. 1986-92), Guild Cath. Lawyers Diocese Palm Beach, Inc. (pres. 1980-81, bd. dirs. 1981—, Monsignor Jeremiah P. O'Mahoney Outstanding Lawyer award 1993), Legal Aid Soc. Palm Beach County, Inc. (bd. dirs. 1981-2000), Univ. Fla. Alumni Assn., Palm Beach County Club (pres. 1983-84), Kiwanis (pres. 1980-81, pres. West Palm Beach found. 1989-2000, dir. 1991—, Citizen of Yr. 1994, George F. Hixon fellowship 1999), KC (grand knight 1978-79), Am. Inns of Ct LIV (West Palm Beach chpt. pres. 1999-2000, bd. dirs. 1995-2000). Roman Catholic. Office: Palm Beach County Cthse 205 N Dixie Hwy West Palm Beach FL 33401-4522 E-mail: wrobleag@pb.seflin.org

WROBLESKI, JEANNE PAULINE, lawyer; b. Phila., Feb. 14, 1942; d. Edward Joseph and Pauline (Popelak) W.; m. Robert J. Klein, Dec. 3, 1979. BA, Immaculata Coll., 1964; MA, U. Pa., 1966; JD, Temple U., 1975. Bar: Pa. 1975. Pvt. practice law, Phila., 1975—; pres., shareholder Jeanne Wrobleski & Assocs., LLC, 1999—. Lectr. on bus. law Wharton Sch., Phila. Mem. Commn. on Women and the Legal Profession, 1986-89; v.p. Center City Residents' Assn.; Eisenhower Citizen Amb. del. to Soviet Union. Bd. dirs. South St. Dance Co., Women in Transition; bd. dirs., mem. exec. com. Temple Law Alumni; del. to Moscow Conf. on Law and Econ. Coop., 1990; del. to jud. conf. 3d Cir. U.S. Ct. Appeals, 1991; mediator U.S. Dist. Ct. (ea. dist.) Pa., 1996. Rhea Liebman scholar, 1974. Mem. AAUW, ABA, Pa. Bar Assn., Phila. Bar Assn. (chmn. women's rights com. 1986, com. on jud. selection and retention, 1986-87, chmn. appellate cts. com. 1992, bus. cts. task force, com. on bus. litigation), Pa. Acad. Fine Arts, Nat. Mus. Women in the Arts, Am. Judicature Soc., Jagiellonian Law Soc., Lawyers Club, Founders Club, The Cosmopolitan Club, Penn Club, Alpha Psi Omega, Lambda Iota Tau. Democrat. Federal civil litigation, General civil litigation. Office: Jeanne Wrobleski & Assocs LLC 1845 Walnut St Fl 24 Philadelphia PA 19103-4708 E-mail: jwrobleski@wwdlaw.com

WROBLEY, RALPH GENE, lawyer; b. Denver, Sept. 19, 1935; s. Matthew B. and Hedvig (Lyon) W.; m. Madeline C. Kearney, June 13, 1959; children: Kirk Lyon, Eric Lyon, Ann Lyon. BA, Yale U., 1957; JD, U. Chgo., 1962. Bar: Mo. 1962. With Bell Tel. Co., Phila., 1957-59; asoc. Stinson, Mag & Fizzell, Kansas City, Mo., 1962-65, mem., 1965-88; ptnr. Bryan, Cave, McPheeters & McRoberts, 1988-92; ptnr., exec. com. Blackwell, Sanders, Peper, Martin LLP, 1992-2000. Bd. dirs. Human Resources Corp., 1971; mem. Civic Coun. Kansas City, 1986—; chmn. Pub. Housing Authority of Kansas City, 1971-74; vice chmn. Mayor's Adv. Commn. on Housing, Kansas City, 1971-74; bd. govs. Citizens Assn., 1965—, vice chmn., 1971-75, chmn., 1978-79; bd. dirs. Coun. on Edn., 1975-81, v.p., 1977-79; bd. dirs., pres. Sam E. and Mary F. Roberts Found., 1974-96; trustee Clearinghouse for Mid Continent Founds., 1977-96, chmn. 1987-89; bd. dirs. Bus. Innovation Ctr., 1984-91, vice-chmn. 1987-91, adv. bd. dirs., 1993-99, Midwest Regional Adv. Bd. Inst. Internat. Edn., 1989-93, Internat. Trade Assn., 1989-92, v.p., 1990; former chmn. bd. dir. Mid-Am. Coalition on Healthcare, 1991-95. Mem. Mo. Bar Assn., Yale Club (pres. 1969-71, outstanding mem. award 1967). Republican. Presbyn. (elder) General corporate, Private international, Mergers and acquisitions. Home: 1015 W 67th Ter Kansas City MO 64113-1942 Office: 2300 Main St Kansas City MO 64108-2416 E-mail: rwrobley@bspmlaw.com

WUERMELING, ULRICH URBAN, lawyer; b. Muenster, Germany, Dec. 24, 1964; s. Georg and Ursula Wuermeling. LLB, U. Bayreuth, Germany, 1992. Atty. Wessing, Frankfurt, Germany, 1996; editor Verlagsgruppe Handelsblatt, Dusseldorf, Germany, 1991; head multimedia law group Wessing, Frankfurt, Germany, 1999—. Communications, Computer, Mergers and acquisitions. Office: Wessing Senckenberganlage 20-22 D-60325 Frankfurt/Main Germany E-mail: u.wuermeling@wessing.com

WUERZNER, ANDREA, lawyer; b. Yverdon, Switzerland, Sept. 7, 1969; d. Peter and Dorothee W. Degree in law, U. Lausanne, Switzerland, 1993, U. N.C., 1998. Bar: Geneva 1995, Zürich 1998. Lawyer Pestalozzi Lachenal Patry, Zürich, 1998—. Contracts commercial, General corporate. Office: Pestalozzi Lachenal Patry Löwenstr 1 8001 Zürich Switzerland Fax: 41.1.217.92.17

WUKITSCH, DAVID JOHN, lawyer; b. Schenectady, N.Y., June 7, 1955; s. Julius and Laura (Isabel) W. BA, SUNY, Albany, 1977; MA, Sch. Criminal Justice, 1978; JD, Union U., 1981. Bar: N.Y. 1982, U.S. Dist. Ct. (no. dist.) N.Y. 1982, U.S. Ct. Appeals (2d cir.) 1986, U.S. Supreme Ct. 1994, U.S. Ct. Appeals (11th cir.) 1999. Law asst. Appellate divsn. N.Y. Supreme Ct., Albany, 1981-83; law clk. to assoc. judge N.Y. Ct. Appeals, 1983-85; assoc. McNamee, Lochner, Titus & Williams P.C., 1985-91, ptnr., 1991—. Cons. Police Found., Washington, 1980-81; atty. Town of New Baltimore, N.Y. Contbr. Albany Law Jour. Law and Tech., 1999. Bd. dirs. Legal Aid Soc. Northeastrn N.Y.; pres. Sr. Svcs. of Albany Found. Mem. ABA (mem. labor and employment sect.), N.Y. State Bar Assn., Justinian Soc. Roman Catholic. Federal civil litigation, Criminal, Labor. Office: McNamee Lochner Titus & Williams PC 75 State St Apt 459 Albany NY 12207-2526 E-mail: wukitsch@mltw.com

WUNSCH, KATHRYN SUTHERLAND, retired lawyer; b. Tipton, Mo., Jan. 30, 1935; d. Lewis Benjamin and Norene Marie (Wolf) Sutherland; m. Charles Martin Wunsch, Dec. 22, 1956 (div. May 1988); children: Debra Kay, Laura Ellen. AB, Ind. U., 1958, JD summa cum laude, 1977; postgrad., Stanford (Calif.) U., 1977. Bar: Calif. 1977, U.S. Dist. Ct. (no. dist.) Calif. 1977. Founder Wunsch and George, San Francisco, 1989-93, Kathryn Wunsch and Assoc. Counsel, San Francisco, 1993-99; ret., 1999. Articles editor Ind. U. Law Rev., 1975-76. Mem. Phi Beta Kappa (v.p. no. calif. 1995-97), Psi Chi. Republican. Avocations: collecting fine art and antiques, theater, opera, gardening, hiking. General corporate, Probate, Real property.

WYATT, CHARLES HERBERT, JR. lawyer; b. Birmingham, Ala., Aug. 18, 1937; s. Charles Herbert and Elizabeth Florida (Farrell) W.; m. Lane Laverne Bradley, Mar. 18, 1966. B.S. in Bus., Jacksonville State U., 1960; J.D., Cumberland U., 1964. Bar: Ala. 1964, U.S. Dist. Ct. (no. dist.) Ala. 1964, U.S. Ct. Appeals (5th cir.) 1975, U.S. Ct. Appeals (11th cir.) 1981, U.S. Supreme Ct. 1984. Ptnr. Cole, Wyatt & Bradshaw, Birmingham, 1964-73; prin. atty. City of Birmingham, 1973— . Chaplain Vulcan Power Squad, U.S. Power Squad, Birmingham, 1983, asst. sec., 1984, adminstrv. officer, 1985, exec. officer, 1987; commdr., Vulcan Power Squadron, 1987—. Mem. Nat. Inst. Mcpl. Law Officers, State of Ala. Standing Com. on Civil Rules and Procedures for Dist. Cts., Sigma Delta Kappa (nat. grand pres. 1973-74). Home: 1300 Beacon Pky E Birmingham AL 35209-7438 Office: City of Birmingham Law Dept 600 City Hall-710 N 20th St Birmingham AL 35203

WYATT, DEBORAH CHASEN, lawyer; b. Atlanta, Apr. 19, 1949; d. S.H. and Catherine Jane (Hudlow) Chasen; m. Richard Haste Wyatt, Jr., Feb. 19, 1972; children: Thomas Clayton, William Tyler. Student, Sweet Briar Col., 1968-70; BA, Tufts U., 1971; JD, U. Va., 1978. Bar: Va. 1978, U.S. Dist. Ct. (we. and ea. dists.) Va. 1978, U.S. Ct. Appeals (4th cir.) 1980, U.S. Ct. Appeals (D.C. cir.) 1984, U.S. Supreme Ct. 1983. Assoc. Lowe & Gordon, Charlottesville, Va., 1978-80; partner Wyatt & Rosenfield, 1980-83, Gordon & Wyatt, Charlottesville, 1984-92, Wyatt & Carter, Charlot-

tesville, 1993-2000, Wyatt & Assocs., PLC, Charlottesville, 2000—. Mem. ATLA, Va. Coll. Criminal Def. Attys. (bd. dirs. 1997—), Charlottesville-Albemarle Criminal Bar Assn., Charlottesville Bar Assn. Avocations: writing, painting. Civil rights, Criminal, Personal injury. Office: Wyatt and Assocs Plc 300 Court Sq Charlottesville VA 22902-5160

WYATT, ROBERT LEE, IV, lawyer; b. Las Cruces, N.Mex., Mar. 9, 1964; s. Robert Lee III and Louise Carole (Bard) W.; m. Vicki Harris Wyatt. BS, Southeastern Okla. State U., 1986; JD, U. Okla., 1989. Bar: Okla. 1989, U.S. Dist. Ct. (we. dist.) Okla. 1990, U.S. Ct. Appeals (10th cir.) 1990, U.S. Dist. Ct. (no. dist.) Okla. 1991, U.S. Ct. Appeals (8th cir.) 1991, U.S. Supreme Ct. 1993. Intern Okla. State Bur. Investigation, Oklahoma City, 1988-89, guest lectr., 1989; dep. spl. counsel Gov. of Okla., 1995; atty. Jones & Wyatt, Enid, Okla., 1989-2000. Mem. criminal justice panel atty. We. Dist. Okla. Contbg. author: Vernon's forms Oklahoma, Criminal Law and Procedure, 1999. Counsel to Fire Civil Svc. Commn. City of Enid, 1998-2000. Mem. ABA (mem. criminal and litigation sects.), Okla. Bar Assn. (mem. ins., mem. criminal law com.), Oklahoma County Bar Assn., Okla. Criminal Def. Lawyers Assn., Nat. Inst. for Trial Advocacy, Nat. Assn. Criminal Defense Lawyers, Luther Bohanon Am. Inn of Ct. (barrister), Phi Delta Phi, Alpha Chi. Democrat. Baptist. General civil litigation, Criminal, Insurance. Home: 408 Timberdale Dr Edmond OK 73034 Office: Wyatt Law Office 228 Robert S Kerr Ave Ste 750 Oklahoma City OK 73102-3420 E-mail: bobwyatt@wyattlaw.com

WYATT, THOMAS CSABA, lawyer; b. Toronto, Ont., Can., Mar. 19, 1952; came to U.S., 1979; s. Charles Wojatsek and Marietta Marcinkova; m. Helen A. Johnson, Dec. 24, 1979; children: J.P. Max, Stephen M. BA, Bishop's U., 1975; BCL, Mcgill U., 1974; JD, U. San Francisco, 1981; LLM, U. Montreal, 1980. Bar: Que. 1975, Calif. 1982, U.S. Dist. Ct. (no. dist.) Calif. 1982, U.S. Ct. Appeals (9th cir.) 1982. Assoc. counsel Can. Gen. Electric, Montreal, 1975-77; solicitor Du Pont Can., Inc., 1977-79; internat. counsel Computerland Corp., Oakland, Calif., 1982-85; sr. counsel Bank of Am., San Francisco, 1985-87, Intel Corp., Santa Clara, Calif., 1987-90; gen. counsel Philips Semiconductors, Sunnyvale, 1990—. Arbitrator Am. Arbitration Assn., San Francisco, 1985—. Bd. dirs. Silicon Valley Law Found., 2000—. Mem. Am. Arbitration Assn., Silicon Valley Assn. of Gen. Counsel (chmn. 1998-2000), Santa Clara County Bar Assn. (bd. trustees 2001—), Knightly Order of Vitez, Knights of Malta. Roman Catholic. Avocations: tennis, adventure travel. Contracts commercial, Computer, Intellectual property. Office: Philips Semiconductors Inc 811 E Arques Ave Rm Ms54 Sunnyvale CA 94085-4523 E-mail: tom.wyatt@philips.com

WYCHE, MADISON BAKER, III, lawyer; b. Albany, Ga., Aug. 11, 1947; s. Madison Baker Jr. and Merle (McKemie) W.; m. Marguerite Jernigan Ramage, Aug. 7, 1971; children: Madison Baker IV, James Ramage. BA, Vanderbilt U., 1969, JD, 1972. Bar: Ga. 1972, U.S. Dist. Ct. (mid. dist.) Ga. 1972, U.S. Ct. Appeals (5th cir.) 1973, S.C. 1976, U.S. Dist. Ct. S.C. 1977, U.S. Ct. Appeals (4th cir.) 1977, U.S. Supreme Ct. 1980, U.S. Ct. Appeals (11th cir.) 1981, U.S. Dist. Ct. (no. dist.) Ga. 1995. Assoc. Perry, Walters, Lippitt & Custer, Albany, 1972-76, Thompson, Ogletree & Deakins, Greenville, S.C., 1976-77, Ogletree, Deakins, Smoak & Stewart, Greenville, 1977-80; ptnr. Ogletree, Deakins, Nash, Smoak & Stewart P.C., 1980—. Bd. dirs. Happy Ho., Inc., Albany. Co-editor Labor and Employment Law for South Carolina Lawyers, 1999. Co-incorporator, sec. State of Tenn. Intercollegiate State Legislature, Nashville, 1967-69; state sec.-treas. Coll. Young Dems., Nashville, 1968; mem. employer and employee rels. com. N.C. Citizens for Bus. and Industry, Raleigh, 1984—; mem. United Way Greenville, vestry Christ Episcopal Ch., Greenville, 1981-85; mem. bd. visitors Clemson U., 1998—; bd. dirs. Blue Ridge Coun., Boy Scouts Am., 1999-2000. Capt. U.S. Army, 1969-77. Recipient Eagle Scouts award Boy Scouts Am., 1961. Mem. ABA, S.C. Bar Assn. (unauthorized practice of law com. 1977-95, chmn. 1982-92, ho. of dels. 1991-98, nominating com. 1992-95, CLE divsn., chmn., 1997-98, exec. com. 1995-99, chmn. seminars subcom. 1995-97), Ga. Bar Assn., Atlanta Bar Assn., Indsl. Rels. Rsch. Assn., S.C. Def. Trial Lawyers Assn., S.C. Andrews Soc. Upper S.C. (bd. dirs. 1979-81, v.p. 1986-87, pres. 1988-90, scholarship chmn. 1998—), Palmetto Soc. (bd. dirs. 1992—), Vanderbilt U. Alumni Assn. (pres. S.C. chpt. 1990-95, bd. dirs. 1994—), The Poinsett Club (bd. dirs.) (Greenville, S.C.), Rotary (bd. dirs. 1982-84, Paul Harris fellow 1986), Commerce Club of Greenville (bd. dirs. 1990—), Phi Delta Phi. General civil litigation, Environmental, Labor. Office: Ogletree Deakins Nash Smoak & Stewart PO Box 2757 Greenville SC 29602-2757

WYCKOFF, E. LISK, JR. lawyer; b. Middletown, N.J., Jan. 29, 1934; m. Elizabeth Ann Kuphal; children: Jenny Adele, Edward Lisk III, Elizabeth Hannah Longstreet. BA, Duke U., 1955; JD, U. Mich., 1960. Bar: N.Y. 1961, U.S. Dist. Ct. (so. and ea. dists.) N.Y. 1962, U.S. Ct. Appeals (2d cir. 1963), U.S. Tax Ct. 1974. Ptnr. Kramer, Levin, N.Y.C. Lectr. Practising Law Inst., 1970—, World Trade Inst., various profl. and bus. orgns. in U.S. and abroad; spl. counsel N.Y. Bankers Assn., 1974-98; counsel N.Y. State Senate Com. Housing and Urban Renewal, 1969-71, N.Y. State Senate Com. Judiciary, 1963-64, Com. Affairs of the City of N.Y., 1962; mem. N.Y.C. Mayor's Taxi Study Commn., 1967 Directing editor, commentator West's McKinney's Forms on Estates and Trusts, 1974—; commentator McKinney's Not-For-Profit Corp. law, 1995—; contbr. articles to profl. jours. Bd. dirs. 1652 Wyckoff House and Assn., Inc., 1982—; trustee Soc. for Preservation of L.I. Antiquities, 1988—, N.Y.C. Hist. House Trust, 1993—, Inner-City Scholarship Fund., Inc. 1993—, The Bard Ctr. Bard Coll., 1994—, Goodspeed Opera Co., 1996—, Florence Gris Wold Mus., 1997—, Wildlife Conservation Soc., 1993—; trustee, pres. Homeland Found., 1989—; mem. Concilium Socalium to Vatican Mus., 1991—; papal hon. Knight Commr. of Order of St. Gregory The Great, 1995. Fellow Am. Coll. Trust and Estate Counsel, Am. Bar Found.; mem. ABA (chair com. on internat. property, estate and trust of law sect. real property, probate and trust law, taxation 1991—), Internat. Fiscal Assn., Internat. Bar Assn., N.Y. State Bar Assn. (exec. com. tax sect., chmn. com. income taxation estates and trusts 1976-80, com. internat. estate planning 1980—), Assn. of Bar of City of N.Y., Holland Soc., St. Nicholas Soc., Knickerbocker Club, Racquet and Tennis Club (N.Y.C.), Mashomack Fish and Game Preserve Club (Pine Plains, N.Y.), Essex Yacht Club (Conn.), N.Y. Yacht Club. Avocations: tennis, sailing. General practice, Non-profit and tax-exempt organizations, Estate taxation. Office: PO Box 67 Old Lyme CT 06371 E-mail: ewyckoff@kramerlevin.com

WYCOFF, WILLIAM MORTIMER, lawyer; b. Pitts., Jan. 1, 1941; s. William Clyde and Margaret (Shaffer) W.; m. Deborah Seyl, Jan. 25, 1963; children: Ann Richardson, Pieter Claesen. AB, Cornell U., 1963; JD, Northwestern U., 1966. Bar: Pa. 1967, U.S. Ct. Appeals (3d cir.) 1967), U.S. Dist. Ct. (we. dist.) Pa. 1967. Assoc., now ptnr. Thorp Reed and Armstrong, Pitts., 1966—. Pres. Children's Home Pitts., 1976-78, 86-88, now bd. dirs.; pres. Pressley Ridge Schs., Pitts., 1988-90, now bd. dirs.: pres. Pressley Ridge Found.; pres., bd. dirs. Pitts. Dance Coun., 1991-94; trustee Pitts. Cultural Trust, 1991-94. Fellow Internat. Acad. Trial Lawyers, Am. Coll. Trial Lawyers; mem. Acad. Trial Lawyers Allegheny County. Avocations: photography, skiing, biking, hiking, golf. Antitrust, General civil litigation, Product liability. Office: Thorp Reed & Armstrong LLP One Oxford Ctr 14th Fl 301 Grant St Pittsburgh PA 15219 E-mail: wwycoff@thorpreed.com

WYLIE, PAUL RICHTER, JR. lawyer; b. Dec. 25, 1936; s. Paul Richter and Alice (Dredge) W.; m. Arlene Marie Klem, Mar. 6, 1982; children: Lynne Catherine, John Michael, Thomas Robert. BSChemE, Mont. State U., 1959; JD, Am. U., 1965. Bar: Utah 1978, Calif. 1970, U.S. Supreme Ct. 1971, Mont. 1990. Patent examiner U.S. Patent and Trademark Office, Washington, 1962-64; asst. gen. patent counsel Dart Industries Inc., L.A., 1967-81; pvt. practice, 1981-86, Pacific Palisades, Calif., 1986-90, Bozeman, Mont., 1990—. Mem. ABA, AIChE, Am. Intellectual Property Law Assn., L.a. Intellectual Property Law Assn., Am. Chem. Soc., Licensing Execs. Soc., Tech. Transfer Soc. Antitrust, Patent, Trademark and copyright. Home: 106 Silverwood Dr Bozeman MT 59715-9255 Office: 1805 W Dickerson St Ste 3 Bozeman MT 59715-4131

WYNN, SIMON DAVID, lawyer, director; b. London, Nov. 6, 1949; came to U.S., 1980; s. Allan Wynn and Sarah Gilmour; m. Nancy Ellen Anderson; 1 child, Alexander Colin. BA, U. Melbourne, Australia, 1972, LLB, 1973; LLM, U. London, 1974. Bar: N.Y. 1981, U.S. Dist. Ct. (ea. and so. dists.) N.Y. 1981. Lectr. law U. New South Wales, Sydney, Australia, 1975-80; barrister, 1977-80; rschr. Ctr. for Rsch. in Institutions and Social Policy, N.Y.C., 1980-84; ptnr. Buss & Wynn, 1985-90; pvt. practice, 1990—; asst. atty. gen. N.Y. State Environ. Protection Bureau, 2001—. Bd. dirs. A.W. Nominees Pty Ltd., Melbourne, 230 W 105 Realty Corp., N.Y.C. Co-author: Racketeering in Legitimate Industry: Two Case Studies, 1983. Arbitrator Sm. Claims Ct., N.Y.C., 1990—. Mem. N.Y. State Bar Assn., N.Y. County Lawyers Assn., Manhattan Soccer Club (treas. 1997—). Avocations: sailing, refereeing soccer. General civil litigation, General corporate, Private international. Home: 230 W 105th St New York NY 10025-3916 E-mail: simon.wynn@oag.state.ny.us

WYNN, STANFORD ALAN, lawyer; b. Milw., May 9, 1950; s. Sherburn and Marjory (Tarrant) W. BBA, U. Wis., Milw., 1972; JD, Case Western Res. U., 1975; LLM in Taxation, U. Miami, 1976. Bar: Wis. 1975, Fla. 1976. Assoc. Walsh and Simon, Milw., 1976-78; atty., asst. dir. advanced mktg. Northwestern Mut. Life Ins. Co., 1978—. Author: The Insurance Counselor-Split Dollar Life Insurance, 1991; cons. editor: The Insurance Counselor-The Irrevocable Life Insurance Trust, 1995. Bd. dirs. Waukesha Estate Planning Coun., 1985-86. Estate planning, Insurance, Estate taxation. Office: Northwestern Mut Life Ins Co 720 E Wisconsin Ave Milwaukee WI 53202-4703

WYNN, THOMAS JOSEPH, lawyer; b. Boston, Nov. 10, 1940; s. Thomas Joseph and Celena M. (Fitzpatrick) W.; m. Elaine M. O'Keefe, Aug. 1, 1964; children— Kristan E., Thomas J. A.B., Providence Coll., 1962; J.D., Suffolk U., 1968, LL.D. (hon.), 1982. Bar: Mass. 1969, U.S. Dist. Ct. Mass. 1973. Account exec., claim mgr. Marsh & McLennan, Boston, 1964-70; ptnr. firm Wynn & Wynn, P.C., Taunton, Mass., 1970— ; dir. Durfee Attleboro Bank, Fall River, Mass. Trustee Suffolk U., Boston, 1984— . Recipient Outstanding Alumni award Suffolk U., 1981. Fellow Am. Bar Found., Mass. Bar Found.; Mem. ABA (ho. of dels. 1981-83), Mass. Bar Assn. (bd. dels. 1976-84, pres. 1981-82), Nat. Conf. Bar Pres., Mass. Bar Found. (trustee 1982-84), New Eng. Bar Assn. (bd. dirs. 1981-83), Assn. Trial Lawyers Am., Internat. Assn. Indsl. Accidents Bds. and Commns. General practice, Personal injury, Real property. Home: 866 Prospect St North Dighton MA 02764-1331

WYNNE, WILLIAM JOSEPH, lawyer; b. Little Rock, July 17, 1927; Student, Little Rock U., 1946-48; JD, U. Ark., 1951. Bar: Ark. 1951, U.S. Dist. Ct. Ark. 1951, U.S. Supreme Ct. 1958; ordained to ministry Presbyn. Ch. Pres. Diversified Drilling Svcs., Inc., Elco Equipment Leasing Co., Inc.; v.p., gen. counsel El Dorado Paper Bag Mfg. Co., Inc.; sr. counsel Murphy Oil Corp., El Dorado, 1951-68; atty. Crumpler, O'Connor & Wynne, 1963—. Adj. prof. law U. Ark., Little Rock; gen. counsel and hearing officer Ark. Oil and Gas Commn. Mem. ABA, Ark. Bar Assn., Union County Bar Assn., Assn. Trial Lawyers Am., Ark. Trial Lawyers Assn., El Dorado C. of C. (Outstanding Young Man 1961-62). Oil, gas, and mineral, General practice. Home: 1501 W Block St El Dorado AR 71730-5300 Office: NBC Pla Ste 308 El Dorado AR 71730 E-mail: wynne2@ipa.net

WYNSTRA, NANCY ANN, lawyer; b. Seattle, June 25, 1941; d. Walter S. and Gaile E. (Cogley) W. BA cum laude, Whitman Coll., 1963; LLB cum laude, Colulmbia U., 1966. Bar: Wash. 1966, D.C. 1969, Ill. 1979, Pa. 1984. With appellate sect., civil divsn. U. S. Dept. Justice, Washington, 1966-67; TV corr. legal news Stas. WRC, NBC and Stas. WTOP, CBS, 1967-68; spl. asst. Corp. Counsel, 1968-70; dir. planning and rsch. D.C. Superior Ct., 1970-78; sp. advisor White house Spl. Action, Office for Drug Abuse Prevention, 1973-74; fellow Drug Abuse Coun., 1974-75; chief counsel Michael Reese Hosp. and Med. Ctr., Chgo., 1978-83; exec. v.p., gen. counsel Allegheny Health Edn. and Rsch. Found., Pitts., 1983-98; pres., CEO Allegheny Health Svcs. Provider's Ins. CO., 1989-98; assoc. prof. Carnegie Mellon U., Sch. Urban and Pub. Affairs, 1985—, Allegheny U. Health Scis., 1991-98. Cons. to various drug abuse programs, 1971-78; health law cons., 1998—. Author: Fundamentals of Health Law, others; contbr. articles to profl. jours. Mem. bd. overseers Whitman Coll., 1993—; mem. bd. elders, East Liberty Presbyn. Ch., 2000—; elder East Liberty Presbyn. Ch., 2000—. Mem. ABA, Nat. Health Lawyers Assn. (bd. dirs. 1985-91, 92-97, 97-99, chair publs. com. 1989-91, audit com. 1991-92, treas. 1992-93, 95-96, exec. com. 1992-99, edn. fund com. 1992-93, mem. nominating com. 1992-93, sec. 1993-95, treas. 1995-96, pres.-elect 1996-97, pres. 1997-98), Am. Health Lawyers Assn. (pres. 1997-98, exec. com. 1997-99, immediate past pres. 1998-99, pub. interest com. 2001—), Am. Soc. Hosp. Attys., others. General corporate, Health, Personal injury.

WYRICK, JERMAINE ALBERT, lawyer; b. Detroit, Oct. 19, 1971; s. Albert and Loretta Wyrick. BA in Polit. Sci., U. Mich., 1993; JD, Wayne State U., 1996. U.S. Dist. Ct. (ea. dist.) Mich., U.S. Ct. Appeals (6th cir.). Pvt. practice, Detroit, 1997—. Bd. dirs. Coalition Affirmative Action Preservation NAACP, 1997—, Legal Redress, Detroit, 1997—, NAACP lectr. Crockett Cmty. Law Sch., 1998. Bd. dirs. N.W. Youth Orgn.; with Angels Night Wayne County Juvenile Ct., 1998, Safe Night Lincoln Br. Libr., 1998, adult reading ptnr. CLEO fellow, Ohio, 1993; recipient Achievement award Coleman A. Young Found., 1989, 90, 91, 92, Disting. Grad. award, 1993, Pro Bono Project award FBA ea. dist. Mich., 1997. Mem. ABA, ATLA, Nat. Bar Assn., Mich. Trial Lawyers Assn., Wolverine Bar Assn., Booker T. Washington Bus. Assn., Econ. Club Detroit, Met. Detroit Optimist Club. Democrat. Mem. Hartford Meml. Bapt. Ch. Avocations: basketball, golf, weightlifting. Civil rights, Criminal, Juvenile. Home: PO Box 44646 Detroit MI 48244 Office: 65 Cadillac Sq Ste 2200 Detroit MI 48226

WYRSCH, JAMES ROBERT, lawyer, educator, author; b. Springfield, Mo., Feb. 23, 1942; s. Louis Joseph and Jane Elizabeth (Welsh) W.; m. B. Darlene Wyrsch, Oct. 18, 1975; children: Scott, Keith, Mark, Brian, Marcia. BA, U. Notre Dame, 1963; JD, Georgetown U., 1966; LLM, U. Mo., Kansas City, 1972. Bar: Mo. 1966, U.S. Ct. Appeals (8th cir.) 1971, U.S. Supreme Ct. 1972, U.S. Ct. Appeals (10th cir.) 1974, U.S. Ct. Appeals (5th cir.) 1974, U.S. Ct. Mil. & Appeals (5th cir.) 1974, U.S. Ct. Mil. & Appeals (5th cir.) 1974, U.S. Ct. Mil. & Apeals 1978, U.S. Ct. Appeals (6th cir.) 1982, U.S. Ct. Appeals (11th cir.) 1984, U.S. Ct. Appeals (7th cir.) 1986, U.S. Ct. Appeals (4th cir.) 1990, U.S. Ct. Appeals (9th cir.) 1998. Assoc. Wyrsch, Hobbs & Mirakian P.C., Kansas City, 1970-71; of counsel, 1972-77; ptnr., 1978—; pres., shareholder, 1988—; adj. prof. U. Mo., 1981—. Mem. com. instrns. Mo. Supreme Ct. 1983—; mem. adv. coun. legal assts. program U. Mo. at Kansas City , 1985-88; mem. cir. ct. adv. com. Jackson COunty, Mo., 1998—; bd. dirs. Kansas City Bar Found. Co-author: Missouri Criminal Trial Practice, 1994; contbr. articles to profl. jours. Mem. U. Mo.-Kansas City Adv Coun., Legal Assts. Program, 1985-88. Capt. U.S. Army, 1966-69. Recipient Joint Svcs. Commendation medal U.S. Army, 1969, U. Mo. Kansas City Svc. award Law Found., 1991-92. Fellow Am. Coll. Trial Lawyers, Am. Bar Found., Mo. Bar Found.; mem. ABA, ATLA, Am. Arbitration Assn. (panel arbitrators 1976-2000), Mo. Bar Assn. (vice-chmn. criminal law com. 1978-79), Kansas City Bar Assn. (chmn. anti-trust com. 1981, chmn. bus. tort, anti-trust, franchise com. 1998), Am. Bd. of Trial Advs. (adv.), Nat. Assn. Criminal Def. Attys., Mo. Assn. Criminal Def. Attys. (sec. 1982), Kansas City Club, Phi Delta Phi, Country Club of Blue Springs. Democrat. Roman Catholic. Antitrust, Criminal. Home: 1501 NE Sunny Creek Ln Blue Springs MO 64014-2044 Office: Wyrsch Hobbs & Mirakian PC 1101 Walnut St Fl 13 Kansas City MO 64106-2134

XING, XUISONG, lawyer; b. Anhui, China; s. Huoshui Xing and Yufang Chen; m. Xiaoli He, Mar. 8, 1965; 1 child, Chuqin. BS, Peking U., Beijing, 1984; LLM, China U. Polit. Scis. & Law, Beijing, 1990. Legal advisor Country Books Pub. Housoe, Beijing, 1990-92; ptnr., exec. com. Global Law Office, 1992—. Arbitrator China Internat. Econ. & Trade Arbitration Commn., Beijing, 1997—. Author: A Textbook on Economic Law, 1991, Transnational Litigation: A Practitioner's Guide, 2000. Mem. London Ct. Internat. Arbitration. Alternative dispute resolution, Banking, General civil litigation. Office: Global Law Office 5/T Towercrest Plz 3 W Rd Beijing 100016 China Fax: 86-10-6467 2012. E-mail: xingxs@globallawoffice.com.cn

YAGER, THOMAS C. judge; b. L.A., Feb. 16, 1918; s. Thomas C. and May M. (McGowan) Y. AB in pol. sci., UCLA, 1939, gen. secondary lifetime tchg. credential, 1940; JD, USC, 1948; LLD, Western State U., Calif., 1972. Reader UCLA Philosophy Dept., 1940; atty. L.A., 1949-57; legal advisor Gov. Calif., 1957, 58; superior ct. sr. judge Calif., 1959-78; founder Cmty. Betterment Svc., L.A. Author numerous legal and religious books; contbr. articles to profl. jours. Founder The Judge Thomas C. Yager Found., L.A., The Cmty. Betterment Svc., L.A.; Major U.S. Army, 1942-46. Office: The Cmty Betterment Svc 108 N Gower St Los Angeles CA 90004-3828 E-mail: pvtsecty@aol.com

YALE, KENNETH P. general counsel, dentist; b. Lincoln, Nebr., Aug. 18, 1956; m. Julia Marie Windsor, Aug. 7, 1982; children: Hilary, Ken, Victoria, George, Lydia. BA, Creighton U., 1978; DDS, U. Md., 1981; CFP, U. Mo., Kansas City, 1984; JD, Georgetown U., 1988. Bar: Va. 1988. Adminstr., clinician USPHS, Kansas City, Mo., 1981-84; cons. Riggs Nat. Bank, Washington, 1984-85; govt. rels. rep. ADA, 1985-87; legis. counsel U.S. Senator Simpson, 1987-89; exec. dir. White House Domestic Policy Coun., 1989-90; chief of staff White House Sci. and Tech. Office, 1990-92; sr. v.p. The Jefferson Group, 1993-96; pres. Jefferson Healthcare, 1997-99; CEO Advanced Health Solutions, Rockville, Md., 1999; v.p. bus. strategies, gen. counsel Eduneering.com, 1999—. Instr. Georgetown U., 1984-85. Author: Section on Healthcare, 1988, Managed Care Compliance Guide, 1999, Healthcare Model Compliance Manual, 2000. Advisor Presdl. campaign, Washington, 1988, 92, 96, 2000. Lt. USPHS, 1981-84. Mem. ABA, ADA. Office: Eduneering.com 10001 Weatherwood Ct Rockville MD 20854-2171 E-mail: kenyale@mindspring.com

YALMAN, ANN, judge, lawyer; b. Boston, June 9, 1948; d. Richard George and Joan (Osterman) Y. BA, Antioch Coll., 1970; JD, NYU, 1973. Trial atty. Fla. Rural Legal Svcs., Immokalee, Fla., 1973-74; staff atty. EEO, Atlanta, 1974-76; pvt. practice Santa Fe, 1976—; probate judge Santa Fe County, 1999—. Part time U.S. magistrate, N. Mex., 1988-96. Commr. Met. Water Bd., Santa Fe, 1986-88. Mem. N.Mex. Bar Assn. (commr. Santa Fe chpt. 1983-86). Home: 441 Calle La Paz Santa Fe NM 87505-2821 Office: 304 Catron St Santa Fe NM 87501-1806

YALOWITZ, KENNETH GREGG, lawyer; b. Moline, Ill., Apr. 9, 1954; s. Jerome M. and Esther F. (Falkoff) Y.; m. Jan A. Albright, Jan. 4, 1976; children: Kevan, James T. BS, Ill. State U., 1976; JD, So. Ill. U., 1979. Bar: Ill. 1979, Mo. 1980, Wash. 1982, U.S. Dist. Ct. (ea. and we. dists.) Wash. 1982, U.S. Ct. Appeals (9th cir.) 1985. Assoc. Peper, Martin, Jensen, Maichel & Hetlage, St. Louis, 1979-82, Nourse & Assocs., Seattle, 1982-86, Hight Green & Yalowitz, Seattle, 1986—. Instr. Bellevue Community Coll., Wash., 1985; bd. dirs. WSBA, chmn. 2000-01. Commr. Issaquah (Wash.) Planning Commn., 1986-94; dir. Luana Water Assn., 1994-97; mem. exec. bd. Issaquah Little League, 1996-99. Mem. ABA, Wash. State Bar Assn., King County Bar Assn., Associated Gen. Contractors (v. chair legal affairs com. 2001-02). Avocations: hiking, skiing, running. Federal civil litigation, Contracts commercial, Construction. Office: Hight Green& Yalowitz 1191 2nd Ave Ste 2110 Seattle WA 98101-2968

YAMAKAWA, DAVID KIYOSHI, JR. lawyer, deceased; b. San Francisco, Jan. 25, 1936; s. David and Shizu (Negishi) Y. BS, U. Calif., Berkeley, 1958, JD, 1963. Bar: Calif. 1964, U.S. Supreme Ct. 1970. Prin. Law Offices David K. Yamakawa Jr., San Francisco, 1964—. Dep. dir. Cmty. Action Agy., San Francisco, 1968-69; dir. City Demonsration Agy., San Francisco, 1969-70; adv. coun. Calif. Senate Subcom. on the Disabled, 1982-83, Ctr. for Mental Health Svcs., Substance Abuse and Mental Health Svcs, Adminstrn. U.S. Dept. Health and Human Svcs., 1995-99; chmn. cmty. residential treatment system adv. com. Calif. Dept. Mental Health, 1980-85, San Francisco Human Rights Commn., 1977-80; pres. Legal Assistance to the Elderly, 1981-83; 2d v.p. Nat. Conf. Social Welfare, 1983-89; v.p. Region IX Nat. Mental Health Assn., 1981-83; cmty. partnership bd. Sch. Social Welfare, U. Calif., Berkeley, 1999—. Vice-chmn. Mt. Zion Hosp. and Med. Ctr., 1986-88; bd. dirs. United Neighborhood Ctrs. of Am., 1977-83, ARC Bay Area, 1988-91, Goldman Inst. on Aging, 1993-99, v.p. 1994-96, vice-chmn. 1996-99, hon. lifetime dir., exec. com., 1999—; trustee Mt. Zion Med. Ctr. U. Calif., San Francisco, 1993-97, UCSF/Mt. Zion, UCSF Stanford Health Care, 1997-2000; chmn. bd. trustees United Way Bay Area, 1983-85; CFO Action for Nature, Inc., 1987—; bd. dirs. Ind. sector, 1986-92, Friends of the San Francisco Human Rights Commn., 1980—, CFO, 1980-85, 94—, vice-chmn. 1985-94; bd. dirs. Father Alfred Boeddeker's La Madre Found., 1982—, v.p. 1994—; bd. dirs. Hispanic Cmty. Found. of the Bay Area, 1989-98, legal counsel, 1989-98; bd. dirs. Kimochi Inc., 1999—, Goldman Inst., 1999—, San Francisco Sr. Ctr., 1999—; bd. dirs. Non-Profit Svcs., Inc., 1987-2000, sec. 1987-90; chmn. 1990-2000; pres. Coun. Internat. Programs, San Francisco, 1987-89, Internat. Inst. San Francisco, 1990-93; citizens adv. com. San Francisco Hotel Tax Fund Grants for the Arts Program, 1991—, acting chmn., 2000—. Recipient John B. Williams Outstanding Planning and Agy. Rels. vol. award United Way of the Bay Area, 1980, Mortimer Fleishhacker Jr. Outstanding Vol. award United Way, 1985, Spl. Recognition award Legal Assistance to the Elderly, 1983, Commendation award Bd. Suprs. City and County of San Francisco, 1983, cert. Honor, 1985, San Francisco Found. award, 1985, 1st Mental Health Awareness award Mental Health Assn., San Francisco, 1990, David Yamakawa Day proclaimed in San Francisco, 1985. Mem. ABA (Liberty Bell award 1986). General practice, Intellectual property, Non-profit and tax-exempt organizations. Office: 582 Market St Ste 410 San Francisco CA 94104-5305 E-mail: attorneyyamakawa@aol.com Died Mar. 01, 2001.

YAMANO, JOHN Y. lawyer; b. Riverside, Calif., Nov. 10, 1959; s. John Yoshiyuki and Junko Yamano; m. Sharon H. Nishi, Apr. 28, 1990. BS in Bus. Adminstrn., U. So. Calif., 1981; JD, U. Calif., Berkeley, 1984. Bar: Calif. 1984, Hawaii 1985, U.S. Dist. Ct. Hawaii 1985, U.S. Ct. Appeals (9th cir.) 1988. Assoc. Case & Lynch, Honolulu, 1984-88, Roeca & Louie, Honolulu, 1988-89; ptnr. McCorriston Miho Miller Mukai, 1989—. Bd. dirs. Hawaii Lawyers Care Pro Bono Svcs. Orgn., 1985-91, treas., 1985-87;

mem. faculty Legal Seminars, Inc., Honolulu, 1987-96; spkr. in field. Author: Hawaii Motor Vehicle Collision Manual Update, 1994; co-author: Hawaii Motor Vehicle Collision Manual, 1990, Hawaii Tort Liability, 1989. Bd. dirs. Hawaii Parkinson Assn., Honolulu, 1998, v.p., 1999—. Named to Outstanding Young Men of Am., 1998. Mem. ABA, Calif. Bar Assn., Hawaii Bar Assn., Alpha Kappa Psi, Phi Kappa Phi, Beta Gamma Sigma. Avocations: golf, tennis. General civil litigation, Constitutional, Insurance. Office: McCorriston Miho Miller Mukai Five Waterfront Pl 500 Ala Moana Blvd Unit 4 Honolulu HI 96813-4920

YAMBRUSIC, EDWARD SLAVKO, lawyer, consultant; b. Conway, Pa., Mar. 9, 1933; s. Michael Misko and Slavica Sylvia (Yambrusic) Y.; m. Natalie Visniak, 1990. BA, Duquesne U., 1957; postgrad., Georgetown U. Law Ctr., 1959-61; JD, U. Balt., 1966; cert., The Hague (Netherlands) Acad. Internat. Law, 1967, 69; diploma, Ctr. Study and Rsch. Internat. Law and Internat. Rels., 1970; PhD in Pub. Internat. Law, Cath. U. Am., 1984. Bar: Md. 1969, U.S. Ct. Customs and Patent Appeals 1972, U.S. Supreme Ct. 1972, U.S. Ct. Internat. Trade 1988. Copyright examiner U.S. Copyright Office, Libr. of Congress, Washington, 1960-69; atty. adviser Office Register of Copyrights, 1969-98; pvt. practice internat. and immigration law, 1969—. Legal counsel Nat. Ethnic Studies Assembly, 1976—, Soc. Fed. Linguists, 1980; pres. AMCRO Internat. Consulting, Inc., 1995—. Author: Treat Interpretation: Theory and Reality, 1987, The Trade-Based Approaches to the Protection of Intellectual Property, 1990; contbr. articles to ofcl. newsletter Nat. Confedn. Am. Ethnic Groups, also legal jours. Pres. Nat. Confedn. Am. Ethnic Groups, Washington; nat. chmn. Croatian-Am. Bicentennial Com. nat. chmn. Nat. Pilgrimage of Croatian-Ams. to Nat. Shrine of Immaculate Conception, Washington; v.p. Croatian Acad. Am. Served to capt. U.S. Army, 1957-59. Duquesne U. Tamburitzans scholar, 1953-57; Hague Acad. Internat. Law fellow, 1970. Mem. ABA, Md. Bar Assn., Internat. Law Assn., Internat. Fiscal Assn., Am. Soc. Internat. Law, Croatian Cath. Union Am., Croatian Frat. Union Am. Republican. Roman Catholic. Certificate issued by the Librarian of Congress in recognition of 40 years of distinguished service to the people of the United States of America, 1957-98. Home and Office: 4720 Massachusetts Ave NW Washington DC 20016-2346

YAMIN, DIANNE ELIZABETH, judge; b. Danbury, Conn., June 4, 1961; d. Raymond Joseph and Linda May (Bucko) Goetz; m. Robert Joseph Yamin, Sept. 3, 1988; children: Samantha Blythe, Rebecca Anne. AB, Lehigh U., 1983; JD, Mercer U., 1986. Bar: Conn. 1986, U.S. Dist. Ct. Conn. 1989. Lawyer Gerald Hecht & Assocs., Danbury, 1986-92; judge State Conn., 1991—. Atty. Yamin & Yamin, Danbury, 1992—; chmn. ethics com. Conn. Probate Assembly, 1994—; mem. Conn. Coun. on Adoptions, 1992—, Conn. Probate Assembly, 1991—. Bd. dirs. Big Bros./Big Sisters, Danbury, 1987-94, Conn Brass Soc., Inc., 1991—, Lions Club Danbury, 1993-94, Friends of Tarrywile Park, Inc., Danbury, 1993-99, Danbury Music Ctr., 1996—, Hispanic Ctr. Greater Danbury, 1999—; pres. coun. women Lehigh Univ., 2000—. Recipient outstanding young citizen award Conn. Jaycees, 1994, pro bono award Conn. Legal Svcs., 1993; named as one of 21 Young Lawyers Leading Us into the 21st Century, ABA Mag., 1995. Mem. ABA, Conn. Bar Assn., Conn. Health Lawyers Assn., Danbury Bar Assn, Omicron Delta Kappa. Republican. Roman Catholic. Avocations: ballet, volunteerism, travel, outdoor activities. Home: 66 Barnum Rd Danbury CT 06811-2938 Office: 155 Deer Hill Ave Danbury CT 06810-7726

YAMIN, MICHAEL GEOFFREY, lawyer; b. N.Y.C., Nov. 10, 1931; s. Michael and Ethel Yamin; m. Martina Schaap, Apr. 16, 1961; children: Michael Jeremy, Katrina. AB magna cum laude, Harvard U., 1953, LLB, 1958. Bar: N.Y. 1959, U.S. Dist. Ct. (so. and ea. dists.) N.Y., U.S. Ct. Appeals (2d cir.) 1966, U.S. Supreme Ct. 1967. Assoc. Weil, Gotshal & Manges, N.Y.C., 1958-65; sr. ptnr. Colton, Hartnick, Yamin & Sheresky, 1966-93, Kaufmann, Feiner, Yamin, Gildin & Robbins, LLP, N.Y.C., 1993—. Trustee Gov.'s Com. Scholastic Achievement, 1976—; mem. Manhattan Cmty. Bd. 6, 1974—88, chmn., 1986—88; mem. Manhattan Borough Bd., 1986—88. Mem. ABA, N.Y. State Bar Assn., Assn. Bar City N.Y., Fed. Bar Coun., Am Fgn. Law Assn. (Am. br.), Internat. Law Assn., Societe de Legislation Comparee, Internat. Bar Assn., Harvard Faculty Club (Cambridge, Mass.), Harvard Club of N.Y.C. (trustee N.Y. Found. 1981—, pres. 1999—, sub-chmn. schs. and scholarships com. 1972-93, bd. mgrs. 1985-88, 93-98, chair house com. 1992-95, v.p. 1995-98, chair comms. com. 1997-99, chair membership svcs. com. 1999-2000), Harvard Alumni Assn. (bd. dirs. 1995-98). General corporate, Mergers and acquisitions, Contracts commercial. Office: 777 3rd Ave New York NY 10017-1401

YANAS, JOHN JOSEPH, lawyer; b. Albany, N.Y., July 18, 1929; m. Mary Faith Casey; children: John J., Joseph J., Kathleen Ann, Mary Patricia. Student Russell Sage Coll., 1947-50; LLB, Albany Law Sch., 1953, LLD, 1989. Bar: N.Y. 1954, U.S. Ct. Appeals (2d cir.) 1962. Assoc. Casey, Honikel and Wisely, Albany, 1954-60; ptnr. Dugan, Casey, Burke & Lyons, Albany, 1960-69; ptnr. Casey, Yanas, Mitchell & Amerling, Albany, 1969-84, Casey, Yanas, Clyne, Mitchell & Amerling, Albany, 1984-88; ptnr. Degraff, Foy, Holt-Harris & Mealey, 1989—; counsel Albany County Pub. Welfare Dist., 1959-60; mem. Albany City CSC, 1970-73, Albany County CSC, 1970-73; justice Albany City Ct., 1973-77; Bank. Trustee Christian Bros. Acad., Albany, 1972—, chair, 1992, Albany Law Sch., 1975—, chair, 1993. Fellow Am. Bar Found., N.Y. Bar Found., ABA; mem. Am. Coll. Real Estate Lawyers, N.Y. State Bar Assn. (chmn. real property law sect. 1974-75, (chmn. com. to confer with N.Y. State Realty Bd. 1975-77, chmn. com. continuing legal edn. 1977-80, treas. 1980-86, chmn. fin. com. 1987, pres.-elect 1988, pres. 1989), Albany County Bar Assn. (pres. 1978). Banking, Probate, Real property. Office: 90 State St Albany NY 12207

YANDLE, STEPHEN THOMAS, dean; b. Oakland, Calif., Mar. 7, 1947; s. Clyde Thomas and Jane Walker (Hess) Y.; m. Martha Anne Welch, June 26, 1971. BA, U. Va., 1969, JD, 1972. Bar: Va. 1972. Asst. dir. admissions U. Va. Law Sch., Charlottesville, 1972-76; from asst. to assoc. dean Northwestern U. Sch. Law, Chgo., 1976-85; assoc. dean Yale U. Law Sch., New Haven, 1985—. Bd. dirs. The Access Group. Commr. New Haven Housing Authority, 1998—; trustee Nat. Assoc. for Law Placement Found. for Rsch. and Edn., 2000—. Capt. U.S. Army, 1972. Mem. Law Sch. Admission Coun. (programs, edn. and prelaw com. 1978-84), Assn. Am. Law Schs. (chmn. legal edn. and admissions sect. 1979, nominations com. 1987, chmn. adminstrn. of law schs. sect. 1991), Nat. Assn. for Law Placement (pres. 1984-85, co-chmn. Joint Nat. Assn. com. on placement 1986-88), New Haven Legal Assistance Assn. (bd. dirs., treas. 1992-98). Office: Yale Law Sch PO Box 208215 New Haven CT 06520-8215 E-mail: stephen.yandle@yale.edu

YANITY, JOSEPH BLAIR, JR. lawyer; b. Homer City, Pa., Nov. 11, 1925; s. Joseph Blair and Perina Maria (Carcelli) Y.; m. Joyce Ann Gilham, Jan. 9, 1954; children: Joseph B., John M., Jennifer A. AB with high honors, Ea. Ky. U., 1949; JD, Washington and Lee U., 1952. Bar: Ohio 1953, U.S. Dist. Ct. (so. dist.) Ohio 1966. Ptnr. Lavelle & Yanity, Athens, Ohio, 1953-78, Yanity & De Veau, Athens, 1978-85; pros. atty. County of Athens, 1958-61; gen. counsel O'Bleness Meml. Hosp., Athens, 1970—. Dir. Bank One of Athens. Mem. Vets. Commn. Athens County, 1961-88; v.p., trustee, Ohio Valley Health Svcs. Found., Athens, 1965—; pres., trustee, Auto Club of South Ctrl. Ohio, Portsmouth, 1970—. Served to 1st lt., U.S. Army, 1943-53, ETO. Recipient Outstanding Alumnus prize Ea. Ky. U., 1976, E.E. Dais award Ohio Valley Health Svcs. Found., 1981. Mem. ABA, Athens County Bar Assn. (pres. 1971), Ohio State Bar Assn., Am. Legion, Symposiarchs Club (pres. 1979), K.C. (grand Knight 1965), Elks (exalted ruler 1961). Avocation: football officiating. General practice, Probate. Home: 7695 Country Club Rd Athens OH 45701-8845 Office: PO Box 748 Athens OH 45701-0748

YANKWITT, RUSSELL MARC, lawyer; b. Massapequa, N.Y., May 20, 1970; s. George Bruce and Adrienne Gail Y. BA, Conn. Coll., 1992; JD, Cornell U., 1996. Bar: N.Y. 1997. Jud. law clk. to hon. Thomas C. Platt U.S. Dist. Ct. (ea. dist.) N.Y., 1996-97; assoc. Skadden Arps Slate Meagher & Flom LLP, N.Y.C., 1997. Federal civil litigation, General civil litigation, Securities. Office: Skadden Arps Slate Meagher & Flom LLP 919 Third Ave New York NY 10022

YANNUCCI, THOMAS DAVID, lawyer; b. Springfield, Ohio, Mar. 30, 1950; s. David Marion and Patricia (Wilson) Y.; m. Lisa Marie Copeland, June 30, 1972; children: Teresa, Andrea, Thomas D. Jr. AB, U. Notre Dame, 1972, JD, 1976. Bar: Ohio 1977, U.S. Ct. Appeals (D.C., 1st, 2d, 3d, 4th, 5th, 6th, 7th, 8th, 11th and 10th cirs.) 1980, U.S. Supreme Ct. 1980, D.C. 1981. Law clk. to presiding justice U.S. Ct. Appeals (D.C. cir.), Washington, 1976-77; trial atty. U.S. Dept. Justice, 1977-80; ptnr. Kirkland & Ellis, 1980—. Editor-in-chief U. Notre Dame Law Rev., 1975-76. Roman Catholic. Antitrust, Federal civil litigation, State civil litigation. Office: Kirkland & Ellis 655 15th St NW Ste 1200 Washington DC 20005-5793 E-mail: thomas_yannucci@dc.kirkland.com

YARBROUGH, EDWARD MEACHAM, lawyer; b. Nashville, Dec. 17, 1943; s. Gurley McTyeire and Miriam (Mefford) Y. BA, Rhodes Coll., 1967; JD, Vanderbilt U., 1973. Bar: Tenn. 1973. Asst. dist. atty. Davidson County, Nashville, 1973-76; ptnr. Hollins, Wagster & Yarbrough, 1976—. Chmn. com. Crime Commn., Nashville, 1981-82; mem. task force House Judiciary Com., Nashville, 1984; chmn. Crimestoppers Inc., Nashville, 1983—; trustee United Way, Nashville, 1983—, Belmont U., 1993—, Cumberland Sci. Mus., 1996—; bd. dirs. Big Bros. Inc., Nashville, 1983-85; mem. nat. devel. bd. Lipscomb U., 2000—; vice chmn. deacons Forest Hills Bapt. Ch. Served to 1st lt. U.S. Army, 1969-71, Vietnam. Decorated Bronze Star; named Best Criminal Def. Atty., Bus. Nashville mag., 1999. Fellow Nat. Speleological Soc. (bd. dirs. 1960—); mem. ABA (bd. dirs. 1985), Tenn. Bar Assn., Nashville Bar Assn. (pres. 1983), Tenn. Criminal Def. Lawyers, Nashville Kiwanis (pres. 1992), Am. Legion, Richland Country Club, City Club (Nashville). Democrat. Baptist. Avocations: cave exploration, photography, skiing, golf, running. State civil litigation, Criminal, Family and matrimonial. Home: 5230 Granny White Pike Nashville TN 37220-1715 Office: Hollins Wagster & Yarbrough 424 Church St Ste 2210 Nashville TN 37219-2303

YARINGTON, BARBARA J. lawyer; b. Omaha, June 8, 1969; d. Charles Thomas and Barbara (Johnson) Yarington. BA, Goucher Coll., 1991; JD, Vermont Law Sch., South Royalton, 1994. Bar: Md. 1994, Wash. 1996. Gen. counsel RMC, Inc., Lexington Park, Md., 1995-96; land use counsel Spencer Cons., Seattle, 1997; land use assoc. Groff & Murphy, PLLC, 1997-99; project mgr. Murray Franklyn Co., Bellevue, Wash., 2000—. Recipient Lee Snyder Lovitt prize, 1991, Janet McBrian award, 1991. Mem. Wash. Athletic Club, Seattle Yacht Club. Avocations: horseback riding, travel, skiing, boating. Office: Murray Franklyn Co 14410 Bel Red Rd Bellevue WA 98007-3942

YARMEY, RICHARD ANDREW, investment manager; b. Kingston, Pa., Aug. 23, 1948; s. Stanley Richard and Rose Mary (Rees) Y.; m. Jeanne Marie Cappelli, Aug. 5, 1972; children: Lynn Rees, Jessica Brett, Kristen Alexandra. BS, U. Scranton, 1970; JD, Cath. U., 1975. Bar: Pa. 1975, D.C. 1976, U.S. Ct. Appeals (5th cir.) 1976, U.S. Tax Ct. 1978, U.S. Ct. Appeals (D.C. cir.) 1980. Contract adjudicator GAO, Washington, 1970-73; program asst. EPA, 1973; assoc. Sharon, Pierson, et al, 1975-82; of counsel Pierson, Semmes et al, 1982-93; prin. Yarmey Capital Mgmt., 1989-95; sr. portfolio mgr. PNC Advisors, 1995—; mgr. Direction Instnl. Investment Group, 2000—. Fin. cons. various pension plans, individuals and bus. concerns, 1976—; TV panelist, speaker, writer on portfolio mgmt.; instr. fin. mgmt. and investments continuing edn. Wilkes U., Wilkes-Barre. Mem. Pa. Bar Assn., Aircraft Owners and Pilots Assn., Alpha Sigma Nu. Democrat. Avocation: cabinetmaking. Office: 201 Penn Ave Scranton PA 18053 also: One PNC Plz Fifth Ave & Wood St Pittsburgh PA 15265-0001 E-mail: richard.yarmey@pncbank.com

YATES, LEIGHTON DELEVAN, JR. lawyer; b. Atlanta, Sept. 4, 1946; s. Leighton Delevan and Stella Louise (Hill) Y.; m. Phyllis Jeanne Hummer, Dec. 22, 1968; children: Leighton Delevan III, Lauren Jeanne. BA, Hampden-Sydney Coll., Va., 1968; JD with high honors, U. Fla., 1973. Bar: Fla. 1974, U.S. Dist. Ct. (middle dist.) Fla. 1975. Assoc. Maguire, Voorhis & Wells, P.A., Orlando, Fla., 1974-77, shareholder, 1978-98, dept. chmn., 1985-90; ptnr. Holland & Knight LLP, 1998—. Bd. dirs. Hubbard Constrn. Co., Winter Park , Fla., 1985—, Blythe Constrn., Inc., Charlotte, NC, 1999—; adminstrv, dir. SunTrust Bank, Orlando, Fla., 1990—. Exec. editor U. Fla. Law Rev., 1973. Mem. Fla. Bd. Bar Examiners, 1992-97, vice chmn., 1995-96, chmn. 1996-97; chmn. Ctrl. Fla. Blood Bank, 1995—, vice chmn., 1980-95; chmn. Orlando Opera Co., 1994, pres., 1993. Fellow Am. Bar Found.; mem. ABA, Fla. Bar Assn., Orange County Bar Assn., Univ. Club of Orlando, Country Club of Orlando, Order of the Coif, Omicron Delta Kappa, Phi Kappa Phi. Republican. Presbyterian. Avocations: scuba diving, cycling, music, reading. E-mail: (home) (office). Banking, General corporate, Mergers and acquisitions. Home: 3218 S Osceola Ave Orlando FL 32806-6251 Office: Holland & Knight LLP 200 S Orange Ave Ste 2600 Orlando FL 32801-3453 E-mail: lyates@cfl.rr.com, lyates@hklaw.com

YATES, LINDA SNOW, financial services marketing executive; b. St. Louis, July 20, 1938; d. Robert Anthony Jerrue and June Alberta (Crowder) Armstrong; m. Charles Russell Snow, Nov. 26, 1958 (div. 1979); children: Cathryn Louise, Christopher Armstrong, Heather Highstone, Sean Webster; m. Alan Porter Yates, July 22, 1983. BBA, Auburn U., 1973, MEd, 1975, EdD, 1998. Cert. profl. sec. Div. head placement div. Solutions Group, Atlanta, 1981-83; employment coord. Fulton Fed. Savs., 1983-84; owner, recruiter Data One, Inc., 1984-85; ops. mgr. Talent Tree Temporaries, 1985-87; legal asst., sec. Rice & Keene, 1987-90; legal word processing asst. Kilpatrick & Cody, 1990-94; pres., owner Power Comm., Cashiers, N.C., 1994-98; regional coord. S.E. region, regional mktg. rep. WorldConnect Comms., Tulsa; dir. mktg. check clear plus divsn. Am. Fin. and Credit Svcs., Inc. Adj. instr. DeKalb Coll., Atlanta, 1980-84, Mercer U., Atlanta, 1981-82; instr. bus. So. Union State Jr. Coll., Valley, Ala., 1974-75; legal sec. Swift, Currie, McGhee & Hiers, Atlanta, 1979-80, Samford, Torbert, Denson & Horsley, Opelika, Ala., 1969-71; dir. acad. planning, chmn. edn. divsn., mem. part-time faculty in ednl. adminstrn. Monterrey Inst. Grad. Studies, Nuevo Leon, Mex. Columnist Neon News Flash, 1995. Mem. Paralegal Assn. Beaufort County (charter mem., sec. 1993-94), Women Bus. Owners, Nat. Assn. Pers. Cons., Internat. Soc. Poets (Disting. mem., Internat. Poet of Merit 1996, Internat. Poetry Hall of Fame 1996), Cashiers Writers Group, Phi Delta Kappa, Alpha Xi Delta. Republican. Episcopalian. Avocations: golf, writing, international travel. Office: PO Box 2441 Cashiers NC 28717-2441

YEAGER, DENNIS RANDALL, lawyer; b. Dallas, Jan. 10, 1941; s. William C. and Katherine (Payne) Y.; m. Jere Jones, Aug. 31, 1963; children: Stephanie Ann O'Donnell, Karen Elizabeth, Brenda Marie. BSS, Loyola U. of South, 1964; LLB, Columbia U., 1967. Bar: N.Y. 1967, D.C. 1979, U.S. Supreme Ct., 1971, U.S. Ct. Appeals (2d cir.) 1972. Assoc. Willkie Farr & Gallagher, N.Y.C., 1967-69; dir., chief exec. officer Nat. Employment Law Project, 1969-75; from assoc. to ptnr. Tufo, Johnston & Allegaert, 1975-80; ptnr. Yeager & Barrett, 1980-93; pvt. practice, 1993—. Chmn. program on bus. errors and omissions ins. Practicing Law Inst., 1983, program on role of outside counsel in bus. investigation, 1985; panelist program on dirs. and officers liabilities, 1988. Mem. Am. Coun. on Germany, N.Y.C., 1995-96. Mem. N.Y. State Bar Assn., Assn. of Bar of City of N.Y., Blue Key, Alpha Sigma Nu. Roman Catholic. Federal civil litigation, State civil litigation, Insurance. Home: 70 W 95th St New York NY 10025-6721 Office: 70 W 95th St New York NY 10025-6721

YEAGER, JEFFREY ALAN, lawyer; b. Toledo, Dec. 8, 1970; s. Albert Wilson and Sheila Ann Y.; m. Amy J. Cubberly, Mar. 5, 1994. BSBA cum laude, Bowling Green (Ohio) State U., 1993; JD with honors, Ohio State U., 1997. Bar: Ohio 1997, U.S. Dist. Ct. (so. dist.) Ohio, 1998, U.S. Ct. Appeals (6th cir.) 1998. Assoc. Squire, Sanders & Dempsey, Columbus, 1997—. Mem. Ohio State Bar Assn., Columbus Bar Assn., Order of Coif. Avocations: art, literature. Federal civil litigation, General civil litigation, State civil litigation.

YEAGER, JOSEPH HEIZER, JR. lawyer; b. Indpls., Jan. 8, 1957; s. Joseph Heizer and Marilyn Virginia (Hillyard) Y.; m. Candance A. Grass, June 2, 1984; children: Samuel, Henry. AB cum laude, Harvard U., 1979; JD cum laude, Ind. U., 1983. Bar: Ind. 1983, U.S. Dist. Ct., (so. and no. dist.) Ind. 1983, U.S. Ct. Appeals (7th cir.) 1986, U.S. Supreme Ct. 1996. Dir. ops. Penn and Schoen Assocs., N.Y.C., 1979-80; assoc. Baker & Daniels, Indpls., 1983-89, ptnr., 1990—. Bd. dirs. Indpls. Legal Aid Soc., 1990-99, pres. 1992-94; chmn. Indpls. Com. for UNICEF, 1986-91; mem. Indpls. Com. for Fgn. Affairs, 1986-91. Mem. Ind. Bar Assn., Indpls. Bar Assn. (litigation sect. exec. com. 1985-86, 1996-2000, chair 1999, mem. jud. evaluation com.), Cen. Ind. Regional Citizens League (bd. dirs. 1997-99). Democrat. Avocation: private pilot. General civil litigation, Contracts commercial, Insurance. Office: Baker & Daniels 300 N Meridian St Ste 2700 Indianapolis IN 46204-1782

YEAGER, KATHLEEN M. court administrator; b. Erie, Pa., Feb. 20, 1953; d. Robert Joseph Cooney and Mary Ann Malthaner; children: Christopher, Patrick. BA in Acctg., Mercychrist Coll., 1989. Cost acct. GE, Erie, Pa., 1989-91; ct. adminstr. County of Erie Ct. Common Pleas, 1991—. Mem. Nat. Asst. Ct. Mgmt., Pa. Assn. Ct. Mgrs., Mid Atlantic Assn. Ct. Mgrs., Inst. Mgmt. Accts. (sec., dir. pub. rels.). Avocations: reading, aerobics, golf, football. Home: 132 E 37th St Erie PA 16504-1522 Office: County of Erie Court Adminstrn Erie PA 16666

YEAGER, MARK LEONARD, lawyer; b. Chgo., Apr. 7, 1950; BA, U. Mich., 1972; JD, Northwestern U., 1975. Bar: Ill. 1975, Fla. 1985. Ptnr. McDermott, Will & Emery, Chgo., 1975—. Mem. ABA. Antitrust, General civil litigation.

YEAGER, RUTH, lawyer; Asst. U.S. Atty., Dept. Justice, Tyler, Tex., chief civil divsn., 1988—; U.S. Atty., Eastern Dist. Tex., 1993-94. Office: US Attys Office 110 N College Ave Ste 700 Tyler TX 75702-0204 E-mail: ruth.yeager@usdoj.gov

YEAST, DANIEL GORDON, lawyer; b. Frankfort, Ky., Jan. 23, 1970; s. Fred Daniel Yeast and Dana Gordon Biscontini. BA, Morehead State U., 1992; JD, U. Ky., 1996. Bar: Ky. 1997, U.S. Dist. Ct. (ea. dist.) Ky. Atty. Travis, Pruitt & Lawless, Somerset, Ky., 1998—. Mem. ABA, Ky. Bar Assn., Pulaski County Bar Assn., Bluegrass Cycling Club. Avocations: fishing, hunting, biking, boating, water sports. General civil litigation, Insurance. Office: Travis Pruitt & Lawless PO Drawer 30 207 E Mt Vernon St Somerset KY 40502

YEGGE, ROBERT BERNARD, law educator, dean; b. Denver, June 17, 1934; s. Ronald Van Kirk and Fairy (Hill) Y. A.B. magna cum laude, Princeton U., 1956; M.A. in Sociology, U. Denver, 1958, J.D., 1959. Bar: Colo. 1959, D.C. 1978. Ptnr. Yegge, Hall and Evans, Denver, 1959-78; with Harding Shultz & Downs successor to Nelson and Harding, 1979—; prof. U. Denver Coll. Law, 1965—, dean, 1965-77, 97-98, dean emeritus, 1977—; asst. to pres. Denver Post, 1971-75; v.p., exec. dir. Nat. Ctr. Preventive Law, 1986-91. Author: Colorado Negotiable Instruments Law, 1960, Some Goals; Some Tasks, 1965, The American Lawyer: 1976, 1966, New Careers in Law, 1969, The Law Graduate, 1972, Tomorrow's Lawyer: A Shortage and Challenge, 1974, Declaration of Independence for Legal Education, 1976. Mng. trustee Denver Ctr. for Performing Arts, 1972-75; chmn. Colo. Coun. Arts and Humanities, 1968-80, chmn. emeritus, 1980—; mem. scholar selection com. Henry Luce Found., 1975—; Active nat. and local A.R.C., chmn. Denver region, 1985-88; trustee Denver Symphony Soc., Inst. of Ct. Mgmt., Denver Dumb Friends League, 1992—, chmn. 2000—, Met. Denver Legal Aid Soc., 1994-99, Colo. Legal Svcs., 2000—, Colo. Acad.; chmn. Colo. Prevention Ctr., 2000—; trustee, vice chmn. Nat. Assembly State Arts Agys.; vice chmn. Mexican-Am. Legal Edn. and Def. Fund, 1970-76. Recipient Disting. Svc. award Denver Jr. C. of C., 1965; Harrison Tweed award Am. Assn. Continuing Edn. Adminstrs., 1985, Alumni Faculty award U. Denver, 1993. Mem. ABA (chmn. lawyers conf. 1987-88, chmn. accreditation commn. for legal asst. programs 1980-90, standing com. legal assts. 1987-92, 98-2001, standing com. delivery legal svcs. 1992-95, 2001—, com. on Gavel award 1995-98, del. to jud. adminstrn. coun. 1989-95, Robert B. Yegge award 1996), Law and Soc. Assn. (life, pres. 1965-70), Colo. Bar Assn. (bd. govs. 1965-77, 97-98), Denver Bar Assn., D.C. Bar Assn., Am. Law Inst., Am. Judicature Soc. (bd. dirs. 1968-72, 75-85, Herbert Harley award 1985), Am. Acad. Polit. and Social Sci., Am. Sociol. Soc., Assn. Am. Law Schs., Order St. Ives, Phi Beta Kappa, Beta Theta Pi, Phi Delta Phi, Alpha Kappa Keta, Omicron Delta Kappa. Home: 3472 S Race St Englewood CO 80110-3138 Office: U Denver Coll Law 1900 Olive St Denver CO 80220-1857

YELENICK, MARY THERESE, lawyer; b. Denver, May 17, 1954; d. John Andrew and Maesel Joyce (Reed) Y. B.A. magna cum laude, Colo. Coll., 1976; J.D. cum laude, Georgetown U., 1979. Bar: D.C. 1979, U.S. Dist. Ct. D.C. 1980, U.S. Ct. Appeals (D.C. cir.) 1981, N.Y. 1982, U.S. Dist. Ct. (so. and ea. dists.) N.Y. 1982, U.S. Supreme Ct. 1992, U.S. Ct. Appeals (5th cir.) 1995. Law clk. to presiding justices Superior Ct. D.C., 1979-81; ptnr. Chadbourne & Parke, LLP, N.Y.C., 1981—. Editor Jour. of Law and Policy Internat. Bus., 1978-79. Mem. Phi Beta Kappa. Democrat. Roman Catholic. Federal civil litigation, State civil litigation. Home: 310 E 46th St New York NY 10017-3002 Office: Chadbourne & Parke LLP 30 Rockefeller Plz Fl 31 New York NY 10112-0129

YEO, JENNIFER, lawyer; d. Mark P. and Mary Y. (Ho) Leong; m. George Y. Yeo; children: Edwina, Edward, William, Frederick. LLB with honors, Nat. U. Singapore, 1981; LLM in Banking Law Studies, Boston U., 1984. Advocate and solicitor, Singapore; solicitor, Eng. and Wales. Legal asst. Lee, Woo & Ptnrs., Singapore, 1982-83, Shook Lin & Bok, Singapore, 1983-87; sr. ptnr. Yeo-Leong & Peh, Singapore, 1987—. Composer: (song) Keindahan Taman, 1977; concerto performance with Singapore Symphony Orch., 1997. Mem. bd. govs. Raffles Girls' Secondary Sch., Singapore; bd. dirs. Tsao Found., Singapore. Recipient 1st prize for piano playing Nat. Music Competition, 1977, Outstanding Student award Morin Ctr. for

Banking Studies, 1985; JAL summer scholar, 1978. Fellow Chartered Inst. Arbitrators, Singapore Inst. Arbitrators; mem. Law Soc., Acad. Law, Internat. Bar Assn. Avocations: playing the piano, gardening, travel. Banking, Intellectual property, Mergers and acquisitions. Office: Yeo-Leong & Peh 20 McCallum St # 12-03 Singapore 069046 Singapore E-mail: jenniferyeo@ylp.com.sg

YERMAN, FREDRIC WARREN, lawyer; b. N.Y.C., Jan. 8, 1943; s. Nat W. and Tina (Barotz) Y.; m. Ann R. Rochlin, May 31, 1965; children: Emily, Deborah. BA, CUNY, 1963; LLB, Columbia U., 1966. Bar: N.Y. 1967. Assoc. Kaye, Scholer, Fierman, Hays & Handler, N.Y.C., 1966-74, ptnr., 1974—, chmn. exec. com., 1990-92. Bd. dirs. Lawyer's Com. for Civil Rights under Law, N.Y. Bd. dirs. United Way Tri-State, N.Y., Legal Aid Soc., N.Y.C.; chmn. Jewish Bd. Family and Children Svcs., N.Y.C., 1994—. Fellow Am. Coll. Trial Lawyers. Home: 31 Sheridan Rd Scarsdale NY 10583-1523 Office: Kaye Scholer Fierman Hays & Handler 425 Park Ave New York NY 10022-3506

YETTER, R. PAUL, lawyer; b. Milw., Aug. 5, 1958; s. Richard and Lobelia (Gutierrez) Y.; m. Patricia D. Yetter, May 6, 1983; children: Chris, Mark, Michael, Joseph, Thomas, Andrew, Daniel. BA, U. Tex., El Paso, 1980; JD, Columbia U., 1983. Bar: Tex. 1983, U.S. Dist. Ct. (so., ea., no. and we. dists.) Tex., U.S. Ct. Appeals (5th cir.); bd. cert. in civil trial law and personal injury trial law Tex. Bd. Legal Specialization. Law clk. to Hon. John R. Brown U.S. Ct. Appeals (5th cir.), Houston, 1983-84; assoc. Baker & Botts, L.L.P., 1984-89, ptnr., 1990-97; name ptnr. Yetter & Warden, L.L.P., 1997—. Chair state judiciary rels. com. State Bar, 1995-96; mem. Funding Parity Task Force, 1995-97; mem. ex officio Jud. Selection Task Force, 1995-97; chair Alliance for Jud. Funding, Inc., 1996—; mem. ex officio contbns. com. Tex. Ctr. for the Judiciary, mem. com. on admissions, So. Dist., Tex., 2000—. Contbr. articles to profl. jours. Recipient Presdl. citation State Bar Tex., 1996; Southwestern Legal Found. rsch. fellow. Fellow Tex. Bar Foun., Houston Bar Found. Federal civil litigation, State civil litigation. Office: Yetter & Warden LLP 600 Travis St Ste 3800 Houston TX 77002-2912

YETTER, RICHARD, lawyer; b. Phila., Mar. 14, 1929; s. Frederick Jacob and Marie (Kircher) Y.; m. Lobelia Gutierrez, Feb. 4, 1955; children: Bruce, Tina Marie, Richard Paul, Erich David. BS, Pa. State U., 1951; JD, Marquette U., 1960. Bar: Wis. 1960, U.S. Dist. Ct. (ea. dist.) Wis. 1960, Tex. 1961, U.S. Dist. Ct. (we. dist.) Tex. 1971, U.S. Ct. Appeals (5th cir.) 1972. Adjuster Md. Casualty Co., El Paso, Tex., 1960-62; pres. Richard Yetter & Assocs. Inc., 1970-90; sole practitioner, 1962-70, 90—. Assoc. judge Mcpl. Ct., El Paso, 1967-71; adj. prof. law Webster U., St. Louis. Pres. Pleasantview Home for Sr. Citizens, Inc., 1968-76; state committeeman Tex. Rep. Com., El Paso, 1968-70; chmn. adv. bd. SBA, Lubbock, Tex., Salvation Army, El Paso; life mem. El Paso County Civil Svc. Commn., 1992-96. Served with USAF, 1951-60. Recipient William Booth award Salvation Army, 1997. Mem. Wis. State Bar, Tex. State Bar, El Paso Bar Assn., El Paso Trial Lawyers Assn. (past bd. dirs.), El Paso Probate Bar Assn. (bd. dirs.), Optimist (life, pres. El Paso), Mil. Order World Wars (life). Methodist. Avocation: walking. Probate, Estate planning. Office: 6070 Gateway Blvd E Ste 501 El Paso TX 79905-2031

YOCKIM, RONALD STEPHEN, lawyer; b. Williston, N.D., Nov. 3, 1949; s. Daniel and Doris Helene Yockim; m. Christine J. Conroy, Dec. 27, 1980 (div.); children: Daniel, Elizabeth, Katherine. BA, Wartburg Coll., Waverly, Iowa, 1971; MA, Mankato State U., 1975; JD, Lewis and Clark U., 1981. Bar: Oreg. 1981, U.S. Dist. Ct. Oreg. 1982, U.S. Ct. Appeals (9th cir.) 1993, U.S. Ct. Fed. Claims 1993, U.S. Supreme Ct. 1995. Water pollution biologist Wis. DNR, Rhinelander, 1974-75; fisheries biologist Agrl. Rsch. Svc., Beltsville, Md., 1975-78; sole practitioner Portland, Oreg., 1981-84; asst. dir. Oreg. Divsn. State Lands, Salem, 1984-86; corp. counsel D.R. Johnson Lumber Co., Riddle, Oreg., 1986-91; atty. Cegavske, Johnson & Yockim, Roseburg, 1991-95; sole practitioner, 1995—. Bd. dirs. Umpqua Indian Devel., Roseburg, 1993-95; mem Cow Creek Gaming Commn., Roseburg, 1993-95; mem. Oreg. Rangeland Adv. Com., Salem, 1985-86; mem adv. bd. Roseburg dist. Bur. Land Mgmt., 1992-94. Chmn. Douglas County Water Adv. Bd., Roseburg, 1990-97; bd. dirs. environ. and natural resources sect. Oreg. State Bar, Salem, 1990-91. Democrat. Lutheran. Avocations: mountain climbing, hunting, fishing, tennis. Administrative and regulatory, Natural resources, Real property. Office: 548 SE Jackson St Ste 7 Roseburg OR 97470-4970

YODOWITZ, EDWARD JAY, lawyer; b. N.Y.C., 1943; BS, Long Island U., 1965; JD, U. Balt., 1969. Bar: N.Y. 1972. Sr. ptnr. Skadden, Arps, Slate, Meagher & Flom, L.L.P., N.Y.C. Chmn. securities litigation seminar Practicing Law Inst., 1984-95; bd. trustees L.I. U., 1990-99. Mem. ABA. Federal civil litigation, Securities. Home: 105 Ocean Ave Lawrence NY 11559-2006 Office: Skadden Arps Slate Meagher & Flom LLP Four Times Sq New York NY 10036-6522 E-mail: eyodowit@skadden.com

YOHALEM, HARRY MORTON, lawyer; b. Phila., Jan. 21, 1943; s. Morton Eugene and Florence (Mishnun) Y.; m. Martha Caroline Remy, June 9, 1967; children: Seth, Mark. BA with honors, U. Wis., 1965; JD cum laude, M in Internat. Affairs., Columbia U., 1969. Bar: N.Y. 1969, D.C. 1981, Calif. 1992, U.S. Supreme Ct. 1985. Assoc. Shearman & Sterling, N.Y.C., 1969-71; asst. counsel to gov. State of N.Y., Albany, 1971-73, counsel office planning svcs., 1973-75; asst. gen. counsel FEA, Washington, 1975-77; mem. staff White House Energy Policy and Planning Office, 1977; dep. gen. counsel for legal svcs. Dept. Energy, 1978-80, dep. under sec., 1980-81; ptnr. Rogers & Wells, 1981-91; gen. counsel Calif. Inst. Tech., Pasadena, 1991—. Editor comments Columbia Jour. Transnat. Law, 1967-68, rsch. editor, 1968-69. Prin. Coun. for Excellence in Govt., Washington, 1990—; pres. Opera Bel Canto, Washington, 1984-87; mem. Lawyers Com. for Arts, Washington, 1981-88; bd. visitors dept. English U. Wis., 1999—. Harlan Fiske Stone scholar Columbia U., 1967, 69. Mem. ABA, Calif. Bar Assn., D.C. Bar Assn. Athenaeum, Phi Kappa Phi, Columbia Club N.Y. General corporate, Education and schools, General practice. Home: 702 E California Blvd Pasadena CA 91106 Office: Calif Inst Tech JPL 180-305 4800 Oak Grove Dr Pasadena CA 91109-8001 E-mail: harry.yohalem@caltech.edu

YOHN, WILLIAM H(ENDRICKS), JR. federal judge; b. Pottstown, Pa., Nov. 20, 1935; s. William H. and Dorothy C. (Cornelius) Y.; m. Jean Louise Kochel, mar. 16, 1963; children: William H. III, Bradley G., Elizabeth J. AB, Princeton U., 1957; JD, Yale U., 1960. Bar: Pa. 1961, U.S. Dist. Ct. D.C. 1961. Ptnr. Wells Campbell Reynier & Yohn, Pottstown, 1961-71; mem., chmn. coms. Pa. House of Reps., Harrisburg, 1968-80; ptnr. Binder Yohn & Kalis, Pottstown, 1971-81; judge Montgomery County Ct. of Common Pleas, Norristown, Pa., 1981-91, U.S. Dist. Ct., ea. dist., 1991—. Asst. D.A., Montgomery County D.A. Office, 1962-65; instr. Am. Inst. of Banking, 1963-66; bd. dirs. Fed. Jud. Ctr., 1999—. Bd. dirs. Greater Pottstown Drug Abuse Prevention Program, 1970-76, Pottstown Meml. Med. Ctr., 1974-95, chmn., 1984-95; mem. exec. com. Yale LAw Sch. Alumni Assn., 1998—. Cpl. USMCR, 1960-66. Mem. Pa. Bar Assn., Montgomery Bar Assn. (bd. dirs. 1967-70). Republican. Office: US Dist Ct 14613 US Courthouse 601 Market St Philadelphia PA 19106-1713

YOHO, BILLY LEE, lawyer; b. Huntington, W.Va., Oct. 24, 1925; s. Wilbert Wiley Yoho Sr. and Nellie Pansy (Bryan) Hawkins; m. Martha Sue Carroll; children: Kevin Richard, Karen Lee; m. Shirley Ann Stone Morris. BA, U. Md., 1950; LLD, U. Md., Balt., 1953. Bar: Md. 1953. Ptnr. Hoyert & Yoho Chartered, Lanham, Md., 1953—; gen. counsel City of College Park, 1959-62; town atty. Town of Colmar Manor, 1956-72; gen. counsel Prince George's Gen. Hosp., Cheverly, 1955-74, MD22 Lions Rsch. Found., Balt., 1988—; ptnr. Hoyert & Yoho Chartered, Lanham, Md., 1987—. Mem. College Park airport program in saving the oldest airport in the world, 1968. With USN, 1943-47. Mem. ABA, Prince George's County Bar Assn. (pres. 1976-77), Md. Assn. Trial Attys., Lions Clubs Internat. (dist. gov. 1989-90, life mem.), NRA, U. Md. Alumni Assn. Democrat. Presbyterian. Avocation: computing, genealogy, Christian study. General corporate, Family and matrimonial, Personal injury. Home: 5950 Westchester Park Dr College Park MD 20740-2802

YONKMAN, FREDRICK ALBERS, lawyer, management consultant; b. Holland, Mich., Aug. 22, 1930; s. Fredrick Francis and Janet Dorothy (Albers) Y.; m. Kathleen VerMeulen, June 9, 1953 (div. Sept. 22, 1980); children: Sara, Margriet, Nina.; m. Barbara Anne Sullivan, Aug. 22, 1981 (div. Mar. 31, 1994); 1 child, Fredrick Ryan; m. Jewel Marie Humphrey, July 4, 1998. BA, Hope Coll., Holland, 1952; JD, U. Chgo., 1957. Bar: N.Y. 1958, Mass. 1968, D.C. 1984. With Winthrop, Stimson, Putnam & Roberts, N.Y.C., 1957-64; sec., gen. counsel Reuben H. Donnelley Corp., 1964-66, Dun & Bradstreet, Inc., N.Y.C., 1966-68; ptnr. Sullivan & Worcester, Boston, 1968-72; gen. counsel Am. Express Co., N.Y.C., 1972-78, exec. v.p., 1975-80; pres. Buck Cons., N.Y.C., 1980-81; mgmt. cons., psychoanalyst, 1981—; counsel Peabody, Lambert & Myers, Washington, 1983-84. Chmn. Outward Bound, Inc., Garrison, N.Y., 1980-81; mem. bd. and chmn. audit com. Kennecott Corp., 1978-81; adj. prof. law Georgetown U., 1976-78; chmn. Georgetown Internat. Law Inst., 1980-81; vis. com. U. Chgo. Law Sch., 1980-82; mem. exec. com. Warner-Amex, 1978-80; bd. dirs. Sageworks Inc., Raleigh, N.C. Bd. dirs. Washington Campus Program, 1976-81; bd. dirs. Young Audiences, 1978-83. With U.S.Army, 1952-54. Recipient Silver Anniversary award Nat. Coll. Athletic Assn., 1977 Mem. ABA, N.Y. State Bar Assn., Rsch. Soc. for Process Oriented Psychology (Zurich) (diplomate). Methodist. Home: 925 Rock Rimmon Rd Stamford CT 06903-1213 E-mail: fyonkman@optonline.net

YOON, HOIL, lawyer; b. Tokyo, Nov. 22, 1943; s. Hakwon and Hoik (Lee) Y.; m. Giyun Kim, June 1, 1968; children: Shinwon E., Eunice J., Grace J., James S. LLB, Seoul Nat. U., 1965, LLM, 1967; JD, Notre Dame U., 1973. Bar: Korea 1967, Ill. 1973, D.C. 1981, U.S. Supreme Ct. 1977, N.Y. 1988. Judge Seoul Civil Dist., Korea, 1970; assoc. Baker & McKenzie, Chgo., 1973-79, ptnr., 1979-87, N.Y.C., 1987-89; sr. and mng. ptnr. Yoon and Ptnrs., Seoul, 1989—; amb. Internat. Economy and Trade of Korea, 2000—. Panelist Am. Arbitration Assn. N.Y.C., 1982—, Korean Comml. Arbitration Bd., 1991—; lectr. Columbia U. Sch. of Law, N.Y.C., 1985-87. Contbr. articles to legal jours. Commr. Korean Ministry Fgn. Affairs Adminstrv. Adjudication Commn., 1990—94; nonstanding commr. Korea Fair Trade Commn., 1996—98; new products adv. com. Korea Stock Exch., 1991—94, mem. stock index futures and options market organizing com., 1995—99, mem. stock index organizing com., 1996—; bd. dirs. Korean-Am. Cmty. Svcs., Inc., 1982—88, U.S.-Korea Soc., Inc., 1984—89. Recipient Presdl. decoration Republic of Korea, 1984. Mem. ABA (chmn. subcom. on Korea 1983-84), Bar Assn. D.C., Chgo. Bar Assn., Assn. of Bar of City of N.Y., Ill. State Bar Assn., N.Y. State Bar Assn., Seoul Bar Assn. (vice chmn. internat. law sect. 1991-92), Korean Bar Assn. (bd. dirs. 1991-92), Korean Patent Attys. Assn., Internat. Bar Assn., Rotary. Contracts commercial, Private international, Antitrust. Home: B-5 Hyundai House 68-13 Samsung-dong Kangnam-ku Seoul 135-090 Republic of Korea Office: 45 Namdaemoonro-4-ka C of C & Industry Bldg # 831 Chung-Ku Seoul 100-743 Republic of Korea E-mail: yoon.hoil@yoonpartners.com

YORAM, RAVED, lawyer; b. Jerusalem, Israel, June 22, 1956; s. Dan and Miryam R.; m. Ayala Levanon Raved, Aug. 24, 1982; children: Tomer, Itai, Roy, Yuval. LLB, Tel Aviv U., Israel, 1982. Israel Bar: 1983; lic. notary Israeli Min. Justice. Mng. ptnr. Raved, Magriso, Beokel & Co., Tel Aviv, Israel, 1990—. Dir. Memet, 1991-96, Hasin Esh, Israel, 2000. Mem. Barelq Governors Yeladim, Israel, 1999—, Um Yafe Um Ehad, 1994—. With Intelligence, 1974-77. Contracts commercial, Real property, Hi-tech and venture. Office: Raved Magriso Benkel & Co 6 Wissotzky St 91213 Tel Aviv Israel E-mail: russell.sleigh@lovells.com

YORK, ALEXANDRA, lawyer; b. Jersey City, Feb. 9, 1939; d. Daniel Simpson and Regina (Norwich) S. BA, Tulane U., 1960; JD, Fordham U., 1976. Bar: N.Y. 1978, N.J., 1984; U.S. Dist. Ct. (so. and ea. dists.) N.Y. 1978, U.S. Dist. Ct. N.J. 1984, U.S. Ct. Appeals (2d cir.) 1987. Vol. Peace Corps, Philippines, 1961-63; legis. adviser Speaker of the Philippine House of Reps., Manila, 1964; speechwriter Mems. U.S. Congress, Washington, 1965; compliance officer U.S. Equal Employment Opportunity Commn., 1966-68; cons. N.Y.C. Dept. Consumer Affairs, 1969; cons., speechwriter N.Y.C. Dept. Air Resources, 1970-72; assoc. Shea and Gould, N.Y.C., 1977-79, Leopold Kaplan P.C., N.Y.C., 1980-86; asst. atty. gen. N.Y. State Dept. of Law, 1987-93; spl. counsel external affairs Congress of Federated States of Micronesia, Pohnpei, 1993-95. Del. Federated States of Micronesia Internat. Climate Change Neg., Geneva, 1994; sr. policy adv. Philippine Sen. Com. Environment, 1996-97; cons. Philippine Dept. Environment and Natural Resources, 1996-97; mem., adv. com. environ. law, Practicing Law Inst., N.Y.C., 1991-93; prof. internat. environ. policy, Ateno de Manila U., Philippines, 1996—; ofcl. del. UN Conf. on Environ. and Devel., Rio de Janiero, 1992; spkr. in field. Contbr. articles on environ. mgmt., internat. environ. law and climate change to profl. jours. Mem. ABA (natural resources sect., energy and environ. sect., internat. law and practice sect. 1990-93, program chair ann. meeting 1991, 92, chair subcom. on Human Rights and Environ., goal IX officer, 1992-93), Assn. of Bar of City of N.Y. (mem. internat. law com. 1990-93, originator spl. com. internat. environ. law 1991, environ. com. 1987-90), Am. Soc. Internat. Law (environ. sect. 1991-92).

YOSHA, LOUIS BUDDY, lawyer; b. Indpls., Aug. 25, 1937; children: Cynthia A., Laura Sue, Alan Bradley, Brandon A. Student, U. Ala.; BA, Ind. U., 1960, JD, 1963; postgrad., U. So. Calif., 1961. Bar: Ind. 1963. Ptnr. Yosha, Kranulik & Levy, Indpls., 1963—. Lectr. in field; faculty Ann Arbor Advocacy Inst. U. Mich. Law Sch. Contbr. articles to profl. jours. Fellow Ind. Trial Lawyers Assn. (bd. dirs.), Internat. Soc. Barristers; mem. ABA, Ind. Bar Assn. (Res Gestae Lit. award 1984), Ind. Trial Lawyers Assn. (pres.-elect), Indpls. Bar Assn., Assn. Trial Lawyers Am., Am. Bd. Trial Advs. Jewish. State civil litigation, Personal injury. Office: Yosha Krahulik & Levy 3500 Depauw Blvd Indianapolis IN 46268-1170 E-mail: buddy@yoshalaw.net

YOSKOWITZ, IRVING BENJAMIN, merchant banker; b. Bklyn., Dec. 2, 1945; s. Rubin and Jennie Y.; m. Carol L. Magil, Feb. 11, 1973; children: Stephen M., Robert J. BBA, CCNY, 1966; JD, Harvard U., 1969; postgrad., London Sch. Econs., 1971-72. Bar: N.Y. 1970, D.C. 1970, Conn. 1982. Programmer IBM, East Fishkill, N.Y., 1966; systems analyst Office Sec. Def., Washington, 1969-71; assoc. Arnold & Porter, 1972-73; atty. IBM, 1973-79, regional counsel Md., to 1979; dep. gen. counsel United Technologies Corp., Hartford, Conn., 1979-81, v.p. and gen. counsel, 1981-86, sr. v.p., gen. counsel, 1986-90, exec. v.p., gen. counsel, 1990-98; sr. ptnr. Global Tech. Ptnrs., L.L.C., Washington, 1998—; sr. counsel Crowell & Moring, 2001—. Bd. dirs. BBA Group, PLC, Equant, N.V. Mem. editorial bd. Harvard Law Rev., 1968-69. With U.S. Army, 1969-71. Knox fellow, 1971-72 Mem. ABA, Am. Corp. Counsel Assn. (bd. dirs. 1982-85), Assn. Gen. Counsel.

YOST, ELLEN G. (ELLEN YOST LAFILI), lawyer; b. Buffalo, May 30, 1945; d. Irwin Arthur and Sylvia Rosen Ginsberg; m. Louis Lafili; children: Elizabeth Anne, Peter Andrew, Benjamin Lewis Yost. AB, Mt. Holyoke Coll., 1966; JD, SUNY, Buffalo, 1983. Bar: N.Y., U.S. Dist. Ct. (we. dist.) N.Y. 1984. Assoc. Jaeckle, Fleischmann & Mugel, Buffalo, 1983-89, Saperston & Day, P.C., Buffalo, 1989—; ptnr. Griffith & Yost, 1991-2000, Fragomen, Del Rey, Bernsen & Loewy, P.C., Buffalo, 2000—. Pres. Buffalo Coun. on World Affairs, 1987-89; bd. dirs. Buffalo World Trade Assn., 1988-90, Legal Svcs. for Elderly, Disabled, Disadvantaged, 1984—. Mem. ABA (co-chair Can. law com. of internat. law and practice sect. 1990-94, vice chair immigration and nationality law com. 1994-95, co-chair 1995-2000, co-chair task force N.Am. Free Trade Agreement 1991-94, immigration coord. com. 1996-2000, coun. internat. law and practice sect. 1998—), Can. Bar Assn., Internat. Bar Assn., N.Y. State Bar Assn. (chmn. U.S. Can. law com. 1987-89, mem. exec. com. internat. law and practice sect. 1987-89, sec. commn. in internat. trade and transactions 1984-87), Am. Immigration Lawyers' Assn. Jewish. Avocations: travel, skiing, sailing. Immigration, naturalization, and customs, Private international. Office: Fragonmen Del Rey Bernsen Et Al 50 Fountain Plz Ste 1320 Buffalo NY 14202-2212 also: Vossendreef 6 1180 Brussels Belgium

YOST, GERALD B. lawyer; b. Harvey, Ill., Dec. 21, 1954; s. Richard Dennis and Marilyn Patricia (Moore) Y.; m. Kay Lynn Benton, Apr. 16, 1977; children: Matthew Brian, Benjamin Gerald, Andrew Richard. BA in Journalsim, Drake U., 1973-76; student, Purdue U., 1975; JD, Hamline U., 1980. Bar: Minn. 1980, U.S. Dist. Ct. Minn. 1980, Wis. 1987. Assoc. Bergman, Street & Ulmen, Mpls., 1980-84; ptnr. Wasserman and Baill, 1984-90, Yost, Stephenson & Sanford, Mpls., 1990-95, Yost & Baill LLP, Mpls., 1996—. Editor: Student Osteo. Med. Assn. Publ. mag., 1976; mem. Law Review Hamline U., 1978-80. Active YMCA, St. Paul. Recipient Am. Jurisprudence award, Lawyers Coop. Pub. Co., St. Paul, 1979. Mem. ABA, Minn. State Bar Assn., Wis. Bar Assn., Phi Alpha Delta, Sigma Delta Chi. Avocations: tennis, racquetball, boating and water skiing, jogging. General corporate, Mergers and acquisitions, Real property. Home: 422 Mt Curve Blvd Saint Paul MN 55105 Office: Yost & Baill LLP 2350 One Fin Plz 120 S 6th St Minneapolis MN 55402-1803 E-mail: gyost@yostbaill.com

YOUNG, BARNEY THORNTON, lawyer; b. Chillicothe, Tex., Aug. 10, 1934; s. Bayne and Helen Irene (Thornton) Y.; m. Sarah Elizabeth Taylor, Aug. 31, 1957; children: Jay Thornton, Sarah Elizabeth, Serena Taylor. BA, Yale U., 1955; LLB, U. Tex., 1958. Bar: Tex. 1958. Assoc. Thompson, Knight, Wright & Simmons, Dallas, 1958-65; ptnr. Rain, Harrell, Emery, Young & Doke, 1965-87; mem. firm Locke Purnell Rain Harrell (A Profl. Corp.), 1987-98; of counsel Locke, Liddell & Sapp LLP, 1999—. Mem. adv. coun. Dallas Cmty. Chest Trust Fund, Inc., 1964-66; bd. dirs. Mental Health Assn. Dallas County, Inc., 1969-72, Trammell Crow Family Found., 1984-87; trustee Hockaday Sch., Dallas, 1971-77, 90—, chmn., 1994-96, Dallas Zool. Soc., 1986-92, Lamplighter Sch., Dallas, 1976-99, chmn., 1983-86, St. Mark's Sch., Dallas, 1970—, pres., 1976-78, The Found. for Callier Ctr. and Comm. Disorders, 1988-99, Friends of Ctr. for Human Nutrition, 1988—, Shelter Ministries of Dallas Found., 1993—, Dallas Hist. Soc., 1993—; bd. dirs. Susan G. Komen Breast Cancer Found., 2000—, Nat. Assn. Ind. Schs., 2000—; mem. Yale Devel. Bd., 1984-91, 1998—. Fellow Tex. Bar Found., Dallas Bar Found.; mem. ABA, Tex. Bar Assn., Dallas Bar Assn., Am. Judicature Soc., Order of Coif, Phi Beta Kappa, Pi Sigma Alpha, Phi Gamma Delta, Phi Delta Phi, Dallas Country Club., Petroleum Club (Dallas), Yale Club (Dallas, N.Y.C.). General corporate, Mergers and acquisitions, Securities. Home: 6901 Turtle Creek Blvd Dallas TX 75205-1251 Office: Locke Liddell & Sapp LLP 2200 Ross Ave Ste 2200 Dallas TX 75201-6776

YOUNG, C. CLIFTON, state supreme court justice; b. Nov. 7, 1922, Lovelock, Nev.; m. Jane Young. BA, U. Nev., 1943; LLB, Harvard U., 1949. Bar: Nev. 1949, U.S. Dist. Ct. Nev. 1950, U.S. Supreme Ct. 1955. Justice Nev. Supreme Ct, Carson City, 1985—, chief justice, 1989-90. Office: Nev Supreme Ct 201 S Carson St Carson City NV 89701-4702*

YOUNG, DEBORAH SCHWIND, lawyer; b. Buffalo, Feb. 28, 1955; d. Richard G. and Rhoda Schwind; m. Thomas Paul Young, May 23, 1981. BA, Dartmouth Coll., 1976; JD, SUNY, Buffalo, 1979. Bar: N.Y. 1980, U.S. Dist. Ct. (we. dist.) N.Y. 1980. Assoc. Harter, Secrest and Emery, Rochester, N.Y., 1979-83; asst. v.p., asst. counsel Chase Lincoln First Bank, 1983-85, v.p., sr. counsel, 1985-92; v.p., sr. assoc. counsel The Chase Manhattan Bank, 1993-96, v.p., asst. gen. counsel, 1997—. Mem. pension com. Rochester Philharm. Orch., 1983-91; mem. Rochester-Monroe County Youth Bd., 1987-88. Mem. N.Y. Bar Assn. Republican. Lutheran. Banking. Office: The Chase Manhattan Bank 1 Chase Sq Rochester NY 14643-0002

YOUNG, DOUGLAS HOWARD, lawyer; b. Bronxville, N.Y., Oct. 16, 1948; s. Joseph Paul and Frances (Lally) Y.; m. Betsy Baker, Apr. 24, 1971; children: Jeffrey D., Kevin C. BA, Gettysburg Coll., 1970; JD magna cum laude, Syracuse U., 1978. Bar: N.Y. 1979, U.S. Dist. Ct. (no. dist.) N.Y. 1979, U.S. Claims Ct. 1992. Ptnr. Melvin & Melvin, Syracuse, N.Y., 1978—. Bd. dirs. Onondaga County Legal Svcs. Corp., Syracuse, pres., 1995-96; village atty. Village of Jordan, N.Y., 1980—. Editor Syracuse Law Rev., 1977-78; contbr. articles to profl. jours. Cub scout leader Boy Scouts Am., Syracuse, 1980-81; umpire Liverpool (N.Y.) Little League, Babe Ruth League, 1981-90, Optimists Basketball, Liverpool, 1985-87; coach Babe Ruth Baseball, Liverpool, 1989-90. Capt. USAF, 1971-76. Named Eagle Scout Boy Scouts Am., 1965. Mem. N.Y. State Bar Assn., N.Y.S. Trial Lawyers Assn., Onondaga County Bar Assn. Episcopalian. Avocations: gardening, golf, outdoor hiking. General civil litigation, Condemnation. Home: 4058 Pawnee Dr Liverpool NY 13090-2853 Office: Melvin & Melvin 217 S Salina St Syracuse NY 13202-1390 E-mail: DYoung@melvinlaw.com

YOUNG, DOUGLAS REA, lawyer; b. L.A., July 21, 1948; s. James Douglas and Dorothy Belle (Rea) Y.; m. Terry Forrest, Jan. 19, 1974; 1 child, Megann Forrest. BA cum laude, Yale U., 1971; JD, U. Calif., Berkeley, 1976. Bar: Calif., 1976, U.S. Dist. Ct. (no. dist.) Calif. 1976, U.S. Ct. Appeals (6th and 9th cirs.) 1977, U.S. Dist. Ct. (ctrl. dist.) Calif. 1979, U.S. Dist. Ct. Hawaii, U.S. Dist. Ct. (so. dist.) Calif., U.S. Supreme Ct. 1982; cert. specialist in appellate law. Law clk. U.S. Dist. Ct. (no. dist.) Calif., San Francisco, 1976-77; assoc. Farella, Braun & Martel LLP, 1977-82, ptnr., 1983—. Spl. master U.S. Dist. Ct. (no. dist.) Calif., 1977-78, 88, 96, 2000; mem. Criminal Justice Act Def. Panel no. dist. Calif.; mem. faculty Calif. Continuing Edn. of Bar, Berkeley, 1982—, Nat. Inst. Trial Advocacy, Berkeley, 1984—, Practicing Law Inst., 1988—; adj. prof. Hastings Coll. Advocacy, 1985—; vis. lectr. law Boalt Hall/U. Calif., Berkeley, 1986; judge pro tem San Francisco Mcpl. Ct., 1984—, San Francisco Superior Ct., 1990—. Author: (with Purver and Davis) California Trial Handbook, ed edit., (with Hon. Richard Byrne, Purver and Davis), 3d edit., (with Purver, Davis and Kerper) The Trial Lawyers Book, (with Hon. Eugene Lynch, Taylor, Purver and Davis) California Negotiation and Settlement Handbook; contbr. articles to profl. jours. Bd. dirs. Berkeley Law Found., 1977-78, chmn., 1978-79; bd. dirs. San Francisco Legal Aid Soc., pres., 1993—; bd. dirs. Pub. Interest Clearinghouse, San Francisco, chmn., 1987—, treas., 1988—; chmn. Attys. Task Force for Children, Legal Svcs. for Children, 1987—; mem. State Bar Appellate Law Adv. Commn., 1994—. Recipient award of appreciation Berkeley Law Found., 1983. Fellow Am. Coll. Trial Lawyers; mem. ABA (Pro Bono Pub. award 1992), San Francisco Bar Assn. (founding chmn. litigation sect. 1988-89, award of appreciation 1989, bd. dirs. 1990-91, pres. 2001), Calif. Acad. Appellate Lawyers, McFetridge Am. Inn of Ct. (master), Lawyers Club San Francisco. Democrat. Federal civil litigation, State civil litigation, Criminal. Office: Farella Braun & Martel 235 Montgomery St Ste 3000 San Francisco CA 94104-2902

YOUNG, GEORGE CRESSLER, federal judge; b. Cin., Aug. 4, 1916; s. George Philip and Gladys (Cressler) Y.; m. Iris June Hart, Oct. 6, 1951; children: George Cressler, Barbara Ann. AB, U. Fla., 1938, LLB, 1940; postgrad., Harvard Law Sch., 1947. Bar: Fla. 1940. Practice in, Winter Haven, 1940-41; asso. firm Smathers, Thompson, Maxwell & Dyer, Miami, 1947; adminstrv., legislative asst. to Senator Smathers of Fla., 1948-52; asst. U.S. atty. Jacksonville, 1952; partner firm Knight, Kincaid, Young & Harris, 1953-61; U.S. dist. judge No., Middle and So. dists. Fla., 1961-73; chief judge Middle Dist., 1973-81, sr. judge, 1981—. Mem. com. on adminstrn. fed. magistrates system Jud. Conf. U.S., 1973-80 Bd. dirs. Jacksonville United Cerebral Palsy Assn., 1953-60. Served to lt. (s.g.) USNR, 1942-46. Mem. Rollins Coll. Alumni Assn. (pres. 1968-69), ABA (spl. com. for adminstrn. criminal justice), Fla. Bar Assn. (gov. 1960-61), Jacksonville Bar Assn. (past pres.), Order of Coif, Fla. Blue Key, Phi Beta Kappa, Phi Kappa Phi, Phi Delta Phi, Sigma Alpha Epsilon. Home: 2424 Shrewsbury Rd Orlando FL 32803-1334 Office: US Dist Ct 635 US Courthouse 80 N Hughey Ave Orlando FL 32801-2278

YOUNG, GEORGE WALTER, lawyer; b. Los Angeles, May 15, 1950; s. George Albert and Edna Margaret (Hill) Y.; m. Marian Eileen Bement, May 29, 1982; children: George Eric, Ryan Walter, John Adam. B.A., UCLA, 1972; J.D., Southwestern U., 1976. Bar: Calif. 1976, U.S. Supreme Ct. 1981. Mem. Young & Young, Los Angeles, 1976-82, Pepper, Hamilton & Scheetz, Los Angeles, 1982-89, ptnr. 1984—; Levinson & Lieberman, Beverly Hills, 1989-93; prin. Young & Young, 1993—. Mem. John Marshall High Sch. Alumni Assn. (pres.), UCLA Alumni Assn., UCLA Bruin Bench. Republican. Presbyterian. Clubs: Los Angeles Athletic. Lodges: Lions, Masons. Federal civil litigation, State civil litigation, Family and matrimonial. Office: Young & Young 550 N Brand Blvd Ste 700 Glendale CA 91203-1900

YOUNG, JAMES EDWARD, lawyer; b. Painesville, Ohio, Apr. 20, 1946; s. James M. and Isabel P. (Rogers) Y. BBA, Ohio U., 1968; JD, Ohio State U., 1972. Bar: Ohio 1972. Law clk. to chief judge U.S. Ct. Appeals, Nashville, 1972-73; chief counsel City of Cleve., 1980-81, law dir., 1981-82; assoc. Jones, Day, Reavis & Pogue, Cleve., 1973-79, ptnr., 1983—. Lawyer; b. Painesville, Ohio, Apr. 20, 1946; s. James M. and Isabel P. (Rogers) Y. BBA, Ohio U., 1968; JD, Ohio State U., 1972. Bar: Ohio 1972; Law clk. to chief judge U.S. Ct. Appeals, Nashville, 1972-73; chief counsel City of Cleve., 1980-81, law dir., 1981-82; assoc. Jones, Day, Reavis & Pogue, 1973-79, ptnr., 1983—. General civil litigation, Environmental. Office: Jones Day Reavis & Pogue 901 Lakeside Ave E Cleveland OH 44114-1190 E-mail: jameseyoung@jonesday.com

YOUNG, JOHN BYRON, retired lawyer; b. Bakersfield, Calif., Aug. 10, 1913; s. Lewis James and Gertrude Lorraine (Clark) Y.; m. Helen Beryl Stone, Dec. 26, 1937; children: Sally Jean, Patricia Helen, Lucia Robin. BA, UCLA, 1934; LLB, U. Calif., Berkeley, 1937. Pvt. practice law Hargreaves & Young, later Young Wooldridge, Bakersfield, 1937-40; dep. county counsel County of Kern, 1940-42; dep. rationing atty. U.S. OPA, Bakersfield and Fresno, Calif., 1942; ptnr. firm Young Wooldridge and predecessors, Bakersfield, 1946-78, assoc. law firm, 1978-91. Bd. dirs., legal counsel Kern County Water Assn., Bakersfield, 1953-76. Mem., chmn. Kern County Com. Sch. Dist. Orgn., Bakersfield, 1950s and 60s; mem. Estate Planning Coun. of Bakersfield, 1960-76, pres., 1965-66. Capt. JAGC, U.S. Army, 1943-46. Mem. Kern County Bar Assn. (prs. 1948, Bench and Bar award 1978). Home: 13387 Barbados Way Del Mar CA 92014-3501 Office: Young Wooldridge 1800 30th St Fl 4 Bakersfield CA 93301-5298

YOUNG, JOHN EDWARD, lawyer; b. Tulsa, July 11, 1935; s. Russell Edward and Frances Lucille (Wetmore) Y.; m. Mary Moore Nason, Dec. 27, 1966; children: Cynthia Nason, Abigail Brackett. BS with honors, Calif. Inst. Tech., 1956; LLB magna cum laude, Harvard U., 1959. Bar: N.Y. 1961, U.S. Dist. Ct. (so. dist.) N.Y. 1973. Assoc. Cravath, Swaine & Moore, N.Y.C., 1960-67, ptnr., 1968-95, resident ptnr. Paris, 1971-73, London, 1990-95, sr. counsel, 1996—. Editor Harvard Law Rev., 1958-59. Trustee Internat. Sculpture Ctr., 1997—, vice chmn., 2000—; trustee Royal Oak Found., 1997—, chmn., 1999—; gov. Am. Crafts Mus., 1997-2000. Sheldon Traveling fellow Harvard U., 1959-60. Mem. Assn. of Bar of City of N.Y., Century Assn., Harvard Club of N.Y.C., N.Y. Yacht Club, City Univ. Club London. Democrat. Episcopal. General corporate, Finance, Securities. Home: 1088 Park Ave New York NY 10128-1132 Office: 380 Madison Ave 7th Fl New York NY 10017-2513 E-mail: jeyoung@attglobal.net

YOUNG, JOHN HARDIN, lawyer, corporate executive; b. Washington, Apr. 25, 1948; s. John D. and Laura Virginia (Gwathmey) Y.; m. Mary Frances (Farley) Crosby. JD, U. Va., 1973; BCL, Oxford U., Eng., 1976. Bar: Va. 1973, D.C. 1974, Pa. 1976, U.S. Dist. Ct. (ea. dist.) Va. 1974, U.S. Dist. Ct. D.C. 1974, Internat. Trade Ct. 1974, U.S. Ct. Fed. Claims 1974, U.S. Ct. Appeals (4th, 5th, Fed. and D.C. cirs.), U.S. Supreme Ct. 1977, U.S. Dist. Ct. Md. 1989; cert. mediator Va. Supreme Ct. 1999-2001. Ptnr. Porter Wright Morris & Arthur, Washington, 1988-92, of counsel, 1992-99; pvt. practice law, 1973-76, 78-81, 1983-88; counsel Sandler, Reiff & Young, P.C., 2001—. Mem. adv. bd. Antitrust Bull.; mem. U.S. Sec. State's adv. com. Pvt. internat. Law, 1987-95; chmn. Va. Retirement Sys. Rev. Bd., 1990-94; asst. atty. gen. Commonwealth of Va., 1976-78; moderator Alexandria Forum, 1993-98, Fedn. Forum/TV Channel 10, 1989-91; gen. counsel various profit and not-for-profit tech. cos. Contbr. articles to profl. jours. and books on litigation, evidence technology contracting and election law. Dem. Nat. Comm. Spl. counsel, 1998-99; counsel State Legislative Redistricting, 2001; nat. chair Dem. Nat. Com. Nat. Lawyers Coun., 1998—; lead Fla. Recount Coun., 2000; counsel various statewide polit. campaigns and counsel for statewide and other election disputes and recounts, 1980-2001. Mem. ABA (chair 1999-2000, adminstrv. law sect., chmn. trade regulaion and competition com., 1983-86, chair dispute resolution com. 1994-96, fellow 2000-), Am. Law Inst., George Mason Am. Inn of Ct., Hon. Soc. Mid. Temple U.K., Comml. Bar Assn. U.K. (overseas mem.), Am. Inns of Ct., Temple Bar Found. (founding mem., bd. dirs.), Phi Alpha Theta (history honors). Episcopalian. Administrative and regulatory, Federal civil litigation, Computer. E-mail: young@gateway.net

YOUNG, MICHAEL ANTHONY, lawyer; b. Lima, Ohio, Sept. 3, 1960; s. William John and Bettye Jean (Day) Y. BS magna cum laude, U. Cen. Fla., 1981; JD with honors, Fla. State U., 1984. Bar: Ga. 1984, Fla. 1985. Assoc. Kilpatrick & Cody, Atlanta, 1984-86, Stokes, Lazarus & Carmichael, Atlanta, 1986-89; pvt. practice, 1989—. Jud. intern U.S. Dist. Ct. (no. dist.) Fla., 1984; weekend atty. Atlanta Legal Aid Soc., 1985-86. Rsch. editor Fla. State U. Law Rev., 1982-84; contbr. articles to legal jours. Dir., pres. ChildKind Found. Mem. ABA, Assn. Trial Lawyers of Am., Fla. Bar Assn., Ga. Bar Assn., Atlanta Bar Assn. Avocations: scuba diving, golf, weightlifting. General civil litigation, Labor, Personal injury. Home: 5275 S Trimble Rd NE Atlanta GA 30342-2174 Office: 17 Executive Park Dr NE Ste 440 Atlanta GA 30329-2222

YOUNG, MICHAEL KENT, dean, lawyer, educator; b. Sacramento, Nov. 4, 1949; s. Vance Lynn and Ethelyn M. (Sowards) Y.; m. Suzan Kay Stewart, June 1, 1972; children: Stewart, Kathryn, Andrew. BA summa cum laude, Brigham Young U., 1973; JD magna cum laude, Harvard U., 1976. Bar: Calif. 1976, N.Y. 1985. Law clk. to Justice Benjamin Kaplan, Supreme Jud. Ct. Mass., Boston, 1976-77; law clk. to Justice William H. Rehnquist U.S. Supreme Ct., Washington, 1977-78; assoc. prof., prof., Fuyo prof. Japanese law Columbia U., N.Y.C., 1978-98; dir. Ctr. Japanese Legal Studies Ctr. for Korean Legal Studies, 1985-98; dir. Program Internat. Human Rights and Religious Liberties Columbia U., 1995-98; dep. legal advisor U.S. Dept. State, Washington, 1989-91, dep. under sec. for econ. affairs, 1991-93, amb. for trade and environ. affairs, 1992-93; dean, Lobingier prof. comparative law and jurisprudence George Washington U. Sch. of Law, 1998—. Vice chair U.S. Commn. on Internat. Religious Freedom, 1999-2000, chair, 2001-; vis. scholar law faculty U. Tokyo, 1978-80, 83; vis. prof. Waseda U., 1989; chmn. bd. advisors Japan Soc.; counsel select subcom. on arms transfers to Bosnia U.S. Ho. of Reps., 1996; mem. steering com. Law Profs. for Dole, 1996; POSCO Rsch. Inst. fellow, 1995-98; mem. com. on internat. jud. rels. U.S. Jud. Conf., 1999—. Fellow Japan Found., 1979-80; Fulbright fellow, 1983-84. Bd. visitors USAF Acad., 2000—. Fellow Am. Bar Found.; mem. Coun. Fgn. Rels. Mem. LDS Ch. Avocations: skiing, scuba diving, photography. Fax: 202-994-5157. E-mail: myoung@law.gwv.edu

YOUNG, ROBERT BRUCE, lawyer; b. Chgo., June 23, 1936; s. James T. and Julia A. (Frey) Y.; m. Janice C. Crowhurst, Aug. 12, 1961; children: Robert W., Wiliam J., Leslie B. BS in Engring., Millikin U., 1959; JD, John Marshall Law Sch., 1978. Bar: Ill. 1978, U.S. Dist. Ct. (no. dist.) Ill. 1978. Assoc. Gifford, Detuno & Gifford, Ltd., Chgo., 1978-90; ptnr. Young & Gildea, Ltd., 1990—. With U.S. Army, 1959-61. Mem. ABA, Ill. Bar Assn., Chgo. Bar Assn., Workers Compensation Lawyers Assn. Personal injury, Workers' compensation. Home: 4056 Ellington Ave Western Springs IL 60558-1205

YOUNG, ROBERT GEORGE, lawyer; b. Atlanta, Mar. 9, 1923; s. Samuel Rollo and Cidney A. (Young) Y.; m. Martha Latimer, Dec. 10, 1949; children: John Latimer, R. Carlisle, S. Scott. AB, Emory U., 1943; LLB, U. Ga., 1949. Bar: Ga. 1949. Assoc. Heyman, Howell and Heyman, Atlanta, 1949-51, Heyman and Abram, Atlanta, 1951-53, Marshall, Greene and Neely, Atlanta, 1953-55; ptnr. Heyman, Abram and Young, 1955-63, Edenfield, Heyman and Sizemore, Atlanta, 1963-69, Webb, Parker, Young and Ferguson, Atlanta, 1970-81, Young & Murphy, 1982-88; pvt. practice Atlanta, 1989—. Asst. county atty. Fulton County (Ga.), 1966-71, county atty., 1971-87, sr. atty., 1987-88. Exec. com. Nat. Assn. R.R. Trial Counsel, 1965-68; treas. Fulton County Rep. Exec. Com., 1962-64; bd. dirs. Atlanta Union Mission. Lt. (j.g.) USNR, 1944-46; PTO. Mem. ABA, Scotch-Irish Soc. U.S., Lawyers of Atlanta Club, University Yacht Club, Capital City Club, Kiwanis, Alpha Tau Omega. General civil litigation. Home and Office: 3561 Ridgewood Rd NW Atlanta GA 30327-2419 E-mail: rgyoung@mindspring.com

YOUNG, ROBERT P., JR. state supreme court justice; Bachelor's degree cum laude, Harvard Coll., 1974; JD, Harvard U., 1977. With Dickinson, Wright, Moon, Van Dusen & Freeman, 1977-1992; v.p., corp. sec., gen. counsel AAA Mich., 1992; appt. Mich. Ct. Appeals 1st Dist., 1995; appt. justice Mich. Supreme Ct., 1998, elected justice, 2000. Mem. Mich. Civil Svc. Commn.; bd. trustees Cen. Mich. U. Office: PO Box 30052 Lansing MI 48909-7552

YOUNG, ROLAND FREDERIC, III, lawyer; b. Norway, Maine, Apr. 8, 1954; s. Roland Frederic Jr. and Marylyn May (Bartlett) Y.; m. Dona Davis Gagliano, Aug. 18, 1979; children: Meghan, Wesley, Taylor. AB, Cornell U., 1976; JD, U. Conn., 1979. Bar: Conn. 1979, U.S. Dist. Ct. Conn., U.S. Tax Ct., U.S. Ct. Appeals (2d cir.). Lectr. Hartford (Conn.) Grad. Ctr., Hartford, Conn., 1992—; ptnr. Howard, Kohn, Sprague & FitzGerald, 1984-91, O'Brien, Tanski & Young, Hartford, 1991—. Lectr. Hartford Grad. Ctr., 1991-98. Author (seminar booklet) Confidentiality of Med. Records, 1989, Limiting Damages, 1990; co-author (seminar booklet) Med. Malpractice in Conn., 1992; editor Conn. Risk Mgmt. Assn., 1986-98. Mem. Nat. Assn. Health Attys., Conn. Def. Lawyers Assn., Conn. Hosp. Assn., Hartford County Bar Assn. (medico-legal liaison com.). Avocations: golf. Federal civil litigation, Health, Personal injury. Office: O'Brien Tanski & Young City Place II 16th Fl Hartford CT 06103 E-mail: rf_young@otylaw.com

YOUNG, SHELDON MIKE, lawyer, author; b. Cleve., Aug. 27, 1926; s. Jack and Rae (Goldenberg) Y.; m. Margery Ann Polster, Dec. 25, 1948 (div. 1988); children: Jeffrey, Martin, Janet; m. Bette Abel Roth, Nov. 11, 1988. BA, Ohio State U., 1948, JD, 1951; LLM, Case Western Res. U., 1962. Bar: Ohio 1951, U.S. Dist. Ct. (no. dist.) Ohio. Gen. counsel Eugene M. Klein & Assocs., Actuaries, Cleve., 1952-72; assoc. Shapiro, Persky & Marken, 1972-74; counsel pension tech. svcs. dept. CNA Ins., Chgo., 1974-76; ptnr. Weiss & Young, Cleve., 1976; of counsel Arter & Hadden, 1977-85, Squire, Sanders & Dempsey, Cleve., 1985-87; pvt. practice, 1987-91, Columbus, Ohio, 1987-93; of counsel Walter & Haverfield, 1993—. Instr. Case Western Res. U. Law Sch., 1962-82, 85, U. Akron Law Sch., 1984, 88. Author: Pension and Profit Sharing Plans, 7 vols., 1977-93; freelance writer for newspapers and mags.; contbr. articles to profl. jours. Served with USN, WWII. Recipient award Nathan Burkan Meml. Copyright Competition, 1951. Mem. ABA (chair obsolete pension rev rul taskforce), Ohio Bar Assn., Cleve. Bar Assn., Columbus Bar Assn., Masons. Jewish. Estate planning, Pension, profit-sharing, and employee benefits. Fax: 614-898-7190. E-mail: yomike@asacomp.com

YOUNG, THOMAS PAUL, lawyer; b. Jamestown, N.Y., Dec. 11, 1955; s. Burdette R. and Ruth Ann Y.; m. Deborah Ann Schwind, May 23, 1981; 1 child, Amanda Marie. BA, SUNY, Geneseo, 1977; JD, Georgetown U., 1980. Bar: N.Y. 1981, U.S. Dist. Ct. (we. dist.) N.Y. 1981. Assoc. Hodgson, Russ, Andrews, Woods & Goodyear, Buffalo, 1980-81; asst. counsel Gannett Co., Inc., Rochester, N.Y., 1982-84; assoc. Underberg & Kessler, 1984-91, sr. atty., 1991-98; of counsel Harter, Secrest & Emery LLP, 1998-2000; gen. counsel, sec. Xelus, Inc., Fairport, N.Y., 2000—. Mem. Perinton (N.Y.) Rep. Com., 1989—; mem. coun. Bethlehem Luth. Ch., Fairport, N.Y., 1984-90; bd. dirs. Geneseo Found., Inc., 1982—; bd. dirs., sec. Martin Luther Found., Rochester, 1986-89; mem. allocations com. United Way Greater Rochester, 1990-95; mem. zoning bd. appeals, Town of Perinton, N.Y., 1997—. Mem. ABA, N.Y. State Bar Assn. General corporate, Mergers and acquisitions, Securities. Office: Xelus Inc 290 Woodcliff Dr Fairport NY 14450-4212 E-mail: tom_young@xelus.com

YOUNG, WILLIAM ALLEN, lawyer; b. Danville, Ill., Aug. 17, 1932; s. John Russell and Marjorie Elizabeth (Brown) Y.; m. Sandra Challice Deitz, June 11, 1960; children: Karen C., David A. BS, U. Ill., 1954, JD, 1958. Bar: Ill. 1958, U.S. Dist. Ct. (cen. dist.) Ill., U.S. Ct. Appeals (7th cir.). Asst. states atty. Vermilion County, Danville, Ill., 1958-60; asst. atty. U.S. Dist. Ct. (cen. dist.) Ill., Danville, 1960-61; atty. City of Danville, 1966-72; ptnr. Young & Parker, Danville, 1972—. Chmn. Vermilion County Rep. Cen. Com., Danville, 1972. Served to 1st lt. U.S. Army, 1955-56, Germany. Mem. Ill. State Bar Assn. (assembly mem. 1984—), Vermilion County Bar Assn. (pres. 1981-82), Jaycees (pres. Danville chpt. 1963-64), Danville C. of C. (v.p. 1972), Rotary Club. Methodist. Lodges: Elks (pres. 1980). Avocations: golf, skiing. Personal injury, Probate, Real property. Home: 6 Lincolnshire Ave Danville IL 61832-1609 Office: Young & Parker 408 N Vermilion St PO Box 687 Danville IL 61834-0687 E-mail: yyoungpark@aol.com

YOUNG, WILLIAM GLOVER, federal judge; b. Huntington, N.Y., Sept. 23, 1940; s. Woodhull Benjamin and Margaret Jean (Wilkes) Y.; m. Beverly June Bigelow, Aug. 5, 1967; children: Mark Edward, Jeffrey Woodhull, Todd Russell. AB, Harvard U., 1962, LLB, 1967; LLD, New Eng. Sch. Law, 2001. Bar: Mass. 1967, U.S. Supreme Ct. 1970. Law clk. to chief justice Supreme Jud. Ct., Mass., 1967-68; spl. asst. atty. gen., 1969-72; chief legal counsel to gov., 1972-74; asso. firm Bingham, Dana and Gould, Boston, 1968-72, ptnr., 1975-78; assoc. justice Superior Ct., Commonwealth of Mass., Boston, 1978-85; judge U.S. Dist. Ct. Mass., 1985-99, chief judge, 1999—. Mem. budget com., 1987-2001, chmn. economy subcom., 1991-2001; lectr. part time Boston Coll. Law Sch., 1968-90, Boston U. Law Sch., 1979—, Harvard Law Sch., 1979—. Served to capt. U.S. Army, 1962-64. Mem. Am. Law Inst., Mass. Bar Assn., Boston Bar Assn., Harvard Alumni (pres. 1976-77) E-mail: william. Office: US Courthouse Rm 5710 Boston MA 02210 E-mail: young@mad.uscourts.gov, bb2Y3@gateway.net

YOUNGBLOOD, DEBORAH SUE, lawyer, speech services professional; b. Fairview, Okla., July 29, 1954; d. G. Dean and Beatrice J. (Hiebert) White. BS with honors, Okla. State U., 1976, MA with honors, 1979; JD cum laude, Boston Coll. Law Sch., 1991; MPH in Health Care Mgmt., Harvard U., 1992. Bar: Colo., N.Mex., U.S. Ct. Appeals (10th cir.). Judicial law clk. Colo. Supreme Ct., 1992-94; assoc. atty. Patton Boggs, L.L.P., Denver, 1994-97, Vaglica & Meinhold, L.L.C., Colorado Springs, 1997-99; pvt. practice atty, speech & lang. pathologist pvt. practice, North Conway, N.H., 1999—. Mem. ABA, Colo. Bar Assn., N.Mex. Bar Assn., Minoru Yasui Am. Inns of Ct. (exec. coun. 1995-97), Phi Kappa Phi. Administrative and regulatory, General civil litigation. Office: SAU 9 19 Pine St North Conway NH 03860-3425 E-mail: youngblood@peoplepc.com

YOUNGBLOOD, ELAINE MICHELE, lawyer; b. Schenectady, N.Y., Jan. 9, 1944; d. Roy W. and Mary Louise (Read) Ortoleva; m. William Gerald Youngblood, Feb. 14, 1970; children: Flagg Khristian, Megan Michele. BA, Wake Forest Coll., 1965; JD, Albany Law Sch., 1969. Bar: Tex. 1970, Tenn. 1978, U.S. Dist. Ct. (no. dist.) Tex. 1971, U.S. Dist. Ct. (so. dist.) Tex. 1972, U.S. Dist. Ct. (mid. dist.) Tenn. 1978, U.S. Dist. Ct. (we. dist.) Tenn. 1998. Assoc. Fanning & Harper, Dallas, 1969-70, Crocker & Murphy, Dallas, 1970-71, McClure & Burch, Houston, 1972-75, Brown, Bradshaw & Plummer, Houston, 1975-76; ptnr. Seligmann & Youngblood, Nashville, 1977-88; pvt. practice, 1988-94; of counsel Ortale, Kelley Herbert & Crawford, 1994—. Contbr. articles to profl. jours. Active Law Day Com. Dallas Bar Assn., 1970—71, Com. for Women in Govt., Dallas, 1969—71; vestry Ch. of Advent, 1991. Fellow: Tenn. Bar Assn. (fee dispute com. 1990—, vice-chair 1996, chair 1997—, CLE com. 1996—, L.A.W. 1996—, bd. dirs. 1996, treas. 1997, blvd. bolt com. 1996—97, publicity, steering com. 1997); mem.: Tenn. Trial Lawyers Assn., Cable Club Nashville (charter), Davidson County Rep. Women's Club, Phi Beta Phi (alumnae liaison 1998—, Christmas Village bd. sec. 1999—, AAU bd.). Republican. Episcopalian. Insurance, Personal injury, Workers' compensation. Address: PO Box 198985 200 Fourth Ave N Fl 3 Noel Pl Nashville TN 37219-8985 E-mail: eyoungblood@ortalekelley.com

YOUNGWOOD, ALFRED DONALD, lawyer; b. N.Y.C., Apr. 27, 1938; s. Milton and Lillian (Ginsburg) Y.; m. Judith Goldfarb, June 24, 1963; children: Jonathan David, Stephen Michael. BA magna cum laude, Yale U., 1959; LLB magna cum laude, Harvard U., 1962. Bar: N.Y. 1962, D.C. 1970, U.S. Tax Ct. 1964, U.S. Ct. Appeals (2d cir.) 1969. Law clk. to judge U.S. Dist. Ct. N.Y., 1962-63; assoc. Paul, Weiss, Rifkind, Wharton & Garrison, N.Y.C., 1964-70, ptnr., 1970—, chair, 1999—. Trustee, treas. exec. com. Ctrl. Synagogue, N.Y.C. Fulbright scholar, London, 1963-64. Fellow Am. Coll. Tax Counsel; mem. ABA, N.Y. State Bar Assn. (chmn. tax sect. 1978-79, exec. com. 1971—, ho. of dels. 1979-80), Assn. of Bar of City of N.Y. Corporate taxation, Taxation, general, Personal income taxation. Home: 1125 Park Ave New York NY 10128-1243 Office: Paul Weiss Rifkind Wharton 1285 Avenue Of The Americas Fl 21 New York NY 10019-6028

YU, BENITA KA PO, solicitor; b. Hong Kong; d. Yu Sai Hung and Yu Shiu So Har Shirley; m. Edmund Kwok; 1 child, Veronica Kwok. BA, U. Oxford, 1986, MA, 1991; law soc. finals 1st class, 1987. Solicitor: Supreme Ct., England, 1989, Wales, 1989, High Ct. Hong Kong Spl. Adminstv. Region, 1994. Articles clk. Norton Rode, London, 1987-89, asst. solicitor, 1989-93, Slaughter and May, Hong Kong, 1994-96, ptnr. Hong Kong, 1996—. Contbg. author: Asia Finance Manual, 2d edit., 1998. Recipient Book prize St. Hugh's Coll., Oxford U., 1984; scholar Hong Kong Govt., 1976-81, Ho Leung Ho Lee, 1983. Mem.: Law Soc. England, Law Soc. Hong Kong, The Oxford and Cambridge Soc. Hong Kong, Company Law Reform (sub-com. standing com.), Hong Kong Golf Assn., Diocesan Old Girls's Assn. (legal sub-com., co-chmn., mem. Careeres & Scholar, sub-com. Diocesan Grad. Singers , standing com. company law reform sub-com.). Avocations: piano, singing, classical music, jazz, golf. Consumer commercial, Mergers and acquisitions, Securities. Office: Slaughter and May 27th Flr Two Exchange Sq Hong Kong China

YUCEL, EDGAR KENT, lawyer, consultant; b. Ankara, Turkey, Aug. 18, 1927; came to U.S., 1948, naturalized, 1958; s. Mustafa Muammer and Refika (Sunkitay) Y.; m. Martha Ellen Diggs, Sept. 8, 1954; 1 child, Edgar Kent. B.S., Galatasaray Lyceum, Istanbul, Turkey, 1948; M.A., U. Ala., 1953, postgrad., 1953-56; J.D., U. Minn., 1962. Bar: Minn. 1962, U.S. Dist. Ct. Minn. 1969. Instr. polit. sci. and econs. U. Ala., Tuscaloosa and Huntsville, 1953-56; project engr. So. Assoc. Engrs., Huntsville, 1956-59, supervising engr. Sperry Univac Co., St. Paul, 1959-62; sr. atty. 3M Co., St. Paul, 1962-69, asst. gen counsel, 1969-81, spl. counsel, 1981—; seminar lectr. St. John's U., Collegeville, Minn., 1976; adj. faculty grad. sch. Coll. St. Thomas, St. Paul, 1986; pro bono atty. So. Minn. Regional Legal Svcs., St. Paul, 1983—. Patentee marking tape. Trustee, gov. Health Central Inc., Mpls., 1972-78; v.p., sec., bd. dirs. Life Scis. Found., Mpls., 1973—; pres. Turkish Cultural Soc., Mpls., 1965-67; vice consul ad honorem Republic of Costa Rica, Mpls., 1964—; del. Internat. Labour Orgns., Tripartite, 1987. Mem. ABA, Minn. Bar Assn., Corp. Counsel Assn. (bd. dirs. 1964-67, pres. 1967-68), Licensing Execs. Soc., Soc. Univ. Patent Adminstrs., Minn. Patent and Trademark Law Assn., Am. Arbitration Assn. (arbitrator 1984—). Clubs: Minneapolis, Minn. Alumni (Mpls). Home: 77 Pond Ave Apt 909 Brookline MA 02445-7114 Office: 3M Ctr 220-11W-01 3M Center # 01 Saint Paul MN 55144-1001

YUDES, JAMES PEYTON, lawyer; b. N.Y.C., July 5, 1950; s. Alfred Edward and Mary (Peyton) Y.; m. Bebbins Rahmeyer, Aug. 11, 1973; children— Meghan, Jeannette. B.S./B.A., Villanova U., 1972, J.D., 1975. Bar: N.J. 1975, U.S. Dist. Ct. N.J. 1975, U.S. Tax Ct. 1979, U.S. Ct. Appeals (3d cir.) 1981, U.S. Supreme Ct. 1981. Jud. law clk. Superior Ct. N.J., 1975-76; assoc. atty. Skoloff & Wolfe, Newark, 1976-78; ptnr. Newman, Yudes & Carey, Cranford, N.J., 1978-79; sr. atty. James P. Yudes, P.C., Counsellors at Law, Mountainside, N.J., 1979— ; mem. Morris county Matrimonial Early Settlement Panel, 1978-80, Middlesex County Matrimonial Early Settlement Panel, 1982, Essex County Matrimonial Early Settlement Panel, 1980-84; mem. Union County Matrimonial Early Settlement Panel, 1978-84, chmn., 1981-84; exec. mem. Inst. for Continuing Legal Edn. N.J., 1982-85; Author: Pre-Nuptial Agreements in New Jersey, 1985. Trustee Family Law Inst. N.J., 1984-85. Fellow Am. Acad. Matrimonial Lawyers (editor newsletter N.J. chpt. 1982-83); mem. Am. Judicature Soc., ABA (family law com. 1976— , exec. mem. mediation com. 1981-84, merit cert. 1980, 81), N.J. State Bar Assn. (legis. coordinator family law sect. 1983-84, exec. com. family law sect. 1981-84, exec. mem. specialization com. 1983-84, family law co-ordinator Supreme Ct. com. of family part 1984-85, Supreme Ct. com. on supervised visitation, awards 1983, cert. recognition for disting. service 1981, 82, 83, 84), Assn. Trial Lawyers N.J. (legis. adv. bd. 1981-84). Republican. Roman Catholic. Family and matrimonial. Office: 80 Morris Ave Springfield NJ 07081-1451

YUN, EDWARD JOON, lawyer; b. Seoul, Republic of Korea, Apr. 2, 1969; s. Alex Sanghyum Yun and Lily Sooja Yun. BA, U. Calif., Berkeley, 1992; JD, N.Y. Law Sch., 1995. Bar: N.Y. 1996, U.S. Dist. Ct (so. and ea. dists.) N.Y. 1997. Assoc. Martin, Clearwater & Bell, N.Y.C., 1995-97,

Dembin & Assocs., P.C., N.Y.C., 1997—. Contbr. articles to profl. jours. Mem. City Bar Chorus, N.Y.C., 1997—. Mem. ABA, Am. Coll. Legal Medicine (assoc. in law), N.Y. State Bar Assn., Assn. of the Bar of the City of N.Y. General civil litigation, General corporate, Health. Home: 98 Riverside Dr Apt 4A New York NY 10024-5323 Office: Dembin & Assocs PC Ste 1400 225 Broadway Rm 1400 New York NY 10007-3001

YURASKO, FRANK NOEL, judge; b. Rahway, N.J., Dec. 22, 1938; s. Frank H. and Estelle (Trudeau) Y.; mm. Mary Byrd, July 23, 1966 (dec. 1991); children: Elizabeth Anne, Suzanne, Frank; m. Rosalee Yurasko, May 1997. BA, Brown U., 1960; cert., London Sch. Econs., 1961; student, Gray's Inn., London, 1960-61; JD, Yale U., 1964. Bar: N.J. 1964, Fla. 1979, U.S. Dist. Ct. N.J. 1965, U.S. Ct. Appeals (3d cir.) 1980, U.S. Supreme Ct. 1969; cert. civil trial atty., N.J. Judge's law clk. N.J. Dept. Judiciary, Trenton, 1964-66; ptnr. Graham, Yurasko, Golden, Lintner & Rothchild, Somerville, N.J., 1966-80; pvt. practice, 1980—. Judge Montgomery Twp. (N.J.) Mcpl. Ct., 1973-84; twp. atty. Hillsborough Twp. (N.J.), 1973—; atty. Green Brook (N.J.) Bd. Adjustment, 1973-2001. Trustee Gill/St. Bernard Sch., Bernardsville, N.J.; mem. alumni bd. trustees Peddie Sch., Hightstown, N.J. Mem. ABA, Am. Jud. Soc., N.J. Bar Assn., Fla. Bar Assn., Somerset County Bar Assn., Mercer County Bar Assn., Assn. Trial Lawyers Am., Trial Attys. N.J., N.J. Fedn. Planning Ofcls., Fed. Bar Assn. Office: PO Box 1041 139 W End Ave Somerville NJ 08876-1809

YURKO, RICHARD JOHN, lawyer; b. Ottawa, Ont., Can., Oct. 30, 1953; came to U.S., 1960; s. Michael and Catherine (Ewanishan) Y.; m. Martha S. Faigen, Apr. 18, 1982; children: Nathan, Daniel. AB summa cum laude, Dartmouth Coll., 1975; JD cum laude, Harvard U., 1979. Bar: Mass. 1979, U.S. Dist. Ct. Mass. 1980, U.S. Ct. Appeals (1st cir.) 1980. Law clk. to Judge James L. King, U.S. Dist. Ct. for So. Dist. Fla., Miami, 1979-80; assoc. Bingham, Dana & Gould, Boston, 1980-85, Widett, Slater & Goldman, P.C., Boston, 1985-87, shareholder, 1987-92, chmn. litigation dept., 1989-91, hiring ptnr., 1992; shareholder Hutchins, Wheeler & Dittmar, 1992-94, chmn. litigation dept., 1992-94; shareholder Yurko & Perry, P.C., 1995—. Contbr. articles to legal jours. Mem. ABA, Mass. Bar Assn., Boston Bar Assn. (chmn. antitrust com.), Phi Beta Kappa. Antitrust, General civil litigation, Contracts commercial. Home: 9 Barnstable Rd Wellesley MA 02481-2802 Office: Yurko & Perry P C 100 City Hall Plz Boston MA 02108-2105

YUSPEH, ALAN RALPH, lawyer, healthcare company executive; b. New Orleans, June 13, 1949; s. Michel and Rose Fay (Rabenovitz) Y.; m. Janet Horn, June 8, 1975. BA, Yale U., 1971; MBA, Harvard U., 1973; JD, Georgetown U., 1978. Bar: D.C. 1978. Mgmt. cons. McKinsey & Co., Washington, 1973-74; adminstrv. asst., legis. asst. Office of U.S. Senator J. Bennett Johnston, 1974-78; atty. Shaw, Pittman, Potts & Trowbridge, 1978-79, Ginsburg, Feldman, Weil and Bress, Washington, 1979-82; gen. counsel Com. on Armed Services-U.S. Senate, 1982-85; ptnr. Preston, Thorgrimson, Ellis & Holman, 1985-88, Miller & Chevalier, Washington, 1988-91, Howrey & Simon, Washington, 1991-97; sr. v.p. ethics, compliance and corp. responsibility HCA-The Healthcare Corp., Nashville, 1997—. Coord. Def. Industry Initiative on Bus., Ethics and Conduct, 1987-97; bd. dirs. Health Care Compliance Assn., Ethics Officer Assn. Editor Law and Policy in Internat. Business jour., 1978-79, Nat. Contract Mgmt. Jour., 1988-92; assoc. editor Pub. Contract Law jour., 1987-91. Chmn. bd. of ethics, City of Balt., 1988-96, mem. planning commn., 1996-97; mem. bd. Housing Authority Balt., 1996-97. 1st lt. USAR, 1971-77. Health. Home: 1812 South Rd Baltimore MD 21209-4506 Office: HCA The Healthcare Co One Park Plaza Nashville TN 37202 E-mail: alan.yuspeh@hcahealthcare.com

YUTHAS, GEORGE ANTHONY, lawyer; b. Superior, Wyo., Dec. 10, 1942; s. Oscar Sigried and Eliza Jane (Hicks) Y.; m. Maryann Zarlengo, Sept. 10, 1972. BA, U. Wyo., 1967; JD, U. Denver, 1972, MBA, 1979. Bar: Colo. 1972, Wyo. 1972. Pvt. practice, Denver, 1972-77; house counsel Pavlakis & Co., 1972-73, R.J. Fulsekor Co., Denver, 1975-77; supr. land Tri-State G & T, Thornton, Colo., 1977-82; mng. atty. Haytt Legal Svcs., Aurora, 1982-86; pvt. practice, 1986—. Cons. Colo.-Wyo. Hotel Assn., Denver, 1975-77. With U.S. Army, 1967-69, Vietnam. Mem. Am. Legion, DAV. Mormon. Bankruptcy, Family and matrimonial, General practice. Home: 2527 Taft Ct Lakewood CO 80215-1100 E-mail: t.yuthas@meiworldcom.net

ZABEL, SHELDON ALTER, lawyer, law educator; b. Omaha, Apr. 25, 1941; s. Louis Julius and Anne (Rothenberg) Z.; m. Roberta Jean Butz, May 10, 1975; children: Andrew Louis, Douglas Patrick, Robert Stewart Warren. AB cum laude, Princeton U., 1963; JD cum laude, Northwestern U., 1966. Bar: Ill. 1966, U.S. Supreme Ct. 1976. Law clk. to presiding justice Ill. Supreme Ct., 1966-67; assoc. Schiff, Hardin & Waite, Chgo., 1967-73, ptnr., 1973—. Instr. environ. law Loyola U., Chgo. Bd. dirs. Chgo. Zool. Soc. Mem. ABA, Chgo. Bar Assn., Chgo. Coun. Lawyers, Order of Coif, Union League Club, Met. Club (Chgo.) Jewish. Avocations: skiing, squash. Environmental, Public utilities. Office: Schiff Hardin & Waite 7200 Sears Tower 233 S Wacker Dr Ste 7200 Chicago IL 60606-6473

ZACHARSKI, DENNIS EDWARD, lawyer; b. Detroit, Feb. 25, 1951; s. Edward J. and Margaret R. (Cendrowski) Z.; m. Susan G. Foster, Aug. 8, 1975; children: Jeffrey Alan, Lauren Michelle. BBA, U. Mich., 1973; JD, Mich. State U., 1977. Bar: Mich. 1977, U.S. Dist. Ct. (ea. dist.) Mich. 1977, U.S. Dist. Ct. (we. dist.) Mich. 1982, U.S. Supreme Ct. 1988, U.S. Ct. Appeals (6th cir.) 1990, Ohio, 1993. Atty. Lacey & Jones, Birmingham, Mich., 1977—. Case evaluator Mediation Tribunal Assn., Detroit; arbitrator Am. Arbitration Assn., Southfield, Mich. Mem. Oakland County Bar Assn., Assn. Trial Def. Counsel, Mich. Trial Def. Counsel. Avocations: golf, skiing, soccer, tennis, cycling. General civil litigation, Insurance, Personal injury. Office: Lacey & Jones 600 S Adams Rd Ste 300 Birmingham MI 48009-6827 E-mail: dzacharski@laceyjones.com

ZACKEY, JONATHAN THOMAS, lawyer; b. Buffalo, Sept. 5, 1952; s. John Felix and Dolores (Rewers) Z.; m. Jennifer Lynn Blecher, March 18, 1995. AB cum laude, Harvard Coll., 1974; JD, Boston U., 1977. Bar: D.C. 1977, U.S. Supreme Ct. 1982, U.S. Dist. Ct. D.C. 1983, U.S. Ct. Appeals (D.C. cir.) 1983, Calif. 1985, U.S. Dist. Ct. (cen., so. and no. dists) Calif. 1986, U.S. Ct. Appeals (9th cir.) 1986, Wash. 1992, U.S. Dist. Ct. Wash. 1992. Exec. counsel Assn. of Trial Lawyers of Am. Products Liability-Medical Malpractice Exchange, 1978-80, chief counsel 1980-84; mng. assoc. Law Offices Sanford M. Gage, Beverly Hills, Calif., 1984-92; ptnr. Erickson & Zackey, Seattle, 1992-95, pres. Law Offices of Jonathan T. Zackey, Seattle, 1995—. Contbr. articles on products liability and med. malpractice to Trial mag., 1978-84. Chmn. Parks and Trails Commn. City of Newcastle, 1995-96. Mem. Assn. Trial Lawyers Am. (asst. to editor Law Reporter 1977, drugs editor Trial mag. 1979-81, mem. Trial com. 1984—, sustaining mem., 1988—, exchange adv. com., 1992—), Calif. Trial Lawyers Assn., Los Angeles Trial Lawyers Assn. (victim's rights com. 1984—), Am. Soc. Law and Medicine, ABA (forum com. on health law 1979-81), D.C. Bar (injury to persons or property and litigation divs.), Wash. State Trial Lawyers Assn. Insurance, Personal injury, Product liability. Office: 800 Bellevue Way NE Ste 400 Bellevue WA 98004-4273

ZAGAMI, ANTHONY JAMES, lawyer; b. Washington, Jan. 19, 1951; s. Placidino and Rosemary Zagami. AA, Prince Georges Community Coll., 1971; BS and Bachelor in Pub. Adminstrn., U. Md., 1973; JD, George Mason U., 1977. Bar: D.C. 1978, U.S. Dist. Ct. D.C. 1979, U.S. Ct. Appeals (D.C. cir.) 1979, U.S. Supreme Ct. 1983. Staff Senate Svc. Dept., Washington, 1968-69; senate engr. Office of the Architect of the Capitol, 1969-77; sales rep., cons. Zagami Realty Co. and Montgomery Realty Co., 1971-76; with pub. rels. for sales div. Army Times Pub. Co., 1973-74; teaching and rsch. asst. to law prof. George Mason U., 1975-76; asst. to sec. to majority U.S. Senate, Washington, 1977-78, staff asst. ofcl. reporters of debates, 1978-81; gen. counsel Joint Com. on Printing, 1981-90, U.S. Govt. Printing Office, Washington, 1990—. Bd. dirs. U.S. Senate Credit Union, chmn., Legal Adv. Com., bd. dir. Mem. ABA, FBA (past pres. Capitol Hill chpt.), Nat. Italian-Am. found., U.S. Capitol Hist. Soc., Senate Staff Club, Phi Alpha Phi. Home: PO Box 75154 Washington DC 20013-0154 Office: US Govt Printing Office Office Of Gen Counsel Washington DC 20401-0001

ZAGARIS, BRUCE, lawyer; b. Modesto, Calif., Sept. 4, 1947; s. Nickolas M. and Dorothy (Chicoine) Z. BA, George Washington U., 1969, JD, 1972, LLM, 1973; LLM, Stockholm U., 1975, Free U., Brussels, 1976. Bar: Oreg. 1973, Idaho 1976, Calif. 1978, U.S. Ct. Appeals (10th cir.) 1978, U.S. Ct. Appeals (4th cir.) 1979, U.S. Supreme Ct. 1982. Law clk. U.S. Dist. Ct., Charleston, W.Va., 1972-73; asst. atty. gen. State of Idaho, Boise, 1973-74; atty., cons. Ada Coun. Govts., Boise, 1974; assoc. Nordic Law Cons., Brussels and Stockholm, 1974-76, Glad Tuttle & White, San Francisco, 1976-77; lectr. U. W.I., Bridgetown, Barbados, 1977-78; ptnr. Berliner & Maloney, Washington, 1978-90, Cameron & Hornbostel, 1992—; of counsel Oppenheimer Wolff & Donnelly, 1990-92; cons. 13 nat. govts., UN; adj. prof. Antioch Sch. Law, Washington, 1983-84, Fordham U.Sch. law, 1990—, Washington coll. sch. law American U., 1993—. Author: International Tax Law, 1978, Foreign Investment in U.S., 1980; editor Internat. Handbook on Drug Control, 1992; editor-in-chief Internat. Enforcement Law Reporter. Mem. Epsilon Housing Trust, Washington, 1984. Grantee Stockholm U., 1974-75, Swedish Inst., 1975, Finnish Govt., 1975-76; Salzburg Seminar fellow, 1975. Mem. ABA (chmn. com. internat. tax law, sect. internat. law, 1989-92, chmn. com. internat. criminal law, criminal justice sect. 1990-93, del. Union Internationales des Avocats 1993—, coordinating com. immigration), Am. Soc. Internat. Law (exec. coun. 1990-92), Washington Fgn. Law Soc. (pres. 1990-91), Internat. Fiscal Assn., Internat. Penal Law Assn. (rep. to orgn. of Am. states), Sigma Chi. Private international, Public international, Corporate taxation. Office: Cameron & Hornbostel 818 Connecticut Ave NW Ste 700 Washington DC 20006-2722

ZAGER, STEVEN MARK, lawyer; b. Memphis, Nov. 16, 1958; s. Jack and Sylvia (Bloomfield) Z.; m. Debra D'Angelo; children: Samantha, Amanda, Kathryn. BA, Vanerbilt U., 1979, JD, 1983. Bar: Tex. 1984, U.S. Dist. Ct. (all dists.) Tex. 1984, U.S. Dist. Ct. Ariz. 1992, U.S. Dist. Ct. (D.C.) 1998, U.S. Ct. Appeals (5th, 6th, and 11th cirs.) 1983, U.S. Ct. Appeals (D.C. cir.) 1991, U.S. Ct. Appeals (Fed. cir.) 1997, U.S. Supreme Ct. 1991. Assoc. Fulbright & Jaworski, Houston, 1983-86, Weil, Gotshal & Manges, Houston, 1986-90, ptnr., 1990-98, head Houston office litigation sect., 1994-96; ptnr., head Austin office bus. litigation group Brobeck, Phleger & Harrison, Austin, 1998—, mng. ptnr., mem. firm ops. com., 2000—. Adj. prof. U. Houston Sch. Law, 1990-95; mem. nat. adv. bd. NALP, 1996—. Contbr. articles to Tex. Bar Jour., Houston Lawyer. Bd. dirs., mem. exec. com. Alley Theatre, Houston, 1988-96, Tex. Accts. and Lawyers for the Arts, Houston, 1984-88; mem. adv. bd. Montgomery Bell Acad., 1996—; bd. dirs. Vol. Legal Svcs. Ctrl. Tex., 2000-01, KLRU, 2001—. Named Oustanding Young Man in Am., U.S. Jaycees, 1983; recipient Frank J. Scurlock award State Bar Tex., 1991, Outstanding Pro Bono Svc. Mem. ABA (litigation sect.), State Bar Tex. (dir. 1997-98), Houston Bar Assn. (sec. 1996-97, v.p. 1997-98, bd. dirs. 1993-96, chair law and arts com. 1994, chair adminstrn. of justice com. 1995, rodeo com. 1997, bd. dirs. 1998, Outstanding Young Lawyer in Houston 1991, Pres.'s award 1996-97, 97-98), Houston Vol. Lawyers Program (bd. dirs. 1997-98, chair 1998), Travis County Bar Assn. (bd. dirs. 2001—, chair bench bar program 2000, mem. jud. affairs com. 1999-2000), Fed. Bar Assn., Masons. Federal civil litigation, State civil litigation, Computer. Office: Brobeck Phleger & Harrison LLP 4801 Plaza on the Lake Austin TX 78746

ZAGORSKY, PETER JOSEPH, lawyer; b. New Britain, Conn., Oct. 27, 1950; s. Edward Joseph and Genevieve Mary (Bogdanski) Z.; m. Jane Elizabeth Bremner, July 14, 1979; children: Kathryn Elizabeth, Kristin Mary, Emily Ann. BA, Hofstra U., 1972; JD, Georgetown U., 1975. Bar: Conn. 1975, U.S. Dist. Ct. Conn. 1976, N.Y. 1986. Assoc. Glazer, Wechsler & Seelig, Stamford, Conn., 1975-77; ptnr. Poulos & Zagorsky, Plainville, Conn., 1977—. Pres., bd. dirs. United Way of Plainville, Conn., 1984; treas., bd. dirs. Visiting Nurse Home Care Service of Central Conn., Inc., New Britain, Conn., 1984. Mem. ABA, Am. Trial Lawyers Assn., Conn. Bar Assn., Conn. Trial Lawyers Assn., Hartford County Bar Assn. State civil litigation, Criminal, General practice. Home: 90 N Mountain Rd Canton CT 06019-2140 Office: 100 E Main St Plainville CT 06062-1954

ZAHARAKO, LEW DALEURE, lawyer; b. Columbus, Ind., Dec. 21, 1947; s. Lewie J. and May (Daleure) Z. B.S., Ind. U.-Bloomington, 1971, J.D., 1974. Bar: Ind. 1974. Investigator, asst. dir. consumer protection div. Ind. Atty. Gen.'s Office, Indpls., 1974-75, dir., 1975-76, chief antitrust sect. 1976, dep. atty. gen. environ. sect. 1976-78; atty. Curry & Zaharako, Columbus, 1978-87; sole practice, Columbus, 1987—; dir. Bartholomew Area Legal Aid, 1992—. Mem. allocation com. United Way, 1981-86. Mem. Ind. Bar Assn., Bartholomew County Bar Assn. (sec.-treas. 1979). Republican. Lodge: Kiwanis (dir. Columbus club 1981-83). Consumer commercial, Contracts commercial, General corporate. Home: 2530 Sandcrest Blvd Columbus IN 47203-3047

ZAHN, DONALD JACK, lawyer; b. Oct. 24, 1941; s. Jerome and Clara (Zinsher) Z.; m. Laurie R. Hyman, Aug. 19, 1966; children: Lawrence, Melissa. AB, NYU, 1963; LLB, Union U., 1966; LLM in Taxation, NYU, 1967. Bar: N.Y. 1966, U.S. Dist. Ct. (no. dist.) N.Y. 1966, U.S. Tax Ct. 1969, U.S. Ct. Appeals (2d cir. 1970), Tex. 1972, U.S. Ct. Appeals (5th and 11th cirs.). Assoc. Bond, Schoeneck and King, Syracuse, N.Y., 1967-71; ptnr. Haynes and Boone, Dallas, 1971-82, Akin, Gump, Strauss, Hauer & Feld, Dallas, 1982-92; assoc. prof. internat. taxation, fed. income taxation, entities taxation, business associations Tex. Wesleyan Sch. Law, Ft. Worth, 1992-99. Vis. prof. fed. income taxation Baylor U. Sch. of Law, 1995, fed. income taxation and bus. orgns. II, 2000, grad. taxation program U. San Diego Sch. of Law, 1996-98; adj. prof. Sch. of Law, So. Meth. U., Dallas, 1972-87, 90-91. Trustee, sec. mem. exec. and fin. com., nominating com. Greenhill Sch., Addison, Tex., 1980-90; trustee, chmn. budget com., mem. fin. com. Jewish Fedn. Greater Dallas, 1978-89; trustee, chmn. Found. Jewish Fedn., Dallas, 1980-89; trustee, v.p., pres. Dallas chpt. Am. Jewish Com., 1980-92; mem. Tex. World Trade Coun., 1986-87, Dallas Mayor's Internat. Com. Mem. State Bar Tex. (sec. 1982-83, chmn. tax sect. 1984-85, newsletter taxation sect. editor 1980-81), Internat. Bar Assn., Internat. Comte (N.Tex. commn.), Southwestern Legal Found. (adv. bd., treas. Internat. and Comparative Law Ctr., lectr. Acad. in Internat. Law), N.Y. State Bar Assn. Jewish. Private international, Mergers and acquisitions, Corporate taxation. Address: 11218 Hillcrest Rd Dallas TX 75230-3501 Office Fax: 214-368-5301

ZAHND, RICHARD H. professional sports executive, lawyer; b. N.Y.C., July 22, 1946; s. Hugo and Rose (Genovese) Z.; m. Phyllis Beth Workman, Aug. 13, 1978; children: Andrew Richard, Melissa Dawn. A.B., NYU, 1968, J.D., 1971. Bar: N.Y. 1972. Assoc. Paul, Weiss, Rifkind, Wharton & Garrison, N.Y.C., 1971-74; staff atty. Madison Square Garden Corp., 1974-75; v.p. legal affairs Madison Square Garden Center, Inc., 1975-79; v.p., gen. counsel Madison Square Garden Corp., 1979-86; v.p. N.Y. Knickerbockers Basketball Club, 1979-86, N.Y. Rangers Hockey Club, N.Y.C., 1979-86; ptnr. Morrison & Foerster, 1986-91; exec. v.p., gen. counsel NHL Enterprises, L.P., 1992—. Served to capt. U.S. Army, 1972. John Norton Pomeroy scholar NYU Law Sch., 1969; Mortimer Bishop scholar NYU Law Sch., 1969; Judge Jacob Markowitz scholar NYU Law Sch., 1970; recipient Am. Jurisprudence prize NYU Law Sch., 1969 Episcopalian. Office: NHL Enterprises LP Fl 46 1251 Ave of the Americas New York NY 10020-1104 E-mail: rzahnd@nhl.com

ZAHRT, WILLIAM DIETRICH, II, lawyer; b. Dayton, Ohio, July 12, 1944; s. Kenton William and Orpha Catharine (Wagner) Z.; m. Patricia Ann Marek, June 10, 1969; children: Justin William, Alitheia Patricia. BS in Physics, Yale U., 1966, JD, 1969, M of Pub. and Pvt. Mgmt., 1990. Bar: N.Y. 1970, Ohio 1972, Tex. 1982, N.C. 1992, U.S. Ct. Appeals (Fed. cir.) 1977. Assoc. Kenyon & Kenyon, N.Y.C., 1969-71, Biebel, French & Nauman, Dayton, 1971-80; sr. patent atty. Schlumberger Well Svcs., Houston, 1980-82; sole practice Kingwood, Tex., 1982-85, 88-90; patent atty. Shell Oil Co., Houston, 1985-88; sr. patent counsel Raychem Corp., Fuquay-Varina, N.C., 1990-97; asst. gen. counsel Advanced Micro Devices, Sunnyvale, Calif., 1997-2000; assoc. gen. counsel, legal dir. intellectual property Palm, Inc., Santa Clara, 2000—. Mem. ABA, Am. Intellectual Property Law Assn., Tex. Bar Assn., Silicon Valley Intellectual Property Law Assn., Dayton Racquet Club, Masons. Anglican. Intellectual property, Patent, Trademark and copyright. Home: 629 Villa Centre Way San Jose CA 95128-5138 Office: Palm Inc M/S 9209 5470 Great America Pkwy Santa Clara CA 95052

ZAISER, KENT AMES, lawyer; b. St. Petersburg, Fla., June 10, 1945; s. Robert Alan and Marion (Brown) Z. AB, Duke U., 1967; postgrad., U. Calif., Berkeley, 1971; JD, U. Fla., 1972. Bar: Fla. 1973, U.S. Dist. Ct. (no. dist.) Fla. 1974, U.S. Supreme Ct. 1978, U.S. Dist. Ct. (so. dist.) Fla. 1980, U.S. Dist. Ct. (mid. dist.) Fla. 1981, U.S. Ct. Appeals (11th cir.) 1981. Rsch. aide Fla. Supreme Ct., Tallahassee, 1973-75, adminstrv. asst. to chief justice, 1975-76; asst. gen. counsel Fla. Dept. Natural Resources, 1976-80; asst. atty. gen. Fla. Dept. Legal Affairs, 1980-85; dep. gen. counsel S.W. Fla. Water Mgmt. Dist., Brooksville, 1985-89, gen. counsel, 1989-92; ptnr. Foley and Lardner, Tallahassee, 1992-93; prin. Kent A. Zaiser, P.A., 1994—. Cons. Fla. State Cts. Adminstr., Tallahassee, 1975; mem. Fla. New Motor Vehicle Arbitration Bd., 1998-99. Contbg. author: Environmental Regulation and Litigation in Florida, 1980-84. Campaign chmn. Vince Fechtel for State Rep. of Fla., Leesburg, 1972. Mem. Tallahassee Bar Assn., Jefferson County Bar Assn., Govs. Club. Democrat. Episcopalian. Home: 3286 Longleaf Rd Tallahassee FL 32310-6406 Office: PO Box 6045 Tallahassee FL 32314-6045

ZAITZEFF, ROGER MICHAEL, lawyer; b. Detroit, June 25, 1940; s. Peter and Mary (Fedchenia) Z.; children: Zachary, Natasha, Zoe, Peter. BA with high honors and high distinction, U. Mich., 1962; MA with distinction, U. Calif., Berkeley, 1963, JD, 1969. Bar: N.Y. 1970, U.S. Dist. Ct. (so. dist.) N.Y. 1975, U.S. Ct. Appeals (2nd cir.) 1975, D.C. 1985. Assoc. Seward & Kissel, N.Y.C., 1969-77, ptnr., 1977-94, Latham & Wakins, N.Y.C., 1994-2000, LeBoeuf Lamb Greene & MacRae, N.Y.C., 2000—. Contbr. articles to profl. jours. Mem. Tribar Opinion Com., 1990-93. Heller grantee U. Mich., 1962; recipient William Jennings Bryan Prize. Mem. ABA, Internat. Bar Assn., Assn. of Bar of City of N.Y., N.Y. State Bar Found., N.Y. County Lawyers Assn. (spl. com. legal opinions in comml. transactions), Phi Beta Kappa. Banking, Finance, Securities. Office: LeBoeuf Lamb Greene & MacRae 125 W 55th St 16th Fl New York NY 10019-5389

ZAK, ROBERT JOSEPH, lawyer; b. Steubenville, Ohio, July 29, 1946; s. Joseph and Pearl (Munyas) Zak; m. Kristy Hubbard Winkler, Sept. 13, 1980; children: Elizabeth Adele, Robert Joseph Jr, Barbara Ann. BS, W.Va. U., 1968, JD, 1975. Bar: WVa 1975, US Dist Ct (so dist) WVa 1975, US Dist Ct (no dist) WVa 1989, US Ct Appeals (4th cir) 1990. Staff atty. Pub. Svc. Commn. of W.Va., Charleston, 1975-76; assoc. Preiser & Wilson L.C., 1976-81, ptnr., 1981-85; sr. ptnr. Zak & Assocs., 1985—. Hearing examiner WVa Bd Regents, Charleston, W.Va., 1987—90; spec asst atty gen State of WVa, Charleston, 1987—90, mem worker's compensation appeals , 1991—97, Charleston, 2001—. With U.S. Army, 1969—71, Vietnam. Fellow: Am Acad Matrimonial Lawyers; mem.: Order Barristers. Republican. Presbyterian. General civil litigation, Family and matrimonial, Personal injury. Office: Zak & Assocs 607 Ohio Ave Charleston WV 25302-2228

ZALESNE, DEBORAH, law educator; b. Phila., Mar. 27, 1966; d. Saul and Rachelle (Brody) Zalesne. BA, Williams Coll., 1988; JD, U. Denver, 1992; LLM, Temple U., 1997. Bar: Colo. 1992. Assoc. Pendleton & Sabian, P.C., Denver, 1992-94; jud. clk. Colo. Supreme Ct., 1994-95; Hon. Abraham L. Freedman tchg. fellow Temple Law Sch., Phila., 1995-97; assoc. prof. law CUNY Sch. Law, Flushing, 1997—. Advisor Russian Commn. on Securities and Exchs., Moscow, 1994. Contbr. articles to profl. jours. Vol., Cmty. Outreach Law Program, N.Y.C., 1999, Jews for Racial and Econ. Justice, N.Y.C., 1999. Securities Law fellow Denver Law Sch., 1991-92. Mem. ABA. Democrat. Office: CUNY Law Sch 65-21 Main St Flushing NY 11367

ZALK, ROBERT H. lawyer; b. Albert Lea, Minn., Dec. 1, 1944; s. Donald B. and Juliette J. (Erickson) Z.; m. Ann Lee Anderson, June 21, 1969; children: Amy, Jenna. BA, Carleton Coll., 1966; JD, U. Minn., 1969. Bar: Minn. 1969, U.S. Dist. Ct. Minn. 1969. Assoc. Popham, Haik, Schnobrich, Kaufman & Doty, Mpls., 1969-72; atty. No. States Power Co., 1972-73, Wright, West & Diessner, Mpls., 1973-84, Fredrikson & Byron P.A., Mpls., 1984-94, Zalk & Assocs., Mpls., 1994-95; ptnr. Zalk & Eayrs, 1995-98, Zalk & Wood, Mpls., 1999, Zalk & Bryant, Mpls., 2000—. Fellow Am. Acad. Matrimonial Lawyers (pres. Minn. chpt. 2000-01), Minn. Bar Assn. (co-chmn. maintenance guideline com. 1991-94), Hennepin County Bar Assn. (co-chmn. family law sect. 1990-91). General civil litigation, Family and matrimonial. Office: Zalk & Bryant Sunset Ridge Bus Park 5861 Cedar Lake Rd Minneapolis MN 55416-1481 E-mail: rzalk@zalkbryant.com

ZALUTSKY, MORTON HERMAN, lawyer; b. Schenectady, Mar. 8, 1935; s. Albert and Gertrude (Daffner) Z.; m. Audrey Englebardt, June 16, 1957; children: Jane, Diane, Samuel BA, Yale U., 1957; JD, U. Chgo., 1960. Bar: Oreg. 1961. Law clk. to presiding judge Oreg. Supreme Ct., 1960-61; assoc. Hart, Davidson, Veazie & Hanlon, 1961-63, Veatch & Lovett, 1963-64, Morrison, Bailey, Dunn, Cohen & Miller, 1964-69; prin. Morton H. Zalutsky, P.C., 1970-76; ptnr. Dahl, Zalutsky, Nichols & Hinson, 1977-79, Zalutsky & Klarquist, P.C., Portland, Oreg., 1980-85, Zalutsky, Klarquist & Johnson, Inc., Portland, 1985-94; Zalutsky & Klarquist, P.C., 1994—. Instr. Portland State U., 1961-64, Northwestern Sch. of Law, 1969-70; assoc. prof. U. Miami Law Sch.; lectr. Practising Law Inst., 1971—, Oreg. State Bar Continuing Legal Edn. Program, 1970, Am. Law Inst.-ABA Continuing Legal Edn. Program, 1973—, 34th, 37th NYU ann. insts. fed. taxation, So. Fed. Tax Inst., U. Miami Inst. Estate Planning, Southwestern Legal Found., Internat. Foun. Employee Benefit Plans, numerous other profl. orgns.; dir. A-E-F-C Pension Plan, 1994-99, chmn., 1989-99. Author: (with others) The Professional Corporation in Oregon, 1970, 82; contbg. author: The Dentist and the Law, 3d edit.; editor-in-chief (retirement plans) Matthew Bender's Federal Tax Service, 1987-90; contbr. to numerous publs. in field. Mem. vis. com. U. Chgo. Law Sch., 1986-88. Mem. ABA (vice chair profl. svcs. 1987-89, mem. coun. tax sect. 1985-87, spl. coord. 1980-85), Am. Law Inst., Am. Bar Retirement Assn. (trustee, bd. dirs., vice chair 1990-91, chair 1991-92), Am. Coll. Employee Benefits Coun. (charter mem.), Am. Coll. Tax Coun. (charter

mem.), Multnomah County Bar Assn., Am. Tax Lawyers (charter mem.), Oreg. Estate Planning Coun. Jewish. Pension, profit-sharing, and employee benefits, Corporate taxation, Estate taxation. Home: 3118 SW Fairmount Blvd Portland OR 97201-1466 Office: 215 SW Washington St Fl 3 Portland OR 97204-2636 E-mail: mort@erisalaw.com

ZAMARIN, RONALD GEORGE, lawyer; b. N.Y.C., May 2, 1946; s. Leonard Leon and Laura Aileen (Gargus) Z.; m. Kathleen Veronica Durkin, July 20, 1968; children: Ryan, Chad, Jennifer. BA, UCLA, 1969, JD, 1972. Bar: Ill. 1972, U.S. Ct. Appeals (7th cir.) 1972, Fed. Trial Bar. Assoc. Isham, Lincoln & Beale, Chgo., 1972-79, ptnr., 1980-88; pvt. practice Des Plaines, Ill., 1988—. Coop. atty. ACLU, Chgo., 1982—; litigating mem. Lawyers Com. for Civil Rights under Law, Chgo., 1974-78. Co-author: Media Law Handbook, 1982. Trustee, treas. Palatine Pub. Libr. Dist. (Ill.), 1980-89; co-chair Citizens Com. for the Palatine Libr., 1990-95, Citizens Com. for the Palatine Park Dist., 1994—; co-founder Palatine Pub. Libr. Found.; mem. Palatine Adv. Bd., 1978-79; mem. bd. commrs. Palatine Boys' Baseball, 1983-98, sec., 1986-98. Mem. ABA (forum com. on comm. law). Republican. Federal civil litigation, State civil litigation, Libel. Home: 553 E Juniper Dr Palatine IL 60067-3771 Office: 575 Lee St Des Plaines IL 60016-4611 E-mail: zamlaw@aol.com

ZAMBOLDI, RICHARD HENRY, lawyer; b. Kittanning, Pa., Nov. 22, 1941; s. Henry F. and Florence E. (Colligan) Z.; m. Maria Therese Reiser, Aug. 12, 1967; children: Elizabeth M., Richard H. Jr., Margaret B. BBA, St. Bonaventure U., 1963; JD, Villanova U., 1966. Bar: U.S. Dist. Ct. (we. dist.) Pa. 1966, Pa. 1968, U.S. Ct. Appeals (3d cir.) 1970, U.S. Supreme Ct. 1981. Law clk. U.S. Dist. Ct. (we. dist.) Pa., Pitts., 1966-67; atty. Nat. Labor Rels. Bd., 1967-68; assoc. Kanehann & McDonald, Allentown, Pa., 1968-69; ptnr. Elderkin Martin Kelly Messina & Zamboldi, Erie, 1969-90, Knox McLaughlin Gornall & Sennett, Erie, 1990—, pres., 1997—. Author (student articles) Villanova Law Rev., 1964-65, editor, 1965-66. Mem. Pa. Bar Assn., Erie County Bar Assn. Republican. Roman Catholic. Labor. Home: 6206 Lake Shore Dr Erie PA 16505-1013 Office: Knox McLaughlin Gornall & Sennett 120 W 10th St Erie PA 16501-1410

ZAMMIT, JOSEPH PAUL, lawyer; b. N.Y.C., May 19, 1948; s. John and Farla (Rudolph) Z.; m. Dorothy Therese O'Neill, June 6, 1970; children: Michael, Paul, Brian. AB, Fordham U., 1968; JD, Harvard U., 1971; LLM, NYU, 1974. Bar: N.Y. 1972, U.S. Dist. Ct. (so. and ea. dists.) N.Y. 1973, U.S. Ct. Appeals (2d cir.) 1973, U.S. Supreme Ct. 1978, U.S. Dist. Ct. (no. dist.) N.Y. 1983, U.S. Ct. Appeals (11th cir.) 1987, U.S. Ct. Appeals (fed. cir.) 1995. Assoc. Reavis & McGrath, N.Y.C., 1971-74; asst. prof. law St. John's U., Jamaica, N.Y., 1974-76, assoc. prof., 1976-78; assoc. Reavis & McGrath, N.Y.C., 1978-79, ptnr., 1979-88, Fulbright & Jaworski L.L.P. (formerly Fulbright Jaworski & Reavis McGrath), N.Y.C., 1989—. Adj. assoc. prof. St. John's U., Jamaica, 1979-83, adj. prof., 1984—; mem. panel comml. arbitrators tech. panel Am. Arbitration Assn., N.Y.C., 1977—. Bd. editors E-commerce Law and Strategy, 1987—; contbr. articles to profl. jours. Mem. ABA, N.Y. State Bar Assn., Assn. of Bar of City of N.Y. (chmn. com. on computer law 1995-98, chmn. comml. liability subcom. 1981-87, fed. cts. com. 1998-2001), Computer Law Assn., Phi Beta Kappa. General civil litigation, Contracts commercial, Computer. Office: Fulbright & Jaworski LLP 666 5th Ave Fl 31 New York NY 10103-0001 E-mail: jzammit@fulbright.com

ZAMORA, ANTONIO RAFAEL, lawyer; b. Havana, Cuba, Jan. 18, 1941; came to U.S., 1960; s. Juan Clemente and Rosario (Munne) Z.; m. Nelly Reggio, Nov. 28, 1963; children— Maria G., Antonio Rafael. License in Diplomatic and Consular Law, U. Havana, 1960; B.A., U. Fla.-Gainesville, 1965, J.D., 1973; M.A., U. Miami, Fla., 1969. Bar: Fla. 1973. Assoc. Shutts & Bowen, Miami, Fla., 1973-78, ptnr., head internat. dept., 1978-82; ptnr. McDermott, Will & Emery, Miami, 1982-83, mng. ptnr., 1983-84; sr. ptnr. Barnett, Alagia, Zamora & Suarez, Miami, 1984—; pres. Terra Nostrum, Inc., Miami, 1982— ; v.p. Corporate Services Inc., Miami, 1984— ; dir. Fla. Internat. Bank, Miami, 1983-84; dir. Internat. Law Conf. for Lawyers of the Americas, 1978, 80. Legal counsel Cuban Am. Nat. Found., Miami, Washington, 1982— ; mem. council advisors Hispanic Coalition, Washington, 1984; pres. Hispanic Am. Voters Edn. Inc., Miami, 1984; sec. Brigada 2506, Miami, 1984. Served to lt. USNR, 1963-65. Mem. Interam. Bar Assn., ABA, Cuban Am. Bar Assn. (v.p. 1976-79, disting. service award 1980, dir. emeritus 1982), Fla. Bar. Republican. Roman Catholic. Clubs: Big Five, American (Miami, Fla.); Ocean Reef (Key Largo, Fla.); Miami Rowing. General corporate, Private international, Real property. Home: 7500 SW 82nd Ct Miami FL 33143-3818

ZANDROW, LEONARD FLORIAN, lawyer; b. Chgo., Aug. 14, 1955; s. Leonard Florian Sr. and Gladiann (Urbanski) Z. BJ, Northwestern U., 1976, MJ, 1977; JD, Boston Coll., 1981. Bar: Mass. 1982, U.S. Dist. Ct. Mass. 1982, U.S. Ct. Appeals (1st cir.) 1982, U.S. Supreme Ct. 1989. Law clk. to presiding justices Mass. Superior Ct., Boston, 1981-82, chief law clk., 1982-83; ptnr. Parker, Coulter, Daley & White, 1983-95; ptnr., founder Brister & Zandrow, 1995—. Assoc. editor Uniform Comml. Code Reporter Digest, 1981; bd. editors Boston Bar Jour., 1994-97, Def. Counsel Jour., 1996—. Mem. personnel bd. Town of Sharon, 1997—2001. Mem. ABA, Internat. Assn. Def. Counsel, Mass. Bar Assn., Boston Bar Assn., Def. Rsch. Inst., Nat. Spinal Cord Injury Assn. (bd. dirs. 1995—, gen. counsel 1997—), Nat. Assn. Railroad Trial Counsel, Catholic Lawyers Guild, Phi Alpha Delta, Kappa Tau Alpha, Sigma Delta Chi. Roman Catholic. Avocations: landscaping, child rearing, scouting. State civil litigation, Personal injury, Appellate. Office: Brister & Zandrow LLP 268 Summer St Boston MA 02210-1108 E-mail: Zandrow@BZ-law.com

ZANOT, CRAIG ALLEN, lawyer; b. Wyandotte, Mich., Nov. 15, 1955; s. Thomas and Faye Blanch (Sperry) Z. AB with distinction, U. Mich., 1977; JD cum laude, Ind. U., 1980. Bar: Ind. 1980, Mich. 1981, U.S. Dist. Ct. (so. dist.) Ind. 1980, U.S. Dist. Ct. (no. dist.) Ind. 1981, U.S. Ct. Appeals (6th cir.) 1985, U.S. Dist. Ct. (ea. dist.) Mich. 1987, U.S. Dist. Ct. (we. dist.) Mich. 1990. Law clk. to presiding justice Allen County Superior Ct, Ft. Wayne, 1980-81; ptnr. Davidson, Breen & Doud P.C., Saginaw, Mich., 1981—. Mem. ABA, Mich. Bar Assn., Ind. Bar Assn., Saginaw County Bar Assn. Roman Catholic. Insurance, Personal injury, Workers' compensation. Home: 547 S Linwood Beach Rd Linwood MI 48634-9432 Office: Davidson Breen & Doud PC 1121 N Michigan Ave Saginaw MI 48602-4762

ZAPHIRIOU, GEORGE ARISTOTLE, lawyer, educator; b. July 10, 1919; came to U.S., 1973, naturalized, 1977; s. Aristotle George and Callie Constantine (Economos) Z.; m. Peaches J. Griffin, June 1, 1973; children: Ari, Marie. JD, U. Athens, 1940; LLM, U. London, 1950. Bar: Supreme Ct. Greece 1946, Eng. 1956, Ill. 1975, Va. 1983. Gen. counsel Counties Ship Mgmt. and R & K Ltd., London, 1951-61; practicing barrister, lectr. City of London Poly., 1961-73; vis. prof. Ill. Inst. Tech.-Chgo. Kent Coll. Law, 1973-76; pvt. practice Northbrook, Ill., 1976-78; prof. law George Mason U. Sch. Law, 1978-94, prof. law emeritus, adj. prof., 1994—. Prof. internat. transactions George Mason U. Internat. Inst., 1992-94; mem. Odin, Feldman & Pittelman P.C., Fairfax, Va., 1994-96; mem. study group on internat. elec. commerce cons. and other pvt. internat. law covs. U.S. Dept. of State. Author: Transfer of Chattels in Private International Law, 1956, U.S. edit., 1981, European Business Law, 1970; co-author: Declining Jurisdiction in Private International Law, 1995; joint editor: Jour. Bus. Law, London, 1962-73; bd. dirs. and bd. editors Am. Jour. Comp. Law of Am. Soc. Comparative Law, 1980-94; contbr. articles to profl. jours. Mem. ABA (sect. internat. law and practice and dispute resolution), Ill. Bar Assn., Chgo. Bar Assn., Am. Arbitration Assn. (panel of comml. arbitrators), George Mason Am. Inn of Ct. (founder, mem. emeritus). Alternative dispute resolution, Contracts commercial, Private international. Home: 400 Green Pasture Dr Rockville MD 20852-4233 Fax: 301-984-1164. E-mail: gzaphiri@gmu.edu

ZARELLA, PETER T. judge; BS, Northeastern U., 1972; JD, Suffolk U., 1975. Bar: Mass. 1976, Conn. 1977, U.S. Ct. Appeals (2d cir.) 1985, U.S. Supreme Ct. 1985, U.S. Dist. Ct. (so. dist. NY) 1990. Pvt. practice, 1979—96; ptnr. Brown, Paindiris & Zarella, Hartford, Conn., 1978—96; judge Superior Ct., 1996—99; % Appellate Ct., 1999—2001; assoc. justice Conn. Supreme Ct., 2001—. Mem. ethics commn. Town of West Hartford, Conn., 1992—95, mem. charter revision commn., 1995—96. Mem.: Conn. Bar Assn. (mem. exec. com. cooml. law and bankruptcy sect. 1985—90, mem. banking law com. 1990—94). Office: Suprteme Ct Bldg PO Drawer N Sta A Hartford CT 06106*

ZASLOWSKY, DAVID PAUL, lawyer; b. N.Y.C., Dec. 30, 1960; s. Daniel N. and Rhoda (Sohn) Z.; m. Lisa Ann Freudenberger, Aug. 26, 1982; children: Amanda Lauren, Michael Joel, Steven Ira. BS in Computer/Info. Sci. summa cum laude, Bklyn. Coll., 1981; JD, Yale U., 1984. Bar: N.Y. 1984, N.J. 1984, U.S. Dist. Ct. (so. and ea. dist.) N.Y. 1985, U.S. Dist. Ct. N.J. 1985, U.S. Cir. Ct. (2d cir.) 1992. Assoc. Baker & McKenzie, N.Y.C., 1984-94, ptnr., 1994—. Author: (with others) Federal Civil Practice, 1989, Transnational Litigation in U.S. Federal Courts, 1991, Litigating International Commercial Disputes, 1996. Mem. ABA (litigation sect.), N.Y. State Bar Assn. (comml. and fed. litigation sect.), Assn. Bar City N.Y. General civil litigation, Contracts commercial. Office: Baker & McKenzie 805 3rd Ave Fl 29 New York NY 10022-7513 E-mail: david.zaslowsky@bakernet.com

ZAVATSKY, MICHAEL JOSEPH, lawyer; b. Wheeling, W.Va., Dec. 15, 1948; s. Mike and Mary (Mirich) Z.; m. Kathleen Hanson, May 28, 1983; children: David, Emily. BA in Internat. Studies, Ohio State U., 1970; MA in Polit. Sci., U. Hawaii, 1972; JD, U. Cin., 1980. Bar: Ohio 1980, U.S. Dist. Ct. (so. dist.) Ohio 1981, U.S. Ct. Appeals (6th cir.) 1985, U.S. Supreme Ct. 1989. Ptnr. Taft, Stettinius & Hollister, Cin., 1980—. Adj. prof. in trial practice and immigration law U. Cin., 1986— Trustee Internat. Visitors Ctr., Cin., 1984-86; bd. dirs. Cin. Charter Com., 1988-91; bd. dirs., mem. steering com. Leadership Cin., 1994-96. Capt. USAF, 1973-77. William Graham fellow U. Cin., 1979, East West Ctr. fellow U. Hawaii, 1970. Mem ABA, Ohio Bar Assn., Cin. Bar Assn., Am. Immigration Lawyers Assn. (chmn. Ohio chpt. 1987-88, 90-93), Potter Stewart Inn of Ct., Order of Coif. Federal civil litigation, State civil litigation, Immigration, naturalization, and customs. Home: 3820 Eileen Dr Cincinnati OH 45209-2013 Office: 1800 Firstar Tower Cincinnati OH 45202

ZAZZALI, JAMES R. judge; b. Newark, June 17, 1937; m. Eileen Fitzsimmons; children: Mara, James Jr., Robert, Courtney, Kevin. BA, JD, Georgetown U. Bar: NJ, NY, DC. Law clk. U.S. Dist. Ct. Judge Lawrence A. Whipple, 1964—65; from asst. prosecutor to chief appellate sect. Essex County Prosecutor's Office, 1965—68; ptnr. Zazzali, Fagella, & Nowak, Newark; atty. gen. State of NJ, 1981—82; gen. counsel NJ Sports and Exposition Authority; assoc. justice NJ Supreme Ct., 2000—. Adj. prof. Seton Hall Law Sch., 1984—; commr. NJ State Commn. of Investigation, 1984—94, chmn., 1990—94; vice-chair Disciplinary Rev Bd., 1984—2000. Democrat. Office: NJ Supreme Ct 151 Bodman Pl Red Bank NJ 07701*

ZEALEY, SHARON JANINE, lawyer; b. St. Paul, Aug. 30, 1959; d. Marion Edward and Freddie Zealey. BS, Xavier U. of La., 1981; JD, U. Cin., 1984. Bar: Ohio 1984; U.S. Dist. Ct. (so. dist.) Ohio 1985; U.S. Ct. Appeals (6th cir.) 1990; U.S. Supreme Ct. 1990. Law clk. U.S. Atty. for S. Dist. of Ohio, Cin., 1982; trust adminstr. Firstar Bank, 1984-86; atty. UAW Legal Svcs., 1986-88; assoc. Manley, Burke Lipton & Fischer, 1988-91; mng. atty. and dep. atty. gen. Ohio Atty. Gen. Office, 1991-95; asst. U.S. atty. criminal div. for So. Dist. Ohio U.S. Attys. Office, 1995-97; United States atty. So. Dist. Ohio, 1997—2000; ptnr. Blank Rome Comisky & McCauley, 2001—. Pro bono svc. Pro Srs., 1987-88; mem. merit selection com. U.S. Ct. Appeals 6th Cir., Bankruptcy Ct.; adj. prof. law, civil rights U. Cin. Vol. lawyer for the poor/Pro Bono Panel participant, 1984—; adv. rev. bd. City of Cin. EEOC, 1989-91; mem. Tall Stacks Commn., Cin., 1991-92, Mayor's Commn. on Children, 1992-93; trustee, bd. visitors U. Cin. Coll. Law, 1992—; mem. BLAC/CBA Round Table, 1988—. Recipient Law Honor scholarship U. Cin. Coll. Law, 1981. Mem. Black Lawyers Assn. of Cin. (pres. 1989-91), Legal Aid Soc. (sec. 1991-92), ABA, Fed. Bar Assn., Ohio Bar Assn., Nat. Bar Assn. (Mem. of Yr. region VI 1990), Cin. Bar Assn. (trustee 1989-94). Democrat. Episcopalian. Office: 1700 PNC Ctr 201 E 5th St Cincinnati OH 45202 Fax: 513-362-8787. E-mail: zealey@blankRome.com

ZEIDMAN, PHILIP FISHER, lawyer; b. Birmingham, Ala., May 2, 1934; s. Eugene Morris and Ida (Fisher) Z.; m. Nancy Levy, Aug. 19, 1956; children: Elizabeth Miriam, John Fisher (dec.), Jennifer Kahn. BA cum laude, Yale U., 1955; LLB, Harvard U., 1958; postgrad., Grad. Sch. Bus. Adminstrn., 1957-58. Bar: Ala. 1958, Fla. 1960, U.S. Supreme Ct. 1961, D.C. 1968, N.Y. 1981. Trial atty. FTC, 1960-61; staff asst. White House Com. Small Bus., 1961-63; spl. asst. to adminstr. SBA, 1961-63, asst. gen. counsel, 1963-65, gen. counsel, 1965-68; spl. asst. to Vice Pres. of U.S., 1968; govt. rels. mgr. Nat. Alliance Businessmen, 1968; founding prin. Brownstein & Zeidman P.C., Washington, 1968-96; sr. ptnr. Rudnick, Wolfe, Epstien & Zeidman, 1996-99; ptnr. Piper Marbury Rudnick & Wolfe, 1999—. Chmn. grants and benefits com. Adminstrv. Conf. U.S., 1968; chmn. food industry adv. com. Dept. Energy, 1979-81; chmn. distbn. and food merchandising subcom. Alliance to Save Energy, 1978; mem. Pres.'s Commn. on Exec. Exch., 1978-81; gen. counsel Internat. Franchise Assn., Am. Bus. Conf.; spl. counsel Japanese Franchise Assn.; advisor to govts. and internat. orgns.; founder EastEuropeLaw, Ltd., Budapest, Hungary. Editor, author: Survey of Laws and Regulations Affecting International Franchising, 1982, 2d edit., 1990, Regulation of Buying and Selling a Franchise, 1983, Legal Aspects of Selling and Buying, 1983, 2nd edit., 1991; cons. editor Global Franchising Alert; assoc. editor Jour. of International Franchising Law and Distribution; contbg. editor Legal Times of Washington, 1978-85; mem. adv. bd. Antitrust and Trade Regulation Report for Bur. Nat. Affairs, 1978-85. Mem. young leadership coun. Dem. Nat. Com.; exec. dir. Dem. platform com., 1972; adviser Nat. Presdl. Campaign of Jimmy Carter, 1976; mem. pres.'s adv. com. John F. Kennedy Ctr. for Performing Arts, 1981; chmn. class coun. Yale Class of 1955; mem. adv. bd. Yale U. Sch. Mgmt.; trustee Yale-China Assn., 1983-89; dir. Appleseed Found., 1994—; mem. adv. bd. DeWitt Wallace Ctr. for Comm., Terry Sanford Inst. Pub. Policy, Duke U., 1994-98. With USAF, 1958-60. Recipient Younger Fed. Lawyer award Fed. Bar Assn., 1965; Jonathan Davenport Oratorical award, 1954; William Houston McKim award, 1955 Mem. ABA (chmn. com. on franchising 1977-81), D.C. Bar Assn., Ala. Bar Assn., Fla. Bar Assn., Fed. Bar Assn., Bar Assn. D.C., Internat. Bar Assn. (chmn. internat. franchising com. 1986-90, mem. coun. sect. bus. law 1996—), Am. Intellectual Property Law Assn. (chmn. franchising com. 1987-90), Assn. Yale U. Alumni (class rep.). Antitrust, Franchising. Office: 1200 19th St NW Washington DC 20036

ZEIGLER, ANN DEPENDER, lawyer; b. Spokane, Wash., June 7, 1947; d. F. Norman and Dorothy (Wolter) dePender; m. Paul Stewart Zeigler, June 20, 1970; 1 child, Kate Elizabeth. BA magna cum laude, Ft. Wright Coll. Holy Names, Spokane, 1969; MFA in Creative Writing, U. Mont., 1975; JD, U. Houston, 1984. Bar: Tex. 1984. Course adminstr. legal communications U. Houston, 1982-84; assoc. Dula, Shields & Egbert, 1984-87; ind. project atty., 1987; assoc. Dow, Cogburn & Friedman, 1987-90; assoc. bankruptcy sect./avoidance litigation Hughes, Watters & Askanase, Houston, 1990—. Co-editor: Insurance Guide-Arts Nonprofits, 1993, Basic Issues in Estate Planning-Representing the Artist, 1994, Leading the Arts Nonprofit: Duties of Officers and Directors, 1999; editl. bd. Houston Lawyer, 1999—, guest editor spl. hist. issue 2001; contbr. articles to profl. jours. Mem. publs. com., writer Tex. Accts. and Lawyers for Arts, Houston, 1988—; mem. Supreme Ct. of Tex. Unauthorized Practice of Law Com., Houston; vol. Houston Lawyers for Hunger Relief, 1988-90. Mem. ABA, State Bar Tex., Houston Bar Assn. (chair law and the arts com. 1996-97, co-chair ann. fiction contest), Can. Bar Assn., Phi Alpha Delta. Democrat. Bankruptcy, General civil litigation, Real property. Home: 4038 Cheena Dr Houston TX 77025-4702 Office: Hughes Watters & Askanase 1415 Louisiana St Fl 37 Houston TX 77002-7360 E-mail: azeigler@hwallp.com

ZEISEL, LAURA, lawyer, educator; b. Bklyn., June 9, 1948; d. Melvin and Shirley Martha (Weinstein) Z.; m. David Seymour Strong, Nov. 20, 1970; children— Sara Zeisel, Elizabeth Pearl. Student Smith Coll., 1966-68; B.A., Washington Sq. Coll., NYU, 1970, postgrad., 1970-72; J.D., SUNY-Buffalo, 1975. Bar: N.Y. 1976, U.S. Dist. Ct. (so. dist.) N.Y. 1976, U.S. Ct. Appeals (2d cir.) 1977, U.S. Dist. Ct. (no. dist.) N.Y. 1979. Atty. Mid-Hudson Legal Services, Poughkeepsie, N.Y., 1975-80; ptnr. Lazar & Zeisel, Poughkeepsie, 1980-82; regional atty. N.Y. State Dept. Environ. Conservation, New Paltz, 1982-85; resident counsel Mid-Hudson br. office Sive, Paget & Riesel, P.C., 1985-88; adj. prof. Marist Coll., Poughkeepsie, 1976— ; mem. Gov.'s Commn. Domestic Violence, Albany, N.Y., 1983-88. Recipient Bennett award Faculty Law and Jurisprudence SUNY, Buffalo, 1975. Mem. N.Y. State Bar Assn., Ulster County Bar Assn., Mid-Hudson Women's Bar Assn. (pres. 1983-84). Democrat. Jewish. Office: 169 Main St New Paltz NY 12561-1119

ZEITLAN, MARILYN LABB, lawyer; b. N.Y.C., Sept. 17, 1938; d. Charles and Florence (Geller) Labb; m. Barrett M. Zeitlan, Apr. 14, 1957; children: Adam Scott, Daniel Craig. BA, Queens Coll., 1958, MS, 1970; JD, Hofstra U., 1978. Bar: N.Y. 1979. Tchr. N.Y.C., 1958-61; pvt. practice matrimonial law, Roslyn, N.Y., 1980—. Assoc. editor: Law Rev., Hofstra U., 1977-78; contbr. articles to profl. jours. Commr. East Hills Environ. Commn., 1971-75; co-founder Roslyn Environ. Assn., 1970; v.p. Roslyn LWV, 1974-75. Hofstra Law Sch. fellow, 1976. Mem. Nassau County Bar Assn., N.Y. State Bar Assn., Phi Beta Kappa. Avocation: horseback riding. Family and matrimonial. Office: 1025 Northern Blvd Ste 201 Roslyn NY 11576-1506

ZELDES, ILYA M. forensic scientist, lawyer; b. Baku, Azerbaidjan, Mar. 15, 1933; came to U.S., 1976; s. Michael B. and Pauline L. (Ainbinder) Z.; m. Emma S. Kryss, Nov. 5, 1957; 1 child, Irina Zeldes Rieser. JD, U. Azerbaidjan, Baku, 1955; PhD in Forensic Scis., U. Moscow, 1969. Expert-criminalist Med. Examiner's Bur., Baku, 1954-57; rsch. assoc. Criminalistics Lab., Moscow, 1958-62; sr. rsch. assoc. All-Union Sci. Rsch. Inst. Forensic Expertise, 1962-75; chief forensic scientist S.D. Forensic Lab., Pierre, 1977-93. Owner Forensic Scientist's Svcs., Pierre, 1977-93. Author: Physical-Technical Examination, 1968, Complex Examination, 1971, The Problems of Crime, 1981; contbr. numerous articles to profl. publs. in Australia, Austria, Bulgaria, Can., Eng., Germany, Holland, India, Ireland, Israel, Rep. of China, Russia, U.S. and USSR. Mem. Internat. Assn. Identification (rep. S.D. chpt. 1979-93, chmn. forensic lab. analysis subcom. 1991-98, firearm and toolmark identification subcom. 2001—), Am. Soc. Crime Lab. Dirs., Am. Assn. Firearm and Toolmark Examiners (emeritus). Avocation: travel. Home: 5735 Foxlake Dr Apt 1 Fort Myers FL 33917-5661 E-mail: ilyaz@iline.com

ZELDES, JACOB DEAN, lawyer; b. Galesburg, Ill., Dec. 10, 1929; s. Louis Herman and Sophia Ruth (Koren) Z.; m. Nancy S. Zeldes, Aug. 23, 1953; children: Stephen, Kathryn, Amy. BS, U. Wis., 1951; LLB, Yale U., 1957. Bar: Conn. 1957, U.S. Dist. Ct. Conn. 1958, U.S. Ct. Appeals (2nd cir.) 1959, U.S. Supreme Ct. 1960, U.S. Tax Ct. 1966. Ptnr. Zeldes Needle & Cooper PC, Bridgeport, Conn. Lt. (j.g.) USNR, 1951-53, Korea. Fellow Am. Bar Found., Am. Coll. Trial Lawyers; mem. ABA Assn. Profl. Responsibility Lawyers, Conn. Bar Assn. (lawyer to lawyer dispute resolution com., spl. counsel Conn. Ho. of Reps., select com. to investigate impeachment of probate judge 1985), Conn. Trial Lawyers Assn., Assn. Trial Lawyers of Am., Nat. Assn. Criminal Def. Lawyers, Conn. Criminal Def. Lawyers Assn., Bridgeport Bar Assn. Democrat. Jewish. Avocations: swimming, hiking, travel. General civil litigation, Criminal. Office: Zeldes Needle & Cooper PC 1000 Lafayette Blvd Fl 5 Bridgeport CT 06604-4725 E-mail: jzeldes@znclaw.com

ZELLER, MICHAEL EUGENE, lawyer; b. Queens, N.Y., June 19, 1967; s. Hans Ludwig and Geri Ann (Schottenstein) Z. BA, Union Coll., 1989; JD, Temple Law Sch., 1992; LLM magna cum laude, U. Hamburg, Germany, 1994. Bar: N.Y. 1992, U.S. Dist. Ct. (so. and ea. dists.) N.Y. 1995, N.C. 1996. Fgn. intern Bryan Gonzalez Vargas y Gonzalez Baz, Mexico City, 1990; student law clk. Hon. Jane Cutler Greenspan, Phila., 1990-91; fgn. clk. DROSTE, Hamburg, 1991, fgn. assoc., translator, 1992-94; freelance translator Charlotte, N.C., 1995—; assoc. Internat. and Corp. Law Group of Moore & Van Allen PLLC, 1995—; owner, restaurateur Salad Garden, L.L.C. and Salad Garden Café, L.L.C., 1998-99; owner Nighttime Entertainment LLC, BGZ Properties, LLC. Vol. atty. Children's Law Ctr. Mem. Charlotte World Affairs Coun., Charlotte Mayor's Internat. Cabinet; bd. dirs. Alemannia Soc., 1996-2000, Young Affiliates of Mint Mus., 1999-2000; bd. dirs., pres. Southgate Commons Homeowners Assn., 1998—. Recipient scholarship Fedn. German/Am. Clubs, 1987; named Vol. Lawyer of the Yr. Children's Law Ctr., 1998. Mem. ABA, N.Y. State Bar Assn., N.C. Bar Assn., Mecklenburg County Bar Assn., Gewerblicher Rechtsschutz und Urheberrecht e.V., European Am. Bus. Forum, Am. Translators Assn., Am. Immigration Lawyers Assn. Avocations: singing, theater, golf, fictional writing. General corporate, Private international, Mergers and acquisitions. Office: 100 N Tryon St Fl 47 Charlotte NC 28202-4003

ZELLER, PAUL WILLIAM, lawyer; b. Eunice, La., Sept. 17, 1948; s. Andrew Albert and Margaret Lucille (Fontenot) Z.; m. Marlene Linda Parrillo, Dec. 17, 1966; children— Paul William, Jr., Jonathan Randolph, Amanda Louise, Joshua Andrew. B.A., La. State U., 1969; J.D., U. Va., 1972. Bar: N.Y. 1973, U.S. Dist. Ct. (so. dist.) N.Y. 1974, U.S. Ct. Appeals (2nd cir.) 1974. Assoc., Debevoise and Plimpton, N.Y.C., 1972-81; asst. corp. counsel Reliance Group, Inc., N.Y.C., 1981-83; asst. v.p. Reliance Group Holdings, Inc., N.Y.C., 1982, v.p., asst. gen. counsel, 1983, v.p., dep. gen. counsel, 1984—; bd. dirs. Empire Gas Corp. Bd. of editors, U. Va. Law Review, 1970-72. Mem. Assn. Bar City of N.Y., Phi Delta Phi. Democrat. Roman Catholic. Contracts commercial, General corporate, Securities. Office: Reliance Group Holdings Inc 55 E 52nd St Fl 29 New York NY 10055-0190

ZELLER, RONALD JOHN, lawyer; b. Phila., Jan. 28, 1940; m. Lucille Bell; children: John, Kevin, Suzanne. BSBA, LaSalle Coll., 1964; JD, Ohio State U., 1967. Bar: Mich. 1968, Fla. 1971. Ptnr. Patton & Kanner, Miami, Fla., 1973-80, of counsel, 1980-89; pres., chief exec. officer Norwegian Cruise Lines, 1980-86; pres. Twenty First Century Mgmt. Group, Inc., Coconut Grove, Fla., 1986-90, Miami Voice Corp., 1990-92; gen. counsel Splty. Mgmt. Co., Delray Beach, Fla., 1992-93, pres., 1994-96; ptnr. Zeller & Assocs., LLC, Palm Beach, 1996—. Dep. chmn. Cruise Lines Internat. Assoc., N.Y.C., 1981-85, chmn., 1986. Trustee United Way Dade County, 1981-86; pres. Cath. Charities, Archdiocese of Miami 1976-78, Broward

County, 1975-76, Excalibur Devel. Ctrs., Inc., 1973-75; mem. citizens bd. U. Miami, 1980-92; mem. exec. bd. New World Sch. Arts, 1986-87; mem. centennial campaign com. Ohio State U. Coll. Law, 1982-92, also mem. nat. coun.; mem. coun. Pres.'s Assocs., LaSalle U., 1982-87; mem. Fla. Postsecondary Edn. Planning Commn., 1986-87; mem. Cmty. Assns. Inst., 1995-2000; chmn. exec. com. Maritime Inst., 1997-99; mem. utility rev. bd. Village of Wellington, 1997-98; mem. gen. counsel Palm Beach Maritime Mus.; mem. Fla. com. Affirm Thy Friendship Campaign, Ohio State U., 1997-2000; mem. cruise line incentive com. Port of Palm Beach, 1997-2000. Mem. ABA (sect. taxation, close corp. com.), Fla. Bar Assn. (lawyers and CPA's com.), Maritime Law Assn. (proctor in admiralty), Pres.' Club Ohio State U. General civil litigation, General corporate, Taxation, general. Office: Zeller & Assocs LLC Esperante Bldg 222 Lakeview Ave Ste 260 West Palm Beach FL 33401 Fax: 561 802-4387. E-mail: zellerlawfirm@juno.com

ZERGER, KIRSTEN LOUISE, lawyer; b. Newton, Kans., Oct. 15, 1950; d. Homer Joshua and Karolyn Louise (Kaufman) Z.; m. Edward Peters Dick, Mar. 28, 1969 (div. 1978); 1 child, Daagya Shanti; m. Sanford Norman Nathan, June 14, 1980; children: Jesse Zerger, Jonathan Kaufman, Joshua Zev. BA with highest distinction, Bethel Coll., 1973; JD, U. Calif.-Berkeley, 1977. Bar: Calif. 1977, U.S. Dist. Ct. (no. dist.) Calif. 1977, U.S. Ct. Appeals (9th cir.) 1987, U.S. Supreme Ct. 1985. Staff atty. United Farm Workers, AFL-CIO, Salinas, Calif., 1977-79; staff atty. Calif. Tchrs. Assn., Burlingame, 1979-85, dep. chief counsel, 1985, chief counsel, 1985-88; pvt. practice, Berkeley, Calif., 1988-93; mediator, facilitator, and trainer, Kansas Inst. for Peace and Conflict Resolution, North Newton, Kansas, 1994-; coll. instr. Bethel Coll., North Newton, Kansas, 1996-; approved mediator, trainer Kans. Supreme Ct., 1998-; speaker edn., profl. confs. Writer on mediation, facilitation and tng. as well as on public sector labor law issues; co-editor book California Public Sector Labor Law, 1989; contbr. articles to profl. jours. Mem. Heartland Mediators Assn., Calif. Bar Assn.(labor and employment law sect., chmn. pub. sector com. 1983-85, membership com. 1982-83, exec. com., 1985-89, treas. 1986-87, vice-chair 1987-88, advisor 1988-89). E-mail: snkz@mtelco.net.

ZERIN, STEVEN DAVID, lawyer; b. N.Y.C., Oct. 1, 1953; s. Stanley Robert and Cecilie Paula (Goldberg) Z.; children: Alexander James, J. Oliver. BS, Syracuse U., 1974; JD, St. Johns U., 1977. Bar: N.Y. 1978, U.S. Dist. Ct. (so. dist.) N.Y. 1985, U.S. Supreme Ct. 1986. Assoc. Gladstein & Isaac, N.Y.C., 1981-82, Sperry, Weinberg, Wels, Waldman & Rubenstein, N.Y.C., 1982-85; ptnr. Wels & Zerin, 1985—. Trustee, mem. bd. govs. Daytop Village. Mem. ABA (exec. mem. and lectr. family law sect.), N.Y. State Bar Assn. (exec. com. family law sect.), Assn. of Bar of City of N.Y. Democrat. State civil litigation, Family and matrimonial, Probate. Home: 12 E 88th St New York NY 10128-0535 Office: Wels & Zerin 600 Madison Ave Fl 22 New York NY 10022-1615

ZERUNYAN, FRANK VRAM, lawyer; b. Istanbul, Turkey, Sept. 17, 1959; came to U.S., 1978; s. Jack Hagop and Ayda (Yagupyan) Z.; m. Jody Lynn Forman, May 18, 1986; children: Daniel, Nicole. French Baccalaureat, Coll. Samuel Moorat, Paris, 1978; BA, Calif. State U., Long Beach, 1982; JD, Western State U., Fullerton, Calif., 1985; postgrad., U. Southern Calif., 1988. Bar: Calif. 1989, D.C., 1995, U.S. Dist. Ct. (cen. dist.) Calif. 1989, U.S. Ct. Internat. Trade 1994, U.S. Supreme Ct., 2000. V.p. law Internat. Mktg. Alliance, Torrance, Calif., 1985-89; pvt. practice L.A., 1989-92; mng. mem. Yacoubian & Zerunyan, P.C., 1992-95; shareholder Sulmeyer, Kupetz, Baumann & Rothman, 1995—. Instr. law Alex Pilibos Sch., L.A., 1993-99; judge pro tem, L.A. Superior Ct. Editor SKB&R Newsletter, 1995—. Bd. dirs. Am. Youth Soccer Orgn., Palos Verdes, Calif., 1995—, referee adminstr., 1995—; bd. dirs., vice-chmn. Daniel Freeman Hosps. Found., 1998—; chmn. scholarship com. Orgn. Istanbul Armenians, Van Nuys, Calif., 1992-94; legal counsel and polity adv. com. Armenian Nat. Com. of Am., Washington, 1993; planning commr. City of Rolling Hills Estates, 2000—. Mem. ABA, Financial Lawyers Conf. Avocations: golf, soccer. Bankruptcy, Contracts commercial, Real property. Office: Sulmeyer Kupetz et al 300 S Grand Ave Ste 1400 Los Angeles CA 90071-3124 E-mail: fzerunyan@skbr.com

ZHAO, QIAN, lawyer; b. Dalian, Liaoning, China, Aug. 24, 1968; LLB, UIBE, Beijing, 1990; JD, NYU, 1998. Bar: N.Y. 1999, People's Rep. China. Ptnr. Haiwen & Ptnr., Beijing, 1990-94; assoc. Sullivan & Cromwell, N.Y.C., 1998-2000, Skadden Arps, Beijing, 2000—. Private international, Mergers and acquisitions, Securities. Office: Skadden Arps Slate Meagher & Flom East Wing Office China World Trade Ctr 100004 Beijing China E-mail: Qzhao@skadden.com

ZICHERMAN, DAVID L. lawyer, educator, financial consultant; b. N.Y.C., Oct. 12, 1961; BA in Psychology magna cum laude, W.Va. U., 1984; JD, MPIA, U. Pitts., 1989. Bar: Del. 1990, Pa. 1990, D.C. 1990. Assoc. Richards, Layton & Finger, Wilmington, Del., 1989-92, Klehr Harrison et al, Phila., 1992-94, Kelly Grimes Pietrangelo & Vakil, P.C., Media, Pa., 1994-97. Adj. prof. Widener U. Law Ctr., Wilmington, 1993-95, fin. cons., Merrill Lynch, 1998—. Editor: State Legislation Forum newsletter, 1991-93; editor Delaware County Legal Jour., 1995-97; contbr. chpt. to book, articles to profl. jours. Bd. dirs. Nat. Tay Sachs and Allied Diseases Assn. Delaware Valley, 1998—; mem. tech. com. Rose Tree Media Edn. Found., 1998—. Avocations: sports, photography, creative writing, travel. Administrative and regulatory, General civil litigation, Insurance. Office: Merrill Lynch PO Box 748 Media PA 19063-0748

ZIEBELL-SULLIVAN, MARTHA JANE, lawyer; b. Ft. Knox, Ky., Feb. 20, 1969; d. John Frederick Ziebell and Leni Wright Hagen; m. Dennis Sullivan, July 24, 1999; 1 child, John. BA in Govt., Smith Coll., 1991; JD, Hamline U., 1994. Bar: Fla. 1997, U.S. Dist. Ct. (mid. dist.) Fla. 1998. Legal transfer specialist Franklin Templeton, St. Petersburg, Fla., 1995-97; assoc. Scott & Fenderson P.A., 1997-98, Law Offices Timothy M. Doud, Largo, Fla., 1998-2000. Mem. ABA, Fla. Bar Assn., St. Petersburg Bar Assn., Inns of Ct. (Canakaris). Republican. Roman Catholic. Bankruptcy, Criminal, Family and matrimonial. Home: 303 E 5th St Hastings MN 55033 Office: The Esquire Group 501 Marquette Ave Ste 1800 Minneapolis MN 55402

ZIEGLER, DONALD EMIL, federal judge; b. Pitts., Oct. 1, 1936; s. Emil Nicholas and Elizabeth (Barclay) Z.; m. Claudia J. Chermak, May 1, 1965; 1 son, Scott Emil. B.A., Duquesne U., 1958; LL.B., Georgetown U., 1961. Bar: Pa. 1962, U.S. Supreme Ct. 1967. Practice law, Pitts., 1962-74; judge Ct. of Common Pleas of Allegheny County, Pa., 1974-78, U.S. Dist. Ct. (we. dist.) Pa., Pitts., 1978—, chief judge, 1994-2001. Mem. Jud. Conf. U.S., 1997-2000. Treas. Big Bros. of Allegheny County, 1969-74. Mem. ABA, Pa. Bar Assn., Allegheny County Bar Assn., Am. Judicature Soc., St. Thomas More Soc. Democrat. Roman Catholic. Club: Oakmont Country. Office: 649 U S Post Office & Courthouse Bldg 7th and Grant St Pittsburgh PA 15219

ZIEGLER, HENRY STEINWAY, lawyer; b. Utica, N.Y., June 21, 1933; s. Frederick J. and Alice (Cantwell) Z.; m. Patricia Blackmore (div.); children: Frederick S., Alicia P., Timothy O.; m. Jourdan Arpelle, Apr. 6, 1991. AB, Harvard U., 1955; LLB, Columbia U., 1958. Bar: N.Y. 1961, U.S. Dist. Ct. (ea. and so. dists.) N.Y. 1962, U.S. Ct. Appeals (2d cir.) 1963, U.S. Tax Ct. 1972. Assoc. Shearman & Sterling, N.Y.C., 1958-67, ptnr., 1967-92; chmn. CEO Deutsche Bank Trust Co., 1995-97, Trust Estate Planning dir., 1998-99; sr. v.p. Fiduciary Trust Co. Internat., N.Y.C., 1999—. Pres. Chamber Music Soc. of Lincoln Ctr., Inc., 1983-89, Christopher D. Smithers Found.; bd. dirs. Lincoln Ctr. for Performing Arts, N.Y.C., 1985-89; hon. trustee St. Lukes-Roosevelt Hosp. Ctr.; bd. regents, Am. Coll. Trust Estate Counsel, 1988-94. With U.S. Army, 1958-60, 61-62. Mem. ABA (fofmer vice chmn. internat. com. on property probate and trust law), Acad. internat. Trust and Estate Law (mem. exec. coun., v.p.), N.Y. State Bar Assn., Assn. Bar City of N.Y., Century Assn., Order St. John of Jerusalem. Republican. Clubs: Racquet and Tennis, Knickerbocker. Avocation: music. Private international, Probate, Estate taxation. Home: 55 Liberty St Apt # 7A New York NY 10005 E-mail: hziegler@ftci.com

ZIFCHAK, WILLIAM C. lawyer; b. 1948; BA, Harvard U., 1970; JD, Columbia U., 1973. Bar: N.Y. 1974, U.S. Ct. Appeals (2d cir.) 1975, U.S. Ct. Appeals (3d cir., D.C. cir.) 1983, U.S. Dist. Ct. (so. dist.) N.Y. 1984. Ptnr., co-chair labor and employment law dept. Kaye, Scholer, Fierman, Hays & Handler, N.Y.C. Planning com. NYU Ann. Nat. Conf. Labor, 1991-97. Contbr. articles to profl. jours. Mem. ABA (sect. labor and employment law 1975—, subcom. antitrust, RICO and labor rels. law), Assn. Bar City of N.Y. (sec. com. labor and employment law 1984-87), N.Y. State Bar (comml.-fed. litig. sect. co-chair labor and employment law com. 1995-97). Alternative dispute resolution, General civil litigation, Labor. Office: Kaye Scholer LLP 425 Park Ave New York NY 10022-3506

ZILLY, THOMAS SAMUEL, federal judge; b. Detroit, Jan. 1, 1935; s. George Samuel and Bernice M. (McWhinney) Z.; divorced; children: John, Peter, Paul, Luke; m. Jane Greller Noland, Oct. 8, 1988; stepchildren: Allison Noland, Jennifer Noland. BA, U. Mich., 1956; LLD, Cornell U., 1962. Bar: Wash. 1962, U.S. Ct. Appeals (9th cir.) 1962, U.S. Supreme Ct. 1976. Ptnr. Lane, Powell, Moss & Miller, Seattle, 1962-88; dist. judge U.S. Dist. Ct. (we. dist.) Wash., 1988—. Judge pro tem Seattle Mcpl. Ct., 1972-80; mem. adv. com. bankruptcy rules U.S. Judicial Conf. Contbr. articles to profl. jours. Mem. Cen. Area Sch. Council, Seattle, 1969-70; scoutmaster Thunderbird Dist. council Boy Scouts Am. Seattle, 1976-84; bd. dirs. East Madison YMCA. Served to lt. (j.g.) USN, 1956-59. Recipient Tuahku Dist. Service to Youth award Boy Scouts Am., 1983. Mem. ABA, Wash. State Bar Assn., Seattle-King County Bar Assn. (treas. 1979-80, trustee 1980-83, sec. 1983-84, 2d v.p. 1984-85, 1st v.p. 1985-86, pres. 1986-87). Office: US Dist Ct 410 US Courthouse 1010 5th Ave Seattle WA 98104-1189

ZIMMERLY, JAMES GREGORY, lawyer, physician; b. Longview, Tex., Mar. 25, 1941; s. George James and Irene Gertrude (Kohler) Z.; m. Nancy Carol Zimmerly, June 11, 1966; children; Mark, Scott, Robin; m. Johanna Bross Huffer, Feb. 14, 1991. BA, Gannon Coll., 1962; MD, U. Md., 1966, JD, 1969; MPH, Johns Hopkins U., 1968; LLD (hon.), Gannon U., 1998. Bar: Md. 1970, D.C. 1972, U.S. Ct. Mil. Appeals 1973, U.S. Supreme Ct. 1973. Ptnr. Acquisto, Asplen & Morstein, Ellicott City, Md., 1970—. Chmn. dept. legal medicine Armed Forces Inst. Pathology, 1971-91; prof. George Washington U., 1972-80; adj. prof. law Georgetown U. Law Ctr., 1972—, Antioch Sch. Law, 1977-80; assoc. prof. U. Md. Sch. Medicine, 1973—; mem. sci. adv. bd. Armed Forces Inst. Path., 1997—; cons. Dept. Def., Dept. Justice, HHS, VA, 1971-91. Editor: Legal Aspects of Medical Practice, 1978-88, Jour. Legal Medicine, 1975-78, Md. Med. Jour., 1977-88, Lawyers' Med. Ency., 1980-90. Chmn. bd. dirs. Balt. Rh Lab., 1984—; med. dir. Monumental Life Ins. Co., 1994—, Aegon Spl. Markets Group, Inc.; chmn. Am. Coll. Legal Med. Found., bd. dirs., 1996—. Fellow Am. Acad. Forensic Scis., Am. Coll. Legal Medicine (pres. 1980-81), Am. Coll. Preventive Medicine; mem. ABA, AMA, Md. Bar Assn., Am. Soc. on Law and Medicine, Am. Coll. Emergency Physicians, Md. Med. Soc. Health, Insurance, Personal injury. Home: 6300 Old National Pike Bluestone Overlook Boonsboro MD 21713 Office: Monumental Life Ins Co 2 E Chase St Baltimore MD 21202-2559 E-mail: JZimmerly@aegonusa.com

ZIMMERMAN, AARON MARK, lawyer; b. Syracuse, N.Y., Jan. 28, 1953; s. Julius and Sara (Lavine) Z. B.S., Syracuse U., 1974, J.D., 1976. Bar: N.Y. 1977, Pa. 1977, D.C. 1978, S.C. 1978, Fla. 1978, U.S. Dist. Ct. S.C. 1978, U.S. Dist. Ct. (no. dist.) N.Y. Corp. atty., asst. sec. Daniel Internat. Corp., Greenville, S.C., 1977-79; ptnr. Abend, Driscoll & Zimmerman, 1979-81; Zimmerman Law Office, Syracuse, 1981— . Bd. dirs. Syracuse Friends Ametuer Boxing, 1982-92. Mem. Am. Arbitration Assn. (arbitrator), Workers Compensation Com. N.Y. State Bar (exec. com. 1984—), Workers Compensation Assn. of Cen. N.Y. (charter mem., dir., treas. 1980-95), N.Y. State Bar, S.C. State Bar, D.C. State Bar, Fla. State Bar, ABA. Lodge: Masons. State civil litigation, Personal injury, Workers' compensation. Home: 602 Standish Dr Syracuse NY 13224-2018 Office: 117 S State St Syracuse NY 13202-1103

ZIMMERMAN, D(ONALD) PATRICK, lawyer; b. Albany, N.Y., Mar. 20, 1942; s. Bernard M. and Helen M. (Eshelman) Z. Student, Lawrenceville Sch., 1960; BA, Rollins Coll., 1964; JD, Dickinson Sch. Law, 1967. Bar: Pa. 1968, U.S. Supreme Ct. 1971. Atty. Legal Aid, 1968-69; pub. defender Lancaster County, Pa., 1969-72; pvt. practice Lancaster, 1974—. Instr. Ct. Common Pleas for Constables, 1976—; solicitor Lancaster County Dep. Sheriff Assn., 1977—, Lancaster County Constable Assn., 1975—; instr. sheriff's dept. Lancaster County for Dep. Sheriffs, 1978-85; of counsel to Dep. Sheriff Assn. Pa., 1979-81; spl. counsel Pa. State Constables Assn., 1981; chmn. Bd. Arbitrators Lancaster County, 1975-81; spl. counsel Legislative Com. to Constable Assn. Pa., 1982. Author: The Pennsylvania Landlord and Tenant Handbook, 1982, revised edit., 1993; editor (with J. Hatfield and A. Taylor) Pennsylvania Constable Handbook, 1998; contbr. articles to profl. jours. Mem. pastoral coun. St. Anthony's Cath. Ch., 1995-98. Recipient Ofcl. Commendation of Merit, Lancaster County Sheriff's Dept., 1979, Ofcl. Commendation of Merit, F.O.P. State Police Lodge 66, 1985, Disting. Svc. award, 1987. Mem. ABA, ATLA, Pa. Bar Assn., Acad. Family Mediators, Lancaster County Bar Assn., Lancaster County Constables Assn. (Outstanding Leadership award 1988, Disting. Svc. award as solicitor 1998, 25 Yrs. Dedicated Svc. award 2000). Family and matrimonial, Landlord-tenant, Personal injury. Office: 214 E King St Lancaster PA 17602-2977

ZIMMERMAN, GOLDA, lawyer, educator; b. Syracuse, N.Y., Sept. 25, 1949; d. Julius and Sara (Lavine) Z.; m. David C. Kapell, Sept. 18, 1977; children: Jermy S., Bethany R. BS in Edn., Boston U., 1971; MS in Ednl. Adminstrn., U. Kasn., 1974; JD, Syracuse U., 1980. Bar: N.Y. 1984, U.S. Dist. Ct. (no. dist.) N.Y. 1984, U.S. Tax Ct. 1984. Elem. tchr. St. John's Sch., Lawrence, Kans., 1971-73; adminstrv. asst. U. Kans., 1973-75; sr. sys. analyst, student data sys. Syracuse U., 1975-77; pvt. practice law Syracuse, 1984—. Adj. prof. adoption law Coll. Law Syracuse U., 1989-99; mem. bd. fisitors Syracuse U. Coll. Law, 1988—; spkr. various groups on adoption, real estate. Author: (with Sandra Crowther) Five Career Education Module for Pre-Service and In-Service Teachers, 1974, Adoption Law in N.Y., 1997; editor-in-chief Adoption Law in New York, 1997. Mem.: Am. Acad. Adoption Attys., Women's Bar Assn. State of N.Y. (N.Y. chpt. 1985—87, state dir. 1987—89), N.Y. State Bar Assn. (real property law sect., com. on problems affecting title and transfer, family law sect.), Onondaga County Bar Assn., Boston U. Alumni Assn. Democrat. Office: 711 E Genesee St # 200 Syracuse NY 13202-2155

ZIMMERMAN, JEAN, lawyer; b. Berkeley, Calif., Dec. 3, 1947; d. Donald Scheel Zimmerman and Phebe Jean (Reed) Doan; m. Gilson Berryman Gray III, Nov. 25, 1982; children: Charles Donald Buffum and Catherine Elisabeth Phebe (twins); stepchildren: Alison Travis, Laura Rebecca, Gilson Berryman. BSBA, U. Md., 1970; JD, Emory U., 1975. Bar: Ga. 1975, D.C. 1976, N.Y. 1980. Asst. mgr. investments FNMA, Washington, 1970-73; assoc. counsel Fuqua Industries Inc., Atlanta, 1976-79; assoc. Sage Gray Todd & Sims, N.Y.C., 1979-84; from assoc. counsel to sr. v.p., gen. counsel, sec. IBJ Whitehall Bank & Trust Co., 1994-99; sr. v.p., gen. counsel, sec., bd. dirs. IBJ Schroder Bus. Credit Corp., 1996-98, Innovest Capital Mgmt., Inc., N.Y.C., 1997-99; sr. v.p., gen. counsel, sec. Innovest Corp., 1997-99; gen. counsel, sec. ArrowSight, Inc. (formerly ParentWatch.com), 2001—. From asst. sec. to sr. v.p., gen. counsel, sec., bd. dirs. IBJ Whitehall Bus. Credit Corp., IBJ Whitehall Capital Corp., IBJ Whitehall Securities, Inc., Delphi Asset Mgmt., Inc., Innovest Asset Mgmt., Inc., N.Y.C., 1997-99; from asst. sec. to v.p., gen. counsel, sec. IBJ Schroder Internat. Bank, Miami, Fla., 1989-98; sr. v.p., gen. counsel, sec. Execution Svcs., N.Y.C., 1991-93. Founder, officer ERA Ga., Atlanta, 1977-79; bd. dirs. Ct. Apptd. Spl. Advs., 1988-94. Named one of Outstanding Atlantans, 1978-79; recipient Disting. Alumni award Emory U. Sch. Law, 1999. Mem. ABA, Assn. of Bar of City of N.Y., Ga. Assn. Women Lawyers (bd. dirs. 1977-79), Am. Soc. Corp. Secs., Inc., LWV, DAR, Assn. Emory Alumni (pres. 1999-2001, bd. govs. 2001—). Computer, General corporate.

ZIMMERMAN, MICHAEL DAVID, lawyer; b. Chgo., Oct. 21, 1943; s. Elizabeth Porter; m. Lynne Mariani (dec. 1994); children: Evangeline Albright, Alessandra Mariani, Morgan Elisabeth; m. Diane Hamilton, 1998. BS, U. Utah, 1966, JD, 1969. Bar: Calif. 1971, Utah 1978. Law clk. to Chief Justice Warren Earl Burger U.S. Supreme Ct., Washington, 1969-70; assoc. O'Melveny & Myers, L.A., 1970-76; assoc. prof. law U. Utah, 1976-78, adj. prof. law, 1978-84, 89-93; of counsel Kruse, Landa, Zimmerman & Maycock, Salt Lake City, 1978-80; spl. counsel Gov. of Utah, 1978-80; ptnr. Watkiss & Campbell, 1980-84; assoc. justice Supreme Ct. Utah, 1984-93, 98-00, chief justice, 1994-98; atty., mediator, arbitrator, of counsel Snell & Wilmer, 2000—. Co-moderator Justice Soc. Program of Snowbird Inst. for Arts and Humanities, 1991, 92, 93, 94, 95, 97, 98; moderator, Tanner lecture panel dept. philosophy U. Utah, 1994; faculty Judging Sci. Program Duke U., 1992, 93; bd. dirs. Conf. of Chief Justices, 1995-98. Note editor: Utah Law Rev., 1968-69; contbr. numerous articles to legal publs. Mem. Project 2000, Coalition for Utah's Future, 1985-96; trustee Hubert and Eliza B. Michael Found., 1994-98, Rowland-Hall St. Mark's Sch., 1997—, Utah Mus. Natural History Found., 1997—; bd. dirs. Summit Inst. for Arts and Humanities, 1998—, chair, 1999—; bd. dirs. Hansen Planetarium, 1998—, Snowbird Inst. for Arts & Humanities, 1989-98, Deer Valley Inst. for Arts & Humanities, 1996-98; bd. dirs. Kanzeon Zen Ctr., 1999—, chair, 2000—; bd. dirs., chair Utah Coun. on Conflict Resolution, 1999—; mem. Pvt. Adjudication Ctr., Duke U., 2000—; co-dir., chair, Registry of Ind. Sci. and Tech. Advisors, 2000—. Named Utah State Bar Appellate Ct. Judge of Yr., 1988; recipient Excellence in Ethics award, Ctr. for Study of Ethics, 1994, Disting. Svc. award Utah State Bar, 1998, Individual Achievement award Downtown Alliance, 1998; participant Justice and Soc. Program of Aspen Inst. for Humanistic Studies, 1988, co-moderator, 1989. Fellow Am. Bar Found.; mem. ABA (faculty mem. appellate judges' seminar 1993), Am. Law Inst., Utah Bar Assn., Salt Lake County Bar Assn., Jud. Conf. U.S. (adv. com. civil rules 1985-91), Utah Jud. Coun. (supreme ct. rep. 1986-91, chair 1994-98), Am. Inns of Ct. VII, Am. Judicature Soc. (bd. dirs. 1995—), Order of Coif, Phi Kappa Phi. Office: Snell & Wilmer 15 West South Temple Ste 1200 Salt Lake City UT 84101

ZIMMERMANN, JOHN JOSEPH, lawyer; b. Chgo., Apr. 30, 1939; s. John Joseph and Ernestine Elizabeth (Leuver) Z.; m. Alice Rose Farrell, July 4, 1964; children: John, Michael, Thomas, Margaret, Kathleen. A.B., DePaul U., 1962, J.D., 1967. Bar: Ill. 1967, U.S. Dist. Ct. (no. dist.) Ill. 1967, U.S. Ct. Appeals (7th cir. 1967. Ptnr. Bradtke & Zimmermann, Mt. Prospect, Ill., 1979— ; village atty. Village of Mt. Prospect, 1968-79, acting village mgr., 1969, 70-71; city atty. City of Wood Dale, Ill., 1975— ; spl. corp. counsel City of Highland Park, Ill., 1979-90, corp. counsel, 1990—; atty. Mt. Prospect Pub. Library, 1982— ; village atty. Village of Mettawa, Ill., 1983—; corp. coun. Village of Schiller Park, Ill., 1993—; dir. Joe Mitchell Buick/GMC Truck, Inc., Mt. Prospect, 1979— ; lectr. Ill. Inst. for Continuing Legal Edn., 1979— , Ill. State Bar Assn., 1988—. Mem. St. Paul of the Cross Sch. Bd. of Edn., Park Ridge, 1972-75, pres., 1974-75; mem. sponsoring com. Ann. Men's Prayer Breakfast, Park Ridge, 1979— . Recipient ofcl. commendation Village of Mt. Prospect, 1971, named hon. citizen, 1974; recipient certs. of appreciation Ill. Inst. Continuing Legal Edn., 1980, Chgo. Bar Assn., 1984, Ill. State Bar Assn., 1988. Mem. Nat. Inst. Mcpl. Law Officers (del., lectr., dir., trustee), Ill. State Bar Assn. (sec. 1983, mem. local govt. sect. council 1981-91), Ill. Home Rule Attys. Com. (charter mem., chmn. 1979), Chgo. Bar Assn. (chmn. local govt. com. 1983-84), Nat. Inst. Municipal Law Officers (bd. dirs. 1991—). Roman Catholic. Government contracts and claims, Real property. Home: 524 Vine Ave Park Ridge IL 60068-4148 Office: Bradtke & Zimmermann 1190 S Elmhurst Rd Mount Prospect IL 60056-4296

ZIMMETT, MARK PAUL, lawyer, educator; b. Waukegan, Ill., July 4, 1950; s. Nelson H. Zimmett and Roslyn (Yastrow) Zimmett Grodzin; m. Joan Robin Urken, June 11, 1972; children: Nora Helene, Lili Eleanor. BA, Johns Hopkins U., 1972; JD, NYU, 1975. Bar: N.Y. 1976, U.S. Dist. Ct. (so. and ea. dists.) N.Y. 1976, U.S. Dist. Ct. (no. dist.) Calif. 1980, U.S. Ct. Appeals (2d cir.) 1980, U.S. Supreme Ct. 1981, U.S. Ct. Appeals (5th cir.) 1986, U.S. Ct. Appeals (9th cir.) 1988. Assoc. Shearman & Sterling, N.Y.C., 1975-83, ptnr., 1984-90; adj. assoc. prof. internat. law NYU, 1986-88; lectr. internat. comml. litig. and arbitration Practicing Law Inst., 2000-01. Author: Letters of Credit, New York Practice Guide Business and Commerical Law, 1990; contbr. articles to profl. jours. Mem. ABA (subcom. on letters of credit, com. on uniform comml. code sect. bus. law), N.Y. State Bar Assn., Assn. of the Bar of the City of N.Y., N.Y. County Lawyers Assn. (com. on bus. bankruptcy law), Citizens Union. Democrat. Jewish. Federal civil litigation, State civil litigation, Private international. Office: 126 E 56th St New York NY 10022-3613

ZIMRING, FRANKLIN E. law educator, lawyer; b. 1942; BA, Wayne State U., 1963; JD, U. Chgo., 1967. Bar: Calif. 1968. Asst. prof. U. Chgo., 1967-69, assoc. prof., 1969-72, prof., 1972-85; co-dir. Ctr. for Studies in Criminal Justice, 1973-75, dir., 1975-86; prof. law dir. Earl Warren Legal Inst., Univ. Calif., Berkeley, 1985—. Author: (with Newton) Firearms and Violence in American Life, 1969; The Changing Legal World of Adolescence, 1982; (with Hawkins): Deterrence, 1973, Capital Punishment and the American Agenda, 1986, The Scale of Imprisonment, 1991, The Search for Rational Drug Control, 1992, Incapacitation: Penal Confinement and the Restraint of Crime, 1995, Crime is Not the Problem, 1997, American Youth Violence, 1998, Punishment and Democracy, 2001. Mem. Am. Acad. Arts and Scis. Office: U Calif Earl Warren Legal Inst Boalt Hall Berkeley CA 94720 E-mail: zimring@law.berkeley.edu

ZIMRING, STUART DAVID, lawyer; b. L.A., Dec. 12, 1946; s. Martin and Sylvia (Robinson) Z.; m. Eve Axelrad, Aug. 24, 1969 (div. 1981); m. Carol Grenert, May 24, 1981; children: Wendy Lynn Grenert, Joseph Noah, Matthew Kevin Grenert, Dov Shimon. BA in U.S. History, UCLA, 1968, JD, 1971. Bar: Calif. 1972, U.S. Dist. Ct. (cen. dist.) Calif. 1972, U.S. Dist. Ct. (no. dist.) Calif. 1984; U.S. Supreme Ct., 1994; cert. specialist in estate planning, probate and trust law. Assoc. Law Offices Leonard Smith, Beverly Hills, Calif., 1971-73; ptnr. Law Offices Smith & Zimring, 1973-76; assoc. Levin & Ballin, North Hollywood, 1976-77; prin. Levin, Ballin, Plotkin, Zimring & Goffin, A.P.C., 1978-91, Law Offices Stuart D. Zimring, North Hollywood, 1991—. Lectr. Los Angeles Valley Coll., Van Nuys, Calif., 1974-82. Author: Inter Vivos Trust Trustees Operating Manual, 1994, Durable Powers of Attorney for Health Care--A Practical Approach to an Intimate Document, 1995, Reverse Mortgages--An Update, 1996, Cultural and Religious Concerns in Drafting Advance Directives, 1996, Drafting for Multi-Cultural Diversity in Advance Directives, 2000. Bd. dirs. Bet Tzedek, Jewish Legal Svcs., L.A., 1975-88, chmn. legal svcs. com., 1978-82; bd. dirs. Brandeis-Bardin Inst., Simi Valley, Calif., 1976-

80; bd. dirs. Bur. Jewish Edn., L.A., 1973-88, chmn. com. on parent and family edn., 1985-87; trustee Adat Ari El Synagogue, L.A., 1982-2000; bd. dirs. Orgn. for the Needs of the Elderly, 1994, 1st v.p. 1995-97, pres., 1997-2001. Recipient Circle award Juvenile Justice Connection Project, L.A., 1989, Wiley W. Manuel award for pro bono legal svcs., 1994, 95, 96, 97, 98. Fellow Nat. Acad. Elder Law Attys. (pres. So. Calif. chpt. 1997, chair nat. tech. com., nat. bd. dirs. 1997—), Am. Coll. Trusts and Estates Coun.; mem. State Bar Calif., San Fernando Valley Bar Assn. (trustee 1979-86). Democrat. Avocations: music, collecting wine, travel, photography. Contracts commercial, Estate planning, Probate. Office: 12650 Riverside Dr North Hollywood CA 91607-3421 E-mail: zimzim@elderlawca.com

ZINCHENKO, VLADIMIR, law educator; b. Smela, Ukraine, Nov. 12, 1948; s. Nikolay Zinchenko and Valentine Starickova; m. Valentine Petrick, June 19, 1971; children: Artem, Alexander, Nikolay. LLM, Kharkiv Law Inst., Ukraine, 1975. Investigator Procurator's Office Sevastopol, Kremea, Ukraine, 1975-77; prof. Ukranian Law Acad., Kharkiv, 1978—; sr. ptnr. Vlad Arsani, 1991—. Mem. Internat. Bar Assn., Assn. Ukrainian Lawyers (chmn. Kharkiv's dept.). Office: Vlad Arsani Artema 43 Kharkiv 61002 Kharkivskaya Ukraine Fax: 143896. E-mail: zin@arsani.kharkiv.com

ZINK, WALTER EARL, II, lawyer; b. Lincoln, Nebr., Nov. 20, 1947; s. Walter Earl and Marjorie Ellen (Hull) Z.; m. Carol Ann Thomas, June 26, 1971; children: Walter, Robert, Carmela. BA in Edn., Nebr. Wesleyan U., 1970; JD with distinction, Nebr. Coll. Law, 1974. Bar: Nebr. 1974, U.S. Dist. Ct. Nebr. 1974. Ptnr. Baylor, Evnen, Curtiss, Grimit & Witt, Lincoln, 1974—. Adj. prof. law Nebr. Coll. Law, Lincoln, 1978-82; brig. gen., asst. adj. gen. Army, NEARNG. Bd. dirs. Camp Kitaki YMCA, Lincoln, 1980-92. Mem. ABA, Nebr. Bar Assn. (vice chmn. young lawyers 1982-83), Fedn. Inst. Corp. Counsel (workers' compensation chair 1995-97), Assn. Def. Trial Attys., Am. Bd. Trial Advocates, Internat. Assn. Def. Counsel (past chair employment law and membership com.), N.G. Assn. U.S., Res. Officers Assn. (v.p. Army 1984-85), Hillcrest Country Club (pres. 1994-96), Blue Key, Kappa Delta Pi. E-mial. Insurance, Military, Workers' compensation. Home: 1420 Broadmoore Dr Lincoln NE 68506-1511 Office: Baylor Evnen Curtiss Grimit & Witt 206 S 13th St Ste 1200 Lincoln NE 68508-2077 E-mail: wzink@baylorlaw.com

ZIPKIN, SHELDON LEE, lawyer, educator; b. Washington, June 10, 1951; s. Sol and Selma (Rumerman) Z.; m. Ellen Linda Reitman, July 1, 1973; children: Saul Moshe, Shana Chaya, Joel Mordechai, Abigail Deborah. Student, Hebrew U., Jerusalem, 1970-71; BA, U. Fla., 1973, MA, Cert. in Urban Studies, 1977; JD, Emory U., 1980. Bar: Ga. 1980, Fla. 1980, U.S. Dist. Ct. (so. dist.) Fla. 1983. Assoc. Gladstone Assocs., Miami, Fla., 1973-75; ptnr. Emory Assocs., Atlanta, 1979-80; dep. consumer adv. Metro Dade County, Miami, 1980-81; asst. pub. defender 11th Jud. Cir., 1981-83; ptnr. Roth & Zipkin, 1984-86; pvt. practice, 1986-87, 88-91; chief consumer litigation sect. Fla. Dept. Legal Affairs, Miami and Tallahassee, 1987-88; ptnr. Roth, Zipkin, Cove & Roth, Miami, 1991-95; pvt. practice law, 1995—. Adj. prof. law U. Miami, St. Thomas U., 1998—; pres., chmn. bd. Analytic Prognostication, Inc., Miami, 1988—. Pres., chmn. bd. dirs. Sta. WDNA-FM Pub. Radio, Miami, 1981-82; mem. consumer adv. coun. Fla. Hosp. Cost Containment Bd., Tallahassee, 1988-89. Fellow Soc. for Applied Anthropology; mem. ABA, ATLA, North Dade Bar Assn. (dir. 1997—), Dade County Bar Assn. (dir. 2000), Fla. Bar Assn. (consumer protection com. 1988—), Omicron Delta Kappa. Democrat. Jewish. Avocations: chess, sailing. General civil litigation, Criminal, General practice. Office: 2020 NE 163rd St North Miami Beach FL 33162-4927 E-mail: zipkin@aol.com

ZIPP, JOEL FREDERICK, lawyer; b. Shaker Heights, Ohio, Feb. 12, 1948; s. Jack David and Eleanor Adele Z.; m. Elizabeth Ann Frieden, Dec. 4, 1976; 1 child, Carlyn Leigh. BS, U. Wis., 1970, MS, 1972; JD, Case Western Res. U., 1975. Bar: Ohio 1975, D.C. 1976, U.S. Ct. Claims, 1976, U.S. Ct. Appeals (D.C. cir.) 1976, U.S. Ct. Appeals (5th cir.) 1979, U.S. Ct. Appeals (11th cir.) 1983, U.S. Supreme Ct. 1983. Trial atty. Fed. Energy Regulation Com., Washington, 1975-79, asst. dir. office of enforcement, 1979; assoc. Morley & Caskin, 1979-80; ptnr. Morley, Caskin & Generelly, 1981-98; mng. ptnr. Cameron McKenna LLP, 1998—; gen. counsel, sec. Portland Natural Gas Transmission Sys., 1993-99. Notes editor Energy Law Jour., 1990-98; bd. dirs. Found. of the Energy Law Jour., 1999—; contbr. articles to profl. jours. Bd. dirs. Westmoreland Children's Ctr., Washington, 1986-88, Found. of the Energy Law Jour., 2000-2001 Smithsonian fellow, 1969. Mem ABA, Energy Bar Assn. (bd. dirs. 1993-96, 2002—, past com. chair 1992, 93 ann. meetings, v.p. 1998-99, pres. 2000-01). Jewish. Avocations: skiing, running, bicycling. Administrative and regulatory, FERC practice, Public utilities. Home: 9216 Burning Tree Rd Bethesda MD 20817-2251 Office: Cameron McKenna LLP 2175 K St NW Washington DC 20037-1831 E-mail: jzipp@cmcklaw.com

ZIPP, RONALD DUANE, judge, priest, real estate broker; b. New Braunfels, Tex., Dec. 7, 1946; s. Nolan William and Irene Alyce (Stiba) Z.; children: Robert Andrew, Kristi Nicole; m. Saundra Zipp, Mar. 5, 1989. BBA, Tex. A&M U., 1968; JD, St. Mary U., San Antonio, 1971; MA, Oxford (Eng.) U., 1997. Bar: Tex. 1971, U.S. Dist. Ct. (so. dist.) Tex. 1972, U.S. Dist. Ct. (we. dist.) Tex. 1974, U.S. Ct. Appeals (5th cir.) 1973, U.S. Supreme Ct. 1974; ordained Anglican clergyman, 1998. Assoc. Kelley, Looney, Alexander & Hiester, Edinburg, Tex., 1971-73; ptnr. Pena, McDonald, Prestia & Zipp, 1973-81; pvt. practice New Braunfels, 1981-82, 89—; real estate broker. Judge Comal County (Tex.) Ct.-at-Law, New Braunfels, 1983—; adj. prof. San Antonio Coll.; real estate broker. Author local newspaper column; contbr. articles to profl. jours. Bd. dirs. New Braunfels Cmty. Svcs., 1992—, prse., 1981-83, 97-98, sec., 1994; bd. dirs. Child Welfare, vice chmn., 1981-82, chmn., 1982-83; dir. Drover-Comal County Fair Assn.; vol. H.O.S.T.S.; vice chmn. Folkfest, 1994, chmn., 1995—; pres. Cmty. Svc. Ctr., 1997; bd. dirs., trustee Sr. Citizens Ctr. and Found.; dir. Comal County Fair Assn.; mentor New Braunfels Ind. Sch. Dist.; clergyman, chancellor Anglican Diocese of S.W. Fellow Coll. of State Bar; mem. ABA, Greater New Braunfels C. of C. (legis. com., resources com., heritage com.), Tex. State Jr. Bar (criminal law com. 1975-76), Tex. Criminal Def. Lawyers' Assn. (bd. dirs. 1976-77, various coms.), Tex. Aggie Bar Assn. (charter), Comal County Bar Assn. (past pres.), Comal County A&M Club (pres., treas.), Hidalgo County Bar Assn. (treas. 1972-75), Opa and Kleine Opa of Wurstfest Assn. (chmn. Folkfest), Hidalgo County A&M Club (pres.), Elks, Kiwanis, Lions (sec. 1996, pres. 1997), Phi Delta Phi. Lutheran/Anglican. Office: 384 Landa St New Braunfels TX 78130-5401 Fax: (830) 629-5754. E-mail: rzipp@nbtx.com

ZIRINSKY, BRUCE R. lawyer; b. N.Y.C., Sept. 6, 1947; BS, Cornell U., 1969; JD, NYU, 1972. Bar: N.Y. 1973, U.S. Dist. Ct. (so. and ea. dists.) N.Y. 1973, U.S. Ct. Appeals (2d cir.) 1974, U.S. Ct. Appeals (1st cir.) 1980, U.S. Ct. Appeals (11th cir.) 1981, U.S. Ct. Appeals (5th cir.) 1986, U.S. Supreme Ct. 1991, U.S. Ct. Appeals (6th cir.), 1995. Mem. Weil, Gotshal & Manges, N.Y.C., 1999; ptnr. Cadwalader, Wickersham & Taft. Mem. ABA (sect. corp., banking and bus. law), N.Y. State Bar Assn. (mem. com. bankruptcy laws banking and bus. law sects. 1979—). Office: Cadwalader Wickersham & Taft 100 Maiden Ln New York NY 10038-4818 E-mail: bruce.zirinsky@cwt.com

ZISMAN, BARRY STUART, lawyer; b. N.Y.C., Sept. 18, 1937; s. Harry and Florence Rita (Tucker) Z.; m. Maureen Frances Brumond, Dec. 30, 1979; children: Michael Glenn, Marlene Ann. AB, Columbia U., 1958, JD, 1961. Bar: D.C. 1962, N.Y. 1965, Tex. 1986, U.S. Dist. Ct. (ea. and so. dists.) N.Y. 1967, U.S. Ct. Appeals (D.C. cir.) 1967, U.S. Dist. Ct. (no. and so. dists.) Tex. 1986, U.S. Ct. Appeals (5th cir.) 1988, U.S. Supreme Ct. 1967. With U.S. Govt., 1962-66; pvt. practice Syosset, N.Y., 1966-71; sr. counsel CBS Inc., N.Y.C., 1972-75; asst. gen. counsel, asst. sec. M. Lowenstein & Sons, 1975-79; gen. counsel Grumman Allied Indsl. Inc., Bethpage, N.Y., 1979-83; asst. gen. counsel Grumman Corp., 1982-83; sr. atty. FDIC, Dallas, 1984-87; of counsel Arter & Hadden, 1987-88, ptnr., 1988, Winstead, McGuire, Sechrest & Minick, Dallas, 1988-90, Arter & Hadden, Dallas and Washington, 1990-91, Rubinstein & Perry, Dallas, 1991-93, The Zisman Law Firm, P.C., Dallas, 1993—. Advisor in field; vice-chmn. Assn. of Bank and Thrift Receivership Coun. Editor and author: Banks and Thrifts: Government Enforcement and Receivership Law, 1991. With U.S. Army, 1961-62. Banking, General civil litigation, General corporate. Home: 905 Murl Dr Irving TX 75062-4441 Office: 200 Renaissance Pl 1412 Main St Fl 23 Dallas TX 75202 E-mail: zislaw@aol.com

ZISSU, ROGER L. lawyer; b. Oceanside, N.Y., Feb. 16, 1939; s. Leonard Zissu and Ruth Zissu Kahn; married. Student, Sorbonne U., Paris, 1958-59, Inst. d'Etudes Politiques, 1958-59; AB summa cum laude, Dartmouth Coll., 1960; LLB cum laude, Harvard U., 1963. Bar: N.Y. 1963, U.S. Dist. Ct. (ea. and so. dists.) N.Y. 1965, U.S. Dist. Ct. (no. dist.) N.Y. 1989, U.S. Ct. Appeals (2d cir.) 1965, U.S. Tax Ct. 1972, U.S. Supreme Ct. 1974. Law clk. U.S. Dist. Ct. Ea. Dist. N.Y., Bklyn., 1963-65; assoc. Davis, Polk & Wardwell, N.Y.C., 1965-70; corp. counsel Vornado, Inc., Garfield, N.J., 1970-73; assoc. Cowan, Liebowitz & Latman PC, N.Y.C., 1973, ptnr., 1974-90, Weiss, David, Fross, Zelnick & Lehrman PC, N.Y.C., 1990-97, Fross, Zelnick, Lehrman & Zissu PC, N.Y.C., 1997—. Lectr. in field. Class agt. Dartmouth Coll. Alumni Fund, Hanover, N.H., 1960—; bd. dirs. Vol. Lawyers for the Arts, 1987-90. Mem. ABA, Assn. of Bar of City of N.Y. (chmn. copyright and literary property com. 1989-92, judiciary com. 1995-98), N.Y. State Bar Assn., Copyright Soc. U.S.A. (trustee 1981, 83-86, 92—, treas. 1988-90, v.p. 1990-92, pres. 1992-94), Dartmouth Club N.Y., Phi Beta Kappa, Alpha Delta Phi. Avocations: swimming, tennis, cross country skiing. Federal civil litigation, State civil litigation, Trademark and copyright. Office: Fross Zelnick Lehrman & Zissu PC 866 United Nations Plz New York NY 10017-1822

ZITO, FRANK R. lawyer, accountant; b. Haverhill, Mass., Mar. 14, 1946; s. Dan and Anne (Grieco) Z.; m. Carol S. Tandy, Sept. 19, 1976. BS, U. Mass., 1969; JD, Suffolk Law Sch., 1972; LLM, NYU, 1973. Bar: Mass. 1972, U.S. Supreme Ct. 1982, U.S. Tax Ct. 1984. Gen. mgr. Sun Ray Baking Co., 1973-79; atty., mem. Tofias Fleishman Shapiro & Co. P.C., Cambridge, Mass., 1979—. Contbr. articles to law jour. Mem. ABA (mem. forum com. 1982-84), Mass. Bar Assn., Am. Inst. CPA's, Mass Soc. CPA's. Construction, Family and matrimonial, Finance. Home: 8 Livermore Rd Belmont MA 02478-4516

ZITZMANN, KELLY C. lawyer, consultant; b. Doylestown, Pa., Dec. 28, 1968; d. John F. Carr, Jr. and Elaina M. McCartney; m. Oliver A. M. Zitzmann, Oct. 28, 1995. AB, Cornell U., 1990; JD cum laude, Bklyn. Law Sch., 1993. Bar: N.Y. 1994. Assoc. Skadden, Arps, et al., N.Y.C., 1993-97; gen. counsel Erie Plastics, Corry, Pa., 1997-98; pres. Zitzmann Cons., LLC, Redding, Conn., 1998—. Recipient Thurgood Marshall award Assn. Bar City N.Y., 1998 Mem. ABA, N.Y. State Bar Assn. Republican. Episcopalian. Avocations: cycling, skiing, scuba diving. Contracts commercial, General corporate, General practice. Office: Zitzmann Cons LLC 35 Hill Rd Redding CT 06896-2314

ZIVIN, NORMAN H. lawyer; b. Chgo., Aug. 10, 1944; s. Alfred E. and Irene (Scher) Z.; m. Lynn F., Dec. 27, 1967; children: Allison, Stephen, Michael. E.M. in Mining Engring., Colo. Sch. Mines, 1965; JD cum laude, Columbia U., 1968. Bar: N.Y. 1968, Ill. 1970, U.S. Supreme Ct. 1975. Assoc. Cooper & Dunham LLP (and predecessor firms), N.Y.C., 1968-70, 71-75, ptnr., 1976—. Mem. Bd. Ethics New Castle (N.Y.), 1974-79. Mem. ABA, Assn. of Bar of City of N.Y., Am. Intellectual Property Law Assn., N.Y. Intellectual Property Law Assn., Soc. Mining Engrs., U.S. Trademark Assn., Fed. Bar Coun., Town Club of Newcastle (pres. 1982-84). Federal civil litigation, Patent, Trademark and copyright. Home: 3 Valley Ln Chappaqua NY 10514-2002 Office: Cooper & Dunham LLP Ste 2200 1185 Avenue Of The Americas New York NY 10036-2615 E-mail: nzivin@cooperdunham.com

ZLAKET, THOMAS A. state supreme court chief justice; b. May 30, 1941; AB in Polit. Sci., U. Notre Dame, 1962; LLB, U. Ariz., 1965. Bar: Ariz. 1965, U.S. Dist. Ct. Ariz. 1967, U.S. Ct. Appeals (9th cir.) 1969, Calif. 1976. Atty. Lesher Scruggs Rucker Kimble & Lindamood, Tucson, 1965-68, Maud & Zlaket, 1968-70, Estes Browning Maud and Zlaket, 1970-73, Slutes Estes Zlaket Sakrison & Wasley, 1973-82, Zlaket & Zlaket, 1982-92; judge pro tempore Pima County (Ariz.) Superior Ct., 1983—; justice Ariz. Supreme Ct., 1992—, vice chief justice, 1996, chief justice, 1997—. Fellow Am. Coll. Trial Lawyers, Am. Bar Found., Ariz. Bar Found.; mem. ABA, Pima County Bar Assn., Am. Bd. Trial Advocates, Ariz. Coll. Trial Advocacy, U. Ariz. Law Coll. Assn., Ariz. Law Rev. Assn. Office: Arizona Supreme Ct 400 W Congress St Tucson AZ 85701-1374*

ZOBEL, RYA WEICKERT, federal judge; b. Germany, Dec. 18, 1931; AB, Radcliffe Coll., 1953; LLB, Harvard U., 1956. Bar: Mass. 1956, U.S. Dist. Ct. Mass., 1956, U.S. Ct. Appeals (1st cir.) 1967. Assoc. Hill & Barlow, Boston, 1967-73, Goodwin, Procter & Hoar, Boston, 1973-76, ptnr., 1976-79; judge U.S. Dist. Ct. Mass., 1979—; dir. Fed. Jud. Ctr., Washington, 1995-99. Mem. ABA, Boston Bar Assn., Am. Bar Found., Mass. Bar Assn., Am. Law Inst. Office: US District Ct 1 Courthouse Way Boston MA 02210-3002

ZOBELL, KARL, lawyer; b. La Jolla, Calif., Jan. 9, 1932; s. Claude E. and Margaret (Harding) ZoB.; m. Barbara Arth, Nov. 22, 1968; children: Bonnie, Elizabeth, Karen, Claude, Mary. Student, Utah State U., 1949-51, Columbia U., 1951-52, AB, 1953, student of law, 1952-54; JD, Stanford U., 1958. Bar: Calif., 1959. Assoc., lawyer Gray, Cary, Ames and Frye, San Diego, 1959-64, ptnr., lawyer, 1964—, chmn., 1989-90; dir., officer San Diego Digital Multimedia Assn., 1994. Bd. dirs., founder La Jolla (Calif.) Bank and Trust Co.; v.p. bd. dirs. Geisel-Seuss Enterprises, Inc. Trustee La Jolla Town Coun., 1962-87, chmn. bd. trustees, 1967-68, pres. 1976-77, 80-81, v.p., 1986-87; trustee La Jollans Inc., 1964-80, founder, 1964, pres. 1965-68, 73-76, 78-79, Dr. Seuss Found., 1992—, James C. Copley Charitable Found., 1992—; mem. charter rev. com. City San Diego, 1968, 73; chmn. City of San Diego Planning Commn., 1988-93; trustee La Jolla Mus. Art, 1964-72, San Diego Mus. Contemporary Art, 1990-92; pres. 1967-70, bd. dirs Scripps Meml. Hosp. Found., 1980-84, bd. overseers, Stanford Law Sch., 1977-80, U. Calif., San Diego, 1974-76. Served to lt. USCG, 1954-57. Fellow Am. Coll. Trust and Estate Counsel; mem. ABA, Calif. Bar, La Jolla Beach and Volleyball Club (pres. 1982—), La Jolla Beach and Tennis Club, Lambda Alpha. Republican. Land use and zoning (including planning), Probate, Real property. Home: Po Box 1 1555 Coast Walk La Jolla CA 92037-3731 Office: Gray Cary Ames & Frye 1200 Prospect St Ste 575 La Jolla CA 92037-3645

ZOBRIST, DUANE HERMAN, lawyer; b. Salt Lake City, Sept. 11, 1940; s. Herman A. and Virginia (Rasmussen) Z.; m. Sharon Ann Jones, June 26, 1964; children— Duane, Melinda, Darren, Brooke, Lindsey. B.A., U. Utah, 1965; J.D., U. So. Calif., 1968. Bar: Calif. 1968. Assoc. Hill-Farrer & Burrill, Los Angeles, 1968-74; sr. ptnr., founder Zobrist-Vienna & McCullough, Los Angeles; ptnr. Carlsmith Ball Wichman Murray Case Mukai & Ichiki. Bd. dirs. San Gabriel Valley council Boy Scouts Am., 1982—, v.p., 1982-85; chmn. maj. gifts Pasadena Boy's Choir, Calif., 1983-85. Mem. Los Angeles Philharmonic Men's Com. Mem. Los Angeles Area C. of C., Calif. State Bar, ABA, Fgn. Law Assn. So. Calif., Fgn. Trade Assn., U.S.-Mex. C. of C. (pres. 1986—, founder, pres. Pacific chpt. 1981-83, bd. dirs., exec. com. 1981—), Brazil Calif. Trade Assn. (trustee 1974—, pres., 1979-81), U. So. Calif. Law Alumni Assn. (pres. 1977-78), U. So. Calif. Legion Lex (trustee 1981-84). Republican. Mem. Ch. of Jesus Christ of Latter-day Saints. Club: Jonathan. Office: Carlsmith Ball Wichman Murray Case Mukai & Ichiki 555 S Flower St Los Angeles CA 90071-2300

ZOFFER, DAVID B. lawyer, consultant; b. N.Y.C., 1947; BA, Hofstra U., 1969; JD, Fordham U., 1972. Bar: N.Y. 1973, U.S. Dist. Ct. (so. and ea. dists.) N.Y. 1974, U.S. Ct. Appeals (2d cir.) 1974, U.S. Supreme Ct. 1978, N.C. 2000; cert. mediator. Asst. dist. atty. frauds bur. N.Y. County Dist. Atty.'s Office, N.Y.C., 1972-76; spl. asst. atty. gen. State of N.Y., 1976-79; sr. v.p. USAU, Inc. (subs. Gen. Reins. Corp.), 1979-90; exec. v.p. Internat. Claims and Litig. Mgmt. Group Inc., Chapel Hill, N.C., 1990—. Mem. faculty Fordham Crisis Mgmt. Strategies Program, N.Y.C., 1994, 7th Annual Tenn. Corp. Counsel Inst., Nashville, 1999, 5th Annual FICC Litig. Mgmt. Coll., Evanston, Ill., 1999; litig. strategies panelist Am. Trucking Assns., New Orleans, 1998; lectr. in field. Mem. Fordham Urban Law Jour., 1971; contbr. articles to profl. jours. Mem. ABA (moderator and chmn. tort and ins. practice conf. 1997, 98, 99), N.Y. Bar Assn., Fedn. Ins. and Corp. Counsel, Def. Rsch. Inst., Am. Corp. Counsel Assn. (chief legal officers' club 1998—), N.C. Bar Assn. (task force on Multidisciplinary practice), N. Hempstead Country Club, Carolina Club, Pi Gamma Mu. Aviation, Insurance, Personal injury. Home: 150 Meadow Run Dr Chapel Hill NC 27514-7786 Office: ICALM Group 6320 Quadrangle Dr Ste 230 Chapel Hill NC 27514-7815 Fax: 919-419-7366. E-mail: dbz@icalmgroup.com

ZOLA, MICHAEL S. lawyer; b. Madison, Wis., Dec. 15, 1942; s. Emanuel and Harriet (Sher) Z.; 1 son, Emanuel David. BS cum laude, U. Wis., 1964; LLB, Columbia U., 1967. Bar: D.C. 1968, Wis. 1968, Calif. 1969, Hawaii 1981, U.S. Dist. Ct. Hawaii 1981, U.S. Dist. Ct. (we. dist.) Wis. 1968, U.S. Dist. Ct. (no. dist.) Calif. 1969, U.S. Ct. Appeals (9th cir.) 1969. Law clk. to judge U.S. Dist. Ct. (we. dist.) Wis., 1967-68; mng. atty. San Francisco Neighborhood Legal Assistance Found., San Francisco, 1968-70; sole practice, Calistoga, Calif., 1970-73; directing atty. Mendocino Legal Services, Ukiah, Calif., 1973-76; state chief of legal services State of Calif., Sacramento, 1976-78, dep. state pub. defender, State of Calif., 1978-79; sole practice, Kailua-Kona, Hawaii, 1980—. Chmn. Mendocino County Dem. Cen. Com., Ukiah, 1975-76; pres. Kona Beth Shalom Congregation, 1991-94; Kona Salvation Army adv. bd., 1993-98. Reginald Heber Smith Poverty Law fellowship, 1968-70. Mem. Hawaii Assn. Criminal Def. Lawyers (bd. dirs. 1989, 91—), Nat. Assn. Criminal Def. Lawyers, Legal Aid Soc. Hawaii (bd. dirs. 1985-86), Rotary Club Kona (pres. 1998-99). Criminal, Family and matrimonial, Personal injury. Office: 75-5744 Alii Dr Ste 223 Kailua Kona HI 96740-1740

ZORIE, STEPHANIE MARIE, lawyer; b. Walla Walla, Wash., Mar. 18, 1951; d. Albert Robert and L. Ruth (Land) Z.; m. Francis Benedict Buda, Apr. 18, 1981 (div. 1985). BA, U. Fla., 1974, JD, 1978. Bar: N.Mex. 1991, Fla. 1978, U.S. Dist. Ct. (so. and mid. dists.) Fla. 1979, U.S. Ct. Appeals (5th cir.) 1979, U.S. Tax Ct. 1980, U.S. Ct. Customs and Patent Appeals 1980, U.S. Customs Ct. 1980, U.S. Ct. Mil. Appeals 1980, U.S. Ct. Claims 1981, U.S. Ct. Internat. Trade 1981, U.S. Ct. Appeals (11th cir.) 1981, U.S. Ct. Appeals (fed. cir.) 1982, U.S. Supreme Ct. 1988; cert. civil ct. mediator Fla. Supreme Ct.; cert. family mediator, N.Mex. Assoc. Richard Hardwich, Coral Gables, Fla., 1978-79, Brown, Terrell & Hogan P.A., Jacksonville, 1979-80, Dorsey, Arnold & Nichols, Jacksonville, 1980-81; sole practice, 1981-84; ptnr. Blakeley & Zorie P.A., Orlando, 1985-86; sole practice, 1986—, Santa Fe. Owner Coyote Cody Co., 1991. Recipient Rep. Claude Pepper award, 1978. Mem. John Marshall Bar Assn., Spanish-Am. Law Students Assn., Phi Alpha Delta (local sec.-treas. 1978-79). Avocations: water sports, needlework, cooking. State civil litigation, Family and matrimonial, Personal injury. Office: PO Box 2898 Santa Fe NM 87504-2898 also: PO Box 372118 Satellite Beach FL 32937-0118

ZORNOW, DAVID M. lawyer; b. N.Y.C., Mar. 31, 1955; s. Jack and Marion (Gilden) Z.; m. Martha Malkin, July 21, 1985; children: Samuel Morris, Hannah Jane, Ethan Lewis. AB summa cum laude, Harvard U., 1976; JD, Yale U., 1980. Bar: N.Y. 1981, U.S. Ct. Appeals (3d cir.) 1982, U.S. Dist. Ct. (so. dist.) N.Y. 1983, U.S. Ct. Appeals (2d cir.) 1984, U.S. Dist. Ct. D.C. 1989, U.S. Ct. Appeals (D.C. cir.) 1989, U.S. Dist. Ct. Ariz. 1990, U.S. Dist. Ct. (ea. dist.) N.Y. 1993. Law clerk to Judge Herbert J. Stern U.S. Dist. Ct. N.J., Newark, 1980-82; assoc. Kramer Levin Kamin Nessen & Frankel, N.Y.C., 1982-83; asst. U.S. atty. so. dist. N.Y. U.S. Atty.'s Office, 1983-87; assoc. counsel Office Ind. Counsel-Iran/Contra Investigation, Washington, 1987-89; ptnr. Skadden Arps Slate Meagher & Flom LLP, N.Y.C., 1989—. Chmn. N.Y.C. Civilian Complaint Rev. Bd., 1994-96; vis. faculty Trial Advocacy Workshop Harvard Law Sch., Cambridge, Mass., 1988. Mem. ABA (com. on white collar crime), Fed. Bar Coun., Assn. of Bar of City of N.Y., N.Y. Coun. Def. Lawyers. Criminal. Office: Skadden Arps Slate Meagher & Flom LLP 4 Times Sq Fl 33 New York NY 10036-6595 E-mail: dzornow@skadden.com

ZOTALEY, BYRON LEO, lawyer; b. Mpls., Mar. 18, 1944; s. Leo John and Tula (Koupis) Z.; m. Theresa L. Cassady, Sept. 7, 1969; children: Nicole, Jason, Krisanthy. BA in Psychology, U. Minn., 1966; MATC, U. St. Thomas, St. Paul, 1968; JD, William Mitchell Coll. of Law, 1970. Bar: Minn. 1970, U.S. Dist. Ct. Minn. 1971, U.S. Ct. Appeals (8th cir.) 1972, U.S. Supreme Ct. 1975. Pres. LeVander, Zotaley & Vander Linden, Mpls., 1970-99, Zotaley Law Offices, Ltd., Hopkins, Minn., 1999—. Arbitrator Minn. No Fault Panel, 1974—; cons. Marthe Properties, Mpls., 1980-90, Theron Properties, Mpls., 1985—. Bd. dirs. Minn. Consumer Alliance, 1994-95; mem. adv. bd. Benilde-St. Margaret's Jr. H.s., 1993-95; bd. trustees St. Mary's Greek Orthodox Ch. Mpls., 1997—, v.p., 1998, pres., 1999—. Mem. ABA, ATLA, Minn. Bar Assn., Hennepin County Bar Assn., Minn. Trial Lawyers Assn. (chmn. Amicus Curiae com. 1980-87, bd. govs. 1982-93, mem. exec. com. 1987-89, emeritus, 1994—). E-mail: b. General corporate, Personal injury, Probate. Home: 5504 Parkwood Ln Edina MN 55436-1728 Office: 310 Wells Fargo Bank Bldg 1011 1st St S Hopkins MN 55343-9413 Fax: 952-933-9034. E-mail: zotaley@worldnet.att.net

ZUBEL, ERIC LOUIS, lawyer; b. Detroit, Nov. 14, 1943; s. Stanley and Virginia (Poplawski) Z.; m. Catherine Hodges, Oct. 6, 1973; children: Conrad, Roland, Kristin. AB, U. Mich., 1966; JD, Golden Gate U., 1971, LLM in Internat. Law with highest hons., 1998. Bar: Nev. 1973, U.S. Dist. Ct. Nev. 1973, U.S. Ct. Appeals (9th cir.) 1973, U.S. Supreme Ct. 1976. Law clk. 8th Jud. Ct., Las Vegas, 1971-73; sole practitioner, 1972—. Contbr. articles to profl. jours. Mem. ABA, ATLA, Nev. Trial Lawyers (bd. govs. 1981-83). Federal civil litigation, State civil litigation, Private international. Home: 13 Windcrest Ln South San Francisco CA 94080-7307 Office: 1900 E Flamingo Rd Ste 296 Las Vegas NV 89119-5116

ZUCKER, DAVID CLARK, lawyer; b. St. Louis, July 29, 1946; s. Clark S. and Georgia L. (Sellers) Z.; m. Karin Wells Waugh, July 10, 1971 (div. Sept. 1985); 1 child, William W.; m. Charlotte Denton, Feb. 8, 1986. B.A., U. Mo., 1968, J.D., 1971; postgrad. Judge Advocate Gen.'s Sch., Charlottesville, Va., 1977-78, Armed Forces Staff Coll., 1981-82. Bar: Mo. 1971, U.S. Ct. Mil. Appeals 1971, U.S. Ct. Appeals (fed. cir.) 1983, U.S. Supreme Ct, 1974, Calif. 1989. Commd. 2d lt. U.S. Army, 1968, advanced through grades to col., 1988, ret., 1988; chief mil. justice, Ft. Leavenworth, Kans., 1971-74; trial atty. Office of Army Chief Trial Atty., Falls Church, Va., 1974-77; dep. chief adminstrv. law Hdqrs. U.S. Army Europe, Heidelberg, W. Ger., 1978-80, internat. logistics atty. contract law, U.S. Army,

Heidelberg, Fed. Rep. of Germany, 1980-81; litigation atty. Office of Judge Advocate Gen., Washington, 1982; chief trial team III, Office of Chief Trial Atty. Hdqrs. Dept. Army, Falls Church, 1982-86; chief, contract law div., Gilbert A. Cuneo prof. govt. contract law, U.S. Army JAG Sch., Charlottesville, Va., 1986-88; sr. staff counsel Hughes Aircraft Co., L.A., 1988—. Mem. ABA, Am. Trial Lawyers Assn., Assn. U.S. Army, Judge Advocates Assn. (bd. dirs. 1983-86), Mo. Bar Assn., Phi Alpha Delta (chpt. vice justice 1969-70). Federal civil litigation, Government contracts and claims, Military. Home: 6 Ringbit Rd E Rolling Hills Estates CA 90274-5242 Office: Hughes Aircraft Co PO Box 956 El Segundo CA 90245-0956

ZUCKER, HOWARD, lawyer; b. N.Y.C., June 21, 1952; s. Morris Milton and Sarah Shirley (Spector) Z.; m. Lynn Carol Bierschenk; children: Lauren Heather, Erica Rachael, Monica Juliet. Student, London Sch. Econs., 1973; BS in Econs. summa cum laude, U. Pa., 1973, JD, 1977. Bar: N.Y. 1978. Ptnr. Hawkins, Delafield & Wood, N.Y.C., 1977—. Author: ABCs of Housing Bonds, 5th edit., 1993. Mem. ABA (chmn. pub. fin. com. of state and local govt. law sect. 1996-98), N.Y. State Bar Assn., Nat. Assn. Bond Lawyers (bd. dirs. 1994-2001, pres.-elect 1998-99, pres. 1999-2000), Omicron Delta Epsilon. Municipal (including bonds), Securities, State and local taxation. Office: Hawkins Delafield & Wood 67 Wall St Fl 11 New York NY 10005-3155

ZUCKERMAN, HERBERT LAWRENCE, lawyer; b. Newark, June 11, 1928; s. David and Adele Zuckerman; m. Janet Albert, Sept. 10, 1950; children: Julia, Elizabeth, William. BSBA, Lehigh U., 1949; JD, Rutgers U., 1953. Acct. Zuckerman & Black, Newark, 1949-56; pvt. practice law, 1956-71; ptnr. Zuckerman, Aronson & Horn, 1971-81; ptnr., v.p. Sills Cummis, 1981-98, sr.counsel, 1998—. Bd. dirs. Am. Jewish Com., 1990—; vol. The Hospice, Glen Ridge, N.J., 1985—. Fellow Coll. of Tax Counsel; mem. ABA, N.J. Bar Assn., Fed. Bar Assn., Essex County Bar Assn., Mental Health Assn. (bd. dirs. 1997—), Mensa. Avocations: tennis, music, theater, opera, reading. Estate taxation, Taxation, general, State and local taxation. Office: Sills Cummis 1 Riverfront Plz Fl 10 Newark NJ 07102-5401 E-mail: hzuckerman@sillscummis.com

ZUCKERMAN, RICHARD KARL, lawyer; b. Bay Shore, N.Y., Feb. 23, 1960; s. Jack Irwin and Dorothy Ann (Sugarman) Z.; m. Jackie Lynn Lachow, Aug. 25, 1984. BA summa cum laude, SUNY, Stony Brook, 1981; JD, Columbia U., 1984. Bar: N.Y. 1985, U.S. Dist. Ct. (ea. and so. dists.) N.Y. 1987. Assoc. Rains & Pogrebin, P.C., Mineola, N.Y., 1984-91, ptnr., 1992—. Editor: Discipline and Discharge in Arbitration, 1998, Discipline and Discharge in Arbitration, 1st supplement, 2000, N.Y. State Public Sector Labor and Employment Law, 2d edit., 1st supplement, 2000; contbg. author: N.Y. State Public Sector Law and Employment Law, 1998; contbr. articles to profl. newsletters. Chairperson ann. fund. SUNY, Stony Brook, 1986-91, bd. dirs. Alumni Assn., 1990-96. Mem. ABA, N.Y. State Bar Assn. (chair labor and employment law sect. com. on govt. employee rels. law 1998—, chair mcpl. law sect., employment rels. com. 1998—, mem. exec. com. labor and employment law sect, 1998—, mem. exec. com. mcpl. law sect., 2001—). Nassau County Bar Assn., N.Y. State Assn. Sch. Attys. (bd. dirs.). Education and schools, Labor. Home: 3187 Ann St Baldwin NY 11510-4509 Office: Rains & Pogrebin PC 210 Old Country Rd Mineola NY 11501-4288

ZUETEL, KENNETH ROY, JR. lawyer; b. L.A., Apr. 5, 1954; s. Kenneth Roy Sr. and Adelle Francis (Avant) Z.; m. Cheryl Kay Morse, May 29, 1976; children: Bryan, Jarid, Christopher, Lauren. BA, San Diego State U., 1974; JD, U. San Diego, 1978. Bar: Calif. 1978 U.S. Ct. Appeals (9th cir.) 1979, U.S. Dist. Ct. (ctrl. dist.) Calif. 1979, U.S. Dist. Ct. (so. and no. dists.) Calif. 1980, U.S. Dist. Ct. (ea. dist.) 1981. Clk. to fed. Judge Martin Pence U.S. Dist. Ct. Hawaii, Honolulu, 1978-79; assoc. litigation Buchalter, Nemer, L.A., 1979-83, Thelen, Marrin, L.A., 1983-88; ptnr. Zuetel & Torigian, Pasadena, Calif., 1988—. Superior ct. arbitrator L.A. Superior Ct., 1982-90, superior ct. settlement officer, 1988-93; judge pro temp L.A. Mcpl. Ct., 1983-94, L.A. Superior Ct., 1989-94; guest lectr. Loyola U. Sch. Law, 1986-95; CEB lectr. Author: Civil Procedure Before Trial, 1992; cons. editor: Cal. Civ. Proc., 1992; contbr. articles to profl. jours. Recipient Recognition award L.A. (Calif.) Bd. Suprs., 1988. Mem. State Bar Calif. (mem. adv. com. continuing edn. 1985-88, trial practice subcom. 1985-88, disciplinary examiner 1986), Los Angeles County Bar Assn. (chair trial atty. project 1982-83, mem. L.A. del. conf. of dels. 1986-96, chair L.A. de. conf. of dels. 1995, exec. com. barristers 1984-88, superior ct. com. 1985-88, civil practice com. 1992-94, exec. com. litigation sect. 1989-90), Pasadena Bar Assn., Inns of Ct. (barrister L.A. chpt. 1991-92), Phi Beta Kappa, Phi Kappa Phi, Phi Alpha Theta, Pi Sigma Alpha. Republican. Presbyterian. General civil litigation, Health. Home: 567 Willow Springs Ln Glendora CA 91741-2974 Office: Zuetel & Torigian 215 N Marengo Ave Ste 195 Pasadena CA 91101-1530 E-mail: ztlaw@pacbell.net

ZUHDI, NABIL (BILL ZUHDI), lawyer, litigator, consultant, producer; b. N.Y.C., June 8, 1955; s. Nazih and Lamya Zuhdi; child from previous marriage: Noah; m. Darla L. Boyd, May 19, 1984. BS, U. Ctrl. Okla., 1979; JD, U. Okla., 1982. Bar: Okla. 1982, U.S. Dist. Ct. (we. dist.) Okla. 1982, U.S. Ct. Appeals (10th cir.) 1989, U.S. Supreme Ct. 1990, Tex. 1991, U.S. Dist. Ct. (no. dist.) Tex. 1998. Assoc. Linn & Helms, Oklahoma City, 1982-85; ptnr. Zuhdi & Denum, 1985-87; assoc. Law Firm Darrell Keith, Ft. Worth, 1994; pvt. practice Oklahoma City, 1987—. Pres. Zuhdi Entertainment Group, Inc., Okla. City, 1986—, Amerisphere, Inc., Okla. City, 1996—; criminal justice act panel We. Dist. Okla., 1985—, spl. death penalty habeas corpus panel, 1998, criminal justice act voluntary panel No. Dist. Tex., 1998. Producer: (concerts) Frank Sinatra, Julio Igleas. Patron Okla. Heart Ctr., Oklahoma City, 1994—. Mem. ABA, ATLA, State Bar Tex., Oklahoma Bar Assn., Oklahoma County Bar Assn., Phi Alpha Delta, Alpha Chi. Republican. Avocations: boxing, film, prodr. of concerts including Frank Sinatra and others. Federal civil litigation, Criminal, Personal injury. Office: PO Box 1077 Oklahoma City OK 73101-1077

ZUKERMAN, MICHAEL, lawyer; b. Bklyn., Oct. 3, 1940; s. Charles Morris and Gertrude Ethel Zukerman; m. Claire J. Goldsmith, June 25, 1961 (div. 1986); children: Steven, Amy; m. Elaine DeMasi, Nov. 21, 1986 (div. 1999); children: Jaclyn, Laura. BS, U. Fla., 1961; LLB, St. John's U., 1964; LLM, NYU, 1966. Bar: N.Y. 1965, Pa. 1983, U.S. Tax Ct. 1984. Credit analyst, loan officer Franklin Nat. Bank, 1964-66; assoc. Jaffin, Schneider, Kimmel & Galpeer, N.Y.C., 1966-67; ptnr. Zukerman, Licht & Friedman and predecessors, 1967-79, Baskin & Sears, P.C., N.Y.C., 1979-85, Graubard, Moskowitz, Dannett, Horowitz & Mollen, N.Y.C., 1985-86, Gersten, Savage, Kaplowitz & Zukerman, N.Y.C., 1986-89; of counsel Olsham, Grundman, Frome & Rosenzweig, 1990-95, Graham &

James, N.Y.C., 1995-2000, Bryan Cave LLP, 2000—; exec. v.p. Brookhill Group, 1986-89. Pres. First Ptnrs. Credit Corp., N.Y.C., 1988-93; bd. dirs. Interjurist LTD, internat. law firm, Dames Moore/Brookhill LLC, 1996-2000, Whitestone Realty Capital, Inc., 1997—. Contbg. editor Real Estate Taxation and Acctg., 1988-93; lectr. on various subjects, 1986—. Contbr. articles to profl. jours. Trustee Temple Beth Torah, Melville, N.Y., 1972-80, YMHA Suffolk County, Hauppague, N.Y., 1980-85; bd. dirs. Dayton Mgmt. Corp., 1974—, Suffolk Jewish Cmty. Planning Bd., Hauppague, 1982-85, Congregation Bnai Elohim, 1994, 2nd v.p., 1995; co-chmn. bus. adv. coun. Town of Greenburgh, 1992. Mem. ABA. E-mail mm. Home: 915 Cherry Ln North Woodmere NY 11501 Office: Bryan Cave LLP 245 Park Ave Rm 2801 New York NY 10167-2897 E-mail: zukerman@BryanCave.com

ZUMBACH, STEVEN ELMER, lawyer; b. Jan. 12, 1950; s. Elmer J. and Mary C. (Frese) Zumbach; m. Kathy J. Case, June 05, 1971; children: Stephanie L., Mathew J. BS, Iowa State U., 1973, PhD, 1980; JD, U. Iowa, 1975. CPA; bar: Iowa 1975. Assoc. Belin Lamson McCormick Zumbach Flynn, P.C., Des Moines, 1977—, ptnr., 1980—. Lectr. law Drake U., Des Moines, 1980—84; mem. Iowa Bd. Regents, 1973—77; trustee, bd. dir. Iowa State U. Found., Ames, Iowa, 1986—. Fellow: Am. coll. Trust and Estate Counsel; mem.: Am. Assn. Agrl. Economists, Iowa Bar Assn., Iowa Soc. CPAs, Polk County Bar Assn., Iowa State U. Alumni Assn. (pres. 1986—87), Greater Des Moines C. of C. (chair C. of C. Fedn. 1993), Order of Coif, Phi Kappa Phi, Omocron Delta Kappa, Gamma Sigma Delta. Republican. Probate, Corporate taxation, Estate taxation. Home: 708 38th St West Des Moines IA 50265-3176 Office: Belin Lamson McCormick Zumbach Flynn PC 666 Walnut St Ste 2000 Des Moines IA 50309-3989

ZWICK, KENNETH LOWELL, lawyer, director; b. Cleve., Oct. 30, 1945; s. Alvin Albert Zwick and Selma (Mack) Durbin; m. Ruth Winifred Epstein, June 21, 1969; children: Tara, Monica. BSME,BS in Mgmt., MIT, 1969; JD, Temple U., 1976. Bar: Pa. 1976. Engr. Raytheon Corp., Norwood, Mass., 1969-71; tech. mgr. On-Line Systems, Inc., Phila., 1971-76; staff atty. Mead Data Cen., Washington, 1976-83; dir. litigation support office U.S. Dept. Justice, 1983-88, dir. mgmt. programs office, 1988—. Mem. ASME (assoc.). Democrat. Jewish. Home: 9316 Wescott Pl Rockville MD 20850-3452 Office: US Dept Justice 3140 Main Justice Bldg Washington DC 20530-0001

ZWIER, LEON, lawyer; b. Melbourne, Victoria, Australia, July 19, 1957; LLB, U. Melbourne, 1980. Bar: barrister, solicitor Supreme Ct. Victoria; practicing cert. Victoria Lawyers Legal Practice Bd. Ptnr. Harding Brereton & Shiff, Melbourne, 1982-88, Lilly Brereton, Melbourne, 1988-90, Barker Gosling, Melbourne, 1990-91, Arnold Bloch Leibler, Melbourne, 1991—. Presenter, lectr. in field. Mem. Law Inst. Victoria, Insolvency Practitioners' Assn. Australia (assoc.). Avocation: skiing. Office: Arnold Bloch Leibler 333 Collins St Melbourne VIC 3000 Australia

Fields of Practice Index

Detroit
Calkins, Stephen
Mamat, Frank Trustick
Shannon, Margaret Anne

Farmington
McFarland, Robert Edwin

Monroe
Bartlett, James Patrick

Mount Pleasant
Lynch, John Joseph

Warren
Bridenstine, Louis Henry, Jr.

MINNESOTA

Edina
Burk, Robert S.

Little Canada
Hardman, James Charles

Minneapolis
Brooks, William Fern, Jr.
French, John Dwyer
Keppel, William James
Marshall, Siri Swenson
Ryan, Thomas J.

Saint Paul
Knapp, John Anthony

MISSISSIPPI

Jackson
Fuselier, Louis Alfred
Mosley, Deanne Marie

MISSOURI

Jefferson City
Bartlett, Alex
Deutsch, James Bernard
Tettlebaum, Harvey M.

Kansas City
Cross, William Dennis
Franke, Linda Frederick
Satterlee, Terry Jean

Saint Louis
Brostron, Judith Curran
Gilhousen, Brent James
Sullivan, Edward Lawrence
Watters, Richard Donald
Withers, W. Wayne

Springfield
McCurry, Bruce

MONTANA

Billings
Sites, James Philip

NEBRASKA

Lincoln
Hewitt, James Watt

Omaha
Krutter, Forrest Nathan
Lee, Dennis Patrick

NEVADA

Las Vegas
Ashleman, Ivan Reno, II
Curran, William P.
Faiss, Robert Dean
Jost, Richard Frederic, III
Lovell, Carl Erwin, Jr.

Reno
Bible, Paul Alfred

NEW HAMPSHIRE

Manchester
Wells, Robert Alfred
Wiebusch, Richard Vernon

North Conway
Youngblood, Deborah Sue

NEW JERSEY

Basking Ridge
DeBois, James Adolphus

Bridgewater
Conroy, Robert John

Hackensack
Navatta, Anna Paula

Livingston
Klein, Peter Martin

Morristown
Barba, Julius William

New Providence
Adler, Nadia C.

Newark
Chaplin, Dolcey Elizabeth
Cummis, Clive Sanford

Princeton
Picco, Steven Joseph
Souter, Sydney Scull
Szwalbenest, Benedykt Jan

Roseland
Eichler, Burton Lawrence
Vanderbilt, Arthur T., II

Secaucus
McNamara, Patrick James

Springfield
Mytelka, Arnold Krieger

Trenton
Isele, William Paul
Pellecchia, John Michael

Vauxhall
Ross, Mark Samuel

Woodbridge
Babineau, Anne Serzan
Barcan, Stephen Emanuel

NEW MEXICO

Albuquerque
Apodaca, Patrick Vincent

Santa Fe
Mills, Thomas C. H.

Taos
Boles, David LaVelle

NEW YORK

Albany
Barsamian, J(ohn) Albert
Piedmont, Richard Stuart
Provorny, Frederick Alan
Teitelbaum, Steven Usher

Ardsley On Hudson
Stein, Milton Michael

Bronx
Stack, Jane Marcia

Brooklyn
Jacobson, Barry Stephen

Buffalo
Harner, Timothy R.

Glens Falls
Lebowitz, Jack Richard

Larchmont
Berridge, George Bradford

New York
Abrams, Robert
Allen, Leon Arthur, Jr.
Block, William Kenneth
Buchman, M. Abraham
Butterklee, Neil Howard
Clapman, Peter Carlyle
Davidson, Sheila Kearney
Diana, Ronald Salvador
Douchkess, George
Filson, Marguerite B.
Fleischman, Edward Hirsh
Gottlieb, Paul Mitchel
Gotts, Ilene Knable
Handler, Arthur M.
Juceam, Robert E.
Lord, Barbara Joanni
Lupkin, Stanley Neil
Marshall, Sheila Hermes
Miller, Richard Allan
Miller, Sam Scott
Most, Jack Lawrence
Naftalis, Gary Philip
Nolan, Terrance Joseph, Jr.
Rossen, Jordan
Schumacher, Harry Richard
Semaya, Francine Levitt
Sorkin, Laurence Truman
White, Katherine Patricia
Wolfe, Richard Barry Michael

Pittsford
George, Richard Neill

Smithtown
Dowis, Lenore

Somers
McGuire, Pamela Cottam

White Plains
Taft, Nathaniel Belmont

Wolcott
Bartlett, Cody Blake

NORTH CAROLINA

Durham
Markham, Charles Buchanan

Fairview
Rhynedance, Harold Dexter, Jr.

Greensboro
Koonce, Neil Wright

Jacksonville
Taylor, Vaughan Edward

Pittsboro
Hubbard, Thomas Edwin (Tim
Hubbard)

Raleigh
Dixon, Wright Tracy, Jr.
Kapp, Michael Keith

NORTH DAKOTA

Bismarck
Anderson, Harold Lloyd
Gerhart, Steven George
Klemin, Lawrence R.

OHIO

Cincinnati
O'Reilly, James Thomas

Cleveland
Gippin, Robert Malcolm
Hardy, Michael Lynn

Columbus
Booker, James Douglas
Fahey, Richard Paul
Feheley, Lawrence Francis
Helfer, Michael Stevens
Maynard, Robert Howell
Morgan, Dennis Richard
Stanton, Elizabeth McCool
Taylor, Joel Sanford

Dayton
Kinlin, Donald James

Dublin
Farrell, Clifford Michael

Howard
Lee, William Johnson

Lancaster
Libert, Donald Joseph

Toledo
Witherell, Dennis Patrick

Washington Township
Post, Alan Richard

OKLAHOMA

Edmond
Loving, Susan Brimer

Oklahoma City
Decker, Michael Lynn
Legg, William Jefferson

Shawnee
Dawson, Cindy Marie

Tulsa
Ferguson, Dallas Eugene
Williamson, Walter Bland

OREGON

Lake Oswego
Nelson, Thomas Howard

Portland
Dotten, Michael Chester
Rutzick, Mark Charles
Sullivan, Edward Joseph

Roseburg
Yockim, Ronald Stephen

PENNSYLVANIA

Blue Bell
Settle, Eric Lawrence
Teklits, Joseph Anthony

Elkins Park
Myers, Kenneth Raymond

Harrisburg
Barto, Charles O., Jr.
Burcat, Joel Robin
Kury, Franklin Leo
Skelly, Joseph Gordon
Van Zile, Philip Taylor, III

Media
Zicherman, David L.

Philadelphia
Collings, Robert L.
Fineman, S. David
Gornish, Gerald
Kendall, Robert Louis, Jr.
Kopp, Charles Gilbert
Morris, Roland
Reiss, John Barlow

Pittsburgh
Bleier, Michael E.
Crayne, Larry Randolph
Klodowski, Harry Francis, Jr.
Leibowitz, Marvin

SOUTH CAROLINA

Charleston
Cannon, Hugh

Columbia
Carpenter, Charles Elford, Jr.
Harvey, Jonathan Matthew
Pollard, William Albert

Greenville
Barash, Anthony Harlan

TENNESSEE

Cordova
Swan, Michael Robert

Hendersonville
McCaleb, Joe Wallace

Johnson City
Epps, James Haws, III

TEXAS

Austin
Brown, Dick Terrell
Colburn, Stuart Dale
Cunningham, Judy Marie
Demond, Walter Eugene
Drummond, Eric Hubert
Golemon, Ronald Kinnan
Maggio-Gonzales, Marissa Ann
Moss, Bill Ralph
Nevola, Roger
Patman, Philip Franklin
Roan, Forrest Calvin, Jr.
Schwartz, Leonard Jay
Smith, Lawrence Shannon
Strauser, Robert Wayne

Dallas
Courtney Westfall, Constance
Dean, David Allen
Dutton, Diana Cheryl
Geiger, Richard Stuart
Hallman, Leroy
Staley, Joseph Hardin, Jr.

Diboll
Ericson, Roger Delwin

Fort Worth
Moros, Nicholas Peter

Houston
Eiland, Gary Wayne
Friedman, J. Kent
Gillmore, Kathleen Cory
Kelly, Hugh Rice
McCreary, Frank E., III
Pope, David Bruce
Rozzell, Scott Ellis
Salch, Steven Charles

Mc Kinney
Dowdy, William Clarence, Jr.

San Antonio
Hollin, Shelby W.
Lutter, Charles William, Jr.

UTAH

Provo
Abbott, Charles Favour

Salt Lake City
Gordon, Robert
Jensen, Dallin W.

VIRGINIA

Alexandria
Duvall, Richard Osgood
Siegel, Kenneth Eric

Arlington
Cohen, Sheldon Irwin
Morris, Roy Leslie

Falls Church
Kirk, Dennis Dean

Herndon
Geldon, Fred Wolman

Mc Lean
Byrnes, William Joseph
Herge, J. Curtis
Olson, William Jeffrey
Raymond, David Walker
Stephens, William Theodore

Midlothian
Hall, Franklin Perkins

Norfolk
Corcoran, Andrew Patrick, Jr.

Norton
Shortridge, Judy Beth

Reston
Platt, Leslie A.
Reicin, Eric David

Richmond
Freeman, George Clemon, Jr.
Gary, Richard David
Hackney, Virginia Howitz

Rosslyn
Carbaugh, John Edward, Jr.

Vienna
Hagberg, Chris Eric

Virginia Beach
Layton, Garland Mason

WASHINGTON

Longview
O'Neill, Thomas Nicholas Stephen

Olympia
Reynolds, Dennis Dean

Seattle
Blom, Daniel Charles
Dolan, Andrew Kevin
Freeman, Antoinette Rosefeldt
Rosen, Jon Howard

Spokane
Weatherhead, Leslie R.

WEST VIRGINIA

Bluefield
Kantor, Isaac Norris

WISCONSIN

Madison
Ehlke, Bruce Frederic
Vaughan, Michael Richard

Milwaukee
Friebert, Robert Howard
Scrivner, Thomas William

WYOMING

Cheyenne
Hathaway, Stanley Knapp

**TERRITORIES OF THE
UNITED STATES**

PUERTO RICO

San Juan
Pierluisi, Pedro R.

AUSTRALIA

Brisbane
Perrett, Ross Graham

Sydney
Grieve, Gordon Thomas

BELGIUM

Brussels
Smith, Turner Taliaferro, Jr.

DENMARK

Copenhagen
Stokholm, Jon Ulrik

NEW ZEALAND

Auckland
Webb, Michael R.

THE PHILIPPINES

Metro Manila
Sumida, Gerald Aquinas

ADDRESS UNPUBLISHED

Anderson, Jon Eric
Babbin, Jed Lloyd
Bagley, William Thompson
Bennett, Steven Alan
Brown, Margaret deBeers
Choukas-Bradley, James Richard
Ginsberg, Ernest
Grange, George Robert, II
Grier, Phillip Michael
Hanzlik, Rayburn DeMara
Hoffman, S. David
Holmes, Michael Gene
Isaacs, Michael Burton
Johnson, Richard Tenney
Kennedy, Thomas J.
Lapidus, Steven Richard
Lea, Lorenzo Bates
Mayer, James Joseph
McGovern, Frances
Nelson, Richard Perry
Oates, Carl Everette
Potter, Tanya Jean
Rivlin, Lewis Allen

Shattuck, Cathie Ann
Tapley, James Leroy
Tavrow, Richard Lawrence
Tolins, Roger Alan
Tucker, William E.
Wagner, Arthur Ward, Jr.
Winslow, John Franklin
Wittig, Raymond Shaffer
Wooldridge, William Charles
Young, John Hardin

ADMIRALTY

UNITED STATES

ALABAMA

Mobile
Quina, Marion Albert, Jr.

ALASKA

Anchorage
Owens, Robert Patrick
Richmond, Robert Lawrence

ARIZONA

Rio Rico
Ryan, John Duncan

CALIFORNIA

Huntington Beach
Nikas, Richard John

Long Beach
Stolpman, Thomas Gerard

Pasadena
Koelzer, George Joseph

San Diego
Hartley, Jason Scott

San Francisco
Danoff, Eric Michael
Donovan, Charles Stephen
German, G. Michael
Meadows, John Frederick
Rosenthal, Kenneth W.
Staring, Graydon Shaw

Walnut Creek
Nolan, David Charles

CONNECTICUT

Brooklyn
Dune, Steve Charles

Danbury
Murray, Stephen James

Stamford
Ligelis, Gregory John

DISTRICT OF COLUMBIA

Washington
Flowe, Benjamin Hugh, Jr.
Hoppel, Robert Gerald, Jr.
Mayer, Neal Michael

FLORIDA

Coral Gables
Buell, Rodd Russell
Keedy, Christian David

Jacksonville
Gabel, George DeSaussure, Jr.
Houser, John Edward
Milton, Joseph Payne
Moseley, James Francis
Rumrell, Richard Gary
White, Edward Alfred

Miami
Hickey, John (Jack) Heyward
Lipcon, Charles Roy
McHale, Michael John
Moore, Michael T.
Peltz, Robert Dwight

Pensacola
Marsh, William Douglas
Wiltshire, William Harrison Flick

Sarasota
Herb, F(rank) Steven

ILLINOIS

Alton
Talbert, Hugh Mathis

Chicago
Johnson, Richard Fred
Kennelly, John Jerome
Marwedel, Warren John

LOUISIANA

Covington
Rice, Winston Edward

Lafayette
Roy, James Parkerson

Lake Charles
Nieset, James Robert

Metairie
Album, Jerald Lewis
Dinwiddie, Bruce Wayland
McMahon, Robert Albert, Jr.

Morgan City
Ramsey, Robert Scott, Jr.

New Orleans
Abaunza, Donald Richard
Desue, Christine L.
Eustis, Richmond Minor
Fendler, Sherman Gene
Futrell, John Maurice
Grant, Arthur Gordon, Jr.
Healy, George William, III
Hurley, Grady Schell
McGlone, Michael Anthony
Pugh, William Whitmell Hill, III
Riess, George Febiger
Rodriguez, Antonio Jose
Sommers, William John, Jr.
Sutterfield, James Ray

MARYLAND

Baltimore
Bartlett, James Wilson, III

MASSACHUSETTS

Manchester
Wolfe, Robert Shenker

MICHIGAN

Clinton Township
Theut, C. Peter

MISSISSIPPI

Biloxi
O'Barr, Bobby Gene, Sr.

MISSOURI

Saint Louis
Dorwart, Donald Bruce
Massey, Raymond Lee

NEW JERSEY

Livingston
Klein, Peter Martin

NEW YORK

Jericho
Semel, Martin Ira

New York
Costello, Joseph Michael
DeOrchis, Vincent Moore
Edelman, Paul Sterling
Glanstein, Joel Charles
Hayden, Raymond Paul
Healy, Nicholas Joseph
Honan, William Joseph, III
Hooker, Wade Stuart, Jr.
Jaffe, Mark M.
Kimball, John Devereux
Kremin, Mark J.
McCormack, Howard Michael
Rosow, Malcolm Bertram
Schmidt, Charles Edward
Stratakis, Christ
Teiman, Richard B.

NORTH CAROLINA

Wilmington
Seagle, J. Harold

OHIO

Cleveland
Baughman, R(obert) Patrick

Columbus
Robol, Richard Thomas

PENNSYLVANIA

Philadelphia
Palmer, Richard Ware

Pittsburgh
Murdoch, Robert Whitten

TENNESSEE

Memphis
Glassman, Richard

TEXAS

Beaumont
Oxford, Hubert, III

Dallas
Adelman, Graham Lewis
Kennedy, Marc J.

Houston
Chandler, George Francis, III
Eckhardt, William Rudolf, III
Gonynor, Francis James
Kline, Allen Haber, Jr.
Lacey, David Morgan
McCarter, Louis Eugene
Nacol, Mae
Pitts, Gary Benjamin
Silva, Eugene Joseph

Humble
Pickle, George Edward

VIRGINIA

Middleburg
Dietz, Robert Sheldon

Norfolk
Clark, Morton Hutchinson
Parsons, Rymn James
Ware, Guilford Dudley

Reston
Maitland, Guy Edison Clay

WASHINGTON

Redmond
Scowcroft, Jerome Chilwell

Seattle
Bagshaw, Bradley Holmes
Davis, Susan Rae
Nye, Daniel Alan
Paul, Thomas Frank
Whitehead, James Fred, III

DENMARK

Copenhagen
Stokholm, Jon Ulrik

ENGLAND

London
Baker, Charles George
Ferrarl, Alexander Domonico

GERMANY

Hamburg
von Teuffel, Nikolai

GREECE

Piraeus
Bowen-Morris, Nigel Vaughan

NEW ZEALAND

Auckland
Laxon, William Allan

SINGAPORE

Singapore
David, James P.

SWEDEN

Stockholm
Arak, Viktor

ADDRESS UNPUBLISHED

Brown, Charles Dodgson
Jackson, Raymond Sidney, Jr.

ALTERNATIVE DISPUTE RESOLUTION

UNITED STATES

ALABAMA

Eufaula
Twitchell, E(rvin) Eugene

Montgomery
Lawson, Thomas Seay, Jr.
McFadden, Frank Hampton

Tuscaloosa
Williams, Roger Courtland

ARIZONA

Scottsdale
Marks, Merton Eleazer

ARKANSAS

Morrilton
Denniston, Jeannie L.

CALIFORNIA

Bakersfield
Gong, Gloria M.

Burlingame
Narayan, Beverly Elaine

Los Angeles
Fisher, Richard N.
Kamine, Bernard S.
Mosk, Richard Mitchell
Weil, Robert Irving

Modesto
Mussman, William Edward, III

Pacific Palisades
Flattery, Thomas Long

Palos Verdes Estates
Pierno, Anthony Robert

San Diego
Mayer, James Hock
Sullivan, Michelle Cornejo

San Francisco
Hoffman, John Douglas
Rosenthal, Kenneth W.
Smith, Robert Michael

San Jose
Bohn, Robert Herbert
Cummins, Charles Fitch, Jr.

San Rafael
Chilvers, Robert Merritt
Roth, Hadden Wing

San Ramon
Welch, Thomas Andrew

COLORADO

Denver
Aisenberg, Bennett S.
Cox, William Vaughan

Golden
Hughes, Marcia Marie

CONNECTICUT

Avon
Widing, Carol Scharfe

Clinton
Hershatter, Richard Lawrence

Greenwich
Storms, Clifford Beekman

Hartford
Dowling, Vincent John
Orth, Paul William

Stamford
Stapleton, James Francis

DISTRICT OF COLUMBIA

Washington
Donegan, Charles Edward
Elcano, Mary S.
Fishburne, Benjamin P., III
Lane, Bruce Stuart
Lewis, David John
Pierson, W. DeVier
Rider, James Lincoln
Thaler, Paul Sanders
Townsend, John Michael
Wilson, Gary Dean

FLORIDA

Fort Myers
Dalton, Anne

Miami
Landy, Burton Aaron

Orlando
Nadeau, Robert Bertrand, Jr.
Sawicki, Stephen Craig
Worthington, Daniel Glen

Sarasota
Phillips, Elvin Willis

Tampa
MacDonald, Thomas Cook, Jr.
Stagg, Clyde Lawrence
Thomas, Wayne Lee

Winter Park
Wagner, Lynn Edward

GEORGIA

Athens
Houser, Ronald Edward

Atlanta
Bird, Francis Marion, Jr.
Croft, Terrence Lee
Hinchey, John William
Linder, Harvey Ronald

Rochelle, Dudley Cecile

Mcdonough
Crumbley, R. Alex

Metter
Doremus, Ogden

HAWAII

Honolulu
Crumpton, Charles Whitmarsh

IDAHO

Boise
Park, William Anthony (Tony)

Idaho Falls
St. Clair, John Gilbert

ILLINOIS

Chicago
Blatt, Richard Lee
Boies, Wilber H.
Cass, Robert Michael
Karon, Sheldon
McMahon, Thomas Michael
Muller, Kurt Alexander
Nugent, Lori S.

Evanston
Morrison, John Horton

Park Ridge
LaRue, Paul Hubert

Rockford
Channick, Herbert S.

INDIANA

Indianapolis
Fels, James Alexander
Wampler, Robert Joseph

KENTUCKY

Louisville
Ballantine, John Tilden
Tannon, Jay Middleton

LOUISIANA

New Orleans
Molony, Michael Janssens, Jr.

MARYLAND

Baltimore
McWilliams, John Michael

Brookeville
Johns, Warren LeRoi

Rockville
Zaphiriou, George Aristotle

MASSACHUSETTS

Boston
Aresty, Jeffrey M.

Weymouth
Fitzsimmons, B. Joseph, Jr.

MICHIGAN

Bloomfield Hills
Morganroth, Fred

Detroit
Ward, George Edward
Wittlinger, Timothy David

Grand Rapids
Enslen, Pamela Chapman

Schoolcraft
Foley, John Francis

MINNESOTA

Minneapolis
Johnson, Paul Owen

Saint Paul
Noonan, James C.
Sarazin, Mary Eileen

MISSISSIPPI

Hernando
Brown, William A.

MISSOURI

Saint Louis
Switzer, Frederick Michael, III

MONTANA

Billings
Toole, Bruce Ryan

NEBRASKA

Omaha
Brownrigg, John Clinton

NEW JERSEY

Hackensack
Goldsamt, Bonnie Blume
Kaps, Warren Joseph
Spiegel, Linda F.

Morristown
Pollock, Stewart Glasson

Red Bank
Michaelson, Peter Lee

Rutherford
Henschel, John James

NEW YORK

Buffalo
Pearson, Paul David

Garden City
Ginsberg, Eugene Stanley

New York
Clemente, Robert Stephen
Davidson, Robert Bruce
DeCarlo, Donald Thomas
Drucker, Jacquelin F.
Filson, Marguerite B.
Freyer, Dana Hartman
Gans, Walter Gideon
Hoffman, David Nathaniel
Kandel, William Lloyd
McDonell, Neil Edwin
Milmed, Paul Kussy
Nicoara, Andra Christina
Rovine, Arthur William
Savitt, Susan Schenkel
Schindler, Steven Roy
Vitkowsky, Vincent Joseph
Zifchak, William C.

Scarsdale
King, Robert Lucien

Uniondale
Eilen, Howard Scott

Valley Stream
Levine, Marilyn Markovich

Westbury
Boes, Lawrence William

NORTH CAROLINA

Fayetteville
Ruppe, Arthur Maxwell

Raleigh
Hunter, Richard Samford, Jr.

OHIO

Cincinnati
Calico, Paul B.

Cleveland
Skulina, Thomas Raymond

Columbus
Hutson, Jeffrey Woodward

Wilmington
Buckley, Frederick Jean

OKLAHOMA

Tulsa
Babiak, Joann U.
Fell, Riley Brown

OREGON

Portland
Tanzer, Jacob

Salem
Gangle, Sandra Smith

PENNSYLVANIA

Philadelphia
Berger, Harold
Blumstein, Edward
Jamison, Judith Jaffe

Plymouth
Musto, Joseph John

RHODE ISLAND

Providence
McAndrew, Thomas Joseph

SOUTH DAKOTA

Rapid City
Shultz, Donald Richard

TENNESSEE

Knoxville
Vines, William Dorsey

Memphis
Williams, J. Maxwell

Nashville
Gannon, John Sexton

TEXAS

Austin
Davis, Robert Larry
Saltmarsh, Sara Elizabeth

Corpus Christi
Coover, Ann E.

Dallas
DelHomme, Beverly Ann
Mighell, Kenneth John
Orleans, Neil Jeffrey

El Paso
Morton, Fred J.

Houston
Moroney, Linda L. S.
Prestridge, Pamela Adair
Shurn, Peter Joseph, III
Susman, Morton Lee
Wright, Paul William

New Braunfels
Pfeuffer, Robert Tug

San Antonio
Javore, Gary William
Pfeiffer, Philip J.

UTAH

Sandy
Western, Marion Wayne

VERMONT

Burlington
Frank, Joseph Elihu

VIRGINIA

Harrisonburg
Wallinger, M(elvin) Bruce

Portsmouth
Lavin, Barbara Hofheins

Richmond
Merhige, Robert Reynold, Jr.

Roanoke
Effel, Laura

Vienna
Titus, Bruce Earl

WASHINGTON

Anacortes
Glein, Richard Jeriel

Bellevue
Sebris, Robert, Jr.

Seattle
Blair, M. Wayne
Cavanaugh, Michael Everett
Loftus, Thomas Daniel
Rasmussen, Frederick Tatum
Smith, James Alexander, Jr.
Wagoner, David Everett

Spokane
Harbaugh, Daniel Paul

WEST VIRGINIA

Huntington
Bagley, Charles Frank, III

WISCONSIN

Green Bay
Grzeca, Michael G(erard)

Milwaukee
Michelstetter, Stanley Hubert
Nelson, Roy Hugh, Jr.

Sun Prairie
Eustice, Francis Joseph

AUSTRALIA

Adelaide
Gaszner, David George

Brisbane
Perrett, Ross Graham

Melbourne
Bartlett, Peter Llewellyn
Gronow, Geoffrey Rees
Meadows, Paul Manvers

Sydney
L'Estrange, Timothy I.

BELGIUM

Liege
Matray, Didier F

CHINA

Beijing
Xing, Xuisong

ENGLAND

London
Bandurka, Andrew Alan
Mackie, David Lindsay
Rochez, Nicholas Dutfield

NEW ZEALAND

Auckland
Laxon, William Allan
Whale, Michael John

NORWAY

Oslo
Moss, Giuditta Cordero

SINGAPORE

Singapore
Shetty, Nishith Kumare

SPAIN

Madrid
Hendel, Clifford James

SWEDEN

Stockholm
Solerud, Hans Gunnar

ADDRESS UNPUBLISHED

Atchison, Rodney Raymond
Bakkensen, John Reser
Bandy, Jack D.
Dubuc, Carroll Edward
Gorske, Robert H.
McQuigg, John Dolph
Pannill, William Presley
Peccarelli, Anthony Marando
Perlman, Richard Brian
Reath, George, Jr.

ANTITRUST

UNITED STATES

ALABAMA

Birmingham
Alexander, James Patrick
Givhan, Robert Marcus
Hardin, Edward Lester, Jr.
Hinton, James Forrest, Jr.
Long, Thad Gladden
Spransy, Joseph William
Stabler, Lewis Vastine, Jr.

ARIZONA

Phoenix
Allen, Robert Eugene Barton
Bouma, John Jacob
Burke, Timothy John
Galbut, Martin Richard
Klausner, Jack Daniel
Price, Charles Steven

Scottsdale
Titus, Jon Alan

ARKANSAS

Little Rock
Anderson, Philip Sidney
Simpson, James Marlon, Jr.

CALIFORNIA

Beverly Hills
Fine, Richard Isaac
Sherwood, Arthur Lawrence

Carlsbad
McCracken, Steven Carl

Lafayette
Sherrer, Charles William

Los Angeles
Barza, Harold A.
Belleville, Philip Frederick
Cohen, Cynthia Marylyn
Creim, William Benjamin
Fredman, Howard S
Fredman, Howard S
Hanson, John J.
Hufstedler, Shirley Mount (Mrs. Seth
  M. Hufstedler)
Olson, Ronald Leroy
Varner, Carlton A.
von Kalinowski, Julian Onesime
Woodland, Irwin Francis

Modesto
Mussman, William Edward, III

Palo Alto
Sherman, Martin Peter

San Diego
Schuck, Carl Joseph
Sullivan, Patrick James

San Francisco
Alexis, Geraldine M.
Allen, Paul Alfred
Boyd, William Sprott
Callan, Terrence A.
Campbell, Scott Robert
Gelhaus, Robert Joseph
Odgers, Richard William
Salomon, Darrell Joseph
Schon, Steven Eliot
Taylor, William James (Zak Taylor)
Trautman, William Ellsworth
Warmer, Richard Craig

San Jose
Anderson, Edward Virgil

Walnut Creek
Pagter, Carl Richard

COLORADO

Denver
Harris, Dale Ray
Hautzinger, James Edward
Kanan, Gregory Brian
Miller, Gale Timothy
Pratt, Kevin Burton
Thomasch, Roger Paul
Timmins, Edward Patrick

Englewood
Figa, Phillip Sam

CONNECTICUT

Darien
Prince, Kenneth Stephen

Fairfield
Huth, William Edward

Farmington
Wiechmann, Eric Watt

Hartford
Dennis, Anthony James

New Haven
Belt, David Levin

Norwalk
Bergere, C(lifford) Wendell, Jr.

Redding
Russell, Allan David

Stamford
Lieberman, Steven Paul

West Hartford
Conard, Frederick Underwood, Jr.

Westport
Amschler, James Ralph

DELAWARE

Wilmington
Magee, Thomas Hugh

DISTRICT OF COLUMBIA

Washington
Atwood, James R.
Barnes, Donald Michael
Bell, Robert Brooks
Berner, Frederic George, Jr.
Blumenfeld, Jeffrey
Bowe, Richard Welbourn
Braverman, Burt Alan
Buffon, Charles Edward
Burchfield, Bobby Roy
Calderwood, James Albert
Calvani, Terry
Cheston, Sheila Carol
Colman, Richard Thomas
Davidow, Joel
deKieffer, Donald Eulette
Denger, Michael L.
Englert, Roy Theodore, Jr.
Ewing, Ky Pepper, Jr.
Fleischaker, Marc L.
Gellhorn, Ernest Albert Eugene
Gold, Peter Frederick
Goodman, Alfred Nelson
Goodman, John M.

Gorinson, Stanley M.
Haines, Terry L.
Heckman, Jerome Harold
Henke, Michael John
Hewitt, Paul Buck
Hills, Carla Anderson
Hobbs, Caswell O., III
Howard, Jeffrey Hjalmar
Jacobsen, Raymond Alfred, Jr.
Jetton, C. Loring, Jr.
Johnson, Shirley Z.
Jordan, Robert Elijah, III
Klarfeld, Peter James
Lavelle, Joseph P.
McDavid, Janet Louise
McDiarmid, Robert Campbell
Miller, John T., Jr.
Moates, G. Paul
Murry, Harold David, Jr.
Pfeiffer, Margaret Kolodny
Rasmussen, Garret Garretson
Rau, Lee Arthur
Rich, John Townsend
Roll, David Lee
Rupp, John Peter
Shenefield, John Hale
Shieber, William J.
Smith, Brian William
Smith, Daniel Clifford
Stock, Stuart Chase
Taurman, John David
Temko, Stanley Leonard
Timberg, Sigmund
Townsend, John Michael
Turnage, Fred Douglas
Vakerics, Thomas Vincent
Wegener, Mark Douglas
Weiss, Mark Anschel
Wiseman, Alan M(itchell)
Wolf, Christopher
Wolff, Elroy Harris
Yannucci, Thomas David
Zeidman, Philip Fisher

FLORIDA

Alachua
Gaines, Weaver Henderson

Boca Raton
Kassner, Herbert Seymore
Kauffman, Alan Charles

Gainesville
Jones, Clifford Alan

Miami
Houlihan, Gerald John
Nachwalter, Michael
Nagin, Stephen Elias
Richman, Gerald F.
Winship, Blaine H.

GEORGIA

Atlanta
Doyle, Michael Anthony
Genberg, Ira
Gladden, Joseph Rhea, Jr.
Grady, Kevin E.
Harrison, Bryan Guy
Killorin, Robert Ware
Lotito, Nicholas Anthony
Rhodes, Thomas Willard

HAWAII

Honolulu
Char, Vernon Fook Leong

IDAHO

Boise
Storti, Philip Craig

ILLINOIS

Barrington
Lee, William Marshall

Chicago
Allen, Henry Sermones, Jr.
Bierig, Jack R.
Bowman, Phillip Boynton
Chefitz, Joel Gerald
Crane, Mark
Donner, Ted A.
Eimer, Nathan Philip
Esrick, Jerald Paul
Finke, Robert Forge
Franch, Richard Thomas
Freeborn, Michael D.
Gibbons, William John
Gordon, James S.
Gustman, David Charles
Hannay, William Mouat, III
Hardgrove, James Alan
Harrold, Bernard
Howell, R(obert) Thomas, Jr.
Hunter, James Galbraith, Jr.
Hyman, Michael Bruce
Johnson, Douglas Wells
Johnson, Lael Frederic
King, Michael Howard
Linklater, William Joseph
Luning, Thomas P.
Lynch, John Peter
McLaughlin, T. Mark
Michaels, Richard Edward
Montgomery, William Adam
Rankin, James Winton
Rovner, Jack Alan
Saunders, George Lawton, Jr.
Silberman, Alan Harvey
Simon, Seymour
Trienens, Howard Joseph

Deerfield
Staubitz, Arthur Frederick

ANTITRUST (continued)

Stern, John Jules
Streicker, James Richard
Tapley, James Leroy
Tasker, Joseph
Tone, Philip Willis
Tubman, William Charles
Walker, Craig Michael
Wooldridge, William Charles
Yeager, Mark Leonard

APPELLATE

UNITED STATES

ARIZONA

Phoenix
Corson, Kimball Jay
Mizrahi, Elan S(hai)
Ulrich, Paul Graham
Wirken, Charles William

CALIFORNIA

Belvedere Tiburon
Allan, Walter Robert

Beverly Hills
Amado, Honey Kessler
Heinke, Rex S.

Costa Mesa
Connally, Michael W.

Long Beach
Tikosh, Mark Axente

Los Angeles
Imre, Christina Joanne
Nordlinger, Stephanie G.
Weatherup, Roy Garfield
Woods, Daniel James

Pacific Palisades
Hunter, M(ilton) Reed, Jr.

Pasadena
Ashley-Farrand, Margalo

Sacramento
Keiner, Christian Mark

San Diego
Bird, Charles Albert

San Francisco
Hoffman, John Douglas
Seabolt, Richard L.

San Rafael
Roth, Hadden Wing

Santa Monica
Genego, William Joseph
Kanner, Gideon

Ventura
Bray, Laurack Doyle

COLORADO

Boulder
Lindenmuth, Noel Charles

Denver
Featherstone, Bruce Alan
Low, Andrew M.
McConnell, Michael Theodore

CONNECTICUT

Brookfield
Secola, Joseph Paul

New Haven
Geisler, Thomas Milton, Jr.

DISTRICT OF COLUMBIA

Washington
Carter, William Joseph
Cooper, Clement Theodore
Dowdey, Landon Gerald
Englert, Roy Theodore, Jr.
Foggan, Laura Anne
Gellhorn, Ernest Albert Eugene
Kent, M. Elizabeth
Kissel, Peter Charles
McKinney, James DeVaine, Jr.
Nickel, Henry V.
Peet, Richard Clayton
Pierson, W. DeVier
Schafrick, Frederick Craig
Weissman, William R.
White-Mahaffey, Virginia L.

FLORIDA

Bartow
Stevenson, Robin Howard

Fort Lauderdale
Bogenschutz, J. David
Hester, Julia A.

Gainesville
Jones, Clifford Alan

Jacksonville
Korn, Michael Jeffrey

Miami
Berger, Steven R.
Curtis, Karen Haynes
Eaton, Joel Douglas
Mehta, Eileen Rose
O'Connor, Kathleen Mary
Rashkind, Paul Michael

Orlando
Hernandez, H(ermes) Manuel
Mason, Steven Gerald
Sheaffer, William Jay

Sarasota
Garland, Richard Roger

Tampa
Pellett, Jon Michael
Polaszek, Christopher Stephen

West Palm Beach
Spillias, Kenneth George

GEORGIA

Athens
Houser, Ronald Edward

Atlanta
Albert, Ross Alan

IDAHO

Boise
Luker, Lynn Michael

Twin Falls
Hohnhorst, John Charles

ILLINOIS

Chicago
Cheely, Daniel Joseph
Kroll, Barry Lewis
Leyhane, Francis John, III
Loew, Jonathan L.
Sullivan, Barry
Trienens, Howard Joseph
Van Demark, Ruth Elaine

Wheaton
Stein, Lawrence A.

Wilmette
Lieberman, Eugene

INDIANA

South Bend
Palmer, Robert Joseph

IOWA

Charles City
Mc Cartney, Ralph Farnham

Des Moines
Finley, Kerry A.
Graziano, Craig Frank

KANSAS

Wichita
Gorup, Geary N.

LOUISIANA

Baton Rouge
Rubin, Michael Harry

New Orleans
Futrell, John Maurice

MARYLAND

Abingdon
Wolf, Martin Eugene

Baltimore
Howell, Harley Thomas
Wilson, Thomas Matthew, III

Westminster
Preston, Charles Michael

MASSACHUSETTS

Boston
Epstein, Elaine May
Zandrow, Leonard Florian

MICHIGAN

Ann Arbor
Walsh, James Joseph

Detroit
Mengel, Christopher Emile
Ward, George Edward

Southfield
Jacobs, John Patrick

MINNESOTA

Minneapolis
Anderson, Alan Marshall
Borger, John Philip

MISSISSIPPI

Madison
Flechas, Eduardo A.

MISSOURI

Clayton
Michenfelder, Albert A.

Kansas City
Deacy, Thomas Edward, Jr.

Saint Louis
Newman, Charles A.
Walsh, Thomas Charles

NEBRASKA

Omaha
O'Connor, Robert Edward, Jr.

NEVADA

Reno
Cornell, Richard Farnham

NEW HAMPSHIRE

Manchester
Middleton, Jack Baer

NEW JERSEY

Hackensack
Vort, Robert A.

Morristown
Pollock, Stewart Glasson

Ocean
Moore, Francis Xavier

Teaneck
Silber, Alan

NEW YORK

Cape Vincent
Stiefel, Linda Shields

Ithaca
Pinnisi, Michael Donato

New York
Cole, Charles Dewey, Jr.
Felder, Raoul Lionel
Hamm, David Bernard
Levy, Herbert Monte
Raab, Sheldon

Pittsford
Rosenhouse, Michael Allan

Syracuse
Cirando, John Anthony

Westbury
Boes, Lawrence William

White Plains
Scialabba, Donald Joseph

NORTH CAROLINA

Raleigh
Hall, John Thomas

Rutherfordton
Byers, Garland Franklin, Jr.

NORTH DAKOTA

Fargo
Crothers, Daniel J.

OHIO

Cincinnati
Faller, Susan Grogan
Hust, Bruce Kevin

Cleveland
Osborne, Frank R.
Whitney, Richard Buckner

Columbus
Cvetanovich, Danny L.

OKLAHOMA

Tulsa
Clark, Joseph Francis, Jr.

OREGON

Portland
Johnson, Mark Andrew

PENNSYLVANIA

Conway
Krebs, Robert Alan

Glenside
Mermelstein, Jules Joshua

Melrose Park
Shmukler, Stanford

Philadelphia
Harvey, Gregory Merrill
Phillips, Dorothy Kay
Solano, Carl Anthony
Wittels, Barnaby Caesar

RHODE ISLAND

Providence
Jones, Lauren Evans

TENNESSEE

Nashville
Trent, John Thomas, Jr.

TEXAS

Austin
Schulze, Eric William

College Station
Kennady, Emmett Hubbard, III

Dallas
Austin, Ann Sheree
Blount, Charles William, III
Freytag, Sharon Nelson
Pruessner, David Morgan
Sloman, Marvin Sherk

Galveston
Vie, George William, III

Houston
Gilbert, Keith Thomas
Owens, Betty Ruth
Schwartz, Charles Walter
Van Kerrebrook, Mary Alice

Mason
Johnson, Rufus Winfield

UTAH

Salt Lake City
Turner, Shawn Dennis

VERMONT

Montpelier
Putter, David Seth

VIRGINIA

Mc Lean
Byrnes, William Joseph

WASHINGTON

Seattle
Mitchell, Robert Bertelson, Jr.
Rummage, Stephen Michael

ENGLAND

London
Dickey, John W.

GERMANY

Berlin
Schoene, Friedrich Tobias

UKRAINE

Kiev
Voitovich, Sergei Adamovich

ADDRESS UNPUBLISHED

Arencibia, Raul Antonio
Beasley, James W., Jr.
Beukema, John Frederick
DeLaFuente, Charles
Kittrell, Pamela R.
Kouba, Lisa Marco
Logan, James Kenneth
Lopez, A. Ruben
Mugridge, David Raymond
Newman, Carol L.
O'Dell, Joan Elizabeth
Ogden, David William
Ostergaard, Joni Hammersla
Pannill, William Presley
Peccarelli, Anthony Marando
Stack, Beatriz de Greiff
Vinar, Benjamin
Weisberg, David Charles

AVIATION

UNITED STATES

ALABAMA

Mobile
Roedder, William Chapman, Jr.

ARIZONA

Phoenix
Toone, Thomas Lee

ARKANSAS

Little Rock
Bohannon, Charles Tad

CALIFORNIA

Los Angeles
Aristei, J. Clark
Baum, Michael Lin
Greaves, John Allen
Hedlund, Paul James
Johnson, Philip Leslie
McGovern, David Carr
Obrzut, Ted
Wood, Willard Mark

San Anselmo
Truett, Harold Joseph, III (Tim Truett)

San Francisco
Dworkin, Michael Leonard

Santa Monica
Bower, Allan Maxwell

COLORADO

Denver
Byrne, Thomas J.

CONNECTICUT

Stratford
McDonough, Sandra Martin

DISTRICT OF COLUMBIA

Washington
Cheston, Sheila Carol
Cobbs, Nicholas Hammer
Jones, Aidan Drexel
Madole, Donald Wilson
Pogue, L(loyd) Welch
Schafrick, Frederick Craig
Trinder, Rachel Bandele
Wray, Robert

FLORIDA

Boca Raton
Wallach, Steven Ernst

Coral Gables
Hoffman, Carl H(enry)

Fort Lauderdale
Denman, James Burton

Melbourne
Trachtman, Jerry H.

Miami
Becerra, Robert John
Marks, Steven Craig
O'Connor, Kathleen Mary
Podhurst, Aaron Samuel

Tampa
Murray, John Michael

GEORGIA

Atlanta
Harkey, Robert Shelton
McGill, John Gardner
Strauss, Robert David

Tucker
Armstrong, Edwin Alan

HAWAII

Honolulu
Char, Vernon Fook Leong
Fried, L. Richard, Jr.

ILLINOIS

Chicago
Geiman, J. Robert
Kennelly, John Jerome
McCabe, Charles Kevin
Rapoport, David E.

INDIANA

Indianapolis
Townsend, Earl C., Jr.

LOUISIANA

New Orleans
Fendler, Sherman Gene

MICHIGAN

Detroit
Torpey, Scott Raymond

NEBRASKA

Omaha
O'Connor, Robert Edward, Jr.

NEVADA

Reno
Hibbs, Loyal Robert

NEW JERSEY

Princeton
Brennan, William Joseph, III

NEW YORK

Cortlandt Manor
Buhler, Gregory Wallace

New York
Barry, Desmond Thomas, Jr.
Chiarchiaro, Frank John
De Vivo, Edward Charles
Fersko, Raymond Stuart
Mentz, Lawrence

NORTH CAROLINA

Chapel Hill
Zoffer, David B.

OHIO

Columbus
Eichenberger, Jerry Alan

PENNSYLVANIA

Philadelphia
Goldberg, Marvin Allen
Prewitt, David Edward

SOUTH CAROLINA

Greenville
Phillips, Joseph Brantley, Jr.

TENNESSEE

Knoxville
Arnett, Foster Deaver

TEXAS

Austin
Papadakis, Myron Philip
Spivey, Broadus Autry

Dallas
Howie, John Robert
Parker, James Francis

San Antonio
Guess, James David

VIRGINIA

Falls Church
Van Oeveren, Edward Lanier

WASHINGTON

Seattle
Gerrard, Keith
McLaughlin, Thomas Jeffrey
Narodick, Kit Gordon
Williams, J. Vernon

WISCONSIN

Marinette
Anuta, Michael Joseph

ENGLAND

London
Dannreuther, David Ion
Dibble, Robert Kenneth
Ferrari, Alexander Domonico
George, Anna-Britt Kristin
Kavanagh, Giles

THE PHILIPPINES

Makati
Agcaoili, Jose Luis Villafranca

Makati City
Salvador, Tranquil, III

UKRAINE

Kyiv
Kolesnyk, Oleg Ivanovich

ADDRESS UNPUBLISHED

Bailey, Francis Lee
Dubuc, Carroll Edward
Johnson, Richard Tenney
Levinson, Kenneth S.

BANKING *See also*
Commercial

UNITED STATES

ALABAMA

Birmingham
Denaburg, Charles L(eon)

Huntsville
Vargo, Robert Frank

ALASKA

Anchorage
Sneed, Spencer Craig

ARIZONA

Phoenix
Gust, John Devens
Spencer, Roger Keith

Tucson
Robinson, Bernard Leo

ARKANSAS

Little Rock
Jiles, Gary D.

Pine Bluff
Strode, Joseph Arlin

CALIFORNIA

Beverly Hills
Fleer, Keith George

Downey
Bear, Henry Louis

Hollywood
Biele, Hugh Irving

Irvine
Marshall, Ellen Ruth

Los Angeles
Clark, R(ufus) Bradbury
Farrar, Stanley F.
Francis, Merrill Richard
Fredman, Howard S
Gyemant, Robert Ernest
Hedlund, Karen Jean
Levine, Thomas Jeffrey Pello
McAniff, Edward John
Millard, Neal Steven
Morgenthaler-Lever, Alisa
Smith, Scott Ormond
Thoren-Peden, Deborah Suzanne
Wessling, Robert Bruce

Pacific Palisades
Share, Richard Hudson

Pasadena
Logan, Francis Dummer

San Carlos
Lee, John Jin

San Diego
Shippey, Sandra Lee

San Francisco
Abbott, Barry Alexander
Block, David Jeffrey
Brandel, Roland Eric
Byrne, Robert William
Coombe, George William, Jr.
Deane, Elaine
Halloran, Michael James
Minnick, Malcolm David
Schochet, Harvey S.
Shenk, George H.
Smith, Robert Michael
Stroup, Stanley Stephenson

San Mateo
Tormey, James Roland, Jr.

COLORADO

Denver
Otten, Arthur Edward, Jr.

Fort Collins
Rogers, Garth Winfield

Littleton
Keely, George Clayton

CONNECTICUT

Bridgeport
Schwartz, Lawrence B.

Hartford
Lotstein, James Irving
Schroth, Peter W(illiam)

Litchfield
Fiederowicz, Walter Michael

Stamford
Padilla, James Earl
Rose, Richard Loomis

Waterbury
Wolfe, Harriet Munrett

Westport
Lindskog, David Richard

DELAWARE

Dover
Twilley, Joshua Marion

Wilmington
Salinger, Frank Max

DISTRICT OF COLUMBIA

Washington
Adams, Lee Stephen
Alexander, Clifford Joseph
Bachman, Kenneth Leroy, Jr.
Bruemmer, Russell John
Collins, John Timothy
Comstock, Robert Francis
Cope, John R(obert)
Eisenberg, Meyer
Horn, Charles M.
Hunt, David Wallingford
Hyde, Howard Laurence
Kaufman, Thomas Frederick
Leibold, Arthur William, Jr.
Levenson, Alan Bradley
Lucas, Steven Mitchell
Lybecker, Martin Earl
Policy, Vincent Mark
Rosenhauer, James Joseph
Smith, Brian William
Stock, Stuart Chase
Trencher, William Mannes
Weinstein, Harris
Weiss, Mark Anschel
Wolff, Paul Martin
Wood, John Martin

FLORIDA

Coconut Grove
Arboleya, Carlos Joaquin

Coral Gables
Paul, Robert
Sacasas, Rene

Deerfield Beach
Buck, Thomas Randolph

Jacksonville
Christian, Gary Irvin
Kent, John Bradford

Jasper
McCormick, John Hoyle

Miami
Berley, David Richard
Garrett, Richard G.
Murai, Rene Vicente
Stumpf, Larry Allen

Naples
McCaffrey, Judith Elizabeth

North Palm Beach
Koffler, Warren William

Orlando
Christiansen, Patrick T.
Jontz, Jeffry Robert
Yates, Leighton Delevan, Jr.

Sarasota
Raimi, Burton Louis

Tampa
Gardner, J. Stephen
Jones, John Arthur
Roberson, Bruce Heerdt

West Palm Beach
Ballot, Alissa E.

Winter Park
Hadley, Ralph Vincent, III

GEORGIA

Atlanta
Carpenter, David Allan
Collins, Steven M.
Crews, William Edwin
Johnson, Benjamin F(ranklin), III
Kessler, Richard Paul, Jr.
Moeling, Walter Goos, IV
Stallings, Ronald Denis

Brunswick
McLemore, Gilbert Carmichael, Jr.

Canton
Hasty, William Grady, Jr.

Macon
Dodson, Carr Glover

Savannah
Searcy, William Nelson

Zebulon
Watson, Forrest Albert, Jr.

HAWAII

Honolulu
Fujiyama, Wallace Sachio
Nakata, Gary Kenji
Okinaga, Lawrence Shoji
Rolls, John Marland, Jr.

Kaneohe
Huber, Thomas P.

ILLINOIS

Chicago
Cohen, Melanie Rovner
Conlon, Steven Denis
Duncan, John Patrick Cavanaugh
Field, Robert Edward
Fishman, Robert Michael
Greenbaum, Kenneth
Hanson, Ronald William
Kaufman, Andrew Michael
Kohn, William Irwin
Kravitt, Jason Harris Paperno
Malkin, Cary Jay
McCrohon, Craig
McDermott, John H(enry)
O'Toole, William George
Prochnow, Herbert Victor, Jr.
Schwartz, Donald Lee

Du Quoin
Atkins, Aaron Ardene

Gurnee
Southern, Robert Allen

Hoffman Estates
Kelly, Anastasia Donovan

Lincolnshire
Bartlett, Robert William

Marengo
Franks, Herbert Hoover

Oak Brook
Ras, Robert A.

Toledo
Prather, William C., III

Watseka
Tungate, James Lester

Wheaton
Stein, Lawrence A.

INDIANA

Huntington
Gordon, William Stout

Indianapolis
Kleiman, Mary Margaret
Neff, Robert Matthew
Talesnick, Stanley

Monticello
Guy, John Martin

Vincennes
Smith, Bruce Arthur

IOWA

Council Bluffs
Pechacek, Frank Warren, Jr.

Iowa City
Downer, Robert Nelson

West Des Moines
Brown, John Lewis

KANSAS

Overland Park
Cohen, Barton Pollock

Wichita
Foote, Richard Van
Guy, James Matheus

KENTUCKY

Bowling Green
Catron, Stephen Barnard

Lexington
Scott, Joseph Mitchell, Jr.

Louisville
Fenton, Thomas Conner
Maggiolo, Allison Joseph

LOUISIANA

New Orleans
Bieck, Robert Barton, Jr.

Claverie, Philip deVilliers
Getten, Thomas Frank
McMillan, Lee Richards, II
Murchison, Henry Dillon
Vance, Robert Patrick

Shreveport
Cox, John Thomas, Jr.

Winnfield
Simmons, Kermit Mixon

MAINE

Portland
Hirshon, Robert Edward
Neagle, Christopher Scott

Yarmouth
Webster, Peter Bridgman

MARYLAND

Annapolis
Michaelson, Benjamin, Jr.

Baltimore
Haines, Thomas W. W.
Isacoff, Richard Irwin
Rafferty, William Bernard
Wasserman, Richard Leo

New Market
Gabriel, Eberhard John

MASSACHUSETTS

Arlington
Keshian, Richard

Boston
Albrecht, Peter Leffingwell
Cherwin, Joel Ira
Fischer, Eric Robert
Loria, Martin A.
Malley, Robert John
Mercer, Richard James
Parker, Christopher William
Smith, Edwin Eric

Lincoln
Gnichtel, William Van Orden

Marion
Worley, Robert William, Jr.

Springfield
Sheils, James Bernard

MICHIGAN

Bloomfield Hills
Williams, J. Bryan

Detroit
Lawrence, John Kidder
Rohr, Richard David

Grosse Pointe
Behringer, Samuel Joseph, Jr.

Kalamazoo
Gordon, Edgar George

Muskegon
Fauri, Eric Joseph

Troy
Allen, James Lee

MINNESOTA

Duluth
Nys, John Nikki

Eden Prairie
Nilles, John Michael

Fridley
Savelkoul, Donald Charles

Saint Paul
Winthrop, Sherman

MISSISSIPPI

Gulfport
Harral, John Menteith

Jackson
Barnett, Robert Glenn
Edds, Stephen Charles
Hammond, Frank Jefferson, III

MISSOURI

Hannibal
Welch, Joseph Daniel

Kansas City
Ayers, Jeffrey David
Deacy, Thomas Edward, Jr.
Graham, Harold Steven
Pelofsky, Joel
Tharp, Tonna K.

Macon
Parkinson, Paul K.

Saint Louis
Graham, Robert Clare, III
Inkley, John James, Jr.

Poscover, Maury B.
Willard, Gregory Dale

MONTANA

Missoula
Bender, Ronald Andrew

NEBRASKA

Lincoln
Guthery, John M.
Johnson, Warren Charles
Perry, Edwin Charles

Omaha
Hamann, Deryl Frederick

NEW HAMPSHIRE

Manchester
Stebbins, Henry Blanchard

NEW JERSEY

Bridgewater
Linett, David

Morristown
O'Grady, Dennis Joseph

Princeton
Szwalbenest, Benedykt Jan

Roseland
Wovsaniker, Alan

Short Hills
Siegfried, David Charles

Somerville
Hutcheon, Peter David

Summit
Pfaltz, Hugo Menzel, Jr.
Woller, James Alan

Union
Greenstein, Richard Henry

Woodbridge
Hoberman, Stuart A.

NEW MEXICO

Albuquerque
Ussery, Albert Travis

Ruidoso
Dutton, Dominic Edward

Socorro
Smith, Leslie Clark

NEW YORK

Albany
Kornstein, Michael Allen
Yanas, John Joseph

Bronxville
Garber, Robert Edward
Veneruso, James John

Buffalo
Lammert, Richard Alan
Swart, Michael

Garden City
Schupbach, Arthur Christopher

Hamburg
Chesbro, Robert Bruce

Hudson
Howard, Andrew Baker

Huntington
Tucker, William P.

Lake George
Hayes, Norman Robert, Jr.

Larchmont
Berridge, George Bradford

Long Island City
Wanderman, Susan Mae

Melville
Lane, Arthur Alan

New York
Barnard, Robert N.
Bergan, Philip James
Bernstein, Donald Scott
Byrnes, Richard James
Caytas, Ivo George
Chen, Wesley
Cohen, Henry Rodgin
Cohen, Marcy Sharon
Cummings, Anthony William
Danilek, Donald J.
Das, Kalyan
Davis, Richard Ralph
Dwyer, Cornelius J., Jr.
Elicker, Gordon Leonard
Fernandez, Jose Walfredo
Fewell, Charles Kenneth, Jr.
Fishman, Mitchell Steven
Freedman, Gerald M.
Garfinkel, Neil B.
Genova, Diane Melisano

Greene, Ira S.
Grew, Robert Ralph
Gross, Richard Benjamin
Gruson, Michael
Halliday, Joseph William
Hauser, Rita Eleanore Abrams
Higgs, John H.
Jock, Paul F., II
Knight, Townsend Jones
Kraemer, Lillian Elizabeth
Kraus, Douglas M.
Lee, In-Young
Lindauer, Erik D.
Lindsay, George Peter
Lynch, Luke Daniel, Jr.
MacRae, Cameron Farquhar, III
Marcus, Eric Peter
McLaughlin, Joseph Thomas
Metzger, Barry
Minsky, Bruce William
O'Connor, William Matthew
Oshima, Michael W.
Patrikis, Ernest T.
Peet, Charles D., Jr.
Puleo, Frank Charles
Quale, Andrew Christopher, Jr.
Quinn, Linda Catherine
Radon, Jenik Richard
Ring, Renee Etheline
Robinson, Irwin Jay
Rocklen, Kathy Hellenbrand
Ross, Michael Aaron
Russo, Thomas Anthony
Schwab, Terrance W.
Semaya, Francine Levitt
Setrakian, Berge
Sheehan, Robert C.
Skigen, Patricia Sue
Solbert, Peter Omar Abernathy
Tallackson, Jeffrey Stephen
Toumey, Donald Joseph
Valat de Córdova, Thierry
Villacorat, Anna Teresa Cruz
Walker, John Lockwood
Wesely, Edwin Joseph
Zaitzeff, Roger Michael

Niagara Falls
Brett, Jay Elliot

Rochester
Galbraith, Robert Lyell, Jr.
Willett, Thomas Edward
Young, Deborah Schwind

Syracuse
Ackerman, Kenneth Edward
Barclay, H(ugh) Douglas
Hubbard, Peter Lawrence

Utica
Kelly, William Wright

White Plains
Serchuk, Ivan

NORTH CAROLINA

Charlotte
Dunn, Jackson Thomas, Jr.
Monge, Jay Parry
Roberts, Manley Woolfolk
Taylor, David Brooke
Walls, George Rodney

Greensboro
Davis, Herbert Owen

Murphy
Bata, Rudolph Andrew, Jr.

Raleigh
Carlton, Alfred Pershing, Jr.
Jernigan, John Lee

Wilmington
Jones, Lucian Cox
Kaufman, James Jay
McCauley, Cleyburn Lycurgus

Winston Salem
Herring, Jerone Carson
Loughridge, John Halsted, Jr.
Strayhorn, Ralph Nichols, Jr.

OHIO

Cincinnati
Bridgeland, James Ralph, Jr.
Coffey, Thomas William

Cleveland
Coquillette, William Hollis
Csank, Paul Lewis
Freimuth, Marc William
Lawniczak, James Michael
Owendoff, Stephen Peter
Stevens, Thomas Charles

Columbus
DeRousie, Charles Stuart
Frasier, Ralph Kennedy
Fultz, Robert Edward
Helfer, Michael Stevens

Lorain
Wiersma, David Charles

OKLAHOMA

Jones
Dean, Bill Verlin, Jr.

Muskogee
Robinson, Adelbert Carl

Oklahoma City
Elder, James Carl

Tulsa
Baker, Gary Hugh

OREGON

Lake Oswego
Byczynski, Edward Frank
Rasmussen, Richard Robert

PENNSYLVANIA

Allison Park
Ries, William Campbell

Exton
Teti, Louis N.

Philadelphia
Auten, David Charles
Berger, Lawrence Howard
Esser, Carl Eric
Genkin, Barry Howard
Hunter, James Austen, Jr.
Loveless, George Group
Maxey, David Walker
Spolan, Harmon Samuel

Pittsburgh
Barrett, Karen Moore
Bleier, Michael E.
Gold, Harold Arthur
Messner, Robert Thomas

Reading
Kline, Sidney DeLong, Jr.
Page, Clemson North, Jr.

Warren
Ristau, Mark Moody

Washington
Posner, David S.

Williamsport
Knecht, William L.

RHODE ISLAND

Providence
Furness, Peter John

SOUTH CAROLINA

Greenville
Barash, Anthony Harlan

TENNESSEE

Cordova
Swan, Michael Robert

Memphis
Glassman, Richard
Winchester, Richard Lee, Jr.

Nashville
Bruce, William Roland

TEXAS

Addison
Kneipper, Richard Keith

Austin
Henderson, George Ervin
Laves, Alan Leonard
Matheson, Daniel Nicholas, III

Boerne
Vaughan, Edward Gibson

Brooks AFB
Tanner, Gordon Owen

Brownsville
Fleming, Tommy Wayne

Dallas
Beuttenmuller, Rudolf William
Birkeland, Bryan Collier
Flanagan, Christie Stephen
Jameson, Gene Lanier
Jones, Lindy Don
Kearney, Douglas Charles
Livingstone, William Edwin, III
Riddle, Michael Lee
Smith, Larry Van
True, Roy Joe
White, James Richard
Zisman, Barry Stuart

Houston
Anders, Milton Howard
Bistline, F. Walter, Jr.
Bridges, David Manning
Goldberg, Charles Ned
LaBoon, Robert Bruce
McCreary, Frank E., III
Paden, Lyman R.
Schroeder, Walter Allen
Shannon, Joel Ingram
Slaydon, Kathleen Amelia
Stuart, Walter Bynum, IV
Weiner, Sanford Alan

La Porte
Armstrong, John Douglas

Liberty
Wheat, John Nixon

Lubbock
Nelson, Jack Odell, Jr.

The Woodlands
Hagerman, John David

Weslaco
Pomerantz, Jerald Michael

UTAH

Saint George
Gallian, Russell Joseph

Salt Lake City
Callister, Louis Henry, Jr.

VIRGINIA

Charlottesville
Hodous, Robert Power

Fairfax
Rust, John Howson, Jr.

Falls Church
Christman, Bruce Lee
Jennings, Thomas Parks

Mc Lean
Walton, Edmund Lewis, Jr.

Reston
Toole, John Harper

Richmond
Buford, Robert Pegram

Roanoke
Densmore, Douglas Warren

Sterling
McBarnette, Bruce Olvin

WASHINGTON

Seattle
Kuhrau, Edward W.
Nye, Daniel Alan
Tune, James Fulcher

WEST VIRGINIA

Charleston
O'Connor, Otis Leslie

WISCONSIN

Milwaukee
Friedman, James Dennis
Schoenfeld, Howard Allen
Schulz, William John
Wiley, Edwin Packard

Racine
Dye, William Ellsworth
Stutt, John Barry

Sun Prairie
Eustice, Francis Joseph

WYOMING

Casper
Lowe, Robert Stanley
McCall, Donn Jay

MEXICO

Coahuila
Hernandez, Juan Ignacio

Mexico City
Ritch, James Earle, Jr.

AUSTRIA

Vienna
Wolf, Richard V.

CHINA

Beijing
Xing, Xuisong

Hong Kong
Lam, Wing Wo

CZECH REPUBLIC

Prague
Brzobohaty, Tomas

DENMARK

Copenhagen
Sogaard, Klaus

ENGLAND

Leeds
Mudd, Philip John

London
Barratt, Jeffrey Vernon
Breakell, David James
Brownwood, David Owen
Cole, Richard A.
Crowley, Laurence Anthony
Dannreuther, David Ion
Dibble, Robert Kenneth
Drury, Stephen Patrick
Kidwell, Mathew Charles
MacRitchie, Kenneth
Moller, Stephen Hans
Quillen, Cecil Dyer, III
Sleigh, Russell Howard Phalf
Woolf, Geoffrey Stephen

FINLAND

Helsinki
Wist, Tarja Tuulia

FRANCE

Paris
Blanchenay, Nicolas

GERMANY

Düsseldorf
Gillessen, Frederick

Stuttgart
Mailaender, Karl Peter

GREECE

Piraeus
Bowen-Morris, Nigel Vaughan

HUNGARY

Budapest
Doughty, Alexander Robert

ITALY

Milan
Plankensteiner, Marco

Rome
Carotenuto, Giovanni

THE NETHERLANDS

Amsterdam
Van Campen, Arnoud Clemens

NEW ZEALAND

Auckland
Webb, Michael R.

PORTUGAL

Lisbon
Calmeiros, Jose Maria Albuquerque
Cid, Tiago

ROMANIA

Bucharest
Pachiu, Laurentiu Victor

SINGAPORE

Singapore
Trahair, Andrew James
Yeo, Jennifer

SOUTH AFRICA

Johannesburg
Schwarz, Harry Heinz

Sandton
Cron, Kevin Richard

SWEDEN

Stockholm
Sarkia, Peter L.

SWITZERLAND

Bern
Friedli, Georg

Geneva
De Pfyffer, Andre

VENEZUELA

Solano Caracas
Garcia-Montoya, Luis Alberto

ADDRESS UNPUBLISHED

Bennett, Steven Alan
Carmody, Richard Patrick
Crook, Donald Martin
Cumberland, William Edwin
Ginsberg, Ernest
Gotlieb, Lawrence Barry
Gregory, George G.
Hackett, Robert John
Harman, Wallace Patrick
Hartmann, Kenneth
Johnson, Leonard Hjalma
Kratt, Peter George
Marker, Marc Linthacum
Millard, John Alden
Ober, Richard Francis, Jr.
Reiter, Glenn Mitchell
Russ, Neil Andrew
Schley, Michael Dodson
Shambaugh, Stephen Ward
Shapiro, Howard Alan
Toomey, Richard Andrew, Jr.
Weil, Peter Henry

BANKRUPTCY *See also* Commercial

UNITED STATES

ALABAMA

Birmingham
Denaburg, Charles L(eon)

ALASKA

Anchorage
Sneed, Spencer Craig

ARIZONA

Flagstaff
Cowser, Danny Lee

Phoenix
Lee, Richard H(arlo)

ARKANSAS

Little Rock
Hughes, Steven Jay
Scott, Isaac Alexander, Jr.

CALIFORNIA

Beverly Hills
Brickwood, Susan Callaghan

Canoga Park
Adams, Anne Claire

Encinitas
Williams, Michael Edward

Hollywood
Biele, Hugh Irving

Los Angeles
Cohen, Cynthia Marylyn
Creim, William Benjamin
Francis, Merrill Richard
Gyemant, Robert Ernest
Havel, Richard W.
Huben, Brian David
Leibow, Ronald Louis
Neely, Sally Schultz
Ohlgren, Joel R.
Ray, David Lewin
Smith, Scott Ormond
Solis, Carlos
White, Robert Joel
Zerunyan, Frank Vram

Newport Beach
Wolf, Alan Steven

Oakland
Allen, Jeffrey Michael
Buckley, Mike Clifford

Pasadena
Katzman, Harvey Lawrence

Sacramento
Felderstein, Steven Howard

San Diego
Godone-Maresca, Lillian
Shapiro, Philip Alan

San Francisco
Holden, Frederick Douglass, Jr.
Millner, Dianne Maxine
Minnick, Malcolm David
Schochet, Harvey S.
Stinnett, Terrance Lloyd

San Jose
Katzman, Irwin

Santa Ana
Heckler, Gerard Vincent

COLORADO

Colorado Springs
Slivka, Michael Andrew

Denver
Brown, James Elliott
Cohen, Jeffrey
DeLaney, Herbert Wade, Jr.
DeMuth, Alan Cornelius
Dowdle, Patrick Dennis
Eklund, Carl Andrew
Keller, Glen Elven, Jr.
Merrick, Glenn Warren
Slavin, Howard Leslie
Tisdale, Douglas Michael

Lakewood
Yuthas, George Anthony

CONNECTICUT

Avon
Grafstein, Joel M.

New Haven
Coan, Richard Morton

Roxbury
Friedman, John Maxwell, Jr.

Stamford
Padilla, James Earl

DELAWARE

Newark
Welsh, Paul Patrick

Wilmington
Melnik, Selinda A.
Patton, James Leeland, Jr.

DISTRICT OF COLUMBIA

Washington
Cohen, Nelson Craig
Foster, Mark Wingate
Mackiewicz, Edward Robert
Mendales, Richard Ephraim

FLORIDA

Boca Raton
Fayette, Kathleen Owens

Brandon
England, Lynne Lipton

Fort Lauderdale
Saunders, Robert M.

Miami
Baena, Scott Louis
Gitlitz, Stuart Hal
Pastoriza, Julio
Scheer, Mark Jeffrey
Stein, Allan Mark

New Port Richey
Focht, Theodore Harold

Orlando
Jontz, Jeffry Robert
Williamson, Michael George

Palm Harbor
Summers-Powell, Alan

Sarasota
Fetterman, James Charles

Tampa
Rydberg, Marsha Griffin

West Palm Beach
Mrachek, Lorin Louis

GEORGIA

Atlanta
Bisbee, David George
Carpenter, David Allan
Cohen, Ezra Harry
Kelley, Jeffrey Wendell
Kessler, Richard Paul, Jr.
Raskin, Daniel Ellis
Rhodes, Thomas Willard

Columbus
Johnson, Walter Frank, Jr.

Roswell
Mimms, Thomas Bowman, Jr.

HAWAII

Honolulu
Adaniya, Kevin Seisho
Chung, Steven Kamsein
Gelber, Don Jeffrey

IDAHO

Boise
Noack, Harold Quincy, Jr.

ILLINOIS

Alton
Struif, L. James

Aurora
Mateas, Kenneth Edward
Patricoski, Paul Thomas

Belleville
Urban, Donald Wayne

Carbondale
Frazier, Dana Sue

Chicago
Berkoff, Mark Andrew
Cohen, Melanie Rovner
Collen, John
Coughlan, Kenneth L.
Cunningham, Thomas Justin
Feinstein, Fred Ira
Fishman, Robert Michael
Gordon, James S.
Hanson, Ronald William
Hoseman, Daniel
Kohn, Shalom L.
Kohn, William Irwin
Murray, Daniel Richard
Peterson, Ronald Roger
Rosenberg, H. James
Sawyier, Michael Tod
Schwartz, Donald Lee
Schwartz, Stuart Randall
Spiotto, James Ernest
Wood, Allison Lorraine

La Grange
Kerr, Alexander Duncan, Jr.

Normal
Bender, Paul Edward

Skokie
Bauer, Michael

Springfield
Narmont, John Stephen

INDIANA

Gary
Boscia, James Dominic

Indianapolis
Ancel, Jerald Irwin
Talesnick, Stanley

Newburgh
Dewey, Dennis James

Valparaiso
Canganelli, Michael Antonio

Vincennes
Smith, Bruce Arthur

IOWA

Iowa City
Trca, Randy Ernest

Shell Rock
Ottesen, Realff Henry

Sioux City
Giles, William Jefferson, III
Poulson, Jeffrey Lee

KANSAS

Wichita
Guy, James Matheus
Johnson, Kevin Blaine

KENTUCKY

Lexington
McKinstry, Taft Avent
Scott, Joseph Mitchell, Jr.

Louisville
Keeney, Steven Harris
Shaikun, Michael Gary

Richmond
Weldon, C. Michael

LOUISIANA

New Orleans
Jones, Philip Kirkpatrick, Jr.
Vance, Robert Patrick

Shreveport
Arceneaux, M(artin) Thomas

MAINE

Bass Harbor
Ervin, Spencer

MARYLAND

Baltimore
Berlage, Jan Ingham
Coppel, Lawrence David
Walker, Irving Edward
Wasserman, Richard Leo

Frederick
Borison, Scott Craig

MASSACHUSETTS

Boston
Albrecht, Peter Leffingwell

Glosband, Daniel Martin
Lamb, Kevin Thomas
Macauley, William Francis
Moreira, Barbara Lyne
Parker, Christopher William
Smith, Edwin Eric

Newton Center
Snyder, John Gorvers

Stoughton
Gabovitch, Steven Alan

MICHIGAN

Ann Arbor
Ellmann, Douglas Stanley

Bloomfield Hills
Cunningham, Gary H.

Detroit
Pirtle, H(arold) Edward
Rochkind, Louis Philipp

Grand Rapids
Curtin, Timothy John
Engbers, James Arend
Mears, Patrick Edward

Grosse Pointe
Behringer, Samuel Joseph, Jr.

Kalamazoo
Pikcunas, Charles Richard

Midland
Battle, Leonard Carroll

MINNESOTA

Duluth
Nys, John Nikki

Edina
Gurstel, Norman Keith

Minneapolis
Baillie, James Leonard
Weil, Cass Sargent
Ziebell-Sullivan, Martha Jane

MISSISSIPPI

Jackson
Edds, Stephen Charles
O'Mara, James Wright

MISSOURI

Cape Girardeau
O'Loughlin, John Patrick

Chesterfield
Radloff, Stuart Jay

Hannibal
Welch, Joseph Daniel

Jefferson City
Turnbull, Reginald Harrison

Kansas City
Carter, J. Denise
Foster, Mark Stephen
Pelofsky, Joel

Maryland Heights
Cooper, Richard Alan

Saint Louis
Anderson, Anthony LeClaire
Willard, Gregory Dale

NEBRASKA

Grand Island
Cuypers, Charles James

Lincoln
Rowe, David Winfield

NEVADA

Las Vegas
Nohrden, Patrick Thomas

NEW HAMPSHIRE

Hollis
Lumbard, Eliot Howland

Portsmouth
Harman, Terrie

Rochester
Jones, Franklin Charles

NEW JERSEY

Flemington
Wolfson, William Steven

Hackensack
Robinson, Sandra Ann

Morristown
O'Grady, Dennis Joseph

Mountainside
Jacobson, Gary Steven

New Brunswick
Miller, Arthur Harold

Newark
Knee, Stephen H.

Parsippany
Chobot, John Charles
Gallagher, Jerome Francis, Jr.

Pitman
Cloues, Edward Blanchard, II

Ridgewood
Trocano, Russell Peter

Roseland
Sarasohn, Peter Radin
Schenkler, Bernard

Somerville
Fuerst, Steven Bernard

Wildwood
Gould, Alan I.

NEW MEXICO

Carlsbad
Byers, Matthew T(odd)

NEW YORK

Armonk
Moss, Eric Harold

Auburn
Gunger, Richard William

Buffalo
Fisher, Cheryl Smith

Garden City
Fischoff, Gary Charles

Hastings On Hudson
Steer, Richard Lane

Jericho
Beal, Carol Ann

New York
Arenson, Gregory K.
Bernstein, Donald Scott
Berzow, Harold Steven
Blackman, Kenneth Robert
Broude, Richard Frederick
Cannell, John Redferne
Carpenter, Randle Burt
Chaitman, Helen Davis
Cook, Michael Lewis
Cowen, Edward S.
Davis, Michael Steven
De Natale, Andrew Peter
Dichter, Barry Joel
Drebsky, Dennis Jay
Dykhouse, David Wayne
Emrich, Edmund Michael
Freedman, Gerald M.
Greene, Ira S.
Gross, Steven Ross
Hahn, Paul Bernard
Halliday, Joseph William
Haynes, Jean Reed
Hershcopf, Gerald Thea
Hirshfield, Stuart
Hirshon, Sheldon Ira
Hughes, Kevin Peter
Jacob, Marvin Eugene
Jerome, John James
Kinzler, Thomas Benjamin
Kraemer, Lillian Elizabeth
Lacy, Robinson Burrell
Langer, Bruce Alden
Lindauer, Erik D.
Mann, Philip Roy
Mayerson, Sandra Elaine
Minkel, Herbert Philip , Jr.
Mittman, Lawrence
Moloney, Thomas Joseph
Novikoff, Harold Stephen
O'Dea, Dennis Michael
Oppenheim, Jeffrey Alan
Perkiel, Mitchel H.
Posner, Louis Joseph
Reilly, Conor Desmond
Sacks, Ira Stephen
Schallert, Edwin Glenn
Scheler, Brad Eric
Schwed, Peter Gregory
Silverberg, Jay Lloyd
Simon, Bruce Harvey
Spivack, Edith Irene
Sylver, Peter T.
Tricarico, Joseph Archangelo

Olean
Heyer, John Henry, II

Smithtown
Holland, Marvin Arthur

Spring Valley
Barr, Harvey Stephen

Syracuse
Ackerman, Kenneth Edward
Hubbard, Peter Lawrence
Rothman, Robert Pierson

White Plains
Posner, Martin Louis

NORTH CAROLINA

Charlotte
Dunn, Jackson Thomas, Jr.

Durham
Carpenter, Charles Francis

Raleigh
Palmer, William Ralph

Winston Salem
Schollander, Wendell Leslie, Jr.

OHIO

Cincinnati
Adams, Edmund John
Bissinger, Mark Christian
Coffey, Thomas William
Hayden, William Taylor
Metz, Jerome Joseph, Jr.
Meyer, Charles Mulvihill

Cleveland
Felty, Kriss Delbert
Foote, Richard Charles
Kopit, Alan Stuart
Lawniczak, James Michael
Meyer, G. Christopher
Morgenstern, Conrad J.

Columbus
Pigman, Jack Richard
Sidman, Robert John
Swetnam, Daniel Richard
Wightman, Alec

Kent
Nome, William Andreas

Toledo
Wicklund, David Wayne

Westerville
Lancione, Bernard Gabe

Worthington
Minton, Harvey Steiger

OKLAHOMA

Muskogee
Williams, Betty Outhier

Oklahoma City
Gibson, Keith Russell
Kline, Timothy Deal
Schwabe, George Blaine, III

Tulsa
Abrahamson, A. Craig
Clark, Gary Carl
Haynie, Tony Wayne
Moffett, J. Denny

OREGON

Portland
Anderson, Herbert Hatfield
Waggoner, James Clyde

PENNSYLVANIA

Blue Bell
Siedzikowski, Henry Francis

Brookville
Smith, Sharon Louise

Center Valley
Smillie, Douglas James

Drexel Hill
West, Kenneth Edward

Johnstown
Kaminsky, Ira Samuel

Mc Murray
Brzustowicz, John Cinq-Mars

Media
McNitt, David Garver

Philadelphia
Aaron, Kenneth Ellyot
Berger, David
Bressler, Barry E.
Gordesky, Morton
Gough, John Francis
Loveless, George Group
Ramsey, Natalie D.
Schorling, William Harrison
Tractenberg, Craig R.

Pittsburgh
Aderson, Sanford M.
Conti, Joy Flowers
Helmrich, Joel Marc
Hollinshead, Earl Darnell, Jr.
Leibowitz, Marvin
Murdoch, David Armor
Sanders, Russell Ronald

Warren
Ristau, Mark Moody

Williamsport
Knecht, William L.

RHODE ISLAND

Providence
Furness, Peter John

SOUTH CAROLINA

Myrtle Beach
Breen, David Hart

TENNESSEE

Chattanooga
Ragan, Charles Oliver, Jr.

Memphis
Matthews, Paul Aaron

TEXAS

Abilene
Boone, Celia Trimble
Hacker, Gary Lee

Austin
Henderson, George Ervin

Bryan
Steelman, Frank (Sitley)

Dallas
Brister, Bill H.
Farquhar, Robert Michael
Johnson, James Joseph Scofield
Miller, Stewart Ransom
Nolan, John Michael
Orleans, Neil Jeffrey
Palmer, Philip Isham, Jr.
Phelan, Robin Eric
Portman, Glenn Arthur

Fort Worth
Mack, Theodore

Houston
Banks, John Robert, Jr.
Ellis, David Dale
Goldberg, Charles Ned
McDaniel, Jarrel Dave
Miller, Gary C.
Prestridge, Pamela Adair
Ray, Hugh Massey, Jr.
Sheinfeld, Myron M.
Sing, William Bender
Slaydon, Kathleen Amelia
Zeigler, Ann dePender

Lubbock
Crowson, James Lawrence

Missouri City
Maddox, Charles J., Jr.

San Antonio
Biery, Evelyn Hudson
Williamson, Deborah Daywood

Tyler
Patterson, Donald Ross

Wichita Falls
Wesbrooks, Perry

VERMONT

Bethel
Obuchowski, Raymond Joseph

Colchester
Garcia, Luis Cesareo

Middlebury
Palmer, Michael Paul

VIRGINIA

Alexandria
Peyton, Gordon Pickett

Danville
Goodman, Lewis Elton, Jr.

Mc Lean
Najjoum, Linda Lemmon

Richmond
Krumbein, Charles Harvey

Roanoke
Farnham, David Alexander

Virginia Beach
Spitzli, Donald Hawkes, Jr.

WASHINGTON

Grandview
Maxwell, John Edward

Kennewick
Hames, William Lester

Seattle
Cullen, Jack Joseph
Sandman, Irvin W(illis)

WEST VIRGINIA

Wheeling
Riley, Arch Wilson, Jr.

WISCONSIN

Madison
Doran, Kenneth John
Walsh, David Graves

Milwaukee
Blain, Peter Charles
Israel, Scott Michael
Schoenfeld, Howard Allen
Sturm, William Charles

WYOMING

Casper
McCall, Donn Jay

Riverton
Girard, Nettabell

AUSTRALIA

Sydney
L'Estrange, Timothy I.
Wong, Christopher Wai C.

CHILE

Santiago
Rosenblut, Alvaro

CHINA

Hong Kong
Bannister, Joe
Rapinet, Crispin William

DENMARK

Copenhagen
Serring, Michael

ENGLAND

Leeds
Mudd, Philip John

London
Crowley, Laurence Anthony
Spencer, Robin Graham Nelson
Woolf, Geoffrey Stephen

FRANCE

Paris
Bougartchev, Kiril Alexandre

HUNGARY

Budapest
Doughty, Alexander Robert

NEW ZEALAND

Auckland
Whale, Michael John

NORWAY

Oslo
Aubert, Fredrik Scheel

SCOTLAND

Glasgow
Burrow, Alistair Stewart

SOUTH AFRICA

Johannesburg
Girdwood, Graham William

THAILAND

Bangkok
Annanon, Songphol

ADDRESS UNPUBLISHED

Carmody, Richard Patrick
Drabkin, Murray
Hargis, V. Burns
Kerner, Michael Philip
Lichtenstein, Sarah Carol
Perlman, Richard Brian
Perlstein, William James
Pickard, Terry Roy
Seifert, Stephen Wayne
Weil, Peter Henry

CIVIL LITIGATION, FEDERAL

UNITED STATES

ALABAMA

Anniston
Woodrow, Randall Mark

Birmingham
Alexander, James Patrick

Max, Rodney Andrew
Newton, Alexander Worthy
Rogers, Ernest Mabry
Smith, Carol Ann
Spotswood, Robert Keeling
Stabler, Lewis Vastine, Jr.

Dothan
Huskey, Dow Thobern

Huntsville
Stephens, Harold (Holman Stephens)

Mobile
Pierce, Donald Fay

Montgomery
Prestwood, Alvin Tennyson
Tindol, Melton Chad

ALASKA

Anchorage
Brown, Harold MacVane
Feldman, Jeffrey Marc
Fortier, Samuel John
Pfiffner, Frank Albert
Richmond, Robert Lawrence

ARIZONA

Phoenix
Beggs, Harry Mark
Beshears, Robert Gene
Bivens, Donald Wayne
Condo, James Robert
Corson, Kimball Jay
Gomez, David Frederick
Grant, Merwin Darwin
Leonard, Jeffrey S.
Ulrich, Paul Graham
Wall, Donald Arthur

Rio Rico
Ryan, John Duncan

Tucson
Hyams, Harold
Kitchen, Charles William
Meehan, Michael Joseph

ARKANSAS

Little Rock
Anderson, Philip Sidney
Dillahunty, Wilbur Harris
Griffin, William Mell, III
Hargis, David Michael
Jones, Stephen Witsell
Light, Robert Vann
Scott, Isaac Alexander, Jr.
Simpson, James Marlon, Jr.

CALIFORNIA

Belvedere Tiburon
Allan, Walter Robert

Beverly Hills
Fine, Richard Isaac

Burbank
Litvack, Sanford Martin

Burlingame
Cotchett, Joseph Winters

Carlsbad
McCracken, Steven Carl

El Segundo
Zucker, David Clark

Emeryville
Blackburn, Robert Parker

Folsom
Goodwin, James Jeffries

Glendale
Young, George Walter

Huntington Beach
Nikas, Richard John

Laguna Hills
Reinglass, Michelle Annette

Long Beach
Haile, Lawrence Barclay
Stolpman, Thomas Gerard

Los Angeles
Angel, Arthur Ronald
Barza, Harold A.
Belleville, Philip Frederick
Bodkin, Henry Grattan, Jr.
Bressan, Paul Louis
Bryan, James Spencer
Chiate, Kenneth Reed
Daniels, John Peter
Fairbank, Robert Harold
Franceschi, Ernest Joseph, Jr.
Gyemant, Robert Ernest
Handzlik, Jan Lawrence
Hart, Larry Calvin
Heller, Philip
Hufstedler, Shirley Mount (Mrs. Seth
    M. Hufstedler)
Lauchengco, Jose Yujuico, Jr.
Levine, Jerome Lester
Long, Gregory Alan
Metzger, Robert Streicher
Miller, Milton Allen
Muhlbach, Robert Arthur
Newman, Michael Rodney
Niles, John Gilbert
Oliver, Dale Hugh

Olson, Ronald Leroy
Patterson, Charles Ernest
Perlis, Michael Fredrick
Riffer, Jeffrey Kent
Straw, Lawrence Joseph, Jr.
Strong, George Gordon, Jr.
von Kalinowski, Julian Onesime
Williams, Richard Thomas
Wine, Mark Philip
Woods, Daniel James

Menlo Park
Dyer, Charles Arnold

Newport Beach
Mandel, Maurice, II
Martens, Don Walter
Millar, Richard William, Jr.

Oakland
Bjork, Robert David, Jr.

Orinda
Roethe, James Norton

Palo Alto
Baron, Frederick David
Fowler, John Wellington
Pasahow, Lynn H(arold)
Phillips, W. Alan
Pooley, James
Tiffany, Joseph Raymond, II

Pasadena
Koelzer, George Joseph
Tanner, Dee Boshard

Redwood City
Kelly, Edward Joseph

Sacramento
Goode, Barry Paul

San Diego
Bayer, Richard Stewart
Buzunis, Constantine Dino
Higgs, Craig DeWitt
Klinedinst, John David
Longstreth, Robert Christy
McDermott, Thomas John, Jr.
Schuck, Carl Joseph
Sullivan, Patrick James
Weaver, Michael James

San Francisco
Alexis, Geraldine M.
Boyd, William Sprott
Callan, Terrence A.
Chambers, Guy Wayne
Finberg, James Michael
Gelhaus, Robert Joseph
Hasson, Kirke Michael
Johns, Richard Seth Ellis
Ladar, Jerrold Morton
Meadows, John Frederick
Ragan, Charles Ransom
Renfrew, Charles Byron
Rosenthal, Kenneth W.
Rubin, Michael
Schon, Steven Eliot
Snow, Tower Charles, Jr.
Suter, Ben
Tonsing, Michael John
Traynor, John Michael
Venning, Robert Stanley
Walcher, Alan Ernest
Wollen, W. Foster
Young, Douglas Rea

San Jose
Gregg, Richard
Morgan, Robert Hall

San Rafael
Kathrein, Reed Richard

Santa Monica
Schlei, Norbert Anthony

Ventura
Bray, Laurack Doyle

Westlake Village
Sullivan, Mark Francis

COLORADO

Boulder
Danielson, Luke Jeffries
Halpern, Alexander
Purvis, John Anderson
Ward, Denitta Dawn

Colorado Springs
Swanson, Victoria Clare Heldman

Denver
Bain, James William
Curtis, George Bartlett
Featherstone, Bruce Alan
Hilbert, Otto Karl, II
Hoffman, Daniel Steven
Husband, John Michael
Jablonski, James Arthur
Johnson, Philip Edward
Kahn, Edwin Sam
Kanan, Gregory Brian
Keller, Glen Elven, Jr.
Law, John Manning
Marquess, Lawrence Wade
Merker, Steven Joseph
Merrick, Glenn Warren
Miller, Gale Timothy
Pascoe, Donald Monte
Roesler, John Bruce
Samuels, Donald L.
Starrs, Elizabeth Anne
Thomasch, Roger Paul
Tisdale, Douglas Michael
Ulrich, Theodore Albert
Wedgle, Richard Jay
Welch, Carol Mae
Wheeler, Malcolm Edward

Seymour
Pardieck, Roger Lee

Valparaiso
Conison, Jay

IOWA

Des Moines
Frederici, C. Carleton
Graves, Bruce
Wharton, John Michael

Marshalltown
Brooks, Patrick William

Sioux City
Mayne, Wiley Edward

KANSAS

Overland Park
Keplinger, Bruce (Donald Keplinger)
Sampson, William Roth
Starrett, Frederick Kent

Prairie Village
Stanton, Roger D.

Shawnee Mission
Badgerow, John Nicholas
Sparks, Billy Schley

Topeka
Dimmitt, Lawrence Andrew
Haney, Thomas Dwight
Hecht, Robert D.
Ochs, Robert Duane
Schroer, Gene Eldon

Wichita
Hund, Edward Joseph
Kennedy, Joseph Winston
Ratner, Payne Harry, Jr.
Woolf, John Paul

KENTUCKY

Bowling Green
Parker, William Jerry
Rudloff, William Joseph

Florence
Busald, E. André

Lexington
Elliott, Robert Lloyd
Fryman, Virgil Thomas, Jr.
Johnson, Brian M.

Louisville
Chauvin, Leonard Stanley, Jr.
Dolt, Frederick Corrance
Ely, Hiram, III
Guethlein, William O.
Partin, C. Fred
Reed, John Squires, II

Newport
Siverd, Robert Joseph

LOUISIANA

Baton Rouge
Rubin, Michael Harry

Covington
Looney, James Holland

Cut Off
Cheramie, Carlton Joseph

Lafayette
Davidson, James Joseph, III

Lake Charles
Davidson, Van Michael, Jr.
Parkerson, Hardy Martell
Veron, J. Michael

New Orleans
Bieck, Robert Barton, Jr.
Bordelon, Alvin Joseph, Jr.
Cheatwood, Roy Clifton
Darden, Marshall Taylor
Fendler, Sherman Gene
Garcia, Patricia A.
Gertler, Meyer H.
Grant, Arthur Gordon, Jr.
Jones, Philip Kirkpatrick, Jr.
Kelly, William James, III
Kupperman, Stephen Henry
Manard, Robert Lynn, III
McGlone, Michael Anthony
Orrill, R. Ray, Jr.
Rosen, William Warren
Sommers, William John, Jr.
Stetter, Roger Alan
Vance, Robert Patrick

Slidell
Shamis, Edward Anthony, Jr.

MAINE

Auburn
Abbott, Charles Henry

Augusta
Johnson, Phillip Edward

Portland
Culley, Peter William
Harvey, Charles Albert, Jr.
Lancaster, Ralph Ivan, Jr.

MARYLAND

Annapolis
Lillard, John Franklin, III

Baltimore
Baker, William Parr
Carbine, James Edmond
Crowe, Thomas Leonard
Dilloff, Neil Joel
Dubé, Lawrence Edward, Jr.
Hansen, Christopher Agnew
Howell, Harley Thomas
Kramer, Paul R.
Loker, F(rank) Ford, Jr.
Pappas, George Frank
Radding, Andrew
Schochor, Jonathan
Sfekas, Stephen James
Strachan, Nell B.
Sturman, Philip
Walker, Irving Edward
White, Pamela Janice

Bethesda
Melamed, Arthur Douglas

Chevy Chase
Weiss, Harlan Lee

Parkville
Hill, Milton King, Jr.

Patuxent River
Fitzhugh, David Michael

Potomac
Meyer, Lawrence George
Mullenbach, Linda Herman

Rockville
Karp, Ronald Alvin

Takoma Park
Browning, Deborah Lea

Towson
Carney, Bradford George Yost
Morrow, Thomas Campbell

MASSACHUSETTS

Boston
Barber, Robert Cushman
Carroll, James Edward
Curley, Robert Ambrose, Jr.
Davis, Christopher Patrick
Dillon, James Joseph
Dougherty, Thomas James
Hieken, Charles
Kavanaugh, James Francis, Jr.
Kociubes, Joseph Leib
Leibensperger, Edward Paul
Macauley, William Francis
Mercer, Richard James
Mone, Michael Edward
Moriarty, George Marshall
Neuner, George William
O'Neill, Timothy P.
Parker, Christopher William
Thornton, Michael Paul
Wilson, Paul Dennis

Chatham
Weidman, Charles Ray

Concord
Perry, Edward Needham

Dedham
Donahue, Michael Christopher

Lexington
Glovsky, Susan G. L.

Medford
Berman, David

Sudbury
Dignan, Thomas Gregory, Jr.

Waltham
Borod, Donald Lee

Weymouth
Fitzsimmons, B. Joseph, Jr.

MICHIGAN

Ann Arbor
Britton, Clarold Lawrence
Walsh, James Joseph

Birmingham
Webster, Robert Byron

Bloomfield Hills
Googasian, George Ara
Pappas, Edward Harvey
Rader, Ralph Terrance
Tallerico, Thomas Joseph
Vocht, Michelle Elise
Weinstein, William Joseph

Detroit
Andreoff, Christopher Andon
Brady, Edmund Matthew, Jr.
Bushnell, George Edward, Jr.
Harris, Patricia Skalny
Longhofer, Ronald Stephen
Saxton, William Marvin
Smith, James Albert

Flint
Hart, Clifford Harvey

Grand Rapids
Enslen, Pamela Chapman
Litton, Randall Gale
Pylman, Norman Herbert, II

VanderLaan, Robert D.

Kalamazoo
Lubben, Craig Henry

Lansing
Baker, Frederick Milton, Jr.
Fink, Joseph Allen
Kritselis, William Nicholas
Rasmusson, Thomas Elmo

Midland
Battle, Leonard Carroll
Gootee, Jane Marie

Northville
Leavitt, Martin Jack

Saint Clair Shores
Sullivan, James A., III

Southfield
Darling, Robert Howard
Fieger, Geoffrey Nels
Jacobs, John Patrick
Miller, Sheldon Lee
Morganroth, Mayer
Turner, Donald Allen

Troy
Alber, Phillip George
Ponitz, John Allan
Schmidt, Michael Francis

MINNESOTA

Crystal
Reske, Steven David

Duluth
Thibodeau, Thomas Raymond

Eden Prairie
Friederichs, Norman Paul

Golden Valley
Hagglund, Clarance Edward

Laporte
Woutat, Paul Gustav

Minneapolis
Bachman, Ralph Walter
Ciresi, Michael Vincent
Eisenberg, Jonathan Lee
French, John Dwyer
Gordon, John Bennett
Hanson, Bruce Eugene
Hanson, Kent Bryan
Hart, B. Clarence
Keppel, William James
Magnuson, Roger James
McGunnigle, George Francis
Meller, Robert Louis, Jr.
Newhall, David Gillette
O'Neill, Brian Boru
Palmer, Deborah Jean
Pentelovitch, William Zane
Reuter, James William
Saeks, Allen Irving
Shroyer, Thomas Jerome
Silver, Alan Irving
Tanick, Marshall Howard
Tourek, Steven Charles

Moorhead
Marquart, Steven Leonard

North Oaks
Woods, Robert Edward

Saint Louis Park
Seaburg, Jean

Saint Paul
Allison, John Robert
Kirsch, Steven Jay
Maclin, Alan Hall
Seymour, Mary Frances

MISSISSIPPI

Gulfport
Hopkins, Alben Norris

Jackson
Clark, David Wright
Currie, Edward Jones, Jr.
Goodman, William Flournoy, III
Harkins, Patrick Nicholas, III
Hauberg, Robert Engelbrecht, Jr.
Henegan, John C(lark)
Howell, Joel Walter, III
Merkel, Charles Michael

Kiln
Thissell, Charles William

MISSOURI

Chesterfield
Stalnaker, Tim

Clayton
Tremayne, Eric Flory

Jefferson City
Bartlett, Alex

Kansas City
Abele, Robert Christopher
Beck, William G.
Beckett, Theodore Charles
Cross, William Dennis
Delaney, Michael Francis
Hubbell, Ernest
Johnson, Mark Eugene
Levings, Theresa Lawrence
Lolli, Don R(ay)

Martucci, William Christopher
McManus, James William
Miller, George Spencer
Palmer, Dennis Dale
Price, James Tucker
Proctor, George Edwin, Jr.
Schult, Thomas P.
Shapiro, Alvin Dale
Sherman, Joseph Allen, Jr.
Stoup, Arthur Harry
Taff, Earl Wayne
Vering, John Albert
Wirken, James Charles
Wolf, Jerome Thomas

Maryland Heights
Cooper, Richard Alan

Rolla
Turley, J. William

Saint Louis
Bonacorsi, Mary Catherine
Brown, Paul Sherman
Clear, John Michael
Collins, James Slade, II
Conran, Joseph Palmer
DeWoskin, Alan Ellis
Erwin, James Walter
Floyd, Walter Leo
Gianoulakis, John Louis
Gilhousen, Brent James
Gilster, Peter Stuart
Grebel, Lawrence Bovard
Kohn, Alan Charles
Mattern, Keith Edward
Moore, McPherson Dorsett
Rabbitt, Daniel Thomas, Jr.
Sestric, Anthony James
Smith, Arthur Lee
Sneeringer, Stephen Geddes
Sugg, Reed Waller
Walsh, Thomas Charles

Springfield
Woody, Donald Eugene

MONTANA

Big Timber
Manos, Christopher Lawrence

Billings
Jones, James Leonard
Malee, Thomas Michael

NEBRASKA

Lincoln
Colleran, Kevin
Thrasher, Louis Michael

Norfolk
Domina, David Alan

North Platte
Baumann, Larry R(oger)

Omaha
Brownrigg, John Clinton
Dolan, James Vincent
Riley, William Jay

NEVADA

Las Vegas
Nelson, Sharon L.
Zubel, Eric Louis

Reno
Barkley, Thierry Vincent
Guild, Clark Joseph, Jr.
Kent, Stephen Smiley

NEW HAMPSHIRE

Concord
Hodes, Paul William

Hollis
Lumbard, Eliot Howland

Manchester
Brown, Stanley Melvin
Richards, Thomas H.

Portsmouth
Shaines, Robert Arthur

NEW JERSEY

Asbury Park
Darnell, Alan Mark

Bridgewater
Dahling, Gerald Vernon

Cherry Hill
Garrigle, William Aloysius
Roth, Kenneth David

Collingswood
Kole, Janet Stephanie

Cranbury
Bronner, William Roche

Cranford
De Luca, Thomas George

Edison
Lavigne, Lawrence Neil

Fairfield
Connell, William Terrence

Hackensack
Horan, John Donohoe

Haddonfield
Fuoco, Philip Stephen

Jersey City
Wind, Jack Jay

Kenilworth
Hoffman, John Fletcher

Liberty Corner
Thompson, T. Jay

Madison
Huettner, Richard Alfred

Middletown
Friedman, Richard Lloyd

Millburn
Kuttner, Bernard A.

Morristown
Bartkus, Robert Edward
Herzberg, Peter Jay
Humick, Thomas Charles Campbell
Szuch, Clyde Andrew
Whitmer, Frederick Lee

Mountainside
Jacobson, Gary Steven

Newark
Cahn, Jeffrey Barton
Cummis, Clive Sanford
Eittreim, Richard MacNutt
Freilich, Irvin Mayer
Kott, David Russell
McGuire, William B(enedict)
Medvin, Alan York
Rak, Lorraine Karen
Schachter, Paul
Simon, David Robert

Parsippany
Kallmann, Stanley Walter

Rochelle Park
Knopf, Barry Abraham

Saddle Brook
Pearlman, Peter Steven

Short Hills
Marshall, John Patrick

Somerville
Sponzilli, Edward George

Summit
Katz, Michael Albert
Saffer, Judith Mack

West Orange
Gordon, Harrison J.

Westfield
Dughi, Louis John, Jr.

Woodbridge
Barcan, Stephen Emanuel

NEW MEXICO

Albuquerque
Bardacke, Paul Gregory
Messersmith, Lanny Dee
Roberts, Randal William

Santa Fe
Burton, John Paul (Jack Burton)
McClaugherty, Joe L.
Schwarz, Michael
Singleton, Sarah Michael
Wertheim, Jerry

NEW YORK

Albany
Powers, John Kieran
Wukitsch, David John

Armonk
Moss, Eric Harold

Brooklyn
Reich, Edward Stuart
Rubenstein, Allen Ira

Buffalo
Fisher, Cheryl Smith
Gorman, Gerald Patrick
Halpern, Ralph Lawrence
Manning, Kenneth Alan
Mattar, Lawrence Joseph
Sampson, John David
Segalla, Thomas Francis

Canaan
Pennell, William Brooke

East Meadow
Hyman, Montague Allan

Farmingdale
Persons, John Wade

Garden City
Kroll, Martin N.

Getzville
DiNardo, Joseph

Glen Cove
Mills, Charles Gardner

Hastings On Hudson
Steer, Richard Lane

Huntington
German, June Resnick

Jericho
Rehbock, Richard Alexander

Lake Sucess
Epstein, Joel Donald

Larchmont
Gaffney, Mark William
McSherry, William John, Jr.
Pelton, Russell Gilbert

Melville
Cahn, Richard Caleb

Mineola
Monaghan, Peter Gerard
Santemma, Jon Noel
Spizz, Harvey Warren

Mount Kisco
Curran, Maurice Francis

New Hyde Park
Levine, Kimberly Anne

New York
Abramowitz, Elkan
Aksen, Gerald
Alcott, Mark Howard
Amsterdam, Mark Lemle
Arenson, Gregory K.
Axinn, Stephen Mark
Baechtold, Robert Louis
Bauer, George A., III
Benedict, James Nelson
Bezanson, Thomas Edward
Bialo, Kenneth Marc
Birnbaum, Edward Lester
Bivona, John Vincent
Blumkin, Linda Ruth
Bodovitz, James Philip
Borstein, Leon Baer
Bosses, Stevan J.
Bradley, E. Michael
Braid, Frederick Donald
Brown, Paul M.
Brown, Peter Megargee
Buchwald, Don David
Burrows, Kenneth David
Burrows, Michael Donald
Carter, James Hal, Jr.
Cayea, Donald Joseph
Chesler, Evan Robert
Clark, Merrell Edward, Jr.
Clary, Richard Wayland
Cohen, Robert Stephan
Cole, Charles Dewey, Jr.
Coleman, Jerome P.
Coll, John Peter, Jr.
Cook, Michael Lewis
Cooper, Michael Anthony
Costello, Robert Joseph
Creel, Thomas Leonard
Cutner, Rolande Regat
Dallas, William Moffit, Jr.
Dankin, Peter Alfred
Davidson, Robert Bruce
De Vivo, Edward Charles
Deffina, Thomas Victor
Dell, Michael John
DeOrchis, Vincent Moore
Dershowitz, Nathan Zev
Diana, Ronald Salvador
Dopf, Glenn William
Douglas, Philip Le Breton
Dunne, Gerard Francis
Ehrenbard, Robert
Elsen, Sheldon Howard
Evans, Martin Frederic
Feldberg, Michael Svetkey
Fensterstock, Blair Courtney
Fersko, Raymond Stuart
Fink, Robert Steven
Fiske, Robert Bishop, Jr.
Fitzpatrick, Joseph Mark
Flamm, Leonard N(athan)
Fletcher, Anthony L.
Forstadt, Joseph Lawrence
Foster, David Lee
Fox, Donald Thomas
Fraser, Brian Scott
Fredericks, William Curtis
Freeman, David John
Gallagher, Brian John
Garfinkel, Barry Herbert
Gitter, Max
Glekel, Jeffrey Ives
Glickstein, Steven
Gold, Stuart Walter
Golomb, David Bela
Greenawalt, William Sloan
Greenbaum, Sheldon Marc
Greenberg, Gary Howard
Greenberg, Ira George
Greenspon, Robert Alan
Haig, Robert Leighton
Hall, John Herbert
Harris, Joel B(ruce)
Hartmann, Carl Joseph
Haynes, Jean Reed
Heller, Robert Martin
Hirsch, Jerome S.
Hollyer, A(rthur) Rene
Horwitz, Ethan
Hritz, George F.
Hughes, Kevin Peter
Hynes, Patricia Mary
Iannuzzi, John Nicholas
Isquith, Fred Taylor
Jackson, Thomas Gene
Jacob, Marvin Eugene
Jacobs, Randall Scott David
Jacobson, Jeffrey E.
Jauvtis, Robert Lloyd
Joffe, Robert David
Joseph, Gregory Paul
Joseph, Leonard
Kalow, David Arthur
Kandel, William Lloyd
Karmali, Rashida Alimahomed
Katz, Jerome Charles

Kaufman, Stephen Edward
Kavaler, Thomas J.
Kazanjian, John Harold
Kenney, John Joseph
Kessler, Jeffrey L.
Kimball, John Devereux
King, Henry Lawrence
Kinzler, Thomas Benjamin
Kobak, James Benedict, Jr.
Kramer, Daniel Jonathan
Krane, Steven Charles
Krasner, Daniel Walter
Kraus, Douglas M.
Kraver, Richard Matthew
Kuh, Richard Henry
Lacy, Robinson Burrell
Langer, Bruce Alden
Lans, Deborah Eisner
Lauer, Eliot
Lee, Jerome G.
Levine, Alan
Lewis, David L.
Linsenmeyer, John Michael
Lowe, John Anthony
Lupert, Leslie Allan
Lustenberger, Louis Charles, Jr.
Malina, Michael
Mandelker, Lawrence Arthur
Martone, Patricia Ann
McCormack, Howard Michael
McGanney, Thomas
McLaughlin, Joseph Thomas
McLean, David Lyle
Meister, Ronald William
Mentz, Barbara Antonello
Mentz, Lawrence
Merritt, Bruce Gordon
Miller, Charles Hampton
Miller, Richard Allan
Miller, Steven Scott
Moloney, Thomas Joseph
Moy, Mary Anastasia
Muccia, Joseph William
Mullaney, Thomas Joseph
Munzer, Stephen Ira
Muskin, Victor Philip
Naftalis, Gary Philip
Nearing, Vivienne W.
Newman, Lawrence Walker
O'Connor, William Matthew
O'Sullivan, Thomas J.
Olasov, David Michael
Oppenheim, Jeffrey Alan
Osgood, Robert Mansfield
Pepper, Allan Michael
Peskin, Stephan Haskel
Phillips, Anthony Francis
Piliero, Robert Donald
Polak, Werner L.
Prutzman, Lewis Donald
Quinn, Yvonne Susan
Raylesberg, Alan Ira
Reibstein, Richard Jay
Reich, Larry Sam
Reilly, John Albert
Reiner, John Paul
Reinthaler, Richard Walter
Rifkind, Robert S(inger)
Ringel, Dean
Rivera, Walter
Robertson, Edwin David
Rogers, Laurence Steven
Rosenberg, David
Rosenberg, Gerald Alan
Rosenfeld, Steven B.
Rosensaft, Menachem Zwi
Rosner, Jonathan Levi
Ross, Gerald Elliott
Rovine, Arthur William
Salomon, Philippe M.
Satine, Barry Roy
Savitt, Susan Schenkel
Schirmeister, Charles F.
Schlau, Philip
Schmidt, Charles Edward
Schulman, Steven Gary
Schumacher, Harry Richard
Schwab, Harold Lee
Schwartz, Barry Fredric
Schwed, Peter Gregory
Seidel, Selvyn
Shanman, James Alan
Shentov, Ognjan V.
Short, Skip
Siffert, John Sand
Silverman, Moses
Skirnick, Robert Andrew
Slade, Jeffrey Christopher
Sladkus, Harvey Ira
Smiley, Guy Ian
Smith, Robert Everett
Smith, Robert Sherlock
Snider, Jerome Guy
Snow, Charles
Sorkin, Laurence Truman
Soyster, Margaret Blair
Stathis, Nicholas John
Stern, Peter R.
Sternman, Joel W.
Stoll, Neal Richard
Swain, Laura Taylor
Taylor, Job, III
Thackeray, Jonathan E.
Tilewick, Robert
Toback, Arthur Malcolm
Urowsky, Richard J.
Waks, Jay Warren
Walinsky, Adam
Weinberger, Harold Paul
Weinstock, Leonard
Wesely, Edwin Joseph
Wishingrad, Jay Marc
Witkin, Eric Douglas
Wolff, Kurt Jakob
Wollan, Eugene
Yankwitt, Russell Marc
Yeager, Dennis Randall
Yelenick, Mary Therese
Yodowitz, Edward Jay
Zimmett, Mark Paul
Zissu, Roger L.
Zivin, Norman H.

Pittsford
Braunsdorf, Paul Raymond

Rochester
Andolina, Lawrence J.
Dolin, Lonny H.

Geiger, Alexander
Kurland, Harold Arthur
Law, Michael R.
Payment, Kenneth Arnold
Smith, Jules Louis
Trueheart, Harry Parker, III
Widor, Aimee L.

Sands Point
Hoynes, Louis LeNoir, Jr.

Southampton
Lopez, David

Spring Valley
Barr, Harvey Stephen

Syracuse
DiLorenzo, Louis Patrick
Gerber, Edward F.
Simmons, Doreen Anne

Troy
Jones, E. Stewart, Jr.

Uniondale
Rivkin, John Lawrence
Sugarman, Robert P.

Waterford
Novotny, F. Douglas

White Plains
Halpern, Philip Morgan
Null, William Seth
Pickard, John Allan

NORTH CAROLINA

Asheville
Cogburn, Max Oliver
Davis, Roy Walton, Jr.

Charlotte
Connette, Edward Grant, III
Raper, William Cranford
Van Hoy, Philip Marshall

Fairview
Rhynedance, Harold Dexter, Jr.

Flat Rock
Brooten, Kenneth Edward, Jr.

Raleigh
Sasser, Jonathan Drew

Tabor City
Jorgensen, Ralph Gubler

Thomasville
Reynolds, Mark Floyd, II

Winston Salem
Barnhill, Henry Grady, Jr.
Comerford, Walter Thompson, Jr.
Porter, Leon Eugene, Jr.

NORTH DAKOTA

Bismarck
Gilbertson, Joel Warren

OHIO

Akron
Cherpas, Christopher Theodore
Ruport, Scott Hendricks
Tipping, Harry A.

Canton
Tzangas, George John

Cincinnati
Calico, Paul B.
Chesser, Stacey C.
Cioffi, Michael Lawrence
Cissell, James Charles
Cunningham, Pierce Edward
DeLong, Deborah
Dornette, W(illiam) Stuart
Frantz, Robert Wesley
Holschuh, John David, Jr.
Maxwell, Robert Wallace, II
Metz, Jerome Joseph, Jr.
Smith, Sheila Marie
Zavatsky, Michael Joseph

Cleveland
Adamo, Kenneth R.
Bell, Steven Dennis
Bixenstine, Kim Fenton
Collin, Thomas James
Crist, Paul Grant
Fisher, Thomas Edward
Goldfarb, Bernard Sanford
Hardy, Michael Lynn
Hoerner, Robert Jack
Kelly, Dennis Michael
Kramer, Edward George
Leiken, Earl Murray
Lewis, John Bruce
Mc Cartan, Patrick Francis
Moore, Kenneth Cameron
Morgenstern, Conrad J.
Skulina, Thomas Raymond
Spurgeon, Roberta Kaye
Strauch, John L.
Stuhldreher, George William
Swartzbaugh, Marc L.
Toohey, Brian Frederick
Weisman, Fred

Columbus
Bartemes, Amy Straker
Cvetanovich, Danny L.
Elam, John Carlton
Ferguson, Gerald Paul
Helfer, Michael Stevens

Hollenbaugh, H(enry) Ritchey
Long, Thomas Leslie
Moul, William Charles
Reid, Nelson Marlin
Robol, Richard Thomas
Sidman, Robert John
Thomas, Duke Winston
Warner, Charles Collins

Dayton
Faruki, Charles Joseph
Saul, Irving Isaac

Portsmouth
Crowder, Marjorie Briggs

Toledo
Allotta, Joseph John
Dane, Stephen Mark
White, Kenneth James

OKLAHOMA

Duncan
Rodgers, Ricardo Juan (Rick Rodgers)

Lawton
Ashton, Mark Alfred

Muskogee
Williams, Betty Outhier

Oklahoma City
Barnes, Robert Norton
Fenton, Elliott Clayton
Kenney, John Arthur
McMillin, James Craig
Nelon, Robert Dale
Paul, William George
Wallace, Thomas Andrew
Woods, Harry Arthur, Jr.
Zuhdi, Nabil (Bill Zuhdi)

Tulsa
Biolchini, Robert Fredrick
Brewster, Clark Otto
Brune, Kenneth Leonard
Davis, G. Reuben
Eagan, Claire Veronica
Eldridge, Richard Mark
Ferguson, Dallas Eugene
Haynie, Tony Wayne
Hughes, William Earle
Kaufman, Ronald C.
Luthey, Graydon Dean, Jr.
Matthies, Mary Constance T.
Strecker, David Eugene

OREGON

Eugene
Fechtel, Edward Ray

Medford
Deatherage, William Vernon
O'Connor, Karl William (Goodyear Johnson)
Thierolf, Richard Burton, Jr.

Portland
Eakin, Margaretta Morgan
Ellis, Barnes Humphreys
Flaherty, Thomas Joseph
O'Neill, Phoebe Joan
Rutzick, Mark Charles
Seymour, Steven Wayne
Stone, Richard James
Westwood, James Nicholson

Salem
Haselton, Rick Thomas

PENNSYLVANIA

Bala Cynwyd
Schwartz, Jeffrey Byron

Bethlehem
Hemphill, Meredith, Jr.

Blue Bell
Siedzikowski, Henry Francis
Teklits, Joseph Anthony

Clarks Summit
Beemer, John Barry

Harrisburg
Feinour, John Stephen

Hazleton
Pedri, Charles Raymond

Lancaster
Lewis, Alvin Bower, Jr.
Nast, Dianne Martha

Lewisburg
Knight, Louise Osborn

Media
List, Anthony Francis
Mulligan, John Thomas

Narberth
Rovner, David Patrick Ryan

New Kensington
Wallace, Henry Jared, Jr.

Norristown
Cowperthwait, Lindley Murray
Gowen, Thomas Leo, Jr.

Orefield
Dimmich, Jeffrey Robert

Philadelphia
Barrett, John J(ames), Jr.

Battis, David Gregory
Berger, David
Berger, Harold
Binder, David Franklin
Brown, William Hill, III
Cooney, J(ohn) Gordon, Jr.
Cramer, Harold
Craven, Charles Warren
Dennis, Edward S(pencer) G(ale), Jr.
Donohue, John Patrick
Durant, Marc
Elkins, S. Gordon
Epstein, Alan Bruce
Fiebach, H. Robert
Garcia, Rudolph
Gordesky, Morton
Hangley, William Thomas
Kessler, Alan Craig
Klein, Howard Bruce
Kraeutler, Eric
Kramer, Gilda Lea
Ledwith, John Francis
Lillie, Charisse Ranielle
Lowery, William Herbert
Madva, Stephen Alan
Mathes, Stephen Jon
McGurk, Eugene David, Jr.
Milbourne, Walter Robertson
Milone, Francis Michael
Minisi, Anthony S.
Parry, William DeWitt
Prewitt, David Edward
Rainville, Christina
Ramsey, Natalie D.
Reich, Abraham Charles
Resnick, Stephanie
Scher, Howard Dennis
Sheils, Denis Francis
Sigmond, Richard Brian
Stuart, Glen R(aymond)
Toll, Seymour I.
Wittels, Barnaby Caesar
Wrobleski, Jeanne Pauline

Pittsburgh
Acheson, Amy J.
Baldauf, Kent Edward
Blenko, Walter John, Jr.
Brown, James Benton
Candris, Laura A.
Caroselli, William R.
Cohen, Robert (Avram)
Hull, John Daniel, IV
Hurnyak, Christina Kaiser
Jones, Craig Ward
Klett, Edwin Lee
Litman, Roslyn Margolis
O'Connor, Edward Gearing
Ober, Russell John, Jr.
Perry, John F.
Pohl, Paul Michael
Raynovich, George, Jr.
Saunders, Martin Johnston
Schmidt, Edward Craig
Schwab, Arthur James
Seymour, Donald Edward
Sherman, Carl Leon
Specter, Howard Alan
Stroyd, Arthur Heister
Van Kirk, Thomas L.

Scranton
Howley, James McAndrew

Southeastern
Husick, Lawrence Alan

Wynnewood
Stapleton, Larrick B.

Wyomissing
Turner, David Eldridge

RHODE ISLAND

Providence
Labinger, Lynette J.
Medeiros, Matthew Francis
Prentiss, Richard Daniel

Warwick
Penza, Joseph Fulvio, Jr.

SOUTH CAROLINA

Charleston
Kahn, Ellis Irvin

Columbia
Babcock, Keith Moss
Livoti, Anthony William
Sheftman, Howard Stephen

Greenville
Coates, William Alexander

Hilton Head Island
McKay, John Judson, Jr.

Mount Pleasant
Laddaga, Beth Jane

SOUTH DAKOTA

Pierre
Gerdes, David Alan

Rapid City
Shultz, Donald Richard

Sioux Falls
Luce, Michael Leigh

TENNESSEE

Chattanooga
Campbell, Paul, III
Cooper, Gary Allan
Gearhiser, Charles Josef

Moore, Hugh Jacob, Jr.

Collierville
Scroggs, Larry Kenneth

Cordova
Swan, Michael Robert

Hendersonville
McCaleb, Joe Wallace

Kingsport
Tweed, Douglas Steven

Knoxville
Hagood, Lewis Russell
Ogden, Harry Peoples

Memphis
Carr, Oscar Clark, III
Chambliss, Prince Caesar, Jr.
Clark, Ross Bert, II
Ledbetter, Paul Mark
Moriarty, Herbert Bernard, Jr.
Noel, Randall Deane
Raines, Jim Neal
Sossaman, William Lynwood

Nashville
Hardin, Hal D.
Patterson, Robert Shepherd
Rush, Stephen Kenneth
Woods, Larry David

Soddy Daisy
Leitner, Paul Revere

Somerville
Wilder, James Sampson, III

TEXAS

Abilene
Suttle, Stephen Hungate

Addison
Lynch, Jeffrey Scott

Arlington
Jensen, John Robert

Austin
Grosenheider, Delno John
Harrison, Richard Wayne
Judson, Philip Livingston
Lochridge, Lloyd Pampell, Jr.
Schwartz, Leonard Jay
Zager, Steven Mark

Baytown
Chavez, John Anthony

Brooks AFB
Tanner, Gordon Owen

Brownsville
Weisfeld, Sheldon

Dallas
Acker, Rodney
Austin, Ann Sheree
Babcock, Charles Lynde, IV
Baggett, Steven Ray
Bickel, John W., II
Case, Thomas Louis
Coleman, Robert Winston
Collins, Michael Homer
Ellis, James Alvis, Jr.
Freytag, Sharon Nelson
Frisbie, Curtis Lynn, Jr.
Gilliam, John A.
Hinshaw, Chester John
Jones, David Stanley
Jones, James Alton
Kearney, Douglas Charles
Keithley, Bradford Gene
Kirby, Le Grand Carney, III
Lowenberg, Michael
Mc Elhaney, John Hess
McAtee, David Ray
McGowan, Patrick Francis
Miller, Stewart Ransom
Mow, Robert Henry, Jr.
Palmer, Philip Isham, Jr.
Palter, John Theodore
Penick, Michael Preston
Pew, John Glenn, Jr.
Prather, Robert Charles, Sr.
Price, John Aley
Ringle, Brett Adelbert
Scuro, Joseph E., Jr.
Selinger, Jerry Robin
Sides, Jack Davis, Jr.
Walkowiak, Vincent Steven
Wilkins, Jerry L.

El Paso
Malone, Daniel Robert

Fort Worth
Dean, Beale
Elliott, Frank Wallace
Hart, John Clifton
Larimore, Tom L.
Mack, Theodore
Randolph, Robert McGehee
Streck, Frederick Louis, III
Watson, Robert Francis

Houston
Amdur, Arthur R.
Atkins, Bruce Alexander
Bagwell, Louis Lee
Ballanfant, Richard Burton
Bayko, Emil Thomas
Beirne, Martin Douglas
Boswell, John Howard
Brinson, Gay Creswell, Jr.
Caldwell, Rodney Kent
Carr, Edward A.
Connelly, George William
Craig, Robert Mark, III
Cunningham, Tom Alan

Essmyer, Michael Martin
Fladung, Richard Denis
Frost, Charles Estes, Jr.
Gomez, Lynne Marie
Gonynor, Francis James
Graham, Michael Paul
Hamel, Lee
Jordan, Charles Milton
Kaplan, Lee Landa
Ketchand, Robert Lee
Kinnan, David Emery
Lacey, David Morgan
Lilienstern, O. Clayton
Lopez, David Tiburcio
McFall, Donald Beury
Michaels, Kevin Richard
Miller, Gary C.
Nunnally, Knox Dillon
Pettiette, Alison Yvonne
Ray, Hugh Massey, Jr.
Reasoner, Harry Max
Rowland, Robert Alexander, III
Schwartz, Charles Walter
Shurn, Peter Joseph, III
Sieger, John Anthony
Silva, Eugene Joseph
Spalding, Andrew Freeman
Stephens, R(obert) Gary
Stuart, Walter Bynum, IV
Susman, Morton Lee
Tabak, Morris
Wallis, Olney Gray
Wray, Thomas Jefferson
Yetter, R. Paul

Humble
Pickle, George Edward

Mcallen
Mills, William Michael

Midland
Estes, Andrew Harper

Missouri City
Maddox, Charles J., Jr.

Nacogdoches
Bias, Dana G.

San Antonio
Allison, Stephen Philip
Biery, Evelyn Hudson
Kaplan, Edward David
Moynihan, John Bignell
Myers, J(oseph) Michael

Waco
Cherry, David Earl

UTAH

Salt Lake City
Christensen, Harold Graham
Orton, R. Willis
Scofield, David Willson
Shea, Patrick A.
Workman, H(arley) Ross

VIRGINIA

Alexandria
Carter, Richard Dennis
Drennan, Joseph Peter
Duvall, Richard Osgood
Georges, Peter John
Sherk, George William
Toothman, John William

Arlington
Alper, Joanne Fogel
Collins, Philip Reilly
Kelly, John James
Weinberg, Robert Lester

Fairfax
Brown, Gary Wayne
Dewhirst, John Ward
Rust, John Howson, Jr.

Falls Church
Kirk, Dennis Dean
Robey, Daniel Lance
Van Oeveren, Edward Lanier

Fredericksburg
Billingsley, Robert Thaine

Great Falls
Railton, William Scott

Herndon
Geldon, Fred Wolman

Mc Lean
Bredehoft, John Michael
Brown, Frank Eugene, Jr.
Najjoum, Linda Lemmon
Walter, Michael Joseph

Midlothian
Hall, Franklin Perkins

Norfolk
Clark, Morton Hutchinson
Corcoran, Andrew Patrick, Jr.

Petersburg
White, William Earle

Portsmouth
Porter, J. Ridgely, III

Richmond
Bing, Richard McPhail
Brooks, Robert Franklin, Sr.
Hall, Stephen Charles
Kearfott, Joseph Conrad
Landin, David Craig
McClard, Jack Edward
McElligott, James Patrick, Jr.

Peluso, Dana C.M.
Rolfe, Robert Martin
Thompson, Paul Michael
Williamson, Thomas W., Jr.

Roanoke
Harris, Bayard Easter
Tegenkamp, Gary Elton
Woodrum, Clifton A., III

Springfield
Chappell, Milton Leroy

Vienna
Razzano, Frank Charles

Virginia Beach
Dumville, S(amuel) Lawrence
Hajek, Francis Paul

Warrenton
Howard, Blair Duncan

WASHINGTON

Bainbridge Island
Morisset, Mason Dale

Redmond
Phillips, Richard Lee

Seattle
Alsdorf, Robert Hermann
Bagshaw, Bradley Holmes
Bringman, Joseph Edward
Corning, Nicholas F.
Freedman, Bart Joseph
Ginsberg, Phillip H(enry)
Gray, Marvin Lee, Jr.
Harris, Thomas V.
McKay, Michael Dennis
McKinstry, Ronald Eugene
Mellem, Roger Duane
Mines, Michael
Riviera, Daniel John
Smith, James Alexander, Jr.
Squires, William Randolph, III
Sullivan, Daniel Frederick
Tausend, Fredric Cutner
Vestal, Josephine Burnet
Yalowitz, Kenneth Gregg

Spokane
Weatherhead, Leslie R.

Tacoma
Mungia, Salvador Alejo, Jr.

WEST VIRGINIA

Charleston
Cowan, John Joseph
Neely, Richard
Robinson, E. Glenn
Slack, John Mark, III

WISCONSIN

Kenosha
Rose, Terry William

Madison
Hildebrand, Daniel Walter
Mitby, John Chester
Whitney, Robert Michael

Milwaukee
Habush, Robert Lee
Levit, William Harold, Jr.
Melin, Robert Arthur
Sostarich, Mark Edward
Terschan, Frank Robert

Racine
Gasiorkiewicz, Eugene Anthony

WYOMING

Casper
Combs, W(illiam) Henry, III

Cheyenne
Bailey, Henry Franklin, Jr.

Cody
Stradley, Richard Lee

Jackson
Schuster, Robert Parks
Shockey, Gary Lee

Wheatland
Hunkins, Raymond Breedlove

ENGLAND

London
Haubold, Samuel Allen

GERMANY

Frankfurt on the Main
Matthew, Leodis Clyde

THE NETHERLANDS

The Hague
Brower, Charles Nelson

ADDRESS UNPUBLISHED

Arencibia, Raul Antonio
Beatie, Russel Harrison, Jr.
Beattie, Donald Gilbert
Blevins, Jeffrey Alexander
Blumenthal, William
Braun, Jerome Irwin
Buehler, John Wilson
Bullard, Rockwood Wilde, III
Comisky, Ian Michael
Cook, Donald Charles
Cox, Marshall
Dubuc, Carroll Edward
Eaton, Larry Ralph
Elderkin, E(dwin) Judge
Erlebacher, Arlene Cernik
Ettinger, Joseph Alan
Fenwick, Lynda Beck
Flanary, Donald Herbert, Jr.
Flynn, Michael
Ginsberg, Marc David
Goddard, Claude Philip, Jr.
Grier, Phillip Michael
Hall, John Hopkins
Harnack, Don Steger
Henderson, John Robert
Henry, DeLysle Leon
Howard, John Wayne
Joelson, Mark Rene
Johnson, Edward Michael
Kiehnhoff, Thomas Nave
King, James Forrest, Jr.
Leydig, Carl Frederick
Lichtenstein, Sarah Carol
Maraziti, Joseph James, Jr.
McInerney, Gary John
Monroe, Murray Shipley
O'Mara, William Michael
Ogden, David William
Pietrzak, Alfred Robert
Reiss, Jerome
Reminger, Richard Thomas
Saltzman, Michael I.
Schneebaum, Steven Marc
Serota, James Ian
Smith, James A.
Smouse, H(ervey) Russell
Springer, Paul David
Stack, Beatriz de Greiff
Stern, John Jules
Tasker, Joseph
Terrell, G. Irvin
Tone, Philip Willis
Twardy, Stanley Albert, Jr.
Vigil, David Charles
Waxman, Seth Paul
Wilson, Hugh Steven
Yeager, Jeffrey Alan
Young, John Hardin

CIVIL LITIGATION, GENERAL

UNITED STATES

ALABAMA

Anniston
Klinefelter, James Louis

Bay Minette
Granade, Fred King

Birmingham
Albritton, William Harold, IV
Boardman, Mark Seymour
Christian, Thomas William
Donahue, Timothy Patrick
Gale, Fournier Joseph, III
Givhan, Robert Marcus
Hardin, Edward Lester, Jr.
Harris, George Bryan
Hinton, James Forrest, Jr.
Long, Thad Gladden
Martin, Cynthia Ann
Nettles, Bert Sheffield
Redden, Lawrence Drew
Scherf, John George, IV
Spotswood, Robert Keeling
Timberlake, Marshall

Dadeville
Oliver, John Percy, II

Florence
Case, Basil Timothy

Mobile
Harris, Benjamin Harte, Jr.
Roedder, William Chapman, Jr.

Montgomery
Laurie, Robin Garrett
Lawson, Thomas Seay, Jr.
McFadden, Frank Hampton
Nachman, Merton Roland, Jr.

Tuscaloosa
Williams, Roger Courtland

Tuscumbia
Munsey, Stanley Edward

ALASKA

Anchorage
Allingham, Lynn Marie

Kodiak
Jamin, Matthew Daniel
Ott, Andrew Eduard

ARIZONA

Flagstaff
Lacey, Henry Bernard

Stoops, Daniel J.

Phoenix
Allen, Robert Eugene Barton
Beggs, Harry Mark
Bodney, David Jeremy
Bouma, John Jacob
Brockelman, Kent
Galbut, Martin Richard
Harrison, Mark Isaac
Johnston, Logan Truax, III
Klausner, Jack Daniel
Lee, Richard H(arlo)
McRae, Hamilton Eugene, III
Mizrahi, Elan S(hai)
Rivera, Jose de Jesus
Rose, David L.
Sherk, Kenneth John
Smock, Timothy Robert
Tennen, Leslie Irwin
Winthrop, Lawrence Fredrick
Wirken, Charles William

Prescott
Gose, Richard Vernie
Perry, John Richard, Jr.

Rio Rico
Ryan, John Duncan

Safford
Van Ry, Bradley Otto

Tucson
D'Antonio, James Joseph
MacBan, Laura Vaden

ARKANSAS

Blytheville
Fendler, Oscar

Crossett
Hubbell, Billy James

Jonesboro
Deacon, John C.

Little Rock
Denton, Deborah S.
Heuer, Sam Tate
Hope, Ronald Arthur
Jiles, Gary D.
Julian, Jim Lee
Light, Robert Vann

CALIFORNIA

Alamo
Madden, Palmer Brown
Thiessen, Brian David

Auburn
Henry, Karen Hawley

Belvedere Tiburon
Allan, Walter Robert
Bremer, William Richard

Berkeley
De Goff, Victoria Joan

Beverly Hills
Amado, Honey Kessler
Burns, Marvin Gerald
Rondeau, Charles Reinhardt
Sherwood, Arthur Lawrence

Burbank
Litvack, Sanford Martin

Burlingame
Narayan, Beverly Elaine

Carlsbad
Koehnke, Phillip Eugene
McCracken, Steven Carl

Claremont
Ferguson, Cleve Robert
Gray, Paul Bryan

Costa Mesa
Boyer, David Dyer
Connally, Michael W.

Cupertino
Jelinch, Frank Anthony
Van Der Walde, Paul D.

Danville
Raines, Richard Clifton

Del Mar
Seitman, John Michael

Encino
Terterian, George

Escondido
Barraza, Horacio

Fremont
Chou, Yung-Ming

Fullerton
Moerbeek, Stanley Leonard

Glendale
MacDonald, Kirk Stewart

Imperial Beach
Merkin, William Leslie

Indio
De Salva, Christopher Joseph

Irvine
Desai, Aashish Y.
Petrasich, John Moris

Long Beach
Roberts, James Donzil

Los Angeles
Adamek, Charles Andrew
Adler, Erwin Ellery
Bosl, Phillip L.
Bringardner, John Michael
Byrd, Christine Waterman Swent
Cathcart, David Arthur
Christopher, Warren
Cohen, Cynthia Marylyn
Field, Richard Clark
Garcia-Barron, Gerard Lionel
Gordon, Jeffrey Sheppard
Hansell, Dean
Heller, Philip
Huben, Brian David
Lange, Joseph Jude Morgan
McGovern, David Carr
Miller, Milton Allen
Morgenthaler-Lever, Alisa
Nordlinger, Stephanie G.
Olivas, Daniel Anthony
Pasich, Kirk Alan
Rothman, Michael Judah
Rutter, Marshall Anthony
Schulman, Robert S.
Scoular, Robert Frank
Shacter, David Mervyn
Shapiro, Robert
Solis, Carlos
Van de Kamp, John Kalar
von Kalinowski, Julian Onesime
Warren, Robert Stephen
Whitaker, Ronald Stephen
White, Robert Joel
Wood, Willard Mark
Woodland, Irwin Francis

Los Gatos
Boccardo, James Frederick
Seligmann, William Robert

Marina Del Rey
Coplan, Daniel Jonathan

Menlo Park
Coats, William Sloan, III

Mill Valley
Nemir, Donald Philip

Modesto
Mussman, William Edward, III

Napa
Kuntz, Charles Powers

Newport Beach
Johnson, Thomas Webber, Jr.
Otto, James Daniel

Oakland
Allen, Jeffrey Michael
Berry, Phillip Samuel

Orange
Sanders, Gary Wayne

Orinda
Roethe, James Norton

Oxnard
McGinley, James Duff

Palm Springs
FitzGerald, John Edward, III

Palmdale
Reichman, Dawn Leslie

Palo Alto
Johnston, Alan Cope

Pasadena
Zuetel, Kenneth Roy, Jr.

Piedmont
McCormick, Timothy Brian Beer

Pleasanton
Harding, John Edward
Scott, G. Judson, Jr.

Sacramento
Brookman, Anthony Raymond
Foster, Douglas Taylor
Houpt, James Edward

San Diego
Brierton, Cheryl Lynn
Brown, LaMar Bevan
Emge, Derek John
Guinn, Stanley Willis
Herring, Charles David
Lathrop, Mitchell Lee
McDermott, Thomas John, Jr.
Noziska, Charles Brant
Shelton, Dorothy Diehl Rees
Von Passenheim, John B.
Weaver, Michael James

San Francisco
Allen, Paul Alfred
Arbuthnot, Robert Murray
Berning, Paul Wilson
Bostwick, James Stephen
Boutin, Peter Rucker
Briscoe, John
Callison, Russell James
Chao, Cedric C.
Danoff, Eric Michael
Deane, Elaine
Donovan, Charles Stephen
Friese, Robert Charles
Johns, Richard Seth Ellis
Kuhl, Paul Beach
Nelson, Paul Douglas
Reding, John Anthony
Richardson, Daniel Ralph
Riley, Benjamin Kneeland
Rowland, John Arthur
Seabolt, Richard L.

Smith, Robert Michael
Sparks, John Edward
Staring, Graydon Shaw
Taylor, William James (Zak Taylor)
Thornton, D. Whitney, II
Trautman, William Ellsworth
Venning, Robert Stanley
Warmer, Richard Craig

San Jose
Bennion, David Jacobsen
Bohn, Robert Herbert
Cummins, Charles Fitch, Jr.
Hernández, Fernando Vargas
McManis, James
Nielsen, Christian Bayard
Patton, David Alan
Smith, Valerie A.

San Marino
Tomich, Lillian

San Rafael
Bloomfield, Neil Jon
Chilvers, Robert Merritt
Roth, Hadden Wing

Santa Ana
Cifarelli, Thomas Abitabile
Frost, Winston Lyle
Heckler, Gerard Vincent
Patt, Herbert Jacob

Santa Barbara
Ah-Tye, Kirk Thomas
Metzinger, Timothy Edward
Moncharsh, Philip Isaac

Santa Cruz
Costello, Donald Fredric

Santa Monica
Bower, Allan Maxwell
Ringler, Jerome Lawrence

Santa Rosa
Gack, Kenneth David

Torrance
Johnson, Einar William

Tracy
Hay, Dennis Lee

Van Nuys
Mikesell, Richard Lyon

Walnut Creek
Schreiber, John T.

Woodland Hills
Flaig, Donald William

Yuba City
Doughty, Mark Anthony

COLORADO

Arvada
Peck, Kenneth E.

Aspen
Shipp, Dan Shackelford

Boulder
Lindenmuth, Noel Charles

Colorado Springs
Purvis, Randall W. B.
Slivka, Michael Andrew
Swanson, Victoria Clare Heldman

Denver
Dowdle, Patrick Dennis
Dunn, Randy Edwin
Fowler, Daniel McKay
Gallegos, Larry Duayne
Green, Jersey Michael-Lee
Harris, Dale Ray
Kaplan, Marc J.
Kintzele, John Alfred
Low, Andrew M.
Malatesta, Mary Anne
Martin, Raymond Walter
McConnell, Michael Theodore
Murane, William Edward
Nesland, James Edward
Smith, Daniel Timothy
Solano, Henry L.
Timmins, Edward Patrick
Tomlinson, Warren Leon
Wheeler, Malcolm Edward
Wollins, David Hart

Englewood
Mitchem, James E.

Golden
Snead, Kathleen Marie

Grand Junction
Griff, Harry

Highlands Ranch
Hagen, Glenn W(illiam)

Sedalia
Ewing, Robert Craig

CONNECTICUT

Bridgeport
Zeldes, Jacob Dean

Brookfield
Secola, Joseph Paul

Danbury
Dornfeld, Sharon Wicks

Fairfield
Denniston, Brackett Badger, III

Farmington
Wiechmann, Eric Watt

Hartford
Bonee, John Leon, III
Orth, Paul William
Space, Theodore Maxwell

Meriden
Lowry, Houston Putnam

New Haven
Belt, David Levin
Carty, Paul Vernon
Todd, Erica Weyer

Norwalk
Feinstein, Stephen Michael

Southport
Sanetti, Stephen Louis

Stamford
McDonald, Cassandra Burns
Mirsky, Ellis Richard
Stapleton, James Francis

Torrington
Leard, David Carl

West Hartford
Swerdloff, Mark Harris

DELAWARE

Dover
Babiarz, Francis Stanley

Wilmington
Kulesza, Joseph Dominick, Jr.
Semple, James William
Stone, F. L. Peter

DISTRICT OF COLUMBIA

Washington
Attridge, Daniel F.
Barnes, Peter
Barnett, Robert Bruce
Bernabei, Lynne Ann
Boss, Lenard Barrett
Buckley, John Joseph, Jr.
Canfield, Edward Francis
Carome, Patrick Joseph
Carter, William Joseph
Cooper, Clement Theodore
Cope, John R(obert)
Eastment, Thomas James
Efros, Ellen Ann
Ellis, Courtenay
Foggan, Laura Anne
Gelb, Joseph Donald
Goodman, John M.
Greenfeld, Alexander
Hassett, Joseph Mark
Jetton, C. Loring, Jr.
Jones, Aidan Drexel
Jones, Allen, Jr.
Jones, George Washington, Jr.
Kendall, David E.
Kent, M. Elizabeth
Klarfeld, Peter James
Kramer, Kenneth Stephen
Loots, James Mason
Martin, Ralph Drury
McDaniels, William E.
Meserve, Richard Andrew
Michaelson, Martin
Moses, Alfred Henry
Murphy, Sean Patrick
Pierson, W. DeVier
Pollock, Stacy Jane
Reid, Inez Smith
Renner, Curtis Shotwell
Rizzo, James Gerard
Sayler, Robert Nelson
Shaffer, David James
Sherman, Lawrence Jay
Shieber, William J.
Statland, Edward Morris
Taylor, William Woodruff, III
Thaler, Paul Sanders
Tompert, James Emil
Watson, Thomas C.
Weinstein, Harris
White-Mahaffey, Virginia L.
Wilson, Gary Dean
Witten, Roger Michael
Wolff, Paul Martin

FLORIDA

Altamonte Springs
Fisher, James Craig

Bartow
Stevenson, Robin Howard

Boca Raton
Beber, Robert H.
Nussbaum, Howard Jay
Silver, Barry Morris
Willis, John Alexander

Clearwater
Blakely, John T.
Pope, Fred Wallace, Jr.

Coral Gables
Buell, Rodd Russell
Gustafson, Anne-Lise Dirks
Hoffman, Carl H(enry)

Daytona Beach Shores
Schott, Clifford Joseph

Fort Lauderdale
Heath, Thomas Clark
Hoines, David Alan
James, Gordon, III
Kreizinger, Loreen I.
Strickland, Wilton L.
Turner, Hugh Joseph, Jr.
Wich, Donald Anthony, Jr.

Fort Myers
Pohl, Michael A.
Terry, T(aylor) Rankin, Jr.

Gainesville
Kurrus, Thomas William

Jacksonville
Bradford, Dana Gibson, II
Bullock, Bruce Stanley
Coker, Howard C.
Korn, Michael Jeffrey
Milton, Joseph Payne
Rumrell, Richard Gary
White, Edward Alfred

Lakeland
Knowlton, Kevin Charles
Wendel, John Fredric

Leesburg
Austin, Robert Eugene, Jr.

Maitland
Bailey, Michael Keith

Miami
Berger, Steven R.
Blackburn, Roger Lloyd
Bronis, Stephen Jay
Critchlow, Richard H.
Curtis, Karen Haynes
Hall, Adam Stuart
Hartz, Steven Edward Marshall
Hickey, John (Jack) Heyward
Korchin, Judith Miriam
Maher, Stephen Trivett
Osman, Edith Gabriella
Peltz, Robert Dwight
Stansell, Leland Edwin, Jr.
Touby, Kathleen Anita
Vento, M. Thérèse
Weinger, Steven Murray

Miami Beach
Ryce, Donald Theodore

Naples
Cardillo, John Pollara

North Miami Beach
Zipkin, Sheldon Lee

North Palm Beach
Lane, Matthew Jay

Orlando
Abbott, Charles Warren
Blackwell, Bruce Beuford
Hartley, Carl William, Jr.
Johnson, Kraig Nelson
Jontz, Jeffry Robert
Kelaher, James Peirce
Metz, Larry Edward
Morgan, Mary Ann
Nadeau, Robert Bertrand, Jr.
Sawicki, Stephen Craig
Spoonhour, James Michael

Palm Beach Gardens
Pumphrey, Gerald Robert

Pensacola
Kelly, John Barry, II
McKenzie, James Franklin
Soloway, Daniel Mark

Pompano Beach
Shulmister, M(orris) Ross

Saint Petersburg
Battaglia, Brian Peter
Henniger, David Thomas
Mann, Sam Henry, Jr.
Ross, Howard Philip

Sanford
Partlow, James Justice

Sarasota
Christopher, William Garth
Garland, Richard Roger

Tallahassee
Barley, John Alvin
Davis, William Howard

Tampa
Alpert, Jonathan Louis
Campbell, Richard Bruce
Gordon, Jeffrey (Jack Gordon)
Hahn, William Edward
Huneycutt, Alice Ruth
MacDonald, Thomas Cook, Jr.
Robinson, John William, IV
Stagg, Clyde Lawrence
Steiner, Geoffrey Blake
Taub, Theodore Calvin

West Palm Beach
Barnhart, Forrest Gregory
Gildan, Phillip Clarke
Mrachek, Lorin Louis
Roberts, George Preston, Jr. (Rusty Roberts)
Spillias, Kenneth George
Stinson, Steven Arthur
Zeller, Ronald John

Winter Park
Wagner, Lynn Edward

GEORGIA

Athens
Tolley, Edward Donald

Atlanta
Altman, Robert
Beckham, Walter Hull, III
Brown, John Robert
Burgoon, Brian David
Carpenter, David Allan
Chilivis, Nickolas Peter
Collins, Donnell Jawan
Collins, Steven M.
Croft, Terrence Lee
Denham, Vernon Robert, Jr.
Fellows, Henry David, Jr.
Genberg, Ira
Harrison, Bryan Guy
Janney, Donald Wayne
Johnson, Benjamin F(ranklin), III
Killorin, Robert Ware
Lackland, Theodore Howard
Longhi, Patrick George
Manley, David Bott, III
McAlpin, Kirk Martin
McGill, John Gardner
Miller, Janise Luevenia Monica
Paquin, Jeffrey Dean
Rhodes, Thomas Willard
Young, Michael Anthony
Young, Robert George

Canton
Hasty, William Grady, Jr.

College Park
Stokes, Arch Yow

Columbus
Harp, John Anderson
McGlamry, Max Reginald

Decatur
Apolinsky, Stephen Douglas
O'Connell, John James, Jr.

Kingsland
Ossick, John Joseph, Jr.

Metter
Doremus, Ogden

Roswell
England, John Melvin

Savannah
Gannam, Michael Joseph
Painter, Paul Wain, Jr.

Statesboro
Brogdon, W.M. "Rowe"

Valdosta
Copeland, Roy Wilson

HAWAII

Honolulu
Chin, Stephanie Anne
Deaver, Phillip Lester
Fong, Peter C. K.
Geshell, Richard Steven
Hart, Brook
Heller, Ronald Ian
Kane, Joelle K.K.S.
Kawachika, James Akio
Lau, Eugene Wing Iu
Mirikitani, Andrew Kotaro
Reinke, Stefan Michael
Sato, Glenn Kenji
Sumida, Kevin P.H.
Yamano, John Y.

Koloa
Blair, Samuel Ray

Lihue
Valenciano, Randal Grant Bolosan

IDAHO

Boise
Green, Cumer L.
Hoagland, Samuel Albert
Noack, Harold Quincy, Jr.
Park, William Anthony (Tony)
Schild, Raymond Douglas
Thomas, Eugene C.

Hailey
Hogue, Terry Glynn

Idaho Falls
Whittier, Monte Ray

Pocatello
Nye, W. Marcus W.

Twin Falls
Hohnhorst, John Charles

ILLINOIS

Belleville
Boyle, Richard Edward

Bloomington
Bragg, Michael Ellis

Chicago
Adelman, Stanley Joseph
Angst, Gerald L.
Barker, William Thomas
Benak, James Donald
Blatt, Richard Lee
Boyle, Gregory Michael
Brand, Mark
Brice, Roger Thomas

Burns, Terrence Michael
Connelly, Mary Jo
Creamer, Robert Allan
Daley, Michael Joseph
Daniels, John Draper
Davis, Scott Jonathan
Donner, Ted A.
Eggert, Russell Raymond
Eimer, Nathan Philip
Elden, Gary Michael
Esrick, Jerald Paul
Feagley, Michael Rowe
Filpi, Robert Alan
Finke, Robert Forge
Formeller, Daniel Richard
Fox, Elaine Saphier
Fox, Kathy Pinkstaff
Frazen, Mitchell Hale
Freerksen, Gregory Nathan
Giampietro, Wayne Bruce
Gilford, Steven Ross
Gustman, David Charles
Halloran, Michael John
Harrold, Bernard
Heinz, William Denby
Henry, Brian Thomas
Herald, J. Patrick
Herman, Sidney N.
Herman, Stephen Charles
Howe, Jonathan Thomas
Howser, Richard Glen
Hyman, Michael Bruce
Janich, Daniel Nicholas
Kamerick, Eileen Ann
Kaminsky, Richard Alan
Karnes, Evan Burton, II
Kim, Michael Charles
Kresse, William Joseph
Kunkle, William Joseph, Jr.
Lochbihler, Frederick Vincent
Luning, Thomas P.
Lynch, John James
Mack, John Melvin
Martin, Alan Joseph
McGonegle, Timothy Joseph
McLaren, Richard Wellington, Jr.
Molo, Steven Francis
Mone, Peter John
Montgomery, William Adam
Neumeier, Matthew Michael
Novak, Mark
O'Toole, William George
Panich, Danuta Bembenista
Pelton, Russell Meredith, Jr.
Pope, Michael Arthur
Price, Paul L.
Rutkoff, Alan Stuart
Saunders, Terry Rose
Schuman, William Paul
Shank, William O.
Sherman, Ian Matthew
Simon, Seymour
Skjold, Benjamin H.
Smith, Stephen Edward
Snyder, Jean Maclean
Stavins, Richard Lee
Stick, Michael Alan
Thomson, George Ronald
Tinaglia, Michael Lee
Tucker, Bowen Hayward
Van Tine, Matthew Eric
Vojcanin, Sava Alexander
Vranicar, Michael Gregory
Weaver, Timothy Allan
Webb, Dan K.
Wilcox, Mark Dean
Wood, Allison Lorraine

Dekalb
Tucker, Watson Billopp

Des Plaines
Jacobs, William Russell, II

Elgin
Roeser, Ronald O.

Jacksonville
Kuster, Larry Donald

La Grange
Kerr, Alexander Duncan, Jr.

Lake Forest
Giza, David Alan

Lisle
May, Frank Brendan, Jr.

Mundelein
Ackley, Robert O.

Oak Brook
Oldfield, E. Lawrence

Oak Park
Schubert, Blake H.

Oakbrook Terrace
Tibble, Douglas Clair

Peoria
Bertschy, Timothy L.
Prusak, Maximilian Michael

Riverwoods
Ford, Michael W.

Rock Island
Wallace, Franklin Sherwood

Rockford
Hunsaker, Richard Kendall

Springfield
Heckenkamp, Robert Glenn
Narmont, John Stephen

Wheaton
Butt, Edward Thomas, Jr.

INDIANA

Columbus
Perkins Senn, Karon Elaine

Danville
Baldwin, Jeffrey Kenton

Evansville
Hayes, Philip Harold
Knight, Jeffrey Lin

Fort Wayne
Pope, Mark Andrew

Indianapolis
Albright, Terrill D.
Blythe, James David, II
Conour, William Frederick
Due, Danford Royce
Kautzman, John Fredrick
McTurnan, Lee Bowes
Moffatt, Michael Alan
Padgett, Gregory Lee
Scaletta, Phillip Ralph, III
Wampler, Robert Joseph
Yeager, Joseph Heizer, Jr.

La Porte
Drayton, V. Michael

Lafayette
Hart, Russell Holiday
Pennell, Stephen Richard

Merrillville
Miller, Richard Allen

South Bend
Reinke, William John

Terre Haute
Bopp, James, Jr.
Kesler, John A.

IOWA

Cedar Rapids
Riley, Tom Joseph

Decorah
Belay, Stephen Joseph

Des Moines
Conlin, Roxanne Barton
Finley, Kerry A.
Norris, Glenn L.

Dubuque
Hammer, David Lindley

Mount Pleasant
Vance, Michael Charles

KANSAS

Kansas City
Holbrook, Reid Franklin
Jurcyk, John Joseph, Jr.

Olathe
Scott, Robert Gene

Overland Park
Branham, Melanie J.
Ruse, Steven Douglas
Smith, Daniel Lynn

Paola
Arnett, Debra Jean

Prairie Village
Sharp, Rex Arthur

Pratt
Stull, Gordon Bruce

Shawnee Mission
Badgerow, John Nicholas
Smith, Edwin Dudley

Topeka
Frost, Brian Standish

Wichita
Franklin, Joni Jeanette
Gorup, Geary N.
Grace, Brian Guiles

KENTUCKY

Crestwood
Ray, Ronald Dudley

Florence
Busald, E. André
Monohan, Edward Sheehan, IV

Lexington
Beshear, Steven L.
Hiestand, Sheila Patricia
Johnson, Brian M.

London
Keller, John Warren

Louisville
Ballantine, John Tilden
Cowan, Frederic Joseph
Ethridge, Larry Clayton
Keeney, Steven Harris
Manly, Samuel
Orberson, William Baxter

Paducah
Nickell, Christopher Shea

Somerset
Yeast, Daniel Gordon

LOUISIANA

Baton Rouge
Gonzales, Edward Joseph, III
Walsh, Milton O'Neal
Wittenbrink, Jeffrey Scott

Bossier City
Jackson, Patrick Richmond

Jefferson
Conino, Joseph Aloysius

Lafayette
Myers, Stephen Hawley
Roy, James Parkerson
Swift, John Goulding

Lake Charles
Sanchez, Walter Marshall
Veron, J. Michael

Metairie
Album, Jerald Lewis
Dinwiddie, Bruce Wayland
Recile, George B.

New Orleans
Abaunza, Donald Richard
Bordelon, Alvin Joseph, Jr.
David, Robert Jefferson
Etter, John Karl
Eustis, Richmond Minor
Fierke, Thomas Garner
Herman, Fred L.
Hoffman, Donald Alfred
Hurley, Grady Schell
Masinter, Paul James
Molony, Michael Janssens, Jr.
Pearce, John Y.
Perry, Brian Drew, Sr.
Pugh, William Whitmell Hill, III
Rodriguez, Antonio Jose
Shields, Lloyd Noble
Sinor, Howard Earl, Jr.
Thomas, Joseph Winand

Shreveport
Politz, Nyle Anthony

MAINE

Bangor
Woodcock, John Alden

Bass Harbor
Ervin, Spencer

Houlton
Sylvester, Torrey Alden

Portland
Culley, Peter William
Hirshon, Robert Edward
Martin, Joel Clark
Schutz, Sigmund D.
Whiting, Stephen Clyde

Sanford
Nadeau, Robert Maurice Auclair

MARYLAND

Abingdon
Wolf, Martin Eugene

Annapolis
Ferris, William Michael

Baltimore
Archibald, James Kenway
Berlage, Jan Ingham
Burch, Francis Boucher, Jr.
Dewey, Joel Allen
Ellin, Marvin
Gillece, James Patrick, Jr.
Hafets, Richard Jay
Kandel, Nelson Robert
Kandel, Peter Thomas
Messina, Bonnie Lynn
Uehlinger, Gerard Paul

Bel Air
Miller, Max Dunham, Jr.

Bethesda
Cohen, Jay Loring
Eisen, Eric Anshel
Moss, Stephen Edward
Nelson, William Eugene

Chevy Chase
Montedonico, Joseph

Greenbelt
Greenwald, Andrew Eric

Lanham Seabrook
McCarthy, Kevin John

North Potomac
Keane, James Ignatius

Oxon Hill
Serrette, Cathy Hollenberg

Towson
Proctor, Kenneth Donald
Vettori, Paul Marion

Westminster
Preston, Charles Michael

MASSACHUSETTS

Amherst
Howland, Richard Moulton

Barnstable
McLaughlin, Edward Francis, Jr.

Boston
Berry, Janis Marie
Brody, Richard Eric
Burns, Thomas David
Carroll, James Edward
Ellis, Fredric Lee
Epstein, Elaine May
Gargiulo, Andrea W.
Goldman, Eric Scot
Gossels, Claus Peter Rolf
Jones, Jeffrey Foster
Kaler, Robert Joseph
Kavanaugh, James Francis, Jr.
Licata, Arthur Frank
McKittrick, Neil Vincent
Moreira, Barbara Lyne
Moriarty, George Marshall
Murray, Philip Edmund, Jr.
O'Neill, Philip Daniel, Jr.
Perry, Blair Lane
Reardon, Frank Emond
Redlich, Marc
Richmond, Alice Elenor
Savrann, Richard Allen
Spelfogel, Scott David
Testa, Richard Joseph
Yurko, Richard John

Burlington
Graves, Robert

Cambridge
Pontikes, Rebecca George

Chelmsford
Grossman, Debra A.
Lerer, Neal M.

Framingham
Herrick, Stewart Thurston

Holyoke
Sarnacki, Michael Thomas

Lynnfield
McGivney, John Joseph

Medford
Berman, David

Newton
Peterson, Osler Leopold

Orleans
Chaplin, Ansel Burt

Salem
Shachok, Mary Ellen

South Easton
Finn, Anne-Marie

Weymouth
Fitzsimmons, B. Joseph, Jr.

Woburn
Lovins, Nelson Preston

Worcester
Donnelly, James Corcoran, Jr.

MICHIGAN

Ann Arbor
Ellmann, Douglas Stanley
Joscelyn, Kent B(uckley)
Niehoff, Leonard Marvin
Walsh, James Joseph

Bingham Farms
Fershtman, Julie Ilene

Birmingham
Delin, Sylvia Kaufman
Wells, Steven Wayne
Zacharski, Dennis Edward

Bloomfield Hills
Baumkel, Mark S.
Cranmer, Thomas William
Cunningham, Gary H.
Janover, Robert H.
Lamping, William Jay
McGarry, Alexander Banting

Charlevoix
Telgenhof, Allen Ray

Dearborn
Demorest, Mark Stuart

Decatur
Kinney, Gregory Hoppes

Detroit
Barr, Charles Joseph Gore
Foley, Thomas John
Lenga, J. Thomas
Mamat, Frank Trustick
McIntyre, Anita Grace Jordan
Nix, Robert Royal, II
Tickner, Ellen Mindy
Torpey, Scott Raymond
Ward, George Edward
Wittlinger, Timothy David

Flint
Hart, Clifford Harvey
Henneke, Edward George

Grand Rapids
Blackwell, Thomas Francis
Neckers, Bruce Warren
Rynbrandt, Kevin Abraham

Grosse Pointe
Goss, James William

Harbor Springs
Turner, Lester Nathan

Lansing
Fink, Joseph Allen
Stackable, Frederick Lawrence

Plymouth
Morgan, Donald Crane

Saginaw
Concannon, Andrew Donnelly

Saint Joseph
Butzbaugh, Elden W., Jr.

South Haven
Waxman, Sheldon Robert

Southfield
Morganroth, Mayer
Sullivan, Robert Emmet, Jr.
Taravella, Christopher Anthony

MINNESOTA

Bemidji
Woodke, Robert Allen

Bloomington
Jackson, Renee Leone

Brooklyn Center
Neff, Fred Leonard

Hallock
Malm, Roger Charles

Hopkins
Hunter, Donald Forrest

Minneapolis
Anderson, Alan Marshall
Baillie, James Leonard
Barnard, Allen Donald
Bland, J(ohn) Richard
Blanton, W. C.
Borger, John Philip
Bruner, Philip Lane
Clary, Bradley G.
Cole, Phillip Allen
Erstad, Leon Robert
Faricy, John Hartnett, Jr.
Gill, Richard Lawrence
Heffelfinger, Thomas Backer
Hoch, Gary W.
Hutchens, Michael D.
Klosowski, Thomas Kenneth
Long, James Jay
McGunnigle, George Francis
McNamara, Michael John
Meshbesher, Ronald I.
Pluimer, Edward J.
Price, Joseph Michael
Rathke, Stephen Carl
Reichert, Brent Larry
Reinhart, Robert Rountree, Jr.
Roe, Roger Rolland, Jr.
Silver, Alan Irving
Voss, Barry Vaughan
Zalk, Robert H.

North Oaks
Woods, Robert Edward

Saint Cloud
Hughes, Kevin John

Saint Louis Park
Rothenberg, Elliot Calvin

Saint Paul
Seymour, Mary Frances

Wayzata
Reutiman, Robert William, Jr.

MISSISSIPPI

Biloxi
Dornan, Donald C., Jr.

Brandon
Obert, Keith David

Gulfport
Allen, Harry Roger
Harral, John Menteith

Jackson
Corlew, John Gordon
Craig, C. York, III
Langford, James Jerry
O'Mara, James Wright

Tupelo
Clayton, Claude F., Jr.
Moffett, T(errill) K(ay)

University
Howorth, David Bishop

MISSOURI

Clayton
Michenfelder, Albert A.

Hannibal
Terrell, James Daniel

Independence
Neilsen, Christina J.

Jackson
Waldron, Kenneth Lynn

Jefferson City
Riner, James William

Kansas City
Beckett, Theodore Cornwall
Conner, John Shull
Deacy, Thomas Edward, Jr.
Eldridge, Truman Kermit, Jr.
Foster, Mark Stephen
Johnston, John Steven
Joyce, Michael Patrick
Lotven, Howard Lee
Martucci, William Christopher
McManus, James William
Newsom, James Thomas
Palmer, Dennis Dale
Rickert, Brian Patrick
Sands, Darry Gene
Shay, David Eugene
Smith, R(onald) Scott
Smithson, Lowell Lee
Stoup, Arthur Harry
Vandever, William Dirk

Marshall
Peterson, William Allen

Saint Louis
Barken, Bernard Allen
Berendt, Robert Tryon
Blanke, Richard Brian
Boggs, Beth Clemens
Burke, Thomas Michael
Carr, Gary Thomas
Floyd, Walter Leo
Fournie, Raymond Richard
Hellmuth, Theodore Henning
Klobasa, John Anthony
Kohn, Alan Charles
Kraft, Carl David
Luberda, George Joseph
Massey, Raymond Lee
McCarter, W. Dudley
McDaniel, James Edwin
Newman, Charles A.
Ramirez, Anthony Benjamin
Ringkamp, Stephen H.
Schramm, Paul Howard
Siegel, Cordell
Switzer, Frederick Michael, III
Walsh, Joseph Leo, III

Springfield
Baxter-Smith, Gregory John
Chamblee, Dana Alicia
FitzGerald, Kevin Michael
Sherwood, Devon Fredrick

MONTANA

Billings
Beiswanger, Gary Lee
Cromley, Brent Reed
Malee, Thomas Michael
Toole, Bruce Ryan

Bozeman
Conover, Richard Corrill
Nelson, Steven Dwayne

Helena
Morrison, John Martin

Missoula
Bender, Ronald Andrew

NEBRASKA

Lincoln
Guthery, John M.
Rowe, David Winfield

Omaha
Fitzgerald, James Patrick
Riley, William Jay

NEVADA

Las Vegas
Bolton, Jennifer Suzanne
Holman, Kristina Sue
Kirsch, Lynn
Nohrden, Patrick Thomas

Reno
Bible, Paul Alfred
Hibbs, Loyal Robert
Hill, Earl McColl

NEW HAMPSHIRE

Manchester
Middleton, Jack Baer

Nashua
Jette, Ernest Arthur

North Conway
Youngblood, Deborah Sue

Portsmouth
Doleac, Charles Bartholomew
Harman, Terrie
Watson, Thomas Roger

NEW JERSEY

Bridgewater
Conroy, Robert John

Cherry Hill
DeVoto, Louis Joseph
Tomar, William

Clark
Barr, Jon-Henry

Edison
O'Brien, John Graham

Elizabeth
Budanitsky, Sander

Florham Park
Chase, Eric Lewis
Laulicht, Murray Jack

Fort Lee
Abut, Charles C.

Freehold
Brown, Sanford Donald

Glen Rock
Markey, Brian Michael

Hackensack
Spiegel, Linda F.
Vort, Robert A.

Haddonfield
Heuisler, Charles William

Highland Park
Alman, Emily Arnow

Iselin
Goodman, Barry S.

Jersey City
DiSciullo, Alan Michael

Kearny
Brady, Lawrence Peter

Lebanon
Johnstone, Irvine Blakeley, III

Marlton
Pappas, Hercules

Millburn
Diamond, Richard S.

Morris Plains
Pluciennik, Thomas Casimir

Morristown
Clark, Grant Lawrence
O'Grady, Dennis Joseph
Pollock, Stewart Glasson
Rose, Robert Gordon
Szuch, Clyde Andrew

Mount Holly
Mintz, Jeffry Alan

Newark
Cahn, Jeffrey Barton
Creenan, Katherine Heras
Forkas, Robert Jason
Garde, John Charles
Siegal, Joel Davis
Wayne, Robert Andrew

North Haledon
Harrington, Kevin Paul

Princeton
Brennan, William Joseph, III
Negovan, Julie
Souter, Sydney Scull
Sutphin, William Taylor

Red Bank
Waldman, Daniel M.

Roseland
Bennett, John K.
Hern, J. Brooke
Sarasohn, Peter Radin
Smith, Wendy Hope

Rutherford
Henschel, John James

Saddle Brook
Cohn, Albert Linn

Secaucus
Castano, Gregory Joseph

Short Hills
Kaye, Marc Mendell

Shrewsbury
Hopkins, Charles Peter, II

Springfield
Mytelka, Arnold Krieger

Stone Harbor
Taylor, Robert Lee

Teaneck
Hayden, Joseph A., Jr.
Silber, Alan

Trenton
Harbeck, Dorothy Anne
Pellecchia, John Michael

Union
Mark, Michael David

Westfield
Hughes, Kieran Patrick

NEW MEXICO

Albuquerque
Beach, Arthur O'Neal
Bova, Vincent Arthur, Jr.
Buchanan, Deena Lynna
Caruso, Mark John
Lopez, Martin, III
Robb, John Donald, Jr.

Carlsbad
Bruton, Charles Clinton

Deming
Sherman, Frederick Hood

Farmington
Moeller, Floyd Douglas
Strother, Robin Dale

Hobbs
Stout, Lowell

Los Alamos
Herr, Bruce

Roswell
Kraft, Richard Lee

Santa Fe
Bienvenu, John Charles
Brannen, Jeffrey Richard
Casey, Patrick Anthony
Culbert, Peter V.
Garber, Bruce Samuel
Pound, John Bennett

NEW YORK

Albany
Alessi, Robert Joseph
Case, Forrest N., Jr.
Couch, Mark Woodworth
Greagan, William Joseph
Laird, Edward DeHart, Jr.

Amherst
Jones, E. Thomas

Bronx
Aris, Joram Jehudah

Bronxville
Fuller, David Otis, Jr.

Buffalo
Brock, David George
Brown, T. Alan
Feuerstein, Alan Ricky
Fisher, Cheryl Smith
Hayes, J. Michael
Jasen, Matthew Joseph
Manning, Kenneth Alan
Parker, Michelle
Schoenborn, Daniel Leonard

Cortlandt Manor
Buhler, Gregory Wallace

Delhi
Hamilton, John Thomas, Jr.
Hartmann, James M.

Garden City
Balkan, Kenneth J.
Di Mascio, John Philip
Fischoff, Gary Charles
Kroll, Martin N.
Sawyer, James

Glens Falls
Firth, Peter Alan

Great Neck
Samanowitz, Ronald Arthur

Hempstead
Kane, Donald Vincent

Hicksville
Giuffré, John Joseph

Hudson
Davis, Deborah Lynn
Howard, Andrew Baker

Huntington
DeMartin, Charles Peter

Ithaca
Pinnisi, Michael Donato

Katonah
Keeffe, John Arthur

Long Beach
Solomon, Robert H.

Long Island City
Risi, Joseph John

Manlius
Mathewson, George Atterbury

Mineola
Bartol, Ernest Thomas
Good, Douglas Jay

New City
Fenster, Robert David

New Hyde Park
Lee, Brian Edward

New York
Alcott, Mark Howard
Altieri, Peter Louis
Appel, Albert M.
Aron, Roberto
Barasch, Amy Pitcairn
Berger, Michael Gary
Bern, Marc Jay
Bernstein, Robert Jay
Bluestone, Andrew Lavoott
Boddie, Reginald Alonzo
Bodovitz, James Philip
Bower, Thomas Michael
Brown, Peter Megargee
Burke, Kathleen Mary
Burrows, Michael Donald
Carling, Francis

Clark, Bruce E.
Colfin, Bruce Elliott
Coll, John Peter, Jr.
Collins, John F.
Conboy, Kenneth
Cook, Barbara Ann
Crane, Roger Ryan, Jr.
Cuneo, Donald Lane
Dankner, Jay Warren
Davidson, George Allan
Davis, Michael Steven
Derzaw, Richard Lawrence
DiBlasi, Gandolfo Vincent
Drebsky, Dennis Jay
Fallek, Andrew Michael
Filson, Marguerite B.
Finkelstein, Ira Allen
Fleischman, Keith Martin
Fredericks, William Curtis
Freyer, Dana Hartman
Ganz, Howard Laurence
Garland, Sylvia Dillof
Genova, Joseph Steven
Gioiella, Russell Michael
Goldstein, Howard Sheldon
Gordon, Michael Mackin
Grassi, Joseph F.
Green, Eric Howard
Greenberg, Gary Howard
Greenberg, Philip Alan
Haig, Robert Leighton
Handler, Arthur M.
Hershman, Scott Edward
Hirshowitz, Melvin Stephen
Hoff, Jonathan M(orind)
Holman, Bud George
Horkovich, Robert Michael
Hynes, Patricia Mary
Jacobs, Hara Kay
Jaffe, Mark M.
Janowitz, James Arnold
Josephson, William Howard
Juceam, Robert E.
Kamien, Kalvin
Kasowitz, Marc Elliot
Kassebaum, John Philip
Katsh, Salem Michael
Katz, Jerome Charles
Kaye, Richard Paul
Kempf, Donald G., Jr.
Kheel, Robert J.
Kirschbaum, Myron
Klapper, Molly
Kleinberg, Norman Charles
Kneeland, Mishell B.
Kostelanetz, Boris
Kurzweil, Harvey
Landron, Michel John
Laufer, Jacob
LeBlang, Skip Alan
Levine, Ronald Jay
Levinson, Paul Howard
Levy, Herbert Monte
Linsenmeyer, John Michael
Liss, Norman
Lupkin, Stanley Neil
Lynton, Harold Stephen
Madsen, Stephen Stewart
Marcellino, Stephen Michael
Matus, Wayne Charles
McDonell, Neil Edwin
McGrath, Christopher Thomas
Miller, Charles Hampton
Miller, Steven Scott
Milmed, Paul Kussy
Moore, Thomas Ronald (Lord Bridestowe)
Munzer, Stephen Ira
Newman, Fredric Samuel
Nonna, John Michael
Norfolk, William Ray
O'Dwyer, Brian
Oberman, Michael Stewart
Oechler, Henry John, Jr.
Owen, Robert Dewit
Packard, Stephen Michael
Paul, James William
Plevan, Kenneth A.
Polak, Werner L.
Raab, Sheldon
Reimer, Lisa J.
Rivera, Walter
Rogers, Theodore Otto, Jr.
Rolfe, Ronald Stuart
Rubin, Herbert
Russotti, Philip Anthony
Sahid, Joseph Robert
Salman, Robert Ronald
Salomon, Philippe M.
Schallert, Edwin Glenn
Schindler, Steven Roy
Schlain, Barbara Ellen
Schwartz, Barry Steven
Schwartz, James Evan
Seiff, Eric A.
Shaw, Robert Bernard
Sigmond, Carol Ann
Silverman, Arthur Charles
Simmons, Peter Lawrence
Sternman, Joel W.
Steuer, Richard Marc
Struve, Guy Miller
Sussman, Alexander Ralph
Tarnoff, Jerome
Tilewick, Robert
Tulchin, David Bruce
Vassallo, John A.
Viktora, Richard Emil
Vitkowsky, Vincent Joseph
Vladeck, Judith Pomarlen
Wailand, George
Wallach, Eric Jean
Walpin, Gerald
Warden, John L.
Weinschel, Alan Jay
Weiser, Martin Jay
Wexelbaum, Michael
Windle, Sarah Pennyquick
Wishingrad, Jay Marc
Witmeyer, John Jacob, III
Wynn, Simon David
Yankwitt, Russell Marc
Yun, Edward Joon
Zammit, Joseph Paul
Zaslowsky, David Paul
Zifchak, William C.

Newburgh
Liberth, Richard Francis

Niagara Falls
Anton, Ronald David

Nyack
Seidler, B(ernard) Alan

Pleasant Valley
Vasti, Thomas Francis, III

Rochester
Kelly, Paul Donald
Lapine, Felix Victor
Lascell, David Michael
Palermo, Anthony Robert
Smith, Jules Louis

Salamanca
Brady, Thomas Carl

Scarsdale
King, Robert Lucien
Perko, Kenneth Albert, Jr.

Schenectady
Wickerham, Richard Dennis

Smithtown
Spellman, Thomas Joseph, Jr.

Syracuse
Engel, Richard Lee
Michaels, Beverly Ann
Traylor, Robert Arthur
Young, Douglas Howard

Troy
Finkel, Sanford Norman

Uniondale
Eilen, Howard Scott
Sugarman, Robert P.

White Plains
Downes, James J.
Greenspan, Leon Joseph
Greenspan, Michael Evan
Guida, Toni M.
Halpern, Philip Morgan
Null, William Seth
Ryan, Robert Davis

Wolcott
Bartlett, Cody Blake

Woodbury
Taub, Linda Marsha

NORTH CAROLINA

Charlotte
Ayscue, Edwin Osborne, Jr.
Lynch, Craig Taylor
Newitt, John Garwood, Jr.

Durham
Carpenter, Charles Francis
Lewis, David Olin

Greensboro
Clark, David McKenzie

High Point
Baker, Walter Wray, Jr.

Oxford
Burnette, James Thomas

Raleigh
Cole, Sean Andrew Burke
Dixon, Wright Tracy, Jr.
Ellis, Lester Neal, Jr.
Glass, Fred Stephen
Hunter, Richard Samford, Jr.
Kapp, Michael Keith
Millberg, John C.
Wetsch, Laura Johnson

Smithfield
Schulz, Bradley Nicholas

Wilmington
Seagle, J. Harold

NORTH DAKOTA

Bismarck
Edin, Charles Thomas
Klemin, Lawrence R.

Dickinson
Greenwood, Dann E.

Fargo
Crothers, Daniel J.

Grand Forks
Cilz, Douglas Arthur

Mandan
Bair, Bruce B.

Minot
Backes, Orlin William

OHIO

Akron
Lombardi, Frederick McKean
Wolfe, John Leslie

Ashtabula
Lesko, Jane Lynn

Beavercreek
Stadnicar, Joseph William

Celina
Lammers, Thomas Dean

Cincinnati
Bissinger, Mark Christian
Chesley, Stanley Morris
Chesser, Stacey C.
Cioffi, Michael Lawrence
Faller, Susan Grogan
Frantz, Robert Wesley
Holschuh, John David, Jr.
Lutz, James Gurney
Rose, Donald McGregor
Scacchetti, David J.
Terp, Thomas Thomsen
Trauth, Joseph Louis, Jr.
Vander Laan, Mark Alan
Whitaker, Glenn Virgil

Cleveland
Bacon, Brett Kermit
Chandler, Everett Alfred
Crist, Paul Grant
Diamant, Michael Harlan
DiVenere, Anthony Joseph
Duncan, Ed Eugene
Feliciano, José Celso
Gippin, Robert Malcolm
Hoffman, Mark Leslie
Kelly, Dennis Michael
Newman, John M., Jr.
Osborne, Frank R.
Rains, M. Neal
Schaefer, David Arnold
Solomon, Randall Lee
Szaller, James Francis
Turoff, Jack Newton
Vance, Victoria Lynne
Weller, Charles David
Whitney, Richard Buckner
Young, James Edward

Columbus
Binning, J. Boyd
Draper, Gerald Linden
Elam, John Carlton
Hardymon, David Wayne
McDermott, Kevin R.
Ray, Frank Allen
Reid, Nelson Marlin
Roubanes, Barbara Ann
Ryan, Joseph W., Jr.
Swetnam, Daniel Richard
Taggart, Thomas Michael
Taylor, AmySue
Taylor, Joel Sanford
Thomas, Duke Winston
Warner, Charles Collins
Woods, William Hunt

Dayton
Faruki, Charles Joseph
Krebs, Leo Francis
Ross, Elizabeth Lorraine

Dublin
Tenuta, Luigia

Findlay
Kentris, George Lawrence

Jackson
Lewis, Richard M.

Lima
Jacobs, Ann Elizabeth

Newark
Gordon, L(eland) James

Portsmouth
Crowder, Marjorie Briggs

Saint Marys
Huber, William Evan

Sandusky
Bailey, K. Ronald

Toledo
Baker, Richard Southworth
Pletz, Thomas Gregory
Wicklund, David Wayne

Wilmington
Buckley, Frederick Jean

Wooster
Kennedy, Charles Allen

Youngstown
Blair, Richard Bryson

OKLAHOMA

Edmond
Lester, Andrew William

Enid
Jones, Stephen

Norman
Talley, Richard Bates

Oklahoma City
Christiansen, Mark D.
Coats, Andrew Montgomery
Cunningham, Stanley Lloyd
Gibson, Keith Russell
Gordon, Kevin Dell
Necco, Alexander David
Nesbitt, Charles Rudolph
Tompkins, Raymond Edgar
Wilson, Julia Ann Yother
Wyatt, Robert Lee, IV

Poteau
Sanders, Douglas Warner, Jr.

Stroud
Swanson, Robert Lee

Tulsa
Arrington, John Leslie, Jr.
Clark, Joseph Francis, Jr.
Cooper, Richard Casey

Daniel, Samuel Phillips
Davis, G. Reuben
Eagan, Claire Veronica
Eagleton, Edward John
Haynie, Tony Wayne
La Sorsa, William George

Vinita
Johnston, Oscar Black, III

OREGON

Corvallis
Ringo, Robert Gribble

Eugene
Horn, John Harold

La Grande
Joseph, Steven Jay

Lincoln City
Elliott, Scott

Portland
Dailey, Dianne K.
Hart, John Edward
Kennedy, Jack Leland
Maloney, Robert E., Jr.
Rieke, Forrest Neill
Sand, Thomas Charles
Savage, John William
Tanzer, Jacob

PENNSYLVANIA

Allentown
Gross, Malcolm Joseph

Altoona
Serbin, Richard Martin

Bethlehem
Bush, Raymond George

Carlisle
Turo, Ron

Center Valley
Smillie, Douglas James

Doylestown
Elliott, Richard Howard

Easton
Brown, Robert Carroll
Noel, Nicholas, III

Greensburg
Belden, H. Reginald, Jr.
Gounley, Dennis Joseph

Harrisburg
Burcat, Joel Robin
Downey, Brian Patrick
Lappas, Spero Thomas
Skelly, Joseph Gordon
Stefanon, Anthony

Hollidaysburg
Pfaff, Robert James

Horsham
Best, Franklin Luther, Jr.

Hummelstown
Mark, Timothy Ivan

Johnstown
Kaharick, Jerome John

King Of Prussia
DeMaria, Joseph Carminus

Kingston
Shaffer, Charles Alan

Malvern
Griffith, Edward, II
May, Judy Royer

Mc Murray
Brzustowicz, John Cinq-Mars

Media
D'Amico, Andrew J.
Ewing, Robert Clark
Zicherman, David L.

Monroeville
McDowell, Michael David

Moon Township
Corbett, Thomas Wingett, Jr.

Newtown
Kardos, Mel D.

Norristown
Cowperthwait, Lindley Murray

Orefield
Dimmich, Jeffrey Robert

Paoli
Chiacchiere, Mark Dominic

Philadelphia
Baum, E. Harris
Bogutz, Jerome Edwin
Bressler, Barry E.
Calvert, Jay H., Jr.
Cannon, John, III
Connor, Joseph Patrick, III
Cooney, J(ohn) Gordon, Jr.
Cullen, Raymond T.
D'Angelo, Christopher Scott
Damsgaard, Kell Marsh
Elkins, S. Gordon

Fickler, Arlene
Fineman, S. David
Fox, Reeder Rodman
Goldberg, Joseph
Hanselmann, Fredrick Charles
Harvey, Gregory Merrill
Hoffman, Alan Jay
Howard, William Herbert
Lewis, John Hardy, Jr.
Mannino, Edward Francis
Mannino, Robert
McGurk, Eugene David, Jr.
Miller, Leslie Anne
Rainone, Michael Carmine
Resnick, Stephanie
Samuel, Ralph David
Schneider, Richard Graham
Serotta, Judd Adam
Sheils, Denis Francis
Walters, Christopher Kent
Wellington, Ralph Glenn
Whinston, Stephen Alan
Wrobleski, Jeanne Pauline

Pittsburgh
Bogut, John Carl, Jr.
Breault, Theodore Edward
Esposito, Cheryl Lynne
Frank, Frederick Newman
Klodowski, Harry Francis, Jr.
Marsico, Leonard Joseph
Miller, James Robert
Murdoch, Robert Whitten
Perry, Jon Robert
Tarasi, Louis Michael, Jr.
Wycoff, William Mortimer

Reading
Roland, John Wanner

Scranton
Burke, Henry Patrick
Howley, James McAndrew

State College
Nollau, Lee Gordon

Sunbury
Saylor, Charles Horace

Warrendale
Micale, Frank Jude

Wilkes Barre
Lach, Joseph Andrew

RHODE ISLAND

Providence
Donnelly, Kevin William
Esposito, Dennis Harry
Glavin, Kevin Charles
Jones, Lauren Evans
Medeiros, Matthew Francis

Warwick
Reilly, John B.

West Warwick
Bottella, Tammy Ann

SOUTH CAROLINA

Charleston
Barker, Douglas Alan
Hood, Robert Holmes
Patrick, Charles William, Jr.

Columbia
Blanton, Hoover Clarence
Carpenter, Charles Elford, Jr.
Gibbes, William Holman
Gray, Elizabeth Van Doren
Lewis, Ernest Crosby
Strom, J. Preston, Jr.

Greenville
Wyche, Madison Baker, III

Mount Pleasant
Ritter, Ann

North Charleston
Joye, Mark Christopher
Wigger, Jarrel L.

Pawleys Island
Daniel, J. Reese

SOUTH DAKOTA

Rapid City
Shultz, Donald Richard
Stuck, Haven Laurence

TENNESSEE

Chattanooga
Adams, Morgan Goodpasture
Akers, Samuel Lee
Gearhiser, Charles Josef
James, Stuart Fawcett
Jessup, William Eugene
Moore, Hugh Jacob, Jr.

Johnson City
Jenkins, Ronald Wayne

Knoxville
Arnett, Foster Deaver
Cremins, William Carroll
Galyon, Luther Anderson, III
Giordano, Lawrence Francis
Lloyd, Francis Leon, Jr.
Roach, Jon Gilbert
Vines, William Dorsey
Wheeler, John Watson
White, Edward Gibson, II

Memphis
Allen, Newton Perkins
Bland, James Theodore, Jr.
Matthews, Paul Aaron
McLean, Robert Alexander
Rutledge, Roger Keith
Schuler, Walter E.

Nashville
Bramlett, Paul Kent
Cantrell, Luther E., Jr.
Clayton, Daniel Louis
Cooney, Charles Hayes
Harris, Alvin Louis
Jameson, Michael Francis

Signal Mountain
Leitner, Gregory Marc

White House
Ruth, Bryce Clinton, Jr.

TEXAS

Abilene
Boone, Celia Trimble

Addison
Hranitzky, Rachel Robyn

Amarillo
Burnette, Susan Lynn

Austin
Arnett, Richard Lynn
Dowd, Steven Milton
Greig, Brian Strother
Hayes, Burgain Garfield
Lochridge, Lloyd Pampell, Jr.
McConnico, Stephen E.
McCullough, Frank Witcher, III
Neblett, Stewart Lawrence
Rittenberry, Kelly Culhane
Schaffer, Dean Aaron
Spivey, Broadus Autry

Bastrop
Van Gilder, Derek Robert

Beaumont
Oxford, Hubert, III
Scofield, Louis M., Jr.
Waterston, Tass Dever

Brownfield
Moore, Bradford L.

Brownsville
Ray, Mary Louise Ryan
Walsh, Lawrence Adrian

Cleveland
Campbell, Selaura Joy

College Station
Kennady, Emmett Hubbard, III

Corpus Christi
Barrera, Eric Isaac
Leon, Rolando Luis

Dallas
Acker, Rodney
Baggett, Steven Ray
Bickel, John W., II
Bonesio, Woodrow Michael
Byrom, Joe Alan
Case, Thomas Louis
Cromartie, Eric Ross
Crotty, Robert Bell
Davenport, James Kent
Dicus, Brian George
Ellis, Alfred Wright (Al Ellis)
Ellis, James Alvis, Jr.
Hackney, Hugh Edward
Hawkins, Scott Alexis
Holmes, James Hill, III
Johnson, James Joseph Scofield
Johnston, Coyt Randal
Kirby, Le Grand Carney, III
Malorzo, Thomas Vincent
Mc Elhaney, John Hess
McDonald, Michael Scott
Mighell, Kenneth John
Mira, Joseph Lawrence
Moore, Edward Warren
Orleans, Neil Jeffrey
Pruessner, David Morgan
Sloman, Marvin Sherk
Stinnett, Mark Allan
Thompson, Peter Rule
Welch, Shannon Lois Kathleen
Zisman, Barry Stuart

El Paso
Cox, Sanford Curtis, Jr.
Darnell, James Oral
Leachman, Russell DeWitt
McDonald, Charles Edward
Morton, Fred J.

Fort Worth
Cooper, Monika Goeschel
Cottongame, W. Brice
Dean, Beale
Griffith, Richard Lattimore
Kelly, Dee J.
Langenheim, Roger Allen
Law, Thomas Hart
Mullanax, Milton Greg
Randolph, Robert McGehee
Sharpe, James Shelby

Galveston
Neves, Kerry Lane

Harlingen
Pope, William L.

Henderson
Adkison, Ron

Houston
Amann, Leslie Kiefer
Banks, John Robert, Jr.
Barnett, Edward William
Bradie, Peter Richard
Carmody, James Albert
Carroll, James Vincent, III
Carter, John Loyd
Dykes, Osborne Jefferson, III
Eckhardt, William Rudolf, III
Edwards, Blaine Douglass
England, Rudy Alan
Farley, Jan Edwin
Farnsworth, T Brooke
Garten, David Burton
Grossberg, Marc Elias
Holloway, Gordon Arthur
Jones, Frank Griffith
Ketchand, Robert Lee
Kruse, Charles Thomas
LaFuze, William L.
Liles, Kevin Warren
Love, Scott Anthony
Lynch, John Edward, Jr.
Maroney, James Francis, III
McCarter, Louis Eugene
McDaniel, Jarrel Dave
Miller, Gary C.
Montague, H. Dixon
Moroney, Linda L. S.
Nations, Howard Lynn
Owens, Betty Ruth
Pate, Stephen Patrick
Prestridge, Pamela Adair
Reasoner, Barrett Hodges
Roach, Robert Michael, Jr.
Spain, H. Daniel
Spalding, Andrew Freeman
Van Fleet, George Allan
Van Kerrebrook, Mary Alice
Walton, Dan Gibson
Wojciechowski, Marc James
Wright, Paul William
Zeigler, Ann dePender

Huffman
Frazier, William Sumpter

Lamesa
Saleh, John

Longview
Welge, Jack Herman, Jr.

Mcallen
Carrera, Victor Manuel

Midland
Fletcher, Richard Royce

Nacogdoches
Bias, Dana G.

Odessa
Hendrick, Benard Calvin, VII

Orange
Dugas, Louis, Jr.

Rockport
Benningfield, Carol Ann

San Antonio
Armstrong, William Tucker, III
Craddock, Allen T.
Drought, James L.
Hohman, A. J., Jr.
Maloney, Pat, Sr.
Montgomery, James Edward, Jr.
Patrick, Dane Herman
Pipkin, Marvin Grady
Wachsmuth, Robert William
Wallis, Ben Alton, Jr.
Welmaker, Forrest Nolan

Sugar Land
Aldrich, Lovell W(eld)
Greer, Raymond White

The Woodlands
Schlacks, Stephen Mark

UTAH

Logan
Jenkins, James C.

Park City
Kennicott, James W.

Provo
Abbott, Charles Favour

Salt Lake City
Anderson, Robert Monte
Orton, R. Willis
Reeder, F. Robert
Scofield, David Willson
Tateoka, Reid
Turner, Shawn Dennis

VERMONT

Brattleboro
McCarty, William Michael, Jr.

Burlington
Frank, Joseph Elihu
Lisman, Bernard

Colchester
Garcia, Luis Cesareo

Montpelier
Putter, David Seth
Valerio, Matthew F.

Rutland
Cleary, David Laurence
Faignant, John Paul

VIRGINIA

Alexandria
Hirschkop, Philip Jay
McGuire, Edward David, Jr.
Toothman, John William

Arlington
Fowler, David Lucas

Charlottesville
McKay, John Douglas

Fairfax
Keith, John A.C.
Stanley, William Martin

Fredericksburg
Billingsley, Robert Thaine

Harrisonburg
Wallinger, M(elvin) Bruce

Leesburg
Price, Stephen Conwell

Lynchburg
Packert, G(ayla) Beth

Mc Lean
Sparks, Robert Ronold, Jr.

Norfolk
Pearson, John Yeardley, Jr.

Norton
Jessee, Roy Mark

Portsmouth
Moody, Willard James, Sr.

Reston
Anderson, Charles Anthony
Bredehoft, Elaine Charlson

Richmond
Bing, Richard McPhail
Carrell, Daniel Allan
Davenport, Bradfute Warwick, Jr.
DeCamps, Charles Michael
Ellis, Andrew Jackson, Jr.
Framme, Lawrence Henry, III
Hall, Stephen Charles
King, William H., Jr.
Krumbein, Charles Harvey
Levit, Jay J(oseph)
Merhige, Robert Reynold, Jr.
Peluso, Dana C.M.
Robinson, John Victor
Rucker, Douglas Pendleton, Jr.
Rudlin, David Alan
Spahn, Gary Joseph
Walsh, James Hamilton

Roanoke
Barnhill, David Stan
Densmore, Douglas Warren
Effel, Laura
McGarry, Richard Lawrence
Mundy, Gardner Marshall

South Riding
Murray, Michael Patrick

Springfield
Costello, Daniel Brian

Vienna
Titus, Bruce Earl

Virginia Beach
Buzard, David Andrew
Dumville, S(amuel) Lawrence
Swope, Richard McAllister

Warrenton
Howard, Blair Duncan

Woodbridge
Roberts, Charles Bren

WASHINGTON

Bainbridge Island
Otorowski, Christopher Lee

Bellevue
Landau, Felix

Bellingham
Raas, Daniel Alan

Gig Harbor
Thompson, Ronald Edward

Grandview
Maxwell, John Edward

Seattle
Boman, Marc Allen
Cunningham, Joel Dean
Dorn, Trilby C. E.
Freedman, Bart Joseph
Gerrard, Keith
Johnson, Bruce Edward Humble
Lemly, Thomas Adger
Lundgren, Gail M.
McCoid, Nancy Katherine
McCune, Philip Spear
McKay, John
McKinstry, Ronald Eugene
McLaughlin, Thomas Jeffrey
Mitchell, Robert Bertelson, Jr.
Paul, Thomas Hunt
Rummage, Stephen Michael
Sandler, Michael David
Simburg, Melvyn Jay
Wayne, Robert Jonathan
Whitson, Lish

Spokane
Eymann, Richard Charles
Leipham, Jay Edward
Lineberger, Peter Saalfield

Tacoma
Krueger, James A.

WEST VIRGINIA

Bluefield
Evans, Wayne Lewis

Buckhannon
McCauley, David W.

Charleston
Berthold, Robert Vernon, Jr.
Brown, James Knight
Neely, Richard
Robinson, E. Glenn
Teare, John Richard, Jr.
Zak, Robert Joseph

Morgantown
Fusco, Andrew G.

WISCONSIN

Deerfield
Pappas, David Christopher

Germantown
Ehlinger, Ralph Jerome

Madison
Anderson, Michael Steven
Doran, Kenneth John
Peterson, H. Dale
Ragatz, Thomas George
Schmid, John Henry, Jr.
Stoddard, Glenn McDonald

Milwaukee
Clark, James Richard
Daily, Frank J(erome)
Friebert, Robert Howard
Marquis, William Oscar
Nelson, Roy Hugh, Jr.
Pettit, Roger Lee
Terschan, Frank Robert
Trecek, Timothy Scott
Van Grunsven, Paul Robert
Williams, Clay Rule

Oshkosh
Kelly, John Martin
Wilde, William Richard

Racine
Rudebusch, Alice Ann

Rhinelander
Saari, John William, Jr.

WYOMING

Casper
Day, Stuart Reid

Sheridan
Cannon, Kim Decker

TERRITORIES OF THE UNITED STATES

PUERTO RICO

San Juan
Pierluisi, Pedro R.

MEXICO

Coahuila
Hernandez, Juan Ignacio

AUSTRALIA

Brisbane
Perrett, Ross Graham

CHINA

Beijing
Xing, Xuisong

Hong Kong
Rapinet, Crispin William

ENGLAND

London
Carruthers, Andrew James
Dickey, John W.
George, Anna-Britt Kristin
Leadercramer, David Ian
Mendelowitz, Michael Sydney

GERMANY

Berlin
Schoene, Friedrich Tobias

Bonn
Nadler, Andreas

IRELAND

Dublin
Preston, Caroline Mary

THE NETHERLANDS

Amsterdam
Van Campen, Arnoud Clemens

THE PHILIPPINES

Metro Manila
Pasal, Emmanuel Pastores

SINGAPORE

Singapore
Liew, Yik Wee
Shetty, Nishith Kumare

SOUTH AFRICA

Johannesburg
Girdwood, Graham William
Prinsloo, Jojannes Christiaan

SWEDEN

Stockholm
Erlandsson, Asa

SWITZERLAND

Zurich
Koch, Thomas

THAILAND

Bangkok
Annanon, Songphol
Chunhakasikarn, Sasirusm Bulpakdi

ADDRESS UNPUBLISHED

Adams, Samuel Franklin
Arencibia, Raul Antonio
Bailey, Francis Lee
Beasley, James W., Jr.
Beldock, Myron
Bell, John William
Beukema, John Frederick
Boone, Richard Winston, Sr.
Braun, Jerome Irwin
Brodsky, David Michael
Brown, Margaret deBeers
Buchmann, Alan Paul
Collins, Theodore John
Connell, William D.
Diamond, Paul Steven
Dondanville, John Wallace
Farley, Barbara Suzanne
Feazell, Vic
Fischer, David Jon
Fleischman, Herman Israel
Garcia Barron, Ramiro
Goddard, Claude Philip, Jr.
Gotlieb, Lawrence Barry
Hall, John Hopkins
Harman, Wallace Patrick
Hicks, C. Flippo
Holmes, Michael Gene
Irvine, John Alexander
Jackson, Raymond Sidney, Jr.
Kapnick, Richard Bradshaw
Kennedy, Vekeno
Killeen, Michael John
Klein, Linda Ann
Kouba, Lisa Marco
Landman, Eric Christopher
Levinson, Kenneth Lee
Lipsman, Richard Marc
Lory, Loran Steven
Masquelette, Philip Edward
McCormick, Homer L., Jr.
McFerrin, James Hamil
McNeil Staudenmaier, Heidi Loretta
McQuigg, John Dolph
Mudd, John O.
Neuhaus, Joseph Emanuel
Newman, Carol L.
Norman, Albert George, Jr.
Pannill, William Presley
Paul, Richard Wright
Perrin, Michael Warren
Pomerene, Toni Graven
Quillen, Cecil Dyer, Jr.
Redmond, Lawrence Craig
Richards, Paul A.
Schor, Suzi
Schultz, Dennis Bernard
Seifert, Stephen Wayne
Slive, Steven Howard
Smith, James A.
Smith, Ronald Ehlbert
Streicker, James Richard
Swann, Barbara
Terrell, G. Irvin
Tone, Philip Willis
Wagner, Arthur Ward, Jr.
Walner, Robert Joel
Weisberg, David Charles
Wessel, Peter
White, John Joseph, III
Wilson, Charles Haven
Wilson, Virgil James, III
Wright, Frederick Lewis, II
Yeager, Jeffrey Alan
Yeager, Mark Leonard

CIVIL LITIGATION, STATE

UNITED STATES

ALABAMA

Anniston
Woodrow, Randall Mark

Birmingham
Kracke, Robert Russell
Max, Rodney Andrew
Newton, Alexander Worthy
Rogers, Ernest Mabry
Smith, Carol Ann
Stabler, Lewis Vastine, Jr.
Whiteside, David Powers, Jr.

Cullman
Poston, Beverly Paschal

Demopolis
Dinning, Woodford Wyndham, Jr.

Huntsville
Stephens, Harold (Holman Stephens)

Montgomery
Tindol, Melton Chad

Tuscumbia
Munsey, Stanley Edward

Woodstock
Downs, Bernard Boozer, Jr.

ALASKA

Anchorage
Bankston, William Marcus
Brown, Harold MacVane
Feldman, Jeffrey Marc
Pfiffner, Frank Albert
Richmond, Robert Lawrence
Walther, Dale Jay

Bethel
Cooke, Christopher Robert
Gathright, Howard T.

ARIZONA

Mesa
Squire, Bruce M.

Phoenix
Beggs, Harry Mark
Beshears, Robert Gene
Condo, James Robert
Gomez, David Frederick
Grant, Merwin Darwin
Leonard, Jeffrey S.
Ulrich, Paul Graham
Wall, Donald Arthur

Prescott
Goodman, Mark N.

Scottsdale
Smith, David Burnell

Tucson
Kitchen, Charles William

Yuma
Hossler, David Joseph

ARKANSAS

Harrison
Pinson, Jerry D.

Little Rock
Dillahunty, Wilbur Harris
Griffin, William Mell, III
Hargis, David Michael
Miller, Peter Alexander
Simpson, James Marlon, Jr.

CALIFORNIA

Aptos
Kehoe, Dennis Joseph

Bakersfield
Kind, Kenneth Wayne

Beverly Hills
Fine, Richard Isaac
Horowitz, Stephen Paul
Jaffe, F. Filmore

Burbank
Ajalat, Sol Peter

Burlingame
Cotchett, Joseph Winters

Chula Vista
Appleton, Richard Newell

Costa Mesa
Frieden, Clifford E.

Daly City
Boccia, Barbara

Emeryville
Howe, Drayton Ford, Jr.

Encinitas
Williams, Michael Edward

Encino
Weissman, I. Donald

Folsom
Goodwin, James Jeffries

Fresno
Ramirez, Frank Tenorio

Glendale
Kazanjian, Phillip Carl
Martinetti, Ronald Anthony
Young, George Walter

Huntington Beach
Garrels, Sherry Ann

Imperial Beach
Merkin, William Leslie

Irvine
Cahill, Richard Frederick
Specter, Richard Bruce

Laguna Hills
Reinglass, Michelle Annette

Long Beach
Haile, Lawrence Barclay

Los Angeles
Adler, Erwin Ellery
Barza, Harold A.
Belleville, Philip Frederick
Bodkin, Henry Grattan, Jr.
Bressan, Paul Louis
Bryan, James Spencer
Chiate, Kenneth Reed
Daniels, John Peter
Fairbank, Robert Harold
Fenster, Fred A.
Grush, Julius Sidney
Handzlik, Jan Lawrence
Hart, Larry Calvin
Heller, Philip
Hufstedler, Shirley Mount (Mrs. Seth M. Hufstedler)
Igo, Louis Daniel
Imre, Christina Joanne
Lawton, Eric
Levine, Jerome Lester
Long, Gregory Alan
Lurvey, Ira Harold
Newman, Michael Rodney
Niles, John Gilbert
Olson, Ronald Leroy
Patterson, Charles Ernest
Phillips, Patricia Dominis
Ray, David Lewin
Riffer, Jeffrey Kent
Robison, William Robert
Sloca, Steven Lane
Snyder, Arthur Kress
Straw, Lawrence Joseph, Jr.
Strong, George Gordon, Jr.
Tepper, R(obert) Bruce, Jr.
Weatherup, Roy Garfield
Williams, Richard Thomas
Wine, Mark Philip
Woods, Daniel James

Marina Del Rey
Serena, C. David

Martinez
Williams, Charles Judson

Menlo Park
Dyer, Charles Arnold

Modesto
Schrimp, Roger Martin

Newport Beach
Millar, Richard William, Jr.

Oakland
Bjork, Robert David, Jr.

Palm Desert
Reinhardt, Benjamin Max

Palo Alto
Baron, Frederick David
Fowler, John Wellington
Pooley, James
Tiffany, Joseph Raymond, II

Pasadena
Telleria, Anthony F.

Pomona
Partritz, Joan Elizabeth

Rancho Cordova
McGrath, William Arthur

Redwood City
Kelly, Edward Joseph

Sacramento
Bell, Wayne S.
Brookman, Anthony Raymond
Callahan, Gary Brent
Goode, Barry Paul
Severaid, Ronald Harold

Salinas
Bolles, Donald Scott

San Anselmo
Truett, Harold Joseph, III (Tim Truett)

San Diego
Bayer, Richard Stewart
Boyle, Michael Fabian
Buzunis, Constantine Dino
Higgs, Craig DeWitt
Klinedinst, John David
McDermott, Thomas John, Jr.
Roseman, Charles Sanford
Sceper, Duane Harold
Schuck, Carl Joseph
Weaver, Michael James

San Francisco
Bicksler, Diana Guido
Boyd, William Sprott
Callan, Terrence A.
Coombe, George William, Jr.
Hasson, Kirke Michael
Ladar, Jerrold Morton
Schon, Steven Eliot
Snow, Tower Charles, Jr.
Sparks, John Edward
Traynor, John Michael
Tuthill, James Peirce
Venning, Robert Stanley
Walcher, Alan Ernest
Wollen, W. Foster
Young, Douglas Rea

San Jose
Cory, Charles Johnson
Gregg, Richard
Hannon, Timothy Patrick
Morgan, Robert Hall
Stutzman, Thomas Chase, Sr.

San Rafael
Chilvers, Robert Merritt
Kathrein, Reed Richard

San Ramon
Welch, Thomas Andrew

Santa Ana
Mosich, Nicholas Joseph

Santa Barbara
Bauer, Marvin Agather
Dickey, Denise Ann
McCollum, Susan Hill
Willey, Charles Wayne

Santa Cruz
Costello, Donald Fredric

Santa Monica
Kanner, Gideon

Sherman Oaks
Joyce, Stephen Michael

Torrance
Ward, Anthony John

Tustin
Madory, Richard Eugene

Ventura
Gartner, Harold Henry, III

Visalia
Feavel, Patrick McGee

Walnut Creek
Pinkerton, Albert Duane, II
Skaggs, Sanford Merle

West Covina
Ebiner, Robert Maurice

Westlake Village
Sullivan, Mark Francis

COLORADO

Aspen
McGrath, J. Nicholas

Boulder
Danielson, Luke Jeffries
Lindenmuth, Noel Charles
Purvis, John Anderson

Breckenridge
Katz, Jeri Beth

Colorado Springs
MacDougall, Malcolm Edward

Delta
Wendt, John Arthur Frederic, Jr.

Denver
Aisenberg, Bennett S.
Bain, James William
Bryans, Richard W.
Casebolt, James Stanton
Cohen, Jeffrey
Cox, William Vaughan
Curtis, George Bartlett
DeLaney, Herbert Wade, Jr.
Featherstone, Bruce Alan
Hoffman, Daniel Steven
Husband, John Michael
Johnson, Philip Edward
Kahn, Edwin Sam
Kanan, Gregory Brian
Law, John Manning
Lerman, Eileen R.
Merker, Steven Joseph
Miller, Gale Timothy
Oxman, Stephen Eliot
Pratt, Kevin Burton
Quiat, Marshall
Samuels, Donald L.
Starrs, Elizabeth Anne
Thomasch, Roger Paul
Wedgle, Richard Jay
Welch, Carol Mae
Williams, Michael Anthony

Englewood
Epstein, Joseph Marc
Figa, Phillip Sam

Fort Collins
Johnson, Donald Edward, Jr.

Frisco
Helmer, David Alan

Golden
Carney, Deborah Leah Turner

Montrose
Overholser, John W.

CONNECTICUT

Bridgeport
Goldberger, Robert R.
Sheldon, Robert Ryel
Williams, Ronald Doherty

Bristol
Hayes, Margaret Mary

Fairfield
LaFollette, Ernest Carlton
Osis, Daiga Guntra

Glastonbury
Taalman, Juri E.

Greenwich
Fogarty, James Robert

Hartford
Fain, Joel Maurice
Pepe, Louis Robert
Sussman, Mark Richard

New Haven
Geisler, Thomas Milton, Jr.

Norwich
Masters, Barbara J.

Plainville
Zagorsky, Peter Joseph

Roxbury
Friedman, John Maxwell, Jr.

Shelton
Ryan, William Joseph, Jr.

Stamford
Benedict, Peter Behrends
Cacace, Michael Joseph
Livolsi, Frank William, Jr.

Trumbull
Brennan, Daniel Edward, Jr.

West Hartford
Elliot, Ralph Gregory

Westport
Kanaga, Lawrence Wesley

Willimantic
Schiller, Howard Barry

Windham
Lombardo, Michael John

DELAWARE

Newark
Welsh, Paul Patrick

Wilmington
Carey, Robert George
Davis, James Francis
Johnston, William David
Kimmel, Morton Richard
Klayman, Barry Martin
Whitney, Douglas E., Sr.

DISTRICT OF COLUMBIA

Washington
Bellinger, Edgar Thomson
Bonner, Walter Joseph
Burch, John Thomas, Jr.
Cash, Roderick William, Jr.
Hassett, Joseph Mark
Liebman, Ronald Stanley
Nace, Barry John
Norton, Randell Hunt
Policy, Vincent Mark
Potenza, Joseph Michael
Rider, James Lincoln
Snyder, Allen Roger
Tompert, James Emil
Tompkins, Joseph Buford, III
Trimble, Stephen Asbury
Tufaro, Richard Chase
Work, Charles Robert
Yannucci, Thomas David

FLORIDA

Altamonte Springs
Heindl, Phares Matthews
Hoogland, Robert Frederics

Bal Harbour
Evans, Thomas William

Boca Raton
Golis, Paul Robert
Kauffman, John Alan Charles
Kenwood, Joel David
Kline, Arlene Karin
Sax, Spencer Meridith

Brandon
Tittsworth, Clayton (Magness)

Coconut Grove
McAmis, Edwin Earl

Coral Gables
Anthony, Andrew John
David, George A.
Glinn, Franklyn Barry
Keedy, Christian David
Stack, Charles Rickman

Crestview
Duplechin, D. James

Fort Lauderdale
Bustamante, Nestor
Denman, James Burton
Haliczer, James Solomon
Kelly, John Patrick
Rose, Norman
Weissman, Jeffrey Mark

Fort Myers
Clarkson, Julian Derieux
Stanley, Bruce McLaren, Sr.

Gulfport
Allen, John Thomas, Jr.

Hollywood
Phillips, Gary Stephen

Jacksonville
Bradford, Dana Gibson, II
Callender, John Francis
Cowles, Robert Lawrence
Gabel, George DeSaussure, Jr.
O'Neal, Michael Scott, Sr.
Pillans, Charles Palmer, III

Longboat Key
Pulvermacher, Louis Cecil

Maitland
Edwards, James Alfred
Trees, Philip Hugh

Melbourne
Trachtman, Jerry H.

Miami
Berman, Bruce Judson
Blumberg, Edward Robert
Cohen, Jeffrey Michael
Critchlow, Richard H.
Diaz, Benito Humberto
Eaton, Joel Douglas
Ferrell, Milton Morgan, Jr.
Lazenby, Robert Alfred
Lipton, Paul R.
Miller, Raymond Vincent, Jr.
Nachwalter, Michael
Palahach, Michael
Richman, Gerald F.
Schiffrin, Michael Edward
Scott, Thomas Emerson, Jr.
Spector, Brian Fred
Starr, Ivar Miles
Stieglitz, Albert Blackwell
Welbaum, R(ome) Earl
Wiseheart, Malcolm Boyd, Jr.
Wright, Robert Thomas, Jr.

Naples
McDonnell, Michael R. N.

North Palm Beach
Lane, Matthew Jay

Orlando
deBeaubien, Hugo H.
Dempsey, Bernard Hayden, Jr.
Eagan, William Leon
Hill, Brian Donovan
Losey, Ralph Colby
Motes, Carl Dalton
Reinhart, Richard Paul
Weiss, Christopher John
Wilson, William Berry

Palm Beach
Hastings, Lawrence Vaeth

Palm Beach Gardens
Blum, Irving Ronald

Saint Petersburg
Boydstun, Charles Bryant, Jr.
Wein, Stephen Joshua

Sarasota
Blucher, Paul Arthur
Rossi, William Matthew

Tampa
Butler, Paul Bascomb, Jr.
Gilbert, Richard Allen
Murray, John Michael
Rydberg, Marsha Griffin
Somers, Clifford Louis
Thomas, Wayne Lee
Vento, John Sebastian
Waller, Edward Martin, Jr.

Vero Beach
O'Haire, Michael

West Palm Beach
Chopin, Susan Gardiner
Farina, John
Stinson, Steven Arthur

Winter Park
Ackert, T(errence) W(illiam)
Godbold, Gene Hamilton

GEORGIA

Atlanta
Blank, A(ndrew) Russell

Boynton, Frederick George
Branch, Thomas Broughton, III
Collins, Donnell Jawan
Doyle, Michael Anthony
Duffey, William Simon, Jr.
Farnham, Clayton Henson
Fleming, Julian Denver, Jr.
Kelley, Jeffrey Wendell
Lore, Stephen Melvin
Paquin, Jeffrey Dean
Powell, Douglas Richard
Rumsey, D(avid) Lake, Jr.
Thomas, James Joseph, II
Wellon, Robert G.
Wood, L. Lin, Jr.

Augusta
Dickert, Neal Workman
Miller, Alfred Montague
Wheale, Duncan Douglas

Columbus
Patrick, James Duvall, Jr.

Conyers
Snapp, William Dorsey

Fayetteville
Johnson, Donald Wayne

Macon
Brown, Stephen Phillip
Dodson, Carr Glover

Marietta
Ingram, George Conley

Mcdonough
Crumbley, R. Alex

Newnan
Franklin, Bruce Walter

Ocilla
Pujadas, Thomas Edward

Snellville
Giallanza, Charles Philip

Statesboro
Franklin, James Burke

Tucker
Armstrong, Edwin Alan

HAWAII

Honolulu
Chuck, Walter G(oonsun)
Chung, Steven Kamsein
Devens, Paul
Duffy, James Earl, Jr.
Fujiyama, Wallace Sachio
Fukumoto, Leslie Satsuki
Iwai, Wilfred Kiyoshi
Kobayashi, Bert Takaaki, Jr.
Kuniyuki, Ken Takaharu
Morse, Jack Craig
Portnoy, Jeffrey Steven
Potts, Dennis Walker
Schraff, Paul Albert
Taylor, Carroll Stribling
Turbin, Richard

IDAHO

Lewiston
Tait, John Reid

ILLINOIS

Anna
Plesko, Jeffrey Michael

Belleville
Coghill, William Thomas, Jr.
Cook, James Christopher

Carbondale
Frazier, Dana Sue

Champaign
Rawles, Edward Hugh

Chicago
Adducci, James Dominick
Adelman, Stanley Joseph
Beatty, William Glenn
Bellows, Laurel Gordon
Biebel, Paul Philip, Jr.
Boies, Wilber H.
Bresnahan, Arthur Stephen
Brown, Donald James, Jr.
Burdelik, Thomas L.
Burke, John Michael
Burke, Thomas Joseph, Jr.
Cherners, Robert Marc
Cherney, James Alan
Chester, Mark Vincent
Cicero, Frank, Jr.
Ditkowsky, Kenneth K.
Eaton, J(ames) Timothy
Episcope, Paul Bryan
Feagley, Michael Rowe
Fina, Paul Joseph
Fowler, Don Wall
Franch, Richard Thomas
Franklin, Richard Mark
Freehling, Paul Edward
Getzoff, William Morey
Gibbons, William John
Griffith, Donald Kendall
Guilfoyle, Robert Thomas
Halloran, Michael John
Hamblet, Michael Jon
Hardgrove, James Alan
Harper, Steven James
Harrington, James Timothy
Hecht, Frank Thomas
Herald, J. Patrick

Howlett, Michael Joseph, Jr.
Hunter, James Galbraith, Jr.
Johnson, Garrett Bruce
Kroll, Barry Lewis
Kuhlman, Richard Sherwin
Leyhane, Francis John, III
Lipton, Lois Jean
Marick, Michael Miron
McGahey, John Patrick
McGonegle, Timothy Joseph
Miller, Douglas Andrew
Montgomery, Julie-April
Mulroy, Thomas Robert, Jr.
Nash, Gordon Bernard, Jr.
Nowacki, James Nelson
Palmer, Robert Towne
Pattishall, Beverly Wyckliffe
Pavalon, Eugene Irving
Peterson, Donald George
Richter, Tobin Marais
Rundio, Louis Michael, Jr.
Samuels, Lawrence Robert
Schoumacher, Bruce Herbert
Schwab, Stephen Wayne
Serritella, William David
Starkman, Gary Lee
Stavins, Richard Lee
Strom, Michael A.
Toohey, James Kevin
Torshen, Jerome Harold
Van Demark, Ruth Elaine

Danville
Blan, Kennith William, Jr.

Deerfield
Lane, William Edward

Des Plaines
Zamarin, Ronald George

Edwardsville
Schum, Randolph Edgar

Elmwood Park
Spina, Anthony Ferdinand

Evanston
Schulte, Bruce John

Freeport
Eden, Robert Elwood

Galesburg
Mustain, Douglas Dee

Hazel Crest
Gurion, Henry Baruch

Joliet
Miller, Randal J.

La Salle
McClintock, Thomas Lee

Lake Forest
Emerson, William Harry

Libertyville
DeSanto, James John

Mattoon
Horsley, Jack Everett

Mount Vernon
Harvey, Morris Lane

Palatine
Victor, Michael Gary

Park Ridge
Franklin, Randy Wayne

Peoria
Sinn, David Randall
Winget, Walter Winfield

Rockford
Knight, William D., Jr.

Schaumburg
Shapiro, Edwin Henry

Skokie
Plotnick, Paul William

Springfield
Londrigan, James Thomas

Taylorville
Spears, Ronald Dean

Wheaton
Copeland, Charlene Carole
Dudgeon, Thomas Carl

INDIANA

Beech Grove
Brown, Richard Lawrence

Bloomington
Grodner, Geoffrey Mitchell

Boonville
Neff, Mark Edward

Columbus
Harrison, Patrick Woods

Evansville
Berger, Charles Lee
Clouse, John Daniel

Hammond
Ruman, Saul I.

Indianapolis
Belknap, Jerry P.
Elberger, Ronald Edward
Fisher, James R.

Saddle Brook
Pearlman, Peter Steven

Short Hills
Marshall, John Patrick

Somerville
Sponzilli, Edward George

South Amboy
McDonnell, William John

Trenton
Doherty, Robert Christopher
Gogo, Gregory

Warren
Kraus, Steven Gary

West Orange
Gordon, Harrison J.
McNaboe, James Francis

Westfield
Dughi, Louis John, Jr.

Wildwood
Gould, Alan I.

Woodbury
Adler, Lewis Gerard

Woodcliff Lake
Phillips, John C.

NEW MEXICO

Alamogordo
Bloom, Norman Douglas, Jr.

Albuquerque
Bardacke, Paul Gregory
Roberts, Randal William

Santa Fe
McClaugherty, Joe L.
Schwarz, Michael
Singleton, Sarah Michael
Wertheim, Jerry
Zorie, Stephanie Marie

Socorro
Smith, Leslie Clark

NEW YORK

Albany
Osterman, Melvin Howard
Powers, John Kieran

Armonk
Moss, Eric Harold

Brooklyn
Nicholson, Michael
Reich, Edward Stuart

Buffalo
Barber, Janice Ann
De Marie, Anthony Joseph
Goldberg, Neil A.
Gorman, Gerald Patrick
Mattar, Lawrence Joseph
Pajak, David Joseph
Sampson, John David
Segalla, Thomas Francis

Canaan
Pennell, William Brooke

Chestnut Ridge
Burns, Richard Owen

Commack
Steindler, Walter G.

Dansville
Vogel, John Walter

Dix Hills
Tucker, Robert Henry

Farmingdale
Persons, John Wade

Getzville
DiNardo, Joseph

Glens Falls
Cullum, James Edward
Meyer, Martin Arthur

Gouverneur
Leader, Robert John

Great Neck
Salzman, Stanley P.

Jackson Heights
Goldblum, A. Paul

Jericho
Corso, Frank Mitchell

Lake Sucess
Epstein, Joel Donald

Larchmont
Gaffney, Mark William
McSherry, William John, Jr.

Melville
Cahn, Richard Caleb

Mineola
Bernstein, Kenneth Alan
Monaghan, Peter Gerard
Raab, Ira Jerry
Spizz, Harvey Warren

Mount Kisco
Curran, Maurice Francis

New Hyde Park
Levine, Kimberly Anne

New Rochelle
Herman, William Charles

New York
Abramowitz, Elkan
Amsterdam, Mark Lemle
Bauer, George A., III
Benedict, James Nelson
Bezanson, Thomas Edward
Birnbaum, Edward Lester
Borstein, Leon Baer
Bradley, E. Michael
Braid, Frederick Donald
Brecker, Jeffrey Ross
Brown, Paul M.
Brown, Peter Megargee
Buchwald, Don David
Burrows, Kenneth David
Burrows, Michael Donald
Chesler, Evan Robert
Cohen, Robert Stephan
Cole, Charles Dewey, Jr.
Coll, John Peter, Jr.
Dallas, William Moffit, Jr.
Damashek, Philip Michael
Dankin, Peter Alfred
Deffina, Thomas Victor
Dell, Michael John
Dopf, Glenn William
Douglas, Philip Le Breton
Ehrenbard, Robert
Elsen, Sheldon Howard
Feder, Saul E.
Feldberg, Michael Svetkey
Fensterstock, Blair Courtney
Fiske, Robert Bishop, Jr.
Fletcher, Anthony L.
Forstadt, Joseph Lawrence
Garfield, Martin Richard
Garfinkel, Barry Herbert
Garland, Sylvia Dillof
Gitter, Max
Goldstein, Kenneth B.
Golomb, David Bela
Greenawalt, William Sloan
Greenbaum, Sheldon Marc
Greenberg, Ira George
Gurfein, Richard Alan
Haig, Robert Leighton
Hall, John Herbert
Harris, Joel B(ruce)
Haynes, Jean Reed
Heisler, Stanley Dean
Hirsch, Jerome S.
Hirshowitz, Melvin Stephen
Hollyer, A(rthur) Rene
Hritz, George F.
Hughes, Kevin Peter
Iannuzzi, John Nicholas
Isquith, Fred Taylor
Jacobowitz, Harold Saul
Jacobs, Randall Scott David
Jacobson, Sandra W.
Joseph, Gregory Paul
Kahn, Alan Edwin
Katz, Jerome Charles
Kaufman, Stephen Edward
Kavaler, Thomas J.
Kinzler, Thomas Benjamin
Kuh, Richard Henry
Langer, Bruce Alden
Lans, Deborah Eisner
Laquercia, Thomas Michael
Lesman, Michael Steven
Lesser, William Melville
Levine, Melvin Charles
Loscalzo, Anthony Joseph
Lupert, Leslie Allan
Lustenberger, Louis Charles, Jr.
Mandelker, Lawrence Arthur
Mantel, Allan David
McGrath, Christopher Thomas
Meister, Ronald William
Merritt, Bruce Gordon
Miller, Charles Hampton
Miller, Steven Scott
Moloney, Thomas Joseph
Muccia, Joseph William
Mullaney, Thomas Joseph
Muskin, Victor Philip
Neff, Michael Alan
Nemser, Earl Harold
North, Steven Edward
O'Connor, William Matthew
O'Dea, Dennis Michael
O'Sullivan, Thomas J.
Olasov, David Michael
Oliveri, Paul Francis
Pepper, Allan Michael
Phillips, Anthony Francis
Polak, Werner L.
Probstein, Jon Michael
Prutzman, Lewis Donald
Quinn, Yvonne Susan
Rabin, Jack
Raylesberg, Alan Ira
Reibstein, Richard Jay
Reich, Larry Sam
Reiner, John Paul
Rifkind, Robert S(inger)
Rikon, Michael
Rivera, Walter
Rosenberg, Gary Marc
Rosenberg, Gerald Alan
Rosenfeld, Steven B.
Rosenzweig, Theodore B.
Rosner, Jonathan Levi
Rothman, Bernard
Salomon, Philippe M.
Salvan, Sherwood Allen
Satine, Barry Roy
Scheinkman, Alan David
Schlau, Philip
Schnurman, Alan Joseph
Schwab, Harold Lee
Shanman, James Alan
Siffert, John Sand
Silverman, Moses
Simon, Michael Scott
Slade, Jeffrey Christopher
Sladkus, Harvey Ira
Smiley, Guy Ian

Smith, Edwin Lloyd
Smith, Robert Everett
Smith, Robert Sherlock
Snider, Jerome Guy
Steigman, Ernest R.
Stern, Peter R.
Sternman, Joel W.
Toback, Arthur Malcolm
Walinsky, Adam
Weinberger, Harold Paul
Weinstock, Leonard
Wesely, Edwin Joseph
Wilensky, Saul
Williamson, Walter
Witkin, Eric Douglas
Wolff, Kurt Jakob
Wollan, Eugene
Yeager, Dennis Randall
Yelenick, Mary Therese
Zerin, Steven David
Zimmett, Mark Paul
Zissu, Roger L.

Newark
Reid, James Edward

Newburgh
Milligram, Steven Irwin

Oyster Bay
Robinson, Edward T., III

Patchogue
Cartier, Rudolph Henri, Jr.
Tona, Thomas

Pittsford
Braunsdorf, Paul Raymond

Riverhead
Twomey, Thomas A., Jr.

Rochester
Dolin, Lonny H.
Fox, Edward Hanton
Geiger, Alexander
Harris, Wayne Manley
Kurland, Harold Arthur
Law, Michael R.
Payment, Kenneth Arnold
Trueheart, Harry Parker, III

Saratoga Springs
Willig, William Paul

Syracuse
Gerber, Edward F.
Simmons, Doreen Anne
Zimmerman, Aaron Mark

Waterford
Novotny, F. Douglas

White Plains
Bender, Joel Charles
Halpern, Philip Morgan
Nesci, Vincent Peter
Null, William Seth
Weiss, Terri Lynn

NORTH CAROLINA

Asheville
Cogburn, Max Oliver
Davis, Roy Walton, Jr.
Frue, William Calhoun

Cary
Montgomery, Charles Harvey

Charlotte
Bragg, Ellis Meredith, Jr.
Cannon, Thomas Roberts
Connette, Edward Grant, III
Raper, William Cranford

Dunn
Pope, Patrick Harris

Eden
Doss, Marion Kenneth

Kinston
Jones, Paul Lawrence

Raleigh
Palmer, William Ralph
Parker, John Hill
Sasser, Jonathan Drew

Tabor City
Jorgensen, Ralph Gubler

Thomasville
Reynolds, Mark Floyd, II

Winston Salem
Barnhill, Henry Grady, Jr.
Comerford, Walter Thompson, Jr.
Porter, Leon Eugene, Jr.

NORTH DAKOTA

Bismarck
Snyder, Robert John

Dickinson
Herauf, William Anton

OHIO

Akron
Cherpas, Christopher Theodore
Ruport, Scott Hendricks
Tipping, Harry A.

Canton
Herbert, David Lee
Plakas, Leonidas Evangelos

Sandrock, Scott Paul

Cincinnati
Calico, Paul B.
Cunningham, Pierce Edward
Davis, Robert Lawrence
DeLong, Deborah
Dornette, W(illiam) Stuart
Maxwell, Robert Wallace, II
Metz, Jerome Joseph, Jr.
Zavatsky, Michael Joseph

Cleveland
Birne, Kenneth Andrew
Bixenstine, Kim Fenton
Brunn, Thomas Leo, Sr.
Climer, James Alan
Crist, Paul Grant
Kelly, Dennis Michael
Kondzer, Thomas Allen
Kopit, Alan Stuart
Leiken, Earl Murray
Mc Cartan, Patrick Francis
Moore, Kenneth Cameron
Morgenstern, Conrad J.
Spero, Keith Erwin
Spurgeon, Roberta Kaye
Strauch, John L.
Stuhldreher, George William
Swartzbaugh, Marc L.
Weisman, Fred

Columbus
Bartemes, Amy Straker
Belton, John Thomas
Cline, Richard Allen
Cvetanovich, Danny L.
Ferguson, Gerald Paul
Hollenbaugh, H(enry) Ritchey
Hutson, Jeffrey Woodward
Long, Thomas Leslie
Moul, William Charles
Starkoff, Alan Gary
Taggart, Thomas Michael
Thomas, Duke Winston

Dayton
Roberts, Brian Michael
Saul, Irving Isaac

Dublin
Farrell, Clifford Michael

Findlay
Kostyo, John Francis

Hamilton
Olivas, Adolf

Jefferson
Geary, Michael Philip

Mentor
McCarter, William Kent

Springboro
Sharts, John Edwin, III

Toledo
White, Kenneth James

Wadsworth
McIlvaine, James Ross

Willard
Thornton, Robert Floyd

Wooster
Kennedy, Charles Allen

OKLAHOMA

Bartlesville
Huchteman, Ralph Douglas

Broken Arrow
Frieze, H(arold) Delbert

Duncan
Rodgers, Ricardo Juan (Rick Rodgers)

Muskogee
Williams, Betty Outhier

Oklahoma City
Epperson, Kraettli Quynton
Fenton, Elliott Clayton
High, David Royce
Kenney, John Arthur
Paul, William George
Willey, Benjamin Tucker, Jr.
Woods, Harry Arthur, Jr.

Tulsa
Abrahamson, A. Craig
Brewster, Clark Otto
Davis, G. Reuben
Eagan, Claire Veronica
Eldridge, Richard Mark
Hughes, William Earle
Luthey, Graydon Dean, Jr.
Spiegelberg, Frank David

OREGON

Eugene
Fechtel, Edward Ray

Hillsboro
Uffelman, John Edward

Medford
Deatherage, William Vernon

Portland
Eakin, Margaretta Morgan
Ellis, Barnes Humphreys
Flaherty, Thomas Joseph
O'Neill, Phoebe Joan
Seymour, Steven Wayne
Stone, Richard James

Westwood, James Nicholson

Salem
Feibleman, Gilbert Bruce
Haselton, Rick Thomas
Robertson, Joseph David

PENNSYLVANIA

Allentown
Brown, Robert Wayne

Altoona
Serbin, Richard Martin

Bala Cynwyd
Schwartz, Jeffrey Byron

Beaver
Petrush, John Joseph

Bethlehem
Hemphill, Meredith, Jr.

Bryn Mawr
Hankin, Mitchell Robert

Chambersburg
Cleaver, David Charles

Clarks Summit
Beemer, John Barry

Feasterville Trevose
Osterhout, Richard Cadwallader

Glenside
Mermelstein, Jules Joshua

Harrisburg
Barto, Charles O., Jr.
Feinour, John Stephen
Maleski, Cynthia Maria

Hazleton
Pedri, Charles Raymond
Schiavo, Pasco Louis

Hollidaysburg
Evey, Merle Kenton
Pfaff, Robert James

Indiana
Kauffman, Thomas Andrew

Lancaster
Lewis, Alvin Bower, Jr.

Media
Cramp, John Franklin
List, Anthony Francis
Mulligan, John Thomas

Morrisville
Hershenson, Gerald Martin

Narberth
Rovner, David Patrick Ryan

New Castle
Mojock, David Theodore

New Kensington
Wallace, Henry Jared, Jr.

Norristown
Cowperthwait, Lindley Murray
Gowen, Thomas Leo, Jr.

North Wales
Brady, George Charles, III

Philadelphia
Abraham, Richard Paul
Barrett, John J(ames), Jr.
Battis, David Gregory
Binder, David Franklin
Brown, William Hill, III
Cooney, J(ohn) Gordon, Jr.
Craven, Charles Warren
Ficbach, H. Robert
Fodera, Leonard V.
Garcia, Rudolph
Gordesky, Morton
Herman, Charles Jacob
Kormes, John Winston
Kramer, Gilda Lea
Ledwith, John Francis
Lillie, Charisse Ranielle
Mathes, Stephen Jon
McGurk, Eugene David, Jr.
Milbourne, Walter Robertson
Milone, Francis Michael
Minisi, Anthony S.
Mulvey, W. Michael
Parry, William DeWitt
Phillips, Dorothy Kay
Scher, Howard Dennis
Sheils, Denis Francis

Pittsburgh
Acheson, Amy J.
Cohen, Robert (Avram)
Feldstein, Jay Harris
Holsinger, Candice Doreen
Hurnyak, Christina Kaiser
Jones, Craig Ward
Klett, Edwin Lee
Litman, Roslyn Margolis
Lucchino, Frank Joseph
O'Connor, Edward Gearing
Ober, Russell John, Jr.
Pohl, Paul Michael
Seymour, Donald Edward
Sherman, Carl Leon
Stroyd, Arthur Heister

Pottsville
Tamulonis, Frank Louis, Jr.

Scranton
Howley, James McAndrew

White Oak
Pribanic, Victor Hunter

Wyomissing
Turner, David Eldridge

RHODE ISLAND

Jamestown
Parks, Albert Lauriston

Providence
Prentiss, Richard Daniel

SOUTH CAROLINA

Charleston
Kahn, Ellis Irvin
Spitz, Hugo Max

Columbia
Babcock, Keith Moss
Sheftman, Howard Stephen

Hilton Head Island
McKay, John Judson, Jr.

SOUTH DAKOTA

Sioux Falls
Luce, Michael Leigh

TENNESSEE

Chattanooga
Akers, Samuel Lee
Campbell, Paul, III
Cooper, Gary Allan

Collierville
Scroggs, Larry Kenneth

Johnson City
Culp, James David

Knoxville
Hagood, Lewis Russell
London, James Harry
Ogden, Harry Peoples

Memphis
Carr, Oscar Clark, III
Chambliss, Prince Caesar, Jr.
Ledbetter, Paul Mark
Moriarty, Herbert Bernard, Jr.
Noel, Randall Deane

Nashville
Hardin, Hal D.
Patterson, Robert Shepherd
Yarbrough, Edward Meacham

Soddy Daisy
Leitner, Paul Revere

Somerville
Wilder, James Sampson, III

Trenton
Malone, Gayle

TEXAS

Abilene
Suttle, Stephen Hungate

Addison
Lynch, Jeffrey Scott

Amarillo
McDougall, Gerald Duane

Arlington
Jensen, John Robert

Austin
Brown, Dick Terrell
Colburn, Stuart Dale
Grosenheider, Delno John
Harrison, Richard Wayne
Hernandez, Mack Ray
Judson, Philip Livingston
Phillips, Travis N.
Shapiro, David L.
Wester, Ruric Herschel, Jr.
Zager, Steven Mark

Brownwood
Bell, William Woodward

College Station
Hoelscher, Michael Ray

Corpus Christi
Alberts, Harold

Dallas
Babcock, Charles Lynde, IV
Baggett, Steven Ray
Bickel, John W., II
Blount, Charles William, III
Callahan, Tena Toye
Coleman, Robert Winston
Collins, Michael Homer
Ellis, James Alvis, Jr.
Freytag, Sharon Nelson
Gilliam, John A.
Hartnett, Will Ford
Jones, David Stanley
Jones, Lindy Don
Lowenberg, Michael
McAtee, David Ray
Mow, Robert Henry, Jr.
Mueller, Mark Christopher
Palter, John Theodore

Pew, John Glenn, Jr.
Prather, Robert Charles, Sr.
Ringle, Brett Adelbert
Scuro, Joseph E., Jr.
Selinger, Jerry Robin
Sides, Jack Davis, Jr.
Siegel, Mark Jordan
Walkowiak, Vincent Steven
Wilkins, Jerry L.

Denton
Narsutis, John Keith

Edinburg
Peña, Aaron, Jr.

El Paso
Malone, Daniel Robert

Fort Worth
Crumley, John Walter
Dean, Beale
Elliott, Frank Wallace
Hart, John Clifton
Larimore, Tom L.
Randolph, Robert McGehee

Garland
Irby, Holt

Hallettsville
Baber, Wilbur H., Jr.

Houston
Atkins, Bruce Alexander
Bagwell, Louis Lee
Ballanfant, Richard Burton
Bayko, Emil Thomas
Beirne, Martin Douglas
Boswell, John Howard
Brinson, Gay Creswell, Jr.
Carr, Edward A.
Craig, Robert Mark, III
Cunningham, Tom Alan
Frost, Charles Estes, Jr.
Fullenweider, Donn Charles
Gilbert, Keith Thomas
Gomez, Lynne Marie
Graham, Michael Paul
Hamel, Lee
Jordan, Charles Milton
Kaplan, Lee Landa
Ketchand, Robert Lee
Kline, Allen Haber, Jr.
Krebs, Arno William, Jr.
Lacey, David Morgan
Lilienstern, O. Clayton
McFall, Donald Beury
Michaels, Kevin Richard
Nunnally, Knox Dillon
Ray, Hugh Massey, Jr.
Reasoner, Harry Max
Rowland, Robert Alexander, III
Spalding, Andrew Freeman
Stephens, R(obert) Gary
Susman, Morton Lee
Tabak, Morris
Wallis, Olney Gray
Wiese, Larry Clevenger
Yetter, R. Paul

Lubbock
Nelson, Jack Odell, Jr.

Lufkin
Garrison, Pitser Hardeman

Mcallen
Mills, William Michael
Thaddeus, Aloysius Peter, Jr.

Midland
Estes, Andrew Harper

Missouri City
Maddox, Charles J., Jr.

Nacogdoches
Bias, Dana G.

Plano
Shaddock, William Charles

San Angelo
Sutton, John Ewing

San Antonio
Allison, Stephen Philip
Hohman, A. J., Jr.
Kaplan, Edward David
Labay, Eugene Benedict
Maloney, Marynell
Myers, J(oseph) Michael
Solis, Carlos Eduardo

San Saba
Hamilton, Elwin Lomax

Sugar Land
Aldrich, Lovell W(eld)

The Woodlands
Hagerman, John David

Waco
Cherry, David Earl

UTAH

Ogden
Sullivan, Kevin Patrick

Salt Lake City
Christensen, Harold Graham
Orton, R. Willis
Verhaaren, Harold Carl

VERMONT

Burlington
Leddy, John Thomas

Chester
Holme, John Charles, Jr.

VIRGINIA

Alexandria
Carter, Richard Dennis
Rosenthal, Edward Scott

Arlington
Alper, Joanne Fogel

Fairfax
Arnold, William McCauley
Saul, Ira Stephen

Falls Church
Robey, Daniel Lance

Fredericksburg
Billingsley, Robert Thaine

Great Falls
Preston, Charles George

Mc Lean
Brown, Frank Eugene, Jr.
Church, Randolph Warner, Jr.
Najjoum, Linda Lemmon
Walton, Edmund Lewis, Jr.

Petersburg
Shell, Louis Calvin
Spero, Morton Bertram

Radford
Davis, Richard Waters
Turk, James Clinton, Jr.

Richmond
Allen, Wilbur Coleman
Brooks, Robert Franklin, Sr.
Hall, Stephen Charles
Kearfott, Joseph Conrad
Krumbein, Charles Harvey
McClard, Jack Edward
Pearsall, John Wesley
Peluso, Dana C.M.
Williamson, Thomas W., Jr.

Roanoke
Tegenkamp, Gary Elton
Woodrum, Clifton A., III

Vienna
Razzano, Frank Charles

Virginia Beach
Hajek, Francis Paul

WASHINGTON

Anacortes
Glein, Richard Jeriel

Centralia
Buzzard, Steven Ray

Longview
O'Neill, Thomas Nicholas Stephen

Renton
Swanson, Arthur Dean

Seattle
Bagshaw, Bradley Holmes
Bringman, Joseph Edward
Cornell, Kenneth Lee
Corning, Nicholas F.
Ginsberg, Phillip H(enry)
McKay, Michael Dennis
Mellem, Roger Duane
Mines, Michael
Moren, Charles Verner
Smith, James Alexander, Jr.
Sullivan, Daniel Frederick
Tausend, Fredric Cutner
Vestal, Josephine Burnet
Waitt, Robert Kenneth
Walter, Michael Charles
Wechsler, Mary Heyrman

Spokane
Anderson, Robert Edward

Tacoma
Mungia, Salvador Alejo, Jr.

WEST VIRGINIA

Charleston
Cowan, John Joseph
Neely, Richard
Robinson, E. Glenn
Slack, John Mark, III

Romney
Saville, Royce Blair

WISCONSIN

Appleton
Chudacoff, Bruce Michael
Murray, John Daniel
Siddall, Michael Sheridan

Black River Falls
Lister, Thomas Edward

Green Bay
Grzeca, Michael G(erard)
Schober, Thomas Leonard

Kenosha
Higgins, John Patrick
Rose, Terry William

La Crosse
Sleik, Thomas Scott

Madison
Hildebrand, Daniel Walter
Mitby, John Chester
Pernitz, Scott Gregory
Whitney, Robert Michael

Milwaukee
Gaines, Irving David
Habush, Robert Lee
Israel, Scott Michael
Levit, William Harold, Jr.
Melin, Robert Arthur
Sostarich, Mark Edward

Oshkosh
Curtis, George Warren

Rhinelander
McEldowney, Todd Richard

Wausau
Grischke, Alan Edward
Kammer, Robert Arthur, Jr.

WYOMING

Casper
Combs, W(illiam) Henry, III

Cheyenne
Bailey, Henry Franklin, Jr.

Jackson
Schuster, Robert Parks
Shockey, Gary Lee

ADDRESS UNPUBLISHED

Adams, Thomas Lawrence
Bakkensen, John Reser
Beatie, Russel Harrison, Jr.
Beattie, Donald Gilbert
Blevins, Jeffrey Alexander
Bossio, Salvatore
Buehler, John Wilson
Carrol, Robert Kelton
Cook, Donald Charles
Cox, Marshall
Elderkin, E(dwin) Judge
Erlebacher, Arlene Cernik
Fekete, George Otto
Fenwick, Lynda Beck
Flanary, Donald Herbert, Jr.
Flynn, Michael
Ginsberg, Marc David
Hall, John Hopkins
Hawkins, Carmen Doloras
Henderson, John Robert
Hoffman, Alan Craig
Horn, Andrew Warren
Howard, John Wayne
Kapner, Lewis
Landman, Eric Christopher
Lapidus, Steven Richard
Lichtenstein, Sarah Carol
McInerney, Gary John
O'Mara, William Michael
Peccarelli, Anthony Marando
Pietrzak, Alfred Robert
Reith, Daniel I.
Reminger, Richard Thomas
Rochlin, Paul R.
Saliterman, Richard Arlen
Saltzman, Michael I.
Smith, James A.
Smouse, H(ervey) Russell
Stanisci, Thomas William
Stern, John Jules
Terrell, G. Irvin
Vigil, David Charles
Vinar, Benjamin
Yeager, Jeffrey Alan

CIVIL RIGHTS

UNITED STATES

ALABAMA

Birmingham
Gilliland, Scott Alan
Whiteside, David Powers, Jr.

Montgomery
Prestwood, Alvin Tennyson

ALASKA

Fairbanks
Schendel, William Burnett

ARKANSAS

Little Rock
Boe, Myron Timothy
Jones, Stephen Witsell

CALIFORNIA

Encino
Kaufman, Albert I.

Fullerton
Talmo, Ronald Victor

Los Angeles
Rosenbaum, Mark Dale

Newport Beach
Mandel, Maurice, II

Oakland
Wallace, Elaine Wendy

San Francisco
German, G. Michael
Rubin, Michael

COLORADO

Denver
Breeskin, Michael Wayne
Martin, Raymond Walter
Roesler, John Bruce

CONNECTICUT

Hartford
Dempsey, Edward Joseph

Stamford
Margolis, Emanuel
Spitzer, Vlad Gerard

DISTRICT OF COLUMBIA

Washington
Bernabei, Lynne Ann
Beyer, Wayne Cartwright
Christensen, Karen Kay
Katsurinis, Stephen Avery
Kramer, Andrew Michael
Leckar, Stephen Craig
Loots, James Mason
Payton, John
Shaffer, David James
Sherman, Lawrence Jay
Snyder, Allen Roger
Wolf, Christopher

FLORIDA

Boca Raton
Silver, Barry Morris

Largo
Trevena, John Harry

Miami
Connor, Terence Gregory
Kurzban, Ira Jay
Maher, Stephen Trivett

Miami Lakes
Cohen, Ronald J.

Pensacola
Kelly, John Barry, II
Soloway, Daniel Mark

Saint Petersburg
Escarraz, Enrique, III

Stuart
Watson, Robert James

Tallahassee
Minnick, Bruce Alexander

Tampa
Bowen, Paul Henry, Jr.
Brown, Frank Edward

West Palm Beach
Roberts, George Preston, Jr. (Rusty Roberts)

GEORGIA

Atlanta
González, Carlos A.

Augusta
Cooney, William J.

ILLINOIS

Carbondale
Frazier, Dana Sue

Chicago
Badel, Julie
Brice, Roger Thomas
Farber, Bernard John
Futterman, Ronald L.
Hecht, Frank Thomas
Lipton, Lois Jean
Skjold, Benjamin R.

INDIANA

Indianapolis
Kashani, Hamid Reza
Klaper, Martin Jay

IOWA

Des Moines
Conlin, Roxanne Barton

KANSAS

Shawnee Mission
Badgerow, John Nicholas

KENTUCKY

Lexington
Hiestand, Sheila Patricia

LOUISIANA

Harvey
Hantel, Philip Edward

New Orleans
Desmond, Susan Fahey
Rawls, John D.

MARYLAND

Baltimore
Granat, Richard Stuart

Glyndon
Renbaum, Barry Jeffrey

Silver Spring
McDermitt, Edward Vincent

MASSACHUSETTS

Boston
Brody, Richard Eric
Hrones, Stephen Baylis
Neumeier, Richard L.

Dedham
Donahue, Michael Christopher

Newton
Lazarus, Norman F.

MICHIGAN

Detroit
Nemeth, Patricia Marie
Wyrick, Jermaine Albert

Grand Rapids
Rynbrandt, Kevin Abraham

Okemos
Schneider, Karen Bush

Saint Clair Shores
Danielson, Gary R.

South Haven
Waxman, Sheldon Robert

Southfield
Turner, Donald Allen

MINNESOTA

Minneapolis
Corwin, Gregg Marlowe

MISSISSIPPI

Jackson
Fuselier, Louis Alfred

Oxford
Lewis, Ronald Wayne

MISSOURI

Saint Charles
Green, Joseph Libory

Saint Louis
Carius, Jeffrey Rapp

NEBRASKA

Lincoln
Cope, Thom K.

NEVADA

Las Vegas
Holman, Kristina Sue

NEW JERSEY

Fairfield
Connell, William Terrence

Hackensack
Latimer, Stephen Mark

Haddonfield
Fuoco, Philip Stephen
Graziano, Ronald Anthony

Liberty Corner
Thompson, T. Jay

Newark
Weinberg, Shelley Ann

Salem
Petrin, Helen Fite

NEW MEXICO

Carlsbad
Bruton, Charles Clinton

Los Alamos
Herr, Bruce

Santa Fe
Bienvenu, John Charles
Farber, Steven Glenn
Schwarz, Michael

NEW YORK

Bronx
Stack, Jane Marcia

Buffalo
Feuerstein, Alan Ricky

Floral Park
Chatoff, Michael Alan

Garden City
Lilly, Thomas Joseph

Glen Cove
Mills, Charles Gardner

Huntington
German, June Resnick
Levitan, Katherine D.

Kew Gardens
Reichel, Aaron Israel

Mineola
Millman, Bruce Russell

New York
Boddie, Reginald Alonzo
Dershowitz, Nathan Zev
Diamond, David Howard
Dugan, Sean Francis Xavier
Flamm, Leonard N(athan)
Fleischman, Keith Martin
Iannuzzi, John Nicholas
Jauvtis, Robert Lloyd
Kennedy, Michael John
Lansner, David Jeffrey
Rossen, Jordan
Shen, Michael

Rochester
Andolina, Lawrence J.

Syracuse
Heath, Joseph John
Rosenthal, Alan

NORTH CAROLINA

Charlotte
Connette, Edward Grant, III

Durham
Fisher, Stewart Wayne
Thompson, Sharon Andrea

Raleigh
Sasser, Jonathan Drew
Wetsch, Laura Johnson

OHIO

Cincinnati
Smith, Sheila Marie

Cleveland
DiVenere, Anthony Joseph
Kramer, Edward George
Lewis, John Bruce

Columbus
Pressley, Fred G., Jr.

Toledo
Dane, Stephen Mark

OKLAHOMA

Edmond
Lester, Andrew William
Loving, Susan Brimer

Oklahoma City
Court, Leonard

Tulsa
Matthies, Mary Constance T.

OREGON

Lincoln City
Elliott, Scott

Tigard
Lowry, David Burton

PENNSYLVANIA

Easton
Noel, Nicholas, III

Harrisburg
Lappas, Spero Thomas

Johnstown
Kaharick, Jerome John

Philadelphia
Elkins, S. Gordon
Epstein, Alan Bruce
Fodera, Leonard V.
Goldberg, Joseph
McHugh, James Joseph
Rainville, Christina

Satinsky, Barnett
Whinston, Stephen Alan

Pittsburgh
Harty, James Quinn
Lyncheski, John E.
Pushinsky, Jon
Saunders, Martin Johnston

Stroudsburg
Muth, Michael Raymond

RHODE ISLAND

Providence
Labinger, Lynette J.

SOUTH CAROLINA

Columbia
Livoti, Anthony William

TENNESSEE

Clarksville
Love, Michael Joseph

Nashville
Lyon, Philip K(irkland)

TEXAS

Austin
Arnett, Richard Lynn
Hamilton, Dagmar Strandberg
Schulze, Eric William

Dallas
Jones, James Alton

Edinburg
Peña, Aaron, Jr.

El Paso
McDonald, Charles Edward

Eldorado
Kosub, James Albert

Galveston
Vie, George William, III

Houston
Clore, Lawrence Hubert
Miller, Brian Charles
Wray, Thomas Jefferson

Orange
Dugas, Louis, Jr.

San Antonio
Armstrong, William Tucker, III
Maloney, Marynell
Moynihan, John Bignell

VIRGINIA

Alexandria
Rosenthal, Edward Scott

Charlottesville
Hazelwood, Kimball Ellen
Wyatt, Deborah Chasen

Mc Lean
Bredehoft, John Michael

Norfolk
Drescher, John Webb

Reston
Bredehoft, Elaine Charlson

Roanoke
Harris, Bayard Easter

Virginia Beach
Swope, Richard McAllister

WASHINGTON

Mercer Island
Halverson, Lowell Klark

Seattle
Rosen, Jon Howard

WEST VIRGINIA

Charleston
Teare, John Richard, Jr.

WISCONSIN

Madison
Barnhill, Charles Joseph, Jr.

KUWAIT

Safat
Ammouna, Sami Saed

SPAIN

Madrid
Lincke, Karl Heinrich

ADDRESS UNPUBLISHED

Atkins, Robert Alan
Beldock, Myron
D'Agusto, Karen Rose
King, James Forrest, Jr.
Portnoy, Sara S.
Rabkin, Peggy Ann
Shattuck, Cathie Ann
Vallianos, Carole Wagner
Wilson, Charles Haven

COLLECTIONS. *See*
Commercial, consumer.

COMMERCIAL FINANCING. *See*
Commercial, contracts.

COMMERCIAL, CONSUMER

UNITED STATES

ALABAMA

Birmingham
Denaburg, Charles L(eon)

Mobile
Armstrong, Gordon Gray, III

ALASKA

Anchorage
Sneed, Spencer Craig

ARIZONA

Prescott
Goodman, Mark N.

ARKANSAS

Fayetteville
Pettus, E. Lamar

Mountain Home
Strother, Lane Howard

CALIFORNIA

Canoga Park
Adams, Anne Claire

Costa Mesa
Frieden, Clifford E.

Del Mar
Seitman, John Michael

Downey
Duzey, Robert Lindsey

Gold River
Andrew, John Henry

Irvine
Goldstock, Barry Philip

Los Angeles
Levine, Thomas Jeffrey Pello
Ohlgren, Joel R.
Porter, Verna Louise
Smith, Scott Ormond

Pacific Palisades
Share, Richard Hudson

San Carlos
Lee, John Jin

San Diego
Guinn, Stanley Willis

San Francisco
Brandel, Roland Eric
Byrne, Robert William

San Jose
Hannon, Timothy Patrick
Small, Jonathan Andrew

Tracy
Hay, Dennis Lee

COLORADO

Delta
Schottelkotte, Michael Roger

Denver
DeMuth, Alan Cornelius
Merrick, Glenn Warren

Pueblo
Kogovsek, Daniel Charles

CONNECTICUT

Groton
Stuart, Peter Fred

West Hartford
Swerdloff, Ileen Pollock

DELAWARE

Wilmington
Ciconte, Edward Thomas
Salinger, Frank Max

DISTRICT OF COLUMBIA

Washington
Cohen, Nelson Craig

FLORIDA

Coral Gables
Dady, Robert Edward

Edgewater
Dunagan, Walter Benton

Fernandina Beach
Manson, Keith Alan Michael

Jacksonville
Coker, Howard C.
Siegel, Edward

Maitland
Trees, Philip Hugh

Miami
Gitlitz, Stuart Hal
Hartz, Steven Edward Marshall
Podhurst, Aaron Samuel
Stein, Allan Mark

Orlando
Christiansen, Patrick T.

Palm Harbor
Summers-Powell, Alan

Tampa
Alpert, Jonathan Louis
Roberson, Bruce Heerdt

GEORGIA

Atlanta
Kessler, Richard Paul, Jr.
Winkler, Allen Warren

HAWAII

Honolulu
Dang, Marvin S. C.
Rolls, John Marland, Jr.
Sato, Glenn Kenji
Tharp, James Wilson

Wailuku
Kinaka, William Tatsuo

ILLINOIS

Aurora
Patricoski, Paul Thomas

Belleville
Gossage, Roza

Carbondale
Wesley, Howard Barry

Chicago
Berkoff, Mark Andrew
Hall, Reed Stanley
Hoseman, Daniel
Hyman, Michael Bruce
Kawitt, Alan
Neumeier, Matthew Michael
Rosenberg, H. James
Schwartz, Stuart Randall
Wood, Allison Lorraine

Crete
Teykl, James Stephen

Moline
Cleaver, William Lehn

INDIANA

Columbus
Zaharako, Lew Daleure

Crawfordsville
Donaldson, Steven Bryan

Evansville
Jewell, John J.

Fort Wayne
Gehring, Ronald Kent

Gary
Boscia, James Dominic

Indianapolis
Hammel, John Wingate
Wellnitz, Craig Otto

IOWA

Shell Rock
Ottesen, Realff Henry

West Des Moines
Brown, John Lewis
McEnroe, Michael Louis

KENTUCKY

Fort Thomas
Whalen, Paul Lewellin

Lexington
McKinstry, Taft Avent

LOUISIANA

Metairie
Johnson, Gregory Scott

MARYLAND

Annapolis
Ruth, John Nicholas

Baltimore
Erwin, H. Robert

New Market
Gabriel, Eberhard John

MASSACHUSETTS

Boston
Garber, Philip Charles
Savrann, Richard Allen

Palmer
Courchesne, Nyles Leopold

MICHIGAN

Birmingham
Harms, Steven Alan

Detroit
Rochkind, Louis Philipp

Grand Rapids
Mears, Patrick Edward

Lapeer
Thomas, Robert Weston

MINNESOTA

Minneapolis
Ventres, Daniel Brainerd, Jr.
Weil, Cass Sargent

Wayzata
Reutiman, Robert William, Jr.

MISSISSIPPI

Pascagoula
Roberts, David Ambrose

MISSOURI

Kansas City
Joyce, Michael Patrick

Saint Louis
Willard, Gregory Dale

NEBRASKA

Kearney
Voigt, Steven Russell

Omaha
Kozlik, Michael David
Lee, Dennis Patrick

NEVADA

Las Vegas
Goodwin, John Robert

NEW JERSEY

Mount Laurel
Burns, Scott David

Newark
Rak, Lorraine Karen

Parsippany
Gallagher, Jerome Francis, Jr.

Ridgewood
Trocano, Russell Peter

NEW MEXICO

Albuquerque
Bova, Vincent Arthur, Jr.

NEW YORK

Dix Hills
Tucker, Robert Henry

Elmsford
Neustadt, Paul

Great Neck
Salzman, Stanley P.

Mineola
Berman, Eric M.

New York
Cohen, Marcy Sharon
Jacobs, Randall Scott David

Syracuse
Gingold, Harlan Bruce
Rothman, Robert Pierson

Westbury
Ciovacco, Robert John

NORTH CAROLINA

Charlotte
Buckley, Charles Robinson, III

Durham
Carpenter, Charles Francis

OHIO

Cincinnati
Vogel, Cedric Wakelee

Cleveland
Felty, Kriss Delbert

Columbus
Frasier, Ralph Kennedy

Shaker Heights
Cherchiglia, Dean Kenneth

Springboro
Sharts, John Edwin, III

OKLAHOMA

Oklahoma City
Gibson, Keith Russell
Schwabe, George Blaine, III

OREGON

Lincoln City
Elliott, Scott

Portland
Waggoner, James Clyde

PENNSYLVANIA

Conway
Krebs, Robert Alan

Jenkintown
Worthington, Sandra Boulton

Lemoyne
Stewart, Richard Williams

Morrisville
Hershenson, Gerald Martin

Pittsburgh
Helmrich, Joel Marc
Messner, Robert Thomas
Sanders, Russell Ronald

Reading
Page, Clemson North, Jr.

RHODE ISLAND

Cranston
Coletti, John Anthony

SOUTH CAROLINA

Charleston
Hood, Robert Holmes

SOUTH DAKOTA

Sioux Falls
Johnson, Richard Arlo

TENNESSEE

Chattanooga
Ragan, Charles Oliver, Jr.

Memphis
Noel, Randall Deane

Nashville
Patterson, Robert Shepherd

TEXAS

Abilene
Sartain, James Edward

Austin
McCullough, Frank Witcher, III

Dallas
Bonesio, Woodrow Michael

Houston
Banks, John Robert, Jr.
Diaz-Arrastia, George Ravelo
Gomez, Lynne Marie

San Antonio
Javore, Gary William

Sugar Land
Greer, Raymond White

Tyler
Patterson, Donald Ross

Weslaco
Pomerantz, Jerald Michael

UTAH

Salt Lake City
Barlow, Peter Hugh

VERMONT

Bethel
Obuchowski, Raymond Joseph

VIRGINIA

Arlington
Walker, Woodrow Wilson

Falls Church
Redmond, Robert

WASHINGTON

Bellingham
Raas, Daniel Alan

Kennewick
Hames, William Lester

Olympia
Walker, Francis Joseph

Spokane
Scanlon, Robert Charles

WEST VIRGINIA

Fairmont
Cohen, Richard Paul
Stanton, George Patrick, Jr.

WISCONSIN

Madison
Doran, Kenneth John

Milwaukee
Israel, Scott Michael
Sturm, William Charles

Racine
Dye, William Ellsworth

AUSTRALIA

Sydney
Wong, Christopher Wai C.

CHINA

Hong Kong
Yu, Benita Ka Po

DENMARK

Copenhagen
Serring, Michael

ENGLAND

London
Ferrarl, Alexander Domonico
Woolf, Geoffrey Stephen

GERMANY

Dusseldorf
Pape, Dieter

GREECE

Athens
Murray, Virginia

ISRAEL

Tel Aviv
Aharoni, Erez

ITALY

Rome
Di Amato, Astolfo

PERU

Lima
Garcia Ruiz-Huidobro, Magali

THE PHILIPPINES

Makati City
Guinto, Bob Lim

SPAIN

Madrid
Lincke, Karl Heinrich

SWEDEN

Uppsala
Stenmark, Anna Romell

ADDRESS UNPUBLISHED

Hargis, V. Burns
Horn, Andrew Warren
Klosk, Ira David
Rodenburg, Clifton Glenn

COMMERCIAL, CONTRACTS

UNITED STATES

ALABAMA

Birmingham
Stewart, Joseph Grier
Trimmier, Charles Stephen, Jr.

Demopolis
Dinning, Woodford Wyndham, Jr.

Mobile
Johnston, Neil Chunn
Peebles, E(mory) B(ush), III
Quina, Marion Albert, Jr.
Roedder, William Chapman, Jr.

ALASKA

Anchorage
Bond, Marc Douglas
Brown, Harold MacVane
Owens, Robert Patrick

ARIZONA

Flagstaff
Lacey, Henry Bernard

Phoenix
Coppersmith, Sam
Kasarjian, Levon, Jr.
Olson, Robert Howard
Spencer, Roger Keith
Tennen, Leslie Irwin

Prescott
Perry, John Richard, Jr.

Scottsdale
Marhoffer, David
Whittington, Thomas Lee

Tucson
McDonough, Lawrence

ARKANSAS

Crossett
Hubbell, Billy James

Little Rock
Hargis, David Michael
Riordan, Deborah Truby
Scott, Isaac Alexander, Jr.

Pine Bluff
Strode, Joseph Arlin

CALIFORNIA

Antioch
Richards, Gerald Thomas

Canoga Park
Adams, Anne Claire

Chatsworth
Weinman, Glenn Alan

Coalinga
Frame, Ted Ronald

Cypress
Olschwang, Alan Paul

Downey
Duzey, Robert Lindsey

El Cajon
Heisner, John Richard

El Segundo
Hunter, Larry Dean

Encinitas
Williams, Michael Edward

Fremont
Chou, Yung-Ming

Glendale
MacDonald, Kirk Stewart

Hollywood
Biele, Hugh Irving

Irvine
Hurst, Charles Wilson

Lake Forest
Ballard, Ronald Michael

Los Angeles
Bennett, Fred Gilbert
Creim, William Benjamin
Francis, Merrill Richard
Huben, Brian David
Hughes, William Jeffrey
Kane, Margaret McDonald
Kupietzky, Moshe J.
Leibow, Ronald Louis
Obrzut, Ted
Seiden, Andy
Solis, Carlos
Wessling, Robert Bruce
Zerunyan, Frank Vram

Mountain View
Bull, Howard Livingston

North Hollywood
Zimring, Stuart David

Oakland
Buckley, Mike Clifford
Leslie, Robert Lorne

Pacific Palisades
Share, Richard Hudson

Palm Springs
FitzGerald, John Edward, III

Palo Alto
Nycum, Susan Hubbell
Prinz, Kristie Dawn

Sacramento
Felderstein, Steven Howard

San Bernardino
Nassar, William Michael

San Clemente
Geyser, Lynne M.

San Diego
Emge, Derek John
Mayer, James Hock

San Francisco
Abbott, Barry Alexander
Collas, Juan Garduño, Jr.
Dworkin, Michael Leonard
Finck, Kevin William
Hinman, Harvey DeForest
Holden, Frederick Douglass, Jr.
Kallgren, Edward Eugene
Kimport, David Lloyd
Mack, John Oscar
Minnick, Malcolm David
Seabolt, Richard L.
Stroup, Stanley Stephenson
Tuthill, James Peirce
Walsh, Joseph Richard

San Mateo
Fishman, Shanti Alice
Tormey, James Roland, Jr.

San Ramon
Freed, Kenneth Alan

Santa Barbara
Metzinger, Timothy Edward

Santa Monica
Homeier, Michael George
McNally, Susan Fowler

Sunnyvale
Ludgus, Nancy Lucke
Wyatt, Thomas Csaba

Tracy
Hay, Dennis Lee

COLORADO

Aurora
Katz, Michael Jeffery

Boulder
Ward, Denitta Dawn

Denver
Aschkinasi, David Jay
Blair, Andrew Lane, Jr.
Brown, James Elliott
Cox, William Vaughan
Dunn, Randy Edwin
Gallegos, Larry Duayne
Horowitz, Robert M.
Keller, Glen Elven, Jr.
Lutz, John Shafroth
Mauro, Richard Frank

Molling, Charles Francis
Slavin, Howard Leslie
Ulrich, Theodore Albert

CONNECTICUT

Bloomfield
Messemer, Glenn Matthew

Brooklyn
Dune, Steve Charles

Fairfield
Huth, William Edward

Greenwich
Putman, Linda Murray

Groton
Jay, William Walton

Litchfield
Fiederowicz, Walter Michael

Meriden
Lowry, Houston Putnam

New Haven
Sobol, Alan J.

Norwalk
Bergere, C(lifford) Wendell, Jr.

Redding
Zitzmann, Kelly C.

Southport
Williams, Michael Peter Anthony

Stamford
Bingham, A. Walker, III
Gold, Steven Michael
Padilla, James Earl
Rose, Richard Loomis
Swerdloff, David Alan

Wethersfield
Terk, Glenn Thomas

DELAWARE

Wilmington
Hatch, Denison Hurlbut, Jr.
Kristol, Daniel Marvin
Melnik, Selinda A.
Patton, James Leeland, Jr.
Semple, James William

DISTRICT OF COLUMBIA

Washington
Babby, Lon S.
Bodansky, Robert Lee
Canfield, Edward Francis
Dempsey, Andrew Francis, Jr.
Fawell, Reed Marquette, III
Flowe, Benjamin Hugh, Jr.
Foster, Mark Wingate
Golden, Gregg Hannan Stewart
Greenberger, I. Michael
Harrison, Earl David
Johnson, David Raymond
Mazo, Mark Elliott
Mendales, Richard Ephraim
Payton, John
Phillips, Leo Harold, Jr.
Rutstein, David W.
Samuelson, Kenneth Lee
Skancke, Nancy J.
Spath, Gregg Anthony
Tufaro, Richard Chase
Vacketta, Carl Lee
Weiner, Kenneth Brian
Wintrol, John Patrick

FLORIDA

Boca Raton
Buckstein, Mark Aaron
Nussbaum, Howard Jay

Boynton Beach
Dembicer, Edwin Herbert

Coral Gables
Dady, Robert Edward

Coral Springs
Polin, Alan Jay

Edgewater
Dunagan, Walter Benton

Fort Lauderdale
Batchelder, Drake Miller
Bustamante, Nestor
Tripp, Norman Densmore

Hollywood
Hollander, Bruce Lee

Jacksonville
Christian, Gary Irvin
Gooding, David Michael
Kent, John Bradford
Prom, Stephen George

Lakeland
Harris, Christy Franklin

Miami
Baena, Scott Louis
Golden, Donald Alan
Granata, Linda M.
Hoffman, Larry J.
McHale, Michael John
Murai, Rene Vicente

Osman, Edith Gabriella
Perez, Luis Alberto
Schiffrin, Michael Edward
Schuette, Charles A.
Stein, Allan Mark
Stuever, Fred Ray
Stumpf, Larry Allen
Touby, Richard

Naples
Emerson, John Williams, II

North Palm Beach
Coyle, Dennis Patrick

Orlando
Hartley, Carl William, Jr.
Leonhardt, Frederick Wayne

Palm Beach Gardens
Scott, Alan Fulton, Jr.

Saint Petersburg
Ross, Howard Philip

Sarasota
Christopher, William Garth
Foreman, Michael Loren

Shalimar
Chesser, David Michael

Tallahassee
Barley, John Alvin

Tampa
Jones, John Arthur
Schwenke, Roger Dean
Whatley, Jacqueline Beltram

Tavernier
Lupino, James Samuel

Vero Beach
Case, Douglas Manning

West Palm Beach
Beall, Kenneth Sutter, Jr.

Winter Park
Ackert, T(errence) W(illiam)
Hadley, Ralph Vincent, III

GEORGIA

Atlanta
Byrne, Granville Bland, III
Calhoun, Scott Douglas
Cargill, Robert Mason
Crews, William Edwin
Hinchey, John William
Lackland, Theodore Howard
Linder, Harvey Ronald
Maines, James Allen
Strauss, Robert David
Veal, Rex R.
Williams, Neil, Jr.
Winkler, Allen Warren

Augusta
Cooney, William J.

Marietta
Ahlstrom, Michael Joseph

Ocilla
Pujadas, Thomas Edward

Perry
Geiger, James Norman

Roswell
Baker, Anita Diane
Mimms, Thomas Bowman, Jr.

Swainsboro
Cadle, Jerry Neal

HAWAII

Honolulu
Asai-Sato, Carol Yuki
Chin, Stephanie Anne
Sato, Glenn Kenji

Kaneohe
Huber, Thomas P.

Paia
Richman, Joel Eser

ILLINOIS

Abbott Park
Brock, Charles Marquis

Chicago
Anderson, J. Trent
Baer, John Richard Frederick
Barnes, James Garland, Jr.
Brand, Mark
Cohen, Melanie Rovner
Coughlan, Kenneth L.
Cunningham, Thomas Justin
Fazio, Peter Victor, Jr.
Field, Robert Edward
Fishman, Robert Michael
Henry, Robert John
Hoseman, Daniel
Johnson, Douglas Wells
Kaplan, Howard Gordon
Karnes, Evan Burton, II
Katz, Stuart Charles
Kohn, William Irwin
Kravitt, Jason Harris Paperno
Laidlaw, Andrew R.
Loew, Jonathan L.
Mehlman, Mark Franklin
Miller, Paul J.

Murray, Daniel Richard
Peterson, Ronald Roger
Rohrman, Douglass Frederick
Schwartz, Donald Lee
Schwartz, Stuart Randall
Shank, Suzanne Adams
Staley, Charles Ralls
Steinberg, Morton M.
Wahlen, Edwin Alfred
White, Linda Diane

Elgin
Roeser, Ronald O.

Evanston
Thompson, Michael

Lake Forest
Giza, David Alan

Long Grove
Obert, Paul Richard

Moline
Cleaver, William Lehn

Oakbrook Terrace
Fenech, Joseph Charles
Tibble, Douglas Clair

Peoria
Atterbury, Robert Rennie, III

Springfield
Adami, Paul E.

Toledo
Prather, William C., III

Urbana
Webber, Carl Maddra

INDIANA

Columbus
Zaharako, Lew Daleure

Fort Wayne
Pope, Mark Andrew

Indianapolis
Ancel, Jerald Irwin
FitzGibbon, Daniel Harvey
Kahlenbeck, Howard, Jr.
Kleiman, Mary Margaret
Miller, David Anthony
Talesnick, Stanley
Vandivier, Blair Robert
Yeager, Joseph Heizer, Jr.

Merrillville
Bowman, Carol Ann
Brenman, Stephen Morris

South Bend
Reinke, William John

Terre Haute
Britton, Louis Franklin

Vincennes
Smith, Bruce Arthur

IOWA

Des Moines
Austin, Bradford Lyle

Sioux City
Madsen, George Frank

KANSAS

Overland Park
Cohen, Barton Pollock

Wichita
Foote, Richard Van
Johnson, Kevin Blaine

KENTUCKY

Bowling Green
Catron, Stephen Barnard

Lexington
Lester, Roy David
McKinstry, Taft Avent
Scott, Joseph Mitchell, Jr.

Louisville
Fenton, Thomas Conner
Shaikun, Michael Gary
Vincenti, Michael Baxter

Richmond
Weldon, C. Michael

LOUISIANA

Baton Rouge
Richards, Marta Alison

Metairie
Hardy, Ashton Richard

New Orleans
Claverie, Philip deVilliers
Danner, William Bekurs
Garcia, Patricia A.
Getten, Thomas Frank
Miller, Gary H.
Pugh, William Whitmell Hill, III
Sher, Leopold Zangwill
Wedig, Regina Scotto

Shreveport
Bryant, J(ames) Bruce
Chastain, Merritt Banning, Jr.

MAINE

Portland
Martin, Joel Clark
Stauffer, Eric P.

MARYLAND

Baltimore
Baker, William Parr
Kandel, Nelson Robert
Katz, Martha Lessman
Kuryk, David Neal
Mogol, Alan Jay
Rafferty, William Bernard
Wasserman, Richard Leo

Bethesda
Goodwin, Robert Cronin
Himelfarb, Stephen Roy
Tanenbaum, Richard Hugh

Easton
Maffitt, James Strawbridge

Rockville
Zaphiriou, George Aristotle

West Bethesda
Scully, Roger Tehan, II

MASSACHUSETTS

Boston
Dello Iacono, Paul Michael
Garber, Philip Charles
Hemnes, Thomas Michael Sheridan
Hester, Patrick Joseph
Huang, Thomas Weishing
Lamb, Kevin Thomas
Rudolph, James Leonard
Shapiro, Sandra
Smith, Edwin Eric
Yurko, Richard John

Brookline
Bursley, Kathleen A.

Framingham
Meltzer, Jay H.

Newton Center
Snyder, John Gorvers

Springfield
Sheils, James Bernard

Wellesley
Marx, Peter A.

MICHIGAN

Ann Arbor
Ellmann, Douglas Stanley

Battle Creek
Markey, James Kevin

Birmingham
Harms, Steven Alan

Bloomfield Hills
Dawson, Stephen Everette
Janover, Robert H.
Lamping, William Jay

Clinton Township
Theut, C. Peter

Dearborn
Dixon, Richard Dean

Detroit
Darlow, Julia Donovan
Dunn, William Bradley
Fromm, Frederick Andrew, Jr.
Nix, Robert Royal, II
Pirtle, H(arold) Edward
Rochkind, Louis Philipp
Thorpe, Norman Ralph

Farmington Hills
Moore, Roy F.

Flint
Powers, Edward Herbert

Grand Rapids
Curtin, Timothy John
Engbers, James Arend
Rynbrandt, Kevin Abraham

Grosse Pointe
Behringer, Samuel Joseph, Jr.

Kalamazoo
Lubben, Craig Henry
Pikcunas, Charles Richard

Muskegon
Fauri, Eric Joseph
Nehra, Gerald Peter

Taylor
Hirsch, David L.

Troy
Berman, Leonard Keith
McKeone, Keri Marie

MINNESOTA

Anoka
Erickson, Phillip Arthur

Austin
Schneider, Mahlon C.

Benson
Wilcox, Donald Alan

Edina
Gurstel, Norman Keith

Hopkins
Hunter, Donald Forrest

Minneapolis
Anderson, Arlene D.
Baillie, James Leonard
Hackley, David Kenneth
Hanbery, Donna Eva
Kuyath, Richard Norman
Weil, Cass Sargent

Rochester
Lantz, William Charles

Saint Cloud
Hughes, Kevin John

Saint Paul
Hansen, Eric Peter
Rebane, John T.

MISSISSIPPI

Jackson
Grant, Russell Porter, Jr.
O'Mara, James Wright

Madison
Flechas, Eduardo A.

MISSOURI

Cape Girardeau
O'Loughlin, John Patrick

Chesterfield
Pollihan, Thomas Henry

Kansas City
Pelofsky, Joel
Tharp, Tonna K.

Maryland Heights
Cooper, Richard Alan

Saint Louis
Carr, Gary Thomas
Cook, Thomas Alfred Ashley
Duesenberg, Richard William
Godiner, Donald Leonard
Hetlage, Robert Owen
Leontsinis, George John
Poscover, Maury B.
Sullivan, Edward Lawrence

MONTANA

Billings
Mitchell, Laura Ann

Helena
Grant, John Halloran

NEBRASKA

Norfolk
Domina, David Alan

Omaha
Fitzgerald, James Patrick
Kozlik, Michael David
Kreifels, Frank Anthony
LaPuzza, Paul James

NEVADA

Las Vegas
Kravitz, Martin Jay
Nasky, H(arold) Gregory
Ritchie, Douglas V.
Singer, Michael Howard

NEW HAMPSHIRE

Portsmouth
Doleac, Charles Bartholomew

NEW JERSEY

Bay Head
Kellogg, James Crane

Bridgewater
Dahling, Gerald Vernon

Cliffside Park
Diktas, Christos James

Edison
Applebaum, Charles

Hackensack
Greenberg, Steven Morey
Sosland, Karl Z.

Jersey City
DiSciullo, Alan Michael

Sandy
Western, Marion Wayne

VIRGINIA

Alexandria
Toothman, John William

Arlington
Walker, Woodrow Wilson

Charlottesville
McKay, John Douglas

Fairfax
Rust, John Howson, Jr.
Sanderson, Douglas Jay

Falls Church
Jennings, Thomas Parks
Thomas, William Griffith

Leesburg
Price, Stephen Conwell

Manakin Sabot
Bright, Craig Bartley

Mc Lean
Brown, Frank Eugene, Jr.
Friedlander, Jerome Peyser, II
Goolrick, Robert Mason

Norfolk
Parker, Richard Wilson
Russell, C. Edward, Jr.
Smith, Richard Muldrow

Reston
Toole, John Harper

Richmond
Bing, Richard McPhail

Roanoke
Farnham, David Alexander
Harrison, David George

WASHINGTON

Bellingham
Packer, Mark Barry

Port Angeles
Gay, Carl Lloyd

Redmond
Scowcroft, Jerome Chilwell

Seattle
Cullen, Jack Joseph
Ginsberg, Phillip H(enry)
Graham, Stephen Michael
Narodick, Kit Gordon
Sandman, Irvin W(illis)
Stokke, Diane Rees
Tune, James Fulcher
Yalowitz, Kenneth Gregg

WEST VIRGINIA

Charleston
Brown, James Knight

WISCONSIN

Beloit
Blakely, Robert George

Madison
Boucher, Joseph W(illiam)
Peterson, H. Dale
Walsh, David Graves

Menomonee Falls
Hurt, Michael Carter

Milwaukee
Levine, Herbert
Martin, Quinn William
Maynard, John Ralph
Rintelman, Donald Brian
Schoenfeld, Howard Allen

Sun Prairie
Eustice, Francis Joseph

WYOMING

Casper
McCall, Donn Jay

Riverton
Girard, Nettabell

TERRITORIES OF THE UNITED STATES

PUERTO RICO

San Juan
Rodriguez-Diaz, Juan E.

MEXICO

Mexico
Quiroz, Lourdes Gabriela

Mexico City
Langarica O'Hea, Lorenza Kristin
Ritch, James Earle, Jr.

ARGENTINA

Buenos Aires
De Rosso, Pablo
Gonzalez, Mariano Pablo

AUSTRALIA

Sydney
Grieve, Gordon Thomas
Jeffares, Paul Reginald

BELGIUM

Brussels
Delsaut, Philippe Patrick
Hoffmann, Maria Elisabeth

CHILE

Santiago
Rosenblut, Alvaro

CZECH REPUBLIC

Prague
Bányaiová, Alena

DENMARK

Copenhagen
Stokholm, Jon Ulrik

ENGLAND

London
Baker, Charles George
Bandurka, Andrew Alan
Breakell, David James
Buckley, Colin Hugh
Drury, Stephen Patrick
Hammerson, Marc Charles
Heard, David James
MacRitchie, Kenneth
Spencer, Robin Graham Nelson

FRANCE

Paris
Blanchenay, Nicolas
Bougartchev, Kiril Alexandre
Gaillot, Laurent D
MacCrindle, Robert Alexander

GERMANY

Frankfurt
Haarmann, Wilhelm

Hamburg
von Teuffel, Nikolai

HUNGARY

Budapest
Balassa, Tamás

INDIA

Calcutta
Deora, Chandra Kumar

New Delhi
Khaitan, Gautam

ISRAEL

Tel Aviv
Yoram, Raved

Tel-Aviv
Bar-on, Ofer

ITALY

Milan
Ricci, Barnaba
Tarchi, Enrico Maria

Milano
Sganzerla, Andrea Benedetio

KENYA

Nairoba
Maosa, Thomas Nyakambi

THE NETHERLANDS

Amstelveen
Tarlavski, Roman

Amsterdam
Van Eeghen, Christiaan Pieter

NORWAY

Oslo
Aubert, Fredrik Scheel

PERU

Lima
Chabaneix, Jean Paul

THE PHILIPPINES

Makati City
Macalaguing, Gene Batalla
Mamuric, Jose Roberto Lota

PORTUGAL

Lisbon
Amendoeira, Rui
Arantes-Pedroso, Filipa De Vilhena

REPUBLIC OF KOREA

Seoul
Yoon, Hoil

ROMANIA

Bucharest
Pachiu, Laurentiu Victor
Voicu, Daniel

SAUDI ARABIA

Riyadh
Taylor, Frederick William, Jr. (Fritz Taylor)

SOUTH AFRICA

Sandton
Cron, Kevin Richard
Schlosberg, Jonathan Harry

SPAIN

Madrid
Martin de Vidales, Nicolas

SWEDEN

Stockholm
Arak, Viktor
Lindquist, Ylva

SWITZERLAND

Bern
Friedli, Georg

Geneva
De Pfyffer, Andre

Zürich
Wuerzner, Andrea

THAILAND

Bangkok
Chunhakasikarn, Sasirusm Bulpakdi

UKRAINE

Kyiv
Kolesnyk, Oleg Ivanovich

ZIMBABWE

Harare
Wood Kahari, Brenda Marie

ADDRESS UNPUBLISHED

Ash, David Charles
Atchison, Rodney Raymond
Berry, Robert Worth
Bloomer, Harold Franklin, Jr.
Brodhead, David Crawmer
Canoff, Karen Huston
Carmody, Richard Patrick
Clabaugh, Elmer Eugene, Jr.
Cornish, Jeannette Carter
Galbraith, Allan Lee

Giusti, William Roger
Hafner, Thomas Mark
Hagerman, Michael Charles
Hernandez, David N(icholas)
Ikeda, Cnythia Yuko
Jamieson, Michael Lawrence
Klaus, Charles
Landy, Lisa Anne
Locke, William Henry
Marker, Marc Linthacum
Maulding, Barry Clifford
McGahren, Eugene Dewey, Jr.
O'Mara, William Michael
Oliver, Samuel William, Jr.
Painton, Russell Elliott
Pallot, Joseph Wedeles
Reath, George, Jr.
Rodenburg, Clifton Glenn
Samuels, Janet Lee
Schultz, Dennis Bernard
Seifert, Stephen Wayne
Stone, Andrew Grover
Tondel, Lawrence Chapman
Voight, Elizabeth Anne
von Sauers, Joseph F.
Weil, Peter Henry

COMMUNICATIONS

UNITED STATES

ARIZONA

Phoenix
Bodney, David Jeremy
Silverman, Alan Henry

Tucson
Meehan, Michael Joseph

ARKANSAS

Little Rock
Riordan, Deborah Truby

CALIFORNIA

Los Angeles
Lederman, Bruce Randolph

Sacramento
Foster, Douglas Taylor

San Francisco
Tobin, James Michael

COLORADO

Denver
Quiat, Marshall

CONNECTICUT

Darien
Beach, Stephen Holbrook

Greenwich
Hurwich, Robert Allan

Hartford
Knickerbocker, Robert Platt, Jr.

Stamford
Apfelbaum, Marc

DISTRICT OF COLUMBIA

Washington
Bartlett, John Laurence
Beisner, John Herbert
Bell, Stephen Robert
Berman, Paul Justin
Besozzi, Paul Charles
Blake, Jonathan Dewey
Blumenfeld, Jeffrey
Braverman, Burt Alan
Brinkmann, Robert Joseph
Carome, Patrick Joseph
Casserly, James Lund
Christensen, Karen Kay
Coursen, Christopher Dennison
Cox, Kenneth Allen
Gastfreund, Irving
Goodman, John M.
Haines, Terry L.
Harris, Scott Blake
Heckman, Jerome Harold
Holtz, Edgar Wolfe
Knauer, Leon Thomas
Krasnow, Erwin Gilbert
Levine, Henry David
Marks, Richard Daniel
McReynolds, Mary Armilda
Michaels, Gary David
Rhyne, Sidney White
Russo, Roy R.
Sanford, Bruce William
Skall, Gregg P.
Spector, Phillip Louis
Tannenwald, Peter
Wiley, Richard Emerson
Woodworth, Ramsey Lloyd

FLORIDA

Orlando
Frey, Louis, Jr.

Saint Petersburg
Bernstein, Howard Mark

GEORGIA

Atlanta
Coxe, Tench Charles
Shapiro, George Howard

ILLINOIS

Chicago
Chudzinski, Mark Adam
Rooney, Matthew A.
Sennet, Charles Joseph

INDIANA

Indianapolis
McKeon, Thomas Joseph

IOWA

Des Moines
Fisher, Thomas George
Fisher, Thomas George, Jr.
Stoffregen, Philip Eugene

KANSAS

Westwood
Devlin, James Richard

KENTUCKY

Louisville
Cowan, Frederic Joseph

LOUISIANA

Metairie
Hardy, Ashton Richard

Shreveport
Bryant, J(ames) Bruce

MARYLAND

Bethesda
Franklin, William Jay

Prince Frederick
Reynolds, Christopher John

Rockville
Millstein, Leo Lee

MASSACHUSETTS

Brookline
Burnstein, Daniel

Framingham
Heng, Gerald C. W.

MICHIGAN

Kalamazoo
Crocker, Patrick David

MINNESOTA

Duluth
Burns, Richard Ramsey

Minneapolis
Tanick, Marshall Howard

Saint Louis Park
Rothenberg, Elliot Calvin

MISSOURI

Chesterfield
Denneen, John Paul

NEW JERSEY

Florham Park
Chase, Eric Lewis

Union
Bottitta, Joseph Anthony

NEW YORK

New York
Bender, John Charles
Briskman, Louis Jacob
Colgan, Jeremy Spencer
Fry, Morton Harrison, II
Joffe, Robert David
Lustbader, Philip Lawrence
McCarthy, Robert Emmett
Redpath, John S(loneker), Jr.
Savell, Polly Carolyn
Sutter, Laurence Brener
Thackeray, Jonathan E.
Varma, Rishi Anand
Welt, Philip Stanley

OKLAHOMA

Tulsa
Ferguson, Dallas Eugene

OREGON

Beaverton
Fulsher, Allan Arthur

Portland
Hinkle, Charles Frederick

PENNSYLVANIA

Clearfield
Falvo, Mark Anthony

Philadelphia
Bogutz, Jerome Edwin
DeBunda, Salvatore Michael
Solano, Carl Anthony

TEXAS

Austin
Drummond, Eric Hubert

VIRGINIA

Arlington
Morris, Roy Leslie

Charlottesville
McKay, John Douglas

Mc Lean
Byrnes, William Joseph

Richmond
Broadbent, Peter Edwin, Jr.

Roanoke
Barnhill, David Stan

WISCONSIN

Madison
Walsh, David Graves

MEXICO

Mexico City
Chacon Lopez Velarde, Ricardo

AUSTRALIA

Melbourne
Bartlett, Peter Llewellyn
Gronow, Geoffrey Rees

Sydney
Simmons, Daniel David

DENMARK

Copenhagen
Lassen, Steen Anker

ENGLAND

London
Fuller, Charles Robert Saunders
Skrein, Stephen Peter Michael
Stokes, Simon Jeremy
Turner, Catrin
Turner, Mark McDougall

FRANCE

Paris
Darlington, Gavin

GERMANY

Frankfurt/Main
Wuermeling, Ulrich Urban

Hamburg
Dieselhorst, Jochen

Munich
Schleifenbaum, Eckhart Johannes

GREECE

Athens
Murray, Virginia

ISRAEL

Jerusalem
Molho, Isaac

Tel Aviv
Aharoni, Erez
Karniel, Yuval

ITALY

Milan
Peron, Sabrina

THE NETHERLANDS

Amsterdam
Schaap, Jacqueline

NORWAY

Oslo
Strømme, Vidar

POLAND

Warsaw
Wierzbowski, Krzysztof Franciszek

PORTUGAL

Lisbon
Arantes-Pedroso, Filipa De Vilhena
Pessanha, Tomas Vasconcelos

SPAIN

Barcelona
Fernandez, Rodolfo

SWEDEN

Stockholm
Malmström, Anders C.
Widmark, Stefan

UKRAINE

Kiev
Konnov, Sergei Vladimirovich
Voitovich, Sergei Adamovich

UNITED ARAB EMIRATES

Dubai
Forsch, Thomas

ADDRESS UNPUBLISHED

Harkless, Angela
Isaacs, Michael Burton
Jameson, Paula Ann
Killeen, Michael John
Norman, Albert George, Jr.

COMPUTER

UNITED STATES

ARIZONA

Phoenix
Bivens, Donald Wayne

CALIFORNIA

Cupertino
Simon, Nancy Ruth

Los Angeles
Metzger, Robert Streicher
Strong, George Gordon, Jr.

Menlo Park
Coats, William Sloan, III

Mountain View
Bull, Howard Livingston

Palo Alto
Hinckley, Robert Craig
Nycum, Susan Hubbell
Sherman, Martin Peter

San Francisco
Chambers, Guy Wayne
Richardson, Daniel Ralph

San Jose
Goldstein, Robin

San Mateo
Fishman, Shanti Alice

Santa Monica
McMillan, M. Sean

Sunnyvale
Wyatt, Thomas Csaba

COLORADO

Colorado Springs
Kubida, William Joseph

Denver
Dorr, Robert Charles

Fort Collins
Fromm, Jeffery Bernard

CONNECTICUT

Darien
Beach, Stephen Holbrook

Monroe
Oliver, Milton McKinnon

Stamford
Gold, Steven Michael
Lieberman, Steven Paul

DELAWARE

Wilmington
Elzufon, John A.

DISTRICT OF COLUMBIA

Washington
Bartlett, John Laurence
Bell, Stephen Robert
Berman, Paul Justin
Brooks, Daniel Townley
Haines, Terry L.
Johnson, David Raymond
Katz, Hadrian Ronald
Marks, Richard Daniel
Peters, Frederick Whitten
Ritter, Jeffrey Blake
Skall, Gregg P.
Spector, Phillip Louis

FLORIDA

Fort Myers
Dalton, Anne

Orlando
Losey, Ralph Colby

Tallahassee
Miller, Morris Henry

GEORGIA

Atlanta
Harrison, Bryan Guy
Maines, James Allen
Marianes, William Byron
Somers, Fred Leonard, Jr.

HAWAII

Honolulu
Schraff, Paul Albert

ILLINOIS

Chicago
Bloom, Christopher Arthur
Kohlstedt, James August
Maher, David Willard
McCrohon, Craig
Schlitter, Stanley Allen
Smedinghoff, Thomas J.
Thomas, Frederick Bradley
Wanke, Ronald Lee

Palatine
Cannon, Benjamin Winton

INDIANA

Indianapolis
Cole, Roland Jay
Dutton, Stephen James
Kashani, Hamid Reza

MAINE

Portland
Stauffer, Eric P.

MARYLAND

Baltimore
Katz, Martha Lessman

Bethesda
Franklin, William Jay
Weinberger, Alan David

North Potomac
Keane, James Ignatius

MASSACHUSETTS

Boston
Aresty, Jeffrey M.
Barber, Robert Cushman
Coolidge, Daniel Scott
Storer, Thomas Perry

Braintree
Paglierani, Ronald Joseph

Brookline
Burnstein, Daniel

Waltham
Barnes-Brown, Peter Newton

Wellesley
Marx, Peter A.

MICHIGAN

Bloomfield Hills
Lamping, William Jay
Stewart, Michael B.

Detroit
Tickner, Ellen Mindy

MINNESOTA

Minneapolis
McNeil, Mark Sanford

MISSOURI

Saint Louis
Rice, Charles Marcus, II

NEVADA

Reno
Ryan, Robert Collins

NEW JERSEY

Monmouth Junction
King, David Roy

New Providence
Maxeiner, James Randolph

Ridgewood
Harris, Micalyn Shafer

Union
Bottitta, Joseph Anthony

Woodbridge
Schaff, Michael Frederick

Woodbury
Adler, Lewis Gerard

NEW YORK

Brooklyn
Bohm, Joel Lawrence

Buffalo
Foschio, Leslie George

Croton On Hudson
Hoffman, Paul Shafer

Long Island City
Wanderman, Susan Mae

Mineola
Weinstock, Benjamin

New York
Bandon, William Edward, III
Black, Louis Engleman
Celedonia, Baila Handelman
Connolly, Kevin Jude
Einhorn, David Allen
Epstein, Michael Alan
Halket, Thomas D(aniel)
Hooker, Wade Stuart, Jr.
Kinney, Stephen Hoyt, Jr.
Lefkowitz, Howard N.
Macioce, Frank Michael
Matus, Wayne Charles
Morris, Francis Edward
Savage, Edward Turney
Spiegel, Jerrold Bruce
Taylor, Job, III
Woods, Christopher John
Zammit, Joseph Paul

Westbury
Nogee, Jeffrey Laurence

White Plains
Pitegoff, Thomas Michael

NORTH CAROLINA

Tarboro
Hopkins, Grover Prevatte

OHIO

Cleveland
Diamant, Michael Harlan
Nave, Michele Garrick

Dayton
Nauman, Joseph George

Miamisburg
Battles, John Martin

PENNSYLVANIA

Bryn Mawr
Stahl, Roy Howard

Lancaster
Gray, Kathleen Ann

Media
Elman, Gerry Jay
Lipton, Robert Stephen

Newtown
Simkanich, John Joseph

Philadelphia
Damsgaard, Kell Marsh

Pittsburgh
Schwab, Arthur James
Silverman, Arnold Barry

TEXAS

Austin
Zager, Steven Mark

Beaumont
Cavaliere, Frank Joseph

Dallas
Farquhar, Robert Michael
Hammond, Herbert J.

Houston
Winer, Stephen I.

Humble
Gaffney, Richard Cook

VIRGINIA

Alexandria
Drennan, Joseph Peter
Greigg, Ronald Edwin
Wieder, Bruce Terrill

Arlington
Doyle, Gerard Francis

WASHINGTON

Redmond
Phillips, Richard Lee

Seattle
Cumbow, Robert Charles
Prentke, Richard Ottesen

AUSTRALIA

Victoria
Ellinson, Dean Avraham

AUSTRIA

Vienna
Frank, Alix

DENMARK

Copenhagen
Langemark, Jesper

ENGLAND

London
Allcock, John Paul Major
Bamford, Timothy James
Stokes, Simon Jeremy
Turner, Catrin
Turner, Mark McDougall

Manchester
Moakes, Jonathan

FRANCE

Paris
Safa, Rachid P.

GERMANY

Frankfurt
Wolff, Florian

Frankfurt/Main
Baeumer, Ulrich J.P.
Wuermeling, Ulrich Urban

Hamburg
Dieselhorst, Jochen

INDIA

New Delhi
Kalha, Baljit Singh

NIGERIA

Victoria Island
Nwasike, Ndi Chuks

PORTUGAL

Lisbon
Pessanha, Tomas Vasconcelos

SCOTLAND

Glasgow
Priest, Andrew David

SINGAPORE

Singapore
Liew, Yik Wee

SPAIN

Barcelona
Fernandez, Rodolfo
Llevat, Jorge

Madrid
Vasquez, Gerard Manuel

SWEDEN

Malmo
Frii, Jonas Erik Werner

UNITED ARAB EMIRATES

Dubai
Forsch, Thomas

ADDRESS UNPUBLISHED

Anani, Tarig
Ash, David Charles
Bierce, William B.
Fernandez, Dennis Sunga
Fischer, David Jon
Hagerman, Michael Charles
Keys, Jerry Malcom
McCobb, John Bradford, Jr.
Miller, John Eddie
Moravsik, Robert James
Pear, Charles E., Jr.
Stone, Andrew Grover
Young, John Hardin
Zimmerman, Jean

CONDEMNATION

UNITED STATES

ALASKA

Anchorage
Weinig, Richard Arthur

CALIFORNIA

Aptos
Kehoe, Dennis Joseph

El Centro
Sutherland, Lowell Francis

El Segundo
Schimmenti, John Joseph

Los Angeles
Salvaty, Benjamin Benedict

Los Gatos
Boccardo, James Frederick

Santa Monica
Kanner, Gideon

Walnut Creek
Skaggs, Sanford Merle

COLORADO

Denver
Bryans, Richard W.

CONNECTICUT

Windham
Lombardo, Michael John

FLORIDA

Boca Raton
Golis, Paul Robert

Orlando
Spoonhour, James Michael

Saint Petersburg
Battaglia, Brian Peter

Sarasota
Blucher, Paul Arthur

GEORGIA

Atlanta
Janney, Donald Wayne

INDIANA

Merrillville
Miller, Richard Allen

LOUISIANA

Lafayette
Davidson, James Joseph, III

MARYLAND

Abingdon
Wolf, Martin Eugene

MASSACHUSETTS

Barnstable
McLaughlin, Edward Francis, Jr.

Boston
Savrann, Richard Allen

Worcester
Bassett, Edward Caldwell, Jr.

MICHIGAN

Detroit
Ward, George Edward

Muskegon
Briggs, John Mancel, III

Saginaw
Martin, Walter

Saint Joseph
Gleiss, Henry Weston

MINNESOTA

Minneapolis
Barnard, Allen Donald

Saint Paul
Spencer, David James

MISSISSIPPI

Kiln
Thissell, Charles William

MISSOURI

Kansas City
Frantze, David Wayne
Smithson, Lowell Lee

NEW JERSEY

Teaneck
Rosenblum, Edward G.

NEW YORK

Mineola
Santemma, Jon Noel

New York
Fischman, Bernard D.
Goldstein, M. Robert
Rikon, Michael
Spivack, Edith Irene

Poughkeepsie
Wallace, Herbert Norman

Rochester
Fox, Edward Hanton

Syracuse
Young, Douglas Howard

NORTH CAROLINA

Raleigh
Davis, Thomas Hill, Jr.

OKLAHOMA

Oklahoma City
Wallace, Thomas Andrew

OREGON

Portland
Maloney, Robert E., Jr.

SOUTH CAROLINA

Columbia
Babcock, Keith Moss

TEXAS

Dallas
Staley, Joseph Hardin, Jr.

Houston
Montague, H. Dixon

San Antonio
Wallis, Ben Alton, Jr.

VERMONT

Burlington
Frank, Joseph Elihu

VIRGINIA

Leesburg
Minchew, John Randall
Price, Stephen Conwell

Richmond
Ellis, Andrew Jackson, Jr.

ADDRESS UNPUBLISHED

McCormick, Homer L., Jr.

CONSTITUTIONAL

UNITED STATES

ALABAMA

Montgomery
Nachman, Merton Roland, Jr.
Tindol, Melton Chad

ARIZONA

Phoenix
Riikola, Michael Edward

Scottsdale
Sears, Alan Edward

CALIFORNIA

Berkeley
Ogg, Wilson Reid

Los Angeles
Bringardner, John Michael

Newport Beach
Mandel, Maurice, II

San Francisco
Hilton, Stanley Goumas

COLORADO

Boulder
Halpern, Alexander

DISTRICT OF COLUMBIA

Washington
Beyer, Wayne Cartwright
Brame, Joseph Robert, III
Burchfield, Bobby Roy
Dowdey, Landon Gerald
Peet, Richard Clayton
Reid, Inez Smith
Williams, Thomas Raymond

FLORIDA

Boca Raton
Kassner, Herbert Seymore

Fort Lauderdale
Benjamin, James Scott

Gainesville
Jones, Clifford Alan

Miami
Rashkind, Paul Michael

Orlando
Mason, Steven Gerald

Sarasota
Blucher, Paul Arthur

Tampa
Thomas, Gregg Darrow

GEORGIA

Atlanta
Bird, Wendell Raleigh
Schroeder, Eric Peter
Shapiro, George Howard
Tewes, R. Scott

HAWAII

Honolulu
Yamano, John Y.

ILLINOIS

Chicago
Barker, William Thomas
Chefitz, Joel Gerald
Giampietro, Wayne Bruce
Wade, Edwin Lee

Joliet
Lenard, George Dean

INDIANA

Terre Haute
Bopp, James, Jr.

KENTUCKY

Louisville
Manly, Samuel

LOUISIANA

Baton Rouge
Riddick, Winston Wade, Sr.

MARYLAND

Silver Spring
McDermitt, Edward Vincent

MASSACHUSETTS

Boston
Burstein, Harvey

MICHIGAN

Ann Arbor
Niehoff, Leonard Marvin

Southfield
Sullivan, Robert Emmet, Jr.

MINNESOTA

Crystal
Reske, Steven David

Saint Louis Park
Rothenberg, Elliot Calvin

MISSOURI

Kansas City
Bryant, Richard Todd

NEBRASKA

Omaha
Rock, Harold L.
Runge, Patrick Richard

NEW YORK

Glen Cove
Lewis, Felice Flanery

New York
Bamberger, Michael Albert
Conboy, Kenneth
Davidson, George Allan
Glekel, Jeffrey Ives
Levitan, David M(aurice)
Levy, Herbert Monte
Wishingrad, Jay Marc

White Plains
Pickard, John Allan

OHIO

Cleveland
Perris, Terrence George

Columbus
Martin, Paige Arlene
McDermott, Kevin R.

OKLAHOMA

Edmond
Lester, Andrew William

OREGON

Portland
Hinkle, Charles Frederick

PENNSYLVANIA

Glenside
Mermelstein, Jules Joshua

Harrisburg
Murren, Philip Joseph

Philadelphia
Serotta, Judd Adam

Pittsburgh
Pushinsky, Jon

TENNESSEE

Clarksville
Love, Michael Joseph

Fayetteville
Dickey, John Harwell

TEXAS

Austin
Hamilton, Dagmar Strandberg
Weddington, Sarah Ragle

Eldorado
Kosub, James Albert

Fort Worth
Sharpe, James Shelby

Galveston
Vie, George William, III

VERMONT

Montpelier
Putter, David Seth

VIRGINIA

Alexandria
Hirschkop, Philip Jay

Charlottesville
Hazelwood, Kimball Ellen

Mc Lean
Sparks, Robert Ronold, Jr.

Richmond
Freeman, George Clemon, Jr.
Ryland, Walter H.

South Riding
Murray, Michael Patrick

WASHINGTON

Seattle
Johnson, Bruce Edward Humble

MEXICO

Mexico City
Ahumada, Ricardo

ADDRESS UNPUBLISHED

Boyd, Thomas Marshall
DeLaFuente, Charles
Diamond, Paul Steven
Howard, John Wayne
Ogden, David William
Swann, Barbara
Twardy, Stanley Albert, Jr.
Waxman, Seth Paul
Wilson, Charles Haven

CONSTRUCTION

UNITED STATES

ALABAMA

Birmingham
Rogers, Ernest Mabry

Eufaula
Twitchell, E(rvin) Eugene

Montgomery
McFadden, Frank Hampton
Wood, James Jerry

ALASKA

Anchorage
Pfiffner, Frank Albert

ARIZONA

Phoenix
Jacques, Raoul Thomas

CALIFORNIA

Carlsbad
Koehnke, Phillip Eugene

Chula Vista
Appleton, Richard Newell

Glendale
MacDonald, Kirk Stewart

Irvine
Suojanen, Wayne William

Los Angeles
Kamine, Bernard S.
Lawton, Eric
Lund, James Louis
Moloney, Stephen Michael
Pieper, Darold D.
Robison, William Robert
Wagner, Darryl William

Marina Del Rey
Smolker, Gary Steven

Morro Bay
Merzon, James Bert

Newport Beach
McGee, James Francis

Oakland
Leslie, Robert Lorne

Redwood City
Wilhelm, Robert Oscar

San Diego
Bleiler, Charles Arthur
Boyle, Michael Fabian

San Francisco
Berning, Paul Wilson
Thiel, Clark T.
Thornton, D. Whitney, II

San Jose
Cory, Charles Johnson

Santa Ana
Heckler, Gerard Vincent

Woodland Hills
Flaig, Donald William

COLORADO

Denver
Bain, James William
Jablonski, James Arthur
Tomlinson, Warren Leon

Highlands Ranch
Hagen, Glenn W(illiam)

CONNECTICUT

Hartford
Dowling, Vincent John
Pepe, Louis Robert

Westport
Lindskog, David Richard

DELAWARE

Wilmington
Cottrell, Paul (William Cottrell)

DISTRICT OF COLUMBIA

Washington
Barnes, Peter
Dempsey, Andrew Francis, Jr.
Fawell, Reed Marquette, III
Lifschitz, Judah
Mitchell, Roy Shaw
Ness, Andrew David
Schor, Laurence
Weiner, Kenneth Brian
West, Joseph D.

FLORIDA

Fort Lauderdale
Bustamante, Nestor

Miami
Greenleaf, Walter Franklin

Orlando
Nadeau, Robert Bertrand, Jr.
Weiss, Christopher John
Wilson, William Berry

Palm Beach Gardens
Scott, Alan Fulton, Jr.

Pompano Beach
Shulmister, M(orris) Ross

Sarasota
Christopher, William Garth
Phillips, Elvin Willis

Tallahassee
Barley, John Alvin

Tampa
Bowen, Paul Henry, Jr.
Campbell, Richard Bruce
Fuller, Diana Lynn

GEORGIA

Atlanta
Croft, Terrence Lee
Genberg, Ira
Groton, James Purnell
Heady, Eugene Joseph
Hinchey, John William
Johnson, Benjamin F(ranklin), III
McGill, John Gardner
Patterson, P(ickens) Andrew
Sweeney, Neal James

HAWAII

Honolulu
Deaver, Phillip Lester
Iwai, Wilfred Kiyoshi
Kane, Joelle K.K.S.
Kobayashi, Bert Takaaki, Jr.
Kupchak, Kenneth Roy

Paia
Richman, Joel Eser

IDAHO

Boise
Storti, Philip Craig

ILLINOIS

Chicago
Angst, Gerald L.
Doyle, John Robert
Hummel, Gregory William
Kim, Michael Charles
Nowacki, James Nelson
Rogers, William John
Schoumacher, Bruce Herbert
Slutzky, Lorence Harley
Vojcanin, Sava Alexander
Vree, Roger Allen

Oakbrook Terrace
Tibble, Douglas Clair

Schaumburg
Frano, Andrew Joseph

INDIANA

Indianapolis
Albright, Terrill D.
Dutton, Clarence Benjamin

South Bend
Reinke, William John

KANSAS

Halstead
Bender, Jack Sinclair, III

KENTUCKY

Louisville
Ethridge, Larry Clayton

LOUISIANA

Lake Charles
Davidson, Van Michael, Jr.

New Orleans
Berkett, Marian Mayer
Brian, A(lexis) Morgan, Jr.
Cheatwood, Roy Clifton
Danner, William Bekurs
Shields, Lloyd Noble
Sinor, Howard Earl, Jr.

MASSACHUSETTS

Belmont
Zito, Frank R.

Boston
Edwards, Richard Lansing

Holyoke
Sarnacki, Michael Thomas

Woburn
Lovins, Nelson Preston

MICHIGAN

Detroit
Candler, James Nall, Jr.

Southfield
Antone, Nahil Peter

Troy
Alber, Phillip George

MINNESOTA

Minneapolis
Bruner, Philip Lane
Hart, B. Clarence
Mayerle, Thomas Michael
Pentelovitch, William Zane
Sand, David Byron

MISSOURI

Kansas City
Beckett, Theodore Cornwall
Conner, John Shull

Saint Louis
Colagiovanni, Joseph Alfred, Jr.
Hetlage, Robert Owen
McCarter, W. Dudley

NEBRASKA

Lincoln
Hewitt, James Watt
Smith, Richard Wendell

NEVADA

Las Vegas
Kirsch, Lynn

Padgett, Anne

Reno
Robison, Kent Richard

NEW HAMPSHIRE

Manchester
Stebbins, Henry Blanchard

NEW JERSEY

Cranford
De Luca, Thomas George

Morristown
Rose, Robert Gordon

Roseland
Hern, J. Brooke
Smith, Wendy Hope

Woodbridge
Sterling, Harold G.

NEW MEXICO

Taos
Boles, David LaVelle

NEW YORK

Albany
Couch, Mark Woodworth

Gouverneur
Leader, Robert John

Greenvale
Halper, Emanuel B(arry)

Hawthorne
Traub, Richard Kenneth

Malverne
Benigno, Thomas Daniel

New York
Brown, Paul M.
Cantor, Louis
Connolly, Kevin Jude
Grassi, Joseph F.
Herbst, Todd L.
Kamien, Kalvin
Kannry, Jack Stephen
Marcellino, Stephen Michael
Salup, Stephen
Scheiman, Eugene R.
Sigmond, Carol Ann
Silverman, Arthur Charles
Viktora, Richard Emil

Rochester
Kurland, Harold Arthur

Scarsdale
King, Robert Lucien

NORTH CAROLINA

Charlotte
Miller, John Randolph
Sink, Robert C.

Raleigh
Davis, Thomas Hill, Jr.

Winston Salem
Tate, David Kirk

OHIO

Akron
Lombardi, Frederick McKean
Ruport, Scott Hendricks

Cincinnati
Bissinger, Mark Christian

Cleveland
Climer, James Alan
Solomon, Randall Lee
Striefsky, Linda A(nn)

Columbus
Eichenberger, Jerry Alan
Gall, John R.
Hutson, Jeffrey Woodward

OKLAHOMA

Broken Arrow
Jones, Ronald Lee

OREGON

Portland
Franzke, Richard Albert
Scott, Lewis Kelly

PENNSYLVANIA

Philadelphia
Donner, Henry Jay
Fox, Reeder Rodman
Howard, William Herbert
Miller, Henry Franklin
Pratter, Gene E. K.
Walters, Christopher Kent

Pittsburgh
Stroyd, Arthur Heister

RHODE ISLAND

Providence
McAndrew, Thomas Joseph

TENNESSEE

Collierville
Scroggs, Larry Kenneth

Knoxville
Galyon, Luther Anderson, III

Memphis
Harvey, Albert C.

Nashville
Harris, Alvin Louis

TEXAS

Austin
Davis, Robert Larry
Greig, Brian Strother
Hayes, Burgain Garfield

Bastrop
Van Gilder, Derek Robert

Dallas
Doke, Marshall J., Jr.
Mira, Joseph Lawrence
Nixon, Charles Richard
Smith, Larry Van
Thau, William Albert, Jr.

Fort Worth
Crumley, John Walter

Houston
Bridges, David Manning
Brown, William Alley
Cooper, Thomas Randolph
Diaz-Arrastia, George Ravelo
Lynch, John Edward, Jr.
Sherman, Robert Taylor, Jr.
Walton, Dan Gibson

San Antonio
Bailey, Maryann George
Javore, Gary William
Wachsmuth, Robert William

UTAH

Salt Lake City
Anderson, Robert Monte
Tateoka, Reid
Verhaaren, Harold Carl

Sandy
Western, Marion Wayne

VERMONT

Rutland
Cleary, David Laurence

VIRGINIA

Chester
Connelly, Colin Charles
Gray, Charles Robert

Fairfax
Arnold, William McCauley

Mc Lean
Molineaux, Charles Borromeo
Stearns, Frank Warren

Richmond
Davenport, Bradfute Warwick, Jr.
McClard, Jack Edward

Roanoke
Barnhill, David Stan

Vienna
Titus, Bruce Earl

WASHINGTON

Seattle
Boman, Marc Allen
Murray, Michael Kent
Petrie, Gregory Steven
Prentke, Richard Ottesen
Squires, William Randolph, III
Yalowitz, Kenneth Gregg

WEST VIRGINIA

Buckhannon
McCauley, David W.

WISCONSIN

Mequon
Burroughs, Charles Edward

Milwaukee
Clark, James Richard

WYOMING

Casper
Reese, Thomas Frank

Wheatland
Hunkins, Raymond Breedlove

CANADA

ONTARIO

Brampton
DeRoma, Nicholas John

AUSTRALIA

Sydney
Wong, Christopher Wai C.

ENGLAND

London
Jalili, Mahir

NIGERIA

Victoria Island
Nwasike, Ndi Chuks

SINGAPORE

Singapore
Shetty, Nishith Kumare

ADDRESS UNPUBLISHED

Bakkensen, John Reser
Canoff, Karen Huston
Dondanville, John Wallace
Hall-Barron, Deborah
Henderson, John Robert
Klein, Linda Ann
Reiss, Jerome
Schultz, Dennis Bernard
Stinchfield, John Edward
Walker, Jordan Clyde, Sr.
Wright, Frederick Lewis, II

CONSUMER CREDIT. *See*
Commercial, consumer.

CONTRACTS. *See*
Commercial, contracts.

CORPORATE, GENERAL

UNITED STATES

ALABAMA

Anniston
Woodrow, Randall Mark

Birmingham
Garner, Robert Edward Lee
Grant, Walter Matthews
Rotch, James E.
Smith, Ralph Harrison
Spransy, Joseph William
Stewart, Joseph Grier
Trimmier, Charles Stephen, Jr.
Wilson, James Charles, Jr.

Dothan
Huskey, Dow Thobern

Huntsville
Vargo, Robert Frank

Mobile
Murchison, David Roderick
Peebles, E(mory) B(ush), III
Quina, Marion Albert, Jr.

Montgomery
Gregory, William Stanley
Wood, James Jerry

Opelika
Hand, Benny Charles, Jr.

ALASKA

Anchorage
Bankston, William Marcus
Bond, Marc Douglas
Fortier, Samuel John

ARIZONA

Kingman
Basinger, Richard Lee

Phoenix
Bauman, Frederick Carl
Case, David Leon
Coppersmith, Sam
Dunipace, Ian Douglas
Hay, John Leonard
Hicks, William Albert, III
Kasarjian, Levon, Jr.
King, Jack A.
Le Clair, Douglas Marvin
Madden, Paul Robert
Martori, Joseph Peter
McRae, Hamilton Eugene, III
Mousel, Craig Lawrence
Moya, Patrick Robert
Rosen, Sidney Marvin
Thompson, Terence William
Williams, Quinn Patrick

Scottsdale
Peshkin, Samuel David

Tucson
Glaser, Steven Jay
Robinson, Bernard Leo
Tindall, Robert Emmett

ARKANSAS

Fayetteville
Pettus, E. Lamar

Little Rock
Anderson, Philip Sidney
Campbell, George Emerson
Catlett, S. Graham
Haley, John Harvey
Marshall, William Taylor
Nelson, Edward Sheffield

Newport
Thaxton, Marvin Dell

Pine Bluff
Ramsay, Louis Lafayette, Jr.

Warren
Claycomb, Hugh Murray

CALIFORNIA

Arcadia
Gelber, Louise C(arp)
Morris, Gary Wayne

Bakersfield
Tornstrom, Robert Ernest

Belvedere Tiburon
Obninsky, Victor Peter

Berkeley
Woodhouse, Thomas Edwin

Beverly Hills
Bordy, Michael Jeffrey
Langer, Simon Hrimes
Roberts, Norman Leslie
Rosky, Burton Seymour
Russell, Irwin Emanuel

Burbank
Davis, J. Alan
Lee, Paulette Wang

Chatsworth
Weinman, Glenn Alan

Claremont
Ferguson, Cleve Robert

Coronado
Adelson, Benedict James

Costa Mesa
Daniels, James Walter
Schaaf, Douglas Allan

Culver City
Tanaka, J(eannie) E.

Cypress
Olschwang, Alan Paul

Downey
Bear, Henry Louis

El Segundo
Gambaro, Ernest Umberto
Hunter, Larry Dean

Emeryville
Ostrach, Michael Sherwood

Fremont
Chou, Yung-Ming

Fresno
Ewell, A. Ben, Jr.

Irvine
Bastiaanse, Gerard C.
Beard, Ronald Stratton
Black, William Rea
Marshall, Ellen Ruth
Shirley, Robert Bryce
Wertheim, Jay Philip
Wintrode, Ralph Charles

La Canada Flintridge
Costello, Francis William
Wallace, James Wendell

Lake Forest
Ballard, Ronald Michael

Larkspur
Burke, Robert Thomas

Los Angeles
Argue, John Clifford
Barnes, Willie R.
Basile, Paul Louis, Jr.
Battaglia, Philip Maher
Blencowe, Paul Sherwood
Carrey, Neil
Castro, Leonard Edward
Christopher, Warren
Clark, R(ufus) Bradbury
De Brier, Donald Paul
Dribin, Leland George
Gipson, Robert Edgar
Girard, Robert David
Grush, Julius Sidney
Hahn, Elliott Julius
Hughes, William Jeffrey
Kane, Margaret McDonald
Katz, Jason Lawrence
Klowden, Michael Louis
Kupietzky, Moshe J.
Lederman, Bruce Randolph
Lesser, Joan L.
Levine, Jerome Lester
May, Lawrence Edward
McDonough, Patrick Joseph
McLane, Frederick Berg
Pearman, Robert Charles
Pircher, Leo Joseph
Power, John Bruce
Shultz, John David
Stauber, Ronald Joseph
Weissman, Barry Leigh

Malibu
Hanson, Gary A.

Menlo Park
Gunderson, Robert Vernon, Jr.
McLain, Christopher M.
Mendelson, Alan Charles
Millard, Richard Steven

Mill Valley
Nemir, Donald Philip

Millbrae
Lande, James Avra

Monte Sereno
Allan, Lionel Manning

Morgan Hill
Foster, John Robert

Newport Beach
Harlan, Nancy Margaret
Jones, Sheldon Atwell
Matsen, Jeffrey Robert
Singer, Gary James

Oak Park
Vinson, William Theodore

Oakland
Anderson, Doris Elaine

Orange
Sanders, Gary Wayne

Pacific Palisades
Flattery, Thomas Long
Lagle, John Franklin

Palo Alto
Climan, Richard Elliot
Cunningham, Brian C.
Deaktor, Darryl Barnett
Hinckley, Robert Craig
Phair, Joseph Baschon
Prinz, Kristie Dawn

Palos Verdes Estates
Pierno, Anthony Robert

Pasadena
Katzman, Harvey Lawrence
Talt, Alan R.
van Schoonenberg, Robert G.
Yohalem, Harry Morton

Rancho Mirage
Goldie, Ray Robert

Riverside
Chang, Janice May

Sacramento
Foster, Douglas Taylor
Severaid, Ronald Harold

Saint Helena
Marvin, Monica Louise Wolf

San Bernardino
Nassar, William Michael

San Clemente
Geyser, Lynne M.

San Diego
Alpert, Michael Edward
Chatroo, Arthur Jay
Dorne, David J.
Edwards, James Richard
Heidrich, Robert Wesley
Mayer, James Hock
Mebane, Julie Shaffer
Shippey, Sandra Lee

San Francisco
Allen, Paul Alfred
Bagatelos, Peter Anthony
Baker, Cameron
Bauch, Thomas Jay
Brandel, Roland Eric
Burden, James Ewers
Campbell, Scott Robert
Collas, Juan Garduño, Jr.
Coombe, George William, Jr.
Devine, Antoine Maurice
Endsley, Meredith Nelson
Feller, Lloyd Harris
Finck, Kevin William

Fledderman, Harry L.
Halloran, Michael James
Kallgren, Edward Eugene
Larson, John William
Latta, Thomas Albert
Mack, John Oscar
Mann, Bruce Alan
McGuckin, John Hugh, Jr.
Millner, Dianne Maxine
Murphy, Arthur John, Jr.
Olejko, Mitchell J.
Palmer, Venrice Romito
Renfrew, Charles Byron
Seegal, John Franklin
Shenk, George H.
Tobin, James Michael
Tuthill, James Peirce
Wild, Nelson Hopkins
Woods, James Robert

San Jose
Doan, Xuyen Van
Gonzales, Daniel S.
Kraw, George Martin

San Marino
Tomich, Lillian

San Mateo
Mandel, Martin Louis

Santa Barbara
Howell, Weldon Ulric, Jr.

Santa Clara
Denten, Christopher Peter

Santa Monica
Boltz, Gerald Edmund
Homeier, Michael George
McMillan, M. Sean
McNally, Susan Fowler
Schlei, Norbert Anthony

Stockton
Taft, Perry Hazard

Studio City
Coupe, James Warnick

Sunnyvale
Ludgus, Nancy Lucke
Schiefelbein, Lester Willis, Jr.

Toluca Lake
Runquist, Lisa A.

Torrance
Petillon, Lee Ritchey

Visalia
Crowe, John T.

Walnut Creek
Nolan, David Charles
Pagter, Carl Richard

COLORADO

Aspen
Peirce, Frederick Fairbanks

Aurora
Hampton, Clyde Robert
Katz, Michael Jeffery

Avon
Marks, Richard Samuel

Castle Rock
Procopio, Joseph Guydon

Colorado Springs
Palermo, Norman Anthony
Rowan, Ronald Thomas

Delta
Wendt, John Arthur Frederic, Jr.

Denver
Aschkinasi, David Jay
Blair, Andrew Lane, Jr.
Bryans, Richard W.
Cohen, Jeffrey
Dunn, Randy Edwin
Eckstein, John Alan
Fanganello, Joseph Michael
Irwin, R. Robert
Jones, Richard Michael
Lerman, Eileen R.
Mauro, Richard Frank
McMichael, Donald Earl
Molling, Charles Francis
Newcom, Jennings Jay
Otten, Arthur Edward, Jr.
Pascoe, Donald Monte
Von Wald, Richard B.

Durango
Sherman, Lester Ivan

Edwards
Calise, Nicholas James

Englewood
Aspinwall, David Charles
Shannon, Malcolm Lloyd, Jr.

Greenwood Village
Lidstone, Herrick Kenley, Jr.

Highlands Ranch
Hagen, Glenn W(illiam)

Lakewood
Scott, Peter Bryan

Littleton
Keely, George Clayton
Ross, William Robert

CONNECTICUT

Avon
Grafstein, Joel M.

Brooklyn
Dune, Steve Charles

Darien
Beach, Stephen Holbrook

Enfield
Berger, Robert Bertram

Greenwich
Brandrup, Douglas Warren
Hurwich, Robert Allan
Nimetz, Matthew
Putman, Linda Murray
Storms, Clifford Beekman

Groton
Stuart, Peter Fred

Hartford
Coyle, Michael Lee
Del Negro, John Thomas
Dennis, Anthony James
Googins, Robert Reville
Gorski, Walter Joseph
Harrison, Thomas Flatley
Lloyd, Alex
Lloyd, James Hendrie, III
Lotstein, James Irving
Middlebrook, Stephen Beach
Richter, Donald Paul
Wetzler, Monte Edwin

Litchfield
Fiederowicz, Walter Michael

New Haven
Behling, Paul Lawrence
Robinson, Dorothy K.

New London
Johnstone, Philip MacLaren

North Grosvenordale
Jungeberg, Thomas Donald

Norwalk
Raikes, Charles FitzGerald
Shertzer, George Edwin

Redding
Russell, Allan David
Zitzmann, Kelly C.

Southbury
Auerbach, Ernest Sigmund

Southport
Sanetti, Stephen Louis

Stamford
Apfelbaum, Marc
Barreca, Christopher Anthony
Bingham, A. Walker, III
Dupont, Wesley David
Gold, Steven Michael
Lieberman, Steven Paul
Rohrer, Dean Cougill
Strone, Michael Jonathan
Swerdloff, David Alan

Waterbury
Wolfe, Harriet Munrett

West Hartford
Guenter, Raymond Albert

Westbrook
Dundas, Philip Blair, Jr.

Winsted
Finch, Frank Herschel, Jr.

DELAWARE

Wilmington
Gamble, Donald Geoffrey Bidmead
Johnston, William David
Kirk, Richard Dillon
Patton, James Leeland, Jr.
Stone, F. L. Peter

DISTRICT OF COLUMBIA

Washington
Argiropoulos, Kathleen O'Neill
Baker, Keith Leon
Barnett, Robert Bruce
Barr, Michael Blanton
Bebchick, Leonard Norman
Beckwith, Edward Jay
Berryman, Richard Byron
Bodansky, Robert Lee
Boone, Theodore Sebastian
Bowe, Richard Welbourn
Boykin, Hamilton Haight
Brooks, Daniel Townley
Brown, David Nelson
Brown, Michael DeWayne
Browne, Richard Cullen
Canfield, Edward Francis
Chanin, Michael Henry
Cohen, Louis Richard
Craft, Robert Homan, Jr.
Dunnan, Weaver White
Eisenberg, Meyer
Elcano, Mary S.
Ellicott, John LeMoyne
Falk, James Harvey, Sr.
Feldhaus, Stephen Martin
Ferrara, Ralph C.
Fox, Paul Walter
Freedman, Jay Weil
Freedman, Walter
Ginsburg, Charles David
Goelzer, Daniel Lee

Goldson, Amy Robertson
Graham, John Stuart, III
Halvorson, Newman Thorbus, Jr.
Hastings, Douglas Alfred
Hirsch, Robert Allen
Hobbs, Caswell O., III
Holtz, Edgar Wolfe
Hunt, David Wallingford
Hyde, Howard Laurence
Isbell, David Bradford
Jones, Allen, Jr.
Jordan, Jon Byron
Klein, Andrew Manning
Kramm, Deborah Lucille
Lanam, Linda Lee
Landfield, Richard
Latham, Weldon Hurd
Lavine, Henry Wolfe
Lybecker, Martin Earl
Madden, Thomas James
Mailander, William Stephen
Michaelson, Martin
Miller, Gay Davis
Morgan, Daniel Louis
Moses, Alfred Henry
Mostoff, Allan Samuel
Muir, J. Dapray
Murphy, Joseph Albert, Jr.
Murphy, Sean Patrick
Murphy, Terence Roche
Nelson, Robert Louis
Petito, Christopher Salvatore
Phillips, Leo Harold, Jr.
Pogue, L(loyd) Welch
Rafferty, James Gerard
Rau, Lee Arthur
Reid, Inez Smith
Ritter, Jeffrey Blake
Roccograndi, Anthony Joseph
Rosenhauer, James Joseph
Russin, Jonathan
Rutstein, David W.
Schmidt, William Arthur, Jr.
Schropp, James Howard
Seeger, Edwin Howard
Shay-Byrne, Olivia
Shuman, Mark Patrick
Smith, Brian William
Sorett, Stephen Michael
Stromberg, Jean Wilbur Gleason
Taylor, Richard Powell
Thomas, Ritchie Tucker
Trimble, Sandra Ellingson
Trinder, Rachel Bandele
Trooboff, Peter Dennis
Watson, Thomas C.
Wilderotter, James Arthur

FLORIDA

Alachua
Gaines, Weaver Henderson

Boca Grande
Brock, Mitchell

Boca Raton
Beber, Robert H.
Beck, Jan Scott
Buckstein, Mark Aaron
Jacobs, Joseph James
Klein, Peter William
Kline, Arlene Karin
Nussbaum, Howard Jay
Reinstein, Joel

Cape Coral
Driscoll, Dawn-Marie

Clearwater
Fine, A(rthur) Kenneth

Coconut Grove
Arboleya, Carlos Joaquin

Coral Gables
Paul, Robert

Daytona Beach
Davidson, David John

Deerfield Beach
Buck, Thomas Randolph

Edgewater
Dunagan, Walter Benton

Fort Lauderdale
Cole, James Otis
Golden, E(dward) Scott
Levitt, Preston Curtis
Schneider, Laz Levkoff

Hollywood
Hollander, Bruce Lee

Jacksonville
Braddock, Donald Layton
Kelso, Linda Yayoi
Kent, John Bradford
Lee, Lewis Swift

Jensen Beach
Stuart, Harold Cutliff

Lake Buena Vista
Schmudde, Lee Gene

Lakeland
Harris, Christy Franklin

Longwood
Rajtar, Steven Allen

Marathon Shores
Michie, Daniel Boorse, Jr.

Marco Island
Arnold, James Leonard

Melbourne
Rosenberg, Priscilla Elliott

Miami
Alonso, Antonio Enrique
Berley, David Richard
Berritt, Harold Edward
Bronis, Stephen Jay
Chabrow, Penn Benjamin
Dreize, Livia Rebbeka
Fishman, Lewis Warren
Fontes, J. Mario F., Jr.
Golden, Donald Alan
Granata, Linda M.
Gross, Leslie Jay
Grossman, Robert Louis
Hoffman, Larry J.
Landy, Burton Aaron
Lyubkin, Rina
Murai, Rene Vicente
Perez, Luis Alberto
Roman, Ronald Peter
Samole, Myron Michael
Stuever, Fred Ray
Touby, Richard
Weiner, Lawrence
Zamora, Antonio Rafael

Naples
Budd, David Glenn

New Port Richey
Focht, Theodore Harold

North Palm Beach
Coyle, Dennis Patrick
Lane, Matthew Jay

Orlando
Blackford, Robert Newton
Capouano, Albert D.
Chong, Stephen Chu Ling
Conti, Louis Thomas Moore
Frey, Louis, Jr.
Hendry, Robert Ryon
Ioppolo, Frank S., Jr.
Pierce, John Gerald (Jerry Pierce)
Worthington, Daniel Glen
Yates, Leighton Delevan, Jr.

Palm Beach
Crawford, Sandra Kay

Parkland
Masanoff, Michael David

Saint Petersburg
Hudkins, John W.
Ross, Howard Philip

Sarasota
Fetterman, James Charles
Herb, F(rank) Steven
Janney, Oliver James
Raimi, Burton Louis

Shalimar
Chesser, David Michael

Tallahassee
Miller, Morris Henry

Tampa
Crawford, Donald Morse
Doliner, Nathaniel Lee
Emerton, Robert Walter, III
Grammig, Robert James
O'Neill, Albert Clarence, Jr.
Roberson, Bruce Heerdt

Tavernier
Lupino, James Samuel

Vero Beach
Case, Douglas Manning

West Palm Beach
Ballot, Alissa E.
Barnett, Charles Dawson
Beall, Kenneth Sutter, Jr.
Gildan, Phillip Clarke
Zeller, Ronald John

GEORGIA

Albany
Moorhead, William David, III

Athens
Davis, Claude-Leonard

Atlanta
Barkoff, Rupert Mitchell
Bisbee, David George
Brecher, Armin George
Byrne, Granville Bland, III
Calhoun, Scott Douglas
Cargill, Robert Mason
Chisholm, Tommy
Coxe, Tench Charles
Durrett, James Frazer, Jr.
Edge, J(ulian) Dexter, Jr.
Fiorentino, Carmine
Gladden, Joseph Rhea, Jr.
Harkey, Robert Shelton
Hasson, James Keith, Jr.
Isaf, Fred Thomas
Jeffries, McChesney Hill, Jr.
Lackland, Theodore Howard
Lee, William Clement, III
Linder, Harvey Ronald
Lower, Robert Cassel
Manley, David Bott, III
Marianes, William Byron
Meyer, William Lorne
Moderow, Joseph Robert
Moeling, Walter Goos, IV
Ortiz, Jay Richard Gentry
Pless, Laurance Davidson
Pryor, Shepherd Green, III
Reed, Glen Alfred
Somers, Fred Leonard, Jr.
Stallings, Ronald Denis
Williams, Neil, Jr.

Augusta
Lee, Lansing Burrows, Jr.

Dunwoody
Callison, James W.

Marietta
Ahlstrom, Michael Joseph
Lurie, Jeanne Flora

Rome
McCrory, Aldous Desmond

Roswell
Baker, Anita Diane

Savannah
Friedman, Julian Richard
Searcy, William Nelson

Sea Island
Revoile, Charles Patrick

HAWAII

Honolulu
Asai-Sato, Carol Yuki
Char, Vernon Fook Leong
Coates, Bradley Allen
Ingersoll, Richard King
Marks, Michael J.
Miller, Clifford Joel
Nakata, Gary Kenji
Okinaga, Lawrence Shoji
Reber, David James
Tharp, James Wilson

Kaneohe
Huber, Thomas P.

IDAHO

Boise
Crossland, Samuel Hess
Schild, Raymond Douglas
Thomas, Eugene C.

Idaho Falls
Whittier, Monte Ray

ILLINOIS

Abbott Park
Brock, Charles Marquis

Arlington Heights
Hoenicke, Edward Henry

Bloomington
Eckols, Thomas Aud

Buffalo Grove
Kole, Julius S.

Chicago
Anderson, J. Trent
Athas, Gus James
Axley, Frederick William
Barack, Peter Joseph
Barnes, James Garland, Jr.
Berry, Richard Morgan
Bloom, Christopher Arthur
Boodell, Thomas Joseph, Jr.
Bowman, Phillip Boynton
Braun, Frederick B.
Burgdoerfer, Jerry
Chester, Mark Vincent
Chudzinski, Mark Adam
Clemens, Richard Glenn
Clinton, Edward Xavier
Coughlan, Kenneth L.
Craven, George W.
Cross, Chester Joseph
Davis, Scott Jonathan
Domanskis, Alexander Rimas
Donohoe, Jerome Francis
Drymalski, Raymond Hibner
Durchslag, Stephen P.
Esrick, Jerald Paul
Fein, Roger Gary
Felsenthal, Steven Altus
Filpi, Robert Alan
Finke, Robert Forge
Frisch, Sidney, Jr.
Garber, Samuel B.
Gates, Stephen Frye
Gavin, John Neal
Gerstein, Mark Douglas
Goldman, Michael P.
Greenbaum, Kenneth
Hamblet, Michael Jon
Hayward, Thomas Zander, Jr.
Head, Patrick James
Heinz, William Denby
Henning, Joel Frank
Henry, Robert John
Hester, Thomas Patrick
Homburger, Thomas Charles
Howell, R(obert) Thomas, Jr.
Janich, Daniel Nicholas
Johnson, Gary Thomas
Johnson, Lael Frederic
Kamerick, Eileen Ann
Kaufman, Andrew Michael
Kirkpatrick, John Everett
Knox, James Edwin
Kohlstedt, James August
Kolmin, Kenneth Guy
Kuntz, William Richard, Jr.
Ladd, Jeffrey Raymond
Landsman, Stephen A.
Lang, Gordon, Jr.
Lauderbale, Katherine Sue
Lorentzen, John Carol
Lubin, Donald G.
Maher, Francesca Marciniak
Malkin, Cary Jay
McCrohon, Craig
McDermott, John H(enry)
McErlean, Charles Flavian, Jr.
McGrath, William Joseph

McLaren, Richard Wellington, Jr.
McMahon, Thomas Michael
Michaels, Richard Edward
Miller, John Leed
Miller, Paul J.
Miller, Ronald Stuart
Murdock, Charles William
Niehoff, Philip John
Peter, Bernard George
Polk, Lee Thomas
Quinlan, William Joseph, Jr.
Rauner, Vincent Joseph
Redman, Clarence Owen
Reich, Allan J.
Reicin, Ronald Ian
Rhind, James Thomas
Rosic, George S.
Ruttenberg, Harold Seymour
Sabl, John J.
Sawyier, Michael Tod
Schreck, Robert A., Jr.
Schulz, Keith Donald
Shank, Suzanne Adams
Shank, William O.
Shindler, Donald A.
Siegel, Howard Jerome
Silets, Harvey Marvin
Smedinghoff, Thomas J.
Steinberg, Morton M.
Swibel, Steven Warren
Thomas, Frederick Bradley
Thomas, Stephen Paul
Thompson, David F.
Veverka, Donald John
Vranicar, Michael Gregory
Wade, Edwin Lee
Wahlen, Edwin Alfred
Wander, Herbert Stanton
Whalen, Wayne W.
Wilson, Roger Goodwin
Winkler, Charles Howard
Wolfe, David Louis

Chicago Heights
Wigell, Raymond George

Crete
Teykl, James Stephen

Decatur
Reising, Richard P.

Deerfield
Gaither, John Francis, Jr.
Oettinger, Julian Alan
Staubitz, Arthur Frederick

Dekalb
Witmer, John Harper, Jr.

Downers Grove
Mason, Peter Ian

Gurnee
Southern, Robert Allen

Hinsdale
Wise, Nancy Joan

Hoffman Estates
Kelly, Anastasia Donovan

La Grange
Kerr, Alexander Duncan, Jr.

Lake Forest
Giza, David Alan

Lake Zurich
Scott, John Joseph

Lansing
Hill, Philip

Lincolnshire
Para, Gerard Albert

Lisle
May, Frank Brendan, Jr.

Long Grove
Obert, Paul Richard

Morris
Rooks, John Newton

North Chicago
de Lasa, José M.

Northbrook
Carter, James Woodford, Jr.
Fox, Michael Edward
Lapin, Harvey I.
Pollak, Jay Mitchell
Sernett, Richard Patrick

Northfield
Denkewalter, Kim Richard

Oak Brook
O'Brien, Walter Joseph, II
Oldfield, E. Lawrence

Oakbrook Terrace
Fenech, Joseph Charles

Palatine
Cannon, Benjamin Winton
Wardell, John Watson

Park Ridge
Hegarty, Mary Frances

Peoria
Atterbury, Robert Rennie, III
Elias, John Samuel
Winget, Walter Winfield

Quincy
Rapp, James Anthony

Rockford
Johnson, Thomas Stuart

Knight, William D., Jr.
Rudy, Elmer Clyde

Schaumburg
Vitale, James Drew

Schiller Park
Congalton, Christopher William

Skokie
Bauer, Michael
Gotkin, Michael Stanley

Taylorville
Austin, Daniel William

Toledo
Prather, William C., III

Urbana
Webber, Carl Maddra

Warrenville
Boardman, Robert A.

INDIANA

Bloomington
Grodner, Geoffrey Mitchell

Columbus
Zaharako, Lew Daleure

Elkhart
Harman, John Royden

Evansville
Baugh, Jerry Phelps
Knight, Jeffrey Lin
Wallace, Keith M.

Fort Wayne
Lawson, Jack Wayne
Shoaff, Thomas Mitchell

Granger
Lambert, George Robert

Huntington
Gordon, William Stout

Indianapolis
Betley, Leonard John
Blythe, James David, II
Coons, Stephen Merle
Deer, Richard Elliott
Dorocke, Lawrence Francis
Dutton, Clarence Benjamin
Dutton, Stephen James
Evans, Daniel Fraley, Jr.
FitzGibbon, Daniel Harvey
Gilliland, John Campbell, II
Hackman, Marvin Lawrence
Kahlenbeck, Howard, Jr.
Kappes, Philip Spangler
Koeller, Robert Marion
Maine, Michael Roland
Neff, Robert Matthew
Patel, Apexa
Patrick, William Bradshaw
Paul, Stephen Howard
Roberts, Patricia Susan
Russell, David Williams
Schwarz, James Harold
Strain, James Arthur
Tabler, Bryan G.
Vandivier, Blair Robert

Merrillville
Bowman, Carol Ann

Newburgh
Dewey, Dennis James

South Bend
Carey, John Leo

Zionsville
Bradley, Charles Harvey, Jr.

IOWA

Burlington
Hoth, Steven Sergey

Council Bluffs
Pechacek, Frank Warren, Jr.

Davenport
Shaw, Elizabeth Orr

Des Moines
Austin, Bradford Lyle
Bennett, Edward James
Brown, Paul Edmondson
Carroll, Frank James
Graves, Bruce
Seitzinger, Edward Francis
Simpson, Lyle Lee

Iowa City
Downer, Robert Nelson

Mason City
Winston, Harold Ronald

Muscatine
Coulter, Charles Roy

Sioux City
Madsen, George Frank

West Des Moines
Brown, John Lewis

KANSAS

Bucyrus
Hoffman, John Raymond

Garden City
Pierce, Ricklin Ray

Halstead
Bender, Jack Sinclair, III

Hutchinson
Swearer, William Brooks

Overland Park
Ellis, Jeffrey Orville
Westerhaus, Douglas Bernard

Shawnee Mission
Snyder, Willard Breidenthal

Topeka
Frost, Brian Standish
Rainey, William Joel

Westwood
Devlin, James Richard

Wichita
Depew, Spencer Long
Johnson, Kevin Blaine
Stephenson, Richard Ismert

KENTUCKY

Bowling Green
Catron, Stephen Barnard

Lexington
Lester, Roy David

Louisville
Bardenwerper, William Burr
Buckaway, William Allen, Jr.
Keeney, Steven Harris
Luber, Thomas J(ulian)
Mellen, Francis Joseph, Jr.
Northern, Richard
Pedley, Lawrence Lindsay
Reed, D. Gary
Tannon, Jay Middleton
Vish, Donald H.
Welsh, Sir Alfred John

Newport
Siverd, Robert Joseph

Owensboro
Miller, James Monroe

Prospect
Aberson, Leslie Donald

LOUISIANA

Baton Rouge
Richards, Marta Alison

Covington
Shinn, Clinton Wesley

Cut Off
Cheramie, Carlton Joseph

Lafayette
Breaux, Paul Joseph
Myers, Stephen Hawley
Skinner, Michael David

Monroe
Curry, Robert Lee, III

New Orleans
Abbott, Hirschel Theron, Jr.
Beahm, Franklin D.
Fierke, Thomas Garner
Miller, Joseph Bayard
Mote, Clyde A
Murchison, Henry Dillon
Page, John Marshall, Jr.
Rinker, Andrew, Jr.
Simon, H(uey) Paul

Shreveport
Cox, John Thomas, Jr.
Jeter, Katherine Leslie Brash
Roberts, Robert, III

MAINE

Brunswick
Owen, H. Martyn

Falmouth
Curran, Richard Emery, Jr.

Portland
Friedrich, Craig William
Keenan, James Francis

Yarmouth
Webster, Peter Bridgman

MARYLAND

Baltimore
Chernow, Jeffrey Scott
Chriss, Timothy D. A.
Cook, Bryson Leitch
Curran, Robert Bruce
Haines, Thomas W. W.
Kandel, Peter Thomas
Katz, Martha Lessman
Mogol, Alan Jay
Moser, M(artin) Peter
Robinson, Zelig
Scriggins, Larry Palmer
Wheatley, Charles Henry, III

Bel Air
Miller, Max Dunham, Jr.

Bethesda
Cohen, Jay Loring
Dickstein, Sidney
Feuerstein, Donald Martin
Garson, Jack A.
Hagberg, Viola Wilgus
Himelfarb, Stephen Roy
Menaker, Frank H., Jr.
Tanenbaum, Richard Hugh
Weinberger, Alan David

Brookeville
Johns, Warren LeRoi

Burtonsville
Covington, Marlow Stanley

Chevy Chase
Schwartzman, Robin Berman

College Park
Gobbel, Luther Russell
Yoho, Billy Lee

Columbia
Maseritz, Guy B.

Easton
Maffitt, James Strawbridge

Lutherville Timonium
Freeland, Charles

New Market
Gabriel, Eberhard John

Prince Frederick
Reynolds, Christopher John

Riverdale
Meyers, William Vincent

Rockville
Katz, Steven Martin
Millstein, Leo Lee
Smith, David Robinson

Towson
Miller, Herbert H.

Westminster
Staples, Lyle Newton

MASSACHUSETTS

Billerica
Lewis, Edwin Leonard, III

Boston
Abbott, William Saunders
Bernhard, Alexander Alfred
Bines, Harvey Ernest
Bohnen, Michael J.
Borenstein, Milton Conrad
Bornheimer, Allen Millard
Buccella, William Victor
Cekala, Chester
Cherwin, Joel Ira
Dello Iacono, Paul Michael
Elfman, Eric Michael
Engel, David Lewis
Fischer, Eric Robert
Goldman, Richard Harris
Greer, Gordon Bruce
Haddad, Ernest Mudarri
Halligan, Brendan Patrick
Hauser, Harry Raymond
Hester, Patrick Joseph
Hines, Edward Francis, Jr.
Jordan, Alexander Joseph, Jr.
Korb, Kenneth Allan
Loeser, Hans Ferdinand
Malley, Robert John
Matzka, Michael Alan
Mooney, Michael Edward
O'Connell, Joseph Francis, III
O'Neill, Philip Daniel, Jr.
Patterson, John de la Roche, Jr.
Redlich, Marc
Rideout, David Edward
Rudolph, James Leonard
Siegel, Steven Richard
Soden, Richard Allan
Spelfogel, Scott David
Stokes, James Christopher
Storer, Thomas Perry
Testa, Richard Joseph
Thibeault, George Walter
Weaver, Paul David
White, Barry Bennett
Williams, Robert Dana
Wolfson, Jeffrey Steven

Braintree
Mullare, T(homas) Kenwood, Jr.

Cambridge
Connors, Frank Joseph

Chestnut Hill
Chyten, Edwin Richard

Fall River
Gordan, Cynthia Lee

Framingham
Meltzer, Jay H.

Gardner
Sans, Henri Louis, Jr.

Holden
Price, Robert DeMille

Hyannis
Horn, Everett Byron, Jr.

Ipswich
Getchell, Charles Willard, Jr.

Lincoln
Schwartz, Edward Arthur

Longmeadow
Quinn, Andrew Peter, Jr.

Lowell
Cook, Charles Addison
Curtis, James Theodore

Natick
Grassia, Thomas Charles

Newton
Frankenheim, Samuel
Glazer, Donald Wayne

Newton Center
Snyder, John Gorvers

Springfield
Weiss, Ronald Phillip

Waltham
Barnes-Brown, Peter Newton
Borod, Donald Lee

Wellesley
Goglia, Charles A., Jr.
Marx, Peter A.

Weston
Bateman, Thomas Robert
Dickie, Robert Benjamin

Worcester
Donnelly, James Corcoran, Jr.
Whipple, Robert Jenks

MICHIGAN

Ada
Mc Callum, Charles Edward

Ann Arbor
Dew, Thomas Edward
Keppelman, Nancy

Battle Creek
Markey, James Kevin

Bloomfield Hills
Berlow, Robert Alan
Cunningham, Gary H.
Gold, Edward David
Janover, Robert H.
Kasischke, Louis Walter
Williams, J. Bryan

Dearborn
Demorest, Mark Stuart

Detroit
Brustad, Orin Daniel
Bushnell, George Edward, Jr.
Calkins, Stephen
Carney, Thomas Daly
Darlow, Julia Donovan
Deason, Herold McClure
Deron, Edward Michael
Felt, Julia Kay
Johnson, Cynthia L(e) M(ae)
Kamins, John Mark
Krsul, John Aloysius, Jr.
Kuehn, George E.
Lewand, F. Thomas
McKim, Samuel John, III
Myers, Rodman Nathaniel
Pearce, Harry Jonathan
Rohr, Richard David
Shaevsky, Mark
Sullivan, Thomas Michael
Thoms, David Moore

Farmington
Cooper, Douglas Kenneth
Harms, Donald C.

Farmington Hills
Moore, Roy F.

Gladwin
Menke, William Charles

Grand Rapids
Engbers, James Arend
Titley, Larry J.

Grosse Pointe
Avant, Grady, Jr.
Phillips, Elliott Hunter

Ishpeming
Steward, James Brian

Jackson
Curtis, Philip James

Kalamazoo
Gordon, Edgar George

Lansing
Gallagher, Byron Patrick, Jr.
Linder, Iris Kay

Livonia
Hoffman, Barry Paul

Midland
Gootee, Jane Marie

Monroe
Lipford, Rocque Edward

Muskegon
Nehra, Gerald Peter

Northville
Leavitt, Martin Jack

Plymouth
Morgan, Donald Crane

Saint Clair Shores
Stevens, Clark Valentine

Southfield
Dawson, Dennis Ray
Kaplow, Robert David
Labe, Robert Brian
Schwartz, Robert H.

Traverse City
Kubiak, Jon Stanley

Troy
Allen, James Lee
Chapman, Conrad Daniel
Dillon, Joseph Francis
Haron, David Lawrence
McGlynn, Joseph Michael
McKeone, Keri Marie
Ponitz, John Allan

Walled Lake
Seglund, Bruce Richard

Warren
Bridenstine, Louis Henry, Jr.

MINNESOTA

Anoka
Erickson, Phillip Arthur

Bayport
Bernick, Alan E.

Bloomington
Broeker, John Milton

Duluth
Nys, John Nikki

Eden Prairie
Nilles, John Michael

Fridley
Savelkoul, Donald Charles

Grand Rapids
Licke, Wallace John

Hopkins
Hoard, Heidi Marie
Hunter, Donald Forrest
Zotaley, Byron Leo

Little Canada
Hardman, James Charles

Minneapolis
Bergerson, David Raymond
Chamberlain, James Robert
Drucker, Christine Marie
Freeman, Todd Ira
Grayson, Edward Davis
Greener, Ralph Bertram
Hackley, David Kenneth
Hanbery, Donna Eva
Kaplan, Sheldon
Klein, William David
Laitinen, Sari K.M.
Lofstrom, Mark D.
Marshall, Siri Swenson
McNamara, Michael John
McNeil, Mark Sanford
Mellum, Gale Robert
Nordaune, Roselyn Jean
Petersen, Mark Allen
Radmer, Michael John
Ryan, Thomas J.
Sanner, Royce Norman
Stageberg, Roger V.
Witort, Janet Lee
Yost, Gerald B.

Rochester
Orwoll, Gregg S. K.

Saint Paul
Chester, Stephanie Ann
Dietz, Charlton Henry
Hansen, Eric Peter
Knapp, John Anthony
LeVander, Bernhard Wilhelm
Maffei, Rocco John
Rebane, John T.
Sheahan, Michael John
Ursu, John Joseph
Winthrop, Sherman

Wayzata
Alton, Howard Robert, Jr.

Woodbury
Norton, John William

MISSISSIPPI

Bay Saint Louis
Bernstein, Joseph

Diamondhead
Reddien, Charles Henry, II

Jackson
Clark, David Wright
Corlew, John Gordon
Travis, Jay A., III

MISSOURI

Cape Girardeau
O'Loughlin, John Patrick

Chesterfield
Fagerberg, Roger Richard
Hier, Marshall David
Pollihan, Thomas Henry

Clayton
Tremayne, Eric Flory

Hillsboro
Howald, John William

Independence
Rice, Guy Garner

Kansas City
Bartunek, Robert R(ichard), Jr.
Blackwood, George Dean, Jr.
Brous, Thomas Richard
Egan, Charles Joseph, Jr.
English, Mark Gregory
Gorman, Gerald Warner
Graham, Harold Steven
Henson, Harold Eugene
Howes, Brian Thomas
Kaufman, Michelle Stark
Rickert, Brian Patrick
Shughart, Donald Louis
Willy, Thomas Ralph
Wrobley, Ralph Gene

Lamar
Geddie, Rowland Hill, III

Macon
Parkinson, Paul K.

Rolla
Thomas, William Herman, Jr.

Saint Louis
Anderson, Anthony LeClaire
Aylward, Ronald Lee
Barken, Bernard Allen
Boggs, Beth Clemens
Brickler, John Weise
Cook, Thomas Alfred Ashley
Cullen, James D.
Dorwart, Donald Bruce
Duesenberg, Richard William
Godiner, Donald Leonard
Graham, Robert Clare, III
Harris, Harvey Alan
Inkley, John James, Jr.
Leontsinis, George John
Luberda, George Joseph
Mattern, Keith Edward
Metcalfe, Walter Lee, Jr.
Miller, Dwight Whittemore
Neville, James Morton
Paule, Donald Wayne
Pickle, Robert Douglas
Poscover, Maury B.
Rose, Albert Schoenburg
Sant, John Talbot
Schoene, Kathleen Snyder
Schramm, Paul Howard
Tierney, Michael Edward
Van Cleve, William Moore
Watters, Richard Donald
Winning, J(ohn) Patrick
Withers, W. Wayne
Wolff, Frank Pierce, Jr.

Springfield
Baxter-Smith, Gregory John
McCurry, Bruce

MONTANA

Billings
Beiswanger, Gary Lee

Missoula
George, Alexander Andrew

NEBRASKA

Lincoln
Hewitt, James Watt
Johnson, Warren Charles
Rembolt, James Earl

Omaha
Barmettler, Joseph John
Dolan, James Vincent
Griffin, Patrick Edward
Hamann, Deryl Frederick
Harr, Lawrence Francis
Kreifels, Frank Anthony
Krutter, Forrest Nathan
Rock, Harold L.
von Bernuth, Carl W.
Vosburg, Bruce David

NEVADA

Las Vegas
Ashleman, Ivan Reno, II
Hinueber, Mark Arthur
Lovell, Carl Erwin, Jr.
Nasky, H(arold) Gregory
Norville, Craig Hubert
Ritchie, Douglas V.
Singer, Michael Howard
Wilson, Joseph Morris, III

NEW HAMPSHIRE

Concord
Potter, Fred Leon

Hanover
Gardner, Peter Jaglom

Manchester
Monson, John Rudolph
Scannell, Timothy C.
Wiebusch, Richard Vernon

Portsmouth
DeGrandpre, Charles Allyson
Shaines, Robert Arthur

Rochester
Jones, Franklin Charles

NEW JERSEY

Basking Ridge
DeBois, James Adolphus

Bridgewater
Ball, Owen Keith, Jr.
Linett, David

Camden
Furey, John J.

Cranbury
Bronner, William Roche
Iatesta, John Michael

East Rutherford
Wadler, Arnold L.

Edgewater
Virelli, Louis James, Jr.

Edison
Goldfarb, Ronald Carl

Elizabeth
Budanitsky, Sander

Far Hills
Corash, Richard

Florham Park
Calabrese, Arnold Joseph
Kandravy, John
Siino, Salvatore G.

Hackensack
Greenberg, Steven Morey
Kaps, Warren Joseph
Masi, John Roger
Strull, James Richard

Iselin
Dornbusch, Arthur A., II

Kenilworth
Connors, Joseph Conlin

Lebanon
Johnstone, Irvine Blakeley, III
Mattielli, Louis

Little Silver
Schmidt, Daniel Edward, IV

Livingston
Klein, Peter Martin

Lyndhurst
Lasky, David

Morristown
Aspero, Benedict Vincent
Barba, Julius William
Gillen, James Robert
Humick, Thomas Charles Campbell

New Brunswick
Miller, Arthur Harold
Scott, David Rodick

New Providence
Adler, Nadia C.

Newark
Creenan, Katherine Heras
Knee, Stephen H.
Liftin, John Matthew
Reich, Laurence

Paramus
Gilbert, Stephen Alan

Parsippany
Chobot, John Charles

Pitman
Cloues, Edward Blanchard, II

Princeton
Burgess, Robert Kyle
Katzenbach, Nicholas deBelleville
Kirstein, Philip Lawrence
Miller, Richard Mark

Ramsey
Ogden, John Hamilton

Ridgewood
Harris, Micalyn Shafer

Saddle Brook
Pearlman, Peter Steven

Secaucus
Fitzpatrick, Harold Francis
Holt, Michael Bartholomew
Israels, Michael Jozef

Somerset
Green, Jeffrey C.

Somerville
Freedman, Stuart Joel
Fuerst, Steven Bernard
Hutcheon, Peter David

Summit
Woller, James Alan

Teaneck
Stone, Sheldon

Tenafly
Spike, Michele Kahn

Cleveland
Baxter, Howard H.
Braverman, Herbert Leslie
Coquillette, William Hollis
Dampeer, John Lyell
Ensign, Gregory Moore
Falsgraf, William Wendell
Freimuth, Marc William
Gherlein, Gerald Lee
Groetzinger, Jon, Jr.
Horvitz, Michael John
Langer, Carlton Earl
Markey, Robert Guy
Marting, Michael G.
Mc Cartan, Patrick Francis
Meyer, G. Christopher
Neff, Owen Calvin
Ollinger, W. James
Owendoff, Stephen Peter
Pearlman, Samuel Segel
Pinkas, Robert Paul
Shore, Michael Allan
Shumaker, Roger Lee
Sogg, Wilton Sherman
Stevens, Thomas Charles
Waldeck, John Walter, Jr.

Columbus
Barrett, Phillip Heston
Brinkman, Dale Thomas
Casey, John Frederick
DeRousie, Charles Stuart
Dunlay, Catherine Telles
Fahey, Richard Paul
Fisher, Fredrick Lee
Frasier, Ralph Kennedy
Schwartz, Robert S.
Starkoff, Alan Gary
Stinehart, Roger Ray
Tarpy, Thomas Michael

Dayton
Taronji, Jaime, Jr.
Watts, Steven Richard

Dublin
Inzetta, Mark Stephen

Hamilton
Meyers, Pamela Sue

Lancaster
Libert, Donald Joseph

Lebanon
Benedict, Ronald Louis

Massillon
Donohoe, James Day

Mount Vernon
Rose, Kim Matthew

North Canton
Dettinger, Warren Walter

Shaker Heights
Cherchiglia, Dean Kenneth

Sharonville
Hanket, Mark John

Sylvania
Kline, James Edward

Toledo
O'Connell, Maurice Daniel
Webb, Thomas Irwin, Jr.

Twinsburg
Kramer, Timothy Eugene

Wickliffe
Kidder, Fred Dockstater

Wooster
Moore, Arthur William

Worthington
Minton, Harvey Steiger

Youngstown
Giannini, Matthew Carlo
Newman, Christopher John

OKLAHOMA

Bartlesville
Roff, Alan Lee

Broken Arrow
Jones, Ronald Lee

Norman
Talley, Richard Bates

Oklahoma City
Barth, J. Edward
Fuller, G. M.
High, David Royce
McBride, Kenneth Eugene
Mock, Randall Don
Paul, William George
Rockett, D. Joe
Stanley, Brian Jordan
Steinhorn, Irwin Harry

Stroud
Swanson, Robert Lee

Tulsa
Arrington, John Leslie, Jr.
Biolchini, Robert Fredrick
Brune, Kenneth Leonard
Cooper, Richard Casey
Cundiff, James Nelson
Eagleton, Edward John
Gaberino, John Anthony, Jr.
Huffman, Robert Allen, Jr.
Kihle, Donald Arthur
Mackey, Steven R.
Moffett, J. Denny

Pritchard, William Winther
Sneed, James Lynde
Spiegelberg, Frank David
Williamson, Walter Bland

OREGON

Albany
Thompson, Orval Nathan

Lake Oswego
Kuntz, Joel Dubois
Rasmussen, Richard Robert

Medford
Shaw, Barry N.

Portland
Abravanel, Allan Ray
Brownstein, Richard Joseph
Burt, Robert Gene
DuBoff, Leonard David
Glasgow, Robert Efrom
Grossmann, Ronald Stanyer
Hanna, Harry Mitchell
Krahmer, Donald Leroy, Jr.
Van Valkenburg, Edgar Walter

PENNSYLVANIA

Allentown
Agger, James H.
Scherline, Jay Alan

Ambler
Albright, Audra A.

Bethlehem
Hemphill, Meredith, Jr.

Blue Bell
Barron, Harold Sheldon
Scudder, Charles Seelye Kellgren

Bradford
Hauser, Christopher George

Grove City
McBride, Milford Lawrence, Jr.

Harleysville
Strauss, Catherine B.

Harrisburg
Hanson, Robert DeLolle

Hollidaysburg
Evey, Merle Kenton

Johnstown
Glosser, William Louis

Kennett Square
Partnoy, Ronald Allen

Lancaster
Duroni, Charles Eugene
Gray, Kathleen Ann
Lewis, Alvin Bower, Jr.

Lehigh Valley
McGonagle, John Joseph, Jr.

Malvern
Cameron, John Clifford
Doerr, John Maxwell
Quay, Thomas Emery

Marietta
Shumaker, Harold Dennis

Mc Murray
Brzustowicz, John Cinq-Mars

Media
Cramp, John Franklin
Harvey, Alice Elease
McNitt, David Garver

Milton
Davis, Preston Lindner

Moon Township
Lipson, Barry J.

Newtown Square
Crowley, James Michael

Norristown
Aman, George Matthias, III

North Wales
Brady, George Charles, III

Paoli
Chiacchiere, Mark Dominic

Philadelphia
Baum, E. Harris
Berger, Lawrence Howard
Bogutz, Jerome Edwin
Chimples, George
Clark, William H., Jr.
Colli, Bart Joseph
Cooper, Wendy Fein
Cramer, Harold
Cross, Milton H.
DeBunda, Salvatore Michael
Del Raso, Joseph Vincent
Doran, William Michael
Drake, William Frank, Jr.
Dubin, Stephen Victor
Gadon, Steven Franklin
Girard-diCarlo, David Franklin
Goldman, Gary Craig
Goldman, Jerry Stephen
Gough, John Francis
Grady, Thomas Michael
Granoff, Gail Patricia
Heisman, Norman M.

Horn Epstein, Phyllis Lynn
Hunter, Jack Duval
Hunter, James Austen, Jr.
Krzyzanowski, Richard L(ucien)
Liu, Diana Chua
Loveless, George Group
McAneny, Eileen S.
Meigs, John Forsyth
O'Brien, William Jerome, II
Pillion, Michael Leith
Promislo, Daniel
Real, Frank Joseph, Jr.
Reiss, John Barlow
Sartorius, Peter S.
Spolan, Harmon Samuel
Stroebel, John Stephen
Subak, John Thomas
Wert, Robert Clifton
Wolff, Deborah H(orowitz)

Pittsburgh
Aderson, Sanford M.
Boswell, William Paret
Conti, Joy Flowers
Crayne, Larry Randolph
Demmler, John Henry
Frank, Ronald William
Hardie, James Hiller
Helmrich, Joel Marc
Herchenroether, Peter Young
Hess, Emerson Garfield
King, Paul Martin
Letwin, Jeffrey William
Messner, Robert Thomas
Murdoch, David Armor
Newlin, William Rankin
Nicoll, John
Nute, Leslie F.
Parker, James Lee
Pugliese, Robert Francis
Reed, W. Franklin
Sutton, William Dwight
Walton, Jon David
Wiley, S. Donald
Wilkinson, James Allan

Reading
Page, Clemson North, Jr.
Roland, John Wanner

Uniontown
Coldren, Ira Burdette, Jr.

Valley Forge
Bovaird, Brendan Peter
Posner, Ernest Gary
Walters, Bette Jean

Wayne
Donnella, Michael Andre
Kalogredis, Vasilios J.

West Chester
Osborn, John Edward

Wilkes Barre
Roth, Eugene
Ufberg, Murray

Wormleysburg
Cherewka, Michael

Wynnewood
Stapleton, Larrick B.

RHODE ISLAND

Barrington
Soutter, Thomas Douglas

Newport
McConnell, David Kelso

Pawtucket
Kranseler, Lawrence Michael

Providence
Carlotti, Stephen Jon
Davis, Andrew Hambley, Jr.
Donnelly, Kevin William
Salvadore, Guido Richard

SOUTH CAROLINA

Charleston
Cannon, Hugh
Clement, Robert Lebby, Jr.

Columbia
Nexsen, Julian Jacobs

Conway
Martin, Gregory Keith

Greenville
Dobson, Robert Albertus, III
Edwards, Harry LaFoy
Graben, Eric Knox
Phillips, Joseph Brantley, Jr.

Hilton Head Island
Hagoort, Thomas Henry
Scarminach, Charles Anthony

Kiawah Island
Coyle, Martin Adolphus, Jr.

Salem
Everett, C(harles) Curtis

SOUTH DAKOTA

Sioux Falls
Johnson, Thomas Jerald

TENNESSEE

Brentwood
Provine, John C.

Chattanooga
Durham, J(oseph) Porter, Jr.

Germantown
Waddell, Phillip Dean

Knoxville
Congleton, Joseph Patrick
Howard, Lewis Spilman
McCall, Jack Humphreys, Jr.
Worthington, Carole Yard Lynch

Lebanon
Blackstock, James Fielding

Memphis
Chambliss, Prince Caesar, Jr.
Friedman, Robert Michael
Jalenak, James Bailey
Kahn, Bruce Meyer
Masterson, Kenneth Rhodes
Rutledge, Roger Keith
Schuler, Walter E.
Tate, Stonewall Shepherd

Murfreesboro
Heffington, Jack Grisham

Nashville
Berry, William Wells
Carr, Davis Haden
Fish, Donald Winston
Mayden, Barbara Mendel
Tuke, Robert Dudley
Woods, Larry David

Parsons
Townsend, Edwin Clay

Signal Mountain
Anderson, Charles Hill

TEXAS

Abilene
Sartain, James Edward
Whitten, C. G.

Austin
Dowd, Steven Milton
Gallerano, Andrew John
Gangstad, John Erik
Godfrey, Cullen Michael
Matheson, Daniel Nicholas, III
Osborn, Joe Allen
Roan, Forrest Calvin, Jr.
Tice, Laurie Dietrich
Tyson, Laura Lanza

Beaumont
Cavaliere, Frank Joseph

Bellaire
Hollrah, David

Brownfield
Moore, Bradford L.

Brownsville
Ray, Mary Louise Ryan

Dallas
Adelman, Graham Lewis
Beuttenmuller, Rudolf William
Blachly, Jack Lee
Blanchette, James Grady, Jr.
Blount, Charles William, III
Brewer, Charles Blake, Sr.
Byrom, Joe Alan
Clossey, David F.
Crowley, James Worthington
Estep, Robert Lloyd
Feld, Alan David
Fishman, Edward Marc
Flanagan, Christie Stephen
Glendenning, Don Mark
Gohlke, David Ernest
Gores, Christopher Merrel
Hallman, Leroy
Kennedy, Marc J.
Malorzo, Thomas Vincent
Marquardt, Robert Richard
Maxwell, Jason P.
McLane, David Glenn
McNamara, Anne H.
Meyer, Ferdinand Charles, Jr.
Miller, Norman Richard
Moore, Marilyn Payne
Newsom, Jan Lynn Reimann
Parker, James Francis
Pleasant, James Scott
Rodgers, John Hunter
Schreiber, Sally Ann
Smith, Milton Clark, Jr.
Spears, Robert Fields
Thompson, Peter Rule
True, Roy Joe
Veach, Robert Raymond, Jr.
Young, Barney Thornton
Zisman, Barry Stuart

Diboll
Ericson, Roger Delwin

Ennis
Swanson, Wallace Martin

Fort Worth
Carr, Thomas Eldridge
Collins, Whitfield James
Larimore, Tom L.
Light, Russell Jeffers
Moros, Nicholas Peter
Watson, Robert Francis
Weekley, Frederick Clay, Jr.

Georgetown
Bryce, William Delf

Houston
Allender, John Roland
Anderson, Eric Severin
Bech, Douglas York

Beirne, Martin Douglas
Berner, Arthur Samuel
Born, Dawn Slater
Cooper, Thomas Randolph
Craig, Robert Mark, III
Crain, Alan Rau, Jr.
Crowl, Rodney Keith
Dilg, Joseph Carl
Ewen, Pamela Binnings
Farley, Jan Edwin
Finch, Michael Paul
Forbes, Arthur Lee, III
Gillmore, Kathleen Cory
Goldman, Nathan Carliner
Gray, Archibald Duncan, Jr.
Harrington, Bruce Michael
Hartrick, Janice Kay
Kelly, Hugh Rice
Kinnan, David Emery
LaBoon, Robert Bruce
Marlow, Orval Lee, II
Maroney, James Francis, III
Martin, Jay Griffith
Murphy, Ewell Edward, Jr.
Myers, Franklin
Nacol, Mae
Nolen, Roy Lemuel
O'Donnell, Lawrence, III
O'Toole, Austin Martin
Paden, Lyman R.
Plaeger, Frederick Joseph, II
Porter, Thomas William, III
Rogers, Arthur Hamilton, III
Sapp, Walter William
Shaddix, James W.
Sieger, John Anthony
Simmons, Stephen Judson
Still, Charles Henry
Szalkowski, Charles Conrad
Watson, John Allen
Wiese, Larry Clevenger
Winer, Stephen I.

Irving
Glober, George Edward, Jr.
Landau, Pearl Sandra

Lancaster
Sewell, Cameron Dee

Lubbock
Crowson, James Lawrence

Mc Kinney
Dowdy, William Clarence, Jr.

Plano
Shaddock, William Charles

Richardson
Jeffreys, Albert Leonidas

San Antonio
Biery, Evelyn Hudson
Bramble, Ronald Lee
Ferguson, Charles Alan
Koppenheffer, Julie B.
Lutter, Charles William, Jr.
Pipkin, Marvin Grady
Steen, John Thomas, Jr.

Sherman
Munson, Peter Kerr

Temple
Pickle, Jerry Richard

Waco
Page, Jack Randall

Wichita Falls
Eberly, Russell Albert

UTAH

Ogden
Mecham, Glenn Jefferson

Salt Lake City
Callister, Louis Henry, Jr.
Gordon, Robert

Spanish Fork
Ashworth, Brent Ferrin

VERMONT

Burlington
Morrow, Emily Rubenstein

South Burlington
Winer, Jonathan Herman

VIRGINIA

Alexandria
Beach, Barbara Purse
Higgins, Mary Celeste
Klewans, Samuel N.
Maloof, Farahe Paul
Paturis, E(mmanuel) Michael
Siegel, Kenneth Eric

Arlington
Fowler, David Lucas
Kelly, John James
McCorkindale, Douglas Hamilton
Morgens, Warren Kendall
Schwartz, Philip

Charlottesville
Dunn, William Wyly
Hodous, Robert Power
Stroud, Robert Edward

Chesapeake
Mastronardi, Corinne Marie

Falls Church
Halagao, Avelino Garabiles

Jennings, Thomas Parks

Glen Allen
Settlage, Steven Paul

Great Falls
Neidich, George Arthur
Preston, Charles George
Rath, Francis Steven

Hampton
McNider, James Small, III

Herndon
Pearlman, Michael Allen

Leesburg
Kushner, Gordon Peter

Lynchburg
Davidson, Frank Gassaway, III

Manakin Sabot
Bright, Craig Bartley

Mc Lean
Brown, Thomas Cartmel, Jr.
Church, Randolph Warner, Jr.
Daniels, Michael Alan
Goolrick, Robert Mason
Greene, Timothy Geddes
LeSourd, Nancy Susan Oliver
Morris, James Malachy
Paist, Mark C.
Raymond, David Walker
Stephens, William Theodore
Walter, Michael Joseph
Walton, Edmund Lewis, Jr.

Midlothian
Hall, Franklin Perkins

Newport News
Kamp, Arthur Joseph, Jr.
Segall, James Arnold

Norfolk
Poston, Anita Owings
Russell, C. Edward, Jr.
Ware, Guilford Dudley

Oakton
Duesenberg, Robert H.

Petersburg
White, William Earle

Portsmouth
Porter, J. Ridgely, III

Reston
Reicin, Eric David

Richmond
Belcher, Dennis Irl
Broadbent, Peter Edwin, Jr.
Buford, Robert Pegram
Carrell, Daniel Allan
Cutchins, Clifford Armstrong, IV
Denny, Collins, III
Elmore, Edward Whitehead
Framme, Lawrence Henry, III
Goodpasture, Philip Henry
Mezzullo, Louis Albert
Minardi, Richard A., Jr.
Musick, Robert Lawrence, Jr.
Pearsall, John Wesley
Redmond, David Dudley
Robinson, John Victor
Starke, Harold E., Jr.
Witt, Walter Francis, Jr.

Roanoke
Bates, Harold Martin
Densmore, Douglas Warren
Farnham, David Alexander
Harrison, David George

South Riding
Murray, Michael Patrick

Springfield
Eley, Randall Robbi

Tysons Corner
Frank, Jacob
Maiwurm, James John

Vienna
Randolph, Christopher Craven

Virginia Beach
Layton, Garland Mason

Winchester
Weiss, Rhett Louis

WASHINGTON

Eastsound
Hoagland, Karl King, Jr.

Montesano
Stewart, James Malcolm

Seattle
Blair, M. Wayne
Blom, Daniel Charles
Graham, Stephen Michael
Hilpert, Edward Theodore, Jr.
Judson, C(harles) James (Jim Judson)
Narodick, Kit Gordon
Palmer, Douglas S., Jr.
Pym, Bruce Michael
Rieke, Paul Victor
Steel, John Murray
Stokke, Diane Rees
Tune, James Fulcher
Whitford, Joseph Peter
Williams, J. Vernon

Tacoma
Krueger, James A.

Walla Walla
Hayner, Herman Henry

Yakima
Wright, J(ames) Lawrence

WEST VIRGINIA

Charleston
Berthold, Robert Vernon, Jr.

Morgantown
Fusco, Andrew G.
Ringer, Darrell Wayne (Dan)

WISCONSIN

Elkhorn
Sweet, Lowell Elwin

Germantown
Ehlinger, Ralph Jerome

Kenosha
Higgins, John Patrick
Richter, David Jerome

Madison
Anderson, Michael Steven
Boucher, Joseph W(illiam)
Hanson, David James
Nora, Wendy Alison
Peterson, H. Dale
Ragatz, Thomas George

Marinette
Anuta, Michael Joseph

Mc Farland
Abbott, William Anthony

Milwaukee
Abraham, William John, Jr.
Bremer, John M.
Donahue, John Edward
Ericson, James Donald
Friedman, James Dennis
Galanis, John William
Holz, Harry George
Iding, Allan Earl
Kurtz, Harvey A.
Levine, Herbert
Martin, Quinn William
Maynard, John Ralph
McGaffey, Jere D.
Mulcahy, Charles Chambers
Rintelman, Donald Brian
Schulz, William John
Williams, Clay Rule

Racine
Coates, Glenn Richard
Du Rocher, James Howard
Dye, William Ellsworth

Sun Prairie
Berkenstadt, James Allan

Waukesha
Hocum, Monica Carroll

WYOMING

Casper
Lowe, Robert Stanley

Cheyenne
Hathaway, Stanley Knapp

TERRITORIES OF THE UNITED STATES

PUERTO RICO

San Juan
Pierluisi, Pedro R.
Rodriguez-Diaz, Juan E.

CANADA

ONTARIO

Brampton
DeRoma, Nicholas John

MEXICO

Coahuila
Hernandez, Juan Ignacio

Mexico
Quiroz, Lourdes Gabriela

Mexico City
Chacon Lopez Velarde, Ricardo
de Uriarte, Horacio Maria
Langarica O'Hea, Lorenza Kristin

ARGENTINA

Buenos Aires
Crivelli, Marcelo
De Rosso, Pablo
Gonzalez, Mariano Pablo

AUSTRALIA

Adelaide
Davis, Glenn Stuart

Melbourne
Galbraith, Colin Robert

Sydney
Brown, John Thomas
Pistilli, Mark Stephen
Simmons, Daniel David

BELGIUM

Brussels
Delsaut, Philippe Patrick
Hoffmann, Maria Elisabeth

Liege
Matray, Didier F

BRAZIL

Sao Paulo
d'Utra Vaz, Marco Antonio

CHILE

Santiago
Allard, Javier
Rosenblut, Alvaro

CHINA

Hong Kong
Shinkle, John Thomas

Shanghai
Qi, Qing Michael

COSTA RICA

San Jose
Castro, Luis D.
Gomez, Jose

CZECH REPUBLIC

Prague
Bányaiová, Alena

DENMARK

Copenhagen
Lassen, Steen Anker
Mogelmose, Henrik

ENGLAND

Birmingham
Graham, Simon
Hull, David Julian

London
Barnes, Oliver William Abbott
Booker, Russell Stuart
Brownwood, David Owen
Buckley, Colin Hugh
Cole, Richard A.
Coppin, Jonathan David
Fuller, Charles Robert Saunders
Goodall, Caroline Mary Helen
Heard, David James
Rosenberg, Daniel P.
Sheach, Andrew Jonathan
Stanley, Ian G.
Walsom, Roger Benham
White, Walter Hiawatha, Jr.

Sheffield
Goulding, Nick

FINLAND

Helsinki
Ahola, Juhani Ilmari
Hentula, Ismo Tapani

FRANCE

Courbevoie
Herzog, Brigitte

Lyon-Villeurbanne
Duflos, Jean-Jacques

Paris
Blanchenay, Nicolas
Poulain de Saint-Pere, Aude

GERMANY

Berlin
Schoene, Friedrich Tobias

Cologne
Wilsing, Hans Ulrich

Dusseldorf
Clev, Heinrich

Düsseldorf
Gillessen, Frederick
Plueckelmann, Katja

Frankfurt
Wolff, Florian

Frankfurt am Main
Harrer, Herbert
Hartmann, Uwe

Frankfurt/Main
Baeumer, Ulrich J.P.

Hamburg
von Teuffel, Nikolai

Munich
Schleifenbaum, Eckhart Johannes

HONG KONG

3 Garden Road
Richardson, David Alexander

Hong Kong
Garvey, Richard Anthony
Graham, David

HUNGARY

Budapest
Balassa, Tamás
Szecsodi, Zsolt

INDIA

New Delhi
Khaitan, Gautam

IRELAND

Cork
Corkery, Garvan

Dublin
Brady, George Eoghan

Dublin 1
Fitzgerald, Eithne Margaret

ISRAEL

Jerusalem
Molho, Isaac

Tel Aviv
Karniel, Yuval

Tel-Aviv
Bar-on, Ofer

ITALY

Mialn
Vecchio, Cesare Giovanni

Milan
Maccioni, Giovanni
Ricci, Barnaba

Rome
Biolato, Giuseppe Vittorio
Di Amato, Astolfo

JAPAN

Osaka
Solberg, Norman Robert

Tokyo
Ishizuka, Nobuhisa
Mikami, Jiro
Thorson, Andrew H.

KENYA

Nairobi
Maema, William Ikutha

THE NETHERLANDS

Amstelveen
Liem, Edwin T.H.
Tarlavski, Roman

Rotterdam
Bolland, Pieter Heyme
van der Horst, Jan

NEW ZEALAND

Auckland
Laxon, William Allan
McNamara, Denis Michael
Owles, Peter Gary
Webb, Michael R.
Whale, Michael John

NIGERIA

Lagus
Muoka, Alexander Nduka

NORWAY

Oslo
Moljord, Kare I.
Thogersen, Kai

Osteras
Drevvatne, Dag

PERU

Lima
Chabaneix, Jean Paul
Garcia Ruiz-Huidobro, Magali
Hernandez, Juan Luis

THE PHILIPPINES

Makati
Agcaoili, Jose Luis Villafranca

Makati City
Banez, Winthrop Hawthorne Redoble
Guinto, Bob Lim
Mamuric, Jose Roberto Lota
Valdecantos, Clarence Darrow Cunan

Metro Manila
Pasal, Emmanuel Pastores
Sumida, Gerald Aquinas

POLAND

Warsaw
Wierzbowski, Krzysztof Franciszek

PORTUGAL

Lisbon
Amendoeira, Rui
Cid, Tiago
Pessanha, Tomas Vasconcelos

REPUBLIC OF KOREA

Seoul
Cho, Chi-Hyoung
Woo, Chang Rok

ROMANIA

Bucharest
Cominos, Theodore Harry, Jr.
Voicu, Daniel

SAUDI ARABIA

Jeddah
Shea, Gerald MacDonald

Riyadh
Taylor, Frederick William, Jr. (Fritz Taylor)

SCOTLAND

Glasgow
Burrow, Alistair Stewart

SINGAPORE

Singapore
Trahair, Andrew James

SOUTH AFRICA

Johannesburg
Franck, Brigitte Broderick

Sandton
Cron, Kevin Richard
Schlosberg, Jonathan Harry

SPAIN

Barcelona
Fernandez, Rodolfo

Madrid
Garrido de las Heras, Miguel
Martin de Vidales, Nicolas
Vasquez, Gerard Manuel

SWEDEN

Gothenburg
Edh, Staffan

Stockholm
Erlandsson, Asa
Lindquist, Ylva

Malmström, Anders C.
Rambe, Lars Joachim
Solerud, Hans Gunnar

SWITZERLAND

Basel
Eulau, Peter H.

Chateau d'Oex
Berman, Joshua Mordecai

Geneva
De Pfyffer, Andre

Zurich
Koch, Thomas

Zürich
Wuerzner, Andrea

UKRAINE

Kiev
Konnov, Sergei Vladimirovich

Kyiv
Grushko, Pavel Gregory
Vronskaya, Anna Alexandrovna

ADDRESS UNPUBLISHED

Adams, Samuel Franklin
Agraz, Francisco Javier, Sr.
Anani, Tarig
Anderson, Geoffrey Allen
Ball, James Herington
Banks, Robert Sherwood
Bartz, David John
Bennett, Steven Alan
Berry, Robert Worth
Bostrom, Robert Everett
Brigham, Henry Day, Jr.
Brodhead, David Crawmer
Bullard, Rockwood Wilde, III
Canoff, Karen Huston
Carlucci, Joseph P.
Cherovsky, Erwin Louis
Clarke, Edward Owen, Jr.
Coleman, John Michael
Coleman, Robert Lee
Collins, Theodore John
Colton, Sterling Don
Coplin, Mark David
Cornish, Jeannette Carter
Cranney, Marilyn Kanrek
Crook, Donald Martin
Crowe, James Joseph
D'Avignon, Roy Joseph
Dixon, Steven Bedford
Donnally, Robert Andrew
Ellison, Noni Lois
Fine, Robert Paul
Fischer, David Charles
Fischer, David Jon
Ford, Ashley Lloyd
Francis, Jerome Leslie
Garcia Barron, Ramiro
Gass, Raymond William
Gilden, Richard Henry
Ginsberg, Ernest
Gordon, David Zevi
Gorske, Robert H.
Greenberg, Ronald David
Gregory, George G.
Grier, Phillip Michael
Griffin, Campbell Arthur, Jr.
Gutman, Richard Edward
Hackett, Robert John
Hackett, Wesley Phelps, Jr.
Harff, Charles Henry
Hargis, V. Burns
Harmon, Gail McGreevy
Harris, Edward Monroe, Jr.
Hartmann, Kenneth
Heider, Jon Vinton
Hennessy, Dean McDonald
Herringer, Maryellen Cattani
Hoffman, S. David
Holtzmann, Howard Marshall
Houle, Jeffrey Robert
Hunt, Ronald Forrest
Huston, Steven Craig
Jacobi, John Albert
Jameson, Paula Ann
Jamieson, Michael Lawrence
Johnson, Leonard Hjalma
Keys, Jerry Malcom
Klaus, Charles
Klosk, Ira David
Koomey, Richard Alan
Koplik, Marc Stephen
Kratt, Peter George
Lea, Lorenzo Bates
Lefkowitz, Alan Zoel
Leibowitt, Sol David
Levy, David
Lightstone, Ronald
Linde, Maxine Helen
Logan, James Kenneth
Lorne, Simon Michael
Lynch, Thomas Wimp
Madden, John Joseph
Maguire, Raymer F., Jr.
Martin, James William
Massad, Stephen Albert
Maulding, Barry Clifford
Mayer, James Joseph
McCabe, Thomas Edward
McGahren, Eugene Dewey, Jr.
McGovern, Frances
McInerney, Gary John
McLendon, Susan Michelle
Mercer, Edwin Wayne
Meyer, Max Earl
Millard, John Alden
Millimet, Erwin
Moravsik, Robert James
Moylan, James Joseph
Natcher, Stephen Darlington
Nelson, Richard Perry

Noddings, Sarah Ellen
O'Brien, James Edward
O'Dell, Joan Elizabeth
Oates, Carl Everette
Ober, Richard Francis, Jr.
Oliver, Samuel William, Jr.
Painton, Russell Elliott
Palizzi, Anthony N.
Pallot, Joseph Wedeles
Patton, James Richard, Jr.
Peck, Mira P.
Porter, Michael Pell
Powers, Elizabeth Whitmel
Prem, F. Herbert, Jr.
Quayle, Marilyn Tucker
Quigley, Leonard Vincent
Rawls, Frank Macklin
Reid, Joan Evangeline
Reiter, Glenn Mitchell
Richards, Paul A.
Rivera, Oscar R.
Rosenn, Harold
Rosner, Seth
Rosseel-Jones, Mary Louise
Ruhm, Thomas Francis
Russ, Neil Andrew
Saliterman, Richard Arlen
Samuels, Janet Lee
Sexton, David Farrington
Shaffer, Richard James
Shambaugh, Stephen Ward
Shapiro, Howard Alan
Sheriff, Seymour
Siegel, Sarah Ann
Silverberg, Mark Victor
Simonton, Robert Bennet
Solberg, Thomas Allan
Speaker, Susan Jane
Spicer, S(amuel) Gary
Springer, Paul David
Stone, Edward Herman
Swacker, Frank Warren
Swift, Aubrey Earl
Tapley, James Leroy
Tavrow, Richard Lawrence
Tierney, Kevin Joseph
Tolins, Roger Alan
Torgerson, Larry Keith
Tubman, William Charles
Voight, Elizabeth Anne
Walker, John Sumpter, Jr.
Walner, Robert Joel
Westphal, Marjorie Lord
Williams, William John, Jr.
Willis, Russell Anthony, III
Wilson, Hugh Steven
Wilson, Rhys Thaddeus
Wohlschlaeger, Frederick George
Wooldridge, William Charles
Wright, Arthur McIntosh
Wunsch, Kathryn Sutherland
Wynstra, Nancy Ann
Zimmerman, Jean

CREDITOR. See
Commercial, consumer.

CRIMINAL

UNITED STATES

ALABAMA

Birmingham
Alford, Margie Searcy
Redden, Lawrence Drew

Cullman
Poston, Beverly Paschal

Florence
Case, Basil Timothy

Mobile
Armstrong, Gordon Gray, III
Pennington, Al

ALASKA

Anchorage
Butler, Rex Lamont
Feldman, Jeffrey Marc
Ross, Wayne Anthony

Bethel
Cooke, Christopher Robert

ARIZONA

Flagstaff
Cowser, Danny Lee

Phoenix
Klahr, Gary Peter
Rose, David L.
Song Ong, Roxanne Kay
Thompson, Joel Erik

Scottsdale
Smith, David Burnell

ARKANSAS

Little Rock
Heuer, Sam Tate

Morrilton
Denniston, Jeannie L.

CALIFORNIA

Belvedere Tiburon
Bremer, William Richard

Fairfield
Honeychurch, Denis Arthur

Fresno
Ramirez, Frank Tenorio

Fullerton
Talmo, Ronald Victor

Glendale
Toscano, Oscar Ernesto
Unger, Charles Joseph

Huntington Beach
Garrels, Sherry Ann

Indio
De Salva, Christopher Joseph

Los Angeles
Berman, Myles Lee
Byrd, Christine Waterman Swent
Garcia-Barron, Gerard Lionel
Handzlik, Jan Lawrence
Lauchengco, Jose Yujuico, Jr.
Rosenbaum, Mark Dale
Shapiro, Robert

Palmdale
Reichman, Dawn Leslie

Paramount
Hall, Howard Harry

Pasadena
Koelzer, George Joseph
Telleria, Anthony F.

Riverside
Schwartz, Bernard Julian

Sacramento
Wishek, Michael Bradley

San Diego
Brown, Douglas Colton
Shelton, Dorothy Diehl Rees

San Francisco
Bondoc, Rommel
Bruen, James A.
Chao, Cedric C.
Cohn, Nathan
Ladar, Jerrold Morton
Philipsborn, John Timothy
Russoniello, Joseph Pascal
Young, Douglas Rea

San Jose
McManis, James

Santa Ana
Harley, Robison Dooling, Jr.

Santa Monica
Genego, William Joseph
Hirsch, Richard Gary

Ventura
Bray, Laurack Doyle

Woodland
Melton, Barry

Yuba City
McCaslin, Leon

COLORADO

Boulder
Flowers, William Harold, Jr.

Breckenridge
Katz, Jeri Beth

Colorado Springs
Fisher, Robert Scott
Walker, Jonathan Lee

Denver
Malatesta, Mary Anne
Nesland, James Edward
Smith, Daniel Timothy
Springer, Jeffrey Alan

Englewood
Coffee, Melvin Arnold

Fort Collins
Johnson, Donald Edward, Jr.

Greenwood Vlg
Fierst, Bruce Philip

CONNECTICUT

Bridgeport
Zeldes, Jacob Dean

Fairfield
Denniston, Brackett Badger, III

New Haven
Carty, Paul Vernon

Norwalk
Feinstein, Stephen Michael

Plainville
Zagorsky, Peter Joseph

Stamford
Lytton, William B(ryan)
Margolis, Emanuel

Waterbury
Marano, Richard Michael

DELAWARE

Wilmington
Malik, John Stephen
Wier, Richard Royal, Jr.

DISTRICT OF COLUMBIA

Washington
Ambrose, Myles Joseph
Barcella, Ernest Lawrence, Jr.
Best, Judah
Bonner, Walter Joseph
Boss, Lenard Barrett
Buckley, John Joseph, Jr.
Chafetz, Marc Edward
Christensen, Karen Kay
Feffer, Gerald Alan
Gainer, Ronald Lee
Geniesse, Robert John
Greenebaum, Leonard Charles
Greenfeld, Alexander
Horn, Stephen
Kendall, David E.
Kent, M. Elizabeth
Kourtesis, Nikolaos Panagiotis
Liebman, Ronald Stanley
Luskin, Robert David
Martin, Ralph Drury
McDaniels, William E.
O'Neil, Thomas Francis, III
Patten, Thomas Louis
Peters, Frederick Whitten
Povich, David
Spaeder, Roger Campbell
Stuart, Pamela Bruce
Taylor, William Woodruff, III
Tompkins, Joseph Buford, Jr.
Tuohey, Mark Henry, III
Turnage, Fred Douglas
Vardaman, John Wesley
Witten, Roger Michael

FLORIDA

Bartow
Stevenson, Robin Howard

Belleair
Cheek, Michael Carroll

Coconut Grove
Denaro, Gregory

Coral Gables
Cano, Mario Stephen

Daytona Beach
Neitzke, Eric Karl

Fernandina Beach
Manson, Keith Alan Michael

Fort Lauderdale
Benjamin, James Scott
Bogenschutz, J. David
Dutko, Michael Edward
Hester, Julia A.
Pascal, Robert Albert
Schreiber, Alan Hickman

Gainesville
Kurrus, Thomas William

Jacksonville
Link, Robert James
McBurney, Charles Walker, Jr.
Pillans, Charles Palmer, III

Largo
Trevena, John Harry

Miami
Becerra, Robert John
Berger, Steven R.
Blake, Stanford
Bronis, Stephen Jay
Ferrell, Milton Morgan, Jr.
Hartz, Steven Edward Marshall
Hirsch, Milton
Houlihan, Gerald John
Pena, Guillermo Enrique
Poston, Rebekah Jane
Quirantes, Albert M.
Rashkind, Paul Michael
Rosen, Michael James
Rothman, David Bill
Scott, Thomas Emerson, Jr.
Weinstein, Alan Edward

Naples
McDonnell, Michael R. N.

North Miami Beach
Zipkin, Sheldon Lee

Orlando
deBeaubien, Hugo H.
Dempsey, Bernard Hayden, Jr.
Hernandez, H(ermes) Manuel
Lubet, Marc Leslie
Mason, Steven Gerald
Sheaffer, William Jay

Saint Petersburg
Russo, Frank
Scott, Kathryn Fenderson
Wein, Stephen Joshua

Stuart
Watson, Robert James

Tallahassee
Davis, William Howard
Morphonios, Dean B.

Tampa
Feegel, John Richard
Medina, Omar F.
Steiner, Geoffrey Blake

GEORGIA

Athens
Houser, Ronald Edward
Tolley, Edward Donald

Atlanta
Altman, Robert
Chilivis, Nickolas Peter
Duffey, William Simon, Jr.
Head, William Carl
Longhi, Patrick George
Lotito, Nicholas Anthony
Miller, Janise Luevenia Monica
Mull, Gale W.
Pilcher, James Brownie
Whitley, Joe Dally
Womack, Mary Pauline

Barnesville
Kennedy, Harvey John, Jr.

Decatur
O'Connell, John James, Jr.

Douglas
Sims, Rebecca Littleton

Gainesville
Hester, Francis Bartow, III (Frank Hester)

Jasper
Marger, Edwin

Kingsland
Ossick, John Joseph, Jr.

Lawrenceville
Harrison, Samuel Hughel

Milledgeville
Bradley, Wayne Bernard

Roswell
England, John Melvin

Valdosta
Bright, Joseph Converse

HAWAII

Honolulu
Cassiday, Benjamin Buckles, III
Hart, Brook
Kuniyuki, Ken Takaharu
Shigetomi, Keith Shigeo
Weight, Michael Anthony

Kailua Kona
Zola, Michael S.

Lihue
Valenciano, Randal Grant Bolosan

ILLINOIS

Aurora
Camic, David Edward
Mateas, Kenneth Edward

Buffalo Grove
Kole, Julius S.

Chicago
Boyle, Gregory Michael
Coulson, William Roy
Crane, Mark
Farber, Bernard John
Hubert, Donald
King, Michael Howard
Kunkle, William Joseph, Jr.
Linklater, William Joseph
Molo, Steven Francis
Murray, Daniel Charles
Nash, Gordon Bernard, Jr.
Senderowitz, Stephen Jay
Silets, Harvey Marvin
Starkman, Gary Lee
Webb, Dan K.

Chicago Heights
Wigell, Raymond George

Decatur
Vigneri, Joseph William

East Alton
Delaney, John Martin, Jr.

Eureka
Harrod, Daniel Mark

Galesburg
McCrery, David Neil, III

Joliet
Lenard, George Dean

La Salle
McClintock, Thomas Lee

Lombard
O'Shea, Patrick Joseph

Murphysboro
Acree, Angela Denise

Oakbrook Terrace
Hicks, James Thomas

Skokie
Plotnick, Paul William

INDIANA

Anderson
Woodruff, Randall Lee

Bedford
Haury, John Carroll

Columbus
Perkins Senn, Karon Elaine

Evansville
Clouse, John Daniel

Fort Wayne
Fleck, John R.

Franklin
Loveall, George Michael

Gary
Lewis, Robert Lee

Indianapolis
Kautzman, John Fredrick

La Porte
Drayton, V. Michael

Shelbyville
Lisher, James Richard

Terre Haute
Kesler, John A.

IOWA

Des Moines
Foxhoven, Jerry Ray

Iowa City
Spies, Leon Fred

Shell Rock
Ottesen, Realff Henry

KANSAS

Garden City
Pierce, Ricklin Ray

Overland Park
Branham, Melanie J.
Spaeth, Nicholas John

Topeka
Haney, Thomas Dwight
Hecht, Robert D.
Schultz, Richard Allen

Wichita
Gorup, Geary N.

KENTUCKY

Covington
Davidson, David Edgar

Frankfort
Chadwick, Robert

Lexington
Fryman, Virgil Thomas, Jr.

Louisville
Manly, Samuel
Partin, C. Fred

LOUISIANA

Baton Rouge
Dixon, Jerome Wayne
Gonzales, Edward Joseph, III
Unglesby, Lewis O.

Covington
Looney, James Holland
Paddison, David Robert

Harvey
Hantel, Philip Edward

Lafayette
Skinner, Michael David

Lake Charles
Sanchez, Walter Marshall

New Orleans
Reed, John Wilson

MAINE

Waterville
Sandy, Robert Edward, Jr.

MARYLAND

Baltimore
Crowe, Thomas Leonard
Gillece, James Patrick, Jr.
Kramer, Paul R.
Radding, Andrew

Glen Burnie
Lilly, John Richard, II

Hyattsville
Matty, Robert Jay

Oxon Hill
Serrette, Cathy Hollenberg

Pocomoke City
Porter, James Harry, Jr.

Potomac
Mullenbach, Linda Herman

Rockville
Gordon, Michael Robert
Van Grack, Steven

Silver Spring
McDermitt, Edward Vincent

Towson
Carney, Bradford George Yost
Morrow, Thomas Campbell

Upper Marlboro
Brennan, William Collins, Jr.

MASSACHUSETTS

Barnstable
McLaughlin, Edward Francis, Jr.
Mycock, Frederick Charles

Boston
Berry, Janis Marie
Burstein, Harvey
Carroll, James Edward
Goldman, Eric Scot
Hrones, Stephen Baylis
McKittrick, Neil Vincent
Sweda, Edward Leon, Jr.

Cambridge
Ta, Tai Van

Lenox
Coffin, Mary McCarthy

Lowell
Bowen, Steven Holmes

Northampton
Vincent, Thomas Philip

Springfield
Bennett, Clarence J.
Burstein, Merwyn Jerome
Maidman, Stephen Paul

Wollaston
Sullivan, William Francis

MICHIGAN

Ann Arbor
O'Brien, Darlene Anne

Bloomfield Hills
Cranmer, Thomas William
McGarry, Alexander Banting

Charlevoix
Telgenhof, Allen Ray

Detroit
Andreoff, Christopher Andon
Pirtle, H(arold) Edward
Wyrick, Jermaine Albert

Grand Rapids
Dodge, David A.

Greenville
Mullendore, James Myers

Inkster
Bullock, Steven Carl

Jackson
Jacobs, Wendell Early, Jr.

Lansing
Rasmusson, Thomas Elmo

Monroe
Bartlett, James Patrick

Saint Clair Shores
Shehan, Wayne Charles

South Haven
Waxman, Sheldon Robert

Southfield
Eklund-Easley, Molly Sue
Morganroth, Mayer

MINNESOTA

Brooklyn Center
Neff, Fred Leonard

Hugo
Flannery, James Patrick

Minneapolis
Heffelfinger, Thomas Backer
Magnuson, Roger James
McNamara, Michael John
Meshbesher, Ronald I.
Nemo, Anthony James
Oleisky, Robert Edward
Peterson, William George
Rathke, Stephen Carl
Timmons, Peter John
Voss, Barry Vaughan
Ziebell-Sullivan, Martha Jane

Plymouth
MacMillan, Peter Alan

Saint Cloud
Seifert, Luke Michael

Stillwater
Hutchinson, Michael Clark

MISSISSIPPI

Gulfport
Owen, Joe Sam

Jackson
Hauberg, Robert Engelbrecht, Jr.

Ocean Springs
Denham, Earl Lamar

Oxford
Lewis, Ronald Wayne

Pascagoula
Roberts, David Ambrose

MISSOURI

Cape Girardeau
Lowes, Albert Charles

Columbia
Moore, Mitchell Jay

Kansas City
Carter, J. Denise
Joyce, Michael Patrick
Lotven, Howard Lee
Reardon, Michael Edward
Rogers, Charles Myers
Wyrsch, James Robert

Keytesville
Wheeler, James Julian

Saint Charles
Green, Joseph Libory

Saint Louis
Marks, Murry Aaron
Ramirez, Anthony Benjamin

Springfield
Sherwood, Devon Fredrick

MONTANA

Bozeman
Nelson, Steven Dwayne

NEBRASKA

Fremont
Line, William Gunderson

Grand Island
Ahlschwede, Earl David

Kearney
Voigt, Steven Russell

Omaha
Runge, Patrick Richard

NEVADA

Las Vegas
Bolton, Jennifer Suzanne
Galliher, Keith Edwin, Jr.
Lukens, John Patrick

Reno
Cornell, Richard Farnham
Robison, Kent Richard
Sage, Larry Guy

NEW HAMPSHIRE

Concord
Hodes, Paul William

NEW JERSEY

Cherry Hill
D'Alfonso, Mario Joseph

Clark
Barr, Jon-Henry

Clifton
Feinstein, Miles Roger
Palma, Nicholas James

Fanwood
Mitzner, Michael Jay

Flemington
Miller, Louis H.

Florham Park
Nittoly, Paul Gerard

Hackensack
Latimer, Stephen Mark
Mullin, Patrick Allen

Haddonfield
Fuoco, Philip Stephen

Metuchen
Vercammen, Kenneth Albert

Middletown
Friedman, Richard Lloyd

Morris Plains
Pluciennik, Thomas Casimir

Mount Laurel
Burns, Scott David

Northfield
Day, Christopher Mark

Ocean
Moore, Francis Xavier
Weisberg, Adam Jon

Old Bridge
Downs, Thomas Edward, IV

Red Bank
Waldman, Daniel M.

Ridgewood
Seigel, Jan Kearney

River Edge
Huegel, Russell J.

South Amboy
McDonnell, William John

Spring Lake
Anderson, James Francis

Teaneck
Hayden, Joseph A., Jr.
Silber, Alan

NEW MEXICO

Albuquerque
Lopez, Martin, III

Farmington
Titus, Victor Allen

Santa Fe
Farber, Steven Glenn

NEW YORK

Albany
Barsamian, J(ohn) Albert
Devine, Eugene Peter
Dulin, Thomas N.
Wukitsch, David John

Batavia
Saleh, David John

Brooklyn
Dorf, Robert Clay
Jacobson, Barry Stephen
Kamins, Barry Michael
Malamud, Alexander

Buffalo
Gorman, Gerald Patrick
Schreck, Robert J.

Carle Place
Mulhern, Edwin Joseph

Cedarhurst
Klein, Irwin Grant

Delhi
Hartmann, James M.

East Northport
Juliano, John Louis

Hempstead
Kane, Donald Vincent

Herkimer
Kirk, Patrick Laine

Jericho
Rehbock, Richard Alexander

Kew Gardens
Schechter, Donald Robert
Sparrow, Robert E.

Mineola
Bernstein, Kenneth Alan
Gulotta, Frank Andrew, Jr.
Rubine, Robert Samuel

New York
Abramowitz, Elkan
Aiello, Robert John
Amsterdam, Mark Lemle
Aron, Roberto
Baumgarten, Sidney
Berger, Michael Gary
Borstein, Leon Baer
Bradley, E. Michael
Buchwald, Don David
Costello, Robert Joseph
Dershowitz, Nathan Zev
Douglas, Philip Le Breton
Elsen, Sheldon Howard
Feldberg, Michael Svetkey
Fink, Robert Steven
Fiske, Robert Bishop, Jr.
Gioiella, Russell Michael
Glekel, Jeffrey Ives
Goldman, Lawrence Saul
Greenberg, Gary Howard
Haynes, George Cleve
Hershman, Scott Edward
Kennedy, Michael John
Kenney, John Joseph
Kostelanetz, Boris
Kuh, Richard Henry
Lauer, Eliot
Laufer, Jacob
Lerner, Max Kasner
Levine, Alan
Levinson, Paul Howard
Lewis, David L.
Lowe, John Anthony
Lupert, Leslie Allan
Lupkin, Stanley Neil

Meister, Ronald William
Naftalis, Gary Philip
Peskin, Stephan Haskel
Raylesberg, Alan Ira
Rosner, Jonathan Levi
Seiff, Eric A.
Seligman, Frederick
Siffert, John Sand
Slade, Jeffrey Christopher
Smith, Morton Alan
Supino, Anthony Martin
Walpin, Gerald
Weinrich, Johnathan Edward
Wildes, Leon
Zornow, David M.

Nyack
Seidler, B(ernard) Alan

Patchogue
Cartier, Rudolph Henri, Jr.

Poughkeepsie
Adin, Richard H(enry)

Rochester
Andolina, Lawrence J.
Lapine, Felix Victor
Rosner, Leonard Allen

Smithtown
Brooks, Sondra

Syracuse
Gerber, Edward F.
Heath, Joseph John
Hildebrandt, George Frederick
Rosenthal, Alan

Troy
Jones, E. Stewart, Jr.

White Plains
Bavero, Ronald Joseph
Greenspan, Leon Joseph
Greenspan, Michael Evan
Pickard, John Allan

NORTH CAROLINA

Charlotte
Batten, Melissa C.
Brackett, Martin Luther, Jr.

Jacksonville
Taylor, Vaughan Edward

Kinston
Jones, Paul Lawrence
Strickland, Annette Webb

Oxford
Burnette, James Thomas

Raleigh
Hall, John Thomas
Suhr, Paul Augustine

Rutherfordton
Byers, Garland Franklin, Jr.

Winston Salem
Alexander, Charles Jackson, II

NORTH DAKOTA

Bismarck
Snyder, Robert John

OHIO

Akron
Cody, Daniel Schaffner
Glinsek, Gerald John

Cincinnati
Cissell, James Charles
Frank, William Nelson
Hust, Bruce Kevin
Scacchetti, David J.
Sims, Victor Dwayne
Whitaker, Glenn Virgil

Cleveland
Bell, Steven Dennis
Chandler, Everett Alfred

Columbus
Belton, John Thomas
Binning, J. Boyd
Cline, Richard Allen
Hollenbaugh, H(enry) Ritchey
Ketcham, Richard Scott
Tyack, Thomas Michael

Fairborn
Wolaver, Stephen Arthur

Findlay
Kentris, George Lawrence

Hamilton
Olivas, Adolf

Hillsboro
Coss, Rocky Alan

Massillon
Beane, Frank Llewellyn

Sandusky
Bailey, K. Ronald

Springfield
Lagos, James Harry

Sylvania
Callahan, John Joseph

Toledo
St. Clair, Donald David

Wadsworth
Paul, Dennis Edward

Xenia
Chappars, Timothy Stephen

OKLAHOMA

Enid
Jones, Stephen

Oklahoma City
Henry, David Patrick
Wyatt, Robert Lee, IV
Zuhdi, Nabil (Bill Zuhdi)

Shawnee
Dawson, Cindy Marie

Tulsa
Brewster, Clark Otto
La Sorsa, William George

Vinita
Johnston, Oscar Black, III

OREGON

Medford
O'Connor, Karl William (Goodyear
   Johnson)

Portland
Birmingham, Patrick Michael
Rieke, Forrest Neill

Vale
Carlson, David Rusco

PENNSYLVANIA

Aliquippa
Palmieri, John Anthony

Carlisle
Turo, Ron

Clarks Summit
Beemer, John Barry

Doylestown
Mellon, Thomas Edward, Jr.

Du Bois
Blakley, Benjamin Spencer, III

Harrisburg
Lappas, Spero Thomas

Indiana
Kauffman, Thomas Andrew

Johnstown
Glosser, William Louis
Kaharick, Jerome John

Lancaster
Minney, Michael Jay
Pyfer, John Frederick, Jr.

Media
List, Anthony Francis

Melrose Park
Shmukler, Stanford

Mercer
Kochems, Robert Gregory

Moon Township
Corbett, Thomas Wingett, Jr.

New Castle
Mangino, Matthew Thomas

Newtown
Kardos, Mel D.

Norristown
Gregg, John Pennypacker

Philadelphia
Dennis, Edward S(pencer) G(ale), Jr.
Durant, Marc
Hoffman, Alan Jay
Klein, Howard Bruce
Kraeutler, Eric
LaCheen, Stephen Robert
Newman, George Henry
Rainville, Christina
Reiff, Jeffrey Marc
Siegel, Bernard Louis
Voluck, Jeffrey M.
Wittels, Barnaby Caesar
Wolf, Bruce

Pittsburgh
Bogut, John Carl, Jr.
Terra, Sharon Ecker

State College
Nollau, Lee Gordon

Stroudsburg
Muth, Michael Raymond

Trevose
McEvilly, James Patrick, Jr.

Uniontown
Davis, James Thomas

White Oak
Pribanic, Victor Hunter

RHODE ISLAND

Providence
McMahon, John Joseph

West Warwick
Pollock, Bruce Gerald

SOUTH CAROLINA

Columbia
Gray, Elizabeth Van Doren
Harpootlian, Richard Ara
Harvey, Jonathan Matthew
Strom, J. Preston, Jr.
Swerling, Jack Bruce

Greenville
Coates, William Alexander
Talley, Michael Frank

SOUTH DAKOTA

Sioux Falls
Johnson, Richard Arlo

TENNESSEE

Chattanooga
Moore, Hugh Jacob, Jr.

Clarksville
Love, Michael Joseph
Smith, Gregory Dale

Fayetteville
Dickey, John Harwell

Hermitage
Burkett, Gerald Arthur

Johnson City
Culp, James David

Knoxville
Giordano, Lawrence Francis
Oberman, Steven
Routh, John William

Memphis
Friedman, Robert Michael
Raines, Jim Neal

Nashville
Hardin, Hal D.
Lane, William Arthur
Yarbrough, Edward Meacham

Springfield
Wilks, Larry Dean

Trenton
Harrell, Limmie Lee, Jr.

White House
Ruth, Bryce Clinton, Jr.

TEXAS

Amarillo
McDougall, Gerald Duane

Austin
Shapiro, David L.

Brownsville
Walsh, Lawrence Adrian
Weisfeld, Sheldon

Canton
White, Jeffery Howell

Corpus Christi
Miller, Carroll Gerard, Jr. (Gerry Miller)

Dallas
Scuro, Joseph E., Jr.
Udashen, Robert Nathan

El Paso
Darnell, James Oral
Leachman, Russell DeWitt

Fort Worth
Alford, Barry James
Cooper, Monika Goeschel

Gainesville
Sullivant, Wesley Benton

Graham
Richie, Boyd Lynn

Houston
Berg, David Howard
Disher, David Alan
Essmyer, Michael Martin
Hamel, Lee
Hocker, Wesley Hardy
Wallis, Olney Gray
Wheelan, R(ichelieu) E(dward)

Huffman
Frazier, William Sumpter

Mason
Johnson, Rufus Winfield

Mc Kinney
Roessler, P. Dee

Mcallen
Connors, Joseph Aloysius, III

Orange
Dugas, Louis, Jr.

San Angelo
Sutton, John Ewing

UTAH

Ogden
Kaufman, Steven Michael
Sullivan, Kevin Patrick

Salt Lake City
Mooney, Jerome Henri

VERMONT

Bellows Falls
Massucco, Lawrence Raymond

Colchester
Garcia, Luis Cesareo

Montpelier
Valerio, Matthew F.

VIRGINIA

Alexandria
Rosenthal, Edward Scott

Arlington
Weinberg, Robert Lester

Charlottesville
Wyatt, Deborah Chasen

Fairfax
Stanley, William Martin

Grundy
McGlothlin, Michael Gordon

Lynchburg
Angel, James Joseph
Light, William Randall
Packert, G(ayla) Beth

Newport News
Saunders, Bryan Leslie

Norfolk
Parsons, Rymn James

Petersburg
Spero, Morton Bertram

Radford
Turk, James Clinton, Jr.

Richmond
Baliles, Gerald L.
Boone, David Eason
Robinson, Thomas Hart

Warrenton
Howard, Blair Duncan

Wytheville
Baird, Thomas Bryan, Jr.

WASHINGTON

Mount Vernon
Moser, C. Thomas

Seattle
McKay, Michael Dennis
Riley, Stewart Patrick
Wayne, Robert Jonathan

Spokane
Weatherhead, Leslie R.

Tacoma
Kram, Peter

WEST VIRGINIA

Charleston
Cowan, John Joseph

Morgantown
Ringer, Darrell Wayne (Dan)

Wheeling
Wilmoth, William David

WISCONSIN

Germantown
Statkus, Jerome Francis

Kenosha
Rose, Terry William

Madison
Foust, Charles William

Milwaukee
Marquis, William Oscar
Orzel, Michael Dale
Sostarich, Mark Edward

Oshkosh
Curtis, George Warren

Wausau
Drengler, William Allan John

WYOMING

Jackson
Spence, Gerald Leonard

TERRITORIES OF THE UNITED STATES

VIRGIN ISLANDS

Saint Thomas
Caffee, Lorren Dale

FRANCE

Paris
Bougartchev, Kiril Alexandre

SPAIN

Barcelona
Martí, Miguel Torrents

ADDRESS UNPUBLISHED

Ascher, Richard Alan
Babbin, Jed Lloyd
Bailey, Francis Lee
Bartz, David John
Beldock, Myron
Brodsky, David Michael
Cacciatore, Ronald Keith
Ching, Louis Michael
Comisky, Ian Michael
Diamond, Paul Steven
English, Gregory Bruce
Ettinger, Joseph Alan
Feazell, Vic
Garry, John Thomas, II
Lopez, A. Ruben
Mitcham, Bob Anderson
Mugridge, David Raymond
Redmond, Lawrence Craig
Saltzman, Michael I.
Schor, Suzi
Sercarz, Maurice Henri
Smouse, H(ervey) Russell
Stockard, Janet Louise
Streicker, James Richard
Twardy, Stanley Albert, Jr.
Waxman, Seth Paul
Wessel, Peter

DEBTOR-CREDITOR. *See*
Commercial, consumer.

DIVORCE. *See* **Family.**

EDUCATION AND SCHOOLS

UNITED STATES

ALABAMA

Anniston
Klinefelter, James Louis

ARIZONA

Phoenix
Ullman, James A.

CALIFORNIA

Malibu
Hanson, Gary A.

Pasadena
Yohalem, Harry Morton

Sacramento
Keiner, Christian Mark

San Francisco
Tonsing, Michael John

Santa Barbara
Ah-Tye, Kirk Thomas

COLORADO

Boulder
Halpern, Alexander

Commerce City
Trujillo, Lorenzo A.

Denver
Breeskin, Michael Wayne
Otten, Arthur Edward, Jr.
Roesler, John Bruce

Englewood
Bolocofsky, David N.

Pueblo
Farley, Thomas T.

CONNECTICUT

New Haven
Robinson, Dorothy K.

DISTRICT OF COLUMBIA

Washington
Goldstein, Michael B.
Medalie, Susan Diane

FLORIDA

Deerfield Beach
Buck, Thomas Randolph

Naples
Rawson, Marjorie Jean

Sarasota
Fetterman, James Charles

Tampa
MacDonald, Thomas Cook, Jr.

GEORGIA

Athens
Davis, Claude-Leonard

Atlanta
González, Carlos A.
Groton, James Purnell

HAWAII

Honolulu
Boas, Frank

IDAHO

Boise
Green, Cumer L.

ILLINOIS

Champaign
Miller, Harold Arthur

Chicago
Slutzky, Lorence Harley

Dekalb
Davidson, Kenneth Lawrence

Lake Forest
Galatz, Henry Francis

INDIANA

Fort Wayne
Pope, Mark Andrew

KANSAS

Hutchinson
Swearer, William Brooks

KENTUCKY

Covington
Wolnitzek, Stephen Dale

MAINE

Yarmouth
Webster, Peter Bridgman

MARYLAND

Glyndon
Renbaum, Barry Jeffrey

Takoma Park
Browning, Deborah Lea

MASSACHUSETTS

Andover
McDaniel, Paul R.

Ashfield
Pepyne, Edward Walter

Boston
Gonson, S. Donald
Gossels, Claus Peter Rolf
Jones, Jeffrey Foster
Lembo, Vincent Joseph
Lyons, Paul Vincent

Medford
Jacobs, Mary Lee

Worcester
Moschos, Demitrios Mina

MICHIGAN

Harbor Springs
Turner, Lester Nathan

MISSOURI

Kansas City
Delaney, Michael Francis
Sands, Darry Gene

Saint Louis
Gianoulakis, John Louis

NEBRASKA

Lincoln
Perry, Edwin Charles

North Platte
Baumann, Larry R(oger)

NEW JERSEY

Freehold
Brown, Sanford Donald

New Brunswick
Scott, David Rodick

Warren
Bernstein, Eric Martin

NEW YORK

Albany
Danziger, Peter
Girvin, James Edward
Osterman, Melvin Howard

Floral Park
Chatoff, Michael Alan

Keeseville
Turetsky, Aaron

Mineola
Millman, Bruce Russell
Pogrebin, Bertrand B.
Zuckerman, Richard Karl

Mount Kisco
Curran, Maurice Francis

New York
Aiello, Robert John
Bear, Larry Alan
Bodner, Marc A.
Liss, Norman
Nolan, Terrance Joseph, Jr.

Pearl River
Riley, James Kevin

Rochester
Lascell, David Michael

NORTH CAROLINA

Cherokee
Martin, Harry Corpening

OHIO

Cleveland
Millstone, David J.

Columbus
Pittner, Nicholas Andrew
Stanton, Elizabeth McCool

Toledo
Pletz, Thomas Gregory

PENNSYLVANIA

Bangor
Spry, Donald Francis, II

Doylestown
Stevens, Paul Lawrence

Lansdale
Sultanik, Jeffrey Ted

Philadelphia
Brier, Bonnie Susan

TENNESSEE

Memphis
deWitt, Charles Benjamin, III

Nashville
Torrey, Claudia Olivia

TEXAS

Abilene
Robinson, Vianei Lopez

Austin
Arnett, Richard Lynn
Schulze, Eric William

Fort Worth
Carr, Thomas Eldridge
Law, Thomas Hart

Houston
Diaz-Arrastia, George Ravelo
Moroney, Linda L. S.

UTAH

Ogden
Mecham, Glenn Jefferson

VIRGINIA

Richmond
Ryland, Walter H.

WISCONSIN

Monroe
Kittelsen, Rodney Olin

Wausau
Dietrich, Dean Richard

WYOMING

Casper
Day, Stuart Reid

ADDRESS UNPUBLISHED

Anderson, Jon Eric
D'Agusto, Karen Rose
Prem, F. Herbert, Jr.
Smith, Ronald Ehlbert

EMINENT DOMAIN. See Condemnation.

ENERGY, FERC PRACTICE

UNITED STATES

CALIFORNIA

Los Angeles
Shortz, Richard Alan
Woodland, Irwin Francis

COLORADO

Denver
Hawley, Robert Cross

DISTRICT OF COLUMBIA

Washington
Beresford, Douglas Lincoln
Berner, Frederic George, Jr.
Brunenkant, Jon Lodwick
Collins, Daniel Francis
Downs, Clark Evans
Eastment, Thomas James
Elrod, Eugene Richard
Feldman, Roger David
Fels, Nicholas Wolff
Fox, Paul Walter
Grady, Gregory
Grenier, Edward Joseph, Jr.
Hollis, Sheila Slocum
Journey, Drexel Dahlke
Kissel, Peter Charles
Mallory, Charles King, III
Mann, Donegan
Manning, Michael J.
Mapes, William Rodgers, Jr.
Mathis, John Prentiss
McBride, Michael Flynn
McDiarmid, Robert Campbell
McKinney, James DeVaine, Jr.
Miller, John T., Jr.
O'Neill, Brian Dennis
Quint, Arnold Harris
Simons, Barbara M.
Skancke, Nancy J.
Zipp, Joel Frederick

ILLINOIS

Chicago
Fazio, Peter Victor, Jr.
Ruxin, Paul Theodore

Lake Forest
Emerson, William Harry

IOWA

Des Moines
Stoffregen, Philip Eugene

MARYLAND

Bethesda
Eisen, Eric Anshel

Chevy Chase
Bruder, George Frederick

MASSACHUSETTS

Boston
Hester, Patrick Joseph

NEW MEXICO

Farmington
Tully, Richard T. C.

NEW YORK

New York
Allen, Leon Arthur, Jr.
Butterklee, Neil Howard
Martin, George J., Jr.

Pittsford
George, Richard Neill

NORTH DAKOTA

Bismarck
Gerhart, Steven George

OREGON

Lake Oswego
Nelson, Thomas Howard

Portland
Dotten, Michael Chester

TENNESSEE

Knoxville
Congleton, Joseph Patrick

TEXAS

Dallas
Armour, James Lott
Keithley, Bradford Gene

Houston
Crowl, Rodney Keith
Hartrick, Janice Kay
Kelly, Hugh Rice
Kruse, Charles Thomas
Martin, Jay Griffith
Ryan, Thomas William

VERMONT

Rutland
Werle, Mark Fred

VIRGINIA

Alexandria
Sczudlo, Walter Joseph

Norfolk
Smith, Richard Muldrow

Richmond
Gary, Richard David

WASHINGTON

Tacoma
Waldo, James Chandler

WISCONSIN

Milwaukee
Kiesling, Donald F., Jr.

ENGLAND

London
Hammerson, Marc Charles

INDIA

New Delhi
Khaitan, Gautam

ADDRESS UNPUBLISHED

Choukas-Bradley, James Richard
Conine, Gary Bainard
Harshman, Raymond Brent
Jacobi, John Albert
Tanenbaum, Jay Harvey

ENERGY, NUCLEAR POWER

UNITED STATES

ALABAMA

Birmingham
Robin, Theodore Tydings, Jr.

CONNECTICUT

Hartford
Knickerbocker, Robert Platt, Jr.

DISTRICT OF COLUMBIA

Washington
Mathis, John Prentiss

McBride, Michael Flynn
Ruddy, Frank

ILLINOIS

Chicago
Rooney, Matthew A.

MARYLAND

Saint Michaels
Brown, Omer Forrest, II

MASSACHUSETTS

Sudbury
Dignan, Thomas Gregory, Jr.

NEW YORK

Dunkirk
Woodbury, Robert Charles

New York
Hayes, Gerald Joseph

Westbury
Nogee, Jeffrey Laurence

NORTH CAROLINA

Raleigh
Glass, Fred Stephen

TENNESSEE

Sevierville
Waters, John B.

TEXAS

Houston
Morgan, Richard Greer

VIRGINIA

Richmond
Rolfe, Robert Martin

ENGLAND

London
Haubold, Samuel Allen

ADDRESS UNPUBLISHED

Eaken, Bruce Webb, Jr.
Fetzer, Mark Stephen
Grisham, Richard Bond

ENTERTAINMENT

UNITED STATES

ARIZONA

Phoenix
Lubin, Stanley
Mousel, Craig Lawrence
Silverman, Alan Henry

CALIFORNIA

Beverly Hills
Fleer, Keith George
Rondeau, Charles Reinhardt
Russell, Irwin Emanuel

Burbank
Davis, J. Alan
Husband, Bertram Paul

Century City
Davis, Donald G(lenn)

Hollywood
Bennett, Bianca Cherie

Irvine
Specter, Richard Bruce

Los Angeles
Biederman, Donald Ellis
Braun, David A(dlai)
Demoff, Marvin Alan
Diamond, Stanley Jay
Donaldson, Michael Cleaves
Lurvey, Ira Harold
Palazzo, Robert Paul
Pasich, Kirk Alan
Robertson, Hugh Duff
Seiden, Andy

Marina Del Rey
Coplan, Daniel Jonathan

Palo Alto
Phillips, W. Alan

San Diego
Hartley, Jason Scott
Von Passenheim, John B.

San Mateo
Mandel, Martin Louis

Santa Ana
Lane, Dominick V.

Santa Monica
Custer, Barbara Ann
Homeier, Michael George
Kranzdorf, Jeffrey Paul
Roberts, Virgil Patrick

Sherman Oaks
Joyce, Stephen Michael

Studio City
Coupe, James Warnick

COLORADO

Colorado Springs
Rowan, Ronald Thomas

Denver
Horowitz, Robert M.

DISTRICT OF COLUMBIA

Washington
Barnett, Robert Bruce
Goldson, Amy Robertson
O'Connor, Charles P.

FLORIDA

Boca Raton
Jacobs, Joseph James

Clearwater
Weidemeyer, Carleton Lloyd

Fort Lauderdale
Benjamin, James Scott

GEORGIA

Atlanta
Coxe, Tench Charles
Smith, Jeffrey Michael

ILLINOIS

Chicago
Durchslag, Stephen P.
Hoffman, Valerie Jane
Lauderdale, Katherine Sue
Sennet, Charles Joseph
Snyder, Jean Maclean

Chicago Heights
Wigell, Raymond George

Oak Brook
Mlsna, Kathryn Kimura

INDIANA

Indianapolis
Elberger, Ronald Edward

LOUISIANA

Shreveport
Bryant, J(ames) Bruce

MARYLAND

Baltimore
Gilbert, Blaine Louis
Hopps, Raymond, Jr.

MASSACHUSETTS

Boston
Albrecht, Peter Leffingwell
Wolfson, Jeffrey Steven

MINNESOTA

Minneapolis
Drucker, Christine Marie
Street, Erica Catherine
Voss, Barry Vaughan

NEVADA

Las Vegas
Goodwin, John Robert

NEW HAMPSHIRE

Concord
Hodes, Paul William

NEW JERSEY

Maplewood
Joseph, Susan B.

Montclair
Brown, Ronald Wellington

Morristown
Schwartz, Howard J.

Woodcliff Lake
Pollack, Jane Susan

NEW YORK

Bethpage
Lemle, Robert Spencer

Brooklyn
Solis, Lino A.

Buffalo
Runfola, Ross Thomas

Chappaqua
Castrataro, Barbara Ann

Great Neck
Luckman, Gregg A.

Kew Gardens
Schechter, Donald Robert

Larchmont
McSherry, William John, Jr.

Mineola
Berman, Eric M.

New York
Barandes, Robert
Berger, Michael Gary
Bernstein, Robert Jay
Colfin, Bruce Elliott
Collyer, Michael
Curtis, Frank R.
DeBaets, Timothy Joseph
Feiman, Ronald Mark
Fry, Morton Harrison, II
Goff, Betsy Kagen
Goldberg, David
Huston, Barry Scott
Indursky, Arthur
Jacobson, Jeffrey E.
Janowitz, James Arnold
Kaminsky, Arthur Charles
Laufer, Jacob
Levinson, Paul Howard
McCarthy, Robert Emmett
Nearing, Vivienne W.
Papernik, Joel Ira
Plotkin, Loren H.
Poster, Michael Sollod
Probstein, Jon Michael
Roberts, Thomas Raymond
Salman, Robert Ronald
Seligman, Delice
Silberman, John Alan
Spanbock, Maurice Samuel
Streicker, Richard Daniel
Traube, Victoria Gilbert
Varma, Rishi Anand
Watanabe, Roy Noboru

Poughkeepsie
Millman, Jode Susan

Rochester
Twietmeyer, Don Henry

Scarsdale
Ellis, James Henry

Westbury
Nogee, Jeffrey Laurence

NORTH CAROLINA

Highlands
Meyerson, Stanley Phillip

OKLAHOMA

Norman
Fairbanks, Robert Alvin

PENNSYLVANIA

Clearfield
Falvo, Mark Anthony

Media
Harvey, Alice Elease

Philadelphia
Berger, Harold
DeBunda, Salvatore Michael
Reiff, Jeffrey Marc

RHODE ISLAND

Cranston
Cervone, Anthony Louis

TENNESSEE

Nashville
Bramlett, Paul Kent
Lyon, Philip K(irkland)
Rush, Stephen Kenneth

TEXAS

Dallas
DelHomme, Beverly Ann
Hammond, Herbert J.

UTAH

Salt Lake City
Mooney, Jerome Henri
Shea, Patrick A.

VIRGINIA

Mount Vernon
Spiegel, H. Jay

Richmond
Goodpasture, Philip Henry

ENGLAND

Birmingham
Hull, David Julian

London
Bamford, Timothy James

ITALY

Milan
Peron, Sabrina

NORWAY

Oslo
Strømme, Vidar

ADDRESS UNPUBLISHED

Carrol, Robert Kelton
Harkless, Angela
Harris, Jay Stephen
Kantrowitz, Susan Lee
Lightstone, Ronald
McLendon, Susan Michelle
Noddings, Sarah Ellen
Nussbaum, Peter David
O'Connor, Edward Vincent, Jr.
Saunders, Lonna Jeanne
Schor, Suzi
Spicer, S(amuel) Gary
Treacy, Vincent Edward
von Sauers, Joseph F.

ENVIRONMENTAL

UNITED STATES

ALABAMA

Birmingham
Alford, Margie Searcy
Gale, Fournier Joseph, III
Palmer, Robert Leslie
Robin, Theodore Tydings, Jr.
Timberlake, Marshall

Mobile
Johnston, Neil Chunn
Pierce, Donald Fay

ALASKA

Anchorage
Linxwiler, James David
Owens, Robert Patrick

Juneau
Tangen, Jon Paul

Kodiak
Ott, Andrew Eduard

ARIZONA

Flagstaff
Gliege, John Gerhardt

Phoenix
Storey, Lee A.
Wolf, G. Van Velsor, Jr.

Scottsdale
Jorden, Douglas Allen

Tempe
Shimpock, Kathy Elizabeth

ARKANSAS

Little Rock
Julian, Jim Lee

CALIFORNIA

Beverly Hills
Bordy, Michael Jeffrey

Fremont
Cummings, John Patrick

La Jolla
Peterson, Paul Ames

Los Angeles
Bonesteel, Michael John

Hansell, Dean
Olivas, Daniel Anthony
Rutter, Marshall Anthony
Straw, Lawrence Joseph, Jr.
Tepper, R(obert) Bruce, Jr.
Wagner, Darryl William

Moraga
Kilbourne, George William

Newport Beach
McGee, James Francis
Otto, James Daniel

Palo Alto
Fowler, John Wellington
Trumbull, Terry Alan

Sacramento
Goode, Barry Paul
Robbins, Stephen J. M.

San Diego
Dawe, James Robert
Longstreth, Robert Christy

San Francisco
Andrews, David Ralph
Bruen, James A.
Corash, Michele B.
McDevitt, Ray Edward
Norris, Cynthia Ann
Reding, John Anthony

Santa Barbara
Metzinger, Timothy Edward

Walnut Creek
Steele, Dwight Cleveland

COLORADO

Aurora
Hampton, Clyde Robert

Boulder
Danielson, Luke Jeffries
Fenster, Herbert Lawrence
Gray, William R.

Cherry Hills Village
Nazaryk, Paul Alan

Denver
Gilbert, Alan Jay
Grant, Patrick Alexander
Holder, Holly Irene
McKenna, Frederick Gregory
Pratt, Kevin Burton
Rockwood, Linda Lee
Sayre, John Marshall
Shepherd, John Frederic

Englewood
Deutsch, Harvey Elliot

Golden
Hughes, Marcia Marie
Snead, Kathleen Marie

CONNECTICUT

Greenwich
Pascarella, Henry William

Hartford
Buck, Gurdon Hall
Davis, Andrew Neil
Harrison, Thomas Flatley
Merriam, Dwight Haines
Sussman, Mark Richard

Stamford
McDonald, Cassandra Burns

DELAWARE

Wilmington
Cottrell, Paul (William Cottrell)
Kirk, Richard Dillon
Klayman, Barry Martin
Waisanen, Christine M.

DISTRICT OF COLUMBIA

Washington
Bernstein, Mitchell Harris
Browne, Richard Cullen
Carr, Lawrence Edward, Jr.
Ewing, Ky Pepper, Jr.
Fleischaker, Marc L.
Frost, Edmund Bowen
Hahn, John Stephen
Haynes, William J(ames), II
Hollis, Sheila Slocum
Holmstead, Jeffrey Ralph
Howard, Jeffrey Hjalmar
Joseph, Daniel Mordecai
Kirsch, Laurence Stephen
Kovacs, William Lawrence
Lettow, Charles Frederick
Lewis, William Henry, Jr.
McCrum, Robert Timothy
McElveen, Junius Carlisle, Jr.
Meserve, Richard Andrew
Mills, Kevin Paul
Nickel, Henry V.
Raul, Alan Charles
Rizzo, James Gerard
Ruddy, Frank
Seeger, Edwin Howard
Shuman, Mark Patrick
Sorett, Stephen Michael
Stoll, Richard G(iles)
Topol, Allan Jerry
Vardaman, John Wesley
Weissman, William R.
Wine, L. Mark

FLORIDA

Boca Raton
Fayette, Kathleen Owens

Jacksonville
Watson, Stacy L.

Key Largo
Mattson, James Stewart

Lake Buena Vista
Schmudde, Lee Gene

Melbourne
Rosenberg, Priscilla Elliott

Miami
Fleming, Joseph Z.
Halsey, Douglas Martin

Miami Lakes
Sharett, Alan Richard

Naples
Humphreville, John David

Orlando
Sims, Roger W.

Tallahassee
Curtin, Lawrence N.

Tampa
Schwenke, Roger Dean
Weaver, Ronald Lee

GEORGIA

Atlanta
Denham, Vernon Robert, Jr.
Killorin, Robert Ware
Kirby, Peter Cornelius
Ortiz, Jay Richard Gentry
Smith, Walton Napier
Stokes, James Sewell

Macon
Ennis, Edgar William, Jr.

Metter
Doremus, Ogden

HAWAII

Honolulu
Lombardi, Dennis M.

ILLINOIS

Chicago
Blatt, Richard Lee
Eggert, Russell Raymond
Feinstein, Fred Ira
Freeborn, Michael D.
Gladden, James Walter, Jr.
Greenspan, Jeffrey Dov
Harrington, James Timothy
Harrold, Bernard
Hesse, Carolyn Sue
Kissel, Richard John
Marwedel, Warren John
McMahon, Thomas Michael
Murray, Daniel Charles
Olian, Robert Martin
Pirok, Edward Warren
Pope, Michael Arthur
Rohrman, Douglass Frederick
Rundio, Louis Michael, Jr.
Schoenfield, Rick Merrill
Shindler, Donald A.
Stick, Michael Alan
Thomson, George Ronald
Zabel, Sheldon Alter

Glen Ellyn
O'Connell, Daniel James

Lombard
Goodman, Elliott I(rvin)

Riverwoods
Ford, Michael W.

Springfield
Immke, Keith Henry

Wheaton
Copeland, Charlene Carole

Wilmette
Lieberman, Eugene

INDIANA

Evansville
Wallace, Keith M.

Indianapolis
Pendygraft, George William
Scaletta, Phillip Ralph, III
Tabler, Bryan G.

Lafayette
Hart, Russell Holiday

IOWA

Davenport
Shaw, Elizabeth Orr

KANSAS

Wichita
Badger, Ronald Kay

KENTUCKY

Frankfort
Chadwick, Robert

Louisville
Guethlein, William O.
Vish, Donald H.

LOUISIANA

Covington
Shinn, Clinton Wesley

New Orleans
Allen, Frank Clinton, Jr.
Malone, Ernest Roland, Jr.
Pearce, John Y.
Rodriguez, Antonio Jose
Sinor, Howard Earl, Jr.
Stetter, Roger Alan
Villavaso, Stephen Donald

MAINE

Augusta
Davis, Virginia Estelle

Bernard
Marchetti, Karin Frances

Portland
Schutz, Sigmund D.

MARYLAND

Baltimore
Fisher, Morton Poe, Jr.
Sack, Sylvan Hanan

Bethesda
Hagberg, Viola Wilgus

Gaithersburg
Sherer, Samuel Ayers

Glen Burnie
Lilly, John Richard, II

Hagerstown
Berkson, Jacob Benjamin

Saint Michaels
Brown, Omer Forrest, II

MASSACHUSETTS

Boston
Cohn, Andrew Howard
Coolidge, Daniel Scott
Davis, Christopher Patrick
Thornton, Michael Paul

Orleans
Chaplin, Ansel Burt

Sudbury
Dignan, Thomas Gregory, Jr.

MICHIGAN

Detroit
Fromm, Frederick Andrew, Jr.

Gaylord
Topp, Susan Hlywa

Midland
Gootee, Jane Marie

Traverse City
Quandt, Joseph Edward

MINNESOTA

Minneapolis
Blanton, W. C.
Erstad, Leon Robert
Gordon, John Bennett
Keppel, William James
Mahoney, Kathleen Mary
O'Neill, Brian Boru
Straughn, Robert Oscar, III

MISSOURI

Kansas City
Beck, William G.
Eldridge, Truman Kermit, Jr.
English, Mark Gregory
Gardner, Brian E.
Price, James Tucker
Proctor, George Edwin, Jr.
Satterlee, Terry Jean
Shay, David Eugene
Smithson, Lowell Lee

Saint Louis
Berendt, Robert Tryon
Gilhousen, Brent James
Hiles, Bradley Stephen
Massey, Raymond Lee
Miller, Dwight Whittemore
Withers, W. Wayne

Yuba City
Doughty, Mark Anthony

COLORADO

Colorado Springs
Kendall, Phillip Alan
Palermo, Norman Anthony
Rouss, Ruth

Commerce City
Trujillo, Lorenzo A.

Denver
Atlass, Theodore Bruce
Crow, Nancy Rebecca
Goddard, Jo Anna
McMichael, Donald Earl
Olsen, M. Kent
Schmidt, L(ail) William, Jr.

Durango
Sherman, Lester Ivan

Lakewood
Scott, Peter Bryan
Thome, Dennis Wesley

Parker
Greenberg, Morton Paul

Pueblo
Altman, Leo Sidney

Rocky Ford
Mendenhall, Harry Barton

CONNECTICUT

Greenwich
Brandrup, Douglas Warren
Selby, Leland Clay

Hartford
Appel, Robert Eugene
Richter, Donald Paul
Toro, Amalia Maria

New London
Johnstone, Philip MacLaren

Ridgefield
Bracken, Nanette Beattie

Stamford
Sarner, Richard Alan

Waterbury
Dost, Mark W.

Westport
Carr, Cynthia
Kosakow, James Matthew

DELAWARE

Wilmington
Grossman, Jerome Kent
Herdeg, John Andrew
Jolles, Janet K. Pilling
Tigani, Bruce William

DISTRICT OF COLUMBIA

Washington
Blazek-White, Doris
Damico, Nicholas Peter
Faley, R(ichard) Scott
McCoy, Jerry Jack
Plaine, Lloyd Leva
Swendiman, Alan Robert

FLORIDA

Boca Raton
Reinstein, Joel

Bradenton
Lopacki, Edward Joseph, Jr.

Clearwater
Hogan, Elwood
Weidemeyer, Carleton Lloyd

Coral Springs
Polin, Alan Jay

Deerfield Beach
Lenoff, Michele Malka

Fort Lauderdale
Golden, E(dward) Scott
Hess, George Franklin, II
Katz, Thomas Owen
Nyce, John Daniel

Gainesville
Tillman, Michael Gerard

Jupiter
Click, David Forrest

Lakeland
Harris, Christy Franklin
Koren, Edward Franz

Miami
Chabrow, Penn Benjamin
Lancaster, Kenneth G.
Scheer, Mark Jeffrey
Weiner, Lawrence

Naples
Bruce, Jackson Martin, Jr.
Rigor, Bradley Glenn

Westman, Carl Edward

North Miami Beach
Slewett, Robert David

Orlando
Lefkowitz, Ivan Martin

Plant City
Sparkman, Steven Leonard

Port Charlotte
Levin, Allen Jay

Sarasota
Conetta, Tami Foley

Tallahassee
Dariotis, Terrence Theodore

Tampa
Ellwanger, Thomas John

West Palm Beach
Henry, Thornton Montagu
Lampert, Michael Allen

GEORGIA

Atlanta
Bird, Francis Marion, Jr.
Bloodworth, A(lbert) W(illiam) Franklin
Calhoun, Scott Douglas
Durrett, James Frazer, Jr.
Hoffman, Michael William
Lamon, Harry Vincent, Jr.
Levy, Bertram Louis
Salo, Ann Sexton Distler
Thrower, Randolph William

Augusta
Lee, Lansing Burrows, Jr.

Rome
McCrory, Aldous Desmond

Savannah
Searcy, William Nelson

HAWAII

Honolulu
Gerson, Mervyn Stuart
Hite, Robert Griffith
Miyasaki, Shuichi
Taylor, Carroll Stribling

IDAHO

Boise
Beal-Gwartney, Tore
Erickson, Robert Stanley

Caldwell
Kerrick, David Ellsworth

Idaho Falls
St. Clair, John Gilbert

ILLINOIS

Alton
Struif, L. James

Belleville
Urban, Donald Wayne

Champaign
Miller, Harold Arthur

Chicago
Abell, David Robert
Acker, Frederick George
Baetz, W. Timothy
Berning, Larry D.
Brown, Alan Crawford
Carr, Walter Stanley
Chandler, Kent, Jr.
Chiles, Stephen Michael
Ellwood, Scott
English, John Dwight
Felsenthal, Steven Altus
Friedman, Roselyn L.
Gelman, Andrew Richard
Gertz, Theodore Gerson
Harrington, Carol A.
Herpe, David A.
Kirkpatrick, John Everett
Lutter, Paul Allen
Marshall, John David
Nitikman, Franklin W.
Pape, Glenn Michael
Pimentel, Julio Gumeresindo
Ryken, Robert Leslie
Schar, Stephen L.
Shank, William O.
Spain, Richard Colby
Stanhaus, James Steven
Trio, Edward Alan
Trost, Eileen Bannon

Crystal Lake
Thoms, Jeannine Aumond

Elmwood Park
Spina, Anthony Ferdinand

Farmer City
Peithmann, William A.

Nashville
Cross, Robert Leonard

Northfield
Denkewalter, Kim Richard

Paris
Fruin, Roger Joseph

Peoria
Coletta, Ralph John

Rockford
Johnson, Thomas Stuart

Springfield
Stuart, Robert Allan, Jr.

INDIANA

Columbus
Crump, Francis Jefferson, III

Elkhart
Harman, John Royden

Evansville
Baugh, Jerry Phelps

Fort Wayne
Fink, Thomas Michael

Fowler
Weist, William Bernard

Granger
Lambert, George Robert

Indianapolis
Ewbank, Thomas Peters
Hetzner, Marc A.
Jewell, George Benson

IOWA

Clarinda
Millhone, James Newton

Council Bluffs
Pechacek, Frank Warren, Jr.

Des Moines
Campbell, Bruce Irving
Simpson, Lyle Lee

Garner
Hovda, Theodore James

Muscatine
Nepple, James Anthony

KANSAS

Concordia
Brewer, Dana

Olathe
Haskin, J. Michael

Overland Park
Cohen, Barton Pollock
Woods, Richard Dale

Wichita
Depew, Spencer Long

KENTUCKY

Florence
Monohan, Edward Sheehan, IV

Lexington
Johnson, Brian M.

Louisville
Duffy, Martin Patrick
Hallenberg, Robert Lewis

Prospect
Aberson, Leslie Donald

LOUISIANA

Jefferson
Conino, Joseph Aloysius

Lake Charles
Shaddock, William Edward, Jr.

Monroe
Curry, Robert Lee, III

New Orleans
Abbott, Hirschel Theron, Jr.
Benjamin, Edward Bernard, Jr.
Berkett, Marian Mayer
Lemann, Thomas Berthelot
McDaniel, Donald Hamilton
Simon, H(uey) Paul

Shreveport
Chastain, Merritt Banning, Jr.

MAINE

Portland
Hunt, David Evans
LeBlanc, Richard Philip

MARYLAND

Baltimore
Lewis, Alexander Ingersoll, III
Moser, M(artin) Peter

Bethesda
Brown, Thomas Philip, III

Nelson, William Eugene

Bowie
Bagaria, Gail Farrell

Columbia
Maseritz, Guy B.

Ellicott City
Henry, Edwin Maurice, Jr.

Gaithersburg
Ballman, B. George

Riverdale
Meyers, William Vincent

Rockville
Katz, Steven Martin
Neuman, Eric Patt

Westminster
Staples, Lyle Newton

MASSACHUSETTS

Boston
Fortier, Albert Mark, Jr.
Fremont-Smith, Marion R.
Kidder, George Howell
Page, George Alfred, Jr.
Pratt, Harold Irving
Stiles, Kevin Patrick
Woodburn, Ralph Robert, Jr.

Holden
Price, Robert DeMille

Marion
Worley, Robert William, Jr.

Newton
Concannon, Thomas Bernard, Jr.

Plymouth
Barreira, Brian Ernest

Springfield
Weiss, Ronald Phillip

Wellesley
Riley, Michael Hylan

West Chatham
Rowley, Glenn Harry

Westfield
Pollard, Frank Edward

Yarmouth Port
Paquin, Thomas Christopher

MICHIGAN

Ann Arbor
Joscelyn, Kent B(uckley)

Bloomfield Hills
Kirk, John MacGregor
Solomon, Mark Raymond
Sommerfeld, David William

Detroit
Deron, Edward Michael
Miller, George DeWitt, Jr.
Rasmussen, Douglas John
Tarnacki, Duane L.
Thoms, David Moore

Farmington
Harms, Donald C.

Flint
Cooley, Richard Eugene

Grand Rapids
Davis, Henry Barnard, Jr.

Grosse Pointe
Goss, James William

Hamtramck
Kaczmarek, Carla

Monroe
Lipford, Rocque Edward

Muskegon
Briggs, John Mancel, III

Saint Clair Shores
Joslyn, Robert Bruce
Stevens, Clark Valentine

Southfield
Kaplow, Robert David
Labe, Robert Brian

Troy
Chapman, Conrad Daniel

MINNESOTA

Duluth
Burns, Richard Ramsey

Edina
Brooks, William James, III

Kenyon
Peterson, Franklin Delano

Minneapolis
Brand, Steve Aaron
Freeman, Todd Ira
Ventres, Judith Martin

Saint Paul
Noonan, James C.
Norton-Larson, Mary Jean
Seymour, McNeil Vernam

MISSISSIPPI

Jackson
Black, D(eWitt) Carl(isle), Jr.
Travis, Jay A., III

MISSOURI

Hillsboro
Howald, John William

Independence
Minton, Kent W.

Jefferson City
Turnbull, Reginald Harrison

Kansas City
Langworthy, Robert Burton
Setzler, Edward Allan
Shughart, Donald Louis
Tanner, Eric Benson
Toll, Perry Mark
Willy, Thomas Ralph

Macon
Parkinson, Paul K.

Saint Louis
Erbs, Thomas J.
Gunn, Michael Peter
Harris, Harvey Alan
Paule, Donald Wayne
Rose, Albert Schoenburg
Sestric, Anthony James
Sherby, Kathleen Reilly
Van Cleve, William Moore

MONTANA

Billings
Thompson, James William

Havre
Moog, Mary Ann Pimley

NEBRASKA

Lincoln
Perry, Edwin Charles
Rembolt, James Earl

Omaha
Hamann, Deryl Frederick

NEVADA

Las Vegas
Chesnut, Carol Fitting
Greene, Addison Kent
Gubler, John Gray

NEW HAMPSHIRE

Hooksett
Rogers, David John

Manchester
Monson, John Rudolph
Wells, Robert Alfred

Portsmouth
DeGrandpre, Charles Allyson

NEW JERSEY

Bay Head
Kellogg, James Crane

Far Hills
Corash, Richard

Hackensack
Deener, Jerome Alan

Mc Afee
Fogel, Richard

Morristown
Sweeney, John Lawrence

Princeton
Beidler, Marsha Wolf
Gorrin, Eugene
Rose, Edith Sprung

Ramsey
Weber, Walter Winfield, Jr.

River Edge
Spiegel, Edna Z.

River Vale
Meyer, Grace Tomanelli

Summit
Cooper, John Weeks

Verona
Hock, Frederick Wyeth

West Orange
Laves, Benjamin Samuel
Richmond, Harold Nicholas

Woodbridge
Lepelstat, Martin L.

Woodcliff Lake
Falcon, Raymond Jesus, Jr.

NEW MEXICO

Albuquerque
Loubet, Jeffrey W.
Tomita, Susan K.

Farmington
Tully, Richard T. C.

Santa Fe
Hickey, John Miller

NEW YORK

Albany
Regal, Evan Charles
Sills, Nancy Mintz

Binghamton
Peckham, Eugene Eliot

Buffalo
McElvein, Thomas Irving, Jr.
Newman, Stephen Michael

Cedarhurst
Klein, Irwin Grant

Corning
Becraft, Charles D., Jr.

Huntington
Hochberg, Ronald Mark

Katonah
Keeffe, John Arthur

Kew Gardens
Adler, David Neil

Long Island City
Risi, Joseph John

Mineola
Bartol, Ernest Thomas
Smolev, Terence Elliot

New York
Barasch, Mal Livingston
Bell, Jonathan Robert
Black, James Isaac, III
Boehner, Leonard Bruce
Clark, Celia Rue
Crary, Miner Dunham, Jr.
Eisen, Edwin Roy
Engel, Ralph Manuel
Etra, Blanche Goldman
Evans, Douglas Hayward
Everett, James William, Jr.
Forger, Alexander Darrow
Gelb, Judith Anne
Heineman, Andrew David
Herbst, Abbe Ilene
Jasper, Seymour
Karan, Paul Richard
Kavoukjian, Michael Edward
Lawrence, Robert Cutting, III
Lesk, Ann Berger
Lingelbach, Albert Lane
Lipsky, Burton G.
Lloyd, James Woodman
Mariani, Michael Matthew
Martin, Malcolm Elliot
Materna, Joseph Anthony
McGrath, Thomas J.
Merrill, George Vanderneth
Molnar, Lawrence
Moore, Thomas Ronald (Lord Bridestowe)
Norden, William Benjamin
Paul, Herbert Morton
Pollan, Stephen Michael
Posner, Louis Joseph
Radin, Sam
Robinson, Barbara Paul
Rubinstein, Kenneth
Saufer, Isaac Aaron
Schlesinger, Sanford Joel
Silberman, John Alan
Spanbock, Maurice Samuel
Steyer, Hume Richmond
Valente, Peter Charles
Van Nuys, Peter
Wimpfheimer, Michael Clark

Pearl River
Riley, James Kevin

Pelham
Hanrahan, Michael G.

Poughkeepsie
Haven, Milton M.

Richmond Hill
De, Meena Indrajit

Riverhead
Twomey, Thomas A., Jr.

Rochester
Buckley, Michael Francis
Clifford, Eugene Thomas
Colby, William Michael
Harter, Ralph Millard Peter
Palermo, Anthony Robert
Trevett, Thomas Neil
Twietmeyer, Don Henry
Vick, Paul Ashton

Rockville Centre
Bennett, James Davison

Schenectady
Parisi, Frank Nicholas

Wickerham, Richard Dennis

Somers
Cowles, Frederick Oliver

South Richmond Hill
Scheich, John F.

Syracuse
Grizanti, Anthony J.
Michaels, Beverly Ann
O'Connor, Michael E.

White Plains
Gjertsen, O. Gerard
Rosenberg, Michael

NORTH CAROLINA

Asheville
Branch, John Wells (Jack Twig)
Lavelle, Brian Francis David

Chapel Hill
Herman-Giddens, Gregory

Charlotte
McBryde, Neill Gregory
Orsbon, Richard Anthony
Preston, James Young
Waggoner, William Johnson
Wood, William McBrayer

Highlands
Meyerson, Stanley Phillip

Jamestown
Schmitt, William Allen

Monroe
Love, Walter Bennett, Jr.

Raleigh
Taylor, Raymond Mason

NORTH DAKOTA

Grand Forks
Cilz, Douglas Arthur

Mandan
Bair, Bruce B.

Minot
Backes, Orlin William

OHIO

Bucyrus
Neff, Robert Clark, Sr.

Cincinnati
Buechner, Robert William
Hoffheimer, Daniel Joseph
Neltner, Michael Martin
Petrie, Bruce Inglis
Ryan, James Joseph
Schwab, Nelson, Jr.
Strauss, William Victor

Cleveland
Braverman, Herbert Leslie
Brucken, Robert Matthew
Hochman, Kenneth George
Horvitz, Michael John
Kurit, Neil
Monihan, Mary Elizabeth
Sogg, Wilton Sherman

Columbus
Casey, John Frederick
Fisher, Fredrick Lee
Martin, Paige Arlene

Dayton
Johnson, C. Terry
Roberts, Brian Michael

Salem
Bowman, Scott McMahan

Warren
Woodall, W. Dallas

Worthington
Minton, Harvey Steiger

OKLAHOMA

Muskogee
Robinson, Adelbert Carl

Oklahoma City
Mock, Randall Don
Ross, William Jarboe

Tulsa
Clark, Gary Carl
Eagleton, Edward John
Hatfield, Jack Kenton
Sneed, James Lynde

OREGON

Albany
Thompson, Orval Nathan

Eugene
Cooper, Michael Lee

La Grande
Joseph, Steven Jay

Pendleton
Rew, Lawrence Boyd

Portland
Bauer, Henry Leland
Froebe, Gerald Allen
Richardson, Campbell
Strader, Timothy Richards

PENNSYLVANIA

Allentown
Frank, Bernard
Noonan, Charles Thomas

Bethlehem
Bush, Raymond George

Bryn Mawr
Frick, Benjamin Charles

Harrisburg
Cicconi, Christopher M.
Hanson, Robert DeLolle
Sullivan, John Cornelius, Jr.

Huntingdon Valley
Kaufman, David Joseph

Johnstown
Glosser, William Louis

King Of Prussia
Gadsden, Christopher Henry
Schneider, Pam Horvitz

Lock Haven
Snowiss, Alvin L.

Media
Emerson, Sterling Jonathan

Milton
Davis, Preston Lindner

Norristown
Sosnov, Amy W(iener)

Philadelphia
Abramowitz, Robert Leslie
Chimples, George
Deming, Frank Stout
Denmark, William Adam
Donner, Henry Jay
Farley, Barbara L.
Goldman, Jerry Stephen
Jamison, Judith Jaffe
Kaier, Edward John
Lombard, John James, Jr.
Meigs, John Forsyth
Rainone, Michael Carmine
Speyer, Debra Gail

Pittsburgh
Connell, Janice T.
Daniel, Robert Michael
Flanagan, Joanna Scarlata
Kabala, Edward John
Ummer, James Walter
Vater, Charles J.

Reading
Linton, Jack Arthur

Stroudsburg
Upright, Kirby Grant

Wormleysburg
Cherewka, Michael

RHODE ISLAND

Providence
Davis, Andrew Hambley, Jr.
Hastings, Edwin H(amilton)
Salvadore, Guido Richard
Silver, Paul Allen

Warwick
Goldman, Steven Jason

SOUTH CAROLINA

Charleston
Branham, C. Michael

Columbia
Gibbes, William Holman
Nexsen, Julian Jacobs
Todd, Albert Creswell, III

Greenville
Dobson, Robert Albertus, III
Edwards, Harry LaFoy
Lynch, J. Timothy

TENNESSEE

Knoxville
Bly, Robert Maurice
Gentry, Mack A.

Memphis
Cook, August Joseph
Jalenak, James Bailey
Kahn, Bruce Meyer
Tate, Stonewall Shepherd

TEXAS

Amarillo
Burnette, Susan Lynn

Austin
Helman, Stephen Jody

Beaumont
Cavaliere, Frank Joseph

Borger
Edmonds, Thomas Leon

Corpus Christi
Stukenberg, Michael Wesley

Dallas
Carpenter, Gordon Russell
Dicus, Brian George
Henkel, Kathryn Gundy
Kroney, Robert Harper
Owens, Rodney Joe
Phelps, Robert Frederick, Jr.
Reid, Rust Endicott
Smith, Frank Tupper

El Paso
Marshall, Richard Treeger
Patterson, Burton Harvey
Yetter, Richard

Fort Worth
Collins, Whitfield James
Curry, Donald Robert
Mullanax, Milton Greg
Tracy, J. David
Willey, Stephen Douglas

Houston
Amann, Leslie Kiefer
Cenatiempo, Michael J.
Collins, Susan Ellen
Eastland, S. Stacy
Friedman, J. Kent
Jeske, Charles Matthew
Koenig, Rodney Curtis
Schwartzel, Charles Boone
Shearer, Dean Paul
Stewart, Pamela L.
Touchy, Deborah K.P.

Mason
Wilkerson, James Neill

Richardson
Conkel, Robert Dale

San Angelo
Carter, James Alfred

San Antonio
Bayern, Arthur Herbert
Netemeyer, Margaret
Oppenheimer, Jesse Halff

Waco
Page, Jack Randall
Ressler, Parke E(dward)

UTAH

Park City
Kennicott, James W.

Salt Lake City
Adams, Joseph Keith

VERMONT

Burlington
Lisman, Bernard
Morrow, Emily Rubenstein

Concord
Norsworthy, Elizabeth Krassovsky

VIRGINIA

Alexandria
McClure, Roger John
McGuire, Edward David, Jr.
Smith, Kevin Hopkins

Ashburn
Gold, George Myron

Charlottesville
Edwards, James Edwin
Kudravetz, David Waller
Middleditch, Leigh Benjamin, Jr.

Lynchburg
Davidson, Frank Gassaway, III

Martinsville
Frith, Douglas Kyle

Mc Lean
Aucutt, Ronald David

Norfolk
Poston, Anita Owings

Petersburg
Baskervill, Charles Thornton

Richmond
Addison, David Dunham
Horsley, Waller Holladay
Mezzullo, Louis Albert
Musick, Robert Lawrence, Jr.
Starke, Harold E., Jr.

Roanoke
Bates, Harold Martin

WASHINGTON

Bellevue
Treacy, Gerald Bernard, Jr.

Bellingham
Packer, Mark Barry

Montesano
Stewart, James Malcolm

Seattle
Blais, Robert Howard
Gores, Thomas C.
Hilpert, Edward Theodore, Jr.
Sweeney, David Brian

Spokane
Riherd, John Arthur
Sayre, Richard Layton

Tacoma
Krueger, James A.

Yakima
Wright, J(ames) Lawrence

WISCONSIN

Appleton
Drescher, Kathleen Ebben

Madison
Roberson, Linda

Middleton
Berman, Ronald Charles

Milwaukee
Iding, Allan Earl
Maynard, John Ralph
Wynn, Stanford Alan

Portage
Bennett, David Hinkley

Racine
Coates, Glenn Richard

Waukesha
Hocum, Monica Carroll
Jastroch, Leonard Andrew

Wauwatosa
Alexander, Robert Gardner

CANADA

ALBERTA

Calgary
Boettger, Roy Dennis

ENGLAND

London
Simon, M. Daniel

GERMANY

Dusseldorf
Palenberg, Hans-Peter

SOUTH AFRICA

Johannesburg
Schwarz, Harry Heinz

SWITZERLAND

Bern
Friedli, Georg

ADDRESS UNPUBLISHED

Buechel, William Benjamin
Easterling, Charles Armo
Fine, Robert Paul
Garry, John Thomas, II
Gray, Brian Mark
Hackett, Wesley Phelps, Jr.
James, Joyce Marie
Keegan, John Robert
Kerner, Michael Philip
Lambert, Samuel Waldron, III
Logan, James Kenneth
Lustig, Robert Michael
McGinty, Brian Donald
Merrill, Abel Jay
O'Brien, Charles H.
Patrick, Marty
Peterson, Howard Cooper
Reiche, Frank Perley
Reid, Joan Evangeline
Rodriguez, Vivian N.
Shook, Ann Jones
Sliger, Herbert Jacquemin, Jr.
Smith, Ronald Ehlbert
Solberg, Thomas Allan
Spitzberg, Irving Joseph, Jr.
Stack, Beatriz de Greiff
Stone, Edward Herman
Sweeney, Deidre Ann
Turner, George Mason
Weisberg, David Charles

Weisman, Paul Howard
Westphal, Marjorie Lord
Willis, Russell Anthony, III
Young, Sheldon Mike

FAMILY AND MATRIMONIAL

UNITED STATES

ALABAMA

Birmingham
Kracke, Robert Russell
Redden, Lawrence Drew

Cullman
Poston, Beverly Paschal

Demopolis
Dinning, Woodford Wyndham, Jr.

Huntsville
Potter, Ernest Luther

Jasper
Thomas, Steven Allen

ALASKA

Anchorage
Ross, Wayne Anthony

Kodiak
Jamin, Matthew Daniel

ARIZONA

Hereford
Lynch, Robert Berger

Phoenix
Rose, David L.
Sterns, Patricia Margaret

Scottsdale
Whittington, Thomas Lee

Tucson
Samet, Dee-Dee

Yuma
Hossler, David Joseph

ARKANSAS

Little Rock
Heuer, Sam Tate
Hope, Ronald Arthur

Searcy
Hughes, Thomas Morgan, III

CALIFORNIA

Alamo
Thiessen, Brian David

Bakersfield
Farr, G(ardner) Neil

Beverly Hills
Amado, Honey Kessler
Horwin, Leonard
Jaffe, F. Filmore

Encino
Kaufman, Albert I.

Foothill Ranch
Cotton, Debra Anne

Fullerton
Bush, William Merritt

Glendale
Toscano, Oscar Ernesto
Young, George Walter

Irvine
Goldstock, Barry Philip

Los Angeles
Igo, Louis Daniel
Lurvey, Ira Harold
Phillips, Patricia Dominis
Rutter, Marshall Anthony

Oakland
Rice, Julian Casavant

Orange
Batchelor, James Kent

Orinda
Casey, Kathleen Heirich

Palmdale
Reichman, Dawn Leslie

Pasadena
Ashley-Farrand, Margalo
Chan, Daniel Chung-Yin
Mehrpoo, Nikoo Nikki

Pleasanton
Staley, John Fredric

Sacramento
Burton, Randall James

Salinas
Bolles, Donald Scott

San Diego
Foerster, Barrett Jonathan
Godone-Maresca, Lillian
Morris, Sandra Joan
Sullivan, Michelle Cornejo

San Francisco
Musser, Sandra G.
Stotter, Lawrence Henry

San Jose
Katzman, Irwin
Smith, Valerie A.
Stutzman, Thomas Chase, Sr.

Seaside
Weingarten, Saul Myer

Selma
Janian, Paulette

Torrance
Moore, Christopher Minor

COLORADO

Colorado Springs
Adams, Deborah Rowland
Evans, Paul Vernon
Fisher, Robert Scott
Lohman, Richard Verne

Delta
Wendt, John Arthur Frederic, Jr.

Denver
Kaplan, Marc J.
Lerman, Eileen R.
McDowell, Karen Ann
McGuane, Frank L., Jr.
Oxman, Stephen Eliot
Quiat, Marshall
Wedgle, Richard Jay

Englewood
Bolocofsky, David N.

Fort Morgan
Higinbotham, Jacquelyn Joan

Golden
Hughes, Marcia Marie

Grand Junction
Griff, Harry

Lakewood
Yuthas, George Anthony

Longmont
Bisgard, Eileen Bernice Reid

CONNECTICUT

Avon
Widing, Carol Scharfe

Bristol
Hayes, Margaret Mary

Danbury
Dornfeld, Sharon Wicks

Fairfield
Osis, Daiga Guntra

Greenwich
Schoonmaker, Samuel Vail, III

Hartford
Spear, H(enry) Dyke N(ewcome), Jr.

Middlefield
Lang, Edward Gerald

New Haven
Coan, Richard Morton
Greenfield, James Robert

Norwich
Masters, Barbara J.

Ridgefield
Fricke, Richard John

South Windham
Asselin, John Thomas

Stratford
McDonough, Sandra Martin

West Hartford
Swerdloff, Ileen Pollock
Swerdloff, Mark Harris

Weston
Strauss, Ellen Louise Feldman

DELAWARE

Wilmington
Kelleher, Daniel Francis
Kulesza, Joseph Dominick, Jr.

DISTRICT OF COLUMBIA

Washington
Ain, Sanford King
Cash, Roderick William, Jr.
Rider, James Lincoln
Statland, Edward Morris

FLORIDA

Boca Raton
Fayette, Kathleen Owens
Sax, Spencer Meridith

Clearwater
Free, E. LeBron

Coral Gables
Cano, Mario Stephen

Daytona Beach
Neitzke, Eric Karl

Fort Lauderdale
Brawer, Marc Harris
Glantz, Wendy Newman
Nyce, John Daniel

Jacksonville
Gooding, David Michael
Siegel, Edward

Miami
Dienstag, Cynthia Jill
Dreize, Livia Rebbeka
Gelb, George Edward
Milstein, Richard Craig
Osman, Edith Gabriella
Pastoriza, Julio
Samole, Myron Michael
Weinstein, Alan Edward

Naples
Rawson, Marjorie Jean

Orlando
Blackwell, Bruce Beuford
deBeaubien, Hugo H.

Palatka
Baldwin, Allen Adail

Palm Beach Gardens
Kahn, David Miller

Saint Petersburg
Scott, Kathryn Fenderson

Sanford
Partlow, James Justice

Tallahassee
Morphonios, Dean B.

Tampa
Stalnaker, Lance Kuebler

West Palm Beach
Chopin, Susan Gardiner

GEORGIA

Atlanta
Cooper, Lawrence Allen
Miller, Janise Luevenia Monica
Mull, Gale W.
Raskin, Daniel Ellis
Wellon, Robert G.

Barnesville
Kennedy, Harvey John, Jr.

Columbus
Grogan, Lynn Langley

Douglas
Sims, Rebecca Littleton

Fayetteville
Fox, Patrick Joseph

Jasper
Marger, Edwin

Lawrenceville
Harrison, Samuel Hughel

Mcdonough
Crumbley, R. Alex

Snellville
Giallanza, Charles Philip

HAWAII

Honolulu
Adaniya, Kevin Seisho
Coates, Bradley Allen

Kailua Kona
Zola, Michael S.

Lihue
Valenciano, Randal Grant Bolosan

Wailuku
Kinaka, William Tatsuo

IDAHO

Boise
Beal-Gwartney, Tore

Hailey
Hogue, Terry Glynn

ILLINOIS

Aurora
Mateas, Kenneth Edward

Belleville
Gossage, Roza

Chicago
Davis, Muller
DuCanto, Joseph Nunzio
Levy, David Henry
Mufler, Kurt Alexander
Pimentel, Julio Gumeresindo
Pritikin, James B.
Ross, Curtis Bennett
Schiller, Donald Charles
Ventrelli, Anita Marie
Veverka, Donald John

Des Plaines
Jacobs, William Russell, II

Eureka
Harrod, Daniel Mark

Galesburg
McCrery, David Neil, III

Hinsdale
Walker, Daniel, Jr.

Mchenry
Gilmore, Carl W.

Moline
Schwiebert, Mark William

Mount Vernon
Harvey, Morris Lane

Mundelein
Ackley, Robert O.

Murphysboro
Acree, Angela Denise

Park Ridge
Franklin, Randy Wayne
Wasko, Steven E.

Rock Island
Wallace, Franklin Sherwood

Springfield
Adami, Paul E.
Narmont, John Stephen
Reed, Robert Phillip

Wheaton
Field, Harold Gregory

Wilmette
Lieberman, Eugene

INDIANA

Anderson
Scott, John Toner

Bedford
Haury, John Carroll

Crawfordsville
Donaldson, Steven Bryan

Evansville
Clouse, John Daniel

Franklin
Loveall, George Michael

Gary
Lewis, Robert Lee

Highland
Goodman, Samuel J.

Indianapolis
Bennett, Maxine Taylor
Blythe, James David, II
Pennamped, Bruce Michael

Valparaiso
Canganelli, Michael Antonio

Warsaw
Walmer, James L.

IOWA

Decorah
Belay, Stephen Joseph

Des Moines
Baybayan, Ronald Alan
Shoff, Patricia Ann

Indianola
Ouderkirk, Mason James

Iowa City
Trca, Randy Ernest

Sioux City
Giles, William Jefferson, III

KANSAS

Lawrence
Brown, David James

Overland Park
Short, Joel Bradley

Paola
Arnett, Debra Jean

Topeka
Frost, Brian Standish
Hejtmanek, Danton Charles

KENTUCKY

Covington
Davidson, David Edgar

Fort Thomas
Whalen, Paul Lewellin

Louisville
Brown, Bonnie Maryetta
Fuchs, Olivia Anne Morris
Silverthorn, Robert Sterner, Jr.
Spalding, Catherine

Somerset
Harlan, Jane Ann

LOUISIANA

Baton Rouge
Stracener, Carol Elizabeth
Wittenbrink, Jeffrey Scott

Covington
Paddison, David Robert

Lake Charles
Ortego, Jim
Sanchez, Walter Marshall

Mandeville
Tranchina, Frank Peter, Jr.

Metairie
Johnson, Gregory Scott

Monroe
Creed, Christian Carl

Shreveport
Rigby, Kenneth

MAINE

Brewer
Ebitz, Elizabeth Kelly

Waterville
Sandy, Robert Edward, Jr.

MARYLAND

Annapolis
Ferris, William Michael
Perkins, Roger Allan

Bethesda
Moss, Stephen Edward

Chestertown
Mowell, George Mitchell

Chevy Chase
Groner, Beverly Anne

College Park
Rosen, Steven
Yoho, Billy Lee

Ellicott City
Henry, Edwin Maurice, Jr.

Oxon Hill
Serrette, Cathy Hollenberg

Rockville
Avery, Bruce Edward
Gordon, Michael Robert

MASSACHUSETTS

Amherst
Howland, Richard Moulton

Belmont
Zito, Frank R.

Boston
Epstein, Elaine May
Gossels, Claus Peter Rolf
Packenham, Richard Daniel
Perera, Lawrence Thacher

Burlington
Graves, Robert

Cambridge
Pontikes, Rebecca George

Chelmsford
Grossman, Debra A.

Lenox
Coffin, Mary McCarthy

Nantucket
Witt, Carol A.

Natick
Marr, David E

Newton
Concannon, Thomas Bernard, Jr.
Monahan, Marie Terry

Northampton
Vincent, Thomas Philip

Palmer
Courchesne, Nyles Leopold

South Hamilton
Campbell, Diana Butt

Wernersville
Worley, Jane Ludwig

RHODE ISLAND

Providence
DiMonte, Vincente A.

SOUTH CAROLINA

Charleston
Farr, Charles Sims

Columbia
Harpootlian, Richard Ara
Sheftman, Howard Stephen

Myrtle Beach
Breen, David Hart

Newberry
Partridge, William Franklin, Jr.

SOUTH DAKOTA

Sioux Falls
Johnson, Richard Arlo

TENNESSEE

Chattanooga
Adams, Morgan Goodpasture

Erwin
Shults-Davis, Lois Bunton

Knoxville
Cremins, William Carroll

Memphis
Rice, George Lawrence, III (Larry Rice)

Nashville
Cobb, Stephen A.
Lane, William Arthur
Yarbrough, Edward Meacham

White House
Ruth, Bryce Clinton, Jr.

TEXAS

Abilene
Boone, Celia Trimble

Austin
Piper, James Walter
Saltmarsh, Sara Elizabeth
Shapiro, David L.
Weddington, Sarah Ragle

Bellaire
Soffar, William Douglas

Bryan
Steelman, Frank (Sitley)

Canton
White, Jeffery Howell

Cleveland
Campbell, Selaura Joy

College Station
Hoelscher, Michael Ray

Conroe
Irvin, Charles Leslie

Dallas
Callahan, Tena Toye
McCurley, Carl Michael
McCurley, Mary Johanna

Fort Worth
Paddock, Michael Buckley

Gainesville
Sullivant, Wesley Benton

Graham
Richie, Boyd Lynn

Houston
Burg, Brent Lawrence
Disher, David Alan
Fullenweider, Donn Charles
Hocker, Wesley Hardy

Longview
Welge, Jack Herman, Jr.

Mc Kinney
Roessler, P. Dee

Rockport
Benningfield, Carol Ann

San Antonio
Cabezas-Gil, Rosa M.
Craddock, Allen T.

Sherman
Munson, Peter Kerr

Sugar Land
Greer, Raymond White

UTAH

Ogden
Kaufman, Steven Michael

VERMONT

Brattleboro
McCarty, William Michael, Jr.

Concord
Norsworthy, Elizabeth Krassovsky

White River Junction
Davis, Emily S.

VIRGINIA

Arlington
Alper, Joanne Fogel
Crouch, Richard Edelin
Malone, William Grady
Polak, Carol Schrier
Schwartz, Philip

Chesapeake
Mastronardi, Corinne Marie

Fairfax
Sanderson, Douglas Jay

Lynchburg
Packert, G(ayla) Beth

Newport News
Segall, James Arnold

Petersburg
Baskervill, Charles Thornton
Spero, Morton Bertram

Portsmouth
Lavin, Barbara Hofheins

Reston
Anderson, Charles Anthony

Richmond
Shields, William Gilbert

Roanoke
Mundy, Gardner Marshall

Virginia Beach
Spitzli, Donald Hawkes, Jr.

Woodbridge
Roberts, Charles Bren

WASHINGTON

Bellevue
Landau, Felix

Grandview
Maxwell, John Edward

Mercer Island
Halverson, Lowell Klark

Seattle
Pritchard, Llewelyn G.
Riviera, Daniel John
Wechsler, Mary Heyrman

Spokane
Anderson, Robert Edward
Lineberger, Peter Saalfield
Scanlon, Robert Charles
Schuchart, Frederick Mark

Tacoma
Kram, Peter

WEST VIRGINIA

Bluefield
Kantor, Isaac Norris

Charleston
Zak, Robert Joseph

Gassaway
Jones, Jeniver James

WISCONSIN

Appleton
Chudacoff, Bruce Michael

Beloit
Blakely, Robert George

Deerfield
Pappas, David Christopher

Delafield
Hausman, C. Michael

Elkhorn
Eberhardt, Daniel Hugo

La Crosse
Sleik, Thomas Scott

Madison
Roberson, Linda

Menomonee Falls
Hurt, Michael Carter

Milwaukee
Loeb, Leonard L.
Meldman, Clifford Kay
Orzel, Michael Dale
Peckerman, Bruce Martin

Rhinelander
McEldowney, Todd Richard

Shawano
Habeck, James Roy

Wausau
Drengler, William Allan John
Molinaro, Thomas J.

ENGLAND

London
Leadercramer, David Ian

ADDRESS UNPUBLISHED

Cook, Donald Charles
Gourvitz, Elliot Howard
Jacobs, Paul Elliot
Kapner, Lewis
Kjos, Victoria
Kolodny, Stephen Arthur
McAlhany, Toni Anne
Mosk, Susan Hines
O'Connor, Edward Vincent, Jr.
Perlman, Richard Brian
Reith, Daniel I.
Rosenn, Harold
Schmidt, Kathleen Marie
Schoenwald, Maurice Louis
Slive, Steven Howard
Smith, Walter Ernest
Tanenbaum, Jay Harvey
Vamos, Florence M.

FINANCE

UNITED STATES

ALABAMA

Birmingham
Garner, Robert Edward Lee

Mobile
Peebles, E(mory) B(ush), III

ALASKA

Anchorage
Wohlforth, Eric Evans

ARIZONA

Phoenix
Bauman, Frederick Carl

ARKANSAS

Little Rock
Nelson, Edward Sheffield

CALIFORNIA

Chatsworth
Weinman, Glenn Alan

Irvine
Farrell, Teresa Joanning

La Canada Flintridge
Wallace, James Wendell

Los Angeles
Leibow, Ronald Louis
Lesser, Joan L.
Obrzut, Ted
Robertson, Hugh Duff
Shortz, Richard Alan

Marina Del Rey
Smolker, Gary Steven

Menlo Park
Kelly, Daniel Grady, Jr.
Millard, Richard Steven

Newport Beach
Wolf, Alan Steven

San Diego
Shippey, Sandra Lee

San Francisco
Alexis, Geraldine M.
Burden, James Ewers
Endsley, Meredith Nelson
Latta, Thomas Albert
Palmer, Venrice Romito

Studio City
Coupe, James Warnick

COLORADO

Basalt
Mersman, Richard Kendrick, III

Castle Rock
Procopio, Joseph Guydon

Denver
Dolan, Brian Thomas
Eckstein, John Alan
Gallegos, Larry Duayne

CONNECTICUT

Westbrook
Dundas, Philip Blair, Jr.

DISTRICT OF COLUMBIA

Washington
Barr, Michael Blanton
Born, Brooksley Elizabeth
Bruemmer, Russell John
Chanin, Michael Henry
Downs, Clark Evans
Fanone, Joseph Anthony
Feldman, Roger David
Niehuss, John Marvin
Petito, Christopher Salvatore
Pogue, L(loyd) Welch
Trimble, Sandra Ellingson
Weiner, Kenneth Brian

FLORIDA

Coral Gables
Kaplan, David Louis

Fort Lauderdale
Batchelder, Drake Miller

Miami
Gross, Leslie Jay
Pearson, John Edward

Naples
McCaffrey, Judith Elizabeth

Orlando
Salzman, Gary Scott

West Palm Beach
Rosen, Marvin Shelby

GEORGIA

Atlanta
Crews, William Edwin
McNeill, Thomas Ray
Moeling, Walter Goos, IV
Schulte, Jeffrey Lewis
Stallings, Ronald Denis
Strauss, Robert David
Veal, Rex R.

ILLINOIS

Chicago
Axley, Frederick William
Crawford, Dewey Byers
Duncan, John Patrick Cavanaugh
Johnson, Gary Thomas
Kaufman, Andrew Michael
Landsman, Stephen A.
Lang, Gordon, Jr.
Malkin, Cary Jay
McErlean, Charles Flavian, Jr.
Mehlman, Mark Franklin
Morrow, John E.
Reich, Allan J.
Reum, James Michael
Schulz, Keith Donald

Deerfield
Bush, Thomas Norman

Lake Zurich
Scott, John Joseph

Warrenville
Boardman, Robert A.

INDIANA

Indianapolis
Hackman, Marvin Lawrence

KENTUCKY

Louisville
Maggiolo, Allison Joseph

LOUISIANA

New Orleans
Ostendorf, Lance Stephen
Rinker, Andrew, Jr.

MARYLAND

Baltimore
Chriss, Timothy D. A.
Scriggins, Larry Palmer

Bethesda
Gottlieb, Jonathan W.

Silver Spring
Hannan, Myles

MASSACHUSETTS

Belmont
Zito, Frank R.

Boston
Bornheimer, Allen Millard
Cohn, Andrew Howard
Jordan, Alexander Joseph, Jr.
Krasnow, Jordan Philip
Malt, Ronald Bradford
Masud, Robert

CONNECTICUT (cont.)
Soden, Richard Allan
Stokes, James Christopher

Lincoln
Gnichtel, William Van Orden

Newton
Glazer, Donald Wayne

MICHIGAN

Detroit
Rohr, Richard David

Farmington Hills
Moore, Roy F.

Grosse Pointe
Barrows, Ronald Thomas

MINNESOTA

Minneapolis
Laitinen, Sari K.M.
Parsons, Charles Allan, Jr.
Potuznik, Charles Laddy

MISSISSIPPI

Jackson
Johnson, Mark Wayne

MISSOURI

Kansas City
Ayers, Jeffrey David
Graham, Harold Steven
Hindman, Larrie C.

Saint Louis
Gillis, John Lamb, Jr.

NEW JERSEY

Cranbury
Iatesta, John Michael

Edison
Lijoi, Peter Bruno

Florham Park
Kandravy, John

Morristown
Gillen, James Robert

Newark
Knee, Stephen H.

Ridgewood
Harris, Micalyn Shafer

Woodbridge
Hoberman, Stuart A.

NEW MEXICO

Albuquerque
Haltom, B(illy) Reid

NEW YORK

Long Beach
Solomon, Robert H.

New York
Andersen, Richard Esten
Bear, Larry Alan
Bergan, Philip James
Bliwise, Lester Martin
Burgweger, Francis Joseph Dewes, Jr.
Bushnell, George Edward, III
Cannell, John Redferne
Caytas, Ivo George
Chang, Ta-kuang
Chilstrom, Robert Meade
Chromow, Sheri P.
Clemente, Robert Stephen
Colgan, Jeremy Spencer
Cummings, Anthony William
Das, Kalyan
Everett, James William, Jr.
Fenster, Marvin
Forry, John Ingram
Freedman, Gerald M.
Genova, Diane Melisano
Gill, E. Ann
Goodwillie, Eugene William, Jr.
Gottlieb, Paul Mitchel
Granoff, Gary Charles
Higgs, John H.
Hirsch, Barry
Hooker, Wade Stuart, Jr.
Janowitz, James Arnold
Kaplan, Carl Eliot
Kaufman, Arthur Stephen
Krouse, George Raymond, Jr.
Lans, Asher Bob
Lewis, Adam McLean
Lindsay, George Peter
Macan, William Alexander, IV
Martin, George J., Jr.
Merrill, George Vanderneth
Moussa, Rhonda K.
Novikoff, Harold Stephen
Olmstead, Clarence Walter, Jr.
Paul, Robert Carey
Phillips, Pamela Kim
Purtell, Lawrence Robert
Rabb, Bruce
Rooney, Paul C., Jr.
Rosenbloom, Lawrence Andrew
Ross, Michael Aaron

Scheler, Brad Eric
Schmidt, Joseph W.
Schorr, Brian Lewis
Seward, George Chester
Shea, Edward Emmett
Silkenat, James Robert
Sperling, Allan George
Stein, Stephen William
Stuart, Alice Melissa
Turner, E. Deane
Vega, Matias Alfonso
Walker, John Lockwood
Welt, Philip Stanley
Wiegley, Roger Douglas
Wolf, Gary Wickert
Young, John Edward
Zaitzeff, Roger Michael

Orangeburg
Seaman, Robert E., III

Rochester
Adair, Donald Robert

NORTH CAROLINA

Charlotte
Monge, Jay Parry
Taylor, David Brooke

Greensboro
Hopkins, John David

OHIO

Cincinnati
Anderson, James Milton
Heldman, James Gardner

Cleveland
Pearlman, Samuel Segel
Pinkas, Robert Paul
Waldeck, John Walter, Jr.

Columbus
Barrett, Phillip Heston
Pigman, Jack Richard
Pittner, Nicholas Andrew

OKLAHOMA

Oklahoma City
Johnson, Robert Max

OREGON

Beaverton
Fulsher, Allan Arthur

Lake Oswego
Rasmussen, Richard Robert

PENNSYLVANIA

Bradford
Hauser, Christopher George

Gladwyne
Booth, Harold Waverly

Harrisburg
Cicconi, Christopher M.

Philadelphia
Auten, David Charles
Doran, William Michael
Flanagan, Joseph Patrick, Jr.
Jones, Robert Jeffries
Mason, Theodore W.
Spolan, Harmon Samuel
Stuntebeck, Clinton A.

Pittsburgh
Ehrenwerth, David Harry
Gold, Harold Arthur
Newlin, William Rankin

SOUTH CAROLINA

Hilton Head Island
Hagoort, Thomas Henry

TENNESSEE

Knoxville
McCall, Jack Humphreys, Jr.

Nashville
Carr, Davis Haden

TEXAS

Austin
Rider, Brian Clayton

Dallas
Veach, Robert Raymond, Jr.
White, James Richard

El Paso
Rash, Alan Vance

Euless
Paran, Mark Lloyd

Houston
Berner, Arthur Samuel
Bilger, Bruce R.
Brunson, John Soles
Ewen, Pamela Binnings
Gover, Alan Shore

O'Toole, Austin Martin
Watson, John Allen
Weber, Fredric Alan
Weiner, Sanford Alan

VERMONT

South Burlington
Winer, Jonathan Herman

VIRGINIA

Arlington
Morris, Roy Leslie

Falls Church
Christman, Bruce Lee

Newport News
Kamp, Arthur Joseph, Jr.

Richmond
Framme, Lawrence Henry, III

Winchester
Weiss, Rhett Louis

WASHINGTON

Seattle
Kuhrau, Edward W.
Tousley, Russell Frederick
Whitford, Joseph Peter

WISCONSIN

Madison
Nora, Wendy Alison

Milwaukee
Galanis, John William

MEXICO

Mexico City
de Uriarte, Horacio Maria

ARGENTINA

Buenos Aires
Gonzalez, Mariano Pablo

AUSTRALIA

Sydney
Machin, Peter William
Shirbin, John Martin

CHINA

Hong Kong
Lam, Wing Wo

CZECH REPUBLIC

Prague
Brzobohaty, Tomas

DENMARK

Copenhagen
Mogelmose, Henrik

ENGLAND

London
Breakell, David James
Dannreuther, David Ion

FINLAND

Helsinki
Tähtinen, Jyrki Juhani

GERMANY

Frankfurt am Main
Hartmann, Uwe

GREECE

Piraeus
Bowen-Morris, Nigel Vaughan

HUNGARY

Budapest
Doughty, Alexander Robert

ISRAEL

Jerusalem
Stern, Doron Daniel

ITALY

Milan
Tarchi, Enrico Maria

Rome
Carotenuto, Giovanni

JAPAN

Tokyo
Ishizuka, Nobuhisa
Mikami, Jiro

THE NETHERLANDS

Amstelveen
Liem, Edwin T.H.

Rotterdam
Bolland, Pieter Heyme

NEW ZEALAND

Auckland
Owles, Peter Gary

PERU

Lima
Chabaneix, Jean Paul
Rebaza, Alberto

THE PHILIPPINES

Makati City
Guinto, Bob Lim

SINGAPORE

Singapore
Trahair, Andrew James

SOUTH AFRICA

Sandton City
Legh, Robert Andrew

SWITZERLAND

Basel
Eulau, Peter H.

ADDRESS UNPUBLISHED

Bloomer, Harold Franklin, Jr.
Bostrom, Robert Everett
Brodhead, David Crawmer
Colton, Sterling Don
Cumberland, William Edwin
Giusti, William Roger
Gutman, Richard Edward
Howell, Donald Lee
Levinson, Kenneth S.
Locke, William Henry
O'Brien, Charles H.
O'Brien, James Edward
Pear, Charles E., Jr.
Pusateri, Lawrence Xavier
Ruhm, Thomas Francis
Shaffer, Richard James
Tondel, Lawrence Chapman
Toomey, Richard Andrew, Jr.
Wohlschlaeger, Frederick George
Wood, Robert Charles
Wright, Robert Payton

FRANCHISING

UNITED STATES

ARIZONA

Phoenix
Hay, John Leonard
Ullman, James A.
Williams, Quinn Patrick
Wirken, Charles William

CALIFORNIA

Los Angeles
Barnes, Willie R.

San Ramon
Freed, Kenneth Alan

COLORADO

Denver
Carson, William Scott

DISTRICT OF COLUMBIA

Washington
Horn, Stephen
Klarfeld, Peter James
McDavid, Janet Louise
Zeidman, Philip Fisher

FLORIDA

Miami
Roman, Ronald Peter

Orlando
Blaher, Neal Jonathan
Chong, Stephen Chu Ling

GEORGIA

Atlanta
Barkoff, Rupert Mitchell
McNeill, Thomas Ray

Augusta
Cooney, William J.

ILLINOIS

Chicago
Baer, John Richard Frederick
Johnson, Douglas Wells
McLaughlin, T. Mark

Lincolnshire
Para, Gerard Albert

INDIANA

Valparaiso
Conison, Jay

MARYLAND

Baltimore
Chernow, Jeffrey Scott
Wilson, Thomas Matthew, III

MASSACHUSETTS

Boston
Siegel, Steven Richard

MICHIGAN

Auburn Hills
Huss, Allan Michael

Lansing
Linder, Iris Kay

MINNESOTA

Minneapolis
Long, James Jay
Pluimer, Edward J.

MISSISSIPPI

Olive Branch
Carnall, George Hursey, II

MISSOURI

Kansas City
Kaufman, Michelle Stark
Palmer, Dennis Dale

Saint Louis
Anderson, Anthony LeClaire

NEW JERSEY

Florham Park
Chase, Eric Lewis

NEW YORK

Buffalo
Bailey, Thomas Charles

Garden City
Kestenbaum, Harold Lee

New York
Rosen, Richard Lewis
Scheiman, Eugene R.

Purchase
Joyce, Joseph James

White Plains
Pitegoff, Thomas Michael

NORTH CAROLINA

Morganton
Simpson, Daniel Reid

Raleigh
Kapp, Michael Keith

Winston Salem
Schollander, Wendell Leslie, Jr.

OHIO

Canton
Sandrock, Scott Paul

Cincinnati
Lutz, James Gurney

Columbus
Buchenroth, Stephen Richard

OKLAHOMA

Tulsa
Slicker, Frederick Kent

OREGON

Lake Oswego
Byczynski, Edward Frank

PENNSYLVANIA

Blue Bell
Siedzikowski, Henry Francis

Philadelphia
Tractenberg, Craig R.

TENNESSEE

Gallatin
Habermann, Ted Richard

TEXAS

Austin
Rittenberry, Kelly Culhane

Houston
Simmons, Stephen Judson

VIRGINIA

Mc Lean
Walter, Michael Joseph

GERMANY

Dusseldorf
Pape, Dieter

NORWAY

Osteras
Drevvatne, Dag

ADDRESS UNPUBLISHED

Coplin, Mark David

GENERAL PRACTICE

UNITED STATES

ALABAMA

Bay Minette
Granade, Fred King

Clanton
Jackson, John Hollis, Jr.

Huntsville
Potter, Ernest Luther

Mobile
Armbrecht, William Henry, III

Montgomery
Ely, Robert Eugene
Stakely, Charles Averett

Tuscaloosa
Williams, Roger Courtland

Tuscumbia
Munsey, Stanley Edward

ALASKA

Anchorage
Allingham, Lynn Marie

Kodiak
Ott, Andrew Eduard

ARIZONA

Hereford
Lynch, Robert Berger

Phoenix
Le Clair, Douglas Marvin

Tucson
McDonough, Lawrence
Tindall, Robert Emmett

ARKANSAS

Blytheville
Fendler, Oscar

El Dorado
Wynne, William Joseph

Fayetteville
Pearson, Charles Thomas, Jr.

Harrison
Pinson, Jerry D.

Jonesboro
Deacon, John C.

Little Rock
Hughes, Steven Jay
Ryan, Donald Sanford
Sherman, William Farrar

Mena
Thrailkill, Daniel B.

Mountain Home
Strother, Lane Howard

Newport
Thaxton, Marvin Dell

CALIFORNIA

Antioch
Richards, Gerald Thomas

Belvedere Tiburon
Obninsky, Victor Peter

Berkeley
Ogg, Wilson Reid

Beverly Hills
Horwin, Leonard
Jaffe, F. Filmore

Burbank
Ajalat, Sol Peter

Del Mar
Seitman, John Michael

El Segundo
Gambaro, Ernest Umberto

Encino
Smith, Selma Moidel

Imperial Beach
Merkin, William Leslie

Los Angeles
Angel, Arthur Ronald
Byrd, Christine Waterman Swent
De Brier, Donald Paul
Van de Kamp, John Kalar
Watson, Glenn Robert
Weissman, Barry Leigh

Martinez
Bray, Absalom Francis, Jr.

Novato
Lewin, Werner Siegfried, Jr.

Palm Desert
Reinhardt, Benjamin Max

Pasadena
Yohalem, Harry Morton

Pleasanton
Harding, John Edward

Rancho Cordova
McGrath, William Arthur

Saint Helena
Marvin, Monica Louise Wolf

Salinas
Bolles, Donald Scott

San Diego
Brierton, Cheryl Lynn
Foerster, Barrett Jonathan
Hofflund, Paul
Shapiro, Philip Alan
Von Passenheim, John B.

San Francisco
Cohn, Nathan
Yamakawa, David Kiyoshi, Jr.

San Jose
Hannon, Timothy Patrick

San Rafael
Drexler, Kenneth

Santa Barbara
Falstrom, Kenneth Edward

Seaside
Weingarten, Saul Myer

Selma
Janian, Paulette

Sherman Oaks
Joyce, Stephen Michael

Sunnyvale
McReynolds, Stephen Paul

Visalia
Crowe, John T.

Walnut Creek
Pinkerton, Albert Duane, II

COLORADO

Aspen
Shipp, Dan Shackelford

Colorado Springs
Donley, Jerry Alan
Evans, Paul Vernon
Rouss, Ruth

Commerce City
Trujillo, Lorenzo A.

Denver
Fanganello, Joseph Michael
Oxman, Stephen Eliot

Fort Collins
Johnson, Donald Edward, Jr.

Frisco
Helmer, David Alan

Hghlnds Ranch
Mierzwa, Joseph William

Lakewood
Yuthas, George Anthony

Montrose
Overholser, John W.

Westcliffe
Snyder, Paul, Jr.

CONNECTICUT

Bethel
Medvecky, Thomas Edward

Bridgeport
Goldberger, Robert R.

Canaan
Capecelatro, Mark John

Glastonbury
Taalman, Juri E.

Greenwich
Brandrup, Douglas Warren

Groton
Stuart, Peter Fred

Hartford
Bonee, John Leon, III
Gale, John Quentin

Lakeville
Rout, Robert Howard

Norwalk
Feinstein, Stephen Michael

Old Lyme
Wyckoff, E. Lisk, Jr.

Plainville
Zagorsky, Peter Joseph

Redding
Zitzmann, Kelly C.

Ridgefield
Fricke, Richard John

Shelton
Ryan, William Joseph, Jr.

Stamford
Benedict, Peter Behrends
Cacace, Michael Joseph
Livolsi, Frank William, Jr.
Spitzer, Vlad Gerard

Stratford
O'Rourke, James Louis

Trumbull
Brennan, Daniel Edward, Jr.

Waterbury
Marano, Richard Michael

West Hartford
Swerdloff, Ileen Pollock

Westport
Cramer, Allan P.

Wethersfield
Terk, Glenn Thomas

Windsor
Morelli, Carmen

Winsted
Finch, Frank Herschel, Jr.

DELAWARE

Dover
Babiarz, Francis Stanley

Wilmington
Kelleher, Daniel Francis
Kulesza, Joseph Dominick, Jr.

Sullivan, Lawrence Matthew

DISTRICT OF COLUMBIA

Washington
Burch, John Thomas, Jr.
Close, David Palmer
Donegan, Charles Edward
Goldson, Amy Robertson
Greenebaum, Leonard Charles
Harrison, Marion Edwyn
Jones, Allen, Jr.
Mayo, George Washington, Jr.
Thaler, Paul Sanders

FLORIDA

Clearwater
Weidemeyer, Carleton Lloyd

Coral Gables
Gustafson, Anne-Lise Dirks

Fort Lauderdale
Nyce, John Daniel

Fort Myers
Dalton, Anne

Gulfport
Allen, John Thomas, Jr.

Largo
Fedor, Allan John

Longboat Key
Pulvermacher, Louis Cecil

Miami
Amber, Laurie Kaufman
Berman, Bruce Judson
David, Christopher Mark
Hirsch, Milton
Milstein, Richard Craig
O'Keefe, Raymond Peter
Samole, Myron Michael
Starr, Ivar Miles
Touby, Richard

Naples
Cardillo, John Pollara
Crehan, Joseph Edward
Westman, Carl Edward

North Miami Beach
Zipkin, Sheldon Lee

Palatka
Baldwin, Allen Adail

Palm Beach Gardens
Pumphrey, Gerald Robert

Tallahassee
Roland, Raymond William

Tampa
Gilbert, Richard Allen

West Palm Beach
Chopin, Susan Gardiner

GEORGIA

Atlanta
Fiorentino, Carmine
Mull, Gale W.
Pless, Laurance Davidson
Pryor, Shepherd Green, III

Barnesville
Kennedy, Harvey John, Jr.

Columbus
Patrick, James Duvall, Jr.

Macon
Brown, Stephen Phillip

Marietta
Ahlstrom, Michael Joseph
Bentley, Fred Douglas, Sr.
Ingram, George Conley

Ocilla
Pujadas, Thomas Edward

Perry
Geiger, James Norman

Savannah
Gannam, Michael Joseph

Statesboro
Franklin, James Burke

HAWAII

Honolulu
Chuck, Walter G(oonsun)
Fong, Peter C. K.
Iwai, Wilfred Kiyoshi

IDAHO

Boise
Hoagland, Samuel Albert
Noack, Harold Quincy, Jr.

Hailey
Hogue, Terry Glynn

Lewiston
Tait, John Reid

Twin Falls
Berry, L. Clyel

ILLINOIS

Aurora
Patricoski, Paul Thomas
Poulakidas, Michael John

Batavia
Drendel, Kevin Gilbert

Belleville
Parham, James Robert

Chicago
Bowman, Phillip Boynton
Chin, Davis
Ditkowsky, Kenneth K.
Farber, Bernard John
Filpi, Robert Alan
Getzoff, William Morey
Henning, Joel Frank
Herman, Stephen Charles
Howe, Jonathan Thomas
Knox, James Marshall
Kohn, Shalom L.
Kresse, William Joseph
Reicin, Ronald Ian
Rosenberg, H. James
Saunders, George Lawton, Jr.
Thompson, David F.
Veverka, Donald John
Vranicar, Michael Gregory

Collinsville
Tognarelli, Richard Lee

East Alton
Delaney, John Martin, Jr.

Elgin
Juergensmeyer, John Eli

Elmwood Park
Spina, Anthony Ferdinand

Galesburg
Mustain, Douglas Dee

Galva
Massie, Michael Earl

Geneva
Landmeier, Allen Lee

Genoa
Cromley, Jon Lowell

Hinsdale
Walker, Daniel, Jr.

Moline
Schwiebert, Mark William

Morris
Rooks, John Newton

Murphysboro
Acree, Angela Denise

Oak Brook
Oldfield, E. Lawrence

Oak Forest
Narko, Medard Martin

Palos Heights
Matug, Alexander Peter

Park Ridge
Franklin, Randy Wayne

Quincy
Rapp, James Anthony

Rockford
Johnson, Thomas Stuart

Schaumburg
Frano, Andrew Joseph

Streator
Harrison, Frank J.

Urbana
Thies, Richard Leon

Watseka
Tungate, James Lester

Waukegan
Bairstow, Richard Raymond

INDIANA

Anderson
Woodruff, Randall Lee

Bloomington
Applegate, Karl Edwin

Boonville
Neff, Mark Edward

Crawfordsville
Donaldson, Steven Bryan

Danville
Baldwin, Jeffrey Kenton

Evansville
Knight, Jeffrey Lin

Fowler
Weist, William Bernard

Indianapolis
Kautzman, John Fredrick

Reuben, Lawrence Mark

Muncie
Smith, Gregory Butler

Newburgh
Dewey, Dennis James

Shelbyville
Lisher, James Richard

South Bend
Casey, Robert Fitzgerald

Terre Haute
Bitzegaio, Harold James
Britton, Louis Franklin
Kesler, John A.

Warsaw
Walmer, James L.

IOWA

Burlington
Hoth, Steven Sergey

Clarinda
Millhone, James Newton

Clinton
Frey, A. John, Jr.

Des Moines
Baybayan, Ronald Alan
Seitzinger, Edward Francis

Greenfield
Howe, Jay Edwin

Mason City
Winston, Harold Ronald

Mount Pleasant
Vance, Michael Charles

Newton
Caldwell, Gilbert Raymond, III

Sioux City
Poulson, Jeffrey Lee

West Des Moines
McEnroe, Michael Louis

KANSAS

Lawrence
Brown, David James
Nordling, Bernard Erick
Smith, Glee Sidney, Jr.

Overland Park
Branham, Melanie J.

Paola
Arnett, Debra Jean

Prairie Village
Sharp, Rex Arthur

Pratt
Stull, Gordon Bruce

Salina
Neustrom, Patrik William

Shawnee Mission
Sparks, Billy Schley

Topeka
Schultz, Richard Allen

Ulysses
Hathaway, Gary Ray

Wichita
Coombs, Eugene G.

KENTUCKY

Florence
Frohlich, Anthony William

Frankfort
Chadwick, Robert

Lexington
Hickey, John King

Louisville
Pettyjohn, Shirley Ellis

Owensboro
Miller, James Monroe

Somerset
Harlan, Jane Ann
Prather, John Gideon
Prather, John Gideon, Jr.

LOUISIANA

Baton Rouge
Stracener, Carol Elizabeth

Lafayette
Foster, David Smith

Lake Charles
Edwards, Margaret A.

Metairie
Johnson, Gregory Scott

NORTH DAKOTA

Dickinson
Herauf, William Anton

Grand Forks
Widdel, John Earl, Jr.

OHIO

Akron
Nolfi, Edward Anthony

Ashtabula
Lesko, Jane Lynn

Athens
Yanity, Joseph Blair, Jr.

Bucyrus
Neff, Robert Clark, Sr.

Celina
Myers, Daniel

Chillicothe
Boulger, William Charles

Cincinnati
Eaton, Janet Ruth
Hoffheimer, Daniel Joseph
Hust, Bruce Kevin
Schwab, Nelson, Jr.
Sims, Victor Dwayne
Vogel, Cedric Wakelee

Cleveland
Boyko, Christopher Allan
Chandler, Everett Alfred
Goldfarb, Bernard Sanford
Kondzer, Thomas Allen
Neff, Owen Calvin
Sanislo, Paul Steve
Spurgeon, Roberta Kaye
Turoff, Jack Newton

Columbus
Casey, John Frederick
Cline, Richard Allen

Dayton
Farquhar, Robert Nichols
Vaughn, Noel Wyandt

Dublin
Lane, James Edward
Tenuta, Luigia

Findlay
Kostyo, John Francis

Franklin
Bronson, Barbara June

Howard
Lee, William Johnson

Jefferson
Geary, Michael Philip

Kent
Nome, William Andreas

Lima
Jacobs, Ann Elizabeth

Mentor
McCarter, William Kent

Mount Vernon
Rose, Kim Matthew

Newark
Gordon, L(eland) James

Painesville
Redmond, Edward Crosby

Saint Marys
Huber, William Evan
Kemp, Barrett George

Springboro
Sharts, John Edwin, III

Toledo
St. Clair, Donald David

Warren
Rossi, Anthony Gerald

Westerville
Lancione, Bernard Gabe

Willard
Thornton, Robert Floyd

Wilmington
Schutt, Walter Eugene

Youngstown
Ausnehmer, John Edward
Briach, George Gary

OKLAHOMA

Edmond
Loving, Susan Brimer

Enid
Martin, Michael Rex

Kingfisher
Baker, Thomas Edward

Lawton
Ashton, Mark Alfred

Mcalester
Cornish, Richard Pool

Oklahoma City
Boston, William Clayton
Nesbitt, Charles Rudolph
Ross, William Jarboe
Wilson, Julia Ann Yother

Poteau
Sanders, Douglas Warner, Jr.

Stroud
Swanson, Robert Lee

OREGON

Eugene
Cooper, Michael Lee
DuPriest, Douglas Millhollen

Medford
Thierolf, Richard Burton, Jr.

Pendleton
Rew, Lawrence Boyd

PENNSYLVANIA

Allentown
Somach, Richard Brent

Clearfield
Falvo, Mark Anthony

Doylestown
Elliott, Richard Howard
Mellon, Thomas Edward, Jr.

Du Bois
Blakley, Benjamin Spencer, III

Easton
Scheer, Joel Martin

Feasterville Trevose
Osterhout, Richard Cadwallader

Harrisburg
Hanson, Robert DeLolle
Maleski, Cynthia Maria
Skelly, Joseph Gordon

Hazleton
Schiavo, Pasco Louis

Kingston
Meyer, Martin Jay

Lancaster
Duroni, Charles Eugene
Pyfer, John Frederick, Jr.

Mc Keesport
Kessler, Steven Fisher

Narberth
Mezvinsky, Edward M.

New Castle
Mangino, Matthew Thomas

North Wales
Brady, George Charles, III

Paoli
Durham, James W.

Philadelphia
Girard-diCarlo, David Franklin
Hoffman, Alan Jay
Moses, Bonnie Smith
O'Brien, William Jerome, II
Wolf, Bruce

Pittsburgh
Bogut, John Carl, Jr.
Herchenroether, Peter Young
Holsinger, Candice Doreen
Litman, Roslyn Margolis
McLaughlin, John Sherman
Pushinsky, Jon
Sanders, Russell Ronald
Terra, Sharon Ecker

Pottsville
Jones, Joseph Hayward

Sewickley
Mance, Jack Michael

Trevose
McEvilly, James Patrick, Jr.

Wernersville
Worley, Jane Ludwig

York
Hoffmeyer, William Frederick

RHODE ISLAND

Cranston
Coletti, John Anthony

Newport
McConnell, David Kelso

Pawtucket
Kranseler, Lawrence Michael

Providence
Esposito, Dennis Harry
Tammelleo, A. David

Warwick
Penza, Joseph Fulvio, Jr.

West Warwick
Pollock, Bruce Gerald

SOUTH CAROLINA

Charleston
Clement, Robert Lebby, Jr.

Columbia
Lewis, Ernest Crosby

Greenville
Talley, Michael Frank

Greenwood
Hughston, Thomas Leslie, Jr.

Hilton Head Island
Scarminach, Charles Anthony

TENNESSEE

Athens
Higgins, Kenneth Dyke

Chattanooga
Jessup, William Eugene

Clarksville
Smith, Gregory Dale

Humboldt
Boyte, George Griffin

Johnson City
Culp, James David
Epps, James Haws, III

Knoxville
Giordano, Lawrence Francis
Routh, John William
Swanson, Charles Walter

Memphis
Allen, Newton Perkins
Manire, James McDonnell
Rutledge, Roger Keith

Nashville
Cantrell, Luther E., Jr.
Torrey, Claudia Olivia
Woods, Larry David

Newport
Bell, John Alton
Campbell, Roy Timothy, Jr.

Oak Ridge
Wilkinson, Robert Warren

Trenton
Harrell, Limmie Lee, Jr.

TEXAS

Austin
Weddington, Sarah Ragle
Wester, Ruric Herschel, Jr.

Bellaire
Soffar, William Douglas

Belton
Burrows, Jon Hanes

Brownsville
Fleming, Tommy Wayne

Brownwood
Bell, William Woodward

Cleveland
Campbell, Selaura Joy

Corpus Christi
Alberts, Harold

Dallas
Levin, Hervey Phillip
Mueller, Mark Christopher
Parker, James Francis
Ringle, Brett Adelbert
Sloman, Marvin Sherk

Denton
Narsutis, John Keith

Fort Worth
Mullanax, Milton Greg
Paddock, Michael Buckley

Garland
Irby, Holt

Georgetown
Bryce, William Delf

Houston
Bradie, Peter Richard
Cooper, Thomas Randolph
Ellis, David Dale
Forbes, Arthur Lee, III
Gutheinz, Joseph Richard, Jr.
Plaeger, Frederick Joseph, II

Lufkin
Garrison, Pitser Hardeman

Richardson
Jeffreys, Albert Leonidas

Rockport
Benningfield, Carol Ann

Round Mountain
Moursund, Albert Wadel, III

San Antonio
Hollin, Shelby W.
Oppenheimer, Jesse Halff
Wallis, Ben Alton, Jr.
Welmaker, Forrest Nolan

Yoakum
Kvinta, Charles J.

UTAH

Park City
Schiesswohl, Cynthia Rae Schlegel

Salt Lake City
McConkie, Oscar Walter
Scofield, David Willson

VERMONT

Burlington
Leddy, John Thomas

Chester
Holme, John Charles, Jr.

VIRGINIA

Alexandria
Beach, Barbara Purse

Arlington
Glazier, Jonathan Hemenway
Walker, Woodrow Wilson

Chester
Gray, Charles Robert

Danville
Conway, French Hoge

Fairfax
Stanley, William Martin

Falls Church
Hartshorn, Roland DeWitt
Kirk, Dennis Dean
Redmond, Robert

Grundy
McGlothlin, Michael Gordon

Lynchburg
Angel, James Joseph
Light, William Randall

Manassas
Scriven, Wayne Marcus

Mc Lean
Friedlander, Jerome Peyser, II
Morris, James Malachy

Mechanicsville
d'Evegnee, Charles Paul

Newport News
Saunders, Bryan Leslie

Norfolk
Ware, Guilford Dudley

Portsmouth
Lavin, Barbara Hofheins

Reston
Anderson, Charles Anthony

Richmond
Pearsall, John Wesley
Robinson, Thomas Hart
Witt, Walter Francis, Jr.

Roanoke
Woodrum, Clifton A., III

Springfield
Chappell, Milton Leroy
Costello, Daniel Brian

Tazewell
Mullins, Roger Wayne

Virginia Beach
Spitzli, Donald Hawkes, Jr.

WASHINGTON

Anacortes
Glein, Richard Jeriel

Bellingham
Serka, Philip Angelo

Centralia
Buzzard, Steven Ray

Montesano
Stewart, James Malcolm

Seattle
Ellis, James Reed
Pritchard, Llewelyn G.

Spokane
Anderson, Robert Edward
Scanlon, Robert Charles

Tacoma
Barline, John
Hostnik, Charles Rivoire

WEST VIRGINIA

Beckley
Kennedy, David Tinsley

Gassaway
Jones, Jeniver James

Romney
Saville, Royce Blair

WISCONSIN

Appleton
Drescher, Kathleen Ebben

Deerfield
Pappas, David Christopher

Germantown
Statkus, Jerome Francis

Madison
Mitby, John Chester

Menomonee Falls
Hurt, Michael Carter

Milwaukee
Donahue, John Edward
Friebert, Robert Howard
Michelstetter, Stanley Hubert
Orzel, Michael Dale
Peranteau, Mary Elizabeth

Monroe
Kittelsen, Rodney Olin

Oshkosh
Kelly, John Martin

Portage
Bennett, David Hinkley

Wausau
Drengler, William Allan John

WYOMING

Cheyenne
Hathaway, Stanley Knapp

Riverton
Girard, Nettabell

CHINA

Hong Kong
Stender, Neal A.

FRANCE

Paris
Safa, Rachid P.

NIGERIA

Lagos
Oyadongha, Kerepamo Peter

NORWAY

Osteras
Drevvatne, Dag

PERU

Lima
Girbau, Miguel Angel

THE PHILIPPINES

Makati
Agcaoili, Jose Luis Villafranca

Makati City
Salvador, Tranquil, III

SAUDI ARABIA

Central Province
Elfaki, Mohamed Ahmed Mohamed

SWITZERLAND

Zurich
Koch, Thomas

ADDRESS UNPUBLISHED

Bierbower, James J.
Burgess, Hayden Fern (Poka Laenui)
Donnally, Robert Andrew
Easterling, Charles Armo
Falkiewicz, Christina L.
Feldkamp, John Calvin
Fleischman, Herman Israel
Garry, John Thomas, II
Hubbard, Michael James
Jorgensen, Erik Holger
Levinson, Kenneth Lee

North Chicago
de Lasa, José M.

Northbrook
Dilling, Kirkpatrick Wallwick

Palatine
Victor, Michael Gary

Springfield
Morse, Saul Julian

INDIANA

Hammond
Diamond, Eugene Christopher

Indianapolis
Betley, Leonard John
Gilliland, John Campbell, II
Horn, Brenda Sue
Kemper, James Dee

KANSAS

Kansas City
Holbrook, Reid Franklin

Overland Park
Ellis, Jeffrey Orville

Prairie Village
Stanton, Roger D.

KENTUCKY

Louisville
Reed, D. Gary

LOUISIANA

Baton Rouge
Riddick, Winston Wade, Sr.

Lafayette
Breaux, Paul Joseph

Metairie
Ford, Robert David

New Orleans
Beahm, Franklin D.
David, Robert Jefferson

MARYLAND

Baltimore
Moser, M(artin) Peter
Pretl, Michael Albert
Sfekas, Stephen James
Wheatley, Charles Henry, III
Zimmerly, James Gregory

Chevy Chase
Montedonico, Joseph

MASSACHUSETTS

Boston
Haddad, Ernest Mudarri
Murray, Philip Edmund, Jr.
Reardon, Frank Emond
White, Barry Bennett

Cambridge
Crawford, Linda Sibery

Springfield
Fein, Sherman Edward

Worcester
Donnelly, James Corcoran, Jr.

MICHIGAN

Detroit
Felt, Julia Kay
Johnson, Cynthia L(e) M(ae)
Shannon, Margaret Anne

Southfield
Schwartz, Robert H.

MINNESOTA

Bloomington
Broeker, John Milton

Hallock
Malm, Roger Charles

Minneapolis
Hanson, Bruce Eugene
Struthers, Margo S.

Saint Paul
LeVander, Bernhard Wilhelm

MISSISSIPPI

Greenville
Martin, Andrew Ayers

MISSOURI

Jefferson City
Tettlebaum, Harvey M.

Kansas City
Blackwood, George Dean, Jr.
Brous, Thomas Richard
Kaufman, Michelle Stark
Toll, Perry Mark

Saint Charles
Weber, William Randolph

Saint Louis
Brostron, Judith Curran
Schoene, Kathleen Snyder
Watters, Richard Donald

NEVADA

Las Vegas
Ashleman, Ivan Reno, II

NEW JERSEY

Berlin
Goldstein, Benjamin

Bridgewater
Conroy, Robert John

Metuchen
Frizell, David J.

New Providence
Adler, Nadia C.

Roseland
Eichler, Burton Lawrence

Trenton
Isele, William Paul

Woodbridge
Schaff, Michael Frederick

NEW MEXICO

Santa Fe
Pound, John Bennett

NEW YORK

Bronxville
Recabo, Jaime Miguel

Brooklyn
Malamud, Alexander

Buffalo
Greene, Robert Michael

New York
Appel, Albert M.
Burke, Kathleen Mary
Cohen, Joshua Robert
Diamond, David Howard
Glass, Joel
Hoffman, David Nathaniel
Huston, Barry Scott
Kaufman, Robert Max
Kornreich, Edward Scott
Paul, Eve W.
Regan, Susan Ginsberg
Scher, Stanley Jules
Seay, J. David
Yun, Edward Joon

Poughkeepsie
Adin, Richard H(enry)

Rochester
Fox, Edward Hanton
Madden, Neal D.

Schenectady
Sokolow, Lloyd Bruce

NORTH CAROLINA

Raleigh
Glass, Fred Stephen
Simpson, Steven Drexell

Wilmington
Kaufman, James Jay

Winston Salem
Brett, Anthony Harvey
Porter, Leon Eugene, Jr.

OHIO

Athens
Hedges, Richard Houston

Chesterland
Durn, Raymond Joseph

Cincinnati
Wales, Ross Elliot

Cleveland
Weller, Charles David

Columbus
Allen, Richard Lee, Jr.
DeRousie, Charles Stuart
Dunlay, Catherine Telles
Fisher, Fredrick Lee
Wightman, Alec

Dublin
Maloon, Jerry L.

Howard
Lee, William Johnson

Toledo
Witherell, Dennis Patrick

Warren
Rossi, Anthony Gerald

OKLAHOMA

Oklahoma City
Gordon, Kevin Dell

Tulsa
Gaberino, John Anthony, Jr.

OREGON

Portland
Anderson, Herbert Hatfield
Cooney, Thomas Emmett
Hart, John Edward

PENNSYLVANIA

Bala Cynwyd
Schwartz, Jeffrey Byron

Blue Bell
Settle, Eric Lawrence

Bryn Mawr
Henry, Ronald George

Erie
Tupitza, Thomas Anton

Harrisburg
Barto, Charles O., Jr.
Maleski, Cynthia Maria

Haverford
Stiller, Jennifer Anne

Malvern
Cameron, John Clifford

Philadelphia
Brier, Bonnie Susan
Calvert, Jay H., Jr.
Campbell, Amy Tannery
Cramer, Harold
Esser, Carl Eric
Flanagan, Joseph Patrick, Jr.
Gornish, Gerald
Kraeutler, Eric
Lowery, William Herbert
McAneny, Eileen S.
Morris, Roland
Reiss, John Barlow

Pittsburgh
Conti, Joy Flowers
Geeseman, Robert George
Hough, Thomas Henry Michael
Kabala, Edward John
Lyncheski, John E.
Perry, John F.
Springer, Eric Winston
Thurman, Andrew Edward
Wilkinson, James Allan

Plymouth
Musto, Joseph John

Wayne
Kalogredis, Vasilios J.

RHODE ISLAND

Providence
Tammelleo, A. David

Woonsocket
Roszkowski, Joseph John

SOUTH CAROLINA

Columbia
Pollard, William Albert

North Charleston
Laddaga, Lawrence Alexander

SOUTH DAKOTA

Pierre
Gerdes, David Alan

TENNESSEE

Kingsport
Tweed, Douglas Steven

Knoxville
Arnett, Foster Deaver

Memphis
Schuler, Walter E.

Nashville
Torrey, Claudia Olivia
Tuke, Robert Dudley
Yuspeh, Alan Ralph

TEXAS

Abilene
Robinson, Vianei Lopez

Austin
Schaffer, Dean Aaron

Burleson
Johnstone, Deborah Blackmon

Dallas
Gerberding Cowart, Greta Elaine
Newsom, Jan Lynn Reimann

Fort Worth
Griffith, Richard Lattimore
Hayes, Larry B.

Harlingen
Pope, William L.

Houston
Blackshear, A.T., Jr.
Crocker, Samuel Sackett
Eiland, Gary Wayne
Farley, Jan Edwin
Rogers, Arthur Hamilton, III

San Antonio
Cruse, Rex Beach, Jr.

Temple
Clements, Jamie Hager
Pickle, Jerry Richard

VERMONT

Saint Johnsbury
Marshall, John Henry

VIRGINIA

Alexandria
Carter, Richard Dennis
Franklin, Jeanne F.
Klewans, Samuel N.

Arlington
Mossinghoff, Gerald Joseph

Great Falls
Neidich, George Arthur

Mc Lean
Brown, Thomas Cartmel, Jr.

Norfolk
Poston, Anita Owings

Reston
Platt, Leslie A.

Richmond
Hackney, Virginia Howitz
Pope, Robert Dean

Roanoke
Lemon, William Jacob

WASHINGTON

Seattle
Dolan, Andrew Kevin
Hutcheson, Mark Andrew
Petrie, Gregory Steven
Waldman, Bart
Williams, Rebecca Lynn

Spokane
Connolly, K. Thomas
Riherd, John Arthur

WEST VIRGINIA

Bluefield
Evans, Wayne Lewis

Wheeling
Riley, Arch Wilson, Jr.
Wilmoth, William David

WISCONSIN

Germantown
Ehlinger, Ralph Jerome

Madison
Hanson, David James

Mequon
Burroughs, Charles Edward

Milwaukee
Biehl, Michael Melvin
Friedman, James Dennis
Van Grunsven, Paul Robert

Waukesha
Hocum, Monica Carroll

ENGLAND

London
White, Walter Hiawatha, Jr.

ADDRESS UNPUBLISHED

Billauer, Barbara Pfeffer
Boone, Richard Winston, Sr.
Burgess, Hayden Fern (Poka Laenui)
Fine, Robert Paul
McFerrin, James Hamil
McLendon, Susan Michelle
Nelson, Richard Perry
Quayle, Marilyn Tucker

Wynstra, Nancy Ann

IMMIGRATION, NATURALIZATION, AND CUSTOMS

UNITED STATES

ARIZONA

Eloy
O'Leary, Thomas Michael

Mesa
Gunderson, Brent Merrill

Phoenix
Song Ong, Roxanne Kay

CALIFORNIA

Bakersfield
Gong, Gloria M.

Fremont
Cummings, John Patrick

Los Angeles
Loewy, Peter Henry

Pasadena
Chan, Daniel Chung-Yin
Mehrpoo, Nikoo Nikki

San Diego
Snaid, Leon Jeffrey

San Francisco
Baker, Steven Wright

San Jose
Doan, Xuyen Van

Studio City
Miller, Charles Maurice

Visalia
Atkins, Thomas Jay

COLORADO

Denver
Heiserman, Robert Gifford

CONNECTICUT

New Haven
Gildea, Brian Michael

DISTRICT OF COLUMBIA

Washington
Ambrose, Myles Joseph
Denniston, John Baker
Engel, Tala
Lublinski, Michael
Mitchell, Carol Ann
Outman, William Dell, II
Stern, Elizabeth Espin

FLORIDA

Coral Gables
Cano, Mario Stephen

Fort Lauderdale
Caulkins, Charles S.
Pascal, Robert Albert

Gainesville
White, Jill Carolyn

Miami
Dreize, Livia Rebbeka
Kurzban, Ira Jay
Poston, Rebekah Jane

Orlando
Johnson, Kraig Nelson
Neff, A. Guy

GEORGIA

Savannah
Gerard, Stephen Stanley

HAWAII

Honolulu
Oldenburg, Ronald Troy

ILLINOIS

Chicago
Anderson, Paul Stewart
Meltzer, Robert Craig
Paprocki, Thomas John
Ruttenberg, Harold Seymour

Rosemont
Mirabile, Thomas Keith

Springfield
Heckenkamp, Robert Glenn
Morse, Saul Julian

Wheaton
Butt, Edward Thomas, Jr.
Dudgeon, Thomas Carl

INDIANA

Granger
Lambert, George Robert

Indianapolis
Due, Danford Royce
Fels, James Alexander
Hammel, John Wingate
Hays, Thomas Clyde
Koch, Edna Mae
Lisher, John Leonard
McKeon, Thomas Joseph
Roberts, Patricia Susan
Schreckengast, William Owen
Yeager, Joseph Heizer, Jr.

Lafayette
Hart, Russell Holiday

Shelbyville
McNeely, James Lee

South Bend
Norton, Sally Pauline
Palmer, Robert Joseph

IOWA

Des Moines
Brown, Paul Edmondson
Duckworth, Marvin E.
Hill, Luther Lyons, Jr.
Seitzinger, Edward Francis
Wharton, John Michael

Dubuque
Hammer, David Lindley

Marshalltown
Brooks, Patrick William

Sioux City
Mayne, Wiley Edward

KANSAS

Overland Park
Ellis, Jeffrey Orville
Ruse, Steven Douglas

KENTUCKY

Bowling Green
Rudloff, William Joseph

Covington
Wolnitzek, Stephen Dale

London
Keller, John Warren

Louisville
Orberson, William Baxter
Reed, D. Gary

Somerset
Yeast, Daniel Gordon

LOUISIANA

Baton Rouge
Dixon, Jerome Wayne
Riddick, Winston Wade, Sr.
Walsh, Milton O'Neal

Covington
Rice, Winston Edward

Lafayette
Judice, Marc Wayne
Swift, John Goulding

Lake Charles
Nieset, James Robert

Metairie
Ford, Robert David
McMahon, Robert Albert, Jr.

New Orleans
Abaunza, Donald Richard
Brian, A(lexis) Morgan, Jr.
Eustis, Richmond Minor
Futrell, John Maurice
Hurley, Grady Schell
Ostendorf, Lance Stephen
Sutterfield, James Ray

MAINE

Bangor
Woodcock, John Alden

Portland
Hirshon, Robert Edward
Lancaster, Ralph Ivan, Jr.
Whiting, Stephen Clyde

MARYLAND

Annapolis
Ruth, John Nicholas

Baltimore
Ebersole, Jodi Kay
Hansen, Christopher Agnew
Messina, Bonnie Lynn
Sturman, Philip
Zimmerly, James Gregory

Bethesda
Schimel, Richard E.

Burtonsville
Covington, Marlow Stanley

Chevy Chase
Weiss, Harlan Lee

Lutherville Timonium
White, William Nelson

Parkville
Hill, Milton King, Jr.

MASSACHUSETTS

Boston
Burns, Thomas David
Goldman, Eric Scot
Halström, Frederic Norman
Neumeier, Richard L.
O'Connell, Joseph Francis, III
Richmond, Alice Elenor

Canton
Masiello, Thomas Philip, Jr.

Chelmsford
Lerer, Neal M.

Hyannis
Horn, Everett Byron, Jr.

Longmeadow
Quinn, Andrew Peter, Jr.

Manchester
Wolfe, Robert Shenker

South Easton
Finn, Anne-Marie

Woburn
Lovins, Nelson Preston

Worcester
Balko, George Anthony, III

MICHIGAN

Bingham Farms
Fershtman, Julie Ilene

Birmingham
Zacharski, Dennis Edward

Detroit
Gunderson, Michael Arthur
Smith, James Albert

East Lansing
Vincent, Adrian Roger

Flint
Henneke, Edward George

Grand Rapids
Spies, Frank Stadler

Harper Woods
Gilbert, Ronald Rhea

Lansing
Baker, Frederick Milton, Jr.
Fink, Joseph Allen
Kritselis, William Nicholas
Sinas, George Thomas

Mount Clemens
Farrell, John Brendan

Pontiac
Pierson, William George

Saginaw
Gallagher, Edward John, II
Zanot, Craig Allen

Saint Clair Shores
Caretti, Richard Louis

Southfield
Gordon, Louis

Troy
Kruse, John Alphonse

MINNESOTA

Edina
Vukelich, John Edward

Golden Valley
Hagglund, Clarance Edward

Laporte
Woutat, Paul Gustav

Marine On Saint Croix
Hoke, George Peabody

Minneapolis
Degnan, John Michael
Erstad, Leon Robert
Faricy, John Hartnett, Jr.
Greener, Ralph Bertram
Hoch, Gary W.
Johnson, Paul Owen
Price, Joseph Michael

Reichert, Brent Larry
Reuter, James William
Sanner, Royce Norman
Witort, Janet Lee

Moorhead
Marquart, Steven Leonard

Saint Paul
Kirsch, Steven Jay
Maclin, Alan Hall

MISSISSIPPI

Biloxi
Dornan, Donald C., Jr.

Brandon
Obert, Keith David

Gulfport
Allen, Harry Roger
Dukes, James Otis
Harral, John Menteith

Jackson
Currie, Edward Jones, Jr.
Langford, James Jerry

MISSOURI

Cape Girardeau
Lowes, Albert Charles

Hannibal
Terrell, James Daniel

Kansas City
Abele, Robert Christopher
Bryant, Richard Todd
Conner, John Shull
Franke, Linda Frederick
Henson, Harold Eugene
Levings, Theresa Lawrence
Milton, Chad Earl
Rickert, Brian Patrick
Shay, David Eugene
Taff, Earl Wayne
Todd, Stephen Max

Saint Louis
Boggs, Beth Clemens
Brown, Paul Sherman
Kraft, Carl David
Marquitz, Kevin John
McDaniel, James Edwin
Reeg, Kurtis Bradford

MONTANA

Billings
Jones, James Leonard

Helena
Morrison, John Martin

NEBRASKA

Lincoln
Zink, Walter Earl, II

North Platte
Dawson, Kimberli Dawn

Omaha
Fuller, Diana Clare
Harr, Lawrence Francis
Krutter, Forrest Nathan

NEVADA

Las Vegas
Padgett, Anne

Reno
Barkley, Thierry Vincent
Pagni, Albert Frank

NEW HAMPSHIRE

Concord
Potter, Fred Leon

Manchester
Hutchins, Peter Edward
Peltonen, John Ernest

NEW JERSEY

Basking Ridge
O'Carroll, Anita Louise

Cherry Hill
Garrigle, William Aloysius

Edison
O'Brien, John Graham

Fairfield
Connell, William Terrence

Hackensack
Kiel, Paul Edward
Pollinger, William Joshua

Little Silver
Schmidt, Daniel Edward, IV

Maplewood
Joseph, Susan B.

Millburn
Madden, Edward George, Jr.

Morris Plains
Pluciennik, Thomas Casimir

Morristown
Gillen, James Robert

Newark
Eittreim, Richard MacNutt
Garde, John Charles
Kott, David Russell
McGuire, William B(enedict)

North Haledon
Harrington, Kevin Paul

Oakhurst
Widman, Douglas Jack

Paramus
Gilbert, Stephen Alan

Parsippany
Kallmann, Stanley Walter

Princeton
Brennan, William Joseph, III

Rutherford
Henschel, John James

Short Hills
Kaye, Marc Mendell

Shrewsbury
Hopkins, Charles Peter, II

Somerville
Freedman, Stuart Joel

Warren
Kraus, Steven Gary

West Orange
McNaboe, James Francis

NEW MEXICO

Albuquerque
Beach, Arthur O'Neal
Roberts, Randal William

Santa Fe
Culbert, Peter V.

NEW YORK

Albany
Laird, Edward DeHart, Jr.

Bronxville
Garber, Robert Edward

Brooklyn
Steinberg, Jerome Leonard

Buffalo
Barber, Janice Ann
Brock, David George
De Marie, Anthony Joseph
Goldberg, Neil A.
Parker, Michelle
Schoenborn, Daniel Leonard
Segalla, Thomas Francis

Elmsford
Neustadt, Paul

Garden City
Balkan, Kenneth J.

Glens Falls
Firth, Peter Alan

Hawthorne
Traub, Richard Kenneth

Melville
Schoenfeld, Michael P.

New York
Anderson, Eugene Robert
Barry, Desmond Thomas, Jr.
Birnbaum, Sheila L.
Bivona, John Vincent
Bower, Thomas Michael
Brady, Bruce Morgan
Calhoun, Monica Dodd
Cayea, Donald Joseph
Chiarchiaro, Frank John
Cohen, Joshua Robert
Cunha, Mark Geoffrey
Davis, Michael Steven
DeCarlo, Donald Thomas
DeOrchis, Vincent Moore
Dopf, Glenn William
Dunham, Wolcott Balestier, Jr.
Evans, Martin Frederic
Fitzpatrick, Garrett Joseph
Foster, David Lee
Gabay, Donald David
Garbarini, Chas. J.
Glass, Joel
Grady, Maureen Frances
Hamm, David Bernard
Hayden, Raymond Paul
Hayes, Gerald Joseph
Henderson, Donald Bernard, Jr.
Hersh, Robert Michael
Horkovich, Robert Michael
Jacobowitz, Harold Saul
Juceam, Robert E.
Kazanjian, John Harold
Kirschbaum, Myron
Klapper, Molly
Kleinberg, Norman Charles
Kroll, Sol
Laquercia, Thomas Michael

LeBlang, Skip Alan
Lederer, Peter David
Lesman, Michael Steven
Lesser, William Melville
Lynch, Luke Daniel, Jr.
Marcellino, Stephen Michael
Marshall, Sheila Hermes
McCormack, Howard Michael
McCormick, Hugh Thomas
Mentz, Lawrence
Nonna, John Michael
Oliveri, Paul Francis
Ornitz, Richard Martin
Packard, Stephen Michael
Quinlan, Guy Christian
Reilly, Conor Desmond
Riley, Scott C.
Rosow, Malcolm Bertram
Scher, Stanley Jules
Schlau, Philip
Schmidt, Charles Edward
Schnurman, Alan Joseph
Seitelman, Mark Elias
Semaya, Francine Levitt
Shanman, James Alan
Short, Skip
Shoss, Cynthia Renēe
Smith, Edwin Lloyd
Squire, Walter Charles
Steigman, Ernest R.
Tract, Marc Mitchell
Wakefield, Susannah Jane
Warshauer, Irene C.
Weiser, Martin Jay
West, Stephen Kingsbury
Williamson, Walter
Wilson, Thomas William
Wollan, Eugene
Yeager, Dennis Randall

Newark
Reid, James Edward

Newburgh
Milligram, Steven Irwin

Patchogue
Tona, Thomas

Rochester
Lascell, David Michael

Scarsdale
Perko, Kenneth Albert, Jr.

Smithtown
Spellman, Thomas Joseph, Jr.

Uniondale
Rivkin, John Lawrence

Westbury
Whiteman, Robert Gordon

White Plains
Klein, Paul E.
Madden, M. Stuart
Taft, Nathaniel Belmont

NORTH CAROLINA

Asheville
Davis, Roy Walton, Jr.
Starnes, Oscar Edwin, Jr.

Chapel Hill
Zoffer, David B.

Durham
Lewis, David Olin

Greensboro
Gabell, Margaret M.

Marion
Burgin, Charles Edward

New Bern
Kellum, Norman Bryant, Jr.

Raleigh
Cole, Sean Andrew Burke
Dixon, Wright Tracy, Jr.
Millberg, John C.
Trott, William Macnider

Smithfield
Schulz, Bradley Nicholas

Winston Salem
Comerford, Walter Thompson, Jr.
Osborn, Malcolm Everett

NORTH DAKOTA

Bismarck
Edin, Charles Thomas
Gilbertson, Joel Warren

OHIO

Akron
Wolfe, John Leslie
Wright, Bradley Abbott

Aurora
Hermann, Philip J.

Canton
Herbert, David Lee

Cincinnati
Hill, Thomas Clark
Meyers, Karen Diane
Neltner, Michael Martin

Cleveland
Brunn, Thomas Leo, Sr.
Duncan, Ed Eugene

Maher, Edward Joseph
Toohey, Brian Frederick

Columbus
Allen, Richard Lee, Jr.
Draper, Gerald Linden
Ryan, Joseph W., Jr.
Schwartz, Robert S.
Woods, William Hunt

Dublin
Lane, James Edward

Independence
Rutter, Robert Paul

Lebanon
Benedict, Ronald Louis

Toledo
Tuschman, James Marshall

Willoughby
Cruikshank, David Earl

Youngstown
Blair, Richard Bryson

OKLAHOMA

Jones
Dean, Bill Verlin, Jr.

Mcalester
Neal, Charles D., Jr.

Norman
Sweeney, Everett John

Oklahoma City
Gordon, Kevin Dell
Wyatt, Robert Lee, IV

Tulsa
Atkinson, Michael Pearce
Clark, Joseph Francis, Jr.

OREGON

Medford
Deatherage, William Vernon

Portland
Cooney, Thomas Emmett
Dailey, Dianne K.
Hill, Christopher T.
Kennedy, Jack Leland

Salem
Robertson, Joseph David

PENNSYLVANIA

Allentown
Scherline, Jay Alan

Gladwyne
Booth, Harold Waverly

Harleysville
Strauss, Catherine B.

Harrisburg
Feinour, John Stephen
Hafer, Joseph Page

Hollidaysburg
Pfaff, Robert James

Horsham
Best, Franklin Luther, Jr.

Hummelstown
Mark, Timothy Ivan

King Of Prussia
DeMaria, Joseph Carminus
Stevens, Capri R.

Kingston
Shaffer, Charles Alan

Malvern
Griffith, Edward, II

Media
Cramp, John Franklin
Zicherman, David L.

New Castle
Mojock, David Theodore

Newtown Square
Crowley, James Michael

Orefield
Dimmich, Jeffrey Robert

Philadelphia
Aaron, Kenneth Ellyot
Connor, Joseph Patrick, III
Craven, Charles Warren
Fineman, S. David
Garcia, Rudolph
Goldberg, Marvin Allen
Hanselman, Fredrick Charles
Heinzen, Bernard George
Herman, Charles Jacob
Howard, William Herbert
Ledwith, John Francis
Lowery, William Herbert
Milbourne, Walter Robertson
Palmer, Richard Ware
Pratter, Gene E. K.
Resnick, Stephanie
Wagner, Thomas Joseph

Pittsburgh
Bochicchio, Vito Salvatore
Ober, Russell John, Jr.
Perry, John F.
von Waldow, Arnd N.

Sewickley
Mance, Jack Michael

Wyomissing
Turner, David Eldridge

RHODE ISLAND

Warwick
Reilly, John B.

SOUTH CAROLINA

Columbia
Carpenter, Charles Elford, Jr.
Livoti, Anthony William
Oswald, Billy Robertson
Painter, Samuel Franklin

Greenville
Lynch, J. Timothy

SOUTH DAKOTA

Pierre
Gerdes, David Alan

Sioux Falls
Luce, Michael Leigh

TENNESSEE

Chattanooga
Campbell, Paul, III
Cooper, Gary Allan

Johnson City
Jenkins, Ronald Wayne

Knoxville
Johnson, Steven Boyd
London, James Harry
Wheeler, John Watson
White, Edward Gibson, II

Memphis
Buchignani, Leo Joseph
Glassman, Richard
Russell, James Franklin

Nashville
Jameson, Michael Francis
Youngblood, Elaine Michele

Signal Mountain
Anderson, Charles Hill

TEXAS

Austin
Grosenheider, Delno John
Rittenberry, Kelly Culhane
Roan, Forrest Calvin, Jr.
Schaffer, Dean Aaron

Beaumont
Oxford, Hubert, III
Scofield, Louis M., Jr.

Corpus Christi
Carnahan, Robert Narvell
Evans, Allene Delories
Fancher, Rick
Leon, Rolando Luis

Dallas
Davenport, James Kent
Ellis, Alfred Wright (Al Ellis)
Geiger, Richard Stuart
LaBrec, David John
Newsom, Jan Lynn Reimann
Pruessner, David Morgan

Fort Worth
Cottongame, W. Brice
Dent, Edward Dwain
Hart, John Clifton
Paddock, Michael Buckley
Wagner, James Peyton

Houston
Dykes, Osborne Jefferson, III
Eckhardt, William Rudolf, III
Krebs, Arno William, Jr.
Love, Scott Anthony
Miller, Brian Charles
Pate, Stephen Patrick
Sherman, Robert Taylor, Jr.
Sorrels, Randall Owen
Wojciechowski, Marc James

Lubbock
Nelson, Jack Odell, Jr.

Mcallen
Mills, William Michael

Midland
Fletcher, Richard Royce

Odessa
Hendrick, Benard Calvin, VII

San Antonio
Brennan, James Patrick, Sr.
Ferguson, Charles Alan
Henry, Peter York
Patrick, Dane Herman
Solis, Carlos Eduardo

Temple
Pickle, Jerry Richard

The Woodlands
Schlacks, Stephen Mark

UTAH

Salt Lake City
Barlow, Peter Hugh
Larson, Bryan A.

VERMONT

Rutland
Faignant, John Paul
O'Rourke, William Andrew, III
Werle, Mark Fred

VIRGINIA

Fairfax
Brown, Gary Wayne

Norton
Shortridge, Judy Beth

Radford
Davis, Richard Waters

Richmond
Allen, Wilbur Coleman
Ellis, Andrew Jackson, Jr.
Esposito, Mark Mario
Spahn, Gary Joseph

Virginia Beach
Dumville, S(amuel) Lawrence
Swope, Richard McAllister

Wytheville
Baird, Thomas Bryan, Jr.

WASHINGTON

Bellevue
Zackey, Jonathan Thomas

Longview
Barlow, John Aden

Olympia
Hoglund, John Andrew

Renton
Swanson, Arthur Dean

Seattle
Blom, Daniel Charles
Burns, Robert William
Harris, Thomas V.
Levy, Barbara Jo
Loftus, Thomas Daniel
Mines, Michael
Waitt, Robert Kenneth
Whitehead, James Fred, III

Spokane
Pontarolo, Michael Joseph
Riherd, John Arthur

WEST VIRGINIA

Huntington
Bagley, Charles Frank, III

Wheeling
Wilmoth, William David

WISCONSIN

Appleton
Lonergan, Kevin
Siddall, Michael Sheridan

Fond Du Lac
English, Dale Lowell

Green Bay
Schober, Thomas Leonard

Kenosha
Higgins, John Patrick

Madison
Pernitz, Scott Gregory
Schmid, John Henry, Jr.

Milwaukee
Bremer, John M.
Gaines, Irving David
Galanis, John William
Wynn, Stanford Alan

Oshkosh
Wilde, William Richard

Rhinelander
Saari, John William, Jr.

Wausau
Kammer, Robert Arthur, Jr.

WYOMING

Rock Springs
Rolich, Frank Alvin

AUSTRALIA

Melbourne
Begg, Derek Jonathon

ENGLAND

London
Bandurka, Andrew Alan
George, Anna-Britt Kristin
Mendelowitz, Michael Sydney
Rochez, Nicholas Dutfield
Spencer, Robin Graham Nelson
Stanley, Ian G.

GREECE

Athens
Murray, Virginia

INDIA

New Delhi
Kalha, Baljit Singh

IRELAND

Dublin 1
Fitzgerald, Eithne Margaret

KENYA

Nairoba
Maosa, Thomas Nyakambi

SINGAPORE

Singapore
David, James P.

SOUTH AFRICA

Johannesburg
Prinsloo, Jojannes Christiaan

ADDRESS UNPUBLISHED

Bandy, Jack D.
Bell, John William
Berman, Richard Bruce
Blazzard, Norse Novar
Brown, Margaret deBeers
Buehler, John Wilson
Dondanville, John Wallace
Eaton, Larry Ralph
Fekete, George Otto
Flanary, Donald Herbert, Jr.
Griffith, Steven Franklin, Sr.
Hawkins, Carmen Doloras
Howell, Ally Windsor
Johnson, Edward Michael
Kennedy, Vekeno
Klein, Judah Baer
Kouba, Lisa Marco
Levinson, Kenneth Lee
Levy, David
Lory, Loran Steven
Massey, Kathleen Marie Oates
McGuffey, Carroll Wade, Jr.
Parker, John Francis
Parker, Robert Marc
Rosseel-Jones, Mary Louise
Russo, Donna Marie
Stanisci, Thomas William
Tierney, Kevin Joseph
Vinar, Benjamin

INTELLECTUAL PROPERTY

UNITED STATES

ALABAMA

Birmingham
Hinton, James Forrest, Jr.
Long, Thad Gladden

ARIZONA

Phoenix
Allen, Robert Eugene Barton
Corson, Kimball Jay
Meschkow, Jordan M.
Sutton, Samuel J.

Tempe
Shimpock, Kathy Elizabeth

ARKANSAS

Pine Bluff
Strode, Joseph Arlin

CALIFORNIA

Cerritos
Sarno, Maria Erlinda

Claremont
Ansell, Edward Orin

Cupertino
Simon, Nancy Ruth

Irvine
Stone, Samuel Beckner

La Jolla
Karlen, Peter Hurd

Los Angeles
Biederman, Donald Ellis
Braun, David A(dlai)
Donaldson, Michael Cleaves
Scoular, Robert Frank
Seiden, Andy
Weisberg, Seth David
Wine, Mark Philip

Marina Del Rey
Coplan, Daniel Jonathan

Menlo Park
Coats, William Sloan, III
Halluin, Albert Price
Mendelson, Alan Charles

Newport Beach
Knobbe, Louis Joseph

Pacific Palisades
Flattery, Thomas Long

Palo Alto
Johnston, Alan Cope
Prinz, Kristie Dawn
Radlo, Edward John
Sherman, Martin Peter

Pasadena
van Schoonenberg, Robert G.

San Bernardino
Nassar, William Michael

San Diego
Chatroo, Arthur Jay
Lathrop, Mitchell Lee
Mebane, Julie Shaffer

San Francisco
Reding, John Anthony
Richardson, Daniel Ralph
Riley, Benjamin Kneeland
Salomon, Darrell Joseph
Thiel, Clark T.
Traynor, John Michael
Yamakawa, David Kiyoshi, Jr.

San Jose
Anderson, Edward Virgil
Hernández, Fernando Vargas
McManis, James
Simon, James Lowell
Small, Jonathan Andrew

San Mateo
Fishman, Shanti Alice

Santa Clara
Zahrt, William Dietrich, II

Seal Beach
Hennen, Thomas Waldo

Sunnyvale
Wyatt, Thomas Csaba

CONNECTICUT

Greenwich
Putman, Linda Murray

Hartford
Morrison, Francis Henry

DELAWARE

Wilmington
Devine, Donn
Huntley, Donald Wayne
Magee, Thomas Hugh
Whitney, Douglas E., Sr.

DISTRICT OF COLUMBIA

Washington
Buffon, Charles Edward
Cantor, Herbert I.
Dinan, Donald Robert
Efros, Ellen Ann
Greenberger, I. Michael
McDaniels, William E.
Pfeiffer, Margaret Kolodny
Price, Griffith Baley, Jr.
Sayler, Robert Nelson
Shieber, William J.
Sokal, Allen Marcel
Spath, Gregg Anthony
Wilson, Gary Dean
Woodworth, Ramsey Lloyd

FLORIDA

Miami
Nagin, Stephen Elias
Spector, Brian Fred

Miami Lakes
Dominik, Jack Edward

Tampa
Thomas, Gregg Darrow

GEORGIA

Atlanta
Fleming, Julian Denver, Jr.

ILLINOIS

Chicago
Altman, Louis
Benak, James Donald
Chin, Davis
Hilliard, David Craig
Karon, Sheldon
Lloyd, Robert Allen
Manzo, Edward David
Ropski, Gary Melchior
Rupert, Donald William
Schur, Gerald
Smedinghoff, Thomas J.
Snyder, Jean Maclean
Wick, Lawrence Scott

Evanston
Thompson, Michael

Libertyville
Fato, Gildo E.

Oak Brook
Mlsna, Kathryn Kimura

Skokie
Gotkin, Michael Stanley

INDIANA

Indianapolis
Knebel, Donald Earl

Merrillville
Kinney, Richard Gordon

IOWA

Des Moines
Fisher, Thomas George

KANSAS

Overland Park
Sampson, William Roth

LOUISIANA

New Orleans
Etter, John Karl
Miller, Gary H.

MARYLAND

Baltimore
Berlage, Jan Ingham
Dewey, Joel Allen
Haines, Thomas W. W.
Hopps, Raymond, Jr.
Pappas, George Frank

Potomac
Troffkin, Howard Julian

MASSACHUSETTS

Boston
Cekala, Chester
Coolidge, Daniel Scott
Deutsch, Stephen B.
Lambert, Gary Ervery
Matzka, Michael Alan
Patterson, John de la Roche, Jr.
Perry, Blair Lane
Storer, Thomas Perry

Braintree
Mullare, T(homas) Kenwood, Jr.

Brookline
Bursley, Kathleen A.

Lexington
Dulchinos, Peter

MICHIGAN

Bloomfield Hills
Stewart, Michael B.

Dearborn
Dixon, Richard Dean

Troy
Cantor, Bernard Jack
McKeone, Keri Marie

MINNESOTA

Bloomington
Jackson, Renee Leone

Minneapolis
Anderson, Alan Marshall
DiPietro, Mark Joseph
Kamrath, Alan Dale
Sawicki, Zbigniew Peter
Street, Erica Catherine

MISSOURI

Kansas City
Tyler, John Edward, III

Saint Louis
Evans, Lawrence E.

NEBRASKA

Omaha
Vosburg, Bruce David

NEVADA

Reno
Kent, Stephen Smiley

NEW HAMPSHIRE

Concord
Rines, Robert Harvey

Hanover
Gardner, Peter Jaglom

Manchester
Scannell, Timothy C.

NEW JERSEY

Florham Park
Laulicht, Murray Jack

Haddonfield
Heuisler, Charles William

Morristown
Schwartz, Howard J.

New Brunswick
Biribauer, Richard Frank

Roseland
Hern, J. Brooke

NEW YORK

Bronxville
Fuller, David Otis, Jr.

Brooklyn
Dorf, Robert Clay

Ithaca
Pinnisi, Michael Donato

New York
Bandon, William Edward, III
Bender, John Charles
Brecher, Howard Arthur
Celedonia, Baila Handelman
Clary, Richard Wayland
Cohen, Myron
Connolly, Kevin Jude
Crane, Roger Ryan, Jr.
Faber, Robert Charles
Hamburg, Charles Bruce
Jaglom, Andre Richard
Karmali, Rashida Alimahomed
Katsh, Salem Michael
Kurnit, Richard Alan
Matus, Wayne Charles
Milgrim, Roger Michael
Oberman, Michael Stewart
Paul, Eve W.
Pegram, John Braxton
Plevan, Kenneth A.
Plottel, Roland
Shentov, Ognjan V.
Spiegel, Jerrold Bruce
Weinberger, Harold Paul
Weinschel, Alan Jay
Woods, Christopher John

NORTH CAROLINA

Durham
Jenkins, Richard Erik

OHIO

Akron
Kreek, Louis Francis, Jr.

Cincinnati
Chesser, Stacey C.

Cleveland
Adamo, Kenneth R.
Burge, David Alan
Collin, Thomas James
Crehore, Charles Aaron

Columbus
Ferguson, Gerald Paul

Miamisburg
Battles, John Martin

OKLAHOMA

Oklahoma City
Kenney, John Arthur

OREGON

Ashland
Fine, J. David

Portland
Van Valkenburg, Edgar Walter

PENNSYLVANIA

Allentown
Simmons, James Charles

Malvern
Quay, Thomas Emery

Media
Elman, Gerry Jay

Philadelphia
Cullen, Raymond T.
Frank, George Andrew
Pillion, Michael Leith

Pittsburgh
Beck, Paul Augustine
Colen, Frederick Haas
Johnson, Barbara Elizabeth

SOUTH CAROLINA

Charleston
Barker, Douglas Alan

TENNESSEE

Signal Mountain
Leitner, Gregory Marc

TEXAS

Borger
Edmonds, Thomas Leon

Dallas
Hammond, Herbert J.
Malorzo, Thomas Vincent
Moore, Edward Warren

Houston
Crocker, Samuel Sackett
Fladung, Richard Denis
Frost, Charles Estes, Jr.
Kirk, John Robert, Jr.
LaFuze, William L.
Pravel, Bernarr Roe
Shurn, Peter Joseph, III
Tripp, Karen Bryant
Vaden, Frank Samuel, III

Plano
Levine, Harold

Tyler
Alworth, Charles Wesley

UTAH

Salt Lake City
Nydegger, Rick D.

VIRGINIA

Arlington
Litman, Richard Curtis
Swift, Stephen Christopher

Fairfax
Dewhirst, John Ward

Falls Church
Brady, Rupert Joseph

Leesburg
Kushner, Gordon Peter

Mc Lean
Edgell, George Paul
LeSourd, Nancy Susan Oliver

Richmond
Merhige, Robert Reynold, Jr.
Robinson, John Victor

WASHINGTON

Redmond
Phillips, Richard Lee

Seattle
Cumbow, Robert Charles
Mitchell, Robert Bertelson, Jr.
Simburg, Melvyn Jay

WISCONSIN

Madison
Bremer, Howard Walter

Milwaukee
Nelson, Roy Hugh, Jr.

CANADA

ONTARIO

Toronto
Chester, Robert Simon George

MEXICO

Mexico
Quiroz, Lourdes Gabriela

AUSTRALIA

Adelaide
Gaszner, David George

Melbourne Victoria
Reid, William Owen

Victoria
Ellinson, Dean Avraham

BELGIUM

Brussels
Hoffmann, Maria Elisabeth

CHINA

Hong Kong
Stender, Neal A.

Taipei
Tsai, Jaclyn Yu-Ling

DENMARK

Copenhagen
Langemark, Jesper
Lassen, Steen Anker

ENGLAND

Bucks
Assim, Gary Dean

London
Allcock, John Paul Major
Bamford, Timothy James
Davies, Isabel Milner
Gilbert, Penny Xenia
Stokes, Simon Jeremy
Turner, Catrin

Manchester
Moakes, Jonathan

GERMANY

Dusseldorf
Harmsen, Christian

Frankfurt/Main
Baeumer, Ulrich J.P.

Hamburg
Dieselhorst, Jochen

Munich
Geissler, Bernhard Heilo

HUNGARY

Budapest
Markó, József

INDIA

New Delhi
Kalha, Baljit Singh

IRELAND

Cork
Corkery, Garvan

ISRAEL

Haifa
Permut, Scott Richard

Jerusalem
Molho, Isaac

Tel Aviv
Karniel, Yuval

ITALY

Milan
Holden, Julia
Tarchi, Enrico Maria

Rome
Fusco, Marta Angela
Salce, Valerio

KENYA

Nairobi
Maema, William Ikutha

THE NETHERLANDS

Amsterdam
Schaap, Jacqueline

The Hague
Van Nispen, Constant J.J.C.

NIGERIA

Lagus
Muoka, Alexander Nduka

PERU

Lima
Garcia Ruiz-Huidobro, Magali
Girbau, Miguel Angel

THE PHILIPPINES

Makati City
Macalaguing, Gene Batalla

Metro Manila
Pasal, Emmanuel Pastores

SAUDI ARABIA

Central Province
Elfaki, Mohamed Ahmed Mohamed

SCOTLAND

Glasgow
Priest, Andrew David

SINGAPORE

Singapore
Liew, Yik Wee
Yeo, Jennifer

SPAIN

Barcelona
Llevat, Jorge

SWEDEN

Stockholm
Rambe, Lars Joachim
Widmark, Stefan

THAILAND

Bangkok
Annanon, Songphol

UKRAINE

Kiev
Konnov, Sergei Vladimirovich

UNITED ARAB EMIRATES

Dubai
Forsch, Thomas

WALES

Cardiff
Lindsey, Michael

ZIMBABWE

Harare
Wood Kahari, Brenda Marie

ADDRESS UNPUBLISHED

Beck, Stuart Edwin
Carten, Francis Noel
Fiorito, Edward Gerald
Harkless, Angela
Herrell, Roger Wayne
Ikeda, Cynthia Yuko
Keys, Jerry Malcom
Leydig, Carl Frederick
Middleton, James Boland
Miller, John Eddie
Noddings, Sarah Ellen
Quillen, Cecil Dyer, Jr.
Sprung, Arnold
von Sauers, Joseph F.

INTERNATIONAL, PRIVATE

UNITED STATES

ALABAMA

Birmingham
Baker, David Remember
Smith, Ralph Harrison
Trimmier, Charles Stephen, Jr.
Wilson, James Charles, Jr.

ALASKA

Anchorage
Allingham, Lynn Marie
Nosek, Francis John

ARIZONA

Phoenix
Grant, Merwin Darwin
Rivera, Jose de Jesus
Rosen, Sidney Marvin
Sterns, Patricia Margaret
Tennen, Leslie Irwin

Scottsdale
Peshkin, Samuel David

Tucson
Tindall, Robert Emmett

CALIFORNIA

Bakersfield
Tornstrom, Robert Ernest

Berkeley
Woodhouse, Thomas Edwin

Beverly Hills
Langer, Simon Hrimes
Roberts, Norman Leslie
Rondeau, Charles Reinhardt

Cypress
Olschwang, Alan Paul

El Segundo
Gambaro, Ernest Umberto

Fremont
Cummings, John Patrick

Irvine
Bastiaanse, Gerard C.
Beard, Ronald Stratton

La Canada Flintridge
Costello, Francis William

Long Beach
Tikosh, Mark Axente

Los Angeles
Burke, Robert Bertram
Castro, Leonard Edward
De Brier, Donald Paul
Hahn, Elliott Julius
Hughes, William Jeffrey
Levine, Thomas Jeffrey Pello
Lund, James Louis
Millard, Neal Steven
Mosk, Richard Mitchell
Oliver, Dale Hugh
Power, John Bruce
Weiser, Frank Alan
Weissman, Barry Leigh

Millbrae
Lande, James Avra

Monte Sereno
Allan, Lionel Manning

Newport Beach
Mallory, Frank Linus

Oak Park
Vinson, William Theodore

Palo Alto
Radlo, Edward John

Pasadena
Chan, Daniel Chung-Yin

San Diego
Chatroo, Arthur Jay
Edwards, James Richard
Snaid, Leon Jeffrey

San Francisco
Baker, Cameron
Baker, Steven Wright
Chao, Cedric C.
Collas, Juan Garduño, Jr.
Danoff, Eric Michael
Devine, Antoine Maurice
Donovan, Charles Stephen
Finck, Kevin William
Freud, Nicholas S.
Gresham, Zane Oliver
Heng, Donald James, Jr.
Hinman, Harvey DeForest
Kimport, David Lloyd
Offer, Stuart Jay
Ragan, Charles Ransom
Shenk, George H.
Walsh, Joseph Richard

San Jose
Doan, Xuyen Van
Kraw, George Martin

San Rafael
Kathrein, Reed Richard

Santa Barbara
Israel, Barry John

Santa Monica
McMillan, M. Sean
Schlei, Norbert Anthony

Sunnyvale
Wehde, Albert Edward

Visalia
Atkins, Thomas Jay

Walnut Creek
Nolan, David Charles

COLORADO

Castle Rock
Procopio, Joseph Guydon

Denver
Jones, Richard Michael
Rich, Robert Stephen
Ulrich, Theodore Albert

Littleton
Ross, William Robert

CONNECTICUT

Bloomfield
Messemer, Glenn Matthew

Fairfield
Huth, William Edward

Greenwich
Nimetz, Matthew

Hamden
Eisner, Lawrence Brand

Hartford
Schroth, Peter W(illiam)

Meriden
Lowry, Houston Putnam

Southbury
Auerbach, Ernest Sigmund

Stamford
Ligelis, Gregory John

Westbrook
Dundas, Philip Blair, Jr.

Westport
Lindskog, David Richard

DELAWARE

Greenville
Long, Linda Ann

Wilmington
Gamble, Donald Geoffrey Bidmead
Melnik, Selinda A.

DISTRICT OF COLUMBIA

Washington
Ackerson, Nels J(ohn)
Atwood, James R.
Baker, Keith Leon
Barr, Michael Blanton
Batla, Raymond John, Jr.
Berryman, Richard Byron
Bierman, James Norman
Blake, Jonathan Dewey
Boone, Theodore Sebastian
Bregman, Arthur Randolph
Brown, David Nelson
Buechner, Jack W(illiam)
Burt, Jeffrey Amsterdam
Cassidy, Robert Charles, Jr.
Chanin, Michael Henry
Clagett, Brice McAdoo
Cymrot, Mark Alan
Danas, Andrew Michael
Davidow, Joel
deKieffer, Donald Eulette
Dinan, Donald Robert
Ellicott, John LeMoyne
Ellis, Courtenay
Feldhaus, Stephen Martin
Fishburne, Benjamin P., III
Fisher, Bart Steven
Flowe, Benjamin Hugh, Jr.
Fox, Paul Walter

Geniesse, Robert John
Gold, Peter Frederick
Gulland, Eugene D.
Harris, Scott Blake
Harrison, Donald
Harrison, Earl David
Harrison, Marion Edwyn
Heron, Julian Briscoe, Jr.
Horlick, Gary Norman
Houlihan, David Paul
Jetton, C. Loring, Jr.
Johnson, Oliver Thomas, Jr.
Kessler, Judd Lewis
Knauer, Leon Thomas
Kramer, William David
Kriesberg, Simeon M.
Lamm, Carolyn Beth
Landfield, Richard
Lavine, Henry Wolfe
Leonard, Will Ernest, Jr.
Lucas, Steven Mitchell
Mazo, Mark Elliott
Mendales, Richard Ephraim
Mendelsohn, Martin
Mirvahabi, Farin
Mitchell, Carol Ann
Mitchell, Roy Shaw
Murphy, Terence Roche
Norberg, Charles Robert
Outman, William Dell, II
Palmeter, N. David
Phillips, Leo Harold, Jr.
Pomeroy, Harlan
Raul, Alan Charles
Rehm, John Bartram
Ritter, Jeffrey Blake
Rosenhauer, James Joseph
Ruddy, Frank
Russin, Jonathan
Schwaab, Richard Lewis
Sherzer, Harvey Gerald
Spector, Phillip Louis
Stayin, Randolph John
Stuart, Pamela Bruce
Thomas, Ritchie Tucker
Timberg, Sigmund
Townsend, John Michael
Trooboff, Peter Dennis
Vakerics, Thomas Vincent
Verrill, Charles Owen, Jr.
Wegener, Mark Douglas
Weiss, Mark Anschel
Work, Charles Robert
Wray, Robert
Zagaris, Bruce

FLORIDA

Boca Grande
Brock, Mitchell

Coral Gables
Paul, Robert
Sacasas, Rene

Fort Lauderdale
Barnard, George Smith
Pascal, Robert Albert
Turner, Hugh Joseph, Jr.

Lake Wales
Wales, Gwynne Huntington

Miami
Berley, David Richard
Ersek, Gregory Joseph Mark
Fontes, J. Mario F., Jr.
Hudson, Robert Franklin, Jr.
Landy, Burton Aaron
Poston, Rebekah Jane
Zamora, Antonio Rafael

Miami Lakes
Dominik, Jack Edward

Naples
Emerson, John Williams, II

North Palm Beach
Koffler, Warren William

Orlando
Hendry, Robert Ryon
Ioppolo, Frank S., Jr.
Johnson, Kraig Nelson
Neff, A. Guy

Sarasota
Partoyan, Garo Arakel

Tampa
Grammig, Robert James
Vento, John Sebastian

Vero Beach
Case, Douglas Manning

West Palm Beach
Barnett, Charles Dawson
Hill, Thomas William, Jr.

GEORGIA

Atlanta
Booth, Gordon Dean, Jr.
Branch, Thomas Broughton, III
Cargill, Robert Mason

Sea Island
Revoile, Charles Patrick

HAWAII

Honolulu
Boas, Frank
Cassiday, Benjamin Buckles, III
Ingersoll, Richard King
Miller, Clifford Joel

ILLINOIS

Abbott Park
Brock, Charles Marquis

Chicago
Athas, Gus James
Barack, Peter Joseph
Barnes, James Garland, Jr.
Bloom, Christopher Arthur
Blount, Michael Eugene
Boodell, Thomas Joseph, Jr.
Breakstone, Donald S.
Burgdoerfer, Jerry
Cass, Robert Michael
Chudzinski, Mark Adam
Cicero, Frank, Jr.
Cunningham, Robert James
Franklin, Richard Mark
Goldman, Louis Budwig
Henry, Frederick Edward
Hunt, Lawrence Halley, Jr.
Kamerick, Eileen Ann
Martin, Alan Joseph
Masters, Paul Holmes
Meltzer, Robert Craig
Michaels, Richard Edward
Morrow, John E.
Partridge, Mark Van Buren
Prochnow, Herbert Victor, Jr.
Rizowy, Carlos Guillermo
Smith, Stephen Edward
Stevenson, Adlai Ewing, III
Thomas, Stephen Paul

Deerfield
Staubitz, Arthur Frederick

Evanston
Thompson, Michael

Naperville
Larson, Mark Edward, Jr.

North Chicago
de Lasa, José M.

Northbrook
Carter, James Woodford, Jr.

Oakbrook Terrace
Fenech, Joseph Charles

Palatine
Cannon, Benjamin Winton
Wardell, John Watson

Peoria
Atterbury, Robert Rennie, III

INDIANA

Indianapolis
FitzGibbon, Daniel Harvey
Patel, Apexa
Russell, David Williams

Lafayette
O'Connell, Lawrence B.

IOWA

Burlington
Hoth, Steven Sergey

KENTUCKY

Louisville
Northern, Richard
Welsh, Sir Alfred John

LOUISIANA

Covington
Rice, Winston Edward

New Orleans
Jones, Philip Kirkpatrick, Jr.
Ostendorf, Lance Stephen
Perry, Brian Drew, Sr.

MARYLAND

Baltimore
Chaplin, Peggy Louie
Robinson, Zelig

Bethesda
Daniels, Michael Paul
English, William deShay
Goodwin, Robert Cronin

Chevy Chase
Schwartzman, Robin Berman

Rockville
Millstein, Leo Lee
Zaphiriou, George Aristotle

West Bethesda
Scully, Roger Tehan, II

MASSACHUSETTS

Boston
Aresty, Jeffrey M.
Bernhard, Alexander Alfred
Bines, Harvey Ernest
Gonson, S. Donald
Greer, Gordon Bruce
Huang, Thomas Weishing
Huang, Vivian Wenhuey Chen
Kaler, Robert Joseph
Kopelman, Leonard

Licata, Arthur Frank
Loeser, Hans Ferdinand
Masud, Robert
O'Neill, Philip Daniel, Jr.
Stokes, James Christopher
Thibeault, George Walter
White, Barry Bennett

Brookline
Burnstein, Daniel

Cambridge
Ta, Tai Van

Carlisle
Hensleigh, Howard Edgar

Ipswich
Getchell, Charles Willard, Jr.

Lincoln
Gnichtel, William Van Orden

Lynnfield
McGivney, John Joseph

Waltham
Barnes-Brown, Peter Newton
Borod, Donald Lee

Wellesley
Fuller, Robert L(eander)

MICHIGAN

Ada
Mc Callum, Charles Edward

Birmingham
Elsman, James Leonard, Jr.

Clinton Township
Theut, C. Peter

Detroit
Darlow, Julia Donovan
Lawrence, John Kidder
Thorpe, Norman Ralph

Troy
Dillon, Joseph Francis

MINNESOTA

Minneapolis
Kozachok, Stephen K.
Lofstrom, Mark D.
McNeil, Mark Sanford
Ryan, Thomas J.

Saint Paul
Maffei, Rocco John
Oh, Matthew InSoo

MISSOURI

Chesterfield
Hier, Marshall David

Kansas City
Wrobley, Ralph Gene

Saint Louis
Leontsinis, George John

NEBRASKA

Grand Island
Cuypers, Charles James

NEVADA

Las Vegas
Zubel, Eric Louis

NEW JERSEY

Montclair
Brown, Ronald Wellington

New Brunswick
Biribauer, Richard Frank

New Providence
Maxeiner, James Randolph

Ramsey
Ogden, John Hamilton

Short Hills
Marshall, John Patrick
Siegfried, David Charles

Summit
English, Jerry Fitzgerald

NEW MEXICO

Albuquerque
Messersmith, Lanny Dee
Schuler, Alison Kay

NEW YORK

Brooklyn
Johnson, Donald Raymond

Buffalo
Heilman, Pamela Davis
Yost, Ellen G. (Ellen Yost Lafili)

Canaan
Pennell, William Brooke

Cortlandt Manor
Buhler, Gregory Wallace

Hillsdale
Lunde, Asbjorn Rudolph

Larchmont
Berridge, George Bradford

New York
Aksen, Gerald
Allen, Leon Arthur, Jr.
Andersen, Richard Esten
Barnard, Robert N.
Bernard, Richard Phillip
Bidwell, James Truman, Jr.
Blume, Lawrence Dayton
Brumm, James Earl
Bryan, Barry Richard
Burak, H(oward) Paul
Byrnes, Richard James
Cable, Paul Andrew
Carpenter, Randle Burt
Carter, James Hal, Jr.
Chang, Ta-kuang
Chilstrom, Robert Meade
Cho, Tai Yong
Clapman, Peter Carlyle
Connor, John Thomas, Jr.
Cooper, Stephen Herbert
Cuneo, Donald Lane
Cutner, Rolande Regat
Davidson, Robert Bruce
de Sampigny, Guillaume
Detjen, David Wheeler
Devine, Michael Buxton
Dlugoff, Marc Alan
Duerbeck, Heidi Barbara
Edelman, Paul Sterling
Ehrenbard, Robert
Elicker, Gordon Leonard
Epstein, Melvin
Ercklentz, Enno Wilhelm, Jr.
Fernandez, Jose Walfredo
Fersko, Raymond Stuart
Fewell, Charles Kenneth, Jr.
Fisher, Robert I.
Fleischman, Edward Hirsh
Forry, John Ingram
Fox, Donald Thomas
Franklin, Robert Stambaugh
Fredericks, Wesley Charles, Jr.
Freyer, Dana Hartman
Gallagher, Brian John
Gans, Walter Gideon
Ganz, David L.
Garfinkel, Barry Herbert
Gettner, Alan Frederick
Gillespie, Jane
Goodwillie, Eugene William, Jr.
Grant, Stephen Allen
Greenspon, Robert Alan
Greeven, Rainer
Halket, Thomas D(aniel)
Hamel, Rodolphe
Harris, Joel B(ruce)
Hauser, Rita Eleanore Abrams
Hayden, Raymond Paul
Hayes, Gerald Joseph
Herold, Karl Guenter
Higgs, John H.
Hritz, George F.
Hurlock, James Bickford
Jacobs, Paul
Jones, Douglas W.
Katsos, Barbara Helene
Kessler, Jeffrey L.
Kies, David M.
Kimball, John Devereux
King, Henry Lawrence
Knight, Townsend Jones
Kojevnikov, Boris Oleg
Komaroff, Stanley
Kramaric, Peter Stefan
Kreitzman, Ralph J.
Krikorian, Van Z.
Lamia, Thomas Roger
Lans, Asher Bob
Larose, Lawrence Alfred
Lederer, Peter David
Lee, In-Young
Linsenmeyer, John Michael
Lowy, George Theodore
Lutringer, Richard Emil
MacRae, Cameron Farquhar, III
Maney, Michael Mason
Marcusa, Fred Haye
Masin, Michael Terry
Matteson, William Bleecker
McDonell, Neil Edwin
McGovern, David Talmage
McLaughlin, Joseph Thomas
Metzger, Barry
Meyer, Mark Alan
Michel, Clifford Lloyd
Milgrim, Roger Michael
Molnar, Lawrence
Muskin, Victor Philip
Nathan, Andrew Jonathan
Newman, Lawrence Walker
Nicoara, Andra Christina
O'Sullivan, Thomas J.
Odell, Stuart Irwin
Olasov, David Michael
Olmstead, Clarence Walter, Jr.
Ornitz, Richard Martin
Osborn, Donald Robert
Oshima, Michael W.
Patrikis, Ernest T.
Paul, Robert Carey
Pavia, George M.
Peet, Charles D., Jr.
Perkins, Roswell Burchard
Pettibone, Peter John
Pierce, Morton Allen
Piliero, Robert Donald
Quale, Andrew Christopher, Jr.
Rabb, Bruce
Radon, Jenik Richard
Radway, Robert J.
Rankin, Clyde Evan, III
Resnicow, Norman Jakob
Rosensaft, Menachem Zwi
Rovine, Arthur William
Rubin, Herbert

Sassoon, Andre Gabriel
Saunders, Mark A.
Savell, Polly Carolyn
Schaab, Arnold J.
Schwab, Terrance W.
Schwartz, Stephen Jay
Seidel, Selvyn
Setrakian, Berge
Seward, George Chester
Shea, Edward Emmett
Shecter, Howard L.
Short, Skip
Silkenat, James Robert
Solbert, Peter Omar Abernathy
Stein, Stephen William
Steyer, Hume Richmond
Stone, David Philip
Thalacker, Arbie Robert
Tran, Julie Hoan
Valat de Córdova, Thierry
Vega, Matias Alfonso
Vig, Vernon Edward
Vitkowsky, Vincent Joseph
Wald, Bernard Joseph
Wang, Albert Huai-En
Weiner, Earl David
Wise, Aaron Noah
Wynn, Simon David
Ziegler, Henry Steinway
Zimmett, Mark Paul

Purchase
Joyce, Joseph James

Rochester
Blyth, John E.

Scarsdale
Beuchert, Edward William

Somers
Cowles, Frederick Oliver

Syracuse
Bogart, William Harry
Fitzpatrick, James David

Westbury
Whiteman, Robert Gordon

White Plains
Pitegoff, Thomas Michael

NORTH CAROLINA

Cary
Taylor, Marvin Edward, Jr.

Charlotte
Roberts, Manley Woolfolk
Zeller, Michael Eugene

Raleigh
Edwards, James Malone

Winston Salem
Coffey, Larry B(ruce)
Loughridge, John Halsted, Jr.

OHIO

Cincinnati
Bridgeland, James Ralph, Jr.
Stith, John Stephen
Wales, Ross Elliot

Cleveland
Baxter, Howard H.
Coquillette, William Hollis
Groetzinger, Jon, Jr.

Columbus
Robol, Richard Thomas

Dublin
Inzetta, Mark Stephen

North Canton
Dettinger, Warren Walter

OKLAHOMA

Bartlesville
Roff, Alan Lee

Tulsa
Baker, Gary Hugh
Cundiff, James Nelson

OREGON

Ashland
Fine, J. David

Portland
Abravanel, Allan Ray

PENNSYLVANIA

Ambler
Albright, Audra A.

Blue Bell
Scudder, Charles Seelye Kellgren

Greensburg
Heubel, William Bernard

Hershey
Simmons, Bryan John

Moon Township
Lipson, Barry J.

Narberth
Mezvinsky, Edward M.

Newtown Square
Crowley, James Michael

Philadelphia
Cannon, John, III
D'Angelo, Christopher Scott
Donohue, John Patrick
Doran, William Michael
Krzyzanowski, Richard L(ucien)
Palmer, Richard Ware
Whiteside, William Anthony, Jr.

Pittsburgh
Frank, Ronald William
Sutton, William Dwight

Valley Forge
Bovaird, Brendan Peter
Posner, Ernest Gary
Walters, Bette Jean

Wayne
Donnella, Michael Andre

West Chester
Osborn, John Edward

RHODE ISLAND

Barrington
Soutter, Thomas Douglas

TENNESSEE

Brentwood
Provine, John C.

Knoxville
Bly, Robert Maurice

Memphis
McLean, Robert Alexander

TEXAS

Austin
Dyer, Cromwell Adair, Jr.
Godfrey, Cullen Michael

Bellaire
Hollrah, David

Brownsville
Walsh, Lawrence Adrian

Dallas
Adelman, Graham Lewis
Armour, James Lott
Birkeland, Bryan Collier
Clossey, David F.
Doke, Marshall J., Jr.
Hackney, Hugh Edward
Hinshaw, Chester John
Kennedy, Marc J.
Moore, Marilyn Payne
Zahn, Donald Jack

Fort Worth
Elliott, Frank Wallace
Langenheim, Roger Allen

Houston
Amdur, Arthur R.
Bilger, Bruce R.
Bistline, F. Walter, Jr.
Brunson, John Soles
Carmody, James Albert
Chandler, George Francis, III
Crain, Alan Rau, Jr.
DeMent, James Alderson, Jr.
Dilg, Joseph Carl
Dula, Arthur McKee, III
Estes, Carl Lewis, II
Glass, Douglas B.
Goldman, Nathan Carliner
Gray, Archibald Duncan, Jr.
Hitchcock, Bion Earl
Lawson, Ben F.
Lopez, David Tiburcio
Marlow, Orval Lee, II
Murphy, Ewell Edward, Jr.
Porter, Thomas William, III
Salch, Steven Charles
Sapp, Walter William
Sherman, Robert Taylor, Jr.
Silva, Eugene Joseph
Wright, Paul William

Mcallen
Carrera, Victor Manuel

San Antonio
Bramble, Ronald Lee

Stephenville
Batson, David Warren

UTAH

Spanish Fork
Ashworth, Brent Ferrin

VIRGINIA

Alexandria
Higgins, Mary Celeste

Arlington
Glazier, Jonathan Hemenway
Morgens, Warren Kendall
Schwartz, Philip

Charlottesville
Dunn, William Wyly

Great Falls
Rath, Francis Steven

Herndon
Pearlman, Michael Allen

Leesburg
Kushner, Gordon Peter

Mc Lean
Daniels, Michael Alan
Kondracki, Edward John
Molineaux, Charles Borromeo

Mechanicsville
d'Evegnee, Charles Paul

Oakton
Vernava, Anthony Michael

Rosslyn
Carbaugh, John Edward, Jr.

WASHINGTON

Redmond
Scowcroft, Jerome Chilwell

Seattle
Nye, Daniel Alan
Palmer, Douglas S., Jr.
Sandler, Michael David
Simburg, Melvyn Jay
Tousley, Russell Frederick

WISCONSIN

Milwaukee
Meldman, Robert Edward
Wiley, Edwin Packard

WYOMING

Cody
Johnson, Wallace Harold

CANADA

ONTARIO

Toronto
Chester, Robert Simon George

MEXICO

Mexico City
Ritch, James Earle, Jr.

AUSTRALIA

Sydney
Brown, John Thomas

BRAZIL

Sao Paulo
d'Utra Vaz, Marco Antonio

CHINA

Beijing
Zhao, Qian

Hong Kong
Rapinet, Crispin William
Shinkle, John Thomas
Stender, Neal A.

ENGLAND

London
Cole, Richard A.
Dickey, John W.
Jalili, Mahir
Langer, Marshall J.
Quillen, Cecil Dyer, III
Rosenberg, Daniel P.
Sleigh, Russell Howard Phalf
White, Walter Hiawatha, Jr.

FRANCE

Courbevoie
Herzog, Brigitte

Paris
Citrey, Eric Jean-Pierre
Fix, Brian David
Gaillot, Laurent D
Poulain de Saint-Pere, Aude
Safa, Rachid P.

GERMANY

Koln
Reufels, Martin J.

ITALY

Milan
Holden, Julia

Rome
Fusco, Marta Angela

JAPAN

Osaka
Solberg, Norman Robert

Tokyo
Thorson, Andrew H.

THE NETHERLANDS

The Hague
Brower, Charles Nelson

NEW ZEALAND

Auckland
McNamara, Denis Michael

NORWAY

Oslo
Moss, Giuditta Cordero

THE PHILIPPINES

Metro Manila
Sumida, Gerald Aquinas

POLAND

Cracow
Kasper, Horst Manfred

REPUBLIC OF KOREA

Seoul
Cho, Chi-Hyoung
Yoon, Hoil

ROMANIA

Bucharest
Cominos, Theodore Harry, Jr.
Jardine, Bryan Wilson

SAUDI ARABIA

Jeddah
Shea, Gerald MacDonald

Riyadh
Taylor, Frederick William, Jr. (Fritz Taylor)

SINGAPORE

Singapore
David, James P.

SPAIN

Madrid
Hendel, Clifford James
Vasquez, Gerard Manuel

THAILAND

Bangkok
Chunhakasikarn, Sasirusm Bulpakdi

ZIMBABWE

Harare
Wood Kahari, Brenda Marie

ADDRESS UNPUBLISHED

Agraz, Francisco Javier, Sr.
Anani, Tariq
Bateman, David Alfred
Berry, Robert Worth
Bloomer, Harold Franklin, Jr.
Crocker, Saone Baron
D'Avignon, Roy Joseph
Garcia Barron, Ramiro
Gilden, Richard Henry
Greenberg, Ronald David
Grisham, Richard Bond
Hafner, Thomas Mark
Hoffman, Ira Eliot
Holtzmann, Howard Marshall
Joelson, Mark Rene
Koplik, Marc Stephen
Landy, Lisa Anne
Lipsman, Richard Marc
McCobb, John Bradford, Jr.

Miller, John Eddie
Neuhaus, Joseph Emanuel
Patton, James Richard, Jr.
Potter, Tanya Jean
Prem, F. Herbert, Jr.
Quigley, Leonard Vincent
Schneebaum, Steven Marc
Silberman, Curt C.
Swacker, Frank Warren
Tasker, Joseph
White, John Joseph, III
Williams, William John, Jr.
Williamson, Edwin Dargan

INTERNATIONAL, PUBLIC

UNITED STATES

CALIFORNIA

Beverly Hills
Langer, Simon Hrimes

Century City
Davis, Donald G(lenn)

Los Angeles
Christopher, Warren
Mosk, Richard Mitchell

San Francisco
Baker, Steven Wright
Philipsborn, John Timothy

Santa Barbara
Israel, Barry John

CONNECTICUT

Southbury
Auerbach, Ernest Sigmund

Stamford
Rose, Richard Loomis

DISTRICT OF COLUMBIA

Washington
Bachman, Kenneth Leroy, Jr.
Batla, Raymond John, Jr.
Bregman, Arthur Randolph
Buechner, Jack W(illiam)
Clagett, Brice McAdoo
Cymrot, Mark Alan
deKieffer, Donald Eulette
Dembling, Paul Gerald
Dempsey, David B.
Denniston, John Baker
Fisher, Bart Steven
Gainer, Ronald Lee
Horlick, Gary Norman
Johnson, Oliver Thomas, Jr.
Jordan, Jon Byron
Kessler, Judd Lewis
Kriesberg, Simeon M.
Leonard, Will Ernest, Jr.
Mendelsohn, Martin
Miller, Gay Davis
Mirvahabi, Farin
Norberg, Charles Robert
Palmeter, N. David
Pomeroy, Harlan
Scheman, L. Ronald
Tomlinson, Margaret Lynch
Trooboff, Peter Dennis
Weisgall, Jonathan Michael
Zagaris, Bruce

FLORIDA

Miami
Kurzban, Ira Jay
Schuette, Charles A.

Satellite Beach
Tasker, Molly Jean

West Palm Beach
Hill, Thomas William, Jr.

GEORGIA

Jasper
Marger, Edwin

HAWAII

Honolulu
Boas, Frank

ILLINOIS

Chicago
Block, Neal Jay
Lynch, John Peter
Rizowy, Carlos Guillermo
Wade, Edwin Lee

INDIANA

Indianapolis
Patel, Apexa

KANSAS

Shawnee Mission
Snyder, Willard Breidenthal

KENTUCKY

Lexington
Hickey, John King

MARYLAND

Bethesda
Sheble, Walter Franklin

Crownsville
Irish, Leon Eugene

Gaithersburg
Sherer, Samuel Ayers

Saint Michaels
Brown, Omer Forrest, II

Takoma Park
Browning, Deborah Lea

MASSACHUSETTS

Boston
Kopelman, Leonard

Carlisle
Hensleigh, Howard Edgar

Weston
Bateman, Thomas Robert

MICHIGAN

Southfield
Antone, Nahil Peter

NEW HAMPSHIRE

Hollis
Merritt, Thomas Butler

NEW JERSEY

Morristown
Fishman, Richard Glenn

NEW YORK

New York
Debo, Vincent Joseph
Frank, Lloyd
Fry, Morton Harrison, II
Ganz, Marc David
Hauser, Rita Eleanore Abrams
Kailas, Leo George
Karls, John Spencer
Krikorian, Van Z.
Metzger, Barry
Nicoara, Andra Christina
Sassoon, Andre Gabriel
Wallach, Evan Jonathan
Welt, Philip Stanley

NORTH CAROLINA

Flat Rock
Brooten, Kenneth Edward, Jr.

OHIO

Cleveland
Feliciano, José Celso

PENNSYLVANIA

Narberth
Mezvinsky, Edward M.

Philadelphia
Heinzen, Bernard George
Krzyzanowski, Richard L(ucien)

Pittsburgh
Van Kirk, Thomas L.

TEXAS

Austin
Dyer, Cromwell Adair, Jr.

VIRGINIA

Alexandria
Higgins, Mary Celeste

Great Falls
Rath, Francis Steven

Portsmouth
Porter, J. Ridgely, III

WYOMING

Cody
Johnson, Wallace Harold

ENGLAND

London
Mackie, David Lindsay

GERMANY

Frankfurt on the Main
Matthew, Leodis Clyde

ITALY

Milan
Plankensteiner, Marco

THE NETHERLANDS

The Hague
Brower, Charles Nelson

ADDRESS UNPUBLISHED

Burgess, Hayden Fern (Poka Laenui)
Hoffman, Ira Eliot
Lichtenstein, Natalie G.
Mercer, Edwin Wayne
Patton, James Richard, Jr.
Quayle, Marilyn Tucker
Schneebaum, Steven Marc
Williamson, Edwin Dargan
Winslow, John Franklin

JUVENILE

UNITED STATES

ALASKA

Anchorage
Butler, Rex Lamont

ARIZONA

Phoenix
Klahr, Gary Peter

CALIFORNIA

Woodland
Melton, Barry

COLORADO

Englewood
Bolocofsky, David N.

Longmont
Bisgard, Eileen Bernice Reid

CONNECTICUT

Danbury
Dornfeld, Sharon Wicks

Weston
Strauss, Ellen Louise Feldman

FLORIDA

Fort Lauderdale
Hester, Julia A.

Jacksonville
McBurney, Charles Walker, Jr.

HAWAII

Honolulu
Shigetomi, Keith Shigeo

ILLINOIS

Chicago
Muller, Kurt Alexander
Tucker, Bowen Hayward

Mundelein
Ackley, Robert O.

INDIANA

Indianapolis
Walker, Ross Paul

IOWA

Des Moines
Lawyer, Vivian Jury

KENTUCKY

Louisville
Spalding, Catherine

LOUISIANA

Baton Rouge
Dixon, Jerome Wayne

La Place
Cicet, Donald James

Lafayette
Saloom, Kaliste Joseph, Jr.

MASSACHUSETTS

South Hamilton
Campbell, Diana Butt

MICHIGAN

Detroit
Wyrick, Jermaine Albert

MINNESOTA

Minneapolis
Oleisky, Robert Edward

Rochester
Baker, Gail Dyer

MISSOURI

Saint Louis
Stewart, Allan Forbes

NEW MEXICO

Alamogordo
Bloom, Norman Douglas, Jr.

NEW YORK

New York
Lansner, David Jeffrey
Reiniger, Douglas Haigh
Rothberg, Glenda Fay Morris
Vachss, Andrew Henry

Syracuse
Engel, Todd Sanford

NORTH DAKOTA

Grand Forks
Anderson, Damon Ernest

OHIO

Ashtabula
Lesko, Jane Lynn

Dayton
Vaughn, Noel Wyandt

PENNSYLVANIA

Mercer
Kochems, Robert Gregory

Monroeville
Cohen, Laura

RHODE ISLAND

Providence
McMahon, John Joseph

TENNESSEE

Clarksville
Smith, Gregory Dale

Fayetteville
Dickey, John Harwell

Hermitage
Burkett, Gerald Arthur

TEXAS

Canton
White, Jeffery Howell

Dallas
Callahan, Tena Toye

VERMONT

Concord
Norsworthy, Elizabeth Krassovsky

VIRGINIA

Newport News
Saunders, Bryan Leslie

ADDRESS UNPUBLISHED

Lory, Loran Steven
Schmidt, Kathleen Marie

Shattuck, Cathie Ann

LABOR *See also* Workers' compensation; Pension

UNITED STATES

ALABAMA

Birmingham
Alexander, James Patrick
Gilliland, Scott Alan
Spotswood, Robert Keeling
Spransy, Joseph William
Whiteside, David Powers, Jr.

Eufaula
Twitchell, E(rvin) Eugene

Mobile
Tidwell, William C., III

ALASKA

Fairbanks
Andrews, Mark
Schendel, William Burnett

ARIZONA

Phoenix
Brockelman, Kent
Gomez, David Frederick
Lubin, Stanley
Wall, Donald Arthur

Tempe
Shimpock, Kathy Elizabeth

Tucson
Kaucher, James William

ARKANSAS

Little Rock
Boe, Myron Timothy
Gunter, Russell Allen
Jiles, Gary D.
Jones, Stephen Witsell

CALIFORNIA

Auburn
Henry, Karen Hawley

Beverly Hills
Florence, Kenneth James

Glendale
Martinetti, Ronald Anthony

Irvine
Black, William Rea
Desai, Aashish Y.
Ristau, Kenneth Eugene, Jr.

Lafayette
Sherrer, Charles William

Laguna Hills
Reinglass, Michelle Annette

Los Angeles
Bressan, Paul Louis
Bryan, James Spencer
Carr, Willard Zeller, Jr.
Cathcart, David Arthur
Emanuel, William Joseph
Fisher, Richard N.
Gross, Allen Jeffrey
Hahn, Elliott Julius
Moloney, Stephen Michael
Oliver, Anthony Thomas, Jr.
Saxe, Deborah Crandall
Silbergeld, Arthur F.
Solo, Gail Dianne
Thoren-Peden, Deborah Suzanne
Whitaker, Ronald Stephen

Oakland
Wallace, Elaine Wendy

Palm Springs
FitzGerald, John Edward, III

Palo Alto
Wheeler, Raymond Louis

Sacramento
Bell, Wayne S.
Shelley, Susanne Mary

San Diego
Bleiler, Charles Arthur
Foerster, Barrett Jonathan

San Francisco
Boutin, Peter Rucker
Gelhaus, Robert Joseph
Hilton, Stanley Goumas
Libbin, Anne Edna
Rubin, Michael
Tonsing, Michael John

Torrance
Johnson, Einar William

Walnut Creek
Burnison, Boyd Edward
Lederman, Henry David
Steele, Dwight Cleveland

Westlake Village
Sullivan, Mark Francis

COLORADO

Boulder
Ward, Denitta Dawn

Denver
Breeskin, Michael Wayne
Hautzinger, James Edward
Husband, John Michael
Jablonski, James Arthur
Marquess, Lawrence Wade
Martin, Raymond Walter
Merker, Steven Joseph
Solano, Henry L.
Timmins, Edward Patrick
Tomlinson, Warren Leon

Golden
Snead, Kathleen Marie

Placerville
Reagan, Harry Edwin, III

CONNECTICUT

Bloomfield
Messemer, Glenn Matthew

Clinton
Hershatter, Richard Lawrence

Fairfield
LaFollette, Ernest Carlton

Hartford
Dempsey, Edward Joseph
Orth, Paul William

New Haven
Sobol, Alan J.

North Grosvenordale
Jungeberg, Thomas Donald

Stamford
Barreca, Christopher Anthony
Spitzer, Vlad Gerard

Trumbull
Brennan, Daniel Edward, Jr.
Czajkowski, Frank Henry

DELAWARE

Dover
Babiarz, Francis Stanley

Wilmington
Lynn, James Torrence, III
Wier, Richard Royal, Jr.

DISTRICT OF COLUMBIA

Washington
Axelrod, Jonathan Gans
Bagby, Thomas Richard
Bernabei, Lynne Ann
Brame, Joseph Robert, III
Donegan, Charles Edward
Elcano, Mary S.
Esslinger, John Thomas
Flowe, Carol Connor
Foster, C(harles) Allen
Goldsmith, Willis Jay
Groner, Isaac Nathan
Horne, Michael Stewart
Kilgore, Peter George
Kramer, Andrew Michael
Loots, James Mason
Lopatin, Alan G.
Lorber, Lawrence Zel
Mackiewicz, Edward Robert
McElveen, Junius Carlisle, Jr.
Miller, Gay Davis
O'Connor, Charles P.
Postol, Lawrence Philip
Quigley, Thomas J.
Sacher, Steven Jay
Shaffer, David James
Sherman, Lawrence Jay
Stern, Elizabeth Espin
Uehlein, E(dward) Carl, Jr.
Wilder, Roland Percival, Jr.

FLORIDA

Clearwater
McCormack, John Robert

Coral Gables
Sugarman, Robert Alan

Coral Springs
Saltman, Stuart Ivan

Fort Lauderdale
Caulkins, Charles S.

Jacksonville
Coffman, Daniel Ray, Jr.
Thomas, Archibald Johns, III

Miami
Connor, Terence Gregory
Fleming, Joseph Z.
Korchin, Judith Miriam

Miami Beach
Ryce, Donald Theodore

Miami Lakes
Cohen, Ronald J.
Sharett, Alan Richard

Orlando
Lopez-Campillo, Juan Carlos

Pensacola
Kelly, John Barry, II

Sarasota
Rossi, William Matthew

Tallahassee
Minnick, Bruce Alexander

Tampa
Blue, James Monroe
Brown, Frank Edward
Lane, Robin
McAdams, John P.
Robinson, John William, IV

Winter Park
Wagner, Lynn Edward

GEORGIA

Athens
Davis, Claude-Leonard

Atlanta
Bradley, Phillip Alden
Harkey, Robert Shelton
Kneisel, Edmund M.
Newman, Stuart
Remar, Robert Boyle
Rochelle, Dudley Cecile
Young, Michael Anthony

College Park
Stokes, Arch Yow

Conyers
Snapp, William Dorsey

Macon
Ennis, Edgar William, Jr.

Savannah
Bowman, Catherine McKenzie
Gerard, Stephen Stanley

HAWAII

Honolulu
Jossem, Jared Haym
Reinke, Stefan Michael

IDAHO

Boise
Mauk, William Lloyd
Storti, Philip Craig

ILLINOIS

Belleville
Parham, James Robert

Chicago
Adelman, Steven Herbert
Badel, Julie
Braun, Frederick B.
Brice, Roger Thomas
Brittain, Max Gordon, Jr.
Burkey, Lee Melville
Dombrow, Anthony Eric
Feinberg, Gary H.
Fox, Elaine Saphier
Freeborn, Michael D.
Giampietro, Wayne Bruce
Gladden, James Walter, Jr.
Greenfield, Michael C.
Hoffman, Valerie Jane
Kaminsky, Richard Alan
Panich, Danuta Bembenista
Pelton, Russell Meredith, Jr.
Peter, Bernard George
Redman, Clarence Owen
Reed, Keith Allen
Rutkoff, Alan Stuart
Schoonhoven, Ray James
Slutzky, Lorence Harley
Smith, Arthur B., Jr.
Taylor, Roger Lee
Tinaglia, Michael Lee
Van Tine, Matthew Eric

Dekalb
Davidson, Kenneth Lawrence

Edwardsville
Carlson, Jon Gordon

Lake Forest
Galatz, Henry Francis
Palmer, Ann Therese Darin

Lombard
Goodman, Elliott I(rvin)

Rock Island
Wallace, Franklin Sherwood

Skokie
Bauer, Michael

Winnetka
Bishop, Mahlon Lee

INDIANA

Bloomington
Winzenreid, James Ernest

Columbus
Perkins Senn, Karon Elaine

Indianapolis
Boldt, Michael Herbert
Gilliland, John Campbell, II
Klaper, Martin Jay
Maine, Michael Roland
Moffatt, Michael Alan
Reuben, Lawrence Mark
Walker, Ross Paul

Shelbyville
McNeely, James Lee

IOWA

Cedar Rapids
O'Brien, David A.

Des Moines
Shoff, Patricia Ann

KANSAS

Overland Park
Westerhaus, Douglas Bernard
Willard, James Robert

KENTUCKY

Louisville
Cutler, Irwin Herbert
Fenton, Thomas Conner
Hopson, Edwin Sharp

LOUISIANA

New Orleans
Angelico, Dennis Michael
Desmond, Susan Fahey
Hearn, Sharon Sklamba
Kelly, William James, III
Malone, Ernest Roland, Jr.
Molony, Michael Janssens, Jr.

Shreveport
Cox, John Thomas, Jr.

MAINE

Bath
Watson, Thomas Riley

MARYLAND

Baltimore
Dubé, Lawrence Edward, Jr.
Gillece, James Patrick, Jr.
Hafets, Richard Jay
Isacoff, Richard Irwin
Pokempner, Joseph Kres
White, Pamela Janice

Crownsville
Irish, Leon Eugene

Potomac
Mullenbach, Linda Herman

MASSACHUSETTS

Boston
Bloom, Howard Martin
Deutsch, Stephen B.
Eisenberg, Andrew Lewis
Lyons, Paul Vincent
Miller, Stacy Lorraine
Moreira, Barbara Lyne
Reardon, Frank Emond
Sweda, Edward Leon, Jr.

Concord
Perry, Edward Needham

Lowell
Cook, Charles Addison

Needham
Coleman, Richard William

Springfield
Sullivan, Frederick Lawrence

Woburn
Kuelthau, Paul Stauffer

Worcester
Felper, David Michael

MICHIGAN

Ann Arbor
Ellmann, William Marshall

Bingham Farms
Fershtman, Julie Ilene

Birmingham
Wells, Steven Wayne

Bloomfield Hills
Cranmer, Thomas William
Vocht, Michelle Elise

Dearborn
Demorest, Mark Stuart

Detroit
Entenman, John Alfred
Glotta, Ronald Delon
Mamat, Frank Trustick
Nemeth, Patricia Marie
Saxton, William Marvin

Sullivan, Thomas Michael

Farmington
McFarland, Robert Edwin

Fremont
Price, Russell Eugene

Grand Rapids
Enslen, Pamela Chapman
Khorey, David Eugene
Stadler, James Robert

Jenison
Kruse, Pamela Jean

Kalamazoo
Freeberg, Edward Ronald

Northville
Leavitt, Martin Jack

Okemos
Schneider, Karen Bush

Saint Clair Shores
Danielson, Gary R.

Southfield
McClow, Roger James

Troy
Berman, Leonard Keith

Walled Lake
Seglund, Bruce Richard

Warren
Bridenstine, Louis Henry, Jr.

MINNESOTA

Bloomington
Boedigheimer, Robert David
Broeker, John Milton

Brooklyn Center
Neff, Fred Leonard

Edina
Burk, Robert S.

Grand Rapids
Licke, Wallace John

Minneapolis
Corwin, Gregg Marlowe
Hackley, David Kenneth
Mahoney, Kathleen Mary
Nelson, Richard Arthur
Reinhart, Robert Rountree, Jr.

Saint Cloud
Hughes, Kevin John

MISSISSIPPI

Jackson
Fuselier, Louis Alfred

Oxford
Lewis, Ronald Wayne

MISSOURI

Chesterfield
Stalnaker, Tim

Independence
Neilsen, Christina J.

Jefferson City
Riner, James William

Kansas City
Delaney, Michael Francis
Foster, Mark Stephen
Kilroy, William Terrence
Martucci, William Christopher
Sands, Darry Gene
Sears, Kelley Dean
Tyler, John Edward, III
Vering, John Albert

Saint Louis
Bonacorsi, Mary Catherine
Carius, Jeffrey Rapp
Gianoulakis, John Louis
Hiles, Bradley Stephen
Jaudes, Richard Edward
Mattern, Keith Edward
McDaniel, James Edwin
Sullivan, Warren Gerald
Switzer, Frederick Michael, III
Webb Anderson, JoAnn Marie
Welch, David William

MONTANA

Billings
Mitchell, Laura Ann

Missoula
Bender, Ronald Andrew

NEBRASKA

Lincoln
Cope, Thom K.

Omaha
Miller, Roger James

NEVADA

Las Vegas
Hinueber, Mark Arthur
Holman, Kristina Sue
Nelson, Sharon L.

NEW JERSEY

Florham Park
Nittoly, Paul Gerard

Fort Monmouth
Desai, Jignasa

Haddonfield
Suflas, Steven William

Liberty Corner
Apruzzese, Vincent John
Thompson, T. Jay

Morristown
Stanton, Patrick Michael

New Providence
Hurley, Lawrence Joseph

Newark
Goldstein, Marvin Mark
Schachter, Paul

Roseland
Bennett, John K.
Hinsdale, Beth A.
Ploscowe, Stephen Allen
Sarasohn, Peter Radin

Somerville
Sponzilli, Edward George

Summit
Katz, Michael Albert
Saffer, Judith Mack

Warren
Bernstein, Eric Martin

Woodcliff Lake
Pollack, Jane Susan

NEW MEXICO

Las Cruces
Neumann, Rita Nunez

Los Alamos
Herr, Bruce

Taos
Boles, David LaVelle

NEW YORK

Albany
Barsamian, J(ohn) Albert
Couch, Mark Woodworth
Devine, Eugene Peter
Girvin, James Edward
Osterman, Melvin Howard
Wukitsch, David John

Bronx
Stack, Jane Marcia

Buffalo
Brydges, Thomas Eugene
Odza, Randall M.
Oppenheimer, Randolph Carl
Salisbury, Eugene W.

Chestnut Ridge
Burns, Richard Owen

Cutchogue
O'Connell, Francis Joseph

Floral Park
Cardalena, Peter Paul, Jr.

Garden City
Fishberg, Gerard
Ginsberg, Eugene Stanley
Lilly, Thomas Joseph
Schwarz, Carl A., Jr.

Hastings On Hudson
Steer, Richard Lane

Huntington
Liput, Andrew Lawrence

Mineola
Millman, Bruce Russell
Pogrebin, Bertrand B.
Zuckerman, Richard Karl

New Hyde Park
Levine, Kimberly Anne

New York
Altieri, Peter Louis
Ballon, Charles
Bassen, Ned Henry
Braid, Frederick Donald
Budd, Thomas Witbeck
Burstein, Neil Alan
Carling, Francis
Coleman, Jerome P.
Cook, Barbara Ann
Cooperman, Robert N.
Diamond, David Howard
Drucker, Jacquelin F.
Fallek, Andrew Michael
Flamm, Leonard N(athan)
Friedman, Eugene Stuart
Ganz, Howard Laurence
Glanstein, Joel Charles

Gordon, Michael Mackin
Hartmann, Carl Joseph
Jacobs, Roger Bruce
Jauvtis, Robert Lloyd
Kandel, William Lloyd
McMahon, James Charles
Miller, Gordon David
Nolan, Terrance Joseph, Jr.
O'Dwyer, Brian
Oechler, Henry John, Jr.
Paul, James William
Pompa, Renata
Reibstein, Richard Jay
Rogers, Theodore Otto, Jr.
Rossen, Jordan
Sachs, Joshua Michael
Safon, David Michael
Salup, Stephen
Savitt, Susan Schenkel
Shen, Michael
Simon, Bruce Harvey
Soyster, Margaret Blair
Spelfogel, Evan J.
Swain, Laura Taylor
Vladeck, Judith Pomarlen
Waks, Jay Warren
Wallach, Eric Jean
Watanabe, Roy Noboru
Weinrich, Johnathan Edward
Witkin, Eric Douglas
Zifchak, William C.

Pittsford
Rosenhouse, Michael Allan

Rochester
Smith, Jules Louis
Wild, Robert Warren

Sands Point
Hoynes, Louis LeNoir, Jr.

Syracuse
DiLorenzo, Louis Patrick
Gaal, John
King, Bernard T.

Valley Stream
Levine, Marilyn Markovich

NORTH CAROLINA

Cary
Brooks, David Victor

Charlotte
Belthoff, Richard Charles, Jr.
Van Hoy, Philip Marshall

Cherryville
Huffstetler, Palmer Eugene

Durham
Fisher, Stewart Wayne
Thompson, Sharon Andrea

High Point
Sheahan, Robert Emmett

Raleigh
Davis, Thomas Hill, Jr.
Trott, William Macnider
Wetsch, Laura Johnson

Thomasville
Reynolds, Mark Floyd, II

Winston Salem
Early, James H., Jr.

OHIO

Akron
Rooney, George Willard
Tipping, Harry A.

Athens
Hedges, Richard Houston

Cincinnati
DeLong, Deborah
Maxwell, Robert Wallace, II
Smith, Sheila Marie

Cleveland
Bloch, Marc Joel
Duvin, Robert Phillip
Ensign, Gregory Moore
Goldfarb, Bernard Sanford
Katz, Mark David
Kramer, Edward George
Leiken, Earl Murray
Lewis, John Bruce
Millisor, Kenneth Ray
Millstone, David J.
Pace, Stanley Dan
Ross, Harold Anthony
Strimbu, Victor, Jr.

Columbus
Bartemes, Amy Straker
Feheley, Lawrence Francis
Morgan, Dennis Richard
Moul, William Charles
Pressley, Fred G., Jr.
Stanton, Elizabeth McCool
Tarpy, Thomas Michael
Warner, Charles Collins

Toledo
Allotta, Joseph John
Dane, Stephen Mark
O'Connell, Maurice Daniel

Youngstown
Newman, Christopher John

OKLAHOMA

Oklahoma City
Bridges, Annita Marie

Court, Leonard
Puckett, Tony Greg

Tulsa
Matthies, Mary Constance T.
Pritchard, William Winther
Strecker, David Eugene

OREGON

Medford
O'Connor, Karl William (Goodyear Johnson)

Portland
Cooper, Nancy M.
Scott, Lewis Kelly
Seymour, Steven Wayne
Smith, Lester V., Jr.

PENNSYLVANIA

Bethlehem
Bush, Raymond George

Blue Bell
Teklits, Joseph Anthony

Doylestown
Stevens, Paul Lawrence

Elkins Park
Furman, Marc

Erie
Zamboldi, Richard Henry

Lansdale
Sultanik, Jeffrey Ted

Monroeville
McDowell, Michael David

New Castle
Flannery, Harry Audley

New Kensington
Wallace, Henry Jared, Jr.

Philadelphia
Baccini, Laurance Ellis
Bernard, John Marley
Bildersee, Robert Alan
Brown, William Hill, III
Dichter, Mark S.
DuPriest, Joanna G.
Epstein, Alan Bruce
Fritton, Karl Andrew
Gilberg, Kenneth Roy
Girard-diCarlo, David Franklin
Goldman, Gary Craig
Kraemer, Michael Frederick
Lillie, Charisse Ranielle
Mannino, Robert
Milone, Francis Michael
O'Reilly, Timothy Patrick
Satinsky, Barnett
Sigmond, Richard Brian
Whiteside, William Anthony, Jr.

Pittsburgh
Bellisario, Domenic Anthony
Brown, James Benton
Candris, Laura A.
Dugan, John F.
Harty, James Quinn
Hough, Thomas Henry Michael
Lucchino, Frank Joseph
Lyncheski, John E.
Orsatti, Ernest Benjamin
Post, Peter David
Ritchey, Patrick William
Saunders, Martin Johnston
Scheinholtz, Leonard Louis

Reading
Roland, John Wanner

Valley Forge
Walters, Bette Jean

RHODE ISLAND

Jamestown
Parks, Albert Lauriston

Providence
Labinger, Lynette J.
McAndrew, Thomas Joseph

SOUTH CAROLINA

Greenville
Hutson, Melvin Robert
Wyche, Madison Baker, III

TENNESSEE

Chattanooga
Phillips, John Bomar

Knoxville
Hagood, Lewis Russell

Memphis
Clark, Ross Bert, II
Conrad, Anne McGrew
Sossaman, William Lynwood

Nashville
Gannon, John Sexton
Lyon, Philip K(irkland)
Thomas, Robert Paige

Signal Mountain
Anderson, Charles Hill

TEXAS

Abilene
Robinson, Vianei Lopez

Amarillo
Cross, Janis Alexander

Austin
Greig, Brian Strother
Schwartz, Leonard Jay

Conroe
Abney, Joe L.
Irvin, Charles Leslie

Corpus Christi
Carnahan, Robert Narvell

Dallas
Austin, Ann Sheree
Case, Thomas Louis
Hackney, Hugh Edward
Jones, David Stanley
Jones, James Alton
McDonald, Michael Scott
Motley, Susan Denara
Nixon, Charles Richard
Thompson, Peter Rule

El Paso
Malone, Daniel Robert

Eldorado
Kosub, James Albert

Houston
Brown, William Alley
Carroll, James Vincent, III
Clore, Lawrence Hubert
Lopez, David Tiburcio
Roven, John David
Ryan, Thomas William
Shaddix, James W.
Tabak, Morris
Wray, Thomas Jefferson

Longview
Jones, Christopher Don

San Antonio
Bettac, Robert Edward
Hollin, Shelby W.
Moynihan, John Bignell
Pfeiffer, Philip J.
Putman, Michael (James Putman)

VIRGINIA

Alexandria
Franklin, Jeanne F.

Arlington
Cohen, Sheldon Irwin

Great Falls
Railton, William Scott

Harrisonburg
Wallinger, M(elvin) Bruce

Manassas
Scriven, Wayne Marcus

Mc Lean
Bredehoft, John Michael
Kruchko, John Gregory

Portsmouth
Moody, Willard James, Sr.

Reston
Reicin, Eric David

Richmond
Burtch, Jack Willard, Jr.
DeCamps, Charles Michael
Levit, Jay J(oseph)
Marstiller, Philip S.
McElligott, James Patrick, Jr.
Thompson, Paul Michael

Roanoke
Effel, Laura
Harris, Bayard Easter

Springfield
Chappell, Milton Leroy

Vienna
Hagberg, Chris Eric

WASHINGTON

Bellevue
Hannah, Lawrence Burlison
Sebris, Robert, Jr.

Seattle
Cavanaugh, Michael Everett
Freeman, Antoinette Rosefeldt
Hutcheson, Mark Andrew
Lemly, Thomas Adger
Rasmussen, Frederick Tatum
Riviera, Daniel John
Rosen, Jon Howard
Squires, William Randolph, III
Vestal, Josephine Burnet
Waldman, Bart

WEST VIRGINIA

Charleston
Dissen, James Hardiman
Slack, John Mark, III
Teare, John Richard, Jr.

WISCONSIN

Hudson
Lundeen, Bradley Curtis

La Crosse
Sleik, Thomas Scott

Madison
Ehlke, Bruce Frederic
Stoddard, Glenn McDonald

Milwaukee
Levy, Alan M.
Michelstetter, Stanley Hubert
Mulcahy, Charles Chambers
Patzke, John Charles
Pettit, Roger Lee
Scrivner, Thomas William
Whyte, George Kenneth, Jr.

Wausau
Dietrich, Dean Richard

ENGLAND

Cardiff
Warren, Martin Hugh

London
Burd, Michael
Fifield, Guy
Hunter, Ian Dalzell
Jeffreys, Simon Baden
Leadercramer, David Ian
Nesbitt, Sean Milo
Roskill, Julian Wentworth

FRANCE

Lyon-Villeurbanne
Duflos, Jean-Jacques

Paris
Doumenge, Arnaud
Poulain de Saint-Pere, Aude

GERMANY

Dusseldorf
Pape, Dieter

Koln
Reufels, Martin J.

HUNGARY

Budapest
Balassa, Tamás
Szecsodi, Zsolt

THE PHILIPPINES

Makati City
Valdecantos, Clarence Darrow Cunan

SPAIN

Barcelona
Martí, Miguel Torrents

Madrid
García-Perrote, Ignacio

SWEDEN

Stockholm
Erlandsson, Asa

VENEZUELA

Las Mercenes
Pro-Risquez, Juan C.

WALES

Cardiff
Williams, Audrey Marina

ADDRESS UNPUBLISHED

Anderson, Jon Eric
Atkins, Robert Alan
Bartz, David John
Blevins, Jeffrey Alexander
Branstetter, Cecil Dewey, Sr.
Brehl, James William
Carrol, Robert Kelton
Cohen, Norton Jacob
Gass, Raymond William
Gleeson, Paul Francis
Hagerman, Michael Charles
Harris, Randolph Burton
Holmes, Michael Gene
Kennedy, Thomas J.
Killeen, Michael John
King, James Forrest, Jr.
Kleiman, Bernard
Koomey, Richard Alan
Maulding, Barry Clifford
Mosk, Susan Hines
Mudd, John O.
Nussbaum, Peter David

Portnoy, Sara S.
Rabkin, Peggy Ann
Richman, Stephen Charles
Rodenburg, Clifton Glenn
Sapp, John Raymond
Serumgard, John R.
Torkildson, Raymond Maynard
Treacy, Vincent Edward
Vallianos, Carole Wagner
Valois, Robert Arthur

LAND USE AND ZONING

UNITED STATES

ARIZONA

Phoenix
Thompson, Joel Erik

Scottsdale
Jorden, Douglas Allen

Sun City
Hauer, James Albert

CALIFORNIA

Beverly Hills
Burns, Marvin Gerald

Claremont
Ferguson, Cleve Robert

Costa Mesa
Kramer, Kenneth Scott

Irvine
Hurst, Charles Wilson

La Jolla
ZoBell, Karl

Los Angeles
Salvaty, Benjamin Benedict
Tepper, R(obert) Bruce, Jr.
Weiser, Frank Alan

Los Gatos
Seligmann, William Robert

Pacific Palisades
Hunter, M(ilton) Reed, Jr.

Sacramento
Robbins, Stephen J. M.

San Diego
Dawe, James Robert

San Francisco
Briscoe, John
Corash, Michele B.
Gresham, Zane Oliver
Hoffman, John Douglas

San Jose
Gonzales, Daniel S.

Walnut Creek
Skaggs, Sanford Merle

COLORADO

Aspen
McGrath, J. Nicholas

Basalt
Mersman, Richard Kendrick, III

Denver
Petros, Raymond Louis, Jr.

Englewood
Deutsch, Harvey Elliot

Westcliffe
Snyder, Paul, Jr.

CONNECTICUT

Hartford
Buck, Gurdon Hall
Davis, Andrew Neil
McCracken, Gregory William
Merriam, Dwight Haines

Mystic
Valentine, Garrison Norton

Wilton
Healy, James Casey

DELAWARE

Wilmington
Devine, Donn
Waisanen, Christine M.

DISTRICT OF COLUMBIA

Washington
Glasgow, Norman Milton
Rosenberg, Ruth Helen Borsuk

FLORIDA

Fort Lauderdale
Moss, Stephen B.

Key Largo
Mattson, James Stewart

Lutz
Hayes, Timothy George

Miami
Mehta, Eileen Rose

Naples
Anderson, R(obert) Bruce
Humphreville, John David

Plant City
Sparkman, Steven Leonard

Saint Petersburg
Bernstein, Howard Mark

Satellite Beach
Tasker, Molly Jean

Tampa
Taub, Theodore Calvin
Weaver, Ronald Lee

West Palm Beach
Sklar, William Paul

GEORGIA

Atlanta
Stokes, James Sewell

Watkinsville
Wright, Robert Joseph

HAWAII

Honolulu
Kupchak, Kenneth Roy
Lombardi, Dennis M.

Kula
Rohlfing, Frederick William

ILLINOIS

Chicago
Domanskis, Alexander Rimas
Greenspan, Jeffrey Dov
Ungaretti, Richard Anthony

Lake Forest
Covington, George Morse

INDIANA

Fort Wayne
Lawson, Jack Wayne

KENTUCKY

Lexington
Murphy, Richard Vanderburgh

Louisville
Bardenwerper, William Burr

LOUISIANA

New Orleans
Villavaso, Stephen Donald

MAINE

Bernard
Marchetti, Karin Frances

Portland
Neagle, Christopher Scott

MARYLAND

Annapolis
Shannonhouse, Royal Graham, III

Chestertown
Mowell, George Mitchell

Gaithersburg
Ballman, B. George
Sherer, Samuel Ayers

Westminster
Preston, Charles Michael

MASSACHUSETTS

Boston
Hawkey, G. Michael
Krasnow, Jordan Philip
Shapiro, Sandra

Dennis Port
Singer, Myer R(ichard)

Natick
Marr, David E

MICHIGAN

Birmingham
Wells, Steven Wayne

Bloomfield Hills
Birnkrant, Sherwin Maurice

Harbor Springs
Smith, Wayne Richard

Southfield
Sullivan, Robert Emmet, Jr.

Three Rivers
Warnock, William Reid

MINNESOTA

Minneapolis
Barnard, Allen Donald
Straughn, Robert Oscar, III
Thorson, Steven Greg

MISSOURI

Clayton
Michenfelder, Albert A.

Kansas City
Gardner, Brian E.
Moore, Stephen James

NEVADA

Las Vegas
Curran, William P.

NEW JERSEY

Edison
Applebaum, Charles

Freehold
Brown, Sanford Donald

Hackensack
Duus, Gordon Cochran
Navatta, Anna Paula

Montville
Buzak, Edward Joseph

Newark
Neuer, Philip David

Newton
Cox, William Martin

Princeton
Sutphin, William Taylor

Scotch Plains
Kraus, Robert H.

Springfield
Grayson, Bette Rita
Mytelka, Arnold Krieger

Union
Greenstein, Richard Henry

Willingboro
Guest, Brian Milton

Woodcliff Lake
Phillips, John C.

NEW YORK

Amherst
Murray, William Michael

Melville
Rathkopf, Daren Anthony

New York
Cook, Robert S., Jr.
Greene, Norman L.

Syracuse
Sparkes, James Edward

NORTH CAROLINA

Asheville
Starnes, Oscar Edwin, Jr.

Cary
Montgomery, Charles Harvey

OHIO

Akron
Schrader, Alfred Eugene

Canton
Barnhart, Gene
Tzangas, George John

Chesterland
Durn, Raymond Joseph

Cincinnati
Trauth, Joseph Louis, Jr.

Dayton
Farquhar, Robert Nichols

Painesville
Aveni, Anthony Joseph

OKLAHOMA

Oklahoma City
Epperson, Kraettli Quynton

Tulsa
Schuller, Stephen Arthur

OREGON

Coquille
Lounsbury, Steven Richard

Eugene
DuPriest, Douglas Millhollen

Portland
Sullivan, Edward Joseph

PENNSYLVANIA

Pittsburgh
Murrin, Regis Doubet

RHODE ISLAND

Westerly
Nardone, William Andrew

SOUTH CAROLINA

Charleston
Robinson, Neil Cibley, Jr.

TEXAS

Houston
Wall, Kenneth E., Jr.

La Porte
Armstrong, John Douglas

VIRGINIA

Alexandria
Beach, Barbara Purse

Leesburg
Minchew, John Randall

Mc Lean
Stearns, Frank Warren

Richmond
Bates, John Wythe, III
Redmond, David Dudley

WASHINGTON

Bainbridge Island
Morisset, Mason Dale

Mount Vernon
Moser, C. Thomas

Olympia
Miller, Allen Terry, Jr.

Seattle
McCune, Philip Spear
Murray, Michael Kent
Walter, Michael Charles
Wilson, Richard Randolph

WISCONSIN

Madison
Rankin, Gene Raymond

Waukesha
Macy, John Patrick

MEXICO

Mexico City
Langarica O'Hea, Lorenza Kristin

GERMANY

Bonn
Nadler, Andreas

ADDRESS UNPUBLISHED

Baldwin, Carolyn Whitmore
Bateman, David Alfred
Pomerene, Toni Graven

LANDLORD-TENANT *See
also* **Commercial**

UNITED STATES

ARIZONA

Scottsdale
Marhoffer, David

CALIFORNIA

Costa Mesa
Daniels, James Walter
Kramer, Kenneth Scott

Irvine
Farrell, Teresa Joanning
Goldstock, Barry Philip

Los Angeles
Porter, Verna Louise

Palo Alto
O'Brien, Bradford Carl

Riverside
Chang, Janice May

San Diego
Meyer, Paul I.

Torrance
Johnson, Einar William

COLORADO

Aspen
Peirce, Frederick Fairbanks

CONNECTICUT

Waterbury
Muroff, Elena Marie

DELAWARE

Wilmington
Kristol, Daniel Marvin

FLORIDA

Miami
Wiseheart, Malcolm Boyd, Jr.

West Palm Beach
Layman, David Michael

GEORGIA

Atlanta
Foreman, Edward Rawson
Patterson, P(ickens) Andrew
Womack, Mary Pauline

HAWAII

Wailuku
Kinaka, William Tatsuo

ILLINOIS

Chicago
Garber, Samuel B.
Homburger, Thomas Charles
Kawitt, Alan
Staley, Charles Ralls
Ungaretti, Richard Anthony
Vree, Roger Allen
White, Linda Diane

INDIANA

Evansville
Jewell, John J.

Indianapolis
Dorocke, Lawrence Francis

KENTUCKY

Louisville
Vincenti, Michael Baxter

LOUISIANA

New Orleans
Sher, Leopold Zangwill

MARYLAND

Silver Spring
Hannan, Myles

MASSACHUSETTS

Boston
Hawkey, G. Michael

Salem
Wasserman, Stephen Alan

MICHIGAN

Bloomfield Hills
Berlow, Robert Alan
Dawson, Stephen Everette

Detroit
Candler, James Nall, Jr.

MINNESOTA

Minneapolis
Hanbery, Donna Eva
Mayerle, Thomas Michael

Rochester
Lantz, William Charles

Saint Paul
Spencer, David James

MISSOURI

Kansas City
Frantze, David Wayne

NEBRASKA

Omaha
Griffin, Patrick Edward

NEW JERSEY

Hackensack
Navatta, Anna Paula

NEW YORK

Chittenango
Baum, Peter Alan

Commack
Somer, Stanley Jerome

Hudson
Davis, Deborah Lynn

Jericho
Beal, Carol Ann

New York
Fenster, Marvin
Goldstein, Kenneth B.
Hackett, Kevin R.
Intriligator, Marc Steven
Levine, Melvin Charles
Rahm, David Alan
Rosenberg, Gary Marc
Sanseverino, Raymond Anthony
Schwartz, Barry Steven
Simon, Michael Scott
Smith, Vincent Milton
Uram, Gerald Robert
Vernon, Darryl Mitchell

NORTH CAROLINA

Winston Salem
Tate, David Kirk

OHIO

Shaker Heights
Barz, Patricia

Twinsburg
Kramer, Timothy Eugene

OKLAHOMA

Oklahoma City
Johnson, Robert Max

OREGON

Cannon Beach
Hillestad, Charles Andrew

PENNSYLVANIA

Lancaster
Zimmerman, D(onald) Patrick

Malvern
Doerr, John Maxwell

Philadelphia
Bressler, Barry E.
Goldman, Gary Craig
Panzer, Mitchell Emanuel
Pillion, Michael Leith

TENNESSEE

Knoxville
Ritchie, Albert

TEXAS

Dallas
Fishman, Edward Marc
Hawkins, Scott Alexis

Houston
Hollyfield, John Scoggins

Irving
Landau, Pearl Sandra

VIRGINIA

Glen Allen
Settlage, Steven Paul

Richmond
Bates, John Wythe, III

ITALY

Rome
Biolato, Giuseppe Vittorio

NORTHERN IRELAND

Belfast
White, Rowan McMurray

ADDRESS UNPUBLISHED

Assael, Michael
Rivera, Oscar R.
Speaker, Susan Jane
Walker, Jordan Clyde, Sr.

LEGISLATIVE

UNITED STATES

ALABAMA

Birmingham
Harris, George Bryan

Mobile
Murchison, David Roderick

ALASKA

Fairbanks
Andrews, Mark

ARIZONA

Phoenix
Cure, Carol Campbell
Riikola, Michael Edward
Wolf, G. Van Velsor, Jr.

ARKANSAS

Little Rock
Sherman, William Farrar

CALIFORNIA

Gold River
Andrew, John Henry

Los Angeles
McDonough, Patrick Joseph
Memel, Sherwin Leonard

Palo Alto
Trumbull, Terry Alan

Sacramento
Micheli, Christopher Michael

Stockton
Taft, Perry Hazard

COLORADO

Denver
McLain, William Allen
Rigg, John Brownlee, Jr.
Safran, Hubert Mayer
Solano, Henry L.

Littleton
Ross, William Robert

DELAWARE

Wilmington
Salinger, Frank Max

DISTRICT OF COLUMBIA

Washington
Ackerson, Nels J(ohn)
Besozzi, Paul Charles
Bonvillian, William Boone
Boone, Theodore Sebastian
Brinkmann, Robert Joseph
Brown, Michael DeWayne
Buechner, Jack W(illiam)
Casserly, James Lund
Cassidy, Robert Charles, Jr.
Columbus, R. Timothy
Cortese, Alfred William, Jr.
Coursen, Christopher Dennison
Evans, Donald Charles, Jr.
Gold, Peter Frederick
Goldstein, Michael B.
Heron, Julian Briscoe, Jr.
Johnson, Shirley Z.
Katsurinis, Stephen Avery
Kautter, David John
Kennedy, Jerry Wayne
Kovacs, William Lawrence
Kramer, William David
Lanam, Linda Lee
Lobel, Martin
Lopatin, Alan G.

Mallory, Charles King, III
Mendelsohn, Martin
Navarro, Bruce Charles
Pate, Michael Lynn
Peet, Richard Clayton
Rehm, John Bartram
Richmond, David Walker
Sacher, Steven Jay
Sackler, Arthur Brian
Stayin, Randolph John
Violante, Joseph Anthony
Weisgall, Jonathan Michael
Wiseman, Alan M(itchell)

FLORIDA

Jensen Beach
Stuart, Harold Cutliff

Satellite Beach
Tasker, Molly Jean

Tallahassee
Barnett, Martha Walters
Curtin, Lawrence N.

GEORGIA

Atlanta
Kirby, Peter Cornelius

Dunwoody
Callison, James W.

HAWAII

Honolulu
Mirikitani, Andrew Kotaro

Kula
Rohlfing, Frederick William

IDAHO

Boise
Thomas, Eugene C.

ILLINOIS

Chicago
Kissel, Richard John
Miller, John Leed

Springfield
Londrigan, James Thomas
Morse, Saul Julian

INDIANA

Danville
Baldwin, Jeffrey Kenton

Indianapolis
Allen, David James
Miller, David Anthony

IOWA

Des Moines
Brown, Paul Edmondson
Luchtel, Keith Edward

KENTUCKY

Crestwood
Ray, Ronald Dudley

MARYLAND

Baltimore
Wheatley, Charles Henry, III

Bethesda
English, William deShay
Pankopf, Arthur, Jr.
Sheble, Walter Franklin

MASSACHUSETTS

Boston
Lembo, Vincent Joseph
Sweda, Edward Leon, Jr.

MICHIGAN

Detroit
Ward, George Edward

MINNESOTA

Little Canada
Hardman, James Charles

Minneapolis
Brooks, William Fern, Jr.

Saint Paul
Knapp, John Anthony

MISSISSIPPI

Jackson
Diaz, Oliver E., Jr.

MONTANA

Bozeman
Harris, Christopher Kirk

NEBRASKA

Omaha
Fuller, Diana Clare

NEVADA

Las Vegas
Faiss, Robert Dean

NEW JERSEY

Trenton
Pellecchia, John Michael

NEW MEXICO

Santa Fe
Carpenter, Richard Norris

NEW YORK

Albany
Ruggeri, Robert Edward

Buffalo
Pajak, David Joseph

Floral Park
Chatoff, Michael Alan

Lancaster
Walsh, J(ohn) B(ronson)

Mineola
Tannenbaum, Bernard

New York
Bear, Larry Alan
Ganz, David L.
Lewis, David L.
Mandelker, Lawrence Arthur
Miller, Sam Scott
Weinrich, Johnathan Edward

Rochester
Rosenbaum, Richard Merrill

NORTH CAROLINA

Raleigh
Trott, William Macnider

OHIO

Columbus
Long, Thomas Leslie
Morgan, Dennis Richard

PENNSYLVANIA

Bryn Mawr
Henry, Ronald George

Harrisburg
Murren, Philip Joseph

Philadelphia
Serotta, Judd Adam
Wagner, Thomas Joseph

Pittsburgh
Hull, John Daniel, IV

TENNESSEE

Nashville
Bruce, William Roland

TEXAS

Austin
Cunningham, Judy Marie
Strauser, Robert Wayne

Beaumont
Waterston, Tass Dever

Dallas
Dean, David Allen
Geiger, Richard Stuart

Houston
Brady, Norman Conrad

Lubbock
Crowson, James Lawrence

UTAH

Salt Lake City
Holtkamp, James Arnold
McConkie, Oscar Walter

VIRGINIA

Alexandria
Campbell, Thomas Douglas
Sczudlo, Walter Joseph

Arlington
Collins, Philip Reilly

Falls Church
Golden, Wilson
Thomas, William Griffith

Mc Lean
Greene, Timothy Geddes
Raymond, David Walker
Stephens, William Theodore

Middleburg
Dietz, Robert Sheldon

Reston
Platt, Leslie A.

Richmond
Hackney, Virginia Howitz

Rosslyn
Carbaugh, John Edward, Jr.

WASHINGTON

Seattle
Dolan, Andrew Kevin

WISCONSIN

Madison
Bremer, Howard Walter
Vaughan, Michael Richard

BELGIUM

Brussels
Smith, Turner Taliaferro, Jr.

ADDRESS UNPUBLISHED

Bagley, William Thompson
Boyd, Thomas Marshall
Hanzlik, Rayburn DeMara
Mudd, John O.
Perlstein, William James
Reeder, James Arthur
Rivlin, Lewis Allen
Trotta, Frank P., Jr.
Wittig, Raymond Shaffer

LIBEL

UNITED STATES

ALABAMA

Mobile
Pennington, Al

ARIZONA

Phoenix
Bodney, David Jeremy
Silverman, Alan Henry

ARKANSAS

Little Rock
Miller, Peter Alexander

CALIFORNIA

Beverly Hills
Heinke, Rex S.

Laguna Hills
Mathews, Stanton Terry

Los Angeles
Battaglia, Philip Maher
Riffer, Jeffrey Kent

Palo Alto
Tiffany, Joseph Raymond, II

Sacramento
Houpt, James Edward

COLORADO

Denver
Cooper, Paul Douglas
Kahn, Edwin Sam
Low, Andrew M.
Murane, William Edward

CONNECTICUT

Stamford
Lytton, William B(ryan)

West Hartford
Elliot, Ralph Gregory

DISTRICT OF COLUMBIA

Washington
Carome, Patrick Joseph
Greenfeld, Alexander

Horne, Michael Stewart
Isbell, David Bradford
Payton, John

FLORIDA

Miami
Vento, M. Thérèse

Tampa
Thomas, Gregg Darrow

GEORGIA

Atlanta
Glaser, Arthur Henry
Schroeder, Eric Peter

HAWAII

Honolulu
Portnoy, Jeffrey Steven

ILLINOIS

Chicago
Clifford, Robert A.
Gilford, Steven Ross
Herman, Sidney N.
Sennet, Charles Joseph

Des Plaines
Zamarin, Ronald George

MASSACHUSETTS

Boston
Dougherty, Thomas James

MICHIGAN

Ann Arbor
Niehoff, Leonard Marvin

MINNESOTA

Minneapolis
Borger, John Philip
Magnuson, Roger James

MISSISSIPPI

Jackson
Diaz, Oliver E., Jr.
Henegan, John C(lark)

MISSOURI

Kansas City
Milton, Chad Earl

NEVADA

Las Vegas
Faiss, Robert Dean
Hinueber, Mark Arthur

NEW JERSEY

Newark
Eittreim, Richard MacNutt

NEW YORK

Albany
Danziger, Peter

Glen Cove
Mills, Charles Gardner

New York
Abelman, Arthur F.
Bamberger, Michael Albert
Cayea, Donald Joseph
Curtis, Frank R.
Gold, Stuart Walter
Kennedy, Michael John
Kurnit, Richard Alan
Ringel, Dean
Robertson, Edwin David
Scheiman, Eugene R.
Schlain, Barbara Ellen
Schwartz, Renee Gerstler
Soyster, Margaret Blair
Udell, Richard
Wallach, Evan Jonathan

White Plains
Madden, M. Stuart

NORTH CAROLINA

Charlotte
Ayscue, Edwin Osborne, Jr.

Marion
Burgin, Charles Edward

OHIO

Cincinnati
Faller, Susan Grogan

Toledo
Pletz, Thomas Gregory

OKLAHOMA

Norman
Sweeney, Everett John

Oklahoma City
Nelon, Robert Dale

OREGON

Portland
Hinkle, Charles Frederick

PENNSYLVANIA

Allentown
Gross, Malcolm Joseph

Harrisburg
Sullivan, John Cornelius, Jr.

Philadelphia
Beasley, James Edwin
Harvey, Gregory Merrill
McHugh, James Joseph
Shestack, Jerome Joseph
Solano, Carl Anthony
Toll, Seymour I.

TENNESSEE

Chattanooga
Phillips, John Bomar

Nashville
Rush, Stephen Kenneth

TEXAS

Dallas
Babcock, Charles Lynde, IV
Mc Elhaney, John Hess

Fort Worth
Sharpe, James Shelby

Houston
Miller, Brian Charles

UTAH

Salt Lake City
Shea, Patrick A.

VIRGINIA

Hampton
Smith, Stephen Mark

Richmond
Rudlin, David Alan

WASHINGTON

Seattle
Johnson, Bruce Edward Humble

CANADA

ONTARIO

Toronto
Chester, Robert Simon George

AUSTRALIA

Melbourne
Bartlett, Peter Llewellyn
Gronow, Geoffrey Rees

ENGLAND

London
Skrein, Stephen Peter Michael

ITALY

Milan
Peron, Sabrina

NORWAY

Oslo
Strømme, Vidar

SINGAPORE

Singapore
Shetty, Nishith Kumare

ADDRESS UNPUBLISHED

DeLaFuente, Charles
Kapnick, Richard Bradshaw
Saunders, Lonna Jeanne
Swann, Barbara

MALPRACTICE. *See*
Personal injury.

**MERGERS AND
ACQUISITIONS**

UNITED STATES

ALABAMA

Birmingham
Baker, David Remember
Grant, Walter Matthews
Rotch, James E.
Stewart, Joseph Grier

ARIZONA

Phoenix
Bauman, Frederick Carl
Moya, Patrick Robert

CALIFORNIA

Irvine
Black, William Rea
Wertheim, Jay Philip
Wintrode, Ralph Charles

Los Angeles
Blencowe, Paul Sherwood
Farrar, Stanley F.
Havel, Richard W.
McAniff, Edward John
McLane, Frederick Berg
Shultz, John David

Menlo Park
Kelly, Daniel Grady, Jr.

Palo Alto
Climan, Richard Elliot
Deaktor, Darryl Barnett
Phair, Joseph Baschon

San Diego
Alpert, Michael Edward
Edwards, James Richard

San Francisco
Baker, Cameron
Block, David Jeffrey
DeMuro, Paul Robert
Feller, Lloyd Harris
Holden, Frederick Douglass, Jr.
Larson, John William
Mann, Bruce Alan
Wood, Robert Warren

San Ramon
Freed, Kenneth Alan

Santa Clara
Denten, Christopher Peter

COLORADO

Denver
Newcom, Jennings Jay
Ruppert, John Lawrence

Edwards
Calise, Nicholas James

Greenwood Village
Lidstone, Herrick Kenley, Jr.

Littleton
Keely, George Clayton

CONNECTICUT

Darien
Prince, Kenneth Stephen

Hartford
Davis, Andrew Neil
Lotstein, James Irving
Wetzler, Monte Edwin

Stamford
Dupont, Wesley David
Jensen, Frode, III

DISTRICT OF COLUMBIA

Washington
Bierman, James Norman
Bowe, Richard Welbourn
Bruemmer, Russell John
Czarra, Edgar F., Jr.
Fishburne, Benjamin P., III
Jacobsen, Raymond Alfred, Jr.
Mazo, Mark Elliott
Rafferty, James Gerard
Repper, George Robert
Stock, Stuart Chase

FLORIDA

Boca Raton
Beck, Jan Scott

Jacksonville
Lee, Lewis Swift

Melbourne
Rosenberg, Priscilla Elliott

Miami
Ersek, Gregory Joseph Mark
Grossman, Robert Louis
Wright, Blandin James

Orlando
Blackford, Robert Newton
Capouano, Albert D.
Conti, Louis Thomas Moore
Heinle, Richard Alan
Yates, Leighton Delevan, Jr.

Sarasota
Janney, Oliver James

Tampa
Doliner, Nathaniel Lee

GEORGIA

Atlanta
Burgoon, Brian David
Jeffries, McChesney Hill, Jr.
McNeill, Thomas Ray
Pless, Laurance Davidson
Schulte, Jeffrey Lewis
Stewart, Jeffrey B.

HAWAII

Honolulu
Reber, David James

ILLINOIS

Chicago
Anderson, J. Trent
Athas, Gus James
Blount, Michael Eugene
Clemens, Richard Glenn
Crawford, Dewey Byers
Davis, Scott Jonathan
Duncan, John Patrick Cavanaugh
Fein, Roger Gary
Gerstein, Mark Douglas
Goldman, Louis Budwig
Gordon, Phillip
Howell, R(obert) Thomas, Jr.
Kaplan, Jared
Kuntz, William Richard, Jr.
McGrath, William Joseph
Morrow, John E.
Reum, James Michael
Rizowy, Carlos Guillermo
Rosic, George S.
Sabl, John J.
Schulz, Keith Donald
Scogland, William Lee
Thomas, Frederick Bradley
Wander, Herbert Stanton

Deerfield
Bush, Thomas Norman
Gaither, John Francis, Jr.

Downers Grove
Mason, Peter Ian

Northbrook
Sernett, Richard Patrick

INDIANA

Indianapolis
Deer, Richard Elliott
Kahlenbeck, Howard, Jr.
Strain, James Arthur

KENTUCKY

Louisville
Mellen, Francis Joseph, Jr.
Tannon, Jay Middleton

LOUISIANA

New Orleans
McMillan, Lee Richards, II

MAINE

Portland
Stauffer, Eric P.

MARYLAND

Baltimore
Robinson, Zelig

Bethesda
Menaker, Frank H., Jr.

MASSACHUSETTS

Billerica
Lewis, Edwin Leonard, III

Boston
Bohnen, Michael J.

Gonson, S. Donald
Halligan, Brendan Patrick
Malt, Ronald Bradford
Patterson, John de la Roche, Jr.
Williams, Robert Dana

Braintree
Mullare, T(homas) Kenwood, Jr.

Springfield
Weiss, Ronald Phillip

MICHIGAN

Ada
Mc Callum, Charles Edward

Battle Creek
Markey, James Kevin

Detroit
Deason, Herold McClure
Lawrence, John Kidder

Farmington
Cooper, Douglas Kenneth

MINNESOTA

Minneapolis
Bergerson, David Raymond
Kaplan, Sheldon
Kozachok, Stephen K.
Mellum, Gale Robert
Stageberg, Roger V.
Yost, Gerald B.

Saint Paul
Rebane, John T.

MISSOURI

Chesterfield
Denneen, John Paul

Kansas City
Wrobley, Ralph Gene

Saint Louis
Cook, Thomas Alfred Ashley
Dorwart, Donald Bruce
Gillis, John Lamb, Jr.
Tierney, Michael Edward

NEBRASKA

Omaha
Griffin, Patrick Edward

NEW HAMPSHIRE

Concord
Potter, Fred Leon

NEW JERSEY

Bridgewater
Ball, Owen Keith, Jr.

Florham Park
Kandravy, John
Siino, Salvatore G.

Monmouth Junction
King, David Roy

Newark
Vajtay, Stephen Michael, Jr.

Pitman
Cloues, Edward Blanchard, II

Princeton
Burgess, Robert Kyle
Miller, Richard Mark

Roseland
Wovsaniker, Alan

NEW YORK

Buffalo
Harner, Timothy R.
Lippes, Gerald Sanford

Fairport
Young, Thomas Paul

Liverpool
Wolfson, Warren David

New York
Atkins, Peter Allan
Backman, Gerald Stephen
Bialkin, Kenneth Jules
Brown, Meredith M.
Burak, H(oward) Paul
Bushnell, George Edward, III
Butler, Samuel Coles
Cotter, James Michael
de Sampigny, Guillaume
Detjen, David Wheeler
Dorado, Marianne Gaertner
Dubin, James Michael
Duffy, W. Leslie
Dunn, M(orris) Douglas
Everett, James William, Jr.
Feit, Glenn M.
Fortenbaugh, Samuel Byrod, III
Fredericks, Wesley Charles, Jr.
Fried, Donald David
Friedman, Robert Laurence
Friedman, Samuel Selig

Gettner, Alan Frederick
Gillespie, Jane
Gruson, Michael
Haje, Peter Robert
Hall, John Herbert
Heller, Robert Martin
Hendry, Andrew Delaney
Hiden, Robert Battaile, Jr.
Hoff, Jonathan M(orind)
Holley, Steven Lyon
Howe, Richard Rives
Hyun, Jung-Wen
Karls, John Spencer
Kassebaum, John Philip
Katz, Ronald Scott
Keene, Lonnie Stuart
Kempf, Donald G., Jr.
Kern, George Calvin, Jr.
Kessel, Mark
Kies, David M.
Komaroff, Stanley
Lamia, Thomas Roger
Landes, Robert Nathan
Larose, Lawrence Alfred
Leonard, Edwin Deane
Levin, Ezra Gurion
Lewis, Adam McLean
Lowy, George Theodore
Mestres, Ricardo Angelo, Jr.
Morphy, James Calvin
Mullman, Michael S.
Nance, Allan Taylor
Nash, Paul LeNoir
Norfolk, William Ray
Parent, Louise Marie
Perkins, Roswell Burchard
Perlmuth, William Alan
Phillips, Pamela Kim
Pierce, Morton Allen
Pisano, Vincent James
Poster, Michael Sollod
Purtell, Lawrence Robert
Quale, Andrew Christopher, Jr.
Reid, Edward Snover, III
Resnicow, Norman Jakob
Rice, Donald Sands
Romney, Richard Bruce
Rosenblum, Scott S.
Rubinstein, Frederic Armand
Ruegger, Philip T., III
Rusmisel, Stephen R.
Schmidt, Joseph W.
Schorr, Brian Lewis
Schwartz, Barry Fredric
Seifert, Thomas Lloyd
Serota, Susan Perlstadt
Shecter, Howard L.
Sheehan, Robert C.
Siegel, Jeffrey Norton
Siller, Stephen I.
Skigen, Patricia Sue
Stone, David Philip
Sussman, Alexander Ralph
Tanenbaum, Gerald Stephen
Thalacker, Arbie Robert
Toumey, Donald Joseph
Tract, Marc Mitchell
Tran, Julie Hoan
Valat de Córdova, Thierry
Vega, Matias Alfonso
Volk, Stephen Richard
Warden, John L.
Washburn, David Thacher
Wells, Andrew Norman
West, Stephen Kingsbury
Wiegley, Roger Douglas
Wilson, Paul Holliday, Jr.
Wolf, Gary Wickert
Yamin, Michael Geoffrey

Rochester
Adair, Donald Robert
Doyle, Justin P

Rye
Roberts, Thomas Alba

Suffern
Stack, Daniel

Syracuse
Bullock, Stephen C.

White Plains
Serchuk, Ivan

NORTH CAROLINA

Charlotte
Bernstein, Mark R.
McBryde, Neill Gregory
Newitt, John Garwood, Jr.
Zeller, Michael Eugene

Greensboro
Davis, Herbert Owen
Hopkins, John David

Raleigh
Edwards, James Malone
Powell, Durwood Royce

Winston Salem
Gunter, Michael Donwell

OHIO

Cincinnati
Anderson, James Milton
Lindberg, Charles David
Meranus, Leonard Stanley
Olson, Robert Wyrick

Cleveland
Langer, Carlton Earl
Markey, Robert Guy
Marting, Michael G.
Nave, Michele Garrick

Columbus
Brinkman, Dale Thomas
Stinehart, Roger Ray

Dayton
Taronji, Jaime, Jr.

Hamilton
Meyers, Pamela Sue

North Canton
Dettinger, Warren Walter

Toledo
Webb, Thomas Irwin, Jr.

Wickliffe
Kidder, Fred Dockstater

OKLAHOMA

Oklahoma City
Rockett, D. Joe

Tulsa
Slicker, Frederick Kent

OREGON

Beaverton
Fulsher, Allan Arthur

Portland
Krahmer, Donald Leroy, Jr.

PENNSYLVANIA

Blue Bell
Barron, Harold Sheldon

Harrisburg
Cicconi, Christopher M.

Media
Harvey, Alice Elease

Philadelphia
Clark, William H., Jr.
Colli, Bart Joseph
Dubin, Stephen Victor
Genkin, Barry Howard
Gough, John Francis
Grady, Thomas Michael
McAneny, Eileen S.
Promislo, Daniel
Sartorius, Peter S.
Strasbaugh, Wayne Ralph
Stuntebeck, Clinton A.

Pittsburgh
Aderson, Sanford M.
Barrett, Karen Moore
Bleier, Michael E.
Frank, Ronald William
Hardie, James Hiller
Newlin, William Rankin
Wilkinson, James Allan

Valley Forge
Bovaird, Brendan Peter

Wilkes Barre
Roth, Eugene

RHODE ISLAND

Pawtucket
Kranseler, Lawrence Michael

Providence
Donnelly, Kevin William

SOUTH CAROLINA

Charleston
Clement, Robert Lebby, Jr.

Hilton Head Island
Hagoort, Thomas Henry

Salem
Everett, C(harles) Curtis

TENNESSEE

Chattanooga
Durham, J(oseph) Porter, Jr.

Knoxville
Howard, Lewis Spilman

Nashville
Carr, Davis Haden
Mayden, Barbara Mendel

TEXAS

Addison
Kneipper, Richard Keith

Austin
Gangstad, John Erik
Laves, Alan Leonard

Dallas
Feld, Alan David
Gohlke, David Ernest
Gores, Christopher Merrel
Miller, Norman Richard
Rodgers, John Hunter
Spears, Robert Fields
Young, Barney Thornton
Zahn, Donald Jack

Ennis
Swanson, Wallace Martin

Houston
Bech, Douglas York
Bilger, Bruce R.
Born, Dawn Slater
Finch, Michael Paul
Gover, Alan Shore
Grace, James Martin, Jr.
Lawson, Ben F.
Myers, Franklin
O'Donnell, Lawrence, III
O'Toole, Austin Martin
Sheinfeld, Myron M.
Still, Charles Henry
Szalkowski, Charles Conrad

Stephenville
Batson, David Warren

UTAH

Salt Lake City
Callister, Louis Henry, Jr.

VIRGINIA

Arlington
McCorkindale, Douglas Hamilton

Charlottesville
Stroud, Robert Edward

Herndon
Pearlman, Michael Allen

Richmond
Broadbent, Peter Edwin, Jr.
Goodpasture, Philip Henry

Tysons Corner
Maiwurm, James John

WASHINGTON

Seattle
Pym, Bruce Michael

WISCONSIN

Milwaukee
Holz, Harry George
Rintelman, Donald Brian

Racine
Coates, Glenn Richard

MEXICO

Mexico City
Chacon Lopez Velarde, Ricardo

ARGENTINA

Buenos Aires
Crivelli, Marcelo

AUSTRALIA

Melbourne
Galbraith, Colin Robert

Sydney
Grieve, Gordon Thomas
Jeffares, Paul Reginald
Pistilli, Mark Stephen
Simmons, Daniel David

AUSTRIA

Vienna
Frank, Alix
Mayr, Andreas W.
Wolf, Richard V.

BELGIUM

Brussels
Delsaut, Philippe Patrick

Liege
Matray, Didier F

CHINA

Beijing
Zhao, Qian

Hong Kong
Yu, Benita Ka Po

Shanghai
Qi, Qing Michael

Taipei
Tsai, Jaclyn Yu-Ling

CZECH REPUBLIC

Prague
Bányaiová, Alena

DENMARK

Copenhagen
Mogelmose, Henrik
Sogaard, Klaus

ENGLAND

Birmingham
Graham, Simon
Hull, David Julian

London
Astleford, Peter David
Barnes, Oliver William Abbott
Booker, Russell Stuart
Buckley, Colin Hugh
Coppin, Jonathan David
Fuller, Charles Robert Saunders
Goodall, Caroline Mary Helen
Heard, David James
Kidwell, Mathew Charles
Rawlinson, Mark Stobart
Rosenberg, Daniel P.
Sheach, Andrew Jonathan
Stanley, Ian G.

Sheffield
Goulding, Nick

FINLAND

Helsinki
Ahola, Juhani Ilmari
Hentula, Ismo Tapani
Tähtinen, Jyrki Juhani
Wist, Tarja Tuulia

FRANCE

Neuilly sur Seine
Raffin, Marie-Hélène J.

Paris
Blanchenay, Nicolas
Citrey, Eric Jean-Pierre
Darlington, Gavin
Fix, Brian David
Gaillot, Laurent D

GERMANY

Cologne
Wilsing, Hans Ulrich

Dusseldorf
Clev, Heinrich

Düsseldorf
Gillessen, Frederick
Plueckelmann, Katja

Frankfurt
Haarmann, Wilhelm
Wolff, Florian

Frankfurt am Main
Hartmann, Uwe

Frankfurt/Main
Wuermeling, Ulrich Urban

Munich
Schleifenbaum, Eckhart Johannes

Stuttgart
Mailaender, Karl Peter

HONG KONG

Hong Kong
Garvey, Richard Anthony
Graham, David

IRELAND

Dublin
Brady, George Eoghan

Dublin 1
Fitzgerald, Eithne Margaret

ISRAEL

Jerusalem
Stern, Doron Daniel

ITALY

Mialn
Vecchio, Cesare Giovanni

Milan
Ricci, Barnaba

Rome
Di Amato, Astolfo
Salce, Valerio

JAPAN

Osaka
Solberg, Norman Robert

Tokyo
Ishizuka, Nobuhisa
Thorson, Andrew H.

KENYA

Nairoba
Maosa, Thomas Nyakambi

THE NETHERLANDS

Amstelveen
Liem, Edwin T.H.
Tarlavski, Roman

Amsterdam
Viersen, Arnoud C.

Rotterdam
Bolland, Pieter Heyme
van der Horst, Jan

NEW ZEALAND

Auckland
McNamara, Denis Michael
Owles, Peter Gary

NORWAY

Oslo
Moljord, Kare I.
Moss, Giuditta Cordero
Thogersen, Kai
Thyness, Erik

Skoyen, Oslo
Wille, Hans Georg

Vika
Ravnaas, Ernst

PERU

Lima
Hernandez, Juan Luis
Rebaza, Alberto

THE PHILIPPINES

Makati City
Banez, Winthrop Hawthorne Redoble
Mamuric, Jose Roberto Lota

PORTUGAL

Lisbon
Pessanha, Tomas Vasconcelos

REPUBLIC OF KOREA

Seoul
Cho, Chi-Hyoung
Choi, Unghwan Raphael

ROMANIA

Bucharest
Jardine, Bryan Wilson
Pachiu, Laurentiu Victor

SAUDI ARABIA

Jeddah
Shea, Gerald MacDonald

SCOTLAND

Glasgow
Burrow, Alistair Stewart

SINGAPORE

Singapore
Yeo, Jennifer

SOUTH AFRICA

Johannesburg
Franck, Brigitte Broderick

Sandton
Schlosberg, Jonathan Harry

Sandton City
Legh, Robert Andrew

SPAIN

Madrid
Garrido de las Heras, Miguel
Hendel, Clifford James
Lincke, Karl Heinrich
Martin de Vidales, Nicolas

Rueda, Pedro Antonio

SWEDEN

Gothenburg
Edh, Staffan

Malmo
Frii, Jonas Erik Werner

Stockholm
Lindquist, Ylva
Malmström, Anders C.
Rambe, Lars Joachim
Sarkia, Peter L.

SWITZERLAND

Basel
Eulau, Peter H.

Chateau d'Oex
Berman, Joshua Mordecai

UKRAINE

Kiev
Voitovich, Sergei Adamovich

Kyiv
Vronskaya, Anna Alexandrovna

VENEZUELA

Solano Caracas
Garcia-Montoya, Luis Alberto

ADDRESS UNPUBLISHED

Ball, James Herington
Bierce, William B.
Blumenthal, William
Bostrom, Robert Everett
Coplin, Mark David
Crook, Donald Martin
D'Avignon, Roy Joseph
Davis, Clarence Clinton, Jr.
Ellison, Noni Lois
Fischer, David Charles
Hanzlik, Rayburn DeMara
Herringer, Maryellen Cattani
Ikeda, Cnythia Yuko
Kapnick, Richard Bradshaw
Lefkowitz, Alan Zoel
Lorne, Simon Michael
Madden, John Joseph
Massad, Stephen Albert
Meyer, Max Earl
Millimet, Erwin
Mitchell, William Graham Champion
O'Brien, James Edward
Oliver, Samuel William, Jr.
Song, Bing
Tierney, Kevin Joseph
Voight, Elizabeth Anne
Wilson, Hugh Steven
Wilson, Rhys Thaddeus
Wohlschlaeger, Frederick George
Wright, Arthur McIntosh

MILITARY

UNITED STATES

ALABAMA

Birmingham
Norris, Robert Wheeler

ARIZONA

Eloy
O'Leary, Thomas Michael

ARKANSAS

Little Rock
Sherman, William Farrar

CALIFORNIA

El Segundo
Zucker, David Clark

San Diego
Brown, Douglas Colton

Santa Ana
Harley, Robison Dooling, Jr.

FLORIDA

Fernandina Beach
Manson, Keith Alan Michael

Jensen Beach
Stuart, Harold Cutliff

MILITARY

GEORGIA

Newnan
McBroom, Thomas William, Sr.

INDIANA

South Bend
Casey, Robert Fitzgerald

KANSAS

Halstead
Bender, Jack Sinclair, III

KENTUCKY

Crestwood
Ray, Ronald Dudley

Lexington
Hickey, John King

MARYLAND

Annapolis
Ferris, William Michael

Glen Burnie
Lilly, John Richard, II

Rockville
Avery, Bruce Edward

MASSACHUSETTS

Boston
O'Connell, Joseph Francis, III

MINNESOTA

Minneapolis
Newhall, David Gillette

NEBRASKA

Lincoln
Zink, Walter Earl, II

NEW JERSEY

Summit
Katz, Michael Albert

NEW YORK

New York
Issler, Harry

NORTH CAROLINA

Jacksonville
Taylor, Vaughan Edward

OHIO

Dayton
Kinlin, Donald James

PENNSYLVANIA

Melrose Park
Shmukler, Stanford

Philadelphia
Wert, Robert Clifton

Pittsburgh
Orsatti, Ernest Benjamin

RHODE ISLAND

Providence
McMahon, John Joseph

TENNESSEE

Newport
Bell, John Alton

TEXAS

Mason
Johnson, Rufus Winfield

VIRGINIA

Arlington
Cohen, Sheldon Irwin

Norfolk
Parsons, Rymn James

Sterling
McBarnette, Bruce Olvin

Virginia Beach
Buzard, David Andrew

MUNICIPAL (include BONDS)

UNITED STATES

ALABAMA

Birmingham
Foster, Arthur Key, Jr.
Haskell, Wyatt Rushton

Montgomery
Gregory, William Stanley

ALASKA

Anchorage
Wohlforth, Eric Evans

ARIZONA

Flagstaff
Gliege, John Gerhardt

Phoenix
Hicks, William Albert, III
Olson, Robert Howard

ARKANSAS

Little Rock
Bohannon, Charles Tad
Campbell, George Emerson

CALIFORNIA

Los Angeles
Hedlund, Karen Jean
Watson, Glenn Robert

Palo Alto
Trumbull, Terry Alan

San Diego
de Sousa, Paula Cristina Pacheco

San Francisco
McDevitt, Ray Edward

CONNECTICUT

Hartford
Lloyd, James Hendrie, III

Westport
Saxl, Richard Hildreth

DISTRICT OF COLUMBIA

Washington
Collinson, Dale Stanley
Graham, John Stuart, III
Journey, Drexel Dahlke
Samuelson, Kenneth Lee

FLORIDA

Coral Gables
Kaplan, David Louis

Jacksonville
McWilliams, John Lawrence, III

Naples
Anderson, R(obert) Bruce

Orlando
Frey, Louis, Jr.

Plant City
Buchman, Kenneth William

West Palm Beach
Spillias, Kenneth George

GEORGIA

Atlanta
Meyer, William Lorne
Mobley, John Homer, II

ILLINOIS

Batavia
Drendel, Kevin Gilbert

Chicago
Chester, Mark Vincent
Hummel, Gregory William
Ladd, Jeffrey Raymond

Pitt, George
Quinlan, William Joseph, Jr.
Spiotto, James Ernest

Crystal Lake
Thoms, Jeannine Aumond

Danville
Hubbard, Fred Leonhardt

Elgin
Juergensmeyer, John Eli

Jacksonville
Kuster, Larry Donald

INDIANA

Boonville
Neff, Mark Edward

Indianapolis
Horn, Brenda Sue
Paul, Stephen Howard

Lafayette
O'Connell, Lawrence B.

KANSAS

Shawnee Mission
Gaar, Norman Edward

KENTUCKY

Louisville
Maggiolo, Allison Joseph

LOUISIANA

Baton Rouge
Richards, Marta Alison

New Orleans
Beck, William Harold, Jr.
Judell, Harold Benn

MAINE

Brunswick
Owen, H. Martyn

MASSACHUSETTS

Boston
Kopelman, Leonard

Worcester
Moschos, Demitrios Mina

MICHIGAN

Detroit
Deason, Herold McClure
Kamins, John Mark
Lewand, F. Thomas
Ward, George Edward

Flint
Cooley, Richard Eugene

Walled Lake
Seglund, Bruce Richard

MINNESOTA

Minneapolis
Thorson, Steven Greg

MISSISSIPPI

Jackson
Edds, Stephen Charles

MISSOURI

Kansas City
Gilmore, Webb Reilly
Lotven, Howard Lee
Moore, Stephen James

Saint Louis
Arnold, John Fox
Brickler, John Weise

NEBRASKA

Omaha
Barmettler, Joseph John

NEVADA

Las Vegas
Jost, Richard Frederic, III

NEW JERSEY

Clifton
Mohammed, Sohail

Medford
Kondracki, Edward Anthony

Montville
Buzak, Edward Joseph

Newark
Scally, John Joseph, Jr.

Roseland
Vanderbilt, Arthur T., II

Secaucus
Castano, Gregory Joseph
Fitzpatrick, Harold Francis
Israels, Michael Jozef

Warren
Bernstein, Eric Martin

NEW YORK

Albany
Girvin, James Edward

Amherst
Murray, William Michael

Buffalo
McElvein, Thomas Irving, Jr.

Cedarhurst
Taubenfeld, Harry Samuel

Garden City
Kroll, Martin N.

Ithaca
Theisen, Henry William

New York
Bach, Thomas Handford
Ganzi, Victor Frederick
Gill, E. Ann
Miller, Arthur Madden
Nicholls, Richard H.
Tarnoff, Jerome
Zucker, Howard

Orangeburg
Rivet, Diana Wittmer

Pearl River
Riley, James Kevin

Salamanca
Brady, Thomas Carl

Stamford
Becker, Carl Frederick

Westbury
Boes, Lawrence William

NORTH CAROLINA

Charlotte
Buckley, Charles Robinson, III

Raleigh
Carlton, Alfred Pershing, Jr.

OHIO

Akron
Schrader, Alfred Eugene
Trotter, Thomas Robert

Cleveland
Boyko, Christopher Allan
Currivan, John Daniel
Kramer, Eugene Leo

OREGON

Ashland
Fine, J. David

Portland
Abravanel, Allan Ray

PENNSYLVANIA

Bryn Mawr
Henry, Ronald George

Erie
Tupitza, Thomas Anton

Lancaster
Gray, Kathleen Ann

Lansdale
Sultanik, Jeffrey Ted

Norristown
Aman, George Matthias, III

Philadelphia
Carson, Timothy Joseph
Jones, Robert Jeffries
Mason, Theodore W.

Pittsburgh
Demmler, John Henry

RHODE ISLAND

Jamestown
Parks, Albert Lauriston

Newport
McConnell, David Kelso

TENNESSEE

Knoxville
Congleton, Joseph Patrick
Roach, Jon Gilbert

Nashville
Trent, John Thomas, Jr.

TEXAS

Houston
Anderson, Eric Severin
McCreary, Frank E., III
Wall, Kenneth E., Jr.
Weber, Fredric Alan

VIRGINIA

Richmond
Pope, Robert Dean

Roanoke
Tegenkamp, Gary Elton

Springfield
Eley, Randall Robbi

WASHINGTON

Bellevue
Hannah, Lawrence Burlison

Seattle
Ellis, James Reed
Gottlieb, Daniel Seth
Spitzer, Hugh D.
Walter, Michael Charles

Spokane
Koegen, Roy Jerome

WISCONSIN

Milwaukee
Levy, Alan M.

Shawano
Habeck, James Roy

Waukesha
Macy, John Patrick

ADDRESS UNPUBLISHED

Choukas-Bradley, James Richard
Clarke, Edward Owen, Jr.
Howell, Donald Lee
Mangler, Robert James
Ostergaard, Joni Hammersla
Pitcher, Griffith Fontaine

NATIVE AMERICAN

UNITED STATES

ALASKA

Anchorage
Fortier, Samuel John

Fairbanks
Andrews, Mark

ARIZONA

Phoenix
Storey, Lee A.

MINNESOTA

Minneapolis
Heffelfinger, Thomas Backer

NEW MEXICO

Albuquerque
Slade, Lynn Heyer

Carlsbad
Bruton, Charles Clinton

OREGON

Medford
Thierolf, Richard Burton, Jr.

WASHINGTON

Bellingham
Raas, Daniel Alan

Tacoma
Hostnik, Charles Rivoire

ADDRESS UNPUBLISHED

McNeil Staudenmaier, Heidi Loretta

NATURAL RESOURCES

UNITED STATES

ARIZONA

Flagstaff
Lacey, Henry Bernard

COLORADO

Cherry Hills Village
Nazaryk, Paul Alan

Denver
Dolan, Brian Thomas
Shepherd, John Frederic

Greenwood Vlg
Ramsey, John Arthur

DISTRICT OF COLUMBIA

Washington
Manning, Michael J.
McCrum, Robert Timothy

LOUISIANA

Lafayette
Durio, William Henry

MICHIGAN

Traverse City
Quandt, Joseph Edward

MINNESOTA

Minneapolis
Blanton, W. C.

MISSOURI

Saint Louis
Sullivan, Edward Lawrence

NEW MEXICO

Albuquerque
Slade, Lynn Heyer

Santa Fe
Carpenter, Richard Norris

OHIO

Columbus
Maynard, Robert Howell

OREGON

Roseburg
Yockim, Ronald Stephen

TENNESSEE

Knoxville
Howard, Lewis Spilman

TEXAS

Houston
Gray, Archibald Duncan, Jr.

Midland
Martin, C. D.

UTAH

Salt Lake City
Barusch, Lawrence Roos
Jensen, Dallin W.
Kirkham, John Spencer

VIRGINIA

Richmond
Denny, Collins, III

WYOMING

Cody
Johnson, Wallace Harold

AUSTRALIA

Sydney
Machin, Peter William
Pistilli, Mark Stephen

NON-PROFIT AND TAX-EXEMPT ORGANIZATIONS

UNITED STATES

ARIZONA

Phoenix
Dunipace, Ian Douglas

CALIFORNIA

Los Angeles
Bringardner, John Michael

Rancho Mirage
Goldie, Ray Robert

San Francisco
Olejko, Mitchell J.
Yamakawa, David Kiyoshi, Jr.

Toluca Lake
Runquist, Lisa A.

Visalia
Atkins, Thomas Jay

COLORADO

Lakewood
Thome, Dennis Wesley

CONNECTICUT

Old Lyme
Wyckoff, E. Lisk, Jr.

DISTRICT OF COLUMBIA

Washington
Beckwith, Edward Jay
Frost, Edmund Bowen
McCoy, Jerry Jack
Medalie, Susan Diane
Nelson, Robert Louis
Oyler, Gregory Kenneth
Schmidt, William Arthur, Jr.
Swendiman, Alan Robert
Watkins, Charles Morgan

GEORGIA

Atlanta
Bird, Wendell Raleigh

ILLINOIS

Chicago
Howe, Jonathan Thomas
Paprocki, Thomas John

INDIANA

Indianapolis
Cole, Roland Jay

Terre Haute
Bopp, James, Jr.

KANSAS

Kansas City
Jurcyk, John Joseph, Jr.

Shawnee Mission
Snyder, Willard Breidenthal

KENTUCKY

Louisville
Buckaway, William Allen, Jr.

MAINE

Bernard
Marchetti, Karin Frances

MARYLAND

Crownsville
Irish, Leon Eugene

Glyndon
Renbaum, Barry Jeffrey

MASSACHUSETTS

Boston
Haddad, Ernest Mudarri

MICHIGAN

Detroit
Tarnacki, Duane L.

Grosse Pointe
Phillips, Elliott Hunter

MINNESOTA

Minneapolis
Greener, Ralph Bertram

Saint Paul
Norton-Larson, Mary Jean

MISSOURI

Kansas City
Langworthy, Robert Burton
Tyler, John Edward, III
Willy, Thomas Ralph

Saint Louis
Van Cleve, William Moore
Wolff, Frank Pierce, Jr.

NEW YORK

Buffalo
Heilman, Pamela Davis

New York
Davidson, George Allan
Finch, Edward Ridley, Jr.
Halprin, Henry Steiner
Josephson, William Howard
Kaufman, Robert Max
Kobrin, Lawrence Alan
Kornreich, Edward Scott
Malkin, Michael M.
Paul, Eve W.
Regan, Susan Ginsberg
Small, Jonathan Andrew
Solomon, Stephen L.

NORTH CAROLINA

Raleigh
Simpson, Steven Drexell

OHIO

Cleveland
Dampeer, John Lyell
Leavitt, Jeffrey Stuart

Toledo
Witherell, Dennis Patrick

Wilmington
Schutt, Walter Eugene

PENNSYLVANIA

Allentown
Frank, Bernard

Harrisburg
Murren, Philip Joseph

King Of Prussia
Gadsden, Christopher Henry

Norristown
Sosnov, Amy W(iener)

Philadelphia
Berger, Lawrence Howard

Pittsburgh
Johnson, Robert Alan

TEXAS

Fort Worth
West, Robert Grady

UTAH

Salt Lake City
Kennard, Raeburn Gleason

VIRGINIA

Charlottesville
Middleditch, Leigh Benjamin, Jr.

Mc Lean
Herge, J. Curtis
LeSourd, Nancy Susan Oliver
Olson, William Jeffrey

WISCONSIN

Milwaukee
Melin, Robert Arthur

ADDRESS UNPUBLISHED

Grange, George Robert, II
Vallianos, Carole Wagner

OIL, GAS, AND MINERAL

UNITED STATES

ALABAMA

Mobile
Armbrecht, William Henry, III
Harris, Benjamin Harte, Jr.

ALASKA

Anchorage
Linxwiler, James David

Juneau
Tangen, Jon Paul

ARIZONA

Prescott
Gose, Richard Vernie

ARKANSAS

El Dorado
Wynne, William Joseph

CALIFORNIA

Bakersfield
Tornstrom, Robert Ernest

San Francisco
Hinman, Harvey DeForest
Norris, Cynthia Ann

COLORADO

Aurora
Hampton, Clyde Robert

Denver
Hawley, Robert Cross
Irwin, R. Robert
Jones, Richard Michael
Shepherd, John Frederic

Englewood
Shannon, Malcolm Lloyd, Jr.

DISTRICT OF COLUMBIA

Washington
Allan, Richmond Frederick
Eastment, Thomas James
Ellis, Courtenay
Graham, John Stuart, III
Jordan, Robert Elijah, III
Manning, Michael J.

FLORIDA

Miami
Wright, Blandin James

ILLINOIS

Pinckneyville
Johnson, Don Edwin

KANSAS

Lawrence
Nordling, Bernard Erick

Pratt
Stull, Gordon Bruce

Ulysses
Hathaway, Gary Ray

Wichita
Depew, Spencer Long

KENTUCKY

Louisville
Pedley, Lawrence Lindsay

LOUISIANA

Baton Rouge
Johnson, Joseph Clayton, Jr.

Cheneyville
Ewin, Gordon Overton

Lafayette
Durio, William Henry
Foster, David Smith
Mansfield, James Norman, III

Lake Charles
Shaddock, William Edward, Jr.

New Orleans
Darden, Marshall Taylor
Miller, Joseph Bayard
Mote, Clyde A
Pearce, John Y.
Sommers, William John, Jr.

Shreveport
Arceneaux, M(artin) Thomas
Roberts, Robert, III

MICHIGAN

Gaylord
Topp, Susan Hlywa

Mount Pleasant
Lynch, John Joseph

MISSISSIPPI

Jackson
Grant, Russell Porter, Jr.
Hughes, Byron William

NEW MEXICO

Albuquerque
Addis, Richard Barton
Haltom, B(illy) Reid

Farmington
Tully, Richard T. C.

NEW YORK

Babylon
Hennelly, Edmund Paul

Buffalo
Jacobs, Charles P.

New York
Elicker, Gordon Leonard
Greeven, Rainer
Harley, Colin Emile
Owen, Robert Dewit
Stein, Stephen William

Olean
Heyer, John Henry, II

White Plains
Berlin, Alan Daniel

OHIO

Canfield
Hill, Thomas Allen

Columbus
Wightman, Alec

OKLAHOMA

Kingfisher
Baker, Thomas Edward

Oklahoma City
Barnes, Robert Norton
Christiansen, Mark D.
Cunningham, Stanley Lloyd
Decker, Michael Lynn
Legg, William Jefferson
Nesbitt, Charles Rudolph
Stanley, Brian Jordan
Towery, Curtis Kent
Willey, Benjamin Tucker, Jr.

Tulsa
Brune, Kenneth Leonard
Fell, Riley Brown
Kihle, Donald Arthur
Mackey, Steven R.
Pritchard, William Winther
Sneed, James Lynde
Spiegelberg, Frank David
Williamson, Walter Bland

PENNSYLVANIA

Pittsburgh
Boswell, William Paret

SOUTH CAROLINA

Newberry
Partridge, William Franklin, Jr.

TEXAS

Abilene
Hacker, Gary Lee

Austin
Dowd, Steven Milton
Godfrey, Cullen Michael
Leaverton, Mark Kane
Lochridge, Lloyd Pampell, Jr.
Patman, Philip Franklin

Boerne
Vaughan, Edward Gibson

Borger
Edmonds, Thomas Leon

Conroe
Irvin, Charles Leslie

Dallas
Armour, James Lott
Blachly, Jack Lee
Collins, Michael Homer
Keithley, Bradford Gene
Wilkins, Jerry L.

Fort Worth
Kelly, Dee J.

Hallettsville
Baber, Wilbur H., Jr.

Houston
Anders, Milton Howard
Anderson, Doris Ehlinger
Brown, William Alley
Carroll, James Vincent, III
Crowl, Rodney Keith
Dykes, Osborne Jefferson, III
England, Rudy Alan
Farnsworth, T Brooke
Frost, Charles Estes, Jr.
Kinnan, David Emery
Lawson, Ben F.
Martin, Jay Griffith
Morgan, Richard Greer
Plaeger, Frederick Joseph, II
Pope, David Bruce
Ryan, Thomas William
Shaddix, James W.
Wiese, Larry Clevenger

Lancaster
Sewell, Cameron Dee

Midland
Martin, C. D.

San Antonio
Labay, Eugene Benedict
Maloney, Pat, Sr.

Sterling City
Durham, Drew Taylor

VIRGINIA

Charlottesville
Dunn, William Wyly

WEST VIRGINIA

Charleston
Brown, James Knight

WYOMING

Casper
Lowe, Robert Stanley
Reese, Thomas Frank

MEXICO

Mexico City
de Uriarte, Horacio Maria

ARGENTINA

Buenos Aires
De Rosso, Pablo

AUSTRALIA

Adelaide
Davis, Glenn Stuart

Sydney
Machin, Peter William

ENGLAND

London
Baker, Charles George
Barratt, Jeffrey Vernon
Hammerson, Marc Charles
Kidwell, Mathew Charles

FRANCE

Paris
MacCrindle, Robert Alexander

THE NETHERLANDS

Rotterdam
van der Horst, Jan

PORTUGAL

Lisbon
Amendoeira, Rui

VENEZUELA

Las Mercenes
Pro-Risquez, Juan C.

ADDRESS UNPUBLISHED

Conine, Gary Bainard
Giusti, William Roger
Harshman, Raymond Brent
Hwang, Roland
Koplik, Marc Stephen
Lynch, Thomas Wimp
Quigley, Leonard Vincent
Shambaugh, Stephen Ward
Swift, Aubrey Earl
Tucker, William E.

PATENT

UNITED STATES

ALABAMA

Birmingham
Robin, Theodore Tydings, Jr.

ARIZONA

Phoenix
Flickinger, Don Jacob
Meschkow, Jordan M.
Phillips, James Harold
Sutton, Samuel J.

Sun City
Hauer, James Albert

CALIFORNIA

Berkeley
Woodhouse, Thomas Edwin

Cerritos
Sarno, Maria Erlinda

Claremont
Ansell, Edward Orin

Cupertino
Simon, Nancy Ruth

Emeryville
Blackburn, Robert Parker

Irvine
Stone, Samuel Beckner
Weissenberger, Harry George

Los Angeles
Bailey, Craig Bernard
Green, William Porter
Klein, Henry

Newport Beach
Knobbe, Louis Joseph
Martens, Don Walter

Palm Springs
Harris, Michael David

Palo Alto
Cunningham, Brian C.
Pasahow, Lynn H(arold)
Pooley, James
Radlo, Edward John

San Francisco
Chambers, Guy Wayne
Smegal, Thomas Frank, Jr.

San Jose
Anderson, Edward Virgil
Goldstein, Robin
Simon, James Lowell
Small, Jonathan Andrew

Santa Clara
Zahrt, William Dietrich, II

Seal Beach
Hennen, Thomas Waldo

Stevenson Ranch
Bovasso, Louis Joseph

Van Nuys
Mikesell, Richard Lyon

COLORADO

Colorado Springs
Kubida, William Joseph

Denver
Carson, William Scott
Dorr, Robert Charles

Fort Collins
Fromm, Jeffery Bernard

CONNECTICUT

Monroe
Oliver, Milton McKinnon

Westport
Dunham, Christopher Cooper
Razzano, Pasquale Angelo

DELAWARE

Wilmington
Huntley, Donald Wayne
Magee, Thomas Hugh

DISTRICT OF COLUMBIA

Washington
Cantor, Herbert I.
Goodman, Alfred Nelson
Hefter, Laurence Roy
Holman, John Clarke
Lavelle, Joseph P.
McCann, Clifton Everett
Potenza, Joseph Michael
Price, Donald Douglas
Repper, George Robert
Schwaab, Richard Lewis
Sokal, Allen Marcel
Spencer, George Henry

FLORIDA

Sarasota
Partoyan, Garo Arakel

GEORGIA

Atlanta
Lee, William Clement, III
Tewes, R. Scott

Norcross
Anderson, Albert Sydney, III

Valdosta
Sinnott, John Patrick

ILLINOIS

Barrington
Lee, William Marshall

Chicago
Altman, Louis
Amend, James Michael
Berenzweig, Jack Charles
Boehnen, Daniel A.
Flannery, John Francis
Geren, Gerald S.
Jacover, Jerold Alan
Kozak, John W.
Krupka, Robert George
Lloyd, Robert Allen
Maher, David Willard
Manzo, Edward David
Nicolaides, Mary
Rauner, Vincent Joseph
Roper, Harry Joseph
Ropski, Gary Melchior
Rupert, Donald William
Schlitter, Stanley Allen
Schneider, Robert Jerome
Schur, Gerald
Sheppard, Berton Scott
Smith, Herman Eugene
Sternstein, Allan J.
Vittum, Daniel Weeks, Jr.
Wanke, Ronald Lee

Deerfield
Birmingham, William Joseph
Scott, Theodore R.

Lansing
Hill, Philip

Libertyville
Fato, Gildo E.

INDIANA

Indianapolis
Emhardt, Charles David
Pendygraft, George William

Merrillville
Kinney, Richard Gordon

KENTUCKY

Louisville
Reed, John Squires, II

MARYLAND

Potomac
Troffkin, Howard Julian

MASSACHUSETTS

Boston
Cekala, Chester
Deutsch, Stephen B.
Hieken, Charles
Lambert, Gary Ervery
Neuner, George William

Braintree
Paglierani, Ronald Joseph

Framingham
Kriegsman, Edward Michael

Lexington
Glovsky, Susan G. L.

MICHIGAN

Bloomfield Hills
Rader, Ralph Terrance
Stewart, Michael B.

Dearborn
Dixon, Richard Dean

Detroit
Rohm, Benita Jill

Grand Rapids
Litton, Randall Gale
Smith, H(arold) Lawrence

Southfield
Taravella, Christopher Anthony

Troy
Cantor, Bernard Jack

MINNESOTA

Eden Prairie
Friederichs, Norman Paul

Minneapolis
DiPietro, Mark Joseph
Eisenberg, Jonathan Lee
Gill, Richard Lawrence
Kamrath, Alan Dale
Sawicki, Zbigniew Peter

Saint Louis Park
Seaburg, Jean

MISSOURI

Saint Louis
Evans, Lawrence E.
Gilster, Peter Stuart
Moore, McPherson Dorsett

MONTANA

Bozeman
Conover, Richard Corrill
Wylie, Paul Richter, Jr.

NEVADA

Reno
Ryan, Robert Collins

NEW HAMPSHIRE

Concord
Rines, Robert Harvey

NEW JERSEY

Bridgewater
Dahling, Gerald Vernon

Edgewater
Virelli, Louis James, Jr.

Edison
Fink, Edward Murray

Iselin
Dornbusch, Arthur A., II

Madison
Huettner, Richard Alfred

New Brunswick
Shirtz, Joseph Frank

Princeton
Plevy, Arthur L.

Red Bank
Michaelson, Peter Lee

NEW YORK

Brooklyn
Rubenstein, Allen Ira

Huntington
Robinson, Kenneth Patrick

Larchmont
Pelton, Russell Gilbert

New York
Baechtold, Robert Louis
Bosses, Stevan J.
Cohen, Myron
Creel, Thomas Leonard
Dunne, Gerard Francis
Einhorn, David Allen
Faber, Robert Charles
Fitzpatrick, Joseph Mark
Hamburg, Charles Bruce
Horwitz, Ethan
Jordan, Frank J.
Kalow, David Arthur
Katsh, Salem Michael
Lee, Jerome G.
Martone, Patricia Ann
Morris, Francis Edward
Neuner, Robert
Pegram, John Braxton
Pfeffer, David H.
Plottel, Roland
Reilly, John Albert
Rogers, Laurence Steven
Shentov, Ognjan V.
Smith, Robert Blakeman

Stathis, Nicholas John
Vassil, John Charles
Zivin, Norman H.

NORTH CAROLINA

Durham
Jenkins, Richard Erik

OHIO

Akron
Kreek, Louis Francis, Jr.

Cleveland
Burge, David Alan
Crehore, Charles Aaron
Fisher, Thomas Edward
Hoerner, Robert Jack

Columbus
Gall, John R.

Cuyahoga Falls
Jones, John Frank

Dayton
Nauman, Joseph George

OREGON

Gleneden Beach
Arant, Eugene Wesley

Portland
Noonan, William Donald

PENNSYLVANIA

Allentown
Simmons, James Charles

Bala Cynwyd
Chovanes, Eugene

Hershey
Simmons, Bryan John

Media
Elman, Gerry Jay
Lipton, Robert Stephen

Moon Township
Alstadt, Lynn Jeffery

Newtown
Simkanich, John Joseph

Philadelphia
Beam, Robert Charles
Dorfman, John Charles
Frank, George Andrew
Quinn, Charles Norman
Seidel, Arthur Harris

Pittsburgh
Baldauf, Kent Edward
Beck, Paul Augustine
Blenko, Walter John, Jr.
Colen, Frederick Haas
Raynovich, George, Jr.
Silverman, Arnold Barry

Southeastern
Husick, Lawrence Alan

Valley Forge
Posner, Ernest Gary

TEXAS

Bastrop
Van Gilder, Derek Robert

Dallas
McGowan, Patrick Francis
Mondul, Donald David
Moore, Stanley Ray

Houston
Caldwell, Rodney Kent
Dula, Arthur McKee, III
Fladung, Richard Denis
Hitchcock, Bion Earl
Kaplan, Lee Landa
Kirk, John Robert, Jr.
Pravel, Bernarr Roe
Tripp, Karen Bryant
Vaden, Frank Samuel, III

Humble
Gaffney, Richard Cook

Irving
Glober, George Edward, Jr.

Plano
Levine, Harold

Tyler
Alworth, Charles Wesley

UTAH

Brigham City
McCullough, Edward Eugene

Salt Lake City
Cornaby, Kay Sterling
Workman, H(arley) Ross

VERMONT

Essex Junction
Walsh, Robert Anthony

VIRGINIA

Alexandria
Georges, Peter John
Greigg, Ronald Edwin
Wieder, Bruce Terrill

Arlington
Litman, Richard Curtis
Mossinghoff, Gerald Joseph
Scafetta, Joseph, Jr.
Swift, Stephen Christopher

Fairfax
Dewhirst, John Ward

Falls Church
Brady, Rupert Joseph

Great Falls
Railton, William Scott

Mc Lean
Edgell, George Paul
Kondracki, Edward John
Shapiro, Nelson Hirsh

Mount Vernon
Spiegel, H. Jay

WISCONSIN

Kenosha
Richter, David Jerome

Madison
Bremer, Howard Walter
Long, Theodore James

CZECH REPUBLIC

Prague
Kroft, Michal

ENGLAND

Bucks
Assim, Gary Dean

London
Allcock, John Paul Major
Gilbert, Penny Xenia

GERMANY

Dusseldorf
Harmsen, Christian

Munich
Geissler, Bernhard Heilo

INDIA

Calcutta
Garodia, Aniruddh

ITALY

Rome
Fusco, Marta Angela

THE NETHERLANDS

The Hague
Van Nispen, Constant J.J.C.

POLAND

Cracow
Kasper, Horst Manfred

REPUBLIC OF KOREA

Seoul
Oh, Seung Jong

SAUDI ARABIA

Central Province
Elfaki, Mohamed Ahmed Mohamed

WALES

Cardiff
Lindsey, Michael

ADDRESS UNPUBLISHED

Adams, Thomas Lawrence
Beck, Stuart Edwin
Carten, Francis Noel
Corle, James Thomas

Fernandez, Dennis Sunga
Fiorito, Edward Gerald
Gray, Brian Mark
Herrell, Roger Wayne
Leydig, Carl Frederick
Peters, R. Jonathan
Sprung, Arnold

**PENSION,
PROFIT-SHARING, AND
EMPLOYEE BENEFITS**

UNITED STATES

ALABAMA

Birmingham
Shanks, William Ennis, Jr.

ARIZONA

Phoenix
Ehmann, Anthony Valentine

CALIFORNIA

Elverta
Betts, Barbara Lang

Irvine
Maldonado, Kirk Francis
Marshall, Ellen Ruth

Los Angeles
Ballsun, Kathryn Ann
Carrey, Neil
Cathcart, David Arthur
Chadwick, William Jordan
Gordon, David Eliot
Saxe, Deborah Crandall

Pacific Palisades
Dean, Ronald Glenn

San Francisco
Foster, David Scott
Gibson, Virginia Lee
Hasson, Kirke Michael
Homer, Barry Wayne
Hurabiell, John Philip, Sr.
Wolfe, Cameron Withgot, Jr.

San Jose
Kraw, George Martin

Sunnyvale
Ludgus, Nancy Lucke

Torrance
Smiley, Stanley Robert

COLORADO

Denver
Crow, Nancy Rebecca
Marquess, Lawrence Wade
Solano, Henry L.

Fort Morgan
Higinbotham, Jacquelyn Joan

Placerville
Reagan, Harry Edwin, III

CONNECTICUT

Stamford
Strone, Michael Jonathan

Trumbull
Czajkowski, Frank Henry

DELAWARE

Wilmington
Hatch, Denison Hurlbut, Jr.

DISTRICT OF COLUMBIA

Washington
Cummings, Frank
Damico, Nicholas Peter
Faley, R(ichard) Scott
Flowe, Carol Connor
Goldsmith, Willis Jay
Kautter, David John
Lopatin, Alan G.
Lorber, Lawrence Zel
Mackiewicz, Edward Robert
Morgan, Daniel Louis
Oliphant, Charles Frederick, III
Quintiere, Gary Gandolfo
Sacher, Steven Jay
Stauffer, Ronald Eugene
Watkins, Charles Morgan
Wilder, Roland Percival, Jr.

FLORIDA

Bradenton
Lopacki, Edward Joseph, Jr.

Coral Gables
Sugarman, Robert Alan

Fort Lauderdale
Caulkins, Charles S.

Miami Lakes
Cohen, Ronald J.

Oldsmar
Hirschman, Sherman Joseph

Orlando
Lefkowitz, Ivan Martin

Saint Petersburg
Escarraz, Enrique, III

Tampa
O'Neill, Albert Clarence, Jr.
Robinson, John William, IV
Watson, Roberta Casper

GEORGIA

Atlanta
Brecher, Armin George
Lamon, Harry Vincent, Jr.

Savannah
Gerard, Stephen Stanley

ILLINOIS

Chicago
Chandler, Kent, Jr.
Daley, Susan Jean
Dombrow, Anthony Eric
Dubbs, John William, III
Fellows, Jerry Kenneth
Freeman, Richard Lyons
Glick, Paul Mitchell
Greenfield, Michael C.
Janich, Daniel Nicholas
Kaplan, Jared
Krueger, Herbert William
Margolin, Stephen M.
McErlean, Charles Flavian, Jr.
Miller, Stephen Ralph
Pape, Glenn Michael
Peter, Bernard George
Polk, Lee Thomas
Rizzo, Ronald Stephen
Ruttenberg, Harold Seymour
Scogland, William Lee
Siske, Roger Charles
Thompson, David F.
Tinaglia, Michael Lee
Wolfe, David Louis

East Alton
Delaney, John Martin, Jr.

Oak Brook
Barnes, Karen Kay

Winnetka
Bishop, Mahlon Lee

INDIANA

Indianapolis
Boldt, Michael Herbert
Karwath, Bart Andrew
Kemper, James Dee
Roberts, Patricia Susan

Valparaiso
Conison, Jay

IOWA

Muscatine
Nepple, James Anthony

KANSAS

Topeka
Rainey, William Joel

KENTUCKY

Louisville
Gilman, Sheldon Glenn
Hallenberg, Robert Lewis

Salyersville
Arnett, William Grover

LOUISIANA

New Orleans
Angelico, Dennis Michael
Hearn, Sharon Sklamba
Malone, Ernest Roland, Jr.

MAINE

Brewer
Ebitz, Elizabeth Kelly

MARYLAND

Baltimore
Curran, Robert Bruce
Dubé, Lawrence Edward, Jr.
Isacoff, Richard Irwin

Cambridge
Jenkins, Robert Rowe

Chevy Chase
Schwartzman, Robin Berman

MASSACHUSETTS

Cambridge
Downey, Richard Ralph

Needham
Coleman, Richard William

Newburyport
Maslen, David Peter

Newton
Walker, Paul Howard

Worcester
Felper, David Michael

MICHIGAN

Ann Arbor
Keppelman, Nancy

Decatur
Kinney, Gregory Hoppes

Detroit
Brustad, Orin Daniel

Grand Rapids
Titley, Larry J.

Grosse Pointe
Phillips, Elliott Hunter

Jackson
Curtis, Philip James

Kalamazoo
Freeberg, Edward Ronald

Muskegon
McKendry, John H., Jr.

Southfield
McClow, Roger James

MINNESOTA

Duluth
Burns, Richard Ramsey

Minneapolis
Freeman, Todd Ira
Nelson, Richard Arthur

Woodbury
Norton, John William

MISSISSIPPI

Jackson
Black, D(eWitt) Carl(isle), Jr.

MISSOURI

Chesterfield
Stalnaker, Tim

Kansas City
Brous, Thomas Richard
Toll, Perry Mark

Saint Louis
Crowe, Robert Alan
Stewart, Allan Forbes

NEVADA

Las Vegas
Greene, Addison Kent

NEW JERSEY

Basking Ridge
O'Carroll, Anita Louise

Camden
Furey, John J.

Florham Park
Witman, Leonard Joel

Mc Afee
Fogel, Richard

Morristown
Capezza, Michelle

Newark
Reich, Laurence
Weinberg, Shelley Ann
White, Cheryl Denney

South Orange
Delo, Ellen Sanderson

NEW MEXICO

Albuquerque
Ramo, Roberta Cooper

Deming
Sherman, Frederick Hood

NEW YORK

Buffalo
Kotaska, Gary F.
Newman, Stephen Michael

Cutchogue
O'Connell, Francis Joseph

Flushing
Schwartz, Estar Alma

Garden City
Lilly, Thomas Joseph
Schwarz, Carl A., Jr.

Glens Falls
McMillen, Robert Stewart

Huntington
Hochberg, Ronald Mark

Long Island City
Wanderman, Susan Mae

Mineola
Pogrebin, Bertrand B.

New York
Budd, Thomas Witbeck
Calhoun, Monica Dodd
Carling, Francis
Curtis, Susan Grace
Dell, Michael John
Friedman, Eugene Stuart
Glanstein, Joel Charles
Kroll, Arthur Herbert
Macris, Michael
O'Dwyer, Brian
Pompa, Renata
Robinson, Marvin Stuart
Serota, Susan Perlstadt
Simon, Bruce Harvey
Simone, Joseph R.
Swain, Laura Taylor
Thompson, Loran Tyson
Wallach, Evan Jonathan
Watanabe, Roy Noboru

Purchase
Lalli, Michael Anthony

Rochester
Colby, William Michael
Wild, Robert Warren

Syracuse
King, Bernard T.

Tarrytown
Mach, Joseph David

White Plains
Klein, Paul E.
Taft, Nathaniel Belmont

NORTH CAROLINA

Charlotte
Harris, Charles Marcus

Winston Salem
Gunter, Michael Donwell

OHIO

Akron
Stark, Michael Lee
Wolfe, John Leslie

Cincinnati
Kammerer, Matthew Paul

Cleveland
Leavitt, Jeffrey Stuart
Ollinger, W. James

Columbus
Kusma, Kyllikki
Tarpy, Thomas Michael

Sharonville
Hanket, Mark John

Toledo
Allotta, Joseph John

OKLAHOMA

Bartlesville
Huchteman, Ralph Douglas

OREGON

Portland
Brownstein, Richard Joseph
Froebe, Gerald Allen
Grossmann, Ronald Stanyer
Zalutsky, Morton Herman

Tigard
Lowry, David Burton

PENNSYLVANIA

Allison Park
Ries, William Campbell

Philadelphia
Abramowitz, Robert Leslie
Bernard, John Marley
Bildersee, Robert Alan
Cannon, John, III
Donner, Henry Jay
Drake, William Frank, Jr.

Elliott, Homer Lee
Gadon, Steven Franklin
Gilberg, Kenneth Roy
Lichtenstein, Robert Jay
O'Reilly, Timothy Patrick
Sigmond, Richard Brian
Thomas, Lowell Shumway, Jr.
Whiteside, William Anthony, Jr.

Pittsburgh
Candris, Laura A.
Geeseman, Robert George
Johnson, Robert Alan
Kabala, Edward John
Scheinholtz, Leonard Louis

Reading
Linton, Jack Arthur

Scranton
Preate, Robert Anthony

SOUTH CAROLINA

Charleston
Bell, James L.

Greenville
Lynch, J. Timothy

TENNESSEE

Nashville
Gannon, John Sexton
Little, Hampton Stennis, Jr.

TEXAS

Dallas
Cowart, T(homas) David
Crowley, James Worthington
Fenner, Suzan Ellen
Gerberding Cowart, Greta Elaine
McLane, David Glenn
Pingree, Bruce Douglas

Fort Worth
Tracy, J. David
Willey, Stephen Douglas

Houston
Dworsky, Clara Weiner
Seymour, Barbara Laverne

Richardson
Conkel, Robert Dale

VIRGINIA

Charlottesville
Hodous, Robert Power

Lynchburg
Davidson, Frank Gassaway, III

Richmond
Anutta, Lucile Jamison
Dray, Mark S.
Levit, Jay J(oseph)
McElligott, James Patrick, Jr.
Musick, Robert Lawrence, Jr.

WASHINGTON

Longview
O'Neill, Thomas Nicholas Stephen

Seattle
Birmingham, Richard Joseph
Petrie, Gregory Steven

Spokane
Connolly, K. Thomas

WEST VIRGINIA

Beckley
Stacy, Don Matthew

Fairmont
Cohen, Richard Paul

WISCONSIN

Hudson
Lundeen, Bradley Curtis

Middleton
Berman, Ronald Charles

Milwaukee
Donahue, John Edward
Kurtz, Harvey A.
Levy, Alan M.

FRANCE

Lyon-Villeurbanne
Duflos, Jean-Jacques

SPAIN

Madrid
García-Perrote, Ignacio

ADDRESS UNPUBLISHED

Goldberger, Allen Sanford
Hammond, Glenn Barry, Sr.
Hardy, Robert Paul
Henry, DeLysle Leon
Keegan, John Robert
Klafter, Cary Ira
Koomey, Richard Alan
Portnoy, Sara S.
Pustilnik, David Daniel
Scharf, Robert Lee
Simonton, Robert Bennet
Sliger, Herbert Jacquemin, Jr.
Stinchfield, John Edward
Treacy, Vincent Edward
Wood, Robert Charles
Young, Sheldon Mike

PERSONAL INJURY *See also* **Insurance**

UNITED STATES

ALABAMA

Birmingham
Alford, Margie Searcy
Boardman, Mark Seymour
Christian, Thomas William
Dobbs, Carney H.
Donahue, Timothy Patrick
Ferguson, Harold Laverne, Jr.
Hardin, Edward Lester, Jr.
Martin, Cynthia Ann
Newton, Alexander Worthy
Norris, Robert Wheeler
Palmer, Robert Leslie
Scherf, John George, IV

Huntsville
Griffin, Malvern Ulysses

Jasper
Thomas, Steven Allen

Mobile
Armstrong, Gordon Gray, III
Pennington, Al

Montgomery
Ely, Robert Eugene

Opelika
Hand, Benny Charles, Jr.

Woodstock
Downs, Bernard Boozer, Jr.

ALASKA

Anchorage
Butler, Rex Lamont
Ross, Wayne Anthony
Walther, Dale Jay
Weinig, Richard Arthur

ARIZONA

Flagstaff
Stoops, Daniel J.

Mesa
Squire, Bruce M.

Phoenix
Begam, Robert George
Beshears, Robert Gene
Cure, Carol Campbell
Klahr, Gary Peter
Leshner, Stephen I.
O'Steen, Van
Plattner, Richard Serber
Riikola, Michael Edward
Rivera, Jose de Jesus
Sherk, Kenneth John
Toone, Thomas Lee
Winthrop, Lawrence Fredrick

Safford
Van Ry, Bradley Otto

Scottsdale
Smith, David Burnell

Tucson
D'Antonio, James Joseph
Grand, Richard D.
Hyams, Harold
Kaucher, James William
MacBan, Laura Vaden
Osborne, John Edwards
Samet, Dee-Dee

Yuma
Hossler, David Joseph

ARKANSAS

Crossett
Hubbell, Billy James

Fayetteville
Pearson, Charles Thomas, Jr.

Fort Smith
Karr, Charles

Harrison
Pinson, Jerry D.

Little Rock
Denton, Deborah S.

Eubanks, Gary Leroy, Sr.
Miller, Peter Alexander
Ryan, Donald Sanford

Mena
Thrailkill, Daniel B.

Searcy
Hughes, Thomas Morgan, III

CALIFORNIA

Aptos
Kehoe, Dennis Joseph

Belvedere Tiburon
Bremer, William Richard

Berkeley
De Goff, Victoria Joan

Beverly Hills
Horowitz, Stephen Paul

Chula Vista
Appleton, Richard Newell

Cupertino
Jelinch, Frank Anthony

El Centro
Sutherland, Lowell Francis

Encino
Kaufman, Albert I.
Terterian, George
Weissman, I. Donald

Escondido
Barraza, Horacio

Folsom
Goodwin, James Jeffries

Fresno
Ramirez, Frank Tenorio

Fullerton
Moerbeek, Stanley Leonard

Glendale
Kazanjian, Phillip Carl
Martinetti, Ronald Anthony

Indian Wells
Weinberg, Steven Jay

Irvine
Desai, Aashish Y.
Graves, Patrick Lee

Laguna Hills
Mathews, Stanton Terry

Long Beach
Roberts, James Donzil
Stolpman, Thomas Gerard

Los Angeles
Angel, Arthur Ronald
Aristei, J. Clark
Baum, Michael Lin
Bonesteel, Michael John
Chiate, Kenneth Reed
Franceschi, Ernest Joseph, Jr.
Garcia-Barron, Gerard Lionel
Greaves, John Allen
Hedlund, Paul James
Lange, Joseph Jude Morgan
Lauchengco, Jose Yujuico, Jr.
Lawton, Eric
Moloney, Stephen Michael
Muhlbach, Robert Arthur
Shacter, David Mervyn
Solo, Gail Dianne

Los Gatos
Boccardo, James Frederick

Marina Del Rey
Serena, C. David

Moraga
Kilbourne, George William

Napa
Kuntz, Charles Powers

Newport Beach
Wentworth, Theodore Sumner

Oakland
Berry, Phillip Samuel
Bjork, Robert David, Jr.
Heywood, Robert Gilmour
Mendelson, Steven Earle

Oxnard
O'Hearn, Michael John

Pacific Palisades
Dean, Ronald Glenn

Paramount
Hall, Howard Harry

Pasadena
Telleria, Anthony F.

Pleasanton
Harding, John Edward
Scott, G. Judson, Jr.

Redwood City
Kelly, Edward Joseph

Riverside
Darling, Scott Edward

Sacramento
Birney, Philip Ripley

Brookman, Anthony Raymond
Burton, Randall James
Callahan, Gary Brent
Hassan, Allen Clarence
Sevey, Jack Charles
Ubaldi, Michael Vincent

San Anselmo
Truett, Harold Joseph, III (Tim Truett)

San Clemente
Fisher, Myron R.

San Diego
Bleiler, Charles Arthur
Boyle, Michael Fabian
Brown, LaMar Bevan
Buzunis, Constantine Dino
Godone-Maresca, Lillian
Higgs, Craig DeWitt
McClellan, Craig Rene
Reed, T. Michael
Roseman, Charles Sanford
Shapiro, Philip Alan
Shelton, Dorothy Diehl Rees
Wolfe, Deborah Ann

San Francisco
Arbuthnot, Robert Murray
Bicksler, Diana Guido
Bostwick, James Stephen
Cohn, Nathan
Dryden, Robert Eugene
German, G. Michael
Kuhl, Paul Beach
Nelson, Paul Douglas
Rowland, John Arthur
Walker, Walter Herbert, III

San Jose
Bennion, David Jacobsen
Bohn, Robert Herbert
Gregg, Richard
Hernández, Fernando Vargas
Katzman, Irwin
Nielsen, Christian Bayard
Smith, Valerie A.
Stein, John C.
Towery, James E.

San Mateo
O'Reilly, Terence John

Santa Ana
Cifarelli, Thomas Abitabile
Patt, Herbert Jacob

Santa Barbara
Bauer, Marvin Agather
Dickey, Denise Ann
Moncharsh, Philip Isaac

Santa Cruz
Costello, Donald Fredric

Santa Monica
Carlson, Jeffery John
Morgan, Kermit Johnson
Ringler, Jerome Lawrence

Santa Rosa
Gack, Kenneth David

Torrance
Deason, Edward Joseph
Ward, Anthony John

Tustin
Madory, Richard Eugene
Posey, Janette Robison

Ventura
Gartner, Harold Henry, III

Visalia
Feavel, Patrick McGee

West Covina
Ebiner, Robert Maurice

Yuba City
Doughty, Mark Anthony
McCaslin, Leon

COLORADO

Arvada
Peck, Kenneth E.

Aspen
Shipp, Dan Shackelford

Boulder
Flowers, William Harold, Jr.
Gray, William R.
Purvis, John Anderson

Colorado Springs
Evans, Paul Vernon
Fisher, Robert Scott
Slivka, Michael Andrew
Swanson, Victoria Clare Heldman

Denver
Aisenberg, Bennett S.
Casebolt, James Stanton
Cooper, Paul Douglas
DeLaney, Herbert Wade, Jr.
Fowler, Daniel McKay
Hoffman, Daniel Steven
Kaplan, Marc J.
Kintzele, John Alfred
Miller, J(ohn) Kent
Safran, Hubert Mayer
Springer, Jeffrey Alan

Englewood
Epstein, Joseph Marc
Karr, David Dean
Nixon, Scott Sherman

Golden
Carney, Deborah Leah Turner

Grand Junction
Griff, Harry

Greeley
Conway, Rebecca Ann Koppes

Greenwood Vlg
Fierst, Bruce Philip

Sedalia
Ewing, Robert Craig

CONNECTICUT

Bridgeport
Sheldon, Robert Ryel
Williams, Ronald Doherty

Bristol
Hayes, Margaret Mary

Brookfield
Secola, Joseph Paul

Fairfield
Osis, Daiga Guntra

Glastonbury
Taalman, Juri E.

Hartford
Bartolini, James Daniel
Fain, Joel Maurice
Gale, John Quentin
Toro, Amalia Maria
Young, Roland Frederic, III

New Haven
Carty, Paul Vernon
Goetsch, Charles Carnahan
Todd, Erica Weyer

South Windham
Asselin, John Thomas

Stamford
Benedict, Peter Behrends

Stratford
O'Rourke, James Louis

Torrington
Leard, David Carl
Wall, Robert Anthony, Jr.

Waterbury
Marano, Richard Michael

West Hartford
Swerdloff, Mark Harris

Weston
Strauss, Ellen Louise Feldman

Westport
Cramer, Allan P.

Willimantic
Schiller, Howard Barry

Windham
Lombardo, Michael John

Windsor
Morelli, Carmen

DELAWARE

Wilmington
Carey, Robert George
Ciconte, Edward Thomas
Elzufon, John A.
Kelleher, Daniel Francis
Kimmel, Morton Richard
Wier, Richard Royal, Jr.

DISTRICT OF COLUMBIA

Washington
Gelb, Joseph Donald
Kourtesis, Nikolaos Panagiotis
Lenhart, James Thomas
Madole, Donald Wilson
Martin, Ralph Drury
Nace, Barry John
Norton, Randell Hunt
Olender, Jack Harvey
Povich, David
Statland, Edward Morris
Trimble, Stephen Asbury
Walker, Betty Stevens
Wheeler, Anne Marie
Wilson, Michael Moureau

FLORIDA

Altamonte Springs
Fisher, James Craig
Heindl, Phares Matthews
Hoogland, Robert Frederics

Boca Raton
Kitzes, William Fredric
Silver, Barry Morris
Willis, John Alexander

Boynton Beach
Dembicer, Edwin Herbert

Bradenton
Groseclose, Lynn Hunter

Bushnell
Hagin, T. Richard

Clearwater
Blakely, John T.
Free, E. LeBron

Coral Gables
Anthony, Andrew John
Buell, Rodd Russell
David, George A.
Glinn, Franklyn Barry
Hoffman, Carl H(enry)
Stack, Charles Rickman

Crestview
Duplechin, D. James

Daytona Beach
Neitzke, Eric Karl

Daytona Beach Shores
Schott, Clifford Joseph

Fort Lauderdale
Denman, James Burton
Haliczer, James Solomon
Heath, Thomas Clark
James, Gordon, III
Kreizinger, Loreen I.
Rose, Norman
Roselli, Richard Joseph
Spellacy, John Frederick
Strickland, Wilton L.
Wich, Donald Anthony, Jr.

Fort Myers
Pohl, Michael A.
Stanley, Bruce McLaren, Sr.
Terry, T(aylor) Rankin, Jr.

Gainesville
Kurrus, Thomas William

Gulfport
Allen, John Thomas, Jr.

Hollywood
Phillips, Gary Stephen

Jacksonville
Bullock, Bruce Stanley
Callender, John Francis
Coker, Howard C.
Gooding, David Michael
Kaunitz, Karen Rose Koppel
Link, Robert James
Milton, Joseph Payne
O'Neal, Michael Scott, Sr.
Rumrell, Richard Gary
White, Edward Alfred

Leesburg
Austin, Robert Eugene, Jr.

Maitland
Bailey, Michael Keith

Melbourne
Trachtman, Jerry H.

Miami
Baumberger, Charles Henry
Blackburn, Roger Lloyd
Blumberg, Edward Robert
Cohen, Jeffrey Michael
Diaz, Benito Humberto
Fox, Gary Devenow
Greenberg, Stewart Gary
Hickey, John (Jack) Heyward
Lipcon, Charles Roy
Marks, Steven Craig
Miller, Raymond Vincent, Jr.
Moore, Michael T.
Palahach, Michael
Peltz, Robert Dwight
Podhurst, Aaron Samuel
Schwartz, Bruce S.
Stansell, Leland Edwin, Jr.
Stieglitz, Albert Blackwell
Touby, Kathleen Anita

Naples
Cardillo, John Pollara
Crehan, Joseph Edward
McDonnell, Michael R. N.

Orlando
Abbott, Charles Warren
Blackwell, Bruce Beuford
Cunningham, James Owen
Hill, Brian Donovan
Kelaher, James Peirce
Metz, Larry Edward
Mooney, Thomas Robert
Morgan, Mary Ann
Sawicki, Stephen Craig

Palm Beach
Hastings, Lawrence Vaeth

Palm Beach Gardens
Blum, Irving Ronald
Scott, Alan Fulton, Jr.
Telepas, George Peter

Panama City
Kapp, John Paul

Pensacola
Levin, Fredric Gerson
Marsh, William Douglas
McKenzie, James Franklin
Soloway, Daniel Mark
Wiltshire, William Harrison Flick

Saint Petersburg
Mann, Sam Henry, Jr.
McKeown, H. Mary
Scott, Kathryn Fenderson

Satellite Beach
Burger, Robert Theodore

Stuart
Watson, Robert James

Tallahassee
Davis, William Howard
Fonvielle, Charles David
Roland, Raymond William

Tampa
Emerton, Robert Walter, III
Feegel, John Richard
Gordon, Jeffrey (Jack Gordon)
Hahn, William Edward
Lane, Robin
Medina, Omar F.
Oehler, Richard Dale
Somers, Clifford Louis
Steiner, Geoffrey Blake
Vessel, Robert Leslie

Tavernier
Lupino, James Samuel

West Palm Beach
Barnhart, Forrest Gregory
McAfee, William James
Roberts, George Preston, Jr. (Rusty Roberts)

GEORGIA

Athens
Tolley, Edward Donald

Atlanta
Beckham, Walter Hull, III
Blank, A(ndrew) Russell
Cooper, Lawrence Allen
Fiorentino, Carmine
Glaser, Arthur Henry
Head, William Carl
Longhi, Patrick George
Lore, Stephen Melvin
McAlpin, Kirk Martin
Pilcher, James Brownie
Powell, Douglas Richard
Rumsey, D(avid) Lake, Jr.
Smith, Walton Napier
Wellon, Robert G.
Womack, Mary Pauline
Wood, L. Lin, Jr.
Young, Michael Anthony

Augusta
Dickert, Neal Workman
Miller, Alfred Montague

Canton
Hasty, William Grady, Jr.

Columbus
Harp, John Anderson
McGlamry, Max Reginald
Patrick, James Duvall, Jr.

Decatur
Apolinsky, Stephen Douglas
O'Connell, John James, Jr.

Fayetteville
Fox, Patrick Joseph
Johnson, Donald Wayne

Macon
Brown, Stephen Phillip

Milledgeville
Bradley, Wayne Bernard

Newnan
Franklin, Bruce Walter

Roswell
England, John Melvin

Snellville
Giallanza, Charles Philip

Statesboro
Brogdon, W.M. "Rowe"
Franklin, James Burke

Tucker
Armstrong, Edwin Alan

Valdosta
Bright, Joseph Converse
Copeland, Roy Wilson

Watkinsville
Wright, Robert Joseph

HAWAII

Honolulu
Crumpton, Charles Whitmarsh
Duffy, James Earl, Jr.
Fried, L. Richard, Jr.
Fukumoto, Leslie Satsuki
Geshell, Richard Steven
Kawachika, James Akio
Kuniyuki, Ken Takaharu
Morse, Jack Craig
Potts, Dennis Walker
Shigetomi, Keith Shigeo
Sumida, Kevin P.H.
Turbin, Richard
Umebayashi, Clyde Satoru

Kailua Kona
Zola, Michael S.

Koloa
Blair, Samuel Ray

IDAHO

Boise
Luker, Lynn Michael

Mauk, William Lloyd
Park, William Anthony (Tony)

Caldwell
Kerrick, David Ellsworth

Idaho Falls
Whittier, Monte Ray

Twin Falls
Berry, L. Clyel

ILLINOIS

Alton
Talbert, Hugh Mathis

Aurora
Poulakidas, Michael John

Belleville
Boyle, Richard Edward
Cook, James Christopher
Gossage, Roza
Heiligenstein, Christian E.
Urban, Donald Wayne

Bloomington
Bragg, Michael Ellis
Kelly, Timothy William

Carbondale
Wesley, Howard Barry

Champaign
Rawles, Edward Hugh

Chicago
Beatty, William Glenn
Brown, Donald James, Jr.
Burdelik, Thomas L.
Burke, John Michael
Burns, Terrence Michael
Cheely, Daniel Joseph
Clifford, Robert A.
Cohen, Stephen Bruce
Connelly, Mary Jo
Doyle, John Robert
Episcope, Paul Bryan
Fina, Paul Joseph
Fox, Kathy Pinkstaff
Frazen, Mitchell Hale
Guilfoyle, Robert Thomas
Henry, Brian Thomas
Howser, Richard Glen
Johnson, Richard Fred
Knox, James Marshall
Kunkle, William Joseph, Jr.
Lidaka, Maris V.
Mack, John Melvin
McCabe, Charles Kevin
McGahey, John Patrick
Miller, Douglas Andrew
Napleton, Robert Joseph
Novak, Mark
Pavalon, Eugene Irving
Pimentel, Julio Gumeresindo
Pirok, Edward Warren
Power, Joseph Aloysius, Jr.
Rapoport, David E.
Rogers, William John
Schoenfield, Rick Merrill
Scudder, Theodore Townsend, III
Serritella, William David
Sherman, Ian Matthew
Skjold, Benjamin R.
Strom, Michael A.
Weaver, Timothy Allan

Collinsville
Tognarelli, Richard Lee

Danville
Blan, Kennith William, Jr.
Young, William Allen

Des Plaines
Jacobs, William Russell, II

Edwardsville
Carlson, Jon Gordon
Schum, Randolph Edgar

Elgin
Juergensmeyer, John Eli

Galesburg
McCrery, David Neil, III

Hazel Crest
Gurion, Henry Baruch

Hinsdale
Walker, Daniel, Jr.

Jacksonville
Kuster, Larry Donald

Joliet
Miller, Randal J.

La Salle
McClintock, Thomas Lee

Libertyville
DeSanto, James John
Rallo, Douglas

Lombard
O'Shea, Patrick Joseph

Mattoon
Horsley, Jack Everett

Mount Vernon
Harvey, Morris Lane

Oak Forest
Narko, Medard Martin

Peoria
O'Brien, Daniel Robert

Prusak, Maximilian Michael
Sinn, David Randall

Rockford
Sullivan, Peter Thomas, III

Springfield
Adami, Paul E.
Heckenkamp, Robert Glenn
Londrigan, James Thomas

Taylorville
Spears, Ronald Dean

Waukegan
Henrick, Michael Francis

Western Springs
Young, Robert Bruce

Wheaton
Dudgeon, Thomas Carl

INDIANA

Anderson
Scott, John Toner
Woodruff, Randall Lee

Bedford
Haury, John Carroll

Bloomington
Applegate, Karl Edwin
Grodner, Geoffrey Mitchell

Columbus
Harrison, Patrick Woods

Evansville
Berger, Charles Lee

Franklin
Loveall, George Michael

Gary
Lewis, Robert Lee

Hammond
Ruman, Saul I.

Indianapolis
Bennett, Maxine Taylor
Conour, William Frederick
Due, Danford Royce
Fels, James Alexander
Fisher, James R.
Hammel, John Wingate
Hays, Thomas Clyde
Hovde, F. Boyd
Hovde, Frederick Russell
Koch, Edna Mae
Lisher, John Leonard
Montross, W. Scott
Schreckengast, William Owen
Wellnitz, Craig Otto
Yosha, Louis Buddy

La Porte
Drayton, V. Michael

Lafayette
Layden, Charles Max

Merrillville
Miller, Richard Allen

Seymour
Pardieck, Roger Lee

Shelbyville
Lisher, James Richard

South Bend
Norton, Sally Pauline

IOWA

Cedar Rapids
O'Brien, David A.
Riley, Tom Joseph
Wilson, Robert Foster

Clinton
Frey, A. John, Jr.

Coralville
McAndrew, Paul Joseph, Jr.

Council Bluffs
Jennings, Dean Thomas

Davenport
Bush, Michael Kevin

Des Moines
Conlin, Roxanne Barton
Cortese, Joseph Samuel, II
Doyle, Richard Henry, IV
Foxhoven, Jerry Ray
Lawyer, Vivian Jury

Indianola
Ouderkirk, Mason James

Iowa City
Spies, Leon Fred
Trca, Randy Ernest

Keokuk
Hoffman, James Paul

Marshalltown
Brooks, Patrick William

Sioux City
Giles, William Jefferson, III

KANSAS

Kansas City
Holbrook, Reid Franklin
Jurcyk, John Joseph, Jr.

Overland Park
Barnett, James Monroe
Keplinger, Bruce (Donald Keplinger)
Smith, Daniel Lynn
Starrett, Frederick Kent

Pittsburg
Short, Timothy Allen

Prairie Village
Sharp, Rex Arthur

Salina
Neustrom, Patrik William

Shawnee Mission
Smith, Edwin Dudley

Topeka
Hejtmanek, Danton Charles
Ochs, Robert Duane
Schroer, Gene Eldon

Wichita
Badger, Ronald Kay
Franklin, Joni Jeanette
Grace, Brian Guiles
Hund, Edward Joseph
Ratner, Payne Harry, Jr.

KENTUCKY

Covington
Davidson, David Edgar

Lexington
Elliott, Robert Lloyd

Louisville
Ballantine, John Tilden
Dedman, Anne Goddard
Faller, Rhoda Dianne Grossberg
Orberson, William Baxter
Rose, Charles Alexander
Silverthorn, Robert Sterner, Jr.
Spalding, Catherine
Welsh, Sir Alfred John

Paducah
Nickell, Christopher Shea

Salyersville
Arnett, William Grover

Somerset
Prather, John Gideon, Jr.

LOUISIANA

Baton Rouge
Unglesby, Lewis O.
Wittenbrink, Jeffrey Scott

Bossier City
Jackson, Patrick Richmond

Covington
Paddison, David Robert

Lafayette
Judice, Marc Wayne
Roy, James Parkerson

Lake Charles
Townsley, Todd Alan

Metairie
Album, Jerald Lewis
Dinwiddie, Bruce Wayland
Recile, George B.

Minden
Johnson, James McDade

Monroe
Creed, Christian Carl

Morgan City
Ramsey, Robert Scott, Jr.

New Orleans
Allen, Frank Clinton, Jr.
David, Robert Jefferson
Desue, Christine L.
Herman, Fred L.
Hoffman, Donald Alfred
Manard, Robert Lynn, III
McGlone, Michael Anthony
Orrill, R. Ray, Jr.
Rawls, John D.
Riess, George Febiger
Thomas, Joseph Winand

Shreveport
Politz, Nyle Anthony
Rigby, Kenneth

Slidell
Shamis, Edward Anthony, Jr.

MAINE

Bangor
Woodcock, John Alden

Bath
Watson, Thomas Riley

Brewer
Ebitz, Elizabeth Kelly

Houlton
Sylvester, Torrey Alden

Portland
Rundlett, Ellsworth Turner, III
Whiting, Stephen Clyde

Sanford
Nadeau, Robert Maurice Auclair

MARYLAND

Annapolis
Dembrow, Dana Lee
Klein, Robert Dale

Baltimore
Archibald, James Kenway
DeVries, Donald Lawson, Jr.
Ebersole, Jodi Kay
Ellin, Marvin
Kuryk, David Neal
Loker, F(rank) Ford, Jr.
Pretl, Michael Albert
Sack, Sylvan Hanan
Schochor, Jonathan
Summers, Thomas Carey
Uehlinger, Gerard Paul
Zimmerly, James Gregory

Bethesda
Himelfarb, Stephen Roy
Schimel, Richard E.

Burtonsville
Covington, Marlow Stanley

Cambridge
Jenkins, Robert Rowe

Chevy Chase
Montedonico, Joseph

College Park
Rosen, Steven
Yoho, Billy Lee

Elkton
Scott, Doris Petersen

Greenbelt
Greenwald, Andrew Eric

Hagerstown
Berkson, Jacob Benjamin
Gilbert, Howard William, Jr.

Hyattsville
Matty, Robert Jay

Lanham Seabrook
McCarthy, Kevin John

Lutherville Timonium
White, William Nelson

Rockville
Karp, Ronald Alvin
Michael, Robert Roy
Van Grack, Steven

Upper Marlboro
Brennan, William Collins, Jr.
Vaughan, James Joseph Michael

MASSACHUSETTS

Bedford
Nason, Leonard Yoshimoto

Boston
Berry, Janis Marie
Brody, Richard Eric
Burns, Thomas David
Curley, Robert Ambrose, Jr.
Edwards, Richard Lansing
Ellis, Fredric Lee
Halström, Frederic Norman
Howard, Gregory Charles
Hrones, Stephen Baylis
Leibensperger, Edward Paul
Licata, Arthur Frank
McKittrick, Neil Vincent
Mone, Michael Edward
Murray, Philip Edmund, Jr.
Neumeier, Richard L.
O'Neill, Timothy P.
Richmond, Alice Elenor
Steward, Martin John
Zandrow, Leonard Florian

Braintree
Riccio, Frank Joseph

Cambridge
Crawford, Linda Sibery
Pontikes, Rebecca George

Canton
Masiello, Thomas Philip, Jr.

Chelmsford
Grossman, Debra A.
Lerer, Neal M.

Holyoke
Sarnacki, Michael Thomas

Lowell
Bowen, Steven Holmes

Malden
Finn, Marvin Ruven

Manchester
Wolfe, Robert Shenker

Natick
Marr, David E

Newton
Peterson, Osler Leopold

North Dighton
Wynn, Thomas Joseph

Pittsfield
Doyle, Anthony Peter

Salem
Shachok, Mary Ellen
Wasserman, Stephen Alan

Somerset
Sabra, Steven Peter

South Easton
Finn, Anne-Marie

Springfield
Bennett, Clarence J.
Burke, Michael Henry
Burstein, Merwyn Jerome
Fein, Sherman Edward

Wollaston
Sullivan, William Francis

Worcester
Balko, George Anthony, III
Bassett, Edward Caldwell, Jr.

MICHIGAN

Ann Arbor
O'Brien, Darlene Anne

Birmingham
Elsman, James Leonard, Jr.
Zacharski, Dennis Edward

Bloomfield Hills
Baumkel, Mark S.
Googasian, George Ara
Victor, Richard Steven
Weinstein, William Joseph

Detroit
Barr, Charles Joseph Gore
Brady, Edmund Matthew, Jr.
Foley, Thomas John
Glotta, Ronald Delon
Gunderson, Michael Arthur
Harris, Patricia Skalny
Labadie, Dwight Daniel
Spencer, William Thomas

East Lansing
Vincent, Adrian Roger

Grand Rapids
Blackwell, Thomas Francis
Neckers, Bruce Warren
Pylman, Norman Herbert, II
Spies, Frank Stadler

Greenville
Mullendore, James Myers

Harper Woods
Gilbert, Ronald Rhea

Lansing
Kritselis, William Nicholas
Sinas, George Thomas
Stackable, Frederick Lawrence

Mount Clemens
Farrell, John Brendan

Pontiac
Pierson, William George

Rapid City
Ring, Ronald Herman

Saginaw
Concannon, Andrew Donnelly
Martin, Walter
Zanot, Craig Allen

Saint Clair Shores
Caretti, Richard Louis
Sullivan, James A., III

Saint Joseph
Butzbaugh, Elden W., Jr.
Gleiss, Henry Weston

Southfield
Berg, Stephanie A.
Darling, Robert Howard
Fieger, Geoffrey Nels
Fraiberg, Matthew Aaron
Goodman, Barry Joel
Gordon, Louis
Leib, Jeffrey M.
McClow, Roger James
Miller, Sheldon Lee
Thurswell, Gerald Elliott
Turner, Donald Allen

Troy
Kruse, John Alphonse
Ponitz, John Allan

Walled Lake
Connelly, Thomas Joseph

West Bloomfield
Gelman, Sandor M.

MINNESOTA

Bemidji
Woodke, Robert Allen

Bloomington
Boedigheimer, Robert David

Duluth
Thibodeau, Thomas Raymond

Edina
Vukelich, John Edward

Hopkins
Zotaley, Byron Leo

Hugo
Flannery, James Patrick

Minneapolis
Bland, J(ohn) Richard
Degnan, John Michael
Gordon, Corey Lee
Hutchens, Michael D.
Johnson, Dennis Robert
Johnson, Paul Owen
Meshbesher, Ronald I.
Nemo, Anthony James
Peterson, William George
Roe, Roger Rolland, Jr.
Timmons, Peter John

Plymouth
MacMillan, Peter Alan

Rochester
Orwoll, Gregg S. K.

Saint Cloud
Seifert, Luke Michael

Saint Louis Park
Seaburg, Jean

Saint Paul
Kirsch, Steven Jay
O'Leary, Daniel Brian
Sheahan, Michael John

MISSISSIPPI

Batesville
Cook, William Leslie, Jr.

Biloxi
Dornan, Donald C., Jr.
O'Barr, Bobby Gene, Sr.

Gulfport
Allen, Harry Roger
Dukes, James Otis
Owen, Joe Sam

Hernando
Brown, William A.

Jackson
Diaz, Oliver E., Jr.
Howell, Joel Walter, III
Merkel, Charles Michael

Madison
Flechas, Eduardo A.

Meridian
Primeaux, Lawrence

Ocean Springs
Denham, Earl Lamar
Luckey, Alwyn Hall

Tupelo
Clayton, Claude F., Jr.

MISSOURI

Cape Girardeau
Lowes, Albert Charles

Clayton
Ritter, Robert Thornton

Columbia
Moore, Mitchell Jay
Schwabe, John Bennett, II

Independence
Neilsen, Christina J.
Terry, Jack Chatterson

Jackson
Waldron, Kenneth Lynn

Jefferson City
Riner, James William

Kansas City
Beckett, Theodore Cornwall
Borel, Steven James
Hubbell, Ernest
Koelling, Thomas Winsor
McManus, James William
Miller, George Spencer
Redfearn, Paul L., III
Sherman, Joseph Allen, Jr.
Smith, R(onald) Scott
Stoup, Arthur Harry
Vandever, William Dirk
Wirken, James Charles

Rolla
Turley, J. William

Saint Ann
Johnson, Harold Gene

Saint Charles
Green, Joseph Libory

Saint Louis
Baldwin, Brent Winfield
Blanke, Richard Brian
Brostron, Judith Curran
Burke, Thomas Michael
Collins, James Slade, II
Cox, Dallas Wendell, Jr.
Fournie, Raymond Richard

Grebel, Lawrence Bovard
Marks, Murry Aaron
Marquitz, Kevin John
Michener, John Athol
Phoenix, G. Keith
Ramirez, Anthony Benjamin
Ringkamp, Stephen H.
Ritter, Robert Forcier
Roskin, Preston Eugene
Siegel, Cordell
Sugg, Reed Waller
Walsh, Joseph Leo, III
Webb Anderson, JoAnn Marie
Williams, Theodore Joseph, Jr.

Springfield
FitzGerald, Kevin Michael
Woody, Donald Eugene

MONTANA

Billings
Jones, James Leonard
Malee, Thomas Michael

Havre
Goldstein, Mort

Helena
Grant, John Halloran
Morrison, John Martin

Missoula
Morales, Julio K.

NEBRASKA

Bellevue
Schroeder, Van Ace

Lincoln
Guthery, John M.

Omaha
Schrempp, Warren C.

NEVADA

Las Vegas
Galliher, Keith Edwin, Jr.
Kravitz, Martin Jay
Lovell, Carl Erwin, Jr.
Lukens, John Patrick
Padgett, Anne

Reno
Kent, Stephen Smiley
Pagni, Albert Frank
Robison, Kent Richard

NEW HAMPSHIRE

Keene
Gardner, Eric Raymond

Manchester
Dugan, Kevin F.
Hutchins, Peter Edward
Middleton, Jack Baer
Peltonen, John Ernest
Thornton, Edward Robert, Jr.

Nashua
Jette, Ernest Arthur

Portsmouth
Tober, Stephen Lloyd
Watson, Thomas Roger

Wolfeboro
Mertens, Edward Joseph, II
Walker, George William

NEW JERSEY

Asbury Park
Darnell, Alan Mark

Atlantic City
Paarz, Robert Emil

Berlin
Goldstein, Benjamin

Cherry Hill
D'Alfonso, Mario Joseph
DeVoto, Louis Joseph
Tomar, William

Clifton
Palma, Nicholas James

Cranford
Messing, Sara Virginia Drick

East Brunswick
Haws, Robert John

Edison
Lavigne, Lawrence Neil
O'Brien, John Graham

Englewood
Milstein, Edward Philip

Fanwood
Mitzner, Michael Jay

Flemington
Miller, Louis H.
Wolfson, William Steven

Hackensack
Kiel, Paul Edward
Masi, John Roger

Pollinger, William Joshua

Haddonfield
Andres, Kenneth G., Jr.
Graziano, Ronald Anthony

Jersey City
Amadeo, Natial Salvatore
Nevins, Arthur Gerard, Jr.

Kearny
Brady, Lawrence Peter

Laurel Springs
Wood, Leonard James

Lebanon
Johnstone, Irvine Blakeley, III

Livingston
Harris, Brian Craig
Rinsky, Joel Charles
Sukoneck, Ira David

Marlton
Pappas, Hercules

Metuchen
Vercammen, Kenneth Albert

Millburn
Kuttner, Bernard A.

Mount Holly
Mintz, Jeffry Alan

Mountainside
Weiseman, Jac Burton

Newark
Medvin, Alan York

Newton
Morgenstern, Robert Terence

North Haledon
Harrington, Kevin Paul

Northfield
Day, Christopher Mark

Oakhurst
Widman, Douglas Jack

Ocean
Weisberg, Adam Jon

Pilesgrove Township
Crouse, Farrell R.

Ridgewood
Seigel, Jan Kearney

River Edge
Huegel, Russell J.

Rochelle Park
Knopf, Barry Abraham

Roseland
Smith, Wendy Hope

Saddle Brook
Cohn, Albert Linn

Short Hills
Kaye, Marc Mendell

Shrewsbury
Hopkins, Charles Peter, II

Somerville
Lieberman, Marvin Samuel

Trenton
Doherty, Robert Christopher
Gogo, Gregory
Harbeck, Dorothy Anne

Warren
Kraus, Steven Gary

West Orange
Gordon, Harrison J.
McNaboe, James Francis

Woodcliff Lake
Phillips, John C.

NEW MEXICO

Albuquerque
Beach, Arthur O'Neal
Caruso, Mark John

Deming
Sherman, Frederick Hood

Farmington
Moeller, Floyd Douglas
Strother, Robin Dale
Titus, Victor Allen

Hobbs
Stout, Lowell

Roswell
Kraft, Richard Lee

Ruidoso
Dutton, Dominic Edward

Santa Fe
Brannen, Jeffrey Richard
Casey, Patrick Anthony
Culbert, Peter V.
Farber, Steven Glenn
McClaugherty, Joe L.
Murphy, Dennis Patrick
Zorie, Stephanie Marie

NEW YORK

Albany
Case, Forrest N., Jr.
Dulin, Thomas N.
Laird, Edward DeHart, Jr.
Napierski, Eugene Edward
Powers, John Kieran
Santola, Daniel Ralph

Bronx
Aris, Joram Jehudah

Brooklyn
Dorf, Robert Clay
Reich, Edward Stuart
Steinberg, Jerome Leonard

Buffalo
Barber, Janice Ann
Brock, David George
Brown, T. Alan
De Marie, Anthony Joseph
Feuerstein, Alan Ricky
Goldberg, Neil A.
Hayes, J. Michael
Jasen, Matthew Joseph
Parker, Michelle
Sampson, John David
Schoenborn, Daniel Leonard
Schreck, Robert J.

Carle Place
Mulhern, Edwin Joseph
Seiden, Steven Jay

Chestnut Ridge
Burns, Richard Owen

Dansville
Vogel, John Walter

Delhi
Hamilton, John Thomas, Jr.

East Northport
Juliano, John Louis

Farmingdale
Persons, John Wade

Flushing
Schwartz, Estar Alma

Garden City
Sawyer, James

Glens Falls
Cullum, James Edward
Firth, Peter Alan
Meyer, Martin Arthur

Hempstead
Kane, Donald Vincent

Hicksville
Giuffré, John Joseph

Hudson
Howard, Andrew Baker

Huntington
DeMartin, Charles Peter

Jackson Heights
Goldblum, A. Paul

Jericho
Corso, Frank Mitchell

Kew Gardens
Reichel, Aaron Israel
Sparrow, Robert E.

Melville
Schoenfeld, Michael P.

Mineola
Bernstein, Kenneth Alan
Raab, Ira Jerry
Rubine, Robert Samuel

New Hyde Park
Lee, Brian Edward

New York
Aiello, Robert John
Bern, Marc Jay
Birnbaum, Edward Lester
Bivona, John Vincent
Bluestone, Andrew Lavoott
Brady, Bruce Morgan
Brecker, Jeffrey Ross
Coffinas, Eleni
Cohen, Joshua Robert
Costello, Joseph Michael
Damashek, Philip Michael
Dankner, Jay Warren
Deffina, Thomas Victor
Edelman, Paul Sterling
Fisher, Bertram Dore
Fitzpatrick, Garrett Joseph
Garbarini, Chas. J.
Garfield, Martin Richard
Gioiella, Russell Michael
Glass, Joel
Golomb, David Bela
Grady, Maureen Frances
Green, Eric Howard
Gurfein, Richard Alan
Hirschhorn, Herbert Herman
Huston, Barry Scott
Issler, Harry
Jacobowitz, Harold Saul
Kalamaras, James
Lantier, Brendan John
Laquercia, Thomas Michael
LeBlang, Skip Alan
Lesman, Michael Steven
Lesser, William Melville
Loscalzo, Anthony Joseph
McGrath, Christopher Thomas
North, Steven Edward
Oliveri, Paul Francis

Peskin, Stephan Haskel
Pittoni, Luke M.
Relkin, Ellen
Ritter, Ann L.
Rosenzweig, Theodore B.
Russotti, Philip Anthony
Salvan, Sherwood Allen
Scher, Stanley Jules
Schnurman, Alan Joseph
Schwartz, Stephen Jay
Schwartz, Steven T.
Seitelman, Mark Elias
Shandell, Richard Elliot
Singer, Jeffrey
Smiley, Guy Ian
Steigman, Ernest R.
Warshauer, Irene C.
Weinstock, Leonard
Weiser, Martin Jay
Weitz, Harvey
Wilensky, Saul
Williamson, Walter

Newark
Reid, James Edward

Newburgh
Milligram, Steven Irwin

Ossining
Daly, William Joseph

Patchogue
Tona, Thomas

Pleasant Valley
Vasti, Thomas Francis, III

Poughkeepsie
Kranis, Michael David

Rochester
Dolin, Lonny H.
Geiger, Alexander
Kelly, Paul Donald
Law, Michael R.
Trevett, Thomas Neil

Salamanca
Brady, Thomas Carl

Saratoga Springs
Willig, William Paul

Schenectady
Taub, Eli Irwin

Smithtown
Brooks, Sondra
Spellman, Thomas Joseph, Jr.

South Richmond Hill
Scheich, John F.

Staten Island
Humphries, Edward Francis

Syracuse
Bogart, William Harry
Butler, John Edward
Hildebrandt, George Frederick
King, Bernard T.
Michaels, Beverly Ann
Rosenthal, Alan
Zimmerman, Aaron Mark

Troy
Finkel, Sanford Norman
Jones, E. Stewart, Jr.

West Babylon
Weinreb, Michael Leonard

Westbury
Whiteman, Robert Gordon

White Plains
Downes, James J.
Greenspan, Michael Evan
Guida, Toni M.
Levine, Steven Jon
Madden, M. Stuart
Nesci, Vincent Peter
Ryan, Robert Davis
Scialabba, Donald Joseph

NORTH CAROLINA

Chapel Hill
Zoffer, David B.

Charlotte
Brackett, Martin Luther, Jr.
Raper, William Cranford

Dunn
Pope, Patrick Harris

Durham
Fisher, Stewart Wayne
Lewis, David Olin
Markham, Charles Buchanan

Fayetteville
Townsend, William Jackson

Greensboro
Clark, David McKenzie
Koonce, Neil Wright

High Point
Baker, Walter Wray, Jr.

Jamestown
Schmitt, William Allen

Marion
Burgin, Charles Edward

New Bern
Kellum, Norman Bryant, Jr.

Oxford
Burnette, James Thomas

Pittsboro
Hubbard, Thomas Edwin (Tim Hubbard)

Raleigh
Hunter, Richard Samford, Jr.
Millberg, John C.
Palmer, William Ralph
Suhr, Paul Augustine

Smithfield
Schulz, Bradley Nicholas

Tarboro
Hopkins, Grover Prevatte

Winston Salem
Alexander, Charles Jackson, II
Early, James H., Jr.

NORTH DAKOTA

Bismarck
Gilbertson, Joel Warren
Snyder, Robert John

Dickinson
Greenwood, Dann E.
Herauf, William Anton

OHIO

Akron
Cherpas, Christopher Theodore
Cody, Daniel Schaffner
Glinsek, Gerald John
Schrader, Alfred Eugene

Aurora
Hermann, Philip J.

Beavercreek
Stadnicar, Joseph William

Canton
Plakas, Leonidas Evangelos

Chillicothe
Boulger, William Charles

Cincinnati
Chesley, Stanley Morris
Davis, Robert Lawrence
Gehrig, Michael Ford
Harris, Jerald David
Holschuh, John David, Jr.
Lutz, James Gurney
Neltner, Michael Martin
Nippert, Alfred Kuno, Jr.
Ralston, James Allen
Scacchetti, David J.
Whitaker, Glenn Virgil
Woodside, Frank C., III

Cleveland
Bacon, Brett Kermit
Birne, Kenneth Andrew
DiVenere, Anthony Joseph
Domiano, Joseph Charles
Duncan, Ed Eugene
Friedman, Hyman
Hoffman, Mark Leslie
Maher, Edward Joseph
Sanislo, Paul Steve
Spero, Keith Erwin
Szaller, James Francis
Trapp, Mary Jane
Turoff, Jack Newton
Vance, Victoria Lynne
Weinberger, Peter Henry
Weisman, Fred

Columbus
Allen, Richard Lee, Jr.
Belton, John Thomas
Binning, J. Boyd
Gerling, Joseph Anthony
Martin, Paige Arlene
Radnor, Alan T.
Ray, Frank Allen
Roubanes, Barbara Ann
Starkoff, Alan Gary
Taylor, AmySue
Tyack, Thomas Michael

Dayton
Krebs, Leo Francis

Dublin
Farrell, Clifford Michael
Lane, James Edward
Maloon, Jerry L.

Findlay
Kentris, George Lawrence

Hamilton
Olivas, Adolf

Independence
Rutter, Robert Paul

Jackson
Lewis, Richard M.

Lima
Jacobs, Ann Elizabeth

Sandusky
Bailey, K. Ronald

Springfield
Lagos, James Harry

Toledo
St. Clair, Donald David
Tuschman, James Marshall

White, Kenneth James

Wadsworth
McIlvaine, James Ross
Paul, Dennis Edward

Willard
Thornton, Robert Floyd

Wooster
Kennedy, Charles Allen

Xenia
Chappars, Timothy Stephen

Youngstown
Ausnehmer, John Edward
Blair, Richard Bryson
Carlin, Clair Myron
Giannini, Matthew Carlo

OKLAHOMA

Duncan
Rodgers, Ricardo Juan (Rick Rodgers)

Lawton
Ashton, Mark Alfred

Norman
Fairbanks, Robert Alvin
Sweeney, Everett John

Oklahoma City
Fenton, Elliott Clayton
Henry, David Patrick
Wallace, Thomas Andrew
Zuhdi, Nabil (Bill Zuhdi)

Tulsa
Atkinson, Michael Pearce

OREGON

Central Point
Richardson, Dennis Michael

Corvallis
Ringo, Robert Gribble

Eugene
Cooper, Michael Lee

Hillsboro
Uffelman, John Edward

Portland
Flaherty, Thomas Joseph
Hart, John Edward
Hill, Christopher T.
Kennedy, Jack Leland
Rieke, Forrest Neill
Savage, John William
Schuster, Philip Frederick , II
Sokol, Larry Nides

Salem
Feibleman, Gilbert Bruce

Tigard
Lowry, David Burton

PENNSYLVANIA

Aliquippa
Palmieri, John Anthony

Allentown
Altemose, Mark Kenneth
Scherline, Jay Alan

Altoona
Serbin, Richard Martin

Beaver
Petrush, John Joseph

Conway
Krebs, Robert Alan

Doylestown
Mellon, Thomas Edward, Jr.

Drexel Hill
West, Kenneth Edward

Easton
Brown, Robert Carroll

Harrisburg
Angino, Richard Carmen
Hafer, Joseph Page
Stefanon, Anthony

Hazleton
Pedri, Charles Raymond
Schiavo, Pasco Louis

Hummelstown
Mark, Timothy Ivan

Indiana
Kauffman, Thomas Andrew

Jenkintown
Worthington, Sandra Boulton

Kingston
Meyer, Martin Jay
Shaffer, Charles Alan

Lancaster
Zimmerman, D(onald) Patrick

Leola
Eaby, Christian Earl

Malvern
Griffith, Edward, II

Mc Keesport
Kessler, Steven Fisher

Media
D'Amico, Andrew J.
Tomlinson, Herbert Weston

New Castle
Mojock, David Theodore

Newtown
Kardos, Mel D.

Norristown
Gowen, Thomas Leo, Jr.

Paoli
Chiacchiere, Mark Dominic

Philadelphia
Abraham, Richard Paul
Beasley, James Edwin
Binder, David Franklin
Blumstein, Edward
Buccino, Ernest John, Jr.
Coleman, Robert J.
Collings, Robert L.
Connor, Joseph Patrick, III
Goldberg, Joseph
Goldberg, Marvin Allen
Hanselmann, Fredrick Charles
Heslin, Gary Phillip
Kanter, Seymour
Kormes, John Winston
Lipson, Heather Joy
McHugh, James Joseph
Messa, Joseph Louis, Jr.
Miller, Leslie Anne
Mulvey, W. Michael
Parry, William DeWitt
Prewitt, David Edward
Reiff, Jeffrey Marc
Rhoads, Nancy Glenn
Samuel, Ralph David
Seidel, Richard Stephen
Voluck, Jeffrey M.

Pittsburgh
Bellisario, Domenic Anthony
Bochicchio, Vito Salvatore
Breault, Theodore Edward
Caroselli, William R.
Cohen, Robert (Avram)
Esposito, Cheryl Lynne
Feldstein, Jay Harris
Hurnyak, Christina Kaiser
Lucchino, Frank Joseph
Meyers, Jerry Ivan
Miller, James Robert
Murdoch, Robert Whitten
Perry, Jon Robert
Schmidt, Edward Craig
Specter, Howard Alan
Tarasi, Louis Michael, Jr.
Terra, Sharon Ecker

Pottsville
Tamulonis, Frank Louis, Jr.

State College
Nollau, Lee Gordon

Sunbury
Saylor, Charles Horace

Trevose
McEvilly, James Patrick, Jr.

Uniontown
Davis, James Thomas

Warrendale
Micale, Frank Jude

Washington
Richman, Stephen I.

White Oak
Pribanic, Victor Hunter

Wilkes Barre
Lach, Joseph Andrew

RHODE ISLAND

Cranston
Cervone, Anthony Louis

Pawtucket
Vacca, Anthony

Providence
Glavin, Kevin Charles
Jones, Lauren Evans
Tammelleo, A. David

Warwick
Penza, Joseph Fulvio, Jr.

West Warwick
Bottella, Tammy Ann
Pollock, Bruce Gerald

SOUTH CAROLINA

Charleston
Bell, James L.
Hood, Robert Holmes
Kahn, Ellis Irvin
Patrick, Charles William, Jr.
Spitz, Hugo Max

Columbia
Blanton, Hoover Clarence
Harpootlian, Richard Ara
Harvey, Jonathan Matthew
Oswald, Billy Robertson

Greenville
Talley, Michael Frank

Hilton Head Island
McKay, John Judson, Jr.

Langley
Bell, Robert Morrall

Mount Pleasant
Laddaga, Beth Jane

Myrtle Beach
Breen, David Hart

North Charleston
Joye, Mark Christopher
Wigger, Jarrel L.

Pawleys Island
Daniel, J. Reese

SOUTH DAKOTA

Belle Fourche
Day, Michael W.

TENNESSEE

Brentwood
Day, John Arthur

Chattanooga
Adams, Morgan Goodpasture
Gearhiser, Charles Josef
James, Stuart Fawcett

Knoxville
Cremins, William Carroll
Johnson, Steven Boyd
Lloyd, Francis Leon, Jr.
London, James Harry
Oberman, Steven
Ownby, Jere Franklin, III
Routh, John William
Swanson, Charles Walter
Vines, William Dorsey
White, Edward Gibson, II

Memphis
Buchignani, Leo Joseph
Friedman, Robert Michael
Harvey, Albert C.
Ledbetter, Paul Mark
Rice, George Lawrence, III (Larry Rice)
Taylor, Jerry F(rancis)

Nashville
Bramlett, Paul Kent
Cantrell, Luther E., Jr.
Clayton, Daniel Louis
Cooney, Charles Hayes
Jameson, Michael Francis
Lane, William Arthur
Youngblood, Elaine Michele

Newport
Bell, John Alton
Campbell, Roy Timothy, Jr.

Parsons
Townsend, Edwin Clay

Soddy Daisy
Leitner, Paul Revere

Somerville
Wilder, James Sampson, III

Springfield
Wilks, Larry Dean

Trenton
Harrell, Limmie Lee, Jr.

TEXAS

Addison
Lynch, Jeffrey Scott

Arlington
Jensen, John Robert

Austin
McConnico, Stephen E.
Pena, Richard
Probus, Michael Maurice, Jr.
Spivey, Broadus Autry
Sulak, Timothy Martin

Beaumont
Scofield, Louis M., Jr.
Waterston, Tass Dever

Bellaire
Soffar, William Douglas

Burleson
Johnstone, Deborah Blackmon

College Station
Hoelscher, Michael Ray

Conroe
Abney, Joe L.

Corpus Christi
Barrera, Eric Isaac
Carnahan, Robert Narvell
Fancher, Rick
Leon, Rolando Luis
Miller, Carroll Gerard, Jr. (Gerry Miller)

Dallas
Burns, Sandra
DelHomme, Beverly Ann
Ellis, Alfred Wright (Al Ellis)
Girards, James Edward

Hawkins, Scott Alexis
Holmes, James Hill, III
Howie, John Robert
Johnston, Coyt Randal
Mighell, Kenneth John
Penick, Michael Preston
Siegel, Mark Jordan
Stinnett, Mark Allan
Terry, David William
Welch, Shannon Lois Kathleen

Edinburg
Peña, Aaron, Jr.

El Paso
Darnell, James Oral
Marshall, Richard Treeger

Fort Worth
Cottongame, W. Brice
Dent, Edward Dwain
Griffith, Richard Lattimore
Hayes, Larry B.
Streck, Frederick Louis, III
Wagner, James Peyton

Gainesville
Sullivant, Wesley Benton

Galveston
Neves, Kerry Lane

Houston
Berg, David Howard
Boswell, John Howard
Brinson, Gay Creswell, Jr.
Essmyer, Michael Martin
Holloway, Gordon Arthur
Kline, Allen Haber, Jr.
Krebs, Arno William, Jr.
Love, Scott Anthony
McCarter, Louis Eugene
McFall, Donald Beury
Nacol, Mae
Nations, Howard Lynn
Nunnally, Knox Dillon
O'Brien, Eva Fromm
Pate, Stephen Patrick
Pettiette, Alison Yvonne
Pitts, Gary Benjamin
Roach, Robert Michael, Jr.
Scholl, Stephen Gerrard
Sorrels, Randall Owen
Spain, H. Daniel
Stephens, R(obert) Gary

Huffman
Frazier, William Sumpter

Longview
Jones, Christopher Don

Mc Kinney
Dowdy, William Clarence, Jr.

Mcallen
Carrera, Victor Manuel
Thaddeus, Aloysius Peter, Jr.

Midland
Fletcher, Richard Royce

Odessa
Hendrick, Benard Calvin, VII

Plano
Robinson, Timothy Stephen

Rowlett
Lyon, Robert Charles

San Antonio
Bailey, Maryann George
Branton, James LaVoy
Cabezas-Gil, Rosa M.
Henry, Peter York
Hohman, A. J., Jr.
Kaplan, Edward David
Maloney, Marynell
Maloney, Pat, Sr.
Myers, J(oseph) Michael
Patrick, Dane Herman
Putman, Michael (James Putman)
Solis, Carlos Eduardo
Welmaker, Forrest Nolan

Sugar Land
Aldrich, Lovell W(eld)

Tyler
Ellis, Donald Lee

Wichita Falls
Wesbrooks, Perry

UTAH

Logan
Jenkins, James C.

Ogden
Kaufman, Steven Michael
Sullivan, Kevin Patrick

Provo
Abbott, Charles Favour

Salt Lake City
Barlow, Peter Hugh
Larson, Bryan A.

Sandy
Bush, Rex Curtis

VERMONT

Bellows Falls
Massucco, Lawrence Raymond

Brattleboro
McCarty, William Michael, Jr.

Burlington
Lisman, Bernard

Montpelier
Valerio, Matthew F.

Rutland
Cleary, David Laurence
Faignant, John Paul
O'Rourke, William Andrew, III

VIRGINIA

Alexandria
Drennan, Joseph Peter
Hirschkop, Philip Jay

Arlington
Malone, William Grady

Ashburn
Gold, George Myron

Charlottesville
Chandler, Lawrence Bradford, Jr.
Wyatt, Deborah Chasen

Chester
Gray, Charles Robert

Danville
Conway, French Hoge

Fairfax
Brown, Gary Wayne
Keith, John A.C.
Saul, Ira Stephen

Falls Church
Halagao, Avelino Garabiles
Hartshorn, Roland DeWitt
Redmond, Robert
Robey, Daniel Lance
Van Oeveren, Edward Lanier

Grundy
McGlothlin, Michael Gordon

Hampton
Smith, Stephen Mark

Lynchburg
Angel, James Joseph
Light, William Randall

Manassas
Scriven, Wayne Marcus

Martinsville
Frith, Douglas Kyle

Mc Lean
Friedlander, Jerome Peyser, II
Santoni, Cynthia Lee

Newport News
Segall, James Arnold

Norfolk
Drescher, John Webb

Norton
Jessee, Roy Mark
Shortridge, Judy Beth

Petersburg
Shell, Louis Calvin

Portsmouth
Bangel, Herbert K.
Blachman, Michael Joel
Moody, Willard James, Sr.

Radford
Davis, Richard Waters
Turk, James Clinton, Jr.

Reston
Bredehoft, Elaine Charlson

Richmond
Allen, Wilbur Coleman
DeCamps, Charles Michael
Esposito, Mark Mario
Landin, David Craig
Robinson, Thomas Hart
Shields, William Gilbert
Spahn, Gary Joseph
Williamson, Thomas W., Jr.

Roanoke
McGarry, Richard Lawrence
Mundy, Gardner Marshall

Virginia Beach
Buzard, David Andrew
Hajek, Francis Paul

Woodbridge
Roberts, Charles Bren

WASHINGTON

Bainbridge Island
Otorowski, Christopher Lee

Bellevue
Landau, Felix
Zackey, Jonathan Thomas

Centralia
Buzzard, Steven Ray

Gig Harbor
Thompson, Ronald Edward

Hoquiam
Kessler, Keith Leon

Kennewick
Hames, William Lester

Longview
Barlow, John Aden

Mount Vernon
Moser, C. Thomas

Olympia
Chambers, Thomas Jefferson
Hoglund, John Andrew

Renton
Barber, Mark Edward
Swanson, Arthur Dean

Richland
Barr, Carlos Harvey

Seattle
Burns, Robert William
Cornell, Kenneth Lee
Corning, Nicholas F.
Crump, David L.
Cunningham, Joel Dean
Davis, Susan Rae
Harris, Thomas V.
Levy, Barbara Jo
Loftus, Thomas Daniel
Lundgren, Gail M.
McCoid, Nancy Katherine
Moren, Charles Verner
Peterson, Jan Eric
Scott, Brian David
Sullivan, Daniel Frederick
Wayne, Robert Jonathan
Whitehead, James Fred, III
Whitson, Lish

Spokane
Eymann, Richard Charles
Harbaugh, Daniel Paul
Leipham, Jay Edward
Pontarolo, Michael Joseph
Schuchart, Frederick Mark

Tacoma
Hostnik, Charles Rivoire
Kram, Peter

WEST VIRGINIA

Beckley
Stacy, Don Matthew

Bluefield
Evans, Wayne Lewis
Kantor, Isaac Norris

Charleston
Berthold, Robert Vernon, Jr.
McKowen, Laurie Garrigan
Zak, Robert Joseph

Fairmont
Stanton, George Patrick, Jr.

Morgantown
Ringer, Darrell Wayne (Dan)

WISCONSIN

Appleton
Chudacoff, Bruce Michael
Lonergan, Kevin
Murray, John Daniel
Siddall, Michael Sheridan

Black River Falls
Lister, Thomas Edward

Delafield
Hausman, C. Michael

Fond Du Lac
English, Dale Lowell

Green Bay
Grzeca, Michael G(erard)

Madison
Pernitz, Scott Gregory
Steingass, Susan R.
Whitney, Robert Michael

Milwaukee
Daily, Frank J(erome)
Habush, Robert Lee
Marquis, William Oscar
Pettit, Roger Lee
Slavik, Donald Harlan
Terschan, Frank Robert
Trecek, Timothy Scott
Van Grunsven, Paul Robert

Oshkosh
Curtis, George Warren
Kelly, John Martin
Wilde, William Richard

Portage
Bennett, David Hinkley

Racine
Gasiorkiewicz, Eugene Anthony
Rudebusch, Alice Ann
Stutt, John Barry

Rhinelander
McEldowney, Todd Richard
Saari, John William, Jr.

Wausau
Grischke, Alan Edward
Kammer, Robert Arthur, Jr.
Molinaro, Thomas J.

WYOMING

Casper
Combs, W(illiam) Henry, III
Day, Stuart Reid

Cheyenne
Bailey, Henry Franklin, Jr.

Jackson
Shockey, Gary Lee
Spence, Gerald Leonard

Rock Springs
Rolich, Frank Alvin

Wheatland
Hunkins, Raymond Breedlove

AUSTRIA

Vienna
Frank, Alix

PERU

Lima
Girbau, Miguel Angel

SOUTH AFRICA

Johannesburg
Prinsloo, Jojannes Christiaan

ADDRESS UNPUBLISHED

Ascher, Richard Alan
Atkins, Robert Alan
Bandy, Jack D.
Beattie, Donald Gilbert
Bell, John William
Berman, Richard Bruce
Billauer, Barbara Pfeffer
Boone, Richard Winston, Sr.
Bossio, Salvatore
D'Agusto, Karen Rose
Embry, Stephen Creston
Ettinger, Joseph Alan
Feazell, Vic
Fekete, George Otto
Fleischman, Herman Israel
Flynn, Michael
Griffith, Steven Franklin, Sr.
Hall-Barron, Deborah
Hoffman, Alan Craig
Hoffman, S. David
Horn, Andrew Warren
Howell, Ally Windsor
Kjos, Victoria
Klein, Linda Ann
Landman, Eric Christopher
Lippes, Richard James
Massey, Kathleen Marie Oates
McAlhany, Toni Anne
McGuffey, Carroll Wade, Jr.
Mugridge, David Raymond
Parker, Robert Marc
Perrin, Michael Warren
Rawls, Frank Macklin
Reminger, Richard Thomas
Rochlin, Paul R.
Rosseel-Jones, Mary Louise
Schmoll, Harry F., Jr.
Smith, Patricia A.
Stanisci, Thomas William
Subin, Florence
Tanenbaum, Jay Harvey
Vigil, David Charles
Wagner, Arthur Ward, Jr.
Weill, (Lige) Harry, Sr.
Wessel, Peter
White, John Joseph, III
Wilson, Virgil James, III
Wynstra, Nancy Ann

PROBATE *See also* Estate planning; Taxation, estate

UNITED STATES

ALABAMA

Bay Minette
Granade, Fred King

Birmingham
Foster, Arthur Key, Jr.

Huntsville
Griffin, Malvern Ulysses

Jasper
Thomas, Steven Allen

Mobile
Holland, Lyman Faith, Jr.

ALASKA

Kodiak
Jamin, Matthew Daniel

ARIZONA

Hereford
Lynch, Robert Berger

Kingman
Basinger, Richard Lee

Mesa
Gunderson, Brent Merrill

Phoenix
Lowry, Edward Francis, Jr.
Smith, Susan Kimsey
Swartz, Melvin Jay

Prescott
Perry, John Richard, Jr.

Scottsdale
Case, Stephen Shevlin
Roberts, Jean Reed

Yuma
Hunt, Gerald Wallace

ARKANSAS

Blytheville
Fendler, Oscar

Little Rock
Haught, William Dixon
Stockburger, Jean Dawson

Morrilton
Denniston, Jeannie L.

Pine Bluff
Ramsay, Louis Lafayette, Jr.

Searcy
Hughes, Thomas Morgan, III

Warren
Claycomb, Hugh Murray

CALIFORNIA

Anaheim
Ross, Roger Scott

Antioch
Richards, Gerald Thomas

Arcadia
Gelber, Louise C(arp)

Belvedere Tiburon
Obninsky, Victor Peter

Berkeley
Ogg, Wilson Reid

Beverly Hills
Horowitz, Stephen Paul
Rosky, Burton Seymour

Downey
Bear, Henry Louis

Elverta
Betts, Barbara Lang

Fresno
Sherr, Morris Max

Fullerton
Roberts, Mark Scott

Granada Hills
Weitkamp, Fredrick John

Grass Valley
Hawkins, Richard Michael

Hayward
Smith, John Kerwin

La Canada Flintridge
Wallace, James Wendell

La Jolla
Shannahan, William Paul
ZoBell, Karl

Long Beach
Tikosh, Mark Axente

Los Angeles
Ballsun, Kathryn Ann
Gallo, Jon Joseph
Nordlinger, Stephanie G.
Rae, Matthew Sanderson, Jr.

Martinez
Bray, Absalom Francis, Jr.

Monterey
Gaver, Frances Rouse

Morgan Hill
Foster, John Robert

Morro Bay
Merzon, James Bert

Newport Beach
Allen, Russell G.
Mallory, Frank Linus

North Hollywood
Kreger, Melvin Joseph
Zimring, Stuart David

Palm Desert
Reinhardt, Benjamin Max

Palo Alto
Miller, Michael Patiky

Palos Verdes Estates
Toftness, Cecil Gillman

Pasadena
Ashley-Farrand, Margalo
Katzman, Harvey Lawrence
Taylor, John David

Pomona
Partritz, Joan Elizabeth

Sacramento
Burton, Randall James
Goodart, Nan L.

San Clemente
Fisher, Myron R.

San Diego
Hofflund, Paul
Payne, Margaret Anne

San Francisco
Byrne, Robert William
Guggenhime, Richard Johnson
Hurabiell, John Philip, Sr.
Manning, Jerome Alan
Thomas, William Scott
Wild, Nelson Hopkins

San Jose
Morgan, Robert Hall

San Marino
Tomich, Lillian

Santa Ana
Patt, Herbert Jacob

Santa Barbara
McCollum, Susan Hill

Santa Monica
Levin, Marvin Eugene

Selma
Janian, Paulette

Torrance
Moore, Christopher Minor
Smiley, Stanley Robert
Ward, Anthony John

Tustin
Posey, Janette Robison

Ukiah
Sager, Madeline Dean

West Covina
Ebiner, Robert Maurice

COLORADO

Colorado Springs
Donley, Jerry Alan
Kendall, Phillip Alan
Lohman, Richard Verne
Purvis, Randall W. B.
Rouss, Ruth

Delta
Schottelkotte, Michael Roger

Denver
Atlass, Theodore Bruce
Goddard, Jo Anna
McMichael, Donald Earl
Olsen, M. Kent
Safran, Hubert Mayer
Schmidt, L(ail) William, Jr.

Lakewood
Scott, Peter Bryan
Thome, Dennis Wesley

Longmont
Flanders, Laurence Burdette, Jr.

Pueblo
Altman, Leo Sidney

Rocky Ford
Mendenhall, Harry Barton

CONNECTICUT

Bethel
Medvecky, Thomas Edward

Bridgeport
Goldberger, Robert R.

Canaan
Capecelatro, Mark John

Clinton
Hershatter, Richard Lawrence

Enfield
Berger, Robert Bertram

Greenwich
Pascarella, Henry William
Selby, Leland Clay

Hartford
Berall, Frank Stewart
Bonee, John Leon, III
Gale, John Quentin
Toro, Amalia Maria

Lakeville
Rout, Robert Howard

Middlefield
Lang, Edward Gerald

Mystic
Valentine, Garrison Norton

Ridgefield
Bracken, Nanette Beattie

Southport
Williams, Michael Peter Anthony

Stamford
Sarner, Richard Alan

Waterbury
Dost, Mark W.

Westport
Kosakow, James Matthew
Saxl, Richard Hildreth

Windsor
Morelli, Carmen

DELAWARE

Dover
Twilley, Joshua Marion

Wilmington
Herdeg, John Andrew
Jolles, Janet K. Pilling

DISTRICT OF COLUMBIA

Washington
Beckwith, Edward Jay
Bellinger, Edgar Thomson
Blazek-White, Doris
Close, David Palmer
Comstock, Robert Francis
Damico, Nicholas Peter
Freedman, Jay Weil
Freedman, Walter
Plaine, Lloyd Leva
Rhyne, Sidney White
Swendiman, Alan Robert

FLORIDA

Bradenton
Lopacki, Edward Joseph, Jr.

Brandon
Tittsworth, Clayton (Magness)

Clearwater
Blakely, John T.
Free, E. LeBron
Hogan, Elwood

Coral Gables
Gustafson, Anne-Lise Dirks

Deerfield Beach
Lenoff, Michele Malka

Fort Lauderdale
Gardner, Russell Menese
Hess, George Franklin, II
Hoines, David Alan
Katz, Thomas Owen
Levitt, Preston Curtis
Moss, Stephen B.

Fort Myers Beach
Shenko, William Edward, Jr.

Jacksonville
Lee, Lewis Swift

Jasper
McCormick, John Hoyle

Jupiter
Click, David Forrest

Lakeland
Koren, Edward Franz

Lutz
Hayes, Timothy George

Marathon Shores
Michie, Daniel Boorse, Jr.

Miami
Amber, Laurie Kaufman
Greenleaf, Walter Franklin
Lancaster, Kenneth G.
Milstein, Richard Craig
Skolnick, S. Harold
Weiner, Lawrence

Naples
Bruce, Jackson Martin, Jr.
Budd, David Glenn
Westman, Carl Edward

North Miami Beach
Slewett, Robert David

Orlando
Worthington, Daniel Glen

Palatka
Baldwin, Allen Adail

Palm Beach Gardens
Kahn, David Miller

Palm Harbor
Summers-Powell, Alan

Pompano Beach
Shulmister, M(orris) Ross

Port Charlotte
Levin, Allen Jay

Saint Petersburg
Lang, Joseph Hagedorn
Mann, Sam Henry, Jr.

Sarasota
Conetta, Tami Foley
Foreman, Michael Loren

Sebring
McCollum, James Fountain

Tallahassee
Boyd, Joseph Arthur, Jr.
Dariotis, Terrence Theodore

Tampa
Ellwanger, Thomas John
Gardner, J. Stephen
Jones, John Arthur
Oehler, Richard Dale
Stalnaker, Lance Kuebler

Vero Beach
O'Haire, Michael

West Palm Beach
Farina, John
Henry, Thornton Montagu

GEORGIA

Albany
Moorhead, William David, III

Atlanta
Bird, Francis Marion, Jr.
Bloodworth, A(lbert) W(illiam) Franklin
Levy, Bertram Louis
Salo, Ann Sexton Distler

Augusta
Lee, Lansing Burrows, Jr.

Brunswick
McLemore, Gilbert Carmichael, Jr.

Columbus
Johnson, Walter Frank, Jr.

Douglas
Sims, Rebecca Littleton

Newnan
McBroom, Thomas William, Sr.

Roswell
Baker, Anita Diane

Savannah
Friedman, Julian Richard
Gannam, Michael Joseph

Swainsboro
Cadle, Jerry Neal

HAWAII

Honolulu
Coates, Bradley Allen
Dang, Marvin S. C.
Gerson, Mervyn Stuart
Hite, Robert Griffith
Taylor, Carroll Stribling

IDAHO

Boise
Erickson, Robert Stanley
Schild, Raymond Douglas

Idaho Falls
St. Clair, John Gilbert

ILLINOIS

Alton
Coppinger, John Bampfield
Struif, L. James

Anna
Plesko, Jeffrey Michael

Aurora
Lowe, Ralph Edward

Batavia
Drendel, Kevin Gilbert

Chicago
Abell, David Robert
Acker, Frederick George
Baetz, W. Timothy
Berning, Larry D.
Brown, Alan Crawford
Carr, Walter Stanley
Cross, Chester Joseph
English, John Dwight
Freeman, Richard Lyons
Friedman, Roselyn L.
Gelman, Andrew Richard
Gutstein, Solomon
Harrington, Carol A.
Herpe, David A.
Kaplan, Howard Gordon
Kirkpatrick, John Everett
Kohlstedt, James August
Kresse, William Joseph
Lidaka, Maris V.
Lutter, Paul Allen
Marshall, John David
Martin, Siva
Nicolaides, Mary
Nitikman, Franklin W.
Ryken, Robert Leslie
Schar, Stephen L.
Spain, Richard Colby
Stanhaus, James Steven
Trio, Edward Alan
Trost, Eileen Bannon

Collinsville
Tognarelli, Richard Lee

Crete
Teykl, James Stephen

Crystal Lake
Thoms, Jeannine Aumond

Danville
Hubbard, Fred Leonhardt
Young, William Allen

Du Quoin
Atkins, Aaron Ardene

Freeport
Eden, Robert Elwood

Genoa
Cromley, Jon Lowell

Lake Bluff
Kennedy, John Foran

Morris
Rooks, John Newton

Murphysboro
McCann, Maurice Joseph

Nashville
Cross, Robert Leonard

Northbrook
Pollak, Jay Mitchell

Oak Brook
O'Brien, Walter Joseph, II

Palatine
Wardell, John Watson

Palos Heights
Matug, Alexander Peter

Paris
Fruin, Roger Joseph

Park Ridge
Hegarty, Mary Frances

Peoria
Coletta, Ralph John

Pinckneyville
Johnson, Don Edwin

Springfield
Reed, Robert Phillip
Stuart, Robert Allan, Jr.

Streator
Harrison, Frank J.

Taylorville
Austin, Daniel William

Watseka
Tungate, James Lester

Waukegan
Bairstow, Richard Raymond

Wheaton
Stein, Lawrence A.

INDIANA

Anderson
Scott, John Toner

Columbus
Crump, Francis Jefferson, III

Evansville
Baugh, Jerry Phelps

Fort Wayne
Fink, Thomas Michael
Gehring, Ronald Kent

Fowler
Weist, William Bernard

Huntington
Gordon, William Stout

Indianapolis
Bennett, Maxine Taylor
Dutton, Clarence Benjamin
Ewbank, Thomas Peters
Johnson, George Weldon
Koeller, Robert Marion
Padgett, Gregory Lee
Patrick, William Bradshaw

Merrillville
Brenman, Stephen Morris

Monticello
Guy, John Martin

Muncie
Smith, Gregory Butler

IOWA

Cedar Rapids
Wilson, Robert Foster

Clarinda
Millhone, James Newton

Council Bluffs
Jennings, Dean Thomas

Des Moines
Hill, Luther Lyons, Jr.
Zumbach, Steven Elmer

Garner
Hovda, Theodore James

Indianola
Ouderkirk, Mason James

Iowa City
Downer, Robert Nelson

Mason City
Heiny, James Ray
Winston, Harold Ronald

Mount Pleasant
Vance, Michael Charles

Muscatine
Coulter, Charles Roy

KANSAS

Concordia
Brewer, Dana

Hutchinson
Swearer, William Brooks

Lawrence
Brown, David James
Nordling, Bernard Erick
Smith, Glee Sidney, Jr.

Olathe
Haskin, J. Michael

Onaga
Stallard, Wayne Minor

Overland Park
Woods, Richard Dale

Topeka
Hejtmanek, Danton Charles
Horttor, Donald J.

Ulysses
Hathaway, Gary Ray

Wichita
Badger, Ronald Kay
Coombs, Eugene G.

KENTUCKY

Bowling Green
Parker, William Jerry

Lexington
Bagby, William Rardin

Louisville
Buckaway, William Allen, Jr.
Chauvin, Leonard Stanley, Jr.
Duffy, Martin Patrick
Fuchs, Olivia Anne Morris
Gilman, Sheldon Glenn
Hallenberg, Robert Lewis
Pettyjohn, Shirley Ellis

Somerset
Prather, John Gideon
Prather, John Gideon, Jr.

LOUISIANA

Baton Rouge
Stracener, Carol Elizabeth

Cheneyville
Ewin, Gordon Overton

Covington
Shinn, Clinton Wesley

Lafayette
Durio, William Henry
Mansfield, James Norman, III

Lake Charles
Shaddock, William Edward, Jr.

New Orleans
Berkett, Marian Mayer
Coleman, James Julian
Lemann, Thomas Berthelot
Page, John Marshall, Jr.
Rinker, Andrew, Jr.
Wedig, Regina Scotto

Shreveport
Rigby, Kenneth

Slidell
Singletary, Alvin D.

Winnfield
Simmons, Kermit Mixon

MAINE

Portland
Hunt, David Evans
LeBlanc, Richard Philip

Westbrook
Gagan, James Ephriam

MARYLAND

Annapolis
Michaelson, Benjamin, Jr.

Shannonhouse, Royal Graham, III

Baltimore
Lewis, Alexander Ingersoll, III

Bowie
Bagaria, Gail Farrell

Elkton
Scott, Doris Petersen

Oxon Hill
Fields, Richard Lawrence

Rockville
Katz, Steven Martin
Neuman, Eric Patt

Towson
Miller, Herbert H.

MASSACHUSETTS

Arlington
Keshian, Richard

Boston
Coolidge, Francis Lowell
Fortier, Albert Mark, Jr.
Fremont-Smith, Marion R.
Goldman, Richard Harris
Huang, Vivian Wenhuey Chen
Kidder, George Howell
Page, George Alfred, Jr.
Perera, Lawrence Thacher
Pratt, Harold Irving
Preston, Jerome, Jr.
Stiles, Kevin Patrick
Woodburn, Ralph Robert, Jr.

Gardner
Sans, Henri Louis, Jr.

Lexington
Dulchinos, Peter

Marion
Worley, Robert William, Jr.

Newton
Monahan, Marie Terry

Pittsfield
Doyle, Anthony Peter

Plymouth
Barreira, Brian Ernest

Salem
Shachok, Mary Ellen

South Hamilton
Campbell, Diana Butt

Watertown
Kaloosdian, Robert Aram
Karaian, Norma Maksoodian

Wellesley
Riley, Michael Hylan

West Chatham
Rowley, Glenn Harry

Westfield
Pollard, Frank Edward

Weston
Freeman, Florence Eleanor

Worcester
Whipple, Robert Jenks

Yarmouth Port
Brown, Robert G.
Paquin, Thomas Christopher

MICHIGAN

Ann Arbor
Dew, Thomas Edward
Ellmann, William Marshall

Birmingham
Sweeney, Thomas Frederick

Bloomfield Hills
Kirk, John MacGregor

Detroit
Labadie, Dwight Daniel
Miller, George DeWitt, Jr.
Rasmussen, Douglas John
Ward, George Edward

Fenton
Hildner, Phillips Brooks, II

Flint
Henneke, Edward George

Fremont
Price, Russell Eugene

Grand Rapids
Davis, Henry Barnard, Jr.

Hamtramck
Kaczmarek, Carla

Harbor Springs
Smith, Wayne Richard

Howell
Parker, Robert Ernser

Ishpeming
Steward, James Brian

Jackson
Curtis, Philip James

Kalamazoo
Gordon, Edgar George

Lansing
Gallagher, Byron Patrick, Jr.
Stackable, Frederick Lawrence

Saginaw
Martin, Walter

Saint Clair Shores
Shehan, Wayne Charles

Southfield
Eklund-Easley, Molly Sue
Leib, Jeffrey M.
May, Alan Alfred

Troy
McGlynn, Joseph Michael

MINNESOTA

Benson
Wilcox, Donald Alan

Fergus Falls
Lundeen, David F.

Hopkins
Zotaley, Byron Leo

Kenyon
Peterson, Franklin Delano

Marine On Saint Croix
Hoke, George Peabody

Minneapolis
Brand, Steve Aaron
Nordaune, Roselyn Jean
Rachie, Cyrus
Saeks, Allen Irving
Ventres, Judith Martin

Saint Paul
Chester, Stephanie Ann
LeVander, Bernhard Wilhelm
Noonan, James C.
Seymour, McNeil Vernam
Sheahan, Michael John

MISSISSIPPI

Jackson
Chadwick, Vernon Henry
Travis, Jay A., III

MISSOURI

Chesterfield
Fagerberg, Roger Richard

Columbia
Parrigin, Elizabeth Ellington

Independence
Minton, Kent W.

Kansas City
Blackwood, George Dean, Jr.
Clarke, Milton Charles
Gorman, Gerald Warner
Langworthy, Robert Burton
Setzler, Edward Allan
Tanner, Eric Benson

Marshall
Peterson, William Allen

Rolla
Thomas, William Herman, Jr.

Saint Louis
Cullen, James D.
Erbs, Thomas J.
Gunn, Michael Peter
Klobasa, John Anthony
Mulligan, Michael Dennis
Paule, Donald Wayne
Sherby, Kathleen Reilly

MONTANA

Billings
Thompson, James William

Havre
Goldstein, Mort

Missoula
George, Alexander Andrew
Morales, Julio K.

NEBRASKA

Lincoln
Rembolt, James Earl
Smith, Richard Wendell

NEVADA

Las Vegas
Chesnut, Carol Fitting
Greene, Addison Kent
Gubler, John Gray

Reno
Hibbs, Loyal Robert

NEW HAMPSHIRE

Manchester
Wells, Robert Alfred

Portsmouth
DeGrandpre, Charles Allyson

Wolfeboro
Walker, George William

NEW JERSEY

Atlantic Highlands
Marshall, Anthony Parr

Cherry Hill
Liebman, Emmanuel

Englewood
Gelber, Linda Cecile

Glen Ridge
Connolly, Joseph Thomas

Hackensack
Strull, James Richard

Hackettstown
Mulligan, Elinor Patterson

Highland Park
Alman, Emily Arnow

Morristown
Aspero, Benedict Vincent
Sweeney, John Lawrence

Newark
Day, Edward Francis, Jr.

Newton
Morgenstern, Robert Terence

Princeton
Beidler, Marsha Wolf
Sutphin, William Taylor

Ramsey
Weber, Walter Winfield, Jr.

River Edge
Spiegel, Edna Z.

Salem
Petrin, Helen Fite

South Plainfield
Santoro, Frank Anthony

Summit
Cooper, John Weeks
Pfaltz, Hugo Menzel, Jr.

Vauxhall
Ross, Mark Samuel

Verona
Hock, Frederick Wyeth

West Orange
Laves, Benjamin Samuel

Willingboro
Guest, Brian Milton

NEW MEXICO

Albuquerque
Bova, Vincent Arthur, Jr.
Buchanan, Deena Lynna
Messersmith, Lanny Dee
Ramo, Roberta Cooper
Tomita, Susan K.

Carlsbad
Byers, Matthew T(odd)

Roswell
Bassett, John Walden, Jr.

Santa Fe
Hickey, John Miller
Wertheim, Jerry

NEW YORK

Albany
Piedmont, Richard Stuart
Regal, Evan Charles
Sills, Nancy Mintz
Yanas, John Joseph

Amherst
Jones, E. Thomas

Andover
Hutter, Robert Grant

Ardsley
Glauberman, Melvin L.

Ballston Spa
Brown, Ifigenia Theodore

Bedford
Atkins, Ronald Raymond

Binghamton
Beck, Stephanie G.
Peckham, Eugene Eliot

Bronx
Aris, Joram Jehudah

Buffalo
Newman, Stephen Michael

Pearson, Paul David

Cape Vincent
Stiefel, Linda Shields

Commack
Braun, Robert Alan

Dobbs Ferry
Juettner, Diana D'Amico

Flushing
Chang, Lee-Lee

Garden City
Dent, Thomas Augustine
Jones, Lawrence Tunnicliffe
Sawyer, James

Getzville
DiNardo, Joseph

Glen Cove
Lewis, Felice Flanery

Glens Falls
Meyer, Martin Arthur

Hicksville
Giuffré, John Joseph

Huntington
Munson, Nancy Kay

Islandia
Pruzansky, Joshua Murdock

Ithaca
Theisen, Henry William

Jericho
Beal, Carol Ann

Kew Gardens
Adler, David Neil

Mineola
Bartol, Ernest Thomas
Smolev, Terence Elliot

New York
Barasch, Mal Livingston
Bell, Jonathan Robert
Black, James Isaac, III
Bryant, George McEwan
Christensen, Henry, III
Crary, Miner Dunham, Jr.
Danilek, Donald J.
Davidoff, Richard Sayles
Duetsch, John Edwin
DuLaux, Russell Frederick
Engel, Ralph Manuel
Etra, Blanche Goldman
Evans, Douglas Hayward
Friedman, Elaine Florence
Gelb, Judith Anne
Herbst, Abbe Ilene
Hirshowitz, Melvin Stephen
Jasper, Seymour
Josephson, William Howard
Kahn, Alan Edwin
Karan, Paul Richard
Kavoukjian, Michael Edward
Klipstein, Robert Alan
Knight, Townsend Jones
Kroll, Arthur Herbert
Lawrence, Robert Cutting, III
Lerner, Max Kasner
Lesk, Ann Berger
Levitan, David M(aurice)
Lingelbach, Albert Lane
Lloyd, James Woodman
Mariani, Michael Matthew
Martin, Malcolm Elliot
Materna, Joseph Anthony
McCaffrey, Carlyn Sundberg
McGrath, Thomas J.
Miller, William Harlowe, Jr.
Molnar, Lawrence
Norden, William Benjamin
O'Neil, John Joseph
Osborn, Donald Robert
Oxman, David Craig
Rado, Peter Thomas
Robinson, Barbara Paul
Rogers, Theodore Otto, Jr.
Saufer, Isaac Aaron
Schizer, Zevie Baruch
Schlesinger, Sanford Joel
Serota, Irving
Shea, James William
Silberman, John Alan
Steyer, Hume Richmond
Tricarico, Joseph Archangelo
Valente, Peter Charles
Van Nuys, Peter
Washburn, David Thacher
Zerin, Steven David
Ziegler, Henry Steinway

Niagara Falls
Brett, Jay Elliot
Levine, David Ethan

Nyack
Seidler, B(ernard) Alan

Ossining
Daly, William Joseph

Oswego
Greene, Stephen Craig

Oyster Bay
Robinson, Edward T., III

Pelham
Hanrahan, Michael G.

Port Chester
Gioffre Baird, Lisa Ann

Poughkeepsie
Dietz, Robert Barron

Purchase
Gioffre, Bruno Joseph

Rochester
Buckley, Michael Francis
Clifford, Eugene Thomas
Frank, Bernard Alan
Harris, Wayne Manley
Harter, Ralph Millard Peter
Whitaker, Benjamin Palmer, Jr.

Rockville Centre
Bennett, James Davison

Schenectady
Parisi, Frank Nicholas
Wickerham, Richard Dennis

Southampton
Platt, Harold Kirby

Stamford
Becker, Carl Frederick

Staten Island
Ferranti, Thomas, Jr.
Fusco, John Anthony

Syracuse
Butler, John Edward
Cirando, John Anthony
Grizanti, Anthony J.
O'Connor, Michael E.
Traylor, Robert Arthur
Wladis, Mark Neil

White Plains
Kurzman, Robert Graham

NORTH CAROLINA

Asheville
Branch, John Wells (Jack Twig)
Frue, William Calhoun
Lavelle, Brian Francis David

Boone
Brown, Wade Edward

Chapel Hill
Herman-Giddens, Gregory

Charlotte
Orsbon, Richard Anthony
Wood, William McBrayer

Jamestown
Schmitt, William Allen

Monroe
Love, Walter Bennett, Jr.

Murphy
Bata, Rudolph Andrew, Jr.

Raleigh
Joyner, Walton Kitchin
Taylor, Raymond Mason

Winston Salem
Vaughn, Robert Candler, Jr.

NORTH DAKOTA

Grand Forks
Widdel, John Earl, Jr.

Mandan
Bair, Bruce B.

OHIO

Akron
Holloway, Donald Phillip
Stark, Michael Lee

Athens
Lavelle, William Ambrose
Yanity, Joseph Blair, Jr.

Bucyrus
Neff, Robert Clark, Sr.

Canton
Barnhart, Gene

Celina
Myers, Daniel

Chillicothe
Boulger, William Charles

Cincinnati
Buechner, Robert William
Cissell, James Charles
Davis, Robert Lawrence
Frank, William Nelson
Hoffheimer, Daniel Joseph
Nippert, Alfred Kuno, Jr.
Porter, Robert Carl, Jr.
Vogel, Cedric Wakelee

Cleveland
Boyko, Christopher Allan
Braverman, Herbert Leslie
Brucken, Robert Matthew
Falsgraf, William Wendell
Foote, Richard Charles
Hochman, Kenneth George
Katcher, Richard
Kondzer, Thomas Allen
Kurit, Neil
Maher, Edward Joseph
Monihan, Mary Elizabeth
Neff, Owen Calvin
Shore, Michael Allan
Shumaker, Roger Lee

Columbus
Sully, Ira Bennett

Dayton
Johnson, C. Terry
Krebs, Leo Francis
Roberts, Brian Michael

Fairborn
Wolaver, Stephen Arthur

Franklin
Bronson, Barbara June

Hartville
McPherson, James Willis, Jr.

Hillsboro
Coss, Rocky Alan

Kent
Nome, William Andreas

Lorain
Wiersma, David Charles

Mount Vernon
Rose, Kim Matthew

Newark
Gordon, L(eland) James
Hite, David L.

Painesville
Aveni, Anthony Joseph
Redmond, Edward Crosby

Salem
Bowman, Scott McMahan

Toledo
Gouttiere, John P.

Warren
Woodall, W. Dallas

Wilmington
Buckley, Frederick Jean
Schutt, Walter Eugene

Wooster
Moore, Arthur William

Youngstown
Briach, George Gary

OKLAHOMA

Kingfisher
Baker, Thomas Edward

Mcalester
Cornish, Richard Pool

Oklahoma City
Fuller, G. M.
High, David Royce
Necco, Alexander David
Ross, William Jarboe
Towery, Curtis Kent
Wilson, Julia Ann Yother

Tulsa
Clark, Gary Carl
Hatfield, Jack Kenton
Steltzlen, Janelle Hicks

OREGON

Albany
Thompson, Orval Nathan

Eugene
Horn, John Harold

Medford
Shaw, Barry N.

Pendleton
Rew, Lawrence Boyd

Portland
Bauer, Henry Leland
Richardson, Campbell
Strader, Timothy Richards

PENNSYLVANIA

Aliquippa
Palmieri, John Anthony

Allentown
Frank, Bernard
Noonan, Charles Thomas

Berwyn
Watters, Edward McLain, III

Brookville
Smith, Sharon Louise

Bryn Mawr
Frick, Benjamin Charles

Doylestown
Elliott, Richard Howard

Greensburg
Gounley, Dennis Joseph

Grove City
McBride, Milford Lawrence, Jr.

Hollidaysburg
Evey, Merle Kenton

Horsham
Best, Franklin Luther, Jr.

Huntingdon Valley
Kaufman, David Joseph

Kennett Square
Temple, L. Peter

King Of Prussia
DeMaria, Joseph Carminus
Gadsden, Christopher Henry
Schneider, Pam Horvitz

Langhorne
Hillje, Barbara Brown

Lemoyne
Stewart, Richard Williams

Lock Haven
Snowiss, Alvin L.

Marietta
Shumaker, Harold Dennis

Mc Keesport
Kessler, Steven Fisher

Media
Emerson, Sterling Jonathan
Tomlinson, Herbert Weston

Milton
Davis, Preston Lindner

Monroeville
Cohen, Laura

Norristown
Sosnov, Amy W(iener)

Philadelphia
Cooper, Wendy Fein
Deming, Frank Stout
Farley, Barbara L.
Jamison, Judith Jaffe
Kaier, Edward John
Lombard, John James, Jr.
Lucey, John David, Jr.
Meigs, John Forsyth
Moses, Bonnie Smith
Speyer, Debra Gail
Wolff, Deborah H(orowitz)
Wright, Minturn Tatum, III

Pittsburgh
Brown, David Ronald
Connell, Janice T.
Daniel, Robert Michael
Flanagan, Joanna Scarlata
Herchenroether, Peter Young
Hess, Emerson Garfield
Hollinshead, Earl Darnell, Jr.
Isabella, Mary Margaret
McLaughlin, John Sherman
Richards, Robert Byam
Sutton, William Dwight
Ummer, James Walter
Vater, Charles J.
Weil, Andrew L.

Pottsville
Jones, Joseph Hayward

Reading
Kline, Sidney DeLong, Jr.

Scranton
Burke, Henry Patrick

Stroudsburg
Upright, Kirby Grant

Uniontown
Coldren, Ira Burdette, Jr.
Davis, James Thomas

Washington
Posner, David S.

York
Hoffmeyer, William Frederick

RHODE ISLAND

Pawtucket
Vacca, Anthony

Providence
Davis, Andrew Hambley, Jr.
Hastings, Edwin H(amilton)
Silver, Paul Allen
Tobin, Bentley

Warwick
Goldman, Steven Jason

Woonsocket
Roszkowski, Joseph John

SOUTH CAROLINA

Charleston
Branham, C. Michael
Farr, Charles Sims

Columbia
Gibbes, William Holman
Nexsen, Julian Jacobs
Todd, Albert Creswell, III

Conway
Martin, Gregory Keith

Pawleys Island
Daniel, J. Reese

SOUTH DAKOTA

Sioux Falls
Johnson, Thomas Jerald

TENNESSEE

Chattanooga
Akers, Samuel Lee

Erwin
Shults-Davis, Lois Bunton

Knoxville
Roach, Jon Gilbert
Worthington, Carole Yard Lynch

Memphis
Allen, Newton Perkins
Bland, James Theodore, Jr.
Buchignani, Leo Joseph
Kahn, Bruce Meyer
Tate, Stonewall Shepherd
Winchester, Richard Lee, Jr.

Nashville
Berry, William Wells
Trautman, Herman Louis

Newport
Campbell, Roy Timothy, Jr.

Oak Ridge
Wilkinson, Robert Warren

Parsons
Townsend, Edwin Clay

Trenton
Malone, Gayle

TEXAS

Amarillo
Burnette, Susan Lynn

Austin
Helman, Stephen Jody
Hernandez, Mack Ray
Osborn, Joe Allen

Bellaire
Jacobus, Charles Joseph

Belton
Burrows, Jon Hanes

Brownsville
Ray, Mary Louise Ryan

Bryan
Steelman, Frank (Sitley)

Corpus Christi
Alberts, Harold
Dohse, Roberta Shellum

Dallas
Blanchette, James Grady, Jr.
Burns, Sandra
Carpenter, Gordon Russell
Dicus, Brian George
Hartnett, Will Ford
Henkel, Kathryn Gundy
Kroney, Robert Harper
Phelps, Robert Frederick, Jr.
Reid, Rust Endicott
Smith, Frank Tupper
Smith, Milton Clark, Jr.
Topper, Robert Carlton

El Paso
Cox, Sanford Curtis, Jr.
Marshall, Richard Treeger
Patterson, Burton Harvey
Yetter, Richard

Electra
Hayers, Paul Hugh

Fort Worth
Carr, Thomas Eldridge
Collins, Whitfield James
Crumley, John Walter
Curry, Donald Robert
Law, Thomas Hart
Weekley, Frederick Clay, Jr.
West, Robert Grady

Georgetown
Bryce, William Delf

Hallettsville
Baber, Wilbur H., Jr.

Houston
Amann, Leslie Kiefer
Cenatiempo, Michael J.
Collins, Susan Ellen
Eastland, S. Stacy
Frost, Charles Estes, Jr.
Jeske, Charles Matthew
Koenig, Rodney Curtis
Schwartzel, Charles Boone
Shearer, Dean Paul
Stewart, Pamela L.
Touchy, Deborah K.P.
Wharton, Thomas H(eard), Jr.

Liberty
Wheat, John Nixon

Longview
Welge, Jack Herman, Jr.

Lufkin
Garrison, Pitser Hardeman

Mason
Wilkerson, James Neill

Mc Kinney
Roessler, P. Dee

New Braunfels
Pfeuffer, Robert Tug

Richardson
Jeffreys, Albert Leonidas

San Angelo
Carter, James Alfred

San Antonio
Bayern, Arthur Herbert
Cabezas-Gil, Rosa M.
Netemeyer, Margaret
Ross, James Ulric

San Saba
Hamilton, Elwin Lomax

Yoakum
Kvinta, Charles J.

UTAH

Salt Lake City
Adams, Joseph Keith

VERMONT

Barre
Koch, Thomas Frederick

Burlington
Morrow, Emily Rubenstein

VIRGINIA

Alexandria
Peyton, Gordon Pickett
Smith, Kevin Hopkins

Arlington
Collins, Philip Reilly
Malone, William Grady

Ashburn
Gold, George Myron

Charlottesville
Edwards, James Edwin
Middleditch, Leigh Benjamin, Jr.

Danville
Conway, French Hoge
Goodman, Lewis Elton, Jr.

Fairfax
Mackall, Henry Clinton

Falls Church
Hartshorn, Roland DeWitt

Mc Lean
Herge, J. Curtis
Morris, James Malachy

Petersburg
Baskervill, Charles Thornton
White, William Earle

Richmond
Addison, David Dunham
Belcher, Dennis Irl
Horsley, Waller Holladay
Warthen, Harry Justice, III

Roanoke
Lemon, William Jacob

WASHINGTON

Bellevue
Treacy, Gerald Bernard, Jr.

Olympia
Walker, Francis Joseph

Port Angeles
Gay, Carl Lloyd

Seattle
Blais, Robert Howard
Gores, Thomas C.
Rieke, Paul Victor
Sweeney, David Brian

Spokane
Sayre, Richard Layton
Schuchart, Frederick Mark

Tacoma
Barline, John

Walla Walla
Hayner, Herman Henry

WEST VIRGINIA

Charleston
O'Connor, Otis Leslie

WISCONSIN

Elkhorn
Eberhardt, Daniel Hugo
Sweet, Lowell Elwin

Hales Corners
Case, Karen Ann

Madison
Everard, Gerald Wilfred
Roberson, Linda

Milwaukee
Iding, Allan Earl

Monroe
Kittelsen, Rodney Olin

Racine
Du Rocher, James Howard

Shawano
Habeck, James Roy

Wauwatosa
Alexander, Robert Gardner

WYOMING

Cody
Stradley, Richard Lee

Laramie
Smith, Thomas Shore

CANADA

ALBERTA

Calgary
Boettger, Roy Dennis

ENGLAND

London
Simon, M. Daniel

INDIA

Calcutta
Deora, Chandra Kumar

ISRAEL

Haifa
Permut, Scott Richard

NIGERIA

Lagos
Oyadongha, Kerepamo Peter

THE PHILIPPINES

Makati City
Macalaguing, Gene Batalla

ADDRESS UNPUBLISHED

Adams, Samuel Franklin
Buechel, William Benjamin
Carlucci, Joseph P.
Clabaugh, Elmer Eugene, Jr.
Dixon, Steven Bedford
Easterling, Charles Armo
Engelhardt, John Hugo
Falkiewicz, Christina L.
Farley, Barbara Suzanne
Galbraith, Allan Lee
Green, Marshall Munro
Hawkins, Carmen Doloras
Hernandez, David N(icholas)
Howell, Ally Windsor
James, Joyce Marie
Jorgensen, Erik Holger
Lambert, Samuel Waldron, III
Maguire, Raymer F., Jr.
Mann, Robert Paul
Martin, Connie Ruth
Martin, James William
Meli, Salvatore Andrew
Merrill, Abel Jay
O'Brien, Charles H.
O'Connor, Edward Vincent, Jr.
O'Dell, Joan Elizabeth
Reiche, Frank Perley
Reid, Joan Evangeline
Reith, Daniel I.
Rodriguez, Vivian N.
Schmidt, Kathleen Marie
Schmoll, Harry F., Jr.
Shook, Ann Jones
Silverberg, Mark Victor
Spitzberg, Irving Joseph, Jr.
Stone, Edward Herman
Subin, Florence
Sweeney, Deidre Ann
Turner, George Mason
Weill, (Lige) Harry, Sr.
Wunsch, Kathryn Sutherland

PRODUCT LIABILITY

UNITED STATES

ALABAMA

Birmingham
Christian, Thomas William

ARIZONA

Phoenix
Begam, Robert George
Condo, James Robert
Leshner, Stephen I.
Plattner, Richard Serber

Safford
Van Ry, Bradley Otto

Tucson
Osborne, John Edwards

ARKANSAS

Fort Smith
Karr, Charles

CALIFORNIA

Danville
Raines, Richard Clifton

Escondido
Barraza, Horacio

Fresno
Runyon, Brett L.

Irvine
Suojanen, Wayne William

Los Angeles
Adamek, Charles Andrew
Aristei, J. Clark
Baum, Michael Lin
Bonesteel, Michael John
Field, Richard Clark
Greaves, John Allen
Hedlund, Paul James
Johnson, Philip Leslie
McGovern, David Carr

Newport Beach
Wentworth, Theodore Sumner

Oakland
Berry, Phillip Samuel

Oxnard
McGinley, James Duff

San Anselmo
Truett, Harold Joseph, III (Tim Truett)

San Diego
Brown, LaMar Bevan
Hartley, Jason Scott
McClellan, Craig Rene

San Francisco
Arbuthnot, Robert Murray
Bruen, James A.
Dryden, Robert Eugene
Fergus, Gary Scott
Walker, Walter Herbert, III

San Jose
Bennion, David Jacobsen
Nielsen, Christian Bayard

San Mateo
O'Reilly, Terence John

Santa Ana
Cifarelli, Thomas Abitabile

Santa Monica
Bower, Allan Maxwell
Carlson, Jeffery John
Ringler, Jerome Lawrence

Walnut Creek
Pagter, Carl Richard

COLORADO

Boulder
Fenster, Herbert Lawrence
Gray, William R.

Denver
Byrne, Thomas J.
Malatesta, Mary Anne
Welch, Carol Mae
Wheeler, Malcolm Edward

Englewood
Nixon, Scott Sherman

CONNECTICUT

Farmington
Wiechmann, Eric Watt

Hartford
Morrison, Francis Henry

Southport
Sanetti, Stephen Louis

Stamford
McDonald, Cassandra Burns

Trumbull
Czajkowski, Frank Henry

DELAWARE

Wilmington
Davis, James Francis

DISTRICT OF COLUMBIA

Washington
Flannery, Ellen Joanne
Gelb, Joseph Donald
Jones, Aidan Drexel
Lewis, David John
Pollock, Stacy Jane
Renner, Curtis Shotwell
Rice, Paul Jackson
Rizzo, James Gerard
Safir, Peter Oliver

FLORIDA

Boca Raton
Wallach, Steven Ernst

Bushnell
Hagin, T. Richard

Fort Lauderdale
Heath, Thomas Clark
James, Gordon, III
Roselli, Richard Joseph
Strickland, Wilton L.
Turner, Hugh Joseph, Jr.

Jacksonville
Bullock, Bruce Stanley
Cowles, Robert Lawrence
Link, Robert James

Leesburg
Austin, Robert Eugene, Jr.

Maitland
Edwards, James Alfred

Miami
Fox, Gary Devenow
Golden, John Dennis
Greenberg, Stewart Gary
Marks, Steven Craig
Scott, Thomas Emerson, Jr.

Orlando
Metz, Larry Edward

Pensacola
Marsh, William Douglas

Sarasota
Herb, F(rank) Steven

Tallahassee
Fonvielle, Charles David

Tampa
Stagg, Clyde Lawrence

West Palm Beach
Barnhart, Forrest Gregory

GEORGIA

Atlanta
Cooper, Lawrence Allen
Head, William Carl

Columbus
Harp, John Anderson
McGlamry, Max Reginald

Newnan
Franklin, Bruce Walter

Savannah
Forbes, Morton Gerald

Statesboro
Brogdon, W.M. "Rowe"

Valdosta
Bright, Joseph Converse

HAWAII

Honolulu
Fried, L. Richard, Jr.

Koloa
Blair, Samuel Ray

IDAHO

Pocatello
Nye, W. Marcus W.

ILLINOIS

Alton
Talbert, Hugh Mathis

Belleville
Boyle, Richard Edward
Heiligenstein, Christian E.

Chicago
Brand, Mark
Burke, Thomas Joseph, Jr.
Cheely, Daniel Joseph
Daniels, John Draper
Eaton, J(ames) Timothy
Formeller, Daniel Richard
Howser, Richard Glen
Matushek, Edward J., III
Mone, Peter John
Mulroy, Thomas Robert, Jr.
Napleton, Robert Joseph
Neumeier, Matthew Michael
Novak, Mark
Price, Paul L.
Rapoport, David E.
Rogers, William John

Rohrman, Douglass Frederick
Toohey, James Kevin
Tucker, Bowen Hayward
Weaver, Timothy Allan

Edwardsville
Carlson, Jon Gordon

Glen Ellyn
O'Connell, Daniel James

Libertyville
Rallo, Douglas

Prospect Heights
Leopold, Mark F.

Rockford
Sullivan, Peter Thomas, III

Wheaton
Butt, Edward Thomas, Jr.

INDIANA

Indianapolis
Hovde, F. Boyd
Hovde, Frederick Russell

Lafayette
Pennell, Stephen Richard

IOWA

Des Moines
Cortese, Joseph Samuel, II

KANSAS

Overland Park
Sampson, William Roth

Wichita
Grace, Brian Guiles
Woolf, John Paul

LOUISIANA

Baton Rouge
Brady, Scott Earl

Lafayette
Swift, John Goulding

Lake Charles
Nieset, James Robert

Metairie
Ford, Robert David
McMahon, Robert Albert, Jr.

New Orleans
Allen, Frank Clinton, Jr.
Desue, Christine L.
Gertler, Meyer H.
Grant, Arthur Gordon, Jr.
Masinter, Paul James
Riess, George Febiger

MAINE

Portland
Culley, Peter William

MARYLAND

Annapolis
Klein, Robert Dale

Baltimore
Archibald, James Kenway
Bartlett, James Wilson, III
Burch, Francis Boucher, Jr.
DeVries, Donald Lawson, Jr.
Dewey, Joel Allen
Ebersole, Jodi Kay
Erwin, H. Robert
Pretl, Michael Albert

Greenbelt
Greenwald, Andrew Eric

Lanham Seabrook
McCarthy, Kevin John

Rockville
Michael, Robert Roy

MASSACHUSETTS

Billerica
Lewis, Edwin Leonard, III

Boston
Dillon, James Joseph
Edwards, Richard Lansing
Ellis, Fredric Lee

Lynnfield
McGivney, John Joseph

Worcester
Balko, George Anthony, III
Bassett, Edward Caldwell, Jr.

MICHIGAN

Ann Arbor
Joscelyn, Kent B(uckley)

Birmingham
Elsman, James Leonard, Jr.

Bloomfield Hills
Baumkel, Mark S.

Detroit
Barr, Charles Joseph Gore
Foley, Thomas John
Lenga, J. Thomas
Torpey, Scott Raymond

Grand Rapids
Blackwell, Thomas Francis
Neckers, Bruce Warren
Spies, Frank Stadler

Saint Joseph
Butzbaugh, Elden W., Jr.

Southfield
Berg, Stephanie A.
Fraiberg, Matthew Aaron
Gordon, Louis

MINNESOTA

Austin
Schneider, Mahlon C.

Minneapolis
Anderson, Arlene D.
Gill, Richard Lawrence
Hanson, Kent Bryan
Hoch, Gary W.
Hutchens, Michael D.
Johnson, Dennis Robert
Klosowski, Thomas Kenneth
Nemo, Anthony James
Price, Joseph Michael
Reichert, Brent Larry
Roe, Roger Rolland, Jr.

Saint Paul
Allison, John Robert
Ursu, John Joseph

MISSISSIPPI

Brandon
Obert, Keith David

Gulfport
Owen, Joe Sam

Jackson
Corlew, John Gordon
Langford, James Jerry
Merkel, Charles Michael

Ocean Springs
Luckey, Alwyn Hall

Tupelo
Clayton, Claude F., Jr.

MISSOURI

Kansas City
Abele, Robert Christopher
Eldridge, Truman Kermit, Jr.
Levings, Theresa Lawrence
Newsom, James Thomas
Redfearn, Paul L., III
Smith, R(onald) Scott
Vandever, William Dirk

Saint Louis
Baldwin, Brent Winfield
Fournie, Raymond Richard
Michener, John Athol
Rabbitt, Daniel Thomas, Jr.
Reeg, Kurtis Bradford
Ringkamp, Stephen H.
Ritter, Robert Forcier
Roskin, Preston Eugene
Walsh, Joseph Leo, III
Williams, Theodore Joseph, Jr.

Springfield
Chamblee, Dana Alicia
FitzGerald, Kevin Michael

NEW HAMPSHIRE

Keene
Gardner, Eric Raymond

Manchester
Hutchins, Peter Edward
Richards, Thomas H.

NEW JERSEY

Cherry Hill
DeVoto, Louis Joseph

Haddonfield
Andres, Kenneth G., Jr.

Livingston
Harris, Brian Craig

Morristown
Bromberg, Myron James

Newark
Garde, John Charles

Somerville
Lieberman, Marvin Samuel

NEW MEXICO

Albuquerque
Caruso, Mark John

Santa Fe
Brannen, Jeffrey Richard
Casey, Patrick Anthony
Murphy, Dennis Patrick

NEW YORK

Albany
Case, Forrest N., Jr.
Danziger, Peter
Greagan, William Joseph
Napierski, Eugene Edward
Santola, Daniel Ralph

Buffalo
Hayes, J. Michael

Flushing
Schwartz, Estar Alma

Melville
Schoenfeld, Michael P.

New Hyde Park
Lee, Brian Edward

New York
Bern, Marc Jay
Bezanson, Thomas Edward
Birnbaum, Sheila L.
Brady, Bruce Morgan
Brecker, Jeffrey Ross
Chiarchiaro, Frank John
Costello, Joseph Michael
Cunha, Mark Geoffrey
Dankner, Jay Warren
De Vivo, Edward Charles
Fallek, Andrew Michael
Garfield, Martin Richard
Grady, Maureen Frances
Greene, Norman L.
Gurfein, Richard Alan
Hamm, David Bernard
Holman, Bud George
Kasowitz, Marc Elliot
Kassebaum, John Philip
Kazanjian, John Harold
Levine, Ronald Jay
Marshall, Sheila Hermes
Newman, Fredric Samuel
Relkin, Ellen
Russotti, Philip Anthony
Schwab, Harold Lee
Schwartz, Steven T.
Seitelman, Mark Elias
Shandell, Richard Elliot
Shelton, Gregory Douglas
Singer, Jeffrey
Wilensky, Saul

Newburgh
Liberth, Richard Francis

White Plains
Ryan, Robert Davis
Scialabba, Donald Joseph

NORTH CAROLINA

New Bern
Kellum, Norman Bryant, Jr.

Pittsboro
Hubbard, Thomas Edwin (Tim Hubbard)

Winston Salem
Barnhill, Henry Grady, Jr.
Maready, William Frank

OHIO

Aurora
Hermann, Philip J.

Cincinnati
Chesley, Stanley Morris
Woodside, Frank C., III

Cleveland
Baughman, R(obert) Patrick
Bixenstine, Kim Fenton
Domiano, Joseph Charles
Schaefer, David Arnold
Vance, Victoria Lynne
Whitney, Richard Buckner

Columbus
Eichenberger, Jerry Alan
Gerling, Joseph Anthony
Hardymon, David Wayne
Radnor, Alan T.
Ray, Frank Allen
Roubanes, Barbara Ann

Youngstown
Carlin, Clair Myron

OKLAHOMA

Oklahoma City
Coats, Andrew Montgomery
Woods, Harry Arthur, Jr.

Tulsa
Atkinson, Michael Pearce
Eldridge, Richard Mark

OREGON

Central Point
Richardson, Dennis Michael

Corvallis
Ringo, Robert Gribble

Portland
Hill, Christopher T.
Maloney, Robert E., Jr.

PENNSYLVANIA

Allentown
Altemose, Mark Kenneth

Easton
Brown, Robert Carroll

Harrisburg
Angino, Richard Carmen
Downey, Brian Patrick
Stefanon, Anthony

Lancaster
Nast, Dianne Martha

Leola
Eaby, Christian Earl

Philadelphia
Barrett, John J(ames), Jr.
Coleman, Robert J.
Cullen, Raymond T.
D'Angelo, Christopher Scott
Damsgaard, Kell Marsh
Fickler, Arlene
Fox, Reeder Rodman
Kramer, Gilda Lea
Lipson, Heather Joy
Madva, Stephen Alan
Mannino, Robert
Messa, Joseph Louis, Jr.
Samuel, Ralph David
Seidel, Richard Stephen
Walters, Christopher Kent

Pittsburgh
Miller, James Robert
Perry, Jon Robert
Specter, Howard Alan
von Waldow, Arnd N.
Wycoff, William Mortimer

Warrendale
Micale, Frank Jude

Wilkes Barre
Lach, Joseph Andrew

RHODE ISLAND

Providence
Glavin, Kevin Charles

SOUTH CAROLINA

Charleston
Bell, James L.
Patrick, Charles William, Jr.

Mount Pleasant
Laddaga, Beth Jane
Ritter, Ann

North Charleston
Joye, Mark Christopher

TENNESSEE

Chattanooga
James, Stuart Fawcett

Knoxville
Ogden, Harry Peoples
Ownby, Jere Franklin, III

Memphis
Harvey, Albert C.

Springfield
Wilks, Larry Dean

TEXAS

Austin
Hayes, Burgain Garfield
Papadakis, Myron Philip
Probus, Michael Maurice, Jr.
Sulak, Timothy Martin

Burleson
Johnstone, Deborah Blackmon

Corpus Christi
Evans, Allene Delories
Fancher, Rick

Dallas
Holmes, James Hill, III
Howie, John Robert
Moore, Edward Warren
Stinnett, Mark Allan
Terry, David William
Walkowiak, Vincent Steven
Welch, Shannon Lois Kathleen

Fort Worth
Hayes, Larry B.
Wagner, James Peyton

Galveston
Neves, Kerry Lane

Houston
Holloway, Gordon Arthur
Jones, Frank Griffith
Nations, Howard Lynn
Pettiette, Alison Yvonne

Roach, Robert Michael, Jr.
Roven, John David
Sorrels, Randall Owen
Spain, H. Daniel

Longview
Jones, Christopher Don

Rowlett
Lyon, Robert Charles

San Antonio
Branton, James LaVoy
Guess, James David
Montgomery, James Edward, Jr.
Putman, Michael (James Putman)

Wichita Falls
Wesbrooks, Perry

VERMONT

Rutland
Werle, Mark Fred

VIRGINIA

Hampton
Smith, Stephen Mark

Norfolk
Bishop, Bruce Taylor
Drescher, John Webb
Pearson, John Yeardley, Jr.

Norton
Jessee, Roy Mark

Richmond
King, William H., Jr.
Marstiller, Philip S.
Walsh, James Hamilton

Roanoke
McGarry, Richard Lawrence

WASHINGTON

Bellevue
Zackey, Jonathan Thomas

Hoquiam
Kessler, Keith Leon

Renton
Barber, Mark Edward

Richland
Barr, Carlos Harvey

Seattle
Cunningham, Joel Dean
Lundgren, Gail M.
McLaughlin, Thomas Jeffrey
Paul, Thomas Frank
Peterson, Jan Eric
Scott, Brian David
Whitson, Lish

WISCONSIN

Appleton
Lonergan, Kevin
Murray, John Daniel

Madison
Anderson, Michael Steven

Milwaukee
Clark, James Richard
Daily, Frank J(erome)
Slavik, Donald Harlan

Wausau
Grischke, Alan Edward

WYOMING

Jackson
Spence, Gerald Leonard

Sheridan
Cannon, Kim Decker

AUSTRALIA

Melbourne
Begg, Derek Jonathon

GERMANY

Koln
Reufels, Martin J.

Munich
Geissler, Bernhard Heilo

IRELAND

Dublin
Preston, Caroline Mary

SOUTH AFRICA

Johannesburg
Girdwood, Graham William

ADDRESS UNPUBLISHED

Connell, William D.
Embry, Stephen Creston
Erlebacher, Arlene Cernik
Kennedy, Vekeno
Manning, Cory E.
Mitchell, William Graham Champion
Paul, Richard Wright
Smith, Patricia A.
Wilson, Virgil James, III

PROFESSIONAL LIABILITY

UNITED STATES

ALABAMA

Birmingham
Nettles, Bert Sheffield

ARIZONA

Phoenix
Bouma, John Jacob
Harrison, Mark Isaac
Smock, Timothy Robert

Tucson
MacBan, Laura Vaden

ARKANSAS

Fort Smith
Karr, Charles

CALIFORNIA

Los Angeles
Lange, Joseph Jude Morgan

Newport Beach
Otto, James Daniel

Sacramento
Birney, Philip Ripley
Hassan, Allen Clarence

San Anselmo
Truett, Harold Joseph, III (Tim Truett)

San Diego
Emge, Derek John
Wolfe, Deborah Ann

San Francisco
Bostwick, James Stephen
Callison, Russell James

San Jose
Towery, James E.

Santa Barbara
Dickey, Denise Ann

COLORADO

Boulder
Flowers, William Harold, Jr.

Denver
McConnell, Michael Theodore
Miller, J(ohn) Kent
Starrs, Elizabeth Anne

Englewood
Nixon, Scott Sherman

DELAWARE

Wilmington
Cottrell, Paul (William Cottrell)

DISTRICT OF COLUMBIA

Washington
Marks, Andrew H.
Sundermeyer, Michael S.
Villa, John Kazar

FLORIDA

Bradenton
Groseclose, Lynn Hunter

Jacksonville
Cowles, Robert Lawrence

Miami
Fox, Gary Devenow
Hall, Adam Stuart

Orlando
Motes, Carl Dalton

Tallahassee
Fonvielle, Charles David

Tampa
Hahn, William Edward

GEORGIA

Atlanta
Smith, Jeffrey Michael

HAWAII

Honolulu
Geshell, Richard Steven

ILLINOIS

Chicago
George, John Martin, Jr.
Heinz, William Denby
Henry, Brian Thomas
Luning, Thomas P.
Lynch, John James
Mone, Peter John
Napleton, Robert Joseph
Price, Paul L.
Rieger, Mitchell Sheridan
Rutkoff, Alan Stuart
Sherman, Ian Matthew
Wilcox, Mark Dean

INDIANA

Indianapolis
Hovde, F. Boyd
Wampler, Robert Joseph

IOWA

Des Moines
Finley, Kerry A.

KANSAS

Shawnee Mission
Smith, Edwin Dudley

LOUISIANA

Lafayette
Judice, Marc Wayne

New Orleans
Beahm, Franklin D.

MARYLAND

Baltimore
Bartlett, James Wilson, III
DeVries, Donald Lawson, Jr.
Summers, Thomas Carey

Rockville
Michael, Robert Roy

MICHIGAN

Detroit
Wittlinger, Timothy David

Saginaw
Concannon, Andrew Donnelly

MINNESOTA

Minneapolis
Bland, J(ohn) Richard
Cole, Phillip Allen
Rathke, Stephen Carl
Saeks, Allen Irving

MISSISSIPPI

Gulfport
Dukes, James Otis

MISSOURI

Kansas City
Koelling, Thomas Winsor

Saint Louis
Baldwin, Brent Winfield

NEW HAMPSHIRE

Keene
Gardner, Eric Raymond

NEW JERSEY

Berlin
Goldstein, Benjamin

East Brunswick
Haws, Robert John

Haddonfield
Heuisler, Charles William

Iselin
Goodman, Barry S.

Jersey City
Nevins, Arthur Gerard, Jr.

Morristown
Bromberg, Myron James

NEW YORK

Buffalo
Brown, T. Alan

Garden City
Balkan, Kenneth J.

New York
Dugan, Sean Francis Xavier
Hoffman, David Nathaniel
Kramer, Daniel Jonathan
Wakefield, Susannah Jane

NORTH CAROLINA

Raleigh
Cole, Sean Andrew Burke

Winston Salem
Maready, William Frank

OHIO

Cincinnati
Woodside, Frank C., III

Cleveland
Domiano, Joseph Charles
Stuhldreher, George William
Trapp, Mary Jane

Columbus
Bloomfield, David Solomon
Draper, Gerald Linden
Gerling, Joseph Anthony
Taylor, AmySue

Dublin
Maloon, Jerry L.

Youngstown
Carlin, Clair Myron

OREGON

Portland
Cooney, Thomas Emmett
Savage, John William

PENNSYLVANIA

Easton
Noel, Nicholas, III

Greensburg
Belden, H. Reginald, Jr.

Harrisburg
Angino, Richard Carmen

Philadelphia
Fodera, Leonard V.
Mannino, Edward Francis
Messa, Joseph Louis, Jr.
Pratter, Gene E. K.
Seidel, Richard Stephen

TENNESSEE

Johnson City
Jenkins, Ronald Wayne

Knoxville
Lloyd, Francis Leon, Jr.

TEXAS

Austin
Moss, Bill Ralph
Probus, Michael Maurice, Jr.

Dallas
Coleman, Robert Winston
Johnston, Coyt Randal
Mow, Robert Henry, Jr.

El Paso
McDonald, Charles Edward

Harlingen
Pope, William L.

Houston
Van Fleet, George Allan
Walton, Dan Gibson

San Antonio
Branton, James LaVoy

VIRGINIA

Arlington
Crouch, Richard Edelin

Norfolk
Pearson, John Yeardley, Jr.

Richmond
Rolfe, Robert Martin
Rucker, Douglas Pendleton, Jr.

WASHINGTON

Renton
Barber, Mark Edward

Seattle
Bringman, Joseph Edward
McCoid, Nancy Katherine

Peterson, Jan Eric
Waitt, Robert Kenneth

AUSTRALIA

Melbourne
Begg, Derek Jonathon

ENGLAND

London
Carruthers, Andrew James
Rochez, Nicholas Dutfield

IRELAND

Dublin
Preston, Caroline Mary

ADDRESS UNPUBLISHED

Paul, Richard Wright
Rosner, Seth

PROPERTY DAMAGE. *See*
Personal injury.

PROPERTY, REAL

UNITED STATES

ALABAMA

Dadeville
Oliver, John Percy, II

Dothan
Huskey, Dow Thobern

Huntsville
Vargo, Robert Frank

Mobile
Holland, Lyman Faith, Jr.
Johnston, Neil Chunn
Meigs, Walter Ralph

ALASKA

Anchorage
Nosek, Francis John

Bethel
Gathright, Howard T.

ARIZONA

Kingman
Basinger, Richard Lee

Phoenix
Cole, George Thomas
Coppersmith, Sam
Jacques, Raoul Thomas
Klausner, Jack Daniel
Lee, Richard H(arlo)
Lowry, Edward Francis, Jr.
Martori, Joseph Peter
Spencer, Roger Keith
Storey, Lee A.

Prescott
Goodman, Mark N.
Gose, Richard Vernie

Scottsdale
Jorden, Douglas Allen
Marhoffer, David
Titus, Jon Alan
Whittington, Thomas Lee

Sun City
Hauer, James Albert

Tucson
D'Antonio, James Joseph
Isaak, Gotthilf Eugene
McDonough, Lawrence

ARKANSAS

Fayetteville
Pearson, Charles Thomas, Jr.
Pettus, E. Lamar

Little Rock
Campbell, George Emerson
Catlett, S. Graham
Haley, John Harvey
Hughes, Steven Jay
Riordan, Deborah Truby

Mena
Thrailkill, Daniel B.

Newport
Thaxton, Marvin Dell

CALIFORNIA

Alamo
Thiessen, Brian David

Anaheim
Ross, Roger Scott

Arcadia
Morris, Gary Wayne

Bakersfield
Kind, Kenneth Wayne

Beverly Hills
Bordy, Michael Jeffrey
Burns, Marvin Gerald
Horwin, Leonard

Burbank
Lee, Paulette Wang

Camarillo
Dunlevy, William Sargent

Coronado
Adelson, Benedict James

Costa Mesa
Boyer, David Dyer
Daniels, James Walter
Frieden, Clifford E.
Kramer, Kenneth Scott

Danville
Raines, Richard Clifton

Elverta
Betts, Barbara Lang

Fresno
Ewell, A. Ben, Jr.

Fullerton
Moerbeek, Stanley Leonard

Hayward
Smith, John Kerwin

Huntington Beach
Garrels, Sherry Ann

Irvine
Farrell, Teresa Joanning
Graves, Patrick Lee
Hurst, Charles Wilson
Petrasich, John Moris
Shirley, Robert Bryce
Wintrode, Ralph Charles

La Jolla
Peterson, Paul Ames
ZoBell, Karl

Los Angeles
Argue, John Clifford
Battaglia, Philip Maher
Grush, Julius Sidney
Kane, Margaret McDonald
Klowden, Michael Louis
Lesser, Joan L.
Lund, James Louis
May, Lawrence Edward
Millard, Neal Steven
Nicholas, Frederick M.
Pearman, Robert Charles
Pircher, Leo Joseph
Porter, Verna Louise
Robertson, Hugh Duff
Robison, William Robert
Rolin, Christopher E(rnest)
Sloca, Steven Lane
Snyder, Arthur Kress
Stauber, Ronald Joseph
Wagner, Darryl William
Watson, Glenn Robert
Wessling, Robert Bruce
Zerunyan, Frank Vram

Los Gatos
Seligmann, William Robert

Marina Del Rey
Smolker, Gary Steven

Mill Valley
Nemir, Donald Philip

Morro Bay
Merzon, James Bert

Newport Beach
Harlan, Nancy Margaret
McGee, James Francis
Wolf, Alan Steven

Oakland
Allen, Jeffrey Michael

Pacific Palisades
Lagle, John Franklin

Palo Alto
O'Brien, Bradford Carl

Pasadena
Talt, Alan R.

Piedmont
McCormick, Timothy Brian Beer

Pleasanton
Staley, John Fredric

Rancho Cordova
McGrath, William Arthur

Rancho Mirage
Goldie, Ray Robert
Lonabaugh, Ellsworth Eugene

Riverside
Darling, Scott Edward

Sacramento
Robbins, Stephen J. M.
Severaid, Ronald Harold

San Carlos
Lee, John Jin

San Clemente
Geyser, Lynne M.

San Diego
de Sousa, Paula Cristina Pacheco
Dorne, David J.
Heidrich, Robert Wesley
Herring, Charles David
Mebane, Julie Shaffer
Meyer, Paul I.
Riley, Kirk Holden

San Francisco
Briscoe, John
Burden, James Ewers
Cheatham, Robert William
Hurabiell, John Philip, Sr.
Johns, Richard Seth Ellis
Kimport, David Lloyd
Mack, John Oscar
McDevitt, Ray Edward
Millner, Dianne Maxine
Riley, Benjamin Kneeland
Suter, Ben

San Jose
Cory, Charles Johnson
Gonzales, Daniel S.
Stutzman, Thomas Chase, Sr.

San Mateo
Tormey, James Roland, Jr.

San Rafael
Bloomfield, Neil Jon

Santa Ana
Beasley, Oscar Homer
Frost, Winston Lyle
Mosich, Nicholas Joseph

Santa Barbara
Egenolf, Robert F.
Willey, Charles Wayne

Santa Monica
Levin, Marvin Eugene
McNally, Susan Fowler

Seaside
Weingarten, Saul Myer

Ukiah
Sager, Madeline Dean

Van Nuys
Mikesell, Richard Lyon

COLORADO

Arvada
Peck, Kenneth E.

Aspen
McGrath, J. Nicholas
Peirce, Frederick Fairbanks

Aurora
Katz, Michael Jeffery

Basalt
Mersman, Richard Kendrick, III

Colorado Springs
Everson, Steven Lee
MacDougall, Malcolm Edward
Palermo, Norman Anthony
Purvis, Randall W. B.

Delta
Schottelkotte, Michael Roger

Denver
Braverman, Janis Ann Breggin
Brown, James Elliott
DeMuth, Alan Cornelius
Dowdle, Patrick Dennis
Fanganello, Joseph Michael
Grant, Patrick Alexander
Holder, Holly Irene
Irwin, R. Robert
Johnson, Philip Edward
Molling, Charles Francis
Pascoe, Donald Monte
Petros, Raymond Louis, Jr.
Sayre, John Marshall
Slavin, Howard Leslie
Tisdale, Douglas Michael

Durango
Sherman, Lester Ivan

Englewood
Deutsch, Harvey Elliot
Mitchem, James E.
Shannon, Malcolm Lloyd, Jr.

Fort Collins
Rogers, Garth Winfield

Frisco
Helmer, David Alan

Montrose
Overholser, John W.

Rocky Ford
Mendenhall, Harry Barton

Westcliffe
Snyder, Paul, Jr.

CONNECTICUT

Avon
Godbout, Arthur Richard, Jr.

Bethel
Medvecky, Thomas Edward

Bridgeport
Schwartz, Lawrence B.

Canaan
Capecelatro, Mark John

Danbury
Murray, Stephen James

Enfield
Berger, Robert Bertram

Farmington
Mandell, Joel

Greenwich
Pascarella, Henry William

Hartford
Buck, Gurdon Hall
Lloyd, James Hendrie, III
McCracken, Gregory William
Merriam, Dwight Haines

Lakeville
Rout, Robert Howard

Mystic
Valentine, Garrison Norton

New Haven
Coan, Richard Morton

New London
Johnstone, Philip MacLaren

Norwich
Masters, Barbara J.

Ridgefield
Bracken, Nanette Beattie
Fricke, Richard John

Shelton
Ryan, William Joseph, Jr.

Southport
Williams, Michael Peter Anthony

Stamford
Cacace, Michael Joseph
Strone, Michael Jonathan

Stratford
McDonough, Sandra Martin

Westport
Amschler, James Ralph
Cramer, Allan P.
Saxl, Richard Hildreth

Wethersfield
Terk, Glenn Thomas

Wilton
Healy, James Casey

Winsted
Finch, Frank Herschel, Jr.

DELAWARE

Dover
Ennis, Bruce Clifford
Twilley, Joshua Marion

Wilmington
Kristol, Daniel Marvin
Tigani, Bruce William

DISTRICT OF COLUMBIA

Washington
Ain, Sanford King
Allan, Richmond Frederick
Barnes, Peter
Bodansky, Robert Lee
Bonvillian, William Boone
Boykin, Hamilton Haight
Brenner, Janet Maybin Walker
Comstock, Robert Francis
Cooper, Clement Theodore
Fawell, Reed Marquette, III
Glasgow, Norman Milton
Harrison, Earl David
Kaufman, Thomas Frederick
Landfield, Richard
Lane, Bruce Stuart
Moses, Alfred Henry
Nichols, Henry Eliot
Policy, Vincent Mark
Rosenberg, Ruth Helen Borsuk
Samuelson, Kenneth Lee
Spath, Gregg Anthony
Stevens, Herbert Francis

FLORIDA

Altamonte Springs
Hoogland, Robert Frederics

Boca Raton
Kassner, Herbert Seymore
Sax, Spencer Meridith

Boynton Beach
Dembicer, Edwin Herbert

Brandon
Tittsworth, Clayton (Magness)

Clearwater
Hogan, Elwood

Walled Lake
Connelly, Thomas Joseph

West Bloomfield
Tobin, Bruce Howard

MINNESOTA

Benson
Wilcox, Donald Alan

Minneapolis
Mayerle, Thomas Michael
Parsons, Charles Allan, Jr.
Straughn, Robert Oscar, III
Thorson, Steven Greg
Ventres, Daniel Brainerd, Jr.
Witort, Janet Lee
Yost, Gerald B.

Rochester
Lantz, William Charles

Saint Paul
Meyer, Theodore James
Spencer, David James
Winthrop, Sherman

MISSISSIPPI

Hernando
Brown, William A.

Jackson
Chadwick, Vernon Henry
Grant, Russell Porter, Jr.
Hammond, Frank Jefferson, III
Hughes, Byron William

MISSOURI

Chesterfield
Pollihan, Thomas Henry

Clayton
Ritter, Robert Thornton

Hillsboro
Howald, John William

Kansas City
Frantze, David Wayne
Hindman, Larrie C.
Howes, Brian Thomas
Levine, Bernard Benton
Moore, Stephen James
Satterlee, Terry Jean
Todd, Stephen Max

Saint Charles
Weber, William Randolph

Saint Louis
Cullen, James D.
Erbs, Thomas J.
Graham, Robert Clare, III
Harris, Harvey Alan
Hellmuth, Theodore Henning
Hetlage, Robert Owen
Inkley, John James, Jr.
Winning, J(ohn) Patrick

MONTANA

Billings
Beiswanger, Gary Lee
Mitchell, Laura Ann

NEBRASKA

Omaha
Barmettler, Joseph John
Kreifels, Frank Anthony
LaPuzza, Paul James

Papillion
Rice, John Edward

NEVADA

Las Vegas
Curran, William P.
Goodwin, John Robert
Norville, Craig Hubert
Singer, Michael Howard

Reno
Hill, Earl McColl
Marshall, Robert William

NEW HAMPSHIRE

Manchester
Stebbins, Henry Blanchard
Thornton, Edward Robert, Jr.

Rochester
Jones, Franklin Charles

Wolfeboro
Walker, George William

NEW JERSEY

Bay Head
Kellogg, James Crane

Boonton
Walzer, James Harvey

Bridgewater
Linett, David

Cherry Hill
Roth, Kenneth David

Chester
Pfaffenroth, Peter Albert

Cliffside Park
Diktas, Christos James

Clifton
Mohammed, Sohail

Cranbury
Iatesta, John Michael

Edison
Applebaum, Charles
Fink, Edward Murray
Goldfarb, Ronald Carl
Lijoi, Peter Bruno

Far Hills
Corash, Richard

Flemington
Wolfson, William Steven

Florham Park
Calabrese, Arnold Joseph

Glen Ridge
Connolly, Joseph Thomas

Glen Rock
Markey, Brian Michael

Hackensack
Duus, Gordon Cochran
Sosland, Karl Z.
Strull, James Richard

Jersey City
D'Alessandro, Daniel Anthony
DiSciullo, Alan Michael

Kearny
Dunne, Frederick R., Jr.

Laurel Springs
Wood, Leonard James

Livingston
Rinsky, Joel Charles
Sukoneck, Ira David

Maplewood
Joseph, Susan B.

Mc Afee
Fogel, Richard

Metuchen
Frizell, David J.

Montclair
Brown, Ronald Wellington

Moorestown
Ewan, David E.

Morristown
Rosenthal, Meyer L(ouis)

Newark
Day, Edward Francis, Jr.
Neuer, Philip David
Wayne, Robert Andrew

Old Bridge
Downs, Thomas Edward, IV

Oradell
Mavroudis, John M.

Princeton
Souter, Sydney Scull

River Vale
Meyer, Grace Tomanelli

Roseland
Eichler, Burton Lawrence

Scotch Plains
Kraus, Robert H.

Secaucus
Castano, Gregory Joseph
McNamara, Patrick James

Sicklerville
Corbisiero Love, Angela M.

South Plainfield
Santoro, Frank Anthony

Springfield
Grayson, Bette Rita

Stone Harbor
Taylor, Robert Lee

Summit
Woller, James Alan

Teaneck
Stone, Sheldon

Tenafly
Spike, Michele Kahn

Union
Mark, Michael David

Willingboro
Guest, Brian Milton

Woodbridge
Babineau, Anne Serzan
Sterling, Harold G.

NEW MEXICO

Albuquerque
Ramo, Roberta Cooper
Ussery, Albert Travis

Roswell
Bassett, John Walden, Jr.

Ruidoso
Dutton, Dominic Edward

Santa Fe
Burton, John Paul (Jack Burton)
Garber, Bruce Samuel
Mills, Thomas C. H.

Seneca
Monroe, Kendyl Kurth

NEW YORK

Albany
Kornstein, Michael Allen
Piedmont, Richard Stuart
Yanas, John Joseph

Andover
Hutter, Robert Grant

Ballston Spa
Brown, Ifigenia Theodore

Bronxville
Veneruso, James John

Brooklyn
Solis, Lino A.

Buffalo
Bailey, Thomas Charles
Greenspon, Burton Edward
Mucci, Gary Louis
Ritchie, Stafford Duff, II

Cedarhurst
Taubenfeld, Harry Samuel

Chittenango
Baum, Peter Alan

Commack
Braun, Robert Alan
Somer, Stanley Jerome

Corning
Becraft, Charles D., Jr.

Cortland
Taylor, Leland Baridon

Delhi
Hamilton, John Thomas, Jr.

Dobbs Ferry
Juettner, Diana D'Amico
Maiocchi, Christine

East Meadow
Adler, Ira Jay
Hyman, Montague Allan

Elmsford
Neustadt, Paul

Flushing
Chang, Lee-Lee

Garden City
Dent, Thomas Augustine
Fischoff, Gary Charles
Jones, Lawrence Tunnicliffe
Kestenbaum, Harold Lee
Schupbach, Arthur Christopher

Glens Falls
McMillen, Robert Stewart

Great Neck
Luckman, Gregg A.
Samanowitz, Ronald Arthur

Greenvale
Halper, Emanuel B(arry)

Hamburg
Chesbro, Robert Bruce

Hudson
Davis, Deborah Lynn

Huntington
Liput, Andrew Lawrence
Munson, Nancy Kay
Tucker, William P.

Islandia
Pruzansky, Joshua Murdock

Ithaca
Barney, John Charles
Theisen, Henry William

Jericho
Kurtzberg, Howard
Semel, Martin Ira

Malverne
Benigno, Thomas Daniel

Manlius
Mathewson, George Atterbury

Melville
Greenberg, Michael J.

Middletown
Kossar, Ronald Steven

Mineola
Cohen, Stanley Dale
Tannenbaum, Bernard
Weinstock, Benjamin

New City
Fenster, Robert David

New York
Abelman, Arthur F.
Alden, Steven Michael
Arouh, Jeffrey Alan
Beckman, Michael
Bennett, Scott Lawrence
Black, James Isaac, III
Bliwise, Lester Martin
Block, William Kenneth
Bodner, Marc A.
Browdy, Joseph Eugene
Bryant, George McEwan
Burgweger, Francis Joseph Dewes, Jr.
Chen, Wesley
Chromow, Sheri P.
Cuiffo, Frank Wayne
Diamond, Bernard Robin
Duetsch, John Edwin
DuLaux, Russell Frederick
Eisen, Edwin Roy
Fenster, Marvin
Finkelstein, Allen Lewis
Ganzi, Victor Frederick
Garfinkel, Neil B.
Goebel, William Horn
Goldstein, Charles Arthur
Goldstein, Eugene E.
Granoff, Gary Charles
Grew, Robert Ralph
Hackett, Kevin R.
Halprin, Henry Steiner
Herbst, Todd L.
Hershcopf, Gerald Thea
Herz, Andrew Lee
Ingram, Samuel William, Jr.
Intriligator, Marc Steven
Jarblum, William
Joseph, Ellen R.
Kalamaras, James
Kalikow, Richard R.
Karim, Yumi Yamada
Karsch, Stephen E.
Kobrin, Lawrence Alan
Kreitzman, Ralph J.
Kuklin, Anthony Bennett
Kumble, Steven Jay
Kuntz, Lee Allan
Lascher, Alan Alfred
Levine, Melvin Charles
Levy, Mark Allan
Lynton, Harold Stephen
Marks, Theodore Lee
Merritt, Raymond Walter
Miller, William Harlowe, Jr.
Montgomerie, Bruce Mitchell
Mullman, Michael S.
Munzer, Stephen Ira
Nance, Allan Taylor
Nathan, Andrew Jonathan
Nelson, John C.
Neveloff, Jay A.
Paul, Robert Carey
Pinover, Eugene Alfred
Plotkin, Loren H.
Pollan, Stephen Michael
Rabin, Jack
Rahm, David Alan
Rahm, Susan Berkman
Richards, David Alan
Rikon, Michael
Robinson, Irwin Jay
Rodman, Lawrence Bernard
Rosen, Richard Lewis
Rosenberg, David
Rosenberg, Gary Marc
Rosenberg, Gerald Alan
Saft, Stuart Mark
Salup, Stephen
Sanseverino, Raymond Anthony
Scala, James Robert
Schwartz, Barry Steven
Schwartz, James Evan
Seifert, Thomas Lloyd
Shenker, Joseph C.
Silverman, Arthur Charles
Simon, Michael Scott
Smith, Vincent Milton
Solomon, Stephen L.
Spivack, Edith Irene
Steinbach, Harold I.
Strauss, Gary Joseph
Strougo, Robert Isaac
Uram, Gerald Robert
Vernon, Darryl Mitchell
Viener, John D.
Weller, Philip Douglas
Wimpfheimer, Michael Clark

Niagara Falls
Brett, Jay Elliot
Levine, David Ethan

Olean
Heyer, John Henry, II

Orangeburg
Rivet, Diana Wittmer

Oswego
Greene, Stephen Craig

Oyster Bay
Robinson, Edward T., III

Port Chester
Gioffre Baird, Lisa Ann

Poughkeepsie
Dietz, Robert Barron
Kranis, Michael David
Wallace, Herbert Norman

Purchase
Gioffre, Bruno Joseph

Riverhead
Twomey, Thomas A., Jr.

Rochester
Blyth, John E.
Clifford, Eugene Thomas
Frank, Bernard Alan
Galbraith, Robert Lyell, Jr.
Madden, Neal D.
Trevett, Thomas Neil
Vigdor, Justin Leonard
Whitaker, Benjamin Palmer, Jr.

Scarsdale
Beuchert, Edward William

Schenectady
Parisi, Frank Nicholas
Sokolow, Lloyd Bruce

South Plymouth
Braswell, Bruce Wayne

Southampton
Platt, Harold Kirby

Stamford
Becker, Carl Frederick

Staten Island
Ferranti, Thomas, Jr.
Fusco, John Anthony
Humphries, Edward Francis

Syracuse
Cirando, John Anthony
Fitzpatrick, James David
Regan, Paul Michael
Sparkes, James Edward
Traylor, Robert Arthur

Utica
Kelly, William Wright

West Babylon
Weinreb, Michael Leonard

Westbury
Ciovacco, Robert John

White Plains
Feder, Robert
Gjertsen, O. Gerard
Guida, Toni M.
Posner, Martin Louis
Rosenberg, Michael
Silverberg, Steven Mark
Topol, Robin April Levitt

Woodbury
Taub, Linda Marsha

NORTH CAROLINA

Asheville
Frue, William Calhoun

Boone
Brown, Wade Edward

Charlotte
Lynch, Craig Taylor
Sink, Robert C.

Durham
Welborn, Reich Lee

Hickory
Smith, Young Merritt, Jr.

Monroe
Love, Walter Bennett, Jr.

Murphy
Bata, Rudolph Andrew, Jr.

NORTH DAKOTA

Bismarck
Edin, Charles Thomas
Klemin, Lawrence R.

Grand Forks
Widdel, John Earl, Jr.

Minot
Backes, Orlin William

OHIO

Canfield
Hill, Thomas Allen

Canton
Barnhart, Gene

Celina
Lammers, Thomas Dean

Chesterland
Durn, Raymond Joseph

Cincinnati
Carroll, James Joseph
Cunningham, Pierce Edward
Heldman, James Gardner
Meranus, Leonard Stanley
Meyer, Charles Mulvihill
Miller, Gail Franklin
Naylor, Paul Donald
Petrie, Bruce Inglis
Strauss, William Victor
Trauth, Joseph Louis, Jr.

Cleveland
Csank, Paul Lewis
Felty, Kriss Delbert
Freimuth, Marc William

Hoffman, Mark Leslie
Owendoff, Stephen Peter
Pearlman, Samuel Segel
Striefsky, Linda A(nn)
Waldeck, John Walter, Jr.

Columbus
Barrett, Phillip Heston
Buchenroth, Stephen Richard
Fultz, Robert Edward
Sully, Ira Bennett

Dublin
Inzetta, Mark Stephen

Franklin
Bronson, Barbara June

Hartville
McPherson, James Willis, Jr.

Lorain
Wiersma, David Charles

Painesville
Aveni, Anthony Joseph

Salem
Bowman, Scott McMahan

Shaker Heights
Barz, Patricia

Toledo
Gouttiere, John P.

Twinsburg
Kramer, Timothy Eugene

Warren
Woodall, W. Dallas

OKLAHOMA

Broken Arrow
Frieze, H(arold) Delbert

Jones
Dean, Bill Verlin, Jr.

Muskogee
Robinson, Adelbert Carl

Oklahoma City
Barth, J. Edward
Elder, James Carl
Epperson, Kraettli Quynton
Fuller, G. M.
Johnson, Robert Max
McBride, Kenneth Eugene
Stanley, Brian Jordan
Willey, Benjamin Tucker, Jr.

Tulsa
Huffman, Robert Allen, Jr.
Mackey, Steven R.
Schuller, Stephen Arthur
Steltzlen, Janelle Hicks

OREGON

Cannon Beach
Hillestad, Charles Andrew

Eugene
DuPriest, Douglas Millhollen
Horn, John Harold

La Grande
Joseph, Steven Jay

Lake Oswego
Byczynski, Edward Frank

Portland
Anderson, Herbert Hatfield
Bauer, Henry Leland
Brownstein, Richard Joseph
Hanna, Harry Mitchell
Schuster, Philip Frederick , II
Waggoner, James Clyde

Roseburg
Yockim, Ronald Stephen

PENNSYLVANIA

Allentown
Brown, Robert Wayne
Somach, Richard Brent

Bradford
Hauser, Christopher George

Bristol
Kashkashian, Arsen

Brookville
Smith, Sharon Louise

Bryn Mawr
Hankin, Mitchell Robert

Drexel Hill
West, Kenneth Edward

Easton
Scheer, Joel Martin

Erie
Tupitza, Thomas Anton

Exton
Teti, Louis N.

Greensburg
Gounley, Dennis Joseph

Grove City
McBride, Milford Lawrence, Jr.

Harrisburg
Kury, Franklin Leo

Kennett Square
Temple, L. Peter

Lancaster
Minney, Michael Jay

Lock Haven
Snowiss, Alvin L.

Malvern
Doerr, John Maxwell

Marietta
Shumaker, Harold Dennis

Media
D'Amico, Andrew J.
Ewing, Robert Clark

New Castle
Mangino, Matthew Thomas

Philadelphia
Auten, David Charles
Cross, Milton H.
Denmark, William Adam
Dubin, Stephen Victor
Finkelstein, Joseph Simon
Goldberg, Richard Robert
Hunter, James Austen, Jr.
Keene, John Clark
Liu, Diana Chua
Maxey, David Walker
Miller, Henry Franklin
O'Brien, William Jerome, II
Panzer, Mitchell Emanuel
Pollack, Michael

Pittsburgh
Brown, David Ronald
Ehrenwerth, David Harry
Gold, Harold Arthur
Hess, Emerson Garfield
Hollinshead, Earl Darnell, Jr.
Letwin, Jeffrey William
Murrin, Regis Doubet
Raynovich, George, Jr.
Reed, W. Franklin
Richards, Robert Byam
Weil, Andrew L.

Reading
Kline, Sidney DeLong, Jr.

Scranton
Burke, Henry Patrick

Washington
Posner, David S.

Wernersville
Worley, Jane Ludwig

Wilkes Barre
Ufberg, Murray

Williamsport
Knecht, William L.

York
Hoffmeyer, William Frederick

RHODE ISLAND

Cranston
Coletti, John Anthony

Providence
Carlotti, Stephen Jon
Tobin, Bentley

West Warwick
Bottella, Tammy Ann

Westerly
Nardone, William Andrew

Woonsocket
Roszkowski, Joseph John

SOUTH CAROLINA

Charleston
Robinson, Neil Cibley, Jr.

Columbia
Lewis, Ernest Crosby

Conway
Martin, Gregory Keith

Greenville
Barash, Anthony Harlan
Edwards, Harry LaFoy

Hilton Head Island
Scarminach, Charles Anthony

TENNESSEE

Erwin
Shults-Davis, Lois Bunton

Germantown
Waddell, Phillip Dean

Knoxville
Ritchie, Albert

Lebanon
Blackstock, James Fielding

Memphis
deWitt, Charles Benjamin, III
Jalenak, James Bailey
Williams, J. Maxwell

Nashville
Bruce, William Roland
Thomas, Robert Paige
Trent, John Thomas, Jr.

TEXAS

Austin
Davis, Robert Larry
Nevola, Roger
Osborn, Joe Allen
Phillips, Travis R.
Rider, Brian Clayton
Tice, Laurie Dietrich
Wester, Ruric Herschel, Jr.

Bellaire
Jacobus, Charles Joseph

Belton
Burrows, Jon Hanes

Boerne
Vaughan, Edward Gibson

Dallas
Beuttenmuller, Rudolf William
Birkeland, Bryan Collier
Fishman, Edward Marc
Levin, Hervey Phillip
Livingstone, William Edwin, III
Martin, Richard Kelley
Miller, Stewart Ransom
Mira, Joseph Lawrence
Mueller, Mark Christopher
Nolan, John Michael
Pleasant, James Scott
Portman, Glenn Arthur
Riddle, Michael Lee
Sandler, Lewis Herbsman
Smith, Larry Van
Smith, Milton Clark, Jr.
Thau, William Albert, Jr.
Topper, Robert Carlton
Walts, William Edward, II
White, James Richard

Denton
Narsutis, John Keith

El Paso
Cox, Sanford Curtis, Jr.
Morton, Fred J.
Rash, Alan Vance

Electra
Hayers, Paul Hugh

Ennis
Swanson, Wallace Martin

Euless
Paran, Mark Lloyd

Fort Worth
Curry, Donald Robert
West, Robert Grady

Houston
Anderson, Doris Ehlinger
Brunson, John Soles
Goldberg, Charles Ned
Hollyfield, John Scoggins
Marlow, Orval Lee, II
Schroeder, Walter Allen
Shannon, Joel Ingram
Simmons, Stephen Judson
Sing, William Bender
Weiner, Sanford Alan
Zeigler, Ann dePender

Irving
Landau, Pearl Sandra

Liberty
Wheat, John Nixon

New Braunfels
Pfeuffer, Robert Tug

Plano
Shaddock, William Charles

Richardson
Davis, M. G.

San Antonio
Barton, James Cary
Koppenheffer, Julie B.
Millet, John Porath
Oppenheimer, Jesse Halff
Pipkin, Marvin Grady
Steen, John Thomas, Jr.

San Saba
Hamilton, Elwin Lomax

Sherman
Munson, Peter Kerr

Spring
Hendricks, Randal Arlan

Sterling City
Durham, Drew Taylor

Waco
Crook, Betty Ross

Weslaco
Pomerantz, Jerald Michael

Yoakum
Kvinta, Charles J.

UTAH

Logan
Honaker, Jimmie Joe
Jenkins, James C.

Ogden
Mecham, Glenn Jefferson

Park City
Kennicott, James W.

Saint George
Gallian, Russell Joseph

Salt Lake City
Anderson, Robert Monte
Barusch, Lawrence Roos
Cornaby, Kay Sterling
Jensen, Dallin W.
Kirkham, John Spencer

VERMONT

Barre
Koch, Thomas Frederick

Chester
Holme, John Charles, Jr.

VIRGINIA

Alexandria
Maloof, Farahe Paul
McClure, Roger John
McGuire, Edward David, Jr.
Sherk, George William
Smith, Kevin Hopkins

Charlottesville
Kudravetz, David Waller

Chester
Connelly, Colin Charles

Danville
Goodman, Lewis Elton, Jr.

Fairfax
Keith, John A.C.
Mackall, Henry Clinton
Sanderson, Douglas Jay
Saul, Ira Stephen

Falls Church
Christman, Bruce Lee
Thomas, William Griffith

Glen Allen
Settlage, Steven Paul

Great Falls
Preston, Charles George

Leesburg
Minchew, John Randall

Martinsville
Frith, Douglas Kyle

Mc Lean
Stearns, Frank Warren

Newport News
Kamp, Arthur Joseph, Jr.

Norfolk
Land, Charles Edwards
Parker, Richard Wilson
Russell, C. Edward, Jr.

Reston
Toole, John Harper

Richmond
Bates, John Wythe, III
Redmond, David Dudley
Rucker, Douglas Pendleton, Jr.
Swartz, Charles Robert
Witt, Walter Francis, Jr.

Roanoke
Lemon, William Jacob

Springfield
Costello, Daniel Brian

Virginia Beach
Layton, Garland Mason

Winchester
Weiss, Rhett Louis

Wytheville
Baird, Thomas Bryan, Jr.

WASHINGTON

Bellingham
Packer, Mark Barry
Serka, Philip Angelo

Gig Harbor
Thompson, Ronald Edward

Olympia
Miller, Allen Terry, Jr.

Port Angeles
Gay, Carl Lloyd

Seattle
Blair, M. Wayne
Cornell, Kenneth Lee
Cullen, Jack Joseph
Kuhrau, Edward W.
Leen, David Arthur

Murray, Michael Kent
Palmer, Douglas S., Jr.
Rieke, Paul Victor
Stokke, Diane Rees
Sweeney, David Brian
Tousley, Russell Frederick
Williams, J. Vernon
Wilson, Richard Randolph

Spokane
Lineberger, Peter Saalfield

WEST VIRGINIA

Charleston
O'Connor, Otis Leslie

Fairmont
Stanton, George Patrick, Jr.

Gassaway
Jones, Jeniver James

Romney
Saville, Royce Blair

Wheeling
Riley, Arch Wilson, Jr.

WISCONSIN

Appleton
Drescher, Kathleen Ebben

Beloit
Blakely, Robert George

Elkhorn
Eberhardt, Daniel Hugo
Sweet, Lowell Elwin

Madison
Rankin, Gene Raymond

Mc Farland
Abbott, William Anthony

Milwaukee
Abraham, William John, Jr.
Biehl, Michael Melvin
Bremer, John M.
Gaines, Irving David
Levine, Herbert

Racine
Du Rocher, James Howard
Stutt, John Barry

Waukesha
Jastroch, Leonard Andrew

WYOMING

Laramie
Smith, Thomas Shore

AUSTRALIA

Sydney
Brown, John Thomas

COSTA RICA

San Jose
Gomez, Jose

FRANCE

Paris
Schultze, Pascal

GERMANY

Dusseldorf
Rauh, Theo

HUNGARY

Budapest
Szecsodi, Zsolt

INDIA

Calcutta
Deora, Chandra Kumar
Garodia, Aniruddh

ISRAEL

Haifa
Permut, Scott Richard

Tel Aviv
Aharoni, Erez
Yoram, Raved

ITALY

Milan
Maccioni, Giovanni

Rome
Biolato, Giuseppe Vittorio

JAPAN

Tokyo
Mikami, Jiro

THE NETHERLANDS

Amsterdam
Van Eeghen, Christiaan Pieter

NIGERIA

Lagos
Oyadongha, Kerepamo Peter

Lagus
Muoka, Alexander Nduka

NORTHERN IRELAND

Belfast
White, Rowan McMurray

ROMANIA

Bucharest
Jardine, Bryan Wilson
Voicu, Daniel

ADDRESS UNPUBLISHED

Arkin, L. Jules
Ascher, Richard Alan
Ash, David Charles
Assael, Michael
Atchison, Rodney Raymond
Baldwin, Carolyn Whitmore
Ball, James Herington
Bateman, David Alfred
Brehl, James William
Carlucci, Joseph P.
Clabaugh, Elmer Eugene, Jr.
Colton, Sterling Don
Conine, Gary Bainard
Cumberland, William Edwin
Dixon, Steven Bedford
Donnally, Robert Andrew
Eaken, Bruce Webb, Jr.
Engelhardt, John Hugo
Falkiewicz, Christina L.
Fenwick, Lynda Beck
Fetzer, Mark Stephen
Francis, Jerome Leslie
Galbraith, Allan Lee
Gordon, David Zevi
Gregory, George G.
Griffith, Steven Franklin, Sr.
Hackett, Wesley Phelps, Jr.
Hall-Barron, Deborah
Harman, Wallace Patrick
Hartmann, Kenneth
Hernandez, David N(icholas)
Holtzschue, Karl Bressem
Hwang, Roland
Hybl, William Joseph
Johnson, Leonard Hjalma
Jorgensen, Erik Holger
Klein, Judah Baer
Lapidus, Steven Richard
Locke, William Henry
Lustig, Robert Michael
Marcus, Kenneth Ben
Martin, Connie Ruth
Martin, James William
McCormick, Homer L., Jr.
McGinty, Brian Donald
Meli, Salvatore Andrew
Mitlak, Stefany (Lynn)
Mosk, Susan Hines
Oates, Carl Everette
Patrick, Marty
Pear, Charles E., Jr.
Peck, Mira P.
Peterson, Howard Cooper
Pickard, Terry Roy
Poliakoff, Gary A.
Rivera, Oscar R.
Rogovin, Lawrence H.
Shaffer, Richard James
Siegel, Sarah Ann
Silverberg, Mark Victor
Simonsen, Gregory Mark
Smith, Walter Ernest
Speaker, Susan Jane
Stinchfield, John Edward
Torgerson, Larry Keith
Walker, Jordan Clyde, Sr.
Wright, Robert Payton
Wunsch, Kathryn Sutherland

**REAL ESTATE
DEVELOPMENT.** *See*
Property, real.

SALES OF GOODS. *See*
Commercial, contracts.

SECURITIES

UNITED STATES

ALABAMA

Birmingham
Baker, David Remember
Garner, Robert Edward Lee
Rotch, James E.
Wilson, James Charles, Jr.

Montgomery
Carter, Gordon Thomas

ALASKA

Anchorage
Bankston, William Marcus

ARIZONA

Phoenix
Bivens, Donald Wayne
Dunipace, Ian Douglas
Galbut, Martin Richard
Hicks, William Albert, III
Madden, Paul Robert
Moya, Patrick Robert
Price, Charles Steven
Thompson, Terence William
Williams, Quinn Patrick

Scottsdale
Titus, Jon Alan

Tucson
Meehan, Michael Joseph

CALIFORNIA

Beverly Hills
Sherwood, Arthur Lawrence

Burlingame
Narayan, Beverly Elaine

Carlsbad
Koehnke, Phillip Eugene

Century City
Davis, Donald G(lenn)

Culver City
Tanaka, J(eannie) E.

El Segundo
Hunter, Larry Dean

Emeryville
Ostrach, Michael Sherwood

Irvine
Wertheim, Jay Philip

Los Angeles
Barnes, Willie R.
Blencowe, Paul Sherwood
Bogen, Andrew E.
Bosl, Phillip L.
Castro, Leonard Edward
Chadwick, William Jordan
Fairbank, Robert Harold
Farrar, Stanley F.
Hedlund, Karen Jean
Klowden, Michael Louis
McAniff, Edward John
McLane, Frederick Berg
Power, John Bruce
Presant, Sanford Calvin
Shortz, Richard Alan

Menlo Park
Gunderson, Robert Vernon, Jr.
Kelly, Daniel Grady, Jr.
Mendelson, Alan Charles
Millard, Richard Steven

Monte Sereno
Allan, Lionel Manning

Newport Beach
Jones, Sheldon Atwell
Singer, Gary James

Oakland
Anderson, Doris Elaine

Pacific Palisades
Lagle, John Franklin

Palo Alto
Climan, Richard Elliot
Cunningham, Brian C.
Deaktor, Darryl Barnett
Phair, Joseph Baschon

Pasadena
van Schoonenberg, Robert G.

San Diego
Alpert, Michael Edward
Sullivan, Patrick James

San Francisco
Block, David Jeffrey
Boutin, Peter Rucker
Campbell, Scott Robert
Cheatham, Robert William
Devine, Antoine Maurice
Feller, Lloyd Harris
Finberg, James Michael
Friese, Robert Charles
Halloran, Michael James

Larson, John William
Latta, Thomas Albert
Mann, Bruce Alan
Murphy, Arthur John, Jr.
Palmer, Venrice Romito
Seegal, John Franklin
Snow, Tower Charles, Jr.
Sparks, Thomas E., Jr.
Suter, Ben

Santa Barbara
Howell, Weldon Ulric, Jr.

Toluca Lake
Runquist, Lisa A.

Torrance
Petillon, Lee Ritchey

COLORADO

Denver
Blair, Andrew Lane, Jr.
Eckstein, John Alan
Hilbert, Otto Karl, II
Lutz, John Shafroth
Mauro, Richard Frank
Newcom, Jennings Jay
Wollins, David Hart

Edwards
Calise, Nicholas James

Greenwood Village
Lidstone, Herrick Kenley, Jr.

CONNECTICUT

Fairfield
Denniston, Brackett Badger, III

Greenwich
Hurwich, Robert Allan
Nimetz, Matthew

Hartford
Wetzler, Monte Edwin

Stamford
Bingham, A. Walker, III
Dupont, Wesley David
Hubschman, Henry A.
Jensen, Frode, III

Waterbury
Wolfe, Harriet Munrett

DISTRICT OF COLUMBIA

Washington
Alexander, Clifford Joseph
Brown, David Nelson
Chafetz, Marc Edward
Cohen, Louis Richard
Collins, John Timothy
Craft, Robert Homan, Jr.
Eisenberg, Meyer
Flagg, Ronald Simon
Freedman, Jay Weil
Goelzer, Daniel Lee
Greenberger, I. Michael
Hart, Christopher Alvin
Horn, Charles M.
Hunt, David Wallingford
Hyde, Howard Laurence
Johnson, Philip McBride
Jordan, Jon Byron
Klein, Andrew Manning
Leckar, Stephen Craig
Lenhart, James Thomas
Levenson, Alan Bradley
Lucas, Steven Mitchell
Lybecker, Martin Earl
Mixter, Christian John
Mostoff, Allan Samuel
Muir, J. Dapray
Murphy, Sean Patrick
Schropp, James Howard
Shuman, Mark Patrick
Sonde, Theodore Irwin
Stevens, Herbert Francis
Stromberg, Jean Wilbur Gleason
Trager, Michael David
Trimble, Sandra Ellingson
Unger, Peter Van Buren
Wenner, Charles Roderick

FLORIDA

Boca Raton
Buckstein, Mark Aaron
Klein, Peter William

Fort Lauderdale
Schneider, Laz Levkoff

Jacksonville
Kelso, Linda Yayoi
McWilliams, John Lawrence, III

Largo
Fedor, Allan John

Miami
Berritt, Harold Edward
Critchlow, Richard H.
Ersek, Gregory Joseph Mark
Fontes, J. Mario F., Jr.
Garrett, Richard G.
Granata, Linda M.
Grossman, Robert Louis
Hall, Adam Stuart
Hoffman, Larry J.
Lyubkin, Rina

Naples
McCaffrey, Judith Elizabeth

New Port Richey
Focht, Theodore Harold

North Palm Beach
Coyle, Dennis Patrick

Orlando
Blackford, Robert Newton
Blaher, Neal Jonathan
Heinle, Richard Alan
Ioppolo, Frank S., Jr.
Pierce, John Gerald (Jerry Pierce)

Palm Beach
Crawford, Sandra Kay

Sarasota
Janney, Oliver James
Raimi, Burton Louis

Tallahassee
Minnick, Bruce Alexander

Tampa
Alpert, Jonathan Louis
Grammig, Robert James

GEORGIA

Atlanta
Albert, Ross Alan
Beckham, Walter Hull, III
Bradley, Phillip Alden
Burgoon, Brian David
Byrne, Granville Bland, III
Collins, Steven M.
Isaf, Fred Thomas
Jeffries, McChesney Hill, Jr.
Meyer, William Lorne
Prince, David Cannon
Schulte, Jeffrey Lewis
Stewart, Jeffrey B.
Williams, Neil, Jr.

HAWAII

Honolulu
Reber, David James

ILLINOIS

Chicago
Axley, Frederick William
Barack, Peter Joseph
Bellows, Laurel Gordon
Blount, Michael Eugene
Burgdoerfer, Jerry
Clemens, Richard Glenn
Clinton, Edward Xavier
Conlon, Steven Denis
Crawford, Dewey Byers
Donohoe, Jerome Francis
Fein, Roger Gary
Futterman, Ronald L.
Garber, Samuel B.
Gates, Stephen Frye
George, John Martin, Jr.
Gerstein, Mark Douglas
Goldman, Louis Budwig
Goldman, Michael P.
Gordon, Phillip
Greenbaum, Kenneth
Henry, Robert John
Johnson, Gary Thomas
Johnson, Lael Frederic
Kolmin, Kenneth Guy
Kravitt, Jason Harris Paperno
Kuntz, William Richard, Jr.
Lang, Gordon, Jr.
Lochbihler, Frederick Vincent
Maher, Francesca Marciniak
McDermott, John H(enry)
McGrath, William Joseph
Miller, Paul J.
Miller, Ronald Stuart
Murdock, Charles William
Niehoff, Philip John
Quinlan, William Joseph, Jr.
Reich, Allan J.
Reum, James Michael
Rhind, James Thomas
Rosic, George S.
Sabl, John J.
Samuels, Lawrence Robert
Schreck, Robert A., Jr.
Schuman, William Paul
Thomas, Stephen Paul
Wander, Herbert Stanton
Winkler, Charles Howard

Deerfield
Gaither, John Francis, Jr.
Oettinger, Julian Alan

Dekalb
Tucker, Watson Billopp

Downers Grove
Mason, Peter Ian

Gurnee
Southern, Robert Allen

Lake Zurich
Scott, John Joseph

Naperville
Larson, Mark Edward, Jr.

Oak Brook
Ras, Robert A.

Oak Park
Schubert, Blake H.

Rosemont
Mirabile, Thomas Keith

Schiller Park
Congalton, Christopher William

Warrenville
Boardman, Robert A.

INDIANA

Indianapolis
Coons, Stephen Merle
Dutton, Stephen James
Kleiman, Mary Margaret
Koeller, Robert Marion
Neff, Robert Matthew
Padgett, Gregory Lee
Strain, James Arthur

IOWA

Des Moines
Austin, Bradford Lyle
Bennett, Edward James

KANSAS

Prairie Village
Stanton, Roger D.

Shawnee Mission
Gaar, Norman Edward

Topeka
Rainey, William Joel

KENTUCKY

Louisville
Pedley, Lawrence Lindsay

LOUISIANA

New Orleans
Bieck, Robert Barton, Jr.
Kupperman, Stephen Henry
McMillan, Lee Richards, II

MARYLAND

Baltimore
Burch, Francis Boucher, Jr.
Chernow, Jeffrey Scott
Scriggins, Larry Palmer

Bethesda
Dickstein, Sidney
Feuerstein, Donald Martin

Columbia
Maseritz, Guy B.

MASSACHUSETTS

Boston
Bines, Harvey Ernest
Bohnen, Michael J.
Engel, David Lewis
Fischer, Eric Robert
Halligan, Brendan Patrick
Jordan, Alexander Joseph, Jr.
Korb, Kenneth Allan
Leibensperger, Edward Paul
Malley, Robert John
Masud, Robert
Matzka, Michael Alan
Soden, Richard Allan
Thibeault, George Walter
Williams, Robert Dana

Framingham
Meltzer, Jay H.

Newton
Glazer, Donald Wayne

Weston
Bateman, Thomas Robert
Dickie, Robert Benjamin

MICHIGAN

Charlevoix
Telgenhof, Allen Ray

Detroit
Kamins, John Mark
Shaevsky, Mark
Tickner, Ellen Mindy

Grosse Pointe
Avant, Grady, Jr.

Lansing
Linder, Iris Kay

Traverse City
Kubiak, Jon Stanley

MINNESOTA

Minneapolis
Bergerson, David Raymond
Cole, Phillip Allen
Kozachok, Stephen K.
Laitinen, Sari K.M.
Mellum, Gale Robert
Palmer, Deborah Jean
Petersen, Mark Allen
Pluimer, Edward J.
Potuznik, Charles Laddy
Radmer, Michael John
Sanner, Royce Norman
Stageberg, Roger V.

North Oaks
Woods, Robert Edward

Woodbury
Norton, John William

MISSOURI

Chesterfield
Denneen, John Paul
Hier, Marshall David

Kansas City
Ayers, Jeffrey David
Gilmore, Webb Reilly

Lamar
Geddie, Rowland Hill, III

Saint Louis
Arnold, John Fox
Brickler, John Weise
Clear, John Michael
Conran, Joseph Palmer
Gillis, John Lamb, Jr.
Pickle, Robert Douglas
Schoene, Kathleen Snyder
Smith, Arthur Lee
Sneeringer, Stephen Geddes
Tierney, Michael Edward

NEBRASKA

Lincoln
Johnson, Warren Charles

Omaha
Rock, Harold L.
von Bernuth, Carl W.
Vosburg, Bruce David

NEVADA

Las Vegas
Nasky, H(arold) Gregory
Norville, Craig Hubert
Ritchie, Douglas V.

NEW JERSEY

Bridgewater
Ball, Owen Keith, Jr.

Camden
Furey, John J.

Florham Park
Siino, Salvatore G.

Little Silver
Schmidt, Daniel Edward, IV

Lyndhurst
Lasky, David

Monmouth Junction
King, David Roy

Newark
Liftin, John Matthew

Princeton
Burgess, Robert Kyle
Kirstein, Philip Lawrence
Szwalbenest, Benedykt Jan

Roseland
Wovsaniker, Alan

Somerville
Hutcheon, Peter David

NEW MEXICO

Albuquerque
Apodaca, Patrick Vincent
Schuler, Alison Kay

Seneca
Monroe, Kendyl Kurth

NEW YORK

Ardsley On Hudson
Stein, Milton Michael

Armonk
Moskowitz, Stuart Stanley

Buffalo
Jacobs, Charles P.
Lammert, Richard Alan
Lippes, Gerald Sanford
Nichols, F(rederick) Harris
Tanous, James Joseph

Fairport
Young, Thomas Paul

Glen Cove
Shields, Craig M.

Great Neck
Rockowitz, Noah Ezra

Jericho
Kurtzberg, Howard

Liverpool
Wolfson, Warren David

Mamaroneck
Du Boff, Michael H(arold)

New York
Abelle, Patsy Caples
Arenson, Gregory K.
Atkins, Peter Allan
Axelrod, Charles Paul
Axinn, Stephen Mark
Bach, Thomas Handford
Backman, Gerald Stephen
Barandes, Robert
Bartlett, Joseph Warren
Bauer, George A., III
Beck, Andrew James
Beckman, Michael
Benedict, James Nelson
Bennett, Scott Lawrence
Bergan, Edmund Paul, Jr.
Bergan, Philip James
Bernard, Richard Phillip
Bialkin, Kenneth Jules
Blackman, Kenneth Robert
Bodovitz, James Philip
Boehner, Leonard Bruce
Brown, Meredith M.
Browne, Jeffrey Francis
Bryan, Barry Richard
Butler, Samuel Coles
Byrnes, Richard James
Caytas, Ivo George
Clemente, Robert Stephen
Cohen, Edward Herschel
Collins, John F.
Conboy, Kenneth
Connor, John Thomas, Jr.
Conrad, Winthrop Brown, Jr.
Cooper, Michael Anthony
Cooper, Stephen Herbert
Costello, Robert Joseph
Cotter, James Michael
Cowan, Wallace Edgar
Cowen, Robert Nathan
Crane, Roger Ryan, Jr.
Cunha, Mark Geoffrey
Davidson, Sheila Kearney
de Saint Phalle, Pierre Claude
de Sampigny, Guillaume
Diamant, Aviva F.
DiBlasi, Gandolfo Vincent
Dorado, Marianne Gaertner
Dubin, James Michael
Duerbeck, Heidi Barbara
Dunham, Wolcott Balestier, Jr.
Dunn, M(orris) Douglas
Epstein, Melvin
Ercklentz, Enno Wilhelm, Jr.
Fass, Peter Michael
Feiman, Ronald Mark
Feit, Glenn M.
Fensterstock, Blair Courtney
Filler, Ronald Howard
Finch, Edward Ridley, Jr.
Finkelstein, Ira Allen
Fisher, Robert I.
Fishman, Mitchell Steven
Fleischman, Edward Hirsh
Fleischman, Keith Martin
Fortenbaugh, Samuel Byrod, III
Frank, Lloyd
Fraser, Brian Scott
Fredericks, William Curtis
Fried, Donald David
Friedman, Bart
Friedman, Robert Laurence
Friedman, Samuel Selig
Gambro, Michael S.
Gillespie, Jane
Glusband, Steven Joseph
Gold, Simeon
Gottlieb, Paul Mitchel
Grant, Stephen Allen
Greenawalt, William Sloan
Gross, Richard Benjamin
Haje, Peter Robert
Heftler, Thomas E.
Hendry, Andrew Delaney
Hersh, Robert Michael
Hershcopf, Gerald Thea
Hershman, Scott Edward
Herzeca, Lois Friedman
Hiden, Robert Battaile, Jr.
Hirsch, Barry
Hirsch, Jerome S.
Hoff, Jonathan M(orind)
Holley, Steven Lyon
Howe, Richard Rives
Hurley, Geoffrey Kevin
Hynes, Patricia Mary
Hyun, Jung-Wen
Isquith, Fred Taylor
Jacob, Marvin Eugene
Jarblum, William
Jock, Paul F., II
Jones, Douglas W.
Kaplan, Carl Eliot
Kaplan, Mark Norman
Karsch, Stephen E.
Katz, Ronald Scott
Kaufman, Arthur Stephen
Kavaler, Thomas J.
Keene, Lonnie Stuart
Kenney, John Joseph
Kern, George Calvin, Jr.
Kessel, Mark
Kies, David M.
Kinney, Stephen Hoyt, Jr.
Kirschbaum, Myron
Koblenz, Michael Robert
Kramer, Daniel Jonathan
Kramer, Morris Joseph
Krasner, Daniel Walter
Kraus, Douglas M.
Krouse, George Raymond, Jr.
Lamia, Thomas Roger
Landes, Robert Nathan
Leonard, Edwin Deane
Levin, Ezra Gurion
Lowe, John Anthony
Lowenfels, Lewis David
Lowy, George Theodore
Lutzker, Elliot Howard
Macioce, Frank Michael
Marcusa, Fred Haye
McGanney, Thomas
McGuire, Eugene Guenard
McLean, David Lyle
Meltzer, Roger
Mentz, Barbara Antonello
Merritt, Raymond Walter
Mestres, Ricardo Angelo, Jr.

Michel, Clifford Lloyd
Miller, Arthur Madden
Miller, Richard Allan
Modlin, Howard S.
Morphy, James Calvin
Morris, Edward William, Jr.
Muccia, Joseph William
Mullaney, Thomas Joseph
Nash, Paul LeNoir
Nemser, Earl Harold
Oshima, Michael W.
Papernik, Joel Ira
Parent, Louise Marie
Parish, J. Michael
Perlmuth, William Alan
Pettibone, Peter John
Pierce, Morton Allen
Pisano, Vincent James
Pompa, Renata
Profusek, Robert Alan
Purtell, Lawrence Robert
Quinn, Linda Catherine
Raab, Sheldon
Reid, Edward Snover, III
Reinstein, Paul Michael
Reinthaler, Richard Walter
Ring, Renee Etheline
Robertson, Edwin David
Rocklen, Kathy Hellenbrand
Rolfe, Ronald Stuart
Romney, Richard Bruce
Rosenbloom, Lawrence Andrew
Rosenblum, Scott S.
Rosensaft, Menachem Zwi
Rubin, Stephen Wayne
Rubinstein, Frederic Armand
Rusmisel, Stephen R.
Russo, Thomas Anthony
Saunders, Mark A.
Savage, Edward Turney
Schallert, Edwin Glenn
Schiff, Kenneth Edmund
Schizer, Zevie Baruch
Schorr, Brian Lewis
Schulman, Steven Gary
Schwartz, Barry Fredric
Shenker, Joseph C.
Siegel, Jeffrey Norton
Siller, Stephen I.
Skirnick, Robert Andrew
Snow, Charles
Snyderman, Marc Ian
Sperling, Allan George
Steinberg, Howard Eli
Stephenson, Alan Clements
Stimmel, Todd Richard
Stone, David Philip
Strom, Milton Gary
Strougo, Robert Isaac
Stuart, Alice Melissa
Supino, Anthony Martin
Sussman, Alexander Ralph
Tanenbaum, Gerald Stephen
Thalacker, Arbie Robert
Thomas, Jeremiah Lindsay, III
Toumey, Donald Joseph
Tricarico, Joseph Archangelo
Underberg, Mark Alan
Urowsky, Richard J.
Viener, John D.
Villacorat, Anna Teresa Cruz
Vogel, Howard Stanley
Wailand, George
Walker, John Lockwood
Walpin, Gerald
Wang, Albert Huai-En
Warwick, Kathleen Ann
Wells, Andrew Norman
West, Stephen Kingsbury
Wilson, Paul Holliday, Jr.
Wolfe, Richard Barry Michael
Wolson, Craig Alan
Yankwitt, Russell Marc
Yodowitz, Edward Jay
Young, John Edward
Zaitzeff, Roger Michael
Zeller, Paul William
Zucker, Howard

Orangeburg
Seaman, Robert E., III

Peconic
Mitchell, Robert Everitt

Purchase
Sharpe, Robert Francis, Jr.

Rochester
Doyle, Justin P
Vigdor, Justin Leonard
Willett, Thomas Edward

Rye
Roberts, Thomas Alba

Scarsdale
Ellis, James Henry

Southampton
Lopez, David

Suffern
Stack, Daniel

Uniondale
Eilen, Howard Scott
Sugarman, Robert P.

NORTH CAROLINA

Burlington
Slayton, John Howard

Charlotte
Harris, Charles Marcus
Miller, John Randolph
Walker, Clarence Wesley

Durham
Welborn, Reich Lee

Greensboro
Clark, David McKenzie

Raleigh
Carlton, Alfred Pershing, Jr.
Powell, Durwood Royce

Winston Salem
Barnhardt, Zeb Elonzo, Jr.

OHIO

Akron
Trotter, Thomas Robert

Chagrin Falls
Streicher, James Franklin

Cincinnati
Heldman, James Gardner
Kammerer, Matthew Paul
Olson, Robert Wyrick
Stith, John Stephen

Cleveland
Csank, Paul Lewis
Dampeer, John Lyell
Langer, Carlton Earl
Markey, Robert Guy
Marting, Michael G.
Stevens, Thomas Charles

Columbus
Brinkman, Dale Thomas
Dunlay, Catherine Telles
McDermott, Kevin R.
Schwartz, Robert S.
Stinehart, Roger Ray

Dayton
Watts, Steven Richard

Lebanon
Benedict, Ronald Louis

Sylvania
Kline, James Edward

Toledo
Webb, Thomas Irwin, Jr.

Wickliffe
Kidder, Fred Dockstater

OKLAHOMA

Oklahoma City
Derrick, Gary Wayne
McMillin, James Craig
Rockett, D. Joe
Steinhorn, Irwin Harry

Tulsa
Biolchini, Robert Fredrick
Kaufman, Ronald C.
Kihle, Donald Arthur
Luthey, Graydon Dean, Jr.
Slicker, Frederick Kent

OREGON

Portland
DuBoff, Leonard David
Krahmer, Donald Leroy, Jr.
Sand, Thomas Charles

PENNSYLVANIA

Allison Park
Ries, William Campbell

Blue Bell
Barron, Harold Sheldon
Scudder, Charles Seelye Kellgren

Malvern
May, Judy Royer

Media
McNitt, David Garver

Philadelphia
Clark, William H., Jr.
Colli, Bart Joseph
Del Raso, Joseph Vincent
Drake, William Frank, Jr.
Esser, Carl Eric
Genkin, Barry Howard
Granoff, Gail Patricia
Hangley, William Thomas
Jones, Robert Jeffries
Promislo, Daniel
Reich, Abraham Charles
Sartorius, Peter S.
Shestack, Jerome Joseph
Speyer, Debra Gail
Stuntebeck, Clinton A.
Wellington, Ralph Glenn
Whinston, Stephen Alan

Pittsburgh
Barrett, Karen Moore
Connell, Janice T.
Ehrenwerth, David Harry
Hardie, James Hiller
Klett, Edwin Lee
Letwin, Jeffrey William
Walton, Jon David

Wynnewood
Stapleton, Larrick B.

RHODE ISLAND

Providence
Carlotti, Stephen Jon

SOUTH CAROLINA

Greenville
Graben, Eric Knox

Salem
Everett, C(harles) Curtis

TENNESSEE

Chattanooga
Durham, J(oseph) Porter, Jr.

Knoxville
McCall, Jack Humphreys, Jr.
Worthington, Carole Yard Lynch

Lebanon
Blackstock, James Fielding

Nashville
Mayden, Barbara Mendel
Tuke, Robert Dudley

TEXAS

Addison
Kneipper, Richard Keith

Austin
Gangstad, John Erik
Laves, Alan Leonard
Matheson, Daniel Nicholas, III
Tyson, Laura Lanza

Dallas
Acker, Rodney
Blachly, Jack Lee
Brewer, Charles Blake, Sr.
Estep, Robert Lloyd
Feld, Alan David
Flanagan, Christie Stephen
Glendenning, Don Mark
Gohlke, David Ernest
Kirby, Le Grand Carney, III
Maxwell, Jason P.
McLane, David Glenn
McNamara, Anne H.
Miller, Norman Richard
Moore, Marilyn Payne
Pleasant, James Scott
Sandler, Lewis Herbsman
Schreiber, Sally Ann
Spears, Robert Fields
Veach, Robert Raymond, Jr.
Young, Barney Thornton

Euless
Paran, Mark Lloyd

Fort Worth
Watson, Robert Francis

Houston
Anderson, Eric Severin
Bech, Douglas York
Berner, Arthur Samuel
Born, Dawn Slater
Carter, John Loyd
England, Rudy Alan
Finch, Michael Paul
Frost, Charles Estes, Jr.
Garten, David Burton
Grace, James Martin, Jr.
LaBoon, Robert Bruce
Myers, Franklin
Nolen, Roy Lemuel
Porter, Thomas William, III
Rogers, Arthur Hamilton, III
Sapp, Walter William
Schwartz, Charles Walter
Still, Charles Henry
Szalkowski, Charles Conrad
Watson, John Allen
Weber, Fredric Alan
Winer, Stephen I.

San Antonio
Brennan, James Patrick, Sr.
Lutter, Charles William, Jr.

VIRGINIA

Arlington
McCorkindale, Douglas Hamilton
Morgens, Warren Kendall

Manakin Sabot
Bright, Craig Bartley

Oakton
Vernava, Anthony Michael

Richmond
Buford, Robert Pegram
Cutchins, Clifford Armstrong, IV
Minardi, Richard A., Jr.
Pope, Robert Dean

Roanoke
Harrison, David George

Springfield
Eley, Randall Robbi

Sterling
McBarnette, Bruce Olvin

Tysons Corner
Maiwurm, James John

Vienna
Randolph, Christopher Craven
Razzano, Frank Charles

SECURITIES

WASHINGTON

Seattle
Alsdorf, Robert Hermann
Graham, Stephen Michael
Mellem, Roger Duane
Pym, Bruce Michael
Rummage, Stephen Michael
Steel, John Murray
Whitford, Joseph Peter

Spokane
Koegen, Roy Jerome

Tacoma
Carlisle, Dale L.

WISCONSIN

Milwaukee
Abraham, William John, Jr.
Peranteau, Mary Elizabeth
Schulz, William John
Williams, Clay Rule

AUSTRALIA

Adelaide
Davis, Glenn Stuart

AUSTRIA

Vienna
Mayr, Andreas W.
Wolf, Richard V.

CHINA

Beijing
Zhao, Qian

Hong Kong
Shinkle, John Thomas
Yu, Benita Ka Po

Taipei
Tsai, Jaclyn Yu-Ling

CZECH REPUBLIC

Prague
Brzobohaty, Tomas

DENMARK

Copenhagen
Sogaard, Klaus

ENGLAND

London
Astleford, Peter David
Barnes, Oliver William Abbott
Booker, Russell Stuart
Brownwood, David Owen
Coppin, Jonathan David
Goodall, Caroline Mary Helen
Hancock, Helen Mathias
Moller, Stephen Hans
Quillen, Cecil Dyer, III

FINLAND

Helsinki
Hentula, Ismo Tapani
Tähtinen, Jyrki Juhani
Wist, Tarja Tuulia

FRANCE

Paris
Darlington, Gavin

GERMANY

Cologne
Wilsing, Hans Ulrich

Düsseldorf
Plueckelmann, Katja

Frankfurt am Main
Harrer, Herbert

HONG KONG

3 Garden Road
Richardson, David Alexander

Hong Kong
Garvey, Richard Anthony

ITALY

Mialn
Vecchio, Cesare Giovanni

THE NETHERLANDS

Amsterdam
Van Campen, Arnoud Clemens

NORWAY

Oslo
Thyness, Erik

PERU

Lima
Hernandez, Juan Luis

THE PHILIPPINES

Makati City
Banez, Winthrop Hawthorne Redoble

REPUBLIC OF KOREA

Seoul
Choi, Unghwan Raphael

SPAIN

Madrid
Garrido de las Heras, Miguel

SWEDEN

Stockholm
Sarkia, Peter L.

SWITZERLAND

Chateau d'Oex
Berman, Joshua Mordecai

UKRAINE

Kyiv
Vronskaya, Anna Alexandrovna

VENEZUELA

Solano Caracas
Garcia-Montoya, Luis Alberto

ADDRESS UNPUBLISHED

Anderson, Geoffrey Allen
Beasley, James W., Jr.
Bierce, William B.
Blazzard, Norse Novar
Brodsky, David Michael
Cherovsky, Erwin Louis
Cranney, Marilyn Kanrek
Ellison, Noni Lois
Fischer, David Charles
Gilden, Richard Henry
Gordon, David Zevi
Griffin, Campbell Arthur, Jr.
Gutman, Richard Edward
Hackett, Robert John
Harff, Charles Henry
Heath, Charles Dickinson
Herringer, Maryellen Cattani
Houle, Jeffrey Robert
Hunt, Ronald Forrest
Huston, Steven Craig
Irvine, John Alexander
Jamieson, Michael Lawrence
Johnson, Edward Michael
Klafter, Cary Ira
Lefkowitz, Alan Zoel
Lorne, Simon Michael
Madden, John Joseph
Massad, Stephen Albert
McCabe, Thomas Edward
Millimet, Erwin
Moylan, James Joseph
Natcher, Stephen Darlington
Ober, Richard Francis, Jr.
Painton, Russell Elliott
Pietrzak, Alfred Robert
Porter, Michael Pell
Powers, Elizabeth Whitmel
Reiter, Glenn Mitchell
Ruhm, Thomas Francis
Samuels, Janet Lee
Schoenwald, Maurice Louis
Sexton, David Farrington
Shapiro, Howard Alan
Song, Bing
Tondel, Lawrence Chapman
Toomey, Richard Andrew, Jr.
Tubman, William Charles
Walker, Craig Michael
Walner, Robert Joel
Williams, William John, Jr.
Williamson, Edwin Dargan
Wilson, Rhys Thaddeus
Wood, Robert Charles

SOCIAL SECURITY. See
Pension.

SPORTS

UNITED STATES

ALABAMA

Opelika
Hand, Benny Charles, Jr.

CALIFORNIA

Irvine
Specter, Richard Bruce

Los Angeles
Demoff, Marvin Alan

San Diego
Meyer, Paul I.

COLORADO

Colorado Springs
Rowan, Ronald Thomas

Denver
Hilbert, Otto Karl, II

DISTRICT OF COLUMBIA

Washington
Babby, Lon S.
Brown, Michael DeWayne

FLORIDA

Lakeland
Wendel, John Fredric

ILLINOIS

Chicago
Cohen, Stephen Bruce

MASSACHUSETTS

Natick
Grassia, Thomas Charles

NEW YORK

New York
Finkelstein, Ira Allen
Galkin, Lee D.
Ganz, Howard Laurence
Goff, Betsy Kagen
Kaminsky, Arthur Charles
Krane, Steven Charles
Wise, Aaron Noah

NORTH CAROLINA

Charlotte
Thigpen, Richard Elton, Jr.

OHIO

Cincinnati
Dornette, W(illiam) Stuart

RHODE ISLAND

Cranston
Cervone, Anthony Louis

TEXAS

Austin
Maggio-Gonzales, Marissa Ann

Spring
Hendricks, Randal Arlan

VIRGINIA

Chesapeake
Mastronardi, Corinne Marie

WASHINGTON

Seattle
Waldman, Bart

THE PHILIPPINES

Makati City
Valdecantos, Clarence Darrow Cunan

ADDRESS UNPUBLISHED

Spicer, S(amuel) Gary
Weisman, Paul Howard

TAXATION, CORPORATE

UNITED STATES

ALABAMA

Birmingham
Shanks, William Ennis, Jr.

Decatur
Blackburn, John Gilmer

Montgomery
Proctor, David Ray

ARIZONA

Phoenix
Ehmann, Anthony Valentine
Everett, James Joseph
Martori, Joseph Peter

Scottsdale
Peshkin, Samuel David

ARKANSAS

Little Rock
Marshall, William Taylor

CALIFORNIA

Coronado
Adelson, Benedict James

Costa Mesa
Schaaf, Douglas Allan

Emeryville
Howe, Drayton Ford, Jr.

Irvine
Goldstein, Michael Gerald

Larkspur
Greenberg, Myron Silver

Los Angeles
Chadwick, William Jordan
Gipson, Robert Edgar
Gordon, David Eliot
Mancino, Douglas Michael
Palazzo, Robert Paul
Pircher, Leo Joseph
Presant, Sanford Calvin
Rath, Howard Grant, Jr.

Newport Beach
Schumacher, Stephen Joseph

San Diego
Riley, Kirk Holden

San Francisco
Caspersen, R(alph) Frederick
Homer, Barry Wayne
Klott, David Lee
Offer, Stuart Jay
Spiegel, Hart Hunter
Wolfe, Cameron Withgot, Jr.
Wood, Robert Warren

Santa Clara
Denten, Christopher Peter

Torrance
Smiley, Stanley Robert

Walnut Creek
Willson, Prentiss, Jr.

COLORADO

Denver
Rich, Robert Stephen
Ruppert, John Lawrence

Parker
Greenberg, Morton Paul

CONNECTICUT

Bridgeport
Schwartz, Lawrence B.

Darien
Dale, Erwin Randolph

Fairfield
LaFollette, Ernest Carlton

Hartford
Coyle, Michael Lee
Lloyd, Alex
Lyon, James Burroughs

New Haven
Behling, Paul Lawrence
Sanborn, Von Eric

Westport
Grodd, Leslie Eric
Sheiman, Ronald Lee

DELAWARE

Wilmington
Baumann, Julian Henry, Jr.
Grossman, Jerome Kent

Hatch, Denison Hurlbut, Jr.

DISTRICT OF COLUMBIA

Washington
Barrie, John Paul
Berrington, Craig Anthony
Chapoton, John Edgar
Collinson, Dale Stanley
Davidson, Daniel Morton
Dunnan, Weaver White
Evans, Donald Charles, Jr.
Halvorson, Newman Thorbus, Jr.
Heffernan, James Vincent
Jacobson, David Edward
Lane, Bruce Stuart
May, Gregory Evers
McClure, William Pendleton
McKeever, Joseph Francis, III
Oyler, Gregory Kenneth
Paul, William McCann
Rafferty, James Gerard
Richmond, David Walker
Robinson, Stephanie
Shay-Byrne, Olivia
Sherman, Gerald Howard
Stauffer, Ronald Eugene
Wellen, Robert Howard
Zagaris, Bruce

FLORIDA

Boca Raton
Beck, Jan Scott
Klein, Peter William
Reinstein, Joel

Fort Lauderdale
Stankee, Glen Allen

Lake Wales
Wales, Gwynne Huntington

Longwood
Rajtar, Steven Allen
Tomasulo, Virginia Merrills

Miami
Hudson, Robert Franklin, Jr.
Ruffner, Charles Louis
Scheer, Mark Jeffrey
Simmons, Sherwin Palmer
Weinstein, Andrew H.
Wright, Blandin James

Oldsmar
Hirschman, Sherman Joseph

Orlando
Conti, Louis Thomas Moore
Lefkowitz, Ivan Martin

Parkland
Masanoff, Michael David

Tampa
Barton, Bernard Alan, Jr.
Levine, Jack Anton

West Palm Beach
Barnett, Charles Dawson

GEORGIA

Atlanta
Cohen, N. Jerold
Edge, J(ulian) Dexter, Jr.
Hasson, James Keith, Jr.

HAWAII

Honolulu
Ingersoll, Richard King
Miyasaki, Shuichi

IDAHO

Boise
Erickson, Robert Stanley

ILLINOIS

Chicago
Banoff, Sheldon Irwin
Block, Neal Jay
Bowen, Stephen Stewart
Craven, George W.
Cunningham, Robert James
Drymalski, Raymond Hibner
Dubbs, John William, III
Ellwood, Scott
Henry, Frederick Edward
Kanter, Burton Wallace
Kaplan, Howard Gordon
Kaplan, Jared
Landsman, Stephen A.
Lipton, Richard M.
Lorentzen, John Carol
Margolin, Stephen M.
McKenzie, Robert Ernest
Michalak, Edward Francis
Palmer, John Bernard, III
Rizzo, Ronald Stephen
Siske, Roger Charles
Swibel, Steven Warren
Wolfe, David Louis

Deerfield
Bush, Thomas Norman

Lake Forest
Palmer, Ann Therese Darin

Naperville
Larson, Mark Edward, Jr.

TAXATION, ESTATE *See also* **Estate planning; Probate**

Los Angeles
Ballsun, Kathryn Ann
Gallo, Jon Joseph
Rae, Matthew Sanderson, Jr.
Rath, Howard Grant, Jr.

Monterey
Gaver, Frances Rouse

Newport Beach
Allen, Russell G.

Palo Alto
Miller, Michael Patiky

Palos Verdes Estates
Toftness, Cecil Gillman

Pasadena
Taylor, John David

Riverside
Darling, Scott Edward

Sacramento
Goodart, Nan L.

San Diego
Payne, Margaret Anne

San Francisco
Caspersen, R(alph) Frederick
Guggenhime, Richard Johnson
Manning, Jerome Alan

COLORADO

Colorado Springs
Kendall, Phillip Alan

Denver
Atlass, Theodore Bruce
Goddard, Jo Anna
Olsen, M. Kent
Schmidt, L(ail) William, Jr.

Longmont
Flanders, Laurence Burdette, Jr.

Pueblo
Altman, Leo Sidney

CONNECTICUT

Greenwich
Selby, Leland Clay

Hartford
Appel, Robert Eugene
Berall, Frank Stewart

New Haven
Behling, Paul Lawrence

Old Lyme
Wyckoff, E. Lisk, Jr.

Stamford
Sarner, Richard Alan

Waterbury
Dost, Mark W.

Westport
Grodd, Leslie Eric
Kosakow, James Matthew
Sheiman, Ronald Lee

DELAWARE

Wilmington
Herdeg, John Andrew
Jolles, Janet K. Pilling

DISTRICT OF COLUMBIA

Washington
Blazek-White, Doris
Faley, R(ichard) Scott
Geske, Alvin Jay
Heffernan, James Vincent
McClure, William Pendleton
McCoy, Jerry Jack
Plaine, Lloyd Leva
Sherman, Gerald Howard

FLORIDA

Fort Lauderdale
Barnard, George Smith
Gardner, Russell Menese

Jacksonville
Braddock, Donald Layton

Miami
Simmons, Sherwin Palmer
Weinstein, Andrew H.

Naples
Bruce, Jackson Martin, Jr.

Sarasota
Conetta, Tami Foley

Tampa
Ellwanger, Thomas John

West Palm Beach
Chopin, L. Frank
Henry, Thornton Montagu

GEORGIA

Albany
Moorhead, William David, III

Atlanta
Bloodworth, A(lbert) W(illiam) Franklin
Cohen, N. Jerold
Thrower, Randolph William

HAWAII

Honolulu
Gerson, Mervyn Stuart
Hite, Robert Griffith
Miyasaki, Shuichi

ILLINOIS

Chicago
Abell, David Robert
Acker, Frederick George
Brown, Alan Crawford
Carr, Walter Stanley
Chiles, Stephen Michael
Cross, Chester Joseph
English, John Dwight
Friedman, Roselyn L.
Gelman, Andrew Richard
Harrington, Carol A.
Herpe, David A.
Kanter, Burton Wallace
Marshall, John David
Nitikman, Franklin W.
Schar, Stephen L.
Siske, Roger Charles
Spain, Richard Colby
Trost, Eileen Bannon

Farmer City
Peithmann, William A.

Lake Bluff
Kennedy, John Foran

Nashville
Cross, Robert Leonard

Oak Brook
Ras, Robert A.

Springfield
Stuart, Robert Allan, Jr.

INDIANA

Fort Wayne
Fink, Thomas Michael

Indianapolis
Ewbank, Thomas Peters
Hetzner, Marc A.
Jewell, George Benson
Johnson, George Weldon
Patrick, William Bradshaw
Ponder, Lester McConnico

IOWA

Clarinda
Millhone, James Newton

Des Moines
Campbell, Bruce Irving
Zumbach, Steven Elmer

KANSAS

Lawrence
Smith, Glee Sidney, Jr.

Topeka
Horttor, Donald J.

Wichita
Sorensen, Harvey R.

KENTUCKY

Louisville
Duffy, Martin Patrick
Fuchs, Olivia Anne Morris

Somerset
Prather, John Gideon

LOUISIANA

New Orleans
Benjamin, Edward Bernard, Jr.
Lemann, Thomas Berthelot
McDaniel, Donald Hamilton

MAINE

Falmouth
Curran, Richard Emery, Jr.

Portland
LeBlanc, Richard Philip

MARYLAND

Baltimore
Cook, Bryson Leitch
Lewis, Alexander Ingersoll, III

Rockville
De Jong, David Samuel

Neuman, Eric Patt

MASSACHUSETTS

Boston
Coolidge, Francis Lowell
Fortier, Albert Mark, Jr.
Metzer, Patricia Ann
Pratt, Harold Irving
Preston, Jerome, Jr.
Woodburn, Ralph Robert, Jr.

Holden
Price, Robert DeMille

Newton
Walker, Paul Howard

Plymouth
Barreira, Brian Ernest

Stoughton
Gabovitch, Steven Alan

Wellesley
Riley, Michael Hylan

West Chatham
Rowley, Glenn Harry

MICHIGAN

Ann Arbor
Dew, Thomas Edward

Birmingham
Sweeney, Thomas Frederick

Bloomfield Hills
Kirk, John MacGregor
Sommerfeld, David William

Detroit
Miller, George DeWitt, Jr.

Hamtramck
Kaczmarek, Carla

Livonia
Fried, William C.

Saint Clair Shores
Joslyn, Robert Bruce

Southfield
Labe, Robert Brian

West Bloomfield
Tobin, Bruce Howard

MINNESOTA

Edina
Brooks, William James, III

Minneapolis
Brand, Steve Aaron

Saint Paul
Seymour, McNeil Vernam

MISSOURI

Kansas City
Bartunek, Robert R(ichard), Jr.
Setzler, Edward Allan
Tanner, Eric Benson

Saint Louis
Mulligan, Michael Dennis
Sherby, Kathleen Reilly

Springfield
Baxter-Smith, Gregory John

MONTANA

Billings
Thompson, James William

Havre
Moog, Mary Ann Pimley

NEBRASKA

Omaha
Kozlik, Michael David

NEVADA

Las Vegas
Hagendorf, Stanley

NEW JERSEY

Atlantic Highlands
Marshall, Anthony Parr

Hackensack
Deener, Jerome Alan

Jersey City
Feder, Arthur A.

Newark
Levin, Simon
Zuckerman, Herbert Lawrence

Ramsey
Weber, Walter Winfield, Jr.

Scotch Plains
Kraus, Robert H.

Secaucus
Israels, Michael Jozef

Summit
Cooper, John Weeks
Pfaltz, Hugo Menzel, Jr.

West Orange
Laves, Benjamin Samuel

Woodbridge
Lepelstat, Martin L.

NEW MEXICO

Albuquerque
Tomita, Susan K.

NEW YORK

Albany
Regal, Evan Charles

Bedford
Atkins, Ronald Raymond

Cortland
Taylor, Leland Baridon

Deer Park
Rolla, Mario F.

Eastchester
Katz, Kenneth Arthur

Garden City
Dent, Thomas Augustine

Huntington
Hochberg, Ronald Mark

Kew Gardens
Adler, David Neil

New York
Barasch, Mal Livingston
Bell, Jonathan Robert
Christensen, Henry, III
Crary, Miner Dunham, Jr.
DuLaux, Russell Frederick
Einstein, Steven Henry
Eisen, Edwin Roy
Engel, Ralph Manuel
Evans, Douglas Hayward
Finch, Edward Ridley, Jr.
Gelb, Judith Anne
Herbst, Abbe Ilene
Karan, Paul Richard
Karim, Yumi Yamada
Kavoukjian, Michael Edward
Klipstein, Robert Alan
Lawrence, Robert Cutting, III
Lesk, Ann Berger
Levitan, David M(aurice)
Lingelbach, Albert Lane
Lloyd, James Woodman
Mariani, Michael Matthew
Martin, Malcolm Elliot
Materna, Joseph Anthony
McGrath, Thomas J.
Norden, William Benjamin
Radin, Sam
Robinson, Barbara Paul
Rubinstein, Kenneth
Saufer, Isaac Aaron
Savage, Michael
Schlesinger, Sanford Joel
Valente, Peter Charles
Whoriskey, Robert Donald
Ziegler, Henry Steinway

Pearl River
Meyer, Irwin Stephan

Poughkeepsie
Haven, Milton M.

Richmond Hill
De, Meena Indrajit

Rochester
Buckley, Michael Francis
Harter, Ralph Millard Peter

Syracuse
Grizanti, Anthony J.
O'Connor, Michael E.

White Plains
Kurzman, Robert Graham

NORTH CAROLINA

Chapel Hill
Herman-Giddens, Gregory

Charlotte
Orsbon, Richard Anthony
Wood, William McBrayer

Winston Salem
Vaughn, Robert Candler, Jr.

OHIO

Cleveland
Brucken, Robert Matthew
Hochman, Kenneth George
Katcher, Richard
Monihan, Mary Elizabeth
Shumaker, Roger Lee

Columbus
Rowland, Ronald Lee

Dayton
Johnson, C. Terry

Fairborn
Wolaver, Stephen Arthur

OKLAHOMA

Oklahoma City
Towery, Curtis Keith

OREGON

Portland
Richardson, Campbell
Zalutsky, Morton Herman

PENNSYLVANIA

Allentown
Noonan, Charles Thomas

Berwyn
Watters, Edward McLain, III

Bryn Mawr
Frick, Benjamin Charles

Huntingdon Valley
Kaufman, David Joseph

Kennett Square
Temple, L. Peter

King Of Prussia
Schneider, Pam Horvitz

Media
Emerson, Sterling Jonathan

Philadelphia
Deming, Frank Stout
Frank, Barry H.
Kaier, Edward John
Lombard, John James, Jr.
Lucey, John David, Jr.

Pittsburgh
Daniel, Robert Michael
Phillips, Larry Edward

Reading
Linton, Jack Arthur

Stroudsburg
Upright, Kirby Grant

SOUTH CAROLINA

Charleston
Branham, C. Michael
Foley, Rion DuBose

Columbia
Todd, Albert Creswell, III

TENNESSEE

Knoxville
Bly, Robert Maurice

Nashville
Berry, William Wells
Little, Hampton Stennis, Jr.
Trautman, Herman Louis

TEXAS

Austin
Helman, Stephen Jody

Corpus Christi
Stukenberg, Michael Wesley

Dallas
Blanchette, James Grady, Jr.
Copley, Edward Alvin
Horwitz, Kenneth Merrill
Hughes, Vester Thomas, Jr.
Jenkins, John Richard, III
Kroney, Robert Harper
Owens, Rodney Joe
Phelps, Robert Frederick, Jr.
Smith, Frank Tupper
Willingham, Clark Suttles

Fort Worth
Willey, Stephen Douglas

Houston
Cenatiempo, Michael J.
Eastland, S. Stacy
Friedman, J. Kent
Jeske, Charles Matthew
Koenig, Rodney Curtis
Osterberg, Edward Charles, Jr.
Schwartzel, Charles Boone
Shearer, Dean Paul
Wharton, Thomas H(eard), Jr.

San Antonio
Bayern, Arthur Herbert
Netemeyer, Margaret

UTAH

Salt Lake City
Adams, Joseph Keith

VIRGINIA

Alexandria
McClure, Roger John
Paturis, E(mmanuel) Michael

Charlottesville
Edwards, James Edwin

Mc Lean
Aucutt, Ronald David

Richmond
Belcher, Dennis Irl
Horsley, Waller Holladay
Warthen, Harry Justice, III

WASHINGTON

Bellevue
Treacy, Gerald Bernard, Jr.

Olympia
Walker, Francis Joseph

Seattle
Gores, Thomas C.

WISCONSIN

Madison
Nora, Wendy Alison

Milwaukee
McGaffey, Jere D.
Wynn, Stanford Alan

Wauwatosa
Alexander, Robert Gardner

WYOMING

Cody
Stradley, Richard Lee

ENGLAND

London
Simon, M. Daniel

GERMANY

Dusseldorf
Clev, Heinrich

REPUBLIC OF KOREA

Seoul
Woo, Chang Rok

SOUTH AFRICA

Johannesburg
Schwarz, Harry Heinz

ADDRESS UNPUBLISHED

Buechel, William Benjamin
Engelhardt, John Hugo
Green, Marshall Munro
James, Joyce Marie
Kahan, Rochelle Liebling
Keller, Thomas Clements
Merrill, Abel Jay
Reiche, Frank Perley
Schacht, Ronald Stuart
Solberg, Thomas Allan
Sweeney, Deidre Ann
Turner, George Mason
Weill, (Lige) Harry, Sr.
Willis, Russell Anthony, III

TAXATION, GENERAL

UNITED STATES

ARIZONA

Phoenix
Case, David Leon
McRae, Hamilton Eugene, III

Scottsdale
Case, Stephen Shevlin

Yuma
Hunt, Gerald Wallace

ARKANSAS

Little Rock
Bohannon, Charles Tad
Catlett, S. Graham
Haley, John Harvey

CALIFORNIA

Burbank
Husband, Bertram Paul

Fresno
Sherr, Morris Max

La Jolla
Shannahan, William Paul

Los Angeles
Argue, John Clifford
Basile, Paul Louis, Jr.
Wasserman, William Phillip

Modesto
Schrimp, Roger Martin

Newport Beach
Matsen, Jeffrey Robert

North Hollywood
Kreger, Melvin Joseph

San Diego
Dorne, David J.
Guinn, Stanley Willis

San Francisco
Foster, David Scott
Freud, Nicholas S.
Maier, Peter Klaus

San Rafael
Bloomfield, Neil Jon

Santa Barbara
Egenolf, Robert F.

COLORADO

Colorado Springs
Everson, Steven Lee

Denver
Crow, Nancy Rebecca
Rich, Robert Stephen

Englewood
Coffee, Melvin Arnold

CONNECTICUT

Hartford
Del Negro, John Thomas

Westport
Carr, Cynthia

DELAWARE

Wilmington
Baumann, Julian Henry, Jr.
Grossman, Jerome Kent
Tigani, Bruce William

DISTRICT OF COLUMBIA

Washington
Barrie, John Paul
Chapoton, John Edgar
Collinson, Dale Stanley
Davidson, Daniel Morton
Feldhaus, Stephen Martin
Geske, Alvin Jay
Kyhos, Thomas Flynn
Mann, Donegan
Morgan, Daniel Louis
Oliphant, Charles Frederick, III
Pomeroy, Harlan
Shay-Byrne, Olivia
Stevens, Herbert Francis
Watkins, Charles Morgan
Wellen, Robert Howard

FLORIDA

Fort Lauderdale
Hoines, David Alan
Katz, Thomas Owen

Fort Myers
Terry, T(aylor) Rankin, Jr.

Lakeland
Koren, Edward Franz

Miami
Chabrow, Penn Benjamin
Simmons, Sherwin Palmer

Orlando
Capouano, Albert D.

Tallahassee
Phipps, Benjamin Kimball, II

Tampa
Barton, Bernard Alan, Jr.
Doliner, Nathaniel Lee
Levine, Jack Anton
O'Neill, Albert Clarence, Jr.

West Palm Beach
Chopin, L. Frank
Lampert, Michael Allen
Zeller, Ronald John

GEORGIA

Atlanta
Durrett, James Frazer, Jr.
Hoffman, Michael William
Lamon, Harry Vincent, Jr.
Thrower, Randolph William

HAWAII

Honolulu
Heller, Ronald Ian

IDAHO

Boise
Green, Cumer L.

ILLINOIS

Chicago
Banoff, Sheldon Irwin
Chin, Davis
Conlon, Steven Denis
Craven, George W.
Cunningham, Robert James
Felsenthal, Steven Altus
Kanter, Burton Wallace
Kolmin, Kenneth Guy
Masters, Paul Holmes
Silets, Harvey Marvin
Von Mandel, Michael Jacques
Winkler, Charles Howard

Lake Forest
Palmer, Ann Therese Darin

Oak Park
Schubert, Blake H.

Peoria
Elias, John Samuel

INDIANA

Indianapolis
Hetzner, Marc A.
Kappes, Philip Spangler

IOWA

Des Moines
Campbell, Bruce Irving

Muscatine
Nepple, James Anthony

KANSAS

Onaga
Stallard, Wayne Minor

Wichita
Sorensen, Harvey R.

KENTUCKY

Lexington
Bagby, William Rardin

Louisville
Luber, Thomas J(ulian)

LOUISIANA

Monroe
Curry, Robert Lee, III

New Orleans
Abbott, Hirschel Theron, Jr.
Hearn, Sharon Sklamba
McDaniel, Donald Hamilton
Nuzum, Robert Weston

MAINE

Portland
Friedrich, Craig William
Hunt, David Evans

MARYLAND

Westminster
Staples, Lyle Newton

MASSACHUSETTS

Boston
Hines, Edward Francis, Jr.
Metzer, Patricia Ann
Page, George Alfred, Jr.
Ritt, Roger Merrill
Solet, Maxwell David

Cambridge
Connors, Frank Joseph
Downey, Richard Ralph

Framingham
Heng, Gerald C. W.

Newburyport
Maslen, David Peter

MICHIGAN

Ann Arbor
Keppelman, Nancy

Birmingham
Sweeney, Thomas Frederick

Bloomfield Hills
Kasischke, Louis Walter

Solomon, Mark Raymond

Detroit
Deron, Edward Michael
Rasmussen, Douglas John

Grand Rapids
Oetting, Roger H.

Grosse Pointe
Goss, James William

Troy
Dillon, Joseph Francis

MINNESOTA

Minneapolis
Klein, William David

MISSISSIPPI

Jackson
Black, D(eWitt) Carl(isle), Jr.
Hammond, Frank Jefferson, III

MISSOURI

Chesterfield
Fagerberg, Roger Richard

Kansas City
Bartunek, Robert R(ichard), Jr.
Egan, Charles Joseph, Jr.
Gorman, Gerald Warner

NEW HAMPSHIRE

Portsmouth
Harman, Terrie

NEW JERSEY

Chester
Pfaffenroth, Peter Albert

Florham Park
Witman, Leonard Joel

Hackensack
Deener, Jerome Alan
Mullin, Patrick Allen

Jersey City
Feder, Arthur A.

Morristown
Fishman, Richard Glenn
Sweeney, John Lawrence

New Brunswick
Shirtz, Joseph Frank

Newark
Costenbader, Charles Michael
Levin, Simon
Vajtay, Stephen Michael, Jr.
Zuckerman, Herbert Lawrence

South Orange
Delo, Ellen Sanderson

West Orange
Richmond, Harold Nicholas

NEW MEXICO

Albuquerque
Hoffman, Patrick Andrew
Loubet, Jeffrey W.

Santa Fe
Hickey, John Miller

NEW YORK

Albany
Teitelbaum, Steven Usher

Binghamton
Peckham, Eugene Eliot

New York
Aidinoff, M(erton) Bernard
Black, Louis Engleman
Brecher, Howard Arthur
Caulfield, Jerome Joseph
Clark, Celia Rue
Cubitto, Robert J.
Dlugoff, Marc Alan
Fass, Peter Michael
Ferguson, Milton Carr, Jr.
Fink, Robert Steven
Finkelstein, Stuart M.
Ganz, Marc David
Gifford, William C.
Hirschfeld, Michael
Kail, Kenneth Stoner
Kolbe, Karl William, Jr.
Kurtz, Jerome
Loengard, Richard Otto, Jr.
MacLean, Babcock
Moore, Thomas Ronald (Lord
  Bridestowe)
Phillips, Barnet, IV
Posner, Louis Joseph
Rooney, Paul C., Jr.
Rosen, Matthew A.
Seigel, Stuart Evan
Serota, Susan Perlstadt
Shorter, James Russell, Jr.
Smith, Morton Alan
Solomon, Andrew P.

Thompson, Loran Tyson
Van Nuys, Peter
White, Harry Edward, Jr.
Whoriskey, Robert Donald
Youngwood, Alfred Donald

Pearl River
Meyer, Irwin Stephan

Purchase
Lalli, Michael Anthony

Rochester
Colby, William Michael
Kraus, Sherry Stokes
Twietmeyer, Don Henry
Wild, Robert Warren

Scarsdale
Liegl, Joseph Leslie

Syracuse
Wladis, Mark Neil

White Plains
Berlin, Alan Daniel
Greenspan, Leon Joseph

NORTH CAROLINA

Asheville
Hamilton, Jackson Douglas
Lavelle, Brian Francis David

Charlotte
Preston, James Young
Thigpen, Richard Elton, Jr.

Raleigh
Simpson, Steven Drexell

Tabor City
Jorgensen, Ralph Gubler

NORTH DAKOTA

Grand Forks
Cilz, Douglas Arthur

OHIO

Cincinnati
Flanagan, John Anthony
Frank, William Nelson
Neumark, Michael Harry
Porter, Robert Carl, Jr.
Ryan, James Joseph

Cleveland
Callahan, Thomas James
Currivan, John Daniel
Doris, Alan S(anford)
Horvitz, Michael John
Ollinger, W. James
Shore, Michael Allan
Sogg, Wilton Sherman

Dayton
Hitter, Joseph Ira

Wooster
Moore, Arthur William

Youngstown
Matune, Frank Joseph

OKLAHOMA

Enid
Jones, Stephen

Oklahoma City
Mock, Randall Don

Tulsa
Moffett, J. Denny

OREGON

Portland
Burt, Robert Gene
Froebe, Gerald Allen
Hanna, Harry Mitchell

PENNSYLVANIA

Bala Cynwyd
Odell, Herbert

Exton
Teti, Louis N.

Philadelphia
Brier, Bonnie Susan
Chimples, George
Cooper, Wendy Fein
Frank, Barry H.
Goldman, Jerry Stephen
Horn Epstein, Phyllis Lynn
Kopp, Charles Gilbert
Lichtenstein, Robert Jay
Strasbaugh, Wayne Ralph
Wiener, Ronald Martin
Wolff, Deborah H(orowitz)

Pittsburgh
Boocock, Stephen William
Geeseman, Robert George
Hitt, Leo N.
Ummer, James Walter

Pottsville
Jones, Joseph Hayward

Uniontown
Coldren, Ira Burdette, Jr.

Wormleysburg
Cherewka, Michael

York
Perry, Ronald

RHODE ISLAND

Warwick
Goldman, Steven Jason

SOUTH CAROLINA

Charleston
Foley, Rion DuBose

Greenville
Dobson, Robert Albertus, III

TENNESSEE

Chattanooga
Jessup, William Eugene

Knoxville
Gentry, Mack A.

Memphis
Bland, James Theodore, Jr.

Nashville
Trautman, Herman Louis

Oak Ridge
Wilkinson, Robert Warren

TEXAS

Austin
Janes, Brandon Chaison
Wood, Donald F.

Corpus Christi
Stukenberg, Michael Wesley

Dallas
Brewer, David Madison
Gerberding Cowart, Greta Elaine
Henkel, Kathryn Gundy
Horwitz, Kenneth Merrill
Jenkins, John Richard, III
Nolan, John Michael
Owens, Rodney Joe
Sinak, David Louis
Wilson, Claude Raymond, Jr.

Fort Worth
Tracy, J. David

Houston
Allender, John Roland
Grossberg, Marc Elias
Hull, Robert Joe
Osterberg, Edward Charles, Jr.
Sheinfeld, Myron M.
Touchy, Deborah K.P.
Wells, Benjamin Gladney

San Antonio
Brennan, James Patrick, Sr.
Cruse, Rex Beach, Jr.

Waco
Page, Jack Randall

UTAH

Salt Lake City
Turner, Shawn Dennis

VIRGINIA

Arlington
Glazier, Jonathan Hemenway

Mc Lean
Aucutt, Ronald David
Susko, Carol Lynne

Richmond
Addison, David Dunham
Denny, Collins, III
Starke, Harold E., Jr.

WASHINGTON

Seattle
Judson, C(harles) James (Jim Judson)

Yakima
Wright, J(ames) Lawrence

WISCONSIN

Middleton
Berman, Ronald Charles

TERRITORIES OF THE UNITED STATES

PUERTO RICO

San Juan
Rodriguez-Diaz, Juan E.

MEXICO

Mexico City
Ahumada, Ricardo

ENGLAND

London
Aleksander, Nicholas P.

FRANCE

Neuilly sur Seine
Raffin, Marie-Hélène J.

Paris
Derouin, Philippe

GERMANY

Dusseldorf
Palenberg, Hans-Peter

Frankfurt
Haarmann, Wilhelm

Munich, Bavaria
Schaefer, Karl P.

ITALY

Milan
Plankensteiner, Marco

NIGERIA

Victoria Island
Nwasike, Ndi Chuks

NORWAY

Vika
Ravnaas, Ernst

PORTUGAL

Lisbon
Calmeiros, Jose Maria Albuquerque
Cid, Tiago

SOUTH AFRICA

Johannesburg
Franck, Brigitte Broderick

SPAIN

Barcelona
Martí, Miguel Torrents

SWEDEN

Uppsala
Stenmark, Anna Romell

THAILAND

Bangkok
Dhanasarnsombat, Prapaipan

UKRAINE

Kyiv
Grushko, Pavel Gregory

ADDRESS UNPUBLISHED

Comisky, Ian Michael
Davis, Clarence Clinton, Jr.
Freund, Samuel J.
Harmon, Gail McGreevy
Houle, Jeffrey Robert
Keller, Thomas Clements
Kerner, Michael Philip
Levy, David
Lipsman, Richard Marc
Meyer, Max Earl
Peterson, Howard Cooper
Rodriguez, Vivian N.
Russ, Neil Andrew
Sliger, Herbert Jacquemin, Jr.
Torgerson, Larry Keith

TAXATION, PERSONAL INCOME

UNITED STATES

ALABAMA

Montgomery
Proctor, David Ray

ARIZONA

Phoenix
Everett, James Joseph

Tucson
Adamson, Larry Robertson

CALIFORNIA

Costa Mesa
Schaaf, Douglas Allan

Larkspur
Greenberg, Myron Silver

Los Angeles
Gipson, Robert Edgar
Gordon, David Eliot
Palazzo, Robert Paul
Presant, Sanford Calvin
Rath, Howard Grant, Jr.

Newport Beach
Schumacher, Stephen Joseph

Palo Alto
Miller, Michael Patiky

San Diego
Riley, Kirk Holden

San Francisco
Caspersen, R(alph) Frederick
Heng, Donald James, Jr.
Thomas, William Scott
Wood, Robert Warren

Santa Barbara
Howell, Weldon Ulric, Jr.

Walnut Creek
Willson, Prentiss, Jr.

COLORADO

Colorado Springs
Everson, Steven Lee

Denver
Ruppert, John Lawrence

Parker
Greenberg, Morton Paul

CONNECTICUT

Darien
Dale, Erwin Randolph

Hartford
Appel, Robert Eugene
Lyon, James Burroughs

Westport
Grodd, Leslie Eric
Sheiman, Ronald Lee

DELAWARE

Wilmington
Baumann, Julian Henry, Jr.

DISTRICT OF COLUMBIA

Washington
Chapoton, John Edgar
Davidson, Daniel Morton
Evans, Donald Charles, Jr.
Heffernan, James Vincent
Jacobson, David Edward
Kautter, David John
Paul, William McCann
Sherman, Gerald Howard

FLORIDA

Fort Lauderdale
Barnard, George Smith
Levitt, Preston Curtis

Lake Wales
Wales, Gwynne Huntington

Longwood
Tomasulo, Virginia Merrills

Miami
Ruffner, Charles Louis
Weinstein, Andrew H.

Oldsmar
Hirschman, Sherman Joseph

Tampa
Levine, Jack Anton

West Palm Beach
Chopin, L. Frank

GEORGIA

Atlanta
Cohen, N. Jerold

ILLINOIS

Chicago
Banoff, Sheldon Irwin
Berning, Larry D.

Block, Neal Jay
Brown, Steven Spencer
Chandler, Kent, Jr.
Dubbs, John William, III
Ellwood, Scott
Fellows, Jerry Kenneth
Lipton, Richard M.
Lutter, Paul Allen
McKenzie, Robert Ernest
Michalak, Edward Francis
Pape, Glenn Michael
Stanhaus, James Steven
Swibel, Steven Warren
Trio, Edward Alan
Von Mandel, Michael Jacques

INDIANA

Indianapolis
Jewell, George Benson
Ponder, Lester McConnico

IOWA

Garner
Hovda, Theodore James

Mason City
Heiny, James Ray

MARYLAND

Lutherville Timonium
Freeland, Charles

Rockville
De Jong, David Samuel

MASSACHUSETTS

Andover
McDaniel, Paul R.

Boston
Elfman, Eric Michael
Fremont-Smith, Marion R.
Mooney, Michael Edward
Ritt, Roger Merrill

Cambridge
Downey, Richard Ralph

Stoughton
Gabovitch, Steven Alan

Worcester
Whipple, Robert Jenks

MICHIGAN

Grand Rapids
Oetting, Roger H.

Livonia
Fried, William C.

Saint Clair Shores
Joslyn, Robert Bruce

Southfield
Kaplow, Robert David

MINNESOTA

Edina
Brooks, William James, III

Minneapolis
Ventres, Judith Martin

Saint Paul
Geis, Jerome Arthur

MONTANA

Havre
Moog, Mary Ann Pimley

NEVADA

Las Vegas
Hagendorf, Stanley

NEW JERSEY

Atlantic Highlands
Marshall, Anthony Parr

Cherry Hill
Liebman, Emmanuel

Princeton
Beidler, Marsha Wolf
Gorrin, Eugene

NEW YORK

Albany
Koff, Howard Michael

Eastchester
Katz, Kenneth Arthur

New York
Agranoff, Gerald Neal
Amdur, Martin Bennett
Caulfield, Jerome Joseph

Christensen, Henry, III
Einstein, Steven Henry
Heitner, Kenneth Howard
Hirschfeld, Michael
Jassy, Everett Lewis
Kahn, Alan Edwin
Kail, Kenneth Stoner
Kalish, Arthur
Koch, Edward Richard
Kurtz, Jerome
Levy, Mark Allan
Lipsky, Burton G.
Macan, William Alexander, IV
MacLean, Babcock
Miller, Arthur Madden
Miller, William Harlowe, Jr.
Nicholls, Richard H.
Paul, Herbert Morton
Phillips, Barnet, IV
Rosen, Matthew A.
Rosow, Stuart L.
Savage, Michael
Scala, James Robert
Shea, James William
Shorter, James Russell, Jr.
Silvers, Eileen S.
Small, Jonathan Andrew
White, Harry Edward, Jr.
Youngwood, Alfred Donald

Pearl River
Meyer, Irwin Stephan

Rochester
Kraus, Sherry Stokes

NORTH CAROLINA

Winston Salem
Osborn, Malcolm Everett

OHIO

Cincinnati
Carroll, James Joseph
Nechemias, Stephen Murray

Cleveland
Callahan, Thomas James
Doris, Alan S(anford)
Leavitt, Jeffrey Stuart
Perris, Terrence George
Toomajian, William Martin

Columbus
Kusma, Kyllikki
Rowland, Ronald Lee

OKLAHOMA

Tulsa
Hatfield, Jack Kenton

OREGON

Lake Oswego
Kuntz, Joel Dubois

Portland
Grossmann, Ronald Stanyer

PENNSYLVANIA

Bala Cynwyd
Odell, Herbert

Berwyn
Watters, Edward McLain, III

Philadelphia
Elliott, Homer Lee
Thomas, Lowell Shumway, Jr.
Whitman, Jules Isidoré
Wiener, Ronald Martin

Pittsburgh
Phillips, Larry Edward
Prosperi, Louis Anthony

Spring House
Rosoff, William A.

RHODE ISLAND

Providence
Olsen, Hans Peter
Reilly, Charles James
Silver, Paul Allen

TENNESSEE

Memphis
Cook, August Joseph

TEXAS

Dallas
Berry, Buford Preston
Copley, Edward Alvin
Hughes, Vester Thomas, Jr.
Pingree, Bruce Douglas
Reid, Rust Endicott
Sinak, David Louis
Willingham, Clark Suttles
Wilson, Claude Raymond, Jr.

Electra
Hayers, Paul Hugh

Houston
Blackshear, A.T., Jr.
Connelly, George William

Disher, David Alan
Estes, Carl Lewis, II
Grossberg, Marc Elias
Stewart, Pamela L.
Wheelan, R(ichelieu) E(dward)

Richardson
Conkel, Robert Dale

San Antonio
Ross, James Ulric

Spring
Hendricks, Randal Arlan

Waco
Ressler, Parke E(dward)

VIRGINIA

Charlottesville
Kudravetz, David Waller

WASHINGTON

Seattle
Birmingham, Richard Joseph

WISCONSIN

Hales Corners
Case, Karen Ann

Milwaukee
Meldman, Robert Edward

ENGLAND

London
Hinshaw, David Love
Langer, Marshall J.

THAILAND

Bangkok
Dhanasarnsombat, Prapaipan

ADDRESS UNPUBLISHED

Assael, Michael
Bost, Thomas Glen
Freund, Samuel J.
Handler, Harold Robert
Marinis, Thomas Paul, Jr.
Schacht, Ronald Stuart
Shook, Ann Jones
Weisman, Paul Howard
Westphal, Marjorie Lord

TAXATION, STATE AND LOCAL

UNITED STATES

ALABAMA

Montgomery
Gregory, William Stanley
Proctor, David Ray

ARIZONA

Phoenix
Le Clair, Douglas Marvin

CALIFORNIA

Irvine
Goldstein, Michael Gerald

Los Angeles
Polley, Terry Lee

Sacramento
Micheli, Christopher Michael

San Francisco
Spiegel, Hart Hunter
Thomas, William Scott

Walnut Creek
Willson, Prentiss, Jr.

COLORADO

Denver
McLain, William Allen

Englewood
Coffee, Melvin Arnold

CONNECTICUT

Hartford
Berall, Frank Stewart
Coyle, Michael Lee
Lyon, James Burroughs

DISTRICT OF COLUMBIA

Washington
Barrie, John Paul
Halvorson, Newman Thorbus, Jr.
Oyler, Gregory Kenneth

FLORIDA

Fort Lauderdale
Stankee, Glen Allen

Jacksonville
McWilliams, John Lawrence, III

Miami
Korchin, Judith Miriam
Ruffner, Charles Louis

Orlando
Spoonhour, James Michael

Tallahassee
Barnett, Martha Walters
Phipps, Benjamin Kimball, II

Tampa
Barton, Bernard Alan, Jr.

GEORGIA

Atlanta
Hoffman, Michael William

Savannah
Friedman, Julian Richard

HAWAII

Honolulu
Heller, Ronald Ian

ILLINOIS

Belleville
Parham, James Robert

Chicago
Lipton, Richard M.
Montgomery, Julie-April
O'Keefe, Kevin Michael
Palmer, John Bernard, III
Peterson, Ronald Roger

Rockford
Rudy, Elmer Clyde

INDIANA

Indianapolis
Paul, Stephen Howard

KANSAS

Topeka
Horttor, Donald J.

KENTUCKY

Louisville
Luber, Thomas J(ulian)

LOUISIANA

Lafayette
Myers, Stephen Hawley

New Orleans
Nuzum, Robert Weston

MARYLAND

Towson
Proctor, Kenneth Donald

MASSACHUSETTS

Boston
Hines, Edward Francis, Jr.
Preston, Jerome, Jr.
Solet, Maxwell David

Wellesley
Fuller, Robert L(eander)

MICHIGAN

Detroit
McKim, Samuel John, III

MINNESOTA

Bayport
Bernick, Alan E.

Saint Paul
Geis, Jerome Arthur

MISSISSIPPI

Jackson
Johnson, Mark Wayne

MISSOURI

Jefferson City
Deutsch, James Bernard

Kansas City
Howes, Brian Thomas

MONTANA

Billings
Sites, James Philip

NEVADA

Las Vegas
Wilson, Joseph Morris, III

NEW JERSEY

Newark
Costenbader, Charles Michael
Levin, Simon
Zuckerman, Herbert Lawrence

Teaneck
Rosenblum, Edward G.

NEW MEXICO

Albuquerque
Buchanan, Deena Lynna
Loubet, Jeffrey W.

NEW YORK

Albany
Koff, Howard Michael
Teitelbaum, Steven Usher

East Meadow
Hyman, Montague Allan

Mineola
Santemma, Jon Noel

New York
Agranoff, Gerald Neal
Block, William Kenneth
Dessen, Stanley Benjamin
Goldstein, M. Robert
Koch, Edward Richard
Shea, James William
Zucker, Howard

NORTH CAROLINA

Charlotte
Thigpen, Richard Elton, Jr.

OHIO

Cincinnati
Nechemias, Stephen Murray

Cleveland
Kramer, Eugene Leo

Dayton
Hitter, Joseph Ira

Youngstown
Matune, Frank Joseph

OKLAHOMA

Oklahoma City
Legg, William Jefferson

OREGON

Coquille
Lounsbury, Steven Richard

Lake Oswego
Nelson, Thomas Howard

PENNSYLVANIA

Pittsburgh
Boocock, Stephen William
Prosperi, Louis Anthony

RHODE ISLAND

Providence
Olsen, Hans Peter
Reilly, Charles James

TEXAS

Austin
Cunningham, Judy Marie
Harrison, Richard Wayne
Janes, Brandon Chaison

Dallas
Bonesio, Woodrow Michael
Wilson, Claude Raymond, Jr.

Fort Worth
Wagner, Andrew Porter

Houston
Hull, Robert Joe
Seymour, Barbara Laverne
Van Kerrebrook, Mary Alice
Wall, Kenneth E., Jr.

San Angelo
Carter, James Alfred

VIRGINIA

Hampton
McNider, James Small, III

Mc Lean
Susko, Carol Lynne

WASHINGTON

Seattle
Hilpert, Edward Theodore, Jr.
Judson, C(harles) James (Jim Judson)

WISCONSIN

Waukesha
Macy, John Patrick

ADDRESS UNPUBLISHED

Bost, Thomas Glen
Drabkin, Murray
Freund, Samuel J.
Harnack, Don Steger
Keller, Thomas Clements

TOXIC TORT

UNITED STATES

ALABAMA

Birmingham
Palmer, Robert Leslie

CALIFORNIA

Fresno
Runyon, Brett L.

Irvine
Suojanen, Wayne William

Moraga
Kilbourne, George William

Oakland
Mendelson, Steven Earle

San Francisco
Fergus, Gary Scott

DISTRICT OF COLUMBIA

Washington
Renner, Curtis Shotwell
Watson, Thomas C.

GEORGIA

Atlanta
Denham, Vernon Robert, Jr.

ILLINOIS

Chicago
Matushek, Edward J., III
Schoenfield, Rick Merrill

Riverwoods
Ford, Michael W.

LOUISIANA

Baton Rouge
Brady, Scott Earl

Lake Charles
Parkerson, Hardy Martell

Shreveport
Politz, Nyle Anthony

MARYLAND

Annapolis
Klein, Robert Dale

Baltimore
Sack, Sylvan Hanan

MASSACHUSETTS

Salem
Wasserman, Stephen Alan

MINNESOTA

Minneapolis
Faricy, John Hartnett, Jr.

MISSOURI

Kansas City
Beck, William G.
Koelling, Thomas Winsor

Saint Louis
Reeg, Kurtis Bradford

NEW YORK

New York
Birnbaum, Sheila L.
Riley, Scott C.
Schwartz, Steven T.

NORTH CAROLINA

Winston Salem
Maready, William Frank

PENNSYLVANIA

Philadelphia
Fickler, Arlene
Lipson, Heather Joy
Madva, Stephen Alan

Pittsburgh
Tarasi, Louis Michael, Jr.

Washington
Richman, Stephen I.

TEXAS

Houston
Edwards, Blaine Douglass
O'Brien, Eva Fromm
Roven, John David

Waco
Cherry, David Earl

VIRGINIA

Norfolk
Bishop, Bruce Taylor

Richmond
King, William H., Jr.

WEST VIRGINIA

Huntington
Bagley, Charles Frank, III

ENGLAND

London
Mendelowitz, Michael Sydney

ADDRESS UNPUBLISHED

Kiehnhoff, Thomas Nave
Manning, Cory E.

TRADEMARK AND COPYRIGHT

UNITED STATES

ARIZONA

Phoenix
Meschkow, Jordan M.
Phillips, James Harold
Sutton, Samuel J.
Ullman, James A.

CALIFORNIA

Beverly Hills
Fleer, Keith George
Heinke, Rex S.

Claremont
Ansell, Edward Orin

Emeryville
Blackburn, Robert Parker

Irvine
Stone, Samuel Beckner
Weissenberger, Harry George

La Jolla
Karlen, Peter Hurd

Larkspur
Burke, Robert Thomas

Los Angeles
Bailey, Craig Bernard
Braun, David A(dlai)

Green, William Porter
Klein, Henry

Newport Beach
Knobbe, Louis Joseph
Martens, Don Walter

Palm Springs
Harris, Michael David

Palo Alto
Hinckley, Robert Craig
Nycum, Susan Hubbell
Pasahow, Lynn H(arold)
Phillips, W. Alan

Sacramento
Houpt, James Edward

San Francisco
Smegal, Thomas Frank, Jr.

San Jose
Goldstein, Robin
Simon, James Lowell

Santa Ana
Lane, Dominick V.

Santa Clara
Zahrt, William Dietrich, II

Seal Beach
Hennen, Thomas Waldo

Stevenson Ranch
Bovasso, Louis Joseph

COLORADO

Colorado Springs
Kubida, William Joseph

Denver
Carson, William Scott
Dorr, Robert Charles
Samuels, Donald L.

Fort Collins
Fromm, Jeffery Bernard

CONNECTICUT

Monroe
Oliver, Milton McKinnon

Westport
Razzano, Pasquale Angelo

DELAWARE

Wilmington
Huntley, Donald Wayne

DISTRICT OF COLUMBIA

Washington
Berman, Paul Justin
Browne, Richard Cullen
Cantor, Herbert I.
Cooper, Alan Samuel
Gastfreund, Irving
Goodman, Alfred Nelson
Hefter, Laurence Roy
Hobbs, J. Timothy, Sr.
Holman, John Clarke
Kramm, Deborah Lucille
Lublinski, Michael
Marks, Richard Daniel
McCann, Clifton Everett
Potenza, Joseph Michael
Price, Donald Douglas
Price, Griffith Baley, Jr.
Repper, George Robert
Schwaab, Richard Lewis
Sokal, Allen Marcel
Spencer, George Henry
Timberg, Sigmund

FLORIDA

Miami
Roman, Ronald Peter
Schiffrin, Michael Edward

Orlando
Blaher, Neal Jonathan

Sarasota
Partoyan, Garo Arakel

GEORGIA

Atlanta
Marianes, William Byron
Schroeder, Eric Peter

Norcross
Anderson, Albert Sydney, III

Valdosta
Sinnott, John Patrick

ILLINOIS

Barrington
Lee, William Marshall

Chicago
Adducci, James Dominick
Altman, Louis
Amend, James Michael

Berenzweig, Jack Charles
Boehnen, Daniel A.
Flannery, John Francis
Geren, Gerald S.
Hannay, William Mouat, III
Hilliard, David Craig
Jacover, Jerold Alan
Kozak, John W.
Krupka, Robert George
Lloyd, Robert Allen
Maher, David Willard
Partridge, Mark Van Buren
Pattishall, Beverly Wyckliffe
Rauner, Vincent Joseph
Roper, Harry Joseph
Ropski, Gary Melchior
Schlitter, Stanley Allen
Schneider, Robert Jerome
Schur, Gerald
Scudder, Theodore Townsend, III
Sheppard, Berton Scott
Sternstein, Allan J.
Vittum, Daniel Weeks, Jr.
Wanke, Ronald Lee
Wick, Lawrence Scott

Deerfield
Birmingham, William Joseph
Scott, Theodore R.

Lansing
Hill, Philip

Libertyville
Fato, Gildo E.

Northbrook
Sernett, Richard Patrick

Skokie
Gotkin, Michael Stanley

INDIANA

Indianapolis
Cole, Roland Jay
Emhardt, Charles David

Merrillville
Kinney, Richard Gordon

KANSAS

Olathe
Scott, Robert Gene

MARYLAND

Baltimore
Hopps, Raymond, Jr.

Potomac
Troffkin, Howard Julian

MASSACHUSETTS

Boston
Hemnes, Thomas Michael Sheridan
Hieken, Charles
Kaler, Robert Joseph
Lambert, Gary Ervery
Neuner, George William
Weaver, Paul David

Braintree
Paglierani, Ronald Joseph

Brookline
Bursley, Kathleen A.

Framingham
Kriegsman, Edward Michael

Lexington
Dulchinos, Peter
Glovsky, Susan G. L.

Watertown
Karaian, Norma Maksoodian

MICHIGAN

Bloomfield Hills
Rader, Ralph Terrance

Detroit
Rohm, Benita Jill

Grand Rapids
Litton, Randall Gale
Smith, H(arold) Lawrence

Southfield
Taravella, Christopher Anthony

Troy
Cantor, Bernard Jack

MINNESOTA

Eden Prairie
Friederichs, Norman Paul

Minneapolis
Kamrath, Alan Dale
Lofstrom, Mark D.
Sawicki, Zbigniew Peter
Street, Erica Catherine

MISSOURI

Kansas City
Milton, Chad Earl

Saint Louis
Evans, Lawrence E.
Forsman, Alpheus Edwin
Gilster, Peter Stuart
Moore, McPherson Dorsett

MONTANA

Bozeman
Conover, Richard Corrill
Wylie, Paul Richter, Jr.

NEVADA

Reno
Ryan, Robert Collins

NEW HAMPSHIRE

Concord
Rines, Robert Harvey

Hanover
Gardner, Peter Jaglom

NEW JERSEY

Edgewater
Virelli, Louis James, Jr.

Madison
Huettner, Richard Alfred

Morristown
Schwartz, Howard J.
Whitmer, Frederick Lee

New Brunswick
Biribauer, Richard Frank

Newark
Cahn, Jeffrey Barton

Princeton
Plevy, Arthur L.

Red Bank
Michaelson, Peter Lee

Summit
Saffer, Judith Mack

NEW YORK

Brooklyn
Rubenstein, Allen Ira

Croton On Hudson
Hoffman, Paul Shafer

Huntington
Robinson, Kenneth Patrick

Larchmont
Pelton, Russell Gilbert

New York
Abelman, Arthur F.
Baechtold, Robert Louis
Bernstein, Robert Jay
Borchard, William Marshall
Bosses, Stevan J.
Burstein, Neil Alan
Celedonia, Baila Handelman
Cohen, Myron
Colfin, Bruce Elliott
Creel, Thomas Leonard
Curtis, Frank R.
DeBaets, Timothy Joseph
Dunne, Gerard Francis
Einhorn, David Allen
Epstein, Michael Alan
Faber, Robert Charles
Fitzpatrick, Joseph Mark
Fletcher, Anthony L.
Genova, Joseph Steven
Goldberg, David
Hamburg, Charles Bruce
Horwitz, Ethan
Jacobs, Hara Kay
Jacobson, Jeffrey E.
Jordan, Frank J.
Kalow, David Arthur
Kane, Siegrun Dinklage
Kobak, James Benedict, Jr.
Kurnit, Richard Alan
Landron, Michel John
Lee, Jerome G.
Lerner, Max Kasner
Malkin, Michael M.
Martone, Patricia Ann
Most, Jack Lawrence
Moy, Mary Anastasia
Nearing, Vivienne W.
Neuner, Robert
Pegram, John Braxton
Pfeffer, David H.
Plevan, Kenneth A.
Plottel, Roland
Price, Robert
Reilly, John Albert
Reiner, John Paul
Rogers, Laurence Steven
Rosenfeld, Steven B.
Sacks, Ira Stephen
Schlain, Barbara Ellen
Smith, Robert Blakeman
Squire, Walter Charles
Stathis, Nicholas John
Steuer, Richard Marc
Udell, Richard
Vassil, John Charles
Woods, Christopher John
Zissu, Roger L.
Zivin, Norman H.

Oneida
Rudnick, Marvin Jack

Purchase
Joyce, Joseph James
Lyons, Gary George

Troy
Netter, Miriam Maccoby

OHIO

Akron
Kreek, Louis Francis, Jr.

Cleveland
Burge, David Alan
Crehore, Charles Aaron
Fisher, Thomas Edward

Columbus
Gall, John R.

Cuyahoga Falls
Jones, John Frank

Dayton
Nauman, Joseph George

OREGON

Gleneden Beach
Arant, Eugene Wesley

PENNSYLVANIA

Allentown
Simmons, James Charles

Bala Cynwyd
Chovanes, Eugene

Moon Township
Alstadt, Lynn Jeffery

Newtown
Simkanich, John Joseph

Philadelphia
Beam, Robert Charles
Dorfman, John Charles
Quinn, Charles Norman
Seidel, Arthur Harris

Pittsburgh
Baldauf, Kent Edward
Beck, Paul Augustine
Blenko, Walter John, Jr.
Colen, Frederick Haas
Schwab, Arthur James
Silverman, Arnold Barry

Southeastern
Husick, Lawrence Alan

SOUTH CAROLINA

Charleston
Barker, Douglas Alan

TEXAS

Addison
Hranitzky, Rachel Robyn

Dallas
Frisbie, Curtis Lynn, Jr.
McGowan, Patrick Francis
Moore, Stanley Ray
Price, John Aley
Selinger, Jerry Robin

Houston
Caldwell, Rodney Kent
Hitchcock, Bion Earl
Kirk, John Robert, Jr.
Pravel, Bernarr Roe
Tripp, Karen Bryant
Vaden, Frank Samuel, III

Plano
Levine, Harold

Tyler
Alworth, Charles Wesley

UTAH

Salt Lake City
Cornaby, Kay Sterling
Workman, H(arley) Ross

VERMONT

Essex Junction
Walsh, Robert Anthony

VIRGINIA

Alexandria
Georges, Peter John
Greigg, Ronald Edwin
Wieder, Bruce Terrill

Arlington
Litman, Richard Curtis
Scafetta, Joseph, Jr.
Swift, Stephen Christopher

Falls Church
Brady, Rupert Joseph

Mc Lean
Edgell, George Paul
Kondracki, Edward John
Shapiro, Nelson Hirsh

Mount Vernon
Spiegel, H. Jay

WASHINGTON

Seattle
Cumbow, Robert Charles

WISCONSIN

Kenosha
Richter, David Jerome

Madison
Long, Theodore James

AUSTRALIA

Victoria
Ellinson, Dean Avraham

COSTA RICA

San Jose
Castro, Luis D.

CZECH REPUBLIC

Prague
Kroft, Michal

ENGLAND

Bucks
Assim, Gary Dean

London
Skrein, Stephen Peter Michael

GERMANY

Dusseldorf
Harmsen, Christian
Rauh, Theo

ITALY

Milan
Holden, Julia

KENYA

Nairobi
Maema, William Ikutha

THE NETHERLANDS

Amsterdam
Schaap, Jacqueline

The Hague
Van Nispen, Constant J.J.C.

POLAND

Cracow
Kasper, Horst Manfred

REPUBLIC OF KOREA

Seoul
Oh, Seung Jong

SCOTLAND

Glasgow
Priest, Andrew David

SPAIN

Barcelona
Llevat, Jorge

WALES

Cardiff
Lindsey, Michael

ADDRESS UNPUBLISHED
Adams, Thomas Lawrence
Beck, Stuart Edwin
Bullard, Rockwood Wilde, III

Carten, Francis Noel
Cornish, Jeannette Carter
Fiorito, Edward Gerald
Gray, Brian Mark
Herrell, Roger Wayne
Huston, Steven Craig
Jameson, Paula Ann
Landy, Lisa Anne
Peters, R. Jonathan
Sprung, Arnold
Vamos, Florence M.

TRANSPORTATION

UNITED STATES

CALIFORNIA

Huntington Beach
Nikas, Richard John

Los Angeles
Pearman, Robert Charles
Pieper, Darold D.

Oakland
Rice, Julian Casavant

San Francisco
Berning, Paul Wilson
Fergus, Gary Scott

COLORADO

Denver
Grant, Patrick Alexander

CONNECTICUT

Danbury
Murray, Stephen James

DISTRICT OF COLUMBIA

Washington
Basseches, Robert Treinis
Calderwood, James Albert
Esslinger, John Thomas
Feldman, Roger David
Goldman, Stanley Irwin
Hirsch, Robert Allen
Mayer, Neal Michael
Mills, Kevin Paul
Moates, G. Paul
Rice, Paul Jackson
Taylor, Richard Powell

FLORIDA

Miami
Moore, Michael T.

GEORGIA

Atlanta
Booth, Gordon Dean, Jr.

Dunwoody
Callison, James W.

IDAHO

Kamiah
Mills, Lawrence

ILLINOIS

Chicago
Benak, James Donald
Daley, Michael Joseph
Herman, Stephen Charles
Marwedel, Warren John
Murray, Daniel Richard
Pirok, Edward Warren

LOUISIANA

Lafayette
Saloom, Kaliste Joseph, Jr.

MARYLAND

Baltimore
Chaplin, Peggy Louie

Bethesda
Pankopf, Arthur, Jr.

MICHIGAN

Farmington
McFarland, Robert Edwin

MISSOURI

Saint Louis
Newman, Charles A.
Williams, Theodore Joseph, Jr.

NEW JERSEY

Livingston
Harris, Brian Craig

Millburn
Madden, Edward George, Jr.

Secaucus
Holt, Michael Bartholomew

NEW YORK

New York
McMahon, James Charles
Oechler, Henry John, Jr.

White Plains
Nesci, Vincent Peter

NORTH CAROLINA

Cherryville
Huffstetler, Palmer Eugene

OHIO

Akron
Wright, Bradley Abbott

Cincinnati
Nippert, Alfred Kuno, Jr.

Cleveland
Skulina, Thomas Raymond

Columbus
Turano, David A.

PENNSYLVANIA

Philadelphia
Wellington, Ralph Glenn
Wert, Robert Clifton

TENNESSEE

Memphis
Russell, James Franklin

TEXAS

Dallas
Staley, Joseph Hardin, Jr.

Houston
Scholl, Stephen Gerrard

VIRGINIA

Alexandria
Siegel, Kenneth Eric

Norfolk
Bishop, Bruce Taylor
Corcoran, Andrew Patrick, Jr.

WISCONSIN

Green Bay
Schober, Thomas Leonard

ENGLAND

London
Dibble, Robert Kenneth
Drury, Stephen Patrick

FINLAND

Helsinki
Ahola, Juhani Ilmari

INDIA

Calcutta
Garodia, Aniruddh

THE PHILIPPINES

Makati City
Salvador, Tranquil, III

VENEZUELA

Las Mercenes
Pro-Risquez, Juan C.

ADDRESS UNPUBLISHED

Tavrow, Richard Lawrence

TRIAL. *See* Civil Litigation; Criminal.

TRUSTS. *See* Probate.

UTILITIES, PUBLIC

UNITED STATES

ALABAMA

Birmingham
Harris, George Bryan
Timberlake, Marshall

Montgomery
Laurie, Robin Garrett

ARIZONA

Tucson
Glaser, Steven Jay

CALIFORNIA

Fresno
Ewell, A. Ben, Jr.

Los Angeles
Clark, R(ufus) Bradbury

Orinda
Roethe, James Norton

San Francisco
Odgers, Richard William

CONNECTICUT

Hartford
Taylor, Allan Bert

Norwalk
Shertzer, George Edwin

Stamford
Rohrer, Dean Cougill

DISTRICT OF COLUMBIA

Washington
Batla, Raymond John, Jr.
Beresford, Douglas Lincoln
Besozzi, Paul Charles
Collins, Daniel Francis
Downs, Clark Evans
Jacobson, David Edward
Mallory, Charles King, III
Mathis, John Prentiss
O'Neill, Brian Dennis
Philion, Norman Joseph, III
Simons, Barbara M.
Zipp, Joel Frederick

FLORIDA

Orlando
Kantor, Hal Halperin

West Palm Beach
Gildan, Phillip Clarke

ILLINOIS

Chicago
Fazio, Peter Victor, Jr.
Hester, Thomas Patrick
Lorentzen, John Carol
Ruxin, Paul Theodore
Zabel, Sheldon Alter

INDIANA

Indianapolis
Allen, David James
Belknap, Jerry P.
Deer, Richard Elliott

IOWA

Des Moines
Fisher, Thomas George, Jr.
Graziano, Craig Frank
Stoffregen, Philip Eugene

KANSAS

Bucyrus
Hoffman, John Raymond

Topeka
Dimmitt, Lawrence Andrew

KENTUCKY

Owensboro
Miller, James Monroe

MARYLAND

Baltimore
Rafferty, William Bernard
Rettberg, Charles Clayland, Jr.

Bethesda
Gottlieb, Jonathan W.

Chevy Chase
Bruder, George Frederick

MASSACHUSETTS

Boston
Jones, Jeffrey Foster

Lowell
Cook, Charles Addison

MICHIGAN

Detroit
Smith, James Albert

MINNESOTA

Fergus Falls
Lundeen, David F.

MISSISSIPPI

Bay Saint Louis
Bernstein, Joseph

MISSOURI

Kansas City
English, Mark Gregory

Saint Louis
Godiner, Donald Leonard
Smith, Arthur Lee

NEBRASKA

Omaha
Dolan, James Vincent

NEVADA

Reno
Marshall, Robert William

NEW JERSEY

Basking Ridge
Jones, William Johnson

Roseland
Vanderbilt, Arthur T., II

Woodbridge
Babineau, Anne Serzan

NEW MEXICO

Santa Fe
Carpenter, Richard Norris

NEW YORK

Albany
Alessi, Robert Joseph

Glens Falls
Lebowitz, Jack Richard

New York
Dunn, M(orris) Douglas
Fischman, Bernard D.
Joseph, Leonard
Parish, J. Michael
Schwartz, Renee Gerstler
White, Katherine Patricia

Pittsford
George, Richard Neill

NORTH CAROLINA

Charlotte
Walker, Clarence Wesley

OHIO

Columbus
Ryan, Joseph W., Jr.

Newark
Hite, David L.

Washington Township
Post, Alan Richard

OKLAHOMA

Tulsa
Arrington, John Leslie, Jr.
Gaberino, John Anthony, Jr.
Huffman, Robert Allen, Jr.
Hughes, William Earle

OREGON

Portland
Dotten, Michael Chester

PENNSYLVANIA

Bryn Mawr
Stahl, Roy Howard

Elkins Park
Myers, Kenneth Raymond

Monroeville
McDowell, Michael David

New Castle
Flannery, Harry Audley

Philadelphia
Gornish, Gerald
Kendall, Robert Louis, Jr.
Satinsky, Barnett
Stuart, Glen R(aymond)

Pittsburgh
Boswell, William Paret
Crayne, Larry Randolph
Demmler, John Henry
Reed, W. Franklin

Wayne
Donnella, Michael Andre

RHODE ISLAND

Providence
Prentiss, Richard Daniel

TENNESSEE

Memphis
Williams, J. Maxwell

Sevierville
Waters, John B.

Trenton
Malone, Gayle

TEXAS

Austin
Brown, Dick Terrell
Demond, Walter Eugene
Drummond, Eric Hubert
Smith, Lawrence Shannon

Dallas
Meyer, Ferdinand Charles, Jr.

El Paso
McCotter, James Rawson

Houston
Gover, Alan Shore
Hartrick, Janice Kay
Rozzell, Scott Ellis

UTAH

Salt Lake City
Gordon, Robert
Holtkamp, James Arnold
Reeder, F. Robert

VERMONT

Saint Johnsbury
Marshall, John Henry

South Burlington
Winer, Jonathan Herman

VIRGINIA

Norfolk
Smith, Richard Muldrow

Richmond
Flippen, Edward L.
Gary, Richard David

WISCONSIN

Madison
Hanson, David James

AUSTRALIA

Sydney
Shirbin, John Martin

ENGLAND

London
Phillips, Robert John

ADDRESS UNPUBLISHED

Bagley, William Thompson
Branstetter, Cecil Dewey, Sr.
Buchmann, Alan Paul
Eaken, Bruce Webb, Jr.
Gorske, Robert H.
Heath, Charles Dickinson
Howell, Donald Lee
Mayer, James Joseph
McGovern, Frances
Norman, Albert George, Jr.
Ostergaard, Joni Hammersla

Pallot, Joseph Wedeles
Powers, Elizabeth Whitmel

WATER. *See* **Property, real.**

WILLS. *See* **Probate.**

**WORKERS'
COMPENSATION** *See also*
Labor; Personal injury

UNITED STATES

ALABAMA

Birmingham
Albritton, William Harold, IV
Dobbs, Carney H.
Donahue, Timothy Patrick
Ferguson, Harold Laverne, Jr.

Dadeville
Oliver, John Percy, II

Mobile
Harris, Benjamin Harte, Jr.

Montgomery
Ely, Robert Eugene
Wood, James Jerry

ARIZONA

Tucson
Samet, Dee-Dee

CALIFORNIA

Daly City
Boccia, Barbara

Oakland
Heywood, Robert Gilmour

Pasadena
Stolzberg, Michael Meyer

Pleasant Hill
Otis, Roy James

Pomona
Partritz, Joan Elizabeth

Sacramento
Hassan, Allen Clarence

Seal Beach
Weitzman, Marc Herschel

Yuba City
McCaslin, Leon

COLORADO

Denver
Kintzele, John Alfred

Greeley
Conway, Rebecca Ann Koppes

CONNECTICUT

South Windham
Asselin, John Thomas

Stratford
O'Rourke, James Louis

Torrington
Leard, David Carl

Willimantic
Schiller, Howard Barry

DELAWARE

Wilmington
Ciconte, Edward Thomas

FLORIDA

Altamonte Springs
Fisher, James Craig
Heindl, Phares Matthews

Bushnell
Hagin, T. Richard

Coral Gables
Glinn, Franklyn Barry

Crestview
Duplechin, D. James

Jacksonville
Houser, John Edward

Orlando
Marshall, Valerie Ann
Mooney, Thomas Robert

Saint Petersburg
Escarraz, Enrique, III

Tampa
Medina, Omar F.
Polaszek, Christopher Stephen
Stiles, Mary Ann

GEORGIA

Fayetteville
Fox, Patrick Joseph
Johnson, Donald Wayne

Milledgeville
Bradley, Wayne Bernard

Savannah
Bowman, Catherine McKenzie

HAWAII

Honolulu
Turbin, Richard
Umebayashi, Clyde Satoru

IDAHO

Boise
Luker, Lynn Michael
Mauk, William Lloyd

Lewiston
Tait, John Reid

Twin Falls
Berry, L. Clyel

ILLINOIS

Belleville
Heiligenstein, Christian E.

Carbondale
Wesley, Howard Barry

Chicago
Episcope, Paul Bryan
Haskins, Charles Gregory, Jr.
Kane, Arthur O.
Knox, James Marshall

Joliet
Miller, Randal J.

Libertyville
Rallo, Douglas

Marengo
Franks, Herbert Hoover

Peoria
O'Brien, Daniel Robert

Rockford
Hunsaker, Richard Kendall
Sullivan, Peter Thomas, III

Western Springs
Young, Robert Bruce

INDIANA

Indianapolis
Walker, Ross Paul

South Bend
Norton, Sally Pauline

IOWA

Cedar Rapids
O'Brien, David A.
Wilson, Robert Foster

Coralville
McAndrew, Paul Joseph, Jr.

Des Moines
Cortese, Joseph Samuel, II
Duckworth, Marvin E.
Shoff, Patricia Ann

Keokuk
Hoffman, James Paul

KANSAS

Olathe
Scott, Robert Gene

Overland Park
Smith, Daniel Lynn

Pittsburg
Short, Timothy Allen

Salina
Neustrom, Patrik William

Wichita
Franklin, Joni Jeanette

KENTUCKY

Lexington
Hiestand, Sheila Patricia

Paducah
Nickell, Christopher Shea

Salyersville
Arnett, William Grover

LOUISIANA

Morgan City
Ramsey, Robert Scott, Jr.

MAINE

Bath
Watson, Thomas Riley

Houlton
Sylvester, Torrey Alden

MARYLAND

Baltimore
Uehlinger, Gerard Paul

Chevy Chase
Groner, Samuel Brian

Hagerstown
Gilbert, Howard William, Jr.

Upper Marlboro
Vaughan, James Joseph Michael

MASSACHUSETTS

Bedford
Nason, Leonard Yoshimoto

Boston
Steward, Martin John

Canton
Masiello, Thomas Philip, Jr.

Malden
Finn, Marvin Ruven

Somerset
Sabra, Steven Peter

Springfield
Bennett, Clarence J.
Fein, Sherman Edward

Worcester
Felper, David Michael

MICHIGAN

Detroit
Glotta, Ronald Delon
Labadie, Dwight Daniel
Spencer, William Thomas

Grand Rapids
Stadler, James Robert

Saginaw
Gallagher, Edward John, II
Zanot, Craig Allen

Southfield
May, Alan Alfred

MINNESOTA

Plymouth
MacMillan, Peter Alan

Saint Cloud
Seifert, Luke Michael

Saint Paul
O'Leary, Daniel Brian

MISSISSIPPI

Batesville
Cook, William Leslie, Jr.

Biloxi
O'Barr, Bobby Gene, Sr.

MISSOURI

Cape Girardeau
McManaman, Kenneth Charles

Columbia
Schwabe, John Bennett, II

Independence
Terry, Jack Chatterson

Kansas City
Franke, Linda Frederick

Marshall
Peterson, William Allen

Saint Louis
Burke, Thomas Michael
Carius, Jeffrey Rapp
Roskin, Preston Eugene

MONTANA

Missoula
Morales, Julio K.

NEBRASKA

Lincoln
Zink, Walter Earl, II

NEW HAMPSHIRE

Hooksett
Rogers, David John

NEW JERSEY

Basking Ridge
O'Carroll, Anita Louise

Jersey City
Nevins, Arthur Gerard, Jr.

Livingston
Sukoneck, Ira David

Mountainside
Weiseman, Jac Burton

Newark
Weinberg, Shelley Ann

Northfield
Day, Christopher Mark

Ocean
Weisberg, Adam Jon

Somerville
Lieberman, Marvin Samuel

Trenton
Gogo, Gregory

NEW MEXICO

Farmington
Strother, Robin Dale
Titus, Victor Allen

Hobbs
Stout, Lowell

NEW YORK

New York
DeCarlo, Donald Thomas
Douchkess, George
Loscalzo, Anthony Joseph
Shen, Michael
Wolfe, Richard Barry Michael

Niagara Falls
Levine, David Ethan

Schenectady
Taub, Eli Irwin

Syracuse
Zimmerman, Aaron Mark

NORTH CAROLINA

Cary
Brooks, David Victor

Durham
Markham, Charles Buchanan

Eden
Doss, Marion Kenneth

OHIO

Cincinnati
Harris, Jerald David

Cleveland
Baughman, R(obert) Patrick
Birne, Kenneth Andrew
Sanislo, Paul Steve

Columbus
Butler, Robert Anthony
Taggart, Thomas Michael

Toledo
Baker, Richard Southworth

Youngstown
Ausnehmer, John Edward

OKLAHOMA

Oklahoma City
Bridges, Annita Marie

Tulsa
Strecker, David Eugene

OREGON

Hillsboro
Uffelman, John Edward

Portland
Schuster, Philip Frederick , II

Salem
Robertson, Joseph David

PENNSYLVANIA

Allentown
Altemose, Mark Kenneth

Beaver
Petrush, John Joseph

Gibsonia
Benson, Stuart Wells, III

Harrisburg
Hafer, Joseph Page

Leola
Eaby, Christian Earl

Morrisville
Hershenson, Gerald Martin

Narberth
Rovner, David Patrick Ryan

New Castle
Flannery, Harry Audley

Philadelphia
Abraham, Richard Paul
Heslin, Gary Phillip
Mulvey, W. Michael

Pittsburgh
Bochicchio, Vito Salvatore
Breault, Theodore Edward
Caroselli, William R.
Harty, James Quinn
Leibowitz, Marvin

Pottsville
Tamulonis, Frank Louis, Jr.

Washington
Richman, Stephen I.

SOUTH CAROLINA

Charleston
Spitz, Hugo Max

Columbia
Blanton, Hoover Clarence
Oswald, Billy Robertson
Painter, Samuel Franklin

Langley
Bell, Robert Morrall

North Charleston
Wigger, Jarrel L.

TENNESSEE

Knoxville
Johnson, Steven Boyd
Ownby, Jere Franklin, III
Wheeler, John Watson

Memphis
Russell, James Franklin

Nashville
Clayton, Daniel Louis
Cooney, Charles Hayes
Youngblood, Elaine Michele

TEXAS

Austin
Colburn, Stuart Dale
Pena, Richard

Conroe
Abney, Joe L.

Dallas
Levin, Hervey Phillip

Fort Worth
Streck, Frederick Louis, III

Houston
Pitts, Gary Benjamin

Mcallen
Thaddeus, Aloysius Peter, Jr.

San Antonio
Craddock, Allen T.
Henry, Peter York

VERMONT

Bellows Falls
Massucco, Lawrence Raymond

Rutland
O'Rourke, William Andrew, III

VIRGINIA

Mechanicsville
d'Evegnee, Charles Paul

WASHINGTON

Richland
Barr, Carlos Harvey

Seattle
Scott, Brian David

Spokane
Harbaugh, Daniel Paul

Pontarolo, Michael Joseph

WEST VIRGINIA

Beckley
Stacy, Don Matthew

Fairmont
Cohen, Richard Paul

WISCONSIN

Black River Falls
Lister, Thomas Edward

Delafield
Hausman, C. Michael

Fond Du Lac
English, Dale Lowell

Hudson
Lundeen, Bradley Curtis

Madison
Ehlke, Bruce Frederic
Schmid, John Henry, Jr.

Racine
Rudebusch, Alice Ann

Wausau
Molinaro, Thomas J.

SPAIN

Madrid
García-Perrote, Ignacio

ADDRESS UNPUBLISHED

Berman, Richard Bruce
Branstetter, Cecil Dewey, Sr.
Cohen, Norton Jacob
Embry, Stephen Creston
Goldberger, Allen Sanford
Harris, Randolph Burton
Hoffman, Alan Craig
McFerrin, James Hamil
McGuffey, Carroll Wade, Jr.
McQuigg, John Dolph
Parker, John Francis
Rochlin, Paul R.
Seagull, Keith Allen

OTHER

UNITED STATES

ALABAMA

Birmingham
Norris, Robert Wheeler *Ethics*

Mobile
Meigs, Walter Ralph *Maritime*

ALASKA

Anchorage
Bond, Marc Douglas *Recreation*

ARIZONA

Phoenix
Gust, John Devens *Agricultural*

Scottsdale
Roberts, Jean Reed *Elder*

CALIFORNIA

Burbank
Husband, Bertram Paul *Equine law*

Los Angeles
Ray, David Lewin *Receivership*
Saxe, Deborah Crandall *Wrongful discharge*

Newport Beach
Jones, Sheldon Atwell *Investment*

San Francisco
Bagatelos, Peter Anthony *Contracts commercial*
Gibson, Virginia Lee *Environmental*
Norris, Cynthia Ann *Business*

COLORADO

Golden
Outerbridge, Cheryl *Mining and minerals*

Greenwood Vlg
Ramsey, John Arthur *Litigation*
Ramsey, John Arthur *UST*

CONNECTICUT

West Hartford
Conard, Frederick Underwood, Jr. *Contracts commercial, trust and estates*

DELAWARE

Greenville
Long, Linda Ann *Government relations*

Wilmington
Gamble, Donald Geoffrey Bidmead *Public affairs*

DISTRICT OF COLUMBIA

Washington
Johnson, Philip McBride *Commodities*
Mathers, Peter Robert *Food and drug*
Scheman, L. Ronald *International finance*
Scheman, L. Ronald *International corporate*
Seeger, Edwin Howard *Foreign trade*

FLORIDA

Longwood
Tomasulo, Virginia Merrills *Tax-exempt organizations*

West Palm Beach
Beall, Kenneth Sutter, Jr. *Agriculture*

ILLINOIS

Chicago
Bernick, David M. *Litigation*
Gordon, Phillip *International Real E*
Hannay, William Mouat, III *Unfair trade regulation*
Nicolaides, Mary *Elder*
Schreck, Robert A., Jr. *Acquisitions*
Senderowitz, Stephen Jay *Commodities*

Galva
Massie, Michael Earl *Agriculture*

INDIANA

Indianapolis
McKeon, Thomas Joseph *Arson, fraud*

IOWA

West Des Moines
McEnroe, Michael Louis *Agriculture*

LOUISIANA

Harvey
Hantel, Philip Edward *Human rights*

MARYLAND

Baltimore
Strachan, Nell B. *Education and schools*

Bethesda
Bozentka, Lynn M. *Commercial leasing*
Bozentka, Lynn M. *Corporate litigation*
Garson, Jack A. *Technology law*
Rosenberg, Mark Louis *Taxation*
Rudolph, Daniel A. *Business litigation*
Rudolph, Daniel A. *Employment litigatio*

Bowie
Bagaria, Gail Farrell *Elder*

North Potomac
Keane, James Ignatius *Management consulting*

MASSACHUSETTS

Boston
Huang, Vivian Wenhuey Chen *Business*

Weston
Freeman, Florence Eleanor *Church law*

MICHIGAN

Auburn Hills
Huss, Allan Michael *Warranty, consumer lemon law*

Bloomfield Hills
Birnkrant, Sherwin Maurice *Municipal (excluding bonds)*

Howell
Parker, Robert Ernser *State and Federal civil litigation*

MISSOURI

Kansas City
Hindman, Larrie C. *Native American*
Tharp, Tonna K. *Equine law*

Saint Louis
Rice, Charles Marcus, II *Artificial intelligence*

NEVADA

Las Vegas
Chesnut, Carol Fitting *Elder*

Reno
Bible, Paul Alfred *Gaming*

NEW HAMPSHIRE

Manchester
Wiebusch, Richard Vernon *Commercial litigation*

NEW JERSEY

River Edge
Spiegel, Edna Z. *Elder Law*

Tenafly
Spike, Michele Kahn *Art*

Trenton
Harbeck, Dorothy Anne *Election*

NEW YORK

Huntington
Robinson, Kenneth Patrick *Technology*

New York
de Saint Phalle, Pierre Claude *Investment companies*
Filler, Ronald Howard *Commodities*
Glusband, Steven Joseph *Commodities*

Gold, Simeon *Restructuring*
Harley, Colin Emile *Equipment leasing*
Heftler, Thomas E. *Commodities*
Kailas, Leo George *Commodities*
Kreitzman, Ralph J. *Administrative and r*
Neuner, Robert *Banking*
Rubin, Stephen Wayne *Mergers and acquisitions*
Seligman, Delice *Art*
Shoss, Cynthia Renée *International taxation*
Silvers, Eileen S. *International taxation*
Vernon, Darryl Mitchell *Animal welfare*
Wildes, Leon *Consular*

OHIO

Cincinnati
Eaton, Janet Ruth *Mental health*

Columbus
Woods, William Hunt *Fidelity and surety*

Hillsboro
Coss, Rocky Alan

Portsmouth
Crowder, Marjorie Briggs *Insurance*

OREGON

Portland
DuBoff, Leonard David *Art*

PENNSYLVANIA

Greensburg
Belden, H. Reginald, Jr. *Business litigation*

Langhorne
Hillje, Barbara Brown *Elder*

Moon Township
Alstadt, Lynn Jeffery *Trade regulation*

Philadelphia
Dorfman, John Charles *Trade regulation, unfair competition*
Newman, George Henry *Forfeiture*

Pittsburgh
Frank, Frederick Newman *Election*
Murrin, Regis Doubet *Condominium and cooperative law*

TENNESSEE

Kingsport
Tweed, Douglas Steven *Employment*

Nashville
Thomas, Robert Paige *Government relations*

TEXAS

Austin
Moss, Bill Ralph *Ethics*

Baytown
Chavez, John Anthony *Trade*

Dallas
LaBrec, David John *State and federal civil litigation*

Houston
Gilbert, Keith Thomas *Election*

UTAH

Park City
Schiesswohl, Cynthia Rae Schlegel *Religion*

WASHINGTON

Olympia
Reynolds, Dennis Dean *Indian*

Seattle
Levy, Barbara Jo *Sexual abuse litigation*

Spokane
Sayre, Richard Layton *Legislative*

WISCONSIN

Milwaukee
Whyte, George Kenneth, Jr. *Employment litigation*

AUSTRIA

Vienna
Mayr, Andreas W. *Venture capital*

CHINA

Shanghai
Qi, Qing Michael *Corporate finance*

CZECH REPUBLIC

Prague
Kroft, Michal *Information Technolo*

ENGLAND

London
Astleford, Peter David *Financial*
Hinshaw, David Love *International and English taxation*
Turner, Mark McDougall *E-business*

FRANCE

Paris
Derouin, Philippe *European and French Commercial & Corporate*
Doumenge, Arnaud *Labor Litigation*

GERMANY

Dusseldorf
Palenberg, Hans-Peter *Initial public offer*

ISRAEL

Tel Aviv
Yoram, Raved *Hi-tech and venture*

KUWAIT

Safat
Ammouna, Sami Saed *Contract and Others*

NORWAY

Oslo
Thogersen, Kai *IT and Telecomms*

Skoyen, Oslo
Wille, Hans Georg *Energy*

ADDRESS UNPUBLISHED

Cherovsky, Erwin Louis *Corporate finance*
Hubbard, Michael James
Moylan, James Joseph *Commodities*
Redmond, Lawrence Craig *Election*
Regenstreif, Herbert *Religion*
Royal, Carl Andrew *Commodities*
Siegel, Sarah Ann *Alternative dispute*
Walker, Craig Michael *Technology*

Professional Index

ARBITRATION AND MEDIATION

UNITED STATES

ALABAMA

Birmingham
Furman, Howard *mediator, arbitrator, lawyer*

ALASKA

Anchorage
Anderson, Kathleen Gay *mediator, hearing officer, arbitrator, trainer*

CALIFORNIA

Arcadia
Mc Cormack, Francis Xavier *lawyer, former oil company executive*

Beverly Hills
Factor, Max, III *arbitrator, mediator*

Lafayette
Cossack, Jerilou *labor arbitrator, mediator*

Los Angeles
Fenning, Lisa Hill *lawyer, mediator, former federal judge*

Petaluma
Castagnola, George Joseph, Jr. *lawyer, mediator, secondary education educator*

Rolling Hills Estates
Rumbaugh, Charles Earl *arbitrator, mediator, educator, lawyer, speaker, judge*

Stanford
Mann, J. Keith *arbitrator, law educator, lawyer*

Van Nuys
Arabian, Armand *arbitrator, mediator, lawyer*

COLORADO

Denver
Carrigan, Jim R. *arbitrator, mediator, retired federal judge*

FLORIDA

Daytona Beach
Barker, Robert Osborne (Bob Barker) *mediator, educator*

GEORGIA

Atlanta
Ordover, Abraham Philip *lawyer, mediator*

MARYLAND

Greenbelt
Jascourt, Hugh D. *lawyer, arbitrator, mediator*

MICHIGAN

Dearborn
Kahn, Mark Leo *arbitrator, educator*

Lansing
Burns, Marshall Shelby *arbitrator, lawyer, retired judge*

Northville
Hariri, V. M. *arbitrator, mediator, lawyer, educator*

Southfield
Gordon, Arnold Mark *lawyer*

NEW YORK

New York
Hallingby, Jo Davis *lawyer, arbitrator*

SOUTH CAROLINA

Saint Helena Island
Scoville, Laurence McConway, Jr. *arbitrator, mediator*

TEXAS

Austin
White, Michael Lee *lawyer*

Dallas
Leeper, Harold Harris *arbitrator*

UTAH

Salt Lake City
Zimmerman, Michael David *lawyer*

VIRGINIA

Lynchburg
Healy, Joseph Francis, Jr. *lawyer, arbitrator, retired airline executive*

Manassas
Weimer, Peter Dwight *mediator, lawyer, corporate executive*

Petersburg
Everitt, Alice Lubin *labor arbitrator*

ENGLAND

London
de Lacy, Richard Michael *arbitrator*

ADDRESS UNPUBLISHED

Ashe, Bernard Flemming *arbitrator, educator, lawyer*
Baker, Patricia (Jean) *lawyer, mediator*
Gaunt, Janet Lois *arbitrator, mediator*
Henke, Robert John *lawyer, mediator, consultant, engineer*

EDUCATION

UNITED STATES

ALABAMA

Birmingham
Langum, David John *law educator, historian*
Nelson, Leonard John, III *lawyer, educator*
Riegert, Robert Adolf *law educator, consultant*
Weeks, Arthur Andrew *lawyer, law educator*

Montgomery
Honey, William Chipman *lawyer, educator*

Orange Beach
Adams, Daniel Fenton *law educator*

Tuscaloosa
Hoff, Timothy *law educator, priest*
Randall, Kenneth C. *dean, law educator*

ARIZONA

Tempe
Furnish, Dale Beck *lawyer, educator*
Matheson, Alan Adams *law educator*
Schatzki, George *law educator*
Spritzer, Ralph Simon *lawyer, educator*
White, Patricia Denise *dean, law educator*

Tucson
Falbaum, Bertram Seymour *law educator, investigator*
Fortman, Marvin *law educator, consultant*
Massaro, Toni Marie *dean, law educator*

ARKANSAS

Fayetteville
Copeland, John Dewayne *law educator*

Little Rock
Wright, Robert Ross, III *law educator*

CALIFORNIA

Berkeley
Barnes, Thomas G. *law educator*
Barton, Babette B. *lawyer, educator*
Berring, Robert Charles, Jr. *law educator, law librarian, former dean*
Buxbaum, Richard M. *law educator, lawyer*
Dwyer, John P. *law educator, dean*
Kadish, Sanford Harold *law educator*
Kagan, Robert Allen *law educator*
Kay, Herma Hill *law educator*
Messinger, Sheldon L(eopold) *law educator*
Moran, Rachel *lawyer, educator*

Pakter, Walter Jay *legal scholar and educator, aviation lawyer*
Samuelson, Pamela Ann *law educator*
Scheiber, Harry N. *law educator*
Zimring, Franklin E. *law educator, lawyer*

Beverly Hills
Shire, Harold Raymond *law educator, writer, scientist*

Claremont
Gann, Pamela Brooks *academic administrator*

Costa Mesa
Rose, I. Nelson *lawyer, educator*

Davis
Bartosic, Florian *law educator, lawyer, arbitrator*
Johnson, Kevin Raymond *lawyer, educator*
Perschbacher, Rex Robert *dean, law educator*
Shimomura, Floyd Dudley *lawyer, educator*
Wolk, Bruce Alan *law educator*

Fresno
Roberson, Clifford Eugene *law educator, lawyer*

Fullerton
Bakken, Gordon Morris *law educator*
Frizell, Samuel *law educator*

La Habra
Hyslop, Richard Stewart *law educator*

La Jolla
Siegan, Bernard Herbert *lawyer, educator*

Larkspur
Ratner, David Louis *retired law educator*

Los Angeles
Abrams, Norman *law educator, university administrator*
Arlen, Jennifer Hall *law educator*
Bauman, John Andrew *law educator*
Bice, Scott Haas *dean, lawyer, educator*
Blumberg, Grace Ganz *law educator, lawyer*
Follick, Edwin Duane *law educator, chiropractic physician*
Jordan, Robert Leon *lawyer, educator*
Mandel, Joseph David *academic administrator, lawyer*
Pugsley, Robert Adrian *law educator*
Rabinovitz, Joel *lawyer, educator*
Raeder, Myrna Sharon *lawyer, educator*
Sobel, Lionel Steven *law educator*
Spitzer, Matthew Laurence *law educator, dean*
Sumner, James DuPre, Jr. *lawyer, educator*
Treusch, Paul Ellsworth *law educator, lawyer*
Varat, Jonathan D. *dean, law educator*

Malibu
Phillips, Ronald Frank *retired academic administrator*

Menlo Park
Brest, Paul A. *law educator*

Monterey
Kadushin, Karen Donna *law school dean*

Orange
Doti, Frank John *law educator, consultant*

Orinda
Hetland, John Robert *lawyer, educator*

Pacific Palisades
Jones, Edgar Allan, Jr. *law educator, arbitrator, lawyer*

Pomona
Palmer, Robert Alan *lawyer, educator*

Ridgecrest
Long, Andre Edwin *law educator, lawyer*

Sacramento
Barilla, Frank (Rocky Barilla) *lawyer, consultant, educator*
Malloy, Michael Patrick *law educator, writer, consultant*
Rich, Ben Arthur *lawyer, educator*

San Diego
Barton, Thomas Donald *lawyer, educator*
Smith, Steven Ray *law educator*

San Francisco
Duffy, Donna Jan *law educator, lawyer*
Folberg, Harold Jay *lawyer, mediator, educator, university dean*
Henke, Dan *law educator*
Kane, Mary Kay *dean, law educator*
Knapp, Charles Lincoln *law educator*
Lee, Richard Diebold *law educator, legal publisher, consultant*
McKelvey, Judith Grant *lawyer, educator, university dean*
Wilson, John Pasley *law educator*

Santa Barbara
Baker, Gordon Edward *political science educator*

Santa Clara
Alexander, George Jonathon *law educator, former dean*
Blawie, James Louis *law educator*

Santa Rosa
DeMitchell, Terri Ann *law educator*

Saratoga
Roush, George Edgar *lawyer*

Stanford
Babcock, Barbara Allen *law educator, lawyer*
Barton, John Hays *law educator*
Kelman, Mark Gregory *law educator*
Rhode, Deborah Lynn *law educator*
Sullivan, Kathleen Marie *dean, law educator*
Williams, Howard Russell *lawyer, educator*

Walnut
McKee, Catherine Lynch *law educator, lawyer*

Woodland Hills
Barrett, Robert Matthew *law educator, lawyer*

COLORADO

Boulder
Bruff, Harold Hastings *dean*
DuVivier, Katharine Keyes *lawyer, educator*
Fiflis, Ted James *lawyer, educator*
Getches, David Harding *law educator, state environmental executive, lawyer*
Nagel, Robert Forder *legal educator, lawyer*
Vigil, Daniel Agustin *academic administrator*
Waggoner, Michael James *law educator*

Denver
Dauer, Edward Arnold *law educator*
Nanda, Ved Prakash *law educator, university official*
Walker, Timothy Blake *lawyer, educator*
Yegge, Robert Bernard *law educator, dean*

Grand Junction
Lachance, Paul Arthur *legal educator, consultant*

CONNECTICUT

Derby
McEvoy, Sharlene Ann *law educator*

Hamden
Margulies, Martin B. *lawyer, educator*

Hartford
Blumberg, Phillip Irvin *law educator*
Newton, Nell Jessup *dean, law educator*
Paul, Jeremy Ralph *law educator*

New Haven
Ackerman, Bruce Arnold *law educator, lawyer*
Clark, Elias *law educator*
Ellickson, Robert Chester *law educator*
Fiss, Owen M. *law educator, educator*
Freed, Daniel Josef *law educator*
Goldstein, Abraham Samuel *lawyer, educator*
Hansmann, Henry Baethke *law educator*
Kronman, Anthony Townsend *law educator, dean*
Marshall, Burke *law educator*
Priest, George L. *law educator*
Rose-Ackerman, Susan *law and political economy educator*
Simon, John Gerald *law educator*
Wedgwood, Ruth *law educator, international affairs expert*
Yandle, Stephen Thomas *dean*

New London
Dupont, Ralph Paul *lawyer, educator*

Storrs Mansfield
Tucker, Edwin Wallace *law educator*

Torrington
Lippincott, Walter Edward *law educator*

DELAWARE

Newark
Elson, Charles Myer *law educator*

Wilmington
Ott, William Griffith *law educator, writer*

DISTRICT OF COLUMBIA

Washington
Aaronson, David Ernest *law educator, lawyer*
Barron, Jerome Aure *law educator*
Bednar, Richard John *lawyer, law educator*
Carrow, Milton Michael *lawyer, educator*
Carter, Barry Edward *lawyer, educator, administrator*
Clark, LeRoy D. *legal educator, lawyer*
Craver, Charles Bradford *legal educator*
Dobranski, Bernard *law educator*
Goldblatt, Steven Harris *law educator*
Gostin, Lawrence O. *lawyer, educator*
Guttman, Egon *law educator*
Jamar, Steven Dwight *law educator*
Kmiec, Douglas William *law educator, columnist*
Kovacic, William Evan *law educator*
Lubic, Robert Bennett *lawyer, arbitrator, law educator*
Milstein, Elliott Steven *law educator, academic administrator*

Peroni, Robert Joseph *law educator, lawyer*
Phillips, Karen Borlaug *economist, railroad industry executive*
Rohner, Ralph John *lawyer, educator, university dean*
Rothstein, Paul Frederick *lawyer, educator*
Saltzburg, Stephen Allan *law educator, consultant*
Sargentich, Thomas Oliver *law educator, researcher*
Schaffner, Joan Elsa *law educator*
Solomon, Lewis David *law educator*
Starrs, James Edward *law and forensics educator, consultant*
Vaughn, Robert Gene *law educator*
Wallace, Don, Jr. *law educator*

FLORIDA

Amelia Island
Bell, Mildred Bailey *law educator, lawyer*

Coral Gables
Rosenn, Keith Samuel *lawyer, educator*
Swan, Alan Charles *law educator*

Davie
Richmond, Michael Lloyd *lawyer, educator*

Fort Lauderdale
Anderson, John Bayard *lawyer, educator, former congressman*
Cane, Marilyn Blumberg *lawyer, educator*
Jarvis, Robert Mark *law educator*
Joseph, Paul R *law educator*
Mintz, Joel Alan *law educator*

Fort Myers
Zeldes, Ilya M. *forensic scientist, lawyer*

Gainesville
Gordon, Michael Wallace *law educator*
McCoy, Francis Tyrone *law educator*
Mills, Jon *dean, law educator*
Taylor, Grace Elizabeth Woodall (Betty Taylor) *law educator, law library administrator*
Van Alstyne, W. Scott, Jr. *lawyer, educator*

Jacksonville
Schupp, Robert Warren *law educator*

Jupiter
del Russo, Alessandra Luini *retired law educator*

Miami
Anderson, Terence James *law educator*
Klein, Irving J. *law educator*
Matthews, Douglas Eugene *lawyer, educator, consultant*
Moreno, Fernando *lawyer, educator*
Robinson, Thomas Adair *law educator, consultant*

North Miami
Bonham-Yeaman, Doria *law educator*

Opa Locka
Light, Alfred Robert *lawyer, political scientist, educator*

Pompano Beach
Service, John Gregory *law educator*

Saint Petersburg
Carrere, Charles Scott *law educator, judge*
Jacob, Bruce Robert *law educator*
Swygert, Michael I(rven) *legal educator*

Tallahassee
D'Alemberte, Talbot (Sandy D'Alemberte) *academic administrator, lawyer*
McHugh, William F. *legal educator*
Schroeder, Edwin Maher *law educator*

Tampa
Petrila, John Philip *health law educator*

GEORGIA

Athens
Beaird, James Ralph *law educator, dean*
Cooper, James Russell *retired law educator*
Huszagh, Fredrick Wickett *lawyer, educator, information management company executive*
Kurtz, Paul Michael *lawyer, educator*
Player, Mack Allen *legal educator*
Ponsoldt, James Farmer *law educator*
Shipley, David Elliott *dean, lawyer*
Spurgeon, Edward Dutcher *law educator, foundation administrator*

Atlanta
Bross, James Lee *law educator*
Hay, Peter Heinrich *law educator, dean*
Hunter, Howard Owen *academic administrator, law educator*
Knowles, Marjorie Fine *lawyer, educator, dean*
Landau, Michael B. *law educator, musician, writer*
Marvin, Charles Arthur *law educator*
Podgor, Ellen Sue *law educator*

HAWAII

Honolulu
Bloede, Victor Carl *lawyer, academic executive*
Callies, David Lee *lawyer, educator*
Miller, Richard Sherwin *law educator*
Van Dyke, Jon Markham *law educator*

IDAHO

Moscow
Vincenti, Sheldon Arnold *law educator, lawyer*

ILLINOIS

Carbondale
Lee, Mark Richard *lawyer, educator*

Champaign
Boyle, Francis Anthony *law educator*
Kindt, John Warren *lawyer, educator, consultant*
Mc Cord, John Harrison *lawyer, educator*
Mengler, Thomas M. *dean*
Nowak, John E. *law educator*
Stone, Victor J. *law educator*

Chicago
Alschuler, Albert W. *law educator*
Appel, Nina Schick *law educator, dean*
Baird, Douglas Gordon *law educator, dean*
Bandes, Susan Anne *lawyer*
Closen, Michael Lee *law educator*
Decker, John Francis *lawyer, educator*
Eglit, Howard Charles *educator, lawyer, arbitrator*
Francis, Clinton William *legal educator*
Garth, Bryant Geoffrey *law educator, foundation executive*
Gerber, David Joseph *legal educator, lawyer*
Helmholz, R(ichard) H(enry) *law educator*
Hermann, Donald Harold James *lawyer, educator*
Herzog, Fred F. *law educator*
Hutchinson, Dennis James *law educator*
Landes, William M. *law educator*
Levmore, Saul *law educator, dean*
McGovern, Peter John *law educator*
Meltzer, Bernard David *law educator*
Merrill, Thomas Wendell *lawyer, law educator*
Perritt, Henry Hardy, Jr. *law educator*
Peterson, Randall Theodore *law educator*
Presser, Stephen Bruce *lawyer, educator*
Scheller, Arthur Martin, Jr. *law educator*
Schulhofer, Stephen Joseph *law educator, consultant*
Shaman, Jeffrey M. *law educator*
Steinman, Joan Ellen *lawyer, educator*
Stone, Geoffrey Richard *law educator, lawyer*
Van Zandt, David E. *dean*

Highland Park
Ruder, David Sturtevant *lawyer, educator, government official*

Hoffman Estates
Williams, Richard Nesbitt *lawyer, educator*

Palatine
Hildebrandt, Sharrie L. *legal technology educator, paralegal*

Park Ridge
Devience, Alex, Jr. *law educator*

Saint Charles
Alfini, James Joseph *dean, educator, lawyer*

South Holland
Wolf, Wayne Lowell *criminal justice educator, researcher*

Urbana
Uchtmann, Donald Louis *lawyer, law educator*

INDIANA

Bloomington
Aman, Alfred Charles, Jr. *dean*
Bradley, Craig MacDowell *law educator*
Dilts, Jon Paul *law educator*
Palmer, Judith Grace *university administrator*
Shreve, Gene Russell *law educator*

Fort Wayne
Spielman, Kim Morgan *lawyer, educator*

Indianapolis
Funk, David Albert *retired law educator*
Greenberg, Harold *legal educator*
Jegen, Lawrence A., III *law educator*

Notre Dame
Gunn, Alan *law educator*
O'Hara, Patricia A. *dean, law educator*

Vincennes
McGaughey, Jerry Joseph *lawyer, educator*

West Lafayette
Scaletta, Phillip Jasper *lawyer, educator*

IOWA

Des Moines
Baker, Thomas Eugene *law educator*
Begleiter, Martin David *law educator, consultant*
Edwards, John Duncan *law educator, librarian*

Grinnell
Osgood, Russell King *academic administrator*

Iowa City
Bezanson, Randall Peter *law educator*
Hines, N. William *dean, law educator, administrator*
Stensvaag, John-Mark *legal educator, lawyer*
Wing, Adrien Katherine *law educator*

KANSAS

Lawrence
Levin, Murray Scott *law educator, arbitrator, mediator*
Turnbull, H. Rutherford, III *law educator, lawyer*

Topeka
Concannon, James M. *law educator, university dean*
Elrod, Linda Diane Henry *lawyer, educator*
Griffin, Ronald Charles *law educator*

Wichita
Williams, Jackie N. *law educator, former prosecutor*

KENTUCKY

Highland Heights
Brewer, Edward Cage, III *law educator*
Jones, William Rex *law educator*
Seaver, Robert Leslie *retired law educator*

Lexington
Irtz, Frederick G., II *lawyer*
Michael, Douglas Charles *law educator*
Oberst, Paul *retired law educator*
Underwood, Richard Harvey *law educator*
Vestal, Allan W. *dean, law educator*

Louisville
Eades, Ronald Wayne *law educator*

LOUISIANA

Baton Rouge
Schroeder, Leila Obier *retired law educator*

New Orleans
Baroni, Barry Joseph *law educator, mediator, arbitrator*
Childress, Steven Alan *law educator*
Friedman, Joel William *law educator*
Osakwe, Christopher *lawyer, educator*
Palmer, Vernon Valentine *law educator*
Ponoroff, Lawrence *law educator, legal consultant*
Sherman, Edward Francis *dean, law educator*

MAINE

York
Redfield, Sarah Erlick *law educator*

MARYLAND

Baltimore
Bogen, David Skillen *law educator*
Herr, Stanley Sholom *law educator*
Lasson, Kenneth *law educator, author, lawyer*
McLain, Susan Lynn *law educator*
Neil, Benjamin Arthur *lawyer, educator*
Rothenberg, Karen H. *dean, law educator*

Bethesda
Mannix, Charles Raymond *law educator*

College Park
Pavela, Gary Michael *legal educator, administrator*

Upper Marlboro
Brown, James Milton *law educator*

MASSACHUSETTS

Amherst
Platt, Rutherford Hayes *lawyer, educator, geographer, consultant*

Boston
Abrams, Roger Ian *law educator, arbitrator*
Bae, Frank S. H. *law educator, law library administrator*
Bagley, Constance Elizabeth *law educator, lawyer*
Carter, T(homas) Barton *law educator*
Cass, Ronald Andrew *dean*
Daynard, Richard Alan *law educator*
Fischer, Thomas Covell *law educator, consultant, writer, lawyer*
Freehling, Daniel Joseph *law educator, law library director*
Hall, David *law educator, dean, law educator, department chairman*
Kindregan, Charles Peter *law educator*
McMahon, Thomas John *lawyer, educator*
Park, William Wynnewood *law educator*
Whitters, James Payton, III *lawyer, university administrator*

Cambridge
Andrews, William Dorey *law educator, lawyer*
Bok, Derek *law educator, former university president*
Clark, Robert Charles *dean, law educator*
Dershowitz, Alan Morton *lawyer, educator*
Fisher, Roger Dummer *lawyer, educator, negotiation expert*
Frug, Gerald E. *law educator*
Glendon, Mary Ann *law educator*
Haar, Charles Monroe *lawyer, educator*
Kaplow, Louis *law educator*
Kaufman, Andrew Lee *law educator*
Oldman, Oliver *law educator*
Ray, Stephen Alan *academic administrator, lawyer*
Roe, Mark J. *law educator*
Schauer, Frederick Franklin *law educator*
Steiner, Henry Jacob *law and human rights educator*
Stone, Alan Abraham *law and psychiatry educator, psychiatrist*
Vagts, Detlev Frederick *lawyer, educator*
von Mehren, Arthur Taylor *lawyer, educator*
Warren, Alvin Clifford, Jr. *lawyer*
Warren, Elizabeth *law educator*
Weiler, Paul Cronin *law educator*
Wise, Virginia Jo *law educator, librarian*

Chestnut Hill
Garvey, John Hugh *dean, law educator*

Concord
Beyer, Henry Anthony *lawyer*

Dedham
Lake, Ann W. *law educator*

MICHIGAN

Ann Arbor
Allen, Layman Edward *law educator, research scientist*
Bollinger, Lee Carroll *academic administrator, law educator*
Chambers, David Laurance, III *legal educator*
Duquette, Donald Norman *law educator*
Gray, Whitmore *law educator, lawyer*
Kamisar, Yale *lawyer, educator*
Lehman, Jeffrey Sean *dean, law educator*
Pierce, William James *law educator*
Reed, John Wesley *lawyer, educator*
St. Antoine, Theodore Joseph *law educator, arbitrator*
Waggoner, Lawrence William *law educator*
White, James Boyd *law educator*

Detroit
Lamborn, LeRoy Leslie *law educator*
Slovenko, Ralph *lawyer, educator*
Volz, William Harry *law educator, administrator*

East Lansing
Bitensky, Susan Helen *law educator*
Revelos, Constantine Nicholas *law educator, writer*
Stenzel, Paulette Lynn *business law educator, lawyer*

Grosse Pointe
Centner, Charles William *lawyer, educator*
Grano, Joseph Dante *law educator*

Lansing
Latovick, Paula R(ae) *lawyer, educator*
Rooney, John Philip *law educator*
Stockmeyer, Norman Otto, Jr. *law educator, consultant*
Warren, Joseph Addison, III *law and history educator*

Traverse City
Quick, Albert Thomas *law educator*

MINNESOTA

Minneapolis
Kilbourn, William Douglas, Jr. *law educator*
Kirtley, Jane Elizabeth *law educator*
Schoettle, Ferdinand P. *lawyer, educator*
Sullivan, E. Thomas *dean*

Saint Paul
Daly, Joseph Leo *law educator*
Jones, C. Paul *lawyer, educator*

MISSISSIPPI

Jackson
West, Carol Catherine *law educator*

MISSOURI

Columbia
Peth, Howard Allen *lawyer, educator*
Phillips, Walter Ray *lawyer, educator*
Westbrook, James Edwin *lawyer, educator*

Kansas City
Freilich, Robert H. *lawyer, educator*

Saint Louis
Levin, Ronald Mark *law educator*
Seligman, Joel *dean*

MONTANA

Whitehall
Bernard, Donald Ray *law educator, international business counselor*

NEBRASKA

Lincoln
Gardner, Martin Ralph *law educator*
Lyons, William Harry *law educator*

Omaha
Forbes, Franklin Sim *lawyer, educator*
Mangrum, Richard Collin *law educator*
O'Hara, Michael James *law educator, researcher*

NEVADA

Reno
Stumpf, Felix Franklin *law educator*

NEW HAMPSHIRE

Concord
Harrison, Keith Michaele *law educator*

Exeter
Vogelman, Lawrence Allen *law educator, lawyer*

Hanover
Prager, Susan Westerberg *law educator, provost*

PROFESSIONAL INDEX 823 EDUCATION

NEW JERSEY

Camden
Patterson, Dennis Michael *lawyer, educator*
Robinson, Paul Harper *lawyer, educator*

Montclair
Mullins, Margaret Ann Frances *lawyer, educator*

Newark
Askin, Frank *law educator*
Blumrosen, Alfred William *law educator*
Blumrosen, Ruth Gerber *lawyer, educator, arbitrator*
Burt, Jacquelyn Jean-Marie *law school administrator*
Defeis, Elizabeth Frances *law educator, lawyer*
Raveson, Louis Sheppard *lawyer, educator*

River Edge
Sullivan, Eugene John *lawyer*

NEW YORK

Albany
Unger, Gere Nathan *physician, lawyer*

Brooklyn
Bass, David Steven *lawyer, educational administrator*
Diamond, Murray J. *lawyer*

Dobbs Ferry
McGrath, John Joseph *law educator*

Elmira
Stone, Kathleen Gale *law educator*

Flushing
Zalesne, Deborah *law educator*

Forest Hills
Greenberg, Robert Jay *law educator*

Hempstead
Diamond, David Arthur *law educator*

Hudson
Agata, Burton C. *law educator, lawyer*

Huntington
Glickstein, Howard Alan *law educator*
Pratt, George Cheney *law educator, retired federal judge*

Ithaca
Alexander, Gregory Stewart *law educator, educator*
Barcelo, John James, III *law educator*
Clermont, Kevin Michael *law educator*
Cramton, Roger Conant *law educator, lawyer*
Eisenberg, Theodore *law educator*
Hillman, Robert Andrew *law educator, former academic dean*
Rossi, Faust F. *lawyer, educator*
Seibel, Robert Franklin *law educator*
Simson, Gary Joseph *law educator, educator*
Teitelbaum, Lee E. *dean, law educator*
Wolfram, Charles William *law educator*

Neponsit
Re, Edward Domenic *law educator, retired federal judge*

New York
Abramovsky, Abraham *law educator, lawyer*
Bell, Derrick Albert *law educator, author, lecturer*
Black, Barbara Aronstein *legal history educator*
Carden, Constance *lawyer, law professor*
Chase, Oscar G(ottfried) *law educator, consultant, author*
Chiang, Yung Frank *law educator*
Dorsen, Norman *lawyer, educator*
Dworkin, Ronald Myles *legal educator*
Estreicher, Samuel *lawyer, educator*
Eustice, James Samuel *legal educator, lawyer*
Farnsworth, E(dward) Allan *lawyer, educator*
Feerick, John David *dean, lawyer*
First, Harry *law educator*
Fogelman, Martin *lawyer, law educator*
Goldberg, Victor Paul *law educator*
Goldschmid, Harvey Jerome *law educator*
Grad, Frank Paul *law educator, lawyer*
Greenawalt, Robert Kent *lawyer, law educator*
Greenberg, Jack *lawyer, law educator*
Greenberger, Howard Leroy *lawyer, educator*
Guggenheim, Martin Franklin *law educator, lawyer*
Henkin, Louis *lawyer, law educator*
Hill, Alfred *lawyer, educator*
Kaden, Lewis B. *law educator, lawyer*
Kernochan, John Marshall *lawyer, educator*
King, Lawrence Philip *lawyer, educator*
Leebron, David Wayne *dean, law educator*
Leonard, Arthur Sherman *law educator, journalist*
Liebman, Lance Malcolm *law educator, lawyer*
Lowenfeld, Andreas Frank *law educator, arbitrator*
Lowenstein, Louis *legal educator*
Marcus, Maria Lenhoff *lawyer, law educator*
Maxfield, Guy Budd *lawyer, educator*
Mundheim, Robert Harry *law educator*
Murphy, Arthur William *lawyer, educator*
Redlich, Norman *lawyer, educator*
Rigolosi, Elaine La Monica *lawyer, educator, consultant*
Rubino, Victor Joseph *academic administrator, lawyer*
Sandler, Ross *law educator*
Schwartz, William *lawyer, educator*
Sexton, John Edward *lawyer, dean, law educator*
Siegel, Stanley *lawyer, educator*
Stewart, Richard Burleson *lawyer, educator*
Strauss, Peter L(ester) *law educator*
Teclaff, Ludwik Andrzej *law educator, consultant, author, lawyer*
Wellington, Harry Hillel *lawyer, educator*

Syracuse
Hancock, Stewart F., Jr. *law educator, judge*
Zimmerman, Golda *lawyer, educator*

Uniondale
Kessler, Lawrence W. *law educator, lawyer*

Washingtonville
King, Josephine Yager *law educator*

White Plains
Blank, Philip Bernardini *lawyer, educator*
Doernberg, Donald Lane *law educator*
Munneke, Gary Arthur *law educator, consultant*
Ottinger, Richard Lawrence *dean, law educator*
Sloan, F(rank) Blaine *law educator*

NORTH CAROLINA

Buies Creek
Davis, Ferd Leary, Jr. *law educator, lawyer, consultant*
Whichard, Willis Padgett *law educator, former state supreme court justice*

Chapel Hill
Daye, Charles Edward *law educator*
Dellinger, Anne Maxwell *law educator*
Mann, Richard Allan *law educator*
Nichol, Gene Ray, Jr. *university dean*
Wegner, Judith Welch *law educator, dean*

Charlotte
Chambers, Julius LeVonne *academic administrator, lawyer*

Cullowhee
Wilson, LeVon Edward *law educator, lawyer*

Durham
Admay, Catherine Adcock *law lecturer, researcher*
Havighurst, Clark Canfield *law educator, educator, law educator*
McCusker, Paul Donald *lawyer, educator*
Reppy, William Arneill, Jr. *law educator*
Schwarcz, Steven Lance *law educator, lawyer*

Greensboro
Swan, George Steven *law educator*

Greenville
Stevens, David Boyette *law educator*

Winston Salem
Foy, Herbert Miles, III *lawyer, educator*
Logan, David Andrew *lawyer, educator*
Walker, George Kontz *law educator*
Walsh, Robert K. *dean*

OHIO

Ada
Fenton, Howard Nathan, III *lawyer, educator*
French, Bruce Comly *lawyer, educator*
Lobenhofer, Louis F. *law educator*

Akron
Aynes, Richard L(ee) *law educator*
Blair, Pamela S. *lawyer*

Bowling Green
Holmes, Robert Allen *lawyer, educator, consultant, lecturer*

Cincinnati
Christenson, Gordon A. *law educator*
Martineau, Robert John *law educator*
Tomain, Joseph Patrick *dean, law educator*
Watts, Barbara Gayle *law academic administrator*

Cleveland
Jensen, Erik Michael *law educator*
Sharpe, Calvin William *law educator, arbitrator*
Werber, Stephen Jay *lawyer, educator*

Columbus
Bahls, Steven Carl *law educator, dean*
Blackburn, John D(avid) *legal educator, lawyer*
Burns, Robert Edward *lawyer*
Murphy, Earl Finbar *legal educator*
Quigley, John Bernard *law educator*
Rogers, Nancy Hardin *dean, law educator*

Oxford
Latimer, John Thomas *law educator*

Toledo
Friedman, Howard Martin *law educator*

OKLAHOMA

Oklahoma City
Beveridge, Norwood Pierson *law educator*

Stillwater
Frye, Edward Moses *law educator*

Tulsa
Belsky, Martin Henry *law educator, lawyer*
Frey, Martin Alan *lawyer, educator*

OREGON

Coos Bay
McClellan, Janet Elaine *law educator*

Eugene
Aldave, Barbara Bader *law educator, lawyer*
Frohnmayer, David Braden *academic administrator*
Kirkpatrick, Laird Clifford *law educator*
Kloppenberg, Lisa A. *law educator*
Swan, Peter Nachant *law educator, legal advisor*

Portland
Bernstine, Daniel O'Neal *law educator, university president*
Huffman, James Lloyd *law educator*
Lyons, Allen Ward *lawyer, educator*

PENNSYLVANIA

Devon
Garbarino, Robert Paul *retired administrative dean, lawyer*

Harrisburg
Diehm, James Warren *lawyer, educator*
Sheldon, J. Michael *lawyer, educator*

Philadelphia
Aronstein, Martin Joseph *law educator, lawyer*
Bocchino, Anthony J. *law educator, consultant*
Boss, Amelia Helen *law educator, lawyer*
Burbank, Stephen Bradner *law educator*
Darby, Karen Sue *legal education administrator*
Fitts, Michael Andrew *law educator, dean*
Leech, Noyes Elwood *lawyer, educator*
Pillai, K. G. Jan *law educator, lawyer*
Pollard, Dennis Bernard *lawyer, educator*
Strazzella, James Anthony *law educator, lawyer*
Summers, Clyde Wilson *law educator*

Pittsburgh
Frolik, Lawrence Anton *law educator, lawyer, consultant*
Nasri, William Zaki *legal educator, copyright consultant*
Nordenberg, Mark Alan *law educator, university official*
Rosen, Richard David *lawyer*
Shane, Peter Milo *law educator*

Scranton
Cimini, Joseph Fedele *law educator, lawyer, former magistrate*

Upper Darby
Hudiak, David Michael *academic administrator, lawyer*

Villanova
Frankino, Steven P. *lawyer, law educator*
Maule, James Edward *law educator, lawyer*
Murphy, John Francis *law educator, consultant, lawyer*

Wynnewood
Phillips, Almarin *economics educator, consultant*

RHODE ISLAND

Bristol
Bogus, Carl Thomas *law educator*

Providence
Lipsey, Howard Irwin *law educator, justice, lawyer*

SOUTH CAROLINA

Columbia
Felix, Robert Louis *law educator*
McCullough, Ralph Clayton, II *lawyer, educator*

SOUTH DAKOTA

Vermillion
Davidson, John Henry *legal educator*

TENNESSEE

Knoxville
Davies, Thomas Young, III *lawyer, law educator*
Galligan, Thomas C., Jr. *dean, law educator*

Livingston
Roberts, John M. *law educator, former prosecutor*

Memphis
Coffman, Claude T. *law educator, lawyer*
Davis, Frederick Benjamin *law educator*
White, Nicholas L. *legal educator*

Nashville
Belton, Robert *law educator*
Bloch, Frank Samuel *law educator*
Charney, Jonathan Isa *law educator, lawyer*
Ely, James Wallace, Jr. *law educator*
Soderquist, Larry Dean *lawyer, educator, consultant, writer*
Syverud, Kent Douglas *dean*

TEXAS

Austin
Allison, John Robert *lawyer, educator, author*
Baade, Hans Wolfgang *legal educator, law expert*
Baker, Mark Bruce *lawyer, educator*
Jentz, Gaylord Adair *law educator*
Laycock, Harold Douglas *law educator, writer*
Markovits, Richard Spencer *lawyer, educator*
Mersky, Roy Martin *law educator, librarian*
Powers, William Charles, Jr. *dean, law educator*
Sampson, John J. *law educator*
Sutton, John F., Jr. *law educator, dean, lawyer*

Dallas
Attanasio, John Baptist *dean, law educator*
Bromberg, Alan Robert *law educator*
Busbee, Kline Daniel, Jr. *retired law educator, lawyer*
Elkins-Elliott, Kay *law educator*
Galvin, Charles O'Neill *law educator*
Garner, Bryan Andrew *law educator, consultant, writer*
Lowe, John Stanley *lawyer, educator*

Fort Worth
Ingram, Denny Ouzts, Jr. *lawyer, educator*

Houston
Alderman, Richard Mark *legal educator, lawyer, television and radio commentator*
Douglas, James Matthew *law educator*
Douglass, John Jay *lawyer, educator*
Graving, Richard John *law educator*
Kelso, R. Randall *law educator*
Rapoport, Nancy B. *dean, law educator*

Lancaster
Pratt, John Edward *law educator*

Lubbock
Skillern, Frank Fletcher *law educator*

Plano
Hemingway, Richard William *law educator*

Pottsboro
Thomas, Ann Van Wynen *law educator*

San Antonio
Beyer, Gerry Wayne *law educator, lawyer*
Castleberry, James Newton, Jr. *retired law educator, dean*
Johnson, Vincent Robert *law educator, educator*
Reams, Bernard Dinsmore, Jr. *lawyer, educator*
Schlueter, David Arnold *law educator*

San Marcos
Parkin-Speer, Diane *English law educator*

Waco
Mc Swain, Angus Stewart, Jr. *retired law educator*

UTAH

Provo
Fleming, Joseph Clifton, Jr. *dean, law educator*
Hansen, H. Reese *dean, educator*

VERMONT

South Royalton
Chase, Jonathon B. *law educator*
Rudnick, Rebecca Sophie *lawyer, educator*

VIRGINIA

Arlington
Anthony, Robert Armstrong *law educator, lawyer*
Grady, Mark F. *dean, law educator*

Blacksburg
Jensen, Walter Edward *lawyer, educator*

Charlottesville
Abraham, Kenneth Samuel *law educator*
Bonnie, Richard Jeffrey *law educator, lawyer*
Ellett, John Spears, II *retired taxation educator, accountant, lawyer*
Howard, Arthur Ellsworth Dick *law educator*
Jeffries, John Calvin, Jr. *law educator*
Kitch, Edmund Wells *lawyer, educator, private investor*
Martin, David Alan *law educator*
Meador, Daniel John *law educator*
Menefee, Samuel Pyeatt *lawyer, anthropologist*
O'Neil, Robert Marchant *university administrator, law educator*
Scott, Robert Edwin *dean, law educator*
White, George Edward *law educator, lawyer*
Whitehead, John Wayne *law educator, organization administrator, author*

Fairfax
Rubenstein, Richard Edward *law educator*

Gloucester Point
Theberge, Norman Bartlett *educator, lawyer*

Lexington
Grunewald, Mark Howard *law educator*
Kirgis, Frederic Lee *law educator*
Partlett, David F. *dean, law educator*

Norfolk
Achampong, Francis Kofi *law educator, consultant*

Richmond
Bryson, William Hamilton *law educator*

Virginia Beach
Jones, Robert Griffith *lawyer, mayor*
Kerr, Gerald Lee, III *lawyer, paralegal educator*

Williamsburg
Marcus, Paul *law educator*
Reveley, Walter Taylor, III *dean*

WASHINGTON

Pullman
Michaelis, Karen Lauree *law educator*

Seattle
Anderson, Gene S. *lawyer*
Burke, William Thomas *law educator, lawyer*
Knight, W.H., Jr. (Joe Knight) *dean, law educator*
Price, John Richard *lawyer, law educator*
Starr, Isidore *law educator*

WEST VIRGINIA

Martinsburg
Day, Michael Gordon *law educator*

Morgantown
Fisher, John Welton, II *law educator, magistrate judge, university official*
Selinger, Carl M. *law educator, dean*

WISCONSIN

Madison
Baldwin, Gordon Brewster *law educator, lawyer*

EDUCATION

Davis, Kenneth Boone, Jr. *dean, law educator*
Foster, George William, Jr. *lawyer, educator*

Milwaukee
Eisenberg, Howard Bruce *law educator*
Geske, Janine Patricia *law educator, former state supreme court justice*
Kircher, John Joseph *law educator*

Stoughton
Wetzel, Volker Knoppke *law educator*

WYOMING

Kemmerer
Sundar, Vijendra *lawyer educator*

Laramie
Selig, Joel Louis *lawyer, educator*

TERRITORIES OF THE UNITED STATES

PUERTO RICO

San Juan
Ramos, Carlos E. *law educator*

Santa Maria Ponce
Cuprill, Charles *retired legal educator*

BELGIUM

Brussels
Garabedian, Daniel *lawyer, educator*

ENGLAND

Bedfordshire
Montgomery, John Warwick *law educator, theologian*

London
Wohl, James Paul *lawyer, educator, author*

GERMANY

Bayreuth
Otto, Harro *law educator*

Duisburg
Reuter, Michael F.M. *law educator*

ITALY

Rome
Morrone, Corrado Lucio *lawyer*

JAPAN

Tokyo
Taniguchi, Yasuhei *law educator*

NIGERIA

Port Harcourt
Uche, Jack-Osimiri *law educator*

SPAIN

Madrid
Lobreto-Lobo, Rafael *law educator*

SWITZERLAND

Zürich
Forstmoser, Peter Bruno *lawyer, educator*

UKRAINE

Kharkivskaya
Zinchenko, Vladimir *law educator*

ADDRESS UNPUBLISHED

Areen, Judith Carol *law educator, university dean*
Barnett, Randy Evan *law educator*
Bernstein, Merton Clay *law educator, lawyer, arbitrator*
Bork, Robert Heron *lawyer, author, educator, former federal judge*
Cunningham, Alice Welt *lawyer, legal educator*
Dunfee, Thomas Wylie *law educator*
Dutile, Fernand Neville *law educator*
Fort, Denise Douglas *law educator, former state official*
Fradella, Henry F. *law educator*
Freedman, Monroe Henry *lawyer, educator, columnist*
Fried, Charles *law educator*
Green, Carol H. *lawyer, educator, journalist*
Hazard, Geoffrey Cornell, Jr. *law educator*
Heymann, Philip Benjamin *law educator, academic director*
Lauderdale, Pat L. *law educator, social scientist*
Lungren, John Howard *law educator, oil and gas consultant, author*

Luskin, Joseph *law educator, researcher*
Maher, John A. *lawyer, law educator*
Manne, Henry Girard *lawyer, educator*
Matheson, Scott Milne, Jr. *dean, law educator*
McCarthy, J. Thomas *lawyer, educator*
Mlyniec, Wallace John *law educator, lawyer, consultant*
Paupp, Terrence Edward *research associate, educator*
Ramsey, Henry, Jr. *university official, lawyer, retired judge*
Reidenberg, Joel R. *law educator*
Sage, Albert Liston, III *lawyer, educator*
Schlueter, Linda Lee *law educator*
Termini, Roseann Bridget *lawyer, educator*
Young, Michael Kent *dean, lawyer, educator*

FINANCE AND REAL ESTATE

UNITED STATES

CALIFORNIA

Encino
Luna, Barbara Carole *financial analyst, accountant, appraiser*

Los Angeles
Bradshaw, Carl John *investor, lawyer, consultant*
Chan, David Ronald *tax specialist, lawyer*

Newport Beach
Harley, Halvor Larson *banker, lawyer*

CONNECTICUT

Hartford
Wilder, Michael Stephen *insurance company executive*

ILLINOIS

Chicago
DeMoss, Jon W. *insurance company executive, lawyer*

Deerfield
Lifschultz, Phillip *financial and tax consultant, accountant, lawyer*

Northbrook
McCabe, Michael J. *insurance executive*
Pike, Robert William *insurance company executive, lawyer*

Wilmette
Rosenbaum, Martin Michael *retired insurance company executive, lawyer*

INDIANA

Indianapolis
Ritz, Stephen Mark *financial advisor, lawyer*

KANSAS

Leawood
Gregory, Lewis Dean *trust company executive*

MARYLAND

Baltimore
Digges, Edward S(imms), Jr. *business management consultant*

Silver Spring
Grubbs, Donald Shaw, Jr. *retired actuary*

MASSACHUSETTS

Gloucester
Means, Elizabeth Rose Thayer *financial consultant, writer, lawyer*

NEBRASKA

Lincoln
Lundstrom, Gilbert Gene *banker, lawyer*

NEW JERSEY

Cherry Hill
Copsetta, Norman George *real estate executive*

NEW YORK

New York
Barbeosch, William Peter *banker, lawyer*
Brown, G(lenn) William, Jr. *bank executive*
Fignar, Eugene Michael *financial company executive, lawyer*
Kaplan, Keith Eugene *insurance company executive, lawyer*
Moore, Andrew Given Tobias, II *investment banker, law educator*
Roche, John J. *lawyer, consultant*
Schlang, David *real estate executive, lawyer*
Seltzer, Jeffrey Lloyd *diversified financial services company executive*

White Plains
Gillingham, Stephen Thomas *financial planner*

Whitestone
Brill, Steven Charles *financial advisor, lawyer*

OHIO

Beachwood
Krone, Norman Bernard *commercial real estate developer, lawyer*

Concord
Conway, Neil James, III *title company executive, lawyer, writer*

Toledo
Batt, Nick *property and investment executive*

PENNSYLVANIA

Philadelphia
Woosnam, Richard Edward *venture capitalist, lawyer*

Scranton
Yarmey, Richard Andrew *investment manager*

TEXAS

Tyler
Guin, Don Lester *insurance company executive*

WASHINGTON

Seattle
Campbell, Robert Hedgcock *investment banker, lawyer*

ADDRESS UNPUBLISHED

McLaughlin, Michael John *retired insurance company executive*
Nelson, Walter Gerald *retired insurance company executive*
Powell, Kathleen Lynch *lawyer, real estate executive*
Rondepierre, Edmond Francois *insurance executive*
Scipione, Richard Stephen *insurance company executive, lawyer, retired*
Shihata, Ibrahim Fahmy Ibrahim *retired bank executive, lawyer, writer*
Weber, John Walter *insurance company executive*
Yoskowitz, Irving Benjamin *merchant banker*

FOUNDATIONS AND ASSOCIATIONS

UNITED STATES

ALABAMA

Montgomery
Hamner, Reginald Turner *lawyer*

CALIFORNIA

Corona
Everett, Pamela Irene *legal management company executive, educator*

Irvine
Fouste, Donna H. *association executive*

Los Angeles
Wainess, Marcia Watson *legal administration consultant*

San Francisco
Neiman, Tanya Marie *legal association administrator*
Soberon, Presentacion Zablan *state bar administrator*

Santa Monica
Gray, Randall Joshua *information services administrator*

COLORADO

Denver
Fevurly, Keith Robert *educational administrator*
Turner, Charles Carre *association executive*

Lakewood
Isely, Henry Philip *association executive, integrative engineer, writer, educator*

CONNECTICUT

Riverside
Coulson, Robert *retired association executive, arbitrator, author*

DISTRICT OF COLUMBIA

Washington
Banzhaf, John F., III *legal association administrator, lawyer*
Bronstein, Alvin J. *lawyer*
Evans, Robert David *legal association executive*
Henderson, Thomas Henry, Jr. *lawyer, legal association executive*
Houseman, Alan William *lawyer*

Kreig, Andrew Thomas *trade association executive*
Lockyer, Charles Warren, Jr. *corporate executive*
Mazzaferri, Katherine Aquino *lawyer, bar association executive*
Mwenda, Kenneth Kaoma *legal consultant, advisor, educator*
Nardi Riddle, Clarine *association administrator, judge*
Peck, Robert Stephen *lawyer, educator*
Rasmus, John Charles *trade association executive, lawyer*
Sterling, Eric Edward *lawyer, legal policy advocate*

FLORIDA

Port Saint Lucie
Weber, Alban *association executive, lawyer*

Tallahassee
Masterson, Stephen Michael *lawyer*

GEORGIA

Atlanta
Kirwan, Allan August *bar executive*

HAWAII

Honolulu
Matayoshi, Coralie Chun *lawyer, bar association executive*

ILLINOIS

Chicago
Hayes, David John Arthur, Jr. *legal association executive*
Pavela, D. Jean *lawyer, law association administrator*
Stein, Robert Allen *legal association executive, law educator*
Wheeler, William Chamberlain, Jr. *association administrator, lawyer*

Park Ridge
Naker, Mary Leslie *legal firm executive*
Schmidt, Wayne Walter *law association executive*

Vernon Hills
Michalik, John James *legal educational association executive*

Waukegan
Hartman, Marshall J. *lawyer*

Wilmette
Geller, William Alan *criminal justice researcher, police and public safety consultant*

INDIANA

Bloomington
Franklin, Frederick Russell *retired legal association executive*

LOUISIANA

Baton Rouge
Pyle, Susan H. *legal association official*

New Orleans
Henderson, Helena Naughton *legal association administrator*

Shreveport
Allen, Marguerite E. *legal association administrator*

MARYLAND

Baltimore
Carlin, Paul Victor *legal association executive*
Eveleth, Janet Stidman *law association administrator*

Lanham Seabrook
Littlefield, Roy Everett, III *association executive, legal educator*

MASSACHUSETTS

Boston
Chenault Minot, Marilyn *legal executive*
Malone, Sue Urwyler *bar association executive*

Waltham
Roosevelt, James, Jr. *health plan executive, lawyer*

MICHIGAN

Lansing
Lobenherz, William Ernest *container company/association executive, lawyer*
Warren, J(ohn) Michael *lawyer*
Winder, Richard Earnest *legal foundation administrator, writer, consultant*

MISSISSIPPI

Jackson
Houchins, Larry *legal association administrator*
Wilson, L(eonard) H(enry) *lawyer*

GOVERNMENT

UNITED STATES

Reback, Joyce Ellen *lawyer*
Roberts, Edward Thomas *lawyer*
Robinson, James Kenneth *federal official*
Rodemeyer, Michael Leonard, Jr. *lawyer*
Rothenberg, Gilbert Steven *lawyer, law educator*
Rusch, Jonathan Jay *lawyer*
Russell, Michael James *lawyer*
Scheige, Steven Sheldon *lawyer*
Schwartzman, Andrew Jay *lawyer*
Sessions, Jefferson Beauregard, III *senator*
Sessions, William Steele *former government official, lawyer*
Shaheen, Michael Edmund, Jr. *lawyer, government official*
Shapiro, Michael Henry *government executive*
Sharfman, Stephen L. *lawyer*
Smith, Duncan Campbell, III *lawyer*
Smith, Dwight Chichester, III *lawyer*
Smith, Jack David *lawyer*
Smyth, Paul Burton *lawyer*
Solomon, Rodney Jeff *lawyer*
Somer-Greif, Penny Lynn *lawyer*
St. Amand, Janet G. *government relations lawyer*
Stanley, Keith Eugene *lawyer*
Stern, Gerald Mann *lawyer*
Stevens, Paul Schott *lawyer*
Stewart, David Pentland *lawyer, educator*
Stucky, Scott Wallace *lawyer*
Svab, Stephen *lawyer*
Timmer, Barbara *United States Senate official, lawyer*
Townsend, Joachim Rudiger (Jack Townsend) *lawyer*
Tyler, Peggy Lynne Bailey *lawyer*
Udall, Thomas (Tom Udall) *congressman*
Wagner, Brenda Carol *lawyer*
Wasserstrom, Ellen *lawyer*
Willmeth, Roger Earl *lawyer*
Winston, Judith Ann *lawyer*
Yambrusic, Edward Slavko *lawyer, consultant*
Zagami, Anthony James *lawyer*
Zwick, Kenneth Lowell *lawyer, director*

FLORIDA

Bartow
Cury, Bruce Paul *lawyer, magistrate, law educator*

Boca Raton
Sparks, William James Ashley *lawyer, educator*

Bradenton
Angulo, Charles Bonin *foreign service officer, lawyer*

Clearwater
Falkner, William Carroll *lawyer*
Tragos, George Euripedes *lawyer*

Coral Gables
Regalado, Eloisa *lawyer*

Fort Lauderdale
Stapleton, John Owen *lawyer*

Gainesville
Huszar, Arlene Celia *lawyer, mediator*

Live Oak
Peters, Lee Ira, Jr. *public defender*

Melbourne
Gougelman, Paul Reina *lawyer*

Miami
de Leon, John Louis *public defender*
Imperato, Joseph John *lawyer, composer*
Kuker, Alan Michael *lawyer*
Lewis, Guy A. *prosecutor*
Maniatty, Philip Ward *lawyer*
Tifford, Arthur W. *lawyer*

North Miami
Dellagloria, John Castle *city attorney, educator*

Orlando
Gold, I. Randall *lawyer*

Pensacola
Johnson, Rodney Marcum *lawyer*

Saint Augustine
Ansbacher, Sidney Franklyn *lawyer*

Tallahassee
Butterworth, Robert A. *state attorney general*
Conners, Patricia A. *lawyer*
Herskovitz, S(am) Marc *lawyer*
Kerns, David Vincent *lawyer*
Kirwin, Thomas F. *prosecutor*
Larson, Sharon D. *lawyer, human resources specialist*
Marshall, Marilyn Josephine *lawyer*
Miller, Gregory R. *lawyer*
Sprowls, Paul Alan *lawyer*
Thiele, Herbert William Albert *lawyer*
Whitney, Enoch Jonathan *lawyer*
Zaiser, Kent Ames *lawyer*

Tampa
Becker, Alison Lea *lawyer*
Cauley, Michael A. *prosecutor*
Wilson, Charles Reginald *lawyer, former prosecutor*

West Palm Beach
Carres, Louis George *lawyer*
Dytrych, Denise Distel *lawyer*
Romano, J. Eric *lawyer*

GEORGIA

Atlanta
Baker, Thurbert E. *state attorney general*
Murphy, Richard Patrick *lawyer*
Parker, Wilmer, III *lawyer, educator*
Raby, Kenneth Alan *lawyer, retired army officer*

Cordele
Christy, Gary Christopher *lawyer*

Decatur
Baker, Herman Dupree *lawyer*
Keyes, Gwendolyn Rebecca *lawyer, educator*

Savannah
Booth, Edmund A., Jr. *prosecutor*

HAWAII

Honolulu
Anzai, Earl I. *state attorney general*
Faust, Anne Sonia *lawyer*
McShane, Rosemary *lawyer*
Moroney, Michael John *lawyer*
Shaw, Abelina Madrid *state official*

IDAHO

Boise
Lance, Alan George *state attorney general*
Moss, Thomas E. *prosecutor*

Eagle
Richardson, Betty H. *lawyer, former prosecutor*

ILLINOIS

Chicago
Abt, Ralph Edwin *lawyer*
Bodenstein, Ira *lawyer*
Dutterer, Dennis Alton *lawyer*
Fitzgerald, Patrick J. *prosecutor*
Gagliardo, Joseph M(ichael) *lawyer*
Gerdy, Harry *lawyer*
Jackowiak, Patricia *lawyer*
Keryczynskyj, Leo Ihor *county official, educator, lawyer*
Krakowski, Richard John *lawyer, public relations executive*
Kuczwara, Thomas Paul *postal inspector, lawyer*
Lassar, Scott R. *prosecutor*
Lefkow, Michael Francis *lawyer*
MacCarthy, Terence Francis *lawyer*
Malinowski, Arthur Anthony *lawyer, labor arbitrator*
Mansfield, Karen Lee *lawyer*
Martin, Kelly Lynn *prosecutor*
Mikva, Abner Joseph *lawyer, retired federal judge*
Millichap, Paul Anthony *lawyer*
Richmond, James Glidden *lawyer*
Tryban, Esther Elizabeth *lawyer*

Deerfield
Kaplan, Alan Michael *lawyer*

Fairview Heights
Grace, (Walter) Charles *prosecutor*

Glen Ellyn
Hudson, Dennis Lee *lawyer, retired government official, arbitrator, educator*

Glenview
Tristano, Sandra *lawyer*

Joliet
Nate, Steven Scott *prosecutor*

Normal
Spears, Larry Jonell *lawyer*

Oak Brook
Miller, Ralph William, Jr. *lawyer*

Peoria
Swain, W. Timothy *lawyer*

Skokie
Pfannkuche, Christopher Edward Koenig *lawyer*

Springfield
Dodge, James William *lawyer, educator*
Ford, Diane *lawyer*
Hulin, Frances C. *prosecutor*
Mool, Deanna S. *lawyer*
Ryan, James E. *state attorney general*

INDIANA

Anderson
Eisele, John Eugene *lawyer*

Dyer
Van Bokkelen, Joseph Scott *prosecutor*

Evansville
Jones, David Leroy *lawyer, educator*

Franklin
Hamner, Lance Dalton *prosecutor*

Indianapolis
Brooks, Susan W. *prosecutor*
Carter, Steve *state attorney general*
Frank, Sarah Myers *lawyer*
Otero, Lettice Margarita *lawyer*
Shadley, Sue Ann *lawyer*

Lafayette
Gerde, Carlyle Noyes (Cy Gerde) *lawyer*

Munster
Amber, Douglas George *lawyer*

IOWA

Cedar Rapids
Larson, Charles W. *prosecutor*
Neumeyer, Debora Hewitt *lawyer*

Des Moines
Burns, Bernard John, III *public defender*
Colloton, Steven M. *prosecutor*
Kelly, Edwin Frost *prosecutor*
Miller, Thomas J. *state attorney general*

Nowadzky, Roger Alan *lawyer, lobbyist*

Dubuque
Ernst, Daniel Pearson *lawyer*

West Des Moines
Johnson, John Paul *lawyer, administrative law judge*

KANSAS

Clearwater
Matlack, Don(ald) (Clyde) *retired lawyer*

Hutchinson
O'Neal, Michael Ralph *state legislator, lawyer*

Olathe
Snowbarger, Vince *former congressman*

Overland Park
Vratil, John Logan *state legislator, lawyer*

Topeka
Stovall, Carla Jo *state attorney general*

Wichita
Flory, James E. *prosecutor*
Randels, Ed L. *lawyer*
Winkler, Dana John *lawyer*

KENTUCKY

Frankfort
Chandler, Albert Benjamin, III *attorney general*
Congleton, Conley Cole, III *lawyer*
Miller, Carl Theodore *lawyer*
Sonego, Ian G. *assistant attorney general*

Lexington
Van Tatenhove, Gregory F. *prosecutor*

Louisville
Barr, James Houston, III *lawyer*
Jewell, Franklin P. *lawyer*
Pence, Stephen Beville *prosecutor*
Smith, R(obert) Michael *lawyer*

Munfordville
Lang, George Edward *lawyer*

LOUISIANA

Baton Rouge
Ieyoub, Richard Phillip *state attorney general*
Parks, James William, II *public facilities executive, lawyer*

Lafayette
Mickel, Joseph Thomas *lawyer*

Marksville
Riddle, Charles Addison, III *state legislator, lawyer*

New Orleans
Jordan, Eddie J. *former prosecutor*
Letten, James *prosecutor*
Ortique, Revius Oliver, Jr. *city official, retired state supreme court justice*

Shreveport
Perlman, Jerald Lee *lawyer*
Washington, Donald W. *prosecutor*

MAINE

Augusta
Rowe, G. Steven *state attorney general, former state legislator*

Portland
Silsby, Paula *prosecutor*

MARYLAND

Annapolis
Duckett, Warren Bird, Jr. *lawyer*

Baltimore
Aisenstark, Avery *lawyer, educator*
Curran, J. Joseph, Jr. *state attorney general*
De Shields-Minnis, Tarra Ramit *lawyer*
DiBiagio, Thomas M. *prosecutor*
Hauhart, Robert Charles *lawyer, educator*

Bethesda
Dozier, Daniel Preston *lawyer*
Rubin, Allan Avrom *lawyer, regulatory agency consultant*

Chevy Chase
Murphy, Brian Charles *lawyer*

Columbia
Closson, Walter Franklin *child support prosecutor*

Gaithersburg
Lastra, Carlos Mariano *lawyer*
McCann, Joseph Leo *lawyer, former government official*

Hyattsville
Rummel, Edgar Ferrand *retired lawyer*

Kensington
Dauster, William Gary *lawyer, economist*

Rockville
Frye, Roland Mushat, Jr. *lawyer*
Parler, William Carlos *lawyer*
Yale, Kenneth P. *general counsel, dentist*

Silver Spring
Becker, Sandra Neiman Hammer *lawyer*
Lederer, Max Donald *lawyer*
Williams, Henry Newton *retired lawyer*

MASSACHUSETTS

Boston
(Guild) Del Bono, Irene Lillian *attorney general*
Donahue, Charlotte Mary *lawyer*
Hayward, Elizabeth *lawyer, artist*
Hoover, David Carlson *lawyer*
Katzmann, Gary Stephen *lawyer*
Nemon, Nancy Susan Schectman *lawyer*
Reilly, Thomas F. *state attorney general*
Starkey, Carol A. *lawyer, prosecutor*
Stern, Donald Kenneth *former prosecutor*
Sullivan, Michael J. *prosecutor*
Wexler, Barbara Lynne *lawyer*
Wild, Victor Allyn *lawyer, educator*

Framingham
Rikleen, Lauren Stiller *lawyer*

Hanscom AFB
Oulton, Donald Paul *lawyer*
Siegel, Julian Lee *lawyer*

North Quincy
Shapiro, Benjamin Louis *lawyer, association administrator*

Springfield
Susse, Sandra Slone *lawyer*

MICHIGAN

Detroit
Parker, Ross Gail *lawyer*

Grand Rapids
Chiara, Margaret *prosecutor*

Kalamazoo
Cinabro, Robert Henry *lawyer*

Lansing
Granholm, Jennifer Mulhern *state attorney general*
Haggerty, William Francis *lawyer*
Mead, Irene Marie
Styka, Ronald Joseph *lawyer*

Mount Pleasant
Novak, Joseph Anthony *lawyer*

MINNESOTA

Minneapolis
Genia, James Michael *lawyer*
Kuhn, Virginia R. *lawyer*
Munic, Martin Daniel *lawyer*

Rochester
Kauffman, Kreg Arlen *lawyer*

Saint Paul
Bastian, Gary Warren *judge*
Black, Bert *state administrator, lawyer*
Hatch, Mike *state attorney general*
Yucel, Edgar Kent *lawyer, consultant*

MISSISSIPPI

Jackson
Moore, Mike *state attorney general*

Oxford
Greenlee, Jim Ming *prosecutor*

Tylertown
Mord, Irving Conrad, II *lawyer*

West Point
Turner, Bennie L. *state legislator, lawyer*

MISSOURI

Columbia
Arnet, William Francis *lawyer*

Farmington
Pratte, Geoffrey Lynn *lawyer, arbitrator*

Independence
Lashley, Curtis Dale *lawyer*

Kansas City
Graves, Todd Peterson *prosecutor*
Jenkins, Melvin Lemuel *lawyer*

Saint Louis
Carlson, Mary Susan *lawyer*
Gruender, Raymond W. *prosecutor*
Johnson, William Ashton *retired lawyer*
Martin, Carla A. *lawyer, veterinarian*
O'Malley, Kevin Francis *lawyer, writer, educator*

MONTANA

Billings
Aldrich, Richard Kingsley *lawyer*
Mercer, William W. *prosecutor*

Helena
McGrath, Mike *lawyer, attorney general*

NEBRASKA

Columbus
Schumacher, Paul Maynard *lawyer*

Clifton
Shotwell, Charles Bland *lawyer, retired air force officer, educator*

Fairfax
Hopson, Everett George *retired lawyer*

Fairfax Station
Bishop, Alfred Chilton, Jr. *lawyer*
Carver, George Allen, Jr. *retired lawyer*

Fort Belvoir
Brittigan, Robert Lee *lawyer*

Fort Eustis
Smail, Laurence Mitchell *lawyer, educator*

Mc Lean
Cinquegrana, Americo Ralph *lawyer*
Mater, Maud *lawyer*

Midlothian
Nelson, Margaret Rose *lawyer, legal educator*

Mineral
Whitlock, Willie Walker *lawyer*

Norfolk
Corrigan, James Joseph, II *lawyer*

Oakton
Cutchin, James McKenney, IV *lawyer, engineer*

Petersburg
Burns, Cassandra Stroud *prosecutor*

Pulaski
McCarthy, Thomas James, Jr. *lawyer*

Reston
Calhoun-Senghor, Keith *lawyer*

Richmond
Beales, Randolph A. *state attorney general*
Gilmore, James Stuart, III *governor*
McFarlane, Walter Alexander *lawyer, educator*
Pollard, Overton Price *state agency executive, lawyer*

Roanoke
Brownlee, John L. *prosecutor*
Crouch, Robert P., Jr. *prosecutor*

Vienna
Stockstill, Charles James *lawyer, engineer*
Whitaker, Thomas Patrick *lawyer*

Virginia Beach
Schon, Alan Wallace *lawyer, actor*

WASHINGTON

Olympia
Gregoire, Christine O. *state attorney general*
Roe, Charles Barnett *lawyer*
Welsh, John Beresford, Jr. *lawyer*

Seattle
Lundin, John W. *lawyer, urban planner*
Pflaumer, Katrina C. *lawyer*

Tacoma
George, Nicholas *lawyer, entrepreneur*

Tumwater
Edmondson, Frank Kelley *lawyer, legal administrator*

Vancouver
Dodds, Michael Bruce *lawyer*

WEST VIRGINIA

Charleston
Betts, Rebecca A. *lawyer*
Kiss, Robert *state legislator*
Kopelman, Larry Gordon *lawyer*
Mc Graw, Darrell Vivian, Jr. *state attorney general*
Warner, Karl K. *prosecutor*

Huntington
Qualls, Alvie Edward, II *lawyer*

Wheeling
Johnston, Thomas E. *prosecutor*

WISCONSIN

Eau Claire
Frank, John LeRoy *lawyer, government executive, educator*

Keshena
Kussel, William Ferdinand, Jr. *lawyer*

Madison
Chandler, Richard Gates *lawyer*
Kennedy, Debora A. *lawyer*
Lautenschlager, Peggy Ann *prosecutor*
Thomas, Gloria *lawyer, nurse, state program administrator*

Milwaukee
Santelle, James Lewis *prosecutor*
Schmitz, Francis David *lawyer*

Sturgeon Bay
Korb, Joan *lawyer*

WYOMING

Cheyenne
MacMillan, Hoke *state attorney general*
Mead, Matthew Hansen *prosecutor*

Woodhouse, Gay Vanderpoel *state attorney general*

TERRITORIES OF THE UNITED STATES

GUAM

APO AP
Tock, Joseph *lawyer*

Agana
Black, Frederick A.

Hagatra
Troutman, Charles Henry, III *lawyer*

NORTHERN MARIANA ISLANDS

Saipan
Soll, Herbert D. *attorney general of Northern Mariana Islands*

PUERTO RICO

San Juan
Gil, Guillermo *prosecutor*
Rodriguez, Annabelle *state attorney general*

VIRGIN ISLANDS

Charlotte Amalie
Stridiron, Iver Allison *attorney general*

MILITARY ADDRESSES OF THE UNITED STATES

EUROPE

APO
Kammerer, Kelly Christian *lawyer*

CANADA

ONTARIO

Harrow
Kurtz, James P. *administrative law judge*

Ottawa
Buchanan, John MacLennan *Canadian provincial official*

ENGLAND

Beverley
Edles, Gary Joel *lawyer*

FRANCE

Paris
Sureau, Françis Maurice *lawyer*

Villamblard
Barnes, James Neil *lawyer*

INDIA

Songpat
Sharma, Harrish Kumar *lawyer*

THE NETHERLANDS

The Hague
Boukema, Henk Jan *lawyer*

TANZANIA

Arusha
Rapp, Stephen John *international procecutor*

ADDRESS UNPUBLISHED

Alm, Steve *former prosecutor*
Anderson, Suellen *lawyer*
Ashman, Kenneth J. *lawyer*
Barasch, David M. *former prosecutor*
Bettenhausen, Matthew Robert *lawyer*
Block, Richard Raphael *lawyer, arbitrator*
Booher, Alice Ann *lawyer*
Brechbill, Susan Reynolds *lawyer, educator*
Brieger, George *lawyer*
Buchanan, Calvin D. (Buck Buchanan) *former prosecutor*
Buchbinder, Darrell Bruce *lawyer*
Cambrice, Robert Louis *lawyer*
Capp, David A. *former prosecutor*
Carpenter, Susan Karen *public defender*
Condra, Allen Lee *lawyer, state official*
Darr, Carol C. *lawyer*
Davis, Wanda Rose *lawyer*
Del Papa, Frankie Sue *state attorney general*
Dettmer, Michael Hayes *former prosecutor*
Dietel, James Edwin *lawyer, consultant*

Dixon, Harry D., Jr. (Donnie Dixon) *former prosecutor*
Dunst, Isabel Paula *lawyer*
Finelsen, Libbi June *lawyer*
Foster, Lloyd Bennett *lawyer, musician*
French, Daniel J. *former prosecutor*
Gaines, Cherie Adelaide *lawyer*
Geloso-Barone, Rosalia A. *lawyer*
George, Joyce Jackson *lawyer, judge emeritus*
Godbey, Ronald Lee *lawyer*
Green, Jeffrey Steven *lawyer*
Helms, David Alonzo *lawyer, real estate broker*
Hendry, Nancy H. *lawyer*
Jallins, Richard David *lawyer*
Jochner, Michele Melina *lawyer*
Krieger, Frederic Michael *lawyer*
Litman, Harry Peter *lawyer, educator*
Lundy, Sheila Edwards *lawyer*
Lynch, Loretta E. *former prosecutor*
MacDougall, William Roderick *lawyer, county official*
Marr, Carmel Carrington *retired lawyer, retired state official*
Mayer, John William *lawyer*
McCloskey, Jay P. *former prosecutor*
McCormick, David Arthur *lawyer*
McMahon, Thomas Patrick *lawyer, state official*
Messick, Wiley Sanders *retired lawyer*
Metzger, Jeffrey Paul *lawyer*
Modisett, Jeffrey A. *lawyer, state attorney general, business executive*
Monaghan, Thomas Justin *former prosecutor*
Moran, Harold Joseph *retired lawyer*
Murray, Fred F. *lawyer*
Neugarten, Jerrold Lee *lawyer*
Patterson, Michael P. *former prosecutor*
Perkins, Dosite Hugh, Jr. *retired lawyer*
Poppler, Doris Swords *lawyer*
Purcell, Bill *mayor*
Ratti, Ricardo Allen *lawyer*
Reilly, Edward Francis, Jr. *former state senator, federal agency administrator*
Reno, Janet *former attorney general*
Rich, Michael Joseph *lawyer*
Rubinkowski, Conrad Sigmund *lawyer, film critic*
Salten, Frances Claire *retired lawyer*
Shaffert, Kurt *retired lawyer, chemical engineer*
Sherling, Fred W.
Smith, Deirdre O'Meara *lawyer*
Steptoe, Mary Lou *lawyer*
Stiles, Michael *former prosecutor*
Stillman, Elinor Hadley *retired lawyer*
Tisci, Michael Anthony *lawyer*
Weinstein, Arthur Gary *lawyer*
Whitehorn, Jo-Ann H. *lawyer*
Whitehouse, Sheldon *attorney general, lawyer*
York, Alexandra *lawyer*

INDUSTRY

UNITED STATES

ARKANSAS

Little Rock
Gardner, Kathleen D. *gas company executive, lawyer*

DISTRICT OF COLUMBIA

Washington
Moore, Robert Madison *food industry executive, lawyer*

INDIANA

Indianapolis
Greer, Charles Eugene *company executive, lawyer*

MARYLAND

Baltimore
Rheinstein, Peter Howard *health care company executive, consultant, physician, lawyer*

MICHIGAN

Benton Harbor
Hopp, Daniel Frederick *manufacturing company executive, lawyer*

Dearborn
Rintamaki, John M. *automotive executive*

MINNESOTA

Saint Paul
Boehnen, David Leo *grocery company executive, lawyer*
Cohen, Robert *medical device manufacturing and marketing executive*

NEBRASKA

Omaha
Rohde, Bruce C. *food company executive, lawyer*

NEW YORK

New York
Tse, Charles Yung Chang *drug company executive*

OHIO

Miamisburg
Thompson, Holley Marker *lawyer, marketing professional*

PENNSYLVANIA

Bethlehem
Barnette, Curtis Handley *steel company executive, lawyer*

Pittsburgh
Kelson, Richard B. *metal products executive*

TEXAS

Canyon Lake
Franklin, Robert Drury *oil company executive, lawyer*

Paris
Horner, Russell Grant, Jr. *real estate investor, retired energy and chemical company executive, inv*

San Antonio
McCoy, Reagan Scott *oil company executive, lawyer*

VIRGINIA

Richmond
Rudnick, Alan A. *management company executive, corporate lawyer*

ADDRESS UNPUBLISHED

Crawford, William Walsh *retired consumer products company executive*
Jackson, Robbi Jo *agricultural products company executive, lawyer*
Ormasa, John *retired utility executive, lawyer*
Sissel, George Allen *manufacturing executive, lawyer*

JUDICIAL ADMINISTRATION

UNITED STATES

ALABAMA

Ashland
Ingram, Kenneth Frank *retired state supreme court justice*

Birmingham
Goldstein, Debra Holly *judge*
Guin, Junius Foy, Jr. *federal judge*
Hancock, James Hughes *federal judge*
Pointer, Sam Clyde, Jr. *retired federal judge, lawyer*
Shores, Janie Ledlow *retired state supreme court justice*

Gadsden
Sledge, James Scott *judge*

Mobile
Butler, Charles Randolph, Jr. *federal judge*
Cox, Emmett Ripley *federal judge*
Howard, Alex T., Jr. *federal judge*
Pittman, Virgil *federal judge*

Montgomery
Brown, Jean Williams *state supreme court justice*
Carnes, Edward E. *federal judge*
De Ment, Ira *judge*
Dubina, Joel Fredrick *federal judge*
Godbold, John Cooper *federal judge*
Harwood, Robert Bernard, Jr. *judge*
Houston, James Gorman, Jr. *state supreme court justice*
Johnstone, Douglas Inge *judge*
Lyons, Champ, Jr. *judge*
Maddox, Alva Hugh *retired state supreme court justice*
Moore, Roy S. *judge*
See, Harold Frend *judge, law educator*
Steele, Rodney Redfearn *judge*
Stuart, Lyn (Jacquelyn L. Stuart) *judge*
Woodall, Thomas A. *judge*

ALASKA

Anchorage
Branson, Albert Harold (Harry Branson) *judge, educator*
Bryner, Alexander O. *state supreme court justice*
Compton, Allen T. *retired state supreme court justice*
Eastaugh, Robert L. *state supreme court justice*
Fabe, Dana Anderson *state supreme court chief justice*
Singleton, James Keith *federal judge*
von der Heydt, James Arnold *federal judge*

Fairbanks
Kleinfeld, Andrew J. *federal judge*

ARIZONA

Bisbee
Holland, Robert Dale *retired magistrate, consultant*

Phoenix
Broomfield, Robert Cameron *federal judge*
Canby, William Cameron, Jr. *federal judge*
Carroll, Earl Hamblin *federal judge*
Feldman, Stanley George *state supreme court justice*
Hicks, Bethany Gribben *judge, commissioner, lawyer*
Jones, Charles E. *state supreme court justice*

Martone, Frederick J. *state supreme court justice*
McGregor, Ruth Van Roekel *state supreme court justice*
McNamee, Stephen M. *federal judge*
Schroeder, Mary Murphy *federal judge*
Silverman, Barry G. *federal judge*
Strand, Roger Gordon *federal judge*
Weisenburger, Theodore Maurice *retired judge, poet, educator, writer*

Tucson
Browning, William Docker *federal judge*
Druke, William Erwin *lawyer, judge*
Marquez, Alfredo C. *federal judge*
Roll, John McCarthy *judge*
Zlaket, Thomas A. *state supreme court chief justice*

ARKANSAS

Batesville
Harkey, John Norman *judge*

Conway
Hays, Steele *retired state supreme court judge*

El Dorado
Barnes, Harry Francis *federal judge*

Fayetteville
Hendren, Jimm Larry *federal judge*

Little Rock
Arnold, Morris Sheppard *judge*
Arnold, Richard Sheppard *federal judge*
Arnold, W. H. (Dub Arnold) *state supreme court justice*
Corbin, Donald L. *state supreme court justice*
Glaze, Thomas A. *state supreme court justice*
Hannah, Jim *judge*
Imber, Annabelle Clinton *state supreme court justice*
Reasoner, Stephen M. *federal judge*
Smith, Lavenski R. (Vence Smith) *former state supreme court justice*
Thornton, Ray *state supreme court justice, former congressman*
Wilson, William R., Jr. *judge*
Woods, Henry *federal judge*
Wright, Susan Webber *judge*

CALIFORNIA

Fort Bragg
Lehan, Jonathan Michael *judge*

Fresno
Coyle, Robert Everett *federal judge*
Petrucelli, James Michael *judge*
Wanger, Oliver Winston *federal judge*

Glendale
Early, Alexander Rieman, III *judge*

Long Beach
Tucker, Marcus Othello *judge*

Los Angeles
Alarcon, Arthur Lawrence *federal judge*
Armstrong, Orville *judge*
Bufford, Samuel Lawrence *federal judge*
Collins, Audrey B. *judge*
Curry, Daniel Arthur *judge*
Hupp, Harry L. *federal judge*
Kelleher, Robert Joseph *federal judge*
Marshall, Consuelo Bland *federal judge*
Mohr, Anthony James *judge*
Rafeedie, Edward *senior federal judge*
Takasugi, Robert Mitsuhiro *federal judge*
Tevrizian, Dickran M., Jr. *federal judge*
Yager, Thomas C. *judge*

Mendocino
Masterson, William A. *retired judge*

Oakland
Jensen, D. Lowell *federal judge, lawyer, government official*
Newsome, Randall Jackson *judge*
Wilken, Claudia *judge*

Pasadena
Boochever, Robert *federal judge*
Fernandez, Ferdinand Francis *federal judge*
Fisher, Raymond Corley *judge, lawyer*
Goodwin, Alfred Theodore *federal judge*
Hall, Cynthia Holcomb *federal judge*
Johnson, Barbara Jean *retired judge, lawyer*
Kozinski, Alex *federal judge*
Nelson, Dorothy Wright (Mrs. James F. Nelson) *federal judge*
Paez, Richard A. *federal judge*
Rymer, Pamela Ann *federal judge*
Tashima, Atsushi Wallace *federal judge*
Wardlaw, Kim A.M. *federal judge*

Ramona
Jordan, David Francis, Jr. *retired judge*

Riverside
Holmes, Dallas Scott *judge, educator*
Timlin, Robert J. *judge*

Sacramento
Dahl, Loren Silvester *retired federal judge*
Karlton, Lawrence K. *federal judge*
Kolkey, Daniel Miles *judge*
Levi, David F. *federal judge*
Moulds, John F. *federal judge*
Schwartz, Milton Lewis *federal judge*
Van Camp, Brian Ralph *judge*

San Diego
Bowie, Peter Wentworth *judge, educator*
Brewster, Rudi Milton *judge*
Gilliam, Earl B. *federal judge*
Harutunian, Albert T(heodore), III *judge*
Jones, Napoleon A., Jr. *judge*
Lewis, Gerald Jorgensen *judge*
McKeown, Mary Margaret *federal judge*
Rhoades, John Skylstead, Sr. *federal judge*
Thompson, David Renwick *federal judge*
Thompson, Gordon, Jr. *federal judge*
Turrentine, Howard Boyd *federal judge*
Wallace, J. Clifford *federal judge*

San Fernando
Schwab, Howard Joel *judge*

San Francisco
Anderson, Carl West *retired judge*
Baxter, Marvin Ray *state supreme court justice*
Berzon, Marsha S. *federal judge*
Brown, Janice Rogers *state supreme court justice*
Browning, James Robert *federal judge*
Chin, Ming *state supreme court justice*
Conti, Samuel *federal judge*
Fletcher, William A. *federal judge, law educator*
George, Ronald M. *state supreme court chief justice*
Kennard, Joyce L. *state supreme court justice*
Noonan, John T., Jr. *federal judge, law educator*
Schwarzer, William W *federal judge*
Sneed, Joseph Tyree, III *federal judge*
Walker, Vaughn R. *federal judge*
Werdegar, Kathryn Mickle *state supreme court justice*

San Jose
Ingram, William Austin *federal judge*
Maloney, Patrick Raymond *retired judge*
Panelli, Edward Alexander *retired state supreme court justice*
Whyte, Ronald M. *federal judge*
Williams, Spencer Mortimer *federal judge*

San Marino
Mortimer, Wendell Reed, Jr. *judge*

Santa Ana
Barr, James Norman *federal judge*
Ferguson, Warren John *federal judge*
Stotler, Alicemarie Huber *judge*

Santa Barbara
Aldisert, Ruggero John *federal judge*

Santa Monica
Vega, Benjamin Urbizo *retired judge, television producer*

Studio City
Lasarow, William Julius *retired federal judge*

Woodland Hills
Mund, Geraldine *judge*
Pregerson, Harry *federal judge*

COLORADO

Central City
Rodgers, Frederic Barker *judge*

Denver
Bender, Michael Lee *state supreme court justice*
Coats, Nathan B. *judge*
Ebel, David M. *federal judge*
Felter, Edwin Lester, Jr. *judge*
Hobbs, Gregory James, Jr. *state supreme court justice*
Kane, John Lawrence, Jr. *federal judge*
Kirshbaum, Howard M. *retired judge, arbiter*
Kourlis, Rebecca Love *state supreme court justice*
Lucero, Carlos *federal judge*
Martinez, Alex J. *state supreme court justice*
McWilliams, Robert Hugh *federal judge*
Mullarkey, Mary J. *state supreme court chief justice*
Nottingham, Edward Willis, Jr. *federal judge*
Porfilio, John Carbone *federal judge*
Rice, Nancy E. *state supreme court justice*
Rovira, Luis Dario *state supreme court justice*
Satter, Raymond Nathan *judge*

Englewood
Erickson, William Hurt *retired state supreme court justice*

Fort Collins
Gandy, H. Conway *retired judge, state official*

Golden
Scott, Gregory Kellam *judge trial referee, former state supreme court justice, lawyer*

CONNECTICUT

Bridgeport
Eginton, Warren William *federal judge*

Danbury
Yamin, Dianne Elizabeth *judge*

Deep River
Spallone, Jeanne Field *retired state judge*

Hartford
Bieluch, William Charles *judge*
Borden, David M. *state supreme court justice*
Chatigny, Robert Neil *judge*
Droney, Christopher F. *judge*
Katz, Joette *state supreme court justice*
Killian, Robert Kenneth, Jr. *judge, lawyer*
Newman, Jon O. *federal judge*
Norcott, Flemming L., Jr. *state supreme court justice*
Palmer, Richard N. *state supreme court justice*
Peters, Ellen Ash *judge, trial referee, retired state supreme court justice*
Schaller, Barry R. *judge*
Shea, David Michael *state supreme court justice*
Sullivan, William J. *state supreme court justice*
Thompson, Alvin W. *judge*
Vertefeuille, Christine S. *judge*
Zarella, Peter T. *judge*

Middlebury
McDonald, Francis Michael *judge trial referee, retired state supreme court justice*

New Britain
Meskill, Thomas J. *federal judge*

New Haven
Arterton, Janet Bond *judge*
Berdon, Robert Irwin *judge trial referee, retired state supreme court justice*
Burns, Ellen Bree *federal judge*
Cabranes, José Alberto *federal judge*
Calabresi, Guido *federal judge, law educator*
Dorsey, Peter Collins *federal judge*
Walker, John Mercer, Jr. *federal judge*
Winter, Ralph Karl, Jr. *federal judge*

Stamford
Callahan, Robert Jeremiah *retired state supreme court justice, trial referee*

Vernon Rockville
Purnell, Oliver James, III *judge*

Waterbury
Goettel, Gerard Louis *federal judge*

DELAWARE

Dover
Hartnett, Maurice A., III *state supreme court justice*

Georgetown
Holland, Randy James *state supreme court justice*

Wilmington
Ambro, Thomas L. *federal judge*
Balick, Helen Shaffer *retired judge*
Jacobs, Jack Bernard *judge*
Latchum, James Levin *federal judge*
Roth, Jane Richards *federal judge*
Stapleton, Walter King *federal judge*
Veasey, Eugene Norman *state supreme court chief justice*

DISTRICT OF COLUMBIA

Washington
Archer, Glenn LeRoy, Jr. *federal judge*
Bayly, John Henry, Jr. *judge*
Beddow, Richard Harold *judge*
Beghe, Renato *federal judge*
Belson, James Anthony *judge*
Berkley, Burton *federal judge*
Breyer, Stephen Gerald *United States supreme court justice*
Bryson, William Curtis *federal judge*
Burnett, Arthur Louis, Sr. *judge*
Chabot, Herbert L. *judge*
Chiechi, Carolyn Phyllis *federal judge*
Clevenger, Raymond C., III *federal judge*
Cohen, Mary Ann *judge*
Couvillion, David Irvin *federal judge*
Cowen, Wilson *federal judge*
Crawford, Susan Jean *federal judge*
Edwards, Harry T. *federal judge*
Farley, John Joseph, III *federal judge*
Farrell, Michael W. *state supreme court justice*
Flannery, Thomas Aquinas *federal judge*
Friedman, Daniel Mortimer *federal judge*
Gajarsa, Arthur J. *circuit court judge*
Gallagher, George R. *judge*
Garland, Merrick Brian *federal judge*
Gerber, Joel *federal judge*
Gibson, Reginald Walker *federal judge*
Ginsburg, Douglas Howard *federal judge, educator*
Ginsburg, Ruth Bader *United States supreme court justice*
Glickman, Stephen *state supreme court justice*
Goldberg, Stanley Joshua *federal judge*
Green, Joyce Hens *federal judge*
Harris, Stanley S. *judge*
Henderson, Karen LeCraft *federal judge*
Holdaway, Ronald M. *federal judge*
Ivers, Donald Louis *judge*
Jackson, Thomas Penfield *federal judge*
Jacobs, Julian I. *federal judge*
Johnson, Norma Holloway *federal judge*
Kennedy, Anthony McLeod *United States supreme court justice*
Kern, John Worth, III *judge*
Kline, Norman Douglas *federal judge*
Kramer, Kenneth Bentley *federal judge, former congressman*
Laro, David *judge*
Lourie, Alan David *federal judge*
Mack, Julia Cooper *judge*
Margolis, Lawrence Stanley *federal judge*
Marvel, L. Paige *federal judge*
Mayer, Haldane Robert *federal chief judge*
Michel, Paul Redmond *federal judge*
Miller, Christine Odell Cook *judge*
Nebeker, Frank Quill *federal judge*
Newman, Pauline *federal judge*
O'Connor, Sandra Day *United States supreme court justice*
Parr, Carolyn Miller *federal judge*
Plager, S. Jay *federal judge*
Rader, Randall Ray *federal judge*
Randolph, A(rthur) Raymond *federal judge*
Rehnquist, William Hubbs *United States supreme court chief justice*
Robertson, James *judge*
Robinson, Wilkes Coleman *retired federal judge*
Rogers, Judith W. *federal judge*
Ruiz, Vanessa *state supreme court justice*
Scalia, Antonin *United States supreme court justice*
Schall, Alvin Anthony *federal judge*
Schwelb, Frank Ernest *district judge*
Sentelle, David Bryan *federal judge*
Smith, Loren Allan *federal judge*
Smith, Roy Philip *judge*
Steadman, John Montague *appellate court judge*
Steinberg, Jonathan Robert *judge*
Stevens, John Paul *United States supreme court justice*
Sullivan, Eugene Raymond *federal judge*
Swift, Stephen Jensen *federal judge*
Tatel, David Stephen *federal judge*
Terry, John Alfred *state supreme court judge*
Thomas, Clarence *United States supreme court justice*
Turner, James Thomas *judge*
Urbina, Ricardo Manuel *judge*
Wagner, Annice McBryde *judge*
Wagner, Curtis Lee, Jr. *judge*
Washington, Eric T. *state supreme court justice*
Weinstein, Diane Gilbert *federal judge*
Whalen, Laurence J. *federal judge*
Williams, Stephen Fain *federal judge*

FLORIDA

Clearwater
Peters, Robert Timothy *judge*

Coral Gables
Davis, Mattie Belle Edwards *retired county judge*

Daytona Beach
Palmer, William D. *judge*
Rouse, Robert Kelly, Jr. *judge*

Deland
Sanders, Edwin Perry Bartley *judge*

Fort Lauderdale
Gonzalez, Jose Alejandro, Jr. *federal judge*
Roettger, Norman Charles, Jr. *federal judge*

Fort Myers
Shafer, Robert Tinsley, Jr. *judge*

Gulfport
Chipman, Marion Walter *retired judge*

Jacksonville
Black, Susan Harrell *federal judge*
Hill, James Clinkscales *federal judge*
Melton, Howell Webster, Sr. *federal judge*
Nimmons, Ralph Wilson, Jr. *federal judge*
Schlesinger, Harvey Erwin *judge*
Tjoflat, Gerald Bard *federal judge*

Key Biscayne
Kraft, C. William, Jr. *federal judge*

Miami
Barkett, Rosemary *federal judge*
Brown, Stephen Thomas *judge*
Cristol, A. Jay *federal judge*
Davis, Edward Bertrand *retired federal judge, lawyer*
Fay, Peter Thorp *federal judge*
Freeman, Gill Sherryl *judge*
Gold, Alan Stephen *federal judge*
Highsmith, Shelby *federal judge*
King, James Lawrence *federal judge*
Marcus, Stanley *federal judge*
Rosinek, Jeffrey *judge*
Siegel, Paul *judge*
Ungaro-Benages, Ursula Mancusi *federal judge*

Orlando
Fawsett, Patricia Combs *federal judge*
Young, George Cressler *federal judge*

Pensacola
Vinson, C. Roger *federal judge*

Saint Petersburg
Grube, Karl Bertram *judge*
Roney, Paul H(itch) *federal judge*

Tallahassee
Anstead, Harry Lee *state supreme court justice*
Grimes, Stephen Henry *retired state supreme court justice*
Harding, Major Best *state supreme court chief justice*
Lewis, R. Fred *state supreme court justice*
Quince, Peggy A. *state supreme court justice*
Shaw, Leander Jerry, Jr. *state supreme court justice*
Webster, Peter David *judge*

Tampa
Corcoran, Clement Timothy, III *judge*
Dail, Joseph Garner, Jr. *judge*
Kovachevich, Elizabeth Anne *federal judge*
Menendez, Manuel, Jr. *judge*

Venice
Hackett, Barbara (Kloka) *federal judge*

Viera
Rainwater, Tonya B. *judge*

West Palm Beach
Eschbach, Jesse Ernest *federal judge*
Ryskamp, Kenneth Lee *federal judge*
Wroble, Arthur Gerard *judge*

GEORGIA

Atlanta
Benham, Robert *state supreme court justice*
Birch, Stanley Francis, Jr. *federal judge*
Camp, Jack Tarpley, Jr. *federal judge*
Carley, George H. *state supreme court justice*
Carnes, Julie Elizabeth *federal judge*
Deane, Richard Hunter, Jr. *federal judge*
Edmondson, James Larry *federal judge*
Fletcher, Norman S. *state supreme court justice*
Forrester, J. Owen *federal judge*
Hines, Preston Harris *state supreme court justice*
Hull, Frank Mays *federal judge*
Hunstein, Carol *state supreme court justice*
Kravitch, Phyllis A. *federal judge*
Martin, Beverly *federal judge*
O'Kelley, William Clark *federal judge*
Ward, Horace Taliaferro *federal judge*

Augusta
Bowen, Dudley Hollingsworth, Jr. *federal judge*

Brunswick
Alaimo, Anthony A. *federal judge*

Cleveland
Barrett, David Eugene *judge*

Columbus
Laney, John Thomas, III *federal judge*

Jeffersonville
Fitzpatrick, Duross *federal judge*

Lawrenceville
Reeves, Gene *judge*

Macon
Anderson, Robert Lanier, III *federal judge*
Hershner, Robert Franklin, Jr. *judge*
Owens, Wilbur Dawson, Jr. *federal judge*
Phillips, J(ohn) Taylor *judge*

Savannah
Edenfield, Berry Avant *federal judge*

HAWAII

Honolulu
Acoba, Simeon Rivera, Jr. *state supreme court justice, educator*
Choy, Herbert Young Cho *federal judge*
Levinson, Steven Henry *state supreme court justice*
Moon, Ronald T. Y. *state supreme court chief justice*
Nakayama, Paula Aiko *state supreme court justice*
Ramil, Mario R. *state supreme court justice*

IDAHO

Boise
Eismann, Daniel T. *judge*
Kidwell, Wayne L. *state supreme court justice*
McDevitt, Charles Francis *retired state supreme court justice, lawyer*
Nelson, Thomas G. *federal judge*
Trott, Stephen Spangler *federal judge, musician*
Walters, Jesse Raymond, Jr. *state supreme court justice*

ILLINOIS

Belleville
Ferguson, John Marshall *retired federal judge*
Stevens, C. Glenn *judge*

Benton
Foreman, James Louis *retired judge*

Chicago
Alesia, James H(enry) *judge*
Aspen, Marvin Edward *federal judge*
Barliant, Ronald *federal judge*
Bauer, William Joseph *federal judge*
Bilandic, Michael A. *retired state supreme court justice, former mayor*
Conlon, Suzanne B. *federal judge*
Cousins, William, Jr. *judge*
Cudahy, Richard D. *federal judge*
Easterbrook, Frank Hoover *federal judge*
Fairchild, Thomas E. *federal judge*
Fitzgerald, Thomas Robert *judge*
Flaum, Joel Martin *federal judge*
Freeman, Charles E. *state supreme court justice*
Funderburk, Raymond *judge*
Grady, John F. *federal judge*
Hart, William Thomas *federal judge*
Leighton, George Neves *retired federal judge*
Leinenweber, Harry D. *federal judge*
McMorrow, Mary Ann G. *state supreme court justice*
Moran, James Byron *federal judge*
Morrissey, George Michael *judge*
Nordberg, John Albert *federal judge*
Norgle, Charles Ronald, Sr. *federal judge*
Pallmeyer, Rebecca Ruth *federal judge*
Posner, Richard Allen *federal judge*
Rovner, Ilana Kara Diamond *federal judge*
Shadur, Milton Irving *judge*
Sonderby, Susan Pierson *federal judge*
Squires, John Henry *judge*
Williams, Ann Claire *federal judge*

Danville
Garman, Rita B. *judge*

East Saint Louis
Beatty, William Louis *federal judge*
Stiehl, William D. *federal judge*

Edwardsville
Crowder, Barbara Lynn *judge*

Elgin
Kirkland, Alfred Younges, Sr. *federal judge*

Fairview Heights
Harrison, Moses W., II *state supreme court chief justice*

Hennepin
Bumgarner, James McNabb *judge*

Palatine
Roti, Thomas David *judge*

Peoria
Heiple, James Dee *former state supreme court justice*
Mihm, Michael Martin *federal judge*

Rock Island
Kilbride, Thomas L. *judge*

Rockford
Reinhard, Philip G. *federal judge*

Springfield
Lessen, Larry Lee *federal judge*
Miller, Benjamin K. *retired state supreme court justice*
Mills, Richard Henry *federal judge*
Wood, Harlington, Jr. *federal judge*

Waukegan
Brady, Terrence Joseph *judge*

Wheaton
Thomas, Robert R. *judge*

Wilmette
Bowman, George Arthur, Jr. *retired judge*

INDIANA

Boonville
Campbell, Edward Adolph *judge, electrical engineer*

Crown Point
Dywan, Jeffery Joseph *judge*

Evansville
Capshaw, Tommie Dean *judge*
Liberty, Arthur Andrew *judge*

Fort Wayne
Lee, William Charles *judge*

Hammond
Rodovich, Andrew Paul *magistrate*

Indianapolis
Barker, Sarah Evans *judge*
Boehm, Theodore Reed *judge*
Dickson, Brent E(llis) *state supreme court justice*
Dillin, S. Hugh *federal judge*
Fisher, Thomas Graham *judge*
Givan, Richard Martin *retired state supreme court justice*
Hamilton, David F. *judge*
McKinney, Larry J. *federal judge*
Rucker, Robert D. *judge*
Shepard, Randall Terry *state supreme court chief justice*
Sullivan, Frank, Jr. *state supreme court justice*

Kokomo
Stein, Eleanor Bankoff *judge*

Lafayette
Kanne, Michael Stephen *federal judge*

Lagrange
Brown, George E. *judge, educator*

Nashville
Stewart, Judith A. *judge, former prosecutor*

South Bend
Brueseke, Harold Edward *magistrate*
Manion, Daniel Anthony *federal judge*
Ripple, Kenneth Francis *federal judge*

IOWA

Algona
Andreasen, James Hallis *retired state supreme court judge*

Cedar Rapids
Hansen, David Rasmussen *federal judge*
Mc Manus, Edward Joseph *federal judge*

Chariton
Stuart, William Corwin *federal judge*

Council Bluffs
Peterson, Richard William *judge, lawyer*

Des Moines
Cady, Mark S. *state supreme court justice*
Carter, James H. *state supreme court justice*
Fagg, George Gardner *federal judge*
Harris, K. David *state supreme court justice*
Larson, Jerry Leroy *state supreme court justice*
Lavorato, Louis A. *state supreme court chief justice*
Snell, Bruce M., Jr. *state supreme court justice*
Streit, Michael J. *judge*
Ternus, Marsha K. *state supreme court justice*
Vietor, Harold Duane *federal judge*
Wolle, Charles Robert *federal judge*

Ottumwa
McGiverin, Arthur A. *former state supreme court chief justice*

Sioux City
O'Brien, Donald Eugene *federal judge*

KANSAS

Kansas City
Lungstrum, John W. *federal judge*
VanBebber, George Thomas *federal judge*
Vratil, Kathryn Hoefer *federal judge*
Waxse, David John *judge*

Lawrence
Briscoe, Mary Beck *federal judge*
Tacha, Deanell Reece *federal judge*

Topeka
Abbott, Bob *state supreme court justice*
Allegrucci, Donald Lee *state supreme court justice*
Cox, Joseph Lawrence *judge*
Crow, Sam Alfred *federal judge*
Davis, Robert Edward *state supreme court justice*
Larson, Edward *state supreme court justice*
Lockett, Tyler Charles *state supreme court justice*
Marquardt, Christel Elisabeth *judge*
McFarland, Kay Eleanor *state supreme court chief justice*
Rogers, Richard Dean *federal judge*
Saffels, Dale Emerson *federal judge*
Six, Fred N. *state supreme court justice*

Wichita
Brown, Wesley Ernest *federal judge*

KENTUCKY

Bowling Green
Huddleston, Joseph Russell *judge*

Elizabethtown
Cooper, William S. *state supreme court justice*

Frankfort
Graves, John William *state supreme court justice*
Johnstone, Martin E. *state supreme court justice*
Lambert, Joseph Earl *state supreme court chief justice*
Stephens, Robert F. *former state supreme court chief justice*
Stumbo, Janet Lynn *state supreme court justice*
Wintersheimer, Donald Carl *state supreme court justice*

Hopkinsville
Adams, James G., Jr. *judge, lawyer*

Lexington
Forester, Karl S. *district court judge*
Keller, James *state supreme court justice*
Varellas, Sandra Motte *judge*

London
Coffman, Jennifer Burcham *federal judge*
Siler, Eugene Edward, Jr. *federal judge*

Louisville
Boggs, Danny Julian *federal judge*
Heyburn, John Gilpin, II *federal judge*
Martin, Boyce Ficklen, Jr. *federal judge*
Roberts, J. Wendell *federal judge*
Simpson, Charles R., III *judge*

Madisonville
Spain, Thomas B. *retired state supreme court justice*

Richmond
Chenault, James Stouffer *judge*

Wickliffe
Shadoan, William Lewis *judge*

LOUISIANA

Baton Rouge
Parker, John Victor *federal judge*
Polozola, Frank Joseph *federal judge*

Lafayette
Davis, William Eugene *federal judge*
Duhe, John Malcolm, Jr. *federal judge*

Lake Charles
Trimble, James T., Jr. *federal judge*

Metairie
Schwartz, Charles, Jr. *federal judge*
Wicker, Thomas Carey, Jr. *retired judge*

New Orleans
Beer, Peter Hill *federal judge*
Calogero, Pascal Frank, Jr. *state supreme court chief justice*
Dennis, James Leon *federal judge*
Duplantier, Adrian Guy *federal judge*
Duval, Stanwood Richardson, Jr. *judge*
Feldman, Martin L. C. *federal judge*
Johnson, Bernette J. *state supreme court justice*
Kimball, Catherine D. *state supreme court justice*
Knoll, Jeannette Theriot *state supreme court justice*
Livaudais, Marcel, Jr. *federal judge*
Mentz, Henry Alvan, Jr. *federal judge*
Mitchell, Lansing Leroy *retired federal judge*
Porteous, G. Thomas, Jr. *judge*
Sear, Morey Leonard *federal judge, educator*
Traylor, Chet D. *state supreme court justice*
Victory, Jeffrey Paul *state supreme court justice*
Wiener, Jacques Loeb, Jr. *federal judge*

Ponchatoula
Kuhn, James E. *judge*

Shreveport
Payne, Roy Steven *judge*
Politz, Henry Anthony *federal judge*
Stagg, Tom *federal judge*
Stewart, Carl E. *federal judge*

MAINE

Auburn
Clifford, Robert William *state supreme court justice*

Bangor
Rudman, Paul Lewis *state supreme court justice*

Portland
Alexander, Donald G. *state supreme court justice*
Bradford, Carl O. *judge*
Calkins, Susan W. *state supreme court justice*
Carter, Gene *federal judge*
Coffin, Frank Morey *federal judge*
Dana, Howard H., Jr. *state supreme court justice*
Glassman, Caroline Duby *state supreme court justice*
Hornby, David Brock *federal judge*
Lipez, Kermit V. *federal judge, former state supreme court justice*
McKusick, Vincent Lee *former state supreme court justice, lawyer, arbitrator, mediator*
Saufley, Leigh Ingalls *state supreme court justice*

Rockland
Collins, Samuel W., Jr. *judge*

MARYLAND

Annapolis
Battaglia, Lynne Ann *judge*
Cathell, Dale Roberts *state supreme court justice*

Eldridge, John Cole *judge*

Baltimore
Bell, Robert M. *state supreme court justice*
Black, Walter Evan, Jr. *federal judge*
Derby, Ernest Stephen *federal judge*
Garbis, Marvin Joseph *judge*
Harvey, Alexander, II *federal judge*
Legg, Benson Everett *federal judge*
Maletz, Herbert Naaman *federal judge*
Motz, Diana Gribbon *federal judge*
Motz, John Frederick *federal judge*
Niemeyer, Paul Victor *federal judge*
Northrop, Edward Skottowe *federal judge*
Quarles, William Daniel *judge*
Rodowsky, Lawrence Francis *retired state judge*

Greenbelt
Chasanow, Deborah K. *federal judge*
Messitte, Peter Jo *judge*

Rockville
Bernstein, Edwin S. *judge*
Raker, Irma Steinberg *judge*

Towson
Wilner, Alan M. *judge*

Upper Marlboro
Chasanow, Howard Stuart *retired judge, lecturer*
Harrell, Glenn T., Jr. *judge*
Krauser, Sherrie L. *judge*

MASSACHUSETTS

Boston
Boudin, Michael *federal judge*
Bowler, Marianne Bianca *judge*
Bownes, Hugh Henry *federal judge*
Campbell, Levin Hicks *federal judge*
Cordy, Robert J. *judge*
Cowin, Judith A. *judge*
Greaney, John M. *state supreme court justice*
Ireland, Roderick L. *state supreme court justice*
Keeton, Robert Ernest *federal judge*
Lasker, Morris E. *judge*
Lindsay, Reginald Carl *judge*
Lynch, Sandra Lea *federal judge*
Marshall, Margaret Hilary *state supreme court chief justice*
Saris, Patti Barbara *federal judge*
Skinner, Walter Jay *federal judge*
Sosman, Martha B. *judge*
Spina, Francis X. *judge*
Stahl, Norman H. *federal judge*
Stearns, Richard Gaylore *judge*
Tauro, Joseph Louis *federal judge*
Wolf, Mark Lawrence *federal judge*
Woodlock, Douglas Preston *judge*
Young, William Glover *federal judge*
Zobel, Rya Weickert *federal judge*

Cambridge
Abrams, Ruth Ida *retired state supreme court justice*

Dedham
Connolly, Thomas Edward *judge*

Harwich Port
Smith, Ralph Wesley, Jr. *retired federal judge*

Longmeadow
Keady, George Cregan, Jr. *judge*

Springfield
Ponsor, Michael Adrian *federal judge*

Worcester
Gorton, Nathaniel M. *federal judge*

MICHIGAN

Ann Arbor
Pepe, Steven Douglas *federal magistrate judge*

Dearborn
Runco, William Joseph *judge*

Detroit
Callahan, J(ohn) William (Bill Callahan) *judge*
Clay, Eric L. *judge*
Corrigan, Maura Denise *judge*
Duggan, Patrick James *federal judge*
Edmunds, Nancy Garlock *federal judge*
Feikens, John *federal judge*
Friedman, Bernard Alvin *federal judge*
Keith, Damon Jerome *federal judge*
Kelly, Marilyn *state supreme court justice*
Kennedy, Cornelia Groefsema *federal judge*
Lloyd, Leona Loretta *judge*
Millender, Beatrice Pennie *magistrate judge*
Rosen, Gerald Ellis *federal judge*
Ryan, James Leo *federal judge*
Taylor, Anna Diggs *judge*
Woods, George Edward *judge*

Flint
Graves, Ray Reynolds *retired judge*

Grand Rapids
Bell, Robert Holmes *county judge*
Brenneman, Hugh Warren, Jr. *judge*
Hillman, Douglas Woodruff *federal district judge*
Miles, Wendell A. *federal judge*
Quist, Gordon Jay *federal judge*

Kalamazoo
Enslen, Richard Alan *federal judge*

Kentwood
Kelly, William Garrett *judge*

Lansing
Cavanagh, Michael Francis *state supreme court justice*
Harrison, Michael Gregory *judge*
Markman, Stephen J. *judge*
McKeague, David William *judge*

PROFESSIONAL INDEX 831 JUDICIAL ADMINISTRATION

Spence, Howard Tee Devon *judge, arbitrator, lawyer, consultant, insurance executive, government official*
Suhrheinrich, Richard Fred *federal judge*
Taylor, Clifford Woodworth *state supreme court justice*
Young, Robert P., Jr. *state supreme court justice*

Saginaw
Jackson, Darnell *judge*
McGraw, Patrick John *judge*

Saint Clair Shores
Hausner, John Herman *judge*

Traverse City
Weaver, Elizabeth A. *state supreme court justice*

White Lake
Boyle, Patricia Jean *retired state supreme court justice*

MINNESOTA

Anoka
Quinn, R. Joseph *former judge*

Minneapolis
Aldrich, Stephen Charles *judge*
Alton, Ann Leslie *judge, lawyer, educator*
Amdahl, Douglas Kenneth *retired state supreme court justice*
Arthur, Lindsay Grier *retired judge, author, editor*
Davis, Michael J. *judge*
Doty, David Singleton *federal judge*
Lebedoff, Jonathan Galanter *federal judge*
Loken, James Burton *federal judge*
MacLaughlin, Harry Hunter *federal judge*
Murphy, Diana E. *federal judge*
Rosenbaum, James Michael *judge*

Minnetonka
Rogers, James Devitt *judge*

Rochester
Keith, Alexander Macdonald *retired state supreme court chief justice, lawyer*

Saint Paul
Alsop, Donald Douglas *federal judge*
Anderson, Paul Holden *state supreme court justice*
Anderson, Russell A. *state supreme court justice*
Blatz, Kathleen Anne *state supreme court chief justice, state legislator*
Gilbert, James H. *judge*
Kishel, Gregory Francis *federal judge*
Kyle, Richard House *federal judge*
Lancaster, Joan Ericksen *state supreme court justice*
Lay, Donald Pomeroy *federal judge*
Page, Alan Cedric *state supreme court justice*
Renner, Robert George *federal judge*
Stringer, Edward Charles *state supreme court justice*
Tomljanovich, Esther M. *state supreme court justice*
Willis, Bruce Donald *judge*

MISSISSIPPI

Aberdeen
Davidson, Glen Harris *federal judge*
Senter, Lyonel Thomas, Jr. *federal judge*

Columbus
Prather, Lenore Loving *former state supreme court chief justice*

Fulton
Mills, Michael Paul *state supreme court justice*

Gulfport
Russell, Dan M., Jr. *federal judge*

Jackson
Banks, Fred Lee, Jr. *state supreme court presiding justice*
Barksdale, Rhesa Hawkins *federal judge*
Cobb, Kay Beevers *state supreme court justice, former state senator*
Easley, Charles D., Jr. *judge*
Jolly, E. Grady *federal judge*
Lee, Tom Stewart *judge*
McRae, Charles R. (Chuck McCrae) *state supreme court presiding justice*
Pittman, Edwin Lloyd *state supreme court chief justice*
Roberts, James Lamar, Jr. *retired state supreme court justice*
Smith, James W., Jr. *state supreme court justice*
Waller, William Lowe, Jr. *state supreme court justice*

Natchez
Bramlette, David C., III *federal judge*

MISSOURI

Jefferson City
Benton, W. Duane *judge*
Blackmar, Charles Blakey *state supreme court justice*
Covington, Ann K. *former state supreme court justice*
Holstein, John Charles *state supreme court judge*
Limbaugh, Stephen Nathaniel, Jr. *state supreme court chief justice*
Price, William Ray, Jr. *state supreme court judge*
Stith, Laura Denvir *judge*
White, Ronnie L. *state supreme court justice*
Wolff, Michael A. *state supreme court judge*

Kansas City
Bowman, Pasco Middleton, II *federal judge*
Gibson, John Robert *federal judge*
Hunter, Elmo Bolton *federal judge*
Koger, Frank Williams *federal judge*
Whipple, Dean *federal judge*
Wright, Scott Olin *federal judge*

Saint Louis
Barta, James Joseph *judge*
Burger, Joan M. *judge*
Gaertner, Gary M., Sr. *judge*
Hamilton, Jean Constance *judge*
Limbaugh, Stephen Nathaniel *federal judge*
McMillian, Theodore *federal judge*
Seiler, James Elmer *judge*
Shaw, Charles Alexander *judge*
Stohr, Donald J. *federal judge*

MONTANA

Billings
Thomas, Sidney R. *federal judge*

Circle
McDonough, Russell Charles *retired state supreme court justice*

Hamilton
Langton, Jeffrey H. *judge*

Helena
Cotter, Patricia O'Brien *judge*
Gray, Karla Marie *state supreme court chief justice*
Harrison, John Conway *state supreme court justice*
Hunt, William E., Sr. *state supreme court justice*
Leaphart, W. William *state supreme court justice*
Nelson, James C *state supreme court justice*
Regnier, James *state supreme court justice*
Rice, Jim *judge*
Trieweiler, Terry Nicholas *state supreme court justice*

Polson
Turnage, Jean Allen *retired state supreme court chief justice*

NEBRASKA

Lincoln
Beam, Clarence Arlen *federal judge*
Connolly, William M. *state supreme court justice*
Gerrard, John M. *state supreme court justice*
Hastings, William Charles *retired state supreme court chief justice*
Hendry, John *state supreme court justice*
Kopf, Richard G. *federal judge*
McCormack, Michael *state supreme court justice*
Miller-Lerman, Lindsey *state supreme court justice*
Stephan, Kenneth C. *state supreme court justice*
Urbom, Warren Keith *federal judge*
Wright, John F. *state supreme court justice*

Omaha
Shanahan, Thomas M. *judge*
Strom, Lyle Elmer *federal judge*

NEVADA

Carson City
Agosti, Deborah Ann *state supreme court justice*
Leavitt, Myron E. *state supreme court justice*
Maupin, A. William *state supreme court justice*
Rose, Robert E(dgar) *state supreme court chief justice*
Springer, Charles Edward *retired state supreme court chief justice*
Young, C. Clifton *state supreme court justice*

Las Vegas
Becker, Nancy Anne *state supreme court justice*
Pro, Philip Martin *judge*
Rawlinson, Johnnie Blakeney *judge*
Steffen, Thomas Lee *former state supreme court justice, lawyer*

Reno
Brunetti, Melvin T. *federal judge*
Hagen, David Warner *judge*
Hug, Procter Ralph, Jr. *federal judge*
McKibben, Howard D. *federal judge*
Reed, Edward Cornelius, Jr. *federal judge*

NEW HAMPSHIRE

Concord
Barbadoro, Paul James *federal judge*
Brock, David Allen *state supreme court chief justice*
Broderick, John T., Jr. *state supreme court justice*
Dalianis, Linda *judge*
DiClerico, Joseph Anthony, Jr. *federal judge*
Duggan, James E., Jr. *judge*
McAuliffe, Steven James *federal judge*
Nadeau, Joseph P. *judge*

NEW JERSEY

Camden
Irenas, Joseph Eron *judge, director*
Simandle, Jerome B. *federal judge*

Egg Harbor Township
Lashman, Shelley Bortin *retired judge*

Flemington
Verniero, Peter G. *state supreme court justice*

Freehold
D'Amico, John, Jr. *judge*
Newman, James Michael *judge, lawyer*

Hackensack
Cipollone, Anthony Dominic *judge, educator*
Stein, Gary S. *state supreme court justice*

Morristown
Hansbury, Stephan Charles *judge*
LaVecchia, Jaynee *judge*

Newark
Alito, Samuel Anthony, Jr. *federal judge*
Barry, Maryanne Trump *federal judge*
Bissell, John W. *federal judge*
Chesler, Stanley Richard *federal judge*
Debevoise, Dickinson Richards *federal judge*
Fuentes, Julio M. *federal judge*
Garth, Leonard I. *federal judge*
Lechner, Alfred James, Jr. *judge*

Red Bank
O'Hern, Daniel Joseph *retired state supreme court justice*
Zazzali, James R. *judge*

Somerville
Yurasko, Frank Noel *judge*

Trenton
Cooper, Mary Little *federal judge, former banking commissioner*
Cowen, Robert E. *federal judge*
Gindin, William Howard *judge*
Greenberg, Morton Ira *federal judge*
Long, Virginia *state supreme court justice*
Poritz, Deborah T. *state supreme court chief justice, former attorney general*

Warren
Coleman, James H., Jr. *state supreme court justice*

NEW MEXICO

Albuquerque
Conway, John E. *federal judge*
Dal Santo, Diane *writer, retired judge*
Hansen, Curtis LeRoy *federal judge*
Parker, James Aubrey *federal judge*

Los Lunas
Pope, John William *judge, law educator*

Roswell
Baldock, Bobby Ray *federal judge*

Santa Fe
Baca, Joseph Francis *state supreme court justice*
Franchini, Gene Edward *state supreme court justice*
Kelly, Paul Joseph, Jr. *judge*
Maes, Petra Jimenez *state supreme court justice*
Minzner, Pamela Burgy *state supreme court justice*
Serna, Patricio *state supreme court chief justice*
Yalman, Ann *judge, lawyer*

NEW YORK

Albany
Graffeo, Victoria A. *judge*
Kaye, Judith Smith *state supreme court chief justice*
Meader, John Daniel *judge*
Miner, Roger Jeffrey *federal judge*

Binghamton
Regenbogen, Adam *judge*

Bronx
Bamberger, Phylis Skloot *judge*

Brooklyn
Amon, Carol Bagley *federal judge*
Glasser, Israel Leo *federal judge*
Korman, Edward R. *federal judge*
Raggi, Reena *federal judge*
Ryan, Leonard Eames *judge*
Sifton, Charles Proctor *federal judge*
Trager, David G. *federal judge*
Weinstein, Jack Bertrand *federal judge*

Buffalo
Elfvin, John Thomas *federal judge*
Skretny, William Marion *federal judge*

Central Islip
Platt, Thomas Collier, Jr. *federal judge*
Seybert, Joanna *federal judge*
Spatt, Arthur Donald *federal judge*

Geneseo
Wesley, Richard C. *state supreme court justice*

Jamaica
Grayshaw, James Raymond *judge*

Lake George
Austin, John DeLong *judge*

Little Valley
Himelein, Larry M. *judge*

New York
Aquilino, Thomas Joseph, Jr. *federal judge, law educator*
Blinder, Albert Allan *judge*
Buchwald, Naomi Reice *judge*
Cedarbaum, Miriam Goldman *federal judge*
Ciparick, Carmen Beauchamp *state supreme court judge*
Eaton, Richard Kenyon *judge*
Feinberg, Wilfred *federal judge*
Freedman, Helen E. *justice*
Gerber, Robert Evan *judge*
Griesa, Thomas Poole *federal judge*
Gropper, Allan Louis *bankruptcy judge*
Haight, Charles Sherman, Jr. *federal judge*
Jacobs, Dennis *federal judge*
Katzmann, Robert Allen *federal judge*
Kearse, Amalya Lyle *federal judge*
Keenan, John Fontaine *federal judge*
Knapp, Whitman *federal judge*
Koeltl, John George *judge*
Leisure, Peter Keeton *federal judge*
Leval, Pierre Nelson *federal judge*
Martin, John Sherwood, Jr. *federal judge*
McLaughlin, Joseph Michael *federal judge, law educator*
Motley, Constance Baker (Mrs. Joel Wilson Motley) *federal judge, former city official*
Mukasey, Michael B. *federal judge*
Musgrave, R. Kenton *federal judge*
Owen, Richard *federal judge*
Patterson, Robert Porter, Jr. *federal judge*
Pollack, Milton *federal judge*
Preska, Loretta A. *federal judge*
Sack, Robert David *judge, educator*
Sand, Leonard B. *federal judge*
Schwartz, Allen G. *federal judge*
Smith, George Bundy *state supreme court justice*
Sotomayor, Sonia *judge*
Sprizzo, John Emilio *federal judge*
Straub, Chester John *judge*
Titone, Vito Joseph *state supreme court justice*
Ward, Robert Joseph *federal judge*

Penn Yan
Falvey, W(illiam) Patrick *judge*

Poughkeepsie
Rosenblatt, Albert Martin *state appeals court judge*

Rochester
Campbell, Vincent Bernard *judge, lawyer*
Telesca, Michael Anthony *federal judge*
Van Graafeiland, Ellsworth Alfred *federal judge*

Rome
Simons, Richard Duncan *lawyer, retired judge*

Sag Harbor
Pierce, Lawrence Warren *retired federal judge*

Schenectady
Levine, Howard Arnold *state supreme court justice*

Syracuse
McCurn, Neal Peters *federal judge*
Munson, Howard G. *federal judge*
Pooler, Rosemary S. *federal judge*
Scullin, Frederick James, Jr. *federal judge*
Wells, Peter Nathaniel *judge, lawyer*

Utica
Cardamone, Richard J. *federal judge*

White Plains
Brieant, Charles La Monte *federal judge*
Conner, William Curtis *judge*
Hardin, Adlai Stevenson, Jr. *judge*
West, Joseph King *judge*

NORTH CAROLINA

Asheville
Thornburg, Lacy Herman *federal judge*

Charlotte
Mullen, Graham C. *federal judge*
Potter, Robert Daniel *federal judge*
Voorhees, Richard Lesley *federal judge*

Greensboro
Bullock, Frank William, Jr. *federal judge*
Osteen, William L. *federal judge*
Tilley, Norwood Carlton, Jr. *federal judge*

Raleigh
Britt, W. Earl *federal judge*
Butterfield, G. K., Jr. *judge*
Campbell, Hugh Brown, Jr. *judge*
Denson, Alexander Bunn *federal magistrate judge*
Eagles, Sidney Smith, Jr. *judge*
Edmunds, Robert H., Jr. *judge*
Lake, I. Beverly, Jr. *state supreme court chief justice*
Martin, John Charles *judge*
Martin, Mark D. *state supreme court justice*
Mitchell, Burley Bayard, Jr. *state supreme court chief justice*
Orr, Robert F. *state supreme court justice*
Parker, Sarah Elizabeth *state supreme court justice*
Small, Alden Thomas *judge*
Wainwright, George *judge*
Webb, John *retired state supreme court justice*

Wilmington
Fox, James Carroll *federal judge*

Winston Salem
Eliason, Russell Allen *judge*
Ward, Hiram Hamilton *federal judge*

NORTH DAKOTA

Bismarck
Conmy, Patrick A. *federal judge*
Kapsner, Carol Ronning *state supreme court justice*
Maring, Mary Muehlen *state supreme court justice*
Neumann, William Allen *state supreme court justice*
Sandstrom, Dale Vernon *state supreme court judge*
Van Sickle, Bruce Marion *federal judge*
VandeWalle, Gerald Wayne *state supreme court chief justice*

Fargo
Bright, Myron H. *federal judge, educator*
Bye, Kermit Edward *federal judge, lawyer*
Magill, Frank John *federal judge*

Minot
Kerian, Jon Robert *retired judge*

OHIO

Akron
Bell, Samuel H. *federal judge, educator*

Cincinnati
Beckwith, Sandra Shank *judge*

Black, Robert L., Jr. *retired judge*
Engel, Albert Joseph *federal judge*
Jones, Nathaniel Raphael *federal judge*
Nelson, David Aldrich *federal judge*
Painter, Mark Philip *judge*
Panioto, Ronald Angelo *judge*
Perlman, Burton *judge*
Spiegel, S. Arthur *federal judge*
Weber, Herman Jacob *federal judge*

Cleveland
Krupansky, Robert Bazil *federal judge*
Manos, John M. *federal judge*
Matia, Paul Ramon *federal judge*
Moore, Karen Nelson *judge*
Oliver, Solomon, Jr. *judge*
Wells, Lesley B. *judge*

Columbus
Calhoun, Donald Eugene, Jr. *federal judge*
Cole, Ransey Guy, Jr. *judge*
Cook, Deborah L. *state supreme court justice*
Douglas, Andrew *state supreme court justice*
Graham, James Lowell *federal judge*
Holschuh, John David *federal judge*
Leach, Russell *judge*
Moyer, Thomas J. *state supreme court chief justice*
Norris, Alan Eugene *federal judge*
Pfeifer, Paul E. *state supreme court justice*
Resnick, Alice Robie *state supreme court justice*
Sargus, Edmund A., Jr. *judge*
Sellers, Barbara Jackson *federal judge*
Smith, George Curtis *judge*
Stratton, Evelyn Lundberg *state supreme court justice*
Sweeney, Asher William *state supreme court justice*
Sweeney, Francis E. *state supreme court justice*

Dayton
Knapp, James Ian Keith *judge*
Merz, Michael *federal judge*
Petzold, John Paul *judge*

Lisbon
Dailey, Coleen Hall *magistrate, lawyer*

Lucasville
Reno, Ottie Wayne *former judge*

Marion
Rogers, Richard Michael *judge*

Medina
Batchelder, Alice M. *federal judge*

Sandusky
Stacey, James Allen *retired judge*

Toledo
Carr, James Gray *judge*
Potter, John William *federal judge*

OKLAHOMA

Atoka
Gabbard, Douglas, II (James Gabbard) *judge*

Guthrie
Brooks, Larry Roger *judge*

Oklahoma City
Alley, Wayne Edward *federal judge, retired army officer*
Bohanon, Luther L. *federal judge*
Cauthron, Robin J. *federal judge*
Hargrave, Rudolph *state supreme court justice*
Henry, Robert Harlan *federal judge, former attorney general*
Hodges, Ralph B. *state supreme court justice*
Holloway, William Judson, Jr. *federal judge*
Lavender, Robert Eugene *state supreme court justice*
Leonard, Timothy Dwight *judge*
Opala, Marian P(eter) *state supreme court justice*
Russell, David L. *federal judge*
Summers, Hardy *state supreme court justice*
Thompson, Ralph Gordon *federal judge*
Watt, Joseph Michael *state supreme court justice*
West, Lee Roy *federal judge*
Winchester, James R. *judge*

Tulsa
Brett, Thomas Rutherford *federal judge*
Frizzell, Gregory Kent *judge*
Kern, Terry C. *judge*
Seymour, Stephanie Kulp *federal judge*
Taylor, Joe Clinton *judge*

OREGON

Eugene
Hogan, Michael R(obert) *judge*

Portland
Fisher, Ann Lewis *judge*
Frye, Helen Jackson *federal judge*
Galton, Sidney Alan *judge*
Graber, Susan P. *federal judge*
Jones, Robert Edward *federal judge*
King, Garr Michael *federal judge*
Kulongoski, Theodore Ralph *former state supreme court justice*
Leavy, Edward *federal judge*
O'Scannlain, Diarmuid Fionntain *judge*
Panner, Owen M. *federal judge*
Redden, James Anthony *federal judge*
Roth, Phillip Joseph *retired judge*
Skopil, Otto Richard, Jr. *federal judge*
Unis, Richard L. *judge*
Van Hoomissen, George Albert *state supreme court justice*

Saint Helens
Shera Taylor, Diana Marie *judge, lawyer*

Salem
Balmer, Thomas Ancil *judge*
Carson, Wallace Preston, Jr. *state supreme court chief justice*
De Muniz, Paul J. *judge*
Durham, Robert Donald, Jr. *state supreme court justice*
Jolley, William Andrew *judge*
Leeson, Susan M. *state supreme court judge*
Peterson, Edwin J. *retired supreme court justice, law educator*
Riggs, R. William *state supreme court judge*

Sweet Home
Miller, Keith Allan *judge, lawyer*

PENNSYLVANIA

Allentown
Platt, William Henry *judge*

Doylestown
Rufe, Cynthia Marie *judge*

Easton
Van Antwerpen, Franklin Stuart *federal judge*

Erie
Mencer, Glenn Everell *federal judge*
Nygaard, Richard Lowell *federal judge*

Harrisburg
Rambo, Sylvia H. *federal judge*
Saylor, Thomas G. *state supreme court justice*

Johnstown
Smith, D. Brooks *federal judge*

Media
Scholl, David Allen *former federal judge, lawyer*

Orwigsburg
Troutman, E. Mac *federal judge*

Philadelphia
Angell, M(ary) Faith *federal magistrate judge*
Bartle, Harvey, III *federal judge*
Becker, Edward Roy *federal judge*
Buckwalter, Ronald Lawrence *federal judge*
Castille, Ronald D. *state supreme court justice*
Fullam, John P. *federal judge*
Green, Clifford Scott *federal judge*
Jaffe, Paul Lawrence *judge, lawyer*
Joyner, J(ames) Curtis *federal judge*
Ludwig, Edmund Vincent *federal judge*
McKee, Theodore A. *federal judge*
Newcomer, Clarence Charles *federal judge*
Nigro, Russell M. *state supreme court justice*
O'Neill, Thomas Newman, Jr. *federal judge*
Pollak, Louis Heilprin *judge, educator*
Reed, Lowell A., Jr. *federal judge*
Rendell, Marjorie O. *federal judge*
Robreno, Eduardo C. *federal judge*
Scirica, Anthony Joseph *federal judge*
Sloviter, Dolores Korman *federal judge*
Weiner, Charles R. *federal judge*
Yohn, William H(endricks), Jr. *federal judge*

Pittsburgh
Bloch, Alan Neil *federal judge*
Cappy, Ralph Joseph *state supreme court justice*
Cohill, Maurice Blanchard, Jr. *federal judge*
Colville, Robert E. *judge*
Diamond, Gustave *federal judge*
Fitzgerald, Judith Klaswick *federal judge*
Flaherty, John Paul, Jr. *state supreme court chief justice*
Lally-Green, Maureen Ellen *superior court judge, law educator*
Lee, Donald John *federal judge*
Mansmann, Carol Los *federal judge, law educator*
Sensenich, Ila Jeanne *judge*
Skwaryk, Robert Francis *judge*
Standish, William Lloyd *judge*
Weis, Joseph Francis, Jr. *federal judge*
Ziegler, Donald Emil *federal judge*

Scranton
Conaboy, Richard Paul *federal judge*
Kosik, Edwin Michael *federal judge*
Nealon, William Joseph, Jr. *federal judge*
O'Malley, Carlon Martin *judge*
Vanaskie, Thomas Ignatius *judge*

Washington
Mc Cune, Barron Patterson *retired federal judge*

West Conshohocken
Newman, Sandra Schultz *state supreme court justice*

Wilkes Barre
Rosenn, Max *federal judge*
Schwartz, Roger Alan *judge*

Williamsport
McClure, James Focht, Jr. *federal judge*
Muir, Malcolm *federal judge*

RHODE ISLAND

Hope Valley
Williams, Frank J. *chief justice, historian, author*

Providence
Bourcier, John Paul *state supreme court justice*
Flanders, Robert G., Jr. *state supreme court justice*
Goldberg, Maureen McKenna *state supreme court justice*
Hagopian, Jacob *federal judge*
Keough, Joseph Aloysios *judge*
Lagueux, Ronald Rene *federal judge*
Lederberg, Victoria *judge, former state legislator, lawyer*
Lisi, Mary M. *federal judge*
Selya, Bruce Marshall *federal judge*
Torres, Ernest C. *federal judge*
Weisberger, Joseph Robert *state supreme court chief justice*

SOUTH CAROLINA

Camden
Chapman, Robert Foster *federal judge*
Jacobs, Rolly Warren *judge*

Charleston
Hawkins, Falcon Black, Jr. *federal judge*

Columbia
Bristow, Walter James, Jr. *retired judge*
Hamilton, Clyde Henry *federal judge*
Kosko, George Carter *judge*
Pleicones, Costa M. *judge*
Toal, Jean Hoefer *state supreme court justice*

Greenville
Herlong, Henry Michael, Jr. *federal judge*
Smith, Willie Tesreau, Jr. *retired judge, lawyer*
Traxler, William Byrd, Jr. *federal judge*
Wilkins, William Walter, Jr. *federal judge*

Greenwood
Moore, James E. *state supreme court justice*

Marion
Waller, John Henry, Jr. *state supreme court justice*

Myrtle Beach
Harwell, David Walker *retired state supreme court chief justice*

Orangeburg
Williams, Karen Johnson *federal judge*

Roebuck
Burnett, E. C., III *state supreme court justice*

Sumter
Finney, Ernest Adolphus, Jr. *retired state supreme court chief justice*

SOUTH DAKOTA

Pierre
Amundson, Robert A. *state supreme court justice*
Gilbertson, David *state supreme court justice*
Konenkamp, John K. *state supreme court justice*
Sabers, Richard Wayne *state supreme court justice*

Sioux Falls
Piersol, Lawrence L. *federal judge*
Wollman, Roger Leland *federal judge*

TENNESSEE

Chattanooga
Barker, William M. *state supreme court justice*
Edgar, R(obert) Allan *federal judge*
Franks, Herschel Pickens *judge*

Greeneville
Hull, Thomas Gray *federal judge*

Jackson
Todd, James Dale *federal judge*

Johnson City
Kiener, John Leslie *judge*

Knoxville
Anderson, Edward Riley *state supreme court chief justice*
Jarvis, James Howard, II *judge*
Jordan, Robert Leon *federal judge*
Murrian, Robert Phillip *judge, educator*

Memphis
Allen, James Henry, Sr. *magistrate judge*
Gibbons, Julia Smith *federal judge*
Gilman, Ronald Lee *judge*
Holder, Janice Marie *state supreme court justice*
McRae, Robert Malcolm, Jr. *federal judge*
Wellford, Harry Walker *federal judge*

Nashville
Birch, Adolpho A., Jr. *state supreme court justice*
Brown, Joe Blackburn *judge*
Daughtrey, Martha Craig *federal judge*
Drowota, Frank F., III *state supreme court justice*
Echols, Robert L. *federal judge*
Merritt, Gilbert Stroud *federal judge*
Nixon, John Trice *judge*
Wiseman, Thomas Anderton, Jr. *federal judge*

Newport
Porter, James Kenneth *retired judge*

Sevierville
Brackett, Colquitt Prater, Jr. *judge, lawyer*

Signal Mountain
Cooper, Robert Elbert *state supreme court justice*

TEXAS

Amarillo
Johnson, Philip Wayne *judge*
Robinson, Mary Lou *federal judge*

Austin
Baker, James A. *state supreme court justice*
Benavides, Fortunato Pedro (Pete Benavides) *federal judge*
Coronado, Santiago Sybert (Jim Coronado) *judge*
Garwood, William Lockhart *federal judge*
Gonzales, Alberto R. *state supreme court justice, former secretary of state*
Gonzalez, Raul A. *retired state supreme court justice, lawyer*
Hankinson, Deborah G. *state supreme court justice*
Hecht, Nathan Lincoln *state supreme court justice*
Hudspeth, Harry Lee *federal judge*
Jefferson, Wallace B. *judge*
Justice, William Wayne *federal judge*
Keller, Sharon Faye *judge*
Nowlin, James Robertson *federal judge*
O'Neill, Harriet *state supreme court justice*
Owen, Priscilla Richman *state supreme court justice*
Phillips, Thomas Royal *state supreme court chief justice*
Pope, Andrew Jackson, Jr. (Jack Pope) *retired judge*
Reavley, Thomas Morrow *federal judge*
Sparks, Sam *federal judge*

Bastrop
Eskew, Benton *judge*

Beaumont
Cobb, Howell *federal judge*

Brownsville
Garza, Reynaldo G. *federal judge*

Bryan
Smith, Steven Lee *judge*

Corpus Christi
Head, Hayden Wilson, Jr. *judge*
Jack, Janis Graham *judge*

Dallas
Higginbotham, Patrick Errol *federal judge*
Leonie, Andrew Drake, III *judge, lawyer*
Sanders, Harold Barefoot, Jr. *federal judge*

Del Rio
Thurmond, George Murat *judge*

Edinburg
Hinojosa, Federico Gustavo, Jr. *judge*

El Paso
Briones, David *judge*
Dinsmoor, Robert Davidson *judge*

Fort Worth
Mahon, Eldon Brooks *federal judge*
McBryde, John Henry *federal judge*
Tillman, Massie Monroe *mediator, retired federal judge*
Wallace, Steven Charles *judge*

Houston
DeMoss, Harold Raymond, Jr. *federal judge*
Gilmore, Vanessa D. *federal judge*
Hanks, George Carol, Jr. *state judge*
Hittner, David *federal judge*
Hughes, Lynn Nettleton *federal judge*
Jones, Edith Hollan *federaljudge*
King, Carolyn Dineen *federal judge*
Lake, Sim *federal judge*
Rosenthal, Lee H. *federal judge*
Smith, Jerry Edwin *federal judge*
Sondock, Ruby Kless *retired judge*
Werlein, Ewing, Jr. *federal judge*

Laredo
Kazen, George Philip *federal judge*

Midland
Morrow, William Clarence *judge, lawyer, mediator*

New Braunfels
Zipp, Ronald Duane *judge, priest, real estate broker*

Richmond
Elliott, Brady Gifford *judge*

San Antonio
Garza, Emilio M(iller) *federal judge*
King, Ronald Baker *federal judge*

Sherman
Brown, Paul Neeley *federal judge*

Temple
Skelton, Byron George *federal judge*

Tyler
Guthrie, Judith K. *federal judge*
Parker, Robert M. *federal judge*
Steger, William Merritt *federal judge*

UTAH

Provo
Harding, Ray Murray, Jr. *judge*
Schofield, Anthony Wayne *judge*

Salt Lake City
Anderson, Stephen Hale *federal judge*
Clark, Glen Edward *judge*
Durham, Christine Meaders *state supreme court justice*
Durrant, Matthew B. *state judge*
Greene, John Thomas *judge*
Howe, Richard Cuddy *state supreme court chief justice*
McKay, Monroe Gunn *federal judge*
Murphy, Michael R. *federal judge*
Rigtrup, Kenneth *state judge, arbitrator, mediator*
Russon, Leonard H. *state supreme court justice*
Sam, David *federal judge*
Wilkins, Michael Jon *state supreme court justice*
Winder, David Kent *federal judge*

VERMONT

Brattleboro
Oakes, James L. *federal judge*

Burlington
Parker, Fred I. *federal judge*

Montpelier
Dooley, John Augustine, III *state supreme court justice*
Gibson, Ernest Willard, III *retired state supreme court justice*
Skoglund, Marilyn *state supreme court justice*

Waterbury Center
Amestoy, Jeffrey Lee *state supreme court chief justice*

Woodstock
Billings, Franklin Swift, Jr. *federal judge*

VIRGINIA

Abingdon
Widener, Hiram Emory, Jr. *federal judge*
Williams, Glen Morgan *federal judge*

Alexandria
Luttig, J. Michael *federal judge*

Annandale
Hollis, Daryl Joseph *judge*

Charlottesville
Crigler, B. Waugh *federal judge*
Michael, James Harry, Jr. *federal judge*
Wilkinson, James Harvie, III *federal judge*

Chesterfield
Davis, Bonnie Christell *judge*

Covington
Stephenson, Roscoe Bolar, Jr. *state supreme court justice*

Danville
Kiser, Jackson L. *federal judge*

Fairfax
Williams, Marcus Doyle *judge*

Falls Church
Barton, Robert L(eroy), Jr. *judge, educator*
Morse, Marvin Henry *judge*

King George
Revercomb, Horace Austin, III *judge*

Lynchburg
Burnette, Ralph Edwin, Jr. *judge*

Manassas
Van Broekhoven, Rollin Adrian *federal judge*

Norfolk
Adams, David Huntington *judge*
Bonney, Hal James, Jr. *federal judge*
Clarke, J. Calvitt, Jr. *federal judge*
Jackson, Raymond A. *federal judge*
Morgan, Henry Coke, Jr. *judge*
Prince, William Taliaferro *retired federal judge*

Richmond
Compton, Asbury Christian *state supreme court justice*
Gregory, Roger Lee *judge*
Hassell, Leroy Rountree, Sr. *state supreme court justice*
Lemons, Donald W. *judge*
Poff, Richard Harding *state supreme court justice*
Russell, Charles Stevens *state supreme court justice, educator*
Tice, Douglas Oscar, Jr. *federal bankruptcy judge*
Williams, Richard Leroy *federal judge*

Roanoke
Turk, James Clinton *federal judge*

Salem
Koontz, Lawrence L., Jr. *state supreme court justice*
Pearson, Henry Clyde *judge*

Virginia Beach
Keenan, Barbara Milano *state supreme court justice*

WASHINGTON

Bellevue
Andersen, James A. *retired state supreme court justice*

Everett
Bowden, George Newton *judge*

Mercer Island
Noe, James Alva *retired judge*

Olympia
Alexander, Gerry L. *state supreme court chief justice*
Bridge, Bobbe J. *state supreme court justice*
Guy, Richard P. *retired state supreme court justice*
Ireland, Faith *state supreme court justice*
Johnson, Charles William *state supreme court justice*
Madsen, Barbara A *state supreme court justice*
Owens, Susan *judge*
Sanders, Richard Browning *state supreme court justice*
Smith, Charles Z. *state supreme court justice*

Richland
Shea, Edward Francis *federal judge*

Seattle
Beezer, Robert Renaut *federal judge*
Bladen, Edwin Mark *lawyer, judge*
Dimmick, Carolyn Reaber *federal judge*
Dwyer, William L. *federal judge*
Farris, Jerome *federal judge*
Fletcher, Betty Binns *federal judge*
Gould, Ronald Murray *judge*
Mc Govern, Walter T. *federal judge*
Rothstein, Barbara Jacobs *federal judge*
Tallman, Richard C. *federal judge, lawyer*
Wright, Eugene Allen *federal judge*
Zilly, Thomas Samuel *federal judge*

Spokane
Quackenbush, Justin Lowe *federal judge*

Tacoma
Bryan, Robert J. *federal judge*

Yakima
McDonald, Alan Angus *federal judge*
Suko, Lonny Ray *judge*

WEST VIRGINIA

Beckley
Faber, David Alan *federal judge*

Charleston
Albright, Joseph P. *state supreme court justice*
Brewer, Lewis Gordon *judge, lawyer, educator*
Copenhaver, John Thomas, Jr. *federal judge*
Davis, Robin Jean *state supreme court justice*
Goodwin, Joseph R. *judge*
Haden, Charles Harold, II *federal judge*
Hallanan, Elizabeth V. *federal judge*
King, Robert Bruce *federal judge*
Marland, Melissa Kaye *judge*
Maynard, Elliott *state supreme court justice*
McGraw, Warren Randolph *state supreme court chief justice*
Michael, M. Blane *federal judge*
Starcher, Larry Victor *state supreme court justice*

Elkins
Maxwell, Robert Earl *federal judge*

WISCONSIN

Madison
Abrahamson, Shirley Schlanger *state supreme court chief justice*
Bablitch, William A. *state supreme court justice*
Bartell, Angela Gina Baldi *judge*
Bradley, Ann Walsh *state supreme court justice*
Crabb, Barbara Brandriff *federal judge*
Crooks, N(eil) Patrick *state supreme court justice*
Heffernan, Nathan Stewart *retired state supreme court chief justice*
Martin, Robert David *judge, educator*
Prosser, David Thomas, Jr. *state supreme court justice, former state representative*
Shabaz, John C. *federal judge*
Sykes, Diane S. *state supreme court justice*
Wilcox, Jon P. *state supreme court justice*

Milwaukee
Evans, Terence Thomas *federal judge*
Reynolds, John W. *federal judge*
Shapiro, James Edward *judge*

WYOMING

Casper
Downes, William F. *judge*

Cheyenne
Brimmer, Clarence Addison *federal judge*
Brorby, Wade *federal judge*
Golden, T. Michael *state supreme court justice*
Hill, William U. *state supreme court justice*
Kite, Marilyn S. *state supreme court justice, lawyer*
Lehman, Larry L. *state supreme court justice*
Voight, Barton R. *judge*

Cody
Patrick, H. Hunter *judge*

TERRITORIES OF THE UNITED STATES

GUAM

Hagatna
Siguenza, Peter Charles, Jr. *territory supreme court justice*
Unpingco, John Walter Sablan *federal judge*

PUERTO RICO

San Juan
Acosta, Raymond Luis *federal judge*
Andreu-Garcia, Jose Antonio *territory supreme court chief justice*
Casellas, Salvador E. *judge*
Corrada del Rio, Baltasar *supreme court justice*
Fuster, Jaime B. *supreme court justice*
Fusté, José Antonio *federal judge*
Gierbolini-Ortiz, Gilberto *federal judge*
Hernandez-Denton, Federico *supreme court justice*
Negron-Garcia, Antonio S. *territory supreme court justice*

VIRGIN ISLANDS

Christiansted
Finch, Raymond Lawrence *judge*
Resnick, Jeffrey Lance *federal magistrate judge*

THE NETHERLANDS

The Hague
Allison, Richard Clark *judge*
Wald, Patricia McGowan *retired federal judge*

ADDRESS UNPUBLISHED

Albritton, William Harold, III *federal judge*
Askey, William Hartman *US magistrate, judge, lawyer*
Barrett, James Emmett *judge*
Bertelsman, William Odis *federal judge*

Boudreau, Daniel J. *state supreme court justice*
Brown, Robert Laidlaw *state supreme court justice*
Butzner, John Decker, Jr. *federal judge*
Callow, Keith McLean *judge*
Callow, William Grant *retired state supreme court justice*
Carrico, Harry Lee *state supreme court chief justice*
Castagna, William John *federal judge*
Ceci, Louis J. *former state supreme court justice*
Clark, Russell Gentry *retired federal judge*
Cochran, George Moffett *retired judge*
Coffey, John Louis *federal judge*
Cohn, Avern Levin *district judge*
Cook, Julian Abele, Jr. *federal judge*
Cyr, Conrad Keefe *federal judge*
Daugherty, Frederick Alvin *federal judge*
Davis, Marguerite Herr *judge*
Day, Roland Bernard *retired chief justice state supreme court*
Dela Cruz, Jose Santos *retired state supreme court justice*
Eaton, Joe Oscar *federal judge*
Edwards, Ninian Murry *judge*
Enoch, Craig Trively *state supreme court justice*
Fadeley, Edward Norman *retired state supreme court justice*
Fecteau, Francis Roger *judge*
Flynn, Peter Anthony *judge*
Garibaldi, Marie Louise *former state supreme court justice*
Gibson, Floyd Robert *federal judge*
Gillette, W. Michael *state supreme court justice*
Goetz, Clarence Edward *retired judge, retired chief magistrate judge*
Golden, Elliott *judge*
Grant, Isabella Horton *retired judge*
Griffin, Robert Paul *former United States senator, state supreme court justice*
Hamblen, Lapsley Walker, Jr. *judge*
Hawkins, Michael Daly *federal judge*
Hayek, Carolyn Jean *retired judge*
Hightower, Jack English *former state supreme court justice, congressman*
Howard, George, Jr. *federal judge*
Ideman, James M. *federal judge*
Joiner, Charles Wycliffe *judge*
Karwacki, Robert Lee *judge*
Kauger, Yvonne *state supreme court chief justice*
Klein, Harriet Farber *judge*
Lee, Dan M. *retired state supreme court justice*
Linn, Richard *federal judge*
Lively, Pierce *federal judge*
Magnuson, Paul Arthur *federal judge*
Mai, Harold Leverne *retired judge*
McCormick, Michael Jerry *judge*
McKee, Roger Curtis *retired federal judge*
Metzner, Charles Miller *federal judge*
Muecke, Charles Andrew (Carl Muecke) *federal judge*
Murray, Florence Kerins *retired state supreme court justice*
Nangle, John Francis *federal judge*
Nesbit, Phyllis Schneider *judge*
Neuman, Linda Kinney *state supreme court justice*
Newbern, William David *retired state supreme court justice*
Newman, Theodore Roosevelt, Jr. *judge*
Payne, Mary Libby *retired judge*
Porter, James Morris *retired judge*
Pusateri, James Anthony *judge*
Reinhardt, Stephen Roy *federal judge*
Rice, Walter Herbert *federal judge*
Ross, Donald Roe *federal judge*
Roszkowski, Stanley Julian *retired federal judge*
Schade, George August, Jr. *judge*
Schroeder, Gerald Frank *state supreme court justice*
Schultz, Louis William *retired judge*
Shearing, Miriam *state supreme court justice*
Silberman, Laurence Hirsch *federal judge*
Souter, David Hackett *United States supreme court justice*
Stahl, Madonna *retired judge*
Staker, Robert Jackson *federal judge*
Stanton, Louis Lee *federal judge*
Suttle, Dorwin Wallace *federal judge*
Sweet, Robert Workman *federal judge*
Talmadge, Philip Albert *former state supreme court justice, former state senator*
Torruella, Juan R. *federal judge*
Trout, Linda Copple *state supreme court chief justice*
Utter, Robert French *retired state supreme court justice*
Vollmer, Richard Wade *federal judge*
Wathen, Daniel Everett *state supreme court chief justice*
Watson, Jack Crozier *retired state supreme court justice*
Wood, Diane Pamela *judge*

LIBRARY

UNITED STATES

ALABAMA

Birmingham
Sinclair, Julie Moores Williams *law librarian, consultant*

Montgomery
Hughes, Judy Anne *law library administrator, researcher, educator*

ARIZONA

Phoenix
Schneider, Elizabeth Kelley *law librarian*

ARKANSAS

Fayetteville
Ahlers, Glen-Peter, Sr. *law library director, educator, consultant*

CALIFORNIA

Fairfield
Moore, Marianna Gay *law librarian, consultant*

Hacienda Heights
Pearson, David Brooksbank *lawyer, educator*

Los Angeles
Iamele, Richard Thomas *law librarian*
Raffalow, Janet Terry *law librarian*

Oakland
Stromme, Gary L. *law librarian*

San Jose
Kuklin, Susan Beverly *law librarian, lawyer*

Santa Ana
Storer, Maryruth *law librarian*

Santa Clara
Hood, Mary Dullea *law librarian*

COLORADO

Denver
Estes, Mark Ernest *law librarian*

DISTRICT OF COLUMBIA

Washington
Asmuth, Gretchen *law librarian, records manager*
Goldberg, Jolande Elisabeth *law librarian, lawyer*
Mahar, Ellen Patricia *law librarian*
McGuirl, Marlene Dana Callis *law librarian, educator*
Shaffer, Roberta Ivy *law librarian*

FLORIDA

Orlando
Diefenbach, Dale Alan *law librarian, retired*

GEORGIA

Athens
Puckett, Elizabeth Ann *law librarian, law educator*

ILLINOIS

Carbondale
Matthews, Elizabeth Woodfin *law librarian, law educator*

Chicago
Lefco, Kathy Nan *law librarian*

INDIANA

Notre Dame
Payne, Lucy Ann Salsbury *law librarian, educator, lawyer*

Valparaiso
Persyn, Mary Geraldine *law librarian, law educator*

KENTUCKY

Lexington
Levy, Charlotte Lois *law librarian, educator, consultant, lawyer*

MASSACHUSETTS

Boston
Wellington, Carol Strong *law librarian*

Cambridge
Duckett, Joan *law librarian*

Concord
Bander, Edward Julius *law librarian emeritus, lawyer*

Greenfield
Lee, Marilyn (Irma) Modarelli *library director*

Leominster
Lambert, Lyn Dee *library media specialist, law librarian*

Sherborn
Borgeson, Earl Charles *law librarian, educator*

Springfield
Dunn, Donald Jack *law librarian, law educator, dean, lawyer*

Winthrop
Brown, Patricia Irene *retired law librarian, lawyer*

MINNESOTA

Minneapolis
Howland, Joan Sidney *law librarian, law educator*

MISSOURI

Kansas City
McKinney, Janet Kay *law librarian*

NEW JERSEY

Newark
Bizub, Johanna Catherine *law librarian*

NEW MEXICO

Santa Fe
Bejnar, Thaddeus Putnam *law librarian, lawyer*

NEW YORK

Brooklyn
Robbins, Sara Ellen *law librarian, educator, lawyer*

Huntington
Jordan, Daniel Patrick, Jr. *law librarian*

Ithaca
Hammond, Jane Laura *retired law librarian, lawyer*

Jamaica
Tschinkel, Andrew Joseph, Jr. *law librarian*

New York
Davey, John H. *law librarian*
Gilligan, Mary Ann *law librarian*
Goodhartz, Gerald *law librarian*
Groh, Jennifer Calfa *law librarian*
Marke, Julius Jay *law librarian, educator*
Merkin, David *reference librarian*
Qian, Jin *law librarian*

Staten Island
Klingle, Philip Anthony *law librarian*

Syracuse
Pellow, David Matthew *lawyer*

Troy
Burch, Mary Seelye Quinn *law librarian, consultant*

NORTH CAROLINA

Chapel Hill
Gasaway, Laura Nell *law librarian, educator*

OHIO

Akron
Chrisant, Rosemarie Kathryn *law library administrator*

Cleveland
Podboy, Alvin Michael, Jr. *law library director, lawyer*

RHODE ISLAND

Providence
Svengalis, Kendall Frayne *law librarian*

SOUTH CAROLINA

Columbia
Cross, Joseph Russell, Jr. *law librarian*

SOUTH DAKOTA

Pierre
Miller, Suzanne Marie *state librarian, educator*

TENNESSEE

Nashville
Winstead, George Alvis *law librarian, biochemist, educator, consultant*

VIRGINIA

Lexington
Wiant, Sarah Kirsten *law library administrator, educator*

Williamsburg
Cooper, William Lewis *research librarian, lawyer, consultant*
Whitehead, James Madison *law librarian*

WASHINGTON

Seattle
Hazelton, Penny Ann *law librarian, educator*
O'Connor, Gayle McCormick *law librarian*

Spokane
Murray, James Michael *librarian, law librarian, legal educator, lawyer*

Tacoma
Steele, Anita Martin (Margaret Anne Martin) *law librarian, legal educator*

WYOMING

Cheyenne
Carlson, Kathleen Bussart *law librarian*

BELGIUM

Brussels
Roox, Kristof *lawyer, educator*

ADDRESS UNPUBLISHED

Citron, Beatrice Sally *law librarian, lawyer, educator*
Gee, Robert Neil *law librarian*
Johnson, Carolyn Jean *retired law librarian*
Lidsky, Ella *retired law librarian*
Parks, Jane deLoach *retired law librarian, legal assistant*

MEDIA

UNITED STATES

CALIFORNIA

La Canada
Paniccia, Patricia Lynn *journalist, writer, lawyer, educator*

Oakland
Dailey, Garrett Clark *publisher, lawyer*

DISTRICT OF COLUMBIA

Washington
Shanks, Hershel *editor, writer*
Stern, Carl Leonard *former news correspondent, federal official*

ILLINOIS

Chicago
Allen, Richard Blose *legal editor, lawyer*
Anderson, Karl Stephen *editor*
Breen, Neil Thomas *publishing executive*
Judge, Bernard Martin *editor, publisher*
King, Jennifer Elizabeth *editor*
Ream, Davidson *law publications administrator, writer*

Vernon Hills
Strother, Jay D. *legal editor*

INDIANA

Noblesville
Feigenbaum, Edward D. *legal editor, publisher, consultant*

NEVADA

Reno
Hengstler, Gary Ardell *publisher, editor, lawyer*

NEW JERSEY

Marlboro
Nates, Jerome Harvey *publisher, lawyer*

Newark
Steinbaum, Robert S. *publisher, lawyer*

NEW YORK

New York
Benton, Donald Stewart *publishing company executive, lawyer*
Rogers, Thomas Sydney *communications executive*

NORTH CAROLINA

Cashiers
Yates, Linda Snow *financial services marketing executive*

PENNSYLVANIA

Philadelphia
Hale, Zan *editor, publisher*

TEXAS

El Paso
Miller, Roger Wayne *court reporter*

VIRGINIA

Charlottesville
Parrish, David Walker, Jr. *legal publishing company executive*

WISCONSIN

Milwaukee
Kritzer, Paul Eric *media executive, communications lawyer*

ADDRESS UNPUBLISHED

Quade, Victoria Catherine *editor, writer, playwright, producer*
Roberts, Delmar Lee *editor*

OTHER

UNITED STATES

ALABAMA

Birmingham
Goodrich, Thomas Michael *engineering and construction executive, lawyer*
Johnson, Joseph H., Jr. *lawyer*

ALASKA

Anchorage
Hayes, George Nicholas *lawyer*

ARIZONA

Phoenix
Griller, Gordon Moore *legal administrator*

Tempe
Bender, Paul *lawyer, educator*
Bucklin, Leonard Herbert *lawyer*

ARKANSAS

Little Rock
Hearne, Mary *retired legal secretary, artist*

CALIFORNIA

Berkeley
Harris, Michael Gene *optometrist, educator, lawyer*

Glendale
Fluharty, Jesse Ernest *lawyer*

Irvine
Hancock, S. Lee *business executive*
Hilker, Walter Robert, Jr. *lawyer*
Weissbard, Samuel Held *lawyer*

Lafayette
Davies, Paul Lewis , Jr. *retired lawyer*

Los Altos
Riter, Bruce Douglas *lawyer*

Los Angeles
Glushien, Morris P. *lawyer, arbitrator*
Parks, George Brooks *land development consultant, university dean*
Pollock, John Phleger *lawyer*
Ray, Gilbert T. *lawyer*
Roney, John Harvey *lawyer, consultant*
Sellers, Carol *lawyer*

Marina Del Rey
Annotico, Richard Anthony *legal administration, real estate investor*

Modesto
Murphy, John Thomas *lawyer*

Newport Beach
Caldwell, Courtney Lynn *lawyer, real estate consultant*
Lawless, William Burns *lawyer, academic administrator*
Wagner, John Leo *lawyer, former magistrate judge*

North Fork
Flanagan, James Henry, Jr. *lawyer, business educator*

Pacific Palisades
Verrone, Patric Miller *lawyer, writer*

Palm Springs
Kimberling, John Farrell *retired lawyer*

Palo Alto
Casillas, Mark *lawyer*

Riverside
Sklar, Wilford Nathaniel *retired lawyer, real estate broker*

Sacramento
Root, Gerald Edward *legal administration*
Scheidegger, Kent Stephen *lawyer*

San Bernardino
Eskin, Barry Sanford *court investigator*

San Francisco
Brick, Ann Veta *lawyer*
Enersen, Burnham *lawyer*
Johnson, Gardiner *lawyer*
Shapiro, Gary John *lawyer*

San Leandro
Newacheck, David John *lawyer, writer*

San Mateo
Kane, Robert Francis *lawyer, former ambassador, consultant*

Santa Ana
Dillard, John Martin *lawyer, pilot*

Santa Barbara
Gaines, Howard Clarke *retired lawyer*

Santa Monica
Kirkland, John C. *lawyer*

Tustin
Kraft, Henry Robert *lawyer*

Van Nuys
Boyd, Harry Dalton *lawyer, former insurance company executive*

Walnut Creek
Van Voorhis, Thomas *lawyer*

West Hollywood
Lyon, John David *lawyer, computer products company executive*

Westlake Village
Levinson, Christopher Gregory *legal administrator*

COLORADO

Denver
Cockrell, Richard Carter *retired lawyer*
Husney, Elliott Ronald *lawyer, financier*
Keatinge, Robert Reed *lawyer*
Lamm, Richard Douglas *lawyer, former governor of Colorado*
Seawell, Donald Ray *lawyer, publisher, arts center executive, producer*
Smead, Burton Armstrong, Jr. *retired lawyer*

Littleton
Spelts, Richard John *lawyer*

CONNECTICUT

Branford
Greenblatt, Morton Harold *retired assistant attorney general*

Greenwich
Cantor, Samuel C. *lawyer, company executive*

Hartford
Cain, George Harvey *lawyer, business executive*
Cullina, William Michael *lawyer*
Pinney, Sidney Dillingham, Jr. *lawyer*
Sorokin, Ethel Silver *lawyer*

New Haven
Gewirtz, Paul D. *lawyer, legal educator*

Redding
Gooch, Anthony Cushing *lawyer*

Stamford
Della Rocco, Kenneth Anthony *lawyer*
Yonkman, Fredrick Albers *lawyer, management consultant*

Weston
Aibel, Howard J. *lawyer, arbitrator/mediator*

DISTRICT OF COLUMBIA

Washington
Alexander, Clifford L., Jr. *management consultant, lawyer, former secretary of army*
Barnard, Robert C. *lawyer*
Bear, Dinah *lawyer*
Bolton, John Robert *lawyer, government official*
Canfield, Andrew Trotter *lawyer, writer*
Condrell, William Kenneth *lawyer*
Crumlish, Joseph Dougherty *lawyer*
Dorsen, David M(ilton) *lawyer*
Ensenat, Donald Burnham *lawyer, former ambassador*
Ginsburg, Martin David *lawyer, educator*
Greif, Joseph *lawyer*
Gutman, Harry Largman *lawyer, educator*
Hartnett, Mary *lawyer*
Hemmendinger, Noel *retired lawyer*
Hennessy, Ellen Anne *lawyer, benefits compensation analyst, educator*
Herz, Charles Henry *lawyer*
Hobelman, Carl Donald *lawyer*
Huebner, Emily Zug *judicial administrator*
Jones, Theodore Lawrence *lawyer*
Kahn, Edwin Leonard *lawyer*
Kimmitt, Robert Michael *executive, banker, diplomat*
Knab, Karen Markle *lawyer*
Kramer, Gerson Balfour *lawyer*
Krumholz, Mimi *human resources administrator*
Lehr, Dennis James *lawyer*
Loevinger, Lee *lawyer, science writer*
Marinaccio, Charles Lindbergh *lawyer, consultant*
Marks, Jonathan Bowles *lawyer, mediator, arbitrator*
Medalie, Richard James *lawyer*
Mishkin, Barbara Friedman *lawyer*
Moler, Elizabeth Anne *lawyer*
Monk, Carl Colburn *lawyer, academic administrator*
Pickering, John Harold *lawyer*
Rhodes, Alice Graham *lawyer*
Rosenthal, Ilene Goldstein *lawyer*
Schmidt, Richard Marten, Jr. *lawyer*
Sclafani, Frances Ann *lawyer, federal agency executive*
Singer, Daniel Morris *lawyer*
Solomon, Frederic *lawyer*
Sterrett, Samuel Black *lawyer, former judge*
Walker, Richard Henry *lawyer*
Waz, Joseph Walter, Jr. *government relations consultant, author*
Whiting, Richard Albert *lawyer*

Worthy, K(enneth) Martin *retired lawyer*

FLORIDA

Arcadia
McGavic, Mitzie W. *court clerk*

Boca Raton
Garlick, Michael *lawyer*

Boynton Beach
Babler, Wayne E. *lawyer, retired telephone company executive*

Bradenton
Clements, Allen, Jr. *retired lawyer*
Thomas, Ella Cooper *lawyer*

Gainesville
Kaimowitz, Gabe Hillel *civil rights lawyer*

Hobe Sound
Simpson, Russell Gordon *lawyer, former mayor, counselor to not-for-profit organizations*

Jacksonville
Halverson, Steven Thomas *lawyer, construction executive*

Key West
Eden, Nathan E. *lawyer*

Leesburg
Fechtel, Vincent John *legal administrator*

Lutz
Timchak, Louis John, Jr. *lawyer, real estate executive*

Palm Beach
Cummings, William Roger *international tax consultant, property management executive*
Grogan, Robert Harris *lawyer*

Panama City
Patterson, Christopher Nida *lawyer*

Sarasota
Davis, Louis Poisson, Jr. *lawyer, consultant*
Hull, J(ames) Richard *retired lawyer, business executive*
Kimbrough, Robert Averyt *lawyer*
Mackey, Leonard Bruce *lawyer, former diversified manufacturing corporation executive*
Ruiz-Suria, Fernando *lawyer*
Wise, Warren Roberts *retired lawyer*

Sun City Center
Fuller, Samuel Ashby *lawyer, mining company executive*

Tallahassee
Griffith, Elwin Jabez *lawyer, university administrator*
Holcomb, Lyle Donald, Jr. *retired lawyer*

Tampa
Kelly, Thomas Paine, Jr. *lawyer*

Wellington
Evangelista, Donato A. *retired lawyer, computer and infosystems manufacturing company executive*

GEORGIA

Athens
Hellerstein, Walter *lawyer*

Atlanta
Howell, Arthur *lawyer*
Phillips, William Russell, Sr. *lawyer*
Robinson, Willie Edward *lawyer*
Rusher, Derwood H., II *lawyer*
Stamps, Thomas Paty *lawyer, consultant*

Roswell
Broome, Barry Dean *lawyer, estate and financial planning consultant*

HAWAII

Honolulu
Gay, E(mil) Laurence *lawyer*
Robinson, Harlo Lyle *lawyer*

Kahului
Richardson, Robert Allen *retired lawyer, educator*

ILLINOIS

Chicago
Baker, Bruce Jay *lawyer*
Baker, James Edward Sproul *retired lawyer*
Berolzheimer, Karl *lawyer*
Bienen, Leigh Buchanan *lawyer*
Blume, Paul Chiappe *lawyer*
Brandt, William Arthur, Jr. *consulting executive*
Clark, David Keith *lawyer, real estate developer*
Johnson, Katherine Anne *health research administrator, lawyer*
McWhirter, Bruce J. *lawyer*
Morris, Norval *criminologist, educator*
O'Leary, Daniel Vincent, Jr. *lawyer*
Schulman, Jerry Allen *lawyer*

Des Plaines
Robison, Charles Bennett *legal consultant*

Naperville
Nortell, Bruce *lawyer*

River Forest
Marcello, Frank F. *lawyer, educator*

Riverwoods
Smith, Carole Dianne *lawyer, editor, writer, product developer*

Skokie
Sachs, Irving Joseph *lawyer, accountant, pension consultant*

Springfield
Bergschneider, David Philip *legal administrator*

Willowbrook
Walton, Stanley Anthony, III *lawyer*

INDIANA

Gary
Isla, Exu Reidemer Q. *corrections professional, lawyer*

Indianapolis
Badger, David Harry *lawyer*
Hiner, Leslie Davis *lawyer, political consultant*

Lafayette
Lazarus, Bruce I. *restaurant and hotel management educator*

IOWA

Cedar Rapids
Gray, William Oxley *retired lawyer*

KANSAS

Overland Park
Callahan, Michael Thomas *lawyer, construction consultant*

Wichita
Ayres, Ted Dean *lawyer, academic counsel*

KENTUCKY

Highland Heights
Dieffenbach, Charles Maxwell *emeritus law educator, lawyer*

Lexington
Turley, Robert Joe *lawyer*
Westin, Richard Axel *law educator, lawyer, consultant*

LOUISIANA

Mandeville
Olivier, Jason Thomas *lawyer*

New Orleans
Bronfin, Fred *lawyer*
Butcher, Bruce Cameron *lawyer*

Shreveport
Hetherwick, Gilbert Lewis *lawyer*

MARYLAND

Annapolis
Evans, William Davidson, Jr. *lawyer*
Jones, Sylvanus Benson *adjudicator, consultant, lawyer*

Baltimore
Gray, Elizabeth Chretien *criminal justice educator, real estate salesperson*
Katz, Laurence M. *legal educator*

Bethesda
Risik, Philip Maurice *lawyer*
Schifter, Richard *lawyer*

Chevy Chase
Meyerson, Christopher Cortlandt *law scholar*

Gaithersburg
Flickinger, Harry Harner *organization and business executive, management consultant*

Kensington
Mathias, Joseph Marshall *lawyer, judge*

Potomac
Affeldt, David Allan *lawyer, legal consultant*
Peter, Phillips Smith *lawyer*

Silver Spring
McKenna, William Francis *lawyer*

MASSACHUSETTS

Auburndale
Bernard, Michael Mark *lawyer, city planning consultant*

Belmont
Simpson, Russell Avington *retired law firm administrator*

Boston
Auerbach, Joseph *lawyer, educator, retired*
Feisel, Lyle Dean *lawyer*
Gabovitch, William *lawyer, accountant*
Hunsaker, Roderick Cason *lawyer, insurance company executive*
Looney, William Francis, Jr. *lawyer*
Meyer, Michael Broeker *lawyer, consultant*
Schoenfeld, Barbara Braun *lawyer, investment executive*
Sears, John Winthrop *lawyer*

Brighton
Ratto, Eugene Joseph *lawyer, commercial arbitrator and mediator, real estate broker, consultant*

Lexington
Davidson, Frank Paul *retired macroengineer, lawyer*

Nantucket
Lobl, Herbert Max *lawyer*

Newton Center
Soifer, Aviam *educator, former university dean*

Springfield
McCarthy, Charles Francis, Jr. *lawyer*
Miller, J(ohn) Wesley, III *lawyer, writer*

MICHIGAN

Ann Arbor
DeVine, Edmond Francis *lawyer*

Birmingham
Lesser, Margo Rogers *legal consultant*

Bloomfield Hills
Jones, John Paul *probation officer, psychologist*

Detroit
Johnson, Clark Cumings *lawyer, educator*

Farmington Hills
Meyer, Philip Gilbert *lawyer*
Rosenfeld, Martin Jerome *management consultant to law firms, educator*

Frankfort
Gerberding, Miles Carston *lawyer*

Grand Rapids
Halliday, William James, Jr. *lawyer*

Lansing
Ewert, Quentin Albert *lawyer, consultant*
Glicksman, Elliot Boris *educator, lawyer*

Muskegon
Van Leuven, Robert Joseph *lawyer*

MINNESOTA

Eagan
Todd, John Joseph *lawyer*

Minneapolis
Grinnell, Joseph Fox *financial company executive*
Hale, James Thomas *retail company executive, lawyer*
Skare, Robert Martin *lawyer, director*

Saint Paul
Rothman, Mitchell Lewis *lawyer, educator*

MISSISSIPPI

Greenwood
Osborne, Solomon Curtis

MISSOURI

Independence
Mortimer, Anita Louise *minister*

Kahoka
Jones, Mary D. *court clerk*

Kansas City
Bevan, Robert Lewis *lawyer*
Bradshaw, Jean Paul, II *lawyer*
Cooper, Corinne *communications consultant, lawyer*
English, R(obert) Bradford *marshal*

Saint Louis
Chackes, Kenneth Michael *lawyer, legal educator*
Ellis, Dorsey Daniel, Jr. *lawyer, educator*
Gilroy, Tracy Anne Hunsaker *lawyer*
Kuhlmann, Fred Mark *lawyer, business executive*
Lane, Frank Joseph, Jr. *lawyer*
Peper, Christian Baird *lawyer*

MONTANA

Missoula
Bowman, Jean Louise *lawyer, civic worker*

NEBRASKA

Lincoln
Alexis, Carl Odman *lawyer, earth scientist*

Omaha
Caporale, D. Nick *lawyer*

NEW HAMPSHIRE

New Durham
Kosko, Susan Uttal *legal administrator*

Portsmouth
Volk, Kenneth Hohne *lawyer*

West Lebanon
Isaacs, Robert Charles *retired lawyer*

NEW JERSEY

Cherry Hill
Rose, Joel Alan *legal consultant*

Flemington
Weinblatt, Seymour Solomon *lawyer*

Jersey City
Frisch, Harry David *lawyer, consultant*

Keyport
Colmant, Andrew Robert *lawyer*

Little Falls
Lieb, L. Robert *lawyer*

Moorestown
Slemmer, Carl Weber, Jr. *retired lawyer*

Newark
Simmons, Peter *law and urban planning educator*

Princeton
Kozlowski, Thomas Joseph, Jr. *lawyer, trust company executive*
Ufford, Charles Wilbur, Jr. *lawyer*

Summit
Caming, H. W. William *lawyer, consultant*

Tenafly
Badr, Gamal Moursi *legal consultant*

Westfield
Bobis, Daniel Harold *lawyer*
Stewart, Robert Campbell *lawyer*

Woodcliff Lake
Morrione, Melchior S. *management consultant, accountant*

NEW MEXICO

Albuquerque
Long, Stephen Carrel Mike *lawyer*
Rivera, Rhonda Rae *lawyer, labor artibrator*
Stevenson, James Richard *radiologist, lawyer*

NEW YORK

Albany
Baum, Joseph Thomas *lawyer*

Amagansett
Frankl, Kenneth Richard *retired lawyer*

Brooklyn
Karmel, Roberta Segal *lawyer, educator*
Tsismenakis, Georgia *lawyer, tax accountant*

Carmel
Laporte, Cloyd, Jr. *lawyer, retired manufacturing executive*

Chappaqua
Hurford, Carol *retired lawyer*

Garden City
Kaplan, Joel Stuart *lawyer*

Great Neck
Molinaro, Valerie Ann *lawyer*

Hastings On Hudson
Thornlow, Carolyn *law firm administrator, consultant*

Hawthorne
Jacobs, Jeffrey Lee *lawyer, education network company executive*

Ithaca
Palmer, Larry Isaac *lawyer, educator*

Jamaica
Shapiro, Irving *lawyer*

Long Beach
Levine, Samuel Milton *lawyer, retired judge, mediator, arbitrator*

Long Island City
Mathers, Allen Stanley *judge, arbitrator, consultant*

Mineola
Albicocco, Santa *county official*
Tankoos, Sandra Maxine *court reporting services executive*
Taub, Stephen Richard *lawyer*

Mount Kisco
Harris, Isaac Ron *lawyer*

New Rochelle
Asante, Samuel Kwadwo Boaten *lawyer, international official*
Gunning, Francis Patrick *lawyer, insurance association executive*

New York
Ames, John Lewis *lawyer*
Arther, Richard Oberlin *polygraphist, educator*
Bigelow, Robert Wilson *trial lawyer*
Brossman, Mark Edward *lawyer*
Cooper, George *writer, consultant*
Corbin, Sol Neil *lawyer*
Costikyan, Edward N. *lawyer*
David, Reuben *lawyer*
Derwin, Jordan *lawyer, consultant, actor*
Farber, Donald Clifford *lawyer, educator*
Fink, Rosalind Sue *lawyer*
Fishman, Fred Norman *lawyer*
Freund, Fred A. *retired lawyer*
Hagan, Peter Anthony *lawyer*
Hornblass, Jerome *lawyer, mediator, arbitrator, former judge*

Hull, Philip Glasgow *lawyer*
Jinnett, Robert Jefferson *lawyer*
Junkerman, William Joseph *retired lawyer*
Kaplan, Madeline *legal administrator*
Katsoris, Constantine Nicholas *lawyer, consultant*
King, Audrey *lawyer, mediator*
Kleckner, Robert George, Jr. *lawyer*
Knight, Robert Huntington *lawyer, bank executive*
Landau, Walter Loeber *lawyer*
Lazerus, Gilbert *lawyer*
Lindenbaum, Samuel Harvey *lawyer*
Maneker, Morton M. *lawyer*
Mosenson, Steven Harris *lawyer*
Nordquist, Stephen Glos *lawyer*
Roberts, Burton Bennett *lawyer, retired judge*
Rosensaft, Lester Jay *management consultant, lawyer, business executive*
Ross, Matthew *lawyer*
Schmertz, Eric Joseph *lawyer, educator*
Shepherd, John Michael *lawyer*
Shientag, Florence Perlow *lawyer*
Sidamon-Eristoff, Constantine *lawyer*
Stratton, Walter Love *lawyer*
Taylor, John Chestnut, III *lawyer*
Terry, Frederick Arthur, Jr. *lawyer*
Thompson, Marttie Louis *lawyer*
Toobin, Jeffrey Ross *writer, legal analyst*
Wender, Ira Tensard *lawyer*
Werner, Robert L. *lawyer, consultant*
Wilcox, John Caven *lawyer, corporate consultant*
Witherwax, Charles Halsey *lawyer, arbitrator, mediator*
Wolf, Diane R. *law consultant*
Wolfe, James Ronald *lawyer*
Zukerman, Michael *lawyer*

Rego Park
Turner, Laurence H. *lawyer, engineer*

Sands Point
Busner, Philip H. *retired lawyer*

Scarsdale
Macchia, Vincent Michael *lawyer*

Schenectady
Levine, Sanford Harold *lawyer*

Syracuse
Hayes, David Michael *lawyer*

Troy
Beeler, Patricia *court administrator*

Yonkers
Scholl, Judith Lois *lawyer*

NORTH CAROLINA

Chapel Hill
Brower, David John *lawyer, urban planner, educator*

Durham
Horowitz, Donald Leonard *lawyer, educator, researcher, political scientist, arbitrator*

Raleigh
Graham, William Edgar, Jr. *lawyer, retired utility company executive*

Research Triangle Park
Diosegy, Arlene Jayne *lawyer, consultant*

NORTH DAKOTA

Bismarck
Nelson, Keithe Eugene *state court administrator, lawyer*

OHIO

Beachwood
Donnem, Roland William *lawyer, hotel owner, developer*

Chagrin Falls
Freedman, Howard Joel *lawyer*

Cincinnati
Krass, Marc Stern *lawyer*
McClain, William Andrew *lawyer*
Nelson, Frederick Dickson *lawyer*

Cleveland
Jaffe, Donald Nolan *lawyer*
Schatz, William Bonsall *lawyer*

Columbus
McConnaughey, George Carlton, Jr. *retired lawyer*
McCutchan, Gordon Eugene *retired lawyer, insurance company executive*
Vorys, Arthur Isaiah *lawyer*

Dayton
Rapp, Gerald Duane *lawyer, manufacturing company executive*

Maumee
McBride, Beverly Jean *lawyer*

Mentor
Gambol, Robert Alan *lawyer*

Milford Center
McDonald, Alan Thomas *lawyer*

Norwalk
Fresch, Marie Beth *court reporting company executive*

Oxford
Brown, Edward Maurice *retired lawyer, business executive*

Troy
Bazler, Frank Ellis *retired lawyer*

OKLAHOMA

Oklahoma City
Allen, Robert Dee *lawyer*
Busey, Phil Gordon *lawyer*
Davenport, Gerald Bruce *lawyer*
Hanna, Terry Ross *lawyer, small business owner*
Taliaferro, Henry Beauford, Jr. *lawyer*

Tulsa
Estill, John Staples, Jr. *lawyer*
Thompson, Anne *court administrator*
Wheeler, Charles Vawter *lawyer*

OREGON

Astoria
Haskell, Donald McMillan *lawyer*

Portland
Funk, William F. *lawyer, educator*
Lavigne, Peter Marshall *environmentalist, lawyer, educator*

PENNSYLVANIA

Allentown
Coe, Ilse G. *retired lawyer*

Ambler
Rodgers, Richard M. *management consultant, lawyer*

Bethlehem
Styer, Jane M. *computer consultant*

Chadds Ford
Bainbridge, John Seaman *retired law school administrator, law educator, lawyer*

Erie
Yeager, Kathleen M. *court administrator*

Harrisburg
Arnold, Elizabeth Appleby *law clerk, billboard designer*

Lake Harmony
Polansky, Larry Paul *court administrator, consultant*

Philadelphia
Benn, Sara Kitchen *lawyer, educator*
Coyne, Charles Cole *lawyer*
Glassmoyer, Thomas Parvin *lawyer*
Kelley, George Lawrence, Jr. *lawyer*
Kunz, Michael E. *court administrator*
Mullinix, Edward Wingate *lawyer*
Murphy, Daniel Ignatius *lawyer*
Murphy, William Patrick *lawyer, editor, writer*
Nofer, George Hancock *lawyer*
Price, Robert Stanley *lawyer*
Reiter, Joseph Henry *lawyer, retired judge*

Pittsburgh
Hill, John Howard *lawyer*

Towanda
Rockefeller, Shirley E. *court clerk*

Wayne
Wilson, Bruce Brighton *retired transportation executive, lawyer*

RHODE ISLAND

Little Compton
Caron, Wilfred Rene *retired lawyer*

Pawtucket
Hendel, Maurice William *lawyer, consultant*

Providence
Kean, John Vaughan *retired lawyer*
Kersh, DeWitte Talmadge, Jr. *lawyer*

Wakefield
Rothschild, Donald Phillip *lawyer, arbitrator*

SOUTH CAROLINA

Columbia
Day, Richard Earl *lawyer, educator*

SOUTH DAKOTA

Sioux Falls
Haas, Joseph Alan *court administrator, lawyer*

TENNESSEE

Knoxville
Smartt, John Madison *lawyer*

Memphis
Richards, Janet Leach *lawyer, educator*
Soutendijk, Dirk Rutger *lawyer, corporate executive*

Nashville
Conner, Lewis Homer, Jr. *lawyer*
Madu, Leonard Ekwugha *lawyer, human rights officer, newspaper columnist, politician, business executive*

TEXAS

Abilene
Stevenson, Deydra *court administrator*

Argyle
Mark, Richard Steve *lawyer, educator, consultant*

Austin
Dougherty, John Chrysostom, III *retired lawyer*
Ehrle, William Lawrence *lawyer, association executive*
Goldstein, E. Ernest *lawyer, consultant*
Stephen, John Erle *lawyer, consultant*

Carrollton
Riggs, Arthur Jordy *retired lawyer*

Dallas
Burke, William Temple, Jr. *lawyer*
Hanson, Arnold Philip *lawyer*
Kipp, John Theodore *lawyer, rancher*

El Paso
Delgado, Graciela *court interpreter*

Fort Worth
Quinn, Francis Xavier *arbitrator, mediator, author, lecturer*

Houston
Caddy, Michael Douglas *lawyer*
Heinrich, Randall Wayne *lawyer*
Sales, James Bohus *lawyer*

Huntsville
Stowe, Charles Robinson Beecher *management consultant, educator, lawyer*

Mc Kinney
Eubanks, Patrice D. *court administrator*

New Braunfels
Reimer, Bill Monroe *lawyer*

Richardson
Wald, Michael H. *lawyer, educator*

San Antonio
Kehl, Randall Herman *executive, consultant, lawyer*

Waco
Thomson, Basil Henry, Jr. *lawyer, university general counsel*

Wimberley
Brinsmade, Lyon Louis *retired lawyer*

UTAH

Salt Lake City
Kimball, Spencer Levan *lawyer, educator*
Moss, Frank Edward *lawyer, former senator*

VERMONT

Randolph Center
Casson, Richard Frederick *lawyer, travel bureau executive*

Shelburne
Kurrelmeyer, Louis Hayner *retired lawyer*

VIRGINIA

Alexandria
Fugate, Wilbur Lindsay *lawyer*
Hawkins, Edward Jackson *lawyer*
Huckabee, Harlow Maxwell *lawyer, writer*
Montague, Robert Latane, III *lawyer*
Pyle, Howard *lawyer, consultant*
Walkup, Charlotte Lloyd *lawyer*

Arlington
Johnson, Charles Owen *retired lawyer*
Muchow, David John *lawyer, consultant*
Pomeranz, Morton *lawyer, educator*

Charlottesville
Cohen, Edwin Samuel *lawyer, educator*

Culpeper
Dulaney, Richard Alvin *lawyer*

Disputanta
Will, Joseph Henry Michael *lawyer, retired military officer*

Fairfax
Baird, Charles Bruce *lawyer, consultant*

Falls Church
Ward, Joe Henry, Jr. *retired lawyer*

Mc Lean
Hoffmann, Martin Richard *lawyer*
Newman, William Bernard, Jr. *consultant*

Richmond
Schwarzschild, Patricia Michaelson *lawyer*

Roanoke
Skolrood, Robert Kenneth *lawyer*

Warrenton
Brooke, Edward William *lawyer, former senator*

WASHINGTON

Kennewick
Sullivan-Schwebke, Karen Jane *lawyer*

Newcastle
Erxleben, William Charles *lawyer, consultant*

Seattle
Diamond, Josef *lawyer*
Stearns, Susan Tracey *lighting design company executive, lawyer*

Spokane
Powers, Mark Gregory *consultant, lawyer*

WEST VIRGINIA

Martinsburg
Hill, Philip Bonner *lawyer*

Parkersburg
Keltner, Robert Earl *lawyer, researcher, business executive*

WISCONSIN

Madison
Bugge, Lawrence John *lawyer, educator*
MacDougall, Priscilla Ruth *lawyer*
Skilton, Robert Henry *law educator, lawyer*

Milwaukee
Hill, John Glenwood, Jr. *university counsel, lawyer*

Platteville
Van Buren, David Paul *criminal justice educator*

Waukesha
Gesler, Alan Edward *lawyer*
Armstrong, Jack Gilliland *lawyer*

MILITARY ADDRESSES OF THE UNITED STATES

EUROPE

APO
Frame, Nancy Davis *lawyer*

ARGENTINA

Buenos Aires
Williams, Maureen Sylvia *legal administration*

BELGIUM

Antwerpen
Schillebeeckx, Jan Paul *radiologist*

Brussels
Fernandez, Cani *lawyer*

CHINA

Shanghai
Chen, Zhensheng *lawyer*

ENGLAND

Leeds
Cantrill, Patrick *lawyer, trade association executive*

London
Elliott, Nicholas Blethyn *barrister*
Fraser, Orlando *barrister*
Green, Richard *lawyer, psychiatrist, educator*
Hamblen, Nicholas *barrister*
Hancock, Christopher Patrick *barrister*
Jarvis, John Manners *barrister, judge*
Malek, Hodge Mehdi *lawyer*

MONACO

Monaco
Fitzgerald, Michael Edward *barrister, solicitor*

SOUTH AFRICA

Sandton City
Canny, Anthony *lawyer*

ADDRESS UNPUBLISHED

Ansley, Shepard Bryan *lawyer*
Avery, James Thomas, III *lawyer, management consultant*
Baum, Stanley David *lawyer*
Beloff, Michael Jacob *barrister*
Beresin, Marta Ilene *lawyer*
Bersin, Alan Douglas *lawyer, school system administrator*
Bertram, Manya M. *retired lawyer*
Carroll, Joseph J(ohn) *lawyer*
Casella, Peter F(iore) *patent and licensing executive*
Charles, Robert Bruce *lawyer*
Cook, S. Alan *lawyer, accountant*
Crawford, Muriel Laura *lawyer, author, educator*
Cremins, James Smyth *political party official, lawyer*
Dickerson, Claire Moore *lawyer, educator*
Everdell, William *retired lawyer*
Fink, Norman Stiles *lawyer, educational administrator, fundraising consultant*
Fino, Teresa Cristina *legal secretary, business owner*
Fowler, Donald Raymond *retired lawyer, educator*
Fowler, Flora Daun *retired lawyer*
Fox, Eleanor Mae Cohen *lawyer, educator, writer*
Frankel, James Burton *lawyer*
Futter, Victor *lawyer*

Gerwin, Leslie Ellen *lawyer, public affairs and community relations executive*
Gipstein, Milton Fivenson *lawyer, psychiatrist*
Gusman, Robert Carl *lawyer*
Hayes, Byron Jackson, Jr. *retired lawyer*
Hoffman, Darnay Robert *management consultant*
Holt, Marjorie Sewell *lawyer, retired congresswoman*
Keaty, Robert Burke *lawyer, writer, business consultant*
Kelepecz, Betty Patrice *protective services official, lawyer*
Kirven, Gerald *lawyer*
Kordons, Uldis *lawyer*
Korsinsky, Eduard *lawyer*
Krongard, Howard J. *lawyer*
Landon, William J. *intelligence officer*
Locke, John Howard *retired lawyer*
Long, Charles Thomas *lawyer, history educator*
Mayson, Preston B., Jr. *retired lawyer*
McGraw, Patrick Allan *lawyer*
Minor, Clara Mae *election judge*
Morgan, Timi Sue *lawyer*
Murphy, Kathleen Mary *former law firm executive*
Murphy, Lewis Curtis *lawyer, former mayor*
Reeder, Robert Harry *retired lawyer*
Renfro, William Leonard *futurist, lawyer, inventor, entrepreneur*
Richardson, John Carroll *lawyer, tax legislative consultant*
Rivers, Kenneth Jay *retired judicial administrator, consultant*
Robinson, Theodore Curtis, Jr. *lawyer*
Segel, Karen Lynn Joseph *lawyer, taxation specialist*
Sigety, Charles Edward *lawyer, family business consultant*
Steele, Eric Henry *lawyer*
Strutin, Kennard Regan *lawyer, educator, legal information consultant*
Terry, John Hart *retired utility company executive, congressman*
Weston, Michael C. *lawyer*
Winslow, Julian Dallas *retired lawyer, historian, writer*
Witt, John William *lawyer*
Zerger, Kirsten Louise *lawyer*

PARAPROFESSIONAL

UNITED STATES

CALIFORNIA

Los Angeles
Arbit, Beryl Ellen *legal assistant*
Arnkra, Joe *legal administrator, writer*
Monorieff, Dorothy *retired paralegal*
Wilson, Mable Jean *paralegal*

Sacramento
Willis, Dawn Louise *paralegal, small business owner*

COLORADO

Boulder
LaVelle, Betty Sullivan Dougherty *legal professional*

CONNECTICUT

Westbrook
Vogell, Connie *paralegal*

DISTRICT OF COLUMBIA

Washington
Townsend, Brian Douglas *paralegal*

GEORGIA

Atlanta
Banks, Linda T. *legal assistant, massage therapist*
Smith, Eleanor Van Law *paralegal*

INDIANA

Highland
Forsythe, Randall Newman *paralegal, educator*

KANSAS

Leawood
Johnston, Jocelyn Stanwell *paralegal*

LOUISIANA

Metairie
Quidd, David Andrew *paralegal*

MARYLAND

Baltimore
Hughes, Margo Gibson *legal assistant*

MICHIGAN

Detroit
Rogers, Hon Paulletto *researcher, writer*

MISSISSIPPI

Hattiesburg
Boatner, Jerra *legal assistant*

MISSOURI

Camdenton
Clark, Mark Jeffrey *paralegal, researcher*

Washington
Schmelz, Brenda Lea *legal assistant*

MONTANA

Bozeman
Piazza, Rosanna Joy *paralegal*

Great Falls
Speer, John Elmer *paralegal, reporter, counselor*

NEW HAMPSHIRE

Concord
Rapp, Elaine *paralegal*

NEW JERSEY

Haddonfield
Smith, Carol J. *legal secretary, medical transcriptionist*

Passaic
Johnson, Sakinah *paralegal*

Wildwood
Callinan, Patricia Ann *legal secretary*

NEW YORK

Bronx
Morganti, Peter Anthony *paralegal*

Garden City
Caputo, Kathryn Mary *paralegal*

Manchester
Gillis, Joan *legal administrative assistant*

New York
Tighe, Maria Theresa *project manager*

NORTH CAROLINA

Cary
Stell, Camille Stuckey *paralegal, educator*

OHIO

Columbus
Larzelere, Kathy Lynn Heckler *paralegal*

PENNSYLVANIA

Moon Township
Murray, Mary P. *law clerk*

SOUTH CAROLINA

Columbia
Wilson, Karen Wilkerson *paralegal*

TENNESSEE

Chattanooga
Williams, Rosemary Helen *paralegal*

TEXAS

Dallas
Flood, Joan Moore *paralegal*
Ku, Anchi H. *legal assistant*

Fort Worth
Reade, Kathleen Margaret *paralegal, author*

Grand Prairie
Avery, Reigh Kessen *legal assistant*

Lockhart
Shomette, Donna M. Dixson *paralegal*

UTAH

Manti
Petersen, Benton Lauritz *paralegal*

WASHINGTON

Seattle
Tessier, Dennis Medward *paralegal, lecturer, legal advisor, consultant*

WEST VIRGINIA

Wellsburg
Viderman, Linda Jean *paralegal, corporate executive*

WISCONSIN

Madison
Barnick, Helen *retired judicial clerk*

ADDRESS UNPUBLISHED

Edwards, Priscilla Ann *paralegal, business owner*
Myhand, Wanda Reshel *paralegal, legal assistant*
Rubinstein, Esta *paralegal*
Vetter, Joanne Reiniger *paralegal*

THE DETROIT COLLEGE OF LAW